American Men & Women of Science

1998-99 • 20th Edition

A Biographical Directory of Today's Leaders in Physical, Biological and Related Sciences.

Volume 3 • G-I

R.R. BOWKER
A Unit of Reed Elsevier Business Information
New Providence, New Jersey

Published by R.R. Bowker, A Unit of Reed Elsevier Business Information

Copyright© 1998 by Reed Elsevier Inc. All rights reserved. Except as permitted under the Copyright Act of 1976, no part of *American Men and Women of Science* may be reproduced or transmitted in any form or by any means stored in any information storage and retrieval system, without prior written permission of R.R. Bowker, 121 Chanlon Road, New Providence, New Jersey, 07974.

International Standard Book Number
    Set: 0-8352-3748-6
    Volume 1:   0-8352-3749-4
    Volume 2:   0-8352-3775-3
    Volume 3:   0-8352-3776-1
    Volume 4:   0-8352-3778-8
    Volume 5:   0-8352-3779-6
    Volume 6:   0-8352-3781-8
    Volume 7:   0-8352-3782-6
    Volume 8:   0-8352-3783-4

International Standard Serial Number: 0192-8570
Library of Congress Catalog Card Number: 6-7326
Printed and bound in the United States of America.

R.R. Bowker has used its best efforts in collecting and preparing material for inclusion in this publication but does not warrant that the information herein is complete or accurate, and does not assume, and hereby disclaims, any liability to any person for any loss or damage caused by errors or omissions in *American Men and Women of Science*, whether such errors or omissions result from negligence, accident or any other cause.

8 Volume Set

ISBN 0-8352-3748-6

American Men & Women of Science

1998-99 • 20th Edition

The 20th edition of *AMERICAN MEN & WOMEN OF SCIENCE* was prepared by the R.R. Bowker Database Publishing Group in collaboration with the Publication Systems Department.

Senior Staff of the Database Publishing Group includes:

Senior Vice President & Chief Operating Officer, R.R. Bowker
Neal Goff

Publisher
Nan Hudes

Vice President, Database Publishing
Leigh Yuster-Freeman

Editorial:
Director: *Owen O'Donnell*
Managing Editor: *Karen Hallard*
Senior Editor: *Alison J. Butkiewicz*
Associate Editors: *Angela Krakow*
Elizabeth McCarthy

Research:
Director: *Judy Redel*
Senior Managing Editor: *Tanya Hurst*
Senior Editor: *Beverly Heath*

Tampa Division:
Director: *Valerie Harris*
Production Manager: *Debra Wilson*
Associate Coordinator: *Jennifer Rodgers*

Contents

Advisory Committee vi

Preface vii

Major Honors & Awards ix

Statistics xi

Sample Entry xvii

Abbreviations xviii

Biographies 1

Advisory Committee

Dr. Charles Henderson Dickens
Former Executive Secretary, Federal Coordinating Council for Science, Engineering & Technology
Office of Science & Technology Policy

Dr. Oscar Nicolas Garcia
NCR Distinguished Professor & Chair, Department of Computer Science & Engineering
Wright State University

Dr. Michael J. Jackson
Executive Director
Federation of American Societies for Experimental Biology

Dr. Shirley Mahaley Malcom
Head, Directorate for Education and Human Resources Programs
American Association for the Advancement of Science

Ms. Beverly Fearn Porter
Assistant to the Executive Director for Society Relations
American Institute of Physics

Dr. William Eldon Splinter
Former Vice Chancellor for Research
University of Nebraska-Lincoln

Dr. Dael Lee Wolfle
Professor Emeritus, Graduate School of Public Affairs
University of Washington

Dr. Ahmed H. Zewail
Linus Pauling Professor of Chemistry & Physics
California Institute of Technology

Preface

American Men and Women of Science remains without peer as a chronicle of North American and Canadian scientific endeavor and achievement. The present work is the twentieth edition since it was first compiled as *American Men of Science* by J. McKeen Cattell in 1906. In its ninety-two year history, *American Men and Women of Science* has profiled the careers of over 300,000 scientists and engineers. Since the first edition, the number of American scientists and the fields they pursue has grown immensely. This edition alone lists full biographies for 119,618 engineers and scientists, 4184 of which are listed for the first time. Although the book has grown, our stated purpose is the same as when Dr. Cattell first undertook the task of producing a biographical directory of active American scientists. It was his intention to record educational, personal and career data which would make "a contribution to the organization of science in America" and "make men [and women] of science acquainted with one another and with one another's work." It is our hope that this edition will fulfill these goals.

The biographies of engineers and scientists constitute seven of the eight volumes and provide birthdate, birthplace, field of specialty, education, honorary degrees, current position, professional and concurrent experience, awards, memberships, research information and addresses for each entrant when applicable. The eighth volume, the discipline index, organizes biographees by field of activity. This index, adapted from the National Science Foundation's Taxonomy of Degree and Employment Specialties, classifies entrants by 192 subject specialties listed in the table of contents of Volume 8. The index lists scientists and engineers by state within each subject specialty, allowing the user to easily locate a scientist in a given area. Also included are statistical information and charts showing the distribution of *AMWS* listees by age and discipline and and annotated listing of the recipients of the Nobel Prizes, the Craaford Prize, the Charles Stark Draper Prize, the National Medals of Science and Technology, the Fields Medal and the Alan T. Waterman Award since the last edition.

While the scientific fields covered by *American Men and Women of Science* are comprehensive, no attempt has been made to include all American scientists. Entrants are meant to be limited to those who have made significant contributions in their field. The names of new entrants were submitted for consideration at the editors' request by current entrants and by leaders of academic, government and private research programs and associations. Those included met the following criteria:

1. Distinguished achievement, by reason of experience, training or accomplishment, including contributions to literature, coupled with continuing activity in scientific work;

or

2. Research activity of high quality in science as evidenced by publication in reputable scientific journals; or, for those whose work cannot be published due to governmental or industrial security, research activity of high quality in science as evidenced by the judgement of the individual's peers;

or

3. Attainment of a position of substantial responsibility requiring scientific training and experience.

This edition profiles living scientists in the physical and biological fields, as well as public health scientists, engineers, mathematicians, statisticians, and computer scientists. The information is collected by means of direct communication whenever possible. All entrants receive forms for corroboration and updating. New entrants receive questionnaires and verification proofs before publication. The information submitted by entrants is included as completely as possible within the boundaries of editorial and space restrictions. If an entrant does not return the form and his or her current location can be verified in secondary sources, the full entry is repeated. References to the previous edition are given for those who do not return forms and cannot be located, but who are presumed to be still active in science or engineering. Entrants known to be deceased are noted as such and a reference to the previous edition is given. Scientists and engineers who are not citizens of the United States or Canada are included if a significant portion of their work was performed in North America.

The information in *American Men & Women of Science* is available on magnetic tape. For information, contact Bowker Electronic Publishing (888-BOWKER-2). *American Men and Women of Science* is also available for online searching through Lexis®-Nexis® (800-227-4908) and through DIALOG, a service of Knight-Ridder Information, Inc. (800-334-2564). The online products allow fielded as well as key word searches of all elements of a record, including field of interest, experience, and location. An ERL-compliant CD-ROM is available through SilverPlatter Information (800-343-0064). Mailing lists are available through Reed Elsevier Business Information Lists (John Panza, Account Manager, Bowker Files, 245 W 17th St, New York, NY, 10011; 212-337-7164).

A project as large as publishing *American Men and Women of Science* involves the efforts of a great many people. The editors take this opportunity to thank the twentieth edition advisory committee for their guidance, encouragement and support. Appreciation is also expressed to the many scientific societies who provided their membership lists for the purpose of locating former entrants whose addresses had changed, and to the tens of thousands of scientists across the country who took time to provide us with biographical information. We also wish to thank Donna Brinkmann and Carol Carr of Reed Technology & Information Services, Inc. for their assistance in the successful production of this directory.

Comments, suggestions and nominations for the twenty-first edition are encouraged and should be directed to The Editors, *American Men and Women of Science*, R.R. Bowker, 121 Chanlon Road, New Providence, New Jersey, 07974.

Karen Hallard
Managing Editor

Major Honors & Awards

Nobel Prizes
Nobel Foundation, Royal Swedish Academy of Sciences & Nobel Assembly of the Karolinska

The Nobel Prizes were established in 1900 (and first awarded in 1901) to recognize those people who "have conferred the greatest benefit on mankind."

1995 Recipients

Chemistry:
Paul Josef Crutzen, Mario Jose Molina & Frank Sherwood Rowland
Awarded "for their work in atmospheric chemistry, particularly concerning the formation and decomposition of ozone."

Physics:
Martin Lewis Perl
Frederick Reines
Awarded to Perl "for the discovery of the tau lepton" and to Reines "for the detection of the nutrino."

Physiology or Medicine:
Edward B. Lewis, Christiane Nusslein-Volhard & Eric F. Wieschaus
Awarded "for their discoveries concerning the genetic control of early embryonic development."

1996 Recipients

Chemistry:
Robert Floyd Curl, Harold Walter Kroto & Richard Errett Smalley
Awarded "for their discovery of fullerenes, carbon atoms bound in the form of a ball."

Physics:
David Morris Lee, Douglas Dean Osheroff & Robert Coleman Richardson
Awarded "for their discovery of superfluidity in helium-3."

Physiology or Medicine:
Peter Charles Doherty & Rolf Martin Zinkernagel
Awarded "for their discoveries of how the immune system recognizes virus-infected cells."

1997 Recipients

Chemistry:
Paul Delos Boyer, Jens Christian Skou & John Ernest Walker
Awarded to Boyer & Walker "for their elucidation of the enzymatic mechanism underlying the synthesis of adenosine triphosphate (ATP)" and to Skou "for the first discovery of an ion-transporting enzyme, NA^+, K^+-ATPase."

Physics:
Claude Nessin Cohen-Tannoudji, Steven Chu & William Daniel Phillips
Awarded "for their development of methods to cool and trap atoms with laser light."

Physiology or Medicine:
Stanley Ben Prusiner
Awarded to Prusiner for his discovery of prions, a new genre of infectious agents.

Crafoord Prize
Royal Swedish Academy of Sciences

The Crafoord Prize was introduced in 1982 to award scientists in disciplines not covered by the Nobel Prize, namely mathematics, astronomy, geosciences and biosciences.

1995 Recipients

Willi Dansgaard & Nicholas John Shackleton
Awarded "for their fundamental work on developing and applying isotope geological analysis methods for the study of climatic variations during the Quaternary period."

1996 Recipient

Robert McRedie May
Awarded to May "for his pioneering ecological research concerning theoretical analysis of the dynamics of populations, communities and ecosystems."

1997 Recipients

Fred Hoyle & Edwin Ernest Salpeter
Awarded "for their pioneering contributions involving the study of nuclear reactions in stars and stars' development."

Charles Stark Draper Prize
National Academy of Engineering

The Draper Prize, awarded biennially, was introduced in 1989 to recognize engineering achievement.

1995 Recipients

John Robinson Pierce & Harold A. Rosen
Awarded for developing communications satellite technology.

1997 Recipients

Vladimir Haensel
Awarded to Haensel for inventing "Platforming" — platinum reforming to convert petroleum into high-performance fuels.

National Medal of Science
National Science Foundation

The National Medals of Science were established by the United States Congress in 1959 and have been awarded by the President of the United States since 1962. The National Science Foundation's selection criteria are based on the "total impact of an individual's work on the present state of physical, biological, mathematical, engineering, behavioral, or social sciences."

1995 Recipients

Thomas Robert Cech
Hans Georg Dehmelt
Peter Goldreich
Hermann A(nton) Haus
Isabella Lugoski Karle
Louis Nirenberg
Alexander Rich
Roger N. Shepard

1996 Recipients

Wallace Broecker
Norman Ralph Davidson
James L(oton) Flanagan
Richard M. Karp
Chandra Kumar Naranbhai Patel
Ruth Patrick
Paul Anthony Samuelson
Stephen Smale

1997 Recipients

William K. Estes
Darleane Christian Hoffman
Harold Sledge Johnston
Marshall N. Rosenbluth
Martin Schwarzschild (deceased)
James Dewey Watson
Robert A. Weinberg
George West Wetherill
Shing-Tung Yau

Fields Medal
International Mathematical Union

The Fields Medals were established in 1936 by Canadian mathematician John Fields to acknowledge outstanding research by young mathematicians. The medals are awarded every four years at the International Congress of Mathematicians.

1994 Recipients

Jean Bourgain
Pierre Louis Lions
Jean-Christophe Yoccoz
Efim Isaakovich Zelmanof

Awarded to Bourgain for his insights into the geometry of infinite dimensional spaces. Awarded to Lions for advances in non-linear partial differential equations. Awarded to Yoccoz for analyzing the end results of complicated sequences of circle maps. Awarded to Zelmanov for solving the unrestricted Burnside problem.

National Medal of Technology
U.S. Department of Commerce

The National Medals of Technology were created as part of the 1980 Stevenson-Wydler Technology Innovation Act and were first awarded in 1985. They are bestowed by the President of the United States to recognize individuals and companies for their development or commercialization of technology or for their contributions to the establishment of a technologically-trained workforce.

1995 Recipients

Praveen Chaudhari
Jerome John Cuomo
Richard Joseph Gambino
Edward R. McCracken
Sam B. Williams
Alejandro Zaffaroni
Procter & Gamble Company
3M

1996 Recipients

Charles Huron Kaman
Stephanie Louise Kwolek
James C. Morgan
Peter Henry Rose
Johnson & Johnson

1997 Recipients

Norman R. Augustine
Vinton Gray Cerf
Ray Milton Dolby
Robert Elliot Kahn
Robert Steven Ledley

Alan T. Waterman Award
National Science Foundation & National Science Board

Established by the United States Congress in 1975, the Waterman Award is given annually to an outstanding researcher, aged 35 or younger, in any field of science or engineering supported by the National Science Foundation.

1995 Recipient

Matthew P.A. Fisher
Awarded to Fisher "for his pioneering contributions to the theory of disordered superconductors."

1996 Recipient

Robert Mebane Waymouth
Awarded to Waymouth for discovering new ways to make polymers.

1997 Recipient

Eric Allin Cornell
Awarded to Cornell for creation of Bose-Einstein condensate (BEC).

Statistics

Statistical distribution of entrants in *American Men & Women of Science* with U.S. mailing addresses is illustrated on the following five pages. The regional scheme for geographical analysis is diagrammed in the map below. A table enumerating the geographic distribution can be found on page xvi, following the charts. The statistics are compiled by tallying all occurrences of a major index subject. Each scientist may choose to be indexed under as many as four categories; thus, the total number of subject references is greater than the number of entrants in *AMWS*.

All Disciplines

	Number	Percent
Northeast	56,006	34%
Southeast	41,313	25%
North Central	19,699	12%
South Central	12,169	7%
Mountain	11,675	7%
Pacific	25,703	15%
TOTAL	**166,565**	**100%**

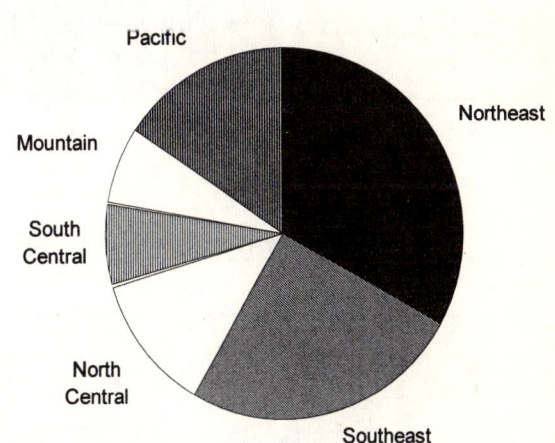

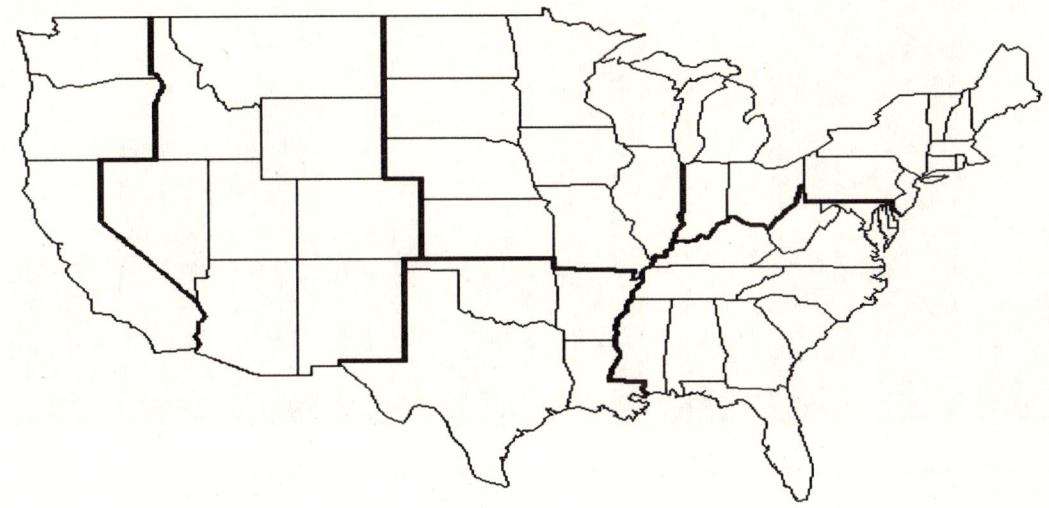

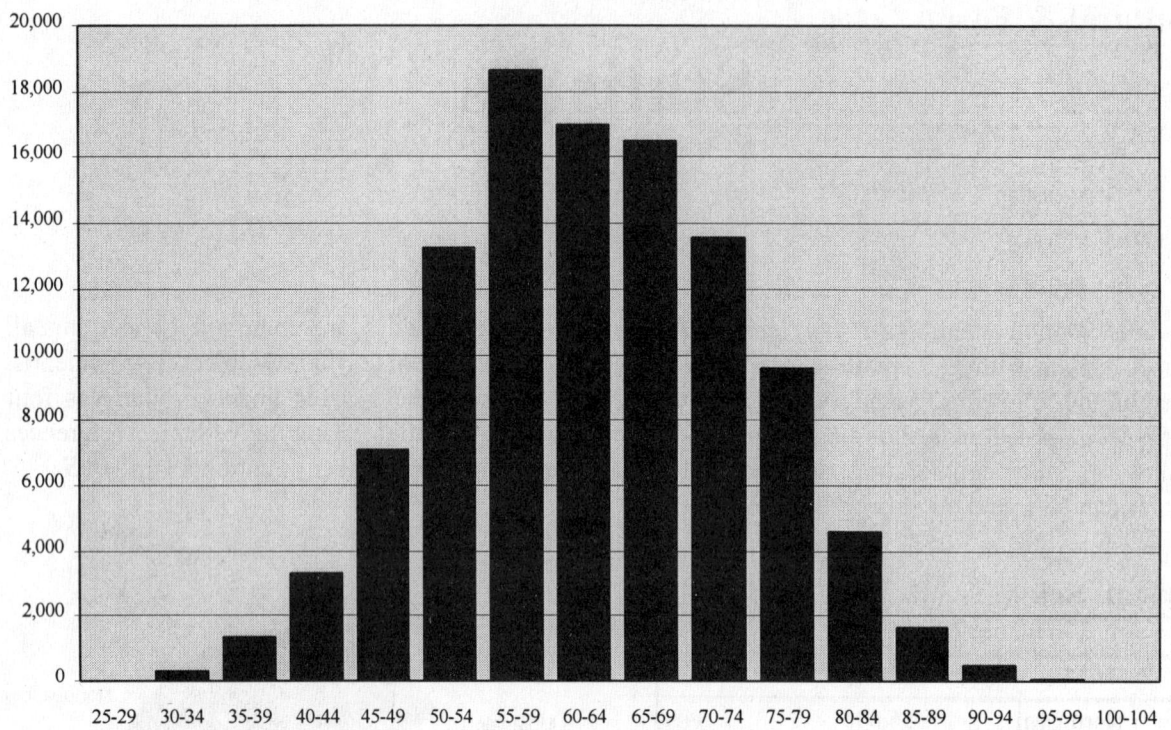
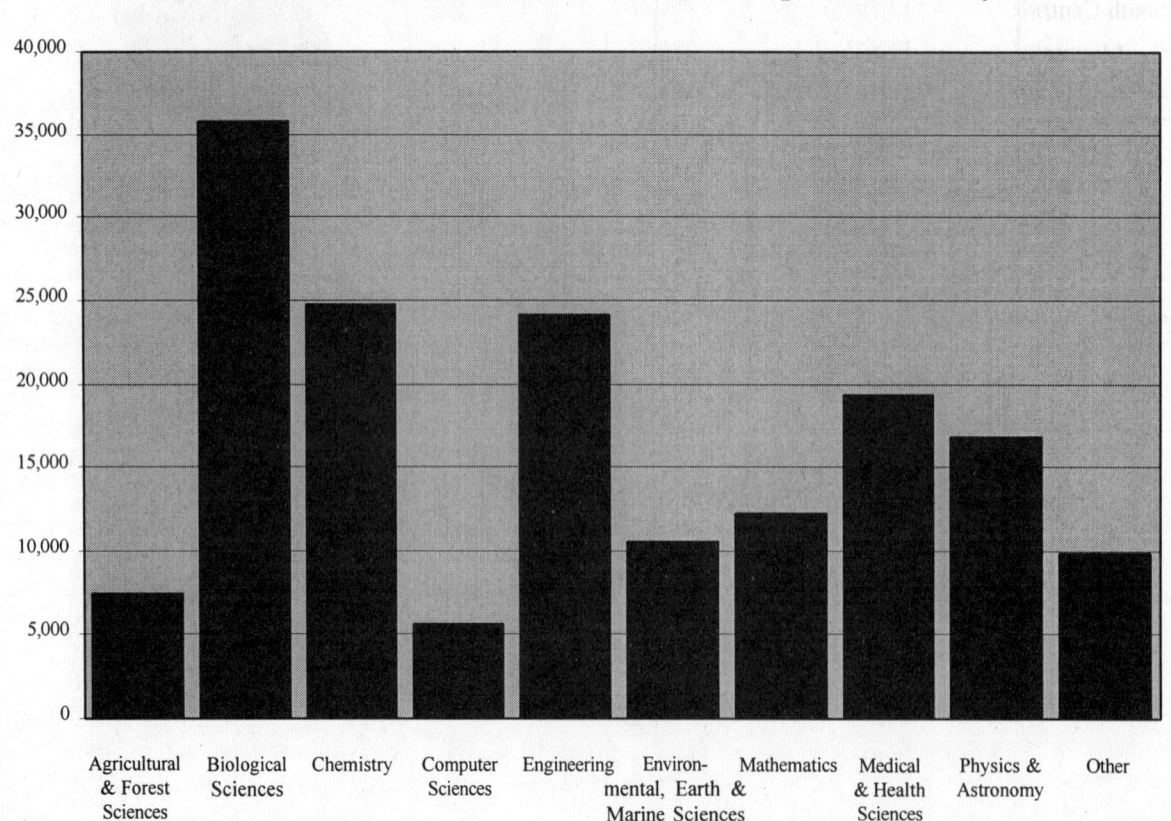

Agricultural & Forest Sciences

	Number	Percent
Northeast	1,585	21%
Southeast	2,053	27%
North Central	1,171	16%
South Central	635	8%
Mountain	739	10%
Pacific	1,305	17%
TOTAL	**7,488**	**100%**

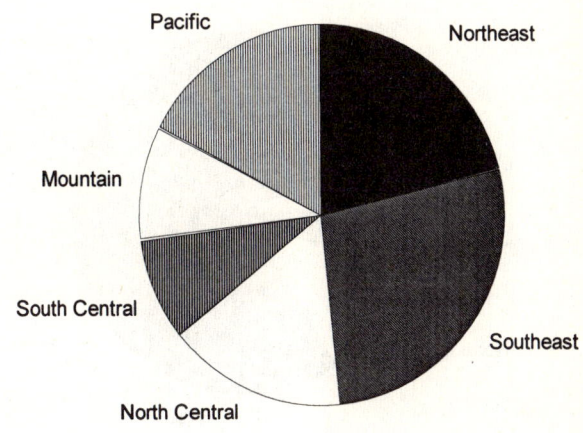

Biological Sciences

	Number	Percent
Northeast	11,671	33%
Southeast	9,045	25%
North Central	4,918	14%
South Central	2,741	8%
Mountain	2,125	6%
Pacific	5,277	15%
TOTAL	**35,777**	**100%**

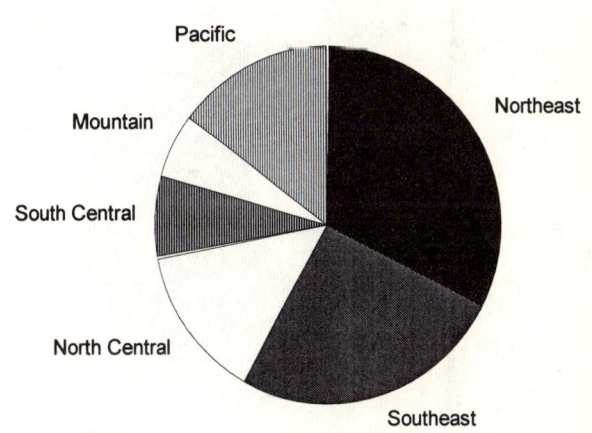

Chemistry

	Number	Percent
Northeast	9,296	38%
Southeast	6,196	25%
North Central	2,964	12%
South Central	1,724	7%
Mountain	1,381	6%
Pacific	3,139	13%
TOTAL	**24,700**	**100%**

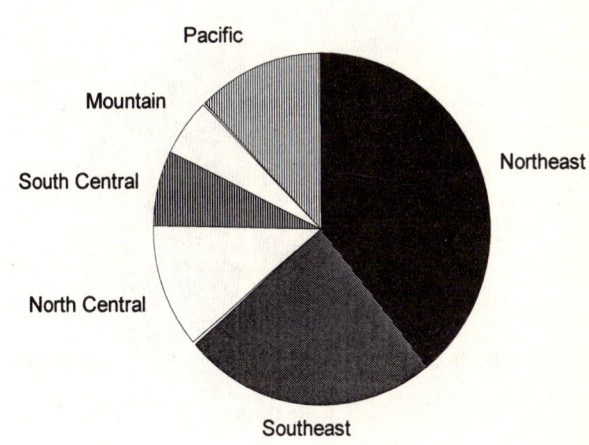

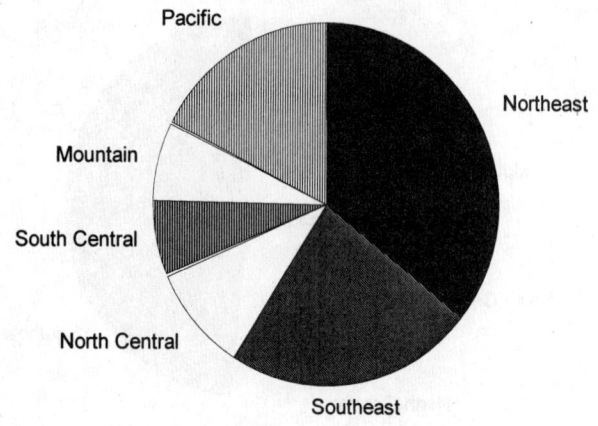

Computer Sciences

	Number	Percent
Northeast	1,983	35%
Southeast	1,278	23%
North Central	556	10%
South Central	378	7%
Mountain	423	7%
Pacific	1,034	18%
TOTAL	**5,652**	**100%**

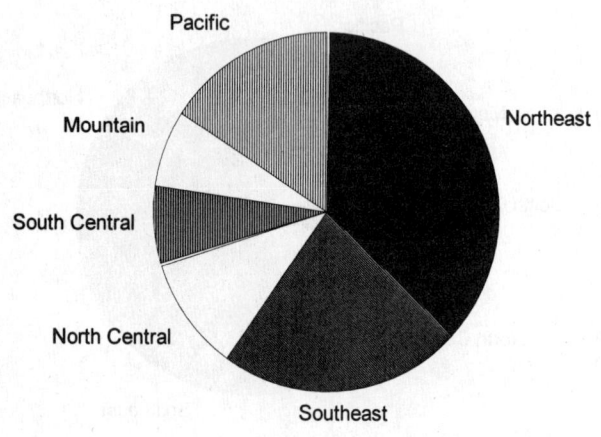

Engineering

	Number	Percent
Northeast	8,780	36%
Southeast	5,487	23%
North Central	2,501	10%
South Central	1,742	7%
Mountain	1,760	7%
Pacific	3,883	16%
TOTAL	**24,153**	**100%**

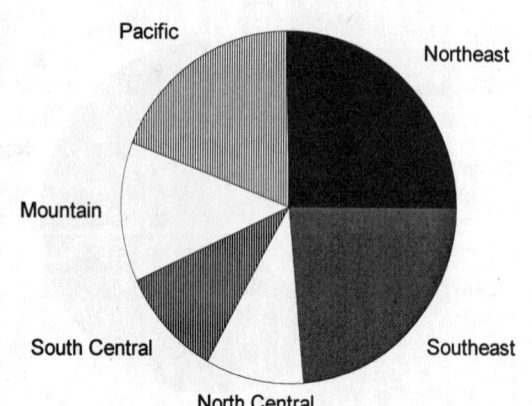

Environmental, Earth & Marine Sciences

	Number	Percent
Northeast	2,654	25%
Southeast	2,507	24%
North Central	984	9%
South Central	1,008	10%
Mountain	1,365	13%
Pacific	2,008	19%
TOTAL	**10,526**	**100%**

Mathematics

	Number	Percent
Northeast	4,292	35%
Southeast	2,865	23%
North Central	1,552	13%
South Central	933	8%
Mountain	760	6%
Pacific	1,901	15%
TOTAL	**12,303**	**100%**

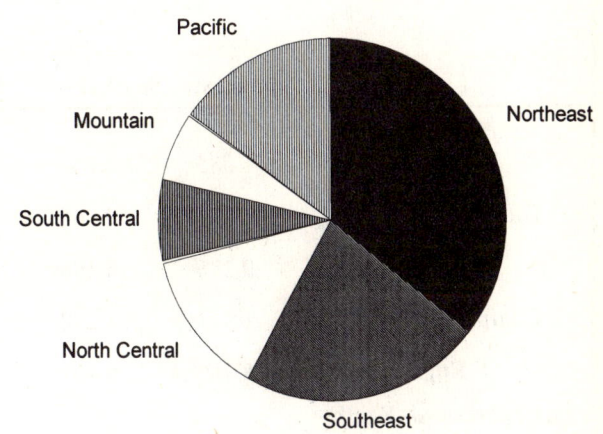

Medical & Health Sciences

	Number	Percent
Northeast	6,883	36%
Southeast	5,139	27%
North Central	2,471	13%
South Central	1,494	8%
Mountain	804	4%
Pacific	2,501	13%
TOTAL	**19,292**	**100%**

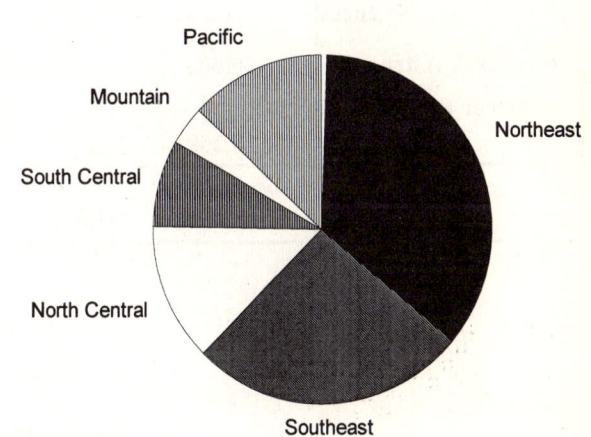

Physics & Astronomy

	Number	Percent
Northeast	5,603	33%
Southeast	3,776	22%
North Central	1,545	9%
South Central	904	5%
Mountain	1,674	10%
Pacific	3,307	20%
TOTAL	**16,809**	**100%**

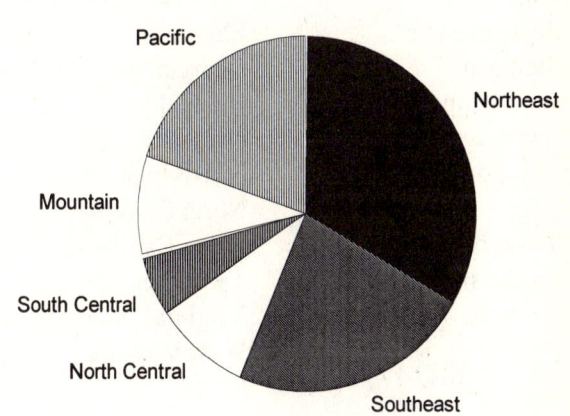

Geographic Distribution of Scientists by Discipline

	Northeast	Southeast	North Central	South Central	Mountain	Pacific	TOTAL
Agricultural & Forest Sciences	1,585	2,053	1,171	635	739	1,305	**7,488**
Biological Sciences	11,671	9,045	4,918	2,741	2,125	5,277	**35,777**
Chemistry	9,296	6,196	2,964	1,724	1,381	3,139	**24,700**
Computer Sciences	1,983	1,278	556	378	423	1,034	**5,652**
Engineering	8,780	5,487	2,501	1,742	1,760	3,883	**24,153**
Environmental, Earth & Marine Sciences	2,654	2,507	984	1,008	1,365	2,008	**10,526**
Mathematics	4,292	2,865	1,552	933	760	1,901	**12,303**
Medical & Health Sciences	6,883	5,139	2,471	1,494	804	2,501	**19,292**
Physics & Astronomy	5,603	3,776	1,545	904	1,674	3,307	**16,809**
Other Professional Fields	3,259	2,967	1,037	610	644	1,348	**9,865**
TOTAL	**56,006**	**41,313**	**19,699**	**12,169**	**11,675**	**25,703**	**166,565**

Geographic Definitions

Northeast
Connecticut
Indiana
Maine
Massachusetts
Michigan
New Hampshire
New Jersey
New York
Ohio
Pennsylvania
Rhode Island
Vermont

Southeast
Alabama
Delaware
District of Columbia
Florida
Georgia
Kentucky
Maryland
Mississippi
North Carolina
South Carolina
Tennessee
Virginia
West Virginia

North Central
Illinois
Iowa
Kansas
Minnesota
Missouri
Nebraska
North Dakota
South Dakota
Wisconsin

South Central
Arkansas
Louisiana
Texas
Oklahoma

Mountain
Arizona
Colorado
Idaho
Montana
Nevada
New Mexico
Utah
Wyoming

Pacific
Alaska
California
Hawaii
Oregon
Washington

Sample Entry

American Men & Women of Science (AMWS) is an extremely useful reference tool. The book is most often used in two ways: to find more information about a particular scientist and to locate a scientist in a specific field.

To locate information about an individual, the biographical section is most helpful. It encompasses the first seven volumes and lists scientists and engineers alphabetically by last name. The fictitious biographical listing shown below illustrates every type of information an entry may include.

The Discipline Index, volume 8, can be used to easily find a scientist in a specific subject specialty. This index is first classified by area of study; within each specialty entrants are divided further by state of residence.

Name — REED, SAMANTHA J(EAN), — **Field of Specialty**: OCEANOGRAPHY, MARINE BIOLOGY. *Current Pos:* SR ASSOC OCEANOGRAPHER, DEPT NAVY, 86- — **Current Position**

Personal Data: b Brooklyn, NY, Nov 9, 42; — **Birthdate**

m 67, James A. Mayer; — **Marriage/Spouse data**

c Steven C & Lillian M. — **Children's Name(s)**

Educ: Univ Notre Dame, BS, 63, MS, 65, Fla State Univ, PhD(oceanog), 70. — **Education**

Hon Degrees: DSc, Univ Calif, Davis, 79. — **Honorary Degrees**

Honors & Awards: Henry Bryant Bigelow Medal, Oceanog, 92; — **Honors & Awards**

Prof Exp: Asst prof oceanog, 71-73, assoc prof oceanog & biol, Harvard Univ, 73-75. — **Professional Experience**

Concurrent Pos: Consult, New England Aquarium, 74-78; vis lect, Wash Univ, 77. — **Concurrent Experience**

Mem: AAAS, Am Soc Naval Engrs, Sigma Xi, Oceanog Soc (vpres 82-83). — **Memberships**

Res: Ocean pollution prevention, water treatment and analysis, ecology of marine plankton and sponges, author of 13 publications. — **Research and Publications**

Mailing Address: 121102 Smithfield Way, Boca Raton, FL 33431. — **Mailing Address**

Fax: 407-555-5939; — **Fax Number**

E-Mail: sreed@usnavy.mil.fla — **E-Mail Address**

Abbreviations

AAAS—American Association for the Advancement of Science
abnorm—abnormal
abstr—abstract
acad—academic, academy
acct—account, accountant, accounting
acoust—acoustic(s), acoustical
ACTH—adrenocorticotrophic hormone
actg—acting
activ—activities, activity
addn—addition(s), additional
Add—Address
adj—adjunct, adjutant
adjust—adjustment
Adm—Admiral
admin—administration, administrative
adminr—administrator(s)
admis—admission(s)
adv—adviser(s), advisory
advan—advance(d), advancement
advert—advertisement, advertising
AEC—Atomic Energy Commission
aerodyn—aerodynamic
aeronaut—aeronautic(s), aeronautical
aerophys—aerophysical, aerophysics
aesthet—aesthetic
AFB—Air Force Base
affil—affiliate(s), affiliation
agr—agricultural, agriculture
agron—agronomic, agronomical, agronomy
agrost—agrostologic, agrostological, agrostology
agt—agent
AID—Agency for International Development
Ala—Alabama
allergol—allergological, allergology
alt—alternate
Alta—Alberta
Am—America, American
AMA—American Medical Association
anal—analysis, analytic, analytical
analog—analogue
anat—anatomic, anatomical, anatomy
anesthesiol—anesthesiology
angiol—angiology
Ann—Annal(s)
ann—annual
anthrop—anthropological, anthropology
anthropom—anthropometric, anthropometrical, anthropometry

antiq—antiquary, antiquities, antiquity
antiqn—antiquarian
apicult—apicultural, apiculture
APO—Army Post Office
app—appoint, appointed
appl—applied
appln—application
approx—approximate(ly)
Apr—April
apt—apartment(s)
aquacult—aquaculture
arbit—arbitration
arch—archives
archaeol—archaeological, archaeology
archit—architectural, architecture
Arg—Argentina, Argentine
Ariz—Arizona
Ark—Arkansas
artil—artillery
asn—association
assoc(s)—associate(s), associated
asst(s)—assistant(s), assistantship(s)
assyriol—Assyriology
astrodyn—astrodynamics
astron—astronomical, astronomy
astronaut—astronautical, astronautics
astronr—astronomer
astrophys—astrophysical, astrophysics
attend—attendant, attending
atty—attorney
audiol—audiology
Aug—August
auth—author
AV—audiovisual
Ave—Avenue
avicult—avicultural, aviculture

b—born
bact—bacterial, bacteriologic, bacteriological, bacteriology
BC—British Colombia
bd—board
behav—behavior(al)
Belg—Belgian, Belgium
Bibl—Biblical
bibliog—bibliographic, bibliographical, bibliography
bibliogr—bibliographer
biochem—biochemical, biochemistry
biog—biographical, biography
biol—biological, biology
biomed—biomedical, biomedicine

biomet—biometric(s), biometrical, biometry
biophys—biophysical, biophysics
bk(s)—book(s)
bldg—building
Blvd—Boulevard
Bor—Borough
bot—botanical, botany
br—branch(es)
Brig—Brigadier
Brit—Britain, British
Bro(s)—Brother(s)
byrol—byrology
bull—Bulletin
bur—bureau
bus—business
BWI—British West Indies

c—children
Calif—California
Can—Canada, Canadian
cand—candidate
Capt—Captain
cardiol—cardiology
cardiovasc—cardiovascular
cartog—cartographic, cartographical, cartography
cartogr—cartographer
Cath—Catholic
CEngr—Corp of Engineers
cent—central
Cent Am—Central American
cert—certificate(s), certification, certified
chap—chapter
chem—chemical(s), chemistry
chemother—chemotherapy
chg—change
chmn—chairman
citricult—citriculture
class—classical
climat—climatological, climatology
clin(s)—clinic(s), clinical
cmndg—commanding
Co—County
Co—Companies, Company
co-auth—co-author
co-dir—co-director
co-ed—co-editor
co-educ—co-education, co-educational
col(s)—college(s), collegiate, colonel
collab—collaboration, collaborative
collabr—collaborator

xviii

ABBREVIATIONS

Colo—Colorado
com—commerce, commercial
Comdr—Commander
commun—communicable, communication(s)
comn(s)—commission(s), commissioned
comndg—commanding
comnr—commissioner
comp—comparitive
compos—composition
comput—computation, computer(s), computing
comt(s)—committee(s)
conchol—conchology
conf—conference
cong—congress, congressional
Conn—Connecticut
conserv—conservation, conservatory
consol—consolidated, consolidation
const—constitution, constitutional
construct—construction, constructive
consult(s)—consult, consultant(s), consultantship(s), consultation, consulting
contemp—contemporary
contrib—contribute, contributing, contribution(s)
contribr—contributor
conv—convention
coop—cooperating, cooperation, cooperative
coord—coordinate(d), coordinating, coordination
coordr—coordinator
corp—corporate, corporation(s)
corresp—correspondence, correspondent, corresponding
coun—council, counsel, counseling
counr—councilor, counselor
criminol—criminological, criminology
cryog—cryogenic(s)
crystallog—crystallographic, crystallographical, crystallography
crystallogr—crystallographer
Ct—Court
Ctr—Center
cult—cultural, culture
cur—curator
curric—curriculum
cybernet—cybernetic(s)
cytol—cytological, cytology
Czech—Czechoslovakia, Czech Republic

DC—District of Columbia
Dec—December
Del—Delaware
deleg—delegate, delegation
delinq—delinquency, delinquent
dem—democrat(s), democratic
demog—demographic, demography
demogr—demographer
demonstr—demontrator
dendrol—dendrologic, dendrological, dendrology
dent—dental, dentistry
dep—deputy
dept—department
dermat—dermatologic, dermatological, dermatology

develop—developed, developing, development, developmental
diag—diagnosis, diagnostic
dialectol—dialectological, dialectology
dict—dictionaries, dictionary
Dig—Digest
dipl—diploma, diplomate
dir(s)—director(s), directories, directory
dis—disease(s), disorders
Diss Abst—Dissertation Abstracts
dist—district
distrib—distributed, distribution, distributive
distribr—distributor(s)
div—division, divisional, divorced
DNA—deoxyribonucleic acid
doc—document(s), documentary, documentation
Dom—Dominion
Dr—Drive

E—East
ecol—ecological, ecology
econ(s)—economic(s), economical, economy
economet—econometric(s)
ECT—electroconvulsive or electroshock therapy
ed—edition(s), editor(s), editorial
ed bd—editorial board
educ—education, educational
educr—educator(s)
EEG—electroencephalogram, electroencephalographic, electroencephalography
Egyptol—Egyptology
EKG—electrocardiogram
elec—electric, electrical, electricity
electrochem—electrochemical, electrochemistry
electroph—electrophysical, electrophysics
elem—elementary
embryol—embryologic, embryological, embryology
emer—emeriti, emeritus
employ—employment
encour—encouragement
encycl—encyclopedia
endocrinol—endocrinologic, endocrinology
eng—engineering
Eng—England, English
engr(s)—engineer(s)
enol—enology
Ens—Ensign
entom—entomological, entomology
environ—environment(s), environmental
enzym—enzymology
epidemiol—epidemiologic, epidemiological, epidemiology
equip—equipment
ERDA—Energy Research & Development Administration
ESEA—Elementary & Secondary Education Act
espec—especially
estab—established, establishment(s)
ethnog—ethnographic, ethnographical, ethnography
ethnogr—ethnographer

ethnol—ethnologic, ethnological, ethnology
Europ—European
eval—evaluation
Evangel—Evangelical
eve—evening
exam—examination(s), examining
examr—examiner
except—exceptional
exec(s)—executive(s)
exeg—exegeses, exegesis, exegetic, exegetical
exhib(s)—exhibition(s), exhibit(s)
exp—experiment, experimental
exped(s)—expedition(s)
explor—exploration(s), exploratory
expos—exposition
exten—extension

fac—faculty
facil—facilities, facility
Feb—February
fed—federal
fedn—federation
fel(s)—fellow(s), fellowship(s)
fermentol—fermentology
fertil—fertility, fertilization
Fla—Florida
floricult—floricultural, floriculture
found—foundation
FPO—Fleet Post Office
Fr—French
Ft—Fort

Ga—Georgia
gastroenterol—gastroenterological, gastroenterology
gen—general
geneal—genealogical, genealogy
geod—geodesy, geodetic
geog—geographic, geographical, geography
geogr—geographer
geol—geologic, geological, geology
geom—geometric, geometrical, geometry
geomorphol—geomorphologic, geomorphology
geophys—geophysical, geophysics
Ger—German, Germanic, Germany
geriat—geriatric
geront—gerontological, gerontology
Ges—Gesellschaft
glaciol—glaciology
gov—governing, governor(s)
govt—government, governmental
grad—graduate(d)
Gt Brit—Great Britain
guid—guidance
gym—gymnasium
gynec—gynecologic, gynecological, gynecology

handbk(s)—handbook(s)
helminth—helminthology
hemat—hematologic, hematological, hematology
herpet—herpetologic, herpetological, herpetology
HEW—Department of Health, Education & Welfare

xix

ABBREVIATIONS

Hisp—Hispanic, Hispania
hist—historic, historical, history
histol—histological, histology
HM—Her Majesty
hochsch—hochschule
homeop—homeopathic, homeopathy
hon(s)—honor(s), honorable, honorary
hort—horticultural, horticulture
hosp(s)—hospital(s), hospitalization
hq—headquarters
HumRRO—Human Resources Research Office
husb—husbandry
Hwy—Highway
hydraul—hydraulic(s)
hydrodyn—hydrodynamic(s)
hydrol—hydrologic, hydrological, hydrologics
hyg—hygiene, hygienic(s)
hypn—hypnosis

ichthyol—ichthyological, ichthyology
Ill—Illinois
illum—illuminating, illumination
illus—illustrate, illustrated, illustration
illusr—illustrator
immunol—immunologic, immunological, immunology
Imp—Imperial
improv—improvement
Inc—Incorporated
in-chg—in charge
incl—include(s), including
Ind—Indiana
indust(s)—industrial, industries, industry
Inf—Infantry
info—information
inorg—inorganic
ins—insurance
inst(s)—institute(s), institution(s)
instnl—institutional(ized)
instr(s)—instruct, instruction, instructor(s)
instrnl—instructional
int—international
intel—intellligence
introd—introduction
invert—invertebrate
invest(s)—investigation(s)
investr—investigator
irrig—irrigation
Ital—Italian

J—Journal
Jan—January
Jct—Junction
jour—journal, journalism
jr—junior
jurisp—jurisprudence
juv—juvenile

Kans—Kansas
Ky—Kentucky

La—Louisiana
lab(s)—laboratories, laboratory
lang—language(s)
laryngol—larygological, laryngology
lect—lecture(s)

lectr—lecturer(s)
legis—legislation, legislative, legislature
lett—letter(s)
lib—liberal
libr—libraries, library
librn—librarian
lic—license(d)
limnol—limnological, limnology
ling—linguistic(s), linguistical
lit—literary, literature
lithol—lithologic, lithological, lithology
Lt—Lieutenant
Ltd—Limited
m—married
mach—machine(s), machinery
mag—magazine(s)
maj—major
malacol—malacology
mammal—mammalogy
Man—Manitoba
Mar—March
Mariol—Mariology
Mass—Massechusetts
mat—material(s)
mat med—materia medica
math—mathematic(s), mathematical
Md—Maryland
mech—mechanic(s), mechanical
med—medical, medicinal, medicine
Mediter—Mediterranean
Mem—Memorial
mem—member(s), membership(s)
ment—mental(ly)
metab—metabolic, metabolism
metall—metallurgic, metallurgical, metallurgy
metallog—metallographic, metallography
metallogr—metallographer
metaphys—metaphysical, metaphysics
meteorol—meteorological, meteorology
metrol—metrological, metrology
metrop—metropolitan
Mex—Mexican, Mexico
mfg—manufacturing
mfr—manufacturer
mgr—manager
mgt—management
Mich—Michigan
microbiol—microbiological, microbiology
micros—microscopic, microscopical, microscopy
mid—middle
mil—military
mineral—mineralogical, mineralogy
Minn—Minnesota
Miss—Mississippi
mkt—market, marketing
Mo—Missouri
mod—modern
monogr—monograph
Mont—Montana
morphol—morphological, morphology
Mt—Mount
mult—multiple
munic—municipal, municipalities
mus—museum(s)
musicol—musicological, musicology
mycol—mycologic, mycology

N—North
NASA—National Aeronautics & Space Administration
nat—national, naturalized
NATO—North Atlantic Treaty Organization
navig—navigation(al)
NB—New Brunswick
NC—North Carolina
NDak—North Dakota
NDEA—National Defense Education Act
Nebr—Nebraska
nematol—nematological, nematology
nerv—nervous
Neth—Netherlands
neurol—neurological, neurology
neuropath—neuropathological, neuropathology
neuropsychiat—neuropsychiatric, neuropsychiatry
neurosurg—neurosurgical, neurosurgery
Nev—Nevada
New Eng—New England
New York—New York City
Nfld—Newfoundland
NH—New Hampshire
NIH—National Institute of Health
NIMH—National Institute of Mental Health
NJ—New Jersey
NMex—New Mexico
No—Number
nonres—nonresident
norm—normal
Norweg—Norwegian
Nov—November
NS—Nova Scotia
NSF—National Science Foundation
NSW—New South Wales
numis—numismatic(s)
nutrit—nutrition, nutritional
NY—New York State
NZ—New Zealand

observ—observatories, observatory
obstet—obstetric(s), obstetrical
occas—occasional(ly)
occup—occupation, occupational
oceanog—oceanographic, oceanographical, oceanography
oceanogr—oceanographer
Oct—October
odontol—odontology
OEEC—Organization for European Economic Cooperation
off—office, official
Okla—Oklahoma
olericult—olericulture
oncol—oncologic, oncology
Ont—Ontario
oper(s)—operation(s), operational, operative
ophthal—ophthalmologic, ophthalmological, ophthalmology
optom—optometric, optometrical, optometry
ord—ordnance
Ore—Oregon
org—organic

ABBREVIATIONS

orgn—organization(s), organizational
orient—oriental
ornith—ornithological, ornithology
orthod—orthodontia, orthodontic(s)
orthop—orthopedic(s)
osteop—osteopathic, osteopathy
otol—otological, otology
otolaryngol—otolaryngological, otolaryngology
otorhinol—otorhinologic, otorhinology

Pa—Pennsylvania
Pac—Pacific
paleobot—paleobotanical, paleobotany
paleont—paleontology
Pan-Am—Pan-American
parasitol—parasitology
partic—participant, participating
path—pathologic, pathological, pathology
pedag—pedagogic(s), pedagogical, pedagogy
pediat—pediatric(s)
PEI—Prince Edward Islands
penol—penological, penology
periodont—periodontal, periodontic(s)
petrog—petrographic, petrographical, petrography
petrogr petrographer
petrol—petroleum, petrologic, petrological, petrology
pharm—pharmacy
pharmaceut—pharmaceutic(s), pharmaceutical(s)
pharmacog—pharmacognosy
pharamacol—pharmacologic, pharmacological, pharmacology
phenomenol—phenomenologic(al), phenomenology
philol—philological, philology
philos—philosophic, philosophical, philosophy
photog—photographic, photography
photogeog—photogeographic, photogeography
photogr—photographer(s)
photogram—photogrammetric, photogrammetry
photom—photometric, photometrical, photometry
phycol—phycology
phys—physical
physiog—physiographic, physiographical, physiography
physiol—physiological, phsysiology
Pkwy—Parkway
Pl—Place
polit—political, politics
polytech—polytechnic(s)
pomol—pomological, pomology
pontif—pontifical
pop—population
Port—Portugal, Portuguese
Pos—Position
postgrad—postgraduate
PQ—Province of Quebec
PR—Puerto Rico
pract—practice
practr—practitioner
prehist—prehistoric, prehistory

prep—preparation, preparative, preparatory
pres—president
Presby—Presbyterian
preserv—preservation
prev—prevention, preventive
prin—principal
prob(s)—problem(s)
proc—proceedings
proctol—proctologic, proctological, proctology
prod—product(s), production, productive
prof—professional, professor, professorial
Prof Exp—Professional Experience
prog(s)—program(s), programmed, programming
proj—project(s), projection(al), projective
prom—promotion
protozool—protozoology
Prov—Province, Provincial
psychiat—psychiatric, psychiatry
psychoanal—psychoanalysis, psychoanalytic, psychoanalytical
psychol—psychological, psychology
psychomet—psychometric(s)
psychopath—psychopathologic, psychopathology
psychophys—psychophysical, psychophysics
psychophysiol—psychophysiological, psychophysiology
psychosom—psychosomatic(s)
psychother—psychoterapeutic(s), psychotherapy
Pt—Point
pub—public
publ—publication(s), publish(ed), publisher, publishing
pvt—private

Qm—Quartermaster
Qm Gen—Quartermaster General
qual—qualitative, quality
quant—quantitative
quart—quarterly
Que—Quebec

radiol—radiological, radiology
RAF—Royal Air Force
RAFVR—Royal Air Force Volunteer Reserve
RAMC—Royal Army Medical Corps
RAMCR—Royal Army Medical Corps Reserve
RAOC—Royal Army Ordnance Corps
RASC—Royal Army Service Corps
RASCR—Royal Army Service Corps Reserve
RCAF—Royal Canadian Air Force
RCAFR—Royal Canadian Air Force Reserve
RCAFVR—Royal Canadian Air Force Volunteer Reserve
RCAMC—Royal Canadian Army Medical Corps
RCAMCR—Royal Canadian Army Medical Corps Reserve
RCASC—Royal Canadian Army Service Corps

RCASCR—Royal Canadian Army Service Corps Reserve
RCEME—Royal Canadian Electrical & Mechanical Engineers
RCN—Royal Canadian Navy
RCNR—Royal Canadian Naval Reserve
RCNVR—Royal Canadian Naval Volunteer Reserve
Rd—Road
RD—Rural Delivery
rec—record(s), recording
redevelop—redevelopment
ref—reference(s)
refrig—refrigeration
regist—register(ed), registration
registr—registrar
regt—regiment(al)
rehab—rehabilitation
rel(s)—relation(s), relative
relig—religion, religious
REME—Royal Electrical & Mechanical Engineers
rep—represent, representative
Repub—Republic
req—requirements
res—research, reserve
rev—review, revised, revision
RFD—Rural Free Delivery
rhet—rhetoric, rhetorical
RI—Rhode Island
Rm—Room
RM—Royal Marines
RN—Royal Navy
RNA—ribonucleic acid
RNR—Royal Naval Reserve
RNVR—Royal Naval Volunteer Reserve
roentgenol—roentgenologic, roentgenological, roentgenology
RR—Railroad, Rural Route
Rte—Route
Russ—Russian
rwy—railway

S—South
SAfrica—South Africa
SAm—South America, South American
sanit—sanitary, sanitation
Sask—Saskatchewan
SC—South Carolina
Scand—Scandinavia(n)
sch(s)—school(s)
scholar—scholarship
sci—science(s), scientific
SDak—South Dakota
SEATO—Southeast Asia Treaty Organization
sec—secondary
sect—section
secy—secretary
seismog—seismograph, seismographic, seismography
seismogr—seismographer
seismol—seismological, seismology
sem—seminar, seminary
Sen—Senator, Senatorial
Sept—September
ser—serial, series
serol—serologic, serological, serology
serv—service(s), serving

xxi

ABBREVIATIONS

silvicult—silvicultural, silviculture
soc(s)—societies, society
soc sci—social science
sociol—sociologic, sociological, sociology
Span—Spanish
spec—special
specif—specification(s)
spectrog—spectrograph, spectrographic, spectrography
spectrogr—spectrographer
spectrophotom—spectrophotometer, spectrophotometric, spectrophotometry
spectros—spectroscopic, spectroscopy
speleol—speleological, speleology
Sq—Square
sr—senior
St—Saint, Street(s)
sta(s)—station(s)
stand—standard(s), standardization
statist—statistical, statistics
Ste—Sainte
steril—sterility
stomatol—stomatology
stratig—stratigraphic, stratigraphy
stratigr—stratigrapher
struct—structural, structure(s)
stud—student(ship)
subcomt—subcommittee
subj—subject
subsid—subsidiary
substa—substation
super—superior
suppl—supplement(s), supplemental, supplementary
supt—superintendent
supv—supervising, supervision
supvr—supervisor
supvry—supervisory
surg—surgery, surgical
surv—survey, surveying
survr—surveyor
Swed—Swedish
Switz—Switzerland
symp—symposia, symposium(s)
syphil—syphilology
syst(s)—system(s), systematic(s), systematical

taxon—taxonomic, taxonomy
tech—technical, technique(s)
technol—technologic(al), technology
tel—telegraph(y), telephone
temp—temporary
Tenn—Tennessee
Terr—Terrace
Tex—Texas
textbk(s)—textbook(s)
text ed—text edition
theol—theological, theology
theoret—theoretic(al)
ther—therapy
therapeut—therapeutic(s)
thermodyn—thermodynamic(s)
topog—topographic, topographical, topography
topogr—topographer
toxicol—toxicologic, toxicological, toxicology
trans—transaction(s)
transl—translated, translation(s)
translr—translator(s)
transp—transport, transportation
treas—treasurer, treasury
treat—treatment
trop—tropical
tuberc—tuberculosis
TV—television
Twp—Township

UAR—United Arab Republic
UK—United Kingdom
UN—United Nations
undergrad—undergraduate
unemploy—unemployment
UNESCO—United Nations Educational Scientific & Cultural Organization
UNICEF—United Nations International Childrens Fund
univ(s)—universities, university
UNRRA—United Nations Relief & Rehabilitation Administration
UNRWA—United Nations Relief & Works Agency
urol—urologic, urological, urology
US—United States
USAAF—US Army Air Force
USAAFR—US Army Air Force Reserve
USAF—US Air Force
USAFR—US Air Force Reserve
USAID—US Agency for International Development
USAR—US Army Reserve
USCG—US Coast Guard
USCGR—US Coast Guard Reserve
USDA—US Department of Agriculture
USMC—US Marine Corps
USMCR—US Marine Corps Reserve
USN—US Navy
USNAF—US Naval Air Force
USNAFR—US Naval Air Force Reserve
USNR—US Naval Reserve
USPHS—US Public Health Service
USPHSR—US Public Health Service Reserve
USSR—Union of Soviet Socialist Republics

Va—Virginia
var—various
veg—vegetable(s), vegetation
vent—ventilating, ventilation
vert—vertebrate
Vet—Veteran(s)
vet—veterinarian, veterinary
VI—Virgin Islands
vinicult—viniculture
virol—virological, virology
vis—visiting
voc—vocational
vocab—vocabulary
vol(s)—voluntary, volunteer(s), volume(s)
vpres—vice president
vs—versus
Vt—Vermont

W—West
Wash—Washington
WHO—World Health Organization
WI—West Indies
wid—widow, widowed, widower
Wis—Wisconsin
WVa—West Virginia
Wyo—Wyoming

Yearbk(s)—Yearbook(s)
YMCA—Young Men's Christian Association
YMHA—Young Men's Hebrew Association
Yr(s)—Year(s)
YT—Yukon Territory
YWCA—Young Women's Christian Association
YWHA—Young Women's Hebrew Association

zool—zoological, zoology

AMERICAN MEN & WOMEN OF SCIENCE

G

GAAFAR, SAYED MOHAMMED, VETERINARY PARASITOLOGY. *Current Pos:* RETIRED. *Personal Data:* b Tanta, Egypt, Jan 18, 24; nat US; m 49; c 4. *Educ:* Cairo Univ, BVSc, 44; Kans State Col, MS, 49, PhD, 50; Agr & Mech Col Tex, DVM, 55. *Honors & Awards:* Fel, NSH, 64; Career Develop Award, NIH, 68; Japanese Soc Prom Sci Award, 87. *Prof Exp:* Veterinarian, Vet Serv, Egypt, 44-46; asst parasitologist, Vet Path Lab, Egypt, 46-47, parasitologist, 50-51; veterinarian, Rutheford Vet Hosp, 52-54; instr, Agr & Mech Col Tex, 55-56, asst prof, 56-58; asst prof vet sci, Purdue Univ, 58-60, assoc prof, 60-63, prof parasitol, 63-90. *Concurrent Pos:* Vis prof, King Saud Univ, Saudi Arabia, Zagagig Univ, Egypt & Osaka Preferred Univ, Safai City, Osaka, Japan; consult & vis prof, Karestart Univ, Bangkok, Thailand; chief ed, Vet Parasitol. *Mem:* Am Soc Trop Med & Hyg; Am Asn Pathologists; Am Asn Vet Parasitologists; Am Soc Parasitol; Am Vet Med Asn; World Fed Parasitologists; World Asn Advan Vet Parasitol; World Vet Asn; Coun Biol Eds. *Res:* Resistance against parasites as affected by dietary supplements and other organisms; surveys on parasitic infestations; immunopathology of helminth parasites in domestic animals; biology of ectoparasitism in domestic animals; immunology of ectoparasitism. *Mailing Add:* 2620 Newman Rd West Lafayette IN 47906

GAAL, ILSE LISL NOVAK, SYMBOLIC LOGIC, ALGEBRA. *Current Pos:* lectr, 64-78, RES ASSOC, UNIV MINN, 60-, ASSOC PROF MATH, 78- *Personal Data:* b Vienna, Austria, Jan 17, 24; nat US; m 52; c 2. *Educ:* Hunter Col, AB, 44; Radcliffe Col, MA, 44, PhD(math), 48. *Prof Exp:* Asst, Mass Eye & Ear Infirmary, 44-46; instr math, Wellesley Col, 48-50; Jewett fel, 50-52; instr, Cornell Univ, 52-53, asst prof, 54-59; res assoc, Yale Univ, 59-60. *Concurrent Pos:* Pres, NCent Sect, Math Asn Am, 85-86. *Mem:* Am Math Soc; Math Asn Am; Asn Symbolic Logic; Asn Women Math; Sigma Xi. *Res:* Mathematical logic; Galois theory. *Mailing Add:* Math Dept Univ Minn 127 Vincent Hall Minneapolis MN 55455

GAAL, ROBERT A P, PETROLEUM GEOLOGY, ENGINEERING GEOLOGY. *Current Pos:* RETIRED. *Personal Data:* b Los Angeles, Calif, Mar 31, 29; m 53, Margaret Lorraine Stephens. *Educ:* Univ Calif, Los Angeles, BA, 53; Univ Southern Calif, MA, 58, PhD(geol), 66. *Prof Exp:* Regional petrol geologist, REDECO, Philippines, 59-61; marine geologist, Allan Hancock Found, 61-62; instr geol, Whittier Col, 62-64; cur mineral, Natural Hist Mus, Los Angeles County, 62-66; staff scientist & oceanogr, TRW Syst, 66-69, chief geologist, 69-73; res scientist gemology, Gemological Inst Am, 73-78; sr marine geologist, Calif State Lands Comn, 78-82, geophysicist, 82-93. *Concurrent Pos:* Res assoc, Natural Hist Mus, Los Angeles County, 66-76; consult geol, various co, 73-97. *Mem:* Am Inst Mining & Metall; Sigma Xi; AAAS; Mineral Soc Am; Am Soc Oceanog (vpres, 69). *Res:* Instrumentation and techniques for detection and identification of properties of natural and synthetic gem materials, especially cathodoluminescence and thermoluminescence especially diamonds; marine geology; nearshore processes; oil seeps; shoreline erosion; marine minerals; offshore petroleum development and geothermal energy; petroleum geology. *Mailing Add:* 4408 Lucera Circle Palos Verdes Peninsula CA 90274

GAAL, STEVEN ALEXANDER, applied mathematics, for more information see previous edition

GAALSWYK, ARIE, APPLIED MATHEMATICS. *Current Pos:* assoc prof, 60-70, chmn dept, 75-80, PROF MATH, AUGUSTANA COL, SDAK, 70- *Personal Data:* b Alvord, Iowa, June 14, 18; m 43; c 3. *Educ:* Luther Col, BA, 42; Univ Wis, MS, 47; Univ Minn, PhD(math), 63. *Prof Exp:* Instr math, Luther Col, 47-48; prin scientist, Mech Div, Gen Mills, Inc, Minn, 50-59; res assoc math, Univ Minn, 59-60. *Concurrent Pos:* Consult, Raven Indust, SDak, 60- *Mem:* Am Math Soc; Am Meteorol Soc. *Res:* Combustion shock waves; mathematical models for problems in mechanics and geophysics. *Mailing Add:* Dept Math Augustana Col Sioux Falls SD 57197-0001

GAAR, KERMIT ALBERT, JR, MEDICAL PHYSIOLOGY. *Current Pos:* from asst prof to assoc prof, 69-77, PROF PHYSIOL, SCH MED, LA STATE UNIV, SHREVEPORT, 77-, DIR ANIMAL CARE, 70- *Personal Data:* b Tyler, Tex, Jan 24, 34; m 58; c 4. *Educ:* Univ Miss, BS(biol) & BS(pharm), 58; Univ Ark, MS, 65, PhD(physiol), 67. *Prof Exp:* From instr to asst prof physiol, Sch Med, Univ Miss, 67-69. *Mem:* Am Physiol Soc. *Res:* Dynamics of control of the body fluids, particularly the microcirculatory and interstitial fluid dynamics as these relate to the pulmonary circulation and pulmonary edema formation. *Mailing Add:* Dept Physiol & Biophys La State Univ Med Ctr PO Box 33932 Shreveport LA 71130-3932

GAARDER, NEWELL THOMAS, ELECTRICAL ENGINEERING. *Current Pos:* assoc prof, 67-76, PROF ELEC ENG, UNIV HAWAII, 76- *Personal Data:* b La Crosse, Wis, Feb 17, 39; m 63; c 1. *Educ:* Univ Wis, BA, 61; Stanford Univ, MS, 62, PhD(elec eng), 65. *Prof Exp:* Res engr, Stanford Res Inst, 63-65; asst prof, Cornell Univ, 65-67. *Mem:* AAAS; Inst Elec & Electronics Engrs. *Res:* Statistical decision theory; statistical communication theory; information sciences. *Mailing Add:* Univ Hawaii 2540 Dole St Honolulu HI 96844

GAARENSTROOM, STEPHEN WILLIAM, ANALYTICAL CHEMISTRY. *Current Pos:* SR STAFF RES SCIENTIST, GEN MOTORS RES & DEVELOP CTR, 77- *Personal Data:* b Minneapolis, Minn, Sept 20, 50; m 81, Nancy Maledon; c Dale & Amy. *Educ:* Carleton Col, BA, 72; Purdue Univ, PhD(anal chem), 77. *Concurrent Pos:* Assoc ed, J Vac Sci Technol, 86-88; ed bd, Surface & Interface Analyst, 89-95; div chmn, Am Vacuum Soc, 89-90; ed bd, J Electron Spectros, 91-; comt chmn, Am Soc Testing & Mat, 92-95; ed, Surface Sci Spectra, 95- *Mem:* AAAS; Am Soc Testing & Mat; Am Chem Soc; Am Vacuum Soc; Asn Anal Chemists; Am Soc Mat Int. *Res:* Surface analysis; electron spectroscopy; information content of spectra. *Mailing Add:* Dept Analytical Chem Gen Motors Res & Develop Ctr Warren MI 48090-9055. *Fax:* 810-986-0817

GABALLAH, SAEED S, BIOCHEMISTRY, MOLECULAR BIOLOGY. *Current Pos:* HEAD NEUROPSYCHIAT LAB, VET ADMIN HOSP, DOWNEY, 65- *Personal Data:* US citizen; m 60; c 3. *Educ:* Cairo Univ, BS, 46; Univ Wis, PhD(biochem), 54. *Prof Exp:* Asst prof, Cairo Univ, 55-57; res assoc biochem, Col Med, Univ Ill, 57-61, asst prof, 62-63; asst prof, Chicago Col Osteop, 63-65. *Mem:* AAAS; Brit Biochem Soc; Am Chem Soc; NY Acad Sci. *Res:* Medical and biological research, especially central nervous system; organ and cell structure. *Mailing Add:* 221 W Sheridan Pl Lake Bluff IL 60044

GABAY, JONATHAN GLENN, CUSTOM COMPUTER DESIGN, REAL TIME ACQUISITION & CONTROL. *Current Pos:* SR TECHNOL ED, MILLER FREEMAN PUBL, 90- *Personal Data:* b Queens, NY, Apr 10, 56; m 88. *Educ:* State Univ NY, Stony Brook, BSEE, 80. *Prof Exp:* Sr technol specialist, Tech Data Specialists, 78-81; sr design engr, Amecom Div, Litton Datalog, 81-84 & Add Div, NCR, 84-85; sr technol ed, Hearst Bus Publ, 85-88, VNU Publ, 88-89 & CMP Publ, 89-90. *Concurrent Pos:* Consult, Computer Design, 84-, Eagle Telephonics, 88-89, Hydro Systs, Plus Logic & Viewlogic, 90- & Melard Systs & Hydro Systs, 91- *Res:* Specialty computer system design; tactical and efficient computer/human interfaces and specialty applications; evaluating state-of-the-art computer aided engineering tools and services for ASICS, PLDs, PCB and other engineering related design automation tools. *Mailing Add:* 124 N Bicycle Path Selden NY 11784

GABAY, SABIT, BIOCHEMISTRY, PHARMACOLOGY. *Current Pos:* CONSULT. *Personal Data:* b Istanbul, Turkey, Mar 18, 22; nat US; div; c Irwin, Nelson & Janis. *Educ:* Galatasaray Col, Turkey, BA, 43; Istanbul Univ, BS, 46; Tex A&M Univ, MS, 54; Univ Madrid, PhD(biochem), 58. *Hon Degrees:* Dr, Mex Nat Inst Culture, Col Behav Sci, 76. *Honors & Awards:* Gold Medal Award, Soc Biol Psych, 82. *Prof Exp:* Res asst, Tex A&M Univ, 53-54; res biochemist, Univ Southern Calif, 55-59; sr res biochemist, Columbia Univ & Rockland State Hosp, 59-61; chief biochem res labs, Vet Admin Med Ctr, Brockton, Ma, 61-85. *Concurrent Pos:* Del Amo Found sr res fel, Univ Madrid, Postgrad Med Sch, 57-59; travel award, Sweden, Denmark, Spain, Italy, USSR, ROMANIA, France, Hungary, Japan, Mexico, Arg, Venezuela, Turkey, Can & Nigeria, 58-85; secy-gen, Int Conf Phenothiazine Metab, France, 62; asst prof, Boston Univ, 62-70; consult, Mo Psychiat Inst, 68-74 & Marcy State Hosp, 70-80; asst prof pharmacol, Harvard Univ, Sch Dent Med, 70-77; Nat Acad Sci exchange prof, Romanian Univs, 71; secy-gen exec comt, World Fedn Biol Psychiat, 74-78; vis prof neuropharm, Ahmadu Bello Univ, Zaria, Nigeria, 77, Ramon & Cajal Ctr, Madrid, Spain, 83; adj prof psychiat, Brown Univ, 78-88; adj prof biochem, Univ VI, St Thomas, 86-92; chmn, Int Biomed Adv Group, 93- *Mem:* Soc Biol Psychiat (pres, 76); Int Soc Neurochem; Int Soc Biochem Pharmacol; Am Soc Neurochem; Asn Res Nerv & Ment Dis; fel Am Col Neuropsychopharmacol; Am Soc Exp Pharmacol & Therapeut; Am Soc Biochem & Molecular Biol. *Res:* Neurobiochemistry; biochemical psychopharmacology and neuropharmacology encompassing drug enzymology and their metabolic mechanisms; molecular pharmacology; drug-protein binding; development of neuropharmacologic agents. *Mailing Add:* 1001 Cloverlea Rd Ruxton MD 21204-6812. *Fax:* 410-832-8777

GABB, TIMOTHY PAUL, LOW CYCLE FATIGUE, THERMAL MECHANICAL FATIGUE. *Current Pos:* RES METALLURGIST, LEWIS RES CTR, NASA, 83- *Personal Data:* b Thibodaux, La, Jan 22, 58. *Educ:* La State Univ, BS, 81, MS, 83; Case Western Reserve Univ, PhD(mat sci), 88. *Mem:* Metall Soc. *Res:* The mechanical property/microstructural relationships of advanced high temperature materials; metallic and metal matrix composite materials. *Mailing Add:* 6474 Willow Dr Cleveland OH 44131

GABBARD, FLETCHER, NUCLEAR PHYSICS. *Current Pos:* from asst prof to assoc prof, Univ Ky, 59-70, prof physics, 70-89, chmn, Dept Physics & Astron, 73-85, EMER PROF PHYSICS, UNIV KY, 89- *Personal Data:* b Sand Gap, Ky, Sept 13, 30; m 57; c 2. *Educ:* Univ Ky, BS, 51; Rice Univ, MA, 57, PhD(physics), 59. *Prof Exp:* Physicist, US Naval Ord Lab, 51-52 & Nat Bur Stand, 52-53. *Mem:* AAAS; Am Phys Soc; Sigma Xi; Am Asn Physics Teachers. *Res:* Energy levels in light nuclei; neutron induced reactions; neutron producing reactions in medium weight nuclei. *Mailing Add:* 350 Lakes Creek Rd Mc Kee KY 40447. *E-Mail:* fgabb@harold.eastky.com

GABBARD, GLEN OWENS, PSYCHOANALYSIS, PSYCHOTHERAPY. *Current Pos:* Resident psychiat, Karl Menninger Psychiat, 75-78, staff psychiatrist, C F Menninger Hosp, 78-84, sect chief, 84-89, med dir, 89-94, vpres clin, 91-94, CALLAWAY DISTINGUISHED PROF, KARL MENNINGER SCH PSYCHIAT, 94- *Personal Data:* b Charleston, Ill, Aug 8, 49; 1985, Joyce Davidson. *Educ:* Eastern Ill Univ, BS, 72; Rush Univ, MD, 75. *Honors & Awards:* Sigmund Freud Award, Am Soc Psychoanal Physicians, 92; Distinguished Lectr Award, Am Psychiat Asn, 95; Burlingame Award, Inst Living, 97; Strecker Award, Inst Pa. *Concurrent Pos:* Clin prof psychiat, Sch Med, Univ Kans, 91-; assoc ed, J Am Psychoanal Asn, 94-; vis lectr, Harvard Med Sch, 96-97; vchair, Comn Psychother, Am Psychiat Asn, 96-; C. *Mem:* Fel Am Psychiat Asn; fel Am Col Psychiatrists; Am Col Psychoanalysts; AMA; Am Psychoanal Asn. *Res:* Length of stay in psychiatric hospital patients and link to outcome; psychotherapy of borderline personality disorder; major textbooks on treatments of psychiatric disorders; psychodynamic psychiatry; borderline personality disorder. *Mailing Add:* Menninger Clin Box 829 Topeka KS 66601-0829

GABBE, JOHN DANIEL, PHYSICS. *Current Pos:* RETIRED. *Personal Data:* b Johannesburg, Rep SAfrica, JulY 19, 29; m 56; c 2. *Educ:* NY Univ, BA, 50, PhD(physics), 57; Univ Ill, MS, 51. *Prof Exp:* Mem tech staff, AT&T Bell Labs, 56-97. *Mem:* Am Phys Soc; Am Asn Artificial Intelligence; Int Neurol Net Soc. *Res:* Machine learning and intelligent computerized design aids; geophysics, statistical data analysis; associative memory retrieval. *Mailing Add:* 14 Laurelwood Dr Little Silver NJ 07739

GABBIANI, GIULIO, CYTOSKELETON, WOUND HEALING. *Current Pos:* asst prof, 69-75, PROF PATH, DEPT PATH, UNIV GENEVA, SWITZ, 75- *Personal Data:* b Cremona, Italy, Mar 19, 37; m 63; c 3. *Educ:* Univ Pavia, Italy, MD, 61; Inst Exp Med & Surg, Univ Montreal, Can, PhD(endocrinol), 65. *Prof Exp:* Asst prof, Inst Exp Med & Surg, Univ Montreal, Can, 65-67 & 68-69; res assoc, Dept Path, Harvard Med Sch, Boston, 67-68. *Mem:* Am Asn Pathologists; Am Soc Cell Biol; Int Acad Path; NY Acad Sci; Soc Exp Biol & Med; Swiss Soc Cellular & Molecular Biol. *Res:* Biology of cytoskeletal elements, acting in particular, in relation to wound healing and vascular pathology. *Mailing Add:* Dept Path Univ Geneva CMU One ru Michel Servet Geneva 4 CH-1211 Switzerland. *Fax:* 4122-702-5746

GABEL, ALBERT A, VETERINARY SURGERY. *Current Pos:* RETIRED. *Personal Data:* b Fremont, Ohio, Mar 3, 30; m 54; c 6. *Educ:* Ohio State Univ, DVM, 54, MSc, 59; dipl, Am Col Vet Surg. *Honors & Awards:* Borden Award, 54. *Prof Exp:* Ambulatory clinician vet med, Col Vet Med, Ohio State Univ, 54-55, instr, 57-60, from asst prof to prof vet surg, 60-89. *Concurrent Pos:* Univ develop fund grant, 58-59; Wyeth Lab res grant, 61-63; chmn eng res group, Ohio State Univ, Col Vet Med. *Mem:* Am Col Vet Surg; Am Vet Med Asn. *Res:* Anesthesia and orthopedics of horses; exercise physiology in horses; evaluation of fitness; experimental training methods and effects of drugs on performance. *Mailing Add:* 7190 Coffman Rd Dublin OH 43017

GABEL, JAMES RUSSEL, PROTOZOOLOGY, NATURAL HISTORY. *Current Pos:* RETIRED. *Personal Data:* b Pottstown, Pa, Aug 21, 18; m 44; c 1. *Educ:* Pa State Col Lock Haven, BS, 47; Univ Pa, PhD(zool), 53. *Prof Exp:* Asst instr zool, Univ Pa, 47-53; asst prof, Fisk Univ, 53-56; assoc prof, WLiberty State Col, 56-59; from asst prof to prof biol, San Francisco State Univ, 59-84. *Mem:* Nature Conserv; Mountain Lion Preserv Asn; Nat Wildlife Fed. *Res:* Protozoan parasitology; histology; desert biology; tarantula studies. *Mailing Add:* 440 Monticello St San Francisco CA 94127-2861

GABEL, JOSEPH C, LYMPHATIC SYSTEMS. *Current Pos:* PROF & CHMN ANESTHESIOL, MED SCH, UNIV TEX, 80- *Educ:* Ohio State Univ, MD, 64. *Res:* Mechanisms, causes and therapy of pulmonary edema. *Mailing Add:* Dept Anesthesiol Univ Calif Sch Med 10833 Box 951778 Los Angeles CA 90095-1778. *Fax:* 310-794-6047

GABEL, RICHARD ALLEN, ORGANIC CHEMISTRY. *Current Pos:* RES CHEMIST ORG CHEM, DIV SYNTEX, ARAPAHOE CHEM, INC, 78- *Personal Data:* b Sterling, Colo, Nov 4, 46; m 70; c 3. *Educ:* Colo State Univ, BS, 69, PhD(org chem), 79; Univ Wis-Madison, MS, 71. *Mem:* Am Chem Soc. *Res:* Displacement of methoxyl group by carbon, nitrogen, oxygen and silicon nucleophiles on o-methoxyphenyloxazolines; regio specific motalation and introduction of an electrophile or addition of a nucleaphile followed by oxidation of pyridyloxazolines. *Mailing Add:* Syntex Chemicals Inc 2075 N 55th St Boulder CO 80301-2803

GABELMAN, IRVING J(ACOB), ELECTRONICS, COMPUTER SCIENCE. *Current Pos:* PRES, TECH ASSOCS, 76- *Personal Data:* b Brooklyn, NY, Nov 12, 18; m 49, Leah; c Alan & Philip. *Educ:* Brooklyn Col, BA, 38; City Col New York, BEE, 45; Polytech Inst Brooklyn, MEE, 48; Syracuse Univ, PhD(elec eng), 61. *Prof Exp:* Radio engr, Watson Labs, Red Bank, NJ, US Dept Air Force, 45-51; electronic scientist, Rome Air Develop Ctr, Griffiss AFB, 51-59, dir advan studies, 59-66, chief plans, 67-70, chief scientist, 71-76. *Concurrent Pos:* US mem, avionics panel, Adv Group Aeronaut Res & Develop, NATO, 63-69, dep chmn, 69-71, chmn, 71- *Mem:* Fel AAAS; fel Inst Elec & Electronics Engrs. *Res:* Switching circuits, especially threshold element logical design; electronic computers. *Mailing Add:* 225 Dale Rd Rome NY 13440

GABELMAN, JOHN WARREN, GEOPHYSICS & GEOCHEMISTRY, STRATIGRAPHY & SEDIMENTATION. *Current Pos:* PRES, JOHN W GABELMAN & ASSOCS INC, 83- *Personal Data:* b Manila, Philippine Islands, May 18, 21; US citizen; m 45, Olive A Thompson; c Barbara G (Williams) & Joan L (Brink). *Educ:* Colo Sch Mines, Geol Eng, 43, MS, 48, DSc, 49. *Honors & Awards:* Cert Merit, Energy Minerals Div, Am Asn Petrol Geologists, 93; Pres Award, Am Asn Petrol Geologists-Energy Minerals Div, 95. *Prof Exp:* Jr mining engr, NJ Zinc Co, 43-44, jr geologist, 46; tech mate, USN, 44-46; instr geol, Colo Sch Mines, 46-49; geologist, Colo Fuel & Iron Corp, 49-51; geologist, Western Mining Dept, Am Smelting & Refining Co, 52-54; dist geologist, Grand Junction Opers Off, US AEC, 54-58, geologist adv Latin-Am, Div Raw Mat, 58-61, chief, Resource Appraisal Br, 61-71, staff engr, Div Prod & Mat Mgt, 71-73, prog mgr geothermal, Div Appl Technol, 73-75; mgr explor res, Utah Int Inc, San Francisco, 75-83. *Concurrent Pos:* US AEC rep, Fed Map Coord Comt, 64-73, Panel; chair Uranium Subcomt, Geosat Comt, Inc, 75-83, vpres, Geosat Comt, 80-83; chair Uranium Comt, Energy Minerals Div, Am Asn Petrol Geol, 75-83 Uranium Geol, Int Atomic Energy Agency, 68-73 & Coun Environ Qual, 72-73. *Mem:* Fel Geol Soc Am; emer mem Am Asn Petrol Geologists; Soc Mining Engrs; fel Soc Econ Geologists; Am Geophys Union; Asn Explor Geochemists; Legion of Honor. *Res:* Mineral ore deposition, structural geology, aerial mapping, tectonics, metallotectonics, spectral remote sensing and mineralogy/petrography by optical and electron microscopy; author of 118 technical publications. *Mailing Add:* 23 Portland Ct Danville CA 94526

GABELMAN, WARREN HENRY, PLANT GENETICS. *Current Pos:* from asst prof to assoc prof, 49-60, chmn dept, 65-73, PROF HORT, UNIV WIS-MADISON, 60- *Personal Data:* b Tilden, Nebr, Apr 18, 21; m 45, Alberta Timmas. *Educ:* Univ Nebr, BSc, 42; Yale Univ, PhD, 49. *Hon Degrees:* DSc, Univ Nebr, 76; Dr, Krakow Agr Univ, 88. *Honors & Awards:* Marion Meadows Award, Am Soc Hort Sci, 66, 69, 73 & 79; Genetics & Plant Breeding Award, Nat Coun Com Plant Breeders, 80. *Prof Exp:* Asst hort, Exp Sta, Univ Nebr, 38-42; fel, Plant Genetics Chg Veg Breeding Prog, Conn Exp Sta, 46-49. *Concurrent Pos:* Vchmn, Vegetable Systs Deleg China, Comt Scholarly Commun with People's Repub China, Nat Acad Sci, 77; mem, USDA Plant Genetic Resources Bd, 75-81. *Mem:* Fel AAAS; fel Am Soc Hort Sci (pres, 78-79); Genetics Soc Am; Crop Sci Soc; Sigma Xi. *Res:* Cytoplasmic inheritance of male sterility in corn, onions, beets, and carrots; biosynthesis of carotenes in carrots; genetics of mineral nutrition efficiencies in higher plants; betalaine synthesis in beets. *Mailing Add:* 1133 Risser Rd Madison WI 53705. *Fax:* 608-262-4743

GABELNICK, HENRY LEWIS, CHEMICAL & BIOMEDICAL ENGINEERING. *Current Pos:* dir extramural progs, Contraceptive Res & Develop Conrad prog, 86-89, dep dir, Conrad Prog, 89-90, PROF OBSTET-GYNEC, EASTERN VA MED SCH, 86-, DIR CONRAD PROG, 90- *Personal Data:* b Boston, Mass, May 10, 40; m 87, Clare Donaher; c Deborah, Tamar & Joel. *Educ:* Mass Inst Technol, BS, 61, MS, 62; Princeton Univ, PhD(chem eng), 66. *Prof Exp:* Sr chem engr, Res Dept, Monsanto Co, Mass, 66-68; chem engr, Biomed Eng Br, NIH, 68-75, biomed engr, Contraceptive Develop Br, 75-86. *Concurrent Pos:* Expert consult, UN Develop Prog, Haifa, Israel, 73, WHO Spec Prog Human Reproduction, 78- *Mem:* Am Inst Chem Engrs; Am Chem Soc; NY Acad Sci; Sigma Xi; Am Pub Health Asn. *Res:* Kinetics of drug distribution in vivo; biomaterials; drug delivery systems; formulation of contraceptive drugs; development of barrier contraceptives; prevention of heterosexual transmission of human immunodefiency virus and other sexually transmitted diseases. *Mailing Add:* 11612 Danville Dr North Bethesda MD 20852-3716. *Fax:* 703-524-4770; *E-Mail:* hgabelnick@conrad.org

GABER, BRUCE PAUL, PHYSICAL BIOCHEMISTRY. *Current Pos:* dept head, Biomolecular Eng Br, 84-90, DEPT HEAD, CTR BIOMOLECULAR SCI & ENG, 90- *Personal Data:* b Chicago, Ill, Oct 15, 41; m 66, 85; c 2. *Educ:* Hendrix Col, BA, 63; Univ Southern Calif, PhD(biochem), 68. *Prof Exp:* Fel, IBM Watson Res Lab, Columbia Univ, 68-70 & IBM T J Watson Res Ctr, 70-71; asst prof chem, Univ Mich, Dearborn, 71-75; sr res assoc chem, Univ Ore, 75-77; res assoc prof biochem, Sch Med, Univ Va, 77-80; consult, 77-80; staff scientist biophys optics sect, Naval Res Lab, Wash, DC, 80-84. *Mem:* Biophys Soc; Am Soc Biochem & Molecular Biol; Molecular Graphics Soc; Sigma Xi. *Res:* Physical biochemistry of biomembranes; molecular modeling of membranes; protein engineering. *Mailing Add:* Interactions Prog Ctr Biol Molecular Sci & Eng Naval Res Lab Code 6930 Washington DC 20375-0001. *Fax:* 202-404-8897

GABIS, DAMIEN ANTHONY, FOOD MICROBIOLOGY. *Current Pos:* Assoc dir, 71-73, vpres, 73-87, PRES, SILLIKER LABS, 87-, CHIEF EXEC OFFICER, 90- *Personal Data:* b Steubenville, Ohio, Feb 26, 42; m 65; c 3. *Educ:* Col Steubenville, BA, 64; Univ Ky, MS, 67; NC State Univ, PhD(food sci), 70. *Concurrent Pos:* Adj assoc prof biol, Ill Inst Technol, 78- *Mem:* Am Soc Microbiol; Inst Food Technologists; Can Soc Microbiol; Int Asn Milk, Food & Environ Sanit; Am Mgt Asn. *Res:* Analytical methods of detection of salmonella and all Enterobacteriaceae in foods; campylobacter. *Mailing Add:* Silliker Labs Group Inc 900 Maple Rd Homewood IL 60430

GABLE, JAMES JACKSON, JR, INTERNAL MEDICINE. *Current Pos:* RETIRED. *Personal Data:* b Oklahoma City, Okla, Apr 3, 18; m 41; c 5. *Educ:* Univ Okla, BS, 40, MD, 42; Am Bd Internal Med, dipl, 53. *Prof Exp:* From asst prof to assoc prof, Sch Med, Univ Okla, 50-72, clin prof med, 72- *Concurrent Pos:* Attend physician, Vet Admin Hosp, 53-; chief med serv, Presby Hosp, 62-67, mem trustees, 64. *Mem:* Fel Am Col Physicians; NY Acad Sci. *Res:* Clinical aspects of internal medicine. *Mailing Add:* 2618 NW 65th St Oklahoma City OK 73116-4921

GABLE, MICHAEL F, INVERTEBRATE BIOLOGY, AMPHIPOD TAXONOMY. *Current Pos:* From asst prof to assoc prof, 72-82, PROF BIOL, EASTERN CONN STATE UNIV, 82- *Personal Data:* b Lancaster, Pa, June 1, 45. *Educ:* Univ Fla, BS, 67; Univ NH, MS, 69, PhD(zool), 72. *Concurrent Pos:* Consult; curtorial affil, Yale Peabody Mus, 88- *Mem:* Am Soc Parasitologists; Crustacean Soc; Soc Integrative & Comp Biol; Sigma Xi. *Res:* Systematics of Bermuda marine amphipod crustaceans. *Mailing Add:* Dept Biol Eastern Conn State Univ Willimantic CT 06226-2295. *Fax:* 860-465-5213; *E-Mail:* gable@ecsu.ctstateu.edu

GABLE, RALPH WILLIAM, PHYSICAL CHEMISTRY. *Current Pos:* AT DEPT CHEM, EASTERN MICH UNIV. *Personal Data:* b San Antonio, Tex, Sept 27, 29; m 53; c 3. *Educ:* Univ Tex, BS, 50; Duke Univ, MA, 53, PhD(phys chem), 56. *Prof Exp:* From asst prof chem to assoc prof, Pfeiffer Col, 55-60, head dept, 55-60; from asst prof to assoc prof, 60-83, PROF CHEM, DAVIDSON COL, 83- *Concurrent Pos:* Res assoc, Fla State Univ, 68-69; vis scientist, Oak Ridge Nat Lab, 78-79; proj seraphim, fel, Dept Chem, Eastern Mich Univ, 85-86. *Mem:* AAAS; Am Chem Soc; Am Asn Univ Prof; NY Acad Sci; AAAS. *Res:* Ion exchange; water structure; water pollution; chemical education; history of chemistry; computers. *Mailing Add:* PO Box 537 Davidson NC 28036

GABLER, ROBERT EARL, PHYSICAL GEOGRAPHY. *Current Pos:* RETIRED. *Personal Data:* b Lodi, Ohio, Nov 22, 27; m 50; c 3. *Educ:* Univ Ohio, BS, 49; Pa State Univ, MS, 51; Columbia Univ, EdD(sci), 57. *Prof Exp:* High sch teacher, Ohio, 50-55; lectr geog, Hunter Col, 55-57; from asst prof to prof, Western Ill Univ, 57-90, chmn dept, 64-74, dir, NDEA Geog Inst, 65-68, dir int progs, 77-90. *Concurrent Pos:* Consult, Geog Inst Progs, US Off Educ, 65-66; dir coord, Nat Coun Geog Educ, 63-69; mem nominating comt, 68-69, const revision comt, 68-, mem exec bd, 69-, mem joint comt, Nat Coun Geog Educ-Asn Am Geog, 70- *Mem:* Asn Am Geogr. *Res:* Physical geography, especially physiography, with strong regional interests in the geography of Asia; application of geography in American education. *Mailing Add:* 711 E Piper St Macomb IL 61455

GABLER, WALTER LOUIS, BIOCHEMISTRY. *Current Pos:* assoc prof, 69-74, PROF ORAL BIOL & BIOCHEM, DENT SCH, UNIV ORE, 74-, AFFIL BIOCHEM MED SCH, 71-, CHMN BIOCHEM, DENT SCH. *Personal Data:* b Chicago, Ill, May 30, 31; m 52; c 4. *Educ:* Northwestern Univ, DDS, 56, PhD(chem), 64. *Prof Exp:* Instr pedodont, Dent Sch, Northwestern Univ, 58-59, instr biochem, 60-64; asst prof biochem pedodont, Dent Sch, Univ Ore, 64-65, assoc prof, 65-67; assoc prof, Univ Ky, 67-69. *Concurrent Pos:* Nat Heart Inst fel, 61-64; Pharmaceut Mfrs Asn grant, 70-71; Advan Inst Dent Res grant, 71; partic, Northwest Environ Health Conf, 71; Epilepsy Found Am grant, 71-72; vis scientist, Ore Regional Primate Res Ctr. *Mem:* AAAS; Int Asn Dent Res; NY Acad Sci. *Res:* Biochemistry of inflammation; metabolism of collagen; drug metabolism during pregnancy. *Mailing Add:* 2 Bartok Pl Lake Oswego OR 97035

GABLIKS, JANIS, VIROLOGY, TOXICOLOGY. *Current Pos:* RETIRED. *Personal Data:* b Nitaure, Latvia, Nov 1, 24; nat US; m 50, Lilija Bune; c Ingrid & Nora. *Educ:* Baltic Univ, Ger, DDS, 49; Rutgers Univ, MS, 57, PhD, 63. *Prof Exp:* Dent surgeon, Int Refugee Orgn Eutin, Ger, 49-51; asst path & virol, E R Squibb & Sons, NJ, 52-55; asst biochem, Bur Biol Res, Rutgers Univ, 56-57; res assoc virol, Schering Co, 57-60; instr bact, Rutgers Univ, 60-63; asst prof cell biol, Mass Inst Technol, 63-67; assoc prof biol, Northeastern Univ, 67-74, prof, 74-89. *Concurrent Pos:* Res assoc, Nat Inst Environ Health, 74-75; vis scientist, Latriau Univ, Riga, 87, 89. *Mem:* Am Soc Microbiol; NY Acad Sci; Sigma Xi; AAAS; Tissue Cult Asn. *Res:* Bacterial toxins; carcinogens; nutrition and viral infections; insecticides; fish viruses; application of cell cultures in toxicology, viral vaccines, antiviral agents; influenza virus. *Mailing Add:* 103 Cabot St Newton MA 02158

GABOR, ANDREW JOHN, NEUROLOGY, NEUROPHYSIOLOGY. *Current Pos:* DIR EEG LAB, SACRAMENTO MED CTR & PROF NEUROL, SCH MED, UNIV CALIF, DAVIS, 69- *Personal Data:* b Budapest, Hungary, July 2, 35; m 61; c 3. *Educ:* George Washington Univ, BA, 56, MS, 58; Duke Univ, PhD(anat), 62, MD, 64. *Prof Exp:* Instr neuroanat, Med Ctr, Duke Univ, 62-64 & 66, resident neurol, 65-67; clin assoc, EEG & Clin Neurophysiol Br, NIH, 67-69. *Mem:* Am Neurol Asn; Am Acad Neurol; Am Epilepsy Soc; Am EEG Soc. *Res:* Clinical neurology and clinical and electrographic manifestations of seizure disorders; cortical organization with special reference to the underlying mechanisms of epilepsy. *Mailing Add:* Dept Neurol Univ Calif Davis Med Ctr 2315 Stockton Blvd Sacramento CA 95817-2201

GABOR, JOHN DEWAIN, CHEMICAL ENGINEERING. *Current Pos:* Asst chem engr, 57-64, CHEM ENGR, ARGONNE NAT LAB, 64- *Personal Data:* b Chicago, Ill, Aug 8, 32; m 61, Mary L Dickinson; c Cathryn C & John D. *Educ:* Univ Ill, BS, 54; Cornell Univ, PhD(chem eng), 57. *Concurrent Pos:* Vis assoc prof, Univ Ill, Chicago Circle, 79-86. *Mem:* Am Inst Chem Engrs. *Res:* Fluidization; heat transfer; fluid mechanics; process development for nuclear fuel reprocessing; chemical reactors; nuclear reactor safety. *Mailing Add:* Argonne Nat Lab D331 9700 S Cass Ave Argonne IL 60439. *Fax:* 630-252-7139

GABOR, THOMAS, PHYSICAL CHEMISTRY, SOL-GEL. *Current Pos:* res specialist, 69-81, SR RES SPECIALIST, CERAMIC TECHNOL CTR, INDUST & ELECTRONIC SECT & INDUST CONSUMER SECT, CENT RES LABS, 3M CO, 81- *Personal Data:* b Budapest, Hungary, June 28, 25; US citizen; m 63, Janet Hecht; c Allen & Andrew. *Educ:* Univ Sci, Hungary, BSc, 48; Univ London, PhD(phys chem), 59. *Prof Exp:* Res chemist org chem, Alco Gand, Belg, 49-50; Taubmans Chems Co, Australia, 51-52 & Monsanto Chem Co, Australia, 53-54; chemist res labs, Westinghouse Elec Corp, 60-63 & Battelle Mem Inst, 64-69. *Res:* Crystal growth; surface chemistry; cvo, fiber coating, sol-gel. *Mailing Add:* 2667 Meyer Ln St Paul MN 55119. *Fax:* 612-733-0648

GABOUREL, JOHN DUSTAN, PHARMACOLOGY. *Current Pos:* from assoc prof to prof, 64-89, EMER PROF PHARMACOL, MED SCH, UNIV ORE, 89- *Personal Data:* b San Francisco, Calif, Oct 16, 28; m 51, Carol Roberts; c Michele, Linda, Allison, Candice & John. *Educ:* Univ Calif, BS, 50; Univ San Francisco, MS, 51; Univ Rochester, PhD(pharmacol), 57. *Prof Exp:* Res assoc, Atomic Energy Proj, Univ Rochester, 55-57; from instr to asst prof pharmacol, Med Sch, Stanford Univ, 57-64. *Concurrent Pos:* Consult toxicol, Univ Rochester, 56-; vis prof, Walter & Eliza Hall, Inst Med Res, Melbourne, Australia, 73-74. *Mem:* Am Soc Pharmacol & Exp Therapeut. *Res:* Cancer research; immunosuppressants, drug effects on lymphocyte function; adrenal steroid effects on lymphoid tissue growth and metabolism; metabolism of atropine; anticonvulsants; ocular pharmacology; effects of vitamin A and other retinoids on cultured retinal pigment epthiliem; particular interest in differences between cultures derived from persons with inherited dystrophies such as retinitis pigmentosa. *Mailing Add:* 6825 SW Raleighwood Way Univ Ore Med Sch Portland OR 97225

GABRIDGE, MICHAEL GREGORY, MICROBIOLOGY. *Current Pos:* PRES & CHIEF EXEC OFFICER, UNIV TECHNOL CORP, 96- *Personal Data:* b Detroit, Mich, Mar 12, 43; m 65; c 2. *Educ:* Mich State Univ, BS, 65, MS, 66; Univ Mich, PhD(microbiol), 71. *Prof Exp:* Res microbiologist, US Pub Health Serv, 67-68; asst prof microbiol, Med Sch, Univ Ill, 71-76, assoc prof, 76-80; sr scientist cell biol, Cell Sci Ctr, Lake Placid, NY, 80-96. *Concurrent Pos:* Vis scientist infectious dis, Clin Res Ctr, London, 77-78; curric coordr basic med sci, Med Sch, Univ Ill, 78-80; adj prof, Dept Path, Med Sch, Univ Vt, 80-83, Dept Biol, State Univ NY, Plattsburgh, 80-; pres, Bionique, Inc, 82-90; dir, Biotech Inst, Univ Fla, 90- *Mem:* Am Soc Microbiol; Tissue Cult Asn; Am Asn Univ Profs; AAAS; Sigma Xi. *Res:* Pathogenesis of respiratory infections; trachea explant culture; mycoplasmas; in-vitro models for cytotoicity, instrumentation for tissue culture. *Mailing Add:* Univ Technol Corp 3101 Iris Ave Boulder CO 80301

GABRIEL, BARBRA L, ELECTRON MICROSCOPY, PROTEIN BIOPHYSICS. *Current Pos:* ASSOC PROF, JAMES MADISON UNIV, 92- *Personal Data:* b Chicago, Ill, Dec 28, 53. *Educ:* Elmhurst Col, BS, 75; Univ Chicago, PhD(biophys), 88. *Prof Exp:* Asst prof physics, Elmhurst Col, 77-88; res assoc, Univ Pa, 88-89 & Univ Va, 89-91; dir electron micros, Musculoskeletal Sci Res Inst, 91-92. *Concurrent Pos:* Consult educ, Argonne Nat Lab, 77-82; dir electron micros, Packer Eng, 81-86. *Mem:* Biophys Soc; Electron Micros Soc Am. *Res:* Structural analysis of proteins using electron microscopy. *Mailing Add:* Rte 2 Box 457 Elkton VA 22827

GABRIEL, CEDRIC JOHN, SOLID STATE PHYSICS. *Current Pos:* RETIRED. *Personal Data:* b Gustine, Calif, Mar 25, 35; m 64; c 2. *Educ:* Fresno State Col, AB, 56; Univ Calif, Berkeley, PhD(physics), 64. *Prof Exp:* Res physicist, Naval Ord Lab, Corona, 64-70; res physicist, Naval Ocean Systs Ctr, 70-95. *Mem:* AAAS; Am Phys Soc. *Res:* Nuclear quadrupole resonance spectroscopy; magnetoptics in solids; photo detection; chemical dynamics. *Mailing Add:* 3778A Balboa Terr San Diego CA 92117

GABRIEL, EDWARD GEORGE, GENETICS, CELL BIOLOGY. *Current Pos:* ASSOC PROF BIOL, LYCOMING COL, WILLIAMSPORT, PA, 77- *Personal Data:* b Batavia, NY, Jan 26, 46; m 70; c 4. *Educ:* Alfred Univ, BA, 68, MS, 69; Ohio State Univ, MS, 74, PhD(genetics), 77. *Concurrent Pos:* Genetic counr, Williamsport Hosp, 78- *Mem:* Genetics Soc Am; AAAS; Am Genetics Soc. *Res:* NOR staining of squirrel chromosomes; chromosome banding techniques in humans. *Mailing Add:* Lycoming Col 700 College Pl Lycoming Col Williamsport PA 17701-5157

GABRIEL, EDWIN Z, COMPUTER SCIENCE, ENERGY TECHNOLOGY & MATERIAL HANDLING. *Current Pos:* PRES & OWNER, GABRIEL COMPUT CO & GABRIEL ENG CONSULTS, 73- *Personal Data:* b Union City, NJ, Aug 26, 13; m 46, Dorothy Draper. *Educ:* Newark Col Eng, BSME, 36, ME, 39, MSEE, 52. *Prof Exp:* Heating engr, Webster Tallmadge & Co, NJ, 38-39; efficiency & mech engr, Prudential Ins Co Am, 39-41; asst mech engr, US Engr Off, NY, 41-42, Manhattan dist, Mass, 42-43; assoc mech engr, Watson Labs, USAF, NJ, 45-48, Cambridge Res Ctr, 48-50; electronic engr, Signal Corps Eng Labs, NJ, 50-52; proj engr, Curtiss-Wright Corp, 52-53; proj engr & consult, Kearfott Co, Inc, 53-55; asst prof elec eng, Univ Lehigh, 55-56; asst prof elec & mech eng, Villanova Univ, 56-60; asst prof elec eng, Fairleigh Dickinson Univ, 60-62; assoc prof, Weapons Dept, US Naval Acad, 62-64; writing textbk, 64-65; independent comput design, develop & mfr, 65; proj engr avionics lab, Electronics Command, US Army, 65-73. *Concurrent Pos:* Teacher physics, Monmouth Univ, 78-79. *Mem:* Am Soc Mech Engrs; Am Soc Eng Educ; Inst Elec & Electronics Engrs; Am Helicopter Soc. *Res:* Study and design of automatic controls and analog and digital components and systems; use of teaching aids for effective presentation of the principles in math, physics and electric circuit analysis; personnel rescuing and cargo retrieval apparatus; educational computers for high school and college teachers and students; eye pointing and head tracking control system; granted 30 US patents. *Mailing Add:* 91 Mt Tabor Way Ocean Grove NJ 07756

GABRIEL, GARABET J(ACOB), ELECTRICAL ENGINEERING, PHYSICS. *Current Pos:* asst prof, 65-69, ASSOC PROF ELEC ENG, UNIV NOTRE DAME, 69-, STAFF MEM, RADIATION LAB, 65- *Personal Data:* b Basrah, Iraq, Feb 15, 35; US citizen. *Educ:* St Louis Univ, BS, 56; Ill Inst Technol, MS, 60; Northwestern Univ, PhD(elec eng, physics), 64. *Prof Exp:* Engr, Motorola Inc, Ill, 56-57; instr elec eng, Ill Inst Technol, 57-61; res asst microwave physics, Northwestern Univ, 61-64; staff scientist, Hallicrafters Co, 64-65. *Concurrent Pos:* Res assoc, Res Inst, Chicago Med Sch, 60. *Mem:* Inst Elec & Electronics Engrs. *Res:* Electromagnetic and applied mathematics; theoretical and experimental work on microwaves and optics; statistical electrodynamics; high speed electromagnetic transients on superconducting coils and boundaries; statistical theoretical analysis of radiation scattering in fluctuating media. *Mailing Add:* Dept Elec Comp Eng Univ Notre Dame Notre Dame IN 46556

GABRIEL, JOHN R, APPLIED MATHEMATICS, COMPUTER SCIENCE. *Current Pos:* vis res fel, Solid Sci Div, Argonne Nat Lab, 62-65, asst head, Comput Ctr, Appl Math Div, 65-69, assoc comput scientist, 69-80, comput scientist, 80-87, sci adv, Comput Appln Ctr, 87-93, SCI ADV, SPEC TECHNOL, DECISION & INFO SCI DIV, ARGONNE NAT LAB, 93- *Personal Data:* b Leeds, Eng, Apr 30, 31; c 2, Marian Howe; c Mary A & Catherine L. *Educ:* Univ Otago, NZ, BS(pure & appl math) & BS(physics & radio physics), 52, MS, 53. *Prof Exp:* Asst lectr physics, Univ Otago, NZ, 54-55, Imp Chem Industs fel, 55-57; theoret physicist, Inst Nuclear Sci, NZ, 57-58; sr spec res fel theoret physics, UK Atomic Energy Authority, Eng, 58-62. *Concurrent Pos:* Independent consult; mem bd dir, MH Gabriel & Assoc Inc. *Mem:* Fel Brit Inst Physics & Phys Soc; Inst Elec & Electronics Engrs Comput Soc; Inst Elec & Electronics Engrs; Asn Comput Mach; NY Acad Sci. *Res:* Data fusion; automated inference systems for plant design and safety qualification; data management for small businesses; group theory and quantum mechanics; numerical linear algebra; military intelligence; organizational cybernetics. *Mailing Add:* MH Gabriel & Assoc 19W 680 97th St Lemont IL 60439. *Fax:* 630-739-5577; *E-Mail:* gabriel@eid.anl.gov

GABRIEL, KAIGHAM (KEN) J, MICROELECTROMECHANICAL SYSTEMS, ROBOTIC SYSTEMS. *Current Pos:* DIR, ELECTRON TECHNOL OFF, DEFENSE ADVAN RES PROJ AGENCY, VA, 91- *Educ:* Univ Pittsburgh, BS, 77; Mass Inst Technol, MS, 79, ScD, 83. *Prof Exp:* Mem tech staff, Photonic Networks & Components Res Dept, Mach Perception Res Dept & Robotic Systs Res Dept, AT&T Bell Labs, 85-91. *Concurrent Pos:* Vis assoc prof, Inst Indust Sci, Univ Tokyo, 89-90; mem staff, Naval Res Labs Nanoelectron Process Facil. *Res:* Photonic networks; nanoelectronics. *Mailing Add:* Electron Technol Off Defense Advan Res Proj Agency 3701 N Fairfax Dr Arlington VA 22203-1714

GABRIEL, KARL LEONARD, PHARMACOLOGY, TOXICOLOGY. *Current Pos:* CONSULT. *Personal Data:* b Philadelphia, Pa, July 27, 29; wid; c Sandra L, Carol A (Jones), David J, Debra L (Evans) & Carolyn B. *Educ:* Univ Pa, AB, 51, VMD, 56; Jefferson Med Col, PhD, 64; Drexel Inst Technol, MS, 65. *Prof Exp:* Asst dir, Indust Biol Res & Testing Lab, Inc, Pa, 56-61; vpres & dir res, AME Assocs, 65-66; assoc prof biol sci & environ eng, Drexel Inst Technol, 66-71; from assoc prof to prof pharmacol, Med Col Pa, 71-84, assoc prof community & preventive med & res assoc prof psychiat, 80-84. *Concurrent Pos:* From instr to asst prof, Sch Vet Med, Univ Pa, 60-65; vis asst prof, Med Col Pa, 65-71; pres, Biosearch, Inc, 68-; dipl, Am Bd Toxicol; consult var chem & pharmaceut co. *Mem:* Soc Toxicol; Am Soc Pharmacol & Exp Therapeut; NY Acad Sci; Am Asn Lab Animal Sci; Sigma Xi; fel Am Col Clin Pharm. *Res:* General pharmacology-toxicology; biomathematics; pesticide toxicology and carcinogenicity; product safety evaluations; skin pharmacology and toxicology. *Mailing Add:* PO Box 368 Ft Washington PA 19034-0368. *Fax:* 215-423-9210

GABRIEL, LESTER H, CIVIL ENGINEERING. *Current Pos:* from asst prof to assoc prof civil eng, 57-67, chmn dept, 63-68, PROF CIVIL ENG, CALIF STATE UNIV, SACRAMENTO, 67- *Personal Data:* b Brooklyn, NY, Mar 17, 28; m 50; c 2. *Educ:* Cooper Union, BSCE, 49; Polytech Inst Brooklyn, MSCE, 56; Univ Calif, Berkeley, PhD, 71. *Prof Exp:* Civil engr, US Bur Reclamation, 49-51; struct engr, Farkas & Barron, 51-52 & Severud-Elstad-Krueger, 52-55; sr struct engr, Kaiser Engrs, 55-57. *Concurrent Pos:* Dir, Appl Res & Design Ctr, NSF sci fel, Calif, 61-; mem comt on soil-struct interaction, Transp Res Bd, Nat Acad Sci-Nat Res Coun, 64-76. *Mem:* Am Soc Civil Engrs; Am Concrete Inst; Am Soc Eng Educ. *Res:* Soil structure interaction for static and dynamic loads on buried structures; concrete materials and materials of manufacture. *Mailing Add:* 4841 Tono Way Sacramento CA 95841-4338

GABRIEL, MORDECAI LIONEL, BIOLOGY, ACADEMIC ADMINISTRATION. *Current Pos:* instr, Brooklyn Col, 45-50, from asst prof to prof biol, 50-89, chmn dept, 65-71, dean, Sch Sci, 71-77, actg vpres acad affairs, 81-82, assoc provost acad affairs, 82-89, EMER PROF BIOL, BROOKLYN COL, 89- *Personal Data:* b New York, NY, Mar 18, 18; m 45; c 2. *Educ:* Yeshiva Col, BA, 38; Columbia Univ, AM, 38, PhD(zool), 43. *Prof Exp:* Asst zool, Columbia Univ, 38-41, lectr, 41-42; instr genetics, Univ Conn, 43-45. *Concurrent Pos:* Fac fel, Ford Found, 54-55; vis prof, Columbia Univ, 55; Fulbright lectr, Tel-Aviv Univ, 59-60. *Mem:* AAAS; Soc Vert Paleont; Am Soc Zool; Soc Study Evolution; Am Asn Anat; NY Acad Sci. *Res:* Comparative myology of Plectognath fishes; meristic variation of fishes; embryology of polydactylism in fowl. *Mailing Add:* Dept Biol Brooklyn Col Brooklyn NY 11210

GABRIEL, OSCAR V, ATOMIC PHYSICS. *Current Pos:* SR ENGR, LOCKHEED MARTIN, 96- *Personal Data:* b Manila, Philippines, Apr 22, 46; m 73; c 1. *Educ:* Univ Philippines, BS, 66; Univ Pittsburgh, MS, 72, PhD(physics), 81. *Prof Exp:* Instr physics, Univ Philippines, 66-69; asst prof, Ateneo de Manila Univ, 73-78; asst prof physics, Univ Richmond, 81-83; Villanova Univ, 83-85; sr engr, GE Aerospace, 85-96. *Mem:* Am Phys Soc; Sigma Xi. *Res:* Theoretical study of inner-shell atomic processes at high energies by analytic perturbation theory and computer-assisted investigation of the same processes; radar systems engineering. *Mailing Add:* 202 Ramblewood Pkwy Mt Laurel NJ 08054

GABRIEL, R OTHMAR, BIOCHEMISTRY. *Current Pos:* RETIRED. *Personal Data:* b Vienna, Austria, Jan 10, 25; US citizen; m 49; c 2. *Educ:* Univ Vienna, PhD(chem), 54. *Prof Exp:* Res assoc biochem, Univ Vienna, 54-58; assoc, Med Ctr, Columbia Univ, 58-60; vis scientist, NIH, 60-64; res biochemist, Civil Serv, 64-65; clin asst prof, Med & Dent Sch, Georgetown Univ, 61-64; prof lectr, 64-65; assoc prof, 65-70, prof, 70-90, actg chmn, 86-88, emer prof biochem, 90. *Concurrent Pos:* Vol scientist, NIH, 90- *Mem:* Am Soc Biol Chemists. *Res:* Structure and function of carbohydrate containing cell surface components; precursors for the biosynthesis of polysaccharides; mechanism of enzyme action. *Mailing Add:* 7401 Westlake Terr Apt 1101 Bethesda MD 20817. *Fax:* 301-670-0425

GABRIEL, RICHARD FRANCIS, NUMERICAL ANALYSIS, DIFFERENTIAL EQUATIONS. *Current Pos:* dir, Comput Ctr, 62-72, prof, 72-87, EMER PROF MATH, SETON HALL UNIV, 87- *Personal Data:* b New Rochelle, NY, Nov 30, 20; m 48, Jeanne M French; c Michael J & Patricia M. *Educ:* Fordham Univ, AB, 43; Columbia Univ, MA, 47; Rutgers Univ, PhD(math), 55. *Prof Exp:* Instr math, Pub Sch, 46-47; educ therapist, Vet Admin, 47-48; instr math, St Francis Col, NY, 48-50; assoc prof & asst dir comput ctr, Rutgers Univ, 50-62. *Concurrent Pos:* NSF grant, 57; consult, Esso Res Eng Co & State Rehab Comput; chmn, NSF Numerical Analysis & Electronic Comput Conf, USAR, 58-62; prin investr, NIH Biomed Comput, Seton Hall Univ, 62-65; bd gov, Math Asn Am, 82-85. *Mem:* AAAS; Soc Indust & Appl Math; NY Acad Sci; Asn Comput Mach; Am Math Soc; Math Asn Am. *Res:* Complex variable; numerical analysis; electronic digital computers; evaluation of programming systems and equipment configurations. *Mailing Add:* 24 Gen Stanton Lane Charleston RI 02813

GABRIEL, TONY A, NUCLEAR PHYSICS. *Current Pos:* DIR, OAK RIDGE DETECTOR CTR, OAK RIDGE NAT LAB, 90-, GROUP LEADER, NUCLEAR ANALYSIS & SHIELDING SECT, ENG PHYSICS & MATH DIV, 93- *Personal Data:* b Nov 12, 42. *Honors & Awards:* Outstanding Serv Award, Protect & Shielding Div, Am Nuclear Soc, 85. *Mem:* Fel Am Phys Soc; Am Nuclear Soc. *Res:* Computer science; material science; fusion and fission reactor neutronics; radiation protection; cancer radiotherapy; detector development and analysis; artificial intelligence; non-nuclear fuel alternatives; high energy physics. *Mailing Add:* 9608 W Lyttleton Lane Knoxville TN 37922

GABRIEL, WILLIAM FRANCIS, ELECTRICAL ENGINEERING, ELECTROMAGNETICS. *Current Pos:* CONSULT S/F ASSOC, LANDOVER, MD, 86- *Personal Data:* b Sault Ste Marie, Mich, Oct 17, 25; m 48, Evelyn L; c Dean W & Linda A. *Educ:* Univ Wis, BS, 45, MS, 48, PhD(elec eng), 50. *Honors & Awards:* Microwave Prize, Inst Elec & Electronics Engrs, 66. *Prof Exp:* Electronic scientist, Naval Res Lab, 50-59; sr res engr, Stanford Res Inst, 59-61; consult, Aero Geo Astro Corp, Va, 61-64; sr engr, NASA Goddard Space Flight Ctr, Md, 64-67; engr, Scanwell Labs, Inc, Va, 67-69; mem staff, Delex Systs, Inc, Arlington, Va, 69-70; head, Antenna Systs Staff, Naval Res Lab, Washington, 70-86. *Concurrent Pos:* AP-S distinguished lectr, Inst Elec & Electronics Engrs, 80-82. *Mem:* Fel Inst Elec & Electronics Engrs; Aerospace & Electronic Syst Soc. *Res:* Adaptive array antenna systems; microwave components; instrumentation; superresolution spectral estimation techniques. *Mailing Add:* 3822 Parkland Dr Fairfax VA 22033

GABRIELE, ORLANDO FREDERICK, RADIOLOGY. *Current Pos:* RETIRED. *Personal Data:* b North Providence, RI, June 6, 27; m 60; c 4. *Educ:* Brown Univ, BA, 50; Yale Univ, MD, 54. *Prof Exp:* Instr radiol, Sch Med, Yale Univ, 57-59, lectr, 59-65, asst prof, 65-66; from assoc prof to prof, Sch Med, Univ NC, Chapel Hill, 66-72; prof radiol & chmn dept, WVa Univ, 72-89. *Mem:* Radiol Soc NAm; Am Col Radiol; Am Roentgen Ray Soc; Asn Univ Radiologists. *Res:* Cardiovascular radiology. *Mailing Add:* 5 Chapel Ridge Ct Pittsburgh PA 15238

GABRIELE, THOMAS L, ELECTRICAL ENGINEERING. *Current Pos:* dir software, 84-90, sr syts analyst, 90-92, ENG FEL, BECTON DICKINSON, 92- *Personal Data:* b York, Pa, Sept 7, 40; m 65; c 3. *Educ:* Lehigh Univ, BSEE, 62; Johns Hopkins Univ, MS, 64; PhD(elec eng), 68. *Prof Exp:* Eng specialist, Martin Marietta Corp, 66-67; prin engr, Commun Div, Bendix Corp, Baltimore, 67-80, supvr, comput aided design, 80-84. *Mem:* Inst Elec & Electronics Engrs. *Res:* Pattern recognition; automated decision systems; computer assisted analysis; microprocessor based systems design. *Mailing Add:* Becton Dickinson PO Box 999 Glencoe MD 21152

GABRIELSE, GERALD, ATOMIC PHYSICS. *Current Pos:* PROF PHYSICS, LYMAN LAB, HARVARD UNIV, 87- *Educ:* Calvin Col, BS, 73; Univ Chicago, MS, 75, PhD, 80. *Honors & Awards:* Manne Siegbahn Mem lectr, Stockholm, Sweden, 93. *Prof Exp:* Res assoc, Univ Wash, Seattle, 78-82, res asst prof, 82-85, from asst prof to assoc prof, 85-87. *Concurrent Pos:* Chaim Weizmann fel, 79-82; invited lectr, Int Conf Quantum Electronics XIV, 86, Optical Soc Am, 86 & 90, Am Phys Soc, 87 & 93, Univ Mo distinguished vis prof prog, 87, Italian Phys Soc, 91, AAAS, 93, Soc Physics Students, 93. *Res:* Atomic physics; author of 88 publications. *Mailing Add:* Lyman Lab Harvard Univ Cambridge MA 02138

GABRIELSE, HUBERT, GEOLOGY. *Current Pos:* Geologist, Geol Surv Can, 53-70, head, Cordilleran Subdiv, 70-79, res scientist, 79-91, EMER RES SCIENTIST, GEOL SURV CAN, 91- *Personal Data:* b Golden, BC, Mar 1, 26; m 55, Jean Freeman; c Peter & Nancy. *Educ:* Univ BC, BASc, 48, MASc, 50; Columbia Univ, PhD(geol), 55. *Honors & Awards:* J Willis Ambrose Medal, Geol Asn Can. *Mem:* Geol Soc Am; NY Acad Sci; fel Geol Asn Can; Royal Soc Can. *Res:* Regional stratigraphy, structure and tectonics. *Mailing Add:* 101-605 Robson St Vancouver BC V6B 5J3 Can. *Fax:* 604-666-1124

GABRIELSEN, ANN EMILY, IMMUNOLOGY. *Current Pos:* RETIRED. *Personal Data:* b Brooklyn, NY, Apr 18, 25. *Educ:* Brooklyn Col, BA, 46; Univ Minn, MA, 53, PhD(microbiol), 70. *Prof Exp:* Res fel pediat, Univ Minn, 61-67, res specialist, 67-70; prin res scientist immunol, Kidney Dis Inst, NY State Dept Health, 70-83. *Mem:* Am Asn Immunologists. *Res:* Complement; autoimmune disease. *Mailing Add:* Empire State Plaza Sta PO Box 2241 Albany NY 12220-0241

GABRIELSEN, BERNARD L, CIVIL & STRUCTURAL ENGINEERING. *Current Pos:* from asst prof to assoc prof, 65-77, prof, 77-, EMER PROF CIVIL ENG & CHMN, SAN JOSE STATE UNIV. *Personal Data:* b Woodland, Wash, May 29, 34; m 66, Shirley Stockland; c 3. *Educ:* Ore State Univ, BS, 56; Stanford Univ, MS, 61, PhD(civil eng), 66. *Prof Exp:* Engr-scientist, Lockheed Missiles & Space Co, 58-61; sr engr, Western Develop Labs, Philco Corp, 61-63; actg asst prof civil eng, Stanford Univ, 63-65. *Concurrent Pos:* Consult legal prof. *Mem:* Am Soc Civil Engrs; Am Concrete Inst; Am Acad Forensic Sci. *Res:* Structural research on the dynamic failure of building panels; application of statistics to structural problems. *Mailing Add:* 17255 Holiday Dr Morgan Hill CA 95037-6527

GABRIELSEN, BJARNE, ORGANIC CHEMISTRY. *Current Pos:* MEM ASSOC, DEPT CHEM, UNIV FLA, GAINESVILLE, 80- *Personal Data:* b Brooklyn, NY, Oct 22, 41. *Educ:* Wagner Col, BS, 62; State Univ NY Stony Brook, MS, 64, PhD(phys org chem), 69. *Prof Exp:* From instr to assoc prof chem, Wagner Col, 70-80. *Mem:* Am Chem Soc. *Res:* Synthesis of labelled organic compounds of biological interest; pyrilium/pyridinium chemistry, specifically modification of amino groups; new experiments in teaching organic chemistry; organic chemistry under high pressure. *Mailing Add:* 4222 Garnet Dr Middletown MD 21769-7543

GABRIELSEN, TRYGVE O, RADIOLOGY. *Current Pos:* from instr to assoc prof, 62-71, PROF RADIOL, MED SCH, UNIV MICH, ANN ARBOR, 71- *Personal Data:* b Vest-Agder, Norway, Mar 27, 30; US citizen; m 55; c 4. *Educ:* Univ Washington, BS, 53, MD, 56. *Honors & Awards:* Asn Univ Radiologists Travel Award, 68. *Prof Exp:* Asst chief diag radiol, Brooke Army Med Ctr, 60-62. *Mem:* Am Asn Neurol Surg; Radiol Soc NAm; Asn Univ Radiol; Am Soc Neuroradiol; Am Soc Head & Neck Radiol. *Res:* Diagnostic radiology, particularly neuroradiology. *Mailing Add:* Dept Radiol Univ Mich Ann Arbor MI 48109

GABRIELSON, RICHARD LEWIS, PLANT PATHOLOGY. *Current Pos:* From asst plant pathologist to assoc plant pathologist, 60-76, PLANT PATHOLOGIST, WESTERN WASH EXP STA, WASH STATE UNIV, 76- *Personal Data:* b Riverside, Calif, Feb 12, 31; div; c 4. *Educ:* San Diego State Col, BA, 52; Univ Calif, Davis, PhD(plant path), 61. *Mem:* Am Phytopath Soc; Sigma Xi. *Res:* Etiology, epidemiology and control of vegetable diseases. *Mailing Add:* 1800 E 67th St No 126 Tacoma WA 98404-4245

GABROVSKY, PETER N, THEORY OF COMPUTABILITY, LOGIC PROGRAMMING. *Current Pos:* ASSOC PROF, CALIF STATE UNIV, 89- *Personal Data:* b Sofia, Bulgaria, Nov 3, 44; US citizen; m 74, Pamela W Kemper; c Vanessa, Alexander, Natasha, Juliana & Isabella. *Educ:* Warsaw Univ, MS, 68; Syracuse Univ, PhD(comput sci), 76. *Prof Exp:* Programmer, US PX, 68-69; sr assoc programmer, IBM, 69-79; exec vpres, United Mo Bank, 79-85; assoc prof, Univ Maine, 85-89. *Concurrent Pos:* Ed, J Modern Logic, 89-94. *Mem:* Asn Comput Mach; Inst Elec & Electronics Engrs; Am Asn Artificial Intel. *Res:* Abstract theory of computability; various non-standard logics and their applications on computer programming. *Mailing Add:* Dept Comput Sci Calif State Univ Northridge CA 91330-8281. *Fax:* 818-677-2140

GABRUSEWYCZ-GARCIA, NATALIA, CELL BIOLOGY, CYTOLOGY. *Current Pos:* PROF BIOL, ONONDAGA COMMUNITY COL, 72- *Personal Data:* b Kiev, Ukraine, Nov 14, 34; US citizen; m 61, A Mariano; c Mariano S. *Educ:* Univ Sao Paulo, BS, 58; Columbia Univ, PhD(zool), 64. *Prof Exp:* Instr histol & cytol, Univ Sao Paulo, 58-59; res assoc pharmacol, State Univ NY Upstate Med Ctr, 64-72. *Concurrent Pos:* USPHS grant, 64-67. *Mem:* Am Soc Cell Biol. *Res:* Structure and nucleic acids metabolism of chromosomes, especially of polytene chromosomes. *Mailing Add:* Dept Biol Onondaga Community Col Syracuse NY 13215

GABUZDA, THOMAS GEORGE, HEMATOLOGY. *Current Pos:* from asst prof to assoc prof, 65-73, PROF MED, JEFFERSON MED COL, 73- *Personal Data:* b Freeland, Pa, Apr 27, 30; m 57; c 3. *Educ:* Lehigh Univ, BA, 51; Harvard Univ, MD, 55; Am Bd Internal Med, dipl, 63, cert hematol, 76, cert med oncol, 85. *Prof Exp:* From intern to asst resident med, Mass Gen Hosp, 55-57; USPHS fel, Med Dept B, Bispebjerg Hosp, Copenhagen, Denmark, 59-60; chief resident med, Lemuel Shattuck Hosp, Boston, 60-61; from res fel to res assoc, Med Sch, Harvard Univ, 61-64, instr, 64-65. *Concurrent Pos:* USPHS fel, Curtis Hemat Lab, Peter Bent Brigham Hosp, Boston, 61-63, asst med, Hosp, 61-64, jr assoc, 64-65; assoc mem, Cardeza Found Hemat Res, 65; chief, Div Hemat, Lankenau Hosp, Philadelphia, 70-95, chief, Div Hemat Onc, 95-; assoc med staff, Thomas Jefferson Univ Hosp, 75-; adj prof comp med, Sch Vet Med, Univ Pa, 75-81. *Mem:* Am Col Physicians; Am Soc Hemat; AMA; Am Fedn Clin Res. *Res:* Normal and abnormal hemoglobins; hemoglobin synthesis; ferritin; iron metabolism. *Mailing Add:* 164 N Latches Lane Bala Cynwyd PA 19004. *Fax:* 610-645-2262

GABY, WILLIAM LAWRENCE, BACTERIOLOGY. *Current Pos:* RETIRED. *Personal Data:* b Hot Springs, NC, June 15, 17; m 40; c 2. *Educ:* Univ Tenn, BA, 39, MS, 40; St Louis Univ, PhD(bact), 56; Am Bd Microbiol, dipl. *Honors & Awards:* Commercial Solvents Award, 52. *Prof Exp:* Sr bacteriologist, State Dept Pub Health, Tenn, 40-41; bacteriologist, Winthrop Chem Co NY, 41-42; sr bacteriologist, Bristol Labs, Inc, 46-49; from asst prof to assoc prof bact, Hahnemann Med Col & Hosp, 49-64; chmn, Dept Health Sci, ETenn State Univ, 64-80, prof microbiol, 64-83. *Mem:* AAAS; Am Soc Microbiol; Am Soc Biol Chemists; Am Asn Immunologists; fel Am Acad Microbiologists. *Res:* Dissociation of bacteria; antigen; antibody response; penicillin production and antibiotic activity; mold mutation and metabolism; lipid and phospholipid role in metabolism. *Mailing Add:* 1408 College Heights Dr Johnson City TN 37604-7124

GACS, PETER, INFORMATION THEORY. *Current Pos:* assoc prof, 84-92, PROF COMPUT SCI, BOSTON UNIV, 92- *Personal Data:* b Budapest, Hungary, May 9, 47; m 72; c 3. *Educ:* Roland Eotvos Univ, Budapest, MS, 70; J W Goeth Univ, WGer, PhD(math), 78. *Prof Exp:* Res assoc math, Math Inst Hungary Acad Sci, 70-77; asst prof, J W Goeth Univ, WGer, 77-78; res assoc comput sci, Stanford Univ, 79; asst prof math & comput sci, Univ Rochester, 80-84. *Concurrent Pos:* Vis prof, Institut fur Statistik, G August Univ, WGer, 75; vis scientist, IBM Almaden Res Ctr, 88-89, DIMACS, 92, CWI, Amsterdam, 93; var NSF grants. *Mem:* Asn Comput Mach; Am Math Soc; Inst Elec & Electronics Engrs. *Res:* Development of new techniques in Multi-terminal Information Theory (Shannon's Theory), including upper bound on common information; exact formulas connecting randomness tests with complexity; new ways to estimate descriptional complexity from below; fault-tolerant cellular automate. *Mailing Add:* Dept Comput Sci Boston Univ 111 Cummington St Boston MA 02215-2411

GADAMER, ERNST OSCAR, APPLIED MATHEMATICS. *Current Pos:* RETIRED. *Personal Data:* b Berlin, Ger, Nov 1, 24; Can citizen; m 54, Elisabeth Falkenbach; c Oliver & Alexander. *Educ:* Univ Frankfurt, dipl physics, 51; Univ Toronto, MA, 56, PhD(aerophys), 62. *Prof Exp:* Res fel, Inst Aerophys, Univ Toronto, 56-61; asst res officer hypersonics, Nat Res Coun Can, 61-62; asst prof eng anal, McMaster Univ, 62-77, assoc prof math sci, 77-90. *Concurrent Pos:* Data reduction engr, de Havilland Can Co, Ont, 58-59. *Res:* Low density aerodynamics; applied mathematics. *Mailing Add:* 37 Park St E Upper Floor Dundas ON L9H 1C9 Can

GADBERRY, HOWARD M(ILTON), TECHNOLOGY FORECASTING, CHEMICAL ENGINEERING. *Current Pos:* assoc chem engr, 46-50, sr chem engr, 50-54, head indust chem sect, 54-58, asst mgr, Div Chem & Chem Eng, 58-61, asst dir, Econ Develop Div, 61-63, SR ADV TECH, MIDWEST RES INST, 63- *Personal Data:* b Kansas City, Mo, July 25, 22; m 52; c 2. *Educ:* Univ Kans, BS, 43. *Prof Exp:* Chemist, Phillips Petrol Co, 43-46. *Mem:* Am Chem Soc; Am Inst Aeronaut & Astronaut; Sigma Xi; Am Asn Textile Chemists & Colorists; Am Ord Asn. *Res:* Advanced industrial technology; economic forecasting and modeling; energy resources and economics; technological forecasting; time-series analysis and forecasting; economic analysis of new technology; technology diffusion and history. *Mailing Add:* 4823 W 96th Terr Shawnee Mission KS 66207

GADDIS, MONICA LOUISE, CARDIOVASCULAR PHYSIOLOGY, EXERCISE PHYSIOLOGY. *Current Pos:* RES ASSOC PHYSIOL, BALL MEM HOSP, 92- *Personal Data:* b Toledo, Ohio, Nov 25, 55; m 79. *Educ:* Ind Univ, Bloomington, BS, 78, MS, 80, PhD(exercise physiol), 84. *Prof Exp:* Res assoc physiol, Sch Med, Ind Univ, 83-92. *Mem:* Am Physiol Soc. *Res:* Reflex control of venous capacitance; influences of chemoreceptor and baroreceptor control upon vascular capacitance. *Mailing Add:* 13885 W 58th Terr 2401 University Dr Shawnee KS 66216

GADDUM-ROSSE, PENELOPE, BIOLOGICAL STRUCTURE. *Current Pos:* Fel biol struct, 66-68, from res assoc to res asst prof, 69-74, asst prof, 74-81, ASSOC PROF BIOL STRUCT, SCH MED, UNIV WASH, 81- *Personal Data:* b Sept 4, 41; Brit citizen. *Educ:* Univ Wales, BSc, 62; Univ Liverpool, PhD(reprod physiol), 65. *Mem:* Am Asn Anat; Soc Study Reprod; Soc Study Fertil. *Res:* Mammalian fertilization; mechanisms of gamete transport. *Mailing Add:* Dept Biol Struct Univ Wash Sch Med SM-20 Seattle WA 98195

GADDY, JAMES LEOMA, CHEMICAL ENGINEERING. *Current Pos:* prof chem eng & head dept, 80-88, distinguished prof chem eng, 88-92, EMER DISTINGUISHED PROF CHEM ENG, UNIV ARK, 92-; PRES, BIOENGINEERING RESOURCES INC, 83- *Personal Data:* b Jacksonville, Fla, Aug 16, 32; m 52, Betty Maricella; c James & Teresa. *Educ:* La Polytech Univ, BS, 55; Univ Ark, MS, 68; Univ Tenn, PhD(chem eng), 72. *Honors & Awards:* Merck Lectr. *Prof Exp:* Process engr, Ethyl Corp, Baton Rouge, La, 55-60; eng supvr, Ark, La Gas, 60-64, proj mgr, 64-67; from assoc prof to prof chem eng, Univ Mo, Rolla, 67-80. *Concurrent Pos:* Consult, McDonnell Aircraft, 73-75, Aerojet Nuclear, 73-75, Monsanto Co, 73-75, UN, 77-79, Basler Hofmann, 77-78, Thermonetics Corp, 77-78, Banyon Eng, 77-78, Quaker Oats Co, 77-, Pritchard Co, 80-, Proctor & Gamble, 82-, Tenn Valley Authority, 83-, & Ethyl Corp, 83-; fac fel, Swiss Fed Inst Technol. *Mem:* Am Inst Chem Engrs; Am Chem Soc; AAAS; Am Soc Eng Educ; Sigma Xi. *Res:* Biochemical engineering; process analysis; author of over 500 publications. *Mailing Add:* Bioeng Resources Inc 1650 Emmaus Rd Fayetteville AR 72701. *Fax:* 501-521-2749; *E-Mail:* jlgaddy@aol.com

GADDY, OSCAR, ELECTRICAL ENGINEERING. *Current Pos:* res asst, Univ Ill, 59-62, from asst prof to prof, 62-93, assoc head dept, 71-84, EMER PROF ELEC ENG, UNIV ILL, URBANA-CHAMPAIGN, 93- *Personal Data:* b Republic, Mo, July 18, 32; m 53, Mary M Vaeth; c Oscar F, John A & William L. *Educ:* Univ Kans, BS, 57, MS, 59; Univ Ill, PhD(elec eng), 62. *Prof Exp:* Instr & res asst elec eng, Univ Kans, 57-59. *Mem:* Fel Inst Elec & Electronics Engrs; Sigma Xi. *Res:* Optical communication; quantum electronics; electron devices; infrared devices; subnanosecond optical pulse generation and detection. *Mailing Add:* 609 Evergreen Ct E Urbana IL 61801

GADE, DANIEL W, CULTURAL GEOGRAPHY & ECOLOGY, BIOGEOGRAPHY. *Current Pos:* from asst prof to assoc prof, 66-79, dir Latin Am studies, 78-87, PROF GEOG, UNIV VT, 79- *Personal Data:* b Niagara Falls, NY, Sept 28, 36; m 65, Mary Killgore; c Christopher P. *Educ:* Valparaiso Univ, BA, 59; Univ Ill, MA, 60; Univ Wis-Madison, MS, 62, PhD(geog), 67. *Prof Exp:* Vis instr geog, Univ Ore, 65-66. *Concurrent Pos:* Soc Sci Res Coun fel, Peru, 70; Nat Geog Soc res grant, Peru, 78; Fulbright res award, Madagascar, 83, Brazil, Arg, Uruguay, 93; Spain-US joint comt res grant, Spain, 88-89. *Mem:* Asn Am Geog; Conf Latin Am Geographers; Am Geog Soc; Soc Ethnobiol; Soc Econ Bot; Int Mountain Soc. *Res:* Past and present ecological relationships of primitive and folk societies; ethnobotany and ethnozoology; process of plant and animal domestication; Latin America; settlement geography; environmental conservation. *Mailing Add:* Dept Geog Old Mill Bldg Univ Vt Burlington VT 05405. *E-Mail:* dgade@zoo.uvm.edu

GADE, EDWARD HERMAN HENRY, III, MATHEMATICS. *Current Pos:* assoc prof math, 66-96, EMER PROF MATH, UNIV WIS, OSHKOSH, 96- *Personal Data:* b St Joseph, Mo, Feb 19, 36; m 60; c 2. *Educ:* Valparaiso Univ, BA, 58; Purdue Univ, MS, 60; Univ Pittsburgh, PhD(math), 65. *Res:* Summability methods analysis. *Mailing Add:* 1015 Maricopa Dr Oshkosh WI 54904

GADE, SANDRA ANN, PHYSICS. *Current Pos:* Asst prof, 66-74, assoc prof, 74-80, PROF PHYSICS, UNIV WIS, OSHKOSH, 80- *Personal Data:* b Waterbury, Conn, Oct 27, 37; m 60; c 2. *Educ:* Valparaiso Univ, BS; Univ Pittsburgh, PhD(physics), 66. *Mem:* Am Phys Soc. *Res:* Atomic physics; nuclear magnetic and electron paramagnetic resonance. *Mailing Add:* Dept Physics Univ Wis Oshkosh WI 54901. *Fax:* 920-424-7317

GADEBUSCH, HANS HENNING, MEDICAL MICROBIOLOGY. *Current Pos:* sr dir antibiotic eval & develop, 87-90, SR DIR MICROBIOL ADMIN, MERCK & CO, 90- *Personal Data:* b Charlottenburg, Ger, Jan 8, 24; nat US; m 49; c 7. *Educ:* Univ Detroit, BS, 49; Univ Mich, MS, 51, PhD, 65. *Prof Exp:* Asst bact, Univ Mich, 49-51; res microbiologist, Irwin, Neisler & Co, Ill, 51-53; clin bacteriologist, Detroit Dept Health, 53; chief bacteriologist, Vet Admin Hosp, 53-57, coordr gen med res, 57-62, head microbiol-immunol res sect, 57-66; chief med microbiol, Squibb Inst Med Res, 66-71, asst dir dept microbiol, 71-79; mgr, New Antibiotic Res, Merck Sharp & Dohme Res Labs, 79-87. *Mem:* AAAS; Am Soc Microbiol; Soc Exp Biol & Med; NY Acad Sci; fel Am Acad Microbiol; fel Infectious Dis Soc Am. *Res:* Microbiology; immunology; biochemistry; analytical chemistry; new drugs from nature research; animal models of human disease. *Mailing Add:* 711 Jade Rd Morrisville PA 19067-3011

GADEK, FRANK JOSEPH, ORGANIC CHEMISTRY. *Current Pos:* assoc prof, 68-80, PROF ORG CHEM, ALLENTOWN COL, 80- *Personal Data:* b Troy, NY, Oct 1, 41; m 70. *Educ:* Siena Col, NY, BS, 63; Cath Univ Am, PhD(org chem), 69. *Prof Exp:* Asst, Cath Univ Am, 68. *Concurrent Pos:* Frederick Gardner Cottrell res grant-in-aid, 71-72. *Mem:* Am Soc Enol; Am Chem Soc; Sigma Xi; Am Asn Univ Professors. *Res:* Synthesis and the investigation of the properties of new heterocyclic aromatic compounds which are analogs of azulene and quinoline using organometallic reagents and novel dehydrogenating agents; french hybrid wines, deacidification and total phenols; chemical deacidification of wines; use of pectic enzymes in wine making. *Mailing Add:* 4744 East Mill Hill Rd East Greenville PA 18041

GAD-EL-HAK, MOHAMED, FLUID MECHANICS, TURBULENCE. *Current Pos:* PROF AEROSPACE & MECH ENG, UNIV NOTRE DAME, 86- *Personal Data:* b Tanta, Egypt, Feb 11, 45; m 76, Dilek Karaca; c Kamal & Yasemin. *Educ:* Ain-Shams Univ, Egypt, BSc, 66; Johns Hopkins Univ, PhD(fluid mech), 73. *Prof Exp:* Instr mech eng, Ain-Shams Univ, 66-68; Whitehead fel, Johns Hopkins Univ, 68-73; sr lectr fluid mech, Univ Southern Calif, 73-74; asst prof eng sci & systs, Univ Va, 74-76; sr res scientist, Flow Res Co, 76-86. *Concurrent Pos:* Vis prof, Univ Grenoble, France, 91-92; ed, J Am Inst Aeronaut & Astronaut & Appl Mech Reviews; distinguished fac fel, Naval Undersea Warfare Ct, Newport, RI, 93; except prof, Univ Politiers, France, 94. *Mem:* Am Physical Soc; fel Am Soc Mech Engrs; Am Inst Aeronaut & Astronaut; Am Chem Soc; hon mem Sigma Xi. *Res:* Basic fluid mechanics; turbulence research especially experimental; development of unique flow visualization techniques; flow control. *Mailing Add:* Dept Aeronaut & Mech Eng Univ Notre Dame Notre Dame IN 46556. *Fax:* 219-631-8341; *E-Mail:* mohamed.gad-el-hak.1@nd.edu

GADEN, ELMER L(EWIS), JR, CHEMICAL ENGINEERING. *Current Pos:* RETIRED. *Personal Data:* b Brooklyn, NY, Sept 26, 23; m 64; c 3. *Educ:* Columbia Univ, BS, 44, MS, 47, PhD(chem eng), 49. *Hon Degrees:* DrEngr, Rensselaer Polytech Inst, 87. *Honors & Awards:* Egleston Medal, Columbia Univ, 86; Founders Award, Am Inst Chem Engrs, 88. *Prof Exp:* Biochem eng head, Chas Pfizer & Co, 48-49; from asst prof to prof chem eng, Columbia Univ, 49-74, chmn dept, 60-69 & 71-74; dean eng, math & bus admin, Univ Vt, 75-79; Chem Eng Dept, Univ Va, 79-94, chmn, Eng Dept, 85-88. *Concurrent Pos:* Tech dir, Biochem Processes, Inc, 59-71. *Mem:* Nat Acad Eng; Am Chem Soc; Am Inst Chem Engrs; Am Soc Eng Educ. *Res:* Biochemical engineering; fermentation; renewable energy resources. *Mailing Add:* Chem Eng Dept Thornton Hall Univ Va Charlottesville VA 22903-2442

GADH, RAJIT, COMPUTER AIDED DESIGN FOR ASSEMBLING & DISASSEMBLING, VIRTUAL REALITY DESIGN. *Current Pos:* ASST PROF MECH ENG, UNIV WIS-MADISON, 92-, DIR, I-CARVE LAB, 92- *Educ:* Indian Inst Technol, MB, 84; Cornell Univ, MS, 86; Carnegie Mellon Univ, PhD(mech eng), 91. *Honors & Awards:* Ralph R Teetor Educ Award, Soc Automotive Engrs, 93; Eng Found Res Initiation Award, 94; Career Award, NSF, 95. *Prof Exp:* Design & software engr, Formteck Inc, 88-89; sr engr, Carnegie Group Inc, 89-90, proj leader, 90-91; vis fac, Univ Calif, Berkeley, 91-92. *Mem:* Inst Elec & Electronics Engrs; Am Soc Mech Engrs; Am Soc Elec Engrs. *Res:* Computer aided design; virtual environments for design in manufacturing and virtual prototyping. *Mailing Add:* Univ Wis 1513 University Ave Madison WI 53706-1572

GADI, INDER KUMAR, CANCER CYTOGENETICS, EVOLUTIONARY BIOLOGY. *Current Pos:* LAB DIR, CLIN CYTOGENETICS, LAB CORP AM, 88- *Personal Data:* m 83, Renu Bhasin; c Rohit & Anuj. *Educ:* Panjas Univ, BSc, 70; Banarash Univ, MSc, 72, PhD(zool), 77. *Prof Exp:* Postdoctoral fel, Zool Soc San Diego, 79-80, Howard Med Sch, 80-84; instr genetics, Univ Med & Dent NJ, 84-85, asst prof surg, 85-88. *Concurrent Pos:* Lab dir, Roche Biomed Labs, 88- *Mem:* Am Soc Human Genetics. *Mailing Add:* 1912 Alexander Dr Durham NC 27709

GADOL, NANCY, experimental biology, for more information see previous edition

GADSBY, DWIGHT MAXON, AQUACULTURE, ECONOMICS OF RESOURCE CONSERVATION. *Current Pos:* agr economist, Div Trade Anal, 63-65, SUPVRY ECONOMIST, DIV ECON RES SERV, USDA, 65- *Personal Data:* b Dickens, Iowa, Oct 2, 32; m 61, Jermaine M Folkman; c Winston Maxon & Alessandra Mae. *Educ:* Iowa State Univ, BS, 54, MS, 60. *Prof Exp:* Fulbright scholar, Univ Padova, 61-62; assoc agr econ, Dept Econ, Iowa State Univ, 62-63. *Concurrent Pos:* Coordr & lectr, USDA, 71-73 & 90. *Mem:* AAAS; Soil Conserv Soc Am. *Res:* Analysis of the economics of natural resource development; quantitative measurement of the impacts associated with rural economic development and associated community improvements. *Mailing Add:* 4711 Medora Dr Suitland MD 20746. *Fax:* 202-219-0418

GADSDEN, RICHARD HAMILTON, SR, CLINICAL BIOCHEMISTRY, CLINICAL & FORENSIC TOXICOLOGY. *Current Pos:* Instr org chem & biochem, 54-56, from asst prof to prof, 56-92, EMER PROF BIOCHEM, PATH & LAB MED & DIR CLIN CHEM, MED UNIV SC, 92- *Personal Data:* b Denver, Colo, June 30, 25; m 53, Emily Mercer; c Grier (Brown), Richard H Jr, Frank M, Philip E, E L Anne & Johnathan L. *Educ:* Col Charleston, BS, 50; Med Col SC, MS, 52, PhD(biochem), 56. *Hon Degrees:* DLitt, Col Charleston, 87. *Honors & Awards:* Outstanding Contrib Educ, Am Asn Clin Chemists, Clin Scientist of Yr, 84. *Concurrent Pos:* Consult clin biochemist, Vet Admin Admin, US Naval Hosp, Med Univ SC; consult, Col Am Pathologists. *Mem:* Fel AAAS; Am Chem Soc; fel Am Inst Chemists; Am Asn Clin Chemists; fel Asn Clin Scientists; Sigma Xi. *Res:* Clinical chemistry; toxicology; clinical medicine; forensic toxicology. *Mailing Add:* Dept Path & Lab Med Med Univ SC Charleston SC 29425. *E-Mail:* gadsdrhs@musc.educ

GADWOOD, ROBERT CHARLES, MEDICINAL CHEMISTRY. *Current Pos:* res scientist, 86-89, Sr Res Scientist, 89-96, SR SCIENTIST, UPJOHN CO, 96- *Personal Data:* b Milwaukee, Wis, May 18, 52; m 75; c 2. *Educ:* Marquette Univ, BS, 74; Univ Wis, PhD(chem), 78. *Prof Exp:* NIH fel, Univ Pittsburgh, 78-80; asst prof chem, Northwestern Univ, 80-86. *Mem:* Am Chem Soc; AAAS. *Res:* Synthesis of new therapeutically useful agents. *Mailing Add:* Pharmacia & Upjohn Co 7246-209-6 301 Henrietta St Kalamazoo MI 49001-0199. *E-Mail:* robert.c.gadwood@am.pnu.com

GADZUK, JOHN WILLIAM, THEORETICAL SOLID STATE PHYSICS, SURFACE PHYSICS. *Current Pos:* PHYSICIST, NAT BUR STAN/NAT INST STAND & TECHNOL, 68- *Personal Data:* b Philadelphia, Pa, Mar 28, 41; m 68, 92, Anita Yergy; c Wendy. *Educ:* Mass Inst Technol, BS, 63, MS, 65, PhD(solid state physics), 68. *Honors & Awards:* Arthur S Fleming Award, 78. *Prof Exp:* Instr physics, Mass Inst Technol, 67-68. *Concurrent Pos:* Nordita vis prof, Chalmers Univ, Goteborg, Sweden, 78-88. *Mem:* Fel Am Phys Soc; Am Vacuum Soc. *Res:* Theory of solids; solid surfaces; chemisorption; photoemission; electron spectroscopies of solids; chemical dynamics at surfaces. *Mailing Add:* Surface Sci Div Nat Inst Stand & Technol Gaithersburg MD 20899. *Fax:* 301-926-6937; *E-Mail:* gadzuk@nist.gov

GAEDKE, RUDOLPH MEGGS, NUCLEAR PHYSICS. *Current Pos:* from asst prof to assoc prof, Trinity Univ, Tex, 67-75, chmn dept, 68-76 & 85-88, dir instnl res & planning, 76-80, assoc vpres acad affairs, 80-84, chmn dept, 85-88, PROF PHYSICS, TRINITY UNIV, TEX, 75- *Personal Data:* b Dallas, Tex, Apr 4, 38; m 60; c 3. *Educ:* Rice Univ, BA, 60; Univ SC, PhD(physics), 65. *Prof Exp:* Asst prof physics, Trinity Univ, Tex, 65-67; sr staff mem, Electro-Nuclear Div, Oak Ridge Nat Lab, 67. *Concurrent Pos:* Res scientist, Tex A&M Univ, 91. *Res:* Nuclear reaction induced by heavy ions; gamma spectroscopy; educational administration; elementary particles. *Mailing Add:* Dept Physics Trinity Univ 715 Stadium Dr San Antonio TX 78212

GAENSLER, EDWARD ARNOLD, SURGERY, PHYSIOLOGY. *Current Pos:* From instr to assoc prof, 48-62, PROF SURG, SCH MED, BOSTON UNIV, 62- *Personal Data:* b Vienna, Austria, Feb 5, 21; nat US; m 53; c 2. *Educ:* Haverford Col, BS, 42; Harvard Univ, MD, 45. *Honors & Awards:* Edward Livingston Trudeau Gold Medal, 81. *Concurrent Pos:* USPHS fel, 48-50; Trudeau fel, 55-59; lectr, Harvard Med Sch & Sch Med, Tufts Univ, 60-; vis thoracic surgeon, Boston City Hosp & Univ Hosp; NIH res career award, 64- *Mem:* Fel Am Col Surg; fel Am Col Chest Physicians; Am Thoracic Soc; Am Soc Thoracic Surg; Am Fedn Clin Res. *Res:* Pulmonary physiology; physiology in thoracic surgery; chest radiology and pathology; interstitch and occupational lung disease. *Mailing Add:* Boston Univ Sch Med 80 E Concord St Boston MA 02118-2394

GAER, MARVIN CHARLES, PURE & APPLIED MATHEMATICAL ANALYSIS. *Current Pos:* PATENT ATTY, 79- *Personal Data:* b Milwaukee, Wis, Apr 28, 35; m 60, Eleanor Putterman; c Arthur, Joseph & Herschel. *Educ:* Univ Wis, BS, 57, MS, 62; Univ Ill, PhD(math), 68; Univ Md, JD, 78. *Prof Exp:* Physicist, Allen-Bradley Co, Wis, 57-58; comput analyst, AC Electronics Div, Gen Motors Corp, 58-62; from instr to asst prof math, Univ Del, 67-75; math analyst, BDM Corp, Va, 77-79. *Concurrent Pos:* Adj assoc prof math, Drexel Univ, 81-82; mathematician, US Naval Air Develop Ctr, Pa, 83-96. *Mem:* Am Math Soc; Math Asn Am; Soc Indust & Appl Math; Sigma Xi. *Res:* Mathematical analysis and its applications primarily in the area of signal processing in oceanographic acoustics. *Mailing Add:* 1756 Morris Dr Cherry Hill NJ 08003-3363

GAERTNER, ALFRED LUDWIG, FORMULATIONS, GRANULATION. *Current Pos:* scientist, 88-92, opers mgr, 92, HEAD FORMULATIONS RES & DEVELOP, GENENCOR INT, 93- *Personal Data:* b Wildberg, Ger, Apr 20, 53; m 88, Debbra Hodgson; c Alexander, Joanna, Emma & Hannah. *Educ:* Univ Tuebingen, MS, 81, PhD(inorg biochem), 84. *Prof Exp:* Instr chem, Univ Tuebingen, 84-85; postdoctoral fel, Massey Univ, 85-86, Univ BC, 86-88. *Concurrent Pos:* Instr chem, Massey Univ, 85-86. *Mem:* Soc Biol Chem; Am Chem Soc; AAAS; Controlled Release Soc. *Res:* Development and application of formulations technology of bioactive products; development of new formulations, analytical method development and transfer of these techniques into production; products include proteins and enzymes produced by recombinant technologies. *Mailing Add:* 925 Page Mill Rd Palo Alto CA 94304. *Fax:* 650-845-6525; *E-Mail:* agaertner@genencor.com

GAERTNER, FRANK HERBERT, BIOCHEMISTRY, MICROBIOLOGY. *Current Pos:* dir molecular genetics, 83-89, DIR NEW TECHNOL RES, MYCOGEN CORP, 89- *Personal Data:* b San Rafael, Calif, July 12, 38; m 62; c Sherry, Sheila & Sharleen. *Educ:* Univ Ariz, BS, 61, MS, 62; Purdue Univ, PhD(microbiol), 66. *Prof Exp:* Res biologist biochem, Univ Calif, San Diego, 66-69; from asst prof to assoc prof biochem, Oak Ridge Grad Sch Biomed Sci, 69-81; sr scientist molecular genetics, Salk Inst Biotechnol Indust Assocs, 81-83. *Concurrent Pos:* USPHS fel, NIH, 66-68; NSF grant, 77-80; cofounder & dir, MBX Systs, 90- *Mem:* Am Soc Microbiol; Fedn Am Socs Exp Biol. *Res:* Unique catalytic and structural properties of multienzyme clusters; regulation of the metabolism of aromatic compounds; plasmid gene expression in molds, yeast and bacteria. *Mailing Add:* Mycogen Corp Dept Molecular Genetics 5501 Oberlin Dr San Diego CA 92121

GAERTNER, RICHARD F(RANCIS), MATERIALS SCIENCE, CHEMICAL ENGINEERING. *Current Pos:* PRES, TECHNOL MGT INC, 95- *Personal Data:* b Pittsburgh, Pa, Aug 10, 33; m 62, Nancy Keary; c Barbara, Richard, Linda & Catherine. *Educ:* Univ WVa, BS, 55, MS, 57; Univ Ill, PhD(chem eng), 59. *Prof Exp:* Res assoc, Gen Elec Res Lab, Gen Elec Co, 59-68, mgr tech mkt, Polymer Prod Oper, 68-69, mgr, Mfg Plastics Dept, 69-71, mgr eng, Laminating Metals Dept, 71-72, mgr tech planning, Chem & Metall Div, 72-75; res dir chem & fiber technol, Owens-Corning Fiberglas Corp, 75-79, dir strategic tech planning, 79-86; dir, Ctr Advan Technol Develop, Iowa State Univ, 86-95. *Mem:* Am Inst Chem Engrs; Am Chem Soc; Sigma Xi. *Res:* Heat transfer associated with change of phase; boiling phenomena; process engineering of polymers; glass reinforced plastic composites; glass reinforcements and yarns; research administration. *Mailing Add:* 204 Beachers Brook Lane Cary NC 27511-5507

GAERTTNER, MARTIN R, ELECTRICAL ENGINEERING. *Current Pos:* RES SCIENTIST, ENG & RES STAFF, FORD MOTOR CO, 73- *Personal Data:* b Winchester, Mass, Apr 21, 44. *Educ:* Rensselaer Polytech Inst, BS, 65; Cornell Univ, PhD(exp physics), 70. *Mem:* Am Phys Soc. *Res:* Electromagnetic compatibility; high vacuum technology (radio frequency sputtering and ion bombardment evaporative deposition of thin films); electron tunneling; development of superconducting quantum interference detectors. *Mailing Add:* 2601 Detroit St Dearborn MI 48124

GAFARIAN, ANTRANIG VAUGHN, MATHEMATICAL STATISTICS, PROBABILITY. *Current Pos:* RETIRED. *Personal Data:* b Fresno, Calif, Dec 26, 24; c 2. *Educ:* Univ Mich, BS(eng math) & BS(mech eng), 47; Univ Calif, Los Angeles, PhD(math), 59. *Prof Exp:* Aerodynamicist, NAm Aviation, Inc, 47-51 & Northrop Aircraft, Inc, 51-52; aerodynamics engr, Aerophysics Develop Corp, 52-53; mem tech staff, Hughes Aircraft Co, 56-59; sr mathematician, Syst Develop Corp, 59-66, sr scientist, 66-69, head math & opers res prog staff, 67-69, mgr, Transp & Telecommun Dept, 69-73; prof indust & syts eng, Univ Southern Calif, 73-90. *Concurrent Pos:* Teacher phys sci exten prog, Univ Calif, Los Angeles, 56-65; assoc prof, Calif State Univ, Northridge, 61-65. *Mem:* Opers Res Soc Am; Inst Indust Engrs; Sigma Xi. *Res:* Application of the mathematical theory of probability and mathematical statistics to the analysis of random phenomena. *Mailing Add:* 1033 Ocean Ave No 304 Santa Monica CA 90403

GAFFAR, ABDUL, IMMUNOCHEMISTRY, THERAPEUTICS FOR ORAL DISEASE. *Current Pos:* res microbiologist, Colgate-Palmolive Res Ctr, 67-70, sr res microbiologist, 70-73, res assoc, 73-75, sr assoc, 80, CORP RES FEL & ASSOC DIR, COLGATE-PALMOLIVE RES CTR, 81-, VPRES ADVAN TECHNOL, GLOBAL TECHNOL GROUP, 92- *Personal Data:* b Dec 10, 40; US citizen; c 1, Maria C; c Vousuf A. *Educ:* Univ Karachi, BS, 56; Brigham Young Univ, MS, 65; Ohio State Univ, PhD(immunol), 67. *Prof Exp:* Res assoc biochem, Pakistan Res Coun, 60-63; res asst bact, Brigham Young Univ, 64-65; res asst immunol, Ohio State Univ, 65-67. *Concurrent Pos:* Bd overseer, Forsythe Den Ctr, Boston, Mass. *Mem:* AAAS; NY Acad Sci; Am Soc Microbiol; Am Chem Soc. *Res:* Immunochemistry of tissue antigens and microbial products; bone/tooth chemistry; oral diseases; granted 105 patents; author of 110 publications. *Mailing Add:* Colgate-Palmolive Res Ctr 909 River Rd Piscataway NJ 08855. *E-Mail:* abdulgaffar@colpal.com

GAFFEN, DIAN JUDITH, CLIMATE VARIABILITY & TRENDS, BOUNDARY-LAYER METEOROLOGY. *Current Pos:* RES METEOROLOGIST, NAT OCEANIC & ATMOSPHERIC ADMIN, AIR RESOURCES LAB, 89- *Personal Data:* b Boston, Mass, Feb 10, 59. *Educ:* Univ Calif, Berkeley, BA, 81; San Jose State Univ, MS, 84; von Karman Inst, Belg, dipl, 85; Univ Md, College Park, PhD(meteorol), 92. *Honors & Awards:* Prof Dr Vilho Vaisala Award, World Meteorol Orgn, 94. *Prof Exp:* Fel, Belg Am Educ Found, 84-85. *Mem:* Am Meteorol Soc; Am Geophys Union. *Res:* Climatology and variability of atmospheric water vapor; long-term meteorological observations; data continuity for climate studies. *Mailing Add:* Nat Oceanic & Atmospheric Admin Air Resources Lab 1315 East-West Hwy Silver Spring MD 20190

GAFFEY, CORNELIUS THOMAS, BIOPHYSICS. *Current Pos:* RETIRED. *Personal Data:* b Philadelphia, Pa, Aug 24, 28; m 55. *Educ:* La Salle Col, BA, 49; Univ Tenn, MS, 51; Purdue Univ, PhD(biophys), 58. *Prof Exp:* Asst physiol, Purdue Univ, 51-52, instr physics, 58; biophysicist physics, Donner Lab, Lawrence Berkeley Lab, Univ Calif, 58-92. *Mem:* Biophys Soc; Radiation Res Soc; Soc Neurosci; Tissue Cult Asn; Soc Exp Biol & Med. *Res:* Effects of irradiation on the nervous system; computer analysis of brain electrical activity; microelectrode techniques with central nervous system tissue cultures; excitation phenomenon in plant cell membranes; effects on non-ionizing radiation on biological systems. *Mailing Add:* 15 Roslyn Ct Oakland CA 94618

GAFFEY, MICHAEL JAMES, PLANETARY ASTRONOMY, REMOTE SENSING. *Current Pos:* PROF GEOL, RENSSELAER POLYTECH INST, 84- *Personal Data:* b Meadville, Pa, Dec 1, 45; m 73. *Educ:* Univ Iowa, BA, 68, MS, 70; Mass Inst Technol, PhD(planetary sci), 74. *Honors & Awards:* Asteroid named in honor, 3545 Gaffey. *Prof Exp:* Mem res staff planetary astron, Mass Inst Technol, 74-77; asst astronr planetary astron, Inst Astron, 77-80; asst researcher planetary geosciences, 80-81; assoc res planetary geosci, Hawaii Inst Geophys, Univ Hawaii, 81-84. *Concurrent Pos:* Consult, Lunar & Planetary Rev Panel, NASA, 77-79. *Mem:* Fel Meteoritical Soc; Am Astron Soc; Am Geophys Union; AAAS. *Res:* Surface mineralogy of minor planets by remote sensing; early solar system processes from study of minor planets; utilization of extraterrestrial resources; remote sensing for terrestrial resources. *Mailing Add:* Dept Geol Rensselaer Polytech Inst Troy NY 12180

GAFFEY, WILLIAM ROBERT, biostatistics, biometry; deceased, see previous edition for last biography

GAFFIELD, WILLIAM, NATURAL PRODUCTS CHEMISTRY. *Current Pos:* RES CHEMIST, WESTERN REGIONAL RES CTR, USDA, 64- *Personal Data:* b Chicago, Ill, Dec 26, 35; m 61; c 2. *Educ:* Univ Ill, Urbana, Champaign, BS, 57; Univ Iowa, PhD(org chem), 63. *Prof Exp:* Res assoc org chem, Univ NH, Durham, 62-64. *Concurrent Pos:* Vis res chemist, Nat Cancer Inst, NIH, Bethesda, 74-75; ed, J Nat Toxins, 93- *Mem:* Fel Royal Soc Chem; Am Chem Soc; Am Soc Pharmacog; AAAS. *Res:* Structure-terata relationships of plant alkaloids; chiroptical determination of natural product configuration and conformation. *Mailing Add:* Western Regional Res Ctr Agr Res Serv USDA Albany CA 94710

GAFFNEY, BARBARA LUNDY, ORGANIC CHEMISTRY, BIOCHEMISTRY. *Current Pos:* res assoc, Inst Microbiol, 69-70, lectr chem, Douglass Col, 70-84, ASSOC PROF, RUTGERS UNIV, 85- *Personal Data:* b Houston, Tex, Dec 31, 44; m 66. *Educ:* Rutgers Univ, BA, 66, PhD(org chem), 70. *Honors & Awards:* Joseph Hyman Award, Am Chem Soc, 89. *Mem:* Am Chem Soc; Biophys Soc. *Res:* Synthesis and characterization of modified oligonucleotides. *Mailing Add:* Dept Chem Rutgers Univ Piscataway NJ 08855. *Fax:* 201-932-5312

GAFFNEY, EDWIN VINCENT, CANCER, IMMUNOLOGY. *Current Pos:* PRES, DECONNES RES INST. *Educ:* Cath Univ, PhD(cell biol), 68. *Prof Exp:* Assoc prof cell biol, Pa State Univ, 71-89; dir res sci, Baptist Med Ctrs, 90- *Mailing Add:* DeConnes Res Inst 1500 Poly Dr Suite 202 Billings MT 59102

GAFFNEY, JEFFREY STEVEN, PHYSICAL ORGANIC CHEMISTRY, ATMOSPHERIC CHEMISTRY. *Current Pos:* CHEMIST, GROUP LEADER, ENVIRON RES DIV, ARGONNE NAT LAB, 89- *Personal Data:* b San Bernardino, Calif, July 28, 49; m 90, Nancy A Marley; c 3. *Educ:* Univ Calif, Riverside, BS, 71, MS, 73, PhD(chem), 75. *Prof Exp:* Res assoc, Dept Chem, 75-77, from assoc chemist to chemist, dept energy & environ, Brookhaven Nat Lab, 77-85; staff mem, Isotope & Nuclear Chem Div, Los Alamos Nat Lab, 85-88. *Concurrent Pos:* US Info Agency Am Participant to Mex, 88, Can, 89; adj res chemist & fac adj, NMex Inst Technol & Mining, Socorro, NMex, 92- *Mem:* Am Chem Soc; Am Asn Aerosol Res; Am Geophys Union. *Res:* Gas chromatography/mass spectrometry; isotope ratio mass spectrometry; gas phase kinetics; atmospheric chemistry; air pollution monitoring; mass spectroscopy of fragile molecules of biological interest; organic geochemistry; combustion chemistry; radiochem. *Mailing Add:* Bldg 203 Environ Res Div Argonne Nat Lab 9700 S Cass Ave Argonne IL 60439. *Fax:* 630-252-8895

GAFFNEY, PATRICK M, AQUACULTURE GENETICS, BIVALVE GENETICS. *Current Pos:* asst prof marine biol, 87-93, ASSOC PROF MARINE BIOL & BIOCHEM, COL MARINE STUDIES, UNIV DEL, 93- *Personal Data:* b New Orleans, La, Dec 3, 51; m 78, Perrin D Smith; c Alison, Conor & Nathaniel. *Educ:* Univ Calif, Berkeley, AB, 73; State Univ NY, PhD(biol sci), 86. *Prof Exp:* Fel, State Univ NY, 86-87. *Concurrent Pos:* Fulbright fel, 73. *Mem:* Genetics Soc Am; Nat Shellfisheries Asn; Soc Study Evolution; World Aquacult Soc; Int Asn Genetics Aquacult; Am Soc Molecular Marine Biol & Biotechnol. *Res:* Genetics of marine organisms, emphasizing population genetics of bivalves and applications of genetics to aquaculture. *Mailing Add:* Univ Del 700 Pilotown Rd Lewes DE 19958-1298. *Fax:* 302-645-4028; *E-Mail:* pgaffney@bach.udel.edu

GAFFNEY, PAUL COTTER, MEDICINE. *Current Pos:* From instr to assoc prof, 51-62, dean admis sch med, 77-78, PROF PEDIAT, SCH MED, UNIV PITTSBURGH, 61-; EXEC DIR, MED ALUMNI ASN, 81- *Personal Data:* b Du Bois, Pa, May 12, 17; m 44; c 7. *Educ:* Univ Pittsburgh, BS, 40, MD, 42. *Concurrent Pos:* Sr staff, Childrens Hosp, Philadelphia, Pa, 53-, med dir, 78-81. *Res:* Hematology. *Mailing Add:* Dept Pediat Childrens Hosp Pittsburgh M-250 Univ Pittsburgh 3705 Fifth Ave Pittsburgh PA 15213-2002

GAFFNEY, PAUL G, II, OCEANOGRAPHY, ATMOSPHERIC SCIENCES. *Current Pos:* exec officer, Naval Res Lab, 83-84, cmndg officer, Naval Oceanog Command Facil, 84-86, dir resources & capt naval oceanog, Naval Res Lab, 86-89, asst chief naval res, 89-91, CMNDG OFFICER, NAVAL RES LAB, 91-95, CMNDG OFFICER NAVAL METEOROL & OCEANOG, NAVAL RES LAB, 95-, CHIEF NAVAL RES, 96- *Personal Data:* b Attleboro, Mass, May 30, 46; m 74; c 1. *Educ:* US Naval Acad, BS, 68; Cath Univ Am, MSE, 69; Jacksonville Univ, MBA, 86. *Prof Exp:* Res asst ocean eng, Cath Univ Am, 68-69; opers officer minesweeping, US Navy, 69-71; adv ocean hydrography, Vietnamese Navy Combat Hydro Surv Team, 71-72; ocean serv officer, Fleet Weather Cent, Rota, Spain, 72-75; exec asst to oceanogr USN, 75-78; res fel Soviet naval affairs, Naval War Col, 78-79; cmndg officer hydrography, Oceano Unit Four, Indonesian Surv, 79-80; actg dir earth sci res, Off Naval Res, 80-81; mil asst int security affairs, Off Asst Secy Defense, 81-83. *Mem:* Explorers Club; Oceanic Soc; Sigma Xi. *Res:* Field hydrographic survey operations in remote areas; mechanical properties of cables. *Mailing Add:* Chief Naval Res 800 N Quincy St Suite 907 Arlington VA 22207

GAFFNEY, PETER EDWARD, MICROBIOLOGY. *Current Pos:* PRES, GA ENVIRON ASSOC, 81- *Personal Data:* b Carbondale, Pa, Nov 24, 31; m 55, Joan Miller; c Lori, Peter Jr & Catherine. *Educ:* Univ Scranton, BS, 53; Syracuse Univ, MS, 54; Rutgers Univ, PhD(environ sci), 58. *Prof Exp:* From asst prof to assoc prof appl biol res & eng exp sta, Ga Inst Technol, 58-65; assoc prof microbiol, Ga State Univ, 65-88. *Concurrent Pos:* Fulbright lectr, Trinity Col, Dublin, 67-68; consult indust microbiol; pres, Southeast Labs, Inc, 71-78; chmn, Analttical Serv, Inc, 78-83; exec secy, Ga Acad Sci, 88-90. *Mem:* AAAS; Am Soc Microbiol; Water Pollution Control Fedn; Sigma Xi; NY Acad Sci; fel Am Acad Microbiol. *Res:* Microbiol physiology; growth kinetics; stream pollution; waste treatment; microbial deterioration of industrial products; industrial fermentations; effects of chlorobiphenyls on waste treatment processes. *Mailing Add:* 2965 Pharr Ct S No 415 Atlanta GA 30305

GAFFNEY, THOMAS EDWARD, PHARMACOLOGY. *Current Pos:* RETIRED. *Personal Data:* b East St Louis, Ill, Nov 5, 30; m 54; c 3. *Educ:* Univ Mo, AB, 51, MS, 53; Univ Cincinnati, MD, 57. *Honors & Awards:* Myrtle Wreath Achievement Award, Hadassah Res, 80. *Prof Exp:* Intern, Harvard Med Serv, Boston City Hosp, 58-59; asst resident medicine, Mass Gen Hosp, 59-60; instr pharmacol & asst med, Col Med, Univ Cincinnati, 60-61; clin assoc, Cardiol Br, Nat Heart Inst, 61-62; from asst prof to prof med, Col Med, Univ Cincinnati, 62-72; prof pharmacol & med & chmn, Dept Basic & Clin Pharmacol, Med Univ SC, 72-93. *Concurrent Pos:* Clinician, Outpatient Dept & attend physician, Cincinnati Gen Hosp, 62-64, dir, Hypertension Clin, 64-72; from assoc prof to prof pharmacol, Col Med, Univ Cincinnati, 62-72, dir, Div Clin Pharmacol, 62-72; res career develop award, Cincinnati Gen Hosp, 62-; mem med adv bd, Coun High Blood Pressure Res, Am Heart Asn; vis scientist toxicol, Mass Spectrometry Lab, Karolinska Inst, Stockholm, 69-70; mem & chmn prog rev comt pharmacol & toxicol, Nat Inst Gen Med Sci. *Mem:* Soc Exp Biol & Med; Am Soc Pharmacol & Exp Therapeut; Am Fedn Clin Res; Protein Soc; Am Soc Clin Invest; Am Clin & Climat Assoc. *Res:* Clinical cardiovascular pharmacology; hypertension. *Mailing Add:* 348 Sugar Hollow Rd Fairview NC 28730-9560

GAFFORD, LANELLE GUYTON, VIROLOGY, MEDICAL MYCOLOGY. *Current Pos:* RETIRED. *Personal Data:* b Columbia, Miss, Feb 27, 30. *Educ:* Univ Miss, BS, 51, MS, 55, PhD(microbiol), 69. *Prof Exp:* From instr to prof microbiol, Med Ctr, Univ Miss, 57-83. *Mem:* Am Soc Microbiol; Am Soc Exp Path; Med Mycol Soc Am; AAAS; Soc Gen Microbiol. *Res:* Biochemistry of avian poxvirus replicaton and hyperolasia; chemical characterization of fowlpox virus; physicochemical characterization of the viral DNA and mapping of the genome. *Mailing Add:* 1042 Meadowbrook Rd Jackson MS 39206

GAGE, ANDREW ARTHUR, SURGERY, ADMINISTRATION. *Current Pos:* PROF SURG, SCH MED, STATE UNIV NY, BUFFALO, 72-; DEP INST DIR, ROSWELL PARK MEM INST, BUFFALO, NY, 87- *Personal Data:* b Buffalo, NY, May 7, 22. *Educ:* Univ Buffalo, MD, 44. *Prof Exp:* Staff surgeon, Vet Admin Med Ctr, 53-68, chief surg serv, 68-84, chief staff, 71-86. *Concurrent Pos:* Assoc dir clin affairs, Roswell Park Mem Inst, 86-87. *Mem:* Int Cardiovasc Soc; Soc Vascular Surg; Am Heart Asn; Soc Cryobiol; Am Col Surg. *Res:* Pacemaker work; cryosurgery; long term assistance of failing heart. *Mailing Add:* Roswell Park Cancer Inst 666 Elm St Buffalo NY 14263-0001

GAGE, CLARKE LYMAN, ORGANIC CHEMISTRY. *Current Pos:* from asst prof to prof, 52-86, EMER PROF CHEM, ST LAWRENCE UNIV, 86- *Personal Data:* b Mason City, Iowa, Apr 20, 21; m 44; c Michael, Timothy & Barnard. *Educ:* Antioch Col, BS, 44; Ohio State Univ, PhD(chem), 51. *Prof Exp:* Res chemist, Polystyrene Copolymers, Monsanto Chem Co, 43-44; asst porphyrins, C F Kettering Found, 46; Vernay fel, 52. *Mem:* Am Chem Soc; Hist Sci Soc; Brit Soc Hist Sci; Sigma Xi. *Res:* History of science (chemistry). *Mailing Add:* 6 Elm St Canton NY 13617

GAGE, DONALD S(HEPARD), ELECTRICAL ENGINEERING. *Current Pos:* RETIRED. *Personal Data:* b Evanston, Ill, June 10, 30; m 56, Jean Ann Veirs; c Rebecca, Nancy & Catherine. *Educ:* Northwestern Univ, BSEE, 53; Stanford Univ, MSEE, 54, PhD(elec eng), 58. *Prof Exp:* Asst elec eng, Stanford Univ, 55-58; from asst prof to assoc prof, Northwestern Univ, 58-62; assoc prof, Mich State Univ, 63-66; from assoc prof to prof elec eng, Univ Colo, Colorado Springs, 66-77, prof elec eng & comput sci, Denver, 77-91. *Concurrent Pos:* NSF fel, 53-55; consult, IBM, Boulder, Colo, 74; Hewlett Packard Corp, Colorado Springs, 84-85. *Mem:* Inst Elec & Electronics Engrs. *Res:* Explanation of semiconductor devices through an understanding of applied solid state physics with special interest in avalanche and transient radiation effects; automated material measurements at 94 gigahertz. *Mailing Add:* 2014 Hercules Dr Colorado Springs CO 80906-1129

GAGE, FREDERICK WORTHINGTON, CHEMISTRY. *Current Pos:* RETIRED. *Personal Data:* b Cleveland, Ohio, Dec 27, 12; m 74, Jonne Grisman; c Frederick W & Richard C. *Educ:* Ill Wesleyan Univ, BS, 34; Northwestern Univ, MS, 37. *Prof Exp:* Res supvr, Columbia-Southern Chem Corp, 36-54; tech dir, Dayton Chem Prod Labs, Inc, Whittaker Corp, 54-58, tech dir & vpres, 58-70, gen mgr, Dayton Coatings & Chem Div, 70-80; consult, Delphi Group, 80-88. *Mem:* Am Chem Soc. *Res:* Rubber reinforcing pigments; caustic soda; general analytical methods; preparation of calcium carbonate and calcium silicate; use as rubber pigments; purification caustic soda; purification titanium tetrachloride; rubber to metal bonding agents. *Mailing Add:* 6650 Carinthia Dr Dayton OH 45459

GAGE, KENNETH SEAVER, GEOPHYSICS, METEOROLOGY. *Current Pos:* physicist, 76-90, PROG LEADER, TROP DYNAMICS & CLIMATE, AERONOMY LAB, ENVIRON RES LABS, NAT OCEANIC & ATMOSPHERIC ADMIN, 90- *Personal Data:* b Boston, Mass, Nov 11, 42; m 69, Molly Miller; c Randall J & Blythe M. *Educ:* Brandeis Univ, AB, 64; Univ Chicago, MS, 66, PhD(geophys fluid dynamics), 68. *Prof Exp:* Asst prof meteorol, Univ Md, College Park, 68-72; vis assoc prof, Eng Exp Sta & Meteorol Dept, Univ Wis-Madison, 72-73; mem staff, Meteorol Dept, Control Data Corp, 73-76. *Concurrent Pos:* Assoc ed, J Appl Meteorol, 82-90,

Radio Sci, 87-92; ed, J Geophys Res Atmospheres, 88-92. *Mem:* Am Meteorol Soc; Am Geophys Union. *Res:* Geophysical fluid dynamics; hydrodynamic stability and turbulence theory; atmospheric turbulence and gravity waves; remote probing of the atmosphere; radar meteorology; atmospheric propagation of electromagnetic waves; mesoscale processes; tropical dynamics and climate variability; development and application of wind profiler technology to tropical atmospheric and climate research; structure of precipitating cloud systems in the tropics. *Mailing Add:* Aeronomy Lab Environ Res Labs Boulder CO 80303. *Fax:* 303-497-5373; *E-Mail:* kgage@al.noaa.gov

GAGE, L PATRICK, MOLECULAR BIOLOGY, BIOCHEMISTRY. *Current Pos:* dir, Dept Molecular Genetics, 82-83, vpres & dir biol res & develop, 83-84, VPRES & DIR EXPLOR RES, ROCHE RES CTR, 84- *Personal Data:* b Endicott, NY, May 4, 42; m 65, 85; c 4. *Educ:* Mass Inst Technol, SB, 64; Univ Chicago, PhD(biophys), 69. *Prof Exp:* USPHS fel, Dept Embryol, Carnegie Inst, Washington, DC, 69-71; asst mem, Roche Inst Molecular Biol, 71-76, assoc mem cell biol, 77-80, head, Lab Recombinant DNA Res, 80-82. *Concurrent Pos:* Adj assoc prof, Biochem PhD Prog, City Univ New York, 75-76; mem adv panel develop biol, NSF, 77-80; adj assoc prof cell biol, Sch Med, NY Univ, 77-; chmn biotechnology adv comt, Pharmaceut Mfrs Asn; bd mem, Life Sci Res Found. *Mem:* Soc Develop Biol; NY Acad Sci; Am Soc Biol Chemists; Am Soc Cell Biol; Sigma Xi; Indust Biotechnology Asn. *Res:* Responsible for all pharmaceutical discovery research, including synthetic chemistry, pharmacology, chemotherapy, immunology, virology, oncology, molecular genetics and biological chemistry; research in support of the fine chemicals, animal health and diagnostics businesses of the company; special interest in biotechnology, molecular immunology and virology. *Mailing Add:* Genetics Inst 87 Cambridge Park Dr Cambridge MA 02140-2387. *Fax:* 617-498-8880

GAGE, TOMMY WILTON, PHARMACOLOGY, PHYSIOLOGY. *Current Pos:* prof pharmacol & chmn dept, 69-92, PROF & VCHMN, COL DENT, BAYLOR UNIV, 92- *Personal Data:* b Stamford, Tex, Oct 6, 35; m 56, Loyce M Voss; c Sharon, Stephen, Susan & Stacey. *Educ:* Univ Tex, Austin, BS, 57; Baylor Univ, DDS, 61, PhD(physiol), 69. *Honors & Awards:* Cooley Trophy, Tex Dent Asn. *Prof Exp:* NIH spec fel, 66-69. *Concurrent Pos:* Mem, Coun on Dent Therapeut, Am Dent Asn, 85-90. *Mem:* Am Asn Dent Sch; Am Dent Asn; Int Asn Dent Res; Am Soc Pharmacol & Exp Therapeut; fel Am Col Dentists; Am Asn Dent Res. *Res:* Cellular responses to oxygen and oxygenating agents, limited to tissues in the oral cavity; pain related to the oral cavity. *Mailing Add:* Dept Oral & Maxillofacial Surg & Pharmacol Baylor Col Dent PO Box 660677 Dallas TX 75266-0677. *Fax:* 214-828-8346

GAGEN, JAMES EDWIN, ORGANIC CHEMISTRY. *Current Pos:* asst prof, 67-74, ASSOC PROF CHEM, UNIV TENN, MARTIN, 74- *Personal Data:* b Elyria, Ohio, Dec 27, 35; m 59; c 4. *Educ:* Kent State Univ, BS, 57; Case Western Res Univ, MS, 64, PhD(org chem), 67. *Prof Exp:* Chemist, B F Goodrich Chem Co, 59-65. *Mem:* Am Chem Soc; Sigma Xi. *Res:* Aromatic substitution by sulfonyl peroxides. *Mailing Add:* Rte 4 Box 351 Martin TN 38237-8972

GAGER, FORREST LEE, JR, ORGANO-ANALYTIC CHEMISTRY, NATURAL PRODUCTS CHEMISTRY. *Current Pos:* RETIRED. *Personal Data:* b Philadelphia, Pa, Apr 23, 22; Wid; c Judith (Perlman) & Brian M. *Educ:* Haverford Col, BS, 49; Ind Univ, AM, 51. *Prof Exp:* Res chemist, Merck & Co, Inc, 51-55; res chemist, Philip Morris, Inc, 55-57, supvr org sect, 57-59, res assoc, 59-60, res scientist, 60-63, sr scientist, 63-85. *Concurrent Pos:* Vis fel, Univ Manchester, 65-66; vis instr, Sweet Briar Col, 85. *Mem:* AAAS; Am Chem Soc; Royal Soc Chem; Sigma Xi; NY Acad Sci; Chromaty Soc. *Res:* Chemistry of natural products; flavors and aromas; tobacco chemistry; chromatography; biosynthesis; isotope tracer techniques. *Mailing Add:* PO Box Z Sweet Briar VA 24595

GAGER, WILLIAM BALLANTINE, PHYSICS. *Current Pos:* ASSOC PROF PHYSICS, JACKSONVILLE UNIV, 67- *Personal Data:* b Columbus, Ohio, April 18, 28; m 56; c 2. *Educ:* Bowdoin Col, AB, 49; Ohio State Univ, MS, 51, PhD(physics), 56. *Prof Exp:* Physicist, Nat Bur Stand, 56-58 & Battelle Mem Inst, 58-67. *Mem:* Am Phys Soc. *Res:* Paramagnetic resonance; nuclear magnetic resonance; very low temperatures; solid state physics. *Mailing Add:* 10135 Lakeview Rd W Jacksonville FL 32225

GAGGIOLI, RICHARD A, MECHANICAL ENGINEERING. *Current Pos:* PROF MECH ENG, MARQUETTE UNIV, 90- *Personal Data:* b Lake Forest, Ill, Dec 3, 34; m 57; c 5. *Educ:* Northwestern Univ, BSME, 57, MS, 58; Univ Wis, PhD(mech eng), 61. *Prof Exp:* NSF fel chem eng, Univ Wis, Madison, 61-62, from asst prof to assoc prof mech eng, 62-69; res mem, US Army Math Res Ctr, 65-67; prof mech eng, Marquette Univ, 69-81, chmn dept, 69-72; dean eng & archit, Catholic Univ Am, 81-84; prof mech eng, Univ Lowell, 84-89. *Concurrent Pos:* Vis fel, Battelle Mem Inst, 68-69. *Mem:* Am Soc Mech Engrs; Am Soc Heating, Refrig & Air Conditioning Engrs. *Res:* Applied thermodynamics; energy engineering; applied mathematics. *Mailing Add:* Dept Mech Eng Olin Rm 201 PO Box 1881 Marquette Univ Milwaukee WI 53201-1881

GAGLIANO, NICHOLAS CHARLES, PEDIATRICS, PREVENTIVE MEDICINE. *Current Pos:* assoc prof pediat, La State Univ, 60-70, assoc prof prev med, 64-70, prof pediat & prev med, 70-, prof pub health, 77-, PROF FAMILY MED, 80-, EMER PROF PEDIAT, LA STATE UNIV, 88- *Personal Data:* b New Orleans, La, Apr 5, 27; m 51; c 2. *Educ:* Loyola Univ, La, BS, 48; La State Univ, MD, 52; Am Bd Pediat, dipl, 61. *Prof Exp:* From intern to resident, Charity Hosp La, New Orleans, 52-55; practicing pediatrician, 55-60. *Concurrent Pos:* Asst proj dir collab child develop prog, Charity Hosp La, 61-64; med dir, Pediat Emergency Rm, Charity Hosp, New Orleans, 76-; vchmn & assoc dir, Residency Training Prog, Dept Pediat, La State Univ, 84-88. *Mem:* Am Acad Pediat. *Res:* Preventive and ambulatory pediatrics. *Mailing Add:* La State Univ Sch Med Dept Pediat 1542 Tulane Ave New Orleans LA 70112-2865

GAGLIANO, SHERWOOD MONEER, PHYSICAL GEOGRAPHY, GEOLOGY. *Current Pos:* PRES, COASTAL ENVIRON, INC, 73- *Personal Data:* b New Orleans, La, Dec 10, 35; m 61. *Educ:* La State Univ, BS, 59, MA, 63, PhD(geog), 67. *Prof Exp:* Supvr sediment lab, Coastal Studies Inst, La State Univ, 60-64; field investr, Coastal Geol, 64-65; instr coastal morphol, 65-67; asst prof coastal geog to assoc prof, 67-73; asst prof marine sci, Univ, 69-73; instr geog & anthrop to asst prof, 63-68. *Concurrent Pos:* Vis geologist, Am Geol Inst, 71; spec lectr, La State Univ, 73- *Mem:* Soc Am Archeol; Geol Soc Am; Soc Econ Paleontologists & Mineralogists; US Quaternary Soc; Sigma Xi. *Res:* Coastal zone management; resource management; regional planning; environmental sciences; sedimentology; geomorphology and archeology of riverine and coastal areas; archeology of early man. *Mailing Add:* 929 E Lakeview Baton Rouge LA 70810-4619

GAGLIARDI, GEORGE N(ICHOLAS), CHEMICAL ENGINEERING. *Current Pos:* Chem engr process develop, Am Cyanamid Co, 52-56, res engr, 56-59, group leader process res agr chem, 59-66, mgr process develop, Agr Div, 66-68, PROD MGR PESTICIDES, AM CYANAMID CO, 68- *Personal Data:* b Brooklyn, NY, May 17, 30; m 56; c 6. *Educ:* Pratt Inst, BChE, 52; NY Univ, MChE, 61. *Mem:* Am Inst Chem Engrs; Am Chem Soc. *Res:* Process research on and manufacture of organic chemicals scaleup; techniques. *Mailing Add:* 16 Vanderveer Dr Trenton NJ 08648-3151

GAGLIARDI, L JOHN, CHEMICAL PHYSICS, BIOPHYSICS. *Current Pos:* Asst prof, 66-74, ASSOC PROF PHYSICS, RUTGERS UNIV, 74- *Personal Data:* b Camden, NJ, Dec 13, 35; m 61, 84; c 5. *Educ:* Villanova Univ, BS, 57; Temple Univ, MA, 65, PhD(physics), 71. *Mem:* Am Phys Soc; Am Asn Physics Teachers. *Res:* Mechanism of protonic transfer and hydration in aqueous systems; protonic charge transfer mechanisms and cell division; membrane electrical stress and cell division. *Mailing Add:* Dept Physics Rutgers Univ Camden Campus 311 N Fifth St Camden NJ 08102-1205

GAGLIARDI, ROBERT M, ELECTRICAL ENGINEERING. *Current Pos:* asst prof, 61-70, assoc prof, 70-80, PROF ENG, UNIV SOUTHERN CALIF, 80- *Personal Data:* b New Haven, Conn, Apr 7, 34; m 57; c 3. *Educ:* Univ Conn, BSEE, 56; Yale Univ, MS, 57, PhD(elec eng), 60. *Prof Exp:* Staff engr, Hughes Aircraft Co, 60-61. *Concurrent Pos:* Consult, Hughes Aircraft Co, 61- *Mem:* Inst Elec & Electronics Engrs. *Res:* Problems of communication theory, information theory, telemetry and data handling system studies. *Mailing Add:* Dept Elec Eng Univ Southern Calif Los Angeles CA 90007

GAGLIARDI, UGO OSCAR, COMPUTER SCIENCES. *Current Pos:* PRES, GEN SYST GROUP INC, 75-; CHMN BD, CTR SOFTWARE TECHNOL, 85- *Personal Data:* b Naples, Italy, July 23, 31; US citizen. *Educ:* Univ Naples, dipl, 51, Dr Ing(elec eng), 54. *Prof Exp:* Dir comput lab, Elec Syst Div, US Air Force, 65-66; res fel comput eng, Harvard Univ, 66-68; vpres eng, Interactive Sci, Inc, 68-70; dir engr, Honeywell Inc, 70-75. *Concurrent Pos:* Fulbright Scholar, Columbia Univ, 55-56; lectr, Harvard Univ, 66-74, prof prac comput eng, 74-83, Gordon McKay prof, 83-; mem, Nat Acad Panel Inst Comput Sci & Technol, Nat Inst Stand & Technol, 85-, chmn, 89- *Res:* Software engineering; computer systems architecture; architecture of very large distributed computer systems; queueing theory; applications to computer systems design. *Mailing Add:* Gen Systs Group 5 Manor Pkwy Salem NH 03079-2842

GAGNA, CLAUDE EUGENE, IMMUNOLOGY, PATHOLOGY. *Current Pos:* POSTDOCTORAL FEL, DEPT OPHTHAL, UNIV MED & DENT NJ, 94-, FEL, DEPT PHYSIOL, 94- *Personal Data:* b New York, NY, Sept 16, 56. *Educ:* St Peter's Col, BS, 79; Fairleigh Dickinson Univ, MS, 83; NY Univ, PhD(anat-biochem), 90. *Honors & Awards:* Leonardo DaVinci Award Sci, 79. *Prof Exp:* Res asst biochem, NY Univ Dent Ctr, 84-90, from instr to assoc prof anat, Basic Med Sci, 88-92, instr molecular biol, 91-93. *Concurrent Pos:* Teaching fel basic med sci, NY Univ, 82-86; biomed consult, Herbert Law Firm, 90-; fel, NIH-Nat Eye Inst, 94. *Mem:* Fel Am Inst Chemists; Am Asn Anatomists; Asn Res Vision & Ophthal; NY Acad Sci; Genetics Soc Am; Protein Soc; AMA; Sigma Xi; Royal Soc Chem. *Res:* Examination of structure and function of left-handed Z-DNA, Z-RNA and Z-helical proteins in both normal and diseased human tissues; development of nonsurgical molecular biological techniques to turn off harmful genes; histology; bioinorganic chemistry. *Mailing Add:* 157 Morningside Lane Palisades Park NJ 07650

GAGNE, JEAN-MARIE, SPECTROSCOPY, OPTICS. *Current Pos:* assoc prof, 65-80, PROF PHYSICS & ENG & HEAD, OPTICAL LAB, POLYTECH SCH, UNIV MONTREAL, 80-, HEAD, DEPT PHYS ENG, 70-, ASSOC PROF, 96- *Personal Data:* b Alma, Que, July 12, 32; m 59; c 1. *Educ:* Univ Montreal, BSc, 58, MSc, 59; Univ Paris, DSc(physics), 65. *Prof Exp:* Asst prof physics, Polytech Sch, Univ Montreal, 59-63; fel spectros, Aime-Cotton Lab, 63-65. *Mem:* AAAS; Can Asn Physicists; Optical Soc Am; Spectros Soc Can; Soc Photo-Optical Instrument Eng. *Res:* Hyperfine structure in line spectra and influence of isotopes on the hyperfine of atomic spectral lines; essentials of a problem os spectroscopy, especially Fabry-Perot spectrometers; detection of flux and spectrometers photon noise and detection noise. *Mailing Add:* Polytech Sch Univ Montreal Centre Ville CP 6079 succ A Montreal PQ H3C 3A7 Can

GAGNE, RAYMOND J, SYSTEMATIC ENTOMOLOGY. *Current Pos:* RES ENTOMOLOGIST, SYST ENTOM LAB, USDA, 65- *Personal Data:* b Meriden, Conn, Aug 27, 35; m 63; c 2. *Educ:* Univ Conn, BA, 61; Iowa State Univ, MS, 63; Univ Minn, PhD(entom), 67. *Concurrent Pos:* Ed, Proceedings Entom Soc Washington, 84-87. *Mem:* AAAS; Entom Soc Am. *Res:* Systematics of Diptera, particularly gall midges. *Mailing Add:* Systematic Entomol C/O Lab USDA US Nat Mus NHB168 Washington DC 20560

GAGNE, ROBERT RAYMOND, ELECTROCATALYSIS. *Current Pos:* DIR CORP DEVELOP, HYPERION CATALYSIS INT, 81- *Personal Data:* b Fitchburg, Mass, Mar 25, 48. *Educ:* Worchester Polytech Inst, BS, 69; Stanford Univ, PhD(chem), 74. *Prof Exp:* Asst prof chem, Calif Inst Technol, 74-81. *Mem:* Am Chem Soc; AAAS; Electrochem Soc; Royal Soc Chem. *Res:* Inorganic chemistry; homogeneous catalysis; electrocatalysis; electron transfer mechanisms; fuel cells and the conversion of solar energy to electricity and fuels. *Mailing Add:* 140 E Arrow Hwy San Dimas CA 91773

GAGNEBIN, ALBERT PAUL, METALLURGY. *Current Pos:* RETIRED. *Personal Data:* b Torrington, Conn, Jan, 23, 09; m 35; c 2. *Educ:* Yale Univ, BS, 30, MS, 32. *Honors & Awards:* Simpson Gold Medal, Am Foundrymen's Soc, 52; Charles F Rand Mem Gold Medal, Am Inst Mining Metall & Petrol Engrs, 77. *Prof Exp:* Res metallurgist, Res Lab, Int Nickel Co, 32-49, metallurgist in charge ductile iron, Res & Develop Div, 49-55, asst mgr, Nickel Sales Dept, 54-56, mgr, 56-58, asst vpres, 57-58, vpres & mgr, Primary Nickel Dept 58-64, exec vpres, 64-88. *Concurrent Pos:* Vpres, Int Nickel Co Can, Ltd, 60-64, exec vpres, 64-67, pres, Inco Ltd, 67-72, chmn, 72-74, dir, 74-88. *Mem:* Nat Acad Eng; Am Foundrymen's Soc; Am Soc Mech Engrs; Am Inst Mining, Metall & Petrol Engrs; Am Soc Metals. *Res:* Development of nickel containing materials. *Mailing Add:* 42 Cheshire Sq Little Silver NJ 07739

GAGNON, CAMILIEN JOSEPH XAVIER, PLANT PATHOLOGY, PLANT BIOCHEMISTRY. *Current Pos:* RETIRED. *Personal Data:* b Saint-Maurice, Que, Nov 11, 29; m 60; c 3. *Educ:* Laval Univ, BA, 52, BScA, 56; Cornell Univ, MSc, 60, McGill Univ, PhD(plant path), 65. *Prof Exp:* Res officer, Forestry Lab, Agr Can, 56-65; res scientist, Forest Res Lab, Dept Forestry, 65-69; res scientist, Res Sta, Agr Can, 69-90, asst dir, 72-90. *Mem:* Can Soc Plant Pathologists. *Res:* Assessment of crop losses due to diseases; epidemiology of forage crop diseases; root rots of forage legumes; etiology and resistance. *Mailing Add:* 3155 Chambord St Ste-Foy PQ G1W 2Y2 Can

GAGNON, CLAUDE, REPRODUCTIVE BIOLOGY & MEDICINE, MALE INFERTILITY. *Current Pos:* assoc prof, 84-89, PROF SURG UROL, MCGILL UNIV, 89-, DIR, UROL RES LABS, ROYAL VICTORIA HOSP, 84- *Personal Data:* b Montreal, Que, Jan 12, 50; m 73; c 3. *Educ:* Univ Montreal, BSc, 70, MSc, 71, PhD(biochem), 74. *Prof Exp:* Fel Neuropharmacol Bictr, Univ Basal, Switz, 74-76 & neuroendocrinol, NIH, Bethesda, 76-78; from asst prof to assoc prof pharmacol, Laval Univ, Que, 78-84. *Concurrent Pos:* Dir, Cell & Molecular Bioregulation Unit, Chul, Laval Univ, 81-84; young investr award, Univ Researchers, Que, Can, 87; pres, Biomed Res Consult, Can 160366, 88-93; chmn, Urol Res Comt, McGill Univ, 88-; vpres, Can Fertil & Andrology Soc, 93-; chmn res coun, Immucon Inc Res & Develop. *Mem:* Am Fertil Soc; Am Soc Cell Biol; Soc Study Reproduction; Am Soc Andrology; Can Fertil & Andrology Soc (pres, 95-96); Can Biochem Soc. *Res:* Regulation of male infertility; mechanisms controlling sperm motility and fertilizing capacity; new pathologies and molecular defects that may explain male infertility; new approaches to improve male infertility potential. *Mailing Add:* Urol Res Lab Royal Victoria Hosp Rm H6-46 McGill Univ 687 Pine Ave Montreal PQ H3A 1A1 Can

GAGNON, EUGENE GERALD, ELECTROCHEMISTRY, ELECTROCHEMICAL ENGINEERING. *Current Pos:* assoc sr res chemist, Electrochem Dept, 70-77, sr res scientist, 77-80, STAFF RES SCIENTIST, RES LAB, GEN MOTORS CORP, 80- *Personal Data:* b Revere, Mass, Feb 20, 36; m 67, Mary A; c Mark, Brian & Michelle. *Educ:* Loyola Col, Que, BSc, 57; Stevens Inst Technol, MS, 60; Pa State Univ, PhD, 70. *Prof Exp:* Asst, Stevens Inst Technol, 58-60; res chem eng, Socony Mobil Oil Co, 60-66; res asst, Pa State Univ, 66-69; asst res dir, C&D Batteries Div, Eltra Corp, 69-70. *Concurrent Pos:* Instr, Rutgers Univ, 64-66; consult, Harry Diamond Labs, Army Mat Command, 68-69; adj prof math, Lawrence Inst Technol, 73; vchmn, Electrochem Soc, 84-86, chmn, 86-88, mem bd dir, 86-88; div ed, J Electrochem Soc, 82-90. *Mem:* Am Chem Soc; Electrochem Soc (secy-treas, 78-84); Sigma Xi; Soc Tribologists & Lubrication Engrs. *Res:* Electrochemical studies on air cathodes; mathematical modeling in porous electrodes; fundamental studies on lead-acid batteries; kinetics of porous silver/silver oxide electrodes at low temperatures in KOH batteries; development of zinc-nickel oxide battery for electric vehicles; improved lead acid battery manufacturing processes; oil reclamation. *Mailing Add:* 6644 Wanita Ct Utica MI 48317. *Fax:* 313-986-2244

GAGNON, LEO PAUL, PHARMACY. *Current Pos:* CONSULT. *Personal Data:* b Milford, NH, Oct 25, 29; m 57; c 6. *Educ:* Mass Col Pharm, BS, 52; Purdue Univ, MS, 54, PhD, 57. *Prof Exp:* Res pharmacist, Pharm Res Lab, Miles Labs, Inc, 56-58, group leader, 58-59, sect head, 59-63; chief, Norwich Prod Develop Sect, Norwich Pharm Co, 63-; Prod Develop Lab, Menthalatum Co. *Mem:* AAAS; Soc Cosmetic Chem; Am Pharmaceut Asn; Acad Pharmaceut Sci; NY Acad Sci; Sigma Xi. *Res:* Pharmaceutical product development; ethical and proprietary medicinals. *Mailing Add:* 170 Cherrywood Dr Williamsville NY 14221

GAGNON, REAL, ANATOMY. *Current Pos:* RETIRED. *Personal Data:* b Montreal, Que, May 9, 24; m 52; c 3. *Educ:* Univ Montreal, BA, 45, MD, 51; Univ Mich, PhD(anat), 55. *Prof Exp:* From asst prof to assoc prof, Univ Montreal, 54-64, prof anat, 64- *Mem:* Can Asn Anat; Fr Asn Anat. *Res:* Gross anatomy; human embryology; anthropology. *Mailing Add:* 1170 Champigny St Lawrence PQ H4L 4P4 Can

GAGOLA, STEPHEN MICHAEL, JR, FINITE GROUPS. *Current Pos:* DEPT MATH, KENT STATE UNIV. *Personal Data:* b Buffalo, NY, June 25, 47; m 76; c 3. *Educ:* State Univ NY, Buffalo, BA & MA, 69; Univ Wis, PhD(math), 74. *Prof Exp:* Res fel, Mich State Univ, 74-76; asst prof, Tex A&M Univ, 76- *Mem:* Math Asn Am. *Res:* Characters of finite groups and in applying character theory to problems both within and outside of group theory. *Mailing Add:* Dept Math Kent State Univ Kent OH 44242

GAGOSIAN, ROBERT B, GEOPHYSICS, GEOCHEMISTRY. *Current Pos:* From asst scientist to sr scientist, Woods Hole Oceanog Inst, 72-82, chmn, Dept Chem, 82-87, assoc dir res, 87-92, sr assoc dir & dir res, 92-93, actg dir, 93-94, DIR, WOODS HOLE OCEANOG INST, 94- *Personal Data:* b Medford, Mass, Sept 17, 44; m, Susan; c Travis & Alex. *Educ:* Mass Inst Technol, SB, 66; Columbia Univ, PhD(org chem), 70. *Concurrent Pos:* Vis lectr, Dept Geol & Geophys, Yale Univ, 75; vis scholar, Univ Washington, 83, Australian Inst Marine Sci, 83; vis fel, Australian Nat Univ, 87; William Evans fel, Univ Otago, New Zealand, 87. *Mem:* AAAS; Am Chem Soc; Geochem Soc Am; Am Geophys Union; Europ Asn Org Geochemists; Sigma Xi. *Mailing Add:* Woods Hole Oceanog Inst Woods Hole MA 02543

GAHERTY, GEOFFREY GEORGE, MACINTOSH CONSULTING & TRAINING. *Current Pos:* COMPUT CONSULT, 87- *Personal Data:* b Montreal, PQ, Mar 7, 41; m 85; c 1. *Educ:* McGill Univ, BSc, 64; Univ Toronto, MA, 66, PhD(anthrop), 70. *Prof Exp:* Actg asst prof anthrop, Univ Calif, Santa Barbara, 68-70; asst prof, Univ Waterloo, 70-71; tutor sci & music, Cool Sch, Fac Med, McMaster Univ, 71-72, asst prof anthrop, 72-75; intern, Toronto Inst Human Rels, 76-79, resident, 79-81, supvr assoc, 81-85; assoc staff therapist, Bioenergetic Psychother Inst, 80-84; instr, Sch Continuing Studies, Univ Toronto, 87-93. *Res:* Comparative osteology of contemporary and prehistoric populations of Africa, Europe and Southeast Asia. *Mailing Add:* 48 Lonsdale Rd Toronto ON M4V 1W5 Can

GAHL, WILLIAM A, HUMAN GENETICS RESEARCH. *Current Pos:* med staff fel, Interinst Genetics Prog, NIH, 81-84, sr staff fel, Sect Human Biochem Genetics, Human Genetics Br, Nat Inst Child Health & Human Develop, 84-86, actg chief, Human Genetics Br, 88, bur chief, 88-94, MED OFFICER & HEAD, SECT HUMAN BIOCHEM GENETICS, HUMAN GENETICS BR, NAT INST CHILD HEALTH & HUMAN DEVELOP, NIH, 86- *Personal Data:* b Waukesha, Wis, Mar 11, 50; m 73, Mary E Schmitt; c Theresa, Rosemary, Christopher & Steven. *Educ:* Mass Inst Technol, BS, 72; Univ Wis, MD, 76, PhD(oncol res), 81; Am Bd Pediat, cert, 81; Am Bd Med Genetics, cert, 84. *Prof Exp:* Intern, Dept Pediat, Univ Wis Hosps, Madison, 76, resident, 77-78, chief resident, 79, instr, 80-81. *Concurrent Pos:* Fel, McArdle Labs Cancer Res, Madison, Wis, 80-81; mem, Nat Med Adv Bd, Cystinosis Found, 84-; dir, Interinst Genetics Prog, Clin Ctr, NIH, 89-; assoc ed, Am J Human Genetics, 90- *Mem:* Soc Inherited Metab Dis; Am Soc Human Genetics; Soc Pediat Res; Soc Study Inborn Errors Metab; Am Soc Clin Invest; Am Fedn Clin Res. *Res:* Biochemistry, molecular biology, diagnosis and treatment of inborn errors of metabolism, lysosomal membrane transport, Hermansky-Pudlak syndrome. *Mailing Add:* Heritable Disorders Br Bldg 10 Rm 9S-241 Nat Inst Child Health & Human Develop 9000 Rockville Pike Bethesda MD 20892. *Fax:* 301-402-0234; *E-Mail:* bgahl@helix.nih.gov

GAHLER, ARNOLD ROBERT, analytical chemistry, environmental chemistry; deceased, see previous edition for last biography

GAI, ELIEZER, GUIDANCE & NAVIGATION SYSTEMS, FAULT TOLERANT CONTROL SYSTEMS. *Current Pos:* Leader, Systs Sci Div, C S Draper Lab, 84-88, mgr, Internal Res & Develop Prog, 86-88, dir, Decision & Control Systs, 88-91, DIR TACTICAL SYSTS PROG OFF, C S DRAPER LAB, 95- *Personal Data:* b Haifa, Israel, Jan 3, 44; US citizen; c Tali. *Educ:* Technion, Israel, BSc, 65, MSc, 71; Moss Inst Technol, PhD(instrumentation control), 74. *Honors & Awards:* Barry Carlton Award, Inst Elec & Electronics Engrs, 80. *Concurrent Pos:* Chmn, Guidance & Control Tech Comt, Am Inst Aeronaut & Astronout, dep dir aeorospace sci, 86-87. *Mem:* Fel Am Inst Aeronaut & Astronaut. *Mailing Add:* 22 Roosevelt Rd Newton MA 02159. *Fax:* 617-258-3777; *E-Mail:* egai@draper.com

GAIDIS, JAMES MICHAEL, ORGANOMETALLIC CHEMISTRY. *Current Pos:* res chemist, W R Grace & Co, Cambridge, 71-73, group leader, 73-74, CHEMIST, W R GRACE & CO, WASHINGTON RES CTR, COLUMBIA, MD, 74- *Personal Data:* b Baltimore, Md, Oct 17, 40; m 63; c 3. *Educ:* Harvard Univ, AB, 63; Univ Wis-Madison, PhD(inorg chem), 67. *Prof Exp:* Res chemist, Dow Chem Co, 67-70. *Mem:* Am Chem Soc; Am Soc Testing & Mat. *Res:* Silicon chemistry; industrial chemistry; materials science. *Mailing Add:* 15012 Kenwood Ct Woodbine MD 21797

GAIDIS, MICHAEL CHRISTOPHER, SUPERCONDUCTIVITY & DEVICES. *Current Pos:* MEM TECH STAFF, JET PROPULSION LAB, PASADENA, CA, 95- *Personal Data:* b Madison, Wis, Mar 10, 67; m 90. *Educ:* Mass Inst Technol, BS(elec eng), BS(physics) & MS, 89; Yale Univ, MS, 90, PhD(appl physics), 94. *Prof Exp:* Res asst III-V semiconductors,

Lincoln Lab, Mass Inst Technol, 86-89, res asst, Elec Eng Lab, 88-89; res asst superconductivity, Yale Univ, 89-94. *Mem:* Am Phys Soc. *Res:* Superconducting single-photon x-ray detectors, primarily for astronomy applications (in conjunction with NASA); rapid thermal annealing of ion-implanted indium phosphide. *Mailing Add:* Jet Propulsion Lab 4800 Oak Grove Dr MS168-314 Pasadena CA 91109. *Fax:* 203-432-4283

GAIDOS, JAMES A, PHYSICS. *Current Pos:* from asst prof to assoc prof, 71-79, PROF PHYSICS, PURDUE UNIV, WEST LAFAYETTE, 79- *Personal Data:* b Clarksburg, WVa, July 15, 36; m 59, 88; c 2. *Educ:* WVa Univ, AB, 58; Univ Wis, PhD(physics), 63. *Prof Exp:* Res assoc physics, Univ Wis, 63-65; asst prof, Hamilton Col, 65-68. *Res:* Elementary particles. *Mailing Add:* Dept Physics Purdue Univ West Lafayette IN 47907-1396

GAIK, GERALDINE CATHERINE, HEALTH SCIENCES. *Personal Data:* b Chicago, Ill, July 6, 42; m 72. *Educ:* Mundelein Col, BS, 64; Loyola Univ, MS, 67; Northwestern Univ, PhD(anat), 72. *Prof Exp:* Asst prof gross anat & histol, Sch Dent Med, Univ Pittsburgh, 72-76; asst prof anat, Sch Dent, Loyola Univ, 76-93. *Concurrent Pos:* Nat Inst Dent Res grant, 75; res grant, Univ Pittsburgh, 75; res grant, Nat Inst Dent Res, 78-80, Dept Health, Educ & Welfare, 78-80 & Pub Health Serv, 78-80; res comt grant, Sch Dent, Loyola Univ, 81. *Mem:* Sigma Xi; Asn Anatomists; Am Asn Anatomists; Soc Neurosci. *Res:* Morphological and experimental work on the development of the avian trigeminal ganglion and the synaptic morphology in the ventral horn gray matter of the spinal cord in paraplegic monkeys. *Mailing Add:* 2532 Belmeade Dr Carrollton TX 75006

GAIL, MITCHELL H, MATHEMATICAL STATISTICS. *Current Pos:* res assoc cell biol, Nat Cancer Inst, 69-72, med statist investr, Clin & Diag Trials Sect, 72-85, chief, Biostatist Br, Div Cancer Etiology, HEAD, EPIDEMIOL METHODS SECT, DIV CANCER ETIOLOGY, NAT CANCER INST, NIH, 85-, CHIEF, BIOSTATIST BR, DIV CANCER EPIDEMIOL & GENETICS, 95- *Personal Data:* b Lexington, Ky, July, 10, 41; m 70. *Educ:* Harvard Univ, BA, 62, MD, 68; George Washington Univ, MMath, 72, PhD(math statist), 77. *Honors & Awards:* Spiegelman Gold Medal, Am Pub Health Asn, 79; Snedecor Award, Am Statist Asn, 86-90; Howard M Temin Award for AIDS Res, 93; Charles Odoroff Mem Lectr, Univ Rochester, 96. *Prof Exp:* Researcher, Biochem Dept, Harvard Med Sch, 64-65 & Mass Gen Hosp, Lab Comput Sci, 68; intern, Peter Bent Brigham Hosp, Boston, 68-69. *Concurrent Pos:* Surgeon, USPHS, 69-; chmn prog comt, Soc Clin Trials, 81, mem bd, 81-85; biostatist prog chmn, Wash Statist Soc, 82; chmn, Am Statist Asn, 86, sesquicentennial prog chmn, 87-89, bd dirs, 94-96; adj prof, Dept Biostatist, Johns Hopkins Univ, 88-; vis prof internal med, Univ Va, 89; vis lectr, Univ Pittsburgh, 91; bd counr, Div Comput Resources & Technol, NIH, 94. *Mem:* Inst Med-Nat Acad Sci; Fel Am Statist Asn (pres, 95); Biometric Soc; Soc Epidemiol Res; Am Soc Clin Invest; Soc Clin Trials; Int Statist Inst; fel AAAS; Int Chinese Statist Asn. *Res:* Statistical methodology for the design and analysis of clinical trials and epidemiological studies; clinical trials in oncology; diagnostic tests; observational studies. *Mailing Add:* 4521 Albemarle St NW 6130 Exec Blvd, Exec Plaza N Rm 403 Washington DC 20016

GAILANI, SALMAN, MEDICINE, CANCER. *Current Pos:* MED ONCOL & NEMATOL, SANDRIDGE PROF CTR. *Personal Data:* b Baghdad, Iraq, May 25, 26; US citizen; m 56; c 3. *Educ:* Univ Baghdad, MB & ChB, 49. *Prof Exp:* Sr cancer res internist, Roswell Park Mem Inst, 61-65, assoc cancer res internist, 65-69, assoc chief med, 69-78; res asst prof med & res assoc prof pharmacol, Grad Sch, State Univ NY, Buffalo, 70-78; dir oncol, St Catherine Hosp, 78-85. *Concurrent Pos:* Clin assoc prof med, Chicago Med Sch, 78- & Ind Univ, 78- *Mem:* Am Soc Hemat; Am Fedn Clin Res; Am Asn Cancer Res; Am Soc Clin Oncol; Am Inst Nutrit. *Res:* Cancer chemotherapy; nutrition. *Mailing Add:* Sandridge Prof Ctr 9116 Columbia Ave Munster IN 46321-2907

GAILAR, NORMAN MILTON, PHYSICS. *Personal Data:* b Hornell, NY, Feb 20, 18; m 69. *Educ:* Syracuse Univ, BA, 48, MS, 50; Ohio State Univ, PhD(physics), 58. *Prof Exp:* Physicist, Nat Bur Stands, 50-52 & Naval Res Lab, 52-53; from asst prof to prof physics, Univ Tenn, Knoxville, 58-85. *Mem:* Optical Soc Am. *Res:* Molecular and infrared spectroscopy; molecular structure. *Mailing Add:* 2709 Reagan Rd Knoxville TN 37931

GAILAR, OWEN H, PHYSICS. *Current Pos:* ASSOC PROF NUCLEAR PHYSICS, PURDUE UNIV, 62- *Personal Data:* b Rochester, NY, Nov 10, 25; m 52, Ruth; c Steven & Jeanna. *Educ:* Univ Rochester, BS, 46; Purdue Univ, MS, 49, PhD(exp nuclear physics), 56. *Prof Exp:* Asst physics, Purdue Univ, 46-56; supvr reactor physics, statics, Combustion Eng, Inc, 57-62. *Concurrent Pos:* Physicist, Nat Bur Stand, 51-52; consult, Pac Gas & Elec Co Calif, Commonwealth Edison, 69-70, Mex Elec Co & Int Asn Energy Economists; adj instr, Fresno City Col. *Res:* Reactor design; application of digital computers to reactor design and analysis; integration of power reactors into utility grids; nuclear fuel cycle; reactor physics; computer applications. *Mailing Add:* 345 W San Carlos Fresno CA 93704

GAILEY, FRANKLIN BRYAN, behavior-ethology; deceased, see previous edition for last biography

GAILLARD, MARY KATHARINE, GAUGE THEORIES, SUPER GRAVITY. *Current Pos:* PROF PHYSICS, UNIV CALIF, BERKELEY, 81-, FAC SR STAFF, LAWRENCE BERKELEY LAB, 81- *Personal Data:* b New Brunswick, NJ, April 1, 39; c Alain, Dominique & Bruno. *Educ:* Hollins Col, BA, 60; Columbia Univ, MA, 61; Univ Paris-sud, Orsay, France, DrSci(theory physics), 64 & 68. *Honors & Awards:* Prix Thibaud, 77; Loeb Lectr Physics, Harvard Univ, 80; Warner-Lambert Lectr, Univ Mich, 84; E O Lawrence Mem Award, 88; JJ Sakura Prize, 93. *Prof Exp:* Asst res, Nat Ctr Sci Res, 64-68, assoc res, 68-73, head res, 73-79, dir res, 80-81. *Concurrent Pos:* Vis scientist, Europ Orgn Nuclear Res, Geneva, 64-81, Nat Accelerater Lab Firm, Batovia, Fl, 73-74, & 83, Inst Theory Physics, Univ Calif, Santa Barbara, 85; chancellor's distinguished lectr, Univ Calif, Berkeley, 81; sci dir, Les Houches Summer Sch, 81; mem, Tech Assessment Comt Univ Progs, Dept Educ, 82; prin investr, NSF, 82-; mem, Subpanel New Facil, HEPAP, 83; vis comt, Fermilab, 83-85, Astrophys Adv Comt, 85-88, Physics Adv Comt, 86-90; adv comt, Theoretical Advan Study, Inst Elem Particle Physics, 83-88; chair, Comt Status Women Physics, Am Phys Soc, 85, mem, Exec Comt, Div Particles & Fields, 90-; adv bd, Inst Advan Studies, Univ Calif, Santa Barbara, 85-88; mem, Subcomt Oversight Rev, NSF Theoret Physics Prog, 88; mem, Rev Comt, Argonne Nat Lab High Energy Physics Div, 88-90; ser ed, Springer-Verlag, 88-; mem, High Energy Physics Adv Panel, Dept Energy, 91- *Mem:* Nat Acad Sci; AAAS; fel Am Acad Arts & Sci; fel Am Phys Soc. *Res:* Elementary particle theory, phenomenology of gauge theories, physics of the early universe, unification of fundamental interactions, super collider physics, effective theories of particle physics based on superstring theories. *Mailing Add:* Lawrence Berkeley Lab 50A-3115 Berkeley CA 94720. *Fax:* 510-486-6808; *E-Mail:* gaillard@lbl.gov

GAIN, RONALD ELLSWORTH, MYCOLOGY, BACTERIOLOGY. *Current Pos:* ASSOC PROF BACT & MYCOL, MARSHALL UNIV, 69- *Personal Data:* b Glendale, Calif, Dec 8, 40; m 61; c 4. *Educ:* Wilmington Col, BS, 62; Miami Univ, MS, 65; WVa Univ, PhD(microbiol), 68. *Prof Exp:* Scientist microbiol, Worcester Found Exp Biol, 68-69. *Concurrent Pos:* Consult, Redi-Prod Corp, 74- *Mem:* Mycol Soc Am; Am Soc Microbiol; Sigma Xi. *Res:* Effect of iodine antiseptic formulations on bacterial endospores. *Mailing Add:* Biol Sci Marshall Univ 400 Halgreer Blvd Huntington WV 25755-0001

GAINER, FRANK EDWARD, ANALYTICAL CHEMISTRY. *Current Pos:* Sr analytical chemist, Analytical Develop Dept, 67-73, antibiotic assay coordr, Antibiotic Assay Dept, 73-80, MGR ANTIBIOTIC ANALYTICAL AND QUAL CONTROL, ELI LILLY & CO, 80- *Personal Data:* b Waynesboro, Ga, June 18, 38; m 61; c 3. *Educ:* Morehouse Col, BS, 60; Tuskegee Inst, MS, 62; Iowa State Univ, MS, 64, PhD(chem), 67. *Mem:* Am Chem Soc; Sigma Xi. *Res:* Coordination of analytical chemical requirements associated with antibiotic development and production; chemical and microbiological assay development, lab automation, and computerization. *Mailing Add:* 1810 W Kessler Blvd Indianapolis IN 46208

GAINER, HAROLD, NEUROBIOLOGY. *Current Pos:* res physiologist, Nat Inst Child Health & Human Develop, NIH, 69-73, chief sect functional neurochem, 73-80, lab chief, Lab Neurochem & Neuroimmunol, Nat Inst Child Health & Human Develop, 83-86, LAB CHIEF, LAB NEUROCHEM, NAT INST NEUROL DIS & COMMUN DIS, NIH, 87-, DIR, BASIC NEUROSCI PROG, 90- *Personal Data:* b New York, NY, Aug 6, 35; m 65, Ruth S; c Vivian, Ben & Jesse. *Educ:* City Col New York, BS, 56; Univ Calif, Berkeley, PhD(physiol), 59. *Prof Exp:* Res fel physiol, Univ Calif, Berkeley, 59-60; USPHS res fels electrophysiol, Columbia Univ, 60-63; from asst prof to assoc prof zool, Univ Md, 63-69. *Concurrent Pos:* Lectr, Sch Med, Univ Calif, San Francisco, 59-60; USPHS res grant, 63-; vis prof, Tel Aviv Univ, 69; prefector, George Washington Univ, Neurosci Training Prog, 75-83. *Mem:* AAAS; Am Physiol Soc; Am Soc Neurochem; Neurosci Soc; Sigma Xi. *Res:* Regulation of the biochemical morphological properties of neurons; neurobiology of neuronal cytoskeletal proteins and neuropeptides. *Mailing Add:* NIH Nat Inst Neurol Dis & Commun Dis Lab Neurochem Bldg 36 Rm 4D-20 Bethesda MD 20892-0001. *Fax:* 301-496-1339

GAINER, JOHN LLOYD, CHEMICAL ENGINEERING. *Current Pos:* from asst prof to assoc prof, 66-82, PROF CHEM ENG, UNIV VA, 82- *Personal Data:* b Grafton, WVa, July 19, 38; m 81, Susan Smith; c 2. *Educ:* Univ WVa, BSChE, 60; Mass Inst Technol, MS, 61; Univ Del, PhD(chem eng), 64. *Prof Exp:* Res chem engr, silicones div, Union Carbide Corp, 64-66. *Concurrent Pos:* Vis fel, Karolinska Inst, Sweden, 71-72; vis researcher, ICI Pharmaceut, Eng, 90. *Mem:* Am Inst Chem Engrs; Am Chem Soc; Am Soc Eng Educ; Sigma Xi. *Res:* Diffusion in liquids; surface chemistry; biological mass transfer; oxygen transport and atherosclerosis; treatment of diseases with carotenoids; biotechnology. *Mailing Add:* Dept Chem Eng Univ Va Thornton Hall Charlottesville VA 22903-2442

GAINER, JOSEPH HENRY, VIROLOGY. *Current Pos:* VET MED OFFICER, FOOD & DRUG ADMIN, 73- *Personal Data:* b Atlanta, Ill, Oct 24, 24; m 54, Bridget Ginty; c Karen, Lisa, Patricia, Kelly, David & Erin. *Educ:* Ohio State Univ, DVM, 46, MS, 47; Univ Mich, MS, 58. *Prof Exp:* Instr, Ohio State Univ, 47-49; res asst comp path, Mayo Clin, 49-50; res assoc med, Univ Chicago, 50-51; asst prof vet sci, Univ Ark, 51-53; vet virologist, Fla Dept Agr, 59-66; sr vet officer, Nat Cancer Inst, 66; virologist & vet dir, Nat Inst Environ Health Sci, USPHS, 67-73. *Concurrent Pos:* Adj prof animal sci, NC State Univ, 67-73. *Mem:* Am Soc Virol; Conf Res Workers Animal Dis; Am Soc Microbiol; Am Vet Med Asn; Int Acad Path; Am Asn Immunologists. *Res:* Ovine ketosis; experimental tuberculosis chemotherapy; radiation sickness; salmonellosis; chemical warfare; equine infectious anemia; metals and viral infections; encephalomyocarditis virus infections of animals; microbial resistance; interferons; experimental radiowave heating; iron deficient neutropenia in baby pigs; bioavailability of oxy tetracycline and amoxicillin in goats; gene control of caprine interferon. *Mailing Add:* 12408 Willow Green Ct Potomac MD 20854-3044. *Fax:* 301-504-9273

GAINER, MICHAEL KIZINSKI, STELLAR PHOTOMETRY, X-RAY DIFFRACTION ANALYSIS. *Current Pos:* RETIRED. *Personal Data:* b St Louis, Mo, Feb 26, 33; m 55; c 8. *Educ:* WVa Univ, BS, 55, MS, 56. *Prof Exp:* Physicist, US Army Ballistics Res Lab, 56-62; asst prof, St Vincent Col, 62-66, assoc prof physics, 66- *Concurrent Pos:* Consult, US Army Res Off, 62-74; guest lectr, Ind Univ Pa, 76; chairperson physics, St Vincent Col, 84-; secy, Western Pa Sect, Am Asn Physics Teachers, 84-86, vpres, 86-88, pres, Western Pa Sect, Am Asn Physics Teachers, 88- *Mem:* Am Asn Physics Teachers; Astron Soc Pac. *Res:* Stellar photometry; x-ray diffraction analysis; shock wave-metal interactions; author of various publications. *Mailing Add:* RD 3 PO Box 415 Blairsville PA 15717

GAINES, ALAN MCCULLOCH, GEOCHEMISTRY, RESEARCH ADMINISTRATION. *Current Pos:* assoc prog dir, NSF, 76-79, prog dir geochem, 79-88, asst to dir sci & technol, 92-93, HEAD RES GRANTS SECT, NSF, 88- *Personal Data:* b Asheville, NC, Nov 13, 38; m 58, 75, Ruth L Norman; c Sean F, Fredericka V, Eric E & Lindsay N. *Educ:* Univ Chicago, BS, 60, MS, 63, PhD(geochem), 68. *Prof Exp:* Lectr chem, Univ Ill, Chicago, 60-62; lectr phys sci, Univ Chicago, 62-64, from res asst to res assoc geochem, 64-69; asst prof geochem, Univ Pa, 69-76. *Mem:* Fel AAAS; fel Mineral Soc Am; Am Geophys Union; Sigma Xi. *Res:* Kinetics and mechanisms of mineral reactions; geochemistry of carbonate minerals; crystal growth mechanisms. *Mailing Add:* Div Earth Sci NSF Arlington VA 22230. *E-Mail:* againes@nsf.gov

GAINES, ALBERT L(OWERY), FISSION & FUSION POWER PLANTS, EQUIPMENT DESIGN FOR FABRICATION AND MAINTENANCE. *Current Pos:* PRES, A GAINES CO, CONSULT, 84- *Personal Data:* b Selma, Ala, Feb 28, 20; m 42, Dorothy Conley; c Albert L, John B, Richard A & William S. *Educ:* Auburn Univ, BME, 46; Univ Mo, MS, 50. *Prof Exp:* Mech engr, Phillips Petrol Co, Okla, 47; asst prof mech eng, Auburn Univ, 47-48; mech engr, Humble Oil & Refining Co, Tex, 48; instr mech eng, Univ Mo, 49-50; develop engr, Union Carbide Nuclear Co Div, Union Carbide Corp, Tenn, 50-56; supvr, Thermo Group, Combustion Eng, Inc, Chattanooga, 56-58, supvr, Spec Prod Eng Sect, 59-60, supvr, Proposition Eng Sect, 60-66, mgr desalination eng, Conn, 66-67, mgr mech design sect, Nuclear Power Dept, 67-69, exec asst to dir power systs eng, 69-70, proj mgr, Waterford Steam Elec Sta Nuclear Plant, 70-76, proj mgr, Advan Develop Dept, 76-84. *Mem:* Am Soc Mech Engrs. *Res:* Design of large, heavy components for power systems; design of fuel assemblies and mechanisms for fission and fusion power plants; evaluation of project specifications and plans, including research and development; numerous patents-high pressure vessels, nuclear fuel structure and supports, superconductor magnet structures, etc. *Mailing Add:* 410 Leyswood Dr Greenville SC 29615

GAINES, DONALD FRANK, INORGANIC CHEMISTRY. *Current Pos:* from asst prof to assoc prof, 69-75, PROF INORG CHEM, UNIV WIS-MADISON, 75- *Personal Data:* b Caldwell, Idaho. July 26, 36; m 60; c 2. *Educ:* Col Idaho, BS, 58; Indiana Univ, PhD(inorg chem), 63. *Prof Exp:* Res assoc inorg chem, Indiana Univ, 63-64 & Univ Manchester, Eng, 64-65. *Mem:* Am Chem Soc; Royal Soc Chem. *Res:* Boron hydrides; organo-group III compounds; boron-group III and IV compounds; boron-nitrogen compounds; metallo-borane complexes; organo group II compounds. *Mailing Add:* Dept Chem Univ Wis 1101 University Ave Madison WI 53706

GAINES, EDWARD EVERETT, ENERGETIC PARTICLE RADIATION IN SPACE, MAGNETOSPHERIC PHYSICS. *Current Pos:* RES SCIENTIST, LOCKHEED MISSILES & SPACE CO, 77- *Personal Data:* b Cleveland, Tenn, Jan 11, 37; m 60; c 1. *Educ:* Univ Chicago, BS, 58; Wash State Univ, MS, 61. *Prof Exp:* Physicist, US Naval Radiol Defense Lab, 60; scientist, Palo Alto Res Labs, 60-65, sr scientist, 65-77. *Mem:* Am Geophys Union. *Res:* Measurement of penetrating particle radiations in space. *Mailing Add:* 737 Kendall Ave Palo Alto CA 94306

GAINES, EDWARD M(CCULLOCH), FORESTRY. *Current Pos:* RETIRED. *Personal Data:* b Pullman, Wash, Sep 30, 13; m 34, Dorothy M Hougland; c Edward E & Alan M. *Educ:* Wash State Col, BS, 34. *Prof Exp:* Forester, Nat Forest Admin, Forest Serv, USDA, 35-41, state & pvt forestry, 41-46, res ctr leader, 46-65, prog mgr res, 65-67, asst dir res Pac Southwest Forest Exp Sta, 67-74. *Mem:* Fel AAAS; Soc Am Foresters. *Res:* Forestry and related resources (water, range, etc). *Mailing Add:* 1423 Blvd Park Dr Lacey WA 98503

GAINES, GEORGE LOWEREE, JR, PHYSICAL CHEMISTRY. *Current Pos:* RES PROF, RENSSELAER POLYTECH INST, 91- *Personal Data:* b New Haven, Conn, Mar 7, 30; m 54, Margaret Greene; c Barbara, George III & Elizabeth. *Educ:* Yale Univ, BS, 50, MS, 52, PhD(chem), 54. *Prof Exp:* Chemist, E I du Pont de Nemours & Co, 50-51; asst chem res, Yale Univ, 52-54; phys chemist, Res & Develop Ctr, Gen Elec Co, 54-90. *Concurrent Pos:* Lectr, Rensselaer Polytech Inst, 70-83. *Mem:* Am Chem Soc. *Res:* Surface chemistry; ion exchange; silicate minerals; adsorption; monolayers; photosynthesis; polymer surface props. *Mailing Add:* 972 Charlton Rd Scotia NY 12302

GAINES, GORDON BRADFORD, SURFACE PHYSICS. *Current Pos:* RETIRED. *Personal Data:* b Fitzgerald, Ga, Aug 10, 23; c 1. *Educ:* Univ Ga, BS, 48, MS, 49; Capital Univ, MBA, 75. *Prof Exp:* Res engr phys electronics, Battelle Mem Inst, 50-52, asst div chief, solid state devices, 52-62, res assoc, Electronic Mat & Devices Div, 62-65, from fel to sr fel, 65-69, chief, Electronic Mat & Devices Div, 69-87,sr researcher, 73-78, res leader, 78-87. *Res:* Physical electronics; electron physics; solid state materials and devices; gas discharges; electron paramagnetic resonance, dielectrics. *Mailing Add:* 966 Faculty Dr Columbus OH 43221

GAINES, J H, ENGINEERING MECHANICS, AERONAUTICAL ENGINEERING. *Current Pos:* from asst prof to assoc prof aeronaut & mech eng, 66-72, PROF AEROSPACE ENG & ENG MECH, UNIV TEX, ARLINGTON, 72- *Personal Data:* b Luling, Tex, Mar 30, 31; m 52; c 3. *Educ:* Univ Tex, Austin, BS, 57, MS, 59, PhD(eng mech), 66. *Prof Exp:* Instr eng mech, Univ Tex, Austin, 58-59; struct engr, Gen Dynamics, Ft Worth, 59-61; lectr civil eng, Grad Sch, Southern Methodist Univ, 61; instr eng mech, Univ Tex, Austin, 61-66. *Concurrent Pos:* Consult, LTV Aerospace Corp, 68-70. *Mem:* Am Soc Civil Engrs; Am Inst Aeronaut & Astronaut; Am Soc Eng Educ. *Res:* Solid mechanics; structural analysis; vibrations; dynamics of structures. *Mailing Add:* Aerospace Eng Dept Univ Tex PO Box 19018 Arlington TX 76019

GAINES, JACK RAYMOND, ORGANIC CHEMISTRY. *Current Pos:* assoc prof, 57-66, PROF ORG CHEM, SDAK SCH MINES & TECHNOL, 66- *Personal Data:* b Bozeman, Mont, May 9, 27; m 57; c 2. *Educ:* Mont State Col, BS, 49, MS, 50, PhD(chem), 56. *Prof Exp:* Instr chem & physics, Western Mont Col Educ, 50-51; res chemist, Phillips Petrol Co, 56-57. *Mem:* Am Chem Soc; Sigma Xi. *Res:* Basic organic chemistry research in heterocyclic compounds and medicinal chemistry; preparation of new plant growth regulators; production of a road de-icer from various biomass sources. *Mailing Add:* Dept Chem & Chem Eng SDak Sch Mines & Technol 501 E St Joseph St Rapid City SD 57701

GAINES, JAMES ABNER, ANIMAL SCIENCE & NUTRITION. *Current Pos:* RETIRED. *Personal Data:* b San Antonio, Tex, Aug 5, 27; m 57; c 9. *Educ:* Agr & Mech Col Tex, BS, 49, MS, 54; Iowa State Univ, PhD(animal breeding, genetics), 57. *Prof Exp:* Assoc prof animal sci, Va Polytech Inst & State Univ, 56-89. *Concurrent Pos:* Mem staff, US AID, Argentina. *Mem:* Am Soc Animal Sci; Sigma Xi; Genetics Soc Am. *Res:* Animal genetics and husbandry; statistics; beef cattle crossbreeding. *Mailing Add:* 2705 Poverty Creek Rd Blacksburg VA 24060

GAINES, JAMES R, SOLID STATE PHYSICS. *Current Pos:* PROF PHYSICS, UNIV HAWAII, 87- *Personal Data:* b Cincinnati, Ohio, Sept 8, 35; c 2. *Educ:* Berea Col, AB, 56; Washington Univ, PhD(physics), 61. *Honors & Awards:* Spark Mastunaga Award for Renewable Energy Achievements, State & Hawaii, 91. *Prof Exp:* From asst prof to prof physics, Ohio State Univ, 61-87. *Concurrent Pos:* Consult, Avco Corp, 64-65; Alfred P Sloan fel, 64-67; vis scientist, AEC, Saclay, France, 65-66; lectr, Col France, 65-66; consult, Malaker Industs, 65-66; vis distinguished scholar, Univ Pa, 67; consult, Gardner Cryogenics Corp, 68-69, Lawrence Livermore Lab, 77- & Los Alamos, 77-; vpres & dir mat res, KMS Fusion, 89-91. *Mem:* Fel Am Phys Soc. *Res:* Nuclear magnetic resonance on liquid and solid tritium, solid hydrogen, deuterium oxide, heavy water at temperatures below four degrees Kelvin; properties of semiconductors. *Mailing Add:* Dept Physics Univ Hawaii Honolulu HI 96822

GAINES, LINDA LURIE, SCIENCE POLICY & LIFECYCLE ANALYSIS, EFFICIENT USE OF RESOURCES. *Current Pos:* res assoc, 76-77, asst environ scientist, 77-83, SYSTS ANALYST, ARGONNE NAT LAB, 76-, ENVIRON SCIENTIST, 83- *Personal Data:* b New York, NY, July 6, 47; m 71, Irwin; c Rebecca & Katherine. *Educ:* Radcliffe Col, BA, 69; Columbia Univ, MA, 71, MPhil, 74, PhD(physics), 77. *Prof Exp:* Res asst, Univ Chicago, 75-76. *Mem:* Sigma Xi; Arms Control Asn. *Res:* Problem solving applied to efficient use of resources; recycling and alternative materials usage. *Mailing Add:* Environ Sci Div Bldg 207 Argonne Nat Lab Argonne IL 60439. *E-Mail:* lgaines@anl.gov

GAINES, MICHAEL STEPHEN, POPULATION BIOLOGY. *Current Pos:* PROF, BIOL DEPT, UNIV MIAMI. *Personal Data:* b New York, NY, Jan 18, 43. *Educ:* Tulane Univ, BS, 64; Ind Univ, MA, 65, PhD(zool), 70. *Prof Exp:* Asst prof systs & ecol, Univ Kans, 70-75, assoc prof, 75- *Concurrent Pos:* Res grant, NSF. *Mem:* Am Soc Study Evolution; Ecol Soc Am; Am Soc Mammalogists. *Res:* Population regulation of fluctuating vole populations; integrating genetics and ecology. *Mailing Add:* Dept Biol Univ Miami PO Box 248106 Miami FL 33124-8106

GAINES, ROBERT D, BIOCHEMISTRY. *Current Pos:* RETIRED. *Personal Data:* b Bozeman, Mont, Sept 4, 33; m 57; c 2. *Educ:* Mont State Col, BS, 55, PhD(biochem), 60. *Prof Exp:* Res chemist, Minn Mining & Mfg Co, 54-57; sr chemist, Pillsbury Co, 60-61; from asst prof to assoc prof chem, Cent Wash State Col, 61-68, chmn dept, 62-66, prof, 68-, chmn dept, 77- *Res:* Carbohydrate chemistry; plant metabolism; microbial and animal physiology. *Mailing Add:* 511 E Fifth Ellensburg WA 98926

GAINES, ROBERT EARL, MATHEMATICS. *Current Pos:* Assoc prof, 67-77, PROF MATH & HEAD DEPT, COLO STATE UNIV, 77- *Personal Data:* b Champaign, Ill, Aug 16, 41; m 61; c 1. *Educ:* Univ Ill, Urbana, BS, 62, MS, 63; Univ Colo, Boulder, PhD(math), 67. *Concurrent Pos:* Vis Prof, Inst Math, Univ Catholique de Louvain, 75. *Mem:* Math Asn Am; Am Math Soc. *Res:* Boundary value problems for nonlinear ordinary differential equations; periodic solutions of nonlinear parabolic equations; mathematical economics. *Mailing Add:* 2533 Terry Lake Rd Ft Collins CO 80524

GAINES, TINSLEY POWELL, ANALYTICAL CHEMISTRY, SOILS & SOIL SCIENCE. *Current Pos:* RETIRED. *Personal Data:* b Elberton, Ga, Feb 3, 39; m 68, Wanda K; c Stacey A & Sarah T. *Educ:* Univ Ga, BS, 61. *Honors & Awards:* Outstanding Res Award, Sigma Xi, 83. *Prof Exp:* Chemist, Coastal Plain Exp Sta, Univ Ga, 65-91. *Concurrent Pos:* Pres, Tifton Phys Soil

Testing Lab, Inc, 82. *Mem:* Fel Asn Off Analy Chemists; Am Soc Agron; Coun Soil Testing & Plant Analy; Sigma Xi; fel Am Inst Chemists. *Res:* Development of analytical chemical methods for soil and plant analysis; chemical analysis of soil and plant tissue; developed over 7000 rootzone mixes for golf greens and athletic fields in the US and over 50 foreign countries. *Mailing Add:* 1412 Murray Ave Tifton GA 31793. Fax: 912-382-7292

GAINEY, LOUIS FRANKLIN, JR, PHYSIOLOGY, INVERTEBRATE ZOOLOGY. *Current Pos:* from asst prof to assoc prof, 76-89, chmn dept, 81-87 & 91-95, PROF, DEPT BIOL, UNIV SOUTHERN MAINE, PORTLAND, 89- *Personal Data:* b New Orleans, La, Nov 18, 47; c 4. *Educ:* Fla State Univ, BS, 69, MS, 72, PhD(physiol), 76. *Mem:* Soc Integrative & Comp Biol; AAAS; Sigma Xi. *Res:* Osmoregulation of bivalved molluscs; effects of toxic dinoflagellates on bivalve mollusks; effects of neuropeptides on bivalve mollusk cilia and muscle. *Mailing Add:* Dept Biol Univ Southern Maine 96 Falmouth St PO Box 9300 Portland ME 04104-9300. *E-Mail:* gainey@usm.maine.edu

GAINS, LAWRENCE HOWARD, ORGANIC CHEMISTRY, CHEMICAL EDUCATION. *Current Pos:* res chemist, 79-85, sr res chemist, 85-92, MGR ORGAN CHEM, LORILLARD RES CTR, LORILLARD, INC, 92- *Personal Data:* b Brooklyn, NY, June 25, 48; m 83, Karen L Coates; c Rachel S & Isaac M. *Educ:* Univ Pa, BS, 70; Univ Ariz, MS, 77, PhD(chem), 80. *Prof Exp:* Res chemist, Nabisco Res Ctr, 70-72; instr organ chem, Univ Ariz, 78-79. *Concurrent Pos:* Lectr, Guilford Col, 81- *Mem:* Sigma Xi; Am Chem Soc; AAAS. *Res:* Synthetic chemistry, specializing in anaerobic and anhydrous techniques as applied to organo-metallic chemistry; transition metal complexes and natural product syntheses particularly syntheses of flavorants. *Mailing Add:* 405 Quicksilver Ct Greensboro NC 27455-9213. *Fax:* 910-373-6640

GAINTNER, JOHN RICHARD, MEDICINE. *Current Pos:* PRES & CHIEF EXEC OFFICER, ALBANY MED CTR & PROF MED, ALBANY MED COL, 83- *Personal Data:* b Lancaster, Pa, Feb 18, 36; m 61; c 3. *Educ:* Lehigh Univ, BA, 58; Johns Hopkins Univ, MD, 62; Am Bd Internal Med, dipl, 71. *Honors & Awards:* Borden Res Award, 62. *Prof Exp:* NIH fel hemat, Johns Hopkins Univ Hosp, 66-67; from asst prof to assoc prof med, Sch Med, Univ Conn Health Ctr, Farmington, 67-77; assoc dean clin affairs, 74-75; chief staff, Univ Hosp, 69-75; assoc dean admin, Sch Med, Johns Hopkins Univ, 77-80, assoc prof med, 77-83, vpres & dept dir, 81-83. *Mem:* Fel Am Col Physicians; Am Med Asn; Med Admin Conf; fel Am Col Physician Exec; Soc Med Aminrs. *Res:* Health care delivery; medical administration; hematology, coagulation and blood platelets; malaria. *Mailing Add:* 375 Longwood Ave Boston MA 02215

GAIR, JACOB EUGENE, GEOLOGY. *Current Pos:* RETIRED. *Personal Data:* b Pittsfield, Mass, Apr 1, 22; m 44, Peggy L Davis; c Cynthia, Philip J & Daniel T. *Educ:* Univ Rochester, AB, 46; Johns Hopkins Univ, PhD(geol), 49. *Prof Exp:* Asst prof geol, Univ Ore, 49-52; geologist, US Geol Surv, 52-87. *Concurrent Pos:* Ed Econ Geol. *Mem:* Geol Soc Am; Soc Econ Geol. *Res:* Petrography and stratigraphy of Precambrian iron ranges of northern Michigan, and of iron and gold region of Minas Gerais, Brazil; structural geology; central Appalachians; petrography; volcanic rocks; iron exploration of Turkey; tungsten exploration of North Carolina; massive sulfide deposits of southern Appalachians; mineral investigations in Eastern Desert of Egypt; mineral assessments of public and Indian lands and Piedmont to Blue Ridge belts in Georgia, North Carolina and South Carolina. *Mailing Add:* 9609 Hillridge Dr Kensington MD 20895

GAISSER, THOMAS KORFF, PARTICLE PHYSICS, COSMIC RAY PHYSICS. *Current Pos:* from asst prof to assoc prof, 70-79, PROF PHYSICS, BARTOL RES INST, UNIV DEL, 79- *Personal Data:* b Evansville, Ind, Mar 12, 40; m 64, Julia Haig; c 1. *Educ:* Wabash Col, BA, 62; Univ Bristol, Eng, MSc, 65; Brown Univ, PhD(physics), 67. *Prof Exp:* Res assoc physics, Mass Inst Technol, 67-69; NATO fel, Cambridge Univ, Eng, 69-70. *Concurrent Pos:* Vis scientist, Brookhaven Nat Lab, 76 & Univ Rome, Italy, 90; vis prof, Univ Wis-Madison, 84. *Mem:* fel Am Phys Soc; Sigma Xi. *Res:* Cosmic rays and high energy physics and astrophysics; particle phenomenology. *Mailing Add:* Bartol Res Inst Univ Del Newark DE 19716

GAIT, ROBERT IRWIN, MINERALOGY, CRYSTALLOGRAPHY. *Current Pos:* asst cur, 67-71, assoc cur, 71-78, CUR MINERAL, ROYAL ONT MUS, TORONTO, 78- *Personal Data:* b Johannesburg, SAfrica, Sept 12, 38; Can citizen. *Educ:* Univ Witwatersrand, BSc, 58, Hons, 59; Univ Man, MSc, 64; PhD(mineral), 67. *Honors & Awards:* Mineral named in honor, Gaitite, 80. *Prof Exp:* Geologist diamond prospecting, Williamson Diamonds Ltd, Tanzania, 60-62. *Concurrent Pos:* Mineral res grant, Dept Univ Affairs, Ont, 69-70 & 70-71; hon dir, Can Gemmological Asn, Toronto. *Mem:* Mineral Asn Can (secy, 73); fel Mineral Soc Am; Geol Soc SAfrica; Mineral Asn SAfrica. *Res:* New minerals; mineral localities; pyrite and quartz crystallography. *Mailing Add:* Dept Earth Sci Royal Ont Mus 100 Queens Park Toronto ON M5S 2C6 Can. *Fax:* 416-586-5814; *E-Mail:* rom!rommin!robert@zoo.toronto.ca

GAITHER, ROBERT BARKER, MECHANICAL ENGINEERING. *Current Pos:* assoc prof, 62-66, chmn dept, 64-92, PROF MECH ENG, UNIV FLA, 66- *Personal Data:* b North Bay, Ont, Aug 12, 29; US citizen; m 54, Konstanze Zielke; c Patricia & Vivienne. *Educ:* Auburn Univ, BME, 51; Univ Ill, MSME, 57, PhD(mech eng), 62. *Honors & Awards:* Centennial Medalion, Am Soc Mech Engrs, 80; Centennial Medalion, Am Soc Eng Educ. *Prof Exp:* Instr mech eng, Univ Ill, 57-62. *Concurrent Pos:* Officer, USN, 51-54. *Mem:* Am Soc Mech Engrs (pres, 81-82); Am Soc Eng Educ; Sigma Xi. *Res:* Statistical thermodynamics; gas dynamics; plasma diagnostics; transport properties; engineering education. *Mailing Add:* 2100 NW 63rd Terr Gainesville FL 32605

GAITHER, THOMAS WALTER, BOTANY. *Current Pos:* Teaching asst life sci, Univ Iowa, 64-66, gen bot, 66-67 & mycol, 67-68; assoc prof, 68-80, PROF GEN BIOL, GEN BOT & NONVASCULAR PLANT MORPHOL, SLIPPERY ROCK STATE COL, 80- *Personal Data:* b Great Falls, SC, Nov 12, 38; m 68; c 1. *Educ:* Claflin Col, BS, 60; Atlanta Univ, MS, 64; Univ Iowa, PhD(bot), 68. *Mem:* AAAS; Mycol Soc Am; Bot Soc Am; Sigma Xi. *Res:* Ultrastructure of myxomycetes; morphology and development of capillitium; ultrastructural changes in angiosperm leaves throughout the growing season; mycology. *Mailing Add:* Dept Biol Slippery Rock Univ Slippery Rock PA 16057

GAITHER, WILLIAM SAMUEL, ACADEMIC ADMINISTRATION. *Current Pos:* PRES & TRUSTEE, INNER-CITY CONSORTIUM, INC; PRIN, GAITHER & ASSOCS. *Personal Data:* b Lafayette, Ind, Dec 3, 32; m 59, Robin C McGraw; c Sarah C (Setton). *Educ:* Rose Polytech Inst, BScE, 56; Princeton Univ, MSE, 62, MA, 63, PhD(civil eng), 64. *Honors & Awards:* Norman J Sollenberger Award, 83; William Chapin Award, 85. *Prof Exp:* Chief party, Ayrshire Collieries Corp, Ind, 54, construct inspector, 55; from field engr to res engr, Dravo Corp, Pa, 56-60; from field eng to field supt, Meyer Corp, Wis, 60-61; grad asst, Princeton Univ, 61-63, lectr, 64; assoc prof coastal eng, Univ Fla, 64-65; from supv engr to chief engr, port & coastal develop, Pipeline Div, Bechtel Corp, 65-67; from assoc prof to prof civil eng, Univ Del, 67-84, dean Col Marine Studies, 70-84; prof & pres, Drexel Univ, 84-87; vchmn, Roy F Weston Inc, 87-89; pres & trustee, Weston Inst, 88-93. *Concurrent Pos:* Arthur Le Grand Doty fel, 61-62; Ford Found fel port planning, 62-64; dir, Roy F Weston Co, Inc, 74-90, Mutual Assurance Co, 85-, Philadelphia Elec Co, 85-90, Univ City Sci Ctr, 84- & Penjerdel Coun, 84-; mem, Marine Bd, Nat Res Coun, 75-81, Drexel Univ, 84-87 & Weston Inst, 88-93. *Mem:* Am Soc Civil Engrs; Soc Naval Archit & Marine Engrs; AAAS; Am Soc Eng Educ. *Res:* Marine structures; ocean engineering; marine transportation systems; marine and environmental organization and policy; energy and environmental education programs to reach inner-city youth. *Mailing Add:* 3601 Baring St Philadelphia PA 19104-2332

GAITZ, CHARLES M, PSYCHIATRY, GERONTOLOGY. *Current Pos:* CLIN PROF PSYCHIAT, BAYLOR COL MED, 78-, CLIN PROF PSYCHIAT, MED SCH, UNIV TEX, HOUSTON, 83- *Personal Data:* b Victoria, Tex, May 7, 22; m 89, Arlene; c J P, Debra (Cohen) & R S. *Educ:* Rice Univ, BA, 42; Univ Tex Med Br, Galveston, MD, 46. *Honors & Awards:* Joseph T Freeman Award, Clin Med Sect, Geront Soc Am, 86; Jack Weinberg Mem Award for Geriat Psychiat, Am Psychiat Asn, 95. *Prof Exp:* Resident psychiat, Johns Hopkins Hosp, 49-52; clin asst prof, Baylor Col Med, 52-78, dir residency training, 62-65; chief, Adult Outpatient Clin, Tex Res Inst Ment Scis, TDMHMR, 60-65, chief, Geront Res Sect, 65-80, head, Clin Servs Div, 78-80, asst dir, 80-85, head, Geront Ctr, 80-85, head, Mem Family Pract Ctr, 85-92; med dir, Partial Hospitalization Spec Care Prog, Sam Houston Mem Hosp, 92-94. *Concurrent Pos:* Consult psychiat, Jewish Home for Aged, Houston, 56-; NIMH grants, 66-69 & 69-72, mem soc probs res rev comt, NIMH, 71-75; mem health sect, White House Conf Aging, 71; pres med staff, Houston Int Hosp, 72-73; mem coun res & develop, Am Psychiat Asn, 75-79, coun aging, 81-86; mem panel aging, President's Comn Ment Health, 77-78. *Mem:* Fel Am Psychiat Asn; fel Am Col Psychiatrists; Group Advan Psychiat; fel Geront Soc (pres, 76-77); fel Am Geriat Soc. *Res:* Delivery of health services to aged persons; relationship of leisure and mental health; treatment of senile dementia; issues faced by aging physicians. *Mailing Add:* 6550 Mapleridge Suite 208 Houston TX 77081

GAJAN, RAYMOND JOSEPH, ANALYTICAL CHEMISTRY, ORGANIC CHEMISTRY. *Current Pos:* RETIRED. *Personal Data:* b Missoula, Mont, Sept 30, 20; m 50; c 3. *Educ:* Univ Mont, BA, 43; Canisius Col, MS, 48. *Prof Exp:* Chemist, Nat Aniline Div, Allied Chem & Dye Corp, 43-49; inspection equip agency, US Army Chem Ctr, Md, 50-54, chem & radiol lab, 54-57; US Bur Mines, Md, 57-60; res chemist, Div Food Chem, Bur Sci, US Food & Drug Admn, 60-71, res chemist, 71-74, sr scientist, div chem & physics, 74-82, sr scientist, div chem technol, off sci, Bur Foods, 82-86. *Mem:* Sigma Xi; Am Chem Soc; fel Asn Off Analytical Chem. *Res:* Development of electroanalytical procedures for the determination of pesticide residues, drugs, food additives and other contaminants when present in foods in less than microgram amounts. *Mailing Add:* 13109 Magellan Ave Rockville MD 20853-3045

GAJDOSIK, RICHARD LEE, FUNCTIONAL ANATOMY & KINESIOLOGY, MOTION & MOVEMENT ANALYSIS. *Current Pos:* instr & clin dir, Univ Mont, 76-79, from asst prof to assoc prof, 79-92, dir, 80-83, chmn, 89-93, PROF ANAT & PHYS THER, UNIV MONT, 93- *Personal Data:* b Baltimore, Md, Oct 4, 49; m, Carol E Giller; c Robyn S & Kelli C. *Educ:* Univ Ky, BS, 71; Univ Cincinnati, MS, 74; Univ NC, Chapel Hill, PhD(cell biol & anat), 89. *Prof Exp:* Asst dir & phys therapist, Bethesda N Hosp, 71-72; dir & phys therapist, Barrett Hosp, 75-76. *Concurrent Pos:* Prin investr, Found Phys Ther, 86-88, Murdock Charitable Trust, 92. *Mem:* Am Phys Ther Asn; Sigma Xi. *Res:* Study of functional anatomy, reliability and validity of therapeutic tests and measurements and skeletal muscle active force and extensibility with special reference to tissue adaptions to therapeutic interventions; author or co-author of more than 25 original research reports, special interest articles and book chapters. *Mailing Add:* Dept Phys Ther Univ Mont Missoula MT 59812-0001. *Fax:* 406-243-2795

GAJDUSEK, DANIEL CARLETON, pediatrics, virology, for more information see previous edition

GAJENDAR, NANDIGAM, SOFTWARE SYSTEMS, COMPUTER SCIENCE. *Current Pos:* asst prof math, 70-73, assoc prof, 73-80, PROF COMPUT SCI & SYSTS ANALYST, INFORM RESOURCE CTR, GRAMBLING STATE UNIV, 80- *Personal Data:* b Nellore, India, Nov 29, 40; m 74, Shobha; c Uday. *Educ:* Sri Venkateswara Univ, India, BA, 59, MS, 61; Indian Inst Technol, Kharagpur, PhD(appl math), 65. *Prof Exp:* Lectr math, Indian Inst Technol, 65-70. *Concurrent Pos:* Grant, Manned Spacecraft Ctr, NASA, 70-71. *Mem:* Asn Comput Mach; Inst Elec & Electronics Engrs. *Res:* Computer software design and application development; numerical applications to structural problems. *Mailing Add:* Dept Math & Comput Sci Grambling State Univ Grambling LA 71245. *Fax:* 318-274-3297

GAJEWSKI, FRED JOHN, CHEMISTRY. *Current Pos:* dir tech opers, Azoplate Corp, 70-73, dir tech opers, 70-77, TECH CONSULT, AZOPLATE DIV, AM HOECHST CORP, 77- *Personal Data:* b New York, NY, May 2, 12; m 39; c 2. *Educ:* NY Univ, BS, 34, PhD(chem), 38. *Prof Exp:* Asst chem, NY Univ, 34-37; res chemist, Calco Chem Co, 37-38; area supvr res & develop, GAF Corp, 38-55, mgr process res & develop, 55-60, tech dir, Antara Div, 60-62, asst to vpres & gen mgr dyestuff & chem div, 62-64, tech adminr res & develop, 64-68, dir shareholder rels, 68-70. *Mem:* AAAS; Am Chem Soc; fel Am Inst Chem. *Res:* Surfactants; acetylene derivatives; dyestuffs; pigments; intermediates; metal carbonyls; metal powders; graphic arts. *Mailing Add:* Azoplate Corp 30 Westbrook Rd Westfield NJ 07090

GAJEWSKI, JOSEPH J, ORGANIC CHEMISTRY. *Current Pos:* from asst prof to assoc prof chem, 66-74, PROF CHEM, IND UNIV, BLOOMINGTON, 74- *Personal Data:* b Hammond, Ind, Nov 7, 39; m 62; c 2. *Educ:* Loyola Univ Chicago, BS, 61; Univ Wis, PhD(org chem), 65. *Prof Exp:* NSF fel org chem, Columbia Univ, 65-66. *Concurrent Pos:* Alfred P Sloan fel, 71-73. *Mem:* Am Chem Soc; Royal Soc Chem. *Res:* Energetics and stereochemistry of chemical reactions; application of molecular orbital theory to organic chemistry. *Mailing Add:* Dept Chem Ind Univ Bloomington IN 47405

GAJEWSKI, RYSZARD, RESEARCH ADMINISTRATION, PLASMA PHYSICS. *Current Pos:* PRES & CHIEF EXEC OFFICER, WAVEBAND CORP, 96- *Personal Data:* b Warsaw, Poland, Feb 23, 30; US citizen; m 54, Ewa Syruczek; c Hania & Piotr. *Educ:* Warsaw Tech Univ, MS, 54; Inst Physics, Polish Acad Sci, PhD(physics), 58. *Prof Exp:* Var teaching pos, 50-67; prof physics, Warsaw Tech Univ, 67-68; DSR staff mem, Mass Inst Technol, 69-71; vis assoc prof, Brandeis Univ, 71-72; sr staff mem, Am Sci & Eng, 72-73, dir res, 73-76; dir, Div Advan Energy Projs, Dept Energy, 77-90; from pres to sr vpres res & develop, Phys Optics Corp, 90-95. *Concurrent Pos:* Head lab plasma theory, Inst Nuclear Res, Warsaw, 58-68; Alfred P Sloan fel, Mass Inst Technol, 59-60; fel, Case Inst Technol, 60-61; vis scientist, Boeing Sci Res Labs, 61 & 64; mem comt peaceful uses nuclear energy, Polish Acad Sci, 64-68; vis scientist, Inst Plasma Physics, Jutphaas, Neth, 69. *Mem:* AAAS; Am Phys Soc. *Res:* Plasma equilibrium and stability in laboratory and astrophysical magnetic fields; atoms in super strong magnetic fields; research administration. *Mailing Add:* WaveBand Corp 375 Van Ness Ave Suite 1105 Torrance CA 90501

GAJEWSKI, W(ALTER) M(ICHAEL), MECHANICAL & NUCLEAR ENGINEERING. *Current Pos:* RETIRED. *Personal Data:* b Hartford, Conn, Apr 4, 23; m 49; c 3. *Educ:* Univ Conn, BEE, 49, MS, 51. *Prof Exp:* Engr, Bettis Atomic Power Lab, 51-55, sr engr & fel engr, 56, supvry engr, 56-59, sect mgr, 59-66, plant mgr, 66-68, asst proj mgr, Westinghouse-Bettis Atomic Power Plant, Pa, 68-70; eng mgr, Fast Flux Test Fac Proj, Hanford Eng Lab, Westinghouse Hanford Co, 70-72, mgr reactor opers eng, 72-85, asst mgr eng, 85-88. *Concurrent Pos:* Consult, Nuclear/Gen Eng Area. *Mem:* Inst Elec & Electronics Soc; fel Am Soc Mech Engrs; Nat Mgt Asn. *Res:* General engineering; reactor plant analysis and systems design; overall reactor plant design, development and evaluation; experimental/ research reactor operations. *Mailing Add:* 3103 S Everett Pl Kennewick WA 99337

GAJJAR, JAGDISH T(RIKAMJI), ELECTROOPTICS, ELECTRICAL ENGINEERING. *Current Pos:* asst prof to assoc prof, 70-84, PROF ELEC ENG & COMPUT SCI, UNION COL, SCHENECTADY, NY, 84- *Personal Data:* b Bombay, India, May 23, 40; m 66, Chandrika P; c Neha & Arish. *Educ:* Univ Bombay, BE, 60 & 61; Univ Okla, MEE, 63; Univ Houston, PhD(elec eng), 70. *Prof Exp:* Proj engr, Fischbach & Moore Systs Inc, Tex, 63-64; instr elec eng, Univ Tulsa, 66-67; teaching fel, Univ Houston, 67-70. *Concurrent Pos:* Prin investr, NSF eng res initiation grant, 71-72; consult, GE Corp Res & Develop Ctr, 77-86; Fulbright faculty fel, 85-86. *Mem:* Inst Elec & Electronics Engrs; Optical Soc Am. *Res:* Optical information processing; system theory and system diagnostics; applied instrumentation; atmospheric probing; rating factor communications on power systems; coding theory. *Mailing Add:* 8 Twin Brook Ct Clifton Park NY 12065. *Fax:* 518-388-6789; *E-Mail:* nsfet:gajjanj@unioncs.union.edu

GAKENHEIMER, WALTER CHRISTIAN, PHARMACEUTICAL CHEMISTRY. *Current Pos:* tech dir, 71-77, MGR RES QUAL ASSURANCE, LATIN AM DIV, ICI AMERICAS, 77- *Personal Data:* b Baltimore, Md, July 28, 16; m 41, 63. *Educ:* Univ Md, BS, 38, MS, 41, PhD(pharmaceut chem), 43. *Honors & Awards:* L S Williams Award. *Prof Exp:* Asst instr pharm, Univ Md, 38-42; synthetic org res chemist, Minerec Corp, Md, 42-45; sr chemist pharmaceut res, Merck & Co, Inc, 45-50, mgr tech serv, 50-53, mgr med mkt, 53-57; sci asst to pres, Stuart Co, 57-59, admin vpres, 59-63; tech dir int div, Atlas Chem Industs, Inc, 63-71. *Mem:* AAAS; Am Chem Soc; Drug Info Asn; NY Acad Sci. *Res:* Pharmaceutical research and development; synthesis of aminoalkanols of pharmacological interest. *Mailing Add:* 413 Stafford Rd Wilmington DE 19803-2955

GAL, ANDREW EUGENE, SYNTHETIC ORGANIC & NATURAL PRODUCT CHEMISTRY. *Current Pos:* RETIRED. *Personal Data:* b Budapest, Hungary, July 14, 18; nat US; m 51, Eva M; c Anthony A, Monica J & Cynthia A. *Educ:* Swiss Fed Inst Technol, Chem Eng, 43, ScD(org chem), 47. *Honors & Awards:* Spec Recognition Award, USPHS, 76. *Prof Exp:* Res chemist, Cruet Labs, France, 48-50 & Roques, 50-53; sr chemist, Nat Drug Co, 53-62; supvr org chem, Hazleton Labs, 62-64; res chemist, Lab Neurochem, Nat Inst Neurol Dis & Stroke, 64-73, chief, Sect Neurochem Methodol, Nat Inst Neurol & Commun Dis & Stroke, 73-89. *Mem:* Am Chem Soc. *Res:* Synthesis of organic chemicals; synthetic estrogens; carbohydrates/ alkaloids; barbituric acids; heterocyclic compounds; sphingolipids; radiochemicals; diagnostic reagents; analytical biochemistry; neurochemistry. *Mailing Add:* 707 Ware St SW Vienna VA 22180

GAL, GEORGE, ORGANIC CHEMISTRY. *Current Pos:* RETIRED. *Personal Data:* b Pecel, Hungary, July 18, 21; m 45; c 1. *Educ:* Pazmany Peter Univ, Hungary, PhD(chem), 44. *Prof Exp:* Res chemist explosives, Nitrochem Factory, Hungary, 44-46; pharmaceut, United Pharmaceut Factory, 46-52, mgr res, 52-56; sr res chemist, Merck Sharp & Dohme Labs, 57-80, sr res fel, 80-86. *Mem:* Am Chem Soc. *Res:* Reduction with complex metalhydrides; synthesis of amino alcohols, amino acids, heterocyclic compounds, steroids, antibiotics and peptides. *Mailing Add:* 5 Timberline Way Watchung NJ 07060

GAL, JOSEPH, STEREOSLELECTIVE DRUG METABOLISM & ANALYSIS. *Current Pos:* ASSOC PROF MED & PHARMACOL, SCH MED, UNIV COLO, 83- *Educ:* Univ Calif, Davis, PhD(chem), 71. *Mailing Add:* Med Clin Pharmacol Dept Univ Colo Health Sci 4200 E Ninth Ave Denver CO 80220-3706

GAL, SUSANNAH, MOLECULAR BIOLOGY, CELL BIOLOGY. *Current Pos:* res assoc, Plant Res Lab, Dept Energy, 91-94, ASST PROF, MICH STATE UNIV, 94- *Personal Data:* b Battle Creek, Mich, Oct 29, 58; m 85, Hilton E Baxter; c Christine A & Katrin M. *Educ:* Johns Hopkins Univ, PhD(biochem), 86. *Prof Exp:* Fel biotechnol, Nat Cancer Inst, NIH, 86-87; fel, Friedrich Miescher Inst, 87-91. *Mem:* Sigma Xi; Int Soc Plant Molecular Biol; Am Soc Plant Physiol. *Res:* Plant molecular biology; targeting and processing of proteins in the endomembrane system of plants; plant proteases. *Mailing Add:* Dept Biol Sci State Univ NY Binghamton NY 13902-6000

GALA, RICHARD R, PHYSIOLOGY, ENDOCRINOLOGY. *Current Pos:* assoc prof, 71-76, PROF PHYSIOL, SCH MED, WAYNE STATE UNIV, 76- *Personal Data:* b Bayonne, NJ, July 2, 35; m 95, Callie Hoxie; c Leslie B & Richard R II. *Educ:* Rutgers Univ, BS, 57, PhD(neuro-endocrinol), 63. *Prof Exp:* Asst reproductive physiol, Univ Maine, 57-58; asst bact, Rutgers Univ, 58-60; res assoc endocrinol & biochem, Sch Med, Univ Louisville, 63-65; asst prof physiol, Sch Med, Boston Univ, 65-71. *Concurrent Pos:* Fel endocrinol & biochem, Sch Med, Univ Louisville, 63-65; vis scientist, Nat Inst Res Dairying, Shinfield, Reading, Eng, 79-80; vis distinguished scientist, Meiji Univ, Kanagawa, Japan, 88; vis res investr, Lab Immunol, Nat Inst Allergy & Infectious Dis, NIH, Bethesda, Md, 91-92 & 95-96. *Mem:* AAAS; Soc Exp Biol & Med; Brit Endocrine Soc; Endocrine Soc; Am Physiol Soc; Int Soc Neuroendocrinology; Soc Neuroscience. *Res:* Relationship between nervous system and anterior pituitary; reproductive physiology; mammary gland physiology and tumorigensis; endocrine-immune interrelationships; sex difference autoimmune diseases. *Mailing Add:* Dept Physiol Wayne State Univ Sch Med Detroit MI 48201. *Fax:* 313-577-5494; *E-Mail:* rrgala@med.wayne.edu

GALABURDA, ALBERT MARK, NEUROLOGY, NEUROANATOMY. *Current Pos:* ASST NEUROLOGIST, BETH ISRAEL HOSP, 76-, DIR BEHAV NEUROL. *Personal Data:* b Santiago, Chile, July 20, 48; US citizen. *Educ:* Boston Univ, AB & MD, 71. *Prof Exp:* Intern, Boston City Hosp, 71-72, resident internal med, 72-73, resident neurol, 73-76, asst vis neurologist, 76-77. *Concurrent Pos:* Mem, Am Bd Internal Med, 75 & Am Bd Psychiat & Neurol, 77. *Mem:* Am Acad Neurol; AAAS; Pan-Am Med Asn; NY Acad Sci; Soc Neurosci; Am Neurol Asn; Am Asn Anat; Behav Neurol Soc; Int Neurophysical Soc. *Res:* Neuroanatomical research in the fields of cytoarchitectonics, language and behavior. *Mailing Add:* Behav Neurol Unit Beth Israel Hosp 330 Brookline Ave K253 Boston MA 02215. *Fax:* 617-667-7011

GALAMBOS, JANOS, STATISTICS. *Current Pos:* from asst prof to assoc prof, 70-73, PROF MATH, TEMPLE UNIV, 73- *Personal Data:* b Zirc, Hungary, Sept 1, 40; m 64, Eva Santa. *Educ:* Eotvos Lorand Univ, Budapest, MSc & PhD(probability), 63. *Prof Exp:* Asst prof porbability & statist, Eotvos Lorand Univ, 63-65; lectr math, Univ Ghana, 65-69 & Univ Ibadan, 69-70. *Concurrent Pos:* vis res fel, Statist Lab, Cambridge Univ, 68; vis prof, Iowa State Univ, 73-74, Goethe Univ, Frankfurt, 74-75, Australian Nat Univ, 78, Keio Univ, Yokohama, 85 & Univ Beijing, 89; fel, Humboldt Found, Bonn, 74-75. *Mem:* Hungarian Acad Sci; Am Math Soc; fel Inst Math Statist; Int Statist Inst. *Res:* Order statistics; distributions; probabilistic number theory; probabilistic inequalities; engineering applications of statistics. *Mailing Add:* Dept Math TU 038-16 Temple Univ Philadelphia PA 19122-2585. *E-Mail:* janos@euclid.math.temple.edu

GALAMBOS, JOHN THOMAS, MEDICINE, GASTROENTEROLOGY. *Current Pos:* DIR, DIV DIGESTIVE DIS, PVT PRACT, 92- *Personal Data:* b Budapest, Hungary, Oct 29, 21; nat US; c 3. *Educ:* Univ Ga, BS, 48; Emory Univ, MD, 52. *Honors & Awards:* Clin Achievement Award, Am Col Gastroenterol, 91. *Prof Exp:* Intern med, Barnes Hosp, St Louis, 52-53;

resident, Billings Hosp, Chicago, 53-54; USPHS res fel, Chicago, 54-55; fel med, Sch Med, Emory Univ, 55-57, assoc, 57-58, from asst prof to assoc prof, 58-67, prof med, 67-92, in-chg gastroenterol teaching prog, 58-92, dir, Dept Med, Div Digestive Dis, 68-92. *Concurrent Pos:* Dir gastroenterol clin, Grady Mem Hosp, 57; assoc physician, Emory Univ Hosp, 58; consult, Vet Admin Hosp, Atlanta, Ga. *Mem:* AAAS; NY Acad Sci; Am Col Gastroenterol(pres, 75-); Am Gastroenterol Asn; Am Col Physicians; Am Asn Study Liver Dis; Int Asn Study Liver. *Res:* Liver function and alcoholic liver disease; portal hypertension and varices and nutrition in alcoholic liver disease; viral hepatitis. *Mailing Add:* 95 Collier Rd Suite 475 Atlanta GA 30309. *E-Mail:* 75104.573@compuserve.com

GALAMBOS, ROBERT, PHYSIOLOGY, PSYCHOLOGY. *Current Pos:* prof, 68-81, EMER PROF NEUROSCI, SCH MED, UNIV CALIF, SAN DIEGO, 81-; RES SCIENTIST, CHILDREN'S HOSP RES CTR, SAN DIEGO, 81- *Personal Data:* b Lorain, Ohio, Apr 20, 14; m 39; c 3. *Educ:* Oberlin Col, AB, 35, MA, 36; Harvard Univ, AM, 38, PhD, 41; Univ Rochester, MD, 46; Yale Univ, MA, 62. *Hon Degrees:* MD, Univ Goteborg, Sweden, 71. *Prof Exp:* Instr & jr investr physiol, Harvard Med Sch, 42-43; intern, Emory Univ Hosp, 46, asst prof anat, Med Sch, 46-47; res fel, Psycho-Acoust Lab, Harvard Univ, 47-51; chief, Dept Neurophysiol, Walter Reed Army Inst Res, 51-62; Higgins Prof psychol & physiol, Yale Univ, 62-68. *Mem:* Nat Acad Sci; Am Acad Arts & Sci; Am Physiol Soc; Acoust Soc Am. *Res:* Hearing; obstacle avoidance by bats; neurophysiology of learning. *Mailing Add:* Dept Neurosci 0608 Univ Calif San Diego 9500 Gilman Dr La Jolla CA 92093-0608

GALAMBOS, THEODORE V, CIVIL ENGINEERING. *Current Pos:* JAMES L RECORD PROF STRUCT ENG, UNIV MINN, 81- *Personal Data:* b Budapest, Hungary, Apr 17, 29; US citizen; m 57; c 4. *Educ:* Univ NDak, BS, 53, MS, 54; Lehigh Univ, PhD(civil eng), 59. *Hon Degrees:* DSc, Tech Univ Budapest, 82. *Honors & Awards:* Norman Medal, Am Soc Civ Engrs, 83. *Prof Exp:* Stress analyst, Babcock & Wilcox Co, 54-56; from res asst to res assoc, Lehigh Univ, 56-59, from asst prof to assoc prof civil eng, 59-65; prof, Washington Univ, 65-68, chmn, Dept Civil Eng, 70-78, Harold R Jolley prof civil eng, 68-81. *Concurrent Pos:* Chmn Column Res Coun, 70-74; mem, struct stability res coun. *Mem:* Nat Acad Eng; hon mem Am Soc Civil Engrs; Int Asn Bridge & Struct Engrs; earthquake Eng Res Inst. *Res:* Inelastic behavior of metal structures and structural elements; static instability of members and frames; probability-based structural design; testing of large concrete structure under dynamic load. *Mailing Add:* Civil Eng Dept Univ Minn 500 Pillsbury Dr SE Minneapolis MN 55455

GALAN, LOUIS, AERONAUTICAL MANAGEMENT, ASTRONAUTICAL MANAGEMENT. *Current Pos:* RETIRED. *Personal Data:* b Pineres, Asturias, Spain, Aug 10, 28; nat US; m 59; c 2. *Educ:* Mass Inst Technol, BS, 51; Univ Mich, MS, 54 & 55. *Prof Exp:* Prog mgr, Apollo lunar exp, Mars Viking siesmometer, Toronto Zoo Ride Vehicle, Bendix Corp Aerospace Systs Div, 58-75, res engr, diesel fuel injection, Bendix Res Labs, 75-77; res engr energy systs, Environ Res Inst Mich, 77-81; dir eng, Photon Sources Inc, 81-84; dir eng, Appl Intelligent Systs, 84-87; res engr, Environ Res Inst Mich, 87-93. *Mem:* Am Soc Prof Engrs; Soc Mfg Engrs. *Mailing Add:* 4030 W Loch Alpine Dr Ann Arbor MI 48103

GALANIS, NICOLAS, HEAT & MASS TRANSFER. *Current Pos:* from asst prof to assoc prof, Univ Sherbrooke, 70-81, head dept, 81-84, assoc dean, 85-86, PROF THERMODYN HEAT TRANSFER, UNIV SHERBROOKE, 81- *Personal Data:* b Athens, Greece, May 6, 39; Can citizen; m 66; Vivienne Birt; c 2. *Educ:* Nat Tech Univ, Greece, dipl eng, 64; Cornell Univ, MS, 67, PhD(thermal eng), 70. *Honors & Awards:* R R Teetor Award, Soc Automotive Engrs, 72. *Prof Exp:* Proj engr, Thermomech Consults, Athens, 64. *Concurrent Pos:* Sci consult, Dept Econ Coord, Ctr Planning & Econ Res, Athens, Greece, 76; res assoc, Univ Queensland, Australia, 77; consult, BEAK Consult Ltd, Can, 78-79; res assoc, Ctr Nat de la Recherche Sci, France, 79-80; prin investr & adminr res contracts, Ministere de L'energie et des Ressources du Que, 80 & 93; vis scientist, Laboratoire Thermique Materiaux Batiments, Toulouse, France, 90 & 93. *Mem:* Eng Inst Can; fel Can Soc Mech Eng (vpres, 80-81); Solar Energy Soc Can; Tech Chamber Greece. *Res:* Modelling, simulation and experimentation related to energy needs of buildings and to the utilization of heat pumps, solar and wind energy; author of over 50 technical publications. *Mailing Add:* Mech Eng Dept Fac Appl Sci Univ Sherbrooke 2500 University Blvd Sherbrooke PQ J1K 2R1 Can. *Fax:* 819-821-7163

GALANTER, MARC, PSYCHIATRY, ALCOHOL & DRUG ABUSE. *Current Pos:* PROF PSYCHIAT & DIR, DIV ALCOHOLISM & DRUG ABUSE, NY UNIV SCH MED, 87-; RES SCIENTIST, COLLABORATING CTR, WHO, 87- *Personal Data:* b New York, NY, Sept 17, 41; m 64, Wynne L Roberts; c Cathryn & Margit. *Educ:* Columbia Univ, BA, 63; Albert Einstein Col Med, MD, 67; Am Bd Psychiat & Neurol, dipl. *Honors & Awards:* Psychopharmacol Award, Am Psychol Asn, 72; MacArthur Medal, Asn Med Educ & Res, 94; Gold Achievement Award, Am Psychiat Asn, 93. *Prof Exp:* Intern, Univ Calif, Los Angeles Hosp, 67-68; resident psychiat, Bronx Munic Hosp Ctr, Albert Einstein Col, 68-71, clin instr, 72-74, dir, Drug & Alcohol Consult Serv, 72-75, asst prof, 74-78, dir, Div Alcoholism & Drug Abuse, 75-87, from assoc prof to prof dept, 78-87. *Concurrent Pos:* Fel comm psychiat, Bronx Munic Hosp Ctr, Albert Einstein Col Med, 72-73; career teacher, Nat Inst Alcohol Abuse & Alcoholism, Nat Inst Drug Abuse, 73-76; clin assoc, Lab Clin Psychopharmacol, NIMH, Washington, 70-72; instr psychiat, Residency Prog, St Elizabeth's Hosp; chmn, Nat Conf Alcohol & Drug Abuse Educ, 77; dir, Lab Alcohol & Drug Abuse, WHO; ed, Official Sci Procs, Nat Coun Alcoholism, 78-; assoc ed, J Alcohol Clin & Exp Res, Am J Addictions, 79; J Substance Abuse Treat, 95-; ed-in-chief, Substance Abuse J, 78- *Mem:* Fel Am Psychiat Asn; AAAS; Am Soc Addiction Med; Am Bd Psychiat & Neurol; Res Soc Alcoholism (secy, 83-85); World Psychiat Asn; Am Acad Psychiatrists, Alcoholism & Addictions (vpres, 87-89, pres, 91-93); NY Acad Med. *Mailing Add:* 285 Central Park W New York NY 10024-3006

GALAS, DAVID JOHN, MOLECULAR GENETICS. *Current Pos:* vpres res & develop, 93-95, EXEC VPRES, DARWIN MOLECULAR CORP, 95- *Personal Data:* b St Petersburg, Fla, Feb 25, 44; m 67; c 2. *Educ:* Univ Calif, Berkeley, AB, 67; Univ Calif, Davis, MS, 68, PhD(physics), 72. *Prof Exp:* Sr scientist, Biomed Div, Lawrence Livermore Lab, Univ Calif, Berkeley, 74-77; supvr res, Dept Molecular Biol, Univ Geneva, Switz, 77-81; from asst prof to assoc prof, Dept Molecular Biol, Univ Southern Calif, 81-83, dir dept, 85-89, prof, 88-93; dir health & environ res, US Dept Energy, 89-93. *Mem:* AAAS; Am Phys Soc; Genetics Soc Am. *Res:* Molecular genetics of transposition and the mechanisms and consequences of these recombination processes; molecular interactions of DNA with proteins and their consequences in gene control and recombination. *Mailing Add:* Darwin Molecular Corp 1631 220th St SE Bothell WA 98021

GALASKA, LOUISE, PUBLIC HEALTH & EPIDEMIOLOGY. *Current Pos:* DEP DIR, DIV CANCER PREV CONTROL, NAT CTR CHRONIC DIS PREV & HEALTH PROM, CTR DIS CONTROL, 93- *Educ:* Barat Col, BA; Univ NC, Chapel Hill, MPA. *Prof Exp:* Dir, Tuberc Control Prog, State Wis; dir sexually transmitted dis/HIV Prev Prog, Chicago Dept Health. *Mailing Add:* Div Cancer Prev Control Ctr Dis Control 4770 Buford Hwy NE MS-K52 Atlanta GA 30341-3724

GALASSO, FRANCIS SALVATORE, SOLID STATE CHEMISTRY, MATERIAL SCIENCES. *Current Pos:* RETIRED. *Personal Data:* b Monson, Mass, Apr 26, 31; m 50, Lois Wood; c Cynthia (Egulf) & Gary. *Educ:* Univ Mass, BS, 53; Univ Conn, MS, 57, PhD(chem), 60. *Honors & Awards:* Cert Recognition, NASA. *Prof Exp:* Res asst solid state chem, Univ Conn, 56-60; res scientist, Res Labs, United Aircraft Corp, 60-62, res supvr mat synthesis group, 62-67, chief mat synthesis sect, 67-74; from prin scientist to sr mat scientist, United Technol Res Ctr, 74-85, mgr, Mat Synthesis Sect, 85-91. *Concurrent Pos:* Sci & eng adv to US Rep Emilio Daddario, Conn; consult, NASA space exp; vis prof, Univ Conn, 85- *Mem:* Am Chem Soc; fel Am Ceramic Soc; Am Inst Mining, Metall & Petrol Eng; Sigma Xi. *Res:* X-ray crystallography; superconducting, pyrolytic, laser, ferroelectric and ferromagnetic, fiber and composite, thermoelectric and infrared optical materials; single crystal growth; perovskite type oxides; laser processing; ceramics; carbon-carbon composite coatings. *Mailing Add:* 13 Green Manor Rd Manchester CT 06040-3342

GALASSO, GEORGE JOHN, MICROBIOLOGY, VIROLOGY. *Current Pos:* EXEC DIR, NAT FOUND BIOMED RES, 96- *Personal Data:* b New York, NY, June 3, 32; m 58, Joan C Walsh; c Catherine J, Gregory J & George J. *Educ:* Manhattan Col, BS, 54; Univ NC, PhD(microbiol), 60. *Honors & Awards:* Super Serv Award, Pub Health Serv; Asst Secy Health's Award Except Achievement, Dept Health & Human Serv & Secy's Spec Citation; Cavaliere della Republica Italiana, Repub Italy. *Prof Exp:* Trainee virol, Univ NC, 60-62, res assoc, 62-63, res asst prof, 63-64; assoc prof, Sch Med, Univ Va, 64-68; mem grants assocs prog, NIH, 68-69, chief, Infectious Dis Br & head, Antiviral Substances Prog, 69-77, chief, Develop & Appln Br, Nat Inst Allergy & Infectious Dis, 77-83, assoc dir, Extramural Affairs, 83-96. *Concurrent Pos:* Sect ed, Antiviral Res, ed, Antiviral Agents & Virus Dis of Man; ed, Int J Exp CLin Chemother; dir, Cong Authorized Found, NIH. *Mem:* Am Soc Microbiol; Infectious Dis Soc; Am Acad Microbiol; Int Soc Antiviral Res; Int AIDS Soc; AAAS. *Res:* Interferon and antiviral research; viral inhibition; antiviral substances; vaccine development; infectious diseases. *Mailing Add:* 636 Crocus Dr Rockville MD 20850-2045

GALATIANOS, ANTHONY ATHANASSIOS, MANAGEMENT INFORMATION SYSTEMS, DIGITAL CELLULAR COMMUNICATION. *Current Pos:* PROF COMPUT SCI, STATE UNIV NY, OLD WESTBURY, 83- *Personal Data:* b Delphi, Greece, Aug 24, 52; US citizen. *Educ:* City Univ NY, BA, 81, MA, 83, MS, 84, PhD(comput sci) & MPhil, 92. *Concurrent Pos:* Adj asst prof, City Univ NY, Laguaria Community Col & Baruch Col, 83. *Mem:* Asn Comput Mach; Inst Elec & Electronics Engrs; NY Acad Sci; AAAS. *Res:* Management information systems. *Mailing Add:* 1724 Parsons Blvd Flushing NY 11357

GALATZER-LEVY, ROBERT M, PSYCHOANALYSIS, CHILD & ADOLESCENT PSYCHOANALYSIS. *Current Pos:* PSYCHIATRIST, PRIVATE PRACTICE, 79-; FAC, CHICAGO INST PSYCHOANALYSIS, 89- *Personal Data:* b New York, NY, July 26, 44; m 74, Jeanne; c Daniel, Isaac, Ben, David & Emma. *Educ:* NY Univ, BS, 64, MS, 65; Wash Univ, MD, 71. *Concurrent Pos:* Lectr, Univ Chicago, 74- *Mem:* Am Psychoanal Asn; Am Acad Child & Adolescent Psychiat; Am Acad Psychiat & Law. *Res:* Effectiveness of psychoanalysis; applications of dynamic systems theory to psychoanalysis and clinical psychoanalysis; human development; forensic psychiatry. *Mailing Add:* 122 S Michigan Ave Suite 1407 Chicago IL 60603-6107. *Fax:* 312-922-5084; *E-Mail:* gala@midway.uchicago.edu

GALAWAY, RONALD ALVIN, BIO-ORGANIC CHEMISTRY. *Current Pos:* asst prof, 75-80, ASSOC PROF CHEM, LOMA LINDA UNIV, LA SIERRA CAMPUS, 80- *Personal Data:* b Oakland, Calif, June 23, 43; m 67. *Educ:* Pac Union Col, BS, 66; Univ Calif, Riverside, MS, 72, PhD(chem), 75. *Mem:* Am Chem Soc. *Res:* Investigation into the mode of action of soybean lipoxygenase and prostaglandin synthetase complex from bovine source. *Mailing Add:* 4950 Via Campeche Riverside CA 92507-5501

GALAYDA, JOHN NICOLAS, PHYSICS. *Current Pos:* DIR, APS ACCELERATOR SYSTS DIV, ARGONNE NAT LAB, 90- *Personal Data:* b Newark, NJ, Nov 29, 48; m 70; c 2. *Educ:* Lehigh Univ, BA, 70; Rutgers Univ, PhD(physics), 77. *Prof Exp:* Asst physicist accelerator physics, Brookhaven Nat Lab, 77-80, assoc physicist, 80-90. *Mem:* Fel Am Phys Soc. *Res:* Accelerator physics. *Mailing Add:* Bldg 401 Argonne Nat Lab 9700 S Cass Ave Argonne IL 60439. *Fax:* 630-252-4240

GALBIATI, LOUIS J, ELECTRICAL ENGINEERING, MATHEMATICS. *Current Pos:* RETIRED. *Personal Data:* b Vineland, NJ, Feb 17, 29; m 53; c 4. *Educ:* Johns Hopkins Univ, BE, 51; Cornell Univ, MS, 56, PhD(elec eng), 60, MEd, 67. *Prof Exp:* Engr, Gen Elec Co, Pa, 51-54; instr elec eng, Cornell Univ, 54-56; prin engr, Kimble Glass Co, Ohio, 56-58; scientist, Aero Lab, Cornell Univ, 59, asst 59-60; prof elec eng & head, Dept Eng, Merrimack Col, 60-62; mgr space payloads, Radio Corp Am, Mass, 62; mem tech staff, Mitre Corp, Mass, 62-68; proj mgr & asst controller, Serv Technol Corp, 68-71; leader, RCA Corp, 72-74; dean instr, Hartford State Tech Col, 74-76; dir eng technol, Univ Ark, 76-78; dean eng technol, State Univ NY Col Technol, Utica-Rome, 78-96. *Concurrent Pos:* Mem instrumentation eng staff, Avco Corp, Mass, 61-62; Merrimack Col rep, Comt Comput Ctr, New Eng Col, 61-62; mem, Andover Sch Comt, 65-68. *Mem:* Am Soc Eng Educ; Inst Elec & Electronics Engrs; Am Geophys Union; Instrument Soc Am. *Res:* Tropospheric control systems; arcs and magnetic fields; microprocessors; solar energy; machine vision. *Mailing Add:* 14 White Pine Rd New Hartford NY 13413

GALBRAITH, DAVID ALLAN, conservation biology, herpetology, for more information see previous edition

GALBRAITH, DONALD BARRETT, DEVELOPMENTAL GENETICS. *Current Pos:* NSF res grants genetics, Trinity Col, Conn, 64-70, assoc prof, 70-77, chair, biol dept, 87-93, PROF BIOL, TRINITY COL, CONN, 77- *Personal Data:* b McDonald, Pa, Mar 10, 37; div, Noreen L Channels; c Barbara, Barrett & Pamela. *Educ:* Grove City Col, BS, 58; Brown Univ, ScM, 60, PhD(biol), & fel, 62. *Prof Exp:* Res assoc, Brown Univ, 63. *Concurrent Pos:* Vis assoc prof oral biol, Univ Conn Health Ctr, 73; vis prof oral biol, Univ Conn Health Ctr, 80, 87. *Mem:* AAAS; Am Genetic Asn; Am Soc Zool; Int Pigment Cell Soc; Sigma Xi; Pan Am Soc Pigment Cell Res. *Res:* Developmental genetics; experimental embryology; radiation biology; expression of color loci in mice; epithelial-mesenchymal interactions. *Mailing Add:* Dept Biol Trinity Col Hartford CT 06106. *Fax:* 860-297-2538; *E-Mail:* donald.galbraith@mail.trincoll.edu

GALBRAITH, HARRY WILSON, ORGANIC CHEMISTRY. *Current Pos:* HEAD, GALBRAITH LABS, INC, 50- *Personal Data:* b Detroit, Mich, Apr 8, 18. *Educ:* Wayne State Col, BS, 40, MS, 42; Purdue Univ, PhD(org chem), 49. *Prof Exp:* Asst res chemist, Children's Fund, Mich, 40-43; asst, Cornell Univ & Purdue Univ, 43-46; analyst chem, Purdue Univ, 46-50. *Mem:* Am Chem Soc; Microchem Soc. *Res:* Organic microanalysis. *Mailing Add:* PO Box 51610 Knoxville TN 37950-1610

GALBRAITH, JAMES NELSON, JR, GEOPHYSICS. *Current Pos:* RETIRED. *Personal Data:* b Philadelphia, Pa, Apr 26, 36; m 83; c 2. *Educ:* Mass Inst Technol, SB, 58, PhD(geophys), 63. *Prof Exp:* Sr scientist, Geosci Inc, 63-67, vpres, 67-70; sr res geophysicist, Mobil Res & Develop Corp, 70-73, assoc geophys adv, 73-78, geophys coordr, 78-81, geophys mgr, 81-86, mgr seismic processing, 86-88, mgr geophys applns, Mobil Explor & Prod Serv, Inc, 88-93. *Mem:* Am Geophys Union; Soc Explor Geophys; Seismol Soc Am; Inst Elec & Electronics Engrs; Europ Asn Explor Geophysicists. *Res:* Computer applications to geophysical problems, including time series analysis and optimum single and multichannel filtering of seismic and magnetic data and solution to boundry value problems. *Mailing Add:* 4220 Irvin Simmons Dr Dallas TX 75229

GALBRAITH, ROBERT MICHAEL, MICROBIOLOGY, IMMUNOLOGY. *Current Pos:* From asst prof to assoc prof microbiol & immunol, Med Univ SC, Charleston, 77-80, from asst prof to assoc prof, Dept Path, 79-80, assoc prof, Dept Med, 81-85, vchmn clin affairs, Dept Microbiol & Immunol, 85-, PROF, DEPT MICROBIOL & IMMUNOL, MED UNIV SC, CHARLESTON, 84-, CHMN DEPT, 87-, PROF DEPT MED, 85- *Personal Data:* b Dec 1, 47. *Educ:* London Univ, MD, 71; Am Bd Internal Med, cert, 83. *Honors & Awards:* Claude B Brown Mem Lectr, 79. *Concurrent Pos:* Dir, Microbiol & Immunol Grad Prog, Med Univ SC; chmn, Multidisciplinary Task Force, Part II Hematopoietic & Immune Sect, Nat Bd Med Exams, 90-, chmn, 89-90; med dir, Liver Transplant Prog, Med Univ SC, Charleston, 90- *Mem:* Fel Am Col Physicians; Am Fedn Clin Res; Am Asn Immunologists; Am Soc Immunol Reprod; Am Soc Microbiologists; Asn Med Lab Immunologists; Clin Immunol Soc; AMA. *Res:* Microbiology; immunology. *Mailing Add:* Dept Microbiol & Immunol Med Univ SC 171 Ashley Ave Charleston SC 29425-0001. *Fax:* 803-792-2464

GALBRAITH, RUTH LEGG, TEXTILES. *Current Pos:* RETIRED. *Personal Data:* b Lecompte, La, Nov 5, 23; m 50; c 1. *Educ:* Purdue Univ, BS, 45, PhD(textile chem), 50. *Prof Exp:* Chemist orlon res, E I du Pont de Nemours & Co, 45-46; textile chemist detergent res, Gen Elec Co, 46-47; asst chem, Purdue Univ, 47-48; prof textiles, Univ Tenn, 50-55; from assoc prof to prof, Univ Ill, Urbana, 56-70; prof & head, Dept Consumer Affairs, Auburn Univ, 70-73, dean, Sch Home Econ, 73-85. *Concurrent Pos:* Mem nat adv comt, Fed Flammable Fabrics Act, 71-73; mem exec bd, Am Home Econ Asn, 75-76 & 78-80; mem, Comt of Nine, USDA, 81-83. *Mem:* Hon mem Am Soc Testing & Mat; Am Asn Textile Chemists & Colorists; Am Chem Soc; Am Home Econ Asn. *Res:* Textile chemistry; detergents; textile fiber and fabric properties. *Mailing Add:* 368 Singleton Auburn AL 36830

GALBRAITH, WILLIAM, BIOCHEMICAL PHARMACOLOGY. *Current Pos:* SR RES PHARMACOLOGIST, E I DU PONT DE NEMOURS & CO, INC, 79- *Personal Data:* b Detroit, Mich, Mar 3, 45; m 67; c 2. *Educ:* Western Reserve Univ, BA, 66; Univ Mich, Ann Arbor, MS, 68, PhD(biochem), 71. *Prof Exp:* Sr biochemist, Riker Labs, 3M Co, 71-75, res specialist biochem pharmacol, 75-79. *Mem:* Am Chem Soc; Sigma Xi; NY Acad Sci; AAAS. *Res:* Biochemistry of the lung, mucus production and secretion; lysosomal enzymes and relation to drug effects; lectins, glycoproteins, carbohydrates and mucopolysaccharides; molecular basis of drug action. *Mailing Add:* Alpha-Beta Tech 1 Innovation Dr Worcester MA 01605

GALDES, ALPHONSE, COMPUTATIONAL CHEMISTRY, BIOCHEMISTRY. *Current Pos:* sr chemist, 84-87, mgr pharmaceut res, BOC Group Tech Ctr, 87-90, sect mgr healthcare, 90-93, DIR BIOL RES, OHMEDA PPD, BOC GROUP INC, 93- *Personal Data:* b Malta, May 10, 52; m 76, Bridget Agius; c Annelise & Andrew. *Educ:* Univ Malta, BSc, 73, MSc, 75, Univ Oxford, PhD, 79. *Prof Exp:* Res fel, Harvard Med Sch, 79-81, res assoc, 81-84. *Concurrent Pos:* Rhodes scholar, 75. *Mem:* NY Acad Sci; AAAS; Am Soc Biochem Molecular Biol; Drug Info Asn. *Res:* Computer assisted design; protein structure and function; pharmacology. *Mailing Add:* 14 Cambridge Ctr Cambridge MA 02142-2005. *Fax:* 617-679-2616

GALDI, ADRIANNE, RADIOLOGICAL HEALTH. *Current Pos:* DIR, DIV ENFORCEMENT I, OFF COMPLIANCE, FOOD & DRUG ADMIN. *Personal Data:* b Apr, 1953. *Educ:* Lowell Tech Inst, BS; Univ Lowell, MS. *Prof Exp:* Regulatory officer, X-ray Prod Br, Div Compliance, Bur Radiol Health, 77-83; sr sci reviewer, Off Device Eval, 83-87, chief, Radiol Devices Br, 87-91, chief, Conventional Therapeut & Radiol Devices Br, 91; actg dir, Div Compliance Progs, Off Compliance & Surveillance. *Mem:* Radiation Res Soc; Am Asn Clin Chem. *Res:* In-vitro diagnostics; diagnostic equipment; general surgery devices. *Mailing Add:* Off Compliance Div Enforcement I (HFZ-320) 2098 Gaither Rd Rockville MD 20850. *Fax:* 301-594-4636

GALDIKAS, BIRUTE, PRIMATOLOGY. *Current Pos:* INVESTR OF ORANGUTANS, BORNEO, 71- *Personal Data:* m 81, Pak Bohap bin Jalan; c Binti, Frederick & Jane. *Concurrent Pos:* Lectr, Simon Fraser Univ, Vancouver; founder orangutan found. *Res:* Author of one book; contributed various articles to professional journals. *Mailing Add:* Camp Leakey Pangkalanbun Borneo Indonesia

GALDSTON, MORTON, MEDICINE. *Current Pos:* asst, 42-46, instr, 46-50, asst prof clin med, 50-54, asst prof med, 54-55, ASSOC PROF MED, NY UNIV MED CTR, 55-, RES ASSOC, 46- *Personal Data:* b New York, NY, Nov 2, 12; m 41; c 3. *Educ:* NY Univ, BS, 32, MD, 37. *Prof Exp:* NY Acad Med Bowen-Brooks scholar med, Johns Hopkins Hosp, 41-42. *Concurrent Pos:* From clin asst vis physician to vis physician, Goldwater Mem Hosp, 43-62; jr asst physician, Cardiac Clin, Lenox Hill Hosp, 48-52, sr asst physician, 52-58; asst vis physician, French Hosp, NY, 49-54, asst attend physician, 54-58; asst vis physician, NY Univ Hosp, 52-64, assoc vis physician, 64-; assoc vis physician, Bellevue Hosp, 55- *Mem:* Am Physiol Soc; Harvey Soc; Soc Clin Invest; Am Heart Asn; fel NY Acad Med. *Res:* Clinical research; physiology of respiration; circulation in general and of heart and kidneys; essential and experimental hypertension; humans under stress. *Mailing Add:* Dept Med NY Univ Med Ctr 550 First Ave New York NY 10016-6402. *Fax:* 212-263-8442

GALE, CHARLES, VETERINARY VIROLOGY. *Current Pos:* RETIRED. *Personal Data:* b Wyandotte, Mich, July 7, 26; wid; c 2. *Educ:* Mich State Univ, DVM, 52; Univ Minn, MPH, 55, PhD(virol), 58. *Prof Exp:* Instr vet bact & virol, Univ Minn, 52-56, asst head, Diag Lab, 53-56; from asst res prof to assoc res prof, Ohio Agr Exp Sta, 56-62, assoc prof & adv, Grad Sch, Ohio State Univ, 60-62; sr res virologist, Eli Lilly & Co, 62-71, res assoc, 71-91. *Concurrent Pos:* Mem Conf Vet Diagnosticians; bd mem, Am Col Vet Microbiol; instr, Eve Div, Indianapolis Univ. *Mem:* Am Vet Med Asn; Conf Res Workers Animal Dis; Am Asn Avian Path; US Animal Health Asn; Tissue Cult Asn; Am Soc Virol; AAAS. *Res:* Viral respiratory diseases, especially of cattle and companion animals; biological and pharmaceutical evaluations. *Mailing Add:* 6627 Pleasant Pkwy Indianapolis IN 46219

GALE, CHARLES C, JR, PHYSIOLOGY. *Current Pos:* RETIRED. *Personal Data:* b Cleveland, Ohio, Sept 28, 26; m 58; c 2. *Educ:* Ariz State Univ, BA, 51; Univ Pa, PhD(physiol), 60; Univ Stockholm, Fil Lic, 63, Fil Dr(physiol), 64. *Prof Exp:* From asst instr to instr physiol, Sch Med, Univ Pa, 56-61; NIH res fel, Royal Vet Col, Sweden, 61-64; res asst prof, Sch Med, Univ Wash, 64-65, from asst prof to assoc prof, 65-75, prof physiol, 75-82, prof biophys, 77-82. *Mem:* Am Physiol Soc; Int Soc Biometeorol; Endocrine Soc. *Res:* Neuroendocrinology, role of the central nervous system in regulation of the pituitary gland; thermoregulation, interaction of central nervous and endocrine systems; reproduction, gestation and lactation. *Mailing Add:* 3028 NW Market No 1 Seattle WA 98107

GALE, DAVID, MATHEMATICAL ECONOMICS. *Current Pos:* vis Miller prof, 65-66, prof, 66-91, EMER PROF MATH, ECON & OPER RES, UNIV CALIF, BERKELEY, 91- *Personal Data:* b New York, NY, Dec 13, 21; m 54; c 2. *Educ:* Swarthmore Col, BS, 43; Univ Mich, MA, 47; Princeton Univ, PhD(math), 49. *Honors & Awards:* Medal Achievement Award, Am Electronics Asn, 96. *Prof Exp:* Mem staff, Radiation Lab, Mass Inst Technol, 43-45; instr math, Princeton Univ, 49-50; from asst prof to prof, Brown Univ, 50-66, chmn dept, 61-66. *Concurrent Pos:* NSF res grant, 52-53; Fulbright res scholar, Denmark, 53-54; consult, Rand Corp, 55-68; Guggenheim fel & vis prof, Univ Osaka, 62-63, 81; NSF sr fel, Univ Copenhagen, 68-69; fel, Ctr Adv

Study Behav Sci, Stanford Univ, 75-76. *Mem:* Nat Acad Sci; Am Math Soc; Mat Asn Am; Economet Soc; Am Acad Arts & Sci. *Res:* Mathematical economics; theory of games; geometry of convex sets; combinatorial problems; semiconductor electronics. *Mailing Add:* Dept Math Univ Calif 909 Evans Hall Berkeley CA 94720

GALE, DOUGLAS SHANNON, II, INTERFACING, COMPUTING FACILITIES MANAGEMENT. *Current Pos:* ADJ PROF & ASST VPRES, DEPT INFO SYSTS & SERV, GEORGE WASHINGTON UNIV, 95- *Personal Data:* b Kansas City, Mo, Aug 16, 42; m 65; c 2. *Educ:* Univ Kans, BS, 64; Univ Minn, MS, 66; Kans State Univ, PhD(physics), 72. *Prof Exp:* Instr physics, St Cloud State Univ, 66-69; asst prof physics, East Tex State Univ, 72-76, assoc prof, 76-79; dir, decentralized comput serv, Cornell Univ, 79-88; dir, comput resource ctr, Univ Nebr, Lincoln, 88-95. *Mem:* Am Phys Soc; Am Asn Physics Teachers; Inst Elec & Electronics Engrs. *Res:* Nuclear physics concerned with quasi-molecular resonances in heavy ion interactions, and heavy ion induced transfer reactions; microcomputer applications; experimental atomic physics, particularly optical and x-ray emission induced by low energy heavy ion bombardment. *Mailing Add:* George Washington Univ Info Systs & Serv Rm B151 801 22nd St NW Washington DC 20052

GALE, GEORGE OSBORNE, MICROBIOLOGY, SCIENCE ADMINISTRATION. *Current Pos:* RETIRED. *Personal Data:* b Brooklyn, NY, May 3, 31; m 53; c 2. *Educ:* Hofstra Univ, BA, 53; Purdue Univ, MS, 57. *Prof Exp:* Res asst microbiol, Purdue Univ, 54-56; biochemist, Lederle Labs, Am Cyanamid Co, 56-59, res bacteriologist, Agr Div, 59-64, group leader, Clin Develop Lab, 64-91, mgr nutrit & physiol, 70-73, mgr, Agr Div, 73-91. *Mem:* AAAS; Am Soc Microbiol; Am Soc Animal Sci; NY Acad Sci. *Res:* Reproductive physiology; bacterial resistance to antibiotics; chemotherapy of experimental infections; veterinary toxicology; herbicides; fungicides; insecticides; plant growth regulants. *Mailing Add:* 4 Sandtown Terr Trenton NJ 08690

GALE, GLEN ROY, PHARMACOLOGY. *Current Pos:* RETIRED. *Personal Data:* b Florence, SC, Dec 1, 29; m 53; c 4. *Educ:* Duke Univ, BA, 50, MA, 52, PhD(pharmacol), 54. *Honors & Awards:* Inventors Award, Dept Com, 80. *Prof Exp:* Physiologist, Vet Admin Hosp, Durham, 53-55; res assoc pharmacol, Duke Univ, 57-59, assoc, 59-65; pharmacologist, Vet Admin Hosp, Durham, NC, 59-65; from asst prof to prof pharmacol, Med Univ SC, 65-93; res career scientist, Vet Admin Med Ctr, Charleston, SC, 80-93. *Concurrent Pos:* USPHS res grant, 61-93; pharmacologist, Vet Admin Hosp, 65-80. *Mem:* AAAS; Sigma Xi; Am Soc Pharmacol & Exp Therapeut; Soc Exp Biol & Med; NY Acad Sci; Am Asn Univ Professors. *Res:* Mechanisms of action of antimicrobial agents and antitumor drugs; synthesis and evaluation of platinum complexes as antineoplastic agents; biochemical pharmacology; experimental chemotherapy; heavy metal toxicology. *Mailing Add:* 1000 Fort Sumpter Dr Charleston SC 29412

GALE, HAROLD WALTER, STRATEGIC COMMUNICATION. *Current Pos:* SR STAFF ENGR, DEFENSE & SPACE SYST, COMMAND SUPPORT DIV, TRW CORP, 80- *Personal Data:* b Syracuse, NY, Mar 19, 39. *Educ:* Syracuse Univ, BS, 60; Air Force Inst Technol, MS, 68; Purdue Univ, PhD(eng), 74. *Prof Exp:* Proj engr, USAF Rocket Propulsion Lab, 60-64, div chief develop eng, Plant Reproduction Off, 64-66, proj engr, Foreign Technol Div, 67-71, dep div chief, Ballistic Missile Off, 74-76, staff develop engr, Hq Syst Command, 76-80. *Concurrent Pos:* Adj prof, Air Force Inst Technol, 69-70. *Mem:* Am Inst Aeronaut & Astronaut; Inst Elec & Electronics Engrs; Armed Forces Commun & Electronics Asn. *Res:* Interaction of electromagnetohydrodynamics processes with terrestrial systems and their utilization in dynamic multi-dimensional systems for national large-scale command and control; technical management. *Mailing Add:* 54631 Broadmoor St Alexandria VA 22315

GALE, HENRY H, MUSCLES. *Current Pos:* ASST PROF MED PHYSIOL, SCH MED, CREIGHTON UNIV, 66- *Educ:* Univ Ill, Chicago, PhD(physiol), 66. *Mailing Add:* Dept Physiol Creighton Univ 2500 California St Omaha NE 68178

GALE, JAMES LYMAN, EPIDEMIOLOGY, PUBLIC HEALTH. *Current Pos:* fel prev med, Univ Wash, 67-69, asst prof, 69-72, assoc prof epidemiol & int health, 72-78, assoc dean, 73-76, PROF EPIDEMIOL UNIV WASH, 78-,; DIR, NORTHWEST CTR PUB HEALTH PRACT, 91-; HEALTH OFFICER, KITTITAS CO, WASH, 91- *Personal Data:* b Boston, Mass, Dec 31, 34; m 66; c 4. *Educ:* Harvard Univ, AB, 57; Columbia Univ, MD, 61; Univ Wash, MS, 69. *Prof Exp:* Intern, Bellevue Hosp, New York, 61-62; resident, Bellevue & Mem Hosps, 62-64; epidemic intel serv officer, USPHS, 64-67. *Concurrent Pos:* Consult, Tri-Serv Gen Hosp, Taipei, Taiwan, 69-70; vis assoc prof, Sch Med, Nat Taiwan Univ, 69-72; USPHS career develop award, 69-74. *Mem:* Am Pub Health Asn; Infectious Dis Soc Am; Int Epidemiol Asn; Am Venereal Dis Asn; Soc Epidemiol Res. *Res:* Epidemiology of infectious disease; adverse effects of vaccines. *Mailing Add:* Dept Epidemiol SC-36 Univ Wash 3900 Seventh Ave NE Seattle WA 98195-0001

GALE, LAIRD HOUSEL, PHYSICAL ORGANIC CHEMISTRY. *Current Pos:* Res technologist radiation chem, Martinez Res Lab, Shell Oil Co, 59-62, res chemist, Emeryville Res Ctr, Shell Develop Co, 62-66, chemist-exchange scientist, Shell Res Ltd, Thornton, Eng, 66-67, sr res chemist, Shell Develop Co, Tex, 62-74, staff res chemist, 74-80, STAFF RES CHEM, BIOL SCI RES LAB, SHELL DEVELOP CO, 80- *Personal Data:* b San Francisco, Calif, Jan 24, 35; m 61; c 2. *Educ:* San Diego State Col, BS, 56; Univ Calif, PhD(org chem), 59. *Mem:* Am Chem Soc; Am Inst Chemists; Sigma Xi. *Res:* Radiation chemistry and free radical chemistry; combustion chemistry; surface analysis techniques, including x-ray photoelectron spectroscopy, auger electron spectroscopy and secondary ion mass spectroscopy; heterogeneous catalysis; mass spectroscopy. *Mailing Add:* 3601 Sagewood Lane Modesto CA 95356-1725

GALE, NORD LORAN, MICROBIOLOGY, BIOCHEMISTRY. *Current Pos:* from asst prof to assoc prof, 68-79, PROF LIFE SCI, UNIV MO, ROLLA, 80- *Personal Data:* b Phoenix, Ariz, Feb 21, 38; m 60; c 3. *Educ:* Brigham Young Univ, MS, 64, PhD(bact), 67. *Prof Exp:* Mem tech staff microbiol, TRW Inc, Calif, 66-68. *Mem:* Soc Environ Geochem & Health; Am Soc Microbiol. *Res:* Autotrophy; microbial membrane transport; distribution, physiology and toxicity of heavy metals; waste treatment. *Mailing Add:* Dept Life Sci Univ Mo Rolla 1101 McCutcheon Rd Rolla MO 65401-2631

GALE, PAULA JANE, CHEMICAL PHYSICS. *Current Pos:* RES ASSOC, MASON LAB, YALE UNIV, 75- *Personal Data:* b Joplin, Mo, July 26, 46. *Educ:* Randolph-Macon Woman's Col, BA, 68; Brandeis Univ, PhD(chem), 76. *Prof Exp:* Analytical chemist, Process Res, Inc, Mass, 69. *Mem:* Am Soc Mass Spectros. *Res:* Atomic and molecular scattering. *Mailing Add:* Bristol Myers Squibb PO Box 4500 Princeton NJ 08543-4500

GALE, PAULA M, WETLANDS, NUTRIENT CYCLING. *Current Pos:* res assoc, 88-91, RES ASST PROF, SOIL & WATER SCI, UNIV FLA, 91- *Personal Data:* b Kansas City, Kans, Oct 18, 56. *Educ:* Univ Ark, BS, 83, PhD(soil biochem), 88. *Prof Exp:* Lab asst, Agron Dept, Univ Ark, 82-83, grad asst, 83-84, res asst, 84-88. *Mem:* Sigma Xi; Am Soc Agron; Soil Sci Soc Am; Coun Agr Sci & Technol. *Res:* Nutrient (carbon, nitrogen, phosphorus and sulfur), cycling and management in both agricultural and nonagricultural settings including on-site disposal and management of non-hazardous wastes in both upland and wetland environments; modeling nutrient transformations associated with land applied plant, industrial and animal residues for the purpose of predicting plant availability of these nutrients. *Mailing Add:* Agr Dept Univ Tenn Martin TN 38238-0001

GALE, ROBERT JAMES, ELECTROCHEMISTRY, SOIL REMEDIATION. *Current Pos:* ASSOC PROF CHEM, LA STATE UNIV, 81- *Personal Data:* b Swindon, Eng, Apr 18, 42; m 71; Julia M Herdman; c Juliet E & Thomas E. *Educ:* Imperial Col, London Univ, BS, ARCS, 63; McGill Univ, Montreal, PhD(chem), 73. *Prof Exp:* Sr chemist, Wilkinson Sword Ltd, London, 64-67; engr, RCA Victor Co Ltd, Montreal, 67-68. *Concurrent Pos:* Vpres, Electrokinetics Inc, Baton Rouge, 89-93. *Mem:* Electrochem Soc. *Res:* Electrokinetic processes for soil decontamination, molten salt research for electric vehicle battery development and the use of high frequencies for future electroanalytical applications. *Mailing Add:* Chem Dept La State Univ Baton Rouge LA 70803-0001. Fax: 504-388-3458

GALE, ROBERT PETER, IMMUNOBIOLOGY, MEDICINE. *Current Pos:* Intern med, Univ Calif, Los Angeles, 70-71, resident, 71-72, fel, 72-74, SCHOLAR IMMUNOL, UNIV CALIF, LOS ANGELES, 72-, ASST PROF MED, 74- *Personal Data:* b New York, NY, Oct 11, 45. *Educ:* Hobart Col, AB, 66; State Univ NY Buffalo, MD, 70; Am Bd Internal Med, dipl, 74; Univ Calif, Los Angeles, PhD, 78. *Concurrent Pos:* Scholar, Leukemia Soc Am, 77- *Mem:* Am Asn Cancer Res; Am Soc Clin Oncol; Am Soc Hematol; Sigma Xi; Soc Exp Biol & Med. *Res:* Bone marrow transplantation; leukemia research. *Mailing Add:* Salick Health Care Inc 8201 Beverly Blvd Los Angeles CA 90048-4520

GALE, STEPHEN BRUCE, ENVIRONMENTAL ENGINEERING, INDUSTRIAL WASTE. *Current Pos:* sales mgr, 78-, PRES, NIAGARA ENVIRON ASSOCS, 81-; PRES, NIAGRA FIBERGLASS INC, 81- *Personal Data:* b Syracuse, NY, June 21, 40; m 63; c 3. *Educ:* Syracuse Univ, BSChE, 62; MS, 64, PhD(sanit eng), 69. *Prof Exp:* Sanit engr, Air Pollution Eng Div, US Army Environ Hyg Agency, 69-72; tech dir & sales mgr, Andco Environ Processes Inc, 72-78. *Mem:* Am Inst Chem Engrs. *Res:* Kinetics of oxidation of sulfites by dissolved oxygen; kinetics of photochemical oxidation of sulfur dioxide in dilute gas-air mixtures; air pollution instrumentation; electrochemical removal of chromates and other heavy metals from waste water effluents. *Mailing Add:* Niagra Fiberglass Inc 88 Okell St Buffalo NY 14220

GALE, WILLIAM ARTHUR, COMPUTATIONAL LINGUISTICS, TEXT INTERPRETATION. *Current Pos:* RETIRED. *Personal Data:* b Houston, Tex, June 23, 39; m 68, Lynn Platt; c Marion E & Rebekah E. *Educ:* Rice Univ, BA, 61, MA, 66, PhD(physics), 68. *Prof Exp:* Mem tech staff, Bell Commun Res, 69-73; mem tech staff, AT&T Bell Labs, 73- *Concurrent Pos:* Dir, Soc Artificial Intel & Statist, 87-93. *Mem:* Am Asn Artificial Intel; Am Statist Asn; Soc Artificial Intel & Statist. *Res:* Artificial intelligence; statistics; computational linguistics; economics. *Mailing Add:* 17 Essex Ave Maplewood NJ 07040

GALEANO, SERGIO F(RANCIS), ENVIRONMENTAL ENGINEERING. *Current Pos:* SR CONSULT, GA PACIFIC CORP, 90- *Personal Data:* b Havana, Cuba, Apr 7, 34; US citizen; wid; c 3. *Educ:* Univ Havana, MS, 57; Univ Fla, MSE, 64, PhD(bioenviron eng), 66. *Prof Exp:* Proj engr, Ingenieria Vame SAm, 56-58; chief design sect, Comision Nacional Acueductos, 59-60, head eng div, 60-61; process develop eng, Owens-Ill, Inc, 66-69, proj mgr new systs develop, 69-71, dir, Chem Div, 77-82, dir, Environ

& Occup Health Div, Owens Health Div, 82. *Concurrent Pos:* Intersoc Bd Environ Eng. *Mem:* Am Inst Chem Engrs; Acad Environ Engrs; Sigma Xi; Nat Soc Prof Engrs; Am Soc Civil Engrs. *Res:* Deep well hydrology; water supply systems; environmental control; process development drying systems. *Mailing Add:* 1707 Yarborough Dr Peachtree City GA 30269-3620

GALEENER, FRANK LEE, solid state physics; deceased, see previous edition for last biography

GALEHOUSE, JON SCOTT, NEOTECTONICS, EARTHQUAKE STUDIES. *Current Pos:* from asst prof to assoc prof, 67-75, chmn dept, 73-76, PROF GEOL, SAN FRANCISCO STATE UNIV, 75- *Personal Data:* b Doylestown, Ohio, Feb 16, 39; m 59, Barbara Adams; c Scott & Jennifer. *Educ:* Col Wooster, BA, 62; Univ Calif, Berkeley, PhD(geol), 66. *Prof Exp:* NSF fel, 66-67. *Concurrent Pos:* Am Chem Soc Petrol Res Fund grant, 67-69; Personal Mobility grant, NSF, 72-73; res grants, US Geol Surv, 79-94. *Mem:* AAAS; Geol Soc Am; Soc Sedimentary Geol; Am Geophys Union; Int Asn Sedimentologists; Sigma Xi. *Res:* Marine sedimentation and provenance of terriginous deposits in the ocean; creep rates on active faults. *Mailing Add:* Dept Geosci San Francisco State Univ 1600 Holloway Ave San Francisco CA 94132-1722. *Fax:* 415-338-7705

GALES, ROBERT SYDNEY, ACOUSTICS. *Current Pos:* RETIRED. *Personal Data:* b Boston, Mass, Dec 12, 14; m 42, Dorothea Frances Yocum; c Robert Timothy, Patricia Frances & Michael Jeffery. *Educ:* Univ Calif, Los Angeles, AB, 38, MA, 42. *Prof Exp:* Asst physics, Univ Calif, Los Angeles, 40-42; assoc physicist & group leader, Div War Res, Univ Calif, 42-45; from physicist & leader, Psychol Physics Br to head, Listening Div, Naval Electronics Lab, 46-67; head listening div, Naval Undersea Ctr, 67-77; supvry physicist, Naval Ocean Systs Ctr, 77-80; staff scientist, Comput Sci Corp, 81-83; consult, SEACO Div Sci Appln Int Corp, 87-88. *Concurrent Pos:* Consult acoust, 48-; mem, Nat Res Coun Comt Hearing, Bioacoustics and Biomechanics, 52-80. *Mem:* Acoust Soc Am (pres, 75-76); Inst Noise Control Eng; Sigma Xi. *Res:* Hearing aids; audio masking; measurements and methods of detection of underwater sounds; noise measurement; voice communication; effects of noise on human performance. *Mailing Add:* 1645 Los Altos Rd San Diego CA 92109

GALETTO, WILLIAM GEORGE, FOOD CHEMISTRY. *Current Pos:* res chemist, Res & Develop Lab, 68-78, mgr tech dept, 78-80, RES MGR, FLAVOR DIV, McCORMICK & CO, 80- *Personal Data:* b Grass Valley, Calif, Oct 5, 39; m 62; c 2. *Educ:* Chico State Col, BS, 61; Univ Calif, Davis, PhD(agr chem), 67. *Prof Exp:* Res asst flavor chem, Dept Enol, Univ Calif, Davis, 62-67; res chemist, Western Regional Res Lab, USDA, 67-68. *Concurrent Pos:* Nat Acad Sci Res Coun assoc 67-68. *Mem:* AAAS; Am Chem Soc; Inst Food Technol; Am Soc Enol. *Res:* Stereochemistry of sesquiterpene lactones; synthesis of natural products; flavor chemistry; gas chromatographic separation of diastereoisomers; enzymatic flavor development. *Mailing Add:* 2712 Crystal Lane Baldwin MD 21013-9115

GALEY, JOHN APT, REACTOR PHYSICS. *Current Pos:* RETIRED. *Personal Data:* b Oak Park, Ill, May 27, 28; m 52, Shirley A Belling; c John A Jr, Anne E (Lyon), Jennifer L (Falvo), Michael D & Bradford C. *Educ:* Yale Univ, BS, 50; Univ Chicago, MS, 54, PhD(physics), 59. *Prof Exp:* Res assoc physics, Notre Dame Univ, 59-60; sr scientist, Bettis Atomic Power Lab, Westinghouse Elec Corp, 60-92. *Res:* Photonuclear work; 100 million electron volt betatron; low energy physics; Van de Graff accelerators; experimental reactor physics. *Mailing Add:* 267 Toura Dr Pleasant Hills PA 15236

GALEY, WILLIAM RALEIGH, PHYSIOLOGY, BIOPHYSICS. *Current Pos:* from asst prof to assoc prof, 72-84, PROF PHYSIOL, SCH MED, UNIV NMEX, 84-, DIR, BIOMED SCI GRAD PROG, 94- *Personal Data:* b Boise, Idaho, July 26, 43; m 83, Cristina Beato; c Ryan, Reid, Cristina & Scott. *Educ:* Lewis & Clark Col, BS, 65; Univ Ore, PhD(biochem), 69. *Prof Exp:* NIH & Mass Heart Asn fels biophys, Harvard Med Sch, 69-71; sr biophysicist, Alza Corp, 71-72. *Concurrent Pos:* Consult, Alza Corp, 72-73, Bell & Howell Corp, 73-74 & Vick Corp, 76-; Fulbright fel, Port, 83 & Turkey, 86; consult med educ, trial lawyers; mem, Basic Sci Educ Forum; vis prof, Panum Inst, Denmark, 83 & St Georges Univ, 93-96. *Mem:* Am Physiol Soc; Biophys Soc; Sigma Xi; AAAS. *Res:* Effect of disease on water and nonelectrolyte transport in cells; electrolyte and water secretion by the exocrine pancreas; cell physiology; medical education. *Mailing Add:* Dept Physiol Univ NMex Sch Med 915 Stanford Dr Albuquerque NM 87131-5196. *Fax:* 505-277-8738; *E-Mail:* bgaley@medusa,unm,edu

GALIBOIS, ANDRE, PHYSICAL METALLURGY, OPERATIONS RESEARCH. *Current Pos:* from asst prof to assoc prof, 65-76, dir eng physics, 71-79, head mines & metall, 76-85, PROF MINES & METALL, LAVAL UNIV, 76-, ASST DIR DEPT, 70- *Personal Data:* b Quebec, Que, Apr 21, 38; m 69; c 1. *Educ:* Laval Univ, BA, 57, BASc, 61, DSc(metall), 64. *Prof Exp:* Lectr eng mech, Laval Univ, 64; Ford Found res fel metall & mat sci, Univ Toronto, 64-65. *Concurrent Pos:* Mem, Defense Res Bd Can, 69-, fac coun, Laval Univ, 66-, Phys Metall Subcomt, Can Nat Adv Comt Res Mining & Metall, 69-; sr partner, Opers Res Consult Firm, 69- *Mem:* Am Soc Metals; Can Inst Mining & Metall. *Res:* Martensitic transformation and tempering mechanism in extra low carbon steels; grain boundaries migration and grain growth in high purity lead, tin and aluminum and in material doped with impurities; operations research applied to mining ventures. *Mailing Add:* Dept Mining & Metall Univ Laval Quebec PQ G1K 7P4 Can

GALIL, FAHMY, TEXTILE CHEMISTRY. *Current Pos:* technol mgr, 69-81, SR SPECIALIST, MONSANTO FIBERS CO, 81- *Personal Data:* b Talkha, Egypt, Oct 20, 25; m 59; c 2. *Educ:* Univ Cairo, BSc, 47, MSc, 54; Manchester Col Sci & Technol, Eng, PhD(polymer sci), 58. *Prof Exp:* Textile chemist, Misr Spinning & Weaving Co, Egypt, 47-50; asst eng, Univ Cairo, 50-58, lectr, 58-64, assoc prof, 64-68; res fel polymers, Univ Mainz, 68-69. *Concurrent Pos:* Humboldt Found fel, Reutlingen, Ger, 62-64. *Mem:* Am Chem Soc; sr mem Am Asn Textile Chemists & Colorists; corp mem Brit Soc Dyers & Colourists. *Res:* Flammability of textile materials; information management systems; theory of dyeing; polymer structure. *Mailing Add:* 2411 Circle Dr SE PO Box 2204 Decatur AL 35603

GALIL, KHADRY AHMED, PERIODONTAL RESEARCH, RESINS & ACID ETCHING. *Current Pos:* asst prof anat, 73-76, ASSOC PROF ANAT & OEAL SURG, UNIV WESTERN ONT, CAN, 76- *Personal Data:* b Egypt, 1942; Can citizen; m 75; c 1. *Educ:* Alexandria Univ, DDS, 64, DrOralSurg, 67; Univ Western Ont, PhD(anat), 73, MSC Periodont, Univ Mich, 87. *Prof Exp:* Asst prof oral surg, Univ Alexandria, Egypt, 64-67; vis prof orthodont, Univ Mich, 69. *Concurrent Pos:* Pvt pract periodontics, Univ Hosp London, Ont. *Mem:* Int Asn Dent Res; Can Dent Asn; fel Acad Gen Dent; Can Asn Dent Res; fel Int Acad Dent; Can Acad Periodont. *Res:* Wound healing. *Mailing Add:* Med Sci Bldg Univ Western Ont London ON N6A 5C1 Can

GALIL, ZUI, COMPUTER SCIENCE. *Current Pos:* chmn, 89-94, PROF, DEPT COMPUT SCI, COLUMBIA UNIV, 82-, DEAN & MORRIS & AIMA A PROF ENG, SCH ENG & APPL SCI, 95- *Personal Data:* b Tel-Aviv, Israel, June 26, 47; US citizen; c 1. *Educ:* Tel-Aviv Univ, BSc, 70, MSc, 71; Cornell Univ, PhD(comput sci), 75. *Prof Exp:* Chmn, Comput Sci Dept, Tel-Aviv Univ, 79-82, prof, 81. *Concurrent Pos:* Res assoc, Dept Math, Cornell Univ, 73-78, Univ Calif, Berkeley, 79-82; researcher, IBM Res Ctr, 75-79; vis prof, Tokyo Univ, 80; chmn, Asn Comput Mach, SIGACT, 83-87; chair, Found Track, 13th World Comput Cong; ed-in-chief, J Algorithms, 88-; managing ed, SIAM J Comput, 91- *Mem:* Fel Asn Comput Mach. *Mailing Add:* Columbia Univ W 116th St & Broadway New York NY 10027

GALIN, DAVID, NEUROPSYCHOLOGY, PSYCHOPHYSIOLOGY. *Current Pos:* asst prof in residence, 68-75, ASSOC PROF IN RESIDENCE, LANGLEY PORTER INST, UNIV CALIF, SAN FRANCISCO, 75- *Personal Data:* b New York, NY, Mar 6, 36; c 2. *Educ:* Antioch Col, BS, 57; Albert Einstein Col Med, MD, 61. *Prof Exp:* Res assoc, NIMH, 62-65; fel, Fels Res Inst, 65-68. *Res:* Brain mechanisms related to behavior, particularly consciousness and subjective experience, neurodevelopment and specialization and interaction of the two cerebral hemispheres. *Mailing Add:* Dept Psychiat Univ Calif 513 Parnassus Ave San Francisco CA 94122-2722

GALIN, MELVYN PHILIP, MANAGEMENT OF SCIENTIFIC & TECHNICAL INFORMATION, COMPUTER NETWORK MANAGEMENT. *Current Pos:* PRES & CHIEF EXEC OFFICER, INST EDUC SERVS INC, 85- *Personal Data:* b Savannah, Ga, Sept 8, 31. *Educ:* Ga Inst Technol, BS, 54; Ind Univ, MBA, 56, DBA(mgmt), 67. *Prof Exp:* Mgt specialist, Off Secy Defense, 56-60; adj prof finance econ investment, Northeastern Univ, 72-80, mgt investments, Middlesex Community Col, 80-86; div prin info systs, Mitre Corp, 84-92, spec asst to pres, 86-92. *Concurrent Pos:* Staff, Govs Mgt Task Force, 75, team leader, 79, adv, 89; exec secy, Govs Adv Comt Info Technol, 76-92; chmn, Govs Adv Comt Human Resources, 80-83; mem, Energy Adv Bd Mass, 90-92. *Res:* Management and use of scientific and technical information in industry and the management of computer systems and network; corporate mergers and acquisitions. *Mailing Add:* 108 Johnston St Savannah GA 31405-5605

GALIN, MILES A, OPHTHALMOLOGY. *Current Pos:* ADJ PROF POLYMER SCI, UNIV LOWELL, 82- *Personal Data:* b New York, NY, Jan 6, 32; m 53; c 4. *Educ:* NY Univ, AB, 51, MD, 55; Nat Bd Med Examrs, dipl, 56, Am Bd Ophthalmol, dipl, 60. *Honors & Awards:* William Warner Hoppin Award, NY Acad Med, 59; Dr Ignacia Barraguer Mem Award, 68; Dr Henry Balconi Mem lectr, NY, 67; Binkhorst Award, Am Intra-Ocular Implant Soc, 78; Rayner Reddy Found lectr, UK Intraocular Implant Soc, 79; Dr P Siva Gold Medal, 82; Temoignage d' Honneur, Can Implant Asn, 75; Edward A Weisser Mem lectr, 76; Sr Hon Award, Am Acad Ophthal. *Prof Exp:* Intern, Mt Sinai Hosp, New York, 55-56; asst ophthalmol surg, Cornell Univ Med Col, 56-58, instr surg, 58-61, from clin asst prof to asst prof ophthalmol surg, 61-66; chmn, Dept Ophthalmol, NY Med Col, 66-73, prof, 66-79, dir res & planning, 73-79. *Concurrent Pos:* From asst resident surgeon to resident surgeon ophthalmol, NY Hosp, 56-59, surgeon to out patients, 59-61, from asst attend surgeon to assoc attend surgeon, 61-66; prin & co-investr, Nat Soc Prev Blindness, Nat Soc Combat Blindness & US Pub Health Serv, Cornell Univ Med Col, 59-66, career scientist, Health Res Coun, 63-66, Nat Soc Prev Blindness & Nat Soc Combat Blindness, NY Med Col, 66-67, US Pub Health Serv, 66-, Susan Greenwall Found, 68-75, Nat Inst Allergy & Infectious Dis, 68-, exchange scientist to USSR, US-Soviet Health Exchange, 69-71 & 74, United Health Found, 69, Am Cancer Found, 71-73 & Am Heart Found, 69-71; consult ophthalmol, Mem Hosp, 60-66; attend ophthalmologist & chief, Flower & Fifth Ave Hosp, Metrop Hosp & Bird S Coler Hosp, 66-79, Blythedale Children's Hosp, 68-73, Westchester Co Med Ctr, 75-79, Med Arts Ctr Hosp, 78- & Cabrini Med Ctr, 82-; consult ophthalmol, St Francis Hosp, 75- & Dept Surg, Catholic Med Ctr Brooklyn & Queens, 76-; first Hermann Hosp lectr, Tex, 67; consult, Fed Aviation Admin, Regional Med Prog, Medicaid Adv Comt Qual Vision Care, Social Security Admin & Nat Multiple Sclerosis Found; hearing examr, Social Security Admin; mem bd dirs, Better Vision Inst; US ed, Annali de Ottalmologia; mem tech adv comt, Bur Handicapped Children; mem bd dirs, Pan Am Implant Asn, 85-; tech consult, Regional Med Prog. *Mem:* AAAS; Am Acad Ophthal & Otolaryngol; AMA; Asn Res Vision & Ophthal; NY Acad Med; NY Acad Sci; Am Intraocular Implant Soc; Asn Univ Prof Ophthalmol; Israel Ophthalmol Soc; Royal Soc Med. *Res:* Glaucoma physiology and implant toxicity. *Mailing Add:* 345 E 37th St 3rd Fl New York NY 10016-3217. *Fax:* 212-922-1423

GALINDO, ANIBAL H, ANESTHESIOLOGY, NEUROPHYSIOLOGY. *Current Pos:* PROF ANESTHESIOL, SCH MED, UNIV MIAMI, 74- *Personal Data:* b Buga, Colombia, Sept 11, 29; m 51; c 4. *Educ:* Rosary Col, Bogota, BSc, 46; Nat Univ Colombia, MD, 52; McGill Univ, PhD(physiol, neurophysiol), 68. *Prof Exp:* Internship, Univ Bogota Hosp, 52-53; pvt pract, 53-54; resident anesthesia, San Jose Hosp, Nat Univ Colombia, 54-56, instr, Univ, 58-59; vis scientist, Nat Inst Neurol Dis & Blindness, 59-63, head sect neuroanesthesia, 60-63; asst prof anesthesiol, Sch Med, McGill Univ, 64-68; from assoc prof to prof, Sch Med, Univ Wash, 68-74, chief, Div Neurosurg Anesthesiol, 72-74. *Mem:* Am Physiol Soc; Am Soc Pharmacol & Exp Therapeut. *Res:* Pharmacology of anesthetic drugs; effect of various anesthetics on cardiac excitability, cerebral and hepatic circulation; neuropharmacology, especially the effects of muscle relaxants and anesthetics on synaptic transmission. *Mailing Add:* 6500 Caballero Blvd Coral Gables FL 33146-3223

GALINDO-LEAL, CARLOS ENRIQUE, CONSERVATION ECOLOGY. *Current Pos:* res assoc, Appl conserv biol, 91-94, CTR DIR, TROP RES PROG, UNIV BC, 95- *Personal Data:* b Feb, 27, 57; div. *Educ:* Univ Autonoma Metrop, BSc, 79; Univ BC, MSc, 84, PhD(ecol), 91. *Prof Exp:* Res assoc, Inst Ecol, 87-88. *Concurrent Pos:* Adv, Ministry Environ Mex, 87, Ministry Agr Mex, 92. *Mem:* Am Soc Nammalogists. *Res:* Impacts of forestry activities on wildlife and with the maintenance of endangered species; research and conservation of tropical ecosistems. *Mailing Add:* Dept Biol Sci Stanford Univ 116 Gilbert Stanford CA 94305-5020. *Fax:* 650-723-5920; *E-Mail:* galindo@leland.stanford.edu

GALINSKY, ALVIN M, PHARMACEUTICAL CHEMISTRY. *Current Pos:* RETIRED. *Personal Data:* b Chicago, Ill, Oct 14, 31. *Educ:* Univ Ill, BS, 54, MS, 57, PhD(pharmaceut chem), 62. *Prof Exp:* From instr to asst prof org medicinals, Col Pharm, Columbia Univ, 60-63; from asst prof to assoc prof phys pharm, Duguesne Univ, 63-68, prof pharm & assoc chmn dept, Sch Pharm, 68- *Mem:* AAAS; Am Asn Cols Pharm; Am Pharmaceut Asn; Sigma Xi. *Res:* Structure-activity relationships; local anesthetics; dosage form, design and bioavailability; kinetics and stability of pharmaceutical dosage forms. *Mailing Add:* 137 Golden Isles Dr Hallandale FL 33009

GALINSKY, IRVING, CYTOLOGY, GENETICS. *Current Pos:* RETIRED. *Personal Data:* b New York, NY, June 15, 21; m 48; c 2. *Educ:* McGill Univ, BSc, 44, MSc, 45; Univ Wis, PhD(cytogenetics), 48. *Prof Exp:* Asst, Univ Wis, 45-48; Hite cancer fel, Univ Tex, 48-49; Nat Cancer fel, Col Med, Baylor Univ, 49-51; res assoc bact genetics, Cold Spring Harbor Lab, 51-53; asst prof genetics & cytol, Univ Del, 53-54; res assoc, Biochem Res Found, 54-59; prof biol, Hofstra Univ, 59-92, chmn dept, 63-92. *Mem:* AAAS; Genetics Soc Am; Am Genetic Asn; Am Asn Cancer Res. *Res:* Cytology of meiosis and mitosis; bacterial genetics; cancer research; mitotic abnormalities in plant and animal cells. *Mailing Add:* 46 Glen Way Cold Spring Harbor NY 11724

GALINSKY, RAYMOND ETHAN, PHARMACEUTICS, PHARMACOKINETICS. *Current Pos:* ASST PROF PHARMACEUT, UNIV UTAH, 83- *Personal Data:* b Hartford, Conn, Jan 27, 48. *Educ:* Univ Calif, Berkeley, BA, 70; Univ Calif, San Francisco, PharmD, 75. *Prof Exp:* Resident clin pharm, hosps & clins, Univ Calif, San Francisco, 75-76; instr, Philadelphia Col Pharm & Sci, 77-78; res fel pharmaceut, Sch Pharm, State Univ NY, Buffalo, 78-80, res asst prof, 80-83. *Concurrent Pos:* NIH Grant & First Award, Nat Inst Aging, 87; adj asst prof pharmacol & toxicol, Col Pharm, Univ Utah, 87- *Mem:* AAAS; Am Soc Clin Pharmacol & Therapeut; Am Col Clin Pharm; NY Acad Sci; Am Soc Pharmacol & Exp Therapeut; Am Asn Pharmaceut Scientists. *Res:* Effect of aging and hepatic disease on the pharmacokinetics and pharmacodynamics of drugs with emphasis on the factors controlling nonlinear conjugation reactions. *Mailing Add:* Dept Indust & Phys Pharmaceut Purdue Univ 1336 Robert Heine Bldg West Lafayette IN 47907-1336. *Fax:* 765-494-7880

GALISON, PETER LOUIS, HISTORY & PHILOSOPHY OF EXPERIMENTATION, HISTORY & PHILOSOPHY OF QUANTUM FIELD THEORY. *Current Pos:* prof hist sci & physics, 92-93, chair, Dept Hist Sci, 93-97, MALLINCKRODT PROF HIST SCI & PHYSICS, HARVARD UNIV, 94- *Personal Data:* b New York, NY, May 17, 55; m, Caroline A Jones; c 2. *Educ:* Harvard Univ, BA & MA, 77, PhD(physics & hist sci), 83; Cambridge Univ, MPhil, 78. *Prof Exp:* From asst prof to prof philos & physics, Stanford Univ, 82-92. *Concurrent Pos:* Howard Found fel, 85; vis asst prof, Hist Dept, Princeton Univ, 85; presidential young investr award, NSF, 86-91; Marta Sutton Weeks fac scholar humanities, 89-92; fel, Ctr Advan Study Behav Sci, 89-90; co-chmn prog hist sci, 90-92; coun mem, Hist Sci Soc, 93-95; bd dirs, Ctr Philos & Hist Sci, Boston Univ, 93-96; vis, Inst Advan Study, 94-95; fel, John D & Catherine T MacArthur Found, 97. *Mem:* Nat Acad Sci; fel Am Acad Arts & Sci; Am Phys Soc; Int Soc Hist Sci; fel AAAS; Sigma Xi. *Res:* History and philosophy of modern physics with special attention to the development of experimentation and instrumentation in the twentieth century; links between the development of science and art and architecture and philosophy. *Mailing Add:* Dept Hist Sci Harvard Univ Sci Ctr 235 Cambridge MA 02138

GALITZ, DONALD S, PLANT PHYSIOLOGY. *Current Pos:* assoc prof, 68-75, PROF BOT, NDAK STATE UNIV, 75- *Personal Data:* b Chicago, Ill, May 28, 35; m 60; c 2. *Educ:* Monmouth Col, BA, 56; Univ Ill, MS, 60, PhD(agron), 61. *Prof Exp:* Asst prof biol sci, Western Ill Univ, 61-67. *Concurrent Pos:* Res assoc, Dept Agron, Univ Ill, 67-68. *Mem:* Am Soc Plant Physiologists; Weed Sci Soc Am. *Res:* Plant physiology and biochemistry; plant metabolism, specifically nitrogen metabolism; stress physiology and physiology of seeds; weed physiology. *Mailing Add:* Dept Bot NDak State Univ Main Campus Fargo ND 58105

GALIVAN, JOHN H, BIOCHEMISTRY, EXPERIMENTAL THERAPEUTICS. *Current Pos:* DIR, MOLECULAR MED & ASSOC DIR, WADSWORTH LABS, NY STATE DEPT HEALTH, 94- *Personal Data:* b Albany, NY, June 19, 39; m 65; c 4. *Educ:* Union Univ, NY, BS, 60; State Univ NY Albany, MS, 63; Albany Med Col, PhD(biochem), 67. *Prof Exp:* Res asst biochem, Albany Med Col, 64-67, assoc prof, 78-82, adj prof, 89; NIH fel, Scripps Clin & Res Found, 67-70; sr res scientist, Div Lab & Res, NY State Dept Health, 70-77, res scientist IV, 77-81, res scientist VI, 81-91, chair, Lab Path, 91-92, dir, Div Clin Sci, 92-94. *Concurrent Pos:* Exp Therapeut Study Sect, NIH, 85-89; ad hoc consult, Nat Cancer Inst, 83-97; prof biomed sci, Albany Sch Pub Health, State Univ NY, 85-; ed, Cellular Pharmacol, 92-; adj prof biochem & molecular biol, Albany Med Col, 85-; dir, NY State Dept Health Breat Cancer Tax Checkoff, Int Folic Acid Symp, 89, 93 & 97. *Mem:* AAAS; Am Chem Soc; Am Asn Cancer Res; Am Soc Biol Chem & Molecular Biol; Soc Pharmaceut Exp Therapeut. *Res:* Enzymology; folate and vitamin B12 metabolism; cancer; experimental therapeutics; cancer diagnostics. *Mailing Add:* Wadsworth Ctr Lab Res NY State Dept Health Empire State Plaza Albany NY 12201. *Fax:* 518-474-3439; *E-Mail:* jhg01@health.state.ny.us

GALKOWSKI, THEODORE THADDEUS, ORGANIC CHEMISTRY. *Current Pos:* from asst prof to assoc prof, 52-60, PROF CHEM, PROVIDENCE COL, 60-, COORDR RES, 67- *Personal Data:* b Worcester, Mass, Nov 9, 21; m 49; c 2. *Educ:* Col of the Holy Cross, BS, 47, MS, 48; Ohio State Univ, PhD(chem), 51. *Prof Exp:* Org chemist, Nat Bur Stand, 51-52. *Mem:* AAAS; Am Chem Soc; fel Am Inst Chemists. *Res:* Structure of starch; proof of structure of carbohydrates; synthesis of Carbon-14 labeled carbohydrates; configurations of branched carbohydrates; carbohydrates in natural products. *Mailing Add:* Dept Chem Providence Col Providence RI 02918-0002

GALL, CARL EVERT, CHEMICAL ENGINEERING. *Current Pos:* from asst prof to assoc prof, 64-92, assoc chmn undergrad, Chem Eng Dept, 87-92, EMER PROF CHEM ENG, UNIV WATERLOO, 92- *Personal Data:* b Burlington, Ont, Can, Dec 17, 31; m 55; c 4. *Educ:* Univ Toronto, BASc, 55; Queen's Univ, Ont, MSc, 62; Univ Minn, PhD(chem eng), 66. *Prof Exp:* Lectr chem, Royal Mil Col, 53-54; tech rep, Imp Oil Ltd, 55-56; asst prof math, Haile Sellassie I Univ, 56-59; asst prof, Royal Mil Col, 59-61, asst prof chem eng, 61-62; res fel, Univ Minn, 62-64. *Res:* Control science; applied mathematics; chemical reaction engineering. *Mailing Add:* Dept Chem Eng Univ Waterloo Waterloo ON N2L 3G1 Can

GALL, DONALD ALAN, COMPUTER SCIENCE, BIOMEDICAL ENGINEERING. *Current Pos:* PRES, OMEGA COMPUT SYSTS, INC, 73- *Personal Data:* b Reddick, Ill, Sept 13, 34; m 73, Kathleen M Insognia; c Christopher, Keith, Elizabeth & Kelly. *Educ:* Univ Ill, BS, 56; Mass Inst Technol, SM, 58, MechE, 60, ScD, 64. *Honors & Awards:* Taylor Medal, Int Conf Prod Res, 71. *Prof Exp:* Exp res engr, Gen Motors Corp, 56-57; staff engr, Dynatech Corp, 59-60, mgr control systs, 62-63; asst prof automatic controls, Carnegie-Mellon Univ, 64-68, assoc prof mech eng, 68-69; res asst prof surg, Sch Med, Univ Pittsburgh, 68-69, res assoc prof surg & anesthesiol, 69-73. *Concurrent Pos:* Eng specialist, Thompson Ramo Wooldridge, Inc, 60-62. *Mem:* AAAS; Am Soc Mech Eng. *Res:* Medical computer systems; biological servomechanisms; computerized information systems; development of generalized data base management systems. *Mailing Add:* Omega Comput Systs Inc 3875 N 44th St No 200 Phoenix AZ 85018

GALL, ERIC PAPINAEU, RHEUMATOLOGY, MEDICAL EDUCATION. *Current Pos:* PROF & CHMN, DEPT INTERNAL MED, CHICAGO MED SCH, 94-, PROF MICROBIOL & IMMUNOL, 94- *Educ:* Univ Pa, AB, 62, MD, 66. *Honors & Awards:* Addie Thomas Distinguished Serv Award, Arthritis Health Prof Health Asn, 88. *Prof Exp:* Resident, Univ Cincinnati & Univ Pa, 71-73; prof med rheumatology, Univ Ariz, 73-74, chief, Rheumatology Allergy Immunol Div, 83-94, prof orthop, 83-94 & prof family & com med, 83-94. *Concurrent Pos:* Fel rheumatology, Univ Pa, 73; mem, House Deleg, Nat Arthritis Found, 81-88 & 97-, bd trustees, 81-85, vchmn, 82-83; dir, Univ Ariz Arthritis Ctr, 85-94; pres, Rheumatology Rehab Sect, Am Col Physicians, 92-95, bd dirs, 92-95. *Mem:* Sigma Xi; fel Am Col Physicians; Arthritis Health Prof Asn (pres, 82-83). *Mailing Add:* Finch Univ Health Sci/Chicago Med Sch 3333 Green Bay Rd North Chicago IL 60064

GALL, GRAHAM A E, FISH GENETICS. *Current Pos:* from asst to assoc prof, 66-78, PROF ANIMAL SCI, UNIV CALIF, DAVIS, 78-, ANIMAL GENETICIST, EXP STA, 66- *Personal Data:* b Moose Jaw, Sask, Sept 2, 36; m 60; c 3. *Educ:* Univ Alta, BSc, 60, MSc, 63; Purdue Univ, PhD(animal genetics), 66. *Prof Exp:* Res asst genetics, Univ Alta, 63 & Purdue Univ, 63-66. *Concurrent Pos:* Genetics consult, Calif Dept Fish & Game, 67-85; mem, Peer Rev Panel, Aquaculture, USDA, 82, 84, 85, 87-90; managing ed, Aquaculture, 85-; secy treas, Int Aquaculture Genetic Asn, 85- *Mem:* Am Fisheries Soc; AAAS; World Aquaculture Soc; Am Genetics Soc. *Res:* Genetics and breeding of fish; application of modern breeding methods to fish farming; population biology and management of Pacific salmon. *Mailing Add:* 641 Cleveland St Davis CA 95616-8521

GALL, JAMES WILLIAM, PHYSICAL CHEMISTRY, HAZARDOUS WASTE TREATMENT. *Current Pos:* res scientist, Phillips Petrol Co, 69-80, sr res scientist chem, 80-85, supvr, 85-91, MGR, FUEL & LUBRICANT ANAL, PHILLIPS PETROL CO, 91- *Personal Data:* b Taylorville, Ill, Apr 22, 42; m 66; c 3. *Educ:* Ohio State Univ, PhD(phys chem), 69. *Prof Exp:* Teaching asst chem, Ohio State Univ, 64-65. *Res:* Photochemistry; gas phase kinetics; chemistry of atmospheric pollutants; interaction of aqueous polymer solutions; thermodynamics and vapor-liquid equilibrium; oxidation; environmental services; hazardous waste treatment, incineration. *Mailing Add:* Phillips Res Ctr 87-D Phillips Petrol Co Bartlesville OK 74004

GALL, JOSEPH GRAFTON, CELL BIOLOGY. *Current Pos:* STAFF MEM, CARNEGIE INST, 83-, AM CANCER SOC PROF DEVELOP GENETICS, 84- *Personal Data:* b Washington, DC, Apr 14, 28; m 55, 82, Diane M Dwyer; c Lawrence F & Barbara G. *Educ:* Yale Univ, BS, 48, PhD(zool), 52. *Honors & Awards:* EB Wilson Medal, Am Soc Cell Biol, 83; V D Mattia Award, Roche Inst Molecular Biol, 89. *Prof Exp:* From instr to assoc prof zool, Univ Minn, 52-64; prof biol, Yale Univ, 64-83. *Concurrent Pos:* Trustee, Yale Univ, 89-95. *Mem:* Nat Acad Sci; Am Acad Arts & Sci; Am Soc Cell Biol (pres, 67-68); Genetics Soc Am; Soc Develop Biol (pres, 84-85); Am Philos Soc. *Res:* Chromosome structure and function; nucleic acid metabolism; gene structure. *Mailing Add:* Carnegie Inst 115 W University Pkwy Baltimore MD 21210. *Fax:* 410-243-6311

GALL, MARTIN, MEDICINAL CHEMISTRY, ORGANIC CHEMISTRY. *Current Pos:* chem sect mgr, Neuromuscular Blocking Agent GI, 90-92, JR PROJ MGR, OHMEDA, 92- *Personal Data:* b New York, NY, Oct 22, 44; m 68, Allyson M Cook; c Ari B, Rachel E & Jonathan M. *Educ:* Trinity Col, Conn, BS, 66; Mass Inst Technol, PhD(org chem), 71. *Prof Exp:* Sr res scientist, Cent Nerv Syst Chem, Upjohn Co, 71-89; dir, Life Environ Sci Div, Syracuse Res Corp, 89-90. *Mem:* Am Chem Soc; Chem Soc; Sigma Xi. *Res:* Synthesize and evaluate new chemical substances which have clinical psychotherapeutic value; study new heterocyclic syntheses; metallation and reaction; central nervous system diseases research; neuromuscular blocking agents; discover novel 5-HT3 antagonists as antiemetics; develop new clinically effective drugs. *Mailing Add:* Anaquest Inc 100 Mountain Ave Murray Hill NJ 07974. *Fax:* 908-771-6161

GALL, ROBERT LAWRENCE, MESOSCALE METEOROLOGY, SYNOPTIC METEOROLOGY. *Current Pos:* DIR, MESOSCALE MICROSCALE METEOROL, NAT CTR ATMOSPHERIC RES, 91- *Personal Data:* b Philadelphia, Pa, July 20, 45; m 74, Linda; c Christopher & Scott. *Educ:* Pa State Univ, BS, 67; Univ Wis, MS, 69, PhD(meteorol), 72. *Prof Exp:* From Asst prof to prof atmospheric sci, Univ Ariz, 72-91. *Mem:* Fel Am Meteorol Soc. *Res:* Studies of the dynamics of cyclones, fronts, tornadoes and hurricanes; numerical simulation of these systems; dynamics of the monsoon system over Mexico. *Mailing Add:* Nat Ctr Atmospheric Res PO Box 3000 Boulder CO 80307-3000

GALL, WALTER GEORGE, ORGANIC CHEMISTRY. *Current Pos:* RETIRED. *Personal Data:* b Passaic, NJ, Mar 11, 29; div; c 2. *Educ:* Carnegie Inst Technol, BS, 50, MS, 50; Univ Rochester, PhD(chem), 53. *Prof Exp:* Res chemist org high polymer chem, Exp Sta, E I Du Pont de Nemours & Co, 53-62, sr res chemist, 63-69, res assoc, Plastics Prod & Resins Dept, 69-81. *Mem:* Sigma Xi; Am Chem Soc; fel Am Inst Chem. *Res:* Bridgehead nitrogen heterocycles; quinolizine; high polymer chemistry; stereospecific polymerizations; high temperature polymers; mineral-filled polymers; polymer flammability. *Mailing Add:* 11838 Via Hacienda El Cajon CA 92019-4099

GALL, WILLIAM EINAR, NEUROSCIENCES. *Current Pos:* RES DIR, NEUROSCI RES PROG, NEUROSCI INST, 81- *Personal Data:* b Warsaw, NY, Apr 12, 42; m 67, Sally Moore. *Educ:* Hamilton Col, AB, 63; Rockefeller Univ, PhD(life sci), 69. *Prof Exp:* Res assoc, Rockefeller Univ, 69-72, from asst prof to assoc prof develop & molecular biol, 72-92. *Mem:* Soc Neurosci; AAAS; Harvey Soc; Am Asn Immunologists. *Res:* Theoretical neurobiology. *Mailing Add:* Neurosci Inst 10640 John Jay Hopkins Dr San Diego CA 92121. *Fax:* 619-626-2099; *E-Mail:* wegall@nsi.edu

GALLAGER, ROBERT G, COMMUNICATIONS, DATA NETWORKS. *Current Pos:* From asst prof to assoc prof, 60-67, FUJITSU PROF ELEC ENG, DEPT ELEC ENG & COMPUTER SCI, MASS INST TECHNOL, 67-, CO-DIR, LAB INFO & DECISION SYSTS, 86- *Personal Data:* b Philadelphia, Pa, May 29, 31; m 81, Marie Tarnowski; c Douglas, Ann & Rebecca. *Educ:* Univ Pa, SB, 53; Mass Inst Technol, SM, 57, ScD, 60. *Honors & Awards:* Shannon Award, Info Theory Soc, Inst Elec & Electronics Engrs, 83; Medal of Honor, Inst Elec & Electronics Engrs, 90. *Concurrent Pos:* Consult, Codex Corp & Lincoln Labs. *Mem:* Nat Acad Sci; Nat Acad Eng; fel Inst Elec & Electronics Engrs. *Res:* Data communication networks; information and communication theory; wireless communication. *Mailing Add:* Mass Inst Technol Rm 35-206 Cambridge MA 02139. *E-Mail:* gallager@lids.mit.edu

GALLAGHER, ALAN C, ATOMIC & MOLECULAR PHYSICS. *Current Pos:* PHYSICIST, NAT BUR STAND, 67- *Personal Data:* b Oak Park, Ill, June 14, 36; div; c 4. *Educ:* Purdue Univ, BES, 58; Columbia Univ, PhD(physics), 64. *Prof Exp:* Res assoc physics, IBM Watson Lab, 64; JOINT INST FOR LAB ASTROPHYS, UNIV COLO, BOULDER, 64- *Concurrent Pos:* Lectr, Univ Colo, 67-71; adj prof, 71- *Mem:* Fel Am Phys Soc. *Res:* Electron, atom and molecular collisions and radiation processes. *Mailing Add:* JILA Univ Colo Boulder CO 80309

GALLAGHER, BRENT S, PHYSICAL OCEANOGRAPHY. *Current Pos:* asst prof, 67-71, ASSOC PROF PHYS OCEANOG, UNIV HAWAII, 71- *Personal Data:* b Greenfield, Mass, Nov 3, 39; m 58; c 2. *Educ:* Univ Calif, Los Angeles, BS, 62; Scripps Inst, Univ Calif, PhD(oceanog), 65. *Prof Exp:* Asst res oceanogr, Inst Geophys & Planetary Physics, Univ Calif, San Diego, 66-67. *Concurrent Pos:* Consult, US Naval Radiological Defense Labs, 67-68. *Res:* Nonlinear aspects of ocean waves; fine-scale structure of physical variables in the ocean. *Mailing Add:* Dept Nat Sci Univ Hawaii 200 W Kawili St Hilo HI 96720-4075

GALLAGHER, BRIAN BORU, NEUROLOGY. *Current Pos:* PROF NEUROL, MED COL GA, 77- *Personal Data:* b Chicago, Ill, Sept 2, 34; m 58, 78; c 2. *Educ:* Univ Notre Dame, BS, 56; Univ Chicago, PhD(biol psychol), 60, MD, 63. *Prof Exp:* Intern med, Univ Chicago, 63-64; resident neurol, Yale Univ-New Haven Hosp, 65-67; from instr to assoc prof, Sch Med, Yale Univ, 67-73; assoc prof pharmacol & neurol, Georgetown Univ, 73-77. *Mem:* AAAS; Am Acad Neurol; Am Soc Neurochem; Soc Neurosci; NY Acad Sci; Sigma Xi. *Res:* Neuropharmacology and neurochemistry of epilepsy. *Mailing Add:* Dept Neurol Med Col Ga Sch Med Augusta GA 30912-0001. *Fax:* 706-721-6757

GALLAGHER, CHARLES CLIFTON, ATMOSPHERIC SCIENCE, PHYSICS. *Current Pos:* Physicist plasma physics, Cambridge Res Lab, 60-74, PHYSICIST STRATOSPHERE, AIR FORCE GEOPHYS LAB, 74-; DIR, GEOPHYS TECHNOL DIV, PLANS & PROG DIRECTORATE, PHILLIPS LAB, 93- *Personal Data:* b Boston, Mass, Feb 17, 37. *Educ:* Boston Col, BS, 58, MS, 60; Northeastern Univ, MS, 67. *Mem:* Am Phys Soc; Sigma Xi. *Res:* Trace gas content of stratosphere studied as a function of altitude, latitude and time using chemiluminescence analysers and gas chromatography and with air samples obtained cryogenically, utilizing balloon-borne samplers. *Mailing Add:* Phillips Lab 29 Randolph Rd Hanscom AFB MA 01731-3010

GALLAGHER, DAVID ALDEN, ELECTRON-TUBE PHYSICS. *Current Pos:* ENG SPECIALIST, ELECTRONIC SYST DIV, NORTHROP CORP, 77- *Personal Data:* b Chicago, Ill, April 20, 49; m 72, Eileen Reminiec; c Drew & Melissa. *Educ:* Univ Ill, Chicago, BS, 71; Univ Ill, Urbana, MS, 73, PhD(physics), 77. *Mem:* Am Phys Soc. *Res:* Fast-wave and millimeter- wave electron tubes, such as the peniotron, gyrotron, ortron and folded-waveguide traveling wave tube; development of both small and large signal theories of beam-wave interactions, their application to simulating tube performance and the conceptualization, development and evaluation of electron tubes. *Mailing Add:* 715 E Charles Arlington Heights IL 60004. *Fax:* 847-590-3177

GALLAGHER, GEORGE ARTHUR, ORGANIC CHEMISTRY. *Current Pos:* RETIRED. *Personal Data:* b Paterson, NJ, Feb 11, 23; m 48, Josephine Dugan; c Stephen F & Thomas J. *Educ:* Cornell Univ, AB, 43; Univ Pa, MS, 50, PhD(chem), 54. *Prof Exp:* Chemist, Socony Mobil Oil Co, Inc, 46-47; res chemist, Atlantic Refining Co, 47-53; chemist, Org Chem Dept, E I du Pont de Nemours & Co, 54-57, chemist, Elastomer Chem Dept, 57-67, personnel adminr, 67-72, lab adminr, 72-77, personnel mgr, 77-85, mgr, Spec Compensation & Benefits, 85. *Mem:* Am Chem Soc. *Res:* Elastomer research. *Mailing Add:* 832 Surrey Lane Media PA 19063

GALLAGHER, JAMES A, POLYMER CHEMISTRY. *Current Pos:* QUAL ASSURANCE MGR, CTR EXCELLENCE ENVIRON ENG & SCI, UNIV DETROIT MERCY, 93- *Personal Data:* b Chicago, Ill, July 12, 26; m 57; c 4. *Educ:* St Louis Univ, BS, 49; Univ Mo, MA, 51, PhD(org chem), 55. *Prof Exp:* Chemist, Lubrizol Corp, Ohio, 51-52, Esso Res & Eng Co, 55-64; chemist, BASF Wyandotte Corp, 65-69, supvr polymer res, 69-71, mgr urethane appln, 72-73, asst to dir urethane chem res & develop, 74-79, asst to vpres res & develop, 80-85, res assoc, 86-91. *Concurrent Pos:* Consult, Polymer Technol, Inc Univ Detroit Mercy, 91- & Technol partnership, Grosse Eli Mish. *Mem:* Am Chem Soc; Sigma Xi. *Res:* Synthetic resin development; synthesis and applications research on organic polymers, chiefly for surface coating, including cure mechanisms, surface chemistry; flammablity of upholstered furniture. *Mailing Add:* 8439 Glengarry Rd Grosse Ile MI 48138. *Fax:* 313-993-1409

GALLAGHER, JANE CHISPA, PLANKTON ECOLOGY, POPULATION GENETICS. *Current Pos:* From asst prof to assoc prof, 78-90, PROF BIOL, CITY COL NY, 90- *Personal Data:* b Frankfurt, Ger, Jan 27, 50; m 77, Bruce A Huber; c Juliana. *Educ:* Stanford Univ, BS, AM, 73; Univ RI, PhD(oceanog), 79. *Mem:* Am Soc Limnol & Oceanog; Phycological Soc Am (secy, 97-); Sigma Xi; Soc Study Evolution; AAAS. *Res:* Ecology and physiology of marine plankton; species succession and population genetics of microalgae. *Mailing Add:* Biol Dept City Col New York Convent Ave 138 St New York NY 10031-9198

GALLAGHER, JOEL PETER, NEUROPHARMACOLOGY, NEUROPHYSIOLOGY. *Current Pos:* from asst prof to assoc prof, 75-85, PROF PHARMACOL & TOXICOL, UNIV TEX MED BR, GALVESTON, 86- *Personal Data:* b Chicago, Ill, Dec 12, 42; m 74; c 3. *Educ:* Col St Thomas, BS, 64; Univ Ill, BS & RPh, 67; Loyola Univ, Chicago, PhD(pharmacol), 72. *Prof Exp:* Community pharmacist, Westchester Apothecary, 67-71; res assoc pharmacol & NIH fel, Loyola Univ Chicago, 71-72, instr neurol & pharmacol, 72-73, NIH fel neurol & pharmacol, 73- 74, NIH fel neurophysiol, 74-75, adj asst prof, 75. *Mem:* Soc Neurosci; Am Soc Pharmacol & Exp Therapeut; Acad Gen Pract Pharm; AAAS. *Res:* Analysis of the site and mechanism of action of drugs and the mechanism of normal and diseased physiological processes occurring at central synapses thought to be involved in the process of anxiety and space motion sickness. *Mailing Add:* Dept Pharmacol Univ Tex Med Br (MS-J-31) Galveston TX 77555-1031. *Fax:* 409-772-9642

GALLAGHER, JOHN JOSEPH, JR, ROCK MECHANICS, BASIN ANALYSIS. *Current Pos:* PRES, STRUCT GEOL & TETONICS INT, 91- *Personal Data:* b Boston, Mass, Oct 7, 40; m 68; c 4. *Educ:* Boston Col, BS, 62; Univ Mo, MA, 65; Texas A&M Univ, PhD(geol), 71. *Prof Exp:* Acting br chief, US Army CEngrs Sch, 66-68; res assoc tectonophysics, Cities Serv Exploration & Prod Res Lab, 71-75, mgr structural geol, 75-78; sr geol assoc, int exploration, Cities Serv Int Co, 78-80; mgr basin studies, Cities Serv Res

& Technol, 80-83; mgr tectonics, Occidental Int Exploration & Prod Co, 83-85; mgr integr explor res, Atlantic Richfield Res & Tech Serv Lab, 85-87, consult explor res, 87-91. *Concurrent Pos:* Mem, Marine Geol Comt, Am Assoc Petrol Geol, 87-, Geophys Comt, Int Comt; adj prof, Univ Tulsa, OK, 72-82; bd trustees, Int Basement Tectonics Assoc, 72-, chmn, 85-90. *Mem:* Am Geophysical Union; Int Basement Tectonics Asn; Geol Soc Am; Am Asn Petrol Geologists; Am Inst Prof Geologists; Sigma Xi. *Res:* Salt tectonics; application of dynamic structural geology and technophysics to oil and gas exploration; scanning electron microscopic fractographic study of fractured sand grains; photoelastic study of stress concentrations in granular-media and thrust-fault analog; oil and gas basin evaluation worldwide; computer applications to remote sensing interpretation. *Mailing Add:* 7140 Crooked Oak Dr Dallas TX 75248-2231

GALLAGHER, JOHN LESLIE, MARINE BOTANY. *Current Pos:* assoc prof marine studies, 80-85, PROF MARINE BIOL & BIOCHEM, UNIV DEL, 85- *Personal Data:* b West Grove, Pa, Nov 4, 35; c 2. *Educ:* Univ Del, BSAg, 57, MS, 59, PhD(biol sci), 71. *Prof Exp:* Instr biol, West Nottingham Acad, 59-68; instr, Univ Del, 68-69; res assoc marine bot, Marine Inst, Univ Ga, 71-76, actg dir, 75-77, assoc marine scientist, 76-79. *Concurrent Pos:* Adj asst prof agron, Univ Ga, 75-79 & adj asst prof bot, 76-79. *Mem:* Ecol Soc Am; Am Soc Limnol & Oceanog; Estuarine Res Fedn (treas, 78-79); Bot Soc Am; Brit Ecol Soc; Am Inst Biol Sci. *Res:* Ecology and physiology of salt marsh autotrophs; tissue culture and transformation of halophytes; development of saline agroecosystems. *Mailing Add:* Col Marine Studies Univ Del Newark DE 19717-0001. *Fax:* 302-645-4028; *E-Mail:* jackg@chopinudel.edu

GALLAGHER, JOHN M(ICHAEL), JR, ELECTRICAL & NUCLEAR ENGINEERING. *Current Pos:* NUCLEAR REGULATORY COMN, 91- *Personal Data:* b Charleston, WVa, Feb 26, 27; m 53; c 6. *Educ:* Rensselaer Polytech Inst, BEE, 51; Mass Inst Technol, MS, 54, EE, 56. *Prof Exp:* Asst & res engr, Dynamic Analytical & Control Lab, Mass Inst Technol, 51-56; sr engr comput analysis group, Atomic Power Dept, Westinghouse Elec Co, 56-59, supvry eng systs transient analysis group, 59-63, mgr systs analysis, 63-67, mgr control & elec systs, 67-69, consult engr, 70-75, mgr instrumentation & control develop, Nuclear Energy Systs, 75-88, consult engr, Control & Elec Systs, 88-90. *Concurrent Pos:* Mem int electro-tech comn, Am Nat Standards Inst. *Mem:* Am Nuclear Soc; Inst Elec & Electronics Engrs. *Res:* Development, design and testing of instrumentation; control electrical equipment and systems for nuclear power plants; distributed computer systems for control and for expert system advice for nuclear and fossil power plants. *Mailing Add:* US Nuclear Regulatory Comm MS 843 Washington DC 20535

GALLAGHER, JOHN SILL, ASTROPHYSICS. *Current Pos:* PROF, ASTRON, UNIV WIS-MADISON, 91- *Personal Data:* b Boston, Mass, Mar 26, 47; m 70; c 2. *Educ:* Princeton Univ, AB, 69; Univ Wis-Madison, PhD(astron), 72. *Prof Exp:* Vis asst prof & res assoc astrophys, Univ Nebr-Lincoln, 72-74; asst prof astrophys, Univ Minn, Minneapolis, 74-77; assoc prof astron, Univ Ill, Urbana, 77-80, prof astron, 80-84, astronr, Kitt Peak Nat Observ, 84-86, dir, Lowell Observ, 86-89. *Concurrent Pos:* Assoc ed, Astrophys J, 86-; dir at large, AURA, Inc, 87- vpres, 89-; Aspen Theoret Astrophys Org Comt, 82- *Mem:* Int Astron Union; Am Astron Soc. *Res:* Observable properties of novae and related binary stars; stellar populations and evolution of extragalactic systems; gas content and structural form of galaxies. *Mailing Add:* Dept Astron Univ Wis 475 N Charter St Madison WI 53706

GALLAGHER, MARGIE LEE, EXPERIMENTAL BIOLOGY. *Current Pos:* asst prof & asst scientist, 80-85, assoc prof & assoc scientist, 85-89, PROF & SCIENTIST, E CAROLINA UNIV, GREENVILLE, 89- *Educ:* Univ Tenn, BS, 69; Univ Fla, MS, 71; Univ Calif, PhD(nutrit), 76. *Prof Exp:* Postdoctoral res, Maine Heart Asn, 76; res asst prof, Univ Maine, Orono, 77-79. *Concurrent Pos:* Vet Admin Ctr, Togus, Maine, 76; numerous grants, 81-; reviewer, Sea Grant Proposals, Nat Oceanic & Atmospheric Admin, proposals, USDA; vis scientist, Israel & Italy, 84, Galilee Inst Technol, Kiryat Shomona, Israel, 85; consult, Charles Sockriter Farmes, Byrd Seafood Co, Inc, Int Nutrit, Inc, & Ospry Seafoods. *Mem:* Sigma Xi; Am Dietetic Asn; Am Fisheries Soc; Am Inst Nutrit; NY Acad Sci. *Res:* Nutrition; experimental biology; numerous technical publications. *Mailing Add:* East Carolina Univ Greenville NC 27858. *Fax:* 919-757-4267

GALLAGHER, MICHAEL TERRANCE, TRANSPLANTATION IMMUNOLOGY, TUMOR IMMUNOLOGY. *Current Pos:* asst res scientist, 80-82, ASSOC RES SCIENTIST IMMUNOL, DEPT CLIN & EXP, CITY OF HOPE NAT MED CTR, 82- *Personal Data:* Gadsden, Ala, Nov 26, 43; m 73; c 2. *Educ:* Univ Houston, BS, 66; Northwestern Univ, MS, 70; Baylor Col Med, PhD(immunol), 74. *Prof Exp:* Instr immunol, Div Exp Biol, Baylor Col Med, 74-75, asst prof, 75-80. *Mem:* Am Asn Cancer Res; Am Asn Immunologists; Int Soc Exp Hematol; The Transplantation Soc. *Res:* Transplantation immunology, particularly bone marrow transplantation and graft-vs-host disease; tumor immunology with emphasis on natural killer cells; differentiation of hemopoietic stem cells; the role of the reticuloendothelial system in autoimmune hemolytic anemia. *Mailing Add:* Dept Health Sci East Tenn State Univ PO Box 70731 Johnson City TN 37614

GALLAGHER, NEAL CHARLES, ELECTRICAL ENGINEERING, OPTICS. *Current Pos:* PROF & CHMN, DEPT ELEC & COMPUT ENG, UNIV DEL. *Personal Data:* b Baltimore, Md, Jan 9, 49; m 71; c 2. *Educ:* Loyola Col, Md, BS, 71; Princeton Univ, MA & MSE, 73, PhD(elec eng), 74. *Prof Exp:* Asst prof, Case Western Res Univ, 74-76; from asst prof to assoc prof elec eng, Purdue Univ, 76-92. *Mem:* Inst Elec & Electronics Engrs; Optical Soc Am. *Res:* Statistical communication theory; digital holography. *Mailing Add:* Dept Elec Eng Univ Del 142 Evans Newark DE 19716

GALLAGHER, NEIL IGNATIUS, INTERNAL MEDICINE, HEMATOLOGY. *Current Pos:* RETIRED. *Personal Data:* b Cleveland, Ohio, Oct 12, 26; m 56; c 4. *Educ:* Santa Clara Univ, BS, 47; Univ Ariz, MA, 51; St Louis Univ, MD, 54; Am Bd Internal Med, dipl, 62, cert hemat, 72. *Prof Exp:* Intern, St Louis City Hosp, Mo, 54-55; asst resident, St Louis Univ Hosp, 55-57; fel hemat, Vet Admin Hosp, St Louis, 57-59, clin investr, 59-61, chief radioisotope lab, 61-68, from assoc chief of staff to chief of staff res, 63-67, chief of med, 66-68; from instr to prof, internal med & vchmn dept, Sch Med, St Louis Univ, 59-73, staff mem, 59-87; staff mem internal med, St Mary's Hosp, 87-94. *Concurrent Pos:* Staff physician, Univ Group Hosps, 59-94; dir, St Louis Univ Med Serv, Vet Admin Hosp, 61-75. *Mem:* Am Fedn Clin Res; Am Soc Hemat; Int Soc Hemat; Soc Exp Biol & Med; fel Am Col Physicians. *Res:* Cell proliferation; humoral regulation of erythropoiesis; pathophysiology of dyserythropoiesis. *Mailing Add:* 869 Rampart Dr St Louis MO 63122

GALLAGHER, PATRICK KENT, INORGANIC CHEMISTRY, THERMAL ANALYSIS. *Current Pos:* DOW PROF MAT CHEM & ENG, DEPT CHEM & MAT SCI & ENG, OHIO STATE UNIV, 90- *Personal Data:* b Waukegan, Ill, Mar 17, 31; m 53, Marianne R Maske; c Michael K & John P. *Educ:* Univ Wis, BS, 52, MS, 54, PhD(inorg chem), 59. *Honors & Awards:* Mettler Award, NAm Thermal Analysis Soc, 76; DuPont Award, Thermal Analysis, Int Confedn Thermal Analysis, 82; Kurnikov Medal, Acad Sci, USSR, 85; Semiconductor Int Res Award, 86; Netzsch, Gessel Thermal Anal, 96. *Prof Exp:* Mem tech staff inorg chem, Bell Labs, 59-89. *Concurrent Pos:* Chmn comt E-37, Am Soc Testing & Mat, 74-76. *Mem:* Fel NAm Thermal Analysis Soc (pres, 75, vpres, 74); Int Confedn Thermal Anal (vpres, pres-elect, 80, pres, 82, treas, 87); Am Chem Soc; fel Am Ceramic Soc; fel AAAS; Mat Res Soc. *Res:* Synthesis, reactivity and characterization of inorganic materials, particularly oxides for electronic ceramics; applications of thermal analysis. *Mailing Add:* Dept Chem Ohio State Univ 100 W 18th Ave Columbus OH 43210-1173. *Fax:* 614-292-3010; *E-Mail:* gallagher.8@osu.edu

GALLAGHER, PATRICK XIMENES, MATHEMATICS. *Current Pos:* PROF MATH, COLUMBIA UNIV, 72- *Personal Data:* b Elizabeth, NJ, Jan 2, 35; m 61; c 2. *Educ:* Harvard Univ, AB, 56; Princeton Univ, PhD(math), 59. *Prof Exp:* Asst math, Princeton Univ, 57-59; instr, Mass Inst Technol, 59-61; asst prof, Columbia Univ, 62-64; mem, Inst Advan Study, 64-65; from assoc prof to prof math, Barnard Col, 65-72. *Mem:* Am Math Soc. *Res:* Analytic number theory; finite groups. *Mailing Add:* Dept Math Columbia Univ 299 Broadway 517 Math MC 4439 New York NY 10027-6902

GALLAGHER, RICHARD HUGO, CIVIL ENGINEERING. *Current Pos:* PROF IN RESIDENCE, UNIV ARIZ, 95- *Personal Data:* b New York, NY, Nov 17, 27; m 52, Terese M Doyle; c Marylee, Richard, William, Dennis & John. *Educ:* NY Univ, BCE, 50, MCE, 55; State Univ NY, Buffalo, PhD(civil eng), 66. *Hon Degrees:* Dr Tech, Tech Univ Vienna, 87; Dr Univ Col Swansea, Wales, 87; Shanghai Univ Technol, Shanghai, 92. *Honors & Awards:* Worcester Reed Warner Medal, Am Soc Mech Engrs, 85, Am Soc Mech Engrs Medal, 93; Structural Dynamics & Mat Award, Am Inst Aeronaut & Astronaut, 90; Benjamin Garver Lamme Award, Am Soc Eng Educ, 90; Gold Medal, Am Asn Comput Mech Mech, 95. *Prof Exp:* Civil engr, US Dept Com, Civil Aeronaut Admin, 50-52; struct designer, Tex Co, 52-55; struct engr, Bell Aerosysts Co, 55-59, group leader struct res, 59-65, asst chief engr, 65-67; prof civil eng, Cornell Univ, 67-78, chmn, Dept Stuct Eng, 70-78; dean, Col Eng, Univ Ariz, 78-84; vpres & dean fac, Worcester Polytech Inst, 84-88; pres, Clarkson Univ, 88-95. *Concurrent Pos:* Consult, Adv Group Aeronaut Res & Develop, NATO, 60-62; founding ed, Int J Numerical Methods Eng, 67- *Mem:* Nat Acad Eng; fel Am Inst Aeronaut & Astronaut; fel Am Soc Mech Engrs; hon fel Am Soc Civil Engrs; Am Soc Eng Educ. *Res:* Solid mechanics, particularly the development of finite element techniques; development of methods of optimum design. *Mailing Add:* 6735 Camino Padre Isidora Tucson AZ 85718. *Fax:* 520-621-8191; *E-Mail:* gallagher@ame.arizona.edu

GALLAGHER, THOMAS FRANCIS, RYDBERG ATOMS, AUTOIONIZATION. *Current Pos:* prof, 84-91, JESSE W BEAMS PROF PHYSICS, UNIV VA, 91- *Personal Data:* b Bronxville, NY, Nov 19, 44; m 74; c 1. *Educ:* Williams Col, AB, 66; Harvard Univ, AM, 68, PhD(physics), 71. *Honors & Awards:* Davidson-Germer Prize, Phys Soc, 96. *Prof Exp:* Res assoc physics, Dept Physics, Harvard Univ, 71, Univ Utah, 71-72; physicist, Molecular Physics Lab, Stanford Res Inst, 72-78, sr physicist, 78-83, prog mgr, 83-84. *Concurrent Pos:* Vis scientist, Atomic Physics Serv, CEN Saclay, 77, Inst Electronics Found, Univ Paris Sud, 80; prof assoc, Lab Aime Colton, Univ Paris Sud, 88. *Mem:* Fel Am Phys Soc; fel Am Optical Soc. *Res:* Highly excited atoms to study quantitatively otherwise relatively inaccessible phenomena; examples are atoms in strong microwave fields; resonant collisional energy transfer and correlation of the electrons in autoionizing states. *Mailing Add:* Dept Physics Univ Va Charlottesville VA 22901

GALLAGHER, WILLIAM J(OSEPH), MECHANICAL ENGINEERING, TECHNICAL & CORPORATE MANAGEMENT. *Current Pos:* pres & chief exec officer, 87-94, VCHMN BD & CHIEF EXEC OFFICER, NUMATEC, INC, 94- *Personal Data:* b Allentown, Pa, Jan 13, 31; m 56, Elizabeh Worrell; c Sharon (Helgasson). *Educ:* Drexel Inst, BS, 53; Lehigh Univ, MS, 55; Univ Pittsburgh, PhD, 62. *Prof Exp:* Engr, Pa Power & Light Co, 53-54; assoc engr thermal & hydraul design, Westinghouse Elec Corp, 57-62, sr engr, 62-64; supvr, Bettis Atomic Power Lab, 64-66; mgr eng, NUS Corp, 66-69, dir tech opers Europe, Ger, 69-71; managing dir, Nuklear Ingenieur Serv GmbH, 71-74; vpres & gen mgr, Eng Consult Div, NUS Corp, 74-75, exec vpres, 82-87, pres, NUS Int, 87, sr vpres, Environ Systs & Consult Serv Group, 75-82, asst to pres, 78-87. *Concurrent Pos:* Mem & chmn, Ger Govt Adv Comts Nuclear Power, 71-74. *Res:* Nuclear reactor heat transfer and fluid flow. *Mailing Add:* 4400 Westover Pl NW Washington DC 20016. *Fax:* 301-652-8399

GALLAGHER, WILLIAM J, CONDENSED MATTER PHYSICS. *Current Pos:* Staff sci & eng comput technol, 78-83, MGR, EXPLOR CRYOGENICS RES GROUP, IBM THOMAS J WATSON RES CTR, 83- *Educ:* Creighton Univ, BS, 74; Mass Inst Technol, PhD(physics), 78. *Concurrent Pos:* Dir, Consortium Superconducting Electronics. *Mem:* Inst Elec & Electronics Eng; fel Am Phys Soc. *Res:* Compound geometrical resonances and reduced Josephson currents observed when tunneling into superconducting proximity effect bilayers. *Mailing Add:* IBM T J Watson Res Ctr PO Box 218 Yorktown Heights NY 10598

GALLAHER, DANIEL DAVID, DIETARY FIBER, ZINC ABSORPTION. *Current Pos:* ASSOC PROF FOOD & NUTRIT, NDAK STATE UNIV, 83- *Personal Data:* b July 30, 52; m 79; c 2. *Educ:* Univ Calif, Davis, PhD(nutrit), 84. *Concurrent Pos:* Prin investr, Nat Cancer Inst grant. *Mem:* Am Inst Nutrit; Inst Food Technol; Am Diabetes Asn; Sigma Xi. *Res:* Influence of dietary fiber on gastro intestinal function; effects of fiber on bile acid metabolism and blood glucose control. *Mailing Add:* Dept Food Sci 225 Food Sci N Ctr Univ Minn 1334 Eckles Ave St Paul MN 55108-1040. *Fax:* 612-625-5272

GALLAHER, EDWARD J, GAMMA AMINOBUTYRIC ACID-BENZODIAZEPINE MECHANISMS, BEHAVIOR GENETICS. *Current Pos:* RES PHARMACOLOGIST, DEPT VET AFFAIRS, PORTLAND, ORE, 79-; ASST PROF, ORE HEALTH SCI UNIV, 86- *Personal Data:* b New York, NY, Mar 27, 46; m 65, Janet Handy; c Deborah & Gary. *Educ:* Univ Wash, PhD(parmacol), 76. *Mem:* AAAS; Am Soc Pharmacol Therapeut; Res Soc Alcoholism. *Res:* Behavioral assessment of tolerance and physical dependence in laboratory rodents; selective breeding for diazepam sensitivity; behavioral models of anxiety; behavior genetics; psychopharmacology. *Mailing Add:* Res Serv 151W Vet Affairs Med Ctr Portland OR 97201-2964. *Fax:* 503-273-5351; *E-Mail:* gallaher@ohsu.edu

GALLAHER, LAWRENCE JOSEPH, PHYSICS, COMPUTER SCIENCE. *Current Pos:* RETIRED. *Personal Data:* b St Louis, Mo, May 31, 25; m 54, Grietje Scheffers; c 7. *Educ:* Rensselaer Polytech Inst, BS, 50; Washington Univ, PhD(physics), 55. *Prof Exp:* Lectr physics, Univ Minn, 55; from asst prof to assoc prof, Ohio Univ, 55-63; res scientist, Ga Inst Technol, 63-80, sr res scientist, 80-85; res scientist, Lockheed, 85-90. *Mem:* Am Phys Soc; Asn Comput Mach. *Res:* Applications of digital computers. *Mailing Add:* 3892 Brenton Way NE Atlanta GA 30319

GALLAHER, WILLIAM RICHARD, VIROLOGY, CELL BIOLOGY. *Current Pos:* asst prof microbiol, 73-80, ASSOC PROF MICROBIOL & IMMUNOL, LA STATE UNIV MED CTR, 80- *Personal Data:* b Englewood, NJ, Dec 28, 44; div; c 4. *Educ:* St Peters Col, NJ, BS, 66; Harvard Univ, PhD(microbiol & molecular genetics), 72. *Prof Exp:* Res assoc membrane biol, Scheie Eye Inst, Univ Pa, 71-73. *Concurrent Pos:* Grantee investr, Cancer Asn Greater New Orleans, 74-76, La Heart Asn, 78-80 & Nat Inst Allergy & Infectious Dis, 78- *Mem:* Am Soc Microbiol; Tissue Cult Asn; Am Soc Virol. *Res:* Biochemistry and genetics of mammalian cell membranes related to cell regulation and sensitivity to viral infection; identification of cellular receptors for animal viruses. *Mailing Add:* Dept Microbiol La State Univ 1901 Perdido St New Orleans LA 70112

GALLANDER, JAMES FRANCIS, FOOD SCIENCE. *Current Pos:* RETIRED. *Personal Data:* b Peoria, Ill, Apr 17, 37; m 63; c 1. *Educ:* Ohio State Univ, BS, 60, PhD(food technol), 64. *Prof Exp:* From instr to prof fruit & veg processing, Ohio Agr Res & Develop Ctr, 62-92. *Mem:* Inst Food Technologists; Am Soc Enol. *Res:* Freezing and canning of pomological crops; wine fermentation. *Mailing Add:* 249 Imgard St Wooster OH 44691

GALLANT, DONALD, PSYCHIATRY, NEUROLOGY. *Current Pos:* From instr to assoc prof, 61-68, PROF PSYCHIAT & NEUROL, SCH MED, TULANE UNIV, 69- *Personal Data:* b Brooklyn, NY, Aug 9, 29; m 54; c 1. *Educ:* Tulane Univ, BS, 51, MD, 55. *Honors & Awards:* Robert C Lancaster Award for Humanitarian Efforts in Psychiat, 85. *Concurrent Pos:* Prin investr, Tulane Psychopharmacol Serv Ctr grant, 62-; consult, La State Alcoholism Prog, 62- *Mem:* Am Col Neuropsychopharmacol; Am Psychiat Asn. *Res:* Investigation and evaluation of neuropsychopharmacologic compounds; alcoholism. *Mailing Add:* Acad Fac Tulane Med Ctr Hosp 1415 Tulane Ave New Orleans LA 70112-2605

GALLANT, ESTHER MAY, SKELETAL MUSCLE, MALIGNANT HYPERTHERMIA. *Current Pos:* from asst prof to assoc prof, 82-93, PROF VET BIOL, COL VET MED, UNIV MINN, 93- *Personal Data:* b Auburn, NY, 43. *Educ:* Ind Univ, PhD(bot), 70. *Prof Exp:* Asst prof vet anat, pharmacol & physiol, Iowa State Univ, 74-78; sr res fel & assoc consult, Dept Pharmacol, Mayo Clin, 79-82. *Mem:* AAAS; Am Phys Soc; Biophys Soc; Am Asn Anatomists. *Res:* Skeletal muscle physiology; mechanical and electrophysiological studies of normal and diseased muscles. *Mailing Add:* Dept Vet Path biol Univ Minn Col Vet Med St Paul MN 55108

GALLANT, JONATHAN A, MOLECULAR BIOLOGY. *Current Pos:* From asst prof to assoc prof, 61-70, PROF GENETICS, UNIV WASH, 70- *Personal Data:* b New York, NY, Sept 23, 37; m 61; c 3. *Educ:* Haverford Col, BS, 57; Johns Hopkins Univ, PhD(biochem), 61. *Concurrent Pos:* NIH res grants, 62-65, 66-70 & 71-; NIH spec fel, Inst Biophys & Biochem, Paris, France, 64-65; dir sci & gas, Grosser Seattle, 69-; Guggenheim fel, 71. *Mem:* AAAS; Genetics Soc Am; Fedn Am Sci. *Res:* Accuracy in translation and transcription; regulation of enzyme synthesis; regulation of RNA synthesis; biology of aging. *Mailing Add:* Genetics SK50 3900 Seventh Ave NE Seattle WA 98195-0001

GALLARDO-CARPENTIER, ADRIANA, PHARMACOLOGY. *Current Pos:* Asst prof, 77-81, ASSOC PROF PHARMACOL, COL MED, HOWARD UNIV, 81- *Personal Data:* b Sept 13, 30; m. *Educ:* Univ Chile, DDS, 55. *Mem:* Am Soc Pharmacol & Exp Therapeut. *Res:* Effects of alcohol on the hypothalamus and on the heart. *Mailing Add:* 4116 Bennett Dr Annadale VA 22003-3401. *Fax:* 202-806-4453

GALLATI, WALTER WILLIAM, ZOOLOGY. *Current Pos:* assoc prof sci, 57-59, PROF BIOL, INDIANA UNIV, PA, 59-, CHMN DEPT, 83- *Personal Data:* b Brooklyn, NY, Dec 7, 27; m 58; c 2. *Educ:* Drew Univ, AB, 50; Univ Miami, MS, 52; Ohio State Univ, PhD(zool), 57. *Prof Exp:* Asst zool, Univ Miami, 50-51; asst zool, Ohio State Univ, 52-54, from asst instr to instr, 54-57. *Mem:* AAAS; Am Soc Parasitol; Am Micros Soc; Am Inst Biol Sci; Sigma Xi. *Res:* Parasitology. *Mailing Add:* 104 Shady Dr Indiana PA 15701

GALLAWAY, BOB MITCHEL, CIVIL ENGINEERING. *Current Pos:* Instr war training in eng, Tex A&M Univ, 43-44, instr eng drawing & descriptive geom, 44-46, asst prof, 46-48, from asst prof to assoc prof civil eng, 48-59, Brackett Prof, 78-80, PROF CIVIL ENG, TEX A&M UNIV, 59- *Personal Data:* b Kosciusko, Miss, Oct 14, 16; m 41; c 3. *Educ:* Tex A&M Univ, BS, 43, MS, 46, ME, 56. *Honors & Awards:* Reed Frank Erskine Award, 93. *Concurrent Pos:* Res engr & head hwy mat dept, Tex Transp Inst; mem, Hwy Res Bd; pres, Consult & Res Serv, Inc, 67-; mem bd consults study 4-10, Nat Coop Hwy Res Prog; mem, Transp Ctr, Univ PR. *Mem:* Nat Soc Prof Engrs; Am Soc Testing & Mat; Am Soc Eng Educ; Am Concrete Inst; Asn Asphalt Paving Technol; Sigma Xi; fel Am Soc Civil Engrs. *Res:* Materials research with particular interest in asphalt paving, portland cement, concrete and soil stabilization; skid resistance; waste solids utilization; synthetic aggregate. *Mailing Add:* 2904 Par Dr Bryan TX 77802

GALLE, KURT R(OBERT), MECHANICAL ENGINEERING. *Current Pos:* RETIRED. *Personal Data:* b Newton, Kans, July 19, 25; m 46; c 2. *Educ:* Purdue Univ, BS, 46, BS, 47, MS, 49, PhD(mech eng), 51. *Prof Exp:* Instr mech eng, Purdue Univ, 48-50; res engr, Boeing Co, Wash, 51-58, sr group engr, 58-60; assoc prof mech eng, Univ Wash, 60-86. *Mem:* Am Inst Aeronaut & Astronaut; Instrument Soc Am; Am Soc Eng Educ; Biomed Eng Soc; Simulation Coun; Sigma Xi. *Res:* Instrumentation research in bioengineering; systems analysis and simulation. *Mailing Add:* 8027 43rd Ave NE Seattle WA 98115

GALLEGLY, MANNON ELIHU, PLANT PATHOLOGY, PHYTOPHTHORA. *Current Pos:* From asst prof to prof plant sci, 49-86, dir div plant sci, 70-86, EMER PROF PLANT SCI, 86- *Personal Data:* b Mineral Springs, Ark, Apr 11, 23; m 47, Mary E Smith; c Michael E, Susan J (Ambrose) & Thomas W. *Educ:* Univ Ark, BS, 45; Univ Wis, MS, 46, PhD(plant path), 49. *Honors & Awards:* Campbell Award, AAAS, 60. *Concurrent Pos:* Consult, US/AID, EAfrica, 69-71. *Mem:* Fel Am Phytopath Soc; Potato Asn Am; Sigma Xi. *Res:* The genus Phytophthora: taxonomy, sexuality, diseases; physiologic specialization and resistance to tomato and potato late blight. *Mailing Add:* 401 Brooks Hall Div Plant Sci WVa Univ Morgantown WV 26506-6057

GALLEGOS, EMILIO JUAN, PHYSICAL & ANALYTICAL CHEMISTRY. *Current Pos:* RETIRED. *Personal Data:* b Del Norte, Colo, June 24, 32; m 63; c 1. *Educ:* Regis Col, BS, 54; Kans State Univ, PhD(phys chem), 61. *Honors & Awards:* Outstanding Paper Award, Geochem Soc, 72. *Prof Exp:* Res chemist, Chevron Res Corp, Stand Oil Co, 61-62, sr res assoc, 62-92. *Mem:* Am Chem Soc; Sigma Xi; Am Soc Mass Spectros. *Res:* Mass spectrometry; electron and optical microscopy; plasma; coal, shale and petroleum analysis; organic geochemistry; gas chromatography; mass spectrometry; computer. *Mailing Add:* 5618 Barrett Ave El Cerrito CA 94530

GALLELLI, JOSEPH F, PHARMACY. *Current Pos:* staff pharmacist, Pharmaceut Develop Serv, 61-62, chief, 62-70, CHIEF, PHARM DEPT, CLIN CTR, NIH, BETHESDA, MD, 70- *Personal Data:* b Brooklyn, NY, Mar 23, 36; m; c 5. *Educ:* Long Island Univ, BS, 57; Temple Univ, MS, 59, PhD(phys pharm), 62. *Honors & Awards:* Abbott Award, Am Soc Hosp Pharmacists, 70. *Prof Exp:* Grad & teaching asst, Dept Pharm, Temple Univ, Sch Pharm, 57-58; jr investr, Pharmaceut Prod Develop Dept, Wyeth Inst Med Res, Radnor, Pa, 58-59; instr, Dept Pharm, Temple Univ, 59-60, Wyeth Labs teaching fel, Sch Pharm, 59-61. *Concurrent Pos:* Chmn, Res Comt, Am Soc Hosp Pharmacists, 67-69 & Parenteral Prods Subcomt, Drug Standards Div, USP, 80-95; contrib ed, J Drug Intel, 67-70; clin instr pharm pract, Univ Md, Sch Pharm, 73-; assoc clin prof, Howard Univ, Col Pharm & Pharmacol Sci, 79-; mem, Drug Standards Consult Panel, 87-91. *Mem:* Am Pharmaceut Asn; Sigma Xi; Acad Pharmaceut Sci; Am Soc Hosp Pharmacists; Dist Columbia Soc Hosp Pharmacists; Int Pharmaceut Fedn; Am Asn Pharmaceut Scientists; Asn Mil Surgeons US. *Res:* Drug stability and assay development; formulation and stability of parenteral products; chemical kinetics and clinical pharmacokinetics; over 60 publications. *Mailing Add:* Warren Grant Magnuson Clin Ctr NIH Pharm Dept Bldg 10 Rm 2C146 Bethesda MD 20892

GALLEN, WILLIAM J, MEDICINE. *Current Pos:* RETIRED. *Personal Data:* b Columbus, Ohio, July 4, 24; m 54; c 7. *Educ:* Ohio State Univ, BA, 45, MD, 48; Am Bd Pediat, dipl, 57, cert cardiol, 61. *Prof Exp:* From intern to resident, Harper Hosp, Detroit, 48-51; resident pediat, Milwaukee Children's Hosp, 53-55; instr, Johns Hopkins Hosp, 55-56; Nat Heart Inst trainee, Karolinska Inst, Sweden, 56-57; from instr to prof pediat, Med Col Wis, 57-86. *Concurrent Pos:* Fel, Crippled Children's Bur, Johns Hopkins

Univ Hosp, 55-56; dir, Cardiac Diag Unit, Milwaukee Children's Hosp, 57-86; dir, Fairchild Cardiac Study Ctr, 57-86, chief, Dept Pediat, 70-72 & med serv, 72-74; vchmn, Dept Pediat, Med Col Wis, 81. *Mem:* Am Col Cardiol; Am Acad Pediat; Am Heart Asn. *Res:* Pediatrics; pediatric cardiology. *Mailing Add:* Childrens Hosp Wisc PO Box 1997 Milwaukee WI 53201-1997

GALLENBERG, LORETTA A, pharmacology, toxicology, for more information see previous edition

GALLER, BERNARD AARON, INTELLECTUAL PROPERTY PROTECTION. *Current Pos:* From instr to assoc prof math, Univ Mich, 55-66, assoc dean, Col Lit, Sci & Arts, 75-79, prof comput & commun sci, 66-84, assoc dir, Comput Ctr, 66-90, prof elect eng & comput sci, 85-94, assoc dir, Res Systs, Info Tech Div, 90-92, EMER PROF, UNIV MICH, ANN ARBOR, 94- *Personal Data:* b Chicago, Ill, Oct 3, 28; m 51, Enid Harris; c Bruce, Elaine, Glenn & Marilyn. *Educ:* Univ Chicago, PhB, 46, BS, 47, PhD(math), 55; Univ Calif, Los Angeles, AM, 49. *Honors & Awards:* Distinguished Serv Award, Asn Comput Mach, 80 & Am Fedn Info Processing Soc, 84. *Concurrent Pos:* Ed-in-chief, Anns Hist Comput, 78-87; chmn, Software Patent Inst, 92-94, pres, 94- *Mem:* Fel Asn Comput Mach (pres, 68-70). *Res:* Digital computers; intellectual property; automatic programming; computer analysis of musical sound; mathematical logic; linear programming; distributed systems. *Mailing Add:* 1056 Ferdon Rd Ann Arbor MI 48104. *Fax:* 313-668-9998; *E-Mail:* galler@umich.edu

GALLER, JANINA REGINA, CHILD PSYCHIATRY. *Current Pos:* Assoc chairperson, Dept Child Psychiat, Sch Med, Boston Univ, 80-85, dir, Residency Training Psychiat, 82-86, PROF PSYCHIAT, BOSTON UNIV, 82-, PROF PUB HEALTH, SCH PUB HEALTH, 84-, DIR, CTR BEHAV DEVELOP, SCH MED, 85- *Personal Data:* b Uppsala, Sweden; US citizen; m 70; c 3. *Educ:* Sophie Newcomb Col, BS, 69; Albert Einstein Col Med, MD, 72. *Honors & Awards:* Blanche Ittleson Award, Am Psychiat Asn, 85; Irving B Harris Award, Soc Behav Pediat, 92. *Concurrent Pos:* Mem adv coun, Nat Inst Child Health & Human Develop/NIH. *Mem:* Am Inst Nutrit; Am Psychiat Asn; Am Acad Child Psychiat; Am Psychosomatic Soc. *Res:* Effects of malnutrition on brain development in animals, and in human populations in Barbados and Mexico. *Mailing Add:* Ctr Behav Develop Boston Univ Med Ctr Solomon Carter Fuller MHC Boston MA 02118. *Fax:* 617-638-4843

GALLER, WILLIAM SYLVAN, sanitary engineering, operations research; deceased, see previous edition for last biography

GALLETTA, GENE JOHN, CYTOLOGY, PLANT PHYSIOLOGY. *Current Pos:* RES PLANT GENETICIST, AGR RES SERV, USDA, 77- *Personal Data:* b Philadelphia, Pa, July 3, 29; m 57; c 2. *Educ:* Univ Md, BS, 51; Rutgers Univ, MS, 53; Univ Calif, PhD(genetics), 59. *Honors & Awards:* G Darrow Small Fruit Res Award, Am Soc Hort Sci. *Prof Exp:* Asst hort, Rutgers Univ, 51-53; asst pomologist, Univ Calif, 53-54 & 56-59, pomologist, 56; from asst prof to prof hort sci, NC State Univ, 59-77, mem fac genetics, 70-77. *Mem:* Fel Am Soc Hort Sci; Am Genetic Asn; Am Pomol Soc; NAm Strawberry Growers Asn; Int Soc Hort Sci. *Res:* Small fruit crop breeding and genetics; plant and fruit morphology; inheritance of quantitative characters and disease resistance; plant propagation; fruit culture. *Mailing Add:* 8707 Graystone Lane Laurel MD 20708

GALLETTI, PIERRE MARIE, TISSUE ENGINEERING, ARTIFICIAL ORGANS. *Current Pos:* chmn, Div Biol & Med Sci, 68-72, vpres biol & med, 72-91, PROF MED SCI, BROWN UNIV, 67-, UNIV PROF, 91- *Personal Data:* b Monthey, Switz, June 11, 27; US citizen; m 59, Sonia Aidan; c Marc H. *Educ:* St Maurice Col, Switz, BA, 45; Univ Lausanne, MD, 51, PhD(physiol), 54. *Hon Degrees:* Roger Williams Col, 79, Univ Nancy, France, 82, Univ Ghent, Belg, 89. *Honors & Awards:* Lilienthal lectr, Mt Sinai Hosp, NY, 64; Hastings lectr, NIH, 79; John H Gibbon Jr Award, Am Soc ExtraCorporeal Technol Inc, 80; Runzi Prize, 88; Eng Pres Lectr, Am Inst Med Biol, 96. *Prof Exp:* Instr physiol, Univ Lausanne, 52-54; resident med, Zurich, 54-57; fel cardiovasc res, Cedars of Lebanon Hosp, Los Angeles, 57-58; from asst prof to prof physiol, Sch Med, Emory Univ, 58-67. *Concurrent Pos:* Int Union Against Cancer fel, Tumor Ctr, Palermo, 64-65; mem, Physiol Training Comt, NIH, 68-72; mem, Vet Admin Nephrol Rev Bd, 72-76; mem, cardiol adv comt, Nat Heart & Lung Inst, 76-79; chmn, Consensus Develop Conf Clin Appln Biomat, Biomed Eng Instrumentation Br, Div Res Serv & Off Med Appln Res & Devices & Technol Br Task Group, Devices & Technol Br, Div Heart & Vascular Dis, NIH, 81-82; Data Rev Bd, Clin Eval Ventricular Assist Devices, Nat Heart, Lung & Blood Inst, 81- & Sorin Biomed Tucin, Italy, Bd Dirs, 84-; sci adv comt I Stat, Princeton, NJ, Cardiopulmonics, Salt Lake City, Utah & Cytotherapeutics Inc, Providence, RI. *Mem:* Am Physiol Soc; Am Soc Artificial Internal Organs; Am Col Cardiol; foreign assoc Royal Acad Med Belg; Acad Med Italy; Swiss Physiol Soc; Int Soc Artificial Organs; Am Ins Med Biol Eng (pres, 94-); foreign mem Royal Acad Med Brussels; Swiss Acad Med. *Res:* Cardiorespiratory physiology; artificial heart, lung, kidney, liver and pancreas; physiology of death and resuscitation; bioengineering of artificial organs; tissue engineering; cell transplantation. *Mailing Add:* Div Biol & Med Brown Univ PO Box GB 393 Providence RI 02912. *Fax:* 401-863-1753

GALLEZ, BERNARD, hydraulic engineering; deceased, see previous edition for last biography

GALLI, JOHN RONALD, GENERAL PHYSICS. *Current Pos:* from asst prof to assoc prof, 63-72, chmn dept, 64-70, & 83-95, PROF PHYSICS, WEBER STATE UNIV, 72-, DEAN COL SCI, 95- *Personal Data:* b Salt Lake City, Utah, Oct 10, 36; m 60, 78, Cheryl Corley; c Shawnee (Petersen), Sherri, Debora, Diana & John D. *Educ:* Univ Utah, BS, 58, MA, 60, PhD(physics), 63. *Prof Exp:* Physicist, Naval Weapons Ctr, China Lake, Calif, 58-59 & Aerojet-Gen Corp Div, Gen Tire & Rubber Co, 63. *Mem:* Am Asn Physics Teachers. *Res:* High pressure physics, mechanical properties of solids; chaotic dynamics; fractal geometry; rotational dynamics. *Mailing Add:* Col Sci Weber State Univ Ogden UT 84408-2501

GALLI, PAOLO, PHYSICAL CHEMISTRY, INDUSTRIAL CHEMISTRY. *Current Pos:* PRES TECHNOL, MONTELL USA, ELKTOWN, MD. *Personal Data:* b Bassano del Grappa, Italy, Aug 29, 36; m, Anna M Marcon; c Giulia, Stefano & Massimo. *Educ:* Univ Padua, Italy, PhD(indust chem), 62. *Prof Exp:* Adj prof chem, Univ Bologna, Italy, 62-84; from adj prof to prof macromolecular sci, Univ Ferrara, Italy, 62-85; vpres, Himont Inc, Wilmington, Del, 85. *Concurrent Pos:* Dir res, Giulio Natta Res Ctr, Ferrara, 77-83; gen mgr, Montedison Spa, Milan, 83-85. *Res:* Industrial chemistry; holder of 30 patents infield; contributed articles to professional journals. *Mailing Add:* Montell USA Inc 912 Appleton Rd Elkton MD 21921

GALLIAN, JOSEPH A, ALGEBRA, MATHEMATICAL SCIENCE. *Current Pos:* From asst prof to assoc prof, 72-80, PROF MATH SCI, UNIV MINN, DULUTH, 80- *Personal Data:* b Pennsylvania, Jan 5, 42; c 3. *Educ:* Slippery Rock State Univ, BA, 66; Notre Dame Univ, PhD(math sci), 71. *Honors & Awards:* Allendoerfer Award, Math Asn Am, Trevor Evans Award. *Mem:* Am Math Asn; Math Asn Am. *Res:* Graph theory; finite groups. *Mailing Add:* Dept Math & Stat Univ Minn-Duluth Duluth MN 55812-2496. *Fax:* 218-726-8399; *E-Mail:* jgallian@umn.edu

GALLIE, THOMAS MUIR, COMPUTER SCIENCE. *Current Pos:* res instr math, Duke Univ, 54-55, from asst prof to prof, 56-71, dir, Comput Lab, 58-64, dir, Comput Sci Prog, 71-72, prof, 71-89, EMER PROF COMPUT SCI, DUKE UNIV, 89- *Personal Data:* b New York, NY, Aug 25, 25; m 91, Elizabeth Button; c 4. *Educ:* Harvard Univ, AB, 47; Univ Tex, MA, 49; Rice Univ, PhD(math), 54. *Prof Exp:* Pvt sch teacher, 49-50; asst, Rice Inst, 51-54. *Concurrent Pos:* Res engr, Humble Oil & Refining Co, 54 & 55-56; visitor, Swiss Fed Inst Technol, Zurich, 62-63 & 73-74; head educ res & training sect, Off Comput Activities, NSF, 68-69; vpres, Microelectronics Ctr NC, 80-81. *Mem:* Asn Comput Mach; Math Asn Am; Sigma Xi. *Res:* Numerical analysis. *Mailing Add:* Dept Comput Sci Duke Univ Durham NC 27708-0251. *E-Mail:* tmg@cs.duke.edu

GALLIGAN, JAMES M, PHYSICAL METALLURGY, SOLID STATE PHYSICS. *Current Pos:* PROF METALL, UNIV CONN, 72- *Personal Data:* b Far Rockaway, NY, May 13, 31; m 58; c 2. *Educ:* Polytech Inst Brooklyn, BMetE, 55; Univ Ill, MS, 57; Univ Calif, Berkeley, PhD(metall), 63. *Honors & Awards:* Von Humboldt Sr Sci Award, 86. *Prof Exp:* Res asst elec eng, Univ Ill, 55-57; res engr metall, E C Bain Lab, US Steel Corp, 57-58 & Lawrence Radiation Lab, Univ Calif, 58-62; from asst prof to assoc prof metall, Columbia Univ, 63-67; scientist, Brookhaven Nat Lab, 67-72. *Concurrent Pos:* Consult, Brookhaven Nat Lab, 65-67, 72-78, Stanley Tool Co, Plumb Tool Co, 73-77 & Aerospace Corp; vis scientist, Max Planck Inst Physics, 67; vis prof, Calif Inst Technol, 78-79, Inst Metall Physics, Gottingen, Cath Univ Chile & Univ Puebla, Mex. *Mem:* Am Inst Mining, Metall & Petrol Engrs; Am Phys Soc; Am Inst Mech Engrs; Sigma Xi; NY Acad Sci. *Res:* Defects in solids; hardening of crystals; superconductivity; metallurgical properties; nuclear materials; scanning tunneling microscopy of materials. *Mailing Add:* 144 Maple Rd Storrs Mansfield CT 06268

GALLIGAN, JOHN D(ONALD), PHYSICAL CHEMISTRY, METALLURGY. *Current Pos:* CONSULT, 92- *Personal Data:* b Washington, DC, Oct 9, 32; m 58; c Charles, Thomas, Monica, Ted & Martin. *Educ:* Manhattan Col, BS, 55; Emory Univ, PhD, 58. *Prof Exp:* Chemist, Harris Res Labs, Washington, DC, 57-58, sr chemist, 58-62; proj chemist, Gillette Safety Razor Co, Boston, 62-65, vpres, Gillette Res Inst, Wash, DC, 65-72, vpres res & develop, Personal Care Div, Chicago & Boston, 72-83, group dir, Boston Res & Develop Labs, 83-91. *Mem:* AAAS; Am Chem Soc; Am Asn Textile Chemists & Colorists; Soc Cosmetic Chemists; Am Inst Chemists. *Res:* Surface and polymer chemistry; lubrication; adsorption; electrochemistry; adhesion; chemical modification of textiles; metallurgy. *Mailing Add:* 30 Bakers Hill Rd Weston MA 02193-1761

GALLIN, ELAINE K, CELLULAR PHYSIOLOGY. *Current Pos:* res assoc, 76-80, HEAD, CELL PHYSIOL PROJ, ARMED FORCES RADIOBIOL RES INST, 81-, PROJ LEADER, 82- *Personal Data:* b New York, NY, Dec 16, 43; m, John I; c Alice & Michael. *Educ:* Cornell Univ, BS, 65; Hunter Col, MS, 70; City Univ NY, PhD(biol), 71. *Prof Exp:* Fel, Johns Hopkins Med Sch, 72-74, Columbia Med Sch, 74-75. *Concurrent Pos:* Adj assoc prof, Physiol Dept, Uniformed Serv Univ Health Sci, 78-90, Georgetown Univ Med Sch, 83-90; cong sci fel, Biophys Soc, 88-89, chair, Pub Policy Comt, 89-90; mem, Physiol Study Sect, NIH, 94- *Mem:* Biophys Soc; Am Phys Soc; Soc Gen Phys. *Res:* Characterization of ion transport mechanisms in macrophages; leukocyte-endothelial cell interactions; effects of ionizing radiation of leukocyte function and vascular integrity. *Mailing Add:* Off Int Health Prog US Dept Energy 19901 Germantown Rd Germantown MD 20874. *Fax:* 301-903-1413

GALLIN, JOHN I, EXPERIMENTAL BIOLOGY. *Current Pos:* clin assoc, Lab Clin Invest, Nat Inst Allergy & Infectious Dis, NIH, 71-74, sr investr, 75-91, head, Bact Dis Sect, 78-86, DIR, DIV INTRAMURAL RES, NAT INST ALLERGY & INFECTIOUS DIS, NIH, 85-, CHIEF, LAB HOST DEFENSES, 91- *Personal Data:* b New York, NY, Mar 25, 43; m 66, Elaine Klimerman; c Alice J & Michael L. *Educ:* Amherst Col, BA, 65; Cornell Univ, MD, 69. *Hon Degrees:* Dr, Amherst Col, 88. *Honors & Awards:* Squibb Award, Infectious Dis Soc Am, 84; Jeffrey Modell Found Lifetime Achievement Award, 90. *Prof Exp:* Intern med, Bellevue Hosp, NY, 69-70, asst resident, 70-71, sr chief med res, 74-75. *Concurrent Pos:* Teaching asst, Sch Med, NY Univ, 70-74, instr, 74-81; consult infectious dis, Med Ctr, USN, Bethesda, Md, 72-, Allergy Clin Immunol Serv, Walter Reed Army Med Ctr, Washington, DC, 82-; assoc ed, J Immunol, 79-83, sect ed, 85-89; mem numerous comt & panels, NIH, 81-; mem, Ad Hoc Working Group, Immunocompetence in Space, NASA, 85, Infectious Dis Adv Coun, Merck, Sharp & Dohme Int, 85-90. *Mem:* Inst Med-Nat Acad Sci; Am Soc Clin Invest; Am Fedn Clin Res; fel Infectious Dis Soc Am; Am Asn Immunologists; Am Soc Cell Biol; Sigma Xi; Soc Leukocyte Biol; Asn Am Physicians. *Res:* Leukocyte (phagocyte) function; inflammation. *Mailing Add:* Dir Warren G Magnuson Clin Ctr NIH 9000 Rockville Pike Bethesda MD 20892

GALLINI, JOHN B(ATTISTA), CHEMICAL ENGINEERING. *Current Pos:* RETIRED. *Personal Data:* b Detroit, Mich, June 5, 34; m 57, Nancy Shea; c 8. *Educ:* Univ Detroit, BChE, 56; Univ Mich, MS, 58, PhD(chem, eng), 61. *Prof Exp:* Res engr, plastics dept, Yerkes Film Res & Develop, E I du Pont de Nemours & Co, Inc, 59-65, group mgr venture develop sect, film dept, 65-66, staff eng, 66-72, res assoc, Spruance Fibers Res & Develop, 72-85. *Mem:* Am Chem Soc; Int Exec Sev Corp; Nat Exec Serv Corp. *Res:* High polymers; polymerization kinetics; physical and molecular properties of polymers; processing technology for thermoplastic materials; Kevlar polymerization, solvent recovery and spinning; coextrusion of film products; processes for nylon, Surlyn, Kapton, and polyacrylonintrile films; Vexar net products; Crofon fiber optics; flammability of nylon resins. *Mailing Add:* 2425 Triton Rd Richmond VA 23235-3337

GALLISTEL, CHARLES RANSOM, BEHAVIORAL PHYSIOLOGY, PHYSIOLOGICAL PSYCHOLOGY. *Current Pos:* PROF, UNIV CALIF, LOS ANGELES, 89- *Personal Data:* b Indianapolis, Ind, May 18, 41; m 69; c 1. *Educ:* Stanford Univ, BA, 63; Yale Univ, PhD(psychol), 66. *Prof Exp:* From asst prof to prof psychol, Univ Pa, 66-89, chmn dept, 81-84. *Concurrent Pos:* Chair, publ bd, Psychonomic Soc, 87-89, Animal Res Comt, Fed of Behav, Psychol & Cognitive Sci. *Mem:* Soc Neurosci; fel Ctr Advan Study Behav Sci; fel Soc Exp Psychologists; fel AAAS; Psychonomic Soc. *Res:* Neural systems in the diencephalon that mediate motivation and reinforcement; electrical self-stimulation of the brain; organization of action; the theory of learning. *Mailing Add:* Dept Psychol Univ Calif Los Angeles 1285 Franz Hall Box 951563 405 Hilgard Ave Los Angeles CA 90095-1563

GALLIVAN, JAMES BERNARD, PHYSICAL CHEMISTRY. *Current Pos:* Res chemist, 65-70, sr res chemist, 70-73, proj leader, 73-77, mgr paper chem res & develop, 77-79, tech dir paper chem, 79-81, mgr new prod, mining chem, 81-83, MGR PHOSPHINE CHEM, AM CYANAMID CO, 84- *Personal Data:* b Sydney, NS, Aug 9, 38; m 61; c 4. *Educ:* St Francis Xavier Univ, BSc, 60, MA, 62; Notre Dame Univ, PhD(radiation chem), 65. *Mem:* AAAS; Am Chem Soc; Chem Inst Can; Tech Asn Pulp & Paper Indust; Am Mining Cong. *Res:* Radiation chemistry; electronic spectroscopy; chemicals for paper industry; analytical chemistry and instrumental analysis; mining chemicals; phosphing chemicals. *Mailing Add:* 45 Cranbury Rd Norwalk CT 06851-2616

GALLIZIOLI, STEVE, WILDLIFE MANAGEMENT. *Current Pos:* RETIRED. *Personal Data:* b Riva, Italy, July 25, 24; US citizen; m 49, Claire Posilippo; c Laura, Debra & Maryann. *Educ:* Ore State Univ, BS, 50. *Honors & Awards:* Am Motors Conserv Award, 67; Special Conserv Award, Nat Wildlife Fedn, 79; McCulloch Conserv of Yr, 86. *Prof Exp:* Dist wildlife biologist, Ariz Game & Fish Dept, 50-55, res biologist, 55-57, res supvr, 57-66, res chief, 66-78, chief, Wildlife Mgt Div, 79-83. *Concurrent Pos:* Partic, Food & Agr Orgn, UN, Assignment to Venezuela, 69; observ, Int Asn Fish & Wildlife Agencies, San Jose, Costa Rica, 78. *Mem:* Wildlife Soc; Outdoor Writers Asn Am. *Res:* Population dynamics of mule deer; investigation of factors controlling Gambel and scaled quail populations; development of inventory technique for Gambel quail, whitewing doves. *Mailing Add:* 17116 E Oro Grande Fountain Hills AZ 85269. *E-Mail:* asteveg@juno.com

GALLO, ANTHONY EDWARD, JR, neurosurgery, for more information see previous edition

GALLO, AUGUST ANTHONY, ORGANIC CHEMISTRY, MEDICINAL CHEMISTRY. *Current Pos:* asst prof, 80-86, ASSOC PROF, DEPT CHEM, UNIV SOUTHWESTERN LA, 86- *Personal Data:* b Rochester, NY, Feb 14, 51; m 83, Sandra Checchi; c Christopher James & Andrea Elizabeth. *Educ:* St John Fisher Col, BS, 73; Vanderbilt Univ, PhD(org chem), 78. *Prof Exp:* Res assoc org med chem, Univ Calif, San Francisco, 78-80. *Concurrent Pos:* Pres, Univ Southwestern La Sigma Xi Club, 85-86 & 96-97; chem sect head, La Acad Sci, 93- *Mem:* Sigma Xi; Am Chem Soc; NY Acad Sci. *Res:* Synthesis of biologically important molecules and collaborative biological testing of these compounds; synthesis of novel heterocycles; organo-sulfur chemistry and new synthetic methodology; natural products chemistry. *Mailing Add:* Dept Chem Univ Southwestern La PO Box 44370 Lafayette LA 70504-4370. *Fax:* 318-482-5676; *E-Mail:* gallo@usl.edu

GALLO, CHARLES FRANCIS, SUPERCONDUCTIVITY, XEROGRAPHY. *Current Pos:* PRES, FOUNDER & CHIEF SCIENTIST, SUPERCONIX INC, 88- *Personal Data:* b Mt Vernon, NY, July 22, 35; wid; c Bonnie. *Educ:* Rensselaer Polytech Inst, BS, 57. *Honors & Awards:* Sci Award, Bausch & Lomb, 50. *Prof Exp:* Coop prog, Gen Elec & RPI, 54-57; jr engr, Res Labs, Westinghouse Elec Corp, 57-62, eng specialist, 62-64; sr physicist, Xerox Corp, Rochester, 64-67, assoc scientist, 67-68, scientist, 68-81; res specialist, 3M Corp, 81-88. *Concurrent Pos:* Sci consult, Inner City Schs, Rochester, NY; lectr, George Washington Univ, 75, Univ Western Ont, 74 & 76, World Electrotech Cong, Moscow, 77 & Purdue Univ, 80, Univ Southampton, 82, Univ Kyushu, 84. *Mem:* Am Phys Soc; Japan Inst Electrostatics; Electrostatics Soc Am; Mat Res Soc; Am Asn Crystal Growth. *Res:* Superconductivity; transport properties thermoelectricity-solids; energy conversion; xerography; coronas; gas discharges; light sources; injection electroluminescence; optical radiation; work function; astrophysics; facsimile systems; alphanumeric printers; electrostatics; charge exchange; solid state physics. *Mailing Add:* 2440 Lisbon Ave Lake Elmo MN 55042. *Fax:* 612-222-0049

GALLO, DUANE GORDON, ANALYTICAL CHEMISTRY, BIOCHEMISTRY. *Current Pos:* RETIRED. *Personal Data:* b Aberdeen, SDak, May 15, 26; m 52; c 10. *Educ:* Univ NDak, BS, 51, MS, 53, PhD(biochem), 55. *Prof Exp:* Asst, Univ NDak, 52-55; from asst sr chemist to sr chemist, Mead Johnson & Co, 57-61, group leader, 61-68, sr res assoc, 68-70, prin investr, 70-73, sr prin investr, 73-75, prin res assoc, 75-78, prin res scientist, 78-87. *Mem:* AAAS; Am Soc Pharmacol & Exp Therapeut; Soc Exp Biol & Med. *Res:* Phosphatide and cholesterol synthesis and metabolism; lipid metabolism; endocrinology; reproductive physiology and biochemistry; drug analysis and metabolism. *Mailing Add:* 10221 Upper Mount Vernon Rd Evansville IN 47712-9603

GALLO, LINDA LOU, BIOCHEMISTRY, NUTRITION. *Current Pos:* res asst biochem, George Washington Univ, 62-69, asst res prof, 69-75, from asst prof to assoc prof, 75-86, PROF BIOCHEM, GEORGE WASHINGTON UNIV, 86- *Personal Data:* b Smithtown, WVa, Aug 20, 37; m 57; c 2. *Educ:* WVa Univ, BS, 59; George Washington Univ, MS, 63, PhD(biochem), 69. *Prof Exp:* Chemist anal chem, Food & Drug Admin, 59-62. *Concurrent Pos:* Sanders fel biochem, George Washington Univ, 62-64; prin investr, NIH grant, 75-88; consult, Cafritz Hosp, 72-75, Anheuser Busch, 75 & Lederle Labs, 84, Wyeth-Ayerst, 86-88; mem, Arteriosclerosis Coun, Am Heart Asn. *Mem:* Sigma Xi; Am Heart Asn; Grad Women Sci; NY Acad Sci; Soc Exp Biol & Med. *Res:* Cholesterol absorption; atherosclerosis; lipoprotein metabolism; lipid metabolism; cachexia. *Mailing Add:* Dept Biochem George Washington Univ Med Sch 2300 I St NW Washington DC 20037-2337. *Fax:* 202-994-8974

GALLO, RICHARD LOUIS, DEVELOPMENTAL BIOLOGY, DERMATOLOGY. *Current Pos:* instr, 92-96, ASST PROF, HARVARD MED SCH, 96- *Personal Data:* b New York, NY, Dec 9, 58; c Max & Lauren. *Educ:* Univ Chicago, BA, 80; Univ Rochester, MD & PhD (biophys), 86. *Honors & Awards:* Arch of Derma Award, AMA, 91. *Prof Exp:* Instr, John Hopkins Hosp, 80-87. *Mem:* Am Soc Cell Biol; Soc Pediat Dermat; AAAS; Soc Invest Dermat. *Res:* Basic mechanisms of epithelial-mesenchymal interactions; regulation and modes of communication of cell surface molecules in development and wound repair. *Mailing Add:* Boston Childrens Hosp Enders 9 Boston MA 02115. *E-Mail:* gallo@al.tch.harvard.edu

GALLO, ROBERT C, CELL BIOLOGY, BIOCHEMISTRY. *Current Pos:* DIR, INST HUMAN VIROL, MED BIOTECHNOL CTR, BIOTECHNOL INST, UNIV MD, 95-, PROF MED, DEPT MICROBIOL & IMMUNOL, SCH MED, 95-, HEAD, TUMOR BIOL PROG, BALTIMORE CANCER CTR, 95- *Personal Data:* b Waterbury, Conn, Mar 23, 37; m 61; c 2. *Educ:* Providence Col, BA, 59; Jefferson Med Col, MD, 63. *Hon Degrees:* Numerous from US & foreign univs, 74-90. *Honors & Awards:* Bryan Priestman Award, 72; Edward Rhodes Stitt Award & Lectr, Asn Mil Surgeons US, 82; Medal of Honor, Am Cancer Soc, 83; Hermann Beerman Award, Soc Invest Dermat, 84; Runme Shaw Mem Lectr, Acad Med, Singapore, 86; Perey Lectr, McMaster Univ, 86; Henry S Kaplan Mem Lectr, Stanford Univ, 87; Richard & Hinda Rosenthal Found Award, Am Col Physicians, 88; Maxwell Finland Award & Lectr, Infectious Dis Soc Am, 90; Karl Landsteiner Mem Award, Am Asn Blood Banks, 90; Ciba Corning Award Lectr, Asn Clin Biochemists, 93; Dale E McFarlin Award, Int Retroviol Asn, 94; Kalinka Award, Asn Against HIV/AIDS, 96; William & Myrtle Harris Distinguished Lectr, Calif Inst Technol, 96; Gustav-Embden Lectr, Klinikum der Johann Wolfgang Goethe-Univ, 96. *Prof Exp:* Clin clerk, Metab Sect, Yale Univ Med Sch, 62-63; from intern to resident med, Univ Chicago, 63-65; clin assoc, Med Br, Nat Cancer Inst, NIH, 65-68, sr investr, 68-69, head, Sect Cellular Control Mech, Human Tumor Cell Biol Br, 69-72, chief, Lab Tumor Cell Biol, 72-95. *Concurrent Pos:* Consult, M D Anderson Hosp & Tumor Inst, 70-71; consult virol, Roswell Park; consult microbiol, Univ SC; blood consult, Hahneman Med Sch Cancer Ctr; vis prof, Univ Minn, 71; lectr, numerous US & foreign univs, 71-90; adj prof, Dept Genetics, George Washington Univ, 72-, Dept Biol, Johns Hopkins Univ, 85-, Dept Microbiol, Immunol & Parasitol, Cornell Univ, 86-, Dept Molecular Genetics & Microbiol, Univ Med & Dent NJ, 87 & Dept Microbiol, Rutgers Univ, 88-; mem, numerous sci comts & panels, govt agencies & nat socs. *Mem:* Nat Acad Sci; Inst Med-Nat Acad Sci; Am Soc Hemat; Am Fedn Clin Res; Am Asn Cancer Res; AAAS; Am Soc Clin Invest; Biochem Soc; Am Soc Biochem & Molecular Biol; Int Soc Hemat; fel Am Acad Microbiol; Leukemia Soc Am; Sigma Xi; Am Asn Physicians; Molecular Med Soc. *Res:* Oncology, especially leukemia; tumor viruses; molecular biology; hematology; mechanisms involved in control of cell growth and differentiation and in particular how these apply in neoplasia; viral oncogenesis; human oncogenesis; role of inciting agents; virology; author of more than 1050 publications. *Mailing Add:* Univ Md Biotechnol Inst 725 W Lombard St Baltimore MD 21201

GALLO, ROBERT VINCENT, ENDOCRINOLOGY. *Current Pos:* asst prof, 70-78, ADJ ASSOC PROF PHYSIOL, SCH MED, UNIV CALIF, SAN FRANCISCO, 78- *Personal Data:* b New York, NY, Aug 18, 41. *Educ:* Columbia Col, BA, 62; Purdue Univ, PhD(biol), 68. *Prof Exp:* NIH fel, Sch Med, Univ Calif, Los Angeles, 68-70. *Concurrent Pos:* NIH grant, Sch Med, Univ Calif, San Francisco, 78-81. *Mem:* AAAS; Endocrine Soc; Int Soc Neuroendocrinol; Am Physiol Soc. *Res:* Reproductive neuroendocrinology. *Mailing Add:* Dept Physiol Univ Conn Box U-42 75 No Eagleville Storrs Mansfield CT 06269-0002

GALLOP, PAUL MYRON, PROTEIN CHEMISTRY. *Current Pos:* BIOCHEMIST, LAB HUMAN BIOCHEM, CHILDREN'S HOSP MED CTR, 72-, DIR, LAB HUMAN BIOCHEM, DEPT ORTHOP SURG, 81- *Personal Data:* b New York, NY, Nov 24, 27; m 64; c 3. *Educ:* Univ Pa, AB, 48; Mass Inst Technol, PhD(biophys), 53; Harvard Med Sch, MSc, 73. *Honors & Awards:* Career. *Prof Exp:* Instr biophys, Mass Inst Technol, 53-54; biophysicist, L I Jewish Hosp, 54-59; vis asst prof, Albert Einstein Col Med, 57-59, from assoc prof to prof biochem, 59-72; chmn, Dept Oral Biol, Sch Dent Med, Harvard Univ, 740, prof biol chem, Div Health Sci & Technol, Harvard-Mass Inst Technol, 76-, dep dir, Med Scientist Training Prog, Sch Med, 79- *Concurrent Pos:* Mem study sect, Adult Develop & Aging Res and Training Comt, NIH, Md, 73-77; mem, aging rev comt, Nat Inst Aging, 74- *Mem:* AAAS; Am Chem Soc; Biophys Soc; Am Soc Biol Chem; Orthop Res Soc; Geront Soc. *Res:* Collagen structure; proteolytic enzymes; collagenase; mechanism of enzyme action; peptide synthesis; connective tissue structure; mass spectrometry; posttranslational modifications; glycohemoglobins; vitamin K-dependent proteins; molecular basis of clinical disorders. *Mailing Add:* Dept Biol Chem Harvard Med Sch Childrens Hosp 300 Longwood Ave Enders 9 Boston MA 02115. *Fax:* 617-355-6823

GALLOPO, ANDREW ROBERT, ORGANIC CHEMISTRY, BIOCHEMISTRY. *Current Pos:* SR RES CHEMIST, SMITH KLINE BEECHAM, 90- *Personal Data:* b Passaic, NJ, Mar 23, 40. *Educ:* Rutgers Univ, AB, 62; Brown Univ, PhD(org chem), 67. *Prof Exp:* NIH fel, Univ Wis, 66-68; asst mgr, Philip Hunt Chem Corp, 68-69; from asst prof to assoc prof chem, Montclair State Col, 69-81; sr scientist, Warner Lambert, 81-88; res assoc, Am Cyanamid, 89-90. *Mem:* Am Chem Soc; Am Asn Dent Res. *Res:* Organic chemical kinetics; enzymic kinetics; enzyme purification; drug delivery systems; oral care products. *Mailing Add:* 133 Wessington Ave Garfield NJ 07026

GALLO-TORRES, HUGO E, GASTROINTEROLOGY. *Current Pos:* med officer, Div Cardio-Renal Drug Prod, 87, MED OFFICER, DIV GASTROENTEROL & COAGULATION DRUG PROD, FOOD & DRUG ADMIN, 87- *Personal Data:* US citizen; c 3. *Educ:* San Marcos Univ, Lima, BSc, 54, MD, 63; Columbia Univ, MS, 64; Tulane Univ, PhD(biochem), 68; Am Bd Nutrit, cert, 78. *Prof Exp:* Resident med, Cent Army Hosp, Lima, 62-63; instr med, Charity Hosp La, 64-68; sr biochemist, Dept Biochem Nutrit, Hoffmann-La Roche Inc, 68-89 & 72-73, res group chief, 74-78; res sect head, Roche Res Ctr, 79-80, sr res physician, Dept Med Res, 81-83, asst med dir, Gastroenterol & Rheumatology, 83-85; dir gastroenterol, Serono Labs, Inc, 85-86. *Concurrent Pos:* Physician, Specialized Clin Diag Neuro-endocrine Dis, Lima, 62-63; WHO fel nutrit, Incap, Guatemala, 64; NIH fel, Tulane Univ, 64-67; vis biochemist, Dept Vitamin & Nutrit Res, Hoffmann-La Roche & Co, Ltd, Basel, Switz, 70-72 & Dept Pharmacl, Roche Prod Ltd, Welwyn, Eng, 71; adj prof, Dept Home Econ, Hunter Col, 77-; adj prof med, Dept Med, Div Gastroenterol & Nutrit, Sch Med & Health Sci, George Washington Univ, 87- *Mem:* Fel Am Col Gastroenterol; Am Gastroenterol Asn; Am Physiol Soc; Am Acad Cert Med Nutritionists. *Res:* Internal medicine, especially gastrointestinal, cardiovascular and bronchopulmonary disorders; clinical nutrition; experimental physiology. *Mailing Add:* Div Gastroenterol & Coagulation Drug Prod Food & Drug Amin HFD-180 5600 Fishers Lane Rm 645 Rockville MD 20857

GALLOWAY, ETHAN CHARLES, ORGANIC CHEMISTRY, POLYMER CHEMISTRY. *Current Pos:* RETIRED. *Personal Data:* b Howell, Mich, Oct 31, 30; m 73, Patricia Winner; c Heather, Samantha & Meagan. *Educ:* Mich State Univ, BSc, 51; Univ Calif, Berkeley, PhD(chem), 54. *Prof Exp:* Res chemist, Dow Chem Co, 54-58, mem staff, Tech Serv & Develop Dept, 58-60, head polymer intermediates, 60-61, head specialty chem, 61-62; dir res, Plastics Div, Nopco Chem Co, 62-65; mgr prod develop, Stauffer Chem Co, 65-66, asst dir, Eastern Res Ctr, 66-67, dir, 67-69, dir res, 69-70, vpres & dir res, 70-78, vpres corp planning & develop, 78-81, exec vpres technol, 81-85; exec vpres technol, Chesebrough-Ponds Inc, 85-88; sr vpres & pres new bus develop, Loctite Corp, 88-90; pres & chief exec officer, Edison Polymer Innovation Corp, 90-96. *Concurrent Pos:* Pres, Indust Res Inst, New York, 78-79; bd dira, Neogen, 84-88; chmn, Coun Chem Res, Washington, DC, 88. *Mem:* Am Chem Soc; Sci Res Soc Am; Indust Res Inst; Coun Chem Res. *Res:* Polymer science and engineering; transfer of technology from universities to industry. *Mailing Add:* 6549 Thornbrook Circle Hudson OH 44236. *Fax:* 216-656-1149

GALLOWAY, GORDON LYNN, INORGANIC CHEMISTRY. *Current Pos:* PROF & DIR PROG GEN CHEM, MICH STATE UNIV, 89- *Personal Data:* b Pottstown, Pa, Sept 25, 36; m 62; c 2. *Educ:* Franklin & Marshall Col, BS, 57; Mich State Univ, PhD(inorg chem), 62. *Prof Exp:* Mem staff, Los Alamos Sci Lab, 61-63; asst prof chem & asst to dean col, St Lawrence Univ, 63-67; from asst prof to prof chem, Denison Univ, 67-89, chmn dept, 73-75. *Concurrent Pos:* Partic, NSF res prog col teachers, 64 & grant, 64-66; W B King vis prof gen chem, Iowa State Univ, 72-73; mem ed bd, J Chem Educ, 70- *Mem:* AAAS; Am Chem Soc; Sigma Xi; Am Asn Univ Profs. *Res:* Chemistry of the interaction of metal ions with organic molecules; analysis of the role of trace elements in health and disease. *Mailing Add:* 1364 Jolly Rd Okemos MI 48864-4046

GALLOWAY, JAMES NEVILLE, ENVIRONMENTAL CHEMISTRY. *Current Pos:* asst prof environ chem, 76-80, assoc prof, 80-88, PROF ENVIRON SCI, UNIV VA, 88- *Personal Data:* b Annapolis, Md, Oct 26, 44; m 68, Nancy E Hodge; c 2. *Educ:* Whittier Col, BA, 66; Univ Calif, San Diego, PhD(chem), 72. *Prof Exp:* Consult chem oceanog, Southern Calif Coastal Water Res Proj, 72; pres, Shenandoah Crafts, Inc, 72-74; assoc environ chem, Cornell Univ, 74-76. *Concurrent Pos:* Pres, Bermuda Biol Stat Res Inc. *Mem:* Am Geophys Union. *Res:* The effect of acid deposition on aquatic ecosystems, the long range transport of atmospheric microcontaminants, the chemistry of natural waters, and air-sea exchange. *Mailing Add:* Environ Sci Dept Univ Va Clark Hall Charlottesville VA 22903

GALLOWAY, KENNETH FRANKLIN, ELECTRONICS ENGINEERING, RADIATION EFFECTS PHYSICS. *Current Pos:* DEAN, SCH ENG & PROF ELEC ENG, VANDERBILT UNIV, 96- *Personal Data:* b Columbia, Tenn, Apr 11, 41; m 59; c 2. *Educ:* Vanderbilt Univ, AB, 62; Univ SC, PhD(physics), 66. *Prof Exp:* Res assoc to assoc prof, Ind Univ, Bloomington, 66-72; res physicist, Naval Weapons Support Ctr, Crane, Ind, 72-74; proj leader, Electronic Tech Div, Nat Bur Stand, 74-77, chief, Semiconductor Devices & Circuits Div, 81-85, Semiconductor Electronics Div, 85-86; head & prof elec & comput eng, Univ Ariz, Tucson, 86-96. *Concurrent Pos:* Sci & technol fel, US Dept Com, 79-80; prof elec eng, Univ Md, College Park, 80-86; gen chmn, Nuclear & Space Radiation Effects Conf & Hardened Electronics & Radiation Technol Conf, Inst Elec & Electronics Engrs, 85, chmn, USA Engr Res & Develop Comt, 94-; mem, Nuclear & Plasma Sci Soc Admin Comt, Inst Elec & Electronics Engrs, 87-90, exec vchmn, Nuclear & Plasma Sci Soc Radiation Effects Comt, 88-91, vpres, Nuclear & Plasma Sci Soc, 89, chmn, Radiation Effects Comt, 91-94. *Mem:* Am Phys Soc; fel Inst Elec & Electronics Engrs; Electrochem Soc; fel AAAS; Am Soc Eng Educ; Sigma Xi. *Res:* Radiation effects on semiconductor devices; measurement techniques for semiconductor devices and circuits. *Mailing Add:* Sch Eng Vanderbilt Univ Box 1826 Sta B Nashville TN 37235. *Fax:* 615-343-8006; *E-Mail:* kfg@vuse.vanderbilt.edu

GALLOWAY, MATTHEW PETER, NEUROPHARMACOLOGY OF MONOAMINES. *Current Pos:* PROF PSYCHIAT & PHARMACOL, WAYNE STATE UNIV 84- *Personal Data:* b Albany, NY, June 19, 53; m 75; c 3. *Educ:* St Louis Univ, PhD(biochem), 81. *Prof Exp:* Fel, Yale Univ Sch Med, 81-84. *Concurrent Pos:* Prin investr, Nat Inst Drug Abuse, Wayne State Univ, 85-, NIMH, 85-88, co-investr, Nat Inst Neurol Dis & Stroke, 89-92, Nat Inst Alcohol Abuse & Alcoholism, 92- *Mem:* Soc Neurosci. *Res:* Neurochemical analysis factors regulating dopamine and serotonin release and synthesis using microdialysis and brain slices; mechanism of action for drugs of abuse and psychotropic medications. *Mailing Add:* Dept Psychiat 2309 Scott Hall Wayne State Univ Sch Med 540 E Canfield Detroit MI 48201. *Fax:* 313-577-7617

GALLOWAY, RAYMOND ALFRED, PHYSIOLOGY. *Current Pos:* From asst prof to assoc prof, 58-69, PROF PHYSIOL, UNIV MD, 69-, PROF BOT, 76- *Personal Data:* b Arbutus, Md, May 12, 28. *Educ:* Univ Md, BS, 52, MS, 56, PhD(bot), 58. *Mem:* Bot Soc Am; Am Soc Plant Physiol; Phycol Soc Am. *Res:* Enzymology; heterotrophy in estuarine algae; physiology of algae; CO_2 metabolism. *Mailing Add:* 138 N Brand Blvd Suite 21 Glendale CA 91203

GALLOWAY, ROBERT L, INSTRUMENTATION, MEDICAL IMAGING. *Current Pos:* Asst prof, 85-93, ASSOC PROF BIOMED ENG & NEUROSURG, VANDERBILT UNIV, 93- *Personal Data:* b Lynchburg, Va, 1955. *Educ:* Duke Univ, BS, 77, PhD(biomed eng), 83; Univ Va, MS, 79. *Mailing Add:* Vanderbilt Univ Box 1653B Nashville TN 37235

GALLOWAY, ROBERT THOMAS, AEROSPACE ENGINEERING. *Current Pos:* STAFF MEM, TRAINING SYSTS DIV, NAVAL AIR WARFARE CTR, ORLANDO. *Honors & Awards:* DeFlorez Training Award, Am Inst Aeronaut & Astronaut, 94. *Mailing Add:* 2173 Mohawk Trail Maitland FL 32751-3950

GALLOWAY, WILLIAM DON, PSYCHOPHYSICS. *Current Pos:* SUPVRY RES PSYCHOLOGIST, CDRH, FOOD & DRUG ADMIN, 70- *Personal Data:* b Dickson, Tenn, Dec 28, 39. *Educ:* Univ Fla, BA, 61; La State Univ, MA, 63; Univ Md, PhD(exp psychol), 70. *Prof Exp:* Res asst, Human Resources Res Off, Ft Benning, Ga, 63-64; res asst animal perception, Inst Behav Res, 66-68; res asst psychol, Sch Med, Johns Hopkins Univ, 68-70. *Mem:* Am Psychol Asn. *Res:* Animal psychophysics, psychopharmacology, behavioral toxicology and teratology; behavioral effects on non-ionizing radiation. *Mailing Add:* 12790 Twin Brook Pkwy Rm 32 Rockville MD 20852

GALLOWAY, WILLIAM EDMOND, PETROLEUM GEOLOGY. *Current Pos:* Elliott prof, 85-93, MORGAN DAVIS PROF GEOL SCI, UNIV TEX, AUSTIN, 93-; SR RES SCIENTIST, TEX BUR ECON GEOL, 75- *Personal Data:* b Waco, Tex, Oct 8, 44; m 66, Rosemary Mauk; c Jennifer & Doug. *Educ:* Tex A&M Univ, BS, 66; Univ Tex, Austin, MA, 68, PhD(geol), 71. *Honors & Awards:* A I Levorsen Award, Am Asn Petrol Geologists, 77 & 86, Wallace Pratt Mem Award, 83. *Prof Exp:* Res scientist assoc, Tex Bur Econ Geol, 70; res scientist, Explor Res Div, Continental Oil Co, 70-73, res group leader, 73-75, dir geol sect, 75. *Concurrent Pos:* Consult energy supply, Off Technol Assessment, US Cong, 77-78; lectr, Continuing Educ Prog, Am Asn Petrol Geologists, 77-, distinguished lectr, 85-86; vis prof, Univ Bergen, 80 & 90; Klabzuba vis prof, Univ Okla, 81. *Mem:* Am Asn Petrol Geologists; Int Asn Sedimentologists; Sigma Xi; Am Geol Inst; Soc Econ Paleontologists & Mineralogists. *Res:* Clastic depositional systems; origin and geologic setting of petroleum deposits and sedimentary uranium ores; sedimentary deagenesis; basin hydrogeology; basin analysis; seismic and sequence stratigraphy. *Mailing Add:* Dept Geol Sci Univ Tex Austin TX 78712-1026. *Fax:* 512-471-9425

GALLOWAY, WILLIAM JOYCE, PHYSICS, AERONAUTICAL ENGINEERING. *Current Pos:* CONSULT, 82- *Personal Data:* b Chicago, Ill, Sept 15, 24; m 46; c 2. *Educ:* Univ Calif, Los Angeles, BS, 49, MS, 50, PhD(physics), 53. *Honors & Awards:* Arch T Colwell Merit Award, Soc Automotive Engrs, 73; Silver Medal in Noise, Acoust Soc Am, 88. *Prof Exp:* Physicist, Res Staff, Eng Labs, Signal Corps, 51-52; vpres, Bolt Beranek & Newman, Inc, 53-82. *Concurrent Pos:* Chmn, Comt Hearing Bioacoust & Biomech, Nat Res Coun, 79; designated eng rep aircraft acoust, Fed Aviation Admin, 82- *Mem:* Nat Acad Eng; Inst Noise Control Engrs (vpres, 78-80); fel Acoust Soc Am (vpres, 83-84); Sigma Xi. *Res:* Acoustics; cavitation in liquids; aircraft, rocket and traffic noise. *Mailing Add:* 19343 Olivos Dr Tarzana CA 91356

GALLUCCI, ROBERT RUSSELL, ORGANIC CHEMISTRY, POLYMER SCIENCE. *Current Pos:* GE CRD, 76-82, GENERAL ELECTRIC PLASTICS, 82- *Personal Data:* b New York, NY, Sept 26, 50; c 1. *Educ:* City Col New York, BS, 72; Princeton Univ, MA, 74. *Concurrent Pos:* Instr polymer blends short course. *Mem:* Am Chem Soc; Soc Plastics Engrs. *Res:* Mechanisms; polymer synthesis; polymer blends. *Mailing Add:* Gen Elec Plastics One Lexan Lane Mt Vernon IN 47620-9367

GALLUN, ROBERT LOUIS, ENTOMOLOGY, GENETICS. *Current Pos:* prof, 71-82, EMER PROF ENTOM, AGR RES STA, PURDUE UNIV, 82- *Personal Data:* b Milwaukee, Wis, Feb 21, 24; m 49; c 2. *Educ:* Mich State Univ, BS, 48, MS, 50; Purdue Univ, PhD, 60. *Prof Exp:* Entomologist, Bur Entom & Plant Quarantine, Agr Res Serv, USDA, 50-52, res entomologist, 53-72, res leader & tech adv, 72-82. *Concurrent Pos:* Assoc prof entom, Purdue Univ, 70-71. *Mem:* Entom Soc Am; Am Soc Agron; Am Genetic Asn; Crop Sci Soc Am; Sigma Xi. *Res:* Host plant resistance to insects; biological races and genetics of the Hessian fly. *Mailing Add:* 214 Spring Valley Lane West Lafayette IN 47906

GALM, JAMES MICHAEL, FORENSIC ENGINEERING. *Current Pos:* SR RES ENGR, CYBEREX, INC, 91- *Personal Data:* b Chardon, Ohio, Apr 12, 62. *Educ:* Case Western Res Univ, BS, 84, MS, 87, PhD(elec eng), 91. *Prof Exp:* Res asst, Case Western Res Univ, 84-90. *Concurrent Pos:* Chief exec officer, PGM Diversified Indusrs, Inc, 86- *Mem:* Inst Elec & Electronics Engrs; Nat Soc Prof Engrs. *Res:* Solid state power electronics and systems; modeling and failure analysis of electric power systems and components. *Mailing Add:* Cyberex Inc 7171 Industrial Park Blvd Mentor OH 44060

GALMARINO, ALBERTO RAUL, MATHEMATICS. *Current Pos:* from asst prof to assoc prof, 63-78, PROF MATH, NORTHEASTERN UNIV, 78- *Personal Data:* b Buenos Aires, Arg, Sept 23, 28; m 61; c 1. *Educ:* Univ Buenos Aires, Lic math, 55; Mass Inst Technol, PhD(math), 61. *Prof Exp:* Instr algebra & topology, Univ Buenos Aires, 57-58; res assoc math, North eastern Univ, 61-62; assoc prof, Univ Buenos Aires, 62-63. *Concurrent Pos:* Math consult, Argentine Navy, 62. *Mem:* Am Math Soc; Argentine Math Soc. *Res:* Probability theory; stochastic processes; theory of games; mathematical analysis. *Mailing Add:* Dept Math Northwestern Univ Boston MA 02115

GALONSKY, AARON IRVING, NUCLEAR PHYSICS. *Current Pos:* assoc prof physics, Mich State Univ, 64-66, dir cyclotron lab, 67-69, assoc dir, 79-80, PROF PHYSICS, MICH STATE UNIV, 66- *Personal Data:* b Brooklyn, NY, Apr 18, 29; m 51, Marion Weber; c Marc, Lee Anne & Bruce. *Educ:* Brooklyn Col, BA, 50; Univ Wis, MS, 51, PhD, 54. *Prof Exp:* Physicist, Oak Ridge Nat Lab, 54-59; group leader, Midwest Univs Res Asn, 59-64. *Concurrent Pos:* Guest prof, Inst Nuclear Physics, Nuclear Res Lab, Julich, WGer, 75-76; Japan Soc Prom Sci fel, Tokyo Inst Technol, 88. *Mem:* Fel Am Phys Soc. *Res:* Nuclear reactions; scattering; radiation shielding; neutrons; neutron halo nuclei. *Mailing Add:* Dept Physics Mich State Univ East Lansing MI 48824. *E-Mail:* galonsky@nscl.msu.edu

GALOSY, RICHARD ALLEN, PSYCHOPHYSIOLOGY, NEUROBIOLOGY. *Personal Data:* b St Louis, Mo, Feb 6, 46. *Educ:* Univ Mo-St Louis, BA, 68; Western Wash State Col, Bellingham, MS, 70; Univ NC, Chapel Hill, PhD(psychophysiol), 74, St Louis Univ; JD, 86. *Prof Exp:* From asst prof to assoc prof neurobiol, Univ Tex Health Sci Ctr, Dallas, 75-82; chmn bd, Anal Data Methods, Inc, 89-93. *Concurrent Pos:* Moss fel, Univ Tex Health Sci Ctr Dallas, 74-75, Tex Heart Asn fel, 75, prin investr cardiovasc adjust behav stress, 76-79, sympathetic stimulation & cardiovasc dynamics, 77-78, central nervous syst control hypertension, 79-81; atty, Schramm & Pines, 86- *Mem:* Soc Neurosci; Soc Psychophysiol Res; AAAS; Am Psychol Asn. *Res:* Neural control of cardiovascular function; effect of environmental stress on cardiovascular function. *Mailing Add:* 19471 Babler Forest Rd Wildwood MO 63005

GALPER, JONAS BERNARD, BIOCHEMISTRY, CELL BIOLOGY. *Current Pos:* ASST PROF CARDIOL, BRIGAM & WOMEN'S HOSP, HARVARD MED SCH, 82- *Educ:* Albert Einstein Col Med, PhD(biochem), 70, MD, 71. *Mailing Add:* Dept Med Cardiovasc Div Harvard Med Sch Brigham & Womens Hosp 75 Francis St Boston MA 02115. *Fax:* 617-732-5132

GALPERIN, BORIS, PHYSICS, OCEANOGRAPHY. *Current Pos:* ASSOC PROF PHYS & OCEANOG, UNIV SFLA, 89- *Personal Data:* b Kiev, Ukraine, Nov 25, 52; US citizen; div; c michael & Daphne. *Educ:* Latvian State Univ, Riga, BA & MA, 75; Technion-Israel Inst Technol, PhD(civil eng), 82. *Prof Exp:* Vis res staff mem, Princeton Univ, 83-84, res staff mem, 84-89. *Concurrent Pos:* Consult, Hydro Qual, Inc, 87-; Cambridge Hydrodynamics, Inc, 94- *Mem:* Am Phys Soc; Am Geophys Union; Am Meteorol Soc. *Res:* Computational fluid dynamics, physical oceanography and turbulence theory, in attempt to understand and quantify and predict the effect of human activities on global and local climate and the effect of climate on human activities. *Mailing Add:* Dept Marine Sci Univ SFla 140 Seventh Ave S St Petersburg FL 33704. *Fax:* 813-893-9189; *E-Mail:* boris@marine.usf.edu

GALPERIN, IRVING, PHYSICAL CHEMISTRY, MATERIALS SCIENCE. *Current Pos:* SR STAFF ENGR, MAXWELL LABS, INC, 78- *Personal Data:* b Buffalo, NY, Dec 3, 26; m 58. *Educ:* Alfred Univ, AB, 48; Canisius Col, MS, 52; Western Res Univ, PhD(phys chem), 57. *Prof Exp:* Chemist, Continental Can Corp, Ill, 58-60, Visking Div, Union Carbide Corp, 60-62, Plastics Div, NJ, 62-64; sr chemist, Interchem Corp, Clifton, 64-67; mem tech staff, Bell Tel Labs, 67-69; group mgr, Gen Cable Corp, 69-74; mat mgr, Hatfield Div, CCS Industs, NJ, 74-76; mat eng mgr, Cable Hydro Div, ITT, Calif, 76-78. *Mem:* Am Chem Soc; Sigma Xi; Instrument Soc Am; Am Inst Chemists; Soc Advan Mat Process Eng. *Res:* Electrochemistry; structure and properties of polymers; materials engineering. *Mailing Add:* 3942 Country Trails Rd Bonita CA 91902-3024

GALSKY, ALAN GARY, PLANT PHYSIOLOGY, MICROBIOLOGY. *Current Pos:* Assoc prof, 69-76, PROF BIOL, BRADLEY UNIV, 76- *Personal Data:* b Chicago, Ill, Mar 6, 42; m 66. *Educ:* Roosevelt Univ, BS, 64; Northwestern Univ, MS, 67, PhD(biol), 69. *Mem:* Am Soc Plant Physiologists; Sigma Xi. *Res:* Role of 3', 5'-cyclic adenosine monophosphate in plants; mechanism of gibberellic acid action; production of plant hormones by phytopathogenic bacteria; biochemical aspects of crown-gall tumor formation. *Mailing Add:* Dept Biol Bradley Univ Peoria IL 61625-0001

GALSTAUN, LIONEL SAMUEL, CHEMICAL ENGINEERING, PHYSICAL CHEMISTRY. *Current Pos:* CONSULT, 83- *Personal Data:* b Kediri, Java, Dec 17, 13; US citizen; wid. *Educ:* Univ Dayton, BS, 33; Mass Inst Technol, SM, 34, PhD(phys chem), 36. *Prof Exp:* Res chemist petrol, Tidewater Oil Co, 36-41, sr res engr refining, 41-45, supvr res, 46-58; sr investr chem, US Strategic Bombing Surv, 45-46; prin engr, Bechtel Corp, 58-62, mgr appl technol chem eng, 62-66, mgr process serv, Bechtel Assocs Prof Corp, 66-76, mgr process design, Bechtel Group Inc, 76-78, sr prin engr, 78-83. *Mem:* Fel Am Inst Chem Engrs; Am Chem Soc; NY Acad Sci; Sigma Xi. *Res:* Fundamental properties of lubricants; processes for manufacture of high octane aviation gasoline components; optimization of refinery operations; desalting of sea water; conversion of coal to fluid fuels; design of prototype process plants from pilot data. *Mailing Add:* 3530 Henry Hudson Pkwy E Bronx NY 10463

GALSTER, RICHARD W, ENGINEERING GEOLOGY. *Current Pos:* CONSULT ENG GEOLOGIST, 85- *Personal Data:* b Seattle, Wash, May 13, 30; m 51; c 2. *Educ:* Univ Wash, Seattle, BS, 52, MS, 56. *Honors & Awards:* Holdredge Award, Asn Eng Geol, 92; Burwell Award, Geol Soc Am, 93. *Prof Exp:* Geologist, Grant Co Pub Utility Dist, Wash, 54-55; geologist, US Engrs, Seattle, 55-85, chief, Geol Sect, 73-85. *Concurrent Pos:* Chmn, Eng Geol Div, Geol Soc Am, 77-78; mem, design rev team to People's Repub China, 80; mem, US Comn Large Dams; mem, US Comt Rock Mechs, Nat Res Coun, 86-89. *Mem:* Asn Eng Geol (secy, 80-81, vpres, 81-82, pres, 82-83); fel Geol Soc Am; Int Asn Eng Geol; Am Inst Prof Geologists. *Res:* Engineering geology; hydrogeology; rock mechanics; geotechnical foundation analysis; seismotectonics; rock excavation design. *Mailing Add:* 546 Adler St Edmonds WA 98020-0908

GALSTER, WILLIAM ALLEN, NEUROMUSCULAR PHYSIOLOGY. *Current Pos:* DIR ELECTROMYOGRAPHY LAB, VET ADMIN MED CTR, SALT LAKE CITY, 88- *Personal Data:* b Kenosha, Wis, Apr 11, 32; m 55, Rita Lorenz; c Richard, Christine, David, Marjorie & Patrick. *Educ:* Univ Wis, Madison, BS, 58, MS, 61. *Prof Exp:* Chemist, Wis State Lab Hyg, 56-57; asst prof biol, St Benedict's Col, 61-64; asst prof comp physiol & coordr anal serv, Univ Alaska, 64-73, assoc zoochemist, Inst Arctic Biol, 73-76; biomed dir, Flammability Res Ctr, Med Col, Univ Utah, 76-80, group leader, molec biol & biochem, Utah Biomed Test Lab, 80-82, res prof, clin chem, Med Technol Dept, 82-84, res coord, Dept Neurol, Med Col, Univ Utah, 84-88. *Concurrent Pos:* Comt combustion toxicol, Am Acad Sci, 79-80. *Mem:* AAAS; Am Soc Mammal; Am Zool Soc; Am Inst Chem; Int Soc Mammalian Hibernation. *Res:* Bioenergetics of natural populations of mammals; gluconeogenesis and lipolysis during cold stress; hibernation periodicity and energetics; acclimatization to high altitude; natural resistance to toxic substances; inhalation toxicology; carcinogenesis; immunosuppression; autoimunogenic neuromuscular disease. *Mailing Add:* 4192 Holloway Dr Salt Lake City UT 84124

GALSTON, ARTHUR WILLIAM, PLANT PHYSIOLOGY. *Current Pos:* prof plant physiol, Yale Univ, 55-65, chmn, Dept Bot, 61-62, dir, Div Biol Sci, 65-66, chmn, Dept Biol, 85-88, prof biol, 65-90, Eaton prof bot, 74-90, EMER PROF BIOL, FORESTRY & ENVIRON SCI, YALE UNIV, 90- *Personal Data:* b New York, NY, Apr 21, 20; m 41; c William A & Beth D. *Educ:* Cornell Univ, BS, 40; Univ Ill, MS, 42, PhD(bot). 43. *Hon Degrees:* LLD, Iona Col, New Rochelle, NY, 80 & Hebrew Univ, Jerusalem, 92. *Honors & Awards:* Merit Award, Bot Soc Am; Medal, NY Acad Sci. *Prof*

Exp: Res fel biol, Calif Inst Technol, 43-44, sr res fel, 47-50, assoc prof biol, 51-55. *Concurrent Pos:* Guggenheim fel, Med Nobel Inst, Stockholm, 50-51; consult, Cent Res Dept, E I du Pont de Nemours & Co, Inc, 55-77; chmn, Comt on Meetings, AAAS, 58-60; mem, metab biol panel, NSF, 59-60; Fulbright fel, Australia, 60-61; mem, Nat Res Coun, 64-76 & 84-87; NSF sr fac fel, Univ London, 68; Einstein fel, Hebrew Univ, Jerusalem, 80, fel, Wolfson Col, Cambridge, 83; Riken scientist, Japan, 88. *Mem:* Am Soc Plant Physiologists (secy, 55-57, vpres, 57-58, pres, 62-63); Bot Soc Am (pres, 67-68); Am Soc Biol Chem Molecular Biol; Fedn Am Scientists; fel AAAS; Am Acad Arts & Sci. *Res:* Plant growth hormones; photobiology; polyamines; differentiation and morphogenesis; circadian rhythms as related to photoperiodism. *Mailing Add:* Dept Biol Yale Univ PO Box 208103 New Haven CT 06520-8103. *E-Mail:* agalston@minerva.cis.yale.edu

GALSWORTHY, SARA B, IMMUNOLOGY, BACTERIOLOGY. *Current Pos:* Asst prof, 74-81, ASSOC PROF MICROBIOL, UNIV WESTERN ONT, 81- *Personal Data:* b Frankfort, Ind, July 1, 38; Can citizen; m 63, Peter; c Alice. *Educ:* Pomona Col, BA, 60; Univ Wis, PhD(physiol chem), 65. *Mem:* Can Soc Microbiologists; Am Soc Microbiol; Can Soc Immunologists. *Res:* Listeria monocytogens infections; mechanisms of virulence; regulation of monocytopoiesis. *Mailing Add:* Dept Microbiol & Immunol Univ Western Ont London ON N6A 5C1 Can

GALT, CHARLES PARKER, JR, INVERTEBRATE ZOOLOGY, MARINE BIOLOGY. *Current Pos:* asst prof, 73-78, ASSOC PROF BIOL, CALIF STATE UNIV, 78- *Personal Data:* b Defiance, Ohio, Dec 27, 42. *Educ:* Univ Calif, Santa Barbara, BA, 65; Univ Wash, MS, 70, PhD(zool), 72. *Prof Exp:* Asst prof biol, Fla State Univ, 72-73. *Mem:* AAAS; Am Soc Limnol & Oceanog; Am Soc Zoologists; Marine Biol Asn UK; Sigma Xi. *Res:* Ecology; functional morphology; bioluminescence of pelagic tunicates of class larvacea; natural history and feeding biology of zooplankton. *Mailing Add:* Dept Biol Calif State Univ Long Beach 3702 Csulb Long Beach CA 90840-0004

GALT, JOHN (ALEXANDER), RADIO ASTRONOMY. *Current Pos:* res scientist, 59-90, ENEST SCIENTIST, DOM RADIO ASTROPHYS OBSERV, 90- *Personal Data:* b Toronto, Ont, Mar 8, 25; m 55, Rena M Smith; c Sheila J & David R. *Educ:* Univ Toronto, BA, 49, MA, 52, PhD(physics), 56. *Prof Exp:* Geophysicist, Govt Can, 49-50; res physicist, Du Pont of Can, 56-57; researcher, Jodrell Bank, Univ Manchester, 57-59. *Concurrent Pos:* Guest prof, Chalmers Tech Univ, Gothenburg, Sweden, 72-73. *Mem:* AAAS; Am Astron Soc; Can Astron Soc; Can Asn Physicists; Royal Astron Soc; Royal Astron Soc Can. *Res:* Physics; spectroscopy; high pressures; electronics; optics; radio astronomy; twenty-one centimeter research; long baseline interferometry, pulsars; radio telescope arrays; OH/IR stars, computers. *Mailing Add:* Dom Radio Astrophys Observ Box 248 Penticton BC V2A 6K3 Can

GALT, JOHN KIRTLAND, SOLID STATE SCIENCE. *Current Pos:* RETIRED. *Personal Data:* b Portland, Ore, Sept 1, 20; m 49; c 1. *Educ:* Reed Col, AB, 41; Mass Inst Technol, PhD(physics), 47. *Prof Exp:* Res assoc, Mass Inst Technol, 45-47; Nat Res Coun fel, Bristol, Eng, 47-48; mem tech staff, Bell Tel Labs, NJ, 48-61, dir solid state electronics res, 61-74; dir solid state sci res, Sandia Labs, 74-78, vpres, 78-85; prin scientist, Aero Space Corp, 85-90; consult, 90-97. *Concurrent Pos:* Mem, Nat Acad Comt Adv to Air Force Syst Command, 71-77, mem, Air Force Sci Adv Bd, 75-91. *Mem:* Nat Acad Eng; fel Inst Elec & Electronics Engrs; fel AAAS; fel Am Phys Soc. *Res:* Mechanical and magnetic properties of solids; band structure of metals; lasers, nonlinear optics, luminescence and optical properties of solids. *Mailing Add:* 10501 Lagrima De Oro NE 820 Albuquerque NM 87111

GALTON, PETER MALCOLM, VERTEBRATE ANATOMY, PALEONTOLOGY. *Current Pos:* from asst prof to prof biol, 70-92, PROF BASIC SCI, COL CHIROPRACTIC, UNIV BRIDGEPORT, 92- *Personal Data:* b London, Eng, Mar 14, 42, UK; US citizen; m 93, Carol A Yoon. *Educ:* Univ London, BSc, 64, PhD(zool), 67, DSc, 82. *Prof Exp:* Cur assoc vert paleont, Peabody Mus & mem res staff geol, Yale Univ, 67-70. *Concurrent Pos:* Cur affil vert paleont, Peabody Mus, Yale Univ, 85- *Mem:* Palaeont Soc WGer; Sigma Xi; Soc Vert Paleont. *Res:* Problems of interpreting dinosaurs as living animals; osteology, functional anatomy, systematics, classification, origins, evolution and interrelationships of different dinosaurs; Mesozoic zoogeography and continental drift. *Mailing Add:* Col Chiropractic Univ Bridgeport Bridgeport CT 06601

GALTON, VALERIE ANNE, ENDOCRINOLOGY. *Current Pos:* from instr to assoc prof, 61-75, PROF PHYSIOL, DARTMOUTH MED SCH, 75- *Personal Data:* b Louth, Eng, May 6, 34; m 77; c 2. *Educ:* Univ London, BSc, 55, PhD(physiol), 58. *Prof Exp:* Res assoc endocrinol, Nat Inst Med Res, London, 55-58 & Thorndike Mem Lab, Harvard Med Sch, 59-61. *Concurrent Pos:* Milton res fel med, Harvard Med Sch, 59-60; Life Ins med res fel, 61-63; USPHS res grants, 62-, res career develop award, 65-70. *Mem:* Endocrine Soc; Am Thyroid Asn. *Res:* Mode of action of the thyroid hormones, nature of their peripheral metabolism and relation between hormonal action and metabolism. *Mailing Add:* Dept Physiol Dartmouth Med Sch 1 Medical Ctr Dr Lebanon NH 03756-0001

GALUSHA, JOSEPH G, JR, ANIMAL BEHAVIOR, ETHOLOGY. *Current Pos:* assoc prof, 75-81, PROF BIOL, WALLA WALLA COL, 81- *Personal Data:* b Battle Creek, Mich, Feb 1, 45; m 68, Marilyn Stream; c 2. *Educ:* Walla Walla Col, BA, 68; Andrews Univ, MA, 72; Oxford Univ, DPhil(ethology), 75. *Prof Exp:* Instr biol, Maplewood Acad, 68-71; res asst, Oxford Univ, 72-75. *Concurrent Pos:* Prof biol, Loma Linda Univ, 88-92. *Mem:* Asn Study Animal Behav; Brit Ornithologists Union; Am Ornithologists Union; Animal Behav Soc; Pac Seabird Group; Int Soc Human Ethol. *Res:* Factors relating to density-dependent behavior of social animals; sociobiology of group structure; theoretical aspects of adoption. *Mailing Add:* Dept Biol Sci Walla Walla Col College Place WA 99324-1198. *E-Mail:* galujo@wwc.edu

GALVIN, AARON A, ELECTRONICS ENGINEERING. *Current Pos:* RETIRED. *Personal Data:* b Brooklyn, NY, Apr 13, 32; m 56; c 3. *Educ:* Mass Inst Technol, BS & MS, 55. *Prof Exp:* Engr, Lincoln Lab, Mass Inst Technol, 55-59, group leader, 59-68; vpres advan develop, Aerospace Res, Inc, 68-78; dir, ADT New Eng Res Lab, 78-94, vpres, 82-87; consult, 88-97. *Mem:* Fel Inst Elec & Electronics Engrs. *Res:* Radar; advanced radar system development, particularly optimal signal processing; radar and ultrasonic intrusion alarms; microprocessor security and energy management; mammography. *Mailing Add:* 5610 Kiowa Circle Boynton Beach FL 33437

GALVIN, CYRIL JEROME, JR, COASTAL ENGINEERING, COASTAL PROCESSES. *Current Pos:* COASTAL ENG CONSULT, 78- *Personal Data:* b Jersey City, NJ, June 16, 35. *Educ:* St Louis Univ, BS, 57; Mass Inst Technol, SM, 59, PhD(geol), 63. *Honors & Awards:* Huber Res Prize, Am Soc Civil Eng, 69, Norman Medal, 70. *Prof Exp:* Res asst, Hydrodyn Lab, Mass Inst Technol, 59-63; phys oceanogr, US Army Coastal Eng Res Ctr, 63-70, chief, Coastal Processes Br, 70-78. *Concurrent Pos:* US Geol Surv, 57, 58; res resident, Math Res Ctr, Univ Wis, 65-66; vis assoc prof geol sci, Northwestern Univ, 72. *Mem:* Am Shore & Beach Preserv Asn; Am Geophys Union; Am Soc Civil Engrs; Int Asn Hydraul Res; Soc Sedimentary Geol; Soc Hist Technol. *Res:* Longshore currents, navigation channels, coastal structures, sea level change; wave climate, sediment transport on beaches; tidal inlets and barrier islands; Iridium anomaly at K/T boundary; history of 19th century science. *Mailing Add:* PO Box 623 Springfield VA 22150

GALVIN, FRED, MATHEMATICS, COMBINATORICS. *Current Pos:* assoc prof, 75-78, PROF MATH, UNIV KANS, 78- *Personal Data:* b St Paul, Minn, Nov 10, 36; m 73, Gabriella Bogats; c David & Jane. *Educ:* Univ Minn, BA, 58, MA, 61, PhD(math), 67. *Prof Exp:* Actg instr math, Univ Calif, Berkeley, 65-67, lectr, 67-68; asst prof, Los Angeles, 68-75. *Mem:* Math Asn Am. *Res:* Elementary and recreational mathematics, combinatorics and classical set theory. *Mailing Add:* Dept Math Univ Kans 405 Snow Hall Lawrence KS 66045-2142

GALVIN, ROBERT W, MANAGEMENT. *Current Pos:* Mem staff, 40-50, sr officer, 59-90, CHMN, EXEC COMT, MOTOROLA INC, 90- *Personal Data:* b Marshfield, Wis, Oct, 1922. *Honors & Awards:* Nat Medal of Technol, 91. *Mailing Add:* Motorola Inc 1303 E Algonquin Rd Schaumburg IL 60196-1065

GALVIN, THOMAS JOHN, INFORMATION SCIENCE. *Current Pos:* PROF INFO SCI & POLICY & DIR, INFO SCI DOCTORAL PROG, SYRACUSE UNIV NY, ALBANY, 89- *Personal Data:* b Arlington, Mass, Dec 30, 32; m 56, Marie C Schumb; c Siobhan Marie. *Educ:* Columbia Univ, AB, 54; Simmons Col Boston, SM, 56; Case Western Res Univ, PhD, 73. *Honors & Awards:* Isadore Gilbert Mudge Award, Am Libr Asn, 72; Ida & George Eliot Prize, Med Libr Asn, 88. *Prof Exp:* Dir, Abbot Pub Libr, 56-59; asst dir, Simmons Col Libr, 59-62; assoc dir & prof, Sch Libr Sci, 62-74; dean & prof, Sch Libr & Info Sci, Univ Pittsburgh, 74-85; exec dir, Am Libr Asn Chicago, 85-89. *Concurrent Pos:* Grad fel, Case Western Res Univ, 65-66; external examr, Univ Ibadan, Nigeria, 76-78; trustee, Thayer Pub Libr Braintree Mass, 73-74. *Mem:* Asn Libr & Info Sci Educ; Am Soc Info Sci; Am Libr Asn (pres, 79-80). *Res:* Author several books and numerous articles. *Mailing Add:* Rockefeller Col Syracuse Univ NY Draper 118 135 Western Ave Albany NY 12222

GALYEAN, MICHAEL LEE, RUMINANT NUTRITION. *Current Pos:* asst prof, 77-80, ASSOC PROF NUTRIT, NMEX STATE UNIV, 80-, PROF, ANIMAL NUTRIT, 86- *Personal Data:* b Bentonville, Ark, Sept 2, 51; m 73; c 3. *Educ:* NMex State Univ, BS, 73; Okla State Univ, MS, 75, PhD(animal nutrit), 77. *Mem:* Am Soc Animal Sci; Am Dairy Sci Asn; Am Inst Nutrit. *Res:* Manipulation of rumen fermentation; metabolic profile of stressed ruminants; nonprotein nitrogen utilization; grain processing for livestock; rate of passage of nutrients through the gastrointestinal tract of ruminants. *Mailing Add:* WTex A&M Univ Box 998 Canyon TX 79016-0001. *Fax:* 806-656-2733

GAMBAL, DAVID, NEUROSCIENCE, NUTRITION. *Current Pos:* assoc prof, 65-68, chmn dept, 76-79, PROF BIOCHEM, SCH MED, CREIGHTON UNIV, 68- *Personal Data:* b Old Forge, Pa, Dec 16, 31; m 60, F Anne Warfield; c Mark, Scott & Todd. *Educ:* Pa State Univ, BS, 53; Purdue Univ, MS, 56, PhD(biochem), 57. *Prof Exp:* Asst, Purdue Univ, 53-57; fel, McCollum-Pratt Inst, Johns Hopkins Univ, 57-59; from asst prof to assoc prof biochem, Vet Med Res Inst, Iowa State Univ, 59-65. *Concurrent Pos:* Grantee, NIH, 60-80, vis res scientist, 87-88. *Mem:* AAAS; Am Chem Soc; Soc Exp Biol & Med; Am Soc Biochem & Molecular Biol; Sigma Xi. *Res:* Isolation and characterization of proteins; hormonal control of cellular metabolism; arachidonic metabolism in brain; vitamin D and bone calcification. *Mailing Add:* Dept Biomed Sci Sch Med Creighton Univ 2500 California St Omaha NE 68178. *Fax:* 402-280-2690; *E-Mail:* dgambal@creighton.edu

GAMBERT, STEVEN ROSS, GERONTOLOGY, ENDOCRINOLOGY. *Current Pos:* PROF MED, NEW YORK MED COL, 83-, CHMN, DEPT MED, 94- *Personal Data:* b New York, NY, Aug 22, 49; m 72; c 2. *Educ:* Univ Col, NY Univ, BA, 71; Columbia Univ Col Physicians & Surgeons, MD, 75. *Honors & Awards:* Geriat Med Acad Award, Nat Inst Aging. *Prof Exp:* Resident med, Dartmouth Med Sch, 75-77; Fel endocrinol, Harvard Med Sch, 77-79; asst prof med, Med Col Wis, 79-81, assoc prof med & physiol, 81-83. *Concurrent Pos:* Consult, Res Planning Panel, Nat Inst Aging, 81 & Wis Dept Health & Social Serv, 81-; co-chmn res comt, Milwaukee Admin on Aging, Long Term Care Geront Ctr, 81-; chief med serv, Ruth Taylor Geriat Inst; dir geriat, Westchester County Med Ctr. *Mem:* Fel Geront Soc Am; fel Am Geriat Soc; fel Am Col Physicians; Endocrine Soc; fel Am Aging Asn (pres, 84). *Res:* Endocrine aspects of aging, primarily involving thyroid hormone economy; neuroendocrine changes; health care delivery. *Mailing Add:* Dept Med NY Med Col Valhalla NY 10595

GAMBESCIA, JOSEPH MARION, internal medicine, gastroenterology; deceased, see previous edition for last biography

GAMBILL, JOHN DOUGLAS, PSYCHOPHARMACOLOGY, PSYCHIATRY. *Current Pos:* res fel, 72-74, PSYCHIAT RESEARCHER, SCH MED, BOSTON UNIV, 75-, ASST PROF PSYCHIAT, 76- *Personal Data:* b Rochester, Minn. *Educ:* Northwestern Univ, BA, 63; Univ Minn, MD, 68. *Prof Exp:* Intern gen med, USPHS Hosp, San Francisco, 68-69; resident psychiat, Mass Gen Hosp, Harvard Univ, 69-72. *Concurrent Pos:* Mem US-USSR health exchange psychiat, Inst Psychiat, Moscow, 74; consult, Boston City Hosp Alcoholism Clin, 75-; lectr psychobiol, Sch Med, Boston Univ, 76-, GRS grant, 77-; staff psychiatrist, Bedford Va Hosp, 78- *Res:* Biological basis of mental illness. *Mailing Add:* 29 Stults Rd Belmont MA 02178

GAMBILL, ROBERT ARNOLD, MATHEMATICS. *Current Pos:* assoc prof math, 60-66, PROF MATH & ASST HEAD DEPT, 66- *Personal Data:* b Indianapolis, Ind, Feb 20, 27; m 50; c 2. *Educ:* Butler Univ, AB, 50; Purdue Univ, MS, 52, PhD(math), 54. *Prof Exp:* Head theoret anal br, Math Div, US Naval Avionics Facil, 54-58; sr mathematician, Gen Motors Corp, 58-60. *Mem:* Am Math Soc; Math Asn Am; Soc Indust & Appl Math. *Res:* Ordinary and functional differential equations; calculus of variations; optimal control. *Mailing Add:* Div Math Purdue Univ West Lafayette IN 47907

GAMBINO, RICHARD JOSEPH, MAGNETIC RECORDING, MAGNETO-OPTICS. *Current Pos:* PRIN RES SCIENTIST, ADJ PROF & LAB DIR MAGHETO OPTICAL MAT, STATE UNIV NY, STONY BROOK, 93- *Personal Data:* b New York, NY, May 17, 35; m 55; c 4. *Educ:* Univ Conn, BA, 57; Polytech Inst NY, MS, 76. *Honors & Awards:* Morris N Llebmann Mem Award, Inst Elec & Electronics Engrs, 92; Nat Medal of Technol, 95. *Prof Exp:* Phys scientist, US Army Signal Res Lab, Ft Monmouth, 56-60; Metallurgist, Pratt & Whitney Aircraft Div, United Aircraft Corp, 60-61; res staff mem, T J Watson Res Ctr, IBM, Yorktown Heights, 61-93. *Concurrent Pos:* Mem, Thin Film Div Bd, Am Vacuum Soc, 86-88. *Mem:* Am Vacuum Soc; Mat Res Soc; fel Inst Elec & Electronics Engrs; Inst Elec & Electronics Engrs Magnetic Soc; Sigma Xi. *Res:* Magnetic and superconducting properties of thin films of crystalline and amorphous metallic materials; magneto-optical and magneto-transport properties. *Mailing Add:* Dept Mat Sci & Eng State Univ NY 148 Sycamore Circle Stony Brook NY 11790

GAMBINO, S(ALVATORE) RAYMOND, CLINICAL PATHOLOGY, CLINICAL CHEMISTRY. *Current Pos:* asst prof, 61-69, dir clin chem labs, 69-77, PROF PATH, COL PHYSICIANS & SURGEONS, COLUMBIA UNIV, 69- *Personal Data:* b Brooklyn, NY, Oct 13, 26; m 53, Madeline Russo; c Catherine & Stephen. *Educ:* Antioch Col, BS, 48; Univ Rochester, MD, 52. *Honors & Awards:* Ward Burdick Award, Am Soc Clin Path, 90. *Prof Exp:* Assoc pathologist, St Luke's Hosp, Milwaukee, Wis, 57-61. *Concurrent Pos:* Asst prof, Marquette Univ, 59-61; dir labs, Englewood Hosp, NJ, 61-69; attend pathologist, Presbyterian Hosp, NY, 69-77; chief pathologist & dir labs, St Luke's-Roosevelt Hosp Ctr, 78-82; founder & ed educ med letter, Lab Report for Physicians, 79- *Mem:* AAAS; Am Soc Clin Path; NY Acad Med; Am Asn Clin Chemists; Col Am Path. *Res:* Measurement and interpretation of blood pH, blood gases, serum bilirubin, and iron metabolism; diagnostic laboratory methodology. *Mailing Add:* Exec Vpres Quest Diag, Inc Teterboro NJ 07608. *Fax:* 201-393-5903; *E-Mail:* doclab@aol.com

GAMBLE, DEAN FRANKLIN, ORGANIC CHEMISTRY, INFORMATION SCIENCE. *Current Pos:* RETIRED. *Personal Data:* b McDonald, Pa, Aug 6, 20; m 46, Mary Wolff; c Thomas D, Susan J & Elizabeth F. *Educ:* Pa State Univ, BS, 42, PhD(chem), 53. *Prof Exp:* Chem librn, NIH, 53-56, head, Sect Doc, Records & Pubs, Cancer Chemother, Nat Serv Ctr, Nat Cancer Inst, 56-60; dir, Dept Sci Info, Miles Labs Inc, Ind, 60-66, actg dir, Info Dept, 66-71; head, Food & Nutrit Info & Educ Mat Ctr, 71-72, dep dir libr serv, 72-76; mem dir's staff, Nat Agr Libr, 76-81. *Mem:* Am Chem Soc. *Res:* Chemical documentation; information processing, storage and retrieval. *Mailing Add:* 481 Almond St Luray VA 22835

GAMBLE, FRANCIS TREVOR, OPTICAL PATTERN RECOGNITION, LASER HOLOGRAPHY. *Current Pos:* from asst prof to assoc prof, Denison Univ, 63-70, chmn dept, 69-70 & 83-89, dean students, 70-79, PROF PHYSICS, DENISON UNIV, 70- *Personal Data:* b Montpelier, Vt, July 10, 28; m 51; c 3. *Educ:* Colgate Univ, AB, 58; Univ Conn, MA, 60, PhD(physics), 63. *Prof Exp:* Res asst physics, Univ Conn, 62-63. *Concurrent Pos:* Consult, Battelle Mem Inst, 64-70 & 80-; consult-evaluator, Comn Insts Higher Educ, N Central Asn, 74-; vis prof chem, Ohio State Univ, 84 & 85. *Mem:* Am Asn Physics Teachers; Am Phys Soc; NY Acad Sci; Optical Soc Am; Sigma Xi; Int Soc Opt Eng. *Res:* Laser holography; optical information processing and pattern recognition; optical system design. *Mailing Add:* Physics & Astron Dept Denison Univ PO Box M Granville OH 43023-0613

GAMBLE, FRED RIDLEY, JR, SOLID STATE SCIENCE. *Current Pos:* OWNER, CHANNEL CROSSINGS, 88- *Personal Data:* b Dallas, Tex, Apr 24, 41; m 64; c 2. *Educ:* Harvard Univ, BA, 64; Stanford Univ, PhD(chem physics), 68. *Prof Exp:* Sr chemist, Syva Corp, 68-71; group leader chem physics, Exxon Res & Eng Co, 71-75, dir, Phys & Mat Sci Lab, 75-81, mgr, mat technol div, 81-83, vpres & dir res, Schlumberger, 83-87; vpres & chief tech officer, Superconductor Technologies, Inc, 87-88. *Mem:* Am Chem Soc; fel Am Phys Soc. *Res:* New superconducting materials; intercalation compounds; interactions between metals and molecules. *Mailing Add:* 125 Harbor Way Suite 21 Santa Barbara CA 93109

GAMBLE, JAMES LAWDER, JR, PHYSIOLOGY, BIOCHEMISTRY. *Current Pos:* RETIRED. *Personal Data:* b Boston, Mass, Jan 8, 21; m 48; c 6. *Educ:* Harvard Univ, BS, 43, MD, 45. *Prof Exp:* Intern pediat, Univ Hosp, Johns Hopkins Univ, 45-46, asst resident, Sch Med, 48-50; clin investr physiol, Brookhaven Nat Lab, 50-52; NIH fel pediat & biochem, Sch Med, Johns Hopkins Univ, 53-57, Am Heart Asn estab investr pediat & physiol, 57-62, from asst prof to assoc prof physiol, 62-89. *Mem:* Soc Pediat Res; Am Pediat Soc; Am Physiol Soc. *Res:* Electrolyte and fluid space physiology; mitochondrial electrolytes and ion transport. *Mailing Add:* 3306 Eastern Ave Highland Town Baltimore MD 21224

GAMBLE, MICHAEL IRVING, ELECTRONIC WARFARE, IMPULSE ELECTRONICS. *Current Pos:* VPRES BUS DEVELOP & PLANNING, ARGO SYSTS INC, 96- *Personal Data:* b Everett, Wash, Dec 19, 35; m 57, Charlotte Anne Albrecht; c Michael S & Paula M. *Educ:* Univ Wash, BS, 58. *Prof Exp:* Mgr spec progs, Avco Corp, 62-73; mgr high power laser progs, Boeing Co, 73-80, dir strategic defense progs, 80-91; chief exec officer, Power Spectra Inc, 91-96. *Concurrent Pos:* Consult, Gamble Consult Group Inc, 96- *Mem:* Assoc fel Am Inst Aeronaut & Astronaut. *Res:* Effects of electromagnetic impulses on detectors and circuits. *Mailing Add:* 10566 Creston Dr Los Altos CA 94024-7417

GAMBLE, ROBERT OSCAR, MATHEMATICS, COMPUTER SCIENCE. *Current Pos:* RETIRED. *Personal Data:* b Greensboro, NC, Nov 20, 35; m 63, Kelley M; c 3. *Educ:* Duke Univ, BSME, 59; Clemson Univ, MS, 63, PhD(math), 71; Univ SC, MS, 88. *Prof Exp:* Develop engr, Celanese Fibers Co, SC, 59-62; instr math, Winthrop Col, 63-66, assoc prof, 70-90; asst prof comput sci, Coastal Carolina Univ, 90-94. *Concurrent Pos:* Adj prof, Park Col. *Mem:* Asn Comput Mach; Math Asn Am. *Res:* Investigation of ring-theoretic properties of matrices over finite local rings; public-key cryptosystems. *Mailing Add:* 4 Mariners Ct Port Royal SC 29935

GAMBLE, THOMAS DEAN, PATTERN RECOGNITION, NEURAL NETS. *Current Pos:* SR STAFF SCIENTIST, ENSCO INC, 80- *Personal Data:* b Bellefonte, Pa, Aug 26, 47; m 69; c 3. *Educ:* Univ Mich, BS, 69; Univ Calif, Berkeley, PhD(physics), 78. *Prof Exp:* Physicist magneto tellurics, Earth Sci Div, Lawrence Berkeley Labs, 78-80. *Mem:* Soc Explor Geophysicists. *Res:* Signal analysis; pattern recognition; magnetotellurics; statistics. *Mailing Add:* 5400 Port Royal Rd Springfield VA 22151-2388. *Fax:* 703-321-4529; *E-Mail:* gamble@ensco.com

GAMBLE, WILBERT, BIOCHEMISTRY. *Current Pos:* from asst prof to assoc prof, 68-76, PROF BIOCHEM & BIOPHYS, ORE STATE UNIV, 76- *Personal Data:* b Greenville, Ala, June 19, 32; m 57, Zeferene Tucker; c Priscilla A. *Educ:* Wayne State Univ, BS, 55, PhD, 60. *Honors & Awards:* Lehnard Fink Medal. *Prof Exp:* Asst physiol chem, Wayne State Univ, 55-59, NIH res fel, 59-62. *Concurrent Pos:* Vis assoc prof & NIH spec fel, Johnson Res Found, Univ Pa, 68-69; assoc, Danforth Found, 69; Fulbright fel, Univ Sci & Technol, Ghana, 71-72; vis res worker, Nat Heart, Lung & Blood Inst, 76-77, IPA investr, 83-84 & 90-91. *Mem:* AAAS; Am Chem Soc; Am Soc Biochem & Molecular Biol. *Res:* Enzymes and metabolism of vascular tissue; computer simulation; mechanism of action of polychlorinated biphenyls; atherosclerosis. *Mailing Add:* Dept Biochem & Biophys Ore State Univ Corvallis OR 97331

GAMBLE, WILLIAM LEO, STRUCTURAL ENGINEERING. *Current Pos:* from asst prof to assoc prof, 63-73, PROF CIVIL ENG, UNIV ILL, URBANA, 73- *Personal Data:* b Elkhart, Kans, Nov 25, 36; m 62; c 3. *Educ:* Kans State Univ, BS, 59; Univ Ill, Urbana, MS, 61, PhD(civil eng), 62. *Prof Exp:* Res asst struct, Univ Ill, Urbana, 59-62; Fulbright res fel, div bldg res, Commonwealth Sci & Indust Res Orgn, Australia, 62-63; sr engr, Bechtel Corp, 64-65. *Concurrent Pos:* Vis lectr, Univ Canterbury, Christchurch, NZ, 73-74; consult, distress concrete structures. *Mem:* Am Concrete Inst; Am Soc Civil Engrs; Am Soc Testing & Mat; Prestressed Concrete Inst. *Res:* Strength and behavior of reinforced concrete floor slab systems; long-term behavior of prestressed concrete bridges; prestressed concrete piling. *Mailing Add:* Dept Civil Eng Univ Ill 205 N Mathews Ave Urbana IL 61801-2374

GAMBOA, GEORGE JOHN, BEHAVIORAL ECOLOGY. *Current Pos:* ASSOC PROF BIOL, OAKLAND UNIV, 80- *Personal Data:* b Boise, Idaho, Jan 21, 46; m 67; c 1. *Educ:* Idaho State Univ, BS, 68; Ariz State Univ, MS, 74; Univ Kans, PhD(biol), 79. *Prof Exp:* Asst & res asst zool, Ariz State Univ, 72-74; asst biol, Univ Iowa, 74-75; asst res fel social behav, Univ Kans, 75-78, res fel, 78-79. *Mem:* AAAS; Entom Soc Can; Int Union Study Social Insects. *Res:* Evolution of insect social behavior; behavioral ecology of social hymenoptera. *Mailing Add:* Bio Sci Dept Oakland Univ Rochester MI 48309-4401

GAMBORG, OLUF LIND, TRANSGENIC PLANTS & PLANT BIOTECHNOLOGY, MOLECULAR BIOLOGY & SCIENCE COMMUNICATION. *Current Pos:* VIS PROF & SPECIALIST BIOTECHNOL, UNIV CALIF, 91- *Personal Data:* b Denmark, Nov 9, 24; Can & US citizen; m 53, Gertrude K Christensen; c Brian, Cheryl (Kirchmeyer) & Linda (Barghi). *Educ:* Univ Alta, BSc, 56, MSc, 58; Univ Sask, PhD(plant biochem), 62. *Honors & Awards:* Gold Medal, Can Soc Plant Physiologists, 77. *Prof Exp:* Sr res officer, Plant Biotechnol Inst, Nat Res Coun, Can, 58-79; res dir, Int Plan Res Inst, 79-83; sr sci consult, Genentech Inc, 83-84; sr staff consult, United Energy Corp, 84-85; assoc dir, tissue cult for crops proj, Colo State Univ, 85-91. *Concurrent Pos:* Consult, McCormack & Co Inc, 86-95; Govt Columbia, 88, N Yemen, 89, Plant Sci Inc, 91-, Appl Phytol Inc, 95-; consult, USAID, India, 88 & Winrock Int Indonesia, 89 & 90-91. *Mem:* Can Soc Plant Physiologists (vpres, 75, pres, 76); Int Asn Plant Tissue Cult; Int Soc Plant Molecular Biol; Am Soc Agron; Scand Soc Plant Physiol. *Res:* Plant cell, tissue and organ culture, plant biotechnology, gene transfer, transgenic plants and gene expressing; plant molecular biology; biochemistry, biotic and abiotic stress in plants; plant micropropagation in tropical and temperate species; somatic embryogenesis use in propagation; published comprehensive book for lab training and reference in plant biotechnology. *Mailing Add:* 1404 Solana Dr Belmont CA 94002-3654. *Fax:* 650-592-6688; *E-Mail:* ucdogamborg@batnet.com

GAMBRELL, CARROLL B(LAKE), JR, INDUSTRIAL ENGINEERING, ENGINEERING MANAGEMENT. *Current Pos:* vpres acad affairs, 67-78, PROF, UNIV CENT FLA, 67- *Personal Data:* b Birmingham, Ala, Dec 1, 24; m 44; c 2. *Educ:* Clemson Univ, BS, 49; Univ Fla, MS, 52; Purdue Univ, PhD, 58; Fla Southern Col, BA, 77. *Prof Exp:* Instr, Clemson Univ, 49-51; asst prof indust eng, Lamar Univ, 52-55; from instr to asst prof, Purdue Univ, 55-59. *Concurrent Pos:* Consult to var govt agencies & comts & var pvt industs, 46-; vis prof to var univs in US, 66-79; mem bd dirs, Regional Energy Training & Res Orgn, Inc, Cocoa, Fla, 71-76, Univ Cent Fla Found, Inc, 74-78, Winter Park Mem Hosp, 75- & Embry-Riddle Aeronaut Univ, 75-; distinguished lectr, Am Inst Indust Engrs, 73-; mem, Engrs Coun Prof Develop. *Mem:* Am Soc Eng Educ; fel Am Inst Indust Engrs; Sigma Xi. *Res:* Human engineering; system simulation; operations research; economic analysis. *Mailing Add:* Univ Res Off Mercer Univ 1400 Coleman Ave Macon GA 31207-1000

GAMBRELL, SAMUEL C, JR, ENGINEERING MECHANICS. *Current Pos:* from asst prof to assoc prof, Univ Ala, Tuscaloosa, 65-73, dir, Solid Mech Div, 69-76, asst dean eng & dir, Bur Eng Res, 76-83, dir eng placement, 78-83, PROF ENG MECH, UNIV ALA, TUSCALOOSA, 73- *Personal Data:* b Owings, SC, Sept 15, 35; m 57; c 3. *Educ:* Clemson Univ, BS, 57, MS, 61; WVa Univ, PhD(eng mech), 65. *Prof Exp:* From instr to asst prof eng mech, Clemson Univ, 59-62; instr, WVa Univ, 62-63. *Concurrent Pos:* Consult indust & legal firms. *Mem:* Am Soc Eng Educ; Soc Exp Mech; Nat Soc Prof Engrs; Sigma Xi. *Res:* Experimental stress analysis; photoelasticity; fatigue; experimental mechanics. *Mailing Add:* 71 Coventry Tuscaloosa AL 35404

GAMBS, GERARD CHARLES, UTILIZATION OF FLY ASH IN CONCRETE & CONCRETE PRODUCTS. *Current Pos:* CONSULT ENGR, 83- *Personal Data:* b Columbus, Ohio, May 2, 18; m 71, Eileen Goggin; c 2. *Educ:* Ohio State Univ, BEM, 40. *Prof Exp:* Jr mining engr, Pittsburgh Coal Co, 40-42; maj atomic bomb proj, US Army CEngrs, 42-46; asst prof, Eng Exp Sta, Ohio State Univ, 46-47; asst vpres, Consol Coal Co, 47-69; bus mgr, Gibbs & Hill, Inc, 69-70; vpres, Ford, Bacon & Davis Inc, 70-83. *Concurrent Pos:* Mem bd dirs, Onan Corp, 71-83, Tipperary Corp, 73-86, Ford, Bacon & Davis, Inc, 73-83. *Mem:* Am Inst Mining Metall & Petrol Engrs; Am Soc Mech Engrs; Am Nuclear Soc; Am Coal Asn. *Res:* Energy; utilization of fly ash in concrete and concrete products; granted 2 US patents. *Mailing Add:* 1725 York Ave Apt 33C New York NY 10128

GAMBS, ROGER DUANE, ETHOLOGY, ANIMAL BEHAVIOR. *Current Pos:* PROF BIOL, CALIF POLYTECH STATE UNIV, 74- *Personal Data:* b Bozeman, Mont. *Educ:* Univ Idaho, BS, 63, MS, 65; Univ Mont, PhD(ethology), 73. *Prof Exp:* Instr biol, Wis State Univ, Whitewater, 65-67; prof zool, Ariz Western Col, 71-72. *Mem:* Am Soc Ichthologists & Herpetologists; Animal Behavior Soc; Cooper Ornithological Soc; Am Ornithologists Union; Am Soc Mammalogists; Wildlife Soc. *Res:* Avian mobbing behavior; functional role of vertebrate vocalizations; evolutionary significance of avian social organizations; social behavior in Tule Elk; effects of wildlife on Blue Oak regeneration; small mammal ecology. *Mailing Add:* Dept Biol Sci Calif Polytech State Univ 1 Polyview Dr San Luis Obispo CA 93407-0001

GAME, JOHN CHARLES, GENETICS OF DNA REPAIR, PULSED-FIELD GEL ELECTROPHORESIS. *Current Pos:* fel, 72-73, asst specialist, 78-82, STAFF SCIENTIST, LAWRENCE BERKELEY LAB, UNIV CALIF, BERKELEY, 82- *Personal Data:* b Tonbridge, Eng, Dec 14, 46. *Educ:* Oxford Univ, Eng, DPhil, 71. *Prof Exp:* Postdoctoral fel genetics, Biol Dept, York Univ, Ont, 71-72; res scientist, Nat Inst Med Res, London, 74-78. *Mem:* Genetics Soc Am. *Res:* Processes of genetic recombination, meiosis, and the repair of DNA using the yeast Saccharomyces cerevisiae; botany including plants of California and Polynesia. *Mailing Add:* Donner Lab Lawrence Berkeley Lab Berkeley CA 94720

GAMELIN, THEODORE W, ANALYSIS & FUNCTIONAL ANALYSIS. *Current Pos:* PROF MATH, UNIV CALIF, LOS ANGELES, 68- *Personal Data:* b Decorah, Iowa, Sept 24, 39; m 61; c 4. *Educ:* Yale Univ, BS, 60; Univ Calif, Berkeley, PhD(math), 63. *Prof Exp:* Clemoore instr math, Mass Inst Technol, 63-65, asst prof, 67-68; prof, Nat Univ La Plata, Arg, 65-66. *Concurrent Pos:* Sloan Found fel, 69-71. *Mem:* Am Math Soc. *Res:* Function algebras; algebras of analytic functions. *Mailing Add:* Dept Math Univ Calif Los Angeles CA 90095-1555

GAMELLI, RICHARD L, MEDICINE, SCIENCE EDUCATION. *Current Pos:* PROF SURGERY, STRICH SCH MED, DIR, SHOCK-TRAUMA INST & CHIEF BURN CTR, FOSTER G MCGAW HOSP, LOYOLA UNIV MED CTR, 90- *Personal Data:* b Springfield, Mass, Jan 18, 49; c 3. *Educ:* St Michael's Col, Colchester, Vt, AB, 70; Univ Vt, MD, 74; Am Bd Surgery, dipl. *Honors & Awards:* Dr James E DeMeules 1st Annual Res Award, Dept Surg, Univ Vt, 90. *Prof Exp:* Straight surg intern, Med Ctr Hosp, Vt, 74-75, surg resident PG-II, PG-III, PG-IV, 75-79; form asst prof to prof surg, Univ Vt Col Med, 79-90, dir surg res labs, Dept Surg, 85-90, dir house staff training prog, 85-89, vchmn, Dept Surg, 85-90, chmn sect gen surg, 89. *Concurrent Pos:* Attend surgeon, Med Ctr Hosp Vt, 79-90, dir & founder burn prog, 80-90, dir, Nutrit Support Servs, 80-88, dir, Resident Teaching Conf, 83-90, assoc surgeon-in-chief, 85-89, dir, Burn-Shock-Trauma Serv, 88-90; grantee, NIH, 81-84, 89-93, Ethicon Inc 88-90, Genetech, Inc, 88-89, Amgen Inc, 89-90, Univ Ill, Chicago, 91; Dr John C Hartnett lectr, St Michael's Col, 83; chmn qual assurance comt burn ctr, Loyola Univ Med Ctr, 90-, infection control comt, 90-, res comt coun, 90-, surg res comt, 91-, intensive care unit comt, 91-, EMS bldg comt, 91-, med chmn nutrit comt, 92-, managed care task force, 93-, commitment to teaching task force, 93-; mem, Spec Study Sect, NIH, 91, physicians adv coun, Marianjoy Rehab Hosps & Clins, 93. *Mem:* Fel Am Chem Soc; Am Burn Asn; NAm Burn Asn (pres, 91); Shock Soc; Soc Univ Surgeons; Soc Leukocyte Biol; Surg Infection Soc; John H Davis Soc (secy-treas, 90-92, pres, 93). *Mailing Add:* Surg Loyola Univ Strich Sch Med 2160 S First Ave Maywood IL 60153-3304

GAMLIEL, AMIR, REMEDIATION OF SOILS FROM ORGANIC CONTAMINANTS, SIMULATION OF SUBSURFACE HYDROLOGY. *Current Pos:* SR HYDROGEOLOGIST, ENVIRON CONSULT ENGRS, INC, 92- *Personal Data:* b Petach-Tickva, Israel, Mar 28, 50; m 75, Edna; c Uri, Irrit & Tami. *Educ:* Technion Univ, Haifa, Israel, BS, 77, MS, 80; Kent State Univ, BS, 84; Univ Mich, PhD(civil & environ eng), 89. *Prof Exp:* Hydrologist, Tahal, Israel, 79-81; hydrogeol, Kent State Univ, 81-83; civil engr, Babcox & Wilcox, 84-85; res engr, Gen Motors, 89-92. *Mem:* Am Soc Civil Eng; Am Geophys Union; Nat Ground Water Asn. *Res:* Improvement and optimization of vapor extraction for subsurface remediation from toxic volatile organic compounds; moving grid finite element algorithms for solving the non-linear coupled set of partial differential equations governing multiphase flow porous media; modeling groundwater flow in a steep-sloped nuclear waste site. *Mailing Add:* Teladine Brown Eng 300 Sparkman Dr Huntsville AL 35805. *Fax:* 615-691-0611

GAMMAGE, RICHARD BERTRAM, CHEMICAL HEALTH & SAFETY, HEALTH PHYSICS. *Current Pos:* res scientist oxide surfaces, 67-70, HEALTH PHYSICIST & GROUP LEADER, MONITORING TECHNOL & INSTRUMENTATION & SOLID STATE RADIATION DOSIMETRY, OAK RIDGE NAT LAB, 70- *Personal Data:* b Whitby, Eng, Nov 5, 37; m 64. *Educ:* Univ Exeter, BSc, 60, PhD(chem), 64. *Prof Exp:* NSF fel, Univ Fla, 64-67. *Concurrent Pos:* Res assoc, Imp Col, Univ London, 64; mem, Comt Int Intercomparisons Environ Dosimeters, 76-. *Mem:* Am Chem Soc; The Chem Soc; Am Indust Hyg Asn; Health Physics Soc. *Res:* Monitoring devices and measurements of indoor air pollutants, especially formaldehyde; real or near real-time monitoring devices for fugitive emissions from synthetic fossil fuels; solid state integrating radiation dosimeters; calcareous absorbents; ceramic oxides; lunar fines and their surface properties. *Mailing Add:* 202 Scenic Dr Oak Ridge TN 37830

GAMMAL, ELIAS BICHARA, ANATOMY, OBSTETRICS & GYNECOLOGY. *Current Pos:* fel med res, Collip Lab, 62-66, lectr obstet & gynec, 67, lectr anat, 68-69, asst prof, 69-73, assoc prof, 73-80, PROF ANAT, UNIV WESTERN ONT, 80-, ASST PROF OBSTET & GYNEC, 67- *Personal Data:* b Cairo, Egypt, Nov 18, 30; Can citizen; m 61; c 5. *Educ:* Ain Shams Univ, Cairo, MB, ChB, 55; Univ Western Ont, PhD(med res), 66. *Prof Exp:* Intern, Ain Shams Univ Hosps, Egypt, 56-57; St Joseph's Infirmary, Atlanta, Ga, 57-58, resident obstet & gynec, 58-61; fel gynec cancer, Emory Univ, 61-62. *Concurrent Pos:* Vis prof anat & reproduction biol, Univ Hawaii, 80-81. *Mem:* Am Asn Anatomists; Can Asn Anatomists; Can Invests in Reprod; assoc Soc Obstetricians & Gynecologists Can. *Res:* Placental trophoblast; endothelial differentiation and proliferation. *Mailing Add:* Dept Anat Univ Western Ont Health Sci Ctr London ON N6A 5C1 Can. *Fax:* 519-661-3936

GAMMEL, GEORGE MICHAEL, PARTICLE BEAMS, ACCELERATOR DESIGN. *Current Pos:* SCIENTIST, VARIAN CORP, 95- *Personal Data:* b Los Alamos, NMex, Sept 26, 52; m 78; c 1. *Educ:* Mich State Univ, BS & MS, 74; Cornell Univ, PhD(appl physics), 79. *Prof Exp:* Res asst appl physics, Lab Plasma Studies, Cornell Univ, 75-78; from asst scientist to assoc scientist, Accelerator Dept, Brookhaven Nat Lab, 80-83; staff mem, Princeton Plasma Physics Lab, 83-90; staff scientist, Grumman Corp, 90-95. *Mem:* Am Physics Soc. *Res:* High current electron beam studies; particle beam fusion research; neutral beam development; plasma diagnostics; accelerator technology. *Mailing Add:* 21 Leo Rd Marblehead MA 01945-2001

GAMMEL, JOHN LEDEL, THEORETICAL PHYSICS. *Current Pos:* chmn dept, 74-82, PROF PHYSICS, ST LOUIS UNIV, 74- *Personal Data:* b Austin, Tex, July 9, 24; m 47; c 5. *Educ:* Univ Tex, BS, 44, MA, 46; Cornell Univ, PhD(theoret physics), 50. *Prof Exp:* Tutor physics, Univ Tex, 42-45, instr math, 45-46; asst physics, Cornell Univ, 46-50; mem staff, Los Alamos Sci Lab, 50-63; prof physics, Tex A&M Univ, 63-67; mem staff, Los Alamos Sci Lab, NMex, 67-74. *Concurrent Pos:* Instr, Univ Calif, Los Angeles, 52; Fulbright fel, 57-58; mem staff, Atomic Energy Res Estab, Harwell, Eng, 61-62; vis prof, Univ Western Ontario, Can, 79-80. *Mem:* Fel AAAS. *Res:* Theoretical nuclear physics. *Mailing Add:* 1408 Ruth Ave St Louis MO 63122

GAMMELL, PAUL M, MEDICAL ULTRASOUND, NONDESTRUCTIVE EVALUATION. *Current Pos:* NAVAL SURFACE WARFARE CTR, 83- *Personal Data:* b Attleboro, Mass, Feb 27, 39; div. *Educ:* Univ Md, BS, 63; Am Univ, MS, 66; Catholic Univ Am, PhD(physics), 71. *Prof Exp:* Res assoc, Dept Chem, Purdue Univ, 71-74; Sci Res Coun sr vis fel, Dept Chem, Southampton Univ, 73; dir res, Med Div, Radionics, Ltd, 74-76; mem tech staff, Jet Propulsion Lab, Calif Inst Technol, 76-82. *Concurrent Pos:* Clin asst prof, Dept Radiol, Sch Med, Univ Southern Calif, 77-82. *Mem:* Sigma Xi; Am Soc Nondestructive Testing; Am Soc Testing Mat; Acoust Soc Am; Inst Elec & Electronics Engrs. *Res:* Ultrasonic physics and signal processing, particularly as applied to diagnostic medical ultrasound and to nondestructive evaluation. *Mailing Add:* 1113 Cresthaven Dr Silver Spring MD 20903

GAMMILL, RONALD BRUCE, ORGANIC CHEMISTRY. *Current Pos:* SCIENTIST ORG CHEM, UPJOHN CO, 77- *Personal Data:* b Louisville, Miss, July 10, 48; m 6; c 2. *Educ:* Millsaps Col, BS, 73; Univ SC, PhD(org chem), 76. *Prof Exp:* Am Cancer Soc fel, Univ Pittsburgh, 76-77. *Mem:* Am Chem Soc. *Res:* New synthetic methods; alkylations; synthesis of novel molecules with biological activity. *Mailing Add:* 6704 Pleasant View Dr Kalamazoo MI 49002-1004

GAMMON, JAMES ROBERT, BIOLOGY, ECOLOGY. *Current Pos:* From asst prof to assoc prof, 61-73, PROF ZOOL, DEPAUW UNIV, 73-, CHAIR, 87- *Personal Data:* b Sparta, Wis, Apr 24, 30; m 53, 81; c 4. *Educ:* Wis State Col, Whitewater, BS, 56; Univ Wis, MS, 57, PhD(zool, bot), 61. *Mem:* Am Fisheries Soc; Am Soc Limnol & Oceanog. *Res:* Fish ecology; river ecology; role of external metabolites in aquatic ecology. *Mailing Add:* Dept Biol Sci DePauw Univ 118 Olin Greencastle IN 46135

GAMMON, NATHAN, JR, SOIL CHEMISTRY, PLANT NUTRITION. *Current Pos:* RETIRED. *Personal Data:* b Cheyenne, Wyo, June 22, 14; m 41, 89, Bonnie Godding; c 2. *Educ:* Univ Md, BS, 36, MS, 39; Ohio State Univ, PhD(soils), 41. *Prof Exp:* Asst soils, Univ Md, 36-39; asst agron, Ohio Exp Sta, 38-42; prof, Inst Food & Agr Sci, Univ Fla, 46-80, emer prof soil chem, 80-94 SCI. *Mem:* AAAS; Am Chem Soc; Soil Sci Soc Am; Am Soc Agron; Sigma Xi. *Res:* Ion exchange; plant nutrition; pasture soils and fertility maintenance; flame photometry; micronutrients; pecan and peach production; movement and availability of and factors influencing Cu, Zh, Fe, B, Mo and Mn in soils. *Mailing Add:* 1403 NW 11 Rd Gainesville FL 32605

GAMMON, RICHARD ANTHONY, MICROBIOLOGY. *Current Pos:* from asst prof to assoc prof, 64-77, PROF BIOL & COORDR NURSING PROG, GANNON COL, 77- *Personal Data:* b Lackawanna, NY, May 6, 37; m 63; c 2. *Educ:* St Bonaventure Univ, BS, 59, PhD(biol), 65. *Prof Exp:* Asst biol, St Bonaventure Univ, 60-64. *Concurrent Pos:* Res asst, Am Sterilizer Co, 66-; NIH res grant, 66-68. *Mem:* AAAS; Am Soc Microbiol. *Res:* Bacteriophages for the thermophile, Bacillus coagulans; kinetics of ethylene oxide sterilization. *Mailing Add:* Dept Biol Gannon Univ 109 W Sixth St Erie PA 16501-1049

GAMMON, RICHARD HARRISS, PHYSICAL CHEMISTRY, ASTRONOMY. *Current Pos:* PROF OCEANOG, UNIV WASH, 89- *Personal Data:* b Washington, DC, Apr 6, 43; m 73; c 1. *Educ:* Princeton Univ, BA, 65; Harvard Univ, MA, 66, PhD(phys chem), 70. *Prof Exp:* NSF fel astron, Univ Calif, Berkeley, 70-71; res assoc astron & chem, Nat Radio Astron Observ, 71-73; vis prof astrochem, Radio Astron Ctr, Mackenzie Univ, Sao Paulo, Brazil, 74-76; vis fel radio astron, Battelle Observ, Pac Northwest Labs, 76-78; affil prof astron & chem, Univ Wash, 78; dir sci, Pac Sci Ctr, 78-80; Nat Oceanic & Atmospheric Admin, 80-89. *Mem:* Am Astron Soc; AAAS; Brazilian Astron Soc. *Res:* Molecular spectroscopy; chemistry of interstellar space. *Mailing Add:* 18035 53rd Ave NE Seattle WA 98155

GAMMON, ROBERT WINSTON, PHOTON CORRELATION SPECTROSCOPY, BRILLOUIN SCATTERING. *Current Pos:* asst prof, Inst Molecular Physics, 72-76, assoc prof, 76-92, PROF PHYS, INST PHYS SCI & TECHNOL, UNIV MD, 92- *Personal Data:* b Washington, DC, Sept 1, 40; m 57, Roberta H Bradley; c John & Sharon. *Educ:* Johns Hopkins Univ, AB, 61, Calif Inst Technol, MS, 63, PhD(physics), 67. *Prof Exp:* Mem tech staff, Hughes Res Labs, 62-63; res assoc physics, Johns Hopkins Univ, 66-67; from asst prof to assoc prof, Cath Univ Am, 67-72. *Concurrent Pos:* Consult Naval Res Labs, 72-86, Nat Bur Stand, 74-78, Telecommun Res & Action Ctr, 80-82, IBM Res Lab, Zurich, 78-79; prin investr, zeho (critical fluid light scattering exp) space shuttle, NASA Microgravity Sci & Appl Div, 84-97; co-investr, critical point facil-thermal equilibrium exp, Int Mat Lab Space Shuttle Flight, 89-91. *Mem:* Am Phys Soc; Optical Soc Am. *Res:* Quantum optics, especially laser light scattering spectroscopy; experimental solid state physics, especially elasticity near phase transitions; thermodynamics, especially experimental critical phenomena in fluids generally and with reduced gravity; laser light scattering. *Mailing Add:* Inst Phys Sci & Technol Univ Md College Park MD 20742. *Fax:* 301-314-9404; *E-Mail:* rg2@umail.umd.edu

GAMMON, WALTER RAY, DERMATOLOGY. *Current Pos:* CLIN PROF DERMAT, E CAROLINA UNIV SCH MED, GREENVILLE, NC, 93- *Personal Data:* b Danville, Va, Oct 25, 42; m 66; c 2. *Educ:* NC State Univ, BS, 67; Univ NC, MD, 71; Am Bd Internal Med, cert, 74; Am Bd Dermat, cert, 79, cert dermat immunol & diag & lab immunol, 85. *Prof Exp:* Intern med, Barnes Hosp, St Louis, 71-72, jr asst resident med & dermat, NC Mem Hosp, Chapel Hill, 73-74; from instr to prof dermat & med, Sch Med, Univ NC, Chapel Hill, 76-93. *Concurrent Pos:* Vis prof & lectr, numerous univs, 76-91; NIH res grants, 77-94; mem, Task Force Immunopath, Am Acad Dermat, 85-88, Task Force Manpower, 86-89 & Spec Grants Rev Comt, Nat Inst Arthritis & Musculoskeletal & Skin Dis, 88. *Mem:* Am Acad Dermat; fel Am Col Physicians; Am Dermat Soc Allergy & Immunol; Am Fedn Clin Res; AMA; Am Soc Cell Biol; Am Soc Dermat Allergy & Immunol; Am Venereal Dis Asn; Soc Invest Dermat; Am Dermat Asn. *Res:* Author of more than 150 technical publications. *Mailing Add:* Eastern Dermat 1705 W Sixth St Greenville NC 27834. *Fax:* 919-966-3921

GAMO, HIDEYA, OPTICAL PHYSICS, ELECTRONICS ENGINEERING. *Current Pos:* prof, 68-91, EMER PROF ELEC ENG, UNIV CALIF, IRVINE, 91- *Personal Data:* b Ueda, Japan, Apr 1, 24; m 56, Yasko Ejima; c Yuriko & Kay. *Educ:* Univ Tokyo, BS, 46, DSc(physics), 58. *Prof Exp:* Res assoc & lectr, Univ Tokyo, 48-58; res consult physicist, T J Watson Res Ctr, IBM Corp, 58-59, res physicist, 59-63; vis prof elec eng, Univ Rochester, 63-64, prof, 64-68. *Concurrent Pos:* Mem adv comt, Elec, Comput & Systs Div, NSF, 79-81; overseas ed, Japanese J Appl Physics, 82-; specialist, Chinese Univ Develop Proj, World Bank, 85; vis prof, Japanese Nat Defense Acad, Xian Jiaotong Univ, China, 85 & Tokyo Univ Sci, 89. *Mem:* Sr mem Inst Elec & Electronics Engrs; fel Optical Soc Am; Am Phys Soc; Phys Soc Japan; AAAS; fel Soc Photo-Optical Instrumentation Engrs; Japanese Soc Appl Physics; Inst Electronic Info & Commun Engrs, Japan; Sigma Xi. *Res:* Faraday rotation in a circular wave guide; intensity correlation interferometry; statistical properties of laser radiation; laser propagation through turbulent atmosphere; optical-electronic devices such as infrared isolator and photovoltaic detector; gas laser plasma; optical communication and information processing; passive unidirectional system; matrix theory of partial coherence; unconventional imaging systems; nonlinear optics of organic materials; physical optics of electron waves; ferroelectric thin films and applications to electro-optical memory. *Mailing Add:* Univ Calif 2283 Engr Gateway Westwing/Elec/Comp Eng Irvine CA 92717-0001

GAMOTA, GEORGE, LOW TEMPERATURE PHYSICS. *Current Pos:* PROF PHYSICS & DIR, INST SCI & TECHNOL, UNIV MICH, ANN ARBOR, 81- *Personal Data:* b Lviv, Western Ukraine, May 6, 39; US citizen; m 61; c 3. *Educ:* Univ Minn, BPhysics, 61, MS, 63; Univ Mich, PhD(physics), 66. *Prof Exp:* Res assoc & lectr, Univ Mich, 66-67; mem tech staff, Bell Labs, Murray Hill, NJ, 67-75; res specialist, Off Under Secy Defense, Res & Eng, Dept Defense, 75-77, dir res, 78-81. *Concurrent Pos:* Mem, Adv Coun Res, 73-75; mem, NJ Gov's Comn to Evaluate Capital Needs of NJ, 75; chmn & founder, Sci & Technol Coun for Congressman M Rinaldo, 74-75; exec secy, Defense Sci Bd Study Fundamental Res in Univs, 76; mem, Pres Sci Adv Fed Coord Coun on Sci & Eng Technol, 76-77; exec secy, Defense Shale Oil Task Group, 78; chmn, Defense Comt Res, 78; mem, Panel Pub Affairs, Am Phys Soc, 81-84; sr corp consult, Sci Appln Int Corp, 81-; mem, Nat Res Coun Off Sci & Eng Personnel Adv Panel, 84; mem, NSF Policy Res & Anal/Sci Resource Studies Adv Comt, 85; mem, Adv Subcomt Electronics, Space Systs & Technol Adv Comt, NASA, 79-, Res Designee Adv Comt, 83 & Space Commercialization Comt, 84; bd adv, Nat Coalition Sci & Technol, 81. *Mem:* Fel AAAS; Am Phys Soc; Ukrainian Am Engrs Soc; Sigma Xi; Inst Elec & Electronics Engrs; Am Defense Preparedness Asn; NY Acad Sci. *Res:* Solid state physics; hydrodynamics; liquid crystals; quantum liquids and solids; soliton like waves in helium; charged particle beams. *Mailing Add:* Mitre Corp 202 Burlington Rd Mail Stop M115 Bedford MA 01730

GAMOW, RUSTEM IGOR, BIOENGINEERING, PHYSIOLOGY. *Current Pos:* asst prof bioeng, 68-73, assoc prof aerospace, 73-76, ASSOC PROF CHEM ENG, UNIV COLO, BOULDER, 76- *Personal Data:* b Washington, DC, Nov 4, 35; m 61. *Educ:* Univ Colo, BA, 61, MBS, 63, PhD(microbiol), 67. *Prof Exp:* Teaching asst phys sci, Univ Colo, 61-63; NIH res fel biol, Calif Inst Technol, 67-68. *Concurrent Pos:* Vis prof, Dept Biochem, Univ Fla, 76; NSF res grant, 78-80; Food & Drug Admin res grant, 78-81. *Mem:* Am Soc Microbiol; Am Soc Plant Physiol; Am Inst Chem Engrs; Biomed Eng Soc. *Res:* Bacteriophage, kinetics; conformational changes in proteins; light response of Phycomyces; exercise physiology. *Mailing Add:* 186 Canon Park Boulder CO 80302-9640

GAMSON, BERNARD W(ILLIAM), CHEMICAL ENGINEERING. *Current Pos:* VPRES, HARVEY ALUMINUM CO, TORRANCE, 70- *Personal Data:* b Chicago, Ill, Aug 18, 17; m 52; c 4. *Educ:* Ill Inst Technol, BS, 38; Univ Mich, MS, 39; Univ Wis, PhD(chem eng), 43. *Prof Exp:* Develop engr, Socony Vacuum Oil Co, NJ, 39-41; res engr, War Prod Bd, Wis, 42-43; group leader, Great Lakes Carbon Corp, 43-49, chief process engr, 49-51, dir res & develop, 51-55; mgr nuclear fuel, Gen Elec Co, 55-56; assoc dir, Res Ctr, Borg-Warner Corp, Ill, 56-60, vpres res & eng, oil field prod, Byron Jackson Div, Calif, 60-65; consult chem engr & scientist, 65-70. *Mem:* Am Chem Soc; Am Inst Chem Engrs. *Res:* Petroleum refining; petro- and heavy chemicals; metallurgy of iron, aluminum and light metals; carbon technology; thermodynamics; sulfur recovery; nuclear reactor technology; oil well logging; thermoelectrics. *Mailing Add:* 11124 Hunt Club Dr Potomac MD 20854-2522

GAMZU, ELKAN R, DRUG DEVELOPMENT. *Current Pos:* vpres develop, 89-90, PRES & CHIEF OPER OFFICER, CAMBRIDGE NEUROSCI, 90- *Personal Data:* b Liverpool, Eng, Jan 27, 43; US citizen; m 65; c 2. *Educ:* Hebrew Univ, Jerusalem, Israel, BA, 67; Univ Pa, MA, 68, PhD(psychiat), 71. *Prof Exp:* Sr pharmacologist, Hoffman-LaRoche, Nutley, NJ, 71-77, res group chief, 78-85; assoc dir clin res, Warner-Lambert, Ann Arbor, Mich, 85-87; sr dir clin therapeut, Parke-Davis/Warner-Lambert, 87-89, vpres drug develop, 89. *Concurrent Pos:* Mem bd gov, NY Acad Sci, 85-86. *Mem:* Fel Am Psychol Asn; fel Am Acad Neurol; Soc Neurosci; Am Soc Pharmacol & Exp Therapeut. *Res:* Techniques to permit rapid, efficient development of safe and efficacious treatment of psychiatric and neurological diseases. *Mailing Add:* Cambridge Neurosci One Kendall Sq Bldg 700 Cambridge MA 02139-1562. *Fax:* 617-225-2741

GAN, JOSE CAJILIG, BIOCHEMISTRY. *Current Pos:* from asst prof to assoc prof, 68-74, PROF BIOCHEM, MED BR, UNIV TEX, GALVESTON, 80- *Personal Data:* b Iloilo, Philippines, Nov 30, 33; m 60, Norma Estoque; c Yvonne G (Bennett) & Karen. *Educ:* Univ Wis, BS, 57; Univ Iowa, MS, 59; Univ Ill, PhD(biochem), 64. *Prof Exp:* Asst res physiologist, Univ Calif, Berkeley, 64-66; asst res biochemist, Hormone Res Lab, Med Ctr, Univ Calif, San Francisco, 66-68. *Concurrent Pos:* San Francisco Heart Asn fel, 65-67. *Mem:* AAAS; Am Soc Biol Chem & Molecular Biol; Soc Exp Biol & Med. *Res:* Plasma protein and amino acid metabolism; biosynthesis, chemistry and biological activity of glycoproteins; erythrocyte glucose and plekydrogenase as marker of chemical exposure. *Mailing Add:* Dept Human Biol Chem & Genetics Univ Tex Med Br Galveston TX 77550

GAN, K K, EXPERIMENTAL HIGH ENERGY PHYSICS. *Current Pos:* ASST PROF, DEPT PHYSICS, OHIO STATE UNIV, 90- *Personal Data:* b Johore, Malaysia, Nov 5, 58; US citizen. *Educ:* Imp Col London, BS, 80; Purdue Univ, PhD(physics), 85. *Honors & Awards:* Outstanding Jr Investr Award, Dept Energy, 91. *Prof Exp:* Fel, Stanford Linear Accelerator Ctr, 86. *Mem:* Am Physics Soc; Nat Physics Soc. *Res:* Study the fundamental constituents of matter. *Mailing Add:* 2685 Wickliffe Rd Columbus OH 43221

GAN, RONG ZHU, HEMODYNAMICS & CARDIOPULMONARY CIRCULATION, BIOMECHANICS & FINITE ELEMENT METHODS. *Current Pos:* res asst, Dept Biomed Eng, 89-92, instr & teaching asst, Depts Mech Eng & Biomed Eng, 89-92, SR RES ASSOC II, DEPT BIOMED ENG, MEMPHIS STATE UNIV, 92- *Personal Data:* m 76, Xiao D Ji; c Julie Y. *Educ:* Huazhong Univ Sci & Technol, BS, 68, MS, 81; Univ Alta, MS, 88; Memphis State Univ, PhD(biomed eng), 92. *Prof Exp:* Asst prof, Dept Bioeng, Huazhong Univ Sci & Technol, 81-85; teaching asst, Dept Math, Univ Alta, 85-88. *Mem:* Biomed Eng Soc. *Res:* Hemodynamics in pulmonary circulation; study of the steady and pulsatile blood flows in the dog lung; finite element modeling of the calcaneus and experimental testing of the calcaneus fractures. *Mailing Add:* 11401 Spring Hollow Rd Oklahoma City OK 73120. *Fax:* 901-678-4180

GANAPATHY, RAMACHANDRAN, NUCLEAR & COSMOCHEMISTRY, INORGANIC & ANALYTICAL CHEMISTRY. *Current Pos:* BAKER FEL, J T BAKER INC, 76- *Personal Data:* b Tellicherry, India, Jan 16, 39; US citizen; m 71; c 1. *Educ:* Univ Madras, BSc, 59; Univ Ark, PhD(chem), 67. *Prof Exp:* Sci officer nuclear chem, Atomic Energy Estt India, 60-63; sr res assoc cosmochem, Enrico Fermi Inst, Univ Chicago, 67-76. *Mem:* Geochem Soc. *Res:* Cosmochemistry: composition of meteorites; search for major meteorite impacts on the earth; high-purity chemicals. *Mailing Add:* Mallinckrodt-Baker Inc 222 Red School Lane Phillipsburg NJ 08865

GANAPOL, BARRY DOUGLAS, NUCLEAR ENGINEERING, EARTH SCIENCE. *Current Pos:* from asst prof to assoc prof, 76-85, PROF NUCLEAR ENG, UNIV ARIZ, 76- *Personal Data:* b San Francisco, Calif, May 15, 44. *Educ:* Univ Calif, Berkeley, BS, 66 & PhD(eng sci), 71; Columbia Univ, MS, 67. *Prof Exp:* Nuclear engr reactor physics, Swiss Fed Inst Reactor Res, 71-72; vis scientist, Ctr Nuclear Studies, Saclay, France, 72-74; nuclear engr reactor safety, Argonne Nat Lab, 74-76. *Concurrent Pos:* Consult, E G & G, 90, Argonne Nat Lab, 76-78, Los Alamos Nat Lab, 79-85, Swiss Fed Inst Reactor Res, 80-81, Sci Appln Inc, 81- 83; NASA summer fel, 87-89; fel, Air Force Off Sci Res, 84; Meyerhoff vis prof, Weizmann Inst Sci. *Mem:* Fel Am Nuclear Soc; Soc Indust & Appl Math; AAAS; Sigma Xi. *Res:* Particle transport theory; fast reactor safety; applied mathematics; remote sensing. *Mailing Add:* Dept Nuclear Aerospace & Mech Eng Univ Ariz Tucson AZ 85721

GANAS, PERRY S, ELECTRON-ATOM COLLISIONS, NUCLEAR SHELL MODEL CALCULATIONS. *Current Pos:* From asst prof to assoc prof, 70-82, PROF PHYSICS, CALIF STATE UNIV, LOS ANGELES, 82- *Personal Data:* b Brisbane, Australia, June 20, 37. *Educ:* Univ Queensland, BSc, 61; Univ Sydney, PhD(physics), 68. *Prof Exp:* Postdoctoral res assoc instr, Univ Fla, 68-70. *Concurrent Pos:* Vis prof physics, Univ Fla, 79-80 & Univ Calif, Los Angeles, 87, 91 & 92; lectr physics, Univ Southern Calif, 85-86; instr physics, Santa Monica Col, 88 & East Los Angeles Col, 89- *Res:* Atomic physics; nuclear physics; electron-atom collisions; nuclear shell model calculations; author of numerous publications on theoretical atomic, molecular and nuclear physics. *Mailing Add:* Physics Dept Calif State Univ Los Angeles CA 90032. *Fax:* 213-343-2497; *E-Mail:* pganas@calstatela.edu

GANAWAY, JAMES RIVES, VETERINARY MEDICINE, MICROBIOLOGY. *Current Pos:* RETIRED. *Personal Data:* b East St Louis, Ill, Jan 2, 27; m 50; c 3. *Educ:* Univ Mo-Columbia, BS & DVM, 53; Johns Hopkins Univ, MPH, 58; Am Bd Vet Pub Health, dipl, 60. *Prof Exp:* Base veterinarian, USAF, 53-56,; assoc virologist, Sch Hyg & Pub Health, Johns Hopkins Univ, 56-58; virologist, Armed Forces Inst Path, Walter Reed Army Med Ctr, 58-61; microbiologist, Comp Path Sect, Lab Aids Br, Div Res Serv, NIH, 61-80; dir vet med, MicroBiol Assocs, 80-87. *Mem:* Am Vet Med Asn; Am Soc Microbiol; Am Asn Lab Animal Sci. *Res:* Investigations of the naturally occurring diseases of laboratory animals and their comparative aspects with human diseases, with emphasis on the infectious diseases, their etiology, pathogenesis, control and/or prevention. *Mailing Add:* 11620 Moorestown Pl Gaithersburg MD 20878

GANCARZ, ALEXANDER JOHN, TECHNICAL MANAGEMENT. *Current Pos:* Staff mem, Los Alamos Nat Lab, 77-79, assoc group leader, Isotope Geochem Group, 80-81, dep group leader, 82-84, dep div leader, Isotope & Nuclear Chem Div, 85-89, div leader, Isotope & Nuclear Chem Div, 90-93, DIV DIR, CHEM SCI & TECHNOL DIV, LOS ALAMOS NAT LAB, 93- *Personal Data:* b Miami, Fla, Jan 15, 48. *Educ:* Princeton Univ, AB, 70; Calif Inst Technol, PhD, 76. *Mem:* Am Chem Soc; Geochem Soc; Am Geophys Union. *Res:* Isotope geochemistry; nuclear weapons physics and diagnostics; natural analogues for high-level nuclear waste repositories; separations chemistry; high precision mass spectrometry. *Mailing Add:* 2016 Calle Le Jano Los Alamos NM 87501

GANCHOFF, JOHN CHRISTOPHER, ANALYTICAL CHEMISTRY, INORGANIC CHEMISTRY. *Current Pos:* asst prof, 66-74, PROF CHEM, ELMHURST COL, 74- *Personal Data:* b Wauwatosa, Wis, Aug 15, 33; m 66; c 2. *Educ:* Marquette Univ, BS, 55, MS, 57; Ga Inst Technol, PhD(chem), 63. *Prof Exp:* Asst prof chem, Rutgers Univ, 62-66. *Concurrent Pos:* Rutgers Univ & Res Coun grants, 63-64. *Mem:* Am Chem Soc. *Res:* Titrations, especially with spectrophotometric end point location, in both aqueous and non-aqueous solvents using complexing agents as titrants. *Mailing Add:* Dept Chem Elmhurst Col Elmhurst IL 60126

GANCHROW, DONALD, NEUROANATOMY, NEUROPSYCHOLOGY. *Current Pos:* SR ASSOC PROF ANAT & ANTHROP, SACKLER FAC MED, TEL AVIV UNIV, 85- *Personal Data:* b Brooklyn, NY, Dec 30, 40; m 67, Judith Ruth Jay; c Dov Amir & Raviv Tal. *Educ:* Brooklyn Col, BS, 61; Duke Univ, PhD(psychol), 69. *Prof Exp:* Nat Acad Sci-Nat Res Coun vis scientist, Behav Sci Div, Pioneering Res Lab, US Army Natick Labs, Mass, 69-71; NINDS spec fel anat, Univ Wis-Madison & Univ Calif, San Francisco, 71-74; from lectr to sr lectr & fel anat & embryol, Hadassah Med Sch, Hebrew Univ, Jerusalem, 75-85. *Concurrent Pos:* Nat Inst Neurol Dis & Stroke spec res fel, 72-74; vis asst prof, Dept Anat, Univ Conn Med Ctr, Farmington, 80-81; vis researcher, Dept Neurobiol, Barrow Neurol Inst, St Joseph's Hosp & Med Ctr, Phoenix, AZ, 93-94; adj prof, Dept Psychol, Ariz State Univ, Tempe, 93-94. *Mem:* Am Asn Anatomists; Sigma Xi; NY Acad Sci; Am Chem Soc. *Res:* Evolution of sensory systems in mammals; trigeminal and gustatory and somesthetic nervous systems; regeneration in central nervous system of mammals; anatomy, electrophysiology, behavior. *Mailing Add:* Dept Anat & Anthropol Sackler Fac Med Tel Aviv Univ Ramat Aviv 69978 Tel Aviv Israel. *Fax:* 972-3-6408287; *E-Mail:* anatom12@post.tau.ac.il

GANCY, ALAN BRIAN, PHYSICAL CHEMISTRY, INORGANIC CHEMISTRY. *Current Pos:* PRES, GANCY CHEM CORP, 82-; PRES & CHIEF EXEC OFFICER, AIRCOMFORT INC, 93- *Personal Data:* b New Haven, Conn, Jan 28, 32. *Educ:* Trinity Col, BS, 53; Yale Univ, MS, 54, PhD(phys chem), 56; Syracuse Univ, MBA, 79. *Prof Exp:* Res chemist, Am Cyanamid Co, Conn, 56-57; from res chemist to sr res chemist, FMC Corp, NJ, 57-65; from res chemist to sr res chemist, Tyco Labs, Inc, 65-70; dir tech develop, Indust Chem Div, Allied Chem Corp, 70-74, dir advan technol, 74-79, consult chemist, 81. *Concurrent Pos:* Adj prof orgn & mgt, Syracuse Univ, 79, vis prof, 80. *Mem:* Am Chem Soc; Electrochem Soc; AAAS; Asn Consult Chemists; Am Inst Chemists. *Res:* Development, testing, manufacture and sale of specialty chemicals, including environmentally safe proprietary deicing agents. *Mailing Add:* 3317 Meadowbriar Lane Baldwinsville NY 13027-1513

GANDELMAN, RONALD JAY, PSYCHOBIOLOGY. *Current Pos:* Asst prof, 71-74, ASSOC PROF PSYCHOL, RUTGERS UNIV, 74- *Personal Data:* b New Haven, Conn, Feb 20, 44. *Educ:* Univ Pittsburgh, BS, 66; Univ Mass, MS, 67, PhD(psychol), 69. *Concurrent Pos:* Nat Inst Child Health & Human Develop fel, NIH, Univ Conn, 69-71. *Mem:* Int Soc Res Aggression; Int Soc Develop Psychobiol; Int Acad Sex Res; Int Soc Psychoneuroendocrinol. *Res:* Hormones and behavior; developmental psychobiology. *Mailing Add:* Dept Psychol Rutgers Univ New Brunswick NJ 08903

GANDER, FREDERICK W(ILLIAM), CHEMICAL ENGINEERING. *Current Pos:* Res eng, Yerkes Res Lab, 46-53, res supvr, 53-55, res mgr, 55-57, lab dir, 57-62, res & develop mgr, 62-70, RES FEL, FILM DEPT, EXP STA, E I DU PONT DE NEMOURS & CO, INC, 70- *Personal Data:* b New York, NY, Jan 14, 21; m 42; c 3. *Educ:* Mass Inst Technol, SB, 42, SM, 46. *Mem:* Am Chem Soc; Am Inst Chem Engrs. *Res:* Polymer synthesis; chemical modification of polymers; polymer fabrication. *Mailing Add:* 2700 Bayshore Blvd No 524 Dunedin FL 34698-1611

GANDER, GEORGE WILLIAM, EXPERIMENTAL PATHOLOGY. *Current Pos:* from asst prof to assoc prof, 63-74, PROF EXP PATH, MED COL, VA COMMONWEALTH UNIV, 74- *Personal Data:* b Hamilton, Mont, June 27, 30; m 58; c 3. *Educ:* Mont State Col, BS, 53; Cornell Univ, MS, 55, PhD(dairy chem), 59. *Prof Exp:* Res assoc dairy chem, Univ Conn, 59-61; res assoc path, Albany Med Col, 61-63. *Mem:* Am Chem Soc; Am Soc Exp Path; NY Acad Sci; Reticuloendothelial Soc; Sigma Xi. *Res:* Mechanism of action of pyrogens; computers in clinical laboratory. *Mailing Add:* Dept Path Med Col Va Va Commonwealth Univ PO Box 662 Richmond VA 23298-1900

GANDER, JOHN E, BIOCHEMISTRY, ENZYMOLOGY. *Current Pos:* prof & chmn, 84-89, PROF MICROBIOL & CELL SCI, UNIV FLA, GAINESVILLE, 89- *Personal Data:* b Roundup, Mont, Mar 9, 25; m 51, Dorothy Hoffman; c Sharon L, Peggy C & Linda K (Baker). *Educ:* Mont State Univ, BSc, 50; Univ Minn, MSc, 54, PhD(agr biochem), 56. *Prof Exp:* Asst prof chem, Mont State Univ, 55-58; from asst prof to assoc prof biochem, Ohio State Univ, 58-64; from assoc prof to prof biochem, Univ Minn, St Paul, 68-84. *Concurrent Pos:* Res career develop award, USPHS & NIH, 65-71. *Mem:* Am Soc Biol Chem & Molecular Biologists; Am Chem Soc; Am Soc Microbiologists; AAAS; Complex Carbohydrates Soc; Sigma Xi. *Res:* Structure, function and biosynthesis of galactofuranosyl-containing fungal glycoproteins and glycopeptides; mechanism of galactofuranosidase catalyzed reaction. *Mailing Add:* Microbiol & Cell Sci Dept Univ Fla 1147 Bldg 981 PO Box 110700 Gainesville FL 32611-0700. *Fax:* 904-392-5922; *E-Mail:* john@micro.1fas.ufl.edu

GANDER, ROBERT JOHNS, POLYMER CHEMISTRY, ORGANIC CHEMISTRY. *Current Pos:* RETIRED. *Personal Data:* b Eagle River, Wis, Sept 12, 18; m 48, Hilda Woetzel; c Mark R & Malcolm J. *Educ:* Univ Wis, BS, 40, MS, 42; Univ Ill, PhD(org chem), 44. *Prof Exp:* Asst Nat Defense Res Comt proj, Univ Wis, 40-42; Off Sci Res & Develop synthetic rubber proj, Univ Ill, 42-45; chemist, Firestone Plastics Co, 45-50; asst dir surg adhesives res, Johnson & Johnson Prod Inc, 50-66, mgr polymer res, Domestic Operating Co, 66-78, sr res fel, 78-87. *Mem:* Am Chem Soc; Math Asn Am. *Res:* Monomer and polymer synthesis; technology of vinyl chloride resins, plasticized vinyl films, pressure-sensitive adhesives, biomedical plastics, polymeric dental materials; retinoic acid derivatives. *Mailing Add:* PO Box 82 Whitehouse NJ 08888-0082

GANDERS, FRED RUSSELL, BIOSYSTEMATICS, POPULATION BIOLOGY. *Current Pos:* From asst prof to assoc prof, 73-86, PROF BOT, UNIV BC, 86- *Personal Data:* b Bremerton, Wash, Mar 10, 45. *Educ:* Wash State Univ, BA & BS, 67; Univ Calif, Berkeley, MA, 69, PhD(bot), 75. *Concurrent Pos:* Vis prof, Bot, Univ Hawaii, 89-90. *Mem:* Soc Study Evolution; Bot Soc Am; Am Soc Plant Taxonomists (secy, 79-80). *Res:* Biosystematics and evolution of plants, effects of mating systems on genetic variability in natural plant populations, the function and evolution of mating systems in plant populations; adaptive radiation and evolution of Hawaiian Bidens. *Mailing Add:* Dept Bot Univ BC 2075 Westbrook Pl Vancouver BC V6T 1W5 Can

GANDHI, HARENDRA SAKARLAL, PHYSICAL CHEMISTRY, CHEMICAL ENGINEERING. *Current Pos:* MGR CHEM ENG DEPT, SCI RES LABS, FORD MOTOR CO, 67- *Personal Data:* b Calcutta, India, May 2, 41; m 66, Yellow Sheth; c Sangeeta & Anand. *Educ:* Univ Bombay, BChE, 63; Univ Detroit, MS, 66, DEng, 71. *Honors & Awards:* Ralph R Teetor Award, Soc Automotive Engrs; Exxon Award, 92. *Prof Exp:* Chem engr eng equipment design, Shwayder Chem, 64-65; specialty coating chemist, Specialty Coating Inc, 65-67. *Concurrent Pos:* Adv, UN/Govt India Proj on Emission Control from Indian vehicles; adj prof chem eng, Wayne State Univ. *Mem:* Am Inst Chem Engrs; Am Chem Soc; Soc Automotive Engrs. *Res:* Heterogeneous catalysis; reaction kinetics; pollution prevention and coating chemistry; author of over 60 publications; granted 30 patents. *Mailing Add:* Sci Res Labs Ford Motor Co PO Box 2053 Dearborn MI 48121

GANDHI, OM P, ELECTROMAGNETIC FIELDS, MICROWAVES. *Current Pos:* assoc prof, elec eng, 67-73 res prof bioeng, 75-78, PROF ELEC ENG, UNIV UTAH, 73- *Personal Data:* b Multan, India, Sept 23, 34; US citizen; m 63; c 3. *Educ:* Univ Delhi, BS, 52; Indian Inst Sci, Bangalore, dipl elec commun eng, 55; Univ Mich, MSEE, 57, ScD(elec eng), 60. *Honors & Awards:* Distinguished Res Award, Univ Utah, 79. *Prof Exp:* Assoc res engr microwave tubes, Electron Physics Lab, Univ Mich, 58-60; res specialist solid-state devices, Philco Corp, 60-62; dep dir & head microwave devices, Cent Electronics Eng Res Inst, Pilani, India, 62-66. *Concurrent Pos:* Consult, Walter Reed Army Inst Res, 73-77 & 90, BSD Corp, 77-81, Equitable Environ Health, Inc, 78-80, Dosimeter Corp, 79-80 & 84-86, Remic Corp, 82, Hughes Aircraft Co & Univ Utah Res Inst, 83-, G E Milwaukee, 86-87, NIOSH, 86- & EG&G, Idaho, 86-88, SCEEE 82, 89-90, ERC Bioserv Corp, 90-91; mem, Int Union Radio Sci Comn B, 77-, Diag Radiol Sect, NIH, 78-81, Panel Eng Aspects of Pecision Acquisition of Vehicle Entry Phased Array Warning Syst, Air Force Radar Systs, Nat Acad Eng, 78-79, Panel Biol Effect Precision Acquisition of Vehicle Entry Phased Array Warning Syst, 78-79, chmn, Comt Man & Radiation, Inst Elec & Electronics Engrs, 80-82; mem, Panel Assessment Possible Health Effects Ground Wave Emergency Network (GWEN) Nat Res Coun, Nat Acad Sci, 90-91; co-chmn, Inst Elec & Electronics Engrs SCC 28 Subcomt IV Safety Levels Radiation 3KHZ-3006HZ, 88- *Mem:* Bioelectromagnetic Soc; Int Microwave Power Inst; fel Inst Elec & Electronics Engrs. *Res:* Electromagnetic energy biological effects; biomedical and energy applications of microwaves, antennas and microwave communications; author over 200 journal articles. *Mailing Add:* Dept Elec Eng 3032 Merrill Eng Bldg Salt Lake City UT 84112

GANDLER, JOSEPH RUBIN, PHYSICAL ORGANIC CHEMISTRY. *Current Pos:* from asst prof to assoc prof, 81-87, PROF CHEM, CALIF STATE UNIV, FRESNO, 87- *Personal Data:* b Brooklyn, NY, Dec 2, 49; m 74; c 2. *Educ:* Brooklyn Col, BS, 71; Univ Calif, Santa Cruz, PhD(chem), 78. *Prof Exp:* NIH fel, State Univ NY, Buffalo, 78-79, Brandeis Univ, 79-81. *Mem:* Am Chem Soc. *Res:* Acid-base catalysis; beta-elimination and proton transfer reactions. *Mailing Add:* Dept Chem Calif State Univ 2555 E San Ramon Fresno CA 93740-8034. *E-Mail:* joseph_gandler@csufresno.edu

GANDOLFI, A JAY, TOXICOLOGY. *Current Pos:* res asst prof toxicol & anesthesiol, 78-85, assoc prof, 85-89, PROF ANESTHESIOL, PHARMACOL & TOXICOL, UNIV ARIZ, 89- *Personal Data:* b San Mateo, Calif, Dec 11, 46; m 68, Judith A Monks; c Christopher, Matthew & Jason. *Educ:* Univ Calif, Davis, BA, 68; Ore State Univ, PhD(biochem), 72. *Prof Exp:* Trainee drug metab, Ore State Univ, 68-72; resident fel anesthetic toxicol, Mayo Clin Found, 72-75; sr res scientist inhalation toxicol, Pac Northwest Labs, Battelle Mem Inst, 75-77. *Concurrent Pos:* Res fel, Mayo Clin Found, 74-75. *Mem:* Soc Toxicol; Am Soc Pharmacol & Exp Therapeut; Am Soc Anesthesiol. *Res:* Biochemical pharmacology and toxicology of foreign compounds to man and animals with emphasis on the metabolism and disposition of the foreign agent and effect of agent on structure and function of endogenous biological components. *Mailing Add:* Univ Ariz Dept Anesthesiol Tucson AZ 85724. *Fax:* 520-626-2385; *E-Mail:* gandolfi@u.arizona.edu

GANDOUR, RICHARD DAVID, PHYSICAL ORGANIC CHEMISTRY, BIO-ORGANIC CHEMISTRY. *Current Pos:* asst prof, 75-80, assoc prof, 80-87, PROF CHEM, LA STATE UNIV, BATON ROUGE, 87- *Personal Data:* b Sistersville, WVa, Feb 12, 45; m 71, 85; c 1. *Educ:* Wheeling Jesuit Col, BS, 67; Rice Univ, PhD(org chem), 72. *Prof Exp:* From teaching assoc to res assoc chem, Univ Kans, 71-75. *Concurrent Pos:* Vis scientist, Ind Univ, 89-90; vis prof, Univ Calif, Los Angeles, 90. *Mem:* Am Chem Soc; fel AAAS; Sigma Xi; Am Soc Biochem & Molecular Biol. *Res:* Bio-organic chemical dynamics; design, synthesis and mechanistic studies of chemical models of enzymatic catalysis; structural bioorganic chemistry; molecular recognition; chemistry and biology of carnitine. *Mailing Add:* Dept Chem La State Univ Blacksburg VA 24061-0212

GANEM, BRUCE, SYNTHETIC ORGANIC & NATURAL PRODUCTS CHEMISTRY. *Current Pos:* from asst prof to prof, 74-93, FRANZ & ELISABETH ROESSLER PROF CHEM, CORNELL UNIV, 93- *Personal Data:* b Boston, Mass, Feb 7, 48; m 87; c Beth Carlson. *Educ:* Harvard Univ, BA, 69; Columbia Univ, PhD(org chem), 72. *Prof Exp:* Fel chem, Stanford Univ, 73-74. *Concurrent Pos:* Consult, CIBA-GEIGY Corp, 78-, Cambridge Neurosci, 90- & Purdue Pharma, 93. *Mem:* Am Chem Soc; fel Royal Soc Chem; Am Soc Biochem & Molecular Biol. *Res:* Methods and reactions, including new organic reagents, for the synthesis of rare and natural products and biologically important molecules. *Mailing Add:* Dept Chem Baker Lab Cornell Univ Ithaca NY 14853. *E-Mail:* bruceganem@qmchem.mail.cornwell.edu

GANESAN, ADAYAPALAM T, molecular biology, genetics; deceased, see previous edition for last biography

GANESAN, ANN K, MOLECULAR GENETICS. *Current Pos:* NIH fel radiol, Med Ctr, Stanford Univ, 65-66, res assoc, 66-71, res assoc biol, 71-75, sr res assoc, 75-91, SR RES SCIENTIST, STANFORD UNIV, 91- *Personal Data:* b Denver, Colo, July 25, 33; m 63. *Educ:* Wilson Col, BA, 54; Univ Wis, MS, 59; Stanford Univ, PhD(genetics), 61. *Prof Exp:* Res assoc microbiol, Palo Alto Med Res Found, 61-62; res assoc biochem, Syntex Inst Molecular Biol, 62-65. *Concurrent Pos:* Mem, NIH Study Sect, 86-90. *Mem:* Am Soc Microbiol; Genetics Soc Am. *Res:* Biochemical genetics of bacteria and cultured mammalian cells, with emphasis on DNA repair. *Mailing Add:* Dept Biol Stanford Univ Stanford CA 94305-5020

GANESAN, DEVAKI, INTERNAL MEDICINE, PHARMACOLOGY. *Current Pos:* MED DIR, GEN MOTORS, 85- *Personal Data:* b Bangalore, India, Feb 1, 40; m 67; c 2. *Educ:* Univ Mysore, India, MBBS, 63; Univ Poona, India, MD, 66. *Prof Exp:* Rotating intern med, surg, obstet & gynec, Bangalore Med Col, India, 62, asst surgeon, 63; lectr pharmacol, Armed Forces Med Col, 63-66; fel cardiovasc, Okla Med Res Found, 67-72, res assoc, Dept Biochem, 70-85, staff scientist, 72-74, asst mem & instr cardiovasc, 74-85. *Mem:* Am Fedn Clin Res; fel Am Heart Asn. *Res:* Lipid transport and lipoprotein metabolism in relation to atherogenesis, hyperlipidemias and physiology of fat absorption; characterization of lipolytic enzymes. *Mailing Add:* 12420 Maple Ridge Rd Oklahoma City OK 73120

GANESAN, SUBRAMANIAM, COMPUTER ARCHITECTURE-PARALLEL PROCESSING, REAL TIME MICROPROCESSOR SYSTEMS. *Current Pos:* assoc prof, 86-93, PROF ENG & CHMN DEPT, OAKLAND UNIV, 93- *Personal Data:* b Tiruchi, India, July 6, 47; m 75, Shanthi; c Krishna. *Educ:* Madras Univ, BE, 68; Indian Inst Sci, MTech, 71, PhD(eng), 81. *Prof Exp:* Scientist, Nat Aeronaut Lab, India, 71-83; asst prof, Western Mich Univ, 84-86. *Concurrent Pos:* Vis scholar, Ruhr Univ, Ger, 79-80, Concordia Univ, Can, 83-84. *Mem:* Sr mem Inst Elec & Electronics Engrs. *Res:* Multiprocessor architecture, realtime digital signal processing system for automotive and medical applications. *Mailing Add:* Dept Comput Sci & Eng Oakland Univ Rochester MI 48309. *Fax:* 248-370-4261

GANFIELD, DAVID JUDD, IMMUNOLOGY, BIOCHEMISTRY. *Current Pos:* dir labs, 83-87, PRES, DELMONT LABS, INC, SWARTHMORE, PA, 87- *Personal Data:* b Dubuque, Iowa, Jan 21, 41; m 64, Mong Ching Wong; c Ken & Tim. *Educ:* Parsons Col, BS, 63; Iowa State Univ, PhD(biochem), 71. *Prof Exp:* Chemist biochem, Nat Animal Dis Ctr, USDA, 63-71; from instr to asst prof biochem, Med Sch, Thomas Jefferson Univ, 71-77; res scientist immunol, Exp Sta, E I Du Pont De Nemours & Co Inc, 77-80, res scientist immunol, Du Pont Glenolden Lab, Pa, 80-82. *Concurrent Pos:* HEW trainee immunol, Thomas Jefferson Univ, 71-74; adj asst prof biochem, 77-82. *Mem:* AAAS; Am Chem Soc; Am Soc Microbiol; Sigma Xi; Parenteral Drug Asn. *Res:* Mechanisms of lymphocyte regulation affecting the immune response; characterization of lymphocyte receptors; separation of lymphocyte subpopulations; genetic control of the immune response; characterization of immunomodulators therapeutic use of staphylocuccus aureus antigens. *Mailing Add:* 2233 Jamaica Dr Wilmington DE 19810. *E-Mail:* 104065.2435@compuserve.com

GANGAROSA, EUGENE J, EPIDEMIOLOGY. *Current Pos:* prof & dir, MPH Prog, 82-89, PROF INT HEALTH, EMORY UNIV, 89- *Personal Data:* b Rochester, NY, Aug 7, 26; m 50; c 4. *Educ:* Univ Rochester, AB, 50, MD, 54, MS, 55. *Prof Exp:* Asst prof med & microbiol, Sch Med, Univ Md, 61-64; chief, Epidemic Intel Serv, Ctr Dis Control, 64-65, chief, Enteric Dis Sect, Bact Dis Br, Epidemiol Prog, 65-70, chief, Enteric Dis Br & dep dir, Bact Dis Div, Epidemiol Br, Ctr Dis Control, 70-78; dean fac, Health Sci, Am Univ Beirut, Lebanon, 78-81. *Concurrent Pos:* Vis assoc prof, Jefferson Med Col, 62; dir, Pakistan Med Res Ctr, Lahore, 62-64; consult, 81- *Mem:* Infectious Dis Soc; Am Epidemiol Soc. *Res:* Clinical investigation; cholera; shigellosis; salmonellosis; botulism; food poisoning; traveler's diarrhea, gastroenterology; hematology; drug toxicity. *Mailing Add:* 5305 Greencastle Way Stone Mountain GA 30087

GANGAROSA, LOUIS PAUL, SR, PHARMACOLOGY. *Current Pos:* assoc prof oral biol, 68-71, assoc prof pharmacol, 68-72, PROF ORAL BIOL, MED COL GA, 71-, PROF PHARMACOL, 72- *Personal Data:* b Rochester, NY, June 8, 29; m 50; c 4. *Educ:* Univ Rochester, BA, 52, MS, 61, PhD(pharmacol), 65; Univ Buffalo, DDS, 55. *Honors & Awards:* C V Mosby Award, 55. *Prof Exp:* Pvt pract, 55-61; asst prof dent res, Univ Rochester, 65-68, from instr to asst prof pharmacol, 65-68. *Concurrent Pos:* Lectr, Eastman Dent Ctr, 63-65, clin res assoc, 65-68; res grant, Nat Inst Dent Res, 67-71 & 81-83, consult training grant comt, 69-71, mem training comt, 71-73; chmn OTC panel on dentrices & dent care agents, Food & Drug Admin, 73-78. *Mem:* Am Soc Pharmacol & Exp Therapeut; Int Asn Dent Res; Am Dent Asn; Am Asn Dent Sch; Soc Exp Biol & Med; fel Am Col Dentists. *Res:* Dental research; local anesthetics; sympathomimets; dental drugs; Iontophoretic medication; antiviral chemotherapy; chronic pain. *Mailing Add:* Sch Dent Med Col Ga Augusta GA 30912- 1128. *Fax:* 706-721-6276

GANGEMI, FRANCIS A, MOLECULAR PHYSICS, QUANTUM PHYSICS. *Current Pos:* from assoc prof to prof, 67-95, chmn dept, 72-95, EMER PROF PHYSICS, OHIO NORTHERN UNIV, 95- *Personal Data:* b Syracuse, NY, Feb 20, 29; m 78, Charleen K Krofft; c Damien, Emily, Maria & Joseph. *Educ:* Univ Notre Dame, BS, 54; Cath Univ Am, MS, 59, PhD(physics), 62. *Prof Exp:* Asst prof physics, Univ Portland, 62-65; assoc prof, Southern Ore Col, 65-67. *Concurrent Pos:* NSF grant, Cornell Conf Relativity, 63; NSF res grant, 63-64. *Mem:* Am Phys Soc; Sigma Xi; Asn Process Philos Educ; fel Relig Humanists. *Res:* Quantum chemistry; theoretical calculation of dipole movements of polyatomic molecules; particle physics; philosophy of science; improving teaching techniques. *Mailing Add:* Dept Physics Ohio Northern Univ Ada OH 45810

GANGI, ANTHONY FRANK, GEOPHYSICS, SEISMOLOGY. *Current Pos:* assoc prof, 67-70, actg head dept, 76-78, PROF GEOPHYS, TEX A&M UNIV, 70- *Personal Data:* b Newark, NJ, Feb 19, 29; m 92, Beverly Goebel; c Robert, Theresa, Stephen & John. *Educ:* Univ Calif, Los Angeles, BS, 53, MS, 54, PhD(physics, geophys), 60. *Honors & Awards:* Basic Res Award, Rock Mechanics, US Nat Comt, 79. *Prof Exp:* Sr electronics technician, Inst Geophys, Univ Calif, Los Angeles, 54-60; mem tech staff, Space Electronics Corp, Calif, 60-62; mgr, Antenna Dept, Space-Gen Corp, 62-64; assoc prof geophys, Mass Inst Technol, 64-67. *Concurrent Pos:* Shell Fel Geophys, 56-57; mgr, Tamu Seismic Studies Lab, 73-77; NATO vis prof, Instituto Nazionale Geofisca, Rome, 75-76; vis prof geophys, Univ Fed Bahia, Salvador, Brazil, 81-82. *Mem:* Inst Elec & Electronics Engrs; Am Geophys Union; Seismol Soc Am; Soc Explor Geophys; Sigma Xi. *Res:* Seismology; elastic and radio-wave propagation; antenna and antenna-array theory; boundary-value problems and mathematical physics; theoretical geophysics; theoretical tectonophysics and rock mechanics; data analysis. *Mailing Add:* Dept Geophys Tex A&M Univ College Station TX 77843-3114. *Fax:* 408-845-6780; *E-Mail:* gangi@tamu.edu

GANGJEE, ALEEM, MEDICINAL CHEMISTRY. *Current Pos:* from asst prof to assoc prof, 79-88, PROF MEDICINAL CHEM, SCH PHARM, DUQUESNE UNIV, PITTSBURGH, 88- *Personal Data:* b Calcutta, India, July 30, 48; US citizen; m 72; c 2. *Educ:* Indian Inst Technol, BS, 69, MS, 71; Univ Iowa, PhD(med chem), 75. *Prof Exp:* Fel biochem, Univ Iowa, 75-76, trainee med chem, State Univ NY Buffalo, 76-79. *Mem:* Am Chem Soc; Am Asn Pharmaceut Scientists; Sigma Xi; NY Acad Sci. *Res:* Medicinal organic chemistry; structure-activity relationships; design of biologically active compounds; antitumor agents related to folates; cardiovascular agents and cholinergic agents; synthetic organic chemistry, stereochemistry and heterocyclic chemistry. *Mailing Add:* Sch Pharm Duquesne Univ Pittsburgh PA 15282

GANGLOFF, PIERRE, GEOMORPHOLOGY. *Current Pos:* Chmn, Dept Geog, 77-78, PROF GEOMORPHOL, UNIV MONTREAL, 65- *Personal Data:* b Mulhouse, France, July 20, 41; Can citizen; m 65; c 5. *Educ:* Univ Strasbourg, BA, 64, PhD(geomorphol), 70. *Concurrent Pos:* Ed, J Geog Physique et Quaternaire, 79. *Res:* Holocene geomorphological evolution of landscapes; quaternary paleogeography; geomorphological mapping; ecological mapping. *Mailing Add:* Dept Geog Univ Montreal 520 Chaemim de La Cot-Ste-Cathrine Montreal PQ H2V 2B8 Can

GANGLOFF, RICHARD PAUL, MECHANICAL ENGINEERING. *Current Pos:* PROF MAT SCI & ENG, UNIV VA, 86- *Personal Data:* b Pittsburgh, Pa, Aug 4, 48; m 70; c 1. *Educ:* Lehigh Univ, BS, 70, MS, 72, PhD(mat sci), 74. *Honors & Awards:* Henry Marion Howe Medal, Am Soc Metals; Award of Merit, Am Soc Testing & Mat. *Prof Exp:* Metallurgist, Corp Res & Develop, Gen Elec Co, 74-80 & Corp Sci Labs, Exxon Corp, 80-86. *Mem:* Am Soc Metals; Am Inst Mining, Metall & Petrol Engrs; fel Am Soc Testing & Mat; Sigma Xi; fel Am Soc Metals Int. *Res:* Hydrogen embrittlement; fatigue; fracture mechanics; titanium and aluminum alloys; deformation and fracture; stress corrosion cracking; liquid metal embrittlement. *Mailing Add:* Dept Mat Sci Bldg 303 Univ Va Charlottesville VA 22903-2442. *Fax:* 804-982-5799; *E-Mail:* rp87u@virginia.edu

GANGOLLI, RAMESH A, PHYSICAL MATHEMATICS. *Current Pos:* from asst prof to assoc prof, 62-67, PROF MATH, UNIV WASH, 67- *Personal Data:* b Bangalore, India, Feb 26, 35. *Educ:* Bombay Univ, BA, 54; Cambridge Univ, BA, 57; Mass Inst Technol, PhD(math), 61. *Honors & Awards:* Paul Levy Prize, 66; NSF Sabbatical Award, 67. *Prof Exp:* Instr math, Mass Inst Technol, 61-62. *Concurrent Pos:* Vis lectr, Tata Inst, Bombay, 64, vis prof, 67, 71, 78, Polish Acad Sci, 67, State Univ NY, Albany, 72-73, ETH, 73, Australian Nat Univ, 87; Sloan fel, 66-68; assoc ed, J Indian Math Soc, 73-, Pac J Math, 85-; chmn, Math Dept, Univ Wash, 81-85, 91- *Mem:* Am Math Soc. *Res:* Mathematics. *Mailing Add:* Math Dept GN-50 Univ Wash Seattle WA 98195-0001

GANGSTAD, EDWARD OTIS, ENVIRONMENTAL SCIENCES. *Current Pos:* RETIRED. *Personal Data:* b Chippewa Falls, Wis, Dec 18, 17; m 45; c 4. *Educ:* Univ Wis, BS, 42, MS, 47; Rutgers Univ, PhD(agron), 50. *Prof Exp:* Asst biochem, Univ Wis, 46-47; asst agron, Rutgers Univ, 47-50; agronomist, Everglade Exp Sta, USDA, Fla, 50-51, res agronomist, 51-53, assoc agronomist, 53-54; from agronomist to prin agronomist, Tex Res Found, 54-66; mgt agronomist, Off Chief Engrs, US Army, Resource Mgt, Opers Div, Washington, DC, 66-69, chief, Aquatic Plant Control Prog, 69-75, botanist, 75-85. *Mem:* AAAS; Am Soc Agron; Weed Sci Soc Am; Am Inst Chem Engrs; Am Soc Civil Engrs. *Res:* Plant growth, breeding, production and utilization; forage crops for livestock production in the Southwest; management of military lands; aquatic plant control; pest control program. *Mailing Add:* 7909 Greeley Blvd Springfield VA 22152

GANGULEE, AMITAVA, PHYSICAL METALLURGY, SOLID STATE PHYSICS. *Current Pos:* PRES, LOGIC, SCI & INNOVATIONS, 89- *Personal Data:* b Rajshahi, India, Apr 26, 41; m, Suzanne G Lorant; c 2. *Educ:* Univ Calcutta, BE, 61; Brown Univ, ScM, 64; Mass Inst Technol, ScD(metall, mat sci), 67; Pace Univ, MBA, 89. *Prof Exp:* Metallurgist, Steel & Allied Prod Ltd, India, 61-62; consult, Metal Eng & Treatment Co, 62-63; mem staff, div sponsored res, Mass Inst Technol, 67; sr assoc metallurgist, components div, IBM Corp, 67-68, res staff mem, T J Watson Res Ctr, 68-86; consult, 87-89. *Concurrent Pos:* Assoc dir, ENSM, Paris, 80. *Mem:* Am Phys Soc; Am Inst Mining, Metall & Petrol Engrs; Inst Mgt Sci. *Res:* Magnetic and transport properties of solids; thermodynamics; x-ray diffraction; relation of structure with properties of solids; optimization; operations research. *Mailing Add:* 194 Wayside Inn Rd Sudbury MA 01776. *Fax:* 781-275-8790

GANGULI, MUKUL CHANDRA, HYPERTENSION, RENAL PHYSIOLOGY. *Current Pos:* ASSOC INVESTR, MINN MED RES FOUND, 96- *Personal Data:* b Comilla, Bengal, India, Feb 28, 38; US citizen; m 70; c 3. *Educ:* Univ Calcutta, India, BSc, 56, BVSc & AH, 61; Agra Univ, India, MVSc, 63; Univ Minn, PhD(nutrit & biochem), 68. *Prof Exp:* Tech asst physiol, Nat Dairy Res Inst, India, 63-64; res asst nutrit, Univ Minn, 64-68; assoc nutrit, Iowa State Univ, 68-70; res assoc nutrit, Univ Minn, 70-96. *Mem:* Sigma Xi; Am Physiol Soc. *Res:* Sodium and prostaglandins and their relationship to the kidney and hypertension; protective role of dietary potassium and dietary fatty acids against sodium chloride hypertension; measurement of renal medullary blood flow and cardiac output in different types of experimental rat hypertension. *Mailing Add:* 825 S Eighth St Ste 824 Minneapolis MN 55404

GANGULY, ASHIT K, RESOURCE MANAGEMENT. *Current Pos:* Sr scientist, Schering-Plough Corp, 68-70, prin scientist, 70-71, res fel, 71-79, assoc dir to dir 79-84, VPRES, SCHERING-PLOUGH CORP, 84- *Personal Data:* b New Delhi, India, Aug 9, 34; m 66; c 1. *Educ:* Delhi Univ, BSc(Hons), 53, MSc, 55, PhD(chem), 59; Univ London, PhD(chem), 62. *Honors & Awards:* Khaira Lectr, Indian Asn Cultivation Sci, 75; Seshadri Mem Award, Delhi Univ, 82; Charles Sabat Lectr, Rutgers Univ, 87; Outstanding Scientist Award, Asn Scientists Indian Origin Am, 91. *Concurrent Pos:* Adj prof, Stevens Inst Technol, Hoboken, NJ, 74-; mem, Med Chem Study Sect, NIH, 86-; mem bd trustees, Bloomfield Col, NJ, 89- *Mem:* Fel Royal Soc Chem; Am Chem Soc; NY Acad Sci. *Res:* Structural elucidation and synthesis of natural products of biological importance; biosynthesis, mutasynthesis and synthesis of macrolide and penem antibodies; synthesis of dual antagonists of platelet aggregation factor and histamine; antiviral and antitumor research. *Mailing Add:* Schering-Plough Res Inst 15-3 Bldg K (3750) Kenilworth NJ 07033-0539

GANGULY, BISHWA NATH, PHYSICS. *Current Pos:* SCIENTIST XEROGRAPHY, JOSEPH C WILSON CTR TECHNOL, XEROX CORP, 73- *Personal Data:* b Patna, India, Jan 2, 42; US citizen; m 66; c 2. *Educ:* Patna Univ, BSc, 60, MSc, 62; Poona Univ, PhD(physics), 66. *Prof Exp:* Fel, Univ Toronto, 67-68; res assoc, La State Univ, Baton Rouge, 68-69; scientist solid state physics, Oak Ridge Nat Lab, 69-71; res asst prof physics, Univ Ill, Urbana, 71-73. *Mem:* Am Phys Soc; Can Asn Physicists. *Res:* Theory of electronic states and conduction mechanisms in amorphous materials, particularly in organic crystals and polymers; superconductivity in metal hydrides; photo-generation and -conduction in amorphous materials. *Mailing Add:* 51 Parkhurst Rd Dayton OH 45440

GANGULY, JIBAMITRA, GEOLOGY, GEOCHEMISTRY. *Current Pos:* from asst prof to assoc prof, 75-86, PROF, DEPT GEOSCI, UNIV ARIZ, 86- *Personal Data:* b Calcutta, India, Oct 24, 38; m 66; c Rajib & Sujoy. *Educ:* Univ Calcutta, BSc, 58; Jadavpur Univ, India, MSc, 60; Univ Chicago, PhD(geophys sci), 67. *Prof Exp:* Sci off, Atomic Energy Estab, India, 61-62; mem res staff, Yale Univ, 67-69, Jadavpur Univ, India, 69-71, & Birla Inst Technol & Sci, India, 71; mem res staff, Inst Geophys & Planetary Physics, Univ Calif, Los Angeles, 72-75. *Concurrent Pos:* Mem, Comt Thermodyn, Int Mineral Asn. *Mem:* Am Geophys Union; fel Mineralogical Soc Am. *Res:* Phase equilibria and kinetic studies in geochemical systems; thermodynamics and crystal chemistry of rock forming minerals. *Mailing Add:* Dept Geosci Univ Ariz Tucson AZ 85721. *Fax:* 520-621-2672; *E-Mail:* ganguly@geo.arizona.edu

GANGULY, PANKAJ, HEMATOLOGY, CELL PHYSIOLOGY. *Current Pos:* PROG DIR, BLOOD DIS & RESOURCES, NIH, BETHESDA, MD, 87-, LEADER, THROMBOSIS & HEMOSTASIS GROUP, BLOOD DIV, NAT HEART, LUNG & BLOOD INST, 92- *Personal Data:* b Calcutta, India, Dec 31, 39; m 70; c 1. *Educ:* Univ Calcutta, BSc, 59, MSc, 61, PhD(biophys), 65. *Prof Exp:* Res assoc biophys, Blood Res Lab, Am Nat Red Cross, Washington, DC, 66-67; res scientist phys biochem, Am Red Cross, Bethesda, Md, 67-71; assoc mem hematol, Univ Tenn Ctr Health Sci, Memphis, 72-81, prof biochem, 82-84; prof biochem, Univ PR, San Juan, 84-87. *Concurrent Pos:* Fel Biophys Div, Saha Inst Nuclear Physics, Calcutta, 65-66; assoc prof biochem, Univ Tenn Ctr Health Sci, Memphis, 72- *Mem:* AAAS; Am Heart Asn; Biophys Soc; Am Soc Biol Chemists; Am Soc Hematol. *Res:* Blood platelets, their role in hemostasis and thrombosis blood coagulation factors; clinical conditions membrane receptors; protein structure. *Mailing Add:* Thrombosis Br NIH RKL II Bldg Rm 10176 Bethesda MD 20892-7950. *E-Mail:* gangulyp@gwgate.nhlbi.nih.gov

GANGULY, RAMA, BIOCHEMISTRY. *Current Pos:* ASSOC PROF MED, UNIV S FLA, 81- *Personal Data:* b Calcutta, India. *Educ:* Univ Calcutta, BSc, 57, MSc, 59, PhD(biochem), 64. *Prof Exp:* Res fel biochem, Cent Sci & Indust Res, Govt India, 59-64; from res officer to sr res officer immunol, Indian Coun Med Res, 64-71; assoc immunol, Dept Med & Med Microbiol, Col Med, Univ Fla, 71-74, instr, 75-76; asst prof to assoc prof infectious dis, Sch Med, WVa Univ, 76-81. *Concurrent Pos:* Mem spec grants rev comt, Nat Inst Dent Res, NIH, 82-86. *Mem:* Am Soc Microbiol; Indian Sci Cong; Indian Soc Microbiol; Am Asn Immunologists; Am Acad Microbiol; Infectious Dis Soc Am. *Res:* Infectious diseases and immunology; cell-mediated immunity and secretory immunology; action of antibiotics on the immunologic functions of the host; development of vaccines; marrophage functions, nutrition and aging. *Mailing Add:* Dept Int Med VAR-151 James A Haley Vet Admin Hosp Univ SFla 13000 Bruce B Downs Blvd Tampa FL 33612. *Fax:* 813-972-7623

GANGULY, SUMAN, IONOSPHERIC ATMOSPHERE STUDIES, RADIO ENGINEERING. *Current Pos:* PRES & SCIENTIST, PHYSICS & ELECTRONICS, CTR REMOTE SENSING, VA, 85- *Personal Data:* b Dacca, India, Feb, 9, 42; US citizen. *Educ:* Calcutta Univ, BS, 60, MS, 62, PhD(physics), 70. *Prof Exp:* Res fel ionospheric res, Bose Res Inst, Calcutta, 62-69, Delhi Univ, 70-72; res assoc, Delhi Univ, 70-72, Calcutta Univ, 72-74; Leverhulme fel, Royal Soc London, Lancaster Univ, UK, 75-76; res assoc, Cornell Univ, 76-79; sr res assoc, Rice Univ, 79-85. *Concurrent Pos:* Adj prof, Elec Eng Dept, Case Western Res Univ, Cleveland, 78-79; prin investr over 30 proj, NSF, NASA, USAF, Army & Navy, 79-; scientist, Comput Dept, Harvey Mudd Col, Claremont, Calif, 82-83; vis scientist, Max Planck Inst Aeronomie, WGer & Max Planck Inst Extraterrestrial Physics, Munchen, WGer, 83, Harvey Mudd Col, Claremont, Calif, 85-87. *Mem:* Am Geophys Union; Inst Elec & Electronics Engrs; Instrumentation Soc Am; Int Soc Optical Eng; Armed Forces Communs & Electronics Asn. *Res:* Radio science; radio engineering; atmosphere science; plasma physics; ionospheric research and ionospheric modification; communication; electronics; signal and image processing; over 100 publications and reports. *Mailing Add:* Ctr Remote Sensing PO Box 9244 McLean VA 22102. *E-Mail:* remote703@aol.com

GANGWAL, SANTOSH KUMAR, SYNTHETIC FUELS. *Current Pos:* SR CHEM ENGR, RES TRIANGLE INST, 77- *Personal Data:* b Calcutta, India, Mar 26, 47; m 74; c 2. *Educ:* Ind Inst Technol, Tech, 68; Univ Waterloo, MASc, 71, PhD(chem eng), 77. *Prof Exp:* Res assoc chem eng, Va Polytech Inst & State Univ, 76, fel, 77. *Concurrent Pos:* Adj prof, Appalachian State Univ, 79-, Duke Univ, 80- *Mem:* Am Chem Soc; Am Inst Chem Eng. *Res:* Coal gasification; synthetic fuels; heterogeneous catalysis; chromatography. *Mailing Add:* 105 S Coslett Ct Cary NC 27513

GANGWAR, ANSHUMALI, FINANCIAL & TECHNICAL INFORMATION SYSTEMS, MINERAL ECONOMICS & OPERATIONS RESEARCH. *Current Pos:* LEAD SR ANALYST INFO SYSTS, ASARCO, 86- *Personal Data:* b Aligarh, India, July 29, 45, US citizen; m 73, Inger E Buus; c Hans B. *Educ:* Agra Univ, India, BS, 62; Indian Sch Mines, BS, 66; Columbia Univ, MS, 69, Eng ScD(mining eng), 73. *Prof Exp:* Engr trainee, Sendra Bansjora Colliery, India, 66-68; safety officer, Cent Kooridih Colliery, India, 68; teaching asst, Columbia Univ, 69-71, preceptor, 71-73, lectr, 73-75; tech systs analyst, Asarco, 72-77, lead sr analyst info systs, 78-80; assoc prof mineral econs, Colo Sch Mines, 80-88. *Concurrent Pos:* Consult, Sigma Tech Inc, 75-80, Asarco Inc, 80-86. *Mem:* Soc Mining Engrs; Inst Cert Comput Profs. *Res:* Information systems for business planning and development. *Mailing Add:* 197 Shenandoah Blvd Toms River NJ 08754-1788

GANGWER, THOMAS E, PHYSICAL CHEMISTRY. *Current Pos:* Res assoc basic chem, 73-75, ASSOC CHEMIST, DEPT ENERGY & ENVIRON. *Personal Data:* b Scranton, Pa, Oct 20, 46; m 69; c 3. *Educ:* Lebanon Valley Col, BS, 68; Univ Notre Dame, PhD(phys chem), 73. *Mem:* AAAS; Am Chem Soc. *Res:* Study of basic coal chemistry and of basic and applied radiation chemistry and photochemistry; microprocessor interfacing and machine language programming. *Mailing Add:* 739 Battle Front Trail Knoxville TN 37922-6657

GANGWERE, STANLEY KENNETH, ZOOLOGY, ENTOMOLOGY. *Current Pos:* from instr to assoc prof, 55-67, dir, Northwoods Biol Sta, 80-85, PROF BIOL, WAYNE STATE UNIV, 67-, ASSOC CHMN BIOL SCI, 85-, DIR, BIOL STA, 90- *Personal Data:* b Canton, Ohio, Nov 12, 25; m 49, Jacqueline D Williams; c Leslie A. *Educ:* Univ Mich, AB, 50, MS, 52, PhD(zool), 57. *Prof Exp:* Asst, Univ Mich, 51-55. *Concurrent Pos:* Fulbright sr lectr, Univ Valencia, 61; Fulbright res scholar, Span Entom Inst, Madrid, 62; sr lectr, La Plata Nat Univ, Arg Fulbright Prog, 74-; mem Adv Screening Comt, Coun Int Exchange Scholars, Washington, 75-; mem, Species Survival Comn, Int Union Conserv Nature & Natural Resources, Switz, 91- *Mem:* Pan Am Acridological Soc (pres, 77-79, exec secy, 80-85); Orthopterists Soc. *Res:* Ecology, biogeography and feeding behavior in orthopteroid insects, especially of Mediterranean subregion and related islands. *Mailing Add:* Dept Biol Sci Wayne State Univ Detroit MI 48202. *Fax:* 313-577-6891

GANIS, FRANK MICHAEL GANGAROSA, BIOCHEMISTRY & MEDICAL ADMINISTRATION, EDUCATIONAL & RESEARCH ADMINISTRATION. *Current Pos:* RETIRED. *Personal Data:* b Rochester, NY, Nov 26, 24; m 49, Josephine Ferraro; c 2. *Educ:* Univ Rochester, AB, 49, PhD(biochem), 56. *Prof Exp:* Asst, Univ Rochester, 50-51, res assoc, 51-56, from instr biochem, 56-62, from instr to asst prof radiation biol, 59-62; dir labs, Clin Study Ctr, Univ Md, Baltimore, 62-66, asst prof biochem, Sch Med & chmn, Dept Biochem, Sch Dent, 66-73; assoc dean sci, Univ Hartford, 73-75; dean, Sch Health Sci, Western Carolina Univ, 76-78; dean acad affairs, Ohio Col Podiatric Med, 78-85, vpres, 80-85, prof biochem, 78-84. *Concurrent Pos:* USPHS fel, Univ Rochester, 56-58; adj clin res assoc, Cleveland Clin Found, 84-90; consult. *Res:* Intermediary metabolism of steroid hormones. *Mailing Add:* 8696 Camelot Dr Chesterland OH 44026

GANLEY, JAMES POWELL, OPHTHALMOLOGY, UVEITIS. *Current Pos:* assoc prof, 80-82, asst dean med affairs, 81-88, HEAD, DEPT OPHTHAL, MED CTR, LA STATE UNIV, SHREVEPORT, 80-, PROF OPHTHAL, 82- *Personal Data:* b Altadina, Calif, Apr 25, 37; m 65, Anne H Hunter; c Anne, Susan, Katherine & Elizabeth. *Educ:* Mt St Mary's Col, Md, BS, 59; Georgetown Univ, MD, 63; Johns Hopkins Univ, MPH, 69, DrPH, 72. *Prof Exp:* Intern, Wash Hosp Ctr, Washington, DC, 63-64; resident ophthal, Upstate Med Ctr, State Univ NY, Syracuse, 65-68; resident prev med, Johns Hopkins Univ, 69-71; sr staff fel, Nat Eye Inst, NIH, 71-74; asst prof ophthal, Sch Med, Univ Ariz, 74-80. *Concurrent Pos:* Mem, Sci Adv Panel, Onchocerciasis Control Prog, WHO, 74-79, Ophthal Drugs Adv Comt, Food & Drug Admin, 76-83, adv comt, La Dept Health & Human Resources, 80-, Epidemiol & Dis Control Study Sect-1, NIH, 82-86, Comt Res, Regulatory Agencies & Fed Systs, Am Acad Ophthal, 86- & assoc secy, 90-92, Reviewers Res, NIH, 90-94; mem bd dirs, La Asn Blind, 80-96, chmn, Human Serv Prog Comt, 85-88, first vchmn & secy, Exec Bd, 89-91, chmn, 91-93; asst dean med affairs, La State Univ Med Ctr, 81-88; mem, bd dir, Northwest La Eye Bank, 87-88 & Shreveport Med Soc, 90-96, first vpres, 94, pres, 95; ed, Opthal Epidemiol, 94- *Mem:* Int Soc Geog Ophthal (pres, 82-88, treas, 90-); Am Acad Ophthal; Am Col Epidemiol; Am Col Prev Med; Int Eye Found; Am Uveitis Soc. *Res:* Ophthalmic epidemiology; uveitis; onchocerciasis; ocular malignant melanoma. *Mailing Add:* Dept Ophthal La State Univ Med Ctr 1501 Kings Hwy Shreveport LA 71130. *Fax:* 318-674-6000

GANLEY, OSWALD HAROLD, BACTERIOLOGY, PHYSIOLOGY. *Personal Data:* b Amsterdam, Holland, Jan 28, 29; nat US; m 55, Gladys Dickens; c 2. *Educ:* Hope Col, AB, 50; Univ Mich, MS, 51, PhD, 53; Harvard Univ, MPA, 65. *Prof Exp:* Asst med bact, Walter Reed Inst Res, 53-55; res assoc allergy & immunol, Merck Inst, 55-60, asst dir sci rels, Merck Sharp & Dohme Res Labs, 60-64; fel sci & pub policy, Harvard Univ, 64-65; spec asst to sci dir, AID, Md, 65-66; chief, Tech Div, Int Sci & Technol Affairs, US Dept State, Washington, DC, 66-69, sci counr, Am Embassy, Rome & Bucharest, 69-73, dir, Off Soviet & E Europ Sci & Technol Affairs, US Dept State, 73-75, dep asst secy of state for sci & technol affairs, 75-78; res assoc, J F Kennedy Sch Govt, Harvard Univ, 78-80, exec dir prog info resources policy, 80-93, lectr pub policy, 80-93. *Mem:* Asn Mil Surgeons US; Am Soc Microbiol; fel Am Acad Microbiol; Am Physiol Soc; Cosmos Club. *Res:* Shock, surgical infections, allergy and host resistance; foreign policy; computers/communication and information. *Mailing Add:* 408 N Estes Dr Chapel Hill NC 27514

GANLEY, W PAUL, GALVANO LUMINESCENCE. *Current Pos:* PROF PHYSICS, ERIE COMMUNITY COL, 74- *Personal Data:* b North Tonawanda, NY, Apr 1, 34; div. *Educ:* State Univ NY, Buffalo, BA, 55, PhD(physics), 60. *Prof Exp:* Physicist, Cornell Aeornaut Lab, 60-61; asst prof physics, Bryn Mawr Col, 61-66; assoc prof & chmn, dept physics, Wilson Col, Pa, 66-72; res physicist, Aeronaut Lab, Cornell Univ, 72-74. *Concurrent Pos:* Asst ed, Am J Physics, 61-66; consult, Calspan Corp, 77. *Mem:* Am Asn Physics Teachers. *Res:* Applied physics; solid state luminescence; acoustics and noise pollution; coherent optics and automatic target recognition; gamma-ray spectroscopy. *Mailing Add:* Dept Physics Erie Community Col S Campus 4140 Southwestern Blvd Orchard Park NY 14127

GANN, DONALD STUART, PHYSIOLOGY, SURGERY. *Current Pos:* PROF SURG & ASSOC CHMN, DEPT SURG, UNIV MD SCH MED, 88-, PROF PHYSIOL, UNIV MD SCH MED, 89- *Personal Data:* b Baltimore, Md, Feb 25, 32; m 59; c 4. *Educ:* Dartmouth Col, AB, 52; Johns Hopkins Univ, MD, 56. *Hon Degrees:* MA, Brown Univ, 80. *Prof Exp:* Investr endocrinol, Nat Heart Inst, 58-60; instr surg, Med Col Va, 63-64; from sr instr to assoc prof surg, Western Res Univ, 64-70; assoc prof surg, Sch Med, Johns Hopkins Univ, 70-74, prof biomed eng, 70-79, prof emergency med, 74-79, dir dept emergency med, 73-79, dir div surg, 74-78, prof surg, 75-79,; dir div emergency med & trauma, 78-79; prof surg & chmn dept, RI Hosp, Brown Univ, 79-88. *Concurrent Pos:* Spec fel, Nat Heart Inst, 63-64, res career develop award, 65-67; from sr instr to prof physiol, Western Res Univ, 64-70, prof & dir biomed eng, 67-70; asst surgeon, Univ Hosp Cleveland, 64-70; surgeon, Johns Hopkins Hosp, 70-79; chief surgeon, RI Hosp, 79-88; chief, Sect Endocrine Surg, Univ Md Hosp, 88- & Sect Trauma Surg, 90- *Mem:* Am Physiol Soc; Am Surg Asn; Am Col Surg; Am Asn Surg Trauma (secy, 81-86, pres, 87-88); Biomed Eng Soc (pres, 71-72); Endocrine Soc; Cent Soc Clin Res. *Res:* Endocrine physiology; electrolyte metabolism; mathematical models in biology and medicine; neuroendocrinology. *Mailing Add:* Dept Surg Univ MD Med Ctr 22 S Greene St Baltimore MD 21201-1544. *Fax:* 301-328-0687

GANN, RICHARD GEORGE, PHYSICAL CHEMISTRY, COMBUSTION. *Current Pos:* chief prog chem, 76-79, head, explor fire res, 80-81, CHIEF, FIRE SCI DIV, NAT INST STAND & TECHNOL, 81- *Personal Data:* b Hartford, Conn, Sept 20, 44; div; c Eric S & Michael B. *Educ:* Trinity Col, Conn, BS, 65; Mass Inst Technol, PhD(phys chem), 70. *Prof Exp:* Res assoc, Univ Pittsburgh, 70-72; res chemist, Naval Res Lab, 72-76. *Concurrent Pos:* Chair, Tech Study Group, Cigarette Safety Act, 84; sr exec fel, Harvard Univ, JFK Sch of Govt. *Mem:* Am Chem Soc; Combustion Inst. *Res:* Development of scientific understanding and engineering measurement methods for fire research. *Mailing Add:* Bldg 224 Room B-250 Nat Inst Stand & Technol Gaithersburg MD 20899. *Fax:* 301-975-4052; *E-Mail:* rgcann@enm.nist.gov

GANNON, JOHN D, COMPUTER SCIENCE. *Current Pos:* From asst prof to assoc prof, 75-88, PROF, DEPT COMPUT SCI, UNIV MD, 88-, CHAIR, 95- *Educ:* Brown Univ, AB, 70, MS, 72; Univ Toronto, PhD(comput sci), 75. *Concurrent Pos:* Prog dir software eng, NSF, 88-89 & 93. *Mem:* Asn Comput Mach. *Mailing Add:* Dept Comput Sci Univ Md College Park MD 20742. *Fax:* 301-405-6707; *E-Mail:* gannon@cs.umd.edu

GANNON, MARY CAROL, NUTRITIONAL BIOCHEMISTRY. *Current Pos:* Chemist, 73-83, NUTRIT BIOCHEMIST, DIV METAB RES, VET ADMIN MED CTR, 83-, DIR, METAB RES LAB, 89-; ASSOC PROF, UNIV MINN, 95- *Personal Data:* US citizen. *Educ:* Univ Minn, BS, 72, PhD(nutrit), 83. *Mem:* Am Inst Nutrit; Am Diabetes Asn; Inst Food Technologists; Europ Diabetes Asn. *Res:* Effect of ingestion of various foods and macronutrients on intermediary metabolism. *Mailing Add:* Metab Res Lab 111G Vet Admin Med Ctr One Veterans Dr Minneapolis MN 55417-2300

GANO, JAMES EDWARD, ORGANIC CHEMISTRY, PHOTOCHEMISTRY. *Current Pos:* From asst prof to assoc prof, 67-76, PROF CHEM, UNIV TOLEDO, 76- *Personal Data:* b Cleveland, Ohio, Sept 6, 41; m 65, Carole Korenevich; c Heather & Andrew. *Educ:* Miami Univ, AB, 63; Univ Ill, MS, 66, PhD(chem), 67. *Concurrent Pos:* Am Chem Soc res grant, 68-70; vis res assoc, Univ Calif, Los Angeles, 74-75; Res Corp res grant, 75-78; dir, Instrumentation Ctr Arts & Sci; dir, Ohio Crystallog Consortium. *Mem:* Am Chem Soc; Am Inst Chemists; Sigma Xi. *Res:* Novel new organic materials; nonlinear optical materials, stilbenes. *Mailing Add:* Dept Chem Univ Toledo Toledo OH 43606. *Fax:* 419-530-4033; *E-Mail:* jgano@uoft02.utoledo.edu

GANO, RICHARD W, CHEMICAL ENGINEERING. *Current Pos:* Res eng, chem res dept, 78-79, res & develop eng, plastics technol eng, mfg eng, MFG SPECIALIST, ELASTOMER & POLYMER PROD DEPT, DUPONT, 79- *Personal Data:* b Wilmington, Del, Jan 4, 56; m 80; c 2. *Educ:* Univ Del, BS, 78; Univ Va, MS, 79. *Mem:* Am Inst Chem Eng; Sigma Xi. *Res:* Catalytic hydrogemation; aerobic permentation. *Mailing Add:* 2582 Park Creek Dr Memphis TN 38139

GANO, ROBERT DANIEL, ORGANIC CHEMISTRY. *Current Pos:* RETIRED. *Personal Data:* b Norfolk, Va, Jan 27, 22; m 53, Marilyn Walseth; c Robert D Jr, Richard W, James H & John W. *Educ:* Univ Richmond, BS, 43; Univ NC, MA, 48. *Prof Exp:* Jr chemist, E I du Pont de Nemours & Co, Inc, 43-44, process chemist, 45-75, sr process chemist, 75-79, sr res & develop chemist, 79-88. *Mem:* Am Chem Soc; Sigma Xi. *Res:* Aromatic nitro, amino and sulfonic acids; azo organic derivatives; new pharmaceutical CPDS (local anesthesics/antimalierials). *Mailing Add:* 1709 Shadybrook Rd Wilmington DE 19803

GANONG, WILLIAM FRANCIS, NEUROENDOCRINOLOGY. *Current Pos:* from asst prof to prof physiol, Sch Med, Univ Calif, San Francisco, 55-82, fac res lectr, 68, chmn dept, 70-87, Lange prof physiol, 82-91, EMER LANGE PROF, SCH MED, UNIV CALIF, SAN FRANCISCO, 91- *Personal Data:* b Northampton, Mass, July 6, 24; m 48, Ruth Jackson; c William F III, Susan (Hardie), Anna (Tokunnga) & James E. *Educ:* Harvard Univ, AB, 45, MD, 49. *Hon Degrees:* DSc, Med Col Ohio, 95. *Honors & Awards:* Boylston Med Soc Prize, 49; IFI Golden Hippocrates Award, Italy, 70; Asn Chmn Departments Physiol Award, 78, 88; A A Berthold Medal, Ger, 85; Lifetime Achievement Award, Coun High Blood Pressure, Am Heart Asn, 95. *Prof Exp:* From intern to jr asst resident med, Peter Bent Brigham Hosp, 49-51; res fel surg, Harvard Med Sch, 52-55, dir, Surg Res Lab, 53-55. *Concurrent Pos:* Co-ed, Frontiers in Neuroendocrinol, 69-, ed-in-chief, Neuroendocrinol, 79-84; mem, US Nat Comt, Int Union Physiol Sci, 75-81, chmn, 76-79; mem, life sci adv comt, NASA, 80-86, comt on space biol & med, NAS, 86-90. *Mem:* Endocrine Soc; Asn Chmn Departments Physiol (pres, 76-77); Int Soc Neuroendocrinol (vpres, 76-80); fel AAAS; Am Soc Pharmacol & Exp Therapeut; Soc Exp Biol & Med; Am Physiol Soc (pres, 77-78); Sigma Xi; Soc Neurosci (treas, 84-85). *Res:* Neuroendocrinology; interrelation between endocrine and brain function. *Mailing Add:* 710 Hillside Ave Albany CA 94706-1022. *Fax:* 510-526-4803; *E-Mail:* wfg@regis.berkeley.edu

GANOTE, CHARLES EDGAR, PATHOLOGY. *Current Pos:* PROF PATH, ETENN STATE UNIV, 89-, GRAD FAC MEM, 91- *Personal Data:* b Blanchester, Ohio, Feb 9, 37. *Educ:* Univ Cincinnati, BS, 60; Vanderbilt Univ, MD, 63. *Prof Exp:* Instr path, Sch Med, Vanderbilt Univ, 62-63, intern 65-66; staff assoc, Sect Path Anat, Lab Exp Path, Nat Inst Arthritis & Metab Dis, 66-69; consult pathologist, Baxter Labs, 69; from asst prof to prof path, Med Sch, Northwestern Univ, 69-89. *Concurrent Pos:* Res fel, Sch Med, Vanderbilt Univ, 62-63; asst resident path, NIH, 66; chief, Electron Micros Labs & attend staff, Northwestern Mem Hosp, 69-89; res fel, Cardiothoracic Inst, Inst Cardiol, London, 73-74; vis prof, Nat Heart, Lung & Blood Inst, 79-80; anat path staff mem, Vet Admin Hosp, Mountain Home, Tenn, 89-; mem coun, Int Soc Heart Res, 91- *Mem:* Am Asn Pathologists & Bacteriologists; Am Soc Exp Path; Int Soc Heart Res. *Res:* Author of more than 80 technical publications. *Mailing Add:* Dept Path ETenn State Univ Col Med PO Box 10001 Johnson City TN 37614-0002

GANOZA, M CLELIA, BIOCHEMISTRY, MOLECULAR BIOLOGY. *Current Pos:* assoc prof, 68-74, PROF, BANTING & BEST MED RES, UNIV TORONTO, 74-, PROF MED GENETICS & MICROBIOL, 96. *Personal Data:* b Lima, Peru, Oct 24, 37; m, Andrew J Becker; c Monica. *Educ:* Rollins Col, BS, 59; Duke Univ, PhD(biochem), 63. *Honors & Awards:* Ayerst Award, Can Fedn Biol Chemists, 76. *Prof Exp:* Post doctoral fel biopolymers, Rockefeller Univ, 63-66, res assoc, 66-68. *Concurrent Pos:* USPHS res fel, Duke Univ, 59-63; assoc, Med Res Coun Can, 69-74, career investr, 74-94; vis scientist, Nat Cancer Inst, NIH, 86; vis prof, Max Planck Inst Molecular Genetics, 95- *Mem:* Fel Am Royal Soc; fel Royal Soc Sci; fel Royal Soc Can; Am Fedn Biol Chemists; Can Fedn Biol Chemists; NY Acad Sci; Sigma Xi. *Res:* Biochemistry; molecular biology; author of numerous publications. *Mailing Add:* Banting & Best Dept Med Res Univ Toronto 112 College St Toronto ON M5G 1L6 Can

GANS, CARL, ZOOLOGY. *Current Pos:* prof zool & chmn dept, 71-75, PROF BIOL, UNIV MICH, 75- *Personal Data:* b Hamburg, Ger, Sept 7, 23; nat US; m 61, Kyoko Andow. *Educ:* NY Univ, BME, 44; Columbia Univ, MS, 50; Harvard Univ, PhD(biol), 57. *Hon Degrees:* Dr, Univ Antwerp, 85. *Honors & Awards:* Gold Medal, Royal Soc Zool Anvers, 85. *Prof Exp:* Asst proj mgr, Babcock & Wilcox Co, NY, 47-51, serv engr, 51-55, contract engr, 55; fel biol, Univ Fla, 57-58; from asst prof to prof biol, State Univ NY, Buffalo, 58-71, chmn dept, 70-71. *Concurrent Pos:* Res assoc, Carnegie Mus, Pa, 52-53, Dept Amphibians & Reptiles, Am Mus Natural Hist, 59-, Mus Zool, Univ Kans, 82-; Guggenheim Mem fel, Dept Zool, Univ Brazil, 53-54; Field Asn Dept Physics, Univ Sydney & Australian Mus, 78-79; consult, Buffalo Mus Sci, 59-66, Buffalo Zool Park, 59-71, Time-Life, Ins, 65-67, Royal Soc Zool Anvers, 69-73; res fel, Dept Zool, Univ Leiden, Holland, vis prof, Dept Zool, Univ Tel Aviv, vis res, Dept Zool, Univ Bristol, sabbatical, 65-66; sr res sci & cur, Mus Zool, Univ Mich, 71-; prof, Nat Mus Natural Hist, Paris, 85; vis prof, Dept Biol, Univ Instelling Antwerpen, Belg, 85-86. *Mem:* Asn Am Anatomists; Am Soc Mech Eng; Soc Study Evolution; Am Soc Ichthyologists & Herpetologists; Am Soc Biomech; Sigma Xi; fel AAAS; Am Inst Biol Sci; Am Soc Zoologists; Am Physiol Soc. *Res:* Behavioral aspects, functional morphology and systematics of reptiles and amphibians; respiration, feeding and burrowing adaptation; concepts of motor coordination; early evolution of vertebrates; herpetology. *Mailing Add:* Dept Zool Univ Tex Austin TX 78712. *E-Mail:* casolus@uts.cc.utexas.edu

GANS, DAVID, MATHEMATICS. *Current Pos:* from instr to assoc prof, 46-74, EMER PROF MATH, WASH SQUARE COL, NY UNIV, 74- *Personal Data:* b New York, NY, Apr 10, 07; m 45. *Educ:* NY Univ, BS, 28, PhD(math), 48; Harvard Univ, AM, 30. *Prof Exp:* Instr math, NY Univ, 28-42 & Univ Ill, 45. *Concurrent Pos:* Fac fel, Fund Adv Ed, 53-54. *Mem:* Math Asn Am; Am Math Soc. *Res:* Modern geometry, especially euclidean, non-euclidean, projective. *Mailing Add:* 828 Dublin St New Orleans LA 70118-1024

GANS, EUGENE HOWARD, PHARMACY, CHEMISTRY. *Current Pos:* PRES, HASTINGS ASSOCS, 87-; CHMN CENT RES, MEDICIS PHARMACEUT, 95- *Personal Data:* b New York, NY, Dec 17, 29; m 54, Roslyn Phillips; c Lois (Kemp). *Educ:* Columbia Univ, BS, 51, MS, 53; Univ Wis, PhD(chem), 56. *Prof Exp:* Lab asst, Col Pharm, Columbia Univ, 51-53; sr scientist group leader, Hoffman-LaRoche, Inc, NJ, 56-60; head, New Prod

Develop Sect, Vick Div Res & Develop Labs, Richardson-Merrell, NY, 60-64, asst dir develop, 64-67, dir, 67-71; assoc dir, Alza Inst Pharmaceut Chem, 71-72; dir invest res, Proctor & Gamble Inc, 72-76; vpres & dir res & develop, Vicks Personal Care, Richardson-Vicks Div, 76-87. *Concurrent Pos:* Chmn proprietary drug task group, Antimicrobial II Rev Panel, Food & Drug Admin, 76-81; chmn, Food & Drug Admin Task Group, Non-Prescription Drug Mfr Asn. *Mem:* Am Pharmaceut Asn; Am Chem Soc; Sigma Xi; NY Acad Sci; Soc Investigative Dermat; Am Acad Dermat. *Res:* Optimizing pharmaceutical and consumer product research and development; corporate research and development management; development of superior drug, toiletry, cosmetic and proprietary products; advanced therapeutic and drug delivery systems; development and management of scientific personnel; synergizing research and development and marketing operations. *Mailing Add:* 5101 N Casa Blanca Dr No 223 Scottsdale AZ 85251

GANS, JOSEPH HERBERT, PHARMACOLOGY. *Current Pos:* RETIRED. *Personal Data:* b Hartford, Conn, Dec 29, 22; c 3. *Educ:* Univ Pa, VMD, 46; Jefferson Med Col, PhD(physiol), 58. *Prof Exp:* Prof pharmacol, Vet Col, State Univ NY, Cornell Univ, 57-61; assoc prof, Sch Med, Ind Univ, 61-67; assoc prof, Col Med, Univ Vt, 67-69, prof, 69-87. *Mem:* AAAS; Am Physiol Soc; Am Soc Pharmacol & Exp Therapeut; Am Soc Nephrology; Soc Exp Biol & Med; Sigma Xi. *Res:* Chemically induced tissue injury and carcinogenesis; role of nucleic acids; kidney function and metabolism. *Mailing Add:* 3625 Terra Granada Apt 1-A Walnut Creek CA 94595

GANS, MANFRED, OXIDATION PROCESSES, SYNTHETIC FIBERS. *Current Pos:* PRES, TECHNOL EVAL & DEVELOP ASN, INC, 86- *Personal Data:* b Borken, Ger, Apr 27, 22; US citizen; m 48; c 2. *Educ:* Univ Manchester, Eng, Hon, 50; Mass Inst Technol, SM & BSr Tech, 51. *Honors & Awards:* Chem Eng Pract Award, Am Inst Chem Engrs, 93. *Prof Exp:* Sr vpres technol, Halcon-Sci Design Co, 51-85. *Concurrent Pos:* Consult, UN Develop Proj, 78- & UN Indust Develop Orgn, 81- *Mem:* Fel Am Inst Chem Engrs. *Res:* Development of oxidation processes for petrochemicals; creation of applied research institutes for chemical and refinery industries in developing countries. *Mailing Add:* 348 Highwood Ave Leonia NJ 07605. *Fax:* 201-792-5677

GANS, PAUL JONATHAN, CHEMICAL PHYSICS. *Current Pos:* from asst prof to assoc prof, 62-73, from asst chmn to chmn dept, 65-70, PROF CHEM, NY UNIV, 73- *Personal Data:* b Chicago, Ill, May 1, 33; m 59; c 2. *Educ:* Ohio State Univ, BSc, 54; Case Inst Technol, PhD(chem), 59. *Prof Exp:* Res assoc chem, Univ Ill, 59-62, instr, 61-62. *Mem:* AAAS; Am Chem Soc; Am Phys Soc; Asn Comput Mach. *Res:* Statistical mechanics; phase transitions; polymeric systems; digital computation; Monte Carlo techniques. *Mailing Add:* Dept Chem New York Univ 4 Washington Pl New York NY 10003-6621

GANS, ROGER FREDERICK, FLUID MECHANICS, DYNAMICS. *Current Pos:* from asst prof to assoc prof mech & aerospace sci, chmn dept, 84-92, PROF, MECH ENG, UNIV ROCHESTER, 86- *Personal Data:* b New York, NY, May 5, 41. *Educ:* Mass Inst Technol, BS, 63; Univ Calif, Los Angeles, MS, 68, PhD(geol), 69. *Prof Exp:* Res assoc geophys & planetary sci, Calif Inst Technol, 69-71; instr appl math, Mass Inst Technol, 71-73, res assoc aeronaut & astronaut, 73-74. *Concurrent Pos:* PI vanow NSF, 76-84; govt & indust consult; sabbatical, Aberdeen Proving Ground & Marshall Space Flight Ctr, 82-83. *Mem:* Am Geophys Union; AAAS; Am Acad Mech; Am Soc Mech Eng; Am Phys Soc. *Res:* Boundary layer theory; lubrication; experimental fluid dynamics; nonlinear dynamics. *Mailing Add:* Mech Engr Prof Univ Rochester Rochester NY 14627. *Fax:* 716-256-2509; *E-Mail:* gans@me.rochester.edu

GANSCHOW, ROGER ELMER, MOLECULAR GENETICS. *Current Pos:* STAFF SCIENTIST, CINCINNATI CHILDREN'S HOSP RES FOUND, 68- *Personal Data:* b Buffalo, NY, Mar 21, 37; m 59, Leonore Hoelty-Nickel; c Pamela & Tod. *Educ:* Valparaiso Univ, BA, 59; State Univ NY Buffalo, PhD(biol), 67. *Prof Exp:* Am Cancer Soc fel biochem, Sch Med, Stanford Univ, 67-68. *Concurrent Pos:* Asst prof, Med Sch, Univ Cincinnati, 68-71, assoc prof, 71-76, prof, 76-; Nat Inst Arthritis & Metab Dis res grant, 70-; assoc ed, Genetics, 78-; mem, Mammalian Genetics Study Sect, NIH, 80-82, Biol Sci I Study Sect, 92-96. *Mem:* Am Soc Biochem & Molecular Biol; Genetics Soc Am; Endocrinol Soc. *Res:* Regulation of mammalian gene expression. *Mailing Add:* Dept Pediat Children's Hosp Res Found 3333 Burnet Ave Cincinnati OH 45229-3039. *Fax:* 513-559-4317; *E-Mail:* ganschow@chmcc.org

GANT, FRED ALLAN, PHYSICAL CHEMISTRY, THERMODYNAMICS. *Current Pos:* RETIRED. *Personal Data:* b Howard, Ala, Aug 7, 36; m 70; c 2. *Educ:* Univ Ala, BS, 62, MS, 65, PhD(phys chem), 67. *Prof Exp:* Chemist, Cent Labs, Swift & Co, 60-61; asst prof chem, Mobile Col, 66-67; prof, Jacksonville State Univ, 67-97. *Concurrent Pos:* Chmn, Health Careers Comt. *Mem:* Am Chem Soc (pres, Ala Sect, 78-79). *Res:* Thermodynamic studies of inorganic compounds using a copper block calorimeter; fused salt; reaction calorimetry; atomic absorption and gas chromatography. *Mailing Add:* Dept Chem Jacksonville State Univ Jacksonville AL 36265-1573

GANT, KATHY SAVAGE, PHYSICS, HEALTH PHYSICS. *Current Pos:* Guest appointment, Atomic & Molecular Physics, 72-76, RES STAFF, CIVIL DEFENSE, RADIOL EMER PLANNING & TECHNOL, EMER PREPAREDNESS EXERCISES, OAK RIDGE NAT LAB, 76- *Personal Data:* b Nashville, Tenn, Jan 5, 47; m 69; c 2. *Educ:* Austin Peay State Univ, BA, 69; Univ Tenn, Knoxville, MS, 71, PhD(physics), 76. *Concurrent Pos:* AEC radiol sci & protection fel, 69-71; USPHS radiol health fel, 71-74; Oak Ridge Assoc Univ grad res partic, 75-76. *Mem:* Sigma Xi; Health Physics Soc. *Res:* Radiation effects; radiological emergency planning; civil defense; emergency technology; electron mobilities and attachment rates in polyatomic gases; excimer formation; fluorescence; emergency preparedness exercises; design of federal radiological exercises. *Mailing Add:* 523 E Scott Ave Knoxville TN 37917-5641

GANT, NORMAN FERRELL, JR, MATERNAL FETAL MEDICINE. *Current Pos:* Fel reproductive physiol, Univ Tex Health Sci Ctr, Dallas, 68-69 & 72-73, from asst prof to assoc prof, 68-76, chmn dept, 77-83, PROF OBSTET & GYNEC, UNIV TEX HEALTH SCI CTR, DALLAS, 76- *Personal Data:* b Wichita Falls, Tex, Feb 16, 39. *Educ:* NTex State Univ, BA, 62; Univ Tex Southwestern Med Sch, MD, 64, MD(obstet & gynec), 68; Am Col Obstet & Gynec, dipl; FRCOG. *Concurrent Pos:* Prin investr, NIH grant, 74- & Robert Wood Johnson grant, 75-80; co-investr, NIH grant, 74-79 & 77-82; co-prin investr, 87, 88 & 92; exec dir, Am Bd Obstet & Gynec, 93- *Mem:* AMA; fel Am Col Obstetricians & Gynecologists; Soc Gynec Invest; Endocrine Soc; Soc Perinatal Obstetricians; Int Soc Study Hypertension Pregnancy. *Res:* Maternal-fetal medicine; pregnancy induced hypertension; endocrinology of pregnancy; definition of the pathophysiology of pregnancy-induced hypertension and a search for the etiology of this hypertensive complication of pregnancy; anti-phosphor lipid antibody syndromes and their relationship to high risk pregnancy. *Mailing Add:* 2915 Vine St Univ Tex Southwestern Med 5323 Harry Hines E Dallas TX 75204-1069

GANTEN, DETLEV, MOLECULAR BIOLOGY, PHARMACOLOGY. *Current Pos:* STAFF, MAX DELBRUCK CTR MOLECULAR MED, BERLIN-BUCH, 91; PROF CLIN PHARMACOL, FREE UNIV BERLIN, 93- *Personal Data:* b Luneburg, Fed Repub Ger, Mar 28, 41; m, Ursula; c 2. *Educ:* Univ Tubingen, Fed Repub Ger, MD, 68; McGill Univ, Montreal, Can, PhD, 73; Univ Heidelberg, Habilitation, 74. *Honors & Awards:* Chavez Award, Int Soc Hypertension, 81; Sechenev Mem Medal, USSR Acad Med Sci, 81; Wissenschaftspreis, Ger Hypertension League, 82; Heilmeyer Medal, Ger Soc Advan Int Med, 90; Max Planck Sci Award, 90; Okamoto Award, Japan, 90; CIBA Award, Coun High Blood Pressure Res, Am Heart Asn. *Prof Exp:* Mem staff, Nephrological Sect, Hotel Dieu Hosp, Univ Montreal, Can, 69-73; prof, Dept Pharmacol, Univ Heidelberg, 73-91. *Concurrent Pos:* Deleg, Concerted Action Comt Biol Europ Community, Ger Res Found & Fed Govt; mem, Coun High Blood Pressure Res, Am Heart Asn; regional ed, Clin & Exp Hypertension; ed, Current Topics Neuroendocrinol; vis lectr, Univ Vancouver, Univ Wash & Univ Portland, 85. *Mem:* Am Heart Asn; Int Soc Hypertension; NY Acad Sci; Am Soc Pharmacol & Exp Therapeut; Europ Neurosci Asn; Europ Soc Clin Invest. *Res:* Molecular biology and pharmacology of neuropeptides; renin-angiotensin system; transgenic animals; pathophysiology of hypertension. *Mailing Add:* Max Delbruck Ctr Molecular Med Robert-Rossle Str 10 13125 Berlin Germany. *Fax:* 6221-563944

GANTHER, HOWARD EDWARD, TRACE ELEMENTS, HEAVY METALS. *Current Pos:* SR SCIENTIST, DEPT NUTRIT SCI, UNIV WIS, 93- *Personal Data:* b Adrian, Mo, Jan 17, 37; m 64; c 2. *Educ:* Univ Mo, BS, 58; Univ Wis, MS, 61, PhD(biochem), 63. *Honors & Awards:* Mead Johnson Award, Am Inst Nutrit, 75. *Prof Exp:* Res assoc biol chem, Univ Mich, Ann Arbor, 63-64; assoc staff scientist, Jackson Lab, Bar Harbor, Maine, 64-65; asst prof biochem, Med Sch, Univ Louisville, 65-69; assoc prof, Univ Wis-Madison, 69-73, chmn dept, 82-85, prof nutrit sci, 73-90; prof prev med & community health, Univ Tex Med Br, Galveston, 91-93. *Mem:* Am Soc Biol Chemists; Am Inst Nutrit. *Res:* Selenium biochemistry; nutrition, metabolism, toxicity, interactions, functions and anticarcinogenicity; toxicology of heavy metals (mercury, cadmium); functions of glutathione and other sulfur compounds. *Mailing Add:* Dept Nutrit Sci Univ Wis 1415 Linden Dr Madison WI 53706

GANTNER, GEORGE E, JR, medicine, pathology; deceased, see previous edition for last biography

GANTT, ELISABETH, PLANT PHYSIOLOGY, BIOLOGICAL STRUCTURE. *Current Pos:* PROF PLANT BIOL, UNIV MD, 88- *Personal Data:* b Gakovo, Yugoslavia, Nov 26, 34; m 58, R Raymond; c 1. *Educ:* Blackburn Col, BA, 58; Northwestern Univ, MSc, 60, PhD(biol), 63. *Honors & Awards:* Darbaker Prize, Bot Soc, 81; Career Advan Award, NSF, 90; G M Smith Medal, Nat Acad Sci, 94. *Prof Exp:* NIH res assoc microbiol, Med Sch, Dartmouth Col, 63-66; NIH res assoc microbiol, Radiation Biol Lab, Smithsonian Inst, 66-88. *Concurrent Pos:* Mem bd fels & assocs, Nat Res Coun, 73-76; vis sr scientist, NIBB, Okazaki, Japan, 82; vis prof plant biol, Cornell Univ, 83. *Mem:* Nat Acad Sci; fel AAAS; Am Inst Biol Sci; Am Soc Photobiol; Am Soc Plant Physiologists (secy, 85-87, vpres, 88, pres, 88-89); Phycol Soc Am (vpres, 77, pres, 78); Japan Soc Plant Physiologists. *Res:* Structure of photosynthetic apparatus; localization and characterization of phycobiliproteins; membrane structure. *Mailing Add:* Dept Microbiol Univ Md College Park MD 20742. *Fax:* 301-314-9082

GANTT, RALPH RAYMOND, BIOCHEMISTRY. *Current Pos:* PROF DIR/CHEMIST, NAT CANCER INST, 66- *Personal Data:* b Chicago, Ill, Apr 2, 36; m 58. *Educ:* Blackburn Col, BA, 58; Univ Ill, Chicago, PhD(biochem, org chem), 64. *Prof Exp:* Am Cancer Soc fel, Dartmouth Med Sch, 63-66. *Mem:* Am Chem Soc; Tissue Cult Asn; Am Soc Biol Chemists. *Res:* Nucleic acid and protein synthesis; carcinogenesis. *Mailing Add:* Nat Cancer Inst NIH Bldg EPN Rm 530 Bethesda MD 20892-0001

GANTZ, RALPH LEE, weed science, entomology, for more information see previous edition

GANTZEL, PETER KELLOGG, PHYSICAL CHEMISTRY. *Current Pos:* RETIRED. *Personal Data:* b Pasadena, Calif, June 23, 34; m 56; c 3. *Educ:* Univ Colo, BA, 56; Univ Calif, Los Angeles, PhD(crystallog), 62. *Prof Exp:* Staff mem, Ga Technol, 62-86. *Mem:* Am Crystallog Asn. *Res:* X-ray diffraction and fluorescence analysis; electron diffraction and microscopy, computer programming for these areas; gamma-ray and optical emission spectroscopy. *Mailing Add:* 8308 Paseo del Ocaso La Jolla CA 92037

GANTZER, MARY LOU, CLINICAL CHEMISTRY, OUTCOMES RESEARCH. *Current Pos:* MGR, CLIN & OUTCOMES RES, BAYER CORP, 96- *Personal Data:* b Minneapolis, Minn, Oct 3, 50. *Educ:* Univ Minn, BChem, 72, MS, 76; Univ Va, PhD(chem), 80. *Prof Exp:* Instr, Biochem Lab, Dept Chem, Univ Va, 80-81; sr res scientist, Diag Div, Miles Inc, 84-86, staff scientist, 86-87, supvr res & develop, Diag Div, 87-93, proj mgr prod develop, 93. *Concurrent Pos:* Mem, People to People Women Mgt Deleg, People's Repub China, 88- *Mem:* Am Chem Soc; Am Asn Clin Chem. *Res:* Clinical chemistry; urinalysis; membrane biochemistry; enzymology; enzyme kinetics; cancer detection; outcomes research. *Mailing Add:* Bayer Corp Diag Div PO Box 70 Elkhart IN 46515. *Fax:* 219-262-7826; *E-Mail:* marylou.gantzer.b@bayer.com

GANZ, AARON, research administration; deceased, see previous edition for last biography

GANZ, CHARLES ROBERT, ANALYTICAL CHEMISTRY, ORGANIC CHEMISTRY. *Current Pos:* PRES, EN-CAS ANALYSIS LABS, 75- *Personal Data:* b Brooklyn, NY, Dec 20, 42; m 63; c 2. *Educ:* NY Univ, BA, 63; Queen's Col, NY, MA, 66; Adelphi Univ, PhD(org chem), 69. *Prof Exp:* Res asst pharmaceut, Pfizer & Co, 63-66; asst chem, Adelphi Univ, 67-68, NASA res fel, 66-67, Petrol Res Fund fel, 68-69; group leader anal res, Ciba-Geigy Corp, 69-75. *Concurrent Pos:* Lectr, Penton Learning Systs, 77- *Mem:* Am Chem Soc; AAAS; Water Pollution Control Fedn; Am Asn Textile Chemists & Colorists. *Res:* Development and improvement of methods for analyzing trace organic and inorganic chemicals in various matrices; development of methods for environmental safety screening of chemical substances; pollutant measurement and detection. *Mailing Add:* 3702 Chiswell Ct Greensboro NC 27410

GAO, HOWARD X, COLLOID SCIENCE, INK FORMULATION. *Current Pos:* MAT SCIENTIST, INT IMAGING MAT INC, 95- *Educ:* Tsinghua Univ, BS, 84; E China Inst Chem Technol, MS, 87; Univ Southern Calif, PhD(chem), 93. *Prof Exp:* Chem lab supvr, E China Inst Chem Technol, 87-89; postdoctoral, Univ Ill, Chicago, 93-95. *Mem:* Am Chem Soc. *Mailing Add:* 310 Commerce Dr Amherst NY 14051. *Fax:* 716-691-1060; *E-Mail:* xinnas_gao@iimak.cemail.compuserve.com

GAO, HUAJIAN, FRACTURE MECHANICS, MECHANICS OF THIN FILM MATERIALS. *Current Pos:* asst prof, 88-94, ASSOC PROF APPL MECH, STANFORD UNIV, 95- *Personal Data:* m 89, Joan H Cheung; c Jonathan M & Elizabeth H. *Educ:* Xian Jiaotong Univ, BS, 82; Harvard Univ, SM, 84, PhD(eng sci), 88. *Honors & Awards:* Young Investr Award, NSF, 93; Alcoa Sci Award, 96. *Prof Exp:* Asst lectr, Xian Jiaotong Univ, 83; postdoctoral fel, Harvard Univ, 88. *Concurrent Pos:* Schlumberger fel, 88; IBM Fac Award, 90; Guggenheim fel, 95; sr vis scientist, Cambridge Univ, 95-96; consult, Intel Inc & Lightspeed Semiconductor Inc. 96; vis assoc prof, Univ Paderborn, Ger & Hong Kong Univ Sci & Technol, 96. *Mem:* Am Soc Mech Engrs; Am Geophys Union; Mat Res Soc; Am Inst Physics; Am Phys Soc; AAAS. *Res:* Micromechanics and fracture; mechanisms of deformation and fracture of materials at multiple length scales. *Mailing Add:* 420 Monroe Dr Palo Alto CA 94306. *E-Mail:* gao@am_sun2.stanford.edu

GAO, JIALI, COMPUTATIONAL CHEMISTRY, MOLECULAR MODELING. *Current Pos:* ASST PROF CHEM, DEPT CHEM, STATE UNIV NY, BUFFALO, 90- *Personal Data:* b Jixi, China, Jan 4, 62. *Educ:* Beijing Univ, China, BS, 82; Purdue Univ, West Lafayette, PhD(org chem), 87. *Prof Exp:* Postdoctoral fel chem, Dept Chem, Harvard Univ, 87-90. *Mem:* Am Chem Soc. *Res:* Quantum mechanical and statistical mechanical studies of organic reactions in solution; protein dynamics; mechanisms of enzyme-catalyzed reactions; molecular modeling. *Mailing Add:* Dept Chem Nat Sci & Math Complex Buffalo NY 14260. *E-Mail:* jiali@tams.chem.buffalo.edu

GAO, KUIXIONG, IMMUNOHISTOCHEMISTRY, LIGHT & ELECTRON MICROSCOPY. *Current Pos:* DIR, TOP-BIO CO, 96- *Personal Data:* b Shanghai, China, May 3, 37; US citizen; m 67; c 2. *Educ:* Nanjing Univ, China, BS, 60, MS, 62; Chinese Acad Sci, Shanghai, PhD(immunol & embryol), 66. *Prof Exp:* Res assoc gas-liquid chromatog & steroids, Shanghai Inst Cell Biol, Chinese Acad Sci, 66-78, asst prof membrane biol, 78-84; asst prof liposome, Dept Biochem, Univ Tenn, 84-86, sr res scientist, Dept Animal Sci, 88-91; res asst prof, Univ Cincinnati, 91-96. *Concurrent Pos:* Consult, J Longevity, China, 82-83 & Zymed Labs, Inc, 91-; vis scientist, Dept Anat, Univ NC, Chapel Hill, 86-87; vis scientist, Dept Physiol, 87-88. *Mem:* NY Acad Sci; Am Soc Cell Biol; Am Soc Electron Micros. *Res:* Immunocytochemical study on antigenic sites in cells; water soluble embedding method for light and electron microscopy; membrane biogenesis; neuromuscular junction study; gas chromatographic analysis of steroids and prostoglanding; embryonic induction; solid core liposomes; one step stain and mount. *Mailing Add:* TOP-BIO Co 4820 Powderhorn Dr Cincinnati OH 45244

GAO, QUANYIN, semiconductor surface chemistry, spectroscopic characterization of bonding structures, for more information see previous edition

GAO, YI-TIAN, PHYSICS, COMPUTER SCIENCE. *Current Pos:* PROF PHYSICS, BEIJING UNIV AERONAUT & ASTRONAUT, CHINA, 96- *Personal Data:* b Beijing, China, May 6, 59. *Educ:* Nankai Univ, China, BSc, 82; City Univ NY, MA, 86; Univ Calif, Los Angeles, MS, 88, PhD, 91. *Honors & Awards:* Julius Goodman Mem Prize Theoret Physics, 91. *Prof Exp:* Postdoctoral res fel, Univ Mich, 91-93; guest scientist, Fermi Nat Accelerator Lab, 93; prof physics & dep dir, Inst Sci & Eng Comput, Lanzhou Univ, China, 93-96. *Concurrent Pos:* Outstanding young fac fel, State Educ Comn, China, 94-97; vis res prof, Lab Computational Physics, Inst Appl Physics & Computational Math, China, 96- *Res:* Theoretical physics. *Mailing Add:* Dept Appl Math & Physics Beijing Univ Aeronaut & Astronaut Beijing 00083 China

GAPOSCHKIN, PETER JOHN ARTHUR, GROUP THEORY, QUANTUM MECHANICS. *Current Pos:* PROGRAMMER ANALYST COMPUT SCI, BUR MGR INFO SYSTS, CITY OF SAN FRANCISCO, 83- *Personal Data:* b Boston, Mass, Apr 5, 40. *Educ:* Mass Inst Technol, BSc, 61; Univ Calif, Berkeley, MA, 65, MA, 66, PhD(physics), 71. *Prof Exp:* Res asst astron, Nat Radio Astron Observ, 62 & Lick Observ, Mt Hamilton, 63; reader math & physics, Univ Calif, Berkeley, 64-71, res asst physics, Lawrence Berkeley Lab, 65-70, teaching asst physics & res asst math, 70; indust physicist, Naval Plant Rep Off, US Navy, Sunnyvale, Calif, 73-75, comput programmer, FNOC, Naval Postgrad Sch, 75-79; sr prog analyst, Informatics PMI, 79-80; instr physics & comput sci, Merritt Col, Oakland, 80-81; instr comput sci, City Col San Francisco, 81-82. *Concurrent Pos:* Asst programmer, Univ Calif, 76-77, programmer, Lawrence Berkeley Lab, 84; co-worker, physics res proj, Stanford Univ, 85- *Mem:* Am Astron Soc; Am Math Soc; Math Asn Am; Asn Comput Mach; Data Processing Mgt Asn; Sigma Xi. *Res:* Group theory. *Mailing Add:* 1442 A Walnut St Suite 371 Berkeley CA 94709-1496

GAPP, DAVID ALGER, COMPARATIVE ENDOCRINOLOGY, IMMUNOHISTOCHEMISTRY. *Current Pos:* asst prof, 78-86, ASSOC PROF BIOL, HAMILTON COL, 86-, CHMN, DEPT BIOL, 90- *Personal Data:* b Washington, DC, Sept 22, 45; m 79; c 2. *Educ:* Col William & Mary, BS, 67, MA, 70; Boston Univ, PhD(biol), 77. *Prof Exp:* Postdoctoral endocrinol, Boston Univ, 77, Jackson Lab, 77-79. *Concurrent Pos:* Lectr biol, Col William & Mary, 68-69; vis colleague, Histochem Dept, Hammersmith Hosp, Royal Postgraduate Med Sch, Univ London, 83. *Mem:* Sigma Xi; Endocrine Soc; Am Soc Zoologists; Am Diabetes Asn; Soc Study Amphibians & Reptiles; AAAS. *Res:* Comparative endocrinology of peptide hormones in the gastro- enteropancreatic endocrine system of reptiles; focus on the presence and distribution of regulatory peptides in turtles; the regulation of insulin secretion from turtle pancreas and gut. *Mailing Add:* Dept Biol Hamilton Col 198 College Hill Rd Clinton NY 13323-1218

GARA, AARON DELANO, RESEARCH ADMINISTRATION. *Current Pos:* PRIN, MICHIGAN GROUP, 93- *Personal Data:* b Lamberton, Pa, Aug 9, 35; m 56, 85; c 4. *Educ:* Drexel Inst Technol, BS, 58; Wash Univ, PhD(physics), 65. *Prof Exp:* Sr res physicist & proj mgr res labs, Gen Motors Corp, 65-83; tech dir, vpres, Newport Corp, 83-93. *Concurrent Pos:* Instr, Lawrence Inst Technol, 72- *Mem:* Fel Optical Soc Am; Soc Photo-Optical Instrument Eng; Am Phys Soc; Int Comn on Optics. *Res:* Optical information processing; optical data storage; electrooptic materials; laser physics; holography. *Mailing Add:* 361 Hilldale Dr Ann Arbor MI 48105

GARA, ROBERT I, FOREST MANAGEMENT, FOREST ENTOMOLOGY. *Current Pos:* PROF FOREST ENTOM, COL FOREST RESOURCES, UNIV WASH, 68- *Personal Data:* b Santiago, Chile, Dec 16, 31; m 58, 79, Marcela Garcia-Huidobro; c Jennifer, Katheryn, Robert Jr & Marcela. *Educ:* Utah State Univ, BS, 53; Oregon State Univ, MS, 62, PhD(entom), 64. *Prof Exp:* Forester, Kirby Lumber Corp, 57-60; res asst forest entom, Boyce Thompson Inst, Plant Res, 60-62, sr scientist, 62-63, proj leader, 63-66; asst prof forest entom, Col Forestry, Syracuse Univ, 66-68. *Concurrent Pos:* Consult, Food & Agr Orgn, Turrialba, Costa Rica, 69-70, Santiago, Chile, 77-78 & Hanoi, VietNam, 90; vis prof, Univ Austral de Chile, Valdivia, 77-78; with USAID, Ecuador, 84-91; consult, Peace Corps, Chile, 89-90. *Mem:* Soc Am Foresters; Entom Soc Am. *Res:* Flight behavior of bark beetles; host selection behavior of forest insects; tropical forest entomology; tropical forestry. *Mailing Add:* Col Forest Resourses Univ Wash Box 352100 Seattle WA 98195. *Fax:* 206-543-3254; *E-Mail:* gara@u.washington.edu

GARABEDIAN, PAUL ROESEL, APPLIED MATHEMATICS. *Current Pos:* PROF MATH, NY UNIV, 59- *Personal Data:* b Cincinnati, Ohio, Aug 2, 27; div. *Educ:* Brown Univ, AB, 46; Harvard Univ, AM, 47, PhD(math), 48. *Honors & Awards:* Birkhoff Prize, Am Math Soc, 83. *Prof Exp:* Nat Res Coun fel, 48-49; asst prof math, Univ Calif, 49-50; from asst prof to prof, Stanford Univ, 50-59. *Concurrent Pos:* Sloan fel, 60-62; Guggenheim fel, 66-67; Sherman Fairchild fel, Calif Inst Technol, 75. *Mem:* Nat Acad Sci; Soc Indust & Appl Math; Am Math Soc; Am Acad Arts & Sci; Am Phys Soc. *Res:* Functions of a complex variable; hydrodynamics; partial differential equations. *Mailing Add:* NY Univ Courant Inst Rm 917 New York NY 10012

GARASCIA, RICHARD JOSEPH, CHEMISTRY. *Current Pos:* from instr to assoc prof, 42-59, chmn dept, 61-66, PROF CHEM, XAVIER UNIV, OHIO, 59- *Personal Data:* b Detroit, Mich, Dec 25, 17; m 42; c 7. *Educ:* Univ Detroit, BS, 40; Univ Mich, MS, 41; Univ Cincinnati, PhD(chem), 50. *Prof Exp:* Instr math, Univ Detroit, 41-42. *Concurrent Pos:* Res chemist, Cook Paint & Varnish Co, Detroit, 41-42. *Mem:* Am Chem Soc. *Res:* Organic synthesis; organic arsenic; phosphorus and antimony compounds; fluorene and acenaphthene chemistry. *Mailing Add:* 1027 Valley Lane Cincinnati OH 45229

GARAVELLI, JOHN STEPHEN, PROTEIN STRUCTURE, BIOMOLECULAR EVOLUTION. *Current Pos:* sr res scientist & database coordr, 89-96, COORDR, NAT BIOMED RES FOUND, 89-, ASSOC DIR, 96- *Personal Data:* b Memphis, Tenn, Sept 7, 47. *Educ:* Duke Univ, BS, 69; Wash Univ, PhD(biochem), 75. *Prof Exp:* Res assoc, Marine Lab, Duke Univ, 75-76; res assoc, Chem Dept, Univ Del, 76-79, lectr gen chem, 79-80; lectr org chem, Tex A&M Univ, 80-81, res assoc, Plant Sci Dept, 81-83; sr res assoc, Extraterrestrial Res Div, Nat Res Ctr, NASA-Ames Res Ctr, 83-85; res assoc & dir comput opers, Agouron Inst, La Jolla, Calif, 86; sr res specialist & syst mgr, Col Pharm, Univ Ill, Chicago, 86-88. *Mem:* AAAS; Am Chem Soc; Int Soc Study Origin of Life; Am Soc Gravitational & Space Biol; Protein Soc; Int Union Pure & Appl Chem. *Res:* Biochemical and biomedical science fields allied with phylogenetics, biogenesis and information theory; protein chemistry; structure and conformation prediction; computer modeling of biomolecules. *Mailing Add:* Box 3783 Washington DC 20007. *E-Mail:* garavelli@nbrf.georgetown.edu

GARAY, ANDREW STEVEN, MOLECULAR CHIRALITY. *Current Pos:* PROF BIOPHYSICS, TEX A&M UNIV, 76- *Personal Data:* b Pecs, Hungary, May 20, 26; nat US; m 68, Margit Toth; c Barnabas, Andras, Borbala, Marton & Ursula. *Educ:* Eotvos Lorand Univ, Budapest, PhD(biochem), 52; Nat Acad, Hungary, DCS, 65. *Prof Exp:* Res scientist pharmaceut, Pharmaceut Res Inst, 53-56; prof plant physiol, Agr Res Sta, Fertod, 56-68; dir biophysics, Biol Res Ctr, Szeged, 68-75. *Concurrent Pos:* Vis prof, Plant Virus Res Inst, Chiba, Japan, 71; Cairo Univ, 72 & Lab D'Optique Phys, Paris, 74; ed, Environ & Radiation Biophysics WGer, 76- *Mem:* Sigma Xi; Am Soc Biophysics; Nat Acad Hungary; Am Phys Soc. *Res:* Origin and role of molecular chirality in biochemical processes. *Mailing Add:* Biochem & Biophys Dept Tex A&M Univ College Station TX 77843

GARAY, GUSTAV JOHN, ENTOMOLOGY, MICROBIOLOGY. *Current Pos:* PROF BIOL, MONROE COMMUNITY COL, 75- *Personal Data:* b Carteret, NJ, May 24, 33; m 58, Marjorie McCarty; c Suzanne M & Gustav C. *Educ:* Columbia Univ, AB, 55; Rutgers Univ, MS, 62, PhD(med entom), 64. *Prof Exp:* Res asst immunol, Rockefeller Univ, 59; res asst entom, Rutgers Univ, 59-64; dir biol div, Ward's Natural Sci Estab, 64-74. *Concurrent Pos:* Sabbatical, Gemencot Imt, 90. *Mem:* Am Soc Microbiol; Sigma Xi; Lepidopterist's Soc; Xerces Soc. *Res:* Mass rearing of insects; laboratory rearing of mosquitoes; Protozoan and Algae culture; photomicrography. *Mailing Add:* 3142 Rush Mendon Rd Honeoye Falls NY 14472-9333

GARAY, LESLIE ANDREW, TAXONOMY. *Current Pos:* EMER CUR, HARVARD UNIV, 88- *Personal Data:* b Hosszuheteny, Hungary, Aug 6, 24; nat US. *Educ:* Tufts Univ, MSc, 61, PhD, 64. *Prof Exp:* Asst, Univ Toronto, 49-51, asst cur, 52-58; cur orchid herbarium oakes ames, Bot Mus, Harvard Univ, 58-88. *Concurrent Pos:* Guggenheim fel, Can, 57-58; mem bd freshman adv, Harvard Univ, 60-63, mem fac arts & sci, 63-, chmn, Int Orchid Comn Classification, Nomenclature & Registration, lectr biol, 65-70; mem, World Orchid Conf, London, 60, Singapore, 63; Int Bot Cong Montreal, Edinburgh, 64; field work in Colombia, Ecuador, Venezuela, Jamaica, Fiji, New Caledonia, New Guinea, Malaya & Ceylon. *Mem:* Int Asn Plant Taxon. *Res:* Taxonomy, phylogeny and evolution of the entire orchid family; orchids of Colombia, Ecuador, Haiti and Okinawa. *Mailing Add:* c/o Harvard Univ Herbaria 22 Divinity Ave Cambridge MA 02138

GARBACCIO, DONALD HOWARD, MECHANICAL ENGINEERING. *Current Pos:* MEM STAFF, C F BRAUN & CO, 77- *Personal Data:* b Paterson, NJ, June 29, 30; m 52; c 4. *Educ:* Newark Col Eng, BSME, 51; Princeton Univ, MSE, 53; Stanford Univ, PhD(eng mech), 55. *Prof Exp:* Res engr, Calif Res Corp, 55-58; sr engr, Rocketdyne Div, NAm Aviation, Inc, 58-60; sr staff mem, Nat Eng Sci Co, 60-64; sr res engr, Sci Eng Assocs Div, Kaman Aircraft Corp, 64-69; sr staff engr, Actron Industs, Inc, 69-77. *Mem:* Am Soc Mech Engrs. *Res:* Structural dynamics; engineering oceanography. *Mailing Add:* 425 Adams St Sierra Madre CA 91024

GARBACZ, ROBERT J, ELECTRICAL ENGINEERING. *Current Pos:* Asst prof, 68-76, ASSOC PROF ELEC ENG, OHIO STATE UNIV, 76-, ASST SUPVR ELECTRO SCI LAB, 55- *Personal Data:* b Buffalo, NY, Sept 12, 33. *Educ:* Univ Buffalo, BS, 55; Ohio State Univ, MS, 57, PhD(electro-magnetic scattering), 68. *Mem:* Inst Elec & Electronics Engrs; Sigma Xi. *Res:* Electromagnetic scattering by antennas; characteristic model expansions of fields scattered by obstacles of arbitrary shape. *Mailing Add:* Dept Elec Eng Ohio State Univ Columbus OH 43210

GARBARINI, EDGAR JOSEPH, CIVIL ENGINEERING. *Current Pos:* RETIRED. *Personal Data:* b Jackson, Calif, Aug 1, 10; m 36; c 2. *Educ:* Univ Calif, Berkeley, BS, 33. *Prof Exp:* Civil engr, Calif Comn, Golden Gate Int Exped, 38-39; engr, Pac Gas & Elec Co, 39-40; engr, Bechtel Group, Inc, 40-84, sr exec consult, 84-95. *Mem:* Nat Acad Eng; fel Am Soc Civil Engrs; Am Soc Mining Engrs. *Mailing Add:* 1170 Sacramento St San Francisco CA 94108-1943

GARBARINI, VICTOR C, HIGH TECHNOLOGY SAFETY ENGINEERING, CHEMICAL CONTAMINATION CONTROL. *Current Pos:* RETIRED. *Personal Data:* b New York, NY, May 24, 26; m 49, Rita Menniti; c Joane, Paul & Victor. *Educ:* Manhattan Col, BS, 44; NY Univ, PhD(chem), 56. *Prof Exp:* Res & chemist, E I du Pont de Nemours & Co, Inc, Del, 51-55; engr, Esso Res & Eng Co, 55-59; mem tech staff, Bell Labs, 59-87. *Concurrent Pos:* Spec safety adv silicon processing technol. *Mem:* Am Chem Soc; Am Soc Safety Engrs; Semiconductor Safety Asn. *Res:* Semiconductor device chemistry; process development and engineering; photolithography; analytical investigations and contamination controls; chemical safety engineering; industrial and commercial process engineering. *Mailing Add:* 3241 Oakland Sq Bethlehem PA 18017-1289

GARBER, ALAN J, BIOCHEMISTRY, CELL BIOLOGY. *Current Pos:* from asst prof to assoc prof med, Baylor Col Med, 74-82, asst prof cell biol, 74-80, prog dir, gen Clin Res Ctr, 77-87, assoc prof biochem & cell biol, 80-82, PROF MED & BIOCHEM & CELL BIOL, BAYLOR COL MED, 82-; CHIEF, DIABETES CLIN, BEN TAUB GEN HOSP, 74- & DIABETES-METAB UNIT, METHODIST HOSP, 85- *Personal Data:* b Philadelphia, Pa, Feb 27, 43; m; c 2. *Educ:* Temple Univ, AB, 64, MD, 68; Fels Res Inst, PhD(physiol chem), 71. *Prof Exp:* Intern med, Temple Univ Hosp, 68-69, resident, 71-72; instr med, Sch Med, Wash Univ, St Louis, 72-74. *Concurrent Pos:* USPHS spec res fel, 72-74; attend physician, Ben Taub Gen Hosp, 74-; investr, Howard Hughes Med Inst, 74-78; counr, Southern Soc Clin Invest, 83-86. *Mem:* Am Fedn Clin Res; Am Diabetes Asn; Endocrine Soc; Southern Soc Clin Invest (pres, 88-89); Am Soc Biochem & Molecular Biol; Am Soc Clin Invest. *Res:* Author of 79 technical publications. *Mailing Add:* Dept Med Biochem & Cell Biol Baylor Col Med 6550 Fannin Suite 1045 Houston TX 77030-2720. *Fax:* 713-790-6211

GARBER, CHARLES A, MATERIALS SCIENCE, POLYMER PHYSICS. *Current Pos:* PRES, STRUCT PROBE, INC, WEST CHESTER, PA, 70- & METUCHEN, NJ, 73- *Personal Data:* b Rock Island, Ill, May 23, 41; m 80. *Educ:* Univ Ill, Urbana, BS, 63; Case Inst Technol, MS, 65, PhD(polymer solid state physics, morphol), 67. *Prof Exp:* Res fel, Case Inst Technol, 63-67; res physicist, Plastics Dept, E I du Pont de Nemours & Co, Inc, Del, 67-70. *Concurrent Pos:* Instr, Cleveland State Univ, 66-67; adj prof, Drexel Inst Technol, 68-69 & Philadelphia Col Textiles & Sci, 69-70; dir, Asn Consult Chemists & Chem Engrs, 77- & Independent Labs Assurance Co, Ltd, 78- *Mem:* Am Chem Soc; Am Inst Chem Eng; Am Phys Soc; Electron Micros Soc Am; Sigma Xi; Soc Cosmetic Chemists; Am Soc Metals. *Res:* Characterization of solid materials with electron optical methods including scanning and transmission electron microscopy, electron probe microanalysis, Auger electron spectroscopy, electron spectroscopy for chemical analysis, thermal analysis and x-ray diffraction. *Mailing Add:* Structure Probe Inc PO Box 656 West Chester PA 19381. *Fax:* 215-436-5409

GARBER, DAVID H, PHYSICS, EDUCATIONAL ADMINISTRATION. *Current Pos:* prog dir, Univ Progs Div, 80-84, CONSULT EDUC & RES PROGS, OAK RIDGE ASSOC UNIV, 84- *Personal Data:* b Norfolk, Va, June 18, 18; m 49; c 2. *Educ:* Univ Pa, AB, 40, AM, 41; Stanford Univ, PhD(physics), 53. *Prof Exp:* Asst physics, Univ Pa, 39-41 & Univ Rochester, 41-42; instr, Stanford Univ, 42-44; physicist, USN Electronics Lab, 44-45; res asst, Stanford Univ, 46-48; instr, Univ Wash, 49-51; res physicist, Cornell Aeronaut Lab, 51-55; sr staff scientist, Gen Dynamics Corp, 55-65; prog mgr, Philco-Ford Corp, 65-66; sci asst to dir, McDonnell Douglas Corp, 66-68, explor sci mgr, 69; consult, Claremont Univ Ctr, 69-70; exec secy Space Sci Bd & consult, Nat Acad Sci, 71-75; asst to vprovost acad admin, Univ Minn, Duluth, 76-80. *Concurrent Pos:* Develop engr, Honeywell, Inc, 41-42; assoc ed, J Spacecraft & Rockets, 67-69; consult, Am Univ, Washington, DC, 75-76. *Mem:* AAAS; Am Asn Physics Teachers; assoc fel Am Inst Aeronaut & Astronaut; Am Phys Soc; Nat Coun Univ Res Admnrs; Sigma Xi. *Res:* Science policy; energy conversion and storage systems; space science and systems; atmospheric physics; atomic nuclear and radiation physics; nuclear magnetic resonance; physical oceanography. *Mailing Add:* 40 Brookside Dr Oak Ridge TN 37830-7670

GARBER, DONALD I, NUCLEAR PHYSICS. *Current Pos:* from asst physicist to assoc physicist, 67-74, PHYSICIST, BROOKHAVEN NAT LAB, 74- *Personal Data:* b Cleveland, Ohio, July 8, 36. *Educ:* Carnegie Inst Technol, BS, 58; Case Inst Technol, MS, 60, PhD(nuclear physics), 64. *Prof Exp:* From instr to asst prof physics, Case Western Res Univ, 64-67. *Mem:* Am Phys Soc. *Res:* Elastic and inelastic scattering of neutrons; polarization measurements of neutrons produced in deuteron reactions; radiative capture; automated nuclear physics publications; interactive computer graphics. *Mailing Add:* 3 Wainscott Lane East Setauket NY 11733

GARBER, EDWARD DAVID, CYTOGENETICS. *Current Pos:* from asst prof to prof, 53-88, EMER PROF BOT, UNIV CHICAGO, 88- *Personal Data:* b New York, NY, Mar 22, 18; m 43, Rosalie Kirshtein; c Joel, Martha & Jane. *Educ:* Cornell Univ, BS, 40; Univ Minn, MS, 42; Univ Calif, PhD(genetics), 49. *Prof Exp:* Asst res scientist & microbial geneticist, Naval Biol Lab, 49-53. *Mem:* Genetics Soc Am; Bot Soc Am; Am Soc Microbiol; Brit Soc Gen Microbiol; Sigma Xi. *Res:* Cytotaxonomy and cytogenetics of sorghum and collinsia; genetics of virulence; fungal genetics. *Mailing Add:* Dept Ecol & Evolution Univ Chicago 5801 Ellis Ave Chicago IL 60637

GARBER, FLOYD WAYNE, HEALTH PHYSICS INSTRUMENTS, MINERALS ASSAY INSTRUMENTS. *Current Pos:* SR SCIENTIST, INTRA SPEC, INC, 92- *Personal Data:* b Winfield, Kan, Aug 31, 41; m 62; c 1. *Educ:* Southwestern Col, BA, 63; Univ Tenn, MS, 65, PhD(physics), 68. *Prof Exp:* Res & develop physicist, EG&G ORTEC, 68-69, detector mfg mgr, 69-80, prog mgr, Wemco I&C Div, 82-83; proj mgr, Technol for Energy Corp, 83-85, dir, Design Eng & Mfg Div, 86-92, corp radiation safety officer, 86-92. *Mem:* Am Phys Soc; Health Physics Soc; Am Soc Mining Engrs; Inst Elec & Electronics Engrs. *Res:* Development, manufacturing and marketing of instruments that measure radiation. *Mailing Add:* 1113 W Outer Dr Oak Ridge TN 37830

GARBER, H(IRSH) NEWTON, OPERATIONS RESEARCH, MANAGEMENT SCIENCE PRACTICE & STRATEGY PLANNING. *Current Pos:* CHMN & PRES, GARBER ASSOCS, INC, 91- *Personal Data:* b Philadelphia, Pa, Mar 16, 30; m 51, Joan Fisher; c 5. *Educ:* Univ Pa, BS, 52; Mass Inst Technol, SM, 53, ScD(elec eng), 56. *Prof Exp:* Oper res analyst, RCA Corp, 56-65, sr scientist, 66-69, mgr opers res, 69-76, dir opers res,

76-86; first vpres & dir mgt sci, Merrill Lynch & Co, Inc, 86-91. *Concurrent Pos:* Chmn, Col Pract Mgt Sci, Inst Mgr Sci, 76-78 & 92-94, pres, 83-84; pres, Inst Mgt Scis, 83-84. *Mem:* Inst Oper Res & the Mgt Sci (pres, 83); Soc Indust & Appl Math; Inst Elec & Electronics Engrs; Sigma Xi. *Res:* Use of scientific methods in the management, planning and operation of industrial, commercial, and government activities. *Mailing Add:* 3 Point Woods Dr North Brunswick NJ 08902-1207. *Fax:* 732-821-3008

GARBER, JOHN DOUGLAS, ORGANIC CHEMISTRY. *Current Pos:* CONSULT, 76- *Personal Data:* b Minneapolis, Minn, May 12, 20; m 43; c 3. *Educ:* Pa State Col, BS, 40; Univ Ill, PhD(chem), 43. *Prof Exp:* Res chemist, Standard Oil Develop Co, 43-47; res dir, E M Wanderman & Co, 47-48; res chemist, Merck & Co, Inc, 48-55, mgr agr & indust org chem develop, 55-64; asst to dir res & develop, Indust Chem Div, Am Cyanamid Co, 64-65, dir, 65-66; gen mgr basic & appl res, Moffett Tech Ctr, CPC Int, Inc, 66-69, sci vpres, Develop Div, 69-73, corp mgr indust res & develop, 73-76. *Mem:* Am Chem Soc. *Res:* Conversion of carbohydrates to furans and their utilization as industrial organics; high temperature polymers and fluids; systemic approaches to plant agricultural chemicals; petrochemicals including specialty resins and organics; food components. *Mailing Add:* 7530 Navigator Circle Carlsbad CA 92009-5404

GARBER, LAWRENCE L, TRANSITION METAL CHEMISTRY. *Current Pos:* from asst prof to assoc prof, Ind Univ, 69-86, chmn, 79-83, asst vchancellor acad affairs, 92-95, PROF CHEM, IND UNIV, SOUTH BEND, 86-, ASSOC VCHANCELLOR ACAD AFFAIRS, 95- *Personal Data:* b Goshen, Ind, July 4, 42; m 65, Carolyn Friedemann; c Natalie Renee. *Educ:* Goshen Col, BA, 63; Mich State Univ, PhD(chem), 67. *Honors & Awards:* Sigma Xi Res Award, 67. *Prof Exp:* Asst prof chem, Goshen Col, 68-69. *Mem:* Am Chem Soc; Sigma Xi. *Res:* Synthesis and characterization of transition metal complexes; water quality studies. *Mailing Add:* Dept Chem Ind Univ South Bend IN 46634-7111. *E-Mail:* lgarber@iusb.edu

GARBER, MEYER, PHYSICS. *Current Pos:* RETIRED. *Personal Data:* b Philadelphia, Pa, June 6, 28. *Educ:* Univ Pa, BS, 49, Univ Ill, MS, 50, PhD(physics), 54. *Prof Exp:* Fulbright fel, Univ Leiden, Neth, 54-55; Nat Res Coun fel, Univ Ottawa, Can, 55-57; prof physics, Mich State Univ, 58-66; physicist, Dept Appl Sci, Brookhaven Nat Lab, 66-, RHIC, 93. *Concurrent Pos:* Mem staff, Div Sponsored Res, Mass Inst Technol, 61-63; vis physicist, Brookhaven Nat Lab, 64. *Mem:* Am Phys Soc; Sigma Xi. *Res:* Low temperature physics. *Mailing Add:* Brookhaven Nat Lab Bldg 902 Upton NY 11973

GARBER, MORRIS JOSEPH, GENETICS, COMPUTER SCIENCES. *Current Pos:* biometrician & prof, 56-80, EMER PROF STATIST, UNIV CALIF, RIVERSIDE, 80- *Personal Data:* b New York, NY, Nov 6, 12; m 43, Gloria R Routman; c David I & Diana L. *Educ:* Agr & Mech Col Tex, PhD(genetics), 51. *Prof Exp:* Asst prof genetics, Agr & Mech Col Tex, 47-56. *Concurrent Pos:* Biometrician, Int Inst Trop Agr, Ibadan, Nigeria, 74-76; statistician, Int Ctr Res, Rice & Beans, Goiania, Goias, Brasil, 80-81. *Mem:* Fel AAAS; Asn Comput Mach; Biomet Soc; Am Statist Asn; Am Genetic Asn. *Res:* Statistical design and analysis in agriculture; computer programming; applied statistics. *Mailing Add:* Dept Statist Univ Calif Riverside CA 92521. *Fax:* 909-787-3286; *E-Mail:* mgarber@ucrstat4.ucr.edu

GARBER, MURRAY S, IMPACT OF COAL MINING ON HYDROLOGIC SYSTEM. *Current Pos:* hydrologist, 83-86, CHIEF HYDROL BR, OFF SURFACE MINING, 86- *Personal Data:* b New York, NY, Nov 10, 34; m 60; c 2. *Educ:* Brooklyn Col, BS, 56; Univ Kans, MS, 62. *Prof Exp:* Hydrologist, US Geol Surv, 56-83. *Mem:* Nat Water Well Asn; fel Geol Soc Am; Am Inst Prof Geologists. *Res:* Impact of coal mining on the hydrologic system. *Mailing Add:* 130 Foxcroft Rd Pittsburgh PA 15220-1704

GARBER, RICHARD HAMMERLE, PLANT PATHOLOGY. *Current Pos:* CONSULT, CALIF PLANTING COTTONSEED DISTRIB, 86- *Personal Data:* b Beaver Falls, Pa, June 22, 21; m 45; c 4. *Educ:* Geneva Col, BS, 47; Colo State Univ, MS, 50; Univ Calif, PhD(plant path), 60. *Prof Exp:* Asst bot & plant path, Colo State Univ, 48-50, resident supt, San Luis Valley Exp Sta, 50-52; plant pathologist, Agr Res Serv, USDA, Univ Calif, 54-86. *Concurrent Pos:* Secy, Cotton Dis Coun, 65-66, chmn, 67-68; mem, US Team, Bi-lateral Conf Plant Protection, Tashkent, Ubekistan, USSR, 80; collabr, Agr Res Serv, USDA; consult, Univ Calif; prog partic, US Dept Can & Peoples Repub China, 95; partic, Australian Cotton Dis Eval, 97. *Mem:* Am Phytopath Soc; Sigma Xi. *Res:* Ecology of plant diseases; seed and soil treatments; fungicides-biological control; new cotton varieties resistant to cotton diseases and nematodes. *Mailing Add:* Calif Planting Cottonseed Distrib 30597 Jack Ave Shafter CA 93263

GARBER, RICHARD LINCOLN, BIOLOGY, MOLECULAR BIOLOGY. *Current Pos:* GENETICS DEPT, UNIV WASH, SEATTLE, 83- *Personal Data:* b Seattle, Wash, May 8, 50; m 78; c 2. *Educ:* Stanford Univ, BS, 72; Yale Univ, MPhil, 76, PhD(biol), 77. *Prof Exp:* Fel biol, Roche Inst Molecular Biol, 77-79. *Concurrent Pos:* Univ Basel, Switz, 79-83. *Mem:* AAAS; Sigma Xi. *Res:* Genetic control of development is studied in fruitfly drosophila; my focus is on the homeotic genes loci which determine the fate of each cell in the organism; control of gene transcription; molecular cloning and nucleic acid sequencing; Japanese silkworm Bombyx mori. *Mailing Add:* Pathogenesis Corp 201 Elliott Ave W STE 150 Seattle WA 98119

GARBER, ROBERT WILLIAM, ANALYTICAL CHEMISTRY, ENVIRONMENTAL CHEMISTRY & RADIOCHEMISTRY. *Current Pos:* PRES, GARBER TECHNOL ASSOC, 94-; SR SCIENTIST, PARALLAX, INC. *Personal Data:* b Philadelphia, Pa, Aug 19, 43; m 66, Sandra Louise Hill; c 2. *Educ:* Philadelphia Col Pharm & Sci, BSc, 65; St Joseph's Col, Pa, MS, 67; Univ Pittsburgh, PhD(anal chem), 75. *Prof Exp:* Environ scientist, Brookhaven Nat Lab, 71-75, chemist air pollution studies, 75-80, res chemist environ studies, 80-88, res chemist, Mat Separation Lab, Nat Fertilizer & Environ Res Ctr, Tenn Valley Authority, 88-94; sr scientist, TN & Assocs, 94-96. *Concurrent Pos:* Adj prof environ chem, Ala A&M Univ, 88- *Mem:* Am Chem Soc. *Res:* Field measurement and analytical methods development for environmental studies, especially air pollution studies; radiochemical laboratory methods; environmental site assessments. *Mailing Add:* 1609 Chandler Rd Knoxville TN 37922

GARBERS, DAVID LORN, BIOLOGICAL CHEMISTRY. *Current Pos:* PROF, HOWARD HUGHES INST, 92- *Personal Data:* b La Crosse, Wis, Mar 17, 44; c 2. *Educ:* Univ Wis, Madison, BS, 66, MS, 70, PhD(biochem), 72. *Prof Exp:* Res assoc physiol, Vanderbilt Univ, 72-74, from asst prof to assoc prof pharmacol, 74-92. *Concurrent Pos:* Investr, Howard Hughes Med Inst, 76-; vis prof, Johns Hopkins Med Sch, 84-85; NIH study sect, 84-87. *Mem:* Nat Acad Sci; Soc Study Reproduction; Am Soc Biol Chemists. *Res:* Molecular biology of fertilization; signal transduction. *Mailing Add:* Howard Hughes Med Inst Univ Tex SW Med Ctr 5323 Harry Hines Blvd Dallas TX 75235-9050

GARBRECHT, WILLIAM LEE, ORGANIC CHEMISTRY. *Current Pos:* RETIRED. *Personal Data:* b Grand Rapids, Mich, Apr 18, 23; m 47; c 3. *Educ:* Kalamazoo Col, AB, 48, MS, 49; Mich State Col, PhD(chem), 53. *Prof Exp:* Org chemist, Eli Lilly & Co, 53-60, develop assoc, 60-68, res assoc, 68-74, res adv, 74-87. *Mem:* Am Chem Soc; AAAS. *Res:* Chemistry of 5-amino tetrazole derivatives; chemistry of ergot alkaloids; chemistry of cephalosporin antibiotics; tetrazole sweeteners. *Mailing Add:* 9411 Poinciana Ct Fort Pierce FL 34951-2946

GARBUNY, MAX, OPTICAL PHYSICS, MOLECULAR PHYSICS. *Current Pos:* develop engr, Westinghouse Elec Corp, 44-46, sr res physicist, 46-52, mgr, Optical Physics Sect, 52-60, CONSULT OPTICAL PHYSICS, SCI & TECHNOL CTR, WESTINGHOUSE ELEC CORP, 60- *Personal Data:* b Koenigsberg, Ger, Nov 22, 12; nat US; m 47, Melitta Lowy; c Vivian J (Prunier), Carole G (Vogel) & Ellen (Garbuny-Best). *Educ:* Tech Univ Berlin, Dipl Ing, 36, Dr Ing, 38. *Prof Exp:* Physicist, Allen-Bradley Co, 39-43; instr physics, Princeton Univ, 43-44. *Concurrent Pos:* Mem nat exec comt, Infrared Info Symposia, 63-70; consult, Sci Adv Panel, US Army, 64-72, mem electronics adv group, Army Electronics Command, 69-74; NY State vis prof, Univ Rochester, 68-69; consult, Edgewood Arsenal, US Army, 72-76. *Mem:* Fel Am Phys Soc; fel Am Optical Soc. *Res:* Atomic physics; microwave devices; spectroscopy; solid state physics; infrared devices; low temperature physics, laser spectroscopy, particularly atomic and molecular resonance phenomena, laser chemistry, remote gas detection and laser engines; development of infrared parametric tunable oscillators; laser induced gas kinetics; laser cooling. *Mailing Add:* 2305 Marbury Rd Pittsburgh PA 15221

GARBUTT, JOHN THOMAS, BIOCHEMISTRY. *Current Pos:* RETIRED. *Personal Data:* b Janesville, Wis, Apr 19, 29; wid; c John Jr, Mary C & Katherine M. *Educ:* Beloit Col, BS, 51; Univ Wis-Madison, MS, 56, PhD(biochem), 58. *Prof Exp:* Sect Leader, Grain Processing Corp, 58-72, Mgr Biochem, 72-95. *Concurrent Pos:* Mem, Indust Adv Comt, Iowa State Univ. *Mem:* Am Chem Soc; AAAS. *Res:* Isolation and application of proteases and amylases for industrial use; industrial applications of carbohydrates and proteins. *Mailing Add:* Grain Processing Corp 1600 Oregon St Muscatine IA 52761-1476

GARCIA, ALBERT B, computer design, network simulation, for more information see previous edition

GARCIA, ALFREDO MARIANO, BIOLOGY, ANATOMY. *Current Pos:* RETIRED. *Personal Data:* b Itati-Corrientes, Arg, Sept 12, 27; US citizen; m 61. *Educ:* Univ Buenos Aires, MD, 53, Dr Med, 58; Columbia Univ, PhD(zool), 62. *Prof Exp:* Res fel hemat, Mt Sinai Hosp, 57-59; instr biol, Columbia Univ, 59, lectr zool, 59-60, instr, 61-62; from asst prof to assoc prof anat, State Univ NY Upstate Med Ctr, 62-74, prof, 74- *Concurrent Pos:* NIH fel, 60-62 & career develop award, 66-70. *Mem:* Histochem Soc. *Res:* Quantitative cytochemistry; fine structure and nucleic acid metabolism of mammalian blood cells. *Mailing Add:* 771 Stevens Rd Tully NY 13159

GARCIA, CARLOS E(RNESTO), APPLIED MATHEMATICS, ENVIRONMENTAL TECHNOLOGIES. *Current Pos:* PROG MGR, ENVIRON TECHNOLOGIES, LOS ALAMOS NAT LAB, 89- *Personal Data:* b Las Vegas, NMex, May 14, 36; m 65, Anita Bencomo; c Marcus E, Camillia A (Sachez), Monica R & Juan C. *Educ:* NMex State Univ, BS, 58, MS, 62, PhD(mech eng), 66, Indust Col Armed Forces, 84. *Prof Exp:* Assoc engr, Douglas Aircraft Co, 58-60; asst mech eng, NMex State Univ, 60-62, instr, 62-65; assoc res engr, NMex Inst Mining & Technol, 65-66, res engr & asst prof fluid dynamics, 66-67; sr scientist, Ling-Temco-Vought, 67-70; tech contract analyst, Atomic Energy Comn, US Dept Energy, 71-73, weapons develop engr, 73-77, sr prog engr, 77-81, chief, Nuclear Mat Mgt Br, 81-83, dir, Environ Safety & Health Div, 84-86, dir, Energy Technologies & Waste Mgt Div, 86-89. *Concurrent Pos:* Tech subcomt chair, Nat Security Indust Asn, Los Alamos, Nat Lab Rep, NMex Environ Alliance. *Mem:* Nat Soc Prof Engrs; Sigma Xi. *Res:* Hydromechanical missile control systems; shock wave phenomena; gas dynamics; thermodynamics; heat transfer; underground nuclear explosions; shock tubes; supersonic wind tunnels; subsonic and supersonic diffusers; boundary layer bleed; thermoelectrics; technical administration; science administration. *Mailing Add:* 45 Sanchez Rd Belen NM 87002. *Fax:* 505-665-8118; *E-Mail:* ceg@lanl.gov

GARCIA, CELSO-RAMON, OBSTETRICS & GYNECOLOGY, REPRODUCTIVE ENDOCRINOLOGY. *Current Pos:* from assoc prof to prof obstet & gynec, Univ Pa, 65-70, William Shippen Jr prof human reproduction & dir div, Sch Med, 70-95, vchmn, Dept Obstet & Gynec, 73-87, dir reproductive surg, 87-95, WILLIAM SHIPPEN JR EMER PROF HUMAN REPRODUCTION, UNIV PA MED CTR, 95- *Personal Data:* b New York, NY, Oct 31, 21; m 50, Shirley Stoddard; c Celso-Ramon Jr & Sarita S. *Educ:* Queens Col, NY, BS, 42; State Univ NY, MD, 45; Am Bd Obstet & Gynec, dipl. *Hon Degrees:* MA, Univ Pa, 71. *Honors & Awards:* Carl Hartman Award, Am Fertil Soc, 61; Pincus Lectr, Sch Med, Wayne State Univ, 74; First John Rock Lectr, Dept Obstet & Gynec, Univ Pa Sch Med, 80. *Prof Exp:* Intern, Norweg Lutheran Hosp, Brooklyn, 45-46; resident path, Cumberland Hosp, 48-49, res fel obstet & gynec, 49-50, resident, 50-53; assoc, Sch Med & Trop Med, Univ PR, 53-54, asst prof, 54-55; res fel gynec, Harvard Med Sch, 55-56; asst dir, Rock Reproduction Clin, Inc, 56-58, co-dir, 58-61; dir training prog physiol of reproduction, Worcester Found Exp Biol, 60-62, sr scientist, 60-65. *Concurrent Pos:* Assoc, San Juan Munic Hosp, 53-55; res fel, Free Hosp Women, 55-57; asst obstetrician & gynecologist, Boston Lying-in Hosp, 56-65; courtesy staff, Faulkner Hosp, 56-57, assoc staff, 57-65; courtesy staff, Free Hosp Women, 57-58, from asst surgeon to assoc surgeon, 58-65; asst, Harvard Med Sch, 58-59, asst obstet & gynec, 59-60, instr, 60-64, clin assoc, 64-65; courtesy staff, Glover Mem Hosp, 58-65 & Newton Wellesley Hosp, 63-65; consult, Worcester State Hosp, 61-65; asst surgeon & chief, Infertil Clin, Mass Gen Hosp, 62-65; chief, Infertil & Endocrine Clin, Hosp Univ Pa, 65-70; consult, Philadelphia Gen Hosp, 65-70 & Pa Hosp, 73-; extraordinary prof, Univ San Luis Potosi, Mex, 74; adj prof biol sci, Drexel Univ, 75-80; Celso-Ramon Garcia endowed prof, Univ Pa, 95. *Mem:* AAAS; Endocrine Soc; Am Fertil Soc (pres); AMA; Asn Planned Parenthood Physicians (pres, 74-75); Sigma Xi; Am Col Surgeons; Am Gynec & Obstet Soc; Soc Gynec Surgeons. *Res:* Reproductive physiology; infertility; menopause; gynecologic surgery; clinical research directed to improvement of the gynecologic health care of women; co-developed first food and drug administration oral contraceptive. *Mailing Add:* 109 Merion Rd Merion Station PA 19066. *Fax:* 215-349-5512, 610-667-3848

GARCIA, EUGENE N, CLINICAL BIOCHEMISTRY, TOXICOLOGY. *Current Pos:* chmn dept health sci, Calif State Univ, 72-77, assoc prof, 72-79, prof, 80-93, EMER PROF CHEM & HEALTH SCI, CALIF STATE UNIV, DOMINGUEZ HILLS, 93- *Personal Data:* b Guadalajara, Mex, Oct 27, 25; US citizen; wid; c Nicholas, Christopher & Peter. *Educ:* Gonzaga Univ, AB, 48; Univ San Francisco, MS, 51; Univ Calif, Los Angeles, PhD(physiol chem), 61. *Prof Exp:* Chemist org synthesis, Calif Corp Biochem Res, 54-55; res asst biochem, Med Ctr, Univ Calif, Los Angeles, 55-60; asst prof, Col Med, Univ Calif, Irvine, 61-69; partner, Programmedia Assocs, Inc, 70-90. *Concurrent Pos:* Consult biomed educ, 69-; lectr, Univ Calif, Los Angeles, 70-84. *Mem:* AAAS; Am Chem Soc; Am Asn Clin Chem; Nat Acad Clin Biochem; NY Acad Sci; Am Inst Chem. *Res:* Ehrlich ascites carcinoma; irradiation effects and development of immunity in mice; lipids in Ehrlich ascites carcinoma; lipoprotein components. *Mailing Add:* ProgramMedia Assocs Inc 15608 Claretta Ave Norwalk CA 90650-6746

GARCIA, HECTOR D, GENETIC TOXICOLOGY. *Current Pos:* SR RES SCIENTIST, KRUG LIFE SCI, 90- *Personal Data:* b Rio Grande City, Tex, Aug 26, 46; m 74, Martha Maldonado; c Mary C, Christina & David. *Educ:* Univ St Thomas, BA, 68; Univ Tex, MS, 75, PhD (molecular biol), 79. *Prof Exp:* Res scientist, Phillip Morris USA, 81-87; consult, Functional Mgt Inst, 87-90. *Res:* Setting safe inhalation exposure limits for airborne contaminants in spacecraft and determining the toxic hazard level of test sample materials flown on manned spacecraft. *Mailing Add:* 1290 Hercules Dr No 120 Houston TX 77058. *Fax:* 281-483-3058

GARCIA, JOHN, CONDITIONED TASTE AVERSION. *Current Pos:* prof, 73-87, EMER PROF PSYCHOL, UNIV CALIF, LOS ANGELES, 87- *Personal Data:* b Santa Rosa, Calif, June 12, 17; m 43; c 3. *Educ:* Univ Calif, Berkeley, BA, 48, MA, 49, PhD(psychol), 65. *Honors & Awards:* Howard Crosby Warren Medal, Soc Exp Psychologists, 78; Distinguished Sci Contrib Award, Am Psychol Asn, 79. *Prof Exp:* Teaching asst psychol, Univ Calif, Berkeley, 49-51; psychologist, US Naval Radiol Defense Lab, San Francisco, 51-58; teacher biol sci, Oakland Pub Schs, Calif, 58-59; asst prof psychol, Calif State Col, Long Beach, 59-65; assoc biologist neurosurg serv, Mass Gen Hosp, 65-68; prof psychol & chmn, Psychobiol Prog, State Univ NY, Stony Brook, 68-71, chmn dept, 71-72; prof, Univ Utah, Salt Lake City, 72-73. *Concurrent Pos:* Consult neurophysiol, Long Beach Vet Admin Hosp, 59-65; lectr psychol, Dept Surg, Harvard Med Sch, Boston, 65-68 & Int Brain Res Sem, Kotor, Yugoslavia, 69; nat lectr, Sigma Xi, Southeastern US, 73-74; distinguished lectr, Univ Ill, 81; pres, Western Psychol Asn, 91-; William James fel, Am Psychol Asn. *Mem:* Nat Acad Sci; fel Soc Exp Psychologists; AAAS; Am Psychol Soc. *Mailing Add:* 1950-A Chilberg Rd Mt Vernon WA 98273

GARCIA, JOSE DOLORES, JR, SCATTERING THEORY, ATOMIC PHYSICS. *Current Pos:* from asst prof to assoc prof, 67-75, PROF PHYSICS, UNIV ARIZ, 75- *Personal Data:* b Santa Fe, NMex, Jan 3, 36; m 60, Margot Weaver; c 2. *Educ:* NMex State Univ, BS, 57; Univ Calif, Berkeley, MA, 59; Univ Wis, PhD(physics), 66. *Prof Exp:* Res officer, Air Force Weapons Lab, 60-63; NASA fel physics, Univ Pittsburgh, 66-67. *Concurrent Pos:* Fulbright grant, 57; consult, Air Force Weapons Lab, Kirtland AFB, 67 & Lawrence Radiation Lab, Livermore, 70-86, Los Alamos Nat Lab, 85-94 & NSF, 95-96. *Mem:* Fel Am Phys Soc; Nat Physics Sci Consortium. *Res:* Atomic bound state theory; atomic scattering theory; use of super computers in theoretical physics. *Mailing Add:* Dept Physics Univ Ariz Tucson AZ 85721. *Fax:* 520-621-4721; *E-Mail:* jdg@physics.arizona.edu

GARCIA, JULIO H, NEUROPATHOLOGY, ELECTRON MICROSCOPY. *Current Pos:* PROF PATH & NEUROL, & DIR ANAT PATH, UNIV ALA, BIRMINGHAM MED CTR, 79- *Personal Data:* b Armenia, Colombia, Dec 22, 33; nat US; m 66; c 2. *Educ:* Col St Bartholomew, Colombia, BS, 51; Nat Univ Colombia, MD, 58; Am Bd Path, dipl, 64. *Honors & Awards:* Humboldt Sr Scientist Award, Fed Rep Ger, 77-78. *Prof Exp:* Intern path, Hosp San Juan de Dios, Colombia, 58-59; resident physician, LI Jewish Hosp, 59-60; resident physician, Kings County Hosp, NY, 60-64; asst prof path, Med Col Va, 64-67; assoc prof path & neurol, Univ Tenn, Memphis, 67-70; assoc prof, Baylor Col Med, 70-71; prof path & head, Neuropath Div, Sch Med, Univ Md, Baltimore, 71-79, dir, Anat Path Labs, 77-79. *Concurrent Pos:* Instr, State Univ NY, 62-64; consult, Eastern State Hosp, Va, 64-66, Off Chief Med Examr, Va, 64-66, Vet Admin Hosp, Richmond, Va, 64-66, Baptist Mem Hosp, Tenn, 67-, WTenn Psychiat Hosp & Inst, 67-, Vet Admin Hosp, Baltimore, 71- & Union Mem Hosp, 72-; USPHS grant, 69 & 73; fel coun cerebrovascular dis, Am Heart Asn, 70, mem res comt I, 71-73; mem stroke adv comt, Joint Comn Accreditation Hosps; mem, NSP-A, Nat Inst Health, 78-82. *Mem:* AAAS; NY Acad Sci; Am Asn Neuropath (vpres, 75-76); Am Asn Path & Bact; Asn Res Nerv & Ment Dis. *Res:* Ultrastructural changes of primates' brain after experimental production of regional ischemia; ultrastructural studies of mechanisms of nerve cell damage after ischemia, shock and trauma; effects of methanol poisoning on the brain; pathology. *Mailing Add:* Div Neuropath Dept Path K-6 Henry Ford Hosp 2799 W Grand Blvd Detroit MI 48202-2689. *Fax:* 313-763-5633

GARCIA, MANUEL MARIANO, BACTERIOLOGY. *Current Pos:* RETIRED. *Personal Data:* b Dumaguete City, Philippines, Nov 25, 38; m 70. *Educ:* Univ Philippines, BSA, 59, MSc, 62; Univ Guelph, PhD(microbiol, bact physiol), 67. *Prof Exp:* Res instr soil microbiol, Univ Philippines, 62-65; res scientist & head, Bact Sect, Animal Dis Res Inst, 67-97. *Mem:* AAAS; Am Soc Microbiol; Can Soc Microbiol; Sigma Xi. *Res:* Growth and survival of animal pathogens in soil; anaerobic bacteria and L-forms; microbial toxins; immunofluorescence; antigens and membranes of fusobacteria; phagocytosis and destruction of anaerobic bacteria by macrophages; microbial vaccines; pathogenesis of necrobacillosis. *Mailing Add:* 26 Castlethorpe Crescent Nepean ON K2G 5P7 Can

GARCIA, MARCELO HORACIO, ENVIRONMENTAL HYDRODYNAMICS & HYDRAULIC MODELING, SEDIMENT TRANSPORT. *Current Pos:* asst prof, 90-96, ASSOC PROF ENVIRON HYDRAUL, DEPT CIVIL ENG, UNIV ILL, 96- *Personal Data:* b Cordoba, Arg, Apr 22, 59; m 84. *Educ:* Nat Univ Litoral, Arg, Dipl Ing, 82; Univ Minn, MSc, 85, PhD(civil eng), 89. *Honors & Awards:* Karl Emil Hilgard Hydraulic Prize, Am Soc Civil Engrs, 96. *Prof Exp:* Res docent hydraul, Nat Univ Litoral, Arg, 82-87; res asst environ, Univ Minn, 83-89, teaching asst fluid mech, 84-86. *Concurrent Pos:* Asst engr, Parano Medio Proj, AyEE, 82-83; vis engr, INCyTH, Arg, 83; consult, Northern States Power Co, Minn, 88-89; vis prof, Hokkaido River Res Found, Japan, 90, Hokkaido Lectr, 90; vis prof, Univ Naaisnal Del Litoral, Arg, 93- *Mem:* Am Geophys Union; Am Soc Civil Engrs; Int Asn Hydraul Res. *Res:* Environmental hydrodynamics; stratified flows; river mechanics; sediment transport; water-sediment interface phenomena and flows through porous media; man-made and natural phenomena. *Mailing Add:* Dept Civil Engr Univ Ill 205 N Mathews Ave Urbana IL 61801. *E-Mail:* mhgarcia@uiuc.edu

GARCIA, MARIA LUISA, MEMBRANE BIOCHEMISTRY, ION CHANNELS. *Current Pos:* fel, Merck Res Labs, 83-84, sr res biochemist, 85-87, res fel, 88-91, SR RES FEL, MERCK RES LAB, 91- *Personal Data:* b Valladolid, Spain, Oct 9, 53; m 82, Gregory J Kaczorowski. *Educ:* Autonoma Univ, Spain, BS, 75, PhD(chem), 79. *Prof Exp:* Fel, Roche Inst Molecular Biol, 79-82, Mt Sinai Hosp, 82-83. *Mem:* NY Acad Sci; Biophys Soc; Am Soc Biol Chemists & Molecular Biologists; Span Chem Soc. *Res:* Biochemistry of ion channel proteins that control the regulation of calcium levels in excitable and non-excitable cells; novel modulators of some of these proteins that may have therapeutic application. *Mailing Add:* 5 Ashbrook Dr Edison NJ 08820. *E-Mail:* mariagarcia@merck.com

GARCIA, MARIANO, MATHEMATICS. *Current Pos:* RETIRED. *Personal Data:* b Naguabo, PR, Sept 13, 18; m 40; c 2. *Educ:* Washington & Jefferson Col, BS, 39, MA, 40; Univ Va, PhD(math), 44. *Prof Exp:* Instr math, Univ Richmond, 44; from asst prof to prof & head dept, Col Agr & Mech Arts, Univ PR, Mayaguez, 44-74; prof math, Hostos Community Col, 74-89. *Mem:* Am Math Soc; Math Asn Am. *Res:* Topology and theory of numbers. *Mailing Add:* 10 Park Ave Apt 4S New York NY 10016

GARCIA, MARIO LEOPOLDO, PHYSICAL CHEMISTRY, COSMETIC CHEMISTRY. *Current Pos:* res scientist phys chem, 66-68, sect head phys chem sect, 68-71, ASSOC DIR PHYS CHEM DEPT, RES LABS, CLAIROL INC, 71- *Personal Data:* b Havana, Cuba, Sept 12, 40; US citizen. *Educ:* Univ Havana, Dr Chem Sci, 64. *Prof Exp:* Mgr phys chem & anal chem dept, Cuban Inst Sugar Cane Derivatives, 64-66. *Concurrent Pos:* Assoc prof phys chem, Univ Havana, 65-66. *Mem:* Soc Rheol. *Res:* Physical chemistry of cosmetic products and their effects on human hair; mechanical, surface and optical properties of hair; structure of human hair; development of instrumental methods of chemical analysis. *Mailing Add:* 1459 Shippan Ave Stamford CT 06902

GARCIA, MEREDITH MASON, MOLECULAR NEUROPHARMACOLOGY. *Current Pos:* fel, Dept Anat & Prog Neurosci, 90-91, res instr, 91-93, ASST PROF, DEPT OTOLARYNGOL & PROG NEUROSCI, TULANE UNIV, 93- *Personal Data:* b Winchester, Mass; m 76, Louis E; c Alberto M. *Educ:* St Mary's Dominican Col, BSc, 84; Tulane Univ, PhD(pharmacol), 90. *Honors & Awards:* William G Carey Sci Award, AAAS, 90. *Prof Exp:* Dir, Radioimmunoassay Lab, Endocrine, Polypeptide & Cancer Inst, Vet Admin Med Ctr, New Orleans, 82-87. *Concurrent Pos:* Pharmaceut Mfrs Asn Found postdoctoral fel pharmacol-morphol, 90-92; Am Cancer Soc Inst res grant, 90-91; Nat Inst Drug Abuse res grant, 91-94; vis scientist, Transgenic Mouse Lab, Dept Molecular Biol, Squibb Inst Med Res, Princeton, 91. *Mem:* Sigma Xi; Am Asn Anatomists; Col Prob Drug Dependence; Am Soc Pharmacol & Exp Therapeut; Int Soc Differentiation; Soc Exp Biol Med; Soc Neurosci. *Res:* Molecular neurobiology of drug abuse; signal transduction at the opiate receptor; regulation of expression of immediate-early genes in the brain; molecular neurobiology of sensory hair cells; role of protein kinase C isoforms in neuronal plasticity in the central auditory system; author of numerous technical publications. *Mailing Add:* Dept Otolaryngol SL-59 Tulane Med Sch, 1430 Tulane Ave New Orleans LA 70112-2699. *Fax:* 504-582-7846; *E-Mail:* mgarcia@mailhost.tcs.tulane.edu

GARCIA, MICHAEL OMAR, VOLCANOLOGY. *Current Pos:* Asst prof, 76-81, ASSOC PROF GEOL, UNIV HAWAII, 81- *Personal Data:* b San Gabriel, Calif, Nov 18, 48; m 77; c 2. *Educ:* Calif State Univ, Humboldt, BA, 71; Univ Calif, Los Angeles, PhD(geol), 76. *Mem:* Geol Soc Am; Am Geophys Union; Minerol Soc Am; Sigma Xi. *Res:* Volcanology; igneous petrology; field, microscopic and chemical analysis of the products of volcanoes including Kilauea and Mauna, Hawaii and Arenal, Costa Rica. *Mailing Add:* Dept Geol & Geophys Univ Hawaii Manoa Honolulu HI 96822-2270

GARCIA, OSCAR NICOLAS, ELECTRICAL ENGINEERING, COMPUTER SCIENCE. *Current Pos:* NCR DISTINGUISHED PROF & CHAIR, DEPT COMPUT SCI & ENG, WRIGHT STATE UNIV, 95- *Personal Data:* b Havana, Cuba, Sept 10, 36; US citizen; m 62, Diane Journigan; c Flora & Virginia. *Educ:* NC State Univ, BSEE, 61, MSEE, 64; Univ Md, PhD(elec eng), 69. *Honors & Awards:* Richard E Merwin Dist Serv Award, IEEE Comput Soc, 88, Meritorious Serv Award, 91; Richard M Emberson Award, Inst Elec & Electronics Engrs, 94. *Prof Exp:* Asst elec eng, NC State Col, 61-62, instr, 62; elec engr, IBM Glendale Develop Labs, 62-63; asst prof elec eng, Old Dominion Univ, 63-66, assoc prof, 69-70; instr, Univ Md, 66-67, res asst, 67-68; from assoc prof to prof elec eng, Dept Comput Sci & eng, Univ SFla, Tampa, 70-78, chmn dept, 75-85; prof elec eng, Dept Elec & Eng & Comput Sci, George Washington Univ, 85-95. *Concurrent Pos:* Prin investr, NSF res initiation grant, 70-71; distinguished vis, Inst Elec & Electronics Engrs, 73-76, mem gov bd, 75-77; prog mgr, Instr Sci Equip Div, NSF, 77-78; prin investr, NSF grants, 80-83 & 90-91; prog dir, Interactive Systs Prog, NSF, 92-95. *Mem:* Fel Inst Elec & Electronics Engrs; Am Soc Eng Educ; Asn Comput Mach; Sigma Xi; Inst Elec & Electronics Engrs Comput Soc (pres, 81-83); fel AAAS. *Res:* Application of coding theory to improved computer reliability and speed; computer architectural design and simulation of digital systems for design and diagnostic tests; artificial intelligence, expert systems, speech recognition. *Mailing Add:* Dept Comp Sci & Eng Wright State Univ 303 Russ Eng Bldg Dayton OH 45435. *Fax:* 937-775-5133; *E-Mail:* ogarcia@nsf.gov

GARCIA, PILAR A, NUTRITION. *Current Pos:* Asst nutrit, 50-55, assoc & instr, 55-57, from asst prof to assoc prof food & nutrit, 57-74, PROF FOOD & NUTRIT, IOWA STATE UNIV, 74- *Personal Data:* b Manila, Philippines, Nov 4, 26. *Educ:* Univ Philippines, BS, 49; Univ Mich, MS, 50; Iowa State Univ, MS, 52, PhD(nutrit), 55. *Mem:* Sigma Xi. *Res:* Human nutrition; energy expenditure of adult women; nutrition and aging of adult women; nutrition during adolescent pregnancy. *Mailing Add:* 2012 Greenbriar Circle Iowa State Univ Ames IA 50014-7820

GARCIA, RAUL, CELL BIOLOGY & PHYSIOLOGY, RECEPTOR PHYSIOLOGY. *Current Pos:* assoc prof, 83-90, PROF MED, UNIV MONTREAL, 90-; LAB DIR, CLIN RES INST MONTREAL, 80- *Personal Data:* b Gijon, Spain, June 15, 35; Can citizen; m 60, Sylvia Weinstein; c Daniel, Cecilia & Francisco. *Educ:* Univ Chile, MD, 60. *Prof Exp:* Asst prof int med, Univ Chile, 63-68; res fel, Clin Res Inst Montreal, 68-70; assoc res prof, Inst Med Sci, Catholic Univ Chile, 70-73; res asst, Clin Res Inst Montreal, 73-80. *Concurrent Pos:* Assoc mem exp med, Univ McGill, 84-; mem, High Blood Pressure Res Coun; staff mem, Hotel-Dieu Hosp. *Mem:* Int Soc Hypertension; Can Soc Hypertension; Am Soc Hypertension; Am Heart Assoc; AAAS. *Res:* Experimental hypertension endocrinology; atrial natriuretic factor, cardiovascular regulation; angiotensin; vasoactive peptides receptor regulation. *Mailing Add:* Clin Res Inst Montreal 110 Pine Ave W Montreal PQ H2W 1R7 Can. *Fax:* 514-987-5688

GARCIA, RICHARD, PARASITOLOGY, MEDICAL ENTOMOLOGY. *Current Pos:* assoc entomologist, 69-93, EMER PROF, UNIV CALIF, BERKELEY, 93- *Personal Data:* b Sebastopol, Calif, Apr 26, 30; m 53; c 2. *Educ:* Univ Calif, Berkeley, BS, 57, PhD(parasitol), 63. *Prof Exp:* USPHS fel arbovirus res, Rocky Mountain Lab, Mont, 63-65; asst res parasitologist, George Williams Hooper Found, Med Ctr, Univ Calif, San Francisco, 65-69. *Mem:* Entom Soc Am; Soc Insect Path; Am Mosquito Control Asn. *Res:* Behavior of bloodsucking arthropods to external stimuli and ecological studies of arboviruses in vector populations; biological control of mosquitoes. *Mailing Add:* Div Biol Univ Calif ESPM Insect Bio 201 Wellman Hall Berkeley CA 94720-3112

GARCIA-BENGOCHEA, FRANCISCO, NEUROSURGERY. *Current Pos:* from assoc prof to prof, 62-76, distinguished serv prof, 70-83, EMER DISTINGUISHED SERV PROF NEUROSURG, COL MED, UNIV FLA, 83- *Personal Data:* b Havana, Cuba, Dec 15, 17; m 53; c 2. *Educ:* Univ Havana, MD, 41; Tulane Univ, MD, 49. *Prof Exp:* Res asst neurol, Col Physicians & Surgeons, Columbia Univ, 44-49, resident neurosurg, Presby Med Ctr, 48-49; instr neurol & neurosurg, Sch Med, Tulane Univ, 49-50, asst prof, 50-51; instr neurosurg, Col Med, Univ Fla, 60-61; asst prof, Sch Med, Univ Kans, 61-62. *Concurrent Pos:* Traveling fel, Sch Med, Univ Havana, 43-45; surgeon, Greystone Brain Res Proj, Columbia Univ, 48-49; neurosurgeon, Charity Hosp New Orleans, Tulane Univ, 49-51; Markle scholar med sci, Sch Med, Tulane Univ, 50-51. *Mem:* Am Asn Neurosurg; Cong Neurol Surg; Neurosurg Soc Am. *Mailing Add:* 4901 Vandiveer Rd Jacksonville FL 32210

GARCIA-CASTRO, IVETTE, ONCOLOGY, CELL CULTURE TECHNIQUES. *Current Pos:* asst dean, 82-87, chair, 85-87, PROF MICROBIOL, UNIV PR, RIO PIEDRAS, 73-, PROF IMMUNOL, APPL MICROBIOL, CELL CULT TECHS, 85- *Personal Data:* b San Juan, PR, June 1, 37. *Educ:* Col Notre Dame Md, BA, 60; Cath Univ Am, MS, 70, PhD(cell biol), 73. *Prof Exp:* Chair, Sci Dept, Notre Dame High Sch, PR, 60-69; sr technician, Microbiol Assocs, Md, 71-73. *Concurrent Pos:* Guest scientist, Walter Reed Army Inst Res, Wash, DC, 81-82 & NIH, 91; pres elec, PR Soc Microbiologists; mem, Supply & Maintenance Plan & Report. *Mem:* Tissue Cult Asn; Am Soc Microbiol; Am Asn Univ Prof. *Res:* Motile response of transformed cells to extracellular matrix components. *Mailing Add:* Dept Biol Univ PR PO Box 22283 Rio Piedras PR 00931

GARCIA-COLIN, LEOPOLDO SCHERER, PHYSICS, THERMAL PHYSICS. *Current Pos:* chmn, Dept Physics & Chem, 74-78, PROF PHYSICS, METROP UNIV, IZTAPALAPA CAMPUS, MEX, 74- *Personal Data:* b Mex, Nov 27, 30; m 57; c 3. *Educ:* Nat Univ Mex, BSc, 53 & 54; Univ Md, PhD(physics), 59. *Hon Degrees:* Dr, Univ Iberoamericana, 91, Univ Puebla, 95. *Honors & Awards:* Sci Award, Acad Sci Res Mex, 65; Nat Prize Physics, Math & Natural Sci, 88. *Prof Exp:* Asst physics, Univ Md, 56-57, asst, Inst Fluid Dynamics & Appl Math, 57-59, res assoc, Inst Fluid Dynamics, 59-60; assoc prof, Nat Polytech Inst, Mex, 60-63; prof, Univ Puebla, 64-66; res prof physics, Nat Nuclear Energy Comn, 66-67; head, Appl Res Div, Mex Petrol Inst, 67-74. *Concurrent Pos:* Res asst, Nat Inst Sci Res, Mex, 53-62; consult, Nuclear Energy Comn, Mex, 60-76; lectr, Sch Mil Eng, 61-62; lectr, Nat Univ Mex, 61-62, part-time prof, 67-84; Van der Waals prof, Univ Amsterdam, 76; mem staff, El Colegio Nacional, Mex, 77; consult, Nat Inst Nuclear Energy, 79-82; distinguished prof, Univ Autonoma Metrop, 83; fel, Latin-Am Acad Sci, 87. *Mem:* AAAS; Am Phys Soc; Am Asn Physics Teachers; Mex Physics Soc; fel Third World Acad Sci. *Res:* Statistical mechanics of equilibrium and non-equilibrium phenomena; superfluids; hydrodynamics of chemically reacting fluids; non-equilibrium thermodynamics; chemical kinetics; formulation of a theory for non-linear non-equilibrium statistical mechanics; non-equilibrium properties of fluids; microscopic theory; glass transition. *Mailing Add:* Dept Physics Univ Autonoma Metrop-Iztapalapa Apdo Postal 55-534 Mexico City 09340 DF Mexico. *Fax:* 52-5-724-4611; *E-Mail:* lgcs@xanum.uam.mx

GARCIA-MUNOZ, MOISES, ASTROPHYSICS. *Current Pos:* res assoc atomic physics, 59-64, SR RES ASSOC, LAB ASTROPHYS & SPACE RES, ENRICO FERMI INST, UNIV CHICAGO, 64- *Personal Data:* b Valencia, Spain, May 21, 22; m 55; c 1. *Educ:* Univ Valencia, MS, 47; Univ Madrid, PhD(nuclear physics), 57. *Prof Exp:* Instr phys chem, Univ Valencia, 49-50, prof, Physics Div, Spanish Atomic Energy Comn, 51-56, investr, 56-59. *Mem:* Fel Am Phys Soc; Am Geophys Union. *Res:* Atomic and molecular processes; space physics. *Mailing Add:* 16465 Woodlawn E Ave South Holland IL 60473

GARCIA-PALMIERI, MARIO R, INTERNAL MEDICINE, CARDIOLOGY. *Current Pos:* from instr to prof, Univ PR, 55-84, assoc, 56-58, dir comprehensive med prog, 56-59, dir outpatient dept, 59-61, head, Dept Med, 61-66, CHIEF SECT CARDIOL, SCH MED, UNIV PR, SAN JUAN, 61-, HEAD DEPT MED, 68-, DISTINGUISHED PROF MED, 84- *Personal Data:* b Adjuntas, PR, Aug 2, 27; m 59; c 1. *Educ:* Univ PR, BS, 47; Univ Md, MD, 51; Am Bd Internal Med, dipl, 58, cert cardiovasc dis, 62. *Prof Exp:* Intern, Fajardo Dist Hosp, 51-52; resident med, Bayamon Dist Hosp, 52-53; asst med, Sch Med, Univ PR, 53-54; Nat Heart Inst fel cardiol, 54-55; head dept med, Fajardo Dist Hosp, 55-56. *Concurrent Pos:* Resident med, San Patricio Vet Admin Hosp, 53-54; ed, Bull PR Med Asn, 60-66; head dept med, Univ Dist Hosp, 61; dir undergrad & postgrad cardiovasc training prog, Sch Med, Univ PR, 61-75; vis prof, Seton Hall Col Med, Sch Med, Univ Fla, 63 & Univ Ala, Birmingham, 81-82; vis lectr, Sch Med, Ind Univ, 63, Brooklyn Jewish Hosp, 64, Cent Univ Venezuela, 64 & Univs Barcelona & Madrid; lectr, Dominican Repub, 66 & 68; consult, San Patricio Vet Admin, Presby, San Jorge, San Juan City, Auxilio Muto & Doctor & Teachers Hosps; lectr cardiovasc epidemiol, Dept Prev Med & Pub Health, Univ PR; fel coun clin cardiol & coun epidemiol, Am Heart Asn; mem, presidential comn ethical aspects med, biomed & behav res, 79-82; mem, adv coun, Nat Inst on Aging, 79-83. *Mem:* AAAS; fel Am Col Physicians; Am Fedn Clin Res; Am Soc Trop Med & Hyg; Am Heart Asn; fel Royal Soc Health; fel Am Col Chest Physicians; Asn Am Med Cols; Asn Prof Med. *Res:* Tropical diseases; study of different electrocardiographical alternations, vectorcardiogram and coronary atherosclerosis. *Mailing Add:* MACP Box DG Caparra Heights San Juan PR 00922

GARCIA-RILL, EDGAR E, NEUROPHYSIOLOGY. *Current Pos:* from asst prof to assoc prof, Univ Ark, 78-87, PROF ANAT, UNIV ARK, 87-, PROF PSYCHIAT, 90- *Personal Data:* b Caracas, Venezuela, Oct 31, 48; Can citizen; m 84, Susan Ebel; c Sarah T. *Educ:* Loyola Col Montreal, BA, 69; McGill Univ, PhD(physiol), 73. *Prof Exp:* Res assoc neuropsychiat, Allan Mem Inst, Montreal, 72-73; fel res anat neurophysiol, Univ Calif, Los Angeles, 74-76, res asst physiol, 76-78. *Concurrent Pos:* Fel Que Med Res Coun, Dept Psychiat, Univ Calif, Los Angeles, 73-74. *Mem:* Soc Neurosci; Can Physiol Soc; Am Asn Anat. *Res:* Neurophysiology of motor-sensory interactions; basal ganglia; locomotion; spinal cord injury; schizophrenia; anxiety disorder. *Mailing Add:* Dept Anat Univ Ark Med Sci 4301 W Markham Little Rock AR 72205

GARCIA-SAINZ, J ADOLFO, SIGNAL TRANSDUCTION, RECEPTORS & SECOND MESSENGERS. *Current Pos:* From asst prof to assoc prof, 80-83, PROF & CHMN BIOCHEM INST PHYSIOL, NAT AUTONOMOUS UNIV MEXICO, 83- *Personal Data:* b Mexico, DF, Mar 10, 52; m 79, Maria E Pasquel; c Jesus, Santiago, Maria & Guadalupe. *Educ:* La Salle Col, BSc, 70; Nat Autonomous Univ Mexico, MD, 76, MSc, 78, PhD(biochem), 81. *Honors & Awards:* Eduardo Liceaga Prize, Nat Acad Med, 84; M Aleman Prize, Found Miguel Aleman, 85; Puebla Sci Prize, 85; Manuel Noriega Morales Prize, Am States Orgn, 90; Maximiliano Ruiz Castaneda Prize, Nat Acad Med, 93. *Concurrent Pos:* Ed, Europ J Pharmacol, 84-; fel, John Guggenheim Found, 85; vpres & pres, Mex Soc Biochem, 87-91. *Mem:* Am Soc Biol Chemists; Am Soc Pharmacol & Exp Therapeut; Biochem Soc; Soc Mex Biochem; Mex Acad Sci. *Res:* Processes involved in signal transduction; receptors, G-proteins, membrane effectors and second messengers are determined using currently available techniques; adrenergic receptors and protein kinase C. *Mailing Add:* Nat Autonomous Univ Mex Apdo 70-248 Mexico City 04510 Mexico. *Fax:* 525-622-56-13; *E-Mail:* agarcia@ifcsun1.ifisiol.unam.mx

GARCIA-SANTESMASES, JOSE MIGUEL, data analysis methods & techniques, expert systems, for more information see previous edition

GARD, DAVID LYNN, CYTOSKELETON, MICROTUBULES. *Current Pos:* SCHOLAR, MED SCH, UNIV CALIF, 82- *Educ:* Calif Inst Technol, PhD(cell biol), 82. *Mailing Add:* Dept Biol Univ Utah Salt Lake City UT 84112. *Fax:* 801-581-4668

GARD, DAVID RICHARD, PHOSPHATE CHEMISTRY. *Current Pos:* Sr res chemist, Monsanto Co, 80-84, res specialist, 84-88, assoc fel, 88-93, FEL, MONSANTO CO, 93- *Personal Data:* b Connersville, Ind, Sept 28, 53; m 80; c Becky & Cathy. *Educ:* Purdue Univ, BS, 75; Univ Ill, PhD(inorganic chem), 81. *Mem:* Am Chem Soc. *Res:* Phosphate chemistry and technology; phase equilibria; new product developement; process development. *Mailing Add:* 13 Steeple Hill Lane 800 N Lindbergh Blvd Ballwin MO 63011-2732. *Fax:* 314-694-2298; *E-Mail:* drgard@ccmail.monsanto.com

GARD, DON IRVIN, ANIMAL NUTRITION. *Current Pos:* RETIRED. *Personal Data:* b Beaver Crossing, Nebr, June 18, 26. *Educ:* Univ Nebr, BS, 50; Okla State Univ, MS, 52; Univ Ill, PhD(animal sci), 54. *Prof Exp:* Dir res & nutrit, Crete Mills, Lauhoff Grain Co, Nebr, 54-57; sr scientist, Eli Lilly & Co, 57-70, res scientist, 70-78, res assoc, 70-90. *Mem:* Am Soc Animal Sci; Poultry Sci Asn; Animal Nutrit Res Coun; World Poultry Sci Asn; Sigma Xi. *Res:* Research utilizing computers to develop new antibiotics and chemo-therapeutic agents for poultry. *Mailing Add:* 3660 N 50 E Greenfield IN 46140-8626

GARD, GARY LEE, FLUORINE CHEMISTRY, OXIDATION CHEMISTRY. *Current Pos:* from asst prof to assoc prof, Portland State Univ, 66-75, chmn dept, 71-77, exec coun, Div Fluorine Chem, 77-80, actg dean, Col Sci & coordr, Environ Sci PhD Prog, 79-81, dept head, 92-94, PROF CHEM, PORTLAND STATE UNIV, 75- *Personal Data:* b Goodland, Kans, Nov 17, 37; m 72, Christina Huprich; c Timothy L, Dolores A, Julie A & Jason L. *Educ:* Univ Wash, BA, 59, BS, 60, PhD(chem), 64. *Prof Exp:* Sr res chemist, Allied Chem Co, 64-66. *Concurrent Pos:* Mem staff, Marine Sci Comn, 79-81; consult, Col Chem Consults Serv, Am Chem Soc, 84-96; adj prof, Ore Grad Ctr, 84-97; Fulbright sr prof award, 89-90; Branford Price Millar Award, 90-91. *Mem:* Am Chem Soc; Sigma Xi. *Res:* Preparation of new oxidizing agents; preparation of new dielectric materials, fuel cell electrolytes, ion conductors, surface active agents, polymers, and complexing systems that contain fluorine; preparative and physical chemical studies of fluorine containing metals and non-metals systems. *Mailing Add:* Dept Chem Portland State Univ Portland OR 97207. *Fax:* 503-725-3888; *E-Mail:* gary@science1.sb2.pdx.edu

GARD, JANICE KOLES, NUCLEAR MAGNETIC RESONANCE SPECTROSCOPY. *Current Pos:* sr res chemist, 84-89, res specialist, 89-92, SR RES SPECIALIST, MONSANTO CO, 92- *Personal Data:* b Phoenix, Ariz, June 4, 54; m 80; c 2. *Educ:* San Diego State Univ, BS, 77; Univ Ill, MS, 80, PhD(phys chem), 84. *Prof Exp:* Anal chemist, Am Testing Inst, 73-77; res asst, Los Alamos Nat Lab, 77. *Concurrent Pos:* Co-chair, St Louis Nuclear Magnetic Resonance Discussion Group, Am Chem Soc, 89-91; lab mgr, Phys Sci Ctr, Nuclear Magnetic Resonance Facil, Creve Coeur, Monsanto Co, 89-91. *Mem:* Am Chem Soc; Sigma Xi. *Res:* Multinuclear, multidimensional nuclear magnetic resonance structural characterization of biological, inorganic, and organic molecules. *Mailing Add:* 13 Steeple Hill Lane Ballwin MO 63011-2732

GARD, NICHOLAS WILLIAM, ecotoxicology, immunotoxicology, for more information see previous edition

GARD, O(LIVER) W(ILLIAM), mechanical engineering; deceased, see previous edition for last biography

GARD, RICHARD, FISHERIES. *Current Pos:* dir div fisheries & natural sci, Univ Alaska Southeast, 75-82, prof fisheries, 78-88, actg dean, Sch Fisheries & Sci, 82-83, EMER PROF FISHERIES, UNIV ALASKA SOUTHEAST, 88- *Personal Data:* b Alhambra, Calif, July 6, 28; m 63; c 2. *Educ:* Univ Calif, AB, 50, MA, 53, PhD(zool), 58. *Prof Exp:* Res zoologist, Univ Calif, 56-58, jr res zoologist, 58, lectr zool, 58-59, from jr res zoologist to asst res zoologist, 59-62; res biologist, US Bur Commercial Fisheries, 62-66; assoc res zoologist, Univ Calif, 69-70, Belvedere Sci Fund grant, 70 & 73-74; res biologist, Nat Marine Fisheries Serv, 71-73; assoc prof fishery & wildlife biol, Colo State Univ, 73-75. *Concurrent Pos:* Prin investr, Belvedere Sci Fund, 69-74, Marine Mammal Comm, 74-76; consult, US Bur Reclamation, 74-75; prin investr, Alaska Sea Grant Prog, 76-79; prin investr, Univ Alaska Juneau Res Coun, 83-85, Alaska Dept Fish & Game, 85-86. *Mem:* Wildlife Soc; Am Fisheries Soc; Am Soc Mammalogists; Soc Marine Mammal; fel Am Inst Fishery Res Biologists. *Res:* Trout stream ecology; life history of sockeye salmon; life history and conservation of the gray whale; age and growth of Arctic char; stock separation of salmonids. *Mailing Add:* 2670 Fritz Cove Rd Juneau AK 99801

GARDELLA, JOSEPH AUGUSTUS, JR, SURFACE SCIENCE & SPECTROSCOPY. *Current Pos:* from asst prof to assoc prof chem, 82-92, res asst prof Stomatology, 87-92, PROF CHEM & BIOMAT, STATE UNIV NY, BUFFALO, 92- *Personal Data:* b Detroit, Mich, Aug 22, 55; m 83. *Educ:* Oakland Univ, BA(philos) & BS(chem), 77; Univ Pittsburgh, PhD(anal chem), 81. *Honors & Awards:* Spec Creativity Award, NSF, 91-93. *Prof Exp:* Fac intern chem, Univ Utah, 81-82. *Concurrent Pos:* Dir, Surface Sci Ctr, State Univ NY, Buffalo, 85-; consult, Air Prod & Chem Inc, 86-; secy, Niagara Frontier Sect, Soc Applied Spectros, 87-; mem, Joint Polymer Educ Comt-Am Chem Soc-Div Polymer Chem, Inc, 87-; co-dir, Indust Univ Ctr Biosurfaces, NSF Indust Univ Coop Res Ctr, 8; prog officer, Chem Div, NSF, Wash, DC, 89-90; fel, Gelb Found, 86-89, Exxon Educ Found, 89-91. *Mem:* Am Chem Soc; Am Vacuum Soc; AAAS; Soc Appl Spectros; Mat Res Soc. *Res:* Study of structure, composition and function of macromolecular surfaces and interfaces; new methods of analysis of polymer surfaces and metal-organic interfaces and thin films; surface modification and characterization of multicomponent polymers; characterization of biological-material interfaces. *Mailing Add:* Dept Chem State Univ NY Buffalo Buffalo NY 14260-3000. *Fax:* 716-829-2960; *E-Mail:* chegard@ubvmsc.cc.buffalo.edu

GARDELLA, LIBERO ANTHONY, PHARMACEUTICAL CHEMISTRY. *Current Pos:* dir qual control, SmithKline Beecham, 80-82, dir pharm develop, 82-88, vpres pharm tech, 88-93, VPRES & DIR PHARM DEVELOP US, SMITHKLINE BEECHAM, 93- *Personal Data:* b Chicago, Ill, July 24, 35; m 65, Eileen DeMarchi; c Lisa, Lee & Mark. *Educ:* Univ Ill, BS, 59, PhD(pharmaceut chem), 62. *Prof Exp:* Fel org chem, Princeton Univ, 62-63; res pharmacist, Pharmaceut Div, Abbott Labs, 63-67, res pharmacist, Hosp Prod Div, 67-69, prog mgr prod develop, 69; dir qual affairs, Arnar-Stone Labs, Am Hosp Supply Corp, 69-80. *Concurrent Pos:* Adj prof pharmaceut, Temple Univ. *Mem:* Am Pharmaceut Asn; Acad Pharmaceut Sci; Am Chem Soc; Am Asn Pharmaceut Scientists. *Res:* Medicinal chemistry; quality control of pharmaceutical dosage forms; formulation of pharmaceutical dosage forms. *Mailing Add:* SmithKline Beecham 709 Swedeland Rd PO Box 1539 King of Prussia PA 19406

GARDENIER, JOHN STARK, MANAGEMENT SCIENCE, SURVEY STATISTICS. *Current Pos:* STATISTICIAN & SOFTWARE ENGR, NAT CTR HEALTH STATIST, 90- *Personal Data:* b Portland, Maine, Apr 10, 37; m 77, Turkan Kumbaraci; c Branda (Marshall), Patricia (Depew), Linda (Sievering-Albrect), Pamela (Antoien), George & Jason. *Educ:* Yale Univ, BA, 59; George Washington Univ, DBusA, 73. *Honors & Awards:* Silver Medal, Dept Transp, 83. *Prof Exp:* Mem tech staff mgt info syst, Comput Sci Corp, 68-69; sr analyst ship costs, CONSULTEC, 69-71; opers res analyst, Personnel Studies, Risk Anal & Marine Safety, USCG, 71-90. *Concurrent Pos:* Sponsor liaison, Maritime Transp Res Bd, Nat Res Coun, 73-83; rep, Int Marine Simulator Forum, 78-87; adj assoc prof, George Washington Univ, 81-82; prof lect, Am Univ, 82-84. *Mem:* AAAS; Soc Comput Simulation; Am Statist Asn; Asn Comput Mach. *Res:* Maritime transportation safety, especially relating to human factors, work demands, training and testing and simulators; alcohol and transportation safety; computer-based simulation, management science; modeling and statistical analysis in managing personnel productivity, effectiveness and economics; software engineering and management for developing computer assisted survey information collection software. *Mailing Add:* 115 St Andrews Dr NE Vienna VA 22180-3660. *Fax:* 301-436-3705; *E-Mail:* jsg6@nchiia.cdc.em.gov

GARDENIER, TURKAN KUMBARACI, MEDICAL STATISTICS. *Current Pos:* STATISTICIAN, US EQUAL EMPLOYMENT OPPORTUNITY COMN, 90- *Personal Data:* b Istanbul, Turkey, Nov 10, 41; m, John S; c Pamela L, George H & Jason C. *Educ:* Vassar Col, AB, 61; Columbia Univ, MA, 62, PhD(statist), 66. *Prof Exp:* Proj dir testing, Sci Res Assocs, 66-67; res scientist statist & opers res, IIT Res Inst, 67-69; asst prof statist & chmn dept, Mid East Tech Univ, 68-70; vis scientist appl math, Brookhaven Nat Lab, 70-71; assoc dir statist, Pfizer Pharmaceut, 71-73; asst prof marine transp, Maritime Col, State Univ NY, 73-77; res assoc biostatist, Rockefeller Univ, 75-76; med statistician, US Environ Protection Agency, 78-81; pres, Pragmatic Corp & Pro-File Comput Inst, 82-90. *Concurrent Pos:* Cent Treaty Orgn res grant, 69; NSF res grant, 70; consult, Col Physicians & Surgeons, Columbia Univ, 73-76 & Dept Energy, 82-84; biostatistician, Ctr Prev Premature Arteriosclerosis, 75-76; asst presiding officer, Maritime Col, State

Univ NY, 75-77; consult, Med Commun-Proj Aldactone, 75-76; systs consult, North Shore Univ Hosp, 75-76; adj asst prof biostatist, Col Physicians & Surgeons, Columbia Univ, 78-80; adj assoc prof statist, George Washington Univ, 79-82; mem comt, Nat Acad Sci; assoc prof, Am Univ, 82-84; subcontractor, Anser Corp, 82-90; res & develop, Prag Mahia Corp. *Mem:* Opers Res Soc Am; Am Statist Asn; AAAS; Soc Risk Anal; Soc Comput Simulation; Biomet Soc. *Res:* Computer applications of medical research; large scale data base design; analysis of time series data, non-parametric statistics, index derivations for patient data; environmental risk estimation; metamodels and preprocessors for simulations. *Mailing Add:* 1000 Salt Meadow Lane McLean VA 22101. *Fax:* 703-356-9636

GARDER, ARTHUR, numerical analysis, for more information see previous edition

GARDIER, ROBERT WOODWARD, PHARMACOLOGY. *Current Pos:* assoc dean grad studies, Wright State Univ, 77-78, dir, Biomed Sci Doctoral Prog, 78-81, prof & dir basic pharmacol & toxicol, 77-93, EMER PROF, SCH MED, WRIGHT STATE UNIV, 93- *Personal Data:* b Scranton, Pa, May 15, 27; m 51, Virginia H Steeves; c Robert Jr, Cynthia & Christopher. *Educ:* Univ Scranton, BS, 49; Univ Tenn, MS, 52, PhD(pharmacol), 54. *Prof Exp:* Pharmacologist, Pitman-Moore Co, 53-58; asst prof pharmacol & dir res anesthesiol, Sch Med, Ind Univ, 59-61; assoc prof pharmacol, Univ Tex Med Br, 61-63; assoc prof pharmacol & anesthesia res dir, Col Med, Ohio State Univ, 63-67, prof, 67-69; dir biol res, Bristol Labs, 69-71; prof pharmacol & anesthesiol, Col Med, Ohio State Univ, 71-77, actg chmn pharmacol, 73-74. *Concurrent Pos:* Mem, Med Div, Inst Nuclear Studies, Oak Ridge, 51, consult, 51-52. *Mem:* AAAS; Soc Pharmacol & Exp Therapeut; Soc Exp Biol & Med; Soc Toxicol. *Res:* Drugs related to anesthesia; autonomic nervous system pharmacology; muscarinic receptor subtypes. *Mailing Add:* Dept Pharmacol & Toxicol Sch Med Wright State Univ Dayton OH 45435

GARDIN, JULIUS M, CARDIOVASCULAR DISEASES, CARDIAC ULTRASOUND. *Current Pos:* from asst prof to assoc prof, 79-89, PROF MED & CARDIOL, UNIV CALIF, IRVINE MED CTR, 89-, CHIEF CARDIOL, 94- *Personal Data:* b Detroit, Mich, Jan 14, 49; m 82, Susan Deanne Kelemen; c Adam Lev, Tova Michal & Margot Anne. *Educ:* Univ Mich, BS, 68, MD, 72; Am Bd Internal Med, dipl. *Prof Exp:* Intern & resident internal med, Univ Mich Affil Hosps, 72-75; fel cardiol, Georgetown Univ Affil Hosps, 75-77; assoc med, Sch Med, Northwestern Univ, 77-78, asst prof, 78-79. *Concurrent Pos:* Guest investr cardiol, Cardiol Br, Nat Heart, Lung & Blood Inst, NIH, 76-77; dir, Cardiopulmonary Resuscitation Comt & Cardiol Noninvasive Lab, Vet Admin, Lakeside Med Ctr, 77-79; dir, Cardiol Noninvasive Lab, Irvine Med Ctr, Univ Calif, 79-; grantee, Am Heart Asn, Calif Affil, 80-82, 83-84, Nat Heart Lung & Blood Inst, 88-; actg chief cardiol, Long Beach, Calif, Vet Admin Med Ctr, 82-84; sec, bd dirs & chmn, Pan-Am Sect, Cardiac Doppler Soc, 84-; assoc ed, Am J Cardiac Imaging, 85-; mem bd dirs, Am Soc Echocardiography, 85-, Coun Geriat Cardiol, 86-; bd dirs & treas, Am Soc Echocardiography, 88-91; fel, Coun Clin Cardiol & Coun Geriat Cardiol, 92-93, fel, Coun Epidemiol, fel, cardiovasc radiol. *Mem:* Fel Am Col Physicians; fel Am Col Cardiol; fel Am Col Chest Physicians; fel Am Heart Asn; Int Cardiac Doppler Soc (vpres, 88-90, pres, 90-92); Am Soc Echocardiography (treas, 89-91, vpres, 91-93, pres, 93-95). *Res:* The application of ultrasound to define anatomy and function of the heart in experimental models, clinical situations and large ipiucmid logic colmorts; geriatric cardiology. *Mailing Add:* Div Cardiol Univ Calif Irvine Med Ctr 101 City Dr S Bldg 53 Orange CA 92668-2901. *Fax:* 714-456-8895

GARDINER, DONALD ANDREW, MATHEMATICAL STATISTICS, EXPERIMENTAL STATISTICS. *Current Pos:* CONSULT STATIST METHODS, 85- *Personal Data:* b Buffalo, NY, Feb 2, 22; m 43, Marie Tropman; c Ellen M, Andrew G & Kathryn C. *Educ:* Univ Buffalo, BS, 43, MBA, 48; NC State Col, PhD(exp statist), 56. *Prof Exp:* Lectr statist, Univ Buffalo, 46-48; asst prof, Univ Tenn, 48-51; asst statistician, NC State Col, 55-56; statistician phys & eng sci, Oak Ridge Nat Lab, Tenn, 56-67, asst dir, Math Div, 67-73; head, Math & Statist Res Dept, Comput Sci Div, Nuclear Div, Union Carbide Corp, 73-83; sr consult statist, Martin Marietta Energy Systs, 83-85. *Concurrent Pos:* Assoc prof, Univ Tenn, 65-73, prof, 73-; vis prof, Fla State Univ, 66-67; ed-elect, Technometrics, 71, ed, 72-74. *Mem:* Fel Am Statist Asn; Sigma Xi; fel AAAS. *Res:* Experimental statistics; design of experiments for physical sciences; statistical analysis of experiments in physical sciences; probability models; computational statistics. *Mailing Add:* 108 Mason Lane Oak Ridge TN 37830. *E-Mail:* dhgardiner@aol.com

GARDINER, JOHN ALDEN, PESTICIDE CHEMISTRY, ANALYTICAL CHEMISTRY. *Current Pos:* Res chemist, Indust & Biochem Dept, 64-67, sr res chemist, 67-69, res supvr, 69-74, res mgr biochem dept, 74-76, asst mgr prod regist, 76-77, MGR REGIST & REGULATORY AFFAIRS, AGR PROD DEPT, E I DU PONT DE NEMOURS & CO, INC, 77- *Personal Data:* b Providence, RI, Feb 9, 38; m 60; c 3. *Educ:* NC Univ, BS, 60; Ohio State Univ, MS, 62, PhD(anal chem), 64. *Mem:* Am Chem Soc; Soc Chem Indust. *Res:* Metabolism/degradation of c-14 pesticides in soil, plants, animals, and water; pesticide residue analysis; assay methods; organic trace analysis. *Mailing Add:* 114 Hitching Post Dr Surrey Park Wilmington DE 19803-1913

GARDINER, JOHN BROOKE, ORGANIC CHEMISTRY. *Current Pos:* RETIRED. *Personal Data:* b Bryn Mawr, Pa, Nov 9, 29; m 56; c 2. *Educ:* Haverford Col, AB, 51; Univ NC, PhD(org chem), 57. *Prof Exp:* Chemist, Prod Res Div, Exxon Chem Technol, 57-59 & high energy propellant proj, 59-64, sr chemist, 64-66, proj leader rubber adhesion, Enjay Polymer Labs, 66-68, staff planner prog & budget, 68-70, res assoc, 71, prog mgr, Enjay New Venture Additives Lab, 70-71, sect head, Linden, 71-92. *Mem:* AAAS; Am Chem Soc; Sigma Xi. *Res:* Optical isomerization; anthracene chemistry; synthetic motor oils; viscosity index improvers for motor oils; synthesis of high energy oxidizers-monomers-binders; scale-up formulation and micro rocket firing; rubber adhesion; microinterferometry; gear oils. *Mailing Add:* 1364 Stony Brook Lane Mountainside NJ 07092-1828

GARDINER, KATHELEEN JANE, HUMAN GENOME ORGANIZATION, MOLECULAR BIOLOGY OF DOWN SYNDROME. *Current Pos:* fel, 84-87, INST FEL, ELEANOR ROOSEVELT INST, 87-; ASST PROF, UNIV COLO, 90- *Personal Data:* b Montreal, Que, June 16, 53; m, Thomas Vere. *Educ:* McGill Univ, BS, 74; Univ Colo, MS, 80, PhD(biophys & genetics), 84. *Prof Exp:* Teacher physics, Seepapitso Second Sch, Govt Botswana, 74-78; instr molecular biol, Univ Colo, 87-93. *Concurrent Pos:* Res career develop award, NIH, 90- *Mem:* Am Soc Human Genetics; AAAS; Human Genome Orgn. *Res:* Isolation and characterization of genes on human chromosome 21 for the study of Down syndrome and genome organizational features and genes on chromosome 3 relevant to leukemia and developmental disease. *Mailing Add:* Eleanor Roosevelt Inst 1899 Gaylord St Denver CO 80206

GARDINER, KEITH M, DESIGN PRODUCTS PROCESSES ORGANIZATIONS & SYSTEMS, MATERIALS SELECTION & EVALUATION. *Current Pos:* PROF INDUST ENG & DIR, CTR MFG SYSTS ENG, LEHIGH UNIV, 88- *Personal Data:* b Stockport, Eng, Mar 30, 33; US citizen; m, Bernice Bult. *Educ:* Univ Manchester, Eng, BSc, 53, PhD(metall), 57. *Prof Exp:* Sect leader nuclear fuels develop, Eng Elec Co Ltd, 56-59; asst dir, F Gardiner Ltd, 59-61; asst mgr mfg methods develop, Rolls-Royce Aero Engine Div, 61-66; sr engr, IBM Corp, 66-87. *Concurrent Pos:* Adj prof mech eng, Univ Vt, 72-80; IBM fac loan prof, Southern Univ La, 78-79; adj prof, State Univ NY, Binghampton, 82-87; mem, Col Fels, Soc Mfg Engrs, 93; int dir, Soc Mfg Engrs, 93-94 & 95-96; ed, J Elec Mfg; assoc ed, J Mfg Systs. *Mem:* Soc Mfg Engrs; Am Soc Mech Eng; Sigma Xi. *Res:* Manufacturing systems engineering aspects of realizing concepts into the marketplace out to end-of-life, measurements and holistic impacts on society. *Mailing Add:* Ctr Mfg Systs Eng Mohler Lab Lehigh Univ 200 W Packer Ave Bethlehem PA 18015-1593. *Fax:* 610-758-6527; *E-Mail:* kg03@lehigh.edu

GARDINER, KENNETH WILLIAM, PHYSICAL CHEMISTRY, ANALYTICAL CHEMISTRY. *Current Pos:* prof appl sci, Col Phys Sci, Univ Calif, 72-77, prof admin, Grad Sch Admin, 72-82, chmn, Appl Sci Prog, 73-77, prof 77-87, prof mgt, Grad Sch Mgt, Riverside, 82-87, EMER PROF ENVIRON SCI, COL NATURAL & AGR SCI, UNIV CALIF, 87- *Personal Data:* b Chicago, Ill, Feb 10, 17; m 42; c 3. *Educ:* Stanford Univ, AB, 39, MA, 40; Mass Inst Technol, PhD(instrument anal chem), 52. *Prof Exp:* Sr res chemist, Lever Bros Co & Firestone Tire & Rubber Co, 41-49; asst, Mass Inst Technol, 50-52; dir res, Gardiner Instrument Res Lab, 52-56; dir res, Gen Chem Lab, Cent Res & Eng Div, Continental Can Co, 56-59; chief res chemist & asst dir, Cent Res Div, Consol Electrodynamics Corp Div, Bell & Howell Co, 59-60; dir chem res, Bell & Howell Res Ctr, 60-64; dir res & eng & gen mgr, Anal Systs Co, Teledyne Systs Corp, 64-70, pres & gen mgr, Teledyne Anal Instruments, Teledyne Inc, 70-72. *Concurrent Pos:* Res assoc, Mass Inst Technol, 53; mem adv panel, Nat Res Coun-Nat Acad Sci for Anal Chem Div, Nat Bur Stand, 72-78, chmn, 77-78. *Mem:* Am Chem Soc; Am Phys Soc. *Res:* Management of technology, technology transfer, methods for measuring technology effectiveness and cost/benefit evaluations of research and development; instrumental analytical chemistry; physical and instrumental methods in research and chemical analysis. *Mailing Add:* 1125 Mesita Rd Pasadena CA 91107

GARDINER, LION FREDERICK, HIGHER EDUCATION DEVELOPMENT. *Current Pos:* lectr, 69-72, asst prof, 72-74, ASSOC PROF ZOOL, RUTGERS UNIV, NEWARK, 74- *Personal Data:* b Glen Cove, NY, June 21, 38; m 71, Jane S Breckenridge. *Educ:* Wheaton Col, Ill, BS, 60; Univ Mich, MS, 64; Univ RI, PhD, 72. *Prof Exp:* Instr biol, Delta Col, Mich, 64-65. *Concurrent Pos:* Fac fel, NJ State Dept Higher Educ, 87-88; co-coordr, grad teaching asst prog, Rutgers Grad Sch, Newark, 90-94. *Mem:* Asn Study Higher Educ. *Res:* Biology of the deep-sea fauna; systematics and biology of the Tanaidacea; marine benthic ecology; development of teaching skills of university faculty and graduate students; liberal education of undergraduates; academic management. *Mailing Add:* Dept Biol Sci Rutgers Univ 101 Warren St Newark NJ 07102-1811. *Fax:* 973-648-5518; *E-Mail:* gardiner@andromeda.rutgers.edu

GARDINER, WILLIAM CECIL, JR, PHYSICAL CHEMISTRY. *Current Pos:* from instr to assoc prof, 60-72, PROF CHEM, UNIV TEX, AUSTIN, 72- *Personal Data:* b Niagara Falls, NY, Jan 14, 33; m 59, 91, Regina Monaco; c Grace, Charlotte & Amy. *Educ:* Princeton Univ, AB, 54; Harvard Univ, PhD(chem), 60. *Honors & Awards:* Alexander von Humboldt Award, 79. *Prof Exp:* Res assoc chem, Max Planck Inst Phys Chem, Gottingen, 55-57. *Concurrent Pos:* Guggenheim fel, Inst Phys Chem, Univ Gottingen, 75-76; Thyssen fel, 81; Lady Davis vis prof, Hebrew Univ Jerusalem, 85; fel, Japan Soc Sci Res, 91. *Mem:* AAAS; Am Phys Soc; Am Chem Soc; Combustion Inst. *Res:* Chemical kinetics; combustion; shock and detonation waves; molecular evolution. *Mailing Add:* Dept Chem Univ Tex Austin TX 78712. *Fax:* 512-471-8696; *E-Mail:* bill@lioness.cm.utexas.edu

GARDLUND, ZACHARIAH GUST, MACROMOLECULAR COMPOSITES, LASER DYES. *Current Pos:* PROF MAT SCI & ENG, UNIV ARIZ, 91- *Personal Data:* b Lake City, Minn, Sept 12, 37; m 63, Sharon Smith; c Karin, Kristina & E Zack. *Educ:* Carleton Col, BA, 59; Univ Ariz, PhD, 64. *Prof Exp:* From assoc sr res chemist to sr res chemist, Gen Motors

Tech Ctr, 64-69, sr res chemist & supvr, Org Chem Sect, 69-77, staff res scientist, 77-87, supvr, Advan Mat Group, Polymers Dept, Res Lab, 77-87, sr staff res scientist, 87-91. *Mem:* Am Chem Soc; Sigma Xi. *Res:* Macromolecular composites; inorganic-organic hybrids; laser dyes; polymer blends; manomer-polymer synthesis. *Mailing Add:* Mat Sci & Eng Dept Univ Ariz Mats Lab 4715 E Fort Lowell Tucson AZ 85712. *Fax:* 520-322-2993; *E-Mail:* zgg@aml.arizona.edu

GARDNER, ALVIN FREDERICK, PATHOLOGY. *Current Pos:* pathologist, Bur Drugs, 63-67, dent officer, Off Drug Surveillance, 67-69, ORAL PATHOLOGIST, BUR DRUGS, FOOD & DRUG ADMIN, DEPT HEALTH & HUMAN SERV, 69- *Personal Data:* b Chicago, Ill, Mar 22, 20; m 82, Ruth M Moskovitz; c Ava L (Mendelson). *Educ:* Emory Univ, DDS, 43; Univ Kansas City, cert, 46; Univ Ill, MS, 57; Georgetown Univ, PhD(path), 59. *Prof Exp:* Res assoc & instr oral path, Univ Ill, 57; resident oral path, Dent & Oral Br, Armed Forces Inst Path, 57-59; assoc prof path & oral path, Sch Dent, Univ Md, 59-63. *Concurrent Pos:* Consult, Vet Admin, 60-; vis scientist, Nat Bur Stand; staff dentist, Kadlec Hosp, Hanford Works, Wash; mem dent serv, Stockton State Hosp, Calif; consult, Stedman's Med Dictionary; NIH, US Army Res & Develop Command, Am Cancer Soc & Sigma Xi res grants. *Mem:* AAAS; Am Nutrit Soc; fel Am Pub Health Asn; Am Med Writers' Asn; Am Dent Asn; Sigma Xi. *Res:* Experimental Lathyrism; disturbances in the metabolism of connective tissue; nutritional disturbance in mesoderm; oral pharmacology, effects of drugs on oral tissues. *Mailing Add:* 2000 Hidden Valley Lane Silver Spring MD 20904

GARDNER, ANDREW LEROY, PLASMA DIAGNOSTICS, MICROWAVE CIRCUITRY. *Current Pos:* from assoc prof to prof, 64-84, EMER PROF PHYSICS, BRIGHAM YOUNG UNIV, 85- *Personal Data:* b Ogden, Utah, Feb 6, 19; m 41, 90, Mavis Bourgeois; c Kayleen, Keith, Lynn, David & Janis. *Educ:* Utah State Univ, BS, 40; Univ Calif, Berkeley, PhD(physics), 55. *Prof Exp:* Commun asst, Idaho Nat Forest, USDA, 41; radio engr, Off Chief Signal Off, US War Dept, 42-44; mem staff, Radiation Lab, Mass Inst Technol, 44-45; res asst & assoc, Inst Eng Res, Univ Calif, 46-54; physicist, Lawrence Radiation lab, 54-64. *Concurrent Pos:* Consult, Inst Plasma Physics, Japan, 62 & Lawrence Radiation Lab, 68-75. *Mem:* Fel Am Phys Soc. *Res:* Experimental plasma physics; microwave circuitry; electronics; high voltage switching. *Mailing Add:* 555 E 2950 N Provo UT 84604. *E-Mail:* gardnera@cougar.netutah.net

GARDNER, ARTHUR WENDEL, GENETICS. *Current Pos:* RETIRED. *Personal Data:* b Cedar City, Utah, Oct 23, 24; m 67, Shirley M Maughan. *Educ:* Utah State Univ, BS, 49; Kans State Univ, MS, 54, PhD(genetics), 56. *Prof Exp:* Instr genetics, Kans State Univ, 55; instr biol, Russell Sage Col, 61-64; asst prof, Washburn Univ, 64-67; from assoc prof to prof, W Ga Col, 67-90, actg head dept, 68-69. *Mem:* AAAS; Am Soc Animal Sci. *Res:* Genetics and physiology of the Syrian hamster. *Mailing Add:* 85 Greenwood Lane Carrollton GA 30117

GARDNER, BERNARD, SURGERY. *Current Pos:* SURG ATTEND, UNIV HOSP, NEWARK, NJ. *Personal Data:* b Brooklyn, NY, Oct 1, 31; m 54; c 3. *Educ:* NY Univ, AB, 52, MD, 56. *Prof Exp:* From asst prof to assoc prof, State Univ NY Downstate Med Ctr, 65-72, prof surg, 72-; dir surg oncol, Kings Co Hosp, 70-; prof surg, Col Med & Dent NJ; chief surg, Hackensack Med Ctr, 83-92. *Concurrent Pos:* Mem bd dirs, Res Found, State Univ NY, 68-; John & Mary R Markle scholar acad med, 68-; vis prof mult insts; mem, Bd Dirs, Southern NY Res Found; mem, Study Sect Cancer Ed, Nat Cancer Inst; chmn, Training Comt, Soc Surg Oncol, 88- *Mem:* Am Surg Asn; Asn Acad Surg; Soc Exp Biol & Med; Soc Univ Surg; Soc Surg Alimentary Tract; Soc Surg Oncol (secy, 88-91). *Res:* Tumor metastases; metabolic effects of tumor, particularly the relationship between tumor growth and calcium and phosphate metabolism; suspension stability of bile and its relationship to the electro-chemistry of the cholesterol-bile salt-lecithin micelle. *Mailing Add:* Univ Med & Dent NJ 185 S Orange Ave MSBG-510 Newark NJ 07103

GARDNER, BRUCE LYNN, AGRICULTURAL ECONOMICS. *Current Pos:* PROF, UNIV MD, 81-; ASST SECY, USDA, WASHINGTON, 89- *Personal Data:* b Solon Mills, Ill, Aug 31, 42; m 64, Mary Agacinski. *Educ:* Univ Ill, BS, 64; Univ Chicago, PhD, 68. *Prof Exp:* Asst prof econ, NC State Univ, Raleigh, 68-75; sr staff economist, Pres Coun Econ Advisors, 75-77; prof, Tex A&M Univ, 77-80. *Concurrent Pos:* Mem bd dirs, Am Agr Econ, 84-87. *Mem:* Fel Am Asn Agr Econ. *Res:* Economics of agricultural policies. *Mailing Add:* 6902 Chansory Lane Hyattsville MD 20782

GARDNER, BRYANT ROGERS, SOIL CHEMISTRY, PLANT NUTRITION. *Current Pos:* RETIRED. *Personal Data:* b McNary, Ariz, Sept 19, 30; m 53; c 8. *Educ:* Ariz State Univ, BS, 58; Univ Ariz, MS, 60, PhD(agr chem), 63. *Prof Exp:* Res assoc, Univ Ariz, 62-63, asst agr chemist, 63-68, assoc agr chemist, 68-73, agr chemist, 73-89. *Mem:* Am Soc Agron. *Res:* Soil fertility; plant physiology. *Mailing Add:* 21420 Via Del Palo Queen Creek AZ 85242

GARDNER, CHARLES OLDA, QUANTITATIVE GENETICS. *Current Pos:* Asst exten agronomist, Univ Nebr, 46-48, from assoc prof to prof, 52-70, chmn, Statist Lab, 57-68, found prof, 70-89, EMER PROF AGRON, UNIV NEBR, 89-, CONSULT, PLANT BREEDING, GENETICS & STATIST, 89- *Personal Data:* b Tecumseh, Nebr, Mar 15, 19; m 47, Wanda M Steinkamp; c Charles Jr, Lynda, Thomas & Richard. *Educ:* Univ Nebr, BSc, 41, MS, 48; Harvard Univ, MBA, 43; NC State Univ, PhD(agron), 51. *Honors & Awards:* Crop Sci Res Award, Crop Sci Soc Am, 78, DeKalb-Pfizer Distinguished Career Award, 84; Distinguished Serv Award, USDA, 88;

Agron Serv Award, Am Soc Agron, 88. *Concurrent Pos:* Asst statistician, NC State Univ, 51-52; vis prof, Univ Wis, 62-63; distinguished professorship, Univ Nebr, 70-89. *Mem:* Fel AAAS (chmn, sect O, 87-88); Genetics Soc Am; fel Am Soc Agron (pres, 81-82); Am Genetic Asn; fel Crops Sci Soc Am (pres, 74-75); Biometric Soc; Sigma Xi. *Res:* Quantitative inheritance studies in plants; insecticide resistance management; biometrical genetics; development of quantitative genetic models and breeding systems for plant improvement. *Mailing Add:* Dept Agron Rm 314 Kiem Hall Univ Nebr Lincoln NE 68583-0915

GARDNER, CHARLES OLDA, JR, PLANT VIROLOGY. *Current Pos:* GRAD ASST, DEPT BIOMETRY, UNIV NEBR, 92- *Personal Data:* b Raleigh, NC, May 27, 49; m 73. *Educ:* Univ Nebr, BS, 71; Univ Fla, PhD(biochem & molecular biol), 76. *Prof Exp:* Res assoc, Dept Genetics, NC State Univ, 77; res assoc, Okla State Univ, 78-81, asst prof, Dept Biochem, 81-87; vis scientist, Dept Agron, Univ Nebr, 87-89; post doctorial fel, Dept Biometry, La State Univ Med Ctr, 90-91. *Mem:* Am Phytopath Soc; Am Plant Physiologists; Sigma Xi. *Res:* Molecular biology of plant viruses; nucleic acid and protein synthesis in plants. *Mailing Add:* Dept Agron Univ Nebr Rm 104 F Miller Hall Lincoln NE 68583-0712

GARDNER, CHESTER STONE, ELECTRICAL ENGINEERING, ELECTRO-OPTICS. *Current Pos:* from asst prof to assoc prof, 73-81, PROF ELEC ENG, UNIV ILL, URBANA, 81- *Personal Data:* b Jamaica, NY, Mar 29, 47; m 68; c 2. *Educ:* Mich State Univ, BS, 69; Northwestern Univ, MS, 71, PhD(elec eng), 73. *Prof Exp:* Mem tech staff, Bell Tel Labs, 69-71; teaching asst elec eng, Northwestern Univ, 71-73. *Concurrent Pos:* Consult, McGraw-Hill Bk Co, 76-77, Caterpillar Tractor Co, 78-, US Army Corp Engrs, 79- & Northern Ill Gas, 81- *Mem:* Optical Soc Am; Inst Elec & Electronics Engrs; Sigma Xi. *Res:* Optical communications; lidar; laser ranging; optical information processing and spread spectrum communications; optical metiology. *Mailing Add:* 1406 W Green St Urbana IL 61801

GARDNER, CLIFFORD S, APPLIED MATHEMATICS. *Current Pos:* prof, 68-90, EMER PROF MATH, UNIV TEX, AUSTIN, 90- *Personal Data:* b Ft Smith, Ark, Jan 14, 24; m 67, Marilyn R Martinez Jackson; c 2. *Educ:* Harvard Col, AB, 44; NY Univ, PhD(math), 52. *Honors & Awards:* Norbert Wiener Prize, 85. *Prof Exp:* Physicist, Nat Adv Comt Aeronaut, 44-46; mathematician, Control Instrument Co, 47-48; physicist, Calif Res & Develop Co, 52-54; physicist, Radiation Lab, Univ Calif, 54-56; res scientist, Courant Inst, NY Univ, 56-62; physicist, Radio Corp Am, 62-64; vis res prof physics, Plasma Physics Lab, Princeton Univ, 64-68. *Mem:* Am Math Soc. *Res:* Differential equations. *Mailing Add:* 8007 Briarwood Lane Univ Tex Austin TX 78758

GARDNER, DANIEL, NEUROPHYSIOLOGY, BIOPHYSICS. *Current Pos:* asst prof, 73-79, assoc prof, 79-89, PROF PHYSIOL, MED COL, CORNELL UNIV, 89-, PROF NEUROSCI, 92- *Personal Data:* b New York, NY, Jan 23, 45; m 67; c 2. *Educ:* Columbia Col, AB, 66; New York Univ, PhD(physiol), 71. *Prof Exp:* Programmer & comput math lectr, Goddard Inst Space Studies, NASA, 62-66; fel physiol, Sch Med, New York Univ, 66-71; sr fel neurophysiol, Sch Med, Univ Wash, 71-73. *Concurrent Pos:* Instr, Workshop Comput Math, Columbia Univ, 63-67; prin investr res grant, NIH, 73- *Mem:* Soc Neurosci; Biophys Soc; Am Physiol Soc; Soc Gen Physiol. *Res:* Biophysics of synaptic transmission between neurons in the nervous system of the marine mollusc aplysia; analysis of biological neural networks; neurophysiology database. *Mailing Add:* Dept Physiol Cornell Univ Med Col 1300 York Ave New York NY 10021-4805. *E-Mail:* dan@aplysia.med.cornell.edu

GARDNER, DAVID ARNOLD, IMFORMATION SYSTEMS. *Current Pos:* res scientist cell biol, Res Div, Bayer Corp, 69-76, tech prod mgr, 76-83, mgr qual assurance develop, Ames Div, 83-87, MGR, INFO SYSTS DIAGNOSTICS DIV, BAYER CORP, ELKHART, 87- *Personal Data:* b Ithaca, NY, June 19, 39; m 59; c 3. *Educ:* Univ Rochester, BS, 61, PhD(biochem), 67; Ind Univ, South Bend, MBA, 83. *Prof Exp:* NIH res fel biochem, Brandeis Univ, 67-69. *Concurrent Pos:* Asst fac fel, Univ Notre Dame, 69-75. *Mem:* Am Asn Clin Chem; NY Acad Sci; Sigma Xi. *Res:* Regulation of cell division in tissue culture; use of cell cultures for the development of clinical diagnostic tests; glycolipid metabolism in cultured mammalian cells; new product development in clinical chemistry; management of technical support group for clinical diagnostic products; development of automated test systems for quality control of medical diagnostic products; automated laboratory information systems. *Mailing Add:* 16243 Marlowe Way Granger IN 46530

GARDNER, DAVID GODFREY, ORAL PATHOLOGY. *Current Pos:* PROF & CHMN DEPT PATH & RADIOL, UNIV TEX, HSC, HOUSTON DENT BR, 84- *Personal Data:* b Darlington, Eng, Feb 24, 36; Can citizen; m 60; c 3. *Educ:* Univ Toronto, DDS, 58; Ind Univ, MSD, 65; Am Bd Oral Path, dipl, 69. *Prof Exp:* Dent officer, Can Army, 58-63; asst prof oral med, Univ BC, 65-66; from assoc prof to prof path, Univ Western Ont, 66-84, chmn div oral path, 70-84. *Concurrent Pos:* Consult oral path & oral med, Children's Psychiat Res Inst, London, Ont, 66-84; mem consult panel, Can Tumour Reference Ctr, Nat Cancer Inst Can, 68-; mem active staff path & dent, Univ Hosp, London, Ont, 72-84; mem staff, Guy's Hosp, London, Eng, 73-74. *Mem:* Fel Am Acad Oral Path (pres, 85-86); Can Acad Oral Path (secy, 66-72, pres, 72-73). *Res:* Disturbances in odontogenesis; odontogenic tumors; disorders of maxillary sinus. *Mailing Add:* Pathol Univ Co Health Sci 4200 E Ninth Ave Denver CO 80220-3706

GARDNER, DAVID MILTON, PHYSICAL CHEMISTRY. *Current Pos:* RETIRED. *Personal Data:* b Cleveland, Ohio, June 21, 28; m 55, Joan G Hutchinson; c Mark A, David W, Nancy J, Jane E & Karen G. *Educ:* Brown Univ, ScB, 50; Univ Pa, MS, 52, PhD(chem), 54. *Honors & Awards:* IR 100 Award, 89. *Prof Exp:* Proj leader, Reaction Motors, Inc, 55-56, sr chemist, 56-57; group leader, Pennwalt Corp, 60-74, sr scientist, 74-82, res mgr, 82-91. *Concurrent Pos:* Lectr, La Salle Col, 66-73, Temple Univ, 92-93. *Mem:* Am Chem Soc; Sigma Xi. *Res:* Thermodynamics; nitrogen; process development; fluorochemicals; organo sulfur compounds. *Mailing Add:* 727 W Valley Forge Rd King of Prussia PA 19406-1572

GARDNER, DAVID R, NEUROPHYSIOLOGY. *Current Pos:* from asst prof to assoc prof, 67-82, assoc undergrad chmn, 79-83, PROF BIOL, CARLETON UNIV, 82-, CHMN DEPT, 83- *Personal Data:* b London, Eng, Aug 10, 42; Can citizen. *Educ:* Southampton Univ, Eng, BSc, 63, PhD(physiol-biochem & neurophys), 66. *Prof Exp:* SRC fel physiol-biochem, Southampton Univ, 66-67. *Concurrent Pos:* Mem bd gov, Carleton Univ, 89- *Mem:* Soc Exp Biol; Soc Neurosci. *Res:* Modes of action of synthetic and natural product pesticides on excitable tissues of invertebrates. *Mailing Add:* Dept Biol Carleton Univ Colonel By Dr Tory Bldg Rm 569 Ottawa ON K1S 5B6 Can

GARDNER, DONALD EUGENE, INHALATION TOXICOLOGY, GENERAL TOXICOLOGY. *Current Pos:* VPRES & CHIEF SCIENTIST, MAN TECH ENVIRON TECHNOL, INC, 89- *Personal Data:* b Council Bluffs, Iowa, Nov 1, 31; m 60, Elly K Peter; c Stephanie, Stephen, Susan & Stuart. *Educ:* Creighton Univ, BS, 55, MS, 58; Univ Cincinnati, PhD(environ health), 71. *Honors & Awards:* Merit Award, Soc Toxicol, Career Achievement Award. *Prof Exp:* Res immunologist, US Biol Labs, Ft Detrick, Frederick, Md, 60-62; res microbiologist, US Biol Proving Ground, Dugway, Utah, 62-64 & Nat Air Pollution Control Admin, 64-71; chief, Biomed Res Br, US Environ Protection Agency, 71-80, dir, Inhalation Toxicol Div, 80-82; dir res, environ sci, Northrop Serv, Inc, 82-89. *Concurrent Pos:* Co-topic leader, Joint Coop Prog US-USSR, US Govt, 73-81; topic leader, US-Poland Joint Agreement, 76-82 & US-Yugoslavia Joint Res Agreement, US Environ Protection Agency, 81-82; adj prof physiol & pharmacol, Sch Med, Duke Univ, 75- & adj assoc prof, NC State Univ, 76-87; mem, Task Force Environ Health, WHO, 76-77; mem sci adv comt, Environ Protection Agency, 80-; consult chem indust, pres, Inhalation Spec Sect, Soc Toxicol, 84-85, Immunotoxicol Spec Sect, 87-88 & Metal Spec Sect, 91; ed, J Inhalation Toxicol; grant & prog sci review comt, Food & Drug Admin, Environ Protection Agency & Nat Inst Environ Health Sci; ed, J Inhalation Toxicol, 88- *Mem:* Soc Toxicol; Am Col Toxicol; NY Acad Sci. *Res:* Environmental and occupational toxicology; immunotoxicology; inhalation toxicology; host defense mechanisms; short-term in vitro for predicting chronic health effects. *Mailing Add:* Inhalation Toxicol Assoc PO Box 97605 Raleigh NC 27624. *Fax:* 919-549-0071

GARDNER, DONALD GLENN, nuclear chemistry, for more information see previous edition

GARDNER, EARL WILLIAM, JR, microbiology, for more information see previous edition

GARDNER, EDWARD EUGENE, SOLID STATE SCIENCE. *Current Pos:* PROF, ELEC & COMPUT ENG DEPT, UNIV COLO, 85- *Personal Data:* b Somerset, Pa, Aug 3, 23; m 48; c 4. *Educ:* Mass Inst Technol, SB, 48; Univ Minn, MA, 50; Cath Univ Am, PhD(physics), 55. *Prof Exp:* Mem res staff, Div Indust, Mass Inst Technol, 48-49; instr gen physics, Va Polytech Inst, 50-51; asst prof, US Naval Acad, 51-55; asst prof elec eng & physics, Lehigh Univ, 55-58; res physicist, Whirlpool Corp, 58-62; adv physicist, 62-69, sr physicist, Systs Prod Div, 69-76, sr physicist, Gen Technol Div, IBM Corp, 76-85. *Concurrent Pos:* Prof, Gen Elec Co, 57; spec lectr, Mich State Univ, 59-; vis prof, Tuskegee Inst, 73-74. *Mem:* Electrochem Soc; Am Phys Soc; Inst Elec & Electronics Engrs; Am Soc Testing & Mat. *Res:* Solid state physics; semiconductor materials and process development; characterization of semiconductor materials; semiconductor materials measurement technique development. *Mailing Add:* 81 Benthaven Pl Boulder CO 80303-6200

GARDNER, ELIOT LAWRENCE, NEUROSCIENCE, PSYCHOPHARMACOLOGY. *Current Pos:* from asst prof to assoc prof, 76-89, DIR, PROG BRAIN & BEHAV, ALBERT EINSTEIN COL MED, 86-, PROF PSYCHIAT & NEUROSCI, 89- *Personal Data:* b Boston, Mass, Dec 31, 40; c 1. *Educ:* Harvard Univ, AB, 62; McGill Univ, MA, 64, PhD(physiol psychol), 66. *Honors & Awards:* Career Scientist Award, Health Res Coun NY, 75. *Prof Exp:* Med officer, Aeromed Div, USAF, 66-69; res fel pharmacol, Albert Einstein Col Med, 69-72; assoc neurol, 72-73; assoc prof biopsychol, City Univ New York, 73-76. *Concurrent Pos:* USPHS fel, 69-72; adj asst prof psychobiol, NY Univ, 70-73; vis asst prof pharmacol, Albert Einstein Col Med, 73-76; adj prof pharmacol, Touro-Technion Biomed Prog, 83-85; USPHS res grants, 74-; vis scientist, Mass Inst Tech, 80. *Mem:* Soc Neurosci; Psychonomic Soc; fel Am Psychol Asn; Brit Brain Res Asn; Int Brain Res Asn. *Res:* Brain function and behavior; neuropharmacology; psychopharmacology; biological psychiatry. *Mailing Add:* Dept Psychiat F-111 Albert Einstein Col Med 1300 Morris Park Ave Bronx NY 10461. *Fax:* 718-918-9274; *E-Mail:* vincent@aecom.yu.edu

GARDNER, ESTHER POLINSKY, NEUROPHYSIOLOGY. *Current Pos:* from asst prof to assoc prof physiol, 73-92, PROF PHYSIOL, & BIOPHYS, SCH MED, NY UNIV, 92- *Personal Data:* b New York, NY, June 14, 41; m 67; c 2. *Educ:* Smith Col, BA, 62; NY Univ, PhD(physiol), 71. *Prof Exp:* Fel physiol, Sch Med, NY Univ, 66-71; sr fel neurophysiol, Sch Med, Univ Wash, 71-73. *Concurrent Pos:* NIH fel, Sch Med, NY Univ, 67-71 & Univ Wash, 71-73; NIH res career develop award, 76-81; Career Scientist Award, Irma T Hirschl Found, 76-81. *Mem:* AAAS; Am Physiol Soc; Soc Neurosci; NY Acad Sci; Int Neural Networks Soc. *Res:* Sensory function of the hand; mechanisms used by single neurons in somatosensory areas of the primate brain to encode spatial and temporal properties of patterned cutaneous stimuli and their relation to sensation. *Mailing Add:* Dept Physiol & Neurosci NY Univ Sch Med 550 First Ave MSB 442 New York NY 10016-6451. *Fax:* 212-263-6964; *E-Mail:* esther_gardner@macmail.med.nyu.edu

GARDNER, FLOYD M, COMMUNICATIONS, ELECTRONICS. *Current Pos:* CONSULT ENGR, 60- *Personal Data:* b Chicago, Ill, Oct 20, 29. *Educ:* Ill Inst Technol, BS, 50; Stanford Univ, MS, 51; Univ Ill, PhD(elec eng), 53. *Mem:* Fel Inst Elec & Electronics Engrs. *Res:* Synchronization of data communication; signal processing; author of books on phase lock techniques and simulation of communications links. *Mailing Add:* Gardner Res Co 1755 University Ave Palo Alto CA 94301. *E-Mail:* 2836063@mcimail.com

GARDNER, FRANK S(TREETER), PHYSICAL METALLURGY. *Current Pos:* RETIRED. *Personal Data:* b Baltimore, Md, Dec 9, 16; m 41, Eleanor Barnum; c Richard B, James S, David R & Thomas W. *Educ:* Mass Inst Technol, SB, 38, ScD(metall), 41. *Prof Exp:* Metallurgist, Am Brake Shoe Co, NJ, 41-46; metallurgist, Gen Elec Co, 46-53, supvr magnetic mat res, Transformer Div, 53-58; proj mgr, Nuclear Metals, Inc, 58-60; dep dir sci, Off Naval Res, 75-81, mat scientist, 60-81, res avd, 81-85. *Mem:* The Metall Soc; Am Soc Metals. *Res:* Metallography; pressure welding; metallurgy of soft magnetic materials; mechanical metallurgy; magnetic transformations; amorphous metals; research programming; lake ecology. *Mailing Add:* 602 Wake Robin Dr Shelburne VT 05482

GARDNER, FRED MARVIN, ELECTRON PHYSICS. *Current Pos:* prof, 70-90, EMER PROF PHYSICS, UNIV HARTFORD, 90- *Personal Data:* b Kansas City, Kans, July 4, 22; m 63, Judith; c Warren F, Charles K, Kevin H & Eric J. *Educ:* St Mary's Col, Minn, BS, 45; St Louis Univ, MS, 52; Univ Notre Dame, PhD(physics), 62. *Prof Exp:* Instr, Christian Bros Mil High Sch, Mo, 45-52; from asst prof to assoc prof physics, St Mary's Col, Minn, 52-62; from res scientist to sr res scientist, United Aircraft Res Labs, 62-69; vpres, High Tech Indust, 69-70. *Mem:* Am Phys Soc; Inst Elec & Electronics Engrs; Am Asn Physics Teachers; Sigma Xi; Gynec Laser Soc; Laser Inst Am. *Res:* Medical lasers. *Mailing Add:* 111 Stockade Rd South Glastonbury CT 06073

GARDNER, FREDERICK ALBERT, FOOD SCIENCE & TECHNOLOGY, MICROBIOLOGY. *Current Pos:* from asst prof to prof, 63-90, EMER PROF POULTRY SCI, TEX A&M UNIV, 90- *Personal Data:* b Middletown Springs, Vt, Nov 23, 27; m 49; c 6. *Educ:* Univ Vt, BS, 53; Agr & Mech Col, Tex, MS, 55; Univ Mo, PhD(poultry sci), 60. *Prof Exp:* Instr poultry sci, Agr & Mech Col, Tex, 54-55; asst, Iowa State Col, 55-56; asst, Univ Mo, 56-58; instr, 58-59. *Mem:* Poultry Sci Asn; Inst Food Technologists; Sigma Xi. *Res:* Chemistry and microbiology of poultry and egg products with specific interest in fundamental product characterization and in the maintenance of product quality. *Mailing Add:* Poultry Sci Dept Texas A&M Univ College Station TX 77843-2471

GARDNER, GERALD HENRY FRASER, MATHEMATICS. *Current Pos:* Keck prof geophys, 90-, EMER PROF, RICE UNIV. *Personal Data:* b Ireland, Mar 2, 26; m 50. *Educ:* Trinity Col, Dublin, BA, 47; Carnegie Inst Technol, MSc, 48; Princeton Univ, PhD(math), 53. *Prof Exp:* Lectr math, Trinity Col, Dublin, 49-54; instr, Cornell Univ, 54-55; asst prof, Carnegie Inst Technol, 55-56; sect head, Explor & Prod, Gulf Res & Develop Co, 56-66, sr scientist, 66-80; prof elec eng & prin investr, Seismic Acoust Lab, Univ Houston, 80-90. *Mem:* Soc Explor Geophysicists; Math Asn Am; Europ Asn Explor Geophysicists; Soc Prof Well Log Analysts. *Res:* Relativity; mathematical physics and seismic exploration. *Mailing Add:* 505 Winterburn Ave Pittsburgh PA 15207

GARDNER, HAROLD WAYNE, BIOCHEMISTRY, LIPID CHEMISTRY. *Current Pos:* CHEMIST, NAT CTR AGR UTILIZATION RES, US DEPT AGR, PEORIA, Ill, 67- *Personal Data:* b Carlisle, Pa, June 19, 35; m 81, Cheryl Pauli; c Scott E, Brooke M, Kelly M, Michael P & Bryce A. *Educ:* Pa State Univ, BS, 57, MS, 63, PhD(biochem), 65. *Prof Exp:* Assoc biochemist, Pineapple Res Inst, 65-66; asst res plant biochemist, Univ Calif, Los Angeles, 66-67. *Concurrent Pos:* Assoc ed, Lipids, 90-96. *Mem:* Am Chem Soc; Am Oil Chemists' Soc; Am Soc Plant Physiologists; Am Soc Biochem & Molecular Biol; Oxygen Soc. *Res:* Oxidation of unsaturated fatty acids by plant systems; lipid hydroperoxides and their reaction products; plant-fungal interactions; prairie ecology. *Mailing Add:* Nat Ctr Agr Utilization Res US Dept Agr Peoria IL 61604. *Fax:* 309-681-6686; *E-Mail:* gardnehw@ncaur1.ncaur.gov

GARDNER, HOWARD EARL, PSYCHOLOGY, NEUROLOGY. *Current Pos:* Lectr educ, 71-86, CO-DIR, PROJ ZERO, HARVARD UNIV, 72-, PROF EDUC, 86-, AFIL PROF PSYCHOL, 87- *Personal Data:* b Scranton, Pa, July 11, 43; m, Ellen Winner; c Kerith, Jay, Andrew & Benjamin. *Educ:* Harvard Univ, AB, 65, PhD, 71. *Hon Degrees:* DEduc, Curry Col, 92; DMus, New Eng Conservancy Mus, 93; LHD, Ind Univ, 95, Salem State Col, 96; DHH, Moravian Col, 96, Macalaster Col, 97. *Honors & Awards:* MacArthur Prize Fel, 81; Grawemeyer Award in Educ, 90. *Concurrent Pos:* Res psychologist, Boston Vct Admin Med Ctr, 78-; prof neurol, Boston Univ Sch Med, 84-87, adj prof, 87-; numerous grants govt & pvt found. *Mem:* AAAS; Nat Acad Educ (vpres); Am Psychol Soc; AAAS. *Res:* Psychology and neurology. *Mailing Add:* Grad Sch Educ Proj Zero Harvard Univ Cambridge MA 02138. *Fax:* 617-495-9709

GARDNER, HOWARD SHAFER, paper chemistry, chemical engineering; deceased, see previous edition for last biography

GARDNER, JAMES A, ATMOSPHERIC SPECTROSCOPY, IONOSPHERE-THERMOSPHERE-MESOSPHERE DYNAMICS. *Current Pos:* ASSOC RES SCIENTIST, LUNAR & PLANETARY LAB, UNIV ARIZ, 96- *Personal Data:* b Salem Mass, Sept 7, 60; m 96, Carol Huffman. *Educ:* Boston Col, BSc, 82, PhD(chem), 89. *Prof Exp:* Geophys res scholar, Southeastern Ctr Elec Eng Educ-Air Force Geophys Lab, 89-91; staff scientist, PhotoMetrics Inc, 91-96. *Mem:* Am Chem Soc; Am Geophys Union. *Res:* Ionospheric spectroscopy; UV-VIS-IR remote sensing; ionospheric dynamics. *Mailing Add:* Univ Ariz PL/GP05 Hanscom AFB MA 01731-3010. *Fax:* 781-377-5571; *E-Mail:* gardner@plh.af.mil

GARDNER, JAMES VINCENT, MARINE GEOLOGY. *Current Pos:* MARINE GEOLOGIST, BR PAC MARINE GEOL, US GEOL SURV, 75- *Personal Data:* b Topeka, Kans, May 28, 40; m 64, 81, Catherine A Burstall; c Brooke M & Lindsay J. *Educ:* Calif State Univ, San Diego, BS, 67; Columbia Univ, MA, 69, PhD(marine geol), 73. *Prof Exp:* Field geologist, Wm Ross Cabeen & Assoc, Peru, 67; geologist, Denver Res Ctr, Marathon Oil Co, 69-70; staff res assoc marine geol, Deep Sea Drilling Proj, Scripps Inst Oceanog, 73-75. *Concurrent Pos:* Mem, Int Decade Ocean Explor Climap Proj, 70-73, corresp mem, 73-80; mem, Deep Sea Drilling Proj Rep, Joint Oceanog Inst Deep Earth Sampling Atlantic Panel, 74-75; vis res scientist, Inst Oceanographic Sci, Godalming, UK, 81-82; vis scholar, Univ Sydney, Australia, 91, vis prof, 93. *Mem:* Fel Geol Soc Am; Am Geophys Union; AAAS; Soc Econ Paleontologists & Mineralogists. *Res:* Marine geology and paleooceanography of equatorial Atlantic, Pacific and Bering Sea; deep-sea sedimentology, high-resolution geophysics and digital side-scan sonar processing and interpretation. *Mailing Add:* Costal & Marine Surv US Geol Surv 345 Middlefield Rd MS 999 Menlo Park CA 94025. *Fax:* 650-354-3191; *E-Mail:* jim@octopus.wr.usgs.gov

GARDNER, JEFFERY FAY, GENETIC REGULATION, RECOMBINATION. *Current Pos:* ASSOC PROF MICROBIOL, UNIV ILL, 78- *Educ:* Marquette Univ, PhD(biol), 75. *Mailing Add:* Dept Microbiol 131 Burrill Hall Univ Ill 407 S Goodwin Urbana IL 61801-3704. *Fax:* 217-244-6697

GARDNER, JERRY DAVID, GASTROENTEROLOGY, INTERNAL MEDICINE. *Current Pos:* Clin assoc physiol & clin nutrit, 68-70, sr staff fel, Digestive Dis Br, 70-73, CHIEF, SECT GASTROENTEROL, NAT INST ARTHRITIS, METAB, DIGESTIVE & KIDNEY DIS, NIH, 73-, CHIEF, DIGESTIVE DIS BR, 77- *Personal Data:* b Chanute, Kans, Jan 15, 41; m 62; c 2. *Educ:* Univ Kans, AB, 62; Univ Pa, MD, 66. *Honors & Awards:* Pollard Prize, Univ Mich, 79; Roche Award, Hoffman-LaRoche, 80. *Mem:* Am Soc Clin Invest; Am Fedn Clin Res; Am Gastroenterol Asn; Am Physiol Soc; AAAS. *Res:* Identification of the biochemical basis of action of gastrointestinal hormones. *Mailing Add:* Gastrointestinal Div St Louis Univ Health Sci Ctr 1402 S Grand Blvd St Louis MO 63104-1028. *Fax:* 314-577-8125

GARDNER, JOHN ARVY, JR, SOLID STATE PHYSICS. *Current Pos:* assoc prof, 73-81, PROF PHYSICS, ORE STATE UNIV, 81- *Personal Data:* b Winona, Miss, Nov 5, 39; m 65; c 2. *Educ:* Rice Univ, BA, 61; Univ Ill, MS, 63, PhD(physics), 66. *Prof Exp:* Res assoc physics, Tech Univ, Munich, WGer, 66-67; asst prof, Univ Pa, 67-73. *Concurrent Pos:* Vis scientist, Univ Warwick, Eng, 79-80 & Max Planck Inst Solid State Res, Stuttgart, WGer, 80-81 & 85. *Mem:* Am Phys Soc; AAAS; Am Ceramic Soc; Mat Res Soc. *Res:* Experimental solid state physics; hyperfine interactions; magnetic and electronic properties of liquid and amorphous semiconductors; ceramics; high temperature semiconductors; high-Tc superconductors. *Mailing Add:* Dept Physics Ore State Univ Weiniger Hall 301 Corvallis OR 97331. *Fax:* 541-737-1683

GARDNER, JOHN HALE, MAGNETIC RESONANCE, PLASMA PHYSICS. *Current Pos:* chmn dept, 61-63 & 64-71, PROF PHYSICS, BRIGHAM YOUNG UNIV, 58- *Personal Data:* b Logan, Utah, Aug 24, 22; m 43, Olga Dotson; c Helen, John Willard, Rebecca, Robert, Eric, Ann Marie & Margaret. *Educ:* Utah State Agr Col, BS, 43; Harvard Univ, AM, 47, PhD(physics), 50. *Prof Exp:* Mem staff, Radiation Lab, Mass Inst Technol, 43-46; from asst prof to prof physics, Brigham Young Univ, 49-58. *Concurrent Pos:* Mem tech staff, Thompson-Ramo-Woolidge Corp, 55-57 & 63-64, consult, Space Tech Labs, 57-63 & 64-68. *Mem:* Fel Am Phys Soc; Am Asn Physics Teachers; fel Brit Inst Physics Eng. *Res:* Soil moisture dynamics; microwave antennas; electromagnetic propagation; magnetic resonance; gaseous electronics; quantum electronics; plasma physics; theoretical physics; laws of physics from inevitable symmetries of nature. *Mailing Add:* Dept Physics 175 ESC Brigham Young Univ Provo UT 84602

GARDNER, JOHN W, PSYCHOLOGY. *Current Pos:* Miriam & Peter Haas Centennial prof pub servs, 89-96, CONSULT PROF, STANFORD UNIV, 96- *Personal Data:* b Los Angeles, Calif, 1912. *Educ:* Stanford Univ, BA & MA; Univ Calif, PhD, 38. *Hon Degrees:* Various from Col & Univs. *Honors & Awards:* Pres Medal Freedom, 64; Public Welfare Medal, Nat Acad Sci; Award Distinguished & Except Serv, Am Bd Prof Psychol. *Prof Exp:* Teacher psychol, Univ Calif, Conn Col for Women & Mt Holyoke Col, 38-41; exec assoc, Carnegie Corp, 46-55, pres, 55-65; secy, Dept HEW, 65-68; chmn, Nat Urban Coalition, 69-70; chmn, Common Cause, 70-77; chair, Organizing Comt, Independant Sector, 78-79, chmn, 80-83. *Concurrent Pos:* Consult, Govt Agencies, 47-65; pres, Carnegie Found Advan Teaching, 55-; mem, Pres Kennedy's Task Force Educ, Pres Carter's Comn Agenda for Eighties & Pres Reagan's Task Force Pvt Sector Initiatives; chmn, Pres Kennedy's Comn Int Educ & Cult Affairs, Pres Johnson's Task Force on Educ, White House Conf Educ, 65 & Pres Comn White House Fel, 76-80. *Mem:* Inst Med-Nat Acad Sci. *Mailing Add:* Sch Educ Stanford Univ Stanford CA 94305-3084

GARDNER, JOSEPH ARTHUR FREDERICK, WOOD CHEMISTRY. *Current Pos:* dean & prof, 65-83, EMER DEAN, FAC FORESTRY, UNIV BC, 84- *Personal Data:* b Nakusp, BC, Aug 17, 19; m 44, Joyce Harper; c Joseph W & Mary L. *Educ:* Univ BC, BA, 40, MA, 42; McGill Univ, PhD, 44. *Prof Exp:* Res assoc, McGill Univ, 44-45; res chemist, Howard Smith Paper Mills, Ont, 45-47; head wood chem sect, Forest Prod Lab, 47-62, dir, 62-65. *Concurrent Pos:* Hon lectr, Univ BC, 53-64, hon prof, 64; mem Can Environ Adv Coun, 84-87. *Mem:* Tech Asn Pulp & Paper Indust; Can Inst Forestry; fel Int Acad Wood Sci; fel Chem Inst Can; Can Pulp & Paper Asn; hon mem Asn BC Prof Foresters; Order Can. *Res:* Chemistry of wood and its components, especially lignin and phenolic extractives. *Mailing Add:* 5537 Wallace St Vancouver BC V6N 2A1 Can

GARDNER, KENNETH DRAKE, JR, INTERNAL MEDICINE. *Current Pos:* RETIRED. *Personal Data:* b San Francisco, Calif, Oct 3, 29; m 54; c 4. *Educ:* Stanford Univ, BMS, 51, MD, 55. *Prof Exp:* Daland res fel clin med, 59-60; instr med, Sch Med, Univ Pa, 60-61; Daland res fel clin med, 61-63; instr med, Sch Med, Stanford Univ, 63-64, asst prof, 64-69; prof, Sch Med, Univ Hawaii, 69-73, assoc dean, 70-73, chmn dept, 71-73, chief, Div Renal Dis, 73-90; prof med, Sch Med, Univ NMex, 73-, asst dean grad med educ, 74- *Concurrent Pos:* Consult, Oversight Subcomt, US House Rep, 79-80; Fifth Cong Sci fel, Fedn Am Socs Exp Biol, 79-80; consult ed, Am J Kidney Dis, 80-; mem, Pub Affairs Comt, Federated Am Socs Exp Med; vchmn, Sci Adv Comt, Polycystic Kidney Res Found; secy-treas, Western Asn Physicians, 89-92, pres, 93-94. *Mem:* Am Fedn Clin Res; fel Am Col Physicians; Am Physiol Soc; Am Soc Nephrology. *Res:* Effect of hormones on molecular movement across collecting tubular walls of the mammalian kidney; clinical renal disease; renal cystic diseases and pathophysiology of human kidney disease. *Mailing Add:* Dept Med Univ NMex Sch Med Albuquerque NM 87131. *Fax:* 505-277-7805

GARDNER, LEONARD ROBERT, GEOLOGICAL & BIOGEOCHEMICAL PROCESSES IN SALT MARSHES, GEOCHEMISTRY OF WEATHERING & SOIL FORMATION. *Current Pos:* PROF GEOL SCI, UNIV SC, 68- *Personal Data:* b East Orange, NJ, Dec 11, 35; m 71, Jennifer Butler; c Leonard, Mariana & Jocelyn. *Educ:* St Peters Col, BS, 58; Pa State Univ, BS, 63, MS, 66, PhD(geol), 68. *Concurrent Pos:* Assoc ed, Geol Soc Am, 88-92. *Mem:* Am Geophys Union. *Res:* Using a combination of field sampling, chemical analyses and simulation modelling, investigated the processes governing the chemical alteration of rock into soil and the decomposition of organic matter and associated nutrient cycling in salt marshes. *Mailing Add:* Geol Dept Univ SC Columbia SC 29208-0001

GARDNER, MURRAY BRIGGS, PATHOLOGY, ONCOLOGY. *Current Pos:* PROF PATH, SCH MED, UNIV CALIF, DAVIS, 81- *Personal Data:* b Lafayette, Ind, Oct 5, 29; m 61, Alice Danielson; c 4. *Educ:* Univ Calif, BA, 51, MD, 54. *Prof Exp:* From asst prof to prof path, Sch Med, Univ Southern Calif, 63-81. *Concurrent Pos:* Pathologist, Univ Southern Calif-USPHS Air Pollution Proj, 63-68; prin investr, NAT Cancer Inst-Univ Southern Calif Res Contract, 68-; dep vet, Los Angeles County, 68-; dir, Acquired Immune Deficiency Syndrome Res, Univ Calif, Davis. *Mem:* AAAS; Int Acad Path; Am Asn Path & Bact. *Res:* RNA tumor virology; etiology and epidemiology of cancer in humans and domestic pets; biological effects of urban air pollution; acquired immune deficiency in man and monkey. *Mailing Add:* 8313 Maxwell Lane Dixon CA 95620

GARDNER, PAUL JAY, HEALTH SCIENCE ADMINISTRATION, HISTOLOGY. *Current Pos:* USPHS trainee, Univ Nebr Med Ctr, Omaha, 63-64, from instr to assoc prof, 64-77, vchmn, Anat Dept, 77-83, interim dean grad studies & res, 83-84, interim vchancellor acad affairs, 91-92, PROF ANAT, UNIV NEBR MED CTR, OMAHA, 77-, ASST VCHANCELLOR ACAD AFFAIRS, 86-, ASSOC DEAN GRAD STUDIES & RES, 92- *Personal Data:* b Wichita, Kans, May 25, 29; m 49; c 4. *Educ:* Univ Wichita, AB, 51, MS, 55; Univ Nebr, PhD(anat), 64. *Prof Exp:* Asst instr anat, Univ Kans, 55-56; prof biol & head dept, Vincennes Univ, 56-60; asst prof biol, Univ Nebr, Omaha, 60-63. *Concurrent Pos:* Exec secy, Cancer Preclin Prog Proj Rev Comt, Grants Rev Bd, Div Extramural Activities, Nat Cancer Inst, NIH, 83-84. *Mem:* Am Soc Cell Biol; Am Asn Anat; Electron Micros Soc; Am Soc Andrology; AAAS. *Res:* Reproductive biology; electron microscopy; ultrastructure and function of male reproductive system. *Mailing Add:* Univ Nebr Med Ctr 600 S 42nd St Omaha NE 68198-6810

GARDNER, PHILLIP JOHN, PHYSICAL CHEMISTRY. *Current Pos:* SR PRIN DEVELOP ENGR, RES & DEVELOP DEPT, COHERENT, INC, 81- *Personal Data:* b Pomona, Calif, July 28, 41; m 63; c 3. *Educ:* Univ Calif, Riverside, BA, 64; Fla State Univ, PhD(phys chem), 69. *Prof Exp:* Mem tech staff, GTE Labs, NY, 69-72, prog mgr, GTE Sylvania Lighting Ctr, Mass, 72-75, eng specialist, GTE Slyvania, Electro-Optics Orgn, 75-81. *Mem:* Am Chem Soc; Am Phys Soc. *Res:* Experimental studies and development of lasers; developmental studies of atomic and molecular arc discharges including electrodeless systems; theoretical and experimental studies of radiative and non-radiative electronic transitions in molecules. *Mailing Add:* Coherent Inc 5100 Patrick Henry Dr Santa Clara CA 95054-0987

GARDNER, REED MCARTHUR, MEDICAL BIOPHYSICS, COMPUTING. *Current Pos:* Asst prof biophys & bioeng, 65-72, assoc prof med biophys & comput, 73-78, PROF MED BIOPHYS & COMPUT, UNIV UTAH, 78-; CO-DIR MED COMPUT, LDS HOSP, 85- *Personal Data:* b St George, Utah, Oct 24, 37; m 59; c 5. *Educ:* Univ Utah, BSEE, 60, PhD(biophys, bioeng), 68. *Concurrent Pos:* Consult, NASA Life Sci Adv Comt, 71 & Nat Libr Med. *Mem:* Inst Elec & Electronics Engrs; Biomed Eng Soc; Am Thoracic Soc; Asn Advan Med Instrumentation. *Res:* Application of bioengineering principles to solution of medical problems; computer applications in intensive care; cardiovascular laboratories and multiphasic screening centers; medical computing with emphasis on decisionmaking and intensive care technology. *Mailing Add:* Biophys Univ Utah Sch Med Salt Lake City UT 84132-0001

GARDNER, RICHARD A, FLUID MECHANICS, HEAT TRANSFER. *Current Pos:* asst prof mech eng, 69-75, ASSOC PROF MECH ENG, WASHINGTON UNIV, 75-, ASST DEPT CHMN, 89- *Personal Data:* b Oak Park, Ill, Dec 6, 41; m 64, Sandra; c Michael, Jennifer & Susan. *Educ:* Purdue Univ, BS, 63, MS, 65, PhD(fluid mech), 69. *Honors & Awards:* Ralph R Teetor Award, Soc Automotive Engrs, 71. *Prof Exp:* From instr to asst prof aeronaut, astronaut & eng sci, Purdue Univ, 68-69. *Concurrent Pos:* Assoc prof, Univ Wyo, 82-83. *Mem:* Am Inst Aeronaut & Astronaut; Am Soc Mech Engrs. *Res:* Magneto-fluid-mechanics; biomagnetic effects; heat transfer. *Mailing Add:* Dept Mech Eng Washington Univ St Louis MO 63130

GARDNER, RICHARD LYNN, biochemistry; deceased, see previous edition for last biography

GARDNER, ROBERT B, METHOD OF EQUIVALENCE, CONTROL THEORY. *Current Pos:* assoc prof, 71-77, assoc chmn, 77-82, PROF MATH, UNIV NC, CHAPEL HILL, 77- *Personal Data:* b Tarrytown, NY, Feb 27, 39; m 62; c 2. *Educ:* Princeton Univ, AB, 59; Columbia Univ, MA, 60; Univ Calif, Berkeley, PhD(math), 65. *Prof Exp:* Res asst math, Univ Calif, Berkeley, 62-65; vis mem, NSF & Sloan grants, Courant Inst Math Sci, NY Univ, 65-67; asst prof, Columbia Univ, 67-70; NSF grant, Inst Advan Study, 70-71; res mathematician & NSF grant, Univ Calif, Berkeley, 71. *Concurrent Pos:* Kenan vis prof, Univ Calif, Berkeley, 77-78; Kenan fel, 84; guest prof, Tech Univ, Berlin, 84, 89, 90, 91 & 93; NSF grants, 86-94; NIH grants, 89-96; vis sr mem, Fields Inst. *Mem:* Am Math Soc; Math Asn Am; Sigma Xi; Soc Indust & Appl Math; sr mem Inst Elec & Electronics Engrs. *Res:* Submanifolds of euclidean spaces; isometries and volume preserving diffeomorphisms; Cauchy problem; non linear wave equations; Backlund transformations; differential systems, method of equivalence and applications, geometric control theory, variational methods; nonlinear normal forms; exact linearization. *Mailing Add:* Dept Math Univ NC Chapel Hill NC 27514. *Fax:* 919-962-2568; *E-Mail:* rbg@math.unc.edu

GARDNER, ROBERT WAYNE, ANIMAL NUTRITION. *Current Pos:* RETIRED. *Personal Data:* b St George, Utah, July 24, 28; m 51; c 5. *Educ:* Utah State Univ, BS, 59; Cornell Univ, MS, 62, PhD(animal nutrit), 64. *Prof Exp:* Res nutritionist, Cornell Univ, 63-64; asst prof dairy sci, Univ Ariz, 64-66; prof animal sci, Brigham Young Univ, 66-85, prof, Benson Agr & Food Inst, 85-93. *Concurrent Pos:* Hon mem, Neuroallergy Comt, Am Col Allergists, 81-85; consult, Biomed & Environ Consults, Inc. *Mem:* Am Soc Animal Sci; Am Dairy Sci Asn; Am Inst Nutrit. *Res:* Energy requirements of animals for milk production; body chemical composition related to growth; interrelationships between selenium, vitamin E and muscular dystrophy; dairy calf nutrition; parturient paresis in dairy cattle; chemicals causing allergic reactions in humans and animals; medical profession in food allergies; completing writing a book on chemical causation and treatment of allergies. *Mailing Add:* 4045 N Canyon Rd Provo UT 84602

GARDNER, ROBIN P(IERCE), CHEMICAL ENGINEERING, NUCLEONICS. *Current Pos:* assoc prof nuclear eng, 67-70, PROF NUCLEAR & CHEM ENG, NC STATE UNIV, 70-, DIR, CTR ENG APPLNS RADIOISOTOPES, 80- *Personal Data:* b Charlotte, NC, Aug 17, 34; m 76, Linda; c Scott C & Christopher R. *Educ:* NC State Col, BChE, 56, MS, 58; Pa State Univ, PhD(fuel technol), 61. *Honors & Awards:* Radiation Indst Award, Am Nuclear Soc, 84; Distinguished Res Award, Alcoa Found. *Prof Exp:* Res asst fuel technol, Pa State Univ, 56-61; scientist, Spec Training Div, Oak Ridge Inst Nuclear Studies, 61-63; res engr & assoc dir, Measurement & Controls Lab, Res Triangle Inst, 63-67. *Concurrent Pos:* Consult, Oak Ridge Inst Nuclear Studies, 63-64; adj asst prof, NC State Univ, 64-; mem, Comt Nuclear Principles & Applns, Hwy Res Bd, Nat Acad Sci-Nat Res Coun, 64-; Centennial Fel, Col Earth & Mineral Sci, Pa State Univ. *Mem:* Fel Am Nuclear Soc; Am Inst Chem Engrs; Am Chem Soc; Am Soc Testing & Mat; Fine Particle Soc; Soc Prof Well Loggers Asn. *Res:* Analysis including Monte Carlo simulation and design of radiation and radioisotope measurement applications such as tracing, ganging, tomography, and analyzers applied to industrial processes. *Mailing Add:* 3005 Randolph Dr Raleigh NC 27609-6941. *Fax:* 919-515-5115; *E-Mail:* gardner@ncsu.edu

GARDNER, RUSSELL, JR, PSYCHIATRIC EDUCATION, PSYCHOANALYSIS. *Current Pos:* PROF PSYCHIAT, DEPT NEUROSCI, SCH MED, UNIV NDAK, 74-, CHMN, DIV PSYCHIAT-BEHAV SCI, 74-, PROF, DEPT FAMILY MED, 80- *Personal Data:* b Granton, Wis, Mar 19, 38; m 60; c 3. *Educ:* MD, Univ Chicago, 62. *Prof Exp:* Instr psychiat, Albert Einstein Col Med, 68-71, asst prof, 71-74. *Concurrent Pos:* Consult, Psychiat Educ Br, NIMH, 76-, mem, Psychiat Educ Rev Comt, 79-82, chmn, 80-82; consult, Jamestown State Hosp, 78- *Mem:* Am Col Psychiatrists; Am Psychiat Asn; Am Psychosomatic Soc; Asn Acad Psychiat. *Res:* Stress effects on medical students, impaired physicians; adult women after childhood incest and confused institutionalized patients; sleep and dream psychophysiology; evolutionary model of manic-depressive disorder. *Mailing Add:* 4 450 Graves Bldg D28 Univ Tex Med Br Galveston TX 77555-0428

GARDNER, SARA A, PHARMACOLOGY, NEUROCHEMISTRY. *Current Pos:* RETIRED. *Personal Data:* b San Diego, Calif, Mar 19, 38; m 74. *Educ:* San Diego State Col, AB, 60; Purdue Univ, West Lafayette, PhD(phys chem), 65. *Prof Exp:* Instr chem, Purdue Univ, 63-64; asst prof, Univ Iowa, 64-65; res assoc neurobiochem, 65-68, from asst prof to assoc prof, 68-73; grants assoc, NIH, 73-74, health scientist adminr, 74-78, dep prog dir, Pharmacol-Toxicol Prog, 78-79, dir, Pharmacol Sci Prog, Nat Inst Gen Med Sci, 79- *Mem:* Int Soc Neurochem; Am Soc Neurochem; Soc Exp Biol & Med; Am Soc Biol Chemists; Am Soc Pharmacol & Exp Therapeut. *Res:* DNA synthesis in developing brain; indoleakylamines in brain. *Mailing Add:* 515 Country Aire Dr Grants Pass OR 97526

GARDNER, SHERWIN, MECHANICAL ENGINEERING, OPERATIONS RESEARCH. *Current Pos:* CONSULT, 93- *Personal Data:* b New York, NY, July 31, 28; m 54; c 2. *Educ:* City Col New York, BME, 50. *Prof Exp:* From jr engr to engr, William L Gilbert Clock Corp, 50-51; engr, Res & Develop Labs, Bulova Watch Co, 54-56; prod engr, Kay Mfg Corp, 56; sr engr & prin engr, Ford Instrument Co, Sperry Rand Corp, 56-58, proj supvr, 58-62, stand mgr, 62-64; proj engr, Booz Allen Appl Res Inc, 64-66, res dir, 66-69, assoc, Booz Allen Systs, Inc, 69-70; asst comnr planning & eval, US Food & Drug Admin, 70-72, dep comnr, 72-79; sr vpres sci & technol, Grocery Mfg Am, 79-93. *Mem:* Inst Food Technologists. *Res:* System engineering analysis; management information systems; organizational and facility planning and evaluation; economic analysis. *Mailing Add:* 5504 Goldsboro Rd Bethesda MD 20817

GARDNER, SYLVIA ALICE, ORGANOMETALLIC CHEMISTRY. *Current Pos:* res chemist, Res Labs, 74-81, sr chemist, Mfg Technol Div, 81-86, TECH ASSOC, EASTMAN KODAK CO, 86- *Personal Data:* b Pittsburgh, Pa, Nov 21, 47. *Educ:* Bucknell Univ, BS, 69; Univ Mass, MS, 71, PhD(inorg chem), 73. *Prof Exp:* Fel, Univ Mass, 73-74. *Concurrent Pos:* Sci secy, VI Int Conf Organometallic Chem, 72-73; adj fac, Rochester Inst Technol, 75- *Mem:* Am Chem Soc; Mat Res Soc. *Res:* Inorganic and organometallic synthetic chemistry; sol-gel chemistry. *Mailing Add:* 50 Smugglers Lane Rochester NY 14617-1412

GARDNER, THOMAS WILLIAM, FLUVIAL GEOMORPHOLOGY IN TECTONIC TERRAINS, REMOTE SENSING OF EARTH RESOURCES. *Current Pos:* from asst prof to prof, 79-92, ASSOC PROF OPTOM, PA STATE UNIV, 92- *Personal Data:* b East Stroudsburg, Pa, Jan 19, 49; m 73, Susan; c Nathan & Blair. *Educ:* Franklin & Marshall Col, BA, 71; Colo State Univ, MS, 73; Univ Cincinnati, PhD(geol), 77. *Prof Exp:* Geologist, Exxon Minerals Co, 78-79. *Concurrent Pos:* Fac assoc, Earth Syst Sci Ctr, Pa State Univ. *Mem:* Geol Soc Am; Am Geophys Union; Am Quarternary Asn. *Res:* Fluvial hydrology, hydrology and geomorphology in disturbed and tectonically active terrains; Quaternary landscape evolution; remote sensing and photogeology. *Mailing Add:* Dept Ophthamol Pa State Univ 500 University Dr Box 850 Hershey PA 17033. *Fax:* 814-865-3191; *E-Mail:* twg@geosc.psu.edu

GARDNER, WALTER HALE, SOIL PHYSICS. *Current Pos:* from asst prof to prof soils, 50-82, prof soils & biophys, 70-72, EMER PROF SOILS & BIOPHYS, WASH STATE UNIV, 82- *Personal Data:* b Beaver, Utah, Feb 24, 17; m 48; c 5. *Educ:* Utah State Univ, BS, 39, MS, 47, PhD(soil physics), 50. *Honors & Awards:* Distinguished Serv Award, Soil Sci Soc Am, 86- *Prof Exp:* Asst soil physics, Cornell Univ, 40-41; spec instr math, Utah State Univ, 48-49. *Concurrent Pos:* Guggenheim fel, 64-65; ed-in-chief, Proc of Soil Sci Soc Am, 65-69; mem, Am Soc Agron-NSF Vis Scientist Prog, 66-68; consult, Int Atomic Energy Agency, Vienna, 71-72; historian, Soil Sci Soc Am, 87- *Mem:* AAAS; fel Am Soc Agron; fel Soil Sci Soc Am (pres, 83-84); AAAS (pres, 85). *Res:* Physics of the soil with emphasis on soil water retention and flow and their effect on plant growth; published a history of soil physics in Advances in Soil Science. *Mailing Add:* 1160 E Telegraph Rd No 10 Wash Utah 84780 Pullman WA 99163

GARDNER, WAYNE SCOTT, PLANT PATHOLOGY, VIROLOGY. *Current Pos:* RETIRED. *Personal Data:* b Clifton, Colo, Jan 11, 20; m 44; c 4. *Educ:* Utah State Univ, BS, 50, MS, 51; Univ Calif, Davis, PhD(plant path), 67. *Prof Exp:* Asst plant path, Utah State, 49-51; instr agr, Mesa Col, 51; plant pathologist, Lab Br, Crops Div, Tech Opers, Dugway Proving Ground, Utah, 51-52, Crops Div, Biol Warfare Facilities, 52-54; agr technician, Agr Div, Columbia-Geneva Steel Div, US Steel Corp, 54-61, Chem Unit, Fairless Works, Pa, 61-63; res asst plant path, Univ Calif, Davis, 63-65, lab technician, 65-67; from assoc prof to prof plant path sci, SDak State Univ, 67-85. *Mem:* Am Phytopath Soc. *Res:* Plant virology and electron microscopy; ultrastructure of plant pathogen, host and environment interaction; effects of air pollutants on plants; cereal and forage crop virus diseases; aerobiology and epiphytology. *Mailing Add:* 135 Leisureville Circle Woodland CA 95776-9424

GARDNER, WAYNE STANLEY, WATER CHEMISTRY, MARINE CHEMISTRY. *Current Pos:* DIR, MARINE SCI INST, UNIV TEX, AUSTIN, 96- *Personal Data:* b Granton, Wis, Sept 13, 41; m 64, Ane K Wohlt; c Linda & Robert. *Educ:* Univ Wis-Stevens Point, BS, 63; Univ Wis-Madison, MS, 64, PhD(water chem), 71. *Prof Exp:* Lt chem, USPHS, 64-66; res assoc, Skidaway Inst Oceanog, Univ Syst Ga, 71-74, asst prof,

74-77; lead chemist, Field Res Group, Columbia Nat Fishery Res Lab, 77-79; phys scientist, Nat Oceanic & Atmospheric Admin, Great Lakes Environ Res Lab, Ann Arbor, Mich, 79-81, head, Ecosyst & Nutrient Dynamics Group, 81-89, sr phys scientist, 89-96. *Mem:* AAAS; Am Soc Limnol & Oceanog; Int Asn Great Lakes Res; Int Asn Theoret & Appl Limnol; Am Geophys Union; fel Am Inst Chemists. *Res:* Aquatic chemistry and transformations of organic compounds and nutrients; biochemistry of aquatic organisms; nutrient and energy transformations; chemical approaches to examine nutrient and biochemical transformation in aquatic systems; author of numerous publications. *Mailing Add:* Univ Tex Austin Marine Sci Inst 750 Channelview Dr Port Aransas TX 78373. *Fax:* 512-749-6777; *E-Mail:* gardner@utmsi.zo.utexas.edu

GARDNER, WESTON DEUAIN, GROSS ANATOMY. *Current Pos:* from instr to prof, 47-79, EMER PROF ANAT, MED COL WIS, 79- *Personal Data:* b Cresco, Iowa, Jan 6, 17; m 44; c 2. *Educ:* Pa State Col, BS, 38; Univ Pittsburgh, MD, 42. *Prof Exp:* Intern, St Francis Hosp, Pittsburgh, 42-43; practicing physician, 45-46; asst anat, Univ Wis, 46-47. *Concurrent Pos:* Dir med educ, Deaconess Hosp, 55-70, asst exec dir, Educ Coun Foreign Med Grads, 60-65; med dir, Curative Workshop Rehab Ctr, Milwaukee, 71-74. *Mem:* Am Asn Anatomists; Asn Med Illusrs; Asn Am Med Cols; Guild Natural Sci Illusrs. *Res:* Embryology of human ear; degeneration studies on the cingulum; repair of bone to experimental fractures; venous patterns of thorax and breast by infrared photographic methods; relation of superficial veins and thorax to breast tumors; development of broncho pulmonary segments in human lungs; segmental veins in human lungs; audiovisual communications; medical illustration. *Mailing Add:* 14905 Wisconsin Dr Elm Grove WI 53122

GARDNER, WILFORD ROBERT, SOIL PHYSICS. *Current Pos:* RETIRED. *Personal Data:* b Logan, Utah, Oct 19, 25; m 49; c 3. *Educ:* Utah State Agr Col, BS, 49; Iowa State Col, MS, 51, PhD(physics), 53. *Honors & Awards:* Am Soc Agron Award, 62. *Prof Exp:* Asst physics, Iowa State Col, 49-51, res assoc, Inst Atomic Res, 51-53; physicist soil physics, US Salinity Lab, USDA, Calif, 53-66; prof soil physics, Univ Wis-Madison, 66-80; head, Dept Soil & Water Sci, Univ Ariz, Tucson, 80-87; dean, Col Natural Resources & dir agr & nat resources progs, Univ Calif, Berkeley, 87-94. *Concurrent Pos:* NSF sr fel, Cambridge Univ, 59; consult ed, Soil Sci, 61-; Fulbright lectr, Univ Ghent, 71-72; Haight traveling prof, Univ Wis, 78; mem, Sci Adv Bd, Environ Protection Agency, 82, Budget & Finance Comt, Am Soc Agron & Comt Irrigation Induced Water Qual Probs, Nat Acad Sci, 85; co-chair orgn comt, USDA-State Exp Sta Symp Plant Water Stress, 84. *Mem:* Nat Acad Sci; fel AAAS; Am Phys Soc; Soil Sci Soc Am; fel Am Soc Agron; Am Geophys Union. *Res:* Measurement of soil moisture by neutron scattering; soil physics; movement of fluids in porous media; soil-water-plant relations; soil salinity; plant biophysics; environmental physics. *Mailing Add:* Col Natural Resources Univ Calif 101 Giannini Hall Berkeley CA 94720

GARDNER, WILLIAM ALBERT, JR, GENITO-URINARY PATHOLOGY, LAB ADMINISTRATION. *Current Pos:* PROF & CHMN PATH, UNIV S ALA COL MED, 81- *Personal Data:* b Sumter, SC, Aug 2, 39; m 60, Ann Medlin; c Elizabeth (Schneider), Lee (Degroft) & William D. *Educ:* Wofford Col, BS, 60; Med Univ SC, MS, 65, MD, 65. *Prof Exp:* Teaching & res asst anat, Med Univ SC, 61-63; intern & path fel, Johns Hopkins Hosp, 65-67; asst & career resident, Duke Univ Med Ctr, 67-68, chief resident & instr path, 68-69; chief, lab serv, path, Vet Admin Med Ctr, Charleston & assoc prof path, Med Univ SC, 69-76, asst prof path, 72-76; chief lab serv path, Vet Admin Med Ctr, Nashville, 76-81; prof & vchmn path, Vanderbilt Univ Sch Med, 76-81. *Concurrent Pos:* Mem House Delegate, Col Am Pathologist, 74-77; vis prof path, Med Univ SC, 76-81; mem working cadre, NCI Nat Prostate Cancer Proj, 77-83; dist comnr, CAP Inspection & Accreditation Prog, 77-81; mem, US-Canadian, IAP educ comt, 78-82; CAP comn, govt rels, 83-85; chmn, Asn Path Chmn Vet Admin, 84-87; coun mem, US/Can Acad Path, 87-91; coun mem, Asn Path, chmn, 88-; ed-in-chief, Yearbook Path & Clin Path, 90-; pres, Ala Asn Pathologists, 91- *Mem:* Am Acad Path; US-Can Acad Path; Am Soc Clin Path; Asn Path Chmn; Col Am Pathologists. *Res:* Origin and pathogensis of prostate cancer; biology and host parasite relationships of trichomonads; etiological agents and natural history of prostatitis and prostate hyperplasia. *Mailing Add:* Dept Path Univ SAla Col Med 2451 Fillinghim St Mobile AL 36617-2238. *Fax:* 334-471-7715

GARDNER, WILLIAM LEE, PHYSICAL CHEMISTRY, INORGANIC CHEMISTRY. *Current Pos:* RES ASSOC, RES LABS, EASTMAN KODAK CO, 68- *Personal Data:* b Carlisle, Pa, June 8, 40; m 65; c 3. *Educ:* Pa State Univ, BS, 62; Purdue Univ, PhD(phys inorg chem), 68. *Mem:* Soc Photog Scientists & Engrs. *Res:* Solution and titration calorimetry; adsorption and surface phenomena within an aqueous medium; properties of photographic gelatin; design and development of radiographic and color photographic materials. *Mailing Add:* 29 Merriam Ave Bronxville NY 10708

GARDNER-CHAVIS, RALPH ALEXANDER, PHYSICAL CHEMISTRY. *Current Pos:* assoc prof, 68-87, EMER PROF CHEM, CLEVELAND STATE UNIV, 87-; DIR, MOLECULAR TECHNOL CORP, 83- *Personal Data:* b Cleveland, Ohio, Dec 3, 22; m 45; c 1. *Educ:* Univ Ill, BS, 43; Western Res Univ, MS, 52, PhD, 59. *Prof Exp:* Chemist, Argonne Nat Labs, 43-47 & Standard Oil Co, Ohio, 49-68. *Concurrent Pos:* Adj prof, Malone Col, 87- *Mem:* Am Chem Soc. *Res:* Infrared spectroscopy, heterogeneous catalysis; quantitative, numerical explanations and predictions of chemical reactions infrared spectroscopy and heterogeneous, homogeneous and enzyme catalysis. *Mailing Add:* Dept Chem Cleveland State Univ 1983 E 24th St Cleveland OH 44115

GARDOCKI, JOSEPH F, PHARMACOLOGY. *Current Pos:* pharmacologist & head neuropsychopharmacol, 60-80, RES FEL, MCNEIL LABS, INC, 80- *Personal Data:* b Brooklyn, NY, Sept 5, 26. *Educ:* Georgetown Univ, PhD, 51. *Prof Exp:* Pharmacologist, Food & Drug Admin, 47-48; pharmacologist, Hazelton Labs, 48-51; sr pharmacologist, Pfizer Therapeut Inst, 52-57; res assoc, Squibb Inst Med Res, 58-59. *Mem:* AAAS; Am Soc Pharmacol & Exp Therapeut; NY Acad Sci. *Res:* Intravenous anesthetics; tranquilizers; diuretics; analgesics; muscle relaxants; neurophysiological correlates of behavior; toxicology; blood chemistry; central nervous system stimulants; bioassay; operant conditioning. *Mailing Add:* 72 Meadow Lane Doylestown PA 18901-4853

GARDON, JOHN LESLIE, POLYMER CHEMISTRY, PHYSICAL CHEMISTRY. *Current Pos:* AT AKZO COATING AM. *Personal Data:* b Budapest, Hungary, June 5, 28; US citizen; m 51; c 2. *Educ:* Swiss Fed Inst Technol, grad, 50; McGill Univ, PhD(phys chem), 52. *Honors & Awards:* Roon Award, Fed Soc Coating Technol, 66. *Prof Exp:* Chemist wood chem, Can Int Paper Co, Hawkesbury, Ont, 55-58; sr chemist textiles, Rohm & Haas Co, 58-60, group leader coatings, 60-62, res assoc polymers, 62-65, res mgr leather finishes, Springhouse, Pa, 65-68; dir, Corp Res Develop Div, M&T chem, Inc, Rahway, NJ, 68-73, dir res & develop, Coating & Ink Div, 73-80; vpres coatings res & develop, Sherwin Williams Co, Chicago, 80- *Concurrent Pos:* Trustee, Paint Res Inst, 74-; chmn, Gordon Res Conf Adhesion, 76- *Mem:* Am Chem Soc (secy, 77-78)); Soc Plastics Engrs; Chem Inst Can; Adhesion Soc; NY Acad Sci; Sigma Xi. *Res:* Polymer synthesis; emulsion polymerization; thermodynamics of polymer solutions; coatings; finishes of textiles, paper and leather; adhesion; lignin; cellulose; polyelectrolytes; membrane separations. *Mailing Add:* 60 Snowshoe Circle Bloomfield Hills MI 48301

GARELICK, DAVID ARTHUR, PHYSICS. *Current Pos:* assoc prof physics, 69-74, PROF PHYSICS, NORTHEASTERN UNIV, 74- *Personal Data:* b Woonsocket, RI, Nov 17, 37; m 60; c 1. *Educ:* Mass Inst Technol, BS, 59, PhD(physics), 63. *Prof Exp:* Res staff, Lab Nuclear Sci, Mass Inst Technol, 63-67; assoc physicist, Brookhaven Nat Lab, 67-69. *Mem:* Am Physics Soc. *Res:* Elementary particles experimentation. *Mailing Add:* Dept Physics Northeastern Univ 360 Huntington Ave Boston MA 02115. *Fax:* 617-373-2943

GAREN, ALAN, DEVELOPMENTAL BIOLOGY. *Current Pos:* PROF MOLECULAR BIOPHYS & BIOCHEM, YALE UNIV, 63-, PROF HUMAN GENETICS, 70- *Personal Data:* b Brooklyn, NY, May 26, 26; m 59; c 5. *Educ:* Univ Colo, BS, 45, PhD(biophys), 53. *Honors & Awards:* Waksman Medal Microbiol, 62. *Prof Exp:* Res chemist, Oak Ridge Nat Lab, 46-48; fel, Nat Found Infantile Paralysis, Cold Spring Harbor, NY, 51-55; res assoc, Purdue Univ, 55-57; sr res assoc, Biol Dept, Mass Inst Technol, 57-60; from assoc prof to prof, Biol Div, Univ Pa, 60-63. *Concurrent Pos:* Guggenheim fel, 70. *Mem:* Nat Acad Sci; fel Am Acad Arts & Sci. *Res:* Genetic and hormonal control of Drosophila development. *Mailing Add:* Dept Molecular Biophys & Biochem Yale Univ Kline Biol Tower New Haven CT 06511

GARETZ, BRUCE ALLEN, PHYSICAL CHEMISTRY. *Current Pos:* asst prof, 78-83, ASSOC PROF PHYS CHEM, POLYTECH UNIV, 83- *Personal Data:* b St Paul, Minn, Nov 24, 49. *Educ:* Harvard Col, AB, 71; Mass Inst Technol, PhD(phys chem), 76. *Prof Exp:* Res assoc & lectr, Dept Chem, Univ Toronto, 76-78. *Concurrent Pos:* Vis prof, Dept Chem, Indian Inst Technol, Kanpur, India, 86; vis scientist, Mass Inst Technol Laser Res Ctr, 84-90; Alfred P Sloan res fel, 84-87. *Mem:* Am Phys Soc; Optical Soc Am; Am Chem Soc. *Res:* Laser spectroscopy; nonlinear optics and multiphoton processes; polarization effects in molecular spectroscopy; laser light scattering; ultrashort pulse spectroscopy. *Mailing Add:* Dept Chem Polytech Univ Brooklyn NY 11201. *Fax:* 718-260-3125; *E-Mail:* bgaretz@duke.poly.edu

GAREWAL, HARINDER SINGH, CANCER PREVENTION & CONTROL, CANCER THERAPEUTICS. *Current Pos:* from asst prof to assoc prof, 85-93, ASST DIR, CANCER PREVENT & CONTROL, CANCER CTR, UNIV ARIZ, 92-, PROF, 94- *Personal Data:* m 77, Kristin; c Jasbir, Raj & Shaun. *Educ:* St Xavier's Col, BS, 68; McGill Univ, PhD(biochem), 72; Harvard Univ, MD, 77. *Honors & Awards:* Career Develop Award, Am Cancer Soc. *Prof Exp:* Chief med resident, Univ Ore, Health Sci Ctr, 80-81. *Concurrent Pos:* Prin investr, Pharmaceut Indust, Nat Cancer Inst, NIH, 86-; Career Develop Award, Am Cancer Soc, 86-89; mem, Cancer Prevent & Control Comt, Am Soc Clin Oncol, 92-; dir, Va Coop Study Core Lab, 94- *Mem:* Fel Am Col Physicians; Am Soc Clin Oncol; Western Soc Clin Invest; Am Soc Clin Nutrit. *Res:* Chemoprevention of aerodigestive tract cancers (oral, lung, gastric); role of antioxidants in disease prevention; cellular and biologic markers of assessing cancer risk; demonstrated role of antioxadants in reversing oral cavity precancerous charges. *Mailing Add:* Ariz Cancer Ctr 1515 N Campbell Ave Tucson AZ 85724

GAREY, CARROLL LAVERNE, CHEMISTRY. *Current Pos:* RETIRED. *Personal Data:* b Ft Collins, Colo, Nov 9, 17; m 41, Edith Filley; c Richard, James & Phillip (deceased). *Educ:* Univ Nebr, BSc, 39, MSc, 47; Purdue Univ, PhD(soils), 52. *Honors & Awards:* Fulbright fel, Finland, 84. *Prof Exp:* Jr engr, State Hwy Dept, Nebr, 40-42; instr soils, Univ Nebr, 46-49; asst prof, Univ Ark, 51-57; res assoc & phys chemist, Inst Paper Chem, Wis, 57-75; mgr, polymer res & develop, Ralston Purina Co, 75-82. *Concurrent Pos:* Consult paper coating & gen paper sci. *Mem:* AAAS; Soc Rheol; Clay Minerals Soc; Am Chem Soc; Tech Asn Pulp & Paper Indust; Sigma Xi. *Res:* Evaluate pigments for paper coatings and fillers; study starches, proteins and polymers in paper manufacture, sizing and conversion; develop natural polymers from protein materials; solve plant production problems in coatings and adhesives field; rheology and physical chemical problems of paper coating suspensions and paper conversion processes; x-ray diffraction in study of cellulose, and structure of paper and coating. *Mailing Add:* 6310 Mesa Verde Dr Lincoln NE 68510

GAREY, MICHAEL RANDOLPH, MATHEMATICS, COMPUTER SCIENCE. *Current Pos:* Mem tech staff, Math Res Ctr, 70-81, dept head, Math Found Comput, 81-88, DIR, MATH SCI RES CTR, AT&T BELL LABS, 88- *Personal Data:* b Manitowoc, Wis, Nov 19, 45; m 65, Jenene G Brandt. *Educ:* Univ Wis-Madison, BS, 67, MS, 69, PhD(comput sci), 70. *Honors & Awards:* Lanchester Prize, Oper Res Soc Am, 79. *Concurrent Pos:* Assoc ed, J Asn Comput Mach, 75-79, ed chief, 79-82, ed, MIT Press Ser, 83-; coun, Asn Comput Mach, 88-96; exec comt, DIMACS, 89-94; bd dirs, Comput Res Asn, 89- *Mem:* Asn Comput Mach; Soc Indust & Appl Math; Oper Res Soc Am. *Res:* Design and analysis of combinatorial algorithms; graph theory; operations research. *Mailing Add:* Bell Labs Lucent Technol 700 Mountain Ave Murray Hill NJ 07974. *E-Mail:* mrg@lucent.com

GAREY, WALTER FRANCIS, COMPARATIVE PHYSIOLOGY. *Current Pos:* RETIRED. *Personal Data:* b Junction City, Ohio, Dec 13, 26; m 50; c 3. *Educ:* Ohio State Univ, BS, 49, MA, 53; State Univ NY, Buffalo, PhD(physiol), 67. *Prof Exp:* Teacher biol & phys sci, Sec Sch, Ohio, Mich & Calif, 49-62; teaching fel, State Univ NY, Buffalo, 62-67; res physiologist, Scripps Inst Oceanog, 67-71, acad adminr, 71-77; dir grants prog, Kroc Found, 77-85. *Mem:* Am Col Rheumatology. *Res:* Comparative physiology of respiration, circulation and acid-base regulation; arthritis; diabetes; multiple sclerosis. *Mailing Add:* 1580 Monarch Dr Santa Ynez CA 93460

GARFIELD, ALAN J, RAY TRACING ALGORITHMS, REAL TIME ANIMATION. *Current Pos:* CHAIR, ART & COMPUT GRAPHICS DEPT, TEIKYO MARYCREST UNIV, 80- *Personal Data:* b Utica, NY; m 79; c 3. *Educ:* Univ Iowa, BA, 71; State Univ NY, Binghamton, MA, 75. *Prof Exp:* Asst prof art hist, Converse Col, 74-76 & Creighton Univ, 76-80; assoc prof comput graphics, Univ Wis-Madison, 90-91. *Concurrent Pos:* Asst prof art hist, SW Mo State Univ, 75-76; pres, Digigraphic Systs, Inc, 84-; consult, McGladdey & Pullen Acct & Dynamic Graphics Inc, 86-90. *Mem:* Asn Comput Mach; Nat Comput Graphics Asn; Spec Interest Group Comput Graphics. *Res:* Exploring ray traced and animation algorithms; significant image research. *Mailing Add:* Dept Comms/Perfect Arts Marycrest Int Univ 1607 W 12th St Davenport IA 52804-4096

GARFIELD, EUGENE, CHEMISTRY, INFORMATION SCIENCE. *Current Pos:* PRES, INST SCI INFO, 56- *Personal Data:* b New York, NY, Sept 16, 25; c 4. *Educ:* Columbia Univ, BS, 49, MS, 54; Univ Pa, PhD(struct ling), 61. *Honors & Awards:* Div Chem Info Sci Award, Am Chem Soc, 77; John Price Wetherill Medal, Franklin Inst; Derek J de Solla Price Mem Award, 84; John Scott Award, 87. *Prof Exp:* Res chemist, Evans Res & Develop Corp, 49-50; chem, Columbia Univ, 50-51; staff mem mach indexing proj, Johns Hopkins Univ, 51-53. *Concurrent Pos:* Lectr, Univ Pa, 63-, adj prof, 70-; consult, Smith, Kline & French Labs, Biol Abstracts, Nat Libr Med & Encycl Americana, 54-58; mem adv comt to cardiovasc lit proj, Nat Acad Sci; founder, publisher and ed, Current Contents, Index Chemicus & Sci Citation Index, Current Bibliog Directory, Chem Substruct Index, Social Sci Citation Index, Arts & Humanities Citation Index, Index to Sci Reviews, Index to Sci & Tech Proceedings, Jour Citation Reports, Automatic Subj Citation Alert; co-founder, former pres & chmn bd, Info Indust Asn, 68-; mem bd dirs, Ann Reviews; ed-in-chief, Scientometrics. *Mem:* Fel AAAS; Am Soc Info Sci; 06276246xxx Writers; NY Acad Sci; Am Chem Soc; Int Sci Policy Found. *Res:* Citation analysis; science policy. *Mailing Add:* Inst Sci Info 3501 Market St Philadelphia PA 19104-3302

GARFIELD, ROBERT EDWARD, PHARMACOLOGY, REPRODUCTIVE PHYSIOLOGY. *Current Pos:* PROF, DEPT OBSTET & GYNECOL & PHYSIOL, DIR REPRODUCTIVE SCI, UNIV TEX MED BR, 91- *Personal Data:* b Douglas, Wyo, Jan 27, 39; m 62, Josette; c John & Patricia. *Educ:* Univ Wyo, BSc, 67, MSc, 69; Univ Alta, PhD(pharmacol), 73. *Prof Exp:* Fel, Dept Physiol, Univ Pa, 73-76; lectr, McMaster Univ, 76-78, from asst prof to prof, 76-91. *Concurrent Pos:* Prin investr, Res Projs, Med Res Coun, Can, 76-; jr fel, Can & Ont Heart Found, 76-77; Can Heart Found scholar, 78-81; sr fel, Ont Heart Found, 81-87; Med Res Coun fel, Univ Paris, 85-86. *Mem:* Sigma Xi; Soc Study Reproduction; Am Physiol Soc; Soc Gynec Invest; Biophys Soc Am; Am Fertil Soc. *Res:* Uterine contractility associated with labor and delivery; factors which regulate smooth muscle; author of 200 publications; 20 patents on treatments and diagnosis of pregnancy; studies of pregnancy. *Mailing Add:* Reproductive Sci J-62 Dept Obstet/Gynec Univ Tex Med Br Galveston TX 77550-2708. *Fax:* 409-772-2261; *E-Mail:* rgarfiel@marlin.utmb.edu

GARFIELD, SANFORD ALLEN, CELL BIOLOGY. *Current Pos:* DIR, SPEC PROGS & PROJ COORDR, NON-INSULIN DEPENDENT DIABETES MELLITUS PRIMARY PREV TRIAL, NAT INST DIABETES DIGESTIVE & KIDNEY DIS, NIH, 86- *Personal Data:* b Feb 21, 43; c 1. *Educ:* Univ Chicago, PhD(develop biol), 74. *Prof Exp:* Assoc prof anat & cell biol, Col Med, Univ Cincinnati, 79-86. *Mem:* AAAS; Am Diabetes Asn. *Mailing Add:* Natcher Bldg 45 Center Dr Rm 5AN24B Bethesda MD 20892

GARFIN, DAVID EDWARD, MOLECULAR BIOLOGY, ELECTRICAL ENGINEERING. *Current Pos:* sr res biochemist, 83-84, group leader, Immunol Res, 84-86, GROUP LEADER, ELECTROPHORESIS & BIOCHEM RES, BIO-RAD LABS, HERCULES, CALIF, 86- *Personal Data:* b Minneapolis, Minn, July 7, 40; m 69, Susan Bettelheim; c Phillip & Daniel. *Educ:* Univ Minn, Minneapolis, BS, 62, MSEE, 64; Univ Calif, Berkeley, PhD(biophys), 72. *Prof Exp:* Res assoc, Univ Calif, San Francisco, 72-78, asst res biochemist, 78-79; mgr prod develop, Tago Inc, Burlingame, Calif, 77-80; head immunol develop & prod, Hana Biol Inc, Emeryville, Calif, 81-82. *Mem:* AAAS; Am Chem Soc; Am Soc Microbiol; Biophys Soc; Electrophoresis Soc; Inst Elec & Electronics Engrs. *Res:* Fractionation and analysis of biological molecules. *Mailing Add:* 112 Kenyon Ave Kensington CA 94708-1027. *Fax:* 510-741-1048

GARFIN, LOUIS, ACTUARIAL SCIENCE. *Current Pos:* RETIRED. *Personal Data:* b Mason City, Iowa, June 7, 17; m 43, Clarice Fagen; c Eugene Arthur & Erica. *Educ:* Univ Iowa, BA, 38, MS, 39, PhD(math), 42. *Prof Exp:* Asst math, Univ Iowa, 39-42; assoc instr radio operating, Training Sch, Army Air Force, Scott Field, 42-43; instr math in charge US Army radio prog, Ill Inst Technol, 43; instr, US Army Pre-Flight Prog, Univ Minn, 43-44; actuary, Ore State Dept Ins, 46-52; from assoc actuary to actuary, Pac Mutual Life Ins Co, 52-64; vpres & Chief Actuary, 64-82; consult actuary, 82-88. *Mem:* Am Math Soc; fel Soc Actuaries; Am Acad Actuaries (vpres, 76-78); Int Actuarial Asn; Sigma Xi. *Res:* Pension funds; theoretical and practical bases and valuation; linear integral equations. *Mailing Add:* 371 Dartmoor St Laguna Beach CA 92651

GARFINKEL, ARTHUR FREDERICK, HIGH ENERGY PHYSICS. *Current Pos:* asst prof, 67-73, assoc prof, 73-78, PROF PHYSICS, PURDUE UNIV, 79- *Personal Data:* b New York, NY, Nov 13, 34; m 63; c 2. *Educ:* Columbia Univ, BA, 56, MS, 58, PhD(physics), 62. *Prof Exp:* Vis scientist, Res Estab Riso, Denmark, 62-64; proj assoc physics, Univ Wis-Madison, 64-67. *Concurrent Pos:* Exchange prof physics, Univ Hamburg, 77-78. *Mem:* Am Phys Soc. *Res:* Experimental particle physics research, primarily making use of counter techniques to study particle reactions; with special interest in proton and antiproton collisions at high energy. *Mailing Add:* Dept Physics Purdue Univ Lafayette IN 47907

GARFINKEL, BORIS, ASTRONOMY. *Current Pos:* sr res assoc & lectr astron, 67-73, emer sr res astronr, 73-83, EMER PROF PHYSICS, YALE UNIV, 83- *Personal Data:* b Moscow, Russia, Nov 18, 04; nat US. *Educ:* City Col New York, BS, Columbia Univ, MA, 27; Yale Univ, PhD(astron), 43. *Honors & Awards:* R H Kent Award, 59. *Prof Exp:* Instr physics, Yale Univ, 43-46; res mathematician, Ballistic Res Lab, Aberdeen Proving Ground, 46-60, dep chief, Comput Lab, 60-63, chief res scientist, 63-67. *Concurrent Pos:* Lectr, Univ Del, 48-56; res assoc, Yale Univ, 58-66, vis prof, 66-67; adv scientist, Lockheed Missile & Space Co, 61-62; Nat Acad Sci sr res assoc, 63-64. *Mem:* Royal Astron Soc; Int Astron Union; Am Astron Soc. *Res:* Celestial mechanics; artificial satellite theory; the ideal resonance problem; astronomical refraction; calculus of variations; Trojan asteroids. *Mailing Add:* 738 Whitney Ave New Haven CT 06511

GARFINKEL, HARMON MARK, MATERIALS SCIENCE. *Current Pos:* pres res & develop, 85-95, CONSULT, ENGELHARD CORP, 95- *Personal Data:* b Brooklyn, NY, May 20, 33; m 56, Lorraine F Plansky; c Elysc & Michelle. *Educ:* Brooklyn Col, BA, 57; Iowa State Univ, PhD(phys chem), 60; Harvard Univ, PMD, 73. *Prof Exp:* Sr chemist, Corning Glass Works, 60-64, mgr phys chem, 64-79, mgr bio org res, 69-73, dir biotech, 73-74, dir appl chem & biol, 74-78, dir res, 78-85. *Mem:* Am Chem Soc; Am Phys Soc; fel Am Inst Chemists; Am Ceramic Soc; NY Acad Sci. *Res:* Developed techniques for improving the strength of ceramics via ion exchange techniques; the fundamentals (kinetics and thermodynamics) of the process. *Mailing Add:* 16599 Traders Crossing Unit 234 Jupiter FL 33477

GARFINKEL, LAWRENCE, EPIDEMIOLOGY, BIOSTATISTICS. *Current Pos:* CONSULT, 90- *Personal Data:* b New York, NY, Jan 11, 22; wid; c Herbert & Martin. *Educ:* City Col New York, BBA, 47; Columbia Univ, MA, 49. *Honors & Awards:* Distinguished Serv Award, Am Cancer Soc, 93. *Prof Exp:* Biostatistician, Am Cancer Soc, 47-59, chief field & spec projs, 59-73, asst vpres, 73-79, vpres epidemiol & statist, 79-90. *Concurrent Pos:* Asst res scientist, Col Dent, NY Univ, 62-69, from asst clin prof to assoc clin prof, 70-79; res consult to sr med investr, Vet Admin Hosp, East Orange, NJ, 65-80; mem epidemiol adv comt, Third Nat Cancer Surv, Nat Cancer Inst, 68-73, mem adv comt, Diet, Nutrit & Cancer Prog, 75-77, mem clearinghouse environ carcinogens, 76-78; assoc prof, Mt Sinai Sch Med, 72; mem cancer com, Am Col Surgeons, 88; mem, Data Mgt Working Group, Nat Cancer Data Base, 89- *Res:* Design and analysis of epidemiologic and pathologic studies in smoking and health; analysis of trends in cancer mortality, morbidity and survival. *Mailing Add:* Am Cancer Soc 1180 Ave of Americas New York NY 10036

GARFINKEL, PAUL EARL, PSYCHIATRY. *Current Pos:* DIR & PSYCHIATRIST IN CHIEF, CLARKE INST PSYCHIAT, UNIV TORONTO, 90-, PROF & CHMN, DEPT PSYCHIAT, 90- *Personal Data:* b Winnipeg, Can, Jan 21, 46; m 67; c 3. *Educ:* Univ Manitoba, MD, 69; FRCP (C), 74; Univ Toronto, MSc, 77. *Honors & Awards:* Paul Christie Mem Award, Ont Ment Health Found, 74; McNeil Award, Can Psychiat Asn, 75. *Prof Exp:* From assoc prof to prof psychiat & vchmn, Dept Psychiat, Univ Toronto, 82-90; phychiatrist-in-chief, Toronto Gen Hosp, 82-90. *Concurrent Pos:* Vis prof, Nat Univ, Dublin, Ireland, 79 & dept psychiat, Univ Manitoba, 81; chief psychosomatic med unit, Clarke Inst Psychiat, 79-82, coordr res, 81-; mem, Health & Welfare Res Comt, Can, 80-82; coordr res, Dept

Psychiat, Univ Toronto, 81-90. *Mem:* Am Psychiat Asn; Psychiat Res Soc; Am Psychosomatic Soc; Soc Neurosci; fel Can Col Neuropharmacol. *Res:* Pathogenetic mechanisms in anorexia neurvosa; treatment of weight disorders; pharmacotherapies of depression. *Mailing Add:* Clarke Inst Psychiat 250 College St Toronto ON M5T 1R8 Can

GARFINKLE, BARRY DAVID, VIROLOGY, MICROBIOLOGY. *Current Pos:* sr microbiologist, Merck Sharp & Dohme, 75-77, mgr biol qual tech serv, 77-81, mgr process validation, 81-83, mgr qual control pharmaceut prod, 83-85, mgr sterile process proj eng, 85-86, sr mgr biol prod technician serv, 86-87, dir quality assurance, 88-90, dir qual mgt validation, 90-91, SR DIR QUALITY MGT VALIDATION, MERCK SHARP & DOHME, 91- *Personal Data:* b Newark, NJ, Oct 3, 46; m 68; c 2. *Educ:* Kans State Univ, BS, 68; Penn State Univ, MS, 70, PhD(microbiol), 72. *Prof Exp:* Res scientist virol, Philip Morris Res Ctr, 74-75. *Concurrent Pos:* NIH spec fel, Cold Spring Harbor, 71; fel, Roche Inst Molecular Biol, 72-74. *Mem:* Am Soc Microbiol; Am Tissue Cult Asn; Pharmaceut Mfg Asn; Parenteral Drug Asn. *Res:* All aspects of research and development of bacterial and viral vaccines; biochemistry. *Mailing Add:* 1274 Georgia Lane Hatfield PA 19440

GARFINKLE, DAVID, GENERAL RELATIVITY. *Current Pos:* asst prof, 91-95, ASSOC PROF PHYSICS, OAKLAND UNIV, 95- *Personal Data:* b New York, NY, Apr 1, 58; m 95, Kimberly L Eddy. *Educ:* Princeton Univ, BA, 80; Univ Chicago, PhD(physics), 85. *Prof Exp:* Res assoc, Wash Univ, 85-87, Univ Fla, 87-89, Univ Calif, Santa Barbara, 89-91. *Mem:* Am Phys Soc; Am Math Soc; Sigma Xi. *Res:* General relativity; black holes, cosmic strings, singularities and numerical relativity. *Mailing Add:* Dept Physics Oakland Univ Rochester MI 48309. *Fax:* 248-370-3408; *E-Mail:* garfinkl@vela.acs.oakland.edu

GARFUNKEL, MYRON PAUL, PHYSICS. *Current Pos:* prof physics, 59-63, chmn, Dept Physics & Astron, 76-82, EMER PROF PHYSICS, UNIV PITTSBURGH, 93- *Personal Data:* b New York, NY, June 17, 23; m 46, Ruth Gottlieb; c Lynn C, Eric L & Glen A. *Educ:* Rutgers Univ, BS, 47, PhD(physics), 51. *Prof Exp:* Physicist, Res Lab, Westinghouse Elec Corp, 51-59. *Mem:* Am Phys Soc; AAAS. *Res:* Solid state physics; cryogenics; superconductivity; microwave acoustics. *Mailing Add:* 123 Fairfax Rd Pittsburgh PA 15221. *Fax:* 412-624-9163; *E-Mail:* garfu@vms.cis.pitt.edu

GARG, ANUPAM, MACROSCOPIC QUANTUM PHENOMENA, SUPERCONDUCTIVITY. *Current Pos:* asst prof, Dept Physics, 88-94, ASSOC PROF, DEPT PHYSICS & ASTRON, NORTHWESTERN UNIV, 94- *Personal Data:* b Amritsar, India, Aug 17, 56; m 88, Neerja Gupta; c Gaurav & Arjun. *Educ:* Indian Inst Technol, Delhi, MS, 77; Cornell Univ, MS, 81, PhD(physics), 83. *Prof Exp:* John D & Catherine T MacArthur res assoc, Univ Ill, Urbana-Champaign, 83-85; res assoc, Inst Theoret Physics, Univ Calif, Santa Barbara, 85-88. *Mem:* Am Phys Soc. *Res:* Macroscopic quantum phenomena super fluidity and superconductivity; reduced symmetry superconductivity; quasicrystals; foundations of quantum mechanics. *Mailing Add:* Dept Physics & Astron Northwestern Univ 2145 Sheridan Rd Evanston IL 60208. *E-Mail:* agarg@nwu.edu

GARG, ARUN, OCCUPATIONAL SAFETY & HEALTH. *Current Pos:* from asst prof to assoc prof, 77-88, PROF INDUST ENG, UNIV WIS, MILWAUKEE, 88-, CLIN PROF, MED COL WIS, 91- *Personal Data:* b Kanpur, India; US citizen; m 74; c Anjali. *Educ:* Inst Technol, Kanpur, India, BS, 69; Villanova Univ, MS, 71; Univ Mich, PE, 73, PhD(indust eng), 76. *Prof Exp:* Mgt, Sch Dent, Univ Mich, 73-76; asst prof indust eng, Univ Miami, 76-77. *Concurrent Pos:* Consult, Med Res Lab, Wright Patterson AFB, Ohio, 72 & Westinghouse Res & Develop Ctr, 77; vis asst prof, Tex Tech Univ, 78. *Mem:* Sr mem Am Inst Indust Engrs; Human Factors Soc; Am Indust Hygiene Asn; Int Indust Ergonomics & Safety. *Res:* Occupational safety and health; ergonomics; occupational biomechanics and work physiology. *Mailing Add:* Indust & Systs Eng Univ Wis PO Box 784 Milwaukee WI 53201. *Fax:* 414-229-6958

GARG, ARUN K, MEDICAL BIOCHEMISTRY, LABORATORY MEDICINE. *Current Pos:* DIR MED BIOCHEM, ROYAL COLUMBIAN & REGIONAL HOSP, 84- *Personal Data:* b Agra, India, July 16, 46; Can citizen; m 70, Lori Ziegler; c Davin. *Educ:* Agra Univ, BSC, 62, MSC, 64; Univ Sask, MSC, 68, PhD(biochem), 70; Univ BC, MD, 77; Royal Col Physicians & Surgeons, FRCP, 80. *Concurrent Pos:* Partner, C J Coody & Assocs, 80-, chmn, 89-; vis assoc prof, Dept Chem, Simon Fraser Univ, 80-84; clin assoc prof, Dept Path, Univ BC, 84-; counr, Can Soc Clin Chemists, 81-83; mem bd dirs, BC Med Soc, 80-; chmn, Sect Clin Path, Can Asn Path, 82-86; dir, med biochem, BC Biomed Lab, 89-; mem bd gov, BC Inst Technol, 92- *Mem:* Can Soc Clin Chemists; Am Col Physicians Execs; Col Am Pathologists; Asn Clin Biochemists UK; Can Med Asn; Can Asn Path; fel, Am Col Pathologists. *Res:* Clinical applications of biochemical methods; role of ADH in Hyponatremia; utilization management, practice guidelines in clinical lab medicine. *Mailing Add:* Dept Path Royal Columbian Hosp 330 E Columbia St New Westminster BC V3L 3W7 CAN. *Fax:* 604-525-7247

GARG, BHAGWAN D, EXPERIMENTAL PATHOLOGY, MORPHOMETRY. *Current Pos:* STAFF RES SCIENTIST, GM RES & DEVELOP CTR, 76- *Personal Data:* b Dhuri Punjab, India, Aug 14, 40; US citizen; m 67, Sharda Jain; c Sunir J & Ravin J. *Educ:* Panjab Univ, India, BS, 61, MS, 62; McMaster Univ, PhD(biol), 66. *Prof Exp:* Res assoc, Case Western Res Univ Sch Med, 66-67; res assoc, Columbia Univ Col Physicians & Surgeons, 67-69; asst prof, Univ Montreal, 69-74; asst prof gross anat, Col Med, Howard Univ, 74-76. *Concurrent Pos:* Lectr, Hunter Col, NY, NY, 68-69, Loyola Col, Montreal, Can, 72-74. *Mem:* Soc Quant Morphol; Int Soc Stereology. *Res:* Toxicologic pathology; health effects and carcinogenic potential of man made fibers. *Mailing Add:* Automotive Safety & Health GM NAO Res & Develop Ctr 30500 Mount Rd Warren MI 48090-9055

GARG, DEVENDRA PRAKASH, ROBOTICS & AUTOMATIC CONTROL SYSTEMS, TECHNOLOGY FORECASTING & ASSESSMENT. *Current Pos:* dir undergrad studies, 77-86, PROF MECH ENG, DUKE UNIV, 72-; DIR, DYNAMIC SYSTS & CONTROL PROG, DIRECTORATE ENG, NSF, 92- *Personal Data:* b Roorkee, India, Mar 22, 34; m 61, Prabha Govil; c Nisha & Seema. *Educ:* Agra Univ, BS, 54; Univ Roorkee, BEng, 57; Univ Wis, MS, 60; NY Univ, PhD(mech eng), 69. *Prof Exp:* Lectr mech eng, Univ Roorkee, 57-62, reader mech eng, 62-65; instr, NY Univ, 65-69; asst prof, Mass Inst Technol, 69-71, assoc prof & chmn, Eng Projs Lab, 71-72. *Concurrent Pos:* Assoc ed, J Dynamic Systs, Measurement & Control, 71-73 & J Interdisciplinary Modeling & Simulation, 77-80; vis lectr mech eng, Mass Inst Technol, 72-76; vis prof mech eng, Univ Roorkee, 78; mem, Organizing & Prog Comt, Int Symp Man Under Vibrations, Suffering & Protection, 79-85; fel, US Dept Transp, 79-80, Nat Aeronaut & Space Admin, 86-87 & US Army Res Off, 88; chmn, Dynamic Systs & Control Div, Am Soc Mech Engrs, 85-86, tech panel, 87-; Fulbright sr scholar, 87-88; vis vchmn, Syst & Design Group Tech Operating Bd, 94-96. *Mem:* Fel Am Soc Mech Engrs; Inst Elec & Electronics Engrs; Sigma Xi; fel Japan Soc Prom Sci. *Res:* Design of controllers for nonlinear systems using computational approach; dynamic modeling, simulation and control of socioeconomic systems; technology forecasting and assessment; high speed ground transportation; robot dynamics and control. *Mailing Add:* Box 90300 Duke Univ Sch Eng Durham NC 27708-0300

GARG, DIWAKAR, MARKETING & FINANCE. *Current Pos:* Sr res engr, Air Prod & Chems Inc, 79-82, prin res engr, 82- 85, sr prin res engr, 85-86, lead develop engr, 86-89, RES ASSOC, AIR PROD & CHEMS INC, 89- *Personal Data:* b Kanpur, India, Sept 11, 52. *Educ:* H B T I, Kanpur, BS, 74; Okla State Univ, Ms, 75; Auburn Univ, PhD(chem eng), 79; Lehigh Univ, MBA, 85. *Concurrent Pos:* New technol develop & mkt. *Mem:* Am Inst Chem Engrs; Am Chem Soc; Am Ceramic Soc; Am Soc Metals. *Res:* Advance coal liquefaction processes; coal products; hydrotreating and hydrocracking; heavy oils upgrading, abrasive, erosive and wear resistant coatings; chemical vapro deposition; reactor design; CVD diamond coatings; PVD coatings; PACVD coatings. *Mailing Add:* Air Prod Chem R2102 7201 Hamilton Blvd Allentown PA 18195

GARG, HARI G, BIOLOGICAL CHEMISTRY. *Current Pos:* asst biochemist surg, Mass Gen Hosp, 71-77, asst biochemist Med, Shriners Burns Inst, 77-89, assoc biochemist surg, 90-93, ASSOC BIOCHEMIST MED, MASS GEN HOSP, 93- *Personal Data:* b Meerut, India, Oct 4, 31; m 60; c 2. *Educ:* Agra Univ, MSc, 52, PhD(chem), 60, DSc, 69. *Honors & Awards:* Khosla Res Prize, Univ Roorkee, 71. *Prof Exp:* Asst prof chem, Govt Uttar Pradesh, India, 52-56; res fel, Govt India, 56-59; fel & pool scientist peptide chem, CSIR, India, 60-62; vis res assoc carbohydrate chem, Ohio State Univ, 62-64; res fel peptide chem, Oxford Univ, 64-65; sci officer, Nucleic Acid Unit, Twyford Labs, London, 65-67; reader org chem, Univ Roorkee, 67-71. *Concurrent Pos:* Prin res assoc, 71-84, prin assoc biol chem, Harvard Med Sch, 84-93. *Mem:* Am Chem Soc; Soc Glycobiology; Indian Chem Soc. *Res:* Synthesis of low molecular weight carbohydrate derivatives of biological significance; the chemistry and structural studies of glycoconjugates. *Mailing Add:* Pulmonary Unit 149 13th St Eight Fl MGH E Charlestown MA 02129

GARG, JAGADISH BEHARI, NUCLEAR PHYSICS. *Current Pos:* PROF PHYSICS, STATE UNIV NY, ALBANY, 66- *Personal Data:* b Kanpur, India, July 7, 29; m 55; c 2. *Educ:* Univ Allahabad, BSc, 48; Univ Lucknow, MSc, 51; Univ Paris, DSc(physics), 58. *Prof Exp:* Physicist, Indian Atomic Energy Dept, 51-55; fel physics, Lab Atomic & Molecular Physics, Col France, 55-58; Turner & Newall fel, Univ Manchester, 58-61; sr res assoc, Columbia Univ, 61-66. *Concurrent Pos:* Dir, Nuclear Accelerator Lab, State Univ NY Albany, 66-72; chmn, Int Conf Statist Properties of Nuclei, 71; vis scientist, Brookhaven Nat Labs, 66-; consult, Oak Ridge Nat Labs, 72-; vis scientist, Australian Atomic Energy Comn, 73, Nuclear Ctr, France, 80. *Mem:* Am Nuclear Soc; fel Am Phys Soc; NY Acad Sci; Sigma Xi; Fedn Am Scientists. *Res:* Reaction mechanism induced by charged particles at intermediate energies; high resolution neutron resonance spectroscopy. *Mailing Add:* Dept Physics State Univ NY Albany NY 12222

GARG, KRISHNA MURARI, MATHEMATICS. *Current Pos:* from asst prof to assoc prof, 66-77, PROF MATH, UNIV ALTA, 77- *Personal Data:* b Lucknow, India, Aug 5, 32; m 66. *Educ:* Lucknow Univ, BSc, 52, MSc, 55, PhD(math), 63. *Prof Exp:* Lectr math, Kanyakubja Col, Lucknow, 57-58, asst prof, 62-63, Govt India Coun Sci & Indust Res sr res fel, 63-64; asst prof, Univ Alta, 64-65; study & res, Inst Henri Poincare, Paris, France, 65-66. *Mem:* Am Math Soc; Math Asn Am; Can Math Cong; Math Soc France. *Res:* Nature of derivates and structure of level sets of real functions in general and nowhere monotone functions in particular. *Mailing Add:* Dept Math Univ Alberta Edmonton AB T6G 2G1 Can

GARG, LAL CHAND, PHARMACOLOGY, PHYSIOLOGY & MEDICINE. *Current Pos:* res assoc, 69-70, instr, 70-71, asst prof, 71-76, assoc prof, 76-86, PROF PHARMACOL, COL MED, UNIV FLA, 86- *Personal Data:* b India, Jan 22, 33; m 59; c 2. *Educ:* Punjab Univ, BS, 54, MS, 56; Univ Fla, PhD(pharmacol), 69. *Prof Exp:* From instr to asst prof pharmacol, Col Vet Med, India, 56-63; asst prof, Punjab Univ, 63-65. *Concurrent Pos:* NIH fac develop award biochem pharmacol, Univ Fla, 79-80. *Mem:* Sigma Xi; Am Soc Pharmacol & Exp Therapeut; NY Acad Sci; Am Soc Nephrol; Am Physiol

Soc; Am Heart Asn. *Res:* Drug-enzyme interactions; renal and electrolyte pharmacology; hypertension. *Mailing Add:* Dept Pharmacol Health Sci Ctr Univ Fla Col Med Box 100267 Gainesville FL 32610-0267. *Fax:* 352-392-9696

GARG, UMESH, NUCLEAR PHYSICS. *Current Pos:* from asst prof to assoc prof, 82-94, ASSOC PROF, UNIV NOTRE DAME, 94-; RES ASSOC, CYCLOTRON INST, TEX A&M UNIV, 78- *Personal Data:* b Bikaner, India, Mar 29, 53; m 80, Anita Padhye; c Noopur N & Neehar N. *Educ:* Birla Inst Technol & Sci, Pilani, India, BSc, 72, MSc, 74; State Univ NY, Stony Brook, MA, 75, PhD(physics), 78. *Prof Exp:* Teaching asst, Dept Physics, State Univ NY, Stony Brook, 74-75, res asst, 75-78. *Concurrent Pos:* Guest scientist, Argonne Nat Lab, 83-; vis prof, Vrije Univ, Amsterdam, Neth, 88-89. *Mem:* Am Phys Soc; Sigma Xi; Am Chem Soc; Indian Physics Asn. *Res:* Gamma-ray spectroscopy following (HI,xn) reactions; giant resonances; heavy-ion reactions; collective properties of nuclei; lifetime measurements. *Mailing Add:* 18254 Westover Dr South Bend IN 46637. *Fax:* 219-631-5952; *E-Mail:* garg@nd.edu

GARGARO, ANTHONY, COMPUTER SCIENCE, SOFTWARE SYSTEMS. *Current Pos:* Comput scientist, 76-80, sr comput scientist, 80-84, LEAD SCIENTIST, COMPUT SCI CORP, 84- *Personal Data:* b Chideock, Eng, Apr 11, 42. *Educ:* Brunel Univ, UK, Dipl, 63. *Concurrent Pos:* Area dir, Spec Interest Groups, Asn Comput Mach, 86- *Mem:* Asn Comput Mach; Brit Comput Soc. *Mailing Add:* Comput Sci Corp 204 W Rte 38 Moorestown NJ 08057-0902

GARGES, SUSAN, GENE REGULATION, PROTEIN CONFORMATION. *Current Pos:* MICROBIOLOGIST, NAT CANCER INST, NIH, 79-, CHIEF, GENETICS SECT, LAB MOLECULAR BIOL, 97- *Personal Data:* b Chelsea, Mass, Jan 9, 53; m 82; c 2. *Educ:* Univ Dayton, BA, 74, MS, 78; Univ Md, PhD(microbiol), 83. *Prof Exp:* Grad teaching asst biol, Univ Dayton, 74-76; fac res asst microbiol, Univ Md, 76-78, grad res asst, 78-79. *Concurrent Pos:* Fac, NIH Grad Sch, Found Advan Educ in Sci, 86- *Mem:* Am Soc Microbiol; AAAS. *Res:* Gene regulation and protein conformation, a genetic approach to the study of the subjects; camp receptor protein (CRP), a transcriptional activator, from Escherichia coli as the model system. *Mailing Add:* Nat Cancer Inst-NIH NIH Bldg 37 Rm 2E06 Bethesda MD 20892. *E-Mail:* sgarges@helix.nih.gov

GARGETT, ANN E, OCEANOGRAPHY. *Current Pos:* RES SCIENTIST, INST OCEAN SCI, 72- *Personal Data:* b Winnipeg, Man, Nov 30, 44. *Educ:* Univ Man, BSc, 66; Univ BC, PhD(physics), 70. *Mem:* Fel Royal Soc Can. *Res:* Oceanography. *Mailing Add:* Inst Ocean Sci Patricia Bay PO Box 6000 Sidney BC V8L 4B2 Can

GARGUS, JAMES L, toxicology; deceased, see previous edition for last biography

GARIBALDI, JOHN ATTILIO, BIOCHEMISTRY. *Current Pos:* Chemist, 46-52, BIOCHEMIST, WESTERN REGIONAL RES LAB, USDA, 55- *Personal Data:* b San Francisco, Calif, Apr 3, 16; m 59; c 2. *Educ:* Univ Calif, BS, 38, PhD(biochem), 58. *Mem:* Am Soc Microbiol. *Res:* Microbial biochemistry; mineral nutrition of microorganisms; process development for the microbial production of antibiotics and vitamins; iron nutrition of microbes; shell egg microbiology. *Mailing Add:* 2311 Alva Ave El Cerrito CA 94530

GARIBALDI, LOUIS, MARINE BIOLOGY. *Current Pos:* assoc dir, 83-88, DIR, NY AQUARIUM, BROOKLYN, 88- *Prof Exp:* Staff mem, New Eng Aquarium & Steinhart Aquarium. *Mem:* Edward H Bean Mem Award, Am Asn Zool Parks & Aquariums, 92. *Mailing Add:* Aquarium for Wildlife Conserv Boardwalk & W Eighth St Brooklyn NY 11224

GARIEPY, CLAUDE, MEAT SCIENCE. *Current Pos:* RES SCIENTIST, AGR CAN, 89- *Personal Data:* b Que, Nov 3, 54. *Educ:* Laval Univ, BScA, 79, MSc, 83, PhD(meat sci), 87. *Prof Exp:* Prof poultry sci, Inst Agr Technol, 79-80; fel meat sci, Lacombe Res Sta, 88-89. *Concurrent Pos:* Assoc prof, Laval Univ & Sherbrooke Univ. *Mem:* Can Soc Animal Sci; Can Meat Sci Asn; Can Inst Food Sci Technol. *Res:* Effects of production factors on the keeping qualities and processing attributes of meat and meat products. *Mailing Add:* Food Res & Develop Ctr 3600 Casavant Blvd W St-Hyacinthe PQ J2S 8E3 Can

GARIEPY, RONALD F, MATHEMATICS. *Current Pos:* PROF MATH, UNIV KY, 70- *Personal Data:* b Mich, Apr 3, 40. *Educ:* Wayne State Univ, PhD(math), 69. *Mem:* Am Math Asn. *Mailing Add:* Math Dept Univ Ky Lexington KY 40506-0027

GARIK, VLADIMIR L, PHYSICAL CHEMISTRY. *Current Pos:* asst prof chem, 64-69, ASSOC PROF CHEM, MONTCLAIR STATE COL, 69- *Personal Data:* b Berlin, Ger, Mar 25, 13; nat US; m 44; c 1. *Educ:* Polytech Inst Brooklyn, BS, 44, MS, 47; Univ Conn, PhD, 53. *Prof Exp:* Assoc prof phys chem, Iona Col, 56-64. *Mem:* Am Chem Soc; Sigma Xi. *Res:* Hydrogenation of nitrocompounds with Raney nickel; kinetics of the decomposition of methyl in propyl ketone. *Mailing Add:* 71 Kensington Ave Clifton NJ 07014-1832

GARIN, DAVID L, ORGANIC CHEMISTRY. *Current Pos:* asst prof, 66-71, ASSOC PROF CHEM, UNIV MO-ST LOUIS, 71-, DIR, CTR SCI & TECHNOL, 88- *Personal Data:* b New York, NY, June 14, 39. *Educ:* City Col New York, BS, 60; Iowa State Univ, PhD(org chem), 64. *Prof Exp:* Van Leer fel, Weizmann Inst Sci, 64, NIH fel, Weizmann Inst Sci & Ind Univ, 64-66. *Concurrent Pos:* Vis scientist, Environ Protection Agency, 79-80; comnr, Miss Hazardous Waste Mgt Comn, 78-81; cong res fel, Am Chem Soc, 80. *Mem:* Am Chem Soc; Nat Coalition Sci & Technol (treas). *Res:* Photochemistry; rearrangement reactions; reaction mechanisms; science and public policy. *Mailing Add:* Dept Chem Univ Mo 8001 Natural Bridge Rd St Louis MO 63121-4499

GARING, JOHN SEYMOUR, MOLECULAR SPECTROSCOPY. *Current Pos:* RETIRED. *Personal Data:* b Toledo, Ohio, Nov 6, 30; m 52, Ione Davis; c John & Susan. *Educ:* Ohio State Univ, BSc, 51, MSc, 54, PhD(physics), 58. *Prof Exp:* Asst physics, Ohio State Univ, 51-53; physicist, Geophys Res Directorate, Air Force Res Div, 58-61, chief, Infrared Physics Br, 61-63; dir, Optical Physics Div, Air Force Geophys Lab, Hanscom AFB, Mass, 63-86. *Mem:* Fel AAAS; fel Optical Soc Am; Am Inst Aeronaut & Astronaut; Sigma Xi. *Res:* Infrared optics and spectroscopy; atmospheric transmission and emission; molecular structure and interactions; spectroscopic and interferometric instrumentation and techniques. *Mailing Add:* 157 Cedar St Lexington MA 02173-6507

GARINO, TERRY JOSEPH, PROCESSING, THIN FILMS. *Current Pos:* PRIN SR MEM TECH STAFF, SANDIA NAT LAB, 87- *Personal Data:* b Staunton, Ill, Oct 5, 60; c Anthony Jing. *Educ:* Mass Inst Technol, PhD(ceramic sci), 87. *Mem:* Am Ceramic Soc; Mat Res Soc. *Res:* Constrained sintering of ceramic thick films; drying of ceramic slurries on substrates; stress effects in ferroelectric thin films; secure magnetic stripes; electro rheological fluids based on ferroelectric powders; micro-machined permanent magnets. *Mailing Add:* Sandia Nat Labs Albuquerque NM 87185-0333. *Fax:* 505-844-4816; *E-Mail:* tjgarin@sandia.gov

GARITO, ANTHONY FRANK, CONDENSED MATTER PHYSICS. *Current Pos:* Res fel, Univ Pa, 64-68, res assoc physics, 68-70, from asst prof to assoc prof, 70-77, PROF PHYSICS, UNIV PA, 77-, TERM CHAIR PROF, 90- *Personal Data:* b New Rochelle, NY; m 63; c 3. *Educ:* Columbia Univ, BS, 62; Univ Pa, PhD, 68. *Concurrent Pos:* DuPont Young fac fel, Univ Pa, 70-73; consult, 72-; vis scholar, Univ Paris, 77 & Soviet Acad Sci, 78; vis prof, Inst Phys & Chem Res, Japan, 85- *Mem:* Am Phys Soc; Optical Soc Am. *Res:* Many-body interactions and instabilities of lower dimensional systems; nonlinear optical phenomena in organic and polymeric systems. *Mailing Add:* Dept Physics Univ Pa Philadelphia PA 19104

GARLAND, CARL WESLEY, PHASE TRANSITIONS, LIQUID CRYSTALS. *Current Pos:* from instr to assoc prof, 53-68, PROF CHEM, MASS INST TECHNOL, 68- *Personal Data:* b Bangor, Maine, Oct 1, 29; m 55, Joan Donaghy; c Leslie & Andrew. *Educ:* Univ Rochester, BS, 50; Univ Calif, PhD(chem), 53. *Prof Exp:* Instr chem, Univ Calif, 53. *Concurrent Pos:* A P Sloan fel, 54-60; sci ed, Optics & Spectros, 60-81, Liquid Crystals, 90-; Guggenheim fel, 63-64; vis prof, Univ Calif, 72, Univ Rome, 74, Kathol Univ Leuven, 77, Ben Gurion Univ, 80, Univ Paris, 81 & 82, Univ Bordeaux, 90. *Mem:* Am Phys Soc; fel Am Acad Arts & Sci. *Res:* Ultrasonic studies of phase transitions and critical points; dynamical and static aspects of cooperative phenomena; high-resolution calorimetry; phase transitions in liquid crystals. *Mailing Add:* Chem Dept Mass Inst Technol 77 Mass Ave Cambridge MA 02139-4307. *Fax:* 617-253-7030

GARLAND, CEDRIC FRANK, EPIDEMIOLOGY, CANCER. *Current Pos:* asst prof, 81-89, ASSOC PROF EPIDEMIOL, SCH MED LA JOLLA, UNIV CALIF, SAN DIEGO, 89-, ASSOC PROF IR, DEPT FAMILY & PREV MED. *Personal Data:* b La Jolla, Calif, Nov 10, 46. *Educ:* Univ Southern Calif, Los Angeles, BA, 67; Univ Calif, Los Angeles, MPH, 70, PhD(pub health), 74, DrPH, 74. *Prof Exp:* Asst prof, Johns Hopkins Univ, Sch Hyg & Pub Health, 74-81. *Concurrent Pos:* Dir Epidemiol Prog, Univ Calif, San Diego, Cancer Ctr, 87- *Mem:* Soc Epidemiol Res; Am Pub Health Asn; fel Am Col Epidemiol; AAAS. *Res:* Epidemiologic studies of breast and colon cancer, melanoma, and diseases of the digestive system; epidemiology of environmentally-induced diseases, studies of effects of vitamin D and calcium on human health. *Mailing Add:* Dept Family & Prev Med Sch Med Univ Calif San Diego 9500 Gilman Dr La Jolla CA 92093-0631

GARLAND, CHARLES E, ORGANIC CHEMISTRY, COLOR SCIENCE. *Current Pos:* RETIRED. *Personal Data:* b Haverhill, Mass, June 5, 26; m 48; c 1. *Educ:* Colby Col, AB, 50; Univ NH, MS, 52. *Prof Exp:* Instr chem, Univ NH, 50-51; res chemist anthraquinone dyes, E I DuPont De Nemours & Co, 51-66, res chemist to sr res chemist color measurement & control, 66-81, indust hyg assoc, 81-86. *Mem:* Am Chem Soc; Am Soc Testing & Mat; Am Indust Hygiene Asn. *Res:* Polarographic reduction of diazonium compounds; research in anthraquinone chemistry leading to new dyes for cotton and polyester fibers; measurement of color in solutions and dyed fabrics and computer shade matching; biological monitoring; permeation testing of safety fabrics; industrial hygiene. *Mailing Add:* Sharpley 314 Brockton Rd Wilmington DE 19803-2412

GARLAND, DONITA L, BIOCHEMISTRY. *Current Pos:* Staff fel, Nat Heart, Lung & Blood Inst, NIH, 75-83, expert, Nat Eye Inst, 83-88, RES CHEMIST, LAB MECHANISMS OCULAR DIS, NAT EYE INST, NIH, 88- *Personal Data:* b Emporia, Kans, 40; m 73; c 1. *Educ:* Washburn Univ, BA, 62; Univ Wash, PhD(biochem), 75. *Mem:* Am Soc Biochem & Molecular Biol; Asn Res Vision & Ophthal. *Res:* Regulation of metabolism of eye lens and mechanisms of cataract formation. *Mailing Add:* 6617 Lone Oak Dr Bethesda MD 20817-1649. *Fax:* 301-496-1759; *E-Mail:* dgarland@helix.nih.gov

GARLAND, GEORGE DAVID, GEOPHYSICS. *Current Pos:* prof physics, 63-87, EMER PROF, UNIV TORONTO, 87- *Personal Data:* b Toronto, Ont, June 29, 26; m 49; c 2. *Educ:* Univ Toronto, BASc, 47, MA, 48; St Louis Univ, PhD(geophys), 51. *Prof Exp:* Lectr geophys, Univ Toronto, 49-52; geophysicist, Dom Observ Can, 52-54; assoc prof geophys, Univ Alta, 54-60, prof, 60-63. *Concurrent Pos:* Secy-gen, Int Union Geod & Geophys. *Res:* Gravity; structure of the earth's crust; magnetic and electric fields of the earth. *Mailing Add:* 5 Mawhiney Ct Huntsville ON P1H 1B7 Can

GARLAND, HOWARD, MATHEMATICS. *Current Pos:* PROF MATH, YALE UNIV, 73- *Personal Data:* b Detroit, Mich, Oct 27, 37; m 61; c 2. *Educ:* Univ Chicago, BS, 57; Wayne State Univ, MS, 59; Univ Calif, Berkeley, PhD(math), 64. *Prof Exp:* Instr math, Yale Univ, 64-65; asst, Inst Advan Study, 65-66; asst prof, Yale Univ, 66-69; assoc prof, Cornell Univ, 69-71; prof, Columbia Univ, 71-72; prof, State Univ NY Stony Brook, 72-73. *Mem:* Am Math Soc. *Res:* Discrete subgroups of Lie groups. *Mailing Add:* Dept Math Yale Univ New Haven CT 06520-8283

GARLAND, JAMES C, EXPERIMENTAL CONDENSED MATTER PHYSICS. *Current Pos:* From asst prof to assoc prof, Ohio State Univ, 70-80, prof & dir, Mat Res Lab,80-85, chmn, Physics dept, 86-90, DEAN, COL MATH & PHYS SCI, OHIO STATE UNIV, 91- *Personal Data:* b Columbia, Mo, Aug 11, 42; c 2. *Educ:* Princeton Univ, AB, 64; Cornell Univ, PhD(physics), 69. *Prof Exp:* NSF fel physics, Cambridge Univ, 69. *Mem:* Fel Am Phys Soc. *Res:* Electronic properties of metals, superconductors and composites; advanced materials. *Mailing Add:* Dept Physics Smith Lab Ohio State Univ Columbus OH 43210

GARLAND, JAMES W, SOLID STATE PHYSICS, THEORETICAL PHYSICS. *Current Pos:* assoc prof, 67-70, PROF PHYSICS, UNIV ILL, CHICAGO CIRCLE, 70- *Personal Data:* b Washington, DC, Aug 1, 33; m 58; c 2. *Educ:* Univ Chicago, MS, 58, PhD(physics), 65. *Prof Exp:* Actg asst prof physics, Univ Calif, Berkeley, 63-65, asst prof, 66-67. *Concurrent Pos:* Alfred P Sloan Found fel, 64-66; vis lectr, Cambridge Univ, 65; consult, Argonne Nat Lab, 67-, assoc physicist, 69-70. *Mem:* Am Phys Soc. *Res:* Theory of metals; semiconductor physics; magnetism; transition metals. *Mailing Add:* 2889 NE Tramwat Pl Albuquerque NM 87122

GARLAND, JOHN KENNETH, TEXT AUTHOR. *Current Pos:* ASSOC PROF CHEM, WASH STATE UNIV, 70- *Personal Data:* b Cadillac, Mich, Dec 27, 35; m 58, Mary Lewis; c Annette (Elwood), Alice (Jaakola), D Sarah, Dan & Jeff. *Educ:* Univ Ill, BS, 57; Univ Kans, PhD(chem), 63. *Prof Exp:* Asst res chemist, Continental Oil Co, Okla, 57-59; asst prof chem, Univ Mo, Columbia, 63-70. *Concurrent Pos:* Adj prof chem, Mont State Univ, 84-85. *Mem:* Am Chem Soc. *Res:* Chemical education; hot atom chemistry, particularly recoil tritium; energy planning; x-ray crystallography. *Mailing Add:* Dept Chem Wash State Univ Pullman WA 99164-4630

GARLAND, MICHAEL MCKEE, SOLID STATE PHYSICS. *Current Pos:* From asst prof to assoc prof, 65-77, PROF PHYSICS, MEMPHIS STATE UNIV, 77- *Personal Data:* b Clarksville, Tenn, Jan 12, 39; m 58; c 2. *Educ:* Austin Peay State Col, BA, 61; Clemson Univ, PhD(physics), 65. *Mem:* Am Asn Physics Teachers; Am Vacuum Soc; Sigma Xi. *Res:* Superconducting behavior of thin films; superconductive tunneling between superimposed films. *Mailing Add:* Dept Physics Memphis State Univ Memphis TN 38152-0001

GARLAND, ROBERT BRUCE, ORGANIC CHEMISTRY. *Current Pos:* CONSULT, ABBOTT LABS, 93- *Personal Data:* b Chicago, Ill, Nov 6, 32; m 55, Janet L Yugue; c Robert B Jr, Linda (Rosenthal), Barbara (Dudzinski) & Angela B. *Educ:* Univ Ill, BS, 53; Mass Inst Technol, PhD(chem), 57. *Prof Exp:* Sr res investr, G D Searle & Co, 59-80, res scientist, Res & Develop Div, 80-93. *Mem:* Am Chem Soc. *Res:* Synthetic organic chemistry; natural products. *Mailing Add:* 2529 Walters Ave Northbrook IL 60062-4444

GARLAND, WILLIAM ARTHUR, medicinal chemistry, for more information see previous edition

GARLAND, WILLIAM JAMES, SYSTEM MODELLING & ANALYSIS, PERFORMANCE SUPPORT SYSTEMS. *Current Pos:* ASSOC PROF NUCLEAR ENG, MCMASTER UNIV, 83- *Personal Data:* b St John's, Nfld, July 26, 48. *Educ:* McMaster Univ, BEng, 70, MEng, 71, PhD(chem eng), 75. *Prof Exp:* Design engr, Ont Hydro, 75-79; supv design engr, Atomic Engegy Can Ltd, 79-83. *Concurrent Pos:* Dept chair, McMaster Univ, 88-94, dir, McMaster Nuclear Reactor, 94-95. *Mem:* Am Nuclear Soc; Can Nuclear Soc. *Res:* Integration of symbolic computation and reasoning into highly computerized numerically based real-time control systems for complex plant process management. *Mailing Add:* Dept Eng Physics McMaster Univ Hamilton ON L8S 4L7 Can. *Fax:* 905-528-4339; *E-Mail:* garlandw@mcmaster.ca

GARLICH, JIMMY DALE, NUTRITION, BIOCHEMISTRY. *Current Pos:* from asst prof to assoc prof, 66-85, PROF POULTRY SCI, NC STATE UNIV, 85- *Personal Data:* b Okawville, Ill, Feb 18, 36; m 65; c 2. *Educ:* Univ Ill, Urbana, BS, 58, MS, 59; Cornell Univ, PhD(animal nutrit), 64. *Prof Exp:* Nat Heart Inst fel human nutrit, Sch Pub Health, Univ Pittsburgh, 64-65 & Sch Med, Univ St Louis, 65-66. *Mem:* Poultry Sci Asn; Am Inst Nutrit. *Res:* Pharmacological effects of amino acids on lipid metabolism in human subjects; effect of plant proteolytic enzyme inhibitors on digestion by chicks; hormonal regulation of calcium metabolism in avian species. *Mailing Add:* Dept Poultry Sci NC State Univ Box 7608 Raleigh NC 27695-7608. *Fax:* 919-515-2625

GARLICK, GEORGE DONALD, GEOCHEMISTRY, PETROLOGY. *Current Pos:* assoc prof, 69-74, PROF GEOL, HUMBOLDT STATE UNIV, 74- *Personal Data:* b Lusaka, Zambia, Nov 29, 34; m 64. *Educ:* Univ Witwatersrand, 56; Calif Inst Technol, PhD(geochem), 65. *Prof Exp:* Geologist, New Consol Gold Fields, SAfrica, 56-59; geochemist, Columbia Univ, 65-66, asst prof geol, 66-69. *Mem:* Am Geochem Soc; Geol Soc Am; Geophys Union; Sigma Xi. *Res:* Oxygen isotope geochemistry and petrology. *Mailing Add:* Dept Geol Humboldt State Univ 1 Harps St Arcata CA 95521-8299

GARLICK, ROBERT L, PROTEIN CHEMISTRY, BIOTECHNOLOGY. *Current Pos:* SR RES SCIENTIST, PHARMACIA & UPJOHN, INC, 85- *Personal Data:* b Cedar Rapids, Iowa, Feb 6, 49; m 79, Diane Nielsen; c Niels W & Elizabeth A. *Educ:* Univ Pacific, AB, 70; Univ Ore, MS, 73; Univ Tex, PhD(zool), 79. *Prof Exp:* Postdoctoral fel, Harvard Med Sch, 79-82, from instr to asst prof med & biochem, 82-84. *Mem:* Am Chem Soc; Am Soc Biochem & Molecular Biol; Protein Soc. *Res:* Folding E Coli-derived recombinant proteins, as well as purifying recombinant proteins from prokangotic as well as enkaryotic lasts. *Mailing Add:* Pharmacia & Upjohn Inc 1410-89-1 Kalamazoo MI 49001. *Fax:* 616-833-4241

GARLID, KEITH DAVID, PHARMACOLOGY. *Current Pos:* assoc prof pharmacol, 71-84, PROF PHARMACOL, MED COL OHIO, 84- *Personal Data:* b Albert Lea, Minn; m; c 1. *Educ:* Gustavus Adolphus Col, BA, 56; Johns Hopkins Univ, Md, 61. *Prof Exp:* Fel biophys, Johns Hopkins Univ, 61-65, asst prof obstet & gynec, 65-71. *Concurrent Pos:* Vis prof phys chem, Norwegian Inst Technol, 80-81, distinguished vis prof biol, Univ Miami, 87. *Mem:* Am Soc Biochem & Molecular Biol; Am Soc Pharmacol & Exp Therapeut; Biophys Soc. *Res:* Membrane biophysics and pharmacology; water structure in biological systems; membrane transport in mitochondria and its relationships to bioenergetics. *Mailing Add:* Dept Chem Biochem & Molecular Biol Ore Grad Inst Sci & Technol Box 91000 Portland OR 97291-1000. *Fax:* 503-690-1464

GARLID, KERMIT L(EROY), NUCLEAR ENGINEERING, CHEMICAL ENGINEERING. *Current Pos:* from asst prof to assoc prof, 60-71, assoc dean, Col Eng, 73-79, actg dean, 80-81, vprovost, 82-86, PROF NUCLEAR & CHEM ENG, UNIV WASH, 71-, CHMN, NUCLEAR ENG, 86- *Personal Data:* b Ellsworth, Wis, May 10, 29; m 54; c 4. *Educ:* Univ Wis, River Falls, BS, 50; Univ Minn, BChE, 56, PhD(chem eng), 61. *Prof Exp:* Engr qual control, Aero Div, Minneapolis-Honeywell Regulator Co, 53-54; instr chem eng, Univ Minn, 56-60. *Concurrent Pos:* Vis prof, Tech Univ, Munich, 68-69; consult, Hanford Atomic Power Oper, Gen Elec Co, 63-68, Pac Northwest Labs, Battelle Mem Inst, 65-68, Electronic Assoc, Inc, 68, Thermodyn, Inc, 70-73, Atlantic Richfield Hanford Co, 71-77, R W Beck & Assoc, 71-75, Adv Comt Reactor Safeguards, 73- & Rockwell Int-Hanford Opers, 77-; vis scientist, Battelle Human Affairs Res Ctr, 76-78♭; vis prof, Norwegian Tech Univ, Trondheim, 80. *Mem:* AAAS; Am Inst Chem Engrs; Am Nuclear Soc; Sigma Xi. *Res:* Control and optimization of chemical processes; nuclear reactor fuel cycle; nuclear reactor safety. *Mailing Add:* 2829 Tenth Ave E Seattle WA 98102

GARMAISE, DAVID LYON, ORGANIC CHEMISTRY. *Current Pos:* SCI LITERATURE CONSULT, 86- *Personal Data:* b Montreal, Que, Mar 26, 23; m 50; c 3. *Educ:* McGill Univ, BSc, 42, PhD(chem), 45. *Prof Exp:* Assoc prof chem, Univ NB, 45-50; Brit Empire Cancer Soc res fel, Univ Wales, 50-52; res sect head, Monsanto Can Ltd, 52-63; mgr org chem res, Abbott Labs Ltd, 63-93. *Mem:* Am Chem Soc; Chem Inst Can; AAAS. *Res:* Synthetic organic chemistry; medicinal chemistry; history of science. *Mailing Add:* 4910 79th Pl Kenosha WI 53142-4570

GARMAN, BRIAN LEE, MATHEMATICS. *Current Pos:* mathematician, 80-85, ASSOC PROF MATH & CHMN DEPT, UNIV TAMPA, 85- *Personal Data:* b Sturgis, Mich, July 6, 45. *Educ:* Cornell Univ, AB, 67; Western Mich Univ, MA, 73, PhD(math), 76. *Prof Exp:* Instr math, Three Rivers High Sch, 67-71; mathematician, Univ Ky, 76-79 & Wesleyan Col, 79-80. *Mem:* Am Math Soc; Math Asn Am; Nat Coun Teachers Math. *Res:* Topological graph theory; mathematical education. *Mailing Add:* Dept Math Univ Tampa Tampa FL 33606

GARMAN, JOHN ANDREW, ORGANIC CHEMISTRY, RESEARCH ADMINISTRATION. *Current Pos:* RETIRED. *Personal Data:* b Berlin, Pa, Aug 2, 21; m 45, 72, Barbara A Etzel; c Justus J & Sarah L (Rocklin). *Educ:* Franklin & Marshall Col, BS, 43; Univ Md, PhD(org chem), 48. *Prof Exp:* Res chemist, Firestone Plastics Co Div, Firestone Tire & Rubber Co, 47-50; res chemist, US Indust Chem Co, 50-53, head org chem sect, 53-54; head org chem sect, Fairfield Chem Div, FMC Corp, 54-55, asst dir, Fairfield Br, Cent Chem Res, 56-57, mgr org chem res, Org Chem Div, 57-58, mgr org chem res, Chem & Plastics Div, 58-62, dir res & develop, Org Chem Div, 62-69; dir res & develop, Great Lakes Chem Corp, 70-83, asst to vpres corp technol, 83-86, patent consult, 86-88. *Mem:* Am Chem Soc. *Res:* Organic synthesis and process development; fine organic chemicals; pharmaceuticals; agricultural chemicals; flame retardants; polymer and plastic additives; bromine chemistry. *Mailing Add:* 1705 Beechwood Ave Baltimore MD 21228

GARMAN, ROBERT HARVEY, TOXICOLOGY, COMPARATIVE PATHOLOGY. *Current Pos:* OWNER & PRES, CONSULTS IN VET PATH, 88- *Personal Data:* b New York City, NY, Aug 20, 41; m 89, Rosalyn Garzarelli; c Raymond J, Andrew N, Kimberly A (Poland) & Robin A (Poland). *Educ:* Cornell Univ, BA, 63, DVM, 66. *Prof Exp:* Vet clinician, Gen

Vet Pract, Warrenton, Va, 66-67; Vet Officer, US Pub Health Serv, NIH, 67-69; fel path, Sch Med & Dent, Univ Rochester, 69-71, instr, 71-73, asst prof path & toxicol, 73-78; sr scientist path, Carnegie-Mellon Inst Res, 78-80, res scientist pathol, Bushy Run Res Ctr, 80-88. *Concurrent Pos:* Adj assoc prof, Univ Pittsburgh, 81- *Mem:* Am Vet Med Asn; Am Col Vet Pathologists; Int Acad Pathol; Am Asn Neuropath; Soc Toxicol Pathologists; NY Acad Sci. *Res:* Spontaneous diseases of animals and models of human disease; toxicologic pathology, including the testng of chemicals for acute, subchronic and chronic effects in animals. *Mailing Add:* 112 Moonlight Dr Murrysville PA 15668. *Fax:* 412-733-3032

GARMANY, CATHARINE DOREMUS, ASTRONOMY. *Current Pos:* fel astron, 76-80, SR INSTR, JOINT INST LAB ASTROPHYS, UNIV COLO, 80-; DIR, FISKE PLANETARIUM & SOMMERS-BAUSCH OBSERV, 91-; CHAIR JOINT INST LAB ASTROPHYSICS, 97- *Personal Data:* b New York, NY, Mar 6, 46; m 2. *Educ:* Ind Univ, BS, 66; Univ Va, PhD(astron), 71. *Honors & Awards:* Annie J Cannon Award, Am Astron Soc-Am Asn Univ Women, 76. *Prof Exp:* Res assoc astron, Univ Va, 71-73. *Mem:* Am Astron Soc; Int Astron Union. *Res:* O-type stars; binaries and stellar atmospheres; stellar kinematics of intermediate age stars. *Mailing Add:* Univ Colo JILA CB 391 Univ Colo Boulder CO 80309

GARMEZY, R(OBERT) H(ARPER), MECHANICAL & ELECTRICAL ENGINEERING. *Current Pos:* RETIRED. *Personal Data:* b Manila, Philippines, Dec 8, 23; c 4. *Educ:* Cornell Univ, BEE, 43, BME, 45; Chrysler Inst Eng, MAE, 47. *Prof Exp:* Instr, Elec Lab, Cornell Univ, 43-44; student engr, Chrysler Corp, 45-47, lab engr, 47-51; head radiator lab, 51-60, dir eng, 60-68, vpres eng, Automotive Div, Blackstone Corp, 68-81. *Concurrent Pos:* Instr, Night Sch, Lawrence Inst Technol, 46-51. *Mem:* Am Soc Mech Engrs; Soc Automotive Engrs; Inst Elec & Electronics Engrs. *Res:* Heat transfer; automotive radiators; heater cores. *Mailing Add:* 96 Gordon St Jamestown NY 14701

GARMIRE, ELSA MEINTS, LASERS. *Current Pos:* DEAN, THAYER SCH ENG, DARTMOUTH, CALIF, 95- *Personal Data:* b Buffalo, NY, Nov 9, 39; m 61; c 2. *Educ:* Radcliffe Col, AB, 61; Mass Inst Technol, PhD(physics), 65. *Honors & Awards:* Achievement Award, Soc Women Engrs. *Prof Exp:* Res fel physics, Mass Inst Technol, 65-66; scientist, Electronics Res Ctr, NASA, 66; res fel elec eng, Calif Inst Technol, 66-74; assoc dir, Univ Southern Calif, 74-81, prof elec eng, 81-95, dir, ctr laser studies, 84-95. *Concurrent Pos:* From part-time res fel to part-time sr res fel appl sci, Calif Inst Technol, 69-74; pres, Laser Images, Inc; consult, Stand Telecommun Labs, Eng, 74; mem tech staff, Aerospace Corp, 75-92; consult, Northrop Corp, 75-77; assoc ed, Optics Lett & Fiber & Integrated Optics; Optical Soc Am rep, Pub Policy Comt, Am Inst Physics. *Mem:* Nat Acad Eng; fel Inst Elec & Electronics Engrs; Optical Soc Am (vpres, 91); fel Am Phys Soc; Inst Elec & Electronics Engrs, Lasers & Electro-optics Soc; Soc Women Engrs. *Res:* Lasers; integrated optics; nonlinear optics; spectroscopy; quantum electronics; author of over 160 publications; awarded 8 patents. *Mailing Add:* Dartmouth Col Thayer Sch Eng Hanover NH 37855-8000

GARMIRE, GORDON PAUL, X-RAY ASTRONOMY, ASTROPHYSICS. *Current Pos:* prof, 80-85, EVAN PUGH PROF ASTRON, PA STATE UNIV, 85- *Personal Data:* b Portland, Ore, Oct 3, 37; m 61, 76; c 4. *Educ:* Harvard Univ, AB, 59; Mass Inst Technol, PhD(physics), 62. *Honors & Awards:* Except Sci Achievement Award, NASA, 78. *Prof Exp:* Mem staff, Div Sponsored Res, Mass Inst Technol, 62-64; asst prof physics, 64-66, assoc prof, 67-68; sr fel, Calif Inst Technol, 66-67; from assoc prof to prof physics, 68-81. *Concurrent Pos:* Mem astron subcomt, NASA, 68-84; Fulbright sr fel & Guggenheim fel, 73-74; consult, Los Alamos Nat Lab, 80-88; chmn, High Energy Astrophys Div, Am Astron Soc, 85; convener, Astron & Space Physics Coun, Univs Space Res Asn, 89- *Mem:* Int Astron Union; Am Astron Soc. *Res:* X-ray and gamma ray astronomy; cosmic rays; high energy astrophysics. *Mailing Add:* Dept Astron 525 Davey Lab Pa State Univ University Park PA 16802-6305

GARMON, LUCILLE BURNETT, HISTORY & PHILOSOPHY OF SCIENCE, CHEMICAL EDUCATION. *Current Pos:* from asst prof to assoc prof physics, WGa Col, 68-74, assoc prof physics & chem, 74-78, actg chmn dept, 82-84, chmn dept, 84-95, PROF CHEM & PHYSICS, WGA COL, 78- *Personal Data:* b Johnstown, Pa, July 1, 36; m 56, Gerald M; c Steven M & Alizon M. *Educ:* Univ Richmond, BS, 56, MS, 60; Univ Va, PhD(chem), 66. *Prof Exp:* Res chemist, Va Inst Sci Res, 57-61; assoc prof chem, ECarolina Col, 64-66; asst prof physics & chem, Auburn Univ, 66-68, fel solid state physics, 66-67. *Concurrent Pos:* Consult, Freeport Kaolin Co, 67-68; vis prof, Chester Col, Eng, 77. *Mem:* AAAS; Am Chem Soc; Am Phys Soc; Am Asn Physics Teachers; Electron Micros Soc Am; Nat Sci Teachers Asn. *Res:* History of science as a means of enhancing science education; electron microscopy; teaching methods in physical and general chemistry. *Mailing Add:* Dept Chem State Univ WGa Carrollton GA 30118-6310. *Fax:* 770-836-6633; *E-Mail:* lgarmon.westga.edu

GARMON, RONALD GENE, ANALYTICAL CHEMISTRY. *Current Pos:* RETIRED. *Personal Data:* b Charlotte, NC, Mar 13, 34; m 55, Betty M Broome; c Karen A, Janet K & Elizabeth J. *Educ:* Univ NC, BS, 58, PhD(chem), 61. *Prof Exp:* From res chemist to sr res chemist, Res Triangle Park Develop Ctr, 61-69, group leader, 68-81; group leader, Monsanto Co, Decatur, Ala, 81-96. *Mem:* Am Chem Soc. *Res:* Analytical chemistry of polymers; radiochemistry; kinetic methods of analysis. *Mailing Add:* 2402 Burningtree Dr SE Decatur AL 35603

GARN, PAUL DONALD, instrumentation, thermal analysis; deceased, see previous edition for last biography

GARN, STANLEY MARION, PHYSICAL ANTHROPOLOGY, NUTRITION. *Current Pos:* prof nutrit, Sch Pub Health & fel, Ctr Human Growth & Develop, 68-93, prof, 72-93, EMER PROF ANTHROP, UNIV MICH, ANN ARBOR, 93- *Personal Data:* b New London, Conn, Oct 27, 22; m 50, Priscilla Crozier; c Barbara & William David. *Educ:* Harvard Univ, AB, 42, AM, 47, PhD(phys anthrop), 48. *Honors & Awards:* Neuhauser Lectr, Soc Pediat Radiol, 81; Raymond Pearl Lectr, Human Biol Coun, 85; Harvey White Lectr, Children's Mem Hosp, 87; Charles R Darwin Lifetime Achievement Award, Am Asn Phys Anthropologists, 94. *Prof Exp:* Res assoc, Mass Inst Technol, 42-44; tech ed, Polaroid Corp, 44-46, consult, 46; instr anthrop, Harvard Univ, 48-52; from assoc prof to prof, Antioch Col, 52-68, chmn, Dept Growth & Genetics, Fels Res Inst, 52-68. *Concurrent Pos:* Res fel, Mass Gen Hosp, 46-50, Forsyth Dent Infirmary, 47-52 & Int Univ Training Prog, 58; vis prof, Univ Chicago, 58, Southern Methodist Univ, 76; mem vis staff, Inst Nutrit Cent Am & Panama, 62; Walker-Ames vis prof, Univ Wash, 86. *Mem:* Nat Acad Sci; Am Soc Naturalists; fel Am Anthrop Asn; Am Asn Phys Anthrop (pres, 66-67); fel Am Acad Arts & Sci; fel Am Acad Pediat; fel Am Soc Clin Nutritionists; Int Asn Dent Res; fel Am Inst Nutrit; Int Orgn Study Human Develop; Human Biol Asn; Int Asn Human Biologists; fel Am Soc Nutrit Sci. *Res:* Growth and development of body tissues; applied physical anthropology; human evolution; interaction of nutrition and genetics on growth development and aging; evolutionary dynamics below the species level in man. *Mailing Add:* Ctr Human Growth 300 N Ingalls Bldg Ann Arbor MI 48109-0406

GARNAR, THOMAS E(DWARD), JR, GEOLOGY, MINERAL ENGINEERING. *Current Pos:* PRIN CONSULT, TICON INC, 85- *Personal Data:* b Vineland, NJ, June 24, 22; m 54. *Educ:* WVa Univ, BS, 50, MS, 51. *Prof Exp:* Asst, WVa Univ, 48-51; res geologist, Res Div, Int Minerals & Chem Corp, 51-56; mining engr, Humphreys Gold Corp, 56-57; develop engr, Pigments Dept, E I du Pont de Nemours & Co, Inc, 57-64, sr res geologist, 64-69, tech supvr, 69-71, res assoc, 71-85. *Mem:* Am Inst Mining, Metall & Petrol Engrs; Soc Econ Geologists; Am Foundrymen's Soc; Sigma Xi. *Res:* Mineralogy and geology of industrial minerals; gravity, electrostatic, high tension, and magnetic concentration of titanium minerals, zircon, aluminum silicates; new uses for mineral products; foundry sand properties. *Mailing Add:* PO Box 417 Keystone Heights FL 32656

GARNEAU, FRANCOIS XAVIER, ORGANIC CHEMISTRY. *Current Pos:* PROF ORG CHEM, UNIV QUE, CHICOUTIMI, 70- *Personal Data:* b Montreal, Que, May 6, 36; m 63; c 3. *Educ:* Concordia Univ Montreal, BSc, 62; Col of the Holy Cross, MSc, 63; Univ Toronto, PhD (organic chem & photochem), 68. *Prof Exp:* Fel, Univ Alta, 68-70. *Mem:* Am Chem Soc; Fr-Can Asn Advan Sci; Chem Inst Can; Int Soc Chem Ecol. *Res:* Plant natural products. *Mailing Add:* Dept De Chem Univ Du Que 555 BL De L Univ Chicoutimi PQ G7H 2B1 Can

GARNER, ALBERT Y, ORGANIC CHEMISTRY, ORGANO-PHOSPHORUS CHEMISTRY. *Current Pos:* RETIRED. *Personal Data:* b Washington, DC, May 8, 25; m 49, Geraldine Hall; c Linda G (Edgar), Christina G (Carroll), Albert G & Edwina G (Graham). *Educ:* Howard Univ, BS, 50, MS, 51; Pa State Univ, PhD(org chem), 56. *Prof Exp:* Instr, Howard Univ, 51-52, res assoc, 52-53; res chemist, Monsanto Chem Co, 56-62, res chemist, Monsanto Res Corp, 62-64, res specialist, 64-65, proj leader & group leader, 65-76, sr res specialist, Monsanto Res Corp, 76-79, sr res specialist, Monsanto Plastics & Resins Co, 79-82, fel, Monsanto Polymer Prod Co, 82-85, fel, Monsanto Chem Co, 86. *Mem:* Am Chem Soc; Am Inst Chem; Sigma Xi. *Res:* Organic and polymer synthesis; reaction mechanisms; organophosphorus chemistry; structure determination; reactive intermediates; reaction injection molding; nylon block copolymers; fire retardancy. *Mailing Add:* 1463 Plumtree Rd Springfield MA 01119-2940

GARNER, ANDREW, CORROSION, METALLURGY. *Current Pos:* ASSOC SCIENTIST CORROSION, PULP & PAPER RES INST CAN, 78-, DIR, VANCOUVER LAB, 89- *Personal Data:* b Manchester, Eng, Oct 23, 45; Can citizen; m 69; c 3. *Educ:* Liverpool Univ, BSc, 68; Univ BC, PhD(metall), 74. *Honors & Awards:* Weldon Medal, Can Paper & Pulp Asn, 85. *Prof Exp:* Metallurgist aluminum, Alcan Industs Ltd, UK, 68-69; sr res engr corrosion, Molybdenum Res, Endako Mines, 75-78. *Mem:* Nat Asn Corrosion Engrs; Am Soc Metals; fel Brit Inst Metallurgists; Tech Asn Pulp & Paper Indust. *Res:* Corrosion in aqueous environments. *Mailing Add:* Pulp & Paper Res Inst Can 3800 Wesbrook Mall Vancouver BC V6S 2L9 Can

GARNER, CYRIL WILBUR LUTHER, PURE MATHEMATICS. *Current Pos:* From asst prof to assoc prof, 64-82, chmn, Dept Math & Statist, 87-94, PROF MATH, CARLETON UNIV, OTTAWA, ONT, 82- *Personal Data:* b Scotland, Ont, Mar 20, 40; m 67, Barbara Carmen. *Educ:* Univ NB, BSc, 61; Univ Toronto, MA, 62, PhD(math), 64. *Concurrent Pos:* Fel, Inst Combinatorics & Applns. *Mem:* Am Math Soc; Can Math Soc. *Res:* Projective geometry; finite geometries and the foundations of geometry with particular emphasis upon hyperbolic geometry; combinatorics. *Mailing Add:* Dept Math Carleton Univ Colonel By Dr Ottawa ON K1S 5B6 Can. *Fax:* 613-520-3536; *E-Mail:* cgarner@math.carleton.ca

GARNER, DANIEL DEE, FORENSIC SCIENCE. *Current Pos:* dir labs, 87-91, VPRES, CELLMARK DIAGNOSTICS, 91- *Personal Data:* b Minford, Ohio, Oct 7, 47; m 68; c 2. *Educ:* David Lipscomb Col, BA, 69; Univ Tenn, PhD(med chem), 73. *Prof Exp:* Lab technologist, Baptist Mem Hosp, 66-69; forensic chemist, Bur Alcohol Tobacco & Firearms, 73-87. *Concurrent Pos:* Med technologist, Howard County Gen Hosp, 73-75; assoc prof lectr, George Washington Univ, 75; assoc prof, Antioch Sch Law, 79- *Mem:* Am Acad Forensic Sci; Am Asn Blood Banks; Am Soc Human Genetics;

Mid-Atlantic Asn Forensic Sci; Am Asn Clin Chemists. *Res:* Characterization of explosives and explosive residues of importance in forensic chemistry; development of identification and characterization techniques. *Mailing Add:* 9631 W Window Way Columbia MD 21046

GARNER, DUANE LEROY, REPRODUCTIVE PHYSIOLOGY, ANIMAL SCIENCE. *Current Pos:* prof & chair, Dept Animal Sci, 85-89, PROF, SCH VET MED, UNIV NEV, RENO, 89- *Personal Data:* b Madera, Calif, Feb 9, 36; m 60, Jane; c Brian, Dean & Evan. *Educ:* Calif State Univ, Fresno, BS, 64; Wash State Univ, MS, 67, PhD(animal sci), 69. *Prof Exp:* Fel reproductive physiol, Dept Dairy Sci, Univ Ill, 69-70, res assoc, 70-72; prof reproductive physiol, Dept Physiol Sci, Okla State Univ, 72-85. *Concurrent Pos:* Spec consult for NIH prog proj rev, NIH, 75, 80, 82, 84, 86, 87, 88, 89 & 90. *Mem:* Soc Study Reproduction; Am Soc Andrology; Am Soc Animal Sci; Soc Analytical Cytol; Am Soc Cell Biol. *Res:* Fluorescent staining of spermatozoa; fertilization, immunobiology of spermatozoa, flow cytometry of spermatozoa; viability assessment of spermatozoa. *Mailing Add:* Sch Vet Med Col Agr Univ Nev-Reno Reno NV 89557-0004. *Fax:* 702-784-1375; *E-Mail:* dgarner@scs.unr.edu

GARNER, GEORGE BERNARD, AGRICULTURAL BIOCHEMISTRY. *Current Pos:* from instr to assoc prof, 53-74, PROF AGR CHEM, UNIV MO, COLUMBIA, 74-, PROF BIOCHEM, 80- *Personal Data:* b Kirksville, Mo, Dec 7, 27; m 48; c 4. *Educ:* Northeast Mo State Teachers Col, BS, 49; Univ Mo, MS, 51, PhD(agr chem), 57. *Prof Exp:* Teacher, Pub Sch, 51-53. *Concurrent Pos:* Fulbright res scholar, 62-63. *Mem:* AAAS; Am Chem Soc; Am Soc Animal Sci; Sigma Xi. *Res:* Rumen nutrition and physiology; nitrate toxicity, fescue toxicosis and physiologically active constituents of forages; analytical methods applicable to agricultural products. *Mailing Add:* Animal Sci Ctr Anal Sci & Biochem Univ Mo Columbia MO 65211-0001

GARNER, HAROLD E, CARDIOVASCULAR DISEASE, ANESTHESIOLOGY. *Current Pos:* PROF VET MED & SURG & ASSOC INVESTR, DALTON RES CTR, UNIV MO-COLUMBIA, 71- *Personal Data:* b Eldorado, Kans, May 8, 35; m 57; c 4. *Educ:* Kans State Univ, BS, 57, DVM, 62, MS, 64; Baylor Col Med, PhD(cardiovasc physiol, biomed eng), 71. *Prof Exp:* Pvt vet pract, 62-65; asst prof, Dept Clin Med, Univ Ill, 66-68; instr, asst prof & spec res fel, Dept Physiol & Surg, Baylor Col Med, 68-71. *Mem:* Am Physiol Soc; NY Acad Sci; Am Soc Vet Anesthesiol; Am Acad Vet Cardiol; Am Vet Med Asn. *Res:* Specific and comparative aspects of equine hypertension-laminitis and human hypertension; automated quantitative administration of volatile anesthetics to animals; equine edotoxemia. *Mailing Add:* Dept Vet Med & Surg Univ Mo Col Vet Med Dalton Res Ctr Columbia MO 65211. *Fax:* 573-882-2950

GARNER, HARRY RICHARD, ELECTROCHEMISTRY. *Current Pos:* CONSULT, M&T HARSHAW, 91- *Personal Data:* b East Liverpool, Ohio, Feb 4, 35; m 57; c 2. *Educ:* Kent State Univ, BS, 57; Western Res Univ, MS, 62. *Prof Exp:* Chemist, Harshaw Chem Co, 57-59, group leader, 59-63, unit mgr, Instrumental Anal Lab, 63-66, from asst sect mgr to sect mgr, Cent Anal Lab, 66-69, tech dir metal finishing res, 69-81, bus mgr, 82-83; vpres & gen mgr, metal finishing, Harshaw-Filtrol, 83-88; vpres & bus dir, Engelhard Corp, 88-90. *Mem:* Am Electroplaters Soc. *Res:* Electrodeposition of metals; analytical chemistry; instrumental analysis; corrosion. *Mailing Add:* 674 Wheatfield Dr Aurora OH 44202

GARNER, HARVEY L(OUIS), COMPUTER ARITHMETIC, COMPUTER SYSTEM DESIGN. *Current Pos:* CONSULT, 88- *Personal Data:* b Lake, Colo, Dec 23, 26; m 50; c 2. *Educ:* Univ Denver, BS, 49, MS, 51; Univ Mich, PhD(elec eng), 58. *Hon Degrees:* MA, Univ Pa. *Prof Exp:* Res assoc, Cosmic Radiation Lab, Univ Denver, 49-51; assoc res engr, Digital Comput Dept, Willow Run Labs, Univ Mich, 51-53, asst head dept, 53-55, from instr to prof elec eng, 55-70, dir info syst lab, 60-64; dir, Moore Sch Elec Eng, 70-77, prof elec eng, Univ Pa, 70-86; dir, MCC, 84-88. *Concurrent Pos:* Nat lectr, Asn Comput Mach, 65; vis prof, Stanford Univ, 76-77. *Mem:* AAAS; Asn Comput Mach; fel Inst Elec & Electronics Engrs. *Res:* Digital computation; machine number systems and arithmetic; integration of hardware and software in digital systems. *Mailing Add:* 7400 Rockberry Cove Austin TX 78750

GARNER, HERSCHEL WHITAKER, VERTEBRATE ZOOLOGY, ECOLOGY. *Current Pos:* asst prof biol, 70-74, ASST PROF BIOL SCI, TARLETON STATE COL, 74- *Personal Data:* b Jacksonville, Tex, June 25, 36; m 59; c 1. *Educ:* Stephen F Austin State Univ, BS, 62; Tex Tech Univ, MS, 65, PhD(zool), 70. *Prof Exp:* Instr biol, Tex Tech Univ, 65-66. *Mem:* AAAS; Am Soc Mammal; Sigma Xi. *Res:* Biology and populations of small mammals. *Mailing Add:* Tarleton State Univ Tarleton Sta Stephenville TX 76402-0001

GARNER, HESSLE FILMORE, GEOMORPHOLOGY. *Current Pos:* prof, 67-76, prof II, 77-87, EMER PROF GEOL, RUTGERS UNIV, 87-; GEOL CONSULT & JUDICATION, 87- *Personal Data:* b Creston, Iowa, Feb 24, 26; m 81, Anita Virgil; c Cynthia, Ana, Craig, Mark, Bruce, Raquel (deceased), Noel, Michelle & Jennifer. *Educ:* Iowa State Col, BS, 50; Univ Iowa, MS, 51, PhD(geol), 53. *Prof Exp:* Asst phys geol, Univ Iowa, 50-51; asst paleont, 52-53; geologist, Richmond Petrol Co Calif, 53, Calif-Ecuador Petrol Co, 54-56; asst prof geol, Univ Ark, 56-60, assoc prof, 61-67. *Concurrent Pos:* Consult, Gulf Oil Co, 58-59, rk Geol Survey Mapping, 60-67. *Mem:* Fel Geol Soc Am; AAAS; Am Asn Petrol Geologists. *Res:* Invertebrate paleontology; paleozoic and mesozoic cephalopoda; tertiary stratigraphy and structure of Ecuador; Andes mountain geomorphology and climatic sedimentation; global drainage development; paleozoic stratigraphy of north Arkansas; global geomorphology; development of fluvial systems and continental clastic deposits; Quaternary paleoclimatology; theories of landform evolution; Ecuadorian geomorphic history. *Mailing Add:* 202 Merrywood Dr Forest VA 24551

GARNER, JACKIE BASS, MATHEMATICS. *Current Pos:* CHAIR, DEPT MATH & STATIST, UNIV ARK, LITTLE ROCK, 92- *Personal Data:* b Jonesboro, La, Aug 21, 34; m 57; c 2. *Educ:* La Polytech Inst, BS, 55; Auburn Univ, MS, 57, PhD(math), 60. *Prof Exp:* From instr to prof math, La Tech Univ, 57-86; prof, Miss State Univ, 86-92. *Concurrent Pos:* NSF res grant, 63-64; appointment, NIH, 76-79, grants, 72-75 & 80-86. *Mem:* Am Math Soc; Math Asn Am. *Res:* Ordinary and partial differential equations. *Mailing Add:* Dept Math & Statist Univ Ark 2801 S University Little Rock AR 72204-1099

GARNER, JAMES G, CYTOGENETICS, MICROBIOLOGY. *Current Pos:* from instr to full prof, 65-76, PROF BIOL, C W POST COL, LONG ISLAND UNIV, 76- *Personal Data:* b Astoria, NY, Dec 21, 38; m 64; c 2. *Educ:* Providence Col, AB, 60; Long Island Univ, MS, 63; St John's Univ, NY, PhD(biol), 67. *Prof Exp:* Teaching fel biol, Long Island Univ, 60-62; teaching asst, St John's Univ, NY, 62-65. *Concurrent Pos:* Mem bd trustees & pub educ comt, Nassau-Suffolk County Chap, Nat Found-March of Dimes; biol consult, John Wiley & Sons, Inc, Publ, McGraw-Hill Book Co & Benjamin/Cummings Publ Co. *Mem:* Am Soc Cell Biol; Sigma Xi. *Res:* Cytogenetics, sex chromatin in vertebrates; Q- and G-banding in human and mammalian chromosomes; microbiology, action of plant hormones on bacteria. *Mailing Add:* Dept Biol C W Post Col Long Island Univ Brookville NY 11548

GARNER, JASPER HENRY BARKDOLL, MYCOLOGY, PLANT PATHOLOGY. *Current Pos:* botanist, Off Air Progs, Environ Protection Agency, 71-72, botanist-microbiologist, spec studies staff, 72-78, biologist, 78-79, ECOLOGIST, ENVIRON CRITERIA & ASSESSMENT OFF, NAT CTR ENVIRON ASSESSMENT, 79- *Personal Data:* b Bulsar, India, Nov 7, 21; US citizen; m 54, Lois M Harman; c Eric L. *Educ:* Manchester Col, BA, 48; Ind Univ, MA, 53; Univ Iowa, PhD(bot), 55. *Prof Exp:* Asst prof bot, Univ Nebr, 55-56; from instr to asst prof, Univ Ky, 56-67; assoc prof, Eastern Tenn State Univ, 67-69; res assoc plant path, NC State Univ, 69-71. *Concurrent Pos:* Univ Ky-Int Coop Admin Prog vis prof, Col Agr & Vet Sci, Univ Indonesia, 57-61; chmn, Task Force Air Qual Criteria Ozone & Other Photochem Oxidants, 75-78 & Health Assessment Cadmium, 77-81 & mem, Task Force Rewriting, Air Qual Criteria, Particulate Mat & Sulfur Oxides, 78-82 & revised Air Qual Criteria, Ozone & other photochem oxidants, 80-84; team mem, Air Qual Criteria, Oxides of Nitrogen, 88-93 & revising, Air Qual Criteria, Ozone & Related Photochem Oxidants, 92-96; proj mgr environ effects & mgr effect particulate matter veg & ecosysts, 94- *Mem:* Mycol Soc Am; Ecol Soc Am; Am Inst Biol Sci. *Res:* Gasteromycetes; forest pathology; interrelationships between natural gas pollution of soil and death of woody plants; vegetational effects of sulfur oxides and ozone; ecological effects of nitrogen oxides; particulate nitrogen deposition and nutrient cycling; sulfur oxides and ozone particularly on forest ecosystems; production, contracting and writing, chapters on effects of ambient air pollutants on vegetation and ecosystems. *Mailing Add:* Environ Criteria & Assessment Off MD-52 Environ Protection Agency Research Triangle Park NC 27711. *Fax:* 919-541-0245; *E-Mail:* garner.jay@epamail.epa.gov

GARNER, LAFORREST D, ORTHODONTICS. *Current Pos:* Asst periodont, Ind Univ, 57-58, res asst, 58-59, from instr to assoc prof, 59-71, PROF ORTHOD, SCH DENT, 71-, ASSOC DEAN, IND UNIV, INDIANAPOLIS, 88-, DIR GRAD & POST GRAD EDUC DENT, 93- *Personal Data:* b Muskogee, Okla, Aug 20, 33; m 64, Alfreida Thomas; c Deana Y, Thomas L & Sanford E. *Educ:* Ind Univ, DDS, 57, MSD, 59, cert, 61. *Concurrent Pos:* Chmn, Dept Orthod, Sch Dent, Ind Univ, 70-, assoc dean dir grad & post grad dent educ minority student serv. *Mem:* Am Dent Asn; Am Soc Dent Children; Int Asn Dent Res; fel Am Col Dent; Sigma Xi; Am Asn Orthod. *Res:* Growth and development; posture of tongue in children with normal occlusions; cleft lip and palate rehabilitation; pedodontics; orthodontics. *Mailing Add:* Sch Dent Ind Univ Indianapolis IN 46202. *Fax:* 317-274-2419

GARNER, LYNN E, TECHNOLOGY IN MATHEMATICS. *Current Pos:* Instr, 64-66, asst prof, 68-74, assoc prof, 74-80, PROF MATH, BRIGHAM YOUNG UNIV, 81- *Personal Data:* b Ontario, Ore, July 19, 41; m 60, Kaye Waite; c Kaylene, Bradley E, Kristen, Alisse & Brian L. *Educ:* Brigham Young Univ, BS, 62; Univ Utah, MS, 64; Univ Ore, PhD(math), 68. *Concurrent Pos:* Math instr, Meridian Sch, 89-96. *Mem:* Am Math Soc; Math Asn Am; Sigma Xi. *Res:* Algebra; commutative algebra; projective and algebraic geometry; number theory; philosophy of mathematics; technology in math and math education. *Mailing Add:* Dept Math Brigham Young Univ Provo UT 84602. *E-Mail:* lynng@math.byu.edu

GARNER, MERIDON VESTAL, MATHEMATICS. *Current Pos:* RETIRED. *Personal Data:* b Belton, Tex, Sept 20, 28; m 56; c 3. *Educ:* Sul Ross State Col, MEd, 56; NTex State Univ, EdD, 63. *Prof Exp:* Assoc prof math, Sul Ross State Col, 56-63; from asst prof to assoc prof, NTex State Univ, 63-94. *Mem:* Math Asn Am. *Res:* Preparation of subject-content material in mathematics for future elementary teachers. *Mailing Add:* Rte 2 Box 2565 Sanger TX 76266-8941

GARNER, REUBEN JOHN, radiation biology, for more information see previous edition

GARNER, ROBERT HENRY, CHEMISTRY. *Current Pos:* asst prof, 59-68, ASSOC PROF CHEM, UNIV ALA, 68-, ASST DEAN, COL SCI, 73- *Personal Data:* b Mobile, Ala, Jan 7, 33; m 61; c 3. *Educ:* Vanderbilt Univ, BA, 54; Rice Inst, PhD(chem), 58. *Prof Exp:* Fel chem, Yale Univ, 58-59. *Mem:* Am Chem Soc. *Res:* Organic chemistry. *Mailing Add:* 9 Dunbrook Tuscaloosa AL 35406

GARNET, HYMAN R, applied mechanics, applied mathematics; deceased, see previous edition for last biography

GARNETT, RICHARD WINGFIELD, JR, PSYCHIATRY. *Current Pos:* RETIRED. *Personal Data:* b Albemarle Co, Va, Mar 27, 15; m 41; c 5. *Educ:* Univ Va, BS, 36, MD, 40, MS, 49. *Prof Exp:* From asst prof to assoc prof, Sch Med, Univ Va, 49-57, actg chmn dept, 56-57 & 63-64, prof, 57-74, clin prof psychiat, 74- *Concurrent Pos:* WHO fel community psychiat, Gt Brit & Western Europe, 63; mem sr fac sem, Harvard Med Sch, 65-67; consult, Vet Admin; sr staff psychiatrist, David C Wilson Psychiat Hosp, 81- *Mem:* Fel Am Psychiat Asn; AMA. *Res:* Psychosomatic medicine; academic and community psychiatry. *Mailing Add:* 917 S Broad St Thomasville GA 31792-6114

GARNSEY, STEPHEN MICHAEL, PLANT VIROLOGY. *Current Pos:* RES PLANT PATHOLOGIST, US HORT RES LAB, AGR RES SERV, USDA, 63- *Personal Data:* b Oceanside, Calif, Aug 3, 37; m 58, Rosalee Zepik; c Michael P & Lisa A. *Educ:* Univ Calif, Riverside, BA, 58, Univ Calif, Davis, PhD(plant path), 64. *Honors & Awards:* Lee M Hutchins Award, Am Phytopathol Soc, 81; Fel, Am Phytopath Soc, 87. *Prof Exp:* Lab technician plant path, Univ Calif, Riverside, 58-59, res asst, Univ Calif, Davis, 59-63. *Concurrent Pos:* Adj prof, Inst Food & Agr Sci, Univ Fla, 83- *Mem:* AAAS; Am Phytopath Soc; Sigma Xi; Am Inst Biol Sci. *Res:* Mechanical transmission, purification and serology of plant viruses; identification and properties of citrus viruses and virus like pathogens; development of virus resistant citrus. *Mailing Add:* Agr Res Serv USDA 2120 Camden Rd Orlando FL 32803-1419

GARODNICK, JOSEPH, DATA COMMUNICATIONS, WIRELESS COMMUNICATIONS. *Personal Data:* b Newark, NJ, Jan 29, 45; m, Ilana Tal; c Richard & Sharon. *Educ:* Rensselaer Polytech Inst, BEE, 66; Polytech Inst New York, MS, 69; City Univ New York, PhD(elec eng), 72. *Prof Exp:* Design engr radio frequency equip, Blonder Tongue Labs, 65-67, design engr digital equip, ITT Avionics, 67-69; res lab asst commun, City Col City New York, 69-72; mem tech staff, Bell Tel Labs, 72; dir commun systs, Goldmark Commun Corp, 72-75; exec vpres, Stern Telecommun Corp, 75-81; chief scientist, Phasecom Corp, 81-86; corp vpres, Fibronics Int Inc, 86-92; exec vpres, InterDigital Commun Corp, 92-94. *Concurrent Pos:* Adj prof, Dept Elec Eng, City Col City Univ New York, 72-81; dir publ bd gov, Commun Soc, 79-83. *Mem:* Inst Elec & Electronics Engrs. *Res:* Digital processing of communication systems; digital phase locked loops; voice encoding; satellite communications; fiber optic data communications; wireless communications; sprad spectrum communications. *Mailing Add:* 56 Wild Goose Way Centerville MA 02668. *Fax:* 508-420-5649; *E-Mail:* jgarodnick@aol.com

GAROIAN, GEORGE, PARASITOLOGY. *Current Pos:* from asst prof to assoc prof, Southern Ill Univ, 56-84, asst chmn dept, 58-61, actg chmn dept, 71-72, chmn dept, 72-73, dir undergrad studies in dept, 73-80, prof, 84-87, EMER PROF ZOOL, SOUTHERN ILL UNIV, 87- *Personal Data:* b Deadwood, SDak, July 23, 27; m 54; c 2. *Educ:* Wash Univ, AB, 49; Univ Ill, MS, 51, PhD(zool), 56. *Prof Exp:* Asst zool, Univ Ill, 49-55, asst vet med, 55-56. *Mem:* Am Soc Parasitologists; Soc Protozoologists. *Res:* Protozoology; helminthology; animal diversity. *Mailing Add:* 705 S Murrie Dr Carbondale IL 62901

GARON, CLAUDE FRANCIS, MICROBIOLOGY, BIOCHEMISTRY. *Current Pos:* chief, Lab Vectors & Pathogens, 85-94, RES MICROBIOLOGIST VIROL, NIH, 71-, CHIEF, ROCKY MOUNTAIN LABS, MICROSCOPY BR & HEAD, BACT PATHOGENESIS SECT, 94- *Personal Data:* b Baton Rouge, La, Nov 5, 42; m 68, Sally Sheffield; c Michele, Anne & Julie. *Educ:* La State Univ, BS, 64, MS, 66; Georgetown Univ, PhD(microbiol), 70. *Honors & Awards:* Lyme Disease Found Prize, 96. *Concurrent Pos:* Fel lab biol viruses, Nat Inst Allergy & Infectious Dis, NIH, 69-71, staff fel, 71-73, sr staff fel, 73-74. *Mem:* Am Soc Microbiol; Micros Soc Am; Am Soc Biochem & Molecular Biol; Am Leptospirosis Res Conf; Pac NW Electron Micros Soc. *Res:* Molecular biology; ultra structure of nucleic acids; to exploit the potential of recombinant DNA technology for the detection and amplification of genes that are important in microbial pathogenesis. *Mailing Add:* Microscopy Rocky Mountain Labs Hamilton MT 59840. *Fax:* 406-363-9372; *E-Mail:* claude_garon@nih.gov

GARON, OLIVIER, COMPARATIVE ANATOMY. *Current Pos:* RETIRED. *Personal Data:* b Quebec, Que, Jan 24, 28; m 55; c 2. *Educ:* Laval Univ, BA, 50; Univ Montreal, DVM, 55, MSc, 61, PhD, 64. *Prof Exp:* Prof anat & biol, Sch Vet Med, Univ Montreal, 57-92, head, Dept Basic Sci, 61-72, dir animal anat & physiol, 72-80, consult, 92-96. *Res:* Domestic and wild animals. *Mailing Add:* 2240 Carillon St Hyacinthe PQ J2S 7S9 Can

GARONE, JOHN EDWARD, human biology, science writing, for more information see previous edition

GAROUTTE, BILL CHARLES, NEUROPHYSIOLOGY. *Current Pos:* asst resident neurol, Univ Hosp, 48 & 51-52, from lectr to prof, 49-86, EMER PROF ANAT & NEUROL, UNIV CALIF, SAN FRANCISCO, 86- *Personal Data:* b Absarokee, Mont, Mar 15, 21; m 48, 89, Rebecca Kasten; c Brian, Susanna, David & Katherine. *Educ:* Univ Calif, AB, 43, MD, 45, PhD(biophys), 54. *Prof Exp:* Intern, San Diego Co Hosp, 45-46. *Concurrent Pos:* Fulbright scholar, Inst Neurol, London, 50-51; vis asst prof, Fac Med, Univ Indonesia, 56-57; vis investr, Inst Brain Res, Tokyo, 63, ext examr, Univ Malaysia, 78, Sci Univ Malaysia, 84. *Mem:* AAAS; Am Epilepsy Soc; Am Electroencephalog Soc; AMA; Am Asn Anat; Sigma Xi; Am Asn Electromyography & Electrodiagnosis. *Res:* Function of the nervous system. *Mailing Add:* 1336 El Camino Real No 245 Millbrae CA 94030-1411. *Fax:* 650-355-8396

GARRARD, CHRISTOPHER S, PULMONARY DISEASE. *Current Pos:* ASSOC PROF MED & ANESTHESIOL, COL MED, UNIV ILL, 77- *Personal Data:* b Wolverhantton, Eng, May 9, 45. *Educ:* Oxford Univ, PhD(physiol), 81. *Mailing Add:* Intensive Therapy Unit John Radcliff Hosp Headington Oxford 0X3 9DU England. *Fax:* 44-1865-220846

GARRARD, THOMAS L, FLIGHT OPERATIONS. *Current Pos:* from scientist to sr scientist, 72-81, MEM PROFESSIONAL STAFF, CALIF INST TECHNOL, 81- *Personal Data:* b Jan 28, 44. *Educ:* Rice Univ, BA, 66; Calif Inst Technol, PhD(physics), 72. *Concurrent Pos:* Exp mgr, Galileo Heavy Element Monitor, 84-; co-investr, Large Isotope Spectrometer Astromag, 89- *Mem:* Life mem Am Phys Soc; life mem Am Geophys Union. *Res:* Studies of interplanetary streaming; identification and study of solar flare data; assisted with accelerator calibrations activity and data analysis planning. *Mailing Add:* Calif Inst Technol 220-47 Downs Lab Pasadena CA 91125

GARRARD, VERL GRADY, PHYSICAL CHEMISTRY, ANALYTICAL CHEMISTRY. *Current Pos:* From instr to assoc prof, 47-86, EMER ASSOC PROF CHEM, UNIV IDAHO, 86- *Personal Data:* b Burley, Idaho, July 21, 23; m 62, Georgia Christensen; c 3. *Educ:* Univ Idaho, BS, 45, MS, 52; Univ Utah, PhD, 67. *Mem:* AAAS; Am Chem Soc; Sigma Xi. *Res:* Chemical kinetics. *Mailing Add:* 422 N 700 E Provo UT 84606

GARRARD, WILLIAM LASH, JR, ENGINEERING MECHANICS. *Current Pos:* Asst prof, 68-76, ASSOC PROF AERONAUT & ENG MECH, UNIV MINN, MINNEAPOLIS, 76- *Personal Data:* b Waco, Tex, Nov 7, 40; m 65. *Educ:* Univ Tex, BS, 62, PhD(eng mech), 68. *Concurrent Pos:* NSF grant, 68-69. *Mem:* Inst Elec & Electronics Engrs. *Res:* Control theory; stability and control of dynamical systems. *Mailing Add:* Dept Aeronaut Univ Minn 1107 Akerman Minneapolis MN 55455

GARRARD, WILLIAM T, MOLECULAR BIOLOGY. *Current Pos:* PROF BIOCHEM, UNIV TEX HEALTH SCI CTR, 74- *Personal Data:* b Seattle, Wash, Sept 16, 42. *Educ:* Univ Calif, Los Angeles, PhD(microbiol), 71. *Mem:* Am Soc Chem Biochemists; Am Soc Cell Biol; Sigma Xi. *Mailing Add:* Dept Molecular Biol & Oncol Univ Tex Southwestern Med Ctr 6000 Harry Hines Blvd Dallas TX 75235-9140. *Fax:* 214-648-1909

GARRATTY, GEORGE, IMMUNOHEMATOLOGY. *Current Pos:* SCI DIR, AM RED CROSS BLOOD PROG, LOS ANGELES, 78-; CLIN PROF PATHOL, UNIV CALIF, LOS ANGELES, 85- *Personal Data:* b London, Eng, July 2, 35; m 69, Eileen Carroll. *Educ:* AIMLS, 58, FIMLS, 60, MRCPath, 80, PhD, 85, FRCPath, 91. *Honors & Awards:* Ivor Dunsford Mem Award, Am Asn Blood Banks, 78, Emily Cooley Mem Award, 89, Morten Grove-Rasmussen Mem Award, 94; Charles R Drew Award, Am Red Cross, 87. *Prof Exp:* Chief med lab scientist hemat, Royal Postgrad Med Sch London, 63-68; res assoc immunohemat, Univ Calif, San Francisco, 68-70, assoc specialist & lectr, 71-78; res assoc, Inst Med Sci, San Francisco, 75-78. *Concurrent Pos:* Lectr, Inner London Educ Authority, 59-68, Paddington Col, London, 59-68 & San Francisco State Univ, 71-78; consult, Irwin Mem Blood Bank, San Francisco, 73-78; mem comt, Tech Manual, Am Asn Blood Banks, 75-82, Sci Prog, 78-81, Stand, 82-89; mem comt, Adv Comt Antiglobulin Sera, Food & Drug Admin, 74-; prog chmn, Calif Blood Bank Syst, 77-78, chmn, Bylaws Comt, 90-; pres, Calif Blood Bank Soc, 85-86. *Mem:* Am Asn Blood Banks; Am Fed Clin Res; Am Asn Immunologists; Am Soc Hematol; Int Soc Blood Transfusion. *Res:* Immune red cell destruction (Alloimmune and Autoimmune); complement; antigen-antibody reactions in immunohematology; flow cytometry. *Mailing Add:* Am Red Cross Blood Prog 1130 S Vermont Ave Los Angeles CA 90006. *Fax:* 231-739-5455; *E-Mail:* garratty@usa.redcross.org

GARRAWAY, MICHAEL OLIVER, PLANT PATHOLOGY. *Current Pos:* asst prof, Ohio State Univ, 68-71, assoc prof, 71-78, PROF BOT PLANT PATH, OHIO STATE UNIV & OHIO AGR RES & DEVELOP CTR, 78- *Personal Data:* b Roseau, Dominica, Brit WI, Apr 29, 34; US citizen; m 66; c 3. *Educ:* McGill Univ, BSc, 59, MSc, 62; Univ Calif, Berkeley, PhD(plant path), 66. *Prof Exp:* Asst res plant pathologist, Univ Calif, Berkeley, 66-68. *Concurrent Pos:* Fred C Gloeckner Found Inc res grant dis of ornamentals. *Mem:* AAAS; Am Phytopath Soc; Am Inst Biol Sci; Can Phytopath Soc; Int Soc Plant Path; Mycol Soc Am. *Res:* Relation of nutrition to rhizomorph initiation and growth in Armillaria mellea (Vahl) Quel; nutritional and environmental factors affecting fungal growth and reproduction; influence of plant nutrition on disease susceptibility; response of maize leaves to biotic and abiotic stresses. *Mailing Add:* Plant Path Ohio State Univ 2021 Coffey Rd Columbus OH 43210-1044

GARRELICK, JOEL MARC, STRUCTURAL DYNAMICS, PHYSICAL ACOUSTICS. *Current Pos:* PRES & SR PRIN SCIENTIST VIBRATION & ACOUST, CAMBRIDGE ACOUST ASSOCS INC, 69- *Personal Data:* b New York, NY, May 20, 41; m 63, Renee Brosell; c Kevin, Jenine & Daniel. *Educ:* City Univ New York, BCE, 63, ME, 65, PhD(mech), 69. *Prof Exp:* Lectr civil eng, City Col New York, 67-68. *Mem:* Am Soc Civil Engrs; fel Acoust Soc Am. *Res:* Theoretical studies in applied mechanics; structural dynamics; underwater acoustics; structure borne noise and vibration. *Mailing Add:* 46 Kenney Lane Concord MA 01742

GARRELL, MARTIN HENRY, ENVIRONMENTAL PHYSICS. *Current Pos:* ASST PROF PHYSICS, ADELPHI UNIV, 70- *Personal Data:* b Brooklyn, NY, Jan 4, 39; m 65. *Educ:* Princeton Univ, AB, 60; Univ Ill, MS, 62, PhD(physics), 66. *Prof Exp:* Volkswagen Found res fel physics, Deutsches Elektronen Synchrotron, 66-68; vis asst prof, Univ Ill, Chicago Circle, 68-70. *Mem:* Am Phys Soc; Sigma Xi. *Res:* Population models; air, water and pesticides pollution; fresh water and marine ecosystems. *Mailing Add:* Dept Physics Adelphi Univ Garden City NY 11530

GARRELS, JAMES I, PROTEIN CHARACTERIZATION, CELLULAR GROWTH REGULATION. *Current Pos:* Am Cancer Soc postdoctoral fel, Cell Biol Group, Cold Spring Harbor Lab, 78-79, staff investr, 79-80, sr staff investr, 80-85, SR STAFF SCIENTIST & DIR, QUEST PROTEIN DATABASE CTR, COLD SPRING HARBOR LAB, 85- *Personal Data:* b Mt Pleasant, Iowa, Feb 14, 48. *Educ:* Calif Inst Technol, BS, 71; Univ Calif, San Diego, PhD(biol), 78. *Concurrent Pos:* NSF res grant, 78-80; NIH res grants, 79-82, 85-90 & 90-; Muscular Dystrophy Asn res grant, 80-84; Cystic Fibrosis Found res grant, 80-81; consult, Millipore Corp, 88- *Mem:* Int Electrophoresis Soc; Am Soc Biochem & Molecular Biol; Am Soc Microbiol. *Res:* Two-dimensional gel electrophoresis of proteins; quantitative computer analysis of two-dimensional gels; construction of protein databases; mammalian cell growth and transformation; author of numerous technical publications. *Mailing Add:* Proteome Inc 111 Hart St Beverly Farms MA 01915-2161. *Fax:* 516-367-8845, 508-922-3971

GARREN, ALPER A, PARTICLE ACCELERATORS, COMPUTER SOFTWARE FOR SYNCHROTRON & BEAM-LINE LATTICES. *Current Pos:* RETIRED. *Personal Data:* b Oakland, Calif, Apr 30, 25. *Educ:* Univ Calif, BA, 45, MA, 50; Carnegie Inst Technol, PhD(physics). *Prof Exp:* Teaching asst, Carnegie Inst Technol, 51-53; staff sr scientist, Lawrence Berkeley Lab, 55-93. *Concurrent Pos:* Vis scientist, Rutherford Lab, 62, Europ Orgn Nuclear Res, 74-75 & 86; staff scientist, Fermi Nat Accelerator Lab, 67-69; vis prof, Univ Tokyo, 79; consult, Superconducting Super Collider, 91-93. *Mem:* Fel Am Phys Soc. *Res:* Lattice design of particle accelerators and storage rings. *Mailing Add:* Lawrence Berkeley Lab B 71H Berkeley CA 94720. *Fax:* 510-486-6485; *E-Mail:* garren@csa.lbl.gov

GARREN, HENRY WILBURN, physiology, endocrinology; deceased, see previous edition for last biography

GARREN, RALPH, JR, HORTICULTURE. *Current Pos:* Asst, Ore State Univ, 50-51, res asst & instr hort, 51-57, from asst prof to prof, 57-86, EMER PROF HORT, ORE STATE UNIV, 86- *Personal Data:* b Rutland, Iowa, June 10, 21; m 42; c 3. *Educ:* Ore State Col, BS, 50, MS, 54; Purdue Univ, PhD, 61. *Concurrent Pos:* Res found fel, Purdue Univ, 57-59. *Mem:* Am Soc Hort Sci; Int Soc Hort Sci. *Res:* Small fruits physiology and production problems. *Mailing Add:* 733 NW Lewisburg Ave Corvallis OR 97330

GARRETSON, CRAIG MARTIN, ELECTROPHYSICS. *Current Pos:* from asst prof to assoc prof, 63-75, coordr, dept eng sci, 66-74, chmn dept physics 75-76 & 79-80, PROF PHYSICS, C W POST COL, LONG ISLAND UNIV, 75- *Personal Data:* b Glendale, NY, Sept 14, 24; m 49, Muriel Ives; c Catherine (Raphael), Christine (Garretson-Persans) & Laura (Fyhr). *Educ:* Cooper Union, BEE, 49; Polytech Inst Brooklyn, MEE, 53, PhD(electrophys), 69. *Prof Exp:* Jr engr, Power Substa, New York City Bd Transp, 46-50; jr engr, Nat Union Radio Corp, 50-51; sr engr, Sylvania Elec Prod, 51-56; engr, Sperry Gyroscope Co, 56-63. *Mem:* Am Asn Physics Teachers; Inst Elec & Electronics Engrs. *Res:* Electron devices; electromagnetic theory. *Mailing Add:* 60 Allan Dr East Norwich NY 11732

GARRETT, ALFRED BENJAMIN, CHEMISTRY. *Current Pos:* asst chem, Ohio State Univ, 29-32, from instr to prof, 35-71, chmn dept chem, 58-62, vpres Univ, 62-69, EMER PROF CHEM, MCPHERSON LAB, OHIO STATE UNIV, 71- *Personal Data:* b Glencoe, Ohio, June 28, 06; m 34; c 3. *Educ:* Muskingum Col, BS, 28; Ohio State Univ, MS, 31, PhD(chem), 32. *Hon Degrees:* DSc, Muskingum Col, 58, Ohio Wesleyan Univ, 62 & Denison Univ, 64. *Honors & Awards:* Am Chem Soc Award, 64; NASA Apollo 11 Award, 70. *Prof Exp:* Teacher pub sch, Pa, 28-29; asst chem, Ohio State Univ, 29-32; assoc prof, Kent State Col, 32-35. *Mem:* Nat Sci Teachers Asn (pres, 69-70); Sigma Xi; Am Chem Soc. *Res:* Photovoltaic cells; ionic equilibria in solution; physical and organic chemistry; low temperature studies of electrolytes; alkyl derivatives of boron hydrides. *Mailing Add:* 6000 Riverside Dr Dublin OH 43017

GARRETT, BARRY B, PHYSICAL CHEMISTRY, INORGANIC CHEMISTRY. *Current Pos:* SR SCIENTIST, OFF RES & DEVELOP (ORD), ARLINGTON, VA, 84- *Personal Data:* b Waco, Tex, Nov 10, 35; m 57; c 2. *Educ:* Univ Tex, BS, 59, MA, 62, PhD(chem), 63. *Prof Exp:* Res assoc, Univ Ill, 63-64; from asst prof to prof chem, Fla State Univ, 64-84. *Concurrent Pos:* Vis prof, Univ Wyo, 75. *Mem:* Am Chem Soc; Am Phys Soc. *Res:* Lattice effects and bonding in solids via electron and nuclear resonance studies. *Mailing Add:* 2100 N Military Rd Arlington VA 22207-3925

GARRETT, BENJAMIN CAYWOOD, OPERATIONS RESEARCH. *Current Pos:* SR TECH ADV, BATTELLE MEM INST. *Personal Data:* b Richmond, Va, Jan 15, 49; m 71; c 2. *Educ:* Davidson Col, BS, 71; Emory Univ, MS & PhD(chem), 75. *Prof Exp:* Chemist, US Army Dugway Proving Ground, Utah, 76-78; asst prof chem, Davidson Col, 78-80; res scientist, Columbus Labs, Battelle Mem Inst, 80-91; chief scientist, Eai Corp, 91- *Mem:* Am Chem Soc. *Res:* Analysis and detection of toxic substances; chemical and biological warfare. *Mailing Add:* 10704 Cogswell Pl Fairfax VA 22039-1823

GARRETT, BOWMAN STAPLES, PHYSICAL CHEMISTRY. *Current Pos:* RETIRED. *Personal Data:* b Baton Rouge, La, July 8, 22; m 44; c 3. *Educ:* Univ La, BS, 40, MS, 42; Univ Ark, PhD, 54. *Prof Exp:* Shift supvr, Flintkote Co, 42; control chemist, Esso Standard Oil Co, 43-45; staff engr, Fuels Lab, Socony-Vacuum Co, 45-49; asst prof chem, Univ Ark, 50-52; sr phys chemist, Rohm & Haas, 53-57, lab head, 57-61, res supvr, 61-66, asst dir res, Res Div, 66-73, mkt mgr Polymers & Resins, Int Div, 73-76, Res & Develop Mgr, Latin Am, 76-78, consult, Latin Am, 78-82. *Mem:* Am Chem Soc. *Res:* Neutron diffraction; polymer physics; industrial polymer applications. *Mailing Add:* 385 Robin Ct Roswell GA 30076

GARRETT, CARLETON THEODORE, CARCINOGENESIS. *Current Pos:* ASSOC PROF PATH, GEORGE WASHINGTON MED CTR, 77- *Educ:* Johns Hopkins Univ, MD, 66; Univ Wis-Madison, PhD(oncol), 77. *Mailing Add:* Dept Path Med Col Va Commonwealth Univ 1101 E Marshall St Richmond VA 23298-0248. *Fax:* 804-828-9749

GARRETT, CHARLES GEOFFREY BLYTHE, PHYSICS. *Current Pos:* RETIRED. *Personal Data:* b Ashford, Kent, Eng, Sept 15, 25; nat US. *Educ:* Cambridge Univ, BA, 46, MA, 50, PhD(physics), 50. *Prof Exp:* Asst low temperature physics, Royal Soc Mond Lab, Cambridge Univ, 46-50; instr physics, Harvard Univ, 50-52; mem tech staff, Bell Labs, 52-60, head, Optical Electronics Res Dept, 60-68 & Mat Sci Res Dept, 68-69, dir, Electron Device Process & Battery Lab, 69-73, dir, Integrated Circuit Lab, 73-79, dir, Common Subsystems Lab, 79-87. *Mem:* Fel Am Phys Soc; fel Inst Elec & Electronics Engrs. *Res:* Solid state; lasers; paramagnetics; surface physics; semiconductor device technology. *Mailing Add:* 7 Fithian Ln East Hampton NY 11937-2605

GARRETT, DAVID L, JR, PHYSICAL CHEMISTRY, POLYMER SCIENCE. *Current Pos:* mgr, Eng Lab, 83-85, dir reliability & test, 85-87, DIR TECHNOL TEST SERV, BOC GEN MOTORS, WARREN, MICH, 87- *Personal Data:* b San Antonio, Tex, Sept 22, 44; m 75; c 4. *Educ:* Morehouse Col, BS, 67; Univ Iowa, MS, 69, PhD(phys chem), 72; Mich State Univ, MBA, 81. *Prof Exp:* Sr res chemist photog, Eastman Kodak Res Labs, 72-77; sr mem eng & res staff, Dept Polymer Sci, Ford Motor Co, 77-80, prin eng & res scientist, 80-83. *Concurrent Pos:* Adj fac phys chem, Rochester Inst Technol, 74-77 & Wayne State Univ, 85; Merrill Europ Study travel fel, France, 65-66. *Mem:* Am Chem Soc; Soc Plastic Indust; Soc Automotive Engrs. *Res:* Composite research; photo-oxidative degradation of paint enamel. *Mailing Add:* 5444 Provincial Dr Bloomfield Hills MI 48302

GARRETT, DAVID WILLIAM, COATING CHEMISTRY, INTERFACE CHEMISTRY. *Current Pos:* RES SCIENTIST, AMOCO PERFORMANCE PRODS, 89- *Personal Data:* b Elyria, Ohio, May 18, 42; m 65, Sharon L Murphy; c Heather, Kimberly, Robert & Timothy. *Educ:* DePauw Univ, BA, 64; Ind Univ, PhD(phys org chem), 69. *Prof Exp:* Fel, Univ Mass, 69-73; res & develop scientist, Owens Corning, 73-89. *Concurrent Pos:* Chmn, Advan Polymer Composites, Soc Plastics Engrs, 92-94. *Mem:* Soc Plastics Engrs. *Res:* Product development on polyphthamide compounds; product development and research on glass fiber sizings. *Mailing Add:* 3077 Bunker Hill Circle Marietta GA 30062

GARRETT, DONALD E(VERETT), CHEMICAL ENGINEERING, PHYSICAL CHEMISTRY. *Current Pos:* PRES, GARRETT ENERGY RES & ENG CO, 75-; PRES, SALINE PROCESSORS, 75-; PRES, LIQUID CHEM CORP, 75- *Personal Data:* b Long Beach, Calif, July 5, 23; m 46; c 4. *Educ:* Univ Calif, BS, 47; Ohio State Univ, MS, 48, PhD(chem eng), 50. *Prof Exp:* Asst chem eng, Ohio State Univ, 47-50; res & develop engr & group leader, Dow Chem Co, Calif, 50-52 & Union Oil Co, 52-55; mgr res, Am Potash & Chem Co, 55-60; pres, Garrett Res & Develop Co, 60-75; exec vpres res & develop, Occidental Petrol Corp, 68-75. *Concurrent Pos:* Pres, Assoc Chem Co, Calif, 60-64; mem gen tech adv comt, Off Coal Res, ERDA & Eng adv comt, Univ Calif, Ohio State Univ & US Dept Interior; adj prof, Univ Calif, Santa Barbara, 85- *Mem:* Am Chem Soc; Am Inst Chem Engrs. *Res:* Inorganic chemistry; research management; crystallization; evaporation; saline mineral processing. *Mailing Add:* Saline Processors Inc PO Box 563 Ojai CA 93023-0563

GARRETT, EDGAR RAY, SPEECH PATHOLOGY. *Current Pos:* From instr to assoc prof speech, NMex State Univ, 48-63, prof in charge speech & dir, Speech & Hearing Ctr, 63-65, head dept speech, 65-85, asst dean, Col Arts & Sci, 69-71, dir commun disorders, 85-90, EMER PROF, NMEX STATE UNIV, 90- *Personal Data:* b Lordsburg, NMex, Aug 14, 21; m 42; c 4. *Educ:* Western NMex Univ, BS, 42; Univ NC, MA, 48; Univ Denver, PhD(speech path), 54. *Honors & Awards:* Sci Exhibit Award, Am Speech & Hearing Asn, 63 & 67. *Concurrent Pos:* Res automated speech correction systs & prog lang for deaf, US Off Educ, 64-74. *Mem:* Fel AAAS; fel Am Speech & Hearing Asn; NY Acad Sci; Sigma Xi. *Res:* Audiology; psychology of learning; programmed instruction; systems analysis of therapy delivery. *Mailing Add:* 6805 Cottontail Lane Las Cruces NM 88005. *E-Mail:* egarrett@nmsu.edu

GARRETT, EPHRAIM SPENCER, III, MICROBIOLOGY, FOOD TECHNOLOGY. *Current Pos:* SPEC ASST, NAT MARINE FISHERIES SERV & LAB DIR, NAT SEAFOOD QUAL & INSPECTION LAB, US DEPT COM, 71- *Personal Data:* b Binghamton, NY, July 20, 37; m 60; c 4. *Educ:* Univ Southern Miss, BS, 62, MS, 64. *Prof Exp:* Res virologist poultry path, Charles Pfizer & Co, 63-65; res microbiologist food technol, US Bur Com Fisheries, 65-68; asst chief seafood inspection serv, US Dept Interior, 68-71. *Concurrent Pos:* US deleg, Food & Agr Orgn-WHO Codex Alimentarius Comn, Codex Comt Food Hyg, 69-; Food & Agr Orgn consult seafood harvesting & processing, 75-76; WHO-Food & Agr Orgn consult seafood microbiol, 77-79; chmn, Trop & Subtrop Technol Fisheries Conf of the Americas, 77. *Mem:* Am Soc Microbiol. *Res:* Presentations dealing with various product quality and safety issues relative to consumer protection in the consumption of fishery products. *Mailing Add:* Nat Seafood Inspect Lab US Dept Com PO Drawer 1207 Pascagoula MS 39568-1207. *Fax:* 228-762-7144; *E-Mail:* spencer.garrett@noaa.gov

GARRETT, HENRY BERRY, SPACE PHYSICS. *Current Pos:* LEAD TECHNOLOGIST, RELIABILITY & QUAL ASSURANCE, JET PROPULSION LAB, CALIF INST TECHNOL, 80- *Personal Data:* b San Francisco, Calif, Feb 15, 48; m 76; c 1. *Educ:* Rice Univ, BA, 70, MS, 73, PhD(space physics, astron), 74. *Honors & Awards:* NASA Award for Exceptional Eng Achievement, 94. *Prof Exp:* Res assoc space physics & astron, Rice Univ, 74; res physicist, Air Force Geophys Lab, 74-80. *Concurrent Pos:* Chmn, Int Asn Geomagnetism & Aeronomy Hist Comt, 78-86; assoc ed, J Spacecraft & Rockets, 87-89; consult, INTELSAT Corp, 89- *Mem:* Am Astron Soc; Am Phys Soc; Am Inst Aeronaut & Astronaut; Am Geophys Union. *Res:* Study of spacecraft changing; theoretical and experimental models of the upper atmosphere from 90 to 500 kilometers, as well as solar forecasting methods; interplanetary meteroid environment and earth space debris. *Mailing Add:* Jet Propulsion Lab MS 301-456 4800 Oak Grove Dr Pasadena CA 91109-8099. *Fax:* 818-393-4699; *E-Mail:* garrett@ix.netcom.com

GARRETT, J MARSHALL, GASTROENTEROLOGY. *Current Pos:* DIR, GASTROENTEROL DEPT, ST VINCENT'S HOSP, 70- *Personal Data:* b Cleveland, Tenn, Nov 18, 32; m 54; c 2. *Educ:* Univ Chattanooga, AB, 56; Univ Tenn, MD, 58; Univ Minn, MS, 64; Am Bd Internal Med, dipl, 67. *Prof Exp:* Intern med, John Gaston Hosp, Memphis, Tenn, 59; staff physician, United Mine Workers Hosp, Wise, Va, 60; resident internal med, Mayo Found, 60-63; chief gastroenterol, Vet Admin Hosp, 64-70; chief of staff, 69-70. *Concurrent Pos:* Fel gastroenterol, Mayo Clin, 63-64; from instr to assoc prof med, Med Ctr, Univ Ala, Birmingham, 64-70, clin assoc prof, 70-; med dir, Montclair Ctr Digestive Dis, Baptist Med, Montclair, Birmingham. *Mem:* AAAS; AMA; Am Fedn Clin Res; Am Gastroenterol Asn; Sigma Xi. *Res:* Motility of the gastrointestinal tract. *Mailing Add:* 880 Montclair Rd No 577 Birmingham AL 35213-1980

GARRETT, JAMES M, ORGANIC CHEMISTRY. *Current Pos:* from asst prof to assoc prof, 67-78, PROF CHEM, STEPHEN F AUSTIN STATE UNIV, 78- *Personal Data:* b Magnolia, Ark, Aug 3, 41; m 66; c 3. *Educ:* Arlington State Col, BS, 63; Univ Tex, PhD(org chem), 66. *Prof Exp:* Fel, Univ Fla, 66-67. *Mem:* Am Chem Soc. *Res:* Synthetic organic photochemistry; chemistry of small ring systems; stable boron cations. *Mailing Add:* Carrizo Creek Box 3220 Nacogdoches TX 75961-9268

GARRETT, JAMES RICHARD, MATHEMATICS. *Current Pos:* RETIRED. *Personal Data:* b Landrum, SC, May 4, 17; m 46, Florence E Creamer; c Lynn, Richard & Ann. *Educ:* Lenoir-Rhyne Col, AB, 40; Calif Inst Technol, BS, 41, MS, 52; Duke Univ, AM, 47, PhD(math), 50. *Hon Degrees:* DS, Lenoir-Rhyne Col, 72. *Prof Exp:* From asst prof to assoc prof math, Ga Inst Technol, 50-60; mgr math serv, Radio Corp Am Missile Test Proj, Patrick AFB, Fla, 60-67; mgr diag & test systs, Info Systs Div, RCA Corp, 67-69, mgr control systs, Comput Div, 69-71; mgr test systs, Univac Div, Sperry Rand Corp, 72; prof math & chmn dept, Lenoir-Rhyne Col, 72-80, dir natural sci & math, 79-97. *Concurrent Pos:* Res assoc, Rich Comput Ctr, Ga Inst Technol, 58-60; consult, 80- *Mem:* Am Math Soc; Math Asn Am; Asn Comput Mach; Soc Indust & Appl Math; Sigma Xi. *Res:* Satellite and missile orbits and trajectories; mathematical problems. *Mailing Add:* 815 S Shannon Ave Indialantic FL 32903

GARRETT, JERRY DALE, EXPERIMENTAL NUCLEAR PHYSICS. *Current Pos:* SCI DIR, HOLIFIELD RADIOACTIVE ION BEAM FACIL, OAK RIDGE NAT LAB, 88- *Personal Data:* b Springfield, Mo, Oct 1, 40; m 65, Anne M Levesque; c Amy C. *Educ:* Univ Mo, Columbia, BS, 62; Univ Pa, MS, 67, PhD(physics), 70. *Honors & Awards:* Ole Romer Award, Danish Ministry Educ. *Prof Exp:* Res assoc physics, Tandem Accelerator Lab, Univ Pa, 70-71; res assoc nuclear physics, Los Alamos Sci Lab, 71-72; from asst physicist to assoc physicist, Brookhaven Nat Lab, 72-75. *Concurrent Pos:* Assoc ed, Nuclear Physics J, 78-; guest scientist, Brookhaven Nat Lab, 78, Daresbury Lab, UK, 84, Joint Inst for Heavy Ion Res, Oak Ridge, 84, 85 & 87; Adv, Int Centre Theoret Physics, Trieste, 84-; mem, NAm Steering Comt Radioactive Ion Beams, 90-; mem Subatomic Grant Selection Comt, Natural Sci & Eng Res Coun Can; nuclear sci adv comt, US Dept Energy, NSF, 92. *Mem:* AAAS; Am Phys Soc; NY Acad Sci; Europ Phys Soc; Danish Phys Soc. *Res:* Nuclear structure studies with radioactive ion beams and the structure of rapidly-rotating nuclei. *Mailing Add:* Oak Ridge Nat Lab PO Box 2008 Bldg 6000 Mail Stop 6368 Oak Ridge TN 37831-6368. *Fax:* 423-524-1268; *E-Mail:* garrett@orph01

GARRETT, L(UTHER) W(EAVER), JR, chemical engineering; deceased, see previous edition for last biography

GARRETT, LANE SAYRE, NEW PRODUCT DEVELOPMENT USING BROAD TECHNOLOGY BASE, ALTERNATIVE ENERGY & PHOTOVOLTAICS. *Current Pos:* PRES, ETA ENG INC, 92- *Personal Data:* b Wilmington, Del, Sept 1, 39; m 61, Ursula E Illing; c Dianna, Alan, Holly & Lorri. *Educ:* Drexel Univ, BSEE, 61; Ariz State Univ, MSE, 70. *Prof Exp:* Proj mgr, Naval Air Develop Ctr, 57-65; dept mgr, Motorola Semiconductor Div, 65-75; mkt develop mgr, Govt Elec Div, 75-76; pres, Ecotronics Inc, 76-79, Ecotronics Labs Inc - Talley Indust, 79-81; gen mgr, Photocomm, Inc, 81-83; pres & gen mgr, SunAmp Systs Inc, 83-86; dir, gen mgr & chief engr, SunAmp Power Co, 86-92. *Concurrent Pos:* Lectr technol trends, Motorola Exec Inst, 71; guest lectr, Sierra Nevada Col, 83-84. *Mem:* Inst Elec & Electronics Engrs; Nat Soc Prof Engrs; Inst Elec Eng; Int Solar Energy Soc. *Res:* Alternative energy, conservation and technology trends; controls for alternative energy and photovoltaic systems and conservation of energy. *Mailing Add:* 8502 E Cactus Wren Rd Scottsdale AZ 85250. *Fax:* 602-948-0912; *E-Mail:* lanegarret@aol.com

GARRETT, MICHAEL BENJAMIN, PHYSICAL INORGANIC CHEMISTRY. *Current Pos:* ASST PROF CHEM, DEL VALLEY COL, 70- *Personal Data:* b San Jose, Calif, Mar 15, 41; m 70. *Educ:* Univ Calif, Berkeley, BA, 63; Univ Ill, Urbana, PhD(inorg chem), 70. *Prof Exp:* Instr chem, Drexel Univ, 69-70. *Concurrent Pos:* Student assoc, Argonne Nat Lab, 66-68. *Mem:* Am Chem Soc; Chem Soc. *Res:* Flash heating and kinetic spectroscopy; spectra of high multiplicity diatomic molecules. *Mailing Add:* Chem Dept Del Valley Col 700 E Butler Ave Doylestown PA 18901-2607

GARRETT, PAUL DANIEL, POLYMER MECHANICAL PROPERTIES, POLYMER INTERFACES. *Current Pos:* Sr res engr, 88-90, res specialist, Phys & Anal Sci Ctr, 90-94, ASSOC FEL, MONSANTO CHEM CO, MONSANTO CO, 94- *Personal Data:* b Highland Park, Ill, Mar 15, 61; m 89, Sharon Johnson; c Alison. *Educ:* Univ Mich, BS, 83; Cornell Univ, MS, 85, PhD(mat sci), 88. *Mem:* Mat Res Soc; Am Chem Soc; Am Phys Soc; Am Soc Mat. *Res:* Deformation and fracture behavior of polymeric materials, including toughened plastics polymer-matrix composites, fibers and coatings; mechanical and thermodynamic behavior of polymeric thin films and interfaces. *Mailing Add:* Monsanto Chem Co 730 Worcester St Springfield MA 01151

GARRETT, PETER WAYNE, FOREST GENETICS. *Current Pos:* res forester genetics, 66-69, proj leader genetics, 69-83, PROJ LEADER ECOL, US FOREST SERV, 84- *Personal Data:* b Petoskey, Mich, Dec 20, 33; m 54, Martha Bird; c 1. *Educ:* Mich State Univ, BS, 58; Univ Mich, MS, 62, PhD(forestry), 69. *Prof Exp:* Asst dist forester, State of Minn, 58-59; res forester, Union Camp Paper Corp, 59-61; asst prof forestry, Mich Technol Univ, 63-66. *Concurrent Pos:* Adj prof forest genetics, Univ NH, 70- *Mem:* Soc Am Foresters. *Res:* Supervising ecology research in Northeast with emphasis on northern hardwood species; regeneration and growth under different harvesting techniques; biodiversity of plant and animal species, migration rates under global change. *Mailing Add:* USDA Forest Serv Northeastern Forest Exp Sta Box 640 Durham NH 03824. *Fax:* 603-868-7604

GARRETT, REGINALD HOOKER, BIOCHEMISTRY, MOLECULAR BIOLOGY. *Current Pos:* from asst prof to assoc prof, 68-82, PROF BIOL, UNIV VA, 82- *Personal Data:* b Roanoke, Va, Sept 24, 39; m 89, Catherine L Touchton; c Jeffrey, Randal & Robert. *Educ:* Johns Hopkins Univ, BS, 64, PhD(biol), 68. *Prof Exp:* Res asst biochem, McCollum-Pratt Inst, Johns Hopkins Univ, 56-64, fel, 68. *Concurrent Pos:* NIH fel, 64-68; Fulbright fel, 75-76; vis fel, Univ Cambridge, 83. *Mem:* Am Soc Biochem & Molecular Biol; Am Soc Microbiol; Am Soc Plant Physiologists; Soc Gen Physiologists; AAAS. *Res:* Enzymology, genetics and regulation of nitrate assimilation; isolation and characterization of Neurospora crassa nit genes; regulation of metabolic potentiality in lower eucaryotes; heterologous expression and characterization of N crassa nitrite reductase; author of one biochemistry text book. *Mailing Add:* Dept Biol Univ Va Charlottesville VA 22903. *Fax:* 804-982-5626; *E-Mail:* rhg@virginia.edu

GARRETT, RICHARD E, MECHANICAL ENGINEERING. *Current Pos:* PROF MECH ENG & HEAD DEPT, UNIV CONN, STORRS, 76- *Personal Data:* b Chester, Pa, Sept 9, 33; m 55; c 2. *Educ:* Univ Del, BSME, 56; Univ Fla, MSME, 63; Purdue Univ, PhD(mech eng), 67. *Prof Exp:* Develop engr, Hamilton Standard Div, United Aircraft Corp, 56-59; asst prof mech eng, Univ Fla, 59-67; from assoc prof to prof, Purdue Univ, 67-76. *Concurrent Pos:* Eng consult, Midwest Appl Sci Corp, 66-68; consult & mem bd dir, TecTran, Inc, 68- *Mem:* Assoc mem Am Soc Mech Engrs; Soc Exp Stress Analysis. *Res:* Computer-aided design and computer graphics; optimization of mechanical devices; bio-medical engineering. *Mailing Add:* 78 Dunham Pond Rd Storrs CT 06268

GARRETT, RICHARD EDWARD, NUCLEAR PHYSICS. *Current Pos:* RETIRED. *Personal Data:* b Roanoke, Va, Feb 17, 22; m 47. *Educ:* Roanoke Col, BS, 42; Ga Inst Technol, MS, 50; Univ Va, PhD(nuclear physics), 53. *Prof Exp:* Instr math & physics, Roanoke Col, 42-43 & 46-48; instr physics, Ga Inst Technol, 48-50 & Univ Va, 50-53; from asst prof to assoc prof physics, Hollins Col, 53-63; assoc prof physics, Univ Fla, 63-74, prof physics & phys sci, 74-89. *Concurrent Pos:* Consult, Radiation Lab, Univ Calif, 58-59; vis lectr, Va Polytech Inst & State Univ, 61; res assoc, Univ Va, 63. *Mem:* AAAS; Am Asn Physics Teachers. *Res:* Nature of nuclear emulsions, physical properties and their use in high energy particle physics; research in teaching development of new material; lecture demonstrations and laboratory experiments. *Mailing Add:* Rte 1 Box 334 Micanopy FL 32667

GARRETT, ROBERT, ENGINEERING. *Current Pos:* DIR SPEC LAWS GROUP, DEPT COM PATENT OFF, 90- *Personal Data:* b Aug 28, 47. *Educ:* Univ Md, BA, 70. *Mailing Add:* Patent Off Park One Suite 4B3 2011 Crystal Dr Arlington VA 22022

GARRETT, ROBERT AUSTIN, urology, for more information see previous edition

GARRETT, ROBERT OGDEN, PHYSICS. *Current Pos:* From asst prof to assoc prof, 64-76, CHMN DEPT & COORDR ENG PROG, BELOIT COL, 70-, PROF PHYSICS, 76- *Personal Data:* b Berkeley, Calif, Jan 11, 33; m 55; c 2. *Educ:* Whitman Col, BA, 54; Cornell Univ, MS, 60; Univ Ore, PhD(physics), 64. *Concurrent Pos:* Res assoc, Univ Ore, 69-70. *Mem:* Am Asn Physics Teachers. *Res:* Pressure broadening of spectral lines of atoms perturbed by foreign gases. *Mailing Add:* 626 Church St Beloit WI 53511

GARRETT, ROBERT ROTH, PHYSICAL CHEMISTRY. *Current Pos:* RETIRED. *Personal Data:* b Asheville, NC, Nov 29, 21; m 53, Jean Mary; c Paul. *Educ:* Duke Univ, BS, 44; Univ Louisville, MS, 51; Cornell Univ, PhD(chem), 57. *Prof Exp:* Asst, Univ Louisville, 50-51, Cornell Univ, 52-56; res chemist, E I DUPONT DE NEMOURS & CO INC, 57-80, res assoc, 80-85, consult, 85-96. *Res:* Phase transitions in high polymers; physical chemistry of elastomers; novel elastomeric adhesives, adhesion problems. *Mailing Add:* 1080 Wood Lane West Chester PA 19382

GARRETT, RUBY JOYCE BURRISS, PHYSIOLOGY, PHARMACOLOGY. *Current Pos:* ADMIN LAW JUDGE, OCCUPATIONAL SAFETY & HEALTH, NC DEPT LABOR, RALEIGH, 84-; PARTNER, VERNON, VERNON, WOOTEN, BROWN, ANDREWS & GARRETT, PA, 87- *Personal Data:* b Greenville, SC, Apr 1, 46; m 69. *Educ:* Univ Tenn, BS, 68; Univ Ky, PhD(physiol, biophys), 71; Univ NC, Chapel Hill, JD, 81. *Prof Exp:* From instr to assoc prof pharmacodyn & toxicol, Univ Ky, 71-79; assoc, Vernon, Vernon, Wooten, Brown & Andrews, PA, 82-86. *Concurrent Pos:* Vis investr, New York Blood Ctr, 73 & 74; grants, Sanders-Brown Res Ctr Aging, 76-78 & Tobacco & Health Inst, 76-79; staff mem, NC Law Rev, 80-81, note & comment ed, 81-82; consult/clerk, OSHA rev bd, NC Dept Labor, Raleigh, 81-83. *Mem:* Am Physiol Soc; Am Soc Cell Biol; Am Pharmaceut Asn; Am Soc Pharmacol & Exp Therapeut. *Res:* Physiological biochemistry; cell membrane structure and function; protein synthesis; author of numerous publications. *Mailing Add:* PO Box 2958 Burlington NC 27216-2958

GARRETT, STEVEN LURIE, FIBER-OPTIC SENSING, THERMOACOUSTICS ENGINES. *Current Pos:* asst prof physics, 81-84, assoc prof, 84-88, PROF PHYSICS, NAVAL POSTGRAD SCH, MONTEREY, CALIF, 88- *Personal Data:* b Los Angeles, Calif, Apr 3, 49; m 74, Gloria Kalisher; c Wendy & Adam. *Educ:* Univ Calif, Los Angeles, BS, 70, MS, 72, PhD, 77. *Honors & Awards:* Rolex Award Enterprise (Environ), Geneva, Switz, 93; Silver Medal Interdisciplinary Acoust (Phys & Eng Acoust), Acoust Soc Am, 93. *Prof Exp:* Res assoc physics, Univ Calif, Los Angeles, 75-77, adj asst prof, 77-78; Hunt fel, Acoust Soc Am, MAPS, Univ Sussex, Eng, 78-79; res fel, Miller Inst, Univ Calif, Berkeley, 79-81. *Concurrent Pos:* Vis scientist, Los Alamos Nat Labs, 80-; consult, Sound Advise, 81-; Rosen prof solid state physics, Technion, Hiafa, Israel, 85. *Mem:* Fel Acoust Soc Am; Optical Soc Am; Am Phys Soc; Am Asn Physics Teachers; Soc Photo-Optical Instrument Engrs; Sigma Xi. *Res:* Acoustics and quantum fluids; transduction; fiber optics sensors; thermoacoustics. *Mailing Add:* Grad Prugin Acous Penn State Univ PO Box 30 State College PA 16804. *Fax:* 408-656-2834

GARRETT, THOMAS BOYD, THEORETICAL CHEMISTRY. *Current Pos:* Res chemist, Armstrong World Indust, Inc, 70-75, from res scientist to sr res scientist, 75-85, res assoc, 85-86, res unit mgr, 86-90, SR PRIN SCIENTIST, ARMSTRONG WORLD INDUST, INC, 90- *Personal Data:* b Pittsburgh, Pa, May 28, 41; m 67; c 1. *Educ:* Carnegie-Mellon Univ, BS, 63; Lehigh Univ, PhD(chem), 70. *Mem:* Am Chem Soc; Sigma Xi; Am Asn Artificial Intel. *Res:* Decision support systems for research and development management. *Mailing Add:* 17 Buttonwood Dr Lititz PA 17543-8843. *E-Mail:* tbgar@delphi.com

GARRETT, WILLIAM NORBERT, ANIMAL NUTRITION. *Current Pos:* Assoc animal husb, 53-56, from asst animal husbandman to assoc animal husbandman, 58-65, assoc prof, 65-69, PROF ANIMAL SCI, UNIV CALIF, DAVIS, 69- *Personal Data:* b Cresson, Pa, June 8, 26; m 54; c 2. *Educ:* Pa State Univ, BS, 50, MS, 51; Univ Calif, PhD(nutrit), 58. *Honors & Awards:* Am Feed Mfrs Asn Nutrit Res Award, Am Soc Animal Sci, 75, Morrison Award, 86. *Concurrent Pos:* Chmn, Dept Animal Sci, Univ Calif. *Mem:* Am Soc Animal Sci (pres, 83-84); Am Inst Nutrit; Coun Agr Sci & Tech; Brit Soc. *Res:* Ruminant nutrition; energy metabolism. *Mailing Add:* 1300 W Eighth St Davis CA 95616

GARRETT, WILLIAM RAY, CHEMICAL PHYSICS. *Current Pos:* physicist, 66-74, chief, Chem Physics Sect, 74-89, SR RES SCIENTIST, OAK RIDGE NAT LAB, 89- *Personal Data:* b Warrior, Ala, Oct 17, 37; m 57; c 3. *Educ:* Univ Ala, BS, 60, MS, 62, PhD(physics), 63. *Prof Exp:* Res assoc physics, Res Inst, Univ Ala, 63-65, asst prof, 65-66. *Mem:* Fel Am Phys Soc; Optical Soc Am; AAAS. *Res:* Theoretical and experimental atomic and molecular physics; monlinear optics; laser physics. *Mailing Add:* MS 6378 Oak Ridge Nat Lab PO Box 2008 Oak Ridge TN 37831. *Fax:* 423-576-2115; *E-Mail:* wrg@ornlstc

GARRETTSON, LORNE KEITH, CLINICAL PHARMACOLOGY, PEDIATRICS. *Current Pos:* ASSOC PROF PEDIAT, EMORY UNIV, 88- *Personal Data:* b Pasadena, Calif, Mar 2, 34; m 63; c 3. *Educ:* Pomona Col, BA, 55; Johns Hopkins Univ, MD, 59. *Prof Exp:* Asst pediat, Emory Univ, 65-68; asst prof, State Univ NY Buffalo, 68-73; assoc prof pediat & pharm, Va Commonwealth Univ, 73-87. *Concurrent Pos:* Vchmn, Accident & Poison Prev Comn, Am Acad Pediat, 74- & mem exec bd, Sect Clin Pharm & Therapeut, 76-79; mem exec bd, Am Asn Poison Control Ctrs, 76-79; consult, Glass Packaging Inst, Closure Comn, 77-79; prin investr, Gen Med Sci, NIH, 78-81. *Mem:* Am Soc Pharmacol & Exp Therapeut; Soc Pediat Res; Am Asn Poison Control Ctrs. *Res:* Age dependent elimination of drugs; pharmacokinetics of effects of drugs; pharmacokinetics of drug interactions. *Mailing Add:* Dept Pediat Emory Univ 69 Butler St SE Atlanta GA 30303-3056. *Fax:* 404-616-6657

GARRICK, LAURA MORRIS, IRON METABOLISM. *Current Pos:* Res asst instr med, 72-76, res instr med, 76-79, RES ASST PROF MED, 79-, STATE UNIV NY, BUFFALO, CLIN ASST PROF BIOCHEM, 86- *Personal Data:* b Chicago, Ill, Sept 8, 45; m 70, Michael; c Amy. *Educ:* Marquette Univ, BS, 67; Univ Va, PhD(biol), 72. *Concurrent Pos:* Richard E Whale fel, 72-73; fel, Maternal & Child Health Serv, State Univ NY, Buffalo, 74-75 & NIH fel, 75-77 & res assoc biochem, 78-86; Howard Hughes fel, Harvard Med Sch, 77-78; prin investr, NSF, 87-90, NIH, 87-90 & 92-94. *Mem:* AAAS; Am Chem Soc; Genetics Soc Am; Am Soc Hematol. *Res:* Control of gene expression; structure and evolution of hemoglobins and their genes; animal models for genetic disease; iron metabolism. *Mailing Add:* Biochem Dept 140 Faber Hall State Univ NY 3434 Main St Buffalo NY 14214. *Fax:* 716-829-2725

GARRICK, MICHAEL D, BIOCHEMISTRY, GENETICS. *Current Pos:* res asst prof pediat, 70, res asst prof biochem, 70-72, from asst prof to assoc prof, 72-79, PROF BIOCHEM, STATE UNIV NY BUFFALO, 79-, RES ASSOC PROF PEDIAT, 76- *Personal Data:* b Newport News, Va, July 25, 38; m 61, 70, Laura V Morris; c Amy R. *Educ:* Johns Hopkins Univ, BA, 59, PhD(biol), 63. *Honors & Awards:* Special Award, Niagara Frontier Assoc Sickle Cell Dis, 75. *Prof Exp:* Asst prof genetics, McCoy Col, Johns Hopkins Univ, 63-64; asst prof biol, Univ Va, 64-70. *Concurrent Pos:* Fel med genetics, Hopkins Med Insts, 63-64. *Mem:* AAAS; Genetics Soc; Am Soc Biochem & Molecular Biol; Am Soc Hemat; NY Acad Sci; Am Inst Biol Sci. *Res:* Biochemical and human genetics; gene action; protein biosynthesis; hemoglobinopathies; iron metabolism; molecular evolution. *Mailing Add:* 48 Bywater Dr Getzville NY 14068-1375. *Fax:* 716-829-2725

GARRICK, RITA ANNE, CELL PHYSIOLOGY, MEMBRANE TRANSPORT. *Current Pos:* ASSOC PROF BIOL, COL LINCOLN CTR, FORDHAM UNIV, 84- *Educ:* Dunbarton Col, BA, 63; Rutgers Univ, MS, 66, PhD(physiol), 71. *Prof Exp:* Asst prof biol, Seton Hall Univ, 72-75; asst prof med, NJ Med Sch, Univ Med & Dent, 76-84. *Concurrent Pos:* Adj assoc prof, Rutgers Univ, 81 & 84, NJ Med Sch, Univ Med & Dent, 84- *Mem:* Am Physiol Soc; NY Acad Sci; Am Soc Zoologists; Sigma Xi; Asn Women in Sci. *Res:* Membrane transport. *Mailing Add:* Dept Nat Sci Fordham Univ Col Lincoln Ctr 113 W 60th St Rm LL813 New York NY 10023-7475. *Fax:* 212-636-6754; *E-Mail:* garrick@mary.fordham.edu, rgarrick@hoh.mbl.edu

GARRIGUS, UPSON STANLEY, ANIMAL SCIENCES, APPLIED ANIMAL SCIENCES. *Current Pos:* asst animal sci, Univ Ill, Urbana, 40-42 & 46-48, from instr to prof, 48-55, head ruminant div, 64-70, assoc head dept, 72-87, prof, 55-87, EMER PROF ANIMAL SCI & INT AGR, UNIV ILL, URBANA, 87- *Personal Data:* b Willimantic, Conn, July 2, 17; m 42, Olive Tyler; c Beth E & Mark T. *Educ:* Univ Conn, BS, 40; Univ Ill, MS, 42, PhD(nutrit), 48. *Prof Exp:* Danforth scholar, 39. *Concurrent Pos:* Mem comt sheep nutrit, Nat Res Coun, 53- & comt use of non-protein nitrogen compounds as protein replacement for animals, 70-; Moorman res travel award, 70; Int Res Travel fel, NFIA, 71; consult agr, Indonesian Univ & consult animal prod, Thailand, 80; consult higher ed, Indonesian Univ, 89. *Mem:* Fel AAAS; fel Am Soc Animal Sci; Am Inst Nutrit; Am Inst Biol Sci; Sigma Xi. *Res:* Use of sulfur, antibiotics, arsenicals and non-protein nitrogen in lamb feeding; pelleting of ruminant rations; commercial ruminant feeding; farm flock feeding; breeding and management of ruminants; world animal agriculture; ruminant nutrition, sheep-goats, beef cattle. *Mailing Add:* 186 Animal Sci Lab Univ Ill 1207 W Gregory Dr Urbana IL 61801. *Fax:* 217-333-8804

GARRIOTT, JAMES CLARK, TOXICOLOGY, PHARMACOLOGY. *Current Pos:* from asst prof to assoc prof pharmacol & path, Dallas, 71-82, assoc prof, Path Dept, 82-96, CHIEF TOXICOLOGIST, BEXAR CO MED EXAMR'S OFF & REGION LAB, 82-; ASSOC PROF, PATH DEPT, HEALTH SCI CTR, UNIV TEX, SAN ANTONIO, 96- *Personal Data:* b Seymour, Ind, Sept 27, 38. *Educ:* Univ Louisville, BA, 60; Ind Univ, PhD(toxicol), 67. *Honors & Awards:* A O Gettler Award, Toxicol Sect, Am Acad Forensic Sci, 92. *Prof Exp:* NIH fel, Inst Marine Sci, Univ Miami, 67-68; toxicologist, Conn State Dept Health, Hartford, 68-70. *Concurrent Pos:* Assoc toxicologist, Southwestern Inst Forensic Sci, 70-73, chief toxicologist, 73-81; consult, Vet Admin Hosp, Dallas, 73-80; affil mem med-dent staff, Bexar Co, Hosp Dist, San Antonio, Tex, 82- *Mem:* AAAS; fel Am Acad Forensic Sci; fel Am Acad Clin Toxicol; Am Chem Soc; Soc Toxicol; Soc Forensic Toxicol. *Res:* Clinical and forensic toxicology; detection and determination of drugs and toxic substances and their metabolites in body specimens; clinical correlation of drug concentrations with their effects. *Mailing Add:* Bexar County Forensic Sci Ctr 7337 Louis Pasteur San Antonio TX 78229-4565. *Fax:* 210-615-2148; *E-Mail:* jcgtox@aol.com

GARRIOTT, MICHAEL LEE, CYTOGENETICS, TOXICOLOGY. *Current Pos:* sr toxicologist, 87-93, RES SCIENTIST, ELI LILLY & CO, 94- *Personal Data:* b Beech Grove, Ind, Jan 9, 51; m 72, Brenda J Nicely; c Randall. *Educ:* Purdue Univ, BS, 73, MS, 76, PhD(mammalian & cytogenetics), 79. *Prof Exp:* Res asst mammalian & cytogenetics, Dept Animal Sci, Purdue Univ, 74-79; fel genetic toxicol, Argonne Nat Lab, 79-82; res investr, G D Searle & Co, 82-87. *Concurrent Pos:* mem Pharmaceut Mfrs Asn, Genetic Toxicol Task Force. *Mem:* Am Genetic Asn; Sigma Xi; Environ Mutagen Soc; Genetic Toxicol Asn. *Res:* Investigations of the effects of drugs, hormones, chemicals, physical agents and environmental stress on mammalian chromosomes; chromosomal aberrations as they adversely affect reproduction; mechanisms; improvement of genetic toxicology tests. *Mailing Add:* 9235 Indian Creek Rd S Indianapolis IN 46259

GARRISON, ALLEN K, PHYSICS. *Current Pos:* SR RES SCIENTIST, GA TECH RES INST, GA INST TECH. *Personal Data:* b Lake Wales, Fla, Oct 24, 31; m 57; c 2. *Educ:* Davidson Col, BS, 53; Duke Univ, PhD(physics), 58. *Prof Exp:* From asst prof to assoc prof, 58-71, prof physics, Emory Univ, 71-88. *Concurrent Pos:* Nat Res Coun fel, Naval Res Lab, 64-65. *Mem:* Am Phys Soc. *Res:* Microwave spectroscopy; solid state physics; electro-optics. *Mailing Add:* Ga Tech Res Inst Ga Tech EMC/EOD Atlanta GA 30332

GARRISON, ARTHUR WAYNE, ENVIRONMENTAL CHEMISTRY, ANALYTICAL CHEMISTRY. *Current Pos:* res chemist, Southeast Water Lab, US Environ Protection Agency, 65-73, supvry res chemist, Environ Res Lab, 73-85, chief, Chem Br, 85-93, RES CHEMIST, NAT EXPOSURE RES LAB, US ENVIRON PROTECTION AGENCY, 93- *Personal Data:* b Greenville, SC, Sept 9, 34; m 78, Frances Mullins; c Arthur Wayne Jr, Bonnie, Christina, Jennifer & Christopher. *Educ:* The Citadel, BS, 56; Clemson Univ, MS, 58; Emory Univ, PhD(org chem), 66. *Honors & Awards:* Silver & Bronze Medal, US Environ Protection Agency. *Prof Exp:* Chemist, Dept Agr Chem, Clemson Univ, 61-62; anal chemist, Pesticide Pollution Lab, Div Water Supply & Pollution Control, USPHS, 62-65. *Concurrent Pos:* Consult, WHO; mem adj fac, Clemson Univ, 83-; vis scientist, Inst Ecol Chem, GSF, Neuherberg, Munich, Ger, 92-93. *Mem:* Am Chem Soc; Sigma Xi; Int Asn Environ Analytical Chem. *Res:* Development of methods for analysis of organic pollutants in water and soil; transformation and transport processes of pollutants in water and soil; environmental chemistry of chiral pollutants. *Mailing Add:* Nat Exposure Res Lab US Environ Protection Agency Athens GA 30605

GARRISON, BARBARA JANE, SURFACE CHEMISTRY. *Current Pos:* from asst prof to assoc prof, 79-86, dept head, 89-94, PROF CHEM, PA STATE UNIV, 86- *Personal Data:* b Big Rapids, Mich, Mar 7, 49; m 78, Nicholas Winograd. *Educ:* Ariz State Univ, BS, 71; Univ Calif, Berkeley, PhD(chem), 75. *Prof Exp:* Res fel chem, Purdue Univ, 75-77, vis asst prof, 78-79; lectr, Univ Calif, Berkeley, 77-78. *Concurrent Pos:* Alfred P Sloan Found fel, 80; vis assoc chem, Calif Inst Technol, 85-86. *Mem:* Am Chem Soc; Am Phys Soc; Am Vacuum Soc. *Res:* Interaction of gases with solid surfaces; keV ion bombardment of solids; etching of semiconductors; molecular beam epitaxial growth of semiconductors and ionization phenomena near metal surfaces; laser ablation of solids. *Mailing Add:* 152 Davey Lab Dept Chem Pa State Univ University Park PA 16802-6302. *E-Mail:* bjg@psu.edu

GARRISON, BETTY BERNHARDT, MULTIPLICATIVE NUMBER THEORY, DISTRIBUTION OF PRIMES. *Current Pos:* instr, 57-59, from asst prof to assoc prof, 62-69, PROF MATH, SAN DIEGO STATE UNIV, 69- *Personal Data:* b Danbury, Ohio, July 1, 32; m 68, John D; c John C. *Educ:* Bowling Green State Univ, BSEd & BA, 54; Ohio State Univ, MA, 56; Ore State Univ, PhD(math), 62. *Prof Exp:* Instr math, Ohio Univ, 56-57. *Mem:* Am Math Soc; Math Asn Am. *Res:* Polynomials with large numbers of prime values; distributions of primes. *Mailing Add:* Dept Math San Diego State Univ San Diego CA 92115-1027

GARRISON, GEORGE WALKER, ELECTRIC PROPULSION & MAGNETOHYDRODYNAMICS, HEAT TRANSFER & FLUID MECHANICS. *Current Pos:* asst dir, Ctr Space Propulsion, 87-90, PROF MECH & INDUST ENG, SPACE INST, UNIV TENN, 83-, EXEC DIR, CTR SPACE TRANSP & APPL RES, 90- *Personal Data:* b Statesville, NC, May 21, 39; m 61, Carole Mayfield; c Renee (Culbertson) & Walker. *Educ:* NC State Univ, BS, 61, MS, 63, PhD(mech eng), 66; Vanderbilt Univ, MBA, 80. *Honors & Awards:* Silver Knight Mgt, Nat Mgt Asn, 92. *Prof Exp:* Sr engr & proj mgr, Aro, Inc, 66-76; sect supvr, Sverdrup Tech Inc, 76-78, br mgr, 78-80, dir, 80-81. *Concurrent Pos:* Pres & chief exec officer, E&M Consults, 82- *Mem:* Fel Am Soc Mech Engrs; Am Inst Aeronaut & Astronaut; Nat Mgt Asn; Am Soc Eng Educ; Sigma Xi. *Res:* Electrical conductivity measurements of potassium seeded nitrogen plasma, developed conductivity algorithms; characterized the operating envelope of a magnetic annular arc. *Mailing Add:* 567 Waters Edge Dr Estill Springs TN 37330-3668

GARRISON, JAMES C, PHARMACOLOGY, BIOPHYSICS. *Current Pos:* Postdoctoral fel, Univ Va, 71-75, from asst prof to prof, 75-85, actg chair, 90-92, PROF PHARMACOL, MED SCH, UNIV VA, 90-, CHAIR, 92- *Personal Data:* b Detroit, Mich, Mar 29, 43; m 85, Claudia Sowa. *Educ:* Union Col, BS, 65; Univ Rochester, PhD(biophys), 71. *Mem:* Sigma Xi; Am Soc Biochem & Molecular Biol; Am Soc Pharmacol & Exp Therapeut. *Res:* Mechanism of action of hormones, growth factors and drugs at the level of the plasma membrane. *Mailing Add:* Dept Pharmacol Univ Va PO Box 448 Charlottesville VA 22908-0001. *Fax:* 804-982-3878; *E-Mail:* jcg8w@virginia.edu

GARRISON, JOHN CARSON, QUANTUM OPTICS, STATISTICAL MECHANICS. *Current Pos:* RETIRED. *Personal Data:* b Lufkin, Tex, May 15, 35; m 57, Hillegonda L Belinfane; c Victoria A & Jennifer S. *Educ:* Purdue Univ, BS, 57, MS, 59, PhD(physics), 61. *Prof Exp:* Sr physicist, Lawrence Livermore Lab, 61-96. *Concurrent Pos:* Lectr, Dept Appl Sci, Univ Calif, Davis, 69-, Physics Dept, Berkeley, 92; vis scientist, Max Planck Inst Quantum Optics, Garching, WGer, 84-85; vis prof, Univ Calif, Berkeley, 93-94. *Mem:* Am Phys Soc; Optical Soc Am; AAAS. *Res:* Quantum optics; topological phases in quantum mechanics and nonlinear optics; theory of amplified spontaneous emission; chaos in laser; quantum phenomena in nonlinear optics; quantum noise theory. *Mailing Add:* L-297 Lawrence Livermore Lab PO Box 808 Livermore CA 94550. *Fax:* 510-643-8497; *E-Mail:* garrison@physics.berkeley.edu

GARRISON, JOHN DRESSER, PHYSICS. *Current Pos:* from asst prof to prof, 56-62, chmn dept, 66-69, PROF PHYSICS, SAN DIEGO STATE UNIV, 62- *Personal Data:* b Salt Lake City, Utah, Aug 9, 22; m 50, 68; c 4. *Educ:* Univ Calif, Los Angeles, BA, 47, MA, 48; Univ Calif, PhD(physics), 54. *Prof Exp:* Instr physics, Yale Univ, 53-56. *Concurrent Pos:* Assoc physicist, Brookhaven Nat Lab, 62-63; consult, Atomic Co. *Mem:* Am Phys Soc. *Res:* Proton-proton scattering; solar energy; nuclear physics; neutron cross sections. *Mailing Add:* Dept Physics San Diego State Univ San Diego CA 92182. *Fax:* 619-594-5485

GARRISON, NORMAN EUGENE, BIOCHEMISTRY, DEVELOPMENTAL BIOLOGY. *Current Pos:* PROF BIOL, ACTG DEPT HEAD & DEAN, JAMES MADISON UNIV, 73- *Personal Data:* b Asheville, NC, Mar 25, 43; m 65, Rose M Jackson; c 2. *Educ:* Mars Hill Col, BS, 65; Wake Forest Univ, MA, 67; Univ Mass, Amherst, PhD(biochem), 73. *Prof Exp:* Instr biol, Mars Hill Col, 66-68; asst prof, Madison Col, 68-70. *Concurrent Pos:* Southern Regional Educ Bd travel grant, 76-77 & 77-78; proj dir, Title VI-A Sci Equip Prog Grant, 78-79 & NSF Instrnl Sci Equipment Prog Grant, 78-80 & 81-84. *Mem:* Sigma Xi. *Res:* Translational control of early embryonic development; human physiology. *Mailing Add:* Col Sci & Math James Madison Univ Harrisonburg VA 22807. *E-Mail:* garrisne@jmu.edu

GARRISON, ROBERT EDWARD, GEOLOGY. *Current Pos:* assoc prof, 68-73, chmn, Earth Sci Bd, 70-80, PROF EARTH SCI, UNIV CALIF, SANTA CRUZ, 73- *Personal Data:* b Dallas, Tex, Oct 25, 32; m 63; c 1. *Educ:* Stanford Univ, BS, 55, MS, 58; Princeton Univ, PhD(geol), 64. *Prof Exp:* Geologist petrol explor, Sunray D-X Oil Co, 59-61; res assoc geol, Princeton Univ, 64-65; asst prof, Univ Calif, Santa Barbara, 65-66; vis asst prof, Univ BC, 66-68. *Concurrent Pos:* Guggenheim fel, 72-73; geologist, US Geol Surv, 73-83. *Mem:* AAAS; Geol Soc Am; Am Asn Petrol Geologists; Soc Econ Paleontologists & Mineralogists. *Res:* Sedimentology and stratigraphy; petrology of carbonate rocks and eugeosynclinal sedimentary rocks; electron microscopy of fine-grained sedimentary rocks. *Mailing Add:* Ocean Sci & Earth Marine Sci Bldg Univ Calif Santa Cruz CA 95064

GARRISON, ROBERT FREDERICK, ASTRONOMY, ASTROPHYSICS & STELLAR SPECTROSCOPY. *Current Pos:* from asst prof to assoc prof, Univ Toronto, 68-78, ASSOC DIR, DAVID DUNLAP OBSERV, CHILE OPER, UNIV TORONTO, 70-, PROF ASTRON, 78-, DIR, SOUTHERN OBSERV, 70- *Personal Data:* b Aurora, Ill, May 9, 36; div; c Forest L, Alexandra & David C. *Educ:* Earlham Col, BA, 60; Univ Chicago, PhD(astron & astrophys), 66. *Honors & Awards:* Bronowski Mem lectr, 88. *Prof Exp:* Res asst astron, Yerkes Observ, 60-61; res assoc, Mt Wilson-Palomar Observ, 66-68. *Concurrent Pos:* Pres, Stellar Classification Comn, Int Astron Union, 85-88, Royal Can Inst, 93-94; Nat lectr, Sigma Xi, 88-90 & Shapley nat lectr, 88- *Mem:* Am Astron Soc; Am Asn Variable Star Observers; Royal Astron Soc Can (vpres, 96-98); Int Astron Union; Can Astron Soc. *Res:* Direct photography of galaxies and H II regions; stellar spectral classification; clusters and associations; Mira variables; galactic structure; stellar spectroscopy; peculiar stars. *Mailing Add:* David Dunlap Observ Univ Toronto Richmond Hill ON L4C 4Y6 Can. *E-Mail:* garrison@astro.utoronto.ca

GARRISON, ROBERT GENE, MEDICAL MICROBIOLOGY. *Current Pos:* RETIRED. *Personal Data:* b Pittsburg, Kans, Aug 30, 25; m 58; c 2. *Educ:* Kans State Col Pittsburg, BA, 49; Kans State Univ, MS, 51, PhD(bact), 54. *Prof Exp:* Asst antibiotics, Sch Med, La State Univ, 51-52; bacteriolosit, Vet Admin Hosp, Grand Island, Nebr, 54-57, scientist, Kansas City, 57-88. *Concurrent Pos:* Asst prof, Sch Med, Univ Kans, 61-67, assoc prof, 67-; clin asst prof, Sch Dent, Univ Mo-Kansas City, 70- *Mem:* Am Soc Microbiologists; Am Pub Health Asn; NY Acad Sci; fel Am Acad Microbiol. *Res:* Physiology of pathogenic fungi; fungal ultrastructure; electron cytochemistry. *Mailing Add:* 4801 E Linwood Ave Kansas City KS 64128

GARRISON, ROBERT J, biometry research, for more information see previous edition

GARRISON, WARREN MANFORD, MOLECULAR RADIOLOGY. *Current Pos:* asst dir, Crocker Lab, 58-62, prin investr, Lawrence Berkeley Lab, 48-77, CONSULT, LAWRENCE BERKELEY LAB, UNIV CALIF, BERKELEY, 77- *Personal Data:* b Seattle, Wash, June 6, 15; m 42; c 2. *Educ:* Univ Calif, Berkeley, BS, 37, MS, 39; NY Univ, PhD(photochem), 42. *Prof Exp:* Res assoc, Metall Lab, Univ Chicago, 42-43, assoc sect chief, Radiation Chem Sect, 43-44; res chemist, Hanford Eng Works, Gen Elec Co, Wash, 45-46; asst prof chem, Univ Wyo, 46-48. *Concurrent Pos:* Consult, E I du Pont de Nemours & Co, 58, Aerojet-Gen Nucleonics Div, Gen Tire & Rubber

Co, 62-64, Battelle Sci Proj, US Army, 77-78 & Am Hosp Supply, 80; chmn, Gordon Res Conf Radiation Chem, 59; State Dept rep, Int Cong Nuclear Energy, Italy, 59. *Mem:* AAAS; Am Chem Soc; Radiation Res Soc; Am Inst Chem. *Res:* Reaction mechanism; radiation chemistry. *Mailing Add:* 1660 Ridgewood Rd Alamo CA 94507-1994

GARRISON, WILLIAM EMMETT, JR, ORGANIC CHEMISTRY, POLYMER CHEMISTRY. *Current Pos:* Res chemist, E I Du Pont de Nemours & Co, Inc, 58-66, sr res chemist, 66-72, res assoc, 72-85, res fel, 85-89, SR RES FEL, POLYMERS, EXP STA, E I DU PONT DE NEMOURS & CO, INC, 89- *Personal Data:* b Media, Pa, Nov 29, 33; m 57, Deloris Meloni; c 6. *Educ:* Juniata Col, BS, 55; Univ Ill, PhD(org chem), 59. *Mem:* Am Chem Soc. *Res:* Polymers; product and process development. *Mailing Add:* Eng Plastics Exp Sta E I du Pont de Nemours & Co Wilmington DE 19898

GARRITY, MICHAEL K, BIOPHYSICS. *Current Pos:* From asst prof to assoc prof, 67-78, PROF PHYSICS, ST CLOUD STATE UNIV, 78- *Personal Data:* b Austin, Minn, Sept 1, 42; m 65, 85. *Educ:* St John's Univ, Minn, BS, 64; Ariz State Univ, MS, 65, PhD(math physics), 68. *Concurrent Pos:* Res fel, Am Soc Eng Educ, Johnson Space Ctr, NASA, 80 & 81; consult med physicist & radiol physics, 86. *Mem:* Am Asn Physics Teachers; Am Asn Med Physicist; Am Soc Therapeut Radiol & Oncol; Am Col Radiol. *Res:* Biomedical instrumentation; formulation of mathematical models; sensory information processing; physics of radiology. *Mailing Add:* Dept Physics & Astron St Cloud State Univ St Cloud MN 56301-4498

GARRITY, THOMAS F, MEDICAL BEHAVIORAL SCIENCE, HEALTH PSYCHOLOGY. *Current Pos:* From instr to assoc prof, 70-81, PROF MED BEHAV SCI, UNIV KY, COL MED, 81-, CHAIR DEPT BEHAV SCI, 88- *Personal Data:* b Philadelphia, Pa, Nov 8, 43; m 69, Ann Rawding; c Jeanne, Beth & Katie. *Educ:* Col Holy Cross, BS, 65; Duke Univ, MA, 67 & PhD(sociol), 71. *Concurrent Pos:* Resident scholar, Nat Heart, Lung & Blood Inst, 76; grant reviewer, Behav Med Study Sect, NIH, 78-79, Vet Admin Merit Review Bd, 81-86; consult, Nat High Blood Pressure Educ Prog, 79-88, Nat Heart Lung & Blood Inst, 74-; reviewer, J Health & Soc Behav, 75-, Soc Sci & Med, 78-,. *Mem:* fel Soc Behav Med; fel Acad Behav Med Res; Am Psychosomatic Soc; Asn Behav Sci & Med Educ. *Res:* Studies of psychosocial factors that influence adherence of patients to preventive and therapeutic regimens; factors that influence translation of life stress into disease; factors that influence behavior adjustment after heart attack. *Mailing Add:* Dept Behav Sci Univ Ky Med Sch 800 Rose St Lexington KY 40536-0001. *Fax:* 606-323-5350; *E-Mail:* bsc108@ukcc.uky.edu

GARRO, ANTHONY JOSEPH, MICROBIOAL GENETICS. *Current Pos:* ASSOC DEAN ACAD AFFAIRS, NJ MED SCH, UNIV Med & Dent NJ, 91- *Personal Data:* b New York, NY, Jan 13, 42; m 63; c 2. *Educ:* Manhattan Col, BS, 63; Columbia Univ, PhD(microbiol), 68. *Prof Exp:* Assoc, Mt Sinai Sch Med & City Col NY, 70-71, from asst prof to prof microbiol, 71-91. *Concurrent Pos:* NIH res fel microbial genetics, Albert Einstein Col Med, 68-70; res grants, Am Cancer Soc, NIH & March of Dimes. *Mem:* AAAS; Am Soc Microbiol; Am Asn Cancer Res; Environ Mutagen Soc; Am Asn Biol Chem; Sigma Xi. *Res:* Mechanisms of chemical carcinogenesis; fetal alcohol syndrome. *Mailing Add:* Acad Affairs Univ Med & Dent NJ NJ Med Sch 185 S Orange Ave Newark NJ 07103-2714. *Fax:* 973-982-7104

GARROD, CLAUDE, THEORETICAL PHYSICS. *Current Pos:* from asst prof to assoc prof, 62-76, PROF PHYSICS, UNIV CALIF, DAVIS, 76- *Personal Data:* b New York, NY, Sept 25, 32; m 55; c 3. *Educ:* NY Univ, AB, 57, PhD(physics), 63. *Prof Exp:* Instr physics, Manhattan Col, 61-62; res scientist, Courant Inst Math Sci, NY Univ, 62-64. *Mem:* Am Phys Soc. *Res:* Quantum theory of many-particle systems. *Mailing Add:* 1421 Tulane Dr Davis CA 95616

GARROU, PHILIP ERNEST, CATALYSIS, ORGANOMETALLIC CHEMISTRY. *Current Pos:* TECHNOL DEVELOP MGR, DOW CHEM CO, 75-, CHIEF SCIENTIST MICRO ELEC, 96- *Personal Data:* b New York, NY, Apr 26, 49; m 69; c 2. *Educ:* NC State Univ, BS, 70; Ind Univ, PhD(inorg chem), 74. *Mem:* Am Chem Soc; Mat Res Soc; Am Ceramics Soc. *Res:* Currently involved in assessing internal and external technology and making recommendations for business opportunities. *Mailing Add:* 111 Ethans Glen Ct 6100 Fairview Rd No 800 Cary NC 27513

GARROW, ROBERT JOSEPH, MATHEMATICS, PHYSICS. *Current Pos:* RETIRED. *Personal Data:* b Buffalo, NY, Dec 24, 29; m 64; c 3. *Educ:* Ohio State Univ, BS, 61; Xavier Univ, MEd, 69. *Prof Exp:* Engr, NAm Aviation, Inc, 57-60; instr math, Ohio State Univ, 60-61; chmn dept, Franklin Univ, 61-71, prof math, 61-93. *Concurrent Pos:* Pres, Montessori Acad, Inc, 72-73, Montessori Child Develop Ctr Inc, 73- & Franklin Educ Serv Inc. *Mem:* Am Soc Eng Educ; Am Math Soc. *Res:* Evaluation of the reliability and validity of an electronics aptitude test; use of the computer as an aid in teaching mathematics and science; design and development of a Montessori school complex; open space school concept consisting of four classrooms and a learning center. *Mailing Add:* 9605 E Bayshore Rd Marblehead OH 43440

GARROWAY, ALLEN N, PHYSICS. *Current Pos:* Nat Res Coun fel, 74-76, RES PHYSICIST, CODE 6120 CHEM DIV, NAVAL RES LAB, 76- *Personal Data:* b Washington, DC, Oct 10, 43. *Educ:* Rensselaer Polytech Inst, BS, 65; Cornell Univ, PhD(exp physics), 72. *Prof Exp:* Sci Res Coun fel nuclear magnetic resonance, Dept Physics, Univ Nottingham, 72-74. *Mem:* Sigma Xi; Am Phys Soc; Fedn Am Scientists; AAAS; Am Chem Soc; Soc Magnetic Resonance Med. *Res:* Nuclear magnetic resonance in the solid state; polymers; NMR imaging. *Mailing Add:* 13404 Kris-Ran Ct Ft Washington MD 20744-6609

GARRUTO, RALPH MICHAEL, NEUROBIOLOGY, BIOMEDICAL ANTHROPOLOGY. *Current Pos:* Fel, Nat Inst Neurol Dis & Stroke, NIH, 72-73, staff fel, 73-75, sr staff fel neurobiol, 75-78, SUPVRY SR RES BIOLOGIST, NAT INST NEUROL DIS & STROKE, NIH, 78- *Personal Data:* b Binghamton, NY, Nov 20, 43; m 69, Judith D Sharp; c Jessica, Jason & John. *Educ:* Pa State Univ, BS, 66, MA, 69, PhD(human biol-anthrop), 73. *Honors & Awards:* Distinguished Achievement Award, Am Dermatoglyphics Asn, 95. *Concurrent Pos:* Adj prof med genetics, Univ SAla, 82-; pres, Am Dermat Asn, 87-88; exec secy, Int Union Anthropol & Ethnol Sci, Comn Aging, 85-; adj sr scientist, Pa State Univ, 85-; bd trustees, Nat Mus Health & Med Found, 90-92; res comt neuroepidemiol, World Fedn Neurol; rep to the Man & the Biosphere Prog, NIH, 93-95. *Mem:* Nat Acad Sci; Am Asn Phys Anthropologists; fel Human Biol Asn (pres/pres elect, 93-96); Soc Epidemiol Res; Soc Study Human Biol; fel Am Col Epidemiol; fel Int Genetic Epidemiol Soc; Soc Neurosci. *Res:* Epidemiology and neurobiology of central nervous system disorders; biology of aging; experimental modelling; retrovirology; physiological and genetic adaptation of human populations to environmental stress. *Mailing Add:* Nat Inst Neurol Dis & Stroke Bldg 376 NIH Frederick Cancer Res & Develop Ctr PO Box B Frederick MD 21702. *Fax:* 301-846-1569

GARRY, PHILIP J, PATHOLOGY, NUTRITION. *Current Pos:* from asst prof to assoc prof path, 74-87, DIR, CLIN NUTRIT LAB, UNIV NMEX, ALBUQUERQUE, 74-, PROF, DEPT PATH, SCH MED, 87- *Personal Data:* b Bancroft, Iowa, Jan 19, 33. *Educ:* Univ Iowa, BA, 61, MS, 65; Ohio State Univ, PhD(biochem & nutrit), 74. *Prof Exp:* Res asst, Dept Pediat, Univ Iowa, 60-62, lab analyst, Dept Biochem, 62-63, asst, 64-65, res assoc, Dept Pediat, 65-66; res assoc, Dept Pediat, Col Med, Ohio State Univ, 66-71, instr, 71-74. *Concurrent Pos:* Prog chmn, Arnold O Beckman Conf, Am Asn Clin Chem, 80; mem, Sci Rev Comt, Clin Nutrit & Early Develop Br, Nat Inst Child Health & Human Serv, 81, Ad Hoc Teaching Nursing Home Rev Comt, Nat Inst Aging, 82, Vitamin & Mineral Workshop, Nat Acad Sci, Nat Bur Stand Proj Session, NIH & Expert Panel Nutrit, Int Fedn Clin Chem, 84, US Dept Com Nat Bur Stand Adv Coun NIH Cancer Chemoprev Prog, 85 & Nutrit Study Sect, NIH, 90-94; corresp ed, Age & Nutrit J, 90. *Mem:* Am Asn Clin Chem; Am Inst Nutrit; Am Soc Clin Nutrit; assoc mem Am Dietetic Asn; fel Am Col Nutrit; Geront Soc Am. *Res:* Author of numerous technical publications. *Mailing Add:* Clin Nutrit Lab Univ NMex Sch Med 2701 Frontier Pl NE No 215 Albuquerque NM 87131-0001. *Fax:* 505-277-2999

GARSCADDEN, ALAN, GASEOUS ELECTRONICS & ELECTRON TRANSPORT THEORY, LASER PHYSICS & LASER APPLICATIONS. *Current Pos:* res physicist, 75-92, assoc chief scientist, Aero Propulsion & Power Lab, 92-95, CHIEF SCIENTIST, WRIGHT LAB, USAF, 95- *Personal Data:* b Glasgow, Scotland, June 10, 37; US citizen; m 62, Avril M Thompson; c Alan G, Andrew K, Avril K & Anne E. *Educ:* Queens Univ, Belfast, BSc, 58, PhD(physics), 62. *Prof Exp:* Res physicist, Aerospace Res Lab, USAF, 62-73, res dir, 73-75. *Concurrent Pos:* Adj prof physics, Air Force Inst Technol, 69-, Univ Okla, 85-87, Univ Tex, Arlington, 91-93; res fel, Aero Propulsion & Power Lab USAF, 88- *Mem:* Fel Am Phys Soc; fel Inst Elec & Electronics Engrs; Nat Res Coun. *Res:* Non equilibrium plasma theory and experiments; numerical solutions of the Boltzmann Transport Equation, vibrational and electron kinetics in gas discharge lasers; thin film depositions, including diamond and high temperature materials; ionization waves in plasmas; plasma processing of materials. *Mailing Add:* WL/CA Wright-Patterson AFB Dayton OH 45433

GARSIA, ADRIANO MARIO, MATHEMATICS. *Current Pos:* PROF MATH, UNIV CALIF, SAN DIEGO, 66- *Personal Data:* b Tunis, Tunisia, Aug 20, 28; nat US; m 55; c 1. *Educ:* Stanford Univ, PhD(math), 57. *Prof Exp:* C L E Moore instr math, Mass Inst Technol, 57-59; asst prof, Univ Minn, 59-61; from assoc prof to prof, Calif Inst Technol, 61-66. *Mem:* Am Math Soc; Math Asn Am. *Res:* Classical analysis; probability theory; classical differential geometry. *Mailing Add:* Dept Math Univ Calif San Diego La Jolla CA 92093-0001

GARSIDE, BRIAN K, OPTO-ELECTRONIC DEVICES & SYSTEMS, FIBER OPTICS. *Current Pos:* PRES, OPTO-ELECTRONICS INC, 78- *Personal Data:* b Ashton-Under-Lyne, Eng, Jan 29, 40; m 63, 83; c 7. *Educ:* Oxford Univ Eng, BA, 62, MA & DPhil, 66. *Prof Exp:* Asst lectr physics, Oxford Univ, 65-66; mem tech staff coherent wave physics, Bell Labs NJ, 66-68; prof lasers & electro optics, McMaster Univ, Hamilton Ont, Can, 68-88. *Concurrent Pos:* Vis prof, Clarendon Lab, Oxford, UK, 75; adv bd mem, Ryerson Polytechnic Univ Toronto, Inst Microstruct Sci, 88-90 & Nat Res Coun, Ottawa, Can, 90-; mem, Grant Selection Comt, Oper Strategic Panel, Nat Sci & Eng Res Coun, Ottawa, Can, 90- *Mem:* Optical Soc Am; Inst Elec & Electronics Engrs; Int Soc Optical Eng; Am Phys Soc; Can Asn Physicists. *Res:* Semiconductor diode laser sources and detectors; fiber optical testing and systems; fiber optical sensor systems. *Mailing Add:* Opto-Electronics Inc Unit 9 2583 Speers Rd Oakville ON L6L 5K9 Can

GARSIDE, CHRISTOPHER, NUTRIENT DISTRIBUTION & CYCLING IN THE MARINE ENVIRONMENT. *Current Pos:* SR RES SCIENTIST, BIGELOW LAB OCEAN SCI, 76- *Personal Data:* b Mar 19, 44. *Educ:* Liverpool Univ, PhD(chem oceanog), 69. *Prof Exp:* Res scientist, Lamont Doherty Geol Observ, 70-71; asst prof, City Univ NY, 71-76. *Concurrent Pos:* Adj fac, Univ New Eng. *Mem:* Am Soc Limnol & Oceanog; Oceanog Soc.

Res: Measurement and modelling of the distribution and fluxes of nutrient elements in the oceans that are responsible for biological primary production, carbon geochemistry and potential control of greenhouse cases. *Mailing Add:* Bigelow Lab Ocean Sci West Boothbay Harbor ME 04575. *E-Mail:* Omnet: c.garside

GARSIDE, EDWARD THOMAS, zoology, for more information see previous edition

GARSIDE, LARRY JOE, ECONOMIC GEOLOGY, VOLCANOLOGY. *Current Pos:* Econ geologist, Nev Bur Mine & Geol, Univ Nev, Reno, 68-85, dep for res, 85-86, chief geologist, 86-87, actg dir & state geologist, 87-89, RES GEOLOGIST, UNIV NEV, RENO, 89- *Personal Data:* b Omaha, Nebr, May 2, 43; m 93, Terri Nelson; c Melissa (Henley) & Kristie (Tacadina). *Educ:* Iowa State Univ, BS, 65; Univ Nev, Reno, MS, 68. *Concurrent Pos:* Exec secy, Nev Oil & Gas Conserv Comn, 74-75; prin investr eng, US Dept Energy, US Geol Surv, Nev Dept Minerals, Army Corps Engrs & US Fish & Wildlife Serv. *Mem:* Geol Soc Am; Soc Econ Geologists; Am Asn Petrol Geologists; Geothermal Resources Coun; Soc Explor Geochemists. *Res:* Epithermal ore deposits; geologic mapping in Mesozoic and Tertiary volcanic terranes of Nevada; Nevada energy resources such as uranium, petroleum, and geothermal energy; author/co-author of over 100 articles and books on Nevada geology. *Mailing Add:* Nev Bur Mines & Geol MS 178 Univ Nev Reno NV 89557-0088. *Fax:* 702-784-1709; *E-Mail:* lgarside@nbmg.unr.edu

GARSKE, DAVID HERMAN, MINERALOGY. *Current Pos:* REF MINERAL SUPPLIER, 70- *Personal Data:* b Kalamazoo, Mich, Mar 2, 37; div; c 1. *Educ:* Mich Technol Univ, BS, 59; Univ Mich, MS, 61, PhD(mineral), 70. *Prof Exp:* Asst prof mineral & geol, SDak Sch Mines & Technol, 65-76. *Mem:* Mineral Soc Am; Mineral Asn Can. *Mailing Add:* 514 Brophy Ave Bisbee AZ 85603

GARST, JOHN ERIC, TOXICOLOGY, MEDICINAL CHEMISTRY. *Current Pos:* RES ASSOC PROF PHARM-TOXICOL, PRIMATE RES INST, NMEX STATE UNIV, HOLLOMAN AFB, 87- *Personal Data:* b Wichita, Kans, Oct 31, 46; m 71; c 2. *Educ:* Univ Kans, BA, 69; Univ Iowa, PhD(med chem), 74. *Prof Exp:* Fel biochem, Yale Univ, 73-74; fel physiol & pharmacol, Med Sch, Vanderbilt Univ, 74-75, fel toxicol, 75-78, res instr, 78; asst prof toxicol & asst prof animal sci, Univ Ill, Urbana, 78-85; assoc prof toxicol, Dept Surg & Med, Vet Med Col, Kans State Univ, 86-87. *Concurrent Pos:* Sect ed, J Animal Sci, 83-86. *Mem:* Am Chem Soc; Soc Toxicol; Am Soc Animal Sci; AAAS. *Res:* Structure-toxicity studies; pharmacology-medicinal chemistry; biochemical toxicology; author of several chapters and numerous articles. *Mailing Add:* 3008 Del Prado Alamogordo NM 88310-3960

GARST, JOHN FREDRIC, CHEMISTRY. *Current Pos:* from asst prof to assoc prof, 63-78, Gen Sandy Beaver teaching prof, 82-85, PROF CHEM, UNIV GA, 78- *Personal Data:* b Jackson, Miss, May 8, 32; m 55, Edna Swindall; c Jennifer L & John F Jr (deceased). *Educ:* Miss State Col, BS, 54; Iowa State Col, PhD(chem), 57. *Prof Exp:* Instr chem, Yale Univ, 57-58; asst prof, Univ Calif, Riverside, 58-63. *Mem:* Am Chem Soc. *Res:* Free radicals; solvent and metal effects on organoalkali systems; Grignard reagent formation; fast reactions in solution. *Mailing Add:* Dept Chem Univ Ga Athens GA 30602. *Fax:* 706-542-9454; *E-Mail:* garst@sunchem.chem.uga.edu

GARSTANG, MICHAEL, METEOROLOGY, OCEANOGRAPHY. *Current Pos:* RES ASSOC MARINE METEOROL, WOODS HOLE OCEANOG INST, 57-; PROF ENVIRON SCI, UNIV VA, 71- *Personal Data:* b Utrecht, Natal, SAfrica, Apr 4, 30; US citizen; m 53; c 2. *Educ:* Univ Natal, BA, 52, MA, 58; Fla State Univ, MS, 61, PhD(meteorol), 64. *Prof Exp:* Asst geog, Univ Natal, 51; indust ed, African Explosives & Chem Industs, Ltd, 52; meteorologist, Brit Colonial Serv, 53-56. *Concurrent Pos:* From asst prof to assoc prof, Fla State Univ, 65-70; mem, Adv Coun to Inst Trop Meteorol, UN Spec Fund Proj, Barbados, 68-70, Univ Corp Atmospheric Res Eval & Goals Comt, 69-70 & Adv Panel to Global Atmospheric Res Prog Anal Group, Nat Ctr Atmospheric Res & Adv Panel Global Atmospheric Res Prog Comt, Adv Comt to Nat Acad Sci, 75-78; vis scientist, Coun Sci & Indust Res, SAfrica, 70; consult, Nat Data Buoy Prog, Lockheed Aircraft Co & Southwest Res Inst, 70-71; prin investr, Trop Meteorol & Oceanog Progs, US Army Res Off, US Dept Defense & Environ Sci Serv Admin, US Forest Serv; chmn, Comt Hurricanes & Trop Meteorol, Am Meteorol Soc, 72-75, past chmn, 75-76; nat coordr, Planetary Boundary Layer Prog, Global Atmospheric Res Prog Atlantic Trop Exp, Nat Acad Sci, 75-78; pres, Simpson Weather Assoc, Inc. *Mem:* Fel Am Meteorol Soc; Sigma Xi; Univ Corp Atmospheric Res; Int Asn Meteorol & Atmoshpheric Physics. *Res:* Tropical meteorology and atmospheric chemistry, especially problems of trace gas exchanges between the surface layer, boundary layer and free atmosphere; rainfall distributions, convective cloud transports, wind energy potential and siting; thunderstorm analysis and short range prediction. *Mailing Add:* Dept Environ Sci Clark Hall Univ Va Charlottesville VA 22903

GARSTANG, ROY HENRY, ASTROPHYSICS, ATOMIC PHYSICS. *Current Pos:* chmn inst, Univ Colo, 66-67, dir, Div Physics & Astrophys, 79-80, actg dir, Fiske Planetarium, 80-81, prof physics, 64-84, prof astrophys, Planetary & Atmospheric Sci, 79-94, FEL JOINT INST LAB ASTROPHYS, UNIV COLO, 64-, EMER PROF PHYSICS, ASTROPHYS, PLANETARY & ATMOSPHERIC SCI, 94- *Personal Data:* b Southport, Eng, Sept 18, 25; m 59, Ann Hawk; c Jennifer K & Susan V. *Educ:* Cambridge Univ, BA, 46, MA, 50, PhD(math), 54, ScD, 83. *Prof Exp:* Jr sci officer, Royal Aircraft Estab, Eng, 45-46; sci officer, Brit Ministry Works, 46-48; res assoc astrophys, Yerkes Observ, Univ Chicago, 51-52; lectr astron, Univ Col, Univ London, 52-60, reader, 60-64; asst dir univ observ, 59-64. *Concurrent Pos:* Ed, Observ Mag, 53-60; astron adv ed, Chambers' Encycl, 60-66; guest worker, Nat Bur Stand, Washington, DC, 61-62, consult, 64-73; chmn comt transition probabilities, Int Astron Union, 64-76, vpres comn 14, 70-73, pres, 73-76; consult, Jet Propulsion Lab, 66-71; Erskine vis fels, Univ Canterbury & vis prof, Univ Calif, Santa Cruz, 71; chmn, Astron Educ Comt, Am Asn Physics Teachers, 87-89. *Mem:* Fel Am Phys Soc; Am Astron Soc; Int Astron Union; Royal Astron Soc; fel Brit Inst Physics; fel Optical Soc Am. *Res:* Spectroscopy; spectrum line intensities; forbidden transitions; spectroscopy of sun, stars and planetary nebulae; light pollution. *Mailing Add:* JILA Univ Colo Boulder CO 80309-0440. *Fax:* 303-492-5235; *E-Mail:* garstang@earthlink.net

GARSTENS, MARTIN AARON, SOLID STATE PHYSICS. *Current Pos:* RETIRED. *Personal Data:* b New York, NY, Mar 9, 11; m 36; c 1. *Educ:* City Col New York, BS, 32; Columbia Univ, MS, 34; Mass Inst Technol, ScD, 41. *Prof Exp:* Physicist, David Taylor Model Basin, 43-45; physicist, Naval Res Lab, Dept Navy, 46-61, Off Naval Res, Washington, DC, 61-74 & Arlington, 74-77. *Concurrent Pos:* Lectr, George Washington Univ, 47-48 & Howard Univ, 62-65. *Mem:* Am Phys Soc. *Res:* Nuclear and electron magnetic resonance; biophysics; foundations of physics. *Mailing Add:* 1801 E Jefferson St Rockville MD 20852-4062

GART, JOHN JACOB, STATISTICS. *Current Pos:* RETIRED. *Personal Data:* b Chicago, Ill, Apr 15, 31; m 61, Sheila Sinclair; c Matthew, Thomas, Jacqueline & Rebecca. *Educ:* DePaul Univ, BSc, 53; Marquette Univ, MS, 55, Va Polytech Inst, PhD(statist), 58. *Prof Exp:* Asst prof biostatist, Sch Hyg & Pub Health, Johns Hopkins Univ, 58-62, assoc prof biostatist & statist, 62-65; mathematician, Nat Cancer Inst, 65-67, head, Math Statist & Appl Math Sect, Biomet Ctr, 67-91. *Concurrent Pos:* Vis res fel, Univ London, 61-62, Va Polytech Inst, 71; adv, WHO, 66 & 80-86, FDA, 72 & 78-81. *Mem:* Fel Am Col Epidemiol; fel Am Statist Asn; fel Inst Math Statist; fel Royal Statist Soc. *Res:* Biometrics; mathematical statistics. *Mailing Add:* 3406 Kenilworth Dr Chevy Chase MD 20815

GARTE, SEYMOUR JAY, CANCER RESEARCH, ENVIRONMENTAL ONCOLOGY. *Current Pos:* Asst environ med, NY Univ Med Ctr, 75-76, assoc res scientist, 76-79, asst prof environ med, 79-87, ASSOC PROF ENVIRON MED, NY UNIV MED CTR, 87- *Personal Data:* b New York, NY, Oct 31, 47; m 69; c 2. *Educ:* City Col New York, BS, 70; City Univ New York, PhD(biochem), 76. *Honors & Awards:* Young Investr Res Award, Nat Cancer Inst, 79. *Concurrent Pos:* Prin investr, NIH grants, 83-; consult, Cahill, Gordon & Reindel, 84-85, Goldman, Hafetz, 87-88; mem, NIH rev panels, 86-; mem sci bd, Cancer Prev Res Inst, 90- *Mem:* Am Asn Cancer Res; Am Chem Soc. *Res:* Molecular biology and biochemistry of environmental carcinogenesis particularly in respect to oncogene activation; biochemical toxicology, chemical carcinogenesis, cell biology and risk assessment. *Mailing Add:* Dept Environ Health NY Univ Sch Med 550 First Ave New York NY 10016-6481

GARTEN, CHARLES THOMAS, JR, RADIOECOLOGY, BIOGEOCHEMISTRY. *Current Pos:* res assoc, Environ Sci Div, Union Carbide Corp, 76-83, RES STAFF MEM, OAK RIDGE NAT LAB, MARTIN MARIETTA ENERGY SYSTS, 84- *Personal Data:* b Huntington, WVa, Mar 27, 48; m 70; c 2. *Educ:* Washington & Lee Univ, BS, 70; Univ Ga, MS, 74. *Prof Exp:* Tech coordr mineral cycling studies, Savannah River Ecol Lab, Univ Ga, 73-76. *Concurrent Pos:* Sect ed, Nuclear Safety, 78-82; assoc ed, J Environ Radioactivity, 93-96. *Mem:* Am Chem Soc. *Res:* Biogeochemistry of long-lived radionuclides; element cycling in terrestrial ecosystems; applications of stable isotopes in ecological studies. *Mailing Add:* Environ Sci Div Oak Ridge Nat Lab Oak Ridge TN 37831-6038

GARTENHAUS, SOLOMON, THEORETICAL PHYSICS. *Current Pos:* from asst prof to assoc prof, 58-64, asst dean grad sch, 72-77, PROF PHYSICS, PURDUE UNIV, 64-, SECY FAC, 80- *Personal Data:* b Ger, Jan 3, 29; m; c 2. *Educ:* Univ Pa, BA, 51; Univ Ill, PhD(physics), 55. *Prof Exp:* Instr, Stanford Univ, 55-58. *Concurrent Pos:* Distinguished vis prof, USAF Acad, 77-78; dir student progs, Univ Hamburg, 79-80. *Mem:* Fel Am Phys Soc; AAAS; NY Acad Sci; Am Asn of Physics Teachers. *Res:* Phase transitions. *Mailing Add:* Dept Physics Purdue Univ West Lafayette IN 47907

GARTH, JOHN CAMPBELL, HIGH ENERGY ELECTRON & PHOTON TRANSPORT IN SOLIDS, MATHEMATICAL METHODS OF PARTICLE TRANSPORT. *Current Pos:* PHYSICIST & DIRECTORATE, SPACE & MISSILES TECHNOL, RADIATION HARDENED ELECTRONICS BR, PHILLIPS LAB, 91- *Personal Data:* b New York, NY, Sept 26, 34; m 60, Nancy McCandless; c Lee M & Lynn V. *Educ:* Princeton Univ, BSE, 56; Univ Ill, MS, 58, PhD(physics), 65. *Prof Exp:* Res asst physics, Univ Ill, 60-64; asst prof, Worcester Polytech Inst, 64-67; res physicist, Air Force Cambridge Res Labs, Rome Air Develop Ctr, Solid State Sci Div, Radiation Hardened Electronics Technol Br, 67-76, physicist, 76-91. *Mem:* Am Phys Soc; Sigma Xi; Am Nuclear Soc; Inst Elec & Electronics Engrs; Am Soc Testing & Mat; Mat Res Soc. *Res:* Theory of kilovolt electron and photon transport in solids, including Boltzmann equation and Monte Carlo techniques; radiation dosimetry for microelectronic devices; electron spin resonance and optical properties of defects in solids; interaction of radiation with matter. *Mailing Add:* Phillips Lab/PL/VTER 3550 Aberdeen Ave SE Kirkland AFB NM 87117. *E-Mail:* garth@plh.af.mil

GARTH, RICHARD EDWIN, GENETICS, BIOLOGY. *Current Pos:* RETIRED. *Personal Data:* b Knoxville, Tenn, Mar 10, 26; m 50; c 6. *Educ:* Emory Univ, AB, 49, PhD(biol), 54; Univ Tenn, MS, 50. *Prof Exp:* Instr biol, Bloomfield Col, 50-51; asst prof, Mt Union Col, 54-55; from asst prof to assoc prof, E Tenn State Col, 55-58; from asst prof to assoc prof Northwestern State Col, La, 58-66; prof biol sci & head dept, Miss State Col Women, 66-69; head, Dept Biol, Univ Tenn, Chattanooga, 69-76, dir, Div Sci & Math, 71-73, prof biol, 76-90. *Concurrent Pos:* Asst prog dir sec sch progs, NSF, 63-64, consult sci personnel & ed, Div, 64- *Res:* Autecology of Spanish moss; hypothalamus-gonadotrophin relationships; blastocyst implantation in rats; avian photoperiodism; physiology of development; molecular genetics. *Mailing Add:* 1413 Sunset Dr Signal Mountain TN 37377

GARTHER, JOHN G, TRANSPLANTATION IMMUNOLOGY, BONE MARROW TRANSPLANTATION. *Current Pos:* PROF PATH & IMMUNOL, UNIV MAN, 96- *Personal Data:* b Mar 3, 51; c 2. *Educ:* McGill Univ, MD, 76; FRCP(C), 80. *Prof Exp:* Assoc prof path, Children's Hosp Winnipeg, 83-97, assoc prof pediat & child health & adj prof immunol, 83-96. *Res:* Graft-versus host disease. *Mailing Add:* Dept Path Univ Man 770 Bannatyne Ave Winnipeg MB R3E 0W3 Can

GARTHWAITE, SUSAN MARIE, CARDIAC DISEASE, ARRHYTHMIA. *Current Pos:* Res scientist, 82-86, GROUP LEADER, G D SEARLE & CO, 86- *Personal Data:* b Lancaster, WI, Jan 24, 50. *Educ:* Alverno Col, Wis, BA, 72; Univ Mo, Columbia, PhD(physiol), 79. *Mem:* Am Physiol Soc; Am Heart Asn. *Res:* Discovery and development of new antiarrhythmic agents, elucidation of mechanisms of cardiac arrhythmias and development of arrhythmia models. *Mailing Add:* Dept Cardiovasc Res G D Searle & Co 4901 Searle Pkwy Skokie IL 60077-2980. *Fax:* 847-982-7512

GARTLAND, WILLIAM JOSEPH, GENETICS, MOLECULAR BIOLOGY. *Current Pos:* grants assoc, Div Res Grants, NIH, 7071, prog admin genetics, Nat Inst Gen Med Scis, 71-76, dir, Off Recombinant DNA Activ, 76-88, chief, Resources & Ctrs Br, Nat Inst Allergy & Infectious Dis, 88-91, SCI REV ADMINR, NAT INST DENT RES, NIH, 91- *Personal Data:* b New York, NY, Apr 15, 41; m 81, Margaret Hamme. *Educ:* Holy Cross Col, BS, 62; Princeton Univ, MA, 64, PhD(biochem sci), 67. *Honors & Awards:* NIH Director's Award, 78; Special Recognition Award, Pub Health Serv, 85. *Prof Exp:* Asst res scientist, NY Univ Med Ctr, 67-69; res biologist, Univ Calif, San Diego, 69-70. *Concurrent Pos:* Exec secy, recombinant DNA Adv Comt, NIH, 74-88, mem exec comt, 76-88; US rep, Comt Recombinant DNA Res, Europ Sci Found, 76-81; consult, NY State Adv Comt Recombinant DNA, 77-88; mem, USDA Agr Recombinant DNA Res Comt, 77-88; US rep, US-Japan Coop Prog Recombinant DNA Res, 81-88; US rep, Orgn Econ Coop & Develop Ad Hoc Comt Experts Safety & Reg Biotechnol, 82-88; US rep, Coun Europe Ad Hoc Comt Experts Genetic Eng, 83-88; US Head, Aids panel US-Japan Coop, Med Sci Prog, 88- *Mem:* AAAS; Am Soc Human Genetics; Am Soc Microbiol. *Res:* Recombinant DNA research; molecular genetics. *Mailing Add:* Nat Inst Dent Res Natcher Bldg Rm 4AN-38E 45 Center Dr MSC 6402 Bethesda MD 20892-6402

GARTLER, STANLEY MICHAEL, GENETICS. *Current Pos:* res asst prof, 57-64, PROF MED & GENETICS, UNIV WASH, 64- *Personal Data:* b Los Angeles, Calif, June 9, 23; m 48. *Educ:* Univ Calif, Los Angeles, BS, 48; Univ Calif, PhD(genetics), 52. *Prof Exp:* Res assoc genetics, Columbia Univ, 52-57. *Concurrent Pos:* USPHS fel, 52-54, sr res fel, 59-, res career award, 64-; NIH merit scholar, 87. *Mem:* Genetics Soc Am (pres, 87); Am Soc Human Genetics; Am Soc Nat; Nat Acad Sci; Am Soc Human Genetics (pres, 87-88). *Res:* Human genetics; mammalian somatic cell genetics. *Mailing Add:* Dept Genetics J-241 Univ Wash Seattle WA 98195

GARTNER, EDWARD A, organic chemistry, for more information see previous edition

GARTNER, LAWRENCE MITCHEL, MEDICINE & PHYSIOLOGY, PEDIATRICS NEONATOLOGY. *Current Pos:* chmn, Dept Pediat, 80-93, PROF PEDIAT, UNIV CHICAGO, 80-, PROF OBSTET & GYNECOL, 95- *Personal Data:* b Brooklyn, NY, Apr 24, 33; m 56, Carol; c Alex & Madeline. *Educ:* Columbia Univ, AB, 54; Johns Hopkins Univ, MD, 58. *Prof Exp:* Intern pediat, Johns Hopkins Hosp, 58-59; resident, Bronx Munic Hosp Ctr, 59-61; from asst instr to instr, Albert Einstein Col Med, 61-63, assoc, 63-64, from asst prof to assoc prof, 64-74, prof pediat, 74-88, dir, Div Neonatology, 70-80, dir, Kennedy Ctr Clin Res Unit, 72-80. *Concurrent Pos:* Chief resident, Bronx Munic Hosp Ctr, 61-62, asst dir premature Ctr, 62-67, dir, 67-; USPHS pediat res trainee, 62-64; Nat Inst Child Health & Human Develop spec fel & career develop award, 64-66; NIH career develop award, 66-74, res grant, 68-; United Health Found res grant, 67-68; Scripps Res fel, Inst Comp Biol, Univ Calif, San Diego, 67; chmn, Dept Pediat, Michael Reese Hosp, 86-89. *Mem:* Perinatal Res Soc; NAm Soc Pediat Gastroenterol (pres); Soc Pediat Res; Am Pediat Soc; Europ Soc Pediat Res; Am Acad Peds; Acad Breastfeeding Med. *Res:* Bilirubin metabolism and physiology of bilirubin transport; management of premature and newborn infants; physiology of the newborn and premature infant; breastfeeding and lactation. *Mailing Add:* Dept Pediat Univ Chicago MC 6060 5841 S Maryland Ave Chicago IL 60637. *Fax:* 773-702-0764

GARTNER, LESLIE PAUL, HISTOLOGY, DENTAL RESEARCH. *Current Pos:* From instr histol to asst prof anat, 70-75, ASSOC PROF ANAT, DENT SCH, UNIV MD, BALTIMORE, 75- *Personal Data:* b Szolnok, Hungary, Mar 18, 43; US citizen; m 71, Roseann Kollar; c Jennifer. *Educ:* Rutgers Univ, AB, 65, MS, 68, PhD(zool), 70. *Concurrent Pos:* Mem, Nat Bd Anat Sci Test Construct Comt, Am Dent Asn. *Mem:* Am Asn Anatomists; Fedn Am Socs Exp Biol; Sigma Xi. *Res:* Histo- and cytochemistry of odontogenesis and palate formation in rodents, as well as the teratogenic effects of radiation on oral embryology; aging and radiation-induced lifespan shortening in insects; development of trisomy 16 mouse; author of several textbooks on anatomy, histology, cell biology, embriology, oral histology, aging in drosophila, and alcohol and pregnancy. *Mailing Add:* Dept Anat Dent Sch Univ Md 666 W Baltimore St Baltimore MD 21201. *Fax:* 410-706-3028; *E-Mail:* lgartner@umabnet.ab.umd.edu

GARTNER, NATHAN HART, TRAFFIC CONTROL, ENGINEERING SYSTEMS ANALYSIS. *Current Pos:* from asst prof to assoc prof, 73-81, PROF CIVIL ENG, UNIV MASS, LOWELL, 81- *Personal Data:* b Cernauti, Romania, Aug 6, 39; US citizen; m 65; c Eran, Doron & Myra. *Educ:* Israel Inst Technol, BSc, 61, MSc, 67, DSc, 70. *Prof Exp:* Lectr eng, Technion, Israel Inst Technol, 70-71; fel transp, Univ Toronto, 71-72; vis asst prof civil eng, Mass Inst Technol, 72-73. *Concurrent Pos:* Vis scientist, Opers Res Ctr, Mass Inst Technol, 73-76, Lab Info & Decision Systs, 79-85, Ctr Transp Studies, 86-91; res fel, Fed Hwy Admin, Washington, DC, 76-78; chmn, Transp Sci Sect, Opers Res Soc Am, 78-79; assoc ed, Transp Sci, 80-89; mem, Transp Res Bd, Nat Acad Sci; assoc ed, Transp Res, 91- *Mem:* Opers Res Soc Am; Inst Transp Engrs. *Res:* Urban traffic control; transportation systems analysis; optimization techniques. *Mailing Add:* 20 Morton Rd Newton MA 02159. *Fax:* 978-934-5032; *E-Mail:* gartner@cae.uml.edu

GARTNER, STEFAN, JR, MICROPALEONTOLOGY, MARINE GEOLOGY. *Current Pos:* assoc prof geol, 75-81, PROF OCEANOG, TEX A&M UNIV, 80- *Personal Data:* b Hungary, Mar 28, 37; US citizen; m 63; c 2. *Educ:* Univ Conn, BA, 60; Univ Ill, MS, 62, PhD(geol), 65. *Prof Exp:* Res geologist, Esso Prod Res Co, 65-68; asst prof marine sci, Univ Miami, 68-72, assoc prof, 72-75. *Mem:* Geol Soc Am; Sigma Xi. *Res:* Biostratigraphic and paleoecologic application of calcareous nannofossils in pelagic and hemipelagic sediments. *Mailing Add:* Dept Oceanog Tex A&M Univ College Station TX 77843-0100

GARTNER, T KENT, DIRECT CELL-CELL INTERACTION, PLATELET AGGREGATION & ADHESION. *Current Pos:* PROF BIOL, MEMPHIS STATE UNIV, 79- *Educ:* Univ Calif, Davis, PhD(bacteriol), 65. *Prof Exp:* Asst prof biol, Univ Calif, Santa Barbara. *Concurrent Pos:* Study sect mem, Heart, Lung & Blood Inst, NIH. *Mem:* AAAS; Am Soc Cell Biol; Am Soc Hemat. *Res:* Role of adhesive glycoproteins in platelet aggregation; adhesion and thrombosis design; synthesis and characterization of peptides which inhibit platelet function; these peptides are models for the design of antithrombosis agents. *Mailing Add:* Dept Biol Memphis State Univ Memphis TN 38152-0001. *Fax:* 901-678-4457

GARTON, DAVID WENDELL, PHYSIOLOGICAL ECOLOGY, POPULATION GENETICS. *Current Pos:* ASST PROF, IND UNIV, 92- *Personal Data:* b Long Beach, Calif, July 14, 53. *Educ:* Univ Ala, Huntsville, BS, 75; La State Univ, MS, 78, MApp Stat, 80, PhD(physiol), 83. *Prof Exp:* Instr biol, Univ Ala, Huntsville, 76-78; teaching & res asst zool & physiol, La State Univ, 76-83; fel, State Univ NY, Stony Brook, 83-85; asst prof, Ohio State Univ, 85-92. *Concurrent Pos:* Adj asst prof, Ohio State Univ. *Mem:* Am Soc Zoologists; Am Soc Limnol & Oceanog; Am Malacological Union; Coun Undergrad Res. *Res:* Ecology, physiology and population genetics of invading invertebrate species in the Laurentian Great Lakes; physiology and genetics of adaptational responses to stressful environments by marine and freshwater invertebrates. *Mailing Add:* Sci 6 Ind Univ Kokomo PO Box 9003 Kokomo IN 46904-9003. *Fax:* 765-455-9276; *E-Mail:* dgarton@indiana.edu

GARTON, RONALD RAY, RESEARCH ADMINISTRATION, GENERAL ENVIRONMENTAL SCIENCES. *Current Pos:* RETIRED. *Personal Data:* b Billings, Mont, Feb 27, 35; m 59. *Educ:* Univ Mont, BA, 58, BS, 63; Mich State Univ, MS, 67, PhD(fisheries, wildlife), 68. *Honors & Awards:* Cert Fisheries Scientist, Am Fisheries Soc, 71; Gold Medal Except Serv for Res, Environ Protection Agency. *Prof Exp:* Res aquatic biologist, Pac Northwest Water Lab, US Environ Protection Agency, 68-72, res aquatic biologist, Western Fish Toxicol Sta, 72-73, chief, 73-81; dir, Freshwater Div, Corvallis Environ Res Lab, 81-86; sr environ scientist, EA Eng, Sci & Technol, Inc, 86-94. *Concurrent Pos:* Mem, Stand Comt, Am Nuclear Soc, 73-; consult, environ. *Mem:* Ecol Soc Am; Am Fisheries Soc; fel Am Inst Fisheries Res Biologists; Soc Environ Toxicol & Chem. *Res:* Effects of thermal pollution on freshwater organisms; effect of pollutants on aquatic species and aquatic ecosystems; environmental risk assessments. *Mailing Add:* 33 McCurdy Lane Port Ludlow WA 98365. *E-Mail:* rrongar@olympus.net

GARTRELL, CHARLES FREDERICK, ORBITAL MECHANICS. *Current Pos:* BUS BEAR SWAMP LUMBER CO WEB SERV, 97- *Personal Data:* b Baltimore, Md, Nov 4, 51; div; c Michael. *Educ:* Univ Md, BA, 73. *Prof Exp:* Task mgr & analyst, Syst Sci Div, Comput Sci Corp, 73-75; systems analyst, RCA Am Commun, 75-78; dep dir, Prog Anal Group, Gen Res Corp, 78-93; prog mgr, Futron Corp, 93-97. *Concurrent Pos:* Lectr, Commun Technol, Georgetown Univ & Future Space Activ, Montgomery Co Pub Sch; prin investr, AI appl for large space syst control; mem, Exec Coun, Am Inst Aeronaut & Astronaut, 87, Astrodyn Tech Comt, 88-91 *Mem:* Am Inst Aeronaut & Astronaut; Optical Soc Am. *Res:* Advanced civilian and military space systems technology covering the next 20-30 years; design and studies of advanced earth observation; radar and communication satellites; orbital transfer vehicles, spacecraft control techniques and systems; spaceflight experimental concept design. *Mailing Add:* 3585 Greenwood Dr Conway SC 29527-6656. *Fax:* 202-488-7863

GARTSHORE, IAN STANLEY, FLUID MECHANICS. *Current Pos:* from asst prof to assoc prof mech eng, 67-79, PROF MECH ENG, UNIV BC, 79- *Personal Data:* b Calgary, Alta, Apr 27, 35; m 62, Anne B Muirhead; c Christine H & John G. *Educ:* Univ BC, BASc, 57; Univ London, MSc, 60; McGill Univ, PhD(mech eng), 65. *Prof Exp:* Sci officer, Nat Phys Lab, UK, 59-60; res officer, Nat Res Coun Can, 61-62; res dir, McGill Univ, 65-67. *Concurrent Pos:* Killam fel, 73-74 & 80-81. *Mem:* Fel Can Aeronaut & Space Inst; Am Inst Aeronaut & Astronaut. *Res:* Laminar and turbulent motion; development of turbulent shear flows; wind effects on structures; wind energy; film cooling of turbine blades; flow in boiler furnaces. *Mailing Add:* Dept Mech Eng Univ BC 2324 Main Mall Vancouver BC V6T 1Z4 Can. *Fax:* 604-822-2403

GARTSIDE, PETER STUART, BIOSTATISTICS. *Current Pos:* asst prof, 73-78, ASSOC PROF BIOSTATIST, DEPT ENVIRON HEALTH, UNIV CINCINNATI, 78- *Personal Data:* b Oldham, UK, Aug 12, 37; US citizen; m 63; c 4. *Educ:* Brigham Young Univ, BS, 67, MS, 69; Univ Calif, Berkeley, PhD(biostatist), 76. *Prof Exp:* Instr, Dept Statist, Brigham Young Univ, 67-69; statistician, Sch Pub Health, Univ Calif, Berkeley, 72-73. *Mem:* Am Statist Asn; Biomet Soc; Am Math Soc; Soc Indust & Appl Math. *Res:* Environmental health research; occupational health research. *Mailing Add:* Dept Environ Health Univ Cincinnati Col Med 231 Bethesda Ave Cincinnati OH 45267

GARTSIDE, ROBERT N(IFONG), CHEMICAL ENGINEERING. *Current Pos:* RETIRED. *Personal Data:* b Fredericktown, Mo, Jan 1, 18; m 59; c Robert J, E Gail (Magin) & Ellen D. *Educ:* Wash Univ, BS, 39. *Prof Exp:* Chem engr, Eastern Lab, Explosives Dept, E I du Pont de Nemours & Co, Inc, 39-42, 46-52, tech asst, Tech Div, 52-53, asst dir, Repauno Process Lab, 53-56, dir, Sales Develop Lab, 56-59, asst dir, Eastern Lab, 59-60, dir, Repauno Develop Lab, 60-67, admin asst, Eastern Lab, Gibbstown, 67-72, sr design consult, Eng Dept, 72-82. *Res:* Process development; administration. *Mailing Add:* 578 High St Woodbury NJ 08096

GARTY, KENNETH THOMAS, ORGANIC CHEMISTRY. *Current Pos:* RETIRED. *Personal Data:* b Chicago, Ill, Nov 4, 16; m 50; c 4. *Educ:* Purdue Univ, BS, 40; Stevens Inst Technol, MS, 47. *Prof Exp:* Chemist res, Bakelite Co, 40-48, group leader, 48-72, proj leader, 52-59, Union Carbide Corp, 59-65, sr chemist, Union Carbide Corp, 72-82. *Mem:* Am Chem Soc. *Res:* Vinyl polymerization and copolymerizations; organosulfur and epoxy polymers; polyethers. *Mailing Add:* 775 Hardgrove Rd Bridgewater NJ 08807-1814

GARVEN, FLOYD CHARLES, organic chemistry; deceased, see previous edition for last biography

GARVER, DAVID L, SCHIZOPHRENIA, PSYCHOPHARMACOLOGY. *Current Pos:* assoc prof, 78-81, PROF PSYCHIAT & PHARMACOL, COL MED, UNIV CINCINNATI, 81- *Personal Data:* b Dayton, Ohio, Feb 3, 39; m 65; c 2. *Educ:* Oberlin Col, BA, 60; Western Reserve Univ Sch Med, MD, 65. *Prof Exp:* Resident psychiat, Univ Colo Med Ctr, 68-71; fel psychiat res, Ill State Psychiat Hosp, 71-72; instr psychiat, Pritzker Sch Med, Univ Chicago, 73-78. *Concurrent Pos:* Asst prof psychiat, Rush Med Sch, 74-78; dir, Lab Psychobiol & Psychopharmacol, Med Univ Cincinnati, 78-, Dept Psychiat, 82- & Psychobiol Treat Unit, Univ Cincinnati Hosp, 78-; chmn, Nat Inst Ment Health Treat Develop & Assessment, 86-; chmn, Educ & Training Comt, Am Col Neuropsychopharmacol, 87; vis prof, dept psychiat, Wash Univ, St Louis, 88- *Mem:* Am Col Neuropsychopharmacol; Psychiat Res Soc (pres, 87-88); Soc Biol Psychiat; Am Psychiat Asn; Soc Neurosci; AAAS. *Res:* Resolution of the biologic heterogeneity within the group of psychotic disorders generally known as schizophrenia; differential drug-response patterns; differential neuroendocrinological response to specific probes; different neurotransmitter patterns in CSF and plasma are utilized to resolve such heterogeneity. *Mailing Add:* Vet Admin Med Ctr "116A" Mental Health Prog 4500 S Lancaster Rd Dallas TX 75216

GARVER, FREDERICK ALBERT, CELL & MOLECULAR BIOLOGY. *Current Pos:* from asst prof to assoc prof, 71-81, PROF, DEPT CELL & MOLECULAR BIOL, MED COL GA, 81-, DIR, HYBRIDOMA FACIL, 89- *Personal Data:* b Marion, Ohio, Oct 22, 36. *Educ:* Ohio State Univ, BS, 59; Univ Colo, PhD(immunol), 69. *Honors & Awards:* Merrell-Dow Award, Soc Perinatal Obstetricians, 82. *Prof Exp:* Postdoctoral fel, Microbiol Dept, Med Ctr, Univ Colo, 63-69 & Immunochem Dept, Max-Planck Inst Exp Med, Gottingen, Ger, 69-71. *Concurrent Pos:* NIH res grants, 80-93; Nat Leukemia Asn res grant, 81-83; mem, Hemoglobin Variants Subcomt, Nat Comt Clin Lab Stand, 82- *Mem:* Am Asn Immunologists; Am Soc Hemat; NY Acad Sci; Reticuloendothelial Soc; Am Soc Biol Chemists; AAAS; Am Asn Univ Professors. *Res:* Indentification of tumor antigens on human leukemia cells; immunochemical identification and characterization of variant hemoglobins; author of more than 100 technical publications. *Mailing Add:* Dept Immunol & Microbiol Med Col Ga Augusta GA 30912-0001. *Fax:* 706-721-7507

GARVER, ROBERT VERNON, MICROWAVE THEORY AND TECHNIQUES. *Current Pos:* SR ENGR, XETA INTL, 80- *Personal Data:* b Minneapolis, Minn, June 2, 32; m 57, Shirley Phillips; c Debra, Douglas, Daniel, Mary & Jennifer. *Educ:* Univ Md, BS, 56; George Washington Univ, MEA, 68. *Prof Exp:* Res physicist microwaves, Harry Diamond Labs, 56-70, physicist fuze proj mgr, 70-75, supvr physicist, 75-79. *Concurrent Pos:* Assoc ed, Inst Elec & Electronics Engrs J Solid-State Circuits, 69-73; consult, Weinschel Eng Co, 70-75. *Mem:* Fel Inst Elec & Electronics Engrs. *Res:* Original ideas in microwave diode switches which served as the basis for all later development of diode switches, limiters, attenuators, and phase shifters. *Mailing Add:* 2393 Bear Den Rd Frederick MD 21701

GARVEY, DANIEL CYRIL, MECHANICAL ENGINEERING. *Current Pos:* VIBRATION & CONTROL SYSTS ENGR, WOODWARD GOVERNOR CO, 70- *Personal Data:* b Chicago, Ill, Nov 25, 40; c Michael D & Erin T. *Educ:* Marquette Univ, BSME, 63; Ill Inst Technol, Chicago, MS, 65. *Honors & Awards:* Arch T Colwell Merit Award, Soc Automotive Engrs, 84; Internal Combustion Engine Award, Am Soc Mech Engrs, 90. *Prof Exp:* Staff Mem, Kearney & Trecker Corp, 60-63, A C Electronics Div, Gen Motors Corp, 65-68. *Mem:* Inst Elec & Electronics Engrs; Soc Automotive Engrs. *Res:* Vibration and control systems. *Mailing Add:* Woodward Governor Co 1000 E Drake Rd Ft Collins CO 80525

GARVEY, GERALD THOMAS, NUCLEAR PHYSICS. *Current Pos:* DIR, LOS ALAMOS MESON PHYSICS FACIL, LOS ALAMOS NAT LAB, 85-, DEP ASSOC DIR, NUCLEAR & PARTICLE PHYSICS PROGS, 84- *Personal Data:* b New York, NY, Jan 21, 35; m 59; c 3. *Educ:* Fairfield Univ, BS, 56; Yale Univ, PhD(physics), 62. *Prof Exp:* Res assoc physics, Yale Univ, 62-63; instr, Princeton Univ, 63-64; asst prof, Yale Univ, 64-66; from asst prof to prof physics, Princeton Univ, 66-76; dir, Physics Div, Argonne Nat Lab, 76-79, assoc dir physical res, 79-80, sr scientist, 76-84; prof physics, Univ Chicago, 78-84. *Concurrent Pos:* Sloan Found fel, 67-69; consult, Brookhaven Nat Lab, 70-71. *Mem:* Am Phys Soc. *Res:* Experimental nuclear physics, particularly reactions and isobaric spin studies; weak interaction in nuclear systems; neutrino physics. *Mailing Add:* Los Alamos Nat Lab MS H846 Box 1663 Los Alamos NM 87545

GARVEY, JAMES F, MOLECULAR BEAMS, VAN DER WAALS CLUSTERS. *Current Pos:* from asst prof to assoc prof, 87-96, PROF CHEM, STATE UNIV NY, BUFFALO, 96- *Personal Data:* b Passaic, NJ, Feb 6, 57; m 87, Pam Lee; c Tricia. *Educ:* Georgetown Univ, BS & MS, 78; Calif Inst Technol, PhD(chem), 85. *Honors & Awards:* Am Inst Chem Award, 78. *Prof Exp:* Postdoctoral fel, Univ Calif Los Angeles, 85-87. *Concurrent Pos:* Consult, Hughes Res, Malibu, Calif, 85-87; Res award, Alfred P Sloan Found, 91; Fulbright Scholar, 94-96. *Mem:* Am Chem Soc; Am Phys Soc; Mat Res Soc; Am Soc Mass Spectrometry. *Res:* Chemical reactions within Van der Waals clusters; photochemistry within metal heyacarbonyl clusters thin film generation via cluster deposition; generation of novel thin films; fullmene ion chemistry. *Mailing Add:* NSM Complex Dept Chem State Univ NY Buffalo NY 14260-3000 *Fax:* 716-645-6963; *E-Mail:* garvey@ubums.cc.buffalo.edu

GARVEY, JUSTINE SPRING, IMMUNOCHEMISTRY. *Current Pos:* from assoc prof to prof immunochem, 74-89, prof, 80-89, EMER PROF BIOL, SYRACUSE UNIV, 90- *Personal Data:* b Wellsville, Ohio, Mar 14, 22; m 46; c 2. *Educ:* Ohio State Univ, BS, 44, MS, 48, PhD(microbiol, chem), 50. *Prof Exp:* Res fel chem, Calif Inst Technol, 51-57, sr res fel, 57-73, res assoc, 73-74. *Concurrent Pos:* Vis prof microbiol, Univ Ill Med Ctr, 73; vis res assoc, Calif Inst Technol, 90- *Mem:* AAAS; Am Asn Immunol; NY Acad Sci. *Res:* Immunological methods; biology of aging; biological and chemical characterization of retained antigen; immunochemistry of metallothionein; role of antigen in immunity. *Mailing Add:* 698 Arden Rd Pasadena CA 91106-4408

GARVEY, R(OBERT) MICHAEL, FREQUENCY AND TIME STANDARDS. *Current Pos:* CONSULT, 90- *Personal Data:* b Winston-Salem, NC, Jan 4, 47; m 75. *Educ:* Davidson Col, BS, 69; Duke Univ, PhD(physics), 75. *Prof Exp:* Res asst physics, Duke Univ, 72-77; mem staff, Nat Bur Standards, 77-79, scientist, Frequency & Time Systs, 79-82, dir, Eng, 82-90. *Mem:* Sigma Xi; Inst Elec & Electronics Engrs. *Res:* Experimental aspects of molecular physics; emphasis on microwave spectroscopy, frequency and time standards, cesium frequency standards, quartz oscillators, frequency and time metrology. *Mailing Add:* 85 Monument Ave Swampscott MA 01907-1947

GARVEY, ROY GEORGE, INORGANIC CHEMISTRY. *Current Pos:* Asst prof, 66-69, ASSOC PROF INORG CHEM, NDAK STATE UNIV, 69- *Personal Data:* b Pocatello, Idaho, Jan 19, 41; m 63; c 3. *Educ:* Univ Utah, BA, 63, PhD(inorg chem), 66. *Mem:* AAAS; Am Chem Soc; Am Crystallog Soc; Sigma Xi. *Res:* Coordination properties of M-D functional groups; kinetics of displacement reactions at transition metal sites; synthesis and physical properties of novel inorganic compounds. *Mailing Add:* Dept Chem NDak State Univ Fargo ND 58105-5516

GARVIN, ABBOTT JULIAN, PATHOLOGY. *Current Pos:* ASSOC PROF PATH, MED UNIV SC, 80-, DIR SURG PATH & CYTOPATH, 85- *Educ:* Med Univ SC, MD, 72, PhD(path), 75. *Mailing Add:* Dept Path & Lab Med Med Univ SC 171 Ashley Ave Charleston SC 29425. *Fax:* 803-792-8033

GARVIN, DAVID, PHYSICAL CHEMISTRY. *Current Pos:* Chemist, Nat Bur Stand, 61-78, chief, Chem Thermodyn Div, 78-81, Chem Thermodyn Data Ctr, 81-86, chemist, 86-89, GUEST RESEARCHER, NAT BUR STAND, 90- *Personal Data:* b Cleveland, Ohio, Aug 25, 23. *Educ:* Yale Univ, BS, 48; Harvard Univ, MA & PhD(chem), 51. *Prof Exp:* Instr chem, Princeton Univ, 51-55, asst prof, 55-61. *Mem:* Am Chem Soc; Am Phys Soc. *Res:* Chemical thermodynamics; information retrieval; chemical kinetics; physical properties, data evaluation. *Mailing Add:* 18700 Walkers Choice Rd No 807 Gaithersburg MD 20879

GARVIN, DONALD FRANK, INDUSTRIAL MICROBIOLOGY. *Current Pos:* RETIRED. *Personal Data:* b Toledo, Ohio, Mar 14, 32; m 51; c 3. *Educ:* Wayne State Univ, BS, 64, MS, 66, PhD(biol), 75. *Prof Exp:* Clin lab technician, Woodward Gen Hosp, Highland Park, Mich, 55-59, asst supvr clin lab, 59-65; sr technologist, William Beaumont Hosp, Royal Oak, Mich, 65-66; res bacteriologist, Wyandotte Chem Corp, 66-75, supvr, BASF Wyandotte Corp, 75-80, supvr regulatory affairs, Diversey Corp, 80-96. *Mem:* Am Soc Microbiol; Am Soc Testing & Mat; Am Chem Soc. *Res:* Identification and isolation of cell wall deficient varients of mycobacterium tuberculosis and clinical L-forms by gas chromotography, polyacrylamide electrophoresis and fluorescent antibody techniques; application research of germicides and fungicides. *Mailing Add:* 2309 23rd St Wyandotte MI 48192

GARVIN, JAMES BRIAN, PLANETARY GEOPHYSICS, RADAR & LASER REMOTE SENSING. *Current Pos:* GEOPHYSICIST GEOL, REMOTE SENSING, PLANETARY & COMETARY SCI, GODDARD SPACE FLIGHT CTR, NASA, 84-, CHIEF SCIENTIST, SHUTTLE LASER ALTIMETER, 90-, PROJ SCIENTIST, EARTH SYST SCI PATHFINDER, GODDARD SPACE FLIGHT CTR, NASA, 95- *Personal Data:* b Poughkeepsie, NY, Mar 10, 56; m 92, Cynthia Slater; c Zachary K & Danika T. *Educ:* Brown Univ, ScB, 78, MS, 81, PhD(geol sci), 84; Stanford Univ, MS, 79. *Prof Exp:* Fel planetary geol, Brown Univ, 84. *Concurrent Pos:* Mem, topog sci working group & mars rover sample return working group, Washington, DC, 88, prin investr, topog profile and res proj grant & co-investr, shuttle laser altimeter exp, NASA, 86; prin investr, Iceland Volcanology, NASA Res proj grant, 88, co-investr, Mars Observer Laser Altimeter Exp, 86-92; co-investr, Venus Data Anal Prog, 93-, Planetary Instrument Design & Develop AOS, 93-, Mars Global Survr, 95-, Radar Sat, NASA, 95- *Mem:* Sigma Xi; Am Geophys Union; Asn Comput Mach. *Res:* Earth and planetary geophysics focusing on the surface processes on Venus, Earth and Mars, and involving radar(microwave), laser and image remote sensing; high resolution altimetry of the earth, moon and mars involving laser and radar systems; terrestrial impact craters from remote sensing datasets; quantitative volcanology of Iceland. *Mailing Add:* NASA Goddard Space Flight Ctr Code 921 Greenbelt MD 20771. *Fax:* 301-286-1616; *E-Mail:* garvin@denali.gsfc.nasa.gov

GARVIN, JEFFREY LAWRENCE, PHYSIOLOGY, EPITHELIAL TRANSPORT. *Current Pos:* assoc staff investr, 88-91, SR STAFF INVESTR, DEPT INTERNAL MED, HYPERTENSION & VASCULAR RES DIV, HENRY FORD HOSP, DETROIT, 91- *Personal Data:* b Pittsburgh, Pa, Dec 1, 57. *Educ:* Univ Miami, BS, 79; Duke Univ, PhD(physiol), 84. *Prof Exp:* Instr med physiol, Dept Physiol, Duke Univ, 80; Nat Kidney Found fel, Lab Kidney & Electrolyte Metab, NIH, 84-85 & 85-88. *Mem:* Am Soc Nephrology; Am Physiol Soc; AAAS; Am Heart Asn. *Res:* Author of more than 30 technical publications. *Mailing Add:* Hypertension & Vascular Res Div Henry Ford Hosp 2799 W Grand Blvd Detroit MI 48202-2689. *Fax:* 313-876-1479

GARVIN, PAUL JOSEPH, JR, HEALTH RISK ASSESSMENT. *Current Pos:* CONSULT, 92- *Personal Data:* b Toledo, Ohio, Nov 16, 28; m 52, Priscilla A Haines; c Peter, Thomas, Paul III, Peggy, Priscilla & Polly. *Educ:* St John's Univ, Minn, BA, 50; Univ Minn, MS, 59. *Prof Exp:* Res assoc, Sterling-Winthrop Res Inst, 54-58; sr res pharmacologist, Baxter Travenol Labs, Inc, 58-73, mgr safety eval, 73-77; dir toxicology, Amoco Corp, 77-78, sr consult environ health, 88-92. *Mem:* Soc Toxicol; Am Soc Pharmacol & Exp Therapeut; Am Indust Hyg Asn; Europ Soc Toxicol; AAAS; NY Acad Sci. *Res:* Health and environmental effects of petroleum products and chemicals; health risk assessment processes. *Mailing Add:* 309 N Wille St Mt Prospect IL 60056. *Fax:* 847-259-8914; *E-Mail:* garvjr@aol.com

GARVIN, PAUL LAWRENCE, MINERALOGY. *Current Pos:* PROF GEOL, CORNELL COL, 69- *Personal Data:* b Dec 5, 39; US citizen; m 64; c 2. *Educ:* Idaho State Univ, BS, 64; Univ Colo, Boulder, PhD(geol), 69. *Prof Exp:* Lectr geol, Idaho State Univ, 64-65. *Concurrent Pos:* Consult, rock & mineral analysis. *Mem:* AAAS; Mineral Soc Am; Nat Asn Geol Teachers. *Res:* Sulfide phase relations; mineralogy and genesis of ore deposits. *Mailing Add:* Dept Geol Cornell Col First St W Mt Vernon IA 52314-1098

GARVINE, RICHARD WILLIAM, PHYSICAL OCEANOGRAPHY. *Current Pos:* ASSOC PROF MARINE STUDIES, UNIV DEL, 77- *Personal Data:* b Pottstown, Pa, Jan 7, 40; m 66; c 2. *Educ:* Mass Inst Technol, BS, 61; Princeton Univ, PhD(aerodyn eng), 65. *Prof Exp:* Theoret aerodynamicist, Space Sci Lab, Gen Elec Co, 65-69; from asst prof to assoc prof mech eng, Marine Sci Inst, Univ Conn, 69-77. *Mem:* AAAS; Am Geophys Union. *Res:* Estuarine dynamics; oceanic fronts; coastal upwelling. *Mailing Add:* Dept Marine Studies Univ Del Newark DE 19717-0001

GARWIN, CHARLES A, ACTUARIAL PROGRAMMING. *Current Pos:* Prog anal, 80-82, SR PROG ANALYSIS, D&B PENSION SERV, 82- *Personal Data:* b Savannah, Ga, Dec 23, 44. *Educ:* Univ Chicago, BS, 64, MS, 65; Univ Calif-Berkeley, PhD(physics), 71. *Mem:* Am Phys Soc; Am Math Soc; Am Math Asn. *Mailing Add:* 1317A Franklin St Santa Monica CA 90404

GARWIN, EDWARD LEE, APPLIED PHYSICS. *Current Pos:* physicist, 62-68, HEAD APPL PHYSICS, STANFORD LINEAR ACCELERATOR CTR, 68-, PROF APPL PHYSICS, 75- *Personal Data:* b Cleveland, Ohio, Mar 22, 33; m 54; c 3. *Educ:* Case Western Res Univ, BS, 54; Univ Chicago, MS, 55, PhD(physics), 58. *Prof Exp:* Res assoc, Univ Chicago, 58-59; res asst prof physics, Univ Ill, 59-60; prof mgr space simulation, Gen Tech Corp, 60-62. *Concurrent Pos:* Consult, Space Technol Labs, Inc, 59-60, Thompson-Ramo-Wooldridge, Inc, 59-60, Gen Tech Corp, 62-64, Rand Corp, 69-74, Searle Cardio-Pulmonary Systs, Inc, 75-77 & Pac Sierra Corp, 79-; sabbatical, Swiss Fed Inst Technol, Zurich, 85-86 & 97. *Mem:* Am Phys Soc; Sigma Xi; Am Vacuum Soc. *Res:* Secondary emission; surface and high energy physics; ultrahigh vacuum; medical electronics and instrumentation; superconductivity; solid state physics; polarized electron sources; high power flashlamps. *Mailing Add:* Stanford Linear Accelerator Ctr PO Box 4349 Bin 72 Stanford CA 94309. *E-Mail:* garwin@slac.stanford.edu

GARWIN, JEFFREY LLOYD, BIOMEDICAL PRODUCT DEVELOPMENT, BIOCHEMICAL PROCESS ENGINEERING. *Current Pos:* chief tech officer, 94-96, DIR, BIOMODA INC, 93-, CHIEF EXEC OFFICER, 96- *Personal Data:* b Chicago, Ill, Nov 18, 49; m 84, June A Bossinger; c 2. *Educ:* Stanford Univ, BS, 71; Yale Univ, MD, 77, PhD(molecular biophys & biochem), 79; Harvard Univ, CSS, 86. *Prof Exp:* Res fel, Dept Microbiol & Molecular Genetics, Harvard Med Sch, 79-81; res scientist, Biogen Inc, 82-84; consult, Biotechnol Prod Develop, 84-86; asst dir clin res, McNeil Consumer Prods Co, 86-90; dir med & qual assurance, Eggland's Best Inc, 90-91, vpres, 91-93; dir sci & technol, R G Vanderweil Engrs Inc, 93-94. *Concurrent Pos:* Sci adv, RhoMed Inc, 88-96, med dir, 93-96; sci adv, Blue Lighting Data Software & Software Inc, 88-; res asst prof med, Med Col Pa, 94-95, adj asst prof, Hahnemann Sch Med, 95-; clin consult, USANA Inc, 96- *Mem:* Am Chem Soc; AAAS. *Res:* Pharmaceuticals, biotechnology, basic biochemical and biomedical science, managed clinical trials; published numerous articles and holds 4 US patents. *Mailing Add:* 135 Fennerton Rd Paoli PA 19301-1145

GARWIN, RICHARD LAWRENCE, EXPERIMENTAL PHYSICS. *Current Pos:* physicist, IBM Watson Lab, Int Bus Machines Corp, 52-65, dir appl res, Thomas J Watson Res Ctr, 65-66, dir IBM Watson Lab, 66-67, fel, 67-93, EMER FEL, THOMAS J WATSON RES CTR, IBM CORP, 93- *Personal Data:* b Cleveland, Ohio, Apr 19, 28; m 47; c 3. *Educ:* Case Western Res Univ, BS, 47, DSc, 66; Univ Chicago, MS, 48, PhD(physics), 49. *Honors & Awards:* Sci Freedom & Responsibility Award, AAAS, 88; Wright Prize, 83; Erice Sci for Peace Prize, 91; R V Jones Intel Award, US Govt, 96; Enrico Fermi Award, 97; Leo Szilard Award, Am Phys Soc. *Prof Exp:* From instr to asst prof physics, Univ Chicago, 49-52. *Concurrent Pos:* Consult, Los Alamos Sci Lab, 49-; adj prof physics, Columbia Univ, 57-; vis scientist, Europ Orgn Nuclear Res, 59-60; consult, President's Sci Adv Comt, 58-62, mem, 62-65 & 69-72; mem, Defense Sci Bd, 66-68, exec comt, Assembly Math & Phys Sci, Nat Res Coun, 74-77, coun, Nat Acad Sci, coun, Inst Strategic Studies, London, 77-85; mem, Defense Sci Bd, 66-69; vis prof appl physics, Harvard Univ, 74; chmn, Solar Energy Res Inst Comt, Nat Res Coun, 75 & Panel Pub Affairs, Am Phys Soc, 78; chmn, Panel Pub Affairs, Am Phys Soc, 78; prof pub policy, Harvard Univ, 79-81; mem, Pugwash Coun, Am Acad Arts & Sci; Andrew D White prof, Cornell Univ, 83-88; chmn, US Govt Sci & Policy Adv Comn, 92-94. *Mem:* Nat Acad Sci; Nat Acad Eng; Inst Med-Nat Acad Sci; fel Am Phys Soc; fel Am Acad Arts & Sci; Coun Foreign Rels; Am Philos Soc. *Res:* Liquid and solid helium; general physics; electronics in communications and displays; avionics; strategic systems; author of over 200 technical publications; awarded 35 US patents. *Mailing Add:* IBM Corp T J Watson Res Ctr PO Box 218 Yorktown Heights NY 10598

GARWOOD, DOUGLAS LEON, PLANT BREEDING, BIOCHEMICAL GENETICS. *Current Pos:* SECY-TREAS & DIR, GARWOOD SEED CO, 80-; TREAS, SEED ENGRS INC, 93-; TREAS & DIR, GOLDEN HARVEST SEEDS, 94- *Personal Data:* b Taylorville, Ill, Feb 8, 44; m 73, Alice Stout; c Mark & Karen. *Educ:* Univ Ill, Urbana-Champaign, BS, 66, MS, 68; Pa State Univ, PhD(genetics), 73. *Prof Exp:* Asst prof to assoc prof plant breeding, Pa State Univ, 73-80. *Concurrent Pos:* Mem, Golden Harvest Seeds Res & Soybean Comts, 82-, Golden Harvest Seeds Mkt Comt, 89-, Golden Harvest Seeds Customer Serv Comt, 92- *Mem:* Am Soc Hort Sci; Am Soc Agron; Crop Sci Soc Am; Nat Sweet Corn Breeders Asn. *Res:* Genetic and biochemical analysis of sugar, starch and phytoglycogen biosynthesis in maize; performance evaluation of field corn hybrids; sweet corn quality evaluation. *Mailing Add:* 1929 N 2050 East Rd Stonington IL 62567-5306. *Fax:* 217-325-3578; *E-Mail:* d_garwood@msn.com

GARWOOD, JOHN ERNEST, CLINICAL, PSYCHOLOGICAL ASSESSMENT. *Personal Data:* b Philadelphia, Pa, Nov 18, 47; 2, Jacqueline Lydston. *Educ:* Reed Col, BA, 70; Portland State Univ, MS, 78; Case Western Res Univ, PhD(clin psychol), 82. *Prof Exp:* Asst prof psychol, clin psychol, Sch Prof Psychol, Pac Univ, 88-96, dir, Psychol Serv Ctr, 89-90, assoc dir, 90-96. *Mem:* AAAS; Am Psychol Asn; Int Soc Study Mult Personality & Dissociation. *Res:* Assessment and treatment of dissociative disorders; applications of and consequences of Godel's theorem to and for psychology. *Mailing Add:* 2600 SE 59th Ave Portland OR 97206-1448

GARWOOD, MAURICE F, chemical engineering, metallurgy; deceased, see previous edition for last biography

GARWOOD, ROLAND WILLIAM, JR, AIR-SEA INTERACTION, OCEAN TURBULENCE. *Current Pos:* adj res prof, 76-79, PROF OCEANOG, NAVAL POSTGRAD SCH, 79-, ASSOC CHMN, DEPT OCEANOG, 90- *Personal Data:* b Bogota, Colombia, Apr 13, 45; US citizen; m 67, Marilyn Goessling; c Dennis, Sarah & Laura. *Educ:* Bucknell Univ, BS, 67; Univ Wash, PhD(oceanog), 76. *Prof Exp:* Comn officer, Nat Oceanic & Atmospheric Admin Corps, 68-71; res & teaching asst, Univ Wash, 71-76. *Concurrent Pos:* Consult ocean modeling & air-sea interactions, Govt & Indust, 76-; prin investr res grants, Office Naval Res, 77-, NSF, 86-; contrib author, US Nat Report, Int Union Geol & Geophys, 79-; assoc ed, J Phys Oceanog, 83-88 & J Geophys Res, 92-96; adj prof marine sci, Univ Calif, Santa Cruz, 95- *Mem:* Am Geophys Union; Am Meteorol Soc; Sigma Xi; Oceanog Soc. *Res:* The ocean surface mixed layer; turbulence, coupled oceanic-atmospheric models; large-eddy simulation of oceanic convection from tropics to polar seas; approximately forty archived publications on oceanic mixing and air-sea interaction. *Mailing Add:* Naval Postgrad Sch Code OCGD Monterey CA 93943. *E-Mail:* garwood@nps.navy.mil

GARWOOD, VICTOR PAUL, AUDIOLOGY. *Current Pos:* from instr to assoc prof, Sch Med, Univ Southern Calif, 50-59, asst dir, 52-59, co-dir, 59-77, chmn, Grad Prog Commun Dis, 67-71, res assoc, Geront Res Inst, 77-79, prof audiol, 59-88, prof, 60-88, EMER PROF AUDIOL & OTOLARYNGOL, SCH MED, UNIV SOUTHERN CALIF, 88- *Personal Data:* b Detroit, Mich, Sept 13, 17; m 42, Dorothy A Olson; c Martha (Hill) & Don Paul. *Educ:* Univ Mich, BA, 39, MS, 48, PhD(speech path, exp phonetics), 52. *Prof Exp:* Clin asst, Speech Clin, Univ Mich, 46-48, chief exam div, 48-50. *Concurrent Pos:* Inst Neurol Dis & Blindness res fel, 57-58, spec res fel, 61-64; res assoc, Deafness Res Lab, Children's Hosp, Los Angeles, 58-61, consult, 64-; consult, Los Angeles County Hosp, 64-; mem hearing aid dispensers exam comt, Bd Med Examrs, State of Calif, 71-79, chmn, 77-79; med consult, Los Angeles Regional Off, Dept Health, 71-87; spec leave, sr audiologist, Audiol Resource Unit, Los Angeles Unified Sch Dist, 72-76. *Mem:* Emer mem Acoust Soc Am; emer mem Am Psychol Asn; fel Am Speech & Hearing Asn; emer mem Sigma Xi; Acad Rehab Audiol. *Res:* Medical audiology; audition; auditory neurophysiology. *Mailing Add:* 1240 Chautauqua Pacific Palisades CA 90272

GARWOOD, WILLIAM EVERETT, CATALYSIS. *Current Pos:* Res chemist, Socony Vacuum Res Labs, Mobil Res & Develop Corp, 42-55, sr chemist, 55-71, res assoc, 71-81, res scientist, 81-87, CONSULT, MOBIL RES & DEVELOP CORP, 87- *Personal Data:* b Kirkwood, NJ, Oct 25, 19; m 46, Betty Spangberg; c John E, Christine L & Deborah A. *Educ:* Univ NC, BA, 42, grad studies, Temple Univ, 47-54. *Concurrent Pos:* US Navy, 44-46; vis scientist, Univ Ill, 69; adj prof, Rowan Col, 90- *Mem:* Am Chem Soc; Catalysis Soc. *Res:* Chemical catalysis; lubricating oil additives; synthetic lubricants; organophosphorus chemistry; hydrodesulfurization; hydrocracking; zeolite-catalyzed reactions; carbonylation; alkylation. *Mailing Add:* Mobil Technol Co Paulsboro NJ 08066

GARY, JAMES H(UBERT), CHEMICAL ENGINEERING. *Current Pos:* head dept, Colo Sch Mines, 60-72, dir & trustee, Res Inst, 70-72, vpres acad affairs, 72-79, dean fac, 77-79, dir & trustee, Res Inst, 81-84, prof, 60-91, EMER PROF, CHEM ENG & PETROL REFINING, COLO SCH MINES, 91- *Personal Data:* b Victoria, Va, Nov 18, 21; m 45, Jane Zerbee, c 4. *Educ:* Va Polytech Inst, BS, 42, MS, 46; Univ Fla, PhD(chem eng), 51. *Honors & Awards:* Halliburton Award, 81; George R Brown Gold Medal, 87. *Prof Exp:* Group engr chem eng, Stand Oil Co, 46-52; asst prof chem eng & res dir eng exp sta, Univ Va, 52-56; from assoc prof to prof, Univ Ala, 56-60. *Concurrent Pos:* Res assoc, Fla Eng Exp Sta, 49-51; consult, US Bur Mines, 57-60; chmn subcomt oil shale alt energy systs, Energy Resources Group, Nat Res Coun, 76-80; chmn oil shale adv comt, Off Technol Assessment, 77-80; mem, Govs Sci & Technol Coun, 80-82. *Mem:* Am Chem Soc; fel Am Inst Chem Engrs; Am Inst Mining, Metall & Petrol Engrs; Am Soc Eng Educ; fel AAAS. *Res:* Desulfurization of petroleum and coal; organic nitrogen removal; distillation; shale oil; heavy oils processing. *Mailing Add:* 1021 18th St Golden CO 80401-1826. *Fax:* 303-278-9615

GARY, NANCY E, INTERNAL MEDICINE, NEPHROLOGY. *Current Pos:* RETIRED. *Personal Data:* b New York, NY. *Educ:* Springfield Col, BS, 58; Med Col Pa, MD, 62. *Prof Exp:* Clin & res fel nephrology, Sch Med, Georgetown Univ, 65-67; chief nephrology, St Vincent's Hosp & Med Ctr, New York, 67-74; from asst prof to prof med, Rutgers Med Sch, Univ Med & Dent NJ, 74-95, assoc dean, 81-95. *Concurrent Pos:* Instr clin med, Sch Med, NY Univ, 68-74; consult ed, Am J Med, 72-; mem, grad fac physiol, Rutgers State Univ, 77-, grad fac toxicol, 82-; fel, Robert Wood Johnson Health Policy, Inst Med, 87-88; pres, Educ Comt Foreign Med Grads; 95. *Mem:* Am Soc Nephrology; fel Am Col Physicians. *Res:* Clinical nephrology; toxic nephrology; medical education. *Mailing Add:* 2401 Pennsylvania Ave NW Ste 475 Washington DC 20037

GARY, NORMAN ERWIN, APICULTURE, ENTOMOLOGY. *Current Pos:* from asst prof to assoc prof, 62-73, PROF ENTOM, UNIV CALIF, DAVIS, 73- *Personal Data:* b Ocala, Fla, Nov 1, 33; m 54; c 2. *Educ:* Univ Fla, BS, 55; Cornell Univ, PhD(apicult), 59. *Honors & Awards:* J I Hambleton Award. *Prof Exp:* Res assoc apicult, Cornell Univ, 59-62. *Concurrent Pos:* Consult, TV & film spec effects with insects. *Mem:* AAAS; Entom Soc Am; Int Bee Res Asn; Animal Behav Soc; Int Union Study Social Insects. *Res:* Behavior of insects, especially honey bees; economic entomology; foraging behavior of honey bees, flight range and distribution; stinging behavior; Africanized bee behavior. *Mailing Add:* Dept Entom Univ Calif Davis CA 95616. *E-Mail:* fzgary@calweb.com

GARY, ROBERT, SOFTWARE DOCUMENTATION, SCIENCE ADMINISTRATION. *Current Pos:* CONSULT, 87- *Personal Data:* b Baltimore, Md, Apr 15, 28; div; c Risa & Eric. *Educ:* Loyola Col, Md, BS, 50; Yale Univ, MS, 51, PhD(chem), 54. *Prof Exp:* Res chemist, E I du Pont de Nemours & Co, 54-60; chemist, Nat Bur Stand, DC, 60-66, phys sci adminstr, 66-67; independent consult, Univ-Govt Rels, 67-70; mem prog planning staff, Nat Adv Comt Oceans & Atmosphere, US Dept Com, 73-77, asst to dir telecommun, 70-73, res appln analyst, 74-76, policy analyst & writer-ed, 77-82; staff leader, Software & Comput Syst Doc, Nat Weather Serv, 82-87. *Res:* Synthetic fibers in non-garment uses; tire research and development; mixed electrolytes; solvent effects; pH standards in ordinary and heavy water; research planning and program development; telecommunications, teleconferencing, applications research, remote sensing, navigation systems, intelligibility of documentation; software and system documentation. *Mailing Add:* 132 Claybrook Dr Silver Spring MD 20902-3115

GARY, STEPHEN PETER, PLASMA PHYSICS. *Current Pos:* staff mem, 77-87, GROUP LEADER, LOS ALAMOS NAT LAB, 87- *Personal Data:* b Cleveland, Ohio, Oct 3, 39; m 66; c 2. *Educ:* Case Western Res Univ, BS, 61; Washington Univ, St Louis, AM, 66, PhD(physics), 67. *Prof Exp:* Instr physics, Webster Col, 64-67; res assoc, Univ Iowa, 67-68; res asst, Univ St Andrews, 68-69; Leverhulme vis fel, Univ Col NWales, 69-70; from asst prof to assoc prof physics, Col William & Mary, 70-76. *Concurrent Pos:* Vis staff mem, Los Alamos Sci Lab, 74-75. *Mem:* Am Phys Soc; Am Geophys Union. *Res:* Linear, nonlinear plasma instabilities; plasma transport; space plasmas. *Mailing Add:* NIS 1 D466 Los Alamos Nat Lab PO Box 1663 Los Alamos NM 87545. *Fax:* 505-665-3332

GARZA, CESAR MANUEL, MANUFACTURING OF MICRO-ELECTRONIC DEVICES, OPTICAL MICRO-LITHOGRAPHY. *Current Pos:* mem tech staff, 84-89, sr mem tech staff, Semiconductor Process & Design Ctr, 89-96, PHOTO BR MGR PROD, TEX INSTRUMENTS, 96- *Personal Data:* b Monterrey, Mex, May 8, 54; US citizen; c 3. *Educ:* Technol Monterrey, BS, 75; Tex Christian Univ, PhD(phys chem), 80. *Prof Exp:* Staff consult, Kurt Salmon Assoc, 80-82; vpres, Lark Luggage, 82-84. *Concurrent Pos:* Lectr microlithography, Semiconductor Training Ctr, Tex Instruments, 88- *Mem:* Am Chem Soc; Int Soc Optical Eng. *Res:* Investigate and develop all viable technologies capable of printing smaller features to achieve a higher level of integration of semiconductor devices; implement process in manufacturing as appropriate. *Mailing Add:* PO Box 655012 MS 374 Dallas TX 75265. *Fax:* 972-995-1916; *E-Mail:* cgarza@epcot.spdc.ti.com

GARZA, CUTBERTO, MATERNAL-INFANT HEALTH, PROTEIN & ENERGY METABOLISM. *Current Pos:* PROF, CORNELL UNIV, 88-, DIR, DIV NUTRIT SCI, 88- *Personal Data:* b San Diego, Tex, Aug 26, 47; m 70, Yolanda Cadena; c Luis Andres, Carlos Daniel & Areil (Abram). *Educ:* Baylor Univ, BS, 69, MD, 73; Mass Inst Technol, PhD(nutrit biochem), 76. *Honors & Awards:* Alan Shawn Feinstein World Hunger Award. *Prof Exp:* From asst prof to prof nutrit & gastrointestinal, Dept Pediat, Baylor Col Med, 76-84, from asst prof to assoc prof physiol, 77-86. *Concurrent Pos:* Mem food & nutrit bd, Inst Med, 90-93; mem bd Sci Counr, DCPC, Nat Cancer Inst, 90-94; chair, Food & Nutrit Bd, 95; assoc dir, Food & Nutrit Prog, UN Univ. *Mem:* Am Soc Clin Nutrit; Int Soc Res Human Milk & Lactation; Am Inst Nutrit, AAAS; Soc Pediat Res; Am Pediat Soc. *Res:* Functional effects of feeding human milk or commercial formula to infants; regulation of lactation performance. *Mailing Add:* Div Nutrit Sci Savage Hall Cornell Univ Ithaca NY 14853

GARZA LOPEZ, ROBERTO ARTURO, STATISTICAL THERMODYNAMICS, NANOCHEMISTRY. *Current Pos:* lectr & researcher, 92-93, vis assoc prof, 93, ASST PROF PHYS CHEM, POMONA COL, 94- *Personal Data:* b Nuevo Laredo, Mex, Sept 27, 61. *Educ:* Tex A&M Univ, BS, 83; Univ Tex, El Paso, MS, 85; Univ Ga, PhD(chem), 91. *Prof Exp:* Res asst, Univ Tex, El Paso, 85, Univ Notre Dame, 87. *Concurrent Pos:* Vis scholar, Stanford Univ, 96- *Mem:* Am Chem Soc; Soc Chem Mex; Sigma Xi. *Res:* Theoretical studies in chemical kinetics with particular application to diffusion; nanomanipulation of vesicles and femtochemistry. *Mailing Add:* 645 N College Ave Claremont CA 91711. *Fax:* 909-621-8410; *E-Mail:* rgaraz@pomona.edu

GARZOLI, SILVIA L, PHYSICAL OCEANOGRAPHY. *Current Pos:* vis res scientist, 80-81, assoc res scientist, 81-85, SR RES SCIENTIST, LAMONT-DOHERTY EARTH OBSERV, COLUMBIA UNIV, 85-; OCEANOGR, ATLANTIC OCEANOG & METEOROL LAB, NAT OCEANOG & ATMOSPHERIC ADMIN, 96- *Personal Data:* b Buenos Aires, Arg, Nov 16, 41. *Educ:* Univ Buenos Aires, MS, 65; Univ La Plata, Buenos Aires, PhD(physics), 68. *Prof Exp:* Assoc res scientist, Argentine Nat Res Coun, Argentine Inst Radioastron, 69-72 & 74-75, Lab Physical Oceanog, France, 75-80; instr, Physics Dept, Buenos Aires Univ Arg, 72-74, assoc prof, 74. *Concurrent Pos:* Consult, Group Experts Sci Aspects Marine Pollution, Orgn Econ Coop & Develop, UN Environ Prog; UNESCO fel, Italy, 75; prin investr, Nat Res Coun Argentina, 88; vis scientist, Univ Miami, 89; prog dir, NSF, 92-94; secy, Phys Oceanog Sect, Am Geophys Union, 96-98. *Mem:* Argentine-NAm Asn Advan Sci Technol & Cult (vpres, 86-90); NY Acad Sci; Am Geophys Union; Int Astron Union; Nat Res Coun Arg; Arg Asn Astron. *Mailing Add:* Atlantic Oceanog & Meteorol Lab Nat Oceanic & Atmospheric Admin 4301 Rickenbacker Causeway Miami FL 33149-1026. *Fax:* 305-361-4412; *E-Mail:* garzoli@aoml.noaa.gov

GARZON, MAX, INTELLIGENT SYSTEMS, NEURAL NETWORKS & CELLULAR AUTOMATA. *Current Pos:* from asst prof to assoc prof, 84-95, PROF COMPUT SCI, UNIV MEMPHIS, 95- *Personal Data:* b Bogota, Columbia, Oct 1, 53; m 75; c 2. *Educ:* Nat Univ, Columbia, BS, 75; Univ Ill, MS, 80, PhD(comput sci), 84. *Prof Exp:* Asst prof math, Nat Univ, Columbia, 82. *Concurrent Pos:* Prin investr, NSF, 86-90; vis prof, LIP-Ecole Normale, Lyon, France, 91-92. *Mem:* Inst Elec & Electronics Engrs; Asn Comput Mach. *Res:* Study models of computation by artificial and natural intelligence, particularly neural networks, automata networks, dynamical systems and their applications to high-performance computing. *Mailing Add:* Math Sci Univ Memphis Memphis TN 38152

GARZON, RUBEN DARIO, ARC INTERRUPTION, SOLID STATE SWITCHING. *Current Pos:* DIR ENG, SQUARE D. *Personal Data:* b Quito, Ecuador, May 1, 37; US citizen; m 62; c 2. *Educ:* Calif State Univ, Los Angeles, BSEE, 68; Pa State Univ, MESc, 73. *Prof Exp:* Develop engr, ITE-Gould, 68-74; proj mgr, Gould-Brown Boueri, 74-79; sr proj mgr, Brown Boveri Elec, 80-85; dir eng, Asea Brown Boveri, 85- *Concurrent Pos:* Prin investr, Energy Res & Develop Admin, US Dept Energy, 74-76, Elec Power

Res Inst, 78-80 & US Dept Energy, 80-81; mem adv panel, NSF Arc Res Proj grant, Univ Mich, 75-77. *Mem:* Sr mem Inst Elec & Electronics Engrs. *Res:* High current, high pressure arc interruption in sulfur hexaflouride circuit breakers; advanced development of switch gear devices using concepts for reduction and interruption of fault currents. *Mailing Add:* 9400 Raven Hollow Rd Brentwood TN 37027

GASARCH, WILLIAM JAN, STRUCTURAL COMPLEXITY THEORY, COMPUTATIONAL LEARNING THEORY. *Current Pos:* Asst prof, 85-91, ASSOC PROF COMPUT SCI, UNIV MD, COLLEGE PARK, 91- *Personal Data:* b New York, NY, Nov 30, 59; m 91, Carolyn Brophy. *Educ:* State Univ NY, Stony Brook, BS, 80; Harvard Univ, MS, 82, PhD(comput sci), 85. *Mem:* Asn Comput Mach. *Res:* View the number of questions one needs to ask to solve a problem to be a measure of that problem complexity. *Mailing Add:* 13228 Copland Ct Silver Spring MD 20904. *Fax:* 301-405-6707; *E-Mail:* gasarch@cs.umd.edu

GASBARRE, LOUIS CHARLES, BOVINE IMMUNOLOGY. *Current Pos:* MICROBIOLOGIST IMMUNOPARASITOL, AGR RES SERV, USDA, 81- *Personal Data:* b Ridgway, Pa, May 15, 48; m 70; c 2. *Educ:* Ind Univ, Pa, BS, 70; Univ Md, MS, 74, PhD(zool), 78. *Prof Exp:* Postdoctoral fel immunol, Res & Training Ctr, WHO, 78-80. *Concurrent Pos:* Mem bd dirs, Am Asn Vet Immunologists, 89- *Mem:* Am Asn Immunologists; Am Asn Vet Immunologists; Am Asn Vet Parasitologists; AAAS. *Res:* Immunology of gastrointestinal nematodes infections of ruminants and definition of cellular immune responses of cattle. *Mailing Add:* Animal Parasitol Inst USDA ARS Bldg 1040 Rm 103 Barc-E Beltsville MD 20705. *Fax:* 301-504-5306

GASCHO, GARY JOHN, SOIL FERTILITY. *Current Pos:* PROF SOIL FERTIL, COASTAL PLAIN EXP STA, UNIV GA, 80- *Personal Data:* b Bad Axe, Mich, Apr 9, 41; m 61, Marilyn Ballagh; c John E & Laura J. *Educ:* Mich State Univ, BS, 63, PhD(soil fertil & plant physiol), 68; Univ Ill, MS, 65. *Honors & Awards:* Outstanding Res Award, Sigma Xi, 83; Carter-Jones Award Outstanding Contrib Soil Sci, 87. *Prof Exp:* From asst prof to prof plant nutrit, Agr Res & Educ Ctr, Univ Fla, 68-80. *Concurrent Pos:* Actg dir, Agr Res & Educ Ctr, Belle Glade, Fla, 79-80; consult. *Mem:* Am Soc Agron; Soil Sci Soc Am; Am Peanut Res & Educ Soc; Coun Agr Sci & Technol; Am Soc Sugarcane Technol; Sigma Xi. *Res:* Peanut nutrition and fertility; sugarcane nutrition and physiology; alternate agronomic crop nutrition; fertility of irrigated crops; fertigation; tissue and soil analysis; nutrition of peanut; foliar feeding. *Mailing Add:* Coastal Plain Exp Sta Box 748 Tifton GA 31793. *Fax:* 912-386-7293; *E-Mail:* gascho@tifton.cpes.peachnet.edu

GASCOIGNE, NICHOLAS ROBERT JOHN, T CELL RECEPTOR STRUCTURE & BIOLOGY, T-CELL DEVELOPMENT. *Current Pos:* asst mem, 87-92, ASSOC PROF, DEPT IMMUNOL, SCRIPPS RES INST, 93- *Personal Data:* b London, Eng, Jan 13, 58; m 86, Stephanie Bremond; c Francesca. *Educ:* Univ Wales, UK, BSc Hons, 80; Univ London, PhD(immunol), 83. *Prof Exp:* Postdoctoral fel molecular immunol, Dept Med Microbiol, Stanford Univ Sch Med, 83-87. *Concurrent Pos:* Scholar, Leukemia Soc Am, 89-94; fac mem, Grad Prog Molecular & Cellular Biol, Scripps Res Inst, 90- *Mem:* Am Asn Immunologists; AAAS. *Res:* Various aspects of T-cell activation, particularly on the genes and structure of the T-cell receptor for antigen; produced soluble form of the receptor for biochemical analysis; measured kinetics of T-cell receptor binding to ligands that cause positive or negative T-cell selection in the thymus. *Mailing Add:* Dept Immunol Scripps Res Inst 10550 N Torrey Pines Rd La Jolla CA 92037-1092. *Fax:* 619-784-9272; *E-Mail:* gascoigne@scripps.edu

GASCOYNE, PETER RUSSELL CHARLES, BIOPHYSICS, SORTING OF CELLS. *Current Pos:* vis scientist, 86-87, asst prof, 87-93, ASSOC PROF EXP PATH, MD ANDERSON CANCER CTR, UNIV TEX, 93- *Personal Data:* b Drayton, Eng, Jan 10, 52; US citizen; m 80, Lynn Marie Maxwell; c Maya Victoria (Upjohn) & Maxwell Peter McKay. *Educ:* Univ Wales, BSc, 73, PhD(biophys), 79. *Prof Exp:* Vis scientist, Marine Biol Lab, Woods Hole, 76-79, postdoctoral fel, 79-82, res assoc, 82-86. *Concurrent Pos:* Assoc prof, Health Sci Ctr, Univ Tex, 94- *Mem:* Am Asn Cancer Res; Eng Med & Biol Soc; Inst Elec & Electronics Engrs; Biophys Soc. *Res:* Aggregate intrinsic biophysical properties of cells represent a phenotypic descriptor of cell structure and function that can be used for cell identification and manipulation; characterize and exploit this marker for biomedical and bioengineering applications through electrical and dielectric approaches. *Mailing Add:* Dept Exp Path No 089 MD Anderson Cancer Ctr Univ Tex 1515 Holcombe Blvd Houston TX 77030. *Fax:* 713-792-5940; *E-Mail:* peter@solace.mdacc.tmc.edu

GASDORF, EDGAR CARL, ANIMAL PHYSIOLOGY. *Current Pos:* From instr to asst prof, 59-66, ASSOC PROF BIOL, BRADLEY UNIV, 66- *Personal Data:* b Decatur, Ind, Nov 27, 31; m 58; c 1. *Educ:* Purdue Univ, BS, 53, MS, 56, PhD(biol sci), 59. *Mem:* AAAS; Ecol Soc Am; Am Inst Biol Sci. *Res:* Reptilian physiological ecology. *Mailing Add:* 60770 W LaSalle Rd Montrose CO 81401

GASH, KENNETH BLAINE, ORGANIC CHEMISTRY. *Current Pos:* assoc prof, 67-77, PROF CHEM, CALIF STATE COL, DOMINGUEZ HILLS, 77- *Personal Data:* b Brooklyn, NY, Jan 2, 33; m 63; c 2. *Educ:* Pratt Inst, BS, 60; Ariz State Univ, PhD(org chem), 68. *Prof Exp:* Lab asst chem, Chas Pfizer & Co, Inc, NY, 50-52, res asst, 56-60; teacher pub schs, NY, 60-63. *Mem:* Am Chem Soc; Sigma Xi. *Res:* Chemistry of carbonium ions, acyl and aroyl-oxonium ions; investigations of linear free energy relationships; synthesis of novel compounds; redesigning undergraduate organic laboratory programs. *Mailing Add:* Calif State Univ Dominguez Hills 1000 E Victoria St Carson CA 90747-0001

GASH, VIRGIL WALTER, PROCESS TECHNOLOGY, AGRICULTURAL CHEMISTRY. *Current Pos:* RETIRED. *Personal Data:* b Rock Falls, Ill, June 28, 19; m 44, Gaynell L Franklin; c Linda & David. *Educ:* Cornell Col, BA, 42; Univ Ill, MS, 47, PhD(chem), 52. *Prof Exp:* Res chemist org chem, William S Merrell Co, 47-50; sr res group leader, Monsanto Co, St Louis, 52-76, mgr res, Monsanto Agr Prod Co, 76-82. *Mem:* Am Chem Soc. *Res:* Fluorocarbons; nitrogen heterocyclics and unsaturated nitrogen compounds; steroids; oxidations; aromatic substitution; alicyclic stereochemistry; functional fluids; agricultural chemistry. *Mailing Add:* 1689 Dawes Rd NE Palm Bay FL 32905

GASIC, GABRIEL J, PATHOLOGY. *Current Pos:* RETIRED. *Personal Data:* b Punta Arenas, Chile, Mar 18, 12; m 53; c 3. *Educ:* Univ Chile, MD, 38. *Honors & Awards:* Paget-Ewing Award, Metastasis Res Soc, 90- *Prof Exp:* Prof biol, Sch Med, Univ Chile, 48-60, dir oncol, 60-65; res assoc, Univ Pa, 60-63, res prof, 66-67, prof path, 67-80; prof, Lab Exp Oncol, Pa Hosp, Philadelphia. *Concurrent Pos:* John Simon Guggenheim Mem Found res fel, 43; Carnegie Inst Res Univ res fel, 44-46; res fel, Rockefeller Univ, 46-47; grants, Rockefeller Found, Damon Runyon Mem Fund, Am Cancer Soc/Nat Cancer Inst, NSF & Pop Coun. *Mem:* AAAS; Am Soc Cell Biol; Histochem Soc; Am Asn Cancer Res; Chilean Acad Sci & Med; Int Soc Thrombosis & Hemostasis. *Res:* Cell surface histochemistry and biology; tumor invasiveness; tumor cell-platelet interactions; growth factors. *Mailing Add:* 221 Richard Way Collegeville PA 19428

GASICH, WELKO E, AERONAUTICAL ENGINEERING. *Current Pos:* CONSULT, 88- *Personal Data:* b Cupertino, Calif, Mar, 28, 22. *Educ:* Stanford Univ, BA, 43, MS, 47. *Prof Exp:* Corp vpres & asst gen mgr technol, Northrop Corp, 61-66, Corp vpres, Ventura Div, 67-71, corp vpres, Aircraft Div, 71-76, corp vpres & group exec, Aircraft Group, 76-79, sr vpres advan projs, 79-85, exec vpres prog, 85-88. *Mem:* Nat Acad Eng; fel Am Inst Aeronaut & Astronaut; fel Soc Automotive Engrs. *Mailing Add:* 3517 Caribeth Dr Encino CA 91436

GASIDLO, JOSEPH MICHAEL, REACTOR PHYSICS, NUCLEAR ENGINEERING. *Current Pos:* resident assoc reactor eng, 59-60, physicist, fast reactors, 60-85, SPECIALIST NUCLEAR CRITICALITY SAFETY, ARGONNE NAT LAB, 65-, NUCLEAR SAFETY NON-REACTOR NUCLEAR FACIL, 87- *Personal Data:* b Detroit, Mich June 29, 35. *Educ:* Wayne State Univ, BSE, 58, MSE, 61. *Prof Exp:* Teaching asst eng mech, Wayne State Univ, 58-59. *Mem:* Am Nuclear Soc. *Res:* Neutron physics of fast breeder reactors specializing in reactivity measurements and reaction rate measurements; criticality safety in handling and processing fissile materials. *Mailing Add:* 1980 McEnzie Ave Idaho Falls ID 83404

GASIORKIEWICZ, EUGENE CONSTANTINE, PLANT SCIENCE, PLANT PATHOLOGY. *Current Pos:* from assoc prof to prof life sci, Univ Wis-Parkside, 68-70, chmn, Div Sci, 68-73, dir, natural sci areas, 68-77, EMER PROF LIFE SCI & ALLIED HEALTH, UNIV WIS-PARKSIDE, 88- *Personal Data:* b Grabiszew, Poland, Mar 11, 20; nat US; m 46; c 2. *Educ:* Marquette Univ, AB, 47, MS, 48; Univ Wis, PhD(plant path), 51. *Prof Exp:* Asst bot, Marquette Univ, 46-48; asst plant path, Univ Wis, 48-51, proj assoc, USDA, 51-52; asst res prof bot, Univ Mass, 52-58, asst prof plant path, Waltham Field Sta, 58-61; horticulturist & plant pathologist, Plant Sci Lab, Biol Res Ctr, S C Johnson & Son, Inc, 61-65; asst prof bot, Univ Wis-Parkside, Racine Campus, 66-67; dir res & tech serv, Can-Am Plant Co, Ltd, 67-68. *Concurrent Pos:* Med malpractice investr, 88- *Mem:* AAAS; Am Phytopath Soc; Am Inst Biol Sci. *Res:* Diseases of greenhouse florist crops; turf and ornamental plants; growth regulants and disease development; pathogen free plants and disease control; ecology of natural areas; Prairie restoration. *Mailing Add:* 236 Old Pine Circle Racine WI 53402

GASIOROWICZ, STEPHEN G, PARTICLE PHYSICS. *Current Pos:* assoc prof, 60-63, PROF PHYSICS, UNIV MINN, MINNEAPOLIS, 63- *Personal Data:* b Gdansk, Poland, May 10, 28; nat US; m 53, Hilde Fromm; c 3. *Educ:* Univ Calif, Los Angeles, AB, 48, MA, 49, PhD(theoret physics), 52. *Prof Exp:* Physicist, Lawrence Radiation Lab, Univ Calif, 52-60; NSF fel, Inst Theoret Physics, Copenhagen & European Orgn Nuclear Res, 57-58; vis scientist, Max Planck Inst Physics & Astrophys, 59-60. *Concurrent Pos:* Consult, Argonne Nat Lab, 61-70; vis scientist, Nordic Inst Theoret Atomic Physics, Copenhagen & Univ Marseille, 64 & Deutsches Elektron-Synchroton, Hamburg, 68-69 & 80; trustee, Aspen Ctr Physics, 80-86; vis prof, Univ Tokyo, 82. *Mem:* Fel Am Phys Soc. *Res:* Elementary particle physics. *Mailing Add:* Sch Physics Univ Minn Minneapolis MN 55455. *Fax:* 612-624-4578; *E-Mail:* gasior@maroon.tc.umn.edu

GASKELL, DAVID R, METALLURGY. *Current Pos:* PROF METALL ENG, PURDUE UNIV, 82- *Personal Data:* b Glasgow, Scotland, Mar 11, 40; m 64; c 3. *Educ:* Glasgow Univ, BSc, 62; McMaster Univ, PhD(metall), 67. *Hon Degrees:* MA, Univ Pa, 72. *Prof Exp:* Metallurgist, LaPorte Chem Ltd, Luton, Eng, 62-64; from asst prof to assoc prof metall, Univ Pa, 67-79, prof metall & geol, 79-82. *Mem:* Am Inst Mining, Metall & Petrol Engrs; Can Inst Mining & Metall; Iron & Steel Inst Japan; Am Soc Metals. *Res:* Physical chemistry of liquid oxide systems; slag-metal chemistry; thermodynamics; chemical and extraction metallurgy. *Mailing Add:* Sch Mat Eng Mat & Elec Eng Bldg Purdue Univ West Lafayette IN 47907. *Fax:* 765-494-1204

GASKELL, PETER, PHYSIOLOGY. *Current Pos:* From asst prof to prof physiol, 55-85, EMER PROF, UNIV MAN, 86- *Personal Data:* b Lancashire, Eng, June 24, 17; m 40; c 3. *Educ:* Univ Western Ont, MD, 50; Univ London, PhD(physiol), 55. *Concurrent Pos:* Med res assoc, Med Res Coun Can, 57-; mem clin invest unit, Winnipeg Gen Hosp, 57-85. *Res:* Peripheral circulation, especially in the limbs; hypertension. *Mailing Add:* 826 Campbell St Winnipeg MB R3N 1C6 Can

GASKELL, ROBERT EUGENE, APPLIED MATHEMATICS. *Current Pos:* chmn dept, 66-72, prof, 66-80, EMER PROF MATH, NAVAL POSTGRAD SCH, 80- *Personal Data:* b Grelton, Ohio, Jan 18, 12; m 40, Jane Weyand; c Ellen (Alcock) & Robert W. *Educ:* Albion Col, AB, 33; Univ Mich, MS, 34, PhD(math), 40. *Prof Exp:* Instr math, Albion Col, 38-39 & Univ Ala, 40-42; res fel mech, Brown Univ, 42-43, res assoc, 43-46; asst prof math, Iowa State Univ, 47-49, assoc prof, 49-51; supvr math servs unit, Boeing Airplane Co, 51-59; prof math, Ore State Univ, 59-66. *Mem:* Fel AAAS; Soc Indust & Appl Math; Math Asn Am; Am Soc Eng Educ. *Res:* Industrial and engineering applications of mathematics. *Mailing Add:* 1207 Sylvan Rd Monterey CA 93940

GASKELL, ROBERT WEYAND, PLANETARY PHYSICS. *Current Pos:* mem tech staff, 84-97, SR ENGR, JET PROPULSION LAB, 97- *Personal Data:* b Providence, RI, July 9, 45; m 67; c 3. *Educ:* Brown Univ, ScB, 67; McGill Univ, PhD(physics), 72. *Prof Exp:* Fel physics, Carleton Univ, 72-74 & Univ Toronto, 74-75; res assoc physics, McGill Univ, 75-77; asst prof physics, Lafayette Col, 77-84. *Mem:* Am Phys Soc. *Res:* Satellite shape and topography; planetary surface simulations. *Mailing Add:* 1865 Sonoma Dr Altadena CA 91001

GASKILL, HERBERT STOCKTON, psychiatry, for more information see previous edition

GASKILL, IRVING E, MATHEMATICS. *Current Pos:* RETIRED. *Personal Data:* b Mt Holly, NJ, Feb 24, 22; m 58, Bertha Mae Kenyon; c Irving Thomas, Robert John & Mary Elizabeth (Horton). *Educ:* Trenton State Teachers Col, BS, 43; Univ Pa, MA, 47. *Prof Exp:* Instr math, Bowling Green State Univ, 47-49; mathematician, Army Map Serv, 51-56 & US Army Engr Math Comput Agency, 56-70; dir math & comput lab, Nat Resource Anal Ctr, 70-75, Fed Preparedness Agency, 75-80. *Mem:* Am Math Soc. *Res:* Mathematical models for computation on electronic computer; economic models; war gaming vulnerability models; nuclear damage assessment models; geodetic network and datum adjustments. *Mailing Add:* 405 Belmont Dr SW Leesburg VA 22075-3510

GASKILL, JACK DONALD, OPTICAL SCIENCES, OPTOELECTRONICS. *Current Pos:* from asst prof to assoc prof, Univ Ariz, 68-75, adminr acad affairs, 80-88, assoc dir, Optical Sci Ctr, 88-93, PROF OPTICAL SCI, UNIV ARIZ, 75-, PROF ELEC & COMPUT ENGR, 88- *Personal Data:* b Ft Collins, Colo, Dec 9, 35; m 56, Sandra Dennison; c Carolyn (Ower) & Cynthia. *Educ:* Colo State Univ, BS, 57; Stanford Univ, MS, 65, PhD(elec eng), 68. *Prof Exp:* Electronics engr, Motorola, Inc, 57-58; res asst elec eng, Stanford Univ, 63-68. *Concurrent Pos:* Consult, US Army Res Off, 70-, Hughes Res Labs, 74-78, Bendix Corp, 78-80, Univ Ala, 89-92 & Lyon & Lyon, 93. *Mem:* Inst Elec & Electronics Engrs; fel Optical Soc Am; fel Soc Photo-Optical Instrument Engrs (vpres/pres elect, 94). *Res:* Fourier optics; holography; medical optics. *Mailing Add:* Optical Sci Ctr Univ Ariz Tucson AZ 85721. *Fax:* 520-621-6778; *E-Mail:* jgaskill@ccit.arizona.edu

GASKIN, DAVID EDWARD, MARINE BIOLOGY & MAMMALS ENTOMOLOGY, LEPIDOPTERA. *Current Pos:* assoc prof, 68-80, PROF MARINE BIOL, DEPT ZOOL, UNIV GUELPH, 80- *Personal Data:* b Croydon, Eng, June 21, 39; m 62, Maureen Wood; c Ross & Paul. *Educ:* Bristol Univ, BSc, 61; Massey Univ, NZ, PhD(entom), 68. *Prof Exp:* Whaling inspector & biologist, Brit Ministry Agr Fisheries & Food-Nat Inst Oceanog, Wormley, Eng, 61-62; asst exp officer fisheries res, Brit Ministry Agr Fisheries & Food, Lowestoft, 62; whale fisheries biologist, Fisheries Res Div, Wellington, NZ, 62-65; lectr zool, Massey Univ, NZ, 65-68. *Mem:* Fel Royal Entom Soc London; NZ Entom Soc; Lepidoptera Soc. *Res:* Ecology and biology of cetaceans; systematics and ecology of the lepidoptera; biogeography. *Mailing Add:* Dept Zool Univ Guelph Guelph ON N1G 2W1 Can. *Fax:* 519-767-1656

GASKIN, FELICIA, BIOCHEMISTRY, NEUROCHEMISTRY. *Current Pos:* PROF PSYCHIAT, MED UNIV VA, 88-, J PRELLOW DARDEN PROF, SCH MED, 88- *Personal Data:* b Carlisle, Pa, Jan 17, 43; m 69, Shu Man Fu; c Kai-Ming & Kai-Mei. *Educ:* Dickinson Col, AB, 65; Bryn Mawr Col, MA, 67; Univ Calif, San Francisco, PhD(biochem), 69. *Prof Exp:* Fel psychiat, Stanford Univ, 69-71; res assoc phys biochem, Rockefeller Univ, 71-72 & Columbia Univ, 72-74; from asst prof to assoc prof path & biophys, Albert Einstein Col Med, 74-82; mem & prof, Okla Med Res Found, Univ Okla, 82-88. *Concurrent Pos:* Nat Inst Neurol Dis & Stroke spec res fel, 72-74; NIH res career develop award, 75-80. *Mem:* Am Chem Soc; Soc Neurosci; Am Asn Neuropath; NY Acad Sci; Am Soc Biochem & Molecular Biol; Am Soc Cell Biol. *Res:* Microtubule assembly; neurofibrous proteins in aging; immunological probes to study Alzheimer's disease; author or coauthor of more than 50 scientific articles in scientific journals and books. *Mailing Add:* Dept Psychiat Med Univ Va Sch Med PO Box 203 Charlottesville VA 22908

GASKIN, JACK MICHAEL, VETERINARY MICROBIOLOGY. *Current Pos:* asst prof vet sci & asst virologist, 73-80, ASSOC PROF, DEPT INFECTIOUS DIS, UNIV FLA, 80- *Personal Data:* b Watertown, NY, Jan 8, 43; m; c 3. *Educ:* Cornell Univ, DVM, 67, PhD(vet microbiol), 73. *Prof Exp:* Vet, NY, 67-73. *Mem:* Am Vet Med Asn. *Res:* Bovine syncytial virus isolations; canine distemper virus in domesticated cats and pigs; herpes virus infection of psittacine birds resembling Pacheio's parrot disease. *Mailing Add:* 2606 NW 67th Terr Gainesville FL 32606

GASKINS, H REX, DEVELOPMENTAL ENDOCRINOLOGY, LOCAL HORMONES & TISSUE DEVELOPMENT. *Current Pos:* ASST PROF IMMUNOL, UNIV ILL, 92- *Personal Data:* b Morehead City, NC, Jan 30, 58; m 87. *Educ:* NC State Univ, BS, 81, MS, 86; Univ Ga, PhD(cell biol), 89. *Prof Exp:* Fel, Am Diabetes Asn, 89-91; fel, Juv Diabetes Found Int, Jackson Lab, 91-92; fel, Ctr Advan Study, Univ Ill, 96. *Mem:* Am Diabetes Asn; Am Asn Immunologists; Soc Exp Biol & Med; AAAS; Juv Diabetes Found Int; Am Soc Microbiol. *Res:* Immunologic mechanisms which underlie pancreatic beta cell destruction in mouse models of diabetes, utilize both classical and molecular genetics techniques to identify genes encoding diabetes susceptibility and determine how their expression in beta cells and macrophages contributes to disease. *Mailing Add:* Dept Animal Sci Univ Ill 1207 W Gregory Dr Urbana IL 61801

GASPAR, MAX RAYMOND, SURGERY, VASCULAR SURGERY. *Current Pos:* SURGEON, HARRIMAN JONES CLIN HOSP, 48-; CHIEF OF STAFF, ST MARY'S HOSP, 67- *Personal Data:* b Sioux City, Iowa, May 10, 15; m 38; c 5. *Educ:* Morningside Col, AB, 36; Univ SDak, BS, 38; Univ Southern Calif, MD, 41; Am Bd Surg, dipl; FACS. *Concurrent Pos:* Clin instr, Univ Calif, Los Angeles, 52-54; assoc clin prof surg, Loma Linda Univ, 53-61, clin prof, 62-65; clin prof, Univ Southern Calif, 65-; dir peripheral vascular serv, Los Angeles Co Hosp, 54-; consult vascular surg, US Naval Hosp, Long Beach. *Mem:* Int Soc Surg; Am Surg Asn; Soc Vascular Surg; Int Cardiovasc Soc; Soc Clin Vascular Surg (pres, 79-81). *Res:* Intestinal anastomosis; vascular surgery. *Mailing Add:* Long Beach Surg Group 1045 Atlantic Long Beach CA 90813-3408

GASPAR, PETER PAUL, PHYSICAL ORGANIC CHEMISTRY, RADIOCHEMISTRY. *Current Pos:* from asst prof to assoc prof, 63-73, PROF CHEM, WASHINGTON UNIV, 73- *Personal Data:* b Brussels, Belg, June 20, 35; US citizen; m 65; c 1. *Educ:* Calif Inst Technol, BS, 57; Yale Univ, MS, 58, PhD(chem), 61. *Honors & Awards:* Frederic Stanley Kipping Award, Organocilicon Chem, 86. *Prof Exp:* NATO fel org chem, Univ Heidelberg, 61-62; res fel chem, Calif Inst Technol, 62-63. *Concurrent Pos:* Res collabr, Brookhaven Nat Lab, 69- *Mem:* Am Chem Soc; Royal Soc Chem. *Res:* Reaction mechanisms; reactive intermediates; photochemistry; gasphase reactions of free atoms and free radicals; organosilicon chemistry; main group organometalic chemistry; archaeometry. *Mailing Add:* Dept Chem Wash Univ St Louis MO 63130-4899

GASPARD, KATHRYN JANE, ENDOCRINOLOGY. *Current Pos:* ASST PROF PHYSIOL & PATHOPHYSIOL, SCH NURSING, MED COL WIS, 81- *Educ:* Med Col Wis, PhD(physiol), 75. *Mailing Add:* Sch Nursing Med Col Wis 1921 E Hartford Ave Milwaukee WI 53212

GASPARINI, FRANCIS MARINO, LOW TEMPERATURE PHYSICS. *Current Pos:* PROF PHYSICS, STATE UNIV NY, BUFFALO, 73- *Personal Data:* b Trieste, Italy, Oct 14, 41; US citizen; m 67; c 2. *Educ:* Villanova Univ, BS, 64; Univ Minn, MS, 66, PhD(physics), 70. *Prof Exp:* Instr physics, Villanova Univ, 66-67; fel, Ohio State Univ, 70-73. *Mem:* Fel Am Phys Soc; AAAS; Sigma Xi. *Res:* Critical aspects of the superfluid transition and surface properties of helium; finite size effects at phase transitions; two-dimensional behavior of He-3. *Mailing Add:* Dept Physics Fronczak Hall State Univ NY Buffalo Amherst NY 14260

GASPAROVIC, RICHARD FRANCIS, APPLIED PHYSICS, SYSTEMS ENGINEERING. *Current Pos:* PRIN STAFF PHYSICIST OCEAN REMOTE SENSING, APPL PHYSICS LAB, JOHNS HOPKINS UNIV, 71- *Personal Data:* b Endicott, NY, Mar 9, 41; m 65; c 2. *Educ:* Fordham Univ, BS, 63; Univ Pa, MS, 64; Rutgers Univ, PhD(physics), 69. *Prof Exp:* Engr electronics, RCA Corp, 69-71. *Mem:* Am Geophys Soc; Am Phys Soc; AAAS. *Res:* Remote sensing of ocean surface; air-sea interaction processes; infrared systems engineering; digital image processing. *Mailing Add:* Johns Hopkins Univ Johns Hopkins Rd Laurel MD 20723

GASPARRINI, CLAUDIA, MICROANALYSIS, MINERALOGY APPLIED TO THE PROCESS OF METAL EXTRACTION & PRECIOUS METALS. *Current Pos:* pres & owner, Jacksonville, Fla, 81-86, PRES & OWNER, MINMET SCI LTD, TORONTO, CAN, 77-, TUCSON, ARIZ, 86- *Personal Data:* b Genova, Italy, Apr 25, 41; Can citizen. *Educ:* Univ Rome, Italy, DSc(earth sci), 65; Univ Cambridge, Eng, dipl, 66. *Honors & Awards:* Cert Appreciation, Int Precious Metals Inst, 96. *Prof Exp:* Sr technician, res asst & res assoc, Univ Toronto, 66-72; phys scientist II, Geol Surv Can, Ottawa, 73; res scientist & mineralogist, Nat Inst Metall, Johannesburg, SAfrica, 74-75; independent consult, 76. *Concurrent Pos:* Mem & vchmn, Process Mineral Comt, Am Inst Mining Engrs, 80; pres & owner, Space Eagle Publ Co Inc, Tucson, Ariz, 89-; mem, Res Bd Adv, Am Biog Inst, 90-; mem, Sci-by-Mail Prog, Mus Sci, Science Park, Boston, 90-92; counr, Europ Soc Appl Geol & Mineral, 96-; adv, Int Precious Metals Inst, China, 96; hon mem, Organizing Comt, Int Conf Precious Metals, Kosice, Slovakia, 95. *Mem:* Can Inst Mining & Metall; Int Precious Metal Inst; Soc Geol Appl Mineral Deposits; Am Asn Women Sci; Europ Soc Appl Geol & Mineral. *Res:* Developed techniques for the microanalysis of minerals; mineralogy as related to the process of extraction; precious metals; author of about 50 publications on microanalysis, ore microcompositions, mineralogy, including books on precious metals. *Mailing Add:* Minmet Sci Ltd 6651 N Campbell No 102 Tucson AZ 85718

GASPER, GEORGE, JR, MATHEMATICAL ANALYSIS. *Current Pos:* from asst prof to assoc prof, 70-76, PROF MATH, NORTHWESTERN UNIV, 76- *Personal Data:* b Hamtramck, Mich, Oct 10, 39; m 67, Brigitta Zemlicka; c Karen & Kenneth. *Educ:* Mich Technol Univ, BS, 62; Wayne State Univ, MA, 64, PhD(math), 67. *Prof Exp:* NSF vis lectr math, Univ Wis, Madison, 67-68; Nat Res Coun Can fel, 68-69; vis asst prof math, Univ Toronto, 69-70. *Concurrent Pos:* NASA traineeship, 66-67; Alfred P Sloan fel, 73-75. *Mem:* Am Math Soc; Soc Indust & Appl Math. *Res:* Analysis; special functions; multipliers; orthogonal expansions; convolution structures; positive kernels; basic hypergeometric series. *Mailing Add:* Northwestern Univ 2033 Sheridan Rd Northwestern Univ Evanston IL 60208-2730. *Fax:* 847-491-8906; *E-Mail:* george@math.nwu.edu

GASS, CLINTON BURKE, MATHEMATICS. *Current Pos:* from assoc prof to prof, DePauw Univ, 54-64, head, Dept Math, Astron & Comput Sci, 60-84, John T & Margaret Deal prof math, 64-86, sr prof, 86-90, EMER PROF MATH, DEPAUW UNIV, 90- *Personal Data:* b Minn, Jan 9, 20; m 41; c 3. *Educ:* Gustavus Adolphus Col, AB, 41; Univ Nebr, MA, 43, PhD(math), 54. *Prof Exp:* Instr math, Univ Nebr, 42-43; from assoc prof to prof, Nebr Wesleyan Univ, 43-47, prof & dean men, 47-53, chmn div natural sci, 53-54. *Concurrent Pos:* Consult pub schs, Indianapolis, 58-59; chmn state math adv comt, Nat Defense Educ Act, 59; assoc prog dir summer insts prog, NSF, Washington, DC, 65-66; math consult, US Dept Defense Overseas Schs, Europe, 69-70; resident dir, semester in Ger & France, DePauw Univ, 77; instr, Challenge Prog, US Dept Defense in Europe, 78-84, 87, 89 & 90. *Mem:* Am Math Soc; Math Asn Am. *Res:* Eigenfunction expansions; mathematical analysis. *Mailing Add:* DePauw Univ 6025 College Ave Greencastle IN 46135-1900

GASS, FREDERICK STUART, MATHEMATICS. *Current Pos:* From asst prof to assoc prof, 68-94, PROF MATH & STATIST, MIAMI UNIV, OXFORD, OHIO, 94- *Personal Data:* b Lincoln, Nebr, Apr 21, 43; m 66, Margery Stoops; c Molly Margaret & David Frederick. *Educ:* DePauw Univ, BA, 64; Dartmouth Col, AM, 66, PhD(math), 69. *Concurrent Pos:* Vis asst prof, Talladega Col, 69-70. *Mem:* Math Asn Am; Asn Symbolic Logic; Am Math Soc; Nat Coun Teachers Math. *Res:* Mathematical logic; recursive function theory; ordinal notation theory. *Mailing Add:* Dept Math Miami Univ Oxford OH 45056-1641

GASS, GEORGE HIRAM, ENDOCRINOLOGY, PHARMACOLOGY. *Current Pos:* CONSULT, 84- *Personal Data:* b Sunbury, Pa, Sept 23, 24; m 48, 90, Marilyn Golla; c Nancy, George & Patricia. *Educ:* Bucknell Univ, BS, 48; Univ NMex, MS, 52; Ohio State Univ, PhD(physiol), 55. *Prof Exp:* Exp biologist, Lederle Labs, Am Cyanamid Co, 48-51; asst chief, Endocrine Br, Div Pharmacol, Food & Drug Admin, 55-59; prof physiol & dir, Endocrinol Pharmacol Res Lab, Southern Ill Univ, 59-79; chmn, Dept Basic Sci, Okla Col Osteop Med & Surg, 79-84. *Concurrent Pos:* Mem, Biol Sci Comt, Grad Sch, USDA, 58-60; sr scientist fel, Alexander von Humboldt Found, WGer, 67-68 & fel; consult, A B Leo Pharmaceut Co, Sweden; Fulbright fel, 72; vis prof, Nat Ctr Toxicol Res, 75, prin investr hormonal carcinogenesis; consult & ed, Endocrine Toxicol, 84-88; adj prof, Sch Osteop Med, Okla Univ. *Mem:* Fel AAAS; Am Physiol Soc; Endocrine Soc; Am Soc Animal Sci; Soc Study Reprod. *Res:* Hormone assay; development of new assay methods; development of knowledge of the physiology and pharmacology of chemical compounds affecting the functions of the endocrine system; carcinogenicity of steroid hormones; mechanism of gastric function. *Mailing Add:* 6718 E 79th St Tulsa OK 74133

GASS, SAUL IRVING, MATHEMATICS. *Current Pos:* chmn dept, 75-79, PROF MGT SCI & STATIST, COL BUS & MGT, UNIV MD, 75- *Personal Data:* b Chelsea, Mass, Feb 28, 26; m 46; c 2. *Educ:* Boston Univ, BS & MA, 49; Univ Calif, PhD, 65. *Honors & Awards:* Jacinto Steinhardt Mem Award. *Prof Exp:* Mathematician, Aberdeen Bombing Mission, 49-51; dir mgt anal, Hqs, USAF, 52-55; appl sci rep, Int Bus Mach Corp, 55-58; chief opers res br, C-E-I-R, Inc, 58-60; sr mathematician, Fed Systs Div, Int Bus Mach Corp, Md, 60-61; systs mgr, 61-66, mgr computer sci & oper res, 66-69; vpres, World Systs Labs, Inc, Md, 69-70; dir opers res, Mathematica, Inc, 70-75. *Concurrent Pos:* Fulbright Scholar, 95-96; vpres int affairs, Inst Opers Res & Mgt Sci, 96-97. *Mem:* Am Fedn Info Processing Socs (secy, 63-65); Soc Indust & Appl Math; Opers Res Soc Am (vpres & pres, 75-77); Math Asn Am; Inst Oper Res Mgt; Am Inst Decision Sci. *Res:* Linear programming; game theory; operations research; digital computer applications. *Mailing Add:* Dept Mgt Sci & Statist Col Bus & Mgt Univ Md College Park MD 20742. *E-Mail:* sgass@mlas.und.edu

GASSAWAY, ALEXANDER RAMSEY, ECONOMIC DEVELOPMENT, WORLD POPULATION & FOOD SUPPLY. *Current Pos:* RETIRED. *Personal Data:* m 66, Carolyn Hoecker; c David & Jon-Peter. *Educ:* Univ Va, BA, 50; George Washington Univ, MA, 57; Clark Univ, PhD(geog), 71. *Prof Exp:* Mil intel res specialist, Eng Strategic Intel Div, Dept Defense, 50-56; grantee, Foreign Field Res, Nat Acad Sci, 58-60; asst prof, Dept Geog, George Washington Univ, 62-66; prof, Dept Geog, Portland State Univ, 66-90. *Concurrent Pos:* Adj prof, Lewis & Clarke Col, 78- *Mem:* Asn Am Geographers. *Res:* Military intelligence-mapping intelligence, utility of terrain for operations; physical and economic geographic influences on sufficiency of food resources in arctic Norway; adequacy of geographic distribution of physician manpower in Oregon; adequacy of pedestrian roadside walkways to serve specific land uses. *Mailing Add:* 2135 SW Boundary Portland OR 97201. *E-Mail:* boag@odin.cc.pdx.edu

GASSAWAY, JAMES D, ELECTRICAL ENGINEERING. *Current Pos:* AT HOWARD INDUSTS, LAUREL, MISS, 90- *Personal Data:* b Fulton, Mass, Aug 17, 32. *Educ:* Univ Miss, BS, 57; Purdue Univ, PhD(elec eng), 64. *Prof Exp:* Design engr, Gen Dynamics Corp, Tex, 57-59; instr elec eng, Purdue Univ, 59-63, asst prof, 63-65; assoc prof, Univ Ala, 65-67; adj prof elec eng, Miss State Univ, 67-80, prof, 80-90. *Concurrent Pos:* Res asst, Am Machine & Foundry, Purdue Univ, 62-63; consult, Wabash Magnetics, Ind, 64 & Radiation Inc, Fla, 68-69. *Mem:* Am Soc Eng Educ; Inst Elec & Electronics Engrs; Sigma Xi. *Res:* Modeling of semiconductor fabrication processes and semiconductor device behavior using digital computer; development of sensitive electronic instruments; thin magnetic films and magnetic properties of rolled sheets; techniques for reduction of limit cycle oscillations in non-linear feedback systems. *Mailing Add:* 2103 Maple Dr Starkville MS 39759

GASSER, CHARLES SCOTT, PLANT MOLECULAR BIOLOGY, MOLECULAR GENETICS. *Current Pos:* asst prof, Dept Biochem & Biophys, 89-92, ASSOC PROF, SECT MOLECULAR & CELLULAR BIOL, UNIV CALIF, DAVIS, 92- *Personal Data:* b Ft Benning, Ga, July 26, 55; m 89. *Educ:* Univ Calif, Davis, BS, 78; Stanford Univ, PhD(biol), 85. *Prof Exp:* Sr res biologist, Monsanto Co, 85-87, res specialist, 87-89, sr res specialist, 89. *Concurrent Pos:* NSF presidential young investr award, 90. *Mem:* Int Soc Plant Molecular Biol; Am Soc Plant Physiol; Tomato Genetics Coop; AAAS; Int Working Group Flowering. *Res:* Immunophilins and prolyl isomerases of higher plants; molecular basis of flower development; flower-specific gene expression. *Mailing Add:* Sect Molecular & Cellular Biol Univ Calif Davis CA 95616-5200

GASSER, DAVID LLOYD, GENETICS, IMMUNOLOGY. *Current Pos:* NIH fel, Univ Pa, 70-72, asst prof, 72-78, assoc prof human genetics, 78-95, PROF GENETICS, UNIV PA, 95- *Personal Data:* b Wadsworth, Ohio, Feb 12, 43; m 68, Gail Barton; c Valerie & Nathan. *Educ:* Univ Akron, BS, 64; Univ Mich, MS, 66, PhD(zool), 70. *Mem:* AAAS; Am Soc Human Genetics; Am Asn Immunologists. *Res:* Genetic control of the immune response; genetics of susceptibility to teratogenic agents. *Mailing Add:* Dept Genetics Univ Pa Sch Med Philadelphia PA 19104-6145. *Fax:* 215-573-5892; *E-Mail:* gasserd@mail.med.upenn.edu

GASSER, HEINZ, crop physiology, plant breeding, for more information see previous edition

GASSER, RAYMOND FRANK, ANATOMY, EMBRYOLOGY. *Current Pos:* Instr embryol, Med Ctr, Univ Ala, 65, from instr to assoc prof, 67-74, assoc dean sch med, 74-75, PROF ANAT, MED CTR, LA STATE UNIV, 74-, DIR, ANAT COMPUT IMAGING LAB, 92- *Personal Data:* b Cullman, Ala, Sept 13, 35; m 61, Eileen Brinkman; c Raymond F Jr & Christopher J. *Educ:* Spring Hill Col, BS, 59; Univ Ala, MS, 62, PhD(anat, physiol), 65. *Concurrent Pos:* Adj cur, Carnegie Collection Human Embryos, Human Develop Anat Ctr, Armed Forces Inst Path, Washington DC, 91- *Mem:* Teratology Soc; Am Asn Clin Anatomists; Am Asn Anatomists. *Res:* Morphogenesis of the head and neck regions in man; morphometrics of neural tube and surrounding structures; effects of physical manipulation on cell differentiation, human embryology. *Mailing Add:* La State Univ Med Ctr Dept Anat 1901 Perdido St New Orleans LA 70112-1393. *Fax:* 504-568-4392; *E-Mail:* rgasse@lsumc.edu

GASSER, WILLIAM, ORGANIC CHEMISTRY. *Current Pos:* from asst prof to assoc prof, 63-71, PROF CHEM, QUINCY UNIV, 71- *Personal Data:* b East Conemaugh, Pa, Nov 22, 23; m 60, Nancy Nabers; c Aurienne, Gabrielle, Nicole & Maria. *Educ:* Waynesburg Col, BS, 47; Univ Mich, MS, 48; Univ Md, MS, 52, PhD(chem), 55. *Prof Exp:* Instr chem, Waynesburg Col, 48-49, from asst prof to assoc prof, 51-53; asst, Univ Md, 49-51 & 53-55; res chemist, Visking Co, Union Carbide Corp, 55-62; mem legal staff, Chas Pfizer & Co, 62-63. *Concurrent Pos:* Consult, Blessing Hosp & Gasser Assoc. *Mem:* AAAS; Am Chem Soc; Sigma Xi. *Res:* Organic synthesis; polymers; patent law. *Mailing Add:* 1828 Maine St Quincy IL 62301

GASSIE, EDWARD WILLIAM, ANIMAL SCIENCE, INFORMATION SCIENCE. *Current Pos:* RETIRED. *Personal Data:* b Addis, La, Nov 29, 25; m 49; c 3. *Educ:* La State Univ, BS, 51, MS, 58, PhD(agr educ), 64. *Prof Exp:* From asst co agent to assoc co agent, La State Univ, Baton Rouge, 51-55, dist supvr, 55-64, assoc prof, 64-68, prof exten educ, 68-88, training specialist, Coop Exten Serv, 64-88, head, Dept Exten & Int Educ, 78-88. *Concurrent Pos:* Mem, Nat Exten Curric Develop Comt, 64- *Res:* Studies of behavioral changes in individuals and groups as a result of planned educational programs and the many variables associated with the extent of these changes. *Mailing Add:* 5833 Georgetown Ave Baton Rouge LA 70808

GASSMAN, MERRILL LOREN, PLANT PHYSIOLOGY, BIOCHEMISTRY. *Current Pos:* from asst prof to assoc prof, 69-82, PROF BIOL SCI, UNIV ILL, CHICAGO, 82- *Personal Data:* b Chicago, Ill, Feb 10, 43; m 67, Beverly S Sacks; c Debra, Sharyl & Aaron. *Educ:* Univ Chicago, SB, 64, SM, 65, PhD(bot), 67. *Prof Exp:* Guest investr & USPHS res fel, Rockefeller Univ, 67-68; res plant physiologist, Int Minerals & Chem Corp, Ill, 68-69; res assoc, Argonne Nat Lab, 69. *Concurrent Pos:* Consult, Int Minerals & Chem Corp, Ill, 69-70; prin investr, NSF grants, 72-87; vis assoc res botanist, Univ Calif, Davis, 76; vis prof bot & microbiol, Ariz State Univ, Tempe, 83; adj instr biol, Oakton Comm Col, Des Plaines, IL, 90-93. *Mem:* AAAS; Am Soc Plant Physiol; Am Soc Biochem & Molecular Biol; Sigma Xi. *Res:* Photo induction of chloroplast development; control systems of porphyrin and chlorophyll metabolism in plants. *Mailing Add:* Dept Biol Sci M/C 066 Univ Ill 845 W Taylor St Rm 3262 Chicago IL 60607. *Fax:* 312-413-2435; *E-Mail:* mxgassman@uic.edu

GAST, ALICE PETRY, CHEMICAL ENGINEERING. *Current Pos:* PROF, DEPT CHEM ENG, STANFORD UNIV. *Honors & Awards:* Initiatives Research, Nat Acad Scis, 92. *Res:* Chemical engineering. *Mailing Add:* Dept Chem Eng Stanford Univ Stanford CA 94305

GAST, JAMES AVERY, OCEANOGRAPHY. *Current Pos:* from asst prof to assoc prof, 61-70, coordr, 61-70, dir marine lab, 64-70, PROF OCEANOG, HUMBOLDT STATE COL, 70- *Personal Data:* b New Rochelle, NY, Apr 28, 29; m 55; c 3. *Educ:* Amherst Col, AB, 53; Univ Wash, MS, 57, PhD(oceanog), 59. *Prof Exp:* Asst, Woods Hole Oceanog Inst, 47-48; asst Univ Wash, 53-58, assoc & actg instr, 58-59, sr oceanogr & exten asst prof, 59-60, res asst prof, 60-61. *Concurrent Pos:* Oceanog consult, 62- *Res:* Oceanographic education; chemical oceanography. *Mailing Add:* 40 E 15th St Arcata CA 95521

GAST, LYLE EVERETT, ORGANIC CHEMISTRY. *Current Pos:* RETIRED. *Personal Data:* b Alden, Ill, Apr 9, 19; m 42, Anna Wright; c Stephen R. *Educ:* Univ Ill, BS, 41; Univ Wis, PhD(org chem), 49. *Prof Exp:* Asst res chemist, Pa Salt Mfg Co, 41-44; res chemist, Northern Regional Labs, USDA, 49-60, head oil coatings invests, 60-77. *Mem:* Am Chem Soc; Am Oil Chemists' Soc. *Res:* Chlorination of organic compounds; fundamental investigations on higher unsaturated fatty acids. *Mailing Add:* 8606 Reese Rd Harvard IL 60033

GAST, ROBERT GALE, SOIL CHEMISTRY. *Current Pos:* ASSOC DEAN & DIR, MICH AGR EXP STA, 83- *Personal Data:* b Philadelphia, Mo, July 28, 31; m 54; c 3. *Educ:* Univ Mo, BS, 53, MS, 56, PhD(soil chem), 59. *Prof Exp:* Asst scientist soil chem, Agr Res Lab, AEC, Tenn, 59-61, assoc prof, 61-68; res assoc soil sci, Mich State Univ, 68-69; prof soil sci, Univ Minn, St Paul, 70-77; head, Dept Agron, Univ Nebr, 77-83. *Concurrent Pos:* Lectr, Oak Ridge Inst Nuclear Studies, 63-70; ed, J Environ Qual, Am Soc Agron, 75-77. *Mem:* Fel Am Soc Agron (pres-elect, 86); Int Soil Sci Soc; Clay Minerals Soc; Soil Sci Soc Am (pres, 82). *Res:* Physical chemistry and mineralogy of soils; nutrient movement. *Mailing Add:* Water Res Mich State Univ 226 Hanna Admin Bldg East Lansing MI 48824

GASTEIGER, EDGAR LIONEL, NEUROPHYSIOLOGY. *Current Pos:* RETIRED. *Personal Data:* b Meadville, Pa, Nov 25, 19; m 49; c 4. *Educ:* Allegheny Col, AB, 42; Univ Ill, MS, 43; Univ Minn, PhD(biophys), 52. *Prof Exp:* Res assoc physiol, Harvard Med Sch, 51-53, assoc, 53-54, asst prof, 54-57; asst prof, Univ Rochester, 57-61; prof phys biol, NY State Vet Col, Cornell Univ, 61-91. *Concurrent Pos:* Res assoc, Mass Gen Hosp, 51-57. *Mem:* AAAS; Am Physiol Soc; Soc Neurosci; Sigma Xi; Biophys Soc. *Res:* Central nervous system; peripheral nerve and muscle physiology; effects of radiation. *Mailing Add:* 304 Ithaca Rd Ithaca NY 14850-4818

GASTIL, R GORDON, GEOLOGY, REGIONAL TECTONICS. *Current Pos:* from asst prof to assoc prof, 59-65, chmn dept, 69-77, PROF GEOL, SAN DIEGO STATE UNIV, 65- *Personal Data:* b San Diego, Calif, June 25, 28; m 58, Janet Manly; c Garth, Mary, George & John. *Educ:* Univ Calif, Berkeley, AB, 50, PhD(geol), 54. *Prof Exp:* Geologist, Shell Oil Co, Alaska, 54 & Can Javelin Ltd, 56-58; lectr geol, Univ Calif, Los Angeles, 58-59. *Concurrent Pos:* Res partic, NSF grants, 60-61, 62-69 & 71; NSF res grants, Baja, Calif, 68-70; mem, Int Geol Field Conf, Am Geol Inst, EAfrica, 69; NSF res grants, Sonora, Mex, 71-72 & 82-88; chmn, Geol Soc Am, 91. *Mem:* AAAS; Geol Soc Am; Soc Econ Paleont & Mineral; Am Geophys Union; Chinese Acad Sci & Earth Sci; Geol Inst Mex. *Res:* Regional structural analysis; geochronology; origin and evolution of continents and ocean basins; emplacement and crystallization of large granitic plotons. *Mailing Add:* Dept Geol San Diego State Univ San Diego CA 92182. *Fax:* 619-594-4372

GASTINEAU, CLIFFORD FELIX, MEDICINE. *Current Pos:* CONSULT INTERNAL MED, MAYO CLIN, 50- *Personal Data:* b Pawnee, Okla, Dec 18, 20; m 51; c 2. *Educ:* Univ Okla, BA, 41, MD, 43; Univ Minn, PhD(med), 50. *Mem:* AAAS; Endocrine Soc; Am Diabetes Asn; fel Am Col Physicians; Sigma Xi. *Res:* Clinical standpoint of diabetes and nutrition. *Mailing Add:* 600 Fourth Ave SW No 504 Rochester MN 55902-3247

GASTL, GEORGE CLIFFORD, TOPOLOGY, ALGEBRA. *Current Pos:* Asst prof, 66-70, ASSOC PROF MATH, UNIV WYO, 70- *Personal Data:* b Shawnee, Kans, Feb 27, 38; m 67. *Educ:* Univ Kans, AB, 60, MA, 62; Univ Wis, PhD(math), 66. *Mem:* Math Asn Am; Am Math Soc. *Res:* Abstract topological spaces; extended topology; uniform spaces; proximity spaces. *Mailing Add:* Dept Math Univ Wyo PO Box 3036 Laramie WY 82071-3036

GASTON, LYLE KENNETH, PHEROMONES. *Current Pos:* CHEMIST & ADJ LECTR TOXICOL & PHYSIOL, UNIV CALIF, RIVERSIDE, 62- *Personal Data:* b Waterloo, Iowa, Nov 7, 30. *Educ:* Iowa State Univ, BS, 53; Univ Calif, Los Angeles, PhD(chem), 60. *Prof Exp:* Fel, Univ Colo, 60-62. *Mem:* Am Chem Soc; Entom Soc Am; AAAS. *Res:* Isolation, identification and synthesis of insect sex pheromones; chemistry and analysis of pesticides and their residues. *Mailing Add:* Div Toxicol & Physiol Rte 2 Box 348 Bishop CA 93514

GASTON, MARILYN HUGHES, PEDIATRICS. *Current Pos:* dir, Div Med, Bur Health Professions, 89-90, DIR, BUR PRIMARY HEALTH CARE, HEALTH RESOURCES & SERVS ADMIN, MD, 90-, ASST SURGEON GEN, DEPT HEALTH & HUMAN SERVS, 90- *Personal Data:* b Cincinnati, Ohio; c Amy Marie & Damon Allen. *Educ:* Miami Univ, AB, 60; Univ Cincinnati, MD, 64; Am Bd Pediat, dipl, 68. *Honors & Awards:* Phyllis Wheatley Award, State of Ohio, 75; Award for Excellence, Pittsburg Sickle Cell Soc, 80; Living Legend Award, Nat Med Asn, 93. *Prof Exp:* Asst dir, Outpatient Dept, Children's Hosp, Ohio, 67-68 & Convalescent Hosp Children, Ohio, 68-69; med dir, Lincoln Heights Health Ctr, Ohio, 69-72; dir, Sickle Cell Screening Clin, Cincinnati Health Dept, 72-76, Comprehensive Sickle Cell Ctr, Children's Hosp Med Ctr, Ohio, 72-76; med expert, Nat Heart, Lung & Bood Inst, NIH, Md, 76-79, dep br chief, comn officer, Sickle Cell Dis Br, Div Blood Dis & Resources, 79-89. *Concurrent Pos:* Instr pediat, Univ Cincinnati Col Med, 67-68, asst clin prof, Div Community Pediat, 68-70, from asst prof to assoc prof pediat, 70-77; pediatrician, Hosp Albert Schweitzer, Haiti, 67, Div Community Pediat, Univ Cincinnati, 68-73, Lincoln Heights Health Ctr, 68-77 & Cincinnati Health Dept, Maternal & Infant Care Proj, 69-73; attend pediatrician, Children's Hosp Med Ctr, 67-76, Cincinnati Gen Hosp, 69-76 & Bethesda Hosp, 74-76; asst clin prof, Cincinnati Tech Col, 74-76, Howard Univ Col Med, 78-91 & Uniformed Servs Univ Health Sci, 87-; co-chair, Nat Sickle Cell Dirs, 74; bd trustees, Child Health Asn, 74-77; vis lectr, Kenyatta Nat Hosp, Kenya, 77; distinguished lectr, King Fahad Hosp Al-Baha, Saudi Arabia, 87; actg nat coordr, Nat Sickle Cell Prog, 88; bd dirs, Univ Cincinnati Found, 89-; life, sci bd, George Wash Univ, 93- *Mem:* Inst Med-Nat Acad Sci; AAAS; Am Acad Pediat; Am Pub Health Asn; Nat Asn Med Minority Educr; Nat Med Asn; NY Acad Sci; Am Soc Hemat; Am Pediat Soc; Am Med Women Asn. *Res:* Sickle cell disease; investigation of cardiac function utilizing non-evasive technologies; prophylactic penicillin in children with sickle cell disease. *Mailing Add:* 4350 East-West Hwy Health Resources & Services Admin Bethesda MD 20814

GASTONY, GERALD JOSEPH, SYSTEMATIC BOTANY. *Current Pos:* Asst prof, 70-76, ASSOC PROF BIOL, IND UNIV, BLOOMINGTON, 76- *Personal Data:* b Cleveland, Ohio, June 2, 40; m 67; c 1. *Educ:* St Louis Univ, AB, 64; Tulane Univ, MS, 66; Harvard Univ, PhD(biol), 71. *Concurrent Pos:* Assoc ed bot, J Rhodora, 72- & Am Fern J, 73- *Mem:* Bot Soc Am; Soc Study Evolution; Am Soc Plant Taxonomists; Int Asn Plant Taxon; Am Fern Soc (secy-treas, 74-77). *Res:* Palynology of tree ferns, both Cyatheaceae and Dicksoniaceae, and their allies; populational genetics of ferns; biosystematic studies of ferns and flowering plants. *Mailing Add:* 3222 N Ramble Rd W Bloomington IN 47408

GASTWIRTH, BART WAYNE, PATHOMECHANICS OF THE FOOT. *Current Pos:* assoc prof & chmn, Dept Orthop Sci & adj assoc prof, Dept Community Health, 81-86, PROF & CHMN, DEPT ORTHOP, SCHOLL COL PODIATRIC MED, 81- *Personal Data:* b Mineola, NY. *Educ:* Ill Col Podiatric Med, DPM, 77; Am Bd Podiatric Orthop, cert, 85. *Prof Exp:* Instr, Dept Med Sci, Ill Col Podiatric Med, 79-80, asst prof, Dept Podiatric Med, 80-81, assoc prof, Dept Orthop Sci, 81. *Concurrent Pos:* Consult, Vet Admin Hosp, Marion, Il, 83- *Mem:* Am Podiatric Med Asn; assoc mem Am Col Foot Surgeons; Am Pub Health Asn. *Res:* Biomechanics of the foot; diseases and surgery of the foot. *Mailing Add:* 3233 N Arlington Heights Rd Arlington Heights IL 60004

GASTWIRTH, JOSEPH L, MATHEMATICAL STATISTICS, STATISTICAL EVIDENCE. *Current Pos:* PROF STATIST, GEORGE WASHINGTON UNIV, 72- *Personal Data:* b New York, NY, Aug 31, 38. *Educ:* Yale Univ, BS, 58; Princeton Univ, MA, 60; Columbia Univ, PhD(math statist), 63. *Prof Exp:* Res assoc statist, Stanford Univ, 63-64; from asst prof to assoc prof, Johns Hopkins Univ, 64-72. *Concurrent Pos:* Vis assoc prof, Harvard Univ, 70-71; vis fac adv, Off Statist Policy, Exec Off of the President, 71-72, consult, 75-; assoc ed, J Statist Asn, 78-88; vis prof, Mass Inst Technol, 79; Guggenheim Found Fel, 85-86; mem, Am Statist Asn, Comn Law & Justice Statist, 88-93. *Mem:* Fel AAAS; fel Inst Math Statist; Int Statist Inst; fel Am Statist Asn; Royal Statist Soc; Indust Rels Res Asn. *Res:* Robust methods of inference; applied probability theory; economic statistics; statistics in law. *Mailing Add:* Dept Statist George Washington Univ Washington DC 20052

GASWICK, DENNIS C, INORGANIC CHEMISTRY. *Current Pos:* PROF CHEM, ALBION COL, 69- *Personal Data:* b Hay Springs, Nebr, Feb 15, 42; m 64, Carolyn Myers; c Christina & Wyatt. *Educ:* Nebr Wesleyan Univ, BA, 64; Ore State Univ, PhD(inorg chem), 68. *Prof Exp:* Res assoc, State Univ NY, Stony Brook, 68-69. *Concurrent Pos:* Vis scholar, Stanford Univ, 76-77; vis prof, Univ Nenchatel, Switz, 83-84; Northwestern Univ, 90-91. *Mem:* Am Chem Soc; Sigma Xi. *Res:* Mechanisms of chromium reactions and their intermediates; synthesis of binuclear chromium-cobalt complexes and the mechanisms of electron transfer reactions in coordination chemistry; kinetics and mechanistic studies of redox and substitution reactions involving complex ions in solution. *Mailing Add:* Dept Chem Albion Col 704 E Porter St Albion MI 49224. *Fax:* 517-629-0509; *E-Mail:* dgaswick@albion.edu

GAT, NAHUM, COMBUSTION, FLUID MECHANICS. *Current Pos:* PRES, OPTO-KNOWLEDGE SYSTS, INC, 91- *Personal Data:* b Poland, Dec 19, 47; Israeli & citizen; m 86, Linda Papermaster; c Joel, Daniel, Aviva & Ilana. *Educ:* Israel Inst Technol, BSc, 69; Univ Cincinnati, MS, 75, PhD(aerospace eng), 78. *Prof Exp:* Teaching asst exp aerospace eng, Univ Cincinnati, 76-78; mem tech staff, Space & Technol Group, TRW Inc, 78-80, sect head, 80-88, sr staff engr, 88-91. *Concurrent Pos:* Adj prof, Calif State Univ, Long Beach, 80-83; pres, Concept Develop Assocs, 86-91. *Mem:* Am Inst Aeronaut & Astronaut; Combustion Inst; Am Soc Mech Engrs; Soc Automotive Engrs; Sigma Xi. *Res:* Spectro-radiometry instrumentation; hyperspectral imaging; signal processing; diagnostics for combustion; medical diagnosis; optics; electro-optics. *Mailing Add:* 1227 Ninth St Hermosa Beach CA 90254. *E-Mail:* oksi@nic.cerf.net

GAT, URI, NUCLEAR ENGINEERING, THERMODYNAMICS. *Personal Data:* b Jerusalem, Israel, June 28, 36; m 61, Ruth Tasse; c Erann & Irit. *Educ:* Israel Inst Technol, BSc, 63; Aachen Tech Univ, Dr Ing, 69; Ky Bd Regist, PE, 72. *Honors & Awards:* Wilhelm Borchers Medaille. *Prof Exp:* Fel scientist nuclear reactor develop, Kernforschungsanlage, Ger, 63-69; asst prof mech eng, Univ Ky, 69-74; mgr, Gas Cooled Fast Reactor Prog, Oak Ridge Nat Lab, 74-80, mgr, Breeder Reactor Prog, 80-82, mgr aerols res, 83-87, reviewer, 87-88, mgr, Robotics Aircraft Paint Removal, 88-91, mgr, High Flux Isotope Reactor Environ Qualification, 89-93. *Mem:* Am Nuclear Soc; Metric Asn; Sigma Xi. *Res:* Liquid metal fast breeder reactor; liquid fuel reactors; molten salt reactors; reactor evaluations; thermochemical equilibrium evaluation and calculation; phase diagrams; kinetics of chlorination of nuclear fuels; flow and heat transfer; metrication; gas cooled reactor; quality assurance; advanced inherently safe reactors; environmental qualification. *Mailing Add:* 238 Gum Hollow Rd Oak Ridge TN 37830-5622. *Fax:* 423-574-2102; *E-Mail:* uri@ornl.gov

GATELY, MAURICE KENT, CYTOKINES, IMMUNOPHARMACOLOGY. *Current Pos:* sr scientist immunopharmacol, 83-85, res investr, 85-88, RES LEADER, HOFFMANN-LA ROCHE, INC, 88- *Personal Data:* b Omaha, Nebr, Feb 3, 46; m 72, Celia Lin; c Lynn C & Mark S. *Educ:* Johns Hopkins Univ, BA, 68, PhD(microbiol), 74, Johns Hopkins Sch Med, MD, 75. *Prof Exp:* Intern pediat, St Louis Children's Hosp 75-76; fel immunol, Harvard Med Sch, 76-79; sr staff fel, cellular Immunol Group Surg Neurol Branch, NIH, Bethesda, Md, 79-83. *Mem:* Am Asn Immunologists; AAAS; NY Acad Sci. *Res:* Identification of factors regulating cytolytic lymphocyte responses and the potential use of such factors in immunotherapy of tumors; author of numerous articles on lymphokines, on the mechanism of lymphocyte-mediated cytolysis and on mechanisms by which human brain tumors evade cellular immune attack. *Mailing Add:* Dept Inflammation-Autoimmune Dis Hoffman-La Roche Inc 340 Kingsland St Rm 3415 Nutley NJ 07110-1199. *Fax:* 973-235-5279

GATENBY, ANTHONY ARTHUR, GENE EXPRESSION, METABOLIC ENGINEERING. *Current Pos:* RES ASSOC, E I DUPONT DE NEMOURS & CO INC, 86- *Personal Data:* b London, Eng, Dec 25, 51; m 75; c 2. *Educ:* Portsmouth Polytech, UK, BSc, 73; Univ London, MSc, 74; Univ Nottingham, PhD(biochem), 77. *Prof Exp:* Res fel, Univ Edinburgh, UK, 77-79; higher sci officer, Plant Breeding Inst, UK, 79-82, sr sci officer, 82-85, prin sci officer, 85; res fel, Univ Wis, 85-86. *Concurrent Pos:* Hon res fel, Inst Enzyme Res, 84-85. *Mem:* Protein Soc. *Res:* The folding and assembly of proteins; protein translocation and secretion through membranes; production of foreign proteins in microorganisms, regulation of translation; metabolic pathway engineering. *Mailing Add:* DuPont Exp Sta PO Box 80328 Wilmington DE 19880-0328. *E-Mail:* gatenbaa@a1.esvax.umc.dupont.com

GATES, ALLEN H(AZEN), JR, REPRODUCTIVE BIOLOGY. *Current Pos:* RETIRED. *Personal Data:* b Rockville, Conn, Nov 7, 29; m 65; c Lisa & Gregory. *Educ:* La State Univ, BS, 51; Univ Edinburgh, Scotland, PhD(genetics), 59. *Prof Exp:* Res asst develop biol, Jackson Lab, Bar Harbor, Maine, 51-53, lab fel reprod biol, 56-59, assoc staff scientist, 59-60; res assoc, Sch Med, Stanford Univ, 60-64, asst prof, 64-70; staff researcher, Syntex Res, Calif, 70-71; asst prof anat, Sch Med, Univ Rochester, 71-75, asst prof genetics, 71-96, asst prof obstet & gynec, radiation biol & biophys, 75-82, asst prof toxicol in radiation biol & biophys, 82-88, asst prof toxicol, Environ Health Sci Ctr, 88-92, asst prof environ med, 92-96. *Concurrent Pos:* Nat Cancer Inst consult, 62-68; prin investr, 63-68 & 78-81. *Mem:* AAAS. *Res:* Mammalian reproduction, development and gentics, superovulation induction and embryo transplantation, toxicological effects of environmental organic mercury, bioeffects of ultrasound from diagnostic exposure levels, ethics of reproductive technologies. *Mailing Add:* 9 Hunters Run Pittsford NY 14534-3413

GATES, BRUCE C(LARK), CHEMICAL ENGINEERING. *Current Pos:* PROF DEPT CHEM ENG & MAT SCI, UNIV CAL, DAVIS, 92- *Personal Data:* b Richmond, Calif, July 5, 40; m 67; c 2. *Educ:* Univ Calif, Berkeley, BS, 61; Univ Wash, PhD(chem eng), 66. *Honors & Awards:* Del Sect Award, Am Chem Soc, 85. *Prof Exp:* From asst prof to assoc prof, Univ Del, 69-77, assoc dir, Ctr Catalytic Sci & Technol, 77-81, prof chem eng, 77-92, dir, Catalytic Sci & Technol, 81-88, H Rodney Shap Prof, 85-92, prof chem, 87-92; Res engr, Chevron Res Co, Calif, 67-69. *Concurrent Pos:* Fulbright res grant, Inst Phys Chem, Univ Munich, 66-67, 75-76 & 83-84. *Mem:* Am Inst Chem Engrs; Am Chem Soc. *Res:* Catalysis; surface chemistry and reaction kinetics; chemical reaction engineering; petroleum and petrochemical processes; catalysis by superacids, zeolites, soluble and supported transition-metal complexes and clusters; catalytic hydroprocessing. *Mailing Add:* Dept Chem Eng Univ Calif Davis CA 95616-5224

GATES, CHARLES EDGAR, AGRICULTURAL STATISTICS. *Current Pos:* PROF, INST STATIST, TEX A&M UNIV, 66- *Personal Data:* b Rapid City, SDak, Mar 6, 26; m 51; c 3. *Educ:* Iowa State Univ, BS, 50; NC State Col, MS, 52, PhD(exp statist), 55. *Prof Exp:* Asst exp statist, NC State Col, 50-53, asst statistician, 53-54; asst prof statist, Univ Minn, St Paul, 56-60, assoc prof, 60-65, prof, 65-66, statistician, Agr Exp Sta, 56-66. *Concurrent Pos:* Inst, Univ Louisville, 55-56. *Mem:* AAAS; Am Statist Asn; Royal Statist Soc; Biomet Soc (secy, E NAm Region, 75-78, pres-elect, 79, pres, 80); Sigma XI. *Res:* Wildlife population estimation; design of agricultural and biological experiments. *Mailing Add:* Statist/OE Teague Res Tex A&M Univ College Station TX 77843-3143

GATES, D(ANIEL) W(ILLIAM), CERAMICS. *Current Pos:* RETIRED. *Personal Data:* b Chicago, Ill, Oct 16, 21; m 45; c 2. *Educ:* Univ Ill, BS, 48; Ga Inst Technol, MS, 51 & 53; Ala A&M Univ, MBA, 82. *Prof Exp:* Mem staff res & develop, Temco, Inc, 47-49; asst, Eng Exp Sta, Ga Inst Technol, 50-53; asst prof ceramics, Clemson Col, 53-54; aero mats res engr, Army Ballistic Missile Agency, NASA, 54-60, mat res engr, George G Marshall Space Flight Ctr, 60-77; instr comput sci, Ala A&M Univ, 80-87. *Mem:* Am Ceramic Soc; Nat Inst Ceramic Engrs; Am Geophys Union; fel Am Inst Chem. *Res:* Geophysical exploration; porcelain enamels; graphite for rockets; materials for space environment; thermal-control coatings for space vehicles. *Mailing Add:* 3026 Crescent Circle SE Huntsville AL 35801

GATES, DAVID G(ORDON), INDUSTRIAL ENGINEERING. *Current Pos:* PROF INDUST ENG, LAMAR UNIV, 63- *Personal Data:* b Kansas City, Mo, Mar 30, 31; m 50; c 2. *Educ:* Univ Ark, BS, 56, MS, 59; Okla State Univ, PhD(eng), 62. *Prof Exp:* Indust engr, Corning Glass Works, 56-57; instr indust eng, Okla State Univ, 60-62; assoc prof, Auburn Univ, 62-63. *Mem:* Am Inst Indust Engrs; Am Soc Eng Educ. *Res:* Methods engineering; work measurement. *Mailing Add:* Dept Indust Eng Lamar Univ Box 10032 Beaumont TX 77710

GATES, DAVID MURRAY, PLANT PHYSIOLOGY, CLIMATOLOGY. *Current Pos:* dir, Biol Sta, 71-86, prof bot, 71-91, EMER PROF BOT, UNIV MICH, ANN ARBOR, 91- *Personal Data:* b Manhattan, Kans, May 27, 21; m 44, Marian Penley; c Murray, Julie, Heather & Marilyn. *Educ:* Univ Mich, BS, 42, MS, 44, PhD(physics), 48. *Honors & Awards:* Gold Medal Ecol, Nat Coun State Garden Clubs, 71; Outstanding Bioclimatologist, Am Meteorol Soc, 71. *Prof Exp:* Asst, Univ Mich, 41-44, res physicist, 42-44; res asst prof physics, Univ Denver, 47-54, assoc prof, 54-55; sci dir & liaison off, Off Naval Res, London, 55-57; asst chief radio propagation, Physics Div, Nat Bur Stand, 57-60, asst chief upper atmosphere & space physics div, 60-61, consult to dir, 61-64; prof natural hist, univ & cur ecol, Univ Mus, Univ Colo, 65; prof biol, Wash Univ, & dir, Mo Bot Garden, 65-71. *Concurrent Pos:* Mem oper anal stand-by unit, Iowa State Col, 53-55 & Univ Denver, 55-; consult, Air Defense Command, Colo, 53-; ed, Radio Propagation & J of Res, 61-63; lectr, Univ Colo, 61-64 & vis prof, 65; chmn environ studies bd, Nat Acad Sci-Nat Acad Eng, 70-73; mem, Nat Sci Bd, 70-76; mem adv panel, Comn Sci & Astronaut, US House Rep, 71-75; mem bd, Conserv Found, 69-86, Nat Audubon Soc, 72-78, Cranbrook Inst Sci, 73-92 & World Wildlife Found, 86-87; mem biometeorol panel, US Nat Comt Int Biol Prog; chmn ad hoc comt environ, Environ Clearinghouse Inc, Washington, DC; mem nat air quality adv comt, USPHS, adv comt biol & med sci, NSF & ad hoc adv comt off ecol, Smithsonian Inst; bd dir, Detroit Edison Co, 79-92; mem bd, Acid Rain Found, 80-92 & L S B Leakey Found, 83-92; distinguished vis scientist, Jet Propulsion Lab, Calif Inst Technol, 89-95. *Mem:* Optical Soc Am; Sigma Xi; Ecol Soc Am; Bot Soc Am; Am Inst Biol Sci (vpres, 74, pres, 75). *Res:* Near and far infrared spectroscopy; upper atmosphere research by infrared; geophysical exploration work; ecology; energy exchange for plants and animals; transpiration; photosynthesis; ecological effects of energy use. *Mailing Add:* Biol Dept Univ Mich Ann Arbor MI 48109-1048

GATES, GERALD OTIS, ECOLOGY. *Current Pos:* from asst prof to prof, 66-77, actg dean, 76-77, vpres, acad affairs, 79-82, ROBERTSON PROF BIOL, UNIV REDLANDS, 77- *Personal Data:* b Brewerton, NY, Oct 18, 39. *Educ:* Univ Ariz, BA, 60, PhD(ecol), 63. *Prof Exp:* Asst prof biol, Univ of the Pac, 63-66. *Res:* Ecology and behavior of amphibians and reptiles. *Mailing Add:* Dept Nat Sci Univ Redlands 1200 E Colton Ave Redlands CA 92374-3755

GATES, HALBERT FREDERICK, INTEGRATED PHYSICAL SCIENCE. *Current Pos:* chmn dept, 69-74, prof, 69-81, EMER PROF PHYSICS, BLOOMSBURG UNIV, PA, 81- *Personal Data:* b Milwaukee, Wis, Oct 30, 19; m 48, Margaret Fritz; c Sandra E, David C & John H. *Educ:* Wis State Teachers Col, BS, 40; Univ Wis, PhM, 44; Mich State Col, PhD(physics), 54. *Prof Exp:* Asst prof physics, Berea Col, 48-50; asst prof & chmn dept, Cornell Col, 54-55; asst prof physics & phys sci, Univ Ill, 55-58; assoc prof physics, Northern Ariz Univ, 58-64, prof & chmn dept, 65-66; prof & chmn dept, Slippery Rock State Col, 67-68. *Mem:* Am Phys Soc; Am Asn Physics Teachers; Sigma Xi. *Res:* Ultrasonics and optics. *Mailing Add:* 1837 E Claremont St Phoenix AZ 85016

GATES, JAMES EDWARD, PHYTOPATHOLOGY, MICROBIOLOGY. *Current Pos:* asst prof, 75-80, ASSOC PROF BIOL, VA COMMONWEALTH UNIV, 80- *Personal Data:* b Chicago, Ill, Jan 6, 43; m 68; c 2. *Educ:* Northern Ill Univ, BSEd, 65, MS, 67; Univ Mo-Columbia, PhD(plant path), 72. *Prof Exp:* Instr biol, Northern Ill Univ, 67-69; asst prof biol, Randolph-Macon Col, 72-75. *Mem:* Sigma Xi; Am Phytopath Soc; Am Soc Microbiol; Mycol Soc Am. *Res:* Genetics of symbiotic development; role of bacteria in formation of acid mine drainage; nitrogen-fixation. *Mailing Add:* Dept Biol Va Commonwealth Univ Box 2012 Richmond VA 23284-9004

GATES, JOHN E(DWARD), materials science, for more information see previous edition

GATES, JOSEPH SPENCER, HYDROGEOLOGY. *Current Pos:* Hydraul engr, US Geol Surv, 56-58, geologist, 58-71, hydrologist, 71-74, hydrologist-in-charge, El Paso field hq, 74-77, proj chief, Rio Grande Environ Study, 71-77, chief, Invest Sect, Utah Dist, 77-94, EMER HYDROLOGIST, US GEOL SURV, 94- *Personal Data:* b Des Moines, Iowa, Jan 18, 35; m 64, Constance M Clemens; c Jennifer A & Karin M. *Educ:* Colo Sch Mines, Geol

E, 56; Univ Utah, MS, 60; Univ Ariz, PhD, 72. *Concurrent Pos:* Geologist, US AID, Cairo, Egypt, 65-67; grad teaching & res assoc, Dept Hydrol & Water Resources, Univ Ariz, 67-71. *Mem:* Geol Soc Am; Am Geophys Union. *Res:* Groundwater geology and hydrology of arid regions. *Mailing Add:* 2560 Cavalier Dr Salt Lake City UT 84121. *Fax:* 801-975-3424; *E-Mail:* jgates@usgs.gov

GATES, LESLIE DEAN, JR, MATHEMATICS. *Current Pos:* RETIRED. *Personal Data:* b Berwyn, Ill, Oct 10, 22; m 50; c 4. *Educ:* Iowa State Col, BS, 47, MS, 50, PhD(math), 52. *Prof Exp:* Instr math, Iowa State Col, 52; mathematician, Armed Forces Spec Weapons Proj, US Dept Defense, 52-54; mathematician, US Naval Proving Grounds, 54-55, head, Appl Math Br, 55-58; mathematician, Atomic Energy Div, Babcock & Wilcox Co, 58-59, chief math sect, 59-61; assoc prof math, Southern Ill Univ, 61- *Mem:* Math Asn Am; Sigma Xi. *Res:* Numerical analysis. *Mailing Add:* 7013 Dax Rd Carbondale IL 62901-4304

GATES, MARSHALL DEMOTTE, JR, ORGANIC CHEMISTRY. *Current Pos:* lectr, 49-52, part-time prof, 52-60, prof chem, 60-81, HAUGHTON EMER PROF, UNIV ROCHESTER, 81- *Personal Data:* b Boyne City, Mich, Sept 25, 15; m 41, Martha Meyer; c 4. *Educ:* Rice Inst, BS, 36, MA, 38; Harvard Univ, PhD(org chem), 41. *Hon Degrees:* DSc, MacMurray Col, 63. *Honors & Awards:* Tishler lectr, Harvard Univ, 53; Welch Found lectr, 60. *Prof Exp:* Asst prof chem, Bryn Mawr Col, 41-43, asst prof chem, 46-49; tech aid, Off Sci Res & Develop, Washington, DC, 43-46. *Concurrent Pos:* Asst ed, J Am Chem Soc, 49-62, ed, 63-69; mem, Comt Drug Addiction & Narcotics, Nat Res Coun, 58-70; mem, President's Comt, Nat Medal Sci, 68-70; vis prof, Dartmouth Col, 82 & 84-86. *Mem:* Am Nat Acad Sci; Am Chem Soc; fel Am Acad Arts & Sci; fel NY Acad Sci. *Res:* Chemistry of natural products and analgesics. *Mailing Add:* 41 W Brook Rd Pittsford NY 14534-1129

GATES, MICHAEL ANDREW, PROTOZOOLOGY, SYSTEMATICS. *Current Pos:* asst prof, 86-89, ASSOC PROF, DEPT BIOL, CLEVELAND STATE UNIV, 90- *Personal Data:* b Corry, Pa, Dec 1, 46; Can citizen; m 74; c 4. *Educ:* Case Western Res Univ, BS, 68; Univ Toronto, MA, 73, PhD(zool), 76. *Prof Exp:* Fel protozool, Brit Mus Natural Hist, London, Eng, 76-77; fel, Cult Ctr Algae & Protozoa, Cambridge, Eng, 77-78; res asst prof zool, Dept Zool, Univ Toronto, 80-85. *Mem:* Am Math Soc; Soc Protozoologists; Am Soc Naturalists; Am Statist Asn; Soc Study Evolution. *Res:* Morphometric variation in ciliated protozoans; ciliate systematics and genetics; theoretical biology, especially the analysis of patterns. *Mailing Add:* Dept Biol Cleveland State Univ Cleveland OH 44115

GATES, OLCOTT, GEOLOGY. *Current Pos:* chmn dept, 66-77, PROF GEOL, STATE UNIV NY COL, FREDONIA, 66- *Personal Data:* b New York, NY, Mar 19, 19; m 42; c 5. *Educ:* Harvard Univ, BS, 41; Univ Colo, MA, 50; Johns Hopkins Univ, PhD, 56. *Prof Exp:* Asst, Woods Hole Oceanog Inst, 46; geologist, US Geol Surv, 49-54; from asst prof geol to assoc prof, Johns Hopkins Univ, 54-63; mem, US Peace Corps, Ghana, 63-65. *Concurrent Pos:* Geologist, Maine Geol Surv. *Mem:* Fel Geol Soc Am; Sigma Xi. *Res:* Volcanology; petrology; structural geology. *Mailing Add:* PO Box 234 Wiscasset ME 04758-0234

GATES, RAYMOND DEE, POLYMER CHEMISTRY. *Current Pos:* RETIRED. *Personal Data:* b Akron, Ohio, Oct 10, 25; m 54, Betty Becker; c David F & Barbara L. *Educ:* Univ Akron, BS, 49, MS, 51, PhD(chem), 61. *Prof Exp:* Res chemist, Firestone Tire & Rubber Co, 51-55, res chemist, Synthetic Rubber & Latex Div, 55-58; inst rubber res, Univ Akron, 58-60; sr res chemist, Chem Div, Int Latex Corp, 60-62, mgr appl polymer res, 62-66; res assoc, PPG Industs, 66-67, res supvr, 67-71; mgr chem servs, Oak Rubber Co, 71-72; mgr, SBR Adhesives Lab, Morgan Adhesives Co, 72-83; chemist, Algan, Inc, 83-91. *Mem:* Am Chem Soc. *Res:* Synthesis of elastomeric polymers and halogenated plastics; polymeric structures and the relationship of structural characteristics to physical properties; mechanism of polymeric network degradation; PVC plastisol compounding; adhesives compounding and characterization; water-based coating studies. *Mailing Add:* 3183 Silver Lake Blvd Cuyahoga Falls OH 44224-3130

GATES, ROBERT LEROY, biochemistry; deceased, see previous edition for last biography

GATES, ROBERT MAYNARD, GEOLOGY. *Current Pos:* From instr to assoc prof, 49-60, PROF GEOL, UNIV WIS-MADISON, 60- *Personal Data:* b Madison, Wis, June 26, 18; m 48; c 2. *Educ:* Univ Wis, BA, 41, MA, 41, PhD(geol), 49. *Concurrent Pos:* Geologist, Conn Geol Surv, 48-78; dir, Wasatch-Uinta Field Camp, 79-87. *Mem:* Fel Geol Soc Am; Mineral Soc Am; Geochem Soc. *Res:* Mineralogy and petrology of igneous and metamorphic rocks; geology of Western Connecticut. *Mailing Add:* 5029 Sheboygan Ave No 205 Madison WI 53705-2821

GATES, RONALD EUGENE, BIOCHEMISTRY. *Current Pos:* RES ASST PROF MED, MED SCH, VANDERBILT UNIV, 80- *Personal Data:* b Milwaukee, Wis, Sept 19, 41; m 69; c 3. *Educ:* St Mary's Col, Minn, BA, 63; Northwestern Univ, PhD(biochem), 68. *Prof Exp:* Fel biochem, St Jude Children's Res Hosp, 71-72; res consult, 73-76; res asst, Dept Pediat, Med Ctr, Univ Tenn, 77-80. *Concurrent Pos:* Fel biochem, Vet Admin Hosp, Kansas City, Mo, 68-70. *Res:* Protein phosphorylation with emphasis on the function of hormones and growth factors; mechanism of action of vitamin A and its binding proteins. *Mailing Add:* Dept Dermat Vanderbilt Univ Sch Med 21st Ave S & Garland Nashville TN 37232-0001

GATES, SYLVESTER J, JR, QUANTUM FIELD THEORY, SUPERSYMMETRICAL THEORIES. *Current Pos:* assoc prof, 84-89, PROF PHYSICS, UNIV MD, 89-; PROF PHYSICS, HOWARD UNIV, 90- *Personal Data:* b Tampa, Fla, Dec 15, 50. *Educ:* Mass Inst Technol, BS, 73, BS, 73, PhD(physics), 77. *Prof Exp:* Jr fel, Harvard Univ, 77-80; res assoc, Calif Inst Technol, 80-82; asst prof appl math, Mass Inst Technol, 82-84. *Concurrent Pos:* Exec tech officer, Nat Soc Black Physicists, 90-92. *Mem:* Nat Soc Black Physicists. *Res:* Study of mathematical models as possible descriptions of the elementary particles and fundamental forces which occur in nature. *Mailing Add:* Dept Physics Rm 4109 Univ Md College Park MD 20742

GATES, WILLIAM HENRY, III, SOFTWARE SYSTEMS, BIOTECHNOLOGY. *Current Pos:* FOUNDER, CHMN BD, CHIEF EXEC OFFICER & DIR, MICROSOFT CORP, 76- *Personal Data:* b Seattle, Wash, Oct 28, 55; m 94, Melinda French. *Honors & Awards:* Nat Medal Technol, US Dept Com Tech Admin, 92. *Mem:* Nat Acad Eng. *Mailing Add:* Microsoft Corp 1 Microsoft Way Redmond WA 98052-8300

GATES, WILLIAM LAWRENCE, METEOROLOGY. *Current Pos:* RETIRED. *Personal Data:* b South Pasadena, Calif, Sept 14, 28; c 3. *Educ:* Mass Inst Technol, SB, 50, SM, 51, ScD, 55. *Prof Exp:* Res meteorologist, Air Force Cambridge Res Ctr, 53-57; asst prof meteorol, Univ Calif, Los Angeles, 57-59, assoc prof, 59-66; res scientist, Rand Corp, 66-76; prof & chmn, Dept Atmospheric Sci, Ore State Univ, 76-89. *Mem:* Am Meteorol Soc; Am Geophys Union; Royal Meteorol Soc. *Res:* Climate dynamics; numerical weather prediction; global environmental change. *Mailing Add:* Lawrence Livermore Nat Lab L-264 PO Box 808 Livermore CA 94551. *Fax:* 510-422-7675; *E-Mail:* gates@pcmdi.llnl.gov

GATEWOOD, BUFORD ECHOLS, AIRCRAFT STRUCTURES. *Current Pos:* RETIRED. *Personal Data:* b Byhalia, Miss, Aug 23, 13; wid; c 1. *Educ:* La Polytech Inst, BS, 35; Univ Wis, MS, 37, PhD(math), 39. *Prof Exp:* Asst math, Univ Wis, 35-39; asst prof, La Polytech Inst, 39-42; asst stress analyst to asst chief struct engr, McDonnell Aircraft Corp, Mo, 42-46; struct res engr, Beech Aircraft, Kans, 46-47; from assoc prof to prof mech & head dept, Air Force Inst Tech, Wright Patterson Base, 47-55, res coordr & res prof, 55-60; prof aeronaut & astronaut eng, Ohio State Univ, 60-78. *Mem:* Am Inst Aeronaut & Astronaut; Am Soc Mech Eng; Math Asn Am; Sigma Xi. *Res:* Shear distribution in diagonal tension beams; thermal stresses in long cylindrical bodies; aircraft structures; buckling of tapered columns; fatigue and thermal stresses. *Mailing Add:* 2150 Waltham Rd Columbus OH 43221-4150

GATEWOOD, DEAN CHARLES, BIOCHEMISTRY. *Current Pos:* Asst gen chem, Sch Dent, Univ Ore Health Sci Ctr, 50-51, asst biochem, 52-53, asst endocrinol, Med Sch, 54-55, from instr to asst prof, 55-63, ASSOC PROF BIOCHEM, SCH DENT, UNIV ORE HEALTH SCI CTR, 63- *Personal Data:* b Iowa City, Iowa, June 29, 25; m 53; c 4. *Educ:* Willamette Univ, BA, 50; Univ Ore, MA, 53. *Mem:* AAAS; Am Chem Soc. *Res:* Etiology of dental caries; biochemistry of selenium and other trace elements; metabolism of oral tissues. *Mailing Add:* 5722 SW Garden Home Rd Portland OR 97219

GATEWOOD, GEORGE DAVID, ASTRONOMY. *Current Pos:* From asst prof to assoc prof astron, 72-89, DIR, ALLEGHENY OBSERV, UNIV PITTSBURGH, 77-, PROF ASTRON, 89- *Personal Data:* b St Petersburg, Fla, May 10, 40; m 59; c 1. *Educ:* Univ SFla, BA, 65, MA, 68; Univ Pittsburgh, PhD(astron), 72. *Honors & Awards:* Nat Space Act Award, 87. *Mem:* Am Astron Soc; Royal Astron Soc; Int Astron Union. *Res:* The determination of stellar distances, luminosities and masses and the detection of extrasolar planetary systems. *Mailing Add:* Allegheny Observ Observ Sta Pittsburgh PA 15214

GATEWOOD, LAEL CRANMER, HEALTH COMPUTER SCIENCE, BIOMETRY. *Current Pos:* scientist health comput sci & biomet, Univ Minn, 67-68, asst prof lab med & biomet & asst dir, Div Health Comput Sci, 71-74, sr assoc prof, Div Health Comput Sci, 74-79, ASSOC PROF LAB MED, PATH & BIOMET, UNIV MINN, MINNEAPOLIS, 74-, DIR, DIV HEALTH COMPUT SCI, 79- *Personal Data:* b Cleveland, Ohio, Nov 16, 38; m 61; c 2. *Educ:* Rockford Col, BA, 59; Univ Minn, Minneapolis, MS, 66, PhD(biomet), 71. *Prof Exp:* Technician biochem res, Mayo Clin, 59-61, technician biophys, 62-67. *Mem:* AAAS; Am Pub Health Asn; NY Acad Sci; Am Asn Med Systs Informatics; Asn Comput Mach; Sigma Xi. *Res:* Biomedical computation; simulation of dynamic physiological systems using both deterministic and stochastic modeling; techniques of quality assurance and data base management for clinical research; application of computers to health care services. *Mailing Add:* Pathol Box 198 Mayo Univ Minn Med Sch 420 Delaware St SE Minneapolis MN 55455-0374

GATHERS, GEORGE ROGER, EXPERIMENTAL SOLID STATE PHYSICS, SHOCK WAVE PHYSICS. *Current Pos:* SELF-EMPLOYED CONSULT, 93- *Personal Data:* b Meridian, Okla, Feb 1, 36; m 69, Christine E Key; c Kevin M. *Educ:* Univ Southern Calif, BS, 60; Univ Calif, Berkeley, PhD(physics), 67. *Prof Exp:* Physicist, Lawrence Livermore Lab, 67-69, group leader physics, 69-70, physicist, 70-93. *Mem:* Am Phys Soc; Am Nuclear Soc. *Res:* Cyclotron resonance in lead; high pressure, high temperature equation of state of materials; shock hydrodynamics; the measurement of the equation of state and electrical properties of liquid metals at very high temperatures and under modest pressures using fast dynamic self-heating methods; criticality safety analysis. *Mailing Add:* 1212 Harvest Rd Pleasanton CA 94566. *E-Mail:* rgathers@aol.com

GATHERUM, GORDON ELWOOD, FORESTRY PHYSIOLOGY, SOILS. *Current Pos:* prof & chmn dept, Ohio State Univ & Ohio Agr Res & Develop Ctr, 69-75, DIR SCH NATURAL RESOURCES, OHIO STATE UNIV, 75-, ASSOC DEAN, COL OF AGR & HOME ECON, 75- *Personal Data:* b Salt Lake City, Utah, Oct 22, 23; m 47; c 2. *Educ:* Univ Wash, Seattle, BS, 49; Utah State Univ, MS 51; Iowa State Univ, PhD(silvicult, plant physiol), 59. *Prof Exp:* Asst range mgt, Utah State Univ, 49-51; asst prof, Tex Technol Col, 51-53; from assoc prof to prof forestry, Iowa State Univ, 53-69. *Mem:* AAAS; Soc Am Foresters; Ecol Soc Am. *Res:* Tree physiology; forest soils. *Mailing Add:* 608 Bobcat Lane Hamilton MT 59840

GATHINGS, WILLIAM EDWARD, IMMUNOLOGY. *Current Pos:* PRES & CHIEF EXEC OFFICER, SOUTHERN BIOTECHNOL ASSOC, INC, 82- *Educ:* University Ala, Birmingham, PhD(biol), 81. *Mailing Add:* South Biotechnol Assoc Inc PO Box 26221 Birmingham AL 35226-0221

GATIPON, GLENN BLAISE, PSYCHOPHARMACOLOGY, NEUROPHYSIOLOGY. *Current Pos:* res assoc, Trauma Clin, Univ Miss, 73-84, chief anesthesiol, 92-97, ASST PROF ANESTHESIOL, PHARMACOL & NEUROSURG, MED CTR, UNIV MISS, 72-, PAIN MED, 97- *Personal Data:* b New Orleans, La, July 10, 40; m 62; c 3. *Educ:* Tulane Univ, BS, 62; La State Univ, Baton Rouge, MS, 64; La State Univ, New Orleans, PhD(physiol), 70, MD, 81. *Prof Exp:* Instr neurophysiol, Sch Med, La State Univ, 70-72. *Concurrent Pos:* Nat Inst Dent Res spec dent res award, Med Ctr, Univ Miss, 73-76; consult pharmacol, Sch Nursing, Univ Southern Miss, 73- *Mem:* Int Asn Dent Res; Soc Neurosci. *Res:* Electrophysiol and computer analysis of single neuron activity; anesthesiology. *Mailing Add:* 326 Rockmoor Trail Marietta GA 30066

GATLAND, IAN ROBERT, THEORETICAL PHYSICS. *Current Pos:* from asst prof to assoc prof, 64-74, PROF PHYSICS, GA INST TECHNOL, 74- *Personal Data:* b London, Eng, Feb 17, 36; m 63; c 4. *Educ:* Univ London, BSc, 57, PhD(theoret physics), 60. *Prof Exp:* Fel theoret physics, European Orgn Nuclear Res, Geneva, 60-61; staff mem physics, Res Inst Advan Study, Md, 61-64. *Mem:* Am Phys Soc; Sigma Xi. *Res:* Atomic collisions; ion-atom, ion-molecular interactions. *Mailing Add:* Dept Physics Ga Inst Technol Atlanta GA 30332

GATLEY, IAN, INFRARED ASTRONOMY, ASTROPHYSICS. *Current Pos:* RES FEL PHYSICS, CALIF INST TECHNOL, 77- *Personal Data:* b Runcorn, Eng, Feb 11, 50; m 76. *Educ:* Univ London, BSc & ARCS, 72; Calif Inst Technol, PhD(physics), 78. *Concurrent Pos:* Co-investr, Kuiper Airborne Observ, NASA, 78- *Mem:* Am Astron Soc. *Res:* Observational infrared astronomy. *Mailing Add:* 6340 N Placita De Eduardo Tucson AZ 85718

GATLEY, WILLIAM STUART, NOISE CONTROL, VIBRATIONS. *Current Pos:* mgr mech eng res, 79-87, CHIEF MECH ENG, MOTOROLA INC, 87- *Personal Data:* b Pueblo, Colo, Jan 24, 32; DIV; c 3. *Educ:* Princeton Univ, AB, 54; Washington Univ, BS, 56, MS, 57; Purdue Univ, PhD, 67. *Honors & Awards:* Guerard Mackey Award, Am Soc Mech Engrs, 73. *Prof Exp:* Res engr drilling, Jersey Prod Res Co, Stand Oil NJ, 57-62; prof mech eng, Univ Mo, Rolla, 66-72 & 73-79; prin acoust consult, Coffeen, Gatley & Assoc, 72-73. *Concurrent Pos:* Prin investr, NSF, 69-72; consult, Gulf Oil Corp, 74-77 & Gen Motors Corp, 76-; adj prof mech eng, Fla Atlantic Univ, 79-87. *Mem:* Am Soc Mech Engrs; Inst Noise Control Eng; Am Soc Eng Educ. *Res:* Noise control; vibrations; mechanical design. *Mailing Add:* 4114 E Sahuaro Dr Phoenix AZ 85028

GATLIN, DELBERT MONROE, III, FISH NUTRITION, NUTRITIONAL BIOCHEMISTRY. *Current Pos:* asst prof, Dept Wildlife & Fisheries Sci, 87-93, ASSOC PROF, GRAD FAC NUTRIT, TEX A&M UNIV, 93- *Personal Data:* b Dallas, Tex, May 22, 58; m 82, Marilyn Martin; c Delbert M IV. *Educ:* Miss State Univ, PhD(nutrit), 83. *Prof Exp:* Asst prof animal nutrit, Univ Ark, Pine Bluff, 85-87. *Mem:* Am Inst Nutrit; Am Fisheries Soc; World Aquacult Soc. *Res:* Basic nutrition of fishes and shellfishes, with emphasis on species cultured for human consumption; determining dietary requirements for and metabolism of various nutrients; nutrition energetics, nutrition-diseases interactions, and nutritional biochemistry of fish as it relates to human health; comprehensive basic nutrition program targeted to improve production efficiency in aquaculture and enhance the quality of resulting products. *Mailing Add:* Dept Wildlife & Fisheries Sci Tex A&M Univ Col Sta TX 77843-2258. *Fax:* 409-845-4096

GATLIN, LILA L, THEORETICAL BIOLOGY, PHYSICAL CHEMISTRY. *Personal Data:* b Hutchinson, Kans; m 47; c 4. *Educ:* Univ Tulsa, BS, 57; Pa State Univ, MS, 59; Univ Tex, Austin, PhD(phys chem), 63. *Prof Exp:* NIH fel, Genet Found, Univ Tex, Austin, 63-64; asst prof phys chem, Drexel Univ, 64-66; vis lectr, Bryn Mawr Col, 66-67; res biophysicist, Space Sci Lab, Univ Calif, Berkeley, 70-74; assoc res geneticist & lectr genetics, Univ Calif, Davis, 74-75; Thomas Welton Stanford fel, Psychol Dept, Stanford Univ, 78-79, vis scholar, Dept Biol Sci, 93-97. *Mem:* AAAS. *Res:* Application of information theory to the living system; information theory and physical research. *Mailing Add:* 80-Q N Cabrillo Hwy No 130 Half Moon Bay CA 94019

GATLING, ROBERT RIDDICK, ANATOMIC PATHOLOGY. *Current Pos:* CHIEF LAB SERV, VET ADMIN MED CTR, 70- *Educ:* Tulane Univ, MD, 41. *Mailing Add:* Dept Path Univ Miss Vet Admin Med Ctr Jackson MS 39216-5199

GATOS, H(ARRY) C(ONSTANTINE), ELECTRONIC MATERIAL, SEMICONDUCTORS. *Current Pos:* leader, Chem & Metall Group, Lincoln Lab, Mass Inst Technol, 55-59, assoc head, Solid State Div, 59-62, head, 62-66, prof electronic mat & molecular eng, 62-90, EMER PROF & SR LECTR ELECTRONIC MAT & MOLECULAR ENG, DEPT MAT SCI ENG & ELEC ENG, MASS INST TECHNOL, 90- *Personal Data:* b Greece, Dec 27, 21; m 50, 87, Ronna Galipeau; c Pamela, Niki & Cobey. *Educ:* Nat Univ Athens, dipl, 45; Ind Univ, AM, 48; Mass Inst Technol, PhD(chem), 50. *Hon Degrees:* DSc, Ind Univ, 83. *Honors & Awards:* Solid State Sci & Technol Award, Electrochem Soc, 75, Acheson Medal, 82; Outstanding Sci Achievement Award, NASA, 75; Golden Cross Order Merit, Polish Peoples Repub, 80; Harry C Gatos Distinguished Lect & Prize, 91; Int Gallium Arsenide & Related Compounds Award, 92; Heinrich Welker Gold Medal, 92. *Prof Exp:* Instr inorg chem, Nat Univ Athens, 42-46; asst metall, Mass Inst Technol, 48-50, res assoc, 50-51, mem res staff, 51-52; res engr, E I du Pont de Nemours & Co, 52-55. *Concurrent Pos:* Consult, var indust & govt orgns; founder & ed-in-chief, Surface Sci, 64-91. *Mem:* Nat Acad Eng; corresp mem & fel AAAS; hon mem Electrochem Soc (pres, 67-68); Am Phys Soc; Am Inst Mining, Metall & Petrol Engrs; corresp mem Am Acad Arts & Sci; Mat Res Soc (pres, 73-75); corresp mem Acad Athens. *Res:* Electrochemistry; electronic materials; semiconductors; applications. *Mailing Add:* 20 Indian Hill Rd Weston MA 02193. *Fax:* 781-891-6656

GATRONE, RALPH CARL, IONIC RECOGNITION, SEPARATIONS CHEMISTRY. *Current Pos:* PROF & CHAIR ORG CHEM, WILKES UNIV, 94- *Personal Data:* b Kingston, Pa, Apr 3, 53; m 76, Colleen G Driscoll; c Laura, Ralph & Erin. *Educ:* Wilkes Col, BS, 75; Univ Buffalo, PhD(synthetic org), 80. *Honors & Awards:* Pollution Prev Award, Dept Energy, 94. *Prof Exp:* Postdoctoral assoc, Stanford Univ, 79-80; res chemist, Allied Signal Corp, 80-86; asst scientist, Argonne Nat Lab, 86-89, scientist, 89-94. *Concurrent Pos:* Consult, Eichrome Indust Int, 89-93; spec term appointment, Argonne Nat Lab, 94-96; chmn, I&EC Div, Am Chem Soc, 96. *Mem:* Am Chem Soc. *Res:* Preparation of crown ethers with ionic recognition properties for the monvalent cations, specifically cesium and lithium. *Mailing Add:* Dept Chem Wilkes Univ Wilkes-Barre PA 18766. *Fax:* 717-831-7862; *E-Mail:* gatrone@wilkes.edu

GATROUSIS, CHRISTOPHER, NUCLEAR CHEMISTRY, PHYSICAL CHEMISTRY. *Current Pos:* chemist, 66-72, from asst div leader to div leader, Nuclear Chem Div, 72-85, ASSOC DIR, CHEM & MATS SCI, LAWRENCE LIVERMORE LAB, UNIV CALIF, 85- *Personal Data:* b Norwich, Conn, Oct 8, 28; c John. *Educ:* DePaul Univ, BS, 57; Univ Chicago, MS, 60; Clark Univ, PhD(nuclear chem), 65. *Prof Exp:* Res asst, Argonne Nat Lab, 56-61; asst scientist, Woods Hole Oceanog Inst, 64-66. *Mem:* Am Phys Soc; Am Chem Soc. *Res:* Mechanisms of nuclear reactions; nuclear spectroscopy; radiochemistry and geochemistry of fallout radionuclides; detection of low level radioactivity. *Mailing Add:* Lawrence Livermore Lab Univ Calif MS-L353 PO Box 808 Livermore CA 94551-0808. *Fax:* 510-423-7040; *E-Mail:* gatrousisi@llnl.gov

GATSKI, THOMAS BERNARD, FLUID DYNAMICS, TURBULENCE. *Current Pos:* res scientist aerocoust, NASA Langley Res Ctr, 77-81, res scientist viscous flow br, 81-90, sr res scientist Theoret Flow, Physics Br, 90-94, SR RES SCIENTIST, AERODYN & ACOUST METHODS BR, NASA LANGLEY RES CTR, 94- *Personal Data:* b Hazleton, Pa, Aug 30, 48; m 70, Rosann; c Megan. *Educ:* Pa State Univ, BS, 70, MS, 72, PhD(aerospace eng), 76. *Prof Exp:* Res assoc turbulence, Div Eng, Brown Univ, 75-77. *Mem:* Am Phys Soc. *Res:* Aerodynamic drag reduction; sound generating mechanisms of turbulent shear flows and their suppression; flow of non-Newtonian fluids; turbulence closure modeling. *Mailing Add:* 721 E Tazewell Way Williamsburg VA 23185. *Fax:* 757-864-8816; *E-Mail:* t.b.gatski@larc.nasa.gov

GATTEN, ROBERT EDWARD, JR, ENVIRONMENTAL PHYSIOLOGY, COMPARATIVE PHYSIOLOGY. *Current Pos:* from asst prof to assoc prof, 78-86, PROF BIOL, UNIV NC, GREENSBORO, 86-, HEAD BIOL, 88- *Personal Data:* b Lexington, Ky, Dec 21, 44; m 68, Florence Fraser; c David & Elizabeth. *Educ:* Col William & Mary, BS, 66, MA, 68; Univ Mich, PhD(zool), 73. *Prof Exp:* Lectr biol, Col William & Mary, 66-67; asst prof biol, Col Wooster, 73-75; asst prof biol, Univ Toledo, 75-78. *Mem:* AAAS; Am Soc Zoologists; Am Soc Ichthyologists & Herpetologists'; Herpetologists League; Soc Study Amphibians & Reptiles. *Res:* Aerobic and anaerobic metabolism in amphibians and reptiles during exercise, diving, and hibernation; thermoregulation in reptiles. *Mailing Add:* Dept Biol Univ NC Greensboro NC 27412-5001. *Fax:* 910-334-5839; *E-Mail:* gatten@iris.uncg.edu

GATTERDAM, PAUL ESCH, AGRICULTURAL CHEMISTRY. *Current Pos:* SR RES CHEMIST, AGR RES CTR, AM CYANAMID CO, 62- *Personal Data:* b La Crosse, Wis, June 27, 29; m 57, Margaret Gutzke; c Hans, Greta & Kort. *Educ:* Univ Wis, BS, 53, MS, 57, PhD(entom), 58. *Prof Exp:* Med entomologist, Agr Res Serv, USDA, 58-60; res asst prof entom, Pesticide Residue Lab, NC State Univ, 61-62. *Mem:* Am Entom Soc. *Res:* Toxicology, persistence, and metabolism of pesticides in or on plants, animals and soil. *Mailing Add:* 15 Pin Oak Dr Trenton NJ 08648. *Fax:* 609-275-3522

GATTI, ANTHONY ROGER, INORGANIC CHEMISTRY, RESEARCH ADMINISTRATION. *Current Pos:* RETIRED. *Personal Data:* b Buffalo, NY, Sept 18, 35; m 57; c 2. *Educ:* Brown Univ, BS, 57; Pa State Univ, PhD(chem), 67. *Prof Exp:* Chemist, Arthur D Little, Inc, Mass, 60-63; from res chemist to sr res chemist & res supvr, Houston Res Lab, Shell Oil Co, 67-73, staff res chemist, 73-80, res supvr, 80-81, dept mgr res, Elastomers

Dept, 81-90, mgr technol acquisition, 90-91. *Mem:* Catalysis Soc. *Res:* Catalysis; the inorganic chemistry and structure of transition metal and noble metal catalysts used in the processing of petroleum products; administration of catalysis and process research; process and product research in thermoplastic elastomers. *Mailing Add:* 21107 Glenwillow Dr Tomball TX 77375

GATTI, PHILIP JOHN, NEUROANATOMY. *Current Pos:* asst prof, 86-92, ASSOC PROF PHARMACOL, HOWARD UNIV COL MED, 92- *Personal Data:* b Jersey City, NJ, June 20, 56; m 93, Jasmine Chen. *Educ:* Villanova Univ, BS, 78; Univ Med & Dent NJ, PhD(pharmacol), 83. *Prof Exp:* Res instr pharmacol, Georgetown Univ Sch Med, 85-86. *Mem:* Am Soc Pharmacol & Exp Therapeut; Soc Neurosci; Am Heart Asn. *Res:* Central neural control of autonomic function; synaptic circuitry of central nervous system pathways identified by neuronal tracers and immunocytochemistry. *Mailing Add:* Dept Pharmacol Howard Univ Col Med Washington DC 20059-0001. *Fax:* 202-806-4453

GATTINGER, RICHARD LARRY, PHYSICS, AERONOMY. *Current Pos:* Asst res off, 64-70, assoc res off physics, 70-77, SR RES OFFICER, NAT RES COUN CAN, 78-; CONTRACTOR, CAN SPACE AGENCY, 96- *Personal Data:* b Neudorf, Sask, June 28, 37; m 62; c 3. *Educ:* Univ Sask, BE, 60, MSc, 62, PhD(physics), 64. *Mem:* Am Geophys Union. *Res:* Observation and interpretation of the atmospheric phenomena classes as airglow and aurora, in near infrared, visible and ultraviolet. *Mailing Add:* 2143 Grafton Crescent Ottawa ON K1J 6K7 Can

GATTO, LOUIS ALBERT, PHYSIOLOGY. *Current Pos:* PROF BIOL, STATE UNIV NY, 78- *Personal Data:* b Montevideo, Repub of Uruguay, Feb 3, 50; nat US. *Educ:* Fordham Univ, MS, 74, PhD(biol), 78. *Mem:* AAAS; Am Soc Zoologists; Sigma Xi; Am Physiol Soc; Am Micros Soc. *Res:* Histophysiology of the respiratory airways in mammals; the pharmacology of their mucosal glands is elucidated by histochemistry and correlated with the viscoelasticity of the mucus. *Mailing Add:* Dept Biol Sci State Univ NY Col-Cortland PO Box 2000 Cortland NY 13045

GATTONE, VINCENT H, II, NEPHROLOGY, HYPERTENSION. *Current Pos:* from asst prof to assoc prof, 86-95, PROF ANAT, CELL BIOL, UNIV KANS MED CTR, 95- *Personal Data:* b Philadelphia, Pa, June 8, 51; m 77, Diane M Wehrle; c Jennifer, Christina, Anthony, Nicholas & Catherine. *Educ:* Ursinus Col, BS, 73; George Washington Univ, MS, 75; Med Col Ohio, PhD(anat), 81. *Prof Exp:* Res fel renal med & hypertension, Sch Med, Ind Univ, 80-83; asst prof anat, M S Hershey Med Ctr, Pa State Univ, 83-86. *Concurrent Pos:* Vis prof, Univ Mich Med Sch, 94-95. *Mem:* Am Asn Anatomists; Soc Neurosci; Am Soc Nephrology; Am Heart Asn; Int Soc Nephrology; Int Pediat Nephrology Asn; AAAS. *Res:* Renal innervation and microvasculature in AIDS nephropathy hypertension; polycystic kidney disease; renal growth factors. *Mailing Add:* Univ Kans Med Ctr Dept Anat Cell Biol 3901 Rainbow Blvd Kansas City KS 66160-7400. *Fax:* 913-588-2710; *E-Mail:* vgattone@kumc.edu

GATZ, ARTHUR JOHN, JR, ECOLOGY. *Current Pos:* from asst prof to assoc prof, 75-88, PROF ZOOL, OHIO WESLEYAN UNIV, 88- *Personal Data:* b Oak Park, Ill, Aug 11, 47; m 86, Michele Moore; c David & Michael. *Educ:* Dickinson Col, AB, 69; Duke Univ, PhD(zool), 75. *Concurrent Pos:* Vis scientist, Environ Sci Div, Oak Ridge Nat Lab, 83-85. *Mem:* AAAS; Ecol Soc Am; Sigma Xi; Animal Behav Soc. *Res:* Population and community ecology of freshwater stream fishes; functional morphology of fishes; population biology of amphibians. *Mailing Add:* Dept Zool Ohio Wesleyan Univ Delaware OH 43015. *E-Mail:* ajgatz@cc.owu.edu

GATZ, CAROLE R, PHYSICAL CHEMISTRY. *Current Pos:* asst prof, 64-68, assoc prof, 68-78, PROF CHEM, PORTLAND STATE UNIV, 78- *Personal Data:* b Omaha, Nebr, Jan 26, 33. *Educ:* Iowa State Univ, BS, 54; Univ Ill, PhD(phys chem), 60. *Prof Exp:* Phys chemist, Stanford Res Inst, 59-64. *Concurrent Pos:* Am Asn Univ Women fel, 70-71. *Mem:* Am Phys Soc; Sigma Xi. *Res:* Quantum chemistry; gas kinetics; atmospheric chemistry. *Mailing Add:* 127 NE 157th Ave Portland OR 97230-4824

GATZ, RANDALL NEAL, physiology, for more information see previous edition

GATZY, JOHN T, JR, PHARMACOLOGY, TOXICOLOGY. *Current Pos:* assoc prof pharmacol & toxicol, 73-83, dir pharmacol grad studies, 81-84, actg chair, 82-83, PROF PHARMACOL & TOXICOL, MED SCH, UNIV NC, CHAPEL HILL, 83- *Personal Data:* b Philadelphia, Pa, June 14, 36; m 58; c 3. *Educ:* Pa State Univ, BS, 58; Univ Rochester, PhD(pharmacol), 63. *Prof Exp:* From instr to asst prof pharmacol, Dartmouth Med Sch, 62-73. *Mem:* Am Soc Pharmacol & Exp Therapeut. *Res:* Bioelectric properties and solute transport of epithlial barriers; cell pharmacology and toxicology; cystic fibrosis. *Mailing Add:* Dept Pharmacol Univ NC Med Sch CB 7365 FLOB Chapel Hill NC 27599-0001. *Fax:* 919-966-5640

GAU, JOHN N, ULTRASONICS, ATOMIC & MOLECULAR PHYSICS. *Current Pos:* Fel physics, 77-79, mem tech staff, 79-81, PROG & PROJ MGR, ANDERSON LAB, UNIV CONN, 81- *Personal Data:* b Boston, Mass, June 17, 45. *Educ:* Iowa State Univ, BS, 67; Univ Nebr, MS, 71, PhD(physics), 75. *Concurrent Pos:* Vis assoc prof physics, Univ Conn, 85- *Mem:* Am Phys Soc; Inst Elec & Electronics Engrs. *Mailing Add:* Telco Am 4755 Fords Rd Colorado Springs CO 80907

GAUCHER, GEORGE MAURICE, SECONDARY METABOLISM, POLYKETIDES. *Current Pos:* from asst prof to prof, 65-97, adj prof chem, 87-95, EMER PROF BIOCHEM, UNIV CALGARY, 97- *Personal Data:* b Edmonton, Alta, Jan 6, 38; m 60, Jean M Andrews; c Peter G, Michelle M, John E & Daniel J. *Educ:* Univ Alta, BSc, 60; Univ Pa, PhD(biochem), 63. *Prof Exp:* Res assoc biochem, Univ Ill, 63-65. *Concurrent Pos:* Smith, Kline & French fel, 63-65; sect ed, Can J Microbiol, 79-82, 84-89, ed, 89-93; mem, Biotechnol Comt, Nat Res Coun, 83-88; William Evans vis fel, Univ Otago, NZ, 87; consult, Merck & Co, Inc, 91-95; ErsKine vis prof, Univ Canterbury, NZ, 92. *Mem:* Am Chem Soc; Can Biochem Soc; Can Soc Microbiologists; Am Soc Microbiol; Soc Indust Microbiol; Am Soc Biochem & Molecular Biol. *Res:* Enzymatic, metabolic, regulatory and genetic aspects of secondary metabolite (polyketide) production by microscopic fungi; mycotoxins; biotransformation technology. *Mailing Add:* Biochem Div Dept Biol Sci Univ Calgary Calgary AB T2N 1N4 Can. *Fax:* 403-289-9311; *E-Mail:* gaucher@acs.ucalgary.ca

GAUD, WILLIAM S, ECOLOGICAL MODELING. *Current Pos:* From asst prof to assoc prof, 70-92, dir, Environ Sci Prog, 91-92, PROF BIOL, NORTHERN ARIZ UNIV, 92-, CHMN, DEPT BIOL SCI, 98- *Personal Data:* b Charleston, SC, June 17, 43. *Educ:* Col Charleston, BS, 65; Univ NC, Chapel Hill, PhD(zool), 70. *Concurrent Pos:* NSF fel syst ecol, Biol Sta, Univ Okla, 71; vis res, Swed Univ Agr Sci, 79-80, 87-88. *Mem:* Ecol Soc Am; Sigma Xi. *Res:* Mathematical modeling of ecosystems and of populations; environmental assessment of the effluent effects of coal-burning electric generating stations and of the transmission of electricity on big-horn sheep populations; nitrogen in pine trees; small game animal foraging behavior and its effects on forest nutrient cycles; insect herbivore-plant interactions; wetlands. *Mailing Add:* 1968 N Crescent Dr Flagstaff AZ 86001. *Fax:* 520-523-7500; *E-Mail:* gaud@nauvax.ucc.nau.edu

GAUDETTE, HENRI EUGENE, GEOLOGY, GEOCHEMISTRY. *Current Pos:* from asst prof to assoc prof, 65-78, PROF GEOL, UNIV NH, 78- *Personal Data:* b Boston, Mass, Jan 26, 32; m 60, Alice C; c Eugene. *Educ:* Univ NH, BA, 59; Univ Ill, MS, 62, PhD(geol), 63. *Prof Exp:* Res assoc clay mineral, Univ Ill, 63-65. *Mem:* Geol Soc Am; Mineral Soc Am; Clay Minerals Soc; Geochem Soc; Am Geophys Union. *Res:* Inorganic geochemistry; distribution of minor and trace elements in rocks and minerals; geochronology and isotope geology; marine geochemistry of estuarine and nearshore systems. *Mailing Add:* Dept Earth Sci Univ NH Durham NH 03824. *Fax:* 603-862-1915; *E-Mail:* h_gaudette@unhh.unh.edu

GAUDETTE, LEO EWARD, INDUSTRIAL TOXICOLOGY, CLINICAL TOXICOLOGY. *Current Pos:* RETIRED. *Personal Data:* b South Bellingham, Mass, Mar 29, 25; m 54; c 2. *Educ:* Col of Holy Cross, BS, 49, MS, 50; Georgetown Univ, PhD(biochem), 57. *Prof Exp:* Chemist, Nat Heart Inst, 54-56; biochemist, Worcester Found Exp Biol, 56-58 & Nat Inst Allergy & Infectious Dis, 58-60; chief lab biochem pharmacol, Joseph E Seagram & Sons, 60-62; head neuropharmacol, Riker Labs, 62-63; tech dir, NEN Biomed Assay Labs, Inc, Mass, 63-75; lab mgr ref lab div, Diamond Shamrock Health Sci, Inc, 75-77; dir, Clin & Occup Med Toxicol, Tabershaw Occup Med Asn, 77-88. *Mem:* AAAS; Am Soc Pharmacol & Exp Therapeut; Am Chem Soc; NY Acad Sci; Am Asn Clin Chemists. *Res:* Drug metabolism, enzymes and mechanisms of action of central nervous system drugs; alcoholism; endocrinological function; isotope methodology, radioimmunoassay. *Mailing Add:* 15 Stanley Rd Medway MA 02053-2151

GAUDIN, ANTHONY J, HERPETOLOGY, MORPHOLOGY. *Current Pos:* asst prof, 70-74, assoc prof, 74-78, PROF BIOL, CALIF STATE UNIV, NORTHRIDGE, 78-, CHMN DEPT, 83- *Personal Data:* b New Orleans, La, Aug 11, 38; m 58; c 2. *Educ:* Univ Southern Calif, AB, 59, MS, 64, PhD(biol), 69. *Prof Exp:* Teacher high sch, 60-64; from instr to asst prof biol, Los Angeles Pierce Col, 64-70. *Concurrent Pos:* NSF sci fac fel, 68-69. *Mem:* Am Soc Ichthyol & Herpet; Soc Study Amphibians & Reptiles; Herpetologists League; Sigma Xi. *Res:* Amphibian embryology and osteology. *Mailing Add:* Dept Biol Calif State Univ 18111 Nordhoff St Northridge CA 91330-8303

GAUDINO, MARIO, RENAL MEDICINE, PHYSIOLOGY. *Current Pos:* dir med compliance, 74-80, assoc dir med serv, 80-89, DIR MED CONSULT SERV, CIBA-GEIGY PHARMACEUT CORP, 89- *Personal Data:* b Buenos Aires, Arg, May 22, 18; nat US; m 47, 84, Judith Jenkins; c David & Brian. *Educ:* Univ Buenos Aires, BS, 34, MD, 44; NY Univ, PhD(physiol), 50. *Prof Exp:* Asst & chief lab & instr physiol, Sch Med, Univ Buenos Aires, 37-44, Arg Nat Cult Comn fel, 45; US Dept State fel, NY Univ, 46-48; asst prof physiol, Med Br, Univ Tex, 49; chmn, Dept Biol Physics, Sch Med, Nat Univ LaPlata, 50-51; res assoc surg, Col Med, NY Univ, 52-55, assoc prof, 55-57; med dir, Abbott Labs, Int Co & Abbott Universal, Ltd, 57-62; assoc med dir, Pfizer Int, Inc, 62-67; assoc dir & dir advan clin res int, Merck Sharp & Dohme Res Labs, 67-71, sr dir clin res int, 71-74. *Concurrent Pos:* Univ fel, NY Univ, 46-49, Dazian Found fel, 46-49; assoc dir med writing & advert, Lederle Labs Div, Am Cyanamid Co, 51-52; estab investr, Am Heart Asn, 54-57; assoc dept med, Northwestern Univ Med Sch, 59; clin asst prof, Med Col, Cornell Univ, 71-77. *Mem:* Soc Exp Biol & Med; Am Physiol Soc; Microcirculatory Soc; fel NY Acad Sci; Am Soc Nephrol; AMA; Am Soc Clin Pharmacol & Therapeut; Am Fedn Clin Res. *Res:* Experimental hypertension; kidney; body and cellular water and electrolyte distribution, exchange and excretion; membrane permeability; biophysics; isotopes; hemodynamics; clinical research; pharmaceutical industry; management. *Mailing Add:* Ciba-Geigy Corp 556 Morris Ave Summit NJ 07901-1398. *Fax:* 908-277-4363

GAUDIOSO, STEPHEN LAWRENCE, MANUFACTURING PROCESS & MATERIALS. *Current Pos:* scientist, Xerox Corp, 73-80, tech specialist/proj mgr, Webster Res Ctr, 80-84, sr tech specialist/core mgr advan prods & technol & advan mat & mfg processes, 84-86, mgr technol develop, 86-88, MGR, MFG TECHNOL PLANNING, XEROX, 88- *Personal Data:* b Rochester, NY, Mar 27, 45; m 69; c 5. *Educ:* Rensselaer Polytech Inst, BS, 67; Univ Mich, Ann Arbor, MS, 69, PhD(phys chem), 72. *Prof Exp:* Presidential intern, Argonne Nat Lab, 72-73. *Mem:* Am Chem Soc; Sigma Xi; Tech Asn Graphic Arts; NY Acad Sci. *Res:* Xerographic process and materials, magnetography, lithography, novel imaging; manufacturing materials and processes. *Mailing Add:* 1077 Everwild View Webster NY 14580-8742

GAUDRY, ROGER, ORGANIC CHEMISTRY. *Current Pos:* RETIRED. *Personal Data:* b Quebec, Que, Dec 15, 13; m 41, Madeleine Vallee; c 5. *Educ:* Laval Univ, BA, 33, BSc, 37, DSc, 40. *Hon Degrees:* Eleven hon doctorates from var univs. *Honors & Awards:* Pariseau Medal, French-Can Asn Advan Sci, 58. *Prof Exp:* Lectr chem fac med, Laval Univ, 40-45; from asst prof to prof, 45-54; asst dir res, Ayerst Labs, Inc & Ayerst, McKenna & Harrison, Ltd, 54-57, dir, 57-63, vpres & dir res, Ayerst, McKenna & Harrison, Ltd, 63-65; rector, Univ Montreal, 65-75; pres, Int Asn Univs, 75-80. *Concurrent Pos:* Vpres, Sci Coun Can, 66-72, pres, 72-75; mem, Acad Latin World, Paris, 67; pres bd, Asn Univs & Cols Can, 69; chmn, Coun UN Univ, 74-76; chmn bd, Network Neural Regeneration & Functional Recovery, 90-96. *Mem:* Am Chem Soc; fel Royal Soc Can; Chem Inst Can (pres, 55-56); Ordre des Chimistes du Quebec. *Res:* Amino acid synthesis and metabolism. *Mailing Add:* Univ Montreal PO Box 6128 Montreal PQ H3C 3J7 Can. *Fax:* 514-343-5744

GAUDY, ANTHONY F, JR, BIOENGINEERING, CIVIL ENGINEERING. *Current Pos:* H Rodney Sharp prof & chmn, Dept Civil Eng, 79-89, EMER PROF, UNIV DEL, 89- *Personal Data:* b Jamaica, NY, June 16, 25; m 55. *Educ:* Univ Mass, BS, 51; Mass Inst Technol, MS, 55; Univ Ill, PhD(eng), 59. *Honors & Awards:* Harrison P Eddy Medal, Water Pollution Control Fedn, 67. *Prof Exp:* Jr engr, Metcalf & Eddy & Alfred Hopkins Assoc, 51; engr, E F Carlson, Inc, 51-52 & Capuano Inc; res asst, Sedgwick Labs, Mass Inst Technol, 53-55; res engr, Nat Coun Stream Improv, 55-57; asst prof sanit eng, Univ Ill, 59-61; from assoc prof to prof, Okla State Univ, 61-68, actg head sch civil eng, 66-67, chmn bioeng & water resources prog, 67-68, Edward R Stapley prof civil eng & dir, Bioeng & Water Resources Prog, 68-79. *Concurrent Pos:* USPHS grant develop grad prog bioenviron eng & res grants, 62-78; vpres, Thomas, Gaudy, McCaskill, Inc, Memphis, Tenn, 70- & Environ Eng Consult Inc, Stillwater, Okla, 74-; Sigma Xi lectr, 71-72. *Mem:* Am Soc Civil Engrs; Water Pollution Control Fedn; Am Water Works Asn; Am Soc Microbiol; Am Chem Soc; Sigma Xi. *Res:* Shock loading, kinetics and mechanism of activated sludge processes; response of biological systems to physical, chemical and biological environment and engineering control of such response. *Mailing Add:* 9335 Merriweather Dr Brooksville FL 34613-4228

GAUFIN, ARDEN RUPERT, ZOOLOGY, LIMNOLOGY. *Current Pos:* instr, 46-49, from assoc prof to prof, 53-77, EMER PROF ZOOL, UNIV UTAH, 77- *Personal Data:* b Salt Lake City, Utah, Dec 25, 11; m 36, Ruth Luny; c 2. *Educ:* Univ Utah, BS, 35, MS, 37; Iowa State Col, PhD(fisheries biol), 51. *Prof Exp:* Instr, Bd Ed, Salt Lake City, 36-43. *Concurrent Pos:* Inspector, Salt Lake City Mosquito Abatement, 35-43 & Terminex of Utah, 39-43; in chg stream sanit res unit, Environ Health Ctr, Cincinnati, 50-53, Salt Lake City Metrop Water Dist, 54-64, NIH, 59-63 & USPHS, 63-65; asst dir biol sta, Univ Mont, 63-75, prof, 68-69; consult, Nat Acad Sci, NIH & Philadelphia Acad Sci. *Mem:* Am Soc Limnol & Oceanog; Am Fisheries Soc; Ecol Soc Am; Entom Soc Am; NAm Benthological Soc. *Res:* Limnological surveys and fisheries investigations; ecology of stoneflies; water pollution research. *Mailing Add:* 5520 Breckenridge Dr Salt Lake City UT 84117

GAUGER, WENDELL LEE, MYCOLOGY. *Current Pos:* from asst prof to assoc prof, 59-67, chmn dept, 65-71, PROF BOT, UNIV NEBR, LINCOLN, 67- *Personal Data:* b Eustis, Nebr, Nov 7, 27; m 52; c 4. *Educ:* Univ Nebr, BS, 51; Univ Idaho, MS, 53; Purdue Univ, PhD(bot), 56. *Prof Exp:* Asst prof bot, Univ Nebr, 56-58; assoc prof biol, Nebr Wesleyan Univ, 58-59. *Mem:* Mycol Soc Am. *Res:* Genetics and variability of fungi. *Mailing Add:* 3501 Everett St Lincoln NE 68506

GAUGHAN, RENATA RYSNIK, PHYSICAL CHEMISTRY. *Current Pos:* sr chemist, Polymer Chem Res Labs, 74-78, sr analyst, Corp New Ventures, 78-80, MKT MGR MONOMERS, ROHM & HAAS CO, 80- *Personal Data:* US citizen. *Educ:* Temple Univ, AB, 66; Univ Pa, PhD(phys chem), 71; Wharton Bus Sch, mgt cert, 80. *Prof Exp:* Res assoc phys chem, Brown Univ, 71-72; res assoc phys & inorg chem, Northwestern Univ, 73-74. *Mem:* Am Chem Soc; Tech Asn Pulp & Paper Indust; Chem Mkt Res Asn. *Res:* Physical chemistry of polymers; polymer synthesis. *Mailing Add:* 1369 Gwynedale Way Lansdale PA 19446-5375

GAUGHAN, ROGER GRANT, POLYMER CHEMISTRY, AVIATION & AUTOMOTIVE FUELS CHEMISTRY. *Current Pos:* STAFF CHEMIST AVIATION FUELS RES, EXXON RES & ENG CO, 90- *Personal Data:* b Elizabeth, NJ, June 16, 51; m 76. *Educ:* NMex Inst Mining & Technol, BS, 74, MS, 76; Univ Utah, PhD(org chem), 80. *Prof Exp:* Res chemist polymer synthesis, Phillips Petrol Co, 80-85. *Mem:* Am Chem Soc; Am Soc Testing & Mats; Soc Automotive Engrs. *Res:* Synthetic organic chemistry and synthesized terpenes; synthesized monomers and subsequently polymerized them; developed automotive fuel additives; developed unleaded aviation gasoline. *Mailing Add:* 501 Ellis Parkway Piscataway NJ 08854-4514. *Fax:* 908-474-2335

GAUGHRAN, GEORGE RICHARD LAWRENCE, ANATOMY. *Current Pos:* from assoc prof to prof, 61-85, vchmn dept, 64-74, EMER PROF ANAT, COL MED, OHIO STATE UNIV, 85- *Personal Data:* b Pa, Oct 19, 19; m 43; c 1. *Educ:* Lehigh Univ, BA, 42; Univ Mich, MS, 47; PhD(zool), 52. *Prof Exp:* Res assoc, Mass Inst Technol, 43; from instr to asst prof anat, Med Sch, Univ Mich, 51-61. *Mem:* Am Asn Anatomists. *Res:* Gross human anatomy. *Mailing Add:* 3630 Grafton Columbus OH 43220-5023

GAUGL, JOHN F, CORONARY FLOW, RESPIRATORY PHYSIOLOGY. *Current Pos:* chmn, Dept Physiol, 71-81, ASSOC PROF MED PHYSIOL, TEX COL OSTEOP MED, 71-; ASSOC PROF, DEPT INTEGRATIVE PHYSIOL, UNIV NTEX HEALTH SCI CTR, 71- *Personal Data:* b Manchester, Conn, May 11, 37; m 87, Lee Hebert; c 3. *Educ:* NTex State Univ, BA, 61, MA, 62; Univ Calif, Berkeley, PhD(physiol), 70. *Prof Exp:* Actg asst prof exercise physiol, Univ Calif, Berkeley, 70-71; chmn, Dept Physiol, 71-81, ASSOC PROF MED PHYSIOL, TEX COL OSTEOP MED, 71- *Mem:* Am Physiol Soc; Am Col Sports Med. *Res:* Controlling factors of right coronary blood flow in dogs; interrelationships between the autonomic nervous system and endogenous opiates in cardiovascular function. *Mailing Add:* Dept Integrative Physiol Univ NTex Health Sci Ctr 3500 Camp Bowie Ft Worth TX 76107-2690

GAUGLER, ROBERT WALTER, BIOCHEMISTRY. *Current Pos:* res asst prof, 80-83, asst res & develop, Naval Med Command, 83-87, EXEC OFFICER, NAVAL MED RES & DEVELOP COMMAND, UNIFORMED SERV UNIV, 87- *Personal Data:* b Paterson, NJ, Aug 12, 40; m 65; c 3. *Educ:* Hope Col, BA, 63; Pa State Univ, MS, 66; Georgetown Univ, PhD(biochem), 73; Roosevelt Univ, MBA, 80. *Prof Exp:* Res chemist biochem, Naval Med Res Inst, 66-68; chief, Lab Res Dept, Nat Naval Dent Ctr, 70-76, res biochemist dent biochem, Naval Dent Res Inst, 76-80. *Mem:* Int Asn Dent Res; Am Chem Soc; Am Soc Microbiol. *Res:* Relationship of bacterial polysaccharides to dental disease; enzymatic degradation of insoluble glucans of streptococcus mutants; fluoride concentrations in dental plaque. *Mailing Add:* 9089 Wexford Dr Vienna VA 22182-2152

GAUHAR, ARUNA, NEUROLOGY, NEUROPATHOLOGY. *Current Pos:* STAFF NEUROPATHOLOGIST, VET ADMIN MED CTR, NORTH CHICAGO, 77- *Personal Data:* b Nagpur, India, Jan 4, 40. *Educ:* Panjab Univ, India, ISc, 56, MB & BS, 61. *Prof Exp:* Resident path, Univ Chicago, 65-67, from instr to asst prof, 69-74; fel neuropath & electron micros, Northwestern Univ & Vet Admin Hosp, Hines, Ill, 67-69, resident neurol, Northwestern Univ, 74-76; assoc prof neurol & neuropath, Chicago Med Sch, 77-80, prof neurol & path, 80-84; consult & assoc prof, Chicago Osteop Col & Hosp, 78-83. *Concurrent Pos:* House physician internal med, Irwin Hosp, New Delhi, India, 62; demonstr path, Christian Med Col, Ludhiana, India, 62, house physician internal med, 63; asst dir autopsy serv, Dept Path, Univ Chicago, 70-72, assoc dir neuropath, 70-74; pvt pract neurol, Baltimore, 84- *Mem:* Am Asn Neuropathologists; Int Acad Path; fel Am Acad Neurol; Sigma Xi. *Res:* Clincial neuropathology and electron microscopy; chromatolysis and axonal reaction in spinal cord motor neurons. *Mailing Add:* 1131 Manor Rd Glen Arm MD 21057

GAUL, RICHARD JOSEPH, ORGANIC CHEMISTRY. *Current Pos:* RETIRED. *Personal Data:* b Pittsfield, Mass, Oct 3, 29; m 53; c 5. *Educ:* Spring Hill Col, BS, 49; Mass Inst Technol, PhD(org chem), 54. *Prof Exp:* Res chemist, Am Cyanamid Co, 54-59; assoc prof chem & actg dir dept, John Carroll Univ, 59-62, dir, 62-65, prof chem, 62. *Mem:* Am Chem Soc. *Res:* Synthetic studies related to penicillin; products derived from acrylonitrile; chemistry of sulfur-nitrogen heterocycles; rocket propellants; structure of terreic acid; synthesis and polarographic behavior of polychlorinated propionitriles, acrylonitriles and derivatives. *Mailing Add:* 9091 Gregory Ct Mentor OH 44060

GAULDEN, MARY ESTHER, RADIOLOGY, RADIOBIOLOGY. *Current Pos:* asst prof, 65-68, assoc prof radiol, 68-96, ADJ PROF, HEALTH SCI CTR, UNIV TEX, DALLAS, 96- *Personal Data:* b Rock Hill, SC, Apr 30, 21; m 56, John Jagger; c Thomas & Yvonne. *Educ:* Winthrop Col, BS, 42; Univ Va, MA, 44, PhD(biol), 48. *Prof Exp:* Res asst cell biol, Univ Ala, 45-46; biologist radiation biol, NIH, 46-47; instr zool, Univ Tenn, 47-49; sr biologist radiation biol, Oak Ridge Nat Lab, 49-65. *Concurrent Pos:* Vis prof, Univ NC, Chapel Hill, 54-55; consult, Oak Ridge Nat Lab, 65-70; acad affil, Med Ctr, Baylor Univ, 75- *Mem:* Fel AAAS; Radiol Soc NAm; Am Soc Cell Biol; Radiation Res Soc; Am Soc Photobiol; Environ Mutagen Soc. *Res:* Effects of low doses of radiation, especially on chromosomes and on man; genotoxicity of chemicals; aneuploidy; Down syndrome. *Mailing Add:* Dept Radiol Univ Tex Southwestern Med Ctr 5323 Hines Blvd Dallas TX 75235-9071. *Fax:* 214-648-7513

GAULDIE, JACK, PATHOLOGY. *Current Pos:* PROF PATH, MCMASTER UNIV, 71- *Educ:* Univ Col, London, PhD(biochem), 68. *Mailing Add:* Dept Path 2N16 McMaster Univ 1200 Main St W Hamilton ON L8N 3Z5 Can. *Fax:* 905-577-0198

GAULT, DONALD E, ASTROGEOLOGY, PLANETARY SCIENCES. *Current Pos:* CHIEF PLANETOLOGIST, MURPHYS CTR PLANETOLOGY, 76- *Personal Data:* b Chicago, Ill, Feb 12, 23; m 47, Mary L Deaver; c Frank L, Kathleen A & Jan M. *Educ:* Purdue Univ, BS, 44. *Honors & Awards:* Medal Except Sci Achievement, NASA, 67; Barringer Medal, Meteoritical Soc, 86; G K Giblert Award, Geol Soc Am 87. *Prof Exp:* Res scientist aerodyn, NASA, 44-59, res scientist ballistics, 59-63, chief planetology br, 63-72, sr staff scientist, Ames Res Ctr, 72-76. *Concurrent Pos:*

Guggenheim fel, Max Planck Inst fur Kern Physik, 72; adj prof, Univ Ariz, 77; Fairchild distinguished scholar, Calif Inst Technol, 78. *Mem:* Am Geophys Union; Meteoritical Soc; fel Geol Soc Am. *Res:* Shock wave dynamics; meteoritics; selenology; impact cratering; comparative planetology. *Mailing Add:* 4229 Parrotts Ferry Rd Vallecito CA 95251

GAULT, N(EAL) L, JR, MEDICINE. *Current Pos:* dean, 72-84, prof, 72-91, EMER PROF INTERNAL MED, MED SCH, UNIV MINN, MINNEAPOLIS, 91- *Personal Data:* b Austin, Tex, Aug 22, 20; m 47, Sarah Diakie; c 3. *Educ:* Univ Tex, BA, 50; Univ Minn, MB, 50, MD, 51. *Honors & Awards:* Supreme Award, Japan Med Asn, 69; Order Rising Sun, Gold Rays with Neck Ribbon, Japan, 92. *Prof Exp:* From instr to assoc prof internal med, Univ Minn, Minneapolis, 53-67, from asst dean to assoc dean, Col Med Sci, 55-67; prof internal med & assoc dean, Sch Med, Univ Hawaii, 67-72. *Concurrent Pos:* Med adv, Seoul Nat Univ, 59-61; consult, Vet Admin Hosp, Minneapolis, 56-67; China Med Bd Ny, Inc, 63, 71 & AID, 64-67; dir postgrad med educ prog, Ryukyu Islands, 67-69; mem coun deans & exec coun, Asn Am Med Col, 74-80; pres, Minn Int Health Vol, 87-; mem, State Minn Bd Continuing Legal Educ, 86; comnr, secy Vet Affairs, Comn Study Health Care Vet in 2010, 90-91. *Mem:* Asn Am Med Cols; AMA. *Res:* Medical education and administration. *Mailing Add:* UMHC PO Box 194 420 Delaware St Minneapolis MN 55455. *Fax:* 612-626-7809; *E-Mail:* gaultool@maroon.tc.umn.edu

GAUM, CARL H, CIVIL ENGINEERING, WATER RESOURCES. *Current Pos:* PRIN ENGR, GAUM & ASSOCS, KENSINGTON, MD, 85- *Personal Data:* b New York, NY, July 29, 22; m 55, Ruth E Banks; c Virginia L (Collison) & Carlann R (Fergusson). *Educ:* Rutgers Univ, BSCE, 49, MSE, 62. *Prof Exp:* Hydraul engr, US Geol Surv, 49-53; consult engr, Gaum Prof Engrs, 53-55; supvry hydraul engr, Philadelphia Dist, US Army Corps Engrs, 55-60, asst chief, Hydrol Br, DC Dist, 60-61 & Basin Planning Br, Ohio River Div, 62-69, asst chief, Interagency & Spec Studies Br & chief tech assistance & int sect, Planning Div, Off Chief Engrs, 69-73, chief cent reports mgt br, Planning Div, Civil Works Directorate, Off Chief Engrs, 70-80; sr water resources engr, Greenhorne & O'Mara Inc, Riverdale, Md, 80-85. *Concurrent Pos:* Planning assoc, Bd Engrs Rivers & Harbors, 61-62; mem, US Comt Large Dams; chmn US sect Publ Comt, Permanent Int Asn Navig Cong, Leningrad, 76, Edinborough, 81, Brussels, 85 & Osaka, 90. *Mem:* AAAS; fel Am Soc Civil Engrs; Nat Soc Prof Engrs; Permanent Int Asn Navig Cong. *Res:* Comprehensive water and related land resource planning, including surface and ground water supplies, water quality, navigation, flood control, sedimentation, drainage, irrigation, fish and wildlife, recreation, power and beach protection; environment; economic evaluation; resources management. *Mailing Add:* 9609 Carriage Rd Kensington MD 20895-3619

GAUMER, ALBERT EDWIN HELLICK, physiological ecology; deceased, see previous edition for last biography

GAUMER, HERMAN RICHARD, MICROBIOLOGY, IMMUNOLOGY. *Current Pos:* DIR, SPEC IMMUNOL LAB, MED CTR LA, NEW ORLEANS, 80-; ASST PROF PATH, LA STATE UNIV MED CTR, 80- *Personal Data:* b Wilmington, Del, Nov 17, 41; m 65; c 2. *Educ:* Dartmouth Col, AB, 64; Univ Del, MS, 67; Univ NC, Chapel Hill, PhD(microbiol), 71. *Prof Exp:* Fel immunol, Univ Colo Med Ctr, 71-73; asst prof microbiol, Sch Dent, Univ Minn, 73-76; asst prof clin immunol, Med Sch, Tulane Univ, 76-80. *Concurrent Pos:* Dir, Flow Cytometry Resource, Charity Hosp. *Mem:* AAAS; Am Soc Microbiol; Sigma Xi. *Res:* Clinical immunology; immunological classification of lymphoproliferative disorders; use of flow cytometry in clinical laboratory. *Mailing Add:* 7324 Beryl St New Orleans LA 70124

GAUMOND, CHARLES FRANK, ACOUSTICS. *Current Pos:* RES PHYSICIST, NAVAL RES LAB, 79- *Personal Data:* b Watertown, NY, Sept 8, 50. *Educ:* Clarkson Univ, BS, 72; Univ Rochester, MA, 76, PhD(physics), 79. *Concurrent Pos:* Adj prof physics, George Mason Univ, 85- *Mem:* Acoust Soc Am; Am Phys Soc; Inst Elec & Electronics Engrs; AAAS; Sigma Xi. *Res:* Acoustical scattering; acoustical imaging; target strength; sonar design and analysis. *Mailing Add:* Naval Research Lab Code 7142 4555 Overlook Ave SW Washington DC 20375-5320

GAUNAURD, GUILLERMO C, ACOUSTICS, APPLIED MECHANICS. *Current Pos:* RES PHYSICIST, NAVAL SURFACE WARFARE CTR, CARDEROCK DIV, W BETHESDA, MD, 71- *Personal Data:* b Havana, Cuba, July 19, 40; US citizen; m 67, Marlene J Johnson. *Educ:* Cath Univ Am, BA, 64, BSME, 66, MS, 67, PhD(acoust), 71. *Honors & Awards:* Bernard Smith Award; Sci Achievement Bronze Medal, Am Defense Preparedness Asn; In-House Lab Independent Res Prog Excellence in Res Award, Naval Surface Warfare Ctr. *Prof Exp:* Sr engr appl mech, McKiernan-Terry Div, Litton Indust, College Park, Md, 68-71. *Concurrent Pos:* Consult engr, Ocean Systs Inc, Div Union Carbide, Arlington, Va, 66-67; res asst, Cath Univ Am, 69-71; lectr acoustics & dynamics, Univ Md Sch Eng, College Park, 84-92; assoc ed, J Ultrasonics, Ferroelectrics & Frequency Control, Inst Elec & Electronics Engrs, 92- *Mem:* Fel Acoust Soc Am; Sigma Xi; NY Acad Sci; Am Phys Soc; sr mem Inst Elect & Electronics Engrs; fel Am Soc Mech Engrs. *Res:* Radiation and scattering theory; absorption in materials; underwater acoustics; physical acoustics; mechanical vibrations and the general response of structures to acoustic mechanical, and electromagnetic excitations; author, researcher, writer and patentee in field; electromagnetism and general mathematical physics. *Mailing Add:* 4807 Macon Rd Rockville MD 20852-2348. *Fax:* 301-227-1020; *E-Mail:* gaunaurd@oasys.dt.navy.mil

GAUNT, ABBOT STOTT, ZOOLOGY. *Current Pos:* from asst prof to assoc prof, 69-86, PROF ZOOL, OHIO STATE UNIV, 86- *Personal Data:* b Lawrence, Mass, July 4, 36; m 63, Sandra L Lovett. *Educ:* Amherst Col, BA, 58; Univ Kans, PhD(zool), 63. *Prof Exp:* Instr biol, Middlebury Col, 63-66, asst prof, 66-67; fel, State Univ NY, Buffalo, 67-68, asst prof, 68-69. *Mem:* Fel AAAS; Soc Study Evolution; fel Am Ornith Union; Wilson Ornith Soc (2nd vpres, 77-79, 1st vpres, 79-81, pres, 81-); Am Soc Zool; Cooper Ornith Soc. *Res:* Avian vocal mechanisms; avian functional anatomy; structure and function of vertebrate muscle. *Mailing Add:* Dept Zool Ohio State Univ 1735 Neil Ave Columbus OH 43210. *Fax:* 614-292-2030; *E-Mail:* agaunt@magnus.acs.ohio-state.edu

GAUNT, JOHN THIXTON, STRUCTURAL ENGINEERING. *Current Pos:* from instr to asst prof struct eng, 64-96, ASSOC HEAD PROF FRESHMAN ENG, PURDUE UNIV, 96- *Personal Data:* b Evansville, Ind, Feb 29, 36; m 58; c 1. *Educ:* Univ Cincinnati, CE, 58; Purdue Univ, MSCE, 59, PhD(struct), 66. *Prof Exp:* Design engr, Int Steel Co, Evansville, Ind, 59-62. *Concurrent Pos:* Lectr, Univ Evansville, 60-62. *Mem:* Am Soc Civil Engrs; Nat Soc Prof Engrs; Am Soc Eng Educ; Sigma Xi. *Res:* Design and behavior of steel structures; structural analysis; guyed towers. *Mailing Add:* 1286 Eng Admin Bldg Purdue Univ West Lafayette IN 47907-1286

GAUNT, PAUL, SOLID STATE PHYSICS. *Current Pos:* RETIRED. *Personal Data:* b Bootle, Eng, Feb 23, 32; m 64; c 2. *Educ:* Univ Sheffield, BSc, 53; Oxford Univ, DPhil(metall), 58. *Prof Exp:* Lectr physics, Univ Sheffield, 57-68; from assoc prof to prof physics, Univ Man, 68-97. *Res:* Physical property and structural changes associated with magnetic and chemical ordering of metals and alloys; hard magnetic materials; electron microscopy; models of magnetic hardening. *Mailing Add:* Dept Physics Univ Man Winnipeg MB R3T 2N2 Can

GAUNT, ROBERT, endocrinology; deceased, see previous edition for last biography

GAUNT, STANLEY NEWKIRK, ANIMAL GENETICS. *Current Pos:* prof dairy sci, 45-80, EMER PROF ANIMAL SCI & GENET, UNIV MASS, AMHERST, 80- *Personal Data:* b Elmer, NJ, June 20, 15; m 39; c 2. *Educ:* Rutgers Univ, BS, 38; NC State Col, PhD(animal genetics & physiol), 55. *Honors & Awards:* DeLaval Exten Award, Am Dairy Sci, 77. *Prof Exp:* Admin asst, Agr Adjust Admin, NJ, 38-39; from asst co agent to assoc co agent, Litchfield Co Exten Serv, Conn, 39-45. *Concurrent Pos:* Researcher, NC State Col, 51-53; res grants, Nat Asn Artificial Breeders, 56, 57-65, Hood Found, 57-65; mem & chmn, Nat Res Comt Milk Compos, 60-67; res grants, Abelard Found, 62-74, George H Walker Res Fund, 73-79, Eastern Artificial Breeders Coop, 65-78 & Agway grant, 66-67; Fulbright res scholar, Denmark, 69; guest lectr univs, Aberdeen, Cambridge, Lisbon, Ljubljana & Thessalonikia, 69; dairy sci & genetics adv to Colanta, Medellin, Antioquia, Colombia, SAm, 79-84. *Mem:* Am Dairy Sci Asn (secy, 51-52); Am Soc Animal Sci; Am Genetic Asn; NY Acad Sci; Sigma Xi. *Res:* Measures of a dairy sire's genetic merit; programs to maximize genetic progress; genetic and environmental influences on non-fat components of milk; relationships between genetic markers to production and reproduction in dairy cattle and the genetics of mastitis. *Mailing Add:* 901 Russell Ave Apt 308 Gaithersburg MD 20877

GAUNYA, WILLIAM STEPHEN, DAIRY HUSBANDRY. *Current Pos:* RETIRED. *Personal Data:* b Conn, Sept 28, 20; m 47; c 3. *Educ:* Univ Conn, BS, 47; Rutgers Univ, MS, 49, PhD, 61. *Prof Exp:* Res assoc dairy husb, Rutgers Univ, 48-49; asst prof dairy husb, Univ Conn, 49-62, from assoc prof to prof animal industs, 72-84. *Mem:* Am Dairy Sci Asn. *Mailing Add:* 12 Argonomy Rd Storrs Mansfield CT 06268. *Fax:* 860-429-4693

GAUR, PRAMOD KUMAR, IN VITRO MEDICAL DIAGNOSTICS, CLINICAL LABORATORY DIAGNOSTICS. *Current Pos:* VPRES RES & DEVELOP URINE CHEM, BAYER CORP, 94- *Personal Data:* b Jaswantnagar, India, Aug 13, 52; US citizen. *Educ:* Kanpur Univ, BSc, 71, MSc, 73; Pittsburg State Univ, MS, 75; Univ Kans, PhD(bot), 79. *Prof Exp:* Res assoc, Univ Wis, 79-80; res fel, Univ Md Med Sch, 80-81; head, Immunol Sect, Stauffer Chem Co, 81-83, sr res immunologist, 83-84; sect mgr, Hybritech Inc, 84-86, res mgr, 86-88; dir immunodiag res & develop, Baxter Diag Inc, 88-90, dir hemostasis res & develop, 90-91, vpres res & develop, 91-92, vpres mkt, 92-93, prod line gen mgr, 93-94. *Concurrent Pos:* Vis scientist, Nat Defense Med Col Taiwan, 81, 84 & 86; vpres, Indian Alumni Clin Chem, 88-90, pres, 90-92. *Mem:* Sigma Xi; AAAS; Am Asn Clin Chem; Am Asn Immunol; Am Asn Cancer Res. *Res:* Immunodiagnostics; cancer diagnostics and blood coagulation; urinalysis; point-of-care diagnostics. *Mailing Add:* Bayer Corp PO Box 70 Elkhart IN 46515. *Fax:* 219-262-6732

GAUR, SIDDHARTHA, REACTION ENGINEERING, HAZARDOUS WASTE TREATMENT. *Current Pos:* DIR, VSLR SCI, 96- *Personal Data:* b Faizabad, India, Sept 3, 62; m 90, Vibha; c Mansi. *Educ:* Aligarh Univ, India, BS, 83; Indian Inst Technol, PhD(chem eng), 89; Colo Sch Mines, MS, 93. *Prof Exp:* Indust develop engr, Indcon Engrs, India, 83-84; sr res officer, Indian Inst Technol, 89-90; vis res prof chem eng, Colo Sch Mines, 90-95, asst prof res, 95-96. *Concurrent Pos:* Fac mem, Energy Div, UN Univ, 96; tech dir, Boundless Corp, Boulder, Colo, 96, vpres, 96-97. *Mem:* Am Inst Chem Engrs; Bioenergy Soc India. *Res:* Conducted and supervised research in the area of mixed waste, polymer recycling, alternate fuels, fossil fuels, batteries, oil spills, metal oxide catalysis, gasifications and reaction kinetics; thermal properties of stock waste fuels. *Mailing Add:* 6434 DeFrame Ave Arvada CO 80004. *E-Mail:* sgaur@hemi.com

GAURI, KHARAITI LAL, GEOCHEMISTRY, SEDIMENTOLOGY. *Current Pos:* from asst prof to assoc prof, 66-73, PROF GEOL, UNIV LOUISVILLE, 73-, CHMN DEPT, 76- *Personal Data:* b Narowal, India, Oct 16, 33; m 64. *Educ:* Panjab Univ, India, BSc, 53, MA, 55; Univ Bonn, PhD(geol), 64. *Prof Exp:* Lectr geog, D A V Col, Jullundher, 55-58; sci assoc geol, Calif Inst Technol, 65-66; sci pool officer, Coun Sci & Indust Res, New Delhi, India, 66. *Concurrent Pos:* Res grants, Geol Soc Am, 67-68, Res Corp, 67-68 & 70-71, Kress Found, 70-71, Am Res Ctr, Egypt, 80-84, Ky Energy Cabinet, 85-86 & NSF, 86-; deleg, Int Conf of Preservation of Stone Statuary, Bologna, Italy, 69, Int Inst Conserv, New York, 70, 2nd Int Symp Deterioration Bldg Stones, Athens, 76, UNESCO/RILEM Int Symp Deterioration & Protection Stone Monuments, 78 & Fourth Int Cong Deterioration & Preserv of Stone Objects, Louisville, 82. *Mem:* Geol Soc Am; Int Inst Conserv. *Res:* Pollutan effects upon masonry materials; conservation of stone statuary. *Mailing Add:* Geol Dept Univ Louisville 2301 S Third St Louisville KY 40206-0001

GAUS, ARTHUR EDWARD, HORTICULTURE. *Current Pos:* exten horticulturist, 54-66, PROF HORT, UNIV MO, COLUMBIA, 66- *Personal Data:* b Maplewood, Mo, Nov 30, 24; m 50; c 3. *Educ:* Univ Mo, BS, 49, MS, 50, PhD, 57. *Prof Exp:* Asst instr hort, Univ Mo, 51-53; exten horticulturist, Kans State Col, 53-54. *Res:* Cost of production in vegetable crops. *Mailing Add:* 808 Hope Pl Columbia MO 65203

GAUS, PAUL LOUIS, PHOTOCHEMISTRY AND ORGANOMETALLIC CHEMISTRY. *Current Pos:* ASST PROF CHEM, COL WOOSTER, 77- *Personal Data:* b Athens, Ohio, Mar 26, 49; m 72; c 2. *Educ:* Miami Univ, BS, 71; Duke Univ PhD(chem), 75. *Prof Exp:* Res assoc chem, State Univ NY Stony Brook, 75-77. *Concurrent Pos:* Counr, Am Chem Soc, 77- *Mem:* Am Chem Soc; Sigma Xi. *Res:* Substitution and electron transfer reactions of transition metal ions; photochemical reactions of organometallic systems. *Mailing Add:* Dept Chem Col Wooster 1189 Beall Ave Wooster OH 44691-2363

GAUSE, DONALD C, COMPUTER SCIENCE. *Current Pos:* adj asst prof comput sci, State Univ NY, Binghamton, 67-68, vis lectr, 68-70, assoc prof, 70-74, prof systs sci, Sch Advan Technol, 74-84, PROF SYSTS SCI, THOMAS J WATSON SCH ENG, STATE UNIV NY BINGHAMTON, 84-; ADJ STAFF, IBM CORP TECHNOL INST & THEIR SUCCESSORS, NY, 80- *Personal Data:* b Elkhart, Ind, May 4, 34; m 56; c 2. *Educ:* Mich State Univ, BS, 56, MS, 57. *Prof Exp:* Assoc engr, Sperry Gyroscope Co, 57-59; proj engr, Gen Motors Truck & Coach, Gen Motors Corp, 59-60, sr proj engr, 60-61, sr res mathematician, Gen Motors Res Lab, 61-62; sr assoc programmer, IBM Corp, 62-63, staff engr, 63-68, mgr prog educ, 68-70. *Concurrent Pos:* Consult, various corps; pres, Ethnotech, Inc, 77-79; nat lectr, Asn Comput Mach; vis lectr, Sch Archit, Swiss Fed Inst, Zurich, Jung Inst, Norwegian Univs & NZ Univs. *Mem:* Asn Comput Mach; Soc Gen Systs Res. *Res:* Adaptive, self-organizing and general systems theory; creative processes; computer modelling and simulation; heuristic programming; decision theory; creative design; management of innovation; user oriented systems design; design methodology. *Mailing Add:* 3 Kingsgate Lane Owego NY 13827

GAUSS, JOHN A, ELECTRONICS ENGINEERING. *Current Pos:* USN, 69-, electronics mat officer, USS Patterson, combat info ctr officer, opers officer, USS Flint, exec officer, USS Conserver, eng duty officer, airborne anti-submarine warfare proj officer, Naval Surface Warfare Ctr, syst chief engr, Cruise Missiles Proj, maj prog mgr, Space & Naval Warfare Syst Command, prog dir & maj prog mgr, Command Systs, 92-94, COMNDR, JOINT INOPERABILITY & ENG ORGN & DEP DIR ENG & INOPERABILITY, DEFENSE INFO SYST AGENCY, USN, DEPT DEFENSE, 94- *Personal Data:* b Salem, Mass; m, Charlotte Crawford. *Educ:* Cornell Univ, BS, 69; Naval Postgrad Sch, MS, PhD(electronics eng). *Mailing Add:* US Dept Defense 701 S Courthouse Rd Arlington VA 22204-2199

GAUSTAD, JOHN ELDON, OBSERVATIONAL ASTRONOMY EDUCATION. *Current Pos:* PROF ASTRON, SWARTHMORE COL, 82- *Personal Data:* b Minneapolis, Minn, May 23, 38; m 80; c 2. *Educ:* Harvard Col, AB, 59; Princeton Univ, PhD(astron), 62. *Prof Exp:* Res assoc astron, Princeton Univ, 62-63; res fel astron, Mt Wilson & Palomer Observ, 63-64; lectr math, Univ Nigeria, 64-67; from asst prof to prof astron, Univ Cal, Berkeley, 67-82. *Concurrent Pos:* Chmn Astron Surv Comt, Nat Acad Sci, 70-72; chmn vis comt, Kitt Peak Nat Observ, 74-76; chmn Dept Astron, Univ Calif, Berkeley, 76-79; assoc dean Col Lett & Sci, 80-82; chmn Dept Astron, Swarthmore Col, 82-86; dir, Sproul Observ, 82-86; Edward Hicks McGill Prof, 90-; vis prof, Wegloyan Univ, 82. *Mem:* Fel AAAS (secy, 85-94); Am Astron Soc; Int Astron Union; Astron Soc Pac (secy, 87-). *Res:* Stellar evolution; infrared astronomy; interstellar matter. *Mailing Add:* Dept Physics & Astron Swarthmore Col 500 College Ave Swarthmore PA 19081-1390. *Fax:* 610-328-7895; *E-Mail:* jgausta1@swarthmore.edu

GAUSTER, WILHELM BELRUPT, SOLID STATE PHYSICS. *Current Pos:* supv, Phys Res Div, Sandia Nat Labs, 79-82, Fusion Technol Div, 82-87, mgr, Exploratory Nuclear Power Systs Dept, 87-89, MGR, NUCLEAR ENERGY SCI & MAT TECHNOL DEPT, SANDIA NAT LABS, 89- *Personal Data:* b Vienna, Austria, Dec 25, 40; US citizen; m 69; c 2. *Educ:* Harvard Univ, AB, 61; Univ Tenn, PhD(physics), 66. *Prof Exp:* Res assoc, Oak Ridge Nat Lab, 66. *Concurrent Pos:* Mem tech staff, Sandia Nat Labs, 66-; adj prof, Univ NMex, 72-73; vis scientist, Kernforschungsanlage J lich, Ger, 74-75. *Mem:* Am Phys Soc. *Res:* Positron annihilation; radiation damage; muon spin rotation; plasma-wall interactions; thermomechanical effects; nuclear technology. *Mailing Add:* Sandia Nat Labs Dept 1112 MS 1415 PO Box 5800 Albuquerque NM 87185-1415

GAUT, ZANE NOEL, CLINICAL PHARMACOLOGY, NUTRITION. *Current Pos:* CONSULT, 85- *Personal Data:* b Nauvoo, Ala, Aug 29, 29; m 55; c 3. *Educ:* Birmingham-Southern Col, BS, 50; Tulane Univ, MD, 54, PhD(biochem), 64. *Prof Exp:* Intern med, St Thomas Hosp, Nashville, Tenn, 54-55; aerospace med specialist, Gen Dynamics Corp, 58-63; asst prof med & biochem, Tulane Univ, 64-66; clin pharmacologist, 66-72, dir clin nutrit, 72-77, asst med dir, 77-78, dir clin res, Endocrinol/Metab, Hoffmann-La Roche, Inc, 78-85. *Concurrent Pos:* NIH res grant, 63-, fel nutrit, 64-; asst attend physician, St Luke's Med Ctr, NY; asst clin prof, Col Physicians & Surgeons, Columbia Univ; referee ed, Prof Soc Exp Biol & Med; attend, Newark Beth Israel Hosp, NJ. *Mem:* AAAS; Am Soc Pharmacol & Exp Therapeut; Am Inst Nutrit; Am Soc Clin Pharmacol & Therapeut; Am Chem Soc. *Res:* Metabolism in human blood platelets; phase I drug evaluation in man; hyperlipidemia; bone disease; obesity. *Mailing Add:* Biomed-Pharmaceut Res 51 Mountain Ave Warren NJ 07059-5337. *Fax:* 908-604-4611

GAUTHIER, DIDIER, CELL BIOLOGY, ECOTOXYCOLOGY. *Current Pos:* lectr, 84-87, asst prof, 87-92, ASSOC PROF BIOCHEM, UNIV MONCTON, 92- *Personal Data:* b Hauterive, Que, Can, Jan 5, 54. *Educ:* Univ Sherbrooke, BSc, 76; Univ Laval, PhD(biochem), 87. *Prof Exp:* Res asst pharmacol, Univ Laval, 80-82, res asst biochem, 82-83. *Concurrent Pos:* Mem, Environ Sci Res Ctr, 88- *Mem:* Can Soc Biochem; Asn Can-Fr Advan Sci. *Res:* Biological markers of water toxycity; Bioadsorption of toxicants by biological biomass. *Mailing Add:* Dept de Chimie et Biochimie Univ de Moncton Moncton NB E1A 3E9 Can. *Fax:* 506-858-4541; *E-Mail:* gauthie@umonctrn.ca

GAUTHIER, FERNAND MARCEL, plant breeding, for more information see previous edition

GAUTHIER, GEORGE JAMES, PHARMACEUTICAL CHEMISTRY. *Current Pos:* res chemist, Med Res Labs, 69-71, CHEMIST, PFIZER CHEM DIV, PFIZER, INC, 71- *Personal Data:* b Franklin, NH, July 22, 40; m 64; c 4. *Educ:* Univ Notre Dame, BSc, 62; Univ NH, PhD(org chem), 66; Univ New Haven, MBA, 75. *Prof Exp:* Res assoc organometallic chem, Frank J Seiler Lab, Off Aerospace Res, USAF Acad, 66-69. *Mem:* Am Chem Soc; Am Soc Brewing Chemists. *Res:* Investigations of nucleophilic additions to pyridinium salts; synthesis and reactions of metallocenes, ruthenocene, ferrocenes. *Mailing Add:* Pfizer Inc Bldg 34 Eastern Point Rd Groton CT 06340-5196

GAUTHIER, GERALDINE FLORENCE, CELL BIOLOGY. *Current Pos:* PROF CELL BIOL, UNIV MASS MED SCH. *Personal Data:* b Haverhill, Mass, May 14, 31. *Educ:* Mass Col Pharm, BS, 54, MS, 55; Radcliffe Col, AM, 56, PhD(anat), 62. *Prof Exp:* Res asst pharmacol, Harvard Med Sch, 56-58, teaching fel anat, 58-59, res fel, 59-62; from instr to asst prof biol, Brown Univ, 62-64; asst prof biol sci, 64-68, assoc prof biol, 68-73, prof biol, Wellesley Col, 73- *Concurrent Pos:* Fel, Am Found Pharmaceut Educ, 54-57; USPHS res award, 63-65, co-recipient, 64-74, prin investr grant, 75-80, 80-85; Muscular Dystrophy Asns Am grant, 69-79; NSF res award, 85-89. *Mem:* AAAS; Am Soc Cell Biol; Histochem Soc; Int Soc Cell Biol. *Res:* Skeletal muscle fibers diversity and muscle cell development. *Mailing Add:* Dept Cell Biol Univ Mass Med Sch 55 Lake Ave N Worcester MA 01655

GAUTHIER, GILLES, BEHAVIORAL ECOLOGY. *Current Pos:* Killam fel, Dept Biol, Univ Laval, 85-87, Nat Sci & Eng Res Coun res fel, 87-91, Nat Sci & Eng Res Coun fel, Dept Biol & Ctr Studies Nordiques, 91-92, PROF, DEPT BIOL & CTR STUDIES NORDIQUES, UNIV LAVAL, 92- *Personal Data:* b Montreal, Que, July 23, 58; c 1. *Educ:* Univ Montreal, BSc, 79; Univ Laval, MSc, 82; Univ BC, PhD(zool), 85. *Mem:* Am Ornithologists Union; Cooper Ornith Soc; Wildlife Soc; Animal Behav Soc. *Res:* Influence of food resources on reproductive strategies and population dynamics in birds; life-history strategies and demography of waterfowl; bioenergetic and plant-herbivore interactions in geese. *Mailing Add:* Dept Biol Univ Laval Ste-Foy PQ G1K 7P4 Can. *Fax:* 418-656-2043; *E-Mail:* gilles.gauthier@bio.ulaval.ca

GAUTHREAUX, SIDNEY ANTHONY, VERTEBRATE ZOOLOGY, ANIMAL BEHAVIOR. *Current Pos:* from asst prof to assoc prof, 70-77, PROF ZOOL, CLEMSON UNIV, 77- *Personal Data:* b Plaquemine, La, Oct 18, 40; m 90, Carroll G Belser; c David J & Renee M. *Educ:* La State Univ, New Orleans, BS, 63; La State Univ, Baton Rouge, MS, 65, PhD(zool), 68. *Prof Exp:* Instr biol, La State Univ, Baton Rouge, 67-68; Stoddard-Sutton res fel zool, Univ Ga, 68-70. *Mem:* Fel Animal Behav Soc (secy, 81-84, pres elect, 85-87, pres, 87-88); fel Am Ornith Union; Am Soc Naturalists; Sigma Xi; fel AAAS; Int Soc Behav Ecol. *Res:* Behavioral ecology; migratory behavior of animals, particularly birds and physiological mechanisms that underlie the behavior; behavioral dominance; radar and telescopic studies of bird migration; circadian rhythms. *Mailing Add:* Dept Biol Sci Clemson Univ Clemson SC 29631. *Fax:* 864-656-0435

GAUTIERI, RONALD FRANCIS, PHARMACOLOGY. *Current Pos:* From asst prof to assoc prof, 60-70, PROF PHARMACOL, TEMPLE UNIV, 70-, CHMN DEPT, 71- *Personal Data:* b Providence, RI, Oct 10, 33; m 62; c 1. *Educ:* RI Col Pharm, BS, 55; Temple Univ, MS, 57, PhD(pharmacol), 60. *Concurrent Pos:* Vis lectr, Am Asn Cols Pharm, 68- *Mem:* AAAS; Acad Pharmaceut Sci; Am Soc Pharmacol & Exp Therapeut; Am Pharmaceut Asn; Am Asn Pharmaceut Scientists. *Res:* Cancer; human placental perfusions; toxicology; teratology; biochemistry; physiology; dental research; gastroenterology; mechanism of action of drugs; fetal pharmacology. *Mailing Add:* 418 Bolton Rd Glenside PA 19038-3206

GAUTREAU, RONALD, PHYSICS. *Current Pos:* PROF PHYSICS, NJ INST TECHNOL, 66- *Personal Data:* b Newark, NJ, Jan 21, 40; m 61, Joan Sharock; c Ronald Jr, Denise & Gregory. *Educ:* Lehigh Univ, BS, 61; Stevens Inst Technol, MS, 63, PhD(physics), 66. *Mem:* Am Phys Soc; Sigma Xi; NY Acad Sci; Gen Relativity & Gravitation Soc. *Res:* Relativity physics with major emphasis on cosmology and the Schwarzschild field; science education. *Mailing Add:* 1464 Lambert St Rahway NJ 07065-2023

GAUTSCH, JAMES WILLARD, RECOMBINANT DNA, GENETIC ENGINEERING. *Current Pos:* CONSULT, 86- *Personal Data:* b Rockford, Ill, Oct 13, 41; m 68; c 2. *Educ:* Univ Denver, BA, 63; Univ Wyo, MS, 68; Univ Calif, Irvine, PhD(molecular biol & biochem), 73. *Prof Exp:* Fel genetics, Jackson Lab, Bar Harbor, Maine, 74-76; fel immunol, Scripps Clin, La Jolla, Calif, 76-78; asst mem molecular biol, 78-86. *Res:* Replication of retroviruses and their effect on host cell growth; mechanisms of gene expression in early mammalian embryo cells. *Mailing Add:* 451 S Granados Ave Solana Beach CA 92075

GAUTSCHI, WALTER, NUMERICAL ANALYSIS. *Current Pos:* PROF MATH & COMPUT SCI, PURDUE UNIV, 63- *Personal Data:* b Basel, Switz, Dec 11, 27; US citizen; m 60, Erika Wuest; c Thomas, Theresa, Doris & Caroline. *Educ:* Univ Basel, PhD, 53. *Prof Exp:* Fel Nat Inst Appl Calculus, Italy, 54-55 & comput lab, Harvard Univ, 55-56; res mathematician, Am Univ, 56-59; mathematician, Oak Ridge Nat Lab, 59-63. *Concurrent Pos:* Res mathematician, Nat Bur Stand, 56-59; vis prof, Tech Univ, Munich, Ger, 70-71 & Univ Wis, 76-77, ETH, Zurich, 96. *Mem:* Am Math Soc; Math Asn Am; Soc Indust & Appl Math; Swiss Math Asn. *Res:* Numerical analysis; special functions; ordinary differential equations; orthogonal polynomials. *Mailing Add:* Dept Comput Sci Purdue Univ West Lafayette IN 47907-1398. *Fax:* 765-494-0739; *E-Mail:* wxg@cs.purdue.edu

GAUVIN, J N LAURIE, THEORETICAL PHYSICS. *Current Pos:* PRES, CGTS INC, 89- *Personal Data:* b Shediac, NB, Oct 8, 29; m 64; c 2. *Educ:* Laval Univ, BSc, 54; Oxford Univ, PhD(theoret physics), 57. *Prof Exp:* From asst prof physics to assoc prof, Laval Univ, 57-70, prof 70-71; dir, Comn Sci Res, Ministry Educ, 71-81, sr adv, secretarial sci develop, 81-89. *Concurrent Pos:* Secy, Que Comt Sci Policy, 71-73. *Mem:* Can Asn Physicists. *Res:* Technology management and strategies. *Mailing Add:* 2650 Chemin St-Louis Quebec PQ G1W 1N3 Can. *Fax:* 418-651-6099

GAUVIN, WILLIAM H, chemical & metallurgical engineering; deceased, see previous edition for last biography

GAVALAS, GEORGE R(OUSETOS), CHEMICAL REACTION ENGINEERING, COAL UTILIZATION. *Current Pos:* From asst prof to assoc prof, 64-75, PROF CHEM ENG, CALIF INST TECHNOL, 75- *Personal Data:* b Athens, Greece, Oct 7, 36; m 80. *Educ:* Nat Tech Univ Athens, dipl eng, 58; Univ Minn, MS, 62, PhD(chem eng), 64. *Honors & Awards:* Wilhelm Award, Am Inst Chem Eng, 83; Wilhelm lectr, Princeton Univ, 87. *Concurrent Pos:* Consult, Phillips Petrol Co, 67- & miscellaneous indust orgn. *Mem:* Am Inst Chem Engrs; Am Chem Soc; Soc Petrol Engrs. *Res:* Chemical reaction engineering and catalysis; applied mathematics; coal combustion; ceramics processing. *Mailing Add:* Dept Chem Eng Calif Inst Technol Pasadena CA 91125-0001

GAVAN, JAMES ANDERSON, anthropology, anatomy; deceased, see previous edition for last biography

GAVANDE, SAMPAT A, SOIL PHYSICS, ENVIRONMENTAL ENGINEERING. *Current Pos:* TEAM LEADER, TEX NATURAL RESOURCE CONSERV COMN, AUSTIN, 92- *Personal Data:* b India; m, Shaila; c Neil & Vikram. *Educ:* Poona Univ, India, BS, 58; Kans State Univ, MS, 62; Utah State Univ, PhD(soil physics, irrig), 66. *Prof Exp:* From res asst to res assoc, Utah State Univ, 62-66; tech officer soil physics, UN Food & Agr Orgn-Inter-Am Inst, Orgn Am States Proj, Turrialba, Costa Rica, 66-69; tech officer soil physics, Trop Soil & Water Mgt, UN Food & Agr Orgn Proj, Nat Agr Ctr, Chapingo, Mex & Trop Agr Ctr, Tabasco, Mex, 69-72; prof soils & irrig & head dept, Grad Sch, Agrarian Autonomas Univ, Saltillo, Mex, 73-75; tech officer soil-water plant relations & co-dir, UN Food & Agr Orgn Proj, Arid Lands Res Ctr, Saltillo, Mex, 75-77; sr scientist, Natural Resources Dept, Radian Corp, 77-82; proj mgr, Foreign Agr Orgn, UN Develop Prog, Paraguay, 87-79; chief, Tech Support Br, Bur Solid Waste, Health Dept Austin, 89-92. *Concurrent Pos:* Soil & water conserv consult, Foreign U N Food & Agr Orgn, Kenya, Chile, India, Iran, Peru, Indonesia & Dominican Repub. *Mem:* Sigma Xi; AAAS; Am Soc Agron; Soil Sci Soc Am; Int Soc Soil Sci; Am Soc Agr Engrs; Am Soc Mining Engrs; Am Soc Testing & Mat. *Res:* Technological and environmental feasibility of waste disposal systems and reclamation of surface mined lands; water conservation and tillage practices; landfill and surface improvements; watershed management and planning. *Mailing Add:* 4501 Upvalley Ct Austin TX 78731-3666. *Fax:* 512-451-1400

GAVASCI, ANNA TERESA, petrology; deceased, see previous edition for last biography

GAVENDA, JOHN DAVID, EXPERIMENTAL SOLID STATE PHYSICS, ELECTROMAGNETIC COMPATIBILITY. *Current Pos:* Asst prof physics & res scientist, Defense Res Lab, 59-62, assoc prof, 62-67, PROF PHYSICS & EDUC, UNIV TEX, AUSTIN, 67- *Personal Data:* b Temple, Tex, Mar 25, 33; m 52, Janie Yeoman; c Victor J & Philip M. *Educ:* Univ Tex, BS, 54, MA, 56; Brown Univ, PhD(physics), 59. *Concurrent Pos:* Sr res fel, Inst Study Metals, Univ Chicago, 63; NATO sr fel sci, Univ Oslo, spring, 69; consult electromagnetic compatibility. *Mem:* AAAS; Am Asn Physics Teachers; fel Am Phys Soc; Inst Elec & Electronics Engrs. *Res:* Electronic properties of metals at low temperatures; physics education; measurement and reduction of electromagnetic emissions from computing equipment. *Mailing Add:* Dept Physics Univ Tex Austin TX 78712. *E-Mail:* gavenda@utaphy.ph.utexas.edu

GAVER, DONALD P, III, BIOFLUID MECHANICS, PULMONARY MECHANICS. *Current Pos:* ASSOC PROF BIOMED ENG, TULANE UNIV, 90- *Personal Data:* b Pittsburgh, Pa, 1959. *Educ:* Calif Inst Technol, BS, 82; Occidental Col, BA, 82; Northwestern Univ, MS, 85, PhD(theoret & appl mech), 88. *Concurrent Pos:* Parker B Francis fel pulmonary mech, 90-93; nat young investr, NSF, 93- *Mem:* Am Phys Soc; Biomed Eng Soc. *Mailing Add:* Dept Biomed Eng Tulane Univ New Orleans LA 70118

GAVER, DONALD PAUL, MATHEMATICS. *Current Pos:* PROF, DEPT OPERS RES, NAVAL POSTGRAD SCH, 74- *Personal Data:* b St Paul, Minn, Feb 16, 26. *Educ:* Mass Inst Technol, SB, 50, SM, 51; Princeton Univ, PhD(math), 56. *Prof Exp:* Mem staff mil opers res, US Navy Opers Eval Group, 51-53; mem systs anal res group, Princeton Univ, 53-56; res mathematician, Res Labs, Westinghouse Elec Corp, 56-60, supvry mathematician, Dept Math, 60, adv math, 62-64; assoc prof math & indust admin, Carnegie-Mellon Univ, 64-70, prof statist & indust admin, 70-74. *Mem:* Opers Res Soc Am; Am Statist Asn; Inst Math Statist. *Res:* Applications of probability and probability models; statistics; operational research. *Mailing Add:* 26780 Paseo Robles Carmel CA 93923-9543

GAVER, ROBERT CALVIN, DRUG METABOLISM, PHARMACOKINETICS. *Current Pos:* SR RES INVESTR II, PHARMACEUT RES & DEVELOP DIV, DEPT METAB & PHARMACOKINETICS, BRISTOL-MYERS CO, 83- *Personal Data:* b Chambersburg, Pa, Oct 2, 38; div; c 2. *Educ:* Pa State Univ, BS, 60; Univ Pittsburgh, PhD(biochem), 64. *Prof Exp:* Res assoc, Univ Ill, 64-67; res scientist, Bristol Labs, Inc, 67-83. *Mem:* AAAS; Am Asn Cancer Res. *Res:* Define the disposition of new therapeutic agents, particularly antihuman agents in animals and humans; development of analytical methodology; isolation and identification of metabolites; pharmacokinetics analyses and protein binding, tissue distribution and bio availability studies. *Mailing Add:* Pharmaceut Res & Develop Div Bristol-Myers Co PO Box 4000 Princeton NJ 08543-4000

GAVIN, DAVID FRANCIS, SYNTHETIC ORGANIC CHEMISTRY. *Current Pos:* SUPVR ORG CHEM RES & DEVELOP, OLIN CORP, 60- *Personal Data:* b Indianapolis, Ind, Jan 4, 39; m 64; c 1. *Educ:* Hofstra Univ, BS, 60; Southern Conn State Col, MS, 66. *Concurrent Pos:* Lectr, Southern Conn State Col, 73-; mgr govt contract R&D, Olin Chem Group. *Mem:* Am Chem Soc; Am Soc Lubrication Engrs; Sigma Xi. *Res:* High performance lubricants and functional fluids based on novel chemical principles. *Mailing Add:* 255 Sorghum Mill Cheshire CT 06410

GAVIN, DONALD ARTHUR, NEUTRON & X-RAY SPECTROMETERS, NUCLEAR REACTOR PHYSICS. *Current Pos:* RETIRED. *Personal Data:* b Albany, NY, Mar 31, 31; m 55; c 7. *Educ:* Holy Cross Col, BS, 53; Univ RI, MS, 55. *Prof Exp:* Supvr critical facil, Knolls Atomic Power Lab, Gen Elec Co, 60-70, prof non-destructive testing, 70-82, sr engr mat anal, 86-91. *Concurrent Pos:* Instr physics, Schenectady Community Col, 78-81; prin investr inserv inspection naval nuclear reactors, 81-83. *Mem:* Am Soc Non Destructive Testing. *Res:* Analyses of materials used in nuclear reactors using neutron transmission; x-ray transmission; real time radiography; in service inspections of naval nuclear reactors. *Mailing Add:* 17 Rivercrest Dr Rexford NY 12148

GAVIN, GERARD BRENNAN, REACTOR PHYSICS, NUCLEAR PHYSICS. *Current Pos:* RETIRED. *Personal Data:* b Long Island City, NY, Aug 28, 23; m 47; c 5. *Educ:* Siena Col, Loudonville, NY, BS, 47. *Prof Exp:* Res asst physics, Knolls Atomic Power Lab, 51-54, physicist, 54-66, physicist reactor measurements, 66-74, proj engr design & construct, 74-75, sr engr nuclear 75-77, physicist prototype test, 77-81, sr physicist prototype test, 81-84. *Res:* Nuclear energy. *Mailing Add:* 51 Nicholas Dr Albany NY 12205

GAVIN, HENRI PHILIPE, VIBRATION CONTROL, ADAPTIVE MATERIALS & STRUCTURES. *Current Pos:* ASST PROF, DUKE UNIV, 95- *Personal Data:* b Lausanne, Switz, May 14, 64; US citizen; m 89, Robin Magee. *Educ:* Princeton Univ, BS, 86; Univ Mich, MS, 88, PhD(civil eng), 94. *Prof Exp:* Res technician, Princeton Univ, 86-87 & 89-91. *Concurrent Pos:* Career grant, NSF, 96. *Mem:* Am Soc Civil Engrs; Am Soc Mech Engrs; Earthquake Eng Res Inst; Soc Exp Mech; Sigma Xi. *Res:* Use of variable-property materials for vibration control applications; earthquake hazard mitigation; dynamics and vibration; electrorheological and magneto rheological materials; earthquake engineering. *Mailing Add:* Dept Civil Eng Duke Univ Durham NC 27708-0287. *E-Mail:* henri.gavin@duke.edu

GAVIN, JAMES RAPHAEL, III, DIABETES. *Current Pos:* SR SCIENTIFIC OFFICER, HOWARD HUGHES MED INST, 91- *Personal Data:* b Nov 23, 45; US citizen; m, Annie; c Hakkim & Lamar. *Educ:* Livingston Col, BS, 66; Emory Univ, PhD(biochem), 70; Duke Univ, MD, 75; Am Bd Internal Med, dipl. *Honors & Awards:* Kelly West Lectr, Univ Okla Health Sci Ctr, 87; George H Howard Jr Lectr Meharry Med Col, 88; Dr Martin L King Jr Lectr, Washington Univ Med, 88; Outstanding Clinician in the Field of Diabetes, Am Diabetes Asn, 90; George H Hamwi Memorial Lectr, Ohio Stae Col Med, 91; Marty Alpern Lectr, Coalition for Diabetes Educ for Minoroties, Henry Ford Hosp, 91; Daniel Hale Williams Award, Chicago Med Asn, 93; Outstanding African Am in Med, Aetna, 93; Edward Hook MD Distinguished Lectr, Univ Va, 94; EE Just Award, Am Soc Cell Biol, 95; Ralph Landes Lectr, Univ NC, 96. *Prof Exp:* Staff assoc, Diabetes Br, NIH, 71-73; intern, Dept Pathol, Duke Univ, 75-76; intern, Dept Internal Med, Barnes Hosp, St Louis, 76-77, resident, 77-78; from asst prof to assoc prof, Washington Univ Sch Med, St Louis, 78-87; prof med & chief, Diabetes Sect, Univ Okla Health Sci Ctr, 87-93, Willliam K Warren prof diabetes studies, 89-91. *Concurrent Pos:* Fel, Hastings Inst Ethics & Life Sci, 71-75; clin fel, Div Metab, Washington Univ Sch Med, St Louis, 78-79, dir, RIA Core Lab, Diabetes, Res & Training Ctr, 78-87; from asst to assoc physician, Barnes Hosp, St Louis, 78-87; vis prof several univs, 85-95; mem, Nat Comt Scientific Progs, Am Diabetes Asn, Inc, 86-89, vchmn, 87-88, chmn, 88-89; actg chief, Sect Endocrinol, Metab & Hypertension, Univ Okla Health Sci Ctr, 88-89; Zollicofer vis prof, Sch Med, Univ NC, 90; chmn, Study Sect Initiative Diabetes in Minorities, Nat Inst Diabetes, Digestive & Kidney Dis, 91, Study Sect Intervention Minorities with Diabetes, 93; Roerig diabetes vis prof, Univ Hawaii Med Ctr, Honolulu, 95. *Mem:* Inst Med-Nat Acad Sci; Am Asn Physicians; Am Diabetes Asn (vpres, 91-92, pres-elect, 92-93, pres, 93-94); Am Fedn Clin Res; Am Soc Acad Black Surgeons; Am Soc Clin Invest; Asn Acad Minority Physicians; Nat Med Asn; Endocrine Soc; Am Clin & Climat Asn. *Res:* Published several articles. *Mailing Add:* Sci Dept Howard Hughes Med Inst 4000 Jones Bridge Rd Chevy Chase MD 20815

GAVIN, JOHN JOSEPH, MICROBIOLOGY. *Current Pos:* RETIRED. *Personal Data:* b New Brunswick, NJ, Oct 21, 22; m 45; c 9. *Educ:* Rutgers Univ, BS, 49, MS, 50, PhD, 64. *Prof Exp:* Head biol control, Smith, Kline & French Labs, Pa, 50-55; chief microbiologist, Food Res Labs, NY, 55-57; Fund Res Therapeut res fel biochem, Norristown State Hosp, 57-64; group leader bact res, Norwich Pharmacol Co & Eaton Labs Div, 64-66; sr scientist & head, Dept Allergy & Immunol, Dome Labs, 66-69; dir biol prod develop, Miles Labs, Inc, 69-71, dir molecular biol res, 71-75, dir allergy res affairs, 75-80, dir res, Hollister Stier Div, 80-84; sr med res & develop specialist, Eng & Econ Res Inc, 84-87, dir sci policy, 87-90. *Concurrent Pos:* Adj assoc prof, Univ Notre Dame, 79-81; adj prof, Eastern Washington Univ, 81-83. *Mem:* AAAS; fel Am Inst Chem; Am Soc Microbiol; Am Chem Soc; NY Acad Sci; Regulatory Affairs Prof Soc. *Res:* Immunology; nucleic acid metabolism; molecular biology. *Mailing Add:* 578 Tulip Poplar Crest Carmel IN 46033

GAVIN, JOSEPH GLEASON, JR, AEROSPACE ENGINEERING & TECHNOLOGY, FUSION POWER. *Current Pos:* RETIRED. *Personal Data:* b Somerville, Mass, Sept 18, 20; m 43, Dorothy Dunklee; c 3. *Educ:* Mass Inst Technol, BS & MS, 42. *Hon Degrees:* ScD, Villanova, NY Regents. *Honors & Awards:* Distinguished Pub Serv Medal, NASA, 71. *Prof Exp:* Design engr, Grumman Aircraft Eng Corp, Bethpage, NY, 46-48, preliminary design group, 48-50, proj engr, 50-56, chief exp projs engr, 56-57, chief missile & space engr, 57-62, dir Lunar Module Prog Apollo, 62-72, vpres, 70-72, pres, 72-76, pres, chief operating officer & dir, 76-85, sr mgt consult, 85-90. *Concurrent Pos:* Chmn bd, Grumman Aircraft Eng Corp, 73-76; chmn, Int Coop Magnetic Fusion Comt, Nat Res Coun, 83-84. *Mem:* Nat Acad Eng; fel Am Inst Aeronaut & Astronaut; fel Am Astron Soc; Aerospace Industs Asn. *Mailing Add:* 341 Spencer Amherst MA 01002-3367

GAVIN, LLOYD ALVIN, MATHEMATICS, STATISTICS. *Current Pos:* assoc prof, 73-84, PROF MATH, CALIF STATE UNIV, SACRAMENTO, 84- *Personal Data:* b New Orleans, La, Apr 20, 43; m 65, Eunice Collins; c Vanessa E, Karen M & Alvin L. *Educ:* Xavier Univ La, BS, 64; Univ Kans, MA, 66; Ill Inst Technol, PhD(math), 73. *Prof Exp:* Asst prof math, Xavier Univ, 70-73. *Concurrent Pos:* Ford Found fel, Ill Inst Technol, 67-68, Whitney Young fel, 67 NDEA fel, 67, 68-70; distinguished dist gov, Toastmasters Int Dist 39, 87-88. *Mem:* Am Math Soc; Math Asn Am; Toastmasters Int. *Res:* Effect of intervention programs on high school and junior high school minorities youth; jacknife statistics. *Mailing Add:* 1213 Cedarbrook Way Sacramento CA 95831-4405. *Fax:* 916-278-5787; *E-Mail:* lagavin@csus.edu

GAVIN, ROBERT M, JR, PHYSICAL CHEMISTRY. *Current Pos:* PRES, MACALESTER COL, 84. *Personal Data:* b Coatesville, Pa, Aug 16, 40; m 62; c 5. *Educ:* St John's Univ, Minn, BA, 62; Iowa State Univ, PhD(chem), 66. *Hon Degrees:* DSc, Haverford Col, 86. *Prof Exp:* From asst prof to prof chem, Haverford Col, 66-84, provost, 80-84. *Concurrent Pos:* Res assoc, Univ Mich, 66; fel, Univ Chicago, 69-70 & Univ Calif, Berkeley, 78-79. *Mem:* Am Chem Soc. *Res:* Molecular structure; spectroscopy; chemical bonding; photochemistry of vision. *Mailing Add:* Macalester Col 1600 Grand Ave St Paul MN 55105-1801

GAVINI, MURALIDHARA B, RADIOCHEMISTRY, GEOCHEMISTRY. *Current Pos:* VPRES & TECH DIR, US TESTING CO INC, 79- *Personal Data:* b India, July 1, 47; m 75; c 1. *Educ:* Andhra Univ, India, BSc, 70, MSc, 72; Univ Ark, Fayetteville, PhD(chem), 76. *Prof Exp:* investr aquatic geochem & atmospheric radiochem, Woods Hole Oceanog Inst, 76-79. *Mem:* Am Chem Soc; Am Nuclear Soc. *Res:* Natural and artifically-produced radionuclides as potential atmospheric tracers; geochemical behavior of artificially produced radionuclides especially transuranium elements in the fresh water environments; technical management; analytical chemistry. *Mailing Add:* 58 Crane Circle New Providence NJ 07974-1107

GAVIS, JEROME, ENVIRONMENTAL CHEMISTRY, ENVIRONMENTAL BIOLOGY. *Current Pos:* RETIRED. *Personal Data:* b Hartford, Conn, June 18, 28; m 54; c 2. *Educ:* Polytech Inst Brooklyn, BChE, 49; Cornell Univ, PhD(chem), 53. *Prof Exp:* Asst prof, Johns Hopkins Univ, 56-60, assoc prof environ eng, 60-90. *Mem:* Am Inst Chem Engrs; Am Chem Soc; Am Soc Limnol & Oceanog; AAAS; Sigma Xi. *Res:* Natural water chemistry; transport phenomena in natural fluid systems; phytoplankton growth and uptake kinetics; interaction of phytoplankton and dissolved metal ions. *Mailing Add:* 2110 South Rd Baltimore MD 21209

GAVLIN, GILBERT, ORGANIC CHEMISTRY, CHEMICAL ENGINEERING. *Current Pos:* PRES, GAVLIN ASSOC INC, 87- *Personal Data:* b Chicago, Ill, Jan 12, 20; m 47, Carolyn Epting; c Suzanne (Cluff) Nancy L & Patricia K (Adamek). *Educ:* Univ Ill, BS, 41; Cornell Univ, PhD(org chem), 48. *Prof Exp:* Res chemist, SAM Labs, Columbia Univ, 43-45 & Tenn Eastman Corp, 45-46; assoc org chemist, Armour Res Found, Ill Inst Tech, 46-47; asst, Cornell Univ, 47-48; res org chemist & dir, Nat Registry Rare Chems, Armour Res Found, 48-54; sr scientist, Richardson Co, 54-56, mgr res dept, 56-64; pres, Poly-Synthetix, Inc, 64-69, Custom Org, Inc, 69-85; tech dir, Safety-Kleen Corp, 85-87. *Mem:* Am Chem Soc; Am Inst Chem Eng; Am Soc Testing & Mat; AAAS. *Res:* Organic fluorine and chlorine compounds; polymer chemistry; mechanism of organic reactions; separation science and technology; mass transfer equipment design. *Mailing Add:* 6500 N Kenton Ave Lincolnwood IL 60646. *Fax:* 312-825-7850; *E-Mail:* ggavlin@worldnet.att.net

GAVORA, JAN SAMUEL, ANIMAL GENETICS & BREEDING, BIOTECHNOLOGY APPLIED IN ANIMAL PRODUCTION. *Current Pos:* SR PRIN RES SCIENTIST, CTR FOOD & ANIMAL RES, AGR CAN, OTTAWA, 71- *Personal Data:* b Brezova pod Bradlom, Slovakia, July 14, 33; Can citizen; m 59, Eva Valachova. *Educ:* Agr Univ, Slovaka, Ing, 57, CSc, 67. *Hon Degrees:* DSc, Agr Univ, Slovaka, 91. *Honors & Awards:* Tom Newman Mem Award, 85; Merit Award, Pub Serv Can, 84; Travel Award, Japan Soc Prom Sci, 88; Cert of Merit, Can Soc Animal Sci, 89. *Prof Exp:* Dir artificial insemination animal breeding, State Breeding Bd, Nitra, Czech, 57-61; dir animal prod, Agr Co-op Farm, V Kostolany, Czech, 62; res scientist animal prod, Inst Sci Agr, Piestany, Czech, 63-66; res scientist poultry breeding, Poultry Res Inst, Ivanka pri Dunaji, Czech, 66-68; fel poultry breeding, Univ Man, 69-70. *Mem:* World's Poultry Sci Asn; Poultry Sci Asn; Can Asn Animal Sci; Genetics Soc Can; Czech Soc Arts & Sci; Agr Inst Can; Int Soc Animal Genetics. *Res:* Genetics of disease resistance; resistance against a neoplastic diseases of chickens, Marek's disease; breeding techniques for simultaneous improvement of production traits and disease resistance; lymphoid leukosis; biotechnology applied in livestock production; use of livestock as bioreactors to produce pharmaceuticals. *Mailing Add:* Bldg No 34 Ctr Food & Animal Res Agri & Agri-Food Can Ottawa ON K1A 0C6 Can. *Fax:* 613-759-1355; *E-Mail:* gavoraj@em.agr.ca

GAW, C VERNON, BIOENGINEERING & BIOMEDICAL ENGINEERING. *Current Pos:* RES & DEVELOP COORDR, INDUST MACH, BARRET CENTRIFUGALS INC, 79- *Personal Data:* b Clinton, Mass, July 12, 42; m 66; c 2. *Educ:* Univ Mass, BS, 68. *Prof Exp:* Electronics engr, Fenwal div, Walter Kidde, 68-74; sr proj engr, IItem Entry Control Div, Damon Corp, 74-79; sr engr, Valtec div, Int Tel & Tel, 79. *Mem:* Inst Elec & Electronics Engrs. *Res:* Liquid phase separation; liquid-solids separation; automatic controls; motion detection. *Mailing Add:* 34 Ford Rd RFD 3 Sterling MA 01564

GAWARECKI, STEPHEN JEROME, GEOLOGY. *Current Pos:* GEOL CONSULT, REMOTE SENSING DYNAMICS, 86- *Personal Data:* b Newark, NJ, July 31, 29; m 54; c 2. *Educ:* Rutgers Univ, BS, 51, MS, 52; Univ Colo, PhD(geol), 63. *Prof Exp:* Staff mining geologist, NJ Zinc Co, Colo & Pa, 52-53; geologist, Doeringsfeld, Amuedo & Ivey, Inc, Colo, 60-62; geologist, US Geol Surv, DC, 62-69, proj chief orbital photo anal, Br Regional Geophysics, 69-72, staff geologist remote sensing activ, 72-79, actg chief, Br Mideastern & Asian Geol & Br Europ & African Geol, Reston, Va, 79-84, chief, Br Resource Anal, 84-86. *Concurrent Pos:* Mem, UN Conf Sci & Technol for Develop, Vienna, 79; lectr geol, Northern Va Community Col, 89. *Mem:* AAAS; Am Soc Photogram & Remote Sensing; Sigma Xi. *Res:* Structural geology; photogeology; remote sensing of environment; regional tectonics; multispectral survey as an exploration tool for base metal deposits in humid tropical environments; tectonic map of North Thailand using ERTS satellite imagery; geologic hazard mitigation. *Mailing Add:* 7018 Vagabond Dr Falls Church VA 22042-3944

GAWER, ALBERT HENRY, PHYSICAL CHEMISTRY. *Current Pos:* ASST PROF CHEM, STATE UNIV NY, NEW PALTZ, 69- *Personal Data:* b New York, NY, July 22, 35. *Educ:* Rutgers Univ, BS, 57; Columbia Univ, AM, 58, PhD(chem), 63. *Prof Exp:* Instr chem, Brooklyn Col, 63-64; asst prof, Barnard Col, Columbia Univ, 64-68. *Mem:* AAAS; Am Chem Soc; Am Phys Soc. *Res:* High resolution nuclear magnetic resonance spectroscopy; chemical applications of Mossbauer effect; instrumental methods of analysis. *Mailing Add:* Dept Chem State Univ NY New Paltz NY 12561

GAWIENOWSKI, ANTHONY MICHAEL, BIOCHEMISTRY, ENDOCRINOLOGY. *Current Pos:* PROF BIOCHEM, UNIV MASS, AMHERST, 63- *Personal Data:* b Newark, NJ, Oct 30, 24; m 55; c 5. *Educ:* Villanova Col, BS, 48; Univ Mo, MS, 53, PhD(biochem), 56. *Prof Exp:* Control chemist, Merck & Co, 48; prof serv rep pharmaceut, Schering Corp, 49-52; res asst, Univ Mo, 53-56; res fel, Univ Tex, 56-57; asst prof, Kans State Univ, 57-63. *Concurrent Pos:* Guest worker, NIH, 69-70; guest scientist, Oak Ridge Asn Univ, 78. *Mem:* Fel AAAS; Am Chem Soc; Endocrine Soc; Sigma Xi; Phytochem Soc. *Res:* Steroid evolution; neurotransmitters; carotene precursors. *Mailing Add:* 902 E Pleasant St Univ Mass Amherst MA 01002-1532

GAWLEY, IRWIN H, JR, CHEMISTRY. *Current Pos:* assoc prof, 55-60, PROF CHEM & DEAN SCH MATH & SCI, MONTCLAIR STATE COL, 60-, VPRES ACAD AFFAIRS, 73- *Personal Data:* b Union City, NJ, Apr 20, 27; m 55; c 2. *Educ:* Montclair State Col, AB, 49, AM 51; Columbia Univ, EdD, 57. *Prof Exp:* Teacher pub schs, NJ, 49-55. *Mem:* AAAS; Am Chem Soc; Nat Asn Res Sci Teaching; Nat Sci Teachers Asn. *Res:* Chemical education; improvement of teaching of chemistry. *Mailing Add:* 177 McCosh Rd Upper Montclair NJ 07043-2105

GAWLEY, ROBERT EDGAR, ORGANIC CHEMISTRY. *Current Pos:* from asst prof to assoc prof org chem, 77-92, PROF, ORG CHEM, UNIV MIAMI, 92- *Personal Data:* b Newark, NJ, Nov 7, 48; m 79, Lorraine O'Brien; c John & James. *Educ:* Stetson Univ, BS, 70; Duke Univ, PhD(org chem), 75. *Prof Exp:* Res assoc med chem, Univ NC, Chapel Hill, 75-77. *Concurrent Pos:* Fogarty Sr Int fel, ETH-Zurich, Switz, 93-94. *Mem:* Am Chem Soc; AAAS; Sigma Xi. *Res:* Synthetic methods; total syntheses; asymmetric synthesis; bioorganic chemistry of marine toxins. *Mailing Add:* Dept Chem Univ Miami PO Box 249118 Coral Gables FL 33124-0431

GAWRON, VALERIE JANE, TEST & EVALUATION, PERFORMANCE MEASUREMENT. *Current Pos:* HUMANS FACTOR ENGR, CALSPAN SRL CORP, 80-, PRIN ENGR, 93- *Personal Data:* b Buffalo, NY, Mar 16, 54. *Educ:* State Univ Col, Geneseo, MA, 75; Univ Ill, PhD(eng psychol), 80; State Univ NY, Buffalo, MBA, 88. *Prof Exp:* Res asst, State Univ Col, Geneseo, 76-77; postdoctoral res assoc, NMex State Univ, 80. *Concurrent Pos:* Test & eval tech chair, Human Factors & Ergonomics Soc, 96-98. *Mem:* Assoc fel Am Inst Aeronaut & Astronaut; fel Human Factors & Ergonomics Soc; Asn Aviation Psychologists; Aerospace Human Factors Asn; Aerospace Med Asn; Am Inst Aeronaut & Astronaut. *Res:* Human performance measurement, development of measures of workload and situation awareness computer aided engineering tools and expert systems; flight test of advanced controls and displays and safety evaluations. *Mailing Add:* 36 Woodward Ave Kenmore NY 14217. *Fax:* 716-631-6990; *E-Mail:* gawron@calspan.com

GAY, BEN DOUGLAS, COMPUTER SCIENCE, ENGINEERING. *Current Pos:* AT MOTOROLA INC, ARLINGTON HEIGHTS, ILL. *Personal Data:* b Salt Lake City, Utah, Jan 11, 42; m 63; c 2. *Educ:* Univ NMex, PhD(numerical gas dynamics), 69. *Prof Exp:* Dir comput sci prog, 73-75, asst prof comput sci & mech eng, Bucknell Univ, 69-, dir, off comput activ, 74- *Mem:* Asn Comput Mach. *Mailing Add:* 200 Maria Dr Barrington IL 60010

GAY, BRUCE WALLACE, JR, ATMOSPHERIC CHEMISTRY, KINETICS. *Current Pos:* sr res chemist, 70-94, dep dir, Atmospheric Chem & Modeling Div, 94-96, PROG MGR, ATMOSPHERIC MODELING DIV, NAT EXPOSURE RES LAB, US ENVIRON PROTECTION AGENCY, 96-, LT COMDR, PUB HEALTH SERV, 70- *Personal Data:* b Ludlow, Mass, July 23, 40; m 68; c 3. *Educ:* Lowell Technol Inst, BS, 62; NMex Inst Mining & Technol, MS, 64. *Honors & Awards:* Spec Sci Achievement Award, US Environ Protection Agency, 74, 76, 82, 84; Bronze Medal, 89. *Prof Exp:* Health serv officer, USPHS, 67-70. *Concurrent Pos:* Teaching asst, Nat Univ Ireland, 64-66. *Mem:* Am Chem Soc; AAAS; Air & Waste Mgt Asn. *Res:* Elucidation of atmospheric reactions to photochemical smog, long path infrared studies of the ambient urban atmosphere, atmospheric reactions of halogenated hydrocarbons and their effect on the earth's ozone layer; detection of naturally occuring hydrocarbons, their reactivity and overall burden to urban hydrocarbon pollution; conducted studies related to the stratospheric ozone hole. *Mailing Add:* Nat Exposure Res Lab Off Res & Develop Environ Protection Agency Mail Drop 80 Research Triangle Park NC 27711. *Fax:* 919-541-1379; *E-Mail:* gay.bruce@epamail.epa.gov

GAY, CAROL VIRGINIA LOVEJOY, BONE CELL BIOLOGY, SKELETAL METABOLISM. *Current Pos:* Res assoc biochem & biophys, Pa State Univ, 72-80, sr proj assoc, 80-83, sr res assoc molecular & cell biol, 80-88, assoc prof, 88-91, PROF POULTRY SCI & CELL BIOL, PA STATE UNIV, 91- *Personal Data:* b Belfast, Maine, Apr 8, 40; m 64, Fred D; c Zachary L. *Educ:* Univ Maine, BA, 62; Pa State Univ, MS, 67, PhD(physiol), 72. *Concurrent Pos:* NIH fel, Pa State Univ, 73-75; res grant, NIH, 77-, res career develop award, 79-84; res grant, USDA, 81-85, Bard, 93- *Mem:* AAAS; Am Soc Cell Biol; Am Physiol Soc; Am Soc Bone & Mineral Res; fel Royal Soc Med. *Res:* Structure and metabolism of mineralized tissues; physiological roles and localization of carbonic anhydrase; mechanism of ocidification of osteoclasts; calcium translocation through osteoblasts. *Mailing Add:* 1905 Buffalo Run Rd Bellefonte PA 16823

GAY, CHARLES FRANCIS, physical chemistry, engineering, for more information see previous edition

GAY, CHARLES WILFORD, EXTENSION ADMINISTRATION, INTERNATIONAL DEVELOPMENT. *Current Pos:* assoc chief party-Morocco, Utah State Univ, 83-86, res asst prof, Range Sci Dept, 86-87, actg dept head/Int Develop, 87-88, res asst prof, 88-89, ASST TO DEAN, ADMIN AFFAIRS & EXTEN, UTAH STATE UNIV, 89- *Personal Data:* b Tulsa, Okla, June 30, 37; m 67, Louise M Kiser; c Timothy L, Patrick N, Beth L Macatee & Richard E Macatee. *Educ:* Okla State Univ, BS, 62, MS, 64. *Prof Exp:* Range exten specialist, NMex State Univ, 64-68, chief party-Paraguay, 68-72; gen mgr, Agr Div, Collier Cobb & Assocs, 72-78; exec vpres, Gay Sales & Serv Corp, 78-83. *Concurrent Pos:* Lectr & consult, Fac Agron & Vet Med, Paraguay, 68-72, Nat Sheep Producers of Ecuador, 90; consult, Ministry Agr, Morocco, 83-86; lectr, Global Nat Res Monitoring & Assessment Conf, 89, Icelandic Soil Conserv Serv, 89; assoc ed, J Arid Soil Res & Rehab, 93- *Mem:* Soc Range Mgt; Soc Am Foresters; Soc Int Develop; Sigma Xi. *Res:* Technology transfer and management of rangeland and range livestock with pastoral societies. *Mailing Add:* Utah State Univ Logan UT 84322-5200. *E-Mail:* chuckg@ext.usu.edu

GAY, DON DOUGLAS, ENVIRONMENTAL SCIENCES, RESEARCH IN PREVENTIVE MEDICINE. *Current Pos:* PRES, SYMPLECTICS, INC, KANSAS CITY, 94- *Personal Data:* b Oklahoma City, Okla, Jan 17, 44; m 66, Mary J Forslund; c Matthew, Meghan & Nathan. *Educ:* Augustana Col, Ill, BA, 66; Univ Iowa, MS, 71, PhD(plant physiol), 75. *Prof Exp:* Res plant physiologist, US Environ Protection Agency, Nev, 74-78; fel & assoc, Dept Prev Med & Environ Health, Univ Iowa, 78-79; sr scientist, Savannah River Lab, SC, 79-86; dir res & develop, Sci Systs Inc, State Col Pa, 86; anal serv dept mgr, Environ Protection Systs, Jackson, Miss, 87; br mgr, Environ Protection Systs, Pensacola, Fla, 88-89; br mgr, Law Environ, 89-92; dir, Chem Sci Dept, Midwest Res Inst, Kansas City, 92-94. *Concurrent Pos:* Vis asst prof biol, Univ Nev, Las Vegas, 75-78; pres, Biosyn, Ltd, 84; fel assoc environ epidemiol, toxicol & chem, Univ Iowa, 78-79; consult asbestos, Environ Monitoring Systs, Inc. *Mem:* Sigma Xi. *Res:* Biochemical pathways in plant, animal and soil systems; analytical instrument development; new technologies and products research and development; biomarkers: identification of and relation to disease processes and hazardous materials exposure; granted 5 US patents. *Mailing Add:* 7428 N Wabash Gladstone MO 64118. *Fax:* 816-468-4170

GAY, FRANK P, POLYMER SCIENCE. *Current Pos:* res chemist, E I du Pont de Nemours, Inc, 53-57, staff scientist, 57-59, res supvr, 59-65, res assoc, Film Dept, 65-79, res assoc, Polymer Prod Dept, 79-86, RES FEL, E I DU PONT DE NEMOURS & CO, INC, 86- *Personal Data:* b Denoya, Okla, Jan 7, 25; m 57; c 2. *Educ:* Ind Univ, BS, 48; Univ Calif, PhD(chem), 51. *Prof Exp:* Asst chem, Univ Calif, 48-51; res chemist, Calif Spray Chem Corp, Stand Oil Co, Calif, 51-53. *Mem:* Am Chem Soc; Sigma Xi. *Res:* Organometallics; polymer physics and degradation; high temperature polymers; polyesters. *Mailing Add:* 527 Hemlock Dr Hockessin DE 19707-9361

GAY, HELEN, BIOLOGY. *Current Pos:* PROF BIOL SCI, UNIV MICH, 62- *Personal Data:* b Pittsfield, Mass, Aug 30, 18. *Educ:* Mt Holyoke Col, BA, 40; Mills Col, MA, 42; Univ Pa, PhD, 55. *Prof Exp:* Asst, Carnegie Inst, Dept Genetics, 42-43; jr prof asst, NIH, 43-45; asst, Dept Genetics, Carnegie Inst, 45-51, res assoc, 54-60, assoc cytogeneticist, 60-62, cytogeneticist, 62. *Concurrent Pos:* Lectr, Adelphi Col, 59-62; guest investr, Brookhaven Nat Lab; cytogeneticist, Carnegie Inst, 62-71. *Mem:* Fel AAAS; Am Soc Nat; Am Soc Zool; Genetics Soc Am; Soc Develop Biol; Am Soc Cell Biol. *Res:* Cytogenetics of Drosophila; cytochemistry; chromosome structure; electron microscopy. *Mailing Add:* Div Biol Sci Univ Mich Ann Arbor MI 48104-0001

GAY, JACKSON GILBERT, THEORETICAL PHYSICS. *Current Pos:* RETIRED. *Personal Data:* b Selma, Ala, Dec 27, 32; m 55, Patricia Varner; c Michael & Leisa. *Educ:* Auburn Univ, BS, 55; Univ Fla, PhD(physics), 63. *Honors & Awards:* John M Campbell Award; Kettering Award. *Prof Exp:* Sr engr, Pratt & Whitney Aircraft Div, United Aircraft Co, 55-60; res assoc physics, Univ Fla, 63-64; sr res physicist, Gen Motors Res Lab, 64-85, sr staff scientist, 85- *Mem:* Am Phys Soc. *Res:* Theory of solid surfaces; Monte Carlo and molecular dynamics simulations of molecular systems. *Mailing Add:* 8208 Camino Del Vernado NW Albuquerque NM 87120

GAY, LLOYD WESLEY, WATERSHED MANAGEMENT. *Current Pos:* assoc prof, 75-76, PROF WATERSHED MGT, SCH RENEWABLE NATURAL RESOURCES, UNIV ARIZ, 76- *Personal Data:* b Bryan, Tex, June 26, 33; m 63; c 4. *Educ:* Colo State Univ, BS, 55; Australian Forestry Sch, Canberra, dipl, 59; Duke Univ, MF, 62, PhD(forest climat), 66. *Prof Exp:* Forester, Apache Nat Forest, Ariz, 55-57; res forester, Cent Sierra Snow Lab, Calif, 60-61; asst prof forest mgt, Ore State Univ, 66-70, from asst prof to assoc prof forest climatol, 70-75. *Concurrent Pos:* Nat Acad Sci-Polish Acad Sci exchangee, Inst Geog, Univ Warsaw, 70, vis scientist, 73; consult, Nat Cellulose & Paper Orgn, Cent Forest Exp Sta, Rome, 70 & 73; res off, Inst Hydrol, Eng, 73; vis scientist, Southwest Watershed Res Ctr, USDA/Agr Res Serv, Tucson, 82; vis prof, Inst Forest Snow & Landscape Res; ETH, Zurich, Switz, 91. *Mem:* Am Meteorol Soc. *Res:* Influence of vegetation on heat balance at earth's surface, especially snow and forest hydrology, forest meteorology and evapotranspiration processes. *Mailing Add:* Sch Renewable Natural Resources Univ Ariz Tucson AZ 85721. *E-Mail:* lgay@ag.arizona.edu

GAY, MICHAEL HOWARD, METABOLISM, PHARMACOKENETICS. *Current Pos:* RES SCIENTIST, UNIROYAL CHEM CO, 90- *Personal Data:* b Tacoma, Wash, July 15, 43; m 65; c Lisa D. *Educ:* Univ Chicago, BA, 66; Wash Univ, PhD(pharmacol), 74. *Prof Exp:* Sr res asst pharmacol, Alcohol & Drug Abuse Res Ctr, McLean Hosp, 75-76; instr, Dept Pharmacol & Med Chem, Northeastern Univ, 76-80, asst prof, Dept Pharmacol, 80-83; sr scientist, Biotek Inc, 83-89. *Concurrent Pos:* Res assoc psychiat, Harvard Med Sch, 75-76; consult, Biotek Inc, 80-83. *Mem:* AAAS; Control Release Soc; Am Chem Soc. *Res:* Neurochemistry of central nervous system depressants; mechanisms of tolerance and physical dependence; pharmacology and sustained drug release technology; metabolism of pesticides. *Mailing Add:* 12 Spindle Hill Rd Apt 2-D Wolcott CT 06716. *Fax:* 203-573-3660

GAY, RENATE ERIKA, IMMUNOHISTOLOGY, COLLAGEN PATHOLOGY. *Current Pos:* res assoc, Inst Dent Res, 76-81, RES ASST PROF DERMAT, UNIV ALA, 81-, ASSOC SCIENTIST, COMPREHENSIVE CANCER CTR & INVESTR, INST DENT RES, 81-, RES ASSOC PROF MED, 84- *Personal Data:* b Halle, EGer, Nov 11, 49; m 73; c 3. *Educ:* Univ Med Sch Munich, MD, 75. *Honors & Awards:* Caral-Nachman Prize, 84. *Prof Exp:* Intern med, Univ Med Sch Munich, 75-76; res specialist biochem, Rutgers Med Sch, 76. *Mem:* Am Rheumatism

Asn; NY Acad Sci; Am Soc Cell Biol. *Res:* Immunohistology and connective tissue pathology in rheumatology; dermatology and cancer research. *Mailing Add:* Ctr Exp Rheumat Clin Rheumat Univ Hosp Gloriastra 25 Zurich CH 8091 Switzerland. Fax: 41-1-255-2962

GAY, RICHARD LESLIE, RADIOACTIVE & HAZARDOUS WASTE MANAGEMENT. *Current Pos:* Mem tech staff chem eng, Atomics Int, Rockwell Int, 76-86, MGR CHEM & PROCESS ENG, ROCKETDYNE DIV, ROCKWELL, 86- *Personal Data:* b Redlands, Calif, Nov 17, 50. *Educ:* Univ Calif, Los Angeles, BS & MS, 73, PhD(eng), 76. *Mem:* Sigma Xi; Combustion Inst; Am Chem Soc; Am Inst Chem Engrs. *Res:* Combustion technology; disposal of hazardous wastes; flue gas desulfurization; energy and resource recovery; volume reduction of radioactive waste; molten salt chemistry; high temperature materials compatibility; energy storage systems; high temperature superconductors; actinide partitioning and transmutation; 7 patents awarded. *Mailing Add:* 10012 Hanna Ave Chatsworth CA 91311-3612. Fax: 818-586-5877

GAY, STEFFEN, CONNECTIVE TISSUE PATHOLOGY, IMMUNOHISTOLOGY. *Current Pos:* vis investr, Inst Dent Res, 76-78, vis asst prof path, 77-78, assoc prof med, Dir Clin Immunol & Rheumat, 78-84, ASSOC PROF, DEPT DERMAT & SCIENTIST, INST DENT RES & COMPREHENSIVE CANCER CTR, 78-, SCIENTIST & PROF MATH, MULTIPURPOSE ARTHRITICS CTR, 84- *Personal Data:* b Geyersdorf, EGe, Mar 22, 48; m 73; c 3. *Educ:* Univ Med Sch Leipzig, EGer, MD, 72. *Honors & Awards:* Alexander-Schmidt-Preis, Ger Soc Thrombosis Res, 75; Int Carol-Nachman Prize Rheumat, 78. *Prof Exp:* Fel path, Univ Med Sch Leipzig, 70-73; resident internal med, Poliklinik Leipzig, 72-73; res fel connective tissue biochem, Max Planck Inst, 73-76. *Concurrent Pos:* Ed-in-chief, J Collagen & Related Res; vis scientist, Dept Biochem, Rutgers Univ, 76; dir, Ctr for Rheumatology, WHO, 84-; assoc ed, Arthritis & Rheumat, 85-; dir, WHO Ctr Rheumatic Dis, 84. *Mem:* Am Asn Pathologists; Am Rheumatism Asn; Ger Path Asn; Ger Rheumatology Asn; NY Acad Sci; Am Soc Cell Biol. *Res:* Biochemistry, immunology, histology and pathology of collagen types, glycoproteins and matrix degrading enzymes in normal and pathological connective tissues; cellular basis and molecular biology of joint destruction in rheumatic diseases. *Mailing Add:* Ctr Exp Rheumat Clin Rheumat Univ Hosp Gloriastra 25 Zurich CH-8091 Switzerland. Fax: 41-1-255-4170

GAY, THOMAS JOHN, ORAL BIOLOGY, PHYSIOLOGY. *Current Pos:* from asst prof to assoc prof, 70-78, PROF ORAL BIOL, HEALTH CTR, UNIV CONN, FARMINGTON, 78- *Personal Data:* b New York, NY, May 19, 40; m 64; c 2. *Educ:* City Col, City Univ New York, BA, 62, PhD(speech sci), 67; Adelphi Univ, MS, 64. *Prof Exp:* Asst prof speech, Hunter Col, 67-69; res scientist speech, Haskins Labs, 69-70. *Mem:* Acoust Soc Am; AAAS; Am Asn Phonetic Sci. *Res:* Articulatory and acoustic phonetics; physiological models of speech production; biological signal processing. *Mailing Add:* 3 Brenthaven Avon CT 06001

GAY, WILLIAM INGALLS, MEDICAL ADMINISTRATION, COMPARATIVE MEDICINE. *Current Pos:* CONSULT, ROW SCI, 88-; CONSULT PVT PRACT. *Personal Data:* b Sussex, NJ, Jan 25, 26; m 48, Millicent R Chapman. *Educ:* Cornell Univ, DVM, 50. *Honors & Awards:* Griffin Award, Am Asn Lab Animal Sci, 71. *Prof Exp:* Pvt pract, 50-52; chief, Dept Animal Husb, Walter Reed Army Med Serv, 52-54; chief, Animal Hosp Sect, NIH, 54-63, asst chief, Lab Aids Br, 61-63, Lab Animal Specialist, Div Res Facil & Resources, 63-66; prog dir comp med, Nat Inst Gen Med, 66-67, chief, Res Grants Br, 67-70, Nat Inst Allergy & Infectious Dis, 70-80, assoc dir, Extramural Progs, 80-88, dir, Animal Resources Prog, Div Res Resources, 80-88. *Mem:* Am Vet Med Asn; Am Asn Lab Animal Sci (pres, 68); AAAS; Found Biomed Res; Int Soc Burn Injuries; Am Col Lab Animal Med (secy-treas, 64-66). *Res:* Laboratory animal medicine; comparative medicine; experimental surgery; medical research administration; grant and contract management. *Mailing Add:* 5200 Chandler St Bethesda MD 20814-2865

GAYER, KARL HERMAN, CHEMISTRY. *Current Pos:* RETIRED. *Personal Data:* b Cleveland, Ohio, Aug 6, 13; m 50; c 3. *Educ:* Case Western Res Univ, BS, 43, MS, 46; Ohio State Univ, PhD(chem), 48. *Prof Exp:* Instr chem, Ohio State Univ, 47-48; from asst prof to assoc prof, Wayne State Univ 48-59, head inorg div, 56-65, prof chem, 59-84. *Concurrent Pos:* Exec secy, dept chem, Wayne State Univ, 56-65. *Mem:* AAAS; Am Inst Chem; Calorimetry Conf; Am Chem Soc; Sigma Xi. *Res:* Thermochemistry; solution calorimetry; thermodynamics of solutions. *Mailing Add:* 7332 Mohansic Bloomfield Hills MI 48301-3552

GAYLES, JOSEPH NATHAN, JR, PHYSICAL CHEMISTRY. *Current Pos:* VPRES, MOREHOUSE SCH MED, 83-, PROF MED, 85- *Personal Data:* b Birmingham, Ala, Aug 7, 37; c 2. *Educ:* Dillard Univ, AB, 58; Brown Univ, PhD(chem), 63. *Hon Degrees:* LLD, Dillard Univ, 83. *Prof Exp:* Res assoc phys chem, Ore State Univ, 63-64; Woodrow Wilson teaching assoc, Morehouse Col, 63-66, asst prof, 64-69, dir med prog, 72-75, prof phys chem, 69-80, pres, Talladega Col, 76-83. *Concurrent Pos:* Res assoc chem, Univ Iowa, 64 & Brown Univ, 66; res staff scientist, IBM Corp, 66-69; Dreyfus scholar, 70-; consult, NIH, 70-, EPA, 72- & NSF, 74-; premed adv, Morehouse Col, 70-77,; Mass Inst Technol bd vistors, 81-88; Woodrow Wilson fel. *Mem:* Am Phys Soc; Am Chem Soc; Am Asn Polit & Social Scientists; Sigma Xi; AAAS. *Res:* Molecular structure and spectroscopy; laser phenomena; liquid crystals. *Mailing Add:* 1515 Austin Rd SW Atlanta GA 30331-2267

GAYLIN, WILLARD, PSYCHIATRY, BIOETHICS. *Current Pos:* prof psychiat & law, Sch Law, Columbia Col & Union Theol Sem, 70-80, CLIN PROF PSYCHIAT, COLUMBIA COL PHYSICIANS & SURGEONS, 80-; PRES, HASTINGS CTR, 70- *Personal Data:* b Cleveland, Ohio, 1925; c 2. *Educ:* Harvard Univ, AB, 47; Western Res Univ, MD, 51. *Honors & Awards:* George E Daniels Medal of Merit for Contrib Psychoanal Med; Elizabeth Cutter Morrow Lectr, Smith Col; Bloomfield Lectr, Med Sch, Case Western Res Univ; Van Giesen Award; Henry Beecher Award. *Prof Exp:* Intern, Cleveland City Hosp, Ohio, 51-52; resident psychiat, Bronx Vet Admin Hosp, NY, 52-54. *Concurrent Pos:* Pvt pract, 54-; from mem fac to clin prof psychiat, Psychoanal Sch, Columbia Univ, 56-; consult, AMA Judicial Coun & Inst of Life, Univ of Paris; mem bd dirs, Field Found, Helsinki Watch, comt Pub Justice & Nat Adv Bd Amnesty Int; lectr, Columbia Col Physicians & Surgeons, 1st commencement, 81; Chubb fel, Yale & vis prof, Harvard Med Sch; vis lectr, Sorbonne, Dartmouth Co, Hampshire Col, Princeton, Calif Inst Technol & Univ Hawaii; mem, Human Rights Comt, Inst Med. *Mem:* Inst Med-Nat Acad Sci; fel Am Psychiat Asn; Am Psychoanal Asn. *Res:* Judicial bias; ethics of behavior control; ethics, law and life sciences; author or editor of 15 books and about 70 articles; human nature; psychology of emotions. *Mailing Add:* Hastings Ctr 255 Elm Rd Briarcliff Manor NY 10510-9974. Fax: 914-478-8212

GAYLOR, DAVID WILLIAM, BIOSTATISTICS. *Current Pos:* CHIEF BIOMET, NAT CTR FOR TOXICOL RES, 72- *Personal Data:* b Waterloo, Iowa, Apr 8, 30; m 54; c 4. *Educ:* Iowa State Univ, BS, 51, MS, 53; NC State Univ, PhD(statist), 60. *Honors & Awards:* Shewell Award, 68 & Wilcoxin Prize, Chem Div, Am Soc Qual Control, 70. *Prof Exp:* Statistician, Hanford Atomic Prod Oper, Gen Elec Co, 53-55, Gen Dynamics/Convair, 55-57, Vallecitos Atomic Lab, Gen Elec Co, 60-62, Res Triangle Inst, 62-68 & Nat Inst Environ Health Sci, 68-72. *Concurrent Pos:* Adj assoc prof, NC State Univ, 67-72; adj prof, Med Sch, Univ Ark, 72- *Mem:* Fel Am Statist Asn; Biomet Soc; fel Soc Risk Anal. *Res:* Statistical design and analysis of experiments; quantitative risk assessment of chemicals. *Mailing Add:* 13815 Abinger Ct Little Rock AR 72212

GAYLOR, JAMES LEROY, MOLECULAR BIOLOGY, NUTRITION. *Current Pos:* corp dir molecular biol, 87-90, CORP DIR SCI & TECHNOL, JOHNSON & JOHNSON, 91- *Personal Data:* b Waterloo, Iowa, Oct 1, 34; m 56, Marilyn Gibson; c Douglas, Ann, Robert & Kenneth. *Educ:* Iowa State Univ, BS, 56; Univ Wis, MS, 58, PhD(biochem), 60. *Prof Exp:* From asst prof to assoc prof biochem, Grad Sch Nutrit, Cornell Univ, 60-69, prof biochem & molecular biol, 69-77, chmn sect, Div Biol Sci, 70-76; prof biochem & chmn dept, Univ Mo, Columbia, 77-80; dir health sci res, E I du Pont de Nemours & Co, Inc, 81-85, dir biol res, 86-87. *Concurrent Pos:* Vis lectr, Univ Ill, 64 & 65; vis mem staff, Dept Biochem, Sch Med, Univ Ore, 66-67; vis prof biochem, Sch Med, Osaka Univ, Japan, 73-74; Guggenheim fel; fel, Arteriosclerosis Coun, Am Heart Asn. *Mem:* Am Chem Soc; Am Soc Biochem & Molecular Biol; Am Inst Nutrit; Am Heart Asn; Am Asn Pharmaceut Scientists; AAAS. *Res:* Biosynthesis cholesterol and other sterols; microsomal electron transport of mixed function oxidases of biosynthetic processes; isolation and purification of microsomal enzymes; reconstitution of microsomal multienzymic systems. *Mailing Add:* Johnson & Johnson 410 George St Rm 1139 New Brunswick NJ 08901-2021. Fax: 732-524-2549

GAYLOR, MICHAEL JAMES, ENTOMOLOGY. *Current Pos:* asst prof, 78-84, ASSOC PROF COTTON ENTOM, AUBURN UNIV, 84- *Personal Data:* b Birmingham, Ala, May 16, 47; m 69, Betty Fuller; c David & Debra. *Educ:* Auburn Univ, BS, 69, MS, 71; Tex A&M Univ, PhD(entom), 75. *Prof Exp:* Asst prof urban entom, Tex Agr Exp Sta, Tex A&M Univ, 75-77. *Mem:* Entom Soc Am; Sigma Xi. *Res:* Management of insect pests of cotton; biological control by indigenous natural enemies. *Mailing Add:* Dept Entom Auburn Univ Auburn AL 36849-3501. Fax: 334-844-5005

GAYLORD, EBER WILLIAM, MECHANICAL ENGINEERING. *Current Pos:* RETIRED. *Personal Data:* b Pittsburgh, Pa, Nov 6, 22; m 62; c 1. *Educ:* Carnegie Inst Technol, PhD(mech eng), 53. *Prof Exp:* Assoc prof mech eng, Carnegie Inst Technol, 53-59; res engr, Gulf Res & Develop Co, 59-84. *Mem:* Am Soc Mech Engrs; Soc Automotive Engrs. *Res:* Experimental fluid mechanics; friction and wear dynamics; interface temperature between rubbing metals; momentum and mass transfer in jets; research and development in petroleum production engineering. *Mailing Add:* 323 W Main Grove City PA 16127

GAYLORD, EDSON I, MECHANICAL ENGINEERING. *Current Pos:* CHMN & PRES, INGERSOLL MILLING MACH CO. *Honors & Awards:* M Eugene Merchant Mfg Medal, Am Soc Mech Engrs/Soc Mfg Engrs, 91. *Mailing Add:* Ingersoll Milling Mach Co 707 Fulton Ave Rockford IL 61103-4069

GAYLORD, NORMAN GRANT, POLYMER CHEMISTRY & TECHNOLOGY. *Current Pos:* PRES, GAYLORD ASSOC, 87- *Personal Data:* b New York, NY, Feb 16, 23; m 45, Marilyn Einhorn; c 4. *Educ:* City Col New York, BS, 43; Polytech Inst Brooklyn, MS, 49, PhD(chem), 50. *Honors & Awards:* Founders Award, Am Acad Optom, 85. *Prof Exp:* Chemist, Elko Chem Works, 43-44, Pa Salt Mfg Co, 45 & Merck & Co, Inc, 46-48; res assoc, Polytech Inst Brooklyn, 48-50; res chemist, Film Dept, E I du Pont de Nemours & Co, 50-55; group leader, Resin Dept, Interchem Corp, 55-56, asst dir, Org Chem Dept, 56-59; vpres, Polymer Div, Western Petrochem Corp, NY, 59-61; pres, Gaylord Res Inst Inc, 61-87. *Concurrent Pos:* Polymer consult, 61-; fel, Res Inst Scientists, Emer, Drew Univ, 87- *Mem:* Am Chem Soc; fel Soc Plastics Eng; Tech Asn Pulp & Paper Industs.

Res: Polymer synthesis; polymerization kinetics; allyl polymerization; stereoregular polymers; organic chemistry of high polymers; block and graft copolymerization; charge transfer polymerization; photopolymerization; polymer modification; controlled release of pharmaceuticals; polymers for contact lenses; reactive processing for polymer blends and alloys. *Mailing Add:* 28 Newcomb Dr New Providence NJ 07974

GAYLORD, RICHARD J, THEORETICAL POLYMER PHYSICS, STATISTICAL MECHANICS. *Current Pos:* asst prof, 74-79, ASSOC PROF POLYMERS, DEPT METALL & MINING ENG, UNIV ILL, URBANA-CHAMPAIGN, 80- *Personal Data:* b Plainfield, NJ, Dec 20, 47; m 70. *Educ:* Polytech Inst Brooklyn, BS, 69; State Univ NY Syracuse, PhD(polymer sci), 73. *Prof Exp:* Res assoc, Polymer Res Inst, Univ Mass, 73-74. *Mem:* Am Phys Soc. *Res:* Statistical mechanics of polymeric systems; bulk polymer deformation; confined chain problems. *Mailing Add:* Dept Metal & Mining Engr 202a Mmb Univ Ill 1304 W Green Urbana IL 61801-2920

GAYLORD, THOMAS KEITH, OPTICAL DATA PROCESSING. *Current Pos:* JULIUS BROWN CHAIR REGENTS PROF ELEC ENG, GA INST TECHNOL, 72- *Personal Data:* b Casper, Wyo, Sept 22, 43; m 66; c 1. *Educ:* Univ Mo, Rolla, BS, 65, MS, 67; Rice Univ, PhD(elec eng), 70. *Honors & Awards:* Curtis W McGraw Award, Am Soc Elec Engrs, 79. *Prof Exp:* Res assoc, Rice Univ, 70-72. *Concurrent Pos:* Ed, Trans Educ, Inst Elec & Electronics Engrs, 78-82. *Mem:* Fel Inst Elec & Electronics Engrs; Sigma Xi; AAAS; fel Optical Soc Am. *Res:* Optical holographic data storage and processing; recording in electro-optic crystals; electromagnetic diffraction; volume gratings; semiconductor devices; instrumentation; optical computing. *Mailing Add:* Sch Elec Eng Ga Inst Technol Atlanta GA 30332-0001

GAYNOR, JOHN DONALD, HERBICIDE DISSIPATION IN SOIL & WATER, NUTRIENT & HERBICIDE FATE IN AGRICULTURAL PRACTICES. *Current Pos:* RES SCIENTIST, GREENHOUSE & PROCESSING CROPS RES CTR, AGR & AGRI-FOOD CAN, 74- *Personal Data:* b Vancouver, BC, Mar 12, 42; m 63, Dianne; c Camille, Donna, Leon, Corrine & Venita. *Educ:* Brigham Young Univ, BSc, 68; Ore State Univ MSc, 70, PhD(soil chem), 73. *Prof Exp:* Rs scientist, Agr Can, 73-74. *Concurrent Pos:* Vis prof, Okayama Univ, 96. *Mem:* Weed Sci Soc Am; Soil Sci Soc Am; Agron Soc Am; Am Chem Soc; Sigma Xi. *Res:* Agricultural practices and systems which minimize nutrient and herbicide loss to surface runoff and subsurface drainage and ground water contamination; evaluation sludge utilization in agriculture with respect to metals. *Mailing Add:* Harrow Res Ctr Harrow ON N0R 1G0 Can. *Fax:* 519-738-2929; *E-Mail:* gaynorj@em.agr.ca

GAYNOR, JOHN JAMES, GENE EXPRESSION, PLANT-PATHOGEN INTERACTIONS. *Current Pos:* ASST PROF BIOL, DEPT BIOL SCI, RUTGERS UNIV, 84- *Personal Data:* b Philadelphia, Pa, Dec 19, 53; m 76; c 4. *Educ:* St Joseph's Col, BS, 75; Rutgers Univ, MS, 78, PhD(plant physiol), 81. *Prof Exp:* Fel, Dept Biol, Yale Univ, 81-82; Lab Plant Molecular Biol, Rockefeller Univ, 82-84. *Concurrent Pos:* Res assoc, Life Sci Div, NASA, 81-82; Henry Rutgers fel, Rutgers Univ, 85-87. *Mem:* Am Soc Plant Physiologists; AAAS; Int Soc Plant Molecular Biol; Bot Soc Am; Sigma Xi. *Res:* Regulation of gene expressions in higher plants; the influence of small effector molecules (ie the phytohormone ethylene) on transcription and in the signal transduction pathway for this horm. *Mailing Add:* Dept Biol Sci Montclair State Univ Upper Montclair NJ 07043

GAYNOR, JOSEPH, CHEMICAL ENGINEERING, IMAGING MATERIALS & PROCESSES. *Current Pos:* PRES, INNOVATIVE TECHNOL ASSOCS, 73- *Personal Data:* b New York, NY, Nov 15, 25; m 51, Elaine Bauer; c Barbara L, Martin S, Paul D & Andrew D. *Educ:* Polytech Inst Brooklyn, BChE, 50; Case Inst Technol, MS, 52, PhD(chem eng), 55. *Honors & Awards:* Indust Res IR-100 Awards, 63, 65. *Prof Exp:* Asst unit opers & plastics lab, Case Inst Technol, 50-55; chem engr, Gen Elec Co, 55-59, chem process engr, 59-64, mgr, Info Mat Systs, 64-66; asst vpres res, Bus Equip Group, Bell & Howell Co, Ill, 66-68, vpres, 68, dir graphic media res, Res Labs, Calif, 68-71; mgr com develop group & mem pres off, Horizons Res Inc, 72-73. *Concurrent Pos:* Plenary lectr, Int Cong Photog Sci; gen chmn, Int Conf Electrophotog, Int Conf Bus Graphics, Int Cong Advan Non-Impact Printing Technol & Gordon Res Conf Phys & Chem Polymeric Films & Coatings. *Mem:* Fel AAAS; fel Am Inst Chem; sr mem Am Soc Photog Scientists & Engrs; Am Chem Soc; NY Acad Sci; Soc Photo-Optic Instrumentation Engrs; Soc Int Develop; fel Int Sci & Technol Soc; fel Soc Imaging Sci & Technol. *Res:* Solubility, diffusion, rheology, adhesion and lubrication of high polymers; engineering properties of high polymers; heat transfer; fluid flow; fluidization; physics and chemistry of the solid state; photochemistry; photoelectricity; unconventional image recording processes; electrophotography; photofabrication; polymeric films and coatings; optical and magnetic data storage discs; non-impact printing technologies; chemical processes. *Mailing Add:* 108 La Brea St Oxnard CA 93035-3928

GAZDA, I(RVING) W(ILLIAM), MECHANICAL ENGINEERING, HEAT TRANSFER. *Current Pos:* Group leader electrode develop, 60-70, sect head electrode develop, 70-74, mgr tech control, 75-79, TECH DIR, GREAT LAKES CARBON CORP, 79- *Personal Data:* b Niagara Falls, NY, Nov 26, 41; m 66; c 1. *Educ:* Rensselaer Polytech Inst, BS, 63, MS, 65, PhD(heat transfer), 69. *Mem:* Am Soc Mech Engrs; Iron & Steel Soc, Am Inst Metall Engrs. *Res:* Heat transfer in fluids; physical and thermal property determinations for ceramics; thermal shock studies on ceramics. *Mailing Add:* SGL Carbon Corp Charlotte NC 28269

GAZDAR, ADI F, CANCER RESEARCH, CELL BIOLOGY. *Current Pos:* SECT HEAD, NAT CANCER INST, 69- *Personal Data:* b Bombay, India, May 15, 37; US citizen; m 69. *Educ:* Univ London, BS & MB, 61. *Mem:* Am Asn Cancer Res; Inst Asn Study Lung Cancer; Am Soc Clin Oncol; Soc Exp Med & Biol. *Res:* Biology of human cancer, especially lung cancer and lymphomas; authored or co-authored approximately 150 publications on cancer research. *Mailing Add:* 5911 Lakehurst Ave Dallas TX 75230

GAZIN, CHARLES LEWIS, geology; deceased, see previous edition for last biography

GAZIS, DENOS CONSTANTINOS, APPLIED MATHEMATICS. *Current Pos:* PRES, GAZIS ASSOC, 95- *Personal Data:* b Salonica, Greece, Sept 15, 30; US citizen; m 74; c 9. *Educ:* Tech Univ, Athens, BS, 52; Stanford Univ, MS, 54; Columbia Univ, PhD(eng mech), 57. *Honors & Awards:* Lanchester Prize, Opers Res Soc Am, 59. *Prof Exp:* Designer engr civil eng, Tech Ministry, Athens, 52-53 & Tippetts & Assocs, NY, 55-57; sr res scientist mech, Gen Motors Res Labs, 57-61; res staff mem, IBM Ctr, Yorktown Hights, 61-79, asst dir, 82-95. *Concurrent Pos:* Instr, Tech Univ, Athens, 52-53; vis prof, Yale Univ, 69-70; dir gen sci, IBM Res Ctr, 71-74, tech adv to IBM chief scientist, IBM Corp Hq, Armonk, NY, 75-77, mem res rev bd, 77-78, 77-78, consult to dir res, IBM Res Ctr, 78-79, asst dir comput sci, 79-82. *Mem:* Opers Res Soc Am; Building Res Bd, Nat Res Coun; Int Platform Asn. *Res:* Operations research; computer science; applications of computers to social and environmental problems. *Mailing Add:* 26 Lake Rd Katonah NY 10536

GAZZANIGA, MICHAEL SAUNDERS, PSYCHOBIOLOGY. *Current Pos:* AT CTR COGNITIVE NEUROSCI, DARTMOUTH COL. *Personal Data:* b Los Angeles, Calif, Dec 12, 39; c 6. *Educ:* Dartmouth Col, AB, 61; Calif Inst Technol, PhD(biol), 64. *Prof Exp:* USPHS res fel psychobiol, Calif Inst Technol, 64-66; from asst prof to assoc prof psychol & chmn dept, Univ Calif, Santa Barbara, 66-69; from assoc prof to prof, Grad Sch, NY Univ, 69-73; prof psychol, State Univ NY, Stony Brook, 73-78, prof soc sci med, 75-78; prof psychiat & dir, Div Cognitive Neurosci, Cornell Med Col, 78-92; prof neurol & dir, Ctr Neurosci, Univ Calif, Davis, 92- *Concurrent Pos:* NIMH res grant, 67-69; State Univ NY Univ-Wide Exchange scholar, 74- *Mem:* Am Physiol Soc; fel Am Psychol Asn; Am Acad Neurol; Int Neuropsychol Asn; NY Acad Sci. *Res:* Studies on human split-brain patient and other neurologic patients addressing the role of language in conscious experience and the cortical mechanisms involved in cognitive processing, visual-motor processing and memory. *Mailing Add:* Ctr Cognitive Neurosci Dartmouth Col 6162 Silsby Hall Hanover NH 03755-3547

GE, WEIKUN, SEMICONDUCTING MICROSTRUCTURES, DEFECTS IN SEMICONDUCTORS. *Current Pos:* SR LECTR PHYSICS, HONG KONG UNIV SCI & TECHNOL, 93- *Personal Data:* b Beijing, China, Mar 25, 42; div; c Cheng & Qiong. *Educ:* Peking Univ, BS, 65; Univ Manchester, UK, PhD(solid state electronics), 83. *Honors & Awards:* Third Degree Prize for Progress in Sci & Technol, Chinese Acad Sci, 88, Second Degree Prize, 89. *Prof Exp:* Engr semiconductor mat devices, Beijing Inst Non-Ferrous Metals, 65-78; postdoctoral fel solid state electronics, Inst Sci Technol, Univ Manchester, 83; assoc prof physics, Inst Semiconductors, Chinese Acad Sci, 84-88; res assoc, Dartmouth Col, 88-91, res assoc prof physics, 91-93. *Mem:* Am Phys Soc; fel Chinese Luminescence Soc. *Res:* Defects in GaAs and Si-for GaAs, local vibrational mode absorption induced by Ga-O-Ga- for Si, new donors and Pd-related defects; optical spectroscopic studies on semiconducting quantum wells and superlattices, especially on band structure of very short-period GaAs-AlAs superlattices; quantum dots physics. *Mailing Add:* Dept Physics Hong Kong Univ Sci & Technol Kowloon Hong Kong People's Republic of China. *Fax:* 852-2358-1652; *E-Mail:* phweikum@usehk.ust.hk

GEACH, GEORGE ALWYN, materials science; deceased, see previous edition for last biography

GEACINTOV, NICHOLAS, CHEMICAL PHYSICS, BIOPHYSICS. *Current Pos:* res scientist solid state physics, 63-69, from asst prof to assoc prof, 69-75, PROF CHEM, NY UNIV, 75- *Personal Data:* b Albi, France, Nov 9, 35; US citizen. *Educ:* State Univ NY Col Forestry, Syracuse, BS, 57, MS, 59, PhD(phys Chem), 61. *Prof Exp:* Res assoc photochem, Polytech Inst Brooklyn, 61-63. *Res:* Photophysics of aromatic molecules and crystals; spectroscopic properties of photosynthetic membranes; structure of carcinogen-nucleic acid complexes. *Mailing Add:* Dept Chem NY Univ New York NY 10003

GEADELMANN, JON LEE, PLANT BREEDING. *Current Pos:* asst prof plant breeding, 72-77, assoc prof, 77-80, PROF AGRON & PLANT GENETICS, UNIV MINN, 80- *Personal Data:* b Anamosa, Iowa, June 4, 44; m 64; c 2. *Educ:* Iowa State Univ, BS, 66, PhD(plant breeding), 70. *Prof Exp:* Asst prof statist, Iowa State Univ, 70-72. *Mem:* Am Soc Agron; Crop Sci Soc Am. *Res:* Population improvement; inbred line development; maize genetics; quantitative genetics. *Mailing Add:* 2030 W Skillman St Paul Roseville MN 55113

GEALER, ROY L(EE), CHEMICAL ENGINEERING, BIOMECHANICS & MATERIALS. *Current Pos:* HARRINGTON ARTHRITIS RES CTR, 87- *Personal Data:* b Detroit, Mich, Oct 23, 32; m 57, Norma Varnen; c Charles & Francine. *Educ:* Wayne State Univ, BS, 54; Univ Mich, MS, 55, PhD(chem eng), 58. *Prof Exp:* Asst combustion res, Univ Mich, 54-58; res engr, Ethyl

Corp, 58-63; prin res eng assoc, Ford Motor Co, 63-68, prin staff engr, 68-78, prin res engr, 78-87. *Mem:* Am Chem Soc; Sigma Xi. *Res:* Development and evaluation of prosthetic materials and devices; automotive industry product and process research, including friction materials, industrial air pollution control, wastewater treatment, energy and fuels. *Mailing Add:* 514 W Marconi Ave Phoenix AZ 85023

GEALT, MICHAEL ALAN, ENVIRONMENTAL MICROBIOLOGY. *Current Pos:* asst prof biol sci, Drexel Univ, 78-84, assoc prof biosci & biotechnol, 84-90, dir, Environ Studies Inst, 93-96, PROF BIOSCI & BIOTECHNOL, DREXEL UNIV, PHILADELPHIA, 90-, DIR, SCH ENVIRON SCI ENG & POLICY, 96- *Personal Data:* b Philadelphia, Pa, Nov 27, 48; m 81, Maryjanet McNamara. *Educ:* Temple Univ, Philadelphia, BA, 70; Rutgers Univ, PhD(microbiol), 74. *Prof Exp:* Res assoc, Col Med & Dent, Rutgers Univ, NJ, 74-76; trainee, Inst Cancer Res, Philadelphia, 76-78. *Concurrent Pos:* Vis scientist, US Environ Protection Agency, Gulf Breeze, Fl, 90-91; chair, Environ & Appl Microbiol Div, Am Soc Microbiol, 95. *Mem:* AAAS; Am Soc Cell Biol; Am Soc Microbiol; Am Mycological Soc; Sigma Xi; fel Am Acad Microbiol. *Res:* Environmental microbiology; exchange of recombinant genetic material between micro-organisms in wastewater and other environments; biodegradation; analysis of genes involved in metabolic pathways. *Mailing Add:* Sch Environ Sci Eng & Policy Drexel Univ 32nd & Chestnut Sts Philadelphia PA 19104. *Fax:* 215-895-2267; *E-Mail:* gealt@duvm.ocs.drexel.edu

GEALY, JOHN ROBERT, GEOLOGY. *Current Pos:* Geologist, Humble Oil & Refining Co, 55-74, GEOLOGIST, ESSO PRODS RES CO, 74- *Personal Data:* b Tokyo, Japan, Dec 4, 30; m 64. *Educ:* Southern Methodist Univ, BS, 51; Yale Univ, MS, PhD(geol), 55. *Mem:* AAAS; Geol Soc Am; Am Asn Petrol Geol; Sigma Xi. *Res:* Regional geology. *Mailing Add:* 366 Tealwood Dr Houston TX 77024

GEALY, MARK W, ATOMIC HYDROGEN TARGETS. *Current Pos:* ASSOC PROF PHYSICS, CONCORDIA COL, MINN, 90- *Educ:* Hastings Col, BA, 78; Univ Denver, MS, 82, PhD(physics), 86. *Prof Exp:* Res assoc, Univ Nebr, Lincoln, 86-90. *Res:* Experimental studies of charge transfer, excitation and ionization in collisions of ions and atoms with atoms and molecules; atomic hydrogen targets. *Mailing Add:* Concordia Col Moorhead MN 56562. *E-Mail:* gealy@cord.edu

GEALY, WILLIAM JAMES, RESEARCH ADMINISTRATION, TECHNOLOGY TRANSFER. *Current Pos:* DIR OFF RES & SPONSORED PROG, NORTHWESTERN UNIV, 80-, ASST VPRES RES, 93- *Personal Data:* b Tokyo, Japan, Sept 7, 25; US citizen; m 45, 70, Marcia Booker; c 4. *Educ:* Univ Mich, BA, 46; Harvard Univ, MA, 51, PhD(geol), 53. *Prof Exp:* Geologist, Stand Oil Co, Calif, 53-56, consult geologist, 56-59; assoc dir develop, Ohio State Univ Res Found, 69-80. *Concurrent Pos:* lectr & asst prof, Southern Methodist Univ, 66-68; adj assoc prof geol, Ohio State Univ, 69-80; interim dir, Technol Commercialization Ctr, Northwestern Univ, 84-85, interim admin, Technol Transf Prog, 89-90 & 93- *Mem:* Geol Soc Am; Am Asn Petrol Geol; Sigma Xi; Soc Res Adminrs; Asn Univ Technol Mgrs; Nat Coun Univ Res Admins. *Res:* Petroleum geology. *Mailing Add:* 803 Milburn St Evanston IL 60201. *Fax:* 847-491-4800

GEANANGEL, RUSSELL ALAN, INORGANIC CHEMISTRY. *Current Pos:* Asst prof, 68-71, assoc prof, 71-77, PROF CHEM, UNIV HOUSTON, 77- *Personal Data:* b Cadiz, Ohio, Aug 2, 41; m 61; c 2. *Educ:* Ohio State Univ, BS, 63, PhD(inorg chem), 68. *Concurrent Pos:* Consult, 80- *Mem:* Am Chem Soc. *Res:* Synthesis and structural characterization of inorganic and organometallic compounds of structural, bonding and materials science interest, including compounds main group elements; multinuclei nuclear magnetic resonance and Mossbauer spectroscopy. *Mailing Add:* Dept Chem Univ Houston Houston TX 77204-5641

GEANKOPLIS, CHRISTIE J(OHN), CHEMICAL ENGINEERING. *Current Pos:* PROF CHEM ENG, UNIV MINN, MINNEAPOLIS, 82- *Personal Data:* b Minneapolis, Minn, June 18, 21. *Educ:* Univ Minn, BChE, 43; Univ Pa, MS, 46, PhD(chem eng), 49. *Prof Exp:* Develop design & process engr, Atlantic Refining Co, 43-47; instr chem eng, Univ Pa, 47-48; from asst prof to prof chem eng, Ohio State Univ, 60-82. *Concurrent Pos:* Consult chem engr, Battelle Mem Inst, 51-78 & Gen Mills Chem, Inc, 66-80, Henkel, Inc, 80-86, H B Fuller, Inc, 88-93 & Omega Source, Inc, 90-92. *Mem:* Am Chem Soc; Am Inst Chem Engrs. *Res:* Diffusion and mass transfer; transport processes; reaction kinetics; biochemical engineering. *Mailing Add:* 151 Amundson Hall Univ Minn 421 Washington Ave SE Minneapolis MN 55455

GEAR, ADRIAN R L, BIOCHEMISTRY. *Current Pos:* ASSOC PROF BIOCHEM, SCH MED, UNIV VA, 67- *Personal Data:* b Pretoria, SAfrica, Aug 31, 39; m 64; c 2. *Educ:* Oxford Univ, BA, 61, MA & DPhil(biochem), 65. *Prof Exp:* Fel biochem, Johns Hopkins Univ, 65-67. *Mem:* Am Soc Biol Chem; NY Acad Sci. *Res:* Mitochondria; blood platelets; survival, function and energy metabolism; mitochondrial biogenesis; ion transport; energy coupling; oxidative phosphorylation. *Mailing Add:* Dept Biochem Jordan Hall Univ Va Sch Med Box 440 Charlottesville VA 22908-0001. *Fax:* 804-924-5069

GEAR, CHARLES WILLIAM, COMPUTER SCIENCE, NUMERICAL SOFTWARE. *Current Pos:* vpres comput sci, 90-92, PRES, NEC RES INST, PRINCETON, 92- *Personal Data:* b London, Eng, Feb 1, 35; m 76, Ann L Morgan; c Kathlyn J & Christopher W. *Educ:* Cambridge Univ, BA, 56; Univ Ill, MS, 57, PhD(math), 60. *Hon Degrees:* Doctorate, Royal Inst Technol, Stockholm, Sweden, 87. *Honors & Awards:* Forsythe Mem Award, Asn Comput Mach, 79. *Prof Exp:* Sr engr comput, IBM Corp, 60-62; prof comput sci, Univ Ill, Urbana, 62-90, dept head, 85-90. *Concurrent Pos:* Consult, Argonne Nat Lab, 66-71 & Inst Comput Appln Sci & Eng, 73-80. *Mem:* Nat Acad Eng; Fel Inst Elec & Electronics Engrs; Soc Indust & Appl Math (pres, 87-88); fel AAAS; fel Am Acad Arts & Sci. *Res:* Numerical analysis; computer graphics; computer software. *Mailing Add:* NEC Res Inst 4 Independence Way Princeton NJ 08540. *Fax:* 609-951-2480; *E-Mail:* cwg@research.nj.nec.com

GEAR, JAMES RICHARD, ORGANIC CHEMISTRY, BIOCHEMISTRY. *Current Pos:* from asst prof to assoc prof, 63-73, PROF CHEM & BIOCHEM, UNIV REGINA, 73- *Personal Data:* b Kindersley, Sask, Apr 26, 35; m 61, Shirlean Magarvey; c Valerie. *Educ:* Univ Sask, BA, 56, MA, 58; McMaster Univ, PhD(biosynthesis), 62. *Prof Exp:* Fel chem, Univ Minn, 62-63. *Concurrent Pos:* Coordr prof progs, Univ Regina, 71-93, head, Dept Chem, 94-97. *Mem:* Fel Chem Inst Can. *Res:* Organic synthesis; biosynthesis and chemistry of natural products. *Mailing Add:* Dept Chem Univ Regina Regina SK S4S 0A2 Can. *E-Mail:* jgear@max.cc.uregina.ca

GEARHART, PATRICIA JOHANNA, ANTIBODY DIVERSITY, B-CELL DEVELOPMENT. *Current Pos:* ASST PROF BIOCHEM, SCH HYG & PUB HEALTH, JOHNS HOPKINS UNIV, 82- *Educ:* Univ Pa, PhD(immunol), 74. *Mailing Add:* Dept Biochem Geront Res Ctr 4940 Eastern Ave Baltimore MD 21224-2780. *Fax:* 410-558-8157

GEARHART, ROGER A, ENGINEERING PHYSICS, SCIENTIFIC MANAGEMENT. *Current Pos:* PHYSICIST, STANFORD LINEAR ACCELERATOR CTR, 68- *Personal Data:* b Chicago, Ill, Nov 27, 35; c 2. *Educ:* Univ Calif, Berkeley, BA, 64. *Prof Exp:* Physicist, Lawrence Berkeley Lab, 60-68. *Concurrent Pos:* Vpres, Danmark Dania, 88-91. *Mem:* Inst Elec & Electronics Engrs. *Res:* High energy physics and nuclear physics using fixed targets at accelerators. *Mailing Add:* Stanford Linear Accel Ctr PO Box 4349 Bin 20 Menlo Park CA 94025

GEARIEN, JAMES EDWARD, MEDICINAL CHEMISTRY, ORGANIC CHEMISTRY. *Current Pos:* Instr chem, Univ Ill, Chicago, 48-50, from asst prof to assoc prof, 50-60, prof chem & chmn dept, 60-88, EMER PROF, COL PHARM, UNIV ILL, CHICAGO, 88- *Personal Data:* b Peoria, Ill, Aug 27, 19; m 48; c 2. *Educ:* Univ Ill, BS, 41; Univ Mich, MS, 42, PhD(pharmaceut chem), 50. *Mem:* Am Chem Soc; AAAS. *Res:* Synthesis of organic medicinals; studies of organic structures and medicinal activity relationships; analgesics and angiotensin analogs. *Mailing Add:* 1301 Pennsylvania Des Plaines IL 60018-1118. *E-Mail:* cliod@aol.com

GEARY, JOHN CHARLES, ASTRONOMY, ELECTRONICS. *Current Pos:* STAFF ASTRONOMER INSTRUMENTATION, SMITHSONIAN ASTROPHYS OBSERV, 78- *Personal Data:* b Chicago, Ill, Jan 2, 45; m 72. *Educ:* Mich State Univ, BA, 67; Univ Ariz, MS, 69, PhD(astron), 75. *Prof Exp:* Staff astronr instrumentation, Max Planck Inst Astron, Heidelberg, 75-78. *Mem:* Am Astron Soc; Soc Photo-Optical Instrumentation Engrs. *Res:* Design and construction of advanced electronic detector systems for astronomical research. *Mailing Add:* Smithsonian Astrophys Observ 60 Garden St Cambridge MA 02138

GEARY, LEO CHARLES, ELECTRICAL & SYSTEMS ENGINEERING. *Current Pos:* cognitant engr, 72-77, prin engr, 77-80, MGR, WESTINGHOUSE, 81- *Personal Data:* b Pittsburgh, Pa, Nov 19, 42; m 65; c 2. *Educ:* Univ Pittsburgh, BS, 64, MS, 65 & PhD(elec eng), 68. *Prof Exp:* Group leader, Gulf Res Develop 68-71, systs engr & systs analyst, 68-72. *Mem:* Inst Elec & Electronics Engrs. *Res:* Research and development of optimal control systems and pattern recognition techniques; design, development and implementation of computer and minor process computer system for data acquisition and process control. *Mailing Add:* 611 Brae Burn Ct Augusta GA 30907

GEARY, NORCROSS D, NEUROBIOLOGY, NEUROENDOCRINOLOGY. *Current Pos:* RES ASSOC, E W BOURNE LAB, NY HOSP, CORNELL MED CTR, WHITE PLAINS, 80- *Personal Data:* b Cambridge, Mass, Sept 6, 47. *Educ:* Harvard Col, BA, 69; Brown Univ, PhD(psychol), 78. *Prof Exp:* Res fel physiol chem & nutrit physiol, Inst Physiol, Ludwig-Maximilians Univ, Munich, Ger, 76-80. *Mem:* Soc Neurosci. *Res:* Neural and physiological control of appetitive behavior, in particular the neuroendocrine bases of food's potencies to reward and to satiate and the contribution of these mechansims to bodyweight regulation. *Mailing Add:* E W Bourne Lab NY Hosp Cornell Med Ctr 21 Bloomingdale Rd White Plains NY 10605

GEBALLE, GORDON THEODORE, URBAN ECOLOGY. *Current Pos:* Assoc res scientist, 81-83, LECTR, SCH FORESTRY & ENVIRON STUDIES, YALE UNIV, 83-, ASST DEAN, 87- *Personal Data:* b Berkeley, Calif, Sept 12, 47; m 71, Shelley; c 3. *Educ:* Univ Calif, Berkeley, BA, 70; Yale Univ, PhD(biol), 81. *Mem:* Am Soc Plant Physiologists; Am Phytopath Soc; AAAS; Sigma Xi; Int Fedn Syst Res. *Res:* Responses of plants to stress; cities as ecosystems; effect of acid precipitation on host-pathogen interactions; soil ecosystems. *Mailing Add:* Sch Forestry & Environ Studies Yale Univ New Haven CT 06511

GEBALLE, RONALD, ATOMIC PHYSICS. *Current Pos:* physicist, Appl Physics Lab, Univ Wash, 43-46, from asst prof to assoc prof, 46-59, chmn dept, 57-73, actg dean, 75-76, assoc dean, Col Arts & Sci, 73-76, vprovost res & dean grad sch, 76-81, PROF PHYSICS, UNIV WASH, 59-, EMER PROF PHYSICS & EMER DEAN GRAD SCH, 85- *Personal Data:* b Redding, Calif, Feb 7, 18; m 40; c 8. *Educ:* Univ Calif, BS, 38, MA, 40, PhD(physics), 43. *Prof Exp:* Physicist, Radiation Lab, Univ Calif, 42-43. *Concurrent Pos:* Consult, Army Res Off, NSF, 57-62; mem citizens comt educ, Wash State Legis, 60; guest scientist, FOM Inst Atomic & Molecular Physics, Neth, 64-65; chmn bd dirs, Pac Northwest Asn Col Physics, 65-70; mem comn, Col Physics, 66-71; secy, Int Conf Physics Electronic & Atomic Collisions, 67-77; mem adv comt grants, Res Corp, 67-73; mem adv panel physics, NSF, 68-73, chmn, 72-73; mem adv panel, Lab Astrophys Div, Inst Basic Stand, Nat Bur Stand, 70-75, chmn, 73-75; mem physics surv comt & chmn panel on educ, Nat Acad Sci-Nat Res Coun, 70-73; mem adv bd, Off Phys Sci, Assembly Math & Phys Sci, 75-; mem-at-large, US Nat Comt, Int Union Pure & Appl Physics, 74-; mem exec comt eval panels, Nat Bur Stand, Nat Acad Sci-Nat Res Coun, 75-; secy-treas, Asn Grad Sch, 78- *Mem:* Fel AAAS; fel Am Phys Soc; Am Asn Physics Teachers (pres, 69-70). *Res:* Atomic collision processes; physics education. *Mailing Add:* Dept Physics Univ Wash Seattle WA 98195

GEBALLE, THEODORE HENRY, LOW TEMPERATURE PHYSICS. *Current Pos:* prof, Dept Appl Physics & Dept Mat Sci & Eng, Stanford Univ, 67-90, chmn, Dept Appl Physics, 75-86, dir, Ctr Mat Res, 76-88, EMER PROF APPL PHYSICS, STANFORD UNIV, 90- *Personal Data:* b San Francisco, Calif, Jan 20, 20; m 41; c 5. *Educ:* Univ Calif, Berkeley, BS, 41, PhD(phys chem), 49. *Honors & Awards:* Oliver E Buckley Solid State Physics Prize, Am Phys Soc, 70; First Bernd Matthias Mem Award, 89; Von Hippel Award, Mat Res Soc, 91; Bodo von Bornes Lectr, Univ Tubingen, Ger, 95; Debye Lectr, Cornell Univ, 96. *Prof Exp:* Res assoc, Low Temperature Lab, Univ Calif, Berkeley, 50-52; mem tech staff, Bell Tel Labs, NJ, 52-68, head, Dept Low Temperature & Solid State Physics, Phys Res Lab, 57-68. *Concurrent Pos:* Consult, Mat Sci Lab, Bell Labs, 68-; Guggenheim fel, Cavendish Lab, Cambridge, Eng, 75; mem, Solid State Physics Deleg, People's Repub China, 75; mem, Nat Comn Superconductivity. *Mem:* Nat Acad Sci; fel Am Phys Soc; Am Acad Arts & Sci; Am Chem Soc; fel AAAS. *Res:* Low temperature physics; superconductivity; materials science; experimental studies of superconductivity and magnetism in intermetallic compounds using heat capacity, transport and optical measurements; thermodynamic and magnetic properties of single crystal cupric sulfate pentahydrate below four degrees Kelvin. *Mailing Add:* Dept Appl Physics Stanford Univ Stanford CA 94305-4085

GEBALLE, THOMAS RONALD, INFRARED SPECTROSCOPY. *Current Pos:* astronr, 81-87, ASSOC DIR, UK INFRARED TELESCOPE, HILO, HAWAII, 87- *Personal Data:* b Seattle, Wash, Nov, 16, 44; m 67; c 2. *Educ:* Univ Calif, Berkeley, BA, 67, PhD(physics), 74. *Prof Exp:* Res fel physics, Univ Calif, Berkeley, 74-75; res scientist, Leiden Univ, 75-77; Carnegie fel, Mt Wilson & Las Campanas Observ, 77-81. *Mem:* Am Astron Soc; Int Astron Union. *Res:* Use of infrared spectroscopy to investigate the solar system, star formation, stellar evolution, interstellar medium and galactic nuclei; design and construction of infrared spectrometers for astronomical use. *Mailing Add:* 1645 Oneawa Pl Hilo HI 96720

GEBAUER, PETER ANTHONY, ORGANIC CHEMISTRY. *Current Pos:* from asst prof to assoc prof, 75-88, PROF CHEM, MONMOUTH COL, ILL, 88-, CHMN DEPT, 77- *Personal Data:* b Albany, Calif, Apr 15, 43; m 67; Janet Siebert; c Matthew & Amy. *Educ:* Harvey Mudd Col, BS, 65; Univ Ill, PhD(org chem), 70. *Prof Exp:* Asst prof chem, Purdue Univ, Indianapolis, 70-75. *Mem:* Am Chem Soc. *Res:* Elimination and substitution reactions employing phosphorus reagents. *Mailing Add:* 700 E Broadway Monmouth IL 61462-1963

GEBBEN, ALAN IRWIN, PLANT ECOLOGY. *Current Pos:* Asst biol, 55-58, from instr to assoc prof, 61-67, chmn dept, 80-85, PROF BIOL, CALVIN COL, 67- *Personal Data:* b Shelbyville, Mich, July 4, 31; m 53; c 4. *Educ:* Calvin Col, AB, 54; Vanderbilt Univ, MAT, 55; Univ Mich, MS, 59, PhD(commonragweed ecol), 65. *Mailing Add:* 3270 Piccadilly Circle SE Grand Rapids MI 49546-4388

GEBBER, GERARD L, PHARMACOLOGY, NEUROPHYSIOLOGY. *Current Pos:* from asst prof to assoc prof pharmacol, 66-75, PROF PHARMACOL, MICH STATE UNIV, 75-, PROF PHYSIOL, 82- *Personal Data:* b New York, NY, Feb 12, 39; m 61, Sandra Rusoff; c Audrey & Elliott. *Educ:* Long Island Univ, 60; Univ Mich, PhD(pharmacol), 64. *Prof Exp:* NIH res fel pharmacol, Univ Pa, 64-65; instr, Tulane Univ, 65-66. *Concurrent Pos:* Merit awardee, NIH, 87- *Mem:* AAAS; Soc Neurosci; Am Physiol Soc; Can Physiol Soc; Am Soc Pharmacol & Exp Therapeut; Inst Elec & Electronics Engrs. *Res:* Central autonomic reflex pathways; central nervous system control of circulation; rhythm generators. *Mailing Add:* Mich State Univ Life Sci Bldg B-426B East Lansing MI 48824-1317. *Fax:* 517-353-8915

GEBBIE, KATHARINE BLODGETT, ASTROPHYSICS. *Current Pos:* DIR, PHYSICS LAB, NAT INST STAND & TECHNOL, 89- *Personal Data:* b Cambridge, Mass, July 4, 32; m 57. *Educ:* Bryn Mawr Col, BA, 57; Univ London, BSc, 60, PhD(astrophys), 65. *Prof Exp:* Res assoc astrophys, Joint Inst Lab Astrophys, Univ Colo, 67-68, lectr physics & astrophys, 74-77; astrophysicist, Nat Bur Stand, 68-85, supvry physicist, 85-89. *Concurrent Pos:* Ed, The Observ, 65-67; adj prof astro-geophys, Univ Colo, 77-89. *Mem:* Int Astron Union; Am Astron Soc; fel Joint Inst Lab Astrophys; Am Phys Soc; Royal Astron Soc. *Res:* Planetary nebulae, stellar atmospheres; physics of solar atmosphere. *Mailing Add:* Physics Lab Nat Inst Stand & Technol Bldg 221, Rm B-160 Gaithersburg MD 20899

GEBBIE, KRISTINE MOORE, PUBLIC HEALTH. *Current Pos:* asst prof, 95-97, ELIZABETH STANDISH GILL ASSOC PROF NURSING & DIR, CTR HEALTH POLICY & HEALTH SERVS RES, COLUMBIA UNIV SCH NURSING, 97-; SR CONSULT PUB HEALTH INITIATIVES, OFF PUB HEALTH & SCI, US DEPT HEALTH & HUMAN SERVS, 94- *Personal Data:* b Sioux City, Iowa, June 26, 43; div; c Anna, Sharon & Eric. *Educ:* St Olaf Col, BS, 65; Univ Calif, Los Angeles, MS, 68; Univ Mich, DPH, 95. *Honors & Awards:* McCormack Award, Asn State & Territorial Health Officials, 88. *Prof Exp:* Instr & lectr, Community & Ment Health Nursing, Sch Nursing, Univ Calif, Los Angeles, 68-71; asst prof nursing, St Louis Univ, 72-77, assoc clin prof, 77-78; coordr ambulatory care, St Louis Univ Hosps, 74-76, asst dir, 76-78; adminr, Ore Health Div & asst dir health, Ore Dept Human Servs, 78-89; secy, Wash State Dept Health, Olympia, 89-93; coordr, Nat AIDS Policy, Washington, 93-94; actg dir, Pub Health Strategies, US Dept Health & Human Servs, 94. *Concurrent Pos:* Adj assoc prof, Dept Psychiat/Ment Health Nursing, Ore Health Sci Univ, 80-; mem, HIV Comt, Asn State & Territorial Health Officials, 85-90, chair, 85-88; mem, Pres Comn Human Immunodeficiency Virus Epidemic, 87-88; distinguished scholar, Am Nurses Found, 89; clin asst prof, Dept Community Health Care Systs, Sch Nursing, Univ Wash, 90-95, affil assoc prof, Dept Health Servs, Sch Pub Health & Community Med, 91-; mem, Bd Health Prom & Dis Prev, 95- *Mem:* Inst Med-Nat Acad Sci; NY Acad Med; Am Pub Health Asn; fel Am Acad Nursing; Am Nurses Asn; Asn Nurses AIDS Care; NAm Nursing Diag Asn. *Mailing Add:* Columbia Univ Sch Nursing 630 W 168th St New York NY 10032

GEBER, WILLIAM FREDERICK, PHYSIOLOGY, PHARMACOLOGY. *Current Pos:* from assoc prof to prof, 65-90, EMER PROF PHARMACOL, MED COL GA, 90- *Personal Data:* b Rahway, NJ, Oct 26, 23; m 46, Joan Rezny; c Sharron. *Educ:* Dartmouth Col, AB, 47; Ind Univ, MS, 50, PhD(physiol), 54. *Prof Exp:* Teaching assoc physiol, Sch Med, Ind Univ, 53-54; res assoc phys med, Med Col, Univ Minn, 54; asst prof physiol, Sch Med, St Louis Univ, 54-58; assoc prof, Sch Med, Univ SDak, 58-65. *Mem:* AAAS; Am Soc Pharmacol & Exp Therapeut; Am Physiol Soc; Soc Toxicol; Am Chem Soc; Teratology Soc. *Res:* Quantitative measurement of blood flow, hyperemea causes, and drug effects in areas of kidney, intestine, muscle and spleen; vascular aging; cardiovascular responses to weightlessness; environmental causes of congenital malformations; drug induced teratogenesis. *Mailing Add:* Dept Pharmacol Med Col Ga Augusta GA 30912

GEBHARD, ROGER LEE, GASTROENTEROLOGY, INTERNAL MEDICINE. *Current Pos:* PROF, MED SCH, UNIV MINN, 77- *Personal Data:* b Sioux City, Iowa, Jan 30, 45; m 66, Gloria Brisson; c Kristin H & Roger K. *Educ:* Univ Minn, BA, 65, MD, 69. *Prof Exp:* Clin res assoc, NIH, 71-73. *Concurrent Pos:* Staff physician, Vet Admin Med Ctr, Minneapolis, Minn, 77- *Mem:* Am Gastroenterol Asn; Am Asn Study Liver Dis; Am Physiol Soc; Am Soc Gastrointestinal Endoscopy. *Res:* Cholesterol metabolism; intestinal function and disease; gallstones and biliary lipids. *Mailing Add:* Minneapolis Vet Admin Med Ctr 111-D One Veteran Dr Minneapolis MN 55417. *Fax:* 612-725-2248

GEBHARDT, BRYAN MATTHEW, CELLULAR & OCULAR IMMUNOLOGY. *Current Pos:* PROF OPHTHAL & MICROBIOL, LA STATE UNIV MED CTR, 78- *Educ:* Tulane Univ, PhD(biol), 67. *Mailing Add:* Dept Ophthal La State Univ Eye Ctr 2020 Gravier St Suite B New Orleans LA 70112-2234. *Fax:* 504-568-4210

GEBHARDT, JOSEPH JOHN, REFRACTORY COMPOSITES DEVELOPMENT. *Current Pos:* SR PHYS CHEMIST, GENERAL SCIENCES INC, 87- *Personal Data:* b New York, NY, Feb 28, 23; wid; c 2. *Educ:* Hobart Col, AB, 44; Carnegie Inst Technol, MSc, 50, DSc(chem), 51. *Prof Exp:* Instr chem, Manhattan Col, 46-47; instr, Carnegie Inst Tech, 47-49, asst, 49-51; sr res chemist, Titanium Div, Nat Lead Co, 51-57; sr res chemist, Am Potash & Chem Corp, 57-59, proj chemist, 59-60; res chemist, Missle & Space Div, Space Sci Lab, Gen Elec Co, 60-69, consult phys chem, Space Syst Div-RSO, 69-86. *Concurrent Pos:* Consult, Materials Applied Inc, 76-86; chmn, Ceramic Metal Systs Div, Am Ceramics Soc, 83. *Mem:* AAAS; fel Am Inst Chem; Am Chem Soc; fel Am Ceramics Soc; Sigma Xi. *Res:* High temperature materials; vapor deposition; solid state reactions; carbon and graphite; composite materials; vapor/solid reactions; formation of ceramic and metallic materials; optical structural properties; carbon-carbon composite processing and properties; inorganic materials processing. *Mailing Add:* 18 Beverly Ave Malvern PA 19355-3006

GEBHART, BENJAMIN, engineering, for more information see previous edition

GEBHART, RONALD, INTERNAL MEDICINE, PRIMARY CARE & INFECTIOUS DISEASES. *Current Pos:* asst assoc chief staff, 84-85, assoc chief staff, 85-95, CHIEF CONSULT, PRIMARY & AMBULATORY CARE, DEPT VET AFFAIRS, 95- *Personal Data:* b Ft Worth, Tex, Apr 10, 45; m 69, Suzanne Parrish; c Skyler P & Douglas B. *Educ:* St Edward's Univ, BS, 67; Med Col Va, MD, 72; Am Bd Internal Med, dipl, 75, dipl infectious dis, 84. *Honors & Awards:* Nat Res Serv Award in Microbiol, 83. *Prof Exp:* Intern, Wilford Hall, USAF Med Ctr, Lackland AFB, Tex, 72-73, resident med, 73-75; staff, Dept Internal Med, USAF Hosp, Torrejon AFB, Spain, 75-76, chief, Internal Med, Lakenhealth, Eng, 76-79, Langley AFB, 79-81; fel infectious dis, Med Col Va, 81-84. *Concurrent Pos:* Physician adv, Automated Med Info Exchange, Vet Health Admin, 86-; mem, Med Care Cost Recovery Prog, Vet Admin Med Ctrs, 91-, Pharm Expert Panel, 91-, Resource Planning Methodol Oversight Comt, 94- *Mem:* Nat Asn Vet Admin Physician Ambulatory Care Mgrs (pres, 90-92); fel Am Col Physicians; Am Soc

Microbiol; Am Fedn Clin Res; Int Soc Human & Animal Mycol; Soc Gen Internal Med; Infectious Dis Soc Am. *Res:* Contributed numerouse publications in fields of medical mycology and health services research. *Mailing Add:* Dept Vet Affairs Vet Admin Hq 810 Vermont Ave NW Washington DC 20420. *Fax:* 202-273-9148; *E-Mail:* gebhart.ron@mail.va.gov

GEBREMICHAEL, ANDEMARIAM, CHEMISTRY. *Current Pos:* vis prof med, 91-95, PROF CHEM & MICROBIOL, DEPT SCI, TUFTS UNIV, 96- *Personal Data:* b Derak, Eritrea, Sept 12, 44. *Educ:* Haile Sellasie Univ, Dira Down, Ethiopa, B, 68; NMex Univ, MS, 73; Boston Univ, PhD(microbiol immunol), 82. *Prof Exp:* Asst chief, Pasteur Inst Ethiopa, 68-70; chief clin labs, All Africa Leprosy Rehab & Training Ctr, 73-74, asst prof, 75; res assoc, Harvard Sch Pub Health, 84-89. *Concurrent Pos:* Fulbright scholar, Univ Asmara, Eritea, 95- *Mem:* AAAS; Am Soc Clin Path. *Mailing Add:* Tufts Univ Sch Med PO Box 913 Boston MA 02120

GECKLE, WILLIAM JUDE, IMAGING PHYSICS, BIOMEDICAL IMAGE PROCESSING. *Current Pos:* assoc physicist, 79-85, PHYSICIST, APPL PHYSICS LAB, JOHNS HOPKINS UNIV, 85-, COORDR COLLAB PROGS IN IMAGE ANALYSIS, 85-, SECT SUPVR, 90- *Personal Data:* b Baltimore, Md, May 26, 55; m 84; c 2. *Educ:* Loyola Col, Baltimore, BS, 77; Mich State Univ, MS, 79. *Prof Exp:* Grad asst, Mich State Univ, 77-79. *Mem:* Inst Elec & Electronics Engrs. *Res:* Development of intelligent processing and modeling techniques applicable to medical imagery; algorithm development for MRI, single photon emission computed tomography, positron-emission tomography, computerized tomography and conventional imaging systems; computer graphics. *Mailing Add:* Appl Physics Lab Johns Hopkins Univ Johns Hopkins Rd Laurel MD 20723

GECZIK, RONALD JOSEPH, PHYSIOLOGY, PHARMACOLOGY. *Current Pos:* PRES, PAUL MICHAEL ASSOC INC, 89- *Personal Data:* b Bronx, NY, Mar 22, 33; m 61; c 3. *Educ:* Fordham Univ, BS, 54, MS, 57, PhD(biol), 59; Seton Hall Univ, JD, 71. *Prof Exp:* Sr res scientist, Colgate-Palmolive Co, 59-62, sr res scientist, Pharmacol Sect, 62-64; asst to dir toxicol, Path Dept, 64-66, mgr biol data, 66-68, dir res admin, Squibb Inst Med Res, 68-73; vpres, Licensing Corp Develop, Carter Wallace, Inc, 73-84; vpres, SNW Inc, 84-89. *Mem:* AAAS; NY Acad Sci; Am Soc Pharmacol & Exp Ther; Licensing Exec Soc; Sigma Xi. *Res:* Dental research, especially caries, periodontal disease and calculus; tissue culture; cytology; regeneration and wound healing; toxicology. *Mailing Add:* 8 Phyllis Place E Brunswick Township Milltown NJ 08850

GEDDES, JOHN JOSEPH, ELECTRICAL ENGINEERING. *Current Pos:* SR ENG, LYONS TECH SYST, 95- *Personal Data:* b Columbus, Ohio, Oct 5, 40. *Educ:* Univ Minn, BSEE, 63; Purdue Univ, MSEE, 68, PhD(elec eng), 71. *Prof Exp:* Design engr circuits, Missle Div, Raytheon Co, 63-66; prin res scientist, Mat Sci Ctr, Honeywell Corp, 71-94; TLC, 94-95. *Mem:* Sr mem Inst Elec & Electronics Engrs; Sigma Xi. *Res:* Magnetics; fiber optics; design and fabrication of Gallium Arsenide devices and monolithic circuits for microwave applications. *Mailing Add:* 5845 Girard Ct Minneapolis MN 55419

GEDDES, KEITH OLIVER, ALGEBRAIC ALGORITHMS, SYMBOLIC COMPUTATION. *Current Pos:* Asst prof, 73-78, ASSOC PROF COMPUT SCI, UNIV WATERLOO, 78- *Personal Data:* b North Battleford, Sask, Nov 4, 47; m 72; c 3. *Educ:* Univ Sask, BA, 68; Univ Toronto, MSc, 70, PhD(comput sci), 73. *Mem:* Asn Comput Mach; Soc Indust & Appl Math; Can Appl Math Soc. *Res:* Algebraic algorithms; systems for symbolic computation, numerical approximation, scientific computation. *Mailing Add:* Dept Comput Sci Univ Waterloo Waterloo ON N2L 3G1 Can

GEDDES, LANELLE EVELYN, PHYSIOLOGY, NURSING. *Current Pos:* assoc prof, 75-78, head, Sch Nursing, 80-91, PROF NURSING, PURDUE UNIV, 78- *Personal Data:* b Houston, Tex, Sept 15, 35; m 62, Leslie A. *Educ:* Univ Houston, BSN, 57, PhD(biophysics), 70. *Prof Exp:* Staff nurse, Houston Independent Sch Dist, 57-62; from instr to asst prof physiol, Baylor Col Med, 72-75. *Concurrent Pos:* Fel physiol, Baylor Col Med, 70-72 & vis asst prof, 75-90; coordr grad prog med & surg, Tex Women's Univ, 74-75. *Mem:* AAAS; NY Acad Sci. *Res:* Evaluation of cardiovascular dynamics and its clinical applications. *Mailing Add:* Sch Nursing Purdue Univ West Lafayette IN 47907

GEDDES, LESLIE ALEXANDER, CARDIOVASCULAR PHYSIOLOGY, BIOMEDICAL ENGINEERING. *Current Pos:* Showalter distinguished prof biomed eng, 74-91, dir, Biomed Eng Ctr, 74-91, EMER SHOWALTER DISTINGUISHED PROF BIOMED ENG, PURDUE UNIV, 91- *Personal Data:* b Port Gordon, Scotland, May 24, 21; nat US; m 45, 51, LaNelle Evelyn Nerger; c James A. *Educ:* McGill Univ, BEng, 45, MEng, 53; Baylor Univ, PhD(physiol), 59. *Hon Degrees:* DSc, McGill Univ, 71. *Honors & Awards:* Nightingale Award, 72; Leadership Biomed Eng Award, Am Soc Advan Med Instrumentation, 85, Laufman-Greatbatch Award, 87; Biomed Eng Award, 85; Career Achievement Award, Inst Elec & Electronics Engrs, 86, Edison Gold Medal, 95. *Prof Exp:* Asst EEG & neurophysiol & demonstr elec eng, McGill Univ, 45-47; consult & supvr tech equip, Montreal Neurol Inst & Royal Victoria Hosp, 46-52; biophysicist, Baylor Col Med, 52, dir, Lab Biophys, 53-57, asst prof physiol, 58-65, prof physiol & chief, Div Biomed Eng, 65-74. *Concurrent Pos:* Consult engr, 49-; partner & consult, Electro-Design Co, 50-52; prof physiol, Dent Col, Univ Tex, 57-74; consult, Nat Found Infantile Paralysis, Southwest Poliomyelitis Respiratory Ctr, 58-60 & USAF, 58-; prof vet physiol & pharmacol, Tex A&M Univ, 65-74, prof biomed eng, 68-74; ed, J Electrocardiol & J Clin Monitoring. *Mem:* Nat Acad Eng; fel Am Col Cardiol; fel Inst Elec & Electronics Engrs; fel Australasian Col Physics & Eng Med Biol; fel AAAS; fel Australian Col Phys Scientists Med; Am Physiol Soc; fel Royal Soc Med; Sigma Xi; fel Alliance Eng Mech & Biol; fel NY Acad Sci; Am Asn Med Instrumentation; Bioelectrochem Soc. *Res:* Electrophysiology; cardiology; biophysical instrumentation. *Mailing Add:* Purdue Univ Biomed Eng Ctr 1293 A A Potter Bldg Rm 204 West Lafayette IN 47907-1293. *Fax:* 765-494-1193; *E-Mail:* geddes@ecn.purdue.edu

GEDDES, WILBURT HALE, MARINE GEOPHYSICS. *Current Pos:* PRES, GEDDES GEOPHYS ASSOCS, 87- *Personal Data:* b Eakly, Okla, Jan 10, 26; m 46; c 5. *Educ:* NC State Col, BS, 49. *Honors & Awards:* Antartic Exploration Medal. *Prof Exp:* Geophysicist airborne magnetics, Marine Geophys Planning Syst Inc, 52-63, dir marine geophys surv, 63-68, dir, Acoust Div, 70-78, dir, Oceanog Off, 78-81, prin scientist, 81-87. *Mem:* Am Geophys Union; Soc Explor Geophysicists; Sigma Xi; Marine Technol Soc. *Res:* Underwater acoustics including propagation through the ocean floor, boundary reflection losses, volume scattering and background noise. *Mailing Add:* 765 E Scenic Dr Pass Christian MS 39571-4620

GEDEON, GEZA S(CHOLCZ), ASTRODYNAMICS. *Current Pos:* RETIRED. *Personal Data:* b Miskolc, Hungary, June 12, 14; US citizen; c 3. *Educ:* Budapest Tech Univ, MS, 37, DSc, 45. *Prof Exp:* Res asst aerodynamics, Aerotech Inst, 39-43; chief test pilot, Repulogepgyar, RT, 43-45; test engr, L Lang Mach & Eng Shop, 47-48; aircraft designer, L Breguet Ateliers d' Aviation, 48-50; lectr math & mech, Ind Tech Col, 50-55; design specialist, Int Harvester Co, 55-56; res scientist, Chance Vought Aircraft, 56-59 & Aeronutronic Div, Ford Motor Co, 59-60; head astrodynamics, Norair Labs, Northrop Corp, 60-62, chief flight mech, space labs, 62-65; staff engr, TRW Syst Inc, 65, mgr analysis mech dept, 65-68, sr scientist, 68-; at West Coast Univ, Los Angeles, Calif. *Concurrent Pos:* Lectr, Univ Calif, Los Angeles, 63-66 & 81- *Mem:* Celestial Mech Inst. *Res:* Astrodynamics related to trajectories, orbit determination and guidance. *Mailing Add:* 16055 Temecula Pacific Palisades CA 90272

GEDULDIG, DONALD, COMPUTER APPLICATIONS, DATA ACQUISITION & ANALYSIS. *Current Pos:* CHIEF SOFTWARE DIV, ARMED FORCES RADIOBIOL RES INST, MED MAT MGT CTR, BETHESDA, 89- *Personal Data:* b New York, NY, Oct 27, 32; m 62, Ulla Gillmer; c Jonas. *Educ:* Cornell Univ, BEE, 55, MS, 57; Columbia Univ, PhD(biophys), 65. *Prof Exp:* Res engr med electronics, RCA Labs, 57-58; res engr, Rockefeller Univ, 58-61; asst res physiologist, Univ Calif, San Diego, 66-68; asst prof biophys, Sch Med, Univ Md, Baltimore, 68-75; assoc prof biophys, Fac Med, Mem Univ Nfld, 75-85. *Concurrent Pos:* NIH fel, Physiol Lab, Cambridge Univ, 65-66; mem Brain Res Inst, Univ Calif, Los Angeles, 66-68; assoc ed, Can J Physiol & Pharmacol, 80-85. *Mem:* Biophys Soc; Soc Gen Physiol. *Res:* Membrane structure and function; transport of ions through membranes; excitation in nerve and muscle; electrophysiological instrumentation; biomedical engineering; computer systems for data acquisition and data analysis; system integration. *Mailing Add:* 053397890 Pl Hyattsville MD 20781. *E-Mail:* geduldig@vax.afrr.usuhs.mil

GEE, ADRIAN PHILIP, BONE MARROW TRANSPLANTATION, COMPLEMENT. *Current Pos:* SR SCIENTIST, BAXTER HEALTHCARE CORP, 87- *Personal Data:* b Whitehead, UK, Apr 30, 52. *Educ:* Univ Birmingham, UK, BSc, 73; Univ Edinburgh, UK, PhD(immunol), 77. *Prof Exp:* Vis fel immunol, Nat Cancer Inst, 78-82; res assoc, dept path, Univ Toronto, 82-83; vis asst prof pediat, Univ Fla, 83-85, assoc prof immunol & med microbiol, 84-87, assoc prof pediat, 85-87, assoc dir res, Div Pediat Hemat, 85-87,. *Concurrent Pos:* Prin investr, Am Heart Asn, 84-86, Am Cancer Soc, 85-87 & Pardee Found, Mich, 85-87; co-prin investr, NIH, 84-87; adj assoc prof, Univ Fla, 87-; Hastilow res scholar; Lady Tata fel. *Mem:* Am Asn Cancer Res; Am Asn Immunologists; NY Acad Sci; Brit Soc Immunol; Inst Biol London. *Res:* Development of procedures to improve bone marrow transplantation; immunomagnetic depletion of subpopulations of cells from marrow to be used for autologous or haplotype-mismatched transplantation. *Mailing Add:* Div Transplant Med Univ SC 7 Richland Med Park Columbia SC 29203. *Fax:* 803-434-3956

GEE, ALLEN, PHYSICAL CHEMISTRY. *Current Pos:* RETIRED. *Personal Data:* b Patterson, Calif, Feb 23, 24; m 55, Mary Wong; c Everett & Beverly. *Educ:* Univ Calif, BS, 47; Mass Inst Technol, PhD(phys chem), 51. *Prof Exp:* Asst chem, Univ Calif, 47; asst protein chem, Mass Inst Technol, 47-50; res assoc, Sugar Res Found, Nat Bur Stand, 51-57; sr process chemist, E I du Pont de Nemours & Co, 57-59; sr proj engr, Tex Instruments, Inc, 59-61; mem tech staff, Hughes Aircraft Co, 61-67, assoc mgr microelectronics lab, Newport Beach Div, 67-69; tech consult & regist investment adv, 70-74. *Mem:* Am Chem Soc; fel Am Inst Chem; Electrochem Soc; NY Acad Sci. *Res:* Serum proteins; bone, teeth and calcium phosphates; infrared and visible spectrophometry; chromatography; waste treatment and water pollution; polymers, sugars, cellulose and synthetic fibers; semiconductors; first Lycra manufacturing plant; surveyor moon lander; early bird synchronized satellite. *Mailing Add:* 2521 Sierra Vista Newport Beach CA 92660

GEE, CHARLES WILLIAM, SCIENCE EDUCATION. *Current Pos:* Asst prof, 67-72, assoc prof, 72-80, PROF BIOL & SCI EDUC, MILLIGAN COL, 80- *Personal Data:* b Des Moines, Iowa, Mar 19, 36; m 59; c 3. *Educ:* Univ Wis, BS, 59; Okla State Univ, MS, 64; Mich State Univ, PhD(sci ed), 67. *Concurrent Pos:* Elem sci consult & staff mem, Eastern Tenn State Univ, 73, 74, 76, 78 & 81. *Mem:* Nat Sci Teachers Asn. *Res:* Experimentation with techniques of science presentation. *Mailing Add:* 510 Rose Ave Johnson City TN 37601

GEE, EDWIN AUSTIN, CHEMICAL ENGINEERING. *Current Pos:* RETIRED. *Personal Data:* b Washington, DC, Feb 19, 20; m 44; c 3. *Educ:* George Washington Univ, BS, 41, MS, 44; Univ Md, PhD(chem eng), 48. *Prof Exp:* Asst chemist, Naval Res Lab, Washington, DC, 41-42; chemist, US Bur Mines, Md, 42-43, phys chemist, 43-44, phys chemist, Ala, 44-45, chem engr, Md, 45-46, metallurgist, Washington, DC, 46-47, asst chief metall div, 47-48; metallurgist & chem engr, E I Du Pont de Nemours & Co, 48-50, supvr res group, 50-51, mgr res sect, 51-53, mgr plants technol, Pigments Dept, 53-57, asst dir sales, 57-60, asst dir, Develop Dept, 57-63, dir, 63-66, mgr res & develop corp diversification, 66-68, gen mgr, Photo Prod Dept, 68-70, vpres, dir & mem exec comt, 70-80; pres, Int Paper Co, 78-81, chmn & chief exec officer, 81-85. *Concurrent Pos:* Mem bd, Buck Hills Falls Co, 77-85, Int Paper Co, 78-85, Am Home Prod Inc, 78-94, Air Prod & Chem Inc, 80-91, Finger Matrix, 84-87, Bell & Howell Corp, 85-88, Oncogene Sci, Inc, 86-, Salomon Bros Fund, 87-94, Bethlehem Steel, 87-92 & Clean Sites, 86- *Mem:* Nat Acad Eng; Am Chem Soc; Nat Soc Prof Engrs; Inst Mining, Metall & Petrol Engrs; Am Soc Metals. *Res:* Organic kinetics; rare metals; titanium and zirconium; extraction of ores; purification of salts; improved method for the acid decomposition of certain silicates; pigments, white and colored; semiconductor materials. *Mailing Add:* PO Box 362 Buck Hill Falls PA 18328

GEE, J BERNARD L, MEDICINE, PHYSIOLOGY. *Current Pos:* assoc prof, 69-81, PROF MED, YALE UNIV, 81- *Personal Data:* b Crewe, Eng, Mar 13, 27; m 57; c 2. *Educ:* Oxford Univ, BA, 48, MSc, 49, MA, 52, BM, ChB, 53; FRCPS, 74. *Prof Exp:* Jr demonstr physiol, Oxford Univ, 48-49; intern surg, Guys Hosp, Univ London, 53-54; intern med, Postgrad Med Sch, Univ London, 56-57; resident, Radcliffe Infirmary, Oxford Univ, 57-59; fel, McGill Univ, 59-61; from instr to asst prof, Sch Med, Univ Wis, 61-64; from asst prof to assoc prof, Sch Med, Univ Pittsburgh, 64-69. *Concurrent Pos:* Consult, Vet Admin Hosps, 68- *Mem:* Am Thoracic Soc; Am Fedn Clin Res; fel Am Col Physicians; Am Physiol Soc; Reticuloendothelial Soc. *Res:* Pulmonary medicine and physiology; exercise and respiratory physiology; metabolic features of alveolar macrophages; occupational lung disease. *Mailing Add:* 38 Turtle Bay Dr Branford CT 06405

GEE, JOHN HENRY, ECOLOGY. *Current Pos:* res fel, 66-67, from asst prof to assoc prof, 67-78, PROF ZOOL, UNIV MAN, 78-, HEAD, ZOOL DEPT, 81- *Personal Data:* b New Westminster, BC, Can, July 25, 36; m 61. *Educ:* Univ BC, BCom, 59, MSc, 61; Univ Sydney, PhD(zool), 67. *Prof Exp:* Scientist, Fisheries Res Bd Can, 61-63. *Concurrent Pos:* Res grants, Fisheries Res Bd Can, Nat Res Coun Can & Univ Manitoba, 67. *Mem:* Can Soc Zoologists. *Res:* Ecology of stream fish; buoyancy regulation in aquatic vertebrates. *Mailing Add:* Dept Zool Univ Man Z320 Duff Roblin Bldg Winnipeg MB R3T 2N2 Can

GEE, LYNN LAMARR, MICROBIOLOGY. *Current Pos:* RETIRED. *Personal Data:* b St Anthony Idaho, June 21, 12; m 33; c 2. *Educ:* Brigham Young Univ, BS, 35; Colo A&M Col, MS, 37; Univ Wis, PhD(bacter), 41. *Prof Exp:* Asst, Brigham Young Univ, 35 & Univ Wis, 41; bacteriologist, Dept State Conserv, Wis, 39-41 & US Civil Serv, 46; soil microbiologist, Purdue Univ, 46-48; prof bact, Tex A&M Univ, 48-54; prof & head dept, Okla State Univ, 54-77. *Concurrent Pos:* Bacteriologist, US Dept Defense, 51-52. *Mem:* Am Soc Microbiol; Am Soc Prof Biol; Am Acad Microbiol; Soc Appl Bact. *Res:* Soil microbiology; aerobiology. *Mailing Add:* 4521 N Classen Ct Stillwater OK 74075-1631

GEE, NORMAN, ELECTRON & ION TRANSPORT, RADIATION CHEM. *Current Pos:* Technologist, 79-84, specialist tech, 84-89, fac serv officer, 89-93, COORD INTROD UNIV CHEM LABS, UNIV ALTA, 93- *Personal Data:* b Ottawa, Ont, Oct 17, 52; m 81, Moira Day; c Kathleen, Domini & Linnet. *Educ:* Univ Alta, BSc, 74 & PhD(radiation chem), 79. *Mem:* Chem Inst Can; Nat Sci Teachers Asn. *Res:* chemistry education; radiation chemistry; thermophysical properties of liquids. *Mailing Add:* Chem Dept Chem Bldg Edmonton AB T6G 2G2 Can. *Fax:* 403-492-8231; *E-Mail:* norman_gee@dept.chem.ualberta.ca

GEE, ROBERT WILLIAM, BIOCHEMISTRY. *Current Pos:* RES ASSOC BIOCHEM, MICH STATE UNIV, 72- *Personal Data:* b Los Angeles, Calif, Jan 24, 36. *Educ:* Univ Southern Calif, PhD(biochem), 67. *Prof Exp:* Fel biochem, Scripps Inst Oceanog, 67-71; vis asst prof plant physiol, Ore State Univ, 71-72. *Mem:* Am Soc Plant Physiologists; Am Chem Soc. *Res:* Studies of plant and animal micro body enzymes, including catalase glycerol phosphate dehydrogenase super oxide dismutase; role of micro bodies in cellular metabolism. *Mailing Add:* 531 Village Dr Lansing MI 48911

GEE, SHERMAN, COMMUNICATIONS, NETWORKING. *Current Pos:* head, Technol Transfer Off, Naval Surface Weapons Ctr, 71-80, actg assoc dir, Navy Technol-Phys Sci & Electronics, 80-81, MGR, COMMAND, CONTROL & COMMUN, OFF NAVAL RES, 82- *Personal Data:* b Canton, China, July 18, 37; US citizen; m 65, Susanna Fang; c Darlene & Michelle. *Educ:* Univ Calif, Berkeley, BS, 60; Mass Inst Technol, MS, 61; Stanford Univ, PhD(elec eng), 65. *Prof Exp:* Res asst radar astron, Stanford Univ, 63-65; adv develop engr, Sylvania Electronic Defense Labs, 61-63 & 65-66; electronic engr, Arnold Eng Develop Ctr, 66-67; electronic warfare engr, Air Force Avionics Lab, 67-69; mgr, Advan Technol Div, MB Assocs, 69-71. *Concurrent Pos:* Spec asst to dir, Nat Tech Info Serv, Dept Com, 76-77; staff specialist, Off Under Secy Defense Res & Eng, 79-80; US nat rep, NATO Coop Res & Develop Proj; assoc tech proj officer, Data Exchange Agreement with Can on Command & Control. *Res:* Electromagnetics; propagation laser instrumentation; radiation and scattering; electronic systems analysis; technological innovation; technology transfer; communications; networks; granted 1 US patent. *Mailing Add:* Off Naval Res 800 N Quincy St Arlington VA 22217

GEE, WILLIAM, OCULAR PNEUMOPLETHYSMOGRAPHY, NONINVASIVE VASCULAR LABORATORY. *Current Pos:* DIR, VASCULAR LAB, LEHIGH VALLEY HOSP, 77-; CLIN PROF SURG, HAHNEMANN UNIV, 86- *Personal Data:* b Riverhead, NY, Nov 4, 31; m 56; c 5. *Educ:* State Univ NY, Brooklyn, MD, 61; Am Bd Surg, cert gen surg, 70, cert vascular surg, 84. *Prof Exp:* Internship & residency, Naval Hosp, St Albans, 61-67; fel, vascular surg, Univ Calif, San Francisco, 72-73; chief, vascular surg, Nat Naval Med Ctr, 73-77. *Concurrent Pos:* Consult, NIH Asymptomatic Carotid Atherosclerosis Study, 85; stroke coun, Am Heart Asn. *Mem:* Soc Vascular Surg; Int Soc Cardiovas Surg; Am Col Surgeons. *Res:* Inventor, Ocular Pneumoplethysmograph; research in the design and development of this instrument from 1967 to present. Sixty four publications related to this and associated research. *Mailing Add:* 2150 Elbow Lane Allentown PA 18103

GEELHOED, GLENN WILLIAM, SURGERY, PHYSIOLOGY. *Current Pos:* from asst prof to assoc prof, 75-86, DIR, SURG RES LABS & TRANSPLANT DIV, GEORGE WASHINGTON UNIV, 75-, CHIEF ENDOCRINE SURG, 75-, PROF SURG, 86- *Personal Data:* b Grand Rapids, Mich, Jan 19, 42; c Donald W & Michael A. *Educ:* Calvin Col, AB, 64, BS, 65; Univ Mich, MD, 68; G W Univ, MPH, 92, MA 93; Univ London, dipl trop med & hyg, 90. *Honors & Awards:* Gold Medal, Southeastern Surg Cong, 75. *Prof Exp:* Asst surg, Peter Bent Brigham Hosp, Harvard Med Sch, 68-70; clin assoc cancer, Nat Cancer Inst, NIH, 70-72 & sr staff investr, 72-75, instr surg, 74-75. *Concurrent Pos:* Clin scholar health care res, Robert Wood Johnson Found, 75-77, assoc dir clin scholar prog, 77-; consult, Nat Cancer Inst, NIH, 75-, Walter Reed Army Hosp, 75-, US Senate Comt on the Judiciary, Mr Kennedy, 77- & WHO, Pan Am Health Orgn, World Bank, UN High Comnr on Refugees, 77-; James IV Traveling Surg Scholar, 86; prof, Int Med Educ; dir, Int Health Ctr; Academic du Cirurgie de Paris, 90; sr Fulbright scholar, African Regional Res Prog, 96. *Mem:* Fel Am Col Surgeons; Asn Acad Surg; Am Physiol Soc; Am Fedn Clin Res; Soc Univ Surgeons; Am Soc Trop Med & Hyg. *Res:* Surgical endocrinology; transplantation and tumor immunology; physiology especially renal, pulmonary and gastrointestinal; shock and trauma; oncology especially breast, melanoma, colon and sarcoma; pathophysiology especially thyroid, parathyroid, adrenal and pancreatic islets; international medical education; health/development international linkage. *Mailing Add:* Off Dean George Washington Univ Ross Hall 103 2300 I Street NW Washington DC 20037. *Fax:* 202-994-0926; *E-Mail:* gwg@gwis2.circ.gwu.edu

GEELS, EDWIN JAMES, ORGANIC CHEMISTRY. *Current Pos:* asst prof, 65-77, PROF CHEM, DORDT COL, 77- *Personal Data:* b Hull, Iowa, Jan 24, 40; m 62; c 2. *Educ:* Calvin Col, BS, 61; Iowa State Univ, PhD(chem), 65. *Prof Exp:* Fel, Iowa State Univ, 65. *Concurrent Pos:* Petrol Res Fund grant, 65-67. *Mem:* Am Chem Soc; Royal Soc Chem. *Res:* Electron transfer and free radical reactions of organic compounds. *Mailing Add:* Chem Dept Dordt College Sioux Center IA 51250-1699

GEER, BILLY W, GENETICS, NUTRITION. *Current Pos:* From asst prof to assoc prof, 63-75, chmn dept, 72-78, coordr, Know-Rush Med Prog, 79-85, PROF BIOL, KNOX COL, ILL, 75- *Personal Data:* b Coin, Iowa, June 6, 35; m 57. *Educ:* Northwest Mo State Col, BS, 57; Univ Nebr, MS, 60; Univ Calif, Davis, PhD(genetics), 63. *Concurrent Pos:* Vis assoc prof, Ore State Univ, 68-69; USPHS spec fel, 68-69; vis prof, Univ Calgary, 77-78 & 84-85; int sci exchange award, Nat Sci & Eng Res Coun Can, 84; vis sci award, Alta Heritage Found Med Res, 85; vis prof & Fulbright sr scholar, Monash Univ, 85. *Mem:* AAAS; Am Soc Zoologists; Am Inst Nutrit; Genetics Soc Am. *Res:* Biochemistry of reproduction; nutritional modification of enzymes; lipid metabolism. *Mailing Add:* Dept Biol Knox Col Galesburg IL 61401. *Fax:* 309-343-9816

GEER, IRA W, SCIENCE EDUCATION, METEOROLOGY. *Current Pos:* Assoc prof, 61-70, chmn dept earth sci, 74-80, PROF METEOROL, STATE UNIV NY COL BROCKPORT, 70- *Personal Data:* b Avoca, NY, Jan 18, 35; m 64; c 2. *Educ:* State Univ NY Col Brockport, BS, 57; Univ NC, MEd, 60; Pa State Univ, EdD, 66. *Concurrent Pos:* UNESCO sci educ adv, Ministry of Educ, Repub Korea, 69-70. *Mem:* Assoc mem Am Meteorol Soc. *Res:* Earth Sciences. *Mailing Add:* Dept Earth Sci State Univ NY Col Brockport NY 14420-2915

GEER, JACK CHARLES, MEDICINE, PATHOLOGY. *Current Pos:* PROF PATH & CHMN DEPT, UNIV ALA, BIRMINGHAM, 75- *Personal Data:* b Galesburg, Ill, Sept 19, 27; m 51; c 5. *Educ:* La State Univ, BS, 50, MD, 56. *Prof Exp:* Asst, Sch Med, La State Univ, 54-55, res assoc, 55-57, from instr to prof path, 57-66; prof, STex Med Sch, Univ Tex, 66-67; prof path, Ohio State Univ, 67-75, chmn dept, 67-72; assoc pathologist, Davidson Labs, 72-75. *Concurrent Pos:* USPHS sr res career develop award, 59-66; vis investr, Rockefeller Inst, 60-61; consult, Spec Ctr Res Atherosclerosis, Bowman-Gray Sch Med, 75-80, NE Regional Primate Ctr, Harvard Univ, 79- *Mem:* Col Am Pathologists; Am Med Asn; Int Acad Path; Am Asn Pathologists & Bacteriologists. *Res:* Experimental pathology; electron microscopy. *Mailing Add:* 3744 Wimbleton Dr Birmingham AL 35223-2730

GEER, JAMES FRANCIS, APPLIED MATHEMATICS. *Current Pos:* PROF MATH, STATE UNIV NY, BINGHAMTON, 69- *Personal Data:* b Syracuse, NY, Oct 3, 40; m 65; c 4. *Educ:* Harpur Col, BA, 62; Univ Va, MA, 64; NY Univ, PhD(math), 67. *Prof Exp:* Mathematician, IBM, 67-69. *Concurrent Pos:* Prin investr, res grants & contracts var industs, NSF, 69-; consult, Math & Physics, IBM, Gen Elec & NASA, 69- *Mem:* Soc Indust & Appl Math; Am Acad Mech. *Res:* Asymptotic, perturbation and numerical methods to solve partial differential equations of mathematical physics, particularly in the areas of fluid mechanics, scattering theory and non-linear oscillations; slender body theory; free boundary value problems. *Mailing Add:* 247 Old Newark Valley Rd Endicott NY 13760

GEER, RICHARD P, POLYMER CHEMISTRY, ORGANIC CHEMISTRY. *Current Pos:* RES CHEMIST, RES CTR, HERCULES INC, 64- *Personal Data:* b LaHarpe, Ill, Sept 23, 38. *Educ:* Univ Ill, Urbana, BS, 60; Univ Rochester, PhD(org chem), 65. *Mem:* Am Chem Soc. *Res:* Polymer and monomer synthesis; free radical chemistry. *Mailing Add:* 1115 Kelly Dr Newark DE 19711

GEER, RONALD L, OCEAN ENGINEERING. *Current Pos:* RETIRED. *Personal Data:* b West Palm Beach, Fla, Sept 2, 26; m 51, Yvonne Chappell; c Ronald L Jr & Mark R. *Educ:* Ga Inst Technol, BME, 51. *Honors & Awards:* Compass Indust Award, Marine Technol Soc, 79; Outstanding Civil Eng Achievement Award, Am Soc Civil Engrs, 80. *Prof Exp:* Proj engr, Deepwater Drilling Prog, Shell Oil Co, New Orleans, 61-63, from staff mech engr to mgr, Marine Tech Group, Head Off Prod Dept, 63-66, chief, Pac Coast, 66-69, sr staff, 67-71, consult, 71-80, sr mech engr consult, Head Off Prod Dept, 80-86. *Concurrent Pos:* Mem vis comt, Dept Ocean Eng, MIT Corp, 78-86; vchmn, Nat Res Coun-Assay Eng, Nat Acad Eng, 79-81, chmn, Marine Bd, 81, mem, Polar Res Bd, 84-86. *Mem:* Nat Acad Eng; hon mem Am Soc Mech Engrs; Am Petrol Inst; Marine Technol Soc. *Res:* Offshore-marine systems engineering; petroleum drilling and production engineering. *Mailing Add:* 14723 Oak Bend Dr Houston TX 77079

GEERING, EMIL JOHN, organic chemistry, for more information see previous edition

GEERS, THOMAS L, STRUCTURAL DYNAMICS, WAVE PROPAGATION & SCATTERING. *Current Pos:* chmn, 85-90, PROF MECH ENG, UNIV COLO, BOULDER,85- *Personal Data:* b El Paso, Tex, Nov. 16, 39; m 61; c 2. *Educ:* Mass Inst Technol, SB, 61, MS, 64, PhD(appl mech-), 67. *Honors & Awards:* Hess Award, Am Soc Mech Engrs, 70. *Prof Exp:* Proj officer, David Taylor Model Basin, 61-63; res engr, Cambridge Acoust Assoc, 64-66; res scientist, Lockheed Palo Alto Res Lab, 66-74, staff scientist, 74-84, mgr, 84-85. *Concurrent Pos:* Consult, 86- *Mem:* fel Am Soc Mech Engrs; Acoust Soc Am; Am Acad Mech; Sigma Xi. *Res:* Structural dynamics and acoustics; analytical and computational methods in structure-medium interaction; asymptotic methods in wave propagation and scattering. *Mailing Add:* Dept Mech Eng Univ Colo Campus Box 427 Boulder CO 80309

GEESAMAN, DONALD FRANKLIN, NUCLEAR STRUCTURE, NUCLEON STRUCTURE. *Current Pos:* Res fel, Argonne Nat Lab, 76-78, asst physicist, 78-80, physicist, 81-91, SR PHYSICIST, ARGONNE NAT LAB, 91- *Personal Data:* b Baltimore, Md, Dec 26, 49; m 74, Janis Graner; c Megan Elizabeth & Matthew Robert. *Educ:* Colo Sch Mines, BS, 71; State Univ NY, Stony Brook, MA, 72, PhD(physics), 76. *Mem:* Fel Am Phys Soc; fel AAAS. *Res:* Nuclear and nucleon structures, primarily using electromagnetic probes. *Mailing Add:* Physics Div Argonne Nat Lab Argonne IL 60439. *Fax:* 630-252-3903; *E-Mail:* geesaman@anl.gov

GEESEMAN, GORDON E, GENETICS, BOTANY. *Current Pos:* RETIRED. *Personal Data:* b Fairview, Ill, Mar 18, 21; m 50; c 1. *Educ:* Univ Ill, BS, 43, MS, 46; Univ Wis, PhD(genetics, agron), 49. *Prof Exp:* With State Dept Agr, Wash, 53-57; asst agronomist, Mont State Col, 57-60; from asst prof to assoc prof genetics & bot, Univ Wis, Stevens Point, 62-90. *Mem:* Nat Autobon Soc; Am Hort Soc; Am Soc Hort Sci. *Res:* Plant physiology, anatomy and genetics; selected economic plants. *Mailing Add:* 583 Darnielle Lane Grants Pass OR 97527

GEESLIN, ROGER HAROLD, MATHEMATICS. *Current Pos:* from asst prof to assoc prof, 60-68, from actg chmn to chmn dept, 69-73 & 74-79, actg dean, Univ Col, 73-74, PROF MATH, UNIV LOUISVILLE, MT SINAI SCH MED, 26- *Personal Data:* b Mt Healthy, Ohio, May 24, 31; m 54; c 3. *Educ:* Kenyon Col, AB, 53; Yale Univ, MA, 57, PhD(math), 58. *Prof Exp:* Instr math, Int Christian Univ, Tokyo, 58-60. *Concurrent Pos:* NSF fel, 53-54. *Mem:* AAAS; Am Math Soc; Math Asn Am; Sigma Xi; Nat Coun Teachers Math. *Res:* Diffusion equations; functional analysis; real and complex variables; applications of computers in mathematics and the teaching of mathematics. *Mailing Add:* 1119 Red Fox Rd Louisville KY 40205

GEFFEN, ABRAHAM, RADIOLOGY. *Current Pos:* from attend radiologist to sr attending radiologist, 49-87, CONSULT RADIOLOGIST, BETH ISRAEL MED CTR, 87-; PROF CLIN RADIOL, MT SINAI SCH MED, 68- *Personal Data:* b Atlanta, Ga, Sept 22, 16; m 48; c 3. *Educ:* Emory Univ, BS, 37; Columbia Univ, MD, 41; Am Bd Radiol, dipl. *Prof Exp:* Asst radiotherapist, Mt Sinai Hosp, NY, 47-49. *Mem:* Am Roentgen Ray Soc; Radiol Soc NAm; fel Am Col Radiol; NY Acad Med; AMA. *Mailing Add:* 28 Disbrow Lane New Rochelle NY 10804

GEFFEN, T(HEODORE) M(ORTON), PETROLEUM RESERVOIR ENGINEERING, OIL RECOVERY RESEARCH. *Current Pos:* PETROL CONSULT, 81- *Personal Data:* b Calgary, Alta, Can, Feb 22, 22; nat US; m 85, Doris Kahn; c William, Maureen & Howard. *Educ:* Univ Okla, BS, 44. *Honors & Awards:* John Franklin Carll Award, Soc Petrol Engrs, 74, Enhanced Oil Recovery Pioneer, 84. *Prof Exp:* Res eng, Petrol & Natural Gas Conserv Bd, Alta, 44-45; petrol engr, Calif Stand Co, 45-46; jr engr, Pan Am Petrol Corp, 46-47, jr res engr, 47-49, res engr, 49-51, tech group leader, 51-53, tech group supvr, 53-55, res group supvr, 55-58, res sect supvr, 58-70; res sect mgr, Amoco Prod Co, 70-76, res consult, 76-81. *Concurrent Pos:* Chmn, Oil Recovery Tech Domain Comt, Am Petrol Inst, 63-64 & Am Petrol Inst-Govt Res Liaison Comt, 64-65; mem bd dirs, Eng Socs Comn Energy, 81-83. *Mem:* Hon mem Am Inst Mining Metall & Petrol Engrs; hon mem Soc Petrol Engrs; Am Asn Petrol Geologists. *Res:* Oil recovery; multiphase fluid flow in porous material; reservoir engineering; enhanced oil recovery. *Mailing Add:* 3314 E 51st St Tulsa OK 74135

GEFTER, MALCOLM LAWRENCE, MOLECULAR BIOLOGY, BIOCHEMISTRY. *Current Pos:* assoc prof, 72-76, PROF BIOL, MASS INST TECHNOL, 76-, EXEC OFFICER, DEPT BIOL. *Personal Data:* b New York, NY, Mar 16, 42. *Educ:* Univ Md, BS, 63; Albert Einstein Col Med, PhD(molecular biol), 67. *Honors & Awards:* Pfizer Award, Am Chem Soc, 75. *Prof Exp:* Asst prof biol sci, Columbia Univ, 69-72. *Mem:* Am Soc Biol Chemists. *Res:* Molecular biology of nucleic acids, including enzymology and genetics of DNA replication and RNA metabolism; genetics and biochemistry of cellular differentiation. *Mailing Add:* ImmunLogic Pharmaceut Corp 610 Lincoln St Waltham MA 02154

GEFTER, WILLIAM IRVIN, INTERNAL MEDICINE. *Current Pos:* RETIRED. *Personal Data:* b Philadelphia, Pa, Jan 29, 15; m 39; c 4. *Educ:* Univ Pa, AB, 35, MD, 39; Am Bd Internal Med, dipl, 47. *Prof Exp:* Intern, Philadelphia Gen Hosp, 39-41, resident med, 41-43; from instr to William J Mullen prof med, Woman's Med Col Pa, 43-66, pres staff, Hosp, 58-60, chief med, Col Div, Philadelphia Gen Hosp, 59-66; prof med, Sch Med, Temple Univ & dir, Dept Med, Episcopal Hosp, Philadelphia, 66-74; dir med educ, St Joseph Hosp, 74-91. *Concurrent Pos:* Consult, Vet Admin Hosp, Philadelphia, 53-66; pres staff, Episcopal Hosp, Philadelphia, 70-72; Clin Prof Med, NY Med Col, 75-91. *Mem:* Fel AMA; fel Am Col Physicians; fel Am Col Cardiol. *Res:* Clinical cardiology; internal medicine; medical education and administration. *Mailing Add:* 167 West Lane Stamford CT 06905

GEGEL, HAROLD L(OUIS), PHYSICAL METALLURGY. *Current Pos:* DIR PROCESSING, UNIVERSAL ENERGY SYSTS (UES) AT BEAVER CREEK, 88- *Personal Data:* b St Louis, Mo, Jan 30, 33; m 57; c 3. *Educ:* Univ Ill, Urbana, BS, 55; Ohio State Univ, MS, 62, PhD(metall eng), 65. *Prof Exp:* Develop engr, Frigidaire Div, Gen Motors Corp, 55-56; proj engr, 56-59, res metallurgist, Air Force Mat Lab, 59-88. *Concurrent Pos:* Prof, Dept Mat Sci & Metall, Univ Cincinnati, 68- *Mem:* Am Soc Metals; Am Inst Mining, Metall & Petrol Engrs; Sigma Xi. *Res:* Alloy design; thermodynamic and electronic factors which control the phase stability of alpha and beta titanium alloys and the correlation of these factors with the important mechanical properties. *Mailing Add:* 6217 McCoppin Mill Rd Hillsboro OH 45133

GEGENHEIMER, PETER ALBERT, NUCLEIC ACID BIOCHEMISTRY, RNA PROCESSING. *Current Pos:* asst prof, 85-91, ASSOC PROF BIOCHEM & BOT, UNIV KANS, LAWRENCE, 91- *Personal Data:* b Tucson, Ariz, Mar 6, 50; m 80. *Educ:* Yale Univ, BS, 72; Wash Univ, St Louis, PhD(molecular biol), 79. *Prof Exp:* Res fel biochem & molecular biol, Univ Calif, San Diego, 80-83; vis res assoc, Univ Colo, Boulder, 83-85. *Mem:* AAAS; Am Soc Biochem Molecular Biol; Int Soc Plant Molecular Biol; Am Soc Plant Physiol; RNA Soc. *Res:* Cellular roles and biochemical mechanisms of RNA processing reactions in bacteria, yeast, plant organelles and plant nuclei; RNA-catalysed RNA processing reactions; structure-function relationships and allosteric regulation of chloroplast adenosine triphosphatase synthase. *Mailing Add:* Univ Kans 2045 Haworth Hall Lawrence KS 66045-2106. *Fax:* 785-864-5321; *E-Mail:* pgesen@ukans.edu

GEHA, ALEXANDER SALIM, CARDIOTHORACIC SURGERY, CARDIOPULMONARY PHYSIOLOGY. *Current Pos:* PROF & DIR CARDIOTHORACIC SURG, CASE WESTERN RES UNIV, SCH MED, 86-; CHIEF, CARDIOTHORACIC SURG, UNIV HOSP CLEVELAND. *Personal Data:* b Beirut, Lebanon, June 18, 36, US citizen; m 67, Diane L Redalen; c Samia, Rula & Nada. *Educ:* Am Univ Beirut, BS, 55, MD, 59; Univ Minn, MS, 67. *Hon Degrees:* MA, Yale Univ, 78. *Prof Exp:* Asst prof cardiothoracic surg, Univ Vt, Col Med, 67-69; from asst prof to assoc prof, Wash Univ, Sch Med, 69-75; from assoc prof to prof & chief, Yale Univ, Sch Med, 75-86. *Concurrent Pos:* Consult cardiothoracic surg, Vet Admin Hosp, WHaven, Conn, 75-86, Waterbury Hosp, Conn, 76-86, Cleveland Vet Admin Hosp, 86-, Cleveland Metrop Gen Hosp, 86-, Mt Sinai Hosp, Cleveland, 90-; mem, Study Sect Surg, Anesthesiol & Trauma, NIH, 81-85; mem, bd dir, Conn Heart Asn, 81-86. *Mem:* Soc Thoracic Surg; Am Asn Thoracic Surg; Am Surg Asn; Am Col Surgeons; Soc Univ Surgeons; Soc Vascular Surg; Sigma Xi; Europ Surg Res Soc. *Res:* Clinical cardiothoracic surgery and cardiovascular research into cardiac hypertrophy and its physiologic effects and characteristics; cardiac and pulmonary transplantation and cardiac preservation and protection, both short-term and long term; cardiac neurophysiology. *Mailing Add:* Div Cardiothoracic Surg Case Western Res Univ & Univ Hosp Cleveland Cleveland OH 44106. *Fax:* 216-844-7597; *E-Mail:* asg5@po.cwru.edu

GEHA, RAIF S, IMMUNOLOGY, ALLERGY. *Current Pos:* asst prof, 76-81, ASSOC PROF PEDIAT, HARVARD MED SCH, 81- *Personal Data:* b Bechmezzine, Lebanon, Oct 12, 45; m 70; c 3. *Educ:* Am Univ, Beirut, BSc, 65, MD, 69. *Prof Exp:* Asst prof pediat, Am Univ, Beirut, 74-76. *Mem:* Soc Pediat Res; Am Asn Immunologist; Am Thoracic Soc; Collegium Int Allergologicum. *Res:* Human TB cell interactions. *Mailing Add:* Dept Pediat Harvard Med Sch Children's Hosp 300 Longwood Ave Boston MA 02115-5737. *Fax:* 781-335-8205

GEHAN, EDMUND A, STATISTICS, CANCER. *Current Pos:* KATHRYN O'CONNOR RES PROF, DEPT BIOMATH, UNIV TEX M D ANDERSON CANCER CTR, HOUSTON, 67- *Personal Data:* b Brooklyn, NY, Sept 2, 29; m 62, Brenda McKeon; c James, Laura, Carole, Diane &

Margery. *Educ:* Manhattan Col, BA, 51; NC State Univ, MS, 53, PhD(exp statist), 57. *Honors & Awards:* Jeffrey A Gottleib Mem Award, 83. *Prof Exp:* From instr to asst prof biostatist, Univ NC, 55-58; math statistician, Biomet Br, Nat Cancer Inst, 58-59, actg head, Biomet Sect, 59-61, head sect, 61-62, math statistician, 64-67. *Concurrent Pos:* Nat Cancer Inst spec fel statist, Birkbeck Col, Univ London, 62-64; mem cancer clin invest rev comt, Nat Cancer Inst, 71-74; fac develop leave, dept biomath & biophys, Univ Pierre & Marie-Curie, Paris, 81; Panelist, Consensus Dev Conf Limb Sparing Treat of Adult Soft Tissue Sarcomas & Osteosarconias, NIH, 84. *Mem:* Biomet Soc (pres-elect, Eastern NAm Region, 71, pres, 72); fel Am Statist Asn; Am Soc Clin Oncol; Int Statist Inst; Soc For Clin Trials; Int Soc Clin Biostats (pres, 87-88). *Res:* Clinical trials in cancer research; statistical methodology with applications in cancer research. *Mailing Add:* Lombardi Cancer Ctr 30800 Reservoir Rd NW Corridor A Washington DC 20007. *Fax:* 713-792-4262

GEHLBACH, FREDERICK RENNER, ECOLOGY. *Current Pos:* From asst prof to assoc prof biol, 63-79, prof, 79-95, EMER PROF BIOL & ENVIRON STUDIES, BAYLOR UNIV, 95- *Personal Data:* b Steubenville, Ohio, July 5, 35; m 60, Nancy Young; c Gretchen & Mark. *Educ:* Cornell Univ, AB, 57, MS, 59; Univ Mich, PhD(zool, conserv), 63. *Honors & Awards:* Samuel T Dana Award, Univ Mich, 63. *Concurrent Pos:* Collabr, Nat Park Serv, 59-; Guggenheim fel, 70-71. *Mem:* Am Soc Ichthyol & Herpet; Ecol Soc Am; Am Ornithol Union. *Res:* Ecology and behavior of southwestern vertebrates; conservation of natural communities and species. *Mailing Add:* Dept Biol Baylor Univ PO Box 97388 Waco TX 76798

GEHLERT, DONALD RICHARD, NEUROANATOMICAL IDENTIFICATION OF PATHWAY & TRANSMITTERS. *Current Pos:* Sr pharmacologist, 89-92, RES SCIENTIST, LILLY RES LABS, 93- *Personal Data:* June 27, 58. *Educ:* Purdue Univ, BS, 81; Univ Utah, PhD(pharmacol), 85. *Prof Exp:* Res assoc, Univ Utah, 85; staff fel, NIH-Nat Inst Gen Med Sci, 85-87, sr staff fel, NIH-Nat Inst Neurol Dis & Stroke, 87-88, unit chief, 88-89. *Concurrent Pos:* Adj assoc prof, Dept Psychiat, Ind Univ Sch Med. *Mem:* Soc Neurosci; Am Soc Pharmacol & Exp Therapeut. *Res:* Understanding the role of neuropeptides in the function of the sympathetic nervous system. *Mailing Add:* Lilly Res Labs Mail Code 0815 Indianapolis IN 46285. *Fax:* 317-637-7944; *E-Mail:* gehlertdonaldr@lilly.com

GEHLSEN, KURT RONALD, TUMOR CELL METASTASIS, CELL ADHESION. *Current Pos:* VPRES, CHIEF TECH OFFICER, MAXIM PHARMACEUT INC, 96- *Personal Data:* b Chicago, Ill, June 17, 56; m 90, Robin Page; c Kai H, Alexie M & Tessa P. *Educ:* Univ Ariz, BS, 80, PhD(anat/physiol), 86. *Prof Exp:* Fel, La Jolla Cancer Res Found, 86-88, res assoc, 88-89; sr scientist, Pharmacia, Inc, 89-90, dir molecular-cell biol, 89-91; vpres & chief opers officer, La Jolla Inst Exp Med, 89-91, dir molecular-cell biol, 90-91; staff scientist, Calif Inst Biol Res, 91-92, assoc staff scientist, 92-96. *Concurrent Pos:* Prin investr, NIH, 91-; res lectr anat, Univ Ariz, 91-; vis lectr, Univ Uppsala, 92; consult var biomed co, 92-; assoc mem, Sidney Kimmel Cancer Ctr, 96- *Mem:* AAAS; Am Soc Cell Biol; Metastasis Soc; Am Asn Cancer Res. *Res:* Molecular mechanisms involved in tumor cell proliferation leading to metastatic dissemination. *Mailing Add:* 6923 Blue Orchid Land Carlsbad CA 92009

GEHMAN, BRUCE LAWRENCE, SOLID STATE PHYSICS, METALLURGY. *Current Pos:* VPRES RES & DEVELOP, LEYBOLD MAT INC, 89- *Personal Data:* b Akron, Ohio, Oct 22, 37; m 60; c 3. *Educ:* Univ Mich, BS, 59; San Diego State Col, MS, 65; Univ Calif, San Diego, MS, 69, PhD(physics), 73. *Prof Exp:* Flight test engr instrumentation, Gen Dynamics Corp, 59-61; staff assoc physics, Gulf Energy & Environ Syst, 61-65; res asst, Univ Calif, San Diego, 65-71; mgr res & develop, Cominco Electronic Mat, 71-86, tech dir, deposition technol, 86-88; vpres bus develop, ISM Technologies, 88-89. *Mem:* Am Soc Testing & Mat; Am Phys Soc; Am Soc Metals; Inst Elec & Electronics Engrs; Int Soc Hybrid Microelectronics. *Res:* Transmission electron spin resonance research in dilute localized magnetic moment systems; specialized metallurgical products for the electronics industry. *Mailing Add:* Leybold Mat Inc 16035 Vineyard Blvd Morgan Hill CA 95037

GEHO, WALTER BLAIR, PHARMACOLOGY, BIOTECHNOLOGY. *Current Pos:* PRES & CHIEF EXEC OFFICER, SDG INC, 93- *Personal Data:* b Wheeling, WVa, May 18, 39; m 62, Marjorie Cooper; c Hans, Alison, Robert, David & Daniel. *Educ:* Bethany Col, BS, 60; Western Res Univ, PhD(pharmacol), 64, MD, 66. *Prof Exp:* Sr instr pharmacol, Case Western Res Univ, 66-67; sect head pharmaceut res, Procter & Gamble Co, 67-81; vpres & dir res, Technol Unlimited, 81-90, pres & chief exec officer, 91-93. *Mem:* AMA; Am Chem Soc. *Res:* Pharmacology of diphosphonates and metabolic bone diseases; targeted drug delivery, liposomes, hepatic directed insulin and the control of glucose metabolism; gene delivery. *Mailing Add:* SDG Inc 146 S Bever St Wooster OH 44691

GEHRELS, NEIL, GAMMA-RAY ASTRONOMY, HIGH ENERGY ASTROPHYSICS. *Current Pos:* Nat Acad Sci, Nat Res Coun res assoc, 81-83, astrophysicist, 83-95, HEAD, GAMMA RAY & COSMIC RAY BR, GODDARD SPACE FLIGHT CTR, NASA, 95- *Personal Data:* b Lake Geneva, Wis, Oct 2, 52; m 80, Ellen Williams; c Thomas W & Emily W. *Educ:* Univ Ariz, BS, 76; Calif Inst Technol, PhD(physics), 81. *Honors & Awards:* Technological Innovation Award, Discover Mag, 92. *Prof Exp:* Res asst, Univ Ariz, 73-76, Max Plank Inst, 74, Calif Inst Technol, 77-81. *Concurrent Pos:* Proj scientist, Compton Gamma-Ray Observ, 91-; chair, High Energy Astrophys Div, Am Astron Soc, 96- *Mem:* Am Astron Soc; fel Am Phys Soc; Am Geophys Union. *Res:* Instrumentation development; observations with current observatories and theoretical interpretation; project scientist for NASAs Compton Gamma Ray Observatory. *Mailing Add:* Code 661 NASA Goddard Space Flight Ctr Greenbelt MD 20771

GEHRELS, TOM, PLANETARY ASTRONOMY. *Current Pos:* assoc prof, 61-67, PROF, LUNAR & PLANETARY LAB, UNIV ARIZ, 67- *Personal Data:* b Neth, Feb 21, 25; nat US; m 51; c 3. *Educ:* Univ Leiden, BSc, 51; Univ Chicago, PhD(astron), 56. *Honors & Awards:* Medal Except Sci Achievement, NASA, 74. *Prof Exp:* Res assoc astron, Ind Univ, 56-61. *Concurrent Pos:* res assoc astron, Univ Chicago, 59-61; V A Sarabhai prof & hon fel, Phys Res Lab, Ahmedabad, India, 78-; gen ed, Space Sci Ser, 82-; corresp mem, Bataafsch Genootschap der Proefondervindelijke Wijsbegeerte, 84- *Mem:* Am Astron Soc; Int Astron Union; hon mem Hiroshima Astron Soc. *Res:* Minor planets; sky surveying; author of numerous publications regarding scannerscopy, ballooning and space programs, polarimetry, and minor planets and related objects. *Mailing Add:* Lunar & Planetary Lab Univ Ariz Tucson AZ 85721

GEHRENBECK, RICHARD KEITH, HISTORY OF PHYSICS. *Current Pos:* from asst prof to assoc prof, 72-88, PROF PHYS SCI, RHODE ISLAND COL, 88- *Personal Data:* b St Paul, Minn, June 8, 34; m 58; c 3. *Educ:* Macalester Col, BA, 56; Univ Minn, MA, 66, PhD(hist of physics), 73. *Prof Exp:* Instr physics & math, Gerard Inst for Boys, Sidon, Lebanon, 57-60; from instr to asst prof physics, Park Col, 62-69; lab coordr physics, Univ Minn, 70-71. *Concurrent Pos:* Area rep, Barnard-Columbia Hist of Physics Lab, 74-78. *Mem:* Am Asn Physics Teachers; Hist of Sci Soc; Sigma Xi. *Res:* History of physics; history of American science; science and society; history of astronomy. *Mailing Add:* 972 Smith St Providence RI 02908

GEHRI, DENNIS CLARK, ENVIRONMENTAL CHEMISTRY. *Current Pos:* MEM SR STAFF, ATOMICS INT DIV, ROCKWELL INT CORP, 67- *Personal Data:* b Beloit, Wis, Jan 28, 37; m 61; c 4. *Educ:* Univ Wis, BS, 59, PhD(phys chem), 68. *Mem:* Am Chem Soc; Sigma Xi; Air Pollution Control Asn. *Res:* Experimental thermodynamics and molecular vibrations of gases; sodium chemistry, particularly interactions of carbon with liquid solium; air pollution control of stationary source and automotive emissions. *Mailing Add:* 12 Meadowlark Lane Agoura Hills CA 91301

GEHRIG, JOHN D, ORAL SURGERY, ANATOMY. *Current Pos:* assoc prof, 54-67, chmn, Dept Oral Surg, 56-70, PROF ORAL SURG, SCH DENT, UNIV WASH, 67-, DIR, GRAD ORAL SURG TRAINING PROG, 70-, DIR ORAL SURG, UNDERGRAD CLIN, 72-, PROF, BIOL STRUCT DEPT, SCH MED, 88- *Personal Data:* b Watson, Minn, Feb 6, 24; m 53; c 7. *Educ:* Univ Minn, DDS, 46, MS, 51; Am Bd Oral Surg, dipl. *Prof Exp:* Prof oral surg, Sch Dent, Univ Kansas City, 52-54. *Concurrent Pos:* Attend, Children's Orthop Hosp, Providence Hosp, Vet Admin Hosp, Seattle & Vet Admin Hosp, Am Lake, Univ Hosp, Univ Wash, Harborview Hosp Med Ctr; consult, Madigan Gen Hosp, Tacoma & US Army Hq Dent Detachment, Ft Lewis; adj prof, Biol Struct Dept, Sch Med, Univ Wash, 75- *Mem:* Am Soc Oral Surg; Am Soc Oral Maxillofacial Surgeons; Am Asn Anatomists; International Asn Study Pain. *Res:* Inferior alveolar nerve regeneration on dogs through a Millipore filter sleeve; comparison of ATb sensitivities with ATb choice; blood and fluid volume changes in oral surgery; evaluation of concurrent methods of dental anesthesia; pain, chronic pain, dental sensory receptor (electron microscopy); vibratory analgesia for local anesthetic administration; topographic brain measures of human pain and pain responsivity; computerized imaging of human skull with measurements; human pain responsivity in a tonic pain model; psychological determinants. *Mailing Add:* Prof Oral & Maxil Surg Univ Wash Sch Med Seattle WA 98195

GEHRIG, ROBERT FRANK, MICROBIOLOGY. *Current Pos:* from asst prof to prof, 62-96, chmn dept, 70-73, 76-78 & 84-87, EMER PROF BIOL, RUSSELL SAGE COL, 97- *Personal Data:* b Manitowoc, Wis, Jan 3, 28; m 54; c 4. *Educ:* Univ Wis, BS, 51, MS, 58, PhD(bact), 61. *Prof Exp:* Asst enzyme chem, Merck Inst Therapeut Res, NJ, 51-53. *Mem:* Am Soc Microbiol. *Res:* Fatty acid metabolism of the filamentous fungi; physiology of penicillia and aspergilli. *Mailing Add:* Dept Biol Russell Sage Col Troy NY 12180

GEHRING, DAVID AUSTIN, INTERNAL MEDICINE, CARDIOLOGY. *Current Pos:* ASSOC MED DIR, COATESVILLE CORRECTIONAL MED SERVS, 97- *Personal Data:* b Bryn Mawr, Pa, Dec 6, 30; m 53, 82, Victoria M Damiano; c David, Paul, Peter, Sue, Barbara, Eric, Theresa, Judy L & Michael A. *Educ:* Univ Pittsburgh, BA, 52, MD, 56; Am Bd Internal Med, dipl. *Honors & Awards:* Pres Medal of Merit, Repub Task Force, 88. *Prof Exp:* Comdr, USN, 56, adv through grades to lt comdr; from intern to resident internal med, US Naval Hosp, USN, Philadelphia, 56-60, mem staff internal med, 60-61; chief, Internal Med Heart Sta, US Naval Hosp, USN, Annapolis, 61-63; cardiologist, KGE Med Group, 63-82; cardiologist & pres, Hobbs Cardiol, PA Hobbs, NMex, 82-86; med dir, Polk Ctr, Pa, 86-91; physician chief grade, Vet Admin Med Ctr, Coatesville, Pa, 91-96, assoc chief staff ambulatory care, 93-96, chief med serv & chief staff, 95-96, cardiologist, 97. *Concurrent Pos:* Testing cardiologist, Anthropometrics United Med Group, 74-82; clin asst prof med, Temple Univ Hosp, Philadelphia, 75-82; adj asst prof med, Jefferson Mem Col, 81-82; chief cardiac rehab unit, Lea Regional Hosp, 82-86; chief med servs, 829th Sta Hosp, USAR, Lubbock, 84-86; consult cardiol, Oil City, Pa, 86-91; mem, ACLS Inst & affil fac Pa Heart Asn, 86-; staff, Franklin Regional Med Ctr, 86-90, Oil City Area Health Ctr, 86-91; mem, Health Care Adv Comt, Congressman William F Clinger, Jr, 23rd dist, Pa, 89-91; teaching staff, St Joseph Hosp, Lancaster, Pa, 91-; eucharistic minister, St Joseph Church, Swedesboro, 92-; clin preceptor, Univ Pa Sch Nursing, 93- *Mem:* Fel Am Col Cardiol; fel Am Col Chest Physicians; fel Am Col Clin Pharmacol; fel & life mem Am Col Physicians; AMA; Am Geriat Soc; St Jude Soc; Am Col Physician Exec. *Mailing Add:* 865 W Red Bank Ave Woodbury NJ 08096-4095

GEHRING, FREDERICK WILLIAM, MATHEMATICS. *Current Pos:* from asst prof to assoc prof, 56-84, chmn dept, 73-75 & 77-84, T H HILDEBRANDT PROF MATH, UNIV MICH, 84-, DISTINGUISHED UNIV PROF, 87-, EMER PROF. *Personal Data:* b Ann Arbor, Mich, Aug 7, 25; m 53, Lois Bigger; c Kalle & Peter. *Educ:* Univ Mich, BSE(elec eng) & BSE(math), 46, MA, 49; Cambridge Univ, PhD(math), 52, ScD, 76. *Hon Degrees:* PhD, Helsinki Univ, 77, Univ Jyvaskula, 90, Norweg Univ Sci & Technol, 97. *Honors & Awards:* Order White Rose, Finland, 86. *Prof Exp:* Benjamin Pierce instr math, Harvard Univ, 52-55. *Concurrent Pos:* Guggenheim & Fulbright fel, 58-59; NSF fel, 59-60; anal ed, Duke Math J, 63-80; ed, D Van Nostrand Publ Co, 63-69, N Holland Publ Co, 70-, Springer-Verlag, 74- & Conformal Geom & Dynamics, Am Math Soc; vis prof, Stanford Univ, 64, Harvard Univ, 64-65, Univ Minn, 71, Mittag Leffler Inst, Sweden, 72 & 90 & Acad Finland, 89-; mem coun, Am Math Soc, 69-75, bd trustees, 83-93; sr vis fel, UK Sci Res Coun, 81; Alexander von Humboldt Prize, 81-82; hon prof, Hunan Univ, People's Repub China, 87-; ed, Bull Am Math Soc, 92; Lars Onsager prof, Norweg Tech Univ, 95. *Mem:* Nat Acad Sci; Math Asn Am; Swiss Math Soc; Finnish Math Soc; Asn Women Math; Am Acad Arts & Sci; Finnish Acad; Am Math Soc; Ger Math Soc; Swedish Math Soc; Europ Math Soc; Royal Norweg Soc Sci & Lett; Royal Norweg Soc Sci & Lett. *Res:* Analysis. *Mailing Add:* 2139 Melrose Rd Ann Arbor MI 48104. *Fax:* 313-763-0937; *E-Mail:* fgehring@math.lsa.umich.edu

GEHRING, HARVEY THOMAS, organic polymer chemistry; deceased, see previous edition for last biography

GEHRING, PERRY JAMES, TOXICOLOGY, PHARMACOLOGY. *Current Pos:* VPRES, RES & DEVELOP, DOWELANCO. *Personal Data:* b Yankton, SDak, Mar 15, 36; m 59, Barbara L Tennis; c Daniel K, Matthew J, Elizabeth L & Heidi L. *Educ:* Univ Minn, Minneapolis, BS & DVM, 60, PhD(pharmacol), 65. *Honors & Awards:* Founder's Award, Chem Indust Inst Toxicol, 83; Merit Award, Soc Toxicol, 83. *Prof Exp:* Res assoc toxicol, Iowa State Univ, 60-61; USPHS fel pharmacol, Univ Minn, Minneapolis, 61-65; pharmacol toxicologist, Dow Chem Co, 65-68; assoc prof pharmacol, Mich State Univ, 68-70; from asst dir to dir toxicol, Dow Chem Co, 70-80, dir life sci, 80-81, vpres agr chem res & develop & dir health & environ res, 81-89. *Concurrent Pos:* Vis prof pharmacol, Mich State Univ, 74-89; adj prof, Dept Pharmacol & Toxicol, Ind Univ. *Mem:* AAAS; Int Union Toxicol(pres,86-89); Soc Toxicol (pres, 80 & 81). *Res:* Toxidynamics; chemical cataractogenesis; metal toxicology; pharmacokinetics; risk assessment. *Mailing Add:* DowElanco 9330 Zionsville Rd Indianapolis IN 46268-1054. *Fax:* 317-337-4955

GEHRING, WALTER J, BIOLOGY, GENETICS. *Current Pos:* PROF, UNIV BASEL, SWITZ, 72- *Personal Data:* b Zurich, Switz, Mar 20, 39; M 64, Elisabeth Lott; c Stephan & Thomas. *Educ:* Univ Zurich, PhD, 65. *Honors & Awards:* Charles Lepold Mayer Prize, Inst France, 86. *Prof Exp:* Res assoc, Univ Zurich, 63-67; post doctoral fel, Yale Univ, 67-69, assoc prof, 69-72. *Concurrent Pos:* Ed, J Exp Zool, 89; Newcomb Cleveland prize, AAAS, 94-95. *Mem:* Nat Acad Sci; Europ Molecular Biol Orgn; Ger Acad Sci; Royal Swed Acad Sci; Swiss Soc Cell & Molecular Biol. *Mailing Add:* Hochfeldstrasse 32 Therwil CH-4106 Switzerland

GEHRIS, CLARENCE WINFRED, BOTANY, PLANT ECOLOGY. *Current Pos:* AT DEPT LARYNGOLOGY OTOLOGY, JOHNS HOPKINS UNIV. *Personal Data:* b Fleetwood, Pa, Oct 25, 17; m 41; c 2. *Educ:* Temple Univ, BS, 38, MEd, 45; Pa State Univ, DEd, 64. *Prof Exp:* Instr pub sch, Pa, 45-62; assoc prof, 62-71, State Univ NY, Brockport, prof biol, 71- *Concurrent Pos:* AAAS-NSF fel, 59-61. *Mem:* Ecol Soc Am; Am Bot Soc; AAAS. *Res:* Bog ecology; peat development; pollen analysis. *Mailing Add:* 8343 Tally Ho Rd Lutherville Timonium MD 21093

GEHRKE, CHARLES WILLIAM, BIOCHEMISTRY. *Current Pos:* assoc prof, 49-53, prof biochem & mgr exp sta chem labs, 54-87, EMER PROF, COL AGR, UNIV MO, COLUMBIA, 87- *Personal Data:* b New York, NY, July 18, 17; m 41, Virginia Horcher; c Charles W, Jon C & Susan G. *Educ:* Ohio State Univ, BA, 39, MSc & BSc, 41, PhD(agr biochem), 47. *Honors & Awards:* Harvey W Wiley Award, Asn Off Anal Chemists, 71; Chromatography Mem Medal, Sci Coun Chromatography, Acad Sci USSR, Moscow, 80; Midwest Award, Am Chem Soc, 86; Dal Nogare Award in Chromatog, 96. *Prof Exp:* Asst bacteriologist, Ohio State Univ, 41, instr, 45-46; food & dairy inspector, Univ Ohio, 41-42; actg prof chem, Mo Valley Col, 42-43, prof & head dept, 43-45, prof chem & head dept, 46-49. *Concurrent Pos:* Co-investr, Apollo 11, 12, 14, 15, 16 & 17 lunar samples; mem, Am Chem Soc Adv Bd Chem Abstracts, 76; Mid Am State Univ Hon Lectr, 78; Sigma Xi res award, Univ Mo, 80. *Mem:* Am Chem Soc; NY Acad Sci; Int Soc Origin Life; fel Asn Off Anal Chemists; Int Asn Off Anal Chemists (pres, 84). *Res:* Physical biochemistry of proteins; gas chromatography of amino acids, genetic molecules and biological substances; analytical methods development; high performance liquid chromatography of RNA and DNA nucleosides; author of 6 books. *Mailing Add:* 708 Edgewood Ave Columbia MO 65203-7410. *Fax:* 573-443-3531

GEHRKE, HENRY, INORGANIC CHEMISTRY. *Current Pos:* From asst prof to assoc prof, 64-72, PROF CHEM, SDAK STATE UNIV, 72- *Personal Data:* b Salina, Kans, May 11, 36; m 56, Alice Bisping; c Stevin, Bruce, Karl & Katherine. *Educ:* Okla State Univ, BS, 58; Univ Iowa, MS, 62, PhD(inorg & org chem), 64. *Mem:* AAAS; Am Chem Soc; Nat Sci Teachers Asn. *Res:* Coordination chemistry of rarer elements; bioinorganic chemistry of molybdenum and rhenium. *Mailing Add:* 334 Marian Ave Brookings SD 57007. *Fax:* 605-688-6364

GEHRKE, ROBERT JAMES, NUCLEAR RADIATION METROLOGY, TECHNICAL MANAGEMENT. *Current Pos:* CONSULTING SCIENTIST, LOCKHEED MARTIN IDAHO TECHNOL CO, IDAHO NAT ENG LAB, 95- *Personal Data:* b Chicago, Ill, Nov 20, 40; m 63, Mary L Irwin; c Marie T, Julie C & Karen M. *Educ:* DePaul Univ, BS, 62; Univ Nev, Reno, MS, 66. *Honors & Awards:* Res & Develop 100 Award, 92. *Prof Exp:* Physicist, Phillips Petrol Co-Idaho Nuclear Corp, Nat Reactor Testing Sta, 65-69, sr physicist, Aerojet Nuclear Co, 69-73; assoc scientist, Idaho Nat Eng Lab, EG&G Idaho, Inc, 73-79, sr scientist, 79-83, sci specialist, 83-85, unit mgr, 85-90, sci specialist, 90-95. *Concurrent Pos:* Contrib ed, Radioactiv & Radiochem, J Appl Measurements; expert witness, Int Atomic Energy Agency, 92. *Mem:* Am Chem Soc; Am Nuclear Soc; Health Physics Soc. *Res:* Applied x-ray and gamma-ray spectroscopy, nuclear radiation metrology, applied radiation measurements, environmental radioanalysis, nuclear structure studies and radiation measurement instrumentation; technical management of a radiation measurement laboratory; prompt gamma neutron activation analysis. *Mailing Add:* Lockheed-Martin Idaho Technol Co PO Box 1625 Idaho Falls ID 83415-2114

GEHRKE, WILLARD H, CHEMICAL ENGINEERING. *Current Pos:* VPRES CO DEVELOP, CURWOOD INC, 68- *Personal Data:* b Belmont, Wis, Jan 21, 20; m 44; c 3. *Educ:* Univ Wis, BS, 42. *Prof Exp:* Chem engr, Monsanto Chem Co, Ohio, 42-47; process engr mfg eng, Marathon Div, Am Can Co, 47-51, supvr, 51, cent mfg eng, 51-53 & process eng, 53-57, mgr, 57-61, asst to vpres res & develop div, 61-62, dir paper prod res & develop, 62-64, dir rigid container res & develop, 64-66, dir fabric bus develop, 66-68. *Concurrent Pos:* Mem, Indust Res Inst. *Mem:* Am Chem Soc; Tech Asn Pulp & Paper Indust. *Res:* Protective packaging films for foods and other products made from polyester, polyolefins, nylon, vinyl and aluminum foil. *Mailing Add:* 21 Meadowbrook Ct Appleton WI 54914-3562

GEHRMANN, JOHN EDWARD, PHARMACOLOGY. *Current Pos:* ASSOC RES PHARMACOLOGIST, UNIV CALIF, DAVIS, 70- *Personal Data:* b Hoboken, NJ, June 25, 41; m 66; c 2. *Educ:* Queens Col, NY, BS, 63; Stanford Univ, PhD(pharmacol), 69. *Prof Exp:* Res assoc psychopharmacol, Brain Res Labs, New York Med Col, 69-70. *Mem:* AAAS; Am Chem Soc; NY Acad Sci; Soc Neurosci. *Res:* Computer based quantitative evaluation of the electroencephalogram; correlations with changes induced by conditioned behavioral responses and drugs acting on the central nervous system; electrophysiological assessment of acute spinal cord injury. *Mailing Add:* 738 Anderson Rd Davis CA 95616-3513

GEHRS, CARL WILLIAM, ECOLOGY, ENVIRONMENTAL TOXICOLOGY. *Current Pos:* life sci synthetic fuels prog coordr, 75-77, RES ECOLOGIST AQUATIC EFFECTS, ENVIRON SCI DIV, OAK RIDGE NAT LAB, 72-, PROG MGR ADV, FOSSIL ENERGY PROG, 75- *Personal Data:* b Elmhurst, Ill, May 4, 41; m 64; c 3. *Educ:* Concordia Teacher's Col, BS, 63; Kans State Teacher's Col, MS, 67; Univ Okla, PhD(aquatic ecol), 72. *Prof Exp:* Biol teacher, Luther High Sch, South Chicago, Ill, 64-69, dean students, 67-69. *Mem:* AAAS; Ecol Soc Am; Sigma Xi; Soc Environ Toxicol & Chem; Soc Int Limnologists. *Res:* Environmental health concerns related to increased coal utilization; aquatic ecology; zooplantion population dynamics; environmental transport, fate and effects of organic contaminants; translation from laboratory to field; risk analysis. *Mailing Add:* 112 Westview Lane Oak Ridge TN 37830

GEHRZ, ROBERT DOUGLAS, ASTROPHYSICS. *Current Pos:* PROF PHYSICS & ASTRON, UNIV MINN, 85-; DIR, MT LEMMON OBSERVING FACIL, 88- *Personal Data:* b Evanston, Ill, Dec 28, 44; m 70; c 2. *Educ:* Univ Minn, BA, 67, PhD(physics), 71. *Prof Exp:* Res assoc physics, Univ Minn, 71-72; from asst prof to prof physics & astron, Univ Wyo, 72-85. *Concurrent Pos:* Vis astronr, Kitt Peak Nat Observ, 69-; consult, Martin Marietta Aerospace, Colo, 74; dir-at-large, Aura, Inc, 76-; mem, NASA first team & NSF astron adv comt, 77-; mem, NASA dost team, 78-, Astron Surv Comt, Nat Acad Sci, 78-81; chmn, NSF Optical/Infrared subcomt, 78-; chmn, Observ Vis Comt, Asn Univ Res Astron, 82-84; adj prof physics & astron, Univ Wyo, 85-; mem NSF adv comt, Astron, 76-79, 87-; NAS comt for planetary & lunar exploration; counr, Am Astron Soc, 86-89. *Mem:* Am Astron Soc; Royal Astron Soc; Sigma Xi; Int Astron Union; fel Explorers Club; AAAS. *Res:* Infrared astronomy; development of infrared instrumentation; construction of a 92 inch infrared telescope; discovery of NeII emission from Novae; infrared observations. *Mailing Add:* Dept Astron Univ Minn 116 Church St SE Minneapolis MN 55455

GEIBEL, JON FREDERICK, REACTION KINETICS. *Current Pos:* res chemist, High Temperature Thermoplastics, 81-85, SUPVR, ENG PLASTICS RES SECT, PHILLIPS RES CTR, 85- *Personal Data:* b White Plains, NY, June 3, 50; m 76. *Educ:* Harvey Mudd Col, BS, 72; Univ Calif, San Diego, MS, 74, PhD(chem), 76. *Prof Exp:* Scholar, Dept Med, Univ Calif, San Diego, 76-77; mem res staff high performance epoxy resins, Eng Res Ctr, Western Elec Co, 77-81. *Mem:* Am Chem Soc; Soc Plastics Eng. *Res:* Hemoglobin model compounds; structure-property relationships in aromatic polysulfide thermoplastics; material processing in microgravity. *Mailing Add:* 2600 Mountain Rd Bartlesville OK 74003-6922

GEIDEL, GWENDELYN, ENVIRONMENTAL GEOCHEMISTRY, ENVIRONMENTAL REGULATION. *Current Pos:* from res technologist I to res technologist II, Univ SC, Columbia, 76-80, res specialist I geochem, 80-82, res asst prof, 82-87, adj prof, 87-95, RES ASSOC PROF GEOL, EARTH SCI & RESOURCES INST, UNIV SC, COLUMBIA, 93- *Personal Data:* b Lowville, NY, May 4, 53; m 76, Frank T Caruccio; c 2. *Educ:* Univ SC, BS, 74, MS, 76, PhD, 82, JD, 89. *Concurrent Pos:* Co-prin investr,

Environ Protection Agency grant, Univ SC, 77-81; prin investr, US Bur Mines grant, Univ SC, 80-85, US Off Surface Mining & Develop Res Grants, 81-86, Hungarian Groundwater Workshop, Environ Law Inst, 90-91; assoc atty, Woodward Leventis Law Firm, Columbia, SC, 89-91; counr atty, 91-96; Rogers, Townsend & Thomas, PC, Columbia, SC, 96- *Mem:* Sigma Xi; Can Land Reclamation Asn; Am Soc Surface Mining & Reclamation; Int Asn Geochem & Cosmochem. *Res:* Environmental and hydrogeological aspects of surface mining with primary emphasis on the prediction of mine drainage quality and ameliorative techniques and environmental legal issues. *Mailing Add:* 3823 Edinburgh Rd Columbia SC 29204

GEIDUSCHEK, E(RNEST) PETER, MOLECULAR BIOLOGY, VIROLOGY. *Current Pos:* chmn biol, 81-83, 94, prof biol, 70-94, RES PROF BIOL, UNIV CALIF, SAN DIEGO, 94- *Personal Data:* b Vienna, Austria, Apr 11, 28; nat US; m 55; c 2. *Educ:* Columbia Univ, AB, 48; Harvard Univ, AM, 50, PhD(chem), 52. *Honors & Awards:* Hilleman Lectr, Univ Chicago, 78; Adriano Buzzati-Traverso Lectr, Rome, 96. *Prof Exp:* Instr, Yale Univ, 52-53 & 55-57; asst prof chem, Univ Mich, 57-59; from asst prof to prof biophys, Univ Chicago, 59-70. *Concurrent Pos:* Guggenheim Found fel, 64-65; res career develop award, USPHS, 62-70; lectr, Europ Molecular Biol Orgn, 77; guest lectr, Ministry Foreign Affairs, France, 91; vis lectr, Technion, Israel, 91; lectr, Brazilian Soc Biochem, 94. *Mem:* Nat Acad Sci; Am Soc Biol Chem; fel AAAS; fel Am Acad Arts & Sci; Am Soc Microbiol; Am Soc Virol; fel Am Acad Microbiol. *Res:* Macromolecular structure; synthesis and function of nucleic acids; physico-chemical methods applicable to large molecules; synthesis and function of nucleic acids; genetic regulation; virus development; biochemistry. *Mailing Add:* Dept Biol & Ctr Molecular Genetics Univ Calif San Diego 9500 Gilman Dr La Jolla CA 92093-0634. *Fax:* 619-534-7073

GEIGER, BENJAMIN, CYTOLOGY, EMBRYOLOGY. *Current Pos:* DEAN, FEINBERG GRAD SCH, 89- *Personal Data:* b Haifa, Israel, Jan 29, 47; m 71, Selly; c 3. *Educ:* Hebrew Univ, MSc, 72; Weizmann Inst Sci, PhD(chem immunol), 77. *Honors & Awards:* John F Kennedy Mem Prize, 77; Levinson Prize, 83; Fedn Europ Biochem Socs Prize, 84. *Prof Exp:* Fel, Univ Calif, San Diego, 77-79, post-grad res assoc, 79; fel, 79-80, sr scientist, 80-82, assoc prof, 83-88, PROF, DEPT CHEM IMMUNOL, WEIZMANN INST SCI, 88- *Mem:* Am Soc Cell Biol; Israeli Soc Biochem; Israeli Soc Cell Biol; Israeli Soc Micros; Europ Molecular Biol Orgn. *Res:* Molecular basis for cell communication and the involvement of the cytoskeleton in cellular interactions. *Mailing Add:* Dept Molecular Cell Biol Weizmann Inst Sci Rehovot 76100 Israel

GEIGER, CLIFFORD G, LOGISTICS, ENGINEERING. *Current Pos:* Dep comdr, Fleet Logistics Support Naval Sea Systs Command, ASST DEP CHIEF, OFF DEP CHIEF NAVAL OPERS LOGISTICS, WASHINGTON, DC, 95- *Educ:* Stevens Inst Technol, BS. *Honors & Awards:* Gold Medal, Am Soc Naval Engrs, 90; Founders Medal, Soc Logistics Engrs, 90. *Concurrent Pos:* Coun, Am Soc Naval Engrs, 91. *Mem:* Am Soc Naval Engrs; Asn Scientists & Engrs. *Mailing Add:* Off Dep Chief Naval Opers Logistics Rm 4E606 2000 Navy Pentagon Washington DC 20350-2000

GEIGER, DAVID KENNETH, BIOINORGANIC & STRUCTURAL CHEMISTRY. *Current Pos:* asst prof chem, 85-91, ASSOC PROF CHEM, COL ARTS & SCI, STATE UNIV NY, GENESCO, 91-, CHAIR, DEPT CHEM, 92- *Personal Data:* b Canton, Ohio, Apr 14, 56; m 81; c 2 Matthew, Mark & Thomas. *Educ:* Franciscan Univ, BA, 78; Univ Notre Dame, PhD(inorg chem), 83. *Prof Exp:* Res assoc, Dept Energy, Notre Dame Radiation Lab, 83-85. *Mem:* Am Chem Soc; Sigma Xi. *Res:* Synthesis and characterization of macrocyclic ligands and their transition metal complexes. *Mailing Add:* Dept Chem State Univ NY Col Arts & Sci Geneseo NY 14454

GEIGER, DONALD R, PHOTOSYNTHESIS, TRANSLOCATION. *Current Pos:* from asst prof to assoc prof, 64-72, PROF BIOL, UNIV DAYTON, 72- *Personal Data:* b Dayton, Ohio, Feb 27, 33. *Educ:* Univ Dayton, BS, 55; Ohio State Univ, MSc, 60, PhD(bot), 63. *Prof Exp:* Teacher, Cathedral Latin Sch, 55-60. *Concurrent Pos:* Prin investr, NSF res grant, 64-67 & 72-; res grant, US AEC, 68-71; prog dir strategies for responsible develop, 74-81. *Mem:* AAAS; Am Soc Plant Physiol; Can Soc Plant Physiol; Australian Soc Plant Physiol; Soc Ecol Restoration. *Res:* Translocation of sugar in higher plants using radioisotope tracer techniques; habitat restoration; photosynthesis and carbon metabolism. *Mailing Add:* Dept Biol Univ Dayton Dayton OH 45469-2320

GEIGER, EDWIN OTTO, BIOCHEMISTRY. *Current Pos:* FERMENTATION MICROBIOLOGIST, PFIZER, 92- *Personal Data:* b Chicago, Ill, Apr 24, 39; m 63; c 4. *Educ:* DePaul Univ, BS, 61; Loyola Univ, MS, 64, PhD(biochem), 66, MBA, 75. *Honors & Awards:* Medal, Am Inst Chem, 61. *Prof Exp:* Fel biochem, Case Western Res Univ, 65-67; sr researcher, CPC Int, 67-75, team leader, 75-76, sect leader, 76-77; mgr corn res, Amstar Corp, 77-85; mgr microbiol devel, BW Biotec Inc, 85-86; sr scientist, Seagrams, 86-92. *Mem:* Am Chem Soc; Sigma Xi. *Res:* Enzyme chemistry; fermentation development; bound enzymes; process development. *Mailing Add:* Pfizer Inc Eastern Point Rd Groton CT 06340

GEIGER, GENE E(DWARD), MECHANICAL ENGINEERING. *Current Pos:* from instr to asst prof mech eng, Univ Pittsburgh, 51-64, assoc res prof, 64-66, assoc prof, 66-71, coordr grad prog, 66-83, PROF MECH ENG, UNIV PITTSBURGH, 71-, ASSOC CHMN, MECH ENG DEPT, 91- *Personal Data:* b Pittsburgh, Pa, Oct 27, 28; m 59, Virginia A Miller; c Gregg T & Amy J. *Educ:* Carnegie Inst Technol, BSME, 50; Univ Pittsburgh, MSME, 55, PhD(mech eng), 64. *Prof Exp:* Res asst residual stress, Mellon Inst, 51. *Concurrent Pos:* Consult, Pa Pub Utility Comn, 64, gas companies Pa, 65-68, knowledge availability syst, Univ Pittsburgh, 65-, Anvil Prod, Inc, 67-68 & Mine Safety Appliances, Inc, 70-75 & 80-81; vis fel, Mellon Inst, 65-69; consult, Berner Int Corp, 75-81, Lectromelt, 79, Sunbeam Corp, 79-80, City of Pittsburgh, 81-90, Schneider Consult Engr, 85-86, Emec Consults, 89- *Mem:* Am Soc Mech Engrs; Nat Soc Prof Engrs. *Res:* Heat transfer; fluid dynamics and power; thermodynamics; energy conservation; fluid power; hydraulics and pneumatics. *Mailing Add:* 113 Greenbrier Dr Carnegie PA 15106. *Fax:* 412-624-1108; *E-Mail:* geiger@civ.pitt.edu

GEIGER, GORDON HAROLD, METALLURGY, MATERIALS SCIENCE. *Current Pos:* CHMN & CHIEF EXEC OFFICER, QUALITECH STEEL CORP, 95- *Personal Data:* b Chicago, Ill, Apr 21, 37; m 74, Ann Davis; c Andrew & Karen. *Educ:* Yale Univ, BE, 59; Northwestern Univ, MS, 61, PhD(mat sci), 64. *Honors & Awards:* Campbell Award, Nat Asn Corrosion Engrs, 66; Stoughton Award, Am Soc Metals, 72. *Prof Exp:* Process engr, Allis-Chalmers Mfg Co, 60-61; res asst, Northwestern Univ, 61-63; res engr, Jones & Laughlin Steel Corp, 64-65; from asst prof to assoc prof metall eng, Univ Wis-Madison, 65-68; from assoc prof to prof mat eng, Univ Ill, Chicago Circle, 69-73; prof metall eng & head dept, Univ Ariz, 73-80; sr proc consult, Inland Steel, 80-81; vpres & tech dir, Chase Manhattan Bank, 82-83; vpres technol, NStar Steel, 83-87, exec vpres, 87-92; sr vpres tech qual, Cargill Inc, 88-92. *Concurrent Pos:* Chmn adv comt steel technol, Off Technol Assessment, US Cong, 78-79. *Mem:* Am Inst Mining, Metall & Petrol Engrs; Am Soc Metals. *Res:* Thermodynamics and transport phenomena in process metallurgy; operations research as applied to metallurgical processes; steelmaking; copper production processes; mineral processing. *Mailing Add:* 4900 Emerson Ave S Minneapolis MN 55440

GEIGER, H JACK, EPIDEMIOLOGY, COMMUNITY MEDICINE. *Current Pos:* Arthur C Logan prof, 78-97, ARTHUR C LOGAN EMER PROF COMMUNITY MED, CITY UNIV NY, MED SCH, CITY COL NY, 97- *Personal Data:* b New York, NY, Nov 11, 25; m 51. *Educ:* Case Western Res Univ, MD, 58; Harvard Univ, MSciHyg, 60. *Prof Exp:* Sci ed, Int News Serv, 49-54; intern med, Sch Med, Harvard Univ, 58-59, NIMH fel Joint Training Prog Soc Sci & Med, Dept Social Rel, 59-61, instr prev med, 61-62, asst med & resident, 62-64, asst prof pub health, Sch Pub Health, 64-65; assoc prev med, Sch Med, Tufts Univ, 65-66, prof, 66-68, prof community health & social med & chmn dept, 68-71; prof, Sch Med, State Univ NY, Stony Brook, 71-80. *Concurrent Pos:* Mem bd gov, Inst Current World Affairs, 61-, chmn, 71; consult, Res Policy Comt, Peace Corps, 62-64, Rockefeller Found, 69-70 & Off Secy, US Dept HEW, 68-; res fel, Thorndike Lab, Boston City Hosp, 64; proj dir, Tufts Univ-Delta Health Ctr, Mound Bayou, Miss & Tufts Univ, Columbia Point Health Ctr, Boston, 65-71; Milbank Mem Fund fac fel, 66-71; mem, Nat Comn Hunger & Malnutrit US, 67-; mem bd, Nat Comn Inquiry Health Servs Americans, 69-71; mem planning comt, White House Conf Youth, 71-; consult, Inst Med-Nat Acad Sci, 80- *Mem:* Inst Med-Nat Acad Sci; fel Am Pub Health Asn; Soc Appl Anthrop; Asn Teachers Prev Med; Asn Am Med Cols; fel AAAS. *Res:* Social medicine and change; community health; cultural factors in the epidemiology of hypertension, rheumatoid arthritis and schizophrenia. *Mailing Add:* 28 Shermerhorn St Brooklyn NY 11201

GEIGER, JAMES STEPHEN, PHYSICS. *Current Pos:* Asst res off, Atomic Energy Can, 56-68, sr res off, 68-86, br mgr nuclear physics, 86-94, EMER RESEARCHER, ATOMIC ENERGY CAN, LTD, 94- *Personal Data:* b Kitchener, Ont, Apr 5, 29; m 56, Gladys E Jowitt; c 4. *Educ:* McMaster Univ, BSc, 51, MSc, 52; Yale Univ, MS, 53, PhD(physics), 57. *Concurrent Pos:* Vis sr scientist, Lab Laser Energetics, Univ Rochester, 76-77. *Mem:* Fel Am Phys Soc; Can Asn Physicists. *Res:* Laser spectroscopy; nuclear physics. *Mailing Add:* PO Box 516 Deep River ON K0J 1P0 Can. *E-Mail:* jgeiger@intranet.ca

GEIGER, JON ROSS, INDUSTRIAL MICROBIOLOGY, BIOTECHNOLOGY. *Current Pos:* sr res biologist, Oline Res Ctr, 81-83, res assoc biotechnol, 83-87, sr res assoc, 87-90, GROUP LEADER BIOTECHNOL & MICROBIOL, OLIN RES CTR, 90- *Personal Data:* b Philadelphia, Pa, Nov 28, 43; m 66, Margaret Jeffrey; c Mike & Doug. *Educ:* Pa State Univ, BS, 65; Univ Conn, PhD(genetics), 76. *Prof Exp:* Teaching asst genetics & biol, Univ Conn, 70-74, NIH cell biol trainee, 74-76, instr, 75; asst prof genetics & microbiol, Smith Col, 76-80. *Concurrent Pos:* Proj dir, Genetics Prog, Smith Col, 77 & Med & Liberal Arts Prog, 78; vis scientist molecular genetics & prin investr spontaneous mutation res, Mass Inst Technol, 80-81; invited guest ed, Am Biol Teacher, 84. *Mem:* AAAS; Am Soc Microbiol; Nat Asn Biol Teachers; Sigma Xi; Soc Indust Microbiol. *Res:* Biodegradation and bioremediation; biocides; industrial microbiology; water sanitization; management of industrial research. *Mailing Add:* Olin Res Ctr PO Box 586 Cheshire CT 06410-0586. *Fax:* 203-271-4351

GEIGER, KLAUS WILHELM, NUCLEAR PHYSICS. *Current Pos:* RETIRED. *Personal Data:* b Berlin, Ger, Apr 26, 21; Can citizen; m 47; c 2. *Educ:* Univ Mainz, PhD, 51. *Prof Exp:* Univ Tubingen, 49; Res asst nuclear physics, Max Planck Inst Chem, Ger, 49-52; fel, Nat Res Coun Can, 52-54, res officer physics, 54-85. *Concurrent Pos:* Guest worker, Nat Res Coun Can, 85-86. *Mem:* Can Asn Physicists. *Res:* Radioactivity; cosmic rays; neutron standardization; neutron dosimetry; neutron spectra; photon dosimetry; electron dosimetry. *Mailing Add:* 865 Chapman Blvd Ottawa ON K1G 1V1 Can

GEIGER, PAUL FRANK, PHARMACOLOGY. *Current Pos:* From asst prof to assoc prof, 67-75, PROF PHARMACOL, NORTHEAST LA UNIV, 75- *Personal Data:* b Meadville, Pa, July 12, 32; m 62; c 2. *Educ:* Univ Tex, BA, 55, BS, 58, MS, 62, PhD(pharmacol), 66. *Mem:* Soc Neurosci; Soc Toxicol. *Res:* Effects of acetylcholine and biogenic amines on cholinesterase on drugs affecting the central nervous system; biochemical seizures; neuropharmacology and toxicology. *Mailing Add:* Div Pharmacol Northeast La Univ 700 University Ave Monroe LA 71209-0001

GEIGER, PAUL JEROME, BIOCHEMISTRY. *Current Pos:* RETIRED. *Personal Data:* b Los Angeles, Calif, Jan 12, 30; m 62. *Educ:* Univ Calif, Berkeley, BS, 51; Johns Hopkins Univ, PhD(biochem), 62. *Prof Exp:* Res engr, Jet Propulsion Lab, Calif Inst Technol, 62, sr scientist, 62-68; res scientist, Biosci Lab, Dow Chem Co, 68-69; NIH res fel pharmacol, Univ Southern Calif, 69, asst prof, 69-73, assoc prof, 73-93. *Concurrent Pos:* Consult, Jet Propulsion Lab, Calif Inst Technol, 71. *Mem:* AAAS; Am Chem Soc; Sigma Xi. *Res:* Enzymology; kinetics of dehydrogenases; sulfhydryl structures; extraterrestrial biology and soil science; life detection on planets; detection of organic substances in arid soils; analytical biochemistry; intermediary metabolism of phosphate compounds; biochemical disorders in disease. *Mailing Add:* 8022 Hill Dr Sebastopol CA 95472

GEIGER, RANDALL L, ELECTRICAL ENGINEERING, MATHEMATICAL STATISTICS. *Current Pos:* PROF ELEC ENG & CHMN, IOWA STATE UNIV, 90- *Personal Data:* b Lexington, Nebr, May 17, 49; m 73; c 3. *Educ:* Univ Nebr, Lincoln, BS, 72, MS, 73; Colo State Univ, PhD(elec eng), 77. *Prof Exp:* Prof elec eng, Tex A&M Univ, 77-90. *Concurrent Pos:* Pres, World Instr Inc, 82-85. *Mem:* Fel Inst Elec & Electronics Engrs; Audio Eng Soc. *Res:* Very-large-scale integration circuit design; analog methodologies; high frequency monolithic filter design; switched capacitor applications; biomedical applications; specialized amplifier design. *Mailing Add:* 2374 220th St Boone IA 50036

GEIGER, WILLIAM EBLING, JR, ANALYTICAL CHEMISTRY. *Current Pos:* assoc prof, 74-77, ASSOC PROF CHEM, UNIV VT, 77- *Personal Data:* b Buffalo, NY, Feb 11, 44; m 65; c 2. *Educ:* Canisius Col, BS, 65; Cornell Univ, PhD(anal chem), 69. *Prof Exp:* Res fel, Northwestern Univ, 69-70; asst prof chem, Southern Ill Univ, 70-74. *Mem:* Am Chem Soc. *Res:* Electroanalytical chemistry; organometallic and transition metal electrochemistry; elucidation of electronic structures by electron spin resonance; radical ion molecular complexes. *Mailing Add:* Dept Chem Univ Vt Cook Sci Complex Burlington VT 05405-0001

GEIGES, K S, ELECTRICAL EQUIPMENT, SAFETY STANDARDS. *Current Pos:* RETIRED. *Personal Data:* b Providence, RI, Aug 24, 08. *Educ:* NJ Inst Technol, BS, 28; Stevens Inst Technol, MS, 43. *Honors & Awards:* Astin-Polk Medal, Am Nat Stand Inst, 78. *Prof Exp:* Vpres, Underwriters Labs, 28-88. *Concurrent Pos:* US Rep, Int Electrotech Comn. *Mem:* Fel Inst Elec & Electronics Engrs. *Mailing Add:* 131 E 18th St Apt 3 Costa Mesa CA 92627

GEIL, PHILLIP H, POLYMER PHYSICS. *Current Pos:* PROF POLYMER DIV, DEPT MAT SCI & ENG, UNIV ILL, 79- *Personal Data:* b Milwaukee, Wis, Sept 26, 30; m 77, Tammar Koehn; c Timothy, Andrew, Judith, Rebecca & Sharon. *Educ:* Wis State Col, Milwaukee, BS, 52; Univ Wis, MS, 54, PhD(physics), 57. *Prof Exp:* Res physicist, E I du Pont de Nemours & Co, 56-62; sr res physicist, Res Triangle Inst, 62-63; from assoc prof to prof polymer sci & eng, Case Western Res Univ, 63-79. *Concurrent Pos:* Ed, J Macromolecular Sci (Physics), 63-; assoc dir, Nat Ctr Composite Mat Res, 86-90. *Mem:* Am Phys Soc; Am Chem Soc; Soc Plastics Eng. *Res:* Polymer physics; relationship of polymer morphology to physical properties; mechanisms of polymer crystallization and deformation; polymer matrix composites; liquid crystal polymers. *Mailing Add:* Polymer Division Dept Mat Sci & Eng Univ Ill 1304 W Green St Urbana IL 61801. *Fax:* 217-333-2736; *E-Mail:* geil@uiuc.edu

GEILKER, CHARLES DON, ASTRONOMY, PHYSICS. *Current Pos:* assoc prof physics & astron, 68-77, PROF PHYSICS, WILLIAM JEWELL COL, 77-, CHMN DEPT, 80- *Personal Data:* b Kingston, Mo, Dec 15, 33; m 58, Neita Frohmuth; c Emily & Eric. *Educ:* William Jewell Col, AB, 55; Vanderbilt Univ, MA, 57; Case Western Res Univ, PhD(astron), 68. *Prof Exp:* Instr radiation physics, USPHS, 57-62; res assoc astron, Observ, Vanderbilt Univ, 62-64. *Mem:* Am Asn Physics Teachers; Health Physics Soc; Sigma Xi; AAAS; Astron Soc Pac. *Res:* Electronic and optical instrumentation; astronomical photoelectric and photographic photometry; microcomputers. *Mailing Add:* 471 E Kansas Liberty MO 64068. *Fax:* 816-514-5027

GEINISMAN, YURI, NEUROBIOLOGY. *Current Pos:* asst prof, 75-77, ASSOC PROF ANAT, MED SCH, NORTHWESTERN UNIV, CHICAGO, 77- *Personal Data:* b Kiev, Ukraine, USSR, Aug 7, 31; US citizen; m 71; c 1. *Educ:* First Moscow Med Univ, MD, 56; USSR Acad Sci, PhD(neuroanat), 62, DMS, 74. *Prof Exp:* Jr sci worker neuroanat, Inst Higher Nerv Activ & Neurophysiol, USSR Acad Sci, 62-66; guest scientist, Dept Anat, Semmelweis Univ Med Sch, Budapest, Hungary, 67-68; sr sci worker neuroanat, Inst Higher Nerv Activ & Neurophysiol, USSR Acad Sci, 68-74. *Mem:* Am Soc Neurosci; Am Asn Anat; AAAS; Sigma Xi. *Res:* Structural and metabolic basis of manifestations of aging process and post-lesion plasticity in the central nervous system. *Mailing Add:* Dept Cell Biol & Anat Northwestern Univ Med Sch 303 E Chicago Ave Chicago IL 60611

GEIS, AELRED DEAN, BIOLOGY. *Current Pos:* RES DIR, WILDBIRD CTRS AM, 91; CONSULT. *Personal Data:* b Chicago, Ill, July 23, 29; m 51; c 1. *Educ:* Mich State Univ, BS, 51, MS, 52, PhD, 56. *Prof Exp:* Instr, Mich State Univ, 53-56; surv statistician, Bur Sport Fisheries & Wildlife, US Fish & Wildlife Serv, Patuxent Wildlife Res Ctr, 56-58, wildlife res biologist & asst chief sect, Migratory Bird Pop Sta, 62-70, migratory bird specialist, Migratory Bird Pop Sta, 70-72, urban wildlife specialist, 72-89. *Mem:* Am Ornithologist Union; Wildlife Soc. *Res:* Wildlife population dynamics, survey methods and biology. *Mailing Add:* PO Box 334 Clarksville MD 21029

GEISBUHLER, TIMOTHY PAUL, NUCLEOTIDE METABOLISM, CHROMATOGRAPHY. *Current Pos:* ASSOC PROF, DEPT PHYSIOL, KIRKSVILLE COL OSTEOP MED. *Personal Data:* b Woodville, Ohio, July 16, 54; m 86. *Educ:* Bowling Green State Univ, BS, 76; Univ Cincinnati, MS, 79; Ohio State Univ, PhD(physiol chem), 83. *Prof Exp:* Res assoc, Univ Mo, 83-86, res asst prof physiol, 86- *Mem:* Am Physiol Soc; Int Soc Heart Res. *Res:* Biochemistry and physiology of diseased heart, with special emphasis on metabolic defects associated with myocardial ischemia; metabolism of nucleotides and nucleosides in healthy and diseased tissues. *Mailing Add:* Dept Physiol Kirksville Col Osteop Med 800 W Jefferson Kirksville MO 63501

GEISE, MARIE CLABEAUX, PHYSICAL ANTHROPOLOGY. *Current Pos:* assoc prof anthrop & chmn dept, 73-80, PROF ANTHROP, STATE UNIV NY COL BUFFALO, 80- *Personal Data:* b Buffalo, NY, July 5, 41. *Educ:* State Univ NY Buffalo, BA, 63, MA, 66, PhD(phys anthrop), 67. *Prof Exp:* Lectr anthrop, Lehman Col, 66-67, from instr to assoc prof, 67-73. *Mem:* AAAS; fel Am Asn Phys Anthrop; Am Anthrop Asn; Human Biol Coun; Int Ref Orgn Forensic Med & Sci. *Res:* Palaeopathology of the pre-Columbian Indians of North America; physical and cultural environmental determinants of disease patterns in skeletal populations; methodology and analysis in osteology; forensic anthropology; biomedical anthropology. *Mailing Add:* Dept Anthrop State Univ NY Col Buffalo NY 14222

GEISER, URS WALTER, ORGANIC CONDUCTORS & SUPERCONDUCTORS, STRUCTURE-PROPERTIES RELATIONSHIPS IN ELECTRONIC MATERIALS. *Current Pos:* Fel, 85-88, asst chemist, 88-92, CHEMIST, ARGONNE NAT LAB, 93- *Personal Data:* b St Gallen, Switz, Nov 10, 56. *Educ:* Univ Bern, Switz, Lic Phil Nat, 80; Wash State Univ, PhD(chem), 85. *Mem:* Am Chem Soc; Am Crystallog Asn; Sigma Xi. *Res:* Crystal structures of organic conductors and superconductors and their relationship with physical properties: conductivity, superconductivity, magnetism. *Mailing Add:* Chem & Mat Sci Div Argonne Nat Lab Argonne IL 60439. *Fax:* 630-252-9151; *E-Mail:* geiser@anchx4.chm.anl.gov

GEISLER, C(HRIS) D(ANIEL), BIOENGINEERING, NEUROPHYSIOLOGY. *Current Pos:* from asst prof to prof, 62-96, EMER PROF ELEC & COMPUT ENG & NEUROPHYSIOL, UNIV WIS-MADISON, 96- *Personal Data:* b New York, NY, Jan 10, 33; m 61; c 2. *Educ:* Mass Inst Technol, BS & MS, 56, ScD, 61. *Prof Exp:* Assoc biocommun, Air Force Res & Develop Command, 60-61; mem tech staff, Bell Tel Labs, 61-62. *Mem:* Fel Am Sci Affiliation; sr mem Inst Elec & Electronics Engrs; fel Acoust Soc; Am Soc Neurosci. *Res:* Quantitative study of the inner ear, including single-neuron recordings and mathematical models; auditory physiology and neurophysiology; sensory prosthesis. *Mailing Add:* Dept Neurophysiol Univ Wis Madison WI 53706. *Fax:* 608-265-3500

GEISLER, FRED HARDEN, MEDICAL PHYSIOLOGY. *Current Pos:* surg resident, 78-79, RES ASSOC MED PHYSIOL, BUFFALO GEN HOSP, NEUROSURG RESIDENT. *Personal Data:* b Chicago, Ill, Mar 2, 47; m 68; c 1. *Educ:* Case Inst Technol, BS, 67; Washington Univ, AM, 69, PhD(physics), 72; State Univ NY Buffalo, MO, 78. *Prof Exp:* Res assoc physics, Brookhaven Nat Lab, 72-74. *Mem:* Sigma Xi; Am Phys Soc; AAAS; AMA. *Res:* Measurement of cardio-pulmonary function in the intensive care hospital unit and patient management utilizing multidimensional computer analysis. *Mailing Add:* 3045 Normandy Pl Evanston IL 60201-1805

GEISLER, GRACE SR, biology, embryology; deceased, see previous edition for last biography

GEISLER, JOHN EDMUND, DYNAMIC METEOROLOGY. *Current Pos:* HEAD DEPT METEOROL, UNIV UTAH. *Personal Data:* b Pittsburgh, Pa, Apr 9, 34; m 74; c 2. *Educ:* Fla State Univ, BS, 59; Univ Ill, PhD(astron), 65. *Prof Exp:* Sr sci officer aeronomy, Radio & Space Res Sta, Slough, Eng, 65-67; res assoc meteorol, Mass Inst Technol, 67-68; from asst prof to assoc prof, 68-75, prof meteorol, Univ Miami, 75- *Concurrent Pos:* Chief scientist meteorol, Off Climate Dynamics, NSF, 75- *Mem:* Am Meteorol Soc. *Res:* Numerical models of large-scale atmospheric waves; climate models. *Mailing Add:* Dept Meteorol Univ Utah 819 Wm Browning Salt Lake City UT 84112-1107

GEISMAN, RAYMOND AUGUST, SR, ANALYTICAL CHEMISTRY, CHEMICAL ENGINEERING. *Current Pos:* RETIRED. *Personal Data:* b St Louis, Mo, Oct 14, 21; m 52, Mary P Abels; c Barbara A, Raymond A Jr & Richard A. *Educ:* Wash Univ, BS, 43, MS, 44 & 54. *Prof Exp:* Anal chemist, Scullin Steel Co, 42-44; prod supvr indust org chem, Monsanto Co, 46-49, asst chief chemist, 49-51, prod supvr indust chem, 51-53, sales engr, 53-55, chief chemist, 55-77, prin engr, 77-87. *Mem:* Am Chem Soc; Am Inst Chem Engrs; Sigma Xi; Instrument Soc Am. *Mailing Add:* 6231 Delor St Louis MO 63109

GEISON, RONALD LEON, BIOCHEMISTRY, NUTRITION. *Current Pos:* CHEMIST, SIGMA CHEM CO, 75- *Educ:* Univ Ill, PhD(nutrit biochem), 65. *Res:* Preparation of synthetic and natural products, lipids. *Mailing Add:* Sigma Chem Co PO Box 14508 St Louis MO 63178-9916. *Fax:* 573-771-3814

GEISS, GUNTHER R(ICHARD), SYSTEMS ANALYSIS, INFORMATION TECHNOLOGY. *Current Pos:* vis assoc prof, Inst Marine Sci, Adelphi Univ, 72, from asst prof to assoc prof, 72-83, prof, Sch Social Work, 83-92, dir, Fac Support Lab, 89-92, PROF, SCH BUS, ADELPHI UNIV, 92- *Personal Data:* b New York, NY, Oct 1, 38; m 62, Carole Fisk; c Christopher & Karin. *Educ:* Polytech Inst Brooklyn, BEE, 59, MEE, 60, PhD(elec eng), 64. *Honors & Awards:* Husita 2 Award. *Prof Exp:* Instr elec technol, Brooklyn Community Col, 60-61; res engr control theory res dept, Grumman Aircraft Eng Corp, 61-64, group leader, 64-69; dir systs sci div, Poseidon Sci Corp, NY, 69-71; mgr NY off, Skills Conversion Proj, Nat Soc Prof Engrs, 71-72. *Concurrent Pos:* Lectr, Polytech Inst New York, 61-75, adj prof, dept elec eng, 75-, adj prof chem eng, 82; chmn, Oil Spillage Bd, Huntington, NY, 71-73; adj prof, Sch Bus, Adelphi Univ, 73-79 & Prog Training for Pub & Community Social Serv, State Univ NY Stonybrook. *Mem:* AAAS; Inst Elec & Electronics Engrs; Sigma Xi; Asn Comput Mach. *Res:* Application of systems theory and computer technology to problems of education and society. *Mailing Add:* 8 Meadowlark Lane Huntington NY 11743-6508. *E-Mail:* geiss@auvax1.adelphi.edu

GEISS, ROY HOWARD, ELECTRON MICROSCOPY. *Current Pos:* RES STAFF, IBM RES LAB, 73- *Personal Data:* b Reading, Pa, Apr 17, 37; div; c 2. *Educ:* Lafayette Col, BS, 59; Cornell Univ, PhD(appl physics), 68. *Prof Exp:* Res physicist, Carpenter Steel Corp, 59-63; sr scientist mat sci, Univ Va, 67-73. *Concurrent Pos:* Mat anal consult, US Army Foreign Sci & Technol Ctr, 72-73. *Mem:* Electron Micro Soc Am; Am Crystallog Asn; Am Soc Metals; Am Inst Mining, Metall & Petrol Engrs. *Res:* Use of transmission electron microscopy to study microstructural parameters of magnetic thin films; analytical electron microscopy including EDS and micro-diffraction; develop new techniques for use of instruments. *Mailing Add:* 15575 Via Veneto Morgan Hill CA 95037

GEISSER, SEYMOUR, MATHEMATICAL STATISTICS. *Current Pos:* PROF STATIST & DIR SCH, UNIV MINN, MINNEAPOLIS, 71- *Personal Data:* b Bronx, NY, Oct 5, 29; m 55, 82, Anne Flaxman; c Mindy, Dan, Georgia & Adam. *Educ:* City Col New York, BA, 50; Univ NC, MA, 52, PhD(math statist), 55. *Prof Exp:* Sr asst scientist, USPHS, 55-57, mathematician, NIMH, NIH, 57-61, chief biomet sect, Nat Inst Arthritis & Metab Dis, 61-65; prof math statist & chmn dept, State Univ NY Buffalo, 65-71. *Concurrent Pos:* Lectr, USDA Grad Sch, 56-60; vis assoc prof, Iowa State Univ, 60; prof lectr, George Washington Univ, 60-65; vis prof, Univ Wis, 64; NSF vis lectr, 66-69; vis prof, Univ Tel-Aviv, Israel, 71, Carnegie-Mellon Univ, 76, Stanford Univ, 77, Univ Orange Free State, 78, Harvard Sch Pub Health, 81, Univ Chicago, 85, Univ Warrick 86 & Stanford Univ, 88; chmn, Panel Occup Safety & Health Statist, Nat Acad Sci, 86-87; Lady Davis vis prof, Hebrew Univ, Jerusalem, Israel, 91 & 94; vis prof, Univ Moderia, Italy, 96. *Mem:* Fel Am Statist Asn; Biomet Soc; fel Inst Math Statist; fel Royal Statist Soc; Int Statist Inst; Bernoulli Soc. *Res:* Biometrics; statistics; research in multivariate analysis; Bayesian inference; predictivism; sample reuse, classification; model selection. *Mailing Add:* Sch Statist 270 Vincent Hall Univ Minn 206 Church St SE Minneapolis MN 55455. *Fax:* 612-624-8868; *E-Mail:* geisser@umnstat.stat.umn.edu

GEISSINGER, LADNOR DALE, COMBINATORICS, APPLICATION GROUP CHARACTERS. *Current Pos:* assoc prof, 67-77, PROF MATH, UNIV NC, CHAPEL HILL, 77- *Personal Data:* b Palm, Pa, Apr 23, 38; m 60, Shirley Burry; c Amy, Eric & Anne. *Educ:* Bluffton Col, BS, 59; Ind Univ, PhD(math), 63. *Prof Exp:* Asst prof math, Purdue Univ, 63-67. *Concurrent Pos:* Vis lectr, Univ Ulm, Ger, 77-78. *Mem:* Am Math Soc; Math Asn Am; Sigma Xi. *Res:* Representation of groups; foundations of combinatorial theory; applications in chemistry and physics of finite symmetry groups. *Mailing Add:* 1105 Old Lystra Rd Chapel Hill NC 27514-9167. *E-Mail:* geissing@math.unc.edu

GEISSLER, PAUL ROBERT, CHEMICAL KINETICS. *Current Pos:* MEM STAFF, EXXON CHEM CO, 76- *Personal Data:* b New York, NY, Jan 19, 32; m 60; c 3. *Educ:* St Peter's Col, BS, 53; Fordham Univ, MS, 56; Univ Wis, PhD(phys chem), 62. *Prof Exp:* From res chemist to sr res chemist, Esso Res & Eng Co, Standard Oil Co, NJ, 62-68, res assoc, 68-76. *Mem:* Am Chem Soc. *Res:* Effect of neutron activation of organic liquids and solutions; radiation chemistry of hydrocarbon alkyl halide solutions; exploratory aromatic research; process optimization via mechanistic and kinetic studies; supercritical fluid chromatography. *Mailing Add:* 3848 Lake Latania Circle Baton Rouge LA 70816-4318

GEISSMAN, JOHN WILLIAM, PALEOMAGNETIST, TECTONOPHYSICIST. *Current Pos:* ASST PROF GEOL, COLO SCH MINES, 80- *Personal Data:* b Rockford, Ill, Oct 29, 52; m 75. *Educ:* Univ Mich, BS, 73, MS, 76, PhD(geol), 80. *Prof Exp:* Student & lectr geol, Univ Mich, 77-79; fel & lectr, Univ Toronto, 79-80. *Concurrent Pos:* Consult, Anaconda Minerals Co, 81-; prin investr, Dept Energy grants, Colo Sch Mines, 81-, NSF grants, 82- *Mem:* Am Geophys Union; Sigma Xi. *Res:* Application of paleomagnetic research to problems in structural geology, economic geology and diagenesis. *Mailing Add:* Univ NMex Main Campus Northrop Hall Albuquerque NM 87131-1116

GEIST, J(OHN) C(HARLES), COMMUNICATIONS. *Current Pos:* RETIRED. *Personal Data:* b Baltimore Co, Md, Sept 20, 15; m 38; c 2. *Educ:* Univ Del, BEE, 37. *Prof Exp:* Test engr, Gen Elec Co, 37-38; jr engr, Hadley Transformer Corp, 39; test engr, Westinghouse Mfg Corp, 40; radio engr, Signal Corps, US Army, 41; systs engr, Link Radio Corp, 46-47; commun engr, Appl Physics Lab, Johns Hopkins Univ, 48; missile systs engr, Vitro Corp Am, 48-58, mgr tech opers, Silver Spring Lab, 58-60, assoc dir, 60-70, vpres, Vitro Labs, 70-80. *Mem:* Sr mem Inst Elec & Electronics Engrs; Am Phys Soc. *Res:* Telemetering; missile guidance; computer applications. *Mailing Add:* 2205 Henderson Ave Silver Spring MD 20902

GEIST, VALERIUS, ZOOLOGY, ETHOLOGY. *Current Pos:* Asst prof, Environ Sci Ctr, Univ Calgary, 68-71, prog dir environ sci, Fac Environ Design, 71-75, assoc prof zool, 71-76, assoc dean, Fac Environ Design, 77-80, prog dir environ sci, Fac Design, 91-94, prof, 76-95, EMER PROF ENVIRON SCI, UNIV CALGARY, 95- *Personal Data:* b Nikolajew, Russ, Feb 2, 38; Can citizen; m 61; c 3. *Educ:* Univ BC, BSc, 60, PhD(zool), 67. *Concurrent Pos:* Nat Res Coun fel, Max Planck Inst Physiol Behav, 67-68; mem, Subcomt Conserv Terrestrial Communities, Can Comt Int Biol Prog, 69-76; Sci Adv Comt, World Wildlife Fund Can, 82-; coun, Can Soc Zoologists, 82-; dir, Alta Soc Prof Biologists; pres, Calgary Chap, Sigma Xi, 85-86; mem, Species Survival Comn, Int Union Conserv Nature & Animals. *Mem:* Wildlife Soc; Can Soc Zool; Can Soc Environ Biol; fel AAAS; Sigma Xi. *Res:* Behavior and evolution of large mammals, especially ungulates; relation between ecology and social behavior; evolution of Ice Age mammals; human biology in relation to environmental design. *Mailing Add:* Fac Environ Design Univ Calgary 2500 University Dr NW Calgary AB T2N 1N4 Can. *Fax:* 250-723-7436

GEISTERFER-LOWRANCE, ANJA A T, CARDIOLOGY. *Current Pos:* POSTDOCTORAL FEL, CARDIOVASC DIV, BRIGHAM & WOMEN'S HOSP, HARVARD MED SCH, 83- *Personal Data:* Can citizen. *Educ:* Univ Guelph, Can, BSc, 82; Univ Va, PhD(physiol), 89. *Prof Exp:* Res asst, Dept Chem, Univ Guelph, 81-83. *Concurrent Pos:* Paul Dudley White fel, 91. *Res:* Author of numerous publications. *Mailing Add:* 4142 Magnolia Ct Kankakee IL 60901. *Fax:* 617-732-7663

GEITZ, R(OBERT) C(HARLES), MECHANICAL ENGINEERING. *Current Pos:* PRES, GEITZ ENG CO, 81- *Personal Data:* b McKeesport, Pa, Oct 23, 19; m 52; c 5. *Educ:* Calif Inst Technol, BS, 41; Univ Pittsburgh, PhD(chem eng), 51. *Prof Exp:* Chem engr, E I du Pont de Nemours & Co, 41-43; partner, Calif Natural Prod, 48-49; sect chief org process develop, Res & Develop Div, Lever Bros, 49-56; group mgr res & develop, Am Mach & Foundry Co, 56-61; pres, Geitz Eng Co, 62-74; pres, 74-81, PROF CHEM ENG, SPRINGFIELD TECH COMMUNITY COL, 68- *Mem:* Sigma Xi; Am Inst Chem Engrs; Am Soc Mech Engrs; Am Chem Soc; AAAS. *Res:* Organic chemical development and manufacture of detergents; product and process development; tobacco sheet and paper; application of mechanical engineering techniques to process industries; laboratory equipment; non-soap bars; process plant design and erection; closed die forging. *Mailing Add:* PO Box 207 Suffield CT 06078

GELATT, CHARLES DANIEL, JR, SOFTWARE SYSTEMS, SOLID STATE PHYSICS. *Current Pos:* PRES, NORTHERN MICROGRAPHICS, INC, 83-; PRES, NMT CORP, 86- *Personal Data:* b La Crosse, Wis, Sept 5, 47; m 69; c 2. *Educ:* Univ Wis-Madison, BA & MS, 69; Harvard Univ, PhD(physics), 74. *Honors & Awards:* Indust Applns Physics Award, Am Inst Physics, 87. *Prof Exp:* Asst prof physics, Harvard Univ, 75-80; mem staff, Thomas J Watson Res Ctr, IBM Corp, 79-82. *Concurrent Pos:* Mem syst bd regents, Univ Wis; bd dirs, Prin Mutual Life Ins Co, Des Moines, Iowa. *Mem:* Am Phys Soc; Inst Elec & Electronics Engrs; Asn Comput Mach; AAAS. *Res:* Theoretical solid state physics; cohesion of transition metal elements and compounds; simulated annealing for optimization; computer graphics. *Mailing Add:* PO Box 2287 La Crosse WI 54602

GELB, ARTHUR, NONLINEAR CONTROL SYSTEMS, ELECTRICAL ENGINEERING. *Current Pos:* PRES, ANALYTIC SCI CORP, 66- *Personal Data:* b New York, NY, Sept 20, 37; m 58; c 3. *Educ:* City Col New York, BEE, 58; Harvard Univ, MS, 59; Mass Inst Technol, DSc, 61. *Prof Exp:* Mgr systs anal, Dynamics Res Corp, 61-66. *Concurrent Pos:* Chmn, MIT Ctr Technol, 87- *Mem:* Fel Inst Elec & Electronics Engrs; fel Am Inst Aeronaut & Astronaut; Sigma Xi. *Res:* Optimal methods of navigation guidance and control; optimal estimation applications; nonlinear control systems. *Mailing Add:* 135 Marsh St Reading MA 02178

GELB, MICHAEL H, CHEMISTRY, BIOCHEMISTRY. *Current Pos:* From asst prof to assoc prof chem, 85-95, PROF CHEM & BIOCHEM, UNIV WASH, SEATTLE, 95- *Personal Data:* m, Heidi Horowitz; c Anna & Max. *Educ:* Univ Calif, Davis, BS, 79; Yale Univ, PhD, 82. *Honors & Awards:* Award for Excellence in Chem, ICI Pharmaceut Group, 91; Pfizer Enzyme Chem Award, Am Chem Soc, 93. *Concurrent Pos:* From adj asst prof to adj assoc prof biochem, Univ Wash, 85-95. *Mem:* Am Chem Soc; Am Soc Biochem & Molecular Biol; Int Union Pure & Appl Chem. *Res:* Mechanistic and medicinal enzymology; lipolytic enzymes; protein prenylation; parasitology; clinical enzymology. *Mailing Add:* Dept Chem & Biochem Univ Wash Box 351700 Seattle WA 98195

GELB, RICHARD LEE, TECHNICAL MANAGEMENT. *Current Pos:* exec vpres, Bristol-Myers Co, 65-67, pres, 67-76, chief exec officer, 72-94, chmn bd, 76-95, EMER CHMN, BRISTOL-MYERS CO, 95- *Personal Data:* b New York, NY, June 8, 24; m 51, Phyllis L Nason; c Lawrence N, Lucy G, Jane E & James M. *Educ:* Yale Univ, BA, 45, Harvard Univ, MBA, 50. *Prof Exp:* staff mem, Clairol Inc, New York, 50-59, pres, 59-64. *Mailing Add:* Bristol-Myers Squibb Co 345 Park Ave New York NY 10154

GELBAND, HENRY, CARDIAC ELECTROPHYSIOLOGY. *Current Pos:* from asst prof to assoc prof pediat & pharmacol, 71-77, PROF PEDIAT & PHARMACOL, SCH MED, UNIV MIAMI, 77-, DIR, DIV PEDIAT CARDIOL, 76- *Personal Data:* b Austria, Aug 31, 36; US citizen; wid; c 3. *Educ:* Washington & Jefferson Col, AB, 58; Jefferson Med Col, MD, 62. *Prof Exp:* Fel pediat cardiol, Col Physicians & Surgeons, Columbia Univ, 67-69, NIH spec res fel pharmacol, 69-71, vis fel pediat, 69-70, assoc pediat, 70-71. *Concurrent Pos:* Instr pediat, Mt Sinai Sch Med, 67-68; consult, Children's Med Servs, Health & Rehab Servs, Fla, 71- & chmn, Cardiac Adv Coun, 85-92; Basil O'Conner Res Award, Nat Found, March of Dimes, 74-76; prin investr, Nat Heart, Lung & Blood Inst, NIH, 76-89; examr for bd cert, Sub-Bd Pediat Cardiol, Am Bd Pediat, 83. *Mem:* Am Heart Asn; fel Am Acad Pediat (treas, 79-80, vchmn, 81-83); fel Am Col Cardiol; emer mem Soc Pediat Res; Am Soc Pharmacol & Exp Therapeut; NAm Soc Pacing & Electrophysiol. *Res:* Measurement of calcium fluxes across myocardial call in developing heart, its relationship to cardiac electro physiology and contractility as well as the use of calcium antagonists as antiarrhythmic agents. *Mailing Add:* Dept Pediat Sch Med Univ Miami PO Box 016960 (R-76) 1601 NW 12th Ave Rom 8008 Miami FL 33136. *Fax:* 305-243-6987

GELBARD, ALAN STEWART, ENZYMOLOGY, NUCLEAR MEDICINE. *Current Pos:* SR RES ASSOC, BIOCHEM DEPT, CORNELL UNIV MED COL, 93- *Personal Data:* b Brooklyn, NY, Mar 28, 34; m 66; c 2. *Educ:* Brooklyn Col, BS, 55; Univ Mass, MS, 56; Univ Wis, Madison, PhD(bact), 60. *Prof Exp:* Instr microbiol, State Univ NY Downstate Med Ctr, 59-62; res assoc, Mem Sloan-Kettering Cancer Ctr, 62-74, assoc, Biophys Lab, 75-78, assoc mem, 79-92. *Concurrent Pos:* Instr, Sloan Kettering Div, Grad Sch Med Sci, Cornell Univ, 69-75, asst prof biophys, 75-81, assoc prof, 81- *Mem:* Am Soc Microbiol; Soc Nuclear Med; AAAS. *Res:* Enzymatic synthesis of amino acids labeled with positron-emitting, short-lived isotopes; development of organ and tumor scanning agents; metabolism and enzyme synthesis during cell cycle of cultured tumor cells; in-vivo studies of tumor and organ metabolism. *Mailing Add:* 17 Bengeyfield Dr East Williston NY 11596-1931

GELBART, ABE, mathematics; deceased, see previous edition for last biography

GELBART, STEPHEN SAMUEL, NUMBER THEORY. *Current Pos:* PROF MATH, WEIZMANN INST SCI, REHOVOT, ISRAEL, 85- *Personal Data:* b Syracuse, NY, June 12, 46; m 68, Mary Glick; c Ben, Ruth & Daniel. *Educ:* Cornell Univ, BA, 67; Princeton Univ, MA, 68, PhD(math), 70. *Prof Exp:* Instr math, Rutgers Univ, Newark, 68-70 & Princeton Univ, 70-71; from asst prof to full prof math, Cornell Univ, 71-85. *Concurrent Pos:* Mem, Inst Advan Study, 72-73; Alfred P Sloan fel, 77-78; vis prof, Hebrew Univ, Jerusalem, 81-82, Tel-Aviv Univ, 83-84; ed, Israel J Math. *Mem:* Am Math Soc; Israel Math Union. *Res:* Automorphic forms, group representations and applications to number theory. *Mailing Add:* Dept Theoret Math Weizmann Inst Sci Rehovot 76100 Israel. *E-Mail:* mtgelbar@weizmann.bitnet

GELBART, WILLIAM M, CHEMICAL PHYSICS. *Current Pos:* assoc prof, 75-79, PROF CHEM, UNIV CALIF, LOS ANGELES, 79- *Personal Data:* b Syracuse, NY, June 12, 46; m 68; c 2. *Educ:* Harvard Univ, BS, 67; Univ Chicago, MS, 68, PhD(chem physics), 70. *Prof Exp:* NSF-NATO fel, Univ Paris, 70-71; Miller Inst fel, Univ Calif, Berkeley, 71-72, asst prof chem, 72-75. *Concurrent Pos:* Alfred P Sloan Found fel, 74-78; Camille & Henry Dreyfus Found teacher-scholar, 76-81; vis prof, Univ Paris, 77-78 & 82-83; mem adv bd, J Statist Physics, 78-82, J Phys Chem, 80-84, Liquid Crystals, 85-, Chem Physics Lett, 86-, Langmuir, 86-, Molecular Physics, 87-; Brotherton vis prof, Univ Leeds, 88. *Mem:* Fel Am Phys Soc; Am Chem Soc. *Res:* Theory of gas-phase molecular relaxation processes and photochemistry; light scattering and optical properties of simple fluids near and away from their critical points; orientational order in liquid crystals, polymeric systems, interfacial films and surfactant solutions. *Mailing Add:* Dept Chem Univ Calif 405 Hilgard Ave Los Angeles CA 90024-1301

GELBAUM, BERNARD RUSSELL, MATHEMATICS. *Current Pos:* RETIRED. *Personal Data:* b New York, NY, Feb 26, 22; m 42, Beatrice Lernev; c Daniel, David, Martin & Ethan. *Educ:* Columbia Univ, AB, 43; Princeton Univ, MA, 47, PhD(math), 48. *Prof Exp:* Instr math, Princeton Univ, 47-48; from asst prof to prof, Univ Minn, 48-64; prof & chmn, Univ Calif, Irvine, 64-68, assoc dean, Sch Phys Sci, 68-71; vpres acad affairs, State Univ NY, Buffalo, 71-74, prof math, 71-96. *Mem:* Am Math Soc. *Res:* Linear spaces; topological algebra; probability; functional analysis. *Mailing Add:* Dept Math State Univ NY Buffalo NY 14214-3093. *Fax:* 716-829-2299; *E-Mail:* mthgelb@newton.math.buffalo.edu

GELBER, RICHARD DAVID, BIOSTATISTICS. *Current Pos:* asst prof, Dept Biostatist, Sch Pub Health & Sidney Farber Cancer Inst, 77-83, ASSOC PROF, DEPT BIOSTATIST, DANA FARBER CANCER INST, HARVARD UNIV, 83- *Personal Data:* b Philadelphia, Pa, May 1, 47; m 69; c 2. *Educ:* Cornell Univ, BS, 69, PhD(oper res), 75; Stanford Univ, MS, 70. *Honors & Awards:* Robert Wenner Prize, 87; Farmitalia Carlo Erba Prize, 87. *Prof Exp:* Res asst prof statist, Sci & Statist Lab, State Univ NY, Buffalo, 75-77. *Concurrent Pos:* Statist & comput consult, Dean of Students Off, Cornell Univ, 73-75. *Mem:* Am Statist Asn; Biomet Soc; Am Soc Clin Oncol. *Res:* Application of statistical techniques to the conduct of clinical trials; special emphasis on sequential techniques; problems of ranking and selection; quality of life assessment; meta-analysis. *Mailing Add:* Div Biostatist Mayer Bldg Dana Farber Cancer Inst 44 Binney St Boston MA 02115

GELBERG, ALAN, ORGANIC CHEMISTRY, INFORMATION SCIENCE. *Current Pos:* chief chem info storage & retrieval staff, Sci Info Facil, Food & Drug Admin, 67-70, dir Mgt & Sci Info Systs Design Div, 70-72, dir, Drug Info Resources Div, Bur Drugs, 72-84, DEP CHIEF, SURVEILLANCE & DATA PROCESSING BR, CTR DRUG EVAL & RES, US FOOD & DRUG ADMIN, 85- *Personal Data:* b New York, NY, May 28, 28; m 57, Iris H Schiff; c Lawrence M, Rachel L & Kitty H. *Educ:* City Col New York, BS, 50; Univ Mo, MS, 53. *Prof Exp:* Asst chem, Univ Mo, 51-52, analy chemist, Agr Exp Sta, 52-53; org chemist, US Army Chem Res & Develop Labs, Md, 55-57, group leader, 57-59, org chemist, Chem Struct Retrieval Prog, 59-61, asst chief, Indust Liaison Off, 61-63; document scientist, Diamond (Alkali) Shamrock Co, 64-67. *Concurrent Pos:* Mem, US Army Chem Corps Info Retrieval Comt, 60-63, liaison rep to mod methods comt, Div Chem Technol, Nat Res Coun, 61-63; mem tech adv bd, J Chem Doc, 69-71; prof lectr, Am Univ, 69-80, adj prof, 81-88; assoc ed, Pesticides Index, 75-79; adj prof, Howard Univ, 89- *Mem:* Am Chem Soc; Sigma Xi; Chem Notation Asn (pres, 70); AAAS; Drug Info Asn. *Res:* Chemical information and structure retrieval; chemical line notations; automatic data processing equipment. *Mailing Add:* 5329 Strathmore Ave Kensington MD 20895. *Fax:* 301-443-9288

GELBKE, CLAUS-KONRAD, NUCLEAR STRUCTURE. *Current Pos:* assoc prof, 77-81, PROF PHYSICS, MICH STATE UNIV, 81-, UNIV DISTINGUISHED PROF, 90- *Personal Data:* b Celle, WGer, May 31, 47. *Educ:* Univ Heidelberg, dipl, 70, Dr rer nat, 73. *Prof Exp:* Vis asst nuclear physics, Max Planck Inst Nuclear Physics, 73-76; physicist nuclear physics, Lawrence Berkeley Lab, 76-77. *Concurrent Pos:* Vis, Brookhaven Nat Lab, 74, Univ Wash, 75; physicist, Lawrence Berkeley Lab, 78-79; Alfred P Sloan fel, 79-83. *Mem:* fel Am Phys Soc. *Res:* Nuclear reactions resulting from nucleus-nucleus collisions, including elastic and inelastic scattering, complete and incomplete fusion reactions, fragmentation reactions, fission and preequilibrium phenomena. *Mailing Add:* Cyclotron Lab & Dept Physics Mich State Univ East Lansing MI 48824

GELBOIN, HARRY VICTOR, BIOCHEMISTRY, CANCER RESEARCH. *Current Pos:* biochemist, NIH, 58-64, head chem sect, Carcinogenesis Studies Br, 64-66, CHIEF LAB MOLECULAR CARCINOGENESIS, NAT CANCER INST, NIH, 66- *Personal Data:* b Chicago, Ill, Dec 21, 29; m 51; c 4. *Educ:* Univ Ill, AB, 51; Univ Wis, MS, 56, PhD, 58. *Prof Exp:* Develop chemist, US Rubber Co, 51-54; asst biochem & cancer res, Univ Wis, 54-58. *Concurrent Pos:* Assoc ed, Cancer Res, 64; keynote speaker, Gordon Res Conf Cancer, 65; prin lectr, Franz Bielschowsky Mem, First Int Symp Molecular Biol, Carcino, NZ, 66; Claude Bernard award-vis prof, Univ Montreal, 70; lectr, Radiol Soc NAm, Ill, 70; prin lectr, US-Japan Coop Med Sci Prog, Charleston, SC, 73; Smith, Kline & French hon lectr, Univ Fla, Gainesville, 74, Univ Mich, 76; vis prof, Georgetown Univ, 78-81 & Hebrew Univ, Jerusalem, 85. *Mem:* Am Asn Cancer Res; Am Soc Biol Chemists; Am Soc Pharmacol & Exp Therapeut; AAAS; Int Soc Study Xenobiotics. *Res:* Biochemical mechanisms of carcinogenesis; drug and carcinogen metabolism; monoclonal antibody analyses of cytochromes P-450 and molecular biology of cytochromes P-450. *Mailing Add:* Lab Molecular Carcinogen NCI NIH Bldg 37 Rm 3E24 9000 Rockville Pike Bethesda MD 20892-0001. *Fax:* 301-496-8419

GELBWACHS, JERRY A, QUANTUM OPTICS, LASERS. *Current Pos:* HEAD OPTICAL PHYS DEPT & SR SCIENTIST, AEROSPACE CORP, 70- *Personal Data:* b New York, NY. *Educ:* City Col NY, BE, 65; Stanford Univ, MS, 66, PhD(elec eng), 70. *Honors & Awards:* Aerospace Corp Pres Sci Award. *Prof Exp:* NSF fel elec eng, 65-68, res asst lasers, Stanford Univ, 68-70. *Mem:* Am Phys Soc; sr mem Inst Elec & Electronics Engrs; fel Optical Soc Am. *Res:* Atomic resonance filters; trace vapor detection; laser remote sensing. *Mailing Add:* Aerospace Corp PO Box 92957 MS M2-253 Los Angeles CA 90009. *Fax:* 310-336-7055; *E-Mail:* gelbwachs@aero.org

GELDERLOOS, ORIN GLENN, ENVIRONMENTAL PHYSIOLOGY. *Current Pos:* from asst prof to assoc prof biol, 70-77, dir, Sci Learning Ctr, 79-83, PROF BIOL SCI, UNIV MICH, DEARBORN, 77-, PROF ENVIRON STUDIES, 81- *Personal Data:* b Grand Rapids, Mich, July 28, 39; m 66, Charlette Snocyink; c David G & Allen B. *Educ:* Calvin Col, BA, 61; Western Mich Univ, MA, 64; Northwestern Univ, PhD(environ biol), 70. *Prof Exp:* Instr high sch, Mich, 62-67. *Concurrent Pos:* NASA bio-space technol training prog, Wallops Island, 68; dir, environ study area, Univ Mich-Dearborn, 70-, dir environ studies prog, 75-; res assoc, Max-Planck Inst Physiol of Behav, Seewiesen, WGer; dir, comprehensive assistance to undergrad sci educ, NSF Grant, 78-82; dir, Rouge River Watershed Educ Proj, NSF grant, 89-93, Global Rivers Environ Educ, Network Teacher Enhancement Prog, 93-98. *Mem:* Animal Behav Soc; AAAS; Sigma Xi; Natural Areas Asn; Soc for Biol Rhythms. *Res:* Biological rhythms; microclimatology; mastery learning; urban ecology; bird migration; environmental physiology; environmental ethics and religion. *Mailing Add:* Dept Nat Sci Univ Mich 4901 Evergreen Rd Dearborn MI 48128-1491. *E-Mail:* ogg@umd@umich.edu

GELDMACHER, R(OBERT) C(ARL), ENGINEERING. *Current Pos:* head, Dept Elec Eng, 66-76, Burchard prof, 66-83, EMER PROF ELEC ENG, STEVENS INST TECHNOL, 83- *Personal Data:* b Elgin, Ill, Apr 22, 17; m 41; c 3. *Educ:* Northern Ill Univ, BE, 42; Purdue Univ, MA, 46; Northwestern Univ, PhD(elec eng), 59. *Prof Exp:* Asst prof eng mech, Purdue Univ, 47-53, assoc prof eng sci, 53-60; prof eng sci & assoc dean eng, NY Univ, 60-66. *Concurrent Pos:* Consult, Picatinny Arsenal, 52- *Mem:* Inst Elec & Electronics Engrs; Soc Indust & Appl Math. *Res:* Magnetomechanical solids; graph theory; network and system analysis and synthesis; applied elasticity. *Mailing Add:* 512 Headquarters Rd Erwinna PA 18920

GELDREICH, EDWIN E(MERY), AQUATIC MICROBIOLOGY. *Current Pos:* CONSULT, 96- *Personal Data:* b Cincinnati, Ohio, May 9, 22; m 50, Loretta M Eibel; c Pamela M & Linda L. *Educ:* Univ Cincinnati, AB, 47, MS, 48. *Honors & Awards:* Kimble Methodol Res Award, 55; Silver Medal, US Environ Protection Agency, 71; Regents' Water Microbiol Lectr, Univ Calif, 79; Res Award, Am Water Works Asn, 84; Bronze Medal, US Environ Prog, 84; Abel Wolman Award Excellence, 89; Allen Hazen lectr, 91. *Prof Exp:* Res bacteriologist, Robert A Taft Sanit Eng Ctr, USPHS, 48-67, res microbiologist, Nat Ctr Urban & Indust Health, 67-68, chief, Bact Sect, Div Water Hyg, Nat Environ Res Ctr, 68-72; chief microbiol, US environ Protection Agency, 72-85, sr res microbiologist, Drinking Water Res Div Werl, 85-95. *Concurrent Pos:* Dir water bacteriol lab eval serv; microbiol consult, Pan-Am Health Orgn, Brazil, spec microbiol consult, 69-88; spec microbiol consult, WHO, 72-; spec microbiol consult, Mediter Pilot study, UN Environ Prog, 76-87; chmn, Am Water Works Asn Organisms Water, 82-85, Joint Task Group, UN Environ Prog, 76-; vis microbiol, Am Soc Microbiol; mem, Task Force Group Drinking Water Qual, WHO, 79-81; mem, Paho Cholera investigation, Peru, 91; outbread invest, 90 & 93. *Mem:* Am Soc Microbiol; Am Water Works Asn; Int Asn Water Qual; fel Am Acad Microbiol. *Res:* Sanitary bacteriology; membrane filter techniques; rapid methods for the enumeration of bacterial indicators of pollution; biological tests for trace impurities in distilled water; microbiological contaminants in water supply; microbial criteria and standards; biofilms in water supply distribution; author 3 books. *Mailing Add:* 7330 Ticonderoga Ct Cincinnati OH 45230. *Fax:* 513-569-7185

GELEHRTER, THOMAS DAVID, MEDICAL GENETICS, CELL BIOLOGY. *Current Pos:* from assoc prof to prof internal med & human genetics, Med Sch, 74-87, dir, Div Med Genetics, 77-87, PROF & CHMN, DEPT HUMAN GENETICS, PROF INTERN MED, MED SCH, UNIV MICH, ANN ARBOR, 87- *Personal Data:* b Liberec, Czech, Mar 11, 36; US citizen; m 59, Barbara Keith; c Eric & Sarah. *Educ:* Oberlin Col, Ohio, BA, 57; Univ Oxford, Eng, MA, 59; Harvard Med Sch, MD, 63. *Honors & Awards:* Merit Award, Nat Cancer Inst, 88-95. *Prof Exp:* Intern & asst resident internal med, Mass Gen Hosp, Boston, 63-65; res assoc molecular biol, Nat Inst Arthritis & Metab Dis, NIH, Bethesda, Md, 65-69; fel med genetics, Univ Wash, Seattle, 69-70; asst prof human genetics, internal med & pediat, Sch Med, Yale Univ, New Haven, Conn, 70-73, assoc prof, 73-74. *Concurrent Pos:* Rhodes scholar, 57-59; vis scientist, Imp Cancer Res Fund Labs, London, 79-80; Macy Found fac scholar, 79-80; mem, Med Knowlege Self-Assessment Prog, Am Col Physicians, Genetics & Molecular Med Subcomt, chair 89-91, mem med adv bd, Gene Screen; bd dir, Am Soc Human Genetics, 93-96; Keeley vis fel, Wadham Col, Univ Oxford, 95, vis fel, Inst Molecular Med, 95. *Mem:* Am Soc Human Genetics; Am Soc Clin Invest; Am Soc Biol Chemists; Am Med Writers Asn; fel AAAS; fel Am Col Med Genetics. *Res:* Hormonal and cytokine regulation of gene expression in normal and transformed hepatocytes; molecular biology of plasminogen activation; biochemical and molecular genetic analysis of the cellular actions of glucocorticoids and cyclic nucleotides. *Mailing Add:* Dept Human Genetics Box 0618 Med Sch Univ Mich 1301 Catherine St Ann Arbor MI 48109-0618. *Fax:* 313-763-5831; *E-Mail:* tdgum@umich.edu

GELENBE, EROL, DISCRETE STOCHASTIC PROCESSES, NEURAL NETWORKS. *Current Pos:* PROF, DUKE UNIV, 93-, CHMN, DEPT ELEC ENG, 94- *Personal Data:* b Istanbul, Turkey, Aug 22, 45; Fr citizen; m 68, Deniz Arman; c Pamir. *Educ:* Mid East Tech Univ, BS, 66; Polytech Univ, NY, MS, 67, PhD(elec eng), 69; Univ Paris, DSc, 73. *Honors & Awards:* Silver Core, Inst Fedn Info Processing, 80. *Prof Exp:* Asst prof, Univ Mich, 70-72; res engr, Nat Inst Res Informatics & Automation, 72-73; prof, Univ Liege, 73-77; assoc prof, Univ Paris XI, 77-84, prof, Univ Paris V, 86-93; exec asst sci & technol, Ministry of Univs, France, 84-86. *Mem:* Fel Inst Elec & Electronics Engrs; Oper Res Soc Am; Inst Elec Engrs (London). *Res:* Electrical engineering; science and technology; computer performance evaluation; neural network models. *Mailing Add:* Duke Univ PO Box 90291 Durham NC 27708-0291

GELERINTER, EDWARD, CHEMICAL PHYSICS, LIQUID CRYSTAL PHYSICS. *Current Pos:* From asst prof to prof, 71-95, EMER PROF PHYSICS, KENT STATE UNIV, 95- *Personal Data:* b New York, NY, Oct 27, 36; m 63, Pearl E Balkin; c 3. *Educ:* City Col New York, BEE, 58; Cornell Univ, PhD(physics), 66. *Concurrent Pos:* Vis prof, Ben Gurion Univ Negev, Israel, 80-81; prin investr grants & contracts, NSF, Binational Sci Found, NIH & NASA, 88-89; Meyerhoff vis prof, Weizmann Inst Sci, Rehovot, Israel. *Mem:* Am Phys Soc; Int Liquid Crystal Soc; Sigma Xi. *Res:* Liquid crystal physics; spin label studies of glass formers: liquids, liquid crystals, polymers, etc. *Mailing Add:* Dept Physics Kent State Univ Kent OH 44242

GELERNTER, HERBERT LEO, PHYSICS, COMPUTER SCIENCE. *Current Pos:* PROF COMPUT SCI, STATE UNIV NY, STONY BROOK, 66- *Personal Data:* b Brooklyn, NY, Dec 17, 29; m 52; c 3. *Educ:* Brooklyn Col, BS, 51; Univ Rochester, PhD(physics), 56. *Prof Exp:* Staff physicist, IBM Res, NY, 56-58, staff physicist & mgr theory automata group, 58-60, sr physicist, 60-64, sr physicist & mgr physics & comput appln res group, 64-66. *Concurrent Pos:* Vis fel, Europ Orgn Nuclear Res, 60-61; mem ad hoc comt on-line data acquisition systs nuclear physics, Nat Res Coun-Nat Acad Sci, 68; Weizmann Mem Found fel, Weizmann Inst, Israel, 72-73. *Mem:* Am Phys Soc; Asn Comput Mach. *Res:* Simulation of intelligent behavior in machines; mathematical biophysics; computer applications in nuclear physics and chemistry; biomedical computer applications research. *Mailing Add:* 17 Old Field Rd A Stony Brook NY 11733

GELFAND, ALAN ENOCH, STATISTICS. *Current Pos:* Asst prof, 69-74, assoc prof, 74-79, PROF STATIST, UNIV CONN, 80- *Personal Data:* b New York, NY, Apr 17, 45; m 73; c 2. *Educ:* City Col New York, BS, 65; Stanford Univ, MS, 67, PhD(statist), 69. *Mem:* Fel Am Statist Asn; Int Statist Inst; Inst Math Statist. *Res:* Bocyerian computation; statistical interference; statistical modeling. *Mailing Add:* 14 Bicknell Rd Ashford CT 06278

GELFAND, DAVID H, MOLECULAR BIOLOGY. *Current Pos:* dir recombinant molecular res, 76-81, VPRES SCI AFFAIRS MOLECULAR GENETICS, CETUS CORP, 81- *Personal Data:* b New York, NY, June 9, 44; m 80; c 1. *Educ:* Brandeis Univ, AB, 66; Univ Calif, San Diego, PhD(biol), 70. *Prof Exp:* Postgrad res assoc biol, Univ Calif, San Diego, 70-72; lab mgr & asst res biochem, Univ Calif, San Francisco, 72-77. *Concurrent Pos:* Mem adv coun, NSF, 80-83. *Mem:* Am Soc Microbiol; AAAS; Am Soc Biol Chemists. *Res:* Isolation, characterization and expression of eukaryotic genes in bacteria, viral oncogenesis, mechanisms of RNA transcription and translation; study of mutations which increase plasmid copy number; isolation/characterization of thermostable DNA polymerases; in vitro DNA amplification. *Mailing Add:* Roche Molecular Syst Inc 1145 Atlantic Ave Alameda CA 94501. *Fax:* 510-814-2910

GELFAND, ERWIN WILLIAM, IMMUNOLOGY, PEDIATRICS. *Current Pos:* CHIEF DIV IMMUNOL & SR SCIENTIST, HOSP FOR SICK CHILDREN, 78- *Personal Data:* b Montreal, Que, Mar 10, 41; c 2. *Educ:* McGill Univ, BSc, 62, MD, 66. *Honors & Awards:* Mead Johnson Award Res Pediat; Queen Elizabeth II Scientist Award. *Prof Exp:* Res assoc, Max Planck Inst Immunobiol, 71-72; from asst prof to assoc prof pediat, Univ Toronto, 72-76. *Concurrent Pos:* Rotating internship, Montreal Children's Hosp, 66-67, jr asst resident, 67-68; sr resident, Children's Hosp Med Ctr, Boston, 68-69, fel med, 69-71; res fel, Harvard Med Sch, Boston, 69-71; Med Res Coun Can fel, 69-72; Queen Elizabeth II res scientist award, 75-81; Mead Johnson res award, 81. *Mem:* Am Fedn Clin Res; Am Asn Immunologists; Can Soc Immunol; Can Med Asn; Am Soc Clin Invest. *Res:* Cell differentiation; immunodeficiency diseases. *Mailing Add:* Dept Pediat Nat Jewish Med & Res Ctr 1400 Jackson St Denver CO 80206-2762

GELFAND, HENRY MORRIS, EPIDEMIOLOGY. *Current Pos:* RETIRED. *Personal Data:* b New York, NY, Jan 7, 20; m 46; c 4. *Educ:* Cornell Univ, BS, 40; Univ Chicago, MD, 50; Tulane Univ, MPH, 56. *Prof Exp:* Intern, USPHS Hosp, Staten Island, NY, 50-51; med entomologist, Liberian Inst, WAfrica, 51-53; assoc prof epidemiol, Sch Med, Tulane Univ, 53-59; chief, Enterovirus Unit, Commun Dis Ctr, 59-63, epidemiol adv, Nat Inst Commun Dis, Delhi, India, 63-65; spec asst res & eval, Smallpox Eradication Prog, Commun Dis Ctr, Ga, 65-68; epidemiologist, Foreign Quarantine Prog, London, Eng, 68-70; chief, Eval Br, Off Pop, USAID & mem staff, Off Int Health, USPHS, 70-72; prof & dir, Epidemiol Prog, Sch Pub Health, Univ Ill, 72-84; adj prof epidemiol, Sch Pub Health, Univ SC, 84. *Concurrent Pos:* Consult, Int Pub Health, WHO & USAID. *Mem:* Am Epidemiol Soc; Am Pub Health Asn; Int Epidemiol Soc; AAAS. *Res:* Epidemiology of infectious diseases; smallpox eradication; foreign quarantine; health programs evaluation; family planning. *Mailing Add:* 4509 Pinyon Dr Virginia Beach VA 23462

GELFAND, ISRAEL M, ALGEBRA ANALYSIS GEOMETRY TOPOLOGY REPRESENTATION THEORY, COMBINATORICS. *Current Pos:* DISTINGUISHED PROF, DEPT MATH, RUTGERS UNIV, 90- *Personal Data:* b Ukraine, Russia, Sept 2, 13; m 79, Tanya Alexeevskaya; c Sergey, Vladimir & Tanya. *Educ:* Moscow State Univ, DSc, 35. *Honors & Awards:* Wolfe Prize, Wolf Found, 78; Wigner Medal Achievements Math Physics, 79; Kyoto Prize, Inamory Found, 89; MacArthur Found Fel, 94. *Prof Exp:* Prof, Moscow Inst Appl Math, Moscow State Univ, 41-90. *Concurrent Pos:* Hon prof, Oxford Univ, 73, Harvard Univ, 76, Paris VI-VII. *Mem:* Nat Acad Sci; Acad Sci; Royal Soc Sweden. *Res:* Invention of Banach algebras; work on inverse problem Gelfand-Levifan equation; 6 volumes of generalized functions work on unitazy representations combinatorial chern-poutrigin classes; papers on cell biology and neurophysiology; generalized hypergeom, functions, non-commutative determinants; author of about 500 papers in almost all areas of mathematics. *Mailing Add:* Dept Math Rutgers Univ Piscataway NJ 08903. *E-Mail:* igelfand@math.rutgers.edu

GELFAND, JACK JACOB, INTELLIGENT SYSTEMS, COGNITIVE SCIENCE. *Current Pos:* res assoc, Princeton Univ, 72-75, res staff astrophys, Dept Astrophys Sci, 75-77, res staff physics, Dept Mech & Aerospace Eng, 77-85, group head, intelligent systs group, David Sarnoff Ctr, 85-89, RES SCIENTIST PSYCHOL, PRINCETON UNIV, 89- *Personal Data:* b Newark, NJ, Aug 5, 44; m 92, Linda Sproehnle; c Morgan. *Educ:* Rutgers Univ, BA, 66, PhD(phys chem), 71. *Prof Exp:* Res staff metall, Solid State Div, RCA, 71-72. *Mem:* Am Asn Artificial Intel; Soc Neurosci; Cognitive Sci Soc. *Res:* Intelligent decision-making system; computer brain modeling; cognitive neuroscience. *Mailing Add:* Dept Psychol Green Hall Princeton Univ Princeton NJ 08544. *Fax:* 609-258-1113; *E-Mail:* jjg@princeton.edu

GELFAND, NORMAN MATHEW, ACCELERATOR PHYSICS. *Current Pos:* MEM STAFF, FERMI NAT ACCELERATOR LAB, 79- *Personal Data:* b New York, NY, Jan 3, 39; m 79, Yona Keshev; c Joseph, Keren & Samuel. *Educ:* Columbia Univ, AB, 59, MA, 61, PhD(physics), 65. *Prof Exp:* Asst prof physics, Univ Chicago, 64-70, assoc prof, 70-80. *Concurrent Pos:* Sloan fel, 65-67; prog officer, NSF, 77-79. *Mem:* Am Phys Soc. *Res:* Computer studies of accelerator lattices; lattice simulations. *Mailing Add:* Fermi Nat Accelerator Lab MS 306 PO Box 500 Batavia IL 60510. *Fax:* 630-840-4552; *E-Mail:* gelfand@fnalv.fnal.gov

GELHAR, LYNN W, CIVIL & ENVIRONMENTAL ENGINEERING. *Current Pos:* from asst prof to assoc prof, 64-73, PROF CIVIL & ENVIRON ENG, MASS INST TECHNOL, 82- *Personal Data:* b July 15, 36. *Educ:* Univ Wis, BS, 59, MS, 60, PhD(civil eng), 64. *Honors & Awards:* Robert E Horton Award, Am Geophys Union, 82; O E Meinzer Award, Geol Soc Am, 87. *Prof Exp:* Civil engr, Soil Conserv Serv, USDA, Madison, Wis, 59-60; jr engr, Fairbanks Morse & Co, Beloit, Wis, 60-61; res asst & instr, Univ Wis-Madison, 61-64; from assoc prof to prof hydrol, NMex Inst Mining & Technol, Socorro, 73-82, prog coordr, 76-82. *Concurrent Pos:* Vis prof, Stanford Univ, Univ Karlsruhe, Sch Mines Paris, Royal Inst Technol, Stockholm, Swiss Fed Inst Technol, Univ Western Australia, Commonwealth Sci & Indust Res Orgn Australia & Lawrence Berkeley Lab; Ford postdoctoral fel, Mass Inst Tecchnol, 64-66 & William E Leonhard prof, 95-96; grad fel, NSF, 64; sabbatical, Stanford Univ, Calif, 71, Univ Karlsruhe & Ecole Mines Paris, 78, Royal Inst Technol, Stockholm, Swiss Fed Inst Technol, Zurich & Univ Western Australia, Perth, 86-87; mem, US Nat Comt, Int Asn Hydrol Sci, 80-85, Groundwater Hydrol Comt, Am Soc Civil Engrs, 72-76, Fluid Dynamics Comt, 74-76 & Porous Media Comt, Int Asn Hydraul Res, 72-77; assoc ed, Hydrol Sci Bull, 81-88 & Water Resources Res, 81-86; Gledden vis sr fel, Univ Western Australia, 87. *Mem:* Fel Am Geophys Union; Sigma Xi. *Res:* Early fluid mechanics studies on turbulent and stratified flows; groundwater hydrology; stochastic theories of transport processes for unsaturated flow; fractured media; chemically heterogeneous media; variable viscosity fluids; biodegradation; multiphase flow; controlled field experiments on macrodispersion in aquifers and unsaturated flow; large-scale supercomputer simulation of flow and transport in heterogeneous porous media; stimulation of insitu biodegradation using gas injection; stochastic subsurface hydrology; groundwater contaminant transport; author of one book & over 140 technical publications. *Mailing Add:* Dept Civil & Environ Eng Mass Inst Technol Rm 48-329 Cambridge MA 02139

GELIEBTER, ALLAN, OBESITY, BULIMIA NERVOSA. *Current Pos:* from asst prof to assoc prof, 76-88, CHMN, DEPT PSYCHOL, TOURO COL, NY, 81-, PROF, 88- *Personal Data:* b Frankfurt, Ger, Jan 22, 47; US citizen; m 95, Stephanie Lazar. *Educ:* City Col NY, BS, 68; Columbia Univ, MA, 70, PhD(psychol), 76. *Prof Exp:* Adj lectr, Dept Psychol, Herbert H Lehman Col, City Univ NY, 74-76, adj asst prof, 76-78. *Concurrent Pos:* Adj instr, Dept Psychol, Touro Col, New York, 75-76; res assoc, Obesity Res Ctr, Dept Med, St Luke's-Roosevelt Hosp Ctr, Columbia Univ, NY, 78-; dir, Weight Control & Eating Dis, 85-; co-chair, Joint Meeting Soc Study Ingestive Behav & Eastern Psychol Asn, NY, 91; prin investr, NIH, 92-96; assoc res scientist, Dept Psychiat, Col Physicians & Surgeons, Columbia Univ, 93- *Mem:* Am Psychol Asn; AAAS; Am Asn Univ Professors; Sigma Xi; NAm Asn Study Obesity; NY Acad Sci; Soc Study Ingestive Behav; Am Soc Clin Nutrit; Am Inst Nutrit. *Res:* Regulation of food intake in obesity and bulimia nervosa; effect of type of exercise on body composition and resting metabolei during dieting in obesity. *Mailing Add:* Dept Med & Psychiat St Luke's-Roosevelt Hosp Ctr WH-100 Amsterdam Ave at 114th St New York NY 10025. *E-Mail:* 4658@columbia.edu

GELINAS, DOUGLAS ALFRED, BOTANY, PHYSIOLOGY. *Current Pos:* Asst prof bot, Univ Maine, 68-74, chair, bot & plant path, 75-82, assoc dean acad affairs, 82-89, ASSOC PROF BOT, UNIV MAINE, ORONO, 74-, CHAIR, DEPT PLANT BIOL & PATH, 90- *Personal Data:* b Nov 18, 40; US citizen. *Educ:* Fitchburg State Col, BS, 63; Purdue Univ, MS, 66, PhD(biol), 68. *Mem:* AAAS. *Res:* Self-paced instruction in biology. *Mailing Add:* Dept Bot Univ Maine Deering Hall Orono ME 04469-0001

GELINAS, ROBERT JOSEPH, COMPUTATIONAL PHYSICS, CHEMICAL KINETICS. *Current Pos:* SR SCIENTIST & MGR, BASIC SCI DIV, SCI APPLICATIONS, INC, 75- *Personal Data:* b Muskegon, Mich, Sept 25, 37; m 60; c 1. *Educ:* Univ Mich, BSE, 60, MSE, 61, PhD(nuclear eng), 65. *Honors & Awards:* Mark Mills Award, Am Nuclear Soc, 65. *Prof Exp:* Physicist & group leader, Lawrence Livermore Lab, 66-75. *Mem:* AAAS; Am Phys Soc; Am Chem Soc; Combustion Inst Int; Sigma Xi. *Res:* Quantum statistical physics; radiation and plasma physics; non-equilibrium physics; chemical kinetics; combustion science; atmospheric physics; reactive fluid dynamics. *Mailing Add:* 1316 Canyon Side Ave San Ramon CA 94583

GELL, MAURICE L, METALLURGY. *Current Pos:* PROF, DEPT METALL, UNIV CONN, 93- *Personal Data:* b Brooklyn, NY, Dec 1, 37; m 60, Joan Hoffman; c Carol & David. *Educ:* Columbia Univ, BA, 59, MA, 60, BS, 61; Yale Univ, MS, 63, PhD(metall), 65. *Honors & Awards:* Eng Mat Achievement Award, Am Soc Metals Int, 86. *Prof Exp:* NSF fel, 65-66; res assoc, Adv Mat Res & Develop Lab, Pratt & Whitney Div, United Technol Corp, 66-67, sr res assoc & group leader, 67-71, group leader, 71-79, asst mgr, 79-81, mgr, Mat Eng Lab, 81-93. *Mem:* Fel Am Soc Metals. *Res:* Mechanical properties of metals including fatigue deformation and fracture, cleavage fracture, hydrogen embrittlement, deformation and fracture of gas turbine engine materials; development of gas turbine alloys; nanostructured materials and coatings; 10 US patents. *Mailing Add:* 27 Franklin Circle Newington CT 06111

GELLAI, MIKLOS, CARDIOVASCULAR & RENAL PHYSIOLOGY. *Current Pos:* SR INVESTR, SMITHKLINE BEECHAM LABS, 92- *Personal Data:* b Enrod, Hungary, Dec 4, 30. *Prof Exp:* Mem staff, SmithKline & French Labs. *Mailing Add:* SmithKline Beecham Labs Dept Pharmacol PO Box 1539 L-521 King of Prussia PA 19406-0939

GELLER, ARTHUR MICHAEL, BIOCHEMISTRY. *Current Pos:* PROF BIOCHEM, UNIV TENN, MEMPHIS, 68- *Personal Data:* b New York, NY, Dec 18, 41; m 84, Malak Kotb; c Suzanne & Laurie. *Educ:* City Col New York, BS, 62; Duke Univ, PhD(biochem), 67. *Prof Exp:* Am Cancer Soc fel, Enzyme Inst, Univ Wis, 67-68. *Concurrent Pos:* Vis scientist, Nat Inst Arthritis, Metab & Digestive Dis, NIH, 76-77; vis prof, Howard Hughes Med Inst, Duke Univ Med Ctr, 85; southeast regional dir & mem bd dirs, Sigma Xi, 84-97. *Mem:* AAAS; Sigma Xi; Am Soc Biol Chemists; Am Asn Univ Professors; Asn Res Vision & Ophthal. *Res:* Biochemistry of the lens; methionine adenosyltransferase; methylation; superantigens. *Mailing Add:* Dept Biochem Univ Tenn Memphis TN 38163. *Fax:* 901-448-7126; *E-Mail:* ageller@physio1.utmem.edu

GELLER, DAVID MELVILLE, BIOCHEMISTRY. *Current Pos:* asst prof, 59-67, ASSOC PROF PHARMACOL, SCH MED, WASHINGTON UNIV, 67- *Personal Data:* b Detroit, Mich, Dec 30, 30. *Educ:* Amherst Col, AB, 52; Harvard Univ, PhD(biochem), 57. *Prof Exp:* NSF fel, Oxford Univ, 57-58; instr biochem, Dept Chem, Univ Ill, 58-59. *Res:* Oxidative and photophosphorylation; phosphorylation mechanisms; serum albumin biosynthesis and secretion. *Mailing Add:* 7337 Maryland Ave St Louis MO 63130-4202

GELLER, EDWARD, NEUROCHEMISTRY. *Current Pos:* Asst biochem, Univ Calif, Los Angeles, 52-55, asst res biol chemist, Med Ctr, 59-65, asst prof, 65-70, ASSOC PROF PSYCHIAT, MED CTR, UNIV CALIF, LOS ANGELES, 70- *Personal Data:* b New York, NY, Dec 6, 28; m 52; c 3. *Educ:* Univ Calif, Los Angeles, AB, 47, BS, 48, MS, 55, PhD(biochem), 56. *Concurrent Pos:* Res biochemist, Vet Admin, 57- *Mem:* Int Soc Neurochem; Am Col Neuropsychopharmacol; Endocrine Soc; Am Soc Neurochem; Int Soc Psychoneuroendocrinol; Sigma XI. *Res:* Relation of biochemistry to mental processes; biochemical correlates of behavior. *Mailing Add:* 22907 Gershwin Dr Woodland Hills CA 91364

GELLER, HARVEY, ANALYTICAL STATISTICS, RESEARCH MANAGEMENT. *Current Pos:* RETIRED. *Personal Data:* b New York, NY, July 6, 21; m 46; c 3. *Educ:* Brooklyn Col, AB, 43. *Prof Exp:* Statistician, Bur Rec & Statist, New York Health Dept, 46-49, Bur Cancer Control, DC Health Dept, 49-51, Div Civilian Health Req, USPHS, 51-53, Off Surgeon Gen, Dept Air Force, 53 & Sch Aviation Med, 54-55; supvry statistician, Chronic Dis Prog, USPHS, 55-59, chief opers studies, Cancer Control Prog, 59-68; head spec cancer surv sect, Nat Cancer Inst, NIH, 68-73, head field liaison sect, Biomet Br, 73-81. *Mem:* AAAS; fel Am Pub Health Asn; Am Statist Asn; Soc Epidemiol Res; Fedn Am Scientists. *Res:* Collection and analysis of cancer morbidity and mortality statistics; testing and evaluation of new cancer screening and diagnostic techniques and instruments; studies in the application of screening tests for cancer. *Mailing Add:* 117 Northway Greenbelt MD 20770

GELLER, HERBERT M, NEUROPHYSIOLOGY, NEUROPHARMACOLOGY. *Current Pos:* PROF PHARMACOL, ROBERT WOOD JOHNSON MED SCH, 85- *Personal Data:* b New York, NY, Feb 20, 45. *Educ:* City Col New York, BEE, 65; Case Western Res Univ, PhD(bioeng), 70. *Prof Exp:* NIH fel physiol, Univ Rochester, 70-72; from asst prof to assoc prof pharmacol, Rutgers Med Sch, 78-85. *Mem:* AAAS; Soc Neurosci; Biophys Soc; Am Physiol Soc; Am Soc Pharmacol & Exp Therapeut. *Res:* Developmental neurobiology of neurol glial interactions, pole of growth fetus and cytokinec in neurol development. *Mailing Add:* Dept Pharmacol Robert Wood Johnson Med Sch 675 Hoes Lane Piscataway NJ 08854-5635. *Fax:* 732-235-4073

GELLER, IRVING, experimental psychology, for more information see previous edition

GELLER, KENNETH N, PHYSICS. *Current Pos:* Assoc prof physics, Drexel Univ, 66-76, assoc prof atmospheric sci, 74-76, assoc dean grad sch, 74-83, dir, Ctr Multidisciplinary Study & Res, 76-83, dir, Off Sponsored Proj, 83-87, PROF PHYSICS & ATMOSPHERIC SCI, DREXEL UNIV, 76-, ASST VPRES RES & TECHNOL MGT, 87- *Personal Data:* b Brooklyn, NY, Sept 22, 30; m 55; c 2. *Educ:* Brooklyn Col, BS, 52; Univ Pa, PhD(physics), 60. *Mem:* AAAS; Am Phys Soc; Technol Transfer Soc; Licensing Exec Soc; Soc Res Adminrs; Asn Univ Tech Managers. *Res:* Study of low energy nuclear reactions; neutron detection techniques; lidar measurements of the atmosphere. *Mailing Add:* 7637 Brookhaven Rd Philadelphia PA 19151-2023

GELLER, MARGARET JOAN, COSMOLOGY. *Current Pos:* ASTROPHYSICIST, SMITHSONIAN ASTROPHYS OBSERV, 83-; PROF ASTRON, HARVARD UNIV, 88- *Personal Data:* b Ithaca, NY, Dec 8, 47. *Educ:* Univ Calif, Berkeley, AB, 70; Princeton Univ, MA, 72, PhD(physics), 75. *Hon Degrees:* DSc, Conn Col, 95. *Honors & Awards:* MacArthur Award, 90; Newcomb-Cleveland Prize, Am Acad Arts & Sci, 90; Helen Sawyer Hogg Prize, Royal Astron Soc Can, 93; Brickwedde lectr, Johns Hopkins Univ, 93; Klopsteg Award, Am Asn Physics Teachers, 96; Bethe Lectr, Cornell Univ, 96. *Prof Exp:* Fel theoret astrophys, Ctr Astrophys, 74-76; res assoc, Harvard Univ, 76-80, asst prof, 80-83. *Concurrent Pos:* Mem Nat Comts, NSF, NASA & Am Astron Soc; trustee, Boston Mus Sci. *Mem:* Nat Acad Sci; Int Astron Union; fel AAAS; Am Astron Soc; fel Am Phys Soc; Am Acad Arts & Sci. *Res:* Nature and history of the galaxy distribution; the origin and evolution of galaxies; x-ray astronomy. *Mailing Add:* Ctr Astrophys 60 Garden St Cambridge MA 02138

GELLER, MARVIN ALAN, METEOROLOGY, PHYSICAL OCEANOGRAPHY. *Current Pos:* adj prof physics earth & space sci, PROF & DIR, INST ATMOSPHERIC SCI, STATE UNIV NY, STONY BROOK, 89- *Personal Data:* b Boston, Mass, Mar 19, 43; m 68, Lynda L Grafinger; c Stephanie & Steven. *Educ:* Mass Inst Technol, BS, 64, PhD(meteorol), 69. *Prof Exp:* From asst prof to assoc prof elec eng & meteorol, Univ Ill, Urbana-Champaign, 69-77; prof meteorol & phys oceanog, Univ Miami, 77-80; res scientist, NASA Goddard Space Flight Ctr, 80-84, chief, Atmosphere's Lab, 84-89. *Mem:* Fel Am Meteorol Soc; Am Geophys Union. *Res:* Atmospheric dynamics with emphasis on atmospheric waves; climate variability studies; upper atmosphere; transport and chemistry. *Mailing Add:* 100 Nicolls Rd State Univ NY Marine Sci Res Ctr Stony Brook NY 11794-0001. *Fax:* 516-632-6251; *E-Mail:* mgeller@ccmail.sunysb.edu

GELLER, MILTON, ANALYTICAL & PHARMACEUTICAL CHEMISTRY. *Current Pos:* sr scientist, Hoffmann La-Roche, Inc, Nutley, 66-78. *Personal Data:* b New York, NY, July 22, 22; m 49; c 2. *Educ:* City Col New York, BS, 44; Brooklyn Col, MA, 60. *Prof Exp:* Anal chemist, Chas Pfizer & Co, Inc, 43-44 & 46-50; chemist, US Signal Corps, 50-51; anal chemist, Chase Chem Co, 51; anal chemist, Nepera Chem Co, 51-58, supvr qual control, 58; sr scientist, Warner Lambert Res Inst, 58-62, sr res assoc, 62-63, dir, Appl Anal Res, 63-66. *Mem:* Am Chem Soc; Am Pharmaceut Asn. *Res:* Methods development for pharmaceutical dosage forms. *Mailing Add:* 4010 Kramer Pl Fairlawn NJ 07410

GELLER, MYER, ELECTROOPTICS. *Current Pos:* RES PHYSICIST, US NAVY ELECTRONICS LAB, 64- *Personal Data:* b Winnipeg, Man, Can, Oct 24, 26; US citizen; m 54. *Educ:* Univ Man, BS, 46; Univ Minn, MS, 48; Mass Inst Technol, PhD(physics), 55. *Prof Exp:* Mem tech staff semiconductors, Hughes Aircraft Co, Calif, 55-60, mem tech staff lasers, 62-64; sr scientist, Electro Optical Systs Inc, Calif, 60-62. *Mem:* Am Phys Soc; Optical Soc Am; Inst Elec & Electronics Eng. *Res:* Coherrent optics, especially stimulated emission devices and non-linear optics; spectroscopy, atomic and plasma physics; optical atmospheric propagation. *Mailing Add:* PO Box 671 La Canada CA 91012

GELLER, NANCY L, MATHEMATICAL STATISTICS, STATISTICS. *Current Pos:* asst prof, 78-80, PROF COMMUNITY & PREV MED, MED COL PA, 80- *Personal Data:* b New York, NY, Nov 3, 44. *Educ:* City Col New York, BS, 65; Case Inst Technol, MS, 67; Case Western Res Univ, PhD(math), 72. *Prof Exp:* Asst prof statist, Univ Rochester, 70-72; asst prof statist, Univ Pa, 72-78. *Mem:* Inst Math Statist; Am Statist Asn; Am Math Soc. *Res:* Nonparametric statistics; use of citations in the study of science; health systems statistics. *Mailing Add:* Biostat Res Branch 2 Rockledge Ctr 8210 MCS 7938 NHL&B Inst Rm 2A11 Bethesda MD 20892-7938. *Fax:* 301-402-6562

GELLER, ROBERT JAMES, SEISMOLOGY. *Current Pos:* ASSOC PROF, TOKYO UNIV, 84- *Personal Data:* b New York, NY, Feb 9, 52; m 78, 90, Emiko Kakiuchi. *Educ:* Calif Inst Technol, BS, 73, MS, 75, PhD(geophys), 77. *Prof Exp:* Res fel geophys, Calif Inst Technol, 77-78; asst prof geophys, Stanford Univ, 78-84. *Concurrent Pos:* Guggenheim fel, 85; vis lectr, Kyoto Univ, 93-; ed, Geophys Res Lett, 94- *Mem:* Am Geophys Union; Seismol Soc Am; Soc Explor Geophysicists; Royal Astron Soc; Sigma Xi. *Res:* Analyzing recordings of earthquake ground motion obtained by highly accurate seismographs to determine the three-dimensional structure of the earth's interior, thereby gaining information on geodynamic processes. *Mailing Add:* Fac Sci Dept Geophys Tokyo Univ Bunkyo-Ku Tokyo 113 Japan. *Fax:* 81-3-3818-3247; *E-Mail:* bob@global.geoph.s.u-tokyo.ac.jp

GELLER, RONALD G, RESEARCH ADMINISTRATION, SCIENCE ADMINISTRATION. *Current Pos:* Res assoc pharmacol, Nat Heart Inst, NIH, 69-71, sr staff fel, 71-72, grants assoc, 72-73, asst chief, Hypertension & Kidney Dis Br, Nat Heart & Lung Inst, 73-75, chief hypertension, 75-78, assoc dir vision res, Nat Eye Inst, 78-87, dir div prog anal, Off Sci Policy & Legis, 87-89, DIR DIV EXTRAMURAL AFFAIRS, NAT HEART LUNG & BLOOD INST, NIH, 89- *Personal Data:* b Peoria, Ill, Jan 15, 43; m 71, Lois; c Andrea, Steven & Lauren. *Educ:* Univ Wis-Madison, BS, 64, PhD(physiol), 69. *Mem:* Am Physiol Soc; Am Heart Asn; Coun High Blood Pressure Res. *Res:* Reflex control of blood pressure; humoral control of blood pressure; physiology and pharmacology of the kallikrein-kinin system. *Mailing Add:* NIH RFL2 Bldg Rm 7100 Bethesda MD 20892-7922. *Fax:* 301-480-3460; *E-Mail:* rg33k@nih.gov

GELLER, SEYMOUR, SOLID STATE PHYSICS & CHEMISTRY. *Current Pos:* prof, 71-90, EMER PROF ELEC ENG, UNIV COLO, BOULDER, 90- *Personal Data:* b New York, NY, Mar 28, 21; m 42; c 2. *Educ:* Cornell Univ, AB, 41, PhD(phys chem), 49. *Prof Exp:* DuPont fel, Cornell Univ, 49-50; res chemist, Benger Lab, E I DuPont de Nemours & Co, 50-52; struct chemist, Bell Tel Labs, Inc, 52-64; struct chemist & group leader, Struct Properties Group, NAm Rockwell Sci Ctr, Calif, 64-71. *Concurrent Pos:* Fac fel, Coun Res & Creative Work, Univ Colo, 77-78, res award, Col Eng & Appl Sci, 79, Croft res prof, 80, res lectr, 85, fac fel, 85-86; Creativity Award, NSF, 83-87. *Mem:* Fel Am Phys Soc; fel Mineral Soc Am; fel Inst Elec & Electronics Engrs; Sigma Xi. *Res:* Relations of properties to crystal structure; crystal chemistry; magnetic, superconducting, and semiconducting materials; solid electrolytes; high pressure phases; phase transitions; structures of inorganic and intermetallic compounds. *Mailing Add:* 3778 Moffit Ctr Boulder CO 80304-1051

GELLER, STEPHEN ARTHUR, HEPATOPATHOLOGY, AUTOPSY PATHOLOGY. *Current Pos:* PROF PATH, UNIV CALIF, LOS ANGELES, 84-; CHMN PATH, CEDARS-SINAI MED CTR, LOS ANGELES, 84- *Personal Data:* b Brooklyn, NY, Apr 26, 39; m 62, Kate DeJong; c David P & Jennifer L. *Educ:* Brooklyn Col, BA, 59; Howard Univ, Washington, DC, MD, 64. *Prof Exp:* From asst prof to assoc prof path, Mt Sinai Sch Med, NY, 71-78, actg chmn, 75-78, vchmn & prof, 78-84. *Concurrent Pos:* Chmn, Anat Path Comt, Col Am Pathologists, 84-85; consult, Off Med Examr, Los Angeles County, 89-; prof lectr, Mt Sinai Sch Med, NY, 90-; pres, Los Angeles Soc Pathologists, 92; vpres, Calif Soc Pathologists, 92- *Mem:* Am Asn Study Liver Dis; Col Am Pathologists; Am Soc Clin Pathologists; US-Can Acad Path; Hans Popper Hepatopath Soc (secy-treas, 89-); Am Asn Hist Med. *Res:* Mechanism of liver injury and hepatocarcinogenesis in a transgenic mouse model for an1pha-l-antitrypsin deficiency; tissue growth factors in liver tumors; manifestations of Epstein-Barr virus infection in human livers after transplantation. *Mailing Add:* Dept Path & Lab Med 8700 Beverly Blvd Los Angeles CA 90048-1865. *Fax:* 310-967-0122; *E-Mail:* geller@csmcmv4x

GELLER, SUSAN CAROL, K-THEORY, CYCLIC HOMOLOGY. *Current Pos:* assoc prof, 81-89, PROF MATH, TEX A&M UNIV, 89-, PROF VET ANAT & PUB HEALTH, 94- *Personal Data:* b Newark, NJ, Oct 27, 48. *Educ:* Case Inst Technol, BS, 70; Cornell Univ, MS, 72, PhD(math), 75. *Prof Exp:* Teaching asst math, Cornell Univ, 70-75; asst prof math, Purdue Univ, W Lafayette, 75-81. *Concurrent Pos:* Fac fel, Bunting Inst Radcliffe Col, Harvard Univ, 80-82; NSF vis prof women, Rutgers Univ, 87-88. *Mem:* Am Math Soc; Math Asn Am; Am Women Math. *Res:* Devise new techniques to compute K-theory of various rings with an emphasis on excision problems, negative K-theory and cyclic homology. *Mailing Add:* Dept Math Texas A&M Univ Col Sta TX 77843-3368. *Fax:* 409-845-6028; *E-Mail:* geller@math.tamu.edu

GELLERT, MARTIN FRANK, BIOCHEMISTRY OF DNA. *Current Pos:* res chemist, 59-69, CHIEF, SECT MOLECULAR GENETICS, LAB MOLECULAR BIOL, NAT INST DIABETES, DIGESTIVE & KIDNEY DIS, NIH, 69- *Personal Data:* b Prague, Czech, June 5, 29; m 55, 74. *Educ:* Harvard Univ, BA, 50; Columbia Univ, PhD(chem), 56. *Honors & Awards:* Merck Award Biochem, Am Soc Biol Chemists, 85; Richard Lounsbery Award, 85. *Prof Exp:* Fel USPHS, Naval Med Res Inst, Md, 57-58; asst prof biochem, Dartmouth Med Sch, 58-59. *Mem:* Nat Acad Sci; AAAS; Am Soc Biochem & Molecular Biol (pres, 93-94); Am Acad Arts & Sci. *Res:* Molecular genetics; enzymes of DNA synthesis and recombination. *Mailing Add:* Lab Molecular Biol Bldg 5 Rm 241 NIDDK NIH Bethesda MD 20892. *Fax:* 301-496-0201

GELLERT, RONALD J, PHYSIOLOGY. *Current Pos:* CLIN SCIENTIST, REPRODUCTIVE GENETICS, SWED HOSP MED CTR, 83- *Personal Data:* b New York, NY, July 24, 35; m 59. *Educ:* NY Univ, BA, 57; Univ Calif, Berkeley, MA, 59, Univ Calif, San Francisco, PhD(physiol), 63. *Prof Exp:* NIH fel, Univ Calif, San Francisco, 63-64, Oxford Univ, 64-65 & Harvard Sch Dent Med, 65-67; sr investr, Pac Northwest Res Found, 67-70; res asst obstet & gynec, Sch Med, Univ Wash, 70-83. *Mem:* AAAS; Endocrine Soc; Soc Study Reproduction. *Res:* Neuroendocrinology of reproductive processes; control of onset of puberty; role of pars tuberalis of the pituitary in physiology of reproduction; pesticides and reproduction; hexachlorophene and neuroendocrine function; mechanism of action of certain anti-ovulatory drugs; vitamin A and reproductive function; xenobiotics and reproductive function, marihuana and reproductive function. *Mailing Add:* 10116 NE 16th Pl Bellevue WA 98004

GELLES, DAVID STEPHEN, MATERIALS SCIENCE, METALLURGY. *Current Pos:* sr engr, 87-88, STAFF ENGR, FUSION MAT, PAC NORTHWEST NAT LAB, 88- *Personal Data:* b Leicester, UK, Mar 19, 45; US citizen; m 74; c Alexander M & Alicia K. *Educ:* Harvey Mudd Col, BSc, 66; Mass Inst Technol, MSc, 68, ScD(phys metall), 71. *Prof Exp:* Sr res fel, Berkeley Nuclear Labs, Berkeley, Glos, UK, 71-74; sr scientist mat develop, Hanford Eng Develop Lab, 74, prin engr, 82-87. *Mem:* Am Soc Metals; Am Inst Metall Engrs; Am Soc Testing & Mat. *Res:* Material response to radiation damage, microstructure/property relationships; ferritic alloy development for breeder reactor applications; ferritic alloy development for fusion reactor applications; 2 US patents. *Mailing Add:* Pac Northwest Nat Lab PO Box 999 P8-15 Richland WA 99352. *Fax:* 509-376-0418; *E-Mail:* ds_gelles@pnl.gov

GELLES, ISADORE LEO, PHYSICS. *Current Pos:* RETIRED. *Personal Data:* b Philadelphia, Pa, Dec 15, 25; m 53; c 3. *Educ:* Temple Univ, BA, 51, MA, 54. *Prof Exp:* Physicist, Pitman-Dunn Lab, Frankford Arsenal, 51-52; acoust engr, Radio Corp Am, 52-53; sr engr semiconductors, Res Div, Philco Corp, 53-54; mem staff microwave & optical spectros, Res Ctr, Int Bus Mach Corp, 56-61; physicist & group supvr, Res Lab, Am-Standard Corp, 61-63; from physicist to sr physicist, Ledgemont Lab, Kennecott Copper Corp, 63-73. *Concurrent Pos:* Consult, 73- *Mem:* Fel AAAS; Am Phys Soc; Sigma Xi; Metall Soc; Am Soc Metals. *Res:* Physical properties of refractory and nonferrous metals; audio spectrum analysis; semiconductor transport properties; magnetic resonance in solids; photoconductivity; ultrasonics in solids; crystal physics; holography. *Mailing Add:* 2423 Chilham Pl Potomac MD 20854

GELLES, S(TANLEY) H(AROLD), PHYSICAL METALLURGY. *Current Pos:* dir, S H Gelles Assocs, 76-86, PRES, GELLES LABS, INC, 86- *Personal Data:* b Boston, Mass, Sept 12, 30; m 56; c 3. *Educ:* Mass Inst Technol, SB, 52, SM, 54, ScD, 57. *Prof Exp:* Asst metall, Mass Inst Technol, 53-57; proj leader phys metall, Nuclear Metals, Inc, Mass, 57-60, proj mgr, 60-63; phys res metallurgist, Ledgemont Lab, Kennecott Copper Corp, 63-68; assoc chief, Battelle Mem Inst, 68-75. *Concurrent Pos:* Consult, Beryllium Comt, Mat Adv Bd, Nat Acad Sci, 64-67; consult, ad hoc comt high pressure technol, Mat Adv Bd, Nat Acad Sci, 72, Beryllium Metal Supply Options, 88-89. *Mem:* Am Inst Mining, Metall & Petrol Engrs; Am Soc Metals; Nat Asbestos Coun; Am Soc Testing Mat. *Res:* Metallurgy of beryllium; phase equilibria; metal deformation; high pressure technology; microstructure/property relations in metals; effect of gravity on microstructural development in alloys. *Mailing Add:* 2485 Wimbledon Rd Columbus OH 43220

GELLHORN, ALFRED, MEDICAL EDUCATION, HEALTH POLICY. *Current Pos:* RETIRED. *Personal Data:* b St Louis, Mo, June 4, 13; m 39; c 4. *Educ:* Washington Univ, MD, 37; Am Bd Internal Med, dipl, 56, cert, 77. *Hon Degrees:* ScD, Amherst Col, 69, City Col NY, 79, State Univ NY, 85, Albany Med Col, 86, Univ Pa, 93. *Prof Exp:* House officer surg, Barnes Hosp, St Louis, Mo, 37-39; house officer gynec, Passavant Hosp, Chicago, 39-40; res fel, Dept Embryol, Carnegie Inst & Johns Hopkins Univ, 40-43; from asst prof physiol to assoc prof pharmacol, Col Physicians & Surgeons, Columbia Univ, 43-46, from assoc prof pharmacol to assoc prof med, 46-58, dir, Inst Cancer Res, 52-68, prof med, 58-68; prof med & pharmacol & dean, Sch Med & dir, Med Ctr, Univ Pa, 68-74; dir, Ctr Biomed Educ, City Col New York, 74-79, vpres health affairs, 74-79; vis prof, Sch Pub Health, Harvard Univ, 80-83; dir med affairs, NY State Dept Health, 83-96. *Concurrent Pos:* Chief, Med Serv, Francis Delafield Hosp, 50-68; from assoc attend physician to attend physician, Presby Hosp, 56-68; vis clin prof, Albert Einstein Col Med, Yeshiva Univ, 56-68; pres, Coun Int Orgn Med Sci, 68-80; mem, Adv Comt, USPHS, Am Cancer Soc & Nat Res Coun; vis prof, Sch Pub Health, Harvard Univ, 80- *Mem:* Inst Med-Nat Acad Sci; Am Asn Cancer Res (pres, 63); Asn Am Physicians; Am Soc Pharmacol & Exp Therapeut; Am Soc Biol Chemists; fel Am Col Physicians. *Res:* Placental physiology; circulatory pharmacology; chemotherapy; infectious disease; clinical research in malignancy; mechanism of action of anti-tumor drugs on clinical cancer chemotherapy; medical aspects of neoplastic disease; lipid metabolism; medical oncology; medical education; medical ethics. *Mailing Add:* Susquehanna Turnpike Durham NY 12422

GELLIS, SYDNEY SAUL, MEDICINE, PEDIATRICS. *Current Pos:* prof & chmn dept, 65-81, prof, 81-88, EMER PROF PEDIAT, TUFTS UNIV, 88-; SR PEDIATRICIAN, NEW ENG MED CTR. *Personal Data:* b Claremont, NH, Mar 6, 14; m 39, Matilda Lichter; c Beth (Crocker) & Stephen. *Educ:* Harvard Univ, AB, 34, MD, 38. *Honors & Awards:* Abraham Jacobi Award, Am Acad Pediat; Howland Award, Am Pediat Soc. *Prof Exp:* Instr pediat, Johns Hopkins Univ, 43-46; asst prof, Harvard Univ, 46-56; prof & chmn dept, Sch Med, Boston Univ, 56-65. *Concurrent Pos:* Consult, Surgeon Gen, 43-47; physician, Children's Med Ctr, Boston, 47-56, consult, 56-; pediatrician-in-chief, Beth Israel Hosp, Boston, 50-56 & New Eng Med Ctr Hosps, 65-81; ed, Year Book Pediat, 52-80; assoc ed, Am J Dis Children; lectr, Harvard Med Sch, 56-93; dir pediat, Boston City Hosp, 56-65, consult pediat, 65-; lectr, Sch Med, Boston Univ, 65-; consult pediat, USAF, 69-79; ed, Pediat Notes, 77- *Mem:* Am Pediat Soc; Soc Pediat Res (secy, 52-58, pres, 58-59); corp mem Fr Soc Pediat; hon mem NZ Pediat Soc. *Res:* Liver disease and jaundice; gamma globulin; hepatitis. *Mailing Add:* 750 Washington St Boston MA 02111. *Fax:* 617-956-2451

GELLMAN, CHARLES, INDUSTRIAL ENGINEERING. *Current Pos:* RETIRED. *Personal Data:* b New York, NY, Dec 18, 16; m 48; c 2. *Hon Degrees:* LHD, New York Col Podiatric Med, 75. *Prof Exp:* Indust specialist, War Dept, 42-45; works mgr, Para Equip Co, 45-47 & Heppe Hudson Co, Inc, 47-50; exec purchasing off & tech adv supply mission, Israel, 50-53; tech dir, Am Technion Soc, 53-55; exec dir & consult, Grand Cent Hosp, New York, 55-63; pres & dir, Jewish Mem Hosp, 63-83. *Concurrent Pos:* Consult, Webb & Knapp Construct Co; pres, Greater New York Hosp Asn, 71-72; chmn, Hosp Asn NY State, 74-75. *Mem:* Am Soc Metals; Soc Automotive Engrs; fel Am Pub Health Asn; fel Royal Soc Health; NY Acad Sci. *Mailing Add:* 12 Birch Lane Green Acres Valley Stream NY 11581

GELLMAN, ISAIAH, SANITATION. *Current Pos:* RETIRED. *Personal Data:* b Akron, Ohio, Feb 19, 28; m 47; c 2. *Educ:* City Col New York, BChE, 47; Rutgers Univ, MS, 50, PhD(sanit), 52. *Prof Exp:* Res assoc sanit, Rutgers Univ, 48-52; process engr air & water, Abbott Labs, 52-56; regional engr pulp & paper-air & water pollution, Nat Coun Stream Improv, 56-67, asst tech dir, NY, 67-69, tech dir, 69-76, exec vpres, 76-87, pres, 87-94. *Concurrent Pos:* Tappi fel & Environ Div Award. *Mem:* Water Pollution Control Fedn; Air Pollution Control Asn; Am Inst Chem Engrs; fel Tech Asn Pulp & Paper Indust. *Res:* Air and water pollution control; water resources development; treatment of gaseous and liquid effluents from pulp and paper production to prevent pollution problems. *Mailing Add:* 7 E 35th St New York NY 10016

GELLMAN, SAMUEL HELMER, BIO-ORGANIC CHEMISTRY, PHYSICAL ORGANIC CHEMISTRY. *Current Pos:* asst prof, 87-93, assoc prof, 93-95, PROF CHEM, UNIV WIS-MADISON, 95- *Personal Data:* b Evanston, Ill, Sept 12, 59; m 90; c 1. *Educ:* Harvard Univ, AB, 81; Columbia Univ, PhD(chem), 86. *Prof Exp:* NIH fel, Calif Inst Technol, 85-87. *Concurrent Pos:* Alfred P Sloan res fel, 93; Arthur C Cope scholar, 97. *Mem:* Am Chem Soc; AAAS; Am Peptide Soc. *Res:* Bio-organic chemistry and biophysics, including the origins of stability and specificity in inter- and intra-molecular non-covalent associations involving biomolecules; protein folding and refolding; protein design; design of new folding polymers. *Mailing Add:* Dept Chem Univ Wis 1101 University Ave Madison WI 53706. *E-Mail:* gellman@chem.wisc.edu

GELL-MANN, MURRAY, THEORETICAL PHYSICS. *Current Pos:* from assoc prof to prof, Calif Inst Technol, 55-67, Millikan prof, Lauritsen Lab High Energy Physics, 67-93, EMER ROBERT ANDREWS MILLIKAN PROF THEORET PHYSICS, CALIF INST TECHNOL, 93-; DIR, SANTA FE INST, 93-, PROF & CO-CHMN SCI BD, 95- *Personal Data:* b New York, NY, Sept 15, 29; wid, 92, Marcia Southwick; c Elizabeth, Nicholas W & Nicholas S. *Educ:* Yale Univ, BS, 48; Mass Inst Technol, PhD(physics), 51. *Hon Degrees:* DSc, Yale Univ, 59, Univ Chicago, 67, Univ Ill, 68, Wesleyan Univ, 68, Univ Turin, 69, Univ Utah, 70, Columbia Univ, 77, Cambridge Univ, Eng, 80. *Honors & Awards:* Nobel Prize Physics, 69; Heineman Prize, Am Inst Physics, 59; Ernest O Lawrence Award, Dept Energy, 66; Franklin Medal, Franklin Inst Philadelphia, 67; Joh J Carty Medal, Nat Acad Sci, 68; Res Corp Award, 69. *Prof Exp:* Mem sch math & physics, Inst Advan Study, 51-52; from instr to assoc prof physics, Inst Nuclear Studies, Univ Chicago, 52-55. *Concurrent Pos:* Mem, Inst Advan Study, 51; vis assoc prof, Columbia Univ, 54; vis prof, Col France & Univ Paris, 59-60, Mass Inst Technol, 63 & Europ Orgn Nuclear Res, Geneva, Switz, 71-72 & 79-80; overseas fel, Churchill Col, Cambridge, Eng, 66; consult, President's Sci Adv Comt, 69-72; chmn, bd trustees, Aspen Ctr Physics, 73-79; citizen regent, Smithsonian Inst, 74-; mem, Sci & Grants Comt, Leakey Found, 77-; dir, J D & C T MacArthur Found, 79-; mem, Coun Foreign Relations; mem bd trustees, Santa Fe Inst, 82-85, co-chmn sci bd, 85-; dir, Advan Physics Corp, 88-; mem bd dirs, Lovelace Inst, 93- *Mem:* Nat Acad Sci; fel Am Acad Arts & Sci; fel Am Phys Soc; foreign mem Royal Soc; hon mem French Phys Soc; Sigma Xi; foreign Pakistan Acad Sci; foreign Indian Acad Sci; Am Philos Soc. *Res:* Elementary particle theory; dispersion or S-matrix theory; the renormalization group; strangeness; the weak interaction; broken symmetry as in the eightfold way; quarks; quantum chromodynamics. *Mailing Add:* Sci Bd Santa Fe Inst 1399 Hyde Park Rd Santa Fe NM 87501. *Fax:* 505-982-0565

GELMAN, ANDREW, APPLIED STATISTICS, BAYESRAN STATISTICS. *Current Pos:* ASSOC PROF STATIST, COLUMBIA UNIV, 96- *Personal Data:* b Philadelphia, Pa, Feb 11, 65. *Educ:* Mass Inst Technol, SB, 85, SB, 86; Harvard Univ, MA, 87, PhD(statist), 90. *Honors & Awards:* Heinz Eulau Award, Am Polit Sci Asn, 95. *Prof Exp:* Asst prof statist, Univ Calif, Berkeley, 90-96. *Concurrent Pos:* Vis asst prof statist, Univ Chicago, 94; Young investr award, NSF, 94. *Mem:* Fel Inst Math Statist; Am Statist Asn; Biomet Soc. *Res:* Statistical modeling, data analysis and computation using Bayesran methods; application areas including sample surveys, political science and public health. *Mailing Add:* Dept Statist Columbia Univ New York NY 10027. *E-Mail:* gelman@stat.columbia.edu

GELMAN, DONALD, FEYNMAN PATH INTEGRALS, VARIATIONAL BOUNDS. *Current Pos:* PROF PHYSICS, C W POST CAMPUS, LONG ISLAND UNIV, 64- *Personal Data:* b Brooklyn, NY, Sept 13, 38; m 62, Doraine Sills; c Sharon B & Deborah L. *Educ:* City Univ NY, BS, 59; NY Univ, MS, 64, PhD(physics), 69. *Prof Exp:* Teaching asst physics, Columbia Univ, 59-61; res physicist, Kollsman Instrument Corp, 61-64; instr sci, NY City Community Col, 64. *Mem:* Am Asn Physics Teachers; Sigma Xi. *Res:* Feynman path integrals and variational bounds in scattering theory; astronomy. *Mailing Add:* Dept Physics CW Post Campus Long Island Univ Brookville NY 11548. *E-Mail:* dgelman@aurora.liunet.edu

GELMAN, HARRY, ANTENNA DESIGN & ANALYSIS, DIGITAL SWITCHING SYSTEMS & NETWORKS. *Current Pos:* sr eng specialist, 79-82, eng mgr, 82-89, SR MEM TECH STAFF, GTE GOVT SYST CORP, 89- *Personal Data:* b New York, NY, May 23, 35; m 57; c 5. *Educ:* City Col New York, BS, 57; NY Univ, PhD(physics), 64. *Prof Exp:* Asst physics, Columbia Univ, 57-58 & NY Univ, 58-59; instr math & physics, US Merchant Marine Acad, 64; staff mem physics, Sandia Corp, 64-66; mem tech staff, Mitre Corp, 66-77; prin scientist, Physical Sci Inc, 77-79. *Concurrent Pos:* Lectr, Northeastern Univ, 67-71. *Mem:* Am Asn Physics Teachers; Am Phys Soc. *Res:* Wave propagation; eikonal methods; theory of scattering; plasma physics; ionospheric physics; quantum theory of fields; special theory of relativity; general relativity; quantum theory of measurement. *Mailing Add:* 25 Collins Ave Reading MA 01867

GELMAN, SIMON, ANESTHESIOLOGY. *Current Pos:* assoc prof, Dept Anesthesiol, Sch Med, Univ Ala Birmingham, 78-81, dir clin res, 79-84, vchmn res, 84-89, PROF, DEPT ANESTHESIOL, SCH MED, UNIV ALA, BIRMINGHAM, 81-, CHMN DEPT, 89-, PROF, DEPT PHYSIOL & BIOPHYS, 89- *Personal Data:* b May 26, 36; c 2. *Educ:* First Leningrad Med Inst, USSR, MD, 59; 25 Oct-Hosp, Leningrad, PhD, 65; Leningrad Dzanelidze Inst First Aid, DSc, 73. *Prof Exp:* Head, Surg Off Polyclin, Siktivkar, USSR, 59-61; physician-resuscitationist, Ctr Treatment Patients Myocardial Infarction, Leningrad, USSR, 64-65; asst prof, Dept Anesthesiol, Leningrad Kirov Advan Training Inst Doctors, 65-73; sr anesthesiologist, Beilinson Med Ctr & Med Sch, Tel-Aviv Univ, Petah Tikva, Israel, 74-75; fel, Dept Anesthesiol, Case Western Res Univ, Cleveland, Ohio, 76-77, resident anesthesiol, Dept Anesthesiol, Univ Hosp, 77-78. *Concurrent Pos:* Mem res comt, Soc Cardiovasc Anesthesiologists, 81-82; vis prof, numerous insts, asns & univs, 81-91; mem sci adv bd, Asn Univ Anesthetists, 85-88 & ASA Comt Res, 88- *Mem:* Israel Soc Anesthesiol; Am Soc Anesthesiologists; Soc Cardiovasc Anesthesiologists; Asn Univ Anesthetists; Int Anesthesia Res Soc; Am Physiol Soc. *Mailing Add:* Dept Anesthesiol Harvard Med Sch Brigham & Woman's Hosp 75 Francis St Boston MA 02115

GELMANN, EDWARD P, MOLECULAR BIOLOGY, GENETICS. *Current Pos:* fel, 78-82, SR INVESTR ONCOL, NAT CANCER INST, NIH, 82-, PROF MED & CELL BIOL, CHIEF DIV MED ONCOL, GEORGETOWN UNIV SCH MED. *Personal Data:* b New York, NY, May 31, 50. *Educ:* Yale Univ, BS, 72; Stanford Univ, MD, 76. *Prof Exp:* Intern & resident internal med, Univ Chicago Hosps & Clins, 76-78. *Mem:* Am Col

Physicians; Am Soc Microbiol; Am Soc Clin Oncol; Am Asn Cancer Res; Am Soc Clin Invest. *Res:* Role of oncogenes in hormone dependent human neoplasma; genetic markers for prostate cancer; medical oncology. *Mailing Add:* Med Oncol Georgetown Univ Hosp 3800 Reservoir NW Washington DC 20007-2196

GELNOVATCH, V, ELECTRICAL ENGINEERING. *Current Pos:* DIR MICROWAVE & SIGNAL PROCESSING DEVELOP DIV, US ARMY ELECTRONICS TECHNOL & DEVICES LAB, 63- *Educ:* Monmouth Col, BS, 63; NY Univ, MS, 66. *Prof Exp:* Signal Corps Sgt, US Army, 56-59. *Concurrent Pos:* Site chief, Holenstadt Microwave Radio Relay Sta, Ger; mem exec & tech comt, Int Solid State Circuits Conf, 68-79; participant, Inst Elec & Electronics Engrs & USSR Popov Soc Exchange Prog, 74; army mem, Adv Group Electron Dev; chmn, Army Millimeter Wave Steering Group, Dept Defense; assoc ed, Microwave J; mem adv bd, Elec Eng Dept & vis prof elec eng, Univ Va; rep, Solid State Circuits Coun. *Mem:* Fel Inst Elec & Electronics Engrs. *Res:* Microwave solid state devices; microwave circuit design; optimization; measurement and synthesis; microwave transistor amplifiers; reflectometer modeling. *Mailing Add:* US Army Res Lab EPSD Directorate AMSRI-EP Ft Monmouth NJ 07703

GELOPULOS, DEMOSTHENES PETER, ELECTRICAL ENGINEERING. *Current Pos:* AT DEPT ENG, VALPARAISO UNIV. *Personal Data:* b Valparaiso, Ind, Apr 24, 38; m 58; c 3. *Educ:* Valparaiso Univ, BS, 60; Univ Notre Dame, MS, 62; Univ Ariz, PhD(elec eng), 67. *Honors & Awards:* Phoenix Outstanding Achievement Award, Inst Elec & Electronics Engrs, 73. *Prof Exp:* Res engr comput, Northrop Nortronics Res Park, 62-63; asst prof elec eng, Univ Akron, 67-68; prof elec eng, Ariz State Univ, 68- *Concurrent Pos:* Consult, TRW, Inc, Euclid, Ohio, 67-68 & Govt Electronics Div, Motorola, 68-69, Ariz Pub Serv Co, 68-78 & Boeing Comput Serv, 77-; prin investr, Res Prog at Ariz State Univ, Elec Power Res Inst, 76- *Mem:* Sr mem Inst Elec & Electronics Engrs. *Res:* Computer simulation of engineering systems; power systems dynamics. *Mailing Add:* Elec Eng Valparaiso Univ Valparaiso IN 46383

GELPERIN, ALAN, NEUROPHYSIOLOGY, BEHAVIORAL BIOLOGY. *Current Pos:* MEM TECH STAFF, BIOL COMPUT RES DEPT, AT&T BELL LABS, 82- *Personal Data:* b Cincinnati, Ohio, July 28, 41; m 82; c 5. *Educ:* Carleton Col, BA, 62; Univ Pa, PhD(zool), 66. *Honors & Awards:* Newcomb-Cleveland Prize, AAAS, 71. *Prof Exp:* From asst prof to prof, Princeton Univ, 68-82. *Concurrent Pos:* Dir, Neural Systs & Behav, Marine Biol Lab, Woods Hole, MA, 77-79; Guggenheim fel, 73. *Mem:* Soc Neurosci; Biophys Soc; Am Physiol Soc. *Res:* Synaptic physiology and learning. *Mailing Add:* 207 Harrison Lane Princeton NJ 08540

GELTMAN, SYDNEY, THEORETICAL PHYSICS. *Current Pos:* PHYSICIST, JOINT INST LAB ASTROPHYS, UNIV COLO, 62- *Personal Data:* b Philadelphia, Pa, May 23, 27; m 53; c 3. *Educ:* Yale Univ, BS, 48, MS, 49, PhD (physics), 52. *Honors & Awards:* A V Humboldt US Sr Scientist Award, 82-83. *Prof Exp:* Physicist, Westinghouse Res Labs, 52-54; appl physics lab, Johns Hopkins Univ, 54-57; National Bur Stands, 57-86. *Concurrent Pos:* Adj prof, Univ Colo, 63-; lectr, Univ Col, London, 66-67; consult Cen Saclay, 78-81, Livermore Nat Lab, 84-85. *Mem:* Fel Am Phys Soc. *Res:* Theory of atomic scattering processes and ionization; atomic radiative processes. *Mailing Add:* Joint Inst Lab Astrophysics Univ Colo Boulder CO 80309-0440

GELUSO, KENNETH NICHOLAS, MAMMALOGY, ECOLOGY. *Current Pos:* asst prof, 77-83, ASSOC PROF BIOL, UNIV NEBR, OMAHA, 83- *Personal Data:* b New York, NY, Dec 10, 45. *Educ:* Univ Vt, BA, 67; Univ Okla, MS, 70; Univ NMex, PhD(biol), 72. *Prof Exp:* Researcher, World Wildlife Fund & Nat Park Serv, 73-77. *Mem:* Am Soc Mammalogists. *Res:* Mammalian biology. *Mailing Add:* Dept Biol Univ Nebr 6000 Dodge St Omaha NE 68182-0001

GEMAN, STUART ALAN, MACHINE & NATURAL VISION, PROBABILITY & STATISTICS. *Current Pos:* PROF APPL MATH, BROWN UNIV, 77- *Personal Data:* b Chicago, Ill, Mar 23, 49; m 78, Hannah Look; c Aaron & Jesse. *Educ:* Univ Mich, BS, 71; Dartmouth Col, MS, 73; Mass Inst Technol, PhD(math), 77. *Mem:* AAAS; Am Math Soc; fel Inst Elec & Electronics Engrs Instrumentation & Measurement Soc; Inst Elec & Electronics Engrs. *Res:* Machine and natural vision; probabilistic image models and their applications to image analysis; neural representations. *Mailing Add:* Appl Math Dept Brown Univ 180 George St PO Box F Providence RI 02912-0001. *E-Mail:* geman@dam.brown.edu

GEMBICKI, STANLEY ARTHUR, CATALYST RESEARCH & DEVELOPMENT, SEPARATION PROCESS RESEARCH & DEVELOPMENT. *Current Pos:* DIR CATALYST RES, UOP RES CTR, 86- *Personal Data:* b Davenport, Iowa, Dec 18, 41; m 70; c 2. *Educ:* Purdue Univ, BS, 64; Dartmouth Col, DE, 69. *Prof Exp:* Mgr catalyst develop, Exp Develop, UOP Inc, 75-78, catalyst res & develop, Process Develop, 78-80, mgr separation technol, Process Res & Develop, 80-86. *Mem:* Am Inst Chem Eng; Am Chem Soc. *Res:* Discovery of new catalysts and research toward new petroleum and petrochemical processes. *Mailing Add:* UOP Res Ctr TIC Box 5016 50 E Algonquin Rd Des Plaines IL 60017-5016

GEMIGNANI, MICHAEL C, TOPOLOGY. *Current Pos:* RETIRED. *Personal Data:* b Baltimore, Md, Feb 23, 38; m 62; c 2. *Educ:* Univ Rochester, BA, 62; Univ Notre Dame, MS, 64, PhD(math), 65; Ind Univ, JD, 80. *Prof Exp:* Instr math, St Mary's Col, Ind, 64-65; asst prof, State Univ NY, Buffalo, 65-68; assoc prof, Univ Notre Dame, 68-72; prof math sci & chmn dept, Ind Univ, Purdue Univ, Indianapolis, 72-81; prof math sci & dean, Col Sci & Humanities, Ball State Univ, Muncie, 81-86; dean, Col Arts & Sci, Univ Maine, 86-88; sr vpres & provost, Univ Houston, Clear Lake, 88-91. *Concurrent Pos:* Consult comput law; chmn, Comt Info Processing, Ind Corp Sci & Technol. *Mem:* Math Asn Am; Am Bar Asn; AAAS; Sigma Xi; Comput Law Asn; Asn Comput Mach. *Res:* Computer related law. *Mailing Add:* 1617 W 11th St Freeport TX 77541

GEMINDER, ROBERT, INSTRUMENTATION & EXPERIMENTAL MECHANICS, MARKETING & MANAGEMENT. *Current Pos:* ENGR CONSULT, 84- *Personal Data:* b Wroclaw, Poland; Aug 3, 35; US citizen; m 59, Judith Strauss; c Minam, Ellen & Shia. *Educ:* Carnegie Mellon Univ, BS, 57. *Honors & Awards:* Seligman Award, Inst Environ Sci, 81. *Prof Exp:* Engr, Ling Temco Yought, 57-59; mgr, Aerojet Gen Corp, 59-65; asst dir, Mech Res Inc, 65-72; dir, Syst Develop Corp, 72-82; vpres, Hughes Tool Corp, 82-84. *Concurrent Pos:* Instr, Citrus Col, 62-65; lectr, ocean seminars, 78; dir mkg, CINC, 95-96. *Mem:* Fel Inst Environ Sci (pres, 75-76); sr mem Instrument Soc Am; Marine Tech Soc. *Res:* Underwater instrumentation; engineering analysis. *Mailing Add:* 50-B Peninsula Ctr Dr Rolling Hills Estates CA 90274

GEMMELL, ROBERT S(TINSON), CIVIL ENGINEERING. *Current Pos:* co-dir, USPHS, 64-65, res grants, 64-68, from asst prof to assoc prof, 64-75, chmn coun urban & regional planning, 75-79, PROF CIVIL ENG, TECHNOL INST, NORTHWESTERN UNIV, 75- *Personal Data:* b Kenton, Ohio, Apr 14, 33; m 55; c 4. *Educ:* Ohio State Univ, BCE, 56, MS, 57; Harvard Univ, PhD(eng), 63. *Prof Exp:* Instr civil eng, Rutgers Univ, 57; lectr & res fel div eng & appl physics & co-dir, USPHS res grant, Harvard Univ, 63-64. *Concurrent Pos:* Off Water Resources res grants, 70-73; res contract, Forest Serv, USDA, 77-79. *Mem:* Am Soc Civil Engrs; Am Water Works Asn; Am Geophys Union; Am Water Resources Asn. *Res:* Coagulation; water treatment processes; water quality management; environmental health engineering; water resources systems; urban systems engineering. *Mailing Add:* Dept Civil Eng Technol Inst Northwestern Univ Evanston IL 60208

GEMMER, ROBERT VALENTINE, PHYSICAL ORGANIC CHEMISTRY, COMBUSTION SCIENCE. *Current Pos:* prog mgr, Gas Res Inst, 85-89, sr prof mgr combustion, 89-93, sr tech mgr indust processes, 93-95, PRIN TECH MGR INDUST PROCESSES, GAS RES INST, 95- *Personal Data:* b Morristown, NJ, Nov 11, 46; m, Claudia Bloomfield; c Sean C & Eric C. *Educ:* Worcester Polytech Inst, BS, 68; Stanford Univ, PhD(org chem), 74. *Prof Exp:* Res asst org chem, Stanford Univ, 68-74; fel, Johns Hopkins Univ, 74-75; res assoc polymer chem, NASA, Ames Res Ctr, 75-77; res chemist polymer chem, Am Cyanamid Co, Stanford, Conn, 77-79; proj mgr, Duracell, Inc, 80-85. *Concurrent Pos:* Resident res assoc, Nat Res Coun, 75-77; trainee, NSF. *Mem:* Am Chem Soc; Am Inst Chem Engrs; Combustion Inst. *Res:* Application of water soluble polymers to water treatment and purification; oxidation of polyhydrocarbons; chemistry of conducting organic materials; alkaline zinc batteries; combustion chemistry and physics. *Mailing Add:* GRI 8600 W Bryn Mawr Ave Chicago IL 60631. *Fax:* 773-399-8170; *E-Mail:* rgemmer@gr:.org

GEMPERLINE, MARGARET MARY CETERA, ANALYTICAL CHEMISTRY. *Current Pos:* RES ASSOC, EAST CAROLINA UNIV, 82- *Personal Data:* b Chicago, Ill, May 31, 53. *Educ:* Ill Benedictine Col, BS, 75; ECarolina Univ, MS, 81. *Prof Exp:* Asst res chemist, CPC Int, Argonne, Ill, 75-77, asst plant chemist, 77-78; sci tech res asst, Ill Legis Coun, 78-79. *Mem:* Am Chem Soc. *Res:* Instrument-computer interfacing; programmed experiments for physically impaired persons. *Mailing Add:* 1000 E Third St Greenville NC 27858-2043

GEMPERLINE, PAUL JOSEPH, MULTICOMPONENT ANALYSIS, COMPUTERIZED DATA ANALYSIS. *Current Pos:* ASST PROF CHEM, E CAROLINA UNIV, 82- *Personal Data:* b Cleveland, Ohio; m 84. *Educ:* Cleveland State Univ, BS, 78, PhD(anal chem), 82. *Concurrent Pos:* Consult, Burroughs Wellcome Co, 84-85. *Mem:* Sigma Xi; Am Chem Soc; Soc Appl Spectros. *Res:* Application of factor analysis to analytical chemistry, chromatographic curve resolution, multicomponent background correction; development of new methods of data analysis. *Mailing Add:* Dept Chem ECarolina Univ Greenville NC 27834

GEMSA, DIETHARD, INFLAMMATION & CYTOKINES, IMMUNITY AGAINST VIRUSES. *Current Pos:* PROF & HEAD IMMUNOL, INST IMMUNOL, PHILIPPS UNIV, MARBURG, GER, 85- *Personal Data:* b Berlin, Ger, Aug 9, 37; m 68, Inken Fischer; c Jan (Ulrich), Kerstin F & Meike C. *Educ:* Univ Freiburg, Ger, MD, 64; Univ Heidelberg, Ger, Priv Doz(immunol), 74. *Prof Exp:* Res fel immunol, Univ Wash, Med Sch, Seattle, 65-67; resident internal med, Univ Mainz, Ger, 68-70; res assoc immunol, Dept Internal Med, Univ Calif, Med Sch, San Francisco, 70-73; asst prof, Inst Immunol, Univ Heidelberg, Ger, 74-82; assoc prof immunopharmacol, Med Sch Hannover, Ger, 83-84. *Concurrent Pos:* Ed-in-chief, Immunobiol, 78- *Mem:* Am Asn Immunologists; Ger Soc Immunol. *Res:* Role of activated monocytes/macrophages in the immune response; inflammation; antiviral defense systems; eicosanoid and cytokine release; tumor cytotoxicity. *Mailing Add:* Inst Immunol Univ Maburg Robert-Koch-Str 17 35033 Marburg Germany. *Fax:* 49-6421-286813; *E-Mail:* gemsa@mailer.uni.marburg.de

GEMSKI, PETER, IMMUNOLOGY, MOLECULAR BIOLOGY. *Current Pos:* RETIRED. *Personal Data:* b Bellingham, Mass, Oct 3, 36; m 92, Lenni J Coplestone; c Thad & Margaret. *Educ:* Brown Univ, AB, 58; Univ RI, MS, 60; Univ Pittsburgh, PhD(microbiol), 64. *Prof Exp:* NIH fels, Lister Inst Prev Med, London, Eng, 64-65 & Dept Med Microbiol, Sch Med, Stanford Univ, 66; res microbiologist, Dept Bact Immunol, Walter Reed Army Inst, 67-74, asst chief, Dept Appl Immunol, 74-80, chief, Dept Biol Chem, 80-87, chief, Dept Molecular Path, 88-96. *Mem:* AAAS; Am Soc Microbiol; fel Infectious Dis Soc. *Res:* Intergeneric bacterial hybridizations; genetic control of lipopolysaccharide biosynthesis; pathogenesis of enteric infections; virulence factors, molecular genetics; molecular and cell biology of bacterial toxins. *Mailing Add:* 160 Oak Hill Rd Sanbornton NH 03269. *Fax:* 202-576-0947

GENACK, AZRIEL Z, ELECTROMAGNETIC CONCEPTS & CLASSICAL WAVE PROPOGATION, SOLID STATE PHYSICS & OPTICS. *Current Pos:* prof, 84-94, DISTINGUISHED PROF PHYSICS, QUEENS COL, 94- *Personal Data:* b NY, 1942; m 66, Ahura Swiatycki; c Yakob, Yitzi, Dani, Avi & Elie. *Educ:* Columbia Univ, BA, 64, PhD(physics), 73. *Prof Exp:* Res assoc, City Univ New York, 73-75; IBM Res Lab, 75-77; sr staff physicist, Exxon Res & Eng Co, 77-84. *Mem:* Fel Am Phys Soc; Optical Soc Am. *Res:* Fundamental measurements of the statistics of electromagnetic waves in random media; observations of short-range, long-range and infinite-range intensity correlation and of intensity and transmission distributions have clarified the universal propogation. *Mailing Add:* Dept Physics Queens Col City Univ New York 65-30 Kissena Blvd Flushing NY 11367. *Fax:* 718-497-3407; *E-Mail:* azg$phys@qcl.qc.edu

GENAIDY, ASHRAF MOHAMED, WORK PHYSIOLOGY, BIOMECHANICS. *Current Pos:* ASST PROF ERGONOMICS, SAFETY & STATIST, WESTERN MICH UNIV, 87- *Personal Data:* b Cairo, Egypt, May 10, 57; m 82; c 1. *Educ:* Cairo Univ, BSc, 80; Univ Miami, MSc, 83, PhD(biomed & indust eng), 87. *Concurrent Pos:* Lectr syst eng, Cairo Univ, 80-81; grad asst ergonomics, Univ Miami, 85-87. *Mem:* Sigma Xi; Human Factors Soc; Ergonomics; Inst Indust Engrs; Am Soc Biomech. *Res:* Ergonomics; safety; biomedical engineering; work methods and work measurement. *Mailing Add:* Univ Cincinnati ML 72 Mech Indust & Nuclear Eng Cincinnati OH 45221

GENCO, JOSEPH MICHAEL, CHEMICAL ENGINEERING, PHYSICAL CHEMISTRY. *Current Pos:* CALDER PROF PULP & PAPER ENG, UNIV MAINE, ORONO, 74-, PROF CHEM ENG, 79- *Personal Data:* b Cleveland, Ohio, Apr 13, 39; m 67; c 1. *Educ:* Case Western Res Univ, BS, 60; Ohio State Univ, MS, 62, PhD(chem eng), 65. *Prof Exp:* Assoc chief, Battelle Mem Inst, 65-74. *Mem:* AAAS; Am Inst Chem Engrs; Am Chem Soc; Tech Asn Pulp & Paper; Sigma Xi. *Res:* Fundamentals of pulping, bleaching and paper-making, pulp and paper technology. *Mailing Add:* 12 Winterhaven Dr Orono ME 04473-1118

GENCO, ROBERT J, IMMUNOCHEMISTRY, MICROBIOLOGY. *Current Pos:* from asst prof to assoc prof, 67-74, dir, Grad Periodont, 68-85, DISTINGUISHED PROF ORAL BIOL & PERIODONT, SCH DENT MED, STATE UNIV NY, BUFFALO, 74-, CHMN, DEPT ORAL BIOL, 77-; STAFF, BUFFALO GEN HOSP, 69- *Personal Data:* b Silver Creek, NY, Oct 31, 38; m 57, Sandra Clarke; c Deborah (Powell), Robert M & Julie (Abford). *Educ:* State Univ NY Buffalo, DDS, 63; Univ Pa, PhD(microbiol), 67. *Hon Degrees:* DSc, Georgetown Univ, 90. *Honors & Awards:* George Thorn Award, 77; William J Gies Found Award, Am Acad Periodont, 83; Seymour J Kreshover lectr, NIH, 85; Gold Medal Res, Am Dent Asn, 91. *Prof Exp:* USPHS fel, 63-66. *Concurrent Pos:* Adv ed, Immunochem, 73-77; dir, Fel Prog Immunol & Periodont, State Univ NY, Buffalo, 74-; Periodont Dis Clin Res Ctr, 78-, assoc dean grad studies & res, Sch Dent Med, 85-, distinguished prof, 89-, interim chmn, Dept Microbiol, Sch Med & Biomed Sci, 90-; basic res in oral sci award, Int Asn Dent Res, 75, res periodont dis award, 81; chmn, Dent Sect, AAAS, 80; res forum, Am Acad Periodont, 84-; chmn, Ad Hoc Comt New Frontiers Oral Health Res, 85-89; mem, Coun Dent Res, Am Dent Asn, 87-90, chmn, 89-90; mem sci adv bd, Nat Inst Dent Res, 87-; ed, J Periodont, 88-; mem, Dent Prod Panel, Food & Drug Admin, 88-92 & 96. *Mem:* Inst Med-Nat Acad Sci; Am Acad Periodont; AAAS; Am Asn Dent Res (vpres, 83, pres-elect, 84, pres, 85); Am Asn Dent Schs; Am Asn Immunologists; Am Asn Microbiologists; Am Dent Asn; Int Asn Dent Res (vpres, 89, pres-elect, 90, pres, 91); NY Acad Sci. *Res:* Structure-function relationships of the various antibody molecules, especially those present in external secretions; host parasite interations in bacterial infectious, neutrophil function; risk factors for chronic infectious diseases. *Mailing Add:* Dept Oral Biol Dent Sch State Univ NY Foster Hall Buffalo NY 14214. *Fax:* 716-829-2387; *E-Mail:* robert_genco@sdm.buffalo.edu

GENCSOY, HASAN TAHSIN, MECHANICAL ENGINEERING. *Current Pos:* from instr to prof, 56-85, EMER PROF MECH ENG, WVA UNIV, 85- *Personal Data:* b Turkey, July 4, 24; US citizen; m 53, Suheyla Akyurek; c Nilgun. *Educ:* Univ Calif, BS, 49; WVa Univ, MS, 51. *Honors & Awards:* Nat Adams Mem Award, Am Welding Soc, 66. *Prof Exp:* Customer engr, Int Bus Mach World Trade Corp, 51-52; prod engr, Bakir Sanayi Ltd, 53-55. *Concurrent Pos:* Consult, Chamber Indust, Turkey, 53-55; design eng consult, pvt cos, Forensic Eng Consult, 74-; consult, WVa Dept Nat Resources. *Mem:* Am Soc Mech Engrs; Am Soc Eng Educ; Sigma Xi. *Res:* Machine design; engineering analysis; engineering systems analysis; similitude in engineering; experimental stress analysis; machine design and stress analysis. *Mailing Add:* 3400 Galt Ocean Dr 902-S Ft Lauderdale FL 33308

GENDEL, STEVEN MICHAEL, MOLECULAR GENETICS, CYANOBACTERIA. *Current Pos:* BR CHIEF, BIOTECH STUDIES BR, CTR FOOD, SAFETY & APPL NUTRIT, FOOD & DRUG ADMIN, 90- *Educ:* Univ Calif, Irvine, PhD(cell biol), 77. *Prof Exp:* Asst prof genetics, Iowa State Univ, 83-90. *Res:* Plasmid molecular biology; nitrogen fixation. *Mailing Add:* Biotech Studies Br Ctr Food, Safety & Appl Nutrit Food & Drug Admin 6502 S Archer Rd Summit-Argo IL 60501

GENDELMAN, HOWARD ELIOT, INFECTIOUS DISEASES. *Current Pos:* PROF MED, PATH & MICROBIOL, UNIV NEBR MED CTR, 93-; CHIEF, LAB VIRAL PATHOGENESIS, DEPT PATH & MICROBIOL, UNIV NEBR MED CTR, 93- *Personal Data:* b Philadelphia, Pa, Mar 18, 54; m 80, Bonnie R Bloch; c Lesley B, Sierra & Adam. *Educ:* Muhlenberg Col, BS, 75; Pa State Univ, MD, 79; Am Bd Internal Med, dipl, 82. *Honors & Awards:* Leo M Davidoff Soc Award, Albert Einstein Col Med, 81; Ray Kroc lectr, Univ Calif, Los Angeles, 87. *Prof Exp:* Res assoc, Pa State Univ, 79, instr neuroanat, 79; resident med, Montefiore Hosp Ctr, Albert Einstein Col Med, 79-82; clin res fel, Dept Neurol & Med, Johns Hopkins Univ Hosp, 82-85; asst prof med, Div Infectious Dis, Johns Hopkins Univ Sch Med, 85-89, lectr, Dept Infectious Dis & Immunol, Sch Pub Health & Hyg, 85-92. *Concurrent Pos:* Prin investr or co-investr numerous grants, 83-; consult, Walter Reed Army Med Ctr, 84, Armed Forces Inst Path, 84, Bethesda Res Labs, 84, Oncor, Inc, 87, Glaxo Res, Inc, 88, Appl Biotechnol, 90, Schering Corp, 90-, Viragen, 90, Advan Biother Concepts, 92- & New Horizons Diag, 92-; spec expert, Lab Molecular Microbiol, Sect Biochem Virol, Nat Inst Allergy & Infectious Dis, NIH, 85-87; co-dir, HIV-Immunopathogenesis Lab, Dept Cellular Immunol, Walter Reed Army Inst Res, 87-92; prin scientist, Henry M Jackson Found Advan Mil Med, Uniformed Servs Univ Health Sci, 88-92, res assoc prof, Dept Path, 90; staff physician infectious dis, Walter Reed Army Med Ctr, 88-92; Carter-Wallace fel, 88-91. *Mem:* Am Col Physicians; AMA; Am Soc Neurol Invest; Am Soc Microbiol; Reticuloendothelial Soc; Clin Immunol Soc; Int Soc Interferon Res; Am Asn Immunol. *Res:* Acquired immunodeficiency syndrome clinical and basic science; development of therapeutics for neurological abnormalities associated with human immunodeficiency virus disease; numerous publications. *Mailing Add:* Dept Path & Microbiol Univ Nebr Med Ctr 600 S 42nd St Omaha NE 68198-5215

GENDERNALIK, SUE AYDELOTT, CHEMISTRY OF ENGINE FUEL RELATIONSHIP IN INTERNAL COMBUSTION. *Current Pos:* RETIRED. *Personal Data:* b Water Valley, Ky; m 46, Edward J. *Educ:* Marygrove Col, BS, 42. *Honors & Awards:* Arch T Colwell Merit Award, Soc Automotive Engrs, 71. *Prof Exp:* Chemist org synthetic chem, Ethyl Corp, 42-44, res chemist anal method develop, 44-52, staff chemist engine fuel res, 52-72, sr res chemist, environ res, 73-81. *Mem:* Am Chem Soc. *Res:* Fuel combustion; engine fuel relationships, particularly as related to exhaust emissions; public health impact of consumer use of lead and manganese; environmental research. *Mailing Add:* 682 N Rosedale Ct Grosse Pointe MI 48236

GENDLER, SANDRA J, MUCINGLYCOPROTEINS, BREAST CANCER BIOLOGY. *Current Pos:* postdoctoral biochem & molecular biol, 84-87, HEAD, MOLECULAR EPITHELIAL CELL BIOL LAB, IMP CANCER RES FUND, 87- *Personal Data:* b Minot, NDak, Sept 21, 44; m 66; c 2. *Educ:* Univ Minn, BA, 66; Univ Ill, MA, 73; Univ Southern Calif, PhD(biochem), 84. *Honors & Awards:* Harry J Deuel Award, Univ Southern Calif, 84. *Prof Exp:* Technician microbiol, Calif State Univ, Long Beach, 75-78; res asst biochem, Univ SCalif, 79-84. *Mem:* Am Soc Cell Biol; Int Soc Differentiation; Am Asn Cancer Res; Europ Asn Cancer Res; Brit Soc Cell Biol; Int Asn Breast Cancer Res; Sigma Xi. *Res:* Molecular studies of the function and regulation of molecules expressed during mammary gland differentiation and carcinogenesis. *Mailing Add:* Dept Biochem & Molecular Biol Mayo Clin S C Johnson Med Res 13400 E Shea Blvd Scottsdale AZ 85259. *Fax:* 602-301-7017

GENEAUX, NANCY LYNNE, acoustics, signal processing; deceased, see previous edition for last biography

GENECIN, ABRAHAM, INTERNAL MEDICINE, CARDIOLOGY. *Current Pos:* RETIRED. *Personal Data:* b Minneapolis, Minn, Aug 21, 18; m 41; c 2. *Educ:* Columbia Univ, AB, 39; Johns Hopkins Univ, MD, 43. *Prof Exp:* From instr to assoc prof med, Sch Med, Johns Hopkins Univ, 44-91. *Concurrent Pos:* Pvt pract. *Mem:* AAAS; AMA; Am Heart Asn; Am Col Physicians. *Res:* Cardiology. *Mailing Add:* 5616 Cross Country Blvd Baltimore MD 21209-4418

GENEGA, STANLEY G, CIVIL ENGINEERING. *Current Pos:* Comdr 2nd lt, US Army, 65, major gen, comdr, Southwestern Div, Dallas, comdr, SAtlantic Div, Atlanta, DIR, CIVIL WORKS HQ, US ARMY CORPS ENGRS WASHINGTON, 92- *Personal Data:* Beth & Stanley Jr. *Educ:* Mass Inst Technol, MS. *Concurrent Pos:* Comdr, Army Engr Dist Savannah; engr consult, Vietnam & Ft Meade Md. *Mailing Add:* Dept Dir Army Civil Works 20 Massachusetts Ave NW Washington DC 20314

GENEL, MYRON, PEDIATRICS, ENDOCRINOLOGY. *Current Pos:* from asst prof to assoc prof pediat, Yale Univ Sch Med, 71-81, dir, Sect Pediat Endocrinol, 71-85, prog dir, Children's Clin Res Ctr, 71-86, PROF PEDIAT, YALE UNIV SCH MED, 81-, ASSOC DEAN GOVT & COMMUNITY AFFAIRS, 85- *Personal Data:* b York, Pa, Jan 6, 36; m 68, Phyllis Berkman; c Elizabeth, Jennifer & Abby. *Educ:* Moravian Col, BS, 57; Univ Pa, MD, 61; Yale Univ, MA, 83. *Hon Degrees:* DSc, Moravian Col, 95. *Honors & Awards:* Jonathan May Award, Am Diabetes Asn, 79. *Prof Exp:* Intern med, Mt Sinai

Hosp, 61-62; resident pediat, Children's Hosp Philadelphia, 62-64; pediatrician, US Army, Teop Res Med Lab, San Juan, PR, 64-66; fel pediat endocrinol, Johns Hopkins Hosp, 66-67; fel genetics & metab dis, Children's Hosp Philadelphia, 67-69; assoc pediat, Sch Med, Univ Pa, 69-71. *Concurrent Pos:* Robert Wood Johnson Health Policy fel, Inst Med-Nat Acad Sci, 82-83; consult health policy, subcomt on Invest & Oversight Comt Sci & Technol, US House Reps, 82-84; chmn, transplant adv comt, Off Comnr, Dept Income Maintenance, State of Conn, 84-92; chmn & organizer Pub Policy Coun, Am Pediat Soc, Assn Med Sch Pediat Dept Chmn & Soc Pediat Res; mem, Health Policy Fel Bd, Inst Med-Nat Acad Sci, 89-95; chmn, Coun Acad Socs, Asn Am Med Cols, 90-91; pres, Conn United Soc Res Excellence, 90-93, chmn, bd dirs, 93-94. *Mem:* Am Acad Pediat; Am Pediat Soc; Asn Am Med Col; Endocrine Soc; Soc Pediat Res; AMA. *Res:* Disorders of growth and sexual development; genetics markers and detection of multiple endocrine neoplasia type 2A. *Mailing Add:* 30 Richard Sweet Dr Woodbridge CT 06525-1126

GENENSKY, SAMUEL MILTON, VISUAL RESEARCH, APPLIED MATHEMATICS. *Current Pos:* dir, 78-83, CONSULT, CTR PARTIALLY SIGHTED, SANTA MONICA HOSP MED CTR, 83- *Personal Data:* b New Bedford, Mass, July 26, 27; m 53; c 2. *Educ:* Brown Univ, BS, 49, PhD(appl math), 58; Harvard Univ, MA, 51. *Prof Exp:* Mathematician, Nat Bur Stand, 51-54; assoc mathematician, Rand Corp, 58-59, res mathematician, 59-78. *Concurrent Pos:* Pres, Coun Citizens With Low Vision, Am Coun for the Blind; mem, Adv Comt Serv Blind & Partially Sighted, Calif Voc Rehab Dept & Adv Comt Low Vision Serv, Am Found for the Blind. *Mem:* Sigma Xi; AAAS; Am Math Soc; fel Am Acad Optom. *Res:* Design of visual aids for disabled persons; closed circuit television system to aid the partially sighted; visual information transfer problems of the partially sighted; classical continuum mechanics, especially elasticity and viscous fluid theory. *Mailing Add:* 1119 23rd St No 6 Santa Monica CA 90403

GENERAZIO, ED, PHYSICS. *Current Pos:* Sr res scientist, NASA, 83-92, technol integration officer, 92-94, BR HEAD, NON DESTRUCTIVE EVALUATION SCI, NASA, 94-, PROG MGR, OFF SAFETY & MISSION ASSURANCE, 96- *Educ:* Univ Mass, BA, 76; Ill Inst Technol, MS, 79; Penn State Univ, Phd(physics), 83. *Res:* Research management. *Mailing Add:* Langley Res Ctr NASA Langley VA 23681. *Fax:* 756-864-4914

GENEROSO, WALDERICO MALINAWAN, GENETICS. *Current Pos:* fel mutagenesis, 67-68, BIOLOGIST MUTAGENESIS, OAK RIDGE NAT LAB, 68- *Personal Data:* b Bauan, Batangas, Philippines, Feb 16, 41; US citizen; m 63; c 2. *Educ:* Univ Philippines, BSA, 60, MS, 62; Univ Mo, Columbia, PhD(genetics), 67. *Prof Exp:* Instr genetics, Univ Philippines, 62-64. *Concurrent Pos:* Consult biol res, Third World Countries. *Mem:* Genet Soc Am; Environ Mutagen Soc; AAAS. *Res:* Chemical and radiation mutagenesis in mice; emphasis on transmissible genetic effects, expression of mutations and mechanisms for chromosome observation formation. *Mailing Add:* 112 Mohawk Rd Oak Ridge TN 37830

GENES, ANDREW NICHOLAS, GEOLOGY, HYDROGEOLOGY. *Current Pos:* asst prof, 66-80, ASSOC PROF GEOL, UNIV MASS, BOSTON, 80- *Personal Data:* b Boston, Mass, Oct 28, 32; m 63, 78, Anne Marr; c Thalia, Carl, Peter, Karen, Jane, Peter & Anne. *Educ:* Boston Univ, AB, 55, AM, 60; Syracuse Univ, PhD(geol), 73. *Prof Exp:* Ed sci, McGraw-Hill Bk Co, 60-66. *Concurrent Pos:* Field mapper, Main State Geol Surv, 73-; chief geologist consult, Hidell-Eyster Assoc, Weytmouth, Mass. *Mem:* Norweg Geol Soc; Am Quaternary Asn. *Res:* Tillite genesis; cirque genesis and upland erosion surface denudation; deglaciation chronology of Northeastern Maine and Greece. *Mailing Add:* Earth Sci 100 Morrissey Blvd Univ Mass/Boston Boston MA 02125. *Fax:* 614-287-6511

GENEST, JACQUES, NEPHROLOGY, ENDOCRINOLOGY. *Current Pos:* sci dir, 67-84, CONSULT, CLIN RES INST MONTREAL, 84- *Personal Data:* b Montreal, Que, May 29, 19; m 53, Estelle Deschamps; c Paul, Suzanne, Jacques Jr, Marie & Helene. *Educ:* Jean de Brebeuf Col, BA, 37; Univ Montreal, MD, 42. *Hon Degrees:* LLD, Queen's Univ, Ont, 66 & Univ Toronto, 70; DSc, Laval Univ, 73, McGill Univ, 79 & Univ Ottawa, 80; DMedSci, Sherbrooke Univ, 74, Mem Univ Nfld, 78, St Francis Xavier Univ, Antigonish, NS, 83, State Univ NY, Buffalo, 84, Rockefeller Univ, 86, Concordia Univ, MTL, 86, Montpellier Univ, France, 89. *Honors & Awards:* Gairdner Award, Univ Toronto, 63; Companion of Can, 67; Flavelle Award, Royal Soc Can, 68; Stouffer Prize, 69; Killam Award, 86; Royal Bank Award, 80; F N G Starr Prize, 82; Izaak Walton Killam Mem Prize, Toronto, 86; Grand Officier, Ordre Nat Que, 91; J H Graham Prize, Royal Col Physicians & Surgeons, Can, 93. *Prof Exp:* Sr intern, Hotel Dieu Hosp, 42, asst resident path, 43-44, chief resident med, 44-45; asst physician, Johns Hopkins Hosp, 45-48; with Rockefeller Inst Med Res, 48-51; med survr, Europ Med Res Ctrs for Que Govt, 51-52; chmn dept med, Fac Med, Univ Montreal & physician-in-chief, Hotel Dieu Hosp, 64-68. *Concurrent Pos:* Archbold fel med, Johns Hopkins Hosp, 45-46, Commonwealth Fund fel, 46-48; lectr, Royal Col, 61; chmn, Med Res Coun Quebec, 64-69; Sims Commonwealth Travelling Prof, 70; specialist & consult hypertension, nephrology & endocrinology; consult, dept nephrology-hypertension, Univ Montreal Hotel-Dieu Hosp, 84- *Mem:* Endocrine Soc; master Am Col Physicians; Am Clin & Climat Asn; Asn Am Physicians; fel Royal Soc Can; Peripatetic Club USA. *Res:* Human arterial hypertension; relationship of kidneys and adrenals to hypertension; electrolytes and renal function. *Mailing Add:* Clin Res Inst Montreal 110 Pine Ave W Montreal PQ H2W 1R7 Can

GENETELLI, EMIL J, SANITARY ENGINEERING, MICROBIOLOGY. *Current Pos:* From instr to asst prof, 62-70, assoc prof, 70-80, PROF ENVIRON SCI, RUTGERS UNIV, 80- *Personal Data:* b Brooklyn, NY, Feb 25, 37; m 60; c 3. *Educ:* Manhattan Col, BCE, 59; Rutgers Univ, MS, 62, PhD(environ sci), 65. *Honors & Awards:* Heukelekian Award Indust Wastewater Treatment. *Mem:* Sigma Xi. *Res:* Microbiology of water and wastewater treatment; water resources; air pollution control; solid waste disposal; aquatic microbiology. *Mailing Add:* 1 Thrush Dr East Brunswick NJ 08816-2725

GENG, SHU, APPLIED STATISTICS. *Current Pos:* assoc prof, 76-84, PROF AGRON & RANGE SCI, UNIV CALIF, DAVIS, 84-, ASSOC DEAN, COL OF AGR & ENVIRON SCI. *Personal Data:* b China, Sept 3, 42; US citizen; m 68; c 2. *Educ:* Nat Taiwan Univ, BS, 64; Kans State Univ, MS, 69, PhD(statist), 72. *Prof Exp:* Statistician, Agr Res & Develop Div, Upjohn Co, 72-76. *Mem:* Biomet Soc; Am Statist Asn; Am Soc Agron. *Res:* Multivariate methods in design and data analysis; simulation models. *Mailing Add:* 223 Hunt Hall Davis CA 95616

GENGENBACH, BURLE GENE, PLANT GENETICS. *Current Pos:* from asst prof to assoc prof, 72-81, PROF PLANT GENETICS, DEPT AGRON, UNIV MINN, ST PAUL, 81- *Personal Data:* b Grand Island, NB, Oct 25, 44; m 67; c 2. *Educ:* Univ Nebr, BS, 66, MS, 68; Univ Ill, PhD(genetics), 71. *Prof Exp:* Res assoc plant physiol, Dept Agron, Univ Ill, 71-72. *Concurrent Pos:* Mem bd dirs, Am Soc Agron & Crop Sci Soc Am, 85-88. *Mem:* Fel Am Soc Agron; fel Crop Sci Soc Am; Genet Soc Am; Am Soc Plant Physiologists; Int Asn Plant Tissue Cell Cult; AAAS. *Res:* Mutant selection in maize cell cultures; selection and genetic studies of cytoplasmic traits of maize; enzymology of pathway regulating amino acid biosynthesis in crop plants; amyloplast differentation in developing maize kernels. *Mailing Add:* Agron 411 Borlaug Hall Univ Minn 1991 Upper Buford Circle St Paul MN 55108-6024

GENGOZIAN, NAZARETH, IMMUNOLOGY, TRANSPLANTATION. *Current Pos:* PROF & DIR, BONE MARROW TRANSPLANT LAB, 92- *Personal Data:* b Racine, Wis, Feb 13, 29; m 48, Leone; c 3. *Educ:* Univ Wis, BS, 51, MA, 53, PhD(immunol), 55. *Prof Exp:* Res assoc, Oak Ridge Nat Lab, 55-56, biologist, 57-60, chief scientist, Oak Ridge Assoc Univs, 60-81; mem, Okla Med Res Found, 81-85; prof, Univ SFla, 85-92. *Concurrent Pos:* USPHS fel, Nat Cancer Inst, 56-57; Ford Found prof, Univ Tenn, 68-76, prof, 72-81; adj prof, Wake Forest Univ, 69-77; transplantation, 71-86. *Mem:* Am Asn Immunologists; Radiation Res Soc; Transplantation Soc; Int Soc Hemat & Graft Eng; Am Soc Hemat. *Res:* Radiation immunology; primatology; bone marrow transplantation; monoclonal antibody; feline immunology; hemat stem cell transplant. *Mailing Add:* Dept Pediat Univ Tenn Med Ctr Thompson Cancer Survival Ctr 1915 White Ave Knoxville TN 37916-2305. *Fax:* 423-541-1733

GENIN, DENNIS JOSEPH, SOLID STATE PHYSICS, ENGINEERING PHYSICS. *Current Pos:* RETIRED. *Personal Data:* b Rockford, Ill, Sept 18, 38; m 60, Patricia M Fudala; c Denise M (Brethen), Louise R (Tompkins) & Aimee L. *Educ:* Beloit Col, BS, 60; Iowa State Univ, PhD(physics), 66. *Prof Exp:* Assoc physics, Argonne Nat Lab, 66-68; sr assoc physicist, Thomas J Watson Res Ctr, IBM, 68-71, staff physicist, 71-75, develop engr, 75-76, proj engr, E Fishkill Facil, 76-84, sr engr, Syst Prod Div, 84-88, sr engr, Gen Technol Div, 88-93. *Mem:* Am Phys Soc; Sigma Xi. *Res:* Electric and magnetic fields in solids using magnetic resonance techniques. *Mailing Add:* One Kellerhause Dr Poughkeepsie NY 12603-5441

GENIN, JOSEPH, SOLID MECHANICS. *Current Pos:* dean, Col Engr, 81-85, DIR, OPTICS & MAT SCI LAB, NMEX STATE UNIV, LAS CRUCES, 85- *Personal Data:* b Norwalk, Conn, Sept 9, 34; m 64, Grace Gale; c Kent, Guy & Hugh. *Educ:* City Col New York, BCE, 54; Univ Ariz, MS, 57; Univ Minn, PhD(solid mech), 63. *Prof Exp:* Instr struct mech, Univ Ariz, 55-58; eng mech, Univ Minn, 58-62; sr engr, Gen Dynamics, Ft Worth, 63-64; from assoc prof to prof aeronaut, astronaut & eng sci, Purdue Univ, 64-72, prof mech eng, 72-81, chmn eng mech, 76-81. *Mem:* Am Soc Eng Educ; Am Inst Aeronaut & Astronaut; Am Soc Mech Engrs; Nat Soc Prof Engrs. *Res:* Solid mechanics; dynamic stability, vibrations, material damping, stress waves, structural mechanics; aeroelasticity, and viscoelasticity. *Mailing Add:* 2012 Crescent Dr Las Cruces NM 88005. *Fax:* 505-646-6111; *E-Mail:* meo315@vaxa.nmxu.edu

GENNARI, F JOHN, NEPHROLOGY, RENAL PHYSIOLOGY. *Current Pos:* PROF MED & DIR NEPHROLOGY UNIT, COL MED, UNIV VT, 79- *Personal Data:* b Jersey City, NJ, May 18, 37; m 58; c 3. *Educ:* Yale Univ, BS, 59, MD, 63. *Prof Exp:* Resident internal med; Univ Va Hosp, 63-66; captain, USAF, 66-68; fel nephrology, Tufts Univ-New Eng Med Ctr, 68-71; from asst prof to assoc prof med, Sch Med, Tufts Univ, 71-79. *Mem:* Am Fed Clin Res; Am Soc Clin Invest; Am Physiol Soc; Am Soc Nephrology. *Res:* Acid-base physiology; biocarbonate reabsorption patterns in the proximal tubule of the kidney in normal and disease states; carbon dioxide generation and diffusion across the tubular epithelium. *Mailing Add:* Dept Med D305 Given Bldg Univ Vt Col Med Burlington VT 05405. *Fax:* 802-656-8595

GENNARO, ALFONSO ROBERT, MEDICINAL CHEMISTRY. *Current Pos:* from instr to assoc prof, 48-65, dir dept, 69-81, PROF CHEM, PHILADELPHIA COL PHARM & SCI, 65- *Personal Data:* b Philadelphia, Pa, Dec 18, 25; m 49; c 5. *Educ:* Philadelphia Col Pharm, BSc, 48; Univ Pa, MSc, 51; Temple Univ, PhD, 56. *Prof Exp:* Chemist, E I du Pont de Nemours & Co, Inc, 51-53; chemist, Pa Salt Mfg Co, 53-55. *Concurrent Pos:* Mem,

Comt Rev, US Pharmacopeia, 65-85, Pa Post-Sec Educ Planning Comn, 74-79 & Gould's Med Dict, 75; ed, Remin Pharm Sci, 80- *Mem:* Int Soc Heterocyclic Chem. *Res:* Synthetic medicinals; drug standards; electronic instrumentation. *Mailing Add:* Dept Chem Philadelphia Col Pharm & Sci 675 S 43rd St Philadelphia PA 19104-4441

GENNARO, ANTONIO LOUIS, VERTEBRATE ECOLOGY. *Current Pos:* from asst prof to assoc prof, Eastern NMex Univ, 66-75, coordr biol sci, Div Natural Sci, 75-77, chair, Biol Dept, 84-91, PROF BIOL, EASTERN NMEX UNIV, 75-; CUR, NATURAL HIST MUS, 67- *Personal Data:* b Raton, NMex, Mar 18, 34; m 81, Marjorie Cox; c Theresa Ann, Carrie Marie & Janelle Elizabeth. *Educ:* NMex State Univ, BS, 57; Univ NMex, MS, 61, PhD(vert ecol), 67. *Prof Exp:* Teacher high sch, NMex, 57-58; dir grad teaching asst biol, Univ NMex, 61-64; asst prof, St John's Univ, Minn, 65-66. *Concurrent Pos:* Consult, Nat Park Serv & NMex Dept Game & Fish, 74- & NMex Environ Inst, 75-; bd trustees, NMex Mus Natural Hist. *Mem:* Am Soc Mammal; Herpetologists League Inc; Sigma Xi. *Res:* Taxonomy and ecology in mammalogy and herpetology and ornithology. *Mailing Add:* 816 W 19th Portales NM 88130. *E-Mail:* marnark@vucca.net

GENNARO, JOSEPH FRANCIS, JR, CELL STRUCTURE. *Current Pos:* CHIEF EXEC OFFICER, JANUARY INT INC, 96- *Personal Data:* b Brooklyn, NY, Apr 9, 24; m 44; c 5. *Educ:* Fordham Univ, BS, 47; Univ Pittsburgh, MS, 49, PhD(zool), 52. *Honors & Awards:* Spec Award, Am Acad Orthop Surgeons, 61; Recognicion Award, AMA, 67; Gustav Ohaus Award Nat Sci Teachers Asn, 76. *Prof Exp:* Asst prof biol, St Johns Univ, Col Pharm, 51-55; instr anat, State Univ NY, Col Med, 53-56; asst prof, Univ Fla, Col Med, 56-64; assoc prof, Univ Louisville, Sch Med, 64-69; assoc prof biol & dir lab cellular biol, NY Univ, Res 69-89; prof anat, Nat Cheng Kung Univ, Col Med, 89-91; prof, Dept Anat & Cell Biol, Col Med, Univ Fla, 89-91. *Concurrent Pos:* Lectr, Univ Pittsburgh, 48 & 50, Inona Col, NY, 76-79, Hunter Col, NY, 78-80, Col of Atlantic, 80, NY Univ Med Ctr, 82, Lake City Community Col, 92 & Santa Fe Community Col, 93-; Res assoc, Brookhaven Nat Lab, 51-56; res fel, Harvard Univ, 64-65 & Smith Kline & Fr Labs, Dept Molecular Pharmacol, 86; vis prof, Dept Anat, Col Med, Nat Cheng Kung Univ, Taiwan, 88-89 & Univ Fla Med Sch, 88 & 90. *Mem:* Am Soc Cell Biol; Int Soc Cryptozool; Int Soc Toxinology; Royal Micros Soc; Am Physiol Soc; Am Micros Soc; Am Asn Anatomists; Biophys Soc. *Res:* Effect of neurotoxins on snaptic function. *Mailing Add:* 4132 NW 13th Ave Gainesville FL 32605

GENNARO, JOSEPH J(OHN), structural engineering, for more information see previous edition

GENNARO, ROBERT NASH, MICROBIOLOGY, BIOLOGY. *Current Pos:* asst prof, 70-76, ASSOC PROF MICROBIOL, UNIV CENT FLA, 76- *Personal Data:* b Raton, NMex, Oct 14, 40; m 76; c 2. *Educ:* NMex State Univ, BS, 63, MS, 65; Tex A&M Univ, PhD(microbiol), 71. *Prof Exp:* Res asst, NMex State Univ, 63-65; instr microbiol, Tex A&M Univ, 65-70. *Mem:* Sigma Xi; Am Soc Microbiol. *Res:* Environmental microbiology; resourse recovery; bioconversion of wastes to methane and alcohol. *Mailing Add:* Dept Molecular Biol Univ Cent Fla Box 25000 Orlando FL 32816-0001

GENNIS, ROBERT BENNETT, BIOPHYSICAL CHEMISTRY. *Current Pos:* asst prof chem, 73-79, assoc prof chem, 79-84, PROF BIOCHEM, UNIV ILL, URBANA, 84- *Personal Data:* b New York, NY, Oct 7, 44; m; c 2. *Educ:* Univ Chicago, BS, 66; Columbia Univ, PhD(chem), 71. *Prof Exp:* Whitney fel, Harvard Univ, 71-73. *Concurrent Pos:* NIH-USPHS career develop grant, 75; Fulbright fel & Guggenheim fel, 89. *Mem:* Biophys Soc; Fed Am Soc Exp Biol; Am Soc Microbiol. *Res:* Protein-lipid interactions; structure and function of lipid requiring enzymes; physical probes of membrane structure and function; membrane-bond electron transport chains. *Mailing Add:* Sch Chem Sci Univ Ill 15 Noyes Lab 505 S Mathews Ave Urbana IL 61801-3617. *Fax:* 217-244-3186

GENOWAYS, HUGH HOWARD, SYSTEMATICS, MAMMALOGY. *Current Pos:* PROF, UNIV NEBR STATE MUS & MUS STUDIES PROG, UNIV NEBR, LINCOLN, 94- *Personal Data:* b Scottsbluff, Nebr, Dec 24, 40; m 63, Joyce E Cox; c Margaret L & Theodore H. *Educ:* Hastings Col, Nebr, AB, 63; Univ Kans, PhD(zool), 71. *Honors & Awards:* C Hart Merriam Award, Am Soc Mammalogist, 87. *Prof Exp:* Res asst, Mus, Tex Tech Univ, 71-72, cur mammals, 72-76, lectr, Mus Sci Prog, 74-76, actg coordr res, 75-76; cur mammals, Carnegie Mus Natural Hist, Pittsburgh, 76-86; dir, Univ State Mus, Univ Nebr, Lincoln, 86-94. *Concurrent Pos:* J William Fulbright scholar, 64; Adj asst prof, dept vet & zool med, Sch Med, Tex Tech Univ, 73-75, dept biol sci, 73-76 & dept path, 75-76; managing ed, J Mammal, Am Soc Mammalogists, 74-78, publ ed, Carnegie Mus Natural Hist, 77-86; mem, Coun Biol Ed; courtesy prof biol sci, Univ Nebr, Lincoln, 87-, chair, Mus Studies Prog, 90-95. *Mem:* Am Soc Mammalogists (pres, 84-86); Am Asn Mus; Sigma Xi; Soc Syst Zoologists; Soc Conserv Biol. *Res:* Systematics, biogeography and ecology of New World mammals, especially rodents and bats; application of computer to data analysis and data retrieval; technology of management and preservation of biological specimens; history of science museums. *Mailing Add:* W436 Nebraska Hall Univ State Mus Univ Nebr Lincoln NE 68588-0514. *Fax:* 402-472-8949; *E-Mail:* hgenoway@unlinfo.unl.edu

GENS, RALPH S, ELECTRICAL ENGINEERING. *Current Pos:* CONSULT, 80- *Personal Data:* b Ger, Nov 25, 24; m 52; c 2. *Educ:* Ore State Univ, BSEE, 49. *Honors & Awards:* Distinguished Serv Award, US Dept Interior, 78; Centennial Medal & William M Harbishaw Award, Inst Elec & Electronics Engrs, 84; Atwood Award, Nat Acad Eng, 90. *Prof Exp:* Asst adminr elec eng, Bonneville Power-Admin, 49-80. *Concurrent Pos:* Chmn, Surge Protective Devices Comt, Inst Elec & Electronics Engrs, 69-70; adv, NSF, 71-76; mem, Elec Comt Papua New Guinea, 81-88. *Mem:* Nat Acad Eng; fel Inst Elec & Electronics Engrs. *Mailing Add:* 76-238 Kea-Kealani Dr Kailua Kona HI 96740-3017. *Fax:* 808-326-7287

GENSAMER, MAXWELL, PHYSICAL METALLURGY. *Current Pos:* Howe prof metall, 50-71, EMER HOWE PROF METALL, COLUMBIA UNIV, 71- *Personal Data:* b Bradford, Pa, June 3, 02; m 50. *Educ:* Carnegie Inst Technol, BS, 24, MS, 31, DSc, 33. *Honors & Awards:* Howe Medal, Am Soc Metals, 32. *Prof Exp:* Plant metallurgist, Am Chain & Cable Co, Pa, 24-29; res metallurgist, Carnegie Inst Technol, 29-45, from asst prof to prof metall eng, 35-45; prof metall & head dept mineral technol, Pa State Univ, 45-47; asst dir res, Carnegie-Ill Steel Corp, 47-50. *Concurrent Pos:* Consult, Esso Res & Eng & US Steel Res Lab. *Mem:* Fel Am Soc Metals; fel Am Inst Mining, Metall & Petrol Engrs. *Res:* Properties of alloys, especially steel as controlled by composition and microstructure; mechanical metallurgy, properties, fracture and failure analysis. *Mailing Add:* 1057 Forest Lakes Dr Apt 309 Naples FL 34105

GENSEL, PATRICIA GABBEY, BOTANY, PALEOBOTANY. *Current Pos:* from asst prof to assoc prof bot, 75-90, PROF BOT, UNIV NC, CHAPEL HILL, 90- *Personal Data:* b Buffalo, NY, Mar 18, 44; m 68; c 1. *Educ:* Hope Col, BA, 66; Univ Conn, MS, 69, PhD(bot), 72. *Prof Exp:* Res asst palynology, King's Col Univ, London, 66-67; res assoc paleobot, Univ Conn, 72-75. *Concurrent Pos:* NSF grants, 74, 77-79, 80-83, 84-87, 88-90 & 92-94. *Mem:* Bot Soc Am; Am Asn Stratig Palynologists; Paleontol Asn; Am Fern Soc. *Res:* Morphology, diversification and evolution of early land vascular plants; studies of Devonian plants; fossil plants, fossil spores-pollen; plant morphology. *Mailing Add:* Dept Biol Univ NC Chapel Hill NC 27599-3280. *E-Mail:* pgensel@unc.edu

GENSHAW, MARVIN ALDEN, PHYSICAL CHEMISTRY. *Current Pos:* PRIN STAFF SCIENTIST, DIAG, DIV MILES LABS, INC, 69- *Personal Data:* b Petoskey, Mich, Sept 24, 39; m 64; c 2. *Educ:* Mich Technol Univ, BS, 61; Univ Pa, PhD(phys chem), 66. *Prof Exp:* Res investr, Univ Pa, 66-69. *Concurrent Pos:* Adj asst prof, Notre Dame Univ, 77-78; mem, Coun Optical Radiation Measurement. *Mem:* Am Chem Soc; Electrochem Soc; Am Asn Clin Chem. *Res:* Physical chemical medical diagnostic tests; reflectance and color theory and measurement; electrochemistry. *Mailing Add:* 2905 Neff St Elkhart IN 46515-4317

GENT, ALAN NEVILLE, PHYSICS, MECHANICS. *Current Pos:* asst dir, Inst Polymer Sci, 64-78, dean grad studies & res, 78-86, prof polymer physics, 61-87, H A Morton prof polymer physics & eng, 87-94, EMER PROF POLYMER PHYSICS & ENG, UNIV AKRON, 94- *Personal Data:* b Leicester, Eng, Nov 11, 27; m 49, Jean M Wolstenholme; c Martin P, P Michael & Andrew J. *Educ:* Univ London, BSc, 46 & 49, PhD(physics), 55. *Honors & Awards:* Corecipient, Mobay Award, 64; Bingham Medal, Soc Rheology, 75; Colwyn Medal, Plastics & Rubber Inst, 77; Int Res Award, Soc Plastics Engrs, 80; 3M Award, Adhesion Soc, 87; Goodyear Medal, Am Chem Soc Rubber Div, 90; High-Polymer Physics Prize, Am Phys Soc, 96. *Prof Exp:* Res asst, John Bull Rubber Co, 44-45, physicist, Brit Rubber Prod Res Asn, 49-58, prin physicist, 58-61. *Concurrent Pos:* Chmn, Gordon Res Conf Elastomers, 66, Gordon Res Conf Cellular Mat, 69, Gordon Res Conf Adhesion, 77 & Gordon Res Conf Composites, 91; vis prof, Queen Mary Col, Univ London, 69-70, McGill Univ, 83 & Univ Minn, 85; consult, Gen Motors & Goodyear Tire & Rubber Co; sci adv, Corp Res, Goodyear Tire & Rubber Co, 94- *Mem:* Nat Acad Eng; Adhesion Soc (pres, 78); Soc Rheology (pres, 81); fel Am Phys Soc. *Res:* Mechanical behavior of elastomers; deformation; fracture; crystallization; adhesion; friction and wear; stress-cracking of polymers. *Mailing Add:* Polymer Sci Univ Akron Akron OH 44325-3909. *Fax:* 330-972-5290; *E-Mail:* angent@goodyear.com

GENT, MARTIN PAUL NEVILLE, CROP PHYSIOLOGY. *Current Pos:* asst scientist, Dept Ecol & Climate, 78-82, ASSOC SCIENTIST, DEPT FORESTRY & HORT, CONN AGR EXP STA, 83- *Personal Data:* b Luton, Eng, July 6, 50; m 72; c 2. *Educ:* Oberlin Col, BA, 71; Yale Univ, PhD(chem), 75. *Prof Exp:* Res assoc biophys, Dept Life Sci, Univ Pittsburgh, 75-78. *Mem:* Crop Sci Soc Am; Plant Physiol Soc; Am Soc Hort Sci. *Res:* Plant response to environment; carbohydrate and nitrogen metabolism in plants; photosynthesis and respiration. *Mailing Add:* Dept Forestry & Hort PO Box 1106 New Haven CT 06504-1106

GENT, MICHAEL, MEDICAL STATISTICS. *Current Pos:* from assoc prof to prof, McMaster Univ, 69-79, chmn dept, 73-79, dean res, 79-84, PROF CLIN EPIDEMIOL & BIOSTATIST, MCMASTER UNIV, 73- *Personal Data:* b Durham, Eng, May 4, 34; m 57; c 2. *Educ:* Univ Durham, BSc, 56, MSc, 60, DSc, 90. *Prof Exp:* Statistician, Imp Chem Indust, Eng, 57-60; sr lectr math, Bradford Inst Technol, Eng, 60-65; from lectr to sr lectr statist, Univ Bradford, 65-69. *Concurrent Pos:* Dir, Clin Trials Methodology Group, Hamilton Civic Hosp Res Ctr. *Mem:* Royal Statist Soc; Am Heart Asn; Can Soc Clin Invest; fel Am Statist Asn; Int Epidemiol Asn; Int Soc Thrombosis & Haemosyasis. *Res:* Multicentre controlled clinical trials; cardiovascular research, particularly thrombosis. *Mailing Add:* Hamilton Civic Hosps Res Ctr 711 Concession St Hamilton ON L8V 1C3 Can. *Fax:* 905-575-2639

GENTER, MARY BETH, PATHOLOGY, NEUROTOXICOLOGY. *Current Pos:* ASST PROF TOXICOL, NC STATE UNIV, 90- *Personal Data:* b Watertown, NY, Mar 2, 62; div. *Educ:* St Lawrence Univ, BS, 84; Duke Univ, PhD(path, toxicol), 88, Am Bd toxicol, dipl, 92. *Prof Exp:* Fel, Chem Indust Inst Toxicol, 88-90. *Mem:* Soc Toxicol; Soc Risk Anal. *Res:* Pathology. *Mailing Add:* Dept Molecular & Cellular Physiol PO Box 670576 Cincinnati OH 45267-0567

GENTHNER, BARBARA ROBYN SHARAK, ANAEROBIC MICROBIAL PHYSIOLOGY, MICROBIAL BIOREMEDIATION. *Current Pos:* ASSOC RES PROF, CTR ENVIRON DIAG & BIOREMEDIATION, UNIV WFLA, 93- *Personal Data:* b Milwaukee, Wis, July 29, 49; m 78, Fred J; c F Nicholas & Elizabeth R. *Educ:* Lawrence Univ, BA, 71; Southern Ill Univ, MS, 78; Univ Ill, PhD(dairy sci), 84. *Prof Exp:* Res scientist, Univ Mo, 82-84; res fel, Battelle Mem Inst, 84-85; sr res scientist, Tech Applns, Inc, 86-87; sr res mgr, Tech Resources, Inc, 87-93. *Concurrent Pos:* Res scientist, Univ NH, 93-; prin investr, Off Naval Res, 93-96, US Environ Protection Agency, 94-97. *Mem:* Am Soc Microbiol; Soc Environ Toxicol & Chem; AAAS. *Res:* Investigate the anaerobic microbial biodegradation of toxic aromatic compounds and to apply this knowledge to environmental bioremediation; isolate and characterize new species of bacteria with physiological potential for bioremediation of toxic aromatic compounds. *Mailing Add:* Ctr Environ Diag & Bioremediation Univ WFla 11000 University Pkwy Pensacola FL 32514. *Fax:* 850-474-3130; *E-Mail:* bgenthne@uwf.edu

GENTHNER, FRED J, MICROBIAL PEST CONTROL AGENTS, MICROBIAL ECOLOGY. *Current Pos:* RES MICROBIOLOGIST, US ENVIRON PROTECTION AGENCY, 85- *Personal Data:* b Chicago, Ill, Mar 24, 52; m 77, Barbara R S. *Educ:* Carthage Col, BS 74; Southern Ill Univ, MS, 77; Univ Ill, PhD(food sci/microbiol), 83. *Prof Exp:* Res assoc, Univ Mo, 82-84 & Ohio State Univ, 84-85. *Mem:* Am Soc Microbiol; Soc Invert Path. *Res:* Develop test methods to evaluate the risk associated with environmental application of microbial pest control agents and genetically engineered microorganisms. *Mailing Add:* US Environ Protection Agency Sabine Island Gulf Breeze FL 32561. *E-Mail:* fgenthner@gulfbr.gbr.gov

GENTILE, ARTHUR CHRISTOPHER, PLANT PHYSIOLOGY. *Current Pos:* RETIRED. *Personal Data:* b New York, NY, Nov 24, 26; m 49, Gloria Ennevor; c Flora. *Educ:* City Col NY, BS, 48; Brown Univ, ScM, 51; Univ Chicago, PhD(bot), 53. *Prof Exp:* Asst biol, City Col NY, 47-48 & Brown Univ, 49-51; asst bot, Univ Chicago, 51-53; univ fel, Duke Univ, 53, Nat Cancer Inst fel, 54-55; plant physiologist, US Forest Serv, 55-56; from asst prof to prof bot, Univ Mass, Amherst, 56-72, from asst dean to assoc dean grad sch, 65-72; dean grad col & vprovost res admin, Univ Okla, 72-74; vpres acad affairs, Univ Nev, Las Vegas, 74-79; exec dir, Am Inst Biol Sci, Arlington, Va, 79-83; dean acad affairs, Ind Univ, Kokomo, 83-88, vchancellor acad affairs, 88-92. *Mem:* Sigma Xi. *Res:* Growth and metabolism of neoplastic plant tissues. *Mailing Add:* 2133 White Tail Run Bloomington IN 47401

GENTILE, DOMINICK E, NEPHROLOGY. *Current Pos:* from asst prof to assoc prof, 69-72, clin assoc prof, 72-80, CLIN PROF MED, UNIV CALIF, IRVINE, 80- *Personal Data:* b Asbury Park, NJ, Jan 12, 32; m 58, Zora Kingson; c 5. *Educ:* Univ Notre Dame, BS, 53; Georgetown Univ, MD, 57. *Prof Exp:* Fel nephrology, Georgetown Univ, 60-62; from instr to asst prof med, Sch Med, Univ Louisville, 64-68, assoc pediat, 67-68; asst prof biophys & physiol, Mt Sinai Sch Med, 68-69. *Mem:* Am Soc Nephrol; Int Soc Nephrol; Biophys Soc; NY Acad Sci. *Res:* Transport physiology and biophysics; renal physiology; kinetic and clinical hemodialysis. *Mailing Add:* 1310 W Stewart Dr Suite 606 Orange CA 92668

GENTILE, JAMES MICHAEL, GENETICS, MOLECULAR BIOLOGY. *Current Pos:* from asst prof to assoc prof, 76-84, HERRICK PROF BIOL, HOPE COL, 84- *Personal Data:* b Chicago, Ill, Aug 31, 46; m 73; c 1. *Educ:* St Mary's Col, Minn, BA, 68; Ill State Univ, MS, 70, PhD(genetics), 74. *Prof Exp:* Teaching asst biol, Ill State Univ, 69-72; researcher genet, Yale Univ Med Sch, 74-76. *Concurrent Pos:* Res contract, Environ Protection Agency, 76-80, Res Corp grant, 77-79; Nat Inst Environ Health Sci grant, 81-; Environ Protection Agency grant, 81-; WHO grant, 84-86. *Mem:* Am Soc Microbiol; Genet Soc Am; Environ Mutagen Soc; AAAS; Am Inst Biol Sci. *Res:* Environmental mutagenesis; in vivo and in vitro metabolism of chemicals to mutagens by both plant and animal systems. *Mailing Add:* Dean Sci Hope Col 137 E 12th St Holland MI 49423-3607

GENTILE, PHILIP, inorganic chemistry, for more information see previous edition

GENTILE, RALPH G, ELECTRICAL ENGINEERING. *Current Pos:* RETIRED. *Personal Data:* b Palermo, Italy, May 13, 14; US nat; m 53; c 4. *Educ:* Univ Rome, Italy, Dr Eng, 38 & 40. *Prof Exp:* Fel aeronaut eng, Rome Inst Advan Studies, 41; res engr, US Govt, 43-44; elec engr, Roger Williams Eng Co, 44-45; chief engr, TRM Elec Co, 45-49; fel nuclear eng, Argonne Nat Lab, 54; res group leader, Monsanto Chem Co, 60-63; mgr, Physics Sect, Babcock & Wilcox Co, 63-79; lectr, Calif Polytech Univ, 79-84. *Mem:* AAAS; Inst Elec & Electronics Engrs; Am Soc Eng Educ; Sigma Xi; AAAS. *Res:* Solid state electronics; industrial instrumentation; energy conversion. *Mailing Add:* Calif Polytech Univ San Luis Obispo CA 93401

GENTILE, RICHARD J, STRATIGRAPHY, ENGINEERING GEOLOGY & PALEONTOLOGY. *Current Pos:* from asst prof to assoc prof, 66-75, PROF GEOL, UNIV MO, KANSAS CITY, 75- *Personal Data:* b St Louis, Mo, June 25, 29. *Educ:* Univ Mo, Columbia, BA, 56, MA, 58; Univ Mo, Rolla, PhD(geol), 65. *Honors & Awards:* Cert Recognition, Sigma Xi, 81. *Prof Exp:* Geologist, Mo Geol Surv, Rolla, 58-65, chief geologist & head of coal geol div, 65-66. *Concurrent Pos:* NSF res grants, 68-69, 70 & 74. *Mem:* Am Asn Petrol Geol; fel Geol Soc Am; Asn Eng Geol; Soc Econ Paleontologists & Mineralogists; Am Inst Prof Geologists; Sigma Xi. *Res:* Nonmetallic mineral resources studies of Missouri; stratigraphy and geologic mapping of Pennsylvanian age strata of western Missouri; geotechnical evaluation of sanitary landfill and quarry sites. *Mailing Add:* Dept Geosci Univ Mo 5100 Rockhill Rd Kansas City MO 64110-2499. *Fax:* 816-235-5535

GENTILE, THOMAS JOSEPH, HIGH ENERGY PHYSICS EXPERIMENTATION. *Current Pos:* STAFF SCIENTIST, MASS INST TECHNOL, LINCOLN LABS, 86- *Personal Data:* b New York, NY, Jan 17, 53. *Educ:* Columbia Univ, BS, 74; Cornell Univ, MS, 78, PhD(physics), 81. *Prof Exp:* Res assoc, Univ Rochester, 81-85 & Ohio State Univ, 85-86. *Mem:* Am Phys Soc. *Res:* Remote sensing and radar imaging. *Mailing Add:* 99 Lincoln Rd Medford MA 02155

GENTLE, KENNETH W, TOKAMAK PHYSICS. *Current Pos:* from asst prof to assoc prof, 66-77, PROF PHYSICS, UNIV TEX, AUSTIN, 77-, CHMN, DEPT PHYSICS, 97- *Personal Data:* b Oak Park, Ill, Oct 27, 40; m 86, Martha Baker. *Educ:* Mass Inst Technol, SB, 62, PhD(physics), 66. *Prof Exp:* Instr physics, Mass Inst Technol, 65-66. *Concurrent Pos:* Fel, Alfred Sloan Found, 73-75. *Mem:* Am Phys Soc; fel Europ Phys Soc. *Res:* Plasma confinement, transport and heating. *Mailing Add:* Dept Physics Univ Tex Austin TX 78712. *E-Mail:* gentle@fusion.ph.utexas.edu

GENTLEMAN, JANE FORER, STATISTICAL ANALYSIS. *Current Pos:* sr res officer statist, Can, Social & Econ Div, 82-91, CHIEF HEALTH & VITAL STAT STUDIES, HEALTH STATIST DIV, STATIST CAN, 96- *Personal Data:* b Washington, DC, Apr 8, 40; m 67; c 2. *Educ:* Univ Chicago, BA, 62, MS, 65; Univ Waterloo, PhD(statist), 73. *Prof Exp:* Statist programmer, Univ Chicago, 62-65; assoc mem tech staff, Bell Tel Labs, 65-68, statist programmer, Imp Col, Univ London, 68-69; from instr to assoc prof, Univ Waterloo, Can, 69-82. *Concurrent Pos:* Ed-in-chief, Health Reports, 96- *Mem:* Inst Statist Inst; Statist Soc Can (pres, 97-); fel Am Statist Asn. *Res:* Data analysis; statistical computing; detection of outliers; analysis of mortality data; vital statistics analysis. *Mailing Add:* Statist Can Coats Bldg 18th Floor Tunney's Pasture Ottawa ON K1A 0T6 Can

GENTLEMAN, WILLIAM MORVEN, COMPUTER SCIENCE, COMP NUMERICAL ANALYSIS. *Current Pos:* res officer, 83-88, PRIN RES OFFICER, NAT RES COUN, 88-, HEAD, SOFTWARE ENG LAB, 90- *Personal Data:* b Calgary, Alta, July 6, 42; div; c 2. *Educ:* McGill Univ, BSc, 63; Princeton Univ, MA, 64, PhD(math), 66. *Honors & Awards:* Ross Medal, 89. *Prof Exp:* Mem tech staff, Bell Tel Labs, 65-69; from asst prof to assoc prof appl anal & comput sci, Univ Waterloo, 69-74, prof comput sci, 74-84. *Concurrent Pos:* Sr res fel, Nat Phys Lab, 68-69, prin res fel, 75-76; vis res officer, Nat Res Coun, 82-83; dir, Consortium Grad Educ Software Eng, 95- *Mem:* Asn Comput Mach; Soc Indust & Appl Math. *Res:* Numerical algorithms and analysis; symbolic algebraic manipulation; software engineering; computer alegebra. *Mailing Add:* Inst Info Technol Nat Res Coun Montreal Rd M-50 Ottawa ON K1A 0R8 Can. *Fax:* 613-952-7151; *E-Mail:* gentlemen@iit.nrc.ca

GENTNER, NORMAN ELWOOD, BIOCHEMISTRY, MICROBIOLOGY. *Current Pos:* Res officer biol, Chalk River Nuclear Labs, Atomic Energy Can Ltd, 71-85, sr research officer, 85-88, sr research officer II, 88-89, HEAD, RADIATION BIOL BR, CHALK RIVER LABS, AECL RES, 89- *Personal Data:* b Carrot River, Sask, Apr 1, 43; div. *Educ:* Univ Sask, BA, 63, Hons, 64; Univ Calif, Davis, PhD(biochem), 68. *Prof Exp:* Lab demonstr, Univ Calif, Davis, 63-64, teaching asst, res asst & assoc biochem, 64-67, fel, 68; fel, Sch Med, Stanford Univ, 69-70. *Concurrent Pos:* Nat Res Coun Can fel, 68; Jan Coffin Childs Mem Fund Med Res fel, 69-70; res student biochem, Atomic Energy Can Ltd, Chalk River, 63-64; mem biol sub-group, Effects of Atomic Radiation, UN Sci Comt; Regant's fel, Univ Calif, Davis, 64. *Mem:* Am Chem Soc; Am Soc Microbiol; Radiation Res Soc; Am Soc Photobiol; Environ Mutagen Soc. *Res:* DNA repair; survival, recovery, and mutation after radiation exposure; individual variation in radiation sensitivity and relation to cancer treatment; DNA repair inhibitors; recombinational repair of DNA lesions and consequences. *Mailing Add:* Radiation Biol Br Chalk River Labs AECL Res Chalk River ON K0J 1J0 Can

GENTNER, ROBERT F, PHYSICAL CHEMISTRY, ATOMIC PHYSICS. *Current Pos:* RES SCIENTIST, ARMAMENT RES & DEVELOP CTR, 80- *Personal Data:* b New York, NY, Oct 31, 38; m 76, Sheila D McGuire. *Educ:* St John's Univ, BS, 60, MS, 62, PhD(phys chem), 68. *Prof Exp:* Res chemist, Picatinny Arsenal, Dover, NJ, 69-80. *Mem:* Am Chem Soc; Am Phys Soc; AAAS. *Res:* Quantum mechanical calculations for atomic systems; detonation physics. *Mailing Add:* Army Res/Develop Ctr Command B 3022 Dover NJ 07801

GENTRY, CLAUDE EDWIN, AGRONOMY. *Current Pos:* Assoc agronomist, 60-69, assoc prof agron, 69-73, PROF AGRON & BIOL, BEREA COL, 73- *Personal Data:* b Oak Hill, WVa, Aug 3, 30; m 55; c 3. *Educ:* Univ Ky, BS, 58, MS, 60, PhD(plant path), 68. *Concurrent Pos:* Fel, Univ Ky, 68. *Mem:* Am Phytopath Soc; Am Soc Agron. *Res:* Alkaloid content of tall fescue; plant pathology, including the interrelationship of Rhizoctonia solani, environment and genotype on the alkaloid content of tall fescue. *Mailing Add:* 129 Highland Dr Berea KY 40403

GENTRY, DONALD WILLIAM, ENGINEERING EDUCATION. *Current Pos:* PROF, DEAN ENG & DEPT HEAD MINING ENG, COLO SCHOOL MINES, 72- *Personal Data:* b St Louis, Mo, Jan 18, 43; m 65, Sheila; c Tara & Chad. *Educ:* Univ Ill, BSE, 65; Univ Nev, MS, 67; Univ Ar, PhD, 72. *Mem:* Nat Acad Eng; Soc Mining, Metall & Explor (pres, 94); Am Inst Mining Metall & Petrol Eng (pres, 96); Sigma Xi. *Res:* Rock mass characterization. *Mailing Add:* 6590 Ridgeview Dr Morrison CO 80465

GENTRY, GLENN ADEN, VIROLOGY. *Current Pos:* from asst prof to assoc prof, 63-68, PROF MICROBIOL, SCH MED, UNIV MISS, 68- *Personal Data:* b Athens, Ga, June 25, 31; m 58, Betty McInnis; c Susan (Saidian) & Linda (Brassell). *Educ:* Maryville Col, BA, 53; Vanderbilt Univ, MS, 56; Univ Miss, PhD(microbiol), 60. *Prof Exp:* Nat Cancer Inst fel, McArdle Mem Lab Cancer Res, 60-63. *Concurrent Pos:* Nat Inst Allergy & Infectious Dis res career develop award, 63-73; Am Cancer Soc & USPHS grants, 63-73; vis prof virol, Glasgow Univ, 70-71. *Mem:* Am Soc Microbiol; Am Asn Exp Path; Sigma Xi. *Res:* Equine and human herpes viruses; pyrimidine metabolism in cell culture and in vivo in mammals; viral antimetabolites; viral physical chemistry; viral genetics. *Mailing Add:* Dept Microbiol Univ Miss Med Ctr Jackson MS 39216-4505. *Fax:* 601-984-1708; *E-Mail:* gentry@fiona.umsmed.edu

GENTRY, IVEY CLENTON, MATHEMATICS. *Current Pos:* From asst prof to assoc prof, 49-56, PROF MATH, WAKE FOREST UNIV, 56- *Personal Data:* b Roxboro, NC, Apr 7, 19; m 43; c 3. *Educ:* Wake Forest Col, BS, 40; Duke Univ, MA, 47, PhD(math), 49. *Mem:* Am Math Soc; Am Math Asn. *Res:* Topology. *Mailing Add:* 5401 Indiana Ave Winston-Salem NC 27106

GENTRY, JOHN TILMON, PUBLIC HEALTH, HOSPITAL ADMINISTRATION. *Current Pos:* RETIRED. *Personal Data:* b St Louis, Mo, Dec 31, 21; m 49; c 5. *Educ:* Washington Univ, AB, 44, BS & MD, 48; Harvard Univ, MPH, 51. *Prof Exp:* Intern, Clins, Univ Chicago, 48-49; resident physician, State Dept Health, NY, 49-50; asst to chief, Epidemiol Br, Communicable Dis Ctr, 51-52, health officer, Great Anchorage Health Dist, Alaska, 52-53; dist state health officer, State Dept Health, NY, 54-57, regional health dir, 57-64; assoc prof pub health admin, 64-68, asst dean prog develop, Sch Pub Health, 64-68; prof pub health admin, Sch Pub Health & dir prog med care & health serv admin, Univ NC, Chapel Hill, 68-74, res prof inst res social sci, 70-74; dir bur health care serv & exec med dir, Medicaid Prog, New York Dept Health, 74-76; comnr health, Erie Co Dept Health, Buffalo, NY, 76-81. *Concurrent Pos:* From clin asst prof to clin assoc prof, State Univ NY Upstate Med Ctr, 55-64; dep chief, Health Div & Chief Med Educ Br, US AID mission, India, 61-63; consult, Nat Comn Community Health Serv, 64-; adj prof, Grad Prog Hosp Admin, Duke Univ, 70-74; adj prof grad sch pub admin, NY Univ, 75- *Mem:* AAAS; fel Am Pub Health Asn. *Res:* Identification of social, psychological and economic factors that enhance or impede the implementation of community health services; epidemiological studies of sarcoidosis and congenital malformations. *Mailing Add:* 258 Atlantic Rd Gloucester MA 01930

GENTRY, KARL RAY, MATHEMATICS. *Current Pos:* ASSOC PROF MATH, UNIV NC, GREENSBORO, 65- *Personal Data:* b Roxboro, NC, Apr 13, 38. *Educ:* Wake Forest Univ, BA, 60; Univ Ga, MA, 62, PhD(math), 65. *Mem:* Am Math Soc. *Res:* General topology. *Mailing Add:* 3022 Darden Rd Greensboro NC 27407

GENTRY, MICHAEL LEE, OPEN INFORMATION SYSTEMS DESIGN, ADVANCED TELECOMMUNICATIONS SYSTEMS. *Current Pos:* Dep & tech dir, Telecommun Automation, US Army, 80-83, sr res consult, Advan Systs Concept Off, 83-85, assoc tech dir, Info Systs Command, 85-87, tech dir, 87-95, SR TECH DIR & CHIEF ENGR, SIGNAL COMMAND, US ARMY, 95- *Personal Data:* b Durant, Okla, Sept 20, 42; m 68, Lois J Jones; c Christopher M & Cynthia L. *Educ:* Okla State Univ, BS, 64; Mass Inst Technol, MS, 66; Univ Ariz, PhD(elec & comput eng), 71. *Concurrent Pos:* Instr math & electronics, Cochise Col, 75-82; mem, Indust Adv Coun, Univ Ariz, 90-93; vchmn & bd dirs, Int Performance, Comput & Commun Conf, 90-; evaluator, NSF, 97. *Mem:* Sr mem Inst Elec & Electronics Engrs; Armed Forces Commun-Electronics Asn. *Res:* Interoperable, non-proprietary, open systems for computing and telecommunications. *Mailing Add:* 1428 El Camino Real Sierra Vista AZ 85635. *E-Mail:* astd@huachuca-emh12.army.mil

GENTRY, ROBERT CECIL, METEOROLOGY. *Current Pos:* RETIRED. *Personal Data:* b Paducah, Ky, Nov 29, 16; m 48, Laura Hartness; c Jane O, Judith L, Robert L & Laura S. *Educ:* Murray State Col, BS, 37; Fla State Univ, PhD, 63. *Honors & Awards:* Gold Medal Award Distinguished Achievement Fed Serv, US Dept Com, 70. *Prof Exp:* Teacher pub sch, Ky, 37-40; res forecaster, US Weather Bur, 42-55, asst dir, Nat Hurricane Res Proj, 55-59, actg dir, 59-61, dir, 61-64, dir, Nat Hurricane Res Lab, 64-74, dir proj stormfury, 66-74; chief res meteorologist, Gen Elec Co, 75-78; adj prof, Clemson Univ, 78-79, res prof, 79-85, adj prof atmospheric physics, 85-91; dir, SC Forestry Asn, 92-94. *Concurrent Pos:* Consult, World Meteorol Orgn, 60-75; cert consult meteorologist, Am Meteorol Soc, 77. *Mem:* Fel Am Meteorol Soc; Am Geophys Union; Sigma Xi. *Res:* Tropical meteorology, especially hurricanes; tornadoes, weather modification. *Mailing Add:* 461 Ridge Rd Salem SC 29676

GENTRY, ROBERT FRANCIS, poultry pathology; deceased, see previous edition for last biography

GENTRY, ROBERT VANCE, GEOCHEMISTRY, NUCLEAR GEOPHYSICS. *Current Pos:* RES PHYSICIST, LECTR & AUTHOR, EARTH SCI ASSOCS, KNOXVILLE, TENN, 86- *Personal Data:* b Chattanooga, Tenn, July 9, 33; m 53, Patricia Ann; c Pattie Lynn, Michael & David. *Educ:* Univ Fla, BS, 55, MS, 56; Columbia Union Col, DSc, 77. *Hon Degrees:* DSc, Columbia Union Col, 77. *Prof Exp:* Nuclear engr, Gen Dynamics/Convair, Tex, 56-57, aerophys engr, 57-58; sr engr, Martin Co, Fla, 58-59; instr math, Univ Fla, 59-61 & Walla Walla Col, 61-62; instr physics, Ga Inst Technol, 62-64; res physicist, Archaeol Res Found, 65-66; from asst prof to assoc prof, Columbia Union Col, 66-84. *Concurrent Pos:* Guest scientist, Chem Div, Oak Ridge Nat Lab, 69-82; grantee, 71-77, res fel grantee, 83- *Mem:* AAAS; Am Phys Soc; Am Geophys Union; fel NSF; NY Acad Sci; Sigma Xi. *Res:* Research, writing and lecturing relative to radioactive halos and their cosmological implications with respect to the creation and age of the earth. *Mailing Add:* 6321 Cate Rd Powell TN 37849. *Fax:* 423-938-6114; *E-Mail:* esa@halos.com

GENTRY, ROGER LEE, OCEANOGRAPHY. *Current Pos:* WILDLIFE BIOLOGIST, MARINE MAMMAL DIV, NAT MARINE FISHERIES SERV, DEPT COM, 74- *Personal Data:* b Bakersfield, Calif, Mar 19, 38; m 72; c Melissa (O'Brien), Erin C & Alison N. *Educ:* Calif State Univ, San Francisco, BA, 63, MA, 66; Univ Calif, Santa Cruz, PhD(biol), 70. *Prof Exp:* Proj leader biol, Stanford Res Inst, 69-70; fel ethol, Univ Adelaide, SAustralia, 70-71; res assoc biol, Univ Calif, Santa Cruz, 71-74. *Concurrent Pos:* Sabbatical to Coastal Marine Studies, Univ Calif, Santa Cruz, 78-80. *Mem:* AAAS; Soc Marine Mammal; Oceanog Soc. *Res:* Social behavior; social organization; and behavioral ecology of vertebrates, especially pinnipeds; diving and foraging behavior of marine vertebrates. *Mailing Add:* 12555 14th Ave NE Seattle WA 98125. *Fax:* 206-526-6615; *E-Mail:* gentry@afsc.noaa.gov

GENTRY, WILLARD MAX, JR, ORGANIC CHEMISTRY. *Current Pos:* RETIRED. *Personal Data:* b Omaha, Nebr, May 2, 23; m 49, Patricia Joy Taylor; c Douglas Willaed, Katherine Joy, Stuart Taylor & Mary Alice. *Educ:* Harvard Univ, AB, 43, AM, 48; Boston Univ, PhD(chem), 51. *Prof Exp:* Chemist, Dow Chem Co, 51-63, group leader, 63-70, anal coordr, 70-71, mgr res planning, 71-83. *Mem:* Am Chem Soc; Sigma Xi. *Res:* Budgeting and project planning for development of new agricultural products and organic chemicals. *Mailing Add:* 19415 Indian Summer Lane Monument CO 80132-9422

GENTRY, WILLIAM RONALD, PHYSICAL CHEMISTRY, CHEMICAL PHYSICS. *Current Pos:* from asst prof to assoc prof, 70-79, PROF CHEM & CHEM PHYSICS, UNIV MINN, 79-, CHAIR, DEPT CHEM, 89- *Personal Data:* b Texarkana, Tex, July 7, 42; m 64, Sharron. *Educ:* Univ Redlands, BS, 64; Univ Calif, Berkeley, PhD(phys chem), 67. *Prof Exp:* Res assoc chem, Mass Inst Technol, 67-68, NSF fel, 68-70. *Concurrent Pos:* Sloan Found res fel, 75-77; pres, Beam Dynamics, 75-; mem, Chem Rev Panel, Air Force Off Sci Res, 80-84; adv ed, Chem Physics Letters, 80-; assoc ed, J Am Chem Soc, 82-; fel, Yamada Sci Found, 86. *Mem:* AAAS; Am Phys Soc; Sigma Xi; Am Chem Soc; Fel Am Phys Soc, 87. *Res:* Chemical dynamics of molecular collisions, including inelastic and reactive processes in the gas phase. *Mailing Add:* Dept Chem Univ Minn Minneapolis MN 55455. *Fax:* 612-626-8659; *E-Mail:* gentry@chemsun.chem.umn.edu

GENTZLER, ROBERT E, CHEMICAL KINETICS. *Current Pos:* Res chemist, Plastics Dept, Wash Lab, 70-80, RES SUPVR, PLASTIC PROD DIV, EXP STA, E I DU PONT DE NEMOURS & CO, INC, 80- *Personal Data:* b York, Pa, Aug 24, 43; m 65; c 2. *Educ:* Dartmouth Col, MA, 67; Univ Mass, PhD(chem), 70. *Mem:* Am Chem Soc. *Res:* Nuclear magnetic resonance studies of probe nuclei in solvation and inorganic complex environments; thermoplastic polymer properties and organic reaction kinetics/catalysis. *Mailing Add:* 26495 Southgate Trail Barrington IL 60010

GENUNG, RICHARD KEITH, ENVIRONMENTAL RESTORATION & WASTE MANAGEMENT. *Current Pos:* DEP DIR ENVIRON RESTORATION & WASTE MGT, MARTIN MARIETTA ENERGY SYSTS, INC, 94- *Personal Data:* b Urbana, Ill, Sept 9, 47; m 85, Donna R McKamey; c Mark A & Linda M. *Educ:* Vanderbilt Univ, BS, 69; Univ Tenn, MS, 71, PhD(chem eng), 76. *Prof Exp:* Res staff, Oak Ridge Nat Lab, 75-85, dir, Waste Mgt Techol Ctr, 85-88, dir, Chem Technol Div, 88-94. *Mem:* Sigma Xi; Nat Mgt Asn; Am Inst Chem Eng. *Res:* Bioprocess engineering research and development; production of fuels and chemicals from biomass and waste materials; development of environmental control technology for aqueous waste streams. *Mailing Add:* 306 Bigtree Dr Knoxville TN 37922-4652

GENUTH, SAUL M, ENDOCRINOLOGY. *Current Pos:* Clin instr med, Case Western Res Univ, 64-70, assoc prof med, 73-78; from asst to assoc med, 64-68, DIR ISOTOPE LAB MED & DIR SALTZMAN INST CLIN INVEST, MT SINAI HOSP, CLEVELAND, 66-; PROF MED, SCH MED, CASE WESTERN RES UNIV, 78- *Personal Data:* b South Norwalk, Conn, Mar 13, 31; m 53; c 2. *Educ:* Harvard Col, AB, 53; Case Western Reserve Univ, MD, 57. *Mem:* Am Fedn Clin Res; Am Diabetes Asn; Endocrine Soc; Am Col Physicians. *Res:* Insulin delivery in diabetes; microvascular complications of diabetes; obesity. *Mailing Add:* Mt Sinai Med Ctr One Mt Sinai Dr Cleveland OH 44106-4191

GENYS, JOHN B, FOREST GENETICS, FORESTRY. *Current Pos:* biologist, Natural Resources Inst, Univ Md, 61-62, res asst prof natural resources, 62-66, res assoc prof, 66-76, chmn, Inland Resources Lab, 78-79, PROF DENDROGENETICS & FOREST SCI, CTR ENVIRON & ESTUARINE STUDIES, UNIV MD, 76- *Personal Data:* b Lithuania, Aug 12, 23; US citizen; m 65; c 2. *Educ:* Univ Göttingen, dipl, 49; Mich State Univ, PhD(forestry, genetics), 60. *Honors & Awards:* Cert Appreciation, US Dept Agr, 87. *Prof Exp:* Forest res aide, Lake States Forest Exp Sta, USDA, 55-57; res asst forest genetics, Mich State Univ, 57-60; instr soil sci, Univ Wis, 60-61. *Concurrent Pos:* Assoc ed, Chesapeake Sci, 63-77; app, Nat Plant Genetic Resources Bd, 82-88. *Res:* Genetic variations in Pinus, Larix, Picea, Prunus and Liriodendron species; selections for productivity, pest and pollution resistance; interspecific pinus hybrids. *Mailing Add:* 8908 Orbit Lane Lanham MD 20706

GENZER, JEROME DANIEL, ORGANIC CHEMISTRY. *Current Pos:* RETIRED. *Personal Data:* b New York, NY, July 23, 25; m 50; c 2. *Educ:* NY Univ, BA, 47; Ind Univ Bloomington, MA, 48. *Prof Exp:* Jr chemist, Warner-Lambert Co, 48-53, from scientist to sr scientist, 53-63, sr res assoc, 63-75, assoc dir & dir chem develop, 77-80. *Mem:* Am Chem Soc. *Res:* Organic synthesis; process research and development of organic chemicals for medicinal use from laboratory through pilot plant in preparation for production, including chemical and equipment design and evaluation and cost evaluation. *Mailing Add:* 27 Washington Ct Livingston NJ 07039

GEOFFROY, GREGORY LYNN, ORGANOMETALLIC CHEMISTRY, UNIVERSITY ADMINISTRATION. *Current Pos:* PROF CHEM, VPRES ACAD AFFAIRS & PROVOST, UNIV MD, COLLEGE PARK, 97- *Personal Data:* b Honolulu, Hawaii, July 8, 46; m 71, Kathleen Carothers; c Susan, Janet, David & Michael. *Educ:* Univ Louisville, BS, 68; Calif Inst Technol, PhD(chem), 74. *Prof Exp:* From asst prof to prof chem, Pa State Univ, University Park, 74-88, dept head, 89, dean, Eberly Col Sci, 89-97. *Concurrent Pos:* Alfred P Sloan Found res fel, 78-80; Camille & Henry Dreyfus teacher scholar award, 77-82; John Simon Guggenheim Found fel, 82-83. *Mem:* Am Chem Soc; fel AAAS; Asn Univs Res Astron. *Res:* Photochemistry of transition metal organometallic compounds; homogeneous catalysis; synthetic organometallic chemistry; heterogeneous catalysis. *Mailing Add:* Univ Md 1119 Main Admin College Park MD 20742

GEOGHEGAN, ROSS, GEOMETRIC GROUP THEORY, FIXED POINT THEORY. *Current Pos:* from asst prof to assoc prof, 72-84, PROF STATE UNIV NY, BINGHAMTON, 84- *Personal Data:* b Dublin, Ireland, July 2, 43; US citizen; m 69, Suzanne Lake; c Niall & Michael. *Educ:* Univ Col Dublin, Ireland, BSc, 63, MSc, 64; Cornell Univ, PhD(math), 70. *Prof Exp:* Mem staff, Inst Advan Study, 70-72. *Concurrent Pos:* Vis asst prof math, Univ Ga, 74-75; mem, Inst Advan Study, 78-79 & 93; vis, Institut des Hautes Etudes Scientifiques, Bures-sur-Yvette, France, 85-86, Math Sci Res Inst, Berkeley, Calif, 89. *Mem:* Am Math Soc; Math Asn Am; Irish Math Soc. *Res:* Geometric topology; homology of groups; fixed point theory; shape theory; infinite-dimensional topology. *Mailing Add:* Dept Math Sci State Univ Ny Binghamton NY 13902-6000. *Fax:* 607-777-2450; *E-Mail:* ross@math.binghamton.edu

GEOGHEGAN, THOMAS EDWARD, M-RNA STRUCTURE, GENE EXPRESSION. *Current Pos:* ASSOC PROF BIOCHEM, UNIV LOUISVILLE, 79- *Educ:* Pa State Univ, PhD(biochem), 75. *Mailing Add:* Dept Biochem Univ Louisville Health Sci Ctr PO Box 35260 Louisville KY 40292-0001. *Fax:* 502-852-6666

GEOGHEGAN, WILLIAM DAVID, CELL BIOLOGY, IMMUNOCHEMISTRY. *Current Pos:* PROG COORDR BIOTECH PROG, MONTGOMERY COL, 94- *Personal Data:* b Milford, Conn, July 2, 43; m 70; c 1. *Educ:* Univ Bridgeport, BA, 70, MS, 72; Ohio State Univ, PhD(anat), 77. *Prof Exp:* Fel cell biol, 77-80, asst prof, Med Col Wis, 80-; at Dept Dermat, Univ Tex Health Sci Ctr. *Concurrent Pos:* Res chemist, Vet Admin, 80- *Mem:* AAAS; Reticuloendothelial Soc; Histochem Soc; Soc Invest Dermat. *Res:* Developed methods for the controlled absorption of proteins to colloidal gold for use in immunochemical assays and immunocytochemistry in light and electron microscopy; immunology of the lung and skin. *Mailing Add:* Dept Biotech Montgomery Col 3200 Hwy 242 W College Park Dr Conroe TX 77384

GEOKAS, MICHAEL C, PANCREATIC ENZYMES, PROTEOLYTIC ENZYMES. *Current Pos:* EMER PROF BIOCHEM, UNIV CALIF DAVIS MED SCH, 90- *Personal Data:* b Villia-Attiha, Greece, Aug 25, 24; m 68. *Educ:* Athens Univ, MD, 51; McGill Univ, MSc, 64, PhD(invest med), 66. *Prof Exp:* Chief med serv, Vet Admin Med Ctr, Martinez, Calif, 74-90. *Mem:* Am Physiol Soc; fel Am Col Physicians; Am Gastroenterol Asn. *Mailing Add:* Univ Calif Davis Med Sch 106 Castle Crest Rd Walnut Creek CA 94595-2707

GEOKEZAS, MELETIOS, INFORMATION SCIENCE, ELECTRICAL ENGINEERING. *Current Pos:* RETIRED. *Personal Data:* b Erythrai, Greece, June 10, 36; US citizen; m 63; c 2. *Educ:* Univ Wash, BS, 60, MS, 63, PhD(elec eng), 68. *Prof Exp:* Res engr, Boeing Co, 61-63 & 65-68; res engr, Honeywell Inc, 68-77, sect chief, 77-79, mgr, 79-80, dir 80-87, dir systs, 87-90, dir advan prog, 90-95. *Mem:* Inst Elec & Electronics Engrs; Am Defense Preparedness Asn. *Res:* Signal processing; pattern recognition. *Mailing Add:* 1387 Hwy 96 St Paul MN 55110

GEORGAKAKOS, KONSTANTINE P, ESTIMATION THEORY, FLASH-FLOOD FORECASTING. *Current Pos:* DIR, HYROL RES CTR, 94- *Personal Data:* b Athens, Greece, Sept 12, 54; m 84; c 1. *Educ:* Nat Tech Univ Athens, Dipl, 77; Mass Inst Technol, MS, 80, ScD, 82. *Prof Exp:* Res asst hydrol & water resources, Mass Inst Technol, 77-82; Nat Res Coun-Nat Oceanic & Atmospheric Admin res assoc hydrol water resources, Hydrol Res Lab, Nat Weather Serv, 82-85, res hydrologist, 85-86; asst prof hydrol & water resources, Univ Iowa, 86-89, assoc prof, Hydrometeorol, 89-94. *Concurrent Pos:* Presidential young investr, NSF, 87-92; mem, Comt Large Scale Exp Hydrol, Am Geophys Union, 84-86, chair precipitation, 90-92 & chair hydrol, Am Meteorol Soc, 91-93; res assoc Nat Res Coun, 82-85; fac scholar, Univ Iowa, 88-91; full res scientist III, Scripps Inst Oceanog, Univ Calif, San Diego, 94- *Mem:* Am Geophys Union; Inst Elec & Electronics Engrs; AAAS; Sigma Xi; Am Meteorol Soc; Am Soc Civil Engrs. *Res:* Design, development and testing of flood and flash-flood forecasting systems that are based on hydrometeorological principles and capable for real-time quantitative probabilistic forecasts; research in precipitation prediction; hydrologic effects of expotential climate change. *Mailing Add:* 12780 High Bluff Dr Suite 250 San Diego CA 92130. *Fax:* 619-792-2519

GEORGAKIS, CHRISTOS, PROCESS CONTROL, CHEMICAL REACTORS. *Current Pos:* assoc prof chem eng, 83-87, CTR DIR, LEHIGH UNIV, 85-, PROF CHEM ENG & PROCESS CONTROL, 87- *Personal Data:* US citizen; m 70, Tina Hinou; c Alexander & Natalie. *Educ:* Nat Tech Univ, Athens, ChE dipl, 70; Univ Ill, MS, 72, Univ Minn, PhD(chem eng), 75. *Prof Exp:* From asst prof to assoc prof chem eng, Mass Inst Technol, 75-83; prof measurement & control, Univ Thessaloniki, 80-83. *Concurrent Pos:* DuPont prof, Mass Inst Technol, 75-76, Edgerton prof, 77-79; Dreyfus Found teacher-scholar, 79-83; vis prof, Rhone Poulenc Industrialization, France, 91 & Delft Univ Technol, 93-94. *Mem:* Am Inst Chem Engrs; Am Chem Soc; Sigma Xi; Soc Indust & Appl Math; AAAS; NY Acad Sci. *Res:* Chemical process modeling; optimization and control; polymerization processes; bioreactors; state estimation; statistical process control. *Mailing Add:* Lehigh Univ 111 Research Dr Bethlehem PA 18015

GEORGAKIS, CONSTANTINE, MATHEMATICS, STATISTICS. *Current Pos:* From instr to asst prof, 62-77, ASSOC PROF MATH, De PAUL UNIV, 77- *Personal Data:* b Vonitsa, Greece, Mar 14, 37; US citizen. *Educ:* DePaul Univ, BS, 61, MS, 63; Ill Inst Technol, PhD(math), 69. *Concurrent Pos:* Dir undergrad res prog, NSF, 68-70. *Mem:* Am Math Soc; Math Soc Am. *Res:* Fourier analysis on groups, probability theory and mathematical statistics. *Mailing Add:* 2219 N Kenmore Ave De Paul Univ Chicago IL 60614-3504

GEORGANAS, NICOLAS D, COMPUTER-COMMUNICATIONS. *Current Pos:* From lectr to assoc prof, Univ Ottawa, 70-80, chmn dept, 81-84, dean eng, 86-93, PROF ELEC ENG, UNIV OTTAWA, 80- *Personal Data:* b Athens, Greece, June 15, 43; Can citizen; m 72; c 2. *Educ:* Nat Tech Univ Athens, Dipl Eng, 66; Univ Ottawa, PhD(control theory), 70. *Concurrent Pos:* Vis prof commun syst archit, IBM CER, La Gaude, France, 77-78 & advan studies, Bull Transac & Inst Nat Res Informatics & Autom, France, 84-85; consult, Dept Commun, Govt Can, 78-83; vis prof broadband network eng, BNR, Ottawa, 93- *Mem:* Fel Inst Elec & Electronics Engrs; NY Acad Sci; Asn Comput Mach. *Res:* Multimedia broadband communications; performance modeling and evaluation of computer systems. *Mailing Add:* Dept Elec Eng Univ Ottawa Ottawa ON K1N 6N5 Can. *Fax:* 613-564-9910; *E-Mail:* georga@trix.genie.uottawa.ca

GEORGE, A(LBERT) R(ICHARD), AEROACOUSTICS, MANUFACTURING ENGINEERING. *Current Pos:* from asst prof to assoc prof, Grad Sch Aerospace Eng, Cornell Univ, 64-72, assoc prof aerospace eng, 72-77, dir, Sibley Sch Mech & Aerospace Eng, 77-87, PROF MECH & AEROSPACE ENG, CORNELL UNIV, 77-, DIR, CORNELL CTR MFG ENTERPRISE, 91- *Personal Data:* b New York, NY, Mar 12, 38; m 59; c 3. *Educ:* Princeton Univ, BSE, 59, MA, 61, PhD(aerospace & mech sci), 64. *Prof Exp:* Res assoc aerospace eng, Princeton Univ, 64. *Concurrent Pos:* Vis asst prof, Univ Wash, 64-65; consult, Southampton Univ, UK, 65-, prin investr, 68-, vis sr res fel, 71-72; head sect, BMW Act, Munich, Ger, 87-88; Nat Res Coun sr assoc, NASA Ames Res Ctr, 88; chmn, Wind Noise Comt, Soc Automotive Engrs. *Mem:* Am Inst Aeronaut & Astronaut; Am Phys Soc; Am Soc Mech Engrs; Soc Automotive Engrs; Am Helicopter Soc; Soc Mfg Engrs. *Res:* Aerodynamics of aircraft and ground vehicles; aerodynamic noise mechanisms; noise control; design and performance of automobiles; sonic boom; manufacturing. *Mailing Add:* Dept Mech & Aerospace Eng 105 Upson Hall Cornell Univ Ithaca NY 14853-7501

GEORGE, ALBERT EL DEEB, PETROLEUM CHEMISTRY, HEAVY OIL RECOVERY. *Current Pos:* res scientist, Energy Res Labs, 72-80, sr res scientist, 80-88, HEAD, BITUMEN & OIL RECOVERY SECT, OTTAWA, 88- *Personal Data:* b Alexandria, Egypt, May 1, 36. *Educ:* Univ Cairo, BSc, 57, MSc, 62, PhD(petrol chem), 67; Enrico Mattei Inst, Milan, Italy, dipl petrol ref, 69. *Prof Exp:* Res asst, Petrol Chem Sect, Nat Res Ctr, Cairo, Egypt, 58-67, res supvr, Petrol Technol Sect, 67-69; Nat Res Coun Can fel, Fuels Res Ctr, 69-72. *Concurrent Pos:* Ital Govt training grant, ENI Petrol Corp, Italy, 68-69; asst dir, Energy Res Prog Off, Energy, Mines & Resources Can, 82-85. *Mem:* Am Chem Soc; Soc Petrol Engrs; Petrol Soc Can Inst Mining & Metall. *Res:* Chemistry of bitumens, heavy oils and synthetic fuels; separation and chemical composition of hydrocarbons nitrogenous and sulfur compounds in petroleum distillates; processing of bitumens and heavy crude oils and their different fractions using high pressure catalytic processes; developing analytical methods for bitumens heavy oils and synthetic fuels; geochemistry of heavy oils and chemistry of enhanced oil recovery. *Mailing Add:* 7 Carmichael Ct Kanata ON K2K 1K1 Can

GEORGE, ANNE DENISE, ORGANIC CHEMISTRY, PHYSICAL ORGANIC CHEMISTRY. *Current Pos:* from asst prof to assoc prof, 78-90, PROF ORG CHEM, NEBR WESLEYAN UNIV, 90- *Personal Data:* b Leeds, Eng, Nov 19, 41; m 68, Thomas A; c 2. *Educ:* Univ Manchester, BSc Hons, 63, PhD(org chem), 66. *Prof Exp:* Fel organometallic chem, Univ Calif, 66-68; res assoc & temp asst prof org chem, Univ Nebr, 68-78. *Mem:* Am Chem Soc; The Chem Soc; Asn Women Sci. *Res:* Mechanisms of nucleophilic aromatic substitutions of abnormal nucleophilic substitutions in allylic systems; physical and synthetic organic chemistry for undergraduate instruction. *Mailing Add:* Nebr Wesleyan Univ 5000 Saint Paul Lincoln NE 68504-2794. *Fax:* 402-465-2179; *E-Mail:* adg@nebrwesleyan.edu

GEORGE, BOYD WINSTON, entomology; deceased, see previous edition for last biography

GEORGE, CARL JOSEPH WINDER, AQUATIC ECOLOGY. *Current Pos:* assoc prof, 67-82, PROF BIOL, UNION COL, NY, 82- *Personal Data:* b Cincinnati, Ohio, Oct 24, 30; m 62. *Educ:* Univ Mich, BS, 56; Harvard Univ, PhD(biol), 60. *Prof Exp:* Asst prof biol, San Fernando Valley State Col, 60-61; asst prof, American Univ Beirut, 61-67, Rockefeller Found grants, 63-67. *Concurrent Pos:* Partic fel, UNESCO Int Cong, Moscow, 66; Smithsonian Inst res support grant fisheries in UAR, 68-72; prin investr lake restoration studies, Environ Protection Agency, 75-79; vis prof, Univ RI, Kingston, 80-81 & Marine Lab, Aberdeen, Scotland, 81; Am field serv, liaison tour ecology of El Nino, 84; sci exhib develop, Schinectody Mus, 86; chmn comn fish, Standard Methods, Am Water Fowl Asn, 88- *Mem:* Am Soc Ichthyol & Herpet; Ecol Soc Am; Am Soc Limnol & Oceanog. *Res:* Vertebrate ecology and general limnology with particular attention to vertebrates of northeastern NY state; ecology of regional and world agriculture; seasonal regional moments of water birds, Upper Hudson Valley. *Mailing Add:* Biol Sci Union Col 807 Union St Schenectady NY 12308-3103

GEORGE, CHARLES REDGENAL, ENTOMOLOGY, PARASITOLOGY. *Current Pos:* assoc prof, 70-74, PROF BIOL, NC CENT UNIV, 74- *Personal Data:* b Faison, NC, July 21, 38; m 61; c 2. *Educ:* A&T Col NC, BS, 60; Okla State Univ, MS, 65; Cornell Univ, PhD(entom), 70. *Prof Exp:* Teacher high sch, NC, 60-64; partic, NSF Acad Year Inst, Okla State Univ, 64-65; instr biol, Fayetteville State Col, 65-66; res asst insect path, Cornell Univ, 66-67. *Mem:* Am Soc Parasitol; Entom Soc Am; Soc Invert Path. *Res:* Effects of malnutrition on growth and mortality of the red rust flour beetle, Tribolium castaneum parasitized by Nosema whitei Weiser. *Mailing Add:* Dept Biol NC Cent Univ 1801 Fayetteville St Durham NC 27707-3129

GEORGE, CLIFFORD EUGENE, ENERGY FROM BIOMASS, ELECTROMAGNETIC POWER APPLICATIONS. *Current Pos:* ASST PROF CHEM ENG, MISS STATE UNIV, 81- *Personal Data:* b Wyandotte, Mich, Mar 16, 42; m 65, Vondell; c 3. *Educ:* Miss State Univ, BSChE, 66, MS, 76, PhD(chem eng), 85. *Prof Exp:* Develop engr, Copolymer Rubber Co, Inc, 66-70; chief process engr, Calumet Industs, 70-78; gen supt, Crosby Chem Co, 78-81. *Mem:* Air & Waste Mgt Asn; Am Inst Chem Engrs; Int Microwave Power Inst; Tech Asn Pulp Paper Indust. *Res:* Improved techniques for the application of electromagnetic energy to industrial applications; energy from biomass processes; contaminated soil remediation. *Mailing Add:* Dept Chem Eng Miss State Univ PO Box 9595 Mississippi State MS 39762-9595

GEORGE, DAVID T, BIOENGINEERING, CARDIOLOGY. *Current Pos:* DIR, FRED A LENNON CARDIOTHORASIC SURG RES LAB, 94- *Educ:* State Univ NY, Buffalo, BS, 83; Univ Pa, MS, 85, PhD(bioeng), 90. *Prof Exp:* asst cardiac mech & skeletal muscle, Philadelphia Heart Inst, 90-94. *Concurrent Pos:* Asst prof surg & biomed eng, Div Cardiothorasic Surgery, Case Western Reserve Univ, 94- *Mem:* Inst Elec & Electronics Engrs; Am Soc Mech Engrs. *Mailing Add:* Case Western Reserve Univ Sch Med 10900 Euclid Ave Cleveland OH 44106-4929

GEORGE, DICK LEON, MATHEMATICS. *Current Pos:* PROF MATH & CHMN DEPT, GA COL MILLEDGEVILLE, 68- *Personal Data:* b Oklahoma City, Okla, Mar 10, 36; m 57; c 2. *Educ:* Okla State Univ, BS, 58; Duke Univ, PhD(math), 62. *Prof Exp:* From instr to asst prof math, NC State Col, 61-63; assoc prof, Charlotte Col, 63-65; assoc prof, Trinity Univ, Tex, 65-68. *Mem:* Am Math Soc; Math Asn Am; Soc Indust & Appl Math. *Res:* Mixed boundary value problems in thermoelasticity. *Mailing Add:* Dept Math Cameron Univ 2800 W Gore Blvd Lawton OK 73505-6320

GEORGE, DONALD WAYNE, PLANT BREEDING, COLD HARDINESS. *Current Pos:* RETIRED. *Personal Data:* b Topeka, Kans, May 1, 21; m 43, Janis Moore Lancaster; c Stephen Thomas & Mark Douglas. *Educ:* Kans State Col, BS, 48, MS, 49. *Prof Exp:* Asst agronomist, Tex Agr Exp Sta, 49-51; asst plant breeder, Univ Ariz, 51-54; agronomist, Pendleton Br Exp Sta, Ore State Univ, 54-65; agronomist, sci & educ admin, USDA & Plant Sci Res Div & Wash State Univ, 65-82. *Mem:* Sigma Xi. *Res:* Cold and frost hardiness; vernalization, photoperiod and temperature influence on development; crown placement; coleoptile tiller and secondary crown development; adaptation to early seeding for erosion-pollution control; post harvest dormancy of wheat. *Mailing Add:* 1610 NW Deane Pullman WA 99163

GEORGE, EDWARD THOMAS, CHEMICAL ENGINEERING. *Current Pos:* RETIRED. *Personal Data:* b North Adams, Mass, Dec 27, 25; m 55; c 4. *Educ:* Worcester Polytech Inst, BS, 47, MS, 49; Yale Univ, DEng, 53. *Prof Exp:* Res scientist, B F Goodrich Chem Co, Ohio, 53-57; eng develop engr, Sci Design Co, NY, 57-59, comput dept mgr, 59-60; res develop mgr & comput dept dir, Quantum, Inc, Conn, 60-62; pres, founder & owner, Conn Sci Ctr, Inc, 62-69; from assoc prof to prof indust eng, Univ New Haven, 70-96. *Concurrent Pos:* Teaching assignments, New Haven Col, 64-70; chmn, Air & Water Conserv Comt, Chamber of Comm, 66- *Mem:* NY Acad Sci; fel Am Inst Chemists. *Mailing Add:* Univ New Haven 300 Orange Ave West Haven CT 06516-1916

GEORGE, ELMER, JR, microbiology, biochemistry, for more information see previous edition

GEORGE, FREDRICK WILLIAM, SEXUAL DIFFERENTIATION. *Current Pos:* Fel endocrinol, 75-77, instr, 77-79, ASST PROF INTERNAL MED, MED SCH, UNIV TEX SOUTHWESTERN, 79-, ASST PROF CELL BIOL, 83- *Personal Data:* b Fairfield, Iowa, Dec 16, 46; m 68; c 2. *Educ:* Iowa State Univ, BS, 69, MS, 72, PhD(zool), 75. *Concurrent Pos:* NIH career develop award. *Mem:* Endocrine Soc; Sigma Xi; Soc Study of Reproduction. *Res:* Fetal endocrinology; sexual differentiation. *Mailing Add:* 6927 Wildgrove Ave Dallas TX 75214

GEORGE, HARVEY, BIOCHEMISTRY, CLINICAL PATHOLOGY. *Current Pos:* DIR DIAG LABS, MASS CTR DIS CONTROL, DEPT PUB HEALTH, COMMONWEALTH OF MASS. *Personal Data:* b New York, NY, Apr 28, 35; div; c 3. *Educ:* Cornell Univ, BA, 57; Univ Tenn, MS, 61, PhD(biochem), 63. *Prof Exp:* Res fel biochem, Sch Med, Tufts Univ, 64-66; sr biochemist, Collab Res, Inc, Mass, 67-68, dir biochem res, 68-70; dir clin labs, Lahey Clin Found, 70-85. *Concurrent Pos:* Asst res prof, Med Sch, Boston Univ, 67-69; assoc prof allied health, Northeastern Univ, Boston. *Mem:* Am Asn Clin Chem; Am Chem Soc; NY Acad Sci; Am Soc Microbiol; Am Soc Clin Path; Am Public Health Asn; Asn Off Anal Chemists. *Res:* Clinical chemistry; protein and nucleic acid biosynthesis; public health and epidemiology. *Mailing Add:* State Lab Inst 305 South St Jamaica Plain MA 02130. *E-Mail:* hgeorge@world.std.com

GEORGE, JAMES E, INORGANIC CHEMISTRY. *Current Pos:* asst prof, 65-69, ASSOC PROF CHEM, DePAUW UNIV, 69- *Personal Data:* b Pittsburgh, Pa, July 25, 38; m 63; c 4. *Educ:* Allegheny Col, BS, 60; Univ Ill, PhD(chem), 64. *Prof Exp:* Asst prof chem, Oberlin Col, 63-65. *Concurrent Pos:* Asst prof chem, Univ Marshal. *Mem:* AAAS; Am Chem Soc. *Res:* Chemical education; structure of coordination compounds; coordination chemistry of biological compounds. *Mailing Add:* Dept Chem DePauw Univ Greencastle IN 46135-1700

GEORGE, JAMES FRANCIS, TESTING & EVALUATION OF DEVELOPMENT SYSTEMS. *Current Pos:* assoc engr, missle res & develop technol & energy, 61-63, sr engr, 63-70, PROJ ENGR, ENERGY & MIL SYSTS DEVELOP, APPL PHYSICS LAB, JOHNS HOPKINS UNIV, 70- *Personal Data:* b Kansas City, Mo, Dec 18, 29; m 57; c 1. *Educ:* Univ Ill, BS, 51; George Washington Univ, MS, 60. *Prof Exp:* Engr bridge design, Howard, Needles, Tummen & Bergendorff, 54-55; bridge engr, Michael Baker Jr, Inc, 55-60. *Mem:* Am Inst Aeronaut & Astronaut. *Res:* Flywheel energy storage systems; surface effect ships for Navy use; ocean thermal energy conversion (OTEC) applications; safety system to prevent damaging fires in shipboard electrical systems. *Mailing Add:* 6453 Via Adventura El Paso TX 79912

GEORGE, JAMES HENRY BRYN, PHYSICAL CHEMISTRY, CHEMICAL ENGINEERING. *Current Pos:* RETIRED. *Personal Data:* b Swansea, Wales, Feb 5, 29; nat US; m 63; c 2. *Educ:* Oxford Univ, BA, 49, MA & PhD(phys chem), 52; Mass Inst Technol, SM, 53. *Prof Exp:* Instr chem eng, Mass Inst Technol, 53; chem engr, Ionics, Inc, 53-54; sr phys chemist, Arthur D Little, Inc, 54-60, group leader, 60-66, sect head phys chem, 66-69, sect head chem systs, 69-74, vpres chem systs, 72-80; pres, George Consult Int Inc, 80-95. *Mem:* Electrochem Soc; Am Chem Soc. *Res:* Thermodynamics; electrochemistry; ion exchange; technology, economics and applications of batteries and fuel cells; electric vehicle; world battery industry studies. *Mailing Add:* 53 Spring Rd Concord MA 01742

GEORGE, JAMES Z, ATOMIC HYPERFINE STRUCTURE, ATOMIC QUANTUM PHYSICS. *Current Pos:* res physicist, Salem, Mass, 78-82, res physicist, Melrose, Mass, 82-86, RES PHYSICIST ATOMIC BEAM RESONATORS, JG RES & TECHNOL, DANVERS, MASS, 87- *Personal Data:* b Lynn, Mass, Dec 29, 22; m 52, Winifred R; c James K & Carolyn A. *Educ:* Northeastern Univ, SB, 48. *Prof Exp:* Physicist mass spectrometry, nuclear radiation physics, NIH, Bethesda, Md, 49-51 & chem div, US Naval Med Res Inst, 51-55; sr physicist atomic beam clock, physics dept, Nat Co, Melrose, Mass, 55-58, sr res physicist tech staff, Malden, Mass, 58-60, mgr atomic beam resonators, dept phys electronics, Melrose, 60-66; pres, Frequency Control Corp, Topsfield, Mass, 66-69; tech consult atomic beam physics, JG Res & Technol, Frequency Electronics Inc, NY & USN, 69-74; dir, atomic res, atomic beam resonators, Frequency Electronics, New Hyde Park, NY, 74-78. *Concurrent Pos:* Consult, USN, 79- *Mem:* Am Phys Soc; Am Inst Physics; NY Acad Sci. *Res:* Hyperfine structure of the "hydrogenic" alkalai atoms; including cesium and rubidium; atomic beam physics. *Mailing Add:* JG Res & Technol One Southside Rd Danvers MA 01923-1408

GEORGE, JOHN ALLEN, entomology, for more information see previous edition

GEORGE, JOHN ANGELOS, AEROSPACE ENGINEERING. *Current Pos:* from asst prof to assoc prof aerospace eng, 59-70, actg chmn dept gen sci, 68-70, PROF AEROSPACE ENG, PARKS COL, ST LOUIS UNIV, 70-, CHMN AEROSPACE ENG & ENG SCI DEPT, 77- *Personal Data:* b Sault Ste Marie, Mich, Sept 10, 34; m 59; c 3. *Educ:* St Louis Univ, BS, 55, PhD(physics), 67; Calif Inst Technol, MS, 56. *Prof Exp:* Flight test engr, McDonnell Aircraft Corp, 58-59. *Concurrent Pos:* Res assoc, St Louis Univ, 65-70. *Mem:* Am Inst Aeronaut & Astronaut; Am Soc Eng Educ. *Res:* Teaching in areas of gas dynamics, aerodynamics and flight mechanics; systems studies for aircraft condition monitoring. *Mailing Add:* Dept Aerospace Eng Parks Col St Louis Univ 500 Falling Springs Rd Cahokia IL 62206-1938

GEORGE, JOHN CALEEKAL, ZOOLOGY, PHYSIOLOGY. *Current Pos:* from assoc prof to prof, 67-86, ACTG CHMN DEPT, UNIV GUELPH, 74-, EMER PROF ZOOL, 86- *Personal Data:* b Kerala, India, June 16, 21; m 50, Achamma Molly; c Vinod, Manoj & Anuppa. *Educ:* Univ Bombay, BSc, 42, PhD(zool), 48. *Honors & Awards:* Guelph Res Award, Sigma Xi, 79; Outstanding Acad Achievement Award, Fed Kerala Associations NAm, 90. *Prof Exp:* Demonstr zool, IY Col, Bombay, India, 45-48; lectr, Inst Sci, Bombay, India, 48; zoologist, Dept Anthrop, Govt India, 48-50; reader & head zool, Univ Baroda, 50-56, prof & head, 57-67. *Concurrent Pos:* Fulbright-Smith-Mundt fel, Univ Pa, 53-54; ed, J Animal Morphol & Physiol,

56-; mem int teamwork embryol & Dutch Govt scholar, Holland, 58; Dorabji Tata travel grant to Holland, 58; Fulbright res scholar & lectr, Wash State Univ, 61-62; ed & founder, Pavo, Indian J Ornith, 63-; res grants, Muscular Dystrophy Asn Am, 64-67 & USDA, 65-67; mem biol res comt, Coun Sci & Indust Res, Govt India, 65-67; food & agr comt, Govt India Atomic Energy Comn, 67; negotiated develop grant, Nat Res Coun Can, 70-74; mem animal biol comt, Nat Res Coun Can, 75-77, chmn, 77, adv, 78; Guelph Res Award, Sigma Xi, 79. *Mem:* Fel NY Acad Sci; fel Zool Soc India; Sigma Xi, (pres, 83). *Res:* Vertebrate anatomy; herpetology; ornithology; environmental physiology; comparative physiology; muscle physiology; avian and insect physiology endocrinology; histochemistry; embryology; pineal physiology; thermal physiology; bird migration. *Mailing Add:* Dept Zool Univ Guelph Guelph ON N1G 2W1 Can. *Fax:* 519-767-1656

GEORGE, JOHN HAROLD, MATHEMATICS. *Current Pos:* from assoc prof to prof, 67-92, EMER PROF MATH, UNIV WYO, 92-; PROF & CHAIR MATH, EMBRY RIDDLE AERONAUT UNIV, 92- *Personal Data:* b Bucyrus, Ohio, Nov 29, 35; m 57, Joanne M Runco; c Randal, Barbara & Tom. *Educ:* Ohio State Univ, BS, 57; Univ Ala, MA, 61, PhD(math), 66. *Prof Exp:* Aerospace scientist, Guid & Control Lab, US Army Ballistic Missile Agency, Ala, 57-60; aerospace scientist & sect chief missile guid & control, Astrionics Lab, Marshall Space Flight Ctr, NASA, 60-66, spec asst to chief res math, Aero-Astrodynamics Lab, Ala, 66-67. *Concurrent Pos:* Sr Humboldt award, 73-74. *Mem:* Math Model Soc; Math Asn Am; Soc Indust & Appl Math. *Res:* Oil shale kinetics and chemical process control; modeling of large scale processes; free boundary problems; statistical forces on ocean structures. *Mailing Add:* Dept Math Embry Riddle Aeronaut Univ 653 Marina Dr Daytona Beach FL 32114. *Fax:* 904-226-7210; *E-Mail:* jgeorge@erav.ab.erau.edu

GEORGE, JOHN LOTHAR, BIOLOGY. *Current Pos:* assoc prof forestry, Pa State Univ, 63-70, wildlife mgt, 70-75, chmn, Wildlife Planning Group, 70-81, prof, 75-81, EMER PROF WILDLIFE MGT, PA STATE UNIV, 81- *Personal Data:* b Milwaukee, Wis, Apr 17, 16; m 44, 63, Janice Chanult; c Carolyn L, John C, Thomas L, David N & Laura E. *Educ:* Univ Mich, BS, 39, MS, 41, PhD(zool), 52. *Honors & Awards:* Creative Res Award, Nat Asn Univ Exten Associations, 72; Outstanding Res Award, NE Wildlife Soc, 81. *Prof Exp:* 4H co camp dir, State Agr Exten Serv, WVa, 39; asst, Univ Mich, 39-42 & 46-47; asst prof zool, Vassar Col, 50-57; assoc cur mammals, NY Zool Soc, 57-58; biologist, Uta US Fish & Wildlife Serv, 58-63. *Concurrent Pos:* Ranger naturalist, Great Smokies Nat Park, 40-41; biologist, US Fish & Wildlife Serv, 46-47; chmn, Comt Ecol Effects of Chem Controls, Int Union Conserv Nature & Natural Resources, Switz, 63-74; trustee, Nat Parks Asn, 69-80; Cong Adv ad hoc comt on environ, US Cong, 70-80; mem, Steering Comt, Symp Continuing Educ, Soc Am Foresters, 73; area chmn, Conserv Award Comt, Wildlife Soc, 75. *Mem:* Wildlife Soc; Wilderness Soc; Am Soc Mammal; Soc Am Foresters. *Res:* Avian ecology; effects of pesticides on wild life; avian and mammal populations and life histories; endangered species; urban wildlife; continuing education; bird roost problems; wildlife airport; agriculture problems. *Mailing Add:* 685 Westerly Pkwy State College PA 16801

GEORGE, JOHN RONALD, CROP PHYSIOLOGY, FORAGE CROP PHYSIOLOGY. *Current Pos:* from asst prof to assoc prof, 69-75, PROF AGRON, IOWA STATE UNIV, 75- *Personal Data:* b Pasco, Wash, Apr 28, 40; m 62, Ethel M Sutton; c Sheryl L & John M. *Educ:* Wash State Univ, BS, 62; Purdue Univ, MS, 64, PhD(crop physiol), 67. *Honors & Awards:* Merit Cert, Am Forage & Grassland Coun, 85. *Prof Exp:* Agronomist, Am Potash Inst, 66-69. *Mem:* Am Forage & Grassland Coun; fel Am Soc Agron; fel Crop Sci Soc Am; fel Nat Asn Cols & Teachers Agr. *Res:* Nitrate accumulation in forage crops; forage production; management and physiology research; establishment, renovation, fertilization and stand dynamics; defoliation management of cool-season and warm-season forage species; the role of warm-season prairie grasses in modern forage-livestock systems. *Mailing Add:* Dept Agron Iowa State Univ Ames IA 50011

GEORGE, KALANKAMARY PILY, SOIL & STRUCTURAL ENGINEERING, PAVEMENT ENGINEERING. *Current Pos:* from asst prof to assoc prof struct eng & soils & res engr, 63-68, PROF CIVIL ENG, UNIV MISS, 68- *Personal Data:* b Kerala, India, June 13, 33; m 58; c Sarah & Anil. *Educ:* Nat Inst Eng, India, BE, 56; Iowa State Univ, MS, 61, PhD(civil eng), 63. *Prof Exp:* Dist asst engr, Pub Works Dept, Kerala, India, 56-59; res assoc soils eng, Eng Exp Sta, Iowa State Univ, 59-63. *Concurrent Pos:* State Hwy Dept res grant & proj dir hwy res, 63-94; NSF grant, 71-74; mem, Transp Res Bd. *Mem:* Am Soc Civil Engrs; Am Soc Fedn Engrs. *Res:* Soil stabilization; pavement mgt; design of soil-cement bases; pavement analysis; soil structure interaction; probabilistic analysis. *Mailing Add:* Dept Civil Eng Univ Miss University MS 38677. *Fax:* 601-234-7191

GEORGE, KATTUNILATHU OOMMEN, HOMEOPATHY. *Current Pos:* DEAN, DIR & PROF HOMEOP MED HEALTH SCI, SAMUEL HAHNEMANN SCH HOMEOP MED, LOS ANGELES INT UNIV, 83- *Personal Data:* b June 30, 43; m 68, Soshmma; c Dommen K. *Educ:* CH Med Col & Hosp, DMS, 65; Calcutta Univ, MBS, 75; Calif Christian Inst, MA, 82. *Prof Exp:* Resident, Hahnemann Mission Hosp, SIndia, 65-67; chief med examr pharmacol, clin med & pharm, Travancore-Cochin Med Coun Homeop Med, India, 67-76; first yr residency, Pub Health Ctr, Calif, 79-80; second yr residency, Family Serv Am, Calif, 79-80; psychoanalyst coun & consult, New Hope Counseling Ctr, Calif, 80-81; consult, Indust Med Clin & Potner's Med Group, Calif, 81-83. *Concurrent Pos:* chief med officer & dir, fel Clin & Pharmaceut, India; med officer, Hahnemann Mission Hosp, India, 65-67; nutrit consult, Biochem Anal Clin, 78-80; prof homeop med, Los Angeles Univ, 79-80; mem fac, Western Univ, Ariz, 82; mem fac, CCI Grad Sch, 82-87. *Mem:* Homeopathic Med Asn Am (pres); Homeop Med Asn India; Soc Ultramolecular Med. *Res:* Comprehensive therapeutics in homeopathy. *Mailing Add:* Hahnemann Res Ctr Inc 18818 Teller Ave Suite 230 Irvine CA 92715

GEORGE, KENNETH DUDLEY, HEALTH PHYSICS, RADIATION DOSIMETRY. *Current Pos:* RETIRED. *Personal Data:* b Eltham, NZ, Oct 31, 16; US citizen; m 43, Mae Johnson; c Gregory & Gillian. *Educ:* Univ Auckland, BSc, 39, MSc, 40. *Prof Exp:* With NZ Dept Sci & Indust Res, 40-44, UK-Can Atomic Energy Proj, Can, 44-48 & 49-50 & US Army Munitions Command, Picatinny Arsenal, 51-64; reactor supvr, Res Ctr, Union Carbide Corp, Tuxedo, NY, 64-66, supt nuclear opers, 66-68, sr res scientist, 68-81. *Mem:* Am Nuclear Soc. *Res:* Medical and industrial applications of radioisotopes and nucleonics; nuclear reactor science. *Mailing Add:* 140 Kingsland Rd Boonton NJ 07005

GEORGE, M COLLEEN, EXERCISE PHYSIOLOGY, CARDIOVASCULAR PHYSIOLOGY. *Current Pos:* CONSULT, PHYSIOL DATA SYSTS LTD, 87- *Personal Data:* b Austin, Tex, Aug 16, 38; m 70. *Educ:* Univ Tex, BS, 60, MEd, 63, EdD, 68; Tex Tech Univ, PhD(physiol), 82. *Prof Exp:* From asst prof to assoc prof phys educ, Tex Tech Univ, 64-70, res asst physiol, Sch Med, 77-81; assoc prof phys educ, N Tex State Univ, 70-76; res dir, Spinal Injury Res & Rehab Group, 85-86. *Concurrent Pos:* Vis prof exercise sci, Ariz State Univ, 84-85. *Mem:* AAAS; Sigma Xi; Am Physiol Soc. *Res:* Motor integration and development of children and the mentally retarded; direct effects of exercise and high altitude on rat myocardium; body composition and exercise tolerance of spinal cord injured humans. *Mailing Add:* 8009 E Del Tiburon Dr Scottsdale AZ 85258-1727

GEORGE, MELVIN DOUGLAS, MATHEMATICS. *Current Pos:* RETIRED. *Personal Data:* b Washington, DC, Feb 13, 36; m 58; c 2. *Educ:* Northwestern Univ, BA, 56; Princeton Univ, PhD(math), 59. *Prof Exp:* Res assoc, Inst Fluid Dynamics & Appl Math, Univ Md, 59-60; from asst prof to prof math, Univ Mo, 60-70, assoc dean grad sch, 67-69; prof math & dean, Col Arts & Sci, Univ Nebr, Lincoln, 70-75; prof math & vpres acad affairs & interim pres, Univ Mo, 94- *Mem:* Am Math Soc; Math Asn Am. *Res:* Mathematical economics; partial differential equations; functional analysis. *Mailing Add:* Pres Off 321 Univ Hall Columbia MO 65211

GEORGE, MICHAEL JAMES, PHYSICS, SHOCK HYDRODYNAMICS. *Current Pos:* MEM STAFF PHYSICS, LOS ALAMOS NAT LAB, UNIV CALIF, 70- *Personal Data:* b Staten Island, NY, Nov 13, 41. *Educ:* Univ NC, BS, 63; Calif Inst Technol, PhD(physics), 69. *Honors & Awards:* Award of Excellence, Dept Energy, 82, 88 & 90. *Prof Exp:* Res fel physics, Calif Inst Technol, 69-70. *Mem:* Sigma Xi. *Res:* Shock wave and detonation physics; cosmic rays and space physics. *Mailing Add:* 505 Oppenheimer Dr Unit 1204 Los Alamos NM 87544-2395

GEORGE, MILON FRED, PLANT PHYSIOLOGY. *Current Pos:* ASST PROF PLANT PHYSIOL, UNIV MO, COLUMBIA, 78- *Personal Data:* b St Cloud, Minn, Jan 19, 44; m 66; c 2. *Educ:* Univ Minn, BS, 66, MS, 73, PhD(plant physiol), 75. *Prof Exp:* Instrumentation engr electronics, McDonnell-Douglas, Santa Monica, Calif, 66-69; asst prof plant physiol, Va Polytech Inst, 75-78. *Mem:* Am Soc Plant Physiologists; AAAS; Am Soc Hort Sci. *Res:* Physiology of plant survival at low temperature. *Mailing Add:* 382 Crown Pt Columbia MO 65203

GEORGE, NICHOLAS, OPTICS, ELECTRICAL ENGINEERING. *Current Pos:* dir, Univ Rochester, 77-81; PROF OPTICS, INST OPTICS, UNIV ROCHESTER, 77-, ASSOC DEAN RES, COL ENG & APPL SCI, 90-, WILSON CHAIR PROF ELECTRONIC IMAGING, 94- *Personal Data:* b Council Bluffs, Iowa, Oct 29, 37; m 66. *Educ:* Univ Calif, Berkeley, BS; Univ Md, MS; Calif Inst Technol, PhD(elec eng & physics). *Prof Exp:* Physicist to sect chief, Nat Bur Stand, Washington, DC; chief, physics sect, Emerson Res Labs, Washington, DC; sr staff physicist, Hughes Aircraft Co, El Segundo, Calif; prof elec eng & appl physics, Calif Inst Technol. *Concurrent Pos:* Consult var Fortune 500 Co; dir-at-large, Optical Soc Am; founding dir, Ctr Optoelectronic Systs Res, 86- & Rochester Imaging Consortium, 91-; with adv bd imaging, sci, Rochester Inst Technol, 85-; founding dir, Ctr Optoelectronic Systs Res, Univ Rochester, 86-, Ctr Electronic Imaging Systs, 91-, prof elec eng, 93- *Mem:* Fel Optical Soc Am; fel Soc Photo-Optical Instrumentation Engrs; Am Phys Soc; Am Asn Univ Profs; Sigma Xi; fel Inst Elec & Electronics Engr. *Res:* Electronic imaging and optoelectronics systems emphasizing automatic pattern recognition, remote sensing and precision meterology; speckle in optical noise with an emphasis on its wavelength dependence and sub-resolution; x-ray diffraction, interference and holography. *Mailing Add:* Inst Optics Univ Rochester Wilson Blvd Rochester NY 14627. *E-Mail:* ngeorge@troi.cc.rochester.edu

GEORGE, PETER KURT, MAGNETIC HEADS, MAGNETIC MATERIALS. *Current Pos:* DIR PERIPHERAL COMP, SEAGATE TECHNOL, 90- *Personal Data:* b Schenectady, NY, Dec 1, 42; m 64; c 2. *Educ:* Univ Mich, BS, 64; Case Inst Technol, MS, 66; Case Western Res Univ, PhD(elec sci appl phys), 69. *Prof Exp:* Postdoctoral elec mat, Delft Tech Univ, 70-71; mem tech staff mat res, Rockwell Int, 71-75; mem tech staff mag res, IBM, 76-77; sr prof design mgr magnetic bubbles, Nat Semiconductor, 77-82; dir peripheral comp, Control Data, 82-90. *Mem:* Inst Elec & Electronics Engrs; Am Inst Physics. *Res:* Developing advanced components for rigid disk drives; magnetoresistive/thin film heads; thin film metal disks. *Mailing Add:* 8741 Sandro Rd S Bloomington MN 55438

GEORGE, PHILIP, BIOPHYSICAL CHEMISTRY, COMPUTATIONAL CHEMISTRY. *Current Pos:* res prof biophys chem, Univ Pa, 55-73, prof biol chem, 73-77, prof, 77-87, EMER PROF BIOL, UNIV PA, 90- *Personal Data:* b Maidstone, Eng, Jan 30, 20; m 46, Kathleen M Hoff; c Francis, Sarah, Emma, Simon, Hannah & Edwin. *Educ:* Cambridge Univ, BA, 41, MA, 44, PhD, 45. *Prof Exp:* Asst tutor, Christ's Col, Cambridge Univ, 45-47; Brotherton res lectr phys chem, Univ Leeds, 47-49; asst dir res, Dept Colloid Sci, Cambridge Univ, 49-55. *Concurrent Pos:* Fel, Christ's Col, Cambridge Univ, 53-55; vis scientist, Inst Cancer Res, Fox Chase Cancer Ctr, 88- *Mem:* Biophys Soc; Am Chem Soc; Am Soc Biol Chem; Hist Sci Soc; Royal Soc Chem; Sigma Xi. *Res:* Coordination chemistry; hemoprotein reactions; biochemical thermodynamics; intermediary metabolism/structural chemistry: energetics; history of chemistry. *Mailing Add:* 4 Herford Pl Lansdowne PA 19050-2408

GEORGE, RAYMOND S, NUCLEAR CHEMISTRY. *Current Pos:* br chief, Nuclear Safeguards & Accountability, US Energy Res & Develop Admin, 75-78, PROG MGR NUCLEAR WEAPONS, US DEPT ENERGY, 78- *Personal Data:* b San Bernardino, Calif, Sept 4, 36; m 63; c 2. *Educ:* Univ Calif, Riverside, BA, 58; Northwestern Univ, PhD(anal chem), 62. *Prof Exp:* Fulbright fel, H C Orsteds Inst, Copenhagen Univ, 62-63; staff mem, Los Alamos Sci Lab, 63-70; sr safeguards engr, Albuquerque Opers Off, Nuclear Mat Mgt Div, US AEC, 71-75. *Concurrent Pos:* Consult solar energy anal & appln. *Res:* Boric acid complexes; inorganic complexation chemistry; analytical research and development; analytical instrumentation; explosives chemistry; crime laboratory establishment and techniques; radiation chemistry; nuclear materials safeguards and accountability; factory automation. *Mailing Add:* 1432 Honeysuckle Ct NE Albuquerque NM 87122

GEORGE, ROBERT, PHARMACOLOGY. *Current Pos:* assoc prof, 61-67, PROF PHARMACOL, CTR HEALTH SCI, UNIV CALIF, LOS ANGELES, 67- *Personal Data:* b Turlock, Calif, Feb 10, 23; m 58; c 2. *Educ:* Univ Ore, AB, 49; Univ Calif, Berkeley, PhD(physiol), 53. *Prof Exp:* Asst physiol, Univ Calif, Berkeley, 50-53; jr res pharmacologist, Univ Calif Med Ctr, San Francisco, 53-56; USPHS fel neuroendocrinol, Maudsley Hosp, Univ London, 56-58; asst res pharmacologist & asst prof pharmacol, 58-61. *Concurrent Pos:* Co-ed, Ann Rev Pharmacol & Toxicol; consult, Nat Inst Drug Abuse & Nat Inst Neurol & Commun Disorders & Stroke. *Mem:* AAAS; Am Soc Pharmacol & Exp Therapeut; Am Physiol Soc; Int Soc Neuroendocrinol. *Res:* Analgesics and neuroendocrine function; neural control of anterior pituitary; diabetes mellitus; pharmacology and pathology of tremor. *Mailing Add:* 18271 Wakecrest Dr Malibu CA 90265-5600

GEORGE, ROBERT EUGENE, RADIOLOGICAL PHYSICS, HEALTH PHYSICS. *Current Pos:* RETIRED. *Personal Data:* b Bowling Green, Ohio, Nov, 24, 29; m 52; c 7. *Educ:* Ohio State Univ, BSc, 52; Univ Rochester, MSc, 61; Purdue Univ, PhD(bionucleonics), 66. *Honors & Awards:* Meritorious Serv Medal, Dept Defense, 72. *Prof Exp:* Chief pharm serv, Naval Hosp, Med Serv Corps, US Navy, Quantico, Va, 53-56, chief pharm serv, Naval Hosp, Newport, RI, 56-60, instr nuclear, chem & biol weapons, Naval Unit, Army Chem Sch, 61-64, res projs group dir, Armed Forces Radiobiol Res Inst, 66-67, chmn, Dept Radiation Biol, 67-72, radiol physicist, Naval Hosp, Bethesda, Md, 72-73; assoc prof, Bionucleonics Dept, Purdue Univ, 73-76; assoc prof & chief radiol physicist, Dept Radiation Oncol, Ind Univ, Indianapolis, 75-89. *Mem:* Radiation Res Soc; Health Physics Soc; Am Asn Physicist in Med; Am Col Radiol. *Res:* Applications of high energy electrons and photons in radiation therapy. *Mailing Add:* 2544 Hawthorne Pl Noblesville IN 46060

GEORGE, ROBERT PORTER, DEVELOPMENTAL BIOLOGY, INVERTEBRATE ZOOLOGY. *Current Pos:* asst prof, 70-75, ASSOC PROF ZOOL, UNIV WYO, 75- *Personal Data:* b San Rafael, Calif, June 18, 37; m 67; c 3. *Educ:* Univ Calif, Berkeley, BA, 61; Univ Hawaii, MS, 67, PhD(microbiol), 68. *Prof Exp:* Res fel bacteriol, Univ Wis-Madison, 68-70. *Mem:* Soc Develop Biol; AAAS; Soc Free Radical Res. *Res:* Transmission and scanning electron microscopy of cellular slime molds; autoradiographic study of stalk formation in Dictyostelium; effect of inhibitors and chemotactic substances on morphogenesis in Dictyostelium; isolation of cell receptors for cyclic-adenosine monophosphate; study of human carnosinase and its inhibitors; protozoan defenses against free radicals. *Mailing Add:* Dept Zool Univ Wyo PO Box 3166 Laramie WY 82071-3166

GEORGE, RONALD BAYLIS, INTERNAL MEDICINE, PULMONARY DISEASES. *Current Pos:* prof med & head Pulmonary Dis Sect, Sch Med, 72-92, PROF & CHMN DEPT MED, LA STATE UNIV MED CTR, SHREVEPORT, 92- *Personal Data:* b Zwolle, La, Nov 17, 32. *Educ:* Univ Ala, BA, 54; Tulane Univ, MD, 58; Am Bd Internal Med, dipl, 65. *Prof Exp:* From asst prof internal med to assoc prof med, Sch Med, Tulane Univ, 66-72. *Mem:* Am Thoracic Soc; Am Col Chest Physicians (pres, 94-95). *Res:* Pulmonary physiology; pneumonias and their x-ray appearance; pulmonary mycoses; lung cancer; obstructive airways disease. *Mailing Add:* Med-Pulmonary Div La State Univ Sch Med PO Box 33932 Shreveport LA 71130-3932

GEORGE, RONALD EDISON, COMPUTER SCIENCE. *Current Pos:* PRES & CHIEF EXEC OFFICER, ACTC TECHNOL, 89- *Personal Data:* b Winnipeg, Man, Can, Oct 1, 37; m 60; c 3. *Educ:* Univ Sask, BEng, 59, MSc, 61; Univ Waterloo, PhD(mgt sci), 78. *Prof Exp:* Lectr mech eng, Univ Sask, 59-61; from anal programmer comput sci to exec dir, Govt of Sask, 61-71; from asst prof to assoc prof comput sci, Univ Guelph, Ont, 74-80; prof, Dept Comput Sci, Univ Calgary, 80-89. *Concurrent Pos:* Consult, Atomic Energy Can, 60; vchmn & bd mem, Sask Govt Comput Ctr, 65-71; adv, S Sask Hosps Bd, 68-71; consult minister health, Study of Psychiat Serv, Govt of Sask, 69. *Mem:* Can Info Processing Soc; Asn Comput Mach; Asn Prof Engrs. *Res:* Management information systems; factors effecting the use of information by senior management. *Mailing Add:* ACTC Technol 350 6715 Eighth St NE Calgary AB T2E 7H7 Can

GEORGE, SARAH B(REWSTER), EVOLUTION, MUSEUM SCIENCE. *Current Pos:* AT UTAH MUS NATURAL HIST, UNIV UTAH, 93- *Personal Data:* b Tacoma, Wash, Nov 16, 56; m 85; c 1. *Educ:* Univ Puget Sound, BS, 78; Ft Hays State Univ, MS, 80; Univ NMex, PhD(biol), 84. *Prof Exp:* Asst cur mammal, Natural Hist Mus Los Angeles Co, 85-90, assoc cur, 90-93. *Concurrent Pos:* Adj asst prof biol, Univ Southern Calif, 85- & Univ Calif, Los Angeles, 89-; mem bd dirs, Am Soc Mammalogists, 85-88, 88-91 & 91-94. *Mem:* Am Soc Mammalogists; Soc Study Evolution; Soc Syst Zool; Asn Women Sci. *Res:* Evolution, systematics, population genetics, conservation biology and taxonomy of small mammals, particularly shrews; museum science and vertebrate collection management. *Mailing Add:* Utah Mus Natural Hist Univ Utah Salt Lake City UT 84112

GEORGE, SIMON, ATOMIC SPECTROSCOPY. *Current Pos:* from asst prof to assoc prof, 61-69, PROF PHYSICS, CALIF STATE UNIV, LONG BEACH, 69- *Personal Data:* b India, May 10, 31; nat US. *Educ:* Univ Travancore, BS, 51; Univ Saugar, MS, 54; Univ BC, PhD(physics), 62. *Prof Exp:* Lectr physics, Hislop Col, Nagpur, 54-55, Gauhati Univ, India, 55-57 & Univ BC, 59-60. *Mem:* Optical Soc Am; Am Asn Physics Teachers; Am Phys Soc. *Res:* Atomic spectroscopy; Fabry Perot interferometry; energy levels in spectra and laser spectroscopy; and physics education. *Mailing Add:* Dept Physics-Astron Calif State Univ 1250 Bellflower Blvd Long Beach CA 90840

GEORGE, STEPHEN ANTHONY, BIOLOGY, NEUROSCIENCE. *Current Pos:* assoc prof biol, 73-83, PROF BIOL, AMHERST COL, 84- *Personal Data:* b Seattle, Wash, May 31, 43; m 69; c Madeleine & Jennifer. *Educ:* Univ BC, BSc, 64; Johns Hopkins Univ, PhD(biophys), 70. *Hon Degrees:* AM, Amherst Col, 84. *Prof Exp:* Asst prof biol sci, Univ Md, Baltimore Co, 70-73. *Concurrent Pos:* Prin investr, NIH grant, 75-; vis scientist develop biol, Nat Inst Med Res, Eng, 77; vis scientist, Univ Col London, 82, Inst Biophys, Beijing, China, 89; adj prof, Neurosci & Behav Prog, Univ Mass. *Mem:* Soc Neurosci; Asn Res Vision & Ophthal. *Res:* Visual system development; nerve cell excitability. *Mailing Add:* Dept Biol Amherst Col Box 2237 Amherst MA 01002-5000. *Fax:* 413-542-7955; *E-Mail:* sageorge@amherst.edu

GEORGE, STEPHEN L, BIOSTATISTICS. *Current Pos:* PROF BIOSTATIST, MED CTR, UNIV TEX, 88- *Personal Data:* b Lubbock, Tex, Dec 11, 43; m 65, Carolyn; c Jessica. *Educ:* Tex Tech Univ, BA, 65; NC State Univ, MS, 67; Southern Methodist Univ, PhD(statist), 69. *Prof Exp:* Asst prof biomet, M D Anderson Hosp & Tumor Inst, Univ Tex, 69-74; dir, Data Ctr, Europ Orgn Res Treat Cancer, 74-75; assoc prof biomet, M D Anderson Hosp & Tumor Inst, Univ Tex, 75-76; dir, Sect Biostatist, St Jude Children's Res Hosp, 76-88. *Concurrent Pos:* Adj asst prof math sci, Rice Univ, 70-75; group statistician, Cancer & Leukemia Group B, Duke Univ Med Ctr, 90- *Mem:* Sigma Xi; fel Am Statist Asn; Int Biomet Soc; Inst Math Statist; Soc Clin Trials; Am Soc Clin Oncol. *Res:* Statistical methods in clinical research; selection problems; sequential analysis; survival studies. *Mailing Add:* Cancer Ctr Biostatist Duke Univ Med Ctr Box 3958 Durham NC 27710. *Fax:* 919-681-8028; *E-Mail:* sgeorge@ccstat.mc.duke.edu

GEORGE, T ADRIAN, INORGANIC CHEMISTRY, ORGANOMETALLIC CHEMISTRY. *Current Pos:* asst prof, 68-74, assoc prof, 74-78, PROF CHEM, UNIV NEBR, LINCOLN, 78- *Personal Data:* b Darlington, Eng, Feb 1, 42; m 68; c Katherine & Thomas. *Educ:* Manchester Col Sci & Technol, BS, 63; Univ Sussex, PhD(chem), 66. *Prof Exp:* Res assoc, Univ Calif, Riverside, 66-68. *Mem:* Royal Soc Chem; Am Chem Soc; Sigma Xi. *Res:* Fixation of dinitrogen using molybdenum complexes as the active specie; preparation of ammonia, hydrazine and organonitrogen compounds from molecular nitrogen. *Mailing Add:* Dept Chem Univ Nebr Lincoln NE 68588-0304. *Fax:* 402-472-9402; *E-Mail:* george@unlinfo.unl.edu

GEORGE, TED MASON, NUCLEAR PHYSICS, ELECTRONICS. *Current Pos:* RETIRED. *Personal Data:* b Lynnville, Tenn, Sept 22, 22; wid. *Educ:* Vanderbilt Univ, BA, 49, MA, 57, PhD(physics), 64. *Prof Exp:* Asst prof physics, Murray State Univ, 56-59 & Furman Univ, 63-64; prof physics & chmn dept, Eastern Ky Univ, 64-88. *Mem:* Am Asn Physics Teachers; Sigma Xi. *Res:* Gamma and beta ray spectroscopy. *Mailing Add:* 5212 Smartt Dr Nashville TN 37220-2030

GEORGE, THOMAS D, MATERIALS SCIENCE, ANALYTICAL CHEMISTRY. *Current Pos:* Mem tech staff, Cent Res Labs, Tex Instruments, 68-69, mgr anal labs, Qual & Reliability Assurance, Components Group, 69-77, opers mgr calculator prod, 77-78, MGR TIME PROD, US CONSUMER GROUP, TEX INSTRUMENTS, 78- *Personal Data:* b Robstown, Tex, Mar 3, 40; m 70. *Educ:* Tex Tech Univ, BS, 62, MS, 65; Northwestern Univ, PhD(mat sci), 68. *Mem:* Electrochem Soc; Sigma Xi. *Mailing Add:* 8009 E Del Tiburon Dr Scottsdale AZ 85258-1727

GEORGE, THOMAS FREDERICK, THEORETICAL CHEMISTRY. *Current Pos:* PROVOST & ACAD VPRES & PROF CHEM & PHYSICS, WASH STATE UNIV, 91- *Personal Data:* b Philadelphia, Pa, Mar 18, 47; m 70. *Educ:* Gettysburg Col, BA, 67; Yale Univ, MS, 68, PhD(chem), 70. *Honors & Awards:* Marlow Medal & Prize, Faraday Div, Royal Soc Chem,

79. *Prof Exp:* Res assoc chem, Mass Inst Technol, 70-71 & Univ Calif, Berkeley, 71-72; from asst prof to prof chem, Univ Rochester, 72-85; prof chem & physics & dean fac natural sci & math, State Univ NY, Buffalo, 85-91. *Concurrent Pos:* Dreyfus Found teacher-scholar, 75-82; Sloan Found res fel, 76-80; organizer, NSF Workshop on Theoret Aspects of Laser Radiation & Its Interaction with Atomic & Molecular Systs, 77; comt mem, US Army Basic Sci Res, 78-81; distinguished vis lectr, Dept Chem, Univ Tex, Austin, 78; mem, Exec Comt, Phys Div, Am Chem Soc, 79-82, 85-88, vchmn, 85-86, chmn, 86-88; vchmn, Sixth Int Conf on Molecular Energy Transfer, Rodez, France, 79; lectr semiclassical methods in molecular scattering & spectroscopy, Adv Study Inst, NATO, Cambridge, Eng, 79; distinguished speaker, Dept Chem, Univ Utah, 80; adv bd mem, J Phys Chem, 80-; distinguished lectr, Air Force Weapons Lab, Kirtland AFB, 80; chmn, Gordon Res Conf, NH, 81; mem prog comt, Fourth-Sixth Int Conf on Lasers & Appl, New Orleans, 81-82, San Francisco, 83 & Int Laser Sci Conf, Dallas, 85; Guggenheim Mem Found fel, 83-84; adj prof chem & physics, State Univ NY, Buffalo, 91-93. *Mem:* Am Chem Soc; fel Am Phys Soc; Royal Soc Chem; fel NY Acad Sci; Sigma Xi; fel Soc Photo-Optical Instrumentation Engrs; Mat Res Soc; Europ Phys Soc; AAAS. *Res:* Theory of laser-induced chemical physics; nonlinear optics; molecular collision dynamics; chemical reactions; energy transfer; molecular clusters; surface and solid state chemistry/physics; high temperature superconductivity; polymers; 457 major publications and 7 edited books. *Mailing Add:* Wash State Univ Off Provost 422 French Admin Bldg Pullman WA 99164-1046

GEORGE, TIMOTHY GORDON, FAILURE ANALYSIS, REFRACTORY METALS. *Current Pos:* sect leader, 83-93, GROUP LEADER HEAT SOURCE TECHNOL, LOS ALAMOS NAT LAB, 83- *Personal Data:* b Pittsburgh, Pa, Dec 12, 58; m 81, Linda C; c 2. *Educ:* Univ Pittsburgh, BS, 80; Univ Phoenix, MA, 90. *Prof Exp:* Staff metallurgist, Kennametal Inc, 80-83. *Concurrent Pos:* Consult, 85- *Mem:* Am Soc Metals; Am Welding Soc. *Res:* Failure analyses of components used in radioisotope space power systems; evaluate materials through investigation of properties at elevated temperatures at high strain rates and in complex strain states; brazing and welding refractory metals. *Mailing Add:* 425 Ridgecrest Ave Los Alamos NM 87544

GEORGE, WILLIAM JACOB, BIOCHEMICAL PHARMACOLOGY. *Current Pos:* asst prof, 70-73, assoc prof, 73-78, PROF PHARMACOL, SCH MED, TULANE UNIV, 78- *Personal Data:* b Houtzdale, Pa, June 19, 38; m 64; c 2. *Educ:* Pa State Univ, BS, 60; Univ Pittsburgh, BS, 64; Univ Mich, PhD(pharmacol), 68. *Honors & Awards:* Merck Found Award, 70. *Prof Exp:* Fel pharmacol, Univ Minn, 68-70. *Concurrent Pos:* Mem, Int Study Group Res Cardiac Metab. *Mem:* AAAS; Am Soc Pharmacol & Exp Therapeut; Am Soc Hemat; NY Acad Sci. *Res:* Drug metabolism; intermediary metabolism; cyclic nucleotides; hormonal control of metabolic processes. *Mailing Add:* Dept Pharmacol Tulane Univ Med Sch 1430 Tulane Ave New Orleans LA 70112-2699

GEORGE, WILLIAM KENNETH, JR, FLUID MECHANICS, TURBULENCE. *Current Pos:* from asst prof to assoc prof mech eng, 74-80, PROF MECH & AEROSPACE ENG, STATE UNIV NY, BUFFALO, 80- *Personal Data:* b Camp Shelby, MS, Apr 19, 45; m 66; c 2. *Educ:* Johns Hopkin Univ, BSE, 67, PhD(mech), 71. *Prof Exp:* Instr aerospace eng, 68-71, res assoc, App Res Lab, Pa State Univ, 71-74. *Concurrent Pos:* Vis scientist, Factory Mutual Res Corp, 74; Ctr Nuclear Studies, Grenoble, 76; Danish Nat Lab, 80-81; vis scientist, Calspan Corp, 87-88; vis prof, DTH, Danish Tech Univ, 88; Fulbright res fel, 88; distinguished fel, Am Soc Eng Educ, 91; vis prof, Univ Glasgow, 95-96, Chalmers Univ, 95-96, KTH Swed Royal Inst, 96. *Mem:* Am Soc Mech Engrs; fel Am Phys Soc; Sigma Xi. *Res:* Fluid mechanics and heat transfer especially turbulent fluids; development experimental techniques, laser Doppler anemometer, measurement and theoretical understanding of turbulent shear flows. *Mailing Add:* Dept Mech & Aerospace Eng 339 Eng E Jarvis Hall State Univ NY Buffalo NY 14260. *E-Mail:* trlbill@eng.buffalo.edu

GEORGE, WILLIAM LEO, JR, PLANT GENETICS, PLANT BREEDING. *Current Pos:* prof hort & head dept, 77-84, ASSOC DEAN & DIR, ACAD PROG, COL AGR, UNIV ILL, 84- *Personal Data:* b Riverside, NJ, June 1, 38; m 60, Marilyn; c Jeffrey W & Deborah L. *Educ:* Del Valley Col, BS, 60; Rutgers Univ, MS, 62, PhD(hort), 66. *Prof Exp:* Res asst genetics, Rutgers Univ, 60-66; asst geneticist, Conn Agr Exp Sta, 66-71; from assoc prof to prof hort, Ohio State Univ & Ohio Agr Res & Develop Ctr, 71-77. *Concurrent Pos:* Res dir, Am Soc Hort Sci, 77-78; vis prof, Univ Fla, Bradenton, 83. *Mem:* Nat Asn State Univs & Land-Grant Cols; fel Am Soc Hort Sci; Sigma Xi; Coun Agr Sci & Technol. *Res:* Genetics and developmental genetics of sexuality and unstable gene systems in higher plants; development of new breeding systems in vegetable crops; genetics and physiology of fruiting in vegetable crops. *Mailing Add:* Col Agr Univ Ill 1301 W Gregory Dr Urbana IL 61801

GEORGE-NASCIMENTO, CARLOS, PROTEIN CHEMICALS. *Current Pos:* prin scientist & mgr, 83-87, SR SCIENTIST, PROTEIN CHEM SECT, CHIRON CORP, EMERYVILLE, CALIF, 87- *Personal Data:* b Santiago, Chile, Aug 28, 45; US citizen; m; c 2. *Educ:* Univ Chile, MS, 67; Baylor Col Med, PhD(biochem), 75. *Prof Exp:* Instr biochem, Sch Chem & Pharm, Univ Chile, 68-70; postdoctoral res fel, Dept Microbiol, Sch Med, Univ Conn, 76-78, instr, 79-80; asst prof, Dept Biochem, Sch Med, Univ PR, 80-83. *Concurrent Pos:* Lectr biochem, Med Sci Campus, Univ PR, 81-83; prin investr, Am Heart Asn & NSF, 81-84; invited prof, Cath Univ, Santiago, Chile, 86, 90 & Univ Chile, Santiago, 88. *Res:* Author of numerous publications. *Mailing Add:* Protein Chem Dept Chiron Corp 4560 Horton St Emeryville CA 94608-2916. *Fax:* 510-655-8453

GEORGE-TAYLOR, MOSUNMOLA ALABA, BIOCHEMISTRY, ENVIRONMENTAL HEALTH. *Current Pos:* res asst, 81-91, res technician, 91-94, ASST PROF CHEM, CLARK ATLANTA UNIV, 94- *Personal Data:* b Lagos, Nigeria, Nov 15, 51; US citizen; c 2. *Educ:* Univ Lagos, Nigeria, BSc, 75; Atlanta Univ, MS, 82; Ga Inst Technol, MS, 87; Clark Atlanta Univ, PhD(biol), 94. *Prof Exp:* Instr chem, Lagos City Col, 75-76, Ikeja Grammar Sch, 77-80. *Concurrent Pos:* Coordr, Allied Health Professions Prog, Clark Atlanta Univ, 95-; res assoc, Morehouse Sch Med, 96- *Mem:* Am Chem Soc; Am Soc Cell Biol. *Res:* Exposing different human female mammary cell lines to electromagnetic fields and monitoring any changes in external features as well as biochemical changes that may occur. *Mailing Add:* Chem Dept Clark Atlanta Univ PO Box 323 James P Brawley Dr at Fair St Atlanta GA 30314. *Fax:* 404-880-6165, 880-6849; *E-Mail:* mgtaylor@cau.edu

GEORGE-WEINSTEIN, MINDY, ANATOMY. *Current Pos:* PROF ANAT, PHILADELPHIA COL OSTEOP MED, 88- *Personal Data:* b Philadelphia, Pa, Feb 5, 53. *Educ:* Thomas Jefferson Univ, BS, 78, PhD(anat), 84. *Prof Exp:* Postdoctoral fel, Dept Biochem & Biophys, Univ Pa, 84-87 & Dept Microbiol, 87-88. *Concurrent Pos:* NIH fel, 84-86 & grant, 90-92; Muscular Dystrophy Asn fel, 86-87. *Mem:* Develop Biol Soc; Am Soc Cell Biol. *Res:* Author of numerous publications. *Mailing Add:* 320 N Bowman Ave Merion PA 19066

GEORGHIOU, GEORGE PAUL, ENTOMOLOGY, TOXICOLOGY. *Current Pos:* jr specialist entom, Univ Calif, Riverside, 58-60, lectr, 60-69, from asst entomologist to assoc, 60-69, head, div toxicol & physiol, 75-83, chmn, dept entom, 83-84, prof entom, 69-93, EMER PROF ENTOM, UNIV CALIF, RIVERSIDE, 93- *Personal Data:* b Famagusta, Cyprus, Nov 23, 25; m 91, Lois Allen; c 2. *Educ:* Cornell Univ, BS, 52, MS, 53; Univ Calif, Berkeley, PhD(entom), 60. *Hon Degrees:* PhD, Univ Thessaloniki, Greece, 81. *Honors & Awards:* Bussart Award, Entom Soc Am, 87; Superior Serv Award, USDA, 89. *Prof Exp:* Govt entomologist, Dept Agr, Cyprus, 54-58. *Concurrent Pos:* Res grants, NIH, 64-67 & 85-, WHO, 65-92, USDA, 66-69 & DAMD, 85-88; consult, Food & Agr Orgn, 73, 74, 75 & 78; mem WHO expert adv panel on vector biol & control, 75-92, Food & Agr Orgn, 76- & AID, 83, 85 & 89; Guggenheim fel, 67-68; fac res lectr, Univ Calif, 87. *Mem:* Fel AAAS; fel Entom Soc Am; Am Chem Soc; Soc Vector Ecol. *Res:* Insect resistance to insecticides; genetics of resistance; insect toxicology; insecticide resistance management. *Mailing Add:* Dept Entom Univ Calif Riverside CA 92521

GEORGHIOU, PARIS ELIAS, ORGANIC CHEMISTRY, ANALYTICAL CHEMISTRY. *Current Pos:* ASSOC PROF CHEM, MEM UNIV NFLD, 75- *Personal Data:* b Cairo, Egypt, July 20, 46; Can citizen; m 71; c 2. *Educ:* Witwatersrand Univ, SAfrica, BSc Hons, 67; McGill Univ, PhD(chem), 73. *Prof Exp:* Instr chem, Dawson Col, Montreal, 72-73; fel, Univ Alta, Can, 73-75. *Concurrent Pos:* Chem Consult to Nat Health & Welfare, Can, Nat Res Coun, Dept Consumer & Corp Affairs. *Mem:* Chem Inst Can; Am Chem Soc. *Res:* Synthesis and mechanisms in organic chemistry; chemical characterization of petroleum and its products; analytical chemistry of trace pollutant gases and respirable particulate matter in indoor air; mutagenicity and carcinogenicity of environmental pollutants and selected organic molecules such as the sterols. *Mailing Add:* Dept Chem Univ Nfld St John's NF A1B 3X7 Can

GEORGHIOU, SOLON, BIOPHYSICS. *Current Pos:* from asst prof to assoc prof physics, 73-83, PROF PHYSICS, UNIV TENN, 83-, ADJ PROF, BIOCHEM, 87- *Personal Data:* b Kato Zodia, Cyprus, Aug 11, 39; US citizen; m 68, Georgia Temenou; c Alexia & Christos. *Educ:* Univ Athens, Greece, BSc, 62; Univ Manchester, MSc, 65, PhD(physics), 68. *Prof Exp:* Res assoc, Univ Minn, 67-69 & Johns Hopkins Univ, 70-73. *Concurrent Pos:* NIH & NSF res grants. *Mem:* Biophys Soc; Am Phys Soc; Am Chem Soc; Am Soc Photobiol. *Res:* Intrinsic and extrinsic fluorescent probes for studying the dynamics and structure of biomolecules and biological assemblies; mechanisms of deexcitation of molecular electronic states; optical, Raman and infrared spectroscopies. *Mailing Add:* Dept Physics Biophys Lab Univ Tenn Knoxville TN 37996-1200. *Fax:* 423-974-7843; *E-Mail:* sgeorghi@utk.edu

GEORGI, HOWARD, THEORETICAL PHYSICS. *Current Pos:* Res fel, Harvard Univ, 71-73, jr fel, Soc Fels, 73-76, Alfred P Sloan Found fel, 76-80, chmn, Physics Dept, 92-95, PROF PHYSICS, HARVARD UNIV, 80- *Personal Data:* b San Bernardino, Calif, Jan 6, 47; c Geoff & Justin. *Educ:* Harvard Col, BA, 67; Yale Univ, PhD, 71. *Honors & Awards:* Sakurai Award, Am Phys Soc. *Concurrent Pos:* Sr fel, Soc Fels, Harvard Univ, 81-, co-chair, Nat Res Coun Comt Women in Sci & Eng. *Mem:* Nat Acad Sci; AAAS; Am Phys Soc. *Res:* Particle theory particularly unified theories of particle interactions at short distances and su(2)xu(1) breaking. *Mailing Add:* Dept Physics Harvard Univ Cambridge MA 02138

GEORGI, JAY R, VETERINARY MEDICINE. *Current Pos:* Asst prof phys biol, NY State Col Vet Med, Cornell Univ, 65-66, from assoc prof to prof, 66-, EMER PROF PARASITOL, NY STATE COL VET MED, CORNELL UNIV. *Personal Data:* b New York, NY, Nov 9, 28; m 52; c 4. *Educ:* Cornell Univ, DVM, 51, PhD, 62. *Mem:* AAAS; Am Vet Med Asn. *Res:* Veterinary clinical parasitology and nematode taxonomy, morphology and bionomics. *Mailing Add:* Diag Lab c/o Col Vet Med PO Box 786 Ithaca NY 14851

GEORGIADE, NICHOLAS GEORGE, PLASTIC SURGERY. *Current Pos:* intern & asst res gen surg, Sch Med, Duke Univ, 49-52, asst res & res plastic surg, 52-54, from instr to assoc prof, 54-64, PROF PLASTIC, MAXILLOFACIAL & ORAL SURG, SCH MED, DUKE UNIV, 64- & CHMN DIV, 75- *Personal Data:* b Lowell, Mass, Dec 25, 18; m 42; c 3. *Educ:* Columbia Univ, DDS, 44; Duke Univ, MD & BS, 49; Am Bd Plastic Surg, dipl; Am Bd Oral Surg, dipl. *Prof Exp:* Intern oral surg, Kings Co Hosp, 44. *Concurrent Pos:* Nat Cancer Inst clin fel, 52-54; consult plastic, maxillofacial & oral surgeon, Vet Admin Hosp, Durham; consult, US Army & USAF; res proj, NIH; mem, Plastic Surg Res Coun; ed, Cleft Palate J, 70-76; vchmn, Am Bd Plastic Surg, 74-75; vchmn, Plastic Surg Residency Rev Comt. *Mem:* Am Soc Plastic & Reconstruct Surg; Am Soc Oral Surg; Am Asn Plastic Surg (secy, 72-75, vpres, 76, pres elect, 77, pres, 78); fel Am Col Surg; Am Soc Maxillofacial Surg (pres, 63); Sigma Xi; Int Soc Aesthetic Plastic Surg. *Res:* Plastic, maxillofacial and oral surgery; tissue preservation; burns; maxillofacial growth and development; numerous publications. *Mailing Add:* Duke Univ Med Cr PO Box 3098 Durham NC 27710-3098

GEORGIADIS, JOHN G, HEAT TRANSFER, FLUID MECHANICS. *Current Pos:* ASSOC PROF, DEPT MECH & INDUST ENG, UNIV ILL, URBANA-CHAMPAIGN, 93- *Personal Data:* b Filiates, Greece, Sept 14, 59; m 87; c Alexis. *Educ:* Nat Tech Univ, Athens, Greece, dipl mech eng, 83; Univ Calif, Los Angeles, MS, 84, PhD(mech eng), 87. *Honors & Awards:* Eng Res Initiation Award, Am Soc Mech Engrs & Eng Found, 88; Presidential Young Invest Award, NSF, 91. *Concurrent Pos:* Investr, Duke/NSF Eng Res Ctr Emerging Cardiovasc Technologies, 89-92; adj assoc prof, Dept Mech Eng & Mat Sci, Duke Univ, 92- *Mem:* Am Soc Mech Engrs; Am Phys Soc. *Res:* Computational fluid mechanics and heat transfer; experimental heat transfer; magnetic resonance imaging flow diagnostics; transport phenomena in random media; bifurcation analysis; cardiovascular fluid mechanics; microscopy. *Mailing Add:* Dept Mech & Indust Eng Univ Ill 140 MEB 1206 W Green St MC-244 Urbana IL 61801. *Fax:* 217-333-1942; *E-Mail:* georgia@uiuc.edu

GEORGIADIS, NICHOLAS J, POPULATION GENETICS, CONSERVATION BIOLOGY. *Current Pos:* RES ASSOC, WASHINGTON UNIV, 90- *Personal Data:* b Nairobi, Kenya, Apr 1, 57; Brit citizen. *Educ:* London Univ, BSc, 80; Syracuse Univ, PhD(biol),87. *Prof Exp:* Res fel, Univ Rochester, 89. *Concurrent Pos:* Res fel, NY Zool Soc-Wildlife Conserv Soc, 89-; mem, Antelope Specialist Group, Int Union Conserv Nature & Natural Resources. *Mem:* Soc Study Evolution; Soc Conserv Biol; Int Union Conserv Nature & Natural Resources. *Res:* Genealogical information from DNA sequences to study processes of evolutionary divergence and the maintenance of biological diversity. *Mailing Add:* 2023 Alfred Ave St Louis MO 63110. *Fax:* 314-935-4432; *E-Mail:* georgiadis@wustlb.wustl.edu

GEORGIAN, VLASIOS, ORGANIC CHEMISTRY. *Current Pos:* from asst prof to assoc prof, 60-90, EMER PROF CHEM, TUFTS UNIV, 90- *Personal Data:* b Quincy, Mass, Sept 5, 19; m 49; c 2. *Educ:* Harvard Univ, SB, 41, MA, 43, PhD(chem), 50. *Prof Exp:* Res chemist, Polaroid Corp, 42-44; asst, Harvard Univ, 45-46; from instr to asst prof chem, Northwestern Univ, 51-57, res assoc, 57-60. *Concurrent Pos:* USPHS fel, Harvard Univ, 50-51; consult, Smith Kline & French Labs, 60-; vis prof, Exten Progs, Harvard Univ, 68-80. *Mem:* Am Chem Soc; Am Acad Arts & Sci; NY Acad Sci; Royal Soc Chem. *Res:* Synthesis of small and strained ring systems; additions to cyclooctatetraene; molecular rearrangements; steroid syntheses and transformations; syntheses of natural products; syntheses of beta lactam antibiotics; tetracycline modifications. *Mailing Add:* 139 Clifton St Belmont MA 02178-2603

GEORGIOU, GEORGE, GENETIC ENGINEERING, ENVIRONMENTAL BIOTECHNOLOGY. *Current Pos:* Asst prof, 86-91, ASSOC PROF CHEM ENG, UNIV TEX, AUSTIN, 91- *Personal Data:* b Athens, Greece, May 18, 59; US citizen; m 84, MaryJean Dotis. *Educ:* Univ Manchester Inst Sci & Technol BSc, 81; Cornell Univ, MS, 83, PhD(chem eng), 87. *Honors & Awards:* Presidential Young Invest Award, NSF. *Concurrent Pos:* Dow Chem Co young fac award, 88. *Mem:* Am Chem Soc; AAAS; Am Soc Microbiol; Am Inst Chem Engrs. *Mailing Add:* Dept Chem Eng Univ Tex Austin TX 78712. *Fax:* 512-471-7963

GEORGIOU, TRYPHON T, CONTROL ENGINEERING & SYSTEMS THEORY. *Current Pos:* vis asst prof, 85-86, ASSOC PROF, DEPT ELEC ENG, UNIV MINN, 89- *Personal Data:* m 80, Efi Foufoula; c Katerina & Thomas. *Educ:* Nat Tech Univ Athens, dipl, 79; Univ Fla, PhD(elec eng), 83. *Prof Exp:* Asst prof, Fla Atlantic Univ, 83-85; from asst prof to assoc prof, Iowa State Univ, 86-89. *Mem:* Inst Elec & Electronics Engrs. *Res:* Robust control; theoretical and software development of design methodologies; systems theory. *Mailing Add:* 2098 Folwell Ave St Paul MN 55108. *Fax:* 612-625-4583; *E-Mail:* georgiou@ee.umn.edu

GEORGOPAPADAKOU, NAFSIKA ELENI, MICROBIAL BIOCHEMISTRY, ENZYMOLOGY. *Current Pos:* res group chief chemother, Roche Res Ctr, 84-85, res investr chemother & pharmacol, 85-88, res leader, Dept Chemother, 88-92, DISTINGUISHED RES LEADER, DEPT CHEMOTHER, ROCHE RES CTR, 92- *Personal Data:* b Thessaloniki, Greece, Jan 6, 50; nat US. *Educ:* Mills Col, BA, 71; Yale Univ, PhD(biochem), 75. *Honors & Awards:* S A Waksman Award, 92. *Prof Exp:* Res fel, Harvard Univ, 76-77; res investr biochem, Squibb Inst Med Res, 77-81, sr res investr microbiol, 81-84. *Mem:* AAAS; Am Chem Soc; Am Soc Microbiol; Am Acad Microbiol; Am Soc Biol Chemists; Am Soc Biochem & Molecular Biol; Sigma Xi. *Res:* Microbial cell wall biosynthesis; proteolytic enzymes; mechanism of enzyme action; antibiotic transport, antibiotic action and design. *Mailing Add:* Dept Molecular Biol Princeton Univ Princeton NJ 08544-0014. *Fax:* 973-235-7373

GEORGOPOULOS, APOSTOLOS P, NEUROPHYSIOLOGY, BEHAVIOR. *Current Pos:* ASSOC PROF NEUROSCI, JOHNS HOPKINS UNIV, 83- *Educ:* Univ Athens, Greece, MD, 68. *Mailing Add:* Brain Sci Ctr One Vetrans Dr Minneapolis MN 55417

GEORGOPOULOS, CONSTANTINE PANOS, BACTERIOPHAGE BIOLOGY, HEAT SHOCK REGULATION. *Current Pos:* from asst prof to assoc prof, 77-82, PROF MOLECULAR BIOL, UNIV UTAH MED CTR, SALT LAKE CITY, 82- *Personal Data:* b Skourichori, Pyrgos, Greece, Jan 27, 42; m 66. *Educ:* Amherst Col, Mass, BS, 64; Mass Inst Technol, PhD(microbiol), 69. *Prof Exp:* Fel biochem, Stanford Univ, 70-71; res assoc molecular biol, Univ Geneva, 72-76. *Concurrent Pos:* Prin investr, NIH Grant, 77-, 84-, NSF Int Travel Award, 86, NSF Intern Exchange grant, 90-; mem, Microbiol, Physiol & Genetics Study Sect, NIH, 85-; vis prof, Dept Molecular Biol, Univ Geneva, 86. *Mem:* Sigma Xi; Am Soc Microbiol; Genetics Am Soc; Am Soc Biochem & Molecular Biol. *Res:* Mechanisms of DNA replication; RNA transcription and morphogenics in bacteria and bacteriophages; regulation and function of the highly conserved stress response in escherichia coli and its role in bacteriophage lambda growth. *Mailing Add:* Anthrop 102 Wm Stewart Salt Lake City UT 84112-1107

GEORGOPULOS, PETER DEMETRIOS, NUCLEAR PHYSICS. *Current Pos:* ASSOC PROF PHYSICS, PA STATE UNIV, DELAWARE CO CAMPUS, 71- *Personal Data:* b Bronx, NY, Oct 1, 44; m 67; c 1. *Educ:* Long Island Univ, BS, 66; Pa State Univ, PhD(physics), 71. *Concurrent Pos:* Regional fac affil, Bartol Res Found, 71-79; vis scientist, Lawrence Livermore Lab, 78 & 79. *Mem:* Am Phys Soc; Am Asn Physics Teachers; Sigma Xi. *Res:* Nuclear structure information obtained by gamma ray studies; statistical properties of matter. *Mailing Add:* Pa State Univ Delaware Co Campus Media PA 19063

GEPNER, IVAN ALAN, DEVELOPMENTAL BIOLOGY, GENETICS. *Current Pos:* Asst prof, 73-80, ASSOC PROF BIOL, MONMOUTH COL, 80- *Personal Data:* b Newark, NJ, Sept 10, 45. *Educ:* Rutgers Univ, BA, 67; Princeton Univ, MS, 69, PhD(biol), 72. *Mem:* Soc Develop Biol; Am Soc Zoologists. *Res:* Cell interactions in development; intercellular adhesion. *Mailing Add:* Dept Biol Monmouth Univ 400 Cedar Ave West Long Branch NJ 07764-1804

GEPPERT, GERARD ALLEN, EXTRACTIVE METALLURGY, ANALYTICAL CHEMISTRY. *Current Pos:* RETIRED. *Personal Data:* b Belleville, Ill, Nov 26, 32; m 56; c 5. *Educ:* St Mary's Univ, Tex, BS, 54. *Prof Exp:* Res chemist extractive metall, Alcoa Res Labs, East St Louis, Ill, 54-72, sr res scientist, 73-75; chief chemist, anal chem, mobile works, Aluminum CoAm, 75-82, Point Comfort Opers, 82-85; consult, 85-87. *Mem:* Am Chem Soc; Metall Soc. *Res:* Refining of bauxite, alumina and alumina chemicals; fire retardant alumina hydrate; quality control and applications of alumina hydrate; alumina extraction from non-bauxitic ores; improvements of the Bayer process. *Mailing Add:* 3720 Claridge Rd S Mobile AL 36608-1752

GERACE, LARRY R, MOLECULAR BIOLOGY. *Current Pos:* from asst prof to assoc prof cell biol & anat, Sch Med, Johns Hopkins Univ, 80-87, ASSOC MEM, DEPT MOLECULAR BIOL, RES INST, SCRIPPS CLIN, 87- *Personal Data:* b West Carthage, NY, Oct 27, 51. *Educ:* Johns Hopkins Univ, BA, 73; Rockefeller Univ, PhD, 79. *Honors & Awards:* R R Bensley Mem Award, 87. *Prof Exp:* Postdoctoral fel, Rockefeller Univ, 79-80. *Concurrent Pos:* NIH res career develop award, 84; managing ed, J Cell Biol, 87-90; sect ed, Current Opinion Cell Biol, 88-90; co-chair, prog comt, Am Soc Cell Biol, 90. *Res:* Author of numerous publications. *Mailing Add:* Dept Molecular Biol Immio Scripps Res Inst 10666 N Torrey Pines Rd La Jolla CA 92037-1092. *Fax:* 619-554-6253

GERACE, MICHAEL JOSEPH, ADHESIVE & SEALANT FORMULATION, NEW PRODUCT DEVELOPMENT & COMMERCIALIZATION. *Current Pos:* PRES, ASTER INC, 86- *Personal Data:* b Brooklyn, NY, Jan 11, 44; m 68, 85; c 3. *Educ:* Long Island Univ, BS, 65; Tufts Univ, PhD(chem), 70. *Prof Exp:* Sr chemist, W R Grace & Co, 75-78; res & develop mgr, Norton Co, 79-81; vpres res & develop, Protective Treatments, 81-86. *Mem:* Am Chem Soc; Adhesives & Sealant Coun; Soc Automotive Engrs; Soc Mfg Engrs. *Res:* Commercialization of automotive and construction adhesives and sealants; plastisols; epoxys; acrylics; hot melts; pressure sensitives; butyls and butyl tapes. *Mailing Add:* 320 Peach Orchard Ave Dayton OH 45419

GERACE, PAUL LOUIS, INORGANIC CHEMISTRY, ELECTROPHOTOGRAPHY. *Current Pos:* RETIRED. *Personal Data:* b Batavia, NY, Aug 20, 34; m 65; c 2. *Educ:* Univ Notre Dame, BS, 56, PhD(chem), 61. *Prof Exp:* Teaching fel chem, Univ Notre Dame, 56-58; res chemist, Solvay Process Div, Allied Chem Corp, NY, 61-66; scientist, Xerox Corp, 66-75, tech specialist & proj mgr, 75-83; res assoc, Amoco Corp, 85-86. *Mem:* Am Chem Soc; Sigma Xi; NY Acad Sci. *Res:* Special materials development and specification, encompassing transfer of product and process technology from research to development to manufacturing; photoconductors and photoreceptors; surface coatings; chemical safety. *Mailing Add:* One Pickthorn Dr Batavia NY 14020-1411

GERACI, JOSEPH E, INTERNAL MEDICINE. *Current Pos:* PROF MED, MAYO GRAD SCH MED, UNIV MINN, ROCHESTER, 62-, CONSULT, MAYO CLIN, 51- *Personal Data:* b Newark, NJ, Feb 24, 16; m 49; c 1. *Educ:* Marquette Univ, MD, 40; Univ Minn, MS, 49. *Mem:* Am Col Physicians; Am Col Chest Physicians; Am Fedn Clin Res; Infectious Dis Soc Am; Am Thoracic Soc. *Res:* Infectious disease. *Mailing Add:* 1760 Eighth St SW Rochester MN 55902-0921

GERAGHTY, JAMES JOSEPH, GEOLOGY. *Current Pos:* ground water geologist, Port Washington, 57-74 & Tampa, 75-78, Annapolis, 78-82, GROUND WATER GEOLOGIST, GERAGHTY & MILLER INC, TAMPA, 78- *Personal Data:* b New York, NY, Nov 20, 20; m 42; c 2. *Educ:* City Col, BS, 49; NY Univ, MS, 53. *Prof Exp:* Geologist, Water Resources Div, Ground Water Br, US Geol Surv, 49-55; ground water geologist, Leggette, Brashears & Graham, 55-57. *Concurrent Pos:* Lectr, Hofstra Col, 52-55, State Univ NY, 58 & NY Univ, 62-; tech adv, UN, 62-74. *Mem:* Geol Soc Am; Am Water Works Asn; Am Asn Petrol Geol; Am Geophys Union; Int Asn Hydrogeol; Am Soc Civil Engrs. *Res:* Ground water geology; hydrology. *Mailing Add:* 3519 Berger Rd Lutz FL 33549

GERAGHTY, MICHAEL A, MATHEMATICS. *Current Pos:* from asst prof to assoc prof math, 64-97 EMER ASSOC PROF MATH, UNIV IOWA, 97- *Personal Data:* b Chicago, Ill, May 15, 30; m 60; c 4. *Educ:* Univ Notre Dame, BSc, 52, PhD(math), 59. *Prof Exp:* Off Naval Res res assoc math, Northwestern Univ, 59-60, asst prof, 60-62; vis assoc prof, Res Inst, Univ Ala, 62-64. *Mem:* Am Math Soc; Math Asn Am. *Res:* Topology. *Mailing Add:* Dept Math Univ Iowa Rm 14 MLH Iowa City IA 52242

GERALD, MICHAEL CHARLES, PHARMACY EDUCATION, PHARMACOLOGY. *Current Pos:* DEAN & PROF PHARMACOL, SCH PHARM, UNIV CONN, 93- *Personal Data:* b New York, NY, Nov 20, 39; m 65, Gloria E Gruber; c Marc J & Melissa S. *Educ:* Fordham Univ, BS, 61; Ind Univ, PhD(pharmacol), 68. *Prof Exp:* USPHS fel psychiat & pharmacol, Univ Chicago, 68-69; from asst prof to assoc prof, Col Pharm, Ohio State Univ, 69-80, actg chmn, 80-81, prof pharmacol, 80-93, assoc dean, 84-93. *Concurrent Pos:* Consult, WHO, 83-84; USP comt rev, 80-85; Gustavus A Pfeiffer Mem Res fel, 83-84; vis assoc prof, Sch Pharm, Univ Wis-Madison, 78; vis prof, Sch Pharm, Univ Concepcion, Chile, 90. *Mem:* NY Acad Sci; AAAS; Am Soc Pharmacol & Exp Therapeut; fel Acad Pharmaceut Sci (secy, 75-77, vchmn, 78-79); Soc Neurosci; Am Asn Cols Pharm. *Res:* Drugs and poisons of Agatha Christie; drug abuse; national drug policy; author of textbooks on general and nursing pharmacology; neuropharmacology; pharmacy education. *Mailing Add:* Sch Pharm Univ Conn Storrs CT 06269-2092. *Fax:* 860-486-1553; *E-Mail:* gerald@uconnvm.uconn.edu

GERALD, PARK S, pediatrics; deceased, see previous edition for last biography

GERALDSON, CARROLL MORTON, SOIL CHEMISTRY. *Current Pos:* From asst prof to prof soil chem, Inst Food & Agr Sci, Agr Res & Educ Ctr, 51-90, EMER PROF SOIL CHEM, GULF COAST RES CTR, UNIV FLA, 91- *Personal Data:* b Manitowoc, Wis, Apr 8, 18; m 49; c 7. *Educ:* St Olaf Col, BA, 40; Univ Wis, PhD(soils, plant physiol), 51. *Honors & Awards:* Vaughan Award, Am Soc Hort Sci, 55; Fla Fruit & Vegetable Award, 56. *Mem:* Am Soc Agron; Am Soc Hort Sci. *Res:* Nutrition of vegetable crops; control of physiological disorders such as black heart of celery and blossom-end rot of tomatoes and peppers; development and utilization of the intensity and balance soil solution testing procedure for evaluating the ionic root environment for optimal production; maintenance of 3-dimensional gradients; establishment in the soil profile by surface application of nutrients with a mulch covering and constant source of water. *Mailing Add:* 1111 99th St NW Bradenton FL 34209

GERARD, CLEVELAND JOSEPH, CONSERVATION, SOIL FERTILITY. *Current Pos:* soil physicist, Tex Agr Exp Sta, 57-89, EMER PROF SOIL PHYSICSIST, 89- *Personal Data:* b Milton, La, Sept 25, 24; m 63; c 2. *Educ:* Southwestern La Inst, BS, 48; Kans State Univ, MS, 50; Agr & Mech Col Tex, PhD(soil physics), 55. *Prof Exp:* Soil scientist, Agr Res Serv, USDA, Ore State Col, 54-57. *Concurrent Pos:* Res award, Tex A&M Univ, 80-81. *Mem:* Soil Sci Soc Am; Int Soil Sci Soc; Int Soil Tillage Res Orgn. *Res:* Soil chemistry; soil physics and soil-plant relationships. *Mailing Add:* 4015 Texas St Vernon TX 76384

GERARD, GARY FLOYD, MOLECULAR BIOLOGY, VIROLOGY. *Current Pos:* DIR RES & DEVELOP, LIFE TECHNOL INC, 85- *Personal Data:* b Saginaw, Mich, June 1, 44; m 66, Kathleen M Ashbaugh; c Christine, Jeffrey & Ann. *Educ:* Pa State Univ, BS, 66; Mich State Univ, PhD(biochem), 72. *Prof Exp:* Res assoc molecular virol, Inst Molecular Virol, Sch Med, St Louis Univ, 71-73, asst prof, 73-77, assoc prof, 77-82; sr scientist, Bethesda Res Lab, 82-85. *Res:* Retro viral and eukaryotic DNA replication. *Mailing Add:* Life Technol Inc 8717 Grovemont Circle Gaithersburg MD 20877. *Fax:* 301-921-9116

GERARD, JESSE THOMAS, ANALYTICAL CHEMISTRY, NUCLEAR CHEMISTRY. *Personal Data:* b Windsor, Ont, Mar 19, 41; m 62; c 2. *Educ:* Univ Windsor, BSc, 64, PhD(anal chem), 68. *Prof Exp:* Res fac mem & co-investr Apollo lunar samples, Dept Chem, Cornell Univ, 68-71; res chemist & Nat Acad Sci-Nat Res Coun inhouse resident res assoc theoret studies br, Lab Space Physics, Goddard Space Flight Ctr, NASA, 71-72; sr res chemist, Anal Sci Div, Res Labs, Eastman Kodak Co, 72-84. *Mem:* Fel AAAS; fel Am Chem Soc; fel Geochem Soc. *Res:* Neutron activation analysis; radiochemistry; x-ray fluorescence analysis; classical chemical analysis; separations; ultra trace, trace, minor and major element analysis. *Mailing Add:* 2255 E Sunset Rd Apt 1118/7 Las Vegas NV 89119-5944

GERARD, PATRICK DALE, NONPARAMETRIC REGRESSION, DESIGN & ANALYSIS OF EXPERIMENTS. *Current Pos:* ASST PROF EXP STATIST, MISS STATE UNIV, 93- *Personal Data:* b Erath, La, Nov 9, 58; m 81. *Educ:* Univ Southwestern La, BS, 79; Va Polytech Inst & State Univ, MS, 81; Southern Methodist Univ, PhD(statist sci), 93. *Prof Exp:* Eng analyst, Gen Dynamics Corp, 82-83; statistician, Boots Pharmaceut Inc, 84-89. *Mem:* Am Statist Asn; Biomet Soc; Sigma Xi. *Res:* Nonparametric regression analysis, specifically kernal regression and locally weighted polynomial regression methods, especially in the areas of agriculture and the biological sciences. *Mailing Add:* Math Miss State Univ Box Ma Mississippi State MS 39762-5921

GERARD, VALRIE ANN, SEAWEED ECOLOGY, AQUACULTURE. *Current Pos:* asst prof, 83-88, ASSOC PROF, STATE UNIV NY STONY BROOK, 88- *Personal Data:* b Amityville, NY, Feb 21, 48. *Educ:* State Univ NY Buffalo, BA, 70; Univ Calif, Santa Cruz, MA, 74, PhD(biol), 76. *Prof Exp:* Killam fel biol, Dalhousie Univ, 76-78; res fel environ eng, Calif Inst Technol, 78-83. *Concurrent Pos:* Lectr, Univ Calif, Santa Cruz, 78, Univ Southern Calif, 79 & 82; vis assoc prof, Univ Calif, Davis, 90. *Res:* Physiological ecology of marine macroalgae; seaweed aquaculture. *Mailing Add:* Marine Sci State Univ NY 100 Nicholls Rd Stony Brook NY 11794-0001

GERARDO, JAMES BERNARD, LASERS, ATOMIC PHYSICS. *Current Pos:* mem res staff, Org 5100, 66-67, supvr plasma physics, 67-74, MGR LASER RES, SANDIA LABS, SANDIA CORP, 74- *Personal Data:* b Toluca, Ill, Oct 18, 36; m 63. *Educ:* Univ Ill, BS, 59, MS, 60, PhD(elec eng), 63. *Prof Exp:* From res asst to res assoc elec eng, Univ Ill, Urbana, 59-67. *Mem:* Fel Am Phys Soc; Optical Soc Am; Mat Res Soc; Inst Elec & Electronic Engrs. *Res:* Laser research and development; molecular physics; gas kinetics. *Mailing Add:* Spec Technols Lab 5520 Ekwill St Suite B Santa Barbara CA 93111

GERASIMOWICZ, WALTER VLADIMIR, SPECTROSCOPY, THERMODYNAMICS. *Current Pos:* AT J P MORGAN, NY, 92- *Personal Data:* b Phoenixville, Pa, July 23, 52. *Educ:* Ursinus Col, BS, 74; Villanova Univ, MS, 77, PhD(phys chem), 81. *Prof Exp:* Res fel, Eastern Regional Res Ctr, USDA, 81-83, staff scientist, 83-92. *Concurrent Pos:* Instr chem, Pa State Univ, Del Co, 79-80, lectr, 80. *Mem:* Am Chem Soc; AAAS; Royal Soc Chem. *Res:* Experimental physical chemistry; metal-ligand interactions; fourier transform infrared; visible and nuclear magnetic resonance spectroscopy; thermodynamic and equilibria studies; vibrational or normal mode analysis. *Mailing Add:* 822 Cherry St Phoenixville PA 19460

GERATZ, JOACHIM DIETER, PATHOLOGY. *Current Pos:* RETIRED. *Personal Data:* b Gloethe, Ger, July 3, 29; US citizen; m 61; c 3. *Educ:* Univ Frankfurt, MD, 53. *Prof Exp:* Asst path, Univ Frankfurt, 54-55; intern, Jefferson Hosp, Roanoke, Va, 55-56; researcher, Univ NC, Chapel Hill, 56-60, from instr to prof, 60-96. *Mem:* AAAS; Int Acad Path; Am Asn Path Am Soc Clin Path; Int Soc Thrombosis & Haemostasis. *Res:* Blood coagulation; inhibitors of proteolytic enzymes; physiology and pathology of the pancreas; antiviral, antiarthritic and anticancer agents. *Mailing Add:* Dept Path Univ NC Med Sch Brinkhous-Bullitt Bldg CB 7525 Chapel Hill NC 27599-7525

GERBA, CHARLES PETER, ENVIRONMENTAL MICROBIOLOGY. *Current Pos:* assoc prof, 81-84, PROF MICROBIOL, UNIV ARIZ, 84- *Personal Data:* b Blue Island, Ill, Sept 10, 45; m 70, Peggy L Gerba; c Peter & Phillip. *Educ:* Ariz State Univ, BS, 69; Univ Miami, PhD(microbiol), 73. *Prof Exp:* Postdoctoral fel virol, Baylor Col Med, 73-74; asst prof, 74-81. *Concurrent Pos:* AAAS fel environ sci, 84; chmn, Div Appl & Environ Microbiol, Am Soc Microbiol, 83-84 & 87-88; consult, Sci Adv Bd, US Environ Protection Agency, 86- *Mem:* Am Soc Microbiol; Int Asn Water Pollution Control & Res; AAAS; Am Water Works Asn; Soc Risk Anal. *Res:* Fate, transport, and removal of pathogenic microorganisms in the environment; new methods for the detection of pathogens in the environment and their removal by water and wastewater treatment. *Mailing Add:* Microbiol Univ Ariz 1501 N Campbell Ave Tucson AZ 85724-0001. *Fax:* 520-621-6366

GERBER, BERNARD ROBERT, POLYMER CHEMISTRY. *Current Pos:* SCI TECH MGT CONSULT, 80- *Personal Data:* b New York, NY, May 31, 35; m 57, 87; c 3. *Educ:* Hunter Col, AB, 55; NY Univ, MS, 58, PhD(phys chem), 64. *Prof Exp:* Operator comput, AEC facil, Inst Math Sci, 55-58; res asst, Rheum Dis Study Group, NY Univ Med Ctr, 58-64; Postdoc res fel, Helen Whitney Found, Inst Molecular Biol, Nagoya Univ, Japan, 64-67; res assoc chem contractile proteins, State Univ NY Downstate Med Ctr, 67-68; asst prof biol, Univ Pa, 68-75; assoc prof phys & org chem & dir sch grad studies, State Univ NY Downstate Med Ctr, 75-79, assoc prof biochem, Sch Med, 75-79; mgr, Databit, 79-80; vpres res, Reseal Cont Corp, 80-85. *Concurrent Pos:* John Polachek Found Med Res fel, 68; prin investr, Biomed Sci support grant, 69-70; NSF instnl grant, 69-71, res grant, 71-78; NY State Instnl grant, 75-80; consult, several cos, 80- *Mem:* AAAS; NY Acad Sci; Biophys Soc; Soc Gen Physiol; Am Inst Chemists. *Res:* Invention and research management of multidose dispensing systems for preservative-free foods, pharmaceuticals and other products; static and dynamic aspects of three-dimensional structure of polymers; self-assembly processes; connective tissue chemistry; bacterial flagella and bacterial motility. *Mailing Add:* 583 Mello Lane Santa Cruz CA 95062-2707

GERBER, DONALD ALBERT, INTERNAL MEDICINE, RHEUMATOLOGY. *Current Pos:* from instr to assoc prof, 69-95, CLIN ASST DEAN, DOWNSTATE MED CTR, STATE UNIV NY, 91-, ADMIN COURSE CO-DIR THIRD YR MED, 93- *Personal Data:* b New York, NY, Apr 10, 32; m 64, Marcia Getz; c Susan E & Andrew J. *Educ:* Columbia Univ, AB, 53, MD, 57; Am Bd Internal Med, dipl, 66. *Prof Exp:* Intern, Osler Med Serv, Johns Hopkins Hosp, Baltimore, Md, 57-58, asst resident & asst med, 58-59; asst resident, Presby Hosp, NY, 59-60; chief, Arthritis Clin, Kings Co Hosp, 72-96. *Concurrent Pos:* Arthritis Found vis fel, Col Physicians & Surgeons, Columbia Univ, 60-63; spec investr, Arthritis Found, 63-66; career scientist award, Health Res Coun, City of New York, 65-75; prin investr res grant, Nat Inst Arthritis, Metab & Digestive Dis, 66-79 & 82-85; chief arthritis, Kings Co Hosp, 72-96. *Mem:* Am Col Rheumatology; Am Fedn Clin Res; Harvey Soc; fel Am Col Physicians. *Res:* Biochemical abnormalities in rheumatoid arthritis and systemic lupus erythematosus; mechanism of action of anti-rheumatic drugs, especially gold thiomalate and D-penicillamine; the role of L-histidine, copper, sulfhydryl groups, hydrogen peroxide, and hypochlorite in rheumatic disease; aggregation of immunoglobulin G; mechanism of action of lupus-inducing drugs. *Mailing Add:* Dept Med Box 42 State Univ NY Health Sci Ctr 450 Clarkson Ave Brooklyn NY 11203-2098

GERBER, GEORGE HILTON, ENTOMOLOGY, PHYSIOLOGY. *Current Pos:* RETIRED. *Personal Data:* b St Walburg, Sask, Mar 19, 42; m 92, Margaret Elliott. *Educ:* Univ Sask, BSA, 64, PhD(entom), 69. *Honors & Awards:* C Gordon Hewitt Award, Entom Soc Can. *Prof Exp:* Res scientist entom, Agr Can, 69-97, sect head, 89-92. *Concurrent Pos:* Assoc ed, Int J Insect Morphol & Embryol, 91- *Mem:* Entom Soc Am; fel Entom Soc Can (pres, 93-94); Can Soc Zoologists; Sigma Xi. *Res:* Reproductive biology and physiology of insects; pest management system for rape crop insects; crop resistance to insect pests. *Mailing Add:* Agr Can Res Sta Winnipeg MB R3T 2M9 Can

GERBER, H JOSEPH, product development; deceased, see previous edition for last biography

GERBER, JAY DEAN, VACCINE RESEARCH & DEVELOPMENT, IMMUNOMODULATIONS. *Current Pos:* PROJ DIR, NORDEN LABS, 85- *Educ:* Univ Kans, PhD(microbiol immunol), 68. *Res:* Immunomodulations. *Mailing Add:* Dept Immunol Smith Kline Beecham Animal Health Ctr PO Box 80809 Lincoln NE 68501-0809. *Fax:* 402-473-2530

GERBER, JOHN FRANCIS, AGRICULTURAL METEOROLOGY, SATELLITE METEOROLOGY. *Current Pos:* RETIRED. *Personal Data:* b Versailles, Mo, Dec 13, 30; m 55; c 3. *Educ:* Univ Mo, BS, 56, MS, 57, PhD(soils), 60. *Prof Exp:* Instr soils, Univ Mo, 59-60; from asst prof to assoc prof, Univ Fla, 60-69, prof fruit crops & climatologist, 69-93, asst dean res, Agr Exp Sta, 71-72, dir Ctr Environ Progs, 73-77, dir, Inst Food & Agr Sci Grants Prog, 77-87. *Concurrent Pos:* Consult, United Fruit Co, 63, Corps Eng, US Army, 65-68, Walt Disney World, Aikins Tech Inc, 67; fac develop grant from Univ Fla & vis prof, Dept Hort, Pa State Univ, 69-70; rev ed, Jour, Am Soc Hort Sci; consult, Org Trop Studies, Environ Protection Agency, USDA, 70-81, NIH, 88; mem, Nat Res Coun Study Panels, 77, 78, 79, bd atmospheric sci & climat; prin investr, Dept Educ, 79-, NASA, 78-80; dir, Biotechnol Inst Res & Develop, USDA, 87-89, Univ Indust Relations, Off Agr Biotechnol, 89-90. *Mem:* Am Soc Hort Sci; Am Meteorol Soc; fel Am Soc Hort Sci; Sigma Xi; AAAS. *Res:* Climatology; cold protection of plants; heat budget studies; agricultural climatology; biotechnology; research administration and science policy. *Mailing Add:* 1126 NW 57th St Gainesville FL 32605

GERBER, JOHN GEORGE, CLINICAL PHARMACOLOGY, INTERNAL MEDICINE. *Current Pos:* from asst prof to assoc prof, 78-89, actg head, Div Clin Pharmacol, 92-93, PROF MED & PHARMACOL, UNIV COLO, 89- *Educ:* Queens Col, BA, 68; Med Col Va, MD, 72. *Concurrent Pos:* Estab investr, Am Heart Asn, 80-85; Burroughs Wellcome clin pharmacol award, 85-90. *Mem:* Am Soc Pharmacol & Exp Therapeut; Am Soc Clin Pharmacol Therapeut; Am Fed Clin Res. *Res:* Drub metabolism in disease states and in the elderly. *Mailing Add:* Health Sci Ctr Campus Box C237 Univ Colo 4200 E Ninth Ave Denver CO 80220. *Fax:* 303-270-3272

GERBER, LEON E, N-DIMENSIONAL GEOMETRY. *Current Pos:* from instr to asst prof, 66-76, ASSOC PROF MATH, ST JOHN'S UNIV, NY, 76- *Personal Data:* b Brooklyn, NY, Sept 5, 41; m 64; c 7. *Educ:* Brooklyn Col, BS, 60; Yeshiva Univ, MA, 62, PhD(math), 68. *Prof Exp:* Programmer, Brookhaven Nat Lab, 60. *Mem:* Math Asn Am. *Res:* Geometry of n-dimensions; numerical analysis; computer graphics. *Mailing Add:* Math & Comput Sci St Johns Univ 8150 Utopia Pkwy Jamaica NY 11439

GERBER, LINDA M, EPIDEMIOLOGY, MEDICAL ANTHROPOLOGY. *Current Pos:* fel & res assoc pub health, Med Col, Cornell Univ, 79-81, asst prof, 82-84, clin asst prof, 84-86, asst prof epidemiol med, 87-95, ASSOC PROF PUB HEALTH, MED COL, CORNELL UNIV, 95- *Personal Data:* b New York, NY, Apr 12, 53; m 82; c 2. *Educ:* State Univ NY, Binghamton, BA, 73; Univ Colo, MA, 76, PhD(anthrop), 78. *Prof Exp:* Res asst psychol, Inst Behav Sci, Univ Colo, 74-75 & instr anthrop, 76; res intern pop, EW Pop Inst, EW Ctr, Hawaii, 76-77; res asst anthrop, Inst Behav Sci, Univ Colo, 75-78, res assoc, 78. *Concurrent Pos:* Res training prog culture change, NIMH, 75-78; postdoctoral fel, Pub Health Serv, 79-81; preceptor, Dept Pub Health, Med Col, Cornell Univ, 80-; res scientist & epidemiologist, Nassau Co Dept Health, 84-86; asst prof clin community & prev med (epidemiol), Sch Med, State Univ NY, Stony Brook 85-87. *Mem:* Fel Human Biol Asn; fel Am Asn Phys Anthropologists; Am Heart Asn; fel Coun Epidemiol; Soc Pub Health Educ. *Res:* Epidemiology of hypertension, with particular interest in body fat and its distribution as risk factors for both hypertension and cardiovascular disease; prevalence and role of microalbuminaria in hypertension. *Mailing Add:* Dept Pub Health Cornell Univ Med Col 411 E 69th St New York NY 10021. *Fax:* 212-746-8544

GERBER, MICHAEL A, PATHOLOGY. *Current Pos:* PROF & CHMN, DEPT PATH, SCH MED, TULANE UNIV, NEW ORLEANS, 87-, DIR, GRAD PROG MOLECULAR & CELL BIOL, 91- *Personal Data:* b Kessel, WGer, Oct 18, 39; m 72; c 1. *Educ:* Gutenberg Gymn, Weisbaden, WGer, MS, 60; Gutenberg Univ, Mainz, WGer, MD, 66; Am Bd Clin & Anat Path, dipl, 72. *Prof Exp:* Internship, Gutenberg Univ, Mainz & Kreiskrankenhaus Bad Harzburg, WGer, 66-67; internship, Middlesex Gen Hosp, New Brunswick, NJ, 67-68, resident path, 68-69; resident path, Mt Sinai Hosp, NY, 69-70, trainee exp path, 70-72; assoc path, Mt Sinai Sch Med & City Hosp Ctr Elmhurst, 72-73; chief electron micros, Vet Admin Hosp, Bronx, NY, 73-74; from asst prof to prof path, Mt Sinai Sch Med, 73-87. *Concurrent Pos:* Mem, Gastrointestinal Drugs Adv Comt, Food & Drug Admin, 82-85; dir path, City Hosp Ctr Elmhurst, NY, 82-87; co-dir cellular & molecular path, Biomed Sci Doctoral Prog, Mt Sinai Sch Med, City Univ New York, 82-87; mem rev comt, Nat Liver Transplant Data Base, NIH, 86-89 & rev comt, Liver Ctr, 90; bk ed, Hepatol, 88-, assoc ed, 89- *Mailing Add:* Dept Path Sch Med Tulane Univ 1430 Tulane Ave Box SL79 New Orleans LA 70112-2699. *Fax:* 504-587-7389

GERBER, NAOMI LYNN HURWITZ, REHABILITATION MEDICINE. *Current Pos:* clin assoc, Arthritis & Rheumatism Br, Nat Inst Arthritis, Metab & Digestive Dis, 73-75, CHIEF, DEPT REHAB MED, CLIN CTR, NIH, BETHESDA, 76-, PHYSICIAN, ARTHRITIS & RHEUMATISM BR, NAT INST ARTHRITIS, DIABETES & DIGESTIVE & KIDNEY DIS, 76- *Educ:* Smith Col, AB, 65; Harvard Univ, MA, 66; Tufts Univ, MD, 71; Am Bd Internal Med, dipl, 75; Am Bd Phys Med & Rehab, dipl, 79. *Honors & Awards:* Women in Sci & Eng Award, 86; Sidney Licht Mem lectr, 89. *Prof Exp:* Res assoc, Med Sch, Tufts Univ, 66-67; intern med, New Eng Med Ctr, Boston, 71-72, resident, 72-73. *Concurrent Pos:* Resident phys med & rehab, George Wash Univ, 75-77, adj assoc prof internal med, 75-; mem, Coun Rehab Rheumatology, Am Rheumatism Asn, 82-, secy, 82-84, pres, 84-86; panel chief orthop surg, NIH, 84-; clin prof phys med & rehab, Georgetown Univ, 88-90; mem, Prof Educ Comt, Arthritis Found, 88-; Kovacs vis fel, Royal Soc Med, Eng, 91. *Mem:* Am Col Rheumatology; Am Acad Phys Med & Rehab; Asn Acad Psychiatrists. *Res:* Evaluation of parameters of gait in children with osteogenins; imperfecta and use of bracing; evaluation of mechanics of motion of one foot pre and post nietatarsal head arthoplasty. *Mailing Add:* Warren Grant Magnuson Clin Ctr NIH Dept Rehab Med Bldg 10 Rm 65235 Bethesda MD 20892

GERBER, SAMUEL MICHAEL, ORGANIC CHEMISTRY & TEXTILE CONSERVATION, DYES & INTERMEDIATES. *Current Pos:* RES ASSOC, RUTGERS UNIV, NEW BRUNSWICK, 85-; CONSULT, COLOR CONSULTS, 83- *Personal Data:* b New York, NY, June 21, 20; m 89, Barbara B Olson; c 2. *Educ:* City Col, BS, 42; Columbia Univ, MA, 48, PhD(chem), 52. *Prof Exp:* Asst chem, Columbia Univ, 47-51; chemist, Am Cyanamid Co, 51-55, asst to tech dir, Org Chem Div, 56-58, group leader, 58-68, chief chemist, Org Chem Div, 68-74; mgr dyes & chem res & develop, Chem Res Div, 74-80; mgr dyes & chem res & develop, Atlantic Chem Corp, 80-81. *Concurrent Pos:* Adj prof, Fashion Inst Technol, NY, 87-92. *Mem:* Am Chem Soc; Brit Soc Dyers & Colourists; The Chem Soc; Am Asn Textile Chemists & Colorists. *Res:* Development and use of dyes, textile chemicals and their intermediates. *Mailing Add:* 745 Schoolhouse Lane Bound Brook NJ 08805-1440. *Fax:* 732-560-9525; *E-Mail:* gerber@superlink.net

GERBERG, EUGENE JORDAN, ENTOMOLOGY. *Current Pos:* RETIRED. *Personal Data:* b New York, NY, June 1, 19; m 41, Josephine Elizabeth Vick; c 5. *Educ:* Cornell Univ, BS, 39, MS, 41; Univ Md, PhD, 54. *Honors & Awards:* Outstanding Award, Med & Vet Entom, Am Regist Prof Entom, 83; Meritorious Serv Award, Am Mosquito Control Asn, 80. *Prof Exp:* Entomol technician, State Conserv Dept NY, 40-41; asst entomologist, USPHS, 41-43; pres, Cornell Chem & Equip Co, 48-79; pres, Am Biochem Lab Inc, 48-81; pres & dir, Insect Control & Res, Inc, 46-90. *Concurrent Pos:* Spec surv, Ministry Agr, Venezuela, 50; coop scientist, USDA, 54-; trop agr specialist, US Mkt & Bus Develop Mission, Nigeria, 61 & Pakistan, 68; consult, WHO, 72, Pan Am Health Orgn, Neth Antilles, 74 & Agency for Int Develop, US Dept of State, Sri Lanka, 77, Thailand, 78; proj leader, EAfrica Aedes Res Unit, Tanzania, WHO, 69 & 70; res assoc, Fla Dept Agr, 72-; pres, Biol Res Inst Am, Inc, 73-90; adj prof, Univ Serv, Univ Health Sci, 86-93, Entom & Nemat Dept, Univ Fla, 90- *Mem:* Entom Soc Am; Am Mosquito Control Asn; Soc Vector Ecol; Am Soc Trop Med & Hyg; Royal Soc Trop Med & Hyg; hon mem Entom Soc Am. *Res:* Tropical and medical entomology; insect ecology; coleoptera; biological control of mosquitoes. *Mailing Add:* 5819 NW 57th Way Gainesville FL 32653

GERBERICH, JOHN BARNES, microbiology; deceased, see previous edition for last biography

GERBERICH, WILLIAM WARREN, METALLURGY, MATERIALS SCIENCE. *Current Pos:* PROF MAT SCI, UNIV MINN, MINNEAPOLIS, 71-, ASSOC HEAD DEPT, 80- *Personal Data:* b Wooster, Ohio, Dec 30, 35; m 59, Susan Goodwin; c Bradley K, Brian K & Beth C. *Educ:* Case Inst Technol, BS, 57; Syracuse Univ, MS, 59; Univ Calif, Berkeley, PhD(mat sci

& eng), 71. *Honors & Awards:* William Spraragen Award, Am Welding Soc, 68. *Prof Exp:* Proj eng metall, Jet Propulsion Lab, Pasadena, Calif, 59-62; sr res scientist, Aeronutronic, Newport Beach, Calif, 62-65; eng specialist, Aerojet Gen Corp, Sacramento, Calif, 65-67; res scientist mat sci, Lawrence Radiation Lab, Univ Calif, Berkeley, 67-71. *Concurrent Pos:* Lectr mat sci, Univ Calif, Berkeley, 67-71; consult, Stand Oil Calif, 68-69 & Meyer Indust, IT&T Corp, 76-; mem, Nat Mat Adv Bd, Nat Res Coun, 73-76 & Bd Publ, Metall Trans, 77-; adv, Minn Pollution Control Agency, 74-76; chmn, Fracture Mech Comt, Am Soc Metals, 78-; vchmn, Fatigue Res Comt, Am Soc Testing & Mat, 78-; bd dir, Acta Metall, 83-86, chmn bd, 86-89; bd dir, Inst Mech Mat, Univ Calif, San Diego, 92-, chmn bd, 94. *Mem:* Am Inst Mining, Metall & Petrol Engrs; fel Am Soc Metals; Am Soc Testing & Mat; Sigma Xi; Mat Res Soc. *Res:* Fracture phenomena including hydrogen embrittlement, ductile-brittle transition phenomena, fatigue crack growth; thin film mechanics including epitaxial interface studies and electron channeling of strain gradients; contact mechanics with antifriction metal and nanoindentation. *Mailing Add:* Dept Chem Eng & Mat Sci Univ Minn Minneapolis MN 55455. *Fax:* 612-626-7246

GERBI, SUSAN ALEXANDRA, CELL BIOLOGY. *Current Pos:* from asst prof to assoc prof, 72-82, PROF BIOL & DIR GRAD PROG MOLECULAR BIOL, CELL BIOL & BIOCHEM, BROWN UNIV, 82-, CHAIR, DEPT MOLECULAR BIOL, CELL BIOL & BIOCHEM, 97. *Personal Data:* b New York, NY, Mar 13, 44; m 76, James T McFlwan. *Educ:* Barnard Col, BA, 65; Yale Univ, MPhil, 68, PhD(biol), 70. *Prof Exp:* Postdoctoral fel, Max Planck Inst Biol Tubingen, WGer, 70-72. *Concurrent Pos:* Childs res grant, 73; USPHS res grant, 74-, career develop award, 75-80; Am Cancer Soc res grant, 77-83 & 86-; NSF res grant, 78, 81 & 82-; vis assoc prof, Duke Univ, 81-82. *Mem:* Am Soc Cell Biol (pres, 93); Soc Develop Biol; Genetics Soc Am; Sigma Xi. *Res:* Structure and function of ribosomal RNA regions conserved during evolution; replication of sciarid amplified DNA puff DNA; control of chromosome movement. *Mailing Add:* 48 Cynthia Rd Seekonk MA 02771

GERBIE, ALBERT B, obstetrics & gynecology, for more information see previous edition

GERDEEN, JAMES C, ENGINEERING MECHANICS. *Current Pos:* PROF MECH ENG, UNIV COLO, 89- *Personal Data:* b Ganado, Mich, July 16, 37; m 60; c 3. *Educ:* Mich Technol Univ, BSME, 59; Ohio State Univ, MSEM, 62; Stanford Univ, PhD(eng mech), 66. *Prof Exp:* Res engr, Appl Mech Div, Battelle Mem Inst, Ohio, 59-63, sr res engr, Adv Solid Mech Div, 65-68; assoc prof eng mech, Mich Technol Univ, 68-76, prof eng mech, 76-89. *Concurrent Pos:* Guest lectr, Ohio State Univ, 67; mem subcomt shells, pressure vessel res comt, Welding Res Coun, 67- *Mem:* Soc Exp Stress Anal; Am Soc Mech Engrs. *Res:* Stress analysis of thin plate and shell structures, particularly pressure vessels; plastic deformation in structures and metal working operations; inelastic behavior and rock mechanics. *Mailing Add:* Univ Colo Campus Box 112 PO Box 173364 Denver CO 80217-3364

GERDES, ANTHONY MARTIN, VENTRICULAR REMODELING IN CARDIAC HYPERTROPHY & FAILURE, CARDIAC PATHOLOGY. *Current Pos:* PROF & CHMN, DEPT ANAT, UNIV SDAK, 93- *Personal Data:* b Dallas, Tex, July 15, 52; m 88, Nancy B Crawford; c Meredith & Caroline. *Educ:* Lamar Univ, BS, 74; Univ Tex, PhD(anat), 78. *Prof Exp:* Fel, La State Univ, 78-80; res asst prof, Univ Ala, Birmingham, 80-82; from asst prof to assoc prof, Univ SFla, 82-92. *Concurrent Pos:* New investr award, NIH, 82; Vis scientist, Univ Munich, Ger, 88, Univ Cincinnati, 91. *Mem:* Am Heart Asn; Am Asn Anatomists; Int Soc Heart Res; Heart Failure Soc Am; Asn Anat, Cell Biol, Neurobiol Chairpersons; AAAS. *Res:* Adaptive and maladaptive growth of heart muscle cells in the progression to failure; first to discover that the shape of contracting muscle cells is abnormally regulated in heart failure. *Mailing Add:* 200 Forest Ave Vermillion SD 57069. *Fax:* 605-677-6381; *E-Mail:* mgerdes@sundance.usd.edu

GERDES, CHARLES FREDERICK, AQUATIC INSECTS, THYSANOPTERA. *Current Pos:* LAB MGR, DEPT PHARMACOL, KIRKSMITH COL OF OSTEOPATH, 82- *Personal Data:* b Keokuk, Iowa, June 25, 45; m 80; c 1. *Educ:* Western Ill Univ, BS, 67, MS, 74; Univ Ill, PhD(entom), 79. *Prof Exp:* Res asst entom, Ill Natural Hist Surv, 77-80; vis asst prof biol, Ill State Univ, 80-81; res assoc biol, Northeast Mo State Univ, 81-84, consult aquatic entom, 82-85. *Mem:* AAAS; Am Registry Prof Entomologists. *Res:* Identification of aquatic insects for environmental impact studies; taxonomic studies of thysanoptera. *Mailing Add:* Dept Pharmacol Kirksmith Col Osteopath 800 W Jefferson Kirksville MO 63501

GERDING, DALE NICHOLAS, INFECTIOUS DISEASES, HOSPITAL EPIDEMIOLOGY. *Current Pos:* CHIEF MED, LAKESIDE VET AFFAIRS MED CTR, 92- *Personal Data:* b Belgrade, Minn, May 16, 40; m 64; c 3. *Educ:* St Johns Univ, Minn, BS, 62; Univ Minn, MD, 68. *Prof Exp:* Space syst analyst, Hughes Aircraft, 62-64; resident med, Peter Bent Brigham Hosp, Boston, 68-69; clin assoc, comput, USPHS, NIH, 69-71; resident med, Dept Med & Lab Med & Path, Univ Minn, 71-73; fel infectious dis, 73-75, instr, Dept Med, 74-75, from asst prof to prof, 75-90; staff physician infectious dis, Vet Admin Med Ctr, 74-75; sect chief, Vet Affairs Med Ctr, 80-92. *Mem:* Fel Infectious Dis Soc Am; Am Soc Microbiol; fel Am Col Physicians. *Res:* The use of molecular biology techniques to characterize hospital infection epidemiology by using plasmid and chromosomal restriction techniques for clostridium difficile; aureus and gentamicin-resistant gram-negatives. *Mailing Add:* Lakeside Vet Affairs Med Ctr 333 E Huron St Chicago IL 60611

GERDING, THOMAS G, TECHNICAL MANAGEMENT, MEDICAL SCIENCES. *Current Pos:* DIR, COL PHARM, DRUG DYNAMICS, UNIV TEX, AUSTIN, 88-; PRES & CHIEF EXEC OFFICER, NEWFORM DEVELOP LABS, INC. *Personal Data:* b Evanston, Ill, Feb 11, 30; m 55, Beverly Starnes; c Mark, David, Gail & Genie. *Educ:* Purdue Univ, BS, 52, MS, 54, PhD(pharm), 60. *Prof Exp:* Instr pharm, Purdue Univ, 57-60, asst prof, 60-61; sr res pharmacist, Pitman-Moore Co Div, Dow Chem Co, 62-63, asst dir prod develop, 63, head prod develop, 63-65; tech dir, Glenbrook Labs Div, Sterling Drug, Inc, 65-67, dir, Prod Develop Div, Sterling-Winthrop Res Inst Div, 67-71; vpres res & develop, Calgon Consumer Prod Co, Merck & Co, 71-77; vpres & dir res & develop, Johnson & Johnson Prod Inc, 77-88. *Concurrent Pos:* Consult, Health Care Indust. *Mem:* Sigma Xi; Am Chem Soc; Am Asn Pharmaceut Scientists. *Res:* Pharmaceutics and wound care and healing; dental devices and medical devices using novel polymeric materials. *Mailing Add:* PO Box 1355 Georgetown TX 78628-1355

GERDOM, LARRY E, SUPERCRITICAL FLUID EXTRACTION, INORGANIC CHROMIUM COMPOUNDS. *Current Pos:* ASSOC PROF CHEM, UNIV MOBILE, 90- *Personal Data:* b Ypsilanti, Mich, May 1, 54; m 78, Victoria Zulewski; c Stefanie L, Mary L & Caleb P. *Educ:* Bob Jones Univ, BS, 76, Miami Univ, MS, 79; Univ Iowa, Phd(chem), 83. *Prof Exp:* Instr, Univ Northern Iowa, 82-83; asst prof chem, SE Mo State Univ, 83-90; chair, Dept Natural Sci, Mobile Col, 91-93. *Concurrent Pos:* Res fel org superconductors, Argonne Nat Lab, 85, x-ray crystal structures, Univ Iowa, 89 & supercritical fluid extraction, USAF, 91-93. *Mem:* Sigma Xi; Am Chem Soc; Nat Asn Adv Pre-Health Professions. *Res:* Supercritical fluid extraction of jet fuels from soil matrices and analysis with gas chromatography; development of on-line supercritical fluid extraction-gas chromatography methods of analysis; synthesis and characterization of coordination compounds of chromium as related to glucose tolerance factor; x-ray crystal structures of small molecules. *Mailing Add:* PO Box 13220 Phys Sci Univ Mobile AL 36663-0220. *Fax:* 334-675-3404

GERDY, JAMES ROBERT, DEVELOPMENTAL BIOLOGY, GENETICS. *Current Pos:* PRES, MEDCORE ASSOCS, 87- *Personal Data:* b Chicago, Ill, Oct 10, 43; m 67; c 1. *Educ:* Lake Forest Col, BS, 65; Northern Ill Univ, MS, 66; Southern Ill Univ, PhD(zool), 75. *Prof Exp:* Instr biol, Col St Francis, 66-69; vis lectr, Valparaiso Univ, 74-75; asst prof biol, Denison Univ, 75-78; mem staff, Smith Kline & French, 78-87. *Mem:* AAAS; Am Inst Biol Sci; Sigma Xi; Am Soc Zoologists; Soc Develop Biol. *Res:* Cell surface studies as related to ontogenic and phylogenetic development; development of genetic regulatory mechanisms; evolutionary embryology. *Mailing Add:* 658 Maple Ct Frankfort IL 60423-9535

GEREBEN, ISTVAN B, PHYSICAL OCEANOGRAPHY, HYDRO ACOUSTICS. *Current Pos:* PRIN ENGR, MARINE ACOUST, INC, 96- *Personal Data:* b Sopron, Hungary, Jan 17, 33; US citizen; m 56, Erzsebet Gombas; c Erzsebet, Balazs, Geza & Agnes. *Educ:* Budapest Tech Univ, Sopton, BS, 55, MS, 56. *Prof Exp:* Res asst geophys, Hungarian Acad Sci, 55-56; field engr, Nat Admin Geophys & Geod Hungary, 56-57; res asst, Lamont Geol Observ, 59-62; res engr, Underseas Div, Westinghouse Elec Corp, 62-66 & Hydrospace Res Corp, 66-67, mgr acoust dept, 67-71; proj dir, Tracor Inc, 71-72; mem tech staff, TRW Systs Group, 72-80, sr oceanogr, 80-93, sr tech mgt, 93-96. *Mem:* Am Geophys Union; NY Acad Sci; US Naval Inst. *Res:* Response of fixed or free floating bodies or structures to ocean wave forces; bearing capacity of ocean bottom sediments; hydrodynamical studies and experimental tests of deep towed bodies; underwater acoustics; submarine silencing; sonar technology; acoustic systems management; towed and fixed surveillance array performance analysis; ocean acoustics; military effectiveness of force structures; effect of active sonars on marine life. *Mailing Add:* 4101 Blackpool Rd Rockville MD 20853

GERECHT, J FRED, CHEMISTRY. *Current Pos:* RETIRED. *Personal Data:* b New York, NY, Nov 8, 15; m 44; c 1. *Educ:* Polytech Inst Brooklyn, BS, 42, MS, 45, PhD(org chem), 48. *Prof Exp:* Lab helper, E R Squibb & Sons, NY, 37-39; technician, Rockefeller Inst, 39-40; chemist, Schering Corp, NJ, 40-41; res chemist, Colgate-Palmolive-Peet Co, 41-49, group leader, Colgate-Palmolive Co, 49-57, res assoc, 57-79. *Concurrent Pos:* Instr, Fairleigh Dickenson Univ, 60-63; instr, Rutgers Univ, 63-73, adj prof, 73-79; adj prof, Somerset County Col, 79-86. *Mem:* Am Chem Soc; Am Oil Chemists Soc. *Res:* Synthesis, polymerization and oxidation of fatty acids; thermal polymerization of olefinic materials; sulfation, sulfonation and carbonium ion reactions. *Mailing Add:* 1236 Crim Rd Bridgewater NJ 08807-2350

GEREN, COLLIS ROSS, PROTEIN CHEMISTRY. *Current Pos:* from asst prof to assoc prof, 76-83, chair, 86-91, PROF CHEM, UNIV ARK, 83-, DEAN GRAD SCH & ASSOC VCHANCELLOR RES, 87- *Personal Data:* b Miami, Okla, Mar 28, 45; m 67; c 2. *Educ:* Northeastern Okla State Univ, BS, 67; Kans State Col Pittsburg, MS, 72; Okla State Univ, PhD(biochem), 74. *Prof Exp:* Teacher high sch sci, Picher, Okla Pub Schs, 67-70; res assoc, Dept Biochem, Med Ctr, Univ Kans, 74-76. *Concurrent Pos:* Coordr, Ark Biotechnol Ctr, 87- *Mem:* Am Soc Biol Chemists; Am Chem Soc; Sigma Xi; Am Asn Univ Prof; Int Soc Toxinology. *Res:* Venoms of North American spiders and snakes: venoms are fractionated, their major toxic components identified, and characterized both as to structure and function, and possible uses for isolated venom components are examined. *Mailing Add:* Dept Chem & Biochem Univ Ark Fayetteville AR 72701

GERENCSER, GEORGE A, EPITHELIAL TRANSPORT CENTER, CHLORIDE PUMP. *Current Pos:* Assoc prof, 80-85, PROF PHYSIOL, SCH MED, UNIV FLA, 85- *Educ:* Ind Univ, PhD(physiol), 71. *Res:* Anion-ATP asc. *Mailing Add:* Dept Physiol J Hillis Miller Health Ctr Univ Fla Med Col PO Box 100274 Gainesville FL 32610

GERENCSER, MARY ANN (AIKEN), BACTERIOLOGY. *Current Pos:* RETIRED. *Personal Data:* b Macon, Ga, Mar 24, 27; m 57. *Educ:* Ga Col Milledgeville, BS, 48; Smith Col, MA, 50; Univ Ky, PhD(bact), 58. *Prof Exp:* Technician, Ga State Dept Health, 50-51; res technician, Commun Dis Ctr, USPHS, 51-54; res asst bact, Univ Ky, 54-57; dir, Consol Labs, 57-59; supvr clin lab microbiol, Michael Reese Hosp, Chicago, Ill, 59-61; res assoc microbiol, Sch Med, WVa Univ, 62-92. *Mem:* Am Soc Microbiol. *Res:* Clinical microbiology; genus Actinomyces; taxonomy; serology; dental microbiology. *Mailing Add:* 1103 Wingate St Dublin GA 31021-3026

GERENCSER, VINCENT FREDERIC, BACTERIOLOGY. *Current Pos:* RETIRED. *Personal Data:* b New Brunswick, NJ, Jan 17, 27; m 57. *Educ:* Fordham Univ, BS, 51; Univ Ky, PhD(bact), 58. *Prof Exp:* Asst bact, Univ Ky, 52-57; res assoc microbiol, Col Med, Univ Ill, 57-59, instr, 59-61; from asst prof to assoc prof microbiol, Sch Med, WVa Univ, 61-92. *Mem:* AAAS; Am Soc Microbiol; Brit Soc Gen Microbiol; Sigma Xi. *Res:* Aquatic microbiology; microbial ecology; taxonomy; genetics; morphology; cytology. *Mailing Add:* 1103 Wingate St Dublin GA 31021

GERETY, ROBERT JOHN, IMMUNOLOGY, PEDIATRICS. *Current Pos:* CHIEF HEPATITIS BR, BUR BIOLOGICS, FOOD & DRUG ADMIN, 73- *Personal Data:* b Jersey City, NJ, Oct 16, 39; m 67; c 3. *Educ:* Rutgers Univ, BA, 62; George Washington Univ, MD, 70; Stanford Univ, MA & PhD(immunol), 71. *Prof Exp:* Res assoc med microbiol, Stanford Univ, 70-71; res assoc viral immunol, Div Virol, NIH, 71-73. *Concurrent Pos:* Chmn, Comt License Biologics US, 72-; contracts consult, Nat Heart, Lung & Blood Inst, NIH, 73-; consult, WHO, 75-; chmn, Hepatitis Coord Comt, NIH, 75-80; chmn, Comt Assess Primate Usage Infectious Dis Res, 78. *Mem:* Am Asn Immunologists; Am Acad Pediat; Sigma Xi; Am Asn Microbiologists. *Res:* Viral hepatitis; immunology; in vitro serologic tests; pediatrics; vaccine production, testing and usage policies; biological standardization. *Mailing Add:* ImmunoLogic Pharmaceut Corp 610 Lincoln St Waltham MA 02154. *Fax:* 781-466-6050

GEREZ, VICTOR, ELECTRICAL ENGINEERING, MECHANICAL ENGINEERING. *Current Pos:* assoc prof & dept head, 83-84, PROF ELECT ENG, MONT STATE UNIV, 84- *Personal Data:* b Santander, Spain, Apr 11, 34; Mexican citizen; m 84; c 2. *Educ:* Nat Univ Mexico, EE, 57; Univ Calif, MEE, 69, PhD(elect eng), 72. *Prof Exp:* Res eng, Fed Elect Bd, 65-73; dept head & prof elect eng, Col Eng Nat Univ Mex, 73-76; dept dir power eng, Inst Elect Res, 77-83. *Concurrent Pos:* Lectr, Ibero Am Univ, 59-65; col eng, 59-68, 77-83, dept head control eng, Col eng, Nat Univ Mex 72-73. *Mem:* Inst Elec & Electronics Engrs; Am Asn Eng Educ; Int Asn Sci Technol Develop. *Res:* Power system transmission planning and operation; Pollution Flashover Phenomenon in Transmission systems; electrical engineering education. *Mailing Add:* Dept Elec Eng Mont State Univ Bozeman MT 59717-3780

GERFEN, CHARLES OTTO, PHYSICAL CHEMISTRY. *Current Pos:* res chemist, Inorg Res Dept, Mallinckrodt Chem Works, 51-55, group leader, 55-57, asst dir, 57-60, dir gen res, 60-63, spec prod dept, 63-71 & narcotics & dangerous drugs, 71-73, dir govt rels, 73-76, DIR SPEC CORP PURCHASES, MALLINCKRODT, INC, 76- *Personal Data:* b Breese, Ill, Apr 10, 20; m 48; c 4. *Educ:* Ill State Univ, normal, BS; Univ Mo, PhD(chem), 51. *Prof Exp:* Chemist, Atmospheric Nitrogen Corp, Ky, 42-43. *Mem:* AAAS; Am Chem Soc; Am Inst Chem. *Res:* Chemistry of group IV and V elements, niobium, tantalum; titanium; zirconium and hafnium; ore beneficiation; chemistry of opium and opiates. *Mailing Add:* 37 Portland Dr St Louis MO 63131

GERFEN, CHARLES R, NEUROPHYSIOLOGY. *Current Pos:* CHIEF, LAB NEUROPHYSIOL, NIMH, 93- *Personal Data:* b St Louis, Mo, July 26, 53. *Educ:* Amherst Col, BA, 75; Northwestern Univ, PhD(anal), 81. *Mailing Add:* Lab Neurophysiol NIMH Bldg 36 2D-30 Bethesda MD 20892

GERGELY, JOHN, BIOCHEMISTRY. *Current Pos:* BIOCHEMIST, MASS GEN HOSP, 69-; DIR DEPT MUSCLE RES, BOSTON BIOMED RES INST, 70- *Personal Data:* b Budapest, Hungary, May 15, 19; nat US; m 45; c 8. *Educ:* Univ Budapest, MD, 42; Leeds Univ, PhD(phys chem), 48. *Prof Exp:* From asst prof pharmacol to asst prof biochem, Univ Budapest, 42-48; asst prof biochem, New Sch Soc Res, 48-50; Nat Heart Inst sr trainee, Univ Wis, 50-51; res assoc med, 51-62, asst prof, 62-71, assoc prof, 71-80, PROF BIOL CHEM, HARVARD MED SCH, 80- *Concurrent Pos:* NIH spec res fel, 48-50; estab investr, Am Heart Asn, 51-58; from asst biochemist to assoc biochemist, Mass Gen Hosp, 54-69; tutor biochem sci, Harvard Med Sch, 57-72; dir dept muscle res, Retina Found, 61-70. *Mem:* Am Soc Biol Chem; Biophys Soc; Am Chem Soc; NY Acad Sci; Brit Biochem Soc. *Res:* Biochemistry of muscle contraction; enzymes; nuclear magnetic resonance; physical chemistry of proteins; electron spin resonance. *Mailing Add:* Dept Muscle Res Boston Biomed Res Inst 20 Staniford St Boston MA 02114-2500. *Fax:* 617-523-6649

GERGELY, PETER, structural & earthquake engineering; deceased, see previous edition for last biography

GERGELY, TOMAS ESTEBAN, RADIO SPECTRUM MANAGEMENT, SOLAR PHYSICS. *Current Pos:* ELECTROMAGNETIC SPECTRUM MGR, NSF, 86- *Personal Data:* b Budapest, Hungary, Oct 14, 43; US citizen; m 70, Ana Lajmanovich; c Gabriela S, Esteban A & Daniel M. *Educ:* Univ Buenos Aires, Licenciado physics, 67; Univ Md, PhD(astron), 74. *Prof Exp:* Asst prof, Nat Technol Univ, Arg, 74; researcher, Inst Radio Astron, Arg, 74-75; res assoc, Univ Md, 76-82, assoc res scientist; 82-85; astrophysicist, NASA Hq, 85-86. *Concurrent Pos:* Adv, US Deleg World Admin Radio Conf, 87, 92 & 95. *Mem:* Am Astron Soc; Int Union Sci Radio. *Res:* Maintaining access of the scientific community to the radio spectrum; solar and coronal physics related to solar radio bursts and coronal mass ejections. *Mailing Add:* NSF 4201 Wilson Blvd Arlington VA 22230. *E-Mail:* tgergely@tnsf.gov

GERGIS, SAMIR D, ANESTHESIOLOGY. *Current Pos:* res fel, Col Med, Univ Iowa, 68, from instr to assoc prof, Dept Anesthesia, 69-76, actg head dept, 77-78, dir, Clin Serv, Hosps & Clins, 78-80, PROF, DEPT ANESTHESIA, COL MED, UNIV IOWA, IOWA CITY, 76-, VCHMN CLIN AFFAIRS, DEPT ANESTHESIA, UNIV IOWA HOSPS & CLINS, 85- *Personal Data:* US citizen. *Educ:* Cairo Univ, Egypt, MB, 54, MD(anesthesia), 62; FACA, 71. *Prof Exp:* House officer, Cairo Univ Hosps, Egypt, 55, resident, Dept Anesthesia, 57-58; fel, Anesthesiol Ctr, WHO & Univ Copenhagen, Denmark, 63. *Concurrent Pos:* Mem, Subcomt Neuromuscular Transmission, Am Soc Anesthesiologists, 86- & Comt Surg Anesthesia, 91; bd mem, Asn Anesthesia Clin Dirs. *Mem:* Int Anesthesia Res Soc; AMA; Am Soc Anesthesiologists; NY Acad Sci; Am Soc Pharmacol & Exp Therapeut; Soc Exp Biol & Med; AAAS; Nat Soc Med Res; Am Soc Clin Pharmacol & Therapeut; Asn Anesthesia Clin Dirs. *Res:* Neuromuscular physiology and pharmacology; clincial research in anesthesia. *Mailing Add:* Dept Anesthesia Univ Hosp Iowa City IA 52242-0001

GERGOVA, KATIA M, CARBON CHEMISTRY. *Current Pos:* CONSULT, 96- *Personal Data:* b Sofia, Bulgaria. *Educ:* St Kliment Ohridsky Univ, MSc, 81; Inst Org Chem, Bulgarian Acad Sci, PhD(tech sci), 91. *Prof Exp:* Res assoc, Pa State Univ, 91-96. *Mem:* Am Chem Soc. *Res:* Preparatian, adsorption properties, porous structure and applications of activated carbons produced from coal (lignites to anthracites) and natural precursors as wood, fruit stones, shells; fuel science, jet fuel, characterization of solid carbons produced by the thermal decomposition of various liquid fuels. *Mailing Add:* 3080 Westover Dr Ferguson PA 16801. *Fax:* 814-865-3075

GERHARD, EARL R(OBERT), CHEMICAL ENGINEERING, ENVIRONMENTAL ENGINEERING. *Current Pos:* RETIRED. *Personal Data:* b Louisville, Ky, Aug 9, 22; m 47; c 5. *Educ:* Univ Louisville, BChE, 43, MChE, 47; Univ Ill, PhD(chem eng), 53. *Prof Exp:* From asst prof to assoc prof, Univ, Louisville, 51-64, prof chem eng, 64-, chmn dept, 69-73, assoc dean, 73-80, dean, 80- *Mem:* Am Chem Soc; Am Soc Eng Educ; Am Inst Chem Engrs; Nat Soc Prof Engrs. *Res:* Transport phenomenon; reaction kinetics; coal research; kinetics and reactor design; environmental impacts and assessment. *Mailing Add:* 5723 Prince William St Louisville KY 40207

GERHARD, GLEN CARL, BIOENGINEERING & BIOMEDICAL ENGINEERING. *Current Pos:* VIS PROF, UNIV ARIZ, 90- *Personal Data:* b Albion, NY, Mar 1, 35; m 57; c 4. *Educ:* Syracuse Univ, BEE, 56; Ohio State Univ, MSc, 58, PhD(elec eng), 63. *Prof Exp:* Engr, Gen Elec Co, 56; asst elec eng, Ohio State Univ, 56-57; develop engr, Eastman Kodak Co, 57; res asst elec eng, Ohio State Univ, 57-58, instr elec eng & res assoc electron devices, 58-62; res engr, Electronics Lab, Gen Elec Co, 62-63 & 64-67; from asst prof to prof elec eng, Univ NH, 67-90, dir, Biomed Ear Nose & Throat Ctr, 81-90. *Concurrent Pos:* Consult, Gen Elec Co, 67-68, Kidder Press Div, Moore Bus Forms, 68-70, Hewlett-Packard, 87-89; assoc dir, Clin Eng Ctr, Univ NH, 73-81, dir, 81-; vis assoc prof elec eng & surg, Univ Ariz, 81-82; legal expert witness, 76- *Mem:* Inst Elec & Electronics Engrs; Eng Med & Biol Soc; Sigma Xi; Asn Advan Med Instrumentation; Am Soc Eng Educ. *Res:* Biomedical instrumentation; physiological transducers and sensors; electrosurgery; neurosurgical instrumentation; prosthetic devices; clinical engineering; analog VLSI circuits. *Mailing Add:* Dept Elect & Comp Eng Univ Ariz Tucson AZ 85721

GERHARD, LEE C, STRATIGRAPHY, RESEARCH ADMINISTRATION. *Current Pos:* STATE GEOLOGIST & DIR, KANS GEOL SURV, UNIV KANS, 87- *Personal Data:* b Albion, NY, May 30, 37; m 64; c 1. *Educ:* Syracuse Univ, BS, 58; Univ Kans, MS, 61, PhD(geol), 64. *Prof Exp:* Explor geologist, Sinclair Oil & Gas Co, 64-65, region stratigrapher, 65-66; from asst prof to assoc prof geol, Southern Colo State Col, 66-72; asst dir & actg dir, WIndies Lab & assoc prof, Dickinson Univ, St Croix, 72-75; asst state geologist, NDak Geol Surv, 75-78, state geologist & dir, 78-81; explor mgr, Rocky Mountain div, Supron Energy Corp, 81-82; Getty Prof geol eng, Colo Sch Mines, 82-87. *Concurrent Pos:* Assoc prof geol, Univ NDak, 75-78, prof, 78-81, chmn dept, 78-81. *Mem:* Hon mem Am Asn Petrol Geologists; Geol Soc Am; Asn Am State Geologists; Sigma Xi. *Res:* Structural geologic history; carbonate petrography; stratigraphy; sedimentary petrology. *Mailing Add:* 1628 Alvamar Dr Lawrence KS 66047-1714. *E-Mail:* lgerhard@ukans.edu

GERHARD, WALTER ULRICH, VIROLOGY, IMMUNOLOGY. *Current Pos:* res assoc viral immunol, 74-77, ASSOC PROF VIRAL IMMUNOL, WISTAR INST, 78- *Personal Data:* b Zurich, Switz. *Educ:* Univ Zurich, Med Prac, 69, Dr med, 71. *Prof Exp:* Fel virol, Inst Immunol, Basel, 71-72; fel immunol, Dept Path, Univ Pa, 73-74. *Mem:* Am Asn Immunologists. *Res:* Antigenic drift of influenza virus; pathogenesis of multiple sclerosis. *Mailing Add:* Wistar Inst Anat & Biol 36th St & Spruce St Philadelphia PA 19104-4268. *Fax:* 215-898-3868

GERHARDT, DON JOHN, HIGH PRESSURE FLUIDS, COMPRESSORS. *Current Pos:* eng mgr, 84-88, CHIEF ENGR, INGERSOLL-RAND, 89- *Personal Data:* b Evansville, Ind, Oct 30, 43; m 68; c 3. *Educ:* Purdue Univ, BSME, 65; Univ Detroit, MS, 67; Univ Mich, PhD(bioeng), 75, MBA, 82. *Prof Exp:* Test engr, Gen Motors Proving Grounds, 65, design engr, Pontiac Div, 66-67, res engr, Res Labs, 68; eng supvr, Ford Motor Co, 72-83. *Concurrent Pos:* Researcher, Hwy Safety Inst, Univ Mich, 69-70, lectr, Med Sch, 70-71; mem, Noise Reduction Comt, Soc Automotive Engrs, 79-80, Chassis Design Comt, 82-83 & Electronics Comt, 85-88; appointee, Exhaust & Emissions, Motor Vehicle Mfrs Asn, 79-80. *Mem:* Am Soc Mech Engrs; Inst Elec & Electronics Engrs; Soc Automotive Engrs; Nat Soc Prof Engrs; Am Soc Metals; Vol Tech Assistance. *Res:* Impact of science on people and environment; product safety; advanced industrial equipment; expert computer systems; microprocessor control theory; advanced compressors; sound and vibration analysis; high pressure fluids; electroencephalogram computer analysis; neuroscience; holder of 3 US patents. *Mailing Add:* 3474 Tanglebrook Trail Clemmons NC 27012

GERHARDT, GEORGE WILLIAM, ORGANIC CHEMISTRY. *Current Pos:* CONSULT, 85- *Personal Data:* b Shaler Twp, Pa, Nov 7, 15. *Educ:* Univ Pittsburgh, BS, 36, PhD(chem), 51. *Prof Exp:* From fel to adv fel, Mellon Inst, 36-59; asst tech dir, Stoner-Mudge Div, Mobil Finishes Co, Inc, 59-66; asst tech dir, Mobil Chem Co, 66-71, lab dir, 71-73, mgr com develop & customer serv, Packaging Coatings Dept, 73-81. *Concurrent Pos:* Mem comt on packaging, Nat Res Coun, 75-78. *Mem:* Am Chem Soc; Inst Food Technol; Fedn Soc Paint Technol; Master Brewers Asn Am. *Res:* Organic coatings; packaging; resin manufacture. *Mailing Add:* 2733 Cole Rd Wexford PA 15090-7810

GERHARDT, H CARL, JR, ACOUSTIC COMMUNICATION, NEUROETHOLOGY. *Current Pos:* from asst prof to assoc prof, 71-80, PROF, DIV BIOL SCI, UNIV MO, COLUMBIA, 81- *Personal Data:* b Newport News, Va, May 23, 45; m 86, Dayna Glanz; c 2. *Educ:* Univ Ga, BS, 66; Univ Tex, Austin, MA, 68, PhD(zool), 70. *Prof Exp:* Res assoc animal commun, Cornell Univ, 70-71. *Concurrent Pos:* NIH res career develop award, 76-81; vis prof, Gesamthochschule, WGer, 78, Dept Zool, Univ Melbourne, 81-82, 84 & 90, Univ Vienna, 84; res scientist develop award, NIMH, 89-94; presidential award res & creativity, Univ Mo. *Mem:* Fel Animal Behav Soc; Int Soc Neuroethology (secy, 84-87); Soc Study Evolution; Am Soc Ithyologists/Herpetologists; Int Soc Behav Ecol; Soc Neurosci. *Res:* Sound pattern recognition in animals, using synthetic acoustic signals to identify pertinent properties of the vocalizations of animals; neurobiological mechanisms and evolution of acoustic communication. *Mailing Add:* Div Biol Chem Univ Mo 117 Schweitzer Hall Columbia MO 65211-0001. *Fax:* 573-882-0123; *E-Mail:* bioscarl@mizzou1.missouri.edu

GERHARDT, HEINZ ADOLF AUGUST, AERONAUTICAL & ASTRONAUTICAL ENGINEERING. *Current Pos:* from eng to mgr advan aerodesign, 62-91, PRIN ENGR, NOTHROP CORP, HAWTHORNE, 91- *Personal Data:* b Biederkopf, Ger, Jan 31, 34; m 62, Heide Hanne Waltraud von Ryschkowsky; c Heinrich, Friederiks & Helmar. *Educ:* Tech Univ Darmstadt, MS, 61. *Honors & Awards:* Aerodyn Award, Am Inst Aeronaut & Astronaut, 94. *Prof Exp:* Engr, Heinkel AG, Munich, 62. *Mem:* Assoc fel Am Inst Aeronaut & Astronaut; Soc Automotive Engrs; Ger Soc Aeronaut & Astronaut. *Res:* Granted patents in field. *Mailing Add:* 278 Calle de Madrid Redondo Beach CA 90277

GERHARDT, JON STUART, MECHANICAL ENGINEERING. *Current Pos:* STAFF MEM, STAND TESTING LAB, 95- *Personal Data:* b Springfield, Ohio, June 5, 43; m 70, Claudia Sadler; c Kirsten & Benjamin. *Educ:* Univ Cincinnati, BScME, 66, MS, 68, PhD(mech eng-math), 71. *Prof Exp:* Coop engr, Whirlpool Corp, 61-66; res assoc & instr, Univ Cincinnati, 69-71; asst prof eng technol, Univ NC, Charlotte, 71-73; proj engr, Duff-Norton Co, 73; sr develop engr, Gencorp, Inc, 73-77, group leader rubber prod eng, 77-79, mgr tech staff develop, 79-84, mgr prod eng & res ctr admin, 84-87, dir res, Gen Tire Inc, 87-95. *Concurrent Pos:* Mem bd dirs, Am Soc Mech Engrs; lectr, Univ Akron, 77-; chmn bd, Chapel Hill Christian Schs. *Mem:* Am Soc Mech Engrs; Soc Automotive Engrs; Am Chem Soc. *Res:* Measurement and analysis of complex dynamic systems; interaction of tire dynamics and vehicles that produce ride quality attributes. *Mailing Add:* 3835 Greentree Rd Cuyahoga Falls OH 44224. *Fax:* 330-798-3374

GERHARDT, KLAUS OTTO, ORGANIC CHEMISTRY, ANALYTICAL CHEMISTRY. *Current Pos:* res anal chemist, 69-77, sr res chemist, 77-88, RES ASSOC PROF BIOCHEM, UNIV MO-COLUMBIA, 88- *Personal Data:* b Drengfurt, Ger, Aug 6, 35. *Educ:* Tech Univ Berlin, Diplom Chemiker, 64, Dr rer nat(anal chem), 67. *Prof Exp:* Fel, Univ Mo-Columbia, 67-68; asst prof phys & gen chem, Lincoln Univ, Mo, 68-69. *Mem:* Am Chem Soc. *Res:* Analytical methods of gas-liquid chromatography and high pressure liquid chromatography for fatty acids, amino acids, nucleosides, and biological markers for the detection of cancer; mass spectrometry. *Mailing Add:* Rm 4 Agr Bldg Univ Mo Columbia MO 65211

GERHARDT, LESTER A, ELECTRICAL & SYSTEMS ENGINEERING. *Current Pos:* assoc prof, Systs Div, Rensselaer Polytech Inst, 69-74, chmn dept, 75-86, dir comput integrated mfg, 86-91, PROF ELEC SYSTS ENG, RENSSELAER POLYTECH INST, 74-, ASSOC DEAN ENG, 91- *Personal Data:* b Bronx, NY, Jan 28, 40; m 61; c 2. *Educ:* City Col New York, BEE, 61; State Univ NY Buffalo, MS, 64, PhD(commun systs), 69. *Prof Exp:* Sr elec engr avionics systs, Bell Aerospace Corp, 61-64, sect head signal & info processing res, 64-69. *Concurrent Pos:* Asst to dir advan res & consult, Bell Aerospace Corp, 69-75; consult, USAF-Rome Air Develop Ctr, 72- & Gen Elec Co, 78-; appointed panel mem, Adv Group Aerospace Res & Develop, NATO, US rep, Collab Res Panel. *Mem:* Sigma Xi; fel Inst Elec & Electronics Engrs. *Res:* Adaptive systems research with applications to communications, control and pattern recognition; voice and image processing; digital, signal and information processing. *Mailing Add:* Dept Comput Sci Rensselaer Polytech Inst Troy NY 12180

GERHARDT, MARK S, computer science, real-time systems architecture, for more information see previous edition

GERHARDT, PHILIPP, MICROBIOLOGY, BACTERIOLOGY. *Current Pos:* chmn dept, Mich State Univ, 65-75, prof, 65-92, assoc dean res & grad study, osteop med, 75-87, EMER PROF MICROBIOL, MICH STATE UNIV, 92- *Personal Data:* b Milwaukee, Wis, Dec 30, 21; m 45, Vera M Armstrong; c Ellen D (Brown), Stephen P & Doris M (Hodardsworth). *Educ:* Univ Wis, PhB, 43, MS, 47, PhD(bact), 49; Am Bd Microbiol, dipl. *Prof Exp:* Asst prof bact, Ore State Univ, 49-51; chief lab, Div Biol Develop, Pine Bluff Arsenal, 51-52; from asst prof to prof microbiol, Med Sch, Univ Mich, 53-65. *Concurrent Pos:* Dir, Ribi Immunol Chem Res Inc, 85-; adj sr scientist, Mich Biotech Inst, 85-; ed-in-chief, Methods Gen & Molecular Bact, 94. *Mem:* Int Union Microbiol Soc (pres, 82-86); hon mem Am Soc Microbiol (secy, 61-67, vpres, 73-74, pres, 74-75); fel Am Acad Microbiol; Soc Gen Microbiol; fel AAAS; Sigma Xi; hon mem Polish Med Soc. *Res:* Spore resistance mechanisms, fermentations; membranes and permeability; spores; dialysis culture. *Mailing Add:* Dept Microbiol Mich State Univ East Lansing MI 48824-1101. *Fax:* 517-353-8957; *E-Mail:* microbiol@msu.edu

GERHARDT, REID RICHARD, ENTOMOLOGY. *Current Pos:* asst prof, 73-78, ASSOC PROF AGR BIOL, UNIV TENN, KNOXVILLE, 78- *Personal Data:* b Monmouth, Ill, May 2, 41; m 65; c 2. *Educ:* Va Polytech Inst, BS, 63, MS, 65; NC State Univ, PhD(entom), 72. *Prof Exp:* Instr biol, Radford Col, 64-66. *Mem:* Entom Soc Am. *Res:* Effect of insect pests on livestock; biology and ecology of biting diptera. *Mailing Add:* Entom Path Dept 205 Plant Sci Bldg Univ Tenn Knoxville TN 37901

GERHART, JAMES BASIL, NUCLEAR PHYSICS, HISTORY OF SCIENCE. *Current Pos:* from asst prof to assoc prof, 56-65, PROF PHYSICS, UNIV WASH, 65- *Personal Data:* b Pasadena, Calif, Dec 15, 28; m 58, Genevra Thomesen; c James E & Sara E. *Educ:* Calif Inst Technol, BS, 50; Princeton Univ, MA, 52, PhD(physics), 54. *Honors & Awards:* Millikan Medal, Am Asn Physics Teachers, 85 & Distinguished Serv Award, 83; Gerhart Lectr, Pac NW Asn Col Physics, 96. *Prof Exp:* Asst physics, Princeton Univ, 50-54, instr, 54-56. *Concurrent Pos:* Chmn, Pac NW Asn Col Physics, 70-72 & exec officer, 72-94; gov bd, Am Inst Physics, 72-78 & 80-82. *Mem:* Fel AAAS; fel Am Phys Soc; Am Asn Physics Teachers (secy, 71-77, vpres, 77, pres-elect, 78, pres, 79); Am Inst Physics; Pac NW Asn Col Physics. *Res:* Beta and gamma ray spectroscopy; nuclear scattering and reactions; science education. *Mailing Add:* Dept Physics Univ Wash Seattle WA 98195. *Fax:* 206-685-0636; *E-Mail:* gerhart@phys.u.washington.edu

GERHART, JOHN C, BIOCHEMISTRY. *Current Pos:* Asst prof molecular biol & virol, Univ Calif, Berkeley, 62-67, assoc prof, 67-73, prof molecular biol & res biochemist, 73-89, PROF MOLECULAR & CELL BIOL, VIRUS LAB, UNIV CALIF, BERKELEY, 89- *Personal Data:* b Cincinnati, Ohio, Mar 27, 36; m 64. *Educ:* Harvard Univ, AB, 58; Univ Calif, Berkeley, PhD(biochem), 62. *Mem:* Nat Acad Sci; Soc Develop Biol; Am Soc Cell Biol. *Res:* Cell growth and regulation; control of enzyme activity; metazoan development. *Mailing Add:* Dept Molecular Biol Univ Calif 2120 Oxford St Bldg LSA Rm 301 Berkeley CA 94720

GERHOLD, GEORGE A, PHYSICAL CHEMISTRY. *Current Pos:* from asst prof to assoc prof, 70-76, PROF CHEM, WESTERN WASH UNIV, 76- *Personal Data:* b Kewanee, Ill, Mar 17, 37; m 58. *Educ:* Univ Ill, BS, 58; Univ Wash, Seattle, PhD(chem), 63. *Prof Exp:* NSF fel chem, Univ Col, Univ London, 63-65; asst prof, Univ Calif, Davis, 65-70. *Res:* Electronic and crystal spectra; excitons. *Mailing Add:* Dept Chem Western Wash Univ Bellingham WA 98225-5996

GERHOLD, HENRY DIETRICH, FOREST GENETICS, URBAN FORESTRY. *Current Pos:* from instr to assoc prof, 56-69, chmn dept, Sch Forest Resources, 85-92, PROF FOREST GENETICS, PA STATE UNIV, 69- *Personal Data:* b Mahwah, NJ, Feb 1, 31; m 56, Marilyn Quigley; c Maureen, David & heidi. *Educ:* Pa State Univ, BS, 52, MF, 54; Yale Univ, PhD(forest genetics), 59. *Prof Exp:* Soil conserv aid, Soil Conserv Serv, USDA, 49, fire control aid, Forest Serv, Mont, 51, forester, Idaho, 52-53; res forester, Northeastern Forest Exp Sta, 54-55. *Concurrent Pos:* NSF travel grant, World Consult Forest Genetics, UN Food & Agr Orgn, 63; NATO sr sci fel, 70; chmn, Northeastern Forest Tree Improv Conf, 70-72; chmn, Genetic Resistance Dis & Insects Subj Group, Int Union Forest Res Orgns, 66-74, dep coordr, Div 2, 74-79. *Mem:* Soc Am Foresters; Sigma Xi; Int Soc Arboricult; Am Forestry Asn; Am Chestnut Found. *Res:* Forest genetics; genetics of Christmas trees and landscape trees; resistance to diseases, insects and air pollutants. *Mailing Add:* 816 S Sparks St State College PA 16801. *Fax:* 814-865-3725

GERICH, JOHN EDWARD, DIABETES, COUNTER-REGULATION. *Current Pos:* PROF MED & PHYSIOL, MAYO MED SCH, ROCHESTER, MINN, 79- *Educ:* Georgetown Univ, MD, 69. *Res:* Insulin resistance. *Mailing Add:* Univ Rochester Med Ctr Col Elmwood Ave Box Med CRC Rochester NY 14642

GERICKE, OTTO REINHARD, PHYSICS. *Current Pos:* physicist, US Army Mat Res Agency, 58-63, res physicist, 63-66, chief appl physics br, 66-69, head nondestructive testing br, 69-78, SUPVRY RES PHYSICIST, US ARMY MAT TECHNOL LAB, 78- *Personal Data:* b Detmold, Ger, Sept 7, 21; US citizen; m 52; c 1. *Educ:* Univ Gottingen, BS, 44, MS, 50. *Honors & Awards:* Cert Outstanding Achievement, Sci Conf, US Army, 62. *Prof Exp:* Physicist, Siemens-Reiniger Co, Ger, 51-54 & Siemens & Halske Co, 54-58. *Mem:* Soc Nondestructive Test; Acoust Soc Am. *Res:* Nondestructive testing; studies of various types of physical phenomena to determine their potential usefulness for nondestructive evaluation of materials including ultrasonic spectroscopy; holography and imaging, image enhancement; computer-based ultrasonic signal processing. *Mailing Add:* 7 Crest Circle Medfield MA 02052

GERIG, JOHN THOMAS, BIO-ORGANIC CHEMISTRY. *Current Pos:* assoc prof, 66-77, PROF CHEM, UNIV CALIF, SANTA BARBARA, 77- *Personal Data:* b Windham, Ohio, Nov 7, 38; m 61; c 2. *Educ:* Col Wooster, BA, 60; Brown Univ, PhD(chem), 64. *Honors & Awards:* Res Career Develop Award, Pub Health Serv, 73-78. *Prof Exp:* Asst org chem, Brown Univ, 60-64; res fel, Calif Inst Technol, 64-66. *Mem:* Am Chem Soc; AAAS; Int Soc Magnetic Res; Am Soc Biol Chemists; Molecular Biol & Protein Soc. *Res:* Nuclear magnetic resonance spectroscopy; protein chemistry; enzymatic reactions. *Mailing Add:* Dept Chem Univ Calif Santa Barbara CA 93106-0001. *Fax:* 805-893-4120

GERIG, THOMAS MICHAEL, STATISTICS. *Current Pos:* Assoc prof, 75-80, PROF STATIST, NC STATE UNIV, 80- *Personal Data:* b Washington, DC, May 25, 42; m 66; c 2. Victoria Harbour; c Alison & Stephanie. *Educ:* George Washington Univ, AB, 65; Univ NC, Chapel Hill, PhD(statist), 71. *Mem:* Am Statist Asn; Inst Math Statist. *Res:* Multivariate analysis; categorical data; statistical computing. *Mailing Add:* 3215 Kenly Ct Raleigh NC 27607. *Fax:* 919-515-7591; *E-Mail:* gerig@stat.ncsu.edu

GERIK, JAMES STEPHEN, SOILBORNE FUNGI, FUNGAL VECTORS OF VIRUSES. *Current Pos:* RES PLANT PATHOLOGIST, HOLLY SUGAR CORP, TRACY, CALIF, 91- *Personal Data:* b Waco, Tex, Sept 24, 56; m 88, Martha Kavnagh. *Educ:* Tex A&M, BS, 77, MS, 79; Univ Calif, Berkeley, PhD(plant path), 84. *Prof Exp:* Res assoc, Univ Wis-Madison, 84-85; postdoctoral, Agr Res Serv, USDA, Salinas, Calif, 85-87, res plant pathologist, 87-91. *Mem:* Am Phytopath Soc; Mycol Soc Am; Am Soc Sugarbeet Technologists; AAAS. *Res:* Ecological and epidemiological aspects of soilborne sugarbeet diseases and fungal vectors of soilborne viruses. *Mailing Add:* PO Box 60 Tracy CA 95378. *Fax:* 209-835-1317; *E-Mail:* gerik@holonet.net

GERIN, JOHN LOUIS, VIROLOGY, BIOCHEMISTRY. *Current Pos:* PROF MICROBIOL & HEAD DIV MOLECULAR VIROL & IMMUNOL, GEORGETOWN UNIV MED CTR, 78- *Personal Data:* b St Paul, Minn, Sept 28, 37; m 60; c 1. *Educ:* Georgetown Univ, BS, 59; Univ Tenn, Knoxville, MS, 61, PhD(zool), 64. *Prof Exp:* Res scientist, Sci Div, Abbott Lab, 64-66, group leader biochem & biophys virol, 66-67; head, Rockville Lab, Molecular Anat Prog, Oak Ridge Nat Lab, 67-78. *Mem:* AAAS; Am Soc Microbiol; Am Asn Immunol; Am Soc Microbiol; Infectious Dis Soc Am. *Res:* Biochemical and biophysical characteristics of animal viruses, especially human respiratory viruses and hepatitis-viruses; purification of viral antigens for vaccine production; antivirals; viral diagnostic. *Mailing Add:* Div Molec Virol & Immunol/Georgetown Univ Sch Med 5640 Fishers Lane Rockville MD 20852-1770. *Fax:* 301-881-0810

GERING, ROBERT LEE, ZOOLOGY, SCIENCE EDUCATION. *Current Pos:* INDEPENDENT RESEARCHER & DEVELOP EDUC PROD, 65-; PRES, INFO APPLNS, INC, 66- *Personal Data:* b Parker, SDak, Feb 18, 20; m 45; c 2. *Educ:* Univ Utah, AB, 47, MA, 48, PhD(invert zool), 50. *Honors & Awards:* Res Award, Am Cancer Soc, 51. *Prof Exp:* Chmn nat sci div & biol dept, Bethel Col, 48-53; asst dir ecol res proj, Univ Utah, 53-54; assoc prof biol, Wells Col, 54-59, prof & chmn dept, 59-65. *Concurrent Pos:* Vis prof, Ward's Natural Sci Estab, 63-64 & Univ Rochester, 65-66; prof biol, Rochester Inst Technol, 66-68; coord computerized multi-media instr, Nat Technol Inst for Deaf, 68-69. *Res:* Advanced audio-visual systems; morphology and behavior study of spiders; genetics. *Mailing Add:* 2169 Baird Rd Penfield NY 14526-2419

GERJUOY, EDWARD, ATOMIC COLLISION THEORY, ENVIRONMENTAL LAW. *Current Pos:* prof, 64-82, EMER PROF PHYSICS, UNIV PITTSBURGH, 82- *Personal Data:* b Brooklyn, NY, May 19, 18; m 40, Jacqueline Reid; c Neil & David. *Educ:* City Col New York, BS, 37; Univ Calif, MA, 40, PhD(physics), 42; Univ Pittsburgh, JD, 77. *Prof Exp:* Res physicist, Off Sci Res & Develop, Columbia Univ, 42-46; asst dir, Sonar Anal Group, 46; asst prof physics, Univ Southern Calif, 46-49, assoc prof, 49-52; from assoc prof to prof, Univ Pittsburgh, 52-58; mem res staff, Gen Atomic Div, Gen Dynamics Corp, 58-61 & E H Plesset Assocs, 61-62; dir plasma & space appl physics, Defense Electronics Prod Div, RCA, 62-64, Environ Hearing Bd, 80-87. *Concurrent Pos:* Consult, Westinghouse Res Labs, Rand Corp, Inst Defense Anal, Lockheed Electronics Div, Inst Energy Anal, Oak Ridge, Tenn, 52-75, Environ Protection Agency, 77-81; mem, Adv Comt, Army Res Off, Nat Acad Sci, 65-68; mem, Health Physics Vis Comt, Oak Ridge Nat Lab, 68-74; vis fel, Joint Inst Lab Astrophys, Colo, 70; ed, Comments Atomic & Molecular Physics, 72-74; consult & counsr legal-tech issues, 76-, assoc of law firm, 78-80; mem coun, Sect Sci & Technol, Am Bar Asn, 78-80, 84-86 & 87-91; mem & chmn, Panel Public Affairs, Am Phys Soc, 78-81 & 94-96, Comt Int Freedom Scientists, 82-85; ed-in-chief, Jurimetrics, 81-87, sr ed, 87-88; mem, Nat Conf Lawyers & Scientists, AAAS, Am Bar Asn, 86-92; mem nat bd, Comt Concerned Scientists, 86-; mem coun, Rose Schmidt, Hasley & DiSalle, Law Firm, 87- *Mem:* Fel AAAS; fel Am Phys Soc; Am Bar Asn. *Res:* Atomic collision theory; technical-legal subjects especially courtroom use of scientific evidence. *Mailing Add:* Dept Physics Univ Pittsburgh Pittsburgh PA 15260. *E-Mail:* gerjuoy@vms.cis.pitt.edu

GERKE, JOHN ROYAL, DRINKING AND WASTEWATER, MARINE AQUACULTURE. *Current Pos:* INSTR, TILLAMOOK BAY COMMUNITY COL, 82-; OWNER & MGR, JOHN R GERKE PHD APPL SCI LAB, 82- *Personal Data:* b New York, NY, May 29, 27; m 48; c Arthur E, Robert H, Steven F & Carol R. *Educ:* Duke Univ, BA, 47; Univ Ill, MS, 49; Rutgers Univ, PhD, 64. *Prof Exp:* Res asst, State Water Surv, Ill, 48-51; sr scientist, E R Squibb & Sons, 51-64, Squibb fel, 62-64; sr microbiologist, Hoffman La Roche, NJ, 64-67; assoc prof microbiol, Pac Univ, 67-76; mem staff, World Book-Childcraft Int, Inc, 76-82. *Mem:* Am Chem Soc; Am Soc Microbiol; Inst Food Technologists; Audubon Native Plant Soc. *Res:* Ocular diseases, pseudomonas diseases; analytical microbiology; microbiological chemistry; microbiological transformation of steroids; antibiotics; water bacteriology and chemistry; marine aquaculture. *Mailing Add:* 1775 Vista View Dr Tillamook OR 97141

GERKEN, GEORGE MANZ, HEARING, BRAIN FUNCTION. *Current Pos:* assoc prof, 73-83, PROF COMMUN DISORDERS, UNIV TEX, DALLAS, 84-; RES SCIENTIST, CALLIER CTR COMMUN DISORDERS, 70- *Personal Data:* b Hackensack, NJ, July 12, 33; m 56; c 2. *Educ:* Mass Inst Technol, BS, 55; Univ Chicago, PhD(physiol psychol), 59. *Prof Exp:* Asst prof psychol, Univ Va, 59-67; res assoc, Callier Ctr Commun Disorders, 67-70, dir grad studies, 74-77. *Concurrent Pos:* Vis prof otolaryngol, Univ Tex Southwestern Med Ctr, 88-90. *Mem:* Am Speech-Lang Hearing Asn; Psychonomic Soc; Soc Neurosci; Am Audiol Soc; Acoustical Soc Am; Asn Res Otolaryngol. *Res:* Brain function; neuropsychology; hearing. *Mailing Add:* Univ Tex Dallas/Sch Human Develop 1966 Inwood Rd Dallas TX 75235

GERKING, SHELBY DELOS, ECOLOGY, FISH BIOLOGY. *Current Pos:* prof, 67-83, chmn dept, 67-74, EMER PROF ZOOL, ARIZ STATE UNIV, 83- *Personal Data:* b Elkhart, Ind, Nov 16, 18; m 43; c 3. *Educ:* DePauw Univ, AB, 40; Ind Univ, PhD(zool), 44. *Honors & Awards:* Mercer Award, Ecol Soc Am, 55; Silver Medal, Am Fisheries Soc; Hickman Lectr, DePauw Univ, 88. *Prof Exp:* Res assoc physiol, Ind Univ, Bloomington, 44-46, instr zool, 46-49, from asst prof to prof, 49-67, dir biol sta, 59-67, assoc dir water resources res ctr, 63-67. *Concurrent Pos:* Mem, Off Sci Res & Develop, 44; res assoc lake & stream surv, State Dept Conserv, Ind, 46-53; Ciba grant, 59; NSF grant & sci fac fel, 59; coordr, mem & dep convenor, Int Biol Prog Biol Basis of Freshwater Fish Prod, Nat Res Coun, Eng, 66; mem adv panel environ biol, NSF, 66-68; Ariz State Univ rep founding insts, Inst Ecol, 64-78; staff mem, jury panel for limnetic prize, inst limnol, Czech Acad Sci & Dept Agron, France, 72; mem Ecol Adv Comt, Sci Adv Bd, Environ Protection Agency, 75-78; consult, Commonwealth Edison, Chicago, 75-78 & Elec Power Res Inst, 84 & 85; vis scientist biol, Euratom Ispra, Italy, 74-75 & Dept Zool, Univ Cape Town, SAfrica, 82; consult, Lake Ohrid Yugoslavia Proj, Smithsonian Inst, 75-78; partic, Symp Lake Metab/Lake Mgt, Univ Uppsala, Sweden, 77; assoc ed, Environ Biol Fishes, J Fish Biol, Marine Ecol Progress Series. *Mem:* Fel AAAS; fel Am Inst Fishery Res Biol; Am Soc Zool; Am Fisheries Soc (vpres, 82-86, pres, 87-88); Ecol Soc Am (treas, 69-71); Int Soc Limnol; Am Soc Ichthy & Herp; Am Soc Limnol & Oceanog; Int Soc Limnol; Sigma Xi. *Res:* Fish populations in lakes and streams; fish nutrition; fish production; temperature tolerance; fish reproduction and stress. *Mailing Add:* 418 E Alameda Dr Tempe AZ 85282-3821

GERLACH, A(LBERT) A(UGUST), APPLIED MATHEMATICS. *Current Pos:* dir res, 70-71, head signal processing br, 71-85, SUPVRY RES PHYSICIST, US NAVAL RES LAB, WASHINGTON, DC, 85- *Personal Data:* b Columbus, Ohio, May 22, 20; m 43; c 5. *Educ:* Ohio State Univ, BS, 42; Ill Inst Technol, MS, 48 & 50, PhD, 58. *Prof Exp:* Sr engr & asst to chief engr, Rowe Eng Corp, 46-48; sr engr, Motorola, Inc, 48; res engr, Armour Res Found, Ill Inst Technol, 48-53; exec engr & mgr, Res Sect, Cook Res Labs Div, Cook Elec Co, 53-61, from asst dir labs to assoc dir labs, Tech-Ctr Div, 61-69, dir res, 69-70. *Mem:* Inst Elec & Electronics Engrs; Acoust Soc Am. *Res:* Circuit and network theory; theory of modulation; integral transforms; information theory and computers; electronic instrumentation; underwater acoustics and signal processing. *Mailing Add:* 123 Quay St Alexandria VA 22314

GERLACH, EBERHARD, MATHEMATICS. *Current Pos:* ASSOC ED, MATH REVIEWS, UNIV MICH, ANN ARBOR, 71- *Personal Data:* b Berlin, Ger, Mar 10, 34; m 66; c 2. *Educ:* Ind Univ, AM, 59; Univ Kans, PhD(math), 64. *Prof Exp:* Res asst math, Univ Kans, 62-64; asst prof, Univ BC, 64-71. *Concurrent Pos:* Fel, Univ Edinburgh, 69-70. *Mem:* Am Math Soc; Math Asn Am; Can Math Soc; Sigma Xi. *Res:* Functional analysis, in particular, Hilbert spaces, linear operators; operator algebras and operator spaces. *Mailing Add:* 904 Bruce St Ann Arbor MI 48103. *Fax:* 313-996-2916; *E-Mail:* epg@math.ams.org

GERLACH, EDWARD RUDOLPH, ANALYTICAL CHEMISTRY. *Current Pos:* chmn dept, 77-80, MEM FAC CHEM, MUSKINGUM COL, 57- *Personal Data:* b McConnelsville, Ohio, June 27, 31; m 51; c 5. *Educ:* Muskingum Col, BS, 56; Ohio State Univ, MS, 62; Walden Univ, PhD, 81. *Prof Exp:* Fac mem chem, biol & math, Batavia, Ohio schs, 56-57. *Concurrent Pos:* Res grants, Ohio Acad Sci, 65-66 & 68-69; NSF grants, 73-79; partic dept energy, Citizen's Energy Workshops, 77-79; consult hazardous chem safety, 80- *Mem:* Am Chem Soc; Coblentz Soc; Nat Sci Teachers Asn. *Res:* Trace elements in strip mine soils; zinc and copper in body fluids; laboratory and home air pollution. *Mailing Add:* 164 W High New Concord OH 43762

GERLACH, HOWARD G, JR, CLINICAL CHEMISTRY. *Current Pos:* Res chemist, Exp Sta, E I du Pont de Nemours & Co, 66-73, nat training supvr, 73-78, training mgr, Automatic Clin Anal Div, 78-80, TECH SUPPORT MGR, PROD MGT, MED PROD DEPT, E I DU PONT DE NEMOURS & CO, INC, WILMINGTON, 81- *Personal Data:* b Cheektowaga, NY, Nov 30, 40; m 64; c 2. *Educ:* Cleveland State Univ, BS, 63; Case Western Res Univ, PhD(org chem), 66. *Mem:* Am Chem Soc; Royal Soc Chem; Am Soc Training & Develop; Am Asn Clin Chem. *Res:* Identification and synthesis of alkaloids; photochromic agents; photopolymerization systems; non-silver photographic systems; international sales & divestitures of businesses. *Mailing Add:* 2603 Pennington Dr Wilmington DE 19810

GERLACH, JOHN LOUIS, DEVELOPED & IMPROVED ANALYTICAL CHEMICAL METHODS, DEVELOPED CORROSION TESTS. *Current Pos:* MGR RES & DEVELOP, NCH CORP, 67- *Personal Data:* b Quincy, Ill; c 3. *Educ:* Univ Ill, BS, 51; Univ Iowa, MS, 56; Univ Cincinnati, MS, 67. *Prof Exp:* Anal chemist, Corn Prod Co, 51-53; sr res chemist & proj leader, Nalco Chem Co, 57-66. *Mem:* Am Chem Soc; Nat Asn Corrosion Engrs; Am Water Works Asn. *Res:* Innovate and develop products to prevent scale and corrosion in boilers, cooling tower-condenser systems, chill water, and automotive cooling systems; develop new products for the clarification of water and industrial wastes; develop new inhibited acid cleaners; holder of three United States patents. *Mailing Add:* 1011 Sam Hill Irving TX 75062-3646

GERLACH, JOHN NORMAN, HYDROMETALLURGY. *Current Pos:* LEAD DESIGN CHEMIST, CHEM DIV, 87- *Personal Data:* b Portland, Ore, Aug 24, 47. *Educ:* Portland State Univ, BS, 69; Univ Calif, Riverside, PhD(chem), 74. *Prof Exp:* Phys scientist, US Army, 70-71; sr chemist, Kennecott Copper Corp, 74-78; res chemist, Phelps Dodge Corp, 79-87. *Mem:* Am Chem Soc; AAAS; Metall Soc, Am Inst Mining, Metall & Petrol Engrs. *Res:* Copper, silver, gold, nickel, cobalt, vanadium and molybdenum extractive metallurgy; solvent extraction, electrochemical processing, leaching, mineral flotation, smelter pollution control, in-situ mining and engineering economics; facilities of all scales, from laboratories to commercial plants. *Mailing Add:* Moly Corp PO Box 124 Mountain Pass CA 92366

GERLACH, ROBERT LOUIS, ELECTRON OPTICS, SURFACE SCIENCE. *Current Pos:* proj scientist, 74-85, DIR, RES & DEVELOP, PHYS ELECTRONICS DIV, PERKIN-ELMER CORP, 85- *Personal Data:* b Guthrie, Okla, Nov 16, 40; m 62; c 4. *Educ:* Northwestern Univ, BS, 64; Cornell Univ, PhD(appl physics), 69. *Honors & Awards:* IR 100 Award, Indust Res Mag, 80 & 81. *Prof Exp:* Mem tech staff surface anal, Sandia Corp, 68-73; sr engr instrument develop, Varian Assoc, 73-74. *Mem:* Am Phys Soc; Am Vacuum Soc; Electron Micros Soc Am. *Res:* Development of surface analysis instruments such as the scanning Auger microprobe, x-ray photoelectron spectrometer and secondary ion spectrometer. *Mailing Add:* 7451 NE Evergreen Pkwy Hillsboro OR 97124

GERLACH, TERRENCE MELVIN, GEOLOGY, GEOCHEMISTRY. *Current Pos:* RES GEOLOGIST & GEOCHEMIST, US GEOL SURV, 89- *Personal Data:* b New London, Wis. *Educ:* Univ Wis, BS, 64, MS, 67; Univ Ariz, PhD(geol), 74. *Prof Exp:* Field geologist, Oliver Mining Co, 65; consult geochem, Anaconda Corp, 73-74; res geologist & geochemist, Sandia Labs, 76-89. *Mem:* Am Geophys Union; Geol Soc Am. *Res:* Chemical thermodynamics of igneous processes. *Mailing Add:* US Geol Surv CVO 5400 McArthur Blvd Vancouver WA 98661

GERLING, MAX O, MATHEMATICS. *Current Pos:* PROF MATH, EASTERN ILL UNIV, 78- *Personal Data:* b Ellendale, NDak, Jan 30, 45; m 69, Petra; c Andy, Susie, Danny & Bobby. *Educ:* NDak State Univ, BA, 67; Ill State Univ, MA, 73; Fla State Univ, PhD(math educ), 77. *Prof Exp:* Math teacher, Lehr High Sch, NDak, 68-71; instr, Ill State Univ, 73, Tallahassee Community Col, 73-78. *Concurrent Pos:* Prin investr, Proj Math Develop Children, NSF, 74-77. *Mem:* Nat Coun Teachers Math; Math Asn Am; Planetary Soc. *Res:* Mathematics education; computer applications to education; mathematical education software. *Mailing Add:* Eastern Ill Univ 503 Hall Ct Charleston IL 61920. *E-Mail:* cfmog@eiu.edu

GERLOFF, GERALD CARL, BOTANY. *Current Pos:* Proj assoc, 48-49, from asst prof to prof, 49-86, EMER PROF BOT, UNIV WIS-MADISON, 86- *Personal Data:* b Aurora, Nebr, Jan 26, 20; m 49, 61; c 2. *Educ:* Univ Nebr, BS, 41; Univ Wis, PhD(soils), 48. *Mem:* AAAS; Am Soc Plant Physiol. *Res:* Mineral nutrition of plants, plant physiology and nutritional ecology. *Mailing Add:* 5 Montauk Pl Madison WI 53711

GERLT, JOHN ALAN, BIOCHEMISTRY. *Current Pos:* PROF CHEM & BIOCHEM, UNIV MD, 84- *Personal Data:* b Sycamore, Ill, July 28, 47; m 86, Jennifer M Quirk. *Educ:* Mich State Univ, BS, 69; Harvard Univ, AM, 70, PhD(biochem), 74. *Prof Exp:* asst prof chem, Yale Univ, 75-81, assoc prof chem, 81-84. *Concurrent Pos:* Jane Coffin Childs Mem Fund fel med res, 74-75; Career Development Award, NIH, 78-83; Alfred Sloan fel, 81-85. *Mem:* Am chem Soc; Am Soc Biochem & Molecular Biol; Protein Soc. *Res:* Electrophilic catalysis in enzyme-catalyzed reactions. *Mailing Add:* 419 Roger Adams Lab Univ Ill Urbana IL 61821. *Fax:* 217-244-7426; *E-Mail:* jg14@umail.umd.edu

GERMAIN, LUCIE, SKIN TISSUE ENGINEERING, STEM CELLS. *Current Pos:* ASST PROF, LAVAL UNIV, 91- *Personal Data:* b Blind River, Can, May 9, 58. *Educ:* Univ Laval, Que, BACC, 81; Laval Univ, Que, PhD(exp med), 86. *Concurrent Pos:* Scholar, Found Res, State Que, 91-; grant, Med Res Coun Can, 93. *Mem:* Soc Investigative Dermat; Soc Micros Can; Can Fedn Biol Soc. *Res:* Involved in research on skin and the culture of epidermal sheet for the treatment of burn patients; also implicated in tissue engineering of skin, blood vessel by culture; also worked on cancer, cell proliferation and differentiation. *Mailing Add:* LOEX Hosp du St-Sacrement 1050 Chemin Ste-Foy Quebec PQ G1S 4L8 Can. *Fax:* 418-682-8000; *E-Mail:* 3021lger@vml.ulaval.ca

GERMAIN, RONALD N, IMMUNOLOGY. *Current Pos:* sr investr, 82-87, CHIEF, LYMPHOCYTE BIOL SECT, LAB IMMUNOL, NAT INST ALLERGY & INFECTIOUS DIS, NIH, 87- *Personal Data:* b New York, NY, Oct 29, 48. *Educ:* Brown Univ, ScB & ScM, 70; Harvard Univ, PhD & MD, 76. *Prof Exp:* From instr to assoc prof path, Harvard Med Sch, 76-82. *Concurrent Pos:* Milton Fund Award, 77-78; assoc ed, J Imunol & J Reticuloendothiol Sos, 80-84, J Molecular & Cellular Immunol, 81-83; scholar grant, Am Cancer Soc, 81-82; guest investr, Lab Molecular Genetics, Nat Inst Child Health & Human Develop, NIH, 81-82; mem, Adv Comt Clin Invest Immunol & Immunother, Am Cancer Soc, 85-87 & Clin Rev Subpanel, Nat Inst Allergy & Infectious Dis, NIH, 87-88; dep ed, J Immunol, 87- *Mem:* Am Asn Immunologists; Sigma Xi. *Mailing Add:* Lymphocyte Biol Sect Lab Immunol NIAID NIH Bldg 10 Room 11N311 Bethesda MD 20892-1892. *Fax:* 301-496-0222

GERMAN, DWIGHT CHARLES, NEUROSCIENCE. *Current Pos:* asst prof, Dept Physiol, 75-79, from asst prof to assoc prof, Dept Physiol & Psychiat, 76-89, PROF, DEPT PSYCHIAT, UNIV TEX SOUTHWESTERN MED CTR, 89- *Personal Data:* b Elmhurst, Ill, May 28, 44; m, Haghani; c Charles & Farrah. *Educ:* Southern Methodist Univ, BA, 66; Univ Okla, MS, 67, PhD(biol psychol), 72. *Prof Exp:* Fel neurophysiol, dept physiol, Univ Wash Med Sch, 72-75. *Concurrent Pos:* Prin investr, NIMH res grants, 76- & NIH, 83-; res affil, Regional Primate Res Ctr, Med Sch, Univ Wash, 84; ed adv bd, Life Sciences, 85-89, Brain Res Bull, 89-93 & J Neural Trans, 89-; adj prof, Bayzor Col Dent, 92- *Mem:* Soc Neurosci; AAAS; Sigma Xi; Int Brain Res Orgn. *Res:* Structure and function of brain catecholamine-containing neurons; role of catecholamine containing neurons in normal and pathological behavior; Parkinsons disease schizophrenia and Alzheimers disease research. *Mailing Add:* Psychiat Univ Tex Southwestern Med Sch 5323 Harry Hines Blvd Dallas TX 75235-7200

GERMAN, JAMES LAFAYETTE, III, HUMAN CYTOGENETICS. *Current Pos:* DIR HUMAN GENETICS, NY BLOOD CTR, 68- *Personal Data:* b Grayson Co, Tex, Jan 2, 26; m 56, Margaret Fohring; c James L IV & Ann E. *Educ:* La Polytech Inst, BS, 45; Southwestern Med Col, MD, 49; Am Bd Internal Med, dipl, 58. *Prof Exp:* Intern, Cook Co Hosp, Chicago, Ill, 49-51; res physician internal med, Vet Admin Hosp, McKinney, Tex, 52-55; clin assoc, NIH, 56-58; res assoc & asst physician, Rockefeller Inst, 58-62, asst prof & assoc physician, 63; assoc prof anat & pediat, Med Col, Cornell Univ, 65-75. *Concurrent Pos:* Mem, Corp Marine Biol Lab, Woods Hole, Mass; clin prof pediat, Cornell Univ Med Col, 75-; adj prof, Rockefeller Univ, 75-86; consult genetics, Dept Path, Mem Hosp Cancer & Allied Dis, NY, 76-96; prof genetics, Cornell Univ Grad Sch Med Sci, 93-; vis prof, Univ Geneva, 82. *Mem:* Am Soc Human Genetics; Europ Soc Human Genetics; Genetics Soc Am; Am Soc Cell Biol; Sigma Xi; Harvey Soc; Am Soc Clin Invest; fel Japan Soc Promotion Sci. *Res:* Genetics of human cancer; human genetics. *Mailing Add:* NY Blood Ctr 310 E 67th St New York NY 10021

GERMAN, RANDALL MICHAEL, MATERIAL SCIENCE. *Current Pos:* FOUNDER, XFORM INC, TROY, 89-; BRUSH CHAIR MAT, PA STATE UNIV, UNIVERSITY PARK, 91- *Personal Data:* m 68, Carol J Hosmer; c Eric & Garth. *Educ:* San Jose State Univ, BS, 68; Ohio State Univ, MS, 71; Univ Calif, Davis, PhD(mat sci), 75. *Honors & Awards:* Tech Develop Award, Japan Inst Metals. *Prof Exp:* Mat scientist, Battelle Columbus Labs, 68-69; mem tech staff, Sandia Nat Lab, Livermore, Calif, 69-77; dir res & develop, Mott Metall Corp, Farmington, Conn, 77-78; dir res, J M Ney Co, Bloomfield, Conn, 78-80; Hunt prof, Rensselaer Poly Inst, Troy, NY, 80-91. *Concurrent Pos:* Chmn, Am Powder Metall Inst. *Mem:* Fel Am Soc Metals; Am Powder Metall; Minerals Metals & Mat Soc; Am Ceramic Soc; Mat Res Soc. *Res:* Research and teaching focus is on particulate materials processing; high performance magnets, tungsten-based composites, aluminum reduction cells, high temperature jet engines; catalytic converters, solder pastes, diamond-intermetallic cutting tools, high surface area capacitors, rapid prototyping systems, chemically inert filters, biomedical microdevices; x-ray telescope collimators, ferrous automotive components, high thermal conductivity microelectronic packages, and cemented carbides wear components; contributed over 320 articles to professional journals; granted patent in field. *Mailing Add:* 118 Res Bldg W Pa State Univ University Park PA 16802-6809. *Fax:* 814-863-8211; *E-Mail:* kmg4@psu.edu

GERMAN, VICTOR FREDERICK, PEDIATRICS. *Current Pos:* asst prof, 81-86, ASSOC PROF, DEPT PEDIAT, UNIV TEX HEALTH SCI CTR, SAN ANTONIO, 86- *Personal Data:* US citizen. *Educ:* Univ Richmond, BS 58; Univ Ill, PhD(org chem), 63. *Hon Degrees:* MD, Univ Chicago, 75. *Prof Exp:* NIH fel, Univ Calif, Berkeley, 63-64; staff mem, Robins rep, Math & Sci Ctr, Richmond Pub Sch, Va Commonwealth Univ, 64-72; intern & resident, Duke Univ, 75-77, asst prof, Div Allergy, 77-81. *Concurrent Pos:* Sr res chemist, A H Robins, 64-72; assoc staff physician, Infant Transport Serv, Univ Calif, 77-79 & Berkeley Health Dept, 80; emergency physician, Med Ctr, Children's Hosp, Oakland Calif, 77-81; fel cardiovasc res & perinatal & pulmonary med, Univ Calif, San Francisco, 77-81; physician, Berkeley Pub

Health, 79-81; assoc staff mem, Dept Pediat, Kaiser Permanent Med Ctr, 80-81. *Mem:* Sigma Xi; Am Physiol Soc; Am Soc Microbiol; Am Thoracic Soc; Am Acad Pediat. *Res:* Mechanisms of gram bacterial adherence to respiratory tract epithelia; alveolar marcophage function (1) in vivo (2) in vitro culture; airway secretions; biosynthesis and release; tracheal submucosal gland physiology gram negative. *Mailing Add:* Dept Pediat Univ Tex Health Sci Ctr 7703 Floyd Curl Dr San Antonio TX 78284-7815. *Fax:* 210-567-2490

GERMANE, GEOFFREY JAMES, MECHANICAL ENGINEERING. *Current Pos:* From asst prof to assoc prof, 79-92, dept chair, 91-95, PROF MECH ENG, BRIGHAM YOUNG UNIV 93- *Personal Data:* b Cleveland Heights, Ohio, July 3, 50; m 76; c 7. *Educ:* Rose Hulman Inst Technol, BS, 72, MS, 75; Brigham Young Univ, PhD(mech eng), 78. *Honors & Awards:* Teetor Award, Soc Automotive Engrs, 81. *Concurrent Pos:* Prin investr, Brigham Young Univ, Utah Power & Light, 79-, US Dept Energy, 80-; consult, Hercules, Inc, 80-81, Utah Power & Light Co, 81-, Collision Safety Eng, 81-90, Carvern Petrochem, 80-84, UHI Corp, 80-, Germane Eng, 91- *Mem:* Soc Automotive Engrs; Sigma Xi. *Res:* Internal combustion engine computer control; alcohol fuels and lean limit combustion; coal-fired power plant fires and explosions prevention; basic combustion and pollutant formation studies of fossil fuels, automotive safety. *Mailing Add:* Brigham Young Univ Dept Mech Eng 242 CB Provo UT 84602

GERMANN, ALBERT FREDERICK OTTOMAR, II, ANIMAL NUTRITION. *Current Pos:* Vpres, 58-77, PRES NUTRIT RES ASSOCS, INC, 77- *Personal Data:* b Cleveland, Ohio, Jan 4, 29; m 54, Jean A Ruprecht; c Gail M (Murphy), Beth D (Berta) & Paula J (Andrews). *Educ:* Purdue Univ, BS, 51, MS, 56, PhD, 58. *Mem:* AAAS; Am Soc Animal Sci. *Res:* Relationship of lysine requirement to protein level of weanling swine; nutrient requirements of the chinchilla and rabbit. *Mailing Add:* 307 W Columbia St South Whitley IN 46787

GERMANN, RICHARD P(AUL), ORGANIC CHEMISTRY, APPLICATION RESEARCH. *Current Pos:* PRES, RAMTEK INT LTD, 73- *Personal Data:* b Ithaca, NY, Apr 3, 18; m 42, Malinda J Plietz; c Cheranne L. *Educ:* Univ Colo, BA, 39. *Hon Degrees:* PhD, Hamilton State Univ, 73. *Prof Exp:* Chief anal chemist, Taylor Refining Co, Tex, 43-44; res develop chemist, Alrose Chem Co Div, Geigy Chem Corp, 52-55; new prod develop chemist, Res Div, W R Grace & Co, Md, 55-60; chief chemist, Soap & Cosmetic Div, G H Packwood Mfg Co, 60-61; coordr chem prod develop, Abbott Labs, Ill, 61-71; consult chemist, 71-72; pres, Germann Int Ltd, 73-82. *Concurrent Pos:* Consult, Chem Dept, Bowling Green State Univ, 88-89. *Mem:* fel AAAS; Am Chem Soc; Am Pharmaceut Asn; Am Asn Textile Chemists & Colorists; Chem Soc London; Com Develop Asn; Chem Mkt Res Asn; Sigma Xi. *Res:* Vitamin nutrition; trace element use in growth of agricultural crops; biocides; pollution control; organic, pharmaceutical, polymer, petroleum, leather, textile, agricultural, dye, paint, detergent, insecticides and biocides, by-product recovery. *Mailing Add:* 6 Vinewood Dr Norwalk OH 44857

GERMANY, ARCHIE HERMAN, ORGANIC CHEMISTRY. *Current Pos:* RETIRED. *Personal Data:* b Dixon, Miss, Nov 18, 17; wid; c Jean (Mosley), Betty (Baugh) & Alice (Nettles). *Educ:* Miss Col, BA, 39; Univ NC, PhD(org chem), 43. *Hon Degrees:* DSc, Miss Col, 83. *Prof Exp:* Lab asst chem, NC, 39-41; res assoc metall lab, Chicago, 43-44; chemist, Clinton Labs, Oak Ridge, 44-46; from assoc prof chem to prof, Miss Col, 46-60, head dept, 60-61, chmn div sci & math, 61-80. *Res:* Synthetic organic chemistry. *Mailing Add:* 803 E Leak Clinton MS 39056

GERMINARIO, RALPH JOSEPH, BIOLOGICAL CHEMISTRY, MOLECULAR ASPECTS OF HUMAN IMMUNODEFICIENCY VIRUS REPLICATION. *Current Pos:* Fel cell genetics, 70-74, STAFF INVESTR, CELL BIOL LAB, LADY DAVIS INST MED RES, 74- *Personal Data:* b Jersey City, NJ, Oct 27, 43; m 76, Susan Colby; c Rachel-Anne C & Giuseppe. *Educ:* Seton Hall Univ, BA, 65, MS, 67; Univ NDak, PhD(microbiol), 70. *Concurrent Pos:* Instr, Dept Biol, Concordia Univ, 75-79, adj prof, 79-; assoc mem, Dept Med, McGill Univ, 78-89, adj prof, 90-91, asst prof, 91-92, assoc prof, 92-, assoc mem, AIDS Ctr, 93- *Mem:* Am Soc Microbiol; Am Soc Cell Biol; NY Acad Sci; Tissue Cult Asn; Can Soc Clin Invest; Cell Cycle Soc; Can Asn Geront. *Res:* Insulin action genetic control; regulation of sugar transport; signal transduction; apoptosis. *Mailing Add:* Lady Davis Inst Med Res 3755 Cote St Catherine Rd Montreal PQ H3T 1E2 Can. *Fax:* 514-340-7502

GERMINO, FELIX JOSEPH, FOOD CHEMISTRY. *Current Pos:* PRES, F GERMINO & ASSOCS INC, 83- *Personal Data:* b New York, NY, July 14, 30; m 52; c 7. *Educ:* Fordham Univ, BS, 52; Univ Chicago, MBA, 74. *Prof Exp:* Food inspector, Food Inspection Serv, USDA, NY, 52; asst chemist, Gen Foods Tech Ctr, 54-59; assoc chemist, Morehead Patterson Res Ctr, Am Mach & Foundry Co, 59-64; proj leader carbohydrate chem, Corn Prod Co, Argo, 64-71; dir, com dev CPC Int, Inc, 64-72; sect leader foods & paper textiles, 65-71, asst mgr, 71-72; assoc dir, Quaker Oats Co, 72-74, dir pet foods, 74-76, vpres res & develop pet foods, 76-78, vpres human foods, 78-82. *Mem:* Am Chem Soc; Inst Food Technol; Indust Res Inst; Coun Foreign Relations; Am Asn Cereal Chem. *Res:* Physical structure of starch; synthesis of polysaccharide derivatives for use in textiles, paper and food related fields; physical chemistry of starch and starch fractions; environmental sciences; food sugar. *Mailing Add:* 12414 83rd Ave Palos Park IL 60464

GERMROTH, TED CALVIN, CELLULOSE & WOOD CHEMISTRY. *Current Pos:* SR RES CHEMIST, EASTMAN CHEM DIV, EASTMAN KODAK, 79- *Personal Data:* b Latrobe, Pa, Feb 21, 52; m 75; c 2. *Educ:* Col William & Mary, Va, BS, 74; Univ Calif, Berkeley, MS, 76, PhD(org chem), 79. *Mem:* Am Chem Soc. *Res:* Derivativization of cellulose and wood products to prepare commercially useful products such as cellulose esters and ethers; wood; pulping; synthetic organic and natural product chemistry. *Mailing Add:* 1974 Cooks Valley Rd Kingsport TN 37664-2914

GERNER, EUGENE WILLARD, CELL BIOLOGY, RADIOBIOLOGY. *Current Pos:* from asst prof to assoc prof, 74-83, PROF, DEPT RADIATION ONCOL & BIOCHEM, HEALTH SCI CTR, UNIV ARIZ, 83- *Personal Data:* b Sheboygan, Wis, Aug 8, 47; m 82, Sandra A Eberlein; c Stephanie, Erica H, Kyle H & Camren. *Educ:* Univ Wis-Madison, BA, 69, MS, 70; Univ Tex Grad Sch Biomed Sci, Houston, PhD(biophys), 74. *Honors & Awards:* Res Award, Radiation Res Soc, 88. *Prof Exp:* Comput programmer, High Energy Physics Dept, Univ Wis-Madison, 67-69, med physicist, Radiol Dept, 69-71; fel biophys, Univ Tex Grad Sch Biomed Sci, Houston, 71-74. *Mem:* Radiation Res Soc; Am Soc Biol Chemists; Am Asn Cancer Res; Am Soc Therapeut Radiol & Oncol. *Res:* Cellular and molecular cancer biology, emphasizing studies on the biochemical controls of mammalian cell cycle kinetics and cellular responses to stress, carcmogenesis. *Mailing Add:* Radiation Oncol Dept Univ Ariz Cancer Ctr Rm 0943 1501 N Campbell Ave Tucson AZ 85724-0001. *Fax:* 520-626-2284; *E-Mail:* gerner@azcc.arizona.edu

GERNS, FRED RUDOLPH, POLYMER CHEMISTRY. *Current Pos:* RETIRED. *Personal Data:* b Mannheim, Ger, Nov 28, 25; nat US; m 56, Eleanor Ulrich; c Jeffrey & Edward. *Educ:* Ohio State Univ, BA, 48; Syracuse Univ, MS, 51; Univ Va, PhD(chem), 59. *Prof Exp:* Jr med chemist, Smith, Kline & French Labs, 52-56; sr org chemist, Burroughs Wellcome & Co, Inc, 59-63; chemist, Chas Pfizer & Co, Conn, 63-65; sr res chemist, Great Lakes Chem Corp, 65-82, res assoc, 82-91. *Mem:* Am Chem Soc; Sigma Xi. *Res:* Nitrogen and sulfur heterocycles; halogen chemistry; polymers; photoresists. *Mailing Add:* 248 Connolly St West Lafayette IN 47906-2724

GERO, ALEXANDER, chemistry; deceased, see previous edition for last biography

GEROCH, ROBERT PAUL, THEORETICAL PHYSICS. *Current Pos:* assoc prof, 71-75, PROF PHYSICS & MATH, ENRICO FERMI INST, UNIV CHICAGO, 75- *Personal Data:* b Akron, Ohio, June 1, 42. *Educ:* Mass Inst Technol, BS, 63; Princeton Univ, PhD(physics), 67. *Prof Exp:* Air Force Off Sci Res fel, Birkbeck Col, 67-68; NSF fel, 68-69; fel physics, Syracuse Univ, 69-70; assoc prof, Univ Tex, Austin, 70-71. *Res:* General relativity. *Mailing Add:* Dept Physics-Math RI 365 Univ Chicago 5640 Ellis Ave Chicago IL 60637

GEROLIMATOS, BARBARA, ENDOCRINOLOGY. *Current Pos:* assoc dir clin & sci affairs, 89-93, DIR CLIN DEVELOP, PFIZER CONSUMER HEALTH CARE, 93- *Personal Data:* b New York, NY, July 13, 50; m 92, Alan M Brown; c Sara & Julia. *Educ:* Fordham Univ, BS, 72; Columbia Univ, MPhil, 76, PhD(biochem), 79. *Prof Exp:* Fel, Dept Surg, Col Physicians & Surgeons, Columbia Univ, 78, NIH fel trainee biochem & endocrinol, Dept Obstet & Gynec, 79-83; med writer, Ayerst Int, 83-84, group leader, 84-86, clin monitor, Ayerst Labs, 86-88; mgr pharmaceut, Boehringer Ingelheim, 88-89. *Concurrent Pos:* Mem & cofounder, Rape Crisis Intervention Prog, Columbia Med Ctr, 78-83; secy, Metrop NY Chap, Asn Women Sci, 82-84, vpres, 84-85, pres, 86-89; chairperson, Career Coun Comt, Scholarship Winners Alumni Asn, IBEW Educ & Cult Fund, 85-90; vchair, Women in Sci Comt, NY Acad Sci, 90-95. *Mem:* Asn Women Sci; NY Acad Sci. *Res:* Drug development and clinical trials in areas of consumer health care products. *Mailing Add:* 350 W 24th St Apt 14G New York NY 10011. *Fax:* 212-573-1186; *E-Mail:* gerolb@pfizer.com

GERONE, PETER JOHN, VIROLOGY. *Current Pos:* DIR, TULANE REGIONAL PRIMATE RES CTR, TULANE UNIV, LA, 71-, ADJ PROF IMMUNOL & MICROBIOL, 73-, ADJ PROF TROP MED, 77- *Personal Data:* b Oakfield, NY, Apr 11, 28; m 51; c 7. *Educ:* State Univ NY, Buffalo, BA, 49, MA, 51; Johns Hopkins Univ, ScD(microbiol), 54. *Honors & Awards:* Dept Army Meritorious Civilian Serv Award, 68. *Prof Exp:* Instr biol, State Univ NY, Buffalo, 50-51; supvry microbiologist, US Army Biol Labs, 54-71. *Concurrent Pos:* Dir, Gulf South Res Inst, 78-89. *Mem:* Int Primatol Soc; Sigma Xi; Am Soc Primatologists; Am Soc Microbiol. *Res:* Infectious diseases in nonhuman primates. *Mailing Add:* Tulane Regional Primate Res Ctr Tulane Univ 18703 Three Rivers Rd Covington LA 70433

GERONIMO, JEFFREY S, PHYSICS, PHYSICAL MATHEMATICS. *Current Pos:* from vis asst prof to assoc prof, 77-91, PROF, SCH MATH, GA INST TECHNOL, 91- *Personal Data:* b Cairo, Egypt, Feb 25, 49; US citizen. *Educ:* State Univ NY, Albany, BS, 72; Rockefeller Univ, PhD(physics), 77. *Prof Exp:* Asst prof, Dept Biophys, Rockefeller Univ, 78-79. *Concurrent Pos:* NSF grantee, 80-84, 87, 88, 90-91 & 94-96; NATO postdoctoral fel, 82-83; vis asst prof, Phys Theoret Ctr Nuclear Sudies, Saclay, France, 82-84; Fulbright grantee, Pierre & Marie Curie Univ, Paris, 96-97. *Mem:* Am Math Soc; Math Asn Am; Soc Indust & Appl Math. *Res:* Applied mathematics in scattering theory, orthogonal polynomials, dynamical systems, interated maps, numerical analysis and wavelets; contributed numerous publications to professional journals. *Mailing Add:* Sch Math Ga Inst Technol Atlanta GA 30332-0160

GEROULD, SARAH, ENVIRONMENTAL TOXICOLOGY ECOSYSTEMS. *Current Pos:* BUR ECOSYST COORDR, DEPT INTERIOR, US GEOL SURV, VA, 94- *Educ:* Univ Wis, MS, 78; Cornell Univ, PhD(nat resources & environ toxicol), 85. *Prof Exp:* Environ toxicologist, US Fish & Wildlife Serv, 85-90; biologist, Off Water Qual, 90-94. *Mem:* Soc Environ Toxicol & Chem. *Mailing Add:* US Geog Surv MS918 Nat Ctr Reston VA 20192. *Fax:* 703-648-6683; *E-Mail:* sgerould@usgs.gov

GEROW, CLARE WILLIAM, ORGANIC POLYMER CHEMISTRY. *Current Pos:* RETIRED. *Personal Data:* b Detroit, Mich, Oct 8, 27; m 51; c 13. *Educ:* Univ Detroit, BS, 51; Iowa State Univ, PhD(org chem), 56. *Prof Exp:* Res polymer chemist, Film Dept, E I du Pont de Nemours & Co, 56-61, tech mkt eval investr, 61-63, res polymer chemist, 63-67, staff scientist, Yerkes Res & Develop Lab, 67-71, staff scientist, Spruance Film Plant, 71-76, res assoc, Spruance Polymer Prod & Res Plant, 76-81, res assoc, 81-84, sr res assoc, Spruance Fibers Plant, 84-90. *Concurrent Pos:* Mem adj fac, Va Commonwealth Univ, 71-89. *Mem:* Am Chem Soc. *Res:* Organogermanium and organosilicon chemistry; polymer chemistry, including polyolefins, polythio ketones and aldehydes and polyimides; modification, formulation and application of barrier coatings to cellulosic and polyester films; polyaramid chemistry. *Mailing Add:* 12809 Walton Lake Dr Midlothian VA 23113

GERPHEIDE, JOHN H, MECHANICAL ENGINEERING, AERONAUTICS. *Current Pos:* PROJ MGR, MAGELLAN. *Personal Data:* b Manitowoc, Wis, Sept 17, 25; m 51; c 3. *Educ:* Calif Inst Tech, BS, 45, MS, 48. *Prof Exp:* Engr, US Naval Ord Test Sta, Inyokern, 46-47; engr, Calif Inst Technol, 48-53, proj engr, 53-59, flight test engr, 54-55, sect mgr spacecraft develop, 60-62, consult Apollo support, 62-63, staff specialist proj planning, 64, proj mgr develop Mars Landing Craft, 67-68, sect mgr syst design & integration, 64-73, proj mgr solar elec propulsion, 73-74, Sea Satellite syst mgr, Jet Propulsion Lab, 74-79, chief engr, flight projs, 79-80, proj mgr, Venus Orbiting Imaging Radar, Jet Propulsion Lab, Calif Inst Technol, 80- *Mem:* Sigma Xi; Planetary Soc. *Res:* Development of advanced designs, new technologies and system approaches to exploration of space. *Mailing Add:* 2165 Queensberry Rd Pasadena CA 91104

GERRARD, JOHN WATSON, PEDIATRICS & ALLERGY. *Current Pos:* RETIRED. *Personal Data:* b Kasenga, Rhodesia, Apr 14, 16; m 41, Betty Whitehead; c 3. *Educ:* Oxford Univ, BA, 38, BM, BCh, 41, DM, 51; FRCP(C), 56; FRCP, 68. *Honors & Awards:* John Scott Award, Philadelphia City Trusts, 62; Enuresis Found Award, 68; Ross Award, Can Pediat Soc, 85. *Prof Exp:* Lectr, Univ Birmingham, 48-51, chief asst, 51-55; head, Dept Pediat, Univ Sask, 55-71, prof, 55-83, emer prof pediat, Univ Hosp, 83-87. *Mem:* Can Pediat Soc; Am Acad Pediat; Am Acad Allergy; Am Col Allergists; Am Acad Environ Med. *Res:* Gastrointestinal and genito-urinary allergies. *Mailing Add:* 809 Colony St Saskatoon SK S7N 0S2 Can

GERRARD, JON M, HEMOSTASIS, THROMBOSIS. *Current Pos:* SECY STATE, WESTERN ECON DIVERSIFICATION, 96- *Personal Data:* b Oct 13, 47; Can citizen; m 72, Naomi Oberholtzer; c Pauline, Charles & Tom. *Educ:* Univ Sask, BA, 67; McGill Univ, Montreal, MMCM, 71; Univ Minn, PhD(med), 78; Am Acad Pediat, cert, 76; FRCP(C), 82. *Honors & Awards:* Scientist Award, Med Res Coun Can, 85; Frederick & Frances Hammerstrom Award, 96. *Prof Exp:* Intern pediat, Univ Minn, 71-72, resident, 72-73, fel, 73-76, from instr to asst prof, 76-80; from asst prof to prof, Dept Pediat & Child Health, Univ Man Winnipeg, 80-93, dir res & clin invest, 84-93, head, Sect Pediat Hemat, 85-93. *Concurrent Pos:* Estab investr, Am Heart Asn, 78; adj prof zool, Univ Man, Winnipeg, 85-91; secy state sci, Res & Develop, Govt Can, 93- *Res:* Blood platelet and a role in bleeding and clotting disorders; basic mechanism of platelet cell biology; applied studies of patients with bleeding disorders; published papers on other blood cells including neutrophils and natural killer cells; bald eagles; published papers and books on bald eagles. *Mailing Add:* RR 1 Box 113 Headingley MB R0H 0J0 Can

GERRARD, THERESA LEE, MONOCYTES, ANTIGEN PRESENTATION. *Current Pos:* SR STAFF FEL, US FOOD & DRUG ADMIN, 84- *Educ:* Med Col Va, PhD(microbiol & immunol), 80. *Mailing Add:* Amgen Boulder 3200 Walnut St Boulder CO 80301. *Fax:* 303-541-1354

GERRARD, THOMAS AQUINAS, GEOLOGY. *Current Pos:* from asst prof to assoc prof, 66-76, PROF GEOL, WITTENBURG UNIV, 76- CHMN DEPT, 73- *Personal Data:* b La Crosse, Wis, Feb 7, 33; m 58; c 3. *Educ:* Univ Cincinnati, BS, 56; Miami Univ, Ohio, MS, 59; Univ Ariz, PhD(geol), 64. *Prof Exp:* Explor geologist, Chevron Oil Co, 64-66. *Concurrent Pos:* Lectr, Tulane Univ, 65-66; geol consult, Minerals Dept, Exxon Co, USA, 69-79. *Mem:* Am Asn Petrol Geol; Soc Econ Paleont & Mineral; Nat Asn Geol Teachers; Sigma Xi; Am Inst Prof Geologists. *Res:* Sedimentary petrology and geochemistry; regional stratigraphy; marine geology. *Mailing Add:* Dept Geol Wittenberg Univ Springfield OH 45501

GERRATH, JOSEPH FREDRICK, BOTANY, PHYCOLOGY. *Current Pos:* Asst prof, 68-80, ASSOC PROF BOT, UNIV GUELPH, 80- *Personal Data:* b Saskatoon, Sask, June 25, 36; m 66; c 2. *Educ:* Univ BC, BA, 59, BSc, 63, MSc, 65, PhD(bot), 68. *Mem:* Can Bot Asn (treas, 75-77); Int Phycol Soc; Phycol Soc Am; Brit Phycol Soc; Sigma Xi. *Res:* Taxonomy and cytology of desmids. *Mailing Add:* Dept Bot Univ Guelph Guelph ON N1G 2W1 Can

GERRING, IRVING, ENVIRONMENTAL SCIENCES, PUBLIC HEALTH ADMINISTRATION. *Current Pos:* RETIRED. *Personal Data:* b Bridgeport, Conn, Apr 16, 09; m 44; c 3. *Educ:* Univ Conn, BS, 31; Columbia Univ, MSPH, 35. *Prof Exp:* Teacher pub sch, Conn, 32; dir, Div Environ Health, Bridgeport, 35-39; assoc pub health engr, USPHS, 41-43, sanitarian, 44-46, exec secy, Pub Health & Med Res Admin, 47-56, exec secy, Parasitol, Radiation & Pop Res Study Sects, 56-71, health scientist adminr, Div Res Grants, NIH, 71-73. *Concurrent Pos:* Spec asst, War Assets Admin, 47. *Mem:* Fel Am Pub Health Asn. *Res:* Bacteriology; public health; air and water pollution; occupational health; food technology. *Mailing Add:* 7 Pinecrest Ct Greenbelt MD 20770

GERRISH, JAMES RAMSAY, GRASSLAND ECOLOGY. *Current Pos:* Res assoc, 81-84, res assoc & supt, 84-87, RES ASST PROF, FORAGE SYST RES CTR, UNIV MO, COLUMBIA, 88- *Personal Data:* b Centralia, Ill, Feb 27, 56; m 78; c 3. *Educ:* Univ Ill, BS, 78; Univ Ky, MS, 81. *Concurrent Pos:* Mem, Am Forage & Grassland Coun. *Mem:* Am Soc Agron. *Res:* Systems analysis of grassland ecosystems grazed by domestic ruminants; plant community dynamics as impacted by grazing behavior. *Mailing Add:* MU FSRC 21262 Genoa Rd Linneus MO 64653

GERRITSEN, ALEXANDER NICOLAAS, METAL PHYSICS, LOW TEMPERATURE PHYSICS. *Current Pos:* vis prof, 54, assoc prof, 56, prof, 60, EMER PROF PHYSICS, PURDUE UNIV, 79- *Personal Data:* b The Hague, Netherlands, Nov 29, 13; m 43, Jacqueline Koelhaas; c Rob & Jeroen. *Educ:* State Univ, Leiden, Drs, 37, Dr, 48. *Prof Exp:* Govt asst physics, State Univ, Leiden, 37, head & instr physics lab, 43, scientist, Found Fundamental Res Matter, 47, sr scientist, 47-56. *Mem:* Fel Am Phys Soc; Netherlands Asn Sci Invest (secy, 48-53). *Res:* Transport phenomena in metals; low temperatures. *Mailing Add:* 100 Wheeler Lane West Lafayette IN 47906

GERRITSEN, FRANCISCUS, coastal & ocean engineering, for more information see previous edition

GERRITSEN, GEORGE CONTANT, PHYSIOLOGY. *Current Pos:* RETIRED. *Personal Data:* b Passaic, NJ, Dec 28, 26; m 50; c 2. *Educ:* Hope Col, AB, 50, Mich State Univ, MS, 55, PhD(physiol), 60. *Prof Exp:* Res instr agr biochem, Mich State Univ, 50-55; sr scientist, Mead Johnson & Co, 60-62; res scientist, Diabetes Res Dept, Upjohn Co, 62-90. *Mem:* AAAS; Am Diabetes Asn; Soc Exp Biol & Med. *Res:* Etiology and pathogenesis of diabetes; hypoglycemic agents; metabolic interrelationships between carbohydrate and lipid metabolism; genetics of diabetic animals and prediabets. *Mailing Add:* 114 Walnut Woods Court Plainwell MI 49080

GERRITSEN, HENDRIK JURJEN, PHYSICS, CHEMISTRY. *Current Pos:* assoc prof, 67-72, PROF PHYSICS, BROWN UNIV, 72- *Personal Data:* b The Hague, Neth, Jan 19, 27; m 72; c 3. *Educ:* State Univ Leiden, BS, 48, PhD(physics, chem), 55. *Prof Exp:* Asst prof low temperature res, State Univ Leiden, 52-55; res physicist, Res Labs, Radio Corp Am, Zurich, 55-57, res physicist & mem tech staff low temperature magnetism, 57-67. *Concurrent Pos:* Assoc prof, Chalmers Univ Technol, Sweden, 61-62; vis prof physics, State Univ Utrecht, Neth, 74 & State Univ Karlsruhe, WGer, 81-82; Int Res & Exchanges Bd Scholar, Lithuanian Soviet Socialist Repub, 84; Fulbright prof, Roshock, Ger, 95-96. *Mem:* Swiss Phys Soc; Sigma Xi; Am Optical Soc; Fedn Am Scientists; Am Friends Serv Comt; Union Concerned Scientists. *Res:* Radio astronomy; microwave properties of solids, particularly at low temperatures and in magnetic materials; gaseous electronics; optics, spectroscopy; nonlinear optics and holography; optical properties of ternary III and V semiconductor layers; plasma dynamics in semiconductors on picosecond time scale; holographic optical elements; liquid crystals; optical properties; experiments and theoretical studies on diffraction gratings. *Mailing Add:* Dept Physics Brown Univ Providence RI 02912. *Fax:* 401-863-2024; *E-Mail:* gerritsen@physics.brown.edu

GERRITSEN, JEROEN, APPLIED AQUATIC ECOLOGY, ECOLOGICAL RISK ASSESSMENT. *Current Pos:* sr scientist, 92, PRIN SCIENTIST, TETRA TECH INC, 93- *Personal Data:* b Leiden, Neth, Nov 6, 51; m 79, Jingyee Kou; c Tristan & Alida. *Educ:* Antioch Co, BS, 74; Johns Hopkins Univ, MA, 76, PhD(ecol & evolution), 78. *Prof Exp:* Res fel, dept zool, Univ Ga, 78-80, proj mgr, Okefenokee Ecosyst Invest, 81-84, res assoc & asst ecologist, Inst Ecol, Univ Ga, 80-87; sr scientist, Versar Inc, 87-92, prog mgr, 89-92. *Concurrent Pos:* Prin investr, NSF grants, 85-87; peer reviewer, Nat Acid Precipitation Assessment Prog, 84; dir, Flow Cytometry Facil, Univ Ga, 85-87; prin investr, contracts, 87- *Mem:* Estuarine Res Fedn; Am Soc Limnol & Oceanog; Ecol Soc Am; NAm Lake Mgt Soc; Soc Environ Toxicol & Chem; Soc Risk Anal. *Res:* Wetland ecology; long-term ecological monitoring and data analysis; watershed and landscape scale response to environmental perturbation; cost-effective methods for biological assessment of aquatic resources; ecological risk assessments. *Mailing Add:* Tetra Tech, Inc 10045 Red Run Blvd No 110 Owings Mills MD 21117. *Fax:* 410-356-9005; *E-Mail:* jgerrits@mail.bcpl.lib.md.us

GERRITSEN, MARY ELLEN, ALLERGY & INFLAMMATION, CARDIOVASCULAR PHYSIOLOGY. *Current Pos:* sr staff scientist, 90-93, PRIN STAFF SCIENTIST, MILES INC, 93- *Personal Data:* b Calgary, Alta, Can, Sept 20, 53; m 80, Thomas Parks; c Odin, Kristen & Madelene. *Educ:* Univ Calgary, BSc, 75, PhD(pharmacol), 78. *Honors & Awards:* Pharm Award, Microcirculatory Soc, 83, Mary Weideman Award, 84. *Prof Exp:* Teaching fel pharmacol, Univ Calif, San Diego, 78-80; from asst prof to assoc prof physiol, NY Med Col, 81-90. *Concurrent Pos:* Ed-in-chief, Microcirculation, Am J Physiol, Circ Res, Cardiovasc Pathobiol. *Mem:*

Microcirculatory Soc; Am Physiol Soc; Am Soc Pharmacol & Exp Therapeut; Am Soc Invest Path; Soc Leukocyte Biol; Am Vascular Biol. *Res:* Hormonal regulation of microvascular endothelial cell function; roles of inflammatory mediators and arachidonic acid metabolites; glucocorticoid and insulin actions on microvascular endothelial cell metabolism; leukocyte adhesion; molecular mechanisms of arthritis; vascular pathology, transcriptional regulation of gene expression. *Mailing Add:* Inst Bone & Joint Disorders Bayer Corp 400 Morgan Lane West Haven CT 06516. *Fax:* 203-937-6923

GERRITY, ROSS GORDON, EXPERIMENTAL PATHOLOGY, CARDIOVASCULAR DISEASES. *Current Pos:* DIR PATH, MED COL GA, 90- *Personal Data:* b Regina, Sask, May 27, 45; m 69; c 3. *Educ:* Univ Sask, BA, 67, MA, 69; Australian Nat Univ, PhD(exp path), 72. *Prof Exp:* Fel path, McMaster Univ, 73-75, asst prof, 75-76; sr staff mem cardiovasc dis res, Cleveland Clin Found, 76-87, St Vincent's Res Ctr, 87-90. *Concurrent Pos:* Fel, Med Res Coun Can, 73-74; consult electron microscopist, McMaster Univ, 73-74, lectr path, 74; res fel, Ont Heart Found, 75-76; dir electron micros facil & microscopist, Fac Health Sci, McMaster Univ, 75-76. *Mem:* Australian Soc Exp Path; Electron Micros Soc Can; fel Am Heart Asn. *Res:* Structure and function of the vascular wall, particularly the relationship between endothelial permeability and vascular disease and the biology of the smooth muscle cell in vivo and in vitro. *Mailing Add:* Dept Path Med Col Ga 1120 15th St BF221 Augusta GA 30912. *Fax:* 706-721-2358

GERRODETTE, TIMOTHY, CONSERVATION BIOLOGY. *Current Pos:* Fishery biologist, Honolulu, 83-89, OPERS RES ANALYST, NAT MARINE FISHERIES SERV, LA JOLLA, 89- *Personal Data:* b May 3, 46; m 96, Pamela Page; c Tien & Tan-ya. *Educ:* Carleton Col, BA, 68; Univ Calif, San Diego, PhD(oceanog), 79. *Mem:* Soc Conserv Biol; Soc Marine Mammal; Wildlife Soc. *Res:* Conservation and management of marine mammals; abundance and population dynamics of rare species. *Mailing Add:* SW Fisheries Sci Ctr F-SWC PO Box 271 La Jolla CA 92038-0271. *Fax:* 619-546-7003; *E-Mail:* timg@ucsd.edu

GERRY, EDWARD T, QUANTUM ELECTRONICS. *Current Pos:* PRES & CHIEF OPER OFFICER, W J SCHAEFFER ASSOCS, 75- *Personal Data:* b Boston, Mass, Sept 7, 38; m 60; c 2. *Educ:* Col William & Mary, BS, 59; Cornell Univ, MS, 62; Mass Inst Technol, PhD(nuclear eng), 65. *Prof Exp:* Chmn, Laser Res Comt, Avco Everett Res Lab, 61-70, dir, Laser Prog Off, 70-71; chief, Laser Technol Div, Advan Res Proj Agency, Dept Defense, 71-75. *Mem:* AAAS; Am Phys Soc. *Res:* Physics of fully ionized plasmas; physics of gas lasers; chemical kinetics. *Mailing Add:* 1549 N 22nd St Arlington VA 22209-1131

GERRY, MICHAEL CHARLES LEWIS, CHEMICAL PHYSICS, SPECTROCHEMISTRY. *Current Pos:* from asst prof to assoc prof, 67-73, PROF CHEM, UNIV BC, 81- *Personal Data:* b Victoria, BC, Nov 8, 39; m 67. *Educ:* Univ BC, BA, 60, MSc, 62; Cambridge Univ, PhD(phys chem), 65. *Honors & Awards:* Union Carbide Award for Chem Educ, Chem Inst, Can, 87; Herzberg Award, Spectros Soc, Can, 88. *Prof Exp:* Fel physics, Duke Univ, 65-67. *Concurrent Pos:* DFG guest prof, Univ Kiel & Munich, 88-89. *Mem:* Royal Soc Chem; Chem Inst Can; Can Asn Physicists. *Res:* Electron spin resonance of irradiated solids; microwave spectroscopy of gases; nuclear quadrupole resonance spectroscopy; high resolution infrared spectroscopy of gases. *Mailing Add:* Dept Chem Univ BC 2036 Main Mall Vancouver BC V6T 1Z1 Can

GERRY, RICHARD WOODMAN, POULTRY NUTRITION. *Current Pos:* RETIRED. *Personal Data:* b Lewiston, Maine, Nov 23, 14; wid; c 3. *Educ:* Univ Maine, BS, 38; Purdue Univ, MS, 46, PhD(animal nutrit), 48. *Prof Exp:* Asst poultry husb, Purdue Univ, 43-48; from assoc prof to prof poultry sci, Univ Maine, Orono, 48-84, emer prof, 85-86. *Mem:* Poultry Sci Asn; World Poultry Sci Asn; Sigma Xi. *Res:* Nutritive value of forest and industrial waste products, potato products, marine products and cereal grains in poultry feed; restricted feeding and watering of growing and laying hens; mineral and vitamin nutrition of poultry. *Mailing Add:* 24 College Heights Orono ME 04473

GERSBACHER, WILLARD MARION, ZOOLOGY, ECOLOGY. *Current Pos:* EMER PROF ZOOL, SOUTHERN ILL UNIV, 66- *Personal Data:* b Springerton, Ill, Mar 25, 06; m 38; c 5. *Educ:* Southern Ill State Norm Univ, EdB, 26; Univ Ill, MA, 28, PhD(zool), 32. *Prof Exp:* Asst zool, Univ Ill, 27-29; instr biol, Southern Ill State Norm Univ, 29-30; prof sci & math & head of dept, Eastern NMex Jr Col, 34-35; instr zool, Eastern Ill Col, 35-36; from asst prof to prof, Southern Ill Univ, 36-66, head dept, 38-55; prof, Southeast Mo State Col, 66-72. *Mem:* AAAS; fel Ecol Soc Am; Am Soc Limnol & Oceanog; Am Micros Soc; Wildlife Soc. *Res:* Ecology of plants and animals; fresh water biology; development of stream and lake communities; methods in biology teaching; nature conservancy. *Mailing Add:* 1709 Colonial Dr Cape Girardeau MO 63701

GERSCH, HAROLD ARTHUR, physics; deceased, see previous edition for last biography

GERSCH, WILL, ENGINEERING SCIENCE. *Current Pos:* PROF STOCHASTIC PROCESSES, UNIV HAWAII, 70- *Personal Data:* b New York, NY, Jan 24, 29. *Educ:* City Col NY, BEE, 50; NY Univ, MS, 56; Columbia Univ, DrEngSc, 61. *Prof Exp:* Jr engr, Res Div, Philco Corp, Ford Motor Co, Pa, 50-51; engr, W L Maxson Corp, NY, 51-53 & Math Inst, NY Univ, 53-56; sr res engr, Electronic Res Lab, Columbia Univ, 56-61; Nat Acad Sci-Nat Res Coun fel eng, Imp Col, Univ London, 61-62; sr res engr, Electronic Res Lab, Columbia Univ, 62-63; assoc prof stochastic processes, Purdue Univ, 63-70. *Concurrent Pos:* Vis prof, Dept Eng Mech, Stanford Univ, 66-67, NIH spec training & res fel neurol, 68-70, consult, 69; res fel, Am Statist Asn, 81-82. *Mem:* AAAS; Soc Indust & Appl Math; Inst Elec & Electronics Engrs. *Res:* Analysis and modeling of time series; applications to dynamical systems; neurophysiology; electroencephalogram and electrocardiogram analysis and modeling; modeling and analysis of econometric data. *Mailing Add:* 1134 Makaiwa St Honolulu HI 96816

GERSCHENSON, LAZARO E, CELL BIOLOGY, PATHOLOGY. *Current Pos:* actg chmn dept, 84-87, PROF PATH, UNIV COLO MED CTR, 77-, CHMN DEPT, 87- *Personal Data:* b Buenos Aires, Arg, Apr 25, 36; m 62, 90, Carol A Kruse; c Mariana, Irene, Jeffrey & Gregory. *Educ:* Univ Buenos Aires, MD, 59, PhD(physiol), 63. *Prof Exp:* Asst res path, Inst Cardiol, Nat Acad Med, Arg, 62-63; fel biochem, Lab Nuclear Med & Radiation Biol, Univ Calif, Los Angeles, 63-66; chief instr biol chem dept, Univ Buenos Aires, 67-68; asst res biochemist, Lab Nuclear Med & Radiation Biol, Univ Calif, Los Angeles, assoc prof path, Med Sch & assoc res biologist, Lab Nuclear Med & Radiation Biol, 71-77. *Concurrent Pos:* Nat Coun Sci Res, Arg foreign res fel, 63-65, career res award, 67-68; vis fel, Oxford Univ, Eng; vis prof, Free Univ, Brussels, Belg. *Mem:* NY Acad Sci; Am Asn Path; Soc Study Reproduction; Am Soc Cell Biol; Endocrine Soc; Int Acad Path. *Res:* Hormonal mechanism of action; cancer research. *Mailing Add:* Dept Path Univ Colo Health Sci Ctr 4200 E Ninth Ave Box 216 Denver CO 80262-0001. *Fax:* 303-466-6795

GERSCHENSON, MARIANA, DNA REPLICATION & REPAIR, TRANSCRIPTIONAL REGULATION. *Current Pos:* FEL ASSOC, EMORY UNIV, 93- *Personal Data:* b Buenos Aires, Arg, Aug 16, 63; m, Daniel E Libutti. *Educ:* Univ Colo, Boulder, BA, 86, PhD(exp path), 93. *Concurrent Pos:* Mentor, Am Assoc Univ Women & Am Soc Biochem Moleular Biol, 93-; lab coordr, Emory Univ, 94. *Mem:* Am Soc Cell Biol; AAAS; Am Soc Biochem & Molecular Biol; Soc Values Higher Educ. *Res:* Genetics and protein chemistry of oxidative phoshonylation (oxphos) in pathological system; proteins involved in oxphos are encoded for by both the mitochondria and nuclear genomes; organelles; diseases associated with these genomes include heart disease and neurodegenarative diseases. *Mailing Add:* NCI NIH Bldg 37 Rm 3B25 Bethesda MD 20892. *Fax:* 301-496-8709

GERSH, MICHAEL ELLIOT, GAS SENSOR, SIGNATURE ANALYSIS. *Current Pos:* VPRES, SPECTRAL SCI INC, 81- *Personal Data:* b Brooklyn, New York, June 3, 43; m 69, Janet Urschel; c David & Ellen. *Educ:* Yale Univ, BS, 65; Univ Wisconsin, PhD, 71. *Prof Exp:* Res assoc, Univ Fl, 71-73; prin scientist, Aerodyne Res Inc, 73-81. *Concurrent Pos:* Mem, Bedford Mass Bd Health, 90-96, chmn, 92-94. *Mem:* Am Phys Soc; Am Chem Soc; AAAS; Sigma Xi. *Res:* Research and development of sensors to characterize gasses and surfaces for industrial processes; aerospace target and background signature phenomenology development and analysis. *Mailing Add:* Spectral Sci Inc 99 S Bedford St Burlington MA 01803-5169. *E-Mail:* gersh@spectral.com

GERSHBEIN, LEON LEE, MAMMALIAN LIVER REGENERATION MECHANISMS, TUMORIGENESIS INDUCTION & MODERATION. *Current Pos:* DIR, NORTHWEST INST MED RES, 58- *Personal Data:* b Chicago, Ill, Dec 22, 17; m 56, Ruth Zelman; c l D, Marcia R (Rabinowitz) & Carla A (Solar). *Educ:* Univ Chicago, SB, 38, SM, 39; Northwestern Univ, PhD(chem), 44. *Prof Exp:* Res assoc org chem, Northwestern Univ, 45-47; asst prof biochem, Col Med, Univ Ill, 47-53; assoc prof, Ill Inst Technol, 53-59. *Concurrent Pos:* Adj prof, Ill Inst Technol, 59- *Mem:* AAAS; Am Asn Cancer Res; Am Chem Soc; Intern Soc Study Xenobiotics; fel Nat Acad Clin Biochem; Soc Exp Biol Med. *Res:* Endogenous factors and mixed function oxidase in liver regeneration as affected by pregnancy, metabolites and xenobiotics; ameliorative action of agents on tumor induction by dimethylhydrazine types; composition of human sebaceous lipids according to age, sex and pathology. *Mailing Add:* Northwest Inst Med Res 5645 W Addison St Chicago IL 60634

GERSHBERG, HERBERT, INTERNAL MEDICINE, ENDOCRINOLOGY. *Current Pos:* from instr to asst prof physiol & med, 50-65, dir endocrine serv, 61-67, ASSOC PROF MED, COL MED, NY UNIV MED CTR, 65-; CONSULT MED, OFF PROF MED CONDUCT, NY STATE BD HEALTH. *Personal Data:* b New York, NY, Dec 1, 17; m 68, Beatrice Gottler; c Viviane, Denise & Danielle. *Educ:* City Col New York, BS, 37; Univ Md, MS, 37; Med Col Va, MD, 41. *Prof Exp:* Fel physiol chem, Sch Med, Yale Univ, 46-48; fel internal med, Col Med, NY Univ, 48-50. *Concurrent Pos:* Practice internal med, 50-; dir diabetes & endocrine clin, Bellevue Hosp, 61-, assoc attend, 65-; dir training grant endocrinol, NIH, 61-67; consult, WHO, Geneva, 64, endocrinol, NY Downtown Hosp, Cornell, Human Growth Hormone Found & med & endocrinol, numerous hosps; assoc attend, Univ Hosps, 65-; reviewing ed, numerous sci pub; prof endocrinol, Univ Miami Med Sch, 70. *Mem:* Soc Exp Biol & Med; Endocrine Soc; Am Physiol Soc; Am Diabetes Asn; Am Col Physicians; Sigma Xi. *Res:* Metabolism, nutrition and endocrinology; pituitary, adrenal cortex and renal function; diabetes; parathyroid; growth hormone; over 130 publications. *Mailing Add:* 614 Second Ave New York NY 10016. *Fax:* 212-684-4290

GERSHENGORN, MARVIN CARL, MOLECULAR MECHANISMS. *Current Pos:* PROF MED, CORNELL UNIV MED COL, 83- *Personal Data:* b New York, NY, May 26, 46; m 69; c 1. *Educ:* City Col City Univ NY, BS, 67; NY Univ, MD, 71. *Honors & Awards:* Van Meter Prize, Am Thyroid Asn, 85. *Prof Exp:* Resident med, Strong Mem Hosp, Univ Rochester, 71-73;

clin assoc endocrinol, NIH, 73-76; from asst prof to assoc prof med, NY Univ Sch Med, 76-83. *Mem:* Am Soc Clin Invest; Endocrine Soc; Am Fedn Clin Res; Am Thyroid Asn; Am Soc Biol Chemists; Am Physiol Soc. *Res:* To understand the molecular mechanisms of hormone action. *Mailing Add:* Div Molecular Med NY Hosp Cornell Med Ctr 525 E 68th St New York NY 10021. *Fax:* 212-746-6289

GERSHENOWITZ, HARRY, HISTORY OF SCIENCE, PHILOSOPHY OF SCIENCE. *Current Pos:* PROF SCI, GLASSBORO STATE COL, 65- *Personal Data:* b New York, NY, Mar 27, 26. *Educ:* St John's Univ, NY, BS, 48; Long Island Univ, BA, 54, MS, 57; Columbia Univ, EDD(sci educ), 67; Am Bd Pharm, dipl. *Prof Exp:* Instr biol, Panzer Col, 55-58; instr sci, Fairleigh Dickinson Univ, 58-62; asst prof biol, Wilkes Col, 62-65. *Mem:* Am Technion Soc; Nat Sci Teachers Asn; Am Inst Aeronaut & Astronaut; Nat Hist Soc. *Res:* The Darwinian Age. *Mailing Add:* Dept Life Sci Rowan Col NJ Glassboro NJ 08028-1701

GERSHENSON, HILLEL HALKIN, MATHEMATICS. *Current Pos:* ASSOC PROF MATH, UNIV MINN, MINNEAPOLIS, 68- *Personal Data:* b New York, NY, Mar 27, 35; m 62; c 3. *Educ:* Univ Wis, BA, 55, MA, 57; Univ Chicago, PhD(math), 61. *Prof Exp:* Instr math, Princeton Univ, 61-63; asst prof, Cornell Univ, 63-68. *Concurrent Pos:* Vis lectr, Aarhus Univ, 66-67. *Mem:* Am Math Soc. *Res:* Algebraic topology; homological algebra. *Mailing Add:* Dept Math 127 Vincent Hall Univ Minn 206 Church St SE Minneapolis MN 55455-0488

GERSHENZON, M(URRAY), SOLID STATE ELECTRONICS. *Current Pos:* PROF MAT SCI & ELEC ENG, UNIV SOUTHERN CALIF, 66-, CHAIR MAT SCI, 93- *Personal Data:* b Brooklyn, NY, Nov 17, 28; m 52, Rosalie Grayer; c Jonathan, Ruth & Leora. *Educ:* City Col New York, BS, 49; Columbia Univ, AM, 53, PhD(chem), 57. *Prof Exp:* Mem tech staff solid state physics, Bell Tel Labs, NJ, 57-66. *Mem:* Am Phys Soc; Inst Elec & Electronics Engrs; Mat Res Soc; Am Asn Crystal Growers. *Res:* Radiative recombination in semiconductors; molecular beam epitaxy. *Mailing Add:* Dept Mat Sci Univ Southern Calif Univ Park Los Angeles CA 90089-0241. *Fax:* 213-740-7797

GERSHINOWITZ, HAROLD, PHYSICAL CHEMISTRY. *Current Pos:* CONSULT, 66- *Personal Data:* b New York, NY, Aug 31, 10; m 35. *Educ:* City Col New York, BS, 31; Harvard Univ, AM, 32, PhD(chem), 34. *Prof Exp:* Harvard Parker traveling fel, Princeton Univ, 34-35; res assoc chem, Columbia Univ, 35-36 & Harvard Univ, 36-38; petrol technologist, Shell Oil Co Inc, Mo, 38-39, dir res lab, Houston, 39-42, dir mfg res east of Rockies, 42-45, dir explor & prod res div, 45-51, vpres explor & prod tech div, 51-53, pres, Shell Develop Co, 53-62, chmn res coun & res coordr, Royal Dutch/Shell, 62-65. *Concurrent Pos:* Dir, Bataafse Petrol Maatschappij NV & Shell Int Res Maatschappij NV, Shell Res, Ltd & Shell Res NV, 62-65; consult, Orgn Econ Coop & Develop, Paris, 66-70; affil, Rockefeller Univ, 67-78, adj prof, 78-81; chmn environ studies bd, Nat Acad Sci-Nat Acad Eng, 67-70. *Mem:* Fel AAAS; Am Chem Soc; Sigma Xi. *Res:* Economics and administration of research; reaction kinetics from standpoint of quantum and statistical mechanics. *Mailing Add:* 25 Sutton Pl S Apt 9-G New York NY 10022-2441

GERSHMAN, LEWIS C, CARDIOLOGY, BIOPHYSICS. *Current Pos:* PROF MED & ASSOC PROF PHYSIOL, ALBANY MED COL, 73- *Personal Data:* b Cleveland, Ohio, Mar 11, 38; m 64, Barbara Breen; c John & Joseph. *Educ:* Princeton Univ, AB, 62; State Univ NY Downstate Med Ctr, MD & PhD(physiol, biophys), 68. *Prof Exp:* Intern med & pediat, Kings County Hosp & State Univ NY Downstate Med Ctr, 68-69; resident internal med, 69-70; instr med, Col Med, Univ Rochester, 72-73. *Concurrent Pos:* Staff physician med, Vet Admin Hosp, Bath, NY, 72-73; staff physician, Vet Admin Med Cntr, Albany, 73-; vis res fel, Mass Gen Hosp, 90; staff internist/cardiologist, Bethesda Naval Hosp, 91. *Mem:* Biophys Soc; Am Fedn Clin Res; NY Acad Sci; AAAS; Sigma Xi; Am Heart Asn. *Res:* Biochemistry of muscle proteins; particularly actin and actin-associated proteins. *Mailing Add:* Vet Admin Med Cntr Holland Ave Albany NY 12208

GERSHMAN, LOUIS LEO, ANALYTICAL CHEMISTRY. *Current Pos:* Chemist, 48-58, supv chemist, 60-66, LAB DIR, US FOOD & DRUG ADMIN, 67- *Personal Data:* b Nov 5, 20; US citizen; wid, Mildred (deceased); c Linda. *Educ:* City Col New York, BS, 41; Polytech Inst, Brooklyn, MS, 57. *Mem:* Am Chem Soc; fel Asn Off Anal Chem. *Res:* Infrared determination of endrin residues. *Mailing Add:* 151 Coolidge Ave Watertown MA 02172

GERSHMAN, MELVIN, BACTERIOLOGY. *Current Pos:* asst prof bact, 58-63, assoc prof microbiol & animal path, 63-77, PROF MICROBIOL, UNIV MAINE, 77- *Personal Data:* b Hartford, Conn, Aug 24, 27; m 50; c 2. *Educ:* Ohio State Univ, BSc, 54; Univ Mass, MSc, 57. *Prof Exp:* Instr bact, Smith Col, 56-57 & Springfield Hosp Nursing Sch, Mass, 57. *Mem:* Am Soc Microbiol; Sigma Xi. *Res:* Diagnostic bacteriology; enteric diseases; mycoplasma; phage typing. *Mailing Add:* 6 Frost Lane Orono ME 04473

GERSHOFF, STANLEY NORTON, NUTRITION. *Current Pos:* prof nutrit & chmn, Grad Dept Nutrit, Tufts Univ, 77-81, dir, Nutrit Inst, 77-81, prin investr, USDA-Human Nutrit Res Ctr, 77-84, DEAN, SCH NUTRIT, TUFTS UNIV, 81-, PRIN INVESTR, USDA-HUMAN NUTRIT RES CTR, 84- *Personal Data:* m. *Educ:* Univ Wis, BA, 43, MS, 48, PhD(biochem), 51. *Honors & Awards:* Borden Award Nutrit, Am Inst Nutrit, 72; Martha F Trulson Lectr, Am Diabetic Asn, 77. *Prof Exp:* Res asst, Dept Biochem, Univ Wis-Madison, 47-51, res assoc, 51-52; res assoc, Dept Nutrit, Sch Pub Health, Harvard Univ, 52-56, from asst prof to assoc prof, 56-77. *Concurrent Pos:* Consult, Unicef, Thailand, Pakistan & Indonesia, 74-80; vis lectr, Sch Pub Health, Harvard Univ, 77-85; counr, Am Soc Clin Nutrit, 79-82; hon prof nutrit & food hyg, WChina Univ Med Sci, 87; mem, numerous comts, coun & bds. *Mem:* Am Inst Nutrit; Am Soc Clin Nutrit; Brit Nutrit Soc; Sigma Xi. *Mailing Add:* Sch Nutrit Tufts Univ 39825 Morning Dove Pl Davis CA 95616-9757. *Fax:* 530-750-0307

GERSHON, ANNE A, MEDICINE, INFECTIOUS DISEASE. *Current Pos:* PROF PEDIAT, COL PHYSICIANS & SURGEONS, COLUMBIA UNIV, 86- *Personal Data:* b Pa, Aug 30, 38; m 61, Michael D; c 3. *Educ:* Smith Col, AB, 60; Cornell Univ, MD, 64. *Hon Degrees:* DSc, Smith Col, 93. *Prof Exp:* Resident training, NY Hosp, 65-66, resident pediat, 66-68; fel infectious dis, Sch Med, NY Univ, 68-70, form instr to prof pediat, 70-85. *Concurrent Pos:* Fel training, Oxford Univ, 65-66. *Mem:* Am Acad Pediat; Soc Pediat Res; Infectious Dis Soc Am; Am Soc Microbiol; Sigma Xi; Am Soc Clin Invest; Pediat Infectious Dis Soc; Am Soc Virol; Am Pediat Soc. *Res:* Viral infections of man and immunologic responses to these infections; viral vaccines; herpesvirus infections; varicella vaccine; author of over 150 publications. *Mailing Add:* Columbia Univ Col Physicians & Surgeons 630 W 168th St New York NY 10032-3702

GERSHON, ELLIOT SHELDON, GENETICS. *Current Pos:* unit chief, 74-78, chief sect psychogenetics, Biol Psychiat Br, 78-84, CHIEF, CLIN NEUROGENETICS BR, NIMH, 84-; MED DIR, USPHS, 80- *Personal Data:* b Brooklyn, NY, June 5, 40; m 67; c 2. *Educ:* Harvard Univ, AB, 61, Harvard Med Sch, MD, 65. *Honors & Awards:* Anna Morika Found Prize, 79. *Prof Exp:* Intern med, Mt Sinai Hosp, 65-66; resident psychiat, Mass Ment Health Ctr, 66-69; clin assoc, Lab Clin Sci, NIMH, 69-71; dir res, Jerusalem Ment Health Ctr, 71-74. *Concurrent Pos:* Teaching fel, Harvard Med Sch, 66-69; consult, Peter Bent Brigham Hosp, 68-69 & Prince George's Co Health Dept, Md, 69-70; mem sci adv bd, Israel Ctr Psychobiol, 72-74; mem fac psychiat, Wash Sch Psychiat, 76- & NIMH Staff Col, 77-; sci adv bd, Found Depression & Manic-Depression, 78-, prof adv bd, Jerusalem Ment Health Ctr, 78-; dir, Off Sci, Alcohol Drug Abuse & Mental Health Admin, 86-87. *Mem:* Am Psychiat Asn; Am Psychopath Asn; Am Col Neuropsychopharmacol; AAAS. *Res:* Manic-depressive illness; genetics; psychopharmacology; psychobiology. *Mailing Add:* NIH Bldg 10 Rm 3N218 9000 Rockville Pike Bethesda MD 20892. *Fax:* 301-402-0859; *E-Mail:* esg@cu.nih.gov

GERSHON, HERMAN, BIOCHEMISTRY. *Current Pos:* SCIENTIST, DEPT CHEM, FORDHAM UNIV, 86- *Personal Data:* b Brooklyn, NY, Jan 27, 21; m 55, Muriel Tobkes; c Judith F (Raskin) & Robin S. *Educ:* Brooklyn Col, BA, 42; Fordham Univ, MS, 47; Univ Colo, PhD(biochem), 50. *Prof Exp:* Chemist, Food Res Labs, Inc, 42-43 & Dr R J Block Lab, 46-47; biochemist, Vet Admin Hosp, Northport, NY, 50-51; dir res & develop, Pharmaceut & Fine Chem, United Org Corp, 51-55; biochem res, Pfister Chem Works, Inc, 55-62; sr org chemist, Boyce Thompson Inst Plant Res, Inc, 62-84; collabr, USDA, Ithaca, NY, 85. *Concurrent Pos:* Adj scientist, NY Bot Garden, 87- *Mem:* Fel AAAS; Am Chem Soc; fel NY Acad Sci; Sigma Xi. *Res:* Amino acid antagonists; synthesis of pyrimidines, quinolines, and fluorinated metabolite analogues; mode of action of antifungal agents. *Mailing Add:* 60 Brewer Rd Monsey NY 10952-4008

GERSHON, MICHAEL DAVID, NEUROBIOLOGY. *Current Pos:* PROF & CHMN ANAT, COL PHYSICIANS & SURGEONS, COLUMBIA UNIV, 75- *Personal Data:* b New York City, NY, Mar 3, 38; m 61; c 3. *Educ:* Cornell Univ, AB, 58, MD, 63. *Honors & Awards:* Jacob Javits Award, Nat Inst Neurol Commun Disorders & Stroke, 85. *Prof Exp:* USPHS res fel, Cornell Univ, 63-64, instr anat, Med Col, 64-65; USPHS res assoc, Dept Pharmacol, Oxford Univ, 65-66; from asst prof to prof anat, Dept Anat, Med Col, Cornell Univ, 66-75. *Concurrent Pos:* Mem, Neurol Disorders Prog Proj, Gastrointestinal Drug Adv Comn, Food & Drug Admin, 73-75; prin investr, Neural Control Gastrointestinal Activ, 76, Neurol A Study; vis prof, Grass Found, 81. *Mem:* Am Asn Anatomists (pres, 95-96); Am Soc Cell Biol; Am Physiol Soc; Am Soc Pharmacol & Exp Therapeut; Soc Neurosci; Sigma Xi; Asn Anat Chmn (pres, 85-86); AAAS; Am Gastroenterol Asn; Am Soc Pharmacol & Exp Therapeut; Endocrine Soc; NY Acad Sci; Int Soc Develop Neurosci; Soc Neurosci. *Res:* Cellular biology patterns of neural organization and factors that govern the development of the intrinsic nervous system of the gut (enteric nervous system). *Mailing Add:* Col Physicians & Surgeons Columbia Univ 630 W 168th St New York NY 10032

GERSHON, SAMUEL, PSYCHOPHARMACOLOGY. *Current Pos:* ASSOC VCHANCELLOR RES, HEALTH SCI, UNIV PITTSBURGH, 88- *Personal Data:* b Poland, Dec 13, 27; US citizen; c 2. *Educ:* Univ Sydney, BBS, 50; Univ Melbourne, DPM, 56; Royal Col Psychiatrists, FRC, 73. *Prof Exp:* Dep psychiat supt, Ballaret Ment Hosp, 54-60; chief psychopharmacol sect, Schizophrenia & Psychopharmacol Joint Res Proj, Univ Mich, 60-63; prin res scientist, Inst Psychiat, Univ Miss, 63-65; dir neuropsychopharmacol res unit, Dept Psychiat, NY Med Sch, 65-79; prof & chmn psychiat, Dept Psychiat, Sch Med, Wayne State Univ, 79-88; dir admin, Lafayette Clin, Mich Dept Ment Health, 79-88. *Concurrent Pos:* Assoc prof physiol, pharmacol & psychiat, Miss Inst Psychiat, Univ Miss, 63-65, vis prof, 75-; distinguished prof, Lakeland AFB, US Air Force Med Ctr, 75-; res assoc prof, Dept Psychiat, NY Univ Med Sch, 65-68, res prof, 68-70, prof, 71-79; res collaborator, Med Dept, Brookhaven Nat Lab Assoc Univ, 78-79. *Mem:* Fel Am Col Neuropsychopharmacol; Am Soc Clin Pharmacol & Therapeut; Am Col Clin Pharmacol; Psychiat Res Soc. *Res:* Biological psychiatry; gerontology; psychopharmacol. *Mailing Add:* Psychiat Univ Pittsburgh Sch Med Pittsburgh PA 15261-0001

GERSHON, SOL D, CHEMISTRY, PRODUCT DEVELOPMENT & ORAL PRODUCTS. *Current Pos:* exec dir, 74-77, consult, Soc Cosmetic Chemists, 74- *Personal Data:* b Chicago, Ill, Oct 18, 10; m 34, Esther R Goodman; c Elaine (Quaroni) & Barbara (Weinstein). *Educ:* Univ Ill, PhC, 30; Univ Chicago, BS, 34, MS, 35, PhD(chem), 38. *Honors & Awards:* Medal Award, Soc Cosmetic Chemists; Fairchild Scholar. *Prof Exp:* Asst chem, Col Pharm, Univ Ill, 30-38, from instr to assoc, 38-42, asst prof, 42-43; res chemist, Pepsodent Co, 43-47, dir new prods develop, Pepsodent Div, Lever Bros Co, 47-48, res mgr, 49-52, asst dir res prod improv & develop, 52-60, develop mgr household prod, 60-63, assoc res dir, 63-65, asst dir develop, 65-68, tech planning dir, Edgewater, 68-74. *Mem:* Am Chem Soc; Am Oil Chemists Soc; hon mem Soc Cosmetic Chemists (vpres, 51, pres, 52); Am Pharmaceut Asn; Int Asn Dent Res; fel Am Inst Chem; hon pres, Int Fedn Soc Cosmetic Chem. *Res:* Chemotherapy; synthesis of organic medicinals; drug assay; carbohydrates; cosmetic, dentifrice, detergent and edible product development. *Mailing Add:* 1363 Mercedes St Teaneck NJ 07666

GERSHOWITZ, HENRY, HUMAN GENETICS. *Current Pos:* RETIRED. *Personal Data:* b New York, NY, Sept 22, 24; m 49; c 4. *Educ:* Brooklyn Col, BA, 49; Calif Inst Technol, PhD(genetics), 54. *Prof Exp:* Res fel immunogenetics, Univ Wis, 54-56; res assoc, 57-61, from asst prof to assoc prof, 61-70, prof human genetics, Univ Mich, Ann Arbor, 70-88. *Concurrent Pos:* Consult, Blood Bank, Univ Hosp, Mich, 57-75; consult, Nat Legal Labs, 79-89, dir, 89- *Mem:* AAAS; Am Soc Human Genetics; Am Asn Immunol; Genetics Soc Am; Am Asn Blood Banks; Sigma Xi. *Res:* Blood group inheritance and correlations; genetic control of immunoglobulin structure and antibody specificity; paternity tests. *Mailing Add:* 2019 Winsted Blvd Ann Arbor MI 48103

GERSON, LOWELL WALTER, EPIDEMIOLOGY, GERONTOLOGY. *Current Pos:* assoc prof epidemiol, 78-82, ASSOC DIR, DIV COMMUNITY HEALTH SCI, NORTHEASTERN OHIO UNIV COL MED, 81-, PROF EPIDEMIOL, 82- *Personal Data:* b New York, NY, Sept 26, 42; m 64, Francine Goldstein; c Stacey & Jeremy. *Educ:* Case Western Res Univ, BA, 64, MA, 66, PhD(med sociol), 70. *Honors & Awards:* Hon Paramedic Akron. *Prof Exp:* Asst prof sociol, John Carroll Univ, 68-70; asst prof med sociol, Mem Univ Nfld, 70-74, assoc prof, 74-75; assoc prof clin epidemiol, McMaster Univ Med Ctr, 75-78. *Concurrent Pos:* Mem, Non Med Use of Drug Sci Rev Comt, Can, 74-76, Nat Health Welfare Can Sci Rev Comn, 74-81 & Exec Comt, Can Liver Found Liver Epidemiol, 79-; prof, Kent State Univ, 80-; adj assoc prof, Grad Sch Univ Pittsburgh, 81-88; adj prof, Univ Akron, 84-; adj grad fac, Kent State Univ, 80-; mem, Ohio Acad Family Pract Res, CHC, 82; vis fel, South Australia Health Comn, 86; chair, Task Force on Acad Base Pub Health, Ohio Pub Health Asn, 88-89; mem rev panel, Health Care Financing Admin, 89. *Mem:* Am Pub Health Asn; Asn Teachers Prev Med; Int Epidemiol Asn; Soc Epidemiol Res; Geront Soc Am; Soc Acad Emergency Med. *Res:* Health services research, primarily ambulatory care; geriatric emergency medicine. *Mailing Add:* 7385 La Costa Dr Hudson OH 44236. *Fax:* 440-325-7943; *E-Mail:* lwg@neoucom.edu

GERSON, ROBERT, PHYSICS. *Current Pos:* PROF PHYSICS, UNIV MO, ROLLA, 62- *Personal Data:* b New York, NY, Dec 5, 23; m 48; c 3. *Educ:* City Col NY, BChE, 43; NY Univ, PhD(physics), 54. *Prof Exp:* Physicist, Erie Resistor Corp, Pa, 53-56; sr physicist, Clevite Res Ctr, Ohio, 56-62. *Mem:* Am Phys Soc; AAAS; Am Asn Physics Teachers; Sigma Xi. *Res:* Dielectric and semiconducting materials; ferroelectricity; ferroelectric-ferromagnetic interaction; electrets; Mossbauer effect; ion implantation; development of novel educational methods for mathematical concepts. *Mailing Add:* 27 McFarland Dr Rolla MO 65401

GERSPER, PAUL LOGAN, SOIL MORPHOLOGY, SOIL MINERALOGY. *Current Pos:* asst prof morphology & soil pedologist, Univ Calif, Berkeley, 68-75, asst dean, Col Agr Sci, 72-74, chmn, Dept Conserv & Resource Studies, 76-80, ASSOC PROF PEDOLOGY, UNIV CALIF, BERKELEY, 75-, ASSOC PEDOLOGIST, AGR EXP STA, 75-, ASSOC PROF, DEPT PLANT & SOIL BIOL, 80- *Personal Data:* b Columbus, Ohio, Oct 12, 36; m 56; c 4. *Educ:* Ohio State Univ, BSc, 61, MSc, 63, PhD(soil sci), 68. *Prof Exp:* Res assoc soil sci, Ohio State Univ, 61-68. *Mem:* Am Soc Agron; Soil Sci Soc Am; Am Polar Soc; Ecol Soc Am; Nat Geog Soc; Am Land Res Asn; Nature Conserv. *Res:* Soil morphology, development and classification; interactions of soil forming factors and their effects on soil development; soil-plant relationships; soil resource evaluation; land use planning. *Mailing Add:* Environ Sci Univ Calif Berkeley CA 94720-0001

GERST, IRVING, COMBINATORIAL IDENTITIES. *Current Pos:* prof, 61-82, EMER PROF APPL MATH STATE UNIV NY, STONY BROOK, 82- *Personal Data:* b New York, NY, May 30, 12; wid; c 2. *Educ:* City Col NY, BS, 31; Columbia Univ, MA, 32, PhD(math), 47. *Prof Exp:* Teacher, Bd Educ, NY, 38-42; instr, USAF Tech Sch, Keesler Field, Miss, 42-44; tech consult, Transportation Corps, US Army Serv Forces, NY, 44-46; mathematician & head appl anal group, Control Instrument Co Div, Burroughs Corp, 46-58; sr proj mem & leader networks group, Radio Corp Am, 58-61. *Concurrent Pos:* Lectr, City Univ NY, 58-61; consult, Sperry-Rand, Inc, 61-63. *Mem:* Am Math Soc; Math Asn Am. *Res:* Network theory; complex variable; functional equations; operational methods; number theory; combinatorics. *Mailing Add:* State Univ NY 38 E 85th St No 7A New York NY 10028-0905

GERST, JEFFERY WILLIAM, ZOOLOGY, PHYSIOLOGY. *Current Pos:* Asst prof physiol, 73-77, ASST PROF ZOOL, N DAK STATE UNIV, 77- *Personal Data:* b San Francisco, Calif, Apr 23, 44; m 66; c 2. *Educ:* Chico State Col, BA, 66, MA, 68; Univ Nebr Lincoln, PhD(zool), 73. *Mem:* Am Soc Zoologists; Sigma Xi. *Res:* Compensatory changes in physiology elicited by changes in the external environment; transport enzyme systems; water-mineral balance. *Mailing Add:* Dept Zool NDak State Univ Main Campus Fargo ND 58105

GERST, PAUL HOWARD, SURGERY, PHYSIOLOGY. *Current Pos:* instr surg, 62-64, ASST PROF SURG, COL PHYSICIANS & SURGEONS, COLUMBIA UNIV, 64-; DIR SURG, BRONX-LEBANON HOSP CTR, 64-; PROF SURG, ALBERT EINSTEIN COL MED, 72- *Personal Data:* m 57; c 3. *Educ:* Columbia Univ, AB, 48, MD, 52. *Prof Exp:* Instr physiol, Univ Pa, 55-56. *Concurrent Pos:* USPHS res fel, 55-56 & res career develop award, 63-64; Am Col Surgeons award, 60-63. *Mem:* Am Col Surgeons; Am Asn Thoracic Surg; Am Physiol Soc; Biophys Soc; Am Col Chest Physicians. *Res:* Thoracic and cardiovascular diseases. *Mailing Add:* Dept Surg Bronx Lebabon Hosp Ctr 1650 Grand Concourse Bronx NY 10457

GERSTEIN, BERNARD CLEMENCE, PHYSICAL CHEMISTRY. *Current Pos:* Res assoc phys chem, Iowa State Univ, 60-61, from asst prof to assoc prof, 61-74, prof chem, 75-92, EMER PROF, IOWA STATE UNIV, 92- *Personal Data:* b Monticello, NY, Oct 18, 32; m 58, Mary Clarice Coffey; c Gregory, Mark, William, Beth & Garth. *Educ:* Purdue Univ, BS, 53; Iowa State Univ, PhD(phys chem), 60. *Concurrent Pos:* Vis assoc prof, Calif Inst Technol, 72-73; vis lectr, Univ Paris, 81, Univ Lille, 92, Tokushima Univ, 95 & Tokyo Inst Tech, 96; vis lectr, Univ de Lille, 92, Tokushima Univ Tokyo Inst Technol, 96; vis prof, Univ Utah, 95. *Mem:* AAAS; Am Chem Soc; Am Phys Soc. *Res:* Heterogeneous catalysis in insulators and semiconductors; applications of pulsed NMR to the study of electronic structures of molecules and solids. *Mailing Add:* Iowa State Univ 3756 Gilman Ames IA 50011-3111. *E-Mail:* bernie@ameslab.gov

GERSTEIN, GEORGE LEONARD, NEUROBIOLOGY. *Current Pos:* asst prof biophys, 64-66, assoc prof biophys & physiol, 66-69, PROF BIOPHYS & PHYSIOL, UNIV PA, 69- *Personal Data:* b Berlin, Ger, Apr 12, 33; div; c 2. *Educ:* Harvard Univ, BA, 52, MA, 54, PhD(physics), 58. *Prof Exp:* NIH fel biophys, Mass Inst Technol, 58-60, instr physics, 60-61, res assoc commun sci, 61-63; mem staff, Ctr Comput Technol, 63-64. *Concurrent Pos:* Mem, Neurol A Study Sect, 67-71 & Comput & Biomath Sci Study Sect, NIH, 72-76. *Mem:* AAAS; Physiol Soc; Soc for Neurosci. *Res:* Electrical activity of the nervous system; auditory system; mathematical analysis and computer simulation in neurophysiology. *Mailing Add:* Dept Neurosci Univ Pa Sch Med Richards Bldg A306/6085 Philadelphia PA 19104-6085. *Fax:* 215-573-5851; *E-Mail:* george@mulab.physiol.upenn.edu

GERSTEIN, LARRY J, MATHEMATICS. *Current Pos:* From asst prof to assoc prof, 67-78, PROF MATH, UNIV CALIF, SANTA BARBARA, 78- *Personal Data:* b Leavenworth, Kans, Aug 28, 40; m 69; c 2. *Educ:* Columbia Col, AB, 62; Univ Notre Dame, MS, 63, PhD(math), 67. *Concurrent Pos:* Vis asst prof, Mass Inst Technol, 70-71; vis assoc prof, Univ Notre Dame, 72-73; hon res fel, Harvard Univ, 78-79; vis prof, Dartmouth Col, 85-86, 92-93. *Mem:* Am Math Soc; Math Asn Am. *Res:* Number theory; quadratic forms. *Mailing Add:* Dept Math Univ Calif Santa Barbara CA 93106. *Fax:* 805-893-2385; *E-Mail:* gerstein@math.ucsb.edu

GERSTEL, DAN ULRICH, BOTANY, CYTOLOGY. *Current Pos:* asst prof agron, 50-53, assoc prof, 53-56, prof field crops, 56-63, Reynolds prof, 64-80, EMER REYNOLDS PROF CROP SCI & GENETICS, NC STATE UNIV, 80- *Personal Data:* b Berlin-Dahlem, Ger, Oct 23, 14; nat US; m 38; c 2. *Educ:* Univ Calif, Davis, BS, 40; Univ Calif, Berkeley, MS, 42, PhD(genetics), 45. *Prof Exp:* Asst bot, Univ Calif, 42-44, assoc genetics, 44-46; assoc geneticist, Res Inst, Stanford Univ, 47 & Natural Rubber Plant Res Sta, USDA, 47-49; res fel, Calif Inst Technol, 49-50. *Concurrent Pos:* Vis prof, Weizmann Inst, 61-62; NC-Israel exchange prof, Bet Dagan, Israel, 79. *Mem:* Genetics Soc Am. *Res:* Cytogenetics and speciation of Nicotiana, Gossypium and Parthenium; interspecific hybridization and genetic instability; origin and breeding of cultivated crops. *Mailing Add:* 1314 Crabapple Lane Raleigh NC 27607

GERSTEN, JEROME WILLIAM, physical medicine & rehabilitation, animal physiology; deceased, see previous edition for last biography

GERSTEN, JOEL IRWIN, THEORETICAL SOLID STATE PHYSICS. *Current Pos:* from asst prof to assoc prof, 70-77, PROF PHYSICS, CITY COL NY, 77- *Personal Data:* b New York, NY, Mar 18, 42; m 64; c 4. *Educ:* City Col NY, BS, 62; Columbia Univ, MA, 63, PhD(physics), 68. *Prof Exp:* Mem tech staff physics, Bell Labs, 68-70. *Concurrent Pos:* Consult, Bell Labs, 70-73; fel, Inst Advan Studies, Hebrew Univ Jerusalem, 78-79. *Mem:* Am Phys Soc. *Res:* Theoretic atomic physics; radiation processes; low energy electron diffraction; nonlinear optical processes; solid state physics; surface physics. *Mailing Add:* Dept Physics City Col NY 138 Convent Ave New York NY 10031-9198

GERSTEN, STEPHEN M, TOPOLOGY, ALGEBRA. *Current Pos:* mem staff, 74-76, PROF MATH, UNIV UTAH, 76- *Personal Data:* b Utica, NY, Dec 2, 40. *Educ:* Princeton Univ, AB, 61; Cambridge Univ, PhD(math), 65. *Prof Exp:* Instr math, Princeton Univ, 63-64 & Rice Univ, 64-65; NSF fel, Oxford Univ, 65-66; from asst prof to assoc prof, Rice Univ, 66-74. *Mem:* Am Math Soc. *Res:* Algebraic topology; homological algebra; projective class groups and Whitehead groups of algebras and geometric applications. *Mailing Add:* 464 E 200 S Salt Lake City UT 84111

GERSTENHABER, MURRAY, MATHEMATICS, LAW. *Current Pos:* from asst prof to assoc prof, 53-61, PROF MATH, UNIV PA, 61-, LECTR LAW, 73-. *Personal Data:* b Brooklyn, NY, May 6, 27; m 56, Ruth P Zager; c Jeremy, David & Rachel. *Educ:* Yale Univ, BS, 48; Univ Chicago, MS, 49, PhD(math), 51; Univ Pa, JD, 73. *Prof Exp:* Jewett fel, 51-53. *Concurrent Pos:* Mem, Inst Advan Study, 57-59, 62, 65-66 & 81-82; mem staff, Inst Defense Anal, 61-62; ed, Bull Am Math Soc, 65-71. *Mem:* Am Math Soc; Math Asn Am; fel AAAS. *Res:* Algebra; deformation of algebras; algebraic cohomology theory; probabilistic inference in law. *Mailing Add:* 237 Hamilton Rd Merion Station PA 19066-1102. *Fax:* 610-667-8470; *E-Mail:* murray@math.upenn.edu

GERSTING, JOHN MARSHALL, JR, APPLIED MATHEMATICS, COMPUTER SCIENCE. *Current Pos:* PROF COMPUT SCI, UNIV HAWAII, HILO, 92-. *Personal Data:* b Cincinnati, Ohio, Nov 1, 40; m 62; c 2. *Educ:* Purdue Univ, BS, 62; Ariz State Univ, MS, 64, PhD(eng sci), 70. *Prof Exp:* Analyst math modeling, Lewis Res Ctr, NASA, 62; analyst trajectory simulation, US Govt, Washington, DC, 64-66; fac assoc eng, Ariz State Univ, 66-70; asst prof eng & comput sci, Ind Univ-Purdue Univ, Indianapolis, 70-74, assoc prof, 75-79, prof comput sci, 79-92. *Mem:* Asn Comput Mach; Am Phys Soc. *Res:* Computational methods; stiff differential systems; hydrodynamic stability; database management systems; relational and hierarchical databases; search techniques. *Mailing Add:* 2405 Kalanianaole Apt Ph9 Hilo HI 96720

GERSTING, JUDITH LEE, COMPUTER SCIENCE EDUCATION, FAULT-TOLERANT COMPUTING. *Current Pos:* PROF COMPUT SCI & CHAIR DEPT, UNIV HAWAII, HILO, 91-. *Personal Data:* b Springfield, Vt, Aug 20, 40; m 62; John Jr; c Adam & Jason. *Educ:* Stetson Univ, BS, 62; Ariz State Univ, MA, 64, PhD(math), 69. *Prof Exp:* From asst prof to assoc prof comput sci, Ind Univ-Purdue Univ, 70-79, prof, 79-91. *Concurrent Pos:* Assoc prof comput sci, Univ Cent Fla, 80-81; staff scientist, Indianapolis Ctr Advan Res, 82-84; vis prof comput sci, Univ Hawaii, Hilo, 90-91. *Mem:* Asn Comput Mach; Inst Elec & Electronics Engrs Comput Soc. *Res:* Fault-tolerant computing systems. *Mailing Add:* Univ Hawaii 200 W Kawili St Hilo HI 96720

GERSTL, SIEGFRIED ADOLF WILHELM, REMOTE SENSING, SPACE SCIENCE. *Current Pos:* MEM STAFF PHYSICS, LOS ALAMOS NAT LAB, 74-. *Personal Data:* b Ger, Aug 5, 39; US citizen; c 2. *Educ:* Univ Stuttgart, Dipl, Phys, 64; Univ Karlsruhe, PhD(physics), 67. *Prof Exp:* Scientist physics, Univ Stuttgart, 64-65; scientist nuclear physics, Univ Karlsruhe, 65-68; sr engr appl physics, Westinghouse Advan Reactors Div, 68-71; mem staff physics, Argonne Nat Lab, 71-74. *Concurrent Pos:* Mem, nat prog comt mem, Am Nuclear Soc, 72-82, NASA satellite instrument panels, 86-; prin investr, NASA & Dept Energy. *Mem:* Am Nuclear Soc; Am Geophys Union; AAAS; Am Soc Photog. *Res:* Physics of satellite remote sensing; modeling of atmospheric optics and imaging; atmospheric correction algorithms; spectral and angular signatures of earth reflectance features; radiation beam propagation for solar and laser radiation; computational solutions to radiative transfer equation. *Mailing Add:* 15 El Nido St Los Alamos NM 87544

GERSTLE, FRANCIS PETER, JR, MATERIALS SCIENCE. *Current Pos:* mem tech staff composite mat, Sandia Labs, 72-73, mem tech staff mech mat, 73-74, supvr composite mat, 74-83, supvr ceramics develop, 84-89, SUPVR CERAMICS & GLASS PROCESSING, SANDIA LABS, 89-. *Personal Data:* b Louisville, Ky, June 23, 42; m 67, 87; c 2. *Educ:* St Joseph's Col, Ind, BA, 64; Mass Inst Technol, SB, 65, SM, 66; Duke Univ, PhD(mech eng & mat sci), 72. *Prof Exp:* Tech staff mem test facil design, Sandia Labs, 66-68; instr & res asst mech eng & mat sci, Duke Univ, 68-71. *Concurrent Pos:* Comt mem characterization org matrix composites, Nat Mat Adv Bd, 78-80; chmn, Gordon Res Conf Composites, 81; comt mem, Lightweight Mil Combat Vehicles, Nat Mat Adv Bd, 81-83; comt mem panel, Nat Acad Sci, 84. *Mem:* Soc Eng Sci; Am Soc Mech Engrs; Soc Advan Mat & Process Eng; Soc Exp Stress Anal. *Res:* Analysis and characterization of filamentary composite materials; design of composite structures, especially pressure vessels; interfacial and residual viscoelastic effects in seals. *Mailing Add:* Dept 2476 Mail Stop 0959 Sandia Labs Albuquerque NM 87109

GERSTLE, KURT H, STRUCTURAL ENGINEERING. *Current Pos:* From instr to assoc prof, 57-70, PROF CIVIL ENG, UNIV COLO, BOULDER, 70-. *Personal Data:* b Munich, Ger, Nov 11, 23; US citizen; m 51; c 4. *Educ:* Univ Calif, Berkeley, BS, 49, MS, 52; Univ Colo, PhD(civil eng), 56. *Honors & Awards:* Wason Medal, Am Concrete Inst, 64; Moisseiff Award, Am Soc Civil Engr, 84; Higgins Lectureship, Inst Steel Construct, 89. *Concurrent Pos:* NSF sci fac fel, Brown Univ, 59-60; vis prof struct eng, SEATO Grad Sch Eng, Thailand, 63-64; Fulbright lectr, Munich Tech Univ, 70-71; vis prof, Norwegian Tech Univ, Trondheim, 78; Alexander von Humboldt sr scientist award, 78-79; Erskine fel, Canterbury Univ, Christchurch, NZ, 86. *Mem:* Am Soc Civil Engrs; Am Concrete Inst; Sigma Xi. *Res:* Elastic and inelastic analysis and behavior of structures; behavior of reinforced concrete structures. *Mailing Add:* Univ Colo Campus Box 428 Boulder CO 80309-0428

GERSTMAN, HUBERT LOUIS, AUDIOLOGY, SPEECH SCIENCES. *Current Pos:* ASSOC PROF OTOLARYNGOL, DEPT SURG, STATE UNIV NY, STONYBROOK, 89-. *Personal Data:* b Buffalo, NY, Feb 20, 34; m 59; c 3. *Educ:* State Univ NY Col, Geneseo, BS, 55; Pa State Univ, MEd, 60, DEd(audiol), 62. *Prof Exp:* Asst prof Speech, Univ Akron, 63-65; instr oral biol, Sch Dent Med, 72-87, ASSOC PROF OTOLARYNGOL & PHYS MED, TUFTS UNIV, SCH MED, 65-. *Concurrent Pos:* HEW fel, St Elizabeth Hosp, 62-63; chief, Speech, Hearing & Lang Ctr, New Eng Med Ctr Hosp, 65-; pres, Mass Speech-Lang-Hearing Asn, 68; pres, Acoust Corp Am, 71-83; ed-treas, Assoc Serv Prog Commun Disorders, 77- & pres, 83-; chmn, Bd Prof Advisors, VNA, Boston, 78-; mem, Prof Serv Bd, Am Speech-Lang-Hearing Asn, 82-84 & Standards Coun, 86-; vpres & pres elec, Nat Alliance Stuttering; mgt consult, 87-89. *Mem:* Fel Am Speech & Hearing Asn; Acoust Soc Am; Am Cleft Palate Asn; Am Auditory Soc; Sigma Xi. *Res:* Speech perception and hearing aids; management of hearing, speech and language impairment; use of artificial speech devices for non-vocal; test and measurement in psycho-acoustic experiments; administration and management of practices and clinical programs. *Mailing Add:* 11234 NE 146th St Kirkland WA 98034

GERSTNER, ROBERT W(ILLIAM), STRUCTURAL ENGINEERING. *Current Pos:* From asst prof to assoc prof, 60-69, PROF STRUCT MECH, UNIV ILL, 69-. *Personal Data:* b Chicago, Ill, Nov 10, 34; m 58; c 2. *Educ:* Northwestern Univ, BS, 56, MS, 57; Univ Ill(civil eng), 60. *Concurrent Pos:* NSF res grant, 64-66. *Mem:* AAAS; Am Soc Civil Engrs; Am Concrete Inst; Am Soc Eng Educ. *Res:* Interface adjustment techniques and numerical methods in solution of problems in structural mechanics and elasticity; stress distributions in layered and sandwich systems. *Mailing Add:* 2628 W Agatite Gerstner & Assoc Chicago IL 60625

GERTEIS, ROBERT LOUIS, INORGANIC CHEMISTRY. *Current Pos:* RETIRED. *Personal Data:* b San Diego, Calif, Sept 1, 36; m 62, Ann Montgomery; c Stephen & Mark. *Educ:* Univ Wichita, BS, 58; Univ Ill, MS, 61, PhD(inorg chem), 63. *Prof Exp:* Res chemist, Esso Res & Eng Co, 63-68; res scientist, NJ Zinc Co, Palmerton, 68-76, sr res scientist, 76-77; sr res scientist, G&W Natural Resource Group, Bethlehem, 77-81; chief chemist, Gold Fields Mining Corp, Golden CO, 81-83, mgr anal serv, 83-92, mgr, Com Testing & Eng, 92-94. *Mem:* Am Chem Soc. *Res:* Analysis of gold, titanium and zinc ores. *Mailing Add:* 28806 Clover Lane Evergreen CO 80439

GERTEISEN, THOMAS JACOB, ORGANIC CHEMISTRY. *Current Pos:* VPRES QUAL CONTROL, GENZYME PHARM. *Personal Data:* b Owensboro, Ky, Oct 21, 43; m 74; c 2. *Educ:* Brescia Col, BA, 66; Univ Tenn, Knoxville, PhD(chem), 70. *Prof Exp:* Asst prof chem, Brescia Col, 70-75; chem res, Sci Adv Bd, US Environ Protection Agency, Chicago, 75-76; asst prof chem, Univ Pittsburgh, Bradford, 76-78; asst prof chem, Columbus Col, 78-81; chem mgr qual assurance, Cutter Labs, 81. *Mem:* Am Chem Soc; Am Soc Qual Control; Am Inst Chemists; Asn Off Anal Chemists. *Res:* Physical properties of fused ring organic compounds; instrumental analysis--infrared hydrogen-bonding studies, mass spectroscopy, nuclear magnetic resonance; gas chromatographic analysis of trace organic contaminants. *Mailing Add:* One Oceanside Terr Swampscott MA 01907

GERTH, FRANK E, III, ALGEBRA, NUMBER THEORY. *Current Pos:* from asst prof to assoc prof, 74-87, PROF MATH, UNIV TEX, AUSTIN, 87-. *Personal Data:* b San Antonio, Tex, Oct 8, 45. *Educ:* Rice Univ, BA, 67; Princeton Univ, MA, 71, PhD(math), 72. *Prof Exp:* Mem prof staff eng, TRW Systs, 68-70; asst math, Princeton Univ, 70-72; instr, Univ Pa, 72-74. *Mem:* Am Math Soc. *Res:* Ideal class groups of algebraic number fields. *Mailing Add:* Dept Math Univ Tex Austin TX 78712

GERTJEJANSEN, ROLAND O, FOREST PRODUCTS. *Current Pos:* from instr to assoc prof, 63-75, PROF FOREST PROD, COL NATURAL RESOURCES, UNIV MINN, ST PAUL, 75-. *Personal Data:* b Vesta, Minn, May 7, 36; m 57; c 3. *Educ:* Univ Minn, BS, 61, MS, 62, PhD(wood sci), 66. *Prof Exp:* Technologist, Univ Forest Prod Lab, 62-63. *Concurrent Pos:* Forest prod consult. *Mem:* Tech Asn Pulp & Paper Indust; Forest Prod Res Soc; Soc Wood Sci & Technol. *Res:* Design and development of new wood base composites; physical and mechanical properties of wood fiber and particle products; evaluation of alternative raw materials for particleboard. *Mailing Add:* Dept Forest Prod 203 Kaufert Lab Univ Minn 2004 Folwell Ave St Paul MN 55108-6128

GERTLER, MENARD M, INTERNAL MEDICINE. *Current Pos:* assoc prof, 58-66, dir cardiovasc res, 58-86, PROF MED, RUSK INST, NY UNIV, 66-. *Personal Data:* b Saskatoon, Sask, May 21, 19; nat US; m 43, Anna Paull; c Barbara L & Stephanie (Schiffer). *Educ:* Univ Sask, BA, 40; McGill Univ, MD, CM, 43, MSc, 46; NY Univ, DSc, 58. *Prof Exp:* Demonstr physiol, Med Sch, McGill Univ, 45-47; resident cardiol & exec dir coronary res proj, Mass Gen Hosp, 47-50; instr med, Col Physicians & Surgeons, Columbia Univ, 50-54. *Concurrent Pos:* Asst, Presby Hosp, NY, 50-54; asst attend physician & physician-in-chg cardiovasc dis, Francis Delafield Div, Columbia Presby Med Ctr, 51-54; consult & lectr, St Albans Naval Hosp; attend physician med, NY Univ Med Ctr, 74-; adj prof med, McGill Univ. *Mem:* Am Chem Soc; fel Am Col Physicians; Am Fedn Clin Res; NY Acad Sci; NY Acad Med; Am Heart Asn. *Res:* Cardiovascular disease and biochemistry; atherosclerosis and epidemiology of heart disease; biochemistry of congestive heart failure. *Mailing Add:* Rusk Inst 400 E 34th St New York NY 10016. *Fax:* 212-689-9253

GERTNER, SHELDON BERNARD, PHARMACOLOGY. *Current Pos:* from asst prof to assoc prof, 57-67, PROF PHARMACOL, NJ MED SCH, UNIV MED & DENT NJ, NEWARK, 67-. *Personal Data:* b New York, NY, Feb 16, 27; m 60, Doreen Kiel; c David, Patricia & Jonathan. *Educ:* Brooklyn Col, BS, 48; Yale Univ, PhD, 53. *Prof Exp:* Rockefeller fel, Nat Inst Med Res, London, Eng, 53-55; fel, Inst Super di Sanita, Rome, Italy, 55; assoc, Col Physicians & Surgeons, Columbia Univ, 55-57. *Mem:* AAAS; Am Soc Pharmacol & Exp Therapeut; Pharmacol Soc Can; Soc Exp Biol & Med; Am Soc Hypertens. *Res:* Autonomic pharmacology; histaminergic neurotransmission; catecholamines in rape victims. *Mailing Add:* Dept Pharmacol NJ Med Sch UMDNJ 185 S Orange Ave Newark NJ 07103-2714

GERTZ, SAMUEL DAVID, PATHOLOGIC ANATOMY. *Current Pos:* lectr, 76-78, SR LECTR, DEPT ANAT, HADASSAH MED SCH, HEBREW UNIV, JERUSALEM, 78-, CHMN DEPT, 90- *Personal Data:* b Baltimore, Md, June 19, 47; m 73; c 3. *Educ:* Yeshiva Univ, BA, 68; Univ Md, MS, 71, PhD(anat), 75; Hebrew Univ, MD, 87. *Prof Exp:* Grad instr, Dept Anat, Sch Dent, Univ Md, 69-71, grad instr, Dept Anat, Sch Med, 71-75, res asst, 72-75, res assoc vascular path, Dept Neurol, 75-76, from instr to asst prof, 76-78. *Mem:* Soc Neurosci; AAAS; Israel Soc Electron Micros; Israel Soc Anat Sci (secy, 77-78); Am Asn Anatomists. *Res:* Clinical and cardiac morphological findings in patients treated with tissue plasminogen activator during acute myocardial infarction; hemodynamic factors in rupture of atheroscleratic plague; role of coronary vasospasm in the pathogenesis of myocardial infarction. *Mailing Add:* Dept Anat Hadassah Med Sch PO Box 12272 Jerusalem 91120 Israel. *Fax:* 972-2-757451

GERTZ, STEVEN MICHAEL, ENVIRONMENTAL SCIENCES, WASTE MANAGEMENT. *Current Pos:* VPRES & GEN MGR, BURNS & ROE ENVIRON SERV INC, 89- *Personal Data:* b Philadelphia, Pa, Feb 15, 43; m 67, Thea G Sigismund; c Shira J & Amira R. *Educ:* Philadelphia Col Pharm & Sci, BS, 65; Drexel Univ, MS, 68, PhD(environ eng), 73. *Prof Exp:* Environ sanitarian, Philadelphia Dept Pub Health, 65-67, indust sanitarian, 68-69; sr biophysicist, Radiation Mgt Corp, 72-74; partner, Porte-Gertz Consults, Inc, 74-80; vpres, Environ Consult & Testing Serv, Inc, 80-81; vpres & assoc div mgr, Weston Inc, 81-89. *Mem:* Am Soc Testing & Mat; Hazardous Mat Control Res Inst; Health Physics Soc; Acad Cert Hazard Control Mgrs; Acad Cert Hazardous Mat Mgrs. *Res:* Management of interdisciplinary environmental programs; environmental monitoring; hazardous waste management; emergency environmental response; health physics; health and safety (chemical); statistics. *Mailing Add:* 306 Bangor Rd Bala Cynwyd PA 19004. *Fax:* 610-354-9347

GERVAIS, FRANCINE, INFLAMMATION, AMYLOIDOSIS. *Current Pos:* RES ASSOC, MONTREAL GEN HOSP RES INST, 82- *Personal Data:* b Montreal, Que, Oct 10, 51; m 76; c 1. *Educ:* Univ Montreal, BSc, MSc,77, PhD(microimmunol), 80-82. *Prof Exp:* Fel hemat, Res Ctr, Sacre-Coeur Hosp, Montreal, 80-82. *Concurrent Pos:* Asst prof, McGill Univ, Dept Exp Med, 83-88; fel immunol, Bristol-Myers, 82; chmn, Animal Care Comt, 89-; assoc prof, McGill Univ, Dept Exp Med, 90- *Mem:* Am Asn Immunol; Reticulocredotheliol Soc; Can Soc Immunologists. *Res:* Role of the anyloid enhancing factor in the pathogenesis of amyloidosis (secondary type and Alzheimer's disease); genetic control of susceptibility to murine AIDS (MAIDS). *Mailing Add:* Dept Except Med Montreal Gen Hosp Res Inst 1650 Cedar Ave Montreal PQ H3G 1A4 Can. *Fax:* 514-933-7146

GERVAIS, PAUL, AGRONOMY. *Current Pos:* prof forages, 62-84, res officer, 84-86, EMER PROF, LAVAL UNIV, 86- *Personal Data:* b St Barthelemy, Que, Aug 27, 15; m 55, Denise Brunet; c Bernard, Jacques, Marie & Danielle. *Educ:* Laval Univ, BSA, 37; McGill Univ, MSc, 48; Univ Wis, PhD, 58. *Honors & Awards:* Agron Merit Award, Que, 80. *Prof Exp:* Res officer cereals & forages, Exp Farm, Can Dept Agr, Lennoxville, 39-60 & legumes & pastures, 60-62. *Mem:* Am Soc Agron; Can Soc Agron (pres, 63-64); Crop Sci Soc Am. *Res:* Management and physiology of forage crops. *Mailing Add:* Dept Plant Sci Laval Univ Quebec PQ G1K 7P4 Can

GERVAY, JOSEPH EDMUND, NATURAL PRODUCTS CHEMISTRY, MATERIALS SCIENCE. *Current Pos:* RETIRED. *Personal Data:* b Dec 29, 31; US citizen; m 56, Helen Hedri; c Michael S. *Educ:* Univ Montreal, BS, 61; Univ BC, MS, 63, PhD(org chem), 65. *Prof Exp:* From res chemist to sr res assoc, Res & Develop Div, Electronics Dept, E I du Pont de Nemours & Co, Inc, 66-84, res assoc, 84-91, sr res assoc, 91-93, consult, 94-96. *Mem:* Am Chem Soc; Soc Photog Sci & Eng. *Res:* Oxo reaction, Fischer-Tropsch synthesis, phenol oxidations and biosynthesis of alkaloids and steroids in vivo and in vitro using isotopic labels; photopolymers; principles, processes and materials; photoresists, unconventional photographic systems; photographic chemistry; organic reaction mechanism; photopolymer systems; electronic materials; electroless plating processes; printed circuit board manufacture; permanent protective coatings; polymer chemistry; solder mask coating; flex printed circuits. *Mailing Add:* 1101 Crestover Rd Wilmington DE 19803

GERWE, RAYMOND DANIEL, CHEMISTRY. *Current Pos:* RETIRED. *Personal Data:* b Cincinnati, Ohio, May 28, 04; m 33; c 2. *Educ:* Univ Miami, Ohio, BS, 27; Univ Cincinnati, MA, 29, PhD(org chem), 32. *Prof Exp:* Instr chem, Oxford Col, 27-28; head res & develop sect, Kroger Food Found, 32-38; dir res, Fla Div, FMC Corp, 38-70. *Concurrent Pos:* Consult, Citrus Processing, 73-; past chmn-Fla sect, Inst Food Technol. *Mem:* Am Chem Soc; Inst Food Tech; Sigma Xi. *Res:* Food technology, processing and chemistry; chemical education; photochemistry as applied to organic chemistry. *Mailing Add:* 2131 Reaney Rd Lakeland FL 33803

GERWE, RODERICK DANIEL, regulatory advocacy for chemical industry, risk & exposure assessment, for more information see previous edition

GERWICK, BEN CLIFFORD, JR, CIVIL ENGINEERING. *Current Pos:* prof, 71-89, EMER PROF CIVIL ENG, UNIV CALIF, BERKELEY, 89-; CHMN, BEN C GERWICK INC, CONSULT ENGRS, SAN FRANCISCO, 88- *Personal Data:* b Berkeley, Calif, Feb 22, 19; m 96, Ellen Chaney; c Beverly (Brian), Virginia (Wallace), Ben C III & William. *Educ:* Univ Calif, BS, 40. *Honors & Awards:* Turner Award & Corbetta Award, Am Concrete Inst, 74; Karp Award, Am Soc Civil Engrs, 76, Pres Award & Peurifoy Award, 89; Lockheed Award, Marine Technol Soc, 77; Blakeley Smith Medal, Soc Naval Architects & Marine Engrs, Franklin Inst, Frank P Brown Medal, 81; Freyssinet Medal, Int Fedn Prestressing, 82; Emil Morsch Medal, Deutsche Beton Verein, 82; Swedish Concrete Award, 85; Distinguished Serv Award, Deep Found Inst, 96. *Prof Exp:* USN, 40-45; mem staff, Ben C Gerwick, Inc, San Francisco, 46-52, pres, 52-70; exec vpres, Santa Fe-Pomeroy, Inc, 68-71. *Concurrent Pos:* Sponsoring mgr, Richmond-San Rafael Bridge substruct, 53-56 & San Mateo-Hayward Bridge, 64-66; lectr construct eng, Stanford Univ, 62-68; consult major bridge & marine construct projs; consult construct engr ocean struct & concrete offshore struct in North Sea, Japan, MidEast, Australia, Southeast Asia & Arctic; chmn marine bd, Nat Res Coun, 78-80; mem, US Arctic Res Comn, 90-95. *Mem:* Nat Acad Eng; hon mem Am Soc Civil Engrs; fel Am Concrete Inst; Fedn Int Precontrainte (pres, 74-78); Fr Construct Soc; Prestressed Concrete Inst (pres, 57-58); Soc Naval Architects & Marine Engrs; Royal Swed Acad Tech Sci; Norweg Acad Tech Sci; Ger Engrs Soc. *Res:* Marine, ocean and arctic structures; concrete structures; deep foundations; author of 2 books on advanced construction technology. *Mailing Add:* 601 Montgomery St Rm 400 San Francisco CA 94111

GERWICK, BEN CLIFFORD, III, PLANT PHYSIOLOGY, WEED SCIENCE. *Personal Data:* b Berkeley, Calif, Mar 2, 53; m 74; c 2. *Educ:* Alaska Methodist Univ, BA, 74; Wash State Univ, PhD(bot), 78. *Prof Exp:* Instr phys educ, Alaska Methodist Univ, 74; res assoc plant physiol, Univ Ga, 78-79; sr res biologist, Dow Chem, 79-86, leader, 86-90; tech leader, herbicide res, Dow Elanco, 90-92. *Concurrent Pos:* NSF fel, 78-79. *Mem:* Am Soc Plant Physiologists; Sigma Xi; Weed Sci Soc. *Res:* Discovery of new herbicides and herbicide; mode-of-actions. *Mailing Add:* 5727 Country Club Dr Oakland CA 94618

GERWIN, BRENDA ISEN, MOLECULAR BIOLOGY. *Current Pos:* sr staff fel, Nat Cancer Inst, 71-73, CHEMIST, NAT CANCER INST, 73- *Personal Data:* b Boston, Mass, May 2, 39; m 60, Robert; c David, Daniel & Joel. *Educ:* Radcliffe Col, BA, 60; Univ Chicago, PhD(biochem), 64. *Prof Exp:* Res assoc biochem, Rockefeller Inst, 64-66; instr, Sch Med, Case Western Res Univ, 66-69; biochemist, Molecular Anat Prog, Oak Ridge Nat Lab, 69-71. *Mem:* Am Soc Biochem & Molecular Biol; Am Soc Microbiol; Sigma Xi; AAAS; Am Chem Soc. *Res:* cancer research; enzymology; cell biology. *Mailing Add:* Bldg 37 Rm 2C15 Nat Cancer Inst Bethesda MD 20892. *Fax:* 301-496-0497

GERWIN, RICHARD A, PLASMA INSTABILITIES, PLASMA TRANSPORT. *Current Pos:* staff mem, Plasma Focus Group, Los Alamos Nat Lab, 71-73, Magnetic Fusion Theory Group, 73-79, group leader, 79-89, STAFF MEM, MAGNETIC FUSION THEORY GROUP, LOS ALAMOS NAT LAB, 89- *Personal Data:* b Chicago, Ill, March 13, 34; m 60; c 2. *Educ:* Univ Chicago, BA, 54, BS, 56, MS, 57; Eindhoven Tech Univ, DSc, 66. *Prof Exp:* Staff mem, Plasma Physics, Boeing Sci Res Lab, 59-71. *Concurrent Pos:* Vis scientist, Inst Fundamental Res on Matter, Neth, 64-66; vis prof, dept nuclear eng, Univ Wash, Seattle, 85. *Mem:* Fel Am Phys Soc. *Res:* Theoretical plasma physics within the context of the magnetic fusion energy goals; magnetic confinement of hot plasmas sufficient to obtain useful energy from fusion reactions; plasma thrusters. *Mailing Add:* 50 Tesuque Los Alamos NM 87544

GERY, IGAL, IMMUNOLOGY. *Current Pos:* SECT HEAD EXP IMMUNOL, NAT EYE INST, NIH, 81- *Educ:* Hebrew Univ, Jerusalem, PhD, (immunol), 63. *Res:* Autoimmunity in the eye. *Mailing Add:* Sect Except Immunol Nat Eye Inst NIH Bldg 10 Rm 10N208 Bethesda MD 20892-1858. *Fax:* 301-402-0485

GESCHKE, CHARLES MATTHEW, COMPUTER SCIENCE. *Current Pos:* PRES, ADOBE SYSTS, 87- *Personal Data:* b Cleveland, Ohio, Sept 11, 39; m 64; c 3. *Educ:* Xavier Univ, Ohio, AB, 62, MS, 63; Carnegie-Mellon Univ, PhD(comput sci), 72. *Prof Exp:* Instr math, John Carroll Univ, 63-68; res scientist comput sci, Palo Alto Res Ctr, Xerox Corp, 72-80, mgr, Imaging Sci Lab, 80-87. *Mem:* Nat Acad Eng; Math Asn Am; Asn Comput Mach. *Res:* Programming languages; machine design for efficient emulation of higher level languages; computer imaging and graphics. *Mailing Add:* 345 Park Ave San Jose CA 95110. *Fax:* 408-537-6000

GESCHWIND, STANLEY, PHYSICS. *Current Pos:* RETIRED. *Personal Data:* b Brooklyn, NY, Nov 22, 21; m 57; c 3. *Educ:* City Col New York, BS, 43; Univ Ill, MS, 47; Columbia Univ, PhD(physics), 51. *Prof Exp:* Res physicist, Columbia Univ, 51-52; physicist, Bell Labs, Murray Hill, 52-66, head, Quantum & Solid State Physics Dept, 66-83. *Mem:* Fel Am Phys Soc; Sigma Xi. *Res:* Microwave spectroscopy; millimeter wave generation; magnetism; paramagnetic resonance; optical spectra of solids; microwave optical double resonance in solids; light scattering. *Mailing Add:* Dept Phys Clark Univ 950 Main St Worcester MA 01610

GESELL, THOMAS FREDERICK, HEALTH PHYSICS, RADIATION DOSIMETRY. *Current Pos:* PROF HEALTH PHYSICS, IDAHO STATE UNIV, 91- *Personal Data:* b East Cleveland, Ohio, Apr 28, 40; m 64; c Diane Wilson; c Rick, Barbara & Eric. *Educ:* San Diego State Univ, BS, 65; Univ Tenn, MS, 68, PhD(physics), 71. *Prof Exp:* From asst prof to assoc prof health physics, Sch Pub Health, Univ Tex Health Sci Ctr, Houston, 71-81; chief, Dosimetry Br, Radiol & Environ Sci Lab, Dept Energy, Idaho Falls, Idaho, 81-88, dir, 88-91. *Concurrent Pos:* Health physics fel, 65-68, radiol health fel, 68-71, consult, Tex State Dept, Health Resources, 73-81, Houston Lighting & Power Co, 73-76 & US Environ Protection Agency, 74-81; adj assoc prof, Rice Univ, 75-81; staff mem, President's Comn on the Accident at Three Mile Island, 79-80; mem, sci comts, Nat Coun Radiation Protection & Measurements, 80-; Health Physics Soc Stand Comt, 81-87; assoc ed, Health

Physics J, 85-90, Dept Energy Liaison to Idaho State Gov, 89, consult; mem, Coun Nat Labs, Environ, Safety & Health Panel, Univ Calif, 95. *Mem:* Health Physics Soc. *Res:* Measurement of ionizing radiation, especially beta dosimetry, and personnel and environmental dosimetry; evaluation of human exposure to radionuclides in the environment. *Mailing Add:* Dept Physics Idaho State Univ Campus Box 8106 Pocatello ID 83209. *Fax:* 208-236-4649; *E-Mail:* gesell@physics.isu.edu

GESELOWITZ, DAVID B(ERYL), BIOMEDICAL ENGINEERING. *Current Pos:* PROF BIOENG, PA STATE UNIV, 71-, PROF MED, 82- *Personal Data:* b Philadelphia, Pa, May 18, 30; m 53; c 3. *Educ:* Univ Pa, BS, 51, MS, 54, PhD(elec eng), 58. *Honors & Awards:* Centennial Medal, Inst Elec & Electronics Engrs, 84; Career Achievement Award, Inst Elec & Electronics Engrs/EMRS Soc. *Prof Exp:* From asst prof to assoc prof, Univ Pa, 58-71. *Concurrent Pos:* Consult, Provident Mutual Life Ins Co, 59-71; Burroughs Corp, 61-64 & Vet Admin Hosp, Washington, DC, 62-74; NIH fel & vis assoc prof, Mass Inst Technol, 65-66; ed, Trans Biomed Eng, Inst Elec & Electronics Engrs, 67-71; chmn electrocardiog comt, Am Heart Asn, 76-81; Guggenheim fel & vis prof, Duke Univ, 78-79; circulatory syst devices panel, Food & Drug Admin, 83-87; vis prof, Univ Okla, 87-88. *Mem:* Nat Acad Eng; Biomed Eng Soc; fel Inst Elec & Electronics Engrs; Int Soc Comput Electrocardiogrpahy; fel Am Col Cardiol; fel AAAS; fel Am Inst Med & Biol Eng. *Res:* Electrocardiography; cardiac electrophysiology; artificial hearts. *Mailing Add:* 232 Hallowell Bldg Pa State Univ University Park PA 16802. *Fax:* 814-863-0490; *E-Mail:* dbgz@psu.edu

GESHNER, ROBERT ANDREW, PHYSICS, MATHEMATICS. *Current Pos:* RETIRED. *Personal Data:* b Chicago, Ill, Feb 8, 28; m 52, Nancy A Beebe; c Phyllis & Glenn. *Educ:* Cornell Univ, AB, 52. *Honors & Awards:* Inst Printed Circuits President's Award, 66. *Prof Exp:* Engr, Western Elec Co, 52-56; dept head photog & printed wire develop, Gen Dynamics Corp, 55-61; prin engr, Govt & Commercial Systs Div, RCA Corp, 61-64, head, Microphotolithography Lab, 74-80, mgr, Solid State Technol Ctr, Advan Mask Technol, 80-83, mgr, Solid State Div, Photomask Technol Opers, 83-85, dir, GE/RCA Phototech Opers, 85-88. *Concurrent Pos:* Consult photolithography. *Mem:* Sr mem Inst Elec & Electronics Engrs. *Res:* Printed wiring manufacturing and artwork; microelectronic packaging; solid state device microphotolithography involving optics, metrology, microphotographic processes, laser and electron beam lithography and inspection sampling plans. *Mailing Add:* 6 Rocky Glenn Way Lebanon NJ 08833

GESKIN, ERNEST S, MECHANISM OF WATERJET MACHINING, WATERJET MACHINING TECHNOLOGY. *Current Pos:* spec lectr, 84-85, assoc prof, 86-89, PROF THERMAL SCI & MFG, NJ INST TECHNOL, 89- *Personal Data:* b Dnepropetrovsk, USSR, June 4, 35; US citizen; m 64, Doris Oskerenko; c Ellen. *Educ:* Dnepropetrovsk Inst Metall, USSR, MS, 57; Moscow Inst Steel & Alloys, PhD(metall), 67. *Honors & Awards:* Cert Recognition, Minerals, Metals & Mat Soc, 89; Cert Recognition, Am Soc Mech Engrs, 90 & 91. *Prof Exp:* Engr, Inst Automation, USSR, 56-67, mgr lab, 67-74; assoc res prof thermal sci, George Washington Univ, 77-78; assoc prof, Clarkson Col Technol, 79-80; res scientist, Revere Copper & Bass, 81-83. *Mem:* Metall Soc; Waterjet Technol Asn; Sigma Xi. *Res:* Development of the formalism of nin-equilibrium thermodynamics; second law analysis and variational methods; application of the second law techniques to development of manufacturing technologies; technology and fundamentals of waterjet machining. *Mailing Add:* Mech Engr Dept 323 Martin Luther King Blvd Newark NJ 07102. *Fax:* 732-549-0922; *E-Mail:* geskin@admin1.njit.edu

GESNER, BRUCE D, ORGANIC POLYMER CHEMISTRY. *Current Pos:* PRES, QUALITEL CONSULT GROUP, 90- *Personal Data:* b Fall River, Mass, May 7, 38; m 91, B Phyllis Whittiker; c Bruce D Jr, Michael S, Jacqueline M (Nurtan) & Jeannine C. *Educ:* Bradford Durfee Col Technol, BS, 60; Univ Idaho, PhD(org chem), 63. *Prof Exp:* Polymer chemist, Bell Tel Lab, 63-69, supvr mat & microconnections group, 69-71, supvr mat chem group, 71-78, field rep, Bell Labs, 78-83, div mgr field liaison, Bellcore, 84; div mgr technol introd & support, Pac Bell, 84-90. *Concurrent Pos:* Adj prof, Morris Brown Col, Atlanta, GA, 73; nat defense act fel, 60-63. *Mem:* Am Chem Soc; AAAS; Sigma Xi. *Res:* Organic reactions mechanisms, composition and structure of polyblends; time dependent relationship of conformationally mobile structures. *Mailing Add:* 1300 Fountain Springs Circle Danville CA 94526-5625

GESSAMAN, JAMES A, PHYSIOLOGICAL ECOLOGY, AVIAN PHYSIOLOGY. *Current Pos:* Asst prof physiol, 68-73, assoc prof, 73-89, PROF BIOL, UTAH STATE UNIV, 90- *Personal Data:* b Dayton, Ohio, Dec 10, 39; m, Deborah Johnson; c Jeffrey, Elizabeth & Janel. *Educ:* Univ Ill, Urbana, MS, 64, PhD(zool), 68. *Res:* Bioenergetics; thermoregulation; hawk migration. *Mailing Add:* Dept Biol Utah State Univ Logan UT 84322-0001. *Fax:* 435-750-1575; *E-Mail:* fajimg@cc.usu.edu

GESSAMAN, MARGARET PALMER, NONPARAMETRIC STATISTICS, DISCRIMINATION. *Current Pos:* from asst prof to assoc prof, 70-76, head dept, 73-80, PROF MATH, UNIV NEBR, OMAHA, 76-,. *Personal Data:* b Florence, Ariz, Oct 7, 34; m 65. *Educ:* Mont State Univ, BS, 56, MS, 65, PhD(statist), 66. *Prof Exp:* Asst prof math, Ithaca Col, 67-70. *Concurrent Pos:* Mem, Math Achievement Comt, Col Level Exam Bd, Educ Testing Serv, 75-80. *Mem:* Am Math Soc; Am Statist Asn; Asn Comput Mach; Inst Math Statist. *Res:* Nonparametric statistics, discrimination and density estimation and statistical decision theory. *Mailing Add:* 60th & Dodge St Univ of Nebr Omaha NE 68182-0243

GESSEL, IRA MARTIN, ENUMERATIVE COMBINATORICS. *Current Pos:* from asst prof to assoc prof, 84-90, PROF MATH & COMPUT SCI, BRANDEIS UNIV, 90- *Personal Data:* b Philadelphia, Pa, Apr 9, 51; m 89, Elizabeth A Levin. *Educ:* Harvard Univ, AB, 73; Mass Inst Technol, PhD(math), 77. *Prof Exp:* Fel, T J Watson Res Ctr, IBM, 77-78; instr appl math, Mass Inst Technol, 78-80, asst prof, 80-84. *Concurrent Pos:* Vis asst prof math, Univ Calif, San Diego, 78; chair, Dept Math, Brandeis Univ, 96-98. *Mem:* Am Math Soc; Math Asn Am; Asn Comput Mach. *Res:* Enumerative combinatorics; problems involving counting permutations, paths and graphs. *Mailing Add:* Dept Math Brandeis Univ Waltham MA 02254-9110

GESSEL, STANLEY PAUL, forestry, soils; deceased, see previous edition for last biography

GESSER, HYMAN DAVIDSON, PHYSICAL CHEMISTRY. *Current Pos:* assoc prof, 55-67, PROF CHEM, UNIV MAN, 67- *Personal Data:* b Montreal, Que, Apr 24, 29; m 52, Esther M Shtern; c 3. *Educ:* Loyola Col, Can, BSc, 49; McGill Univ, PhD(phys chem), 52. *Honors & Awards:* Borden Award, 83. *Prof Exp:* Fel photochem, Univ Rochester, 52-54; Nat Res Coun Can fel, Ottawa, Can, 54-55. *Concurrent Pos:* Res fel, Israel Inst Technol, 61-62; UN Develop Prog tech asst expert, Ctr Indust Res, Israel, 68-69. *Mem:* Am Chem Soc; fel Chem Inst Can; Chem Soc; Sigma Xi. *Res:* Atomic, thermal and photochemical kinetics; gas chromatography; surface reactions; liquid fuels from natural gas. *Mailing Add:* Dept Chem Univ Man Winnipeg MB R3T 2N2 Can. *Fax:* 204-275-0905; *E-Mail:* hgesser@cc.umanitoba.ca

GESSERT, CARL F, PHARMACOLOGY. *Current Pos:* asst prof pharmacol, 62-67, actg chmn dept, 67-69, ASSOC PROF PHARMACOL, COL MED, UNIV NEBR, OMAHA, 67- *Personal Data:* b St Louis, Mo, Apr 14, 23; m 58; c 2. *Educ:* Wash Univ, AB, 49; Univ Wis, PhD(biochem), 55. *Prof Exp:* Res asst, Sch Med, Wash Univ, 55-58, res instr, 58-62. *Mem:* Affil Am Soc Pharmacol & Exp Therapeut; Sigma Xi. *Res:* Pharmacology of neurotransmitters. *Mailing Add:* 6620 Burt St Omaha NE 68132-2628

GESSERT, WALTER LOUIS, PHYSICS. *Current Pos:* from assoc prof to prof, 61-86, EMER PROF PHYSICS & ASTRON, EASTERN MICH UNIV, 86- *Personal Data:* b Detroit, Mich, May 26, 19; m 44; c 3. *Educ:* Eastern Mich Univ, BS, 44; Wayne State Univ, MS, 47; Mich State Univ, PhD(physics), 54. *Prof Exp:* Instr gen physics, Wayne State Univ, 46-50; asst ultrasonics res, Mich State Univ, 51-54; physicist tire noise, US Rubber Co, 54-57, group leader in chg passenger tire design, 57-61. *Concurrent Pos:* Teacher musical acoust, Eastern Mich Univ, 86- *Mem:* Acoust Soc Am; Am Asn Physics Teachers; Optical Soc Am; Sigma Xi. *Res:* Ultrasonics; instrumentation; optics. *Mailing Add:* Dept Physics-Astron Eastern Mich Univ 712 Oxford Rd Ypsilanti MI 48197

GESSLER, ALBERT MURRAY, RUBBER CHEMISTRY. *Current Pos:* Chemist rubber, Standard Oil Develop Co, 42-58, res assoc, Esso Res & Eng Co, 58-66, SR RES ASSOC SYNTHETIC RUBBER, CHEM RES DIV, EXXON CHEM CO, 66- *Personal Data:* b Staten Island, NY, Nov 10, 18; m 43; c 2. *Educ:* Cornell Univ, BS, 42. *Concurrent Pos:* Chmn, NY Rubber Group, 65; chmn elastomers, Gordon Res Conf, 71. *Mem:* Brit Inst Rubber Indust; Am Chem Soc. *Res:* Elastomer and high polymer chemistry and technology; reinforcement with carbon blacks. *Mailing Add:* 448 Orchard St Cranford NJ 07016

GESSLER, JOHANNES, FLUID MECHANICS, HYDRAULICS. *Current Pos:* asst prof civil eng, 66-70, assoc prof, 70-88, PROF CIVIL ENG, COLO STATE UNIV, 88- *Personal Data:* b Basel, Switz, Oct 19, 36; m 62; c 4. *Educ:* Swiss Fed Inst Technol, BS, 60, PhD(hydraul), 65. *Prof Exp:* Jr engr, Swisselectra, Basel, 60-61; res engr, Lab Hydraul Res, Swiss Fed Inst Technol, 61-66. *Mem:* Am Soc Civil Engrs; Swiss Eng & Archit Soc; Int Asn Hydraul Res. *Res:* River mechanics, especially sediment transport; ophmization techniques of water supply systems. *Mailing Add:* 3205 Shore Rd Ft Collins CO 80524-1687

GESSNER, ADOLF WILHELM, CHEMICAL ENGINEERING, ENVIRONMENTAL ENGINEERING. *Current Pos:* ASSOC, CHEN PATENTS, SILVER SPRING, MD, 85- *Personal Data:* b Berlin, Ger, Aug 26, 28; m 53, Alice Lee Chen; c 2. *Educ:* Williams Col, BA, 52; Mass Inst Technol, ScD(chem eng), 54. *Prof Exp:* Process engr, Chemische Werks Huls, WGer, 54-55; develop engr, Jones & Laughlin Steel Corp, Pa, 55-57; process engr & mgr chem eng sect, Sci Design Co, NY, 57-61; sr develop engr, Lummus Co, NJ, 61-67; supvr process develop, Foster Wheeler Corp, 67-70; dir eng & develop, Givaudan Corp, Clifton, 70-80; sr process coordr, Lurgi Corp, River Edge, NJ, 80-82; sr engr, Synthetic Fuels Corp, Washington DC, 82-86; chief, tech assessment br, US Dept Energy, Morgantown, WVa, 86-87; mgr, Environ Eng & Develop Lab, Versar Inc, Columbia, Md, 87-91. *Concurrent Pos:* Lectr, Polytech Inst Brooklyn, 61-63, adj prof, 63- *Mem:* Am Chem Soc; Am Inst Chem Engrs; Sigma Xi. *Res:* Thermodynamics; unit operations; pollution prevention research and development. *Mailing Add:* 3013 Birchtree Lane Silver Spring MD 20906-3035

GESSNER, FREDERICK B(ENEDICT), MECHANICAL ENGINEERING. *Current Pos:* from asst prof to assoc prof, 67-76, PROF MECH ENG, UNIV WASH, 77- *Personal Data:* b Newark, NJ, June 11, 37; m 62; c 4. *Educ:* Lehigh Univ, BS, 59; Purdue Univ, MS, 60, PhD(mech eng), 64. *Prof Exp:* Res scientist, Res Div, Am Radiator & Standard Sanit Corp, 63-65; asst prof mech eng, Va Polytech Inst, 65-67. *Concurrent Pos:* NASA res grants, 66-67 & 76-; consult res div, Am Radiator & Standard Sanit Corp,

66-67; NSF res grants, 68-71 & 73-79; assoc ed, J Fluids Eng, 75-78; Off Naval Res grant, 76- *Mem:* Am Soc Mech Engrs; Sigma Xi; Am Soc Eng Educ; Am Inst Aeronaut & Astronaut. *Res:* Fluid mechanics; heat transfer; turbulence; secondary flow in non-circular ducts; subsonic flow in diffusers; pressure-flow behavior in distensible tubes; fluid dynamic studies of flow in the lower urinary tract; Reynolds stress modeling of corner flows; supersonic corner flows; hot-wire measurement techniques for complex flows. *Mailing Add:* Dept Mech Eng Univ Wash Box 352600 Seattle WA 98195-0001

GESSNER, IRA HAROLD, PEDIATRIC CARDIOLOGY. *Current Pos:* resident, 60-61, chief resident, 62, from instr to assoc prof, 62-70, PROF PEDIAT, COL MED, UNIV FLA, 70- *Personal Data:* b Rockville Center, NY, June 23, 31; m 59; c 3. *Educ:* State Univ Iowa, AB, 52; Univ Vt, MD, 56; Am Bd Pediat, dipl, 64, cert cardiol, 66. *Prof Exp:* Intern pediat, Ohio State Univ, 56-57. *Concurrent Pos:* Mem coun cardiovasc dis in the young, Am Heart Asn; Am Heart Asn advan res fel, Univ Fla, 62-64 & Wenner-Gren Inst, Stockholm, 64-65; NIH career develop award, 67; mem sub-bd pediat cardiol, Am Bd Pediat, 73-79. *Mem:* Soc Pediat Res; Teratology Soc; Am Acad Pediat; fel Am Col Cardiol; Am Heart Asn; Am Pediat Soc. *Mailing Add:* Div Pediat Cardiol Med Col Univ Fla J Hillis Health Ctr Box 100296 Gainesville FL 32611-2002

GESSNER, PETER K, PHARMACOLOGY. *Current Pos:* asst prof pharmacol, 62-67, assoc prof, 67-75, PROF PHARMACOL, STATE UNIV NY BUFFALO, 75- *Personal Data:* b Warsaw, Poland, May 3, 31; m 59; c 2. *Educ:* Univ London, BSc, 55, PhD(biochem), 58. *Prof Exp:* Res assoc, Res Div, Cleveland Clin, 58-61, asst staff mem, 61-62. *Concurrent Pos:* Career teacher alcoholism & substance abuse, Nat Inst Alcohol Abuse & Alcoholism/Nat Inst Drug Abuse, 78-82. *Mem:* Am Soc Pharmacol & Exp Therapeut. *Res:* Characterization of drug interactions including investigation of concurrent changes in the metabolic fate of the drugs and other biochemical events to determine mechanism; study of interaction of drugs and ethanol; study of withdrawal phenomena; evaluation of instruction; phenomenology and mechanism of action of hallucinogens; study of absorption on activated charcoal; pharmacological action and metabolic fate of disulfiram and diethyldithiocarbamate. *Mailing Add:* Dept Pharmacol & Therapeut SUNY Buffalo 122 Faber Hall 3435 Main St Buffalo NY 14214-3000. *Fax:* 716-829-2801

GESSNER, ROBERT V, MYCOLOGY, MICROBIOLOGY. *Current Pos:* from asst prof to assoc prof, 78-88, PROF, DEPT BIOL SCI, WESTERN ILL UNIV, 88- *Personal Data:* b Elizabeth, NJ, Apr 17, 48; m 81. *Educ:* Rutgers Univ, BS, 70; Univ RI, MS, 72, PhD(biol sci), 75. *Prof Exp:* Fel marine mycol, Inst Marine Sci, Univ NC, Chapel Hill, 75-76, res assoc & instr, 76-78. *Mem:* Mycol Soc Am; Brit Mycol Soc; Am Soc Microbiol; Am Phytopath Soc; Int Soc Arboricult. *Res:* Ecology, physiology and morphology of fungi; morels; arboriculture; salt-marsh and marine fungi. *Mailing Add:* Dept Biol Sci Western Ill Univ 900 W Adams St Macomb IL 61455-1396. *Fax:* 309-298-2270; *E-Mail:* mfrvg@uxa.ecn.bgu.edu

GESSNER, TERESA, BIOCHEMICAL PHARMACOLOGY, TOXICOLOGY. *Current Pos:* RETIRED. *Personal Data:* b Stanislawow, Poland, Sept 28, 33; US citizen. *Educ:* Univ London, BSc, 56, PhD(org chem), 59. *Prof Exp:* Res chemist, B F Goodrich Co, Cleveland, 59-62; res assoc med chem, State Univ NY Buffalo, 62-64, from instr to asst prof biochem pharmacol, 64-71; sr cancer res scientist, Dept Exp Therapeut, Roswell Park Mem Inst, 72-75, assoc cancer res scientist, 75-95. *Concurrent Pos:* From res asst prof to res assoc prof pharmacol, Roswell Park Grad Div, State Univ NY Buffalo, 71-77, res prof, 77-, dir grad studies, 74-76; mem, Nat Bladder Cancer Proj Study Sect, 77- *Mem:* Biochem Soc Gt Brit; Am Chem Soc; Am Soc Pharmacol & Exp Therapeut. *Res:* Metabolism of drugs, carcinogens and other xenobiotics; metabolic conjugations; drug interactions. *Mailing Add:* Dept Exp Therapeut Roswell Park Cancer Inst 666 Elm St Buffalo NY 14263-0001

GESSOW, ALFRED, ROTORCRAFT ENGINEERING. *Current Pos:* prof & dir, Ctr Rotorcraft Educ Res, 80-93, EMER PROF, UNIV MD, 93- *Personal Data:* b Jersey City, NJ, Oct 13, 22; m 47, Elaine Silverman; c Laura B (Goldman), Miles J, Lisa G (Michelson) & Andrew J. *Educ:* City Col New York, BCE, 43; NY Univ, MAero Eng, 44. *Honors & Awards:* Nikolsky Hon Lectureship, Am Helicopter Soc, 85, Alexander Klemin Award, 96; Fed Avaiation Admin Award, 90. *Prof Exp:* Aeronaut res scientist, Langley Res Ctr, Nat Adv Comt Aeronaut, Va, 44-49, head fluid & space physics sect, NASA HQ, 59-61, chief fluid physics br, 61-67, asst dir res div, 67-71, chief aerodyn & fluid mech, Aerodyne & Vehicle Systs Div, Off Advan Res & Technol, 71-80. *Concurrent Pos:* Lectr, Grad Exten Ctr, Univ Va, Hampton, 45-58; founding ed, Am Helicopter Soc, 55; helicopter consult to France & Ger, Adv Group Aeronaut Res & Develop, 59; exec secy adv comt fluid mech, NASA, 59-63, mem res & tech subcomt fluid mech, 67-, mem subcomt electrophys & adv coun basic res, 68-; adj prof, NY Univ, 68 & Cath Univ Am, 70-; chmn indust & prof adv coun, Dept Aerospace Eng, Pa State Univ, 70-; invited prof, Korean Inst Advan Sci, Seoul, Korea, 80; mem, Bd Army Sci & Technol, Nat Acad Sci, 80-86; chmn dept aerospace eng, Univ Md, 80-93; mem, Army Sci Bd, 86-92. *Mem:* Fel Am Inst Aeronaut & Astronaut; hon fel Am Helicopter Soc; Am Soc Eng Educ. *Res:* Rotating-wing aerodynamics; fluid physics; electrophysics; aerodynamics; computational aerodynamics; helicopter aerodynamics, flight mechanics and design. *Mailing Add:* 7308 Durbin Terr Bethesda MD 20817. *Fax:* 301-314-9001; *E-Mail:* ag7@umail.umd.edu

GEST, HOWARD, MICROBIOLOGY. *Current Pos:* chmn dept, 66-70, prof microbiol, 66-78, DISTINGUISHED PROF MICROBIOL, DEPT BIOL, IND UNIV, BLOOMINGTON, 78-, ADJ PROF, DEPT HIST PHILOS SCI, 83- *Personal Data:* b London, Eng, Oct 15, 21; nat US; wid, Theodore, Michael & Donald; c 3. *Educ:* Univ Calif, Los Angeles, BA, 42; Wash Univ, PhD(microbiol), 49. *Prof Exp:* Asst metall lab, Univ Chicago, 43; from jr chemist to assoc chemist, Clinton Labs, Tenn, 43-46; asst radiol, Sch Med, Wash Univ, 46-49; from instr to assoc prof microbiol, Sch Med, Western Reserve Univ, 49-59; prof microbiol, Henry Shaw Sch Bot, Wash Univ, 59-64, dept zool, 64-66. *Concurrent Pos:* USPHS spec res fel, Calif Inst Technol, 56-57; mem adv panel metab biol, NSF, 63-66; NSF sr fel, Nat Inst Med Res, London, 65-66; mem, Study Sect Bact & Mycol, NIH, 66-68, chmn, Study Sect Microbiol Chem, 68-69 & Study Sect Microbiol Physiol & Genetics, 88-90; mem comt microbiol probs man in extended space flight, Nat Acad Sci-Nat Res Coun, 67-69; Guggenheim fel, Imp Col, Univ London, Univ Stockholm & Univ Tokyo, 70; vis prof, Univ Tokyo & Japanese Soc Promotion Sci, 70; Guggenheim fel, Univ Calif, Los Angeles & Imp Col, Univ London, 80; distinguished fac lect award, Ind Univ, 87. *Mem:* Hon mem Am Soc Microbiol; Am Soc Biochem & Molecular Biol; Brit Soc Gen Microbiol; Am Acad Microbiol; fel AAAS. *Res:* Physiology and intermediary metabolism of microorganisms; photosynthesis; metabolism of molecular hydrogen and nitrogen; electron transport mechanisms; metabolic regulatory mechanisms; biogeochemistry. *Mailing Add:* Biol Dept Ind Univ Bloomington IN 47405-6800. *Fax:* 812-855-6705

GESTELAND, RAYMOND FREDERICK, GENE REGULATION, TRANSLATION. *Current Pos:* INVESTR & PROF HUMAN GENETICS, HOWARD HUGHES MED INST, UNIV UTAH,78- *Personal Data:* b Madison, Wis, April 2, 38; m 60; c 4. *Educ:* Univ Wis, BS, 60, MS, 61; Harvard Univ, PhD(biochem), 65. *Prof Exp:* NSF fel, Inst Molecular Biol, Univ Geneve, 62-66; asst dir res, Cold Spring Harbor, NY, 67-78. *Res:* Regulation of gene expression and the mechanism of decoding, including nonsense suppressors, tRNA structure and context effects. *Mailing Add:* Dept Human Genetics Howard Hughes Med Inst Univ Utah 6160 Eccles Genetics Bldg Salt Lake City UT 84112. *Fax:* 801-585-3910

GESTELAND, ROBERT CHARLES, NEUROPHYSIOLOGY, ELECTRICAL ENGINEERING. *Current Pos:* assoc dean biomed sci, 89-93, PROF CELL BIOL, NEUROBIOL & ANAT, UNIV CINCINNATI MED CTR, 85-, VPRES RES & UNIV DEAN ADVAN STUDIES, 93- *Personal Data:* b Madison, Wis, July 1, 30; wid; c Matthew, Wendy & Caroline. *Educ:* Univ Wis, BS, 53; Mass Inst Technol, SM, 57, PhD(neurophysiol), 61. *Prof Exp:* Engr, Gen Radio Co, 53-54; mem staff, Harvard-Peabody-Smithsonian Exped, Kalahari Desert, 57-58; mem res staff, Electronics Res Lab, Mass Inst Technol, 61-62, res assoc biol, 62-65; mem res staff life sci, Sci Eng Inst, 62-65; assoc prof elec eng & biol, Northwestern Univ, 65-67, assoc prof to prof biol sci, 67-80, prof neurobiology & physiol, 80-85. *Concurrent Pos:* Consult, Arthur D Little Co, Inc, Mass Ment Health Ctr, Invention Group Inc & Unilever NV; pres, Taste & Smell Consult Group, Inc, Evanston, Ill, 79-87; NIH Javits, Pepper Investr. *Mem:* AAAS; Am Phys Soc; Soc Neurosci; Asn Chemoreception Sci. *Res:* Sensory neurophysiology; electrode processes; electronic circuit theory. *Mailing Add:* 318 Chenora Ct Cincinnati OH 45215. *Fax:* 513-556-0128; *E-Mail:* robert.gesteland@uc.edu

GESUND, HANS, STRUCTURAL ENGINEERING. *Current Pos:* dir grad studies civil eng, 84-88, chmn, Dept Civil Eng, 87-92, PROF STRUCT ENG, UNIV KY, 58- *Personal Data:* b Vienna, Austria, Sept 18, 28; nat US; m 51, Irmgard Orth; c Peter & Ann. *Educ:* Yale Univ, BEng, 50, MEng, 53, DEng, 58. *Prof Exp:* Instr civil eng, Yale Univ, 53-58. *Concurrent Pos:* Consult struct eng, Conn. *Mem:* Fel Am Soc Civil Engrs; Am Soc Eng Educ; Int Asn Bridge & Struct Engrs; fel Am Concrete Inst; Am Soc Testing Mat; Sigma Xi. *Res:* Structural design; reinforced concrete; structural mechanics; limit and ultimate load design; design of concrete slabs; author of more than 50 publications.. *Mailing Add:* Dept Civil Eng Univ Ky Lexington KY 40506-0281

GETCHELL, THOMAS VINCENT, PHYSIOLOGY, BIOPHYSICS. *Current Pos:* PROF, DEPT PHYSIOL & BIOPHYS, UNIV KY, 89-, ASSOC DEAN RES & BASIC SCI, UNIV KY, 89- *Personal Data:* b Erie, Pa, Nov 16, 39; c 2. *Educ:* Gannon Col, BA, 63; Villanova Univ, MS, 66; Northwestern Univ, PhD(neurosci), 69. *Prof Exp:* Instr, Biol Dept, Gannon Col, 63-64; assoc physiol, Med Sch & assoc mem, Monell Chem Senses Ctr, Univ Pa, 69-72; NIH spec fel neurophysiol, Yale Univ, 73-74, asst prof, Dept Physiol, 74-78; from assoc prof to prof, Dept Anat & Cell Biol, Wayne State Univ, 78-89, chairperson, Neurosci Prog, 81-85, assoc dean, Grad Sch, 86-89. *Concurrent Pos:* Vis scientist, Roche Inst Molecular Biol, 76, 88-89, NIH sr fel, 88-89; assoc prog dir, Sensory Physiol & Perception Prog, Directorate Biol, Behav & Social Sci, NSF, 78-79; adj prof, Sch Med, Wayne State Univ, 80-89; mem, Commun Sci Study Sect, NIH, 81-82, mem & chmn, Sensory Dis & Lang Study Sect, 82-86, mem, Bd Friends, Nat Inst Deafness & Other Commun Dis, NIH, 91- & Nat Adv Bd, 91-95; assoc ed, Behav & Brain Sci, 84-; exec chairperson, Asn Chemoreception Sci, 89-90. *Mem:* AAAS; Am Physiol Soc; Asn Chemoreception Sci; Asn Neurosci Depts & Progs; Asn Res Otolaryngol; Europ Chemoreception Res Orgn; NY Acad Sci; Soc Neurosci; Sigma Xi. *Res:* Author of numerous publications. *Mailing Add:* Dean's Ofc PMMN 140 Col Med Univ Ky 800 Rose St Lexington KY 40536-0001. *Fax:* 606-233-6805

GETHMANN, RICHARD CHARLES, GENETICS. *Current Pos:* asst prof, 71-76, ASSOC PROF BIOL, UNIV MD, BALTIMORE COUNTY, 77- *Personal Data:* b Yakima, Wash, June 8, 41; m 74; c 2. *Educ:* Wash State Univ, BS, 64; Ore State Univ, MS, 66; Univ Chicago, PhD(biol), 70. *Prof Exp:* NSF fel genetics, Univ Calif, San Diego, 70-71. *Mem:* Genetics Soc Am. *Res:* Chromosome behavior in Drosophila. *Mailing Add:* Dept Biol Sci Univ Md Baltimore County 5401 Wilkens Ave Catonsville MD 21228-5329

GETHNER, JON STEVEN, ANALYTICAL INSTRUMENTATION, PROCESS ANALYTICAL CHEMISTRY. *Current Pos:* PRES, ADAPTIVE ANALYZER TECHNOLOGIES, 91- *Personal Data:* b Chicago, Ill, July 12, 46; m 83. *Educ:* Univ Chicago, SB, 68; Columbia Univ, MPhil, 73, PhD(chem), 76. *Prof Exp:* Systs engr, IBM Corp, 68-70; staff fel biophysics, NIH, 76-78; res chemist, Corp Res Lab, Exxon Res & Eng Corp, 78-80, staff chemist, 80-91. *Mem:* Am Phys Soc; Biophys Soc; Am Chem Soc. *Res:* Hydrodynamics of particles in solution; nucleation phenomena; biological self-assembly systems; intermolecular interactions; laser light scattering; structure and properties of gel and polymer networks; coal physical chemistry; FTIR spectroscopy; NIR and FTIR analyzer systems; real-time chemical process measurement. *Mailing Add:* Adaptive Analyzer Technologies 610 River St Hoboken NJ 07030. *E-Mail:* 76154.1011@compuserve.com

GETOOR, RONALD KAY, MATHEMATICS. *Current Pos:* PROF MATH, UNIV CALIF, SAN DIEGO, 66- *Personal Data:* b Royal Oak, Mich, Feb 9, 29; m 59; c 1. *Educ:* Univ Mich, AB, 50, MS, 51, PhD(math), 54. *Prof Exp:* Instr math, Princeton Univ, 54-56; from asst prof to prof, Univ Wash, 56-66. *Concurrent Pos:* NSF fel, 59-60; vis prof, Stanford Univ, 64-65. *Mem:* Am Math Soc; fel Inst Math Statist. *Res:* Probability theory, especially general theory of Markov processes and their associated potential theory. *Mailing Add:* 9500 Gilman Dr Univ Calif San Diego La Jolla CA 92093-0112

GETSINGER, WILLIAM J, MICROWAVES, TRANSMISSION LINE ANALYSIS. *Current Pos:* CONSULT, 84- *Personal Data:* b Waterbury, Conn, Jan 24, 24. *Educ:* Univ Conn, BS, 49, Stanford Univ, MS, 59, EE, 62. *Prof Exp:* Design engr, Technicraft Labs, 49-50 & 52-57, Westinghouse Elec Corp, 50-52; sr res engr, Stanford Res Inst, 57-62; staff mem, Lincoln Labs, Mass Inst Technol, 62-69; br mgr, proj mgr & sr scientist, Comsat Labs, 69-84. *Mem:* Fel Inst Elec & Electronics Engrs. *Res:* Microwave discontinuity analysis. *Mailing Add:* 6662 Bozman Neavitt Rd Bozman MD 21612

GETTING, IVAN ALEXANDER, PHYSICS. *Current Pos:* CONSULT, 77- *Personal Data:* b New York, NY, Jan 18, 12; m, Helen Avery; c Nancy G (Resch), Ivan C & Peter A. *Educ:* Mass Inst Technol, BS, 33; Oxford Univ, DPhil(astrophys), 35. *Hon Degrees:* DSc, Northeastern Univ, 54, Univ Southern Calif, 86. *Honors & Awards:* Naval Ord Develop Award, 45; President's Medal of Merit, 48; Except Serv Award, USAF, 60; Kitty Hawk Award, Los Angeles Chamber Com, 75; Pioneer Award, Inst Elec & Electronics Engrs, 75, Founder's Medal, 89. *Prof Exp:* Jr fel, Harvard Univ, 35-40; mem, Radiation Lab, Mass Inst Technol, 40-45, prof, 45-50; asst develop planning, Dep Chief Staff Develop, USAF, 50-51; vpres eng & res, Raytheon Co, 51-60; pres & trustee, The Aerospace Corp, 60-77. *Concurrent Pos:* Mem sci adv bd, USAF, 45-; mem, Res & Develop Adv Coun, Sig Corps, 52-60; consult, var panels of the Pres Sci Adv Comt, 61-75; chmn, Naval Warfare Panel, 71-75; consult, Nat Security Coun, 75-77; mem, Undersea Warfare Comn, Navy Studies bd & panels, Nat Acad Sci. *Mem:* Nat Acad Eng; fel Am Phys Soc; fel Inst Elec & Electronics Engrs (pres, 78); Am Acad Arts & Sci; hon fel Am Inst Aeronaut & Astronaut. *Res:* Particle accelerators; nuclear physics; radar; fire control; gaseous discharges; astrophysics; multivibrator high speed router; automatic tracking of targets by radar; rapid scanning radar antennas; satellite systems. *Mailing Add:* 1760 Ave Del Mundo No 103 Coronado CA 92118-3036. *Fax:* 619-435-3953; *E-Mail:* ivanag@webtv.net

GETTING, PETER ALEXANDER, NEUROSCIENCE, ELECTROPHYSIOLOGY. *Current Pos:* from asst prof to assoc prof, 80-85, PROF PHYSIOL, UNIV IOWA, 85- *Personal Data:* b Boston, Mass, Nov 28, 44; m 69; c 2. *Educ:* Mass Inst Technol, BS, 67; Univ Calif, Berkeley, PhD(biophys), 71. *Prof Exp:* Fel neurophysiol, Univ Wash, 71-73; asst prof biol, Stanford Univ, 73-80. *Concurrent Pos:* Mem, adv comt, Friday Harbor Labs, 82-83; mem, Neurobiol II Study Sect, NIH, 83- *Mem:* Soc Neurosci; AAAS; Am Physiol Soc; Int Soc Neuroethology. *Res:* Description of neuronal circuitry mediating behavior using intra and extra-cellular recording techniques; biophysical approaches applied to mechanisms of neuronal excitability and synaptic transmission; neuronal control of mammalian respiration. *Mailing Add:* 417 Monroe St Iowa City IA 52246

GETTINS, PETER GREGORY WOLFGANG, MULTINUCLEAR MAGNETIC RESONANCE, PROTEASE INHIBITORS. *Current Pos:* PROF BIOCHEM, UNIV ILL, CHICAGO. *Personal Data:* b Sunderland, UK, Nov 8, 53; US citizen. *Educ:* Oxford Univ, BA, 76 & DPhil(biochem), 79. *Prof Exp:* Asst molecular biophys, Yale Univ, 79-83, res scientist, 83-84; from asst prof to assoc prof biochem, Vanderbilt Univ Sch Med, 84-93. *Mem:* Am Soc Biochem & Molecular Biol; Am Chem Soc; AAAS; Int Soc Magnetic Resonance. *Res:* Structure and function relationships of proteins with particular emphasis on human plasma protease inhibitors; use of spectroscopic methods; nuclear magnetic resonance; electron paramagnetic resonance; fluorescence; sit-directed; mutagenesis. *Mailing Add:* Dept Biochem Univ Ill 1819-53 W Polk St Chicago IL 60612. *Fax:* 312-413-8769; *E-Mail:* pgettins@uic.edu

GETTLER, JOSEPH DANIEL, PHYSICAL ORGANIC CHEMISTRY. *Current Pos:* from instr to asst prof, 46-54, ASSOC PROF CHEM, NY UNIV, 54- *Personal Data:* b Brooklyn, NY, Mar 5, 16; m 55; c 4. *Educ:* Columbia Univ, BA, 37, MA, 39, PhD(chem), 43. *Prof Exp:* Res chemist, Air Reduction Co, 43-46. *Concurrent Pos:* Adj assoc prof chem, Columbia Univ, 74-; tech adv, Syn-Zyme Labs. *Mem:* Am Chem Soc; Royal Soc Chem; Sigma Xi. *Res:* Solution kinetics; condensation reactions; molecular rearrangements; statistical analysis. *Mailing Add:* 209 Jennifer Lane Yonkers NY 10710

GETTNER, MARVIN, PHYSICS. *Current Pos:* PHYSICIST, DEPT ENERGY, WASHINGTON, 90- *Personal Data:* b Rochester, NY, July 21, 34; m 59; c 3. *Educ:* Univ Rochester, BS, 56; Univ Pa, PhD(physics), 61. *Prof Exp:* Res assoc physics, Univ Pa, 60-61; from asst prof to prof physics, Northeastern Univ, 61-90. *Concurrent Pos:* Vis scientist, Rutherford Lab, Eng, 68-69, vis scientist, Max Planck Inst, Cern, Geneva, 76-77; prin investr, high energy exp group, NSF, 72- *Mem:* Fel Am Phys Soc. *Res:* Experimental study of high energy electron-position collision to reveal the fundamental nature of matter, forces and energy; techniques used include radiation and nuclear particle detectors, real time data acquisitions, digital electronics and large scale data analysis. *Mailing Add:* 9642 Shadow Oak Dr Gaithersburg MD 20879

GETTY, ROBERT J(OHN), chemical engineering; deceased, see previous edition for last biography

GETTY, WARD DOUGLAS, PLASMA WAVE PROPAGATION, EXPERIMENTAL PLASMA PHYSICS. *Current Pos:* assoc prof, 66-77, PROF ELEC ENG, UNIV MICH, ANN ARBOR, 77- *Personal Data:* b Detroit, Mich, Aug 8, 33; m 55; c 4. *Educ:* Univ Mich, BS(math) & BS(elec eng), 55, MS, 56; Mass Inst Technol, ScD(elec eng), 62. *Prof Exp:* Asst prof elec eng, Mass Inst Technol, 62-66. *Concurrent Pos:* Ford Found fel, 62-64; consult, Raytheon Co, 63-66; vis scientist, Princeton Plasma Physics Lab, 73-74, Lawrence Livermore Lab, 79, IBM, East Fishkill, 91. *Mem:* Inst Elec & Electronics Engrs; Am Phys Soc; Sigma Xi. *Res:* Plasma physics in application to materials processing; electron beam sources. *Mailing Add:* Dept Elec-Comp Eng Univ Mich Ann Arbor MI 48109. *E-Mail:* getty@engin.umich.edu

GETZ, GODFREY S, BIOCHEMISTRY, PATHOLOGY. *Current Pos:* asst prof path & res assoc biochem, Univ Chicago, 64-67, assoc prof, 67-72, assoc dean col & div biol sci, 74-77, actg dean, Div Biol Sci, 93-95, PROF PATH & BIOCHEM, UNIV CHICAGO, 72-, CHMN, DEPT PATH, 88- *Personal Data:* b Johannesburg, SAfrica, June 18, 30; m 55; c 4. *Educ:* Univ Witwatersrand, MB, BCh, 54, BSc, 55; Oxford Univ, DPhil(biochem), 63. *Prof Exp:* Lectr chem path, Witwatersrand Univ, 56 & 59-63; demonstr biochem, Oxford Univ, 56-59; res assoc, Harvard Med Sch, 63-64. *Concurrent Pos:* Donald N Pritzker distinguished serv prof, Univ Chicago. *Mem:* Am Soc Biochem & Molecular Biol; Sigma Xi; Am Asn Investigative Path. *Res:* Lipoprotein biogensis and function in relation to atherosclerosis and Alzheimer's disease; mitochondrial biogenesis. *Mailing Add:* Dept Path Mc 3083 Univ Chicago 5841 S Maryland Ave Chicago IL 60637-1470. *Fax:* 773-702-1119; *E-Mail:* getz@mort.bsd.uchicago.edu

GETZ, LOWELL LEE, ECOLOGY. *Current Pos:* RETIRED. *Personal Data:* b Chesterfield, Ill, Sept 21, 31; m 53, Mary R; c Colleen M & Allison L. *Educ:* Univ Ill, BS, 53; Univ Mich, MS, 59, PhD(zool), 60. *Prof Exp:* Res assoc ecol, Univ Mich, 59-61; instr zool, Univ Conn, 61-62; from asst prof to assoc prof, 62-69; prof, Univ Ill, Urbana, 69-97, head, Dept Ecol, Ethology & Evolution, 75-80 & 88-95. *Mem:* Am Soc Mammal; Brit Ecol Soc; Ecol Soc Am; Soc Study Evolution; Sigma Xi; fel AAAS. *Res:* Ecology of mammals and mollusks. *Mailing Add:* 606 E Healey St Champaign IL 61820. *E-Mail:* lowell_getz@qms1.life.uiuc.edu

GETZ, MICHAEL JOHN, CELL BIOLOGY, MOLECULAR BIOLOGY. *Current Pos:* from instr to asst prof biochem, Mayo Med Sch, 76-81, assoc prof cell biol, 81-85, consult path, anat & molecular med, Mayo Clin & Found, 77-80, consult cell biol, 80-85, PROF BIOCHEM & MOLECULAR BIOL, MAYO MED SCH, 87-, CONSULT BIOCHEM & MOLECULAR BIOL, MAYO CLIN & FOUND, 85- *Personal Data:* b Peoria, Ill, Apr 28, 44; m 64; c 2. *Educ:* WTex State Univ, BSc, 67, MSc, 68; Univ Tex Grad Sch Biomed Sci, PhD(molecular biol), 72. *Prof Exp:* Nat Cancer Inst fel molecular biol, Beatson Inst Cancer Res, Glasgow, Scotland, 72-74; Mayo Found fel exp path, Mayo Clin & Mayo Found, 74-75, assoc consult path, anat & molecular med, 75-77. *Concurrent Pos:* Am Cancer Soc res grant, 76-78; res grant, NIH, Pub Health Serv, 78-94; biol sci study sect, Pub Health Serv, NIH, 90- *Mem:* AAAS; Am Soc Cell Biol. *Res:* Regulation of gene expression by peptide growth factors; mechanisms of cell proliferation and chemical carcinogenesis. *Mailing Add:* Dept Biochem & Molecular Biol Mayo Clin & Found 200 SW First St Rochester MN 55905-0001

GETZ, WAYNE MARCUS, POPULATION MODELING, OLFACTION IN INSECTS. *Current Pos:* PROF ENVIRON SCI, DEPT ENVIRON SCI, POLICY & MGT, UNIV CALIF BERKELEY, 79- *Personal Data:* b Johannesburg, SAfricia, Apr 26, 50; US citizen; m 72, Jennifer Gonski; c Stacey & Trevor. *Educ:* Univ Witwatersrand, SAfrica, BSc, 71, BSc Hons, 72, PhD, 76. *Honors & Awards:* US Sr Sci Award, Alexander von Humboldt Found, Ger, 92. *Prof Exp:* res scientist, Nat Resource Inst Math Sci, Coun Sci & Indust Res, 74-79. *Concurrent Pos:* Fel, Col Natural Resources, Univ Colo, 76; vis mech eng, Univ Calif, Berkeley, 77; dir, Resource Modelers Asn, 91-94. *Mem:* Resource Modelers Asn (pres, 95-96); Entom Soc Am; Int Soc Ecol Modeling; Soc Math Biol; Int Neural Network Soc; AAAS. *Res:* Dynamical systems theory and simulation modeling to problems in resource management, population genetics, ecology, evolutionary theory, and neural processing; behavior, learning, kin recognition and olfaction in honey bees. *Mailing Add:* Dept Environ Sci Policy & Mgmt Univ Calif Berkeley CA 94720-0001

GETZEN, FORREST WILLIAM, PHYSICAL CHEMISTRY, SOLUTION THERMODYNAMICS. *Current Pos:* from assoc prof to prof, 61-85, EMER PROF CHEM, NC STATE UNIV, 85- *Personal Data:* b Stuart, Fla, Feb 28, 28; m 56, Evangeline Sferes; c Thompson Hart, Katherine Anna & Peter Lindsay. *Educ:* Va Mil Inst, BS, 50; Mass Inst Technol, PhD(chem), 56. *Prof Exp:* Instr chem, Va Mil Inst, 50-51; asst, Mass Inst Technol, 53-55; res engr, Humble Oil & Refining Co, 56-61. *Concurrent Pos:* Mem, US Eng Team, Kabul, Afghanistan, 65-67. *Mem:* AAAS; Am Chem Soc; Am Inst Mining Metall & Petrol Eng; fel Am Inst Chem; Sigma Xi. *Res:* Fluid phase behavior; compressibility of gaseous argon; interfacial phenomena; surface and colloid chemistry; solution thermodynamics. *Mailing Add:* 2009 Banbury Rd Raleigh NC 27608

GETZEN, RUFUS THOMAS, GROUNDWATER HYDROLOGY. *Current Pos:* HYDROLOGIST, US DEPT INTERIOR, GEOL SURV, 71- *Personal Data:* b Columbia, SC, Apr 11, 44; m 68. *Educ:* Wake Forest Col, AB, 65; Univ SC, MS, 69; Univ Ill, PhD(geol), 74. *Mem:* Nat Water Well Asn; AAAS; Soc Econ Paleontologists & Mineralogists. *Res:* Hydrologic effects of petrofabrics. *Mailing Add:* 505 Broderick St San Francisco CA 94117

GETZENDANER, MILTON EDMOND, PESTICIDE CHEMISTRY. *Current Pos:* RETIRED. *Personal Data:* b Grandview, Wash, Apr 17, 18; m 41; c 2. *Educ:* Whitman Col, AB, 40; Univ Wash, MS, 45; Univ Tex, PhD(biochem), 49. *Prof Exp:* Res chemist, Univ Wash, 44-46; res scientist concentration growth factor, Univ Tex, 48-49; biochemist, Hanford Works, Gen Elec Co, 49-53; agr chem research, Dow Chem Co, 53-59, group leader residue res, Bioprod Dept, 59-69, res dir residue res, Agr Organics Dept, 69-75, assoc scientist govt regist, Health & Environ Res, 76-81. *Concurrent Pos:* Jr chemist, Chem Warfare Serv, US Army, 43-46. *Mem:* Am Chem Soc; Am Soc Testing & Mat; Asn Off Analytical Chem. *Res:* Effect of radiation on bacterial growth; metabolite destruction by ionizing radiations; concentration of growth factor; lignin research; methods for and analysis of agricultural chemical residues; protocols for studies on crops, animals, soil, water, elucidating residues of agricultural chemicals to establish safety; registration and tolerances for agricultural products through United States Environmental Protection Agency; global registration coordinator. *Mailing Add:* 6008 Melbourne Indianapolis IN 42608-1054

GETZIN, PAULA MAYER, GENERAL COMPUTER SCIENCES. *Current Pos:* asst prof, 69-77, ASSOC PROF CHEM, KEAN COL, 77- *Personal Data:* b New York, NY, Oct 6, 41; c 2. *Educ:* Radcliffe Col, BA, 61; Columbia Univ, MA, 62, PhD(chem), 67; Stevens Inst Technol, MS(computer sci), 86. *Prof Exp:* Fel chem, Rutgers Univ, 67-69. *Concurrent Pos:* mem, Highland Park Bd Educ, 80-87. *Mem:* Am Chem Soc; Sigma Xi; Asn Comput Mach. *Res:* Theoretical chemical calculations. *Mailing Add:* 423 Lincoln Ave Highland Park NJ 08904-2628

GEUMEI, AIDA M, CLINICAL PHARMACOLOGY, INTERNAL MEDICINE. *Current Pos:* CLIN ASSOC PROF INTERNAL MED, SOUTHWESTERN MED SCH, DALLAS, 78-; DIR PULMONARY DEPT, HENDERSON MEM HOSP, 78- *Educ:* Univ Alexandria, Egypt, PhD(pharmacol), 65. *Prof Exp:* CLIN ASSOC PROF INTERNAL MED, SOUTHWESTERN MED SCH, DALLAS, 78- *Mailing Add:* RR 7 Henderson TX 75652

GEURTS, MARIE ANNE H L, PALYNOLOGY. *Current Pos:* adj prof, 78-82, PROF GEOG & PALYNOLOGY, UNIV OTTAWA, 82- *Personal Data:* b Leopoldville, Congo, June 4, 47. *Educ:* Cath Univ Louvain, SC, 69, DcSc, 75. *Prof Exp:* Asst geog & physics, Cath Univ Louvain, 69-76; researcher, Nat Ctr Geomorphol Res, Belg, 76-78. *Concurrent Pos:* Traveling fel, Belg Ministry Educ, 76. *Mem:* Belg Asn Geol; Asn French Speaking Palynologists; Can Palynologists. *Res:* Contemporary pollen spectra and palynostratigraphy in Yukon territory and Northwest territories (Canada); formation and stratigraphy of continental limestone in Belgium, France, Spain and Canada (tufa or travertine). *Mailing Add:* Dept Geog Univ Ottawa Ottawa ON K1N 6N5 Can. *E-Mail:* magad@aex.1.uottowa.ca

GEUSIC, JOSEPH EDWARD, SOLID STATE PHYSICS, OPTICS. *Current Pos:* PRES, GEUSIC INFORMATION SERVS INC, 95- *Personal Data:* b Nesquehoning, Pa, Nov 21, 31; m 53, Irene Jean Hosak; c Patricia, Mark, Michael, Mary Ellen, Robert & Joseph. *Educ:* Lehigh Univ, BS, 53; Ohio State Univ, MS, 55, PhD(physics), 58. *Honors & Awards:* Quantum Electronics Award, Inst Elec & Electronics Engrs, 92; R W Wood Prize, Optical Soc Am, 93. *Prof Exp:* Res assoc, Physics Dept, Ohio State Univ, 55-58; mem tech staff, AT&T Labs, 58-62, supvr solid state laser group, 62-66, head, Solid State Optical Device Dept, 66-70, head, Magnetics Dept, 70-84, head, Semiconductor Laser Dept, 84-94. *Mem:* Fel Inst Elec & Electronics Engrs; Am Phys Soc; Sigma Xi. *Res:* First report of paramagnetic spectra; invention and development of Nd/YAG laser, barium sodium niobate nonlinear optical material; first demonstration of continuous operating optical parametric oscillator; developer of semiconductor lasers for terrestrial and undersea lightwave communication systems, magnetic bubble materials and devices; granted 30 patents in field and over 62 articles published. *Mailing Add:* 261 Lorraine Dr Berkeley Heights NJ 07922-2341. *Fax:* 732-771-0282; *E-Mail:* josephgeusic@micron.com

GEVANTMAN, LEWIS HERMAN, PHYSICAL CHEMISTRY. *Current Pos:* RETIRED. *Personal Data:* b New York, NY, Sept 12, 21; m 48, Leatrice; c Sandra (Cay) & Janis (Mara). *Educ:* Johns Hopkins Univ, BE, 42; Univ Notre Dame, PhD(chem), 51. *Prof Exp:* Chem operator, Bethlehem Steel Co, 42 & Johns Hopkins Univ, 42-43; assoc chemist, Clinton Labs, Oak Ridge Nat Labs, 43-46; supvry chemist, Radiation Chem, US Naval Radiol Defense Lab, 51-64; sr sci adv, US Mission, UN Int Atomic Energy Agency, 64-67; prog mgr off standard ref data, Nat Inst Standards & Technol, 67-83, sr prog analyst, 72-73, consult, 83-97. *Concurrent Pos:* Consult, Nuclear Sci & Eng Corp, 56-60 & mem staff, Coun Environ Qual, 79-80; secy, Solubility Data Proj, Int Union Pure & Appl Chem, 80-92. *Mem:* Sigma Xi; Am Chem Soc; Int Union Pure & Appl Chem. *Res:* Effect of ionizing radiation on the rates of chemical reactions; distribution of absorbed energy in matter and energy transfer mechanisms; radiation dosimetry; nuclear weapons effects; chemical kinetics; solid state; scientific data evaluation and management. *Mailing Add:* 11608 Toulone Dr Potomac MD 20854

GEVARTER, WILLIAM BRADLEY, SIMULATION OF MOTIVATED HUMAN DECISION MAKING. *Current Pos:* CONSULT COGNITIVE SCI & ARTIFICIAL INTEL, GEVARTER & ASSOCS, 90- *Personal Data:* b Brooklyn, NY, July 19, 27; m 71; c 5. *Educ:* Univ Mich, BS, 51; Univ Calif, Los Angeles, MS, 55; Stanford Univ, PhD(aeronaut & astronaut eng), 66. *Prof Exp:* Staff engr, Lockheed Missiles & Space Co, 57-66; adv engr, Int Bus Mach, 66-67; mem tech staff, Bellcom, Div Bell Labs, 67-71; opers res analyst, NASA Hq, Wash, DC, 70-75, mgr automation res & technol, 75-81, res assoc artificial intel, 81-83, computer scientist, Ames Res Ctr, 84-90. *Concurrent Pos:* Mem, Robotics & Automation Coun, Inst Elec & Electronics Engrs, 84-85. *Mem:* Inst Elec & Electronics Engrs. *Res:* Artificial intelligence; cognitive science; robotics; expert systems; simulation of human decision making considering emotions; author of publications on artificial intelligence and robotics. *Mailing Add:* Saint Helena Santa Rosa CA 95403

GEWANTER, HERMAN LOUIS, SYNTHETIC ORGANIC & NATURAL PRODUCTS CHEMISTRY. *Current Pos:* RETIRED. *Personal Data:* b Bronx, NY, May 26, 27; m 66, Arline Zullow; c Richard M & Daniel S. *Educ:* Long Island Univ, BS, 52; Univ Fla, PhD(fluorocarbons), 62. *Prof Exp:* Chemist, Standard Chem Prod, Inc, 52-56; res asst, Univ Fla, 56-61; proj leader org Synthesis, Res & Develop Chem Div, Union Carbide Corp, 62-66; staff scientist tech serv & prod develop, Pfizer Inc, 66-69, mgr tech serv, Tech Serv Ctr, 69-92. *Concurrent Pos:* Consult, H L Gewanter Assocs. *Mem:* AAAS; Sigma Xi; Am Chem Soc; Steel Struct Painting Coun; NY Acad Sci; Am Oil Chemists Soc. *Res:* Fluorocarbon chemistry; alkyl amines and polyalkylene amines and derivatives; polymer intermediates; detergent additives; chelation; citrates, gluconates, itaconates, erythorbates, 2-ketogluconates, fumarates, sorbitol and derivatives and applications; detergent formulation and iron oxide removal under ecologically acceptable conditions. *Mailing Add:* 143 Hoyt St Apt 6N Stamford CT 06905

GEWARTOWSKI, J(AMES) W(ALTER), ELECTRONICS ENGINEERING. *Current Pos:* RETIRED. *Personal Data:* b Chicago, Ill, Nov 10, 30; m 56, Marion Wakeman; c Marion, Diane, Patricia, John & Karen. *Educ:* Ill Inst Technol, BS, 52; Mass Inst Technol, SM, 53; Stanford Univ, PhD(elec eng), 58. *Honors & Awards:* Thompson Mem Award, Inst Radio Eng, 60. *Prof Exp:* Res asst, Electronics Lab, Stanford Univ, 54-57; mem tech staff, AT&T Bell Labs, 57-62, supvr microwave source group, 62-71, supvr microwave integrated circuits, Amplifiers & Dielec Resonators Group, 81-84, supvr SL receiver & optical relay group, 84-89. *Mem:* Fel Inst Elec & Electronics Engrs; Sigma Xi. *Res:* Microwave solid state circuits and lightwave receivers. *Mailing Add:* 2908 Edgemont Dr Allentown PA 18103

GEWERTZ, BRUCE LABE, MEDICINE, VASCULAR SURGERY. *Current Pos:* assoc prof, Univ Chicago, 81-88, fac dean med educ, 89-92, PROF SURG, UNIV CHICAGO, 88-, DALLAS B PEMISTER PROF & CHMN, DEPT SURG, 92- *Personal Data:* b Philadelphia, Pa, Aug 27, 49; c Samantha, Barton & Alexis. *Educ:* Pa State Univ, BS, 69; Jefferson Med Sch, MD, 72. *Honors & Awards:* Collier Award. *Prof Exp:* Surg res, Univ Mich, 72-77; asst prof surg, Southwestern Med Sch, 77-81. *Concurrent Pos:* Ed, J Surg Res, 90-; teaching scholar, Am Heart Asn, 78-81. *Mem:* Soc Vascular Surg; Soc Univ Surgeons; Am Surg Asn (pres, 82-83); Am Col Surgeons; Am Physiol Soc; Soc Clin Surg. *Res:* Regulation of blood flow in the intestine, kidneys and spinal cord. *Mailing Add:* Dept Surg MC5029 5841 S Maryland Ave Chicago IL 60637. *Fax:* 773-702-2140

GEWIRTZ, ALLAN, MATHEMATICS, COMPUTER SCIENCES. *Current Pos:* prof math, 68-96, asst dean, Sch Gen Studies, Brooklyn Col, 71-74, dean, Continuing Higher Educ, 81-84, EMER PROF, BROOKLYN COL, 96- *Personal Data:* b Brooklyn, NY, May 30, 31; m 54, Roberta Katz; c Andrew, Eric, Gregory & Pamela. *Educ:* Brooklyn Col, BS, 59, MA, 64; City Univ New York, PhD(math), 67. *Prof Exp:* Stand engr, Western Elec Corp, 59-61; electronics proj leader, Veeco Instruments Corp, 61-64; assoc prof math, Pace Univ, 64-68. *Concurrent Pos:* Consult, microcomputers, 82-; Treas Freehold Area Hosp, 88-89; vchmn, Centrastate Med Ctr, 90-93, chmn, Centrastate Healthcare Syst, 94-; pres, New Vista Group, Inc, 96- *Mem:* Math Asn Am; fel NY Acad Sci; AAAS. *Res:* Combinatorial mathematics, including graph theory, block designs and game theory; low and direct current detection, including mass spectrometry and ion gauges; microcomputer applications in mathematics; medical quality assurance. *Mailing Add:* 63 Blenheim Rd Englishtown NJ 07726. *Fax:* 908-536-2451

GEWIRTZ, DAVID A, EXPERIMENTAL CHEMOTHERAPY. *Current Pos:* Fel, Dept Med, 77-80, from instr to asst prof, 80-88, ASSOC PROF PHARMACOL, MED COL VA, 88- *Personal Data:* b Ger, Aug 28, 48; US citizen; m 74; c 3. *Educ:* Brooklyn Col, BS, 70; City Univ NY, Mt Sinai, PhD(physiol), 77. *Mem:* Am Asn Cancer Res; Am Soc Pharmacol Exp Ther. *Res:* Analysis of the biochemical factors conferring intrinsic resistence to chemotherapy in the hepatoma cell; studies of the biochemical pharmacology of antineoplastic drugs in MCF7 breast tumor cells. *Mailing Add:* Pharm Va Commonwealth Univ Sch Med Richmond VA 23298-1900. *Fax:* 804-371-8079

GEWURZ, HENRY, IMMUNOLOGY. *Current Pos:* PROF IMMUNOL & CHMN, DEPT IMMUNOL & MICROBIOL, ST LUKE'S MED CTR, 71- *Personal Data:* b Barcelona, Spain, June 1, 36. *Educ:* Johns Hopkins Univ, MD, 62. *Mem:* Am Fedn Clin Res; Am Asn Physicians; Am Asn Immunologists; Am Soc Clin Invest. *Mailing Add:* Dept Immunol & Microbiol Rush Med Col Presby-St Luke's Med Ctr 1653 W Congress Pkwy Chicago IL 60612-3684. *Fax:* 312-942-2808

GEYER, JOHN CHARLES, sanitary engineering; deceased, see previous edition for last biography

GEYER, MARK ALLEN, NEUROSCIENCES, PSYCHOPHARMACOLOGY. *Current Pos:* staff res assoc psychol, 70-72, asst res psychobiologist, dept psychiat, 73-78, from asst prof to assoc prof psychiat, 79-89, PROF PSYCHIAT, SCH MED, UNIV CALIF, SAN DIEGO, 89- *Personal Data:* b Portland, Ore, Dec 19, 44. *Educ:* Univ Ore, BA, 66; Univ Iowa, MA, 68; Univ Calif, San Diego, PhD(psychol), 72. *Prof Exp:* Res asst psychol, Univ Iowa, 66-68, res asst pharmacol, 68 & 68-70. *Concurrent Pos:* Founding partner, San Diego Instruments; NIMH res sci develop awardee, 83- *Mem:* Soc Biol Psychiat; Soc Neurosci; Am Col Neuropsychopharmacol. *Res:* Behavioral, histochemical and pharmacological studies of noradrenergic, dopaminergic and serotonergic neurons in mammalian brain; studies of drugs of abuse. *Mailing Add:* Dept Psychiat M-003 Univ Calif San Diego Med Sch 9500 Gilman Dr La Jolla CA 92093-5003

GEYER, RICHARD ADAM, OCEANOGRAPHY, GEOPHYSICS. *Current Pos:* RETIRED. *Personal Data:* b New York, NY, Oct 27, 14; m 40, Anna Thomson; c Sandra & Rick Jr. *Educ:* NY Univ, BS, 37, MS, 40; Princeton Univ, MA, 50, PhD(geophys), 51. *Prof Exp:* Res geophys & geol, Standard Oil Co, NJ, 38-42; physicist-in-chg degaussing range, Bur Ord, US Navy Dept, RI, 42-44, sr field instr, Oceanog Inst, Woods Hole, 44-45; sr res geophysicist, Humble Oil & Refining Co, 45-48, head oceanog sect, 49-54; chief geophysicist, Gravity Dept, Geophys Serv, Inc, Tex Instruments, Inc, 54-59, mgr, 59-66; head, Dept Oceanog, Tex A&M Univ, 66-76, dir, geosci Develop Progs, 76-80, prof oceanog, 66-80, emer prof, 80-92; pres, Geophys Assocs, Inc, 81-91. *Concurrent Pos:* Instr, Princeton Univ, 39-42; adj asst prof, Univ Houston, 48-61; ed, Soc Explor Geophys, 49-51; mem oceanwide surv panel, Comt Oceanog, Nat Acad Sci, 61-; tech dir oceanog, Geosci Dept, Geophys Serv, Inc, Tex Instruments, Inc, 63-66; vchmn, President's Comn Marine Sci Eng & Resources, 67-69; chmn adv comt, Int Decade Ocean Explor, NSF, 70-; consult, US Coast & Geodetic Surv; ed, Submersibles & Their Use in Oceanog Eng & Marine Pollution; adj prof, Offshore Technol Res Ctr, Tex A&M Univ, 89- *Mem:* Hon mem Soc Explor Geophys; Nat Ocean Indust Asn; Marine Technol Soc. *Res:* Exploration geophysics; application of oceanographic science to marine engineering operations and to military aspects of underwater sound. *Mailing Add:* 22 Woodstone Sq Austin TX 78703

GEYER, ROBERT PERSHING, BIOCHEMISTRY. *Current Pos:* Fel, 46-48, from asst prof to assoc prof, 49-71, PROF NUTRIT, SCH PUB HEALTH, HARVARD UNIV, 71-, CHMN DEPT, 77- *Personal Data:* b Racine, Wis, Sept 28, 18; m 45; c 2. *Educ:* Univ Wis, BS, 41, MS, 43, PhD(biochem), 46. *Hon Degrees:* MA, Harvard. *Concurrent Pos:* Mem, Coun Thrombosis, Am Heart Asn & Int Conf Biochem of Lipids; mem blood dis & resources adv bd, Nat Heart & Lung Inst, 74-76 & 79-83; consult, 84-88; co-chair 2nd & 3rd Int Symp on Artificial Blood Substitutes. *Mem:* Fel AAAS; Am Chem Soc; Am Asn Cancer Res; Am Inst Nutrit; Tissue Cult Asn; Sigma Xi; Soc Exp Biol Med; Mat Res Soc. *Res:* Development and study of artificial blood substitutes; nutritional, biochemical and chemical studies on oils and fats; parenteral nutrition and the metabolic fate of parenteral nutrients; tissue culture biochemistry. *Mailing Add:* 53 Brington Rd Harvard Univ Brookline MA 02146-6012

GEYER, STANLEY J, LABORATORY MEDICINE. *Current Pos:* PROF PATH, SCH MED, GEORGETOWN UNIV, 90-, DIR, DEPT LAB MED, HOSP, 90-, DIR, AUTOPSY PATH, 91- *Personal Data:* b Pittsburgh, Pa, July 25, 49. *Educ:* Jefferson Med Col, MD, 74; Am Bd Path, cert, 78. *Prof Exp:* Resident path, Med Ctr, NY Univ, 74-75 & Univ Health Ctr Pittsburgh, 75-76; postdoctoral fel exp path & immunol, Dept Path, Sch Med, Univ Pittsburgh, 76-77, from asst prof to assoc prof path, 77-84, asst dean vet affairs, 82-84; staff pathologist & chief, Autopsy Sect, Pittsburgh Vet Admin Med Ctr, 77-79, chief, Lab Serv, 79-82, transfusion officer & chief, Blood Bank, 81-83, chief staff, 82-84; assoc prof path & assoc dean, Sch Med, Univ Wash, 84-90. *Concurrent Pos:* Chief staff, Seattle Vet Admin Med Ctr, 84-90; fac mem, Health Systs Specialist Training Prog, Vet Admin Cent Off, 84-90, chmn, Data Mgt Task Force Support Peer Rev, 85-86 & Nat Qual Care Work Force, 88-89; mem, Nat Adv Comt Peer Rev Orgn Vet Admin, 85-90 & Task Force Physician Staffing Needs Vet Admin, Inst Med, 88- *Mem:* Am Asn Neuropathologists; AAAS; Am Asn Immunologists; Fel Col Am Pathologists; NY Acad Sci; Soc Med Decision Making; Group Res Path Educ; Acad Clin Lab Physicians & Scientists; Am Soc Clin Pathologists. *Mailing Add:* Dept Lab Med W Penn Hosp 4800 Friendship Ave Pittsburgh PA 15224-1722. *Fax:* 412-578-7390

GEYLING, F(RANZ) TH(OMAS), COMPUTER MODELING PHYSICAL DESIGN. *Current Pos:* mem tech staff, mech res, 54-60, head analytical mech & eng physics, 60-70, DISTINGUISHED MEM TECH STAFF, MAT RES & ENG, BELL TEL LABS, 70- *Personal Data:* b Tientsin, China, Sept 7, 26; nat US; m 61; c 4. *Educ:* Stanford Univ, BS, 50, MS, 51, PhD(eng mech), 54. *Prof Exp:* Instr, Stanford Univ, 50-52. *Mem:* Am Soc Mech Engrs; Am Phys Soc; AAAS. *Res:* Computer fluid mechanics; modelling of material processes; structural mechanics and stress analysis; process modelling and manufacturability studies relating to material science and physical devices. *Mailing Add:* 6706 Cypress Pt N Austin TX 78746

GEYMAN, JOHN PAYNE, FAMILY MEDICINE. *Current Pos:* chmn dept, 76-90, prof, 76-90, EMER PROF FAMILY MED, SCH MED, UNIV WASH, 90-; IN PRACT, INTER ISLAND MED CTR, FRIDAY HARBOR, WASH. *Personal Data:* b Santa Barbara, Calif, Feb 9, 31; m 56, Eugenia Deichlelr; c John M, James C & William S. *Educ:* Princeton Univ, AB, 52; Univ Calif, San Francisco, MD, 60; Am Bd Family Pract, dipl. *Honors & Awards:* Thomas Johnson Award, Am Acad Family Physicians, 80; Curtis Hames Res Award, 90. *Prof Exp:* Intern, Los Angeles Co Gen Hosp, 60-61; resident, Sonoma Co Hosp, Santa Rosa, 61-63; pvt pract, Mt Shasta, 69-71; dir, Family Pract Residency Prog, Community Hosp Sonoma Co, 69-71 & Davis Family Residency Network Prog, Univ Calif, 72-; chmn, Div Family Pract & assoc prof community & family med, Univ Utah, 71-72; prof family pract & vchmn dept, Sch Med, Univ Calif, Davis, 72-76. *Concurrent Pos:* Asst clin prof ambulatory & community med, Univ Calif, 72-; consult, Am Acad Family Physicians, 72-; Family Med, NIH, 72-77 & Residency Assistance Prog, 75-80; ed, J Family Pract, 73-90, J Am Bd Family Pract, 90-; chmn, Pictorial Comt, Am Bd Family Pract, 74-77; consult, Am Acad Family Physicians, 72-, Family Med, NIH, 72-77 & Residency Assistance Prog, 75-80. *Mem:* Fel Am Acad Family Physicians; Soc Teachers Family Med; AMA; Inst Med Nat Acad Sci. *Res:* Family practice curriculum development and evaluation; role of family physician; changing trends in medical education and clinical practice. *Mailing Add:* Dept Family Med Univ Wash Seattle WA 98195

GEZON, HORACE MARTIN, MICROBIOLOGY, EPIDEMIOLOGY. *Current Pos:* EPIDEMIOLOGIST & MICROBIOLOGIST, ATLANTIC ANTIBODIES, 75- *Personal Data:* b Grand Rapids, Mich, Nov 12, 14; m 39, Elizabeth Brownlee; c Philip & Margaret. *Educ:* Calvin Col, AB, 38; Univ Chicago, MD, 40. *Prof Exp:* From instr to asst prof pediat, Univ Chicago, 47-52; from assoc prof epidemiol to prof epidemiol & microbiol, Univ Pittsburgh, 52-66; prof pediat, Sch Med, Boston Univ, 66-75, chmn, Dept Pediat, 66-70. *Concurrent Pos:* Res fel pediat path, Univ Chicago, 46-47; vis prof, Am Univ, Beirut, 50-51; consult to Surgeon Gen, US Army; dir, Comn Enteric Infections, Armed Forces Epidemiol Bd, 63-70; dir pediat serv, Boston City Hosp, 66-70; lectr pediat, Harvard Med Sch, 67-; lectr microbiol, Harvard Sch Pub Health, 67-69; consult pediat, Children's Hosp, 67-; clin prof pediat, Sch Med, Tufts Univ, 76-81; consult pediat. *Mem:* Soc Pediat Res; Am Epidemiol Soc; Am Pediat Soc. *Res:* Action of antibiotics on bacteria; epidemiology of streptococcal, staphylococcal, enteric diseases of human and chlamydial, corynebacterial and mycobacterial diseases of goats; bacterial metabolism; pediatrics. *Mailing Add:* 15 Western Ave Gorham ME 04038

GFELLER, EDUARD, NEUROANATOMY, PSYCHIATRY. *Current Pos:* PVT PRACT, 87- *Personal Data:* b Aarburg, Switz, Sept 11, 37; nat US; m 59, 74; c 2. *Educ:* Univ Berne, DrMed, 64. *Prof Exp:* From instr to asst prof neuroanat, Johns Hopkins Univ, 65-72; from asst prof to assoc prof psychiat, Sch Med, Univ Ala, Birmingham, 74-78; prof psychiat & neurosci, Col Med, Univ Fla, 78-87. *Concurrent Pos:* Fel endocrinol, Univ Berne, 64-65; chief, Psychiat Serv, Vet Admin Hosp, Birmingham, 75-77; chief staff, Vet Admin Hosp, Tuscaloosa, 77-78; chief psychiat serv, Vet Admin Hosp, Gainesville, 78-. *Mem:* AAAS; Am Asn; Sigma Xi. *Res:* Catecholamine metabolism in brain; etiology and genetics of schizophrenia. *Mailing Add:* 589 W State Rd 434 Longwood FL 32750

GHADIRI, M REZA, CHEMISTRY. *Current Pos:* ASST PROF, SCRIPPS RES INST, CALIF, 89- *Personal Data:* b Tehran, Iran, Dec 8, 59; m 86, Franaz Amirfarzaneh. *Educ:* Univ Wis, BA, 82, PhD(chem), 87. *Honors & Awards:* Beckman Young Investr Award, Arnold & Mabel Beckmand Found, 91; Pure Chem Award, Am Chem Soc, 95. *Prof Exp:* Postdoctoral fel, Rockefeller Univ, 87-89. *Concurrent Pos:* Searle scholar, 91. *Mem:* AAAS; Am Chem Soc. *Mailing Add:* 5133 Seagrove Ct San Diego CA 92130

GHAFFAR, ABDUL, CELLULAR IMMUNOBIOLOGY, CANCER IMMUNOLOGY. *Current Pos:* ASSOC PROF IMMUNOL, SCH MED, UNIV SC, 78- *Personal Data:* b Macchli Shaher, India, July 6, 42; m 66, Anita Christensen; c Tariq, Omar & Yasmeen. *Educ:* Univ Karachi, BSc, 62; Univ London, MPhil, 70; Univ Edinburgh, PhD(immunol), 73. *Prof Exp:* Res asst, Univ Edinburgh, 70-72, res fel, 73-75; res asst prof, Univ Miami, 75-78; staff investr, Comprehensive Cancer Ctr, State Fla, 75-78. *Concurrent Pos:* Asst ed, J Reticuloendothelial Soc. *Mem:* Brit Soc Immunol; Am Asn Immunologists; Reticuloendothelial Soc; Am Soc Microbiol; Royal Col Pathologists. *Res:* Cellular immunology; cancer immunology; immunosuppression and immunopotentiation; macrophage functions and immunoregulation. *Mailing Add:* Dept Microbiol & Immunol Univ SC Sch Med Columbia SC 29208-0001. *E-Mail:* ghaffar@med.sc.com

GHAI, GEETHA R, BIOCHEMICAL PHARMACOLOGY, CARDIOVASCULAR PHARMACOLOGY. *Current Pos:* ASST DIR, CTR ADVAN FOOD TECHNOL INST, COOK COL, NEW BRUNSWICK, NJ, 93- *Personal Data:* b Madras, India, Jan 7, 46; m 68, Rajendra; c Pranav & Nirupa. *Educ:* Gujarat Univ, India, BSc Hons, 65; Calcutta Univ, India, MSc, 68; Baroda Univ, India, PhD(microbiol), 72; Rutgers Univ, NJ, MBA, 93. *Prof Exp:* Res assoc pharmacol, Dept Pharmacol & Exp Therapeut, State Univ NY, Buffalo, 75-78; res assoc pharmacol, Dept Pharmacol, Univ Southern Ala, Mobile, 78-80; asst prof, 80-83; res scientist, Res Dept, Pharmacol Div, Ciba-Geigy, Summit, NJ, 83-87; sr res scientist, 87-93. *Concurrent Pos:* Reviewer, NJ Affil Peer Rev Comt, Am Heart Asn, 89-91; speaker, NJ Asn Biomed Res. *Mem:* Am Soc Pharmacol & Exp Therapeut. *Res:* Biotechnology and molecular biology-related advances; reception technology. *Mailing Add:* Cook Col Rutgers Univ PO Box 231 New Brunswick NJ 08903-0231. *E-Mail:* geetha@cafti.rutgers.edu@smtp

GHALI, AMIN, CIVIL ENGINEERING. *Current Pos:* PROF CIVIL ENG, UNIV CALGARY, CAN. *Honors & Awards:* Le Prix A B Sanderson Award, Can Soc Civil Eng, 92. *Mailing Add:* Dept Civil Eng Univ Calgary Calgary AB T2N 1N4 Can

GHALY, THARWAT SHAHATA, GEOLOGY, PETROLOGY. *Current Pos:* PROF GEOL, E TEX STATE UNIV, 67- *Personal Data:* b Cairo, Egypt, Oct 12, 39; m 65; c 2. *Educ:* Ain Shams Univ, Cairo, BSc, 59; Glasgow Univ, PhD(igneous & metamorphic petrol), 65. *Prof Exp:* Instr geol, Fac Sci, Ain Shams Univ, Cairo, 59-61; res asst, Glasgow Univ, 62-65; mineralogist, Thermal Syndicate Ltd, Wallsend, Eng, 66-67. *Mem:* Geol Soc Am; Geol Soc London; Geol Soc Glasgow. *Res:* Igneous and metamorphic petrology with mineralogy and geochemistry; structures, petrology and metamorphic differentiation of Precambrian rocks. *Mailing Add:* 2820 Bois D Arc 5 Commerce TX 75428

GHANAYEM, BURHAN I, TOXICOLOGY. *Current Pos:* vis postdoctoral fel, Nat Inst Environ Health Sci, NIH, 83-84, staff fel, 84-86, sr staff fel, 86-88, TOXICOLOGIST, NAT INST ENVIRON HEALTH SCI, NIH, RESEARCH TRIANGLE PARK, NC, 88- *Personal Data:* b Kufrzibad, Jordan, Mar 11, 52; US citizen; m 79; c 3. *Educ:* Cairo Univ, Egypt, BS, 75; NTex State Univ, MS, 79; Univ Tex Med Br, PhD(pharmacol-toxicol), 83. *Prof Exp:* Pharmacist, Kuwait, 75-77; res technician, Tex Col Osteop Med, Ft Worth, Tex, 77-79; res assoc, Univ Tex Med Br, Galveston, 79-80, asst lab supvr, 80-81, res assoc, 81-83. *Concurrent Pos:* Instr, Durham Tech Community Col, NC, 85-90. *Mem:* Soc Toxicol; Am Soc Pharmacol & Exp Therapeut. *Res:* Metabolism of environmental chemicals and their toxicity; mechanisms of chemical-induced carcinogenicity. *Mailing Add:* NIEHS NIH PO Box 12233 Research Triangle Park NC 27709-2233. *Fax:* 919-541-1460

GHANDAKLY, ADEL AHMAD, ELECTRIC ENERGY SYSTEMS. *Current Pos:* ASSOC PROF ELEC ENG, UNIV TOLEDO, 79- *Personal Data:* b Alexandria, Egypt, Mar 15, 45; Can citizen; m 81. *Educ:* Univ Alexandria, BSc, 67; Univ Calgary, MSc, 73, PhD(elec eng), 75. *Prof Exp:* Instr elec eng, Univ Alexandria, 67-69; design engr, Pub Utility, Egypt, 69-71; res asst, Univ Calgary, 71-75; sr design engr, Montreal Energy Co, 75-77; asst prof, Univ New Orleans, 77-79. *Concurrent Pos:* Consult, Siemens-Allis Co, 77-79, La Power & Light, 78 & Detroit Edison Co, 79- *Mem:* Inst Elec & Electronics Engrs; Asn Prof Engrs. *Res:* Computer applications to power system studies and control; power system design; control of large motor drives; study and design of solar and wind energy systems. *Mailing Add:* 6201 Garden Rd Maumee OH 43537

GHANDEHARI, MOHAMMAD HOSSEIN, MATERIALS SCIENCE & ENGINEERING METALLURGY. *Current Pos:* RES SCIENTIST, SCI & TECHNOL DIV, UNOCAL, CALIF, 80- *Personal Data:* b Tehran, Iran, Sept 29, 43; m 64; c 2. *Educ:* Weber State Col, BS, 68; Univ Utah, PhD(chem), 70. *Prof Exp:* Asst prof chem, Tehran Univ Technol, Iran, 70-73; instr & res assoc, Univ Utah, 73-75; res chemist, Fansteel Res Ctr, 75-80. *Mem:* Inst Elec & Electronics Engrs; Mat Res Soc; Am Chem Soc; Electrocham Soc. *Res:* Powder metallurgy of rare earth magnets; electrometallurgy of rare earth metals in molten salts; ceramics processing; rare earth metals and alloys; high temperature superconductors; fuel cells. *Mailing Add:* Moly Corp Inc 67750 Bailey Rd Mountain Pass CA 92366

GHANDHI, SORAB KHUSHRO, ELECTRICAL ENGINEERING. *Current Pos:* RETIRED. *Personal Data:* b Allahabad, India, Jan 1, 28; US citizen; m 81, Cecilia M Tymann; c Khushro, Rustom & Behram. *Educ:* Benares Hindu Univ, BSc, 47; Univ Ill, MS, 48, PhD, 51. *Prof Exp:* Mem tech staff, Electronics Lab, Gen Elec Co, 51-60; res mgr, Philco Corp, Ford Motor Co, 60-63; prof electrophys, Rensselaer Polytech Inst, 63-92, chmn, Div Electrophys, 67-74. *Concurrent Pos:* Consult, Sprague Elec Co, Mass, Analog Devices, Mass, RCA, Pa & Stauffer Chem Co, Am Cyanamid; ed, Solid-State Electronics J. *Mem:* Sigma Xi; fel Inst Elec & Electronics Engrs. *Res:* Solid state devices, processes and materials; microelectronics. *Mailing Add:* 2716 Cita Ave Escondido CA 92029-5816. *Fax:* 518-276-6261; *E-Mail:* ghandhi@rpi.ecse.edu

GHARRETT, ANTHONY JOHN, FISH BIOCHEMICAL & POPULATION GENETICS. *Current Pos:* from asst prof to assoc prof, 76-88, PROF FISHERIES, UNIV ALASKA, FAIRBANKS, 88-, DIR, FISHERIES DIV, 94- *Personal Data:* b Seattle, Washington, Dec 23, 45; m 76, Jessica Romm. *Educ:* Calif Inst Technol, BS, 67; Ore State Univ, MS, 73, PhD(genetics), 75. *Prof Exp:* NIH fel trainee genetics & cell biol, Univ Minn, 74-76. *Concurrent Pos:* Prin investr, Alaska Sea Grant Col Prog, Univ Alaska, 77-; vis assoc prof, Univ Mich, 85-86; tech comt mem, Western Regional Aquacult Consortium, 86-92; Interagency Personnel Act Assignment, Nat Marine Fisheries Soc, Auke Bay Lab, 86-90. *Mem:* AAAS; Sigma Xi; Pac Fishery Biologists; Am Inst Fishery Res Biologists; Am Fisheries Soc. *Res:* Biochemical genetics of salmonid; population genetics, stock separation and identification; genetic marking; mitochondrial DNA studies of salmonids; quantitative genetics and salmon population structure. *Mailing Add:* Univ Alaska Fairbanks 11120 Glacier Hwy Juneau AK 99801. *Fax:* 907-965-6447; *E-Mail:* ffajg@aurora.alaska.gov

GHASSEMI, MASOOD, ENVIRONMENTAL ENGINEERING, CHEMICAL ENGINEERING. *Current Pos:* SUPVR, ENVIRON COMPLIANCE, LOCKHEED MISSILES & SPACE CO, SUNNYVALE, CALIF, 89- *Personal Data:* b Tehran, Iran, Mar 7, 40; m 68. *Educ:* Univ Wash, BS, 61, MS, 63, PhD(environ eng), 67. *Prof Exp:* Proj engr, Havens & Emerson Engrs, Ohio, 67-68; mem tech staff, Atomics Int, N Am Rockwell Corp, 68-73; mem tech staff, TRW Chem Eng Div, 73-75, sr proj engr, TRW Environ Eng Div, 75-83; prin & tech dir, Meesa, San Pedro, Calif, 83-85; chief hazardous waste engr, Chem Hill, Santa Ana, Calif, 85-87; dir, Solid & Hazardous Waste Mgt Prog, URS Consults Inc, Long Beach, Calif, 87-89. *Concurrent Pos:* Sr lectr, Univ Southern Calif, 72-76. *Mem:* Hazardous Mat Control Res Inst; Am Chem Soc; Sigma Xi. *Res:* Hazardous waste management; environmental assessment of new energy technologies; water and wastewater treatment technologies; environmental impact assessment. *Mailing Add:* 962 El Cajon Way Palo Alto CA 94303-3408

GHATE, SUHAS RAMKRISHNA, computer simulation & modeling, for more information see previous edition

GHAUSI, MOHAMMED SHUAIB, ELECTRICAL ENGINEERING. *Current Pos:* DEAN, COL ENG, UNIV CALIF, DAVIS. *Personal Data:* b Kabul, Afghanistan, Feb 16, 30; m 61; c 2. *Educ:* Univ Calif, Berkeley, BS, 56, MS, 57, PhD(elec eng), 60. *Honors & Awards:* Inst Elec & Electronics Engrs Medal. *Prof Exp:* From asst prof to prof elec eng, NY Univ, 60-74; prof elec & comput eng & chmn dept, Wayne State Univ, 74-78; dean eng & John F Dodge prof eng, Oakland Univ, 78- *Concurrent Pos:* Sect head, Elec Sci & Analysis, NSF, 72-74. *Mem:* Fel Inst Elec & Electronics Engrs, circuits & systs soc (pres, 76-77); NY Acad Sci; Inst Elec & Electronics Engrs. *Res:* Electronic circuits and systems; author of numerous publications. *Mailing Add:* Sch Eng Univ Calif Davis CA 95616

GHAZALI, MASOOD RAHEEM, CLINICAL NEUROLOGY, NEUROPATHOLOGY. *Current Pos:* MED FEL SPECIALIST, UNIV MINN, 92- *Personal Data:* b Hyderabad, Andhra Pradesh, India, July 16, 66. *Educ:* Bd Intermediate, India, PreMed(inter), 83; Armed Forces Med Col, India, MB BS, 88; Educ Comn Foreign Med Grad, FMGEMS, 91. *Prof Exp:* Rotating intern, SCent HQ Hosp, SecBad, India, 88-89; pvt pract med, Hyderabad, India, 90-92. *Concurrent Pos:* Consult mem, Imtiyaz Gen Hosp, 89-92. *Mem:* Am Med Asn; Am Acad Neurol. *Res:* Frontiers of medical genetics and molecular biology; clinical neurology, neuropathology; the final answer to the clinicians hypothesis of disease mechanisms; origin and course of brain tumors. *Mailing Add:* 4210 Meghan Lane St Paul MN 55122. *Fax:* 612-625-7950

GHAZANSHAHI, SHAHIN D, ELECTRICAL ENGINEERING, BIOMEDICAL ENGINEERING. *Current Pos:* ASSOC PROF ELEC ENG, CALIF STATE UNIV, FULLERTON, 85- *Personal Data:* b Tehran, Iraq, May 1, 52; m 72, Mohammad Sarkarati; c Farshid & Nushin. *Educ:* Tehran Univ, BS, 75, MS, 77; Univ Southern Calif, MSc, 81, PhD(biomed eng), 84. *Prof Exp:* Res fel biomed, Univ Southern Calif, 84-85. *Mem:* Inst Elec & Electronics Engrs; Biomed Eng Soc. *Res:* Biomedical engineering; mathematical modeling; system identification; statistical and stochastic analysis; respiratory system modeling. *Mailing Add:* Dept Elec Eng Calif State Univ Fullerton CA 92634. *Fax:* 714-449-7162

GHAZARIAN, JACOB G, BIOCHEMISTRY, NUTRITION. *Current Pos:* asst prof, 75-80, ASSOC PROF BIOCHEM, MED COL WIS, 80- *Personal Data:* b Baghdad, Iraq, Nov 28, 37; US citizen; m 65; c 1. *Educ:* Murray State Univ, BSc, 63; Memphis State Univ, MSc, 67; Univ Neb, Lincoln, PhD(biochem), 71. *Prof Exp:* Vis scientist biochem, Univ Tenn, Memphis, 70-71; fel, Univ Wis-Madison, 71-74, proj assoc, 74-75. *Concurrent Pos:* Prin investr, NSF grants, 66-78, NIH fel, 71-74 & NIH grant, 76-79; NIH career develop award, 76-81. *Mem:* Sigma Xi; Am Soc Bone & Mineral Res; Int Soc Supramolecular Biol; Am Chem Soc; AAAS. *Res:* Physiochemical and immunological characterization of kidney and liver mitochondrial and microsomal hydroxylases (monooxygenases) associated with the orderly control of the vitamin D endocrine system. *Mailing Add:* Dept Biochem Med Col Wis 8701 Watertown Plank Rd Milwaukee WI 53226-3548. *Fax:* 414-257-2008

GHEBREHIWET, BERHANE, MOLECULAR IMMUNOLOGY, BIOCHEMISTRY. *Current Pos:* asst prof, Dept Med, 79-85, assoc prof, Dept Med & Path, 85-92, PROF DEPT MED & PATH, SCH MED, STATE UNIV NY, STONY BROOK, 92- *Personal Data:* b Asmara, Eritrea, Sept 28, 46; US citizen. *Educ:* Sch Vet Med, Warsaw, Poland, DVM, 71; Vet Sch, Alfort, France, MSc, 73; Univ Paris, DSc(immunol), 74. *Honors & Awards:* Sigma Xi. *Prof Exp:* Res assoc molecular immunol, Scripps Clin & Res Found, 74-80. *Mem:* AAAS; NY Acad Sci; Am Asn Immunol; Am Chem Soc; Am Asn Vet Immunol; Am Fedn Clin Res; Soc Leukocyte Biol; Clin Immunol Soc. *Res:* Complement and the interaction of complement with cell surface receptors; role of complement in inflammation; immunobiology and molecular biology of complement receptors and cell surface molecules. *Mailing Add:* Dept Med Health Sci Ctr State Univ NY Level 16 Rm 40 Stony Brook NY 11794-8161

GHEITH, MOHAMED A, GEOLOGY, MINERALOGY. *Current Pos:* lectr, Boston Univ, 58-59, from asst prof to assoc prof, 59-69, chmn dept, 64-75, dir, Spec Int HealthPProgs, 78-85, dir, Spec External Progs Mid East, 78-86, PROF GEOL, BOSTON UNIV, 69- *Personal Data:* b Kherbeta, Kom Hamada, Egypt, Feb 11, 25; c 2. *Educ:* Cairo Univ, BSc, 45; Univ Minn, MS, 50, PhD(geol), 51. *Prof Exp:* Demonstr geol, Cairo Univ, 45-46; lectr, Ain-Shams, Cairo, 52-57. *Concurrent Pos:* Consult, Bur Mining & Com, Egypt, 54-57; fel, Sch Advan Studies, Mass Inst Technol, 57-59; distinguished vis prof, Kuwait Univ, 73, Am Univ, Cairo, Cairo Univ, Alexandria Univ, Tanta & Mansoura Univ, 73-74 & Univ Qatar, Egypt, 83; deleg, Nubian Arabian Shield Geol & Mineralization Conf, Saudi Arabia, 78, Morocco, 82. *Mem:* Fel Geol Soc Am; Am Crystallog Asn; Nat Asn Geol Teachers;

Mineral Soc Am; Geol Soc Egypt; AAAS. *Res:* Geochemistry of iron oxides and oxide hydrates; geochronology of Northeast Africa; crystallography, genesis, stability relations and synthesis of some phosphate minerals and silicates; science education; archeological geology. *Mailing Add:* 21 Windsor Rd Billerica MA 01821

GHEN, DAVID C, SONAX UNDERWATER ACOUSTICS, NAVAL ASW ANALYSIS. *Current Pos:* corp scientist, 84-87, DEPT MGR, ANALYSIS & TECHNOL INC, 87- *Personal Data:* b Pittsburgh, Pa, Feb 7, 39; m 60; c 2. *Educ:* Muskingum Col, BS, 61; Penn State Univ, MS, 62. *Prof Exp:* Sr analyst, Analysis & Technol Inc, 74-76, group mgr, 76-77, br mgr, 77-78, prin sci, 78-79, chief scientist, 79-80; res specialist, Shearwater Inc, 80-84. *Mem:* Am Acoust Soc. *Res:* Development and evaluation of submarine tactics and associated system performance requirements. *Mailing Add:* 84 Ocean View Ave Mystic CT 06355

GHENT, ARTHUR W, ECOLOGY, BIOMETRICS. *Current Pos:* from asst prof to assoc prof, 64-69, prof quant biol, 70-76, PROF ENTOM & ZOOL, UNIV ILL, URBANA, 76- *Personal Data:* b Toronto, Ont, Sept 8, 27; m 90, Joy Wiele; c Jennifer, David & Tove. *Educ:* Univ Toronto, BScF, 50, MA, 54; Univ Chicago, PhD(zool), 60. *Prof Exp:* Res officer, Forest Insect Lab, Can Dept Agr, 50-59; asst prof zool, Univ Okla, 60-64. *Concurrent Pos:* Biostatistics ed, Am Midland Naturalist. *Res:* Insect and molluscan ecology and behavior; forest ecology; nonparametric methods. *Mailing Add:* Dept Ecol Ethology & Evolution Univ Ill 515 Morrill Hall Urbana IL 61801

GHENT, EDWARD DALE, GEOLOGY, METAMORPHIC PETROLOGY. *Current Pos:* from asst prof to assoc prof, 67-75, head dept, 87-92, PROF GEOL, UNIV CALGARY, 75- *Personal Data:* b Little Rock, Ark, Oct 4, 37; m 62, Gretchen Kluter. *Educ:* Yale Univ, BS, 59; Univ Calif, Berkeley, PhD(geol), 64. *Prof Exp:* Asst prof geol, San Jose State Col, 64; lectr, Victoria Univ, Wellington, 64-67. *Mem:* Mineral Asn Can; Geol Soc Am; Mineral Soc Am; Am Geophys Union. *Res:* Metamorphic petrology; geochemistry; electron microprobe analysis. *Mailing Add:* Dept Geol Univ Calgary Calgary AB T2N 1N4 Can. *Fax:* 403-284-0074; *E-Mail:* ghent@geo.ucalgary.ca

GHENT, KENNETH SMITH, MATHEMATICS. *Current Pos:* from assoc prof to prof math, 47-77, EMER PROF MATH, UNIV ORE, 77-, DIR INT STUDENT SERV, 74- *Personal Data:* b Hamilton, Ont, June 29, 11; nat US; m 42, Helen Majorie Tillman; c Robert Charles, Dorothy Claire (Turch) & Margaret Elizabeth (Morgan). *Educ:* McMaster Univ, BA, 32; Univ Chicago, SM, 33, PhD(math), 35. *Prof Exp:* From instr to asst prof math, Univ Ore, 35-42; physicist, 11th Naval Dist, USN, 42-45. *Mem:* Am Math Soc; Math Asn Am. *Res:* Algebra and number theory; sums of values of polynomials multiplied by constants. *Mailing Add:* 982 Lincoln St Eugene OR 97401

GHEORGHIU, PAUL, PHYSICS, INSTRUMENTATION. *Current Pos:* PRES, PAUL SIGMA INC, 78- *Personal Data:* b Rumania, June 27, 16; US citizen; m 46; c 1. *Educ:* Signal Corps Mil Acad, BSEE, 37; Polytech Sch, lic es sc, 40; Advan Prof Sch, dipl life sci, 55. *Prof Exp:* Asst prof physics & electronics, Signal Corps Mil Acad, 42-43; ed, Asn Free Press, 48-56; proj engr electronics, Manson Labs, 57-59 & Bulova Res & Develop Electronics, Bulova Watch Co, 59-60; sr systs engr res & develop, Transitron Electronic Corp, 60-62; dir bio-med & electronic res, Advan Res Ctr, Hi-G, Inc, Conn, 62-66; vpres, Med Electrosci, Inc, NY, 66-70; mgr indust controls div, Opto Mechanisms, Inc, NJ, 70-72; pres, Today's Technol Assoc, 72-74; mgr advan res & develop, Scott Electronics Div, NCR Corp, 74-78. *Concurrent Pos:* Secy, Joint Mil Comt Defense Res, 40-42; sr staff scientist, Frequency Electronics; consult, Lorad Electronics & Math Assocs Inc. *Mem:* Sr mem Inst Elec & Electronics Engr; Int Fedn Med Electronics & Biol Eng; NY Acad Sci; Int Soc Cybernet Med. *Res:* Metrology of standards and traceability; medical electronics, electro-chemical and solid state switching techniques; life sciences; bio-engineering; environmental technology; applied physics; communication in their design; production and marketing; management of advanced electronics; international marketing; cybernetics; operations research; computer sciences. *Mailing Add:* 2402 Loyal Lane Bel Air MD 21015

GHERARDI, GHERARDO JOSEPH, pathology, for more information see previous edition

GHERING, MARY VIRGIL, ENZYMOLOGY, CHEMISTRY GENERAL. *Current Pos:* RETIRED. *Personal Data:* b Grand Rapids, Mich, July 18, 10. *Educ:* Cent Mich Univ, AB, 35; Marquette Univ, MS, 48; St Thomas Inst, PhD, 68. *Prof Exp:* High sch teacher, Mich, 36-38, Nottawa Twp Sch Unit, 41-42 & Marywood Acad, 42-43; pub sch teacher, 43-49; from asst prof to prof chem, Aquinas Col, 49-68; chmn dept phys sci, 59-63; libm, St Thomas Inst, 68-87. *Mem:* Am Chem Soc; Am Inst Chemists. *Res:* Effect of six vitamins of B complex upon the growth of Fusarium solani in a synthetic medium; effect of low velocity electrons upon the activity of trypsin. *Mailing Add:* 153 Lakeside Dr NE Grand Rapids MI 49503-3895

GHERING, WALTER L, ACOUSTICS. *Current Pos:* RETIRED. *Personal Data:* b Edinboro, Pa, Nov 3, 30. *Educ:* US Naval Acad, BS, 56; Pa State Univ, BS, 61, MS, 63, PhD(physics), 68. *Prof Exp:* Res physicist, Babcock and Wilcox Res Ctr, 68-73, res specialist, 73-87. *Mem:* Inst Noise Control Eng. *Res:* Acoustic instrumentation, noise and vibration control; engineering physics (sonic cleaning and structural vibrational response prediction); industrial instrumentation (two-phase flow measurement and high-temperature pressure sensors). *Mailing Add:* 2460 S Linden Ave Alliance OH 44601

GHERNA, ROBERT LARRY, BACTERIOLOGY, BIOCHEMISTRY. *Current Pos:* Sr scientist bact, Am Type Cult Collection, 66-67, asst cur, 73-74, from actg head to head, Dept Comput Sci, 76-85, HEAD, DEPT BACT, AM TYPE CULT COLLECTION, 74- *Personal Data:* b Los Angeles, Calif, Nov 15, 37; m 62; c 3. *Educ:* Univ Southern Calif, AB, 60, PhD(bact), 64. *Concurrent Pos:* Fel, Stanford Univ, 64-66; adj assoc prof microbiol, Univ Md, 76-79. *Mem:* Am Soc Microbiol; Sigma Xi; US Fedn Cult Collections (vpres, 78); Am Inst Biol Sci; NY Acad Sci. *Res:* Bacterial physiology; general microbiology; bacterial systematics; sulfur and heterocyclic metabolism. *Mailing Add:* 27 Maryland Ave Gaithersburg MD 20877

GHEZ, ANDREA MIA, ASTRONOMY, PHYSICS. *Current Pos:* asst prof, 94-97, ASSOC PROF PHYSICS & ASTRON, UNIV CALIF, LOS ANGELES, 97- *Personal Data:* b New York, NY, June 16, 65; m 93, Tom La Tourette. *Educ:* Mass Inst Technol, BS, 87; Calif Inst Technol, MS, 89, PhD, 93. *Honors & Awards:* Young Investr Award, NSF, 94; Anne Jump Cannon Award, 94; Fullam Dudley Award, 95. *Prof Exp:* Hubble postdoctoral fel, Univ Ariz, 92-93; vis res scholar, Inst Astron, Eng, 94. *Concurrent Pos:* Sloan fel, 96; Packard fel, 96. *Mem:* Am Astron Soc. *Res:* Discovered young formation of low mass stars in multiple star systems; production of first diffraction-limited image with Keck 10-m telescope; showed dynamically the existance of a massive black hole at the center of our galaxy. *Mailing Add:* Dept Astron Univ Calif 405 Hilgard Ave Los Angeles CA 90095

GHEZZO, MARIO, INTEGRATED CIRCUITS. *Current Pos:* STAFF PHYSICS, CORP RES DEVELOP CTR, GEN ELEC CO, 69- *Personal Data:* b Trieste, Italy, Nov 20, 37; US citizen; m 73. *Educ:* Univ Trieste, Dr physics, 62. *Prof Exp:* Staff, Res Lab, Sprague Elec Co, Mass, 66-69. *Concurrent Pos:* Lectr, integrated circuit yield enhancement, Rensselaer Polytech Inst. *Mem:* Electrochem Soc; Inst Elec & Electronics Engrs. *Res:* Development of a 1 micron complementary metal-oxide semiconductor bulk process for very large scale integration circuit applications; investigation of advanced metal oxide semiconductor field effect transistor structures and integration in a viable integrated circuit process; yield and productivity enhancement of integrated circuits. *Mailing Add:* Gen Elec Co Corp Res Develop Bldg KW-B1309 PO Box 8 Schenectady NY 12301

GHIA, KIRTI N, FLUID DYNAMICS, APPLIED MECHANICS. *Current Pos:* from asst prof to assoc prof, 69-78, PROF FLUID DYNAMICS, UNIV CINCINNATI, 78- *Personal Data:* b Bombay, India. *Educ:* Gujarat Univ, India, BS, 60; Ill Inst Technol, MS, 65, PhD(mech & aerospace eng), 69. *Prof Exp:* Res engr, Premier Automobiles Ltd, India, 60-61; res asst fluid dynamics, Ill Inst Technol, 61-62, instr, 62, asst, 62-69. *Concurrent Pos:* Consult, Huyck Corp, 65-67, Kenner Prod Co, Cincinnati, 72-76, Gen Elec Co, Cincinnati, 73-, Air Force Flight Dynamics Lab, Wright Patterson AFB, 76-, Naval Ship Res & Develop Ctr, Bethesda, 77- & Reynolds Metal Co, Ala, 78-; co-prin ininvestr, NSF grants, 72-79, Aerospace Res Lab, 72-75, Gen Elec Co grants, 74-75 & 76-77 & Off Sci Res grants, 78-79. *Mem:* Am Inst Aeronaut & Astronaut; Am Soc Mech Engrs; Am Soc Eng Educ; Sigma Xi. *Res:* Analysis and numerical solutions of three-dimensional viscous internal flow problems; use of numerical coordinate transformations and higher-order spline techniques and direct solvers in the solution of navier-stokes equations. *Mailing Add:* Dept Aerospace Eng & Eng Mech Univ Cincinnati Matl Loc 70 Cincinnati OH 45221

GHIARA, PAOLO, IMMUNOLOGY. *Current Pos:* res asst immunopharmacol, 83-87, SR INVESTR IMMUNOPHARMACOL, SCLAVO, RES CTR, 87- *Personal Data:* b Naples, Italy, Apr 18, 58; m 84; c 2. *Educ:* Classic Lyceum A Genovesi, Naples, Bachelor, 76; Nat Music Conserv, Livorno, dipl, 80; Univ Naples, MSc, 82. *Prof Exp:* Internal student pharmacol, Inst Exp Pharmacol, Univ Naples, 79-82, fel, 82-83. *Concurrent Pos:* Fel, Wellcome Res Labs, Beckenham, UK, 85; Ludwig Inst, Epalinges, 87. *Mem:* Gruppo di Coop Immunol; Am Asn Immunologists. *Res:* Immunopharmacology of the inflammatory process; cDNA cloning and expression of interleukin-1 beta; structure-activity relationships of interleukin-1; identification and characterization of membrane receptors for interleukin-1. *Mailing Add:* Via Fiorentina Siena I-53100 Italy. *Fax:* 39-577-243-564

GHIDONI, JOHN JOSEPH, PATHOLOGY, AUTOPSY PATHOLOGY & CARDIOVASCULAR PATHOLOGY, 69- *Current Pos:* PROF PATH, UNIV TEX MED SCH SAN ANTONIO, 69- *Personal Data:* b Yonkers, NY, Feb 22, 31; m 56; c 6. *Educ:* Fordham Univ, BSc, 53; State Univ NY, MD, 57. *Prof Exp:* Intern, Brooklyn Hosp, 57-58; resident path, Bronx Munic Hosp Ctr, NY, 58-62; instr, Albert Einstein Col Med, 62-63; asst prof, Baylor Col Med, 65-69, dir lab exp path, 66-69. *Concurrent Pos:* USPHS fel, Albert Einstein Col Med, 61-62, spec fel, 62-63; consult path, Vet Admin Hosp, Houston, Tex, 67-69. *Mem:* Electron Micros Soc Am; Int Acad Path; Am Soc Cell Biol; Am Asn Path. *Res:* Amyloidosis; epithelial metaplasia; cell injury by proton particles; effects of isoproteronal on salivary gland; cardiovascular prostheses; cellular dedifferentiation and differentiation. *Mailing Add:* Dept Path-Cell Bio Univ Tex Med Sch 7703 Floyd Curl Dr San Antonio TX 78284-7750. *E-Mail:* ghidoni@uthscsa.edu

GHIL, MICHAEL, ATMOSPHERIC SCIENCES, GEOPHYSICS. *Current Pos:* dir, Climate Dynamics Ctr, 86-92, chmn, Dept Atmospheric Sci, 88-92, PROF ATMOSPHERIC SCI, UNIV CALIF, LOS ANGELES, 85-, DIR, INST GEOPHYS PLANET PHYSICS, 92- *Personal Data:* b Budapest, Hungary, June 10, 44; m 82, Michele J Denizot; c Emmanuel A & Mirella J. *Educ:* Technion-Israel Inst Technol, BSc, 66, MSc, 71; NY Univ, MS, 73, PhD(math), 75. *Honors & Awards:* Condorcet Medal, Ecole Normale

Superieure, Paris, 96. *Prof Exp:* Res assoc, NASA Goddard Inst Space Studies, NY, 75-76; res asst prof math, Courant Inst Math Sci, New York, 76-79, res assoc prof atmospheric sci, 79-82, res prof, 82-86. *Concurrent Pos:* Adj asst prof atmos sci, Columbia Univ, 75-79; vis prof meteorol, Stockholm Univ, 78; dir, Int Sch Physics, Varenna, Italy, 83; vis prof geophysics, Cath Univ Louvain, Belg, 84-85; distinguished vis scientist, Jet Propulsion Lab, Calif Inst Technol/NASA, Pasadena, Calif, 88-; mem, Climate Res Comt, Nat Res Coun, 89-; chair, Waves & Stability Comt, Am Meteorol Soc, 90-92; Guggenheim fel, 91-92; spec creativity award, NSF, 93-95; bd gov, Weizmann Inst Sci, Rehovot, Israel, 95-; Condorcet vis prof, Ecole Normale Superieure, Paris, 95; Elf-Aquitaine CNRS vis prof, Acad Sci, Paris, 96; vis prof, Col France, Paris, 97. *Mem:* Fel Am Geophys Union; Soc Indust & Appl Math; Sigma Xi; fel Am Meteorol Soc. *Res:* Climate dynamics; data assimilation and sequential estimation; dynamical system theory; large-scale atmospheric dynamics; wind-driven and thermohaline ocean circulation; coupled ocean-atmosphere system; celestial mechanics; applied mathematics and statistics. *Mailing Add:* Dept Atmospheric Sci Univ Calif 7127 MSB Los Angeles CA 90095-1565. Fax: 310-206-5219

GHIORSO, ALBERT, PHYSICS. *Current Pos:* physicist, 46-69, DIR HEAVY ION LINEAR ACCELERATOR, DEPT CHEM, LAWRENCE BERKELEY LAB, UNIV CALIF, BERKELEY, 69- *Personal Data:* b Vallejo, Calif, July 15, 15; m 42; c 2. *Educ:* Univ Calif, BS, 37. *Hon Degrees:* PhD, Gustavus Adolphus Col, 66. *Prof Exp:* Mem staff, Metall Lab, Univ Chicago, 42-46. *Mem:* Am Phys Soc. *Res:* Transuranium elements; co-discoverer of elements 95-106, inclusive; nuclear properties of heavy element isotopes; fission counters; electronic apparatus for measurement of nuclear radiations; reactions induced by heavy ions; systematics of radioactive decay. *Mailing Add:* 687 Vincente Ave Berkeley CA 94707

GHIORSO, MARK STEFAN, AQUEOUS GEOCHEMISTRY, IGNEOUS PETROLOGY. *Current Pos:* From asst prof to assoc prof, 80-88, PROF GEOL, UNIV WASH, 88- *Personal Data:* b San Francisco, Calif, Oct 21, 54. *Educ:* Univ Calif, Berkeley, AB, 76, MA, 78, PhD(geol), 80. *Concurrent Pos:* Presidential young investr award, NSF, 85-90. *Mem:* Geol Soc Am; Mineral Soc Am; Am Geophys Union; Geochem Soc; Am Math Asn. *Res:* Thermodynamic modelling and properties of silicate liquids; mass transfer in hydrothermal and geothermal systems; experimental determination of the kinetics of mineral dissolution; diffusion in silicate liquids. *Mailing Add:* 3900 Seventh Ave NE Univ Wash Seattle WA 98195-0001

GHIRARDELLI, ROBERT GEORGE, ORGANIC CHEMISTRY. *Current Pos:* vis asst prof, Duke Univ, 62-68, sr res assoc chem, 68-71, adj assoc prof, 72-81, ADJ PROF, DUKE UNIV, 82- *Personal Data:* b San Francisco, Calif, Nov 12, 30; m 57, Virginia Holder; c Mark, Linda (Smith), Alice, Thomas & David. *Educ:* Univ San Francisco, BS, 52; Calif Inst Technol, PhD(chem), 56. *Prof Exp:* Asst, Calif Inst Technol, 56-57 & Ga Inst Technol, 57-58; asst prof chem, Robert Col, Istanbul, 58-60; chief, Org Chem Br, US Army Res Off, 60-67, assoc dir, Chem Div, 67-74, assoc dir, Chem & Biol Sci Div, 74-77, dir, Chem & Biol Sci Div, 77-94. *Mem:* Fel AAAS; Am Chem Soc. *Res:* Stereochemistry; reaction mechanisms; macrocyclic polyethers; circular dichroism. *Mailing Add:* Duke Univ Paul M Gross Chem Lab PO Box 90354 Durham NC 27708-0354

GHIRON, CAMILLO A, BIOPHYSICS. *Current Pos:* asst prof physiol & res assoc biochem, 64-66, from asst prof to prof, 66-91, EMER PROF BIOCHEM, SCH MED & SCH AGR, UNIV MO-COLUMBIA, 91- *Personal Data:* b Turin, Italy, Nov 11, 32; US citizen; m 59; c 3. *Educ:* Mass Inst Technol, SB, 54; Univ Utah, PhD(molecular biol), 64. *Prof Exp:* Res asst neurosurg, Sch Med, NY Univ, 56-57; res asst biophys, Brookhaven Nat Lab, 57-60; res assoc chem, Univ Minn, 63-64. *Concurrent Pos:* Partic, AEC Training Prog Radiation Phys Chem, Univ Minn, 63-64; Nat Heart Inst sr fel, Biol Div, Oak Ridge Nat Lab, 71-72; asst prof phys biochem, Ill Inst Technol, 93- *Mem:* AAAS; Radiation Res Soc; Biophys Soc; Am Chem Soc; Brit Biochem Soc; Sigma Xi. *Res:* Radiation inactivation kinetics of enzymes; photodynamic action; photophysics; dynamic topography of proteins. *Mailing Add:* 2130 N Lincoln Park W Apt 10 S Chicago IL 60614

GHISELIN, MICHAEL TENANT, ZOOLOGY. *Current Pos:* RES FEL, CALIF ACAD SCI, 83- *Personal Data:* b Salt Lake City, Utah, May 13, 39. *Educ:* Univ Utah, BA, 60; Stanford Univ, PhD(biol), 65. *Honors & Awards:* Pfizer Prize, Hist Sci Soc, 70. *Prof Exp:* Fel systs, Marine Biol Lab, 65-67; from asst prof to assoc prof zool, Univ Calif, Berkeley, 67-78; Guggenheim fel, 78-79, fel Mac Arthur Prize, 81-86. *Concurrent Pos:* Res prof biol, Univ Utah, 80-83. *Mem:* AAAS; Soc Syst Zool; Am Soc Nat; Paleont Soc; Soc Study Evolution. *Res:* Comparative invertebrate anatomy; evolutionary biology; history, methodology and philosophy of biology. *Mailing Add:* Calif Acad Sci Golden Gate Park San Francisco CA 94118-4599. Fax: 415-750-7090; *E-Mail:* mghiselin@calacademy.org

GHISTA, DHANJOO NOSHIR, biomedical engineering, surgery, for more information see previous edition

GHOLSON, LARRY ESTIE, ENTOMOLOGY. *Current Pos:* MGR AGR DEVELOP, WESTERN SUGAR CO, 87- *Personal Data:* b San Luis Obispo, Calif, July 13, 49; m. *Educ:* US Merchant Marine Acad, BS, 71; Calif Polytech State Univ, MS, 75; Iowa State Univ, PhD(entom), 78. *Prof Exp:* Lab instr entom, zool & natural hist, Calif Polytech State Univ, 74-75; res assoc entom, Iowa State Univ, 76-78; asst prof entom, NMex State Univ, 78-80; ext specialist, crop sci, NC State Univ, Raleigh, 80-81; ext specialist, Integrated Pest Mgt, Univ Wyo, 81-87. *Concurrent Pos:* Mem comt pest detection & surv Entom Soc Am, 78-80; tech adv, major cereal grain prod, Egypt, 79; mem, Int Agr Liason Off, State of Wyo, Trade Mission, Egypt, Saudi Arabia & Jordan, 85, Saudi Arabia & Jordan, 86; dir, Beet Sugar Develop Found, 87-91. *Mem:* Entom Soc Am; Sigma Xi; Am Phytopath Soc; AAAS; Am Soc Sugar Beet Technologists. *Res:* Integrated crop production strategies for forages and small grains in Wyoming and the Middle East; development of sugar beet production technology. *Mailing Add:* 772 16th St Boulder CO 80302

GHOLSON, ROBERT KARL, BIOCHEMISTRY. *Current Pos:* res assoc, 62-66, assoc prof, 66-69, PROF BIOCHEM, OKLA STATE UNIV, 69- *Personal Data:* b McLeansboro, Ill, Feb 13, 30; m 52; c 3. *Educ:* Univ Chicago, BA, 50; Univ Ill, BS, 55, PhD(biochem), 58. *Prof Exp:* Res assoc biochem, Okla State Univ, 58-59; res assoc med sch Univ, Univ Mich, 59-61 & Kyoto Univ, 61-62. *Mem:* Am Soc Biol Chem; Am Chem Soc; Sigma Xi; NY Acad Sci. *Res:* Biosynthesis of pyridine nucleotides; plant-pathogen interactions. *Mailing Add:* 1008 W Brooke Ave Stillwater OK 74075

GHONEIM, MOHAMED MANSOUR, ANESTHESIA, PSYCHOPHARMACOLOGY. *Current Pos:* from asst prof to assoc prof, 67-72, PROF ANESTHESIA, UNIV IOWA, 76- *Personal Data:* b Egypt, Feb 6, 34; US citizen; m 66. *Educ:* Ain Shams Univ, Cairo, Egypt, MB, ChB, 57; FRCA, 63. *Prof Exp:* Sr house officer, anesthesia Nuffield Dept Anaesthetics, Oxford, Eng, 63-64; lectr, Assiut Univ, Egypt, 64-65. *Mem:* Am Soc Anesthesiologists; Am Soc Pharmacol & Exp Therapeut; Asn Univ Anesthetists; Royal Col Anaesthetists Eng. *Res:* Psychopharmacology, particularly the effects of drugs on human cognition and memory; psychological outcomes of anesthesia and surgery; effects of general anesthetics on human memory. *Mailing Add:* Dept Anesthesia Univ Iowa Hosp Col Med 200 Hawkins Dr Iowa City IA 52242-0001

GHONEIM, YOUSSEF AHMED, CONTROL SYSTEM DESIGN, AUTOMOTIVE APPLICATIONS. *Current Pos:* sr res engr, 85-90, STAFF RES ENGR AUTOMOTIVE INDUST, GEN MOTORS RES LABS, 90- *Personal Data:* b Cairo, Egypt. *Educ:* Cairo Univ, Egypt, BSc, 76, MSc, 78; McGill Univ, Montreal, Can, MEng, 80, PhD(elec eng), 85. *Prof Exp:* Res engr teaching, Cairo Univ, 76-78; teaching asst, McGill Univ, 79-85. *Mem:* Inst Elec & Electronics Engrs. *Res:* Vehicle traction; chassis control; analytical and experimental investigation. *Mailing Add:* 20672 Windham Macomb Township MI 48044

GHOSAL, KANCHAN, MEMBRANES & POLYMER BARRIERS, EMULSION POLYMERS & LATEX FILM FORMATION. *Current Pos:* SR DEVELOP ENGR, REICHHOLD CHEM, 94- *Personal Data:* b Nagpur, India, Apr 3, 63; m 92, Adite Banerjee. *Educ:* Inst Technol, India, BS, 85; Univ Akron, MS, 89; NC State Univ, PhD(chem eng), 94. *Prof Exp:* Process engr, JK Synthetics Ltd, India, 85-87. *Mem:* Am Inst Chem Engrs; Am Chem Soc; Am Soc Testing & Mat; Sigma Xi. *Res:* Transport of small molecules through polymers with application in barrier films and membrane separation; crosslinking and film formations from emulsion polymers; development of novel emulsion polymers. *Mailing Add:* 2800 Avent Ferry Rd No 204 Raleigh NC 27606

GHOSE, HIRENDRA M, PHYSICAL CHEMISTRY, INORGANIC CHEMISTRY SURFACE PHYSICS & TRIBOLOGY. *Current Pos:* dir, Sci & Technol, 78-87, PROF CHEM & CHMN, DEPT PHYSICS SCI, CUYAHOGA COMMUNITY COL, 70-; CONSULT, NSF, ENVIRON PROTECTION AGENCY, NASA & NAT EDUC TRAINING PROG, 76-; PRES, GHOSE & ASSOCS, 78- *Personal Data:* b Patna, India; US citizen; m 60; c 3. *Educ:* Bihar Nat Col, Patna, BSc, 49; Sci Col Patna, MSc, 53; Mont State Col, PhD(phys chem), 60. *Prof Exp:* Demonstr physics, Bihar Nat Col, Patna, 49-51, prof chem, 53-55; instr, Skidmore Col, 59-60; sr res scientist, Glidden Co, 60-67; res supvr, Addressograph Multigraph Corp, 67-70. *Concurrent Pos:* Vis lectr, State Univ NY, Col Plattsburgh, 59-60; consult, Friends Psychiat Res Inst, Spring Grove Ment Hosp, Baltimore, Md, 66-67; consult environ, chem & educ areas; pres, Ghose Industs Inc, 72-78. *Mem:* Am Chem Soc; Am Vacuum Soc; Soc Tribologists & Lubrication Engrs. *Res:* Surface reactivity, fluid chemistry, Auger Emission Spectroscopy; interaction of lubricant antiwear additives with alloy and ceramic surfaces; published books and technical papers in the fields of physics, chemistry, mathematics, high technology science, engineering and also published a fiction book in 1992. *Mailing Add:* Dept Phys Sci 2900 Community College Ave Cleveland OH 44115. *Fax:* 216-987-4758

GHOSE, RABINDRA NATH, BIOPHYSICS, PHYSICS. *Current Pos:* PRES & CHMN BD, TECHNOL RES INT, 83- *Personal Data:* b Howrah, India, Sept 1, 25; US citizen; m 64, Dorothy Stewart; c Geoffrey M. *Educ:* Univ Jadavpur, Calcutta, BEE, 46; Indian Inst Sci, Bangalore, dipl, 48; Univ Wash, MS, 52; Univ Ill, MA & PhD(elec eng), 54, EE, 56, LLB, 70; Golden Gate Univ, MBA, 86. *Honors & Awards:* Hind Rattan Award, Minister Finance, India, 92. *Prof Exp:* Instr elec eng, Jadavpur Univ, India, 46-49; tech officer & chief tech instr, Hq Western Command Indian Signals, 49-51; mem tech staff, Radio Corp Am, 54-56 & Space Tech Lab, 56-59; dir, Res & Adv Develop, Space-Gen Corp, 59-63; chmn bd, Am Nucleonics Corp, 63-83. *Concurrent Pos:* Mem grad fac, Univ Southern Calif, 58-59; reviewer sci proposals, NSF, 62; session chmn, Int Conf Microwaves, Commun & Info Theory, 64; mem res & tech adv bd, NASA, 74-76; mem, div adv group, Air Force Sci Adv Bd, 80-84; mem, adv comt & panel chmn, Defense Intel. *Mem:* Fel AAAS; fel Inst Elec & Electronics Engrs; fel Am Phys Soc; fel Inst Elec Engrs London; fel Inst Phys; fel Inst Engrs India; fel Am Phys Soc; fel Inst Elec & Telecommun Eng. *Res:* Electromagnetic field theories; microwaves; nuclear science antennas; biomedical instrumentations. *Mailing Add:* 8167 Mulholland Terr Los Angeles CA 90046. *Fax:* 818-880-5694

GHOSE, SUBRATA, MINERAL PHYSICS. *Current Pos:* res assoc prof, Univ Wash, 72-75, res prof mineral, 75-77, actg prof geol sci, 77-78, PROF MINERAL PHYSICS, UNIV WASH, 78- *Personal Data:* b Jamshedpur, India; m 67; c 2. *Educ:* Univ Calcutta, MSc, 55; Univ Chicago, MS & PhD(mineral), 59. *Honors & Awards:* Sr US Scientist Award, Alexander von Humboldt Found, Ger. *Prof Exp:* Res assoc, Univ Pittsburgh, 59-61 & Univ Bern, 61-63; sr res assoc, Swiss Fed Inst Technol, 63-65; asst prof chem, Worcester Polytech Inst, 65-67; Nat Res Coun-Nat Acad Sci sr res fel, Goddard Space Flight Ctr, NASA, Md, 67-71; vis lectr crystallog, Univ Calif, Berkeley, 71-72. *Concurrent Pos:* Vis prof, Univ Sci & Med, Grenoble, France, 80-81; vis prof, Univ Kyoto, Kyoto, Japan, 86, Univ Bayreuth, Bayreuth, Ger, 90; adj prof mat sci & eng & geophys, Univ Wash. *Mem:* Fel Mineral Soc Am; Mineral Asn Can; Am Crystallog Asn; Am Geophys Union. *Res:* Crystal chemistry of rock-forming silicates, phosphates and borates; cation order-disorder and thermodynamics and kinetics of crystalline solutions; physics of minerals; lattice dynamics; structural and magnetic phase transitions. *Mailing Add:* 4110 NE 165th St Seattle WA 98155

GHOSE, TARUNENDU, PATHOLOGY. *Current Pos:* assoc prof, 69-77, PROF PATH & ASSOC PROF MICROBIOL, DALHOUSIE UNIV, 77- *Personal Data:* b Begusarai, India, May 25, 28. *Educ:* Univ Calcutta, BS, 45, MB, BS, 50; Indian Cancer Res Ctr, Bombay, PhD(exp path & oncol), 59; FRCP, 74. *Honors & Awards:* Med Res Coun Prize, India, 59. *Prof Exp:* House surgeon & registr, R G Kar Med Col Hosp & Chittaranjan Cancer Hosp, Calcutta, 50-54; asst med officer & res officer, Indian Cancer Res Ctr & Tata Mem Hosp, Bombay, 55-58, 59-61; med officer, Nat Acad Sci, US, 58-59; univ fel, Univ Aberdeen, 61-62, lectr path, 63-65; univ fel, Univ Leeds, 63; sr lectr, Monash Univ, Australia, 65-68. *Concurrent Pos:* Sr registr, Aberdeen Royal Infirmary, 63-65; assoc pathologist, Prov NS; head, Sect Immunopath, Victoria Gen Hosp, Halifax, NS, 69-; mem, Grant Rev Panels, Med Res Coun, Can & Cancer Res Soc, Montreal. *Mem:* Path Soc Gt Brit & Ireland; Am Asn Cancer Res. *Res:* Cancer immunology; immunopathology of respiratory and joint diseases. *Mailing Add:* Dept Path Dalhousie Univ Halifax NS B3H 4H7 Can

GHOSH, AMAL KUMAR, SOLID STATE PHYSICS. *Current Pos:* res assoc, Esso Res & Eng Co, 70-74, res assoc, Exxon Res Ctr, 74-75, SR RES ASSOC, EXXON RES CTR, 75- *Personal Data:* b Thaton, Burma, June 21, 31; m 61; c 3. *Educ:* Univ Calcutta, BS, 51, MS, 54, PhD(physics), 61 *Prof Exp:* Res assoc, Univ Notre Dame, 58-60; resident res assoc, Argonne Nat Lab, 60-62, asst physicist, 62-65; mem sci staff, Itek Corp, 66-70. *Mem:* Am Phys Soc. *Res:* Optical properties of solids; radiation effects; photoimaging and semiconductor devices. *Mailing Add:* Diabetes Ctr Univ Pa 4450 Remo Crescent Philadelphia PA 19020-2932

GHOSH, AMAL KUMAR, biochemistry; deceased, see previous edition for last biography

GHOSH, AMIT KUMAR, MECHANICAL METALLURGY, MATERIALS SCIENCE. *Current Pos:* mem tech staff mat, 76-80, mgr metalls processing, Sci Ctr, 80-88, PRIN SCIENTIST, ROCKWELL INT CORP, 88-; PROF MAT SCI & ENG, UNIV MICH, 88- *Personal Data:* b India; m 70; c 2. *Educ:* Univ Calcutta, BEng, 66; Univ Ill, Champaign, MS, 68; Mass Inst Technol, PhD(metall & mat sci), 72. *Honors & Awards:* Marcus Grossman Award, Am Soc Metals, 76; Rockwell Indust Res & Develop Award, Dept Defense, 83 & NASA, 84; Quad Chap Award, Am Soc Metals, 85. *Prof Exp:* Trainee steel mfg, Hindustan Steel Ltd, India, 64-65; sr res metallurgist metal forming, Res Labs, Gen Motors Corp, 72-76. *Concurrent Pos:* Consult, Battelle Labs, Mich Tech Univ, 78-79, EG&G, Boeing, Rockwell, GM, Allison, Allied Signal, Northrop, Crucible & Marko; instr, Am Soc Metals Acad Metals Course, 81-; dir Metall Soc, Am Inst Mining, Metall & Petrol Engrs; prin investr, Dept Defense Progs. *Mem:* Fel Am Soc Metals; Am Inst Mining, Metall & Petrol Engrs; Am Deep Drawing Res Group; Mat Res Soc. *Res:* Conventional metal working; superplastic forming and forging; constitutive relations in metal deformation; workability in deformation processing; ductile fracture; diffusion bonding; metal matrix composites; titanium aluminides; silicide intermetallics and composites. *Mailing Add:* Dept Mat Sci & Eng Univ Mich 2102 Dow Bldg Ann Arbor MI 48109-2136. *Fax:* 313-763-4788; *E-Mail:* amit_ghosh@um.cc.imich.edu

GHOSH, ARATI, MEMBRANE TRANSPORT-PROTEIN, ELECTRON MICROSCOPY. *Current Pos:* RES SCIENTIST TOXICOL/ENVIRON POLLUTION, NJ STATE DEPT HEALTH, TRENTON, 85- *Personal Data:* b Raipvr, MP, India, Mar 1, 36; US citizen; m 60; c 1. *Educ:* Calcutta Univ, India, BSc, 55, MSc, 57, PhD(biochem), 63. *Prof Exp:* Sr man power fel microbiol, Calcutta Univ, India, 58-63, sr UGC fel, 63-64; postdoctoral fel neurochem, Univ Western Ont, London, Can, 64-66; res assoc microbial genetics, Waksman Inst Microbiol, Rutgers Univ, NJ, 67-73; res specialist microbial cell physiol, Rutgers Med Sch, Univ Med & Dent NJ, Piscataway, 73-85. *Concurrent Pos:* Vis scientist, Nat Inst Med Res, Mill Hill, London, UK, 77. *Mem:* Am Soc Cell Biol; Electron Micros Soc Am. *Res:* Membrane structure and membrane regulation of microbial protein secretion; mechanism of action of antibiotics on cell membrane; electron microscopic analysis of environmental pollution (asbestos). *Mailing Add:* 8 Constitution Ct East Brunswick NJ 08816

GHOSH, ARUP KUMAR, PHYSICS, MATERIAL SCIENCE. *Current Pos:* res assoc, 76-78, asst physicist, 78-79, ASSOC PHYSICIST, BROOKHAVEN NAT LAB, 80- *Personal Data:* b Calcutta, India, May 31, 50; m 72; c 2. *Educ:* Univ Delhi, BSc, 69, MSc, 71; Univ Rochester, PhD(physics), 76. *Prof Exp:* Res assoc physics, Univ Rochester, 76. *Mem:* Am Phys Soc. *Res:* Superconductivity; A-15 material preparation; transport properties of superconductors and amorphous material; superconductors and amorphous material; amorphous silicon. *Mailing Add:* 7 Darthmouth Rd Shoreham NY 11786. *E-Mail:* ghosh@magadd2nov.add.bnl.gov

GHOSH, ASOKE KUMAR, SPACE SCIENCE, PLASMA PHYSICS. *Current Pos:* dir prog develop & spec projs plasma, energy & electronics, 77-85, DIR SPACE & PHOTONICS DIV, MPB TECHNOL, 85- *Personal Data:* b Dacca, India, June 17, 38; Can citizen; m 64, Chandralekha Maulik; c Tanima, Sumonto & Emon. *Educ:* Calcutta Univ, BSc, 56, MSc, 59; Jadavpur Univ, PhD(plasma physics), 64. *Prof Exp:* Sr lectr physics, N Bengal Univ, 62-63; mem sci staff plasmas, laser electronics, RCA Ltd, Can, 65-77. *Res:* Plasma physics; gas discharge; lasers; microwave; solar energy; pollution monitoring devices; ARC technology; heat pipe application; devices; laser applications (zone crystallization); iodine laser; microgravity; remote sensing; photonics. *Mailing Add:* 151 Hymus Point Claire PQ H9R 1E9 Can. *Fax:* 514-695-7492

GHOSH, BHASKAR KUMAR, MATHEMATICAL STATISTICS. *Current Pos:* from asst prof to assoc prof, 61-68, chmn dept, 81-85, PROF MATH, LEHIGH UNIV, 68- *Personal Data:* b Dibrugarh, India, Feb 10, 36; m 60, Graf; c Monica, Anita & Rebecca. *Educ:* Univ Calcutta, BSc, 55; Univ London, PhD(statist), 59. *Prof Exp:* Res asst statist, Univ Col, Univ London, 58-59; statistician, Atomic Power Construct, Ltd, Eng, 59-60; asst lectr statist & math, Chelsea Col, Univ London, 60-61. *Concurrent Pos:* Consult, Pa Power & Light Co, 62-63; IT&T Corp, 64; Beryllium Corp, 65 & Howmet Aluminum Corp, 79, BOC Group, 84-; vis prof, Mass Inst Technol, 68, Va Polytech Inst, 78-80, Univ Munster, WGer, 86-87; Humboldt Sr US Scientist, 86-87. *Mem:* Fel Inst Math Statist; fel Royal Statist Soc. *Res:* Probability; sequential analysis; statistical inference. *Mailing Add:* Dept Math Lehigh Univ Bethlehem PA 18015. *Fax:* 610-758-6553; *E-Mail:* bkg0@lehigh.edu

GHOSH, BIJAN K, PHYSIOLOGY, ELECTRON MICROSCOPY. *Current Pos:* Asst res prof, Waksman Inst, 68-73, assoc prof, 73-79, PROF PHYSIOL, ROBERT WOOD JOHNSON MED SCH, UNIV MED & DENT NJ & HON PROF, WAKSMAN INST MICROBIOL, RUTGERS UNIV, 79- *Personal Data:* b India, 35; US citizen; m 60; c 1. *Educ:* Calcutta Univ, India, BSc, 55, MSc, 57, DSc(microbiol & physiol), 63. *Concurrent Pos:* Vis prof, Univ Amsterdam, 73; vis lectr, Chinese Acad Sci, 85. *Mem:* Can Soc Biochem; Am Soc Chem Biol; Am Soc Microbiol; Electron Micros Soc Am. *Res:* The mechanism of regulation of protein secretion by membrane; nature of bacterial membrane compartments; application of quantitative electron microscopy to study microbial physiology and molecular biology. *Mailing Add:* Dept Physiol & Biophys UMDNJ Robert Wood Johnson Med Sch 675 Hoes Lane Piscataway NJ 08854. *Fax:* 732-463-4288

GHOSH, CHITTA RANJAN, IMMUNOLOGY, MICROBIOLOGY. *Current Pos:* LAB SCIENTIST, OMAHA-DOUGLAS COUNTY HEALTH DEPT, 80- *Personal Data:* b Mulghar, India, Mar 1, 36. *Educ:* Univ Calcutta, BVS, 57; Univ Ky, PhD(microbiol), 69. *Prof Exp:* Vet surgeon, Govt WBengal, India, 58-63; instr obstet & gynec, Sch Med, Tufts Univ, 69-74; immunologist, St Joseph's Hosp, 73-75; immunologist, dept path, Sch Med, Creighton Univ, 75-80. *Concurrent Pos:* Immunologist, St Margarets Hosp, 69-74. *Mem:* Am Soc Microbiol. *Res:* Autoimmune diseases; clinical immunology and serology; immunology of cancer. *Mailing Add:* 1308 N 40th St Omaha NE 68131

GHOSH, DIPAK K, SKIN CARE RESEARCH, DERMATOLOGICAL RESEARCH. *Current Pos:* DIR RES & DEVELOP, CHESEBROUGH-POND'S RES LAB, 78- *Personal Data:* b Kalupur, WBengal, India, Feb 21, 47; m 76; c 2. *Educ:* Jadavpur Univ, India, BS, 67, PhD(pharm), 73; Banaras Hindu Univ, India, MS, 69. *Prof Exp:* Sr res chemist pharmaceut, Tata-Fison Labs, India, 69-70; res fel pharm, Rutgers Univ, 73-74; sr scientist pharmaceut, Block Drug Co, NJ, 74-78. *Mem:* Am Pharmaceut Asn; Soc Cosmetic Chemists; Royal Soc Chem. *Res:* Development, evaluation and clinical testing of dermatological semisolid formulations; cough and cold medicine; antacid, analgesic and other over the counter products; several US patents. *Mailing Add:* 73 Field Rock Rd Monroe CT 06468

GHOSH, HARA PRASAD, GENETIC ENGINEERING & BIOTECHNOLOGY. *Current Pos:* from asst prof to assoc prof, 69-76, chmn, 83-91, PROF BIOCHEM, MCMASTER UNIV, 76- *Personal Data:* b India, June 1, 37; m 68; c 2. *Educ:* Calcutta Univ, BSc Hon, 57, MSc, 59, PhD(biochem), 63. *Prof Exp:* Fel biochem, Univ Calif, Davis, 64-66 & Univ Wis-Madison, 66-67. *Concurrent Pos:* Med Res Coun Can scholar, 69-74; mem, Molecular Biol & Virol Grants Panel, Nat Cancer Inst Can, 82-84, Molecular Biol Grants Panel, Med Res Coun Can, 83-85; vis prof biol, Mass Inst Technol, 84-85, Univ Col, London, 92. *Mem:* Am Soc Biol Chemists; Can Biochem Soc; Am Soc Microbiol; Am Soc Virol. *Res:* Virus entry and assembly: membrane fusion, protein targeting, cloning, construction and expression of chimeric genes and engineered mutagenesis; introduction and expression of foreign genes in mammalian cells and tissues; retroviruses and vectors. *Mailing Add:* Dept Biochem McMaster Univ 1200 Main St W Hamilton ON L8N 3Z5 Can. *Fax:* 905-522-9033; *E-Mail:* ghosh@fhs.mcmaster.ca

GHOSH, MRIGANKA M(OULI), WATER CHEMISTRY, ENVIRONMENTAL & REMEDIATION ENGINEERING. *Current Pos:* PROF & GOODRICH CHAIR OF EXCELLENCE, DEPT CIVIL & ENVIRON ENG, UNIV TENN, KNOXVILLE, 90- *Personal Data:* b Calcutta, India, Nov 5, 35; m 67, Rajyasnee nee Sarker; c Rupa. *Educ:* Indian Inst Technol, Kharagpur, BTech, 58; Univ Ill, Urbana, MS, 62, PhD(sanit eng), 65. *Prof Exp:* Jr engr, Hindusthan Steel Ltd, India, 58-59, asst engr, 59-60; grad asst civil eng, Univ Ill, Urbana, 61-65, asst prof, 65-66; reader, Jadavpur Univ, India, 66-68; from asst prof to prof, Univ Maine, 68-76; prof civil eng, Univ Mo, 76-84; prof environ eng, Pa State Univ, 84-90. *Concurrent*

Pos: Consult, Calcutta Metrop Planning Orgn, 66-68, Edward C Jordan & Co, 69-70, city of Somersworth, 69- & city of Dover, 71-; ed, J Environ Engr Div, Am Soc Civil Engrs, 78-80. *Mem:* Am Water Works Asn; Am Soc Civil Engrs (exec secy, 80-84); Water Pollution Control Fedn; Am Chem Soc; Int Asn Water Qual; Asn Environ Eng Profs. *Res:* Chemistry of iron and manganese in natural waters; role of yellow organic acids in natural waters; physical chemical parameters affecting the removal of colloids by porous media; removing trace organics from drinking waters; bioremediation of contaminated soils; photochemistry of chlorinated organics. *Mailing Add:* Dept Civil & Environ Eng Univ Tenn Knoxville TN 37996-2010. *Fax:* 423-974-2669; *E-Mail:* mghosh@utk.edu

GHOSH, SAKTI P, MATHEMATICAL STATISTICS, COMPUTER SCIENCE. *Current Pos:* mem res staff, T J Watson Res Ctr, 62-68, MEM RES STAFF, RES LAB, IBM CORP, 68- *Personal Data:* b Calcutta, India, Feb 6, 35. *Educ:* Univ Calcutta, BSc, 55, MSc, 57; Univ Calif, Berkeley, PhD(statist), 62. *Honors & Awards:* Spec Award For Model Curric, Comput Socs Group, Inst Elec & Electronics Engrs, 77; IBM Res Div Award, 78; Invention Achievement Award, IBM, 82. *Prof Exp:* Statistician, State Statist Bur, Govt WBengal, India, 58-59; asst statistician, Univ Calif, Berkeley, 59-62. *Concurrent Pos:* Adj asst prof, NY Univ, 64-; co-chmn, Int Symposium Very Large Data Bases, 76; prog co-chmn & mem, Steering Comt, Nat Comput Conf, 78; invited US rep, SE Asia Comput Conf, Manila, 78; adj prof, San Jose State Univ, 82-; ed, Software Eng, Inst Elec & Electronics Engrs, 84- *Mem:* Fel Inst Elec & Electronics Engr, 90. *Res:* Sampling theory; information retrieval theory; information sciences; computer language; coding theory; information and data conversion; manufacturing research; statistical database management. *Mailing Add:* IBM Corp Monterey & Cottle Rds San Jose CA 95193

GHOSH, SAMBHUNATH, ENVIRONMENTAL ENGINEERING, BIOENGINEERING. *Current Pos:* prof & chmn, Civil Eng Dept, 85-89, PROF CIVIL & ENVIRON ENG, UNIV UTAH, 89-; PRES, ENVIROENERGETICS, 89- *Personal Data:* b Calcutta, India, Aug 1, 35; US citizen; m 61, Anima Paul; c Monica (Driggers) & Dipankar. *Educ:* Univ Calcutta, BS, 56; Univ Ill, Urbana, MS, 63; Ga Inst Technol, PhD(civil & environ eng), 70. *Honors & Awards:* Monie A Ferst Mem Res Award, Sigma Xi; John Ericsson Award in Renewable Energy, Sci & Technol, US Dept Energy, 93, Gold Medal; George Bradley Gascoigne Medal, Water Environ Fedn, 96. *Prof Exp:* Jr engr civil eng, Pub Works Dept, State of Assam, India, 56-57; asst engr struct & sanit eng & asst construct engr, Durgapur Steel Proj, Hindustan Steel, Govt India, 58-61; grad res asst environ eng, Univ Ill, Urbana, 61-63; res assoc, Univ NC, Chapel Hill, 63-64; engr sanit eng, Wiedeman & Singleton, Ga, 64-65; trainee environ & civil eng, Ga Inst Technol, 65-69, fel civil eng, 70; mgr bioeng res, Inst Gas Technol, Ill Inst Technol, 70-85. *Concurrent Pos:* Consult, Aqua Tech, Atlanta, Ga, 69-70; vis lectr, Dept Environ Eng, Ill Inst Technol, 71-72; US deleg, sci exchange visit People's Repub China, US Nat Acad Sci & Chinese Asn Sci & Technol, 82; mem, Nat Prog Vis Scientists People's Repub China, US Nat Acad Sci, 86-87; adj prof bioeng, Univ Utah, 89-91; Fulbright res & lectr award, Nat Environ Eng Res Inst, Nagpur, India, 90-91; prof, Tohoku Univ, Japan, 94; fel, Japan Soc Prom Sci, 94-95. *Mem:* Am Soc Civil Engrs; Int Asn Water Pollution Res; Water Pollution Control Fedn; Soc Indust Microbiol; Sigma Xi; Water Environ Fedn; Int Asn Water Qual; Am Chem Soc; Am Soc Microbiol. *Res:* Water and wastewater treatment; solid and hazardous wastes engineering; bioremediation of soils and sediments; anaerobic digestion; treatability studies; process development; pilot studies; process commercialization; biomass and renewable energy; author of numerous publications. *Mailing Add:* Dept Civil Eng Merrill Eng Bldg Univ Utah Salt Lake City UT 84112-1180

GHOSH, SANJIB KUMAR, PHOTOGRAMMETRY, GEODESY. *Personal Data:* b Calcutta, India, Sept 9, 25; m 51, Tapati Bose; c Sanjoy & Sujoy. *Educ:* Univ Calcutta, BSc, 45; Int Training Ctr Aerial Surv, Delft, Neth, Photog Engr, 57; Ohio State Univ, PhD(photogram), 64. *Honors & Awards:* Presidential Award, Am Soc Photogram, 71 & 79. *Prof Exp:* Survr, Surv India, 48-60; from res asst to res assoc photogram, 60-61; from instr to assoc prof photogram & geod, Ohio State Univ, 62-79; prof photogram, Lava Univ, 79-92. *Concurrent Pos:* Mem panel experts photogram, UNESCO, 66-; vis prof, Fed Univ Parana, Brazil, 76-77; invited prof, Hosei Univ, Japan, 77-78; UN consult, 80-; external examr, Univ Teknologi Malaysia, Lagos Univ, Nigeria, Univ Delhi, India, Univ Rajasthan, India; invited prof, Inst Agr & Vet, Hassan II, Morocco, 87-88; Univ Sao, Paolo Brazil, 89; UN Fel, 56-57. *Mem:* Am Soc Photogram; fel Am Cong Surv & Mapping; Int Soc Photogram; Geog Soc India; Brit Photogram Soc; Can Inst Surv. *Res:* Geometric and physical aspects of photogrammetry; orientation of photogrammetric models; aerial triangulation; photogrammetric system calibration; un-conventional photogrammetry; remote sensing. *Mailing Add:* 6344 Thorncrest Dr Galloway OH 43119

GHOSH, SATYENDRA KUMAR, STRUCTURAL ENGINEERING, EARTHQUAKE ENGINEERING. *Current Pos:* struct engr, 74-75, sr struct engr, 75-79, PRIN STRUCT ENGR, PORTLAND CEMENT ASN, 79- *Personal Data:* b Berhampore, India, Sept 17, 45; m 73; c 2. *Educ:* Univ Calcutta, BE, 66; Univ Waterloo, MASc, 69, PhD(struct eng), 72. *Prof Exp:* Res & teaching asst civil eng, Univ Waterloo, 67-69, 70-72 & Univ Pittsburgh, 69-70; fel, Univ Waterloo, 72-73, res assoc, 73, adj prof, 73-74. *Concurrent Pos:* Partner, Elan Assocs, Waterloo, Ont, 72-73; consult, Peter Sheffield & Assocs, Toronto, 73; partic earthquake eng workshop, NSF, Univ Calif, Berkeley, 77; mem joint comts, Am Concrete Inst & Am Soc Civil Eng, 77- *Mem:* Am Concrete Inst; Am Soc Civil Engrs. *Res:* Analysis and design of earthquake resistant reinforced concrete building structures.. *Mailing Add:* 1811 E Cree Lane Mt Prospect IL 60056

GHOSH, SUBIR, STATISTICAL PLANNING OF EXPERIMENTS. *Current Pos:* asst prof, 80-85, ASSOC PROF STATIST, UNIV CALIF, RIVERSIDE, 85- *Personal Data:* b Calcutta, India, Aug 26, 50; m 78. *Educ:* Univ Calcutta, BS, 68, MS, 70, Colo State Univ, PhD(statist), 76. *Prof Exp:* Res asst statist, Colo State Univ, 72-75 & fel, 76; researcher math statist, Indian Statist Inst, India, 71, vis fel, 76-77 & lectr, 77-80. *Mem:* Inst Math Statist; Am Statist Asn. *Res:* Statistical planning or design of experiments; search design; robustness of design against the unavailability of data; linear models; planning with correlated data; optimum designs; sampling methods. *Mailing Add:* Dept Statist Univ Calif Univ Calif Riverside CA 92521

GHOSH, SWAPAN KUMAR, IMMUNOLOGY, BIOCHEMISTRY. *Current Pos:* assoc prof, 88-92, PROF IMMUNOL, IND STATE UNIV, 92- *Personal Data:* b Calcutta, India, Jan 1, 42; m 70, Rita Mitra; c Tista & Pritha. *Educ:* Univ Calcutta, India, BSc, 62, MSc, 64, PhD(biochem), 69. *Prof Exp:* Lectr biochem, Med Col Calcutta Univ, 66-68; asst prof biochem, Med Col, NBengal Univ, 68-70; USPHS fel pharmacol, Med Ctr, Univ Ill, 71-72; sr res assoc neurochem, State Univ NY, Buffalo, 73-75; Nat Cancer Inst fel immunol, Roswell Park Mem Inst, 76-78, cancer res scientist III, 79-88. *Concurrent Pos:* Adj asst prof immunol, State Univ NY, Buffalo, 85; Assoc prof Immunol, Ind Univ, Terre Haute Med Ctr, 90- *Mem:* Sigma Xi; Am Asn Immunologists. *Res:* Immunological aspects of tumor metastasis; biochemical and immunological characterization of mammalian cell surfaces; mechanism of generation of tumor variants; idiotype-induced cell-mediated immunity; pregnancy-induced protection against mammary carcinogenesis. *Mailing Add:* Dept Life Sci Ind State Univ 6th & Cherry Terre Haute IN 47809. *Fax:* 812-237-4480; *E-Mail:* lsghosh@scifac.indstate.edu

GHOSH, VINITA JOHRI, MODELLING, COMPUTER SIMULATIONS. *Current Pos:* PHYSICS ASSOC, MULTILAYER SYSTS, BROOKHAVEN NAT LAB, 80- *Personal Data:* m, Arup K; c 2. *Educ:* Univ Rochester, PhD(physics), 79. *Concurrent Pos:* Tech ed, Phys Rev, 80-81. *Mem:* Am Phys Soc. *Res:* Theoretical and computer simulation studies of superconducting materials, photo-voltaic materials, and the study of mubmicroscopic defects using positron spectroscopy. *Mailing Add:* Bldg 480 Brookhaven Nat Lab Upton NY 11971

GHOSHAL, NANI GOPAL, COMPARATIVE ANATOMY, NEUROANATOMY. *Current Pos:* instr, 63-66, from asst prof to assoc prof, 67-74, PROF VET ANAT, IOWA STATE UNIV, 74- *Personal Data:* b Dacca, India, Dec 1, 34; m 71, Chhanda Banerjee; c Nupur. *Educ:* Bengal Vet Col, Calcutta, GVSc, 55; PG (ICAR), 57; Royal (Dick) Sch Vet Studies, Edinburgh, DTVM, 61; Fac Vet Med, Hannover, Dr med vet, 62; Iowa State Univ, PhD(anat), 66. *Honors & Awards:* Raymond Star Gold Medal, Govt W Bengal, India, 55. *Prof Exp:* Vet asst surgeon, Civil Vet Dept, Govt W Bengal, India, 55; demonstr comp vet anat, Bengal Vet Col, Calcutta, 55-56; res asst, MB Govt Col Vet Sci & Animal Husb, Mhow, 56-59; pool scientist, Indian Coun Agr Res, New Delhi, 63. *Concurrent Pos:* Tollygunj Calcutta Scholar, 54, Ger Acad Exchange Serv Scholar, Govt WGer, 61; adj prof, Inst Agron & Vet, Hassan II, Rabat, Morocco, 83-88; consult, Minn-Morocco Proj, USAID, 84-88. *Mem:* AAAS; Am Asn Vet Anat; fel Royal Zool Soc Scotland; World Asn Vet Anat; Pan Am Asn Anat; Am Asn Anat; NY Acad Sci; Sigma Xi. *Res:* Gross anatomy; functional anatomy; brain temperature regulation; author and co-author of textbooks, grants and awards. *Mailing Add:* 1070 Dept Vet Anat Col Vet Med Iowa State Univ Ames IA 50011-2020. *Fax:* 515-294-3932

GHOSHTAGORE, RATHINDRA NATH, MATERIALS SCIENCE, SEMICONDUCTOR INTEGRATED CIRCUITS. *Current Pos:* CONSULT GUEST RESEARCHER, SEMICONDUCTOR ELECTRONICS DIV, NAT INST STAND & TECHNOL, 94- *Personal Data:* b Sribari, Bangladesh, July 8, 37; m 67, Srirupa Sen; c Ujjal & Ipsita. *Educ:* Univ Calcutta, BS, 57, MS, 60; Mass Inst Technol, ScD(ceramics), 65. *Honors & Awards:* Ambica C Sen Gold Medal, Univ Calcutta, 60. *Prof Exp:* Sr physicist, Fundamental Res Lab, Xerox Corp, NY, 65-66; mem tech staff mat & processes, Fairchild Res & Develop Lab, Calif, 66-67; sr engr, Westinghouse Res Labs, 68-74, fel scientist, 74-79, adv scientist, 79-80, adv engr & prog mgr, Westinghouse Advan Technol Lab, 80-91; res fac, Univ Md, 92-93. *Concurrent Pos:* Fac physics & chem, Towson State Univ, 93-94. *Mem:* Fel Am Phys Soc; Electrochem Soc; sr mem Inst Elec & Electronics Engrs. *Res:* Insulators and semiconductors; chemical vapor deposition of thin solid films in amorphous, polycrystalline, epitaxial and glassy state; diffusion in semiconductors; process development and fabrication of advanced silicon integrated circuits. *Mailing Add:* 10315 Castlefield St Ellicott City MD 21042-5866. *Fax:* 301-948-4081; *E-Mail:* rho@apollo.ecel.nist.gov

GHOWSI, KIUMARS, solid liquid interfaces phenomena, high electric field breakdown in solids & liquids, for more information see previous edition

GHOZATI, SEYED-ALI, ELECTRICAL ENGINEERING, COMPUTER SCIENCE. *Current Pos:* asst prof, 76-81, ASSOC PROF COMPUT SCI, QUEENS COL, 81- *Personal Data:* b Tehran, Iran, Oct 19, 44. *Educ:* Tehran Univ, BS, 67; Columbia Univ, MS, 72, MPH & PhD(elec eng, comput sci), 76. *Prof Exp:* Teaching asst, Dept Elec Eng & Comput Sci, Columbia Univ, 71-76, assoc consult work, 76. *Concurrent Pos:* City Univ grants, 78-79, 80-81, 81-82. *Mem:* Inst Elec & Electronics Engrs; Sigma Xi. *Res:* Stochastic systems; simulation; microprocessors. *Mailing Add:* Dept Comput Sci City Univ NY-Queens Col Flushing NY 11367-1597

GHUMAN, GIAN SINGH, GEOENVIRONMENTAL SCIENCE. *Current Pos:* assoc prof, 67-71, PROF EARTH SCI, SAVANNAH STATE COL, 71- *Personal Data:* b Barchuhi, India, July 7, 29; m 48; c 3. *Educ:* Punjab Univ, India, BS, 52, MS, 55; Univ Calif, Davis, PhD(soil sci), 67. *Honors & Awards:* Presidential Achievement Award, 82. *Prof Exp:* Res asst fertilizer exp, Dept Agr, Punjab Univ, India, 55-57; asst prof soil chem, Shri Karan Narinder Col Agr, India, 57-62. *Concurrent Pos:* Dir, NASA Res Proj Kennedy Space Ctr, 74-77; dir, Marshland Res Proj, SE Atlantic Coast, Environ Protection Agency, 79-83; dir, heavy metal compos, Munic Wastewate Res Proj, 84-85; dir, Release rates of Toxic Metals from Coastal Soils Res Proj, 88-89. *Mem:* AAAS; Am Soc Agron; Soil Sci Soc Am; Int Soc Soil Sci; Clay Minerals Soc; Environ Geochem & Health Soc. *Res:* Availability of iron and manganese as affected by soil treatments; investigations on mineral manganocalcite; clay minerals and mineralization in surface and ground waters; water quality and marine sediments; heavy metals in estuaries. *Mailing Add:* Dept Math & Physics Savannah State Col St Col Br Savannah GA 31404-9710

GIACCHETTI, ATHOS, SPECTROSCOPY. *Current Pos:* RETIRED. *Personal Data:* b Florence, Italy, Jan 1, 21; US citizen; m 48, Alfa Borri; c Paula & Mauro. *Educ:* Univ Florence, Dr(physics), 47. *Prof Exp:* Asst prof physics, Nat Univ South, Arg, 48-53; head, Spectros Sect, Nat AEC, 53-58; assoc prof atomic spectros, La Plata Nat Univ, 58-60; Orgn Am States fel & vis prof, Purdue Univ, 60-61; assoc physicist, Argonne Nat Lab, 61-71; specialist, Dept Sci Affairs, Orgn Am States, 71-86. *Concurrent Pos:* Vis scientist, Aime Cotton Lab, Nat Ctr Sci Res, France, 69-70; hon prof, Univ La Plata, 80. *Mem:* Optical Soc Am. *Res:* Atomic spectroscopy; spectrochemistry; standard wave lengths; term analysis. *Mailing Add:* 617 Taney Ave Frederick MD 21702

GIACCO, ALEXANDER FORTUNATUS, SCIENCE ADMINISTRATION. *Current Pos:* MANAGING DIR, AXESS CORP, 91- *Personal Data:* b San Giovanni di Gerace, Italy; m, Edith Brown; c 5. *Educ:* Va Polytech Inst, BS, 42. *Hon Degrees:* DBus, William Carey Col, 80; LLD, Widener Univ, 84, Cath Univ Am, 90; DBus Admin, Goldey Beacom Col, 84; LHD, Mt St Marys Col, 88. *Honors & Awards:* Order of Merit, Ital Repub, 85. *Prof Exp:* Mgt, prod, mkt & planning positions, Hercules Inc, 42-71, mem bd dirs, 71-73, gen mgr, Hercules Europe, 73-74, vpres, 74-76, exec vpres, 76-77, chief exec officer & 6th pres, 77-80, chmn bd, 80-87; chmn, Himont Inc, 83-91, chief exec officer, 87-90. *Concurrent Pos:* Chmn, econ develop comt, Del Round Table; dep chmn, Propulsion Comt Guided Missiles & Jet-Assisted Take-Off, Am Defense Preparedness Asn; mem, Adv Coun Japan-US Econ Rel, adv bd, New Ctr Hist Chem; mem bd dirs, Montedison, SpA, 83-90, Marvin & Palmer Assocs, 87-, Ferruzzi Finanziaria, 88-91, China Trust Bank, 88- & Carlisle Plastics, 91-93. *Mem:* Nat Acad Eng; Am Asn Soverign Mil Order; Soc Chem Indust; Soc Plastics Indust; Soc Automotive Engrs. *Res:* One patent on the design of solid rocket propellant grains. *Mailing Add:* Axess Corp 100 Interchange Blvd Newark DE 19711. *Fax:* 302-452-6610

GIACCONI, RICCARDO, ASTROPHYSICS. *Current Pos:* DIR GEN, EUROP SOUTHERN OBSERV, 92- *Personal Data:* b Genoa, Italy, Oct 6, 31; nat US; m 57; c 3. *Educ:* Univ Milan, PhD(physics), 54. *Hon Degrees:* DSc, Univ Chicago, 83; Laurea ad Honoreum Astron, Univ Padua, 84. *Honors & Awards:* Helen B Warner Prize, Am Astron Soc, 66; Como Prize, Ital Phys Soc, 67; Rontgen Prize Astrophys, Physikalisch-Medizinische Gessellschaft, Ger, 71; Medal for Except Sci Achievement, NASA, 71 & 80, Distinguished Pub Ser Award, 72; Richtmyer Mem Lectr, Am Asn Physics Teachers, 75; Space Sci Award, Am Inst Aeronaut & Astronaut, 76; Elliot Cresson Medal, Franklin Inst, 80; Catherine Wolfe Bruce Gold Medal, Astron Soc Pac, 81; Dannie Heineman Prize Astrophys, Am Astron Soc/Am Inst Physics, 81; Henry Norris Russell lectr, Am Astron Soc, 81; Gold Medal, Royal Astron Soc, 82; A Cressy Morrison Award, NY Acad Sci, 82; Wolf Prize in Physics, 87. *Prof Exp:* Asst prof physics, Univ Milan 54-56; Fulbright fel, Ind Univ, 56-58; res assoc, Princeton Univ, 58-59; exec vpres & mem bd dirs, Am Sci & Eng, Inc, Mass, 59-73; prof astron & assoc dir, High Energy Astrophys Div, Ctr Astrophys, Harvard Univ, 73-81; dir, Space Telescope Sci Inst, Baltimore, 81-92. *Concurrent Pos:* Vis comt, Asn Univ Res Astron, 71-75, Univ Padova & Univ Chicago; counr, Am Astron Soc, 79-82; pres, Comt 48, Int Astron Union, 82-86; prof physics & astron, Johns Hopkins Univ, 82-92; mem adv comt, Max-Planck Inst Physics & Astrophys; vis comt, Asn Univ Res Astron, 71-75; prof physics, Univ Milan, Italy, 91- *Mem:* Nat Acad Sci; Am Acad Arts & Sci; fel AAAS; Am Phys Soc; Int Astron Union; Comt Space Res; Am Astron Soc; fel Royal Astron Soc. *Res:* X-ray astronomy; fields and particles. *Mailing Add:* Karl-Schwarzchild-Str 2 85748 Garching Germany

GIACOBBE, F W, INDUSTRIAL GASES RELATED RESEARCH & DEVELOPMENT-FUNDAMENTALS, MATERIALS & PROPERTIES. *Current Pos:* SR SCIENTIST, CHICAGO RES CTR, AM AIR LIQUIDE INC, 82- *Personal Data:* b Meriden, Conn, June 4, 43; m 68, Elizabeth; c James, Matthew & David. *Educ:* Cent Conn State Col, BS, 65, MS, 68; Pa State Univ, Dr, 71. *Prof Exp:* Asst prof physics, Shippensburg State Col, 71-75, chmn, Phys Dept, 73-75; mgr gases res/res scientist, Gases Group Res Ctr, Chemetron Corp, 75-78; pres & dir res & develop, Hanover Res & Develop, Inc, 78-82. *Mem:* Am Phys Soc; Am Chem Soc; Mat Res Soc; Am Ceramic Soc; Am Soc Metals. *Res:* Development of new uses for common and rare gases in industrial applications; general thermodynamics; chemical thermodynamics; physical chemistry; physical adsorption; methods of gas separation and purification; thermal plasma arc physics; production and properties of high temperature ceramic superconductors. *Mailing Add:* Chicago Res Ctr Am Air Liquide Inc 5230 South East Ave Countryside IL 60525

GIACOBBE, THOMAS JOSEPH, ORGANIC CHEMISTRY, BIOORGANIC CHEMISTRY. *Current Pos:* group leader agr chem process develop, 78-81, group leader polyethylene pilot plant, 81-84, GROUP LEADER NEW PROD RES, MOBIL CHEM CO, 84- *Personal Data:* b Newark, NJ, June 25, 41; m 65; c 3. *Educ:* Bowdoin Col, BA, 63; Univ Vt, PhD(chem), 68. *Prof Exp:* NIH fel, Univ Wis-Madison, 68-69; spec assignments dept, Dow Chem Co USA, 69-71, res biol chemist, 71-72, herbicide proj mgr, 72-76, mgr agr chem process develop, 76-78. *Concurrent Pos:* Fel, Univ Wis, 68-69; instr, Univ Calif Exten, 76. *Mem:* Am Chem Soc. *Res:* Synthetic organic chemistry; structure-activity correlations; physical organic and process chemistry; lubrication chemistry; agricultural chemistry. *Mailing Add:* Nassau Ct Skillman NJ 08558-9611

GIACOBINI, EZIO, AGING & DEVELOPMENT OF NERVOUS SYSTEM. *Current Pos:* PROF PHARMACOL & CHMN DEPT, SCH MED, ILL UNIV, 82- *Educ:* Univ Turin, Italy, MD, 53; Karolinska Inst, Sweden, PhD(physiol), 59. *Mailing Add:* 4 Tour de Champel 52 Geneva 1206 Switzerland

GIACOLETTO, L(AWRENCE) J(OSEPH), ELECTRONICS. *Current Pos:* prof, 60-87, EMER PROF ELEC ENG, MICH STATE UNIV, 87- *Personal Data:* b Clinton, Ind, Nov 14, 16; m 41, Maxine Dicks; c Carol (Heiser). *Educ:* Rose-Hulman Inst Technol, BS, 38; Univ Iowa, MS, 39; Univ Mich, PhD(electronics), 52. *Prof Exp:* Univ Iowa, 38-39; asst elec mach, Univ Mich, 39-41; res engr, Labs Div, Radio Corp of Am, NJ, 46-56; res mgr, Electronics Dept, Sci Lab, Ford Motor Co, 56-60. *Concurrent Pos:* Pres, CoRes Inst, Okemos, Mich. *Mem:* Fel AAAS; fel Inst Elec & Electronics Engrs. *Res:* Theory, design and application of solid state devices; electronics; power electronics. *Mailing Add:* 4465 Wausau Rd Okemos MI 48864-2741. *Fax:* 517-349-0675

GIACOMELLI, FILIBERTO, EXPERIMENTAL PATHOLOGY. *Current Pos:* prof, 78-94, EMER PROF PATH, WAYNE STATE UNIV, 94- *Personal Data:* b Pisa, Italy, Nov 18, 28; m 58. *Educ:* Univ Pisa, MD, 54. *Prof Exp:* Asst med path, Univ Pisa, 56-57 & Univ Rome, 57-63; asst gen path, Univ Pisa, 63-66; asst prof path, Ind Univ, Indianapolis, 66-67; assoc, Columbia Univ, 67-68; from asst prof to assoc prof path, New York Med Col, 68-78. *Concurrent Pos:* NIH fel, Columbia Univ, 61-63. *Mem:* Am Asn Path; Am Heart Asn; Am Soc Cell Biol; Electron Micros Soc Am; AAAS; NY Acad Sci. *Res:* Light and electron microscopy; cytochemistry of normal and abnormal tissues; ultrastructure and biology of hypertensive and diabetic cardiovascular disease in experimental animals; metabolic and morphological correlates. *Mailing Add:* Dept Path 540 E Canfield Ave Detroit MI 48201

GIACOMETTI, LUIGI, BIOLOGY. *Current Pos:* prog dir corneal dis & cataract, Nat Eye Inst, 73-77, EXEC SECY VISUAL SCI BR, DIV RES GRANTS, NIH, 77- *Personal Data:* b Gubbio, Italy, Jan 21, 26; US citizen; m 55; c 2. *Educ:* Brown Univ, MSc, 62, PhD(biol), 64. *Prof Exp:* Asst scientist, Ore Regional Primate Res Ctr, 64-67, assoc scientist, 67-69, sci dir, Ore Zool Res Ctr, 69-73. *Concurrent Pos:* Asst prof, Johns Hopkins Univ, 74. *Mem:* AAAS; Am Asn Anat. *Res:* Anatomy. *Mailing Add:* 13519 Cleveland Dr Rockville MD 20850

GIAEVER, IVAR, BIOPHYSICS, PHYSICS. *Current Pos:* INST PROF SCI, RENSSELAER POLYTECH INST, 89- *Personal Data:* b Norway, Apr 5, 29; nat US; m 52, Inger Skramstad; c John, Anne, Guri & Trine. *Educ:* Norweg Inst Technol, Siv Ing, 52; Rensselaer Polytech Inst, PhD(theoret physics), 64. *Hon Degrees:* Numerous hon doctorate degrees. *Honors & Awards:* Nobel Prize in Physics, 73; Oliver E Buckley Prize, Am Phys Soc, 65; Vladimir K Zworkin Award, Nat Acad Eng, 74. *Prof Exp:* Maintenance engr, Norweg Army, 53; patent examr, Norweg Govt, 54; engr, Advan Eng Prog, Gen Elec Co, Can, 54-56; appl mathematician, Gen Elec Co, NY, 56-58, staff mem, Res & Develop Ctr, 58-88. *Concurrent Pos:* Guggenheim fel, Cambridge Univ, 69-70; adj prof, Univ Calif, San Diego, 75; vis prof, Salk Inst Biol Studies, La Jolla, 75; mem, Comt Scholarly Commun with People's Repub China, Nat Acad Sci, 76; prof-at-large, Univ Oslo, 88. *Mem:* Nat Acad Sci; Nat Acad Eng; Norweg Prof Engrs; fel Am Phys Soc; Norweg Acad Sci; Inst Elec & Electronics Engrs; Am Acad Arts & Sci; hon mem Norweg Acad Technol; hon mem Am Soc Mech Engrs; Swed Acad Eng; Korean Nat Acad Sci. *Res:* Application of the tools of physics to solve biological problems; determine how mammalian cells recognize each other, and to find out why cancer cells metastasize; understand the process of protein absorption on various materials; develop a microscopic process that can image DNA and protein without damaging the molecules; author of 75 papers; recipient of 34 patents; tissue culture. *Mailing Add:* Rensselaer Polytech Inst Troy NY 12180-3590. *Fax:* 518-276-2825; *E-Mail:* giaevi0rpi.edu

GIALAMAS, STEFANOS, KNOT THEORY, MATHEMATICS EDUCATION. *Current Pos:* DEAN GEN EDUC STUDIES, ILL INST ART, 96- *Personal Data:* b Greece, Sept 29, 55; US citizen; m 86, Sofia Hilentzaris; c Panayiotis & Zacharo. *Educ:* Aristotle Univ Greece, BS, 77; Cork Univ, MS, 79; State Univ NY, Buffalo, MA, 81; Univ Ill, PhD(math), 86. *Prof Exp:* Asst prof, Univ Wis-Oshkosh, 88-89; chair, Math Prog, Columbia Col, 89-92; exec dir, Aristotle Acad, 92-95. *Concurrent Pos:* Educ consult, Synthex Int, 93-; asst prof, Emporia State Univ, 96-98. *Mem:* Am Math Soc; Math Asn Am; Nat Coun Teachers Math; Nat Coun Sci Teachers. *Res:* Knot theory; mathematics and art; history and philosophy of math and science; mathematics education and integration of mathematics and science. *Mailing Add:* 10513 S Sun Valley Ct Palos Hills IL 60465. *Fax:* 312-280-3528; *E-Mail:* gialamas@t500.aii.edu

GIALLORENZI, THOMAS GAETANO, QUANTUM OPTICS. *Current Pos:* head, Optical Tech Br, 70-78, SUPT OPT SCI DIV, NAVAL RES LAB, 78- *Personal Data:* b New York, NY, Feb 28, 43; m 66; c Thomas & Kathy. *Educ:* Cornell Univ, BS, 65, MS, 66, PhD(appl physics), 69. *Honors & Awards:* Award Appl Sci, Sci Res Soc Am, 73; Charles Bassett Award, Instrument Soc Am, 84; Presidential Meritorious & Distinguished Sr Exec Award, 84 & 90; Conrad Award, 85; Harry Diamond Award, Inst Elect & Electronis Engrs, 86, Tyndall Award, 90; US Naval Meritorious Civilian Serv Award, 78; Distinguished Civilian Serv Award, Defense Dept, 87; Michaelson Award, USN League, 95. *Prof Exp:* Res physicist, Gen Tel & Electronics Labs, 69-70. *Concurrent Pos:* Consult to var govt agencies; ed-in-chief, Inst Elec & Electronics Engrs Lightwave Technol J; assoc ed, Proceedings Inst Elec & Electronics Engrs, 89- & Appl Optics, 91-94. *Mem:* Nat Acad Eng; Am Phys Soc; fel Inst Elec & Electronics Engrs; fel Optical Soc Am. *Res:* Fiber and integrated optics; electro optics, optical systems; laser physics. *Mailing Add:* Off Naval Res Lab Code 5600 4555 Overlook Ave SW Washington DC 20375-5000. *Fax:* 202-767-9300

GIAM, CHOO-SENG, PHYSICAL ORGANIC CHEMISTRY, ANALYTICAL CHEMISTRY. *Current Pos:* PROF, TEX A&M UNIV, GALVESTON, 88- *Personal Data:* b Singapore, Apr 2, 31; m 56; c 3. *Educ:* Univ Malaya, BSc, 54, Hons, 55; Univ Sask, MSc, 61, PhD(chem), 63. *Prof Exp:* Govt analyst, Chem Dept, Govt Singapore, 55-58; lectr chem, Univ Malaya, 58-59; res chemist, Imp Oil, Can, 63-64; res assoc chem, Univ Calif, 64-66; prof chem & oceanog, Tex A&M Univ, 66-81; prof chem & geol sci, Univ Tex El Paso, 81-83, dean, Col Sci, 81-83. *Concurrent Pos:* Analyst, Munic Coun, Malaya, 58-59; fels, Nat Res Coun Can, 63-64 & Pa State Univ, 64-65. *Mem:* Am Chem Soc. *Res:* Chemistry of heterocycles, effects of structures of organic compounds on their reactivities; environmental chemistry; nucleophilic reactions and mechanisms of these reactions. *Mailing Add:* Coastal Zone Lab PO Box 1675 Galveston TX 77553-1675

GIAMATI, CHARLES C, JR, COMPUTER SOFTWARE. *Current Pos:* CONSULT COMPUT SYSTS, 92- *Personal Data:* b Akron, Ohio, Aug 26, 27; m 54, Mildred Rogos; c 2. *Educ:* Oberlin Col, AB, 50; Univ Mich, AM, 52; Case Inst Technol, PhD(physics), 62. *Prof Exp:* Physicist, Lewis Res Ctr, NASA, 58-85; sr systs engr, Lockheed Missiles & Space Co, 86-92. *Concurrent Pos:* Lectr, Fenn Col, 61-65, Oberlin Col, 65-66 & Cleveland State Univ, 67-70; Fulbright-Hayes lectr grant, Istanbul Tech Univ, 66-67; chmn, Ohio Sect, Am Phys Soc, 70-71. *Mem:* AAAS; Am Phys Soc. *Res:* Cosmic ray physics; large scintillation and Cerenkov detectors; scattering of nucleons from complex nuclei; nucleon scattering; computer control systems; computer image processing and control systems; computer software and network architecture. *Mailing Add:* 2760 Wagar Rd Rocky River OH 44116. *E-Mail:* eh240@cleveland.freenet.edu

GIAMBRONE, JOSEPH JAMES, MICROBIOLOGY, IMMUNOLOGY. *Current Pos:* PROF POULTRY PATH & VET PATHOBIOL, AUBURN UNIV, 77- *Personal Data:* b Norristown, Pa, June 24, 50; c Joy & Jake. *Educ:* Univ Del, BS, 72, MS, 74; Univ Ga, PhD(microbiol), 77. *Honors & Awards:* Res Award, Poultry Sci Asn. *Concurrent Pos:* Vis scientist, Commonwealth Sci & Indust Res Orgn, Animal Health Div, Parkville, Australia, 86, Animal Health Res Inst, Cairo, Egypt, 93- *Mem:* Poultry Sci Asn; World Vet Poultry Sci Asn; Am Asn Avian Pathologists; World Poultry Sci. *Res:* Determination of various immune mechanisms which render poultry resistant to specific disease; molecular biology of RNA viruses of poultry. *Mailing Add:* Dept Poultry Sci Auburn Univ Auburn AL 36849-3501. *Fax:* 334-844-2641

GIAMEI, ANTHONY FRANCIS, METALLURGY, MATERIALS SCIENCE. *Current Pos:* Res assoc alloy studies, Adv Mat Res & Develop Lab, 66-68, sr res assoc, 68-69, group leader, 69-71, group leader alloy res, Mat Eng & Res Lab, 71-77, sr staff scientist, Pratt & Whitney Aircraft Group, 77-81, PRIN SCIENTIST, UNITED TECHNOL RES CTR, 81- *Personal Data:* b Corning, NY, Oct 14, 40; m 62; c 2. *Educ:* Yale Univ, BE, 62; Northwestern Univ, PhD(mat sci), 67. *Honors & Awards:* George Mead Gold Medal, 81. *Mem:* Am Soc Metals; Am Inst Mining Metall & Petrol Engrs; Sigma Xi. *Res:* Phase transformation morphology and kinetics; quantitative phase analysis by x-ray diffraction; stacking faults in ordered lattices; temperature dependence of strength in intermetallics; influence of structural changes on strength; undirectional solidification; crystal growth; superalloy forming; rapid solidification. *Mailing Add:* PO Box 160 Higganum CT 06441

GIAMMARA, BERVERLY L TURNER SITES, ELECTRON MICROSCOPY, HISTOCHEMISTRY. *Current Pos:* CONSULT, 85- *Personal Data:* b Gove City, Kans, Feb 4, 38; m 56; c 3. *Educ:* Univ Louisville, BLS, 76, MS, 81. *Honors & Awards:* Patent on Silver Methenamine Stain. *Prof Exp:* Lab asst, Col Med, Univ Fla, 60-64; res asst, Sch Med, Univ Louisville, 64-65; electron microscopist, Am Standard Develop & Eng Lab, 65-71; dir, Electron Micros Lab, Grad Prog & Res, Univ Louisville, 78-73. *Concurrent Pos:* Res asst prof, Univ NC, 83-85. *Mem:* Electron Micros Soc Am (chmn); Int Asn Dent Res; Mat Res Soc; Sigma Xi. *Res:* Biological electron microscopy; ultrastructural and histochemical studies of normal and pathologic tissues; material-tissue interactions; multiple grid staining device and epoxy slide embedment. *Mailing Add:* 2205 Weber Ave Louisville KY 40205

GIAMMONA, CHARLES P, JR, OCEANOGRAPHY. *Current Pos:* DEP DIR, STRATEGIC PETROL RESERVE PROG, TEX A&M UNIV, 80-, ASSOC HEAD, ENVIRON ENG, CIVIL ENG DEPT, 80- *Personal Data:* b Chicago, Ill, Aug 22, 48; m 70; c 3. *Educ:* St Mary's Col, BA, 70; Tex A&M Univ, PhD(oceanog), 78. *Prof Exp:* Lectr, Dept Biol, Univ Wis, 70-72; appl oceanographer & res assoc, Tex A&M Univ, 72-79; prog mgr, Oceanog Div, Univ Petrol & Minerals, Saudi Arabia, 79; asst dir, NJ Sea Grant Prog, 79-80. *Concurrent Pos:* Expert witness pollution study, Mississippi River, 72; aquanaut, Hydrolab Underwater Habitat, 73; consult, Hess Oil Co, LGL Environ Consults, 74-78, Cultural Resource Serv, US Army Corps Engrs, 78-; res award, Southern Regional Educ Biol, 77. *Mem:* Sigma Xi; Soc Limnol & Oceanog; Am Soc Civil Engrs. *Res:* Scientific diving and underwater photo interpretation; strategic petroleum reserve sites monitoring studies. *Mailing Add:* Brady Tower 202 E Houston St Suite 500 San Antonio TX 78205

GIAMMONA, SAMUEL T, PEDIATRICS. *Current Pos:* prof, 69-71, ADJ PROF PEDIAT, UNIV CALIF, SAN DIEGO, 71-; CHMN DEPT, DIS CHEST SECT, CHILDREN'S HOSP, 71- *Personal Data:* b Grand Rapids, Mich, Dec 17, 30. *Educ:* Mich State Univ, BS, 51; Yale Univ, MD, 54. *Prof Exp:* Jr instr pediat, Univ Mich, 58-59; asst prof, Med Ctr, Ind Univ, 62-65; assoc prof, Sch Med, Univ Miami, 65-69, sci dir ment retardation prog, 67-69. *Mem:* Am Acad Pediat; Am Fedn Clin Res. *Res:* Pulmonary physiology in infants and other children. *Mailing Add:* Dept Pediat Childrens Hosp SF 3700 California St San Francisco CA 94418-1618

GIAMPAPA, MARK STEVEN, RADIATIVE TRANSFER, DATA ANALYSIS & SPECTRAL DIAGNOSTICS. *Current Pos:* STAFF SCIENTIST, NAT OPTICAL ASTRON OBSERV, 82- *Personal Data:* b Cincinnati, Ohio, Oct 4, 54; m 90, Elizabeth M McNally. *Educ:* Univ Southern Calif, BS, 76; Univ Ariz, PhD(astron), 80. *Honors & Awards:* George Van Biesbroeck Award, 85. *Prof Exp:* Teaching asst astron, Univ Southern Calif, 74-76; teaching asst astron, Steward Observ, Univ Ariz, 76-80, res assoc, 80; postdoctoral fel, Harvard-Smithsonian Ctr Astrophys, 80-82. *Concurrent Pos:* Prin investr, Int Untraviolet Explor Prog, 80-; ed, Second Cambridge Workshop Sun & Cool Stars, 81-82 & Astron Quart, 82-; mem or chair sci organizing comt, Cambridge Workshops Sun & Cool Stars, 85, 91, 93, 95 & 97; vis fel, Smithsonian Astrophys Observ, 82-83; vis scientist, Sch Physics, Univ Sydney, Australia, 87; mem, proposal peer review panel, NASA Sci Progs, 87-90, subcomt space physics, US NASA, 88; Instml Univ Ariz, 96. *Mem:* Am Astron Soc; Int Astron Union. *Res:* Solar-stellar physics; analogs of solar magnetic phenomena such as spots and flares as they occur on other stars; the sun as a star; measurement of stellar magnetic fields, detection of surface features; the delineation of the properties of stellar dynamos; pre-main sequence stars and star formation; high resolution spectroscopy; asteroseismology. *Mailing Add:* Nat Solar Observ 950 N Cherry Ave PO Box 26732 Tucson AZ 85726-6732. *Fax:* 520-318-8278; *E-Mail:* giampapa@noao.edu

GIAMPIETRO, PHILIP FRANCIS, CLINICAL GENETICS. *Current Pos:* fel, 89-92, ASST ATTEND PEDIAT, NY HOSP, 92-; ASST PROF PEDIAT, CORNELL UNIV MED COL, 92- *Personal Data:* b Queens, NY, Oct 29, 56; m 86, Adeline M Kaam; c Jennifer & Grace. *Educ:* State Univ NY, Stony Brook, BS, 78, MD, 86; City Univ New York, PhD(biomed sci), 83. *Prof Exp:* Intern, Univ Hosp, Stony Brook, 86-87; resident, Long Island Jewish Hosp, 87-89. *Concurrent Pos:* Adj fac, Rockefeller Univ, 92-; consult, Cent Suffolk Hosp, 92- *Mem:* Am Col Med Genetics; fel Am Acad Pediat; Am Soc Human Genetics. *Res:* Clinical genetics and syndrome deliniation; Fanconi anemia and Marfan syndrome. *Mailing Add:* Cornell Univ Med Col Div Genetics HT-150 525 E 68th St New York NY 10021. *Fax:* 212-746-8893

GIANARIS, NICHOLAS JAMES, NONDESTRUCTIVE EVALUATION, STATISTICAL METHODS. *Current Pos:* SR TECH SPECIALIST, BOEING CO, 92- *Personal Data:* b Pittsburgh, Pa, Mar 12, 63. *Educ:* Carnegie Mellon Univ, BS, 85; Johns Hopkins Univ, MS, 92, PhD(mat sci & eng), 96. *Prof Exp:* Proj engr, Echoram Technol, 85-88; vpres technol, Carbon Steel Inspection, 88-92. *Concurrent Pos:* Engr, Northrop Corp, 88-89; adj prof, Del Co Community Col, 92; adj prof mat sci & eng, Widener Univ, 92-, eng adv, 96- *Mem:* Am Soc Mat; Mat Res Soc; Minerals, Metals & Mats Soc; Am Soc Nondestructive Testing; Am Helicopter Soc. *Res:* Statistical methods in materials engineering applications; testing, design and manufacture of aerospace and other advanced material structures, components and devices. *Mailing Add:* 3421 W Chester Pike Unit C-12 Newtown Square PA 19073. *Fax:* 610-591-6118; *E-Mail:* nicholas.j.gianaris@ibm.net

GIANELLY, ANTHONY ALFRED, ORTHODONTICS. *Current Pos:* assoc prof, 67-69, PROF ORTHODONT & CHMN DEPT, GRAD SCH DENT, BOSTON UNIV, 69-, RES PROF BIOCHEM & HEAD ORTHODONT SECT, UNIV HOSP, 76- *Personal Data:* b Boston, Mass, Aug 19, 36; m 60; c 2. *Educ:* Harvard Univ, AB, 57, DMD, 61, cert orthodont, 63; Boston Univ, PhD(biochem), 67, MD, 74. *Prof Exp:* Res assoc orthodont, Sch Dent Med, Harvard Univ, 63-64; Nat Inst Dent Res fel, Boston Univ, 64-67. *Concurrent Pos:* Consult, Mass Medicaid Prog, 72- *Mem:* Am Asn Orthod. *Res:* Growth, development and modification of craniofacial region. *Mailing Add:* 92 Windsor Rd Waban MA 02168

GIANETTO, ROBERT, BIOCHEMISTRY. *Current Pos:* RETIRED. *Personal Data:* b Montreal, Que, Aug 7, 27; m 52; c 4. *Educ:* Univ Montreal, BSc, 49, MSc, 51, PhD(biochem), 53. *Prof Exp:* Nat Res Coun Can fel, Cath Univ Louvain, 52-53; from assoc prof to prof biochem, Univ Montreal, 53-88. *Mem:* AAAS; NY Acad Sci; Can Biochem Soc. *Res:* Enzymology; lysosomes. *Mailing Add:* 10872 LeBlanc Montreal North PQ H1H 5C6 Can

GIANG, BENJAMIN YUNWEN, MASS SPECTROMETRY. *Current Pos:* RES ASSOC, ZENECA INC, 91- *Personal Data:* b Hong Kong, May 7, 41; US citizen; m 65, Virginia Liang; c Vernon, Andrew & Leslie. *Educ:* Columbia Union Col, BA, 63; Univ Md, MS, 67; Univ Calif, Davis, PhD(agr chem), 72.

Prof Exp: Chemist, Hazelton Lab, 63-64; staff res assoc, Univ Calif, 66-70. *Concurrent Pos:* Lectr, Univ Calif Exten, 73. *Mem:* Am Chem Soc; Am Soc Mass Spectrometry. *Res:* Use the technique of mass spectrometry in the discovery efforts for new weed controlling agents; identification of unknown molecules. *Mailing Add:* Zeneca Inc 1200 S 47th St Richmond CA 94804-4610. *Fax:* 510-231-1252

GIANINO, PETER DOMINIC, OPTICAL PHYSICS, SOLID STATE PHYSICS. *Current Pos:* res physicist, Cambridge Res Labs, 59-76, RES PHYSICIST, ROME AIR DEVELOP CTR, USAF, 76- *Personal Data:* b East Boston, Mass, May 8, 32; m 54, Marion Celani; c 3. *Educ:* Boston Col, BS, 53; Northeastern Univ, MS, 59. *Honors & Awards:* Marcus O'Day Annual Award, USAF Cambridge Res Labs, 74. *Prof Exp:* Physicist, Sylvania Elec Prod Div, Gen Tel & Electronics Corp, 55-58 & Ewen-Knight Corp, 58-59. *Mem:* Optical Soc Am; Am Asn Physics Teachers; Soc Photo-Optical Instrumentation Engrs; Sigma Xi. *Res:* Antenna pattern synthesis of linear arrays; missile systems; three-level solid state masers; magnetic anisotropy and resonance at low temperatures; secondary electron emission; laser windows; fiber optics; optical signal processing. *Mailing Add:* 570 Lebanon St Melrose MA 02176

GIANNELIS, EMMANUEL P, MATERIALS CHEMISTRY, SYNTHESIS OF NEW MATERIALS. *Current Pos:* asst prof, 87-93, ASST PROF, MAT SCI & ENG, CORNELL UNIV, 93- *Personal Data:* b Rhodes, Greece, Sept 5, 57; m 87, Harriet Koutsouris. *Educ:* Univ Athens, Greece, BS, 80; Mich State Univ, PhD(inorg chem), 85. *Prof Exp:* Res assoc chem, Mich State Univ, 85-86, res assoc chem eng, 86-87. *Concurrent Pos:* Consult, Therm, Inc, 88-90, Corning, Inc, 90- & S Adelman & Assoc, 91- *Mem:* Sigma Xi; AAAS; Am Chem Soc; Am Ceramic Soc; Mat Res Soc; Clay Minerals Soc. *Res:* Physics and chemistry of intercalation; molecular assemblies of electroactive polymers; polymer-ceramic nanocomposites; ceramic thin films; materials for optoelectronic packaging; sensing devices; materials for optical waveguides and photonics. *Mailing Add:* Bard Hall Ithaca NY 14853-1501. *Fax:* 607-255-9680; *E-Mail:* emmanuel@msc.cornell.edu

GIANNETTI, RONALD A, BEHAVIORAL MEDICINE, COMPUTER SOFTWARE DEVELOPMENT. *Current Pos:* Chair fac, 88-91, DEAN PSYCHOL, FIELDING INST, SANTA BARBARA, 91- *Personal Data:* b Chicago, Ill, May 21, 46; m 75, Carolyn Openshaw; c Anthony. *Educ:* Univ Calif, Berkeley, AB, 67, PhD(psychol), 73. *Prof Exp:* Treat team leader, Vet Admin Hosp, Salt Lake City, 73-74, patient evaluator, 74-75, eval coordr, 76-78; from asst prof to assoc prof, Eastern VA Med Sch, 78-85, prof, dept psychiat, 85-88. *Concurrent Pos:* Instr, Col Med Univ Utah, 74-77, res asst prof, 77-78; dir, internship training, Eastern Va Med Sch, 78-81; chair, Va Consortium Prof Psychol, 79-88; consult, Vet Admin Med Ctr, Hampton, Va, 82-88. *Mem:* Fel Am Psychol Asn; fel Soc Personality Assessment; Soc Comput in Psychol; fel Am Psychol Soc. *Res:* Applications of computer technology to problems of mental health care delivery, particularly computer based patient evaluation. *Mailing Add:* Fielding Inst 2112 Santa Barbara St Santa Barbara CA 93105. *Fax:* 805-687-4590; *E-Mail:* rongian@fielding.edu

GIANNINI, A JAMES, CLINICAL TOXICOLOGY, BIOPSYCHIATRY. *Current Pos:* assoc prof, 78-84, PROF & VCHMN PSYCHIAT, NORTHEAST OHIO MED COL, 84-; PROF PSYCHIAT, OHIO STATE UNIV, 84- *Personal Data:* b Youngstown, Ohio, June 11, 47; m 75; c 2. *Educ:* Youngstown State Univ, BS, 70; Univ Pittsburgh, MD, 74. *Honors & Awards:* Bronze Award, Brit Med Asn, 82. *Prof Exp:* Chief res consult, Pa Justice Comn, 74-75; fel psychiat, Yale Univ, 75-78. *Concurrent Pos:* Sr consult, Fair Oaks Hosp, 70-, Regent Hosp, 79-, Smith Kline-Bechman Laboratories, 82; co-dir, Wed Clin Yale New Haven Hosp, 76-78; clin assoc prof psychiat, Ohio State Univ, 82-84; chmn, Natl Adv Comm on Rape, NIH, 83-84; Mahoning Co Ment Health Bd, 83-87; psychiat & toxicol Western Res Care Syst, 84-; mem, Adv Comn NIDA, 84-; consult, sci adv bd, Neurodata Inc, Los Angeles, 88-; forensic psychiatrist, Mahoning Co Prosecutor's Off, Youngstown, OH, 89-; med dir, Chem Abuse Ctrs Inc, 89-; examnr, LaTrohs Univ, Bundvora, Australia, 89-91; Am partic, Drug Abuse Prog, US Info Agency, Cyprus, Italy & Yugoslavia, 90- *Mem:* Soc Neurosci; Sigma Xi; fel Am Col Clin Pharmacol; Am Acad Clin Psychiat; Acad Psychosom Med; fel, Am Psychiat Asn. *Res:* Physiology of psychopathological processes; cocaine addiction; psychosis; premenstrual syndrome; anorexia nervosa. *Mailing Add:* 721 Boardman Poland Rd Apt 200 Youngstown OH 44512

GIANNINI, GABRIEL MARIA, PHYSICS. *Current Pos:* pres, G M Giannini & Co, Inc, 44-57, dir res lab & pres, Giannini Sci Corp, 57-65, PRES, GIANNINI INST, 65- *Personal Data:* b Rome, Italy, Oct 21, 05; nat US; m 31; c 3. *Educ:* Univ Rome, Dr(physics), 29. *Prof Exp:* Student engr, Radio Corp of Am, Victor Mfg Co, Camden, 30-31; res engr, Curtis Inst Music, Philadelphia, 31-34, John D Rockefeller, Jr & Riverside Church, NY, 33-35; res engr & co-exec, Transducer Corp, 36-39; cost control engr, Vultee Aircraft Corp, Calif, 39-41; staff asst coordr, Off Vpres In Chg Mfg, Lockheed Aircraft Corp, 41-43. *Concurrent Pos:* Instr, Eve Sch, Univ Calif, 41-43; pres & chief engr, Autoflight Corp, 44-47; mem, Nat Air Coun, 48- *Mem:* Acoust Soc Am; Am Phys Soc; Soc Automotive Engrs; assoc fel Am Inst Aeronaut & Astronaut; sr mem Inst Elec & Electronics Engrs; assoc fel Royal Aeronaut Soc UK; Am Soc Mech Engrs; Am Soc Naval Engrs; Marine Technol Soc; US Naval Inst. *Res:* Reaction power plants and automatic flight equipment; plasma technology; underwater electrical equipment. *Mailing Add:* 51555 Madison St Indio CA 92201-9740

GIANNINI, MARGARET JOAN, PEDIATRICS. *Current Pos:* dir rehab develop, 81-91, dep asst chief med dir prosthetics & rehab, 88-91, CONSULT, VET ADMIN, WASHINGTON, 91- *Personal Data:* b Camden, NJ, May 27, 21; m 48; c 4. *Educ:* Hahnemann Med Col, MD, 45; Am Bd Pediat, dipl, 50. *Prof Exp:* From assoc prof to prof pediat, NY Med Col, 48-79, dir, Univ Affil Ment Retardation Inst, 50-79; dir, Nat Inst Handicapped Res, Washington, DC, 79-81. *Concurrent Pos:* Consult, Bur Handicapped Children, NY Health Dept, 60-; mem, State Wide Planning Comt Ment Retardation & NY State Dept Ment Hyg, 64; mem bd dirs, Avard Learning Ctr; mem adv bd, Ment Retardation Sect, Headstart Proj, Massive Econ Neighborhood Develop; mem adv coun, Asn Help Retarded Children; chmn, Int Sem Ment Retardation; chmn, Ment Retardation Task Force State Wide Planning Voc Rehab Serv, NY State Dept Educ. *Mem:* Inst Med-Nat Acad Sci; fel Am Acad Pediat; Asn Univ Affil Facil. *Res:* Mental retardation. *Mailing Add:* 40 Rockledge Dr Pelham Manor NJ 10803

GIANNOTTI, RALPH ALFRED, ORGANIC CHEMISTRY. *Current Pos:* from asst prof to assoc prof, 70-84, PROF CHEM, STATE UNIV NY AGR & TECH COL FARMINGDALE, 84- *Personal Data:* b Long Island City, NY, May 12, 42; m 64; c 4. *Educ:* St John's Univ, BS, 63, MS, 65, PhD(org chem), 69. *Prof Exp:* Res asst org chem, St John's Univ, 64-69; res assoc, Mass Inst Technol, 69-70. *Concurrent Pos:* Adj prof chem, Nassau Community Col, 72- *Mem:* Am Chem Soc; Coblentz Soc; NY Acad Sci. *Res:* Synthesis and characterization of polypeptides with known repeating sequence of amino acids; solid phase peptide synthesis; proteins. *Mailing Add:* Dept Chem State Univ NY Col Tech Farmingdale 1250 Melville Rd Farmingdale NY 11735-1313

GIANNOVARIO, JOSEPH ANTHONY, ANALYTICAL CHEMISTRY, NON-METALLIC MATERIALS. *Current Pos:* Res chemist, Space Div, Gen Elec Co, 74-77, proj scientist life sci, Space Systs, 77-79, sr scientist life sci, 79-81, TEAM LEADER SYSTS ENG, SPACE LAB 4, MATSCO DIV, GEN ELEC CO, 81- *Personal Data:* b Brooklyn, NY, Mar 18, 48; m 70; c 2. *Educ:* Villanova Univ, BS, 70, MS, 74, PhD(anal chem), 75. *Mem:* Am Chem Soc. *Res:* Air pollution analysis by gas chromatography; free flow, continuous particle electrophoresis-space applications; life sciences support-space shuttle environmental systems. *Mailing Add:* 10 Sycamore Ct Paoli PA 19301

GIANOLA, UMBERTO FERDINANDO, SYSTEMS DESIGN, SYSTEMS SCIENCE. *Current Pos:* CONSULT, 88- *Personal Data:* b Birmingham, Eng, Oct 29, 27; m 52; c 3. *Educ:* Univ Birmingham, Eng, BSc, 48, PhD, 51. *Prof Exp:* Consult, Royal Aircraft Estab, Eng, 51; res fel, Univ BC, 51-53; mem tech staff, Bell Labs, 53-63, head solid state digital device dept, 63-69 & ocean res dept, 69-71, dir Ocean Systs Studies Ctr, 71-84, Defense Systs Ctr, 84-85, Govt Systs Planning Ctr, 85-88. *Mem:* Sci Res Soc Am; fel Inst Elec & Electronics Engrs; Sigma Xi. *Res:* Electron optics; nuclear radiation detectors; solid state devices for memory, logic and communication systems; ocean acoustics and antisubmarine warfare surveillance systems. *Mailing Add:* 1212 Hunt Dr Vero Beach FL 32963-2411

GIANTS, THOMAS W, POLYMERIC OPTICAL MATERIALS, CONDUCTIVE POLYMERS. *Current Pos:* mem tech staff, 88-93, SR MEM TECH STAFF, MECH & MAT SCI CTR, AEROSPACE CORP, 93- *Personal Data:* b Lowell, Mass, Jan 3, 40. *Educ:* Lowell Technol Inst, BS, 61, MS, 66; Tufts Univ, PhD(org-anal chem), 71. *Prof Exp:* Instr chem, Boston State Col, 70-72; res assoc org polymer chem, Univ Ariz, 72-73; res chemist, Hughes Aircraft Co, 73-78, head mat chem sect, 78-86, sr staff engr, 86-88. *Mem:* Am Chem Soc; Sigma Xi; Mat Res Soc. *Res:* Structure-property relationships in polymer systems; polymeric thin films; synthesis and characterization of high temperature materials involving organic and organometallic polymers; nuclear magnetic resonance spectrometry; conformational analysis. *Mailing Add:* Aerospace Corp MS M2/250 PO Box 92957 Los Angeles CA 90009-2957. *Fax:* 310-336-5846; *E-Mail:* tom__giants@qmail2.aeri.org

GIANTURCO, MAURIZIO, ORGANIC CHEMISTRY. *Current Pos:* head tech res & develop sect, 63-68, dir corp res dept, 68-73, asst to vpres, 73-75, asst to sr vpres, 75-76, vpres sci, 76-81, SR VPRES SCI, COCA-COLA CO, 81- *Personal Data:* b Potenza, Italy, Dec 2, 28; m 54; c 2. *Educ:* Univ Rome, DrChem, 51. *Prof Exp:* Instr org chem, Univ Rome, 51-52; sr res assoc, Univ Ill, 53-56; res chemist, Tenco, Inc, 56-61, head fundamental res sect, 61-63. *Concurrent Pos:* Donegani res fel, 51-52; Fulbright fel, 52-53. *Mem:* Am Chem Soc; Inst Food Technol; NY Acad Sci; AAAS; Am Inst Chemists; Am Inst Food Technol. *Res:* Organic natural products; infrared and mass spectrometry. *Mailing Add:* Coca Cola Co PO Drawer 1734 Atlanta GA 30301

GIAQUINTA, ROBERT T, PLANT PHYSIOLOGY, BIOCHEMISTRY & BIOTECHNOLOGY. *Current Pos:* res scientist, E I Du Pont de Nemours & Co, Inc, 75-79, res supvr plant physiol, 79-81, res mgr, Cent Res & Develop Dept, 81-84, res mgr, 85-87, MGR BIOTECH BUS DEVELOP, AGR PROD DEPT, E I DU PONT DE NEMOURS & CO, INC, 87- *Personal Data:* b Lawrence, Mass, Feb 22, 47; m 70; c 2. *Educ:* Merrimack Col, BA, 68; Univ Dayton, MS, 70, PhD(plant physiol), 72. *Honors & Awards:* Charles A Shull Award, Am Soc Plant Physiologists, 85. *Prof Exp:* Res assoc fel plant biochem, Purdue Univ, 72-74. *Concurrent Pos:* Mem exec comt, Am Soc Plant Physiol, 83-86; mem ed bd, J Plant Physiol, 83-; chmn, Plant Growth Regulator Soc Am, 85-86. *Mem:* Am Soc Plant Physiologists; Plant Growth Regulation Soc Am. *Res:* Mechanism and control of photosynthate translocation in crop plants; loading and unloading of assimilates in the phloem and the cellular events governing assimilate partitioning within the plant. *Mailing Add:* 13 High Meadow Lane Newark DE 19711

GIARDINI, ARMANDO ALFONZO, mineralogy; deceased, see previous edition for last biography

GIAROLA, ATTILIO JOSE, MICROWAVE, ANTENNAS & OPTOELECTRONICS. *Current Pos:* dean grad sch, State Univ Campinas, 75-86, prof, 75-95, acad vpres, 80-82, EMER PROF ELEC ENG, STATE UNIV CAMPINAS, 95- *Personal Data:* b Jundiai, Brazil, Oct 26, 30; m 55, Nilva J Niero; c Adriana & Ronald. *Educ:* Univ Sao Paulo, BS, 54; Univ Wash, MS, 59, PhD(elec eng), 63. *Prof Exp:* Instr elec eng, Aeronaut Inst Technol, Brazil, 55-57, assoc prof, 63-65; instr, Seattle Univ, 57-60 & Univ Wash, 60-62; res engr, Boeing Co, 62-63, res scientist, 65-68; assoc prof elec eng, Tex A&M Univ, 68-74. *Concurrent Pos:* Chmn, Nat Electronics Conf, Brazil, 64, Intern Symp Microwave Tech Indust Develop, Brazil, 85; vis prof, Univ Sao Paulo, 65; consult, Capes, Brazil, 79-, FAPESP, 85-, & CNPQ, 87-; Unicamp prof, 87-93, emer prof, 93-; assoc ed, J Brazilian Telecommun Soc, 87- *Mem:* Sr mem Inst Elec & Electronics Engrs; Brazilian Microwave Soc (vpres, 85-87, pres, 87-89); Brazilian Telecommunication Soc. *Res:* Solid state and microwave devices; parametric devices; optical devices; traveling wave tubes; frequency selective limiters; elastic-, spin-, and magnetoelastic-delay lines; bioeffects of electromagnetic radiation; electromagnetic wave propagation; antennas; planar structures such as strip, microstrip and fin lines; patch antennas; dispersion in optical fibers; dielectric waveguides, dielectric grating waveguides, optoelectronic devices. *Mailing Add:* Faculdade de Eng Eletrica e de Computacao-DMO Unicamp CP 6101 Campinas SP 13083-970 Brazil

GIAROLI, JOHN NELLO, ORAL SURGERY. *Current Pos:* from asst prof to assoc prof, 60-76, PROF ORAL & MAXILLOFACIAL SURG, COL DENT, UNIV TENN, MEMPHIS, 76- *Personal Data:* b Memphis, Tenn, Feb 14, 28; wid; c Cindy, John, Eddie, Linda, Nancy & Mark. *Educ:* Memphis State Univ, BS, 50; Univ Tenn, DDS, 53. *Prof Exp:* Instr, Loyola Univ, New Orleans, 55-56; intern, Charity Hosp, New Orleans, La, 56-57; resident, Confederate Mem Hosp, Shreveport, 57-59. *Concurrent Pos:* Chief, Dent Serv, St Francis Hosp; consult, LeBonheur Children's Hosp, Baptist Mem Hosp Cent, Baptist Mem Hosp E, St Joseph Hosp, Methodist Hosp N & Methodist Hosp Cent. *Mem:* Am Dent Asn; Am Soc Dent Children; Am Acad Oral Med; Am Soc Advan Gen Anesthesia Dent; Int Dent Fedn; Am Soc Oral & Maxillofacial Surg; Am Dent Soc Anesthesiol; Int Fedn Dent Anesthesiol; Am Asn Univ Prof; Am Col Oral & Maxillofacial Surgeons. *Mailing Add:* Dept Oral Surg Col Dent Univ Tenn Memphis TN 38101

GIARRUSSO, FREDERICK FRANK, CHEMISTRY. *Current Pos:* HEAD INT BUS, MALLINCKRODT CHEM, 93- *Personal Data:* b Little Falls, NY, May 23, 36; m 62. *Educ:* Ariz State Univ, BS, 58; Univ Mich, PhD(chem), 66. *Prof Exp:* Jr res chemist, Merck & Co, Inc, 58-61; fel natural prod, Calif Inst Technol, 65-66; res chemist, Gen Elec Res & Develop Ctr, NY, 66-68; sr res scientist, Squibb Inst Med Res, 68-71, sect head, Chem & Biol Res Admin, 71-74, head, Preclinical Res Admin, 74-76; mgr, Sci Admin Res & Develop, 76-80, dir, comput lab systs, res & develop, Revlon Health Care Group, 80-; mem staff, Tripos Assoc, Mo; mgr bus develop, Res & Develop Systs, Digital Equip Corp, 88-93. *Mem:* AAAS; Am Chem Soc; Chem Soc; Drug Info Asn (vpres, 80-81). *Res:* Synthetic organic and natural product chemistry; steroids; the application of computers to biological and chemical research. *Mailing Add:* 930 Tahoe Blvd Suite 802-150 Incline Village NV 89451

GIBALA, RONALD, METALLURGY. *Current Pos:* PROF & CHMN DEPT MAT SCI & ENG, UNIV MICH, ANN ARBOR, 84- *Personal Data:* b New Castle, Pa, Oct 3, 38; c 4. *Educ:* Carnegie Inst Technol, BS, 60; Univ Ill, MS, 62, PhD(metall eng), 64. *Honors & Awards:* Alfred Noble Prize, Am Soc Civil Engrs, 69. *Prof Exp:* From asst prof to prof metall, Case Western Res Univ, 64-84, prof macromolecular sci, 77-84, co-dir, Mat Res Lab, 81-84; prog dir metall, NSF, 82-83. *Concurrent Pos:* NSF res grant, 66-71 & 76-; Dept Energy res contract, 67-89; USAF Off Sci Res grant, 71-75, 90-; vis prof, Centre d'Etudes Nucleaires de Grenoble, 73-74; res consult, Gen Motors Corp Res Labs, 77-82. *Mem:* Fel Am Soc Metals; Am Inst Mining Metall & Petrol Engrs; Sigma Xi; AAAS; Mat Res Soc; Am Ceramics Soc. *Res:* Physical metallurgy; defects in solids; internal friction; mechanical properties of solids. *Mailing Add:* Mat Sci Univ Mich 2300 Hayward Ann Arbor MI 48109-2136

GIBALDI, MILO, PHARMACOLOGY. *Current Pos:* prof & dean Sch Pharm, 78-95, assoc vpres health sci, 82-95, EMER PROF & DEAN PHARMACEUT, UNIV WASH, 95- *Personal Data:* b New York, NY, Dec 17, 38; m 60; c 1. *Educ:* Columbia Univ, BS, 60, PhD(pharmaceut), 63. *Hon Degrees:* DSc, Col Pharmaceut Sci, Columbia Univ, 76. *Prof Exp:* Asst prof pharm, Columbia Univ, 63-66; from asst prof to assoc prof, State Univ NY, Buffalo, 66-69, prof pharmaceut, 69-78. *Concurrent Pos:* NIH res grant, 67-70; consult, Hoffman-La Roche, Ciba Geigy, Beohringen Ingelheim, Ricker/3M, Ortho, Searle, 66-; investr, NIGNIS/NIH Prog Proj Grant, 83-; mem, Panel on Generic Drugs, Food & Drug Admin, 86. *Mem:* Inst Med-Nat Acad Sci; fel AAAS; Am Pharmaceut Asn; fel Acad Pharmaceut Sci; Am Asn Cols Pharm; Am Chem Soc; Acad Soc Clin Pharmacol; NY Acad Sci; Am Soc Pharamacol & Exp Therapeut; Sigma Xi. *Res:* Drug absorption; physical-chemical and biological properties of bile salts; dissolution phenomena; pharmacokinetics; author of series of textbooks. *Mailing Add:* Univ Wash Pharmaceut-Box 357610 Seattle WA 98195-7610

GIBB, JAMES WOOLLEY, BIOCHEMICAL PHARMACOLOGY. *Current Pos:* from asst prof to assoc prof, 67-75, PROF PHARMACOL, UNIV UTAH, 75-, CHMN PHARMACOL & TOXICOL, 74- *Personal Data:* b Magrath, Alta, Apr 19, 33; m 56, LaVon Robinson; c 2. *Educ:* Univ Alta, BS, 58, MS, 61; Univ Mich, PhD(pharmacol), 65. *Prof Exp:* Res assoc pharmacol, Nat Heart Inst, 65-67. *Concurrent Pos:* Vis res prof, Pharmakologisches Inst, Univ Innsbruck, 73-74. *Mem:* AAAS; NY Acad Sci; Am Soc Pharmacol & Exp Therapeut; Soc Neurosci; Am Soc Clin Pharmacot Therapeut. *Res:* Biosynthesis of catecholamines and indoleamines; neurochemistry; drug abuse; neuropeptides. *Mailing Add:* Dept Pharmacol & Toxicol Univ Utah Salt Lake City UT 84112

GIBB, RICHARD A, GEOPHYSICS, GEODEY & GEOLOGY. *Current Pos:* res scientist, Energy Mines & Resources Can, 65-82, chief scientist gravity & geodynamics, Earth Physics Br, 83-86, chief aeromagnetics, gravity & geodynamics, geophys div, 86-95, CHIEF GRAVITY, GEODETIC SURV DIV, GEOMATICS CAN, 95- *Personal Data:* b Fraserburgh, Scotland, Feb 16, 36; m 60, Maureen Miller; c Petra, Paul & Sarah. *Educ:* Aberdeen Univ, BSc, 58; Univ Birmingham, MSc, 59, PhD(geol), 61; Carleton Univ, Ottawa, BA, 75. *Prof Exp:* Geophysicist, Bur Mineral Resources, Geol & Geophys, Australia, 62-65. *Concurrent Pos:* Secy subcomt gravity, Assoc Comt Geod & Geophys, Can, 67-72; prog mgr, geophysics activ, Can Nuclear Fuel Waste Mgt Prog, 83-87; ed, Can Geophys Bull; assoc ed, JGR-Solid Earth, 90-93. *Mem:* Can Geophys Union; Am Geophys Union. *Res:* Solid-earth geophysics, physical geodesy tectonophysics, potential field methods and interpretation; application of geophysical methods to research areas of Canadian Nuclear Fuel Waste Management Program. *Mailing Add:* Natural Resources Can Geomatics Can Geodetic Surv Div Ottawa ON K1A 0E9 Can. *Fax:* 613-992-1468; *E-Mail:* gibb@geod.nrean.gc.ca

GIBB, THOMAS ROBINSON PIRIE, ANALYTICAL CHEMISTRY, MARINE CHEMISTRY. *Current Pos:* assoc prof & dir sponsored res, 52-58, prof, 58-80, EMER PROF CHEM, TUFTS UNIV, 80- *Personal Data:* b Belmont, Mass, Feb 10, 16; m 39, 83, Reen D Meergans; c Roberta-Louise & Paul A. *Educ:* Bowdoin Col, BS, 36; Mass Inst Technol, PhD(org-metallic chem), 40. *Prof Exp:* Instr, Mass Inst Technol, 40-43, asst prof, 43-46; dir chem res, Metal Hydrides, Inc, 46-51. *Concurrent Pos:* Consult, Chem Warfare Serv Develop Lab, Mass Inst Technol, 44-46, Oak Ridge Nat Lab, 51-52 & Gen Elec Co, 58-60; vis prof, Univ Fla, 63; hon res assoc, Univ Col, Univ London, 64; guest investr, Woods Hole Oceanog Inst, 70. *Mem:* Fel AAAS; Am Chem Soc. *Res:* Instrumental analysis; inorganic hydrides; structural inorganic; trace-constituents of sea water; foam separation; exotic air pollutants; hydrides for neutron shielding and hydrogen storage. *Mailing Add:* 55 Main St Dover MA 02030

GIBBARD, BRUCE, EXPERIMENTAL HIGH ENERGY PHYSICS. *Current Pos:* assoc physicist, Brookhaven Nat Lab, 78-80, physicist head, Data Acquisition Group, Accelerator Dept, 80-81, physicist, 81-90, PHYSICIST & HEAD, HIGH ENERGY & NUCLEAR PHYSICS COMPUT GROUP, PHYSICS DEPT, BROOKHAVEN NAT LAB, 90- *Personal Data:* b Detroit, Mich, Oct 18, 42; m 66. *Educ:* Univ Mich, BS, 64, MS, 66, PhD(physics), 70. *Prof Exp:* Jr vis scientist physics, Europ Orgn for Nuclear Res, 70-72; sr res assoc & instr lab nuclear studies & physics dept, Cornell Univ, 72-78. *Mem:* Am Phys Soc. *Res:* Strong interactions involving neutrons in the initial and/or final states; electroproduced multiparticle final states; neutrino-induced reactions, high energy pp interactions; techniques and instrumentation for data acquisition and processing. *Mailing Add:* Physics Dept Bldg 510C Brookhaven Nat Lab PO Box 5000 Upton NY 11973. *E-Mail:* gibbard@bnl.gov

GIBBARD, H FRANK, PHYSICAL CHEMISTRY, ELECTROCHEMISTRY. *Current Pos:* DIR RES, POWER CONVERSION INC, ELMWOOD PARK, NJ, 86- *Personal Data:* b Norman, Okla, Dec 27, 40; m 57; c 4. *Educ:* Univ Okla, BS, 62; Mass Inst Technol, SM, 64, PhD(phys chem), 67. *Prof Exp:* Res assoc, Mass Inst Technol, 66-67; from asst prof to assoc prof chem, Southern Ill Univ, Carbondale, 67-76; sr staff scientist, Gould Labs, 76-78, prin scientist, 78-80, Gould phys chem fel, 80-86. *Mem:* Electrochem Soc; AAAS; Am Chem Soc. *Res:* Electrochemistry; thermal properties of battery systems; physical chemistry of solutions of electrolytes and nonelectrolytes; primary and secondary batteries; calorimetry. *Mailing Add:* H Power Corp 60 Montgomery St Belleville NJ 07109

GIBBENS, ROBERT PARKER, RANGE MANAGEMENT. *Current Pos:* RETIRED. *Personal Data:* b Ness City, Kans, Nov 15, 28. *Educ:* Ft Hays Kans State Col, BS, 50, MS, 52; Univ Wyo, PhD(range mgt), 72. *Prof Exp:* Asst specialist range mgt, Sch Forestry, Univ Calif, Berkeley, 55-67; specialist, Plant Sci Div, Univ Wyo, 67-72; fel animal sci, SDak State Univ, 72-74; range scientist, Agr Res Serv, USDA, 74-93. *Mem:* AAAS; Soc Range Mgt; Ecol Soc Am. *Res:* Structure and function of rangeland ecosystems and rangeland ecosystem modelling; grazing management strategies; rangeland revegetation; rangeland plant phenology. *Mailing Add:* 2701 Fairway Dr Las Cruces NM 88011

GIBBINS, BETTY JANE, CHEMISTRY, SCIENCE EDUCATION. *Current Pos:* from assoc prof to prof, 58-84, EMER PROF CHEM, LAKE ERIE COL, 84- *Personal Data:* b Canton, Ohio, May 7, 23. *Educ:* Mt Union Col, BA, 45; Ohio State Univ, MS, 47, PhD(chem), 53. *Prof Exp:* Asst, Res Lab, Goodyear Tire & Rubber Co, 45-46; instr chem, Col Wooster, 48-51; asst prof, Franklin & Marshall Col, 53-58. *Mem:* AAAS; Sigma Xi; Am Chem Soc. *Res:* Molecular additive compounds and phase diagrams. *Mailing Add:* 405 Bank St Apt 5 Painesville OH 44077

GIBBINS, SIDNEY GORE, INORGANIC CHEMISTRY. *Current Pos:* RETIRED. *Personal Data:* b Mt Vernon, NY, Feb 24, 26; m 53; c 3. *Educ:* Calif Inst Technol, BS, 49; Univ Wash, Seattle, PhD(chem), 55. *Prof Exp:* Res chemist, E I du Pont de Nemours & Co, NY, 55-57, Olin Mathieson Chem Corp, Calif, 57-59, Nat Eng Sci Co, 59-61 & Aerospace Corp, 61-64; asst prof chem, NMex Highlands Univ, 64-65; asst prof chem, Univ Victoria, BC, 65-69, assoc prof, 69-87. *Mem:* Am Chem Soc. *Res:* Boron, silicon and transition metal hydrides; hydrogen peroxide; hydrazine; instrumental analysis; mass and infrared spectrometry; nuclear magnetic resonance; gas chromatography; high vacuum techniques. *Mailing Add:* 701 Fieldston Rd Bellingham WA 98225-8707

GIBBON, NORMAN CHARLES, MECHANICAL ENGINEERING. *Current Pos:* RETIRED. *Personal Data:* b Buffalo, NY, June 16, 29; m 60; c 2. *Educ:* Iowa State Univ, BS, 57; State Univ NY, Buffalo, MBA, 72. *Prof Exp:* Engr, Union Carbide, 57-62, proj engr, 62-64, sect engr, 64-67, div engr, 67-70, supvr, 70-77, proj mgr, Linde Div, 77-91. *Res:* Thermal insulation; vacuum technology; heat transfer; cryogenic equipment development. *Mailing Add:* 4342 E River Rd Grand Island NY 14072

GIBBONS, ASHTON FRANK ELEAZER, REPRODUCTIVE PHYSIOLOGY, ENDOCRINOLOGY. *Current Pos:* CHMN & PROF, DEPT BIOL SCI, OAKWOOD COL, 82- *Personal Data:* b Mahaicony, Guyana, Apr 20, 35; US citizen; m 63; c 2. *Educ:* Atlantic Union Col, BA, 62; Boston Univ, MA, 67, PhD(reproductive physiol), 70. *Prof Exp:* Res asst endocrinol, Worcester Found Exp Biol, 63-65, 66-67; sr res asst, 68-70, res assoc, 70-72, dir summer res training prog, 73-78, staff scientist, 73-78. *Concurrent Pos:* Vis prof biol, Atlantic Union Col, 73-74; NIH res fel, 79, 80 & 85; extramural assoc, NIH, 89. *Mem:* NY Acad Sci; Soc Study Fertility; Soc Study Reproduction; Radiation Res Soc; Am Soc Zoologists; Am Physiol Soc; Sigma Xi; Int Soc Hypertension Blacks. *Res:* Early development; radiation biology of early mammal development; physiology of hypertension; cardiovascular physiology. *Mailing Add:* Dept Biol Oakwood Col Huntsville AL 35896-0001. *Fax:* 205-726-7409

GIBBONS, BARBARA HOLLINGWORTH, BIOCHEMISTRY, MOLECULAR BIOLOGY. *Current Pos:* Asst researcher, 67-75, assoc res cytol, 75-82, RESEARCHER, UNIV HAWAII, 82- *Personal Data:* b Newark, Del, Jan 17, 32; m 61, Ian; c 2. *Educ:* Mt Holyoke Col, AB, 53; Harvard Univ, PhD(biochem), 63. *Mem:* Am Soc Cell Biol. *Res:* Molecular genetics of dynein ATPases; molecular mechanism of motility in sperm flagella. *Mailing Add:* Pac Biomed Res Ctr Univ Hawaii Honolulu HI 96813-5593. *Fax:* 808-599-4817

GIBBONS, DAVID LOUIS, PHYSICAL CHEMISTRY, FUEL TECHNOLOGY. *Current Pos:* RES SCIENTIST, MARATHON OIL CO, 76- *Personal Data:* b Cleveland, Ohio, May 11, 46; m 70; c 2. *Educ:* Univ Chicago, BS, 69; Univ Ill, Urbana, PhD(chem), 74. *Prof Exp:* Asst prof chem, Colgate Univ, 74-76. *Mem:* Am Chem Soc; Soc Petrol Engrs; Sigma Xi; Soc Core Analysis. *Res:* Rock and fluid properties. *Mailing Add:* Marathon Oil Co 7400 S Broadway Littleton CO 80160-2609

GIBBONS, DONALD FRANK, BIOMEDICAL ENGINEERING. *Current Pos:* CORP SCIENTIST LIFE SCI LAB, 3M CTR, ST PAUL, MINN, 82- *Personal Data:* b Birmingham, Eng, July 23, 26; m 50, June E; c Kathryn & Peter. *Educ:* Univ Birmingham, BSc, 47, PhD, 50, DSc, 73. *Prof Exp:* Res fel, Univ Chicago, 50-52; res assoc, Royal Mil Col, Can, 52-54; mem tech staff, Bell Tel Labs, 54-62; prof metall, Case Western Res Univ, 62-67, dir, Ctr Study Mat, 62-74, prof biomed eng & exp path, 68-81. *Mem:* Soc Biomat; Am Soc Test & Mat; Biol Eng Soc UK; NY Acad Sci; Acad Surg Res; fel Int Asn Med & Biol Environ. *Res:* Biomaterials; histopathology; improvement of present and development of new materials suitable for biological implantation, including encapsulation of microelectronic circuits and electrode materials; examination of ancient works of art. *Mailing Add:* 6 Blue Goose Rd St Paul MN 55127. *Fax:* 612-786-1519; *E-Mail:* dfgibbons@mmm.com

GIBBONS, IAN READ, MOLECULAR BIOLOGY. *Current Pos:* assoc prof, 67-69, PROF BIOPHYS, PAC BIOMED RES CTR, UNIV HAWAII, 69- *Personal Data:* b Hastings, Eng, Oct 30, 31; m 61, Barbara Hollingworth; c Wendy & Peter. *Educ:* Cambridge Univ, BA, 54, PhD(biophys), 57. *Honors & Awards:* E B Wilson Medal, Am Soc Cell Biol, 94; Int Prize Biol, Japan, 95. *Prof Exp:* Res fel biophys, Univ Pa, 57-58; res fel biol, Harvard Univ, 58-62, lectr, 62-63, asst prof, 64-67. *Mem:* Am Soc Cell Biol; Royal Soc London; Am Soc Biol Chem; Biophys Soc. *Res:* Cell motility; molecular organization of subcellular organelles, especially cilia and flagella. *Mailing Add:* Pac Biomed Res Ctr Univ Hawaii Honolulu HI 96822. *Fax:* 808-599-4817; *E-Mail:* ian@hawaii.edu

GIBBONS, J WHITFIELD, POPULATION ECOLOGY, HERPETOLOGY. *Current Pos:* Res assoc, 68-73, SR ECOLOGIST, SAVANNAH RIVER ECOL LAB, 73-; PROF ECOL, UNIV GA, 85- *Personal Data:* b Montgomery, Ala, Oct 5, 39; m 63; c 4. *Educ:* Univ Ala, BS, 61, MS, 63; Mich State Univ, PhD(zool), 67. *Concurrent Pos:* Dir, NSF Undergrad Res Participation Proj, 69, 70 & 92-93; adj prof, Wake Forest Univ, 86, Mich State Univ, 88; res assoc, Smithsonian Inst, 86; NIH fel ecol, Savannah River Ecol Lab. *Mem:* Am Soc Ichthyologists & Herpetologists; Ecol Soc Am; Sigma Xi; Herpetologists' League (pres, 89-90). *Res:* Population dynamics and ecology of fish, amphibians and reptiles; reproductive ecology and evolution of reptiles; effects of thermal effluents on natural populations of animals; effects of artificial elevation of environmental temperatures on animal populations, particularly vertebrates; life history phenomena in reptile and amphibian populations. *Mailing Add:* Savannah River Ecol Lab Drawer E Aiken SC 29802

GIBBONS, JAMES F, ELECTRICAL ENGINEERING. *Current Pos:* from asst prof to prof, Stanford Univ, 57-83, dean, Sch Eng, 84, Frederick Emmons Terman dean, Sch Eng, 84-96, REID WEAVER DENNIS PROF ELEC ENG, STANFORD UNIV, 83-, SPEC COUN TO PRES FOR INDUST RELATIONS. *Personal Data:* b Leavenworth, Kans, Sept 19, 31; m 54; c 3. *Educ:* Northwestern Univ, BS, 53; Stanford Univ, MS, 54, PhD(elec eng), 56. *Honors & Awards:* Jack A Morton Award, Inst Elec & Electronics Engrs, 80; Award Solid State Sci & Technol, Electrochem Soc, 89. *Prof Exp:* Fulbright fel, Cambridge Univ, 56-57. *Concurrent Pos:* Mem tech staff, Bell Tel Labs, Inc, 56; consult, Shockley Transistor Corp, 57-63, Fairchild Camera & Instrument Co, 64-71, Avantek, Inc, 64-, Electronics Br, Atomic Energy Res Estab, Harwell, Eng, 70-71, Acad Educ Develop, 73-75, Technol Aids Basic Educ Develop, Alaska Natives Found, 73-75, Gen Elec Co, United Technols, Inc & Micropower Systs, Inc, 77-; NSF sr fel, 63-64; Fulbright lectr, 63-64; assoc ed, Transactions Electron Devices, Inst Elec & Electronics Engrs, 64-70; mem grad fel panel, NSF, 64-70, chmn eng fel panel, 68-70; mem bd dirs, Avantek, Inc, 67- & comt higher educ, HEW, 69-74; vis prof, Nuclear Physics Dept, Oxford Univ, 70-71 & Univ Tokyo, 71; mem, US Sci Team Exchanges on Ion Implantation & Beam Processing, Japan, 71, People's Repub China, 76, USSR, 77 & 79, Australia, 81; founder & chmn, Solar Energy Res Assocs, 75-; bd dirs, Lockheed Corp, Raychem Inc & Technol Strategies & Alliances; sci adv bd, KRI, Int. *Mem:* Nat Acad Sci; Nat Acad Eng; Royal Swed Acad Eng Sci; fel Inst Elec & Electronics Engrs; Sigma Xi; Norweg Acad Tech Sci; fel Am Acad Arts & Sci. *Res:* Transistor circuits; solid state devices; ion implantation in semiconductors; semiconductor device analysis; process physics and solar energy. *Mailing Add:* Terman Bldg Rm 214 Stanford Univ Stanford CA 94305

GIBBONS, JAMES JOSEPH, ANALYTICAL CHEMISTRY, PHYSICAL CHEMISTRY. *Current Pos:* MGR, ANALYTICAL SERV, DAYCO TECH CTR, 85-, ENVIRON COORDR, DAYCO PROD, INC, 87- *Personal Data:* b Springfield, Mo, Oct 31, 46. *Educ:* Drury Col, AB, 68; La State Univ, Baton Rouge, PhD(analytical & inorg chem), 74. *Hon Degrees:* DLitt, Xavier Univ, Calcutta, India, 76. *Prof Exp:* Res chemist, Hoffman-Taff Div, Syntex Pharmaceut, 69-70; teaching asst gen chem, La State Univ, 71-74; dir, Drury Res Inst, 74-84, lectr gen chem, Drury Col, 74-75, from asst prof to assoc prof chem, 76-84, coordr, Dept Chem, Math & Physics, 78-79. *Concurrent Pos:* Vis scientist lectr chem, Jadavpur Univ & distinguished scientist exchange prog, Kalyani Univ, India, 75-76, 80-81 & 82-83; vis assoc prof chem, Univ Okla, 83. *Mem:* AAAS; Am Chem Soc; fel Am Inst Chemists; Sigma Xi; NY Acad Sci. *Res:* Solution chemistry of electrolytes in mixed solvents; materials testing of rubber and plastic compounds; polymer synthesis and characterization of properties; hazardous waste treatment and disposal of polymers. *Mailing Add:* Mgr Analytical Serv Dayco Prod Inc 511 E Normal PO Box 3258 Springfield MO 65807

GIBBONS, JEAN DICKINSON, STATISTICAL ANALYSIS. *Current Pos:* RETIRED. *Personal Data:* b St Petersburg, Fla, Mar 14, 38; m 58, 74. *Educ:* Duke Univ, AB, 58, MA, 59; Va Polytech Inst, PhD(statist), 63. *Prof Exp:* Asst prof math, Mercer Univ, 58-60; asst prof math & statist, Univ Cincinnati, 61-63; from asst prof to assoc prof statist, Univ Pa, 63-70; prof statist, Univ Ala, 70-95. *Concurrent Pos:* Res prof; consult; Fulbright scholar. *Mem:* Fel Am Statist Asn; Int Statist Inst. *Res:* Performance of nonparametric tests based on ranks of observations; ranking and selection procedures. *Mailing Add:* 4400 N A1A No 301 Hutchinson Island FL 34949

GIBBONS, JOHN HOWARD, SCIENCE, TECHNOLOGY POLICY. *Current Pos:* ASST TO PRES SCI & TECHNOL & DIR, OFF SCI & TECHNOL POLICY, EXEC OFF PRES, 93- *Personal Data:* b Harrisonburg, Va, Jan 15, 29; m 55, Mary A Hobart; c Virginia N (Barber), Diana C (Albers) & Mary M. *Educ:* Randolph-Macon Col, BS, 49; Duke Univ, PhD(physics), 54. *Hon Degrees:* ScD, Randolph-Macon Col, Va, 77; DHL, Ill Inst Technol, 94; DSc, Mt Sinai Med Sch, 95, Univ Del, 96, Duke Univ, 97. *Honors & Awards:* Distinguished Serv Award, Fed Energy Admin, 74; Pub Serv Award, Fedn Am Scientists, 90; Szilard Award, Am Physics Soc, 91; Officer's Cross of the Order of Merit, Fed Repub Ger, 91; Philip Hauge Abelson Prize, AAAS, 92. *Prof Exp:* Res assoc nuclear physics, Duke Univ, 53-54; physicist, Oak Ridge Nat Lab, 54-75, group leader, Geophys Lab, 65-69, dir, Environ Prog, 69-73; dir, Off Energy Conserv, Fed Energy Admin, 73-74; prof physics & dir energy environ & resources, Univ Tenn, 74-79; dir, Off Technol Assessment, US Cong, 79-93. *Concurrent Pos:* Chmn, Conserv Panel, Off Technol Assessment, US Cong, 75, Control & Abatement Technol Panel, 76, Panel Nat Energy Plan Policy Anal, 77 & Panel Residential Energy Conserv Assessment, 77-79; mem, Comt Measurements Energy Consumption, Nat Acad, 76, chmn, Demand Conserv Panel, Comt Nuclear & Alternative Energy Systs, 76-79 & Panel Energy, Natural Resources & Environ, 77-78; vice co-chmn, Task Force Fuel Utilization & Conserv, Nat Coal Policy Proj, Ctr Strategic Studies, Georgetown Univ, 77-79; Sigma Xi nat lectr, 78-79; mem, Bd Sci & Technol Int Develop, Nat Res Coun, 79-87; mem, Energy & Resources Comt, Aspen Inst, 79-92; mem, Coun Foreign Rels, 90-92; mem, Carnegie Comn Sci, Technol & Govt Task Force on Long Term Goals & Priorities in Sci & Technol, 90-92. *Mem:* Nat Acad Eng; fel Am Phys Soc; Sigma Xi; fel AAAS. *Res:* Supply and efficiency; resource flows and environmental impacts including global climate change and technological options to resolve such problems; technology and economic growth; science and public policy; author of numerous publications. *Mailing Add:* PO Box 497 The Plains VA 22171. *E-Mail:* jgibbons@ostp.eop.gov

GIBBONS, JOSEPH H(ARRISON), CHEMICAL ENGINEERING. *Current Pos:* assoc prof, 63-74, chmn dept, 77-93, PROF CHEM ENG, UNIV SC, 74-, ASSOC DEAN ENG, 91- *Personal Data:* b Turbeville, SC, Sept 4, 34; m 56, Geneva Floyd; c Karen & Lisa. *Educ:* Univ SC, BS, 56; Univ Pittsburgh, MS, 58, PhD(heat transfer), 61. *Prof Exp:* From jr engr to sr engr, Westinghouse Elec Corp, 56-63. *Mem:* Am Inst Chem Engrs; Am Soc Eng Educ; Am Chem Soc; Nat Soc Prof Engrs. *Res:* Heat transfer and fluid dynamics. *Mailing Add:* Dept Chem Eng Univ SC Columbia SC 29208-0001. *Fax:* 803-777-0027

GIBBONS, LARRY V, INDUSTRIAL HYGIENE, HAZARDOUS WASTE ANALYSIS. *Current Pos:* PRES & LAB DIR, APPL RES & DEVELOP LAB, ARDL, INC, 71- *Personal Data:* b Harrisburg, Ill, Mar 18, 32; m 54; c 4. *Educ:* Wash Univ, AB, 54; Southern Ill Univ, MS, 58, PhD(physiol), 70. *Honors & Awards:* b Harrisburg, Ill, Mar 18, 32. *Prof Exp:* Res supvr, Biol Lab, UMC Industs, 58-63, res dir, Unidynamics, 70-71; sr physiologist, adv space craft design, McDonnell Douglas, 63-68; assoc dir res, Intersci Res Inst, 68-70. *Mem:* Sigma Xi; Am Chem Soc; Am Physiol Soc; Air Pollution Control Asn. *Mailing Add:* ARDL Inc PO Box 1566 Mt Vernon IL 62864-1566

GIBBONS, LOUIS CHARLES, PETROLEUM CHEMISTRY. *Current Pos:* RETIRED. *Personal Data:* b Lost Springs, Wyo, Aug 8, 14; m 40, Margaret Shook; c 1. *Educ:* Univ Ohio, Athens, BS, 36; Ohio State Univ, MS, 38, PhD(org chem), 40. *Prof Exp:* Chemist, Nat Adv Comt Aeronaut, Va, 41, head org synthesis sect, Ohio, 42-45, chief fuels br, 45-50, assoc chief fuels & combustion res div, 50-55; res chem supvr, Ohio Oil Co, 55-61, assoc res dir, Marathon Oil Co, Colo, 61-70, res adv, Ohio, 70-72, assoc res dir, 72-75, res assoc, Colo, 75-79. *Mem:* Am Chem Soc. *Res:* Synthesis and combustion of hydrocarbons; paraffinic hydrocarbons derived from tetrahydrofuryl alcohol; tertiary oil recovery; aircraft fuels; petroleum chemistry. *Mailing Add:* 133 Sherbrook Rd Mansfield OH 44907

GIBBONS, MATHEW GERALD, ATMOSPHERIC PHYSICS, NUCLEAR PHYSICS. *Current Pos:* RETIRED. *Personal Data:* b Oakland, Calif, Jan 21, 19. *Educ:* St Mary's Col, Calif, BS, 40; Univ Calif, Berkeley, MA, 45, PhD(physics), 53. *Prof Exp:* Instr chem, St Mary's Col, Calif, 40-42, instr physics, 42-45, asst prof & dept head, 45-56; res physicist, US Naval Radiol Defense Lab, San Francisco, 56-64, phys sci adminr, 64-69, sci ed optics & spectros, 60-76. *Res:* Nuclear magnetic resonance; atmospheric transmission of visible and near infrared radiation; nuclear reactor hazards; nuclear weapon effects. *Mailing Add:* 3535 Coolidge Ave Apt 45 Oakland CA 94602-3304

GIBBONS, MICHAEL FRANCIS, JR, BIOLOGICAL ANTHROPOLOGY, ANATOMY. *Current Pos:* instr, 72-74, asst prof, 74-79, ASSOC PROF ANTHROP, UNIV MASS, 79- *Personal Data:* b Laconia, NH, Mar 20, 41. *Educ:* Yale Univ, BA, 63, MPhil, 70, PhD(anthrop), 74. *Prof Exp:* Teaching fel anat, Yale Univ, 71-72. *Concurrent Pos:* Vis prof anthrop & biol, Univ Alaska, 77-78; vis scientist, Mass Audubon Soc, 78-79; Ford prof, Univ Mass, 86-87; res assoc, Peabody Mus, Andover, 92- *Mem:* Soc Vert Paleont; fel Am Anthrop Asn; Sigma Xi; Am Geol Inst; AAAS; Am Asn Anatomists. *Res:* Time and evolution; evolution of speech sound generation potential; regional anatomy of the head and neck in primates; human and primate paleontology; mammalian reproductive systems; forensic osteology. *Mailing Add:* Anthrop Harbor Campus Univ Mass Boston MA 02125-3393. *Fax:* 617-265-7173

GIBBONS, PATRICK C(HANDLER), QUASICRYSTALS, NANOCLUSTERS. *Current Pos:* from asst prof to assoc prof, 76-89, PROF PHYSICS, WASH UNIV, 89- *Personal Data:* b Washington, DC, Dec 18, 43; m 68, Jane E Forsell; c Elizabeth, Jonathan, Jane C & Katherine. *Educ:* Georgetown Univ, BS, 65; Harvard Univ, PhD(physics), 71. *Prof Exp:* From instr to asst prof physics, Princeton Univ, 71-76. *Mem:* Am Phys Soc. *Res:* Electron microscopy and electron energy loss studies of quasicrystals, nanoclusters and crystalline C60. *Mailing Add:* Campus Box 1105 St Louis MO 63130

GIBBONS, RONALD J, MICROBIOLOGY, BACTERIAL PHYSIOLOGY. *Current Pos:* Res assoc microbiol, Harvard Univ, 59-61, assoc bact, 61-64, asst prof, 64-65, assoc staff mem, 65-67, SR STAFF MEM, FORSYTH DENT CTR, HARVARD UNIV, 67-, CLIN PROF ORAL BIOL, 74-, DIR, FORSYTH DENT CTR, 91- *Personal Data:* b New York, NY, Dec 10, 32; m 59; c Sarah J, David P & John A. *Educ:* Wagner Col, BS, 54; Univ Md, MS, 56, PhD(microbiol), 58. *Hon Degrees:* Dr Odontol, Univ Goteborg, Sweden, 77; MD, Univ Utrecht, Holland, 80. *Honors & Awards:* Res Award, Int Asn Dent Res, 67; Dent Caries Award, Int Asn Dent Res, 90; Distinguished Scientist Award, Int Asn Dent Res, 92. *Concurrent Pos:* Res fel bact, Forsyth Dent Ctr, Harvard Univ, 58-59. *Mem:* Am Soc Microbiol; Int Asn Dent Res; Am Dent Asn. *Res:* Microbiological ecology; physiology and ecology of bacteria indigenous to mucous membranes of man; microbiology of mixed anaerobic infections, dental caries and periodontal disease; adhesion of bacteria to host tissues. *Mailing Add:* 10 Moores Isle Lane Kittery Point ME 03905

GIBBS, ALAN GREGORY, APPLIED MATHEMATICS. *Current Pos:* GRAD DEGREE ELEC ENG, UNIV WASH, 96- *Personal Data:* b Weaverville, Calif, Feb 23, 39; m 69. *Educ:* Stanford Univ, BS, 60, MS, 61, PhD(nuclear eng), 65. *Prof Exp:* Sr res scientist, Pac Northwest Labs, Battelle Mem Inst, 65-80; fac mem, Ore State Univ, 80-92. *Concurrent Pos:* Lectr, Ctr Grad Study Richland, Wash, 67-68; Battelle vis prof, Univ Wash, 68-69. *Mem:* Sigma Xi. *Res:* Mathematics of transport theory, neutron scattering theory, nuclear reactor theory; statistical mechanics; stochastic processes; atmospheric physics. *Mailing Add:* PO Box 70190 Seattle WA 98107

GIBBS, ANN, NUCLEAR CHEMISTRY. *Current Pos:* SR FEL NUCLEAR CHEM, SAVANNAH RIVER PROJ, 66- *Personal Data:* b Corpus Christi, Tex, May 19, 40. *Educ:* Univ Tex, BA, 62; Univ Ark, MS, 64, PhD(nuclear chem), 66. *Honors & Awards:* Award Merit, Am Soc Testing & Mat, 92. *Prof Exp:* Res assoc marine chem, Inst Marine Sci, Univ Tex, 60-63; res asst accelerators, Univ Ark, 62-66. *Mem:* Am Nuclear Soc; Am Chem Soc; Am Phys Soc; AAAS; Am Soc Testing & Mat. *Res:* Spectroscopy of transuranium elements and non-destructive analysis of plutonium; analytical chemistry of heavy water and transuranium elements. *Mailing Add:* Savannah River Site Westinghouse Savannah River Co Aiken SC 29808

GIBBS, CHARLES HOWARD, DENTAL RESEARCH, BIOMEDICAL ENGINEERING. *Current Pos:* asst prof, 74-80, ASSOC PROF BASIC DENT SCI, COL DENT, UNIV FLA, GAINESVILLE, 80- *Personal Data:* b Salt Lake City, Utah, Dec 24, 40; m 64; c 2. *Educ:* Univ Utah, BSME, 64; Case Western Res Univ, MS, 66, PhD(eng), 69. *Prof Exp:* Proj engr, Eng Design Ctr, Case Western Res Univ, 64-71, asst clin prof & sr res assoc, 71-74. *Concurrent Pos:* Prin investr, Nat Inst Dent Res res grants, 71- *Mem:* Am Inst Dent Res; Am Dent Asn; Sigma Xi. *Res:* Jaw movements, occlusion, forces on teeth and jaw; tooth mobility; biomedical engineering applied to dentistry. *Mailing Add:* 1918 SW 48th Ave Gainesville FL 32608

GIBBS, CLARENCE JOSEPH, JR, VIROLOGY. *Current Pos:* virologist arbovirus sect, Lab Trop Virol, Nat Inst Allergy & Infectious Dis, 59-63, DEP CHIEF LAB CNS STUDIES & CHIEF LAB SLOW, LATENT & TEMPERATE VIRUS INFECTIONS, NAT INST NEUROL & COMMUN DIS & STROKE, 63-, NEUROVIROL COORDR, INTRAMURAL RES, 74- *Personal Data:* b Washington, DC, Dec 10, 24. *Educ:* Cath Univ Am, AB, 50, MS, 52, PhD, 62; Univ Mass, MD. *Hon Degrees:* DSc, Cath Univ Am. *Honors & Awards:* Nat Inst Allergy & Infectious Dis. *Prof Exp:* Med bacteriologist clin path, Div Vet Med, Walter Reed Army Inst Res, 52-55; virologist, Dept Hazardous Opers, Div Commun Dis, 55-59. *Concurrent Pos:* Assoc prof epidemiol, Sch Pub Health & Hyg & assoc prof neurol, Sch Med, Johns Hopkins Univ; Nat Soc Med Sci fel comn; mem comt virol, Nat Comn Med Sci. *Mem:* Am Asn Immunol; World Fedn Neurol; AAAS; Am Soc Trop Med & Hyg; Am Asn Path; Sigma Xi. *Res:* Virus induced immunopathology; zoology, epidemiology and immunogenicity of arboviruses; aging process in man; behavioral changes in man and animals associated with infectious processes; oncogenic and tumor viruses; disease patterns in primitive populations; hemorrhagic fevers; ecology of infectious diseases; viral epidemiology. *Mailing Add:* 326 E St NE Washington DC 20002

GIBBS, DANIEL, neurobiology, insect physiology, for more information see previous edition

GIBBS, DAVID LEE, CLINICAL MICROBIOLOGY, PUBLIC HEALTH. *Current Pos:* asst dir new drug develop, 80-81, assoc dir clin microbiol, 81-86, SR ASSOC DIR CLIN RES, PFIZER PHARMACEUT, INC, 86- *Personal Data:* b San Francisco, Calif, July 5, 48. *Educ:* Cornell Univ Med Ctr, PhD(microbiol), 74; Am Bd Med Microbiol, dipl, 80. *Prof Exp:* Fel public health & med microbiol, Ctr Dis Control, 74-76; consult smallpox prog, WHO, India, 75; instr med, Med Col, Cornell Univ, 77-78, asst prof, 78-79; dir clin microbiol, Santa Clara Valley Med Ctr, 79-80. *Concurrent Pos:* Vis prof, Fed Univ Bahia, Brazil, 77-79; US dir, Commun Dis Ctr, Brazil, 77-79. *Mem:* Am Soc Microbiol. *Res:* Antibiotics; clinical microbiology and immunology methods. *Mailing Add:* 219 E 42nd St New York NY 10017

GIBBS, DOON LAURENCE, SOLID STATE PHYSICS. *Current Pos:* asst physicist, 83-84, ASSOC PHYSICIST, BROOKHAVEN NAT LAB, 84- *Personal Data:* b Urbana, Ill, Feb 5, 54. *Educ:* Univ Utah, BS, 77; Univ Ill, MS, 79; PhD(physics), 82. *Prof Exp:* Res asst, Univ Ill, 78-82. *Mem:* NY Acad Sci. *Res:* Magnetic x-ray scattering studies of the magnetic structure and phase transitions of solids using synchrotron radiation; surface x-ray scattering studies of solids. *Mailing Add:* Phys Dept 510B Brookhaven Nat Lab PO Box 5000 Upton NY 11973. *E-Mail:* doon@solids.phys.bnl.gov

GIBBS, FINLEY P, PHYSIOLOGY, ANATOMY. *Current Pos:* ASSOC PROF ANAT, SCH MED, UNIV MO COLUMBIA, 81- *Personal Data:* b Washington, DC, Aug 15, 40; m 63; c 3. *Educ:* Univ Calif, Berkeley, AB, 63; Univ Ore, PhD(physiol), 68. *Prof Exp:* Asst prof, Sch Med & Dent, Univ Rochester, 68-75, assoc prof anat & physiol, 75-81. *Mem:* Am Physiol Soc; Endocrine Soc; Am Asn Anatomists. *Res:* Control of ACTH secretion, the control of metatonin secretion and mechanisms involved with the biological clock (circadian rhythms); neuroendocrinology. *Mailing Add:* Dept Anat Sch Med Univ Mo Columbia MO 65212-0001

GIBBS, GERALD V, MINERALOGY. *Current Pos:* prof mineral, 67-81, UNIV DISTINGUISHED PROF, VA POLYTECH INST & STATE UNIV, 81- *Personal Data:* b Hanover, NH, June 28, 29; m 59; c 4. *Educ:* Univ NH, BA, 55; Univ Tenn, MS, 57; Pa State Univ, PhD(mineral), 62. *Honors & Awards:* Roebling Gold Medalist, 86. *Prof Exp:* Res assoc mineral, Univ Chicago, 61-62; res mineralogist, Linde Co, Union Carbide Corp, NY, 62-63; from asst prof to assoc prof mineral, Pa State Univ, 63-67. *Concurrent Pos:* NSF fel, 60-61 & 64-82, NASA grants, 71-73; vis distinguished prof, Ariz State Univ, 79, 83; vis res sci, Sch Higher Educ, 86. *Mem:* Mineral Soc Am (pres, 81); Am Crystallog Asn; fel Am Geophys Union. *Res:* Silicate mineralogy; bonding in minerals; mathematical crystallography. *Mailing Add:* Dept Geol Sci Va Polytech Inst & State Univ PO Box 0420 Blacksburg VA 24063-0001

GIBBS, GORDON EVERETT, PEDIATRICS. *Current Pos:* assoc prof pediat, 54-56, prof & chmn dept, 56-66, res prof pediat, 66-81, EMER PROF PEDIAT, COL MED, UNIV NEBR, 81- *Personal Data:* b Cordova, Ill, Sept 25, 11; m 41; c 4. *Educ:* Univ Redlands, AB, 32; Univ Calif, MA, 35, PhD(physiol), 39, MD, 42. *Honors & Awards:* Bronze Star Medal, US Army, 44; Meritorious Serv Medal, USAF, 71. *Prof Exp:* From intern to resident, Univ Hosp, Univ Calif, 42-47; assoc prof pediat res, Univ Md, 50-54. *Concurrent Pos:* Sr fel pediat, Nat Res Coun, Calif, 47-49 & Univ Ill, 49-50; prin investr, NIH grants. *Mem:* Am Pediat Soc; Soc Exp Biol & Med; Am Diabetes Asn; Am Acad Pediat; Sigma Xi. *Res:* Juvenile diabetes; experimental diabetes in monkeys; effect of diet, insulin and hypophysectomy on retinal and renal complications; cystic fibrosis of the pancreas; clinical research; numerous published articles. *Mailing Add:* 88120 Ave 73 Thermal CA 92274

GIBBS, HAROLD CUTHBERT, PARASITOLOGY. *Current Pos:* PROF ANIMAL PATH & WILDLIFE RESOURCES, UNIV MAINE, ORONO, 71-, CO-OP PROF FOREST RESOURCES, 77- *Personal Data:* b Barbados, BWI, Apr 29, 28; m 54; c 4. *Educ:* McGill Univ, BSc, 51, MSc, 56, PhD, 58; Ont Vet Col, DVM, 55. *Prof Exp:* Pathologist, Can Wildlife Serv, 57-58; hon asst prof parasitol, Macdonald Col, McGill Univ, 58-63, assoc prof, 63-71. *Concurrent Pos:* Lectr, Univ Ottawa, 57-58; res officer, Animal Path Labs, Can Dept Agr, 58-62; sr parasitologist, Averst, McKenna & Harrison, 62-63. *Mem:* Am Soc Parasitol; Wildlife Dis Asn; Am Vet Med Asn; Sigma Xi. *Res:* Helminthology. *Mailing Add:* 588 Kennebec Rd Hampden ME 04444-9704

GIBBS, HYATT MCDONALD, NONLINEAR OPTICS, OPTICAL BISTABILITY. *Current Pos:* dir, Optical Circuitry Coop, 84-91, PROF OPTICAL SCI, UNIV ARIZ, 80- *Personal Data:* b Hendersonville, NC, Aug 6, 38. *Educ:* NC State Univ, BS(elec eng) & BS(eng physics), 60; Univ Calif, Berkeley, PhD(physics), 65. *Honors & Awards:* Michelson Medal, Franklin Inst, 84. *Prof Exp:* Actg asst prof physics, Univ Calif, Berkeley, 65-67; mem tech staff, Bell Labs, 67-80. *Concurrent Pos:* Exchange scientist, Philips Res Labs, Eindhoven, Neth, 75-76; vis lectr, Princeton Univ, 78-79; Franklin Inst fel. *Mem:* Fel Am Phys Soc; fel Optical Soc Am; sr mem Inst Elec & Electronics Engrs; fel AAAS. *Res:* Spin exchange; time reversal; polarization of lead and thallium; self-induced transparency pulse breakup, peak amplification, pulse compression, degeneracy, Faraday rotation, self focusing, pulse collisions; neoclassical theory tests; subnatural linewidth fluorescence; optical transistor, optical bistability; superfluorescence; energy transfer and Anderson localization; laser spectroscopy; coherent optics; optical turbulence; nonlinear optical signal processing. *Mailing Add:* Optical Sci Ctr Univ Ariz Tucson AZ 85721. *Fax:* 520-621-4323

GIBBS, JAMES GENDRON, JR, NEUROBIOLOGY, PSYCHIATRY. *Current Pos:* res assoc, 72-73, asst prof, 73-78, ASSOC PROF PSYCHIAT, CORNELL UNIV MED COL, 78- *Personal Data:* b Charleston, SC, Dec 28, 38; m 64; c 2. *Educ:* Trinity Col, BS, 60; Med Col SC, MD, 64. *Prof Exp:* Intern, Univ Hosp, Univ Mich, 64-65; med officer, US Army, 65-67; resident psychiat, NY Hosp-Cornell Med Ctr, 68-72. *Concurrent Pos:* Fel, Found Fund Res Psychiat, 72-73; Glorney-Raisbeck fel, NY Acad Med, 73-74; NIMH res scientist develop award, 74-80; Irma T Hirschl career scientist award, 79-84. *Mem:* Am Physiol Soc; Am Psychiat Asn; Asn Res Nervous & Ment Dis; Soc Neurosci. *Res:* Physiological mechanisms of motivated behaviors. *Mailing Add:* Dept Psychol Cornell Univ Med Col Ny Hosp Cornell Univ Med Ctr White Plains NY 10605-1596

GIBBS, LOIS MARIE, ENVIRONMENTAL SCIENCE. *Current Pos:* ENVIRONMENTALIST, CITIZENS CLEARINGHOUSE FOR HAZARDOUS WASTES, VA. *Honors & Awards:* Goldman Environ Award, Goldman Environ Found, 90. *Mailing Add:* Citizens Clearinghouse PO Box 6806 Falls Church VA 22040

GIBBS, MARTIN, PLANT PHYSIOLOGY. *Current Pos:* RETIRED. *Personal Data:* b Philadelphia, Pa, Nov 11, 22; m 50, S Karen Kvale; c Steven, Michael, Robert, Janet & Laura. *Educ:* Philadelphia Col Pharm, BS, 43; Univ Ill, PhD(plant physiol), 47. *Honors & Awards:* Charles Reid Barnes Award; Adolph E Gude Award; Martin Gibbs Medal. *Prof Exp:* Asst chem, Univ Ill, 43-44, asst bot, 44-45, asst agron, 45-47; mem, Dept Biol, Brookhaven Nat Lab, 47-56; assoc prof biochem, Cornell Univ, 56-60, prof, 60-64; chmn dept, Brandeis Univ, 65-68, prof biol, 64-78, prof photobiol, 78-93, Abraham & Gertrude Burg prof life sci, 85-93. *Concurrent Pos:* Vis prof, Univ Pa, 54 & Queens Col, 58; vis scientist, Res Inst Adv Study, Md, 59 & 60; consult, NSF, 61-64 & 67-70 & NIH, 64-67; ed, Physiologie Vegetale, 68-71; nat lectr, 69, Sci Res Soc Am-Sigma Xi; consult, NATO Fel Bd; ed in chief, Plant Physiol, 63-92, ed, Annual Rev, 67-70; vis prof, Univ Calif, Riverside, 77-91. *Mem:* Nat Acad Sci; Acad Sci France; Am Soc Plant Physiol; Am Soc Biol Chem; Am Acad Arts & Sci; Russ Soc Plant Physiol. *Res:* Photosynthesis; carbohydrate metabolism of higher plants and algae. *Mailing Add:* Dept Biol Brandeis Univ Waltham MA 02254. *Fax:* 781-736-2688

GIBBS, MARVIN E, CHEMICAL ENGINEERING. *Current Pos:* CHMN & CHIEF EXEC OFFICER, ENVIRON RECYCLING INC, ST LOUIS. *Personal Data:* b St Louis, Mo, Dec 30, 34; m 88, Margaret Stout; c Jennifer & Deborah. *Educ:* Washington Univ, St Louis, BS, 56, PhD(chem eng), 60. *Prof Exp:* Sr res engr, Monsanto Co, St Louis, 60-66, res specialist, 66-67, res group leader, 67-70, mfg supt, Tex, 70-77, res mgr, 77-78, dir planning & control, 78-80, dir res & develop, 80-91, technol dir, 91-94. *Mem:* Am Inst Chem Engrs. *Res:* Process research, using special techniques, including and reaction kinetics, to provide all necessary information for large scale production. *Mailing Add:* 13445 Kings Glen Dr St Louis MO 63131

GIBBS, NORMAN EDGAR, computer science, for more information see previous edition

GIBBS, PETER (GODBE), PHYSICS. *Current Pos:* assoc prof physics, 57-62, from actg chmn to chmn dept, 67-76, PROF PHYSICS, UNIV UTAH, 62-, ASSOC RES PROF CERAMIC ENG, 56- *Personal Data:* b Salt Lake City, Utah, Dec 7, 24; m 53; c 3. *Educ:* Univ Utah, BS, 47, MS, 49, PhD(physics), 51. *Honors & Awards:* Purdy Prize, Am Ceramic Soc, 62. *Prof Exp:* Res assoc physics, Univ Ill, 51-52, instr, 52-54; Fulbright lectr theoret physics, Univ Ceylon, 54-55. *Concurrent Pos:* Fulbright lectr, Univ Sao Paulo, 63; consult, Atomics Int Div, NAm Aviation, Inc, 58-63, Dept Sci Affairs, Orgn Am States, 63 & Stanford Res Inst, 65-67; res assoc physics, Univ Calif, Berkeley, 77-78. *Mem:* Fel AAAS; NY Acad Sci; Biophys Soc; fel Am Phys Soc; Am Asn Physics Teachers; Sigma Xi. *Res:* Solid state and biological physics. *Mailing Add:* 3125 Kennedy Dr No 905 Salt Lake City UT 84108

GIBBS, R DARNLEY, botany; deceased, see previous edition for last biography

GIBBS, RICHARD LYNN, ATOMIC PHYSICS, PLASMA PHYSICS. *Current Pos:* From asst prof to assoc prof, 66-74, PROF PHYSICS, LA TECH UNIV, 74- *Personal Data:* b Buffalo, NY, May 12, 39; m 59; c 3. *Educ:* Univ of the South, BA, 61; Clarkson Col Technol, MS, 63, PhD(physics), 66. *Mem:* AAAS; Am Phys Soc; Am Asn Physics Teachers. *Res:* Atomic and molecular structure calculations; mathematical physics; experimental plasma measurements. *Mailing Add:* Dept Physics La Tech Univ PO Box 3187 Tech Sta Ruston LA 71270. *E-Mail:* gibbs@uchep.uchicago.edu

GIBBS, ROBERT JOHN, PHYSICAL CHEMISTRY, SCIENCE ADMINISTRATION. *Current Pos:* RETIRED. *Personal Data:* b New York, NY, Aug 14, 26; m 52; c 5. *Educ:* Fordham Univ, BS, 48, MS, 49, PhD(phys org chem), 52. *Prof Exp:* Res assoc phys chem, Sch Med, Univ Va, 52-54; mem staff, Mass Inst Technol, 54-56; chemist, Eastern Utilization Res & Develop Div, USDA, 56-64; grants assoc, Div Res Grants, USPHS, 64, asst to extramural opers & procedures officer, Off Dir, NIH, 64-69, opers anal off, 69-71, chief gen res support br, Div Res Resources, 71-74; asst vpres planning & develop, Univ DC, Washington, 74-78, admin & serv, 78-83. *Mem:* Fel AAAS; Am Chem Soc; Sigma Xi. *Res:* Science administration; kinetics of protein denaturation; physical properties of proteins; structural proteins of muscle. *Mailing Add:* 19630 White Rock Dr Sun City West AZ 85375-5723

GIBBS, RONALD JOHN, GEOCHEMISTRY. *Current Pos:* PROF, COL MARINE STUDIES, UNIV DEL, 74-. DIR, COLLOIDAL CTR, 85- *Personal Data:* b Joliet, Ill, Dec 26, 33. *Educ:* Northwestern Univ, Ill, BS, 57, MS, 60; Univ Calif, San Diego, PhD(oceanog), 65. *Prof Exp:* Asst prof geol, Univ NMex, 65-66 & Univ Calif, Los Angeles, 66-70; assoc prof, Northwestern Univ, Ill, 70-74. *Mem:* AAAS; Geol Soc Am; Clay Minerals Soc. *Res:* Environmental studies, pollution, sedimentology; clay mineralogy; geochemistry of dissolved and suspended loads of river systems; oceanic processes affecting discharged materials of river systems & pollution transport. *Mailing Add:* Col Marine Studies Univ Del Newark DE 19717-0001

GIBBS, SAMUEL JULIAN, DENTAL RADIOLOGY, RADIOBIOLOGY. *Current Pos:* from asst prof to assoc prof, 70-92, PROF DENT & RADIOL, VANDERBILT UNIV, 92- *Personal Data:* b Amory, Miss, Apr 1, 32; m 58, Emily J Starnes; c Samuel P, Stephen J & Julie A. *Educ:* Emory Univ, DDS, 56; Univ Rochester, PhD(radiation biol), 69; Am Bd Oral & Maxillofacial Radio, dipl, 81. *Prof Exp:* Pvt pract, Ala, 59-63. *Concurrent Pos:* Consult, Vet Admin Hosp, Nashville, Tenn, 70-; dir, Am Bd Oral & Maxillofacial Radiol, 83-88, vpres, 84-87, pres, 88. *Mem:* Fel Am Acad Dental Radiol (vpres, 79-80, pres, 80-81); Radiation Res Soc; Int Asn Dent Res; Am Dent Asn; Am Col Radiol; Radiol Soc NAm. *Res:* Experimental dental radiology; hazards of diagnostic radiology. *Mailing Add:* Dept Radiol & Radiol Sci Vanderbilt Univ Med Ctr Nashville TN 37232. *Fax:* 615-322-3764; *E-Mail:* gibbsxsj@ctrvax.vanderbilt.edu

GIBBS, SARAH PREBLE, CELL BIOLOGY, PHYCOLOGY. *Current Pos:* from asst prof to assoc prof, 66-74, PROF BIOL, MCGILL UNIV, 74- *Personal Data:* b Boston, Mass, May 25, 30; div; c Elizabeth D & Christopher H. *Educ:* Cornell Univ, AB, 52, MS, 54; Radcliffe Col, PhD(cell biol), 62. *Honors & Awards:* Darbaker Prize, Bot Soc Am, 75. *Prof Exp:* NIH fel biol, Harvard Univ, 61-62; NIH fel bact, Edinburgh Univ, 62-63, res assoc animal genetics, 63-65. *Concurrent Pos:* Mem fel comt, Nat Res Coun Can, 75-78; mem, Cell & Genetics Grant Comt, Natural Sci & Eng Res Coun Can, 82-85, Life Sci Sch & Fel Comt, 93-96. *Mem:* Can Soc Cell & Molecular Biol (pres, 72-73); Am Soc Cell Biol; Phycol Soc Am; fel AAAS; fel Royal Soc Can; Int Soc Evolutionary Protistology. *Res:* Cell biology, molecular organization of chloroplasts, evolution of algal chloroplasts from eukaryotic endosymbionts. *Mailing Add:* Dept Biol McGill Univ 1205 Docteur Penfield Ave Montreal PQ H3A 1B1 Can. *Fax:* 514-398-5069

GIBBS, TERRY RALPH, mechanical engineering, nuclear engineering, for more information see previous edition

GIBBS, THOMAS W(ATSON), METALLURGY, MATERIALS ENGINEERING. *Current Pos:* res mettallurgist, 65-68, res supvr, 68-71, venture specialist, 71-75, consult mgr mat engr, 75-79, MGR CONSULT SERVICES, E I DU PONT DE NEMOURS & CO, INC, 79- *Personal Data:* b Alexandria, Va, Sept 27, 32; m 54; c 3. *Educ:* Mass Inst Technol, SB, 54, SM, 55, ScD(metall), 64. *Prof Exp:* Assoc scientist, Avco Corp, 57-59, sr scientist, 59-64, staff scientist, 64-65. *Mem:* Am Soc Metals; Nat Asn Corrosion Engrs. *Res:* Mechanical properties; high temperature metallurgy; high intensity arcs; mechanical testing; materials engineering; fiber metallurgy; composite materials; semiconductor preparation and properties; dimensional stability; wear; foundry metallurgy. *Mailing Add:* 2527 Deepwood Dr Wilmington DE 19810

GIBBS, WILLIAM EUGENE, POLYMER ENGINEERING. *Current Pos:* vpres & dir res & develop, Plastics Div, 78-85, SCI & TECH CONSULT, AM HOECHST CORP, 85- *Personal Data:* b Akron, Ohio, Sept 23, 30; m 48; c 5. *Educ:* Univ Akron, BS & MS, 56, PhD(chem), 59. *Prof Exp:* Res chemist, Inst Rubber Res, Univ Akron, 53-55 & Goodyear Tire & Rubber Co, 55-58; res chemist, Air Force Mat Lab, 58-59, group leader, 59-62, chief, Polymer Br, 62-66, dir, 66-70; vpres & dir res & develop, Foster Grant Co, Inc, 70-78. *Concurrent Pos:* Mem, Comt Fire Toxicol, Nat Acad Sci. *Mem:* Am Chem Soc. *Res:* Synthesis and properties of polymers; physical chemistry of polymers; mechanisms of polymerizations and degradation. *Mailing Add:* 317 Jule Dr Chesapeake VA 23322-3615

GIBBS, WILLIAM ROYAL, STUDY OF THE STRONG INTERACTION. *Current Pos:* PROF PHYSICS, NMEX STATE UNIV, 93- *Personal Data:* b Dublin, Tex, July 6, 34; m 55, Valerie Barnes; c Victor & Gail. *Educ:* Univ Tex, BS, 55, MA, 57; Rice Univ, PhD(physics), 61. *Prof Exp:* Res assoc physics, Univ Neuchatel, 61-62; group leader T-5, Los Alamos Nat Lab, 73-75 & 89-90, mem res staff, 62-90, lab assoc, 90-94. *Mem:* Fel Am Phys Soc. *Res:* Nuclear reaction mechanisms; hadron-nucleus interaction. *Mailing Add:* Dept Physics NMex State Univ Las Cruces NM 88003

GIBEAULT, VICTOR ANDREW, ORNAMENTAL HORTICULTURE. *Current Pos:* COOP EXTEN SPECIALIST TURF & LANDSCAPE, COOP EXTEN SERV, UNIV CALIF, RIVERSIDE, 69- *Personal Data:* b Pawtucket, RI, Oct 21, 41; m 65; c 2. *Educ:* Univ RI, BS, 63, MS, 65; Ore State Univ, PhD(farm crops), 71. *Mem:* Am Soc Agron; Weed Sci Soc Am. *Res:* Adaptation of turf grass species and varieties to various habitats; herbicide influence on growth and development of turf grasses. *Mailing Add:* 5675 Via Mensabe Riverside CA 92506

GIBIAN, GARY LEE, SIGNAL PROCESSING, PSYCHOACOUSTICS. *Current Pos:* SR SCIENTIST, PLANNING SYSTS INC, 89- *Personal Data:* b Englewood, NJ, April 17, 49. *Educ:* Mass Inst Technol, BS, 71; Washington Univ, MA, 73, PhD(physics), 80. *Prof Exp:* Teaching asst, Washington Univ, 71-73, res asst, Cent Inst Deaf, 73-76, res asst physiol & biophysics, 76-79; assoc sr res scientist, Gen Motors Res Labs, 79-81, sr res scientist, 81-82; asst prof, Am Univ, Physics Dept, 82-88. *Mem:* Acoustical Soc Am; Audio Engr Soc; Comput Music Assoc. *Res:* Physiological acoustics, cochlear nonlinearites; psychoacoustics, subjective response to transportation noise. *Mailing Add:* 7923 Jones Branch Dr McLean VA 22102

GIBIAN, THOMAS GEORGE, CHEMISTRY. *Current Pos:* PRES, TECH GUID INT, INC, GREENWICH, CONN, 76- *Personal Data:* b Prague, Czech, Mar 20, 22; nat US; m 49; c 4. *Educ:* Univ NC, BSc, 42; Carnegie-Mellon Univ, PhD(chem), 48. *Prof Exp:* Petrol res, Atlantic Ref Co, 48-51; develop engr, Dewey & Almy Chem Div, W R Grace & Co, Md, 51-52, plant mgr, 53-56, gen mgr, Battery Separator Div, 56-57, vpres, Org Chem Div, 57-62 & Chem Group, 62-63, pres, Res Div, 63-66, vpres & tech group exec, 66-74; pres, Chem Construct Corp, NY, 74-76; chmn, Henkel Corp, 80-85. *Concurrent Pos:* Lectr, Drexel Inst Technol, 49-51. *Mem:* Am Chem Soc; Indust Res Inst; Soc Chem Indust; Soc Chimie Industrielle. *Res:* Administration and management. *Mailing Add:* PO Box 219 Sandy Spring MD 20860-0219

GIBILISCO, JOSEPH, DENTISTRY. *Current Pos:* consult, Dept Dent, 56-62, chmn dept dent, Mayo Clin, 62-76, PROF DENT, MAYO MED SCH, 75- *Personal Data:* b Omaha, Nebr, Feb 6, 24; m 51; c 3. *Educ:* Univ Minn, DDS, 48, MSD, 51. *Prof Exp:* Chmn dept oper dent, Creighton Univ, 49-51; assoc prof dent & anat, Univ Ala, 51-54. *Concurrent Pos:* Chmn, Southeastern Minn Health Systs Agency, 76-80 & Minn State Coord Coun, 76- *Mem:* AAAS; Am Dent Asn; Int Asn Dent Res; fel Am Col Dent; Am Acad Oral Med; Sigma Xi. *Res:* Clinical dentistry, particularly oral diagnosis and management of complex craniofacial pain problems. *Mailing Add:* Mayo Clin Rochester MN 55901

GIBLETT, ELOISE ROSALIE, HEMATOLOGY, IMMUNOGENETICS. *Current Pos:* RETIRED. *Personal Data:* b Tacoma, Wash, Jan 17, 21. *Educ:* Univ Wash, BS, 42, MS, 47, MD, 51. *Honors & Awards:* Emily Cooley Award, 75; Karl Landsteiner Award, 76; Philip Levine Award, 78. *Prof Exp:* Clin assoc med, Sch Med, Univ Wash, 55-57, from clin instr to clin prof, 58-67, res prof med, 67-87, emer prof med & emer exec dir, Puget Sound Blood Ctr, 87- *Concurrent Pos:* USPHS fel hemat, Univ Wash & Postgrad Med Sch, London, 53-55; head immunogenetics & assoc dir, Puget Sound Blood Ctr, 55-79, exec dir, 79-87; mem, NIH Genetics Study Sect, Nat Heart, Lung & Blood Res Rev Comt, Nat Blood Resources Comt, Food & Drug Admin Toxicol Adv Comt; USPHS trainee genetics, Case Western Res Univ, 60. *Mem:* Nat Acad Sci; Am Soc Hemat; Am Soc Human Genetics (pres, 73); Am Asn Immunol; Asn Am Physicians. *Res:* Erythrokinetics; genetic polymorphisms of all blood components; blood group antibodies; inherited enzyme defects in immunodeficiency diseases. *Mailing Add:* 6533 53rd St NE Seattle WA 98115

GIBLEY, CHARLES W, JR, ZOOLOGY, EMBRYOLOGY. *Current Pos:* CONSULT, 84- *Personal Data:* b Philadelphia, Pa, Oct 28, 34; m 56; c 4. *Educ:* Villanova Univ, BS, 56; Iowa State Univ, MS, 59, PhD(zool), 61. *Prof Exp:* Lab instr biol, Villanova Univ, 57; res asst zool, Iowa State Univ, 57-61; asst prof biol, Villanova Univ, 61-65; prof histo-embryol, Pa Col Podiatric Med, 63-70, acad dean, 67-74, prof anat, 70-84, vpres acad affairs, 74-84. *Concurrent Pos:* Asst biologist & asst prof, Univ Tex M D Anderson Hosp & Tumor Inst, 65-67. *Mem:* Am Soc Zool; Soc Develop Biol; AAAS; Am Asn Anatomists; Am Soc Cell Biol. *Res:* Experimental embryology; histochemistry and developmental causes underlying the morphogenesis of embryonic and adult kidney in vertebrates. *Mailing Add:* Dept Anat Phila Col Pharm & Sci 600 S 43rd St Woodland Kingsessing Philadelphia PA 19104. *Fax:* 215-596-8764

GIBLIN, DENIS RICHARD, NEUROLOGY. *Current Pos:* ASSOC PROF NEUROL, ALBERT EINSTEIN COL MED, 73- *Personal Data:* b Montreal, Que, Mar 14, 27; m 66, Susan Scharn; c Vanessa & Timothy. *Educ:* McGill Univ, BSc, 48, MD, 52. *Honors & Awards:* A Cressy Morrison Award Nat Sci, NY Acad Sci, 63. *Prof Exp:* Intern, Royal Victoria Hosp, Montreal, 52-53; intern med, Duke Univ Hosp, Durham, NC, 53-54; resident neurol, Montreal Neurol Inst, 54-55 & Peter Bent Brigham Inst, Boston, 55-56; Nuffield traveling fel, London, 56-57. *Res:* Neurophysiology, clinical, evoked somatosensory and visual responses in healthy subjects and patients with neurological disorders; neurophysiology, sensory coding by individual neurons. *Mailing Add:* Dept Neurol Albert Einstein Col Med Bronx NY 10461

GIBLIN, FRANK JOSEPH, BIOCHEMISTRY. *Current Pos:* assoc ocular res, 74-77, asst prof ocular res, inst biol sci, 77-83, ASSOC PROF BIOMED RES, EYE RES INST, OAKLAND UNIV, 83- *Personal Data:* b St Petersburg, Fla, Feb 24, 42; m 65; c 2. *Educ:* Univ Windsor, BASc, 65; State Univ NY Buffalo, PhD(biochem), 74. *Honors & Awards:* Rohto Cataract Res Award, 81; Alcon Res Recognition Award, 85. *Prof Exp:* Engr chem, Procter & Gamble Co, 65-69. *Mem:* AAAS; Sigma Xi; Asn Res Vision & Ophthal. *Res:* Mechanism of formation of cataract in the ocular lens and the possible role of glutathione in maintaining the transparency of this tissue by preventing oxidative damage. *Mailing Add:* Oakland Univ Eye Res Inst Rochester MI 48309

GIBLIN-DAVIS, ROBIN MICHAEL, PHYTOPATHOLOGY, ENTOMOLOGY. *Current Pos:* asst prof, 85-90, ASSOC PROF ENTOM, UNIV FLA, FT LAUDERDALE, 90- *Personal Data:* b Berkeley, Calif, Mar 6, 55; m 82; c 3. *Educ:* Univ Calif, Davis, BS, 77, PhD(entom), 82. *Prof Exp:* Postdoctoral assoc, Univ Calif, Riverside, 82-85. *Mem:* Soc Nematologists; Entom Soc Am; Orgn Trop Am Nematologists. *Res:* The taxonomy, ecology and physiology of nematode parasites and associates of plants (turfgrasses and ornamentals) and insects. *Mailing Add:* Univ Fla 3205 College Ave Ft Lauderdale FL 33314

GIBOFSKY, ALLAN, RHEUMATOLOGY, FORENSIC MEDICINE. *Current Pos:* asst prof to assoc prof med, 79-95, asst prof pub health, 89-92, PROF MED, CORNELL MED COL, NY, 95-,PROF PUB HEALTH, 95- *Personal Data:* b New York, NY, Sept 7, 49; m 82; c 3. *Educ:* Brooklyn Col, NY, 69; Cornell Univ Med Col, MD, 73; Fordham Univ, NY, JD, 85. *Honors & Awards:* Nat Res Serv Award, NIH, 77; Arthritis Found Res Award, 87- *Prof Exp:* Intern pathol, NY Hosp, 73-74, res med, 74-77; res fel immunol, Rockefeller Univ, 77-79. *Concurrent Pos:* Jonas Salk scholar, City NY, 69; adj assoc prof immunol, Rockefeller Univ, 85-; chair by laws comt, Am Soc Histocompatibility & Immunogenetics, 86-90; adj assoc prof law, Fordham Univ, 87-95; mem, Data & Technol Assessment Prog, Am Med Asn, 87-; pres, Med Sci Comt, NY Arthritis Found, 88-92; prof law, Fordham Univ, 95- *Mem:* Fel Am Col Rheumatism (secy-treas, 96-); fel Am Col Legal Med; Am Col Physicians; Am Asn Immunologists; Am Fed Clin Res. *Res:* Immunogenetics of the rheumatic diseases; rheumatic fever. *Mailing Add:* 535 E 70th St New York NY 10021

GIBOR, AHRON, PHYSIOLOGY. *Current Pos:* assoc prof, 66-68, PROF PHYSIOL, UNIV CALIF, SANTA BARBARA, 68- *Personal Data:* b Jaffa, Israel, Sept 16, 25; nat US; m 50; c 2. *Educ:* Univ Calif, BA, 50, MA, 52; Stanford Univ, PhD(biol), 56. *Prof Exp:* Res biologist, Alaska Dept Fish & Game, 57-59; chief biol sect, Resources Res, Inc, 59-60; res assoc physiol, Rockefeller Inst, 60-63, asst prof, 64-66. *Concurrent Pos:* Guggenheim fel, 78-79; vis prof, Kyoto Univ, 85. *Mem:* Am Soc Cell Biol; AAAS. *Res:* General and algal physiology. *Mailing Add:* Dept Biol USCB Santa Barbara CA 93106

GIBORI, GEULA, ENDOCRINOLOGY, REPRODUCTIVE PHYSIOLOGY. *Current Pos:* asst prof, 76-80, assoc prof, 80-86, PROF PHYSIOL, UNIV ILL, 86- *Personal Data:* b Beirut, Lebanon, Aug 8, 45; m 70, Shimon; c Gil, Ilan & Ron. *Educ:* Lebanese Univ, BS, 67; Sorbonne, MS, 68; Tel Aviv Univ, PhD(physiol), 73. *Honors & Awards:* Golden Apple Award, 85 & 93; Am Med Womens Asn Award, 94. *Prof Exp:* Lectr physiol, Univ Tel Aviv, 71-73; fel reproduction, Case Western Res Univ, 73-75 & Univ Mich, 75-76. *Concurrent Pos:* Fulbright Found fel, 73-76, Fulbright award, 73-74; NSF grant, 78-84, NIH grants, 78-; merit award, NIH, 88- *Mem:* Endocrine Soc; Soc Study Reproduction; Soc Study Fertil; Am Physiol Soc; Soc Exp Biol Med; fel AAAS. *Res:* Placental derived regulators and the molecular control of ovarian function. *Mailing Add:* Dept Physiol & Biophys Col Med Univ Ill 901 S Wolcott m/c 901 Chicago IL 60612-7342. *Fax:* 312-996-1414

GIBSON, ATHOLL ALLEN VEAR, SOLID STATE PHYSICS, LOW TEMPERATURE PHYSICS. *Current Pos:* VPRES RES & DEVELOP, NALORAC CRYOGENICS CORP, 84- *Personal Data:* b Eshowe, S Africa, Nov 25, 40; m 70, Edna Mendoza; c 2. *Educ:* Univ Natal, BSc, 61, PhD(physics), 71. *Prof Exp:* Lectr physics, Univ Natal, 63-68 & 69-70; lectr, Nottingham Univ, 70-71; fel, Univ Fla, 71-73, asst prof, 73-76; res assoc, Northwestern Univ, 76-78; asst prof physics, Tex A&M Univ, 78-84. *Concurrent Pos:* Consult, Los Alamos Nat Lab, 82-84. *Mem:* Am Phys Soc. *Res:* Nuclear magnetic resonance as a probe of the solid state and of surfaces at low and very low temperatures and high pressures; nuclear magnetic resonance spectrometer design. *Mailing Add:* 837 Arnold Dr No 600 Martinez CA 94553

GIBSON, AUDREY JANE, MICROBIOLOGY, BIOCHEMISTRY. *Current Pos:* RETIRED. *Personal Data:* b Paris, France, Oct 5, 24; m 51. *Educ:* Cambridge Univ, BA, 46; Univ London, PhD(biochem), 49. *Prof Exp:* Commonwealth Fund fel microbiol, Hopkins Marine Sta, Stanford Univ, 49-50; res assoc, Agr Res Coun Unit Microbiol, Univ Sheffield, 50-51 & 53-63; asst prof microbiol & phys biochem, Johnson Res Found, Pa, 63-65; asst prof microbiol, Cornell Univ, 66-70, assoc prof, 70-79, prof biochem, molecular & cell biol, 79- *Concurrent Pos:* Res assoc, Univ Ill, 61. *Mem:* Soc Biol Chemists; Am Soc Microbiol. *Res:* Growth regulation in photosynthetic prokaryotes; characterization and regulation of transport processes; carbon, phosphate and nitrogen metabolism; membrane giogenesis. *Mailing Add:* 3 Woods End Rd Etna NH 03750. *Fax:* 607-255-2428

GIBSON, BENJAMIN FRANKLIN, V, NUCLEAR PHYSICS, FEW-BODY PHYSICS. *Current Pos:* group leader, 82-86, STAFF PHYSICIST, THEORET PHYSICS DIV, LOS ALAMOS NAT LAB, 72- *Personal Data:* b Madisonville, Tex, Sept 3, 38; m 68, Margaret Ferguson; c 3. *Educ:* Rice Univ, BA, 61; Stanford Univ, PhD(physics), 66. *Honors & Awards:* Award Sr US Scientists, Humboldt Found, 92. *Prof Exp:* Fel, Lawrence Radiation Lab, Univ Calif, 66-68; Nat Res Coun res assoc, Nat Bur Stand, DC, 68-70; res assoc physics, Brooklyn Col, 70-72. *Concurrent Pos:* Detailee, Dept Energy, 80-81; res fel, Japan Soc Prom Sci, 84; Murdoch fel, Inst Nuclear Theory, 92; vis scholar, Univ Melbourne, 86-87, Flinders Univ, 87; assoc ed, Phys Review C, 88-; vchmn, Few-Body Topical Group, Am Phys Soc, 90-92, chmn, 92-93, secy-treas, Div Nuclear Physics, 95- *Mem:* Fel Am Phys Soc. *Res:* Theoretical nuclear, hypernuclear and elementary particle physics; medium energy physics; few-body physics. *Mailing Add:* MS-B283 Los Alamos Nat Lab Los Alamos NM 87545. *Fax:* 505-667-1931; *E-Mail:* gibson@t5.lanl.gov

GIBSON, CARL H, FLUID DYNAMICS, OCEANOGRAPHY. *Current Pos:* asst res engr, 65-66, ASSOC PROF ENG PHYSICS & OCEANOG, UNIV CALIF, SAN DIEGO, 65- *Personal Data:* b Springfield, Ill, Sept 26, 34; div; c 2. *Educ:* Univ Wis, BS, 56, MS, 57; Stanford Univ, PhD(chem eng), 62. *Prof Exp:* Chem engr, Oak Ridge Nat Lab, 57-58; Peace Corps teacher, Osmania Univ, India, 62-64. *Concurrent Pos:* Guggenheim fel, 73. *Mem:* Fel Am Phys Soc; Am Inst Chem Eng; Sigma Xi. *Res:* Turbulence; turbulent mixing of passive and reacting scalar properties; transport phenomena; nuclear reactor engineering; oceanography; atmospheric and oceanic diffusive phenomena. *Mailing Add:* Univ Calif San Diego 2201 Eng Bldg R-011 La Jolla CA 92093

GIBSON, COLVIN LEE, PARASITOLOGY. *Current Pos:* CONSULT, WHO, 74- *Personal Data:* b Detroit, Mich, Apr 12, 18; m 41; c 3. *Educ:* Univ Mich, AB, 40, AM, 41, PhD(zool), 51. *Prof Exp:* Parasitologist, Onchocerciasis Res Proj, Pan-Am Sanit Bur & USPHS, 48-52; parasitologist, Lab Trop Dis, Nat Inst Allergy & Infectious Dis, NIH, 52-57, spec asst to chief extramural progs br, 57-61, chief virus reagents prog, 61-62, chief res reference br, 62-63, sci commun officer, 63, chief res grants br, 63-65, chief parasitol & med entom br, 65-68, asst to dir, NIH, 68-75. *Concurrent Pos:* Ed, Trop Med & Hyg News, 66-87. *Mem:* Am Soc Parasitol; Am Soc Trop Med & Hyg. *Res:* Filarial diseases, especially onchocerciasis; epidemiology of toxoplasmosis. *Mailing Add:* 3307 Harrell St Silver Spring MD 20906

GIBSON, COUNT DILLON, JR, MEDICINE. *Current Pos:* assoc dean, Community Health Progs, 69-80, prof community & prev med & chmn dept, 69-87, PROF HEALTH RES & POLICY, MED CTR, STANFORD UNIV, 88- *Personal Data:* b Covington, Ga, July 10, 21; m 50; c 4. *Educ:* Emory Univ, BA, 42, MD, 44. *Prof Exp:* Asst med, Col Physicians & Surgeons, Columbia Univ, 50-51; from asst prof to assoc prof, Med Col Va, 51-57; prof prev med & chmn dept, Med Sch, Tufts Univ, 58-69. *Mem:* Fel Am Col Physicians; fel Am Pub Health Asn. *Res:* Infectious diseases; medical care. *Mailing Add:* Dept Health Res & Policy Stanford Univ Med Ctr Stanford CA 94305

GIBSON, DAVID F(REDERIC), INDUSTRIAL ENGINEERING. *Current Pos:* from assoc prof to prof indust eng, 72-76, asst dean, 77-83, DEAN, COL ENG, MONT STATE UNIV, 83- *Personal Data:* b West Newton, Mass, Jan 10, 42; m 63, Rebecca Harper; c 2. *Educ:* Purdue Univ, BSIE, 63, MSIE, 64, PhD(indust eng), 69. *Prof Exp:* Indust engr, Naval Ord Plant, Ill, 63; res asst, Purdue Univ, 63-64; proj indust engr & chief methods & stand br, Sacramento Army Depot, 65-66; instr indust eng, Purdue Univ, 68-69; asst prof indust & mgr eng, Mont State Univ, 69-71; dean, Sch Syst Sci, Ark Tech Univ, 71-72. *Concurrent Pos:* Dir, Eng Exp Sta, Mont State Univ, 77- *Mem:* Inst Indust Engrs; Am Soc Eng Educ; Nat Soc Prof Eng; Nat Coun Examrs Eng & Surveyors. *Res:* Management systems analysis and design; computerized planning systems; surface coal mining operations; forest engineering. *Mailing Add:* Col Eng Mont State Univ Bozeman MT 59717. *Fax:* 406-994-6665; *E-Mail:* adedg@mtsuniv1.bitnet

GIBSON, DAVID JOHN, TERRESTRIAL PLANT ECOLOGY, GRASSLAND ECOLOGY. *Current Pos:* asst prof, 92-94, ASSOC PROF PLANT BIOL, SOUTHERN ILL UNIV, 94- *Personal Data:* b Cuckfield, W Sussex, UK, June 16, 58; m 92, Lisa Smith; c Lacey. *Educ:* Univ Reading, UK, BSc, 79; Univ Okla, MS, 81; Univ Wales, UK, PhD(plant sci), 85. *Prof Exp:* Asst scientist, Kans State Univ, 85-88; asst prof biol, Univ WFla, 88-92. *Mem:* Inst Biol; Brit Ecol Soc; Ecol Soc Am; Sigma Xi. *Res:* Primarily plant community and population ecology of grasslands, especially long term studies from permanent plots; concepts of competition, succession, diversity and ecophysiology are of particular interest. *Mailing Add:* Dept Plant Biol Southern Ill Univ Carbondale IL 62901-6509

GIBSON, DAVID MARK, BIOCHEMISTRY. *Current Pos:* assoc prof, 58-61, actg chmn dept biochem, 65-67, prof, 61-75, chmn dept, 67-88, Grace M Showalter prof, 75-92, EMER PROF, BIOCHEM, SCH MED, IND UNIV, 92- *Personal Data:* b Kokomo, Ind, Aug 7, 23; wid, Margaret Lockhart (deceased); c Carl L, John L, Shauna (Koop), Heather (Garrison) & Mark C. *Educ:* Wabash Col, AB, 44; Harvard Univ, MD, 48. *Prof Exp:* Asst prof, Enzyme Inst, Univ Wis, 55-58. *Concurrent Pos:* Res fel biochem, Univ Ill, 50-53 & Enzyme Inst, Univ Wis, 53-58; estab investr, Am Heart Asn, 57-62; Career Develop Award, NIH, 62-67. *Mem:* AAAS; Am Soc Cell Biol; Am Soc Biol Chemists; Biochem Soc Gt Brit; Am Heart Asn. *Res:* Control of fatty acid and cholesterol biosynthesis; regulation of hydroxymethylglutaryl co-enzyme A reductase by reversibile phosphorylation. *Mailing Add:* Dept Biochem Sch Med Ind Univ Indianapolis IN 46202-5122

GIBSON, DAVID MICHAEL, ORGANIC CHEMISTRY. *Current Pos:* sr chemist, 79-86, staff chemist, 86-99, STAFF QUAL CONTROL CHEMIST, EXXON CHEM AMERICAS, 89- *Personal Data:* b Joplin, Mo, Sept 1, 45; m 75; c 2. *Educ:* Southwest Mo Univ, BS, 67; Univ New Orleans, PhD(org chem), 75. *Prof Exp:* Res assoc, Int Paper Co, 75-79. *Mem:* Am Soc Testing & Mat. *Res:* Analytical techniques for analysis of light hydrocarbons and intermediate alcohols. *Mailing Add:* Exxon Chem Americas Chem Plant Lab PO Box 241 Baton Rouge LA 70821

GIBSON, DAVID THOMAS, BIOCHEMISTRY, MICROBIOLOGY. *Current Pos:* From asst prof to prof microbiol, Univ Tex, Austin, 69-88, PROF BIOCATALYSIS & MICROBIOL, UNIV IOWA, 88- *Personal Data:* b Wakefield, Eng, Feb 16, 38; m 63, Janet Peers; c 2. *Educ:* Univ Leeds, BSc, 61, PhD(biochem), 64. *Honors & Awards:* Minnie F Piper Stevens Award, 83; Award in Appl & Environ Microbiol, Procter & Gamble. *Concurrent Pos:* Res grants, NIH, 70-, ENVIRON PROTECTION AGENCY, 86-; NIH grant, 71; consult, Gen Elec, 75-80; assoc ed, Soc Indust Microbiol, 76-79; study sect mem microbial chem, NIH, 77-81. *Mem:* Am Soc Microbiol; Am Chem Soc; AAAS; Soc Indust Microbiol; Sigma Xi. *Res:* Mechanisms used by micro-organisms to oxidize polycyclic aromatic hydrocarbons; mechanisms of enzymatic oxygen fixation. *Mailing Add:* Dept Microbiol Univ Ia Col Med Bowen Sci Bldg Rm 3 733 Iowa City IA 52242-0001

GIBSON, DOROTHY HINDS, ORGANIC CHEMISTRY, ORGANOMETALLIC CHEMISTRY. *Current Pos:* from asst prof to assoc prof, 69-75, PROF CHEM, UNIV LOUISVILLE, 75- *Personal Data:* b Italy, Tex, July 19, 33. *Educ:* Tex Christian Univ, BA, 54, MA, 56; Univ Tex, Austin, PhD(chem), 65. *Prof Exp:* Instr chem, Tex Christian Univ, 56-61; res assoc, Univ Tex, Austin, 64-65 & Univ Colo, 65-69. *Concurrent Pos:* Vchair, chem, Univ Louisville, 78-87, actg chair, 82-83. *Mem:* Sigma Xi; Am Chem Soc. *Res:* Synthesis and properties of transition metal carbonyl complexes; reactive organometallic intermediates; transition metal hydrides as reducing agents. *Mailing Add:* Dept Chem Univ Louisville Louisville KY 40292. *Fax:* 502-852-8149

GIBSON, EARL DOYLE, COMMUNICATIONS ENGINEERING. *Current Pos:* AT SIERRA SEMICONDUCTOR, 88- *Personal Data:* b Putnam, Okla, July 20, 23; m 57; c 4. *Educ:* Okla Inst Technol, BSEE, 49; Univ Md, MSEE, 60. *Prof Exp:* Engr, Gen Elec Co, 49-51 & US Naval Ord Lab, Md, 51-56; chief analysis sect, ACF Industs, Inc, 56-63; sr staff engr, Aerospace Corp, Calif, 63-66; sr staff scientist, Electronics Res Ctr, Rockwell Int, 66-76. *Mem:* Inst Elec & Electronics Engrs. *Res:* Data communications; adaptive equalization; adaptive receivers. *Mailing Add:* 171 Sudbury Dr Milpitas CA 95035

GIBSON, EDWARD F, EXPERIMENTAL NUCLEAR PHYSICS, INSTRUMENTATION. *Current Pos:* from asst prof to assoc prof, 69-78, chmn dept, 79-88, PROF PHYSICS, CALIF STATE UNIV, SACRAMENTO, 78- *Personal Data:* b Colorado Springs, Colo, Apr 2, 37; m 63, Harriette DuShane; c Sascha, Graham, Clark & Eileen. *Educ:* Univ Colo, Boulder, BA, 59, MA, 64, PhD(physics), 66. *Prof Exp:* Physicist, Cryogenic Eng Div, Nat Bur Stand, 58-64; res asst nuclear physics, Univ Colo, 64-66, res assoc, 66; res assoc, Univ Ore, 66-68, scientist in residence, US Naval Radiol Defense Lab, 68-69. *Concurrent Pos:* Consult, Calif Energy Comn, 77-79 & Control Data Corp, 81-86; vis prof, Univ Colo, 80. *Mem:* Am Phys Soc; Sigma Xi. *Res:* Nuclear spectroscopy; nuclear reactions; elastic and inelastic 3He scattering; gamma-ray spectroscopy; nuclear life times; low temperature electrical and thermal conductivity; meson scattering; intermediate energy meson physics; computer assisted instruction. *Mailing Add:* 527 Blackwood St Sacramento CA 95815-3703. *Fax:* 916-278-6664; *E-Mail:* egibson@csus.edu

GIBSON, EDWARD GEORGE, atmospheric physics, engineering, for more information see previous edition

GIBSON, ELEANOR JACK, PERCEPTION, PSYCHOLOGICAL DEVELOPMENT. *Current Pos:* res assoc, 49-66, SUSAN LINN SAGE PROF PSYCHOL, CORNELL UNIV, 72- *Personal Data:* b Peoria, Ill, Dec 7, 10; m 32, James J; c James J & Jean G. *Educ:* Smith Col, BA, 31, MA, 33; Yale Univ, PhD, 38. *Hon Degrees:* Numerous from US univs, 72-96. *Honors & Awards:* Distinguished Scientist Award, Am Psychol Asn, 68, G Stanley Award, 70, Gold Medal, 86; Wilbur Cross Medal, Yale Univ, 73; Howard Crosby Warren Medal, 77; Distinguished Sci Contrib Award, Soc Res Child Develop, 81; Nat Medal Sci, 92. *Prof Exp:* From asst to asst prof, Smith Col, 31-49. *Concurrent Pos:* Fel, Inst Advan Study, Princeton, 59-60; fel, Inst Advan Study Behav Sci, Stanford, Calif, 63-64; Guggenheim fel, 72-73; vis prof, Mass Inst Technol, 73, Inst Child Develop, Univ Minn, 80 & Univ Pa, 84; distinguished vis prof, Univ Calif, Davis, 78; vis scientist, Salk Inst, Calif, 79; div chairperson, AAAS, 83; Montgomery fel, Dartmouth Col, 86; Woodruff vis prof psychol, Emory Univ, 88-90; William James fel, Am Psychol Soc, 89; fel, Inst Advan Study, Ind Univ, 90. *Mem:* Nat Acad Sci; fel AAAS; fel Am Psychol Asn; Soc Exp Psychologists; Soc Res Child Develop; Am Acad Arts & Sci; hon mem Brit Psychol Soc; hon mem NY Acad Sci; Sigma Xi; hon mem Ital Soc Res Child Develop. *Res:* Perceptual development. *Mailing Add:* RR 1 Box 265A Middlebury VA 05753-9705

GIBSON, EVERETT KAY, JR, GEOCHEMISTRY, ANALYTICAL CHEMISTRY. *Current Pos:* aerospace technician, 70-74, planetary scientist space sci, 74-93, SR SCIENTIST, JOHNSON SPACE CTR, NASA, 93- *Personal Data:* b Seagraves, Tex, May 13, 40; m 73, Morgan Shott; c Bradford Pierce. *Educ:* Tex Tech Univ, Bs, 63, MS, 65; Ariz State Univ,

PhD(Geochem), 69. *Honors & Awards:* Sustained Performance Award, Johnson Space Ctr, NASA, 71, 72, & 76; Outstanding Lectr Award, Am Astron Soc, 76; Greatest Achievement Award, Popular Sci Mag, 96; Best Sci Award Time Mag, 96; Outstanding Accomplishment Award, Planetary Soc, 96. *Prof Exp:* Teaching asst chem, Tex Tech Univ, 63-65, instr, 65. *Concurrent Pos:* Res assoc, Nat Acad Sci-Nat Res Coun, Johnson Space Ctr, NASA, 69-70, lunar sample prelim exam team, 69-73, lunar sample anal & planning team, 74-77; consult, Economist, London, 70-75 & Brit Broadcasting Corp, London, 75-80; lunar sample prin investr, NASA, Washington, DC, 71-90; dir, Clear Creek Basin Authority, Harris County, Tex, 74-76; assoc ed, Proc 5th to 9th & 12th Lunar & Planetary Sci Conf, 74-78; adj prof geol, Univ Houston, 74-90, lectr, Sch Continuing Educ, 76-; prin investr planetary geol, 78-88 & NASA Planetary Biol Prog, 83-; Leverhulme sr fel, Open Univ, Eng, 84-85; coun, Meteoritical Soc, 87-90. *Mem:* Meteoritical Soc (secy, 74-80); Am Chem Soc; AAAS; Int Asn Geochem & Cosmochem; Sigma Xi. *Res:* Geochemistry of meteorites and lunar samples; nature of volatiles in terrestrial and extraterrestrial materials; development of analytical methods of analysis for volatile elements; life on mars, Martian geochemical processes; nature of Archean atmosphere and ocean. *Mailing Add:* 1015 Trowbridge Dr Houston TX 77062

GIBSON, FLASH, AQUATIC ENTOMOLOGY. *Current Pos:* ASST PROF BIOL, EASTERN WASH UNIV, 71- *Personal Data:* b Spokane, Wash, Apr 3, 44; m 63; c 2. *Educ:* Eastern Wash Univ, BA, 66; Ore State Univ, MA, 69, PhD(zool), 71. *Mem:* Ecol Soc Am; Am Soc Zoologists; Northwest Sci Asn; Sigma Xi. *Res:* Ecological physiology of aquatic invertebrates of northwestern United States wetlands. *Mailing Add:* Dept Biol Eastern Wash Univ MS 72 Cheney WA 99004-2496

GIBSON, GARY EUGENE, BIOCHEMISTRY. *Current Pos:* from asst prof to assoc prof biochem & neurol, 78-90, PROF NEUROSCI, CORNELL MED SCH, 90- *Personal Data:* b Greeley, Colo, Oct 3, 45; m 73. *Educ:* Univ Wyo, BS, 68; Cornell Univ, PhD(physiol), 73. *Honors & Awards:* Jordi Folch-Pi Award, Am Soc Neurochem, 82. *Prof Exp:* NIH trainee, 73-76, asst res biochemist, Neuropsychiat Inst, Univ Calif, Los Angeles, 76-78. *Mem:* Sigma Xi; Am Soc Neurochem; AAAS; Soc Neurosci; Int Soc Neurochem; Fedn Am Soc Exp Biol & Med. *Res:* Examination of interactions in brain and other tissues of calcium, neurotransmitters and oxidative metabolism during aging, vitamin deficiencies and Alzheimer's disease; vitamin deficiencies and Alzheimer's disease. *Mailing Add:* Dept Biochem & Neurol Cornell Univ Burke Med Res Inst Sturgis Bldg 785 Mamaroneck Ave White Plains NY 10605-2523. *Fax:* 914-946-1722

GIBSON, GEORGE NICHOLAS, ULTRAFAST PHENOMENA, HIGH DENSITY LASERS. *Current Pos:* ASST PROF PHYSICS, UNIV CONN, 93- *Personal Data:* b Boston, Mass, Apr 12, 61. *Educ:* Univ Calif, Berkeley, BA, 83; Univ Ill, PhD(physics), 90. *Honors & Awards:* Early Career Develop Award, NSF, 94. *Prof Exp:* Res assoc, Univ Md, 90-93. *Concurrent Pos:* Vis scientist, AT&T Bell Labs, 90-93; Cottrell scholar, 95. *Mem:* Am Phys Soc; Optical Soc Am; AAAS. *Res:* Behavior of atoms and molecules in high-intensity short-pulse laser fields. *Mailing Add:* Dept Physics U-46 Univ Conn 2152 Hillside Rd Storrs CT 06269. *Fax:* 860-486-3346; *E-Mail:* gibson@main.phys.uconn.edu

GIBSON, GEORGE R, EXPLORATION GEOLOGY, PETROLEUM GEOLOGY. *Current Pos:* GEOL CONSULT, 52- *Personal Data:* b Kendaia, NY, Oct 2, 05. *Educ:* Univ Minn, BA, 30, PhD(geol), 34. *Prof Exp:* Instr geol, Univ Minn, 33-34, Ohio State Univ, 40-41; assoc prof geol, Carleton Col, 34-38; geologist, Socony-Vacuum Co, 38-40, Magnalia Oil Co, 41-43; dist mgr, Richfield Oil, 43-48; mgr explor, Seaboard Petrol, 48-52. *Mem:* Sigma Xi; Earth Scientist; fel Geol Soc Am; Soc Independent Professional Earth Scientists; Am Asn Petrol Geologists; Soc Econ Paleontologists & Mineralogists. *Mailing Add:* PO Box 2296 Midland TX 79702-2296

GIBSON, GERALD W, ORGANIC CHEMISTRY. *Current Pos:* DEAN, ROANOKE COL, 84- *Personal Data:* b Saluda Co, SC, Oct 27, 37; m 68; c 3. *Educ:* Wofford Col, BS, 59; Univ Tenn, PhD(chem), 63. *Prof Exp:* From asst prof to prof chem, Col Charleston, 65-84, chmn dept, 68-82. *Mem:* Am Chem Soc. *Res:* Organolithium compounds; general and organic chemistry problem-solving; Wiswesser line notation; reactions of organolithium compounds with alkyl halides. *Mailing Add:* Pres Maryville Col Maryville TN 37801

GIBSON, GORDON, THEORETICAL PHYSICS. *Current Pos:* sr scientist, Atomic Power Div, Westinghouse Elec Corp, 55-64, fel scientist, Astronuclear Lab, 64-67, adv scientist, 67-74, mgr plasma & nuclear eng dept, 74-84, consult scientist, Advan Energy Systs Div, 84-86, CONSULT SCIENTIST, SOURCE & TECH CTR, WESTINGHOUSE ELEC CORP, 86- *Personal Data:* b McKeesport, Pa, Jan 9, 26; m 55; c 4. *Educ:* Univ Pittsburgh, BS, 49, MS, 52, PhD(physics), 55. *Prof Exp:* Instr physics & res asst, Univ Pittsburgh, 50-55. *Concurrent Pos:* Consult, Lawrence Radiation Lab, Univ Calif, 55-64. *Mem:* Am Phys Soc. *Res:* Neutron cross sections; nuclear rocket reactor; plasma and reactor physics; controlled fusion. *Mailing Add:* 120 Lamar Rd Pittsburgh PA 15241

GIBSON, HAROLD F(LOYD), MILITARY OPTICAL SYSTEMS, LASER USING WEAPONS. *Current Pos:* RETIRED. *Personal Data:* b Retrop, Okla, Feb 24, 21; m 41; c 2. *Educ:* Univ Okla, BS, 43, MS, 48. *Prof Exp:* Physicist, Radiation Lab, Nat Bur Stands, 48-53; physicist, Harry Diamond Labs, 53-56, supvr physicist, 56-62, supvr res & develop, 62-69, chief, Appl Physics Br, 69-76, chief, Components & Mat Lab, 76-80. *Concurrent Pos:* Consult, 80- *Mem:* AAAS; Am Phys Soc. *Res:* Solid state physics; energy sources and conversion techniques; laser materials; applied infrared and laser technology. *Mailing Add:* 10705 Jamaica Dr Silver Spring MD 20902

GIBSON, HAROLD J(AMES), mechanical engineering; deceased, see previous edition for last biography

GIBSON, HARRY GENE, AGRICULTURAL MACHINERY DESIGN, SIMULATION OF OFF-HIGHWAY VEHICLES. *Current Pos:* ASSOC PROF AGR ENG, PURDUE UNIV, 79- *Personal Data:* b Morgantown, WVa, Sept 10, 38; m 56, Pamela S Payne; c Sheree, Harry C, Michael, Patricia, Kirsten & John. *Educ:* WVa Univ, BS, 62, MS, 69. *Prof Exp:* Res proj engr, US Bur Mines, 62-65; supvr mech eng, US Forest Serv, 65-78; mgr plantation harvesting, Jari Forestal e Agropecuaria, 78-79. *Concurrent Pos:* Eng consult, Gibson Eng Consult, 79-; Fulbright scholar, Coun Int Exchange Scholars, 91. *Mem:* Am Soc Agr Engrs; Soc Automotive Engrs; Fluid Power Soc; Coun Forest Eng; Int Soc Trop Foresters. *Res:* Off-highway vehicle design including simulation of agricultural tractors implements; research on quality control in cabinet and furniture (wood). *Mailing Add:* Dept Agr Eng Purdue Univ West Lafayette IN 47907. *Fax:* 765-496-1115; *E-Mail:* gibson@ecn.purdue.edu

GIBSON, HARRY WILLIAM, PHYSICAL ORGANIC CHEMISTRY. *Current Pos:* PROF DEPT CHEM, VA POLYTECH INST & STATE UNIV, 86- *Personal Data:* b Syracuse, NY, May 2, 41; m 62, Elizabeth Hurley; c Katherine J, Mark D & Christine M. *Educ:* Clarkson Col Technol, BS, 62, PhD(chem), 66. *Prof Exp:* Investr chem with Prof Ernest L Eliel, Univ Notre Dame, 65-66; res chemist, Res & Develop Lab, Chem Div, Union Carbide Corp, 66-69; scientist, Res Labs, Xerox Corp, 69-74, sr scientist, 74-82, sr mem res staff, 82-84, sr res scientist & dir allied signal, Eng Mat Res Ctr, 84-86. *Concurrent Pos:* Jones Laughlin scholar, 58-62; fel Nat Defense Educ Act, 62-65; vis lectr, Dept Chem, Univ Ill, 78; mem joint educ comt, Div Polymer Chem & Org Coatings & Plastics, Am Chem Soc, 79-84; co-ed, Polymer Educ Newsletter, Am Chem Soc, 81-83; adj prof, Dept Chem, Univ Rochester, 82-84; chmn, Rochester Sect, Am Chem Soc, 84; vis lectr, dept chem, Univ Ottawa, 85; participant, Mat Sci eng study, Nat Res Coun, Nat Acad Sci, 85. *Mem:* Am Chem Soc; Sigma Xi; Chem Inst Can. *Res:* Chemistry of Reissert and related compounds; chemical modification of polymers; electrical properties of organics; electrically conductive polymers; polymer synthesis and characterization; polyketones; novel polymer architectures-polyrotaxanes. *Mailing Add:* 4789 Susannah Dr Blacksburg VA 24060-8971. *Fax:* 540-231-8517

GIBSON, J MURRAY, ELECTRON MICROSCOPY, SEMICONDUCTOR PHYSICS. *Current Pos:* PROF PHYSICS, UNIV ILL, URBANA, 91- *Personal Data:* b Forres, Scotland, Mar 8, 54; m 80. *Educ:* Univ Aberdsen, Scotland, BSc, 75; Univ Cambridge, Eng, PhD(physics), 78. *Honors & Awards:* Burton Medal, Electron Micros Soc Am. *Prof Exp:* Res fel, Dept Physics, Univ Cambridge, 78 & Res Div, IBM, 78-80; mem tech staff, Iterface Physics Dept, Bell Labs, 80-87, distinguished mem tech staff & head electronics & photonics mat res dept, 87-91. *Mem:* Am Phys Soc; Inst Physics; Electron Micros Soc Am. *Res:* Ultra-high resolution electron microscopy applied to problems in solid-state physics and materials science. *Mailing Add:* Dept Physics Univ Ill 1110 W Green St Urbana IL 61801

GIBSON, JAMES (BENJAMIN), ASTROMETRY, PHOTOMETRY. *Current Pos:* RETIRED. *Personal Data:* b Ellensburg, Wash, June 9, 28; m 68; c 1. *Educ:* Univ Calif, Berkeley, AB, 52. *Prof Exp:* Physicist, Lawrence Livermore Lab, Univ Calif, 53-57; math analyst, Missiles & Space Div, Lockheed Aircraft Corp, 57-58; asst, Lick Observ, Univ Calif, 58-60; astronr, Flagstaff Sta, US Naval Observ, 60-61; res asst astron, Van Vleck Observ, Wesleyan Univ, 61-63, res assoc, 64-67; res asst, Observ, Yale Univ, 68-71; prin observer, Yale-Columbia Southern Observ, 71-74; tech officer astron, Univ Orange Free State, 74-76; consult, 76-78; mem tech staff, Jet Propulsion Lab, 78-86, optical astro engr, ITT, Fed Elec Corp & Jet Propulsion Lab, 86-88, optical astro engr, 88-96. *Concurrent Pos:* Res assoc, Inst Advan Study, 66-67; NASA res grant for eclipse exped, 66-67; vis astronr, Kitt Peak Nat Observ, 66-67; guest investr, Palomar Observ, 81- *Mem:* Fel AAAS; Am Astron Soc; fel Royal Astron Soc; Royal Astron Soc Can; Sigma Xi; Int Astron Union. *Res:* Observational astronomy; astrometry; comet and minor planet positions from photographic plates and charge coupled device frames; intermediate bandwidth photoelectric photometry; systematic errors of trigonometric parallaxes; spectroscopy and spectral classification; airborne optical instrumentation; variable stars in galactic and globular clusters; flare stars. *Mailing Add:* 6838 Greeley St Tujunga CA 91042

GIBSON, JAMES DARRELL, MECHANICAL ENGINEERING. *Current Pos:* dir grad studies, 79-87, PROF MECH ENG, ROSE-HULMAN INST TECHNOL, 72- *Personal Data:* b South Bend, Ind, Apr 8, 34; m; c 3. *Educ:* Purdue Univ, BS, 57, MS, 59; Univ NMex, PhD, 68. *Prof Exp:* Sr engr, Gen Dynamics Corp, 59-63; instr mech eng, Univ NMex, 63-68; assoc prof, Univ Wyo, 68-72. *Concurrent Pos:* NASA-Am Soc Eng Educ fel, Langley Res Ctr, 69, proj dir systems design fel prog, 71, 72 & 73. *Mem:* Am Soc Eng Educ; Inst Noise Control Eng; Am Soc Mech Engrs. *Res:* Vibrations and noise; mechanical design. *Mailing Add:* RR 1 Brazil IN 47834

GIBSON, JAMES EDWIN, PHARMACOLOGY, TOXICOLOGY. *Current Pos:* GLOBAL RES & DEVELOP DIR, DOW ELANCO, 90- *Personal Data:* b Des Moines, Iowa, Aug 22, 41; m 61; c 3. *Educ:* Drake Univ, BA, 64; Univ Iowa, MS, 67, PhD(pharmacol), 69. *Honors & Awards:* Achivement Award, Soc Toxicol. *Prof Exp:* Chemist, Chem Labs, Iowa State Dept Agr, 62-64; jr res scientist pharmacol, Neuropharmacol Div, Abbott Labs, Ill, 64-65; asst prof, Mich State Univ, 69-72, assoc prof pharmacol, 72-76; vpres & dir res, Chem Indust Inst Toxicol, 76-89; dir toxicol affairs, Dow Chem, 89-90. *Concurrent Pos:* Vis prof pharmacol, Univ Mainz, 75-76; US sr scientist award, Alexander von Humboldt Found, 75-76. *Mem:* AAAS; Soc Develop Biol; Am Soc Pharmacol & Exp Therapeut; Soc Toxicol; Teratology Soc. *Res:* Determination and description of drug or chemical induced teratogenicity, embryotoxicity and perinatal toxicity in mammals with particular emphasis on molecular mechanisms of action; teratology. *Mailing Add:* Dow Elanco 9330 Zionsville Rd Indianapolis IN 46268

GIBSON, JAMES H, ENVIRONMENTAL SCIENCES. *Current Pos:* DIR, USDA UVB MONITORING PROG, 95- *Personal Data:* b Morgantown, WVa, May 3, 30; c 2. *Educ:* WVa Univ, BS, 52; Cornell Univ, PhD(anal chem), 57. *Prof Exp:* Chemist, Eastman Kodak Co, NY, 57-60; fel & res assoc, Cornell Univ, 60-61; chief chem div, US Army Chem Corps, Dugway Proving Grounds, Utah, 61-63; assoc prof anal chem, Colo State Univ, 63-80, dir, Natural Resource Ecol Lab, 73-83, coordr, nat atmospheric deposition prog, 78-95. *Concurrent Pos:* Consult, US Army Chem Corps, Dugway Proving Ground, 63-65; NSF grants, 64-70 & 74-78; dir admin & serv, Natural Resource Ecol Lab, Colo State Univ, 71-73; dir grassland biome studies, US/Int Biol Prog, 74-78; chmn, US Grazinglands Comt & mem, US nat comt, Man & Biosphere Prog, UNESCO, 75-76 & 79-, mem comt 14, environ pollution, 82-; chmn, Comt Monitoring & Assessment Trends Acid Deposition, Nat Res Coun, 83-85; prin investr atmospheric deposition, Bur Land Mgt, 79-, USDA, 79- Nat Park Serv, 79-, Nat Oceanog & Atmospheric Admin, 81-, Environ Protection Agency, 83-, US Geol Survey, 83- & US Forest Serv, 85- *Mem:* AAAS; Am Chem Soc. *Res:* Measurements and monitoring of atmospheric deposition; effects in natural ecosystems; administration in areas of systems ecology and environmental sciences. *Mailing Add:* Natural Resources Ecol Lab Colo State Univ Ft Collins CO 80523

GIBSON, JAMES JOHN, ELECTRONICS ENGINEERING. *Current Pos:* CONSULT, SIGNAL SYST RES, 87- *Personal Data:* b St Albans, Eng, Mar 12, 23; US citizen; m 57; c 3. *Educ:* Royal Inst Technol, Sweden, CivIng, 47; Chalmers Inst Technol, Sweden, TekLic, 71. *Hon Degrees:* DEng, Chalmers Inst Technol, Sweden, 85. *Honors & Awards:* David Sarnoff Award, RCA Labs, 85. *Prof Exp:* Res engr electronics, Res Inst Nat Defense, Sweden, 46-52 & RCA Labs, 52-54; group head, Royal Inst Technol, Sweden, 54-56; mem tech staff, RCA LABS, 56-59, fel tech staff electronics, 69-87. *Concurrent Pos:* Fac mem, LaSalle Col, 71-73; mem, Cable Television Adv Comt, 72-75, Nat Quadrophonic Radio Comt, 72-75 & Digital Audio Stand Comt, 78-81; vis prof elec eng, Rutgers Univ, 78-; mem, Fed Commun Comn Adv Comt, tv receiver noise figures, 79-80; mem, Electronic Indust Asn Comt, tv multichannel sound, 82-85; mem admin comt, Inst Elec & Electronics Engrs, Consumer Electronics Soc, 87-89; chmn, Inst Elec & Electronics Engrs Masarulbuka Award subcomt, 87-89. *Mem:* Fel Inst Elec & Electronics Engrs; fel Audio Eng Soc; Soc Motion Picture & Television Engrs; AAAS; Sigma Xi. *Res:* Consumer electronic systems; solid state circuits; communication systems television and frequency modulation broadcast systems; antennas; computer memories. *Mailing Add:* Signal Syst Res 47 Castle Howard Ct Princeton NJ 08540-4025

GIBSON, JOHN E(GAN), ENGINEERING MANAGEMENT. *Current Pos:* COMMONWEALTH PROF & DEAN ENG & APPL SCI, UNIV VA, 73- *Personal Data:* b Providence, RI, June 11, 26; m 50; c 4. *Educ:* Univ RI, BS, 50; Yale Univ, ME, 52, PhD(elec eng), 56. *Prof Exp:* From instr to asst prof elec eng, Yale Univ, 52-57; from assoc prof to prof, Purdue Univ, 57-65, dir, Control & Info Syst Labs, 61-65; dean eng, Oakland Univ, 65-73, John Dodge Prof eng, 70-73. *Concurrent Pos:* Consult, various aerospace & electronics firms & Dept Com, 66-67; adv, Electronics Res Ctr, NASA, Mass, 66-70 & NSF, 81. *Mem:* Fel Inst Elec & Electronics Engrs; Am Soc Elec Engrs; Nat Soc Prof Engrs. *Res:* Nonlinear automatic control; large scale systems; transportation systems; urban system studies, long range planning and management of research and development. *Mailing Add:* 515 Rodes Dr Charlottesville VA 22903

GIBSON, JOHN KNIGHT, HIGH TEMPERATURE CHEMISTRY, ANTINIDE CHEMISTRY. *Current Pos:* RES STAFF, OAK RIDGE NAT LAB, 83- *Personal Data:* b Springfield, Mass, Oct 22, 57; m 82, Tomoko Nagai; c Kentaro. *Educ:* Boston Univ, BA, 79; Univ Calif, Berkeley, PhD(phys chem), 83. *Prof Exp:* Res asst, Lawrence Berkeley Lab, 79-83. *Mem:* Am Chem Soc. *Res:* Thermochemistry; solid state chemistry; high temperature chemistry; physicochemical properties of actinide and lanthanide elements and compounds; transplutonium element chemistry; mass spectrometry; laser ionization; laser ablation; thermal analysis; gas-phase reactions. *Mailing Add:* Chem & Analytical Sci Div Oak Ridge Nat Lab Oak Ridge TN 37831-6375

GIBSON, JOHN MICHAEL, NEUROPHYSIOLOGY, BIOENGINEERING. *Current Pos:* INSTR, ELEC ENG TECHNOL, HARRY-GEORGETOWN TECH COL, 97- *Personal Data:* b Franklin, Ky, Aug 11, 40; m 64. *Educ:* Univ Ky, BSEE, 63, PhD(physiol & biophys), 70. *Prof Exp:* Fel neurophysiol, Univ Wis-Madison, 70-73, asst scientist, 73-80, assoc scientist neurophysiol, 80-84, asst prof biometry, 84-88; asst prof otolaryngology, Med Univ SC, 88-90; instr eng technol, Savannah Tech, 91-95; instr eng technol, Cent Carolina Tech Col, 95-97. *Mem:* Soc Neurosci; Inst Elec & Electronics Engrs; Inst Elec & Electronics Engrs Comput Soc; Inst Elec & Electronics Engrs Med & Biol Soc; Int Neural Network Soc; Asn Comput Soc. *Res:* Computer simulation studies of artificial neural networks and their enhancement through simulated evolution and selection; application of engineering and computer techniques to the biomedical sciences. *Mailing Add:* 1109 Harts Bluff Rd Wadmalaw Island SC 29487

GIBSON, JOHN PHILLIPS, PATHOLOGY, VETERINARY MEDICINE. *Current Pos:* pathologist toxicol, Merrell-Dow Pharmaceut, Inc, 64-70, head, Dept Path & Toxicol, 70-90, dir drug safety assessment, 90-93, CONSULT, MERRELL DOW PHARMACEUT, INC, 94- *Personal Data:* b Pittsburg, Kans, Sept 18, 30; m 53, Mary L Heath; c 2. *Educ:* Kans State Univ, BS, 53, DVM & MS, 59; Ohio State Univ, PhD(vet path), 64. *Prof Exp:* Instr vet bact, Purdue Univ, 59-60; res assoc vet path, Ohio State Univ, 60-64. *Concurrent Pos:* Adj asst prof, Col Med, Univ Cincinnati, 65-90, adj assoc prof lab animal med, 72-90. *Mem:* Am Col Vet Path; Soc Toxicol; Int Acad Path; Soc Toxicol Pathologists; Teratol Soc; Am Vet Med Asn. *Res:* Veterinary and comparative pathology; toxicity testing of therapeutic agents; drug safety assessment. *Mailing Add:* 550 Woodbrook Lane Cincinnati OH 45215

GIBSON, JOSEPH W(HITTON), JR, CHEMICAL ENGINEERING. *Current Pos:* RETIRED. *Personal Data:* b Norristown, Pa, Feb 24, 22; m 46, Norma J Stewart; c Joseph W III, Winn S (Goheil) & Philip B. *Educ:* Worcester Polytech Inst, BS, 44. *Honors & Awards:* Olney Medal, Am Asn Textile Chemists & Colorists, 79. *Prof Exp:* Res chem engr fiber & dyeing, E I Du Pont De Nemours & Co, 46-51, res chem engr clothing comfort, 51-52 & 53-57, res chem engr leather-like prods, 52-53, res chem engr end use textiles, 57-67, sr res engr textile res, 67-79, sr tech specialist & group leader, Imaging Systs Mkt, 79-91. *Concurrent Pos:* Postgrad, Princeton Univ & Mass Inst Technol, 44-45; mem, Pantyhose Sizing Comt, Nat Asn Hosiery Mfr, 69-71. *Mem:* Am Chem Soc; hon mem Fiber Soc; Sigma Xi; Am Asn Textile Chemists & Colorists; Int Platform Asn. *Res:* Technical evaluations of photopolymer printing plates; preparation and evaluation of end use textiles; clothing comfort with human subjects; dyeing of synthetic fibers. *Mailing Add:* 1215 Hillside Blvd Carrcroft Wilmington DE 19803

GIBSON, JOYCE CORREY, BIOCHEMISTRY. *Current Pos:* MGR ATHEROSCLEROSIS BIOCHEM, CIBA-GEIGY CORP, NJ, 86- *Personal Data:* b Jan 5, 48; c 2. *Educ:* Mt Holyoke Col, AB, 70; Harvard Univ, MSc, 72, DSc(nutrit), 74. *Prof Exp:* Res asst, Dept Nutrit, Harvard Univ, 70, Dept Cell Cult, Strangeways Lab, Eng, 71; NIH postdoctoral fel, Dept Nutrit, Cornell Univ, 74-76; sci officer, Med Prof Unit, St Vincent's Hosp, Univ New South Wales, 76-79; asst prof med, Div Arteriosclerosis & Metab, Mt Sinai Sch Med, 79-83; res assoc prof, Dept Med, Sch Med, Univ Miami, 83-86. *Mem:* Assoc mem Sigma Xi; Am Heart Asn; AAAS; Am Inst Nutrit; Am Inst Clin Nutrit. *Res:* Author of numerous scientific journal articles. *Mailing Add:* Pharmaceut Div Ciba-Geigy Corp 556 Morris Ave Summit NJ 07901-1398. *Fax:* 908-277-5752

GIBSON, KATHLEEN RITA, PHYSICAL ANTRHOPOLOGY, NEUROANATOMY. *Current Pos:* From asst prof to assoc prof, 70-80, PROF ANAT, DENT BR, UNIV TEX HEALTH SCI CTR, HOUSTON, 80- *Personal Data:* b Philadelphia, Pa, Oct 9, 42. *Educ:* Univ Mich, Ann Arbor, BA, 63; Univ Calif, Berkeley, PhD(anthrop), 70. *Concurrent Pos:* Mem, Grad Sch Biomed Sci, Univ Tex, Houston, 71-; lectr anthrop, Rice Univ, 72-76, adj assoc prof, 81- *Mem:* AAAS; Am Anthrop Asn; Am Soc Primatologists; Am Asn Phys Anthrop; Am Anat Asn; Int Primatological Asn; Am Asn Dent Schs. *Res:* Comparative neurology; primate behavior; brain maturation; evolution of language, intelligence and tool use; dental evolution. *Mailing Add:* Dept Gross Anat Univ Tex Dent PO Box 20068 Houston TX 77225-3507

GIBSON, KENNETH DAVID, biochemistry, for more information see previous edition

GIBSON, LEE B, MICROPALEONTOLOGY & PALEONTOLOGY, ENVIRONMENTAL SCIENCES & MARINE GEOLOGY. *Current Pos:* GEOL CONSULT, INDEPENDENT OIL & GAS EXPLOR, 96- *Personal Data:* b Chicago, Ill, Mar 3, 26; m 53, Louise Stresino; c 1. *Educ:* Wash Univ, BA, 49, MA, 52; Univ Okla, PhD(geol, paleobot), 61. *Prof Exp:* Instr geol, Univ NH, 53-54; paleontologist, Creole Petrol Corp, Venezuela, 54-57; sr paleontologist, 57-59; sr res geologist, Mobil Oil Corp, 61-70, res assoc, Field Res Lab, 70-72, chief stratigrapher, Mobil Explor & Producing, 72-84; environ scientist, US Environ Protection Agency, 87-96. *Concurrent Pos:* Consult, 85-87; Rollin D Salisbury fel, Univ Chicago & Univ Okla. *Mem:* Am Asn Petrol Geol; Sigma Xi. *Res:* Paleoecology; application of animal population characteristics to paleoenvironmental interpretation in conjunction with the development of new biostatigraphic methodology; regional and applied biostratigraphy; eustatics, seismic stratigraphy, oil & gas explorationist, environmental science. *Mailing Add:* 10215 Epping Lane Dallas TX 75229

GIBSON, M JEAN, RADIATION THERAPY. *Current Pos:* MED PHYSICIST, COLUMBIA OGDEN REGIONAL MED CTR, 77- *Personal Data:* b Columbia, Utah, Dec 1, 30. *Educ:* Col St Benedict, BA, 56; Univ Iowa, MS, 66, PhD(physics), 69. *Prof Exp:* Asst prof physics, Col St Benedict, 69-75. *Mem:* Am Asn Physicists Med. *Mailing Add:* Ogden Regional Med Ctr 5475 S 500 E Ogden UT 84405. *Fax:* 801-479-2581; *E-Mail:* jgibson@jund.com

GIBSON, MARY MORTON, NEUROPHYSIOLOGY. *Current Pos:* Fel, Univ Wis-Madison, 70-73, ASST SCIENTIST RES AUDITORY & VISUAL NEUROPHYSIOL, DEPT NEUROPHYSIOL & OPHTHAL, 73- *Personal Data:* b Bardstown, Ky, Nov 20, 39; m 64. *Educ:* Univ Ky, BSME, 63, PhD(physiol & biophys), 70. *Mem:* AAAS; Acoust Soc Am; Soc Neurosci. *Res:* Single unit and intracranial and extracranial evoked potential studies of the auditory and visual pathways of animals. *Mailing Add:* 1109 Hartsbluff Rd Wadmalaw Island SC 29487

GIBSON, MELVIN ROY, PHARMACOGNOSY. *Current Pos:* From asst prof to prof, 49-85, EMER PROF, PHARMACOG, WASH STATE UNIV, 85. *Personal Data:* b St Paul, Nebr, June 11, 20. *Educ:* Univ Nebr, BS, 42, MS, 47; Univ Ill, PhD(pharmacog), 49;. *Hon Degrees:* DSc, Univ Nebr, 85. *Honors & Awards:* Nat Kappa Psi Citation for Serv to the Prof of Pharm, 61; R A Lyman Award, Am Asn Cols Pharm, 73. *Concurrent Pos:* Ed, Am J Pharmaceut Educ, 56-61; sr vis fel sci, Orgn Econ Coop & Develop, Neth & Sweden, 62; pres, Am Soc Pharmacog, 64-65; mem, US Pharmacopeia Rev Comt, 70-75; bd dir, Am Found Pharmaceut Educ, 80-85. *Mem:* Fel AAAS; NY Acad Sci; Int Pharmaceut Fedn; Am Inst Hist Pharm; Acad Pharmaceut Sci; Sigma Xi; hon mem Am Found Pharmaceut Educ. *Res:* Public health education for pharmacy students; enzyme-alkaloid relations in plants; sterile plant tissue culture; plant biosynthesis. *Mailing Add:* W 707 Sixth Ave 41 Spokane WA 99204

GIBSON, PETER MURRAY, MATHEMATICS. *Current Pos:* from asst prof to assoc prof, 67-74, PROF MATH, UNIV ALA, HUNTSVILLE, 74- *Personal Data:* b Laurel Hill, NC, Sept 1, 39; m 70. *Educ:* NC State Univ, BS, 61, MS, 63, PhD(math), 66. *Prof Exp:* Instr math, NC State Univ, 66-67. *Concurrent Pos:* Hon fel, Univ Wis-Madison, 74-75. *Mem:* Am Math Soc; Math Asn Am. *Res:* Combinatorial mathematics; linear algebra. *Mailing Add:* Dept Math Sci Univ Ala Huntsville AL 35899-0001

GIBSON, QUENTIN HOWIESON, PHYSIOLOGY, BIOPHYSICAL CHEMISTRY. *Current Pos:* DISTINGUISHED FAC PROF BIOCHEM, RICE UNIV, 96- *Personal Data:* b Aberdeen, Scotland, Dec 9, 18; m 51; c 4. *Educ:* Queen's Univ Belfast, MB, BCh, 41, MD, 44, PhD(biochem), 46, DSc, 51. *Prof Exp:* Demonstr physiol, Queen's Univ Belfast, 41-46, lectr, 46-47; lectr, Sch Med, Univ Sheffield, 47-55, prof biochem & chmn dept, 55-63; prof phys biochem & physiol, Sch Med, Univ Pa, 63-65; greater Philadelphia prof biochem, molecular & cell biol, Cornell Univ, 65-96. *Concurrent Pos:* Fogarty fel, NIH, 88; assoc ed, J Biol Chem. *Mem:* Nat Acad Sci; fel Royal Soc; Brit Physiol Soc; Am Acad Arts & Sci; Am Soc Biol Chem. *Res:* Etiology and biochemistry of idiopathic methemoglobinemia; hemoglobinometry; measurement of rapid reactions; mechanisms of enzyme reactions. *Mailing Add:* Dept Biochem Rice Univ 6100 Main St Houston TX 77005

GIBSON, RAYMOND EDWARD, RADIOPHARMACEUTICAL CHEMISTRY, RECEPTOR PHARMACOLOGY. *Current Pos:* from asst res prof to assoc res prof, Dept Radiol, George Wash Univ Med Ctr, 76-83, sr res scientist, 83-87, sr staff scientist, 87-88, ADJ ASSOC PROF, DEPT RADIOL, GEORGE WASHINGTON UNIV MED CTR, 88-; RES FEL, MERCK, SHARP & DOHME RES LAB, 88- *Personal Data:* b San Juan, PR, Oct 27, 46; m 80; c 2. *Educ:* Univ Calif, Santa Cruz, BA, 69; Univ Calif, Santa Barbara, PhD(chem), 72. *Prof Exp:* NIH postdoctoral fel, Dept Biol, Cornell Univ, 72-74, res assoc, 74-76. *Concurrent Pos:* Bd dir, Radiopharmaceut Sci Coun, Soc Nuclear Med, 88-90. *Mem:* Am Chem Soc; Soc Nuclear Med; AAAS. *Res:* Development of receptor-binding radiopharmaceuticals for clinical diagnosis and for basic pharmaceutical research. *Mailing Add:* Merck Sharp & Dohme Res Lab West Point PA 19486

GIBSON, ROBERT HARRY, ANALYTICAL CHEMISTRY. *Current Pos:* Assoc prof, 65-75, prof chem & chmn dept, 75-, EMER PROF CHEM, UNIV NC, CHARLOTTE. *Personal Data:* b Clover, SC, Jan 25, 38; m 60; c 2. *Educ:* Erskine Col, AB, 60; Columbia Univ, MA, 61, PhD(chem), 65. *Mem:* Am Chem Soc; AAAS; Electrochem Soc; Sigma Xi. *Res:* Electroanalytical chemistry; polarography; electrochemistry of organic compounds. *Mailing Add:* Dept Chem Univ NC 9201 Univ City Blvd Charlotte NC 28223-0001

GIBSON, ROBERT LEE, ASTRONAUTICS. *Current Pos:* Astronaut, NASA, 78-84, pilot, Shuttle Mission 41-B, 84, Shuttle Mission, 61-C, 86, spacecraft comdr, STS-27, 88, STS-47, 92, CHIEF ASTRONAUT OFF, NASA, HOUSTON, 92- *Personal Data:* b Cooperstown, NY, Oct 30, 46; m, Rhea Seddon; c Paul, Julie & Dann. *Educ:* Calif Polytech State Univ, BA, 69. *Mailing Add:* Astronaut Off Johnson Space Center NASA Houston TX 77058

GIBSON, ROSALIND SUSAN, NUTRITIONAL ASSESSMENT, TRACE ELEMENTS. *Current Pos:* PROF APPL HUMAN NUTRIT, DEPT FAMILY STUDIES, UNIV GUELPH, 79- *Personal Data:* b Northumberland, UK, Nov 20, 40; m 63; c 1. *Educ:* Univ London, BSc, 62 & PhD(nutrit), 79; Univ Calif Los Angeles, MS, 65. *Prof Exp:* Res biochemist, Inst Orthop, Univ London, 62-63; nutrit biochemist, Ethio-Swed Children's Nutrit Unit, Addis Ababa, Ethiopia, 65-68; lectr nutrit, Trinity & All Saints Col, 68-71 & Polytech NLondon, 71-78; res assoc nutrit, Dept Pediat, Dalhousie Univ, 77-78. *Concurrent Pos:* Mem health & welfare, Expert Comt Dietary Fibre, 84-85; vis prof, dept human nutrit, Univ Otago, Dunedin, NZ & Inst Med Res, Madang, Papua New Guinea, 86-87; coun mem, Int Union Nutrit Sci, 93- *Mem:* Can Soc Nutrit Sci (treas, 82-85); Can Dietetic Asn; Brit Nutrit Soc; Am Inst Nutrit. *Res:* Trace elements essential in human nutrition; assessment of trace element status of groups at risk for trace element deficiencies; use of hair as index of trace element status; nutritional assessment with emphasis on pre-school children in less industrialized countries. *Mailing Add:* Appl Human Nutrit Dept Family Studies Univ Otago PO Box 56 Dunedin New Zealand. *Fax:* 643-479-7958

GIBSON, SAM THOMPSON, INTERNAL MEDICINE, GOVERNMENT & REGULATORY. *Current Pos:* RETIRED. *Personal Data:* b Covington, Ga, Jan 1, 16; m 42, 86, Madge L Crouch; c Lena S, Stephen C, Judith T (Hammer) & Lucy F. *Educ:* Ga Inst Technol, BS, 36; Emory Univ, MD, 40. *Prof Exp:* Spec res assoc, Harvard Med Sch, 43; asst med dir, Blood Prog, Am Nat Red Cross, 49-51, assoc med dir, 51-53, assoc dir, 53-56, dir, 56-66, sr med officer, 57-67; asst dir, Div Biol Stand, NIH, 67-72; asst dir, Bur Biologics, FDA, 72-74, asst to dir, 74-77, dir, Div Biologics Eval, 77-83, dir, Div Biol Prod Compliance, 83-85, assoc dir sci & technol, Off Compliance, Ctr Drug Eval & Res, 85-88, dir sci & technol, Off Health Affairs, Rockville, MD, 88-89. *Concurrent Pos:* Med house officer, Peter Bent Brigham Hosp, 40-41, asst resident, 46-47, asst, 47-49; Res fel med, Harvard Med Sch, 41-42, Milton fel, 47-49; assoc, Sch Med, George Washington Univ, 49-63, asst clin prof, 63-, asst, Univ Hosp, 49-, clin asst prof med, Uniformed Serv, Univ Health Sci, 80-; consult, Nat Naval Med Ctr, Md, 50-63; adv blood transfusion serv, League Red Cross Socs, 55-66. *Mem:* Int Soc Blood Tranfusion; Am Soc Hemat; Int Soc Hemat; AMA; Am Fedn Clin Res. *Res:* Effect of serum albumin on kidney and liver function in disease; blood banking and plasma fractionation. *Mailing Add:* 5801 Rossmore Dr Bethesda MD 20814-2229

GIBSON, THOMAS ALVIN, JR, health physics; deceased, see previous edition for last biography

GIBSON, THOMAS CHOMETON, internal medicine, cardiology, for more information see previous edition

GIBSON, THOMAS GEORGE, INVERTEBRATE PALEONTOLOGY. *Current Pos:* GEOLOGIST, US GEOL SURV, PALEONT & STRATIG BR, US NAT MUS, 62- *Personal Data:* b Milwaukee, Wis, Aug 10, 34; m 56; c 3. *Educ:* Univ Wis, BS, 56, MS, 59; Princeton Univ, PhD(geol), 62. *Prof Exp:* Geologist, Shell Oil Co, 57. *Mem:* Paleont Soc; Marine Biol Asn UK. *Res:* Distribution and taxonomy of marine mollusca and foraminifera in the tertiary deposits of the Atlantic and Gulf coastal plains and the recent of the Atlantic Shelf. *Mailing Add:* 744 Kentland Dr Great Falls VA 22066

GIBSON, THOMAS RICHARD, POST-TRANSLATIONAL PROCESSING, BIOSYNTHESIS. *Current Pos:* RES ASST PROF, SAN DIEGO STATE UNIV, 86-; PRIN INVESTR, AM HEART ASN, 87- *Personal Data:* b Orange, CA, June 26, 51. *Educ:* Univ Calif, BS, 73, PhD(biochem), 79. *Prof Exp:* Res assoc, Harbor, Univ Calif, Los Angeles, Med Ctr, 79-82. *Mem:* Am Soc Biochem & Molecular Biol; Am Soc Hypertension. *Res:* Atrial Natrionetic Factor is produced in the heart and acts on the kidney; biosynthesis and processing of Atrial Natrionetic Factor. *Mailing Add:* Dept Biol San Diego State Univ 5500 Campanile Dr San Diego CA 92182

GIBSON, THOMAS WILLIAM, ORGANIC CHEMISTRY. *Current Pos:* RETIRED. *Personal Data:* b Petoskey, Mich, Oct 11, 35; m 60; c 5. *Educ:* Aquinas Col, BS, 59; Purdue Univ, PhD(chem), 63. *Prof Exp:* Res chemist, Miami Valley Labs, Procter & Gamble Co, 63-91. *Mem:* Am Chem Soc. *Res:* Organic synthesis, especially as applied to naturally occurring terpenoids; photochemistry of various classes of organic compounds. *Mailing Add:* 6250 Lake Leelanau Dr Traverse City MI 49684-9540

GIBSON, WALTER MAXWELL, EXPERIMENTAL PHYSICS. *Current Pos:* prof physics & chmn dept, 76-84, vpres res & dean grad studies, 84-86, DISTINGUISHED PROF PHYSICS, STATE UNIV NY, ALBANY, 88- *Personal Data:* b Enoch, Utah, Nov 11, 30; m 53, 67; c 7. *Educ:* Univ Utah, BS, 54; Univ Calif, PhD(nuclear chem), 56. *Prof Exp:* Mem tech staff, Bell Tel Labs, 59-76. *Concurrent Pos:* Res collabr, Brookhaven Nat Labs, 60-; adj prof, Rensselaer Polytech Inst, 63-76 & Rutgers Univ, 63-76; ed, Radiation Effects, 84-88. *Mem:* Fel Am Phys Soc; Am Vacuum Soc; Sigma Xi; AAAS. *Res:* Nuclear and solid state physics, principally nuclear fission mechanism studies; principles and application of solid state detectors and interaction of charged particles with crystalline and amorphous media, surfaces, structure and dynamics. *Mailing Add:* Dept Physics State Univ NY 1400 Washington Ave Albany NY 12222. *E-Mail:* gidal@beauty.1.lbl.gov

GIBSON, WILLIAM ANDREW, HISTOCHEMISTRY, CYTOCHEMISTRY. *Current Pos:* INSTR, BIOL DEPT, UNIV NEW ORLEANS. *Educ:* Georgetown Univ, PhD(path), 76. *Prof Exp:* Asst dean grad study & res, Baylor Col Dent, 86- *Mailing Add:* 4708 Jeannette Dr Metairie LA 70003. *Fax:* 504-286-6121

GIBSON, WILLIAM LOANE, mathematical analysis, software engineering, for more information see previous edition

GIBSON, WILLIAM RAYMOND, PHARMACOLOGY. *Current Pos:* RETIRED. *Personal Data:* b Murphysboro, Ill, Oct 21, 23; m 46; c 2. *Educ:* Butler Univ, BS, 48, MS, 56. *Prof Exp:* Pharmacologist, Eli Lilly & Co, 56-63, asst head biol qual control, 63-65, head, Toxicity Dept, 65-77, dir toxicol planning, 77-79; consult toxicol, 79-90. *Concurrent Pos:* Lectr, Butler Univ, 58-61, res assoc toxicol, 80-87. *Mem:* Soc Toxicol; Sigma Xi. *Res:* Pharmacology of anesthetics, sedatives, antihistamines and anticholinergics; toxicology of drugs and agricultural chemicals. *Mailing Add:* 12026 Castle Row Overlook Carmel IN 46032

GIBSON, WILLIAM WALLACE, ENTOMOLOGY. *Current Pos:* from asst prof to assoc prof, 62-68, PROF BIOL, STEPHEN F AUSTIN STATE UNIV, 68- *Personal Data:* b Philadelphia, Pa, Sept 26, 28; m 51; c 3. *Educ:* Univ RI, BS, 51; Kans State Univ, MS, 55, PhD(entom), 57. *Prof Exp:* Jr asst entom & plant path, Univ Exp Sta, Univ RI, 52, asst zool, 52-53; asst entom, Kans State Univ, 53-56; cur insect collection, Rockefeller Found Mex Agr Prog, 56-58; entomologist, Assoc Seed Growers, Inc, 58-61; temporary asst prof biol, Northeast La State Col, 62. *Mem:* Entom Soc Am; Mex Soc Entom; Sigma Xi. *Res:* Biological and ecological investigations of insects; taxonomy of scarab dung beetles. *Mailing Add:* Dept Biol Stephen F Austin State Univ PO Box 13003 Nacogdoches TX 75962-0001

GICLAS, HENRY LEE, ASTRONOMY. *Current Pos:* Res asst astron, Lowell Observ, 31-42, astronr, 42-81, exec officer, 53-75, EMER ASTRONOMER, LOWELL OBSERV, 86- *Personal Data:* b Flagstaff, Ariz, Dec 9, 10; m 36, Bernice Kent; c Henry L Jr. *Educ:* Univ Ariz, BS, 37. *Hon Degrees:* DSc, Northern Ariz Univ, 80. *Concurrent Pos:* Adj prof, Ohio State Univ, 68-81; exec vpres, Raymond Educ Found, Ariz, 71-77, pres, 77-91; adj prof, Northern Ariz Univ, 72-90. *Mem:* Fel AAAS; Int Astron Union; Am Astron Soc. *Res:* Photographic and photoelectric photometry; positional astrometry, comets and minor planets; proper motion survey. *Mailing Add:* 120 E Elm Ave Flagstaff AZ 86001. *Fax:* 520-774-6296

GICLAS, PATRICIA C, BIOCHEMISTRY, IMMUNOPATHOLOGY. *Current Pos:* sr investr, Dept Pediat, Nat Jewish Hosp & Res Ctr, 80-89, CO-DIR, DIAG IMMUNOL LAB, NAT JEWISH CTR IMMUNOL RESPIRATORY MED, 89- *Personal Data:* b Albuquerque, NMex. *Educ:* NMex Inst Mining & Technol, BS, 70; Univ Ariz, PhD(molecular biol), 76. *Prof Exp:* Fel, Scripps Clin & Res Found, 75-77; fel, Nat Jewish Hosp & Res Ctr, 77-79, res assoc, 79-80. *Concurrent Pos:* Instr, Dept Med, Health Sci Ctr, Univ Colo, 79-80, asst prof, Pulmonary Div, 80- *Mem:* AAAS; Am Soc Microbiol; Am Asn Immunologists; NY Acad Sci; Int Soc Develop & Comp Immunol. *Res:* Biochemistry of complement activation and complement-mediated aspects of acute inflammation particularly as related to pulmonary disease; mechanisms of protein synthesis and turnover in acute inflammation. *Mailing Add:* Immunodiagnostic Lab Nat Jewish Ctr Immunol & Respiratory Med 1400 N Jackson Denver CO 80206-2761

GICQUAUD, CLAUDE R, CELL MOTILITY, MEMBRANE BIOLOGY. *Current Pos:* PROF BIOCHEM, UNIV QUE, TROIS-RIVIERES, 75-, DIR, RES GROUP, 83- *Personal Data:* b Grenoble, France, Apr 12, 43. *Educ:* INSA, France, Ingineer, 66; Univ Montreal, Can, MSc, 68, PhD(biol), 72. *Prof Exp:* Postdoctoral, Osaka Univ, Japan, 72-75. *Mem:* Am Soc Cell Biol; Fr Can Asn Advan Sci. *Res:* Cell motility with emphasis on the interactions between the microfilaments and membrane lipids; bidimensional crystallization of proteins. *Mailing Add:* Univ Que CP 500 Trois-Rivieres PQ G9A 5H7 Can. *Fax:* 819-376-5084; *E-Mail:* claude_gicquaud@uqtr.uquebec.cca

GIDAL, GEORGE, EXPERIMENTAL HIGH ENERGY PHYSICS. *Current Pos:* SR STAFF PHYSICIST, LAWRENCE BERKELEY LAB, 66- *Personal Data:* b Munich, Ger, Sept 8, 34; US citizen; m 62; c 2. *Educ:* Columbia Univ, AB, 55, MA, 57, PhD(physics), 60. *Prof Exp:* Res assoc physics, Lawrence Radiation Lab, 60-61; res physicist, Inst Physics, Torino, Italy, 64-65. *Concurrent Pos:* Vis assoc prof, Tel Aviv Univ, 69-70. *Mem:* Am Phys Soc. *Res:* Strong interactions of particles; measurements of interaction mechanisms via details of production and decay distributions; backward inelastic scattering; electron-positron interactions; photon-photon interactions. *Mailing Add:* Lawrence Berkeley Lab 50-346 Univ Calif Berkeley CA 94720

GIDARI, ANTHONY SALVATORE, PHARMACOLOGY, HEMATOLOGY. *Current Pos:* from instr to asst prof med, 72-77, asst prof, 77-80, ASSOC PROF PHARMACOL, STATE UNIV NY DOWNSTATE MED CTR, 80- *Personal Data:* b Cambridge, Mass, Sept 20, 43. *Educ:* Tufts Univ, BS, 65; NY Univ, MS, 70, PhD(physiol, hemat), 72. *Prof Exp:* Asst res scientist hemat & physiol, Lab Exp Hemat, NY Univ, 71-72. *Mem:* Am Soc Pharmacol & Exp Therapeut. *Res:* Biochemistry and physiology of blood cell formation including the regulation of erythropoiesis by the hormone erythropoietin; mechanism of action of vasodilator agents. *Mailing Add:* Dept Pharmacol Box 29 State Univ NY Health Sci Ctr 450 Clarkson Ave Brooklyn NY 11203-2098. *Fax:* 718-270-2241

GIDDA, JASWANT SINGH, AUTONOMIC PHARMACOLOGY, GASTROENTEROLOGY. *Current Pos:* Res scientist pharmacol, 87-92, SR RES SCIENTIST, LILLY RES LAB, ELI LILLY & CO, 92-, GROUP LEADER, 93- *Personal Data:* b Hoshiarpur, Panjab, India, Oct 1, 46; US citizen; m 75; c 2. *Educ:* Panjab Univ, India, BSc, 65, Hons, 67, MSc, 68, PhD(biol), 73. *Prof Exp:* Res scientist neurobiol, Univ Tex, Dallas, 74-78, instr gastroenterol, Health Sci Ctr, San Antonio, 78-81; instr, Harvard Med Sch, 81-84; sr res scientist pharmacol, Bristol-Myers Co, Syracuse, 84-87. *Concurrent Pos:* Lectr pharmacol, Harvard Med Sch, 84-87; asst res prof physiol, State Univ NY, New York, 85-87; adj assoc prof physiol & biol, Ind Univ Med Ctr, Indianapolis. *Mem:* Am Motility Soc; Am Gastroenterol Asn; Am Physiol Soc. *Res:* Understanding the neuromuscular mechanisms which control motility and secretion in the gastrointestinal tract. *Mailing Add:* Eli Lilly & Co Lilly Res Labs 0815 Lilly Corp Ctr Indianapolis IN 46285

GIDDENS, DON P(EYTON), FLUID MECHANICS, GAS DYNAMICS. *Current Pos:* DEAN ENG, WHITING SCH ENG, JOHNS HOPKINS UNIV, 92- *Personal Data:* b Augusta, Ga, Oct 24, 40; m 57, Karen Baldzer; c 4. *Educ:* Ga Inst Technol, BAE, 63, MSAE, 65, PhD(aerospace eng), 66. *Prof Exp:* Assoc aircraft engr, Lockheed-Ga Co, 63; mem tech staff, Aerospace Corp, Calif, 66-67; assoc prof, Ga Inst Technol, 68-70, prof, 77-82, regents prof mech eng, 82-92, dir aero eng, 88-92. *Concurrent Pos:* Fel, NDEA, 63-66; nat lectr, Sigma Xi Res Soc, 84-87. *Mem:* Sigma Xi; fel Am Asn Mech Engrs; Am Inst Aeronaut & Astronaut; Am Soc Eng Educ; fel Am Heart Asn; fel Am Inst Med & Biol Engr. *Res:* Fluid mechanics of the cardiovascular system and the application to medical problems; rarefied gas dynamics; turbulent flows. *Mailing Add:* Johns Hopkins Univ 3400 N Charles St Baltimore MD 21218-2694

GIDDENS, JOEL EDWIN, SOIL MICROBIOLOGY. *Current Pos:* RETIRED. *Personal Data:* b Eastman, Ga, Feb 11, 17; wid; c 3. *Educ:* Univ Ga, BS, 40, MS, 42; Rutgers Univ, PhD(soils), 50. *Prof Exp:* Asst, Univ Ga, 40-42; jr chemist, Southern Regional Res Lab, USDA, 42-45; asst agronomist, Univ Ga, 46-48, 50-52, assoc prof, 52-59, prof agron, 59-85. *Mem:* Fel Am Soc Agron; Soil Sci Soc Am; Am Chem Soc; Am Soc Microbiol; Soil Conserv Soc Am. *Res:* Soil fertility; nitrogen fixation by plants; waste management. *Mailing Add:* 315 Parkway Dr Athens GA 30606

GIDDENS, WILLIAM ELLIS, JR, VETERINARY PATHOLOGY. *Current Pos:* RETIRED. *Personal Data:* b Dublin, Ga, Oct 8, 37; m 61, Kathleen Walsh; c Bryce. *Educ:* Iowa State Univ, DVM, 61; Mich State Univ, PhD(path), 68. *Prof Exp:* NIH fel path, Mich State Univ, 65-67, res instr, 67-68; asst prof, Univ Wash, 68-78, assoc prof path, Div Animal Med, Sch Med, 78-87. *Mem:* Am Col Vet Path; Am Vet Med Asn; Int Acad Path. *Res:* Comparative pathology; respiratory diseases of animals and man; pathogenesis of virus diseases of nonhuman primates. *Mailing Add:* 150 Live Oak Lane Labelle FL 33935

GIDDINGS, GEORGE GOSSELIN, FOOD PROCESSING, FOOD ENGINEERING. *Current Pos:* RADIATION PROCESSING CONSULT, 87- *Personal Data:* b Worcester, Mass, Mar 26, 37; m 66, Gertraud M Borst; c Thomas E & Erika M. *Educ:* Univ Mass, BSc, 63; Mich State Univ, MSc, 69, PhD(food sci & technol), 72. *Prof Exp:* Res food technologist, US Army, Res & Develop Command, Natick, Mass, 63-66; res assoc, Mich State Univ, 66-72; prof food sci, NC State Univ, 72-77; sr tech adv & mgr food technol, Fundacion Chile, 77-81; dir food appl, Radiation Technol, Inc, 81-83; dir food irradiation serv, Isomedix Inc, NJ, 83-87. *Mem:* Am Chem Soc; Inst Food Technologists. *Res:* Meat pigment chemistry and biochemistry; radiation preservation of foods. *Mailing Add:* 61 Beech Rd Randolph NJ 07869. *Fax:* 973-887-1476

GIDDINGS, JOHN CALVIN, physical chemistry; deceased, see previous edition for last biography

GIDDINGS, THOMAS H, JR, ELECTRON MICROSCOPY, MICROBIOLOGY. *Current Pos:* MEM STAFF, DEPT MOLECULAR BIOL, UNIV COLO. *Educ:* Univ Colo, PhD(biol). *Mailing Add:* Dept Molecular & Cellular Develop Biol Univ Colo Boulder CO 80309-0347

GIDDINGS, WILLIAM PAUL, PHYSICAL ORGANIC CHEMISTRY. *Current Pos:* RETIRED. *Personal Data:* b Indianapolis, Ind, May 7, 33; m 61, Rochelle Sherman; c 3. *Educ:* DePauw Univ, BA, 54; Harvard Univ, MA, 56, PhD(phys org chem), 59. *Prof Exp:* Res instr chem, Univ Wash, 59-60; asst prof, Albion Col, 60-62; from asst prof to assoc prof chem, Pac Lutheran Univ, 62-68, chmn dept, 66-70 & 83-89, chmn, Div Natural Sci, 69-75, prof chem, 68-96. *Concurrent Pos:* NSF res grant, 64-66; Petrol Res Fund res grant, 66-69; vis scholar, Dept Civil Eng & Atmospheric Sci, Univ Wash, 76 & Dept Environ Health, 89-90; Exchange pro, Sichuan Union Univ, 86 & 92. *Mem:* Am Chem Soc; Sigma Xi; AAAS; Am Asn Univ Prof. *Res:* Nature of carbonium ion intermediates in solvolysis reactions; atmospheric chemistry of organic compounds. *Mailing Add:* 12211 C St S Tacoma WA 98444

GIDEZ, LEWIS IRWIN, BIOCHEMISTRY. *Current Pos:* asst prof, 58-69, ASSOC PROF BIOCHEM, ALBERT EINSTEIN COL MED, 69- *Personal Data:* b Boston, Mass, Jan 27, 27; m 55; c 5. *Educ:* Iowa State Col, BS, 48; Harvard Univ, PhD(biochem), 53. *Prof Exp:* Asst med biochemist, Med Dept, Brookhaven Nat Lab, 52-58. *Concurrent Pos:* Estab investr, Am Heart Asn, 58-63; career scientist, Health Res Coun, NY, 64-70; exec ed, J Lipid Res, 70- *Mem:* Am Chem Soc; Am Soc Biol Chem. *Res:* Chemistry and metabolism of lipids and lipoproteins. *Mailing Add:* 9650 Rockville Pike Bethesda MD 20814-3998. *Fax:* 301-571-1855

GIDLEY, J(OHN) L(YNN), CHEMICAL & PETROLEUM ENGINEERING. *Current Pos:* VIS PROF PETROL ENG, TEX A&M, 92- *Personal Data:* b Lytle, Tex, Dec 30, 24; m 59; c 7. *Educ:* Univ Tex, BS, 50, MS, 52, PhD(chem eng), 55. *Honors & Awards:* Distinguished Serv Award, Soc Petrol Engrs, 90, John Franklin Carll Award, 92. *Prof Exp:* Sr res engr, Prod Res Div, Humble Oil & Refining Co, 54-63; new uses adv, Stand Oil Co, NJ, 63-64, res assoc, Prod Res Div, Esso Prod Res Co, 64-68; hq supvr engr, Exxon Co, USA, 68-69, from tech adv to sr tech adv, 69-86, consult, 86. *Concurrent Pos:* Distinguished lectr, Soc Petrol Engrs, 80-81, emer distinguished lectr, 89-90. *Mem:* Nat Acad Eng; Am Chem Soc; Soc Petrol Engrs. *Res:* Well stimulation methods; sand control, cementing, perforating; engineering training. *Mailing Add:* 5211 Caversham Dr Houston TX 77096. *Fax:* 713-665-3307

GIDLEY, JAMES SCOTT, CIVIL ENGINEERING, OPERATIONS RESEARCH. *Current Pos:* ASSOC PROF CIVIL ENG & CHMN ENG, GENEVA COL, 90- *Personal Data:* b New Bedford, Mass, Oct 30, 54. *Educ:* Univ RI, BSc, 75; Harvard Univ, MS, 76, PhD(environ eng), 81. *Honors & Awards:* State-of-the-Art Civil Eng Award, Am Soc Civil Engrs, 86. *Prof Exp:*

From asst prof to assoc prof civil eng, WVa Univ, 81-90. *Concurrent Pos:* Vpres, Gidley Labs Inc. *Mem:* Am Soc Civil Engrs; Water Environ Fedn; Am Soc Eng Educ; Am Geophys Union; Asn Ground Water Scientists & Engrs; Am Soc Testing & Mat. *Res:* Optimization methods applied to water resource systems design and gas production from the anaerobic decomposition of organic wastes in sanitary landfills. *Mailing Add:* 141 Nelson Ave New Brighton PA 15066

GIDWANI, RAM N, BIOPHARMACEUTICS, PHYSICAL PHARMACY. *Current Pos:* SR SCIENTIST, IMMUNOBIOL RES INST, JOHNSON & JOHNSON, 88- *Personal Data:* b India, Mar 11, 36; US citizen; m 73; c 2. *Educ:* L M Col Pharm, India, BS, 58; St John's Univ, MS, 59; Univ Alta, PhD(biopharmaceut), 75. *Prof Exp:* Res pharmacist res & develop, Warner Lambert, NJ, 69-70; res pharmacist, Miles Labs, Ind, 70-71; asst prof pharmaceut, Arnold & Marie Schwartz Col Pharm, Brooklyn, NY, 75-77; sr scientist res & develop, Block Drug Co, NJ, 78; sr scientist res & develop, USV Pharmaceut, 78-80; sr scientist, FMC, Maine, 80-82; sr scientist, Sandoz Labs, Neb, 82-86; sr scientist, NIH, Md, 86-88. *Concurrent Pos:* Fel Nuclear Med Res Labs, Univ Calif, Los Angeles, 75. *Mem:* Am Pharmaceut Asn; Acad Pharmaceut Sci; Soc Cosmetic Chemists; Fedn Am Soc Exp Biol. *Res:* Evaluation of solid dispersion systems; differential thermal analysis; solubility; dissolution; bioavailability and pharmacokinetic studies. *Mailing Add:* 43 Gridley Circle Milford NJ 08848

GIEBISCH, GERHARD HANS, PHYSIOLOGY. *Current Pos:* prof & chmn, Dept Physiol, 68-73, STERLING PROF CELLULAR & MOLECULAR PHYSIOL, SCH MED, YALE UNIV, 70- *Personal Data:* b Vienna, Austria, Jan 17, 27; US citizen; m 52, Ilse; c 2. *Educ:* Univ Vienna, MD, 51. *Hon Degrees:* DLitt, Univ Uppsala, 77 & Univ Bern, 79; Dr, Univ Lausanne, 91 & Univ Vienna, 96. *Honors & Awards:* Homer Smith Award, 71; Johannes Muller Medal, Ger Physiol Soc, 80; Alexander von Humboldt Prize, 87; Volhard Medal, Ger Nephrological Soc, 88; Ernst Jung Prize Med, 90; A N Richards Award Int Soc Nephrology, 92; Berliner Award, Am Soc Nephrology, 94. *Prof Exp:* Instr pharmacol, Med Sch, Univ Vienna, 51, asst prof, 56-57; intern, Milwaukee Hosp, 52-53; fel physiol, Med Col, Cornell Univ, 53-54, instr, 55-56, from asst prof to prof, 57-68. *Concurrent Pos:* Estab investr, Am Heart & Asn, 57-62; pub health res career award, 62-68; mem, Physiol Study Sect, NIH, 64-69 & 82-84; NIH career award, 65-68; sect ed, Kidney & Electrolyte Metab, Am J Physiol, Am J Appl Physiol, 67-69; mem, Renal Dis & Urol Training Grant Study Sect, 70-73; hon prof, Univ Lausanne, 74-75; fac scholar award, Josiah Macy, Jr Found, 74-75; mem coun, Soc Gen Physiol, 80-82, Am Physiol Soc, 88-90 & Nat Inst Diabetes, Digestive Dis & Kidney Dis, 88-93; Wellcome vis prof, 83; ed, Physiol Rev, 85-90. *Mem:* Nat Acad Sci; Soc Gen Physiologists (pres, 86-87); Am Physiol Soc; Biophys Soc; Am Soc Nephrology (pres, 71-72); Soc Clin Res; Am Acad Arts & Sci. *Res:* Electrolyte metabolism; renal physiology, particularly studies on single nephrons, employing methods of micropuncture. *Mailing Add:* Dept Cellular & Molecular Physiol Yale Univ Sch Med 333 Cedar St New Haven CT 06520-8026. *Fax:* 203-785-4951

GIEDT, W(ARREN) H(ARDING), MECHANICAL ENGINEERING, MATERIALS SCIENCE. *Current Pos:* prof, 65-83, head dept, 65-69, assoc dean grad study, Col Eng, 72-80, EMER PROF MECH ENG, UNIV CALIF, DAVIS, 83- *Personal Data:* b Leola, SDak, Nov 1, 20; m 50. *Educ:* Univ Calif, Berkeley, BAS, 44, MS, 46, PhD(mech eng), 50. *Honors & Awards:* Jennings Award, Am Welding Soc, 70; Western Elec Award, Am Soc Eng Educ, 71, G Edwin Burks Award, 74; Heat Transfer Mem Award, Am Soc Mech Engrs, 76, James Harry Potter Gold Medal, 85; Thermal Eng Mem Award, Japan Soc Mech Eng, 90. *Prof Exp:* From instr to prof mech eng, Univ Calif, Berkeley, 47-65. *Concurrent Pos:* Serv engr, Babcock & Wilcox Co, 50; consult, Bechtel Corp, 51; proj leader, Detroit Controls Corp, 52-56; consult, Am Standard Corp, 56-65; Lawrence Livermore Nat Lab, 60-, Boeing Co, 62-66 & Sandia Nat Labs, 83-; Fulbright prof, Univ Tokyo, 63; consult, NASA, 64-67; ed, J Heat Transfer, 67-72; fel, Japan Soc Prom Sci, 88. *Mem:* Fel Am Soc Mech Eng; Am Welding Soc; Am Soc Eng Educ. *Res:* Heat transfer; thermodynamics; welding. *Mailing Add:* 111 W Winnie Way Arcadia CA 91007

GIEGEL, JOSEPH LESTER, CLINICAL BIOCHEMISTRY. *Current Pos:* PRES, DIAMEDIX CORP, 85- *Personal Data:* b New York, NY, June 27, 38; m 64; c 3. *Educ:* Univ Miami, BS, 62, PhD(microbiol), 68. *Prof Exp:* Instr dermat & microbiol, Sch Med, Univ Miami, 68-70; dir clin chem res & develop, Dade Div, Am Hosp Supply Corp, 70-85. *Concurrent Pos:* Tech dir, La Huis Clin Labs, Miami, Fla, 68-70. *Mem:* Am Chem Soc; Am Asn Clin Chemists; Sigma Xi. *Res:* Diagnostic procedures of research and development in clinical chemistry and immunology. *Mailing Add:* 8395 SW 78th St Miami FL 33143

GIELISSE, PETER JACOB MARIA, MINERALOGY, CRYSTALLOGRAPHY. *Current Pos:* PROF ENG, FLA STATE UNV, 87- *Personal Data:* b 's-Hertogenbosch, Netherlands, Mar 7, 34; US citizen; m 56; c 2. *Educ:* Boston Col, MS, 59; Ohio State Univ, PhD(mineral), 61. *Prof Exp:* Res engr physics, Comstock & Wescott, Inc, Mass, 57-59; Res Found fel, Ohio State Univ, 59-61; res physicist, Air Force Cambridge Res Labs, Mass, 61-63; res engr solid state physics, Metall Prod Dept, Gen Elec Co, Detroit, 63-68; prof mat & chmn eng, Univ RI, 68-80. *Concurrent Pos:* Res asst geophys, Boston Col, 58-59, instr geol & geophys, 61-63. *Mem:* Am Geophys Union; Am Mineral Soc. *Res:* Thermochemical mineralogy; physical, structural and optical properties of materials; phase equilibria in multi-component systems; crystal synthesis; very high pressure-high temperature materials; semiconductor devices. *Mailing Add:* 5667 Santa Anita Dr Tallahassee FL 32308

GIERASCH, LILA MARY, BIOPHYSICAL CHEMISTRY. *Current Pos:* ROBERT A WELCH PROF BIOCHEM & PHARMACOL, UNIV TEX SOUTHWESTERN, DALLAS, 88-, CHAIR, MOLECULAR BIOPHYS GRAD PROG, MED CTR, 91- *Personal Data:* b Needham, Mass, Sept 18, 48; m 91, John Pylant. *Educ:* Mt Holyoke Col, AB, 70; Harvard Univ, PhD(biophys), 75. *Honors & Awards:* Vincent Du Vigneaud Award, 84; Mary Lyon Award, 85. *Prof Exp:* Teaching fel, Harvard Univ, 72-73; asst prof chem, Amherst Col, 74-79 & Univ Del, 79-81; from assoc prof to prof chem, Univ Del, 81-87. *Concurrent Pos:* A P Sloan fel, 84-86; Guggenheim fel, 86; coun Am Peptide Soc, 93-99; exec coun, Div Biochem, Am Chem Soc, 94- *Mem:* Am Chem Soc; fel AAAS; NY Acad Sci; Biophys Soc; Am Soc Biol Chemists; assoc Int Union Pure Appl Chem; Am Peptide Soc; Biophys Soc (pres elect, 94). *Res:* Conformational analysis of peptides and proteins by nuclear magnetic resonance, CD and other spectroscopic methods; biophysical approaches to protein folding and localization in vivo. *Mailing Add:* Dept Chem Univ Mass Box 34510 Amherst MA 01003-4510. *Fax:* 413-545-0011; *E-Mail:* gierasch@utsw.swmed.edu

GIERASCH, PETER JAY, ASTRONOMY. *Current Pos:* assoc prof, 72-80, PROF ASTRON, CORNELL UNIV, 80- *Personal Data:* b Washington, DC, Dec 19, 40; m 64; c 2. *Educ:* Harvard Univ, BA, 62, PhD(appl math), 68. *Prof Exp:* Asst prof meteorol, Fla State Univ, 69-72. *Concurrent Pos:* Res fel, Alfred P Sloan Found, 75. *Mem:* Am Meteorol Soc; Am Astron Soc; Int Astron Union. *Res:* Atmospheric motions on planets; solar convection. *Mailing Add:* Dept Astron Cornell Univ 426 Space Sci Ithaca NY 14853-6801

GIERE, FREDERIC ARTHUR, MAMMALIAN PHYSIOLOGY. *Current Pos:* prof & chmn, 62-88, EMER PROF & CHMN BIOL DEPT, LAKE FOREST COL, 88- *Personal Data:* b Galesville, Wis, Dec 10, 23; m 55, Hazel M Teien; c Nils F, John E & Martha M (Glende). *Educ:* Luther Col, AB, 47; Syracuse Univ, MS, 51; Univ NMex, PhD(physiol), 53. *Prof Exp:* Instr biol, Luther Col, 47-49; asst zool, Syracuse Univ, 49-51; asst physiol, Univ NMex, 51-53, asst prof, 53-55; assoc prof biol, Luther Col, 55-62. *Concurrent Pos:* Lectr, Univ SDak, 61; consult, Argonne Nat Lab, 67-84; USPHS fel, Inst Work Physiol, Oslo, Norway, 68-69; vis scientist molecular anat prog, Argonne Nat Lab, 77-78 & 84-85; consult, Abbott Labs, 78-82, Nat Bureau Standards, 83; adj prof, Northwestern Univ, 88-, Barat Col, 93-96. *Mem:* Fel AAAS; Am Soc Zool; Am Physiol Soc; Soc Exp Biol & Med; NY Acad Sci; Electrophoresis Soc. *Res:* Water and electrolyte metabolism; 2-D SDS electrophoresis of tissues and urine metabolites, work physiology. *Mailing Add:* N33 W7215 Buchanan St Cedarburg WI 53012-2214

GIERER, PAUL L, ORGANIC CHEMISTRY. *Current Pos:* CONSULT, SOLERA LABS, 92- *Personal Data:* b New York, NY. *Educ:* City Univ NY, BA, 59; Southern Ill Univ, PhD(chem), 72. *Prof Exp:* Chemist, GAF Corp, 63-66; res chemist, Mallinckrodt, Inc, 73-81; tech mgr, Witco Chem Co, 81-83; mgr client servs, Eldib Eng & Res, 83-91. *Mem:* Am Chem Soc. *Res:* Drug chemicals; organometallics; heterocycles. *Mailing Add:* 806 Morris Turnpike Short Hills NJ 07078

GIERING, JOHN EDGAR, PHARMACOLOGY, PHYSIOLOGY. *Current Pos:* RETIRED. *Personal Data:* b Easton, Pa, Feb 8, 29; m 54; c 3. *Educ:* Moravian Col, BS, 51; Purdue Univ, MS, 53, PhD(endocrinol), 57. *Prof Exp:* Sr res scientist, Astra Pharmaceut Prod, Inc, 56-65, head hemat sect, 65-66; head, Dept Develop Pharmacol, Pennwalt Corp, 66-73, mgr int sci opers, 73-76, assoc med dir, Pharmaceut Div, 76-80, dir sci & coordr licensing, Pharmaceut Div, 80-92. *Concurrent Pos:* Mem coun thrombosis, Am Heart Asn. *Mem:* AAAS; affil Am Soc Pharmacol & Exp Therapeut; assoc Pharmacol Soc Can; NY Acad Sci. *Res:* Reproductive physiology; action of sex steroids on uterine enzymes and morphology; blood coagulation; pharmacology of fibrinolytic agents and platelet aggregation; drug screening and evaluation; clinical pharmacology; analgesic drug development. *Mailing Add:* 8936 Main St West Bloomfield NY 14585

GIERING, WARREN PERCIVAL, ORGANOMETALLIC CHEMISTRY. *Current Pos:* asst prof, 71-77, ASSOC PROF CHEM, BOSTON UNIV, 77- *Personal Data:* b Troy, NY, Aug 17, 41; m 67; c 2. *Educ:* Rensselaer Polytech Inst, BS, 63; State Univ NY Stony Brook, PhD(chem), 69. *Prof Exp:* Res assoc chem, Brandeis Univ, 69-71. *Mem:* Am Chem Soc. *Res:* Synthesis and chemistry of reactive pi-complexes of alkenes, alkynes, carbenes, and cyclobutadienes. *Mailing Add:* Dept Chem Boston Univ Boston MA 02215-2507

GIERKE, TIMOTHY DEE, PHYSICAL CHEMISTRY, POLYMER PHYSICS. *Current Pos:* res chemist, E I DuPont de Nemours & Co Inc, 74-80, sr supvr, Cent Res & Develop, 80-84, prod mgr, 84-88, indust mgr, 88-90, venture mgr, 90-92, RES MGR, E I DUPONT DE NEMOURS & CO INC, 92- *Personal Data:* b Spokane, Wash, Dec 27, 46; m 70; c 4. *Educ:* Gonzaga Univ, BS, 69; Univ Ill, PhD(phys chem), 74. *Prof Exp:* Res asst phys chem, Univ Ill, 71-74. *Mem:* Am Phys Soc. *Res:* Physical chemistry of liquid crystals and polymers; optical microscopy; ion containing polymers; Rayleigh light scattering; molecular theories of fluids. *Mailing Add:* 2405 Granby Rd Wilmington DE 19810. *Fax:* 302-695-1513

GIES, ROBERT JAY, PROPULSION PLANT DESIGN, AIRCRAFT CARRIERS. *Current Pos:* assoc engr, Newport News Shipbuilding, 90-94, engr, 94-96, sr engr, 96, ENG SUPVR, NEWPORT NEWS SHIPBUILDING, 96- *Personal Data:* b Washington, DC, July 27, 67; m 93, Louisa Manalal. *Educ:* Old Dominion Univ, BSME, 90, MEng Mgt, 94. *Prof Exp:* Facilities analyst, Old Dominion Univ, 87-90. *Concurrent Pos:* Instr,

Design Apprentice Prog, Newport News Shipbuilding, 94-, instr carrier eng, 95-; bd dirs, Old Dominion Univ, 96-; dir progs, Am Soc Mech Engrs. *Mem:* Assoc mem Am Soc Mech Engrs; assoc mem Am Soc Naval Engrs; assoc mem Soc Naval Architects & Marine Engrs. *Res:* Analysis and research on nuclear and non-nuclear propulsion; installation; alignment; main engines, shafting, bearings, propellers, components for aircraft carriers, naval combatants, and commercial ships. *Mailing Add:* 3820 Point Elizabeth Dr Chesapeake VA 23321-5723. *Fax:* 757-688-2537; *E-Mail:* giesrj@nns.com

GIESE, CLAYTON, CHEMICAL PHYSICS, LASER SPECTROSCOPY. *Current Pos:* assoc prof, 65-74, PROF PHYSICS, UNIV MINN, MINNEAPOLIS, 74- *Personal Data:* b Minneapolis, Minn, July 19, 31; m 85, Joyce A Woods. *Educ:* Univ Minn, BS, 53, PhD(physics), 57. *Prof Exp:* From instr to asst prof physics, Univ Chicago, 57-65. *Mem:* Am Phys Soc. *Res:* Dynamics of molecular and ionic collisions; spectroscopy of molecular beams; properties of superfluid helium. *Mailing Add:* Sch Physics & Astron Univ Minn Minneapolis MN 55455. *E-Mail:* giese@physics.spa.umn.edu

GIESE, DAVID LYLE, APPLIED STATISTICS, ACADEMIC ADMINISTRATION. *Current Pos:* Instr math, 57-63, coordr res, 63-74, from asst prof to assoc prof math, 65-74, PROF MATH & ASST DEAN GEN COL, UNIV MINN, MINNEAPOLIS, 74- *Personal Data:* b Wells, Minn, Aug 18, 33. *Educ:* Univ Minn, BS, 55, MA, 58, PhD(educ psychol), 65. *Mem:* AAAS; Am Educ Res Asn; Psychomet Soc; Asn Instnl Res; Am Statist Asn. *Res:* Application of statistical methods to problems of educational curriculum development and evaluation with emphasis on program evaluation rather than individual achievement. *Mailing Add:* 128 Pleasant St SE 220 APH Gen Col Univ Minn Minneapolis MN 55455-0434

GIESE, GRAHAM SHERWOOD, COASTAL OCEANOGRAPHY. *Current Pos:* from guest investr to RES SPECIALIST, WOODS HOLE OCEANOG INST, 85- *Personal Data:* b Newport News, Va, Oct 13, 31; m 58; c 5. *Educ:* Trinity Col, Conn, BS, 53; Univ RI, MS, 64; Univ Chicago, PhD(geophys sci), 66. *Prof Exp:* Res asst coastal processes, Woods Hole Oceanog Inst, 56-62, asst scientist, 67; from asst prof to assoc prof oceanog, Univ PR, 67-72; assoc scientist oceanog, Marine Consult Assocs, Inc, 72-76; from assoc scientist to sr scientist oceanog, Provincetown Ctr Coastal Studies, 76-83; assoc dir, Marine Sci Res Ctr, State Univ NY, Stonybrook, 83-85. *Mem:* AAAS; Am Geophys Union; Am Meteorol Soc. *Res:* Coastal and near-shore oceanography. *Mailing Add:* PO Box 96 Truro MA 02666

GIESE, JOHN H, MATHEMATICS. *Current Pos:* RETIRED. *Personal Data:* b Chicago, Ill, Mar 10, 15; m 46; c 2. *Educ:* Univ Chicago, BS, 36; Princeton Univ, PhD(math), 40. *Prof Exp:* Instr math, Princeton Univ, 39-40; instr, Rutgers Univ, 40-42; instr, Purdue Univ, 42-44; aerodynamicist, Bell Aircraft Corp, NY, 44-46; mathematician, Ballistic Res Labs, 46-58, chief comput lab, 59-68, chief Appl Math Div, 68-74. *Concurrent Pos:* Instr math, Princeton Univ, 41-42; lectr, Univ Mich, 54-55; prof math, statist & comput sci, Univ Del, 63-77. *Res:* Isohedral polyhedra; elementary geometrical examples for computer graphics; personal computing; numerical analysis. *Mailing Add:* 2123 Sherwood Lane Havre de Grace MD 21078

GIESE, ROBERT FREDERICK, PHYSICS. *Current Pos:* Fel physics, Argonne Nat Lab, 72-75, res asst systs anal, 75-77, asst environ engr systs anal, 77-78, SYSTS ANALYST, ENERGY SYSTS DIV, ARGONNE NAT LAB, 78- *Personal Data:* b Milwaukee, Wis, Apr 2, 43; m 66; c 1. *Educ:* Univ Wis-Madison, BS, 65; Stanford Univ, PhD(physics), 73. *Concurrent Pos:* Woodrow Wilson fel, Stanford Univ, 65-66, teaching asst, 66-67, res asst, 67-72; systs anal, Off Dir, Argonne Nat Lab, 85- *Res:* Systems analysis in energy related fields; simulation of storage within electric utility supply systems. *Mailing Add:* 1144 Dove Ct Naperville IL 60540

GIESE, ROBERT PAUL, PHYSICAL GEODESY, GEOGRAPHICAL INFORMATION SYSTEMS. *Current Pos:* VPRES, GIESE TECH RESOURCES, INC, 93- *Personal Data:* b Green Bay, Wis, June 23, 36; m 75, Jennifer M Brittain. *Educ:* Univ Wis-Madison, BS, 61; Univ Mo, Columbia, MA, 68; Univ Houston, PhD(math), 74. *Prof Exp:* Cartogr, Aeronaut Chart & Info Ctr, USAF, 62-65; comput programmer, Cancer Res Ctr, Columbia, 65-66; instr math, Univ Mo, Columbia, 66-67; comput consult, Robert P Giese Consults, 67-82; vpres, G-Tech Corp, Houston, 82-93. *Concurrent Pos:* Systs analyst, Calif Comput Prods, 68-69; sr res staff mem, Ray Geophys, Houston, 69-71; comput programmer, Dept Biomath, Univ Tex, Houston, 71-73; lectr math, Univ St Thomas, Houston, 75-80, adj prof bus, 80-88; vis lectr, Rice Univ, Houston, 83-84; adj prof, Grad Sch Mgt Systs, Univ Houston, 84-85, Dept Technol, 87-89 & Dept Indust Eng, 90-92. *Mem:* Math Asn Am. *Res:* Applied mathematics; computer science; suitability of nuclear waste storage sites. *Mailing Add:* Giese Tech Resources Inc PO Box 7681 Houston TX 77270-7681. *E-Mail:* giese@flash.net

GIESE, ROGER WALLACE, ORGANIC CHEMISTRY, BIOCHEMISTRY. *Current Pos:* assoc prof, 77-81, PROF, NORTHEASTERN UNIV, 81- *Personal Data:* b St Paul, Minn, Jan 26, 43; m 70; c 3. *Educ:* Hamline Univ, BS, 65; Mass Inst Technol, PhD(org chem), 69; Am Bd Clin Chem, dipl, 77. *Prof Exp:* Assoc on staff med, Peter Bent Brigham Hosp, 69-73. *Concurrent Pos:* Fel, Woodrow Wilson Soc, 65-66 & Am Cancer Soc, 69-71; res fel biol chem, Harvard Med Sch, 69-73, trainee human biochem training prog, 70-73; fac fel clin chem, Barnett Inst Chem Anal, Northeastern Univ, 74-; ed, J Chromatogr, 90-; Ctr Environ Health Sci, Mass Inst Technol, 92- *Mem:* Am Asn Clin Chem; AAAS; Am Chem Soc; Clin Radioassay Soc; Am Soc Mass Spectrometry. *Res:* Ultratrace organic and biological analysis. *Mailing Add:* 122 Mugar Hall Northeastern Univ Boston MA 02115. *Fax:* 617-373-8720

GIESE, RONALD LAWRENCE, FOREST ENTOMOLOGY. *Current Pos:* PROF FORESTRY & CHMN DEPT, UNIV WIS-MADISON, 75- *Personal Data:* b Milwaukee, Wis, June 28, 34; m 54; c 2. *Educ:* Wis State Col, Milwaukee, BS, 56; Univ Wis, MS, 58, PhD(entom, plant ecol), 60. *Prof Exp:* From asst prof to prof entom, Purdue Univ, West Lafayette, 60-75, dir natural resources & environ sci prog, 70-75. *Mem:* Fel AAAS; Soc Am Foresters; Ecol Soc Am; Entom Soc Am; Entom Soc Can. *Res:* Population dynamics; animal and plant ecology; computer science; radiology; bioclimatology; symbioses; forest stand structure and species composition related to insect fauna; mycangia; periodicity; pest management; simulation. *Mailing Add:* Dept Forestry 120 Russell Labs Univ Wis 1630 Linden Dr Madison WI 53706-1520

GIESE, ROSSMAN FREDERICK, JR, CRYSTALLOGRAPHY. *Current Pos:* asst prof geol sci, 66-68, assoc prof, 68-77, actg chmn dept, 70-72, PROF GEOL SCI, STATE UNIV NY, BUFFALO, 77- *Personal Data:* b New York, NY, Jan 7, 36; m 60; c 3. *Educ:* Columbia Univ, BA, 56, MA, 59, PhD(mineral), 62. *Honors & Awards:* Ralph Grim lectr, Univ Ill, 79. *Prof Exp:* Sr physicist, Carborundum Co, 61-66. *Concurrent Pos:* Sr cancer res scientist, Ctr Crystallog Res, Roswell Park Mem Inst, 66-68; sr res assoc, Nat Res Coun, 74-75; res assoc, Nat Ctr Sci Res, France, 75-76. *Mem:* AAAS; Am Crystallog Asn. *Res:* Crystal structure and crystal chemistry of minerals, particularly clays and micas; interatomic forces in silicate minerals; crystal chemistry of water and hydroxyl in minerals. *Mailing Add:* Dept Geol 876 Nat Sci Complex State Univ NY Buffalo NY 14260-3050

GIESECKE, ADOLPH H, MEDICINE, ANESTHESIOLOGY. *Current Pos:* from asst prof to assoc prof, 63-69, chmn dept, 81-92, PROF ANESTHESIOL, UNIV TEX SWESTERN MED CTR, 69- *Personal Data:* b Oklahoma City, Okla, Apr 19, 32; m 54, Veronica Morel; c 4. *Educ:* Univ Tex, MD, 57. *Prof Exp:* Intern, William Beaumont Army Hosp, El Paso, Tex, 57-58; resident, Parkland Mem Hosp, Dallas, 60-63. *Concurrent Pos:* Attend anesthesiologist, Parkland Mem Hosp, Children's Med Ctr & Vet Admin Hosp, Dallas, Tex, 63- & Presby Hosp, 67-; Fulbright lectr & guest prof, Johannes Gutenberg Univ, Ger, 70. *Mem:* AMA; Am Soc Anesthesiol; Int Anesthesia Res Soc; Int Trauma Anesthesiol & Critical Care Soc (pres, 92-95). *Res:* Anesthesia for trauma. *Mailing Add:* Dept Anesthesiol Univ Tex SWestern Med Ctr 5323 Harry Hines Blvd Dallas TX 75235-7200

GIESEKE, JAMES ARNOLD, CHEMICAL ENGINEERING, AEROSOL SCIENCE. *Current Pos:* From res chem engr to sr chem engr, 63-70, assoc fel, 70-74, res leader, 74-87, SECT MGR, BATTELLE COLUMBUS LABS, 87- *Personal Data:* b Granite City, Ill, Oct 16, 36; m 82, Linda Delma; c 3. *Educ:* Univ Ill, BS, 59; Univ Wash, MS, 63, PhD(chem eng), 64. *Mem:* Sigma Xi; Air Pollution Control Asn; Am Inst Chem Engrs; Am Chem Soc; Am Asn Aerosol Res. *Res:* Mechanics and physics of aerosols; dust collection problems; fission product transport analyses related to nuclear reactor safety. *Mailing Add:* 3930 Smiley Rd Hilliard OH 43026

GIESEKER, DAVID, ALGEBRA. *Current Pos:* PROF, DEPT MATH, UNIV CALIF, LOS ANGELES, 75- *Personal Data:* b Oakland, Calif, Nov 23, 43. *Educ:* Redd Col, BS, 65; Harvard univ, MS, 67, PhD(math), 70. *Mem:* Am Math Soc. *Res:* Algebra. *Mailing Add:* Math Dept Univ Calif Los Angeles CA 90095-1555

GIESEKING, JOHN ELDON, SOIL SCIENCE. *Current Pos:* from asst prof to prof soil physics, 34-74, EMER PROF SOIL CHEM, UNIV ILL, URBANA, 74- *Personal Data:* b Altamont, Ill, Oct 1, 05; m 36; c 1. *Educ:* Univ Ill, BS, 26, MS, 27, PhD(soils), 34. *Prof Exp:* Asst soils, Univ Ill, 27-32; asst soil chem, Univ Mo, 32-33. *Concurrent Pos:* Lectr, Univ Nebr, 58; ed, Monogr on Soil Components. *Mem:* AAAS; Am Chem Soc; Am Soil Sci Soc; Int Soc Soil Sci; fel Am Inst Chem. *Res:* Cation and anion exchange studies; mutual flocculation between positive and negative colloids; use of x-rays for diffraction studies; electron microscopy; petroleum cracking catalysts; use of radioactive potassium and phosphorus in cation and anion exchange and fixation studies. *Mailing Add:* 1701 E Main St Urbana IL 61801

GIESEL, JAMES THEODORE, POPULATION BIOLOGY, ECOLOGY. *Current Pos:* asst prof, 70-76, ASSOC PROF ZOOL, UNIV FLA, 76- *Personal Data:* b Toledo, Ohio, Nov 17, 41; m 64; c 1. *Educ:* Mich State Univ, BS, 63; Univ Ore, PhD(biol), 68. *Prof Exp:* Ford Found fel pop biol, Univ Chicago, 69-70. *Mem:* Ecol Soc Am; Genetics Soc Am; Soc Study Evolution. *Res:* Analysis of the temporal aspects of interspecific competition; isozymic analysis of the genetics of natural populations; theoretical analysis of the effects of age distribution in populations with overlapping generations on effective number and selection. *Mailing Add:* Dept Zool Univ Fla PO Box 118525 Gainesville FL 32611

GIESLER, GREGG CARL, NUCLEAR CHEMISTRY, COMPUTER PROGRAMMING. *Current Pos:* STAFF MEM, EXCEL TECH & ENVIRON SERV, 92- *Personal Data:* b Chicago, Ill, Sept 11, 44; m 68, Maryjean A Vik; c Susananne J, Janaanne M, Jonthan C & Jeffrey R. *Educ:* Univ Ill, Urbana, BS, 66; Mich State Univ, PhD(chem physics), 71. *Prof Exp:* Staff mem nuclear chem, Los Alamos Nat Lab, Univ Calif, 72-86, Jomar Systs, 86-88 & Salem Tech Serv, 88-92. *Mem:* Am Chem Soc; Am Phys Soc. *Res:* Pion interactions with complex nuclei; gamma-ray spectroscopy; computer-controlled data acquisition and processing; radiation dosimetry; waste management. *Mailing Add:* G Cubed 660 Navajo Los Alamos NM 87544-2628. *Fax:* 505-845-3115

GIESS, EDWARD AUGUST, SOLID STATE PHYSICS, CERAMICS. *Current Pos:* ADJ PROF ELEC ENG, UNIV NC, CHARLOTTE, 92- *Personal Data:* b Mineola, NY, Sept 12, 29; m 53; c 3. *Educ:* State Univ NY Col Ceramics, Alfred, BS, 51, MS, 52, PhD(ceramics), 58. *Prof Exp:* Ceramic engr, Res Div, Nat Lead Co, 52-55; res staff mem crystal chem, Res Div, Int Bus Mach Corp, 58-84, mfg res, 84-92. *Concurrent Pos:* Exec Comt, Am Asn Crystal Growth, 90- *Mem:* AAAS; fel Am Inst Chem; fel Am Ceramic Soc; Am Phys Soc; Am Asn Crystal Growth (vpres, 81-84). *Res:* Flux melt crystal growth; solid state reactions and sintering; electrooptic and magnetic materials; magnetic bubble garnet liquid phase epitaxy, glass ceramics, superconducting oxides. *Mailing Add:* Univ NC, Charlotte 9201 Union City Blvd, Elec Eng Smith Bldg Charlotte NC 28223. *Fax:* 704-547-3183; *E-Mail:* eageiss@mosaic.uncc.edu

GIESSEN, BILL C(ORMANN), SOLID STATE CHEMISTRY, MATERIALS SCIENCE. *Current Pos:* assoc prof chem, 68-83, PROF CHEM & MECH ENG, NORTHEASTERN UNIV, 73-; ASSOC DIR, BARNETT INST CHEM ANALYSIS & MAT SCI, 74- *Personal Data:* b Pittsburgh, Pa, June 8, 32; m 60; c 1. *Educ:* Univ Gottingen, DSc(metall), 58. *Honors & Awards:* Hume-Rothery Award, Metall Soc, Am Indst Mech Eng, 90. *Prof Exp:* Res assoc metall, Mass Inst Technol, 59-68. *Concurrent Pos:* Vis prof, Mass Inst Technol, 75, Harvard Univ, 76; dir, Encogy Mats Corp, 78-88; secy alloy phase comt, Am Inst Mining, Metall & Petrol Engrs, 70-72; dir & chmn, Cambridge Anal Asn, Inc, 79-89; dir, Marko Mat, Inc, 78-, Cambridge Mkt Analysis Corp, 89- *Mem:* Am Chem Soc; Am Crystallog Soc; Am Inst Mining, Metall & Petrol Engrs; Mat Res Soc (secy, 79-82); Am Soc Metals. *Res:* Physical metallurgy; x-ray crystallography; structural and alloy chemistry, rapid solidification processing, mechanical, electronic and magnetic properties of alloys, metallic glasses; ceramic superconductors; ion nitriding. *Mailing Add:* 22 Centre St Cambridge MA 02139

GIESY, JOHN PAUL, JR, LIMNOLOGY. *Current Pos:* PROF FISHERIES & WILDLIFE & COORDR, ENVIRON EFFECTS RES, PESTICIDE RES CTR, MICH STATE UNIV, 81- *Personal Data:* b Youngstown, Ohio, Aug 9, 48; m 70; c 1. *Educ:* Alma Col, BS, 70; Mich State Univ, MS, 72, PhD(limnol), 74. *Honors & Awards:* Agr Recognition Award, Ciba-Geigy Award; Chevron Distinguished Lectr Award; Vollenweider Lectr Aquatic Sci Award, Nat Water Res Inst Can, 94; Founders Award, Soc Environ Toxicol & Chem, 95. *Prof Exp:* Res assoc limnol, Savannah River Ecol Lab, Univ Ga, 74-81. *Concurrent Pos:* NSF res fel, 69-70; fel, Woodrow Wilson Found, 70; instr ecol, Alma Col, 72; fel, North Cent Res Found, 72-74; instr ecol, Univ SC, 75, Univ Fla & Emory Univ, 78-; mem bd dirs, Soc Environ Toxicol Chem, 86-92, pres int chap, 90-91, chmn bd dirs, 92-93; Fulbright fel, Univ Bayreuth, WGer, 87-88; bd dirs, Int Asn Sci. *Mem:* Ecol Soc Am; Am Soc Limnol Oceanog; Int Soc Theoret Appl Limnol; Soc Environ Toxicol Chem (pres, 90-91); Sigma Xi. *Res:* Cycling of heavy metals; uptake and availability of heavy metals in aquatic systems; aquatic toxicology; pesticides; dioxins; polychloride biphenyls; author of over 250 books, book chapters and journal publications. *Mailing Add:* Fisheries & Wildlife Mich State Univ East Lansing MI 48824

GIETZEN, DOROTHY WINTER, PHYSIOLOGICAL SCIENCES. *Current Pos:* grad student, Dept Nutrit, Univ Calif, Davis, 76-78, res assoc & teaching asst, Dept Animal Physiol, 78-83, postdoctoral fel, Food Intake Lab & Dept Physiol Sci, Sch Vet Med, 83-86, dir res, dir, Neurochem Lab & asst res neurophysiologist, Dept Psychiat, Sch Med, 86-91, asst res neurophysiologist, Dept Physiol Sci, Sch Vet Med, 87-90, assoc res neurophysiologist, Univ, 90-91, EXEC DIR, FOOD INTAKE LAB & SR SCIENTIST, CLIN NUTRIT RES UNIT, UNIV CALIF, DAVIS, 88-, ASST PROF, DEPT PHYSIOL SCI, SCH VET MED, 91- *Educ:* Calif State Univ, Sacramento, BS, 70; Univ Calif, Davis, MS, 78, PhD(physiol), 83. *Prof Exp:* Sch health consult, Placer County Off Educ, Auburn, Calif, 71-76. *Concurrent Pos:* Sch health consult, Rocklin Sch Dist, Calif, 76-78; mem, Animal Resources Comt, Dept Nutrit, Univ Calif, Davis, 89, Space Allocation Comt, 89-90, Dean's Res Coord Coun, Sch Med, 89-91 & Biomed Res Support Grant Selection Adv Comt, 90. *Mem:* Am Inst Nutrit; Am Physiol Soc; Sigma Xi; Soc Neurosci; Soc Study Ingestive Behav; Int Brain Res Orgn; Women Neurosci; AAAS; Am Asn Univ Women. *Mailing Add:* Dept Vet Med Physiol Sci Univ Calif Davis Davis CA 95616-8732. *Fax:* 530-752-7690

GIEVER, JOHN BERTRAM, MATHEMATICS. *Current Pos:* PROF MATH SCI, NMEX STATE UNIV, 59- *Personal Data:* b Omaha, Nebr, Sept 18, 19; m 43; c 3. *Educ:* Creighton Univ, BS, 42; Mass Inst Technol, PhD(math), 48. *Prof Exp:* Instr math, Boston Univ, 48-51, asst prof, 51-52; mem staff, Instrumentation Lab, Mass Inst Technol, 52-53; from asst prof to assoc prof math, Univ Okla, 53-59. *Mem:* Am Math Soc; Asn Symbolic Logic; Math Asn Am. *Res:* Algebraic topology. *Mailing Add:* 475 Milton Ave Las Cruces NM 88005

GIFFEN, MARTIN BRENER, PSYCHIATRY. *Current Pos:* RETIRED. *Personal Data:* b Pittsburgh, Pa, Sept 13, 19; m 41, Margaret Duncan; c Marsha (Chelders) & Cheryl. *Educ:* Univ Mich, AB, 41; Univ Pittsburgh, MD, 45. *Prof Exp:* Chief psychiat, USAF Hosp, Fla, 54-57, Wiesbaden, Ger, 57-61, chmn dept psychiat, Wilford Hall USAF Hosp, Tex, 61-68, dir psychiat residency prog & hosp serv, 65-68, vcomdr, 68; prof psychiat, Univ Tex Med Sch, San Antonio, 68-85, coordr psychiat residency training, Univ Tex Health Sci Ctr, 72-85, clin prof psychiat, 85. *Concurrent Pos:* Consult psychiat, Surgeon Gen, USAF Europe, 57-61, Surgeon Gen, US Air Force, 61-68, US Attorney Western Dist Tex, 63-69 & Wilford Hall USAF Hosp, Tex, 68-; examr, Am Bd Psychiat & Neurol, 71-72. *Mem:* Fel AAAS; fel Am Psychiat Asn; emer fel Am Col Psychiat; Asn Mil Surgeons US; Am Acad Psychiat & Law. *Mailing Add:* Dept Psychiat Univ Tex Med Sch HSC-SA 7703 Floyd Curl Dr San Antonio TX 78284-6200

GIFFEN, ROBERT H(ENRY), ENVIRONMENTAL ASSESSMENT, CORROSION. *Current Pos:* sr engr, Westinghouse Elec Co, 51-57, supvr engr, 57-64, fel engr, 64-66, supvr, 66-69, mgr radiation technol, 69-72, ADV ENGR, BETTIS ATOMIC POWER LAB, WESTINGHOUSE ELEC CORP, 72- *Personal Data:* b Pottsville, Pa, Feb 10, 22; m 49; c 3. *Educ:* Newark Col Eng, BS, 43; Iowa State Col, MS, 47, PhD(chem eng), 51. *Prof Exp:* Control chemist, Gen Chem Co, NJ & Ill, 43-44; chem engr, Los Alamos Sci Lab, Univ Calif, 46; jr res asst, Inst Atomic Res, Iowa State Col, 47-51. *Mem:* Am Inst Chem Engrs. *Res:* Design and development of fluid systems for pressurized water nuclear power plants; environmental assessments. *Mailing Add:* 5188 Priscilla Dr Bethel Park PA 15102

GIFFEN, WILLIAM MARTIN, JR, POLYMER CHEMISTRY. *Current Pos:* RETIRED. *Personal Data:* b Akron, Ohio, June 23, 33; m 61, Janet Roth; c Diane L, William M III & Laura R. *Educ:* Univ Akron, BS, 55, MS, 56, PhD(polymer chem), 61. *Prof Exp:* Asst proj chemist, Amoco Chem Corp, Ind, 61-62; sr res chemist, Gen Tire & Rubber Co, 62-64; sr chemist, Tech Dept, Marbon Chem Div, Borg-Warner Corp, WVa, 64-68, res assoc, Develop Div, 68-70; mem fac, Wash Tech Col, 71-72; sr chemist, Addressograph-Multigraph Corp, Ohio, 72-74; sr chemist, Standard Oil Co, Ohio, 74-85. *Mem:* Am Chem Soc. *Res:* Emulsion, graft, and alkylene oxide polymerizations; cationic and anionic solution polymerizations; vinyl polymerizations and copolymerizations; latex formulation; high impact resins; photo-conductive polymers; latex can and metal coatings; food packaging plastics; reinforced and filled plastics composites; composites for metal replacement; membrane separation of liquid mixtures; polyvinyl chloride blends and alloys. *Mailing Add:* 7250 Darien Dr Hudson OH 44236-1203

GIFFIN, WALTER C(HARLES), INDUSTRIAL ENGINEERING. *Current Pos:* RETIRED. *Personal Data:* b Walhonding, Ohio, Apr 22, 36; m 56, Beverly Neff; c Steven & Rebecca. *Educ:* Ohio State Univ, BIndustEng & MSc, 60, PhD(mass transp), 64. *Prof Exp:* Res engr, Gen Motors Res Labs, 60-61; res assoc opers res, Eng Exp Sta, 61-62, from instr to prof, 62-87, emer prof indust eng, Ohio State Univ, 87-92; prof & chair eng, Univ Southern Colo, 87-92. *Res:* Air traffic control, inventory control and transportation systems; queueing phenomena. *Mailing Add:* 419 S Fairway Dr Pueblo CO 81007

GIFFORD, CAMERON EDWARD, ECOLOGY, PHYSIOLOGY. *Current Pos:* SEA GRANT PROG COORDR, MASS MARATIME ACAD, 92- *Personal Data:* b New Bedford, Mass, Sept 23, 31; m 52; c 2. *Educ:* Earlham Col, BA, 55; Harvard Univ, MA, 59; Univ Ga, PhD(zool), 64. *Prof Exp:* Assoc prof biol & chmn dept, Earlham Col, 61-72, dir, David Worth Dennis Biol Sta, 62-72; res specialist, Environ Systs Lab, Woods Hole Oceanog Inst, 72-76, oil spill res coordr, Ecosyst Ctr, Marine Biol Lab, 76-78; owner & vpres, Gifford & Gifford Inc, DBA H V Lawrence, 77-92. *Mem:* Int Ornith Cong; Sigma Xi. *Res:* Avian physiology; homing behavior in bats; chlorophyll determinations in various marine algae; lipid determinations and migratory behavior in the bobolink; mariculture, investigations for the biological requirements and development of technical systems for mass culturing various phycocolloid producing marcoscopic marine algae. *Mailing Add:* 11 C Chilmark Dr East Falmouth MA 02536

GIFFORD, DAVID STEVENS, ORGANIC CHEMISTRY. *Current Pos:* RETIRED. *Personal Data:* b Glens Falls, NY, Nov 14, 24; m 51; c 4. *Educ:* Dartmouth Col, AB, 49; Univ Conn, PhD(org chem), 60. *Prof Exp:* Res chemist, Naugatuck Chem Div, US Rubber Co, 50-54; asst col instr chem, Univ Conn, 55-56, asst, 56-57, asst col instr, 57-59; res asst, Purdue Univ, 59-61; from asst ed to assoc ed org indexing, Chem Abstr Serv Ohio State Univ, 61-69, sr assoc indexer, 69-73, sr assoc ed, 73-94. *Mem:* AAAS; Sigma Xi. *Res:* Abstracting and indexing terpenes and carbohydrates from Russian and Japanese literature. *Mailing Add:* 110 Brevoort Rd Columbus OH 43214

GIFFORD, ERNEST MILTON, BOTANY, DEVELOPMENTAL PLANT MORPHOLOGY & ANATOMY. *Current Pos:* Jr botanist, Agr Exp Sta, Univ Calif, Davis, 49-51, from instr to assoc prof bot, 50-61, from asst botanist to assoc botanist, 57-61, chmn dept, 63-68, 70-71 & 73-78, prof, 62-87, EMER PROF BOT & BOTANIST, AGR EXP STA, UNIV CALIF, DAVIS, 88- *Personal Data:* b Riverside, Calif, Jan 17, 20; m 42, Jean Duncan; c Jeanette. *Educ:* Univ Calif, Berkeley, AB, 42, PhD(bot), 50. *Honors & Awards:* Cert Merit, Bot Soc Am, 81. *Concurrent Pos:* Merck sr res fel, Harvard Univ, 56-57; NSF res grant, Univ Calif, 58-66 & 79-82; John Simon Guggenheim Mem Found fel, 66-67; Fulbright res scholar, Nat Ctr Sci Res, France, 66-67; NATO sr fel, France, 74; ed-in-chief, Am J Bot, 75-79. *Mem:* Am Inst Biol Sci; Bot Soc Am (vpres, 81, pres, 82); Sigma Xi; Int Soc Plant Morphologists (vpres, 80-84). *Res:* Developmental anatomy and ultrastructure of vascular plants; quantitative studies of lower vascular plant meristems; spermatogenesis in Ginkgo biloba. *Mailing Add:* Sect Plant Biol Univ Calif Davis CA 95616-8537

GIFFORD, FRANKLIN ANDREW, JR, METEOROLOGY. *Current Pos:* CONSULT, 80- *Personal Data:* b Union City, NJ, May 7, 22; m; c 2. *Educ:* NY Univ, BS, 47; Pa State Univ, MS, 54, PhD(meteorol), 55. *Honors & Awards:* Gold Medal, US Dept Com, 63; Outstanding Contrib to Advan Appl Meteorol Award, Am Meteor Soc, 90. *Prof Exp:* Meteorologist, Northwest Airlines, Inc, 45-50; res meteorologist, US Weather Bur, Nat Oceanic & Atmospheric Admin, 50-66, dir, Atmospheric Turbulence & Diffusion Lab, 66-80. *Concurrent Pos:* Mem, Adv Comt Reactor Safeguards, US AEC, 58-68, consult, Adv Comt Reactor Safety, 68-80; consult, Int Atomic Energy Agency, 66-83. *Mem:* Fel Am Meteorol Soc; fel AAAS; Sigma Xi. *Res:* Atmospheric turbulence and diffusion; air pollution; reactor hazards; meteorology of other planets. *Mailing Add:* 109 Gorgas Lane Oak Ridge TN 37831

GIFFORD, GERALD F, RANGELAND HYDROLOGY. *Current Pos:* RETIRED. *Personal Data:* b Chanute, Kans, Oct 24, 39; m 82, Cinda J Lowman. *Educ:* Utah State Univ, BS, 62, MS, 64, PhD(watershed sci), 68. *Prof Exp:* Lectr watershed mgt, Univ Nev, Reno, 65-67; from asst prof to prof range watershed sci & chmn, Watershed Sci Unit, Utah State Univ, 67-84, dir, Inst Land Rehab, 82-84; head, Dept Range, Wildlife & Forestry, Univ Nev, Reno, 84-92, chmn, Dept & Environ & Resource Sci, 92-94. *Concurrent Pos:* Consult, Nat Park Serv, Nat Comn Water Qual, Bur Land Mgt, Amax Coal Co, Smithsonian Inst, Tex Tech Found, Mountain Fuel Supply, Univ Minn Morocco Proj & Off Tech Assessment, 67-; vis prof, Div Land Resources Mgt, Commonwealth Sci & Indust Res Orgn, Alice Springs & Canberra, Australia, 73-74; mem, Wild & Free-Roaming Horses & Burro Comt, Nat Acad Sci, 79-80, Sci Comt Rangeland Hydrol, Soc Range Mgt; assoc ed, J Range Mgt, 82-87, 91- & Arid Soil Res & Rehab, 84-90; AAAS Comt, Arid Lands, 87-90. *Mem:* Am Water Resources Asn; Soil Conserv Soc Am; Soc Wetlands Scientists. *Res:* Man's impact on the hydrologic cycle in arid and semiarid rangeland environments; runoff; erosion; infiltration; evapotranspiration; groundwater recharge. *Mailing Add:* 3880 Squaw Valley Circle Reno NV 89509-5663. *E-Mail:* gifford@equinox.unr.edu

GIFFORD, HAROLD, OPHTHALMOLOGY. *Current Pos:* RETIRED. *Personal Data:* b Omaha, Nebr, Jan 25, 06; m 36; c 3. *Educ:* Univ Nebr, BSc, 30, MD, 31. *Prof Exp:* From instr to assoc prof ophthal, Col Med, Univ Nebr, 36-64, prof, 64-80, emer prof, 80-91. *Concurrent Pos:* Practicing physician. *Mem:* Am Ophthal Soc; fel Am Acad Ophthal & Otolaryngol. *Res:* Clinical research. *Mailing Add:* 3636 Burt St Omaha NE 68131-1946

GIFFORD, JAMES FERGUS, HISTORY OF MEDICINE. *Current Pos:* ASSOC PROF HIST MED, DUKE UNIV, 77- *Personal Data:* b Lynn, Mass, Mar 3, 40; m 63. *Educ:* Dartmouth Col, BA, 61; Andover Newton Theol Sch, BD, 64, STM, 65; Duke Univ, PhD(social & intellectual hist), 69. *Prof Exp:* Assoc prof hist, Guilford Col, 69-77. *Concurrent Pos:* Josiah Macy Jr Found fel, 75-76. *Mem:* Am Asn Hist Med; Orgn Am Historians. *Mailing Add:* 321 S Riverdale Dr Durham NC 27712

GIFFORD, JOHN A, ARCHAEOLOGICAL GEOLOGY, GEOARCHAEOLOGY. *Current Pos:* asst prof archaeol, 83-86, ASSOC PROF ARCHAEOL, UNIV MIAMI, CORAL GABLES, 86- *Personal Data:* b Strasbourg, France, Feb 17, 47; US citizen. *Educ:* Univ Mass, Amherst, BS, 69; Univ Miami, MS, 73; Univ Minn, Minneapolis, PhD(archaeol geol), 78. *Prof Exp:* Assoc dir, Archaeometry Lab, Univ Minn, 78-82. *Mem:* Archaeol Inst Am; Geol Soc Am; Soc Prof Archeol; Soc Archaeol Sci. *Res:* Physical environmental changes affecting coastal cultures, primarily prehistoric in the Mediterranean and Caribbean. *Mailing Add:* Univ Miami 4600 Rickenbacker Causeway Miami FL 33124-8106

GIFFORD, RAY WALLACE, JR, MEDICINE. *Current Pos:* mem staff, 61-67, head dept hypertension & nephrology, 67-85, VCHMN DIV MED, CLEVELAND CLIN FOUND, 78- *Personal Data:* b Westerville, Ohio, Aug 13, 23; m 47, 73; c 4. *Educ:* Otterbein Col, BS, 44; Ohio State Univ, MD, 47; Univ Minn, MS, 52. *Hon Degrees:* DSc, Otterbein Col, 86. *Honors & Awards:* Oscar B Hunter Award, Am Soc Clin Pharmacol & Therapeut, 79; Simon Rodbard Award, Am Col Chest Physicians, 82. *Prof Exp:* Intern, Colo Gen Hosp, Denver, 47-48; resident physician internal med, Univ Hosp, Ohio State Univ, 48-49; fel, Mayo Found, 49-52, consult sect internal med, Mayo Clinic, 52-61, instr med, Mayo Found, Univ Minn, 53-58, asst prof, 58-61. *Concurrent Pos:* Mem, Adv Comt to Dir NIH, 82-86; mem bd trustees, AMA, 86-90. *Mem:* AMA; Am Heart Asn; Am Fedn Clin Res; fel Am Col Physicians; fel Am Col Cardiol; fel Am Col Chest Physicians. *Res:* Hypertension and renal disease. *Mailing Add:* 3479 Glen Allen Dr Cleveland OH 44121

GIFFORD, ROBIN P, COMPUTER ENGINEERING, INDUSTRIAL PHYSICS. *Current Pos:* STAFF MEM, HEWLETT-PACKARD CO. *Honors & Awards:* Indust Appln Prize, Am Inst Physics, 93. *Mailing Add:* Hewlett Packard Co PO Box 10350 Palo Alto CA 94303

GIFFORD, WAYNE ARTHUR, COMPUTATIONAL FLUID DYNAMICS, MATHEMATICIAN MODELING OF POLYMER PROCESSES. *Current Pos:* SCIENTIST, EXTRUSION DIES, INC, 95- *Personal Data:* m 68, Laura Lou Pazmino; c Kimberley Ann & Devon Wayne. *Educ:* Clarkson Univ, BS, 68; Univ Minn, MS, 70, PhD(chem eng), 79. *Prof Exp:* Advan engr, Owens-Corning Sci & Tech Ctr, 79-86; res assoc, Dow Chem Res Ctr, 87-94; Consult, W A Gifford & Assoc, 94-95. *Concurrent Pos:* Invited lectr, Dept Chem Eng, Ohio State Univ, 93, Univ Calif Davis, 96 & Univ Minn, 97; bd dirs, Soc Plastics Engrs, 97- *Mem:* Soc Plastics Engrs; Soc Rheol; Am Soc Mech Engrs; Am Inst Chem Engrs. *Res:* Developing, writing and implementation of fast and efficient 3-D computational fluid dynamics algorithms which are used routinely to design polymer processing equipment. *Mailing Add:* Extrusion Dies Inc 911 Kurth Rd Chippewa Falls WI 54729-1443. *Fax:* 715-726-2205

GIFKINS, ROBERT CECIL, PRIMARY METALLIC CREEP, SUPERPLASTICITY. *Current Pos:* RETIRED. *Personal Data:* b London, Eng, May 30, 18; m 42, Elizabeth Glakner; c Kenneth, Pamela & Roger. *Educ:* London Univ, BSc, 41; Melbourne Univ, DSc, 61. *Honors & Awards:* Silver Medal, Australian Inst Metals, 65; Hofman Prize; Int Metall Soc, 74; R C Gifkins Ann Lectr, 95. *Prof Exp:* Tech asst, Brit Indust Solvents, 36-37; exp officer, Nat Phys Lab, 37-46, Brit Atomic Energy Authority, 46-48; sci officer & chief res officer, Commonwealth Sci & Indust Res Organ 48-78; sr res fel, Imperial Col, 62-63; Southampton Univ, 78-79. *Concurrent Pos:* Vis prof, Univ BC, 69-70; Acta Metallurgica travelling lectr, 91-92. *Mem:* Fel Inst Mat UK; fel Inst Metals & Mat Australia; hon fel Inst Engrs Australia; Australian Inst Metals (pres, 65); hon mem Iron & Steel Inst Japan. *Res:* Contributed over 100 research papers to professional journals. *Mailing Add:* PO Box 257 Somers Australia

GIFT, HELEN C, DENTISTRY. *Current Pos:* res sociologist, 86-88, chief, Health Prom Sect, 88-91, CHIEF, DIS PREV & HEALTH PROM BR, NAT INST DENT RES, NIH, 91- *Personal Data:* b Kingsport, Tenn, Jan 20, 43. *Educ:* Emory Univ, BA, 65, MA, 69, PhD(sociol), 71. *Honors & Awards:* Vol Award, USPHS, 93, Exemplary Serv Award, 95. *Prof Exp:* Dir, Bur Econ Behav & Res, 73-81; assoc res dir, Darcy McManus & Masius, 81-83; dir mkt res, DS Howard & Assoc, 83-86. *Mem:* Int Asn Dent Res; Am Asn Pub Health Dent. *Mailing Add:* NIDR-NIH Bldg 45 Rm 3AN-44D Bethesda MD 20892. *Fax:* 301-480-8254; *E-Mail:* gifth@de45.nidr.nih.gov

GIFT, JAMES J, TOXICOLOGY, ECOLOGY & ENVIRONMENTAL SCIENCES. *Current Pos:* SR TOXICOLOGIST, DIR RISK ASSESSMENT & MGT BUS, CHIEF SCIENTIST, & SR VPRES EA ENG, SCI & TECHNOL INC. *Personal Data:* b July 25, 42; m 67, Audrey Geger; c Craig & Andrea. *Educ:* Harvard Univ, BA, 64; Rutgers Univ, MA, 68, PhD(environ sci), 70. *Mem:* Am Fisheries Soc; Soc Environ Toxicol & Chem; Water Environ Fedn. *Res:* Physiological effects of thermal gradients of numerous marine, estuarine and freshwater fish species, direction of ecological and human health risk assessments. *Mailing Add:* EA Eng Sci & Technol Inc 11019 McCormick Rd Cockeysville-Hunt Valley MD 21031. *Fax:* 410-771-1625

GIGER, ADOLF J, RADIO COMMUNICATIONS, RADIO PROPAGATION. *Current Pos:* CONSULT, GIGER RADIO CONSULT, 90-; CHIEF SCIENTIST, ATI INC, 93- *Personal Data:* b Solothurn, Switz, Jan 4, 27; US citizen; m 58, Maya Pfister; c Alexander, Monica & Peter. *Educ:* Swiss Fed Inst Technol, dipl elec eng, 50, Dr sc tech, 56. *Prof Exp:* Res engr, Inst High Frequency Tech, Swiss Fed Inst Technol, 50-56; mem tech staff, AT&T Bell Labs, 56-58, supvr, 58-71, dept head, 71-89. *Concurrent Pos:* US deleg, Study Group 9, Int Consultative Radio Comt, Geneva, Switz, 77-89. *Mem:* Fel Inst Elec & Electronics Engrs. *Res:* Design and analysis of digital radio relay systems; physics and modeling of microwave propagation; microwave interference analysis and prediction; development of antennas and circuits for interference reduction; consulting on air navigation systems. *Mailing Add:* 27 Olde Farms Rd Boxford MA 01921

GIGLI, IRMA, DERMATOLOGY, IMMUNOLOGY. *Current Pos:* PROF MED & DERMAT & VCHAIR MED SCI, HEALTH SCI CTR, UNIV TEX, 95- *Personal Data:* b Cordoba, Arg, Dec 22, 31. *Educ:* Nat Univ Cordoba, MD, 57. *Honors & Awards:* Stephen Rothman Mem Award, Soc Invest Dermat, 96. *Prof Exp:* Intern med, Cook Co Hosp, Chicago, 57-58, resident dermat, 58-60; fel, NY Univ, 60-61; vis investr immunol, Howard Hughes Med Inst, Miami, Fla, 61-64; investr, Univ Frankfurt, 65-67; res assoc, Harvard Univ, Med Sch, 67-69, from asst prof to assoc prof dermat, 69-75, assoc immunol, 69-76, sr assoc dermat, 71-75; prof dermat & exp med, NY Univ, 76-80, dir, Asthma & Allergic Dis Ctr Immunodermat Studies, 80-91; prof med & chief, Div Dermat, Univ Calif, San Diego, 83-95. *Concurrent Pos:* Med Found award, 68-69; Am Cancer Soc fac res award, 70-72; chief dermat, Peter Bent Brigham Hosp, 71-75; NIH res career develop award, 72-76; Guggenheim award, 74-75; vis scientist biochem, Univ Oxford, 74-75. *Mem:* Inst Med-Nat Acad Sci; Am Asn Immunologists; Am Acad Dermat; Soc Invest Dermat; Asn Am Physicians; Am Soc Clin Invest. *Res:* Immunochemistry and immunobiology or the complement system; studies of skin diseases which may have immunological basis. *Mailing Add:* Health Sci Ctr Inst Molecular Genetics Univ Tex 2121 W Holcombe Blvd Houston TX 77030

GIGLIO, RICHARD JOHN, OPERATIONS RESEARCH, INDUSTRIAL ENGINEERING. *Current Pos:* Engr aerospace eng, 59-60, sr proj engr indust eng & opers res, 63-67, prof, 67-77, HEAD INDUST ENG & OPERS RES, UNIV MASS, 78- *Personal Data:* b Hartford, Conn, Aug 27, 37; m 60; c 2. *Educ:* Mass Inst Technol, BS, 59; Stanford Univ, MS, 62, PhD(opers res), 65. *Concurrent Pos:* Prin investr grants, New Eng Elec Co, 72-73, HEW, 73-76, Army Res & Develop Command, 76-77 & Mass Dept Health, 77-78. *Mem:* Opers Res Soc Am; Inst Mgt Sci. *Res:* Design and analysis of large scale industrial and public systems, especially health related systems. *Mailing Add:* 171 Heatherstone Rd Amherst MA 01002

GIGLIOTTI, HELEN JEAN, BIOCHEMISTRY. *Current Pos:* asst prof, 66-69, assoc prof, 69-73, chmn dept, 77-80, PROF CHEM, CALIF STATE UNIV, FRESNO, 74-, ASST VPRES ACAD AFFAIRS, BUDGET & INSTRUCT RESOURCES, 81- *Personal Data:* b Rochester, NY, July 27, 36. *Educ:* Vassar Col, BA, 58; Univ Mich, PhD(biochem), 63. *Prof Exp:* Res assoc biochem, Scripps Clin & Res Found, 63-66. *Concurrent Pos:* Consult, Cent Calif Med Labs. *Mem:* AAAS; Am Chem Soc; Am Asn Clin Chem. *Res:* Clinical chemistry methods, especially chromatographic and enzymological; plant biochemistry. *Mailing Add:* Chem Dept MS 70 Calif State Univ Fresno CA 93726

GIGLIOTTI, MICHAEL FRANCIS XAVIER, PHYSICAL METALLURGY OF TITANIUM. *Current Pos:* METALLURGIST, GEN ELEC CORP RES & DEVELOP, 70- *Personal Data:* b Springfield, Mass, Oct 10, 44; m 71, Sharon Munkittrick; c Sara & Anna. *Educ:* Boston Col, BS, 66; Dartmouth Col, PhD(eng sci), 70. *Res:* Behavior of titanium alloys at high temperatures; physical properties and non-destructive evaluation of titanium; solidification of eutectic superalloys; metal-mold reactions; processing of metal matrix and intermetallic matrix composites. *Mailing Add:* 41 Kile Dr Scotia NY 12302. *E-Mail:* gigliotti@crd.ge.com

GIGUERE, JOSEPH CHARLES, electrical engineering, for more information see previous edition

GIGUERE, RAYMOND JOSEPH, MICROWAVE HEATING IN ORGANIC SYNTHESIS, INTRAMOLECULAR CYCLIZATIONS. *Current Pos:* asst prof, 88-90, assoc prof, 90-97, PROF ORG CHEM, SKIDMORE COL, 97- *Personal Data:* b Menominee, Mich, Aug 17, 54; m 80, Undine Sarach; c Julia. *Educ:* Kalamazoo Col, BA, 76; Univ Hannover, Ger, Dr rer nat, 80. *Prof Exp:* Fel, Deutsche Forschungs Gemeinschaft, 80-82; NIH res assoc, Mich State Univ, 82-83; asst prof org chem, Mercer Univ, 83-88. *Concurrent Pos:* Prin investr, NIH, 86-89, Am Chem Soc-Petrol Res Fund, 86-88 & 92-94; Camille & Henry Dreyfus Scholar, Camille & Henry Dreyfus Found, 91-93. *Mem:* Am Chem Soc; Coun Undergrad Res. *Res:* Developing the use of microwave heating for organic synthesis; developed synthetic methodology involving intramolecular cyclizations. *Mailing Add:* 84 Lincoln Ave Saratoga NY 12866

GIKAS, PAUL WILLIAM, PATHOLOGY. *Current Pos:* From instr to assoc prof, 60-69, PROF PATH, UNIV MICH MED SCH, ANN ARBOR, 69-, ASST DEAN MED SCH ADMIS, 90- *Personal Data:* b Lansing, Mich, July 23, 28; m 52, Suzanne Haglund; c Sandra (Brooks), Sarah (Malinusky) & Paula (Nagelvoort). *Educ:* Univ Mich, BA, 50, MD, 54. *Concurrent Pos:* Chief lab serv, Vet Admin Hosp, Ann Arbor, 60-68; mem adv comt traffic safety, Dept HEW, 66-68; consult, Armed Forces Inst Path & USPHS, 67-68 & 71. *Mem:* Fel Col Am Pathologists; US-Can Acad Path. *Res:* Pathogenesis of injuries in highway accidents; long term preservation of blood by freezing; correlation of morphologic findings in prostatic carcinoma with imaging techniques. *Mailing Add:* Dept Path Univ Mich Med Sch C4130 Med Sci I C Wing 1301 Catherine Ann Arbor MI 48109-0611. *Fax:* 313-764-4542

GIL, JOAN, PULMONARY PATHOLOGY, IMAGE ANALYSIS. *Current Pos:* PROF PATH, MT SINAI SCH MED, 84- *Personal Data:* b Barcelona, Catalonia, Spain, June 26, 40; m 70, Brigitte Sollereder; c Daniel & Isadora. *Educ:* Univ Barcelona Med Sch, Med, 64, Doctorate Med, 68; Univ Berne Med Sch, Habilitation, 74. *Hon Degrees:* MA, Univ Pa, 83. *Prof Exp:* Mem staff anat, Med Sch, Univ Berne, 66-76; assoc prof med, Univ Miami, 76-77, Univ Pa, 77-84. *Concurrent Pos:* Res career develop award, Nat Heart, Lung & Blood Inst, NIH, 77-82. *Mem:* Int Soc Stereology; Am Thoracic Soc; Am Physiol Soc; NY Acad Sci; Southern Soc Clin Invest. *Res:* Classificatory and image analysis procedures for the computerized diagnosis in image analysis; correlations between structure and function of lung pathology; pulmonary microcirculation; pulmonary micromechanics; experimental lung pathology. *Mailing Add:* Dept Path Box 1194 Mt Sinai Med Ctr 100th St & Fifth Ave New York NY 10029-6574. *Fax:* 212-860-7851; *E-Mail:* joan_gil@smtplink.mssm.edu

GIL, SALVADOR, NUCLEAR ASTROPHYSICS. *Current Pos:* res asst, 79-84, RES ASSOC, NUCLEAR PHYSICS LAB, UNIV WASH, 86- *Personal Data:* b Salta, Arg, Sept 8, 50; c 2. *Educ:* Univ Nat Tucuman, Argentina, BS, 75; Univ Wash Seattle, MS, 80 & PhD(physics), 84. *Prof Exp:* Teaching asst physics, Univ Nat Tucuman, 71-77; res asst nuclear physics, Tandar Cnea, Buenos Aires, 78-79 & 84-86. *Concurrent Pos:* Exchange visitor, Am Field Serv, 68-69; fel Orgn Am States, 82-84; assoc prof, Univ Buenos Aires, 88- *Mem:* Am Phys Soc; Am Teacher Asn; Argentine Physics Asn. *Res:* Heavy ion nuclear physics; sub-barrier fusion, in particular, the spin distribution of the compound nucleus form in heavy ion reactions. *Mailing Add:* Dept Physics Tandar-CNEA Ave Libertador 8250 Buenos Aires 1428 Argentina

GILANI, SHAMSHAD H, TERATOLOGY, CARDIOLOGY. *Current Pos:* From instr to assoc prof, 67-81, PROF ANAT, NJ MED SCH, COL MED & DENT NJ, 81- *Personal Data:* b Lahore, WPakistan, Feb 4, 37; m 70; c 2. *Educ:* Univ Punjab, WPakistan, BS, 55, MS, 58; State Univ NY Buffalo, PhD(exp embryol), 67. *Honors & Awards:* Golden Apple Award, AMA, 73, 82, 84, 85, 86. *Mem:* Am Asn Anat; Teratology Soc; Europ Teratology Soc; Soc Develop Biol; Sigma Xi. *Res:* Analyzing the mechanism of abnormal development of the heart. *Mailing Add:* Anat Dept UMD NJ Med Sch 185 S Orange Ave Newark NJ 07103-2714

GILARDI, EDWARD FRANCIS, ENVIRONMENTAL ENGINEERING, ENVIRONMENTAL SCIENCE. *Current Pos:* PROJ MGR, ROY F WESTON INC, 65- *Personal Data:* b Brooklyn, NY, Apr 26, 36; m 63; c 4. *Educ:* Manhattan Col, BCE, 57; Rutgers Univ, MS, 63, PhD(environ sci), 66. *Prof Exp:* Engr, NY State Conserv Dept, 57-59; res assoc, Rutgers Univ, 59-65. *Mem:* Am Soc Civil Engrs; Air Pollution Control Asn; Am Acad Environ Engrs; Water Pollution Control Asn; Sigma Xi. *Res:* Biological waste treatment; application of wastes to land environment; reaction of air pollutants with building materials. *Mailing Add:* 12 Long Lane Malvern PA 19355-2916

GILARDI, RICHARD DEAN, STRUCTURAL CHEMISTRY. *Current Pos:* res assoc x-ray diffraction, 66-68, RES CHEMIST, NAVAL RES LAB, 68- *Personal Data:* b Wisconsin Rapids, Wis, Feb 23, 40; m 60; c 1. *Educ:* Mass Inst Technol, BS, 61; Univ Md, PhD(phys chem), 66. *Prof Exp:* Chemist, Am Instrument Co, Md, 62-63 & Inst Defense Analysis, Va, 66. *Concurrent Pos:* Consult, Inst Defense Analysis, 65-66. *Mem:* Am Crystallog Asn; Am Chem Soc; Sigma Xi. *Res:* Techniques of diffraction analysis; molecular structure determination by x-ray diffraction; correlation of molecular structure with biological activity; biopolymer structure. *Mailing Add:* Naval Res Lab Code 6030 Washington DC 20375-0001

GILBARG, DAVID, APPLIED MATHEMATICS. *Current Pos:* exec head dept, 59-69, PROF MATH, STANFORD UNIV, 57- *Personal Data:* b Brooklyn, NY, Sept 17, 18; m 41; c 1. *Educ:* City Col New York, BS, 38; Ind Univ, PhD(math), 41. *Prof Exp:* Asst math, Ind Univ, 39-41; physicist, Nat Bur Standards, 41-42; chief, Fluid Dynamics Test Sect, Naval Ord Lab, 42-45, chief, Theoret Mech Subdiv, 45-46; from asst prof to assoc prof math, Ind Univ, 46-57. *Mem:* Am Math Soc; Math Asn Am; Ger Soc Appl Math & Mech. *Res:* Fluid dynamics; partial differential equations. *Mailing Add:* Dept Math Stanford Univ 209 Creekside Dr Palo Alto CA 94306-4507

GILBERT, ALLAN HENRY, SYNTHETIC ORGANIC CHEMISTRY. *Current Pos:* res chemist, 56-65, sect chief detergent solids sect, 65-72, mgr tech serv, 72-75, dir sci res, 75-83, VPRES, SCI AFFAIRS LEVER BROS CO, EDGEWATER, 83- *Personal Data:* b Liverpool, Eng, Oct 20, 29; m 46; c 2. *Educ:* Univ Liverpool, BSc, 51, PhD(org chem), 54. *Prof Exp:* Can Res fel, Univ NB, 54-56. *Mem:* Am Chem Soc; Asn Res Dirs. *Mailing Add:* 200 Beechwood Rd Oradell NJ 07649

GILBERT, ALTON LEE, INFORMATION SCIENCES, RESEARCH MANAGEMENT. *Current Pos:* SR VPRES, SR SCIENTIST & TECH DIR, TECH SOLUTIONS INC, MESILLA PARK, NMEX, 82- *Personal Data:* b Elmira, NY, Apr 13, 42; m 88, Susan M Scott; c David L & Elizabeth A. *Educ:* NMex State Univ, BSEE, 70, MS, 71, ScD(info sci), 73. *Honors & Awards:* Edward Gamble Award, 79. *Prof Exp:* Res engr commun, NMex State Univ, 69-73; res electronics engr info sci, White Sands Missile Range, 73-82. *Concurrent Pos:* Adj assoc prof, Dept Elec Eng, NMex State Univ, 73-84; evaluator res prog, US Army Res Off, 73-82; partner & engr, Gilbert-Roman Eng Asn, 74-77; mem tech review comt, Joint Serv Electronics Prog, 75-82; adv, Tex Tech Control Theory Prog, Off Naval Res, US Navy, 76-82. *Mem:* Inst Elec & Electronics Engrs; Sigma Xi; Comput Soc. *Res:* Real-time applications of pattern recognition and machine intelligence; improvements in communications systems for data transmission and processing; novel computer architectures for data handling in real-time; robotics and artificial intelligence; test and evaluation instrumentation; real-time video tracking. *Mailing Add:* Tech Solutions Inc PO Box 1148 Mesilla Park NM 88047. *Fax:* 505-525-5801; *E-Mail:* gilbert_al@msn.com

GILBERT, ARTHUR CHARLES, VIBRATION ANALYSIS & DESIGN, PRODUCT APPLICATIONS. *Current Pos:* CONSULT, USN DEPT DEFENSE, 88- *Personal Data:* b New York, NY, Sept 23, 26; div, Suzanne Teperson; c Pamela G (Remis) & Randi G (Cutler). *Educ:* NY Univ, BAeroE, 46 MAeroE, 47 ScD(eng), 56. *Prof Exp:* Sr tech exec res & develop & vpres eng, Cent Intel Agency, Bendix & United Aircraft Corp, 61-70; sci adv, Chief Naval Opers, USN, Dept Defense, 70-75; vpres, Data Solutions Corp, 75-77 & Unified Industs, Inc, 77-78; dir, OAO Corp, 78-81; construct engr, Daughters Am Revolution, 82-87; consult, FMC Corp & Litton Corp, 82-88. *Concurrent Pos:* Founder & dir, Auto-Train Corp, 68-79; consult, NIH, 69-70; consult & lectr, Naval War Col, USN, 75-76; expert witness, numerous atty partnerships, 85- *Res:* System analysis and design; structural dynamics; advanced technical planning; engineering management; weapon system requirements analyses and design; aircraft structural failures and patent infringements; helicopter acoustive and vibrations; photoelasticity; author of numerous publications and books. *Mailing Add:* 1201 S Eads St Arlington VA 22202-2840

GILBERT, ARTHUR DONALD, INDUSTRIAL CHEMISTRY. *Current Pos:* RETIRED. *Personal Data:* b Niagara Falls, NY, Aug 12, 16; m 41; c 4. *Educ:* Middlebury Col, AB, 38; Cornell Univ, PhD(org chem), 42. *Prof Exp:* Asst instr chem, Cornell Univ, 39-41; res chemist, Eastern Lab, E I du Pont de Nemours & Co, Inc, 42-50, lab tech head, 50-52, tech specialist, Explosives Dept, Tech Div, 52-55, asst dir, Burnside Lab, 55-56, mgr tech div, Foreign Rels Dept, 56-58, mgr patent & licensing sect, Int Dept, 58-60, asst dir, Eastern Lab, 60-63, dir, Explosives Exp Sta Lab, 63-68, tech specialist, Res & Develop Div Staff, 68-73, patents & licensing specialist, Polymer Intermediates Dept, 73-77. *Mem:* Am Chem Soc; Soc Chem Indust. *Res:* Detonation research; organic polymer intermediate research; fundamental chemistry of organic reactions of nitric acid. *Mailing Add:* Gardenside M-2 Shelburne VT 05482-9805

GILBERT, BARRIE, SEMICONDUCTOR DESIGN, DEVICE DESIGN. *Current Pos:* group leader Techtronics, 64-70 & Analog Devices, 77-80, DIV FEL ANALOG DEVICES, PLESSY RES LABS, 81- *Personal Data:* b Bournemouth, Eng, June 5, 37. *Educ:* Bournemouth Municipal Col, HNC (appl physics), 62. *Prof Exp:* Scientific asst, Signal & Develop Estab, UK Ministry Defense, 54-55; engr, Mullard, 58-64; design engr, Vickers-Armstrong, 64. *Mem:* Fel Inst Elec & Electronics Engrs. *Res:* Circuit design; high performance non-linear analog circuits; translinear principle; translinear multiplier. *Mailing Add:* 1100 NW Compton Dr Suite 301 Beaverton OR 97006

GILBERT, BARRY JAY, PHYSICS. *Current Pos:* Asst prof physics, 68-77, assoc prof, 77-, PROF PHYSICS, RI COL. *Personal Data:* b Brooklyn, NY, Feb 2, 43; m 65; c 2. *Educ:* Polytech Inst Brooklyn, BS, 63; Lehigh Univ, MS, 65, PhD(physics), 68. *Mem:* Am Asn Physics Teachers. *Res:* Theoretical plasma physics. *Mailing Add:* Dept Phys Sci RI Col 600 Mt Pleasant Providence RI 02908-1924

GILBERT, BARRY KENT, PHYSIOLOGY, ELECTRICAL ENGINEERING. *Current Pos:* Res asst physiol & biophys, Mayo Clin, Mayo Found, 71-73, res assoc, 73-75, instr physiol, 75-77, asst prof physiol & biophys, Mayo Med Sch, 78-80, STAFF SCIENTIST, DEPT PHYSIOL

& BIOPHYS, MAYO CLIN, MAYO FOUND, 80- *Personal Data:* b Chicago, Ill, Sept 22, 44; m 73; c 1. *Educ:* Purdue Univ, BS, 65; Univ Minn, PhD(physiol, biophys), 72. *Concurrent Pos:* NIH fel, Nat Heart, Lung & Blood Inst, 72-74; assoc staff scientist physiol & biophys, Mayo Clin/Mayo Found, 75-77, staff scientist, 78-, assoc prof biophys, 80-85, prof, Physiol/Biophys, 86- *Mem:* Am Physiol Soc; Inst Elec & Electronics Engrs; AAAS; Defense Sci Res Coun, Defense Adv Res Proj Agency. *Res:* Application of engineering and computational methods to the solution of computation bound problems in biomedical research and clinical medicine; design of high performance signal processors using gallium arsenide integrated circuits; development of computer aided design (CAD) software for signal processor and integrated circuit design. *Mailing Add:* PO Box 1012 Rochester MN 55903-1012. *Fax:* 507-284-9171; *E-Mail:* gilbert@mayo.edu

GILBERT, BRIAN E, VIROLOGY. *Current Pos:* MEM FAC, DEPT MICROBIOL & IMMUNOL, BAYLOR COL MED, TEX MED CTR, 73- *Personal Data:* b Hollywood, Calif, Jan 31, 42; m 70; c 2. *Educ:* Univ Calif, Berkeley, AB, 64; Univ Calif, Los Angeles, PhD(med microbiol & immunol), 70. *Prof Exp:* Postdoctoral Fel, microbiol, Sch Med, Northwestern Univ, 70-73. *Mem:* Am Soc Microbiol; Am Soc Virol; Int Soc Antiviral Res; AAAS. *Res:* Role of cystine in the morphogenesis of Histoplasma capsulatum; regulation of protein synthesis at the translational level during mouse brain development; antiviral chemotherapy; aerosol therapy for viral respiratory disease. *Mailing Add:* Dept Microbiol & Immunol Baylor Col Med One Baylor Plaza Houston TX 77030-3411

GILBERT, CARTER ROWELL, ICHTHYOLOGY. *Current Pos:* asst cur ichthyol, Fla State Mus & asst prof zool, Univ Fla, 61-72, assoc cur & joint assoc prof & Latin Am Studies, 72-87, CUR ICHTHYOL, FLA MUS NATURAL HIST & PROF ZOOL, UNIV FLA, 87- *Personal Data:* b Huntington, WVa, May 23, 30; m 58; c 2. *Educ:* Ohio State Univ, BSc, 51, MSc, 53; Univ Mich, PhD(zool, ichthyol), 60. *Prof Exp:* Asst zool, Ohio State Univ, 52; asst ichthyol, Div Fishes, Mus Zool, Univ Mich, 58-59; res assoc, US Nat Mus, 59-61. *Concurrent Pos:* Numerous grants, NSF, Am Physiol Soc. *Mem:* Am Soc Ichthyol & Herpet (hon secy, 81-82, secy, 82-90); Japanese Soc Ichthyol; Soc Systematic Zool; Sigma Xi. *Res:* Eastern North American freshwater fishes; sharks; western Altantic marine fishes; Over 65 publications. *Mailing Add:* 620 NW 40th Terr Gainesville FL 32607

GILBERT, DANIEL LEE, PHYSIOLOGY. *Current Pos:* head, Unit Reactive Oxygen Species, Biophys Sect Clin, Neurosci Br, Nat Inst Neurol Dis & Stroke, 92-94, head, Sect Cellular Biophys, Lab Biophys, 63-71, PHYSIOLOGIST, NIH, 62-, HEAD, UNIT ON REACTIVE OXYGEN SPECIES, BASIC NEUROSCI PROG, 94- *Personal Data:* b Brooklyn, NY, July 2, 25; m 64, Claire Plunguian; c Raymond L. *Educ:* Drew Univ, AB, 48; Univ Iowa, MS, 50; Univ Rochester, PhD(physiol), 55. *Honors & Awards:* Bowditch lectr, Am Physiol Soc, 64; Rebeca Gerschman Lectr, Int cell Res Orgn, UNESCO Int Symp, Buenos Aires, 94. *Prof Exp:* Instr physiol, Sch Med & Dent, Univ Rochester, 55-56; from instr to asst prof, Albany Med Col, 56-60; from asst prof to assoc prof, Jefferson Med Col, 60-63. *Concurrent Pos:* Consult, Grad Coun, George Washington Univ, 65-70; mem corp, Marine Biol Lab, Woods Hole; counr, Oxygen Soc, 87-89. *Mem:* Fel AAAS; Biophys Soc; Am Physiol Soc; fel Oxygen Soc; Soc Neurosci; Sigma Xi. *Res:* Oxygen poisoning; Reactive oxygen species; cell permeability; neurophysiology. *Mailing Add:* BNP Ninos Bldg 36 Rm 5A-25 Bethesda MD 20892-4156. *Fax:* 301-496-8765; *E-Mail:* dangil@helix.nih.gov

GILBERT, DAVID ERWIN, ATOMIC SPECTROSCOPY. *Current Pos:* assoc prof physics & chmn dept, 68-74, prof & dean acad affairs, 77-83, PRES, EASTERN ORE STATE COL, 83- *Personal Data:* b Fresno, Calif, June 23, 39; m 60, Carolyn Parker; c Ronald & Joan (Madsen). *Educ:* Univ Calif, Berkeley, AB, 62; Univ Ore, MA, 64, PhD(physics), 68. *Prof Exp:* Teaching asst physics, Univ Ore, 62-65, res asst, 65-68. *Concurrent Pos:* Res assoc, Univ Ore, 69-71; vis scientist, Sect Astrophys, Paris Observ, Meudon, France, 75-76. *Mem:* Sigma Xi. *Res:* Studies of the effects of foreign gas on atomic absorption lines, total line shape studies. *Mailing Add:* Eastern Ore State Col La Grande OR 97850. *Fax:* 541-962-3493; *E-Mail:* gilbertd@eosc.osshe.edu

GILBERT, DAVID MICHAEL, DNA REPLICATION, CELL-CYCLE. *Current Pos:* ASST PROF, HEALTH SCI CTR, STATE UNIV NY, 94- *Personal Data:* b Brockton, Mass, Oct 9, 59; m 88, Katherine Mary Dousa; c Justin, Sarah & Jay. *Educ:* Univ Calif, San Diego, BA, 82; Stanford Univ, PhD(genetics), 89. *Prof Exp:* Postdoctoral, Fac Med, Nat Ctr Sci Res, 89-91 & Roche Inst, 91-94. *Res:* Developed the first cell free system that can initiate mammalian DNA reproduction in a physiologically relevant manner and have shown that recognition of specific replication origins requires nuclear architecture; identified a novel point in gi-phase at which replication origins are selected and are elucidating the mechanism. *Mailing Add:* 4631 Glencliffe Rd Manlius NY 13210. *Fax:* 315-464-8750; *E-Mail:* gilbertd@vax.cs.hscsyr.edu

GILBERT, DEWAYNE EVERETT, CEREAL CROPS, FORAGE CROPS. *Current Pos:* assoc prof, 76-79, head dept, 78-83, PROF AGRON, UNIV NEV, 79-, EXTEN AGRONOMIST, 76- *Personal Data:* b Dixon, Ill, Oct 18, 24; m 50; c 3. *Educ:* Iowa State Col, BS, 50, MS, 56, PhD(argon), 59. *Prof Exp:* Instr agron, Iowa State Col, 55-59; asst prof agron, Ohio State Uinv, 59-63; farm adv bioclimatology, Univ Calif, 63-64 & 73-76, exten specialist, 64-73. *Concurrent Pos:* Head dept, 78-83, exten argonomist, Univ Nev, Reno, 76- *Mem:* Am Soc Agron; Crop Sci Soc Am; Sigma Xi. *Res:* Crop weather interactions; alfalfa. *Mailing Add:* 3358 Dana Way Sparks NV 89431

GILBERT, DON DALE, ANALYTICAL CHEMISTRY. *Current Pos:* from asst prof to assoc prof, 65-75, chair, Chem Dept, 82-87, PROF CHEM, NORTHERN ARIZ UNIV, 75- *Personal Data:* b Ponca City, Okla, June 5, 34; m 63; c 2. *Educ:* Univ Calif, Berkeley, BS, 56; Univ Minn, PhD(anal chem), 59. *Prof Exp:* Res chemist, Anal & Phys Measurement Div, Calif Res Corp, Stand Oil Co Calif, 59-65. *Mem:* Am Chem Soc; fel AAAS; Sigma Xi. *Res:* Liquid chromatography; colorimetry; trace analysis; electroanalytical chemistry. *Mailing Add:* Dept Chem PO Box 5698 Northern Ariz Univ Flagstaff AZ 86011. *E-Mail:* gilbert@nauvax.ucc.nau.edu

GILBERT, DOUGLAS L, ecology; deceased, see previous edition for last biography

GILBERT, EDGAR NELSON, MATHEMATICS. *Current Pos:* MEM TECH STAFF, BELL TEL LABS, 48- *Personal Data:* b Woodhaven, NY, July 25, 23; m 48; c 3. *Educ:* City Col New York, BS, 43; Mass Inst Technol, PhD(math), 48. *Prof Exp:* Asst physics, Univ Ill, 43; staff mem, Radiation Lab, Mass Inst Technol, 44-46. *Mem:* Inst Elec & Electronics Engrs; Soc Indust Appl Math. *Res:* Electromagnetic theory; differential equations; information theory; probability. *Mailing Add:* 39 Knollwood Rd Whippany NJ 07981

GILBERT, EDWARD E, ENTOMOLOGY. *Current Pos:* RETIRED. *Personal Data:* b New York, NY, May 1, 25; m 61; c 5. *Educ:* Southern Methodist Univ, BS & MS, 50; Univ Calif, Berkeley, PhD, 61. *Prof Exp:* Asst prof biol, State Univ NY Stony Brook, 58-65; prof, Northeast Mo State Teachers Col, 65-69; head, Dept Biol, W Ga Col, 69- *Concurrent Pos:* NSF fel, Radioecol Inst, Oak Ridge Inst Nuclear Studies, 63, NSF grant, 67-69. *Mem:* AAAS; Ecol Soc Am; Am Inst Biol Sci. *Res:* Life history biology, particularly Tribolium; taxonomy of Curculionidae. *Mailing Add:* 7074 Park Arms Ct Fairfield Plantation Villa Rica City GA 30180

GILBERT, ELMER G(RANT), ENGINEERING. *Current Pos:* From instr to assoc prof, Univ Mich, 53-63, prof aeronaut eng, 63-94, prof info & mem, Comput, Info & Control Eng Prog, Dept Aerospace Eng, 71-94, EMER PROF AEROSPACE ENG, UNIV MICH, ANN ARBOR, 94- *Personal Data:* b Joliet, Ill, Mar 29, 30. *Educ:* Univ Mich, BSE, 52, MSE, 53, PhD(instrumentation eng), 57. *Honors & Awards:* Richard E Bellman Control Heritage Award, Inst Elec & Electronics Engrs, 96. *Mem:* Nat Acad Eng; Soc Indust & Appl Math; Inst Elec & Electronics Engrs. *Res:* Automatic control; systems theory; optimization. *Mailing Add:* Dept Aerospace Eng Univ Mich 1320 Beal Ave Ann Arbor MI 48109-2118. *Fax:* 313-763-0578; *E-Mail:* elmer-gilber@umich.edu

GILBERT, ETHEL SCHAEFER, public health & epidemiology, for more information see previous edition

GILBERT, EUGENE CHARLES, SYNTHETIC ORGANIC CHEMISTRY, ORGANIC POLYMER CHEMISTRY. *Current Pos:* sr res & develop assoc, PVC Div, BF Goodrich, 79, mfr mgr, 80-83, res & develop mgr, 84-85, bus mgr, Med Prod, 85-90, MGR, POWER MAT, BF GOODRICH, 91- *Personal Data:* b Manchester, NH, Nov 16, 42; m 65; c 2. *Educ:* St Anselm's Col, AB, 65; Univ Notre Dame, PhD(phys org chem), 69. *Prof Exp:* Res assoc org chem, Johns Hopkins Univ, 69-70; from group leader to sr group leader res & develop, Chem Div, Quaker Oats Co, 70-75; prog mgr develop, Chem Div, Chemetron Corp, 75-77; res & develop mgr, Chem Div, Thiokol Corp, 77-79. *Mem:* Am Chem Soc. *Res:* Conformational analysis; thermodynamics; polymer stabilizers; radiation curable coatings; thermoplastic and thermosetting plastics and elastomers; polymer films; synthetic wound dressings; polymer based medical disposables. *Mailing Add:* Great Lakes Chem Corp 3324 Chelsea Ave Memphis TN 38108

GILBERT, FRANCIS EVALO, CHEMISTRY. *Current Pos:* RETIRED. *Personal Data:* b Mattoon, Ill, June 8, 16; m 42; c 2. *Educ:* Univ Ill, BS, 39. *Prof Exp:* Chemist, Cuneo Press, Ill, 39-41 & Eversharp, Inc, 46; chief chemist & dir res, 46-84, vpres, Sanford Ink Co, 67-84. *Mem:* Am Chem Soc. *Res:* Specialty inks, writing, stamping, marking; adhesives, dextrine, gum and rubber types; packaging of above items for retail distribution. *Mailing Add:* Peninsula Regent One Baldwin Ave Apt 717 San Mateo CA 94401-3851

GILBERT, FRANKLIN ANDREW, SR, HORTICULTURE. *Current Pos:* RETIRED. *Personal Data:* b Burlington, NJ, June 8, 19; m 44; c 3. *Educ:* Rutgers Univ, BS, 42, MS, 48, PhD, 52. *Honors & Awards:* Int Dwarf Tree Asn Award, 81. *Prof Exp:* Asst exten specialist pomol, Rutgers Univ, 44-46, instr & res assoc, 46-50; horticulturist, Univ Exp Sta, Peninsula Br Exp Sta, 50-82, from asst prof to prof, 50-82, emer prof horticult, 82-83. *Mem:* Am Soc Hort Sci; Am Pomol Soc. *Res:* Strawberry breeding; apple rootstock studies. *Mailing Add:* 403 W Pine Sturgeon Bay WI 54235-2823

GILBERT, FRED, HUMAN GENETICS. *Current Pos:* ASSOC PROF PEDIAT & CO-DIR HUMAN GENETICS, CORNELL UNIV MED COL, 88- *Personal Data:* b Brooklyn, NY, Nov 24, 41. *Educ:* Mass Inst Technol, BS, 62; Albert Einstein Col Med, MD, 66. *Prof Exp:* Intern & asst resident internal med, Barnes Hosp, Wash Univ Sch Med, 66-68; clin assoc biochem genetics, Nat Heart & Lung Inst, 68-71; fel human genetics & asst biol, Yale Univ & Sch Med, 71-74; asst prof human genetics & assoc pedt, Univ Pa Sch Med, 74-83; assoc prof pediat & human genetics, Mt Sinai Med Sch, NY, 83-88. *Mem:* Am Soc Human Genetics; AAAS. *Res:* Cell biology; differentiation and neurobiology. *Mailing Add:* Cornell Univ Med Col Genetics Dept 1300 York Ave Box 53 New York NY 10021

GILBERT, FRED IVAN, JR, internal medicine, public health; deceased, see previous edition for last biography

GILBERT, FREDERICK EMERSON, JR, PATHOLOGY, CLINICAL CHEMISTRY. *Current Pos:* LAB DIR, COWETA GEN HOSP, NEWNAN HOSP, GILBERT LAB, 73- *Personal Data:* b Birmingham, Ala, June 1, 41; m 62; c 2. *Educ:* Birmingham Southern Col, BS, 63; Univ Ala, MS, 65, MD, 68. *Honors & Awards:* Med Col Ala Res Award, 68. *Prof Exp:* Res assoc biochem, Mem Inst Path, 65-71; chief cytopath, Ctr Dis Control, 71-73. *Concurrent Pos:* Southern Med Asn res fel, 69-70. *Mem:* Am Chem Soc; Am Asn Clin Chemists; Am Soc Clin Path; Col Am Path; Am Soc Hist Med. *Res:* Multiphasic screening to study the diseased codon; inorganic pyrophosphatase and its role in nucleotide metabolism; quality control cytology. *Mailing Add:* 2 Pinehollow Dr Newnan GA 30263-3313

GILBERT, FREDERICK FRANKLIN, FISH & WILDLIFE SCIENCES. *Current Pos:* dir wildlife biol, Wash State Univ, 81-85, prof zool & wildlife biol, 85-88, interim chair natural resource sci, 88-91, PROF NATURAL RESOURCE SCI, WASH STATE UNIV, 88- *Personal Data:* b Toronto, Can, Aug 5, 41; US citizen; m 64, 81; c 3. *Educ:* Acadia Univ, BS, 65; Univ Guelph, MS, 66, PhD(zool), 68. *Prof Exp:* Big game prog leader, Maine Inland Fish & Game, 68-72; from asst prof to assoc prof zool, Univ Guelph, 72-81. *Concurrent Pos:* Asst prof, Univ Maine, 68-72; dir, Ecol Serv Planning, 75-77; chair, Fac Senate, Wash State Univ, 86-88; chair, US Tech Adv Group ISO/TC191, 87- *Mem:* AAAS; Am Soc Mammalogists; Wildlife Soc; Soc Am Foresters; Soc Northwestern Vertebrate Biol. *Res:* Forest management practices in relation to wildlife populations; bioenergetic relationships in natural and perturbed ecosystems; role of environmental factors in modifying population density, behavior and physiology of wildlife species. *Mailing Add:* Dept Natural Resource Sci Wash State Univ Pullman WA 99164-6410

GILBERT, GARETH E, BOTANY. *Current Pos:* From instr to asst prof, 52-61, ASSOC PROF BOT, OHIO STATE UNIV, 61- *Personal Data:* b Fall River, Mass, Sept 30, 21; m 49; c 2. *Educ:* Ohio State Univ, BSc, 48, MSc, 49, PhD(plant ecol), 53. *Mem:* Ecol Soc Am; Sigma Xi. *Res:* Plant ecology. *Mailing Add:* 2324 Shrewsbury Rd Columbus OH 43221

GILBERT, GEORGE LEWIS, INORGANIC CHEMISTRY. *Personal Data:* b Abington, Mass, Sept 10, 33; m 62; c 3. *Educ:* Antioch Col, BS, 58; Mich State Univ, PhD(inorg chem), 63. *Prof Exp:* Res chemist, Lawrence Radiation Lab, Univ Calif, 63-64; chmn, Chem Dept, Denison Univ, 60-74, from asst prof to assoc prof chem, 64-80, actg chmn dept, 67-68, sci coordr, 70-74, coordr, Learning Resources Ctr, 80-83. *Mem:* AAAS; Sigma Xi; Royal Soc Chem. *Res:* Reactions of noble gas compounds; coordination compounds and their structures. *Mailing Add:* Dept Chem Denison Univ PO Box M Granville OH 43023-0613

GILBERT, GORDON R, PHYSICS. *Current Pos:* PROF, DEPT PHYSICS, MESA STATE COL, 77- *Personal Data:* b Toronto, Ont, Nov 22, 50. *Educ:* Unvi Toronto, BS, 72; McGill Univ, MSc, 73, PhD(math)75. *Concurrent Pos:* Killam fel, Can Coun, 93. *Mem:* Royal Soc Can. *Mailing Add:* 628 Sage Ct Grand Junction CO 81506-1955

GILBERT, HARRIET S, HEMATOLOGY. *Current Pos:* prof med & dir, Gen Clin Res Ctr, 86-91, CLIN PROF MED, ALBERT EINSTEIN COL MED, YESHIVA UNIV, BRONX, NY, 91- *Personal Data:* b Philadelphia, Pa, June 22, 30; m 57; c Laura, David & Daniel. *Educ:* Bryn Mawr Col, AB, 51; Columbia Univ, MD, 55; Am Bd Internal Med, dipl, 65; Am Bd Hemat, dipl, 72. *Prof Exp:* From intern to res resident internal med, Mt Sinai Hosp, 55-58, clin asst hemat, 58-63, asst attend hematologist, 63-69; from asst prof to assoc prof med, Mt Sinai Sch Med, 66-81, asst dean res, 77-81, prof med & assoc dean res, 81-86. *Concurrent Pos:* Fel, Mt Sinai Hosp, 58-61, from res asst to res assoc, 61-64; Am Cancer Soc fel, 59-61, grant, 65; consult, Elmhurst Hosp, NY, 64-; attend hematologist, Bronx Vet Hosp, 71-73, consult, 73-; asst dir, Res Activities Comt & Off & asst prog dir, Clin Res Ctr, Mt Sinai Med Ctr, 75-79, assoc dir, 79-; assoc attend hematologist, Mt Sinai Hosp, 69-81; attending hematologist, Mt Sinai Hosp & Med Ctr, 81-; lectr, Mt Sinai Sch Med, 86-; attend Weiler Hosp, Albert Einstein Col Med, 86-, Bronx Munic Hosp Ctr, 86-, Montefiore Med Ctr, 86-; assoc ed, Mt Sinai J Med. *Mem:* Biophys Soc; Harvey Soc; Am Soc Hemat; Am Fedn Clin Res; Am Col Physicians; Am Inst Nutrit. *Res:* Hematology, especially myeloproliferative diseases; biochemical changes, including lipid metabolism, erythrocyte metabolism, histamine and serotonin metabolism and leukocyte membrane development; clinical problems, particularly surgical and neurological complications; chemotherapy in control of myeloproliferative disease; vitamin B-12 binding proteins; automation in hematology. *Mailing Add:* 115 E 72 St New York NY 10021. *Fax:* 212-535-7744; *E-Mail:* hgilbert@buray.net

GILBERT, HIRAM FRAZIER, CATALYSIS OF PROTEIN FOLDING, CHEMISTRY & BIOLOGY OF DISULFIDE BONDS. *Current Pos:* PROF BIOCHEM, BAYLOR COL MED, 77-, ASSOC DEAN, 96- *Personal Data:* b Knoxville, Tenn, Nov 18, 46; m 68, Sandra R; c Meredith L & Nathan F. *Educ:* Univ Tenn, Knoxville, BS, 69; Univ Wis-Madison, PhD(biochem), 75. *Prof Exp:* Am Cancer Soc fel, Brandeis Univ, 75-77. *Concurrent Pos:* NIH career develop award, Baylor Col Med, 82-87; vis prof, Oxford Univ, 86-87; consult, Beckman Instruments, 88-90; chair, Biomed Sci Study Sect, NIH, 89-94; ed, J Biol Chem, 93- *Mem:* Am Chem Soc; Am Asn Biochem & Molecular Biol. *Res:* Role of disulfide bond formation in protein folding and regulation; catalysis of protein folding. *Mailing Add:* Dept Biochem Baylor Col Med Houston TX 77030. *E-Mail:* hgilbert@bcm.tmc.edu

GILBERT, JACK PITTARD, ANALYTICAL CHEMISTRY, GOOD MANUFACTURING PRACTICES. *Current Pos:* RETIRED. *Personal Data:* b Lenior County, NC, Nov 8, 25; m 44, June Valle Cole; c Gary Lee & Carol (Laskowski). *Educ:* Wagner Col, BS, 52. *Prof Exp:* Chemist, Radioactive Lab, Merck Sharp & Dohme Res Lab Div, Merck & Co, Inc, 51-56, suprv anal chem, Pilot Plant Control Lab, 56-67, sr res chemist, 67-73, group leader, 73-76, sect leader anal chem, Microanal & Pilot Plant Control Lab, 76-86, sect leader, Good Mfg Practices, 86-91. *Mem:* Am Chem Soc; Am Microchem Soc. *Res:* Functional group analysis; micro and macro; monaqueous titrations; acid base analysis; spectrophotometer analysis; specific ion analysis and potentiometric titrations; good manufacturing practices, good laboratory practices, and specification. *Mailing Add:* 1441 Kittiwake Dr Punta Gorda FL 33950

GILBERT, JAMES ALAN LONGMORE, INTERNAL MEDICINE. *Current Pos:* dir, Clin Teaching Unit, 70-86, EMER PROF, ROYAL ALEXANDRA HOSP, EDMONTON, 86- *Personal Data:* b Grantown-on-Spey, Scotland, Jan 28, 18; m 44; c 8. *Educ:* Univ Edinburgh, MB & ChB, 41, MD, 47; FRCP, 47 & 65; FRCP(E), 47; FRCPS(C), 50. *Honors & Awards:* I Provincial Award, Excellence in Med, 78. *Prof Exp:* Assoc prof, 57-63, prof med, univ alta, 63- *Mem:* Fel Am Col Physicians; fel Royal Soc Arts; Am Gastroenterol Asn; Can Asn Gastroenterol (pres, 70); Int Soc Res Med Educ (pres, 74). *Res:* Prediabetic syndromes; physiological basis of the dumping syndrome following partial gastrectomy for peptic ulcer; medical education, evaluation in medical education; ethanol metabolism and its complications. *Mailing Add:* 405 Hys Ctr 11010 101st St Edmonton AB T5H 4B9 Can

GILBERT, JAMES FREEMAN, GEOPHYSICS, SEISMOLOGY. *Current Pos:* assoc dir, 76-88, PROF GEOPHYS, INST GEOPHYS & PLANETARY PHYSICS, SCRIPPS INST OCEANOG, UNIV CALIF, SAN DIEGO, 61- *Personal Data:* b Vincennes, Ind, Aug 9, 31; m 59, Sarah Bonney; c Cynthia, Sarah & James. *Educ:* Mass Inst Technol, BS, 53, PhD(geophys), 56. *Hon Degrees:* Dr, Utrecht Univ, 94. *Honors & Awards:* Gold Medal, Royal Astron Soc, 81; Arthur L Day Medal, Geol Soc Am, 85; Balzan Prize, 90; John E Barton distinguished lectr, Ky Geol Surv, 96. *Prof Exp:* Res assoc, Mass Inst Technol, 56-57; asst prof, Inst Geophys, Univ Calif, Los Angeles, 57-59, assoc prof, 60; sr res geophysicist, Tex Instruments, Inc, 60-61. *Concurrent Pos:* Guggenheim fel, Cambridge Univ, 64-65, Guggenheim overseas fel, Churchill Col, Cambridge, 72-73; guest lectr, Veining-Meinesz Geophys Inst, Univ Utrecht, 73 & Acad Sci, USSR, 76; distinguished lectr, Dept Physics, Univ Alta, 80; Sherman Fairchild distinguished scholar, Div Geol & Planetary Sci, Calif Inst Technol, 87; chmn, Grad Dept, Scripps Inst Oceanog, Univ Calif, San Diego, 88-91, fac res lectr, Univ, 91-92. *Mem:* Nat Acad Sci; Am Phys Soc; fel Europ Geophys Soc; fel Am Geophys Union; Seismol Soc Am; Sigma Xi; Am Acad Arts & Sci. *Res:* Elastodynamics; normal mode theory; geophysical problems of inversion and inference; structure of the earth and of earthquake sources; earthquake mechanism; computational geophysics. *Mailing Add:* Dept Geophys Univ Calif 8602 La Jolla Shores Dr La Jolla CA 92093-0225. *Fax:* 619-534-8090; *E-Mail:* fgilbert@ucsd.edu

GILBERT, JAMES ROBERT, WILDLIFE SCIENCE, BIOSTATISTICS. *Current Pos:* asst prof, 75-80, assoc prof, 80-86, PROF WILDLIFE, UNIV MAINE, 86-, CHAIRPERSON, 93- *Personal Data:* b Jefferson, Mo, Feb 16, 46; m 69; c 2. *Educ:* Colo State Univ, BS, 68; Univ Minn, MS, 70; Univ Idaho, PhD(wildlife), 74. *Prof Exp:* Res assoc wildlife, Univ Idaho, 71-73; instr, Cornell Univ, 73-74; res assoc, Univ Wash, 74-75. *Concurrent Pos:* Consult, US Fish & Wildlife Serv, Bur Land Mgt & Fed Hwy Admin; working group grey seals, Int Coun Explor of Sea, 77-79. *Mem:* Wildlife Soc; Am Soc Mammalogists; Biometr Soc; Bear Biologists Asn; Soc Marine Mammal. *Res:* Population dynamics and censusing, especially of large terrestrial and marine mammals. *Mailing Add:* Dept Wildlife Mgt Univ Maine Orono ME 04469-0001

GILBERT, JEROME A, BIOMECHANICS, OSTEOPOROSIS. *Current Pos:* assoc prof, 88-92, PROF BIOL ENG & VET MED, MISS STATE UNIV, 93- *Personal Data:* b Jackson, Miss, Dec 9, 54. *Educ:* Miss State Univ, BS, 77; Duke Univ, PhD(biomed, eng), 82. *Prof Exp:* Vis asst prof mech eng, NC State Univ, Chapel Hill, 82-83, asst prof orthop surg, 83-88. *Mem:* Am Soc Biomech; Sigma Xi; Orthop Res Soc; Am Soc Mech Engrs. *Mailing Add:* Agr & Biol Eng Miss State Univ PO Box 9632 Mississippi State MS 39762-9632

GILBERT, JEROME B, RESEARCH ADMINISTRATION. *Current Pos:* CONSULT ENGR, 91- *Honors & Awards:* Gordon Fair Award, Am Acad Environ Eng, 93. *Mem:* Nat Acad Eng. *Mailing Add:* 324 Tappen Terr Orinda CA 94563

GILBERT, JIMMIE D, ALGEBRA. *Current Pos:* PROF MATH, UNIV SC, SPARTANBURG, 86- *Personal Data:* b Quitman, La, July 12, 34; m 53, 74, Linda Phillips; c Donna, Lisa, Martin, Dan, Beckie & Matt. *Educ:* La Polytech Inst, BS, 56; Auburn Univ, MS, 57, PhD(math), 60. *Prof Exp:* Instr math, Auburn Univ, 57-58; from asst prof to assoc prof, 58-62, prof math, La Tech Univ, 65-86. *Mem:* Am Math Soc; Math Asn Am. *Res:* Linear algebra, author of 15 college mathematics textbooks. *Mailing Add:* Dept Math Univ SC Spartanburg SC 29303. *Fax:* 864-503-5375; *E-Mail:* j.gilbert@mcs.uscs.sc.edu

GILBERT, JOEL STERLING, mechanical engineering, for more information see previous edition

GILBERT, JOHN ANDREW, EXPERIMENTAL STRESS ANALYSIS, APPLIED OPTICS. *Current Pos:* dir civil eng prog, Dept Mech Eng, 85-90, PROF & MECH ENGR, DEPT MECH & AEROSPACE ENG, UNIV ALA, HUNTSVILLE, 85- *Personal Data:* b Ger, Sept 3, 48; US citizen; m 85, Kathleen M Leonard; c Allison, Ben, Rebecca & Richard. *Educ:* Polytech Inst Brooklyn, BS, 71, MS, 73; Ill Inst Technol, PhD(solid mech), 75. *Honors & Awards:* Cert of Recognition, Am Inst Aeronaut & Astronaut, 90; Engr of Yr, Am Soc Civil Engrs, 91. *Prof Exp:* From lectr to assoc prof eng, Univ Wis, Milwaukee, 75-85. *Concurrent Pos:* Consult, Allen Bradley Co, 76-77, 82-85, Appl Power, 79-81, Gen Elec Med Systs Div, 80-81, Waukesha Engine, 81 & AT&T Bell Lab, 81-89; prin investr, Army Res Off Contracts, 80-87 & NSF, 83-85, NASA, 87-; res fel, Am Soc Nondestructive Testing, 87; adj prof mat sci, Univ Ala, Tuscaloosa, 88-, Birmingham, 89-; pres, Optechnol Inc, 89-; dir, Consortium Holography, Appl Mechs & Photonics, 93-; mem eng staff, Center Appl Optics, 95- *Mem:* Fel Soc Exp Mech; Am Acad Mech; Sigma Xi; Brit Soc Strain Measurement; Am Soc Eng Educ; Soc Photo-Optical Instrumentation Engrs; Am Soc Civil Engrs. *Res:* Holographic interferometry and speckle metrology; fiber optic sensing; radial metrology; published over 130 papers and granted 2 patents. *Mailing Add:* Dept Mech & Aerospace Eng Univ Ala Huntsville AL 35899

GILBERT, JOHN BARRY, PHYSICAL CHEMISTRY. *Current Pos:* RETIRED. *Personal Data:* b Hull, Eng, Jan 21, 37; m 59; c 2. *Educ:* Univ Hull, BSc, 57, PhD(chem), 60. *Prof Exp:* Res fel photochem, Univ Alta, 60-62; from res assoc to sr res assoc, Esso Petrol Can, 62-83, res adv, 83-91. *Mem:* Fel Chem Inst Can. *Res:* Petroleum refining; catalytic processes, especially catalytic hydrogenation and hydrocracking; catalytic theory and reactor design theory; environmental protection; petroleum products quality. *Mailing Add:* 1675 Winton Rd Sarnia ON N7V 4C1 Can

GILBERT, JOHN CARL, PHYSICAL ORGANIC CHEMISTRY. *Current Pos:* From asst prof to assoc prof, 65-84, chmn dept, 87-91, PROF CHEM, UNIV TEX, AUSTIN, 84- *Personal Data:* b Laramie, Wyo, Jan 30, 39; m 65, Lucia Albino; c Melissa C. *Educ:* Univ Wyo, BS, 61; Yale Univ, MS, 62, PhD(chem), 66. *Concurrent Pos:* NIH prin investr, Welch Found. *Mem:* Am Chem Soc; Sigma Xi; AAAS. *Res:* Thermal and photochemical isomerization of hydrocarbons; organometallics; carbenes; synthesis; reaction mechanisms. *Mailing Add:* 4402 Balcones Dr Austin TX 78731. *Fax:* 512-471-8696; *E-Mail:* Bitnet: cmax015@utxvms

GILBERT, JOHN JOUETT, FRESHWATER BIOLOGY, INVERTEBRATE ZOOLOGY. *Current Pos:* from asst prof to assoc prof, 67-74, PROF BIOL, DARTMOUTH COL, 74- *Personal Data:* b Southampton, NY, July 18, 37; m 59, Caroline S Colburn; c John S & Anne M. *Educ:* Williams Col, BA, 59; Yale Univ, PhD(biol), 63. *Prof Exp:* NIH fel, Univ Wash, 63-64; asst prof biol, Princeton Univ, 64-67. *Mem:* Am Soc Zool; Am Soc Limnol & Oceanog; Ecol Soc Am; Int Asn Theoret & Appl Limnol. *Res:* Biology of rotifers; ecology; invertebrate biology; sexuality and form-change in ploimate rotifers; biology of freshwater sponges; trophic interactions in and competition among freshwater zooplankton. *Mailing Add:* Dept Biol Sci Dartmouth Col Hanover NH 03755

GILBERT, LAWRENCE IRWIN, ZOOLOGY. *Current Pos:* William Rand Kenan prof zool, 80-82, KENAN PROF & CHAIR BIOL, UNIV NC, CHAPEL HILL, 82- *Personal Data:* b New York, NY, Jan 24, 29; m 52; c 3. *Educ:* Long Island Univ, BS, 50; NY Univ, MS, 55; Cornell Univ, PhD(zool), 58. *Prof Exp:* From asst prof to prof biol sci, Northwestern Univ, Evanston, 58-80. *Concurrent Pos:* NSF sr fel, Univ Berne, 64-65; vis scientist, Am Physiol Soc, 63-; mem, Presidential Task Force Pest Mgt, 71-72; ed, Insect Biochem, 84-; fel, Am Acad Arts & Sci, 90. *Mem:* Soc Growth & Develop; Soc Exp Biol; Am Soc Cell Biol; Entom Soc Am; Sigma Xi. *Res:* Invertebrate endocrinology; biochemical effect of insect hormones; insect physiology; lipid metabolism and transport in insects; endocrine gland ultrastructure; sterols and terpenes in insects. *Mailing Add:* Dept Biol Univ NC CB 3280 Coker Hall Chapel Hill NC 27599-3280

GILBERT, MARGARET LOIS, BOTANY, ECOLOGY. *Current Pos:* from asst prof to assoc prof, 54-61, Nelson C White chair, Natural Sci, 81, PROF BIOL & CHMN, DEPT BIOL SCI & DIV NATURAL SCI, FLA SOUTHERN COL, 61- *Personal Data:* b Wakefield, RI, June 9, 28. *Educ:* Univ RI, BS, 49; Univ Wis, PhD(bot), 53. *Prof Exp:* Asst prof biol, Northwestern State Col, La, 53-54. *Concurrent Pos:* Consult. *Mem:* Bot Soc Am; Ecol Soc Am; Sigma Xi. *Res:* Plant ecology. *Mailing Add:* Dept Biol Fla Southern Col 111 Hollingsworth Dr Lakeland FL 33801-5698

GILBERT, MURRAY CHARLES, PETROLOGY. *Current Pos:* DIR GEOL & GEOPHYS, UNIV OKLA, 90- *Personal Data:* b Lawton, Okla, Jan 21, 36; m 58; c 3. *Educ:* Univ Okla, BS, 58, MS, 61; Univ Calif, Los Angeles, PhD(geol), 65. *Prof Exp:* Asst res geologist, Univ Calif, Los Angeles, 65; fel, Carnegie Inst Geophys Lab, 65-68; from asst prof to prof petrol, Va Polytech Inst & State Univ, 68-83, chmn dept, 75-80; head dept, Tex A&M Univ, 85-90. *Concurrent Pos:* Geologist, Okla Geol Surv, 77-78. *Mem:* Am Geophys Union; Am Asn Petrol Geologists; Geol Soc Am; Mineral Soc Am; Mineral Soc Gt Brit & Ireland. *Res:* Experimental mineralogy and petrology; stability relations of amphiboles, pyroxenes, olivine, and aluminum silicates; sulfide-silicate relations; geology and petrology of Wichita Mountains, Oklahoma and Southern Oklahoma Anlacogen; planetology. *Mailing Add:* 1412 Aspen Lane Norman OK 73072

GILBERT, MYRON B, COMMUNICATIONS SCIENCE, SCIENCE ADMINISTRATION. *Current Pos:* RETIRED. *Personal Data:* b Rochester, NY, Sept 3, 21; m 45; c 3. *Educ:* Cornell Univ, AB, 47; Mass Inst Technol, MS, 49. *Prof Exp:* Meteorologist, Pan Am Grace Airways, 49-57; chief, Systs & Applns Br, Geophys Res Directorate, 57-60, chief, Eval Div, Air Force Cambridge Res Labs, 60-67, dir, Air Force Environ Consult Serv, 67-69; mgr tech commun, Honeywell Info Systs, 69-74; managing ed, Johns Hopkins Appl Tech Digest & ed supvr, Appl Phys Lab, Johns Hopkins Univ, 75-88. *Mem:* Am Meteorol Soc; Am Geophys Union; AAAS; Inst Elec & Electronics Engrs. *Res:* Dissemination of scientific and technical information; writing and publication of scientific reports in the areas of geophysics, mathematics, physics and engineering. *Mailing Add:* 700 Seventh St SW Apt 143 Washington DC 20024

GILBERT, PAUL H, CIVIL ENGINEERING. *Current Pos:* CHMN & SR VPRES, PARSONS BRINCKERHOFF QUADE & DOUGLAS INC, 78- *Educ:* Univ Calif, Berkeley, BS, 58, MS, 60. *Honors & Awards:* Lincoln Arc Welding Award; RicKey Medal, Am Soc Civ Engrs, Construct Mgt Award, 94. *Prof Exp:* Design supvr, prog mgr & unit supvr, Calif State Water Proj. *Concurrent Pos:* Chmn, Career Develop Comt, Parson Brinckerhoff Quade & Douglas Inc, 78-93; lectr, Univ Calif, Berkeley, Stanford Univ, Golden Gate Univ & Sacramento State Univ. *Mem:* Nat Acad Eng; Am Consult Engrs Coun; Am Soc Civil Engrs; Sigma Xi; Soc Am Mil Engrs; Am Underground-Space Asn. *Res:* New technology; special problem-solving; high-level nuclear waste isolation facilities; water system tunnels and affluent outfall system; fixed and movable bridges. *Mailing Add:* Parsons Brinckerhoff Quade & Douglas Inc 999 Third Ave Suite 2200 Seattle WA 98104

GILBERT, PAUL WILNER, MATHEMATICS. *Current Pos:* RETIRED. *Personal Data:* b Rochester, NY, Feb 14, 16; m 41, 89, Kathleen Sullivan; c Emily & James. *Educ:* Univ Rochester, AB, 36, AM, 37; Duke Univ, PhD(math), 40. *Prof Exp:* Instr math, Tex Technol Col, 40-42 & US Mil Acad, 45-46; from instr to prof math, Syracuse Univ, 46-81. *Mem:* Math Asn Am. *Res:* Numerical analysis. *Mailing Add:* 202 Wellington Rd De Witt NY 13214

GILBERT, PERRY WEBSTER, MARINE BIOLOGY, VERTEBRATE MORPHOLOGY. *Current Pos:* exec dir, 67-78, EMER DIR, MOTE MARINE LAB, 78-; PROF NEUROBIOL & BEHAV, CORNELL UNIV, 68- *Personal Data:* b North Branford, Conn, Dec 1, 12; m 38; c 8. *Educ:* Dartmouth Col, AB, 34; Cornell Univ, PhD(zool), 40. *Hon Degrees:* DHumL, York Col, Pa, 78. *Prof Exp:* Instr zool, Dartmouth Col, 34-36; asst, Cornell Univ, 37-40, from instr to prof zool, 40-68. *Concurrent Pos:* Instr, Marine Biol Lab, Woods Hole, 41; Carnegie fel, 49-50; Guggenheim fel, 57, 64; chmn shark res panel, Am Inst Biol Sci, 58-; consult comt polar res, Nat Acad Sci, 59-; leader, Tahiti-Tikehau Exped, 64; chief scientist, Brit Honduras Exped Shark, 69. *Mem:* Fel Am Inst Fishery Res Biologists; Am Soc Zool; Am Soc Ichthyol & Herpet; Am Soc Mammal; Soc Study Evolution. *Res:* Morphology of birds, fish and mammals; development of vertebrate eyeball musculature; structural and functional adaptations of aquatic birds; biology of elasmobranch fishes. *Mailing Add:* Mote Marine Lab 1600 City Island Park Sarasota FL 33577

GILBERT, R(OBERT) J(AMES), mechanical engineering; deceased, see previous edition for last biography

GILBERT, RICHARD A, DRUG DELIVERY SYSTEM & CANCER RESEARCH, INSTRUMENTATION & CONTROL APPLICATIONS. *Current Pos:* chem eng fac, 81-91, CHAIR CHEM ENG, UNIV S FLA, 91- *Personal Data:* b Carthage, NY, Nov 13, 44. *Educ:* John Carroll Univ, MS, 71; Univ SFla, PhD(analytical chem), 81; Villanova Univ, AB, 96. *Prof Exp:* Polymer engr, Stand Prod Inc, 70-74. *Concurrent Pos:* Res engr, Gen Elec Res Lab, 70-96. *Mem:* Am Soc Testing & Mat; Am Vacuum Soc; Am Soc Eng Educ; Sigma Xi. *Res:* Biomedical instrumentation applications; surface science and materials interface applications; instrumentation for environmental monitor and controls; industrial instrumentation and process control. *Mailing Add:* Dept Chem Eng Col Eng Univ SFla Tampa FL 33620

GILBERT, RICHARD CARL, MATHEMATICAL ANALYSIS. *Current Pos:* assoc prof, 63-67, PROF MATH, CALIF STATE UNIV, FULLERTON, 67- *Personal Data:* b Ft Wayne, Ind, Sept 15, 27; m 56; c 3. *Educ:* Harvard Univ, AB, 51; Univ Calif, Los Angeles, PhD(math), 58. *Prof Exp:* Asst, Univ Calif, Los Angeles, 53-55; actg instr math, Univ Calif, Riverside, 55-57, actg asst prof, 57-58, asst prof, 58-63. *Concurrent Pos:* Vis asst prof, Univ Chicago, 61-62; vis assoc prof, Math Res Ctr, Univ Wis, 62-63. *Mem:* Am Math Soc; Math Asn Am; Am Sci Affil. *Res:* Spectral theory of linear operators; ordinary differential equations; functional analysis. *Mailing Add:* 443 Hillcrest Ave Placentia CA 92670-4108

GILBERT, RICHARD DEAN, POLYMER CHEMISTRY. *Current Pos:* assoc prof, 66-68, prof textile chem, 68-90, PROF WOOD & PAPER SCI, NC STATE UNIV, 90- *Personal Data:* b Winnipeg, Man, Mar 14, 20; nat US; m 44, 82, Doris Holland; c Laura L. *Educ:* Univ Man, BSc, 42, MSc, 43; Univ Notre Dame, PhD, 50. *Prof Exp:* Jr res chemist, Polymer Corp, 46-47, res chemist, 50-51; res chemist, Ky Synthetic Rubber Corp, 51-55; group leader, Uniroyal Chem Co, 55-60, sect mgr synthetic rubber & latex, 60-66. *Concurrent Pos:* Consult, Borg-Warner Chem, 69-77, Monsanto, 69-78, Gen Tire, 79, Catawba-Char Lab, 81-, Lord Corp, 85-87, 90-92 & Prod Int, 88. *Mem:* Am Chem Soc; NY Acad Sci; Fiber Soc; Sigma Xi; AAAS. *Res:* High polymers; biodegradable polymers; biopolymers elastomeric fibers; photodegradation of polymers; spin labelling studies of dye diffusion; anisotropic solutions of cellulose; epoxy-graphite fiber composites, polymer blends; block copolymers. *Mailing Add:* Box 8005 NC State Univ Raleigh NC 27695. *Fax:* 919-515-6302; *E-Mail:* gilbert@cfr.cfr.ncsu.edu

GILBERT, RICHARD E(ARLE), CHEMICAL ENGINEERING. *Current Pos:* From asst prof to assoc prof, 58-69, PROF CHEM ENG, UNIV NEBR, 69- *Personal Data:* b Brooklyn, NY, Jan 24, 33; m 57; c 5. *Educ:* Worcester Polytech Inst, BS, 54; Princeton Univ, PhD(chem eng), 59. *Mem:* Am Chem Soc; Am Inst Chem Engrs; Am Soc Eng Educ. *Mailing Add:* Dept Chem Eng Univ Nebr 236 Avery Lincoln NE 68588-0126

GILBERT, RICHARD LAPHAM, JR, CHEMISTRY. *Current Pos:* res chemist, 50-55, group leader process develop, 55-62, group leader phosphorus & nitrogen res, 62-73, group leader prep agr chem, 73-77, SR RES CHEM, AM CYANAMID CO, 77- *Personal Data:* b Schenectady, NY, Oct 5, 16; m 39, 55; c 4. *Educ:* Cornell Univ, BChem, 38. *Prof Exp:* Chem microscopist, Am Cyanamid Co, 38-44, res chemist, 44-48; res chemist, Lion Oil Co, 48-50. *Mem:* Am Chem Soc; Am Inst Chem Eng. *Res:* Process analysis; economic analyses; fermentation products as agricultural chemicals; laboratory construction and ventilation. *Mailing Add:* 08540-4133 Princeton NJ 08540

GILBERT, ROBERT, MEDICINE. *Current Pos:* from instr to assoc prof, 56-72, PROF, DEPT MED, HEALTH SCI CTR, STATE UNIV NY, SYRACUSE, 72- *Personal Data:* b Chicago, Ill, Dec 5, 24; c 1. *Educ:* Univ Ill, BS, 50; Am Bd Internal Med, dipl. *Prof Exp:* Intern, Cook County Hosp, 52-53; resident, Upstate Med Ctr, 53-56. *Mem:* Fel Am Col Physicians; Am Physiol Soc; Fedn Clin Res; Am Heart Asn; Am Thoracic Soc. *Res:* Author of numerous publications. *Mailing Add:* Dept Med Health Sci Ctr State Univ NY 750 E Adams St Syracuse NY 13210

GILBERT, ROBERT L, SOLID STATE PHYSICS. *Current Pos:* from asst prof to assoc prof of physics, 66-77, chmn dept, 70-77, PROF PHYSICS, NORTHEASTERN ILL UNIV, 77- *Personal Data:* b Chicago, Ill, Jan 28, 31; m 55; c 2. *Educ:* Ill Inst Technol, BS, 55, MS, 58, PhD(physics), 67. *Prof Exp:* Physicist, Admiral Corp, 55-57; proj physicist, Nuclear-Chicago Corp, 58-62. *Concurrent Pos:* Consult, Solid State Div, Oak Ridge Nat Lab, 66, fel, 67-68. *Mem:* Am Inst Physics; Sigma Xi. *Res:* Theory of imperfections of solids with emphasis upon optical properties of F-centers in alkali-halides. *Mailing Add:* 1574 Anderson Lane Buffalo Grove IL 60089-1207

GILBERT, ROBERT OWEN, VETERINARY MEDICINE. *Current Pos:* asst prof theriogenol, 88-92, CHIEF THERIOGENOL SECT, COL VET MED, CORNELL UNIV, 90-; DIR, BOVINE RES CTR, CORNELL UNIV, 91- *Personal Data:* b Pretoria, Transvaal, SAfrica, Dec 22, 54; m 77, Kathleen Clarke; c David R & Mary-Anne. *Educ:* Univ Pretoria, BVSc, 77, MMedVet, 85. *Prof Exp:* Asst vet with pvt prac, Ladysmith, Natal, SAfrica, 77-78, Alberton, Transvaal, SAfrica, 78; vet supt, Taurus A I Coop, Irene, SAfrica, 78-81; state vet, A I sect Vet Res Inst, Onderstepoort, SAfrica, 81-84; sr lectr, Dept Genesiol, Univ Pretoria, Onderstepoort, 81-84, assoc prof theriogenol, 86-88. *Concurrent Pos:* Scholar, Witwatersrand Agr Soc, 77; grantee, Dorper Sheep Breeders' Asn, 82, AVMA Found, 85, Univ Pretoria, 86-87, Hoechst, Ger, 87-88, Cornell Univ Col Vet Med, 89-92, Eastern Artificial Insemination Coop, 91, Nat Asn Animal Breeders, 19, NRSA, 91; resident theriogenol, Univ Wis Sch Vet Med, 84-85; head theriogenol clin, Univ Pretoria, 86-88; mem various comts & subcomts, Univ Pretoria, 87, 88, Cornell Univ, 89- *Mem:* S African Vet Asn; Royal Col Vet Surgeons; Soc Theriogenol; Vet in Indust Group; Rural Practitioners Group. *Mailing Add:* Bovine Res Ctr Col Vet Med Cornell Univ T5 0301 Vet Res Tower Ithaca NY 14853

GILBERT, ROBERT PERTSCH, MATHEMATICS. *Current Pos:* UNIDEL CHAIR & PROF MATH, UNIV DEL, 75- *Personal Data:* b New York, NY, Jan 8, 32; m 55; c Carolyn & Jennifer. *Educ:* Brooklyn Col, BS, 52; Carnegie Inst Technol, MS(math) & MS(physics), 55, PhD(math), 58. *Honors & Awards:* Alexander von Humboldt Sr Scientist Award, 75 & 85. *Prof Exp:* From instr to asst prof math, Univ Pittsburgh, 57-60; asst prof, Mich State Univ, 60-61; asst prof, Univ Md, 61-64, res assoc prof, 64-65; prof, Georgetown Univ, 65-66; prof, Ind Univ, Bloomington, 66-75. *Concurrent Pos:* Ed-in-chief, Applicable Analysis, main ed, Complex Variables; ed, J Math Analysis; ed, J Nonlinear Anal, Appl Math J Chinese Acad Sci & Math Methods Appl Sci; consult, Hahn-Meitner Inst, Berlin, 74-75; consult ed, Pitman Press, Eng, 75- *Mem:* Am Math Soc; Soc Indust & Appl Math; Int Soc Anal Appl Comput. *Res:* Classical analysis; symbolic computing; partial differential equations; computational acoustics; physical mathematics. *Mailing Add:* Dept Math Univ Del 105 Rees Hall Newark DE 19716. *Fax:* 302-368-1835; *E-Mail:* gilbert@math.udel.edu

GILBERT, ROBERT PETTIBONE, internal medicine, for more information see previous edition

GILBERT, SARAH, ATOMIC & MOLECULAR PHYSICS, OPTICS. *Current Pos:* GROUP LEADER, NAT INST STAND & TECHNOL, 85- *Personal Data:* b June 8, 55. *Educ:* Univ Mich, PhD(physics). *Mem:* Am Phys Soc; Optical Soc Am. *Mailing Add:* Nat Inst Stand & Technol 325 Broadway Mail Stop 815 03 Boulder CO 30303. *E-Mail:* sgilbert@boulder.nist.gov

GILBERT, SCOTT F, DEVELOPMENTAL BIOLOGY. *Current Pos:* MEM STAFF, SWARTHMORE COL, 80- *Personal Data:* b New York, NY, April 13, 49; m 71, Anne Raunio; c Daniel, Sarah & David. *Educ:* Wesleyan Univ, BA, 71; Johns Hopkins Univ, MA, 76, PhD(biol), 76. *Honors & Awards:* Dwight J Ingle Prize, 84. *Prof Exp:* Fel molecular biol, Univ Wis, 76-78 & immunol, 78-80. *Mem:* Soc Develop Biol; Am Soc Human Genetics; Int Soc Develop Biol; Am Zool Soc; Hist Sci Soc. *Res:* Investigation of developmentally important compounds on mammalian cell surfaces; evolutionary developmental biology. *Mailing Add:* Dept Biol Swarthmore Col Swarthmore PA 19081

GILBERT, SEYMOUR GEORGE, FOOD SCIENCE. *Current Pos:* prof packaging sci, 65-75, PROF II, RUTGERS UNIV, 75- *Personal Data:* b Orange, NJ, Mar 24, 14; m 39; c 4. *Educ:* Rutgers Univ, BS, 35, MS, 38, PhD(plant physiol), 41. *Honors & Awards:* Ebert Award, Am Acad Pharm Sci, 75; Prof Award, Packaging Inst, 75. *Prof Exp:* Asst bot, Rutgers Univ, 36-39, plant physiol, 39-41, res assoc pomol, 41-42; assoc plant physiologist, Field Lab, Tung Invest, US Dept Agr, 42-51; sr chemist in charge malt res sect, Pabst Brewing Co, 51-58; lab mgr & staff asst to res & develop dir, Milprint, Inc, 58-60, res mgr, 60-63, corp tech dir, 63-65; dir, Packaging Inst, 75-78. *Concurrent Pos:* Instr, Univ Fla, 46-51; consult, Nat Res Coun, 74-78. *Mem:* Am Chem Soc; Inst Food Technol; Packaging Inst; Am Soc Testing & Mat. *Res:* Packaging; enzyme technology; plant biochemistry; migration to foods; physical chemistry of foods. *Mailing Add:* 76 Ross Hall Blvd Piscataway NJ 08854

GILBERT, STEPHEN MARC, ELECTRICAL ENGINEERING, MATHEMATICS. *Current Pos:* vpres res & develop, 74-89, DIR NEW PROD DEVELOP, DYNETICS, INC, 89- *Personal Data:* b Long Island, NY, Mar 31, 41; m 62; c 2. *Educ:* NJ Inst Technol, BS, 62; Univ Southern Calif, MS, 64; Cornell Univ, PhD(elec eng), 67. *Prof Exp:* Engr design, Hughes Aircraft Co, 62-64; instr teaching, Cornell Univ, 64-67; supvr res & develop, Bell Tel Labs, 67-71; dept mgr develop, Teledyne Brown Eng Co, 71-74. *Concurrent Pos:* Hughes masters fel, Hughes Aircraft Co, 62-64; Ford fel, Cornell Univ, 64-65, Faraday fel, 65-66, NSF fel, 66-67; instr, Fairleigh Dickenson Univ, 66-67; mem bd dir & chmn acad coun, Southeastern Inst Technol, 75-; assoc prof, Univ Ala, Huntsville, 72-75. *Mem:* Sigma Xi. *Res:* Application of engineering and mathematical principles to radar and communications systems; electronic countermeasures; electronic counter-countermeasures; waveform design; signal processing; system evaluation. *Mailing Add:* 6 Asbury Rd Huntsville AL 35801

GILBERT, SUSAN POND, AXONAL TRANSPORT, CELL MOTILITY. *Current Pos:* RES ASSOC, PA STATE UNIV, 86- *Educ:* Dartmouth Col, PhD(cell biol), 86. *Mailing Add:* Dept Biol Sci Univ Pittsburgh Pittsburgh PA 15260. *Fax:* 412-624-4739

GILBERT, THEODORE WILLIAM, JR, ANALYTICAL CHEMISTRY. *Current Pos:* prof, 60-88, EMER PROF ANALYTICAL CHEM, UNIV CINCINNATI, 88- *Personal Data:* b Attleboro, Mass, Nov 4, 29; m 68, Peggy Chestnut. *Educ:* Mass Inst Technol, BS, 51; Univ Minn, PhD(chem), 56. *Prof Exp:* Res chemist, Oak Ridge Nat Lab, 56-57; asst prof chem, Pa State Univ, 57-60. *Concurrent Pos:* Mem staff, Brookhaven Nat Lab, 66-67. *Mem:* Am Chem Soc. *Res:* Liquid chromatography; ion exchange; trace analysis; analytical solvent extraction. *Mailing Add:* 46 N Liberty St Nantucket MA 02554-2127

GILBERT, THOMAS LEWIS, ENVIRONMENTAL SCIENCE, THEORETICAL CHEMICAL PHYSICS. *Current Pos:* ASSOC DIR, CHICAGO CTR RELIG & SCI, 88- *Personal Data:* b Topeka, Kans, Nov 24, 22; m 46; c 3. *Educ:* Calif Inst Technol, BS, 44, MS, 49; Ill Inst Technol, PhD(theoret physics), 56. *Prof Exp:* Asst, Armour Res Found, 44-46, from asst physicist to assoc physicist, 47-56, res physicist, 56; from asst physicist to physicist, 56-76, SR PHYSICIST, ARGONNE NAT LAB, 76- *Mem:* Am Phys Soc; Sigma Xi; AAAS; Health Physics Soc; Soc Risk Analysis; Soc Sci Study Relig; Inst Relig & Sci. *Res:* Electronic structure of atoms, molecules and solids; interatomic forces; environmental analyses and project management; risk assessment; philosophy of science; relationship of science and religion. *Mailing Add:* 11919 Ford Rd Palos Park IL 60464-1407

GILBERT, THOMAS REXFORD, ANALYTICAL CHEMISTRY. *Current Pos:* asst prof, 81-85, ASSOC PROF CHEM, NORTHEASTERN UNIV, 86-; FAC FEL, BARNETT INST CHEM ANALYSIS & MAT SCI, 87- *Personal Data:* b Rochester, NY, Oct 29, 46; m 83; c 3. *Educ:* Clarkson Col Technol, BS, 68; Mass Inst Technol, PhD(anal chem), 71. *Prof Exp:* Res assoc, New Eng Aquarium, 71-77, assoc dir res, 77-81. *Concurrent Pos:* Res assoc fel chem, Brandeis Univ, 73-77. *Mem:* Am Chem Soc; Soc Appl Spectros; Sigma Xi. *Res:* Environmental analytical chemistry of trace metals; plasma emission spectroscopy; bioanalytical separations. *Mailing Add:* 22 Castle Rd Norfolk MA 02056-1773

GILBERT, W(ILLIAM) D(OUGLAS), MECHANICAL ENGINEERING. *Current Pos:* RETIRED. *Personal Data:* b Kingston, Ont, Feb 13, 10; m 40; c 3. *Educ:* Queen's Univ, BSc, 32; Mass Inst Technol, SM, 35. *Prof Exp:* Lectr mech eng, Queen's Univ, 46-49, from asst prof to assoc prof, 49-59, head dept, 56-69, prof, 59-92. *Concurrent Pos:* Mem, Civilian Atomic Power Dept, Can Gen Elec Co, 56-59; mem, Atomic Energy Can Ltd, Ont, 69-70. *Res:* Two phase fluid flow; thermodynamics. *Mailing Add:* 18 Kensington Ave Kingston ON K7L 3N6 Can

GILBERT, WALTER, MOLECULAR BIOLOGY. *Current Pos:* NSF fel physics, Harvard Univ, 57-58, lectr & res fel, 58-59, asst prof, 59-64, assoc prof biophys, 64-68, prof biochem, 68-72, Am Cancer Soc prof molecular biol, 72-81, sr assoc biochem & molecular biol, 82-84, prof biol, 85-86, H H Timken prof sci, 86-87, chair, Dept Cellular & Develop Biol, 87-93, CARL M LOEB UNIV PROF, DEPT MOLECULAR & CELLULAR BIOL, HARVARD UNIV, 87- *Personal Data:* b Boston, Mass, Mar 21, 32; m 53; c 2. *Educ:* Harvard Univ, AB, 53, AM, 54; Cambridge Univ, PhD(math), 57. *Hon Degrees:* DSc, Univ Chicago & Columbia Univ, 78, Univ Rochester, 79 & Yeshiva Univ, 81. *Honors & Awards:* Nobel Prize in Chem, 80; US Steel Found Award Molecular Biol, Nat Acad Sci, 68; V D Mattia Lectr, Roche Inst Molecular Biol, 76; Smith Kline & Fr Lectr, Univ Calif, Berkeley, 77; Louis & Bert Freedman Award, NY Acad Sci, 77; Charles-Leopold Mayer Prize, Acad Sci, Inst France, 77; Harrison Howe Award, Am Chem Soc, 78; Gairdner Found Award, 79; Albert Lasker Basic Med Res Award, Albert & Mary Lasker Found, 79; Prize Biochem Anal, Ger Soc Clin Chem, 80; Sober Award, Am Soc Biol Chemists, 80. *Prof Exp:* Chmn & prin exec officer, Biogen-N V, 81-84. *Concurrent Pos:* Guggenheim fel, Paris, 68-69; vchair, Myriad Genetics, Inc, 92- *Mem:* Nat Acad Sci; Am Acad Arts & Sci; Am Phys Soc; Am Soc Biol Chem; foreign mem Royal Soc. *Res:* Gene evolution; genetic control mechanisms; repressors; protein-DNA interactions; author and co-author of 98 articles on theoretical physics and molecular biology. *Mailing Add:* Biol Labs 16 Divinity Ave Cambridge MA 02138-2092

GILBERT, WALTER WILSON, INDUSTRIAL CHEMISTRY. *Current Pos:* RETIRED. *Personal Data:* b Johnson City, Tenn, July 10, 22; m 50; c 2. *Educ:* Ga Inst Technol, BS, 44, MS, 47; Univ Wis, PhD(chem), 50. *Prof Exp:* Res chemist, Cent Res Dept, E I Du Pont de Nemours & Co, Inc, 50-63, supvr mat res, 63-67, res mgr, Develop Dept, 67-70, mgr chem res sect, Electrochem Dept, 70-72, lab adminr, Indust Chem Dept, 72, res supvr, Indust Chem Dept, 73-77, res supvr Chem & Pigments Dept, Exp Sta, 78-85. *Mem:* Am Chem Soc; Sigma Xi. *Res:* Reactions under high pressure; catalysis; inorganic crystal growth; tropolone; magnetic materials; compositions for hybrid circuits, industrial chemicals; amines and polyols for polymer intermediates; THF polymerization. *Mailing Add:* 519 Summit Dr Berkeley Ridge Hockessin DE 19707-9647

GILBERT, WILLIAM BEST, AGRONOMY. *Current Pos:* RETIRED. *Personal Data:* b Berea, Ky, Feb 13, 21; m 48; c 2. *Educ:* Berea Col, BS, 42; Univ Ky, MS, 52; NC State Univ, PhD(physiol, ecol), 56. *Prof Exp:* Teacher, Pub Schs, Ky, 45-50; asst, Univ Ky, 50-52; asst, NC State Univ, 52-55, from asst prof to assoc prof, 58-76, prof crop sci, 76- *Concurrent Pos:* Consult, Univ NC Mission, Peru, 55-58. *Mem:* Am Soc Agron. *Mailing Add:* 2001 Hillock Dr Raleigh NC 27612

GILBERT, WILLIAM HENRY, III, ECOLOGY, ENVIRONMENTAL SCIENCES. *Current Pos:* from asst prof to assoc prof, 78-86, PROF, SIMPSON COL, 86-, DEPT HEAD, 95- *Personal Data:* b Glen Ridge, NJ, Nov 30, 39; m 68, Mary A Beecher; c Mary M (Wright) & William H IV. *Educ:* Yale Univ, BA, 62; Univ Mass, Amherst, PhD(ecol), 73. *Prof Exp:* Head, Sci Dept, Ethiopian Ministry Educ, US Peace Corps, 64-66; res trainee ecol, Marine Biol Lab, 69-70; asst prof biol, Colby Col, 70-76; asst prof environ studies, Ottawa Univ, 76-78. *Concurrent Pos:* Lake Red Rock Proj, 84- *Mem:* Ecol Soc Am; Nat Audubon Soc; Nature Conservancy. *Res:* Molluscan ecology and systematics; mathematical models for dispersion patterns and species diversity; bird distribution; environmental studies. *Mailing Add:* Dept Biol & Environ Sci Simpson Col Indianola IA 50125. *Fax:* 515-961-1498; *E-Mail:* gilbert@storm.simpson.edu

GILBERT, WILLIAM IRWIN, PETROLEUM CHEMISTRY. *Current Pos:* RETIRED. *Personal Data:* b Philadelphia, Pa, Mar 6, 15; m 46; c 2. *Educ:* Pa State Col, BS, 36; Princeton Univ, AM, 38, PhD(org chem), 39. *Prof Exp:* Instr chem, Western Md Col, 39-40; res chemist, Gulf Res & Develop Co, Gulf Oil Corp, 40-45, asst head sect new processes, 45-52, head, Petrochem Sect, 52-55, asst dir, Processes Div, 55-61, dir, Petrochem Div, 61-68 & 71-75, Kansas City Lab, 68-71, sr policy adv 75- *Mem:* AAAS; Am Chem Soc. *Res:* Petroleum refining; petrochemicals. *Mailing Add:* 500 Rte 909 No CH19 Longwood at Oakmmont Verona PA 15147

GILBERT, WILLIAM JAMES, algology; deceased, see previous edition for last biography

GILBERT, WILLIAM SPENCER, NUCLEAR PHYSICS. *Current Pos:* physicist, Lawrence Livermore Lab, 54-63, PHYSICIST, LAWRENCE BERKELEY LAB, UNIV CALIF, 63- *Personal Data:* b New York, NY, May 25, 27; m 56; c 2. *Educ:* Univ Calif, AB, 48, PhD(physics), 52. *Prof Exp:* Physicist, Radiation Lab, Univ Calif, 49-52; res engr, Atomic Energy Res Dept, NAm Aviation, Inc, 52-54. *Mem:* Am Phys Soc. *Res:* Accelerator design; radioactivity problems; shielding; experimental areas; superconductivity; cryogenics; superconducting magnets. *Mailing Add:* 2952 Claremont Blvd Berkeley CA 94705

GILBERT-BARNESS, ENID F, PEDIATRICS, DEVELOPMENTAL PATHOLOGY. *Current Pos:* DIR PEDIAT PATH, PATH DEPT, TAMPA GEN HOSP, 92-, PROF PEDIAT & PATH, LAB MED, 93- *Personal Data:* b Sydney, Australia, May 31, 27; nat US; m 54, 87, Lewis A; c Mary M, Elizabeth A, Jennifer E, James C (deceased) & Rebecca D. *Educ:* Univ Sydney, MS, 50, MD, 83; Am Col Pathol, FACP, 63; Royal Col Path, Australia, FRAC Path. *Prof Exp:* From asst prof to assoc prof path, WVa Univ, 63-70; prof path, Univ Wis, 71-92, prof pediat, 72-92. *Concurrent Pos:* Dir Pediat Path, Univ Wis, 71- & surg path, 75-, distinguished med alumni prof, 86-; vis prof, Univ SFla, 78-92; mem, Cancer Educ Comt, 80-83; mem, Study Sect, Nat Heart Lung & Blood Inst, NIH, 80-83; pres, Soc Pediat Path, 86-87; hon fac, Suzhou Med Col, China. *Mem:* Am Soc Clin Path; Soc Pediat Path (pres, 86-87); Teratology Soc; Arthur Purdy Stout Soc; Am Acad Pediat; Int Acad Path; Am Pediat Soc; hon fel Int Pediat Path Asn (pres, 90-92); hon fel SAm Cardiovasc Soc; hon fel Latin Am Pediat Path Asn. *Res:* Genetic and developmental pathology; birth defects and malformation syndromes; sudden infant death syndrome. *Mailing Add:* Tampa Gen Hosp PO Box 1289 Tampa FL 33601. *Fax:* 813-253-4093

GILBERTSEN, RICHARD B, IMMUNOPATHOLOGY. *Current Pos:* res assoc & group leader, Dept Pharmacol, Immunopharmacol Sect, Parke-Davis Pharmaceut Res, Warner-Lambert Co, 80-85, sr res assoc & group leader, 85-89, sr res assoc & group leader, Dept Exp Ther, Immunopath Sect, 89-90, ASSOC RES FEL, DEPT EXP THER, IMMUNOPATH SECT, PARKE-DAVIS PHARMACEUT RES, WARNER-LAMBERT CO, 90- *Personal Data:* US citizen; m 73; c 2. *Educ:* Beloit Col, BS, 69; Duke Univ, PhD(immunol), 74. *Prof Exp:* Res assoc, Med Ctr, Duke Univ, 74-75; proj assoc, Immunobiol Res Ctr, Univ Wis-Madison, 75-76, postdoctoral fel, 76-77; immunopharmacologist, Dept Pharmacol, Anti-Arthritis Proj, Abbott Labs, North Chicago, 77-80. *Mem:* Am Col Rheumatology; Inflammation Res Asn; Am Soc Pharmacol & Exp Therapeut. *Mailing Add:* Pharmacol Dept Parke-Davis Pharmaceut Res 2800 Plymouth Rd Ann Arbor MI 48105-2495. *Fax:* 313-996-4333

GILBERTSON, DONALD EDMUND, PARASITOLOGY, MALACOLOGY. *Current Pos:* RETIRED. *Personal Data:* b Whitehall, Wis, Oct 22, 34; m 57; c 2. *Educ:* Wis State Univ, BS, 59; SDak State Univ, MS, 62; Univ Cincinnati, PhD(zool), 66. *Prof Exp:* Asst zool, SDak State Univ, 60-62 & Univ Cincinnati, 62-65; res fel med parasitol, Sch Pub Health, harvard Univ, 66-68; from asst prof to assoc prof zool, Univ Minn, Minneapolis, 68-84, prof ecol & behav biol, 84- *Concurrent Pos:* Dir, James Ford Bell Mus Natural Hist, 83- *Mem:* AAAS; Am Soc Trop Med & Hyg; Am Soc Parasitol; Sigma Xi. *Res:* Host parasite relationships; protein and nucleic acid metabolism of mollusks; control of disease bearing snails; biochemistry of mollusk body fluids. *Mailing Add:* Rte 3 box 274 Osseo WI 57478

GILBERTSON, MICHAEL, ECOTOXICOLOGY. *Current Pos:* SECY, WATER QUAL BD & BIOLOGIST, INT JOINT COMN, 86- *Personal Data:* b Durham, Eng, Feb 4, 45; Can citizen. *Educ:* Queen's Univ, Belfast, BD, 67, MSc, 69. *Honors & Awards:* Chandler-Misener Award, Int Asn Great Lakes Res, 72. *Prof Exp:* Biologist limnol, Can Ctr Inland Waters, 69-71; biologist pesticides, Can Wildlife Serv, 71-74; biologist contaminants, Environ Protection Serv, Environ Can, 75-81; biologist contaminants, Fish Habitats Mgt, Dept Fisheries & Oceans, Ottawa, 81-86. *Concurrent Pos:* Leader, Can Task Force Polychlorobiphenyls, 75-76 & Can Task Force Mirex, 76-77. *Res:* Effects and movement of chemical contaminants in ecosystems; chick edema disease; polychlorinated dibenzo-p-dioxins in the Great Lakes; transboundary pollution and United States/Canada relations. *Mailing Add:* Int Joint Comn PO Box 32869 Detroit MI 48232-2869

GILBERTSON, ROBERT LEE, MYCOLOGY, FOREST PATHOLOGY. *Current Pos:* PROF PLANT PATH, UNIV ARIZ, 67- *Personal Data:* b Hamilton, Mont, Jan 15, 25; m 48, Patricia Park; c Park L & Joan E. *Educ:* Univ Mont, BA, 49; Univ Wash, MS, 51; State Univ NY, PhD(mycol), 54. *Prof Exp:* Asst, State Univ NY Col Forestry, Syracuse, 51-54; asst prof forestry, Univ Idaho, 54-59; from assoc prof to assoc prof forest bot, State Univ NY Col Forestry, Syracuse, 59-67. *Concurrent Pos:* Consult, US Forest Serv, 57-; vis assoc prof, Biol Sta, Univ Mont, 64, 66 & Univ Minn, 70; chmn, Western Int Forest Dis Work Conf, 80. *Mem:* Mycol Soc Am (pres, 79); Soc Am Foresters; Phytopath Soc Am; Brit Mycol Soc. *Res:* Taxonomy of woodrotting fungi of North America; biology of wood-rotting basidiomycetes of North America, including taxonomy, floristics, genetics of sexuality and vegetative incompatibility, pathological relationships, and ecological significance. *Mailing Add:* 6521 N Camino Padre Isidoro Tucson AZ 85718

GILBERTSON, ROBERT LEONARD, MOLECULAR VIROLOGY, MOLECULAR DETECTION OF PLANT PATHOGENIC ORGANISMS. *Current Pos:* asst prof, 90-94, ASSOC PROF PLANT PATH, UNIV CALIF, DAVIS, 94- *Personal Data:* b Chicago, Ill, Oct 15, 55; m 92, Maria R Rojas. *Educ:* Univ Mass, BS, 78, MS, 81; Colo State Univ, PhD(plant path & weed sci), 85. *Prof Exp:* Res asst, Univ Mass, Amherst, 78-80, exten technician entom, 80-81; res asst, Colo State Univ, 82-85; res assoc, Univ Wis-Madison, 85-87, asst scientist, 87-90. *Concurrent Pos:* Ed, Plant Cell Reports, 92-; consult, Windrock Found, 92. *Mem:* Am Phytopath Soc; Am Soc Virol. *Res:* Investigation of molecular mechanisms by which viruses infect and spread within plants, molecular detection and characterization of plant pathogens, and approaches for developing and engineering plants with resistance to plant pathogens. *Mailing Add:* Dept Plant Path Univ Calif Davis CA 95616-5200. *Fax:* 530-752-5674; *E-Mail:* fzgilber@alcor.ucdavis.edu

GILBERTSON, TERRY JOEL, CLINICAL BIOCHEMISTRY, DRUG METABOLISM. *Current Pos:* res scientist, 72-84, DIR, UPJOHN CO, 85- *Personal Data:* b La Crosse, Wis, May 18, 39; m 67; c 2. *Educ:* Wis State Univ, La Crosse, BS, 62; Univ Minn, Minneapolis, PhD(org chem), 67. *Prof Exp:* Trainee biochem, Univ Minn, St Paul, 67-68; asst prof, SDak State Univ, 68-72. *Concurrent Pos:* Sabbatical, Mayo Clin, 82-83. *Mem:* Am Chem Soc; Am Asn Clin Chemists; NY Acad Sci; Asn Official Anal Chem. *Res:* Development of clinical laboratory assays and synthesis of labeled compounds and drug metabolism; application of these to clinical studies and agriculture. *Mailing Add:* Upjohn Co Kalamazoo MI 49007

GILBEY, STEVE, METALLURGICAL ENGINEERING. *Current Pos:* from res engr to sr res engr, Armco Steel Co, 67-72, res assoc, 72-75, mgr steelmaking res, 75-82, dir process res, 82-93, managing dir, Armco Res & Technol, 93-95, VPRES RES & TECHNOL, ARMCO RES & TECHNOL, 95- *Personal Data:* b Dayton, Ohio, Sept 22, 39. *Educ:* Univ Cincinnati, BS, 62; Ohio State Univ, PhD(metall eng), 66. *Prof Exp:* Res engr steelmaking, Youngstown Steel Co, 66-76. *Concurrent Pos:* Chmn external adv comn, Mat Sci & Eng Dept, Ohio State Univ, 88- *Mem:* Am Iron & Steel Soc; Am Soc Metals Int. *Mailing Add:* Armco Inc Res & Technol 705 Curtis St Middletown OH 45044-5812

GILBOE, DANIEL PIERRE, MICROBIOLOGY, ORGANIC CHEMISTRY. *Current Pos:* RES BIOCHEMIST, VET ADMIN HOSP, 68- *Personal Data:* b Amboy, Ill, Dec 29, 34; m 61. *Educ:* Univ Wis-Madison, BSc, 56, MSc, 59; Univ Minn, PhD(biochem), 67. *Prof Exp:* Chemist, Minn Mining & Mfg Co, 56; res chemist, Archer-Daniels-Midland Co, Minn, 60-63; res assoc, Dept Dairy Sci, Univ Ill, Urbana, 67-68. *Concurrent Pos:* Instr biochem, Univ Minn, 71-74, asst prof, 74-; ed, J Neurochem, 86-93. *Mem:* AAAS; Am Chem Soc; Am Soc Biochem & Molecular Biol; Sigma Xi. *Res:* Hormonal and metabolite regulation of liver glycogen metabolism with particular reference to control of glycogen synthase phosphatase; initiation of liver glycogen synthesis. *Mailing Add:* Vet Affairs Med Ctr Univ Minn One Veterans Dr Minneapolis MN 55417-2300

GILBOE, DAVID DOUGHERTY, BIOCHEMISTRY, ANIMAL PHYSIOLOGY. *Current Pos:* Res asst biochem, 55-58, from instr physiol chem & surg to prof physiol & surg, 58-89, PROF PHYSIOL & NEUROSURG, UNIV WIS-MADISON, 89- *Personal Data:* b Richland Center, Wis, July 13, 29; m 51; c 2. *Educ:* Miami Univ, BA, 51; Univ Wis, MS, 55, PhD(biochem), 58. *Concurrent Pos:* Fulbright lectr, Univ Chile, 70; Neurol & Study Sect, 80-84; ed bd, J Neurochem, 86-93 & J Neurochem Res, 86- *Mem:* Am Chem Soc; Am Physiol Soc; Int Soc Neurochem; Am Soc Biol Chem; Int Soc Cerebral Blood Flow & Metabolism; Am Soc Neurochem. *Res:* Biochemistry of brain function; transport of metabolites; pharmacologic treatment of post ischemia brain injury; nuclear magnetic resonance studies of brain cell pH and metabolism during ischemia and recovery. *Mailing Add:* Dept Neurosurg Univ Wis Med Sch 4630 Med Sci Ctr Madison WI 53706-1532

GILBREATH, SIDNEY GORDON, III, INDUSTRIAL ENGINEERING. *Current Pos:* from assoc prof to prof, Tenn Technol Univ, 68-78, chmn dept, 69-78 & 80-82, prof, 82-91 INTERIM CHMN & DEPT INDUST ENG, TENN TECHNOL UNIV, 91- *Personal Data:* b Atlanta, Ga, Aug 11, 31; m 57; c 3. *Educ:* Univ Tenn, BS, 58, MS, 62; Ga Inst Technol, PhD(indust eng), 67. *Prof Exp:* Indust engr, Robertshaw Corp, 59-60; sales engr, Wallace & Tiernan Inc, 60-61; civil engr, Tenn Valley Authority, 61-62; instr indust eng, Ga Inst Technol, 62-66; asst prof, Va Polytech Inst, 67-68; dir mat mgt, Westmoreland Coal Co, Inc, 78-79, gen mgr, Va Oper, 79-80. *Concurrent Pos:* Consult indust energy & mgt, 68-78. *Mem:* Am Soc Qual Control; Am Inst Indust Engrs (pres, 78-79); Am Soc Eng Educ. *Res:* Statistical sampling; methods engineering; engineering economy; production; inventory control and management; facilities design and material handling. *Mailing Add:* 110 Breen Ln Cookeville TN 38506

GILBREATH, WILLIAM POLLOCK, SPACE BIOLOGY. *Current Pos:* Res scientist, NASA, 62-75 & 77-81, prog mgr hq, 75-76, 82-83 & 86-92, proj mgt, 82-85, CHIEF FLIGHT PROG MGT, HQ, NASA, 93- *Personal Data:* b Portland, Ore, Nov 10, 36; m 65, 93, Anita vonKoor; c Joan & Susan. *Educ:* Reed Col, BA, 58; Univ Wash, PhD(inorg chem), 62. *Mem:* Am Chem Soc; sr mem Am Inst Aeronaut & Astronaut; Sigma Xi. *Res:* Sponsor the development of biological and medical research and technology investigations for spaceflight. *Mailing Add:* 928 Kings Blvd Sun City FL 33573. *Fax:* 202-358-4168

GILBRECH, DONALD ALBERT, ENGINEERING MECHANICS. *Current Pos:* RETIRED. *Personal Data:* b Holly Grove, Ark, Apr 12, 27; m 49; c 3. *Educ:* Univ Ark, BSIE, 53, MS, 54; Purdue Univ, PhD(mech eng), 58. *Prof Exp:* From instr to prof eng mech, Univ Ark, Fayetteville, 53-92. *Mem:* Am Soc Mech Engrs. *Res:* Fluid mechanics, especially instrumentation, acoustics, pulsating flow and gas dynamics; experimental stress analysis; engineering science; computer interfacing. *Mailing Add:* 18076 Countrywood Rd Fayetteville AR 72703

GILBY, STEPHEN WARNER, STEELMAKING. *Current Pos:* res engr, Armco Steel Co, 67-69, sr res engr, 69-72, res assoc, 72-75, mgr steelmaking res, 75-82, dir process res, 82-93, MANAGING DIR RES & TECH, ARMCO STEEL CO, 93- *Personal Data:* b Dayton, Ohio, Sept 22, 39; m 62; c 3. *Educ:* Univ Cincinnati, BS, 62; Ohio State Univ, PhD(metall eng), 66. *Prof Exp:* Res engr steelmaking, Youngstown Steel Co, 66-76. *Concurrent Pos:* Chmn, external adv comn, Mat Sci & Eng Dept, Ohio State Univ, 88-92. *Mem:* Am Iron & Steel Soc; Am Soc Metals Int. *Res:* Steelmaking and continuous casting process development. *Mailing Add:* 2607 Sherman Ave Middletown OH 45044-4839

GILCHRIST, BRUCE, IMPACT OF COMPUTERS ON SOCIETY EMPLOYMENT & ECONOMICS. *Current Pos:* RETIRED. *Personal Data:* b Pontefract, Eng, Aug 4, 30; nat US; m 92, Pamela Vogeley Ruben; c Ian C, James & Andrew. *Educ:* Univ London, BSc, 50, PhD(meteorol), 52. *Prof Exp:* Vis meteorologist, Inst Advan Study, 52-54; mem staff, 54-56; asst prof math & dir comput ctr, Univ Syracuse, 56-59; mgr prog & comput, Res Ctr, Int Bus Mach, 59-61, dir systs eng prog, Corp Staff, 61-63; dir planning, Serv Bur Corp, 63-65; mgr sci opers, Int Bus Mach Data Processing Div, 65-68; exec dir, Am Fedn Info Processing Socs, Inc, 68-73; dir comput activities, Columbia Univ, 73-85, sr adv info strategy, 86-91 dir. *Concurrent Pos:* Consult, US Weather Bur, 55-59; mem panel weather & river serv, Nat Acad Sci/Nat Acad Engrs comt adv Environ Sci Serv Admin, 68-69; panel nat progs comput sci & eng bd, Nat Acad Sci, 68-69; consult, US Off Educ, 71-72 & US Gen Acctg Off, 76-90. *Mem:* AAAS; Asn Comput Mach (secy, 60-62, vpres, 62-64); Am Meteorol Soc; Inst Elec & Electronics Engrs; Am Fedn Info Processing Soc (pres, 66-68). *Res:* Methods and applications of high speed computation; manpower and regulatory aspects of the computer industry; computer industry economics; social impact of computers. *Mailing Add:* PO Box 656 Chappaqua NY 10514

GILCHRIST, RALPH E(DWARD), PETROLEUM ENGINEERING. *Current Pos:* PRES, RALPH E GILCHRIST INC, 79- *Personal Data:* b Milwaukee, Wis, Dec 17, 26; m 55; c 3. *Educ:* Univ Denver, BA, 47; Univ Tex, BS, 50, MS, 51; Pa State Univ, PhD(petrol & natural gas eng), 58. *Prof Exp:* Res engr petrol prod res, Texaco, Inc, 51-52; res assoc petrol & natural gas eng, Pa State Univ, 54-57; asst proj engr petrol prod res, Sinclair Res Labs, Inc, 57-59; res engr, Phillips Petrol Co, 59-66; sr res engr prods, Tenneco Oil Co, 66-69, dir prod res, 69-71; mgr explor & prod res, Southwest Res Inst, 71-73; dean & prof technol, Corpus Christi State Univ, 73-79. *Concurrent Pos:* Lectr, Univ Tulsa, 59-60. *Mem:* Am Inst Mining, Metall & Petrol Engrs; Sigma Xi; Am Soc Oceanog. *Res:* Drilling; production; reservoir engineering; oil and gas recovery. *Mailing Add:* 201 Vanderpool Lane No 126 Houston TX 77024-6139

GILDE, HANS-GEORG, ORGANIC CHEMISTRY. *Current Pos:* RETIRED. *Personal Data:* b Ger, July 8, 33; US citizen; m 57; c 2. *Educ:* Albright Col, BS, 57; Ohio Univ, PhD(org chem), 61. *Prof Exp:* Instr chem, Ohio Univ, 60-61; from asst prof to assoc prof org chem, Marietta Col, 61-70, prof chem, 70-84, Ebenezer Baldwin Andrews Chair chem & natural sci, 84-92. *Concurrent Pos:* Assoc, Danforth Found, 78-84; Harness Fel, 86-89. *Mem:* Am Chem Soc; Sigma Xi. *Res:* Molecular spectroscopy. *Mailing Add:* 106 Grandview Ave Marietta OH 45750

GIL DE LAMADRID, JESUS, MATHEMATICS. *Current Pos:* from asst prof to assoc prof, 57-67, PROF MATH, UNIV MINN, MINNEAPOLIS, 67- *Personal Data:* b San Juan, PR, Aug 20, 26; m 50; c 3. *Educ:* Univ Chicago, BS, 48, MS, 49; Univ Mich, PhD(math), 55. *Prof Exp:* Res assoc, Navy Logistics, George Washington Univ, Wash, 50-52; instr math, Ohio State Univ, 55-57. *Concurrent Pos:* Res assoc & lectr, Yale Univ, 61-62; residence, Centre Univ Int, Paris, 64-65; vis prof, Univ Rennes, 71-72 & Ludwig-Maximilians-Univ, Munich, 74-75 & 78-79. *Res:* Harmonic analysis; representation theory of topological groups and algebras. *Mailing Add:* Dept Math Univ Minn Minneapolis MN 55455

GILDEN, DONALD HARVEY, NEUROLOGY, NEUROBIOLOGY. *Current Pos:* res assoc, Wistar Inst, 71-76, asst prof, 71-76, ASSOC PROF NEUROL, SCH MED, UNIV PA & WISTAR INST, 76- *Personal Data:* b Baltimore, Md, Aug 30, 37; m 66; c 2. *Educ:* Dartmouth Col, BA, 59; Univ Md, MD, 63. *Prof Exp:* Intern, Univ Ill Res & Educ Hosp, 63-64; resident neurol, Univ Chicago Hosps, 64-67; staff neurologist, Walter Reed Army Med Ctr, US Army, 67-69; fel neurovirol, Sch Hyg & Pub Health, Johns Hopkins Univ, 69-71. *Mem:* Am Acad Neurol; Am Asn Immunologists; Am Asn Neuropathologists; Am Soc Microbiol; AAAS. *Res:* Fast and slow virus infection of the central nervous system; virus-induced immunopathology; multiple sclerosis. *Mailing Add:* Dept Neurol Univ Co Health Sci Ctr 4200 E 9th Ave Box B-182 Denver CO 80262-0001

GILDEN, RAYMOND VICTOR, IMMUNOLOGY, GENETICS. *Current Pos:* DIR, MOLECULAR ONCOL PROG, FREDERICK CANCER RES CTR, 76- *Personal Data:* b Chicago, Ill, Aug 4, 35; m 57; c 3. *Educ:* Univ Calif, Los Angeles, AB, 57, MA, 59, PhD(zool), 62. *Prof Exp:* USPHS fel, Calif Inst Technol, 62-63; assoc mem, Wistar Inst, 63-65; vpres res div, Flow Labs, Inc, 65-76. *Mem:* Sigma Xi. *Res:* Tumor viruses. *Mailing Add:* Dyn Corp 1003 W Seventh St Suite 501 Frederick MD 21701

GILDENBERG, PHILIP LEON, NEUROSURGERY, NEUROPHYSIOLOGY. *Current Pos:* DIR, HOUSTON STEREOTACTIC CTR, 91- *Personal Data:* b Hazleton, Pa, Mar 15, 35; m 86, Patricia O'Neill Franklin; c Susan, Steven, Ronald, Laura & Alexandra. *Educ:* Univ Pa, AB, 55; Temple Univ, MD & MS, 59, PhD(neurophysiol), 70. *Prof Exp:* Res assoc neurophysiol, Max Planck Inst Brain Res, 68; staff neurosurgeon, Cleveland Clin Found, 68-72; assoc prof neurosurg, Col Med, Univ Ariz, 72-75; prof & chief div neurosurg, Univ Tex Med Sch, Houston, 75-83. *Concurrent Pos:* Fel, Max Planck Inst Brain Res, 68; asst ed, Progress Neurol & Psychiat, 69-74; adj asst prof, Case Western Reserve Univ, 70-72; assoc ed, Confinia Neurologica, 72-75; ed, Appl Neurophysiol, 74-88, Pain & Headache, 88- & Stereotactic Functional Neurosurg, 89- *Mem:* Fel Am Col Surg; Cong Neurol Surg; Am Asn Neurol Surg; Soc Univ Neurosurg; Am Soc Stereotactic & Functional Neurosurg (secy-treas, 72-); Int Asn Study Pain; World Soc Stereotactic & Func Neurosurg (secy-treas, 76-92, pres, 93-). *Res:* Physiology and stereotactic treatment of involuntary movements; stereotactic techniques in management of brain tumors. *Mailing Add:* 6624 Fannin No 1620 Houston TX 77030. *Fax:* 713-669-0358; *E-Mail:* hsc@dymicro.com

GILDENHORN, HYMAN L, MEDICINE, RADIOLOGY. *Current Pos:* assoc radiologist, 56-57, dir dept, 57-75, CHMN, DIV DIAG RADIOL, CITY OF HOPE MED CTR, 77- *Personal Data:* b Cleveland, Ohio, May 27, 21; m 55. *Educ:* Ohio State Univ, BS, 43, MS, 47; Cornell Univ, MD, 51; Am Bd Radiol, dipl, 56. *Prof Exp:* From intern med to resident radiol, Michael Reese Hosp, Chicago, Ill, 51-55. *Concurrent Pos:* Asst clin prof, Univ Southern Calif, 69-75; mem coun cardiovascular radiol, Am Heart Asn. *Mem:* AMA; Radiol Soc NAm; NY Acad Sci; Int Col Radiol; Sigma Xi. *Res:* Physical factors related to diagnostic roentgenology; clinical research in diagnostic roentgenology; synergism of irradiation and cholesterol diet in production of arteriosclerotic lesions in animals. *Mailing Add:* City of Hope Nat Med Ctr Div Diag Radiol Duarte CA 91010

GILDERSLEEVE, BENJAMIN, ECONOMIC GEOLOGY, GEOLOGICAL MAPPING. *Current Pos:* RETIRED. *Personal Data:* b Damascus, Va, June 7, 07; wid; c Kent Emerson, Larry Benjamin & James Richard. *Educ:* Univ Va, BS, 30, MS, 31; Johns Hopkins Univ, PhD(geol), 39. *Prof Exp:* Field asst, Va Geol Sur, 30-31; jr geol, US Geol Sur, 31-34; from asst geol to assoc geol, Tenn Valley Authority, 34-51; group chief, commodity geologist & head, Bowling Green Field Off, 51, 77. *Mem:* Sigma Xi; fel Geol Soc Am. *Mailing Add:* 837 Ridgecrest Way Bowling Green KY 42104-3822

GILDERSLEEVE, RICHARD E, ELECTRICAL ENGINEERING. *Current Pos:* from instr to assoc prof elec eng, 48-77, ASST DEAN, COL ENG, SYRACUSE UNIV, 77- *Personal Data:* b Flushing, NY, Aug 17, 14; m 48; c 2. *Educ:* Rensselaer Polytech Inst, BEE, 48; Univ Syracuse, PhD(elec eng), 58. *Prof Exp:* Eng asst, Consol Edison Co, 34-41. *Mem:* Am Soc Eng Educ; Inst Elec & Electronics Engrs. *Res:* Microwave antennas. *Mailing Add:* 718 Maple Dr Fayetteville NY 13066

GILDOW, FREDERICK E, PLANT PATHOLOGY. *Current Pos:* asst prof, 83-89, ASSOC PROF PLANT PATH, PA STATE UNIV, 89- *Personal Data:* b Zanesville, Ohio, Dec 24, 48. *Educ:* Ohio Univ, Athens, BS, 70, MS, 74; Cornell Univ, PhD(plant path), 80. *Prof Exp:* Tech asst, Ohio Univ, Athens, 71-72, teaching asst, 72-74; asst prof, Univ Calif, 80-83. *Mem:* Am Phytopath Soc; Am Soc Virol; Entom Soc Am; Sigma Xi. *Res:* Virus-vector interactions regulating virus transmission; study of the mechanism for luteovirus transport through aphid vector cells and the virus-membrane interactions involved in vetor-specificity; ultrastructural studies by electron microscopy and immunocytochemistry; studies of the crytopathology of several aphid-infecting viruses and their effect on plant virus transmission; ultrastructural studies of tomato spotted wilt virus transmission by thrips; author of numerous publications. *Mailing Add:* Dept Plant Path Pa State Univ 319 Buckout Lab University Park PA 16820

GILDSETH, WAYNE, PHYSICAL CHEMISTRY, GENERAL COMPUTER SCIENCE. *Current Pos:* DEAN, SOUTHERN ARK UNIV, 90- *Personal Data:* b Sioux Falls, SDak, July 10, 35; m 60; c 2. *Educ:* Augustana Col, SDak, BA, 57; Iowa State Univ, PhD(phys chem), 64. *Prof Exp:* Prof chem, Pac Lutheran Univ, 64-66; prof chem, Augustana Col, SDak, 66-79; at Univ SDak, Sch Med, 79-83; dean, St Cloud State Univ, 83-90. *Concurrent Pos:* SDak Statehouse fel, 72-73. *Mem:* Am Chem Soc; Asn Comput Mach. *Res:* Electrolytic solution chemistry; ionic complexes. *Mailing Add:* Southern Ark Univ Box 1397 Magnolia AR 71753

GILE, LELAND HENRY, SOIL GENESIS, SOIL CLASSIFICATION. *Current Pos:* INDEPENDENT RES, 76- *Personal Data:* b Alfred, Maine, Feb 23, 20; m 47, Dora Blossom. *Educ:* Univ Maine, BS, 53; Univ Wis, MS, 54. *Honors & Awards:* Kirk Bryan Award, Geol Soc Am, 83; Cert Merit, Arid Zone Res, AAAS, 87. *Prof Exp:* Conserv aide, Soil Conserv Serv, USDA, 46-50, soil scientist, 55-57, res soil scientist, 57-76. *Mem:* Fel AAAS; Soil Sci Soc Am; fel Geol Soc Am; Am Quaternary Asn; Int Soc Soil Sci; Sigma Xi. *Res:* Soil-geomorphic studies in arid and semiarid lands. *Mailing Add:* 2600 Desert Dr Las Cruces NM 88001

GILES, EUGENE, PHYSICAL & BIOLOGICAL ANTHROPOLOGY, FORENSIC ANTHROPOLOGY. *Current Pos:* assoc prof, Univ Ill, 70-73, head dept, 75-80 , 82-83 & 93-94, assoc dean, Grad Col, 86-89, PROF ANTHROP, UNIV ILL, URBANA-CHAMPAIGN, 73- *Personal Data:* b Salt Lake City, Utah, June 30, 33; m 64, Inga Wikman; c Eric G & Edward E. *Educ:* Harvard Univ, AB, 55, AM, 60, PhD(anthrop), 66; Univ Calif, Berkeley, MA, 56. *Prof Exp:* Instr anthrop, Univ Ill, Urbana-Champaign, 64-66; asst prof, Harvard Univ, 66-70. *Concurrent Pos:* NSF fel demog, Australian Nat Univ, 67-68; vis asst prof anthrop, Univ Utah, 69; vis fel prehist, Australian Nat Univ, 78; assoc dean, LAS Col, 95- *Mem:* Fel Am Anthrop Asn; Am Soc Human Genetics; Am Asn Phys Anthropologists (vpres, 79-80, pres, 81-83); Human Biol Asn; fel Am Acad Forensic Sci; fel AAAS. *Res:* Analysis of morphological variation in crania; demography, physical variation and genetic structure of noncosmopolitan human populations in oceania; forensic anthropology; history of physical anthropology. *Mailing Add:* Dept Anthrop 109 Davenport Hall Univ Ill 607 S Mathews Urbana IL 61801. *Fax:* 217-244-3490; *E-Mail:* e-giles1@uiuc.edu

GILES, JESSE ALBION, III, ORGANIC CHEMISTRY. *Current Pos:* RETIRED. *Personal Data:* b New Kensington, Pa, June 2, 31; m 53; c 3. *Educ:* Univ NC, BS, 53; Univ Ala, MS, 55. *Prof Exp:* Res chemist, R J Reynolds Tobacco Co, 54-67, sec head res dept, 67-76, mgr analytical res div, 76-80, dir tech serv, 80-87. *Concurrent Pos:* Abstractor, Chem Abstr, Am Chem Soc, 55-66. *Mem:* Am Chem Soc; Sigma Xi. *Res:* Chemistry of plant natural products; diterpenes; aliphatic sulfur and boron compounds; radiocarbon and tritium tracer techniques. *Mailing Add:* 7720 Whitehorse Dr Clemmons NC 27012-9150

GILES, JOHN CRUTCHLOW, PHYSICS. *Current Pos:* from asst prof to assoc prof, 64-70, PROF PHYSICS, CALIF STATE UNIV, HAYWARD, 70- *Personal Data:* b London, Eng, Jan 15, 34; m 56; c 2. *Educ:* Sheffield Univ, BSc, 55; Univ Exeter, PhD(physics), 58. *Prof Exp:* Nat Res Coun Can fel, Univ BC, 58-60, from instr to asst prof physics, 60-63; lectr, Aberdeen Univ, 63-64. *Mem:* Am Asn Physics Teachers. *Res:* Solid state physics; semiconducting substances; optical and transport properties. *Mailing Add:* 5578 Greenridge Rd Castro Valley CA 94552

GILES, MICHAEL ARTHUR, PHYSIOLOGY, AQUATIC TOXICOLOGY. *Current Pos:* RETIRED. *Personal Data:* b Toronto, Ont, Oct 6, 43; m 74; c 4. *Educ:* Univ Man, BSc, 65; Univ BC, MSc, 69, PhD(zool), 73. *Prof Exp:* Fisheries biologist salmon enhancement, Dept Fisheries, Can, 65-67; res scientist herring biol, Fisheries & Marine Serv Environ Can, 73-74; res assoc & lectr environ biol, Sir George Williams Univ, Montreal, 75-76; res scientist aquatic toxicol, Freshwater Inst Fish & Marine Serv Environ Can, 76-95. *Concurrent Pos:* Teaching fel, Univ BC, 72-73 & 74-75. *Mem:* Can Soc Zoologists. *Res:* Respiratory physiology of fish; physiological toxicology of fish; ontogenetic variation in physiology of fish; aquaculture. *Mailing Add:* 413 Nightingale Rd Winnipeg MB R3J 3G7 Can

GILES, MICHAEL KENT, OPTICAL ENGINEERING, ELECTRICAL ENGINEERING. *Current Pos:* PROF, DEPT ELEC & COMPUT ENG, NMEX STATE UNIV, LAS CRUCES, 82- *Personal Data:* b Logan, Utah, Oct 24, 45; m 68; c 7. *Educ:* Brigham Young Univ, BES, 71, MS, 71; Univ Ariz, MS, 76, PhD(optical sci), 76. *Honors & Awards:* Cert Outstanding Achievement, US Army Dept Chief of Staff for Res Develop & Acquisition, 78. *Prof Exp:* Electronics engr electro-optics, US Naval Weapons Ctr, China Lake, Calif, 71-77; res electronics engr, Electro-optics & Imaging Processing, White Sands Missile Range, 77-80. *Concurrent Pos:* Res physicist optics, USAF Weapons Lab, Albuquerque, NMex, 80-82. *Mem:* Optical Soc Am; Soc Photo-Optical Instrumentation Engrs. *Res:* Image processing (digital and optical); lasers; sensors; visual optics. *Mailing Add:* 211 W Dona Ana Sch Rd Las Cruces NM 88005

GILES, NORMAN HENRY, GENETICS. *Current Pos:* Fuller E Callaway prof 72-86, EMER PROF GENETICS, UNIV GA, 86- *Personal Data:* b Atlanta, Ga, Aug 6, 15, m 39, 69, Doris Vos; c Annette (Brown) & David. *Educ:* Emory Univ, AB, 37; Harvard Univ, MA, 38, PhD(biol), 40. *Hon Degrees:* DSc, Emory Univ, 80. *Honors & Awards:* Thomas Hunt Morgan Medal, Genetics Soc of Am 88. *Prof Exp:* Parker fel, Harvard Univ, 40-41; from instr to prof bot, Yale Univ, 41-61, Eugene Higgins prof genetics, 61-72. *Concurrent Pos:* Prin biologist, Oak Ridge Nat Lab, 47-50; consult biol, Oak Ridge Nat Lab, 51-64 & Brookhaven Nat Lab, 56-64; Fulbright & Guggenheim fels, Univ Genetics Inst, Copenhagen, 59-60; mem genetics study sect, NIH, 60-64, mem genetics training comt, 66-70; Guggenheim fel genetics, Australian Nat Univ, 66; chmn genetics sect, Nat Acad Sci, 76-79. *Mem:* Nat Acad Sci; AAAS; fel Am Acad Arts & Sci; Am Soc Naturalists (pres, 77); Am Inst Biol Sci; Genetics Soc Am (treas, 54-56, vpres, 69, pres, 70); foreign mem Royal Danish Acad Sci & Letters. *Res:* Molecular organization function and regulation of gene clusters and multienzyme complexes, especially in lower eucaryotes. *Mailing Add:* Dept Genetics Univ Ga Athens GA 30602-7223. *Fax:* 706-542-3910

GILES, PETER COBB, PHYSICS. *Current Pos:* SR PHYSICIST, LAWRENCE LIVERMORE LAB, UNIV CALIF, 58- *Personal Data:* b Albany, Calif, Nov 21, 29; div; c 4. *Educ:* Univ Calif, BS, 52, MS, 53, PhD(physics), 58. *Mem:* Am Phys Soc; Sigma Xi. *Res:* Nuclear physics; application of computers and numerical techniques to physical problems. *Mailing Add:* 1881 De Leon Way Livermore CA 94550-5668

GILES, RALPH E, PHARMACOLOGY, BIOCHEMISTRY. *Current Pos:* DIR, TECHNOL ACCESS GROUP, ZENECA PHARMACEUT GROUP, 94- *Personal Data:* b Rahway, NJ, Mar 26, 41; m 63; c 5. *Educ:* Fordham Univ, BS, 62; Univ Minn, PhD(pharmacol), 66. *Prof Exp:* Asst prof pharmacol, Fordham Univ, 66-68; scientist, Warner-Lambert Res Inst, 68-69, sr scientist, 69-72, sr res assoc, 72-75, dir, 75-93, dir res planning, 93-94. *Mem:* NY Acad Sci; Am Soc Pharmacol & Exp Therapeut; Soc Exp Biol & Med; fel Royal Soc Med; Sigma Xi. *Res:* Respiratory pharmacology; ens pharmacology; bronchodilators; experimental production of emphysema; renal pharmacology; catechol-o-methyl transferase. *Mailing Add:* Technol Access Group Zeneca Pharmaceut Group Wilmington DE 19897-0001. *Fax:* 302-886-4354

GILES, ROBERT H, JR, ECOLOGY, WILDLIFE MANAGEMENT. *Current Pos:* from assoc prof to prof forestry, 67-74, PROF WILDLIFE MGT & ENVIRON & URBAN SYST, VA POLYTECH INST & STATE UNIV, 74- *Personal Data:* b Lynchburg, Va, May 25, 33; m 56; c 2. *Educ:* Va Polytech Inst, BS, 55, MS, 58; Ohio State Univ, PhD(wildlife mgt), 64. *Prof Exp:* Dist biologist, Va Comn Game & Inland Fisheries, 58-60; asst prof wildlife mgt, Univ Idaho, 63-67. *Mem:* Wildlife Soc. *Res:* Conservation education evaluation; insecticide-ecology; forest ecology; computer simulation of ecological systems. *Mailing Add:* Dept Wildlife Mgt Va Polytech Inst & State Univ PO Box 0321 Blacksburg VA 24063-0001

GILES, ROBIN, FUZZY REASONING, FOUNDATIONS OF PHYSICS. *Current Pos:* RETIRED. *Personal Data:* b London, Eng, Jan 30, 26; m 54, Jessie McClelland; c Marian, Cynthia & Eleanor. *Educ:* Glasgow Univ, BSc, 46, DSc(found of thermodyn), 66. *Honors & Awards:* Kelvin Medal, Glasgow Univ, 68. *Prof Exp:* From asst lectr to sr lectr physics, Glasgow Univ, 46-66; assoc prof math, Queen's Univ, Ont, 66-69, prof, 69-93. *Concurrent Pos:*

Carnegie fel physics, Inst Theoret Physics, Copenhagen, Denmark, 54-55; res assoc math, Tulane Univ, 63-64. *Mem:* Soc Exact Philos. *Res:* Use of formal languages and nonclassical logic for exact reasoning under uncertainty; application of this to artificial intelligence and to foundations of physics. *Mailing Add:* Dept Math & Statist Queen's Univ Kingston ON K7L 3N6 Can. *E-Mail:* rg1@post.queensu.ca

GILES, ROBIN ARTHUR, physics, for more information see previous edition

GILES, THOMAS DAVIS, MEDICINE, CARDIOLOGY. *Current Pos:* from instr to assoc prof med, Sch Med, Tulane Univ, 64-74, fel cardiol, 68-70, clin assoc prof,74-76, assoc prof, 76-77, PROF MED, DEPT & SCH MED, TULANE UNIV, 77-, DIR CARDIOVASC RES, SCH MED, 81- *Personal Data:* b Greenwood, Miss, Feb 24, 38; c 3. *Educ:* Tulane Univ, MD, 62; Am Bd Internal Med, dipl, 69. *Prof Exp:* Intern med, Charity Hosp, New Orleans, 62-63, resident internal med, 63-66, chief resident, 65-66. *Concurrent Pos:* Vis physician & cardiologist, Charity Hosp La, 69-79; mem, Cardiovasc Task Force, Joint Comn Accreditation Health Care Orgn, 88- *Mem:* Fel Am Col Angiol; fel Am Col Cardiol; Am Col Clin Pharmacol; fel Am Col Physicians; Am Fedn Clin Res; Am Soc Clin Pharmacol & Therapeut; Am Soc Hypertension; Am Soc Pharmacol & Exp Therapeut. *Res:* Cardiomyopathies; congestive heart failure; hypertension; polypeptides and the cardiovascular system; regulation of CNS neurotransmitters and drugs in cardiovascular control. *Mailing Add:* Med Ctr La State Univ 1542 Tulane Ave New Orleans LA 70112-2699

GILETTI, BRUNO JOHN, GEOCHEMISTRY. *Current Pos:* from asst prof to assoc prof geol, 60-67, chmn dept, 77-80, PROF GEOL, BROWN UNIV, 67- *Personal Data:* b New York, NY, Dec 6, 29; m 84; c 2. *Educ:* Columbia Univ, AB, 51, BS, 52, MA, 54, PhD(geol), 57. *Prof Exp:* Res fel, Lamont Geol Observ, Columbia Univ, 57-58; res fel geol & mineral, Oxford Univ, 58-60. *Concurrent Pos:* Assoc physician, Univ Paris, VI, 85. *Mem:* Am Geol Soc; Geochem Soc; Am Geophys Union. *Res:* Kinetics of geological processes, especially diffusion; absolute age determination of geological materials by isotopic analysis; distribution and abundance of radioactive and stable nuclides in the earth and their significance in geology. *Mailing Add:* Dept Geol Sci Brown Univ Providence RI 02912-9127

GILFEATHER, FRANK L, MATHEMATICS. *Current Pos:* PROF & CHMN, DEPT MATH & STATIST, UNIV NMEX, 88- *Personal Data:* b Great Falls, Mont, Sept 29, 42; m; c 2. *Educ:* Univ Mont, BA, 64, MA, 66; Univ Calif, Irvine, PhD(math), 69. *Prof Exp:* Assoc, Off Naval Res, 69-70; asst prof math, Univ Hawaii, 70-74; from assoc prof math to prof math, Univ Nebr, Lincoln, 74-88. *Concurrent Pos:* Prog dir modern analysis, NSF, 83-85; staff dir, Bd Math Sci, Nat Res Coun, 85-87. *Mem:* Am Math Soc; Math Asn Am. *Res:* Operator theory on Hilbert spaces; non self-adjoint operator algebras. *Mailing Add:* 1224 Rockrose Rd NE Albuquerque NM 87121

GILFERT, JAMES C(LARE), ELECTRICAL ENGINEERING. *Current Pos:* From assoc prof to prof, 67-83, chmn dept, 69-83, EMER PROF ELEC ENG, OHIO UNIV, 83-; FOUNDER & PRES, ATHENS TECH SPECIALISTS, INC, 82- *Personal Data:* b Tamaqua, Pa, June 21, 27; m 49; c 3. *Educ:* Antioch Col, BS, 50; Ohio State Univ, MSc, 51, PhD(physics), 57. *Prof Exp:* Res assoc antenna lab, Ohio State Univ, 53-56, from instr to assoc prof elec eng, 57-67. *Concurrent Pos:* Sr tech specialist, NAm Aviation, Inc, 61-67; Am Coun Educ fel, 71-72; vis prof, Chubu Inst Technol, Nagoya, Japan, 73, 80; chmn eng res coun prog, Am Soc Eng Educ, 75-76; design consult, Ohio State Dept Transp, 77- *Mem:* Am Soc Eng Educ; Inst Elec & Electronics Engrs. *Res:* Microprocessor applications; instrumentation; communications. *Mailing Add:* Dept Elec Eng 37 Sunset Dr Athens OH 45701

GILFILLAN, ALASDAIR MITCHELL, PHOSPHOLIPID METABOLISM IN MAST CELL-BASOPHIL SIGNALLING, PROTEIN KINASE C ACTIVATION IN MAST CELL SIGNALLING. *Current Pos:* sr scientist, 87-89, assoc res investr biochem, 89-92, PRIN INVESTR, DEPT PHARMOL, HOFFMANN-LA ROCHE, 87-, RES INVESTR BIOCHEM, DEPT BRONCHOPULMONARY RES, 92- *Personal Data:* b Perth, Scotland, May 2, 56; m 81, Corinne C Kong. *Educ:* Univ Strathclyde, BSc Hons, 77; Univ Manchester, MSc, 79, PhD(pharmacol), 81. *Prof Exp:* Fel assoc biochem, Dept Pediat, Yale Univ, 82-85, assoc res scientist, 85-87. *Mem:* Royal Pharmaceut Soc Gt Brit; Am Soc Biochem & Molecular Biol; Am Soc Cell Biol. *Res:* Signal transduction mechanisms leading to inflammatory mediator release from mast cells; mechanisms of pulmonary surfactant secretion; biology of high affinity ice receptor. *Mailing Add:* Dept Inflammation 340 Kingsland St Nutley NJ 07110-1199. *Fax:* 973-235-6596

GILFILLAN, ROBERT FREDERICK, MICROBIOLOGY. *Current Pos:* CONSULT, 90- *Personal Data:* b Roanoke, Va, Oct 30, 23; m 51; c 3. *Educ:* Univ Tenn, BA, 49, MS, 50, PhD(microbiol, biochem), 56. *Prof Exp:* Asst bact, Univ Tenn, 49-50 & 54-55; asst bact metab, Univ Minn, 50-53; microbiologist, US Dept Defense, Gen Mills, Minn, 53-54; res assoc biol, Oak Ridge Nat Lab, Tenn, 55-56; asst prof bact & virol, Med Col SC, 56-59; asst prof obstet & gynec, Med Sch, Tufts Univ, 59-61; chief virol unit, Found Res Nerv Syst, 61-64; microbiologist, St Margaret's Hosp, Boston, 59-61, chief virologist, 64-70; asst prof obstet & gynec, Sch Med, Tufts Univ, 69-80; chief, Virol Lab, State Lab Inst, Dept Pub Health, Mass, 70-82; assoc prof Vet Med & Pathol, Tufts Sch Vet Med, 82-90. *Concurrent Pos:* Soc Am Bact fel, Sch Med, Yale Univ, 57; res assoc, Sch Med, Univ Boston, 61-64; lectr appl microbiol, Harvard Sch Pub Health, 73- *Mem:* AAAS; Am Soc Microbiol; Sigma Xi. *Res:* Virology; experimental pathology. *Mailing Add:* 2533 Buena Vista Rd Winston-Salem NC 27104

GILFIX, EDWARD LEON, OPERATIONS ANALYSIS & SYSTEMS REQUIREMENTS, MANAGEMENT INFORMATION SYSTEMS DESIGN. *Current Pos:* PRIN ENGR, MISSILE SYSTS DIV, RAYTHEON CO, 67- *Personal Data:* b Cambridge, Mass, Mar 14, 23; m 52, Lores Levita; c Katherine L, David J & Daniel A. *Educ:* Univ Mass, BS, 50; Univ Mich, MS, 51. *Prof Exp:* Mem tech staff, Willow Run Res Ctr, Univ Mich, 51-53; staff mem, Chrysler Corp, 53-55; mgr customer training, Datamatic Corp, 55-62; mem tech staff, Mitre Corp, 62-67. *Res:* Multi-discipline systems analysis, design, and documentation in programs involving air defense missile systems; command and control systems; centralized product assurance data analysis systems; electric utility distribution automation systems. *Mailing Add:* 42 Peacock Farm Rd Lexington MA 02173

GILFORD, DOROTHY MORROW, MATHEMATICAL SCIENCES, POLICY STUDIES. *Current Pos:* PRIN PARTNER, GILFORD ASSOCS, 94- *Personal Data:* b Ottumwa, Iowa, Feb 19, 19; m 50, Leon. *Educ:* Univ Wash, BS, 40, MS, 42. *Prof Exp:* Lectr statist, Brynmawr Col, 44-45; asst prof, George Washington Univ, 45-48; chief, Biomet Br, Civil Aeronaut Admin, 48-51; dep dir, Div Financial Statist, Fed Trade Comn, 51-55; head, Math Statist Br, Off Naval Res, 55-59, Logistics & Statist Br, 59-62, dir, Math Sci Div, 62-68; asst comnr educ statst & dir, Nat Ctr Educ Statist, US Off Educ, 68-74; dir, Human Resource Studies, Nat Acad Sci, 75-78, sr statistician, Comt Nat Statist, 78-88, dir, Bd Int Educ Studies, 88-94. *Concurrent Pos:* Prin investr, Acad Res Productivity, Nat Acad Sci, 79, Statist Family Assistance Progs, 81-83, Statist Aging Pop, 86-88, mem, Panel Teacher Supply & Demand, 86-87; mem, Nat Educ Goals Tech Group, US Dept Educ, 93-94; consult statist, Nat Ctr Educ Statist, 95-97, Nat Acad Sci, 97, Nat Acad Sci, 97. *Mem:* Am Statist Asn (vpres, 74-76); Int Statist Inst; Am Educ Res Asn. *Res:* Design of national and international policy - related statistics programs; policy studies of human resources in science and engineering; studies of supply and demand and quality of science and mathematics teachers; methodology for measuring in-service professional development of teachers. *Mailing Add:* 6602 Rivercrest Ct Bethesda MD 20816-2178. *E-Mail:* gilford@compuserve.com

GILFORD, LEON, MATHEMATICAL STATISTICS, ENGINEERING STATISTICS. *Current Pos:* vpres res & develop, 82-90, CONSULT, CORBO CORP, 90- *Personal Data:* b Warsaw, Poland, Feb 14, 17; nat US; m 50, Dorothy Morrow. *Educ:* Brooklyn Col, AB, 39; George Washington Univ, AM, 49. *Honors & Awards:* Silver Medal, US Dept Com, 56. *Prof Exp:* Math statistician, US Bur Census, 46-55, chief opers res & qual control br, 55-60; sr scientist, Opers Res, Inc, 60-69, prin scientist, 69-71; chief statistician & dir admin data processing, US Tariff Comn, 71-74; spec asst reliability, Energy Res & Develop Admin, 74-76; consult, 76-77; spec asst statist res, US Bur Census, 77-78, actg assoc dir statist stand & methodol, 81. *Concurrent Pos:* Coun mem Am Statist Asn, 68-70; mem, Sub comt Statist Methods, Am Nat Stand Comt Z-1, 76-83; mem adv coun, US Dept Educ, 79; mem adv comt, Energy Info Admin, Dept Energy, 81-84; consult, 81-93; mem bd dirs, Cobro Corp, 83-; mem, Panel on Qual Control, Nat Welfare Progs, Nat Acad Sci, 86-87; mem bd dirs, Planning Sci Inc, 88-89. *Mem:* Fel AAAS; fel Am Statist Asn; Inst Statist. *Res:* Mathematical models of physical and social systems, data collection and processing. *Mailing Add:* 6602 Rivercrest Ct Bethesda MD 20816

GILFOYLE, GERARD PAUL, HEAVY-ION NUCLEAR PHYSICS, ELECTRO-NUCLEAR PHYSICS. *Current Pos:* asst prof, 87-93, ASSOC PROF PHYSICS, UNIV RICHMOND, 93- *Personal Data:* b Harrisburg, Pa, June 13, 57; m 92, Linda E Pattee. *Educ:* Franklin & Marshall Col, BA, 79; Univ Pa, PhD(nuclear physics), 85. *Prof Exp:* Res fel, State Univ NY, Stony Brook, 85-87. *Concurrent Pos:* Vis prof, Univ Pa, 88; prin investr, Res Corp, 89-91; proj dir, NSF, 92; co-prin investr, US Dept Energy, 92- *Mem:* Am Phys Soc; Sigma Xi. *Res:* Interactions and behavior of atomic nuclei at high temperature; understand how even smaller objects, the quarks, interact to form the atomic nucleus. *Mailing Add:* Dept Physics Univ Richmond Richmond VA 23173. *Fax:* 804-289-8482; *E-Mail:* gilfoyle@urvax.urich.edu

GILFRICH, JOHN VALENTINE, ANALYTICAL CHEMISTRY, X-RAY ANALYSIS. *Current Pos:* CONSULT, 82- *Personal Data:* b Springfield, Mass, Sept 14, 27; m 54, Nancy J Tucker; c John T, N Lynn, Beth A, Robert H & Georgia A. *Educ:* Am Int Col, BA, 49. *Prof Exp:* Anal chemist, Nat Bur Stand, 48-50, phys chemist, 50-52; anal chemist, US Naval Ord Lab, 52-60, phys chemist, 60-66; res chemist, Naval Res Lab, 66-71, head, Spectrochem Analytical Sect, 71-77, consult, X-ray Optics Br, 77-81, assoc head, Condensed Matter Physics Br, 81-82. *Concurrent Pos:* Consult, Condensed Matter Physics Br, Naval Res Lab, 83-87. *Mem:* Am Chem Soc; fel Am Inst Chem; Am Crystallog Asn; Sigma Xi; Microbeam Anal Soc; Soc Appl Spectros. *Res:* General analytical chemistry, including application of x-ray diffraction and spectroscopy to analytical problems; application and study of x-ray physics. *Mailing Add:* 8710 Lowell St Bethesda MD 20817-3218

GILGAN, MICHAEL WILSON, SHELLFISH TOXINS, FISH PRODUCT QUALITY. *Current Pos:* RETIRED. *Personal Data:* b Burns Lake, BC, Feb 26, 38; m 60, Norma E Angus; c Brian D, Thomas M & Kathleen J. *Educ:* Univ BC, BSc, 59, MA, 62; Univ Wis, PhD(biochem), 65. *Honors & Awards:* President's Award, Nat Res Coun Can, 88. *Prof Exp:* res scientist, Dept Fisheries & Oceans, 65-95. *Concurrent Pos:* Assoc referee, Asn Off Analytical Chemists, 92; mem, Methods Comt Natural Toxins, Asn Off Anal Chemist Int, 92- *Mem:* AAAS; Sigma Xi; Am Chem Soc; Asn Off Anal Chemists Int. *Res:* Brain and smooth muscle phosphorylases; paralytic shellfish poison; toxins of the mold Fusarium tricinctum; biochemistry and physiology of molt and sex hormones of crustaceans; natural products from starfish; bioactive amines in fish products; chemical indicators of fish product quality; marine toxins in fish and shellfish. *Mailing Add:* 34 Lyngby Ave Dartmouth NS B3A 3T8 Can. *Fax:* 902-426-5342

GILGENBACH, RONALD MATTHEW, ELECTRON BEAM & LASER PLASMA INTERACTIONS, ELECTRON BEAM PHYSICS. *Current Pos:* PROF & LAB DIR, NUCLEAR ENG & RADIOL SCI DEPT, UNIV MICH, 80- *Personal Data:* b Fond Du Lac, Wis, Dec 15, 49; m 80, Catherine Hayden; c Karen & Matthew. *Educ:* Univ Wis, BS 72, MS, 73; Columbia Univ, PhD(elec eng), 78. *Honors & Awards:* Centennial Key Award, Inst Elec & Electronics Engrs, 84, Plasma Sci & Appln Award, 97; Young Mem Eng Achievement Award, Am Nuclear Soc, 87. *Prof Exp:* Mem tech staff, Bell Labs, 74-77; res asst, Plasma Lab, Columbia Univ, 77-78; res scientist, Jaycor, 78-80. *Concurrent Pos:* Contractor, Naval Res Lab, 78-80; vis scientist, Oak Ridge Nat Lab, 79-80, Mass Inst Technol, 80; consult, McDonnell Douglas, 79-80, Gen Motors Res Lab, 85-93; pres young investr, NSF, 84. *Mem:* Inst Elec & Electronics Engrs; fel Am Phys Soc. *Res:* The physics and engineering of intense particle beam and laser interactions with plasmas, gases and materials; applications of electron beams to microwave generation and novel accelerators. *Mailing Add:* Nuclear Eng & Radiol Sci Dept Univ Mich Ann Arbor MI 48109-2104. *E-Mail:* rongilg@umich.edu

GILHAM, PETER THOMAS, ORGANIC CHEMISTRY, BIOCHEMISTRY. *Current Pos:* assoc prof, 62-69, PROF BIOL SCI, PURDUE UNIV, WEST LAFAYETTE, 69- *Personal Data:* b Sydney, Australia, Nov 12, 30; div; c 3. *Educ:* Univ Sydney, BSc, 51, MSc, 53, DSc, 75; Univ NSW, PhD(org chem), 56. *Prof Exp:* BC Res Coun fel, Univ BC, 56-58; Imp Chem Indust res fel org chem, Imp Col, London, 58-59; lectr, Univ Adelaide, 59-60; asst prof enzyme inst, Univ Wis, 60-62. *Concurrent Pos:* Mem subcomt biol chem, Div Chem & Chem Technol, Nat Acad Sci-Nat Res Coun, 64-66. *Mem:* Am Chem Soc; Am Soc Biol Chem. *Res:* Stereochemistry; nucleic acid structure and synthesis. *Mailing Add:* Dept Biol Sci Purdue Univ West Lafayette IN 47907-1968

GILINSKY, VICTOR, THEORETICAL PHYSICS. *Current Pos:* CONSULT, 84- *Personal Data:* b Warsaw, Poland, May 28, 34; US citizen; div; c David & Anessa. *Educ:* Cornell Univ, BEngPhys, 56; Calif Inst Technol, PhD(theoret physics), 61. *Prof Exp:* Mem tech staff, Aerospace Corp, 61; phys scientist, Rand Corp, 61-71, asst dir policy & prog rev, AEC, 71-73, head phys sci dept, 74-75; comnr, US Nuclear Regulatory Comn, 75-84. *Mem:* Am Phys Soc; Inst Strategic Studies. *Res:* Many-body aspects of plasma physics; electromagnetic waves in the atmosphere; nuclear power technology; arms control; science and technology policy. *Mailing Add:* 48 Wellesley Circle Glen Echo MD 20812. *Fax:* 301-320-2783; *E-Mail:* v.gilinsky@genib.gbis.com

GILINSON, PHILIP J(ULIUS), JR, ELECTRICAL ENGINEERING, AEROSPACE ENGINEERING. *Current Pos:* RETIRED. *Personal Data:* b Lowell, Mass, July 28, 14; m 43; c 2. *Educ:* Mass Inst Technol, BS, 36, MS, 52. *Prof Exp:* Engr, Heinze Elec Co, Mass, 36-38, Pac Mills, Inc, 38-40 & Doelcam Corp, 46-47; engr electromagnetics, Instrumentation Lab, Mass Inst Technol, 47-54, asst dir, 54-62, dep assoc dir, 62-73; staff consult, Charles Stark Draper Lab, Inc, 73-80. *Mem:* Sigma Xi; Nat Soc Prof Engrs. *Res:* Development and design of electromagnetic devices in aeronautics and astronautics, particularly inertial guidance in instrumentation systems; development of new precision measurement techniques in electromechanics and viscometer used in polymer chemistry and blood rheology research. *Mailing Add:* 8 Fuller Rd Chelmsford MA 01824

GILJE, JOHN, INORGANIC CHEMISTRY. *Current Pos:* From asst prof to assoc prof, 65-75, prof hons prog, 76-79, PROF CHEM, UNIV HAWAII, 75- *Personal Data:* b Elkader, Iowa, Feb 24, 39; m 70. *Educ:* Univ Minn, BChem, 61; Univ Mich, PhD(inorg chem), 65. *Honors & Awards:* Honeywell Prize in Sci & Eng, 61; Alexander von Humboldt Distinguished Scientist Award, 90. *Concurrent Pos:* Vis prof, Univ Tex, Austin, 72-73; mem organizing comt, US-Japan Organotransition Element Symp, 74, Am Chem Soc/Chem Soc, Japan Chem Cong, 79, Cong Pac Basin Chem Soc, 84; Alexander von Humboldt fel, Tech Univ Braunschwieg, WGer, 80-81; acad vis, Imperial Col Sci & Technol, London, 79-80; vis prof, Univ Goettingen, Ger, 90. *Mem:* Am Chem Soc. *Res:* Organometallic and main group chemistry; synthesis of new materials; F-element chemistry. *Mailing Add:* Dept Chem James Madison Univ Harrisonburg VA 22801

GILKERSON, WILLIAM RICHARD, PHYSICAL CHEMISTRY. *Current Pos:* res fel, 54-55, from asst prof to assoc prof, 55-66, PROF CHEM, UNIV SC, 66- *Personal Data:* b Greenville, SC, June 5, 26; m 56; c 3. *Educ:* Univ SC, BS, 49; Univ Kans, PhD(chem), 53. *Prof Exp:* Res fel chem, Univ SC, 53 & Calif Inst Technol, 53-54. *Mem:* Am Chem Soc. *Res:* Conductance and dielectric properties of electrolytes in solution; ion pairing. *Mailing Add:* Dept Chem Univ SC Columbia SC 29208

GILKESON, M(URRAY) MACK, CHEMICAL ENGINEERING. *Current Pos:* assoc prof, 61-64, PROF ENG, HARVEY MUDD COL, 64- *Personal Data:* b Augusta, Kans, Feb 8, 22; m 44; c 4. *Educ:* Univ Southern Calif, BE, 44; Kans State Univ, MS(chem eng), 47; Univ Mich, MSE, 51, PhD(chem eng), 52; Claremont Grad Sch, PhD(govt), 77. *Prof Exp:* Cost acct, El Dorado Foundry, Inc, 46; asst, Eng Res Inst, Univ Mich, 49-51; from asst prof to assoc prof, Tulane Univ, 52-61. *Concurrent Pos:* Dir, Prog Pub Policy Studies, Claremont Cols, 73-75; vis coordr, Engenharia Clinica-Fed Univ, Brazil, 76-77; prog assoc, NSF Int Prog, 78-80; assoc dir, Am Soc Eng Educ, 84-86; vis prof, Papua, New Guinea, Univ Tech, 87. *Mem:* Am Inst Chem Engrs; Am Soc Eng Educ. *Res:* Contact catalysis; engineering design; overseas development; public policy studies; entrepreneurship. *Mailing Add:* Dept Eng Harvey Mudd Col Claremont CA 91711

GILKESON, RAYMOND ALLEN, SOIL SCIENCE. *Current Pos:* RETIRED. *Personal Data:* b Sutherland, Nebr, Mar 29, 21; m 45; c 3. *Educ:* Univ Nebr, BSc, 49; Wash State Univ, MSc, 51. *Prof Exp:* Soil scientist, Soil Conserv Serv, 51-53; from asst soil scientist to soil scientist, Wash State Univ, 53-73, from asst prof to prof soils, 53-83. *Mem:* Soil Sci Soc Am. *Res:* Soil survey and classification; methods of soil survey of forest and range lands; airphoto interpretation. *Mailing Add:* 60 North St Sequim WA 98382

GILKEY, JOHN CLARK, CRYOBIOLOGY, INSTRUMENT DEVELOPMENT. *Current Pos:* DIR RES, RESEARCH MFG CO, 85- *Educ:* Purdue Univ, PhD(biol), 77. *Concurrent Pos:* Asst res scientist & dir, Biotechnol Div, Life Sci Core Facil Micros, Univ Ariz. *Res:* Physiology and biophysics of fertilization and early development. *Mailing Add:* 2537 E Richards Pl Tucson AZ 85716-1123. *Fax:* 520-626-1042

GILKEY, PETER BELDEN, MATHEMATICS. *Current Pos:* assoc prof, 81-85, PROF MATH, UNIV ORE, 85- *Personal Data:* b Utica, NY, Feb 27, 46; m 78, Carolyn F; c George & Emily. *Educ:* Yale Univ, BS & MA, 67; Harvard Univ, PhD(math), 72. *Prof Exp:* Instr comput sci, NY Univ, 71-72; lectr math, Univ Calif, Berkeley, 72-74; asst prof math, Princeton Univ, 74-80. *Concurrent Pos:* Sloan Found grant, 75; NSF grant, 72- *Mem:* Am Math Soc. *Res:* Differential geometry and global analysis. *Mailing Add:* Dept Math Univ Ore Eugene OR 97403-1222. *E-Mail:* gilkey@euclid.uoregon.edu

GILKEY, RUSSELL, POLYMER CHEMISTRY. *Current Pos:* RETIRED. *Personal Data:* b Hopkinsville, Ky, Nov 19, 20; m 44; c 2. *Educ:* Univ Ky, BS, 43; Univ Ill, PhD(chem), 49. *Prof Exp:* Res chemist, B F Goodrich Co, 43-45; sr res chemist, Tenn Eastman Co, 49-67, res assoc to sr res assoc, 67-79. *Mem:* Am Chem Soc; Sigma Xi. *Res:* Polymers; fibers; plastics; adhesives; protective coatings. *Mailing Add:* 1704 Springfield Ave Kingsport TN 37664-2030

GILL, AYESHA ELENIN, POPULATION GENETICS, MEDICAL GENETICS. *Current Pos:* coordr, Statewide Immunization Info Syst, Immunization Br, Calif Dept Health, 95- *Personal Data:* b Fresno, Calif, Oct 31, 33; div; c Plara & Erika. *Educ:* Univ Calif, Berkeley, BA, 57, BA, 61, PhD(genetics), 72; Am Bd Med Genetics, dipl, 84. *Prof Exp:* Asst prof biol, Univ Calif, Los Angeles, 72-79; from asst prof to assoc prof, Univ Nev, 79-84; res scientist, NY State Dept Health, 84-87; dir followup, Newborn Screening, 87-88; res scientist & statistician, Inst Health Policy Studies, Univ Calif, San Francisco, 89-93; consult, Poverty & Race Res Coun, 94; consult, Inst Health Policy Studies, Univ Calif, San Francisco, 94-95. *Concurrent Pos:* Fel pop biol, Univ Chicago, 71-72; human & med geneticist, State Nev Genetics Prog, 79-81, dir, 81-82. *Mem:* Soc Study Evolution; Am Pub Health Asn. *Res:* Human genetic diseases, care and prevention; newborn screening; population genetics and evolutionary dynamics of natural populations; emphasis on speciation in rodents, using a multivariate approach. *Mailing Add:* 2308 Jefferson Ave Berkeley CA 94703. *E-Mail:* agill1@hw1.canwnet.gov

GILL, BIKRAM SINGH, PLANT GENETICS, AGRICULTURE. *Current Pos:* from asst prof to assoc prof, 79-87, PROF PLANT PATH, KANS STATE UNIV, 87- *Personal Data:* b Dhudike, India; US citizen; c 4. *Educ:* Khalsa Col Amritsar, BS, 63; Punjab Univ Chandigarh, MS, 66; Univ Calif, Davis, PhD(genetics), 73. *Prof Exp:* D F Jones fel genetics, Univ Mo, Columbia, 73-74; res assoc cell biol, Wash Univ, 74-75; res geneticist, Univ Calif, 75-78; prof genetics, Agr Res & Educ Ctr, Univ Fla, 78-79. *Concurrent Pos:* Lectr, Univ Calif, Riverside, 77; vis scientist, Coun Sci & Res Orgn, Div Plant Indust, Canberra, Australia, 86-87; vis prof, US Nat Acad Sci, Ger Dem Repub, 87 & Sci Sem, Peoples Repub China, 87; assoc ed, J Heredity, 84- *Mem:* Genetics Soc Am; Agron Soc Am; Crop Sci Soc Am. *Res:* Cytogenetics of crop plants such as wheat, tomato and sugarcane; molecular biology of mouse cells in tissue culture; giemsa banding and chromosome identification work in plants. *Mailing Add:* Dept Plant Path 4024 Throckmorton Kans State Univ Manhattan KS 66506

GILL, BRUCE DOUGLAS, SYSTEMATICS ECOLOGY & BEHAVIOR OF SCARABAEOIDEA, IDENTIFICATION & REGULATORY ENTOMOLOGY. *Current Pos:* ENTOMOLOGIST, ANIMAL & PLANT HEALTH DIRECTORATE, AGR CAN, 90- *Personal Data:* b Vancouver, BC, May 8, 57. *Educ:* Univ BC, BSc, 80; Carleton Univ, PhD(entom), 86. *Prof Exp:* Asst prof biol, Carleton Univ, 86-87; cur entom, Can Mus Nature, 88-90. *Concurrent Pos:* Res assoc biol, Carleton Univ, 87-95. *Mem:* Coleopterists Soc; Asn Systs Collections; Entom Soc Am; Entom Soc Can; Sigma Xi. *Res:* Taxonomy, systematics, ecology and biogeography of scarab beetles (coleoptera: scarabaeoidea) of the world with particular emphasis upon tropical regions. *Mailing Add:* 36 Warren Ave Ottawa ON K1Y 0R8 Can. *Fax:* 613-759-6938; *E-Mail:* gillbd@em.agr.ca

GILL, C(HARLES) BURROUGHS, METALLURGICAL ENGINEERING, ENVIRONMENTAL ENGINEERING. *Current Pos:* RETIRED. *Personal Data:* b Sudbury, Ont, Apr 8, 21; m 55, Carolyn Somervill; c Catherine & Joseph. *Educ:* Univ Toronto, Ont, BASc, 46; Mo Sch Mines, MS, 47, PhD(metall), 52. *Prof Exp:* Res metallurgist, Mo Sch Mines, 52-55; tech supt, Deloro Smelting & Refining Co, 55-57; prof metall eng, Lafayette Col, 57-89. *Mem:* Am Inst Mining, Metall & Petrol Engrs; Sigma Xi. *Res:* Extractive metallurgy and environmental engineering; published several articles and 2 books. *Mailing Add:* 405 Monroe St Easton PA 18042

GILL, DEREK FRANK, FORENSIC CHEMISTRY, BLENDING & ANALYSIS OF HIGH PURITY GASES & MIXTURES. *Current Pos:* VPRES TECH SERVS, AIRGAS SPECIALTY GASES, 96- *Personal Data:* b Suffolk, Eng, Juy 11, 48; m 79, Dorothy E Lobley. *Educ:* Univ Leeds, UK, BSc, 69, PhD(chem), 72. *Prof Exp:* Head, Chem Dept, Davis Tutors, UK, 72-73; data prep mgr, Attwood Statists, UK, 73-74; higher sci officer, Metrop Police Forensic Lab, 74-78; dept head, Mat Sci Group, Brit Aerospace, UK, 78-80; prin scientist, Mintek, SAfrica, 80-81; head, Specialty Gas Div, Fedgas, SAfrica, 81-88. *Mem:* Am Chem Soc; Royal Soc Chem; Air & Waste Mgt Asn; Instrument Soc Am. *Res:* Preparation and properties of sterically hindered tertiary phosphine complexes of platinum, palladium, ruthenium and osmium; blood alcohol analysis. *Mailing Add:* PO Box 1120 Edgewood NM 87015

GILL, DHANWANT SINGH, STATISTICS, MATHEMATICS. *Current Pos:* assoc prof math, 89-92, COORDR STATIST PROG, CALIF STATE POLYTECH UNIV, 91-, PROF MATH, 92- *Personal Data:* b India, Dec 1, 41; m 70, Raj Preet; c 4. *Educ:* Punjab Univ, India, BA, 60, MA, 63; Miami Univ, MSc, 73; Kans State Univ, PhD(statist), 77. *Prof Exp:* Lectr math, SN Col, Banga, India, 63-66 & SGGS Col, Chandigarh, India, 66-71; grad teacher asst, Miami Univ, 72-74, Oxford, 74-77, Kans State Univ; asst prof statist, NDak State Univ, 77-82, assoc prof, 82-90, dir, Consult Ctr, 86-90, chmn, Dept Statist, 88-90. *Mem:* Am Statist Asn. *Res:* Multivariate statistical analysis; distribution theory, linear statistical models sampling and data analysis. *Mailing Add:* Dept Math Calif State Polytech Univ 3801 W Temple Ave Pomona CA 91768-4033

GILL, DOUGLAS EDWARD, POPULATION BIOLOGY, ECOLOGY. *Current Pos:* Asst prof, 71-76, ASSOC PROF ZOOL, UNIV MD, 76- *Personal Data:* b New York, NY, Jan 25, 44; m 67. *Educ:* Marietta Col, BS, 65; Univ Mich, Ann Arbor, MA, 67, PhD(zool), 71. *Concurrent Pos:* Mem fac, Orgn Trop Studies, 71, coordr, 72 & 79. *Mem:* Am Soc Zoologists; Ecol Soc Am; Soc Study Evolution; Brit Ecol Soc; Am Soc Naturalists. *Res:* Population dynamics of natural populations; dynamics of natural metapopulations of the red-spotted newt; clinal variation in life history traits of frogs; co-evolution of parasites and hosts; evolution of trees. *Mailing Add:* Dept Zool Univ Md College Park MD 20742-0001

GILL, FRANK BENNINGTON, ORNITHOLOGY. *Current Pos:* SR VPRES, NAT AUDUBON SOC, NY, NY. *Personal Data:* b New York, NY, Oct 2, 41; m 65; c 1. *Educ:* Univ Mich, BS, 63, PhD(zool), 69. *Prof Exp:* Asst cur ornith, Acad Natural Sci, Philadelphia, 69-74, dir systs, 73-95, assoc cur ornith, 74-95. *Concurrent Pos:* Adj assoc prof, Univ Pa, 74-; dir, Hawk Mountain Sanctuary, 75-; assoc ed, Am Midland Naturalist, 75-78. *Mem:* Am Ornithologists Union; Am Soc Naturalists; Soc Study Evolution; Soc Syst Zool; Ecol Soc Am. *Res:* Birds; foraging ecology; energetics; speciation and hybridization; geographic variation and evolutionary flexibility; vocal communication. *Mailing Add:* Nat Audubon Soc 700 Broadway New York NY 10003

GILL, GEORGE WILHELM, PHYSICAL ANTHROPOLOGY. *Current Pos:* Instr, 71, from asst prof to assoc prof, 71-85, PROF ANTHROP, UNIV WYO, 85- *Personal Data:* b Sterling, Kans, June 28, 41; m 62, 75; c 4. *Educ:* Univ Kans, BA, 63, MPhil, 70, PhD(anthrop), 71; Am Bd Forensic Anthrop, dipl, 78. *Concurrent Pos:* Sci consult for skeletal identification, Wyo State Law Enforcement Agencies, 72-; sci leader, Easter Island Anthrop Exped, 81; bd dirs, Am Bd Forensic Anthrop, 85-; secy, Phys Anthrop Sect, Am Acad Forensic Sci, 85-87, chmn, 87-88. *Mem:* Am Asn Phys Anthrop; fel Am Acad Forensic Sci. *Res:* Human evolution and skeletal biology of late prehistoric and modern populations, especially North America, Mesoamerica and Polynesia; human osteology and skeletal identification (forensic anthropology), especially racial identification. *Mailing Add:* Dept Anthrop Univ Wyo PO Box 3431 Laramie WY 82071-3431

GILL, GORDON NELSON, ENDOCRINOLOGY. *Current Pos:* NIH res fel, Univ Calif, San Diego, 68-69, asst prof, 69-73, assoc prof, 73-78, chief, Div Endocrinol, 74-95 PROF MED, SCH MED, UNIV CALIF, SAN DIEGO, 78-, CHAIR FAC BIOMED SCI, 95- *Personal Data:* b Montgomery, Ala, Dec 19, 37; m 74, Patricia O'Neil; c Grace, Daniel, Leigh & Deudre. *Educ:* Vanderbilt Univ, BA, 60, MD, 63; FACP. *Prof Exp:* Internship internal med, Vanderbilt Univ Hosp, 63-64; resident internal med, Yale-New Haven Hosp, 64-66; fel, Sch Med, Yale Univ, 66-68. *Concurrent Pos:* Sect ed, Int Encycl Pharmacol & Therapeut, 72-; mem endocrinol study sect, NIH, 76-80. *Mem:* Am Fedn Clin Res; Am Soc Clin Invest; Am Soc Biol Chemists; Endocrine Soc; Asn Am Physicians; fel Am Acad Arts & Sci. *Res:* Mechanisms through which polypeptide hormones and cyclic nucleotides control cell growth and differentiated function. *Mailing Add:* Dept Med 0650 Univ Calif San Diego La Jolla CA 92093-0650

GILL, GURCHARAN S, MATHEMATICS. *Current Pos:* From asst prof to assoc prof, 65-72, PROF MATH, BRIGHAM YOUNG UNIV, 72-, ASSOC CHAIR DEPT, 96- *Personal Data:* b Moga, Punjab, India, Mar 26, 35; US citizen; m 58; c Vilo K, Sheila A, Susan B, Paul S, Stephen M, Janice & David M. *Educ:* Brigham Young Univ, BS, 58; Univ Utah, MS, 60, PhD(math), 65. *Mem:* Am Math Soc; Math Asn Am; Soc Indust & Appl Math; Nat Coun Teachers Math. *Res:* Functional analysis; topology. *Mailing Add:* 595 E 3230 N Provo UT 84604. *Fax:* 801-378-3703; *E-Mail:* gillg@math.byu.edu

GILL, HARMOHINDAR SINGH, plant pathology, mycology, for more information see previous edition

GILL, HAROLD HATFIELD, ANALYTICAL CHEMISTRY. *Current Pos:* Chemist, 51-54, analytical specialist, 54-62, analytical res specialist, 63-68, sect leader, 69-70, RES MGR, DOW CHEM CO, 71- *Personal Data:* b Hays, Kans, Sept 26, 21; m 40; c 3. *Educ:* Kans State Col, BS, 49, MS, 50. *Mem:* Am Chem Soc; fel Am Inst Chemists; AAAS; Sigma Xi. *Res:* Molecular spectroscopy; thermal chemistry; analysis of environmental samples for trace components. *Mailing Add:* 2004 Rapanos Dr Midland MI 48640-5140

GILL, JAMES EDWARD, CYTOCHEMISTRY, CYTOLOGY. *Current Pos:* AT ABBOTT LAB, MOUNTAIN VIEW, CALIF, 92- *Personal Data:* b Berkeley, Calif, Apr 12, 31; m 64, 79; c 3. *Educ:* Univ Calif, Berkeley, AB, 55; Stanford Univ, MS, 58, PhD(physics), 63. *Prof Exp:* Physicist, Film Dept, E I Du Pont de Nemours & Co, 62-65; biophysicist, Biomed Div, Lawrence Livermore Lab, Univ Calif, 65-75; asst prof path, Sch Med & Dent, Univ Rochester, 75-79; Becton Dickson Facs Syst, Mountain View, Calif, 79-89; mem staff, Unipath Co, Mountain View, Calif, 89-92. *Mem:* Int Soc Analytical Cytol. *Res:* Fluorescence cytochemistry for cell identification; flow cytometry for clinical diagnosis and monitoring; molecular physics; cytology; light microscopy. *Mailing Add:* 5440 Patrick Henry Dr Santa Clara CA 95054

GILL, JAMES WALLACE, fermentations, biochemistry & enzymology, for more information see previous edition

GILL, JOHN LESLIE, BIOMETRICS. *Current Pos:* from assoc prof to prof, 64-95, EMER PROF ANIMAL SCI, MICH STATE UNIV, 95- *Personal Data:* b La Harpe, Ill, May 25, 35; m 82, Jelena Bulatovic; c Mark & Jay. *Educ:* Univ Ill, BS, 56; Iowa State Univ, MS, 61, PhD, 63. *Prof Exp:* Res assoc statist, Iowa State Univ, 61-62; assoc prof, Va Polytech Inst, 63-64. *Concurrent Pos:* Vis fel math, Univ NSW, 71; vis prof, Univ Reading, 78, Swiss Fed Inst Technol, 78, Agr Univ, Norway, 84, Tech Univ, Munich, 85, 91, Agr Univ Wageningen, Neth, 85 & Univ Sussex, Eng, 92. *Mem:* Bernoulli Soc; Am Soc Animal Sci; Biomet Soc; Am Statist Asn. *Res:* Design and analysis of experiments in biological research. *Mailing Add:* 2578 Woodhill Dr Okemos MI 48864-2439

GILL, JOHN PAUL, JR, MATHEMATICAL ANALYSIS. *Current Pos:* PROF DEPT MATH, UNIV S COLO, 83- *Personal Data:* b Tuscaloosa, Ala, Feb 16, 37. *Educ:* Univ Ga, BS, 58; Univ Ala, MA, 64; Colo State Univ, PhD(math), 71. *Prof Exp:* Instr math, Murray State Univ, 64-67; assoc prof 71-81, prof math & chmn dept, Univ Southern Colo, 81-83. *Concurrent Pos:* Gov, Rocky Mountain Sect Math Asn Am, 87-90. *Mem:* Am Math Soc; Sigma Xi; Math Asn Am. *Res:* Complex analysis; continued fractions and infinite series. *Mailing Add:* Math Dept Univ S Colo Pueblo CO 81001-4990

GILL, JOHN RUSSELL, JR, HYPERTENSION. *Current Pos:* sr investr, 60-88, chief clin serv, 78-88, EMER SCIENTIST, HYPERTENSION-ENDOCRINE BR, NAT HEART, LUNG & BLOOD INST, NIH, BETHESDA, MD, 88-; CLIN ASSOC PROF MED, GEORGETOWN UNIV, WASHINGTON, DC, 72- *Personal Data:* b Richmond, Va, July 22, 29; m 64; c 3. *Educ:* Univ Va, BA, 50, MD, 54; Am Bd Internal Med, cert, 62. *Prof Exp:* Med intern, St Louis City Hosp, Wash Univ Serv, 54-55; jr asst resident, Duke Hosp, Durham, NC, 55-56, sr asst resident, 56-57; clin assoc, Nat Heart Inst, NIH, 57-59; Nat Found fel, Inst Biol Chem, Univ Copenhagen, Denmark, 59-60. *Concurrent Pos:* Clin asst prof med, Georgetown Univ, 66-72; chmn, Med Records Comt, Clin Ctr, NIH, 74-75; Animal Care & Use Comt, Nat Heart, Lung & Blood Inst, 85-88, mem, Intramural Rev Bd, 78-88; mem, Coun High Blood Pressure Res, Am Heart Asn & Coun Circulation, Sect Renal Dis. *Mem:* Am Fedn Clin Res; Am Soc Clin Invest; Am Physiol Soc; Am Soc Nephrology; Am Soc Hypertension; Endocrine Soc; fel Am Col Physicians. *Res:* Author of numerous publications. *Mailing Add:* Hypertension Endocrine Br Nat Heart Lung & Blood Inst NIH Bldg 10 Rm 8C104 Bethesda MD 20892

GILL, MERTON, psychoanalysis; deceased, see previous edition for last biography

GILL, PIARA SINGH, PHYSICAL CHEMISTRY, PHOTO CHEMISTRY. *Current Pos:* from asst prof to assoc prof, 69-77, PROF CHEM, TUSKEGEE UNIV, 77- *Personal Data:* b Bassuwal, India, Feb 15, 40; m 67; c 2. *Educ:* Panjab Univ, India, BSc, 61, MSc, 62; Kans State Univ, MS, 65, PhD(chem), 67. *Prof Exp:* Fel chem, Univ Houston, 67-68; res assoc, Wright-Patterson AFB, Ohio, 68-69. *Res:* Chemical reactions induced by radiation, specifically the collisional energy transfer from excited ions to neutral molecules; mass-spectrometric studies of ion-molecule reactions. *Mailing Add:* Dept Chem Tuskegee Univ Tuskegee AL 36088-1699

GILL, ROBERT WAGER, ECOLOGY. *Current Pos:* Asst prof biol, 67-71, asst prof biol & statist, 71-74, asst to vchancellor, 74-87, EXEC ASST TO CHANCELLOR, UNIV CALIF, RIVERSIDE, 87- *Personal Data:* b Waterbury, Conn, Jan 19, 40; m 77; c 2. *Educ:* Oberlin Col, BA, 61; Univ Mich, MS, 63, PhD(zool), 67. *Mem:* AAAS. *Res:* Population and community ecology; population genetics; theoretical ecology. *Mailing Add:* Univ Calif 4148 Hinderaker Hall Riverside CA 92521

GILL, RONALD LEE, ON-LINE ISOTOPE SEPARATION, G-FACTOR MEASUREMENTS. *Current Pos:* PHYSICIST, BROOKHAVEN NAT LAB, 79- *Personal Data:* b Mechanicsburg, Pa, Nov 30, 49; m 71; c 2. *Educ:* Pa State Univ, BS, 71; Iowa State Univ, MS, 74, PhD(nuclear chem), 77. *Prof Exp:* Teaching fel, Iowa State Univ, 77-79. *Mem:* Am Phys Soc; Am Chem Soc. *Res:* Nuclear structure studies of short lived isotopically separated fission products. *Mailing Add:* 44 Mary Pitkin Path Shoreham NY 11786

GILL, STEPHEN PASCHALL, ACOUSTICS, SIGNAL PROCESSING. *Current Pos:* FOUNDER & CHIEF SCIENTIST, MAGNETIC PULSE INC, 85- *Personal Data:* b Baltimore, Md, Nov 13, 38; m 61, Margaret Gaskins; c Elizabeth (Olmsted) & Richard Paschall. *Educ:* Mass Inst Technol, BS, 60; Harvard Univ, MA, 61, PhD(appl physics), 64. *Prof Exp:* Physicist, Stanford Res Inst, 64-66, head high energy gas dynamics, 66-68; head high energy gas dynamics, Physics Int Co, 68-70, mgr, Shock Dynamics Dept, 70-72; pres & founder, Artec Assocs, Inc, 72-77, chief scientist & chmn bd, 72-79. *Concurrent Pos:* Pres & founder, Votan, 79-81, chief scientist, 79- *Mem:* Am Math Soc; Am Phys Soc; Inst Elec & Electronics Engrs. *Res:* Applied mathematics; shock wave physics; signal processing; commercial products in speech verification and speech recognition; commercial products in oil well instrumentation. *Mailing Add:* 32 Flood Circle Atherton CA 94027

GILL, THOMAS GRANDON, MANAGEMENT OF INTELLIGENT SYSTEMS. *Current Pos:* ASSOC PROF, FLA ATLANTIC UNIV, 91- *Personal Data:* b Boston, Mass, Apr 26, 55; m 89, Clare E Barres; c Thomas R & Jonathan G. *Educ:* Harvard Univ, AB, 75, MBA, 82, DBA(info systs), 91. *Prof Exp:* Pres, SnCorp Inc, 82-83; vpres tech suprvs, Agribus Assoc, 83-86. *Res:* Adoption of expert systems within organizations and the impact of complexity on individual decision-making. *Mailing Add:* 1190 SW 20th St Boca Raton FL 33486

GILL, THOMAS JAMES, III, PATHOLOGY, IMMUNOLOGY. *Current Pos:* prof path, chmn dept & pathologist in chief, 71-90, PROF HUMAN GENETICS, SCH MED, UNIV PITTSBURGH, 84-, MAUD L MENTEN PROF EXP PATH, 88- *Personal Data:* b Malden, Mass, July 2, 32; m 61, Faith Etoll; c Elizabeth R, Thomas J & Christopher G (deceased). *Educ:* Harvard Univ, AB, 53, AM, 57; Harvard Med Sch, MD, 57; Am Bd Path, dipl, 65. *Honors & Awards:* Smith, Kline & Fr Distinguished Lectr, Hahneman Med Col, 84; Whipple Lectr, Univ Rochester, 84; Distinguished Scientist Award, Southwest Found Biomed Res, 86; Berry Lect, Tex A&M Univ, 95; Muhlbock Lectr, Int Coun Lab Animal Sci, 95. *Prof Exp:* Asst path, Peter Bent Brigham Hosp, 57-58; med intern, NY Hosp-Cornell Med Ctr, 58-59; from asst to sr assoc, Peter Bent Brigham Hosp, 59-71. *Concurrent Pos:* Jr fel, Harvard Univ, 59-62, from res fel to assoc, Med Sch, 59-65, from asst prof to assoc prof, 70-72; Lederle med fac award, 62-65; NIH res career develop award, 65-71; assoc mem comn immunization, Armed Forces Epidemiol Bd, 66-70, mem, 70-72, consult, govt & indust, 66-, Surgeon Gen, US Army, 70-76; mem sci adv bd, St Jude Children's Res Hosp, 69-77; consult, Surgeon Gen, US Army, 70-76; mem, Allergy & Immunol Res Comt, Nat Inst Allergy & Infectious Dis, 73-76; mem, Merit Rev Bd Immuniol, Med Res Serv, Vet Admin, 76-79, bd dirs, Allegheny Co Chap Easter Seal Soc, 72-77, Sci Adv Comt, Damon Runyon-Walter Winchell Cancer Fund, 78-81, Comt Animal Models & Genetic Stocks, Nat Res Coun, 78-86, chmn, 83-86, Comt Rabbit Genetic Resources, 79-80 & Comt Perserv Lab Animal Resources, 85-90; trustee, Am Bd Path, 81-92, pres, 92, life trustee, 93-; mem, Maternal & Child Health Res Comt, Nat Inst Child Health & Human Develop, 92-96, chmn, 95-96. *Mem:* AAAS; Int Soc Immunol Reproduction (pres, 92-95); Am Asn Immunol; Am Soc Reproductive Immunol (vpres, 93-94, pres, 95-96); Transplantation Soc (vpres, 82-84). *Res:* Immunology; genetics; reproductive immunology; immunogenetics and its application to tissue transplantation and reproduction in inbred rats and humans. *Mailing Add:* Dept Path Univ Pittsburgh Sch Med Pittsburgh PA 15261. *E-Mail:* gill@med.pitt.edu

GILL, WILLIAM D(ELAHAYE), SOLID STATE PHYSICS, TECHNICAL MANAGEMENT. *Current Pos:* Res physicist, Res Div, 62-79, MGR & ADVAN PRINTER TECHNICIAN, INFO PROD DIV, INT BUS MACH CORP, 62- *Personal Data:* b Portugal, Jan 18, 35; Can citizen; m 62; c 3. *Educ:* Univ BC, BASc, 60, MASc, 62; Stanford Univ, PhD(mat sci), 69. *Mem:* Am Phys Soc. *Res:* Electronic properties of metallic polymers; transport properties in insulating solids; photoconductivity; photovoltaic effects in heterojunctions; advanced printer technology. *Mailing Add:* 1928 Cowper St Palo Alto CA 94301

GILL, WILLIAM JOSEPH, FOOD SCIENCE. *Current Pos:* OWNER & PRES, SEASONSHIELD & CROWN WINDOW CO, 89- *Personal Data:* b Romulus, Mich, July 17, 44; m 67, Sara Stryker; c Amy J & Aaron W. *Educ:* Mich State Univ, BS, 66, MS, 68; Pa State Univ, PhD(food sci), 76. *Prof Exp:* Food scientist, Mead Johnson & Co, 68-69; sr mgr prod res & develop, H J Heinz & Co, 69-76; corp vpres res & tech servs, Pepsico, Inc, 76-83; corp exec vpres menu & opers develop, Pillsburg Co Burger King Corp, 84-89. *Concurrent Pos:* Mgmt consult, Triangle Group, 83-84. *Mem:* AAAS; Inst Food Technologists; Food Safety Coun; Am Chem Soc; Int Life Sci Inst. *Res:* Processes, materials, packages, quality assurance, scientific and regulatory affairs relative to food and beverage products. *Mailing Add:* Seasonshield & Crown Window Co 355 Center Ct Venice FL 34292

GILL, WILLIAM N(ELSON), CHEMICAL ENGINEERING. *Current Pos:* prof & chmn dept, 86-92, RUSSELL SAGE PROF CHEM ENG, RENSSELAER POLYTECH INST, 89- *Personal Data:* b New York, NY, Sept 13, 28; m 54, 82, Chandlee Lloyd; c Max W, Douglas M, Alison L & Christine M. *Educ:* Syracuse Univ, BS, 51, MA, 55, PhD(chem eng), 60. *Honors & Awards:* Lectr Award, Chem Eng Div Am Soc Elec Engrs, 92. *Prof Exp:* Field engr, Am Blower Corp, 51-55; res assoc, Syracuse Univ, 55-57, from instr to assoc prof chem eng, 57-65; prof & chmn dept, Clarkson Col Technol, 65-71; dean & prof chem eng, State Univ NY, Buffalo, 71-86. *Concurrent Pos:* Consult, Corning Glass Corp, 75, Carborundum Co, Niagara Falls, 76- & NASA; Fulbright-Hays sr scholar, US-UK Educ Comt, 77; Glenn Murphy Distinguished Prof, Iowa State Univ, 80-82; Fulbright Sr Res Scholar, US-Australia Educ Comt, 86-87. *Mem:* Fel Am Inst Chem Engrs. *Res:* Role of transport phenomena in chemical reactions; reverse osmosis studies; dispersion phenomena; crystal growth; semiconductor processing; ultrafiltration of proteins; CVD of interconnects and dielectrics; polymer-ceramic pyrolysis. *Mailing Add:* Chem Eng Dept Rm 102 Ricketts Bldg Renesselaer Polytech Inst Troy NY 12180-3590. *Fax:* 518-276-4030

GILL, WILLIAM ROBERT, AGRONOMY, SOIL DYNAMICS. *Current Pos:* res soil scientist, 55-71, dir, 71-80, COLLABR, NAT SOIL DYNAMICS LAB, USDA, 80- *Personal Data:* b McDonald, Pa, July 21, 20; m 47, Irene Majorkiewicz; c William R Jr, John P, David C, Michael J & Elaine N. *Educ:* Pa State Univ, BS, 42; Univ Hawaii, MS, 49; Cornell Univ, PhD(agron, soils), 55. *Honors & Awards:* John Deere Gold Medal, Am Soc Agr Engrs, 90. *Prof Exp:* Soil scientist, Pineapple Res Inst, Univ Hawaii, 49-50; asst, Cornell Univ, 52-55. *Concurrent Pos:* Adj prof, Grad Fac, Auburn Univ, 57-87; US exchange scientist, USSR, 70. *Mem:* Am Soc Agron; Soil Sci Soc Am; Int Soil Sci Soc; Am Soc Agr Eng. *Res:* Dynamic relations of soil-machine systems with emphasis on tillage and traction in agricultural soils as they influence the efficiency and production of crops and soil physical conditions; agricultural engineering. *Mailing Add:* 283 Hillcrest Dr Auburn AL 36830. *E-Mail:* gillwilr@eng.auburn.edu

GILLAM, BASIL EARLY, mathematics; deceased, see previous edition for last biography

GILLARD, BAIBA KURINS, GLYCOBIOLOGY, CARBOHYDRATE CHEMISTRY. *Current Pos:* asst prof exp med, 83-90, RES ASSOC PROF, BAYLOR COL MED, HOUSTON, TEX, 90- *Personal Data:* b Ger, May 14, 46; m 67, Charles; c Laine. *Educ:* Purdue Univ, BS, 67; Washington Univ, MA, 69, PhD(chem), 72. *Prof Exp:* Robert A Welch Found fel biochem, Baylor Col Med, 72-74; Cystic Fibrosis Found res fel, Sch Med, Univ Calif, Los Angeles, 74-76, adj asst prof & asst res biochemist, Dept Pediat, 75-81, lectr, Dept Chem, 81-83. *Mem:* Am Chem Soc; Am Soc Biol Chem & Molecular Biol; AAAS; Soc Glycobiol. *Res:* Glycosphingolipids; biosynthesis, subcellular localization, trafficking; immune function. *Mailing Add:* Dept Med Baylor Col One Baylor Plaza Houston TX 77030. *Fax:* 713-790-0681; *E-Mail:* bgillard@bcm.tmc.edu

GILLARY, HOWARD L, NEUROPHYSIOLOGY. *Current Pos:* asst prof, 69-74, assoc prof, 74-79, PROF PHYSIOL, UNIV HAWAII, 79- *Personal Data:* b New York, NY, Feb 6, 40. *Educ:* Oberlin Col, AB, 61; Johns Hopkins Univ, PhD(biol), 66. *Prof Exp:* Nat Acad Sci-Nat Res Coun res assoc biophys, Naval Med Res Inst, Md, 65-67; res assoc & USPHS fel biol, Stanford Univ, 67-69. *Mem:* Soc Neurosci. *Res:* Sensory physiology; quantitative electrophysiological studies on labellar taste receptors of the blowfly, eyes of a terrestrial gastropod, and neural control of behavior in the crayfish; photoreceptors in a marine gastropod. *Mailing Add:* Dept Physiol Univ Hawaii Burns Med Sch 1960 East-West Rd Honolulu HI 96822-2319

GILLASPIE, ATHEY GRAVES, JR, plant pathology, for more information see previous edition

GILLE, JOHN CHARLES, ATMOSPHERIC SOUNDING, MIDDLE ATMOSPHERE. *Current Pos:* prog scientist, 72-73, leader, Upper Atmosphere Proj, 73-77, HEAD, GLOBAL ATMOSPHERIC CHG SECT, NAT CTR ATMOSPHERIC RES, 77- *Personal Data:* b Akron, Ohio, Oct 12, 34; m 63, Ellen Fetter; c Sarah & Edward. *Educ:* Yale Univ, BS, 56; Cambridge Univ, BA, 58, MA, 66; Mass Inst Technol, PhD(geophys), 64. *Honors & Awards:* Except Sci Achievement Award, NASA, 82. *Prof Exp:* Res asst meteorol, Harvard Univ, 60-64; from asst prof to assoc prof, Fla State Univ, 64-72. *Concurrent Pos:* Consult, Honeywell Inc, 64-71, IBM Corp, 67-68, Barnes Eng, 71, Arthur D Little, 83 & TRW Corp, 89-92; mem, var adv groups on earth & planetary atmospheres, NASA, 69- & var nat comns, 70-; vis prof astro-geophys, Univ Colo, 70, lectr, 72-94, res prof, 97-; assoc ed, J Atmospheric Sci, 74-80, J Geophys Res, 80-82; vis prof, Geophys Dept, Kyoto Univ, 88. *Mem:* Fel AAAS; Am Geophys Union; fel Am Meteorol Soc. *Res:* Inversion of satellite measurements, especially limb infrared emission to obtain stratosphere and mesosphere temperature and composition; calculation, and measurements of atmospheric infrared, visible radiation; middle atmospheric dynamics, chemistry; retrieval of tropospheric CO and CH4; tropospheric chemistry. *Mailing Add:* Nat Ctr Atmospheric Res PO Box 3000 Boulder CO 80307-3000

GILLELAND, MARTHA JANE, BIOORGANIC CHEMISTRY. *Current Pos:* assoc prof, 72-77, chairperson dept, 74-81, PROF CHEM, CALIF STATE UNIV, BAKERSFIELD, 77- *Personal Data:* b Monroe, La, Sept 9, 40. *Educ:* La Polytech Inst, BS, 62; La State Univ, Baton Rouge, PhD(org chem, biochem), 68. *Prof Exp:* Res assoc biochem, Edsel B Ford Inst Med Res, Mich, 68-69; fel, Northwestern Univ, Evanston, 70-71. *Mem:* Sigma Xi; AAAS; Am Chem Soc. *Res:* Mechanism of enzyme action. *Mailing Add:* 5250 SW Flansberg Ave Waldport OR 97394

GILLEN, KEITH THOMAS, ATOMIC & MOLECULAR COLLISIONS, BEAM-SURFACE INTERACTIONS. *Current Pos:* RETIRED. *Personal Data:* b Cleveland, Ohio, Aug 11, 42; m 90, Denise Kilbourne; c Daniel. *Educ:* Calif Inst Technol, BS, 64; Univ Wis, Madison, PhD(phys chem), 70. *Prof Exp:* Postdoctoral fel, Chem Dept, Univ Calif, Berkeley, 70-73; postdoc fel, SRI Int, 73-75, from chem physicist to sr chem physicist, 75-83, prog mgr 83-90; prog officer, Div Chem, NSF, 88-90. *Concurrent Pos:* Fel Miller Inst, Univ Calif, Berkeley, 70-72; IBM fel, 72-73. *Mem:* AAAS; Am Chem Soc; Am Phys Soc. *Res:* Atomic, molecular and ionic collisions both in the gas phase and on surfaces; mass spectrometric surface analysis techniques. *Mailing Add:* 134 Carmelita Dr Mountain View CA 94040. *E-Mail:* kgillen@earthlink.net

GILLEN, KENNETH TODD, AGING, DEGRADATION. *Current Pos:* mem staff polymer sci, 74-90, sr mem tech staff, 90-91, DISTINGUISHED MEM TECH STAFF, SANDIA LABS, 91- *Personal Data:* b Cleveland, Ohio, Aug 11, 42; m 64; c 2. *Educ:* Univ Calif, Berkeley, BS, 64; Univ Wis-Madison, PhD(chem), 70. *Prof Exp:* Mem staff chem physics, Bell Tel Labs, NJ, 70-72; mem staff electronics, Jeol, Inc, NJ, 72-74. *Mem:* Am Chem Soc; Am Phys Soc. *Res:* Polymers; mechanical properties; viscoelasticity; aging; radiation effects on polymers; permeation. *Mailing Add:* 8104 Northridge Ave NE Albuquerque NM 87109-3017

GILLENWATER, JAY YOUNG, UROLOGY. *Current Pos:* asst prof urol, 65-67, PROF UROL & CHMN DEPT, SCH MED, UNIV VA, 67- *Personal Data:* b Kingsport, Tenn, July 27, 33; m 55; c 3. *Educ:* Univ Tenn, BS, 54, MD, 57. *Prof Exp:* Instr histol & gross anat, Sch Med, Univ Tenn, 56; intern med, Sch Med, Univ Louisville, 60-62. *Concurrent Pos:* USPHS fel renal & cardiovasc dis, Univ Pa Grad Hosp, 64-65; NIH urol training grant, 65-69, study grants, 66-68 & 66-71; lectr, Sch Med, Univ Louisville, 61-62. *Mem:* AAAS; Am Physiol Soc; Am Fedn Clin Res; Am Col Surg; AMA; Am Urol Asn. *Res:* Renal physiology. *Mailing Add:* Dept Urol Univ Va Sch Med Box 422 Charlottesville VA 22908-0001. *Fax:* 804-982-3652

GILLER, E(DWARD) B(ONFOY), NUCLEAR ARMS CONTROL, SCIENCE POLICY. *Current Pos:* dir mil appln, US AEC, Washington, DC, 67-72, asst gen mgr nat sec, 72-75, dep asst adminr nat sec, ERDA, 75-77, joint chiefs of staff, 77-84, CONSULT, JOINT CHIEFS STAFF, DEPT DEFENSE, 84-; VPRES, TRANS MAR INC, 90- *Personal Data:* b Jacksonville, Ill, July 8, 18; m 43, Mildred F Schmidt; c Susan A, Carol E, Bruce C, Penny M & Paul B. *Educ:* Univ Ill, BS, 40, MS, 48, PhD(chem eng), 50. *Prof Exp:* Jr engr petrol ref, Sinclair Oil Co, 40-41; USAF, 41-, chief radiation br, Armed Forces Spec Weapons Proj, 50-54, dir res, Spec Weapons Ctr, 54-59, spec asst to comdr, Off Aerospace Res, 59-64, dir sci & technol, Hq, 64-67. *Concurrent Pos:* Sr scientist, arms control, Pac-Sierra Res Corp, 84- *Mem:* AAAS; Sigma Xi; fel Am Inst Chem; Am Inst chem Engrs. *Res:* Low temperature viscosity of hydrocarbons; heat transfer; gaseous thermal diffusion; atmospheric transmission optics; effects of high intensity radiant energy; nuclear weapons effects; high energy particle physics; government research; arms control treaty negotiation; small particle separation. *Mailing Add:* 216 Wapiti Dr Bayfield CO 81122-9243

GILLES, FLOYD HARRY, NEUROPATHOLOGY, NEUROLOGY. *Current Pos:* BURTON E GREEN PROF PEDIAT NEUROPATH, CHILDREN'S HOSP, 83- *Personal Data:* b Elgin, Ill, Oct 18, 30; div; c 5. *Educ:* Univ Chicago, BA, 51, BS & MD, 55; Am Bd Psychiat & Neurol, dipl, 62; Am Bd Path, dipl & cert neuropath, 74. *Prof Exp:* Intern, Johns Hopkins Hosp, 55-56, asst neurol, Sch Med, 54-59; instr clin neurol, Sch Med, Georgetown Univ, 59-61; neuropathologist, Children's Hosp Med Ctr, Harvard, Med Sch, 62-71, from assoc prof to prof neuropath, 71-83. *Concurrent Pos:* Nat Insts Neurol Dis & Blindness spec fel neuropath, Cent Anatomic Lab, Md, 61-62; asst resident, Baltimore City Hosps, 56-58 & Johns Hopkins Hosp, 58-59; from instr clin neurol to asst prof neuropath, Harvard Med Sch, 62-71; mem path task force, Perinatal Res Br, Nat Inst Neurol Dis & Stroke, 70; assoc neuropath, Beth Israel Hosp, Boston, 71-79, New Eng Deaconess Hosp & New Eng Baptist Hosp, 81-84. *Mem:* Am Asn Neuropath (asst secy-treas, 70). *Res:* Pediatric neuropathology; reaction of fetal brain to insult. *Mailing Add:* Children's Hosp 4650 Sunset Blvd MS 43 Los Angeles CA 90027

GILLES, KENNETH ALBERT, CEREAL SCIENCE, FOOD TECHNOLOGY & INSPECTION. *Current Pos:* CONSULT AGR, MKT & FOOD SAFETY, 89- *Personal Data:* b Minneapolis, Minn, Mar 6, 22; m 44, Beverly E Barrows; c Jeffrey A & Diane E. *Educ:* Univ Minn, BS, 44, PhD(biochem), 52. *Honors & Awards:* W F Geddes Award, Am Asn Cereal Chem. *Prof Exp:* Chem engr, Pillsbury Mills, Inc, 46-49; instr agr biochem, Univ Minn, 49-51; proj leader cereal biochem, Gen Mills, Inc, 52-60 & basic milling res, 60-61; prof cereal technol & chmn dept, NDak State Univ, 61-70, prof cereal chem & vpres agr, 69-81, emer prof, 89; adminr, Fed Grain Inspection Serv, USDA, 81-86; asst secy agr, USDA, 86-89. *Concurrent Pos:* Ed, Cereal Chem, 61-68; chmn, NDak Agr Res & Exten Bd, 72-81; dir, Bd Com Credit Corp, 86-89. *Mem:* Fel AAAS; Am Chem Soc; Am Asn Cereal Chem (pres, 71-72); Inst Food Technol; Asn Oper Millers; Sigma Xi. *Res:* Structure, quantity and functional properties of cereal carbohydrates, lipids, proteins and enzymes; storage, utilization and quality inspection of grains, flour and semolina for domestic and international markets including public policy regulations and oversight; lipids. *Mailing Add:* 100 E Lark Ave McAllen TX 78504-2013. *E-Mail:* kagrochert@juno.com

GILLES, PAUL WILSON, PHYSICAL CHEMISTRY. *Current Pos:* from asst prof to prof, 47-63, DISTINGUISHED PROF CHEM, UNIV KANS, 63- *Personal Data:* b Kansas City, Kans, Jan 13, 21; m 44; c 3. *Educ:* Univ Kans, AB, 43; Univ Calif, PhD(phys chem), 47. *Prof Exp:* Asst chem, Univ Calif, 43-44 & Manhattan Proj, 44-47. *Mem:* AAAS; Am Chem Soc; Am Phys Soc; Sigma Xi. *Res:* High temperature chemistry; thermodynamics; vaporization processes; vapor pressures; properties of refractory borides, carbides and oxides; dissociation energies and stabilities of high temperature gases; x-ray crystallography; mass spectrometray; high molecular weight of boron sulfides. *Mailing Add:* Dept Chem Univ Kans 20 Mallott Lawrence KS 66045-0001

GILLESPIE, ARTHUR SAMUEL, JR, INDUSTRIAL CHEMISTRY. *Current Pos:* res chemist, 67-77, dir corp serv, 77-88, ENVIRON MGR, LITHIUM DIV, FMC CORP, 88- *Personal Data:* b Peking, China, Nov 21, 31; US citizen; m 53; c 3. *Educ:* Wake Forest Univ, BS, 53; Duke Univ, MA, 55. *Prof Exp:* Staff mem, Battery Lab, Sania Corp, 55-56; res engr, Phys Chem Dept, Aluminum Co Am, 56-61; res chemist, Measurements & Controls Lab, Res Triangle Inst, 61-66; sr chemist, Tex Gulf Sulphur Co, 66-67. *Mem:* Am Chem Soc. *Res:* Commercial utilization of mineral wastes; nuclear chemistry and radiochemistry; instrumentation design and development; water resources; water, air and hazardous wastes methods and management; aluminum and lithium chemistry; general corporation management matters; governmental affairs; environmental management. *Mailing Add:* 618 Hillcrest Ave Gastonia NC 28052

GILLESPIE, CLAUDE MILTON, NUCLEAR PHYSICS, RADIATION HYDRODYNAMICS. *Current Pos:* MEM STAFF NUCLEAR WEAPON EFFECTS & PHENOMENOL, NUCLEAR WEAPON DESIGN, INERTIAL FUSION, LOS ALAMOS NAT LAB, 66- *Personal Data:* b Huntsville, Ala, Dec 13, 32; c 2. *Educ:* Ga Inst Technol, BS, 55; Ohio State Univ, PhD(physics), 66. *Mem:* Am Phys Soc; Am Geophys Union. *Res:* Beta and gamma ray spectroscopy; phenomenology and hydrodynamics of explosions; theoretical and experimental nuclear weapon effects; laser fusion; design and testing of nuclear weapons; weapons system analysis. *Mailing Add:* 427 Estante Way Los Alamos NM 87544

GILLESPIE, DANIEL THOMAS, STATISTICAL PHYSICS, MARKOV PROCESSES. *Current Pos:* res physicist, 71-80, MATHEMATICIAN, NAVAL WEAPONS CTR, 80- *Personal Data:* b Springfield, Mo, Aug 15, 38; m 76, Carol A Clarke; c Mark T & Christopher E. *Educ:* Rice Inst, BA, 60; Johns Hopkins Univ, PhD(physics), 68. *Prof Exp:* Res asst physics, Johns Hopkins Univ, 64-68; res assoc, Univ Md, 68-71. *Concurrent Pos:* Instr, Johns Hopkins Univ, 66-68 & Univ Md, 71. *Mem:* Am Phys Soc; Sigma Xi. *Res:* Kinetic theory; Monte Carlo methods; theory and simulation of stochastic processes, especially Markov processes; chemical kinetics of nonequilibrium systems. *Mailing Add:* 812 W Vicki Ave Ridgecrest CA 93555

GILLESPIE, ELIZABETH, PHARMACOLOGY, BIOCHEMISTRY. *Current Pos:* RETIRED. *Personal Data:* b Montreal, Que, May 7, 36. *Educ:* McGill Univ, BSc, 57, PhD(biochem), 66. *Prof Exp:* Res assoc pharmacol, Yale Univ, 68-71; from instr to asst prof med, Johns Hopkins Univ, 71-81; mgr, Respiratory Sect, Mead Johnson & Co, 81-82; sr res scientist cardiovasc biol, Bristol Myers Pharmaceut Res & Develop, 83-89. *Concurrent Pos:* USPHS grant pharmacol, Yale Univ, 66-68. *Mem:* Am Asn Immunol; Am Soc Pharmacol & Exp Therapeut. *Res:* Biochemical pharmacology; immediate hypersensitivity; atherosclerosis cardiovascular disease. *Mailing Add:* 3351 Old Murfreesboro Rd Lebanonle TN 37090-0819

GILLESPIE, GEORGE H, PHYSICS OF PARTICLE ACCELERATORS, ATOMIC COLLISIONS AT HIGH ENERGIES. *Current Pos:* PRES, G H GILLESPIE ASSOC, INC, 88- *Personal Data:* b Dallas, Tex, Sept 9, 45; c James S, Colin H & Ian G. *Educ:* Rice Univ, Houston, Tex, BA & MEE, 68; Univ Calif, San Diego, MS, 69, PhD(physics), 74. *Prof Exp:* Engr, Int Bus Mach, 67; res asst, Los Alamos Sci Lab, 68 & Univ Calif, San Diego, 68-74; staff scientist, Phys Dynamics, Inc, 75-87; assoc, La Jolla Inst, 76-88. *Concurrent Pos:* Consult, Sci Appln Int Corp, 85-88; rev comt, Eng Physics Div Argonne Nat Lab, Univ Chicago, 91-93. *Mem:* Am Phys Soc; AAAS. *Res:* Atomic, electromagnetic and nuclear interactions at intermediate energies; superconducting instruments; physics of particle accelerators; mathematical physics; technology assessment; computer simulations of accelerator beams. *Mailing Add:* G H Gillespie Assoc Inc PO Box 2961 Del Mar CA 92014

GILLESPIE, GEORGE YANCEY, IMMUNOBIOLOGY OF NEOPLASMS, MOLECULAR BIOLOGY OF MACROPHAGES. *Current Pos:* ASSOC PROF, DEPT SURG, UNIV ALA, 87- *Personal Data:* b Greenwood, Miss, Oct 29, 43; m 66, Lady J Campbell; c Jan (Seghers). *Educ:* Univ Miss, BA, 65, MS, 68, PhD(immunol & immunochem), 71. *Prof Exp:* Res asst immunol, dept biol, Univ Miss, 68-71; res fel immunopathol, dept path, Med Ctr, Univ Kans, Kansas City, 71-73, instr path, 73-75; res assoc immunopathol, Scripps Clin & Res Found, La Jolla, Calif, 75-77; res asst prof path, Univ NC, Chapel Hill, 77-81, from res asst prof to res assoc prof surg, dept surg, 81-87. *Concurrent Pos:* Mem core fac & dir, Immuno-Neurooncol Res Prog, Lineberger Cancer, Res Ctr, Univ NC, Chapel Hill, 79-87, dir, tissue cult facil, 84-87; topic ed, Surv Immunol Res, 81-87. *Mem:* AAAS; Am Asn Immunologists; Am Soc Invest Path; Am Soc Microbiol; Soc Biol Therapy; Tissue Cult Asn. *Res:* The role of mononuclear phagocyte-derived growth factors in wound healing, neovascularization and neoplastic cell proliferation; immunobiology and immunotherapy of malignant brain tumors; central nervous system regulation of immune function. *Mailing Add:* Div Neurosurg Dept Surg Univ Ala 1900 University Blvd Birmingham AL 35294-0006. *Fax:* 205-934-7676

GILLESPIE, JAMES HOWARD, VETERINARY SCIENCE, VIROLOGY. *Current Pos:* asst prof poultry dis, 46-48, asst prof bact, 48-50, assoc prof vet bact, 50-56, asst dir lab dis of dogs, 51-61, chmn dept, 72-81, PROF VET BACT, NY STATE COL VET MED, CORNELL UNIV, 56- *Personal Data:* b Bethlehem, Pa, Nov 26, 17; m 41; c 3. *Educ:* Univ Pa, VMD, 39; Am Col Vet Microbiologists, dipl. *Honors & Awards:* Gaines Award, Am Vet Med Asn. *Prof Exp:* Instr poultry dis & asst poultry pathologist, Univ NH, 40. *Concurrent Pos:* USPHS fels, State Vet Res Inst, Amsterdam & Univ Calif, Berkeley, 60-61; exec secy adv comt foot & mouth dis, Nat Acad Sci, 61-; chmn, Nat Acad Sci-Nat Res Coun Foot & Mouth Dis Mission, Arg, 62; chmn animal resources adv comt, Div Res Resources, NIH, 74-75; chmn bd comp virol, WHO, 75-80; consult, Plum Island Animal Dis Ctr, USDA, 75-81; bd mem, Am Col Vet Microbiologists. *Mem:* AAAS; Am Soc Microbiol; Am Vet Med Asn; Conf Res Workers Animal Dis. *Res:* Animal virology and bacteriology; viral diseases of domesticated animals, fin-fish and shellfish. *Mailing Add:* 616-A Vet Res Cornell Univ Dept Microbiol Ithaca NY 14853

GILLESPIE, JERRY RAY, PHYSIOLOGY, PATHOLOGY. *Current Pos:* PROF & HEAD DEPT CLIN SCI, KANS STATE UNIV, 93-, HEAD VET MED TEACHING HOSP, 93- *Personal Data:* b Lincoln, Nebr, Jan 25, 37; m 83, Martha H Johnson; c Cheryl, Rod, Victoria & Justin. *Educ:* Okla State Univ, BS & DVM, 61; Univ Calif, Davis, PhD(comp path), 65. *Honors & Awards:* Fulbright-Hays Award. *Prof Exp:* Asst anat, Okla State Univ, 57-61, supvr animal care, Univ Dairy Barn, 60-61; gen practitioner, Gotherburg Animal Hosp, Nebr, 61-62; asst specialist anat, Sch Med, Univ Calif, Davis, 62-65, from asst prof clin sci to assoc prof, 66-71, assoc dean student serv, 70-72, assoc prof med physiol, 69-75 & vet med physiol, 71-75, prof physiol, Sch Vet Med & Sch Med, 75-93. *Concurrent Pos:* Fel, Cardiovasc Res Inst, San Francisco, 65-66. *Mem:* AAAS; Am Physiol Soc; Am Vet Med Asn; Am Col Cardiol; Am Soc Anesthesiol; Am Asn Higher Ed; Am Asn Vet Clinicians. *Res:* Investigations of respiratory mechanics in healthy animals and those with chronic respiratory diseases. *Mailing Add:* Dept Clin Sci Col Vet Med Kans State Univ Manhattan KS 66506-5606. *Fax:* 785-532-4288; *E-Mail:* gillesp@vetmail.trotnet.vet.ksu.edu

GILLESPIE, JESSE SAMUEL, JR, ORGANIC CHEMISTRY. *Current Pos:* BEIRNE CARTER FOUND, 89- *Personal Data:* b Lynchburg, Va, Dec 20, 21; m 50, Nancy V Blackburn; c Samuel H, Leonard B, William W & Nan W (O'Connell). *Educ:* Va Mil Inst, BS, 43; Univ Va, PhD(chem), 49. *Prof Exp:* Asst prof chem, Univ Richmond, 49-51; sr chemist, Va-Carolina Chem Corp, 51-53, group leader, 53-54, asst div mgr, 54-56, mgr org & agr chem, 56-58; partner, Cox & Gillespie Chemists & Chem Engrs, 58-62; sr chemist, 62-68, actg dir, 68-69, dir, Va Inst Sci Res, Univ Richmond, 69-82, prof chem, 72-82; adv, Thomas F & Kate Miller Jeffress Mem Trust, 82-96. *Concurrent Pos:* Dir sponsored progs, Univ Richmond, 72-82. *Mem:* Am Chem Soc; Sigma Xi. *Res:* Mechanisms of organic reactions; synthetic organic and medicinal chemistry. *Mailing Add:* 303 Hillwood Rd Richmond VA 23226. *Fax:* 804-788-2700

GILLESPIE, JOHN, THEORETICAL PHYSICS. *Current Pos:* ASSOC PROF PHYSICS, LEHMAN COL, CITY UNIV NY, 78- *Personal Data:* b Buffalo, NY, Oct 30, 36. *Educ:* Univ Rochester, BS, 58; Univ Calif, Berkeley, PhD(theoret physics), 63. *Prof Exp:* Physicist, Lawrence Radiation Lab, Univ Calif, 63; res assoc, Columbia Univ, 63-65; res assoc, Stanford Linear Accelerator Ctr, 65-67; mem staff, Theoret Physics Ctr, Polytech Sch, Paris, 67-68; res physicist, AEC, Saclay, France, 68-69; asst prof physics, Boston Univ, 69-72; prof, Inst Nuclear Sci, Univ Grenoble, France, 72-75; instr res, Polytech High Sch, Paris, 75-78. *Concurrent Pos:* Asst prof, Univ Calif, Santa Cruz, 65-66; vis investr biophysics, Sloan-Kettering Inst, NY, 78- *Mem:* AAAS; Am Phys Soc; NY Acad Sci; Europ Phys Soc; Am Asn Physicists Med; Sigma Xi. *Res:* Nuclear theory; elementary particles; medical physics. *Mailing Add:* Dept Physics & Astron Herbert H Lehman Col Bronx NY 10468. *E-Mail:* Bitnet: jrglc@cunyum

GILLESPIE, LAROUX KING, PRECISION MINIATURE MACHINING, DEBURRING & BURR TECHNOLOGY. *Current Pos:* MGR ENG PROJ, ALLIEDSIGNAL AEROSPACE CO, 81- *Personal Data:* b Colorado Springs, Colo, Nov 11, 42; m 66; c 5. *Educ:* Kansas Univ, BS, 65, MS, 68; Utah State Univ, MS, 73. *Honors & Awards:* Nat Award Merit, Soc Mfg Engrs, 74, Albert Sargent Progress Award, 84. *Prof Exp:* Process engr, Bendix Corp, 66-73, sr engr, 73-78, staff engr, 78-81. *Concurrent Pos:* Dir, Soc Mfg Engrs, 77-81; chmn, Worldwide Burr, Technol Comt, 94- *Mem:* Soc Mfg Engrs; Am Soc Mech Engrs. *Res:* Metal cutting; precision miniature machining; burr formation and deburring. *Mailing Add:* Allied-Signal Aerospace Co PO Box 419159 Kansas City MO 64141-6159

GILLESPIE, ROBERT HOWARD, ORGANIC CHEMISTRY. *Current Pos:* RETIRED. *Personal Data:* b Richmond, Ind, Jan 31, 16; m 44, Gertrude C Weber; c Robert H Jr, Mary E & Frank S. *Educ:* Ind Univ, BS, 38; Univ Wis, PhD(org chem), 44. *Prof Exp:* Asst, Nat Defense Res Comt Projs, Univ Wis & Kendall Mills, 40-44, textile chemist, Res Dept, Kendall Mills, 44-55, res chemist, Theodore Clark Lab, 55-59; res assoc, Inst Paper Chem, 59-60; chemist, Forest Prod Lab, Forest Serv, USDA, 60-66, supvr res chemist, 66-87. *Mem:* Fel AAAS; fel Am Inst Chemists; Fiber Soc; fel Am Soc Testing & Mat; Forest Prod Res Soc; Am Chem Soc. *Res:* Organic synthesis; textile development; cellulose chemistry; pressure-sensitive adhesives; rubbers, resins and plastics; non-woven fabrics; chemistry of wood; wood adhesives. *Mailing Add:* 3 Downwind Hilton Head Island SC 29928

GILLESPIE, RONALD JAMES, INORGANIC CHEMISTRY & GENERAL CHEMISTRY. *Current Pos:* from assoc prof to prof, 58-89, EMER PROF CHEM, MCMASTER UNIV, 89- *Personal Data:* b London, Eng, Aug 21, 24; m 50, Madge E Garner; c Ann & Lynn. *Educ:* Univ London, BSc, 45, PhD, 49, DSc, 57. *Hon Degrees:* LLD, Concordia Univ, Montreal & Dalhousie Univ, Halifax, 88; DSc, McMaster Univ, Hamilton, Ont, 93. *Honors & Awards:* Harrison Mem Prize, Chem Soc, 53; Distinguished Serv Award Advan Inorg Chem, Am Chem Soc, 73, Flourine Chem Award, 81; Chem Inst Can, Union Carbide Award for Chem Educ, 76; Chem Inst Can Medal, 77; Silver Jubilee Medal, 78; Nyholm lectr, Royal Soc Chem, 78-79; Henry Marshall Tory Medal, Royal Soc Can, 83; Izaak Walter Killam Mem Prize, Can Coun, 87. *Prof Exp:* Lectr chem, Univ Col, London, 49-58. *Concurrent Pos:* Commonwealth Found fel, Brown Univ, 53-54; vis prof, Univ Manchester, Eng, Univ Sci Tech Languedoc, Montpellier, France, Univ Geneva, Switz, Univ Gottingen, WGer, Australian Nat Univ, Canberra, Univ Melbourne, Australia, Univ Auckland, NZ, Panjab Univ, Chandigarh, India, 65-83; vis fel, Univ Durlem, UK, 95. *Mem:* Am Chem Soc; Chem Inst Can; Royal Soc Chem; fel Royal Inst Chem; fel Royal Soc Can; fel Royal Soc London. *Res:* Inorganic and physical chemistry of nonaqueous solvents; structural inorganic chemistry; fluorine chemistry; chemistry of the nonmetallic elements; chemical education. *Mailing Add:* Dept Chem McMaster Univ 1280 Main St W Hamilton ON L8S 4L8 Can. *Fax:* 905-522-2509; *E-Mail:* gillespie@mcmail.cis.mcmaster.ca

GILLESPIE, TERRY JAMES, AGRICULTURAL METEOROL. *Current Pos:* assoc prof, 68-80, PROF METEOROL, UNIV GUELPH, 80- *Personal Data:* b Vancouver, BC, Jan 5, 41; m 66; c 2. *Educ:* Univ BC, BSc, 62; Univ Toronto, MA, 63; Univ Guelph, PhD(meteorol), 68. *Prof Exp:* Meteorologist, Can Govt Serv, 63-66. *Mem:* Can Meteorol Oceanog Soc. *Res:* Meteorology as applied to agriculture. *Mailing Add:* Dept Meteorol Univ Guelph Guelph ON N1G 2W1 Can. *E-Mail:* tgillesp@lrs.uoguelph.ca

GILLESPIE, THOMAS DAVID, AUTOMOTIVE ENGINEERING. *Current Pos:* RES SCIENTIST VEHICLE RES, TRANSP RES INST, UNIV MICH, 76- *Personal Data:* b New Brighton, Pa, Dec 3, 39; m 63; c 2. *Educ:* Carnegie Inst Technol, BS, 61; Pa State Univ, MS, 65, PhD(mech eng), 70. *Honors & Awards:* L Ray Buckendale Award, Soc Automotive Engrs, 84. *Prof Exp:* Engr glass res, Glass Res Ctr, PPG Indust, 63-64; proj officer res & develop, Armor & Eng Bd, US Army, 64-66; res assoc, Pa State Univ, 70-73; sr develop engr automotive mfg, Ford Motor Co, 73-76. *Concurrent Pos:* Pvt consult, 77- *Mem:* Soc Automotive Engrs; Am Soc Testing & Mat; Am Soc Mech Engrs; Sigma Xi. *Res:* Heavy vehicle braking, handling and ride performances; highway roughness and frictional characteristics. *Mailing Add:* 1083 Bandera Dr Ann Arbor MI 48103

GILLESPIE, WALTER LEE, SCIENCE EDUCATION. *Current Pos:* assoc prog dir, Teacher Educ Sect, NSF, 67-71, prog dir, Div Pre-Col Educ Sci, 71-73, head, Instrnl Improv Implementation Sect, Pre-Col Educ, 73-75, dir, Div Sci Educ Resources Improv, 75-78, dep asst dir sci educ, 78-80, ACTG ASST DIR SCI & ENG EDUC, NSF, 80- *Personal Data:* b Hamilton, Ohio, Jan 6, 30; m 53; c 2. *Educ:* Miami Univ, AB, 52, MA, 54; Univ Ill, PhD(zool), 60. *Prof Exp:* Asst prof zool, Butler Univ, 59-60; from instr to assoc prof biol, Wells Col, 60-67. *Mem:* AAAS; Ecol Soc Am; Am Soc Zool; Am Ornith Union; Arctic Inst NAm; Sigma Xi. *Res:* Bird populations of the subarctic; improvement of science and engineering education programs. *Mailing Add:* 1800 Kimberly Rd Silver Spring MD 20903-1217

GILLESPIE, WILLIAM HARRY, PALEOZOIC PALEOBOTANY, FORESTRY CONSULTING. *Current Pos:* PALEOBOTANIST, COAL RESOURCES BR, US GEOL SURV, 74. *Personal Data:* b Webster Springs, WVa, Jan 8, 31; m 50, Betty I Rasnick; c William A, Linda M, Clifton P, James D & Laura L. *Educ:* Univ WVa, BS, 52, MS, 54. *Prof Exp:* Forest biologist, Plant Pest Control Div, 56-66, from asst dir to dir, 66-69, admin asst, 69-82, asst comnr, 82-86, dir, WVa Div Forestry & state forester, 86-93. *Concurrent Pos:* Instr, WVa Univ, 58-74, adj assoc prof & mem grad fac, 74-87, adj prof, 87- *Mem:* Fel Soc Am Foresters; Bot Soc Am; Int Asn Plant Taxon; Am Asn Petrol Geologists; Am Inst Biol Sci; Geol Soc Am. *Res:* Paleobotany; economic and general botany of the Appalachian area; paleobotany of the Paleozoic of the United States, especially compression floras; control of forest tree diseases; general forest management. *Mailing Add:* 916 Churchill Circle Charleston WV 25314-1747. *Fax:* 304-346-5849

GILLETT, LAWRENCE B, GEOLOGY. *Current Pos:* assoc prof, 62-73, PROF GEOL, STATE UNIV NY COL PLATTSBURGH, 73- *Personal Data:* b Montreal, Que, Aug 22, 31; m 61. *Educ:* McGill Univ, BS, 53, MS, 56; Princeton Univ, MA, 56, PhD(geol), 62. *Prof Exp:* Asst prof geol, Univ NDak, 59-62. *Mem:* Am Geophys Union; Nat Asn Geol Teachers; Can Inst Mining & Metall; Geol Asn Can; Sigma Xi. *Res:* Structures of diabase dikes; petrology of syenites; base metal exploration in Canada; glacial geomorphology; liquid immiscibility. *Mailing Add:* 30 Conroy Rd West Chazy NY 12992-2703

GILLETT, TEDFORD A, FOOD SCIENCE, MEAT SCIENCE. *Current Pos:* RES GROUP LEADER, UNION CARBIDES FOOD SCI INST, 76- *Personal Data:* b Burley, Idaho, Aug 18, 35; m 60; c 5. *Educ:* Univ Idaho, BS, 60, MS, 62; Mich State Univ, PhD(food sci), 66. *Prof Exp:* Res assoc biochem, Mich State Univ, 66-68; asst prof food & animal sci, Utah State Univ, 69-76. *Mem:* Inst Food Technol; Am Meat Sci Asn; Am Soc Animal Sci. *Res:* Body composition; enzyme purification and characterization; meat processing; effect of nitrite upon bioavailability of iron; ham processing and emulsion technology. *Mailing Add:* 9900 Keswick Ave N Stillwater MN 55082

GILLETTE, DEAN, MATHEMATICS. *Current Pos:* PROF, ENG DEPT, HARVEY MUDD COL. *Personal Data:* b Chicago, Ill, Aug 11, 25; m 49; c 1. *Educ:* Ore State Col, BS, 48; Univ Calif, AM, 50, PhD(math), 53. *Prof Exp:* Asst math, Univ Calif, 50-53; mem tech staff, Bell Labs, 56-62, dir, Mil Anal Ctr, 62-66, exec dir, 66-71, exec exec dir systs res, 71-79, exec dir corp studies, Transmission Systs Eng Div, 79- *Mem:* AAAS; Am Math Soc; Soc Indust & Appl Math; Inst Elec & Electronics Engrs; Sigma Xi. *Res:* Systems analysis; operations research. *Mailing Add:* Claremont Grad Sch PO Box 354 The Sea Ranch CA 95497-0354

GILLETTE, EDWARD LEROY, EXPERIMENTAL RADIATION THERAPY, COMPARATIVE ONCOLOGY. *Current Pos:* From instr to assoc prof, 59-71, PROF RADIOL, COLO STATE UNIV, 71-, DIR COMP ONCOL, COL VET MED & BIOMED SCI, 74-, CHMN, DEPT RADIOL HEALTH SCI, 89- *Personal Data:* b Coffeyville, Kans, May 21, 32; m 88, Sharon McChesney; c William, Jeffrey, Timothy & Jennifer. *Educ:* Kans State Univ, BS & DVM, 56; Colo State Univ, MS, 61, PhD(physiol, radiation biol), 65. *Honors & Awards:* Ralston Purina Res Award, 88. *Concurrent Pos:* Advan fel sect exp radiother, Univ Tex M D Anderson Hosp & Tumor Inst, 68-69; vis scientist, Los Alamos Sci Lab, Univ Calif, 72-76; Cancer Res Manpower Rev Comt, NIH, 80-84; counr, Radiation Res Soc, 88-91; adj prof, Duke Univ Med Col, 95- *Mem:* Am Col Vet Radiol (pres, 72-73); Am Vet Med Asn; Radiation Res Soc; Am Soc Therapeut Radiol & Oncol; Am Asn Cancer Res;

Vet Cancer Soc (pres, 82-84); Am Col Vet Internal Med. *Res:* Experimental radiotherapy; hyperthermia and radiation response of spontaneous tumors and normal tissue response. *Mailing Add:* Radiol Health Sci Colo State Univ Ft Collins CO 80523

GILLETTE, FRANK C, JR, AERONAUTICAL ENGINEERING. *Current Pos:* Mech designer, 62-77, chief struct, 77-80, ENG MGR, YF119 PROG, DIR PROJS FOR GOVT ENGINES & SPACE PROPULSION, PRATT & WHITNEY, 80- *Personal Data:* m, Jane; c 3. *Educ:* Univ Fla, BS. *Honors & Awards:* Laurels Award, Aviation Week, 91. *Mem:* Am Inst Aeronaut & Astronaut; Am Soc Mech Engrs. *Res:* Design of the RL10 rocket chamber, the turbine section of the J58; management of the overall structural engineering effort of the J52, TF30, F100 rockets and preliminary design; awarded patents in field. *Mailing Add:* Pratt & Whitney Aircraft Govt Prod Div PO Box 169600 West Palm Beach FL 33410-9600

GILLETTE, JAMES ROBERT, BIOCHEMICAL PHARMACOLOGY. *Current Pos:* biochemist, 54-58, dep chief, 67-71, actg chief, 71-72, CHIEF LAB CHEM PHARMACOL, NAT HEART, LUNG & BLOOD INST, 72-, HEAD SECT DRUG ENZYME INTERACTION, 58- *Personal Data:* b Hammond, Ind, Feb 9, 28; m 53; c 2. *Educ:* Cornell Col, AB, 47; Univ Iowa, MS, 49, PhD(biochem), 54. *Hon Degrees:* DSc, Cornell Col, 79. *Honors & Awards:* Roland T Lakey Hon Lect Award, 67; Claude Bernard Vis Prof Award, Univ Montreal, 71; Bernard B Brodie Award Drug Metab, 78; Alan D Bass lectr, 79. *Prof Exp:* Asst prof biol & chem, Jamestown Col, 49-51. *Mem:* AAAS; Am Soc Biol Chem; Am Chem Soc; Am Soc Pharmacol; Int Soc Study Xenobiotics. *Res:* Metabolism of drugs and other foreign compounds. *Mailing Add:* 5615 Northfield Rd Bethesda MD 20817-6735

GILLETTE, KEVIN KEITH, MATHEMATICS, OPERATIONS RESEARCH. *Current Pos:* sr systs analyst, opers eng, 86-95, SR ENG, MCI, 95- *Personal Data:* b Walla Walla, Wash, July 5, 61; m 83; c 2. *Educ:* Stanford Univ, BS & MS, 82. *Prof Exp:* Sr res analyst, mgt sci, Bank Am, 82-83; res analyst opers res, Am Airlines, 84-86. *Concurrent Pos:* Lectr, Sch Mgt, Univ Tex, Dallas, 85-88, Comput Sci Dept, 88 & 91- *Mem:* Soc Indust & Appl Math. *Res:* Improving accuracy of airline forecasting systems related to flight planning and weather. *Mailing Add:* MCI 2400 N Glenville Rd Richardson TX 75082. *Fax:* 817-967-1145

GILLETTE, MARTHA ULBRICK, NEUROPHYSIOLOGY, CHRONOBIOLOGY. *Current Pos:* vis asst prof physiol & biol, Univ Ill, 78-85, vis assoc prof physiol, 85-88, assoc prof, Dept Physiol & Biophys, 88-90, assoc prof, 90-93, PROF CELL & STRUCT BIOL, PHYSIOL & COLL MED, UNIV ILL, 93- *Personal Data:* b Lincoln, Nebr, Nov 5, 45; m 69, Rhanor; c 2. *Educ:* Grinnell Col, Iowa, BA, 67; Univ Hawaii, MS, 69; Univ Toronto, PhD(zool), 75. *Prof Exp:* Fel neurophysiol, Univ Calif, Santa Cruz, 75-78; Lectr neurophysiol, Div Nat Sci, Univ Calif, Santa Cruz, 78. *Concurrent Pos:* affil, Neural Pattern Array group, Beckman Inst Advan Sci & Technol. *Mem:* Soc Neurosci; Int Soc Neuroethol; Found Biomed Res; Soc Res Biol Rhythms. *Res:* Mechanisms of circadian time-keeping neurons in the mammalian brain, including eletrophysiology, biochemistry and second messenger regulation; mechanisms of melatonin, serotonin and neuropeptide adjustment of clock phase. *Mailing Add:* Dept Cell & Struct Biol Univ Ill B107 Chem & Life Sci Lab 601 S Goodwin Ave Urbana IL 61801. *Fax:* 217-244-1648

GILLETTE, NORMAN JOHN, paleobotany, for more information see previous edition

GILLETTE, P(HILIP) ROGER, SCIENCE & RELIGION. *Current Pos:* RETIRED. *Personal Data:* b Mt Vernon, Iowa, May 12, 17; wid, Bettelaine Dunbar; c Kenneth L & Sandra J. *Educ:* Cornell Col, BA, 37; Univ Ill, BS, 38, MS, 39, PhD(physics), 42. *Prof Exp:* Mem staff, Radiation Lab, Mass Inst Technol, 42-45; proj engr, Sperry Gyroscope Co, NY, 45-48; physicist, Gen Elec Co, 48-50; sr res engr, SRI Int, 50-57, sr res physicist, 57-92. *Concurrent Pos:* Instr philos, Col Notre Dame, 87-88. *Mem:* Am Phys Soc; Inst Elec & Electronics Engrs; AAAS; Sigma Xi. *Res:* Molecular absorption and fluorescence spectroscopy; characteristics and design of pulseforming networks and pulse transformers; weapons, information and training systems design and operations analysis. *Mailing Add:* 2385 Crestview Dr S Salem OR 97302

GILLETTE, PAUL CRAWFORD, PEDIATRIC CARDIOLOGY, CARDIAC ELECTROPHYSIOLOGY. *Current Pos:* PROF & DIR PEDIAT CARDIOL, MED UNIV SC, 84-; CO-DIR, PALMETTO HEART INST, 90- *Personal Data:* b 1942; m 92, Vicki Zeigler; c 2. *Educ:* Univ NC, BA, 65; Med Col SC, MD, 69. *Honors & Awards:* Mitchel Rubin Award Pediat Res, 92. *Prof Exp:* Intern pediat, Baylor Col Med, 69-70, resident, 70-72, fel pediat cardiol, 72-74; fel cell biophys, 74-75, from asst prof to assoc prof pediat cardiol & cell biophys, 75-80, prof pediat cardiol, 80-84. *Concurrent Pos:* Educ grant, Am Acad Pediat, 70; consult, NIH, 77-78, 81 & 82, AMA Residency Rev Comt, 79-, AMA Diag Therapeut; prin investr, Nat Res & Demonstration Ctr, NIH, 77-79, res career develop award, 79-84; chmn, Pacemaker Comt, Am Col Cardiol, 90- *Mem:* Am Col Cardiol; Am Acad Pediat; NAm Soc Pacing & Electrophysiol (pres); Am Heart Asn; Soc Pediat Res. *Res:* Developmental cardiac electrophysiology and pharmacology; developed techniques for electrophysiological study of cardiac arrhythmia in children and treatment with medical, pacing and surgical techniques; studied developmental cardiac physiology and pharmacology and the DNA metabolism of the heart. *Mailing Add:* Cook Children's Heart Ctr 801 Seventh Ave Ft Worth TX 76104. *Fax:* 803-792-3284

GILLETTE, RHANOR, NEUROPHYSIOLOGY. *Current Pos:* ASST PROF NEUROPHYSIOL, DEPT PHYSIOL & BIOPHYS, UNIV ILL, URBANA, 78- *Personal Data:* b Bushnell, Fla, July 7, 43; m 69; c 2. *Educ:* Univ Miami, BS, 67; Univ Hawaii, MS, 69; Univ Toronto, PhD(zool), 74. *Prof Exp:* Fel, Univ Calif, Santa Cruz, 74-78. *Mem:* Soc Neurosci. *Res:* Mechanisms of plasticity in behavior; mechanisms of plasticity in neuron function; evolution of nervous systems. *Mailing Add:* Dept Physiol & Biophys Univ Ill Urbana Co Med 506 S Mathews Ave Urbana IL 61801-3618

GILLETTE, RICHARD F, AVIONIC SYSTEMS, ELECTRONIC COUNTER MEASURES. *Current Pos:* eng specialist, 64-71, prod line mgr, 71-73, prog mgr, 73-75, mgr advan systs, 75-77, dir eng, 77-79, VPRES ENG, NORTHROP CORP DEFENSE SYSTS, 79- *Personal Data:* b Chicago, Ill, July 2, 34; m 54; c 4. *Educ:* Ill Inst Technol, BS, 66; Loyola Univ, MBA, 69. *Prof Exp:* Engr, Beltone Electronics, 55-62; mgr sustaining engr, Knight Div Allied Radio, 62-64. *Mem:* Inst Elec & Electronics Engrs; Nat Soc Prof Engrs; Asn Old Crows. *Res:* Microwave signal detection and analysis; broad band microwave power generation; integrated systems for electronic counter measures. *Mailing Add:* 204 Circle Dr Tower Lakes IL 60010

GILLETTE, RONALD WILLIAM, virology, molecular biology, for more information see previous edition

GILLHAM, JOHN K, POLYMER SCIENCE, THERMOSETTING POLYMERS. *Current Pos:* assoc prof, 65-75, PROF CHEM ENG, PRINCETON UNIV, 75- *Personal Data:* b London, Eng, Aug 7, 30; m 61, Helen; c Matthew, Jane & Martha. *Educ:* Cambridge Univ, BA, 53, MA, 57; McGill Univ, PhD(chem), 59. *Honors & Awards:* Chem of Plastics & Coatings Award, Am Chem Soc, 78; Award in Thermal Anal, NAm Thermal Anal Soc, 78; Doolittle Award, Am Chem Soc, 80; Roon Award, Fedn Socs Coatings Technol, 83 & 89; Ann Int Res Award, Soc Plastics Engrs, 88; Roy W Tess Award in Coatings, Am Chem Soc, 96. *Prof Exp:* Res chemist, Stamford Labs, Am Cyanamid Co, 58-65. *Concurrent Pos:* Vis res chemist, Plastics Prog, Princeton Univ, 64-65; mem, Nat Mat Adv Bd Comts, Washington, 81, 84; vis fel, Japan Soc Prom Sci, 83; vis scholar, Chinese Acad Sci, People's Repub China, 84. *Mem:* Am Chem Soc; Soc Plastics Eng; NAm Thermal Analysis Soc. *Res:* Thermosetting polymers; spiral fractures; dynamic mechanical analysis; development of torsional braid analysis (TBA) technique; development of time-temperature-transformation (TTT) cure diagram; conversion-temperature-property; Tg vs. conversion relationship in thermosetting systems. *Mailing Add:* Dept Chem Eng Princeton Univ Princeton NJ 08544-5263. *Fax:* 609-258-0211

GILLHAM, NICHOLAS WRIGHT, GENETICS, MOLECULAR BIOLOGY. *Current Pos:* from assoc prof to prof, 68-82, JAMES B DUKE PROF ZOOL, DUKE UNIV, 82- *Personal Data:* b New York, NY, May 14, 32; m 56, Carol Collins. *Educ:* Harvard Univ, AB, 54, AM, 55, PhD(biol), 62. *Prof Exp:* USPHS fel, Yale Univ, 62-63; from instr to asst prof biol, Harvard Univ, 63-68. *Concurrent Pos:* Vis prof, Rockefeller Univ, 74-75; mem, President's Panel Med Res, 75 & gov task force on sci & technol, 82; mem study sect genetics, NIH, 76-80; Guggenheim fel, Cold Spring Harbor, 84-85, Duke Univ, 85; vchmn bd dirs & chmn sci comt, Am Type Cult Collection, 90-93, chmn bd dirs, 93-96. *Mem:* Int Soc Plant Molecular Biol; Genetics Soc Am; Sigma Xi. *Res:* Organelle heredity, molecular biology and transformation; genetics and molecular biology of chloroplasts and mitochondria. *Mailing Add:* Duke Univ DCMB Group LSRC Bldg Box 91000 Durham NC 27708-1000. *Fax:* 919-613-8177; *E-Mail:* gillham@acpub.duke.edu

GILLHAM, ROBERT WINSTON, GROUNDWATER RESOURCE & CONTAMINATION, REMEDIATION OF CONTAMINATED GROUNDWATER. *Current Pos:* res asst prof, Univ Waterloo, 74-77, from asst prof to assoc prof, 77-86, chmn, Dept Earth Sci, 93-97, PROF GROUNDWATER, UNIV WATERLOO, 86- *Personal Data:* b Newmarket, Ont, Dec 29, 40; m 63, Virginia Caskie; c David. *Educ:* Univ Toronto, BSA, 63; Univ Guelph, MSc, 68; Univ Ill, PhD(soil physics), 73. *Honors & Awards:* Thomas Roy Award, Can Geotech Soc, 88; Nabor Carrillo lectr, Mex Soc Soil Mech, 94; Miroslaw Ramanowski Medal. *Prof Exp:* Fel soils, Univ Guelph, 73-74; dir, Waterloo Ctr Groundwater Res, 87-92. *Concurrent Pos:* Mem, Working Group Contrib Contaminants Great Lakes by Groundwater, Internal Joint Comt, 84-88, Groundwater Contamination Working Group, Scope, 86-, Comt Hydrol, Nat Res Coun Asn, 88-89; ed-in-chief, J Contaminant Hydrol, 86-91. *Mem:* Am Geophys Union; Am Soc Agron; Asn Groundwater Scientists & Engrs; fel Royal Soc Can. *Res:* Response of aquifers to pumping, groundwater-surface water interactions and migration of contaminants in groundwater; remediation of contaminated aquifers. *Mailing Add:* 11 Crawford St Guelph ON N1G 1Y9 Can

GILLIAM, CHARLES HOMER, HORTICULTURE, PLANT PHYSIOLOGY. *Current Pos:* asst prof, 80-83, ASSOC PROF HORT, AUBURN UNIV, 83- *Personal Data:* b Lexington, Tenn, Oct 14, 52; m 71; c 2. *Educ:* Univ Tenn, Martin, BS, 74; Va Polytech Inst & State Univ, MS, 76, PhD(hort), 77. *Honors & Awards:* R P White Award, Hort Res Inst, 78. *Prof Exp:* Asst prof, Ohio State Univ, 77-80. *Mem:* Am Soc Hort Sci; Int Plant Propagators Soc; Sigma Xi. *Res:* Weed control in nursery crops; improving production efficiency of ornamentals. *Mailing Add:* Dept Hort Auburn Univ Auburn AL 36849-3501

GILLIAM, JAMES WENDELL, SOIL CHEMISTRY. *Current Pos:* From asst prof to assoc prof, 65-76, PROF SOIL CHEM, NC STATE UNIV, 76- *Personal Data:* b Chicota, Tex, July 18, 38; m 58; c 3. *Educ:* Okla State Univ, BS, 60; Miss State Univ, MS, 63, PhD(soil chem), 65. *Mem:* Fel Am Soc Agron; AAAS; fel Soil Sci Soc Am; Sigma Xi. *Res:* Fertilizer reactions in soils; uptake of nutrients by plants and plant analysis; cation exchange reactions of soil organic matter; contribution of fertilizers to contamination of surface waters; nonpoint source pollution; agricultural water management; wetlands and agriculture; effect of buffers and riparian areas on water quality. *Mailing Add:* Dept Soil Sci NC State Univ Box 7619 Raleigh NC 27695-0001

GILLIAM, OTIS RANDOLPH, PHYSICS. *Current Pos:* Instr, 50-51 & 53-55, from asst prof to assoc prof, 56-67, PROF PHYSICS, UNIV CONN, 67- *Personal Data:* b Waverly, Va, Sept 19, 24; m 53; c 3. *Educ:* Randolph-Macon Col, BS, 43; Duke Univ, PhD(physics), 50. *Concurrent Pos:* Consult, Am Optical Co, 66-67, Brookhaven Nat Lab & Picatinny Arsenal. *Mem:* Am Phys Soc; Am Asn Physics Teachers. *Res:* Determination of the structure of matter by microwave methods, paramagnetism and radiation damage. *Mailing Add:* Dept Physics U-46 Univ Conn 2152 Hillside Rd Storrs CT 06269

GILLICH, WILLIAM JOHN, PENETRATION MECHANICS, ARMOR CONCEPT DESIGN & DEMONSTRATION. *Current Pos:* res physicist, Aberdeen Proving Ground, US Army Ballastic Res Lab, 64-71, supv res physicist & chief wave propagation & mat sect, Solid Mech Br, 71, actg chief, 71-73, supv res physicist & chief, Penetration Mech Br, 73-82, SUPV RES PHYSICIST & CHIEF, ARMOR MECH BR, TERMINAL BALLISTICS DIV, US ARMY BALLISTIC RES LAB, ABERDEEN PROVING GROUND, 82- *Personal Data:* b Washington, DC, Jan 8, 35; m 59, Margaret A Mowery; c Michael J, Christopher J & Patrick J. *Educ:* Johns Hopkins Univ, BES, 57, MS, 60, PhD(mech), 64. *Honors & Awards:* R H Kent Award, 81; Am Defense Preparedness Asn Awards. *Prof Exp:* From jr instr to instr mech eng, Johns Hopkins Univ, 57-60, res asst, 61-64; supv res physicist & chief penetration mechanics br, 74-82, Armor Mech Br, 82-97. *Concurrent Pos:* Res asst, Johns Hopkins Univ, 57-64; instr, Ballistic Inst, Univ Del Exten, 69-70. *Mem:* Soc Natural Philos; Am Soc Mech Engrs; Soc Exp Stress Analysis; Army Defence Preparedness Asn. *Res:* Plastic and elastic wave propagation; dynamic continuum mechanics; shock wave reflections; moire technology; penetration mechanics; armor technology. *Mailing Add:* 1000 Dellwood Dr Fallston MD 21047. *Fax:* 410-278-6061; *E-Mail:* wgillich@arl.mil

GILLIES, ALASTAIR J, ANESTHESIOLOGY, PHARMACOLOGY. *Current Pos:* RETIRED. *Personal Data:* b Halifax, Eng, Oct 7, 24; US citizen; m 52; c 4. *Educ:* Univ Edinburgh, BSc, 47, MB, ChB, 48. *Prof Exp:* Resident house surgeon & resident anesthetist, Royal Infirmary, Edinburgh, 48-49; asst res anesthesiol, Mass Gen Hosp, 52; asst anesthetist, Strong Mem Hosp, 54-55; asst prof anesthesiol, Sch Med, Yale Univ, 55-59; prof pharmacol & toxicol, Med Ctr, Univ Rochester, 59-77, prof anesthesiol & chmn dept pharmacol & toxicol, 59-86. *Concurrent Pos:* Fel, Mayo Found, 53; anesthesiologist, Grace-New Haven Community Hosp, 55-59; anesthetist in chief, Strong Mem Hosp, 59-77; consult, Bur Heart Dis, NY State Dept Health. *Mem:* Am Soc Anesthesiol; Asn Univ Anesthetists; NY Acad Sci; Pan-Am Med Asn; Int Anesthesia Res Soc; Brit Med Asn. *Mailing Add:* 443 White Springs Rd Geneva NY 14456

GILLIES, CHARLES WESLEY, PHYSICAL & PHYSICAL ORGANIC CHEMISTRY. *Current Pos:* PROF PHYS CHEM, RENSSELAER POLYTECH INST, 76- *Personal Data:* b Wilmington, Del, Dec 1, 46; m 67, 87; c 3. *Educ:* West Chester State Col, BA, 68; Univ Mich, PhD(phys chem), 72. *Honors & Awards:* Fajans Award, 72. *Prof Exp:* Fel phys chem, Harvard Univ, 73-76. *Concurrent Pos:* Referee, J Am Chem Soc, 72-, J Phys Chem, 78- & J Molecular Spectros; proj dir, Grant Petrol Res Found, 77-80 & Res Corp, US Dept Energy, 81; reviewer, NSF, 78- & Nat Res Coun, 79. *Mem:* Am Chem Soc. *Res:* Applications of microwave spectroscopy to structures and mechanisms; Fourier transform microwave spectroscopy. *Mailing Add:* Dept Chem Rensselaer Polytech Inst 110 Eighth St Troy NY 12180-3522

GILLIES, GEORGE THOMAS, MEDICAL PHYSICS, BIBLIOGRAPHIC STUDIES. *Current Pos:* postdoctoral fel, 80-81, res asst prof, 85-88, RES ASSOC PROF ENG PHYSICS, UNIV VA, 88- *Personal Data:* b Rugby, NDak, Aug 20, 52; m 79; c 1. *Educ:* NDak State Univ, BSc, 74; Univ Va, MSc, 76, PhD(eng physics), 80. *Prof Exp:* Physicist, Int Bur Weights & Measures, 81-83; develop staff mem, Martin Marietta Energy Systs, Inc, 83-85. *Concurrent Pos:* Vis scientist, US Nat Bur Standards, 81, Cavendish Lab, Cambridge Univ, 81-82 & Univ Trieste, 82; prin investr, Video Tumor Fighter Proj, 87- *Mem:* Sr mem Inst Elec & Electronics Engrs; Am Phys Soc; Optical Soc Am. *Res:* Experimental tests of Newtonian gravitation; design of magnetic suspension systems; development of the video tumor fighter which is a method of nonlinear stereotaxis that can deliver hyperthermia to brain tumors. *Mailing Add:* 4310 Beaver Creek Rd Earlysville VA 22901. *E-Mail:* gtg@virginia.edu

GILLIGAN, DIANA MARY, CELL BIOLOGY, HEMATOLOGY. *Current Pos:* FEL, DEPT MED, DUKE UNIV MED CTR, 90- *Educ:* Albert Einstein Col Med, MD & PhD(anat & struct biol), 85. *Prof Exp:* resident, Internal Med, NC Mem Hosp, 85-90. *Mem:* Am Soc Cell Biol; Am Col Physicians; Am Soc Hemat. *Mailing Add:* Div Hemat & Oncol Yale Univ Sch Med 333 Cedar St New Haven CT 06510. *Fax:* 203-785-7232

GILLIGAN, LAWRENCE G, MATHEMATICS. *Current Pos:* PROF MATH, UNIV CINCINNATI, 84- *Personal Data:* b New York, NY, June 19, 48; m; c 2. *Educ:* NY Univ, BA, 69, MA, 73. *Mem:* Am Asn Univ Prof; Am Soc Eng Educ; Am Math Asn Two Yr Col (vpres, 84); Math Asn Am. *Mailing Add:* Univ Cincinnati 2220 Victory Pkwy Cincinnati OH 45206

GILLIKIN, JESSE EDWARD, JR, ANALYTICAL CHEMISTRY, INORGANIC CHEMISTRY. *Current Pos:* Qual assurance control scientist, 78, qual assurance supvr, 79-81, qual assurance specialist, 81-82, QUAL ASSURANCE SUPVR, BURROUGHS WELLCOME CO, 82- *Personal Data:* b Morehead City, NC, Jan 22, 52; m 70; c 2. *Educ:* East Carolina Univ, BA, 74, MS, 76. *Mem:* Am Chem Soc. *Res:* Electroanalytical chemistry, with an emphasis towards computerized laboratory equipment. *Mailing Add:* 13008 Caenen Shawnee Mission KS 66213

GILLILAN, JAMES HORACE, MATHEMATICS. *Current Pos:* ASST PROF MATH, UNIV MO-KANSAS CITY, 66- *Personal Data:* b Kansas City, Mo, Dec 21, 32; m 70. *Educ:* Univ Mo, BA, 54, MA, 55; Univ Ill, PhD(math), 61. *Prof Exp:* Instr math, Univ Mich, 61-63. *Mem:* Am Math Soc. *Res:* Integration theory. *Mailing Add:* Dept Math Univ Mo Kansas City MO 64110

GILLILAND, BOBBY EUGENE, ELECTRICAL ENGINEERING, INSTRUMENTATION. *Current Pos:* From asst prof to assoc prof elec eng, 67-76, from asst dean to assoc dean eng, 73-86, PROF ELEC & COMPUT ENG, CLEMSON UNIV, 76-, SPEC ASST TO PRES, 86- *Personal Data:* b Epps, La, Aug 6, 36; m 59; c 1. *Educ:* La Polytech Inst, BS, 58; Univ Ark, MS, 61, PhD(electronics, instrumentation), 67. *Prof Exp:* Res asst electronics & instrumentation, Univ Ark, Little Rock, 62-67. *Concurrent Pos:* Mem, SC Nuclear Adv Coun, 73-80, chmn, 75-76 & SC Energy Exten Serv Task Force, 78-81. *Mem:* Inst Elec & Electronics Engrs; Am Soc Eng Educ; Nat Soc Prof Engrs; Instrument Soc Am; Sigma Xi. *Res:* instrumentation including digital, textile and biomedical; digital computer control systems; modeling and simulation; innovative graduate engineering education. *Mailing Add:* 411 Shorecrest Dr Clemson SC 29631-1445

GILLILAND, DENNIS CRIPPEN, STATISTICS, MATHEMATICS. *Current Pos:* from asst prof to assoc prof, 66-74, dept chairperson, 85-89, PROF STATIST & PROBABILITY, MICH STATE UNIV, 74- *Personal Data:* b Warren, Pa, July 23, 38; m 57; c 3. *Educ:* Kent State Univ, BA, 59; Mich State Univ, MS, 63, PhD(statist), 66. *Prof Exp:* Develop engr, Goodyear Aerospace Corp, 59-66. *Concurrent Pos:* Lectr, Univ Calif, Berkeley, 66-67; vis scholar, Univ Chicago, 82. *Mem:* Inst Math Statist; Am Statist Asn; Am Soc Qual Control. *Res:* Applied statistics; decision theory; statistics and law. *Mailing Add:* Dept Statist & Probability Mich State Univ East Lansing MI 48824

GILLILAND, FLOYD RAY, JR, ENTOMOLOGY, ZOOLOGY. *Current Pos:* CONTRACT RES & CONSULT, 77- *Personal Data:* b Cotter, Ark, Dec 18, 39; m 62; c 1. *Educ:* Ark Polytech Col, BS, 62; Univ Ark, MS, 64; Miss State Univ, PhD(entom), 67. *Prof Exp:* From asst prof to prof entom, Auburn Univ, 67-77. *Mem:* AAAS; Entom Soc Am. *Res:* Basic and applied studies of cotton insects, especially methods of biological control of cotton insects. *Mailing Add:* PO Box 640008 Pike Road AL 36064-0008

GILLILAND, HAROLD EUGENE, CHEMICAL ENGINEERING, PHYSICAL CHEMISTRY. *Current Pos:* Res scientist, 64-67, res group supvr, Continental Oil Co, 67-80, sect dir, 80-88, MGR RESERVOIR ENG, CONOCO INC, 88- *Personal Data:* b Duncan, Okla, Sept 9, 37. *Educ:* Mass Inst Technol, SB, 59, SM, 61, PhD(chem eng), 65. *Mem:* Am Inst Mining, Metall & Petrol Engrs. *Res:* Heterogeneous catalysis; thermal methods of recovering hydrocarbon resources; petroleum recovery processes; reservoir engineering; drilling and completions. *Mailing Add:* 1503 Kelliwood Oaks Dr Katy TX 77450

GILLILAND, JOE E(DWARD), CHEMICAL ENGINEERING. *Current Pos:* chem engr, 51-57, pilot plant supvr, 57-63, SUPT, SPEC CHEM DEPT, OZARK-MAHONING CO, 63- *Personal Data:* b Alhambra, Calif, Dec 4, 27; m 52; c 2. *Educ:* Tex Tech Col, BS, 49; Okla State Univ, MS, 60. *Prof Exp:* Chem engr, Tex Brine Corp, 49-51. *Mem:* Inst Chem Engrs. *Res:* Inorganic fluorine compounds; crystallization. *Mailing Add:* 5512 S Yorktown Pl Tulsa OK 74105

GILLILAND, JOHN L(AWRENCE), JR, CHEMICAL ENGINEERING. *Current Pos:* RETIRED. *Personal Data:* b Clearfield, Pa, Oct 4, 10; m 35; c 3. *Educ:* Univ Colo, BS, 33. *Honors & Awards:* Award of Merit, Am Soc Testing & Mat. *Prof Exp:* From jr chem engr to chem engr, US Bur Reclamation, 33-51; gen chemist, Ideal Cement Co, 51-64, dir qual control, 64-67, tech dir, 67-70, dir environ qual, Cement Div, Ideal Basic Indust, Inc, 70-77. *Concurrent Pos:* Mem nat adv comt control tech, Nat Air Pollution Control Admin. *Mem:* Am Chem Soc; Am Soc Testing & Mat; Am Acad Environ Engrs. *Res:* Air pollution control; quality control of Portland cement manufacture; environmental controls. *Mailing Add:* 3753 S Granby Way Aurora CO 80014. *E-Mail:* 71233.25@compuserve.com

GILLILAND, ROBERT MCMURTRY, PSYCHIATRY, PSYCHOANALYSIS. *Current Pos:* PVT PRACT. *Personal Data:* b Galveston, Tex, Jan 16, 21; m 44; c 2. *Educ:* Univ Tex, BA, 41; Univ Tex Med Br Galveston, MD, 45. *Prof Exp:* Resident psychiat, Vet Admin Hosp, Waco,

Tex, 46-48 & Univ Tex Med Br Galveston, 48-49; pvt pract psychiat & psychoanalysis, 49-64; prof psychiat, Baylor Col Med, 64- *Concurrent Pos:* Supr analyst, Psychoanalysis Inst, Houston-Galveston, 64- *Mem:* Am Psychoanalysis Asn; Am Psychiat Asn; Int Psychoanalysis Asn. *Mailing Add:* 5300 San Jacinto St Suite 120 Houston TX 77004

GILLILAND, RONALD LYNN, SOLAR & STELLAR VARIABILITY. *Current Pos:* ASSOC ASTROMR, SPACE TELESCOPE SCI INST, 88- *Personal Data:* b Emporia, Kans, July 16, 52. *Educ:* Univ Kans, Lawrence, BA, 74; Univ Calif, Santa Cruz, PhD(astrophys), 79. *Prof Exp:* Fel, Advan Study Prog, High Altitude Observ, Nat Ctr Atmospheric Res, 79-81, staff scientist, 81-88. *Mem:* Am Astron Soc; Int Astron Union. *Res:* Solar and stellar variability from both theoretical and obervational approaches. *Mailing Add:* 1204 Southview Rd Baltimore MD 21218

GILLILAND, STANLEY EUGENE, DAIRY & FOOD MICROBIOLOGY. *Current Pos:* from assoc prof to prof, 76-86, REGENTS PROF ANIMAL SCI, OKLA STATE UNIV, 86- *Personal Data:* b Minco, Okla, June 24, 40; m 60, 90, Jurlean Hall; c 4. *Educ:* Okla State Univ, BS, 62, MS, 63; NC State Univ, PhD(food sci), 66. *Honors & Awards:* Pfizer Award, Am Dairy Sci Asn, 79, Dairy Res Award, 87; Res award, Am Cult Dairy Prod Inst, 91. *Prof Exp:* Assoc prof food sci, NC State Univ, 65-76. *Concurrent Pos:* Elmo Bairman prof, Okla State Univ, 88. *Mem:* Fel Am Acad Microbiol; Inst Food Technol; Am Dairy Sci Asn; Sigma Xi; Am Soc Microbiol. *Res:* Nutrition of lactic starter cultures; growth of high population bacterial starter cultures; antagonisms of starter cultures toward psychrotrophic bacteria & food-borne pathogens; factors which limit the growth and action of starter cultures; microbial dietary supplements; intestinal microecology; health and/or nutritional benefits from lactobacilli as dietary adjuncts. *Mailing Add:* Animal Sci Dept Okla State Univ Stillwater OK 74078-0425. *E-Mail:* seg@okway.okstate.edu

GILLIN, JAMES, CHEMICAL ENGINEERING, PROCESS CHEMISTRY. *Current Pos:* RETIRED. *Personal Data:* b Floral Park, NY, Sept 16, 25; m 49, June Jacobi; c Sheryl (Tuohy) & J Scott. *Educ:* Cornell Univ, BChE, 47, PhD(chem eng), 51. *Prof Exp:* Sr engr chem eng process develop, Merck & Co Inc, 49-52, group leader, 52-56, sect mgr pilot plant, 56-59, mgr, 59-62, dir, 62-64, chem engr res & develop, 64-69, exec dir new drug develop, 69-70, exec dir planning & admin, 70-71, vpres develop, Merck, Sharp & Dohme Res Labs, 71-79, pres, MSD AGVET DIV, 79-87. *Mem:* Nat Acad Eng; Am Chem Soc; Am Inst Chem Engrs; NY Acad Sci; fel Am Inst Chem. *Res:* Ion exchange; vapor phase catalytic oxidation. *Mailing Add:* 11354 Golf View Lane North Palm Beach FL 33408. *Fax:* 561-691-4871; *E-Mail:* giltree@aol.com

GILLINGHAM, JAMES CLARK, HERPETOLOGY. *Current Pos:* from asst prof to assoc prof, 76-84, PROF BIOL, CENT MICH UNIV, 84- *Personal Data:* b Waukesha, Wis, Oct 15, 44; m 67; c 2. *Educ:* Wis State Univ, Oshkosh, BS, 67, MS, 72; Univ Okla, PhD(zool), 76. *Honors & Awards:* Ortenberger Award & Arthur N Bragg Natural Hist Award, Univ Okla, 76. *Prof Exp:* Fac asst biol, Univ Wis, Oshkosh, 67-72; vis instr zool, Univ Okla, 75-76. *Concurrent Pos:* Dir, Cent Mich Biol Sta, 85- *Mem:* Am Soc Zoologists; Animal Behav Soc; Am Soc Icthyologists & Herpetologists; Herpetologists League; Soc Study Amphibians & Reptiles; Sigma Xi. *Res:* Behavioral ecology of amphibians and reptiles; ritualized behavior of snakes; behavioral morphology of reptiles. *Mailing Add:* Dept Biol Cent Mich Univ Mt Pleasant MI 48859-0001

GILLINGHAM, JAMES M, PHARMACEUTICAL CHEMISTRY. *Current Pos:* GILLINGHAM CONSULT, 89- *Personal Data:* b Gallipolis, Ohio, Mar 29, 24; m 48, Carolyn Oakes; c Carol L & James S. *Educ:* Denison Univ, BA, 49; Northwestern Univ, 50. *Honors & Awards:* E Baugh Award Chem, 49. *Prof Exp:* Asst res chemist, Parke, Davis & Co, 50-55; asst sci dir, Warren Teed Prods, 55-59; prod mgr, Diamond Labs, 59-60, dir pharmaceut prods develop, 60-61; vpres, Vale Chem Co, 61-70; mgr pharmaceut prod, Animal Health Div, Am Hoechst Corp, 70-72; dir tech serv & qual assurance, Marion Labs, Inc, 72-76, sr tech adv, regulatory affairs, 76-89. *Concurrent Pos:* Res assoc, Univ Mo, Kansas City. *Mem:* Am Soc Qual Control. *Res:* Research and products development in pharmaceutical and analytical chemistry; production and processing of veterinary and human pharmaceutical products; quality assurance and regulatory compliance of pharmaceutical products and processes; good manufacturing practice regulations. *Mailing Add:* 9706 Overbrook Rd Leawood KS 66206-2310. *Fax:* 913-381-0287; *E-Mail:* pkdp@prodigy.com, jgillingham@pop.umkc.edu

GILLIOM, RICHARD D, ORGANIC CHEMISTRY. *Current Pos:* RETIRED. *Personal Data:* b Bluffton, Ind, June 25, 34; m 58, Patricia Hastings; c Laura, Andrea & Bruce. *Educ:* Southwestern at Memphis, BS, 56; Mass Inst Technol, PhD(org chem), 60. *Prof Exp:* Res chemist, Esso Res Labs, Humble Oil & Refining Co, 60-61; from asst prof to prof chem, Southwestern, Memphis, 61-84; prof chem, Rhodes Col, 84-90. *Concurrent Pos:* Fulbright lectr, Univ Skoplje, 68-69; assoc, Drug Design Div, Univ Tenn Ctr Health Sci, 75; consult, Molecular Design Int, 76-88; res investr, VA Hosp, Memphis, 84-. *Mem:* Am Chem Soc. *Res:* Effects of structure upon reactivity; quantitative structure-activity relationship; computational chemistry. *Mailing Add:* 35 Wakefield Cove Jackson TN 38305

GILLIS, BERNARD THOMAS, organic chemistry, for more information see previous edition

GILLIS, CHARLES NORMAN, PHARMACOLOGY. *Current Pos:* assoc prof anesthesiol & pharmacol, 69-73, PROF ANESTHESIOL PHARMACOL, SCH MED, YALE UNIV, 73- *Personal Data:* b Glasgow, Scotland, Feb 3, 33; US citizen; m 60; c 2. *Educ:* Glasgow Univ, BSC, 54, PhD(pharmacol), 57. *Hon Degrees:* MA, Yale Univ, 73. *Prof Exp:* Asst lectr exp pharmacol, Glasgow Univ, 54-57; asst prof pharmacol, Univ Alta, 57-61; from asst prof to assoc prof pharmacol, Yale Univ, 61-68; head cardiovasc pharmacol, Squibb Inst Med Res, 68-69. *Concurrent Pos:* Estab investr, Am Heart Asn, 64-68; vis assoc prof, Med Sch, Rutgers Univ, 68-69; assoc ed, Biochem Pharmacol, 81-93. *Mem:* Am Soc Pharmacol & Exp Therapeut; Pharmacol Soc Can. *Res:* Cardiopulmonary and autonomic pharmacology; neuropharmacology. *Mailing Add:* Dept Anesthesiol Yale Univ Sch Med 333 Cedar St New Haven CT 06510-3219. *Fax:* 203-737-5220

GILLIS, HUGH ANDREW, MASS SPECTROMETRY, RADIATION CHEMISTRY. *Current Pos:* VPRES ACAD & DEAN SCI, ST FRANCIS XAVIER UNIV, 87- *Personal Data:* b Sydney, NS, Aug 11, 35; Can citizen; m 77; c 2. *Educ:* St Francis Xavier Univ, BSc, 54; Univ Notre Dame, PhD(chem), 57. *Prof Exp:* Gen Elec Co res fel phys chem, Univ Leeds, 57-59; assoc res officer, Nat Res Coun Can, Ottawa, 67-74, sr res officer, Physics Div, 74-81, liaison officer, Off Atlantic Regional Dir, 81-85, sr res officer, Atlantic Res Lab, Nat Res Coun Can, Halifax, NS, 85-87. *Concurrent Pos:* Vis fel, Mellon Inst, Carnegie-Mellon Univ, 60, 65, 67 & 68, Centre D'Etudes Nucleaire De Saclay, France, 73. *Mem:* Can Asn Physicists; Am Chem Soc; fel Chem Inst Can. *Res:* Trapped and solvated electrons in irradiated aqueous, alcoholic and hydrocarbon liquids and solids. *Mailing Add:* St Francis Xavier Univ PO Box 5000 Antigonish NS B2G 2W5 Can

GILLIS, JAMES THOMPSON, SIGNAL PROCESSING & WAVELET WAVEPOCKET ANALYSIS, PRECISION POINTING & CONTROL OF SPACECRAFT. *Current Pos:* mem tech staff, Controls Analysis Dept, 83-88, eng specialist, Precision Pointing Off, 88-93, MGR, SOFTWARE ANALYSIS, AEROSPACE CORP, 93- *Personal Data:* b Boston, Mass, Aug 30, 56; div. *Educ:* Wash Univ, St Louis, BS, 79; Univ Calif Los Angeles, MS, 85, PhD(elec eng), 88. *Prof Exp:* Mem tech staff, Space & Commun Group, Hughes Aircraft, 79-83. *Concurrent Pos:* Res assoc, Systs Res Ctr, Univ Md, 90-91. *Mem:* Inst Elec & Electronics Engrs; Soc Indust & Appl Math; Am Math Soc; Math Asn Am; Am Inst Aeronaut & Astronaut. *Res:* Precision pointing and vibration control of spacecraft and launch vehicles; wavelet and wavepacket analysis and Armax identification. *Mailing Add:* PO Box 3411 El Segundo CA 90245

GILLIS, JOHN ERICSEN, EVOLUTIONARY BIOLOGY. *Current Pos:* ASSOC PROF BIOL, UNIV WIS-LA CROSSE, 84- *Personal Data:* b White Plains, NY, May 16, 43. *Educ:* Univ Pa, BA, 65; Colo State Univ, MS, 68, PhD(zool), 75. *Prof Exp:* Teaching asst zool, Colo State Univ, 68 & 70; asst prof biol, Univ Maine, Ft Kent, 75-76, Allegheny Col, 76-83 & Univ Nebr, Lincoln, 84. *Mem:* AAAS; Soc Study Evolution; Herpetologists League; Soc Study Amphibians & Reptiles; Sigma Xi. *Res:* Amphibian water economy; evolutionary relationships in the Rana pipiens complex; color polymorphisms in grasshoppers; thermal ecology of grasshoppers. *Mailing Add:* Dept Biol Univ Wis La Crosse La Crosse WI 54601

GILLIS, JOHN SIMON, PSYCHOLOGY, PSYCHOPHARMACOLOGY. *Current Pos:* chmn dept, 76-84, PROF PSYCHOL, ORE STATE UNIV, CORVALLIS, 76- *Personal Data:* b Washington, DC, Mar 21, 37; m 59, Mary A Wesolowski; c Holly A, Mark & Scott. *Educ:* Stanford Univ, BA, 59; Cornell Univ, MS, 61; Univ Colo, PhD, 65. *Prof Exp:* Lectr, Dept Psychol, Australian Nat Univ, Canberra, 68-70; sr psychologist, Mendocino State Hosp, Calif, 71-72; assoc prof, Dept Psychol, Tex Tech Univ, Lubbock, 72-76. *Concurrent Pos:* Consult, Vet Admin, Ciba-Geigy Pharm, US Info Agency, UN High Comn Refugees; Fulbright lectr, India, 82-83 & Greece, 92; vis prof, Univ Karachi, 84 & 86, Univ Punjab, Pakistan, 85, Am Univ Cairo, 84-86. *Mem:* Am Psychol Asn. *Res:* Psychology; identifying high risk individuals for drug abuse; effects of psychotherapy; effects of psychoactive drugs. *Mailing Add:* Dept Psychol Ore State Univ Corvallis OR 97331-5303. *Fax:* 541-737-3547; *E-Mail:* gillisj@cla.orst.edu

GILLIS, MARINA N, POLYMER CHEMISTRY. *Current Pos:* res chemist, chem div, Thiokol Corp, 57-81, SR RES CHEMIST, CONGOLEUM CORP, TRENTON, 81- *Personal Data:* b Harrisburg, Pa, Jan 30, 34; m 61. *Educ:* Wilson Col, BA, 55. *Mem:* Am Chem Soc. *Res:* Polymer synthesis; polymer structure and properties; polyethylene sulfide degradation and stabilization; polyacrylates; polyurethanes; polymeric coatings; radiation polymerization; synthesis and reactions of urethane curatives; polysulfides, rotogravure inks, vinyl foams and chemical embossing. *Mailing Add:* 12 Lawndale Rd Yardley PA 19067-3431

GILLIS, MURLIN FERN, VETERINARY MEDICINE, PHYSICS. *Current Pos:* From res scientist to sr res scientist, Pac Northwest Labs, Battelle Mem Inst, 66-71, res assoc, 71-72, res & develop mgr, 72-75, mgr proj develop, 75-80, assoc mgr, Biol Dept, 80-86, RES OPERS MGR, LIFE SCI CTR, PAC NORTHEST LABS, BATTELLE MEM INST, 86- *Personal Data:* b Santa Cruz, Calif, Apr 26, 35; m 71; c 3. *Educ:* Univ Wash, BS, 56; Calif Inst Technol, MS, 59; Wash State Univ, DVM, 63. *Mem:* Am Vet Med Asn. *Res:* Experimental surgery; bioengineering; biomaterials; implantology; fertility control; hyperbaric medicine; bioelectromagnetism; research administration. *Mailing Add:* 2330 Camas Ave Richland WA 99352

GILLIS, PETER PAUL, SOLID MECHANICS, MATERIALS SCIENCE. *Current Pos:* asst prof eng mech, 64-68, assoc prof mat sci, 68-75, PROF MAT SCI, UNIV KY, 75- *Personal Data:* b Newport, RI, Dec 23, 30; m 53, 80, Donna J Place; c Paul C, Andrew P, James M, Mary E, Douglas A Place & Eric M Place. *Educ:* Brown Univ, ScB, 53, ScM, 61, PhD(eng), 64. *Prof Exp:* Prod engr, Fram Corp, RI, 56-57; develop engr, Leesona Corp, 57-58; instr mach design, RI Sch Design, 58-59; res asst eng, Brown Univ, 59-64. *Concurrent Pos:* Consult, Spindletop Res Inc, Ky, 64-66, Lawrence Livermore Lab, 65-73, Sandia Corp, NMex, 67 & Los Alamos Sci Lab, 68-79; Fulbright-Hays res scholar, Physics & Eng Lab, Dept Sci & Indust Res, NZ, 70-71; consult div compliance, Atomic Energy Comn, 70-73; vis scientist, State Univ NY Col Forestry, Syracuse, 71. *Mem:* Am Inst Mining, Metall & Petrol Engrs; fel Am Soc Metals Int; Am Soc Mech Engrs; Fedn Am Scientists; Volunteers Tech Assistance. *Res:* Flow and fracture properties of materials, particularly relations between these characteristics and the microstructure of the material in terms of the concepts of crystal physics. *Mailing Add:* Dept Mat Sci & Eng Univ Ky Lexington KY 40506-0046. *Fax:* 606-323-1929

GILLIS, RICHARD A, PHARMACOLOGY. *Current Pos:* from instr to assoc prof, 67-77, PROF PHARMACOL, SCH MED, GEORGETOWN UNIV, 77- *Personal Data:* b Rochester, NY, Mar 20, 38; m 60; c 1. *Educ:* Miami Univ, BA, 60; McGill Univ, PhD(pharmacol), 65. *Prof Exp:* Instr, Harvard Med Sch, 67. *Concurrent Pos:* Res fel pharmacol, Harvard Med Sch, 65-66. *Mem:* AAAS; Am Soc Pharmacol & Exp Therapeut. *Res:* Cardiovascular and autonomic nervous system pharmacology. *Mailing Add:* Dept Pharmacol NW 408 Med-Dent Georgeton Univ Sch Med 3900 Reservoir Rd NW Washington DC 20007

GILLIS, STEVEN, IMMUNOPHARMACOLOGY. *Current Pos:* EXEC VPRES & DIR RES & DEVELOP, IMMUNEX CORP, SEATTLE, 82-, PRES & CHIEF OPER OFFICER, 88- *Personal Data:* b Philadelphia, Pa, Apr 25, 53; m 76, Anne C Edgar; c Sarah M & Bradley S. *Educ:* Williams Col, BA, 75; Dartmouth Col, PhD, 78. *Honors & Awards:* Int Immunopharmacol Award, 83. *Prof Exp:* Lectr biol, Dartmouth Col, Hanover, NH, 77-78, res assoc, Med Sch, 78-79; assoc researcher, Mem Sloan-Kettering, New York, 79-80; asst prof, Univ Wash, Seattle, 80-83. *Concurrent Pos:* Asst mem, Fred Hutchinson Cancer Ctr, Seattle, 80-82, affil investr, 82-; adj assoc prof, Univ Wash, 82-90, adj prof, 90- *Mem:* Am Asn Immunol; NY Acad Sci; AAAS. *Res:* Recombinant lymphokines and their receptors; contributed articles to professional journals. *Mailing Add:* Corixa Corp 1124 Columbia St Seattle WA 98104-2936

GILLISPIE, GREGORY DAVID, PHYSICAL CHEMISTRY, CHEMICAL PHYSICS. *Current Pos:* NDAK STATE UNIV, CHAIR, 89-, PROF CHEM, 90- *Personal Data:* b Painesville, Ohio, June 23, 49; m 72; c 3. *Educ:* Mich State Univ, BS, 71, PhD(chem), 75. *Prof Exp:* Fel chem, Wayne State Univ, 75-77; asst prof, State Univ NY, Albany, 77-82; from asst prof to assoc prof, chem, 83-90. *Mem:* Am Phys Soc; Am Chem Soc; Int Soc Optical Eng. *Res:* Laser spectroscopy; radiationless transitions; fluorescence; phosphorescence; intramolecular hydrogen bonds. *Mailing Add:* Dakota Technologies 2201-A 12th St N Fargo ND 58102-1803

GILLMAN, DAVID, MATHEMATICS. *Current Pos:* asst prof, 64-69, ASSOC PROF MATH, UNIV CALIF, LOS ANGELES, 69- *Personal Data:* b New York, NY, Sept 6, 38. *Educ:* Univ Wis, BS, 58, MS, 59, PhD(math), 62. *Prof Exp:* Res instr math, Cornell Univ, 62; mem, Inst Advan Study, 62-64. *Res:* Topology. *Mailing Add:* Dept Math Univ Calif Los Angeles CA 90095-1555

GILLMAN, HYMAN DAVID, INORGANIC CHEMISTRY. *Current Pos:* PRES, SPECIALTY CHEM SYSTS. *Personal Data:* b Brooklyn, NY, Dec 21, 41; m 67, Mary Ellen Hays; c Jeffrey H, Joshua G & Heather M. *Educ:* Long Island Univ, BS, 63; Tufts Univ, PhD(inorg chem), 68. *Prof Exp:* Sr res chemist, Pennwalt Chem Corp, 68-81; tech serv mgr, ARCO Chem Co. *Mem:* Am Chem Soc. *Res:* Synthesis of chemicals for the electonics industry; novel chemical for the electonics industry; UV resins and coatings. *Mailing Add:* 521 Pughtown Rd Spring City PA 19475-9720. *Fax:* 610-948-0744

GILLMAN, LEONARD, MATHEMATICS. *Current Pos:* chmn dept, 69-73, prof, 69-87, EMER PROF MATH, UNIV TEX, AUSTIN, 87- *Personal Data:* b Cleveland, Ohio, Jan 8, 17; m 38; c 2. *Educ:* Columbia Univ, BS, 41, MA, 45, PhD(math), 53. *Prof Exp:* Asst math, Columbia Univ, 41-42, lectr, 43; assoc, Tufts Col, 43-45; mem staff, Opers Eval Group, Mass Inst Technol, 45-51; from instr to assoc prof math, Purdue Univ, 52-60; prof & chmn dept, Univ Rochester, 60-69. *Concurrent Pos:* Guggenheim Mem fel, 58-59; mem, Inst Advan Study, 58-60; NSF sr fel, 59-60; vis lectr, Math Asn Am, 61-69; mem comt on regional develop, Nat Acad Sci-Nat Res Coun, 63-65, chmn, 65-66; mem, US Comn on Math Instr, 65-66, chmn, 66-69; US deleg, Int Comn Math Instr, 66-69, organizing comt, First Int Cong Math Educ, 69; math ed, W W Norton Co, 67-80; mem ed bd, Gen Topology & Its Appln, 71- *Mem:* Am Math Soc (assoc secy, 69-71); Math Asn Am (treas, 73-86, pres-elect, 86-87, pres, 87-89); Nat Coun Teachers Math. *Res:* Theory of sets; topology; rings of continuous functions. *Mailing Add:* 1606 The High Rd Austin TX 78746-2236

GILLMOR, CHARLES STEWART, HISTORY OF PHYSICS AND ENGINEERING SINCE SEVENTEEN FIFTY, QUANTITATIVE MEASURES OF SCIENCE GROWTH. *Current Pos:* FROM INSTR TO PROF HIST & SCI, WESLEYAN UNIV, 67- *Personal Data:* b Kansas City, Mo, Nov 6, 38; m 64, Rogene Marie Godding; c Charles S III & Alison (Bogue). *Educ:* Stanford Univ, BS, 62; Princeton Univ, MA, 66, PhD(hist & philos sci), 68. *Honors & Awards:* Antarctic Serv Medal, Nat Acad Sci, 63. *Prof Exp:* Ionospheric physicist, US Nat Bur Stand, Boulder, Colo, 60-62. *Concurrent Pos:* Sr Fulbright res fel, Cavendish Phys Lab, Cambridge Univ, Eng, 76; vis scholar, NASA, Washington, DC, 80-81; NSF sci exchange fel, Ctr Res Terrestrial & Planetary Physics, Paris, 84-85; ed, Transactions, Am Geophys Union, 83-86 & Hist Geophys, 84-94; Hennebach vis prof, Colo Sch Mines, 96-97. *Mem:* Fel Am Phys Soc; Sigma Xi; Am Geophys Union; Hist Sci Soc; Soc Hist Technol; AAAS. *Res:* Writing a history of physics of the ionosphere and magnetosphere from its beginnings about 1900 to the present. *Mailing Add:* Wesleyan Univ Middletown CT 06459-0002. *E-Mail:* sgillmor@wesleyan.edu

GILLMORE, DONALD W(OOD), FUEL ENGINEERING, CHEMICAL ENGINEERING. *Current Pos:* RETIRED. *Personal Data:* b Lorain, Ohio, June 24, 19; m 44, Johanna Mayer; c Susan, Janet & Judith. *Educ:* Williams Col, BA, 41; Pa State Univ, PhD(fuel tech), 54. *Prof Exp:* Asst, Titanium Div, Nat Lead Co, 41-43; res assoc, Inst Gas Tech, 43-44; sr chemist, Butadiene Div, Koppers Co, Inc, 44-45; res chemist, Houdry Process Corp, 45-48; asst & assoc fuel tech div, Pa State Univ, 48-51; supvr carbon res, Pittsburgh Coke & Chem Co, 53-59; mgr tech br, Electro Minerals Div, Carborundum Co, Niagara Falls, 60-67, plant mgr, 67-70; res supvr, US Bur Mines, 70-75; res supvr, Energy Res & Develop Admin, Morgantown Energy Res Ctr, WVa, 75-77; sect leader, Morgantown Energy Technol Ctr, WVa, 77-80, br chief, Dept Energy, 80-85. *Res:* Fuel and coal technology; physical chemistry; activated carbon; electron microscopy; Fischer-Tropsch synthesis; abrasives; electric furnacing; refractories; coal gasification, fluid-bed combustion and gasification; fly ash utilization; strip mine and coal refuse reclamation; coal preparation; oil and gas recovery; in-situ coal gasification. *Mailing Add:* 661 South View St Morgantown WV 26505

GILLOOLY, GEORGE RICE, LUMINESCENT MATERIALS RESEARCH. *Current Pos:* prod engr halophosphors, Gen Elec Co, Cleveland, 57-58, chemist phosphors, 58-64, res chemist, 64-78, sr develop chemist phosphors, 78-90, sr res chemist phosphors, 90, CONSULT PHOSPHORS, GEN ELEC CO, 90- *Personal Data:* b West Chester, Pa, June 6, 30; m 55, Jean Aubrey; c Gregory B & Bryan C. *Educ:* Univ Mich, BS, 53; Dartmouth Col, MA, 57. *Honors & Awards:* Saul Dushman Award, Gen Elec Corp Res & Develop Ctr, 80. *Prof Exp:* Teacher sci, Flat Rock High Sch, 53-54; instr chem, Flint Jr Col, 54-55; teaching fel chem, Dartmouth Col, 55-57. *Concurrent Pos:* Client instr, Kepner-Tregoe, 73-83. *Mem:* Electrochem Soc; Am Chem Soc; fel Am Inst Chemists. *Res:* Luminescence materials research including identifying developing and implementing new phosphors and phosphor improvements; halophosphate lamp phosphors; halophosphate phosphor synthesis. *Mailing Add:* 1375 E Colonial Salisbury NC 28144-2211

GILLOTEAUX, JACQUES JEAN-MARIE A, HISTO-CYTOCHEMISTRY, HISTOLOGY. *Current Pos:* ASSOC PROF MICROS ANAT, COL MED, NORTHEASTERN OHIO UNIV, 79- *Personal Data:* b Mons, July 9, 44; Belg citizen; m 72; c 1. *Educ:* Univ Louvain, BSc, 64, MSc, 66, ScD, 74. *Prof Exp:* Instr biol & chem, Col St Pierre, 66; prof histol, Univ Louvain, 70-71; lectr cell biol, State Univ NY, Stony Brook, 76; asst prof physiol, Upstate Med Ctr, State Univ NY Syracuse, 77-79; adj prof biol, Onondaga Community Col, 79. *Concurrent Pos:* Vis prof, Med Sch, St Georges Univ, 79. *Mem:* Royal Zool Soc Belg; Am Soc Cell Biol; AAAS; Am Asn Anatomists; Histochem Soc. *Res:* Structure and function of contractile cells and tissues; comparative histochemistry and cytochemistry; cell biology related to cardiac tissues and to hormone-induced carcinogenesis. *Mailing Add:* Prog Micro Anat Northeastern Ohio Univ Col Med 4209 State Rte 44 Rootstown OH 44272-9989

GILLOTT, DONALD H, ELECTRICAL ENGINEERING. *Current Pos:* prof elec eng & chmn dept, 68-76, DEAN SCH ENG, CALIF STATE UNIV, SACRAMENTO, 76- *Personal Data:* b Connellsville, Pa, Aug 25, 31; m 70; c 3. *Educ:* Univ Pittsburgh, BS, 56, MS, 59, PhD(elec eng), 63. *Prof Exp:* Jr engr, Latrobe Steel Co, 54-56; from instr to assoc prof elec eng, Univ Pittsburgh, 56-68. *Concurrent Pos:* NSF grant, 64-, travel grant, Europe, 66; design engr, Latrobe Steel Co, 56-58; consult, Power Supply Div, Int Bus Mach Corp, 59-63 & Nat Acad Sci, 63- *Mem:* Am Soc Eng Educ; sr mem Inst Elec & Electronics Engrs. *Res:* Flux penetration in magnetic materials, including effects of saturation and hysteresis. *Mailing Add:* Calif State Univ Sacramento CA 95819

GILLOW, EDWARD WILLIAM, PHYSICAL CHEMISTRY, ANALYTICAL CHEMISTRY. *Current Pos:* CONSULT, 88- *Personal Data:* b Scranton, Pa, Apr 14, 39; m 62; c 3. *Educ:* Pa State Univ, BS, 60; State Univ NY Buffalo, PhD(phys chem), 66. *Prof Exp:* Fel chem, Univ Tex, Austin, 66-68; res chemist, Jackson Lab, E I du Pont de Nemours & Co, Inc, 78-88, Pigments Dept, Exp Sta Lab, 68-70, tech serv chemist, Chestnut Run Lab, 70-72, res chemist, Pigments Dept, Exp Sta, 72-78, res chemist, Chem & Pigments Dept, 78-88. *Res:* Chemical kinetics; analytical methods development; solution chemistry with nonaqueous solvents; chromatography; porosimetry. *Mailing Add:* 1811 Bybrook Rd Wilmington DE 19803

GILLUM, AMANDA MCKEE, DRUG DISCOVERY, INFORMATION MANAGEMENT. *Current Pos:* DIR, BIOL SOLUTIONS, MDL INFO SYST, 96- *Personal Data:* b Rochester, NY, Apr 13, 47; m 68, William; c Jessalyn & Allison. *Educ:* Ind Univ, AB, 69; Mass Inst Technol, PhD(biochem), 76, MS, 87. *Prof Exp:* Scholar, Med Sch, Stanford Univ, 76-78; sr res investr, E R Squibb & Sons, Inc, 78-87; dir, Discovery Biochem, Sterling Winthrop, 87-94. *Mem:* Soc Indust Microbiol; AAAS; Soc

Biomolecular Screening. *Res:* Molecular target-based drug discovery; natural sources of diverse compounds; data and information management systems. *Mailing Add:* 28 Abey Dr Pennington NJ 08534. *Fax:* 609-730-8783; *E-Mail:* amanda@mdli.com

GILLUM, RICHARD FRANK, EPIDEMIOLOGY, CARDIOLOGY. *Current Pos:* SPEC ASST CARDIOVASC EPIDEMIOL, CTR DIS CONTROL & PREV, NAT CTR HEALTH STATIST, 84- *Personal Data:* b Dec 12, 44. *Educ:* Kans State Univ, BA, 67; Northwestern Univ Med Sch, MD, 70; Harvard Univ Sch Pub Health, MS, 76. *Honors & Awards:* Searle Distinguished Res Award; Savage Sci Achievement Award. *Prof Exp:* Clin fel, med, Harvard Med Sch, 70-72; clin asst, Wash, DC, Gen Hosp & Freedman's Hosp, 72-74; res fel, Harvard Med Sch, 74-75; from asst prof to assoc prof med & pub health, Univ Minn Sch Med & Pub Health, 76-84. *Concurrent Pos:* Med officer, Methods Br Nat Ctr Health Serv Res & Develop, 72-73; instr med, Howard Univ Med Sch, 72-74; mem, Exec Comt, Coun Epidemiol, AHA, 79-83, Comt Criteria & Methods, 79-83, Scholarship Comt, Nat Med Fel, Inc, 77- & bd dirs, Am Heart Asn, 79-83; prin investr, Minn Heart Surv, 79-84; fel, Am Col Cardiol, 79-; bd dirs, United Methodist Comt Relief, 80-84; assoc ed, Am J Epidemiol, 93- *Mem:* Fel Am Col Epidemiol; fel Am Heart Asn; fel Am Col Cardiol. *Res:* Epidemiology and prevention of coronary heart disease, stroke, and other cardiovascular diseases; epidemiology, control, and prevention of cardiovascular diseases in minority populations; childhood prevention of hypertension. *Mailing Add:* Off Anal & Epidemiol Nat Ctr Health Stats Ctr Dis Control Prev 6525 Belcrest Rd Hyattsville MD 20782

GILLUM, RONALD LEE, CLINICAL PATHOLOGY. *Current Pos:* PROF PATH, COL MED, UNIV OKLA, 85- *Personal Data:* b Decatur, Ill, Feb 7, 38; m 60; c 3. *Educ:* DePauw Univ, BA, 60; Univ Ill Col Med, MD, 64; Am Bd Path, dipl & cert anat path & clin path, 69 & dipl & cert radioisotopic path, 74. *Prof Exp:* Intern, Ill Cent Hosp, Chicago, 64-65; resident path, Univ Ill Res & Educ Hosps, 65-69, teaching asst, Col Med, 65-67, instr, 67-69; asst prof, Univ Tex Med Br Galveston, 72-75; assoc prof, Univ Tex Med Sch, Houston, 75-77, Col Med, Univ Okla, 77-85; chief path serv, 80-84, DIR CLIN LABS, OKLA MEM HOSP, 84- *Mem:* Am Asn Clin Chemists; Am Soc Clin Pathologists; Acad Clin Lab Physicians & Scientists; AMA; Col Am Pathologists; NY Acad Sci; AAAS. *Res:* Selection and utilization of instrumentation and methods in the clinical laboratory; the place of continuing education in quality control in the clinical laboratory; selection and interpretation of lab tests; nutritional disorders and trace elements. *Mailing Add:* Dept Path Univ Okla Col Med PO Box 26901 Oklahoma City OK 73126-0901

GILMAN, ALBERT F, III, MATHEMATICS. *Current Pos:* asst vpres acad affairs, 69-73, dir comput ctr, 70-72, actg vice chancellor acad affairs, 72, PROF MATH, WESTERN CAROLINA UNIV, 69- *Personal Data:* b Chicago, Ill, June 25, 31; m 64; c 10. *Educ:* Northwestern Univ, BS, 52; Univ Mont, MA, 58; Ind Univ, MA, 62, PhD(math), 63. *Honors & Awards:* NAS Vis Exchange Prof, Bulgarian Acad Sci, 78. *Prof Exp:* From instr to asst prof math, Bowdoin Col, 63-66; from assoc prof to prof math & chmn div sci & math, Col VI, 66-69. *Concurrent Pos:* Exec dir, Republican Study Group, US House of Rep, 73-74; NEH Fel, Univ Chi, 82. *Mem:* Am Math Soc; Math Asn Am. *Res:* Noncommutative schemes; economic models; psephology; politicometrics. *Mailing Add:* Dept Math Western Carolina Univ Cullowhee NC 28723

GILMAN, ALFRED G, BIOCHEMISTRY, PHARMACOLOGY. *Current Pos:* PROF & CHMN DEPT PHARMACOL, UNIV TEX SOUTHWESTERN MED CTR, 81-, RAYMOND WILLIE DISTINGUISHED CHAIR MOLECULAR NEUROPHARMACOL, 87- *Personal Data:* b New Haven, Conn, July 1, 41; m 63; c Kathryn Hedlund; c Amy, Anne & Edward. *Educ:* Yale Univ, BA, 62; Case Western Res Univ, MD & PhD(pharmacol), 69. *Hon Degrees:* DSc, Univ Chicago, 91, Case Western Res Univ, 95. *Honors & Awards:* Nobel Prize in Phys/Med, 94; John J Abel Award Pharmacol, Am Soc Pharmacol & Exp Therapeut, 75, Louis S Goodman & Alfred Gilman Award, Drug Receptor Pharmacol, 90, Torald Sollmn Award, 97; Poul Edvard Poulsson Award, Norweg Pharmacol Soc, 82; Gairdner Found Int Award, 84; Richard Lounsbery Award, Nat Acad Sci, 87; Distinguished Res Award Biomed Sci, Am Asn Med Col, 88; Albert Lasker Basic Med Res Award, 89; Passano Found Award, 90; Basic Sci Res Prize, Am Heart Asn, 90; Am Col Physicians Award, 95; Medal of Honor, Am Cancer Soc, 95. *Prof Exp:* Pharmacol res assoc, Lab Biochem Genetics, Nat Heart & Lung Inst, NIH, 69-71; from asst prof to prof pharmacol, Univ Va, 71-81. *Concurrent Pos:* Mem bd sci counrs, Nat Health, Lung & Blood Inst, NIH, 82-86; ad hoc mem pharmacol study sect, NIH, 73-75, mem, 77-81; mem sci adv comt biochem & chem carcinogenesis, Am Cancer Soc, 82-86; mem sci rev bd, Howard Hughes Med Inst, 86-93; adv gen med sci, Coun NIH, 92-95; vis comt, Sch Med, Case Western Res Univ, 95-99. *Mem:* Nat Acad Sci; Inst Med-Nat Acad Sci; Am Soc Pharmacol & Exp Therapeut; Am Soc Biol Chemist; fel Am Acad Arts & Sci; fel AAAS. *Res:* Author of over 200 technical journal articles. *Mailing Add:* Univ Tex Southwestern Med Ctr Dept Pharmacol 5323 Harry Hines Blvd Dallas TX 75235-9041. *E-Mail:* agilm1@mednet.swmed.edu

GILMAN, DONALD LAWRENCE, METEOROLOGY. *Current Pos:* RETIRED. *Personal Data:* b Hartford, Conn, Oct 15, 31; m 61, 87; c 3. *Educ:* Harvard Univ, AB, 52; Mass Inst Technol, MS, 54, PhD(meteorol), 57. *Prof Exp:* Mem res staff, Meteorol Dept, Mass Inst Technol, 55-58; res meteorologist, Extended Forecast Div, Nat Weather Serv, Nat Oceanic & Atmospheric Admin, 58-64, chief, Develop & Testing Sect, 64-71, chief, Long Range Prediction Group, Nat Meteorol Ctr, 72-79, chief, Prediction Br, Climate Analysis Ctr, 79-89. *Mem:* AAAS; fel Am Meteorol Soc; Am Geophys Union; Sigma Xi. *Res:* Objective techniques of extended and long range forecasting; forecast verification; meteorological statistics. *Mailing Add:* 2319 Kimbro St Alexandria VA 22309-1822

GILMAN, FREDERICK JOSEPH, theoretical high energy physics, for more information see previous edition

GILMAN, J PAUL, ECOLOGY, EVOLUTIONARY BIOLOGY. *Current Pos:* EXEC DIR COMN LIFE SCIENCES, NAT RES COUN/NAT ACAD SCI, 93-, BD AGR, 96- *Educ:* Johns Hopkins Univ, BA, 74, MA, 75, PhD(ecol & evolutionary biol), 79. *Prof Exp:* Legislative asst to Sen Peter Domenici, 79-89, admin asst, 85-91; prof staff mem, Senate Comt Energy & Natural Resources, 81-85; exec asst, Secy Energy, 91-92; assoc dir, Off Mgt & Budget, exec off pres, 92-93. *Concurrent Pos:* Mem, Comt Sci Eng & Pub Policy, AAAS; bd dir, Annapolis Ctr. *Mem:* Ecol Soc Am; AAAS. *Mailing Add:* Bd Agr Nat Res Coun 2101 Constitution Ave NW Washington DC 20418. *Fax:* 202-334-1639; *E-Mail:* pgilman@nas.edu

GILMAN, JANE P, MATHEMATICS. *Current Pos:* from asst prof to assoc prof, Newark Col Arts & Sci, 72-84, chmn dept, 82-90, PROF, DEPT MATH & COMPUT SCI, RUTGERS UNIV, NEWARK, NJ, 84- *Personal Data:* b Washington, DC, April 17, 45; m, Robert; c Sarah & Timothy. *Educ:* Univ Chicago, BS, 65; Columbia Univ, PhD, 71. *Prof Exp:* Instr, State Univ NY, Stony Brook, 71-72. *Concurrent Pos:* Mem, Inst Advan Study, Sch Math, Princeton, NJ, 79-80; mem, Math Sci Res Inst, Berkeley, Calif, 86; vis res mathematician, Princeton Univ, 88-89, vis prof, 90-91; mem, Coun Am Math Soc, 86-88. *Mem:* Am Math Soc; Am Math Asn; Am Women Math. *Res:* Riemann surfaces; fuchsian groups; teichmuller theory; author of over 20 technical research articles. *Mailing Add:* Dept Math & Comput Sci Rutgers Univ Smith Hall Newark NJ 07102

GILMAN, JOHN JOSEPH, PHYSICS, METALLURGY. *Current Pos:* PROF MAT SCI & ENG, UNIV CALIF, LOS ANGELES, 93- *Personal Data:* b St Paul, Minn, Dec 22, 25; wid; c Pamela, Gregory, Cheryl, John, Kathryn, Nicholas & Brian. *Educ:* Ill Inst Technol, MS, 48; Columbia Univ, PhD(metall), 52. *Honors & Awards:* Mathewson Medal, Am Inst Mining, Metall & Petrol Eng, 59; Campbell lectr, Am Soc Metals, 66; Reduction to Pract Award, Metall Soc, 86; IR-100 Awards, 74, 76, 80. *Prof Exp:* Res engr metall, Crucible Steel Co, 48-52; res assoc, Gen Elec Co, 52-60; prof eng, Brown Univ, 60-63; prof physics & metall, Univ Ill, Urbana-Champaign, 63-68; dir, Mat Res Ctr, Allied Chem Corp, 68-78, dir, Corp Develop Ctr, 78-80; mgr corp res, Stand Oil Co, Ind, 80-85; assoc dir, Lawrence Berkeley Lab, 85-87, sr scientist, 87-93. *Concurrent Pos:* Adj prof, Columbia Univ, 68-74; consult, Lawrence Radiation Lab; mem mat res coun, Advan Res Proj Agency, Dept Defense, 68-82. *Mem:* Nat Acad Eng; fel Am Soc Metals; fel Am Inst Mining, Metall & Petrol Eng; fel Am Phys Soc; Mat Res Soc. *Res:* Mechanical behavior of solids; solid state physics; behavior of shock and detonation waves in solids; research management; technical management; chemical reactions in solids. *Mailing Add:* 6532 Boelter Hall Univ Calif Los Angeles CA 90095. *Fax:* 310-706-7353; *E-Mail:* gilman@seas.ucla.edu

GILMAN, JOHN RICHARD, JR, SCIENCE ADMINISTRATION. *Current Pos:* PRES CONSULT, JOHN R GILMAN & ASSOCS, 78- *Personal Data:* b Malden, Mass, July 6, 25; m 60; c 2. *Educ:* Harvard Univ, AB, 46; NY Univ, MSW, 83. *Prof Exp:* At John H Breck, Inc, 47-48, dir publicity, 49-53, asst adv mgr, 50-53, dir new prod, Mkt Res, 55-58, tech dir, 56-62; dir new prod, Acco Labs, Am Cyanamid Corp, 63; exec vpres, treas, pres & dir, August Sauter Am, Inc, New York, 65-78. *Concurrent Pos:* Lectr, Niagara Univ, Niagara Falls, NY, 85 & 86, Newport Col, Newport, RI, 86 & 87. *Mem:* NY Acad Sci; fel Am Orthopsychiat Asn. *Res:* Psychological impediments to creative investigation and to effective administration in science and technology; effective communications within the research and development function, and between research and development and other organizational functions. *Mailing Add:* 12 Evans Lane Hope Valley RI 02832

GILMAN, MARTIN ROBERT, TOXICOLOGY. *Current Pos:* TOXICOLOGIST, HAZELTON LABS, 83- *Personal Data:* b Brooklyn, NY, Mar 28, 37; m 63; c 1. *Educ:* Del Valley Col, BS, 63; Drexel Univ, MS, 68, PhD(toxicol), 71. *Prof Exp:* Consult toxicologist, Gilmar Assocs, 71-72; dir, Cannon Labs, 72-74; Prod Safety Toxicologist, Colgate-Palmolive Co, 74-83. *Mem:* AAAS; NY Acad Sci; Soc Toxicol; Teratol Soc. *Res:* Consumer product safety; Federal Hazardous Substances Act evaluations; food products safety; animal toxicologic study evaluations; human irritation/sensitization; inhalation teratology; animal reproduction. *Mailing Add:* Hazelton Res Prod 1722 Charter Ave Kalamazoo MI 49024

GILMAN, NORMAN WASHBURN, organic chemistry, for more information see previous edition

GILMAN, PAUL BREWSTER, JR, PHYSICAL CHEMISTRY. *Current Pos:* RETIRED. *Personal Data:* b Havana, Cuba, Nov 21, 29; US citizen; m 52; c 4. *Educ:* Univ Mass, BS, 51; Northeastern Univ, MS, 54; Rutgers Univ, PhD(phys chem), 57. *Prof Exp:* From res chemist to sr res assoc, Eastman Kodak Co, 57-89, consult, 89-92. *Mem:* Fel Soc Photog Sci & Eng. *Res:* Photochemistry; photographic science; spectral sensitization; luminescence; photothermographic materials. *Mailing Add:* 261 Hillary Lane Penfield NY 14526

GILMAN, PETER A, CONVECTION THEORY, DYNAMO THEORY. *Current Pos:* sci vis, Advan Study Prog, Nat Ctr Atmospheric Res, 69-70, mem staff, 70-73, chmn, Advan Study Prog, 71-75, head, Solar Variability Sect, 77-87, dir, High Altitude Observ, 87-89, SR SCIENTIST NAT CTR ATMOSPHERIC RES, 73-, ASSOC DIR, 89- *Personal Data:* b Hartford, Conn; m 66, 76; c 4. *Educ:* Harvard Col, BA, 62; Mass Inst Technol, SM, 64,

PhD(meteorol), 66. *Prof Exp:* Asst prof astro-geophys, Univ Colo, Boulder, 66-69. *Concurrent Pos:* Lectr, Univ Colo, Boulder, 70-77, adj prof astrophys, planetary & atmospheric sci, 79-; mem, Solar & Space Physics Comt, Space Sci Bd, Nat Acad Sci, 80-83. *Mem:* AAAS; Am Meteorol Soc; Am Astron Soc; Am Geophys Union; Int Astron Union. *Res:* Fluid dynamics and magneto hydrodynamics of the sun and planets. *Mailing Add:* High Altitude Observ Nat Ctr Atmospheric Res PO Box 3000 Boulder CO 80307

GILMAN, RICHARD ATWOOD, GEOLOGY. *Current Pos:* from asst prof to prof geol, 63-74, dept chmn, 75-87, DISTINGUISHED TEACHING PROF GEOL, STATE UNIV NY COL FREDONIA, 74- *Personal Data:* b Concord, NH, Jan 22, 35; m 58; c 1. *Educ:* Dartmouth Col, AB, 57; Univ Ill, MS, 59, PhD(geol), 61. *Prof Exp:* Instr phys sci, Univ Ill, 61-63. *Concurrent Pos:* Consult, Maine Geol Surv, 62-; res found grant-in-aid, State Univ NY Col Fredonia, 63; NSF fel, 71-72. *Mem:* AAAS; Geol Soc Am; Nat Asn Geol Teachers; Sigma Xi. *Res:* Structural analysis of igneous and metamorphic rocks; field mapping in Southern Maine. *Mailing Add:* 41 Newton St Fredonia NY 14063

GILMAN, ROBERT EDWARD, ORGANIC CHEMISTRY. *Current Pos:* from asst prof to assoc prof, 64-72, PROF CHEM, ROCHESTER INST TECHNOL, 73- *Personal Data:* b Concord, NH, Jan 19, 32; m 54; c 2. *Educ:* Dartmouth Col, AB, 54; Univ Mich, MS, 57, PhD(chem), 59. *Prof Exp:* Res chemist, W R Grace & Co, 58-60; Nat Res Coun Can fel, 60-62; vis asst prof, Williams Col, 62-64. *Concurrent Pos:* NSF sci fac fel, Univ Calif, Los Angeles, 70-71. *Mem:* Am Chem Soc. *Res:* Natural products; stereochemistry; reaction mechanisms; organic synthesis; cyclophane chemistry. *Mailing Add:* 8211 Michael Dr Huntington Beach CA 92647

GILMAN, ROBERT HUGH, DYNAMICAL SYSTEMS, GROUP THEORY. *Current Pos:* From asst prof to assoc prof, 74-82, PROF MATH, STEVENS INST TECHNOL, 82- *Personal Data:* b Utica, NY, July 28, 42; m 69; c 2. *Educ:* Princeton Univ, AB, 64; Columbia Univ, PhD(math), 69. *Hon Degrees:* Hon M Eng, Stevens Inst technol, 87. *Concurrent Pos:* Vis mem, Courant Inst Math Sci, 71-72; mem, Inst Advan Study, 84-85. *Mem:* Am Math Soc; Math Asn Am; Sigma Xi. *Res:* Dynamical systems and computational group theory. *Mailing Add:* 477 Vose Ave South Orange NJ 07079-3018

GILMAN, SID, CLINICAL NEUROLOGY, NEUROPHYSIOLOGY & NEUROPHARMACOLOGY. *Current Pos:* PROF & CHMN DEPT NEUROL, UNIV MICH, 77-, CHIEF, NEUROL SERV, UNIV MICH HOSPS, 77- *Personal Data:* b Los Angeles, Calif, Oct 19, 32; m 62, 84, Carol G Barbour; c 1. *Educ:* Univ Calif, Los Angeles, BA, 54, MD, 57. *Honors & Awards:* Weinstein Goldenson Award, 81; Lucy G Moses Prize in Basic Neurol, 73; Robert B Wartenberg Lestr, Am Acad Neurol, 94. *Prof Exp:* Intern, Univ Calif Hosp, Los Angeles, 57-58; res assoc, NIH, 58-60; resident, Neurol Inst, Boston City Hosp, Mass, 60-63; instr neurol, Harvard Med Sch, 65-66, assoc, 66-68; from asst prof to assoc prof, Col Physicians & Surgeons, Columbia Univ, 68-72, prof neurol, 72-76, H Houston Merritt prof neurol, 76-77. *Concurrent Pos:* Ambrose & Gladys Bowyer Found fel med, 57-58; res fel, Harvard Med Sch at Boston City Hosp, 62-65. *Mem:* Inst Med-Nat Acad Sci; Am Acad Neurol; Am Neurol Asn (pres 88-89); Am Soc Clin Invest; Soc Neurosci; AAAS. *Res:* Disorders of movement and behavior in humans and animals with lesions of the central nervous system; positron emission tomography studies of cerebellar degenerations; dementia; and epilepsy. *Mailing Add:* Dept Neurol TC 1914 Univ Mich 1500 E Med Ctr Dr Ann Arbor MI 48109-0316

GILMAN, STEVEN CHRISTOPHER, IMMUNOPHARMACOLOGY, INFLAMMATION. *Current Pos:* DIR BIOL RES, CYTOGEN CORP, PRINCETON, NJ, 87- *Personal Data:* b Urbana, Ill, Dec 25, 52; m; c 4. *Educ:* Miami Univ, Ohio, BS, 75; Pa State Univ, MS, 77, PhD(microbiol), 79. *Prof Exp:* Res assoc immunol, Scripps Clin & Res Found, 79-82; res scientist immunol, Wyeth Labs, Inc, 82-87. *Concurrent Pos:* Adj res prof, Sch Med, Temple Univ, 83-; assoc ed, Int Arch Pharmacodynamics & Ther, 85-; fel, NIH & Coun Tobacco Res. *Mem:* Am Asn Immunol; Am Soc Microbiol; Inflammation Res Asn; Soc Nuclear Med; Am Rheumatism Asn. *Res:* Regulation of immune responses in disease states such as arthritis and aging; role of hormones and other soluble mediators in bone and joint destruction; monoclonal antibody immunotherapy. *Mailing Add:* Pfizer Cent Res Eastern Pt Rd Groton CT 06340. *Fax:* 609-987-7211

GILMARTIN, MALVERN, BIOLOGICAL OCEANOGRAPHY. *Current Pos:* prof biol oceanog & dir, Ctr Marine Studies & Sea Grant, 78-85, prof zool, 85-91, EMER PROF ZOOL, DEPT ZOOL, UNIV MAINE, 91- *Personal Data:* b Los Angeles, Calif, Nov 14, 26; m 52,74, Noelia Revelante; c Malvern, Dale M, Sheile A, Ian & Darren. *Educ:* Pomona Col, BA, 54; Univ Hawaii, MS, 56; Univ BC, PhD(oceanog), 60. *Prof Exp:* Sr scientist, Inter-Am Trop Tuna Comt, 60-65; assoc prof oceanog, Univ Hawaii, 65-67; prof biol oceanog & dir oceanog, Stanford Univ, 67-69 & 70-74; prog dir biol oceanog, NSF, 69-70; dir, Australian Inst Marine Sci, 74-78. *Concurrent Pos:* Consult, Nat Fishing Inst, Ecuador, 61-64 & Empresa Puertos de Colombia, 63; coordr, Inter-Am El Nino Proj, 62-64; mem, NSF biol oceanog panel, 70-74; NSF R/V Alpha Helix adv bd, 71-74; sr sci adv, Ctr Marine Res, Yugoslavia, 72-, Plank Comt, Int Comn, Sci Explor Mediter Sea, 74-; mem, Comt Oceanog Res, Australia; Comt Great Bar Reef Mar Park Authority; adv, Fish Inst, Makerere Univ, Uganda, 79-81; Fulbright scholar, Yugoslavia, 83-84 & 90. *Mem:* AAAS; Am Soc Limnol & Oceanog; Am Fisheries Soc; Phycol Soc Am; Sigma Xi. *Res:* Primary and secondary aquatic production eutrophication; fisheries; oceanography. *Mailing Add:* Zool Dept 306 Murray Hall Univ Maine Orono ME 04469. *Fax:* 207-581-2537

GILMARTIN, THOMAS JOSEPH, ELECTRO-OPTICAL SYSTEMS. *Current Pos:* assoc proj leader, Lawrence Livermore Nat Lab, 74-75, dep div leader, 75-79, asst prog leader, 79-81, syst group leader, Laser Prog, 81-86, opers mgr, 86-91, dir staff, Instnl Planning, 91-96, DEP DIR ENG & ENVIRON SYSTS, LAWRENCE LIVERMORE NAT LAB, 96- *Personal Data:* b Rochester, NY, Aug 5, 40; m 67; c 2. *Educ:* Georgetown Univ, BS, 62; Purdue Univ, MS, 64, PhD(elec eng), 68. *Prof Exp:* Staff, Optics Div, Lincoln Lab, Mass Inst Technol, 67-74. *Res:* Applications of lasers for laser radar, inertial confinement fusion, and isotope separation; design and integration of systems; performance and cost optimization; program planning. *Mailing Add:* 2408 Sheffield Dr Livermore CA 94550

GILMER, DAVID SEELEY, WILDLIFE POPULATIONS & HABITATS, REMOTE SENSING. *Current Pos:* STA LEADER, BIOL RES DIV, US GEOL SURV, DIXON, CALIF, 94- *Personal Data:* b Manila, Philippines, Dec 1, 37; US citizen; m 63; c 2. *Educ:* US Naval Acad, BS, 59; Univ Mich, MWM, 67; Univ Minn, PhD(ecol), 71. *Prof Exp:* Wildlife res biologist, Northern Prairie Wildlife Res Ctr, US Fish & Wildlife Serv, Jamestown, NDak, 72-79, biologist-in-chg, Wildlife Res Field Sta, 79-85, chief, Sect Pac States Ecol, NPac Wildlife Res Ctr, Dixon, Calif, 85-94. *Concurrent Pos:* Adj prof, Humboldt State Univ, 88-, Calif State Univ, Sacramento, 91-; adj fac, Ore State Univ, Corvallis, 92- *Mem:* Wildlife Soc; Cooper Ornith Soc; Asn Field Ornithologists. *Res:* Waterfowl ecology; raptor ecology; wetland ecology; remote sensing for wildlife habitat and population assessment; biotelemetry. *Mailing Add:* US Geol Surv Biol Res Div Dixon Field Sta 6924 Tremont Rd Dixon CA 95620-9603. *Fax:* 916-678-5039; *E-Mail:* dave_gilmer@nbs.gov

GILMER, GEORGE HUDSON, COMPUTER MODELING OF MATERIALS PROCESSING. *Current Pos:* DISTINGUISHED MEM TECH STAFF, BELL LABS, 72- *Personal Data:* b Hampden-Sydney, Va, Sept 3, 37; m, Wilhelmina Juliana Bernharda Bos; c Juliana W (Scott), George H, Cornelia B & Hendrik C W. *Educ:* Davidson Col, BS, 58; Univ Va, PhD(physics), 62. *Prof Exp:* Res assoc, Cornell Univ, 62-64; from asst prof to assoc prof physics, Washington & Lee Univ, 64-72. *Concurrent Pos:* Vis, Delft Technol Univ, 70-71. *Mem:* Fel Am Phys Soc; Minerals, Metals & Mat Soc. *Res:* Crystal growth theory; grain boundary theory; computer models of crystal growth, atomistic models of semiconductor device processing. *Mailing Add:* 1E-434 AT&T Bell Labs 600 Mountain Ave Murray Hill NJ 07974. *Fax:* 908-582-4228; *E-Mail:* ghg@bell-labs.com

GILMER, PENNY JANE, BIOPHYSICAL CHEMISTRY & IMMUNOCHEMISTRY, SCIENCE EDUCATION. *Current Pos:* from asst prof to assoc prof chem, Fla State Univ, 77-96, interim assoc dean arts & sci, 90-91, assoc chair chem, 91-93, PROF, FLA STATE UNIV, 96- *Personal Data:* b Hackensack, NJ, Aug 19, 43; m 80, Sanford A Safron; c Helena M & Nathaniel S. *Educ:* Douglass Col, BA, 65; Bryn Mawr Col, MA, 67; Univ Calif, Berkeley, PhD(biochem), 72. *Prof Exp:* Fel biophys, Stanford Univ, 73-75, fel immunochem, 75-77. *Concurrent Pos:* Giannini fel, 73-75; NIH fel, 75-77; mem, Comt B, Am Asn Univ Profs; actg asst prof human biol, Stanford Univ, 76; mem, Comt Fac Res, Fla State Univ, 78 & 84; prin invest, Res Corp grant, 89-; co-dir, Funded Teacher Prep Prog, NSF, 91-94 & Funded Teacher Enhancement Prog, 92-95; consult, La Bd Regents & Statewide Syst Initiative, 92-93 & Fla Statewide Syst Initiative, 93-95 & Higher Educ Consortium Math & Sci, 96- *Mem:* Am Chem Soc; fel AAAS; Fedn Am Soc Exp Biol; Asn Women Sci; Sigma Xi. *Res:* Fast reaction kinetics; enzyme mechanisms; membrane-mediated phenomena; cell-surface cabohydrates; cell-cell recognition; sialic acids; science education. *Mailing Add:* Dept Chem Fla State Univ Tallahassee FL 32306-3006. *Fax:* 850-644-8281; *E-Mail:* gilmer@iris1.sb.fsu.edu

GILMER, ROBERT, COMMUTATIVE ALGEBRA, FIELD THEORY. *Current Pos:* from asst prof to prof math, 63-81, ROBERT O LAWTON DISTINGUISHED PROF, 81- *Personal Data:* b Pontotoc, Miss, July 3, 38; m 63, Rachel Colson; c David & Stephen. *Educ:* Miss State Univ, BS, 58; La State Univ, MS, 60, PhD(math), 61. *Prof Exp:* Res instr math, La State Univ, 61-63; vis lectr, Univ Wis, 62-63. *Concurrent Pos:* Res assoc, Off Naval Res, 62-63; vis prof, Miss State Univ, 62; Alfred P Sloan Found fel, 65-67; prin investr, NSF grants, 65-89; assoc ed, Am Math Monthly, 71-73; Fulbright sr scholar res award, Australian-Am Educ Found, 73-74; vis prof, Latrobe Univ, 74; Univ Tex, Austin, 76-77; mem, ed bd, J Commun in Algebra, 74-85; vis res prof, Univ Conn, 74-85. *Mem:* Am Math Soc; Math Asn Am. *Res:* Commutative ring theory; polynomial and power series rings; dimension theory; monoid rings; multiplicative ideal theory. *Mailing Add:* Dept Math Fla State Univ Tallahassee FL 32306-3027. *Fax:* 850-644-4053; *E-Mail:* gilmer@math.fsu.edu

GILMER, ROBERT MCCULLOUGH, PHYTOPATHOLOGY. *Current Pos:* From asst prof to prof, 50-76, head dept, 69-72, EMER PROF PLANT PATH, NY EXP STA, CORNELL UNIV, 76- *Personal Data:* b Lawrence, Kans, Dec 10, 20; m 55. *Educ:* Univ Wis, BS, 47, MS, 48, PhD(phytopath), 50. *Mem:* Am Phytopath Soc. *Res:* Virology of deciduous fruit trees. *Mailing Add:* 20421 Ted Rd Brooksville FL 34601

GILMER, THOMAS EDWARD, JR, SOLID STATE PHYSICS, SEMICONDUCTORS. *Current Pos:* RETIRED. *Personal Data:* b Draper, Va, Mar 4, 25; m 51; c 5. *Educ:* Hampden-Sydney Col, BS, 48; Univ NC, MS, 53, PhD(physics), 56. *Prof Exp:* Instr math, Ky Mil Inst, 48-50; asst, Duke Univ, 53 & Univ NC, 53-54; sr scientist, Exp Inc, Va, 55-56, head solid state physics lab, 57-58; assoc prof physics, Va Polytech Inst & State Univ, 58-62, actg head dept, 59-60, prof physics, 62-89, assoc dean, Col Arts & Sci, 69-79, head dept, 82-89. *Mem:* Am Phys Soc. *Res:* Neutron spectra and cross-sections; ionizing energy loss; magnetic resonance; electrical properties of semiconductors; infrared absorption in solids; photovoltaics. *Mailing Add:* 611 Landsdowne Dr Blacksburg VA 24060

GILMONT, ERNEST RICH, ORGANIC CHEMISTRY. *Current Pos:* CONSULT, ARTHUR D LITTLE, 84- *Personal Data:* b Newton, Mass, July 1, 29; m 65. *Educ:* Middlebury Col, AB, 51, MSc, 52; Mass Inst Technol, PhD(org chem), 56. *Prof Exp:* Sr res chemist, FMC Corp, NJ, 56-58, group leader, 58-61; dir res, US Peroxygen Corp, Calif, 61-62; sr scientist, Millmaster Onyx Corp, Newark, NJ, 62-66, dir res & develop, A Gross & Co Div, 66-70 & tech dir, 70-78, gen mgr copygraphics, 78-84. *Concurrent Pos:* Comnr, Sci Manpower Comn, 74-; lectr, Robert A Welch Found, 75; chmn, Coun Scientific Soc Pres, 64-69; dir, Asn Res Dirs, 84-86. *Mem:* Fel AAAS; Am Chem Soc; fel Am Inst Chem (pres, 73-75); Am Oil Chem Soc; Am Inst Chem Engrs. *Res:* Fatty acids; hydrogenation; organic peroxides; polymerization catalysis; halogenation. *Mailing Add:* Arthur D Little Inc 146 Central Park West New York NY 10023

GILMONT, ROGER, CHEMICAL ENGINEERING. *Current Pos:* ADJ PROF CHEM ENG, POLYTECH INST BROOKLYN, 51-, PRES, GILMONT INSTRUMENTS, INC, 61- *Personal Data:* b New York, NY, Dec 30, 16; m 41; c 1. *Educ:* Cooper Union, BChE, 39; Polytech Inst Brooklyn, MChE, 43, DrChE, 47. *Prof Exp:* Draftsman, US Coast & Geod Surv, Washington, DC, 40-41; jr chem engr, QM Corps, US War Dept, 41; jr mat engr, Nat Bur Standards, 41-42; phys chemist, 42-43; teacher chem eng, City Col New York, 43-44; phys chemist, Gen Foods Corp, NJ, 44-47; tech dir, Emil Greiner Co, 47-55, pres, Manostat Corp, 55-61. *Mem:* AAAS; Am Chem Soc; Am Technion Soc; Instrument Soc Am; Am Inst Chem; Am Inst Chem Engrs; Sigma Xi. *Res:* Thermodynamics; instrument design; food spoilage; correlation of vapor liquid equilibria. *Mailing Add:* 3841 240th St Flushing NY 11363

GILMORE, ALVAN RAY, FORESTRY. *Current Pos:* RETIRED. *Personal Data:* b Pensacola, Fla, Nov 6, 21; m 43; c 2. *Educ:* Univ Fla, BSF, 49; Duke Univ, MF, 50, DF, 61. *Prof Exp:* Instr forestry, Univ Fla, 50-52; asst prof, Ala Polytech Inst, 53-58; assoc prof forestry, Univ Ill, Urbana-Champaign, 58-68, prof, 68-92. *Res:* Forest tree physiology; forest soils; forest ecology. *Mailing Add:* PO Box 865 Dadeville AL 36853

GILMORE, ARTHUR W, RESOURCE MANAGEMENT, OPERATIONS RESEARCH. *Current Pos:* dir, Grad Studies Indust Mgt, 78-89, EMER LECTR, STATE UNIV NY, STONY BROOK, 89- *Personal Data:* b Louisville, Ky, Oct 5, 20; m 48, Beverly M Snow; c David, Beverly, Richard & Paul. *Educ:* Rensselaer Polytech Inst, BAE, 42; Univ Colo, MS, 56. *Prof Exp:* Instr aerodyn eng, Rensselaer Polytech Inst, 42-43; aerodynamicist A, aircraft design, Consol-Vultee Corp, 43-44; asst prof eng autopilot design, Sperry Gyroscope Co, 45-48; section head, dir eng design, Grumman Aerospace Corp, 48-77; asst prof aerodyn eng, Univ Colo, 55-57. *Concurrent Pos:* Mem, res adv comt aerodyn, NASA, 60-63; mem, Nat Comn Eng Manpower, 66-68; consult, Am Asn Eng Socs, 77-84, Long Island Lighting Co, 78-79 & AIL Div, Eaton Corp, 84-85. *Mem:* Assoc Sigma Xi. *Res:* Aerodynamics; engineering economics; production and operations analysis; engineering manpower. *Mailing Add:* 12 Satterly Rd East Setauket NY 11733

GILMORE, EARL C, WHEAT BREEDING. *Current Pos:* RETIRED. *Personal Data:* b Whitney, Tex, Sept 7, 30; m 54, Margaret Breland; c Larry R, John W & Shelley L. *Educ:* Tex A&M Univ, BS, 52, MS, 57; Univ Minn, PhD(genetics), 67. *Prof Exp:* Instr agron, Tex A&M Univ, 57-59; res agronomist, USDA, 59-65 & Dekalb Agr Asn, Inc, 65-66; from asst prof to prof plant breeding, Tex A&M Univ, Vernon, 66-79, res dir resident & prof, Tex Agr Exp Sta, 79-92. *Concurrent Pos:* Consult hybrid wheat, Rohm & Haas Co, 73-74. *Res:* Development of hybrid wheat, breeding wheat and flax; quantitative genetics of agronomic crops; wheat breeding. *Mailing Add:* 5529 Lake Highlands Dr Waco TX 76710

GILMORE, EARL HOWARD, MATHEMATICS. *Current Pos:* RES CHEMIST, HELIUM RES CTR, US BUR MINES, 68- *Personal Data:* b Turkey, Tex, July 9, 23; m 46; c 2. *Educ:* Tex Tech Col, BS, 43, MS, 47; Univ Calif, PhD(chem), 51. *Prof Exp:* Phys chemist, US Naval Ord Test Sta, 50-53; from asst prof to assoc prof chem, Okla State Univ, 53-58; from asst prof to assoc prof math, Tex Tech Col, 58-68. *Concurrent Pos:* Res assoc, Res Found, Okla State Univ, 53-57. *Mem:* Am Chem Soc; Am Phys Soc; Math Asn Am. *Res:* Photoelectric photometry; energy level systems for excited molecule species. *Mailing Add:* 11300 Indian Hill Rd Amarillo TX 79124-2371

GILMORE, FORREST RICHARD, NUCLEAR WEAPONS EFFECTS. *Current Pos:* CONSULT, 90- *Personal Data:* b Cisco, Tex, Aug 25, 22; div; c 2. *Educ:* Calif Inst Technol, BS, 44, PhD(physics), 51. *Prof Exp:* Res analyst, Douglas Aircraft Co, 44-45; instr appl mech & res engr, Calif Inst Technol, 50-53; physicist, Rand Corp, 53-71; sr staff scientist, R&D Assocs, 71-90. *Mem:* Fel Am Phys Soc; Am Optical Soc; Am Geophys Union. *Res:* Atmospheric physics; atomic and molecular physics; radiation; hydrodynamics; nuclear weapons effects. *Mailing Add:* 1123 Ocean Park Blvd No B Santa Monica CA 90405

GILMORE, JAMES EUGENE, ENTOMOLOGY, TEPHRITID FRUIT FLY RESEARCH. *Current Pos:* RETIRED. *Personal Data:* b Tokay, NMex, July 13, 27; m 53; c 2. *Educ:* NMex State Univ, BS, 50; Ore State Univ, MS, 57. *Prof Exp:* County office mgr prod & mkt admin, USDA, 50-54; asst pests of pome & stone fruits, Ore State Univ, 55-57; entomologist, Citrus Insect Invests, Entom Res Div, Calif, 57-64, entomologist & asst to chief, Fruit & Veg Insects Res Br, USDA, Beltsville, Md, 64-69, asst to dir, Entom Res Div, 69-72, asst dir, Calif-Hawaii-Nev Area, Western Region, 72-82, dir, Trop Fruit & Veg Res Lab, Agr Res Serv, Honolulu, HI, 82-90. *Mem:* Entom Soc Am. *Res:* Biology and control of insects and mites attacking citrus and deciduous fruits; insect and mite pathogens for biological control; resistance of mites to chemicals; control, quarantine and eradication of tropical fruit flies. *Mailing Add:* 2841 Holly Ave Clovis CA 93612

GILMORE, JOSEPH PATRICK, PHYSIOLOGY. *Current Pos:* RETIRED. *Personal Data:* b Brooklyn, NY, Sept 30, 28; m 50, Harriet K; c Cathleen, Joanne, Dennis & Gerard. *Educ:* St John's Univ, NY, BS, 51, MS, 52; George Washington Univ, PhD(physiol), 62. *Prof Exp:* Asst zool & physiol, St John's Univ, NY, 50-52; physiologist, Naval Med Field Res Lab, Camp Lejeune, 52-55, head dept physiol, 55-58; physiologist, Lab Cardiovasc Physiol, Nat Heart Inst, 58-64, dep chief, 64-66; from assoc prof to prof physiol, Med Sch, Univ Va, 66-70; prof physiol & biophys & chmn dept, Col Med, Univ Nebr, Omaha, 70-88. *Concurrent Pos:* NIH career develop award, 67; assoc, George Washington Univ, 62-66; mem study sect cardio B, NIH, 68-72; mem, Cardiovascular A Res Study Comt, Am Heart Asn, 64-; mem coun, Soc Exp Biol & Med, 78- mem coun high blood pressure res, Med Adv Bd. *Mem:* Am Physiol Soc; Am Heart Asn; Am Soc Nephrology; Am Soc Pharmacol & Exp Therapeut; fel Am Col Cardiol. *Res:* Electrophysiology of cardiac nerve; renal physiology with particular reference to body salt and water control; renin-angiotensin. *Mailing Add:* 1389 Ventnor Ave Tarpon Springs FL 34689. *E-Mail:* jgilm91240@aol.com

GILMORE, MAURICE EUGENE, MATHEMATICS, ALGEBRAIC TOPOLOGY. *Current Pos:* from instr to assoc prof, 66-78, chmn dept, 75-88, PROF MATH, NORTHEASTERN UNIV, 78- *Personal Data:* b New York, NY, Jan 2, 38; m 64, 91, Cathi Sonneborn; c Peter B, Christopher A & Jessica L. *Educ:* Georgetown Univ, AB, 59; Syracuse Univ, BS, 61; Univ Calif, Berkeley, PhD(math), 67. *Prof Exp:* Teaching asst, Syracuse Univ, 59-61; asst, Univ Calif, Berkeley, 61-66. *Concurrent Pos:* Prof, State Tech Univ, Chile, 68-69; NSF grantee, 79-82, 93-95 & 95- *Mem:* Am Math Soc; Math Asn Am; Nat Coun Teachers Mat. *Res:* Algebraic topology; vector fields; homotopy groups; obstruction theory; differential topology; homotopy theory; three-manifolds; knot theory; mathematics education. *Mailing Add:* Dept Math Northeastern Univ Boston MA 02115. *E-Mail:* gilmore@nev.edu

GILMORE, PAUL CARL, COMPUTER SCIENCE. *Current Pos:* prof & dept head, 77-85, EMER PROF COMPUT SCI, UNIV BC, 90- *Personal Data:* b Can, Dec 5, 25; nat US; m 54; c 2. *Educ:* Univ BC, BA, 49; Cambridge Univ, MA, 51; Univ Amsterdam, PhD(math), 53. *Honors & Awards:* Lanchester Prize, Opers Res Soc Am, 64. *Prof Exp:* Univ res assoc math & Nat Res Coun Can res fel, Univ Toronto, 53-55; asst prof, Pa State Univ, 55-58; staff mathematician, Thomas J Watson Res Ctr, IBM Corp, 58-77, mgr combinatorial math, 64-67, asst to chief scientist, 74-75. *Concurrent Pos:* Vis prof, Univ BC, 71-72; adj prof math statist, Columbia Univ, 72-77; mem, Coun Can Math Soc; mem, Grant Selection Comt Comput & Info Sci Natural Sci & Eng Res Coun Can. *Mem:* Asn Comput Mach; Opers Res Soc Am; Can Info Processing Soc; Can Math Soc. *Res:* Logical foundations of mathematics and computer science. *Mailing Add:* Dept Comput Sci Univ BC 201-2366 Main Mall Vancouver BC V6T 1Z4 Can

GILMORE, ROBERT, NON-LINEAR DYNAMICS & GROUP THEORY. *Current Pos:* PROF PHYSICS, DREXEL UNIV, 81- *Personal Data:* b New York, NY, 1941. *Educ:* Mass Inst Technol, BS(math) & BS(Physis) 62, PhD(physics), 67. *Prof Exp:* Mem tech staff, Inst Defense & Anal, 79-81. *Mem:* Fel Am Phys Soc. *Mailing Add:* Dept Physics & Atmospheric Sci Drexel Univ Philadelphia PA 19104

GILMORE, ROBERT BEATTIE, FUEL TECHNOLOGY & PETROLEUM ENGINEERING, ENVIRONMENTAL SCIENCES. *Current Pos:* RETIRED. *Personal Data:* b 1913; m 40, Kathleen Kuk; c Betsy (McNeil, deceased), Judy (Lepthien), C Patricia & Sally (Shaw). *Educ:* Univ Tulsa, BS, 39. *Honors & Awards:* DeGolyer Medal, Soc Petrol Engrs, 75. *Prof Exp:* Engr, Shell Oil Corp, 34-41; vpres & dir, De Golyer & MacNaughton, 49-61, pres, 62-66, chmn bd, 67-71, sr chmn, 72-77, vchmn exec comt, 78-88. *Concurrent Pos:* Petrol Eng lectr, Univ Tex, Dallas, Oil & Gas Financial Mgt, 79-87; pres, Giloil. *Mem:* Soc Petrol Engrs (pres, 55). *Mailing Add:* 6246 Prestonshire Lane Dallas TX 75225

GILMORE, ROBERT SNEE, NONDESTRUCTIVE TESTING, QUALITY ASSURANCE. *Current Pos:* develop engr, 72-77, RES PHYSICIST, RES & DEVELOP CTR, GEN ELEC CO, 77- *Personal Data:* b Pittsburgh, Pa, Apr 20, 38; m 63; c 2. *Educ:* Rensselaer Polytech Inst, BCE, 60, MS, 64, PhD(geophysics), 67. *Honors & Awards:* IR-100 Award for Comput Assisted Ultrasonic Microscope; fel, Am Soc Nondestructive Testing. *Prof Exp:* Fel Biophys, Rensselaer Polytech Inst, 66-68; group leader ultrasonics, NASA Electronics Res Ctr, 68-70; mem staff, Bioeng Dept, Forsyth Dent Ctr, 70-71. *Concurrent Pos:* Res affil, Mass Inst Technol, 69-71; adj prof mat eng, Rensselaer Polytech Inst, 78-80, bioeng, 82- *Mem:* Fel Am Soc Nondestructive Testing; Sigma Xi. *Res:* Ultrasonic characterization of materials with respect to elastic constants, grain size, composition and suitability for service at high temperatures and stresses; ultrasonic imaging; ultrasonic microscopy; nondestructive testing; ultrasonic spectroscopy and microspectroscopy. *Mailing Add:* Gen Elec Co Corp Res & Develop 1 Research Circle Bldg KWD Rm 246 Niskayuna NY 12309

GILMORE, SHIRLEY ANN, NEUROBIOLOGY, SPINAL CORD. *Current Pos:* From instr to assoc prof, 62-75, PROF ANAT, MED CTR, UNIV ARK, LITTLE ROCK, 75-, CHMN DEPT ANAT, UNIV ARK MED SCI, 84- *Personal Data:* b Connellsville, Pa, Jan 1, 35. *Educ:* Thiel Col, BA, 57; Univ Cincinnati, PhD(anat), 61. *Honors & Awards:* Jacob Javits Neurosci Investr Award, NIH. *Concurrent Pos:* USPHS res fel, Uppsala, 61-62; mem, panel postdoctoral fels, NSF, 71; consult, Associateship Off, Comn Human Resources, Nat Acad Sci, 81; mem Life Sci Panel, Nat Res Coun Assoc Prog; mem, Neurol A study sect, NIH, 88-93, chair, 91-93. *Mem:* AAAS; Am Asn Anat; Am Inst Biol Sci; Am Asn Hist Med; Soc Neurosci. *Res:* Effects of radiation on maturing nervous system; normal maturation and myelin formation in spinal cord; regenerative and reparative capacities of immature spinal cord; glial development and maturation. *Mailing Add:* Dept Anat 510 Univ Ark Med Sci Little Rock AR 72205-7199. *Fax:* 501-686-6382; *E-Mail:* sgilmore@anatomymail.uams.edu

GILMORE, STUART IRBY, SPEECH PATHOLOGY, AUDIOLOGY. *Current Pos:* RETIRED. *Personal Data:* b New York, NY, July 24, 30; c 6. *Educ:* State Univ NY, Albany, BA, 50, MA, 51; Univ Wis, PhD(speech), 62. *Prof Exp:* Instr commun, Talladega Col, 51-53; dir speech path & audiol, Jr League Speech & Hearing Clin, Columbia, 54-60; asst prof speech path, Peabody Col, Vanderbilt Univ, & dir, Bill Wilkerson Speech & Hearing Ctr, 60-62; asst prof speech, Univ Wis, 62-65; prof speech, La State Univ, 65-80; dir clin serv, Jeddah Inst Speech & Hearing, Suadi Arabia, 92-96. *Concurrent Pos:* Consult, 65-, Belle Chasse State Sch, 70-; lectr & supvr, Mayo Clin Sem on Laryngectomy Rehab, 81-85, Int Asn Laryngectomees Voice Inst, 82-85; adj prof, Dept Otorhinolaryngology, La State Univ Med Sch & Earl K Long Hosp. *Mem:* Sigma Xi; fel Am Speech-Lang & Hearing Asn; Comput Users in Speech; Am Cleft Palate Asn. *Res:* Communicative disorders of the aged; measures of speech and language proficiency; psychosocial concomitants laryngectomy. *Mailing Add:* 405 E Worthington Ave Charlotte NC 28203-5343

GILMORE, THOMAS DAVID, ONCOGENES, VIROLOGY. *Current Pos:* ASSOC PROF BIOL, BOSTON UNIV, 87- *Personal Data:* b Uniontown, Pa, Dec 28, 52; m 93, Christine Li. *Educ:* Princeton Univ, AB, 74; Univ Calif, Berkeley, PhD(zool), 84. *Prof Exp:* Fel, McArdle Labs & Jane Coffin Childs fel, Univ Wis, 84-87. *Concurrent Pos:* Prin investr, First Award, NIH, 88-93, Rol Res Grant, 93-; Study Sect, Am Cancer Soc, 91, 93 & NIH, 92. *Mem:* Am Soc Microbiol. *Res:* Role of the rel family of oncogenes in the normal and malignant control of cell growth. *Mailing Add:* Biol Dept Boston Univ 5 Cummington St Boston MA 02215. *Fax:* 617-353-6340

GILMORE, THOMAS MEYER, organic chemistry, for more information see previous edition

GILMORE, WILLIAM FRANKLIN, MEDICINAL CHEMISTRY, PEPTIDES. *Current Pos:* vpres acad affairs, 93-96, EXEC VPRES & VPRES ACAD AFFAIRS, PROF CHEM, W VA INST TECHNOL, 96- *Personal Data:* b Bailey, Miss, Mar 26, 35; m 63, Ann Louise Gauthier; c Kristin Ann & Paul David. *Educ:* Va Mil Inst, BS, 57; Mass Inst Technol, PhD(org chem), 61. *Prof Exp:* Chemist antiradiation drugs, Walter Reed Army Inst Res, 62-63; res assoc peptides, Inst Molecular Biophys, Fla State Univ, 63-64; assoc chemist org synthesis, Midwest Res Inst, 64-65; sr chemist, 65-67; from asst prof to assoc prof pharmaceut chem, Sch Pharm, Univ Miss, 67-71, chmn dept, 69-71, prof med chem, 71-93, chmn dept, 71-80 & 88-93. *Concurrent Pos:* Mem pharmacol & toxicol training comt, Nat Inst Gen Med Sci, 67-70; mem review comt, Nat Asn Bds Pharm Licensure, 80- *Mem:* AAAS; Am Chem Soc; Am Asn Cols Pharm; Sigma Xi; Am Peptide Soc. *Res:* Organic synthesis; mechanism of Favorskii rearrangement; synthesis of radioprotective compounds; synthesis of polypeptides; peptido minetics. *Mailing Add:* 161 Faxette Pike Montgomery WV 25136. *Fax:* 304-442-3059; *E-Mail:* wfgilm@wvit.wvnet.edu

GILMOUR, CAMPBELL MORRISON, BACTERIOLOGY. *Current Pos:* HEAD DEPT BACT, UNIV IDAHO, 70- *Personal Data:* b Scotland, July 2, 16; nat US; m 43; c 3. *Educ:* Univ BC, BSA, 41, MSA, 45; Univ Wis, PhD(bact), 49. *Prof Exp:* Assoc prof bact, Okla Agr & Mech Col, 49-51; from assoc prof to prof, Ore State Univ, 51-67; dir, Ctr Environ Biol, Univ Utah, 67-70. *Concurrent Pos:* Study-lectureship, Rockefeller Found; consult water pollution. *Mem:* Am Soc Microbiol. *Res:* Classification and metabolism of soil microorganisms. *Mailing Add:* 2335 15th St Lewiston ID 83501

GILMOUR, ERNEST HENRY, PALEONTOLOGY. *Current Pos:* vprovost, Grad Studies & Res, 87-89, provost, 89-91, PROF GEOL, EASTERN WASH UNIV, 67- *Personal Data:* b Adin, Calif, Aug 17, 36; m 82, Peggy J Keller; c Ernest H Jr, William B, Nadine M (Madrazo) & Laura L. *Educ:* Univ Southern Calif, BS, 60; Univ Mont, MS, 64; PhD(geol), 67. *Honors & Awards:* Trustees Medal, Nat Acad Sci; Fulbright lectr, Pakistan. *Prof Exp:* Geologist, Cominco Am, Inc, 63; instr, Univ Mont, 64; geologist, US Geol Surv, 64-65; asst prof mineral fuels & geologist, Mont Bur Mines & Geol, 65-67. *Concurrent Pos:* Teaching asst, Univ Southern Calif, 60-61; mem staff, Goudkoff & Hughes, Calif, 67; consult; exchange scientist, Russia. *Mem:* Fel Geol Soc Am; Am Asn Petrol Geol; AAAS; Paleont Soc; Am Inst Mining Engrs; Sigma Xi. *Res:* Carbonate petrology, paleontology and paleoecology; Paleozoic Bryozoa, Coelenterata, Protozoa and Brachiopoda; taxonomic and biostratigraphic studies of Permian bryozoa in western US, Pakistan, USSR, Poland, and Canada. *Mailing Add:* Dept Geol Eastern Wash Univ Cheney WA 99004. *Fax:* 509-359-4386; *E-Mail:* egilmour@ewu.edu

GILMOUR, HUGH STEWART ALLEN, PHYSICAL CHEMISTRY, PHOTOGRAPHY. *Current Pos:* CONSULT, 90- *Personal Data:* b Alta, Can, Apr 25, 26; m 51; c 2. *Educ:* Univ BC, BA, 49; Univ Utah, PhD(chem), 53. *Prof Exp:* Fel chem, Univ Ill, 53-55; res chemist, Eastman Kodak Co, 55-68, res assoc, 68-89. *Mem:* Soc Photog Scientists & Engrs. *Res:* Photosynthesis; photochemistry; color photographic systems; color thermographic systems and media; digital recording media; pollution detectors. *Mailing Add:* 183 Oakdale Dr Rochester NY 14618-1148. *E-Mail:* humar@aol.com

GILMOUR, MARION NYHOLM H, MICROBIOLOGY, DENTAL RESEARCH. *Current Pos:* RETIRED. *Personal Data:* b Vancouver, BC, Jan 29, 28; US citizen; m 51; c 2. *Educ:* Univ BC, BA, 49; Univ Ill, Urbana, MSc, 52, PhD(microbiol), 57. *Prof Exp:* Jr res officer microbial genetics, Atomic Energy Can, Ltd, 49-51; head, Dept Microbiol & res assoc, Eastman Dent Ctr, 57-77; clin instr, Univ Rochester, 60-69, from asst prof to assoc prof dent, 74-90. *Concurrent Pos:* Consult, Nat Inst Dent Res, 71-, mem study sect, 73-75; consult, Microbiol Ore Curriculum Comt, Am Asn Dent Schs. *Mem:* AAAS; Am Inst Biol Sci; Am Soc Microbiol; Int Asn Dent Res; NY Acad Sci. *Res:* Oral microorganism, their physiological amd metabolic capabilities and factors affecting them both in vitro and in vivo. *Mailing Add:* 183 Oakdale Dr Rochester NY 14618

GILMOUR, THOMAS HENRY JOHNSTONE, INVERTEBRATE ZOOLOGY. *Current Pos:* from asst prof to assoc prof, 64-80, PROF INVERT ZOOL, UNIV SASK, 80- *Personal Data:* b Dunoon, Scotland, Sept 27, 36; m 62; c 2. *Educ:* Univ Glasgow, BSc, 60, PhD(zool), 63. *Prof Exp:* Asst lectr zool, Univ Exeter, 63-64. *Mem:* Can Soc Zool; Am Soc Zool. *Res:* Functional morphology of invertebrates. *Mailing Add:* Dept Biol Univ Sask 112 Science Pl Saskatoon SK S7N 5E2 Can

GILMOUR-STALLSWORTH, LISA K, CARDIOVASCULAR MODELLING, CHEMICAL ANALYSIS-HAZARDOUS WASTE. *Current Pos:* INDUST HYG, HOUSTON LIGHTING & POWER, 96- *Personal Data:* b Rochester, NY, Jan 9, 59; m 83, George Stallsworth. *Educ:* Cornell Univ, BS, 80, AB, 81; Univ Tex, Austin, MS, 83, PhD, 91. *Prof Exp:* Engr, Sun Oil Co, 79 & Univ Tex, 81-90; at Baker Hughes, 91-96. *Concurrent Pos:* Environ columnist, Local Newspaper; mem, Round Rock Environ Rd; mentor eng prog; teacher indust hyg. *Mem:* Am Indust Hyg Asn; Am Soc Safety Engrs; Am Bd Indust Hyg; Am Water Works Asn. *Res:* Pharmacologic manipulation of peritoneal mass transfer; engineering analysis of cardiovascular function. *Mailing Add:* 9302 Carvel Houston TX 77036. *E-Mail:* lisa__stallsworth@hlp.com

GILOW, HELMUTH MARTIN, ORGANIC CHEMISTRY. *Current Pos:* MEM STAFF CHEM DEPT, RHODES COL, MEMPHIS. *Personal Data:* b Cedarburg, Wis, Sept 11, 33; m 67; c 1. *Educ:* Wartburg Col, BA, 55; Univ Iowa, MS, 57, PhD, 59. *Prof Exp:* Assoc prof, 59-69, chmn dept, 76-78, prof chem, Southwestern Memphis, 69- *Mem:* Am Chem Soc; Sigma Xi. *Res:* Pyrimidine and purine type derivatives; reactions and properties of beta diketones; substituent effects of positive poles in aromatic substitution; pyrrole chemistry; photochemistry. *Mailing Add:* 877 N Barksdale Memphis TN 38107

GILPIN, MICHAEL JAMES, PURE MATHEMATICS. *Current Pos:* asst prof, 72-80, ASSOC PROF MATH, MICH TECHNOL UNIV, 80- *Personal Data:* b Washington, Iowa, Mar 4, 41; m 66; c 1. *Educ:* Parsons Col, BS, 63; Univ Ariz, MA, 65; Univ Ore, PhD(math), 72. *Prof Exp:* Instr math, Gonzaga Univ, 65-68. *Mem:* Am Math Soc; Math Asn Am. *Res:* Symmetric spaces and symmetric forms of degree greater than three over fields. *Mailing Add:* Dept Math Mich Technol Univ Houghton MI 49931-1295

GILPIN, ROGER KEITH, CHROMATOGRAPHY, SPECTROSCOPY. *Current Pos:* From to asst prof to assoc prof, 78-86, PROF ANALYTICAL CHEM, DEPT CHMN, KENT STATE UNIV, 86- *Personal Data:* b Middlesboro, Ky, Apr 29, 47; m 67; c 4. *Educ:* Ind State Univ, BS, 69; Univ Ariz, PhD(analytical chem), 73. *Prof Exp:* Sr scientist anal chem, McNeil Labs Inc, 73-76, group leader, 76-78. *Concurrent Pos:* Sr tech adv, IBM Instruments, 81-83. *Mem:* Am Chem Soc; Sigma Xi; Soc Appl Spectros; AAAS. *Res:* Fundamental and applied thin layer, gas, and high pressure liquid chromatography; organometallic surface reactions; infrared radiation, electronic spin resonance and nuclear magnetic resonance of chemically modified surfaces; pharmaceutical analysis. *Mailing Add:* 134 Oellman Hall Wright State Univ Dayton OH 45435

GILREATH, JAMES PRESTON, WEED CONTROL, HERBICIDE DEGRADATION. *Current Pos:* Asst prof, 81-86, ASSOC PROF WEED SCI, UNIV FLA, 86- *Personal Data:* b Greenville, SC, Sept 20, 47; m 75, Phyllis Robinson. *Educ:* Clemson Univ, BS, 74, MS, 76; Univ Fla, PhD(hort), 81. *Mem:* Weed Sci Soc Am; Am Soc Hort Sci. *Res:* Development of chemical weed control programs for floriculutral and vegetable crops and investigations into herbicide movement and in soil; herbicide degradation; weed biology. *Mailing Add:* Univ Fla Gulf Coast Res & Educ Ctr 5007 60th St E Bradenton FL 34203. *Fax:* 941-751-7639

GILROY, JAMES JOSEPH, BACTERIOLOGY. *Current Pos:* from asst chmn to chmn dept, 67-70, ASSOC PROF BACT, BOSTON COL, 64- *Personal Data:* b Scranton, Pa, June 5, 26; m 58; c 4. *Educ:* Univ Scranton, BS, 49; Cath Univ Am, MS, 51; Univ Md, PhD(bact), 58. *Prof Exp:* Clin bacteriologist, Children's Hosp, Washington, DC, 52-53; bacteriologist, Army Chem Ctr, Ft Detrick, Md, 53-54; asst bact, Univ Md, 54-57; from asst prof to assoc prof, Colo State Univ, 57-64. *Mem:* Am Soc Microbiol. *Res:* Bacterial metabolism; nutritional requirements for growth of rumen bacteria; nutritional requirements for toxin production by Clostridium perfringens; induction of fermentation enzymes in bacteria; bacterial growth inhibition by d-camphor. *Mailing Add:* Dept Biol Boston Col 140 Commonwealth Ave Chestnut Hill MA 02167-3800

GILROY, JOHN, CEREBROVASCULAR DISEASE, MULTIPLE SCLEROSIS. *Current Pos:* From instr to prof neurol, 63-67, chmn, 68-86, CLIN PROF, WAYNE STATE UNIV, 86- *Personal Data:* b Eng, Mar 29, 25; US citizen; m 52, 75, Marcia Kollenberg; c 3. *Educ:* Univ Durham, MB & BS, 48, MD, 57, FRCP(C), 65; FACP, 71. *Concurrent Pos:* Chmn neurol, William Beaumont Hosp, Royal Oak, Mich. *Mem:* Am Neurol Asn; Am Acad Neurol; Am Soc Neuroimaging. *Res:* Cerebrovascular disease and neuroaudiology; author and co-author of 110 publications. *Mailing Add:* 27177 Lahser Rd Suite 103 Southfield MI 48034-8467

GILRUTH, ROBERT R(OWE), AERONAUTICAL ENGINEERING, AEROSPACE ENGINEERING. *Current Pos:* RETIRED. *Personal Data:* b Nashwauk, Minn, Oct 8, 13; m 37; c 1. *Educ:* Univ Minn, BS, 35, MS, 36. *Hon Degrees:* DSc, Univ Minn, 62, George Washington Univ, 62, Ind Inst Technol, 62; DEng, Mich Technol Univ, 63; LLD, NMex State Univ, 70. *Honors & Awards:* Reed Award, Am Inst Aeronaut & Astronaut, 50; Louis Hill Space Transportation Award, 62; Goddard Mem Trophy, 62; Spirit of St Louis Medal, Am Soc Mech Engrs, 65; Guggenheim Int Astronaut Award, Inst Aeronaut Sci, 66; Space Flight Award, Am Astronaut Soc, 67; James Watts Int Medal, 71; Robert J Collier Trophy, 72; Nat Aviation Club Award for Achievement, 71. *Prof Exp:* Mem, Nat Adv Comt Aeronaut, NASA, 37-43, asst chief, Flight Res Div, 43-45, chief, Pilotless Aircraft Res Div, 45-51, asst dir, Langley Res Ctr, 51-58, dir, Proj Mercury, Space Task Group, NASA, 58-61, dir, Manned Spacecraft Ctr, 61-73, consult to admir, Johnson Space Ctr, 74-76. *Concurrent Pos:* Consult, Res & Develop Bd, 46-58; mem, Sci Adv Bd, US Air Force, 51-57 & Ballistic Missile Defense Comt, 55; mem bd dir, Bunker-Ramo Corp, 74-78; consult aerospace, 78- *Mem:* Nat Acad Sci; Nat Acad Eng; hon fel Am Inst Aeronaut & Astronaut; hon fel Royal Aeronaut Soc. *Res:* Airplane stability and structures; hydrofoil craft; aerodynamics; rocket propulsion; manned space flight; high temperature facilites. *Mailing Add:* 2600 Barracks Rd Charlottesville VA 22901

GILSTEIN, JACOB BURRILL, PHYSICS, RESEARCH ADMINISTRATION. *Current Pos:* RETIRED. *Personal Data:* b NY, Feb 5, 23; m, Ethel Ladov; c Saul, Margot, Zachary, Amy & Judith. *Educ:* City Col New York, BS, 43; NY Univ, MS, 50, PhD, 58. *Prof Exp:* Physicist pilotless aircraft instrumentation, Nat Adv Comt Aeronaut, 46-47; res assoc, Combustion, Rocket Propulsion, Detonation, Res Div, NY Univ, 47-56; physicist, Missiles & Space Vehicles Dept, Gen Elec Corp, Pa, 56-59, physicist systs appln, Defense Systs Dept, 59-61, systs engr, Missile & Space Div, 61-66, mgr aerospace physics lab, Reentry Systs Dept, 66-68, mgr aerospace physics & systs anal, 68; Dept Ballistic Missile Defense, Off Asst Secy Army & dir, Army Advan Ballistic Missile Defense Agency, 68-74; mgr, Advan Syst Eng, Gen Elec Corp, 74-79, prog gen mgr, Advan Systs, 79-84, mgr, Penetration & Defense Systs, 84-87, chief scientist, Strategic Syst Dept, 87-91. *Mem:* Am Phys Soc; assoc fel Am Inst Aeronaut & Astronaut; Sigma Xi; Am Defense Preparedness Asn. *Res:* Instrumentation; combustion studies of jets and rockets; boundary layer theory; detonation in solid explosives; hypersonic aerodynamics; plasma physics; vulnerability and hardening; penetration aids; strategic defense systems; management of high energy laser developments; electronic counter measures. *Mailing Add:* 666 W Germantown Pike Apt 611N Plymouth Meeting PA 19462

GILSTRAP, FRANKLIN EPHRIAM, ENTOMOLOGY. *Current Pos:* Asst prof, 74-80, ASSOC PROF ENTOM, TEX A&M UNIV, 80- *Personal Data:* b Clovis, Calif, Apr 24, 44; m 64; c 1. *Educ:* Fresno State Col, BA, 68; Univ Calif, Riverside, MS, 71, PhD(entom), 74. *Mem:* Entom Soc Am; Can Entom Soc; Int Orgn Biol Control; Acarological Soc Am. *Res:* Biological control of arthropod pests of grain sorghum, wheat, corn and citrus; to obtain, release, establish and evaluate exotic natural enemies developing bio-ecological information for both pests and beneficials. *Mailing Add:* Dept Entom Tex A&M Univ College Station TX 77843-0100

GILTINAN, DAVID ANTHONY, PHYSICS. *Current Pos:* Assoc prof, 68-70, head dept, 69-72, PROF PHYSICS, EDINBORO UNIV PA, 70-, CHAIR, 91- *Personal Data:* b Jamestown, NY, Dec 7, 36; m 67, Janice M Peterson; c Brian D & Kevin P. *Educ:* Case Inst Technol, BS, 59, MS, 63, PhD(physics), 68. *Mem:* Am Soc Eng Educ; Am Asn Physics Teachers. *Res:* Theoretical and nuclear physics; elementary particle reactions; phenomenological computer analysis. *Mailing Add:* Dept Physics & Technol Edinboro Univ Pa Edinboro PA 16444-0001. *E-Mail:* giltinan@edinboro.edu

GILULA, LOUIS ARNOLD, MUSCULOSKELETAL, RADIOLOGY. *Current Pos:* From instr to assoc prof, 73-82, PROF RADIO K, MALLINCKRODT INST RADIOL, WASHINGTON UNIV SCH MED, 82-, PROF ORTHOP SURG & PROF PLASTIC SURG, 96- *Personal Data:* b Lubbock, Tex, Oct 21, 42; m 70, Deborah L Schline; c Tanya & Ian. *Educ:* Univ Ill, Chicago, MD, 67; Am Bd Radiol, dipl, 73. *Concurrent Pos:* Dir, musculoskeletal sect, Mallinckrodt Inst Radiol, Wash Univ Sch Med, 75- *Mem:* Fel Am Col Radiol; Int Skeletal Soc; AMA; Soc Radiol Soc NAm; Asn Univ Radiol; Am Roentgen Ray Soc; hon mem Am Soc Surg Hand. *Res:* Musculoskeletal radiology; three dimensional imaging of the musculoskeletal system; author of more than 350 technical articles & publications and two text books; wrist radiology and anatomy. *Mailing Add:* 250 Dielman Rd St Louis MO 63124

GILULA, NORTON BERNARD, MOLECULAR & CELL BIOLOGY. *Current Pos:* MEM MOLECULAR BIOL, SCRIPPS RES INST, 86-, DEAN GRAD STUDIES, 88- & CHAIR, DEPT CELL BIOL, 91- *Personal Data:* b Dec 9, 44. *Educ:* Southern Ill Univ, BA, 66, MA, 68; Univ Calif, Berkeley, PhD(physiol), 71. *Honors & Awards:* Burton Award, Electron Micros Soc Am, 79. *Prof Exp:* Res fel anat, Harvard Med Sch, 72; postdoctoral fel cell biol, Rockefeller Univ, 72-73, from asst prof to assoc prof, 73-81; prof cell biol, Baylor Col Med, 81-86. *Concurrent Pos:* Assoc ed, Develop Biol, 76-78, J Neurocytol, 77-78; chmn, Biol Sci Sect, NY Acad Sci, 77 & Molecular Biol Study Sect, NIH, 80-81; mem, Sci Adv Bd, Wills Found, 82-, Nat Adv Coun, Nat Inst Gen Med Sci, NIH, 84-87 & Panel Cell Biol, Nat Res Coun, 85-86; ed, Current Opinion Cell Biol, 89- *Mem:* Fel AAAS. *Mailing Add:* Dept Cell Biol MB6 Scripps Res Inst 10666 N Torrey Pines Rd La Jolla CA 92037-1092. *Fax:* 619-554-6945

GILVARG, CHARLES, BIOCHEMISTRY. *Current Pos:* prof chem, Frick Chem Lab, Princeton Univ, 64-70, chmn dept biochem sci, 70-73, prof, 70-89, PROF MOLECULAR BIOL, PRINCETON UNIV, 90- *Personal Data:* b New York, NY, June 13, 25; m 49; c 4. *Educ:* Cooper Union, BChE, 48; Univ Chicago, PhD(biochem), 51. *Honors & Awards:* Paul-Lewis Award, Am Chem Soc, 62. *Prof Exp:* Nat Found Infantile Paralysis fel, 52-54; from instr to prof biochem, Sch Med, NY Univ, 54-64. *Concurrent Pos:* Cancer res scholar, 55-58; USPHS sr res fel, 58-61, career res develop award, 61-64, consult, 62-; Guggenheim Fel, 64-66; LaRoche Fel, 73-74; ed, J Biol Chem, 65-70, 72-78 & Biochem et Biophysica Acta, 78-81. *Mem:* AAAS; Am Soc Biol Chem; Am Chem Soc; Harvey Soc. *Res:* Intermediary metabolism, particularly in microorganisms. *Mailing Add:* Dept Molecular Biol Princeton Univ Princeton NJ 08544-0001. *Fax:* 609-258-2759

GIMARC, BENJAMIN M, THEORETICAL CHEMISTRY. *Current Pos:* from asst prof to assoc prof, 66-78, head dept, 73-76 & 82-85, PROF CHEM, UNIV SC, 78- *Personal Data:* b Nogales, Ariz, Dec 5, 34; m 59, Jerry Dell Watts. *Educ:* Rice Univ, BA, 56; Northwestern Univ, PhD(phys chem), 63. *Prof Exp:* Instr chem, Northwestern Univ, 61-62; res assoc, Johns Hopkins Univ, 62-63, USPHS fel & lectr chem, 63-64; asst prof, Ga Inst Technol, 64-66. *Concurrent Pos:* Vis scholar, Princeton Univ, 76-77, Univ Calif, Berkeley, 85; Nat Acad Sci exchange scientist, Zagreb, Yugoslavia, 78, 82, 84. *Mem:* Am Chem Soc; Am Phys Soc. *Res:* Development of qualitative molecular orbital theory and applications to problems of molecular shapes; relative molecular stabilities; reaction mechanisms; chemical applications of graph theory; strain and resonance in inorganic rings and clusters. *Mailing Add:* Dept Chem Univ SC Columbia SC 29208

GIMBLE, JEFFREY M, IMMUNOBIOLOGY. *Current Pos:* ASST MEM, OKLA MED RES FOUND, OKLAHOMA CITY, 87- *Personal Data:* b Oct 14, 55. *Educ:* Dartmouth Col, BA, 76; Yale Univ, MA, 80, PhD(cell biol), 81, MD, 82. *Prof Exp:* Intern, Dept Internal Med, Barnes Hosp, Wash Univ, St Louis, Mo, 82-83, jr resident, 83-84; med staff fel res, Lab Immunogenetics, Nat Inst Allergy & Infectious Dis, NIH, 84-87. *Concurrent Pos:* Adj asst prof, Dept Microbiol & Immunol, Health Sci Ctr, Univ Okla, Oklahoma City, 88- *Res:* Author of numerous publications. *Mailing Add:* Dept Immunobiol & Cancer Oklahoma Med Res Found 825 NE 13th St Oklahoma City OK 73104-5097. *Fax:* 405-271-8568

GIMBRONE, MICHAEL ANTHONY, JR, EXPERIMENTAL PATHOLOGY, CELL BIOLOGY. *Current Pos:* res assoc, 74-76, from asst prof to assoc prof, 79-85, PROF PATH, HARVARD MED SCH, 85- *Personal Data:* b Buffalo, NY, Nov 16, 43; m 71; c 3. *Educ:* Cornell Univ, AB, 65; Harvard Med Sch, MD, 70. *Honors & Awards:* Exp Path Award, Warner-Lambert Parke-Davis, 82. *Prof Exp:* Intern, resident & res fel, Mass Gen Hosp, 70-72; staff assoc pathophysiol, Nat Cancer Inst, 72-74. *Concurrent Pos:* Mem vis fac, W Alton Jones Cell Sci Ctr, 76-78; consult, Nat Heart, Lung & Blood Inst, NIH, 76-; estab investr, Am Heart Asn, 77-82; head, Vascular Pathophysiol Res Lab, 77-85, dir, vascular res div, Brigham & Women's Hosp, 85- *Mem:* Nat Acad Sci; Am Soc Cell Biol; AAAS; Tissue Cult Asn; Am Soc Hematol; Am Asn Pathologists; Am Heart Asn. *Res:* Cardiovascular pathophysiology, especially atherosclerosis, thrombosis and hypertension; vascular cell biology. *Mailing Add:* Vascular Res Div LMRC 4th Floor Brigham & Womens Hosp 221 Longwood Ave Boston MA 02115-5817. *Fax:* 617-732-5933

GIMELLI, SALVATORE PAUL, PHARMACEUTICAL CHEMISTRY. *Current Pos:* from asst prof to assoc prof, 54-70, PROF CHEM, FAIRLEIGH DICKINSON UNIV, 70-, CHMN DEPT, 77- *Personal Data:* b New York, NY, Feb 22, 19; m 44; c 1. *Educ:* St John's Univ, NY, BS, 41; Fordham Univ, MS, 47; Rutgers Univ, PhD, 66. *Prof Exp:* Chemist, Philco Corp, 42-45; asst chem, Fordham Univ, 45-47; instr, Lafayette Col, 47-50; res chemist pharmaceut, Reed & Carnrick, 50-54. *Mem:* Am Chem Soc. *Res:* Synthetic medicinal products. *Mailing Add:* 42 Terrace Ave Rochelle Park NJ 07662

GIMLETT, JAMES I, optics, geophysics, for more information see previous edition

GIMPLE, GLENN EDWARD, INORGANIC CHEMISTRY. *Current Pos:* INSTRNL COORDR, WOLF CREEK NUCLEAR OPER CORP, 86- *Personal Data:* b Lovewell, Kans, Sept 15, 40; m 62; c 2. *Educ:* Kans State Teachers Col, BA, 62; Univ Kans, PhD(chem), 69. *Prof Exp:* From asst prof to assoc prof chem, Emporia State Univ, 65-86. *Mem:* Am Chem Soc. *Res:* Coordination compounds; use of substituted 2, 2-bipyrimidines as ligands in complexes of transition metals; kinetics and mechanisms of inorganic reactions; electron transfer reactions. *Mailing Add:* 2265 M N Hwy 99 Emporia KS 66801

GIN, W(INSTON), ROCKET PROPULSION. *Current Pos:* res engr, Calif Inst Technol, 57-59, res group supvr, 59-61, asst sect chief, Solid Propellant Eng Sect, 61-63, sect chief, 63-75, sect mgr, Solid Propulsion & Environ Systs Sect, 75-78, sect mgr, Propulsion Systs Sect, Jet Propulsion Lab, 78-82, div staff engr, 82-89, EXEC ASST TO ASSOC DIR, CALIF INST TECHNOL, 89- *Personal Data:* b San Francisco, Calif, Aug 24, 28; m 60, Ellen Ong; c Robert. *Educ:* Univ Ariz, BA, 50, BS, 51; Univ Calif, Los Angeles, MA, 55, MS, 59. *Honors & Awards:* Solid Propellant Rocketry Team Award, Nat Aeronaut & Space Admin, 76. *Prof Exp:* Mem tech staff, Hughes Aircraft Co, 53-57. *Mem:* Am Inst Aeronaut & Astronaut; Sigma Xi. *Res:* Rocket propulsion; gas dynamics; pyrotechnics; chemical processes; granted US patent for apparatus and method for control of a solid rocket fueled vehicle. *Mailing Add:* 1418 Star Ridge Dr Monterey Park CA 91754. *Fax:* 818-354-3122; *E-Mail:* winston.gin@jpl.nasa.gov

GINDLER, JAMES EDWARD, NUCLEAR CHEMISTRY. *Current Pos:* RETIRED. *Personal Data:* b Highland, Ill, Jan 4, 25; m 49, Marguerite Rhodes; c William P, Jeffrey A, Ann E & Gregory S. *Educ:* Eastern Ill State Col, BS, 50; Univ Ill, MS, 51, PhD(chem), 54. *Honors & Awards:* Co-recipient, Genia Czerniak Prize, Ahavat Zion Found, 74. *Prof Exp:* Assoc chemist, Argonne Nat Lab, 53-72, chemist, 72-90, asst div dir, 83-90. *Concurrent Pos:* Vis chemist, Nuclear Res Ctr, Karlsruhe, 64-66. *Mem:* Sigma Xi. *Res:* Heavy element chemistry and nuclear properties; fission product chemistry and spectroscopy; fission process. *Mailing Add:* 625 62nd St Downers Grove IL 60516

GINELL, WILLIAM SEAMAN, ART CONSERVATION SCIENCE, ARCHITECTURAL CONSERVATION. *Current Pos:* head mat sci, 84-90, HEAD ARCHT CONSERV RES, GETTY CONSERV INST, 90- *Personal Data:* b New York, NY, Aug 24, 23; m 46, Sally Friedman; c Richard Scott, Cary David & Carolyn Beth (Plumb). *Educ:* Polytech Inst Brooklyn, BS, 43; Univ Wis, PhD(chem), 49. *Prof Exp:* Asst chem, Substitute Alley Mat Labs, Columbia Univ, 43-44; res chemist, SED, Oak Ridge, Tenn, 44-46; res asst, Univ Wis, 46-49; from assoc chemist to chemist, Brookhaven Nat Lab, 49-58; sr res specialist, Atomics Int Div, NAm Aviation, Inc, 58-61; head inorg chem sect, Aerospace Corp, 61-63; prin scientist, Douglas Aircraft Co, Calif, 63-67; sect chief, McDonnell Douglas Astronaut Co, Huntington Beach, 67-78, prin staff scientist, 78-84. *Concurrent Pos:* Consult, J Paul Getty Mus & McDonnell Douglas Astronau Co. *Mem:* Fel AAAS; Am Soc Testing Mats; Am Inst Conserv; Int Inst Conserv; Asn Preserv Technol. *Res:* Materials science; art conservation science; seismic stabilization of historic structures; stone and earthen architecture conservation; liquid metal chemistry; nuclear and laser radiation damage; semiconductors; infrared materials. *Mailing Add:* Getty Conserv Inst 1200 Getty Ctr Dr Los Angeles CA 90049. *E-Mail:* bginell@getty.edu

GINE-MASDEU, EVARIST, LIMIT THEOREMS IN PROBABILITY THEORY. *Current Pos:* PROF MATH, UNIV CONN, 90- *Personal Data:* b Catalonia, Spain, July 31, 44; m 66, Rosalind Eastaway; c 2. *Educ:* Univ Barcelona, dipl, 66, DSc, 76; Mass Inst Technol, PhD(math), 73. *Honors & Awards:* Venezuelan & Catalan Nat Prizes in Math, 77. *Prof Exp:* Asst prof math, Univ Carabobo, Venezuela, 66-70; lectr math & statist, Univ Calif, Berkeley, 74-75; res assoc, Venezuelan Inst Sci Res, 73-80, head dept, 75-79; assoc prof, Autonomous Univ Barcelona, Spain, 77-80; assoc prof math, La State Univ, 80-82; from assoc prof to prof math, Tex A&M Univ, 82-90. *Concurrent Pos:* Vis prof, Louis Pasteur Univ, France, 78, 87, Ctr Recerca Mat, Barcelona, 90, 92, 93, Univ Paris, Sud, 93; prin investr, NSF, 80-; assoc ed, J Theoret Probab, 89-; prof, Grad Ctr, City Univ NY, Staten Island, 88-90. *Mem:* Fel Inst Math Statist; Bernoulli Soc; Catalan Sci Soc; Int Statist Inst. *Res:* Statistics of directions; central limit theorem in infinite dimensional spaces; limit theorems for empirical processes; bootstrap. *Mailing Add:* Dept Math Univ Conn Storrs CT 06269. *Fax:* 860-486-4238; *E-Mail:* gine@uconnvm.vconn.edu

GINER, JOSE D, ELECTROCHEMISTRY, PHYSICAL CHEMISTRY. *Current Pos:* PRES, GINER INC, 73- *Personal Data:* b Teruel, Spain, Aug 4, 28; US citizen; c Jose L, Isabel, A Silvana, Julia & J Cristina. *Educ:* Univ Valencia, BS & MS, 51; Univ Madrid, Dr(chem), 55. *Prof Exp:* Staff scientist electrochem res, CSIC, Madrid, 55-56; res fel, Univ Erlangen, 56-58 & Univ Bonn, 58-61; proj engr fuel cell res, Pratt & Whitney Aircraft, 61-65; asst dir electrochem res, Tyco Labs, 65-73. *Mem:* Am Chem Soc; Am Inst Chem Engrs; Int Soc Electrochem; Electrochem Soc; Am Soc Testing & Mat. *Res:* Fuel cells; electrocatalysis; batteries; electrochemical sensors; corrosion; general electrode kinetics; biomedical devices. *Mailing Add:* 14 Spring St Brookline MA 02154-4497

GINER, JOSE-LUIS, BIOSYNTHETIC CHEMISTRY, MARINE NATURAL PRODUCTS. *Current Pos:* ASST PROF ORG CHEM, ENVIRON SCI & FORESTRY, STATE UNIV NY, 95- *Educ:* Brandeis Univ, AB, 79, MA, 80; Standford Univ, PhD(chem), 91. *Prof Exp:* Postdoctoral fel, Eidgenossische Tech Sch, Zurich, 91-93, Harvard Med Sch, 93-95. *Mem:* Am Chem Soc. *Res:* Application of biochemistry and physical-organic chemistry to the study of natural products; biosynthesis, especially steroids of marine origin; development of new synthetic methods. *Mailing Add:* Dept Chem Col Environ Sci & Forestry State Univ NY Syracuse NY 13210. *Fax:* 315-470-6856; *E-Mail:* jlginer@syr.edu

GINER-SOROLLA, ALFREDO, ORGANIC CHEMISTRY, BIOCHEMISTRY. *Current Pos:* asst prof, 65-74, assoc prof biochem, Sloan-Kettering Div, Med Col, Cornell Univ, 74-82, ASSOC MEM, SLOAN-KETTERING INST, 67- *Personal Data:* b Vinaros, Spain, Sept 23, 19; m 64; c 1. *Educ:* Univ Madrid, MS, 47, Dr Pharm, 54; Cornell Univ, PhD, 58. *Honors & Awards:* Valencia Sci Prize, 77. *Prof Exp:* Asst tuberc study, Andreu Labs, Barcelona, 47-52; sci adv, Span Div, Farbwerke Hoechst, 52-54; res assoc, Sloan-Kettering Inst, 57-60; vis scientist, Univ Chem Lab, Cambridge Univ, 60-63; assoc, Sloan-Kettering Inst, 63-67. *Concurrent Pos:* Asst, Sch Pharm, Univ Barcelona, 51-54; res fel, Sloan-Kettering Inst, 54-57; vis prof, sr investr, Dept Pharmacol, Immunopharmacol Prog, Col Med, Univ SFLA, 83- *Mem:* Am Chem Soc; Am Asn Cancer Res; AAAS. *Res:* Synthesis of new purine antimetabolites and immunomodulators as antiviral and anticancer agents; carcinogenesis studies of nitrosated DNA and RNA bases and psychotropic and their prevention. *Mailing Add:* Plaza Sant Antoni No 26 Univ SFla 12901 N 30th St Box 9 Vinaros 12500 Spain

GINEVAN, MICHAEL EDWARD, RISK ANALYSIS, ENVIRONMENTAL MONITORING. *Current Pos:* MANAGING PRINCIPAL, STEP 5 CORP, 93- *Personal Data:* b Amsterdam, NY, Oct 22, 46; m 70, Jean Anderson; c Sean M. *Educ:* State Univ NY Albany, BS, 68; Univ Mass, Amherst, MS, 71; Univ Kans, PhD(mat biol), 76. *Honors & Awards:* Distinguished Achievement Medal, Am Statist Asn Sect on Statist & Environ, 93. *Prof Exp:* Res assoc, Environ Res Lab, Univ Kans Ctr Res Inc, 76-78; res assoc, Argonne Nat Lab, 78-79; asst statistician, Div Biol & Med Res, 79-82; biostatistician, Health Effects Br, US Nuclear Regulatory Comn, 82-86, biostatistical consult, 86-87; sr sci adv statist, Environ Corp, 87-88; prin scientist biostatist, Risk Focus Div, Versar, Inc, 88-91; dep dir, Off Epidemiol & Health Surveillance, US Dept Energy, 91-93. *Concurrent Pos:* Courtesy asst prof, Dept Entom, Univ Kans, 77-78; consult environ sci, Terrestial Biomonitoring Prog, Environ Protection Agency, 79-82; mem, Nuclear Regulatory Res Comt, Am Statist Asn, 84-; vchmn, Am Statist Asn, Comt Statist & the Environ, 87-; chmn, Organizing Comt, Eight Annual Am Statist Asn, Conf Radiation & Health, 88-89; mem, Radon Mitigation Subcomt US Environ Protection Agency, Radiation Adv Comt, 87; secy, Am Statist Asn Sect on Statist & the Environ, 89-90; mem, Nat Res Coun Comt Assessment of Possible Health Effects of the Ground Wave Emergency Network, 90-91. *Mem:* Am Statist Asn; Biomet Soc; Soc Epidemiol Res; AAAS; Soc Risk Analysis; Int Environmetrics Soc. *Res:* Statistical aspects of health and environmental issues; computer modeling of carcinogenic risk; design of pesticide residue surveys; estimation of human exposure; development of improved risk estimates for toxic materials. *Mailing Add:* 307 Hamilton Ave Silver Spring MD 20901-3336. *Fax:* 202-429-8762

GING, ROSALIE J, PSYCHIATRY. *Current Pos:* instr, 56-65, ASST PROF PSYCHIAT, MED SCH, UNIV MICH, ANN ARBOR, 65-; CHIEF PSYCHIAT SERV, VET ADMIN HOSP, 60- *Personal Data:* b Detroit, Mich, June 26, 21; c 2. *Educ:* Univ Mich, BA, 42, MD, 45; Am Bd Psychiat & Neurol, dipl, 57. *Prof Exp:* Intern, New Eng Hosp Women & Children, Boston, 46; resident, Pottstown Hosp, Pa, 48; pvt pract, 49; resident psychiat, Philadelphia State Hosp, 50-51, Conn State Hosp, Middletown, 52-53 & Univ Kans Hosp, Kansas City, 53-54; clin instr psychiat, Univ Kans, Kansas City, 55-56. *Concurrent Pos:* Staff psychiatrist, Vet Admin Hosp, Kansas City, 54-56; staff psychiatrist, Vet Admin Hosp, Ann Arbor, 56-58, asst chief psychiat serv, 58-60; mem clin psychopharmacol res rev comt, NIMH, 73-77; mem exec comt coop chemother studies in psychiat, Vet Admin. *Mem:* AMA; fel Am Psychiat Asn. *Res:* Consistency of electroencephalograms of normal subjects and psychiatric patients; correlation of electroencephalograms and multiple physical symptoms; clinical electroencephalography. *Mailing Add:* 2215 Fuller Rd Ann Arbor MI 48105-2300

GINGELL, RALPH, TOXICOLOGY. *Current Pos:* sr toxicologist, 80-88, STAFF TOXICOLOGIST, DEPT TOXICOL, SHELL OIL CO, 88- *Personal Data:* b Pontypool, Gt Brit, July 26, 45; m 76, Janet Tremel. *Educ:* Univ Birmingham, BSc, 66; Univ London, PhD(biochem), 70; Am Bd Toxicol, dipl, 85. *Prof Exp:* Lectr biochem, Brooklands Tech Col, Weybridge, 70-71; assoc prof biochem, Eppley Cancer Res Inst & Dept Biochem, Univ Nebr Med Ctr, Omaha, 71-80; res asst, St Mary's Hosp Med Sch, Univ London. *Concurrent Pos:* Sainsbury res fel, Nat Col Food Technol, Weybridge, Gt Brit, 70-71. *Mem:* Soc Toxicol. *Res:* Metabolism of xenobiotics, including toxicants and carcinogens in mammals in relation to their modes of action; industrial toxicology. *Mailing Add:* Dept Toxicol Shell Chem Co PO Box 4320 Houston TX 77210. *Fax:* 713-241-3325; *E-Mail:* gingell@neosoft.com

GINGER, LEONARD GEORGE, ORGANIC CHEMISTRY. *Current Pos:* PRES, L G GINGER & ASSOCS, 81- *Personal Data:* b Chicago, Ill, Oct 1, 18; m 43; c 6. *Educ:* Northwestern Univ, BS, 39; Univ Chicago, MS, 41; Yale Univ, PhD(org chem), 43. *Prof Exp:* Jr chemist, Merck & Co, NJ, 40-41; Pittsburgh Plate Glass fel, Northwestern Univ, 44, Int, Inc fel, 45-49; asst sci dir, Baxter Int, Inc, 49-53, dir org chem res, 53-57, dir res, 57-59, vpres res & develop, 59-69, sr vpres, 69-81. *Concurrent Pos:* Assoc chemist, Manhattan Proj, Univ Chicago, 44 & Off Sci Res & Develop, Northwestern Univ, 46; consult, Baxter Travenol Labs Inc, 82-84, BW-Biotec, 85-87, Energy Consults, Inc, 87- *Mem:* AAAS; Am Chem Soc; NY Acad Sci; Indust Res Inst. *Res:* Bacterial chemistry; pyrogens; organic synthesis; micro-analytical methods; chemistry of tubercle bacillus; pharmaceuticals; thyroid chemistry; parenteral nutrition; biomedical engineering; medical electronics; blood preservation; microbial enzymes. *Mailing Add:* 2100 Burr Oak Dr L G Ginger & Assocs Glenview IL 60025

GINGERICH, KARL ANDREAS, INORGANIC CHEMISTRY, PHYSICAL CHEMISTRY. *Current Pos:* PROF CHEM, TEX A&M UNIV, 68- *Personal Data:* b Lahr, Germany, Oct 8, 27. *Educ:* Univ Freiburg, dipl, 54, Dr rer nat, 57. *Prof Exp:* Asst, Univ Freiburg, 53-57; res assoc, Univ Ill, 57-58; asst prof chem, Pa State Univ, 58-64; sr chemist, Battelle Mem Inst, 64-68. *Mem:* Am Chem Soc. *Res:* Knudsen cell mass spectrometric and matrix isolation spectroscopic studies of high temperature systems and derived thermodynamic and structural properties. *Mailing Add:* Dept Chem Tex A&M Univ College Station TX 77843-3255

GINGERICH, OWEN (JAY), HISTORY OF ASTRONOMY. *Current Pos:* astrophysicist, 62-86, SR ASTRON, SMITHSONIAN ASTROPHYS OBSERV, 86-; PROF ASTRON & HIST SCI, HARVARD UNIV, 69- *Personal Data:* b Washington, Iowa, Mar 24, 30; m 54, Miriam Sensenig; c Jonathan C, Mark P & Peter E. *Educ:* Goshen Col, BA, 51; Harvard Univ, MA, 53, PhD(astron), 62. *Honors & Awards:* Sigma Xi Nat lectr, 71; George Darwin lectr, Royal Astron Soc, 71; Order of Merit, Com Class, People's Repub Poland, 81; Asteroid named in honor, Gingerich 2658. *Prof Exp:* From instr to asst prof astron & dir observ, Am Univ, Beirut, 55-58; lectr astron, Wellesley Col, 58-59. *Concurrent Pos:* Dir, Cent Bur Astron Telegrams, Int Astron Union, 65-68, assoc dir, 68-79, pres, Comn Hist of Astron, 71-76; counr, Am Astron Soc, 73-76, chmn, Educ Adv Comt, 75-77, chmn, Hist Astron Div, 80 & 83-84; assoc ed, J Hist Astron, 75-; overseas fel, Churchill Col, Cambridge, Eng, 85-86. *Mem:* AAAS; Hist Sci Soc; Am Astron Soc; Am Philos Soc (vpres, 82-85); Int Acad Hist Sci; Am Acad Arts & Sci. *Res:* History of astronomy, especially Copernicus, Tycho, Kepler; history of early scientific printing; science and theology. *Mailing Add:* Ctr Astrophys Harvard-Smithsonian, 60 Garden St Cambridge MA 02138. *Fax:* 617-496-7564; *E-Mail:* ginger@cfs.harvard.edu

GINGERICH, PHILIP DERSTINE, VERTEBRATE PALEONTOLOGY. *Current Pos:* from asst prof to assoc prof, 76-83, dir mus, 81-87, PROF PALEONT, UNIV MICH, 83-, DIR, MUS PALEONT, 89- *Personal Data:* b Goshen, Ind, Mar 23, 46; m 82, B Holly Smith; c Daniel Derstine & Matthew Janney. *Educ:* Princeton Univ, AB, 68; Yale Univ, MPhil, 72, PhD(paleont), 74. *Honors & Awards:* Shuchert Award, Paleont Soc, 81. *Prof Exp:* Asst prof paleont, Univ Mich, 74-75; NATO fel, Univ Montpellier, 75-76. *Concurrent Pos:* J S Guggenheim fel, 83. *Mem:* AAAS; Am Soc Naturalists; Sigma Xi; Soc Study Evolution; Soc Vert Paleont; Paleont Soc. *Res:* Primate evolution; origin and radiation of mammals, especially whales; fossil record and evolution at the species level and rates of evolution. *Mailing Add:* Mus Paleont Univ Mich Ann Arbor MI 48109-1079. *Fax:* 313-936-1380; *E-Mail:* gingeric@umich.edu

GINGERY, ROY EVANS, BIOCHEMISTRY, PLANT PATHOLOGY. *Personal Data:* b Lodi, Ohio, June 3, 42; m 64; c 2. *Educ:* Carnegie-Mellon Univ, BS, 64; Univ Wis, MS, 67, PhD(biochem), 68. *Prof Exp:* Asst prof, USDA & Ohio Agr Res & Develop Ctr, Ohio State Univ, 68-69, res chemist plant path, 69-93. *Mem:* Am Phytopath Soc. *Res:* Nucleic acid metabolism in virus infected plants; biochemical mechanisms of disease resistance in plants. *Mailing Add:* USDA-AGR-NPS Rm 230 Bldg 005 BARC-West Beltsville MD 20705

GINGOLD, KURT, SYNTHETIC INORGANIC & ORGANOMETALLIC CHEMISTRY. *Current Pos:* CONSULT, 86- *Personal Data:* b Vienna, Austria, Aug 7, 29; nat US; m 57, Alice Saltzman; c Betty R & David I. *Educ:* Tulane Univ, BS, 50; Harvard Univ, MA, 52, PhD(chem), 53. *Prof Exp:* Lit chemist, Ethyl Corp, Mich, 53-54; sr info scientist, Am Cyanamid Co, 56-86. *Concurrent Pos:* Vpres, Int Fedn Translr, 63-66, mem coun, 66-77 & 84-93. *Mem:* Am Chem Soc; fel Inst Linguists, London; Am Translr Asn (pres, 63-65). *Res:* Scientific literature; technical writing, editing and translation; organometallic and inorganic chemistry; information science. *Mailing Add:* 35 Windsor Lane Cos Cob CT 06807. *Fax:* 203-869-2742

GINGRAS, BERNARD ARTHUR, ORGANIC CHEMISTRY. *Current Pos:* RETIRED. *Personal Data:* b Montreal, Que, Jan 23, 27; m 52; c 4. *Educ:* Univ Montreal, BSc, 48, MSc, 49, PhD, 52; Oxford Univ, DPhil, 54. *Hon Degrees:* Dr Sci, York Univ, 79. *Prof Exp:* Lectr org chem, Univ Montreal, 51-52; Nat Res Coun Can overseas fel, Oxford Univ, 52 & Merck & Co, Inc, 53; from assoc res officer to sr res officer, Div Appl Chem, Nat Res Coun Can, 54-67, assoc awards officer, 67-70, dir off grants & scholar, 70-72, asst vpres univ res, 72-74, vpres univ grants & scholar, 74-78, vpres external rel, 78-84, exec vpres, 85-87, vpres externternal rel, 87-90. *Mem:* Fel Chem Inst Can; Fr-Can Asn Advan Sci (pres). *Res:* Textiles; fungicides for prevention of deterioration of fibers by microorganisms; photochemical degradation of cellulose; coordination chemistry. *Mailing Add:* 919 Bermuda Ave Ottawa ON K1K 0V8 Can

GINGRASS, RUEDI PETER, PLASTIC SURGERY. *Current Pos:* assoc prof & chmn dept, 71-83, CLIN PROF, PLASTIC SURG, MED COL WIS, 86-; CONSULT, 83- *Personal Data:* b Milwaukee, Wis, May 10, 32; m 58, 83, Julie Welv; c David, Mary, Charles, Sarah & Amy. *Educ:* Univ Mich, AB, 54, MD, 58; Marquette Univ, MS, 63. *Prof Exp:* Asst prof plastic surg & exec dir, Sch Med, Marquette Univ, 67-71. *Concurrent Pos:* NIH head & neck cancer trainee, Duke Univ Med Ctr, 63-66. *Mem:* Am Soc Plastic & Reconstructive Surg; Soc Head & Neck Surg; Am Asn Plastic Surg; Plastic Surg Res Coun. *Res:* Wound healing and wound infection; skin grafting. *Mailing Add:* 9800 W Blue Mound Rd Milwaukee WI 53226-4353

GINGRICH, NEWELL SHIFFER, PHYSICS. *Current Pos:* from asst prof to prof, 37-73, EMER PROF PHYSICS, UNIV MO-COLUMBIA, 73- *Personal Data:* b Orwigsburg, Pa, Jan 29, 06; m 28; c 2. *Educ:* NCent Col, AB, 26; Lafayette Col, MA, 27; Univ Chicago, PhD(physics), 30. *Prof Exp:* Lab instr physics, Lafayette Col, 26-27, instr, 27-28; asst prof, Mt Allison Univ, 30-31; instr, Mass Inst Technol, 31-36. *Concurrent Pos:* Grants-in-aid, AAAS, Rumford Fund, Am Acad Sci & Elizabeth Thompson Sci Fund, Res Corp, NSF; physicist, Naval Ord Lab, 41-43; tech aide, Liaison Off, Off Sci Res & Develop, Washington, DC, 43-44, Oak Ridge Nat Lab, 52-53 & Argonne Nat Lab, 56-58; NSF fel, 59-60. *Mem:* AAAS; fel Am Phys Soc; Am Asn Physics Teachers; Am Crystallog Asn; Sigma Xi. *Res:* Compton effect in x-rays; circuits used with geiger counter work; diffraction of x-rays by elements in liquid state; cosmic rays; atomic distribution in liquids; magnetic structure in crystals; neutron diffraction. *Mailing Add:* 320 Physics Bldg Univ Mo Columbia MO 65203

GINI, MARIA LUIGIA, ARTIFICIAL INTELLIGENCE, ROBOTICS. *Current Pos:* asst prof, 82-88, ASSOC PROF COMPUTER SCI, UNIV MINN, MINNEAPOLIS, 88- *Personal Data:* b Milano, Italy, July 30, 46; m 82, Daniel Boley. *Educ:* Univ Milano, Italy, Doctor(physics), 72. *Prof Exp:* Res assoc computer sci, Politecnico Milano, Italy, 73-76, sr res assoc, 78-82; vis res assoc Artificial Intel, Stanford Univ, 76-77. *Concurrent Pos:* Vis prof, Univ Salerno, Italy, 88-89 & Stanford Univ, 89. *Mem:* Asn Comput Mach; Am Asn Artificial Intel; Comput Prof Social Responsibility; Inst Elec & Electronic Engrs. *Res:* Integration of artificial intelligence with robotics for navigation, exploration and task execution in changing environments; planning and sensing to detect and recover from errors in robotic assembly. *Mailing Add:* 4-192 Elec Eng & Computer Sci Bldg Univ Minn 200 Union St SE Minneapolis MN 55455-0191. *Fax:* 612-625-0572; *E-Mail:* gini@cs.umn.edu

GINIS, ASTERIOS MICHAEL, FOOD SCIENCE, BIOCHEMISTRY. *Current Pos:* sr res food scientist res & develop, 76-80, develop leader, 80-89, DIR, CEREAL PARTNERS WORLDWIDE. *Personal Data:* b Thessaloniki, Greece, Feb 16, 45; m 71; c Michael. *Educ:* Univ Thessaloniki, BS, 68; Univ Wis-Madison, MS, 73, PhD(food sci), 76. *Prof Exp:* Res asst plant breeding, Cereals Inst & Cotton Inst Greece, 66-67; res asst, Univ Wis-Madison, 71-76. *Mem:* Inst Food Technologists; Am Meat Sci Asn; Am Asn Cereal Chemists. *Res:* Basic and exploratory food; product and process development; frozen foods; storage life prediction of foods; breakfast cereals. *Mailing Add:* Romanel-sur-Morges 1122 Switzerland. *Fax:* 41-21-803-0260

GINN, H EARL, INTERNAL MEDICINE, NEPHROLOGY. *Current Pos:* SR VPRES, REN CORP, 90- *Personal Data:* b Tylertown, Miss, July 7, 31; c 2. *Educ:* Baylor Univ, BS, 53; Emory Univ, MD, 57. *Prof Exp:* Intern, Med Ctr, Univ Okla, 57-58; resident internal med, 58-60; instr med, New York Hosp, Med Ctr, Cornell Univ, 60-61; instr med & physiol, Med Ctr, Univ Okla, 62, asst prof med, physiol & urol, 62-65; from asst prof to prof, Sch Med, Vanderbilt Univ, 65-73, prof med, 73-89, prof urol, 65-89; partner & physician, Nashville Nephrology Assoc, 89- *Concurrent Pos:* USPHS fel renal & electrolyte physiol, Cornell Univ, 60-61; NIH career res develop award, Med Ctr, Univ Okla, 64-65 & Univ Hosp, Vanderbilt Univ, 65-; clin investr, Vet Admin Hosp, Med Ctr, Okla, 61-64, chief renal & electrolyte sect, Okla City Vet Admin Hosp & chief kidney sect, Med Ctr, Univ Okla, 63-65; chief nephrology div & chief renal dialysis units, Vanderbilt Univ Hosp, 65-; gen consult, Kidney Dis Control Prog, 67-68; mem coun circulation, Am Heart Asn. *Mem:* Am Physiol Soc; Am Soc Artificial Internal Organs; Am Soc Nephrology; Harvey Soc. *Res:* Renal transplantation; dynamics of hemodialysis; biochemistry of uremia. *Mailing Add:* Nephrol Asn 28 White Bridge Rd No 300 Nashville TN 37205

GINN, ROBERT FORD, CHEMICAL ENGINEERING, MATHEMATICS. *Current Pos:* RETIRED. *Personal Data:* b Alamosa, Colo, Aug 13, 31. *Educ:* Univ Colo, Boulder, BS, 53; Lawrence Univ, MS, 57; Univ Del, MChE, 64, PhD(chem eng), 68. *Prof Exp:* Chem engr, Albert E Reed Paper Group, Eng, 57-58; res engr, Nat Vulcanized Fibre Co, Del, 59-60 & Westvaco Corp, Md, 65-69; sr scientist, Am Can Co, Wis, 69-71; res fel, Inst Paper Chem, 71-77; asst prof chem eng, Mich Technol Univ, 77-97. *Mem:* Am Chem Soc; Soc Rheology; Brit Soc Rheology; Am Inst Chem Engrs; Sigma Xi. *Res:* Polymer science and engineering. *Mailing Add:* Box 866 Rte 1 Houghton MI 49931

GINN, THOMAS CLIFFORD, AQUATIC ECOLOGY, FISHERY BIOLOGY. *Current Pos:* VPRES ENVIRON CONSULT, PTI ENVIRON SERV, 87- *Personal Data:* b Medford, Ore, July 18, 46. *Educ:* Ore State Univ, BS, 68, MS, 70; NY Univ, PhD(aquatic ecol), 77. *Prof Exp:* Res asst radiol physics, X-ray Sci & Eng Lab, Ore State Univ, 69-71; asst res scientist aquatic ecol, Inst Environ Med, NY Univ Med Ctr, 71-77; mgr biol serv, 77-80, dir environ consult, Tetra Tech, Inc, 80-87. *Mem:* Am Fisheries Soc; AAAS; Sigma Xi; Am Inst Fishery Res Biologists; Estuarine Res Fedn; Water Pollution Control Fedn. *Res:* Effects of toxic substances on marine and estuarine biota; response of freshwater ecosystems to lake restoration techniques; toxic responses of freshwater and marine organisms to chlorinated effluents; sewage discharge effects on marine ecosystems. *Mailing Add:* 7904 127th Ave SE Renton WA 98056

GINNARD, CHARLES RAYMOND, ANALYTICAL CHEMISTRY. *Current Pos:* Analytical chemist surface analytical & polymer characterization, 69-78, sect supvr chem anal, 78-83, res adminr, 83-86, personnel adminr, 86-94, RES & DEVELOP MGR, CENT RES & DEVELOP DEPT, E I DU PONT DE NEMOURS & CO, INC, 94- *Personal Data:* b Detroit, Mich, Oct 2, 47; m 69, Christine Fairfield; c Kelly, Janet & Matthew. *Educ:* Wayne State Univ, BS, 69. *Mem:* Am Chem Soc; Sigma Xi. *Res:* Analytical intrumentation and techniques for polymer, chemical and biophysical characterization. *Mailing Add:* Du Pont Cent Res & Develop Exp Sta E228/210 Wilmington DE 19880-0228

GINNINGS, GERALD KEITH, MATHEMATICS, STATISTICS. *Current Pos:* assoc prof, 66-68, PROF MATH, E TENN STATE UNIV, 68- *Personal Data:* b Greensboro, NC, Sept 16, 28; m 58; c 3. *Educ:* Elon Col, BA, 50; Appalachian State Teachers Col, MA, 62; Auburn Univ, EdD(math educ), 66. *Prof Exp:* Teacher electronics, H L Yoh Co Commun, Ft Sill, Okla, 59; field engr, Inter-Continental Ballistic Missile Launching Sites, Radio Corp Am Serv Co, NJ, 59-61; design engr, Martin Co, Colo, 61; asst prof math, Berry Col, 62-65. *Res:* Modern and traditional algebra; breeching the barrier in communications which exists between the applied mathematics areas and the pure areas. *Mailing Add:* 5 Foxborough Johnson City TN 37604

GINNINGS, P(AUL) R(OLL), CHEMICAL ENGINEERING. *Current Pos:* RETIRED. *Personal Data:* b Shreveport, La, June 16, 23; wid; c Pamela G (Huffman) & Lisa G (Waters) (deceased). *Educ:* NC State Col, BS, 48. *Prof Exp:* Jr chemist, Viscose Control Lab, Indust Rayon Corp, 48-49, jr chem engr, Prod Supt Staff, 49-52; res engr, Tire Cords & Fabrics, Res Div, Goodyear Tire & Rubber Co, 52-53, chem engr, De-Icing Res, 53-55, group leader ice-guard res, 55-62, group leader new prod res, 62-65, sect head mat eng res, 65-68, sect head flexible films & sheeting, 68-77, sect head plastics res, Res Div, 77-80, sect head, 80-81, prin engr, Polyester Applications Dept, 81-86. *Concurrent Pos:* Prog chmn, Akron Sect, Soc Plastics Engrs. *Mem:* Am Chem Soc; Soc Plastics Engrs; fel Am Inst Chem. *Res:* Viscose preparation and spinning, textiles as related to tire cords; conductive rubber; de-icing; rain erosion resistance of aircraft materials at high speeds; adhesives; structural laminates for aircraft ice-guards; rubber compounding; plastics processing; acoustical rubbers; solution cast and extruded polyvinyl chloride films; processing of thermoplastic polymers; investigation of polymer blends; research to develop copolyesters suitable for processing into films, sheeting and other articles suitable for industrial food packaging applications; patents issued. *Mailing Add:* 377 Shannon Dr Wadsworth OH 44281

GINNS, JAMES HERBERT, MYCOLOGY, FOREST PATHOLOGY. *Current Pos:* RES MYCOL, CAN DEPT AGR, 69- *Personal Data:* b New Britain, Conn, June 21, 38; m 67. *Educ:* Univ Conn, BS, 60; WVa Univ, MS, 62; NY State Univ, Syracuse, PhD(mycol), 67. *Prof Exp:* Res plant path, WVa Agr Exp Sta, 60-62; res forest path, Southlands Exp Forest, Int Paper Co, 62-64; teacher bot, Col Forestry, NY State Univ, 65-67; res forest path, Can Forest Serv, 67-69. *Concurrent Pos:* Systematic mycol, Can Dept Agr, 69-97; cur, Can Collection Fungus Cultures, 75-82, Nat Mycol Herbarium Can, 88-97; counr, Mycol Soc Am, 77-79; Friends of Farlow Herbarium, 82- *Mem:* Mycol Soc Am (vpres, 95, pres, 96); Sigma Xi; Asn Syst Collections. *Res:* Taxonomy, classical and biochemical of wood; decaying fungi, especially polyporaceae and corticiaceae of the boreal forest. *Mailing Add:* Saunders Bldg Cent Exp Farm Ottawa ON K1A 0C6 Can. *Fax:* 613-759-1599; *E-Mail:* ginnsj@em.agr.ca

GINOCCHIO, JOSEPH NATALE, THEORETICAL NUCLEAR PHYSICS. *Current Pos:* STAFF PHYSICIST, LOS ALAMOS NAT LAB, 75- *Personal Data:* b Summit, NJ, Dec 25, 36; m 64, Anita Stingle; c 2. *Educ:* Lehigh Univ, BS, 58; Univ Rochester, PhD(physics), 64. *Honors & Awards:* Alexander von Humboldt Res Award. *Prof Exp:* Res assoc nuclear physics, Rutgers Univ, 64-66 & Mass Inst Technol, 66-68; assoc prof, Yale Univ, 68-75. *Mem:* Fel Am Phys Soc. *Res:* Study of nuclear structure with shell model and interacting boson model, many-body physics; random phase approximation applied to nuclear bound and scattering states; group theory as used in nuclear physics and many-body physics; four nucleon correlations in nuclei, pion and intermediate energy proton scattering from nuclei. *Mailing Add:* Los Alamos Nat Lab Mail Stop B283 PO Box 1663 Los Alamos NM 87545. *E-Mail:* gino@t5.lanl.gov

GINOS, JAMES ZISSIS, MEDICINAL CHEMISTRY, ORGANIC CHEMISTRY. *Current Pos:* sr res assoc, 80-86, ASSOC LAB MEM, MEM SLOAN-KETTERING CANCER CTR, 86-; RES ASSOC PROF CHEM, MED COL, CORNELL UNIV, 75- *Personal Data:* b Hillsboro, Ill, Feb 1, 23; m 47; c 2. *Educ:* Columbia Col, BA, 54; Stevens Inst Technol, MS, 57, PhD(org chem), 64. *Prof Exp:* Chemist, Colgate-Palmolive Co, NJ, 52-57; chief chemist, Diamond Alkali, NJ, 57-58; chemist, Nopco Chem Co, 59-64; from asst scientist to scientist, Brookhaven Nat Labs, NY, 64-75. *Concurrent Pos:* Asst instr, Newark Col Eng, 59-60; res asst prof, Mt Sinai Sch Med, 68-70. *Mem:* AAAS; Am Chem Soc; Am Soc Pharmacol & Exp Therapeut; Soc Nuclear Med; NY Acad Sci; Am Soc Clin Pharmacol & Therapeut. *Res:* Synthesis of radiopharmaceuticals for use in position emission tomography. *Mailing Add:* 200 Winston Dr Cliffside Park NJ 07010

GINSBERG, ALVIN PAUL, INORGANIC CHEMISTRY. *Current Pos:* MEM TECH STAFF, BELL TEL LABS, 60- *Personal Data:* b Brooklyn, NY, Jan 7, 32. *Educ:* NY Univ, AB, 54; Columbia Univ, AM, 55, PhD(chem), 59. *Prof Exp:* Instr chem, Brown Univ, 59-60. *Mem:* AAAS; Am Chem Soc; Am Phys Soc; Royal Soc Chem. *Res:* Preparation, spectroscopic and magnetic properties of transition metal compounds; applications of valence theory; hydride complexes. *Mailing Add:* 119 Spring Ridge Dr Berkeley Heights NJ 07922-1492

GINSBERG, BARRY HOWARD, DIABETES MELLITUS, ENDOCRINOLOGY. *Current Pos:* MED DIR, WORLDWIDE DIABETES HEALTHCARE, BECTON DICKINSON & CO, 90- *Personal Data:* b Brooklyn, NY, May 9, 45; m 67, Marjorie Kanef; c Susan & David. *Educ:* Harpur Col, State Univ NY, Binghamton, BA, 65; Einstein Col Med, PhD(molecular biol), 71, MD, 72. *Prof Exp:* Resident med, Harvard Univ, 74; asst prof, Univ Iowa, 77-82, asst prof biochem, 78-82, assoc prof, 82-88, prof med & biochem, 88-90. *Concurrent Pos:* Mem bd dirs, Am Diabetes Asn, 82-85. *Mem:* Endocrine Soc; Am Diabetes Asn; Am Fedn Clin Res. *Res:* Devices for diabetes; develoment of a glucose sensor; relationship of diabetes control to complications; computers in medicine. *Mailing Add:* Becton Dickinson & Co One Becton Dr Franklin Lakes NJ 07417-1883. *Fax:* 201-847-4865; *E-Mail:* barry_ginsberg@bdhq.bd.com

GINSBERG, DAVID LAWRENCE, PUBLIC HEALTH PLANNING. *Current Pos:* PARTNER, LARSEN SHEIN GINSBERG & PARTNERS, 95- *Personal Data:* b New York, NY, Sept 21, 32; m 69, Emily Boor; c Stuart S, Daniel P & Laura R. *Educ:* Cornell Univ, BArch, 55. *Prof Exp:* Partner, Perkins & Will, 57-78, exec vpres, 78-79; exec vpres & chief planning officer, Columbia-Presby Health Serv Inc, 79-92; dep to pres, Presby Hosp, 93-95. *Concurrent Pos:* Asst clin prof pub health, Columbia Univ; sr consult, US Global Health Serv. *Mem:* Am Hosp Asn; Am Pub Health Asn; Soc Hosp Planning. *Mailing Add:* 169 W 78th St New York NY 10024-6738

GINSBERG, DONALD MAURICE, SUPERCONDUCTIVITY, LOW TEMPERATURE PHYSICS. *Current Pos:* From res assoc to assoc prof, 59-66, PROF PHYSICS, UNIV ILL, URBANA-CHAMPAIGN, 66- *Personal Data:* b Chicago, Ill, Nov 19, 33; m 57, Joli Lasker; c 2. *Educ:* Univ Chicago, BA, 52, BS, 55, MS, 56; Univ Calif, PhD(physics), 60. *Concurrent Pos:* Alfred P Sloan res fel, 60-64; NSF fel, 66-67; mem, Educ Rev Comt Solid State Div, 77-82, chmn, 79-80, Mat Sci & Technol Div, Argonne Nat Lab, 82-83; vis scientist physics, Am Asn Physics Teachers & Am Inst Physics, 65-71. *Mem:* Fel Am Phys Soc; AAAS; Sigma Xi. *Res:* Superconductivity. *Mailing Add:* Dept Physics Loomis Lab Univ Ill Urbana Champaign 1110 W Green St Urbana IL 61801

GINSBERG, EDWARD S, HIGH ENERGY PHYSICS. *Current Pos:* asst prof, 66-71, ASSOC PROF PHYSICS, UNIV MASS, BOSTON, 71- *Personal Data:* b New York, NY, Oct 4, 38; div; c Lesley, A Benjamin & David. *Educ:* Brown Univ, AB & ScB, 59; Stanford Univ, MS, 61, PhD(physics), 65. *Prof Exp:* Res assoc physics, Univ Pa, 64-66. *Concurrent Pos:* NSF res grant, 67-73. *Mem:* Am Phys Soc; Am Asn Physics Teachers. *Res:* High energy theoretical physics; weak and electromagnetic interactions; radiative convections; planetary science. *Mailing Add:* Univ Mass Boston-Physics 100 Morrissey Blvd Boston MA 02125-3393

GINSBERG, HAROLD SAMUEL, VIROLOGY, MICROBIOLOGY. *Current Pos:* EXPERT SCIENTIST, LAB INFECTIOUS DIS, NIH, 93- *Personal Data:* b Daytona Beach, Fla, May 27, 17; m 49, Marian Reibstein; c Benjamin, Peter R, Ann M & Jane E. *Educ:* Duke Univ, AB, 37; Tulane Univ, MD, 41. *Hon Degrees:* DSc, Tulane Univ, 95. *Honors & Awards:* Alexander von Humboldt Found Sr US Scientist Award, 85; Outstanding Infectious Dis Award, Bristol Myers Squibb, 94. *Prof Exp:* Resident, Mallory Inst Path, Boston City Hosp, 41, asst, 42, intern, 4th Med Serv, Harvard Univ, 42-43, asst resident, Thorndike Mem Lab, 43; asst physician, Hosp & asst, Rockefeller Inst, 46-49, res physician hosp & assoc, 49-51; assoc prof prev med & asst prof med, Sch Med, Western Res Univ, 51-60; prof microbiol & chmn dept, Univ Pa, 60-73; prof med & microbiol & chmn, Col Physicians & Surgeons, Columbia Univ, 73-85; Eugene Higgins prof, 85-93. *Concurrent Pos:* Consult, Nat Inst Allergy & Infectious Dis, Surgeon Gen, USPHS, NASA, 69-73; mem, Comn Acute Respiratory Dis, Armed Forces Epidemiol Bd, 59-71, adv bd, Am Cancer Soc, 70-74 & 75-; mem, Microbiol Comn, Nat Bd Mex Examrs, 72-, chmn, 75-84; ed, J Bact, J Virol, J Exp Med, J Infectious Dis & Intervirol; actg dir, Comprehensive Cancer Ctr, Columbia Univ, 83-85; Fogarty int scholar, 93-94. *Mem:* Nat Acad Sci; Inst Med-Nat Acad Sci; Am Soc Clin Invest; Asn Am Physicians; Harvey Soc; Am Asn Immunol; Am Acad Microbiol (vpres, 70-71, pres, 71-72). *Res:* Biochemistry and genetics of viral infections. *Mailing Add:* Nat Inst Allergy & Infectious Dis NIH Twinbrook II Facil 12441 Parklawn Dr Rockville MD 20852

GINSBERG, JERRY HAL, STRUCTURAL ACOUSTICS & VIBRATION, NONLINEAR ACOUSTICS. *Current Pos:* prof, 80-89, GEORGE W WOODRUFF CHAIR, SCH MECH ENG, GA INST TECHNOL, 89-, DISTINGUISHED PROF, 94- *Personal Data:* b New York, NY, Sept 18, 44. *Educ:* Cooper Union, BSCE, 65; Columbia Univ, MS, 66, EScD(eng mech), 70. *Prof Exp:* Asst prof eng mech, Sch Aero, Astro & Eng Sci, Purdue Univ, 69-74, assoc prof, Sch Mech Eng, 74-80. *Concurrent Pos:* Fulbright Hays advan res fel, US State Dept, 75; assoc prof, Nat Super Sch Elec Mech, Nancy, France, 75-76; consult, Lawrence Livermore Nat Lab, 79-95 & Gen Motors Res Labs, 86-89. *Mem:* Fel Acoust Soc Am; fel Am Soc Mech Engrs; Sigma Xi; Am Acad Mech. *Res:* Acoustics and vibrations involving dynamic response of submerged structures; nonlinear effects in propagation of acoustic waves; high-intensity sound beams; wave propagation in heterogeneous elastic media; dynamics of mechanical systems. *Mailing Add:* Sch Mech Eng Ga Inst Technol Atlanta GA 30332-0405. *E-Mail:* jerry.ginsberg@me.gatech.edu

GINSBERG, JONATHAN I, mathematical analysis, for more information see previous edition

GINSBERG, MARK HOWARD, IMMUNOLOGY, CELL BIOLOGY. *Current Pos:* fel, 75-78, ASST MEM IMMUNOPATH, SCRIPPS CLIN & RES FOUND, 78-, ASSOC MEM, 82- *Personal Data:* b New York, NY, Aug 30, 45; m 68; c 2. *Educ:* State Univ NY Downstate Med Ctr, MD, 70. *Prof Exp:* Intern med, Univ Chicago, 70-71, resident, 71-73, fel rheumatol, 73-75. *Concurrent Pos:* Clin instr, Sch Med, Univ Calif, San Diego, 76-; clin investr, Nat Inst Arthritis, Metab & Digestive Dis, NIH, 77- *Mem:* Am Asn Immunologists; Am Fedn Clin Res; Am Rheumatism Asn; Am Soc Clin Res. *Res:* Role of platelets in inflammation; mechanisms of platelet secretion and adhesion; biology of platelet factor four. *Mailing Add:* Vascular Biol Scripps Res Inst 10550 N Torrey Pines Rd La Jolla CA 92037-1092. *Fax:* 619-784-7343

GINSBERG, MURRY B(ENJAMIN), electronics engineering, for more information see previous edition

GINSBERG, MYRON DAVID, NEUROLOGY. *Current Pos:* ASSOC PROF TO PROF NEUROL & RADIOL, SCH MED, UNIV MIAMI, 79-, DIR, CEREBRALVASCULAR RES CTR, 81- *Personal Data:* b Denver, Colo, Aug 26, 39; m 69; c 2. *Educ:* Wesleyan Univ, BA, 61; Harvard Med Sch, MD, 66. *Prof Exp:* Clin fel, Harvard Med Sch & Boston City Hosp, 66-68; resident & fel neurol, Harvard Med Sch & Mass Gen Hosp, 68-70; staff assoc physiol, Lab Perinatal Physiol, NIH, 70-72; res fel neuropath, Mass Gen Hosp, Boston, 72-73; asst to assoc prof neurol, Sch Med, Univ Pa, 73-79. *Concurrent Pos:* estab investr, Am Heart Asn, 76-81; attend neurologist, Jackson Mem

Hosp; Javits Neurosci Investr award, NIH, 85-92; Am Heart Asn, Nat Res Comt, 86; ed-in-chief, J Cerebral Blood Flow & Metab, 91-97. *Mem:* Am Acad Neurol; Am Physiol Soc; John Morgan Soc; Am Neurol Asn; Int Soc Cerebral Blood Flow & Metab; Soc Neurosci; Sigma Xi. *Res:* Physiology and neuropathology of energy-deprivation states in the central nervous system; cerebral blood flow and metabolism in hypoxic-ischemic encephalopathy. *Mailing Add:* Dept Neurol Sch Med Univ Miami PO Box 016960 Miami FL 33101-6960

GINSBERG, THEODORE, MECHANICAL ENGINEERING. *Current Pos:* SR SCIENTIST MECH ENG, BROOKHAVEN NAT LAB, 74- *Personal Data:* b Brooklyn, NY, Aug 28, 41; m 67; c 2. *Educ:* Pratt Inst, BChE, 63; Pa State Univ, MS, 66, PhD(nuclear eng), 70. *Prof Exp:* Assoc mech engr, Argonne Nat Lab, 70-72; sr lectr nuclear eng, Technion-Israel Inst Technol, 72-74. *Mem:* Am Nuclear Soc; Am Soc Mech Engrs. *Res:* Heat transfer; fluid mechanics; two-phase flow and heat transfer; nuclear reactor safety; experimental thermofluid sciences. *Mailing Add:* Brookhaven Nat Lab Bldg 820-M Upton NY 11973

GINSBERG-FELLNER, FREDDA VITA, MEDICINE, ENDOCRINOLOGY. *Current Pos:* assoc, 67-69, from asst prof to assoc prof, 69-81, DIR PEDIAT ENDOCRINOL, MT SINAI SCH MED, 77-, PROF PEDIAT, 81- *Personal Data:* b New York, NY, Apr 21, 37; m 61; c 2. *Educ:* Cornell Univ, AB, 57; NY Univ, MD, 61. *Honors & Awards:* Paul Lacy Award, Nat Diabetes Res Interchange, 82; Mary Jane Kugel Award, Juv Diabetes Found, 88; Diabetes in Youth Award, Am Diabetes Asn, 91. *Prof Exp:* Intern pediat, Albert Einstein Col Med, 61-62, fel pediat endocrinol, 62-65, asst resident pediat, 63-64, sr resident, 65-66. *Concurrent Pos:* Sr clin pediatrician, Mt Sinai Hosp, 67-69, asst attend pediatrician, 69-74, assoc attend pediatrician, 74-81, attend pediatrician, 81-, dir, Carole & Michael Friedman & Family Young Peoples Diabetes Treat Unit, 84- *Mem:* Am Diabetes Asn; Endocrine Soc; Soc Pediat Res; Am Pediat Soc; Am Fedn Clin Res; Am Acad Pediat. *Res:* Mechanisms of development of type I insulin dependent diabetes mellitus; genetic and immune factors; gestational diabetes; childhood obesity. *Mailing Add:* Dept Pediat Mt Sinai Sch Med One Gustave L Levy Pl Box 1659 New York NY 10029-6574

GINSBURG, ANN, BIOCHEMISTRY, PHYSICAL BIOCHEMISTRY. *Current Pos:* CHIEF, SECT PROTEIN & CHEM, NAT HEART, LUNG & BLOOD INST, NIH, 66- *Personal Data:* b 1932; m 55; c 2. *Educ:* Univ Calif, Berkeley, BA, 54, MA, 55; George Washington Univ, PhD(biochem), 64. *Concurrent Pos:* Bd dirs, Calorimetry Conf. *Mem:* Am Soc Biochem & Molecular Biol; Calorimetry Conf; Biophys Soc; Protein Soc. *Res:* Enzyme structure/regulation; thermodynamics of ligand-protein & protein-protein interactions; protein unfolding/folding. *Mailing Add:* Nat Lung & Blood Inst NIH Bldg 3 Rm 208 Bethesda MD 20892-0340. *Fax:* 301-496-0599

GINSBURG, BENSON EARL, GENETICS. *Current Pos:* PROF BIOBEHAV SCI & CHMN DEPT, UNIV CONN, 69- *Personal Data:* b Detroit, Mich, July 16, 18; m 41; c 3. *Educ:* Wayne State Univ, BS, 39, MS, 41; Univ Chicago, PhD(zool), 43. *Prof Exp:* Instr zool & physiol, Univ Chicago, 43-44, res assoc pharmacol, 44-46, asst prof biol sci, 46-49, from assoc prof to prof natural sci, 49-59, chmn dept, 50-57, assoc dean univ, 57-59, prof biol & head sect, 59-63, William Rainey Harper prof, 63-69. *Concurrent Pos:* Sci assoc, Jackson Lab; fel, Ctr Advan Study Behav Sci, 57-58; consult ed, Encycl Britannica Films, 59-; mem adv comt animal resources, NIH, 65-; mem panel behav biol, Nat Acad Sci-Nat Res Coun, 66-67. *Mem:* Genetics Soc Am; Am Soc Naturalists; Biomet Soc; Am Soc Human Genetics; Am Genetic Asn. *Res:* Gene action in mammalian nervous system; inheritance of emotionality; biological education; zoology. *Mailing Add:* 149 Hillyndale Rd Storrs CT 06268-1804

GINSBURG, DAVID, organic chemistry, for more information see previous edition

GINSBURG, HERBERT, EXPERIMENTAL STATISTICS. *Current Pos:* RETIRED. *Personal Data:* b Schenectady, NY, May 2, 28; m 51; c 3. *Educ:* State Univ NY, BA, 50, MA, 51; NC State Univ, MS, 54. *Prof Exp:* Eng statistician, Westinghouse Elec Corp, 54-61, sr res statistician, Res Labs, 61-63, fel statistician, Bettis Atomic Power Lab, 63-91. *Concurrent Pos:* Adj mem grad fac, Univ Pittsburgh, 62-91. *Mem:* Am Statist Asn; Royal Statist Soc; Sigma Xi. *Res:* Experimental design; empirical model building; teaching. *Mailing Add:* 5738 Wilkins Ave Pittsburgh PA 15217-1214

GINSBURG, JACK MARTIN, PHYSIOLOGY. *Current Pos:* assoc prof, 68-73, PROF PHYSIOL & ASSOC PROF MED, MED COL GA, 73- *Personal Data:* b Philadelphia, Pa, May 31, 28; m 55; c 1. *Educ:* Univ Pa, BA, 49; Tulane Univ, PhD(physiol), 53. *Prof Exp:* Lab asst physiol, Tulane Univ, 50-53; res participant, Biol Div, Oak Ridge Nat Lab, 53-54; instr pharmacol, Tulane Univ, 54-55; instr physiol, Univ Cincinnati, 57-59; asst prof, Col Med, Univ Rochester, 59-68. *Mem:* AAAS; Am Physiol Soc; Am Soc Nephrology; Soc Exp Biol & Med. *Res:* Biological transport; body fluid; electrolytes. *Mailing Add:* Dept Physiol Med Col Ga Augusta GA 30912-0001

GINSBURG, MERRILL STUART, APPLIED SEISMOLOGY, SIGNAL PROCESSING. *Current Pos:* RETIRED. *Personal Data:* b Chicago, Ill, July 20, 35; m 71; c 2. *Educ:* Mass Inst Technol, BS, 59, MS, 60; Univ Utah, PhD(geophys), 63. *Prof Exp:* Sr geophys engr, Geophys Serv Ctr, Mobil Oil Corp, 63-65, sr geophys interpreter, 65-70, assoc geophysicist, Explor Develop Dept, Explor Serv Ctr, 71-72, assoc geophysicist, Gravity-Magnetic Sect, 72-74, geophys specialist, 74-77, staff geophysicist, Gravity Magnetic Sect, Explor Serv Ctr, 71-82; staff geophysicist, Velocity Refraction Modeling Unit, Mobile Explor & Prod Serv, Inc, 82-83, sr staff geophysicist, 83-85, geophys adv, 85-89, geophys adv, Appl Geophys Dept, 89-90, geophys adv, Signal Processing Dept, Seismic Gravity Magnetic Serv Unit, 90-92. *Mem:* Am Geophys Union; Soc Explor Geophys; Europ Asn Explor Geophys; NY Acad Sci; Sigma Xi. *Res:* Gravity and magnetics; applied mathematics; seismic modeling; seismic signal processing; issued one patent. *Mailing Add:* 2918 Country Place Circle Carrollton TX 75006-4708

GINSBURG, NATHAN, biophysics; deceased, see previous edition for last biography

GINSBURG, ROBERT NATHAN, SEDIMENTOLOGY. *Current Pos:* PROF SEDIMENTOLOGY, COMP SEDIMENTOLOGY LAB, ROSENSTIEL SCH MARINE & ATMOSPHERIC SCI, UNIV MIAMI, 70- *Personal Data:* b Wichita Falls, Tex, Apr 26, 25; m 56. *Educ:* Univ Ill, AB, 48; Univ Chicago, MA, 50, PhD(geol), 53. *Honors & Awards:* Cloos lectr, Johns Hopkins, 80; Twenhofel Medal, Soc Econ Paleont & Mineral, 85; Gold Medal, Fla Acad Sci, 76. *Prof Exp:* Asst marine geol, Marine Lab, Univ Miami, 50-54; res geologist, Shell Develop Co, 54-60, sr res assoc geol, 60-65; prof geol & oceanog, Johns Hopkins Univ, 65-70. *Concurrent Pos:* Queen's fel, Australia, 78; distinguished lectr, Am Asn Petrol Geologists, 84 & 85; pres, IUGS Global Sedimentary Geol Comn, 87. *Mem:* Fel Geol Soc Am; fel AAAS; Int Asn Sedimentol (vpres, 82-); hon Soc Econ Paleont & Mineral (pres, 68); hon mem Am Asn Petrol Geologists; Am Geophys Union; Can Soc Petrol Geologists; Soc Sedimentary Geol. *Res:* Recent sediments; coral reefs; ancient and modern algal structures; marine geology. *Mailing Add:* Marine Geol Univ Miami 4600 Rickenbacker Causeway Miami Beach FL 33149

GINSBURG, SEYMOUR, COMPUTER SCIENCE. *Current Pos:* prof, 66-77, FLETCHER JONES PROF COMPUT SCI, UNIV SOUTHERN CALIF, 77- *Personal Data:* b Brooklyn, NY, Dec 12, 27; div; c David & Diane. *Educ:* City Col New York, BS, 48; Univ Mich, MS, 49, PhD(math), 52. *Prof Exp:* Asst prof math, Univ Miami, Fla, 51-55; mathematician, Nat Cash Register Co, 56-59; head systs synthesis & orgn sect, Hughes Res Labs, 59-60 & sr mathematician, Syst Develop Corp, 60-71. *Concurrent Pos:* Guggenheim fel, 74-75. *Mem:* Am Math Soc; Math Asn Am; Asn Comput Mach; fel Inst Elec & Electronics Engrs; Soc Indust & Appl Math. *Res:* Automata; formal language theory; grammar theory; theory of data bases. *Mailing Add:* Comput Sci Dept Univ Southern Calif Los Angeles CA 90089-0781

GINSBURG, VICTOR, BIOCHEMISTRY. *Current Pos:* CHIEF BIOCHEM SECT, NAT INST ARTHRITIS, METAB & DIGESTIVE DIS, 56- *Personal Data:* b Singapore, Mar 22, 30; nat US; m 55; c 2. *Educ:* Univ Calif, BA, 52, PhD, 55. *Concurrent Pos:* Fel, Nat Found, 58-59. *Mem:* Am Chem Soc; Am Soc Biol Chem. *Res:* Carbohydrate biochemistry. *Mailing Add:* 6905 Loch Lomond Dr Bethesda MD 20817. *Fax:* 301-496-2443

GINSBURGH, IRWIN, ENGINEERING PHYSICS. *Current Pos:* CONSULT, 84- *Personal Data:* b Brooklyn, NY, Apr 15, 26; m 46; c 4. *Educ:* City Col NY, BS, 47; Rutgers Univ, PhD(physics), 51. *Honors & Awards:* R & D 100 Award, Indust Res Mag, 68, 69, 71, 72 & 87. *Prof Exp:* Asst, Rutgers Univ, 47-50; res physicist, Amoco Oil Co, Stand Oil Co Inc, 51-57, sr proj physicist, 57-61, sr res supvr, 61-66, res assoc, 66-76, sr res assoc, 76-84. *Concurrent Pos:* Consult & legal expert, fire & explosion, 84- *Mem:* Am Phys Soc; Combustion Inst. *Res:* Engineering physics; fuel technology and petroleum engineering; acoustics; atmospheric chemistry and physics; hydrogen explosions; static electricity; automation; explosions; vapor recovery; air and water conservation; new energy sources. *Mailing Add:* 24125 Clearbank Lane Newhall CA 91321

GINSKI, JOHN MARTIN, PHYSIOLOGY. *Current Pos:* asst prof, Med Units, 60-67, ASSOC PROF PHYSIOL & BIOPHYS, UNIV TENN CTR HEALTH SCI, MEMPHIS, 67- *Personal Data:* b Chicago, Ill, May 26, 26; m 56; c 3. *Educ:* Loyola Univ, Ill, BS, 49, MS, 53, PhD(physiol), 56. *Prof Exp:* Res assoc pharmacol, Univ Chicago, 55-56; res assoc physiol & pharmacol, Col Med, Univ Sask, 57; from instr to asst prof, Col Med, Univ Nebr, 57-60. *Concurrent Pos:* Vis prof, Univ Valle, Columbia, 63-64. *Mem:* AAAS; Am Physiol Soc; Soc Exp Biol & Med. *Res:* Electrolyte exchange across cellular membranes and the correlation of these mechanisms with physiological activity of the cells. *Mailing Add:* Dept Physiol & Biophys Univ Tenn Memphis Sci 894 Union Memphis TN 38163-0001. *Fax:* 901-448-7126

GINSPARG, PAUL H, QUANTUM FIELD THEORY, STATISTICAL PHYSICS. *Current Pos:* STAFF MEM, LOS ALAMOS NAT LAB, 90- *Personal Data:* b Chicago, Ill. *Educ:* Harvard Univ, BA, 77; Cornell Univ, PhD(physics), 81. *Prof Exp:* Jr fel, Soc Fels, Harvard Univ, 81-84, from asst prof to assoc prof physics, 84-90. *Concurrent Pos:* Vis, Prof CEN Saclay, 79-80, Princeton Univ, 82-, Stanford Linear Accelerator Ctr, 87- *Res:* Quantum field theory; string theory; confromal field theory; statistical mechanics. *Mailing Add:* Los Alamos Nat Lab MS-B285 PO Box 1663 Los Alamos NM 87545

GINTAUTAS, JONAS, RESEARCH ADMINISTRATION, SCIENCE EDUCATION. *Current Pos:* DIR BASIC & CLIN RES & PROF NEUROL, BROOKDALE HOSP MED CTR, BROOKLYN, NY, 85- *Personal Data:* b Justinava, Lithuania, Oct 3, 38; US citizen; m 70; c 2. *Educ:* Moscow Pedag Inst, BS & MS, 65; Northwestern Univ, PhD(appl neurosci & speech path);

Autonomy Univ Juarez, MD, 84. *Prof Exp:* Assoc prof speech path, psychol & neurosci, Texas Tech Univ, Health Sci Ctr, 75-77, fel physiol, 77-79, assoc prof anesthesiol & dir res labs, 79-82. *Concurrent Pos:* Vpres med affairs, Albert Int Corp, NY, 86-; ed consult, J Aphasia, Apraxia & Agnosia, 79-. *Mem:* AAAS; Int Anesthesia Res Soc; NY Acad Sci. *Res:* Cardiovascular and smooth muscle physiology; pharmacology; action of calcium channel blocks and local anesthetics; higher cortical function disorders. *Mailing Add:* Brookdale Univ Hosp Med Ctr Linden & Rockaway Brooklyn NY 11212

GINTER, MARSHALL L, ATOMIC & MOLECULAR STRUCTURE, VUV INSTRUMENTATION & RADIATION. *Current Pos:* from asst prof to assoc prof, 66-74, PROF MOLECULAR PHYSICS, UNIV MD, COLLEGE PARK, 74- *Personal Data:* b Chico, Calif, Aug 24, 35; m 57; c Gretchen & Karl. *Educ:* Chico State Col (BS, 58; Vanderbilt Univ, PhD(phys chem), 61. *Prof Exp:* Res assoc phys chem, Vanderbilt Univ, 59-60, dir spectros lab, 61-62; res assoc physics, Univ Chicago, 62-66. *Concurrent Pos:* Consult, Naval Res Lab, Washington, DC, 67-95; guest worker, Nat Bur Standards, Gaithersburg, Md, 84-89; adj prof, Univ Ill, Urbana, 93- *Mem:* Fel Am Phys Soc; Am Chem Soc; fel Optical Soc Am; Sigma Xi. *Res:* Atomic and molecular structure; high resolution electronic spectroscopy; electronic structure of small molecules; atomic and molecular Rydberg states; VUV light sources and instrumentation. *Mailing Add:* Inst Phys Sci & Technol Univ Md College Park MD 20742. *Fax:* 301-314-9404

GINTHER, ROBERT J, INORGANIC CHEMISTRY. *Current Pos:* chemist & head res group, struct & compos luminescent mat, 46-69, head cent mat res activ, 69-73, RES PHYSICIST, MAT SCI DIV, NAVAL RES LAB, 73- *Personal Data:* b Lewiston, Maine, July 19, 17; m 43; c 3. *Educ:* Northeastern Univ, BS, 40. *Prof Exp:* Chemist, Sylvania Elec Prod, Inc, 40-46. *Mem:* Am Phys Soc; Electrochem Soc; Sigma Xi; Am Ceramic Soc (vchmn glass div, 75). *Res:* Luminescence of inorganic crystals and glasses. *Mailing Add:* 3107 Myrtle Ave Temple Hills MD 20748

GINZBERG, ELI, RESOURCE MANAGEMENT, ECONOMICS. *Current Pos:* A Barton Hepburn prof, 35-79, DIR, EISENHOWER CTR CONSERV HUMAN RESOURCES, COLUMBIA UNIV, 50-, DIR, REVSON FEL PROG ON FUTURE CITY NY, 78-, A BARTON HEPBURN EMER PROF ECON & SPEC LECTR, GRAD SCH BUS, 79-, SPEC LECTR, SCH PUB HEALTH, 89- *Personal Data:* b New York, NY, Apr 30, 11; m 46, Ruth Szold; c Abigail, Jeremy & Rachel. *Educ:* Columbia Univ, AB, 31, AM, 32, PhD, 34. *Hon Degrees:* DLitt, Jewish Theol Seminary Am, 66 & Columbia Univ, 82; LLD, Loyola Univ, 69; LHD, Rush Univ, 85, Kirksville Col Osteop Med, 93. *Honors & Awards:* Martin Mem Lectr, Am Col Surgeons, 80. *Concurrent Pos:* Spec asst to chief statistician, US War Dept, 42-44; dir, Resources Anal Div, Surgeon Gen's Off, 44-46; dir, NY State Hosp Study, 48-49, med consult, Hoover Comn, 52; mem, Bd Gov, Hebrew Univ, Jerusalem, 53-59; chmn, Nat Manpower Adv Comt, 62-73 & Nat Comn Manpower; consult, Depts State & Labor & Gen Acctg Off; co-chair, Adv Comt, Job Creation Proj, Nat Comt Full Employment, 84-86. *Mem:* Inst Med-Nat Acad Sci; Am Acad Arts & Sci; fel AAAS; Am Econ Asn; assoc mem Soc Med Consult Armed Forces. *Res:* Author of 100 books in economics. *Mailing Add:* Eisenhower Ctr Conserv Human Resources Columbia Univ New York NY 10027. *Fax:* 212-222-0867

GINZBURG, LEV R, THEORETICAL ECOLOGY. *Current Pos:* assoc prof, 77-83, PROF ECOL & EVOLUTION, STATE UNIV NY, STONY BROOK, 83- *Personal Data:* b Moscow, USSR, Jan 11, 45; m 70, Tatyana Porotova; c Maria & Alexander. *Educ:* Univ St Petersburg, Russia, MS, 67; Agrophys Inst, St Petersburg, PhD(math biol), 70. *Prof Exp:* Res assoc, Agrophys Inst, St Petersburg, 67-70, sr res assoc, 70-75; asst prof math, Northeastern Univ, Boston, Mass, 76-77. *Concurrent Pos:* Pres, Appl Biomath, 82- *Res:* Theoretical ecology, mathematical models in ecology; applied ecology relating to ecological risk analysis as a methodology for environmental impact assessment. *Mailing Add:* Dept Ecol & Evolution State Univ NY 100 Nicholls Rd Stony Brook NY 11794-0001

GINZBURG, VITALY LAZAREVICH, PHYSICS. *Current Pos:* STAFF PN LEBEDEV PHYSICS INST, RUSSIAN ACAD SCI, 40-; PROF, MOSCOW TECH INST PHYSICS, 68- *Personal Data:* b Moscow, Russia, Oct 4, 16; m 46, Nina; c 1. *Honors & Awards:* Lomonosov Prize, 62; Lenin Prize, 66; Vavilov Gold Medal, 95; Big Lomonosov Gold Medal, 95. *Prof Exp:* Prof, Gorky Univ, 45-68. *Mem:* Foreign fel Nat Acad Sci; Acad Sci USSR; Acad Europ; hon fel Indian Acad Sci; NY Acad Sci; foreign fel Indian Nat Sci Acad. *Res:* Contributed articles to professional journals. *Mailing Add:* Lebedev Phys Inst Russ Scis Leninsky Prospect 53 Moscow B-333 Russia

GINZEL, KARL-HEINZ, PHARMACOLOGY. *Current Pos:* PROF PHARMACOL, UNIV ARK MED SCI, LITTLE ROCK, 71- *Personal Data:* b Reichenberg, Czech, June 1, 21; US citizen; m 58; c 2. *Educ:* Univ Vienna, MD, 48. *Prof Exp:* Res asst pharmacol, Vienna, 48-53; res sci officer, Biol Sect, Glaxo Labs, Eng, 54-55; sr lectr neuro-pharmacol, Inst Neurol, Nat Hosp Nerv Dis, London, 57-60; head neuropharmacol sect, Riker Labs, Calif, 60-70. *Concurrent Pos:* WHO res fel pharmacol, Oxford Univ, 52-53; sr res fel neurophysiol & pharmacol, Univ Birmingham, 55-57; res assoc anatomist, Univ Calif, Los Angeles, 69-71; vis prof, Cardiovasc Res Inst, Univ Calif, San Francisco, 76. *Mem:* Am Soc Pharmacol & Exp Therapeut; Brit Physiol Soc; Ger Pharmacol Soc. *Res:* Pharmacology of neuromuscular and ganglionic transmission; introduction to clinical use of succinylcholine; central muscle relaxant agents; respiratory stimulant vanillic acid diethyamide; psychotomimetic drugs; 5-hydroxytryptamine; autonomic and cardiovascular pharmacology; neuropharmacology; sensory stimulants; prostaglandins, nicotine; educational programs on tobacco; expert reviewer of the Surgeon General's Report 87, Nicotine Addiction. *Mailing Add:* Dept Pharmacol Univ Ark Med Sci 4301 W Markham Little Rock AR 72205-7101

GINZTON, EDWARD LEONARD, APPLIED PHYSICS. *Current Pos:* RETIRED. *Personal Data:* b Dnepropetrovsk, Ukraine, Dec 27, 15; US citizen; m 39; c 4. *Educ:* Univ Calif, BS, 36, MS, 37; Stanford Univ, EE, 38, PhD, 40. *Honors & Awards:* Liebmann Mem Prize, Inst Elec & Electronics Engrs, 58, Medal of Hon, 69. *Prof Exp:* Res engr, Sperry Gyroscope Co, NY, 40-46; asst prof appl physics & elec eng, Stanford Univ, 46-47; mem, Bd Dir, Varian Assoc Inc, 48-59, chmn, 59-84, chief exec officer, 59-72, pres, 64-68, chmn, Exec Comt, 84- *Concurrent Pos:* From assoc prof to prof elec eng, Stanford Univ, 47-68, dir, Microwave Lab, 49-59, dir, Proj M, 57-60; co-chmn, Stanford Mid-Peninsula Urban Coalition, 68-72; mem bd dir, Mid-Peninsula Coalition Housing Develop Corp, 70-; chmn, Comt Motor Vehicle Emissions, Nat Acad Sci, 71-74, co-chmn, Comt Nuclear Energy Study, 75-80, mem, Comt Sci & Nat Security, 82-84 & Comt Lab Animals Biomed & Behav Res, 85-88; mem coun, Nat Acad Eng, 74-80; mem bd dir, Stanford Hosp, 75; mem bd trustees, Stanford Univ, 77- *Mem:* Nat Acad Sci; Nat Acad Eng; AAAS; Am Acad Arts & Sci; fel Inst Elec & Electronics Engrs; Nat Acad Econ Res. *Res:* Microwave tube and measurements; linear electron accelerators; circuits. *Mailing Add:* 28014 Natoma Rd Los Altos Hills CA 94022

GIOANNINI, THERESA LEE, BIOORGANIC & ORGANIC CHEMISTRY. *Current Pos:* assoc prof, 90-92, PROF, DEPT NATURAL SCI, BARUCH COL, CITY UNIV NEW YORK, 92-; RES ASSOC PROF, DEPT PSYCHOL, NY UNIV MED CTR, 94- *Personal Data:* b Galesburg, Ill, Nov 21, 49; m 79, Jerrold P Weiss; c 2. *Educ:* St Mary-of-the-Woods Col, BS, 71; NY Univ, MS, 76, PhD(chem), 78. *Prof Exp:* Biochem technician spec chem clin lab, Mercy Hosp, 71-73; asst res scientist chem opiate receptor, NY Univ Med Ctr, 77-84, res asst prof, Dept Psychol, 84-93. *Mem:* Am Chem Soc; AAAS; NY Acad Sci. *Res:* Use of photo affinity labels to investigate biological systems; chemical characterization and isolation of the opiate receptors; examination of biological systems with photophysical probes. *Mailing Add:* Dept Natural Sci Baruch Col City Univ New York 17 Lexington Ave New York NY 10010

GIOGGIA, ROBERT STEPHEN, OPTICS. *Current Pos:* From instr to assoc prof, 67-84, PROF PHYSICS, WIDENER COL, 84- *Personal Data:* b Bronx, NY, Sept 29, 43. *Educ:* NY Univ, BS, 65; Trinity Col, MS, 67; Bryn Mawr Col, PhD(physics), 75. *Mem:* Am Asn Physics Teachers; Am Phys Soc; Sigma Xi; Optical Soc Am. *Res:* Instabilities and chaos in lasers. *Mailing Add:* Dept Physics Widener Col 1 University Pl Chester PA 19013

GIOIA, ANTHONY ALFRED, ARITHMETIC FUNCTIONS. *Current Pos:* assoc prof, 66-74, PROF MATH, WESTERN MICH UNIV, 74- *Personal Data:* b Torrington, Conn, Apr 7, 34; m 78, M Patricia; c 3. *Educ:* Univ Conn, BA, 55; Univ Mo, MA, 61, PhD(math), 64. *Prof Exp:* Instr math, Univ Mo, 59-64; asst prof, Tex Tech Univ, 64-66. *Mem:* Am Math Soc; Math Asn Am; Fibonacci Asn. *Res:* Theory of numbers; arithmetic functions. *Mailing Add:* Dept Math PO Box 536 Galesburg MI 49053-0536

GIOLLI, ROLAND A, NEUROANATOMY, HISTOLOGY. *Current Pos:* from asst prof anat to assoc prof, 64-70, PROF ANAT, NEUROBIOL & BIOL SCI, UNIV CALIF, IRVINE-CALIF COL MED, 74- *Personal Data:* b San Vito, Italy, Feb 22, 34; US citizen; m 63; c 3. *Educ:* Univ Calif, Davis, AB, 56; Univ Calif, Berkeley, PhD(anat), 60. *Prof Exp:* Asst anat, Univ Calif, Berkeley, 57-59, res anatomist, Sch Optom, 60-63. *Concurrent Pos:* Ment Health Training Prog fel, Dept Anat & Brain Res Inst, Univ Calif, Los Angeles, 63-64; Alexander von Humboldt Sr Scientist Award, 82-83. *Mem:* Am Asn Anat; Soc Neurosci. *Res:* Visual system; visual-vestibular mechanisms; oculomotor system; neurotransmitters. *Mailing Add:* Dept Anat & Neurobiol Col Med Univ Calif Irvine CA 92717. *Fax:* 714-824-8549

GIOMETTI, CAROL SMITH, TWO DIMENSIONAL ELECTROPHORESIS, PROTEIN BIOCHEMISTRY. *Current Pos:* fel, Argonne Nat Lab, Ill, 78-82, asst biologist, 82-83, asst biochemist, 83-87, BIOCHEMIST, ARGONNE NAT LAB, ILL, 87- *Personal Data:* b Milford, Conn, Aug 10, 50; m 79, Ronald P; c Brian, Renee & Gregory. *Educ:* Knox Col, Galesburg, Ill, BA, 72; Rush Med Col, Chicago, Ill, MT, 73; Univ Ill, Chicago, PhD(biochem), 78. *Honors & Awards:* Young Clin Chemist Res Award, Am Asn Clin Chem, 84. *Prof Exp:* Teaching asst biochem, Univ Ill, Chicago, 73-78. *Mem:* Am Soc Cell Biol; Electrophoresis Soc; Environ Mutagen Soc; Am Soc Clin Pathologists. *Res:* Two dimensional gel electrophoresis used to detect protein alterations related to genetic variation, toxic exposure and-or pathological processes in human cells and animal model systems; proteins found to be markers for specific abnormalities are characterizied biochemically. *Mailing Add:* Argonne Nat Lab Ctr Mechanistic Biol & Biotechnol Bldg 202 9700 S Cass Ave Argonne IL 60439. *Fax:* 630-252-5517; *E-Mail:* csgiometti@anl.gov

GION, EDMUND, PHYSICS. *Current Pos:* RES PHYSICIST, BALLISTIC RES LAB, ABERDEEN PROVING GROUND, 65- *Personal Data:* b Altheimer, Ark, Sept 27, 29; m 60; c 3. *Educ:* Reed Col, BA, 59; Lehigh Univ, MS, 61, PhD(physics), 65. *Mem:* Am Phys Soc; Am Defense Preparedness Asn. *Res:* Shock tubes; blast waves; non-equilibrium flow phenomena; fluid dynamics. *Mailing Add:* 809 S Washington St Havre De Grace MD 21078

GIONFRIDDO, MAURICE PAUL, AERONAUTICAL ENGINEERING. *Current Pos:* AERO ENGR, ARMY NATICK RES, DEVELOP & ENG CTR, MASS, 57- *Personal Data:* b Medford, Mass, Feb 19, 31; m 56, Joan M Powers; c Marianne E & Linda. *Educ:* Mass Inst Technol, BS, 53, MS, 59. *Honors & Awards:* Aerodyn Decelerator Award, Am Inst Aeronaut & Astronaut, 90. *Prof Exp:* Res asst, Aeroelastic & Struct Res Lab, Mass Inst

Technol, Cambridge, 53-54; aero res engr, Air Force Cambridge Res Ctr, Bedford, Mass, 56-57. *Concurrent Pos:* Mem, Nat Parachute Tech Coun, 91- *Mem:* Fel Am Inst Aeronaut & Astronaut; Sigma Xi. *Res:* Aeronautical engineering. *Mailing Add:* 20 Westminster Way Westborough MA 01581-3410

GIORDANO, ANTHONY B(RUNO), electronics engineering, research administration; deceased, see previous edition for last biography

GIORDANO, ARTHUR ANTHONY, DIGITAL COMMUNICATIONS, DIGITAL SIGNAL PROCESSING. *Current Pos:* VPRES SYSTS, CNR, INC, 85- *Personal Data:* b Boston, Mass, Sept 28, 41; m 64; c 2. *Educ:* Northeastern Univ, BS, 64, MS, 66; Univ Pa, PhD(elec eng), 70. *Prof Exp:* Eng specialist, GTE Sylvania, 70-72; sr tech staff, Stein Assocs, 72-74; eng specialist, GTE Sylvania, 70-72, sr eng specialist, 78-80, radio systs dept mgr, 80-81, survivable systs dept mgr, 81-85. *Concurrent Pos:* Instr, Northeastern Univ, 73-75 & 78-79, Tufts Univ, 80-81 & Northeastern Univ, 81-; vchmn, Comn E, Int Union Radio Sci, 78-81, chmn, 81-84. *Mem:* Int Union Radio Sci; Inst Elec & Electronics Engrs. *Res:* Design and performance evaluation of various radio systems, including waveform design (modulation and coding), channel modeling, receiver design, network design, propagation analysis, digital signal processing, spread spectrum and message handling systems. *Mailing Add:* GTE Labs 40 Sylvan Rd Waltham MA 02254

GIORDANO, NICHOLAS J, THERMAL & SOLID STATE PHYSICS. *Current Pos:* ASST PROF PHYSICS, PURDUE UNIV, 79- *Personal Data:* b Frankfort, Ind, Dec 21, 51; m 73; c 1. *Educ:* Purdue Univ, BS, 73; Yale Univ, PhD(eng & appl sci). *Prof Exp:* Asst prof eng & appl sci, Yale Univ, 77-79. *Concurrent Pos:* Vis scientist, Hahn-Meitner Inst, Berlin, 77. *Mem:* Am Phys Soc. *Res:* Fabrication and properties of microstructures; low frequency noise in solids. *Mailing Add:* Physics Dept Purdue Univ West Lafayette IN 47907

GIORDANO, PAUL M, AGRICULTURAL RESEARCH. *Current Pos:* CONSULT SOIL SCI SPECIALIST, ENVIRON & WASTE MGR, 93- *Personal Data:* b Providence, RI, Apr 4, 36. *Educ:* Univ RI, BS, 59, MS, 60; Univ Conn, PhD(soil chem), 64. *Prof Exp:* Mem staff, Tenn Valley Authority. *Mem:* Soil Sci Soc Am; Am Soc Agron; Nat Mgt Asn. *Mailing Add:* 215 Wesley Ct Florence AL 35630

GIORDANO, THOMAS HENRY, GEOCHEMISTRY. *Current Pos:* Fel geochem, Depts Physics & Earth Sci, 77-79, ASST PROF GEOL, NMEX STATE UNIV, 80- *Personal Data:* b Philadelphia, Pa, Feb 13, 50. *Educ:* Millersville State Col, BA, 72; Pa State Univ, PhD(geochem), 78. *Mem:* Am Chem Soc; Am Geophys Union; Soc Econ Geologists; Geochem Soc. *Res:* Chemical hydrothermal systems; chemical speciation in natural waters; experimental determination of mineral solubilities; transport and deposition of ore minerals. *Mailing Add:* Dept Geol Sci NMex State Univ Box 3AB Las Cruces NM 88003

GIORDANO, TONY, GENE REGULATION, MRNA PROTEIN INTERACTIONS. *Current Pos:* SR RES SCIENTIST, ABBOTT LABS, 91- *Personal Data:* b Cleveland, Ohio, May 8, 60; m 82, Heidi L Spanninger; c Victoria E, Gabrielle M & Dante. *Educ:* New Col Univ SFla, BA, 83; Ohio State Univ, MSc, 84, PhD(molecular genetics), 88. *Prof Exp:* Fel biotechnol, Nat Cancer Inst, NIH, 88-90, staff fel, Nat Inst Aging, 90-91. *Concurrent Pos:* Adj asst prof, Dept Med & Neurosci, Chicago Med Sch, 93- *Mem:* Am Soc Cell Biol; Soc Neurosci. *Res:* Gene regulation in Alzheimer's disease; clone genes novel to the disease. *Mailing Add:* Dir Molecular Biol Symphony Pharmaceut Inc 76 Great Valley Pkwy Malvern PA 19355. *Fax:* 847-937-9195

GIORDMAINE, JOSEPH ANTHONY, OPTICAL PHYSICS, SOLID STATE PHYSICS. *Current Pos:* VPRES, NEC RES INST, 89- *Personal Data:* b Toronto, Ont, Apr 10, 33; m 58; c 3. *Educ:* Univ Toronto, BA, 55; Columbia Univ, AM, 57, PhD(physics), 60. *Prof Exp:* Instr physics, Columbia Univ, 59-61; dir chem physics res, Bell Labs, 71-76, Solid State Electronics, 74-81, Electronic & Photonic Technol, 81-83, III & V Electronic & Display, 83-85, dir, Advan Technol Develop, 85-87, mem tech staff, 61-89. *Concurrent Pos:* Consult, Fairchild Camera & Instrument Corp, 61; lectr, Univ Calif Exten, 64-68; vis prof, Munich Tech Univ, 66; mem comt basic res advan, Army Res Off, Nat Res Coun, 67-72, panel atomic, molecular & electronics physics, Physics Surv Comt, 70-71; adv ed, Optics Commun, 70-75 & J Non-Metals 72-80; mem comt on atomic & molecular physics, Nat Res Coun, 71-74; vis comt, Mass Inst Technol Mat Magnet Lab, 71-73; nomination comt, Am Physical Soc, 73, Frack Isakson Prize Award Comt, 81; prog chmn, Int Quantum Electronics Conf, 76, chmn, 78; assoc ed, Optics Lett, 77-79; mem steering comt, Conf Laser Eng & Appln, 77-79; mem comt employment foreign scientist to US, Nat Res Coun, 79-80, US liason comt, IUPAP, 81-87; ed comt, Ann Rev Mats Sci Asn, 79-, assoc ed, 83-; mem, Inst Imaging Sci Adv Comt, Polytechnic Inst, NY, 81; mem Comn Quantum Electronics, Int Union Rive & Appl Physics, 81-87, vchmn, 86-87. *Mem:* AAAS; fel Am Phys Soc; sr mem Inst Elec & Electronics Eng; Am Astron Soc; Optical Soc Am; Sigma Xi. *Res:* Molecular beams; paramagnetic resonance and relaxation; masers and lasers; nonlinear optical effects; optical properties of solids; radio astronomy; solid state electronics. *Mailing Add:* 710 Prospect Ave Princeton NJ 08540

GIORGI, ANGELO LOUIS, RADIOCHEMISTRY. *Current Pos:* RETIRED. *Personal Data:* b Syracuse, NY, July 18, 17; m 46, Elizabeth M Taylor; c Stephen & Daniel. *Educ:* Syracuse Univ, BS, 39; Univ NMex, MS, 54, PhD, 57. *Prof Exp:* Chemist, Gen Motors Corp, 40-42; jr chemist, US Bur Mines, 42-44; asst chemist, Naval Res Lab, 44-46; mem staff radiochem, Los Alamos Nat Lab, 46-87. *Mem:* Am Phys Soc; Mat Res Soc. *Res:* Superconductivity; study of superconducting properties of refractory carbides and nitrides; magnetism and superconductivity in actinide metals. *Mailing Add:* 151 El Gancho St Los Alamos NM 87544

GIORGI, ELSIE A, HEALTH CARE PLANNING. *Current Pos:* ASSOC CLIN PROF MED, SCH MED, UNIV CALIF, LOS ANGELES, 72- *Personal Data:* b New York, NY, Mar 8, 11. *Educ:* Hunter Col, BA, 31; Col Physicians & Surgeons, Columbia Univ, MD, 49; Am Bd Internal Med, dipl, 56. *Prof Exp:* Asst prof clin med, Cornell Univ Med Col, 57-62; asst prof, Univ Calif, Los Angeles, 62-66; asst prof med, Univ Southern Calif, Sch Med, 66-69; assoc clin prof community & family med, Univ Calif, Col Med, Irvine, 69-72. *Concurrent Pos:* Dir med, NY Infirmary, 60-61; attend physician, Dept Med, Cedars-Sinai Hosp, Los Angeles, 62-; guest lectr, Sch Social Welfare, Univ Calif, Los Angeles, 64-81; attend physician, Los Angeles Co Hospital, Univ Southern Calif Med Ctr, 66-71; assoc mem, Dept Internal Med, Orange Co Med Ctr, 69-; mem staff, St John's Hosp, Calif, 70- *Mem:* Inst Med-Nat Acad Sci; Geront Soc; Am Pub Health Asn. *Mailing Add:* 153 S Laskey Dr Suite 3 Beverly Hills CA 90212

GIORGI, JANIS V(INCENT), FLOW CYTOMETRY, LYMPHOCYTE DIFFERENTIATION. *Current Pos:* ASST PROF IMMUNOL, UNIV CALIF SCH MED, LOS ANGELES, 84- *Personal Data:* b Meadville, Pa, May 23, 47. *Educ:* Univ Fla, Gainesville, BA, 69, Univ NMex, PhD(microbiol & immunol), 77. *Prof Exp:* Fel, Sch Med, Univ NMex, 77-80, asst resident prof path, 80-81; instr surg, immunol, Harvard Med Sch, 81-83. *Concurrent Pos:* Asst surg immunol, Mass Gen Hosp, 81-83. *Mem:* Am Asn Immunologists; Soc Anal Cytol; Clin Cytometry Soc. *Res:* Basic laboratory research on human immunology, especially immune deficiencies, virus-host interactions, and transplantation biology. *Mailing Add:* Dept Med/CIC Univ Calif Sch Med 12-240 Factor Bldg Los Angeles CA 90095-1745

GIORGIO, ANTHONY JOSEPH, HEMATOLOGY, BIOCHEMISTRY. *Current Pos:* PROF MED, CHARLES R DREW POSTGRAD MED SCH, UNIV CALIF, LOS ANGELES, 72-; ASSOC PROF, UNIV SOUTHERN CALIF, 72- *Personal Data:* b Hartford, Conn, Feb 8, 30; m 61; c 3. *Educ:* Boston Univ, AB, 52, MD, 57; Columbia Univ, MSPH, 53; Am Bd Internal Med, dipl; Am Bd Hematol, dipl. *Prof Exp:* Instr med, Univ Utah, 62-66; asst prof pediat, NY Med Col, 67-70; asst prof med, Sch Med, Univ Pittsburgh, 70-72; chief, Hemat Div, Martin Luther King, Jr Gen Hosp, 72-78. *Concurrent Pos:* NIH fel biochem, Univ Utah, 64-66; NIH res grant, 69- *Mem:* Am Inst Nutrit; Am Soc Clin Nutrit; Am Fedn Clin Res; Am Soc Hemat; fel Am Col Physicians. *Res:* Nutritional anemias; vitamin B-12 metabolism; clinical laboratory methodology. *Mailing Add:* 3440 W Lomita Blvd Torrance CA 90505-4801

GIORI, CLAUDIO, POLYMER CHEMISTRY, MEDICAL APPLICATIONS OF PLASTICS. *Current Pos:* POLYMER SPECIALIST, HOLLISTER INC, 87- *Personal Data:* b Milano, Italy, June 2, 38; US citizen; m 63, Serena Mazza; c Nicholas & Robert. *Educ:* Univ Milano, PhD(polymer chem), 62. *Prof Exp:* Res scientist, ENI Res Labs, 63-65 & Fibers Div, Allied Chem Corp, 65-68; res scientist, IIT Res Inst, 68-74, sr scientist, 74-81; sr res scientist, Borg-Warner Corp, 81-87. *Concurrent Pos:* Nat dir, Soc Aerospace Mat & Process Eng, 84-85. *Mem:* AAAS; Am Chem Soc; Soc Aerospace Mat & Process Eng. *Res:* Synthesis of high temperature resistant polymers; kinetics and mechanisms of polymerization; stereospecific polymerization; thermal degradation and stabilization of polymers; polymers for reverse osmosis processes; effect of radiation on polymers; polymers for medical devices. *Mailing Add:* 2975 Orange Brace Rd Riverwoods IL 60015

GIOVACCHINI, PETER L, PSYCHIATRY, PSYCHOSOMATIC MEDICINE. *Current Pos:* from clin asst prof to clin assoc prof, 54-62, CLIN PROF PSYCHIAT, UNIV ILL COL MED, 62- *Personal Data:* b New York, NY, Apr 12, 22; m 45; c 3. *Educ:* Univ Chicago, BS, 41, MD, 44. *Prof Exp:* Res fel psychiat, Univ Chicago Clins, 48-50. *Concurrent Pos:* Consult, Michael Reese Hosp, Chicago, 51-57, Wil Wilmette Family Serv Bur, Ill, 54-, United Charities, Chicago, 55-64 & Res & Educ Hosp, Chicago, 58-; vis prof psychiat, Univ Southern Calif, 68; ed-in-chief, Tactics & Tech Psychoanal Treat, 72-; co-ed, Adolescent Psychiat, 72-81; lectr, Am Psychother Inst, 73- *Mem:* Am Psychoanalytic Asn; fel Am Psychiat Soc; fel Am Orthopsychiat Asn. *Res:* Psychotherapeutic process; characterological disorders; psychosomatic medicine, particularly multiple psychosomatic conditions in the same patients; psychotic states. *Mailing Add:* 270 Locust Rd Winnetka IL 60093-3609. *Fax:* 847-441-7141

GIOVACCHINI, RUBERT PETER, medicine, for more information see previous edition

GIOVANELLA, BEPPINO C, CANCER. *Current Pos:* LAB DIR, CANCER RES LAB, ST JOSEPH'S HOSP, 70- *Personal Data:* b Merano, Italy, June 12, 32; m 71; c 2. *Educ:* Univ Rome, Laurea(biol), 56, Libera Docenza (gen path), 62. *Prof Exp:* Asst cancer res, Regina Elena Inst, Rome, 56-60; res assoc, McArdle Lab, Univ Wis-Madison, 62-70. *Concurrent Pos:* Clin asst prof oncol, Col Med Baylor Univ, 71-75, adj asst prof oncol, 75-77, adj assoc prof, Baylor Col Med, 77- *Mem:* Am Asn Cancer Res; Am Asn Pathologists; NY Acad Sci. *Res:* Radiobiology of tumors; skin carcinogenesis; effects of supranormal temperatures on normal and neoplastic cells; chemotherapy of malignant tumors; immunobiology of neoplastic cells; heterotransplantation of human tumors in nude thymusless mice. *Mailing Add:* Cancer Res Lab St Joseph's Hosp Houston TX 77002

GIOVANELLI, RICCARDO, RADIO ASTRONOMY. *Current Pos:* PROF ASTRON, CORNELL UNIV, 91- *Personal Data:* b Reggio Emilia, Italy, Aug 30, 46; m 77. *Educ:* Univ Bologna, Laurea di Dottorato, 68; Ind Univ, Bloomington, MA, 71, PhD(astron), 76. *Hon Degrees:* Knight of Rep of Italy for J W Merit, 97. *Honors & Awards:* H Draper Medal Astron Physics, Nat Acad Sci, 89. *Prof Exp:* Res asst astron, Univ Bologna, 68-69; vis prof physics, Nat Univ El Salvador, 73-75; staff scientist astron, Univ Bologna, 76-77; vis prof, Univ Okla, 77-78; sr res assoc, Nat Astron & Ionosphere Ctr, 78-91, head, Radio Astron Div, 84-91; dir, Areciho Observ, 87-88. *Mem:* Soc Ital Astron; Am Astron Soc; Int Astron Union; AAAS. *Res:* Structure of the interstellar medium; high velocity hydrogen clouds; interacting galaxies; clusters of galaxies; cosmology. *Mailing Add:* Dept Astron Cornell Univ 412 Space Sci Bldg Ithaca NY 14853

GIOVANIELLI, DAMON V, INTERNAL CONFINEMENT FUSION, NUCLEAR EXPLOSIVES. *Current Pos:* PRES, SUMNER ASSOC, 93-; VPRES, SCI APPL INT CORP. *Personal Data:* b Teaneck, NJ, May 8, 43; m 68, Eleanor Rand; c Kiva & Tina. *Educ:* Princeton Univ, AB, 65; Dartmouth Col, PhD(physics), 70. *Prof Exp:* Instr appl sci, Yale Univ, 70-72; mem staff, Los Alamos Nat Lab, 72-77, alt group leader, 77-79, assoc div leader, 79-80, prog mgr exp inertial fusion, 80-83, dep assoc dir, 83-87, physics div leader, 87-93. *Concurrent Pos:* Mem, Prog Comt, Div Plasma Physics, AM Phys Soc, 78-79; Chief scientist, Technol Inst Sci Collab, 92- *Mem:* Am Phys Soc; Am Asn Physics Teachers; Sigma Xi; fel AAAS; Am Inst Aeronauts & Astronauts. *Res:* Inertial fusion experiments; nuclear explosive experiments; high pressure research. *Mailing Add:* 12 Loma del Escolar Los Alamos NM 87544. *Fax:* 505-984-3251

GIOVINCO, GINA, NURSING. *Current Pos:* ASSOC PROF NURSING, UNIV CENT FLA, 87- *Educ:* Fla State Univ, BSNEd, 63; NY Univ, MA, 66; Univ Pac, PhD(community ment health), 81. *Prof Exp:* Nurse officer, USPHS Hosp, NY, 63-69; instr pediat, Col Med, Univ NMex, 69-70; assoc prof & chmn, Nursing Prog, Temple Univ, 70-75; assoc prof, Hahnemann Col Allied Health, 75-76; nurse dir & adminr, Home Health Lehigh Valley Inc, 76-77; assoc prof & chmn, Dept Nursing, Col Misericordia, 77-80; assoc prof, Grad Prog, Univ Southern Miss, 80-82; asst prof, Reach Proj, Col Nursing, Univ Fla, 82-83, Grad Prog, 83-87. *Concurrent Pos:* Fulbright grante, Univ Jordan, 96-97. *Res:* Contributed numerous publications in field. *Mailing Add:* Sch Nursing Univ Cent Fla HPB410 4000 Central Florida Blvd Orlando FL 32816-2210. *Fax:* 407-823-5675

GIOVINETTO, MARIO BARTOLOME, CLIMATOLOGY, SEA ICE. *Current Pos:* prof & head dept, 73-83, PROF CLIMAT, UNIV CALGARY, 83- *Personal Data:* b La Plata, Arg, May 5, 33; m 66, Lois Jenkins; c Anna. *Educ:* Univ Wis-Madison, MS, 66, PhD(geog), 68. *Prof Exp:* Res asst glaciol, Ohio State Univ, 59-61; res assoc geol, Univ Mich, 59; proj asst glaciol, Univ Wis-Madison, 61-67, actg instr climat, 67-68; from asst prof to assoc prof, Univ Calif, Berkeley, 68-73. *Concurrent Pos:* Mem, Nat Res Coun, 71-74. *Mem:* Am Geophys Union; Int Glaciol Soc. *Res:* Arctic and Antarctic glaciology; physical climatology of glaciers and its implications on paleoclimates. *Mailing Add:* Dept Geog Univ Calgary Calgary AB T2N 1N4 Can. *Fax:* 403-282-6561; *E-Mail:* mgiovine@acs.ucalgary.ca

GIOVINO, GARY A, PATHOLOGY, EPIDEMIOLOGY. *Current Pos:* epidemiologist, Off Smoking & Health, Ctr Dis Control & Prev, 88-91, actg chief, Epidemiol Br, 90-91, CHIEF, EPIDEMIOL BR, OFF SMOKING & HEALTH, CTR DIS CONTROL & PREV, 91- *Personal Data:* b Sept 30, 52; 85, Susan Backus; c Claire & Daniel. *Educ:* Univ Notre Dame, BA, 74; State Univ NY, Buffalo, MS, 79, PhD(exp path & epidemiol), 87. *Prof Exp:* Can-dial oper, Cancer Info Servs, Roswell Park Mem Inst, 77-79, sr med recs clerk tumor registry, 80-82, res affil, Dept Cancer Control Epidemiol, 82-83, counr & asst to dir, Stop Smoking Clin, 83-84; asst res scientist, NY State Dept Health, 84; res assoc, Smoking Res Prog, Dept Psychol, Univ Rochester, 85-88. *Concurrent Pos:* Instr, Dept Psychol, Univ Rochester, 84-87, asst prof, 87-88; consult, US Dept Health & Human Servs, 90-96, Mass Inst Health Policy, 93-95, US Food & Drug Admin, 95, WHO, 96, Ctr Family & Community Health, 96 & Ctr Dis Control & Prev, 96. *Mem:* Soc Res Nicotine & Tobacco; Am Pub Health Asn. *Res:* Patterns, determinants and consequences of tobacco use; disease prevention and health promotion; authored or co-authored over 100 scientific publications. *Mailing Add:* Off Smoking & Health Ctr Dis Control 4770 Buford Hwy NE MSK-50 Atlanta GA 30341-3724. *Fax:* 770-488-5848; *E-Mail:* gag3@cdc.gov

GIPSON, ILENE KAY, CELL BIOLOGY. *Current Pos:* assoc scientist & head, Morphol Univ, 79-84, SR SCIENTIST & HEAD, CORNEA UNIT, SCHEPENS EYE RES INST, BOSTON, 84-; ASSOC PROF OPHTHAL ANAT & CELL BIOL, HARVARD MED SCH, BOSTON, 85- *Personal Data:* b Hoberg, Mo, Oct 13, 44. *Educ:* Drury Col, BA, 66; Univ Ark, MS, 68, PhD(zool), 73. *Honors & Awards:* Alcon Res Award, 85; Merit Award, Nat Eye Inst, 90. *Prof Exp:* Teaching asst zool, Univ Ark, 66-68, res asst plant path, 68-70, asst zool, 70-73; res assoc & instr cell biol cornea, Univ Ore, 74-76, asst prof ophthal, Health Sci Ctr, 76-79; asst prof ophthal, Harvard Med Sch, Boston, 79-85. *Concurrent Pos:* Consult, Vision Res Planning Comt, Nat eye Inst, 76, prin investr NIH Grant, 77-, res career develop award, 78-83, mem, Vision Res Prog Comt, Study Sect, 79-84; Visa Study Sect, 92- *Mem:* Am Soc Cell Biologists; Asn Res Vision & Ophthal; Int Soc Eye Res. *Res:* Motility and adhesion of corneal epithelium; mucin synthesis by stratified epithelia. *Mailing Add:* Schepens Eye Res Inst 20 Staniford St Boston MA 02114-2500. *Fax:* 617-720-1069

GIPSON, MACK, JR, GEOLOGY. *Current Pos:* PROF GEOL, UNIV SC, 86- *Personal Data:* b Trenton, SC, Sept 15, 31. *Educ:* Paine Col, BA, 53; Univ Chicago MS, 61, PhD(geol), 63. *Prof Exp:* Prof & chmn, Dept Geol Sci, Va State Univ, 64-75; res assoc, Exxon Prod Res Co, 75-82; mgr plastic geol & sr plastic geologist, NLER Co, 82-84; explorationist, Aminoil Inc, 84; sr proj specialist, Phillips Petrol, 84-86. *Mem:* Sigma Xi; fel Geol Soc Am; Asn Petrol Geologists; Nat Asn Black Geologists & Geophysicists; Am Geophys Union; Nat Tech Asn; Nat Asn Geol Teachers. *Mailing Add:* Dept Geol Univ SC Columbia SC 29208-0001

GIPSON, PHILIP, WILDLIFE ECOLOGY. *Current Pos:* res assoc wildlife ecol, Univ Ark, Fayetteville, 71-74. *Personal Data:* b Ft Smith, Ark, Jan 2, 43. *Educ:* State Col Ark, BS, 64; Univ Ark, MS, 67, PhD(zool), 71. *Prof Exp:* Teacher sci, Juneau Pub Sch Syst, Alaska, 65-66; asst prof wildlife ecol & exten wildlife specialist, Univ Nebr, Lincoln, 74-76; assoc prof wildlife mgt & asst leader Alaska Coop Wildlife Res Unit, Univ Alaska, 76-84; supvr wildlife res, Ark Game & Fish Comn, Little Rock, 84-87. *Concurrent Pos:* Consult, Ark Dept Planning, 72-73. *Mem:* Wildlife Soc; Am Soc Mammal; Ecol Soc Am; Sigma Xi; Soc Risk Anal. *Res:* Interrelationships of wildlife and agriculture, emphasizing damage assessment and control; predator and prey interactions; wildlife and habitat relationships. *Mailing Add:* 1611 Sunnyslope Lane Manhattan KS 66502-4630. *Fax:* 785-532-7159

GIPSON, ROBERT MALONE, INDUSTRIAL ORGANIC CHEMISTRY. *Current Pos:* Res Chemist, Texaco Chem Co Austin Labs, 65-76, supvr applns res, 76-82, mgr develop, 82-86, mgr tech servs, 86-88, DIR, TEXACO PORT ARTHUR RES LABS, 88-, DIR REFINING & FUELS RES, TEXACO RES & DEVELOP, 91- *Personal Data:* b Odessa, Tex, Apr 9, 39; m 61; c 2. *Educ:* Abilene Christian Col, BS, 61; Univ Tex, MA, 63, PhD(org chem), 65. *Mem:* Am Chem Soc; AAAS. *Res:* Catalysis; process research; surface active agents. *Mailing Add:* 2701 Glacier Dr Port Arthur TX 77640. *Fax:* 409-989-6681

GIRALDO, ALVARO A, IMMUNOPATHOLOGY. *Current Pos:* ASSOC PATHOLOGIST, ST JOHN HOSP, DETROIT, 76-, HEAD, DIV IMMUNOPATH, 78- *Personal Data:* b Colombia, SAm, Jan 7, 45; nat US; c 2. *Prof Exp:* Internship, St Ignacio Univ Hosp, SAm, 67; resident path, Cent Mil Hosp, SAm, 69; internship, St John Hosp, Mich, 70, resident path, 71-74, fel path cancer, Univ Tex Syst Cancer Ctr, M D Anderson Hosp & Tumor Inst, 75. *Concurrent Pos:* Fel immunol, Wayne State Univ, 76-78, adj asst prof, Dept Immunol & Microbiol, Sch Med, 78-88, Dept Path, 80-88, adj assoc prof, Dept Immunol, Microbiol & Path, 88-, vis fel histocompatability & molecular biol, 89-; vis fel cardiovasc path, NIH, 79; vis scholar hematopath, Univ Southern Calif, Los Angeles, 84. *Mem:* Am Soc Clin Pathologists; Int Acad Path; Am Asn Pathologists; Soc Hematopath; NY Acad Sci; AAAS; Soc Cardiovasc Path; Soc Med Lab Immunol; Am Asn Immunologists; Clin Immunol Soc. *Mailing Add:* Dept Immunopath St John Hosp 22101 Moross Rd Detroit MI 48236-2172. *Fax:* 313-881-4727

GIRARD, DENNIS MICHAEL, MATHEMATICS, STATISTICS. *Current Pos:* asst prof ecosyst anal, 69-73, assoc prof math & statist, 73-90, PROF INFO & COMPUT SCI, UNIV WIS-GREEN BAY, 90- *Personal Data:* b Detroit, Mich, July 26, 39; m 62; c 3. *Educ:* Univ Detroit, BS, 61, MA, 62; Ohio State Univ, PhD(math), 68. *Prof Exp:* Aerospace engr, Lewis Res Ctr, NASA, 62-63; asst prof math, Ohio State Univ, 68-69. *Mem:* AAAS; Am Math Soc; Math Asn Am; Am Statist Asn; Biometr Soc; Inst Math Statist; Inst Elec & Electronics Engrs. *Res:* Biomathematics; biostatistics; image analysis; statistical methodology in toxicology. *Mailing Add:* Col Environ Sci Univ Wis Green Bay WI 54301

GIRARD, FRANCIS HENRY, TECHNOLOGY COMMERCIALIZATION, TECHNOLOGY DEVELOPMENT & IDENTIFICATION. *Personal Data:* b Chicago, Ill, Dec 28, 35; m 58; c 3. *Educ:* De Paul Univ, BS, 57 & MS, 59; Northwestern Univ, PhD(chem), 64. *Prof Exp:* Instr chem, Evanston Hosp Sch Nursing, 60; res chemist, Toni Co, 64-67, sr res chemist, 67-69, res supvr 69-71; from asst res dir to res dir, Personal Care Div, Gillette Co, 72-78, dir prod develop, 78-90; dir, New Technol Develop, Toiletries Technol Labs, 90. *Concurrent Pos:* Ed, J Soc Cosmetic Chemists, 83-86. *Mem:* Am Chem Soc; Soc Cosmetic Chemists; Sigma Xi. *Res:* Cosmetic, toiletries and personal care products research and development; cosmetic science particularly chemistry and physics of hair and skin; polymer chemistry; phosphoramidic acid chemistry; guanidine chemistry; intermediary metabolism. *Mailing Add:* Ten Ivy Lane Sherborn MA 01770-1452

GIRARD, G TANNER, NATURAL RESOURCE POLICY, ORNITHOLOGY. *Current Pos:* COMNR, POLLUTION CONTROL BD, STATE OF ILL, 92- *Personal Data:* b Jacksonville, Fla, May 15, 52; m 76, Suellen Hill; c 2. *Educ:* Principia Col, BS, 74; Univ Cent Fla, MS, 76; Fla State Univ, PhD(sci educ), 79. *Prof Exp:* Assoc prof biol & environ sci, Biol Dept, Principia Col, Elsah, Ill, 77-92. *Concurrent Pos:* Mem, Ill Nature Preserves Comn, 87-94, chmn, 89-92; vis prof, Univ del Valle, Guatemala, 88, consult, Surv Proposed Nat Parks, 89; consult, Ill River's Proj, 90- *Mem:* Am Inst Biol Sci; Am Ornithologists Union. *Res:* Ecology; natural resource policy; ornithology; science education; wildlife management. *Mailing Add:* RR 1 Grafton IL 62037

GIRARD, JAMES EMERY, ANALYTICAL CHEMISTRY. *Current Pos:* assoc prof, 79-84, chmn dept, 85-91, PROF, DEPT CHEM, AMERICAN UNIV, 85- *Personal Data:* b Joliet, Ill, July 1, 45; c 6. *Educ:* Lewis Col, BA, 67; Pa State Univ, PhD(org chem), 71. *Prof Exp:* Scholar chem, Pa State Univ,

71-72; fel, Univ Calif, San Diego, 72-73; asst prof chem, Col Holy Cross, 73-76; staff scientist, Gen Elec Corp Res & Develop, 77-79. *Concurrent Pos:* consult & expert witness. *Mem:* AAAS; Am Chem Soc; Sigma Xi. *Res:* High pressure liquid chromatography, gel permeation chromatography, gas chromatography; ion chromatography; pharmaceuticals; environment; supurcritical fluid chromatography; capillary zone electrophoresis. *Mailing Add:* Chem Dept Am Univ 4400 Mass Ave Washington DC 20016

GIRARD, KENNETH FRANCIS, bacteriology, immunology, for more information see previous edition

GIRARDEAU, MARVIN DENHAM, JR, STATISTICAL MECHANICS, QUANTUM MANY-BODY THEORY. *Current Pos:* assoc prof physics, Univ Ore, 63-67, dir, Inst Theoret Sci, 67-69, chmn dept, 74-76, PROF PHYSICS, UNIV ORE, 67-, MEM, INST THEORET SCI, 63-, MEM, CHEM PHYS INST, 81- *Personal Data:* b Lakewood, Ohio, Oct 3, 30; m 56, Susan Brown; c Ellen, Catherine & Laura. *Educ:* Case Inst Technol, BS, 52; Univ Ill, MS, 54; Syracuse Univ, PhD(physics), 58. *Honors & Awards:* Alexander von Humboldt Prize, Fed Repub Germany, 84. *Prof Exp:* NSF fel physics, Inst Advan Study, Princeton Univ, 58-59; res assoc, Brandeis Univ, 59-60; mem staff, Boeing Sci Res Labs, Wash, 60-61; res assoc, Enrico Fermi Inst Nuclear Studies, Univ Chicago, 61-63. *Concurrent Pos:* Prin investr, NSF, 65-78 & Off Naval Res, 81-87; vis prof Nordic Inst Theoret Atomic Physics, Norges Tekniske Hogskole, Trondheim, Norway, 69-70, Univ Colo, 78, Univ Paul Sabatier, Toulouse, France, 79 & Univ Nice, France, 80; vis scientist, Univ Libre, Bruxelles, Belgium, 70, Max Planck Inst, Fed Repub Germany, 84-86; mem, physics rev panel, Nat Res Coun, 79, 81, 84, 85. *Mem:* Fel Am Phys Soc; Sigma Xi. *Res:* Quantum many-body problems; statistical mechanics; atomic molecular and chemical physics; nonperturbative approaches to theory of dynamics and optimal control of strongly driven quantum and classical systems. *Mailing Add:* Inst Theoret Sci Univ Ore Eugene OR 97403-1274. *Fax:* 541-346-5217; *E-Mail:* girardeau@quantum5.uoregon.edu

GIRARDI, ANTHONY JOSEPH, MICROBIOLOGY. *Current Pos:* RETIRED. *Personal Data:* b Philadelphia, Pa, Mar 19, 26; m 58; c 2. *Educ:* Pa State Univ, BS, 49; Univ Pa, PhD(med microbiol), 52. *Prof Exp:* Instr prev med, Sch Med, Yale Univ, 52-53; instr virol, Univ Pa, 53-56; chief res, Microbiol Res Found, 56-59; res assoc, Merck Inst Therapeut Res, 59-63; res assoc, Wistar Inst, 63-70, assoc mem, 70-74; dir, E Tenn Cancer Res Ctr, 74-77; sr mem & head dept virol & immunol, Inst Med Res, 77-85; Info Sci, Info Ventures, 85-91. *Concurrent Pos:* NIH res fel, Sch Med, Yale Univ, 52-53, Nat Cancer Inst grant, 57; res assoc, Children's Hosp, Philadelphia, 53-56; consult, Microbiol Assocs, Inc, 53-56. *Mem:* Tissue Cult Asn; NY Acad Sci; Am Asn Cancer Res; Am Asn Immunol; Sigma Xi. *Res:* Virology; cancer virus; tumor immunology. *Mailing Add:* 14 E Wayne Terr Collingswood NJ 08108

GIRARDOT, JEAN MARIE DENIS, ROLE OF VITAMIN K IN CARBOXYLATION OF BLOOD PROTEIN, CALMODULIN IN BRAIN HIPPOCAMPUS. *Current Pos:* PRES, BIOMED DESIGN INC, 87- *Personal Data:* b Lons Le Saunier, France, Nov 10, 44; m 66, Marie N Byk; c Natacha & Mare. *Educ:* Univ Louis Pasteur, France, BS, 66; Univ Okla, MS, 76, PhD(biochem & molecular biol), 77. *Prof Exp:* Res tech, Neurochem Ctr, Strasbourg, France, 66-70; sr res tech, Merrell Toraude Strasbourg, France, 70-72, Okla Med Res Found, Oklahoma City, 72-74; fel, Univ Louis Pasteur, France, 77-80; asst prof biochem, Found & Dept Biochem, Univ Okla Health Sci Ctr, 80-84; sr res sci, Kimberly Clark Corp, 84-87. *Concurrent Pos:* Grant referee, NSF & NIH, 83-84; asst mem biochem, Okla Med Res Found, 84; consult, Medtronic Heart Valve Div, 88-; prin investr, Small Bus Innovation Res Prog, Nat Heart Blood & Lung Inst, NIH, 89; prin investr, Nat Heart, Blood & Lung Inst, 91-93. *Mem:* Soc Biochem & Molecular Biol; Soc Exp Biol & Med; Soc Biomat. *Res:* Fixation of tissue heart valve replacement; anticalcification of tissue heart valve replacement and other bioprostheses. *Mailing Add:* Pres Biomed Design Inc 430 Tenth St NW S-204 Atlanta GA 30318-5769. *Fax:* 404-874-7973

GIRARDOT, PETER RAYMOND, GENERAL ENVIRONMENTAL SCIENCES. *Current Pos:* dean sci, 66-73, PROF CHEM, UNIV TEX, ARLINGTON, 66- *Personal Data:* b Detroit, Mich, Aug 15, 22; m 53, Rosemary; c 7. *Educ:* Univ Detroit, BS, 44; Univ Mich, MS, 48, PhD(chem), 52. *Prof Exp:* Group leader, Metall Lab, Univ Chicago, 44-45; jet instrumentation, Appl Physics Lab, Johns Hopkins Univ, 45; instr chem, Univ Mich, 50-51; asst, Eng Res Inst, 51-52; proj leader phys & inorg chem, Bjorksten Res Labs, Inc, 52-55; sr res supvr explor inorg chem, Pittsburgh Plate Glass Co, 55-66. *Concurrent Pos:* prof chem, Inst Teknologi, Mara, Malaysia, 86-87. *Mem:* Am Chem Soc; Int Union Pure & Appl Chem; Am Soc Enol & Viticult. *Res:* Inorganic chlorinations; halides, subhalides and polyhalides; extractive metallurgy; high temperature reactions; heavy industrial chemicals; metal cluster compounds; fermentation; chemistry of air pollution. *Mailing Add:* 1220 Academy Arlington TX 76013. *Fax:* 817-273-3808

GIRAUDI, CARLO, CHEMICAL ENGINEERING. *Current Pos:* RETIRED. *Personal Data:* b Turin, Italy, Mar 28, 26; US citizen; m 50, Doris Lang; c Diane M & Carlo F. *Educ:* Milan Polytech Inst, DSc(chem eng), 49. *Prof Exp:* Chem engr, Ultra Chem Works Div, Witco Chem Co, 50-57, plant engr, 57-58, tech dir & vpres 58-61, vpres, res & develop 61-70, group vpres, 70-80. *Mem:* Am Chem Soc; Am Inst Chem Engrs. *Res:* Organic chemistry. *Mailing Add:* 413 Devonshire Dr Venice FL 34293

GIRD, STEVEN RICHARD, PRODUCTION EFFICIENCY OPTIMIZATION, QUALITY CONTROL. *Current Pos:* DIR, NEW PROD DEVELOP, JIM BEAM BRANDS CO, 88- *Personal Data:* b San Diego, Calif, June 15, 43; m 68; c 2. *Educ:* San Diego State Univ, BS, 67, MS, 71. *Prof Exp:* Microanal chemist, RocketDyne-Div NAm Rockwell, 67-69; sr res chemist, Caligrapo, Inc-Div Southern Comfort, 71-79; res chemist & prod mgr, Brown Forman, 79-81; tech dir, Mohawk Liqueur Corp-McKesson Corp, 81-88. *Mem:* Inst Food Technologists. *Res:* Develop and refine flavor systems; use new technologies to create new alcoholic beverages, reduce costs and improve product stability. *Mailing Add:* Jim Beam Brands Co Hwy 245 Clermont KY 40110

GIRERD, RENE JEAN, PATHOLOGY. *Current Pos:* RETIRED. *Personal Data:* b Le Creusot, France, Mar 1, 20; m 49; c 1. *Educ:* Univ Lyon, MD, 53, PhD, 60. *Prof Exp:* Asst, Univ Montreal, 52-53; biochemist, F W Horner Ltd, 53-54; instr med, Univ Southern Calif, 54-55; biologist, Nepera Chem Co, 55-57; sr scientist, Warner-Lambert Res Inst, 57-62; path res, NY Med Col, 62-63 & Albert Einstein Col Med, 63-65; asst prof path, NY Med Col, 66-67; pathologist, Morristown Mem Hosp, 67-68; lab dir, Dover Gen Hosp, NJ, 69-87; forensic pathologist, Morris Co, 78-95. *Mem:* Am Physiol Soc. *Mailing Add:* 4 Gunston Ct Morris Plains NJ 07950

GIRI, JAGANNATH, STRUCTURAL ANALYSIS, FLUTTER ANALYSIS. *Current Pos:* sr group engr, 82-89, staff eng struct dynamics, 89-92 SR TECH SPECIALIST, STRUCT DYNAMICS, BEECH AIRCRAFT CORP, WICHITA, 92- *Personal Data:* b Bharahopur, India, Jan 16, 33; US citizen; m 58, Radha; c Punam, Madhu, Uma & Bala (Krishna). *Educ:* Bihar Inst Technol, India, BS, 57; Univ Maine, Orono, MS, 72; Ga Inst Technol, PhD(struct optimization), 76. *Prof Exp:* Foreman, Prod Planning, Indian Tube Co, 58-62; asst prof mech eng, Regional Inst Technol, 62-70; res engr, Ga Inst Technol, 76-79; sr engr, Cessna Aircraft Co, Wichita, 79-82. *Mem:* Am Inst Aeronaut & Astronaut; Am Soc Mech Engrs. *Res:* Structural analysis; optimization. *Mailing Add:* 2524 N Fox Run Ct Wichita KS 67226. *Fax:* 316-676-4125; *E-Mail:* giri@vax882.mac.may.com

GIRI, LALLAN, EXPERIMENTAL BIOLOGY. *Current Pos:* DIR QUAL CONTROL, CONNAUGHT LABS, INC, 89- *Personal Data:* c 3. *Educ:* Univ Gorakhpur, India, BS, 65; Banaras Hindu Univ, India, MS, 67; Univ Mont, Missoula, PhD(biol sci), 74. *Prof Exp:* Res assoc, Dept Chem, Univ Mont, Missoula, 74-75; group leader protein biochem, Max Planck Inst Molecular Genetics, WGer, 75-78; res biochemist, Dept Biol Chem, Sch Med, Univ Md, 78-79; asst prof, Dept Biochem & Microbiol, Univ Mass, Amherst, 79-83; mgr chem res & develop, Pharmacia LKB Biotechnol Inc, NJ, 83-89. *Concurrent Pos:* Consult, NIH, 84-87 & NSF, 90-91. *Mem:* Am Soc Biol Chemists; Am Soc Biochem & Molecular Biol; NY Acad Sci; AAAS; Sigma Xi. *Res:* Proteins and peptides; process development; fermentation; molecular biology. *Mailing Add:* BW Mfg Co Glaxo Wellcome Co 40 Technology Way West Greenwich RI 02817-1777. *Fax:* 401-392-3796

GIRI, NARAYAN C, MATHEMATICAL STATISTICS, MULTVARIATE ANALYSIS. *Current Pos:* assoc prof, 64-70, PROF MATH & STATIST, UNIV MONTREAL, 70- *Personal Data:* b India, May 1, 28; m 62, Nilima Mandal; c Nabanta & Nandan. *Educ:* Midnapur Col, BSc, 51; Univ Calcutta, MSc, 53; Stanford Univ, PhD(math statist), 61. *Prof Exp:* Statist asst, Jute Agr Res Inst, India, 53-55; res investr biomet, Indian Coun Agr Res, 55-58; asst prof math, Univ Ariz, 61-62 & Cornell Univ, 62-64. *Concurrent Pos:* Grants, US Off Naval Res, 61-63 & 64-70, Nat Res Coun Can, 65-78, & Nat Sci Cong Asn; asst prof, Indian Inst Technol, Kanpur, India, 65-67, assoc prof, 67-68; Que Res Grant, 70-78; mem bd dir, Ctr Res Math, 70-72; ed, J, Can Statist Asn, 72-74; visitor, Indian Statist Inst, Calcutta, India. *Mem:* Hon fel Inst Math Statist; hon fel Am Statist Asn; fel Royal Statist Soc; Can Statist Asn; Int Statist Inst. *Res:* Multivariate analysis; biometry; design of experiments; sample survey; mathematics; published 10 books and about 90 original research papers in reputed statistical journals. *Mailing Add:* Dept Math Univ Montreal Montreal PQ H3C 3J7 Can

GIRI, SHRI N, PULMONARY TOXICOLOGY, BIOCHEMICAL PHARMACOLOGY. *Current Pos:* assoc prof, 74-80, actg chmn, 80-81, PROF PHARMACOL, DEPT PHYSIOL SCI, UNIV CALIF, DAVIS, 80- *Personal Data:* b India, Jan 30, 34; US citizen; m 66; c 2. *Educ:* Univ Allahabad, India, BSc, 55; Mathura, India, BVSc/AH, 59; Mich State Univ, MS, 61; Univ Calif, Davis, PhD(comp pharmacol & toxicol), 65. *Prof Exp:* Fel, Dept Pharmacol, Med Ctr, Univ Calif, San Francisco, 65-67; res assoc, Dept Pharmacol, Stanford Univ, 67-68; asst prof pharmacol, Dept Physiol Sci, Univ Calif, Davis, 68-74; vis scientist, Lab Chem Pharmacol, NIH, 76-77. *Concurrent Pos:* Prin investr, NIH grants, 81- *Mem:* AAAS; Am Soc Pharmacol & Exp Therapeut; Am Soc Toxicol. *Res:* Biochemical mechanism of lung damage in response to lung toxicants; roles of prostaglandins and cyclic nucleotides in health and disease. *Mailing Add:* Dept Vet Pharmacol Toxicol Univ Calif Davis Sch Vet Med Davis CA 95616-5224. *Fax:* 530-752-4698

GIRIFALCO, LOUIS A(NTHONY), SOLID STATE PHYSICS, METALLURGY. *Current Pos:* assoc prof metall eng, Univ Pa, 61-65, dir, Lab Struct Matter, 67-69, chmn, Dept Metall & Mat Sci, 72-74, assoc dean, Col Eng & Appl Sci, 74-79, vprovost res, 79-81, actg provost, 81, prof, 65-82, UNIV PROF MAT SCI & ENG, UNIV PA, 82- *Personal Data:* b Brooklyn, NY, July 3, 28; m 50; c 8. *Educ:* Rutgers Univ, BS, 50; Univ Cincinnati, MS, 52, PhD(phys chem), 54. *Hon Degrees:* DSc, Hahnemann Univ, 96. *Prof Exp:* Res chemist, E I du Pont de Nemours & Co, 54-55; solid state physicist, NASA, 55-59, head, Solid State Physics Sect, Lewis Res Ctr, Ohio, 59-61. *Concurrent Pos:* Pres, Cara Corp, 69-70. *Mem:* AAAS; Am Phys Soc; Am Soc

Metals; Mat Res Soc; Mining, Minerals & Mat Soc. *Res:* Surface chemistry; diffusion in solids; statistical mechanics of solids; lattice vibrations; imperfections in metals; cohesion in metals; theory of alloys. *Mailing Add:* Dept Mat Sci & Eng 403 LRSM Univ Pa 3231 Walnut St Philadelphia PA 19104-6202. *Fax:* 215-573-2128

GIRIJAVALLABHAN, VIYYOOR MOOPIL, ORGANIC CHEMISTRY, MEDICINAL CHEMISTRY. *Current Pos:* sr scientist & fel med res, 75-77, sect leader, 81, assoc dir, infectious dis, 82-87, prin scientist med res, 78-81, DIR, INFECTIOUS DIS & TUMOR BIOL, SCHERING CORP, 88- *Personal Data:* b Kerala, India, May 31, 42; c 2. *Educ:* Univ Kerala, MSc, 65, PhD(org chem), 70. *Honors & Awards:* President's Award, Schering-Plough, 83. *Prof Exp:* Res fel org chem, Regional Res Labs, Hyderabad, India, 65-69; fel, Imp Col, Univ London, 70-74. *Mem:* Am Chem Soc; AAAS; NY Acad Sci. *Res:* Chemical and biological sciences; enzymology and related pharmaceutical sciences such as antibiotics, antivirals, cardiovascular agents; antitumor agents. *Mailing Add:* Schering-Plough Corp Res Ctr 2015 Galloping Hill Rd K-15-3 Kenilworth NJ 07003-0539

GIRIT, IBRAHIM CEM, LOW TEMPERATURE PHYSICS. *Current Pos:* asst prof physics, 89-94, DIR MED INFO SCI, INST PHYSICS ATMOSPHERE, PRINCETON UNIV, 96- *Personal Data:* b Ankara, Turkey, Dec 21, 51; m 76, Emel Zeybek; c Gaglar O & Basar E. *Educ:* Hacettepe Univ, Turkey, BSc, 74; Sussex Univ, Eng, PhD(nuclear physics), 80. *Prof Exp:* Res fel physics, Sussex Univ, 80-82; from asst prof to assoc prof physics, Hacettepe Univ, 82-85; res assoc, Vanderbilt Univ-Univ Tenn, 85-87, Vanderbilt Univ-Orau, 87-89. *Concurrent Pos:* Sci exchange grant, Sci & Eng Res Ctr, London; UN, Tokten consult; sci dir, Smithsonian Info, White House, Washington, DC, 94-96. *Mem:* Am Phys Soc. *Res:* Low temperature nuclear orientation; parity and time reversal violation; mixed symmetry states in vibrational nuclei; bolometric detector development and measurement of 17 KeV neutrino mass. *Mailing Add:* 56 Marion Dr Plainsboro NJ 08536. *E-Mail:* girit@pupcyc2.princeton.edu

GIROLAMI, GREGORY SCOTT, CHEMICAL VAPOR DEPOSITION OF THIN FILMS, CATALYTIC ORGANOTRANSITION METAL COMPOUNDS. *Current Pos:* from asst prof to assoc prof, 83-93, PROF CHEM, UNIV ILL, URBANA-CHAMPAIGN, 93- *Personal Data:* b Honolulu, Hawaii, Oct 16, 56; m 79, Vera V Mainz. *Educ:* Univ Tex, Austin, BS(chem) & BS(physics), 77; Univ Calif, Berkeley, MS, 79, PhD(chem), 81. *Honors & Awards:* Young Investr Award in Chem, Off Naval Res, 86; Sloan Res Award, A P Sloan Found, 88. *Prof Exp:* NATO fel, Imp Col Sci & Technol, 82-83. *Concurrent Pos:* Consult, Quantum Chem, 85-91 & Exxon, 91-95; Dreyfus Teacher-Scholar Award, Henry & Camille, Dreyfus Found, 88; vis scientist, AT&T Bell Labs, 91; NAm Regional ed, J Chem Soc, Dalton Trans, 94- *Mem:* Am Chem Soc; Royal Soc Chem; Mat Res Soc. *Res:* Chemistry of early transition metal alkyl, hydride and porphyrin complexes; development of transition metal complexes as precursors for the chemical vapor deposition of thin films; synthesis of novel magnetic materials based on cyanometallate building blocks; synthesis of molecule-based magnets. *Mailing Add:* Sch Chem Sci A526 Chem/Life Sci Lab Box 4-6 601 S Goodwin Ave Urbana IL 61801-3617. *Fax:* 217-333-2685; *E-Mail:* Girolami@aries.scs.uiuc.edu

GIROLAMI, ROLAND LOUIS, MICROBIOLOGY. *Current Pos:* RETIRED. *Personal Data:* b Milwaukee, Wis, Sept 19, 24; m 49. *Educ:* Univ Wis, BS, 50, MS, 52, PhD(bact), 55. *Prof Exp:* Asst bact, Univ Wis, 51-55; res assoc, Oak Ridge Nat Lab, 55-56; res microbiologist, Res Div, Nat Dairy Prod Corp, 56-57; res microbiologist, Abbott Labs, 57-79, dir qual assurance, Abbott Sci Prod Div, Calif, 69-73, sr microbiologist, 73-85. *Mem:* Am Soc Microbiol; Sigma Xi. *Res:* Clinical microbiology; antimicrobial agents; secondary metabolism. *Mailing Add:* 445 Tanasi Way Loudon TN 37774

GIROTTI, ALBERT WILLIAM, BIOCHEMISTRY, PHOTOBIOLOGY. *Current Pos:* from asst prof to assoc prof, 68-89, PROF BIOCHEM, MED COL WIS, 89- *Personal Data:* b Springfield, Mass, Aug 9, 37; m 69, Margaret Jones; c John. *Educ:* Mass Inst Technol, SB, 59; Univ Mass, MS & PhD(protein chem), 65. *Prof Exp:* Res assoc, Med Col, Cornell Univ, 65-68. *Concurrent Pos:* NSF grants, 71-73 & 82-, NIH grants, 74-79 & 88-; interim chmn biochem, Med Col Wis, 91-92. *Mem:* Am Chem Soc; Am Soc Photobiol (pres, 95-96); Am Soc Biol Chemists; Sigma Xi; Oxygen Soc. *Res:* Mechanisms of lipid peroxidation in cell membranes; antineoplastic effects of phototherapeutic sensitizing agents; oxygen radical biochemistry. *Mailing Add:* Dept Biochem Med Col Wis 8701 Watertown Plank Rd Milwaukee WI 53226-4801. *Fax:* 414-266-8497; *E-Mail:* agirotti@post.its.mcw.edu

GIROU, MICHAEL L, DISTRIBUTED COMPUTING, PARALLEL ALGORITHMS. *Current Pos:* PRES, MT SYSTS CO, 87- *Personal Data:* b St Louis, Mo, July 2, 47; div; c 2. *Educ:* Univ Mo-Columbia, AB, 68, PhD(math), 89. *Prof Exp:* Mgr tech develop, Honeywell Inc, 69-72; pres & chief exec officer, MFD Inc, 73-84; div dir, Presearch Inc, 84-87. *Concurrent Pos:* Adj prof, Univ Tex, Dallas, 90- *Mem:* Am Math Soc; Asn Comput Mach; Soc Indust & Appl Math. *Res:* Algorithms for parallel and distributed computers; general topology. *Mailing Add:* 2538 Big Horn Lane Richardson TX 75080

GIROUARD, FERNAND E, SOLID STATE PHYSICS. *Current Pos:* from asst prof to assoc prof, 64-72, head dept math, Physics & Comput Sci, 67-73 & 85-91, PROF PHYSICS, UNIV MONCTON, 72- *Personal Data:* b St Mary, NB, Sept 19, 38; m 60; c Gisele, Jacqueline & Daniel. *Educ:* St Joseph Univ, BSc, 59; Univ Notre Dame, PhD(physics), 65. *Mem:* Can Asn Physicists; Am Asn Physics Teachers. *Res:* Optical properties of thin films and solids (vacuum ultraviolet to the infrared); solar selective surfaces; electrochromic systems. *Mailing Add:* Dept Physics Univ Moncton Moncton NB E1A 3E9 Can. *Fax:* 506-858-4541; *E-Mail:* girouaf@umoncton.ca

GIROUARD, RONALD MAURICE, PLANT MORPHOLOGY, PLANT PHYSIOLOGY. *Current Pos:* RETIRED. *Personal Data:* b Sudbury, Ont, Mar 22, 36; m 67, Monique Gagnon; c Jean-Pierre & Louise. *Educ:* Univ Toronto, BSA, 60; Ohio State Univ, MSc, 62; Purdue Univ, PhD(hort), 67. *Prof Exp:* Res scientist natural resources, Can-Que Region, Can Forest Serv, 66-95. *Concurrent Pos:* Vis prof plant propagation, Univ Laval, 69-78. *Mem:* Int Plant Propagators Soc; Int Soc Root Res; Am Soc Hort Sci; Am Orchid Soc. *Res:* Root form and stability of outplanted seedlings grown in forestry containers. *Mailing Add:* 3349 Rue-Radison Ste-Foy PQ G1X 2K2 Can. *Fax:* 418-648-5849

GIROUX, GUY, OPTICS. *Current Pos:* RETIRED. *Personal Data:* b Levis, Que, July 13, 26; m 62; c 2. *Educ:* Laval Univ, BA & BPh, 45, BS, 50, MS, 53, DSc(physics), 55. *Honors & Awards:* Queen's Jubilee Medal, 78. *Prof Exp:* Defence serv sci officer, Can Res & Develop Estab, Can, 55-63; Liaison Off, Mass, 63-66; sci consult, Can Res & Develop Estab, 66-67; sect head optical & infrared surveillance, Defence Res Estab, Valcartier, 67-78, dir, Command & Control Div, Res Estab, 78-89. *Res:* Study of semiconductors used as photodetectors; infrared physics; nuclear physics; beta-rays spectroscopy; use of Fourier analysis in optics and noise problems; reentry physics; lasers; optical and infrared surveillance equipment and systems; optical and infrared counter-surveillance; computer simulation; army and navy command & control. *Mailing Add:* 699 Rue Dalquier Ste-Foy PQ G1V 3H4 Can

GIROUX, VINCENT A(RTHUR), ELECTRICAL ENGINEERING. *Current Pos:* RETIRED. *Personal Data:* b Los Angeles, Calif, Nov 26, 21; m 40, Josephine Gieseke; c 8. *Educ:* Univ Calif, Los Angeles, BS, 49; Univ Southern Calif, MSEE, 56. *Prof Exp:* Eng asst, Southern Calif Edison Co, 49-51; eng assoc, Los Angeles Dept Water & Power, 51-57; from asst prof to prof eng, Calif State Univ, Los Angeles, 57-85. *Concurrent Pos:* Lectr, Univ Southern Calif, 60-85. *Mem:* Inst Elec & Electronics Engrs. *Res:* Power system analysis and economics; interruption of large magnitude currents. *Mailing Add:* 322 14th St Santa Monica CA 90402

GIROUX, YVES M(ARIE), STRUCTURAL ENGINEERING. *Current Pos:* Asst civil eng, Laval Univ, 60-62, from asst prof to assoc prof, 64-72, head dept, 67-72, assoc vrector acad & res, 77-78, PROF CIVIL ENG, LAVAL UNIV, 72-, ASST TO RECTOR, 87- *Personal Data:* b Quebec, Que, June 15, 35; m 58; c 3. *Educ:* Laval Univ, BA, 55, BAS, 59; Mass Inst Technol, MS, 60, DSc(struct eng), 66. *Concurrent Pos:* Assoc ed, Can J Civil Engrs, 74-82; Nat Coun Univ Res Admin; founding pres, CESRIO, 87-93; chmn bd, Can-France-Hawaii, Telescope Corp, 88-89; mem, Atomic Energy Control Bd, 95- *Mem:* Can Soc Civil Engrs; Can Asn Union Res Admin (pres, 83-84); Am Soc Eng Educ. *Res:* Numerical analysis of structures; connections for steel structures; research management. *Mailing Add:* 1236 Petitclerc Cap-Rouge Quebec PQ G1Y 3G2 Can. *E-Mail:* yves.giroux@rec.ulaval.ca

GIRSCH, STEPHEN JOHN, PHOTOBIOLOGY. *Current Pos:* MEM STAFF DEPT OPHTHAL, UNIV ROCHESTER MED CTR. *Personal Data:* b Roanoke, Va, May 13, 46; m 71. *Educ:* Pa State Univ, BS, 68; Univ Okla, PhD(biophys), 72. *Prof Exp:* Res fel bioluminescence, Biol Labs, Harvard Univ, 72-74; res assoc, Univ Sussex, 74-75; fel vision, Heinz Steinitz Marine Lab, Israel, 75-76; res fel vision, Dept Molecular Biol, Univ Ore, 76- *Concurrent Pos:* NIH Eye Inst fel, 72; res assoc bioluminescence, Hebrew Univ Jerusalem, 75; vis res fel, Tobias Landau Found, 75. *Mem:* AAAS; Am Chem Soc; Am Soc Photobiol. *Res:* Characterization and comparison of various bioluminescent systems with special emphasis on the chemical mechanisms of light emission; additional studies on visual systems and their interfacing to bioluminescent systems. *Mailing Add:* 56 Highland Pkwy Rochester NY 14620

GIRVIN, EB CARL, GENETICS. *Current Pos:* RETIRED. *Personal Data:* b Georgetown, Tex, Dec 27, 17; m 44, Virginia Lessor; c Eric R & Stacey V. *Educ:* Univ Tex, BA, 40, MA, 41, PhD, 48. *Prof Exp:* Prof biol & zool, Millsaps Col, 48-53; chmn div natural & appl sci, Southwestern, Univ, 67-70, head dept, 53- 81, prof biol, 53-88. *Concurrent Pos:* Mem, Tex State Bd Examr Basic Sci, 60-75. *Mem:* AAAS. *Mailing Add:* 1703 E 16th St Georgetown TX 78626

GIRVIN, JOHN PATTERSON, NEUROSURGERY, SURGICAL TREATMENT OF EPILEPSY. *Current Pos:* From asst prof to prof, 68-84, PROF NEUROSURG & PHYSIOL & CHMN, DEPT CLIN NEUROL SCI, UNIV WESTERN ONT, LONDON, ONT, 84- *Personal Data:* b Detroit, Mich, Feb 5, 34; Can citizen. *Educ:* Univ Western Ont, MD, 58; McGill Univ, PhD(physiol), 65; FRCS(C), 68; Am Bd Neurol Surg, dipl, 85. *Concurrent Pos:* Prof & chmn, dept clin neurol sci, Univ Western Ont, 84-89. *Mem:* Am Asn Neurol Surgeons; Res Soc Neurol Surgeons; Soc Neurosci; Am Epilepsy Asn; AAAS; Royal Col Physicians & Surgeons. *Res:* Neurophysiology of epilepsy, both in laboratory animals and humans; neuroprostheses. *Mailing Add:* London Health Sci Ctr Univ Campus 339 Windermere London ON N6A 5A5 Can

GIRVIN, STEVEN M, THEORETICAL CONDENSED MATTER PHYSICS, MANY-BODY THEORY. *Current Pos:* PROF PHYSICS, IND UNIV, 87- *Personal Data:* b Austin, Tex, Apr 5, 50; m 72; c 2. *Educ:* Bates Col, BS, 71; Univ Maine, MS, 73; Princeton Univ, MS, 74, PhD(physics), 77. *Prof Exp:* Res assoc, Ind Univ & Chalmers Univ, Gothenburg, Sweden, 77-79; physicist, Nat Bureau Standards, 79-87. *Mem:* Am Phys Soc; Sigma Xi. *Res:* Theoretical condensed-matter physics and many-body theory; the two dimensional electron gas inversion layers and superconductivity. *Mailing Add:* Dept Physics Ind Univ Swain Hall W 117 Bloomington IN 47405. *Fax:* 812-855-5533

GIRZ, CECILIA GRIFFITH, SATELLITE METEOROLOGY, WEATHER FORECASTING APPLICATIONS. *Current Pos:* Physicist, Nat Weather Serv, Nat Oceanic & Atmospheric Admin, 70-71 & Nat Hurricane & Exp Meteorol Lab, 72-78, meteorologist, Weather Res Prog, 78-88, dir, 88-90, ACTG CHIEF, SCI DIV, FORECAST SYSTS LAB, NAT OCEANIC & ATMOSPHERIC ADMIN, 90- *Personal Data:* b Cleveland Ohio, June 3, 49; m 71; c 4. *Educ:* Notre Dame Col Ohio, BS, 70; Univ Dayton, MS, 73; Colo State Univ, PhD(atmospheric sci), 87. *Concurrent Pos:* Counr, Am Meteorol Soc, 83-86. *Mem:* Fel Am Meteorol Soc; Am Geophys Union. *Res:* Technique to estimate convective rainfall from geostationary-satellite thermal infrared imagery that could be applied in the tropics and mid-latitudes; quartitative use of imagery in the forecasting of severe weather. *Mailing Add:* Nat Oceanic & Atmospheric Admn ERL/FSL R/E/FSI 325 Broadway Boulder CO 80303

GISH, DUANE TOLBERT, ORIGINS-MOLECULAR BIOLOGY & PALEONTOLOGY. *Current Pos:* assoc dir, 71-81, VPRES, INST CREATION RES, 81- *Personal Data:* b White City, Kans, Feb 17, 21; m 46, Lorraine J Gibson; c Sandra R (Slaughter), Duane R, Darrell G & Laurie J (Knapp). *Educ:* Univ Calif, Los Angeles, BS, 49; Univ Calif, Berkeley, PhD(biochem), 53. *Prof Exp:* Lilly fel, Med Col, Cornell Univ, New York, 53-55, asst prof biochem, 55-56; asst res assoc biochem, Virus Lab, Univ Calif, Berkeley, 56-60; res assoc biochem, Upjohn Co, Kalamazoo, Mich, 60-71. *Concurrent Pos:* Prof, Christian Heritage Col, 71-81. *Mem:* Am Chem Soc; fel Am Inst Chemists; AAAS; fel Creation Res Soc. *Res:* Writing on all aspects of the subject of origins; lecture and debate extensively; amino acid chemistry; peptide synthesis; protein structure determination; nucleoside synthesis. *Mailing Add:* 4300 Summit Dr La Mesa CA 91941. *Fax:* 619-448-3469

GISH, KENNETH WARD, IN-VEHICLE DISPLAYS, VISUAL SCREENING MEASURES. *Current Pos:* SR HUMAN FACTORS PSYCHOLOGIST, SCIENTEX CORP, 93- *Personal Data:* b Nampa, Idaho, July 7, 58; m 89, Nancy L Weisher; c Nickolas. *Educ:* Wash State Univ, BS, 80; Brown Univ, MS, 82; Pa State Univ, PhD(exp psychol), 88. *Prof Exp:* Res psychologist, Naval Air Develop Ctr, 87-93. *Concurrent Pos:* Adj fac, Bucks Co Community Col, 90-93. *Mem:* Human Factors & Ergonomic Soc; Transp Res Bd. *Res:* Evaluation of head-up displays for automotive use, with older driver needs as a high-priority concern; develop vision standards for drivers that relate to driver safety. *Mailing Add:* 1722 Sumneytown Pike PO Box 1367 Kulpsville PA 19443. *E-Mail:* gish@juno.com

GISLASON, ERIC ARNI, ION-MOLECULE COLLISIONS & REACTIONS, ISOTOPE EFFECTS. *Current Pos:* from asst prof to assoc prof, 69-77, acting head, 93-94, PROF CHEM, UNIV ILL, CHICAGO CIRCLE, 77-, HEAD, CHEM DEPT, 94- *Personal Data:* b Oak Park, Ill, Sept 9, 40; wid; c Kristina E & John H. *Educ:* Oberlin Col, AB, 62; Harvard Univ, PhD(chem physics), 67. *Prof Exp:* Nat Ctr Air Pollution Control spec fel chem, Univ Calif, Berkeley, 67-69. *Concurrent Pos:* Vis scientist, FOM Inst Atomic & Molecular Physics, Amsterdam, Neth, 77-78; assoc prof, Univ Paris, Orsay, 85; mem, Am Chem Soc Vis Assocs Prog, 89- *Mem:* Am Phys Soc; Am Chem Soc; Sigma Xi; Coun Chem Res. *Res:* Theoretical studies of molecular collisions; ion-molecule reactions and isotope effects. *Mailing Add:* Dept Chem M/C111 Univ Ill Chicago 845 W Taylor Chicago IL 60607-7061. *Fax:* 312-996-0431; *E-Mail:* gislason@uic.edu

GISLASON, I(RVING) LEE, CHILD & ADOLESCENT PSYCHIATRY. *Current Pos:* from clin asst prof to assoc prof, 77-87, CLIN PROF PSYCHIAT, UNIV CALIF, IRVINE, 87- *Personal Data:* b Nanaimo, BC, July 21, 43; m 69; c 2. *Educ:* Univ BC, MD, 69. *Prof Exp:* Gen practice med, 70-72. *Mem:* Fel Am Acad Child Psychiat; fel Royal Col Physicians & Surgeons Can. *Res:* Infant, adolescent, adult and group psychiatry. *Mailing Add:* 12443 Lewis St 101 Garden Grove CA 92640. *Fax:* 714-289-8701

GISLER, GALEN ROSS, ASTRONOMY, PLASMA & SPACE PHYSICS. *Current Pos:* MEM STAFF, LOS ALAMOS NAT LAB, 81- *Personal Data:* b Clovis, NMex, June 21, 50; m 84; c 2. *Educ:* Yale Univ, BS, 72; Cambridge Univ, PhD(astrophysics), 76. *Prof Exp:* Res assoc astron, Leiden Univ Observ, 76-77; res assoc, Kitt Peak Nat Observ, 77-79; asst scientist astron, Nat Radio Astron Observ, 79-81. *Mem:* Royal Astron Soc; Am Astron Soc. *Res:* Evolution of galaxies and clusters of galaxies; gas dynamics inside and outside galaxies; computational plasma physics; particle acceleration. *Mailing Add:* D468 LANL PO Box 1663 Los Alamos NM 87545

GISOLFI, CARL VINCENT, PHYSIOLOGY. *Current Pos:* From instr to assoc prof, 69-81, PROF EXERCISE SCI, PHYSIOL & BIOPHYS, UNIV IOWA, 81- *Personal Data:* b New York, Nov 15, 42; m 65; c 3. *Educ:* Manhattan Col, BS, 64; Ind Univ, PhD(physiol), 69. *Mem:* Am Physiol Soc; Soc Neurosci; fel Am Col Sports Med (pres). *Res:* Mechanisms enabling man to adapt to stress and the regulation of body temperature during exercise; Work-heat tolerance, heat acclimatization; circulatory response to hyperthermia; body fluid homeostasis; gastrointestinal function during exercise. *Mailing Add:* Dept Physiol & Biophys Exercise Sci Univ Ia Bowen Sci Bldg Rm N420FH Iowa City IA 52242-0001. *Fax:* 319-335-6994

GIST, LEWIS ALEXANDER, JR, organic chemistry, science administration; deceased, see previous edition for last biography

GISZCZAK, THADDEUS, metallurgical engineering; deceased, see previous edition for last biography

GITAITIS, RONALD DAVID, PHYTOBACTERIOLOGY. *Current Pos:* Asst prof, 80-85, ASSOC PROF PLANT PATH, UNIV GA, 85- *Personal Data:* b Wilmington, Del, Apr 25, 50; m 77; c 2. *Educ:* Univ Del, BS, 74; Univ Fla, MS, 76, PhD(plant path), 79. *Mem:* Am Phytopath Soc; Sigma Xi. *Res:* Epidemiologic studies of bacterial plant diseases that occur in southern United States; investigate seed treatments for control of seed-borne bacteria; screen plant germplasm for resistance to plant diseases. *Mailing Add:* 104 Clyde Circle Tifton GA 31794

GITELMAN, HILLEL J, MEDICINE. *Current Pos:* res fel metab, Dept Med, Sch Med, Univ NC, Chapel Hill, 64-66, from asst prof to assoc prof med, 66-73, med dir, Clin Chem Lab, 67-71, PROF MED, DEPT & SCH MED, UNIV NC, 73- *Personal Data:* b Rochester, NY, Dec 23, 32; m; c 4. *Educ:* Princeton Univ, AB, 54; Univ Rochester, MD, 58; Am Bd Internal Med, cert, 66. *Prof Exp:* Intern med, Duke Hosp, Durham, NC, 58-59, jr asst resident, 59-60, resident, 62-63; clin assoc, Nat Inst Arthritis & Metab Dis, NIH, 60-62; trainee & instr med, Dept Med, Med Ctr, Duke Univ, 63. *Concurrent Pos:* Counr, Am Fedn Clin Res, 70-73. *Mem:* Sigma Xi; Southern Soc Clin Invest; Am Fedn Clin Res; Am Physiol Soc. *Mailing Add:* Dept Med Univ NC Sch Med CB 7155 Chapel Hill NC 27514. *Fax:* 919-966-4251

GITHENS, JOHN HORACE, JR, PEDIATRICS, PEDIATRIC HEMATOLOGY. *Current Pos:* assoc dean, 64-73, prof 64-84, EMER PROF PEDIAT, UNIV COLO MED CTR, DENVER, 84- *Personal Data:* b Woodbury, NJ, Jan 2, 22; wid; c James S & Wendy M. *Educ:* Swarthmore Col, BA, 44; Temple Univ, MD, 45; Am Bd Pediat, dipl, 52, dipl pediat hem/onc, 74. *Honors & Awards:* Ross Award in Pediat Educ, 57. *Prof Exp:* From intern to assoc prof pediat, Univ Colo, 51-60; prof & chmn dept, Col Med, Univ Ky, 60-63. *Concurrent Pos:* Mem consult staff, Denver Childrens Hosp; dir, Colo Sickle Cell Ctr, 74-88. *Mem:* Am Acad Pediat; Soc Pediat Res; Am Pediat Soc. *Res:* Pediatric hematology; medical education. *Mailing Add:* 7100 E Severn Pl Denver CO 80220

GITLIN, HARRIS MARTLIN, DRIP IRRIGATION SYSTEMS. *Current Pos:* exten specialist teaching & res, 62-83, EMER EXTEN SPECIALIST, COL TROP AGR, UNIV HAWAII, 83- *Personal Data:* b Columbus, Ohio, Feb 20, 14; m 45; c 1. *Educ:* Ohio State Univ, BSc, 40, BAE, 41; Mich State Univ, MSc, 62. *Prof Exp:* Asst prof, dept agr eng, Ohio State Univ, 46-49; sr res engr, agr res dept, Ford Tractor & Implement Div, 49-59. *Mem:* Am Soc Agr Engrs. *Res:* Crop drying methods of water loss by grain & grass, and methods of accelerating loss; methods and limitations of minimum tillage; haymaking processes and equipment; hydraulics of drip irrigation systems. *Mailing Add:* 1646 Quincy Pl Honolulu HI 96816-2020

GITLITZ, MELVIN H, ORGANOMETALLIC CHEMISTRY, TOXICOLOGY. *Current Pos:* prin scientist, 92-95, MGR MFG TECHNOL, AGRICHEM DIV ELF ATOCHEM NA, KING OF PRUSSIA, PA, 95- *Personal Data:* b Montreal, Que, Feb 28, 40; m 64, Margaret Macdonald; c David & Karin. *Educ:* McGill Univ, BSc, 61; Univ Western Ont, PhD(chem), 65. *Prof Exp:* Sr res chemist, Corp Res Lab, M&T Chem Inc, Rahway, 65-72, res assoc develop div, 72-75, res mgr, 75-76, res mgr chem div, 76-88, sr staff scientist, 88-92. *Mem:* Am Chem Soc. *Res:* Organometallic chemistry and industrial applications of organo metallics; organometallic pesticides and biocides; metal-organic chemical vapor deposition (MOCVD); toxicology of organometallic compounds, agricultural chemicals. *Mailing Add:* 92 Daylesford Blvd Berwyn PA 19312. *Fax:* 610-878-6490

GITNICK, GARY L, GASTROENTEROLOGY. *Current Pos:* from asst prof to assoc prof, 69-79, chief staff, Med Ctr, 90-92, PROF MED GASTROENTEROL, UNIV CALIF, LOS ANGELES, 79-, CHIEF, DIV DIGESTIVE DIS, 93- *Personal Data:* b Omaha, Nebr, Mar 13, 39; c 4. *Educ:* Univ Chicago, BS, 60, MD, 63. *Prof Exp:* Internship & fel internal med, Johns Hopkins Hosp, 63-64; residency internal med, Mayo Clinic, 64-65; res assoc, Sect Infectious Dis & head, Univ Vaccine Develop, NIH, 67-69. *Concurrent Pos:* Residency gastroenterol, Mayo Clin, 67-69; asst proj dir, Clin Res Ctr, Univ Calif, Los Angeles, 69-71. *Mem:* AAAS; Am Asn Study Liver Dis; Am Col Physicians; Am Fed Clin Res; Am Gastroenterol Asn. *Res:* Basic studies regarding the causation of Crohn's disease and ulcerative colitis and a major effort investigating the forms of acute viral hepatitis and the progression of acute hepatitis to chronic liver disease. *Mailing Add:* Dept Med Gastroenterol 10833 Le Conte Ave 10833 Le Conte Ave Los Angeles CA 90024-1602

GITSOV, IVAN, ANIONIC POLYMERIZATION, SELF ASSEMBLING MACROMOLECULES. *Current Pos:* DIR, POLYMER CHARACTERIZATION FACIL, CORNELL UNIV, 93-; ASSOC PROF, COL ENVIRON SCI & FORESTRY, STATE UNIV NY, 96- *Personal Data:* b Sofia, Bulgaria, Nov 27, 54; m 91, Pavlina Toncheva Ivanova; c Ioan Pavel. *Educ:* Univ St K Ohridski, Sofia, Bulgaria, MS, 79; Bulgarian Acad Sci, PhD(polymer chem), 86. *Prof Exp:* Res assoc, Inst Polymers, Bulgarian Acad Sci, Sofia, 79-87; assoc prof res & develop, Inst Spec Chem, Sofia, Bulgaria, 87-93. *Concurrent Pos:* Fel, W M Greve Found, 90. *Mem:* Am Chem Soc. *Res:* Developed methods for synthesis and characterization of novel polymers and copolymers; dendrimers; hyper branched macromolecules. *Mailing Add:* Cornell Univ 46 Baker Lab Ithaca NY 14853. *Fax:* 315-470-6856; *E-Mail:* ig14@cornell.edu

GITTELMAN, BERNARD, ELEMENTARY PARTICLE PHYSICS. *Current Pos:* PROF PHYSICS, CORNELL UNIV, 69- *Personal Data:* b Philadelphia, Pa, Oct 28, 32; m 58; c 3. *Educ:* Mass Inst Technol, BS, 54, PhD(physics), 58. *Prof Exp:* Res assoc physics, Princeton Univ, 58-66 & Stanford Univ, 66-69. *Mem:* Am Phys Soc. *Res:* Electromagnetic interactions of elementary particles. *Mailing Add:* Lab Nuclear Studies Cornell Univ Ithaca NY 14853

GITTELMAN, DONALD HENRY, polymer chemistry, biochemistry; deceased, see previous edition for last biography

GITTES, RUBEN FOSTER, GENITOURINARY SURGERY, ENDOCRINOLOGY. *Current Pos:* PROF SURG, HARVARD MED SCH & CHIEF UROL, PETER BENT BRIGHAM HOSP, 76- *Personal Data:* b Majorca, Spain, Aug 4, 34; US citizen; m 55; c 3. *Educ:* Harvard Univ, AB, 56, MD, 60. *Prof Exp:* Clin assoc surg, Nat Cancer Inst, 63-65; clin asst urol, Mass Gen Hosp, 66-67; asst prof surg & urol, Univ Calif, Los Angeles, 68-69; from assoc prof to prof surg & urol, Univ Calif, San Diego, 71-76. *Concurrent Pos:* Vis asst, Inst Urol, Hosp de Santa Cruz y San Pablo, Barcelona, Spain, 67; mem surg training comt, NIH, 69- *Mem:* AAAS; Asn Acad Surg; Soc Univ Urol; Soc Univ Surg; fel Am Col Surg. *Res:* Experimental hyperparathyroidism; thyrocalcitonin and urinary calcium homeostasis; control of gonadal development; renal transplantation. *Mailing Add:* Scripps Clin & Res Found 10666 N Torrey Pines La Jolla CA 92037-1027

GITTINGS, STEPHEN REED, RESEARCH COORDINATION, ENVIRONMENTAL EDUCATION COORDINATION. *Current Pos:* Asst res scientist, 89-92, GRAD FAC MEM, TEX A&M UNIV, 89-; MGR, FLOWER GARDEN BANKS NAT MARINE SANCTUARY, 92- *Personal Data:* b Meriden, Conn, Apr 26, 57; m 81, Martha Banks; c Allison & Dana. *Educ:* Westminster Col, BS, 79; Tex A&M Univ, MS, 83, PhD(oceanog), 88. *Mem:* Sigma Xi; Int Soc Reef Studies. *Res:* Coral reproduction, reef fish censuses, and resource monitoring. *Mailing Add:* 216 W 26th St Suite 104 Bryan TX 77803. *Fax:* 409-779-2334; *E-Mail:* sgittings@ocean.nos.noaa.gov

GITTINS, ARTHUR RICHARD, ENTOMOLOGY. *Current Pos:* RETIRED. *Personal Data:* b Edmonton, Alta, May 26, 26; m 49; c 2. *Educ:* Univ Alta, BSc, 52; Univ Idaho, MS, 55; Mont State Col, PhD, 63. *Prof Exp:* Entomologist, City Edmonton, Alta, 49-52; from instr to prof entom, Univ Idaho, 55-78, head dept, 69-78, dean grad sch, 78-88, assoc vpres res, 84-88. *Concurrent Pos:* Ed, Idaho Acad Sci J, 89-; chmn, Comn Health & Environ, 89- *Mem:* Am Entom Soc; Soc Syst Zool; Entom Soc Am; Entom Soc Can; fel Royal Entom Soc London. *Res:* Systematic entomology; insect anatomy; insect systematics, biology with special emphasis on solitary wasps. *Mailing Add:* 624 N Lincoln Moscow ID 83843

GITTINS, JOHN, GEOLOGY, GEOCHEMISTRY. *Current Pos:* lectr, 61-63, from assoc prof to prof geol, 63-95, EMER PROF GEOL, UNIV TORONTO, 95- *Personal Data:* b Eng, Aug 12, 32; Can citizen; m 58, Jean M Heptinstall; c 3. *Educ:* McMaster Univ, BSc, 55, MSc, 56; Cambridge Univ, PhD(petrol), 59, ScD, 83. *Prof Exp:* Vis res assoc geochem, Pa State Univ, 59-60, asst prof mineral, 60-61. *Concurrent Pos:* Vis prof, Cambridge Univ, 68-69, 77 & 83-84; Bye fel, Robinson Col, Cambridge, 83-84, 89-90. *Mem:* Royal Hort Soc; Geol Asn Can; Mineral Asn Can; Mineral Soc Gt Brit; Mineral Soc Am. *Res:* Igneous and metamorphic petrology; phase equilibrium; experimental mineralogy and petrology; carbonatites and alkaline rocks; ore genesis. *Mailing Add:* Dept Geol Univ Toronto Toronto ON M5S 3B1 Can

GITTLEMAN, ARTHUR P, COMPUTER SCIENCES. *Current Pos:* from asst prof to prof math, 66-88, PROF COMPUT SCI, CALIF STATE UNIV, LONG BEACH, 88- *Personal Data:* b Brooklyn, NY, Oct 7, 41; m 86, Charlotte Singleton; c Amanda E. *Educ:* Univ Calif, Los Angeles, AB, 62, MA, 65, PhD(math), 69. *Prof Exp:* Asst, Univ Calif, Los Angeles, 62-65, asst, Inst Geophys, 65-66. *Mem:* Math Asn Am; Asn Comput Mach; Inst Elec & Electronics Engrs. *Res:* Programming languages, algorithms and data structures, object-oriented design; java development. *Mailing Add:* Dept Comput Sci Calif State Univ Long Beach CA 90840. *E-Mail:* artg@csulb.edu

GITTLEMAN, JONATHAN I, MAGNETISM, SUPERCONDUCTIVITY. *Current Pos:* RETIRED. *Personal Data:* b Newark, NJ, Feb 5, 26; m 47; c 3. *Educ:* Rutgers Univ, BS, 48, PhD(physics), 52. *Prof Exp:* Instr physics, Rutgers Univ, 52-53; scientist, Franklin Inst, 53-55; mem tech staff, RCA Labs, 55-83, sr mem tech staff, 83-87. *Mem:* Am Phys Soc; Mat Res Soc. *Res:* Electrical, magnetic, thermal and optical properties of metals; superconductors, semiconductors and composites. *Mailing Add:* 15 Bearfort Way Lawrenceville NJ 08648-3625

GITTLER, FRANZ LUDWIG, PHYSICAL CHEMISTRY. *Current Pos:* RETIRED. *Personal Data:* b Breslau, Ger, Mar 12, 24; US citizen; m 51; c 4. *Educ:* Syracuse Univ, BA, 48; Univ Buffalo, MA, 50; Pa State Univ, PhD(phys chem), 54. *Prof Exp:* Sr chemist, Sylvania Elec Prod, Inc, 54-57; scientist, Linde Lab, Union Carbide Corp, 57-58; mem res staff, Bell Tel Labs, 58-89; asst prof, Pa State Univ, Allentown, 80-90. *Concurrent Pos:* Lectr, Pa State Univ, Fogelsville. *Mem:* Am Chem Soc; Electrochem Soc; Inst Elec & Electronics Engr. *Res:* Statistical thermodynamics and thermodynamic properties of substances; chemistry and physics of semiconductor materials, processing and devices. *Mailing Add:* 1141 N Broad St Allentown PA 18104. *E-Mail:* flg1@psuaedu

GITTLESON, STEPHEN MARK, PROTOZOOLOGY, MACINTOSH HARDWARE & SOFTWARE. *Current Pos:* from asst prof to assoc prof, 72-78, PROF BIOL, FAIRLEIGH DICKINSON UNIV, 78- *Personal Data:* b Washington, DC, July 6, 38; m 63. *Educ:* Tulane Univ, BS, 60, MS, 62; Univ Calif, Los Angeles, PhD(zool), 66. *Prof Exp:* Res scholar, Univ Calif, Los Angeles, 66; asst prof zool, Univ Ky, 66-70; res assoc, Stevens Inst Technol, 71-72. *Concurrent Pos:* Partic exec ed training prog, Rockefeller Univ, 70-71 & Heart & Lung Inst, NIH, Stevens Inst Technol, 71-72. *Res:* Cellular effects of narcotic gases; motile behavior of individual and aggregate swimming Protozoa; ecology of underground water Protozoa; applications of computer in education. *Mailing Add:* Sch Natural Sci Fairleigh Dickenson Univ H4440 1000 River Rd Teaneck NJ 07666-1996

GITZENDANNER, L G, MECHANICAL & ELECTRICAL ENGINEERING. *Current Pos:* RETIRED. *Personal Data:* b New York, NY, Mar 27, 19; m 43, 90, Dorothea McNaught Cunningham; c 4. *Educ:* Lehigh Univ, BS, 41. *Honors & Awards:* C A Coffin Award, 46. *Prof Exp:* Develop engr elec mech, Gen Elec Co, 41-46, mgr invest sect, Gen Eng Lab, 46-47, design sect, 47-50, mech develop, 50-55 & mech equip eng, 55-61, consult engr mech eng, Adv Tech Labs, 61-67; mgr disc design eng, Honeywell Info Systs Inc, 67-75; proj mgr, Diablo Systs Inc, 75-77; mgr, Advan Concepts Lab, Magnetic Peripherals Inc, 77-84. *Mem:* Inst Elec & Electronics Engrs; Am Soc Mech Engrs; Nat Soc Prof Engrs. *Res:* Electromechanical development engineering; automation; remotely operated tools for nuclear work; underwater sound; mechanical design; computer peripherals. *Mailing Add:* 4949 NW 31 Terr Oklahoma City OK 73122

GIUFFRIDA, ROBERT EUGENE, ORGANIC CHEMISTRY. *Current Pos:* res dir, 64-80, QUAL CONTROL MGR, ELAN CHEM CO, 80- *Personal Data:* b New York, NY, Aug 23, 28; m 55; c 2. *Educ:* Columbia Univ, BS, 52. *Prof Exp:* Chemist, US Testing Co, 54-55 & Ciba Pharmaceut Prod, 55-60; res dir, Org Prod Inc, 60-64. *Mem:* AAAS; Am Chem Soc; Am Inst Chemists; NY Acad Sci. *Res:* Synthetic organic chemistry; synthetic methods for manufacture of aroma and flavor chemicals. *Mailing Add:* 73 W Trail Stamford CT 06903-2411

GIUFFRIDA, THOMAS SALVATORE, COMMUNICATIONS ENGINEERING, RADIO ASTRONOMY. *Current Pos:* MEM TECH STAFF COMMUN ENG, BELL TEL LABS, 77- *Personal Data:* b Meriden, Conn, Sept 23, 49; m 72. *Educ:* Wesleyan Univ, BA, 71; Mass Inst Technol, PhD(physics), 78. *Concurrent Pos:* Comt mem, Radio Commun Comt, Commun Soc Inst Elec & Electronics Engrs, 78- *Mem:* Am Astron Soc; Sigma Xi. *Res:* System and planning studies for radio facilities to be used in the national communications network; radio interferometry and its application to atmospheric and astronomical measurements. *Mailing Add:* AT&T H02K433 101 Crawfords Corner Rd Holmdel NJ 07733

GIULIANELLI, JAMES LOUIS, SOLAR ENERGY, FUELS. *Current Pos:* dir, Inst Chem Educ, 90-91, assoc prof, 85-93, PROF CHEM, REGIS COL, 93- *Personal Data:* b Beverly, Mass, Aug 7, 40; m 66, Elisabeth A Hansen; c 2. *Educ:* Univ Mass, BS, 62; Univ Wis-Madison, PhD(chem), 69. *Prof Exp:* Res fel, Univ Tex, 69-71; contract prof chem, Univ Los Andes, Venezuela, 71-77; vis asst prof chem, Colo Sch Mines, 77-79, asst prof chem, 79-85. *Concurrent Pos:* Res fel, Jet Propulsion Lab, Calif Inst Technol, Pasadena, 80, consult, 80-81, res fel, 81. *Mem:* Am Chem Soc. *Res:* Separation of sulfur forms in coal; rates and mechanisms by electron spin resonance; technology and applications of solar ponds; transmission of light in solar ponds; hands-on science for children. *Mailing Add:* Math & Sci Regis Univ 3333 Regis Blvd Denver CO 80221-1099. *Fax:* 303-964-5526

GIULIANO, ROBERT MICHAEL, SYNTHETIC ORGANIC & NATURAL PRODUCTS CHEMISTRY. *Current Pos:* asst prof, 82-88, ASSOC PROF CHEM, VILLANOVA UNIV, 88- *Personal Data:* b Altoona, Pa, June 4, 54; m 81; c 3. *Educ:* Pa State Univ, BS, 76; Univ Va, PhD(chem), 81. *Prof Exp:* Postdoctoral assoc chem, Univ Md, 81-82. *Concurrent Pos:* Regional ed, J Carbohydrate Chem, 89-; mem chmn, Carbohydrate Div, Am Chem Soc, 89-; vis assoc prof res, Brown Univ, 90-91. *Mem:* Am Chem Soc; Sigma Xi. *Res:* Synthetic organic and carbohydrate chemistry; synthesis of carbohydrate components of antibiotics; cycloaddition reactions; electrophilic amination. *Mailing Add:* Dept Chem Villanova Univ 800 E Lancaster Ave Villanova PA 19085-1699

GIULIANO, VINCENT E, APPLIED MATHEMATICS. *Current Pos:* mem sr prof staff opers res, 59-67 & 71-83, SR STAFF MEM, ARTHUR D LITTLE, 71-; PRIN, ELECTRONIC PUBL GROUP, 93- *Personal Data:* b Detroit, Mich, Nov 17, 29; m 54; c 8. *Educ:* Univ Mich, AB, 52, MS, 56; Harvard Univ, PhD(appl math), 59. *Prof Exp:* Staff mathematician, Gen Motors Res Ctr, 53-54; res assoc appl math, Comput Lab, Wayne State Univ, 56 & Harvard Univ, 57-59; chief scientist & vpres, Mirror Systs Inc, 83-93. *Concurrent Pos:* Res fel math ling & Gordon McKay vis lectr, Harvard Univ, 60-63; lectr, NATO Advan Study Inst, 63; prof & dean, Sch Info & Libr Studies, State Univ NY Buffalo, 67-71. *Mem:* Inst Elec & Electronics Engrs. *Res:* Information processing research; studies concerning diverse aspects of processing; storage retrieval and use of scientific, biomedical and natural-language information; visual and language pattern-processing problems; evaluatory studies of information systems. *Mailing Add:* 241 Glezen Lane Wayland MA 01778-1520

GIUS, JOHN ARMES, SURGERY. *Current Pos:* from assoc prof to prof, 52-72, EMER PROF SURG, UNIV IOWA, 72-; ATTEND SURGEON & DIR MED EDUC, POMONA VALLEY COMMUNITY HOSP, 71- *Personal Data:* b Fairbanks, Alaska, June 2, 08; m 36; c 1. *Educ:* Univ Ore, BA, 31, MD, 34; Columbia Univ, DSc(med), 39. *Prof Exp:* From instr to assoc prof surg, Med Sch, Univ Ore, 39-52. *Mem:* Soc Univ Surg; Am Col Surg. *Res:* Venous circulation; binary tract diseases. *Mailing Add:* 1798 N Garey St Pomona CA 91767-2918

GIVANT, STEVEN ROGER, ALGEBRAIC LOGIC, MODEL THEORY. *Current Pos:* PROF MATH & COMPUT SCI, MILLS COL, 75- *Personal Data:* b Berkeley, Calif, Sept 1, 43. *Educ:* Univ Calif, Berkeley, BA, 67, MA, 69, PhD(math), 75. *Prof Exp:* Instr, Proj Spec Elem Educ for Disadvantaged, 66-72, dir, San Francisco Bay Area, 72-74; assoc res mathematician, Univ Calif, Berkeley, 75-78. *Concurrent Pos:* Dir & co-prin investr, Mills Summer Math Inst, 91-95. *Mem:* Asn Symbolic Logic; Am Math Soc; Math Asn Am. *Res:* Theory and structure of relation algebras and cylindric algebras; universal horn classes with few models in infinite powers. *Mailing Add:* PO Box 9084 Oakland CA 94613

GIVEN, ROBERT R, ENVIRONMENTAL BIOLOGY. *Current Pos:* staff biologist, Univ Southern Calif, 65-69, asst dir, 69-70, asst prof & dir res, Marine Lab, 70-76, RES SCIENTIST, INST MARINE & COASTAL STUDIES & DIR, CATALINA MARINE SCI CTR, UNIV SOUTHERN CALIF, 76- *Personal Data:* b Los Angeles, Calif, July 20, 32; m 59; c 3. *Educ:* Chico State Col, AB, 53; Univ Southern Calif, MS, 63, PhD(biol), 70. *Prof Exp:* Diver-biologist marine zool, Pomona Col, 57-59; marine biologist, Univ Southern Calif, 59-61, 62-63; diver-biologist, Calif Dept Fish & Game, 63-65. *Mem:* Soc Syst Zool; Sigma Xi; Asn Syst Collections. *Res:* Ecology, taxonomy and distribution of southern California marine invertebrates; training of scientist-divers; manned submersibles on continental shelf; biological effects of marine pollution (benthic, in shore). *Mailing Add:* 30800 Palos Verdes Dr E Rancho Palos Verdes CA 90275-6273

GIVENS, BARBARA, CELL BIOLOGY. *Current Pos:* RES SCIENTIST, PAC BIOMED RES CTR, HONOLULU. *Honors & Awards:* E B Wilson Award, Am Soc Cell Biol, 94. *Mailing Add:* Pac Biomed Res Ctr 41 Ahui St Honolulu HI 96813

GIVENS, EDWIN NEIL, ORGANIC CHEMISTRY. *Current Pos:* SR SCI CTR APPL ENG RES, UNIV KY, 92- *Personal Data:* b St Louis, Mo, Dec 8, 35; m 57, Susie Lackey; c Carolyn & Sally. *Educ:* William Jewell Col, AB, 57; Univ Del, MS, 63, PhD(org chem), 65. *Prof Exp:* Sr res chemist petrol, Mobil Res & Develop Corp, 64-76; sr res chemist coal, Air Prod & Chem Inc, 76-78, sect mgr coal, 78-80, mgr, coal liquid res & develop, 80-84, mgr, res & develop safety & spec serv, 84-89, mgr process syst res, 89-91, mgr res & develop planning, Environ Eng Div, 91-92. *Mem:* Am Chem Soc; NAm Catalysis Soc. *Res:* Coal liquefaction; coal liquids upgrading and hydrotreating; petroleum processing; naphtha reforming; petrochemicals; zeolite synthesis; zeolite catalysis. *Mailing Add:* 3086 Montavesta Rd Lexington KY 40502-2956. *Fax:* 606-257-0302; *E-Mail:* egivens@alpha.caer.uky.edu

GIVENS, IAN, CELL BIOLOGY. *Current Pos:* RES SCIENTIST, PAC BIOMED RES CTR, HONOLULU. *Honors & Awards:* E B Wilson Award, Am Soc Cell Biol, 94. *Mailing Add:* Pac Biomed Res Ctr 41 Ahui St Honolulu HI 96813

GIVENS, JAMES ROBERT, REPRODUCTIVE ENDOCRINOLOGY. *Current Pos:* from instr to asst prof med, Univ Tenn, 64-68, asst dir clin res ctr, 65-69, dep chief, 70-71, co-dir, 71-73, from assoc prof to prof med, 68-89, from assoc prof to prof obstet & gynec, 70-89, dir, Div Reproductive Med, 70-89, EMER PROF MED, 89-, EMER PROF OBSTET & GYNEC, UNIV TENN, MEMPHIS, 89- *Personal Data:* b Huntsville, Ala, Aug 6, 30; m 78, Mary K Gammage. *Educ:* David Lipscomb Col, BS, 52; Vanderbilt Univ, MS, 53; Univ Tenn, Memphis, MD, 56. *Prof Exp:* Internship, Memphis Hosps, 56-57, residency internal med, 59-61; instr med, Tufts Univ, 61-62 & Vanderbilt Univ, 62-64. *Concurrent Pos:* USPHS fel, Tufts Univ, 61-62. *Mem:* Soc Gynec Invests; Endocrine Soc; Am Fedn Clin Res; Am Fertil Soc; Am Col Physicians; Am Med Asn. *Res:* Understanding the inheritance and characterization of the pathophysiology of polycystic ovaries. *Mailing Add:* 1831 Georgia Hwy 112 Sylvester GA 31791

GIVENS, PAUL EDWARD, PACKAGING ENGINEERING, MANPOWER-MACHINE SYSTEMS. *Current Pos:* CHMN & PROF, INDUST & MGT SYSTS ENG DEPT, UNIV SFLA, TAMPA, 87- *Personal Data:* b Pawhuska, Okla, Aug 12, 34; m 57, Ann Piper; c Scott & Mark. *Educ:* Univ Ark, BS, 57; Creighton Univ, MBA, 68; Univ Tex, Arlington, PhD(indust eng), 74. *Honors & Awards:* Edward A Smith Res Award, Edward A Smith Found, 85; Sarchet Award, Am Acad Eng Educr, 96. *Prof Exp:* Div indust engr pipeline opers, Northern Natural Gas Co, 65-67, mgr employee rels, 67-69; mgr personnel, Western Co NAm, 69-72; grad teaching asst indust eng, Univ Tex, Arlington, 72-74; instr mgt, 74; assoc prof, Miss State Univ, 74-80; mgt specialist bus opers, Miss State Coop Exten Serv, 77-80; vpres opers, Cotton Mkt, Staplcotn, Greenwood, Miss, 80-83; dir technol, Ctr Technol Develop, Univ Mo, Rolla, 84-85, assoc prof eng mgt, 83-87, dir, Small Bus Inst, 84-86, assoc dir, Ctr Technol Develop, 85-86. *Concurrent Pos:* Consult manpower planning & develop, LTV Aerospace, 71 & Tech Eng-Archit Mgt Proj, State Mo, 84-85; dir, Mgt Div, Inst Indust Engrs, 78 & 79; pres, Soc Eng & Mgt Systs, Inst Indust Eng, 91-92; bd trustees & vpres prof enhancement, Inst Indust Engrs, 94-96. *Mem:* Fel Inst Indust Engrs; Am Soc Eng Mgt; Am Soc Eng Educ; Acad Mgt; Inst Packaging Profs. *Res:* Long distance education and globalization of technology. *Mailing Add:* Indust Eng 118 Col Eng Univ SFla Tampa FL 33620-9951. *E-Mail:* givens@aunburn.eng.usf.edu

GIVENS, RICHARD SPENCER, ORGANIC CHEMISTRY, BIOANALYTICAL CHEMISTRY. *Current Pos:* from asst prof to assoc prof, Univ Kans, 67-76, chmn dept, 88-95, assoc vchancellor, 95-96, PROF CHEM, UNIV KANS, 76-, ASST PROVOST, 96- *Personal Data:* b Buffalo, NY, May 19, 40; m 66, Susan M Gillett; c Barbara J (Heeb), Elizabeth I (Porter), Marjory L & Eleanor M. *Educ:* Marietta Col, BS, 62; Univ Wis, PhD(org chem), 67. *Prof Exp:* NIH fel org chem, Iowa State Univ, 66-67. *Concurrent Pos:* Assoc dir, Ctr Bioanalytical Res, Univ Kans, 83-88, dir, 89-91; vis foreign scientist, Sci Res Coun, Eng, Univ Sheffield; hon lectr, Mid-Am State Univ, 70-71 & 84-85. *Mem:* Am Chem Soc; Royal Soc Chem; NY Acad Sci; Inter-Am Photochem Soc; fel AAAS; fel Am Inst Chemists. *Res:* Organic photochemistry, both synthetic and mechanistic investigations; mechanisms and applications of chemiluminescence; photochemistry of caged bioactive substrates, nucleotides, amino acids, neurotransmitters and metal ions. *Mailing Add:* Dept Chem 5023 MAL Univ Kans Lawrence KS 66045-0046. *E-Mail:* rgivens@caco3.chem.ukans.edu

GIVENS, SAMUEL VIRTUE, BIOSTATISTICS. *Current Pos:* ASST DIR RES STATIST, HOFFMAN-LA ROCHE INC, 72-, INT DIR BIOSTATIST,. *Personal Data:* b Roanoke, Va, Nov 22, 46; m 68; c 2. *Educ:* Va Polytech Inst & State Univ, BS, 68, MS, 70, PhD(statist), 73. *Prof Exp:* Consult statist, Stochastics Inc, 71-72. *Concurrent Pos:* Teaching asst statist, Va Polytech Inst & State Univ, 72; adj prof statist, Seton Hall Univ, 74- *Mem:* Am Statist Asn; Biomet Soc. *Res:* General problems in the bioassay area and multivariate design of experiments restricted by a cost criterion. *Mailing Add:* 33 Seneca Pl Montclair NJ 07043

GIVENS, WILLIAM GEARY, PHYSICAL CHEMISTRY. *Current Pos:* MEM FAC, DEPT CHEM, GROSSMONT COL, 66- *Personal Data:* b Camden, Ark, Sept 10, 32; m 58; c 2. *Educ:* Rice Inst, BA, 54; Univ Wis, PhD, 59. *Prof Exp:* Res chemist, Jersey Prod Res Co, 59; asst prof chem, Norwich Univ, 59-61 & Exten Div, Univ Wis, 61-62; res chemist, Gen Dynamics/Astronaut, 62-64 & Rocketdyne Div, NAm Aviation, Inc, 64-66. *Mem:* Am Chem Soc. *Mailing Add:* Dept Chem Grossmont Col 800 Grossmont College Dr El Cajon CA 92020

GIVI, PEYMAN, COMBUSTION, COMPUTATIONAL FLUID DYNAMICS. *Current Pos:* from asst prof to assoc prof, 88-93, PROF MECH & AEROSPACE ENG, STATE UNIV NY, BUFFALO, 93- *Personal Data:* b Tehran, Iran, June 26, 58; US citizen; m 83, Suzanne J Pellarin; c Regina J, Carmen J, Julian L & Jerom P. *Educ:* Youngstown State Univ, BE, 80; Carnegie Mellon Univ, ME, 82, PhD(mech eng), 84. *Prof Exp:* Res scientist, Flow Industs Inc, 85-88. *Concurrent Pos:* Prin investr, NASA, NSF, Off Naval Res & Air Force Off Sci Res, 85-; mem panel, Workshops Combustion & Fluid Mech, 85-, several comts, NSF, 89-; vis scholar, NASA Lewis Res Ctr, 88; vis scientist, NASA Langley Res Ctr, 89 & 90; Off Naval Res young investr award, 90-93; NSF presidential young investr award, 90-92; fac adv, Soc Women Engrs, 90-; pres fac fel, 92-95. *Mem:* Combustion Inst; Am Inst Aeronaut & Astronaut; Soc Aerospace Eng; Am Soc Mech Eng. *Res:* Computational fluid mechanics; numerical combustion; use of advanced computational methods and modern supercomputer to understand the complex phenomena of turbulent combustion; turbulence; non-linear system identifications. *Mailing Add:* Dept Mech & Aerospace Eng State Univ NY Buffalo NY 14260-4400. *Fax:* 716-645-3875

GIVLER, ROBERT L, MEDICINE, PATHOLOGY. *Current Pos:* PATHOLOGIST, RES HOSP & MED CTR, KANSAS CITY, 72-; CLIN ASSOC PROF, UNIV MO, KANSAS CITY, 84- *Personal Data:* b Mason City, Iowa, May 8, 31; m 56; c 1. *Educ:* Univ Iowa, MD, 56. *Prof Exp:* Intern, King County Hosps, Seattle, Wash, 56-57; instr path, Univ Iowa, 57-58, asst, 58-61, assoc, 61, from asst prof to assoc prof, 63-72. *Mem:* Col Am Path; Am Soc Clin Path; Int Acad Path. *Res:* Leukemia; lymphoma. *Mailing Add:* Dept Path Res Hosp/Med Ctr Kansas City MO 64132

GIVONE, DONALD DANIEL, ELECTRICAL ENGINEERING. *Current Pos:* PROF ELEC ENG, STATE UNIV NY, BUFFALO, 63- *Personal Data:* b Paterson, NJ, July 10, 36; m 72, Louise Vertino; c Donna M & David D. *Educ:* Rensselaer Polytech Inst, BSEE, 58; Cornell Univ, MS, 61, PhD(elec eng), 63. *Mem:* Sigma Xi. *Res:* Switching circuit theory and logic design; computer technology. *Mailing Add:* Dept Elec & Comput Eng State Univ NY Buffalo NY 14260. *E-Mail:* ddgivone@acsu.buffalo.edu

GIZA, CHESTER ANTHONY, SYNTHETIC ORGANIC CHEMISTRY, ORGANIC STEREOCHEMISTRY. *Current Pos:* ENVIRON SCIENTIST, FOSTER WHEELER CORP, 91- *Personal Data:* b Three Rivers, Mass, May 18, 30; m 61, Yueh-hua Chen; c 2. *Educ:* Univ Mass, Amherst, BS, 55, MS, 58; Univ Notre Dame, PhD(org chem), 68. *Prof Exp:* Asst chem, Univ Mass, Amherst, 54-57; chemist, Union Carbide Res Inst, NY, 59-63; asst chem, Univ Notre Dame, 63-67; lab mgr & chief qual control officer, Newell Specialty Chem Co, 86-88; asst prof, Wheeling Col, 67-70, chmn dept, 74-75, assoc prof org chem, 70-85. *Concurrent Pos:* Chem consult, 71-; vis scientist, WVa Univ, 75, Carnegie-Mellon Univ, Pa, 81. *Mem:* Sigma Xi; Am Chem Soc. *Res:* Synthesis and evaluation of biologically active organic compounds, with special attention to stereochemical aspects of structure; growth-promoting substances. *Mailing Add:* 1501 Walnut Grove Rd Wheeling WV 26003-9632

GIZA, YUEH-HUA CHEN, organic biochemistry; deceased, see previous edition for last biography

GIZIS, EVANGELOS JOHN, BIOCHEMISTRY, FOOD SCIENCE. *Current Pos:* VPRES, QUEENS COL, CITY UNIV NY, 86- *Personal Data:* b Tinos, Greece, Apr 1, 34; m 67, Frances Murray; c John, Alexander & Paul R. *Educ:* Nat Univ Athens, BS; Ore State Univ, PhD(food sci & biochem), 63. *Prof Exp:* Fel food sci, Mich State Univ, 64-65; fel enzymes & pectins, Mellon Inst, 65-66; biochemist, L I Jewish Hosp, Queens Hosp Ctr Affil, Jamaica, NY, 66-70; assoc prof natural sci, City Univ NY, 70-72; vpres, Bor Manhattan Community Col, City Univ NY, 77-85, actg pres, 85-86; prof natural sci & assoc dean fac, Hostos Community Col, City Univ NY, 72-, dean arts & sci, 74-75; adj prof, Dept Nutrit, NY Univ, 76- *Concurrent Pos:* Res collab, Med Dept, Brookhaven Nat Lab, 66-70; res chemist, Vet Admin Hosp, Brooklyn, NY, 70-72. *Mem:* Soc Exp Biol & Med; Am Chem Soc; Inst Food Technol; NY Acad Sci; Am Inst Nutrit. *Res:* Pectinolytic enzymes and pectins; vitamin B12 binders in milk, in normal human and pernicious anemia serum; chromatographic techniques. *Mailing Add:* 427 Ryder Manhasset NY 11030-2761. *Fax:* 718-997-5738; *E-Mail:* van@mkh1.qc.edu

GJEDDE, ALBERT, NEUROPHARMACOLOGY, NEUROLOGY. *Current Pos:* assoc prof, 86-89, PROF NEUROL & NEUROSURG, MONTREAL NEUROL INST, MCGILL UNIV, 89- *Personal Data:* b Copenhagen, Denmark, Jan 10, 46; m 83; c 3. *Educ:* Rungsted Acad, Copenhagen, Artium, 64; Univ Copenhagen, Cand Med, 73, Dr med(physiol), 83. *Prof Exp:* Postdoctoral fel, Dept Neurol, Cornell Univ Med Col, 73-76; postdoctoral fel, Dept Neurosura, Rigshospitalet, Univ Copenhagen, 76-79, from asst prof to assoc prof physiol, Panum Inst, 79-86. *Concurrent Pos:* Assoc dir, McConnell Brain Imaging Ctr, Montreal Neurol Inst, 87-, dir, Positron Imaging Labs, 89-; dir, Int Soc Cerebral Blood Flow & Metab, 87-; dep chief ed J Cerebral Blood Flow Metab, 87-; coordr & prin investr, Med Res Coun Spec Proj Positron Imaging, 89- *Mem:* Int Soc Neurochem; Am Physiol Soc; Soc Neurosci. *Res:* Cerebral blood flow and metabolism; blood-brain transfer of nutrients and water, relationship between blood flow; glucose metabolism and oxygen consumption in the brain of mammals and man; dopaminergic neurotransmission and metabolism of amino acids; disorders of brain metabolism and dopaminergic neurotransmission in humans, including mitochondrial encephalopathiesm; Parkinson's disease; schizophrenia; temporal lobe epilepsy and related disorders; positron emission tomography. *Mailing Add:* Prof Positron Emission Tomography Ctr Aarhus Univ Hosp Bygning 10 Indgang 10C DK 8000 Aarhus Denmark, *Fax:* 45-8949-3020

GJESSING, HELEN WITTON, MICROBIOLOGY. *Current Pos:* from instr to assoc prof, 63-77, PROF BIOL, UNIV VI, 77- *Personal Data:* b Boston, Mass, Nov 22, 27; m 55; c 4. *Educ:* Beloit Col, BA, 50; Univ Mass, MA, 52. *Prof Exp:* Res technician virus, Res Infectious Dis Div, Children's Med Ctr & Sch Med, Harvard Univ, 52-53, res asst, 53-55; res & teaching asst parasitol res & lab instr, Sch Trop Med, San Juan, PR, 55-57. *Concurrent Pos:* Actg dean, Univ VI, 68-69, chmn sci & math div, 69-72 & 76-78; dir minority biomed support prog res grant, NIH, 76-77; dir minority inst sci improvement prog grant, NSF, 78-81. *Mem:* Am Soc Microbiol; Sigma Xi. *Res:* Antibiotic marine bacteria, particularly those in sponges; antibiotic marine sponges. *Mailing Add:* Div Sci & Math Univ Virgin Islands St Thomas VI 00802

GJOSTEIN, NORMAN A, MATERIALS SCIENCE, ELECTRONIC SYSTEMS. *Current Pos:* MATS ENG CONSULT, 96-; ADJ PROF MATS ENG, UNIV MICH, 96- *Personal Data:* b Chicago, Ill, May 26, 31; m 59; c 2. *Educ:* Ill Inst Technol, BS, 53, MS, 54; Carnegie-Mellon Univ, PhD(metall eng), 58. *Honors & Awards:* Shoemaker Award, Am Soc Metals, 90. *Prof Exp:* Res engr, Thompson-Ramo-Wooldridge, Inc, 58-60; sr res scientist, Ford Motor Co, 60-61, prin res scientist assoc, 61-64, staff scientist, 64-69, prin res scientist, 69-73, mgr, Metall Dept, 73-76, mgr Europ res liaison, 76-78, mgr res planning, 78-79, dir long-range & systs res, 79-81, dir, Systs Res Lab, 81-86, dir power train & mat, 86-88, dir, Mat Res Lab, 86-96. *Concurrent Pos:* Mem trustees, Am Soc Metals Int, 91-93; mem bd dir, Eng Soc Detroit, 91-93. *Mem:* Nat Acad Eng; Inst Elec & Electronics Engrs; Am Inst Mech Engrs; Sigma Xi; fel Am Soc Metals Int. *Res:* Physics and chemistry of interfaces and surfaces; composite materials; applications of advanced automotive materials; leed and auger spectroscopy. *Mailing Add:* 544 S Claremont Dearborn MI 48124. *Fax:* 302-277-6442; *E-Mail:* ngjostei@msn.com

GLABE, CHARLES G, CELL BIOLOGY, BIOCHEMISTRY. *Current Pos:* MEM STAFF WORCESTER FEDN EXP BIOL. *Personal Data:* b Columbus, Ohio, Jan 16, 52. *Educ:* Calif State Univ, Sacramento, BA, 73; Univ Calif, Davis, PhD(zool), 77. *Prof Exp:* Res asst, Univ Calif, Davis, 73-77; res assoc, Sch Med, Johns Hopkins Univ, 78- *Concurrent Pos:* Rockefeller Found fel, 78- *Mem:* Am Soc Cell Biol. *Res:* Biochemistry of fertilization, cell adhesion and cell surface interactions. *Mailing Add:* Dept Molecular Biol & Biochem Univ Calif Irvine Irvine CA 92717-0001. *Fax:* 714-856-8551

GLABERSON, WILLIAM I, low temperature physics, for more information see previous edition

GLABMAN, SHELDON, INTERNAL MEDICINE, NEPHROLOGY. *Current Pos:* asst prof, 68-73, ASSOC PROF MED, MT SINAI SCH MED, 73- *Personal Data:* b New York, NY, Apr 13, 32; m 54; c 3. *Educ:* Univ Pa, BA, 53; Chicago Med Sch, MD, 57. *Prof Exp:* Div dialysis unit, Mt Sinai Hosp, 68-86. *Concurrent Pos:* USPHS fel, Med Col, Cornell Univ, 60-62 & Mt Sinai Hosp, 62-65; asst attend med, Mt Sinai Hosp, 68-73, assoc attend, 73-; consult, Lincoln Hosp, New York, 70-72. *Mem:* Am Fedn Clin Res; Am Soc Nephrology; Int Soc Nephrology. *Res:* Renal physiology; hemodialysis; renal transplantation. *Mailing Add:* 1175 Park Ave New York NY 10128-1211

GLADDEN, BRUCE, EXERCISE PHYSIOLOGY, MUSCLE FATIGUE. *Current Pos:* ASSOC PROF EXERCISE PHYSIOL, DIV ALLIED HEALTH, UNIV LOUISVILLE, 78- *Personal Data:* b Hohenwald, Tenn, Jan 27, 51; m 73; c 2. *Educ:* Univ Tenn, Knoxville, PhD(zool), 76. *Mem:* Am Physiol Soc; Am Col Sport Med. *Res:* Muscle fatigue, lactate metabolism; the role of oxygen in muscle performance; substrate utilization. *Mailing Add:* Dept Health & Phys Educ Auburn Univ 2050 Coliseum Auburn AL 36849-5323. *Fax:* 334-844-4025

GLADDING, GARY EARLE, EXPERIMENTAL HIGH ENERGY PHYSICS. *Current Pos:* Res assoc physics, 71-72, from asst prof to assoc prof, 73-85, PROF PHYSICS, UNIV ILL, 86- *Personal Data:* b Brownwood, Tex, Apr 16, 44; m 66, 84; c 2. *Educ:* Univ Ill, BS, 65; Harvard Univ, AM, 68, PhD(physics), 71. *Concurrent Pos:* Vis scientist physics, Europ Orgn for Nuclear Res, 72; NSF fel, 72. *Mem:* Am Phys Soc. *Res:* Counter and proportional wire chamber experiments studying the production of new particles with large transverse momentum. *Mailing Add:* Dept Physics Univ Ill 1110 W Green St Urbana IL 61801

GLADFELTER, WAYNE LEWIS, INORGANIC CHEMISTRY. *Current Pos:* from asst prof to assoc prof, 79-88, PROF CHEM, UNIV MINN, 88- *Personal Data:* b Bryn Mawr, Pa, Feb 16, 53; m 78; c 2. *Educ:* Colo Sch Mines, BS, 75; Pa State Univ, PhD(chem), 78. *Honors & Awards:* Nobel Laureate Signature Award, Am Chem Soc, 80. *Prof Exp:* NSF fel chem, Calif Inst Technol, 78-79. *Mem:* Am Chem Soc; Sigma Xi; Mat Res Soc. *Res:* Synthesis and characterization of metal carbonyls, nitrosyls and organometallic cluster compounds; catalysis organometallic precursors to solid state materials; chemical vapor deposition. *Mailing Add:* Dept Chem Univ Minn Minneapolis MN 55455-0100

GLADFELTER, WILBERT EUGENE, PHYSIOLOGY, NEUROBIOLOGY. *Current Pos:* from instr to assoc prof, 59-96, EMER PROF PHYSIOL, WVA UNIV, 96- *Personal Data:* b York, Pa, April 29, 28; m 52, Ruth Ballantyne; c James, Charles & Mary. *Educ:* Gettysburg Col, AB, 52; Univ Pa, PhD(physiol), 60. *Prof Exp:* Asst instr physiol, Univ Pa, 54-56, 58-59. *Mem:* Am Physiol Soc; Soc Neurosci; Sigma Xi; Soc Integrative & Comp Biol. *Res:* Somatosensory system-spinal cord; regulation of energy exchange; hypothalamus and motor activity. *Mailing Add:* Dept Physiol WVA Univ PO Box 9229 Morgantown WV 26506. *Fax:* 304-293-3850; *E-Mail:* glad@wvnvms.wvnet.edu

GLADMAN, CHARLES HERMAN, MATHEMATICS. *Current Pos:* From instr to assoc prof, 48-83, chmn dept, 65-68, EMER ASSOC PROF MATH, UNIV TEX, EL PASO, 83- *Personal Data:* b Harrison Co, Ohio, May 24, 17; m 47; c 1. *Educ:* Ohio State Univ, BS, 38, MA, 48. *Concurrent Pos:* Mathematician, Schellenger Res Labs, 58-60. *Mem:* AAAS; Math Asn Am; Soc Indust & Appl Math; Sigma Xi. *Res:* Mathematical analysis. *Mailing Add:* Univ Tex El Paso TX 79968-0001

GLADNEY, HENRY M, COMPUTER SCIENCE. *Current Pos:* Res staff mem, 63-68, tech adv to vpres & chief scientist, 68-70, mgr res comput facility, 70-72, mgr, Molecular Dynamics Dept, 72-76, mgr res comput facility, 77-79, RES STAFF MEM COMPUT SCI, ALMADEN RES CTR, INT BUS MACH CORP, 79- *Personal Data:* b Prague, Czech, Feb 8, 38; Can citizen; m 69; c 2. *Educ:* Univ Toronto, BA, 60; Princeton Univ, MA, 62, PhD(chem), 63. *Concurrent Pos:* Res sabbatical, 76-77. *Mem:* Asn Comput Mach; fel Am Phys Soc. *Res:* Laboratory and factory automation; software security; resource control in computer facilities; programming languages; distributed data systems. *Mailing Add:* IBM Almaden Res Ctr 650 Harry Rd Dept K52/802 San Jose CA 95120-6099

GLADROW, ELROY MERLE, PHYSICAL CHEMISTRY. *Current Pos:* RETIRED. *Personal Data:* b Cleveland, Ohio, Sept 2, 15; m 47, Elizabeth Deihl; c Cynthia & Marsha. *Educ:* Heidelberg Col, BS, 38; Iowa State Col, PhD(chem), 48. *Prof Exp:* Res assoc chemist, Nat Defense Res Comt, Manhattan Proj, AEC, 42-47; res chemist, Stand Oil Develop Co, 47-58 & Esso Stand Oil Co, 58-63; res assoc, Exxon Res & Eng Co, 63-70, sr res assoc, 70-79. *Concurrent Pos:* Consult, Exxon Res & Eng Co, 79-80, Ethyl Corp, 83-84. *Res:* Hydrocarbon catalysis; cracking, reforming, hydrocracking, hydrodesulfurization, isomerization, fuel cell; separation and preparation of pure rare earths; uranium fission products chemistry; radiation chemistry. *Mailing Add:* 9884 Spanish Moss Ct Sun City AZ 85373

GLADSTONE, HAROLD MAURICE, MATHEMATICS, COMPUTER SCIENCES. *Current Pos:* asst chmn, 70-71, chmn dept, 71-74, from asst prof to assoc prof, 69-75, PROF CHEM, MIDDLESEX COUNTY COL, 75- *Personal Data:* b Brooklyn, NY, Jan 23, 32; div; c Steven & Roberta. *Educ:* Rensselaer Polytech Inst, BS, 52; Adelphi Univ, MS, 56; Polytech Univ, PhD(org chem), 61. *Prof Exp:* Res chemist, Armstrong Cork Co, 56-57; eve instr, Adelphi Univ, 58-60; res chemist, Esso Res & Eng Co, 61-62; proj mgr, Quantum Inc, 62-63, dir lab, 63-65; mem tech staff, Bell Tel Labs, 65-69. *Mem:* Am Chem Soc. *Res:* Organic synthesis; chaos and fractals; chemistry of hazardous materials; polymers. *Mailing Add:* Dept Chem Middlesex County Col Woodbridge Ave & Mill Rd Edison NJ 08818

GLADSTONE, MATTHEW THEODORE, ORGANIC CHEMISTRY. *Current Pos:* RETIRED. *Personal Data:* b Manchester, NH, Apr 25, 19; m 46; c 3. *Educ:* Univ Chicago, BS, 40, PhD(org chem), 48. *Prof Exp:* Lab asst chem, Univ Chicago, 41-42 & 46-47; res assoc, Gen Elec Co, 47-50; res assoc, Abrasives Div, Tech Dept, Behr-Manning Corp, 51-54, group leader, 54-64;

asst dir res, Coated Abrasives Div, Norton Co, NY, 64-72, res assoc, 74-83; tech consult, Riken-Norton Co, Ltd, Tokyo, 72-74. *Mem:* AAAS; Am Chem Soc; Am Inst Chem. *Res:* Alkyd and phenolic resins; plastics; free radical reactions; reactions of free radicals in solution; decomposition of acetyl peroxide in acids, nitroalkanes and halogenated esters; fluorocarbon polymers; abrasives, epoxy resins; cloth finishing; polyurethanes. *Mailing Add:* 761 Cent Parkway Schenectady NY 12309

GLADSTONE, WILLIAM TURNBULL, FOREST GENETICS, WOOD SCIENCE. *Current Pos:* ED, SOUTHERN J APPL FORESTRY, 89- *Personal Data:* b Syracuse, NY, May 5, 31; m 56; c 2. *Educ:* State Univ NY Col Forestry, Syracuse Univ, BS, 53; Yale Univ, MF, 65; NC State Univ, PhD(forest genetics, wood sci), 69. *Prof Exp:* Asst pulp mill supt, Union Bag Camp Paper Corp, Va, 53-63; asst prof forest genetics, State Univ NY Col Forestry, Syracuse Univ, 68-72; forest geneticist, Weyerhaeuser Co, 72-74, mgr, Southern Forestry Res Ctr, 74-76, mgr trop forestry res, 76-89. *Mem:* Tech Asn Pulp & Paper Indust; Forest Prod Res Soc; Soc Am Foresters. *Res:* Variability and heritability of wood properties; relationships between wood fiber properties and products manufactured from wood; environmental influences on wood properties. *Mailing Add:* Burdin Hill Rd Avoca NY 14809

GLADUE, BRIAN ANTHONY, PSYCHOBIOLOGY, NEUROSCIENCES. *Current Pos:* RES FAC & RES PROF PSYCHOL, UNIV CINCINNATI, 94- *Personal Data:* b Norwich, Conn, Nov 30, 50; m 84, 96; c 2. *Educ:* Northeastern Univ, BA & BS, 73; Mich State Univ, PhD(zool), 79. *Prof Exp:* Instr animal behav, Dept Zool, Mich State Univ, 79; fel psychobiol, Human Sexuality Training Grant, Dept Psychiat, State Univ NY, Stony Brook, 79-81; res fel psychoendocrinol, Long Island Res Inst, 80-81, res scientist, 81-84; prog dir human sexuality & assoc prof psychol, NDak State Univ, 84-93; sr scientist, Am Psychol Asn, 93-94. *Concurrent Pos:* Nat res serv award, NIMH, 79-81. *Mem:* Int Soc Human Ethology; Int Soc Res Aggression; Am Psychol Asn; Am Psychol Soc; Int Acad Sex Res; Asn Politics & Life Sci. *Res:* Gonadal hormone influences on the development of sexual behavior and aggression; psychology of aggression in humans; science policy. *Mailing Add:* Univ Cincin 261 Old Shriners Bldg ML-0840 Cincinnati OH 45267-0840. *Fax:* 513-558-2744; *E-Mail:* brian.gladue@uc.edu

GLADWELL, GRAHAM M L, INVERSE PROBLEMS, CONTACT PROBLEMS. *Current Pos:* PROF CIVIL ENG, UNIV WATERLOO, 69-, PROF APPL MATH, 79- *Personal Data:* b Oxford, Eng, Feb 21, 34; Can citizen; m 58; c 3. *Educ:* Univ London, BSc, 54, PhD(math), 57, DSc, 69. *Honors & Awards:* Cancam Medal, Can Cong Appl Mech, 91. *Prof Exp:* Asst lectr math, Univ Col London, 56-59, lectr, 59-60; lectr, Univ WI, 60-62; lectr mech eng, Mass Inst Technol, 62; lectr aeronaut, Univ Southampton, 62-63, sr lectr vibration theory, Inst Sound & Vibration Res, 63-69. *Concurrent Pos:* Dir, Am Acad Mech, 80-83; ser ed, solid mech & applications, Kluwer Acad Publ, 89- *Mem:* Fel Inst Math & Its Applications; Fel Am Acad Mech; Soc Indust & Appl Math. *Res:* Contact problems in the classical theory of elasticity; theory of vibration, particularly inverse problems in vibration; inverse scattering theory. *Mailing Add:* Dept Civil Eng Univ Waterloo Waterloo ON N2L 3G1 Can

GLADWELL, IAN, MATHEMATICAL SOFTWARE, NUMERICAL ANALYSIS. *Current Pos:* assoc prof, 87-88, PROF & CHMN MATH, SOUTHERN METHODIST UNIV, 88-94, PROF, 95- *Personal Data:* b Bolton, Eng, Oct 20, 44; m 79, Joan Meuing; c Theresa, Sean, Kathleen & Mary. *Educ:* Oxford Univ, BA, 66, PhD(math), 70; Univ Manchester, MS, 67. *Prof Exp:* Teaching asst math, Univ Manchester, 67-69, lectr, 69-80, sr lectr, 80-87. *Concurrent Pos:* Res fel, Dept Computer Sci, Univ Toronto, 75; Royal Soc indust fel, NAG Ltd, Oxford, 86; assoc ed, J Numerical Anal, Inst Math & Applications, 87- *Mem:* Fel Inst Math & Applications; Soc Indust & Appl Math. *Res:* Numerical analysis; mathematical software; parallel computation; knowledge based systems; scientific computation. *Mailing Add:* Math Dept Southern Methodist Univ Dallas TX 75275-0156. *Fax:* 214-768-2355; *E-Mail:* gladwell@seas.smu.edu

GLADYSZ, JOHN A, ORGANIC CHEMISTRY, ORGANOMETALLIC CHEMISTRY. *Current Pos:* assoc prof, 82-85, PROF, UNIV UTAH, 85- *Personal Data:* b Kalamazoo, Mich, Aug 13, 52. *Educ:* Univ Mich, BSChem, 71; Stanford Univ, PhD(org chem), 74. *Honors & Awards:* Arthur C Cope Scholar Award, 88; Organometall Chem Award, Am Chem Soc, 94. *Prof Exp:* Asst prof org chem, Univ Calif, Los Angeles, 74-82. *Concurrent Pos:* Alfred P Sloan Foundation fel, 80-84; Camille & Henry Dreyfus teacher-scholar grant, 80-85; assoc ed, Chem Rev, 84-; consult, Corp Res Labs, Exxon Res & Eng; sr scientist award, Alexander von Humboldt Found, 95. *Mem:* Am Chem Soc; Chem Soc; AAAS. *Res:* Chiral transition metal complexes in asymmetric organic synthesis; mechanisms of asymmetric induction and organometallic transformations; reactions of coordinated ligands; homogeneous catalysis; metal complexes of elemental carbon. *Mailing Add:* Dept Chem Univ Utah Salt Lake City UT 84112. *Fax:* 801-581-8433; *E-Mail:* gladysz@rhenium.chem.utah.edu

GLAENZER, RICHARD H, ELECTRICAL ENGINEERING, PHYSICS. *Current Pos:* SR PROC ENGR SPECIALIST, MEMC ELECTRONIC MATS, 88- *Personal Data:* b St Louis, Mo, Nov 29, 33; m 63; c 4. *Educ:* Wash Univ, St Louis, BS, 60, MS, 64; Carnegie-Mellon Univ, PhD(elec engr), 68. *Prof Exp:* Engr, McDonnell Douglas Corp, 60-62, res assoc, 62-64, res scientist, 67-71; staff engr, McDonnell Douglas Astronaut Co, 71-77; sect mgr, McDonnell Douglas Electronics Co, 77-83; vis prof, Inst Nat de Astrofisica, Optica, & Electronics, 83-84; sr res specialist, Monsanto Co, 84-88. *Mem:* Inst Elec & Electronics Engrs; AAAS. *Res:* Integrated circuits; photodetectors; infrared to visible image conversion; electrical behavior of defects in semiconductor materials and devices. *Mailing Add:* 501 Pearl Dr St Peters MO 63376

GLAESER, HANS HELLMUT, INORGANIC CHEMISTRY. *Current Pos:* from res chemist to sr res chemist, 66-73, res assoc, 73-83, RES FEL, WHITE PIGMENTS & MINERAL PROD, E I DU PONT DE NEMOURS & CO, INC, 83- *Personal Data:* b Chemnitz, Ger, June 30, 34; nat US; m 62, Erika; c Annette & Barbara. *Educ:* Karlsruhe Tech Univ, BS, 55, MS, 58, Dr rer nat, 61. *Prof Exp:* Res fel inorg chem, Wash State Univ, 62-66. *Mem:* Am Inst Metall Engrs. *Res:* Extractive metallurgy, TiO_2 pigment manufacture, thermochemical equilibrium calculations; reaction mechanisms; chlorination technology of ilmenite and other ores. *Mailing Add:* Meadows 11 Meadow Lane Wilmington DE 19807

GLAESER, ROBERT M, BIOPHYSICS. *Current Pos:* lectr med physics, 65-66, from asst prof to assoc prof, 66-76, PROF BIOPHYS, UNIV CALIF, BERKELEY, 76- *Personal Data:* b Kenosha, Wis, July 20, 37; m 60, Rachel Anton; c Steven, Mark & Kathryn. *Educ:* Univ Wis-Madison, BS, 59; Univ Calif, Berkeley, PhD(biophys), 64. *Honors & Awards:* Elizabeth R Cole Award, Biophys Soc, 92. *Prof Exp:* NSF fel, Math Inst, Oxford Univ, 63-64; NIH traineeship biophys, Univ Chicago, 64-65. *Mem:* AAAS; Biophys Soc; Electron Micros Soc Am (pres, 86-); Am Crystallog Asn; Am Soc Cell Biol; Royal Micros Soc. *Res:* Molecular structure and molecular organization of cell membranes; electron optics and the interpretation of electron microscopic images. *Mailing Add:* Univ Calif 363 Donner Labs Berkeley CA 94720-0001. *Fax:* 510-486-6488; *E-Mail:* rmglaeser@lbl.gov

GLAESER, WILLIAM A(LFRED), METALLURGY, TRIBOLOGY. *Current Pos:* prin engr, Battelle Mem Inst, 51-57, proj leader, 57-59, asst chief, Eng Mech Div, 59-64, assoc chief, Exp Physics Div, 64-69, fel lubrication mech, Div Mech & Systs Eng Dept, 69-72, RES LEADER, STRUCT MAT & TRIBOLOGY SECT, COLUMBUS LABS, BATTELLE MEM INST, 72- *Personal Data:* b Utica, NY, Aug 25, 23; m 51; c 3. *Educ:* Cornell Univ, BME, 49; Ohio State Univ, MS, 59. *Prof Exp:* Develop engr, Clark Bros, Inc, 49-51. *Concurrent Pos:* Adj asst prof, Ohio State Univ; chmn, Gordon Conf Friction Lubrication & Wear, 82. *Mem:* Am Soc Metals; Sigma Xi. *Res:* Bearings lubrication and wear phenomena, especially as concerned with unusual environments; metallurgical aspects of wear and friction; solid state physics aspects of wear and friction; near surface microstructures of worn metals and alloys by electron microscopy. *Mailing Add:* 731 Laural Land Dr S Columbus OH 43214

GLAGOV, SEYMOUR, PATHOLOGY. *Current Pos:* From instr to assoc prof, 58-70, PROF PATH, UNIV CHICAGO, 70- *Personal Data:* b New York, NY, Aug 8, 25; m 46; c 1. *Educ:* Brooklyn Col, BA, 46; Univ Geneva, MD, 53; Am Bd Path, dipl, 60. *Concurrent Pos:* Res fel, Am Heart Asn, 58-60; estab investr, Am Heart Asn, 62- *Mem:* Sigma Xi. *Res:* Experimental pathology; pathophysiology and biology of blood vessels; diseases of the liver; human pathology. *Mailing Add:* Dept Path Mc 3083 Univ Chicago 5841 S Maryland Ave Chicago IL 60637-1463. *Fax:* 773-702-3778

GLAHN, RAYMOND PHILIP, IRON ABSORPTION & BIOAVAILABILITY. *Current Pos:* RES PHYSIOLOGIST, AGR RES SERV, USDA, 92- *Personal Data:* b Lancaster, Pa, Oct 3, 61. *Educ:* Pa State Univ, BS, 83, MS, 86, PhD(physiol), 89. *Honors & Awards:* Excellence in Res Ann Award, Am Physiol Soc, 92. *Prof Exp:* Res assoc, Dept Animal/Poultry Sci, Univ Ark, 89-90; res fel, Dept Nephrology, Mayo Clin & Found, 90-92. *Mem:* Am Soc Nutrit Sci. *Res:* Defining mechanisms of iron absorption; developing and applying a caco-2 cell/invitro digestion model to improve food iron availability. *Mailing Add:* US Plant Soil & Nutrit Lab Cornell Univ Tower Rd Ithaca NY 14853. *Fax:* 607-255-1132; *E-Mail:* rpg3@cornell.edu

GLAID, ANDREW JOSEPH, III, BIOCHEMISTRY. *Current Pos:* From asst prof to assoc prof, 54-61, PROF CHEM, DUQUESNE UNIV, 61-, CHMN DEPT, 75- *Personal Data:* b Pittsburgh, Pa, July 14, 23; m 55; c 5. *Educ:* Duquesne Univ, BS, 49, MS, 50; Duke Univ, PhD(biochem), 55. *Mem:* Am Chem Soc; Sigma Xi; Am Asn Univ Prof. *Res:* Kinetics of enzymatic reactions; stereochemistry of biologically active compounds. *Mailing Add:* 668 Fruithurst Dr Pittsburgh PA 15228

GLAJCH, JOSEPH LOUIS, CHROMATOGRAPHY, OPTIMIZATION OF SEPARATIONS. *Current Pos:* res mgr, 91, ASSOC DIR NEW PROD CHEM, DUPONT MERCK PHARMACEUT CO, 92- *Personal Data:* b Buffalo, NY, Jan 26, 54; m 80, Mary E Dickey; c Brent S, Kelly & Scott. *Educ:* Cornell Univ, AB, 75; Univ Ga, PhD(anal chem), 78. *Prof Exp:* Res chemist, E I DuPont de Nemours & Co, Inc, 75-83, group leader life scis, 83-85, res supvr, 85-90. *Concurrent Pos:* Chmn, Gordon Conf Anal Chem, 91; co-instr, Am Chem Soc, 93-, chair anal div, 93. *Mem:* Am Chem Soc. *Res:* General high-performance liquid chromatography, especially systematic method development and column studies; pharmaceutical analysis and formulation development especially for radiopharmaceuticals. *Mailing Add:* Dupont-Merck 331 Treble Cove Rd North Billerica MA 01862-2821. *Fax:* 978-436-7500; *E-Mail:* glajchjl@lldmpc.dnet.dupont.com

GLAMKOWSKI, EDWARD JOSEPH, ORGANIC CHEMISTRY. *Current Pos:* res assoc, 71-77, RES GROUP MGR, HOECHST-ROUSSEL PHARMACEUTICALS, INC, SOMERVILLE, 77- *Personal Data:* b Brooklyn, NY, May 20, 36; m 63; c 3. *Educ:* Fordham Univ, BS, 58; Ohio State Univ, PhD(chem), 63. *Prof Exp:* Sr res chemist, Merck, Sharp & Dohme Res Labs, Rahway, 63-71. *Mem:* Am Chem Soc. *Res:* Indoles and other heterocyclic compounds; analgesic, anti- inflammatory and antipsychotic agents; drugs for the treatment of alzheimer's disease. *Mailing Add:* Seven Owens Dr Warren NJ 07060-6716

GLANCEY, BURNETT MICHAEL, MEDICAL ENTOMOLOGY, ECONOMIC ENTOMOLOGY. *Current Pos:* MED RES ENTOMOLOGIST FIRE ANT PROJ, SCI & EDUC ADMIN-FED RES, USDA, 68- *Personal Data:* b New Orleans, La, May 31, 30; m 56, 81. *Educ:* La State Univ, BS, 55, MS, 58; Cornell Univ, PhD(entomol), 63. *Prof Exp:* Res entomologist mosquito biol, Area Control, Agr Res Serv, 63-68. *Mem:* Sigma Xi. *Res:* Pheromones of fire ants; ant physiology. *Mailing Add:* 1126 St Johns Ave Green Cove Springs FL 32043

GLANCY, DAVID L, CARDIOLOGY. *Current Pos:* chief cardiol & prof med, 72-74, CLIN PROF MED, LA STATE UNIV MED CTR, NEW ORLEANS, 74-; DIR CARDIOL DEPT, UNIV HOSP, 74- *Personal Data:* b Cincinnati, Ohio, Oct 17, 34; m 57; c 3. *Educ:* Emory Univ, BA, 55; Johns Hopkins Univ, MD, 61. *Prof Exp:* Intern & asst resident med, Johns Hopkins Hosp, 61-63; asst & chief resident, Grady Mem Hosp, Atlanta, Ga, 63-65; instr, Emory Univ, 65-66; staff assoc cardiol, Nat Heart & Lung Inst, La State Univ Med Ctr, 66-68, sr investr, 68-69, chief cardiac diag, 69-72. *Concurrent Pos:* Fel coun clin cardiol, Am Heart Asn; founding mem Cardiac Angiography & Interactions. *Mem:* Fel Am Col Cardiol; fel Am Col Physicians; fel Am Col Chest Physicians; Am Fedn Clin Res. *Res:* Clinical cardiology; cardiovascular physiology; cardiac pathology; interventional cardiology. *Mailing Add:* Cardiol Dept Univ Hosp 2021 Perdido St New Orleans LA 70112-1352

GLAND, JOHN LOUIS, SURFACE CHEMISTRY. *Current Pos:* PROF CHEM & CHEM ENG, UNIV MICH, 88- *Personal Data:* b Valparaiso, Ind, Feb 22, 47; m 67; c 2. *Educ:* Wittenberg Univ, BA, 69; Univ Calif, Berkeley, PhD(phys chem), 73. *Honors & Awards:* Giuseppe Parravano Award for Excellence in Catalysis Res. *Prof Exp:* Staff res scientist, Gen Motors Res Labs, 73-82; assoc corp res, Exxon Res & Eng Co, 82-88. *Mem:* Am Chem Soc; Am Phys Soc; Am Vacuum Soc; Sigma Xi. *Res:* Reactions with and over solid surfaces; effects of the geometry and electronic properties of the surface on reactivity; soft x-ray absorption studies of absorbed species and surface reactions using synchrotron radiation; development of fluorescence yield near edge spectroscopy (FYNES) in the soft x-ray region; high resolution electron energy loss spectroscopy; low-energy electron diffraction; auger and electron spectroscopic chemical analysis applied to mechanistic studies of catalysis *Mailing Add:* 11260 Darwood Rd Pinckney MI 48169-8833

GLANDT, EDUARDO DANIEL, THERMODYNAMICS. *Current Pos:* From asst prof to prof, 77-90, Carl V S Patterson prof, 90-96, RP & EC MEVER PROF CHEM ENG, UNIV PA, 96- *Personal Data:* b Buenos Aires, Arg, Mar 4, 45; US citizen. *Educ:* Univ Buenos Aires, BS, 68; Univ Pa, MS, 75, PhD(chem eng), 77. *Honors & Awards:* Victor K Lamer Award, Am Chem Soc, 79. *Concurrent Pos:* Gulf vis prof, Dept Chem Eng, Carnegie-Mellon Univ, 89-90. *Mem:* Nat Acad Eng; Am Chem Soc; Am Phys Soc; AAAS; Am Inst Chem Engrs. *Res:* Classical and statistical thermodynamics: liquids and their mixtures, computer simulations; interfacial phenomena: adsorption, colloids, membranes; heterogeneous media: percolation and gelation phenomena. *Mailing Add:* Dept Chem Eng Univ Pa Philadelphia PA 19104-6393

GLANTZ, RAYMON M, NEUROPHYSIOLOGY. *Current Pos:* asst prof biol, Rice Univ, 69-74, assoc prof biol & elec eng, 74-80, chmn biol, 87-89, PROF BIOL & ELEC ENG, RICE UNIV, 80-, PROF BIOCHEM & CELL BIOL, 89- *Personal Data:* b Brooklyn, NY, July 1, 41. *Educ:* Brooklyn Col, BA, 63; Syracuse Univ, MS, 64, PhD(physiol psychol), 66. *Prof Exp:* Instr physiol, Sch Med, NY Univ, 66-67; res fel neurophysiol, Calif Inst Technol, 67-69. *Concurrent Pos:* Grass Found fel neurophysiol, Woods Hole Marine Biol Lab, 67; vis res assoc, Med Fac, Rotterdam Univ, summers 70-; investr, Woods Hole Marine Biol Lab, 79; adj prof, Molecular Physiol & Biophys, Baylor Col Med, 86- *Mem:* AAAS; Am Soc Zool; Soc Neurosci; Int Soc Neuroethnol. *Res:* Information processing in the invertebrate visual system; neural control of behavior; mechanism of phototransduction; biophysical properties of dendrites; synaptic physiology of neural networks. *Mailing Add:* Dept Biochem Rice Univ PO Box 1892 Houston TX 77251. *Fax:* 713-285-5154; *E-Mail:* glantz@neuron.rice.edu

GLANTZ, STANTON ARNOLD, CARDIOVASCULAR PHYSIOLOGY, INVOLUNTARY SMOKING & TOBACCO CONTROL. *Current Pos:* Sr fel cardiovasc res, 75-77, from asst prof to assoc prof, 77-86, PROF MED, UNIV CALIF, SAN FRANCISCO, 86- *Personal Data:* b Cleveland, Ohio, May 3, 46; m 72; c 2. *Educ:* Univ Cincinnati, BS, 69; Stanford Univ, MS, 70, PhD(appl mech), 73. *Concurrent Pos:* Aerospace engr, NASA Manned Spacecraft Ctr, 69; mem, Cardiovasc Res Inst, Univ Calif, San Francisco, 77-; vis prof med, Univ Vt, 88- *Mem:* Am Heart Asn; Am Physiol Soc; AAAS. *Res:* Mechanics of cardiac function; applied biostatistics; involuntary smoking; bioengineering; statistics; public health policy. *Mailing Add:* Dept Med CVR1 Div Cardiol Univ Calif San Francisco Third & Parnassus Aves San Francisco CA 94143-0124. *Fax:* 415-476-0424

GLANVILLE, JAMES OLIVER, INORGANIC CHEMISTRY, ANALYTICAL CHEMISTRY. *Current Pos:* VPRES RES & DEVELOP, WEN-DON CORP, 78- *Personal Data:* b London, Eng, July 24, 41; m 65; c 2. *Educ:* Univ London, BSc & ARCS, 62; Univ Md, PhD(chem), 67. *Prof Exp:* Res chemist, Res & Develop Dept, Inorg Div, FMC Corp, 68-69; assoc prof chem, Va Western Community Col, 69-76; vis prof chem, Va Tech, 77-78. *Mem:* Am Chem Soc; Am Inst Chemists; Am Soc Testing & Mat; Sigma Xi. *Mailing Add:* Chem Dept Va Polytech Inst State Univ 1008 Evergreen Way Blacksburg VA 24060

GLANZ, FILSON H, ELECTRICAL ENGINEERING. *Current Pos:* asst prof, 65-70, ASSOC PROF ELEC ENG, UNIV NH, 70- *Personal Data:* b Los Angeles, Calif, Aug 7, 34; m 67; c 1. *Educ:* Stanford Univ, BS, 56, MS, 57, PhD(elec eng), 65. *Prof Exp:* Engr, Librascope, Inc, 57-59 & Stanford Res Inst, 61-63. *Mem:* Inst Elec & Electronics Engrs; Sigma Xi. *Res:* Adaptive pattern recognition; information theory; digital signal processing; non-uniform sampling. *Mailing Add:* 25 Orchard Dr Durham NH 03824-2913

GLANZ, PETER K, PHYSICS. *Current Pos:* Asst prof, 71-76, ASSOC PROF PHYSICS, RI COL, 76- *Personal Data:* b Portsmouth, Va, Oct 23, 41; m 63. *Educ:* Bates Col, BS, 63; Bucknell Univ, MS, 65; Univ Conn, PhD(physics), 71. *Concurrent Pos:* Mem, Mus Holography. *Mem:* Nat Asn Sci Teachers; Am Asn Physics Teachers. *Res:* Interferometric holography. *Mailing Add:* Dept Physics RI Col Providence RI 02908

GLANZ, WILLIAM EDWARD, MAMMALOGY, COMMUNITY ECOLOGY OF VERTEBRATES. *Current Pos:* asst prof zool, 79-85, coop asst prof wildlife, 83-85, ASSOC PROF ZOOL & COOP ASSOC PROF, UNIV MAINE, ORONO, 85- *Personal Data:* b Ypsilanti, Mich, Jan 27, 49; m 80. *Educ:* Dartmouth Col, AB, 70; Univ Calif, Berkeley, PhD(zool), 77. *Prof Exp:* Teaching fel trop biol, Smithsonian Trop Res Inst, 77-78; lectr environ studies, Univ Calif, Santa Cruz, 78-79, vis lectr biol, Univ Calif, Los Angeles, 79. *Mem:* Am Soc Mammalogists; Am Ornith Union; AAAS; Asn Trop Biol; Cooper Ornith Soc; Ecol Soc Am. *Res:* Community ecology of mammals and birds in North and South America; seed predation, caching behavior and territoriality in squirrels; population dynamics of mammals in tropical forests. *Mailing Add:* Dept Zool Univ Maine Murray Hall Orono ME 04469-5751

GLAROS, GEORGE RAYMOND, ORGANIC CHEMISTRY. *Current Pos:* ASSOC PROF CHEM, RUSSELL SAGE COL, 72- *Personal Data:* b Minneapolis, Minn, Nov 23, 41; m 67; c 2. *Educ:* Univ Minn, BChem, 65; Univ Nebr, PhD(org chem), 71. *Prof Exp:* Peace Corps lectr chem, Cameroon Protestant Col, 65-67; instr chem, Univ Conn, 71-72. *Mem:* Am Chem Soc. *Res:* Chemistry of sulfoxides; allylic rearrangements. *Mailing Add:* Dept Chem Russell Sage Col Troy NY 12180-2291

GLARUM, SIVERT HERTH, PHYSICAL CHEMISTRY. *Personal Data:* b Providence, RI, June 6, 33; m 59; c 2. *Educ:* Kalamazoo Col, BA, 55; Brown Univ, PhD(chem), 60. *Prof Exp:* Mem tech staff, Bell Labs, 59-93. *Mem:* Am Chem Soc; Am Phys Soc; Sigma Xi. *Res:* Dielectrics; solid state; paramagnetic resonance. *Mailing Add:* 7 Vanderpool Dr Morristown NJ 07960-5808

GLASCOCK, HOMER HOPSON, II, PHYSICS. *Current Pos:* RES PHYSICIST, HARRIS CORP, 90- *Personal Data:* b Hannibal, Mo, Apr 10, 29; m 58; c 3. *Educ:* Univ Mo, BS, 51, MS, 56, PhD(solid state physics), 61. *Honors & Awards:* IR 100 Award, 79. *Prof Exp:* res physicist, Gen Elec Co, 60-90. *Mem:* Am Phys Soc; Inst Elec & Electronics Engrs. *Res:* Solid state and surface physics; physical electronics. *Mailing Add:* 225 Exchange St Mills MA 02054

GLASCOCK, MICHAEL DEAN, ARCHAEOLOGICAL CHEMISTRY, GEOCHEMISTRY. *Current Pos:* SR RES SCIENTIST, UNIV MO, 79-, ASSOC PROF NUCLEAR ENG, 88-, GROUP LEADER, 92- *Personal Data:* b Hannibal, Mo, June 27, 49. *Educ:* Univ Mo-Rolla, BS, 71; Iowa State Univ, PhD(nuclear physics), 75. *Prof Exp:* Res asst nuclear physics, Ames Lab, USAEC, 73-75; res assoc nuclear physics, Univ MD, College Park, 75-78. *Mem:* Am Phys Soc; Sigma Xi; Am Chem Soc; Am Nuclear Soc; Soc Archaeol Scientists. *Res:* Development of applications for neutron activation analysis as an analytical technique for various disciplines including agriculture, archaeology, biology, chemistry, nuclear engineering, geology and physics. *Mailing Add:* 1002 Sheffield Ct Columbia MO 65203. *Fax:* 573-882-6360

GLASEL, JAY ARTHUR, NEUROCHEMISTRY, BIOCHEMISTRY. *Current Pos:* assoc prof, 71-75, PROF BIOCHEM, UNIV CONN HEALTH CTR, 75- *Personal Data:* b New York, NY, Apr 30, 34; m 62, Jean M Stewardson. *Educ:* Calif Inst Technol, BS, 55; Univ Chicago, PhD(chem physics), 59. *Prof Exp:* Asst prof biochem, Columbia Univ, 64-70; vis scientist, Oxford Univ, 70-71. *Concurrent Pos:* NSF fel, Univ Calif, San Diego, 60-61 & Imp Col, Univ London, 61-62. *Mem:* Am Phys Soc; Am Chem Soc; Am Soc Biol Chemists. *Res:* Molecular biology of opioid receptor expression in cells. *Mailing Add:* Dept Biochem Univ Conn Health Ctr Farmington CT 06030. *Fax:* 860-679-2216; *E-Mail:* glasel@panda.uchc.edu

GLASER, DONALD ARTHUR, PHYSICS, MOLECULAR BIOLOGY. *Current Pos:* vis prof, Univ Calif, Berkeley 59-60, prof physics, 60-64, Miller Res Biophysicist, 62-64, prof physics & molecular biol, 64-89, PROF PHYSICS & PROF MOLECULAR & CELL BIOL, DIV NEUROBIOL, UNIV CALIF, BERKELEY, 89- *Personal Data:* b Cleveland, Ohio, Sept 21, 26; m 60. *Educ:* Case Inst Technol, BS, 46, Calif Inst Technol, PhD(physics), 50. *Hon Degrees:* DSc, Case Inst Technol, 59. *Honors & Awards:* Nobel Prize, 60; Charles Vernon Boys Prize, Brit Inst Physics & Phys Soc, 58; Prize, Am Phys Soc, 59; Golden Plate Award, Am Acad Achievement, 89. *Prof Exp:* From instr to prof physics, Univ Mich, 49-59. *Concurrent Pos:* Distinguished res fel, Smith-Kettlewell Inst Vision Res, 83-84. *Mem:* Nat Acad Sci; fel Am Phys Soc; Neurosci Inst; Int Acad Sci; Asn Res Vision & Opthal; NY Acad Sci; AAAS; Am Asn Artificial Intel; Am Soc Microbiol; Fedn Am Scientists; Sigma Xi. *Res:* Nuclear physics; cosmic rays; molecular genetics; neurobiology. *Mailing Add:* Dept Molecular & Cell Biol Univ Calif 337 Stanley Hall Berkeley CA 94720. *Fax:* 510-642-5058

GLASER, EDMUND M, COMPUTER SCIENCE, PHYSIOLOGY. *Current Pos:* PROF PHYSIOL & COMPUT SCI, SCH MED, UNIV MD, BALTIMORE, 70- *Personal Data:* b New York, NY, Oct 17, 27; m 59; c 3. *Educ:* Cooper Union, BEE, 49; Johns Hopkins Univ, MSE, 54, DEng, 60. *Prof Exp:* Electromech engr control systs, Glenn L Martin Co, 50-52; res assoc, Radiation Lab, Johns Hopkins Univ, 52-60; assoc prof physiol, 62-70. *Concurrent Pos:* Fel physiol, Sch Med, Johns Hopkins Univ, 62; consult, Hoover Electronics, 58-59, Electronic Commun, Inc, 60-62, Westinghouse Elec Corp, 62-63, Johns Hopkins Univ, 62-64. *Mem:* AAAS; Soc Neurosci; Inst Elec & Electronics Engrs; Acoust Soc Am; Sigma Xi. *Res:* Sensory neurophysiology, especially auditive, and its relationship to information theory; biological control systems; application of computers to the neurosciences; biomedical engineering. *Mailing Add:* Dept Phys Univ Md Sch Med 655 W Baltimore St Baltimore MD 21201-1559

GLASER, FREDERIC M, QUANTUM PHYSICS. *Current Pos:* ASSOC PROF PHYSICS, PAN AM UNIV, 69- *Personal Data:* b Toledo, Ohio, Dec 7, 35; m 61; c 1. *Educ:* Purdue Univ, BS, 57; Ohio State Univ, PhD(phys chem), 63. *Prof Exp:* Summer res asst, Am Cyanamid Co, 56-59; NSF fel & res assoc physics, Univ Chicago, 63-64; asst prof, Bowling Green State Univ, 64-66; mem staff, Houston Opers, TRW Systs Inc, 66-69. *Mem:* AAAS; Am Phys Soc; Am Chem Soc; Am Math Soc; Soc Indust & Appl Math. *Res:* Theoretical solid state physics; bonding theory of small molecules and ultraviolet spectra; experimental reflectance spectroscopy. *Mailing Add:* Dept Phys & Geol Univ Tex Pan Am Edinburg TX 78539-2999

GLASER, FREDERICK BERNARD, PSYCHIATRY. *Current Pos:* PROF PSYCHIAT & DIR, ALCOHOL & DRUG PROG, E CAROLINA MED SCH, 94- *Personal Data:* b Rochester, NY, Nov 8, 35; div; c 1. *Educ:* Univ Wis, BS, 55; Harvard Univ, MD, 59. *Prof Exp:* Assoc prof psychiat & chief, Sect Drug & Alcohol Abuse, Med Col Pa, 72-75; cong fel health policy, Robert Wood Johnson Found, 74-75; prof psychiat, Fac Med, Univ Toronto, 75-89; prof & dir, Substance Abuse Ctr, Univ Wash, 89-94. *Concurrent Pos:* John & Mary R Markle Found scholar, 68-73; consult treatment, Gov's Coun Drug & Alcohol Abuse, Commonwealth Pa, 72-75; chmn, Demonstration Rev Comt, Nat Inst Drug Abuse, 75-77; assoc ed, Res Advan Alcohol & Drug Problems, 75-89; head psychiat, Addiction Res Found Clin Inst, 75-89; vis lectr, Felton Bequest, Melbourne, Australia, 79. *Mem:* Am Psychiat Asn; Can Psychiat Asn; Royal Col Physicians & Surgeons Can. *Res:* Development and implementation of a systems approach to health care delivery, including alcohol and drug dependence. *Mailing Add:* Dept Psychiat E Carolina Sch Med Greenville NC 27838-4354. *Fax:* 919-830-8585; *E-Mail:* puglaser@ecuum.cis.edu.ecu

GLASER, GILBERT HERBERT, NEUROLOGY. *Current Pos:* RETIRED. *Personal Data:* b New York, NY, Nov 10, 20; m 46, Morfydd M Pugh; c Gareth E & Sara E. *Educ:* Columbia Univ, AB, 40, MD, 43, ScD(med), 51. *Hon Degrees:* MA, Yale Univ, 63. *Honors & Awards:* Lennox Lectr Award, Am Epilepsy Soc, 85; Distinguished Scholar Award, Med Col Va, 86. *Prof Exp:* Intern, Mt Sinai Hosp, NY, 43-44; asst resident neurol, Neurol Inst, 44-45, chief resident, 45-46; res asst, Columbia Univ, 48-50, instr, 50-51, assoc, 51-52; from asst prof to prof Sch Med, Yale Univ, 52-91, head sect, 52-71, chmn dept, 71-86, emer prof neurol, 91. *Concurrent Pos:* Resident psychiat, NY Psychiat Inst, 48-49, sr res scientist, 49-50; consult to Surgeon Gen, Neurol Res Training Grant Comt, USPHS, 56-60, mem, Neurol Res Progs Grant Comt, 68-72, mem, Epilepsy Adv Comt, 74-77; vis prof neurol, Hosp for Sick Children & Univ Col, London, 65-66; Hunan Med Col, Changsha, China, 86; vis prof, Nat Hosp, London, 72 & Park Hosp, Oxford, 73, 74, 75, 78, 81, 84, & 87, Brain Res Inst, Univ Niigato, Japan, 89; mem, Neuropharmacol Adv Comt, Food & Drug Admin, Dept Health, Educ & Welfare, 70-72; ed, Epilepsia, J Neurol Sci, J Nervous & Ment Dis; Fulbright Distinguished Prof, Univ Zagreb, Yugoslavia, 81; vis scholar, Green Col, Oxford Univ, Eng, 87, 88. *Mem:* Am EEG Soc; Am Epilepsy Soc (pres, 63); Am Neurol Asn (1st vpres, 77-78); fel Am Col Physicians; Am Acad Neurol (pres, 73-75); hon mem Asn Brit Neurologists. *Res:* Clinical neurology and neurophysiology; electroencephalography; epilepsy; neuromuscular disorders; metabolic disorders of the nervous system; developmental neurology. *Mailing Add:* 205 Millbrook Rd North Haven CT 06473

GLASER, HAROLD, THEORETICAL PHYSICS. *Current Pos:* RETIRED. *Personal Data:* b Kurseni, Lithuania, Aug 28, 24; US citizen; m 45; c 3. *Educ:* Roosevelt Univ, BS, 48; Northwestern Univ, MS, 49, PhD(physics), 53. *Honors & Awards:* Meritorious Civilian Serv Award, Dept Navy, 65. *Prof Exp:* Instr, Roosevelt Univ, 49-51; sr physicist, Appl Physics Lab, Johns Hopkins Univ, 52-54; head, Theoret Anal Sect, Syst Anal Br, Naval Res Lab, 54-57, physicist, Off Naval Res, 57-64, head, Nuclear Physics Br, 64-66; dep chief solar physics, Off Space Sci & Appln, NASA, 66-67, chief, 67-70; chief planning, Nat Bur Stand, 70-71; Off Sci & Technol, Exec Off of President, 71-72; dep & actg dir, Exp Technol Incentives Prog, Nat Bur Stand, 72; dep dir sci & technol, Off Nat Res & Develop Assessment, NSF, 72-75; dir, Solar Terrestrial Progs, NASA, 75-80; consult, Off Mgt & Budget, 80-81; asst to pres, Lab Affairs, Univ Calif, Berkeley, 81-84; consult, 84-95. *Concurrent Pos:* Res assoc, Univ Southern Calif, 59; consult, Lawrence Livermore Nat Lab, 84. *Mem:* Int Astron Union; Am Phys Soc; Am Geophys Union; Am Astron Soc; Sigma Xi. *Res:* Electromagnetic propagation; noise theory; radio astronomy; solar physics. *Mailing Add:* 1902 Berryman St Berkeley CA 94709

GLASER, HERMAN, PHYSICS. *Current Pos:* from asst prof to prof, 53-93, chmn dept, 75-93, EMER PROF & ADJ PROF PHYSICS, HOFSTRA UNIV, 93- *Personal Data:* b Brooklyn, NY, Nov 11, 23; wid; c Stanley L. *Educ:* Brooklyn Col, BA, 43; Johns Hopkins Univ, PhD(physics), 50. *Prof Exp:* Instr physics, Univ NC, 43-44; physicist, Naval Ord Lab, 44-45; jr instr physics, Johns Hopkins Univ, 45-49; assoc prof, Tex Tech Col, 50-53. *Mem:* Am Phys Soc; Am Asn Physics Teachers; Sigma Xi. *Res:* X-ray spectroscopy; low energy nuclear physics. *Mailing Add:* Dept Physics Hofstra Univ Hempstead NY 11550. *Fax:* 516-463-4939

GLASER, JANET H, CELL CULTURE, CARBOHYDRATE BIOCHEMISTRY. *Current Pos:* vis asst prof microbiol, Univ Ill, 74-75, res asst biochem, 75-85, asst dir, 85-87, ASSOC DIR BIOTECHNOL CTR, UNIV ILL, 87- *Personal Data:* b Eugene, Ore, Mar 9, 44; m 68; c 2. *Educ:* Univ Wash, BS, 66; Univ Calif, San Diego, PhD(biol), 71. *Prof Exp:* Asst human genetics, Sch Med, Wash Univ, St Louis, 71-74. *Mem:* Am Soc Biol Chemists; AAAS. *Res:* Regulation of synthesis of proteoglycans and collagen by chondrocytes in serum-free tissue culture and factor controlling expression of differentiated phenotype. *Mailing Add:* Univ Ill 601 E John Champaign IL 61820. *Fax:* 217-244-0466

GLASER, KEITH BRIAN, IMMUNOPHARMACOLOGY. *Current Pos:* RES SCIENTIST, DIV IMMUNOPHARMACOL, WYETH-AYERST RES, 89- *Personal Data:* b Munich, WGer, May 27, 60; US citizen; c 3. *Educ:* Tex A&M Univ, Galveston, BS, 82; Univ Calif, Santa Barbara, PhD(marine pharmacol), 87. *Prof Exp:* Teaching asst pharmacol, Dept Biol Sci, Univ Calif, Santa Barbara, 83, trainee marine pharmacol, Marine Sci Inst, 83-87; NIH postdoctoral fel, Sch Med, Wash Univ, St Louis, 87; res chemist, Univ Calif, San Diego, 87-88, NIH postdoctoral fel, 88-89. *Concurrent Pos:* Mem, Gordon Res Conf Marine Natural Prod Chem, 84 & Int Conf Therapeut Control Inflammatory Dis, Inflammation Res Asn, 86 & 90. *Mem:* Assoc mem Am Soc Biochem & Molecular Biol. *Res:* Site and mechanism of action of anti-inflammatory and immunomodulatory agents; pharmacological mode of action of anti-inflammatory marine natural products; author of more than 20 technical publications. *Mailing Add:* Res Invest Pharmacologist Immunosci Abbott Labs Abbott Park North Chicago IL 60064-3500. *Fax:* 847-938-5034

GLASER, KURT, CHILD PSYCHIATRY. *Current Pos:* asst prof, 72-81, EMER ASST PROF PEDIAT & PSYCHIAT, MED SCH, JOHNS HOPKINS UNIV, BALTIMORE, 81-; EMER CLIN ASSOC PROF PSYCHIAT, SCH MED, UNIV MD, BALTIMORE, 81- *Personal Data:* b Vienna, Austria, Feb 16, 15; nat US; m 46, Susanne Stein; c Richard, Benjamin, David & Dan. *Educ:* Univ Vienna, 33-38; Univ Lausanne, MD, 39; Univ Ill, MSc, 48. *Prof Exp:* Instr pediat, Col Med, Univ Ill, 45-50; asst chief physician, Med Sch, Hebrew Univ, Israel, 50-54; from clin instr to clin assoc prof pediat & psychiat, Sch Med, Univ Md, Baltimore, 54-81. *Concurrent Pos:* Consult, Dept Pediat & Psychiat, Sinai Hosp, Baltimore, 59-, Ctr Eval Clin Children, Univ Md, 59-75, John F Kennedy Inst, 76-92, Social Security Admin, 85- & Harbel Ment Health Clin, 86-; clin dir, Rosewood State Hosp, Owings Mills, Md, 61-72; dir, Adolescent Unit, Springfield Hosp Ctr, Sykesville, Md, 72-81; staff psychiatrist, Sheppard Pratt Hosp, Baltimore, 84-85. *Mem:* Emer fel Am Acad Pediat; fel Am Psychiat Asn; Am Soc Adolescent Psychiat. *Res:* Growth and development of premature infants; cellular composition of the bone marrow in normal infants and children; problems of child psychiatry, including school phobia, learning disorders, depression and suicide in children and adolescents, maternal deprivation in children; mental retardation. *Mailing Add:* 7200 Third Ave C-101 Sykesville MD 21784-5201. *E-Mail:* kurtglas@aol.com

GLASER, LESLIE, TOPOLOGY. *Current Pos:* assoc prof, 68-71, PROF MATH, UNIV UTAH, 71- *Personal Data:* b DeKalb, Ill, Sept 4, 37; m 58; c 4. *Educ:* DePauw Univ, BA, 59; Univ Wis, MS, 61, PhD(topol), 64. *Prof Exp:* Asst prof math, Rice Univ, 64-68. *Concurrent Pos:* Vis mem, Inst Advan Study, 69-70; Sloan fel, 69-71. *Res:* Point set topology; combinatorial topology. *Mailing Add:* 1757 Herbert Ave Salt Lake City UT 84108

GLASER, LUIS, BIOCHEMISTRY. *Current Pos:* EXEC VPRES & PROVOST, UNIV MIAMI, FLA, 86- *Personal Data:* b Vienna, Austria, Mar 30, 32; US citizen; m 61; c 2. *Educ:* Univ Toronto, BA, 53; Washington Univ, PhD(biochem), 56. *Prof Exp:* From instr to prof biochem, Sch Med, Wash Univ, 56-86, chmn dept, 75-86. *Mem:* Am Soc Biol Chemists; Am Soc Cell Biol; Am Chem Soc; Am Soc Neurosci. *Res:* Mechanisms of sugar synthesis; control of cell growth; bacterial cell wall components; neuronal development; embryonal development. *Mailing Add:* Univ Miami 240 Ash Bldg PO Box 248033 Coral Gables FL 33124-4628. *Fax:* 305-284-3356

GLASER, MICHAEL, BIOCHEMISTRY, NEUROSCIENCES. *Current Pos:* from asst prof to assoc prof, 74-83, PROF BIOCHEM, UNIV ILL, 83- *Personal Data:* b Cleveland, Ohio, Mar 11, 45; m 68; c 2. *Educ:* Univ Calif, Los Angeles, BS, 66; Univ Calif, San Diego, PhD(chem), 71. *Prof Exp:* Fel biochem, Med Sch, Washington Univ, 71-74. *Concurrent Pos:* NIH fel, 71-73; mem, NIH Molecular Cytology Study Sect, 81-85; mem, Ill Heart Asn Grant Rev Comt, 76-77 & Am Heart Asn Physiol Chem B Res Study Comt, 71-81; Ctr Advan Study fel, Univ Ill, 78; NIH res career develop award, 76-81; vis sr scientist, NIH, 91-92. *Mem:* Am Soc Neurochem; Soc Neurosci; Am Soc Biochem & Molecular Biol; Biophys Soc; Am Soc Cell Biol. *Res:* Membrane structure, function and biogenesis; myelin formation and neuronal-glial interactions; fluorescene microscopy and spectroscopy. *Mailing Add:* Dept Biochem Univ Ill 600 S Mathews Ave Urbana IL 61801. *E-Mail:* m-glaser@uiuc.edu

GLASER, MILTON ARTHUR, ORGANIC POLYMER CHEMISTRY. *Current Pos:* CONSULT, 78- *Personal Data:* b New York, NY, Sept 4, 12; m 37; c 3. *Educ:* Tufts Univ, BS, 34. *Honors & Awards:* Outstanding Serv Award, 57; Distinguished Serv Award, 59; Heckel Award, 63; Merit Award,

68; Pregl Award, NY Acad Sci, 86. *Prof Exp:* Engr, Mass, 31-32 & 34-36; chief chemist & dir res, Standard Varnish Works, 36-45; vpres & tech dir, Midland Div, Dexter Corp, Waukegan, 45-64, exec vpres res & develop, 64-70, div vpres res & develop, 70-77. *Concurrent Pos:* Lectr, NDak State Univ, Ill Inst Technol & Univ Mo; pres, Fedn Socs Paint Technol, 56-57; vpres & trustee, Paint Res Inst, 58, pres, 65-66; titular mem org coating sect, Int Union Pure & Appl Chem, 67-; Mattiello lectr, 74. *Mem:* Am Chem Soc; Am Oil Chemists' Soc; Nat Asn Corrosion Eng; fel Am Inst Chemists; Inst Food Technol. *Res:* Organic coatings including alkyd, silicone, epoxy, urethane and phenolic polymers; high-temperature resistant coatings; corrosion resistant coatings for container linings; specialty coatings for severe exposure environments; consult on reasearch and development to improve innovative productivity in laboratories. *Mailing Add:* 171 Wentworth Ave Glencoe IL 60022

GLASER, MYRON B(ARNARD), ELECTRICAL ENGINEERING, ELECTRONICS ENGINEERING. *Current Pos:* PRIN, GLASER ASSOCS, 89- *Personal Data:* b New York, NY, Dec 31, 27; m 85. *Educ:* City Col New York, BEE, 50; Yale Univ, MEng, 51. *Prof Exp:* Assoc proj engr, Sperry Gyroscope Co, 51-53, proj engr, 53-57, sr engr, 57-58, prin engr, Sperry Phoenix Co, 58-62; sr res engr, SRI Int, 62-89. *Concurrent Pos:* Alt deleg, Radio Technol Comn Aeronaut, 64, partic spec comt 117, 68- *Mem:* Inst Elec & Electronics Engrs; Inst Navig. *Res:* Telecommunications and information systems; public safety communications systems; electronic voting systems; geographic information systems; systems planning and implementation assistance; user; systems design & systems science; two United States patents. *Mailing Add:* Glaser Assocs 1909 Milano Way Mountain View CA 94040

GLASER, PETER E(DWARD), ENGINEERING, SOLAR ENERGY & SPACE TECHNOLOGY. *Current Pos:* RETIRED. *Personal Data:* b Czech, Sept 5, 23; nat US; m 55, Eva Graf; c David, Susan & Steven. *Educ:* Leeds Col Tech, Eng, dipl, 43; Charles Univ, Prague, dipl, 47; Columbia Univ, MS, 51, PhD, 55. *Honors & Awards:* Carl F Kayan Medal, Columbia Sch Eng, 74; Farrington Daniels Award, Int Solar Energy Soc, 85; Peter E Glaser Pleuary Lectr, Int Astronaut Fedn, 96; Space Technol Hall Fame, US Space Found, 96. *Prof Exp:* Head, Design Dept, Werner Textile Consults, 49-53; sr res engr, Arthur D Little Inc, 55-61, group leader, 61-66, sect head eng sci, 66-73, vpres eng sci, 73-78, corp vpres, 78-94. *Concurrent Pos:* Mem, Mat Adv Bd, Nat Acad Sci, 58, Study Group Solar Energy, 71; mem, Int Inst Refrig, 59-72; ed-in-chief, J Solar Energy, Int Solar Energy Soc, 71-85; co-investr, Shuttle, Initial Blood Storage Exp, 78-86; pres, Susat Energy Coun, 78-; mem, Solar Power Satellite Adv Panel, Off Technol Assessment, 80-81; chmn, Space Power Comts, Int Astron Fedn, 84-89, Task Force Space Goals, NASA, 86-87 & Lunar Energy Enterprise Case Study Task Force, 88-89. *Mem:* Fel AAAS; Am Soc Mech Engrs; Int Solar Energy Soc (pres, 68-70); fel Am Inst Aeronaut & Astronaut; Int Acad Astronaut; NY Acad Sci. *Res:* Thermal insulation developments for extreme temperatures; design of solar furnace and arc imagining furnace; high temperature research with imagining furnaces; lunar surface research; solar power satellite development; solar heating and cooling; photovoltaic conversion; rural electrification systems using renewable resources; lunar surface missions; commercial space power utility; remote sensing applications; extravehicular activity on the lunar surface; selection of launch sites in Hawaii; space station habitability module appliances; advanced space transportation systems for operation in cis-lunar space; space-based sensor systems to identify CO_2-induced climate changes; space station portable contamination detector; space suit gloves and boot soles for moon and Mars surface missions; dust protection during extravehicular activities on the moon and mars; power relay satellite, high-altitude, long-endurance aircraft using wireless power transmission, space power systems to benefit earth. *Mailing Add:* 62 Turning Mill Rd Lexington MA 02173-1010

GLASER, RAINER, DEAMINATION CHEMISTRY & DNA ALKYLATION, ELECTRON & SPIN DENSITY ANALYSIS. *Current Pos:* ASST PROF, UNIV MO, COLUMBIA, 89- *Personal Data:* b Freudenstadt, Ger, June 18, 57. *Educ:* Univ Tuebingen, dipl chem, 84; Univ Calif, Berkeley, PhD(chem), 87. *Prof Exp:* Res assoc, Yale Univ, 87-89. *Mem:* Am Chem Soc; AAAS. *Res:* Physical and theoretical (bio)organic chemistry research directed at understanding deamination chemistry and its role in the alkylation of DNA. *Mailing Add:* Univ Mo 123 Chem Bldg Columbia MO 65211-0001. *Fax:* 573-882-2754; *E-Mail:* chemrg@mizzou1

GLASER, ROBERT, LEARNING THEORY, COGNITIVE PSYCHOLOGY INSTRUCTION. *Current Pos:* prof psychol, 57-72, prof educ, 64-72, DIR, LEARNING RES & DEVELOP CTR, UNIV PITTSBURGH, 63-, PROF PSYCHOL & EDUC, 72- *Personal Data:* b Providence, RI, Jan 18, 21; c 2. *Educ:* City Col NY, BS, 42; Ind Univ, MA, 47, PhD(psychol measurement & learning theory), 49. *Hon Degrees:* DSc, Univ Leuven, 80, Ind Univ, 84 & Univ Gateborg, 85. *Honors & Awards:* Outstanding Res Field Instrnl Mats Award, Am Educ Res Asn/Am Educ Publ Inst, 70; Distinguished Res Educ Award, Am Educ Res Asn, 76; E L Thorndike Award, Distinguished Psychol Contribs, Am Psychol Asn, 81; Distinguished Sci Award Applns Psychol, 87. *Prof Exp:* Instr psychol, Ind Univ, 48-49; asst prof, Univ Ky, 49-50; res asst prof, Univ Ill, 50-52; sr res scientist, Am Inst Res, 52-56. *Concurrent Pos:* Consult, Ford Found Proj Indust Literacy, 81; vis prof, Japan Soc Prom Sci, 82; mem Comt Res Math, Sci & Technol Educ, Nat Res Coun, 84, Math Sci Educ Bd, 85-87; mem, Forum Res Mgt, Fedn Behav, Psychol & Cognitive Sci, 87-89, bd sci affairs, Am Psychol Asn, 88-, Design & Analysis Comt, Nat Asn Educ Publishers, 83- *Mem:* Am Psychol Asn; Nat Acad Educ (pres, 81-85); Psychonomic Soc; Am Educ Res Asn; AAAS. *Res:* Cognitive analysis of the acquisition of knowledge, the nature of expertise; inference and discovery in science; cognition, learning and instructional systems. *Mailing Add:* Learning Res/Develop Ctr Univ Pittsburgh Pittsburgh PA 15260

GLASER, ROBERT J, organic chemistry, bio-organic chemistry, for more information see previous edition

GLASER, ROBERT JOY, MEDICINE. *Current Pos:* TRUSTEE & DIR MED SCI, LUCILLE P MARKEY CHARITABLE TRUST, 84- *Personal Data:* b St Louis, Mo, Sept 11, 18; m 49, Helen Hofsommer; c Sally L, Joseph II & Robert J Jr. *Educ:* Harvard Univ, SB, 40, MD, 43; Am Bd Internal Med, dipl, 51. *Hon Degrees:* ScD, Temple Univ, Chicago Med Sch, Univ Colo, Univ NH, Mt Sinai Med Sch, Thomas Jefferson Univ & Wash Univ; LHD, Rush Med Col. *Honors & Awards:* Lowell Lectr, Mass Gen Hosp, 65; Stockton Kimball Lectr, 72; Abraham Flexner Award, Assoc Am Med Col, 84; Hubert Humphrey Cancer Res Ctr Award, 85; Merrimon Lectr, 85. *Prof Exp:* Intern med, Barnes Hosp, St Louis, Mo, 44; resident, Peter Bent Brigham Hosp, Boston, Mass, 44-45; resident, Barnes Hosp, St Louis, Mo, 45-47; from instr to assoc prof, Med Sch, Washington Univ, 49-57, asst & assoc dean, 53-57; chief div immunol, 54-57; prof & dean, Univ Colo, 57-63, vpres med affairs, 59-63; prof social med, Harvard Med Sch, 63-65; prof med, dean sch med & vpres med affairs, Stanford Univ, 65-70; vpres, Commonwealth Fund, 70-72; pres, Henry J Kaiser Family Found, 72-83. *Concurrent Pos:* Asst med, Washington Univ, 45-47; Nat Res Coun fel, Med Sch, Washington Univ, 47-49; asst physician, Barnes Hosp, St Louis, 49-57; chief rheumatic fever clin, Washington Univ Clins, 49-57; consult, State of Mo Crippled Childrens Serv, 49-55, Div of Serv for Crippled Children, Univ Ill, 50-57, Vet Admin Hosps, Denver & Grand Junction, Colo & Albuquerque, NMex, 57-63, Fitzsimons Army Hosp, Denver, 57-63, Lowry AFB Hosp, 57-63, Nat Health Res Facil Adv Coun, 58-61, Vet Admin, Mass, 63-65, Harvard Med Servs, Boston City Hosp, 63-65 & Peter Bent Brigham Hosp, Boston, 63-65; vis physician, Univ I Med Serv, St Louis City Hosp, 50, chief serv, 50-53; mem sci adv coun, Rheumatic Fever Res Inst, 56-59; attend physician, Colo Gen Hosp, 57-63; mem grad training grant comt, Nat Inst Allery & Infectious Dis, 58-61; mem, Nat Health Res Facil Adv Coun, 61-65, adv coun, Nat Inst Dent Res, 65-69; pres, Affiliated Hosps Ctr, Inc, Boston, 63-65; Alpha Omega Alpha lectr, Univ Ala, 63, Boston Univ, 63, Univ Colo, 64, Univ WVa, 64, Univ Louisville, 65, Univ Cincinnati, 66, Univ Calif, San Francisco, 67, NY Med Col, 69 & Univ Ind, 70; vpres med affairs & dean, Stanford Univ, 65-70; mem adv comt higher educ, HEW, 67-68, ad hoc adv comt, 67-68, nat adv ment health coun, 70-; mem bd dirs, Kaiser Found Hosps & Health Plan, Inc, 67-79; mem bd, Commonwealth Fund, 69-88, Kaiser Family Found, 70-83, Hewlett-Packard, 71-91, Calif Water Serv Co, 72-93, Dynapol, 72-83, Equitable Life Ins Soc, 79-86, First Boston Inc, 82-88, Resonex, Inc, 84-86, Packard Found, 84-, Alza Corp, 87-, Affymax, 88-, AXS, 91-, Nellcor, 92-, Pharmagenesis, 93- & Hanger Orthop, 93-; mem comt med affairs, Yale Univ, 69-82, mem adv bd, Yale Sch Org & Mgt, 76-84; consult prof med, Stanford Univ, 73- *Mem:* Nat Acad Sci; Inst Med-Nat Acad Sci; Am Fedn Clin Res (secy, 52-53, chmn, 54-55); Am Med Cols (asst secy, 56-60, vpres, 63-64, pres-elect, 67-68; Am Acad Arts & Sci (vpres, 72-76); Am Clin & Climat Asn (vpres, 74-75, pres, 82-83); Fedn Biomed Res; Am Soc Clin Res. *Res:* Experimental streptococcal infections; rheumatic fever; systematically studied the pathogenesis of experimental group A streptococcal respiratory infections in small animals and attempted to develop animal models of acute rheumatic fever; demonstrated the adverse effect of cortisone on streptococcal infections in animals. *Mailing Add:* Lucille P Markley Charitable Trust 525 Middlefield Rd Suite 130 Menlo Park CA 94025

GLASER, ROGER MICHAEL, EXERCISE PHYSIOLOGY. *Current Pos:* Asst prof biol sci, Wright State Univ, 72-74, from asst prof to assoc prof physiol, 74-81, PROF PHYSIOL, SCH MED, WRIGHT STATE UNIV, 81- *Personal Data:* b Brooklyn, NY, Feb 6, 44; m 74. *Educ:* Queens Col, NY, BA, 68, MS, 69; Ohio State Univ, PhD(exercise physiol), 71. *Concurrent Pos:* Fel physiol, Col Med, Ohio State Univ, 71-72; consult pulmonary dis, Wright Patterson AFB Hosp & cardiol, Dayton Vet Admin Hosp, 75- *Mem:* Aerospace Med Asn; Am Physiol Soc; fel Am Col Sports Med; Biomed Eng Soc; Inst Elec & Electronics Engrs; Sigma Xi. *Res:* Examining energy cost, power efficiency, cardiovascular and pulmonary stresses involved with wheelchair locomotion to reduce physiological risks and increase physical work capacity of wheelchair patients for their improved rehabilitation. *Mailing Add:* Rehab Med & Restor Care Dept Wright State Univ Sch Med 3171 Research Blvd Dayton OH 45435

GLASER, RONALD, VIROLOGY, PSYCHONEAROLIMMUNOLOGY. *Current Pos:* chmn, Dept Med Microbiol & Immunol, 78-92, assoc dean res & grad educ, 92-94, PROF, DEPT MED, COL MED, OHIO STATE UNIV, 78-, ASSOC VPRES HEALTH SCI RES, 94- *Personal Data:* b New York, NY, Feb 27, 39; m 79, Janice Kiecolt; c Erik & Andrew. *Educ:* Univ Bridgeport, BA, 62; Univ RI, MS, 64; Univ Conn, PhD(virol), 68. *Honors & Awards:* Leukemia Soc Scholar Award, Leukemia Soc Am, 74; Simson First Found Res Award, 93. *Prof Exp:* Asst prof virol, Life Sci Dept, Ind State Univ, 69-70; asst prof microbiol, Hershey Med Ctr, Pa State Univ, 70-73, from assoc prof to prof, 73-78. *Concurrent Pos:* NIH fel, Baylor Col Med, 68-69; USPHS grant, 74-77 & 77-81; sr mem grad sch, Pa State Univ, University Park, 74-78; fels, Franco-Am Exchange Prog-Fogarty Int Nat Ctr, 75 & 77; guest lectr, Hunan Med Col, China, 86; mem, AIDS Policy Subcomt, Nat Adv Ment Health Coun, NIMH, 87-90; Ida Beam distinguished vis prof, Univ Iowa, 90. *Mem:* AAAS; Am Soc Microbiol; Acad Behav Med Res; Asn Med Lab Immunologists; Psycho Neuro Immunol Res Soc. *Res:* Association of oncogenic herpes viruses and cancer; regulation of the Epstein-Barr virus in human cells and its association with nasopharyngeal carcinoma; neuroimmunology, stress and health. *Mailing Add:* Ohio State Univ Health Sci Res 2175 Graves Hall 333 W Tenth Ave Columbus OH 43210. *Fax:* 614-292-1011; *E-Mail:* glasen.1@osu.edu

GLASER, WARREN, MEDICINE, PHYSIOLOGY. *Current Pos:* CLIN PROF MED, SCH MED & DENT, UNIV ROCHESTER, 72- *Personal Data:* b Brooklyn, NY, Apr 8, 28; m 61; c 2. *Educ:* Columbia Univ, AB, 46, MD, 50. *Prof Exp:* Resident exp med, Oak Ridge Inst Nuclear Studies, 55-56; from instr to assoc prof med, State Univ NY Downstate Med Ctr, 63-72. *Concurrent Pos:* Consult, Med Div, Oak Ridge Inst Nuclear Studies; attend physician, Strong Mem Hosp. *Mem:* Fel Am Col Physicians; Am Fedn Clin Res; fel NY Acad sci; fel NY Acad Med; Sigma Xi. *Mailing Add:* 31 Bristol View Dr Fairport NY 14450-4224

GLASER DE LUGO, FRANK, APPLIED MATHEMATICS. *Current Pos:* from lectr to assoc prof, 70-79, PROF MATH, CALIF STATE POLYTECH UNIV, POMONA, 79- *Personal Data:* US citizen; m 88, Elke Maluschka; c Anya. *Educ:* Loyola Univ, Los Angeles, BA, 63; Calif State Col, Los Angeles, MA, 66; Univ Calif, Riverside, PhD(math), 70. *Prof Exp:* Teaching asst math, Calif State Col, Los Angeles, 65-66 & Univ Calif, Riverside, 66-70. *Concurrent Pos:* Lectr, Univ Madrid, 80, Univ Fes, Morocco, 82, Univ Aalborg, Denmark, 87 & Tech Univ, Istanbul, Turkey, 92. *Mem:* Asn Turkish Am Scientists. *Res:* Developing a theory of means of function relative to a weight function in N-dimensional space, consisting of a generalization of the work of E D Cashwell and C J Everett; translation of Whitney's Singularity Theory and Catastrope Theory by Zeeman into Spanish; non-euclidean geometry; developing a form of non-euclidean geometry called Hyper-polar-geometry. *Mailing Add:* Dept Math Calif State Polytech Univ 3801 W Temple Ave Pomona CA 91768-4039

GLASFORD, GLENN M(ILTON), ELECTRICAL ENGINEERING. *Current Pos:* from instr to prof, 47-86, EMER PROF ELEC ENG, SYRACUSE UNIV, 86- *Personal Data:* b Arcola, Tex, Nov 4, 18; m 48; c 2. *Educ:* Univ Tex, BS, 40; Iowa State Col, MS, 42. *Prof Exp:* Mem staff, Radiation Lab, Mass Inst Technol, 42-45; head, Adv Develop Group, TV Transmitter Dept, Allen B DuMont Labs, 45-47. *Concurrent Pos:* Consult, Gen Elec Co, 48-53 & Int Bus Mach Corp, 57-59. *Mem:* Fel AAAS; fel Inst Elec & Electronics Engrs; Soc Motion Picture & TV Engrs; Am Soc Eng Educ. *Res:* Electronics; physics and application of semiconductor devices; television; radar. *Mailing Add:* Dept Elec & Comput Eng Syracuse Univ Syracuse NY 13244

GLASGOW, DAVID GERALD, POLYMER CHEMISTRY. *Current Pos:* GROUP LEADER POLYMER ENG, UNIV DAYTON RES INST, 93- *Personal Data:* b Apple Creek, Ohio, Aug 25, 36; m 58; c 3. *Educ:* Col Wooster, AB, 58; Univ Cincinnati, PhD(org chem), 63. *Prof Exp:* Sr res chemist, Org Sect, Monsanto Res Corp, 62-65, Polymer Synthesis Sect, 65-68, res group leader, 68-75, sr res group leader, 75-78, sr res specialist, 78-93. *Mem:* Am Chem Soc. *Res:* Polymer synthesis; polyurethanes; polyesters; polyamides; adhesives; elastomers; thermoplastics; organic synthesis; chlorinated and brominated aromatics; specialty carbon substrates; process development. *Mailing Add:* 361 S Village Dr Dayton OH 45459-2129. *Fax:* 937-229-3433

GLASGOW, JOHN CHARLES, APPLIED MECHANICS, STRUCTURAL DYNAMICS. *Current Pos:* head, Dynamics Sect, 63-68, res engr, Short Takeoffs & Landing Propulsion Br, 68-72, sr proj engr, 72-75, SR RES ENGR, WIND ENERGY SYSTS, LEWIS RES CTR, NASA, 63- *Personal Data:* b Nashville, Tenn, Dec 14, 32; m 58; c 3. *Educ:* Univ Notre Dame, BS, 54; St Louis Univ, MS, 60. *Prof Exp:* Struct engr, McDonnell Aircraft Corp, Mo, 54-56, aero loads engr, 56-57, dynamics engr, 57-61; sr engr, Dynamics, NAm Aviation Inc, Ohio, 61-63. *Concurrent Pos:* Instr, Wash Univ, 59-61. *Res:* Large horizontal axis wind turbines associated primarily with structural dynamics and controls aspects of the machines. *Mailing Add:* 5862 Gareau Dr North Olmsted OH 44070

GLASGOW, LOUIS CHARLES, PHYSICAL CHEMISTRY, CHEMICAL PROCESS TECHNOLOGY. *Current Pos:* res chemist textile fibers, Lycra Res & Develop, E I du Pont de Nemours, 73-75, res chemist atmospheric sci, Freon Prod Div, 75-77, sr res chemist, 77-78, sr suprvr, 78-79, supt, Kel-Chlor Plant, 79-80, dir, Sabine River Lab, 80-82, prin consult corp res & develop planning, 82-84, planning mgr, Atomic Energy Div, 84-86, prog mgr nylon, 87-89, lab dir, 89-92, DIR CHEM SCI, DIR, CORP RES & DEVELOP PLANNING, DUPONT CHEM, EI DUPONT DE NEMOURS, 95- *Personal Data:* b Chicago, Ill, Sept 28, 43; m 67; c 2. *Educ:* Univ Ill, BS, 65; Univ Wis, MS, 70, PhD(chem), 71. *Prof Exp:* Fel photochem, Radiation Chem Div, Max Planck Inst, Mulheim, Ger, 70-72; asst prof phys chem, Northeastern Univ, 72-73. *Concurrent Pos:* Bd chem sci & technol, Nat Res Coun. *Mem:* Sigma Xi; Am Chem Soc; fel AAAS. *Res:* Photochemistry; gas phase reactions; resource management; research management and planning. *Mailing Add:* Du Pont Chem E I Du Pont de Nemours & Co Inc Exp Sta 262/225 119 Quintynnes Dr Wilmington DE 19898

GLASHAUSSER, CHARLES MICHAEL, NUCLEAR PHYSICS. *Current Pos:* from asst prof to assoc prof, 69-79, PROF PHYSICS, RUTGERS UNIV, NEW BRUNSWICK, 79- *Personal Data:* b Newark, NJ, Dec 7, 39; m 65, Suellen O'Brien; c Alexander & Allegra. *Educ:* Boston Col, BS, 61; Princeton Univ, PhD(physics), 66. *Prof Exp:* Physicist, Saclay Nuclear Res Ctr, France, 65-67 & Lawrence Radiation Lab, Univ Calif, Berkeley, 67-69. *Concurrent Pos:* Guest prof, Univ Munich, 75-76; physicist, Saclay Nuclear Res Ctr, France, 81 & 85; chmn, Los Alamos Meson Physics Facil Users Group, Inc, 84; vis prof, Univ Paris, Orsay, 91. *Mem:* Fel Am Phys Soc; AAAS. *Res:* Spin dependence in inelastic scattering at intermediate energy; polarization phenomena in nuclear reactions; the delta resonance in nuclei. *Mailing Add:* Dept Physics Rutgers Univ New Brunswick NJ 08903. *Fax:* 732-445-4343; *E-Mail:* glashausser@ruthep.rutgers.edu

GLASHOW, SHELDON LEE, ELEMENTARY PARTICLE PHYSICS. *Current Pos:* prof, 66-78, Mellon prof sci, 87-92, HIGGINS PROF PHYSICS, HARVARD UNIV, 79- *Personal Data:* b New York, NY, Dec 5, 32; m 71; c 4. *Educ:* Cornell Univ, BA, 54; Harvard Univ, AM, 55, PhD(physics), 58. *Hon Degrees:* DSc, Yeshiva Univ, 78, Univ Aix-Marseille, 82, Adelphi Univ, Bar Ilan Univ & Gustavus Adolphus, 89. *Honors & Awards:* Nobel Prize Physics, 79; Oppenheimer Mem Prize, 77; George Ledlie Prize, 78; Castiglione de Sicilia Prize, 83; Erice Sci for Peace Prize, 91; Richt Myer Lect Award, 93. *Prof Exp:* NSF fel, Inst Theoret Phys, Copenhagen Univ, 58-60; res fel physics, Calif Inst Technol, 60-61; asst prof, Stanford Univ, 61-62; assoc prof, Univ Calif, Berkeley, 62-66. *Concurrent Pos:* Sloan fel, 62-66; vis scientist, Niels Bohr Inst, 64 & Europ Orgn Nuclear Res, 68; consult, Brookhaven Nat Lab, 68-; vis prof, Univ Aix-Marseille, 71 & Mass Inst Technol, 74-75 & 79-80; affil sr scientist, Houston, 83-; distinguished univ prof & vis prof physics, Boston Univ, 83-84, distinguished vis scientist, 84; pres, Int Sakharov Comt, 85-88; coun mem, Am Acad Achievement. *Mem:* Nat Acad Sci; fel AAAS; Am Acad Arts & Sci; Sigma Xi; fel Am Phys Soc; Russian Acad Sci; Am Asn Physics Teachers. *Res:* Theory of elementary particles and their interactions; unified picture of strong, weak and electrodynamic interactions; identification of the fundamental constituents of matter. *Mailing Add:* 30 Prescott St Brookline MA 02146

GLASKY, ALVIN JERALD, BIOCHEMISTRY. *Current Pos:* PRES, GLASKY ASSOC, 80-; PRES, CHIEF EXEC OFFICER & CHMN, ADVAN IMMUNOTHERAPEUT, INC, 87- *Personal Data:* b Chicago, Ill, June 16, 33; m 57; c 4. *Educ:* Univ Ill, BS, 54, PhD(biochem), 58. *Prof Exp:* Asst biochem, Univ Ill, 54-56; NSF fel Biochem Inst, Univ Lund, 58-59 & Wenner-Grens Inst, Univ Stockholm, 59; dir biochem res labs, Michael Reese Hosp, Chicago, Ill, 59-62; group leader drug enzym, Dept Pharmacol, Abbott Labs, 62-66; dir res, Int Chem Nuclear Corp, 66-68; pres, chief exec officer & chmn, Newport Pharmaceut Int, Inc, 68-84; exec dir, Am Soc Health Asn, 84-85. *Concurrent Pos:* Asst prof, Col Med, Univ Ill, 59-68; assoc prof, Chicago Med Sch, 68- *Mem:* AAAS; Am Chem Soc; Am Soc Microbiol; Am Pharmaceut Asn; NY Acad Sci; Sigma Xi. *Res:* Mechanisms of drug action; biochemical pharmacology; viral chemotherapy; immunopharmacology; biochemistry of learning and memory. *Mailing Add:* Advan Immunotherapeut 12231 Pevero Tustin CA 92680-1106

GLASNER, MOSES, MATHEMATICS. *Current Pos:* ASSOC PROF MATH, PA STATE UNIV, UNIVERSITY PARK, 75- *Personal Data:* b Cluj, Romania, June 29, 42; US citizen. *Educ:* Univ Calif, Los Angeles, BA, 63, MA, 65, PhD(math), 66. *Prof Exp:* Actg asst prof math, Univ Calif, Los Angeles, 66-67; asst prof, Calif Inst Technol, 67-75. *Mem:* Am Math Soc; Optical Soc Am. *Res:* Global aspects of potential theory; beam propagation methods. *Mailing Add:* 1219 Smithfield Circle State College PA 16801-6426

GLASOE, PAUL KIRKWOLD, CHEMISTRY. *Current Pos:* RETIRED. *Personal Data:* b Northfield, Minn, Nov 22, 13; m 35, 85, Dorothea Q; c Martha G (Hendricks), Sigrid M & Christina K (Koeckeritz). *Educ:* St Olaf Col, AB, 34; Univ Wis, PhD(inorg chem), 38. *Prof Exp:* Asst chem, Univ Wis, 34-38, instr gen chem, 38; instr, Univ Ill, 38-40; res chemist, Eastman Kodak Co, 40-47; from assoc prof to prof chem, Wittenberg Col, 47-51; prof, Carthage Col, 51-52; prof chem, Wittenberg Univ, 52-79, chmn dept, 60-68. *Concurrent Pos:* NSF fac fel, Cornell Univ, 58-59 & King's Col, Univ London, 68-69. *Mem:* Am Chem Soc; Sigma Xi. *Res:* Colloids; chemical analysis of photographic developers; non-aqueous solvents; acidity in heavy water; exchange of deuterium for hydrogen in hydrogen-bonded systems. *Mailing Add:* 8102 Highwood Dr Apt 321 Bloomington MN 55438

GLASPEY, JOHN WARREN, ASTRONOMY. *Current Pos:* CONSULT, 88- *Personal Data:* b Glens Falls, NY, July 18, 44; m 69; c 2. *Educ:* Case Inst Technol, BSc, 66; Univ Ariz, PhD(astron), 71. *Prof Exp:* Res assoc astron, Univ BC, 71-73, lectr & instr, 73-75, res assoc, 75-76; astronomer & engr astron, Univ Montreal, 76-88. *Mem:* Int Astron Union; Am Astron Soc; Can Astron Soc; Astron Soc Pac. *Mailing Add:* McDonalds Univ Observ PO Box 1337 Ft Davis TX 79734

GLASPIE, DONALD LEE, THERMODYNAMICS & HEAT TRANSFER, METAL STAMPING PRODUCT DESIGNING. *Current Pos:* OWNER, GLASPIE CONSULT ENGR, 84- *Personal Data:* b Oxford, Ind, Feb 16, 22; m, Nettie F Martin; c Judy A (Dunn), Karen S (Mosman) & Paula C (Jones). *Educ:* Purdue Univ, BSME, 47; Wichita State Univ, MS, 61. *Prof Exp:* Engr air conditioning, Shelby-Skipwith, Inc, Tenn, 47-52; co-owner, Ozark-York, Inc, Mo, 52-55; engr, Boeing Airplane Co, Kans, 55-63, design engr, New Orleans, 63-66; specialist, Vought Aeronaut Div, LTV, Inc, Dallas, 66-71; owner merch, Glaspie Consult Engr, 71-73; mgr res & develop mech, Glitsch, Inc, Subsid Foster Wheeler, Dallas, 71-83; mgr, Eng Serv Dept, CACI, Inc-Fed, Dallas, 83-84. *Mem:* Am Soc Mech Engrs; Am Soc Heating Refrig & Air Conditioning Engrs. *Res:* Air conditioning systems design for aircraft and buildings; petrochemical tower packing and other internal equipment design; fabrication systems and mechanical equipment design; engineering computer software development. *Mailing Add:* PO Box 998 Marble Falls TX 78654-0998

GLASPIE, PEYTON SCOTT, PHYSICAL ORGANIC CHEMISTRY, SURFACE CHEMISTRY. *Current Pos:* sr chemist process develop-surface chem, Monsanto Polymers & Petrochem Co, 74-78, catalysis group supvr, Monsanto Chem Intermed, Co, 78-81, process technol mgr anal chem, 81-82, mgr personnel planning, Monsanto Corp Res Co, 83-85, mgr, 86-89, MGR EXTERNAL RES & DEVELOP FUNDING, MONSANTO CORP RES CO, 90-, MGR INFO SYSTS, 91- *Personal Data:* b Commerce, Tex, Dec 16, 46; m 72. *Educ:* ETex State Univ, Commerce, BS, 69; Rice Univ, PhD(chem), 74. *Prof Exp:* Asst chem, Rice Univ, 69-74. *Mem:* Am Chem Soc; Catalysis Soc; Sigma Xi. *Res:* Surface chemistry explorations of currently used industrial processes by novel instrument applications; applying the results to better understand the chemical kinetics of the reactions and thereby improve the system; laboratory automation and computer applications. *Mailing Add:* 14678 Los Padres Ct Chesterfield MO 63017-2441

GLASS, ALASTAIR MALCOLM, ELECTRONIC & OPTOELECTRONIC APPLICATIONS. *Current Pos:* mem tech staff, AT&T Bell Labs, 67-78, supvr, 78-83, head device mat & res, 83-87, Mat Res Lab, 87-89, asst dir, 89-91, dir, Passive Components Res Lab, 91-95, DIR, PHOTONIC COMPONENTS RES LAB, BELL LABS, LUCENT TECHNOL, 96- *Personal Data:* b Harrogate, Yorkshire, Eng, Aug 2, 40; m 66; c 4. *Educ:* Univ Col, London, BSc; Univ BC, PhD(physics), 64. *Prof Exp:* Res fel, Univ London, Kings Col, 65-67. *Concurrent Pos:* adv comt, Piezoelec, Off Naval Res, 79-85, mat res, 85, 87; adv comt, Basic Sci Res, 80-83; mat res adv comt, Pa State Univ, 83-; electronic mat working group, NASA, 84-; chair, Nat Mat adv bd comt, Processing Challenges in Compound Semiconductors, 86-88, Conf Lasers & Electrooptics, 92; dir-at-large, Optical Soc Am. *Mem:* Nat Acad Eng; Mat Res Soc; fel Inst Elec & Electronics Engrs; fel Optical Soc Am. *Res:* Development and understanding of new materials and devices for optoelectronic applications, including optical fibers, semiconductor lasers, passive optical components and optical storage. *Mailing Add:* Bell Labs Lucent Technol 700 Mountain Ave Murray Hill NJ 07974

GLASS, ALEXANDER JACOB, PHYSICS, OPTICS. *Current Pos:* PRES & COORDR, KMS FUSION, INC, 81- *Personal Data:* b Pittsfield Twp, NY, Jan 4, 33; m 59; c 3. *Educ:* Rensselaer Polytech Inst, BS, 54; Yale Univ, MS, 55, PhD(physics), 63. *Honors & Awards:* Res Publ Award, US Naval Res Lab, 69. *Prof Exp:* Res staff mem, Res Inst Advan Study, Md, 57-58; res assoc, Yale Univ, 63-64; staff scientist Inst Defense Analysis, 64-66; chief laser physics br, Naval Res Lab, 66-68; prof elec eng, Wayne State Univ, 68-70, chmn dept, 70-73; head theory & design analysis, Lawrence Livermore Lab, 73-78, asst assoc dir lasers, 78-81. *Concurrent Pos:* Fel, Yale Univ, 60; lectr space sci, Cath Univ Am, 65-68 & appl sci, Univ Calif, Davis, 73-; mem, Inst Res Eng Sci, 68-70. *Mem:* Fel Optical Soc Am; Inst Elec & Electronics Engrs; Am Phys Soc. *Res:* Non-linear optics; high power laser design; laser damage; quantum electronics; numerical methods. *Mailing Add:* 206 Hillcrest Rd Berkeley CA 94705-2811

GLASS, ANDREW MARTIN WILLIAM, INFINITE GROUP THEORY, INFINITE AUTOMORPHISM GROUPS. *Current Pos:* from asst prof to assoc prof, 71-81, PROF MATH, BOWLING GREEN STATE UNIV, 81-, CHAIR DEPT, 91- *Personal Data:* b London, Eng, June 7, 44; m 86, Lilly M McGill; c Steven H Sample, Michael G Sample, David W Sample, J Scott Sample, James K Sample & Laura J (Keller). *Educ:* Cambridge Univ, BA, 66, MA, 70; Univ Wis-Madison, PhD(math), 71. *Concurrent Pos:* Vis assoc prof, Univ Alta, Edmonton, 77; Van Vleck prof math, Wesleyan Univ, 82-83; vis prof math, Univ Cambridge, 88, Math Inst, Univ Oxford, 90 & 91. *Mem:* London Math Soc; Cambridge Philosophical Soc; Edinburgh Math Soc. *Res:* Infinite (permutation, automorphism) groups; decidability problems for lattice-ordered groups; relations and identities in algebra; analytic number theory-Catalan's equation. *Mailing Add:* Math Dept Bowling Green State Univ Math Sci Bldg Rm H15 Bowling Green OH 43403. *Fax:* 419-372-6092

GLASS, ARTHUR WARREN, GENETICS. *Current Pos:* Assoc prof, 50-59, head dept, 50-72, PROF BIOL, GUSTAVUS ADOLPHUS COL, 59- *Personal Data:* b Flint, Mich, Mar 14, 21; m 50; c 4. *Educ:* Gustavus Adolphus Col, AB, 43; Univ Minn, MA, 48, PhD, 54. *Mem:* Sigma Xi; Soc Study Evolution. *Res:* Population genetics. *Mailing Add:* 510 Capitol Dr St Peter MN 56082-1302

GLASS, BILLY PRICE, MARINE GEOLOGY, ASTROGEOLOGY. *Current Pos:* from asst prof to assoc prof, 70-83, dept chmn, 86-96, PROF GEOL, UNIV DEL, 83- *Personal Data:* b Memphis, Tenn, Sept 9, 40, Judith A Niggl; c 2. *Educ:* Univ Tenn, BS, 63; Columbia Univ, PhD(marine geol), 68. *Honors & Awards:* Nininger Meteorite Award, 66-67; Antarctic Serv Medal, 79. *Prof Exp:* Res asst marine geol, Lamont Geol Observ, 65-67; res scientist, Goddard Space Flight Ctr, US Army Corps Engrs, 68-70, Nat Res Coun resident res assoc, 70. *Concurrent Pos:* Prin investr, Apollo 12-17 Lunar Samples & NSF, 72-88; mem, US-Japan Antarctic Search for Meteorites, 77-78. *Mem:* Fel Geol Soc Am; fel Meteoritical Soc; Sigma Xi; Am Geophys Union; Int Astron Union; Nat Asn Geol Teachers. *Res:* Correlation and dating of marine sediments; tektites and microtektites; effects of large impacts; impact ejecta and shock metamorphism. *Mailing Add:* 387 Hobart Dr Newark DE 19713. *Fax:* 302-831-4158; *E-Mail:* billy.glass@mvs.udel.edu

GLASS, BRYAN PETTIGREW, MAMMALOGY. *Current Pos:* from asst prof to prof, 46-85, EMER PROF ZOOL, OKLA STATE UNIV, 85- *Personal Data:* b Mandeville, La, Aug 21, 19; m 46; c 2. *Educ:* Baylor Univ, AB, 40; Agr & Mech Col Tex, MS, 46; Okla State Univ, PhD, 52. *Prof Exp:* Asst zool, Agr & Mech Col Tex, 40-42 & 45-46. *Concurrent Pos:* Dir mus, Okla State Univ, 66-85. *Mem:* Am Soc Ichthyologists & Herpetologists; Am Soc Mammal. *Res:* Systematics of Oklahoma rodents; ecology of muskrats in Oklahoma; biology; taxonomy; migration of bats; Ethiopian mammals; Brazilian mammals; author and co-author of several publications. *Mailing Add:* 517 South Willis St Stillwater OK 74074

GLASS, DAVID BANKES, PHARMACOLOGY, BIOCHEMISTRY. *Current Pos:* asst prof, 78-84, ASSOC PROF PHARMACOL, EMORY UNIV, 84- *Personal Data:* b Indianapolis, Ind, Apr 30, 47; m 73; c 1. *Educ:* Purdue Univ, BS, 70; Univ Minn, PhD(pharmacol), 76. *Prof Exp:* Fel biochem, Univ Calif, Davis, 76-77; fel pharmacol, Univ Wash, 77-78. *Concurrent Pos:* Med res fel, Bank of Am-Giannini Found, 76-77; res investr, Am Heart Asn, Ga affil, 80-83. *Mem:* Protein Soc; AAAS; NY Acad Sci; Am Chem Soc; Am Soc Pharmacol & Exp Therapeut; Am Soc Biol Chemists. *Res:* Biochemical pharmacology; biochemistry of protein kinases; peptide synthesis; peptide structure-function studies. *Mailing Add:* Dept Pharmacol Emory Univ Sch Med Atlanta GA 30322-3090. *Fax:* 404-727-0365

GLASS, DAVID CARTER, PSYCHOLOGICAL STRESS, BEHAVIORAL MEDICINE. *Current Pos:* vprovost, State Univ NY, Stony Brook, 82-86 & 89-93, prof, 82-94, spec adv to the provost, 86-89, EMER PROF, STATE UNIV NY, STONY BROOK, 94- *Personal Data:* b New York, NY, Sept 17, 30; m 82, Kathleen Kehoe. *Educ:* NY Univ, AB, 52, MA, 54, PhD(social psychol), 59. *Honors & Awards:* Socio Psychol Prize, AAAS, 71; Am Psychol Asn Award, 88. *Prof Exp:* Postdoctoral fel psychophysiol, NY Univ, 59-62; asst prof social psychol, Ohio State Univ, 62-63; staff social psychologist, Russell Sage Found, 63-66; assoc prof psychol, Rockefeller Univ, 66-68; prof psychol, NY Univ, 68-72; prof & chair psychol, Univ Tex, Austin, 72-76; prof psychol, Grad Ctr, City Univ New York, 76-82. *Concurrent Pos:* Adj assoc prof psychol, Columbia Univ, 65-66, 67-68; staff social psychol, Russell Sage Found, 66-71, vis scholar, 75-76; dir, Lab Biobehav, Grad Ctr, City Univ New York, 77-82; vis prof, Inst Health, Rutgers Univ, 93-96. *Mem:* Sigma Xi; fel Am Psychol Asn; fel AAAS; Acad Behav Med Res (pres, 80-81); Soc Psychophysiol Res; Am Psychosomatic Soc. *Res:* Effects of psychosocial factors on physical illness; depression and professional burnout. *Mailing Add:* 330 E 33rd St Apt 11J New York NY 10016

GLASS, EDWARD HADLEY, ENTOMOLOGY. *Current Pos:* from assoc prof to prof, 48-87, head dept, 69-82, EMER PROF ENTOM, NY STATE AGR EXP STA, 87- *Personal Data:* b Waltham, Mass, Feb 19, 17; m 42; c 2. *Educ:* Mass State Col, BS, 38; Va Polytech Inst, MS, 40; Ohio State Univ, PhD(entom), 43. *Prof Exp:* Asst entomologist, Exp Sta, Va Polytech Inst, 40-41; entomologist, Am Cyanamid Co, NY, 43-48. *Concurrent Pos:* Vis prof, Univ Philippines, 66-67. *Mem:* Fel AAAS; Entom Soc Am; Sigma Xi. *Res:* Biology and control of apple orchard insect pests; insect photoperiodism; tropical rice insects and their control; use of sex pheromones for insect detection and control. *Mailing Add:* 377 White Springs Rd Geneva NY 14456

GLASS, EDWARD NATHAN, THEORETICAL PHYSICS. *Current Pos:* assoc prof, 74-81, PROF PHYSICS, UNIV WINDSOR, 81- *Personal Data:* b New York, NY. *Educ:* Carnegie-Mellon Univ, BS, 59; Syracuse Univ, MS & PhD(physics), 69. *Prof Exp:* Math analyst, Guid Systs, Norden Div United Aircraft Corp, 59-62; vis asst prof physics, Univ Cincinnati & Trenton State Col, 71-73; vis res fel, Princeton Univ, 73-74. *Concurrent Pos:* Fel, Aeronaut Res Lab, Nat Acad Sci, 69-71; vis scholar, Stanford Univ, 81-82; vis prof, Univ Mich, 94-97. *Mem:* Am Phys Soc; Am Asn Physics Teachers; Can Asn Physics. *Res:* General relativity; relativistic astrophysics. *Mailing Add:* Dept Physics Univ Windsor Windsor ON N9B 3P4 Can. *E-Mail:* physeg@ucc.uwindsor.ca

GLASS, GARY BERTRAM, COAL GEOLOGY, AGENCY HEAD-STATE GOVERNMENT. *Current Pos:* staff coal geologist, 71-78, dep dir, 78-81, STATE GEOLOGIST, GEOL SURV WYO, 81- *Personal Data:* b Pittsburgh, Pa, Mar 6, 40; m 87, Judith Cobb; c Gary B Jr, William C & Susan L (Heien). *Educ:* Bucknell, Univ, BS, 62; Lehigh Univ, MS, 64. *Prof Exp:* Capt, US Army CEngrs, 64-67; coal geologist, Pa Topog & Geol Surv, 67-71. *Concurrent Pos:* Lectr coal, Eng Dept, Univ Wyo, 78-80, lectr coal geol, Geol Dept, 79-87; ed, Coal Div, Geol Soc Am, 80-82, Am Inst Prof Geologists, 85-86; comnr, Wyo Oil & Gas Conserv Comn, 81- *Mem:* Am Inst Prof Geologists (vpres, 88); Geol Soc Am; Asn Am State Geologists. *Res:* Bituminous coal fields of Pennsylvania and the subbituminous and bituminous coals and coal geology of Wyoming; economic geology of coal. *Mailing Add:* Wyo State Geol Surv PO Box 3008 Laramie WY 82071

GLASS, GEORGE, HIGH ENERGY PHYSICS, EXPERIMENTAL NUCLEAR PHYSICS. *Current Pos:* MEM STAFF, UNIV TEX, AUSTIN, 92- *Personal Data:* b Vienna, Austria, June 15, 36; US citizen; m 64, Patricia Patterson; c Sarah, Jessica, David & Rebekah. *Educ:* Mass Inst Technol, SB, 59, PhD(physics), 64. *Prof Exp:* Mem res staff physics, Mass Inst Technol, 64-65; res assoc, Northeastern Univ, 65-66; asst prof, Univ Wash, 66-74; mem staff, Tex A&M Univ, 73-92. *Mem:* Am Phys Soc; Am Asn Physics Teachers. *Res:* High energy nuclear physics; particles; electronics; light. *Mailing Add:* 3218C Walnut Los Alamos NM 87544. *Fax:* 505-665-1712; *E-Mail:* mp0gg@lampf.bitnet

GLASS, GEORGE B JERZY, GASTROENTEROLOGY. *Current Pos:* from asst clin prof to assoc clin prof med, 48-54, assoc prof, 54-62, chief sect gastroenterol, 61-69, PROF MED & DIR GASTROENTEROL LAB, METROP MED CTR, NEW YORK MED COL, 62- *Personal Data:* b Warsaw, Poland, Jan 9, 03; nat US; m 33; c 2. *Educ:* Univ Warsaw, MD, 27; Am Bd Internal Med, dipl. *Prof Exp:* Intern, Hosp Wolski, Warsaw, 27-28, resident, 28-29; resident Med Div, Allgemeines Hosp, Univ Vienna, 31-32; resident, Hosp Hotel Dieu, Paris, France, 32-33; asst physician, Hosp Child Jesus, 33-38. *Concurrent Pos:* Fel, Krankenaus am Urban, Berlin, Ger, 30-31; assoc physician, Metrop Hosp, New York, 50-61, vis physician, 62-; Bird S Coler Mem Hosp, 52-; assoc attend physician, Flower & Fifth Ave Hosps, 54-61, attend physician, 62-; assoc clinician, Sloan-Kettering Inst, 60-66; assoc vis physician, James Ewing Hosp, 61-66; consult gastroenterol, New York Infirmary, 67-; assoc consult, Mem Hosp. *Mem:* Asn Am Physicians; Am Fedn Clin Res; Am Physiol Soc; Am Gastroenterol Asn; Am Soc Hemat. *Res:* Physiology and biochemistry of the stomach; intrinsic factor and vitamin B-12 metabolism; chemistry and biological significance of large molecular substances in gastric juices; immunology of atrophic gastritis and pernicious anemia. *Mailing Add:* 120 E 79th St New York NY 10021

GLASS, GRAHAM PERCY, PHYSICAL CHEMISTRY. *Current Pos:* asst prof, 67-73, ASSOC PROF CHEM, RICE UNIV, 73- *Personal Data:* b Birmingham, Eng, July 21, 38; m 65. *Educ:* Univ Birmingham, BSc, 59; Cambridge Univ, PhD(chem), 63. *Prof Exp:* Fel chem, Harvard Univ, 63-65; lectr, Univ Essex, 65-67. *Mem:* Am Phys Soc; Am Chem Soc. *Res:* Reaction kinetics; molecular energy transfer; shock tube chemistry. *Mailing Add:* 2340 Robin Hood Houston TX 77005-2606

GLASS, HIRAM BENTLEY, GENETICS. *Current Pos:* acad vpres, 65-71, distinguished prof, 65-76, EMER DISTINGUISHED PROF BIOL, STATE UNIV NY, STONY BROOK, 76- *Personal Data:* b Laichowfu, Shantung, China, Jan 17, 06; m 34; c 2. *Educ:* Baylor Univ, AB, 26, MA, 29, LLD, 58; Univ Tex, PhD(genetics), 32. *Hon Degrees:* Nine from US univs, 57-77. *Prof Exp:* Teacher pub sch, Tex, 26-28; fel genetics, Nat Res Coun, Univ Oslo, Kaiser-Wilhelm Inst & Univ Mo, 32-34; instr zool, Stephens Col, 34-38; from asst prof to prof biol, Goucher Col, 38-48; from assoc prof to prof, Johns Hopkins Univ, 48-65. *Concurrent Pos:* Res assoc, Teachers Col, Columbia, 36-37; asst ed, Quart Rev Biol, 44-48, assoc ed, 49-57, ed, 58-86; res assoc, Baltimore RH Blood Typing Lab, 47-52; consult, US Dept State, Ger, 50-51; dir surv biol abstracting, Biol Abstracts, 52-54; mem bd trustees, 54-60, pres, 58-60; del, Int Union Biol Scis, 53, 55; ed, Surv Biol Progress, 54-62; mem bd sch comnrs, Baltimore, Md, 54-58; adv, Comt Biol & Med, AEC, 55-63, chmn, 62-63; mem, Comt Genetic Effects Atomic Radiation, Genetics Panel, Nat Acad Sci, 55-64; Davis Washington Mitchell lectr, Tulane Univ, 58; adv, Continuing Comt Conf Sci & World Affairs, 58-64; democratic adv, Coun Comt Sci & Tech, 59-60; adv, Gov Adv Comt Nuclear Energy, Md, 59-65; chmn, Biol Sci Curriculum Study, 59-65; nat lectr, Sigma Xi, 58-59 & bicentennial lectr, 75-76; lectr, Stoneburner, Va Med Col & John Calvin McNair, Univ NC, 63; chmn bd trustees, Cold Spring Harbor Lab, 67-73; chmn, Life Sci Prog, Space Sci Bd Rev, NASA, 70; vis prof, Univ Calif, Santa Cruz, 71-72; dir, Hist & Genetics Proj, Am Philos Soc, 71-82. *Mem:* Nat Acad Sci; AAAS (pres, 69); Genetics Soc Am (vpres, 60); Am Soc Naturalists (secy, 50-53, pres, 65); Nat Asn Biol Teachers (pres, 71); Am Soc Human Genetics (pres, 67); Czech Acad Sci. *Res:* Genetics of Drosophila; human genetics; history of genetics; suppressor genes; Rh blood types. *Mailing Add:* 1066 Eighth St Boulder CO 80302-7106

GLASS, HOWARD GEORGE, PHARMACOLOGY. *Current Pos:* RETIRED. *Personal Data:* b Chicago, Ill, May 25, 09; m 42; c 2. *Educ:* Univ Ill, BS, 32; Northwestern Univ, MS, 35; Univ Chicago, PhD(pharmacol), 42; Marquette Univ, MD, 49. *Prof Exp:* Chemist, Bauer & Balk, Ill, 35-38; res assoc, Toxicity Lab, Off Sci Res & Develop, Chicago, 41-44; instr pharmacol, Sch Med, Univ Okla, 44-46; instr, Marquette Univ, 46-48; pharmacologist, Armour Labs, Ill, 49-53; pharmacologist, Miles-Ames Res Lab, Ind, 53-62; asst dir, Dept Drugs, AMA, 62-75. *Concurrent Pos:* Med consult, 77- *Mem:* Am Soc Pharmacol & Exp Therapeut; Soc Exp Biol & Med. *Res:* Anoxia; respiratory physiology; toxicology of drugs; sedatives; clinical pharmacology of enzymes; antihypertensives; diuretics; antineoplastic agents. *Mailing Add:* 2740 Freedom Heights Colorado Springs CO 80904-5130

GLASS, I(RVINE) I(SRAEL), aerospace engineering, fluids; deceased, see previous edition for last biography

GLASS, JAMES CLIFFORD, MACROMOLECULAR STRUCTURE, HIGH T SUPERCONDUCTORS. *Current Pos:* DEAN SCI, MATH & TECHNOL, EASTERN WASH UNIV, 88-, PROF PHYSICS, 88- *Personal Data:* b Los Angeles, Calif, Sept 20, 37; m 59; c 4. *Educ:* Univ Calif, Berkeley, BA, 60; Calif State Univ, MS, 65; Univ Nev, PhD(physics). *Prof Exp:* Physicist, Rocketdyne, 60-64; sr physicist, Electro-Optical, 64-65; from asst prof to prof physics, NDak State Univ, 68-88, chair physics, 73-85, chair eng sci, 85-88. *Concurrent Pos:* Vis scientist, Kernforschungsanlage Julich, BRD, 77-78. *Mem:* Am Phys Soc; Am Asn Physics Teachers; Sigma Xi. *Res:* Hyperfine interactions: gamma-gamma correlations, Mossbauer in ferroelectrics, superconductors and macromolecules; molecular biophysics: positron annihilation applied to conformational free volume; active transport; enzyme dynamics. *Mailing Add:* E Wash Univ MS 68 Cheney WA 99004-2496

GLASS, JOHN RICHARD, ANALYTICAL CHEMISTRY. *Current Pos:* RETIRED. *Personal Data:* b Lancaster, Pa, Aug 31, 17; m 40, Helen Dudar; c Penelope & James. *Educ:* Elizabethtown Col, BS, 38. *Honors & Awards:* John D Goodell Award, Am Water Works Asn, 43; IR 100 Award, Indust Res Mag, 76. *Prof Exp:* Res chemist water purification, Wallace & Tiernan Co, 39-45; sr res chemist analytical res, Mobil Oil Corp, 45-61, res assoc, 61-82. *Concurrent Pos:* Consult, 82-83. *Mem:* Am Chem Soc. *Res:* Colorimetric and trace metal analysis; analytical instruments. *Mailing Add:* 189 Cedar Rd Mickleton NJ 08056

GLASS, LAUREL ELLEN, DEVELOPMENTAL BIOLOGY, GERIATRIC MEDICINE. *Current Pos:* from instr to prof anat, Sch Med, Univ Calif, San Francisco, 59-89, exec dir, Ctr Deafness, 84-89, prof psychiat, 84-89, EMER PROF ANAT & PSYCHIAT, SCH MED, UNIV CALIF, SAN FRANCISCO, 89- *Personal Data:* b Selma, Calif, Oct 1, 23. *Educ:* Univ Calif, BA, 51; Duke Univ, PhD(exp embryol), 58; Univ Calif, San Francisco, MD, 74. *Prof Exp:* Asst zool, Duke Univ, 53-56; res assoc, Path Res Lab, Vet Admin Hosp, Durham, NC, 57-58. *Concurrent Pos:* Instr anat, Duke Univ, 58. *Mem:* Am Asn Anat; Soc Develop Biol; Am Deafness & Rehab Asn; Self-Help Hard Hearing People; Am Soc Aging; Geront Soc Am. *Res:* Cell interactions during gonadogenesis; macromolecular transfer between maternal body and oocyte or embryo; affective and behavioral effects of acquired hearing loss. *Mailing Add:* 1300 NE 16 Ave No 1408 Portland OR 97232-1454. *Fax:* 503-280-2349; *E-Mail:* 75713.3335@compuserve.com

GLASS, MICHAEL, CHEWING GUM TECHNOLOGY. *Current Pos:* Asst scientist, Warner Lambert Co, 74-76, assoc scientist, 76-78, scientist, 78, sr scientist, 79-81, res assoc, 81, mgr gum base develop, 82, mgr gum develop, 84, DIR GUM DEVELOP WORLDWIDE, WARNER LAMBERT CO, 86- *Personal Data:* b New York, NY, July 29, 50; m 73, Sharon Kohn; c Joseph, Brian & David. *Educ:* Hebert H Lehman Col, BS, 72; Bernard Baruch Col, MBA, 79. *Concurrent Pos:* Mem tech comt, Europ Asn Chewing Gum Industs, 90-; chmn tech comt, Nat Asn Chewing Gum Mgrs, 92- *Mem:* Am Chem Soc; Rubber Div, Am Chem Soc; Inst Food Technologists; Am Asn Candy Technologists. *Res:* Granted over 80 US and foreign patents for unique chewing gums. *Mailing Add:* 10-15 Ellis Ave Fair Lawn NJ 07410-1599. *Fax:* 973-540-5430

GLASS, NATHANIEL E, CONDENSED MATTER PHYSICS, OCEAN PHYSICS & REMOTE SENSING. *Current Pos:* STAFF SCIENTIST, ARETE ASSOCS, 93- *Personal Data:* b Philadelphia, Pa, Mar 2, 49; m 91, Esther Smith. *Educ:* Univ Pa, BA, 70; State Univ NY, Stony Brook, PhD(physics), 76. *Prof Exp:* Res asst, Swiss Fed Inst Technol, Lausanne, 77-80, fel physics dept, Univ Calif, Irvine, 80-83, adj prof, physics dept, Naval Postgrad Sch, 84-87; mem tech staff, Rockwell Int Sci Ctr, 87-93. *Mem:* Am Phys Soc; Sigma Xi; Sci Res Soc. *Res:* Condensed matter theory; lattice dynamics theories of imperfect crystals and of dislocation dynamics; surface electromagnetic waves; acoustic waves; nonlinear optics and superconductivity; ocean physics and remote sensing. *Mailing Add:* 4022 Santa Thomas Pl Newbury Park CA 91320

GLASS, RICHARD STEVEN, ORGANIC CHEMISTRY. *Current Pos:* from asst prof to assoc prof, 70-82, PROF CHEM, UNIV ARIZ, 82- *Personal Data:* b New York, NY, Mar 5, 43; m 70, Susan Stern; c Ethan & Lawrence. *Educ:* NY Univ, BA, 63; Harvard Univ, PhD(chem) 67. *Prof Exp:* NIH fel, Stanford Univ, 66-67; sr res chemist org chem, Hoffmann La Roche, Inc, 67-70. *Concurrent Pos:* Nat Res Serv Awards fel, Nat Heart, Lung & Blood Inst, 88-89. *Mem:* Fel AAAS; Am Chem Soc; Royal Soc Chem; Sigma Xi. *Res:* Total synthesis of natural products; synthetic methods; organosulfur chemistry; biorganic mechanisms; organometallic chemistry; organoselenium. *Mailing Add:* Dept Chem Univ Ariz Tucson AZ 85721-0002. *Fax:* 520-621-8407; *E-Mail:* glass@ccut.arizona.edu

GLASS, RICHARD THOMAS, ORAL PATHOLOGY, FORENSIC ODONTOLOGY. *Current Pos:* From asst prof to assoc prof path, 72-75, CHIEF SECT ORAL PATH, UNIV OKLA, 76-, PROF ORAL PATH & CHMN DEPT, COL DENT, 80- *Personal Data:* b Jacksonville, Fla, March 9, 41; m 91, Patsy Gunsaulis; c 3. *Educ:* Emory Univ, DDS, 65; Univ Chicago, PhD(path), 72; Am Bd Oral Path, dipl. *Concurrent Pos:* Consult, Vet Admin Hosp, Muskogee, Oklahoma City, 72, Fed Aviation Admin & Okla State Med Examr, 73-; staff, Childrens Mem Hosp, Oklahoma City, 72-, Presby Hosp, 80-; oral pathologist, Health Sci Ctr Hosp, Univ Okla, 72- *Mem:* Fel Am Acad Oral Path; Am Dent Asn; Int Asn Dent Res; fel Sigma Xi. *Res:* Cancer of the head and neck; oral mucosal inflammatory diseases; forensic odontology; transmission of disease (infected toothbrush denture). *Mailing Add:* Okla Univ PO Box 26901 Oklahoma City OK 73190

GLASS, ROBERT LOUIS, BIOCHEMISTRY. *Current Pos:* From instr to assoc prof, 56-72, PROF BIOCHEM, UNIV MINN, ST PAUL, 72- *Personal Data:* b Chicago, Ill, May 15, 23; m 46; c 4. *Educ:* Univ Ill, BS, 50; Univ Minn, MS, 54, PhD(agr biochem), 56. *Mem:* Am Chem Soc; Am Oil Chem Soc. *Res:* Lipid biochemistry. *Mailing Add:* 5570 Donegal Dr St Paul MN 55126

GLASS, ROGER I M, MEDICINE, EPIDEMIOLOGY. *Current Pos:* EPIDEMIOLOGIST, CTR DIS CONTROL, 77-, CHIEF, VIRAL GASTROENTERITIS UNIT, 86- *Personal Data:* b Somerville, NJ, Jan 10, 46; c 3. *Educ:* Harvard Col, AB, 67; Harvard Med Sch, MD, 72; Harvard Univ, MPH, 72; PhD, Goteboz, Swed, 84. *Prof Exp:* Mem staff environ epidemiol, Nat Inst Environ Health Sci, 73-74; lectr med, Radcliffe Infirmary, 74; instr med & fel clin epidemiol, Mt Sinai Sch Med, 76-77. *Concurrent Pos:* Scientist, Int Ctr Diarrheal Dis Res, Bangladesh, 75-83; med officer, NIH; clin assoc prof, Dept Pediat, Sch Med, Emory Univ, adj prof, Div Int Health, Sch Pub Health. *Mem:* Soc Epidemiol Res; Am Fedn Clin Res; AAAS; Am Pub Health Asn; Am Epidemiol Soc; Am Soc Virol. *Res:* Epidemiology and laboratory studies of enteric diseases in humans; rotavirus vaccines. *Mailing Add:* Ctr Dis Control 1600 Clifton Rd NE Atlanta GA 30333. *Fax:* 404-639-3645

GLASS, WERNER, CHEMICAL ENGINEERING. *Current Pos:* CONSULT, 86- *Personal Data:* b Berlin, Ger, May 27, 27; US citizen; m 52, Lois Satz; c Alan, Donald & Kenneth. *Educ:* Syracuse Univ, BChE, 50; Mass Inst Technol, SM, 51, ScD(chem eng), 56. *Honors & Awards:* Winquist Medal, Swed Acad Sci. *Prof Exp:* Res engr, Esso Res & Eng Co, Stand Oil Co (NJ), 56-58, group head, 58-59, sr engr, 59-63; asst dir res, Ionics, Inc, 63-64, dep dir res, 64-67; sr engr, Esso Res & Eng Co, 67-68, eng assoc, 68-71; sr staff adv, Exxon Res & Eng Co, 71-86. *Mem:* Am Inst Chem Engrs. *Res:* Planning and evaluation; communication skills. *Mailing Add:* 913 Boulevard Westfield NJ 07090

GLASS, WILLIAM A, RADIOLOGICAL PHYSICS. *Current Pos:* RETIRED. *Personal Data:* b Winfield, Kans, Dec 9, 31; m 56; c 3. *Educ:* Southwestern Univ, BA, 53; Univ Kans, MA & MS, 58. *Prof Exp:* Asst prof physics, Kans State Teachers Col, 58-62; sr res scientist radiol physics, Pac Northwest Labs, Battelle Mem Inst, 63-69, mgr, radiol physics, 72-80, dept mgr, 80-85, asst dir res, 85-86, chief scientist, 86-89, sr adv, 89-91. *Concurrent Pos:* Clin lectr, Univ Wash, 64-69; res collabr, Brookhaven Nat Lab, 69-70; adj prof radiol, Univ Wash, 74- *Mem:* AAAS; Am Phys Soc; Radiation Res Soc. *Res:* Interaction of charged particles in matter; radiation dosimetry; microdosimetry; ionization phenomena; biological effects of ionizing radiation. *Mailing Add:* 1717 S 69th Ave Yakima WA 98908

GLASSBRENNER, CHARLES J, PHYSICS. *Current Pos:* PROF COMPUT SCI, WORCESTER STATE COL, 67- *Personal Data:* b Albany, NY, Apr 9, 28; m 59; c 3. *Educ:* St Bernardine of Siena Col, BS, 50, MS, 56; Univ Conn, PhD(physics), 63; Northeastern Univ, MS, 77. *Prof Exp:* Elec engr, NY State Architects Off, 51-55; physicist, Watervliet Arsenal, NY, 56-57; asst physics, Univ Conn, 57-60; physicist, Res Lab & Knolls Atomic Power Lab, Gen Elec Co, 60-64; sr physicist, Controls for Radiation Inc, Mass, 64-66 & Ion Physics Corp, 66-67. *Mem:* Asn Comput Mach; Am Phys Soc; Sigma Xi. *Res:* Radiation effects on solids; thermal conductivity; mechanical strength of solids; thermodynamics; computer science. *Mailing Add:* 380 Grove St Paxton MA 01612

GLASSCO, WILLIAM SHOEMAKER, RESEARCH IN CHOLINERYICS NICOTINE & MUSCARINE DEVIATIONS, RESEARCH IN OPIATES. *Current Pos:* Technician, 90-91, FEL, MED COL VA, 91- *Personal Data:* b Hartford, Conn, Apr 7, 61. *Educ:* Randolph-Macon Col, BS, 84; Med Col Va, PhD(med chem), 91. *Mem:* Am Chem Soc; Am Inst Chem. *Res:* Developing novel nicotine compounds and novel selective opiate compounds; nicotine-derived analgesics with decreased (non-analgesic) nicotine activity. *Mailing Add:* 2040 Park Ave Richmond VA 23220. *E-Mail:* wglassco@ruby.vcu.edu

GLASSER, ALAN HERBERT, THEORETICAL PLASMA PHYSICS. *Current Pos:* MEM STAFF, LOS ALAMOS NAT LAB, 84- *Personal Data:* b Brooklyn, NY, Sept 8, 43; m 66; c 2. *Educ:* Columbia Col, BA, 65; Univ Calif, San Diego, MS, 67, PhD(physics), 72. *Prof Exp:* Res assoc mem physics, Plasma Physics Lab, Princeton Univ, 72-75, res staff, 75-80; mem fac, Phys Dept, Auburn Univ, 80-84. *Mem:* Sigma Xi; AAAS; Am Phys Soc. *Res:* Equilibrium, stability and transport of magnetically confined plasmas, with an emphasis on the influence of realistic geometry; numerical simulation of fluids. *Mailing Add:* I15K717 LANL PO Box 1663 Los Alamos NM 87545. *E-Mail:* ahg@lani.gov

GLASSER, HAROLD N, CIVIL ENGINEERING, ENVIRONMENTAL ENGINEERING. *Current Pos:* SER ED, SELECTED WORKS OF ARNE NAESS, EL BOSQUE PUMALIN FOUND, 96- *Educ:* Reed Col Portland, BA, 84; Univ Calif, Davis, MS, 90, PhD(civil & environ eng), 95. *Prof Exp:* Asst prof, Dept Humanities & Social Sci, Grad Prog Environ Policy Analysis, NJ Inst Technol, 95-96. *Concurrent Pos:* Consult, Aprovecho Res Inst, Cottage Grove, Ore, 86-87, City Martinez Local Assessment Comt, Calif, 88-92 & Resource Insights, Sacramento, 92-93; Switzer Found environ fel, 90; lectr, Univ Calif, Santa Cruz, 94-95, Schumacher Col, Devon, Eng, 95 & Univ Oslo, Norway, 96; Fulbright lectr tres fel, 96; vis Fulbright prof, Ctr Develop & Environ & Dept Philos, Univ Oslo, 96. *Res:* Methods of environmental policy analysis; multi-attribute decision-theory; theories of rationality and decisionmaking; use of fundamental scientific and engineering; principles to analyze environmental problems; foundations of economic theory; author of numerous publications. *Mailing Add:* 527 43rd St Oakland CA 94609. *E-Mail:* hglasser@igc.apc.org

GLASSER, JAY HOWARD, BIOSTATISTICS, COMMUNITY HEALTH. *Current Pos:* ASSOC PROF BIOMET & COMPUT SCI, UNIV TEX SCH PUB HEALTH HOUSTON, 69- *Personal Data:* b New Haven, Conn, May 6, 35. *Educ:* Univ Conn, BS, 57; Columbia Univ, MS, 60; NC State Univ, PhD(exp statist), 67. *Prof Exp:* From instr to asst prof biostatist, Univ NC, 64-69. *Concurrent Pos:* Consult, HEW, 67-; sr lectr community med, St Thomas's Hosp Sch, Eng, 74-; HEW career develop award, 70. *Mem:* Am Statist Asn; Biomet Soc; fel Am Pub Health Asn; fel Royal Statist Soc; Int Union Sci Study Pop. *Res:* Health services. *Mailing Add:* 5427 Valkeith Dr Houston TX 77096

GLASSER, JOHN WEAKLEY, MATHEMATICAL EPIDEMIOLOGY. *Current Pos:* EIS officer, 88-90, EPIDEMIOLOGIST, CTRS DIS CONTROL, 90-; ASSOC PROF BIOL, EMORY UNIV, 93- *Personal Data:* b Baltimore, Md, Oct 3, 44; m, Jane Elise Hagner; c Matthew F, Joshua A. *Educ:* Princeton Univ, AB, 66; Duke Univ, PhD(zool), 76; Harvard Univ, MPH, 88. *Prof Exp:* Teaching asst, Duke Univ, 71-76; asst prof zool, Univ Ga, 76-83, assoc sci ecol, 83-87. *Mem:* Soc Epidemiol Res; Sigma Xi; Am Soc Naturalists. *Res:* Design and evaluate public health interventions via mathematical models. *Mailing Add:* Nat Immunization Prog Ctrs Dis Control 1600 Clifton Rd Atlanta GA 30333

GLASSER, JULIAN, chemical metallurgy, for more information see previous edition

GLASSER, LEO GEORGE, PHYSICAL OPTICS. *Current Pos:* CONSULT 80- *Personal Data:* b Wilkes-Barre, Pa, July 20, 16; m 41; c 3. *Educ:* Cornell Univ, AB, 38, MA, 40. *Prof Exp:* Asst, Eastman Kodak Co, NY, 38; asst, Nat Geog Soc, Cornell Univ, 38-40; physicist, US Navy Bur Ord, Washington, DC, 40-44; sr physicist, Tenn Eastman Corp, Oak Ridge, 44-45; res engr & supvr eng res lab, E I Du Pont de Nemours, 45-55, res mgr, 56-59, elec res, Mech Develop Lab, 59-60, asst dir eng res lab, 60-63, dir eng physics lab, 63-70, mgr div progs, 70-73, dir eng physics lab, 73-80. *Concurrent Pos:* Dir, Mt Cuba Astron Observ, 71- *Mem:* Optical Soc Am; Sigma Xi; Am Astron Soc. *Res:* Development and application of colorimetric instruments and optical and other analytical instruments for process control; light measurement; refractometry; ultraviolet and infrared spectrophotometry; lasers, holography. *Mailing Add:* 726 Loveville Rd No 84 Hockessin DE 19707

GLASSER, M LAWRENCE, SOLID STATE PHYSICS, APPLIED MATHEMATICS. *Current Pos:* prof math, 77-92, PROF PHYSICS, CLARKSON UNIV, 77- *Personal Data:* b Crookston, Minn, Oct 5, 33; m 56; c 4. *Educ:* Univ Chicago, BA, 53, MS, 55; Univ Miami, MS, 57; Carnegie Inst Technol, PhD(physics), 62. *Honors & Awards:* J Graham Res Award, 78. *Prof Exp:* Instr physics, Univ Miami, 57-58; sr physicist, Battelle Mem Inst, 62-64; asst prof physics, Univ Wis, 64-66; sr physicist, Battelle Mem Inst, 66-67, staff scientist, 67-74; prof appl math, Univ Waterloo, 74-77. *Concurrent Pos:* Consult, Battelle Mem Inst, 64. *Mem:* Am Phys Soc; Math Asn Am; Soc Indust & Appl Math; Am Asn Physics Teachers. *Res:* Theoretical solid state physics; classical mathematical analysis; statistical mechanics. *Mailing Add:* Dept Physics Clarkson Univ Potsdam NY 13699-5820. *Fax:* 315-268-6670; *E-Mail:* laryg@sun.mcs.clarkson.edu

GLASSER, RICHARD LEE, NEUROBIOLOGY. *Current Pos:* From instr to asst prof, 57-65, ASSOC PROF PHYSIOL, SCH MED, UNIV NC, CHAPEL HILL, 65- *Personal Data:* b Baltimore, Md, Mar 26, 27; m 50; c 3. *Educ:* Johns Hopkins Univ, AB, 49; Univ Md, PhD(physiol), 57. *Concurrent Pos:* Vis asst prof, Sch Med, Duke Univ, 59-61. *Mem:* AAAS; Am Physiol Soc; Animal Behav Soc; Soc Neurosci; Soc Values Higher Educ. *Res:* Neurophysiology; neural control of respiration; neural control of cardiovascular activity; neural control of sweat gland activity; memory consolidation mechanisms. *Mailing Add:* Dept Physiol Univ NC Sch Med Res Wing CB No 7545 Chapel Hill NC 27599-7545

GLASSER, STANLEY RICHARD, REPRODUCTIVE BIOLOGY, ENDOCRINOLOGY. *Current Pos:* ASSOC PROF CELL BIOL, BAYLOR COL MED, 72-, DEPT DIR GRAD STUDIES, 75- *Personal Data:* b New York, NY, Dec 2, 26; m 50; c 2. *Educ:* Cornell Univ, BA, 48; Rutgers Univ, PhD(zool), 52. *Honors & Awards:* Medal Pop Res, Franklin Inst of Philadelphia, 72. *Prof Exp:* From instr to asst prof radiation biol, Med Sch, Univ Rochester, 52-62; assoc prof obstet & gynec, Med Sch, Vanderbilt Univ, 62-72. *Concurrent Pos:* Vis asst prof, Ill Wesleyan Univ, 58; lectr, Am Inst Biol Sci-Med Educ Nat Defense, 58-65; vis prof, Baylor Univ, 59; prof obstet & gynec, Maternal Health & Family Planning Prog, Meharry Med Sch, 64-72; prof obstet & gynec, Hahnemann Med Col, 68-77; fel cancer res, Weizmann Inst Rehovat, Israel, 78. *Mem:* Endocrine Soc; Soc Study Reproduction; Brit Soc Study Fertil; Am Physiol Soc; Soc Develop Biol. *Res:* Mammalian reproductive biology; hormone action; biochemistry of decidua and implantation; steroid receptors; uterus, corpus luteum, steroidogenesis; biochemistry of trophoblast growth and differentiation. *Mailing Add:* Dept Cell Biol Baylor Col Med One Baylor Plaza Houston TX 77030-3411. *Fax:* 713-790-1275

GLASSER, WOLFGANG GERHARD, LIGNIN CHEMISTRY, PULP & PAPER CHEMISTRY. *Current Pos:* from asst prof to assoc prof, 72-80, dir, Biobased Mat Ctr, 88-91, PROF WOOD CHEM, VA POLYTECH INST & STATE UNIV, 80-, ASSOC DEAN RES & GRAD STUDIES, 91- *Personal Data:* b Zwickau, Ger, Oct 9, 41; m 69, Heidemarie; c Christine M & Stephan A. *Educ:* Univ Hamburg, Ger, dipl-Holzwirt, 66, Dr rer nat (wood chem), 69. *Honors & Awards:* George Olmsted Award, Am Paper Inst, 74; Sci Achievement Award, Int Union Forestry Res Inst, 86. *Prof Exp:* Res assoc & asst prof chem eng, Univ Wash, Seattle, 69-71. *Concurrent Pos:* Panel chmn, Nat Acad Sci, 74-76; dir, Pulp & Paper Res Inst, Sao Paulo, Brazil, 76; sabbatical, Inst Resquisas Technol, Sao Paulo, Brazil, 76, Centre de Recherches sur les Macromolecules Vegetales, Grenoble, France, 85 & Nat Univ Singapore, 93; publicity chair, Am Chem Soc, 86-89, chmn, 90, prog chmn, 93-, counr, 91- *Mem:* Am Chem Soc; Tech Asn Pulp & Paper Indust; Soc Wood Sci Technol; Sigma Xi. *Res:* Chemistry research with wood; separation of constitutive biopolymers from lignocellulosic resources; use of wood-derived polymers for structural materials and plastics; chemical modification of lignin, xylan and cellulose; author of numerous technical publications; natural polymers and composites; renewable and biodegradable materials. *Mailing Add:* 1302 Highland Circle Blacksburg VA 24060-5623. *Fax:* 540-231-7664; *E-Mail:* wglasser@vt.edu

GLASSGOLD, ALFRED EMANUEL, THEORETICAL PHYSICS, ASTROPHYSICS. *Current Pos:* assoc prof, 63-65, head dept, 69-74, PROF PHYSICS, NY UNIV, 65- *Personal Data:* b Philadelphia, Pa, July 20, 29; m 53, Mihaly; c Judith & Eric. *Educ:* Univ Pa, BA, 50; Mass Inst Technol, PhD(physics), 54. *Prof Exp:* Physicist, Oak Ridge Nat Lab, 54-55; lectr theoret physics, Univ Minn, 55-57; res physicist, Univ Calif, 57-63. *Mem:* AAAS; Am Astron Soc; Int Astron Union; Am Phys Soc. *Res:* Physical properties of interstellar and circumstellar matter involved in dynamical processes relating to stellar birth and death. *Mailing Add:* Dept Physics NY Univ 4 Wash Pl New York NY 10003

GLASSICK, CHARLES ETZWEILER, ORGANIC CHEMISTRY. *Current Pos:* RETIRED. *Personal Data:* b Columbia, Pa, Apr 6, 31; m 52; c 5. *Educ:* Franklin & Marshall Col, BS, 53; Princeton Univ, MA, 55, PhD(chem), 57. *Hon Degrees:* DSc, Univ Richmond, 77; LLD, Dickinson Law Sch, 86. *Prof Exp:* Res chemist, Rohm & Haas Co, 57-62; assoc prof chem, Adrian Col, 62-67; Am Coun Educ fel acad admin, Fresno State Col, 67-68; vpres, Great Lakes Cols Asn, 68-69; assoc dean, Albion Col, 69-71; vpres acad affairs, Univ Richmond, 71-72, vpres & provost, 72-77; pres, Gettysburg Col, 77-89. *Concurrent Pos:* Instr, Temple Univ, 58-62; consult, Nat Endowment for the Humanities, 73-74 & State Coun Higher Educ in Va, 74-76. *Mem:* Am Chem Soc. *Res:* Synthesis of polycyclic aromatics and carcinogenics; plant growth regulatory chemicals and alkaloids. *Mailing Add:* 77 E Andrews Dr Atlanta GA 30305

GLASSLEY, WILLIAM EDWARD, ROCK-WATER INTERACTION, NUCLEAR WASTE DISPOSAL. *Current Pos:* tech area leader, 85-90, TASK LEADER GEOCHEM, LAWRENCE LIVERMORE LAB, 91- *Personal Data:* b Ventura, Calif, July 1, 47; c 2. *Educ:* Univ Calif, San Diego, BA, 69; Univ Wash, MS, 71, PhD(tectonics, petrol), 73. *Prof Exp:* Fel, Mineral-Geol Mus, Univ Oslo, 73-74; asst prof tectonics & petrol, Dept Oceanog, Univ Wash, 74-76; assoc prof geol, Middlebury Col, 76-85. *Mem:* Am Geophys Union; AAAS. *Res:* Evolution of chemical environments in nuclear waste depositories. *Mailing Add:* Dept Earth Sci Lawrence Livermore Nat Lab Livermore CA 94550. *Fax:* 510-422-1002; *E-Mail:* glassley@llnl.gov

GLASSMAN, ARMAND BARRY, LABORATORY MEDICINE, NUCLEAR MEDICINE. *Current Pos:* PROF PATH & RADIOL & DIR CLIN LABS, VANDERBILT UNIV MED CTR, 92- *Personal Data:* b Paterson, NJ, Sept 9, 38; m 58, Alberta C Macri; c Armand P, Steven B & Brian A. *Educ:* Rutgers Univ, BA, 60; Georgetown Univ, MD, 64. *Prof Exp:* Assoc prof & dir clin labs path, Med Col Ga, 71-74, prof & dir, 74-76; prof & med dir, Med Technol & Med Lab Technol & prof & chmn, Lab Med, Med Univ SC, 76-87, prof, Col Grad Studies, 76-87, assoc dean & prof radiol & nuclear med, Col Med, 79-87; prof path & nuclear med, Albert Einstein Col Med, 87-89; vpres & lab dir, Nat Ref Lab, 89-92. *Concurrent Pos:* Consult, Vet Admin Hosp, Augusta, Ga, 71-76, Lab Nuclear Med, Charleston, 76-; sr vpres med affairs, Montefiore Med Ctr, 87-89; consult & med bd, Sci Adv, Nordic Fedn Heart & Lung Asn. *Mem:* Am Col Physicians; Acad Clin Lab Physicians & Scientists; Asn Clin Scientists; Am Asn Blood Banks; Col Am Pathologists & Am Soc Clin Pathologists; Sigma Xi. *Res:* Quantitation and functional characterization of lymphocytes using surface markers, mitogenic responsiveness, carbohydrate metabolism and biomathematical modeling. *Mailing Add:* Univ Tex Md Anderson Cancer Ctr 1515 Holcombe Blvd Box 73 Houston TX 77030-4095

GLASSMAN, EDWARD, genetics, alcohol metabolism, for more information see previous edition

GLASSMAN, IRVIN, ENGINEERING, PHYSICAL CHEMISTRY & COMBUSTION. *Current Pos:* res assoc mech & aerospace eng, Princeton Univ, 50-55, from asst prof to assoc prof, 55-64, prof, 64-86, ROBERT H GODDARD PROF MECH & AEROSPACE ENG, PRINCETON UNIV, 86- *Personal Data:* b Baltimore, Md, Sept 19, 23; m 51, Beverly Wolfe; c Sharilynn (Powell), Diane J (Gienger) & Barbara A (Glassman). *Educ:* Johns Hopkins Univ, BE, 43, DrEng, 50. *Honors & Awards:* Egerton Gold Medal, Combustion Inst, 82; Roe Award, Am Soc Eng Educ, 84. *Prof Exp:* Asst chem eng res, Substitute Alloy Mat Labs, Columbia, 43-46. *Concurrent Pos:* NSF sr fel & vis prof, Univ Naples, 66-67, vis prof, 78-79; chmn, Propulsion & Energetics Panel, Adv Group Aerospace Res & Develop, NATO, 66-79; ed, Combustion Sci & Technol, 68-; mem comt on motor vehicle emissions, Nat Res Coun; Stand Oil Calif vis prof combustion, Stanford Univ, 75- *Mem:* Nat Acad Eng; Am Chem Soc; Combustion Inst; Am Asn Univ Profs. *Res:* Combustion problems in energy, environment, propulsion, fire safety. *Mailing Add:* PO Box 14 Princeton NJ 08542-0014. *Fax:* 609-258-5963; *E-Mail:* glassman@princeton.edu

GLASSMAN, JEROME MARTIN, TOXICOLOGY, BIOSTATISTICS. *Current Pos:* PVT CONSULT, 88- *Personal Data:* b Philadelphia, Pa, Mar 2, 19; m 52, Justine H Rizinsky; c Martin, Lorna & Gary. *Educ:* Univ Pa, AB, 39, MA, 42; Yale Univ, PhD(pharmacol, pub health), 50. *Honors & Awards:* Scouter's Award, 61. *Prof Exp:* Statistician, Bur Census, US Dept Com, Washington, DC, 40-43; hematologist, Div Pharmacol, Food & Drug Admin, 43-45; instr microanat & physiol, Essex Col Med & Surg, 45-46; res assoc, Biol Div, Schering Corp, 46; instr biol sci, Hunter Col, 46-47; asst, Lab Appl Physiol, Yale Univ, 50-51; sr res pharmacologist, Wyeth Labs, 51-59, head, Dept Pharmacodynamics, 59-62; dir, Div Pharmacol, USV Pharmaceut Corp, NY, 62-68, dir biol res, 68-70; dir clin res & pharmacol, Wampole Labs Div, Denver Chem Mfg Co, 70-75; dir clin invest, Wallace Labs Div, Carter Wallace Inc, 75-88. *Concurrent Pos:* Assoc prof, NY Med Col, 63-85. *Mem:* Fel AAAS; Soc Toxicol; fel Am Col Clin Pharmacol Chemother; fel Am Col Clin Pharmacol; fel NY Acad Sci; Am Soc Pharmacol & Exp Therapeut; Sigma Xi. *Res:* Nature of fibrillae of cells; toxicology of dichloro-diphenyl-trichloroethane; toxicology of benzidine and its congeners; adsorbents and anticholinergic drugs; pharmacology of hyaluronidase; cardiotonicity and cardiotoxicity of sympathomimetic amines; inflammation; analgesic agents; local anesthetics; antidiabetic agents; otitis externa; immunologics; anticoagulants; venereal disease; headaches; antibiotics, muscle relaxants, mucolytics; awarded patents in field. *Mailing Add:* 280 Sleepy Hollow Rd PO Box 23 Briarcliff Manor NY 10510-0023

GLASSMAN, SIDNEY FREDERICK, PLANT TAXONOMY, CLASSIFICATION OF PALMS. *Current Pos:* RETIRED. *Personal Data:* b Chicago, Ill, July 30, 19; m 50, Ida Margolis; c Robert & Paula. *Educ:* Univ Ill, BS, 42, MA, 47; Univ Okla, PhD(bot), 50. *Prof Exp:* Instr bot, Univ Wyo, 51-52; asst botanist, Field Mus, Univ Ill, Chicago, 51, from asst prof to assoc prof biol sci, 52-89, res fel, 57, cur herbarium, 55-89, res assoc, 63-89. *Concurrent Pos:* Fel, Nat Res Coun, Caroline Islands, 49; instr, Wilson Jr Col, 53; NSF grantee, 65, 69 & 75-, res trips, Europe, 66, Utrecht & Berlin, 74, Univ Tex & Ill, 80, Kew Gardens, Eng, Univ Strathclyde, Glasgow, 81-, palm collecting trips, Brazil, 65, 69, 76 & 88. *Mem:* Am Soc Plant Taxon; Int Asn Plant Taxon; Int Palm Soc. *Res:* Revision of index of American palms and palm genus Copernicia; grass flora of Chicago region and revision of genus Syagrus; revision of palm genera Attalea, Scheelea, Orbignya and Maximiliana. *Mailing Add:* 8942 Bellefort Ave Morton Grove IL 60053

GLASSOCK, RICHARD JAMES, NEPHROLOGY, TRANSPLANTATION. *Current Pos:* PROF INTERNAL MED & NEPHROLOGY & CHMN DEPT MED, SCH MED, UNIV CALIF, LOS ANGELES, 80- *Educ:* Univ Calif, Los Angeles, MD, 60. *Mailing Add:* Dept Med Univ Ky Ky Clinic J525 Lexington KY 40536-0284. *Fax:* 606-323-1197

GLASSTONE, SAMUEL, nuclear science; deceased, see previous edition for last biography

GLATSTEIN, ELI J, RADIATION ONCOLOGY. *Current Pos:* AT SIMMONS CANCER RES CTR, UNIV TEX SOUTHWEST MED CTR, 92- *Personal Data:* b Muscatine, Iowa, Feb 20, 38. *Educ:* State Univ Iowa, BA, 60; Stanford Univ, MD, 64; Am Bd Radiol, cert, 72. *Honors & Awards:* Presidential Meritorious Exec Rank Award, 85. *Prof Exp:* Intern, NY Hosp, Med Ctr, Cornell Univ, 64-65; Picker Found fel radiobiol, Hammersmith Hosp, London, UK, 70-71, fel, Gray Lab, Mt Vernon Hosp, Northwood, Middlesex, UK, 71-72; resident & fel radiation ther, Sch Med, Stanford Univ, 67-70, asst prof radiol, 72-77, univ adv, 73-77, fac sen, Med Sch Senate, 75-77; cancer expert, Radiol Oncol Br, Nat Cancer Inst, 77-78, actg dir, Clin Oncol Prog, 88-89; chief Radiation Oncol Br, Clin Oncol Prog, Div Cancer Treatment, Bethesda, 78-92, actg dir, Radiation Res Prog, 91-92. *Concurrent Pos:* Consult radiation biol, Lawrence Radiation Lab, Berkeley, 74-76; mem, Cancer Clin Invest Rev Comt, Nat Cancer Inst, 76-78; assoc prof radiol, Uniformed Serv Univ Health Sci, Bethesda, 79-81, prof, 81-; Nat Cancer Inst rep, Am Joint Comt Cancer, 90-92. *Mem:* Am Soc Therapeut Radiologists; Int Soc Lymphology; Brit Inst Radiol; Am Radium Soc; Am Soc Clin Oncol; Int Asn Study Lung Cancer; Radiation Res Soc; Asn Univ Professors; Am Asn Cancer Res; AAAS. *Res:* Radiation effects; normal tissue tolerance; lymphomas-Hodgkin's Disease; genitourinary cancer; sarcomas; pediatric neoplasia; lung cancer; radiation therapy treatment planning; photodynamic therapy; radioimmunoglobin therapy; intraoperative radiotherapy. *Mailing Add:* 4500 Roland Ave Suite 507 Dallas TX 75219. *Fax:* 214-648-7613

GLATZER, LOUIS, MICROBIAL GENETICS, MOLECULAR BIOLOGY. *Current Pos:* ASST PROF BIOL, UNIV TOLEDO, 73- *Personal Data:* b New York, NY, Aug 7, 40; m 65; c 1. *Educ:* Dartmouth Col, AB, 63; NC State Univ, MS, 65; Univ Tex, Austin, PhD(zool, biochem), 70. *Concurrent Pos:* Nat Inst Gen Med Sci fel, Oak Ridge Nat Lab, 70-73. *Mem:* Am Soc Photobiol; Am Soc Microbiol. *Res:* Plasmid genetics; effects of near ultraviolet light irradiation on bacterial systems; molecular biology of recombination; homologies between related and unrelated DNA's. *Mailing Add:* Dept Biol Univ Toledo Toledo OH 43606

GLAUBER, ROY JAY, PHYSICS. *Current Pos:* lectr & Bayard Cutting fel, 52-54, from asst prof to prof, 54-76, MALLINCKRODT PROF PHYSICS, HARVARD UNIV, 76- *Personal Data:* b New York, NY, Sept 1, 25; m 60; c 2. *Educ:* Harvard Univ, SB, 46, AM, 47, PhD(physics), 49. *Honors & Awards:* A A Michelson Award, Franklin Inst, 85; Max Born Medal & Award, Am Optical Soc, 85; Danni Heineman Award, Am Phys Soc, 96. *Prof Exp:* Asst theoret physics, Los Alamos Sci Lab, 44-46; AEC fel, Inst Advan Study, 49-50, mem, 49-51, Jewett fel, 51-52; lectr theoret physics, Calif Inst Technol, 51-52. *Concurrent Pos:* AEC fel, Swiss Fed Inst Technol, 50; Fulbright lectr, Grenoble, France, 54; Guggenheim Mem Found fel, 59; mem bd & ed, J Math & Physics, 61-63, J Nuclear Physics, 72; US-Soviet exchange lectr, Leningrad, 64; consult, Radiation Lab, Univ Calif, Bell Tel Labs, Am Tel & Tel Co & Lewis Res Ctr, NASA, Ohio, Los Alamos Nat Lab; NSF sr fel, 66-67; vis scientist, CERN, Geneva, 67 & 83, guest prof, 72-73; Lorentz prof, Univ Leidan, Holland, 74; vis prof, Nordita, Copenhagen, 74 & Col de France, 83; adj prof physics, Univ Ariz, Tucson, 88-; Alexander von Humboldt res award, Bonn, 89. *Mem:* Fel Nat Acad Sci; fel Am Phys Soc; fel Am Acad Arts & Sci; fel Am Optical Soc. *Res:* Nuclear physics; particle diffraction and diffusion problems; elementary particle theory and high energy physics; quantum optics; statistical mechanics; quantum theory of measurement. *Mailing Add:* Lyman Lab Physics Harvard Univ Cambridge MA 02138-2901

GLAUBERMAN, GEORGE ISAAC, FINITE GROUP THEORY. *Current Pos:* From instr to assoc prof, 65-70, PROF MATH, UNIV CHICAGO, 70- *Personal Data:* b New York, NY, Mar 3, 41; m 89, Roza Zwillinger; c 2. *Educ:* Polytech Inst Brooklyn, BS, 61; Harvard Univ, MA, 62; Univ Wis, PhD(math), 65. *Concurrent Pos:* Sloan Found res fel, 67-69; NSF & Sci Res Coun fel, Univ Oxford, Eng, 71-72; Guggenheim fel & vis sr res fel, Jesus Col, 78-79; vis, Math Inst, Univ Oxford, Eng, 78-79. *Mem:* Am Math Soc; Math Asn Am; NY Acad Sci. *Res:* Algebra, principally the theory of finite groups. *Mailing Add:* Dept Math Univ Chicago 5734 S University Ave Chicago IL 60637

GLAUBMAN, MICHAEL JUDA, PARTICLE PHYSICS, NUCLEAR PHYSICS. *Current Pos:* from asst prof to assoc prof, 59-70, PROF PHYSICS, NORTHEASTERN UNIV, 70- *Personal Data:* b Baltimore, Md, Dec 31, 24; m; c 4. *Educ:* Hebrew Univ, BS, 47; Univ Ill, MA, 50, PhD(physics), 53. *Prof Exp:* Asst physics, Univ Ill, 49-53 & Princeton Univ, 53-55; res assoc, Columbia Univ, 55-56; sr res physicist, Atomics Int Div, NAm Aviation, Inc, 56-59. *Mem:* Am Phys Soc; AAAS. *Res:* Experimental nuclear structure; high energy experimental physics. *Mailing Add:* Dept Physics Northeastern Univ Boston MA 02115. *E-Mail:* glaubman@neohepcas.northeastern.edu

GLAUDEMANS, CORNELIS P, MEDICINE. *Current Pos:* CHIEF, NIH, 67- *Personal Data:* b Semarang, Java, Apr 16, 32; US citizen; m 56; c 6. *Educ:* Fed Univ, Utrecht, Netherlands, BS, 54; McGill Univ, Can, PhD(chem), 58. *Prof Exp:* Vis res scientist, NIH, 62-65; prof chem, Yale Univ, 65-67. *Mailing Add:* 14014 Shippers Lane Rockville MD 20853

GLAUERT, HOWARD PERRY, CHEMICAL CARCINOGENESIS, NUTRITION & CANCER. *Current Pos:* from asst prof to assoc prof, 85-96, PROF NUTRIT & TOXICOL, UNIV KY, 96- *Personal Data:* b St Louis, Mo, June 19, 52. *Educ:* Univ Mo, Columbia, BA, 74; Mich State Univ, PhD(nutrit), 82. *Honors & Awards:* Res Career Develop Award, NIH, 92. *Prof Exp:* Lab technician food sci, Univ Mo, 73-76; grad asst nutrit, Mich State Univ, 76-82; fel environ toxicol, Univ Wis, 82-85. *Concurrent Pos:* Alexander von Humboldt res fel, Ger Cancer Res Ctr, 92. *Mem:* Am Inst Nutrit; Sigma Xi; Soc Toxicol; Am Asn Cancer Res. *Res:* Mechanism by which chemicals induce liver cancer; nutrition and cancer; transgenic models of carcinogenesis. *Mailing Add:* Dept Nutrit & Food Sci Univ Ky 204 Funkhouser Bldg Lexington KY 40506-0054. *Fax:* 606-257-3707; *E-Mail:* nfshpg@ukcc.uky.edu

GLAUNSINGER, WILLIAM STANLEY, SOLID STATE CHEMISTRY, PHYSICAL CHEMISTRY. *Current Pos:* asst prof chem, 72-76, ASSOC PROF CHEM, ARIZ STATE UNIV, 76- *Personal Data:* b Newark, Ohio, May 10, 45; m 67; c 1. *Educ:* Miami Univ, BS, 67; Cornell Univ, PhD(chem), 72. *Prof Exp:* Teaching asst, Cornell Univ, 67-69, res asst, 69-72. *Concurrent Pos:* Res Corp res grant, 74; NSF grant, 76; Phys Res Found grant, 77. *Mem:* Am Chem Soc; AAAS; Am Phys Soc; Int Soc Magnetic Resonance; Sigma Xi. *Res:* Magnetic resonance spectroscopy using electron paramagnetic resonance, nuclear magnetic resonance and electron-nuclear double resonance techniques; theoretical and experimental investigation of metal-ammonia systems; transition metal oxides; rare earth hexaborides; II-VI compounds and alloys; metallic microcrystals; spin-labeled biomolecules. *Mailing Add:* Dept Chem Ariz State Univ Temple AZ 85287-0002

GLAUSER, ELINOR MIKELBERG, PHARMACOLOGY, PHYSIOLOGY. *Current Pos:* from instr to asst prof, 63-70, ASSOC PROF PHARM & MED, SCH MED, TEMPLE UNIV, 70- *Personal Data:* b Philadelphia, Pa, Aug 24, 31; m 52; c 3. *Educ:* Univ Pa, BA, 52; Woman's Med Col of Pa, MD, 57. *Prof Exp:* Assoc res, Dept Med, Woman's Med Col Pa, 61-63. *Concurrent Pos:* Fel physiol, Trudeau Soc, Sch Med, Univ Pa, 58-59; Kate Hurdmead fel exp med, Cambridge Univ, 59-60; fel med, Harvard Med Sch, 60-61; NIH fel, 61-63; Am Thoracic Soc fel, 63-64. *Mem:* AAAS; Am Thoracic Soc; Am Chem Soc; AMA; NY Acad Med. *Res:* Pulmonary physiology, pulmonary pharmacology and chronic pulmonary disease in man. *Mailing Add:* 830 Montgomery Ave #414 Bryn Mawr PA 19010

GLAUSER, FREDERICK LOUIS, PULMONARY MEDICINE. *Current Pos:* chief, Pulmonary Sect, 84-88, CHIEF, PULMONARY DIV, MCGUIRE VET ADMIN MED CTR, MED COL VA, RICHMOND, 87-, PROF, 89- *Personal Data:* b Philadelphia, Pa, June 15, 37; c 2. *Educ:* Ursinus Col, BS, 59; Hahnemann Med Col, MD, 63. *Prof Exp:* Resident internal med, Vet Admin Hosp, Univ Ore, 66-68; resident pulmonary med, 68-69; fel pulmonary dis, Univ Pittsburgh Hosp, 69-70 & Stanford Univ, 70-71; clin pract internal med & pulmonary dis, San Jose Med Clin, Calif, 71-72; asst prof med in line, Pulmonary Div, Sch Med, Univ Calif, Irvine, 72-75, asst prof med in residence, Univ, 75-77. *Concurrent Pos:* Actg dir respiratory ther, Orange County Med Ctr, 72-75; consult, Long Beach Vet Admin Med Ctr, 73-75; chief, Pulmonary Sect B, 75-77, co-dir MICU, 75-76, dir, 76-77; co-dir, MICU, Med Col Va & McGuire Vet Admin Med Ctr, 78-; Nat Heart, Lung & Blood Inst consult, site visits, 80 & 86; chmn, Multidisciplinary Crit Care Comt, Med Col Va, 81-86, mem, 86-; chmn, Crit Care Comt, McGuire Vet Admin Med Ctr, 85-88. *Mem:* Am Physiol Soc; Fedn Am Socs Exp Biol; Microcirculatory Soc. *Mailing Add:* Dept Med Pulmonary Dis Commonwealth Univ Sch Med Richmond VA 23298-1900

GLAUSER, MARK N, MECHANICAL ENGINEERING, AERONAUTICAL ENGINEERING. *Current Pos:* Asst prof, 87-93, ASSOC PROF MECH & AERONAUT, DEPT MECH & AERONAUT ENG, CLARKSON UNIV, 93- *Personal Data:* b Buffalo, NY, Mar 10, 57. *Educ:* State Univ NY, BS, 82, PhD(mech eng), 87. *Concurrent Pos:* Vis sr res sci, Nassau Langley Res Ctr, 94-95; Fulbright scholar, Univ Poiters, France, 95; prog mgr turbulence & internal flows, Off Sci Res, Air Force, 96-97. *Mem:* Am Soc Mech Engrs; Am Inst Aeronaut & Astronaut; Am Phys Soc; Sigma Xi. *Mailing Add:* Dept Mech & Aeronaut Eng Clarkson Univ Box 5725 Potsdam NY 13699-5725. *Fax:* 315-268-6438; *E-Mail:* glauser@sun.soe.clarkson.edu

GLAUSER, STANLEY CHARLES, PHARMACOLOGY. *Current Pos:* CHIEF SECT PHARMACOL, DEPT MED, GRAD HOSP, PHILADELPHIA, PA, 79- *Personal Data:* b Philadelphia, Pa, June 19, 31; m 52; c 3. *Educ:* Univ Pa, BA, 51, MS & MD, 55, PhD(phys chem), 59. *Prof Exp:* Asst phys chem, Sch Med, Univ Pa, 52-54; res assoc, NIH, 57-59; NSF res fel molecular biol, Med Res Coun Unit, Cavendish Lab, Cambridge Univ, 59-60; res assoc biol, Mass Inst Technol, 60-61; asst prof molecular biol & physiol, Sch Med, Univ Pa, 61-65; from assoc prof to prof molecular pharmacol, Sch Med, Temple Univ, 65-79. *Concurrent Pos:* Instr, USDA Grad Sch, 58-59; prof, Hadassah Med Sch, Hebrew Univ, Jerusalem, Israel, 83- *Mem:* AAAS; Am Chem Soc; Am Med Asn; NY Acad Sci; Am Soc Pharmacol & Exp Therapeut. *Res:* Molecular biology; physical chemistry of hemoproteins and other porphyrin-like compounds of biological interest; thermodynamics; kinetics; genetics. *Mailing Add:* 830 Montgomery Ave No 414 Bryn Mawr PA 19010

GLAUZ, ROBERT DORAN, APPLIED MATHEMATICS. *Current Pos:* PROF MATH, UNIV CALIF, DAVIS, 68- *Personal Data:* b Detroit, Mich, Aug 13, 27; m 53; c 3. *Educ:* Univ Mich, BSE, 48, MS, 49; Brown Univ, PhD(appl math), 53. *Prof Exp:* Instr math, Mont State Col, 49-50; asst, Brown Univ, 51-53; mem staff, Los Alamos Sci Lab, Univ Calif, 53-57; eng anal specialist, Aircraft Gas Turbine Div, Gen Elec Corp, 57-58; tech specialist, Aerojet-Gen Corp Div, Gen Tire & Rubber Co, 58-66, mgr eng anal & prog, 66-68. *Mem:* Am Math Soc; Math Asn Am; Asn Comput Mach. *Res:* Viscoelasticity; numerical analysis. *Mailing Add:* 3124 Shelter Cove Pl Davis CA 95616-2630

GLAUZ, WILLIAM DONALD, ENGINEERING SCIENCE, DATA ACQUISITION AND ANALYSIS. *Current Pos:* assoc analyst, 63-64, sr analyst, 64-66, prin analyst, 66-69, head anal & appl math, 69-71, mgr hwy & traffic systs eng, 71-80, DIR SAFETY & ENG ANALYSIS, MIDWEST RES INST, 80- *Personal Data:* b Grand Rapids, Mich, Oct 26, 33; m 56; c 4. *Educ:* Mich State Univ, BS, 56; Purdue Univ, MS, 59, PhD(eng sci), 64. *Prof Exp:* Instr, Purdue Univ, 56-63. *Concurrent Pos:* Consult, Midwest Appl Sci Corp, 59-63; lectr, Univ Mo-Kansas City, 64-79; comt chmn, Hwy Res Bd, Nat Acad Sci-Nat Res Coun. *Mem:* Inst Transp Eng. *Res:* Research management; highway safety; traffic analysis; simulation; digital computation; mechanics; applied mathematics; aerodynamics. *Mailing Add:* 11600 Minor Dr Kansas City MO 64114

GLAVIN, GARY BERTRUN, NEURO-GASTROENTEROLOGY, BRAIN-GUT RELATIONSHIPS. *Current Pos:* Assoc prof pharmacol, 84-88, ASSOC PROF NEUROSURG, UNIV MAN, 87-, PROF PHARMACOL, 88-, DEPT HEAD, PHARMACOL & THERAPEUT, 96- *Personal Data:* b Winnipeg, Man, Feb 2, 49; m 73, Karen Dooley; c Matthew. *Educ:* Univ Man, BA, 71, MSc, 73 & PhD(psychopharmacol), 75. *Concurrent Pos:* Consult, Dept Pharmacol, Laboratorios Del Dr Esteve, SA, Barcelona, Spain; Matsumite Int Res Fel, Kurume, Japan; vis scholar res fel, Harvard Univ; vis fel prof, Dept Pharmacol, Lo Yok Tong, Univ Hong Kong. *Mem:* Am Soc Pharmacol & Exp Therapeut; Soc Neurosci; AAAS; NY Acad Sci; Am Gastroenterol Asn; Can Asn Gastroenterol; Int Brain-Gut Soc; Am Med Sch Pharmacol; Can Pharmacol Soc. *Res:* Role of central and peripheral dopamine in experimental gastroduodenal ulcer disease; monoamine neurochemistry of stress and of focal seizure disorder. *Mailing Add:* Dept Pharmacol Fac Med Univ Man Winnipeg MB R3E 0W3 Can. *Fax:* 204-783-6915; *E-Mail:* glavin@cc.umanitoba.ca

GLAWE, DEAN A, MYCOLOGY. *Current Pos:* PROF, PLANT PATH DEPT, UNIV ILL. *Honors & Awards:* Alexopoulos Prize, Mycol Soc Am, 91. *Mailing Add:* Dept Plant Path Univ Ill 1102 S Goodwin Urbana IL 61801

GLAWE, LLOYD NEIL, INVERTEBRATE PALEONTOLOGY, PALEOCENE FORAMINIFENA & STRATIGRAPHY. *Current Pos:* From asst prof to assoc prof, 64-77 PROF GEOL, NE LA UNIV, 77- *Personal Data:* b Des Moines, Iowa, Aug 21, 32; m 70, Nancy Gholson; c Lori M & John D. *Educ:* Univ Ill, BS, 54; La State Univ, MS, 60, PhD(paleont), 66. *Concurrent Pos:* Res assoc, La Geol Surv, 61, Ala Geol Surv, 64 & Oil & Gas Consult & Contract Geol, 80- *Mem:* Paleont Res Inst; Soc Econ Paleontologists & Mineralogists; Sigma Xi. *Res:* Classification and distribution of Gulf Coast Tertiary Pectinidae; Paleocene/Eocene foraminiferal biostratigraphy and paleoenvironments. *Mailing Add:* 33 E Elmwood Dr Monroe LA 71203

GLAZE, ROBERT P, BIOCHEMISTRY, SCIENCE EDUCATION. *Current Pos:* PRES, GLAZE, INC, 91- *Personal Data:* b Birmingham, Ala, Apr 14, 33; m 58, Barbara Malloy; c David W & Jennifer D (Mitchell). *Educ:* Univ of the South, BS, 55; Univ Rochester, PhD(biochem), 61. *Prof Exp:* Asst prof biochem, Univ Ala, Birmingham, 64-72, from asst dean to assoc dean, Schs Med & Dent, 67-72, dir instnl study prog, 72-73, coordr res grants, 67-76, asst to pres, 73-76, dean admin, 76-77, vpres res & grad studies, 77-81, actg vpres instnl advan, 80-81, vpres res & instnl advan, 81-88, exec dir, UAB Res Found, 88, vpres res develop, 88-90, asst to pres spec prog, 91. *Concurrent Pos:* Fel physiol chem, Sch Med, Johns Hopkins Univ, 61-64; USPHS fel, 62-63 & trainee, 62-64; NSF res grant, 66-68. *Mem:* AAAS; Am Chem Soc; Am Inst Chemists; NY Acad Sci. *Res:* Mitochondrial electron transport; oxidative phosphorylation; phosphate transfer enzymes; uremia. *Mailing Add:* 3610 Dunbarton Dr Birmingham AL 35223-2888. *Fax:* 205-970-0685

GLAZE, WILLIAM H, ENVIRONMENTAL CHEMISTRY. *Current Pos:* PROF & PROG DIR, ENVIRON SCI & ENG PROG, SCH PUBL HEALTH, UNIV CALIF, LOS ANGELES, 84- *Personal Data:* b Sherman, Tex, Nov 21, 34; m 76; c 4. *Educ:* Southwestern Univ Tex, BS, 56; Univ Wis, MS, 58, PhD(chem), 61. *Honors & Awards:* F J Zimmerman Award, Environ Sci, 86. *Prof Exp:* Robert A Welch fel, Rice Univ, 60-61; from asst prof to assoc prof, NTex State Univ, 61-65, assoc dean arts & sci & dir, Inst Environ Studies, 73-75, prof chem, 65-80, dir, Inst Appl Sci, 75-80; prof chem & environ sci, head, Grad Prog Environ Sci & dir, Ctr Energy & Environ Sci, Univ Tex, Dallas, 80-84. *Concurrent Pos:* Robert A Welch res grant organometallic compounds, 63-74; NSF undergrad equip fel consult, 64 & res grant organometallic photochem, 69-71; res grants, Environ Protection Agency, 74- & mem, Sci Adv Bd; Tex Water Develop Bd grant, Tex Dept Health grant & NSF sponsored appointee res exchange prog, Shell Develop Co, 76; James M Montgomery & Metrop Waste Dist Contract, 86-88; res grants, US-Mex Policy Rels, Hewlett Found, Advan Oxidation Processes, La Dept Water & Power, US Environ Protection Agency, San Diego Wastewater Reuse, Western Consortium Pub Health, Hazardous Substances Control, NSF & Eng Res Ctr, 87- *Mem:* Am Chem Soc; Environ Protection Agency. *Res:* Chemistry of water disinfection compounds; reaction kinetics and mechanisms; water purification by activated carbon; trace organics in the environment; mass spectrometry and gas chromatography. *Mailing Add:* Univ NC Cb No 7400 Chapel Hill NC 27599-8140

GLAZENER, EDWARD WALKER, POULTRY HUSBANDRY, HIGHER EDUCATION. *Current Pos:* assoc prof poultry genetics, NC State Univ, 46-49, head dept poultry sci, 55-60, dir instr, Sch Agr & Life Sci, 60-70, actg dean, 70-71, prof poultry sci & genetics, 49-86, dir acad affairs, Sch Agr & Life Sci, 60-86, assoc dean & dir, 74-86, spec asst, 86-88, EMER DIR SPEC ASSIGNMENTS, JEFFERSON SCHOLAR HONORS PROG-COMMUNITY COL PROG DEVELOP, NC STATE UNIV, 88- *Personal Data:* b Raleigh, NC, Feb 3, 22; m 47; c 2. *Educ:* NC State Col, BS, 43; Univ Md, MS, 45, PhD(poultry genetics), 49. *Honors & Awards:* Martin Litwack Vet Progression Award, 86. *Prof Exp:* Asst county agent, Exten Serv, NC State Col, 44; asst prof poultry husb, Univ Md, 46. *Concurrent Pos:* Vis scholar, Pa State Univ, 72; chmn, Coun Higher Educ, Agr Sci, Southern Regional Educ Bd, 74-, Manpower Adv Assessment Comt, USDA, 80-86 & Higher Educ Comt, USDA, 82-84. *Mem:* Fel AAAS; Am Genetic Asn; Poultry Sci Asn; Am Inst Biol Sci; Am Asn Higher Educ. *Res:* Genetics and endocrinology of poultry; thyroid activity as related to strain differences in growing chickens; curriculum development, particularly in agricultural and biological sciences; pre-professional medical sciences. *Mailing Add:* 3424 Lewis Farm Rd Raleigh NC 27607-6725

GLAZER, ALEXANDER NAMIOT, BIOCHEMISTRY, MOLECULAR BIOLOGY. *Current Pos:* prof microbiol, Dept Microbiol & Immunol, 76-89, PROF BIOCHEM & MOLECULAR BIOL, DEPT MOLECULAR & CELL BIOL, UNIV CALIF, BERKELEY, 89- *Personal Data:* b July 7, 35. *Educ:* Univ Sydney, Australia, BSc(Hon), 56, MSc, 57; Univ Utah, PhD(biochem), 60. *Honors & Awards:* Endeavour Prize, British Asn Advan Sci, 56; Darbaker Prize, Bot Soc Am, 80; Sci Reviewing Prize, Nat Acad Sci, 91. *Prof Exp:* Postdoctoral biophys, Weizmann Inst Sci, Israel, 61-62; postdoctoral, Molecular Biol Lab, Med Res Ctr, Cambridge, Eng, 62-63; from asst prof to prof biochem, Sch Med, Univ Calif, Los Angeles, 64-76. *Concurrent Pos:* Assoc mem, Inst Molecular Biol, Univ Calif, Los Angeles, 65-76; mem, NIH Biophys & Biophys Chem A Study Sect, 69-73; chmn, Dept Microbiol & Immunol, Univ Calif, Berkeley, 77-82; expert analyst, Chemtracts in Biochem & Molecular Biol, 89-; sr staff, Div Chem Biodynamics, Lawrence Berkeley Lab, 90- *Mem:* Am Soc Biochem & Molecular Biol; AAAS; Am Soc Microbiol; fel Am Acad Arts & Sci. *Res:* Protein structure-function relationships, enzymology, biophysical chemistry- Examples: assembly of macromolecular complexes (flagella, phycobilisomes), development of fluorescent reagents for cell sorting, cell analyses, and detection of reactive oxygen species and physiologically important antioxidants, methods for DNA detection. *Mailing Add:* 229 Stanley Hall Univ Calif Berkeley CA 94720. *Fax:* 510-643-9290

GLAZER, JUDITH, ELECTRONIC ASSEMBLY, ELECTRONIC PACKAGING. *Current Pos:* mfg develop engr, 89-93, reliability physics engr, 93-95, PROJ MGR, ELECTRONIC ASSEMBLY DEVELOP CTR, HEWLETT PACKARD CO, 95- *Personal Data:* b Cambridge, Eng, Aug 2, 62; US citizen. *Educ:* Univ Calif, Berkeley, BS(elec eng) & BS(met sci eng) 83, MS, 86, PhD(mat sci eng), 89. *Honors & Awards:* Hardy Medal, Metals Minerals & Mats Soc, 93. *Prof Exp:* Printed circuit engr, Hewlett Packard GmbH, Boeblingen, Ger, 91-92. *Mem:* Metals Minerals & Mats Soc; Am Soc Metals; Surface Mount Technol Asn. *Res:* Development of new manufacturing processes for electronics assembly with an emphasis on reliability issues associated with new packages and new solder alloys. *Mailing Add:* Hewlett Packard 1501 Page Mill Rd MS 4U-3 Palo Alto CA 94304-1126

GLAZER, ROBERT IRWIN, PHARMACOLOGY, ONCOLOGY. *Current Pos:* PROF, DEPT PHARMACOL, GEORGETOWN UNIV MED CTR, 89- *Personal Data:* b New York, NY, May 14, 42; m 65, Roxane; c Michele & Jeffrey. *Educ:* Columbia Univ, BS, 65, MS, 67; Ind Univ, PhD(pharmacol), 70. *Prof Exp:* Asst prof pharmacol, Emory Univ, 72-77; head, Appl Pharmacol Sect, Lab Med Chem & Biol, Nat Cancer Inst, 77-85, supvr pharmacologists, Lab Biol Chem, 85-89. *Concurrent Pos:* Nat Cancer Inst fel pharmacol, Sch Med, Yale Univ, 70-72 & res grant, Emory Univ, 73-76; Pharmaceut Mfrs Asn found fac develop award, 73-75; Bristol-Myers Multidrug Resistance Grant, 88-93. *Mem:* AAAS; Am Soc Pharmacol & Exp Therapeut; Am Asn Cancer Res; Am Soc Biochem & Molecular Biol. *Res:* Studies the role of protein phosphorylation and serine and tyrosine protein kinases in differentiation; multidrug resistance and human immunodeficiency virus (HIV) replication. *Mailing Add:* Res Bldg Rm W318 Georgetown Univ Med Ctr 3970 Reservoir Rd Washington DC 20007

GLAZIER, DOUGLAS STEWART, PHYSIOLOGICAL ECOLOGY, EVOLUTIONARY ECOLOGY. *Current Pos:* from asst prof to assoc prof, 80-91, PROF BIOL, JUNIATA COL, 91- *Personal Data:* b Detroit, Mich, Oct 20, 51; m 75, Debra A Kirchhof; c Brynda J & Darron Kirchhof. *Educ:* Oakland Univ, BA, 73; Cornell Univ, PhD(ecol), 79. *Prof Exp:* Teaching asst biol, Oakland Univ, 70-72, res asst, Inst Biol Sci, 71-73; teaching asst biol, ecol & zool, Sect Ecol & Systs, Cornell Univ, 73-78; tech ed, Ecol Soc Am, 79-80. *Concurrent Pos:* Prin investr, Sigma Xi Grants, 76-77, PEW Charitable Trusts, Juniata Col, 90 & Howard Hughes Med Inst Grants, Juniata Col, 91-92 & 94, co-prin investr, NSF Grant, 84-85; hon res fel, Dept Animal & Plant Sci, Univ Sheffield, Eng, 88-89. *Mem:* Am Soc Mammalogists; Am Soc Naturalists; Ecol Soc Am; NAm Benthological Soc; Soc Study Evol; Soc Syst Biologists. *Res:* Physiological and evolutionary ecology of small mammals and freshwater invertebrates; biology of fauna of freshwater springs; biological correlates of geographic ranges; patterns of taxonomic diversity; life-history evolution. *Mailing Add:* Biol Dept Juniata Col Huntingdon PA 16652. *Fax:* 814-641-3685

GLAZIER, ROBERT HENRY, ORGANIC CHEMISTRY. *Current Pos:* assoc prof, 62-70, PROF CHEM, WASHBURN UNIV, 70- *Personal Data:* b Amherst, Mass, Oct 1, 26. *Educ:* Amherst Col, AB, 48; Univ NH, MS, 50; Univ Kans, PhD(chem), 52. *Prof Exp:* Prof chem & chmn dept, Alderson-Broaddus Col, 52-54 & Nebr Wesleyan Univ, 54-61; vis prof, Kalamazoo Col, 61-62. *Mailing Add:* Dept Chem Washburn Univ 1700 SW College Ave Topeka KS 66621-1110

GLAZKO, ANTHONY JOACHIM, chemical pharmacology; deceased, see previous edition for last biography

GLAZMAN, YULI M, SURFACE CHEMISTRY, COLLOID CHEMISTRY. *Current Pos:* RETIRED. *Personal Data:* b Kiev, Russia, Aug 7, 11; m 50, Natalya Tamarova; c Alla. *Educ:* Kiev State Univ, MChem, 34; Ministry Higher Educ, USSR, PhD(chem), 39; USSR Acad Sci, DrChem, 59. *Hon Degrees:* Ministry Higher Educ, USSR, prof chem, 60. *Prof Exp:* From asst prof to assoc prof phys chem, Kiev State Univ, 37-41; assoc prof phys chem & colloid chem, Technol Inst Light Indust, Kiev, USSR, 45-60, prof & chmn dept, 60-74; vis prof chem, Northeastern Univ, 75-77; prof chem eng, Tufts Univ, 75-91. *Concurrent Pos:* Mem acad coun colloid chem, USSR Acad Sci, 60-74; mem acad coun disperse systs stability, Ukrainian SSR Acad Sci, 64-74; chmn, Precipitation & Crystallization Sect, USSR Mendeleyev Chem Soc, 71-75; consult, Polaroid Corp, 76-87 & Drew Chem Corp, 77-80; lectr, Ctr Prof Advan, 79-88. *Mem:* Am Chem Soc. *Res:* Disperse systems stability; adsorption from solution; surfactants and their micelle formation in solution; surface forces in disperse systems; stabilization of coal-oil slurries; over 110 publications. *Mailing Add:* 1788 Beacon St Apt 3A Brookline MA 02146

GLEASON, ANDREW MATTEI, MATHEMATICS. *Current Pos:* From asst prof to prof math, 50-69, Hollis prof math & natural philos, 69-92, EMER HOLLIS PROF MATH & NATURAL PHILOS, HARVARD UNIV, 92- *Personal Data:* b Fresno, Calif, Nov 4, 21; m 59; c 3. *Educ:* Yale Univ, BS, 42. *Hon Degrees:* AM, Harvard Univ, 53. *Honors & Awards:* Cleveland Prize, 52. *Mem:* Nat Acad Sci; Am Math Soc (vpres, 62-63, pres, 81-82); Math Asn Am; Am Acad Arts & Sci; Am Philos Soc. *Res:* Topological groups; Banach algebras. *Mailing Add:* 110 Larchwood Dr Cambridge MA 02138

GLEASON, CLARENCE HENRY, MEDICINAL CHEMISTRY, RESEARCH ADMINISTRATION. *Current Pos:* RETIRED. *Personal Data:* b Montreal, Que, May 19, 22; m 50, Shirley Apple; c Edmund, Monte & Sherry. *Educ:* McGill Univ, BSc, 44, PhD(chem), 47. *Prof Exp:* Lectr, McGill Univ, 44-45; res chemist, Charles E Frosst & Co, 47-62, chief res chemist, 62-69, exec asst to dir res, 69-82, dir res admin & planning, Merck Frosst Labs, 83-87. *Concurrent Pos:* Lectr, Sir George Williams Col, 47-48; dir, Belair Chem Ltd, Can, 64-65. *Mem:* Fel Chem Inst Can; Am Chem Soc; Soc Res Adminr; NY Acad Sci; Can Res Mgt Asn. *Res:* Novel and improved medicinal agents. *Mailing Add:* 7514 Mountbatten Rd Montreal PQ H4W 1J8 Can

GLEASON, EDWARD HINSDALE, JR, EMULSION POLYMERIZATION, PAPER COATINGS. *Current Pos:* RETIRED. *Personal Data:* b North Adams, Mass, May 20, 27; m 50, Virginia Stanley; c Margaret, Jane, Laura & Philip. *Educ:* Northeastern Univ, BS, 53; State Univ NY, PhD(chem), 59. *Prof Exp:* Res chemist, Am Cyanamid Co, 53-56; res chemist, Koppers Co Inc, 59-67, mgr latices res, 67-74; sr proj scientist, Arco/Polymers Inc, 74-80; sci adv, Polysar Latex, 80-88; sr res assoc, BASF Corp, 88-92. *Mem:* Am Chem Soc; Tech Asn Pulp & Paper Indust. *Res:* Polymer chemistry; vinyl polymerization; copolymerization; emulsion polymerization. *Mailing Add:* 5726 Barrington Country Circle 2200 Polymer Dr Ooltewah TN 37363. *E-Mail:* bo___gin@bellsouth.net

GLEASON, GALE R, JR, ENVIRONMENTAL SCIENCE. *Current Pos:* RETIRED. *Personal Data:* b Battle Creek, Mich, Oct 8, 27; m 49; c 4. *Educ:* Cent Mich Univ, BS, 50; Mich State Univ, MS, 51, PhD(fisheries, wildlife), 61. *Prof Exp:* From instr to assoc prof biol, Cent Mich Univ, 54-65; prof biol & chmn dept, Lake Superior State Col, 65-86, chmn, Div Natural Sci, 68-86. *Concurrent Pos:* AEC res fel, 55-57; consult, Mich State Dept Hwy & Transp, 75; proj dir, US Dept Interior Bur Outdoor Recreation, 75-76. *Mem:* Am Soc Limnol & Oceanog. *Res:* Trophodynamics of the St Marys River System, interconnecting waters of Lake Superior and Lake Huron. *Mailing Add:* 3989 Nicolet Rd Sault Ste Marie MI 49783

GLEASON, GEOFFREY, RADIOCHEMISTRY. *Current Pos:* RETIRED. *Personal Data:* b Los Angeles, Calif, Apr 23, 23; m 50, Helen Unger; c Gary Alan & Greta Louise. *Educ:* Univ Southern Calif, BChE, 47. *Prof Exp:* Asst, Am Potash & Chem Co, 48-49; res assoc, Abbott Labs, 49-52, mgr, Oak Ridge Div, 52-58, res scientist, 58-64, sr scientist, Oak Ridge Assoc Univs, 64-79, anal chemist, Oak Ridge Nat Lab, 79-83, anal chemist, Oak Ridge Assoc Univs, 83-87. *Concurrent Pos:* Consult, 87- *Mem:* Am Chem Soc; Sigma Xi. *Res:* Radiochemical separations; analytical chemistry; radiation measurement. *Mailing Add:* 127 Cumberland View Dr Oak Ridge TN 37830. *E-Mail:* jgleason@oxfordnm.usa.com

GLEASON, JAMES GORDON, MECHANICAL ENGINEERING. *Current Pos:* from instr to asst prof mech eng, 40-45, assoc prof mech eng & head aeronaut div, 45-54, PROF MECH & AERONAUT ENG, UNIV ARK, FAYETTEVILLE, 54- *Personal Data:* b Hammondsport, NY, Mar 24, 15; m 40; c 1. *Educ:* Ala Polytech Inst, BS, 38; Univ Ark, MS, 54. *Prof Exp:* Asst instr, Ala Polytech Inst, 37-38, lab technician & instr, 38-40. *Concurrent Pos:* Plant engr, Forrest Park Canning Co, 70; vis res engr, Power Plant Unit,

Boeing Airplane Co, Pratt & Whitney Aircraft & Main Burner Group. *Mem:* Am Soc Eng Educ; Am Soc Mech Engrs; Soc Automotive Engrs; Am Soc Heating, Refrig & Airconditioning Engrs; Nat Soc Prof Engrs. *Res:* Theory of aeronautics; internal combustion engines; aircraft engines; thermodynamics; refrigeration; airconditioning; machine design; compressible fluid flow. *Mailing Add:* 1139 Sunset Dr Fayetteville AR 72701

GLEASON, LARRY NEIL, parasitology; deceased, see previous edition for last biography

GLEASON, RAY EDWARD, BIOSTATISTICS, GENETICS. *Current Pos:* BIOSTATISTICIAN, CLIN RES CTRS, BRIGHAM & WOMEN'S HOSP, 85-, MASS INST TECHNOL, 87- *Personal Data:* b Burlington, Vt, Dec 17, 31; m 64; c 4. *Educ:* Univ Vt, BSc, 54; Univ Mass, MS, 60; Tex A&M Univ, PhD(genetics, statist), 63. *Prof Exp:* Geneticist, Nedlar Farms, Inc, NH, 54-58; trainee, Div Math Biol, Harvard Med Sch & Peter Bent Brigham Hosp, 63-65; res assoc, 69-70, sr investr, Elliott P Joslin Res Lab, Harvard Med Sch & prin assoc med, Med Sch, 70-85. *Concurrent Pos:* Res fel, Elliott P Joslin Res Lab, Harvard Med Sch, 65-68; res assoc, Dartmouth Med Sch, Norris Cotton Cancer Res Ctr, 85-86. *Mem:* Biomet Soc; Boston chap, Am Statist Asn. *Res:* Endocrinology-hypertension, nutrition and biostatistical analysis. *Mailing Add:* 92 Dudley St Medford MA 02155

GLEASON, ROBERT WILLARD, ORGANIC CHEMISTRY. *Current Pos:* From instr to assoc prof, Middlebury Col, 60-72, from actg chmn to chmn dept, 69-77, dean sci, 82-84, chmn, Div Natural Sci, 77-82, dean fac, 84-88, PROF CHEM, MIDDLEBURY COL, 72- *Personal Data:* b Santiago, Chile, Feb 9, 32; US citizen; m 58; c 3. *Educ:* Middlebury Col, BA, 54, MS, 56; Mass Inst Technol, PhD(org chem), 60. *Concurrent Pos:* Vis fac res assoc, Univ Colo, 67-68; vis prof, Univ Cologne, 74-75; C Nuirmiu, VT-EPSCOR, 84- *Mem:* Am Chem Soc; Sigma Xi. *Res:* Oxidation of 1, 1-disubstituted hydrazines; reductions of N-nitrosamines. *Mailing Add:* Dept Chem Middlebury Col Middlebury VT 05753-6000

GLEASON, THOMAS JAMES, ELECTRO-OPTICS, SOLID STATE PHYSICS. *Current Pos:* PRES, GLEASON RES ASSOCS, INC, 82- *Personal Data:* b Louisville, Ky, Sept 23, 41; m 69; c 2. *Educ:* Johns Hopkins Univ, BA, 63, PhD(physics), 68. *Prof Exp:* Res asst low energy nuclear physics, Johns Hopkins Univ, 66-68; physicist basic res, Harry Diamond Labs, US Army, 69-71, res physicist appl physics, 71-74, suprvy physicist, electro-optic systs, 74-77, br chief, 77-80; prog mgr, Syst Planning Corp, 80-82. *Mem:* Am Phys Soc; Sigma Xi. *Res:* Military electro-optic systems; non-linear optical systems; laser devices. *Mailing Add:* 10375 Launcelot Lane Columbia MD 21044

GLEATON, HARRIET ELIZABETH, ANESTHESIOLOGY. *Current Pos:* RETIRED. *Personal Data:* b Altoona, Pa, Aug 25, 37. *Educ:* Temple Univ, MD, 62. *Prof Exp:* Instr anesthesia, Sch Med, Univ Pa, 67-69; asst prof, Pritzker Sch Med, Univ Chicago, 69-71; assoc prof anesthesia, Sch Med, Univ Okla, 71-81, chief anesthesia sect & med dir respiratory ther, Univ Hosp, 71-81; anesthesiologist, Bartlesville Med Part Ctr, 85-92. *Concurrent Pos:* USPHS fel anesthesia res, Sch Med, Univ Pa, 65-67; staff anesthesiologist, Hosp Univ Pa, 67-69; asst attend physician, Michael Reese Hosp & Med Ctr, 69-71, assoc attend physician, 71; consult anesthesia, Vet Admin Hosp, Oklahoma City, 71-81; med dir respiratory ther, Oscar Rose Jr Col, 78-85. *Mailing Add:* 3600 Mountain Rd Bartlesville OK 74003-6905

GLEAVES, EARL WILLIAM, ANIMAL NUTRITION. *Current Pos:* RETIRED. *Personal Data:* b Miami, Okla, Apr 3, 30; m 50; c 3. *Educ:* Okla State Univ, BS, 53, MS, 61, PhD(animal nutrit), 65. *Prof Exp:* Instr poultry nutrit, Okla State Univ, 63-64; form asst prof to prof poultry exten & nutrit, Univ Nebr, Lincoln, 64-91. *Concurrent Pos:* Eval team, Syrian Animal Sci Prog, 78-79; consult, US Feed Grains Coun, Italy, Japan, South Korea, Taiwan & Poland, 82, 85 & 87. *Mem:* Poultry Sci Asn; World Poultry Sci Asn. *Res:* Interrelationships of nutrition and physiology in the domestic fowl. *Mailing Add:* 1318 Scott Lane Miami OK 74354

GLEAVES, JOHN THOMPSON, PHYSICAL CHEMISTRY. *Current Pos:* SR RES CHEMIST, MONSANTO POLYMERS & PETROCHEMICALS, 75- *Personal Data:* b Louisville, Ky, May 2, 46; m 68; c 2. *Educ:* Univ Louisville, BS, 68; Univ Ill, MS, 73, PhD(phys chem), 75. *Mem:* Am Chem Soc. *Res:* Molecular dynamics; application of multiphoton spectroscopic techniques to the study of molecular dynamics; reactions at gas-solid interfaces; infrared and visible chemiluminescence. *Mailing Add:* RR 1 Box 171-A2 Foley MO 63347-9728

GLEBE, BRIAN DOUGLAS, BIOLOGY. *Current Pos:* CONNORS BROTHERS LTD, 93- *Personal Data:* b Kitchener, Ont, Jan 14, 48; m 73; c 3. *Educ:* Univ Guelph, BSc, 71; McGill Univ, PhD(biol), 77. *Prof Exp:* Nat Res Coun fel biol, NAm Salmon Res Lab, 77-78; researcher & fish culturist, 78-85, aquacult coordr, Huntsman Marine Lab, 85-92. *Mem:* Can Soc Zoologists; Am Fisheries Soc. *Res:* Salmon ecology, genetics and aquaculture. *Mailing Add:* PO Box 511 Shamcook Lake Rd St Andrews NB E0G 2X0 Can. *Fax:* 506-529-4774

GLECKMAN, PHILIP LANDON, SOLID STATE LASERS, SOLAR ENERGY. *Current Pos:* DIR RES, TIR TECH INC, 93- *Personal Data:* b Boston, Mass, Nov 16, 61; m 87. *Educ:* Mass Inst Technol, BS, 84; Univ Chicago, MS, 86, PhD(physics), 88. *Prof Exp:* Res asst, Enrico Fermi Inst, Univ Chicago, 85-88, res assoc, 88-90. *Concurrent Pos:* Consult, Philips Corp, 87-88. *Mem:* Optical Soc Am; Sigma Xi. *Res:* Novel concepts in optical design called nonimaging optics to establish a record high concentration of sunlight. *Mailing Add:* 21 Miners Trail Irvine CA 92620

GLEDHILL, BARTON L, VETERINARY MEDICINE, CYTOLOGY. *Current Pos:* ADJ INSTR, CTR SCI EXCELLENCE, CONTRA COSTA COL, 96- *Personal Data:* b Philadelphia, Pa, Sept 29, 36; m 59, Marianne Palmer; c Christopher & Rebecca. *Educ:* Pa State Univ, BS, 58; Univ Pa, VMD, 61; FRVCS, Royal Vet Col Sweden, 62, PhD(vet reproduction), 66; Am Col Theriogenologists, dipl, 73. *Honors & Awards:* Ortho lectr, Mc Master Univ, 84; Tap lectr, Am Fertil Soc, 90. *Prof Exp:* Am Vet Med Res Trust res fel, 61-64; NIH fel, 64-66; from asst prof to assoc prof reproduction, Sch Vet Med, Univ Pa, 69-72; sr staff scientist, Lawrence Livermore Nat Lab, Univ Calif, 73-80, dep div leader, Biomed Sci Div, 80-82, div leader, 82-91, dep assoc dir, Biol & Biotechnol Prog, 91-96. *Concurrent Pos:* Docent, Royal Vet Col Sweden, 66-; NIH spec fel, 68-70; ad hoc mem, Study Sect, NIH, 85- & Study Sect Rev Bd, USDA, 86-; consult, Cytogam, 88-90. *Mem:* Am Vet Med Asn; Soc Study Reproduction; Am Col Theriogenology (pres, 75-76); Environ Mutagen Soc; Soc Anal Cytol (pres, 91-93). *Res:* Male gametogenesis and fertilization; DNA adduct detection; gender preselection; accelerator mass spectrometry; Health Care Technology. *Mailing Add:* Biol & Biotechnol Res Prog L-452 Lawrence Livermore Nat Lab Univ Calif Livermore CA 94550. *E-Mail:* gledhill1@llnl.gov

GLEDHILL, ROBERT HAMOR, POULTRY NUTRITION, MANAGEMENT. *Current Pos:* RETIRED. *Personal Data:* b South Kingstown, RI, Feb 2, 31; m 54; c 3. *Educ:* Univ RI, BS, 52, MS, 54; Purdue Univ, PhD(poultry nutrit), 57. *Prof Exp:* Nutritionist, Archer-Daniels-Midland Co, 57-60; res assoc, Corn Prod Co, 60-61; res nutritionist, Hales & Hunter Co, Ill, 61-66; sr poultry nutritionist, Cent Soya Co, Inc, 66-89. *Mem:* Poultry Sci Asn. *Res:* Nutritional research on broilers, replacement birds, layers and turkeys. *Mailing Add:* 140 W Beech Dr Decatur IN 46733

GLEDHILL, RONALD JAMES, CHEMISTRY OF COLOR PHOTOGRAPHY, INFORMATION SCIENCE. *Current Pos:* RETIRED. *Personal Data:* b Cleveland, Ohio, Nov 23, 14; m 42, Catherine Connery; c George H, Robert H, Anthony C & Mary J (Chmielewski). *Educ:* Ohio State Univ, BA, 39; Univ Minn, PhD(phys chem), 46. *Prof Exp:* Asst chem, Univ Minn, 39-43; res chemist, Eastman Kodak Co, 46-67, res assoc, 67-76. *Mem:* Assoc mem Am Chem Soc. *Res:* Color and constitution of dyes; color photography research; particle-size measurement; technical information retrieval systems. *Mailing Add:* 2 Gibson St Apt 401 North East PA 16428-1058

GLEDHILL, WILLIAM EMERSON, MICROBIOLOGY, BIOCHEMISTRY. *Current Pos:* sci fel, 70-90, CONSULT ENVIRON SCI, MONSANTO CO, 90- *Personal Data:* b Baltimore, Md, Aug 1, 41; c 2. *Educ:* Univ Del, BA, 63, MS, 66; Pa State Univ, PhD(microbiol, biochem), 69. *Prof Exp:* Res microbiologist, Tenneco Chem, Inc, 69-70. *Mem:* Am Soc Microbiol; Soc Indust Microbiol; Soc Environ Toxic Chem; Soap & Detergent Asn; Chem Mfg Asn. *Res:* Microbial physiology and ecology; industrial application of novel microorganisms; environmental impact of synthetic organic chemicals; environmental sciences. *Mailing Add:* 1809 Crystal Pt Columbia MO 65203

GLEESON, AUSTIN M, ELEMENTARY PARTICLE PHYSICS. *Current Pos:* from asst prof to assoc prof, 69-77, PROF PHYSICS, UNIV TEX AUSTIN, 77- *Personal Data:* b Philadelphia, Pa, Apr 5, 38; m 60; c 2. *Educ:* Drexel Inst, BSc, 60; Univ Pa, MSc, 63, PhD(physics), 65. *Prof Exp:* Comput designer, Radio Corp Am, 56-58 & 60-62; tech rep, Burroughs Corp, 58-59; instr physics, Drexel Inst, 59-60 & 62-63; res asst, Univ Pa, 63-65; res assoc, Syracuse Univ, 65-67, asst prof, 67-69. *Concurrent Pos:* Assoc dean, Col Nat Sci, 80-85. *Mem:* Am Inst Physics. *Res:* Strong interaction elementary particle phenomenology. *Mailing Add:* Dept Physics Univ Tex Austin TX 78712. *E-Mail:* gleeson@utaphy.ph.utexas.edu

GLEESON, JAMES NEWMAN, PHYSICAL ORGANIC CHEMISTRY, POLYMER CHEMISTRY. *Current Pos:* Res chemist polymer chem, 68-77, RES CHEMIST PHYS ORG & POLYMER CHEM, AMOCO CHEM CORP, STAND OIL CO, IND, 77- *Personal Data:* b Louisville, Ky, Mar 30, 40; m 74. *Educ:* Bellarmine Col, AB, 62; Xavier Univ, MS, 64; Univ Cincinnati, PhD(phys org chem), 69. *Mem:* Am Chem Soc; Soc Advan Mat & Process Eng. *Res:* Advanced structural materials; non-biological solar photochemistry; technology forecasting; research planning. *Mailing Add:* 2441 Trilium Lane Naperville IL 60540

GLEESON, RICHARD ALAN, CHEMORECEPTION. *Current Pos:* RES SCIENTIST, WHITNEY LAB, UNIV FLA, 83- *Personal Data:* b Pittsburgh, Pa, Sept 26, 47; m 69; c 1. *Educ:* Franklin & Marshall Col, BA, 69; Pa State Univ, MS, 72; Col William & Mary, PhD(marine sci), 78. *Prof Exp:* Postdoctoral fel, Monell Chem Senses Ctr, 78-80, asst mem, 80-83. *Concurrent Pos:* Vis asst prof, Dept Zool, Univ Fla, 80-81. *Mem:* Am Soc Zoologists; Soc Neurosci; Asn Chemoreception Sci. *Res:* Chemosensory neurobiology and behavior of aquatic organisms, particularly crustaceans; pheromonal communication systems; morphology, neurophysiology and biochemistry/cytochemistry of chemoreceptors. *Mailing Add:* Whitney Lab Univ Fla 9505 Ocean Shore Blvd St Augustine FL 32086-8623. *Fax:* 904-461-4008; *E-Mail:* rglee@nervm.nerdc.ufl.edu

GLEESON, THOMAS ALEXANDER, METEOROLOGY. *Current Pos:* From asst prof to assoc prof, 49-59, PROF METEOROL, FLA STATE UNIV, 59- *Personal Data:* b New York, NY, Aug 11, 20; m 42; c 2. *Educ:* Harvard Univ, BS, 46; NY Univ, MS, 47, PhD(meteorol), 50. *Concurrent Pos:* State climatologist, Florida, 84- *Mem:* AAAS; fel Am Meteorol Soc; Am Geophys Union. *Res:* General meteorology and climatology; probability and statistical relations in meteorology. *Mailing Add:* Fla State Univ/Meterol Tallahassee FL 32306

GLEGHORN, G(EORGE) J(AY), (JR), ELECTRICAL ENGINEERING, APPLIED MATHEMATICS. *Current Pos:* RETIRED. *Personal Data:* b San Francisco, Calif, May 27, 27; m 48; c 3. *Educ:* Univ Colo, BS, 47; Calif Inst Technol, MS, 48, PhD(elec eng), 55. *Prof Exp:* Mem tech staff, TRW Space Technol Labs, 54-59, head, Control Dept, 58-60, head launch opers, Pioneer I & V, Explorer VI Satellites, 59-60, prog dir, Able 5 Lunar Probe Satellite, 60-61, prog dir, Orbit Geophys Observ, 61-65, asst dir opers, Space Systs Prog Mgt, 65-66, mgr spacecraft opers, Space Vehicles Div, 66-70, mgr, Defense Space Systs Opers, 70-73, asst gen mgr eng, Space Syst Div, TRW Defense & Space Systs Group, 74-81, vpres & chief engr, TRW Space & Technol Group, 81-91. *Concurrent Pos:* Mem, Nat Weather Serv Modernization Comt, Nat Res Coun, 91- *Mem:* Fel Am Inst Aeronaut & Astronaut; Inst Elec & Electronics Engrs; Sci Res Soc Am; Sigma Xi; Nat Acad Eng; Asn Comput Mach. *Res:* Control system and digital computer analysis and engineering; spacecraft and ballistic missile system engineering; orbital debris studies. *Mailing Add:* 28850 Crestridge Rd Rancho Palos Verdes CA 90275-5063

GLEICH, CAROL S, HEALTH SCIENCES EDUCATION. *Current Pos:* health educ specialist, 77-88, chief, Res Develop Sect, 88-90, CHIEF, SPEC PROJ & DATA ANAL BR, DIV MED & EXEC SECY COUN GRAD MED ED, BUR HEALTH PROFESSIONS, HEALTH RESOURCES & SERV ADMIN, HEALTH & HUMAN SERV, 90- *Personal Data:* b Kewanee, Ill, Jan 18, 35. *Educ:* Univ Iowa, BA, 58, MS, 67, PhD(health sci educ), 72. *Prof Exp:* From instr to asst prof path, Col Med, Univ Iowa, 71-77, dir med technol prog, 72-77. *Concurrent Pos:* Adj assoc prof, Dept Path, Sch Med, Univ Md, 80-90; assoc ed, Am J Allied Health. *Mem:* Am Soc Clin Path; Am Soc Allied Health Prof; Am Soc Clin Lab Sci; Nat Coun Int Health. *Res:* Clinical laboratory manpower and allied health; international consulting on health professions manpower and allied health education; physician manpower, medical education and physician credentialing. *Mailing Add:* 14800 Rocking Spring Dr Rockville MD 20853

GLEICH, GERALD J, IMMUNOLOGY, INTERNAL MEDICINE. *Current Pos:* from instr to asst prof med & microbiol, Mayo Med Sch, Univ Minn, 65-73, assoc prof med, microbiol & immunol, Mayo Grad Sch Med, 73-77, prof med & immunol, 77-82, chmn, Dept Immunol, 82-90, PROF IMMUNOL & MED, MAYO MED SCH, UNIV MINN, 82- *Personal Data:* b Escanaba, Mich, May 14, 31; m 56, 76; c 7. *Educ:* Univ Mich, BA, 53, MD, 56; Am Bd Internal Med, dipl, 65; Am Bd Allergy, dipl, 66. *Prof Exp:* Intern, Philadelphia Gen Hosp, Pa, 56-57; resident internal med, Jackson Mem Hosp, Miami, Fla, 59-61; trainee allergy & immunol, Med Ctr, Univ Rochester, 61-63, instr med & microbiol, Sch Med & Dent, 63-65. *Concurrent Pos:* Consult, Methodist Hosp & St Mary's Hosp, Rochester, Minn, 65-; NIH res grants, 66-; bd sci counrs, Nat Int Allergy & Infectious Dis, 81-83. *Mem:* Am Acad Allergy; Am Fedn Clin Res; Am Asn Immunol; fel Am Col Physicians; Am Soc Clin Invest. *Res:* Antibody formation; hypersensitivity; eosinophils. *Mailing Add:* 401-A Guggenheim Bldg Rochester MN 55905. *Fax:* 507-284-1086; *E-Mail:* gleich@mayo.edu

GLEICHER, GERALD JAY, ORGANIC CHEMISTRY. *Current Pos:* RETIRED. *Personal Data:* b Brooklyn, NY, Jan 31, 39; m 66; c 3. *Educ:* Brooklyn Col, BS, 59; Univ Mich, MS, 61, PhD(chem), 63. *Prof Exp:* Instr chem, Univ Mich, 63; res assoc, Univ Tex, 64-65 & Princeton Univ, 65-66; from asst prof to prof chem, Ore State Univ, 66-96. *Mem:* Am Chem Soc; Royal Soc Chem. *Res:* Free radical reaction mechanisms; quantum chemistry; linear free energy relationships; steric effects. *Mailing Add:* 3713 NW Camas Pl Corvallis OR 97330

GLEIM, CLYDE EDGAR, ORGANIC CHEMISTRY, OPERATIONS RESEARCH. *Current Pos:* CONSULT 78- *Personal Data:* b Wheelersburg, Ohio, July 22, 13; m 49; c 3. *Educ:* Ohio Univ, BS, 35; Ohio State Univ, MS, 38; Pa State Univ, PhD(org chem), 41. *Prof Exp:* Asst inorg chem, Ohio Univ, 35; asst shift chemist, Sharple Solvents Co, Mich, 35-36, res chemist, 36; asst Ohio State Univ, 37-38 & Pa State Univ, 39-41; from res chemist to sr res chemist, Goodyear Tire & Rubber Co, 41-58, head plastics polymerization sect, 58-65 & polymer characterization & specialty polymers sect, 65-67, info analyst, Polyester Div, Fiber Tech Ctr, 67-78. *Concurrent Pos:* Instr night col, Univ Akron, 48-50. *Mem:* Am Chem Soc. *Res:* Amyl naphthalenes and amines; pure hydrocarbons; urethans and derivatives; vinyl, allyl, urea-formaldehyde and phenolformaldehyde resins and rubber adhesives; molding and laminating resins; high molecular weight addition and condensation polymers; mostly saturated polyester polymers and copolymers. *Mailing Add:* 2501 Kensington Rd Akron OH 44333-2056

GLEIM, PAUL STANLEY, SOLID STATE CHEMISTRY, SEMICONDUCTORS. *Current Pos:* CONSULT, SEMICONDUCTOR INDUST, 82- *Personal Data:* b Wheelersburg, Ohio, Dec 20, 23; m 50; c 2. *Educ:* Ohio Univ, BS, 49. *Prof Exp:* Chemist, Res Div, Armco Steel Corp, 51-57; engr, Semiconductor Components Div, Tex Instruments Inc, 57-59, group leader, Germanium Develop Dept, 59-62 & Semiconductor Res & Develop Lab, 62-69, mgr advan prod, Chem Mat Div, 69-72, mgr eng silicon mat, 73-77, mgr eng, Gadolinium Gallium Garnet Components Group, 77-81. *Mem:* Electrochem Soc. *Res:* Semiconductor crystal growth; vapor phase deposition of semiconductors and insulators; processing of semiconductors, especially technology of cutting, lapping, mechanical and chemical polishing; semiconductor fabrication; engineering and manufacturing of advanced silicon materials systems for integrated circuits; processing of gadolinium gallium garnet, especially technology of slicing, lapping, edge beveling, stress relieving and polishing for magnetic bubble memories. *Mailing Add:* Eight Cumberland Pl Richardson TX 75080

GLEIM, ROBERT DAVID, BIO-ORGANIC CHEMISTRY. *Current Pos:* RES CHEMIST, CORP NEW VENTURES, ROHM & HAAS CO, 77- *Personal Data:* b Philadelphia, Pa, Nov 11, 46; m 70. *Educ:* Elizabethtown Col, BS, 68; Brown Univ, PhD(org chem), 73. *Prof Exp:* Fel chem, Case Western Reserve Univ, 74-75; fel pharm, Univ Wis-Madison, 75-77. *Mem:* Am Chem Soc; AAAS; Sigma Xi. *Res:* Application of synthetic techniques to the total synthesis of natural products development of electrically conductive polymers (polyacetylene) with improved stability and enhanced transport properties particularly adriamycin, pre-prostaglandin endoperoxide and bicyclic alkaloids. *Mailing Add:* 1986 Street Rd New Hope PA 18938

GLEISER, CHESTER ALEXANDER, VETERINARY & COMPARATIVE PATHOLOGY. *Current Pos:* PROF PATH & VET PATHOLOGIST, DEPT PATH, UNIV TEX HEALTH SCI CTR, 80- *Educ:* Univ Pa, VMD, 40. *Mailing Add:* 5403 Lancashire San Antonio TX 78230-4121

GLEISER, MARCELO, COSMOLOGY & PARTICLE PHYSICS, STATISTICAL PHYSICS & PHASE TRANSITIONS. *Current Pos:* asst prof, 91-95, ASSOC PROF PHYSICS & ASTRON, DARTMOUTH COL, 95- *Personal Data:* b Rio de Janeiro, Brazil, Mar 19, 59; c Andrew P, Eric I & Tali S. *Educ:* Cath Univ Rio, BSc, 81; Fed Univ Rio, MSc, 82; Univ London, PhD(physics), 86. *Prof Exp:* Res scientist, Fermi Nat Accelerator Lab, 86-88, Inst Theoret Physics, Univ Calif, 88-91. *Concurrent Pos:* Prin investr, NSF, 92-95 & 94-, NASA, 95-97; vis scientist, Univ Calif, Santa Barbara, 92, Fermi Nat Accelerator Lab, 95; co-prin investr, NATO, 94-96; Presidential fac fel award, White House/NSF, 94. *Mem:* Am Phys Soc; AAAS. *Res:* Interface between cosmology and high energy physics; gravitational wave astronomy; nonequilibrium statistical mechanics; numerical and analytical studies of complex nonlinear systems; cosmology and condensed matter physics. *Mailing Add:* Dept Physics Dartmouth Col Hanover NH 03755. *Fax:* 603-646-1446

GLEISSNER, GENE HEIDEN, COMPUTER APPLICATION, SYSTEMS DEVELOPMENT. *Current Pos:* PRES, GLEISSNER ASSOCS, 87- *Personal Data:* b Brooklyn, NY, Feb 1, 28; m 67, Clare Lovitz. *Educ:* Columbia Univ, AB, 47, MA, 48. *Prof Exp:* Lectr math, Columbia Univ, 48-50; dep head programming & coding br, US Naval Weapons Lab, 50-54, head comput div, 55-63, asst dir comput, Comput & Analysis Lab, 63-65, assoc tech dir comput, Math & Logistics, David Taylor Naval Ship Res & Develop Ctr, 65-86, spec asst to dir, Navy Labs Interlab Comput, 74-86; vpres, Integrated Microcomput Systs, Inc, 86-87. *Mem:* Math Asn Am. *Res:* Computer and information systems technology and applications; development and management of computer networks; logistics systems analysis; office automation; systems design; research and development management. *Mailing Add:* 10532 Farnham Dr Bethesda MD 20814-2222

GLEITER, MELVIN EARL, BIOCHEMISTRY, ENVIRONMENTAL CHEMISTRY. *Current Pos:* from asst prof to assoc prof chem, 64-72, PROF CHEM, UNIV WIS-EAU CLAIRE, 72-, CHMN DEPT, 88- *Personal Data:* b Alma, Wis, June 9, 26; m 55; c 2. *Educ:* Wartburg Col, BA, 51; Purdue Univ, MS, 56, PhD(biochem), 58. *Prof Exp:* Sr res biochemist, Monsanto Co, 58-64. *Mem:* Am Chem Soc; AAAS; Sigma Xi. *Res:* Effects of pesticides on environment; air and water pollution analysis; energy and environmental effects; nature conservancy. *Mailing Add:* 2816 Irene Dr Eau Claire WI 54701-6691

GLEMBOTSKI, CHRISTOPHER CHARLES, ENZYMOLOGY, TISSUE CULTURE. *Current Pos:* PROF BIOL, SAN DIEGO STATE UNIV, 86- *Personal Data:* b Sommerville, NJ, Dec 13, 52; m 76. *Educ:* Calif Polyteech State Univ, San Luis Obispo, BS, 73; Univ Calif, Los Angeles, PhD(biochem), 79. *Prof Exp:* Instr biochem & physiol, Univ Colo Med Sch, 80-83; asst prof, pharmacol, Univ Pa Sch Med, 83-86. *Concurrent Pos:* Res fel, Univ Colo Med Sch, 79-83. *Mem:* Sigma Xi; NY Acad Sci. *Res:* Post-translational processing of pro-adrenocorticotropic hormone/endorphin in the pituitary. *Mailing Add:* Dept Biol San Diego State Univ 5500 Campanile Dr San Diego CA 92182-4601. *Fax:* 619-594-6200

GLENDE, ERIC A, JR, TOXICOLOGY. *Current Pos:* Res assoc path, 66-67, physiol, 67-68, asst prof, 68-75, ASSOC PROF PHYSIOL, SCH MED, CASE WESTERN RES UNIV, 75- *Personal Data:* b Fergus Falls, Minn, Nov 12, 38; m 69, 79, Nancy Baker; c Scott, Laura, Eric & Carl. *Educ:* Concordia Col, Moorhead, Minn, BA, 60; Univ NDak, MS, 62, PhD(biochem), 66. *Mem:* Am Physiol Soc; Oxygen Soc. *Res:* Toxic and nutritional liver injury. *Mailing Add:* Dept Physiol Sch Med Case Western Res Univ 2119 Abington Rd Cleveland OH 44106

GLENDENING, NORMAN WILLARD, applied chemistry, surface coatings; deceased, see previous edition for last biography

GLENDENNING, KAREN K, NEUROANATOMY, AUDITORY SYSTEM. *Current Pos:* from asst prof to assoc prof, 74-90, PROF NEUROSCI & PSYCHOL, FLA STATE UNIV, 90- *Personal Data:* b Niagara Falls, NY, Mar 27, 47; c Adam S Kircher. *Educ:* Univ Wash, BS, 67; Ohio State Univ, MA, 69, PhD(physiol psychol), 71. *Honors & Awards:* Fox Found Award, Geraldine Dietz Fox, 93. *Prof Exp:* Postdoctoral res fel, USPHS, 72 & Duke Univ, 72-74. *Concurrent Pos:* Vis prof, Univ Oslo, Norway, 84-85, vis prof physiol, Monash Univ, Clayton, Victoria, Australia, 93. *Mem:* Am Asn Anatomists; Am Asn Mammalogists; Soc Neurosci; Asn Res Otolaryngol. *Res:* Comparative chemical and functional neuroanatomy with emphasis on the hindbrain auditory system. *Mailing Add:* Dept Psychol Fla State Univ Tallahassee FL 32306-1051

GLENDENNING, NORMAN KEITH, THEORETICAL NUCLEAR PHYSICS, THEORETICAL ASTROPHYSICS. *Current Pos:* Physicist, 58-63, head, Nuclear Theory Group, 65-83 & 92-93, chmn div staff comt, 78-90, SR STAFF SCIENTIST, NUCLEAR SCI DIV, LAWRENCE BERKELEY LAB, UNIV CALIF, BERKELEY, 63- *Personal Data:* b Galt, Can, Jan 17, 31; m 63; c 2. *Educ:* McMaster Univ, BSc, 54, MSc, 55; Ind Univ, PhD(physics), 59. *Honors & Awards:* Humboldt Res Award, 94. *Concurrent Pos:* Physicist, Lab Nuclear Physics, Orsay, France, 62-63 & Saclay Nuclear Res Ctr, 62-63; mem, Int Conf Nuclear Struct, Kingston, Ont, 60, Padua, Italy, 62, Gatlinberg, Tenn, 66, Varenna, Italy, 67, Dubna, Russia, 68, Montreal, Que, 69, Argonne, 72, Nashville, 74, Tokyo, Bombay & Calcutta, 77, Hirschegg, Austria, Madison, Wis & Bangalore, India, 78, Roscoff, France, 79, Vancouver, Can, 79, Hirschegg, Austria, 80, 81, 85, 86 & 88, Balaton, Hungary, Fontevraud, France, & Florence, Italy, 83, Darmstadt, WGer & Helsinki, 84, Kyoto, Japan, 87; lectr, Radium Inst, Orsay, France, 62-63; guest prof, Univ Frankfurt, 69, Lab Physique Theorique, France, 67, 73, 76, 79, Univ Pierre & Marie Curie, 80, 81, 83, 85 & 87; chmn, Sci Prog Comt Conf Intermediate Energy Heavy Ion Symp, Berkeley, Calif, 75 & Third Summer Study High Energy Heavy Ion Physics, 76; distinguished alumni lectr, McMaster Univ, 78; Humboldt Res Award, 94. *Mem:* Fel Am Phys Soc. *Res:* Theoretical research in the field of direct nuclear reactions; two-nucleon transfer reactions; microscopic theory of inelastic scattering; nuclear structure; nuclear collisions at relativistic energies; properties and phase transitions in super dense nuclear matter, neutron stars. *Mailing Add:* Lawrence Berkeley Lab Univ Calif Berkeley CA 94720

GLENDINNING, S GAIL, PHYSICS. *Honors & Awards:* Excellence in Plasma Physics Award, Am Phys Soc, 95. *Mailing Add:* 2313 Alice Ct Fremont CA 94539

GLENISTER, BRIAN FREDERICK, PALEOBIOLOGY. *Current Pos:* from asst prof to prof, 59-74, chmn dept, 68-74, A K MILLER PROF GEOL, UNIV IOWA, 74- *Personal Data:* b Albany, Australia, Sept 28, 28; m 56, Anne Marie Treloar; c Alan Edward, Linda Marie & Kathryn Grace. *Educ:* Univ Western Australia, BSc, 49; Univ Melbourne, MSc, 53; Univ Iowa, PhD(geol), 56. *Prof Exp:* Asst, Univ Melbourne, Australia, 50-54 & Univ Iowa, 54-56; sr lectr geol, Univ Western Australia, 56-59. *Mem:* AAAS; Paleont Soc; Soc Econ Paleontologists & Mineralogists; Geol Soc Am; Brit Paleont Asn; Sigma Xi. *Res:* Fossil cephalopods; biostratigraphy. *Mailing Add:* Geol Dept Univ Iowa Iowa City IA 52242-1379. *Fax:* 319-335-1821; *E-Mail:* geology@uiowa.edu

GLENISTER, PAUL ROBSON, FOOD SCIENCE. *Current Pos:* RETIRED. *Personal Data:* b Chicago, Ill, June 18, 18. *Educ:* Chicago Teachers Col, BEd, 39; Univ Chicago, SM, 41, PhD(bot), 43. *Prof Exp:* Teacher biol & bot, Wilson Jr Col, 43-50; researcher, J E Siebel Sons' Co, 50-82. *Mem:* AAAS; Am Soc Brewing Chemists. *Res:* Beer and brewing. *Mailing Add:* 6432 St Calif Ave Chicago IL 60629-2836

GLENN, ALAN HOLTON, INSTRUMENTATION, VALVE NOISE. *Current Pos:* PROD MGR RES & DEVELOP, VALTEK, INC, 75- *Personal Data:* b Brigham City, Utah, May 9, 50; m 74; c 3. *Educ:* Brigham Young Univ, BS, 74, ME, 75, PhD, 87. *Mem:* Assoc mem Am Soc Mech Eng. *Res:* Noise generated in control valves. *Mailing Add:* 650 S Lucerne Dr Salem UT 84653

GLENN, ALFRED HILL, MARINE METEOROLOGY, PHYSICAL OCEANOGRAPHY. *Current Pos:* CONSULT METEOROLOGIST & PRES, A H GLENN & ASSOCS, 46- *Personal Data:* b Yonkers, NY, June 3, 21; m 47. *Educ:* Univ Wis, BS, 42; NY Univ, MA, 43. *Honors & Awards:* Appl Meteorol Award, Am Meteorol Soc, 62; Outstanding Serv to Meteorol Award, Am Meteorol Soc, 71. *Prof Exp:* Jr engr, Holway & Cochrane, Tulsa, 39-41; mem staff, Chicago Bridge & Iron Co, 42; meteorologist, Air Weather Serv, Washington, DC, 45-46. *Concurrent Pos:* Captain, US Army Air Force, 43-45; panel mem oceanog, Res & Develop Bd, 47-48, mem subcomt on oceanog, joint meteorol comt; consult, Am Meteorol Soc. *Mem:* Fel Am Meteorol Soc; fel Royal Meteorol Soc. *Res:* Engineering meteorology and oceanography; hurricane and severe storm forecasting; decision theory applications in meteorological-oceanographic forecasting. *Mailing Add:* New Orleans Lakefront Airport PO Box 26337 New Orleans LA 70126

GLENN, BARBARA PETERSON, RUMINANT NUTRITION. *Current Pos:* RES ANIMAL SCIENTIST, USDA, 82- *Personal Data:* b Lincoln, Nebr; m 75, Donald S; c Kacie & Nathan. *Educ:* Univ Ky, BS, 75, PhD(animal sci), 80. *Prof Exp:* Fac res assoc, Univ Md & USDA, 80-81. *Concurrent Pos:* Secy, Dairy Livestock Comt, Am Soc Animal Sci, 89. *Mem:* Am Soc Animal Sci; Am Dairy Sci Asn; Am Registry Prof Animal Scientists; Coun Agr Sci & Technol. *Res:* Evaluation of nitrogen and carbohydrate utilization by ruminants, specifically dairy cattle; intake, nutrient digestibility and metabolism, rates of passage and nutrient flows to the lower gut have been measured in dairy cattle. *Mailing Add:* Agr Res Serv USDA Bldg 200 Rm 124 Beltsville MD 20705. *Fax:* 301-504-8162; *E-Mail:* bglenn@asrr.arsusda.gov

GLENN, BERTIS LAMON, VETERINARY PATHOLOGY, COMPARATIVE PATHOLOGY. *Current Pos:* From asst prof to assoc prof, 53-67, PROF VET PATH, OKLA STATE UNIV, 67- *Personal Data:* b Duncan, Okla, Sept 9, 22; m 54. *Educ:* Okla State Univ, DVM, 52, MS, 61; Univ Okla, PhD(comp path), 63; Am Col Vet Path, dipl. *Concurrent Pos:* NSF sci fac fel, 61-62; NIH spec fel, 62-63. *Mem:* AAAS; Am Vet Med Asn; NY Acad Sci; Sigma Xi. *Res:* Photosensitivity diseases; liver function; congenital porphyria; genital diseases of the dog caused by hormonal disturbances; cytogenetics of domestic animals. *Mailing Add:* 2020 W Third Ave Stillwater OK 74074

GLENN, EDWARD PERRY, NEW CROPS & AGRONOMIC METHODS TO UTILIZE SALINE WATER SUPPLIES, ELUCIDATE MECHANISM OF SALT TOLERANCE OF HALOPHYTES. *Current Pos:* Rockefeller Found fel, Environ Res Lab, Univ Ariz, 79-81, res assoc, 82-89, assoc res scientist, 89-90, SR RES SCIENTIST & HEAD BIORESOURCES UNIT, ENVIRON RES LAB, UNIV ARIZ, 90-, PROF SOIL, WATER & ENVIRON SCI & PROF WILDLIFE & FISHERIES SCI, 95- *Personal Data:* b Tucson, Ariz, Sept 22, 47; m 69, Sarah Ellis; c Charlotte. *Educ:* Univ Hawaii, BA, 69, MS, 73, PhD(bot), 78. *Mem:* Phycol Soc; AAAS; Am Botan Soc; Am Inst Biol Sci. *Res:* Enhanced food production through development of new crops and agronomic methods; marine agronomy; halophytes; physiology of salt tolerances; greenhouse crops; seaweeds and algae. *Mailing Add:* Environ Res Lab 2601 E Airport Dr Tucson AZ 85706

GLENN, FURMAN EUGENE, ORGANIC POLYMER CHEMISTRY. *Current Pos:* TECHNOL FEL, DUPONT DOWN ELASTOMERS LLE, 92- *Personal Data:* b Gastonia, NC, Nov 3, 44; m 68, Janet Brown; c Furman E Jr, Kevin L & Michael L. *Educ:* NC Col, Durham, BS, 66; Wayne State Univ, PhD(org chem), 73. *Prof Exp:* Res chemist, E I Du Pont de Nemours & Co, Inc, 72-81, area supt, 81-89, sr res assoc, 89-92. *Mem:* Am Chem Soc; Sigma Xi. *Res:* Development and study of nonconventional methods for synthesis of elastomeric block copolymers containing polyurethane segments, development of new methods for control of free radical emulsion polymerizations leading to hydrocarbon synthetic elastomers; study of colloid properties of latices employed in binder and adhesive applications; development of new heat resistant hydrocarbon elastomers; management of diene monomer synthesis and polymerization. *Mailing Add:* 4713 Nottinghamshire Dr Louisville KY 40299. *Fax:* 502-569-2256

GLENN, GEORGE R(EMBERT), SR, CIVIL & GEOTECHNICAL ENGINEERING. *Current Pos:* RETIRED. *Personal Data:* b Anderson, SC, Sept 2, 23; m 44, Virginia Henderson; c 3. *Educ:* Clemson Univ, BCE, 43, MSCE, 57; Southern Baptist Theol Sem, MDiv, 55; Iowa State Univ, PhD, 63. *Prof Exp:* Field engr, Daniel Construct Co, 46-47; resident engr, J E Sirrine Co, 48-50; consult engr, 50-51; instr eng, Speed Sch Sci, Louisville, 51-55; prof eng & head dept, Bluefield Col, 55-57 & Wingate Col, 57-58; asst prof appl sci, Southern Ill Univ, 58-64; asst dean & assoc prof, Col Eng, Rutgers Univ, 64-69, prof civil & environ eng, 70-87, assoc dean, Col Eng, 69-70; vis prof eng, Clemson Univ, 88-90. *Concurrent Pos:* Design engr, 54, 56, 58; with NSF res participation prog, Iowa State Univ, 60, Ford Found grant, 61-63; res civil engr, US Naval Civil Eng Lab, Calif, 64; pres, Am Field Serv, NJ; Mem, Lime-Pozzolan Stabilization Comn, Soils & Geol Div & Physicochem Phenomena In Soils Comn, Transp Res Bd, Nat Res Coun, 80-86 & Stabilization of Soil & Rock with Chem Coun, 87-; on leave, head Civil Eng Technol Dept, Greenville, SC, 80-81. *Mem:* Am Soc Civil Engrs; Am Soc Eng Educ; Sigma Xi; Transp Res Bd. *Res:* Advanced geotechnical engineering; evaluation of soil properties; physico-chemical phenomena in soil stabilization; effect of soil properties upon use as an engineering material in foundations; structures. *Mailing Add:* 7 Drifter Lane Salem SC 29676-4104

GLENN, JAMES FRANCIS, UROLOGY. *Current Pos:* PROF SURG, COL MED, UNIV KY, 87-, CHIEF OF STAFF, 93- *Personal Data:* b Lexington, Ky, May 10, 28; m 48, Gale Morrison; c 4. *Educ:* Univ Rochester, BA, 50; Duke Univ, MD, 53; Nat Bd Med Examrs, dipl, 54; Am Bd Urol, cert, 62; FRCS, 87. *Honors & Awards:* Robert V Day Mem lectr, Western Sect, Am Urol Asn, 69, Hugh Hampton Young Award, 82; William T Belfield lectr, Chicago Urol Soc, 77. *Prof Exp:* Intern gen surg, Peter Bent Brigham Hosp, Boston, 52-54; resident urol surg, Med Ctr, Duke Univ, 56-59, instr, Sch Med, 58-59; asst prof, Yale Univ, 59-61; assoc prof, Bowman Gray Sch Med, 61-63; prof & chief urol, Med Ctr, Duke Univ, 63-80; prof surg & dean, Sch Med, Emory Univ, 80-83; pres, Mt Sinai Sch Med, 83-84, prof urol, 83-87, pres, Med Ctr, Sch Med & Hosp, 83-87. *Concurrent Pos:* Assoc surg, Yale-New Haven Hosp, 59-61; attend urologist, Vet Admin Hosp, W Haven, Conn, 59-61, NC Baptist Hosp, 61-63, Duke Univ Med Ctr, 63-80 & Mt Sinai Hosp, NY, 83-87; consult urologist, Conn State Hosp, 60-61, Vet Admin Med Ctr, Durham, 59-61, Lincoln Hosp, Babies Hosp, Watts Hosp & Durham County Gen Hosp, 63-80, Womack Army Hosp, Ft Bragg, NC, 67-80, Vet Admin Med Ctr, Oteen, NC, 69-80, Atlanta, Ga, 80-83, Bronx, NY, 83-87 & Lexington, Ky, 87-, Comn Handicapped Children, Commonwealth of Ky, 87- & Shriners' Hosp for Crippled Children, Lexington, Ky, 88-; prin investr, Cancer Chemotherapy Prog, NIH, 61-63, Adjuvant Bladder Cancer Study, 64-70; consult, Div Med Sci, Nat Acad Sci-Nat Res Coun, 67-68, mem, Comt Genito-Urinary Syst, 68-71; vis prof, Great Ormond St Hosp for Sick Children & Inst Child Health, Univ London, 72-73; consult, Agency Int Develop, Vietnam Med Sch, AMA, 67-71; consult to surgeon gen, USAF, 75-80; attend surgeon, Emory Univ Hosp, Grady Mem Hosp, Crawford W Long Hosp & Henrietta Egleston Children's Hosp, Atlanta, 80-83 & Univ Ky

Hosp, 87-; dir, Med Care Am Inc, 86-, Nat City Bank, 90-; chmn bd, Cardinal Hill Hosp, Lexington, 88- *Mem:* Am Col Surgeons; Am Acad Pediat; Am Urol Asn; Am Asn Clin Urologists; Soc Pediat Urol; AMA; Am Fedn Clin Res; Int Soc Urol; Am Soc Nephrology; Am Asn Genito-Urinary Surgeons; Am Surg Soc; NY Acad Sci; NY Acad Med; Can Urol Asn; Colombian Urol Soc; German Urol Asn; Pan Am Med Asn; Royal Soc Med; Int Soc Surg; Soc Univ Surgeons; Soc Univ Urologists. *Res:* Adrenal surgery; pediatric urology; genitourinary malignancies. *Mailing Add:* Dept Surg Univ Ky Med Ctr PO Box 1390 Lexington KY 40536-1390. *Fax:* 606-323-1944

GLENN, JEFFREY K, ANALYTICAL BIOCHEMISTRY, FLOW CYTOMETRY. *Current Pos:* sr res scientist, 91-94, PRIN SCIENTIST, ROBERT WOOD JOHNSON PHARMACEUT RES INST, 94- *Personal Data:* b Chicago, Ill, Oct 30, 52; m 87, Sharyn Keith. *Educ:* Northwestern Univ, BA, 74; Univ Wis-Madison, MS, 78, MA 79; Ore Grad Inst Sci & Technol, PhD(biochem), 86. *Prof Exp:* Instr, Ky State Univ, 79-80; fel, Univ Rochester, 85-88; proj leader, DuPont Med Prods, 88-91. *Mem:* Am Chem Soc; AAAS. *Res:* Creation of assays for the detection or quantitation of biological compounds. *Mailing Add:* Ortho Diagnostics Bioanal Develop Dept Robert W Johnson Pharmaceut Res Inst 1001 Rte 202 PO Box 350 Raritan NJ 08869. *Fax:* 908-218-8056

GLENN, JOHN FRAZIER, ELECTROPHYSIOLOGY, STRATEGIC PLANNING. *Current Pos:* US Army, 75-, res psychologist, Hum Eng Lab, 75-79, res psychologist, 80-81, chief, Neurotoxicol Br, Med Res Inst Chem Defense, 81-86, liason officer, Off Asst Surgeon Gen Res & Develop, 87-88, technol staff officer med res, Off Asst Secy Army, 88-89, dep comdr, US Army Res Inst Environ Med, 89-92, staff officer, 86-87, exec asst comdr, med res & develop command, 92-96, DIR MED SYSTS INTEGRATION OFFICE, US ARMY, 96- *Personal Data:* b Dalton, Ga; m 79, Jane M Chisholm; c Michelle R, Ashley G & Amanda C. *Educ:* Univ NC, Chapel Hill, BA, 69; Duke Univ, MA, 70, PhD(biol psychol), 75. *Concurrent Pos:* Adj prof physiol psychol, Antioch Col, 78-79; army lead person, Bd Army Sci & Technol, Nat Res Coun, 89-; chmn, Sci Rev Comt, US Army Res Inst Environ Med, 90-92, Human Subj Res Rev Bd, US Army, 92- *Mem:* Soc Neurosci; NY Acad Sci; AAAS; Brit Brain Res Asn. *Res:* Neurophysiology of taste and hearing, specifically centrifugal control of sensorineural processing; neurotoxicology and experimental therapeutics, including development and application of computerized electroencephalographic methods; cholinergic mechanisms of heat adaption. *Mailing Add:* US Army Med Res & Mat Command Attention: MCMR-MSI 504 Scott St Ft Detrick MD 21702-5012. *E-Mail:* glennj@detrick-emh1.army.mil

GLENN, JOHN HERSCHEL, JR, AERONAUTICS. *Current Pos:* US SEN, OHIO, 75- *Personal Data:* b Cambridge, Ohio, July 18, 21; m 43, Anna M Castor; c Carolyn A & John D. *Educ:* Muskingum Col, BS, 62. *Honors & Awards:* Cong Space Medal Honor, 78. *Prof Exp:* Astronaut, NASA Proj Mercury, 59-65, pilot, Mercury-Atlas 6, 62; vpres corp devel & dir, Royal Crown Cola Co, 66-74. *Concurrent Pos:* Mem, Spec Comt Aging. *Mem:* Soc Exp Test Pilots; hon mem Int Acad Astronaut. *Mailing Add:* US Senate 503 Hart Senate Bldg Washington DC 20510

GLENN, JOSEPH LEONARD, BIOCHEMISTRY. *Current Pos:* From asst prof to assoc prof, 56-66, chmn dept, 75-79, PROF BIOCHEM, ALBANY MED COL, 66- *Personal Data:* b Albany, NY, Jan 20, 29; m 60; c 4. *Educ:* St Lawrence Univ, BS, 50; Syracuse Univ, MS, 52, PhD, 54. *Concurrent Pos:* Nat Heart Inst fel, Enzyme Inst, Univ Wis, 54-56; Lederle Med Fac award, 58-61; USPHS res career develop award, 62-72. *Mem:* Am Soc Biol Chem. *Res:* Cellular metabolism; enzymology. *Mailing Add:* 24 David Ave Troy NY 12180-8443

GLENN, KEVIN CHALLON, BIOLOGY SCIENCE. *Current Pos:* sr res biologist, Monsanto Co, 83-85, res specialist, 85-87, res group leader I, 87-88, assoc sci fel, 88-92, SCI FEL, MONSANTO CO, ST LOUIS, MO, 92-, GROUP LEADER, 95- *Personal Data:* b Albuquerque, NMex, Mar 29, 54; c 2. *Educ:* Calif State Polytech Univ, BS, 75; Univ Calif, Irvine, PhD(biol), 79. *Prof Exp:* Am Heart Asn postdoctoral fel, Univ Wash, Seattle, 79-81; sect leader cell biol, Bethesda Res Labs, Inc, 81-82; staff res scientist, Flow Labs, Inc, Va, 82. *Concurrent Pos:* Adj asst prof, In Vitro Cell Biol & Biotechnol Prog, State Univ NY, Plattsburgh & Miner Inst, Chazy, 87-92; course instr, Molecular Biol Eukaryotic Cells Biotechnol Prog, Univ Col, Washington Univ, St Louis, Mo, 90- *Mem:* Am Heart Asn; Endocrine Soc. *Res:* Discovery of novel therapeutics to treat atherosclerosis and lipid-related risk factors for coronary artery disease. *Mailing Add:* Discovery Res Monsanto Co T2M 800 N Lindbergh Blvd St Louis MO 63167

GLENN, LEWIS ALAN, MECHANICAL ENGINEERING, COMPUTATIONAL PHYSICS. *Current Pos:* physicist, 77-83, assoc div leader theoret & appl mech, Physics Dept, 83-87, SHOCK PHYSICS GROUP LEADER, EARTH SCI DIV, LAWRENCE LIVERMORE NAT LAB, 87- *Personal Data:* b Brooklyn, NY, Nov 17, 36; m 58, Lynn Schneider; c Jeffrey & Stephanie. *Educ:* Polytech Inst NY, BChE, 58; NJ Inst Technol, ME, 61; Univ Southern Calif, PhD(mech eng), 68. *Prof Exp:* Proj engr, US Naval Air Rocket Test Sta, 59-62 & NAm Aviation, Inc, 62-68; staff scientist, Appl Theory, Inc, Los Angeles, 68-71; sr staff scientist, Inst CERAC, Ecublens, Switz, 71-77. *Concurrent Pos:* Consult & fel, NAm Rockwell, 66-68; pres, Glenn Technol Consults. *Mem:* Am Phys Soc; assoc fel Am Inst Aeronaut & Astronaut; Am Acad Mech; Am Geophys Union. *Res:* Continuum mechanics; fracture; dynamic properties of materials. *Mailing Add:* Lawrence Livermore Lab PO Box 808 Livermore CA 94550. *Fax:* 510-423-6907; *E-Mail:* glenn@s54.es.llnl.gov

GLENN, RICHARD A(LLEN), CIVIL ENGINEERING. *Current Pos:* instr eng, Ventura Col, 61-67, dean instr, 67-76, pres col, 76-85, EMER PRES, VENTURA COL, 86- *Personal Data:* b Brooklyn, NY, Mar 16, 25; m 47; c 4. *Educ:* Purdue Univ, BS, 49; Wash Univ, PhD(geol), 53. *Prof Exp:* Geologist & geophysicist, Standard Oil Co, Calif, 53-61. *Mem:* Am Asn Petrol Geol; Sigma Xi. *Res:* Geology and its relationship to the location of economic mineral deposits and to engineering; seismology. *Mailing Add:* 1880 S Rice Rd Ojai CA 93023-3880

GLENN, ROLAND DOUGLAS, CHEMICAL ENGINEERING. *Current Pos:* pres, New York, 72-90, PRES, COMBUSTION PROCESSES INC, DARIEN, CONN, 91- *Personal Data:* b Somerville, Mass; m 39, Eleanor N Greene; c Mary E, Nancy A (Hansen), Sara E (Baker) & Rolene D (Ramsey). *Educ:* Mass Inst Technol, BS & MS. *Prof Exp:* Prod supvr, Union Carbide Corp, South Charleston, WVa, group leader & plant mgr, 53-56, div vpres, New York, 57-68; vpres, Pope, Evans & Robbins, 69-71. *Concurrent Pos:* Sloan fel, Mass Inst Technol; dir, Asn Consult Chemists & Chem Engrs, 74-92; ed, Directory Consult Servs, 78-88. *Mem:* Am Inst Chem Engrs; Am Chem Soc; Asn Consult Chemists & Chem Engrs. *Res:* Chemical engineering. *Mailing Add:* 53 Goodwives River Rd Darien CT 06820-5919

GLENN, ROLLIN COPPER, SOILS. *Current Pos:* chmn dept, 73-77, PROF PLANT SCI, UNIV MAINE, 73- *Personal Data:* b Nov 25, 27; m 53; c 3. *Educ:* Va Polytech Inst & State Univ, BS, 55, MS, 57; Univ Wis, PhD(soils), 59. *Prof Exp:* From asst prof to prof agron, Miss State Univ, 59-73. *Mem:* Am Soc Agron; Soil Sci Soc Am; Soil Conserv Soc Am; Clay Minerals Soc; Int Soc Soil Sci; Sigma Xi. *Res:* Soil chemistry, mineralogy and fertility; soil conservation; turf soils; production agronomy. *Mailing Add:* Poplar Old Town ME 04468

GLENN, WILLIAM GRANT, zoology, for more information see previous edition

GLENN, WILLIAM HENRY, JR, OPTICAL PHYSICS, APPLIED MATHEMATICS. *Current Pos:* CONSULT, 94- *Personal Data:* b Philadelphia, Pa, Dec 22, 37; m 66; c 2. *Educ:* Mass Inst Technol, SB & MS, 60, PhD(physics), 66. *Prof Exp:* Instr physics, Southeastern Mass Tech Inst, 65; sr res scientist, United Technol Res Ctr, 66-68, prin scientist, 68-71, sr prin scientist, 71-90, sr consult scientist, 90-94. *Concurrent Pos:* Lectr, Hartford Grad Ctr, Rensselaer Polytech Inst, 68; assoc ed, Inst Elec & Electronics Engrs J Quantum Electronics, 82-85. *Mem:* Fel Optical Soc Am; Inst Elec & Electronics Engrs. *Res:* Quantum & nonlinear and fiber optics; laser and optical physics; photonics; mathematical modeling. *Mailing Add:* 41 Marjorie Lane Vernon Rockville CT 06066

GLENN, WILLIAM WALLACE LUMPKIN, SURGERY. *Current Pos:* from instr to assoc prof, Sch Med, Yale Univ, 48-61, chief cardiovascular surg, 48-68, chief cardiothoracic surg, 68-75, Charles W Ohse prof surg, 61-85, sr res scientist, 85-87, EMER CHARLES W OHSE PROF SURG, SCH MED, YALE UNIV, 85- *Personal Data:* b Asheville, NC, Aug 12, 14; m 43; c 2. *Educ:* Univ SC, BS, 34; Jefferson Med Col, MD, 38. *Hon Degrees:* MA, Yale Univ, 61, Dr, Univ Cadiz, Spain. *Honors & Awards:* Alton Oschner lectr; Samuel Harvey lectr; George Rosen Mem Award; Gold Heart Award, Am Heart Asn. *Prof Exp:* Intern, Pa Hosp, 38-40; resident surg, Mass Gen Hosp, 40-41; asst physiol, Sch Pub Health, Harvard Univ, 41-43; resident surg, Mass Gen Hosp, 45-46; assoc, Jefferson Med Col, 46-48. *Concurrent Pos:* Pres, Am Heart Asn, 70-71; bd dirs, Charles E Culpepper Found, 78-85; ed, Thoracic & Cardiovasc Surgeon. *Mem:* Am Surg Asn; Am Col Surgeons; AMA; Am Thoracic Asn; Am Soc Artifical Internal Organs. *Res:* Cardiovascular physiology and surgery; physiology of the lymphatics; medical education; cardiothoracic surgery; author or co-author of over 190 publications. *Mailing Add:* 685 Forest Rd West Haven CT 06516

GLENNAN, T(HOMAS) KEITH, education administration, public service; deceased, see previous edition for last biography

GLENNER, GEORGE GEIGER, pathology, alzheimers disease; deceased, see previous edition for last biography

GLENN-LEWIN, DAVID CARL, PLANT ECOLOGY. *Current Pos:* DEAN, FAIRMONT COL LIBERAL ARTS A7 SCI, WICHITA STATE UNIV, 94- *Personal Data:* b Chicago, Ill, Sept 22, 44; m 74, Kathleen; c 3. *Educ:* Knox Col, AB, 65; Cornell Univ, PhD(ecol, evolutionary biol), 72. *Prof Exp:* From asst prof to prof, Iowa State Univ, 72-94, chair bot, 87-90, assoc dean, Col Lib Arts & Sci, 90-91, interim dean, 91-93, spec asst to provost, 93-94. *Concurrent Pos:* Consult, Black & Veatch Eng, 75, 78 & 81; vis prof, York, UK, 80, Utrecht, Neth, 81-82. *Mem:* Ecol Soc Am; Brit Ecol Soc; Int Asn Ecol; Int Assoc Veg Sci. *Res:* Numerical ecology; vegetation science; species diversity and ecosystem structure. *Mailing Add:* Fairmount Col Lib Arts & Sci Campus Box 5 Wichita State Univ Wichita KS 67260-0005. *Fax:* 316-978-3234; *E-Mail:* dglennle@twsuum.uc.twsu.edu

GLESER, LEON JAY, MATHEMATICAL STATISTICS. *Current Pos:* PROF MATH & STATIST, UNIV PITTSBURGH, 89- *Personal Data:* b St Louis, Mo, Dec 17, 39; m 69; c 1. *Educ:* Univ Chicago, BS, 60; Stanford Univ, MS, 62, PhD(statist), 63. *Prof Exp:* Asst prof math statist, Columbia Univ, 63-65; from asst prof to assoc prof statist & biostatist, Johns Hopkins Univ, 65-72; from assoc prof to prof statist, Purdue Univ, 72-89. *Concurrent Pos:* Vis fel, Educ Test Serv, 71-72; assoc ed, J Am Statist Asn, 71-74 & 86- &

Psychometrika, Psychometric Soc, 72-79; vis prof, Sidney Farber Cancer Inst & Sch Pub Health, Harvard Univ, 79-80; vis fac, Nat Bur Stand, 88- *Mem:* Fel Am Statist Asn; fel Inst Math Statist; Psychometric Soc. *Res:* Statistical inference; multivariate statistical analysis; large sample theory; model building and goodness of fit tests; psychometrics; biometrics. *Mailing Add:* Dept Math & Statist Univ Pittsburgh Pittsburgh PA 15260

GLESS, ELMER E, ACAROLOGY. *Current Pos:* asst prof biol, Mont Col Mineral Sci & Technol, 68-70, assoc prof biol sci, 70-72, head dept, 70-88, PROF BIOL SCI, MONT COL MINERAL SCI & TECHNOL, 70- *Personal Data:* b Rogers, Nebr, Feb 3, 28; m 62; c 2. *Educ:* Ariz State Univ, BAEd, 55; Iowa State Univ, MS, 57, PhD(acarology), 68. *Prof Exp:* Med entomologist, USDA, Tex, 58-59 & William Cooper & Nephews, Inc, 59-62; instr biol, Northern Ill Univ, 62-64; field entomologist, Bernice P Bishop Mus, Hawaii, 65-67; res assoc, Iowa State Univ, 67-68. *Mem:* Am Entom Soc; Sigma Xi; Sci Soc. *Res:* Prostigmatid mite biology and taxonomy; water microbiology including bacteria and invertebrate insects. *Mailing Add:* Dept Biol Sci Mont Technol 1300 W Park St Butte MT 59701-8997

GLESS, GEORGE E, ELECTRICAL ENGINEERING, ELECTRIC VEHICLES. *Current Pos:* from instr to assoc prof, 46-64, in charge hybrid comput facil, 66-69, prof, 64-, EMER PROF ELEC ENG, UNIV COLO, BOULDER. *Personal Data:* b Schuyler, Nebr, Jan 15, 17; m 40; c 2. *Educ:* Univ Colo, BS, 40, MS, 48; Iowa State Univ, PhD(elec eng), 63. *Prof Exp:* Student engr, Commonwealth Edison Co, Ill, 40-41, electronic & control engr, 41-46. *Concurrent Pos:* Consult, Elec Vehicle. *Mem:* Am Soc Eng Educ; Inst Elec & Electronics Engrs. *Res:* Computers and control systems; electric vehicles. *Mailing Add:* 2940 13th St Boulder CO 80304

GLESSNER, ALFRED JOSEPH, TECHNOLOGY TRANSFER LICENSING. *Current Pos:* DIR, CTR TECHNOL TRANSFER, UNIV PA, 91- *Personal Data:* b Chester, Pa, Jan 19, 43; m 66, Patricia Smith; c Elizabeth & Matthew. *Educ:* Villanova Univ, BChE, 64; Univ Pa, MS, 67, PhD(chem eng), 69. *Prof Exp:* Res engr, Res & Develop, Sun Oil Co, 69-77, mgr bus develop, Sun Tech, 77-83; dir, Admin & Regulatory Affairs, Adamantech, 84-89. *Mem:* Am Inst Chem Engrs; Am Chem Soc; Licensing Exec Soc; Asn Univ Technol Managers. *Res:* Physical adsorption; thermodynamics; statistical mechanics; molecular sieves; separation processes; solid-liquid phase equilibrium; petroleum refining processes; catalytic reforming; catalytic cracking. *Mailing Add:* 16 Hawthorne Lane Glen Mills PA 19342-1316

GLETSOS, CONSTANTINE, ORGANIC CHEMISTRY, MEDICINAL CHEMISTRY. *Current Pos:* PRIN SCIENTIST ORG CHEM, AM HOME PROD CORP, 68- *Personal Data:* b Stylis, Greece, Aug 5, 34; m 67, Helen D Kerr; c Evangelos R, Rizos W, Vasilios P & Elly H. *Educ:* Nat Univ Athens, dipl chem, 58; Univ BC, MSc, 65, PhD(org chem), 68. *Prof Exp:* Res chemist, Gen Develop Co, Greece, 61-63; anal chemist, Gen Govt Chem Labs, Greece, 63. *Concurrent Pos:* Lab asst, Chropei Co, 57-58; lab dir & instr, Army, 59-61; teaching asst, Univ BC, 63-68; grants, Nat Cancer Inst, Can, 63, Nat Res Coun Can, 65 & Med Res Coun, 68. *Mem:* Can Inst Chemists; Am Chem Soc. *Res:* Isolation of diphosphopyridine nucleotide; steroids; alkaloids; terpenoids; penicillins; cephalosporins; peptides; heterocyclic drugs and intermediates; macrolides. *Mailing Add:* Wyeth Ayerst Labs Chem Develop Dept 401 N Middletown Rd Pearl River NY 10965. *Fax:* 914-732-5560; *E-Mail:* gletsoc@war.wyeth.com

GLEW, DAVID NEVILLE, PHYSICAL CHEMISTRY. *Current Pos:* RETIRED. *Personal Data:* b Stamford, Eng, Sept 27, 28; m 52; c 4. *Educ:* Cambridge Univ, BA, 49, PhD, 52. *Prof Exp:* Fel, Nat Res Coun Can, Ottawa, 52-54; AEC contract with Prof J H Hildebrand, Univ Calif, 54-55; sr lectr chem & dept head,Univ Natal, Durban, SAfrica, 55-57; res chemist, Dow Chem Can, Inc, 57-61, assoc scientist, 61-67, res scientist, 67-91. *Mem:* Royal Soc Chem; fel Chem Inst Can. *Res:* Water and aqueous solution structure, properties and H-bonding; reaction kinetics; thermodynamics and phase equilibria of aqueous systems; materials science and thermoplastic composites. *Mailing Add:* 536 Highbury Park Sarnia ON N7V 2J9 Can

GLEWWE, CARL W(ILLIAM), ALTERNATIVE ENERGY, COMPUTER SCIENCES. *Current Pos:* OWNER & VPRES, LYNN SERVS, INC, 86- *Personal Data:* b St Paul, Minn, May 1, 27; m 53; c 3. *Educ:* Univ Minn, BS, 50, MS, 55, PhD(elec eng), 58. *Prof Exp:* Instr elec eng, Univ Minn, 53-58; syst design engr digital comput, Univac Div, Sperry Rand Corp, 58-61, mgr 61-69, group mgr digital comput, 69-79, dir prog mgt, Mid-Am Solar Energy Ctr, 79-81; vpres eng, Burdick Corp, 82-83; dir eng, Sentech Med Corp, 84-85. *Concurrent Pos:* Sr engr, Gen Mills, Inc, 57-58; dir res, Minn Energy Agency, 77-78. *Mem:* Inst Elec & Electronics Engrs. *Res:* Computer design; alternative energy sources. *Mailing Add:* 2886 Sibley Hills Dr St Paul MN 55121

GLEYSTEEN, JOHN JACOB, SURGERY, GASTROINTESTINAL PHYSIOLOGY. *Current Pos:* ASSOC PROF SURG, UNIV ALA, BIRMINGHAM, 87- *Personal Data:* b Sioux City, Iowa, Jan 3, 41; m 71; c 2. *Educ:* Grinnell Col, BA, 63; Univ Iowa, MD, 67; Am Bd Surg, cert, 76 & 86. *Prof Exp:* Resident gen surg, Univ Ala Med Ctr, Birmingham, 70-75; staff physician surg serv, 75-80, asst chief surg, 80-87, CHIEF SURG, VET ADMIN MED CTR, 87- *Concurrent Pos:* Asst prof surg, Med Col Wis, 75-87. *Mem:* Asn Acad Surg; Am Col Surgeons; Am Gastroenterol Asn; Soc Surg Alimentary Tract. *Res:* Gastrointestinal physiology; gastric motility and emptying; portal hypertension. *Mailing Add:* Va Med Ctr 700 S 19th St Birmingham AL 35233-1927

GLEZEN, WILLIAM PAUL, INFECTIOUS DISEASES, PEDIATRICS. *Current Pos:* assoc prof, 75-77, PROF MICROBIOL & PEDIAT & EPIDEMIOLOGIST, INFLUENZA RES CTR, DEPT MICROBIOL & IMMUNOL, BAYLOR COL MED, HOUSTON, 77-, HEAD, PREV MED SECT, DEPTS MICROBIOL, IMMUNOL & PEDIAT, 89- *Personal Data:* b Oblong, Ill, Mar 15, 31; m 53, Dorothy; c Laurie & Paul. *Educ:* Purdue Univ, BS, 53; Univ Ill, BS, 54, MD, 56. *Prof Exp:* Instr pediat, Sch Med, Univ NC, 61-62; epidemiologist, Kansas City Field Sta, Commun Dis Ctr, USPHS, 62-64; chief respiratory & enteric virus dis unit, 64-65; Instr, Sch Med, Univ Kans, 63-65; from asst prof to assoc prof pediat, Sch Med, Univ NC, Chapel Hill, 65-75. *Concurrent Pos:* Adj prof epidemiol, Univ Tex Sch Pub Health, 83- *Mem:* Am Pediat Soc; Infectious Dis Soc Am; Am Acad Pediat; Am Epidemiol Soc; Soc Pediat Res; Am Soc Virol. *Res:* Epidemiology and pathogenesis of acute respiratory disease; maternal immunization studies; control of preventable infections with vaccines. *Mailing Add:* Dept Microbiol & Immunol Baylor Col Med One Baylor Plaza Houston TX 77030

GLICK, ARNOLD J, THEORETICAL SOLID STATE PHYSICS. *Current Pos:* from asst prof to assoc prof, 61-78, PROF PHYSICS, UNIV MD, COLLEGE PARK, 78- *Personal Data:* b Brooklyn, NY, Nov 7, 31; m 53, 79; c 3. *Educ:* Brooklyn Col, BA, 55; Univ Md, PhD(physics), 61. *Prof Exp:* NSF fel, Weizmann Inst, 59-61. *Concurrent Pos:* NSF fel, Univ Paris, Orsay & Ctr for Nuclear Study, Saclay, France, 67-68; vis prof, Hebrew Univ, 78 & Weizmann Inst, 81-82; Lady Davis fel, Israel Inst Technol, 78. *Mem:* Am Phys Soc. *Res:* Quantum mechanical many body problem; theory of solids and condensed matter. *Mailing Add:* Dept Physics Univ Md College Park MD 20742

GLICK, BERNARD ROBERT, PHOTOSYNTHESIS, NITROGEN FIXATION. *Current Pos:* assoc prof molecular biol, 82-89, PROF MOLECULAR BIOL & BIOTECHNOL, UNIV WATERLOO, 89- *Personal Data:* b New York, NY, April 9, 45; Can citizen; m 68; c 1. *Educ:* City Col New York, BS, 69; Univ Waterloo, MSc, 72, PhD(chem), 74. *Prof Exp:* Fel molecular biol, Univ Toronto, 74-78; res assoc, Nat Res Coun Can, 78-79; group leader, ENS Bio-Logicals, Inc, 79-82. *Mem:* Am Soc Microbiol; Can Soc Microbiol. *Res:* Regulation of PEP carboxylase gene expression in sorghum bicolor and anabaena variabilis; genetic modification of free living diazotrophs; introduction of cellulase genes, chromosomal integration; development of a two-stage airlift fermenter for recombinant microorganisms. *Mailing Add:* Dept Biol Univ Waterloo Waterloo ON N2L 3G1 Can

GLICK, BRUCE, PHYSIOLOGY, IMMUNOLOGY. *Current Pos:* RETIRED. *Personal Data:* b Pittsburgh, Pa, May 5, 27; m 50; c 3. *Educ:* Rutgers Univ, BSc, 51; Univ Mass, MSc, 53; Ohio State Univ, PhD(genetics, physiol), 55. *Prof Exp:* Asst, Univ Mass, 51-52 & Ohio State Univ, 52-55; from asst to prof poultry immunol & physiol, Miss State Univ, 55-86, coordr animal physiol prog, 73-86, prof immunol & head, Poultry Sci Dept, 86-95. *Concurrent Pos:* Merck res award, 78. *Mem:* Fel AAAS; Am Physiol Soc; Am Asn Immunol; fel Poultry Sci Asn; Am Ornith Union; Reticuloendothelial Soc. *Res:* Physiology of lymphoid tissue, especially bursa of Fabricius; cellular interactions in the chickens immune system; kinetics of the lymphomatoid complex; ruiandendritic cells. *Mailing Add:* 100 S Poplar St Seneca SC 29678. *Fax:* 864-656-1033

GLICK, CHARLES FREY, ANALYTICAL CHEMISTRY. *Current Pos:* RETIRED. *Personal Data:* b Allentown, Pa, Apr 21, 17; m 46, Carolyn V Butz; c David C. *Educ:* Lehigh Univ, BS, 38, MS, 40; Mass Inst Technol, PhD(phys chem), 43. *Prof Exp:* Res chemist, E I du Pont de Nemours & Co, NJ, 43-46; supvr phys res lab, Barrett Div, Allied Chem & Dye Corp,; asst head physics lab, Rohm & Haas Co, 53-56, res technologist, 56-59; sect supvr, Physics & Analytical Chem Div, US Steel Corp, 59-82. *Mem:* Am Chem Soc. *Res:* Chemical physics; instrumental methods of organic and inorganic analysis. *Mailing Add:* HC 80 Box 90 Maysville WV 26833-9704

GLICK, DAVID, ANALYTICAL CHEMISTRY. *Current Pos:* EMER PROF PATH, MED SCH, STANFORD UNIV, 73-, MEM STAFF, CANCER BIOL RES LAB, 78- *Personal Data:* b Homestead, Pa, May 3, 08; m 29, 41, 45, 81; c 4. *Educ:* Univ Pittsburgh, BS, 29, PhD(biochem), 32; Am Bd Clin Chem, dipl, 53. *Hon Degrees:* LLD, Univ Glasgow, 80. *Honors & Awards:* Van Slyke Award, 77; Ames Award, 80; Evans Lectr, 81; Glick Lectr, 84- *Prof Exp:* Asst chem, Univ Pittsburgh, 29-32; Hernsheim fel chem, Mt Sinai Hosp, NY, 32-34; chief chemist, Mt Zion Hosp, San Francisco, 34-36; Rockefeller fel, Carlsberg Lab, Denmark, 36-37; chief chemist, Newark Beth Israel Hosp, 37-42; head vitamin & enzyme res, Russell-Miller Milling Co, Minn, 43-46; from assoc prof to prof physiol chem, Univ Minn, 46-61; prof & head div,histochem, Med Sch, Stanford Univ, 61-73; dir, Ctr Histochem Res, 73-78, STAFF SCIENTIST, SRI INT, 78- *Concurrent Pos:* Vis res chemist, Carlsberg Lab, Denmark, 33; fel, Commonwealth Fund, Carlsberg Lab, Denmark, Inst Cell Res, Stockholm, 49, 58-59 & Zool Sta, Naples, 59; consult, Toxicity Lab, Univ Chicago, 45-46, Vet Admin Hosp, Minneapolis, 46-47, Ft Detrick, 57-67 & Vet Admin Hosp, Palo Alto, 61-89; mem cytochem panel, Comt Growth, Nat Res Coun, 51-55; MacFarlane prof exp med, Univ Glasgow, 70-71; ed, Methods Biochem Analysis, 53-88; co-ed, Tech Biochem & Biophys Morphol, 72-77. *Mem:* Fel AAAS; Am Chem Soc; Soc Exp Biol & Med; Am Soc Biol Chem; hon mem Histochem Soc (vpres, 50, 69, pres, 51, 70); Am Soc Cell Biol; hon mem Royal Danish Acad Sci; hon mem Finnish Histochem Soc; hon assoc Int Fedn Socs Histochem & Cytochem (vpres, 68-72, pres 72-76). *Res:* Histochemistry quantitative techniques and applications; biochemistry, enzymes, vitamins. *Mailing Add:* 680 Junipero Serra Blvd Stanford CA 94305-8444

GLICK, DAVID M, PROTEIN CHEMISTRY, ENZYMOLOGY. *Current Pos:* SR RESEARCHER, HEBREW UNIV, 93- *Personal Data:* b San Francisco, Calif, Jan 4, 36; m 61, Jacqueline Zwirn; c Daniel, Naomi & Noah. *Educ:* Oberlin Col, BA, 57; Case Western Res Univ, PhD(biochem), 62. *Prof Exp:* Res assoc biochem, Weizmann Inst, 62-63, Brookhaven Nat Lab, 64-66; from asst prof to assoc prof, Med Col Wis, 66-90; sr scientist, Makor Chems, Jerusalem, Israel, 90-92. *Concurrent Pos:* Fel, Arthritis & Rheumatism Found, 62-64; res assoc, King's Col, London, 63 & State Univ NY, Buffalo, 64; vis prof, Free Univ Brussels, 73-74; vis assoc prof technion, Haifa, 87. *Mem:* Am Chem Soc; Am Soc Biochem Molecular Biol; Biochem Soc London; Israel Biochem Soc. *Res:* Enzymology and biological action of cholinesterases. *Mailing Add:* Dept Biol Chem Hebrew Univ Jerusalem 91904 Israel. *Fax:* 972-2-652-0258; *E-Mail:* dglick@shum.huji.ac.il

GLICK, FORREST IRVING, LOW TEMPERATURE PHYSICS. *Current Pos:* RETIRED. *Personal Data:* b Glasgow, Mont, May 24, 34; m 58, 64, Marvis Osland; c Arthur, Jennifer & Reginald. *Educ:* St Olaf Col, BA, 56; Univ Minn, MS, 59, PhD(physics), 66. *Prof Exp:* Instr physics, Univ Minn, 63-64; from asst prof to prof physics, Mankato State Univ, 64-93, asst to dean, Sch Physics, Eng & Technol, 85-91. *Mem:* Am Asn Physics Teachers; Am Phys Soc. *Res:* Liquid helium; low temperature physics. *Mailing Add:* 215 Haynes St Mankato MN 56001

GLICK, GERALD, INTERNAL MEDICINE, CARDIOLOGY. *Current Pos:* PROF MED, RUSH PRESBY ST LUKE'S MED CTR, 92- *Personal Data:* b Brooklyn, NY, Apr 3, 34; m 63, Sharon Ringel; c David, Bonnie, Douglas & Caroline. *Educ:* Cornell Univ, AB, 55, MD, 58; Am Bd Internal Med, dipl, 66; Am Bd Cardiovasc Dis, dipl, 68. *Prof Exp:* Intern med, Sch Med, Rochester & Strong Mem Hosp, 58-59, resident, 59-60; sr investr, Cardiol Br, Nat Heart Inst, 62-68; assoc prof pharmacol & med & dir, Div Clin Cardiovasc Pharmacol, Baylor Col Med, 68-71; dir, Cardiovasc Inst, Michael Reese Hosp & Med Ctr, 71-78; prof med, Pritzker Sch Med, Univ Chicago, 74-78, clin prof med, 78-90. *Concurrent Pos:* USPHS fel cardiol, 60-62; Am Heart Asn estab investr, 63-69; attend physician, Nat Heart Inst, 63-68; hon med asst, Postgrad Med Sch & Hammersmith Hosp, London, Eng, 64-65; chief electrocardiog, NIH, 66-68. *Mem:* Fel Am Col Physicians; Am Physiol Soc; fel Am Col Cardiol; Am Soc Clin Invest; Am Soc Pharmacol & Exp Therapeut. *Res:* Clinical cardiology and investigations relating to cardiovascular pharmacology, the autonomic nervous control of the cardiovascular system and the determinants of ventricular function. *Mailing Add:* Rush Presby St Luke's Med Ctr 1725 W Harrison Suite 1159 Chicago IL 60612

GLICK, HAROLD ALAN, BIOPHYSICS. *Current Pos:* MEM STAFF, FLEET ANALYSIS CTR, US NAVY, 80- *Personal Data:* b US citizen. *Educ:* Univ Calif, Los Angeles, BS, 64; Univ Chicago, MS, 66; Univ Calif, Riverside, PhD(physics), 76. *Prof Exp:* Res asst physics, Gen Motors Res Lab, 66; instr, Calif State Univ, San Bernadino, 71; NIH fel, Univ Chicago, 76-77; asst prof, Riverside City Col, 78; asst prof physics, Claremont Men's Col, 78-79. *Mem:* Am Phys Soc; Sigma Xi. *Mailing Add:* PO Box 5000 MS 31B Corona CA 91718

GLICK, J LESLIE, BIOTECHNOLOGY. *Current Pos:* CONSULT, 93- *Personal Data:* b New York, NY, Mar 2, 40; c 2. *Educ:* Columbia Univ, AB, 61, PhD(zool), 64. *Honors & Awards:* John S Newberry Prize. *Prof Exp:* USPHS vis res fel biochem, Princeton Univ, 64-65; sr cancer res scientist, Roswell Park Mem Inst, 65-67, assoc cancer res scientist, 67-69; exec vpres, Assoc Biomedic Systs, Inc, 69-72, pres, 72-75, chmn bd, 72-77; pres, Genex Corp, 77-84, chief exec officer, 77-87, chmn bd, 83-85, pres, 85-87; chief exec off, Bionix Corp, 87-93. *Concurrent Pos:* Asst res prof, Roswell Park Div, State Univ NY Buffalo, 67-68, assoc res prof & chmn, 68-70, mem exec comt, Grad Sch, 68-70; res prof, Canisius Col, 68-70, Niagara Univ, 68-70; pres & chmn bd, HTI Corp, 72-75; vpres, Nat Asn Life Sci Indust, 75-76, dir, 75-77; pres, Inst Sci & Social Accountability, Inc, 75-78; pres & dir, Indust Biotechnol Asn, 81-83, dir, 83-84; overseer, Simon's Rock of Bard Col, 84-85, first chmn bd overseers, 85; mem, Biotechnol Tech Adv Comt, US Dept Com, 85-87, trustee, Nat Fac Humanities, Arts & Sci, 85-87; mem, bd ed adv, Strategic Directions, 84-87 & adv coun, High Technol Mkt Rev, 86-87; adj prof, Grad Sch Technol & Mgt, Univ Col, Univ Md, 88-, mem adv panel, 88-, mem, Grad Coun, 92-94; ed-in-chief, Technol Mgt, 92- *Mem:* Am Physiol Soc; NY Acad Sci; Sigma Xi; Int Asn Mgt Technol. *Res:* Technology assessments pertaining to biotechnology; bioethical problems; evaluation systems on performance of research. *Mailing Add:* 10899 Deborah Dr Potomac MD 20854

GLICK, JANE MILLS, MOLECULAR BIOLOGY. *Current Pos:* from asst prof to assoc prof, 77-90, PROF BIOCHEM, MED COL PA, 90- *Personal Data:* b Memphis, Tenn. Nov 26, 43; m 68, John H; c Katherine A & Sarah S. *Educ:* Randolph-Macon Woman's Col, AB, 65; Columbia Univ, PhD(biochem), 71. *Prof Exp:* NIH fel, Lab Biochem, Nat Cancer Inst, 72-73; Cancer Res Found Chicago fel, Radiobiol Res Div, Sch Med, Stanford Univ, 73-74; res assoc, Sch Dent Med, Univ Pa, 74-75, res asst prof & nat res serv fel, Dept Biochem, 75-77. *Concurrent Pos:* Consult, Lab Chem Pharmacol, Nat Heart & Lung Inst, NIH, 71. *Mem:* AAAS; Am Soc Biochem & Molecular Biol; Am Heart Asn; Am Soc Human Genetics. *Res:* Cellular lipid metabolism, lipases; foam cell formation and regression; atherosclerosis. *Mailing Add:* Dept Biochem Prof Inst Human Gene Therapy Univ Pa Med Ctr Rm 409 Stellar Chance Labs 422 Curie Blvd Philadelphia PA 19104-6069. *Fax:* 215-573-8606

GLICK, JOHN H, INTERNAL MEDICINE, MEDICAL ONCOLOGY. *Current Pos:* From asst prof to assoc prof, 74-83, PROF MED, UNIV PA, 83-, DIR, CANCER CTR, 85-, MADLYN & LEONARD ABRAMSON PROF CLIN ONCOL, 88- *Personal Data:* b New York, NY, May 9, 43; m 68; c 2. *Educ:* Princeton Univ, AB, 65; Columbia Univ, MD, 69. *Concurrent Pos:* mem, COCERT, Am Bd Med Specialties, 85-, bd gov, Am Bd Internal Med, 87-89, Instnl Res Grants Review Comn Am Chem Soc, 89-; prin investr, Ctr Support Grant, Univ Pa, NCI, 85-94, Eastern Coop Oncol Group Grant, 91-; chmn, Am Bd Internal Med, Subspec Bd Med Oncol, 87-89. *Mem:* Fel Am Col Physicians; Am Soc Clin Oncol; Am Asn Cancer Res; Am Fedn Clin Res; Am Soc Hemat. *Res:* Development of improved treatment for patients with Hodgkin's disease and breast cancer, including the use of adjuvant therapy in early stage breast cancer; founded the Philadelphia Bone Marrow Transplant Program, which is now testing the efficacy of ABMT in combination with high-dose chemotherapy in the treatment of metastatic breast cancer. *Mailing Add:* Univ Pa Cancer Ctr Hosp Univ Pa Col Med 3400 Spruce St Penn Tower Philadelphia PA 19104

GLICK, JOHN HENRY, JR, CLINICAL CHEMISTRY. *Current Pos:* RETIRED. *Personal Data:* b Cumberland, Md, June 16, 24; m 54; c 5. *Educ:* Cath Univ, AB, 49; St Louis Univ, PhD(biochem), 56. *Prof Exp:* From instr to asst prof biochem, Col Med & Dent NJ, Newark, 56-66; from asst prof to assoc prof biochem in path, Med Ctr, Univ Kans, 66-73, assoc prof path & oncol, 73-89. *Mem:* AAAS. *Res:* Lipoproteins; patient test data analysis. *Mailing Add:* 3518 W 48th Ter Shawnee Mission KS 66205

GLICK, MARY CATHERINE, PEDIATRICS. *Current Pos:* Assoc, Dept Anat & Dept Therapeut Res, Sch Med, Univ Pa, 60-65, from asst prof to assoc prof, Dept Therapeut Res, 65-72, assoc prof, Dept Pediat, 72-75, PROF PEDIAT RES, SCH MED, UNIV PA, PHILADELPHIA, 75- *Educ:* Pa State Univ, BS, 48; Univ Pa, MS, 53, PhD(microbiol), 58. *Concurrent Pos:* Res fel, Lab Carbohydrate Res, Harvard Med Sch, Mass Gen Hosp, 63-64; mem, Grad Group Molecular Biol, Sch Med, Univ Pa, 69-; Exp Biol Sect, breast Cancer Task Force, NIH, 73-76 & Physiol Chem Study Sect, NIH, 77-82; vis prof, Dept Genetics & Dept Biochem, Weizmann Inst Sci, Israel, 71-73; admin chmn, Sci Adv Comt, Daman Runyon-Walter Winchell Cancer Fund, NY, 78-79; assoc ed, Cancer Res, 82-85. *Mem:* Am Soc Biol Chemists; Nat Soc Complex Carbohydrates (pres-elect & pres, 81-82). *Mailing Add:* Dept Pediat Res Univ Pa Sch Med Childrens Hosp 34th St Civi Ctr Blvd Philadelphia PA 19104. *Fax:* 215-590-4298

GLICK, MILTON DON, PHYSICAL CHEMISTRY, INORGANIC CHEMISTRY. *Current Pos:* SR VPRES & PROVOST, ARIZ STATE UNIV, 91- *Personal Data:* b Memphis, Tenn, July 30, 37; m 65, Peggy Porter; c David & Sandy. *Educ:* Augustana Col Ill, AB, 59; Univ Wis, PhD(phys chem), 65. *Prof Exp:* Fel x-ray crystallog, Cornell Univ, 64-66; from asst prof to prof, 66-83, chmn chem dept, Wayne State Univ, 78-83; dean, Col Arts & Sci, Univ Mo, 83-88; provost & interim pres, Iowa State Univ, 88-91. *Res:* X-ray crystallographic studies on compounds of chemical and biological interest; computer applications in chemistry; computer graphics; structure-magnetic correlations; structure-relativity correlations. *Mailing Add:* Off Sr Vpres & Provost Ariz State Univ Tempe AZ 85287-2803. *Fax:* 602-965-0785; *E-Mail:* glick@asu.edu

GLICK, RICHARD EDWIN, PHYSICAL CHEMISTRY. *Current Pos:* from asst prof to assoc prof, 59-66, PROF CHEM, FLA STATE UNIV, 66-, DIR INST FUTURE RESOURCES, 82- *Personal Data:* b Chicago, Ill, Apr 7, 27; div; c 4. *Educ:* Univ Ill, BS, 51; Univ Calif, Los Angeles, PhD(chem), 54. *Prof Exp:* Res chemist, Brookhaven Nat Lab, 54-55; Milton fel, Harvard Univ, 55-56; asst prof chem, Pa State Univ, 56-59. *Concurrent Pos:* Vis scientist, Peymeinade, France, 70-71; pres, Corp Future Resources, UNLTD, Inc, 86-, CFR Bio-Gen Corp, 86. *Mem:* Am Soc Mass Spectrometry; Sigma Xi. *Res:* Bio-mass energy processes and by-product utilization; cosmochemistry; chemical kinetics. *Mailing Add:* 1909 Chowkeebin Ct Tallahassee FL 32301

GLICK, ROBERT L, ROCKET PROPULSION. *Current Pos:* PRIN ENGR, TALLEY DEFENSE SYSTS, 86- *Personal Data:* b Ashland, Ky, Jan 26, 34; m 91, Marilyn G Petty; c Christopher L & Heather L. *Educ:* Purdue Univ, BSME, 55, MSME, 59, PhD(mech eng), 66. *Prof Exp:* Prin engr, Huntsville Div, Thiokol Corp, 63-66, 72-78, Morton Thiokol, 84-85; tech specialist, Cummins Engine Co, Inc, Ind, 66-69; assoc prof mech eng, Univ Kans, 69-72; res engr, Res Inst, Univ Dayton, 78-81; sr researcher, Dept Aeronaut & Astronaut, Purdue Univ, 81-84. *Mem:* Assoc fel Am Inst Aeronaut & Astronaut. *Res:* Steady and nonsteady internal ballistics of solid propellant rockets; thrust modulation and combustion of solid propellants; heat transfer; gas dynamics; material properties. *Mailing Add:* 525 N 101st Pl Mesa AZ 85207

GLICK, SAMUEL SHIPLEY, PEDIATRICS, PUBLIC HEALTH. *Current Pos:* RETIRED. *Personal Data:* b Baltimore, Md, Dec 18, 00; m 27, Bessie Stein; c Leonard B & Harriet G. *Educ:* Johns Hopkins Univ, AB, 20; Univ Md, MD, 25. *Prof Exp:* Intern, Univ Hosp, Univ Md, 25-26; resident, Sydenham Hosp Contagious Dis, Baltimore, 26-27, St Vincent's Infant Home, 27-28 & health off, Dept Health, Baltimore, 28-41; from asst prof to prof, Univ Md, Baltimore, 48-71, emer prof. *Concurrent Pos:* Practicing pediatrician, 28-87; staff pediatrician, Baltimore City Dept Health, 65-87, Johns Hopkins Hosp, Univ Md Hosp, Sinai Hosp. *Mem:* Fel Am Acad Pediatrics; AMA; Am Acad Pediat. *Res:* Nutritional diseases; study of child health services in Maryland; teaching medical students. *Mailing Add:* 3737 Clarks Lane Baltimore MD 21215

GLICK, STANLEY DENNIS, NEUROPHARMACOLOGY. *Current Pos:* PROF & CHMN PHARMACOL & TOXICOL, ALBANY MED COL, 84- *Personal Data:* b New York, NY, Oct 10, 44; m 73. *Educ:* NY Univ, BA, 65; Albert Einstein Col Med, PhD(pharmacol), 69, MD, 71. *Prof Exp:* From asst prof to prof pharmacol, Mt Sinai Sch Med, 71-84. *Mem:* AAAS; Am Soc Pharmacol & Exp Therapeut; Soc Neurosci; NY Acad Sci. *Res:* Changes in drug sensitivity following brain damage; cerebral asymmetry; drug addiction and dependence; basal ganglia function; function of dopamine in brain; function of histamine in brain. *Mailing Add:* Dept Pharmacol & Toxicol A-136 Albany Med Col A-136 47 New Scotland Ave Albany NY 12208-3479

GLICKMAN, DANIEL ROBERT, AGRICULTURE. *Current Pos:* SECY, US DEPT AGR, 95- *Personal Data:* b Wichita, Kans, Nov 24, 44; m 66, Rhoda J Yura; c Jonathan & Amy. *Educ:* Univ Mich, BA, 66; George Washington Univ, JD, 69. *Concurrent Pos:* Officer, Glickman Inc, 70- *Mailing Add:* US Dept Agr Off Secy 14th & Independence Ave SW Rm 200A Washington DC 20250

GLICKMAN, LAWRENCE THEODORE, EPIDEMIOLOGY, VETERINARY MEDICINE. *Current Pos:* DEPT HEAD VET PATH, PURDUE UNIV, 88- *Personal Data:* b New York, NY, May 16, 42; m 67; c 2. *Educ:* State Univ NY, Binghamton, BA, 64, MA, 66; Univ Pa, VMD, 72; Univ Pittsburgh, MPH, 75, DrPH(epidemiol), 77. *Prof Exp:* Res assoc pharmacol, Endo Labs, 66-67; assoc veterinarian, Trooper Vet Hosp, 72-74; asst dir lab animal, Health Ctr, Univ Pittsburgh, 76-77; asst prof epidemiol & head div, NY State Col Vet Med, Cornell Univ, 77-80; assoc prof & chief epidemiol, Sch Vet Med, Univ Pa, 80-88. *Concurrent Pos:* Fel cardiovasc dis, Grad Sch Pub Health, Univ Pittsburgh, 75-76. *Mem:* Am Pub Health Asn; Soc Epidemiol Res; Teachers Vet Prev Med & Pub Health; Am Vet Med Asn; Asn Vet Med Educrs. *Res:* Epidemiology; seroepidemiology; zoonotic diseases; parasitic diseases; nosocomial infections; preventive medicine; comparative medicine. *Mailing Add:* Dept Vet Path Purdue Univ West Lafayette IN 47907

GLICKMAN, ROBERT MORRIS, MEDICINE. *Current Pos:* HERRMAN L BLUMGART PROF MED, HARVARD MED SCH, 90-; PROF MED, DIV HEALTH SCI & TECHNOL, MASS INST TECHNOL, 90- *Personal Data:* b Brooklyn, NY, June 23, 39. *Educ:* Amherst Col, AB, 60; Harvard Med Sch, MD, 64; Am Bd Internal Med, cert, 73. *Prof Exp:* Intern med II & IV, Harvard Med Servs, Boston City Hosp, 64-65, asst resident med, 65-66; res fel med, Harvard Med Sch, 66-68, from instr to assoc prof, 70-77; from assoc prof to Samuel Bard prof med & chmn, Dept Med, Columbia Univ Col Physicians & Surgeons, NY, 77-90. *Concurrent Pos:* Chief, Internal Med Res Br, US Army Med Res & Develop Command, Off Surgeon Gen, 68-70; asst physician, Mass Gen Hosp, 74-75; chief, Div Gastroenterol, Beth Israel Hosp, Boston, 75-77, asst physician, 75-77, physician-in-chief, Dept Med, 90-, chmn, 96-, sr vpres acad & clin strategies, 96-; from assoc to attending physician, Presby Hosp, NY, 77-90, dir med serv, 82-90; chief, Div Gastroenterol, Columbia-Presby Med Ctr, NY, 77-84; ed, Selected Summaries, Gastroenterol, 82-88; assoc ed, Hepatology, 90; sr counr, Asn Am Physicians. *Mem:* Inst Med-Nat Acad Sci; Am Fedn Clin Res; Am Soc Clin Invest(pres-elect, 83-84, pres, 84-85); Asn Am Physicians; fel Am Col Physicians; Am Gastroenterol Asn (pres, 88); fel NY Acad Med. *Mailing Add:* Dept Med Beth Israel Deaconese Med Ctr 330 Brookline Ave Boston MA 02215

GLICKMAN, SAMUEL ARTHUR, organic chemistry; deceased, see previous edition for last biography

GLICKMAN, WALTER A, PHYSICS. *Current Pos:* Asst prof, 64-70, assoc prof, 70-77, PROF PHYSICS, LONG ISLAND UNIV, 77- *Personal Data:* b New York, NY, Sept 8, 38. *Educ:* Alfred Univ, BA, 59; Pa State Univ, MS, 62, PhD(physics), 64. *Res:* Molecular spectroscopy. *Mailing Add:* Dept Physics Long Island Univ 385 1 University Plaza Brooklyn NY 11201-5320

GLICKSMAN, ARVIN SIGMUND, MEDICINE, BIOLOGY. *Current Pos:* DIR RADIATION ONCOL, ROGER WILLIAMS CANCER CTR, 89- *Personal Data:* b New York, NY, Mar 14, 24; m 56, Bernice Grobstein; c Jonathan, Jane, Merrylee & Caroline. *Educ:* Chicago Med Sch, MB, 48, MD, 49. *Prof Exp:* Intern, Kings Co Hosp, Brooklyn, 48-50; resident, Mem Ctr Cancer & Allied Dis, 52-54; from asst to assoc, Radiobiol Sect, Sloan-Kettering Inst Cancer Res, 55-65; assoc dir dept radiation ther, Michael Reese Hosp & Med Ctr, Chicago, 65-67; assoc prof radiol, Mt Sinai Sch Med, 67-70, prof radiother & dir radiother res unit, 70-73; prof med sci & chmn dept radiation med, Brown Univ, 73-90. *Concurrent Pos:* AEC fel med sci, Dept Biochem, Duke Univ, 50-52; guest physician, Brookhaven Nat Lab, 50-52; res fel, Sloan-Kettering Inst Cancer Res, 54-55; asst attend, physician & med consult, Mem Ctr Cancer & Allied Dis, 55-65; asst attend physician, Kings Co Hosp, 55-60, James Ewing Hosp, 59-64, asst vis radiotherapist, 64-65; Dillon fel, Royal Marsden Hosp, London, 61-62; NIH res career develop award, Royal Marsden Hosp & Inst Cancer Res, London, 62-64; asst attend radiotherapist, Mem Hosp, 64-65; dep dir, Radiother Ctr, Mt Sinai Hosp, 67-73; consult radiotherapist, Arden Hill Hosp & Elizabeth A Horton Mem Hosp, 68-; consult radiation ther, Univ Conn Health Ctr, 72-75; dir dept radiation oncol, RI Hosp, 73-84, dir dept radiation med & biol res, 84-89; assoc, Div Div Oncol, Roger Williams Gen Hosp, 74-; physician-consult radiol, Vet Admin Hosp, rovidence, 74-; mem cancer clin invest rev comt, Nat Cancer Inst, 75-79, chmn, community clin oncol prog eval comm, 84-86. *Mem:* AAAS; Radiation Res Soc; Am Asn Cancer Res; NY Acad Med; Am Soc Clin Oncol; Am Soc Therapeut Radiol Oncol. *Res:* Radiobiology; radiation therapy; oncology; internal medicine. *Mailing Add:* Old Blackstone Rd Uxbridge MA 01569. *Fax:* 401-456-6500

GLICKSMAN, LEON ROBERT, MECHANICAL ENGINEERING. *Current Pos:* PROF ARCHIT & MECH ENG, MASS INST TECHNOL, 66- *Personal Data:* m, Judith Kidder; c Shayna, Eric & David. *Educ:* Mass Inst Technol, BS, 59, PhD(mech eng), 64; Stanford Univ, MS, 60. *Honors & Awards:* Robert Knapp Award, Am Soc Mech Engrs, 69, Melville Medal, 70. *Mem:* Am Soc Mech Engrs; Am Soc Heating Refrig & Air Conditioning Engrs; Am Inst Chem Engrs. *Res:* Energy in buildings, including new materials, insulation and air circulation; heat transfer and fluid dynamics of fluidized beds. *Mailing Add:* Mass Inst Tech Rm 4-209 Cambridge MA 02139

GLICKSMAN, MARTIN E, PHYSICAL METALLURGY. *Current Pos:* chmn, Dept Mat Eng, 75-85, JOHN TODD HORTON DISTINGUISHED PROF, RESSELAER POLYTECH INST, 86- *Personal Data:* b New York, NY, Apr 4, 37; m 66, Lucinda. *Educ:* Rensselaer Polytech Inst, BMetE, 57, PhD(phys metall), 61. *Honors & Awards:* Arthur S Flemming Award, 69; Grossman Award, Am Soc Metals, 71; Sci Res Soc Am Award, 67; Nat Crystal Growth Award, Am Asn Crystal Growth, 96. *Prof Exp:* Nat Acad Sci-Nat Res Coun fel, Naval Res Lab, 61-63, res metallurgist, 63-66, actg br head metal physics, 66-69, head transformation & kinetics br, 69-75. *Mem:* Nat Acad Eng; fel Minerals Metals & Mat Soc; fel Am Soc Metals; Sigma Xi; Am Phys Soc; AAAS; Am Inst Aeronaut & Astronaut; fel Metall Soc. *Res:* Solidification and crystal growth of metals and alloys; surface energy studies; defects in metals; thermodynamics of stressed systems; interfacial phenomena in metals; metallurgy of superconductors; lattice vacancies. *Mailing Add:* Dept Mat Sci & Eng Rensselaer Polytech Inst CII 9111 Troy NY 12180. *Fax:* 518-276-2198; *E-Mail:* glickm@rpi.edu

GLICKSMAN, MAURICE, EXPERIMENTAL SOLID STATE PHYSICS. *Current Pos:* univ prof & prof eng, Brown Univ, 69-94, dean Grad Sch, 74-76, dean fac & acad affairs, 76-78, provost & dean fac, 78-86, provost, 86-90, prof physics, 90-94, EMER PROVOST, BROWN UNIV, 90-, PROF ENG RES, 94- *Personal Data:* b Toronto, Ont, Oct 16, 28; nat US; m 49, Yetta Leich; c Howard D, Roslynn S & Marcie A. *Educ:* Univ Chicago, SM, 52, PhD(physics), 54. *Prof Exp:* Researcher nuclear physics, Atomic Energy Proj, Chalk River, Can, 49-50; instr physics, Roosevelt Univ, 53-54; res assoc, Inst Nuclear Studies, Ill, 54; mem tech staff, RCA Labs, NJ, 54-62, head plasma physics, 61-63, dir res, Tokyo Lab, 63-67, head gen res, 67-69. *Concurrent Pos:* Chmn comt mat for radiation detection devices, Nat Res Coun-Nat Mat Adv Bd, 71-74; chmn vis comt elec eng, Univ Pa, 77-84; chmn vis comt grad educ, Vanderbilt Univ, 77-81; mem, Solar Energy Res Inst Univ Adv Panel, 78-79; mem bd trustees, Northeast Radio Observ Corp, 78-94; pres adv comt, Emory Univ, 81-; dir, Ctr Res Libr, 81-86 & chmn, 83-84; trustee, Univ Res Asn, 83-88, vchmn, 86-88, Fermilab Bd, 88-, vchmn 88-89, 94-97 & chmn 89-94; mem higher educ policy adv comt, Online Comput Libr Ctr, Cleveland, Ohio, 84-90, trustee, 93-; chmn, Peer Rev Comt, Nat Renewable Energy Lab Photovoltaics Div, 93-96; dir, Manisses Commun, 93-, Lifespan Corp, 94- *Mem:* Fel Am Phys Soc; fel Inst Elec & Electronics Engrs. *Res:* Nuclear properties; pi-meson scattering; semiconductor alloys; band structure; semiconductor transport properties; galvanomagnetic effects; hot electrons; plasmas in solids; gaseous plasmas; semiconductor luminescence. *Mailing Add:* Box D Brown Univ Providence RI 02912-9104. *Fax:* 401-863-1157; *E-Mail:* maurice_glicksman@brown.edu

GLICKSTEIN, JOSEPH, ANALYTICAL CHEMISTRY. *Current Pos:* prof, 63-86, EMER PROF CHEM, BROOKLYN COL, CITY UNIV NEW YORK, 86- *Personal Data:* b New York, NY, Aug 31, 17; m 41, Virginia LaForge; c David A. *Educ:* Mich State Col, BS, 38; NY Univ, PhD(chem), 51. *Prof Exp:* Asst gastric chem res, Mt Sinai Hosp, NY, 38-40 & City Dept Hosps, New York, 40-42; res engr, Bolsey Res & Develop Corp, 51; proj engr, Electro-Phys Labs, Conn, 52-55; prof chem, Adelphi Univ, 55-63. *Concurrent Pos:* Res collabr, Brookhaven Nat Lab, 58-62. *Mem:* AAAS; Am Chem Soc. *Res:* Instrumentation; electrochemical studies, including polarography; spectrophotometry. *Mailing Add:* Dept Chem Brooklyn Col City Univ NY Brooklyn NY 11210

GLICKSTEIN, MITCHELL, NEUROANATOMY, PHYSIOLOGICAL PSYCHOLOGY. *Current Pos:* from assoc prof to prof psychol, 67-80, SR SCIENTIST MED RES COUN, BROWN UNIV, 80-, PROF NEUROSCI, DEPT ANAT, UNIV COL LONDON, 87- *Personal Data:* b Boston, Mass, July 13, 31; m 76, Lydia Sinclair; c Benjamin & Hannah. *Educ:* Univ Chicago, BA, 51, PhD(psychol), 58. *Prof Exp:* USPHS fel biol, Calif Inst Technol, 58-60; res assoc, Sch Med, Stanford Univ, 60-61; assoc prof physiol & biophys, Sch Med, Univ Wash, 61-66, biol structure, 66-67. *Concurrent Pos:* Sr res assoc, Oxford Univ, 69-70; vis prof, Univ Parma, 83. *Mem:* Physiol Soc; Anat Asn Gt Brit & Ireland; Soc Neurosci; Brain Res Asn. *Res:* Brain mechanisms in vision and movement. *Mailing Add:* Dept Anat Univ Col London Gowers St London WC1E6BT England

GLICKSTEIN, STANLEY S, NUCLEAR PHYSICS, WELDING. *Current Pos:* ADV SCIENTIST, BETTIS ATOMIC POWER LAB, WESTINGHOUSE ELEC CORP, 64- *Personal Data:* b Brooklyn, NY, Nov 12, 33; m 57; c Steven, Barbara, Karen & Cathy. *Educ:* Polytech Inst Brooklyn, BEE, 55; Pa State Univ, MS, 59, PhD(physics), 61. *Prof Exp:* Res assoc physics, Princeton Univ, 61-63, instr, 63-64. *Mem:* Am Welding Soc; Am Phys Soc; Laser Inst Am; Am Soc Nondestructive Testing. *Res:* Neutron radiography; welding arc physics; lasers for materials processing. *Mailing Add:* Bettis Atomic Power Lab Westinghouse Elec Corp PO Box 79 West Mifflin PA 15122

GLIDDEN, RICHARD MILLS, RUBBER CHEMISTRY. *Current Pos:* RETIRED. *Personal Data:* b Irvington, NJ, Nov 3, 24; m 52; c 3. *Educ:* Rutgers Univ, BS, 50. *Prof Exp:* Tech dir, Ames Rubber Corp, 50-75, vpres, 65-75, exec vpres opers, 75-78, pres, 78-85, chmn bd dirs, 85-95. *Mem:* Am Chem Soc. *Res:* Development and manufacture of rubber compounds. *Mailing Add:* 39 Summit Trail Sparta NJ 07871

GLIEDMAN, MARVIN L, SURGERY. *Current Pos:* surgeon-in-chief, combined depts surg, 76-91, ATTENDING SURGEON, MONTEFIORE HOSP & MED CTR, 67- *Personal Data:* b New York, NY, Aug 3, 29; m 54, Schwartz; c Charles & Joanna. *Educ:* Syracuse Univ, BA, 50; State Univ NY, MD, 54. *Honors & Awards:* Dudley Mem Medal, 54; Linder Surg Prize, 54. *Prof Exp:* From asst instr to assoc prof surg, State Univ NY Downstate Med Ctr, 59-66; chmn dept, Albert Einstein Col Med, 72-91. *Concurrent Pos:* Markle scholar acad med, 64-69; asst attend Surgeon, Kings County Hosp, Brooklyn, 60-; chief dept surg, Montefiore Hosp & Med Ctr, 67-76; prof surg, Albert Einstein Col Med, 67- *Mem:* Am Soc Nephrol; NY Acad Sci; Am Col Surg; Am Gastroenterol Asn; Am Soc Artificial Internal Organs; Am Med Asn; Am Surg Asn; Am Med Writers Asn; Asn Advan Med Instrumentation; Soc Surg Alimentary Tract. *Res:* Gastrointestinal surgery and physiology with emphasis on the liver and pancreas, particularly with regard to problems of cirrhosis, diabetes and transplantation. *Mailing Add:* Dept Surg Montefiore Hosp & Med Ctr 111 E 210th St Bronx NY 10467-6028. *Fax:* 718-547-2929

GLIMCHER, MELVIN JACOB, ORTHOPEDIC SURGERY, BIOPHYSICS. *Current Pos:* from asst prof to assoc prof, 59-65, PROF ORTHOP SURG, HARVARD MED SCH, 65-; DIR, ORTHOP RES LABS, CHILDREN'S HOSP MED CTR, 80- *Personal Data:* b Brookline, Mass, June 2, 25; c 3. *Educ:* Purdue Univ, BS(gen sci) & BS(mech eng), 46; Harvard Univ, MD, 50. *Honors & Awards:* William F Neuman Award. *Concurrent Pos:* Res fel, Harvard Med Sch, 56; res fel biol, Mass Inst Technol & fel, Sch Advan Studies, 56-59; chief orthop serv, Mass Gen Hosp, 66-71; orthop surgeon-in-chief, Children's Hosp Med Ctr, 71-80. *Mem:* Electron Micros Soc Am; Orthop Res Soc; Biophys Soc; Am Acad Arts & Sci; Sigma Xi; Am Acad Orthop Surgeons; Am Orthop Asn; An Soc Bone & Mineral Res. *Res:* Biological mineralization; bone and mineral metabolism. *Mailing Add:* Ortho Res Children's Hosp Med Ctr 320 Longwood Ave Boston MA 02115-5737. *Fax:* 617-730-0226

GLIME, JANICE MILDRED, BRYOLOGY, ECOLOGY. *Current Pos:* from asst prof to assoc, 73-84, PROF BIOL SCI, MICH TECHNOL UNIV, 84- *Personal Data:* b Cumberland, Md, Jan 27, 41. *Educ:* Frostburg State Col, BS, 62; WVa Univ, MS, 64; Mich State Univ, PhD(bot), 68. *Prof Exp:* Asst instr botany, Mich State Univ, 68; from instr to asst prof, Plymouth State Col, 68-70, asst prof biol sci, 70-73. *Concurrent Pos:* Assoc ed, Hikobia & J Hattori Bot Lab. *Mem:* Ecol Soc Am; Am Bryol & Lichenological Soc; Am Inst Biol Sci; Brit Bryol Soc; Int Asn Bryol. *Res:* Ecology of streams, especially bryophytes and insects; systems ecology and taxonomy of Fontinalis; experimental bryology; effects of acid rain and heavy metals on byrophytes; bryophyte niche width; geothermal plant communities. *Mailing Add:* Dept Biol Sci Mich Technol Univ Houghton MI 49931. *Fax:* 906-487-3167; *E-Mail:* jmglime@mtu.edu

GLIMM, JAMES GILBERT, SCIENTIFIC COMPUTING. *Current Pos:* vis leading prof, DISTINGUISHED PROF & HEAD, DEPT APPL MATH, STATE UNIV NY, STONY BROOK, 88- *Personal Data:* b Peoria, Ill, Mar 24, 34; m 57; c 1. *Educ:* Columbia Univ, AB, 56, AM, 57, PhD(math), 59. *Honors & Awards:* Phys & Math Sci Award, NY Acad Sci, 79; Dannie Heineman Prize, 80; Steele Prize, Am Math Soc, 93. *Prof Exp:* NSF fel, 59-60; from asst prof to prof math, Mass Inst Technol, 60-68; prof, Rockefeller Univ, 74-82; vis prof, Courant Inst Math, NY Univ, 80-82, prof, 82-89. *Concurrent Pos:* Temp mem, Inst Advan Study, Princeton, NJ, 59-60; Guggenheim fel & vis assoc prof, Courant Inst Math, 64-65 & Aarhus Univ, Denmark, 65-66; vis mem, Courant Inst Math, NY Univ, 63-64, prof, 68-74. *Mem:* Nat Acad Sci; Am Math Soc; Am Acad Arts & Sci; Soc Indust & Appl Math; Soc Petrol Engrs; Int Asn Math Physicists; Am Phys Soc. *Res:* Non-linear differential equations; functional analysis; operators on Hilbert space; mathematical physics; quantum field theory; computational fluid dynamics. *Mailing Add:* Appl Math & Statist 120 E 81st St New York NY 10028

GLINER, GAIL S, MATH EDUCATION. *Current Pos:* PROF, DEPT MATH, METROP STATE COL, DENVER 82- *Personal Data:* b Los Angeles, Calif, Mar 13, 44. *Educ:* Univ Calif, BA, 65; Bowling Green State Univ, MA, 68; Univ Calif, Santa Barbara, PhD(educ psychon), 80. *Mem:* Math Asn Am; Am Educ Res Asn. *Res:* Math education. *Mailing Add:* Metrop State Col Denver PO Box 173362 Campus Box 38 Denver CO 80217

GLINKOWSKI, MIETEK T, PLASMA PHYSICS & ELECTRICAL DISCHARGES, POWER SYSTEM PROTECTION & RELAYING. *Current Pos:* vis prof, 89-90, ASST PROF ELEC POWER ENG, RENSSELAER POLYTECH UNIV, 90- *Personal Data:* b Czestochowa, Poland, Dec 29, 56; m 81, Alexandra Lisowska; c Cassandra. *Educ:* Poznan Polytech, BS & MS, 80; Rensselaer Polytech Inst, MEng, 85, PhD(elec power), 89. *Prof Exp:* Asst vacuum technol, Inst Electroenergy, 80-82, sr asst, 82-84. *Concurrent Pos:* Consult, Consol Edison NY, Joslyn High Voltage Corp, New Eng Elec Serv Co, Gen Elec, Utility Technol Systs & Kinetics Industs Inc. *Mem:* Inst Elec & Electronics Engrs; Inst Elec & Electronics Engrs Power Eng Soc. *Res:* Physics of current interruption in high voltage switching devices; switching phenomena in power systems; power system protection, including protective relaying, intelligent protection, protection of power equipment, testing and design of protection systems. *Mailing Add:* 7 Terrace Pl Troy NY 12180. *Fax:* 518-276-6226; *E-Mail:* glinkm@.rpi.edu

GLINSKI, RONALD P, BIO-ORGANIC CHEMISTRY, PATHOLOGY. *Current Pos:* CONSULT 80- *Personal Data:* b Windsor, Ont, Aug 4, 41. *Educ:* Univ Windsor, BS, 63; Wayne State Univ, PhD(org chem), 67; Univ Mich, MD, 75. *Prof Exp:* Sr res chemist org biochem, Ash Stevens Inc, 66, res supvr, 68-75; resident pathol, Univ Mich, 75-80. *Mem:* Am Chem Soc; Chem Inst Can; AAAS; AMA; NY Acad Sci; Sigma Xi. *Res:* Organic synthesis; carbohydrates; nucleotides; natural products; kinetics; enzymology; process development. *Mailing Add:* 195 Pine Dr Whiteville NC 28472-9801

GLINSMANN, WALTER H, NUTRITION. *Current Pos:* chief, Exp Nutrit Br & dir res, 78-83, chief, Clin Nutrit Br, 83-87, ASSOC DIR CLIN NUTRIT, DIV NUTRIT, CTR FOOD SAFETY & APPL NUTRIT, FOOD & DRUG ADMIN, DEPT HEALTH & HUMAN SERV, 87- *Personal Data:* c 3. *Educ:* Columbia Univ, BA, 56, MD, 60. *Prof Exp:* Asst chief, Dept Metab, Walter Reed Army Inst & attend physician med & endocrinol, Walter Reed Army Hosp, 62-65; prog planner, Growth & Develop Prog, Nat Inst Child Health & Human Develop, NIH, 65-66, guest investr, Clin Endocrinol Br, Nat Inst Arthritis & Metab Dis, 66-67, sr res investr, Lab Biomed Sci, Nat Inst Child Health & Human Develop, 67-68, chief, Sect Physiol Controls, 68-72. *Concurrent Pos:* Pvt consult res planning & prog develop, Growth & Develop Prog, Nat Inst Child Health & Human Develop, NIH, 65. *Mem:* Am Inst Nutrit; Am Soc Clin Nutrit; Am Physiol Soc; Am Diabetes Asn; AAAS. *Mailing Add:* 1321 Fourth St SW Washington DC 20024-2201. *Fax:* 202-484-5051

GLISSON, ALLEN WILBURN, JR, ELECTRICAL ENGINEERING, ELECTROMAGNETIC THEORY. *Current Pos:* Res asst physics, Univ Miss, 72-73, res asst elec eng, 73-78, asst prof elec eng, 78-84, ASSOC PROF ELEC ENG, UNIV MISS, 84- *Personal Data:* b Meridian, Miss, June 26, 51; m 75; c 2. *Educ:* Univ Miss, BS, 73, MS, 75, PhD(elec eng), 78. *Concurrent Pos:* Consult, Northrop Corp, 82, Lincoln Lab, Mass Inst Technol, 83 & TRW, 83-85; Arthur J Schmitt Fac Grant to attend Nat Commun Forum, 83 & 85. *Mem:* Inst Elec & Electronics Engrs; Prof Soc Antennas & Propagation; Prof Soc Microwave Theory & Tech; Sigma Xi; Electromagnetics Soc; Int Union Radio Sci; Prof Soc Electromagnetic Compatibility. *Res:* Radiation and scattering; antennas; mathematical methods; numerical techniques; electromagnetic theory. *Mailing Add:* PO Box 1652 University MS 38677-1652

GLISSON, SILAS NEASE, CARDIOVASCULAR ANESTHESIA. *Current Pos:* asst prof, 72-78, ASSOC PROF ANESTHESIOL & PHARMACOL, LOYOLA UNIV, STRITCH SCH MED, 78- *Personal Data:* b Springfield, Ill, May 8, 41; m 68; c 2. *Educ:* Southern Ill Univ, BA, 64; Loyola Univ Chicago, Stritch Sch Med, PhD(pharmacol), 72. *Prof Exp:* Instr pharmacol, Univ Conn Med Ctr, 71-72. *Concurrent Pos:* Consult, Hines Vet Admin Hosp, 77- *Mem:* Am Soc Anesthesiologists; Am Soc Pharmacol & Exp Therapeut; Int Anesthesia Res Soc; Soc Cardiovasc Anesthesiologists. *Res:* Pharmacology of anesthetic and related drugs; mechanisms of neuroendocrine responses associated with surgery and anesthesia; interaction of the sympathoadrenal, renin-angiotensin and adrenal cortical responses to perioperative stresses; anesthetic pharmacokinetics. *Mailing Add:* Dept Anesthesiol Ward 12-189 Northwestern Univ 303 E Chicago Ave Maywood IL 60611-3072. *Fax:* 312-908-6968

GLITZ, DOHN GEORGE, BIOCHEMISTRY. *Current Pos:* from asst prof to assoc prof, 67-77, PROF BIOL CHEM, MED SCH, UNIV CALIF, LOS ANGELES, 77-, VICE CHAIR, 78- *Personal Data:* b Buffalo, NY, Sept 28, 36; m 66, Beryl Davey; c Rachel. *Educ:* Univ Ill, BS, 58; Univ Wis, MS, 60; Univ Calif, PhD, 64. *Prof Exp:* Chemist, Swift & Co Res Labs, 58. *Concurrent Pos:* Fel, Enzyme Inst, Univ Wis, 63-64; USPHS fel, Virus Res Unit, Cambridge Univ, 64-66; fel, Virus Lab, Univ Calif, Berkeley, 66-67; Guggenheim fel, Friedrich Miescher Inst, Basel, Switz, 74-75; vis scientist, Nat Inst Med Res, London, Eng, 81-82. *Mem:* Am Soc Biol Chem; RNA Soc. *Res:* Nucleic acid biochemistry, including physical and chemical properties; electron microscopy of nucleoproteins and their immune complexes; ribosome structure and function; spliceosome structure; human ribonucleases. *Mailing Add:* Dept Biol Chem Univ Calif Med Sch Los Angeles CA 90095-1737. *Fax:* 310-206-5272; *E-Mail:* dglitz@biochem.medsch.ucla.edu

GLOBENSKY, YVON RAOUL, GEOLOGY. *Current Pos:* RETIRED. *Personal Data:* b Montreal, Que, Feb 6, 37; m 59; c 2. *Educ:* Univ Montreal, BSc, 59; Univ NB, MSc, 62, PhD(geol), 65. *Prof Exp:* Asst dir geol, Geol Explor Serv, Que Ministry Energy & Resources, 64-72, geologist in chg, St Lawrence Lowland of Quebec, 77-84, geologist in chg, Southern Div, 84-88, dir, Montreal Off, Serv Geol, 88-95. *Mem:* Fel Geol Soc Am; fel Geol Asn Can; Paleont Soc; Soc Econ Paleont & Mineral; Geol Soc France. *Res:* Geology of the St Lawrence Lowlands; paleontology, stratigraphy and mineral deposits. *Mailing Add:* 1360 St Jacques St Apt No 305 Montreal PQ H3C 4M4 Can

GLOBUS, ALBERT, NEUROANATOMY, NEUROPHYSIOLOGY. *Current Pos:* PVT PRACT PSYCHIAT. *Personal Data:* b New York, NY, Oct 13, 31; m 51; c 3. *Educ:* Northwestern Univ, BA, 51, MD, 55. *Prof Exp:* Intern, Orange County Hosp, 55-56; pvt pract, Calif, 58-63; guest scientist, Max Planck Inst, 67-68; asst prof human morphol, psychobiol & psychiat, Univ Calif, Irvine-Calif Col Med, 68-74; assoc prof psychiat, Univ Calif, Davis, 74- *Concurrent Pos:* USPHS fel neuroanat, Univ Calif, Los Angeles, 63-67. *Mem:* AMA; Am Asn Anat; Am Psychiat Asn. *Res:* Golgi analysis of cortical anatomy; intracellular physiology of spinal motoneurons; iontophoresis of radioactive amino acids in spinal motoneurons; maternal behavior in primates; psychiatry. *Mailing Add:* 1990 Third St No 600 Sacramento CA 95814

GLOCK, ROBERT DEAN, VETERINARY PATHOLOGY. *Current Pos:* DIR, CENT ARIZ VET LAB, 81- *Personal Data:* b York, Nebr, Nov 1, 36. *Educ:* Iowa State Univ, DVM, 61, PhD(vet path), 71; Am Col Vet Pathologists, dipl, 74. *Prof Exp:* Vet virologist, US Army, 61-63; vet practr, Edgerton Vet Serv, 63-67; NIH fel, Iowa State Univ, 67-70, asst prof, 70-76, prof vet path, 76-81. *Mem:* Am Vet Med Asn; Am Asn Swine Practrs (pres, 76-77); Sigma Xi; Comp Gastroenterol Soc. *Res:* Swine disease research with emphasis on pathogenesis of enteric diseases and Aujeszky's Disease. *Mailing Add:* Diag Lab Colo State Univ Ft Collins CO 80523-0001

GLOCKLIN, VERA CHARLOTTE, DRUG REGULATION, PHARMACOLOGY. *Current Pos:* RETIRED. *Personal Data:* b Edmonton, Alta, Oct 16, 26; US citizen. *Educ:* Univ Toronto, BA, 48; McGill Univ, MSc, 50; Yale Univ, PhD, 59. *Honors & Awards:* Distinguished Career Award, Drug Info Asn, 89. *Prof Exp:* Res technician pharmacol, Western Res Univ, 50-51; res asst, Cancer Res Lab, Univ Fla, 53-55; res assoc, Eye Res Lab, Univ Chicago, 59-66; USPHS med res grant, Inst Neurol Dis & Blindness, 62-66; pharmacologist, Food & Drug Admin, 66-70, supvry pharmacologist, 70-80, asst dir, Off Drug Eval, 80-89. *Concurrent Pos:* Abstractor, Chem Abstr, 55-60. *Mem:* Soc Toxicol; Int Soc Study Xenobiotics; Sigma Xi. *Res:* Neuropharmacology; comparative biochemistry; endocrinology. *Mailing Add:* 4409 Rosedale Ave Bethesda MD 20814-4752

GLOCKNER, PETER G, APPLIED SOLID & CONTINUUM MECHANICS, STRUCTURAL ENGINEERING. *Current Pos:* assoc prof civil eng, Univ Calgary, 62-67, head, Dept Mech Eng, 76-87, prof, civil eng, 67-94, prof mech eng, 76-94, EMER PROF, UNIV CALGARY, 94- *Personal Data:* b Moragy, Hungary, Jan 26, 29; nat Can; m 55, Sarah Kraft; c Marilyn E (Veronica). *Educ:* McGill Univ, BEng, 55; Mass Inst Technol, MSc, 56; Univ Mich, PhD(civil eng), 64. *Honors & Awards:* Gzowski Gold Medal, Eng Inst Can, 72; Moisseiff Award, Am Soc Civil Engrs, 83; Cancam Medal, 93. *Prof Exp:* Struct design engr, C C Parker, Whittaker & Co, Ltd, Alta, 56-58; from asst prof to assoc prof appl mech, Univ Alta, 58-68, asst prof civil eng, 58-62. *Concurrent Pos:* Chmn, Res & Develop Div, Can Soc Mech Eng, 83-85. *Mem:* Am Soc Civil Engrs; Eng Inst Can; Int Asn Shell Struct; Can Soc Mech Eng; Can Soc Civil Engr; Am Acad Mech. *Res:* Fundamentals of continuum mechanics and solid mechanics and their application to linear and nonlinear plate and shell theory and the static and dynamic linear and nonlinear response of plates and shells. *Mailing Add:* Dept Civil Eng or Dept Mech Eng Univ Calgary Calgary AB T2N 1N4 Can

GLOD, EDWARD FRANCIS, ENVIRONMENTAL & ANALYTICAL CHEMISTRY. *Current Pos:* RES SCIENTIST, CHEM WASTE MGT INC, 82- *Personal Data:* b Youngstown, Ohio, June 28, 42; m 71; c 1. *Educ:* Youngstown Univ, BS, 65; Ohio State Univ, MS, 69, PhD(org chem), 71. *Prof Exp:* Res asst, Ohio State Univ, 71-73; surv chemist lab cert, Ohio Dept Health Labs, 73-74, chief, Environ Labs, 74-78; hazardous waste coordr, Ohio Environ Protection Agency, 78-82. *Concurrent Pos:* Mem, Int Joint Comn, 76- *Mem:* Am Chem Soc; Am Soc Testing & Mat. *Mailing Add:* Northrop Grumman Corp 600 Hicks Rd MS H6282 Rolling Meadows IL 60008

GLODE, LEONARD MICHAEL, MEDICAL ONCOLOGY. *Current Pos:* from asst prof to assoc prof, 78-92, PROF MED, DIV MED ONCOL, UNIV COLO HEALTH SCI CTR, 92-, CO-DIR GENE THER PROG, 94-, CO-DIR ADULT ONCOL PROG, 94- *Personal Data:* b Chadron, Nebr, July 19, 47; c 3. *Educ:* Washington Univ, MD, 72. *Prof Exp:* Res assoc microbiol, Lab Microbiol & Immunol, NIH, 74-76; fel med oncol, Dana Farber Cancer Inst, Harvard Med Sch, 76-78. *Concurrent Pos:* Ed-in-chief, Am Soc Clin Oncol, 96- *Mem:* Am Asn Cancer Res; Am Soc Clin Oncol. *Res:* Utility of ligand directed toxins and regulated expression of toxin genes in cancer therapy; novel prostate cancer therapeutics. *Mailing Add:* Dept Med Oncol B171 Univ Colo Health Sci Ctr 4200 E Ninth Ave Denver CO 80262

GLOECKLER, GEORGE, PHYSICS. *Current Pos:* asst prof, 67-74, assoc prof, 74-80, PROF PHYSICS, INST PHYS SCI & TECH, UNIV MD, COLLEGE PARK, 80- *Personal Data:* b Odessa, Russia, Aug 10, 37; US citizen; m 58. *Educ:* Univ Chicago, SB, 60, SM, 61, PhD(physics), 65. *Honors & Awards:* Except Sci Achievement Medal & Group Achievement Award, NASA, 81. *Prof Exp:* Res assoc cosmic ray physics, Univ Chicago, 65-66, Enrico Fermi fel, 66-67. *Concurrent Pos:* Res fel, NASA, 62-64, co-recipient res grant, 68-; Ennco Fermi fel, 64-65; Alfred P Sloan res fel, 69-71; Alexander von Humboldt Sr US Scientist Award, 77-78. *Mem:* Nat Acad Sci; Am Astron Soc; Am Geophys Union; NY Acad Sci; fel Am Phys Soc. *Res:* Cosmic plasma physics and heliospheric physics; cosmic rays; investigation of thermal and suprathermal plasma composition in the heliosphere, magnetospheres of Earth and the outer planets, and near the Giacobini-Zinner comet. *Mailing Add:* 12201 Prospect Landing Mitchellville MD 20721-2503

GLOEGE, GEORGE HERMAN, chemistry; deceased, see previous edition for last biography

GLOERSEN, PER, PHYSICS. *Current Pos:* PHYSICIST, GODDARD SPACE FLIGHT CTR, NASA, 70-, SR SCIENTIST, 80- *Personal Data:* b Washington, Pa, Dec 19, 27; wid; c William B, Peter F & Kathryn A. *Educ:* Johns Hopkins Univ, MA, 52, PhD(physics), 56. *Prof Exp:* Physicist, Gen Elec Space Sci Lab, 56-70. *Mem:* Am Geophys Union. *Res:* Plasma physics, physical properties of radiating shock waves in gases; high resolution molecular spectroscopy in the ultraviolet, visible and infrared; instrumentation; electric propulsion; remote sensing in the microwave regime; analysis of polar sea ice data. *Mailing Add:* NASA Goddard Space Flight Ctr Code 971 Greenbelt MD 20771. *E-Mail:* per@intrepid.gsfc.nasa.gov

GLOGE, DETLEF CHRISTOPH, OPTICAL COMMUNICATIONS. *Current Pos:* mem tech staff optical commun res, 65-75, HEAD, LIGHTWAVE SYSTS DEVELOP, HOLMDEL LAB, BELL LABS, 75- *Personal Data:* b Breslau, Ger, Feb 2, 36; m 69. *Educ:* Brunswick Tech Univ, Dipl Ing, 61, Dr Ing(optical waveguides), 64. *Prof Exp:* Asst prof electronics, Brunswick Tech Univ, 64-65. *Mem:* Fel Inst Elec & Electronics Engrs; fel Optical Soc Am. *Res:* Optical communication systems. *Mailing Add:* 20 Saratoga Dr Colts Neck NJ 07722

GLOGOVSKY, ROBERT L, PHYSICAL CHEMISTRY, BIOCHEMISTRY. *Current Pos:* from asst prof to assoc prof, Elmhurst Col, 65-74, chmn, Chem Dept, 71-89, chmn, Div Nat Sci, 75-78, PROF CHEM, ELMHURST COL, 74- *Personal Data:* b North Chicago, Ill, May 29, 36; m 61; c Cheryl L, Dawn M, Robert L II & Mary S. *Educ:* Northern Ill Univ, BS, 59; Univ Colo, PhD(phys chem), 65. *Prof Exp:* Kettering Found intern chem, Kalamazoo Col, 64-65; prof, State Univ NY, Buffalo, Malaysia, 90-91. *Concurrent Pos:* Pres, Sea Educ Develop Group; Fulbright scholar award, Slovak Tech Univ, Bratislava, 92-93; Malone fel, Nat Coun US-Arab Rels, 93-94; vis prof, Univ Buffalo. *Mem:* AAAS; Am Chem Soc. *Res:* Energy transfer and storage; biophysical chemistry; trace metal uptake in plants; educational and technical training program development. *Mailing Add:* Dept Chem Elmhurst Col Elmhurst IL 60126. *Fax:* 630-279-7558; *E-Mail:* bobj@elmhurst.edu

GLOMB, WALTER L, RADIO COMMUNICATIONS. *Current Pos:* RES ENGR, UNITED TECHNOL RES. *Personal Data:* b Glen Ridge, NJ, Feb 7, 25; m 48; c 6. *Educ:* Columbia Univ, BS, 46, MS, 48. *Prof Exp:* Sr engr, Defense Commun Div, ITT, 50-70, vpres & dir, 70- *Mem:* Fel Inst Elec & Electronics Engrs. *Res:* Radio communication at microwave frequencies via line of sight; tropospheric scatter; satellite communication systems including transmission, switching and system organization. *Mailing Add:* United Technol Res East Hartford CT 06108

GLOMSET, JOHN A, BIOCHEMISTRY, PHYSIOLOGY. *Current Pos:* from res asst prof to res prof, 60-74, MED STAFF, REGIONAL PRIMATE CTR, UNIV WASH, 64-, PROF MED & ADJ PROF BIOCHEM, 74-, INVESTR, HOWARD HUGHES MED INST LAB, 76-, PROF BIOCHEM, 84- *Personal Data:* b Des Moines, Iowa, Nov 2, 28; m 54; c 2. *Educ:* Univ Uppsala, med lic, MD, 60. *Prof Exp:* Docent med chem, Univ Uppsala, 60. *Mem:* Nat Acad Sci; Am Soc Biochem & Molecular Biol; Am Soc Cell Biol; Am Acad Arts & Sci. *Res:* Protein prenylation; phospholipid metabolism. *Mailing Add:* Howard Hughes Med Inst Univ Wash J611F Health Sci Bldg SL15 Seattle WA 98195. *Fax:* 206-543-0858

GLOMSKI, CHESTER ANTHONY, ANATOMY, HEMATOLOGY. *Current Pos:* from asst prof to assoc prof, 66-79, PROF ANAT, SCH MED & DENT, STATE UNIV NY, BUFFALO, 79- *Personal Data:* b Detroit, Mich, June 8, 28; m 66; c 2. *Educ:* Detroit Inst Technol, BS, 51; Wayne State Univ, MS, 53; Univ Minn, PhD(anat), 61; Univ Miss, MD, 65. *Prof Exp:* Teaching asst anat, Sch Med, Univ Minn, 55-61; intern med, St Paul-Ramsey Hosp, St Paul, Minn, 65-66. *Concurrent Pos:* Consult hemat, Health Care Plan, Inc. *Mem:* Am Asn Anat; Am Soc Hemat; Sigma Xi. *Res:* Experimental hypersplenism; Comparative hematology; erythrocyte kinetics by neutron activation analysis; blood dyscrasias; hemopoiesis and low dose X-irradiation. *Mailing Add:* State Univ NY Buffalo Sherman Hall Buffalo NY 14214-3000. *Fax:* 716-829-2915

GLONEK, THOMAS, PHYSICAL CHEMISTRY, INORGANIC PHYSIOLOGY. *Current Pos:* assoc prof biochem, 69-81, ASSOC PROF PHYSIOL, RES RESOURCES CTR, MED CTR, UNIV ILL, 81- *Personal Data:* b Chicago, Ill, Apr 28, 41. *Educ:* Northern Ill Univ, BS, 63; Univ Ill, PhD(biochem), 69. *Mem:* Sigma Xi. *Res:* Nuclear magnetic resonance; second row element chemistry; biochemistry; physiology; medicine. *Mailing Add:* 803 S Highland Ave Oak Park IL 60304

GLOOR, PIERRE, NEUROPHYSIOLOGY. *Current Pos:* RETIRED. *Personal Data:* b Basel, Switz, Apr 5, 23; Can citizen; m 54; c 2. *Educ:* Univ Basel, MD, 49; McGill Univ, PhD(neurophysiol), 57. *Honors & Awards:* Robert Bing Prize, Swiss Acad Med Sci, 62; Michael Found Prize, 80; William G Lennox Award, Am Epilepsy Soc, 81; Herbert Jasper Award, Am EEG Soc, 88; Wilder Penfield Award, Can League Against Epilepsy, 90. *Prof Exp:* Lectr EEG, Mcgill Univ, 55-57, assoc electroencephalographer, 55-61, asst prof exp neurol, 57-62, assoc prof clin neurophysiol, 62-68; chief lab, Montreal Neural Hosp, 61-84, electroencephalographer, 61, neurophysiologist & chief, Neurophysiol Labs, 66-88; prof clin neurophysiol, Montreal Neurol Inst, McGill Univ, 68-88. *Concurrent Pos:* Electroencephalographer, Jewish Gen Hosp, Montreal, 56-61; del, Int Fedn Soc EEG & Clin Neurophysiol, 61-69; physician in charge EEG, Royal Victoria Hosp, Montreal, 62-84. *Mem:* Can Soc EEG (secy, 62-63, pres, 64-65); Can Physiol Soc; Can Neurol Soc; Am EEG Soc (pres, 78-79); Am Epilepsy Soc (pres, 76); Soc Neurosci; Int Brain Res Orgn. *Res:* Neurophysiology of limbic system and hypothalamus; experimental and clinical electroencephalographic studies on epilepsy; physiological basis and history of electroencephalography. *Mailing Add:* Montreal Neurol Inst 3801 University St Montreal PQ H3A 2B4 Can. *Fax:* 514-398-4497

GLOOR, WALTER THOMAS, JR, PHARMACY. *Current Pos:* asst dean, Creighton Univ, 72-80, prof, 72-90, dir, Allied Health Sci Div, 79-82, EMER PROF, SCH PHARM, CREIGHTON UNIV, 90- *Personal Data:* b Norfolk, Nebr, Sept 26, 24; m 48; c 6. *Educ:* Univ Nebr, BS, 50; Univ Wash, PhD(pharmacog), 55. *Prof Exp:* Instr pharm, Col Pharm, Univ Nebr, 50-52; sr scientist pharmaceut chem, Smith Kline & French Labs, 55-56, unit head, Invest Prod Lab Mfg Unit, 56-68; assoc prof pharm, Col Pharm, Univ RI, 68-71 & Sch Pharm, WVA Univ, 71-72. *Res:* Alkaloid biosynthesis in fungi; problems in manufacture of parenterals, tablets and other pharmaceutical forms. *Mailing Add:* 2 Skidmore Circle Bella Vista AR 72715

GLOOSCHENKO, WALTER ARTHUR, WETLANDS, AQUATIC ECOLOGY. *Current Pos:* PRES, ECO-TROPICA CONSULT, 91- *Personal Data:* b Berkeley, Calif, Sept 9, 38; m 67, Val Lanwermeyer; c Claudio. *Educ:* Univ Calif, Berkeley, BS, 60; Univ Calif, Davis, MS, 62; Ore State Univ,

PhD(oceanog), 67. *Prof Exp:* Soil scientist, US Bur Reclamation, 61-62; teacher high sch, Calif, 62-64; asst prof oceanog, Fla State Univ, 67-70; res scientist, Fisheries Res Bd Can, Environ Can, 70-73, res scientist, Nat Water Res Inst, 73-91. *Concurrent Pos:* Adj prof, Dept Land Resource Sci, Univ Guelph, Ont, 78-; vis assoc prof fac environ studies, York Univ, Toronto, 85-92; consult, Environ Impact Develop Projs, Mex, Brazil, Nicaragua, Sri Lanka. *Mem:* Soc Wetland Scientists (pres, 83-84); Soc Conserv Biol. *Res:* Ecology and geochemistry of salt marshes; wetlands ecology; peat; toxic substances; tropical coastal ecology; environmental impact studies. *Mailing Add:* 2790 NE Pilkington Ave Corvallis OR 97330

GLORIEUX, FRANCIS HENRI, PEDIATRIC BONE DISEASES. *Current Pos:* from asst prof to assoc prof, 72-80, PROF SURG, PEDIAT & HUMAN GENETICS, MCGILL UNIV, 80-; DIR RES, SHRINERS HOSP, MONTREAL, 72- *Personal Data:* b Brussels, Belg, June 7, 39; Can citizen; m 64, Jacqueline Serruys; c Stephane, Delphine & Melanie. *Educ:* Univ Louvain, MD, 63; Univ Montreal, MSc, 68; McGill Univ, PhD(human genetics), 72. *Honors & Awards:* Knight, Order of the Crown, Belg, 79; Knight, Order of St John of Jerusalem, 85; Barter Award, Am Soc Bone & Mineral Res, 93. *Prof Exp:* Resident pediat, War Mem Hosp, Brussels, 63-64; Hosp de la Conception, France, 64-65 & Hosp Ste Justine, Montreal, 66-68; res fel biochem genetics, Montreal Childrens Hosp, 69-72. *Concurrent Pos:* Adminr, Found Delarecherche Ensante of Que, 84-88; adj prof pediat, Univ Montreal, 86- *Mem:* Soc Pediat Res; Am Soc Human Genetics; Am Soc Bone & Mineral Res; Am Soc Cell Biol. *Res:* Clinical investigation of pediatric bone diseases; gene mapping; role of proto-oncogenes in skeletal development; gene expression in bone cells. *Mailing Add:* Shriners Hosp 1529 Cedar Ave Montreal PQ H3G 1A6 Can. *Fax:* 514-842-5581

GLORIG, ARAM, OTOLOGY. *Current Pos:* ASSOC DIR, EAR RES INST, 78- *Personal Data:* b Manchester, Eng, June 8, 06; nat US; m 44; c 2. *Educ:* Loma Linda Univ, MD, 38; Am Bd Otolaryngol, dipl, 47. *Prof Exp:* Intern, Mem Assoc Hosp, New London, Conn, 37-38; asst, Path Lab, Los Angeles County Hosp, 38-39; resident, Willard Parker Hosp, NY, 39-40; assoc otolaryngol, Emory Univ, 41-42, asst prof, 46-47; chief audiol & speech correction, Phys Med & Rehab Div, Dept Med & Surg, Vet Admin, Washington, DC, 47-53; assoc prof ear, nose & throat, Univ Southern Calif, 53-64; clin prof otolaryngol, Univ Tex Med Sch, Dallas, 64-77; dir, Callier Hearing & Speech Ctr, 64-77, dean sch human develop, 74-77. *Concurrent Pos:* Dir audiol & speech correction ctr, Walter Reed Army Hosp, 47-52; instr, Univ Md, 48-53; lectr, Episcopal Eye, Ear & Throat Hosp, 49-53; clin instr, George Washington Univ, 51-53; assoc prof, Loma Linda Univ, 54-67; asst prof, Univ Calif, Los Angeles, 55-64; consult to Surgeon Gen, US Army, Off Voc Rehab, Washington, DC, Civil Aeronaut Admin, Vet Admin. *Mem:* Fel Acoust Soc Am; Am Otol Soc; fel Am Speech & Hearing Asn; fel AMA; fel Am Acad Ophthal & Otolaryngol. *Res:* Audiology; psychoacoustics. *Mailing Add:* House Ear Clin 2100 W 3rd St Suite 111 Los Angeles CA 90057-1902

GLORIOSO, JOSEPH CHARLES, III, MOLECULAR VIROLOGY, GENETICS THERAPY. *Current Pos:* from asst prof to assoc prof, 76-84, PROF MICROBIOL & IMMUNOL, UNIV MICH MED CTR 84-, ASST DEAN RES GRAD STUDIES, 88- *Personal Data:* b Louisville, Ky, July 9, 45. *Educ:* Univ Southwestern La, BS, 68, MS 70,State Univ, PhD(microbiol), 74. *Prof Exp:* Post doc, La State Univ Med Ctr, 74-76. *Concurrent Pos:* Spec reviewer Genetic Biol Study Sect, NSF, 81-, mem, Virol Study Sect, NIH, 86-; guest scientist, Ger Cancer Res Ctr, 82-83; mem, Virol study Sect, NIH, 86-; pres, Primagen, 88- *Mem:* Am Soc Microbiol; AAAS; Am Soc Virol; Am Asn Immunologists; Am Soc Gen Microbiol; Am Chem Soc. *Res:* Herpes simplex virus and neurotropic human pathogen; genetic engineering technologies employed to understand molecular basis of herpes simplex virus latency; virus reactivation; neuropathogenesis; development of herpes simplex virus as a gene transfer vector for treatment of autosomal neurologic diseases. *Mailing Add:* Molecular Genetics Biochem Univ Pittsburgh Sch Med Pittsburgh PA 15261-0001. *Fax:* 412-624-8997

GLORIOSO, ROBERT M, COMPUTER SCIENCE, ELECTRICAL ENGINEERING. *Current Pos:* CHIEF EXEC OFF, MARATHON TECHNOL. *Personal Data:* b Danbury, Conn, Apr 18, 40; m 62; c 1. *Educ:* Northeastern Univ, BSEE, 62; Univ Conn, MS, 64, PhD(comput sci), 67. *Prof Exp:* Instr elec eng, Univ Conn, Storrs, 64-67; proj eng comput tech team, US Army Electronics Command, Ft Monmouth, 67-69; assoc prof elec & comput eng, Univ Mass, Amherst, 69-76; mgr appl res & develop & tech dir comput syst develop group, Digital Equip Corp, 76-80, mgr corp res, 80- *Concurrent Pos:* Consult, Conn Res Assocs, 63-72; lectr math, Stevens Inst Technol, Hoboken, 68-69. *Mem:* Sr mem Inst Elec & Electronics Engrs; Asn Comput Mach; Sigma Xi. *Res:* Computer system organization; theory of computer design; human factors in computer system design; intelligent systems. *Mailing Add:* 70 Birch Hill Rd Stow MA 01775

GLOSS, STEVEN PAUL, WATER RESOURCE MANAGEMENT, AQUATIC ECOLOGY. *Current Pos:* DIR, WYO WATER RES CTR, 87- *Personal Data:* b Medford, Ore, May 1, 44. *Educ:* Mt Union Col, BS, 66; SDak State Univ, MS, 69; Univ NMex, PhD(biol), 77. *Prof Exp:* Proj leader, Utah Div Wildlife Res, 69-74; res biol fisheries, US Fish & Wildlife Serv, 78-87. *Mem:* Am Fisheries Soc; Sigma Xi; AAAS; Am Water Resources Asn. *Res:* Water resources; water policy; environmental pollutants. *Mailing Add:* 77 E North Fork Rd Centennial WY 82055

GLOSSER, ROBERT, OPTICAL PROPERTIES OF SOLIDS, MODULATION SPECTROSCOPY. *Current Pos:* assoc prof, 75-90, PROF PHYSICS, UNIV TEX, DALLAS, 90- *Personal Data:* b Johnstown, Pa, Dec 14, 37; m 63, Joan K Thorn; c Jeremy D. *Educ:* Mass Inst Technol, SB, 59; Univ Chicago, MS, 62, PhD(physics), 67. *Prof Exp:* Res scientist, Naval Weapons Ctr, 67-69; lectr physics, Univ Calif, Santa Barbara, 69-71; asst prof, Univ Md, 71-75. *Concurrent Pos:* Consult, Naval Weapons Ctr, 74, Varo, Inc, 84 & 87-93; fac fel, Naval Res Lab, 86, distinguished fac fel, 90. *Mem:* Sigma Xi; Am Phys Soc. *Res:* Application of optical techniques to study the electronic and vibrational structure of solids and to characterize material properties; silicon and III-V compounds and alloys; porous silicon and semiconductor clusters; raman spectroscopy; photoluminescence. *Mailing Add:* 2909 Deep Valley Trail Plano TX 75075. *Fax:* 972-690-2848; *E-Mail:* glosser@utdallas.edu

GLOSTEN, LAWRENCE R, ENGINEERING. *Current Pos:* CHMN, GLOSTEN ASSOC, 58- *Personal Data:* b 1918. *Mem:* Nat Acad Eng. *Mailing Add:* 7751 Hansen Rd Bainbridge Island WA 98110

GLOTH, RICHARD EDWARD, ORGANIC & ORGANOMETALLIC CHEMISTRY. *Current Pos:* Sr res chemist, Hydrocarbon Sect, Goodyear Tire & Rubber Co, 69-76, sr res chemist, Rubber Chem Sect, 76-80, prod rep, Specialty Chem, 81-86, latex & resins, 86-89, PROD REP NITRILE ELASTOMERS, GOODYEAR TIRE & RUBBER CO, 89- *Personal Data:* b Springfield, Mass, Aug 25, 41; m 66, Rena Vengrow; c 3. *Educ:* Univ Mass, Amherst, BA, 63, MS, 69, PhD(org chem), 70. *Mem:* Am Chem Soc. *Res:* Synthesis and reactions of arene-chromium and arene-tungsten tricarbonyls; synthesis of organometallic catalysts; homogeneous and heterogeneous catalysis; accelerations; rubber antioxidants. *Mailing Add:* Chem Div Dept 743 Goodyear Tire & Rubber Co Akron OH 44316-0001. *Fax:* 330-796-2617

GLOVER, ALLEN DONALD, ORGANIC CHEMISTRY. *Current Pos:* from asst prof to assoc prof, 66-91, PROF CHEM, BRADLEY UNIV, 91-, COORDR MED TECHNOL & COOP COORDR SCI, 85-, CHAIR, 88- *Personal Data:* b Kirksville, Mo, Jan 6, 38; m 63, Cynthia Rose; c Sarah Rose. *Educ:* Culver-Stockton Col, AB, 60; Carnegie Inst Technol, PhD(chem), 65. *Prof Exp:* Res fel chem, Calif Inst Technol, 65-66. *Concurrent Pos:* Res assoc, dept org chem, Univ Adelaide, Australia, 73 & dept clin biochem, Univ Otago, Dunedin, NZ, 80 & 87, dept chem, 94. *Mem:* Am Chem Soc; Sigma Xi. *Res:* Chemical education. *Mailing Add:* Dept Chem Bradley Univ Peoria IL 61606

GLOVER, BENJAMIN HOWELL, psychiatry; deceased, see previous edition for last biography

GLOVER, CLAIBORNE V C, III, PROTEIN PHOSPHORYLATION. *Current Pos:* asst prof biochem, 83-92, asst prof genetics, 84-92, PROF BIOCHEM & GENETICS, UNIV GA, 92- *Personal Data:* b Atlanta, Ga, July 8, 47; m 80; c 1. *Educ:* Duke Univ, BA, 69; Ga State Univ, MS, 74; Univ Rochester, PhD(biol), 79. *Prof Exp:* Post-doctoral fel biochem, Stanford Univ, 79-83. *Concurrent Pos:* Biol Sci Study Sect, NIH, 90-94. *Mem:* AAAS; Am Soc Biochem & Molecular Biol; Genetics Soc Am. *Res:* Biochemical, molecular and genetic analysis of protein kinases and their substrates in D melanogaster and S cevevisiae; regulation of nuclear protein function by phosphorylation/dephosphorylation. *Mailing Add:* Dept Biochem Univ Ga Life Sci Bldg Athens GA 30602-7229. *Fax:* 706-542-1738; *E-Mail:* glover@bscr.uga.edu

GLOVER, DAVID VAL, CYTOGENETICS. *Current Pos:* asst prof, 62-65, assoc prof, 65-72, PROF PLANT GENETICS & BREEDING, PURDUE UNIV, 72- *Personal Data:* b Farmington, Utah, May 18, 32; m 54; c 6. *Educ:* Utah State Univ, BS, 54, MS, 59; Univ Calif, PhD(genetics), 62. *Prof Exp:* Asst agron, Utah State Univ, 57-59; asst genetics & plant breeding, Univ Calif, 59-62. *Concurrent Pos:* Vis Scholar, Univ MN, 84- *Mem:* AAAS; Am Genetic Asn; fel Am Soc Agron; Sigma Xi; fel Crop Sci Soc Am; fel AAAS; Coun Agr Sci & Technol. *Res:* Genetics and cytogenetics of crop plants; genetics and biochemistry of maize endosperm gene interactions; carbohydrate, protein and nutritional quality in plant genetics and breeding; autotetraploid inheritance in alfalfa; breeking and physiology of alfalfa; somoclonal genetics. *Mailing Add:* Agron Purdue Univ West Lafayette IN 47907-1968

GLOVER, ELSA MARGARET, PHILOSOPHY OF SCIENCE. *Current Pos:* Asst prof, 67-71, assoc prof, 71-84, PROF PHYSICS, STILLMAN COL, 84- *Personal Data:* b Rochester, NY, Nov 11, 39. *Educ:* Univ Rochester, BS, 61; Purdue Univ, MS, 63, PhD(physics), 67. *Mem:* Sigma Xi; Am Asn Physics Teachers. *Res:* Scientific method and other methods of searching for truth; the relation between physics and metaphysics; the nature of space, time and matter. *Mailing Add:* Dept Math & Sci Stillman Col PO Drawer 1430 Tuscaloosa AL 35403-1430. *Fax:* 205-366-8996

GLOVER, FRED WILLIAM, ARTIFICIAL INTELLIGENCE, MATHEMATICAL PROGRAMMING. *Current Pos:* John King prof, 70-87, US WEST CHAIR SYST SCI, UNIV COLO, BOULDER, 87- *Personal Data:* b Kansas City, Mo, Mar 8, 37; m 88, Diane Tatham; c Dana & Paul. *Educ:* Univ Mo, BBA, 60; Carnegie-Mellon Univ, PhD, 65. *Honors & Awards:* Int Achievement Award, Inst Mgt Sci, 82; Energy Res Award, Energy Res Inst, 83; Outstanding Achievement Award, Am Inst Decision Sci, 84; Distinguished Res Lectr Award, Univ Colo, 88; Res Excellence Priz, Opers Res Soc, 89. *Prof Exp:* Miller res fel, Univ Calif, Berkeley, 65, asst prof, 65-66; assoc prof, Univ Tex, Austin, 66-69; prof, Univ Minn, Minneapolis,

69-70. *Concurrent Pos:* Consult, over 70 US Corps & govt agencies, 65-, US Cong, 84 & Nat Bur Stand, 86; lectr, NATO, France, Italy, Ger, Denmark, 70-89, Inst Decision Sci, 84; chmn, Bd Analysis, Res & Comput, Austin, 71-83; bd dirs, Mgt Systs & Decision Analysis Inst, Boulder, 74-82; partic host vis exchange, Nat Acad Sci, 81; res dir, Artificial Intel Ctr, Boulder, 84-; head res assoc, Global Optimization Space Consternation Ctr, Boulder, 88-; vis res chair eng, Univ Tex, Austin, 89, vis Cockerell family regents chaired professorship, 89; invited distinguished lectr, Swiss Fed Inst Technol, Lausanne, 90-; res prin, US West Joint Res Initiative, Univ Colo, 90-; prin investr, Air Force Off Sci Res, Off Naval Res, 90- *Mem:* Fel AAAS; Am Inst Decision Sci; Am Asn Col Schs Bus; Opers Res Soc Am; Math Prog Soc; Inst Mgt Scis. *Res:* Development of network and netform models for optimization, and of heuristic search methods linking artificial intelligence and mathematical programming. *Mailing Add:* Col Bus & Admin Univ Colo Box 419 Boulder CO 80309

GLOVER, GEORGE IRVIN, ENZYMOLOGY, PROTEIN CHEMISTRY. *Current Pos:* res mgr biocatalysis, 80-83, res mgr protein biochem, bio sci dept, 84-89, SCI FEL, MONSANTO CO, 89-; ASSOC DIR PROTEIN BIOCHEM, SMITH KLINE BEECHAM, 89- *Personal Data:* b Oakland, Calif, Mar 8, 40; m 59; c 2. *Educ:* Univ Calif, Berkeley, BS, 62, PhD(org chem), 66. *Prof Exp:* Sr res chemist, Air Prod & Chem, Inc, 66-67; res collabr protein chem & enzyme, Brookhaven Nat Lab, 67-70; from asst prof to assoc prof, Tex A&M Univ, 70-80. *Concurrent Pos:* NIH fel, 67-69; asst vis scientist, Brookhaven Nat Lab, 69-70. *Mem:* Am Soc Biol Chemists; Am Chem Soc. *Res:* Irreversible enzyme inhibitors; purification, kinetics and active sites of enzymes; synthesis of potential pesticides; medicinal chemistry; protein biochemistry. *Mailing Add:* Dept Protein Biochem UE0432 Smith Kline Beecham Pharmaceut PO Box 1539 King of Prussia PA 19406-0939. *Fax:* 610-270-7359

GLOVER, KENNETH MERLE, ATMOSPHERIC PHYSICS, ELECTRONICS. *Current Pos:* res physicist, Bedford, 62-70, supvry res physicist, Air Force Cambridge Res Labs, Off Aerospace Res, 70-74, CHIEF WEATHER RADAR BR, AIR FORCE GEOPHYS LAB, AIR FORCE SYST COMMAND, L G HANSCOM AFB, 74- *Personal Data:* b Hamilton, Ohio, Oct 11, 28; m 76; c 4. *Educ:* Miami Univ, AB, 58, MS, 60. *Prof Exp:* Res engr, Corp Res Labs, P R Mallory & Co, 60-62. *Mem:* Inst Elec & Electronics Engrs; Am Meteorol Soc; Sigma Xi. *Res:* Radar backscatter cross-sections of dielectric spheres; backscatter from the clear atmosphere; radar observations of the tropopause; radar observations of insects; remote sensing of clear air turbulence; Doppler radar data processing and display; use of Doppler radar in severe storms; atmospheric remote sensing. *Mailing Add:* 42 Jackson Dr Acton MA 01720

GLOVER, LEON CONRAD, JR, ORGANIC CHEMISTRY, POLYMER CHEMISTRY. *Current Pos:* staff chemist, 64-73, mgr, 73-81, TECH DIR, RAYCHEM CORP, 81- *Personal Data:* b Exeter, NH, July 5, 35; m 63, Dagmar M Nielsen; c Kira M, Leon C III & Gail G. *Educ:* Univ Notre Dame, BS, 57; Stanford Univ, PhD(org chem), 62. *Prof Exp:* Chemist, Shell Develop Co, Calif, 62-64. *Concurrent Pos:* Dir, NEAR, Inc, Mountain View, Calif. *Mem:* Am Chem Soc; Sigma Xi; Soc Plastics Engrs. *Res:* Organic peroxides; vanadium catalyzed olefin polymerizations; lithium catalyzed living polymer systems; high temperature polymer synthesis and evaluation; polymer characterization; radiation chemistry; hot melt adhesives development; polymer additives evaluation. *Mailing Add:* 1131 Buckingham Dr Los Altos CA 94024. *Fax:* 650-361-7950

GLOVER, LYNN, III, TECTONICS. *Current Pos:* PROF GEOL, VA POLYTECH INST & STATE UNIV, 70- *Personal Data:* b Washington, DC, Nov 29, 28; m 50. *Educ:* Va Polytech Inst & State Univ, BS, 52, MS, 53; Princeton Univ, PhD(geol), 67. *Prof Exp:* Geologist, US Geol Surv, 53-70. *Mem:* Fel Geol Soc Am; Am Asn Petrol Geol; Soc Econ Paleont & Mineral; Am Geophys Union; Cosmos Club; Explorer's Club. *Res:* Appalachian geology and tectonics. *Mailing Add:* Dept Geol Sci Va Polytech Inst State Univ Blacksburg VA 24061

GLOVER, ROLAND LEIGH, ELECTROCHEMISTRY. *Current Pos:* RETIRED. *Personal Data:* b Peterborough, Ont, Dec 19, 11; nat US; m 68, Mariette deC Bevington. *Educ:* Univ Toronto, BASc, 34, MASc, 35. *Prof Exp:* Asst, Univ Toronto, 34-35; lab technician, Nat Carbon Co Div Union Carbide Corp, Ont, 35-39, develop engr, Ohio, 39-44, head prod & process develop, 44-45, asst supt in chg eng & lab, 45-48, supt, Ont, 49-50, factory mgr, 51-54, asst dir res, Ohio, 54-56, asst to vpres & gen mgr NY, 56-59, gen mgr tech, Union Carbide Consumer Prod Div, 59-62, vpres, 62-73, technol consult, Battery Prod Div, Union Carbide Corp, 73-76. *Concurrent Pos:* Exec secy, Corp Technol Comt, 74-76. *Mem:* Electrochem Soc; fel Chem Inst Can. *Res:* Administration of chemical and electrochemical consumer products. *Mailing Add:* 2145 Lemon Ave Englewood FL 34223

GLOVER, ROLFE ELDRIDGE, III, SUPERCONDUCTIVITY PHASE TRANSITION, THIN METAL FILMS. *Current Pos:* from assoc prof to prof, 61-87, EMER PROF PHYSICS, UNIV MD, COLLEGE PARK, 87- *Personal Data:* b Wilmington, Del, Sept 6, 24; m 57, Barbara Ford Smith; c Rolfe IV, Gordon & Katherine. *Educ:* Bowdoin Col, BA, 48; Mass Inst Technol, BS, 48; Univ Gottingen, PhD(physics), 53. *Prof Exp:* NSF fel, Univ Calif, 55-57; asst prof, Univ NC, 57-61. *Concurrent Pos:* Alfred P Sloan res fel, 58-62; sr US scientist award, Alexander von Humboldt Found, 74-75. *Mem:* Fel Am Phys Soc. *Res:* Superconductivity; phase transitions; amorphous materials; thin films; chemical reactions at low temperatures; field effect in superconductors. *Mailing Add:* Dept Physics Univ Md College Park MD 20742. *E-Mail:* 75523,3225@compuserve.com

GLOVER, ROY ANDREW, NEUROANATOMY, MEDICAL EDUCATION. *Current Pos:* From instr to asst prof, 68-88, ASSOC PROF ANAT, UNIV MICH, ANN ARBOR, 88- *Personal Data:* b Cleveland, Ohio, Apr 7, 41; m 63; c 3. *Educ:* Calvin Col, BS, 63; Ohio State Univ, MSc, 65, PhD(anat), 68. *Honors & Awards:* Richard O'Connor Award for Res Excellence, Arthroscopy Asn NAm, 90. *Mem:* Am Asn Anatomists; Soc Neurosci; Am Asn Advan Sci; Soc Sigma Xi. *Res:* Development neurobiology of the neural tube in neurological mutations; biology of neuroglia; medical education; peripheral nerve degeneration and regeneration; role of substance P in the etiology of knee joint pain and the inflammatory changes accompanying degenerative joint disease; multiple substructure anatomical organ model patent. *Mailing Add:* Dept Anat Univ Mich Ann Arbor MI 48109-0616. *Fax:* 313-763-1166

GLOVER, SANDRA JEAN, ENTOMOLOGY. *Current Pos:* assoc prof, 69-80, PROF BIOL, APPALACHIAN STATE UNIV, 80- *Personal Data:* b Mansfield, La, Jan 19, 39. *Educ:* Northwestern State Univ, BS, 61; Univ Ga, MEd, 65, PhD(entom), 68. *Prof Exp:* Teacher high sch, La, 61-64; asst prof biol, Miss State Col Women, 68; res fel entom, Univ Ga, 68-69. *Concurrent Pos:* Instr, Univ Ga, 64-65 & fel, 68-69. *Mem:* Entom Soc Am; Am Inst Biol Sci; AAAS. *Res:* Insect physiology and behavior. *Mailing Add:* Dept Biol Appalachian State Univ 1 Appalachian State Boone NC 28608-0001

GLOVSKY, M MICHAEL, ALLERGY, CLINICAL IMMUNOLOGY. *Current Pos:* VIS ASSOC CHEM, CALIF INST TECHNOL, 77-; CLIN PROF MED, UNIV SOUTHERN CALIF, LOS ANGELES, 84- *Personal Data:* b Boston, Mass, Aug 15, 36. *Educ:* Tufts Univ, BS, 57, MD, 62. *Concurrent Pos:* Spec NIH res fel, Walter Reed Army Inst Res, 66-69; fel hemat & immunol, Univ Calif, San Francisco, 68-69; fel Kaiser Permanente Med Group, 69-71, chief, Dept Allergy & Clin Immunol, 72-, prin investr, Allergy Res Lab, 70-84, co-dir residency prog allergy & clin immunol, 74-84; head, Asthmat & Allergy Ctr, Huntington Mem Hosp, Pasadena, Calif, 89- *Mem:* AAAS; Reticuloendothelial Soc; Am Asn Immunologists; fel Am Acad Allergy; Am Thoracic Soc. *Res:* Interaction of immunoglobulins and complement; role of complement in human disease; mechanisms of anaphylaxis and allergy; occupational and environmental lung disease. *Mailing Add:* Asthma & Allergy Ctr Huntington Mem Hosp 39 Congress St Suite 301 Pasadena CA 91105-3022. *Fax:* 626-795-0982

GLOWA, JOHN ROBERT, NEUROENDOCRINOLOGY, NEUROSCIENCES. *Current Pos:* PROF PHARMACOL, PSYCHIAT & PSYCHOL, LA STATE UNIV MED CTR, 96- *Personal Data:* b Washington, DC, Sept 10, 46; m, Elizabeth Ellis; c Kathryn. *Educ:* Univ Md, BS, 72, MS, 76, PhD(biopsychol), 79. *Prof Exp:* Grad res asst, Dept Psychol, Univ Md, 75-79; res assoc, Dept Psychiat, Harvard Med Sch, 79-83; sr pharmacologist, Ayerst Labs Res, 83-84; sr staff fel, Clin Neurosci Br, NIMH BUNGm 84-86, Chief, Biopsychol Unit, Clin Neuroendocrinol Br, 87-; spec expert, Lab Med Chem, NIDDK, NIH, 91-; adj res assoc prof, Dept Psychiat, Uniformed Serv Univ Health Sci, Bethesda, Md, 92- *Concurrent Pos:* Fel environ sci, AAAS, 86; vis asst prof, Dept Psychol, Univ Md, 86-87; coordr biopsychol prog & assoc prof, Psychol Dept, Hood Col, Frederick, Md, 86-; res psychologist-in-residence, Dept Psychol, Am Univ, 87- *Mem:* Fel Am Psychol Asn; Am Soc Pharmacol & Exp Therapeut; Behav Pharmacol-Toxicol Soc; Soc Neurosci. *Res:* Behavior pharmacology; behavioral toxicology; neuroendocrine and central nervous system interactions. *Mailing Add:* Dept Pharmacol La State Univ Med Ctr 1501 Kings Hwy Shreveport LA 71130. *E-Mail:* jglowa@lsumc.edu

GLOWACKI, JULIE, ORTHOPEDIC. *Current Pos:* SR INVESTR, DEPT ORTHOP SURG, BRIGHAM & WOMEN'S HOSP, BOSTON, 88- *Personal Data:* b Boston, Mass, Sept 16, 44. *Educ:* Boston Univ, BA, 66; Harvard Univ, PhD, 73. *Prof Exp:* Res fel med, Endocrine Unit, Mass Gen Hosp, Harvard Med Sch, 72-74, assoc med, Med Sch, 74-76, res fel surg, 75-76, assoc biol chem, 75-78, res assoc, Dept Surg, 77-82, asst prof, 82-88, ASSOC PROF, DEPT ORTHOP SURG, HARVARD MED SCH, 89- *Concurrent Pos:* Assoc med, Mass Gen Hosp, 74-76 & asst biochem, Endocrine Unit, 76-77; sr scientist & admin dir, Bay Biochem Res, 75-77; vis scientist, Univ Mex & Nat Inst Nutrit, 76-77; vis investr, Salk Inst, La Jolla, 82-83; vis res biologist, Vet Admin Med Ctr, La Jolla, 82-87; consult, US Army, 89-; mem, Sci-Technol Comt, Am Asn Tissue Banks, 89-91 & Dent Prod Panel, US Food & Drug Admin, 91- *Mem:* Am Asn Dent Res; Am Elasmobr Soc; Am Soc Bone & Mineral Res; Am Soc Cell Biol; Am Soc Zoologists; Endocrine Soc; Int Asn Dent Res; Orthop Res Soc; Plastic Surg Res Coun; Soc Exp Biol & Med. *Res:* Cell biology of osteoclasts, osteoblasts and chondroblasts; clinical use of demineralized bone in craniomaxillofacial orthopedic and periodontal surgery; regulation of bone formation; regulation and mechanisms of bone resorption; pathophysiology of metabolic bone disease; hemangiomas and vascular malformations; mast cell as a bone cell; comparative skeletal and mineral metabolism. *Mailing Add:* Dept Orthop Res Brigham & Women's Hosp 75 Francis St Boston MA 02115

GLOWER, DONALD D(UANE), MECHANICAL ENGINEERING, NUCLEAR ENGINEERING. *Current Pos:* prof & chmn nuclear eng, Ohio State Univ, 64-68, prof & chmn mech eng, 68-76, dean, Col Eng, 76-90, vpres commun & develop, 90-92, EMER VPRES COMMUN & DEVELOP, OHIO STATE UNIV, 92- *Personal Data:* b Shelby, Ohio, July 29, 26; m 53, Betty Stahl; c Donald Jr, Michel, Jacob & Leilani. *Educ:* US Merchant Marine Acad, BS, 46; Antioch Col, MS, 53; Iowa State Univ, MSc, 58, PhD, 60. *Prof Exp:* Asst engr officer, Grace Lines Inc, 47-49; res engr, Battelle Mem Inst, 53-54; asst prof, Col Eng, Iowa State Univ, 54-58, asst prof nuclear eng, 60-61; fel, NSF, 59-60; mem res staff, Sandia Corp, 61-63; head, Radiation Effects Dept, Gen Motors Corp, 63-64. *Mem:* Fel Am Nuclear Soc; Am Soc Eng Educ; fel Am Soc Mech Engrs; Sigma Xi. *Res:* Energy conversion; manufacturing and management systems. *Mailing Add:* 2338 Kensington Dr Columbus OH 43221. *Fax:* 614-488-5913; *E-Mail:* glower.1@osu.edu

GLOWER, DONALD D, JR, CARDIAC MECHANICS, CARDIAC SURGERY. *Current Pos:* res fel surg, 82-84, resident gen & thoracic surg, 84-89, ASST PROF SURG, DUKE UNIV, 89-, ASST PROF BIOMED ENG, 91- *Personal Data:* b Ames, Iowa, Oct 30, 54; m 90, Sue A Masar; c Clare E. *Educ:* Ohio State Univ, BS, 76; Johns Hopkins Univ, MD, 80. *Mem:* Assoc fel Soc Univ Surgs; Soc Thoracic Surg; Am Physiol Soc; Am Heart Asn; Sigma Xi; fel Am Col Cardiol. *Res:* Quantification of cardiac function; cardiac mechanics in aschemia and heart failure; left ventricular oxygen consumption in heart failure; management of aortic dissection; outcome in patients undergoing coronary or valve operations. *Mailing Add:* PO Box 3851 Duke Univ Med Ctr Durham NC 27710. *Fax:* 919-684-8563

GLOWIENKA, JOHN CLEMENT, PLASMA PHYSICS. *Current Pos:* MEM RES STAFF, OAK RIDGE NAT LAB, 80- *Personal Data:* b Milwaukee, Wis, Apr 18, 48; m 74. *Educ:* Rensselaer Polytech Inst, BS, 71, ME, 73, PhD(plasma dynamics), 75. *Prof Exp:* Eng asst elec power, Cent Hudson Gas & Elec Corp, 67-71; res asst plasma dynamics, Rensselaer Polytech Inst, 71-75; electronics engr plasma diag, Technol Div, Simulation Br, Air Force Weapons Lab, 75-78; asst prof plasma physics, Univ Ill, Urbana-Champaign, 78-80. *Mem:* Am Phys Soc; Inst Elec & Electronics Engrs. *Res:* High energy density; magnetically confined plasma diagnostics by heavy ion beam probing; x-ray diagnostics. *Mailing Add:* Dansforth Lane Oak Ridge TN 37830-8753

GLOYD, STEPHEN S, HEALTH POLICY & MANAGEMENT. *Current Pos:* famil pract resident, Univ Wash, 73-76, adj asst prof & asst prof, 90-95, ASSOC PROF, DEPT HEALTH SERVS, UNIV WASH SCH PUB HEALTH & COMMUNITY MED, 95-, ADJ ASSOC PROF, DEPT FAMILY MED, SCH MED, 95- *Personal Data:* b Philadelphia, Pa, Aug 29, 47; m, Ahoua Kone; c Moussa & Salim. *Educ:* Harvard Univ, BA, 69, MPH, 83; Univ Chicago, MD, 73; Am Bd Family Pract, dipl. *Prof Exp:* Physician, NW Hosp Emergency Rm, Seattle, 76-77; staff physican, Boeing Co, Seattle, 77-78; physician, Group Health Coop, Seattle, Burien & Fed Way, 77-79; physician, Sofala Province, Min Health, Mozambique, 79-82; staff physician, SeaMar Community Health Clin, 83-85; proj dir, Mex Rural Health Proj, Univ Wash Collab Univ Guadalajara, Mex, 85-91. *Concurrent Pos:* Consult physician, Fremont Community Health Clin 74-78; instr, Epidemiol & Biostatist, Seattle Midwifery Sch, 83-85; physician, Prison Health Serv, State Wash Dept Corrections, 85-86; mem, Mayor Comt Cent Am, Seattle, 86-87; dir, Int Health Prog, Sch Pub Health & Community Med, Univ Wash, 86-, chair, World Health Day Planning Comt, 89-, mem, Pacific Rim Comt, 93-; med dir, Seattle King Count Dept Pub Health Travel Clin, 86-; pres, Mozambique Health Comt, Seattle, 87-92; W K Kellogg Found Nat fel, 87-90; ed consult, Int J Health Servs, Baltimore, 89-; gov bd mem, Nat Coun Int Health, 94-; proj dir, Seattle & Chimoio, Mozambique, 92-, exec dir, Health Alliance Int, 94-; Fulbright res award, Int Coun Exchange Scholars, US Info Agency, 96-97. *Res:* Effectiveness of prenatal care in Cote d'Ivoire; contributed numerous publications to professional journals. *Mailing Add:* Sch Med Univ Wash Box 357660 Seattle WA 98195-7660

GLOYER, STEWART EDWARD, INDUSTRIAL ORGANIC CHEMISTRY. *Current Pos:* vpres bus mgr, 89-92, VPRES RES & DEVELOP, HUMKO CHEM, DIV WITCO CORP, 83-, VPRES OLEFINS/STYRENIS, SBV POLYMER ADDITIVES, 93- *Personal Data:* b Milwaukee, Wis, May 23, 42; m 67; c 2. *Educ:* Univ Rochester, BS, 64; Univ Mich, MS, 66, PhD(chem), 69; Univ Chicago, MBA, 77. *Prof Exp:* Asst org chem, Univ Mich, 64-69; res chemist, Kraft Res & Develop Div, 69-71, group leader, 71-76, com develop mgr, Humko Sheffield Chem Div, 77-78, tech dir, Humko Sheffield Chem, Div Kraft Inc, 78-80, tech dir, 80-83. *Mem:* Soc Automotive Engrs; Am Chem Soc; Am Oil Chemists Soc; Soc Plastics Engrs. *Res:* Organic nitrogen chemistry; fatty acid chemistry; synthetic lubricant base stocks; additives for plastics; homogeneous and heterogeneous catalysis of organic reactions. *Mailing Add:* 1 American Lane Greenwich CT 06831-2559

GLOYER, STEWART WAYNE, CHEMISTRY. *Current Pos:* RETIRED. *Personal Data:* b Milwaukee, Wis, May 22, 10; m 39; c 3. *Educ:* Beloit Col, BS, 32; Univ Wis, PhD(chem), 39. *Prof Exp:* Res chemist, Coatings & Resins Div, PPG Industs Inc, 39-44, group leader, 44-52, asst dir res, 52-58, assoc dir res & develop, 58-65, div dir coatings develop, 65-68, div tech dir indust prod, 68-75; mgt & tech consult, Coatings Indust, 75-83. *Mem:* Am Chem Soc; Forest Prod Res Soc; fel Am Inst Chemists; Fedn Socs Paint Technol. *Res:* Protective and industrial coatings; resins; automotive finishes; electrocoating; ultraviolet and radiation coatings; coil and container coatings. *Mailing Add:* 1380 W Wisconsin Ave Apt 320 Oconomowoc WI 53066

GLOYNA, EARNEST F(REDERICK), SANITARY & ENVIRONMENTAL ENGINEERING. *Current Pos:* from asst prof to assoc prof civil eng, Univ Tex, Austin, 47-59, prof & dir, Environ Health Eng Labs, 54-70 & Ctr Res Water Resources, 63-73, dean, Col Eng, 70-87, Bettie Margaret Smith chair environ health eng, 82-87, PROF CIVIL ENG, UNIV TEX, AUSTIN, 59-, CHAIRED PROF ENVIRON ENG, 82-; CONSULT ENVIRON ENG, 87- *Personal Data:* b Vernon, Tex, June 30, 21; m 46; c 2. *Educ:* Tex Tech Univ, BS, 46; Univ Tex, MS, 49; Johns Hopkins Univ, DrEng, 52. *Honors & Awards:* Harrison Prescott Eddy Medal, Water Pollution Contron Fedn, 59 & Gordon Maskew Fair Medal, 79; Environ Qual Award, Environ Protection Agency, 77; Gordon Maskew Fair Award, Am Acad Environ Engrs, 82; J J King Prof Eng Achievement Award, 82; Order of Henri Pittier, Nat Conserv Medal, Repub Venezuela, 83; Award for Appln of Sci Knowledge in Pub Affairs, Nat Environ Develop Asn, 83; Simon W Freese Environ Eng Award, Am Soc Civil Engrs, 86; Nat Conserv Achievement Award in Sci, 86 & Nat Wildlife Fedn, 87; Centennial Medal, Am Soc Eng Educators, 93. *Prof Exp:* Jr engr, Tex Hwy Dept, Wichita Falls, 46; off engr, Magnolia Petrol Co, Dallas, Tex, 46-47. *Concurrent Pos:* Res asst, Johns Hopkins Univ, 50-52; guest engr, Brookhaven Nat Lab, 52; consult indust, USAF, USArmy, US Senate, Environ Protection Agency & UN; mem, Sci Adv Bd, US Environ Protection Agency, chmn, 82; gov coun, Nat Acad Eng; dir, Parker Drilling Co, Okla, 78-, bd dirs, US Nat Comt, World Energy Conf, 79-80, Nat Soc Prof Engrs, 81-88, Civil Eng Res Found, Am Soc Civil Engrs, 89-90, Res Found, Water Pollution Control Fedn, 89-90 & Epsey, Huston & Assocs, 90-; mem, Steinman Coun, Nat Soc Prof Engrs, 87- *Mem:* Nat Acad Sci; Nat Acad Eng; hon mem & fel Am Soc Civil Engrs; Asn Environ Eng Prof; Am Acad Environ Engrs (pres, 83); Am Inst Chem Engrs; hon mem Water Pollution Control Fedn (pres, 83-84); Nat Soc Prof Engrs; Am Soc Eng Educ; Am Water Works Asn; Asn Prof Environ Eng (past pres); Sigma Xi; Am Acad Environ Engr (pres,83); Inter Am Sanitary Asn; Nat Soc Prof Engr. *Res:* Water and wastewater treatment; author or editor of 8 books and author or coauthor of about 300 publications; industrial waste minimization; water reuse, water resource management; solid waste disposal; air pollution control; engineering education. *Mailing Add:* Dept Civil Eng Univ Tex Ernest Cockrell Jr Hall 4-200 Austin TX 78712

GLUCK, LOUIS, BIOCHEMISTRY, PEDIATRICS. *Current Pos:* PROF PEDIAT & OBSTET & GYN, COL MED, UNIV CALIF, IRVINE, 84- *Personal Data:* b Newark, NJ, June 18, 24; m 47; c Stephen L, David L, Clifford D & Ferris E. *Educ:* Rutgers Univ, BSc, 48; Univ Chicago, MD, 52; Am Bd Pediat, dipl, 63. *Honors & Awards:* Arvo Ylppo Award, Finland. *Prof Exp:* Intern med, Univ Clin, Univ Chicago, 53; resident pediat, Columbia-Presby Med Ctr, 56-59; instr, Sch Med, Stanford Univ, 59-60; from asst prof to assoc prof pediat, Sch Med, Yale Univ, 60-68; prof, Sch Med, Univ Miami, 68-69; prof reproductive med, Sch Med, Univ Calif, San Diego, 69-84. *Concurrent Pos:* Ed-in-chief, Current Probs Pediat; chmn, State of Calif Area XIII Ment Retardation Bd, 73-75; exec ed, Perinatology & Neonatology J. *Mem:* NY Acad Sci; Soc Study Reproduction; Perinatal Res Soc; Am Pediat Soc; Soc Pediat Res; Sigma Xi. *Res:* Developmental biochemistry; neonatal intensive care; fundamental studies on lung maturity of the fetus; L/S ratio test for lung maturity. *Mailing Add:* Univ Calif Irvine Med Ctr Pediat Dept Univ Calif Irvine Med Ctr Orange CA 92668-2901

GLUCK, RONALD MONROE, SOLID STATE CHEMISTRY & ELECTRONICS. *Current Pos:* Chemist, 57-68, res chemist, 68-75, sr res chemist, 76-81, RES ASSOC, EASTMAN KODAK CO, 81- *Personal Data:* b Brooklyn, NY, Jan 25, 37; m 58; c 3. *Educ:* Polytech Inst Brooklyn, BS, 57; Univ Rochester, MS, 71. *Mem:* Electrochem Soc. *Res:* Materials oriented research and process development for solid state microelectronic image sensors. *Mailing Add:* 55 Sandcastle Dr Rochester NY 14622

GLUCKSTEIN, FRITZ PAUL, INFORMATION COLLECTION & RETRIEVAL. *Current Pos:* RETIRED. *Personal Data:* b Berlin, Ger, Jan 24, 27; US citizen; wid; c 1. *Educ:* Univ Minn, BS, 53, DVM, 55; Am Bd Vet Pub Health, dipl, 66; Univ Md, MLS, 84. *Prof Exp:* Vet meat inspector, USDA, 55-56, asst vet pathologist, 58-59, vet analyst, 59-63; chief, Microbiol Br, Sci Info Exchange, Smithsonian Inst, 63-66; coordr vet affairs, Nat Libr Med, USPHS, 66-93; Consult, Biomed Info Retrieval, 93- *Mem:* Am Vet Med Asn; Am Pub Health Asn; Am Asn Lab Animal Sci; fel Royal Soc Health; Med Libr Asn. *Res:* Foreign animal diseases; laboratory animal science; veterinary public health; analysis and retrieval of scientific information. *Mailing Add:* 11801 Rockville Pike No 812 Rockville MD 20852

GLUCKSTEIN, MARTIN E(DWIN), CHEMICAL ENGINEERING, CHEMICAL PROCESS. *Current Pos:* CONSULT, 92- *Personal Data:* b Brooklyn, NY, May 19, 28; m 51, Marjorie Bliese; c Michael, Daniel, Lora, Joel & Lawrence. *Educ:* Univ Mich, BSE, 50, MSE, 51, PhD, 57. *Prof Exp:* Asst, Eng Res Inst, Univ Mich, 51, res assoc, 52-56, assoc res engr, 56; chem engr, Ethyl Corp, 56-63, res assoc, 63-64, res supvr, 64-86, res & develop mgr, 86-89, mgr process safety, 90-92. *Concurrent Pos:* Instr, Wayne State Univ, 57-62. *Mem:* Fel AAAS; Am Chem Soc; Am Inst Chem Engrs; Sigma Xi. *Res:* Combustion; fuels; lubricants; chemical process safety; catastrophe investigation; risk management. *Mailing Add:* 3955A Saint Andrews Ct Brookfield WI 53045. *Fax:* 414-781-3082

GLUCKSTERN, ROBERT LEONARD, PHYSICS. *Current Pos:* chancellor, 75-82, PROF, UNIV MD, COLLEGE PARK, 75- *Personal Data:* b Atlantic City, NJ, July 31, 24. *Educ:* City Col New York, BEE, 44; Mass Inst Technol, PhD(physics), 48. *Prof Exp:* AEC fel physics, Univ Calif, Berkeley, 48-49 & Cornell Univ, 49-50; res assoc, Yale Univ, 50-51, from asst prof to assoc prof, 51-64; prof & head dept, Univ Mass, Amherst, 64-69, assoc provost, 69-71, vchancellor acad affairs & provost, 71-75. *Concurrent Pos:* Consult, Lawrence Radiation Lab, Livermore, 58-61; Yale Univ fac fel, European Orgn Nuclear Res, Switz, 61-62; consult, Brookhaven Nat Lab, 63-, Los Alamos Nat Lab, 64- & Fermi Nat Accelerator Lab, 68-70 & 84-87; vis prof, Univ Tokyo, 70. *Mem:* Am Phys Soc; Am Asn Physics Teachers. *Res:* Theoretical, nuclear and elementary particle physics; accelerator theory. *Mailing Add:* 3117 Physics Bldg Univ Md College Park MD 20742

GLUECK, BERNARD CHARLES, PSYCHIATRY. *Current Pos:* RETIRED. *Personal Data:* b Baltimore, Md, Aug 26, 14; m 36; c 2. *Educ:* Columbia Univ, AB, 34, CPM, 51; Harvard Med Sch, MD, 38. *Prof Exp:* Instr psychiat, Col Physicians & Surgeons, Columbia Univ, 52-55, assoc psychoanalyst, Psychoanalysis Clin, 51-55; from assoc prof to prof, Univ Minn, 55-60; dir res psychiat, Inst Living, 60-79. *Concurrent Pos:* Lectr, Sch Med, Yale Univ, 66-79; prof, Dept Psychiat, Univ Conn, 78-82. *Mem:* Am Psychosom Soc; fel Am Psychiat Asn; Am Psychopath Asn (treas, 52-64, vpres, 64-65, pres, 66-67); Asn Psychoanal Med; fel Acad Psychoanal. *Res:* Psychoanalysis; computers; behavioral science. *Mailing Add:* 275 Steele Rd B159 West Hartford CT 06117-2752

GLUECK, HELEN IGLAUER, medicine, coagulation; deceased, see previous edition for last biography

GLUNTZ, MARTIN L, ORGANIC CHEMISTRY, FOOD TECHNOLOGY. *Current Pos:* RETIRED. *Personal Data:* b Harrisburg, Pa, Feb 11, 31; m 77, Karen McHenry; c Marti L, Michael, Marcia, Matthew & Mitchell. *Educ:* Lebanon Valley Col, BS, 53; Univ Del, MS, 57, PhD(org chem), 60. *Prof Exp:* Develop chemist, Am Cyanamid Co, NJ, 60-63; plant chemist, Tenneco Colors Div, Tenneco Chem, Inc, Pa, 63-66, mgr res, 66-68, plant mgr, SC, 68-69; chief prod develop technologist, Hershey Food Corp, 69-72, mgr planning & admin, 72-76, prod mgr, Hershey Plant, 76-77, mgr eng liaison, 77-81, dir int tech serv, 81-85, vpres tech serv, Hershey Int, Ltd, 85-96. *Mem:* Am Chem Soc. *Res:* Dyes and dye intermediates; food technology. *Mailing Add:* PO Box 269 Hummelstown PA 17036-0269. *Fax:* 717-566-9292

GLUSHKO, VICTOR, biochemistry, endocrinology, for more information see previous edition

GLUSKER, JENNY PICKWORTH, PHYSICAL BIOCHEMISTRY, X-RAY CRYSTALLOGRAPHY. *Current Pos:* res assoc, Inst Cancer Res, 56-67, asst mem, 67, mem, 67-79, SR MEM, INST CANCER RES, 79- *Personal Data:* b Birmingham, Eng, June 28, 31; nat US; m 55, Donald; c Ann, Mark J & Katharine (Seaboldt). *Educ:* Oxford Univ, BA, 53, MA & DPhil(chem), 57. *Hon Degrees:* DSc, Col Wooster, Ohio, 85. *Honors & Awards:* Garvan Medal, Am Chem Soc, 79; Fankuchen Award, Am Crystall Asn, 95. *Prof Exp:* Res fel x-ray crystallog, Calif Inst Technol, 55-56. *Concurrent Pos:* Res assoc prof, Univ Pa, 69-79, adj prof, 80-; vis fel, Oriel Col, Oxford, UK, 95. *Mem:* AAAS; Am Crystallog Asn; Am Chem Soc; Am Soc Biol Chem; Biophys Soc; Am Phys Soc. *Res:* Infrared spectroscopy; molecular structures in general; mechanisms of enzyme reactions from x-ray crystallographic studies of enzymes and their substrates and inhibitors; studies of polycyclic mutagens and carcinogens and the metabolic products of carcinogens. *Mailing Add:* Inst Cancer Res Fox Chase Cancer Ctr 7701 Burholme Ave Philadelphia PA 19111. *Fax:* 215-728-2863; *E-Mail:* jp_glusker@fccc.edu

GLUSKOTER, HAROLD JAY, GEOLOGY. *Current Pos:* CHIEF, BR COAL GEOL, US GEOL SURV, 85- *Personal Data:* b Chicago, Ill, May 8, 35; m 57; c 3. *Educ:* Univ Ill, BS, 56; Univ Iowa, MS, 58; Univ Calif, Berkeley, PhD(geol), 62. *Prof Exp:* From asst geologist to assoc geologist, Ill State Geol Surv, 62-70, geologist, Coal Sect, 70-78, head, 75-78; sr res assoc, Exxon Prod Res Co, Houston, 78-81, sr res supvr, 81-85. *Concurrent Pos:* Mem, Nat Comt Geochem, 75-80. *Mem:* Geol Soc Am; Am Inst Mining, Metall & Petrol Eng; Soc Econ Paleontologists & Mineralogists; Geochem Soc. *Res:* Geology of the Franciscan Formation, California; inorganic chemistry of coal; coal geology; mineral matter in coal. *Mailing Add:* US Geol Surv 12201 Sunrise Valley Dr MS 956 Reston VA 22092

GLUSMAN, MURRAY, NEUROPSYCHIATRY. *Current Pos:* RETIRED. *Personal Data:* b New York, NY, Dec 31, 14; m 49; c 2. *Educ:* NY Univ, BS, 34, MD, 38. *Prof Exp:* Asst neurol, Col Physicians & Surgeons, Columbia Univ, 49-50, from asst to assoc clin prof psychiat, 50-72, prof clin psychiat, 72-95. *Concurrent Pos:* Chief psychiat res behav physiol, NY State Psychiat Inst, 66-95; dir, Postdoctoral Res Training Prog, Col Physicians & Surgeons, Columbia Univ, 68- *Mem:* Am Acad Neurol; AAAS; Asn Res Nervous & Ment Dis; fel Am Psychiat Asn; Psychiat Res Soc. *Res:* Neural mechanisms in pain; brain mechanisms and emotional behavior; biogenic amines and aggression. *Mailing Add:* 22 Nobska Rd Woods Hole MA 02543

GLYDE, HENRY RUSSELL, THEORETICAL SOLID STATE PHYSICS. *Current Pos:* chmn, 82-89, PROF PHYSICS, UNIV DEL, 82-89 & 91- *Personal Data:* b Calgary, Alta, Oct 31, 37; c 2. *Educ:* Univ Alta, BS, 60; Oxford Univ, PhD(physics), 64. *Prof Exp:* Ciba Found fel, Univ Brussels, 64-65; res fel physics, Univ Sussex, 65-69; physicist, Atomic Energy Can Ltd, 69-71 & 72-75; proj staff, Int Develop Res Ctr, Can, 71-72; from assoc prof to prof physics, Univ Ottawa, 78-82; prof physics & chmn, Univ Alta, 89-91. *Concurrent Pos:* Vis physicist, Nat Res Coun, Can, 68, Atomic Energy Can Ltd, 78, Inst Laue Langevin, France, 75, 76, 81 & 86 & Brookhaven Nat Lab, 77 & 83; chmn theoret physics div, Can Asn Physicists, 74-75, chmn, div physics & soc, 76-78; vis prof, Chulalongkorn Univ, Thailand, 79-84 & State Univ NY, 83. *Mem:* Fel Am Phys Soc; Can Asn Physicists. *Res:* Neutron scattering; theory of metals; solidified inert gases; lattice dynamics; liquid and solid helium. *Mailing Add:* Dept Physics Univ Del Newark DE 19716

GLYMPH, EAKIN MILTON, RUBBER CHEMISTRY. *Current Pos:* RETIRED. *Personal Data:* b Pomaria, SC, Sept 6, 15; m 44; c 3. *Educ:* Clemson Univ, BS, 36; Iowa State Univ, PhD(biophys chem), 41. *Prof Exp:* Res chemist, Firestone Plantations Co, WAfrica, 41-46 & Firestone Tire & Rubber Co, 46-48, head latex group, Res Lab, 48-66, mgr natural rubber res & develop, 66-70, mgr natural rubber res & develop, Firestone Natural Rubber & Latex Co, 70-80. *Mem:* Am Chem Soc. *Res:* Polarography; industrial fermentations; synthetic and hevea rubber latexes; latex preparations and applications. *Mailing Add:* 728 Mt Gilead Dr Murrells Inlet SC 29576

GLYNN, PETER W, MARINE ECOLOGY. *Current Pos:* ZOOLOGIST, SMITHSONIAN TROP RES INST, 67- *Personal Data:* b Coronado, Calif, Apr 20, 33; m 60; c 2. *Educ:* Univ SDak, BS, 55; Stanford Univ, MS, 60, PhD(biol), 63. *Prof Exp:* Asst marine ecol, Univ PR, Mayag ez, 60-67. *Concurrent Pos:* NSF res grant, 63-66. *Mem:* Sigma Xi. *Res:* Structure and interactions in coral reef communities; systematics of marine isopoda, especially sphaeromatids. *Mailing Add:* Div Marine Biol/Fisheries-Rosenstiel Sch Marine & Atmospheric Sci Univ Miami 4600 Rickenbacker Causeway Miami FL 33149-1220

GLYNN, WILLIAM ALLEN, MATHEMATICS. *Current Pos:* RETIRED. *Personal Data:* b Nowata, Okla, Jan 21, 35; m 53; c 2. *Educ:* Northeastern State Col, BS, 60; Okla State Univ, MS, 62, PhD(math), 65. *Prof Exp:* Asst prof, Western Ill Univ, 65-68; assoc prof math & chmn dept, Va Commonwealth Univ, 68-73, prof math sci & chmn dept, 73-75, prof & assoc dean arts & sci, 75-96, assoc dean humanities & sci, 81-96. *Mem:* Math Asn Am. *Res:* Topology. *Mailing Add:* 9307 Classic Rd Glen Allen VA 23060

GNADE, BRUCE E, SEMICONDUCTOR MATERIALS, SEMICONDUCTOR PROCESSING. *Current Pos:* PROG MGR, DARPA, 97- *Personal Data:* b St Charles, Mo, Nov 2, 55; m 82; c 1. *Educ:* St Louis Univ, BA, 76; Ga Inst Technol, PhD(nuclear chem), 82. *Prof Exp:* Mem tech staff mat characterization, Tex Instruments, 82-88, sr mem tech staff, 88-90, mgr advan sci mat, Cent Res Labs, 90-97. *Concurrent Pos:* Adj prof, Physics Dept, Univ NTex, 88- *Mem:* Am Phys Soc; Mat Res Soc. *Res:* Silicon heterostrute materials systems for quantum electronics; thin film ferroelectric materials; silicon surface chemistry; nuclear analytical techniques; low energy nuclear structure. *Mailing Add:* Darpa 3701 Fairfax Dr Arlington VA 22203. *E-Mail:* gnade@resbld.csc.ticomm

GNAEDINGER, JOHN P(HILLIP), CIVIL ENGINEERING, GEOTECHNICAL ENGINEERING. *Current Pos:* pres, Soil Testing Serv, Inc, 48-91, EMER CHMN STS CONSULT LTD, 91- *Personal Data:* b Oak Park, Ill, Jan 11, 26; m 56; c John P Jr & Sarah E (Booras). *Educ:* Cornell Univ, BCE, 46; Northwestern Univ, MS, 47. *Prof Exp:* Struct designer, Shaw Metz & Dolio, Ill, 46-49. *Concurrent Pos:* Pres, Ill Eng Coun, 62; mem, Spec Adv Comt Struct Response to Sonic Boom, comt Radioactive Waste Disposal in Enewetok, Nat Acad Sci-Nat Acad Eng-Nat Res Coun, 64; chmn, Fed Construct Coun, 68-69 & Bldg Res Adv Bd, 69-71; chmn, Careers for Youth Found, 78-94; pres, John P Gnaedinger Res Corp, 80-94; hon mem, Bldg Res Adv Bd; Distinguished Scholar, Nat Acad Sci Exchange Prog, Peoples Repub China, 84; chmn, Shore Protection Stand Comt, Am Soc Civil Engrs, 94, mem, Residential Struct Expansive Soils Comt, 94. *Mem:* Am Soc Testing & Mat; fel Am Soc Civil Engrs; Nat Soc Prof Engrs; fel Asn Soil & Found Engrs (past pres); Sigma Xi; Nat Inst Bldg Sci. *Res:* Soil mechanics and foundation engineering, chemical grating and stabilization of soils; maturity testing of concrete; incinerator residue utilization for pavement construction. *Mailing Add:* 1415 Lakecook Rd Deerfield IL 60015

GNAEDINGER, RICHARD H, FOOD SCIENCE, ANIMAL HUSBANDRY. *Current Pos:* RETIRED. *Personal Data:* b Pocahontas, Ill, Sept 15, 30; m 77, Lorene Robl. *Educ:* Southern Ill Univ, BS, 58; Mich State Univ, MS, 60, PhD(food sci), 62. *Prof Exp:* Food technologist, Bur Com Fisheries, US Fish & Wildlife Serv, 62-63, chemist, 63-68; asst dir pet foods nutrit res, Ralston Purina Co, 68-70; diabetes res, Washington Univ, 70-73; chief chemist, Lab Serv, Mo Dept Health, 73-88, environ specialist, 88-93. *Concurrent Pos:* Pest Control & Financial Serv. *Mem:* Sigma Xi. *Res:* Animal and pet nutrition; animal production; utilization of fish and fishery products; laboratory animal care; body composition; headspace blood alcohol; breath and blood alcohol; issued two patents; lead in drinking water. *Mailing Add:* 508 Alcazar Ct Lady Lake FL 32159

GNANADESIKAN, RAMANATHAN, STATISTICAL ANALYSIS. *Current Pos:* PROF STATIST, RUTGERS UNIV, 91- *Personal Data:* b Madras, India, Nov 2, 32; m 65, Mrudulla Waknis; c Anand & Mukund. *Educ:* Univ Madras, BSc, 52, MA, 53; Univ NC, PhD(math statist), 57. *Honors & Awards:* Founders Award, Am Statist Asn, 96. *Prof Exp:* Res asst math statist, Univ NC, 54-57; sr res statistician, Procter & Gamble Co, 57-59; mem tech staff, Bell Tel Labs, 59-68, head statist & data anal res dept, 68-83, div mgr, info sci res, 84-86, asst vpres math, commun & comput sci res, Bellcore, 86-90, asst vpres info sci & technol, 90-91. *Concurrent Pos:* Consult, Cincinnati Bd Educ, 57-59; lectr & consult, Sch Med, Univ Cincinnati, 58-59; adj assoc prof, Courant Inst Math Sci, NY Univ, 61-63; adv, US Bur Census, 67-69; vis prof, Imp Col Sci & Technol, Univ London, 69; vis prof, Princeton Univ, 71 & Inst Advan Studies, Vienna, Austria, 81; adv comt, NSF, Div Math Sci, 85-88; bd gov, Inst Math & Its Appln, Univ Minn, 86-89; bd trustees, Nat Inst Statist Sci, 91-; bd gov, NJ State Math Coalition, 91-95; math sci educ bd, NAS, 89-92. *Mem:* Fel AAAS; Biomet Soc; fel Am Statist Asn; fel Inst Math Statist (pres, 88-89); Math Asn Am; fel Royal Statist Soc; Int Asn Statist Comput (pres, 81-83); Int Statist Inst. *Res:* Multivariate analysis, especially in the fields of the analysis and design of experiments and related areas of data analysis and theoretical statistics; graphical methods and robust procedures. *Mailing Add:* 425 Fairmount Ave Chatham NJ 07928-1369. *Fax:* 732-445-3428; *E-Mail:* rg@stat.rutgers.edu

GO, MATEO LIAN POA, STRUCTURAL ENGINEERING. *Current Pos:* assoc prof, 59-63, dir prof adv serv ctr, 67-72, chmn dept civil eng, 69-72, PROF ENG, UNIV HAWAII, 63-, CHMN DEPT CIVIL ENG, 81- *Personal Data:* b Amoy, China, Sept 17, 18; m 52; c 3. *Educ:* Cornell Univ, BCE, 42, PhD(struct & transp eng, soil mech), 46; Mass Inst Technol, SMCE, 43. *Prof Exp:* Construct engr, Mahony-Troast Construct Co, NJ, 42, 46-47; mgr, Mateo L P Go Construct Co, Philippines, 47-53, tech consult, Go Occo & Co, 53-54, br mgr, 54-56; asst prof eng, Syracuse Univ, 57-59. *Concurrent Pos:* Spec lectr, Cebu Inst Technol Philippines, 47-50; pres, Eng Assocs, 71. *Mem:* Am Soc Civil Engrs; Am Soc Eng Educ; Am Concrete Inst. *Res:* Airport engineering; space technology; structural mechanics; reinforced concrete; transportation and construction engineering. *Mailing Add:* 2415 Ferdinand Ave Honolulu HI 96822

GO, VAY LIANG, MEDICINE. *Current Pos:* EXEC CHAIR & PROF, DEPT MED, SCH MED, UNIV CALIF, LOS ANGELES, 88- *Personal Data:* b Ozamis City, Philippines, Aug 29, 38; US citizen; m 63; c 3. *Educ:* Univ Santo Tomas, Manila, AA, 58, DR, 63. *Honors & Awards:* 189th Luis Guerrero Mem Lectr, Philippine Soc Gastroenterol, 79; Alimurong Lectr Award, Univ Santo Tomas Alumni Asn, 89. *Prof Exp:* Med internship, Northwestern Hosp, Minneapolis, 64; resident internal med, Mayo Clin & Mayo Found, Rochester, 65-66, fel gastroenterol, 67-68; res assoc, Banting & Best Dept Med Res, Univ Toronto, 69-71; from asst prof to prof med, Mayo Med Sch, 72-88; dir, Div Digestive Dis & Nutrit, Nat Inst Arthritis, Diabetes, Digestive & Kidney Dis, NIH, 85-88. *Concurrent Pos:* Mem, NIH Group Pancreas, 72-74, Immunol Comt, 73-75; mem comt res, Am Gastroenterol Asn, 77-80 & 83-86; consult, Mayo Clin & Mayo Found, 71-88; mem, Fed Drug Admin Adv Comt Gastrointestinal Drugs, 90-94. *Mem:* AAAS; Am Asn Cancer Res; Am Asn Clin Invest; Am Fedn Clin Res; Am Gastroenterol Asn; Am Pancreatic Asn (pres, 78-79 & 88-89); Am Soc Clin Nutrit; Endocrine Soc; Sigma Xi; fel Am Col Physicians. *Res:* Relationship between pancreatic blood flow and vasoactive intestinal polypeptide; effective gastric stimulus and distribution of active hypothalamic sites; role of glucagon in splanchnic hyperemia of chronic portal hypertension. *Mailing Add:* Dept Med UCLA Sch Med Warren Hall No 13-146 Los Angeles CA 90024-1786. *Fax:* 310-824-5990

GOAD, CLYDE CLARENTON, GEODESY. *Current Pos:* geodesist, 75-81, CHIEF GRAVITY, ASTRON & SPACE GEOD DIV, NAT OCEAN SURV, NAT OCEANIC & ATMOSPHERIC ADMIN, 81- *Personal Data:* b Mount Airy, NC, Nov 20, 46; m 69; c 2. *Educ:* NC State Univ, BS, 69; Johns Hopkins Univ, MS, 71; Catholic Univ Am, PhD(aerospace eng), 77. *Prof Exp:* Sr analyst, Wolf Res & Develop Corp, Riverdale, Md, 69-75. *Mem:* Am Geophys Union; Sigma Xi. *Res:* Satellite geodesy-effects of earth and ocean tides on the orbits of artificial satellites; numerical modeling of the geoid of the earth. *Mailing Add:* 744 Northbridge Lane Columbus OH 43235

GOAD, WALTER BENSON, JR, BIOPHYSICS. *Current Pos:* RETIRED. *Personal Data:* b Marlowe, Ga, Sept 5, 25; m 52; c 3. *Educ:* Union Col, BS, 45; Duke Univ, PhD(physics), 54. *Prof Exp:* Mem Staff, T-Div, Los Alamos Nat Lab, 50-89. *Concurrent Pos:* Sr fel biophys, Univ Colo, 64-65, vis prof, 68-; vis scientist, Med Res Coun, Lab Molecular Biol, Cambridge Univ Eng, 70-71; scholar, Eleanor Roosevelt Inst Cancer Res, 77-; fel, Los Alamos Nat Lab, 87- *Mem:* Fel AAAS; fel Am Phys Soc; Sigma Xi. *Res:* Informatics; algorithms for molecular genetics. *Mailing Add:* Los Almos Nat Lab Mail Stop K710 Los Alamos NM 87545

GOANS, RONALD EARL, RADIATION PHYSICS, INSTRUMENTATION. *Current Pos:* LAB THEORET & PHYS BIOL, NAT INST CHILD HEALTH & DEVELOP, NIH, 87- *Personal Data:* b Knoxville, Tenn, Aug 12, 46; m 71; Judy Winegar; c Robert & Ronald E Jr. *Educ:* Univ Tenn, BS, 68, MS, 69, PhD(physics), 74; George Washington Univ, MD, 83. *Honors & Awards:* IR-100 Award, Indust Res-Develop Mag, 78. *Prof Exp:* Instr electronics, Univ Tenn, 69-74; res assoc health physics, Oak Ridge Nat Lab, 74-79 & George Washington Med Sch, 79-83; res assoc, Dept Obstet & Gynec, Providence Hosp, Washington, DC, 83-87. *Concurrent Pos:* Consult, Brazilian Inst Atomic Energy, 76-79; mem, Defense Nuclear Agency Inspection Team for radiol clean-up of Enewetak Atoll, 77-79. *Mem:* Health Physics Soc; Sigma Xi; AMA; Am Burn Asn. *Res:* Radiation instrumentation; optimization techniques; medical ultrasonics; chemical physics; theoretical and experimental research in medical ultrasonics; tissue characterization relevent to burns and to obstetrics & gynecology; biomathematics. *Mailing Add:* 1422 Eagle Bend Rd Clinton TN 37716-4009. *Fax:* 301-402-0263; *E-Mail:* ron@helix.nih.gov

GOATES, JAMES REX, PHYSICAL CHEMISTRY. *Current Pos:* From asst prof to assoc prof, 47-54, chmn dept, 65-68, PROF CHEM, BRIGHAM YOUNG UNIV, 54-, DEAN, COL PHYS & MATH SCI, 81- *Personal Data:* b Lehi, Utah, Aug 14, 20; m 48; c 3. *Educ:* Brigham Young Univ, BS, 42; Univ Wis, PhD(phys & soil chem), 47. *Mem:* Am Chem Soc; Sigma Xi. *Res:* Thermodynamic properties of metallic sulfides; thermodynamics and mechanisms of adsorption; thermodynamics of solutions. *Mailing Add:* Brigham Young Univ Provo UT 84601

GOATES, STEVEN REX, ANALYTICAL CHEMISTRY. *Current Pos:* asst prof, 82-87, ASSOC PROF CHEM, BRIGHAM YOUNG UNIV, 87- *Personal Data:* b Provo, Utah, Nov 8, 51; m 77; c 1. *Educ:* Brigham Young Univ, BSc, 76; Univ Mich, MSc, 77, PhD(chem), 81. *Prof Exp:* Res assoc, Radiation Lab, Columbia Univ, 81-82. *Mem:* Sigma Xi; Am Chem Soc; Am Phys Soc. *Res:* Chemical analysis by laser methods; investigation of supersonic jet spectroscopy and supercritical fluids for chemical analysis; laser spectroscopic interrogation of non-electrolyte solutions; laser photoframentation spectroscopy. *Mailing Add:* Dept Chem Brigham Young Univ 139 Eyring Sci Ctr Provo UT 84602-1022

GOAZ, PAUL WILLIAM, ORAL & MAXILLOFACIAL RADIOLOGY. *Current Pos:* prof oral diag & roentgenol, 78-91, EMER PROF DIAG SCI, BAYLOR COL DENT, DALLAS, 91- *Personal Data:* b Lafayette, Ind, Apr 13, 22; m, Virginia M Fijalkowski; c Mary E (Hecox) & Karan A (Wensowitch). *Educ:* Loyola Univ, Chicago, DDS, 50; Univ Chicago, SM, 53; Okla State Univ, BS, 59. *Prof Exp:* Intern, Zoller Mem Clin, Chicago, 50-51, asst dent surg, 51-53; clin asst dent surg, Sch Med, Univ Okla, 53-54, from instr to asst prof, 54-70; assoc prof oral diag & vchmn dept, Sch Dent, Loyola Univ Chicago, Maywood, 70-78. *Concurrent Pos:* Res fel, Okla Med Res Found & head dent sect, 53-62; pvt pract. *Mem:* Am Acad Oral Maxillofacial Radiol; Am Asn Phys Anthrop; Am Asn Dent Res; Sigma Xi. *Res:* Salivary, bacterial growth factors; clinical testing of potential anticariogenic agents; dental morphology and anthropology; oral and maxillofacial radiology. *Mailing Add:* 10930 Ridge Meadow Dr Dallas TX 75218. *Fax:* 214-828-8346

GOBEL, FREDERICK L, CARDIOVASCULAR DISEASES. *Current Pos:* assoc prof med, 72-80, CLIN ASSOC PROF MED, SCH MED, UNIV MINN, 80- *Personal Data:* b La Crosse, Wis, Jan 8, 35; c 3. *Educ:* Univ Wis, BS, 57, MD, 59. *Honors & Awards:* Mordse J Shapiro Mem Travel Award, 69. *Prof Exp:* Gen pract med, Duluth, Minn, 60-62; chief resident, Med Serv, Vet Admin Hosp, 66; cardiac fel, Dept Med, Sch Med, Univ Minn, 66-69; dir cardiac cath lab med, Cardiovasc Sect, Vet Admin Hosp, 69-77, chief cardiovasc sect, 72-77. *Concurrent Pos:* From instr to asst prof med, Sch Med, Univ Minn, 67-72; pvt practr cardiol, 77- *Mem:* Am Heart Asn; fel Am Col Physicians; fel Am Col Cardiol; fel Coun Clin Cardiol. *Res:* Relationship between myocardial blood flow and myocardial oxygen consumption, and hemodynamic predictors of myocardial blood flow, and how each is altered by medical or surgical therapy. *Mailing Add:* 4521 E Lake Harriet Blvd Minneapolis MN 55409

GOBEL, STEPHEN, CYTOLOGY, NEUROBIOLOGY. *Current Pos:* SCI REV ADMINR, NEUROL SCI STUDY, NIH, 84- *Personal Data:* b New York, NY, Dec 27, 38; m 61, Sharon A Keshner; c Jennifer M & Amy B. *Educ:* NY Univ, DDS, 63. *Honors & Awards:* Commendation Medal, USPH Serv. *Prof Exp:* Dent surgeon, Nat Inst Dent Res, 66-77, chief neurocytology & exp anat sect, 77-84. *Concurrent Pos:* Fel cytol, Col Dent, NY Univ, 63-66. *Mem:* Soc Neurosci; Int Asn Study Pain; Int Asn Dent Res; AAAS; Am Col Sports Med. *Res:* Electron microscopical studies of the neural circuitry of primary and second order neurons in the dorsal horns of the trigeminal system and spinal cord; basic mechanisms underlying pain and other somatic sensations; effects of nerve injury on the spinal cord and brain. *Mailing Add:* 5917 Empire Way Rockville MD 20852. *Fax:* 301-594-7044

GOBER, JAMES WILLIAM, PROKARYOTIC DEVELOPMENT, MICROBIAL GENETICS. *Current Pos:* ASST PROF BIOCHEM, UNIV CALIF, LOS ANGELES, 91- *Personal Data:* b Cambridge, UK, Oct 28, 57; US citizen. *Educ:* Northeastern Univ, BS, 80; Boston Univ, PhD(microbiol), 87. *Prof Exp:* Helen Hay Whitney fel, Columbia Univ, 88-89; Helen Hay Whitney scholar, Stanford Univ, 89-91. *Concurrent Pos:* Sr fel, Am Cancer Soc, Stanford Univ, 91; mem, Molecular Biol Inst, Univ Calif, Los Angeles, 92-, prin investr, NIH grant, 92- *Mem:* Am Soc Microbiol; Genetics Soc Am; AAAS; Sigma Xi. *Res:* Transcriptional regulation during cell differentiation in Caulobacter; genetics and biochemistry of cell cycle and polar gene expression; DNA higher-order structure and transcriptional activation; chromosome structure; regulation of flagellum assembly and cell division. *Mailing Add:* Dept Chem & Biochem Univ Calif 405 Hilgard Ave Los Angeles CA 90024-1301. *Fax:* 310-206-4038; *E-Mail:* jwg@argon.chem.ucla.edu

GOBERSTEIN, SIMON M, ALGEBRA. *Current Pos:* PROF, DEPT MATH & STATIST, CALIF STATE UNIV, CHICO, 81- *Personal Data:* b Saratov, Russia, Aug 20, 49. *Educ:* Univ Saratov, Russia, MS, 71; Univ Ark, PhD(math), 81. *Mem:* Am Math Soc. *Res:* Algebra. *Mailing Add:* Dept Math & Statist Calif State Univ Chico CA 95929-0525

GOBLE, ALFRED THEODORE, OPTICS. *Current Pos:* from lectr to prof, 45-74, chmn dept, 66-71, EMER PROF PHYSICS & RES PROF, UNION COL, NY, 74- *Personal Data:* b River Falls, Wis, Jan 24, 09; m 35, Ethel Frank; c Robert L, Louis F & Jonathan C. *Educ:* Univ Wis, BA, 29, PhD(physics), 33. *Prof Exp:* Asst physics, Univ Wis, 29-33, Univ Alumni Res Found res assoc, 33-34; from instr to asst prof, Univ Tulsa, 34-37; from asst prof to assoc prof, Alfred Univ, 37-46. *Concurrent Pos:* Vis asst prof, Princeton Univ, 42-43; res assoc, Harvard Univ, 44-45; consult, Stand Rolling Mills, Inc, 49-54, Revere Copper & Brass, Inc, 54-72 & Thompson-Ramo-Wooldridge Corp, 55-58; mem tech staff, Space Tech Lab, 58-59, consult, 59-60; consult, Aerospace Corp, 60-64; vis researcher, Clarendon Lab, Oxford, 64-65 & 71-72. *Mem:* Am Phys Soc; Optical Soc Am; Am Asn Physics Teachers. *Res:* Theoretical spectroscopy; intensities in platinum-like spectra; recombination spectra of potassium; cosmic rays; high resolution spectroscopy; isotope shifts. *Mailing Add:* Dept Physics Union Col Schenectady NY 12308. *Fax:* 518-388-6974; *E-Mail:* goblea@gar.union.edu

GOBLE, DAVID FRANKLIN, THEORETICAL PHYSICS. *Current Pos:* asst prof theoret physics, 68-77, ASSOC PROF THEORET PHYSICS, DALHOUSIE UNIV, 77- *Personal Data:* b Pincher Creek, Alta, July 31, 40; m 62; c 2. *Educ:* Univ Alta, BSc, 62, MSc, 63; Univ Toronto, PhD(theoret physics), 67. *Prof Exp:* NATO res fel, Inst Pure & Appl Phys Sci, Univ Calif, San Diego, 67-68. *Mem:* Am Asn Physics Teachers; Can Asn Physicists. *Res:* Development of a microscopic theory of liquid helium four using many-body techniques; explanation of finite size effects in liquid helium four. *Mailing Add:* Dept Physics Dalhousie Univ Halifax NS B3H 4H6 Can

GOBLE, FRANS CLEON, ARCHEOZOOLOGY, COMPARATIVE OSTEOLOGY & ODONTOLOGY. *Current Pos:* ARCHEOLOGIST, DEPT ANTHROP, SCI MUS MINN, 83- *Personal Data:* b Chicago, Ill, July 11, 13. *Educ:* Battle Creek Col, BS, 33; Univ Mich, MS, 34, ScD(zool), 39. *Prof Exp:* Asst, Univ Mich, 34, tech asst histol, 35-38; pathologist, Bur Game, State Conserv Dept, NY, 38-45; pathologist & parasitologist, Sterling-Winthrop Res Inst, 45-51; head lab path, Abbott Labs, 51-52; biol consult, St Thomas, Virgin Islands, 52-53; dir parasitol, Ciba Pharmaceut Co, 54-60, dir chemother, 61-68; dir biol, Smith, Miller & Patch, Inc, 69-72; dir, Dept Infectious Dis, Res & Develop Div, Cooper Labs Inc, 72-78. *Concurrent Pos:* Mem, 4th, 6th, 7th & 8th Int Cong Trop Med & Malaria; mem, 1st Int Cong Chagas Dis, Adv Group Res, Pan-Am Health Orgn, 62, consult & chmn chemother res group, 63-; mem exp adv panel parasitic dis, WHO, 64-79; consult toxicol, 78-, osteol, Crow Canyon Archeol Ctr, 89- *Mem:* Am Anthrop Asn; Am Asn Pathologists; Soc Toxicol; Am Soc Trop Med;

Archaeol Inst Am; Soc Am Archaeol. *Res:* Pathology and chemotherapy of experimental infectious diseases; histology and hematology in subacute and chronic toxicity studies on synthetic organic compounds and antibiotics; identification of animal bones from archeological sites. *Mailing Add:* 1147 S Winthrop St Paul MN 55119

GOBLE, GEORGE G, STRUCTURAL ENGINEERING. *Current Pos:* chmn, Dept Civil & Archit Eng, 77- EMER PROF CIVIL & ARCHIT ENG, UNIV COLO, BOULDER, 92- *Personal Data:* b Eagle, Idaho, Sept 11, 29; m 53; c 2. *Educ:* Univ Idaho, BS, 51; Univ Wash, MS, 57, PhD(struct), 61. *Honors & Awards:* Collingwood Award, Am Soc Civil Engrs, 65; Lincoln Prof Struct Design Award, 66. *Prof Exp:* Prof struct, Case Western Reserve Univ, 61-77. *Concurrent Pos:* Vis prof, Univ Calif, Berkeley, 68- *Mem:* Am Soc Civil Engrs; Am Concrete Inst; Soc Exp Stress Analysis. *Res:* Behavior of civil engineering structures; design of structures; optimum design of structures using mathematical programming; dynamic pile behavior. *Mailing Add:* 3775 Moffit Ct Boulder CO 80304

GOBLE, JAMES H, JR, THIN FILM FABRICATION. *Current Pos:* SUPVR, RES & DEVELOP GROUP, TALANDIC RES CORP, 85- *Personal Data:* b Tex. *Educ:* Univ Tex, Austin, BS, 75; Univ Calif, Berkeley, 82. *Prof Exp:* Nat Res Coun resident res assoc & CDI contractor, Jet Propulsion Lab, 82-85; res assoc, Mass Inst Technol, 81-82. *Mem:* Am Chem Soc; Am Phys Soc; Am Vacuum Soc; AAAS; Int Soc Optical Eng. *Res:* Basic and/or applied research in physics and chemistry of thin film fabrication and characterization for optical and electrical applications. *Mailing Add:* 415 S El Molino Apt 9 Pasadena CA 91101

GOBLIRSCH, RICHARD PAUL, MATHEMATICS. *Current Pos:* assoc prof, 64-77, PROF MATH & ACTG DEAN, COL ST THOMAS, 77- *Personal Data:* b Minneapolis, Minn, Jan 1, 30; m 52; c 3. *Educ:* Col St Thomas, BA, 51; Univ Wis, MA, 52, PhD, 56. *Prof Exp:* Asst math, Univ Wis, 53-56; instr, Univ Va, 56-59; asst prof, Univ Rochester, 59-63; vis asst prof, Univ Colo, 63-64. *Mem:* Am Math Soc; Math Asn Am; Sigma Xi. *Res:* Geometric topology; real variables. *Mailing Add:* 247 Finn St S St Paul MN 55105-1256

GOBRAN, RAMSIS, ORGANIC CHEMISTRY. *Current Pos:* res polymer chemist, Minn Mining & Mfg Co, 59-67, res specialist, 67-72, sr res specialist, 72-74, prod develop mgr, Indust Tape Div, 74-80, researcher, Prod Develop & New Prod Mgr, Disposable Prod, 80-82, div scientist, Disposable Prod Div, 83-84, CORP SCIENTIST, DISPOSABLE PROD DIV, 3M CO, 85- *Personal Data:* b Sinbellawin, Egypt, Feb 20, 32; US citizen; m 59; c 3. *Educ:* Univ Alexandria, BSc, 52; Univ Southern Calif, MS, 57, PhD(chem), 59. *Prof Exp:* Parke Davis Co fel, 57-59, Goodyear Rubber Co fel, 59. *Mem:* Am Chem Soc; Sigma Xi. *Res:* Polymer, photographic and organic heterocyclic chemistry; adhesives. *Mailing Add:* 1026 Brenner Ave St Paul MN 55113-1908

GOBUSH, WILLIAM, MATHEMATIC COMPUTER LANGUAGES, IMPACT MECHANICS. *Current Pos:* appl mathematician, 74-83, mgr aerodyn res, 83-96, PRIN SR ENGR, TITLEIST & FOOTJOY WORLDWIDE, 96- *Personal Data:* b Lawrence, Mass, Apr 14, 45; m 69. *Educ:* Clark Univ, BA, 66; Dartmouth Col, PhD(chem), 70. *Honors & Awards:* Am Chem Soc Award, 66. *Prof Exp:* Post-doctoral fel, Tex A&M Univ, 70-71 & Midland Macromolecular Inst, 71-74. *Mem:* Am Phys Soc; Am Chem Soc. *Res:* Applied math; computer programming in electronic imaging; impact analysis and aerodynamic analysis of rotating bodies and elastomer analysis; granted 28 US patents and 6 foreign patents; authored several journal publications and book articles. *Mailing Add:* 17 Merrymount Dr N Dartmouth MA 02747. *Fax:* 508-979-3903; *E-Mail:* gobush@tfjww.com

GOCHENAUR, SALLY ELIZABETH, MYCOLOGY. *Current Pos:* RETIRED. *Personal Data:* b Cleveland, Ohio, Mar 30, 32. *Educ:* Univ Cincinnati, BS, 58, MS, 60; Univ Wis, PhD(bot), 64. *Prof Exp:* From asst prof to prof microbiol, Adelphi Univ, 64-85. *Concurrent Pos:* Res assoc, Univ Wis, 64-; res collabr, Brookhaven Nat Lab, 68-69. *Mem:* Bot Soc Am; Mycol Soc Am; Brit Mycol Soc; Ecol Soc Am; Sigma Xi. *Res:* Fungal physiology; taxonomy and ecology of soil fungi. *Mailing Add:* 7965 Kimbee Dr Cincinnati OH 45244

GOCHENOUR, WILLIAM SYLVA, VETERINARY MEDICINE. *Current Pos:* RETIRED. *Personal Data:* b East St Louis, Ill, July 18, 16; m 40; c 1. *Educ:* Univ Pa, VMD, 37; Am Bd Pub Vet Health, dipl; Am Bd Microbiol, dipl. *Prof Exp:* Lab vet, Bur Animal Indust, USDA, 37-38; res vet, Pitman Moore Co Div, Allied Labs, Inc, 39; chief vet bact, Med Serv Grad Sch, Walter Reed Army Med Ctr, US Army, 49-53, chief animal stand & liaison br, Off Surgeon Gen, 53-54, chief animal assessment br, Med Unit, Ft Detrick, 54-63, dep dir, Walter Reed Army Inst Res, Walter Reed Army Med Ctr, DC, 63-74; dir animal care serv, Med Ctr, Univ Ky, 74-77. *Mem:* Fel AAAS; Am Pub Health Asn; Am Vet Med Asn; Asn Mil·Surg US. *Res:* Infectious diseases, especially respiratory diseases and the zoonoses. *Mailing Add:* 1286 Oaklawn Park Lexington KY 40517

GOCHFELD, MICHAEL, OCCUPATIONAL HEALTH & ENVIRONMENTAL & ECOLOGICAL RISK ASSESSMENT. *Current Pos:* dir, occup med, 80-95, CLIN PROF, ROBERT WOOD JOHNSON MED SCH, 80- *Personal Data:* m 81, Joanna Burger; c 2. *Educ:* Albert Einstein Col Med, MD, 65; City Univ NY, PhD(environ biol), 75. *Prof Exp:* Res assoc, Rockefeller Univ, 76-77; dir occup & environ health, NJ Dept Health, 78-80. *Concurrent Pos:* Sci consult, NJ Agent Orange Comn, 83-90, Am Legion Agent Orange Panel, 88-; pres, NJ Occup Med Asn. *Mem:* Fel Am Col Occup & Environ Med; fel Am Ornith Asn; Ecol Soc Am; Soc Conserv Biol. *Res:* Developmental methods for evaluation, individual, community and ecosystem exposure to environment contaminants; testing of new models for studying neurobehavioral development. *Mailing Add:* EOHSI 681 Frelinghuysen Piscataway NJ 08855. *Fax:* 732-445-0130; *E-Mail:* gochfeld@eohsi.rutgers.edu

GOCHMAN, NATHAN, BIOCHEMISTRY. *Current Pos:* CLIN CHEMIST, LAB SERV, VET ADMIN HOSP, 72- *Personal Data:* b Brooklyn, NY, Nov 11, 33; m 55; c 2. *Educ:* Brooklyn Col, BS, 55; Northwestern Univ, PhD(chem), 58. *Prof Exp:* Supvr, Bioanal Lab, G D Searle & Co, 58-62; dir clin chem, Technicon Instruments Corp, 62-66, res lab dir, 66-68; clin chemist, Clin Ctr, NIH, 68-72. *Concurrent Pos:* Assoc adj prof chem & pathol, Univ Calif, San Diego, 72-79, adj prof path, 79- *Mem:* AAAS; Am Asn Clin Chem (pres, 78); NY Acad Sci; Am Chem Soc; Sigma Xi. *Res:* Enzymology; analytical biochemistry; drug metabolism; development of methods and instruments for biochemical determinations with emphasis on automation. *Mailing Add:* 6409 E Lookout Lane Anaheim Hills CA 92807-4827

GOCHNAUER, THOMAS ALEXANDER, MICROBIOLOGY. *Current Pos:* RETIRED. *Personal Data:* b Appleton, Wis, July 29, 19; m 50; c 3. *Educ:* Univ Wis, PhD(bact), 50. *Prof Exp:* Res assoc entom & econ zool, Univ Minn, 49-61; chief apicult sect, Entom Res Inst, Can Dept Agr, 61-70, res scientist, Entom Sect, Ottawa Res Sta, 70-92. *Mem:* AAAS; Am Soc Microbiol; NY Acad Sci; Can Soc Microbiol; Soc Invert Path; Sigma Xi. *Res:* Honeybee diseases and control; antibiotics; phages; effects of gamma radiation; detection, distribution and infectivity of B larvae and Ascosphaera apis spores in the honeybee environment. *Mailing Add:* 14 Trinity Dr Nepean ON K2H 6H2 Can

GODAR, EDITH MARIE, ORGANIC CHEMISTRY, ANALYTICAL CHEMISTRY. *Current Pos:* RETIRED. *Personal Data:* b Chicago, Ill, June 19, 21. *Educ:* Rosary Col, BS, 42; Loyola Univ, Ill, MS, 56, PhD(org chem), 59. *Prof Exp:* Res chemist, Res Div, Am Can Co, 43-56; instr chem, Loyola Univ, Ill, 59-68; assoc prof chem, Mary Manse Col, 68-80, chmn dept sci & math, 71-80. *Concurrent Pos:* Instr, Rosary Col, 53-54; sr res chemist, Int Minerals & Chem Corp, 59-68; fel, Univ Detroit, 68. *Mem:* Am Chem Soc; Soc Appl Spectros; Sigma Xi. *Res:* Synthetic organic chemistry; instrumental methods of analysis. *Mailing Add:* 11704 103rd Ave NE Kirkland WA 98034

GODARD, HUGH P(HILLIPS), CHEMICAL ENGINEERING, INDUSTRIAL CHEMISTRY. *Current Pos:* RETIRED. *Personal Data:* b Montreal, Que, Oct 19, 14; m 91; c 1. *Educ:* Univ BC, BASc, 36, MASc, 37; McGill Univ, PhD(indust & cellulose chem), 41. *Honors & Awards:* Frank Newman Speller Award, Nat Asn Corrosion Engrs, 63; Plummer Medal, Eng Inst Can, 56. *Prof Exp:* Chief chemist, Chems & Explosives, Inspection Bd, UK & Can, 41-45; head, Chem Div, Aluminum Labs, Ltd, 45-66, dep dir, Kingston Lab, Alcan Int Ltd Res Ctr, Kingston, 66-73. *Concurrent Pos:* Bd dirs, Nat Asn Corrosion Engrs, 52-55; dir publ, Chem Inst Can, 55-58; ed, Mats Performance, 73-83; pres, Aluminum Corrosion Serv, 73-91; pres, Int Cong Metallic Corrosion, 84. *Mem:* Nat Asn Corrosion Engrs (pres, 59-60). *Res:* Corrosion of aluminum and its prevention. *Mailing Add:* 465-1674 56th St Delta BC V4L 2M5 Can

GODBEE, H(ERSCHEL) W(ILLCOX), CHEMICAL ENGINEERING. *Current Pos:* RES ENGR, OAK RIDGE NAT LAB, 58- *Personal Data:* b Hinesville, Ga, Mar 4, 28; m 52; c 3. *Educ:* Ga Inst Technol, BChE, 52, PhD(chem eng), 64. *Honors & Awards:* Sarge Ozker Award, Am Soc Mech Engrs. *Mem:* Sigma Xi. *Res:* Heat transfer, especially measurement of thermo-physical properties; safe economical treatment of radioactive wastes. *Mailing Add:* 104 Tidewater Rd Oak Ridge TN 37830

GODBEY, JOHN KIRBY, ELECTRONICS ENGINEERING. *Current Pos:* PRES, JOHN K GODBEY ENG CONSULT, INC. *Personal Data:* b Cisco, Tex, Nov 14, 21; m 43; c 3. *Educ:* Southern Methodist Univ, BS, 44; Univ Tex, MS, 47. *Prof Exp:* Res technologist, Field Res Labs, Magnolia Petrol Co, 47-55; sr res technologist, Mobil Oil Corp, 55-68, sr res engr, Mobil Res & Develop Corp, 68- *Mem:* Inst Elec & Electronics Engrs; Am Inst Mining, Metal & Petrol Engrs; Nat Soc Prof Engrs. *Res:* Exploration and production well surveying; drilling methods and instrumentation; automatic control; borehole measurements; pumping well technology. *Mailing Add:* 4339 Hockaday Dr Dallas TX 75229

GODBEY, WILLIAM GIVENS, PHYSICAL CHEMISTRY, NUCLEAR CHEMISTRY. *Current Pos:* EMER PROF, ALASKA PAC UNIV, 85- *Personal Data:* b Georgetown, Tex, Sept 24, 19; wid; c 1. *Educ:* Southwestern Univ, BS(chem) & BS(educ), 40; Univ Mo, MS, 58, PhD(agr chem), 60. *Prof Exp:* Anal dir, Agr Consult Labs, 45-53 & Res Found Labs, Colo Sch Mines, 53-54; chief chemist, Am Smelting & Ref Co, 54-55; from instr to asst prof agr chem, Univ Mo, 55-62; prof chem, Southwest Mo State Col, 62-65; prof chem, Alaska Methodist Univ, 65-77. *Concurrent Pos:* Agr consult, Tex Exp Sta, Dow Chem Co, Rio Grande Valley Cities & Texsun Citrus Growers, 45-51; NIH res grant molecular studies on casein, 60-62. *Mem:* AAAS; fel Am Inst Chem; Am Chem Soc; NY Acad Sci. *Res:* Molecular structure of biochemical macromolecules using electrophoresis, ultra centrifugation and wide and small angle x-ray scattering techniques. *Mailing Add:* PO Box 418 Skagway AK 99840

GODBOLE, SADASHIVA SHANKAR, INSTRUMENTATION & INTERACTIVE SIMULATION. *Current Pos:* sr res engr, Babcock & Wilcox Co, 71-74, group supvr, 74-79, res specialist, 79-87, appln specialist, 87-93, ADV ENGR & EXPERT, BABCOCK & WILCOX CO, 93- *Personal Data:* b Indore, India, Sept 7, 39; m 62; c 2. *Educ:* Victoria Jubilee Tech Inst, India, BE, 58; Va Polytech Inst, MS, 69, PhD(elec eng), 71; George Washington Univ, MEA, 82. *Prof Exp:* Technician, Hindustan Elec Co, India, 58; sect engr, Heavy Elec Ltd, 59-67. *Mem:* Sr mem Inst Elec & Electronics Engrs; Am Soc Mech Engrs. *Res:* Development of math models and simulations for application in design, integration, familarization, demonstration, training, equipment checkout, initial start-up and operation of a new or retrofit system; design of intrumentation and control systems; practical application of electrical, nuclear, thermal, hydraulic and automatic control theory to analytical design and modeling of power plants; industrial processes. *Mailing Add:* 111 Bedford Springs Rd Lynchburg VA 24502

GODCHAUX, WALTER, III, MEMBRANES, LIPIDS. *Current Pos:* assoc prof, 78-90, PROF, UNIV CONN, 91- *Personal Data:* b New Orleans, La, Apr 15, 39; div; c 1. *Educ:* Mass Inst Technol, SB, 60, PhD(biol), 65. *Prof Exp:* NIH fel biochem, Univ Ore, 65-67; fel molecular biol, Sch Med, Yale Univ, 67-70; asst prof biol, Amherst Col, 70-78. *Mem:* Am Soc Biochem & Molecular Biol; Am Soc Microbiol; Am Sigma Xi. *Res:* Eukaryotes: mechanism of protein biosynthesis; biosynthesis of membrane proteins; photoreceptor function; lipids, membranes and motility of gliding bacteria. *Mailing Add:* Box U-131 Univ Conn Storrs CT 06269-2131. *Fax:* 860-486-1936

GODDARD, EARL G(ASCOIGNE), ELECTRONIC SYSTEMS ENGINEERING. *Current Pos:* CONSULT, 78- *Personal Data:* b Mesilla Park, NMex, Nov 10, 17; m 47, Barbara Bacorn; c Robert F (deceased) & James A. *Educ:* NMex State Univ, BS, 39; Stanford Univ, AM & EE, 47. *Honors & Awards:* Centennial Bronze Medal, Inst Elec & Electronics Engrs, 84. *Prof Exp:* Instr elec eng, Rice Univ, 41-43; asst microwave res, Off Res & Inventions proj, Stanford Univ, 46-47; asst prof elec eng, Duke Univ, 47-48; from asst prof to assoc prof electronics, US Naval Post-Grad Sch, Calif, 48-55; sr res engr, Stanford Res Inst, 55-60, mgr field eng training, Microwave Tube Group, Varian Assocs, 61-63; mgr eng, Delcon Div, Hewlett-Packard, 64-65; electronic systs engr, Dalmo Victor Div, Textron, 65-67, engr, 69-72; engr, Appl Technol Div, Itek, 67-69, sr scientist, 72-78. *Concurrent Pos:* Electronic systs consult, 78-84; bd dirs, ECE Acad, Col Eng, NMex State Univ, 91- *Mem:* Goddard Asn Am; Goddard Asn Europ; Nat Geog Soc; Nature Conservancy; US Naval Sailing Asn; Am Asn Retired Persons; Sierra Club. *Res:* Design and application of electronic systems. *Mailing Add:* 2522 Webster St Palo Alto CA 94301-4249

GODDARD, JEROME, MEDICAL ENTOMOLOGY, PUBLIC HEALTH ENTOMOLOGY. *Current Pos:* MED ENTOMOLOGIST, MISS DEPT HEALTH, 89- *Personal Data:* b Booneville, Miss, Apr 12, 57; m 79, Rosella M Blackman; c Jerome II & Joseph D. *Educ:* Univ Miss, BAE, 79, MS, 81; Miss State Univ, PhD(entom), 84. *Prof Exp:* Med entomologist, USAF, 86-89. *Concurrent Pos:* Adj fac, Sch Aerospace Med, USAF, 87-89; clin asst prof prev med, Univ Miss Med Sch, 91-; grad fac, Miss State Univ, 93- *Mem:* Sigma Xi; Am Soc Rickettsiol & Rickettsial Dis; Am Mosquito Control Asn. *Res:* Insect vector ecology and control; ecology of ticks and tick-borne diseases. *Mailing Add:* Bur Environ Health Miss Dept Health PO Box 1700 Jackson MS 39215. *Fax:* 601-960-7688; *E-Mail:* jgoddard@msdh.state.ms.us

GODDARD, JOE DEAN, PHYSICS OF FLUIDS. *Current Pos:* PROF CHEM ENG, UNIV CALIF, SAN DIEGO, 91- *Personal Data:* b Buncombe, Ill, July 13, 36; m 57; c 5. *Educ:* Univ Ill, BS, 57; Univ Calif, PhD(chem eng), 62. *Prof Exp:* Res engr, French Inst Petrol, 62-63; from asst prof to prof chem eng, Univ Mich, Ann Arbor, 63-75; chmn dept, Univ Southern Calif, 76-86, fluor prof chem eng, 76-91. *Concurrent Pos:* NATO fel, 61-62; NSF sr fel, Univ Cambridge, 71; Fulbright fel, Belg, 84. *Mem:* Am Inst Chem Engrs; Soc Rheology (vpres, 89-91, pres, 91-92); Brit Soc Rheology; Am Math Soc; Am Phys Soc. *Res:* Applied mathematics; heat and mass transfer; rheology of complex fluids and particulate systems; fluid mechanics. *Mailing Add:* Dept Ames Univ Calif San Diego 9500 Gillman Dr La Jolla CA 92093-0411

GODDARD, JOHN BURNHAM, INORGANIC CHEMISTRY, ANALYTICAL CHEMISTRY. *Current Pos:* SR DEVELOP ASSOC RES & DEVELOP, PRAXAIR, INC, 93- *Personal Data:* b New Haven, Conn, Nov 7, 42; m 68, Carolyn Kuhr; c Christine & Laura. *Educ:* Mass Inst Technol, BS, 64; Northwestern Univ, PhD(inorg chem), 69. *Prof Exp:* Teaching asst chem, Northwestern Univ, 65-68; from res chemist to sr res chemist, Union Carbide Corp, 68-76, sr scientist, 76-81, proj mgr, metals div, 81-85, mgr anal serv, Linde Div, 85-93. *Mem:* Am Chem Soc; Metall Soc; Sigma Xi. *Res:* Atmospheric gas purification; gas analysis; aerosol particulate analysis; mass spectroscopy methods development. *Mailing Add:* Praxair Inc 175 E Park Dr Tonawanda NY 14151-0044

GODDARD, MURRAY COWDERY, COLOR SCIENCE. *Current Pos:* RETIRED. *Personal Data:* b Cleveland, Ohio, May 14, 24; m 46, Marilyn Hoffman; c 3. *Educ:* Mass Inst Technol, SB, 48; Case Inst Technol, MS, 50. *Prof Exp:* Photog engr, Color Tech Div, Eastman Kodak Co, 50-64, sr physicist, Res Labs, 64-65, res assoc image struct & comput appln, 65-68, res assoc, Res Labs, Comput-Based Learning Systs, 68-74, res assoc, Color Printer Exposure Determination, 74-82. *Mem:* Am Phys Soc; Soc Photog Sci & Eng; Optical Soc Am; Sigma Xi. *Res:* Image structure; computer applications; colorimetry; exposure determination; electronics; individualized learning systems for education and training; color science applied to photography; digital imaging. *Mailing Add:* 614 38th St Anacortes WA 98221

GODDARD, RAY EVERETT, FOREST GENETICS. *Current Pos:* RETIRED. *Personal Data:* b Lakeland, Fla, Sept 28, 22; m 43; c 4. *Educ:* Univ Fla, BSF, 47, MSF, 48; Agr & Mech Col, Tex, PhD(genetics), 60. *Prof Exp:* Silviculturalist, Tex Forest Serv, 48-59; from asst prof & asst geneticist to assoc prof & assoc geneticist, Univ Fla, 59-76, prof forest genetics, Agr Exp Sta, 76- *Mem:* Soc Am Foresters; Am Genetic Asn; Sigma Xi. *Res:* Physiology and genetics of disease resistance in forest trees. *Mailing Add:* 4380 NW 33rd Ct Univ Fla Gainesville FL 32601

GODDARD, STEPHEN, ORNITHOLOGY, ECOLOGY. *Current Pos:* DEP ATTY GEN, DIV ENVIRON QUAL, 95- *Personal Data:* b Ogden, Utah, Jan 5, 37; m 66. *Educ:* Utah State Univ, BS, 60, MS, 62, PhD(biol), 67. *Prof Exp:* Res asst zool, Okla State Univ, 63-66; from asst prof to assoc prof biol, Wis State Univ, River Falls, 66-78; atty, Idaho Dept Fish & Game, 80-95. *Mem:* Wildlife Soc; Wilson Ornith Soc; Am Ornith Union; Am Soc Mammal. *Res:* Ecology and management of game and nongame bird populations. *Mailing Add:* 1410 N Hilton Boise ID 83706

GODDARD, WILLIAM ANDREW, III, SUPERCONDUCTIVITY, REACTION MECHANISMS. *Current Pos:* Arthur Amos Noyes res fel chem, Calif Inst Technol, 64-66, Noyes instr, 66, from asst prof to prof theoret chem, 67-78, prof chem & appl physics, 78-84, CHARLES & MARY FERKEL PROF CHEM & APPL PHYSICS, CALIF INST TECHNOL, 84-, DIR, MATS & PROCESS SIMULATION CTR. *Personal Data:* b El Centro, Calif, Mar 29, 37; m 57; c 4. *Educ:* Univ Calif, Los Angeles, BS, 60; Calif Inst Technol, PhD(eng sci), 64. *Honors & Awards:* Buck Witney Medal, Am Chem Soc, 78, Comput in Chem Award, 88. *Concurrent Pos:* Alfred P Sloan Found res fel, 67-69; mem numerous comts & bds, 72-; vis staff mem, Theoret Physics Div, Los Alamos Nat Lab, NMex, 73-; consult, Argonne Nat Lab, 78-82, Gen Motors Res Labs, 78-, Bell Labs, 79-83, Sandia Nat Lab, 79-84, Gen Elec Res & Develop Ctr, 82-, Shell Develop Co, 82-, Res & Develop Stand Oil Ohio, 84- & var other cos & insts; mem sci adv bd, Triton Biosci, 84-86. *Mem:* Nat Acad Sci; Mat Res Soc; Am Vacuum Soc; Sigma Xi; fel AAAS; fel Am Phys Soc; Am Chem Soc; Int Acad Quantum Molecular Sci. *Res:* New methods of theory including quantum mechanics for the electronic wave functions of large molecules and crystals, force fields to describe the dynamics of atomic motions, molecular dynamics of large molecules and solids and statistical dynamics; implementation of methods in efficient software for high speed calculations; application of methods to important industrial problems in collaboration with industrial engineers and scientists; heterogeneous and homogeneous catalysis; superconductivity; polymers clanco. *Mailing Add:* Beckman Inst Calif Inst Technol Mail Code 139-74 Pasadena CA 91125

GODDIN, C(LIFTON) S(YLVANUS), PROCESS DESIGN. *Current Pos:* CONSULT, GAS PROCESSING, 84- *Personal Data:* b Richmond, Va, July 23, 14. *Educ:* Univ Mich, BS, 36, MS, 37, PhD, 65. *Prof Exp:* Chem engr, Res Dept, Standard Oil Co, Ind, 37-41; sr res assoc, Res Ctr, Amoco Prod Co, 46-84. *Mem:* Am Chem Soc; Am Inst Chem Engrs. *Res:* Geothermal energy; petrochemicals; gas processing; thermodynamics; granted 18 US patents. *Mailing Add:* Hyco Corp 10205 E 47 Pl Tulsa OK 74146

GODDU, ROBERT FENNO, POLYMER CHEMISTRY. *Current Pos:* RETIRED. *Personal Data:* b Winchester, Mass, Oct 5, 25; m 49; c 3. *Educ:* Harvard Univ, AB, 48; Mass Inst Technol, PhD(anal chem), 51. *Prof Exp:* From res chemist to sr res chemist, Hercules Res Ctr, 51-61, res supvr, 61-67, mgr, Fiber & Film Res Div, 67-69, Mat Sci Div, 69-74, New Enterprise Res Div, 74-75, dir res & develop, Coatings & Specialty Prod Dept, 75-78, dir, Plant Develop Labs, 78-80, admin dir, Develop Dept, Hercules Inc, 80-84. *Mem:* Am Chem Soc. *Res:* Near-infrared and infrared spectrophotometry; polymer chemistry processes and fabrication; polymer characterization; water soluble polymers and their applications. *Mailing Add:* 52 Ulverston Dr Kennett Sq PA 19348-2044

GODEC, CIRIL J, UROLOGY & GU ONCOLOGY, PROSTEHTIC DEVICES & NUTRITION. *Current Pos:* ASSOC PROF, DEPT UROL, DOWNSTATE MED CTR, STATE UNIV NY, BROOKLYN, 83- *Personal Data:* b Ljubljana, Slovenia, Feb 16, 37; US citizen; m, Suzanne Smith; c Barbara, Ursula & NIcholas. *Educ:* Univ Ljubljana, MD, 63, PhD, 74. *Prof Exp:* Internship, Univ Ljubljana, 74-75, assoc prof urol, 75-76; resident, Hennepin Co Med Ctr, Minn, 76-79, asst prof 79-83. *Concurrent Pos:* Chmn, Inst Continence Soc, 77 & Long Insland Col Hosp, Brooklyn, NY, 83-88. *Mem:* Am Urol Asn; Int Spina Bifida Soc; NY Acad Med; Int Chem Soc; Soc Clin Urol. *Res:* Development of treatment for urinary incontinency and impotency; genetics of prostatic cancer; neurogenic bladder disfunction; granted US patent. *Mailing Add:* 111 E 85th St New York NY 10028

GODENNE, GHISLAINE D, ADOLESCENT YOUTH PSYCHIATRY. *Current Pos:* fel pediat res, Johns Hopkins Univ, 57-58, from asst prof to assoc prof psychiat, 65-68, asst prof ment hyg, 62-68, pediat, 63-68, assoc prof psychiat, ment hyg & pediat, 68-80, prof psychol & dir, Coun & Psychiat Serv, 73-90, PROF PSYCHIAT, MENT HYG & PEDIAT, JOHNS HOPKINS UNIV, 80-, EMER DIR, COUN & PSYCHIAT SERV, 90-; PROF CLIN PSYCHIAT, UNIV MD, 82- *Personal Data:* b Brussels, Belg, June 2, 24. *Educ:* Univ Louvain, BS, 48, MD, 52. *Honors & Awards:* Decorated Chevalier, Ordre de Leopold, Belgium, 72, Decorated Officer, 85; Christopher Plantin Award, Belg, 90, Nobility Concession Title Baroness, 91. *Prof Exp:* Intern & resident pediat, Providence Hosp, Washington, DC, 52-54; fel pediat, Mayo Clin, Rochester, Minn, 54-57. *Concurrent Pos:* Fulbright grant, 51-52; Parke, Davis & Co res invest grant, 57-58; resident psychiat, Johns Hopkins Hosp, 58-62, dir, Adolescent Psychiat Serv, 64-73, dir, Health Serv, 78-88; consult, Baltimore City Hosps, 59-81, Cyburhome, 60-83, Dept

Ment Health, 64-72, Assoc Cath Charities, Md, 70-77 & Jewish Family & Children Serv, Md, 72-73 & 75-77; NIMH gen pract grant, 61-63, career teaching award, 63-65; chief psychiatrist, Good Shepherd Ctr, Md, 70-74; assoc prof clin psychiat, Univ Md, 78-82; consult, Loyola Col, 90-92. *Mem:* Fel Am Psychiat Asn; fel Am Col Physicians; fel Am Soc Adolescent Psychiat (pres, 81-82); World Fedn Mental Health (vpres); fel Am Pub Health Asn; Am Psychoanalysis Asn; Am Asn Univ Profs; fel Am Orthopsychiat Asn; Int Soc Adolescent Psychiat; fel Am Col Health Asn. *Res:* Clinical papers on adolescence and youth. *Mailing Add:* 15 Edgevale Rd Baltimore MD 21210-2215

GODER, HAROLD ARTHUR, PLANT ECOLOGY. *Current Pos:* PROF BIOL, KEENE STATE COL, 70- *Personal Data:* b North Cape, Wis, July 3, 24; m 57; c 3. *Educ:* Univ Wis, BS, 50, MS, 51, PhD, 55. *Prof Exp:* Assoc prof biol, Wis State Col, 55-70. *Mem:* Ecol Soc Am; Nat Asn Biol Teachers. *Res:* Phytosociological study of Tsuga Canadensis at the termination of its range in Wisconsin; taxonomic survey of the amphibians of New Hampshire. *Mailing Add:* Dept Biol Keene State Col Univ NH 229 Main St Keene NH 03435-0001

GODFREY, ANDREW ELLIOTT, GEOMORPHOLOGY. *Current Pos:* MEM STAFF, INTERMOUNTAIN REGION, US FOREST SERV, 92- *Personal Data:* b Philadelphia, Pa, May 31, 40; m 68; c 2. *Educ:* Franklin & Marshall Col, AB, 64; Johns Hopkins Univ, PhD(geog), 69. *Prof Exp:* Asst prof geol, Vanderbilt Univ, 68-72; mem staff, Ashley Nat Forest, 72-79; mem staff, Fishlake Nat Forest, 79-92. *Concurrent Pos:* Consult geologist, Nat Ecol Found, Nashville, 72-73, Brigham Young Univ, Mus Peoples Cult, Provo, 84-89. *Mem:* AAAS; Geol Soc Am; Am Quaternary Asn; Sigma Xi. *Res:* Climatic and geologic factors of pediment formation; geochemistry of small streams and its relationship to processes of erosion; environmental factors in planning (recreational) land use; rates of cave development in Uinta Mountains; magnitude and frequency of landslides in central Utah; quantitative erosion rates of shale in an arid environment; wind erosion of shale in an arid environment. *Mailing Add:* 5110 Burch Creek Dr Ogden UT 84403-4210. *Fax:* 801-625-5277

GODFREY, BRENDAN BERRY, PLASMA PHYSICS, NUMERICAL ANALYSIS. *Current Pos:* ADJ PROF, UNIV NMEX, 91- *Personal Data:* b Norfolk, Va, July 17, 45; m 72, Kathryn Burke; c Helen, Brendan & Elizabeth. *Educ:* Univ Minn, BS, 67; Princeton Univ, MA, 69, PhD(physics), 70. *Prof Exp:* Off & staff scientist physics, Air Force Weapons Lab, 70-72; staff mem physics, Los Alamos Sci Lab, 72-77, group leader, T-15, 77-79; group leader, Mission Res Corp, 79-88, vpres, 88-89, chief scientist, Weapons Lab, 89-90; dir advan weapons, Phillips Labs, 91-93. *Concurrent Pos:* Adj prof, Univ NMex, 85-93. *Mem:* Fel Am Phys Soc; sr mem Inst Elec & Electronics Engrs. *Res:* Theoretical and computational study of intense relativistic electron beam phenomena with application to microwave sources, accelerator development, and inertial fusion. *Mailing Add:* AL/CC 2509 Kennedy Circle Brooks Air Force Base TX 78235. *Fax:* 505-846-0417; *E-Mail:* godfrey@plk.af.mil

GODFREY, CHARLES S, PHYSICS. *Current Pos:* VPRES & CHIEF SCIENTIST, PHYSICS INT CO, 62- *Personal Data:* b San Francisco, Calif, Aug 12, 18; m 45, 63; c 5. *Educ:* Mass Inst Technol, BS & MS, 41; Univ Calif, PhD(physics), 53. *Prof Exp:* From physicist to div leader physics, Lawrence Radiation Lab, Univ Calif, 53-62. *Res:* Continuum mechanics and explosive phenomena. *Mailing Add:* 1450 Euclid Ave Berkeley CA 94708

GODFREY, DONALD ALBERT, PHYSIOLOGY, BIOCHEMISTRY. *Current Pos:* PROF OTOLARYNGOL, PHYSIOL & ANAT, MED COL OHIO, 88-, RES DIR OTOLARYNGOL, 96- *Personal Data:* b Tarrytown, NY, Aug 26, 44; m 67, Lynn Cottrell; c Tim & Matt. *Educ:* Rensselaer Polytech Inst, BS, 66; Harvard Univ, PhD(physiol), 72. *Prof Exp:* Fel pharmacol, Sch Med, Washington Univ, 72-75, res asst prof, 75-78; res assoc physiol, Cent Inst Deaf, 75-78; from asst prof to assoc prof physiol, Oral Roberts Univ, 78-88. *Concurrent Pos:* NSF fel, Harvard Univ, 66-71; NIH fel, Sch Med, Washington Univ, 72-74; res grant, NIH, 81-; adj prof, Dept Commun Disorders, Col Health & Human Servs, Bowling Green State Univ, 89-; prin investr, res grants, NIH, 81- *Mem:* Sigma Xi; AAAS; Soc Neurosci; Int Brain Res Orgn; Acoust Soc Am; Asn Res Otolaryngol. *Res:* Biochemistry, physiology and anatomy of the central nervous system, especially those parts concerned with special senses, particularly audition and equilibrium. *Mailing Add:* Dept Otolaryngol Med Col Ohio PO Box 10008 Toledo OH 43699-0008

GODFREY, GARY LUNT, ELEMENTARY PARTICLE PHYSICS. *Current Pos:* res assoc physics, 76-80, STAFF PHYSICIST, STANFORD LINEAR ACCELERATOR CTR, 80- *Personal Data:* b San Francisco, Calif, Nov 4, 46. *Educ:* Calif Inst Technol, BS, 68; Univ Calif, Berkeley, PhD(physics), 75. *Prof Exp:* Fel, Lawrence Berkeley Lab, 75. *Res:* Experimental electron-positron storage ring physics using a highly segmented NaI detector known as the Crystal Ball. *Mailing Add:* 20 Tynan Way Portola Valley CA 94028

GODFREY, GEORGE LAWRENCE, SYSTEMATIC ENTOMOLOGY. *Current Pos:* instr natural resources, 93-95, CO-DIR, HASKELL ENVIRON RES STUDIES CTR, HASKELL INDIAN NATIONS UNIV, 94-, CHAIR, DEPT NATURAL & SOC SCI, 96- *Personal Data:* b Shawnee, Okla, Apr 25, 43; m 92, Guy; c 6. *Educ:* Northern State Col, SDak, BS, 65; Cornell Univ, PhD(entom), 70. *Prof Exp:* Res asst insect ecol, Cornell Univ, 65-66; teaching asst ecol, 66-67, res asst systematics, 67-70; asst entomologist, Ill Natural Hist Surv, 70-76, assoc prof scientist, 76-92; res assoc agr entom, Univ Ill, 70--71, from asst prof to assoc prof, 71-93, int prog coordr, Int Soybean Prog, 71-76, affil, Dept Entom, 87-93, affil, Dept Forestry, 93. *Concurrent Pos:* Consult, Mo Bot Garden, 73-75; ed, J Lepidopterists' Soc, 75-77, Smithsonian Inst Libr, 87-88; res affil, Ill State Mus, 93- *Res:* Systematics and life history studies of Lepidoptera, especially of the Noctuidae and Notodontidae; natural resources of Native American lands. *Mailing Add:* Dept Natural & Soc Sci Haskell Indian Nations Univ 155 Indian Ave Lawrence KS 66046. *Fax:* 785-749-8406

GODFREY, HENRY PHILIP, IMMUNOLOGY, EXPERIMENTAL PATHOLOGY & HOST-PARASITE RELATIONSHIP. *Current Pos:* assoc prof 82-88, PROF PATH, NY MED COL, VALHALLA, NY, 88- *Personal Data:* b Poughkeepsie, NY, Aug 7, 41; m 77, Ginger Schnaper; c Thomas O & David S. *Educ:* Harvard Univ, AB, 61, MD, 65; Birmingham Univ (UK) PhD, 80. *Prof Exp:* Intern med, Barnes Hosp, St Louis, Mo, 65-66; surgeon, Div Biol Stand, NIH, 66-70; lectr, Inst Exp Immunol, Univ Copenhagen , 72-75; asst prof path, Sch Basic Health Sci, State Univ NY Stony Brook, 75-82. *Concurrent Pos:* Moseley traveling fel, Harvard Univ, 70-72; hon res fel, Univ Birmingham, 70-78. *Mem:* AAAS; Am Soc Microbiol; NY Acad Sci; Am Asn Immunol; Harvey Soc; Am Soc Invest Path. *Res:* Cellular and biochemical bases of the induction and elicitation of cellular immune response and other forms of chronic inflammation, especially as related to disease processes such as tuberculosis and Lyme disease. *Mailing Add:* Dept Path NY Med Col Basic Sci Bldg Valhalla NY 10595-1690. *Fax:* 914-993-4679; *E-Mail:* hgodfrey@nymc.edu

GODFREY, JOHN CARL, ORGANIC CHEMISTRY, MEDICINAL CHEMISTRY. *Current Pos:* PRES, GODFREY SCI & DESIGN, INC, 79-, CONSULT, MED & ORG CHEM, 90- *Personal Data:* b Cornelius, Ore, Mar 11, 29; m 54, Nancy J Williams; c Laura A (Janda), Helen R (Wilder) & Sabrina G (Novick). *Educ:* Pomona Col, BA, 51; Univ Rochester, PhD(org chem), 54. *Prof Exp:* Res chemist, Shell Develop Co, 54-55; Smith Kline & French fel org chem, Rutgers Univ, 55-57, instr chem, 57-59; res chemist & group leader pharmaceut chem, Bristol-Myers Co, 59-65, dir biochem res, 65-74, dir med chem process labs, 74-75, clin monitor, 75-77, mgr technol eval & new ventures, Bristol Labs Div, 77-79; asst dir clin res, Revlon Health Care Group, USV Pharmaceut Co, 79-85; assoc dir clin res, Rorer Pharmaceut Corp, 85-90. *Concurrent Pos:* Dir, Hill Abrasives Inc, Ontario, NY, 90- *Mem:* Am Chem Soc; Am Soc Microbiol; fel Am Inst Chemists; AAAS; NY Acad Sci. *Res:* Design, organize, monitor, analyze and report clinical evaluations of new drugs in areas of antibiotics, cardiovascular agents, human rhinovirus treatment; synthesis of penicillins; organic synthesis; semisynthetic antibiotics; trace element therapy. *Mailing Add:* 1649 Old Welsh Rd Huntingdon Valley PA 19006-5835

GODFREY, JOHN JOSEPH, SPEECH SCIENCE. *Current Pos:* MEM STAFF, DEPT COMMUN DIS, UNIV TEX, RICHARDSON; DIR, LING DATA CONSORTIUM, UNIV PA, 92- *Personal Data:* b New York, NY, Dec 19, 41; m 76; c 2. *Educ:* Fordham Univ, AB, 65, MA, 66; Georgetown Univ, PhD(ling), 71. *Prof Exp:* Res assoc speech recognition, Aerospace Med Res Lab, US Air Force, Dayton, Ohio, 70-72; res assoc, Univ Dayton Res Inst, 72-74; asst prof speech sci, Univ Tex, Dallas, 75-80, assoc prof, 80- *Concurrent Pos:* Res assoc, Nat Res Coun Nat Acad Sci, 70-72. *Mem:* Acoust Soc Am; Ling Soc Am; Am Asn Phonetic Scis. *Res:* Speech perception in normal and auditorily impaired populations. *Mailing Add:* 37 Linden Ave Haddonfield NJ 08033

GODFREY, MAURICE, HERITABLE DISORDERS OF CONNECTIVE TISSUE, MARFAN SYNDROME. *Current Pos:* asst prof pediat, 90-94, ASSOC PROF PATH & MICROBIOL, UNIV NEBR MED CTR, 92-, ASST PROF, EPPLEY INST CANCER RES, 93-, ASSOC PROF, PEDIAT, 94- *Personal Data:* m 85, Matilde E Almeida; c C Maximilian, R Alessandro & D Guillermo. *Educ:* Monmouth Col, BS, 77; Columbia Univ, PhD(pathobiol & immunol), 86. *Prof Exp:* Fel, Shriners Hosp, Ore Health Sci Univ, 86-89. *Concurrent Pos:* Basil O'Connor scholar, March of Dimes Birth Defects Found, 92-94; mem, Basic Sci Coun, Am Heart Asn. *Mem:* AAAS; NY Acad Sci; Am Soc Human Genetics; Am Fedn Clin Res; Am Heart Asn. *Res:* Biochemical, immunochemical, and molecular characterization of the heritable disorders of connective tissue with a particular emphasis on the Marfan syndrome. *Mailing Add:* 600 South 42nd St Omaha NE 68198-5430. *Fax:* 402-559-7248; *E-Mail:* mgodfrey@unmcvm.unmc.edu

GODFREY, PAUL JEFFREY, COASTAL PLANT ECOLOGY, BIOMETEOROLOGY. *Current Pos:* asst prof, 70-76, ASSOC PROF PLANT ECOL, UNIV MASS, 76- *Personal Data:* b New York, NY, Apr 2, 40; m 68. *Educ:* Univ Conn, BS, 62; Duke Univ, PhD(plant ecol), 69. *Prof Exp:* Biologist, Cape Lookout Nat Seashore, 68-69; biologist, US Nat Park Serv, 69-70. *Concurrent Pos:* Res biologist, US Nat Park Serv, 70-; leader, Nat Park Serv Coop Res Unit, Univ Mass, 73-77; appointee, Barrier Island Study Group, US Dept Interior, 77-79; vis prof, Marine Lab, Duke Univ, 78-81; appointee, UNESCO-Man & Biosphere Coastal Classification Comn, 79- *Mem:* Ecol Soc Am; Brit Ecol Soc; Int Soc Biometeorol; Sigma Xi. *Res:* Coastal ecology of eastern North America: geobotany, biogeography, biometeorology, autecology of Spartina patens and other coastal species, human impacts, and management of beaches and dunes; ecology of central New England forests. *Mailing Add:* Dept Biol Univ Mass Amherst Amherst MA 01003-0002

GODFREY, PAUL RUSSELL, BIOCHEMISTRY. *Current Pos:* CONSULT, 85- *Personal Data:* b Ventnor, NJ, Nov 26, 14; m 40; c 5. *Educ:* William Jewell Col, AB, 38; Purdue Univ, MS, 40, PhD(biochem), 52. *Prof Exp:* Asst prof chem, Ouachita Col, 41-42 & Furman Univ, 42-43; asst chemist, Purdue Univ,

43-46; prof chem, La Col, 46-70; prof chem, Tusculum Col. 70-80, dean fac, 81-85. *Concurrent Pos:* Res partic, Oak Ridge Inst Nuclear Studies, 60 & 61, res assoc, 63; res asst, Sch Med, Tulane Univ, 64, res partic, Case Inst Technol, 65; vis prof, Northwestern State Col La, 66; res chemist, Southern Forest & Range Exp Sta, US Forest Serv, 67, consult, Insul-Therm Co, 87- *Mem:* Am Chem Soc; Sigma Xi. *Res:* Analytical methods and nutritional studies of fluorine and iodine; lipid metabolism. *Mailing Add:* 127 Smokey View Dr Greeneville TN 37743-3704

GODFREY, ROBERT ALLEN, ANALYTICAL CHEMISTRY. *Current Pos:* Chemist prod characterization, 67-73, group leader, 73-76, SECT MGR POLYMER ANALYSIS & PHYSICS, MOBAY CORP, 76- *Personal Data:* b Sharon, Pa, Dec 28, 44; m 67. *Educ:* Thiel Col, AB, 66. *Mem:* Am Chem Soc; Soc Plastics Indust; Am Soc Testing & Mat. *Res:* Materials characterization; spectroscopy; chromatography; polymer characterization. *Mailing Add:* 101 Rivercrest Dr Coraopolis PA 15108

GODFREY, SUSAN STURGIS, MICROBIOLOGY. *Current Pos:* Fel, Dept Biochem, Univ Pittsburgh Sch Med, 73-76, res asst prof develop biol, Dept Biol Sci, 77-80, lab instr microbiol, 80-90, LECTR MICROBIOL, DEPT BIOL SCI, UNIV PITTSBURGH, 90- *Personal Data:* b Philadelphia, Pa, Nov 20, 44; m 71. *Educ:* Wheaton Col, Norton, Ma, AB, 66; Univ Pa, PhD(microbiol), 73. *Concurrent Pos:* Asst res fel, Inst Molecular Biol, Academia Sinica, Taipei, Taiwan, 90. *Mem:* AAAS; Am Soc Microbiol. *Res:* Comparative study aimed at understanding how proteins adapted to extreme environments, particularly such as habitats of the archaea, differ from their more familiar homologues and how this affects their function. *Mailing Add:* Dept Biol Sci Univ Pittsburgh A-234 Langley Hall Pittsburgh PA 15260-0001. *Fax:* 412-624-4759; *E-Mail:* ssg1@vms.cis.pitt.edu

GODFREY, THOMAS NIGEL KING, PHYSICS, COMPUTER SCIENCE. *Current Pos:* RETIRED. *Personal Data:* b Madison, Wis, Dec 11, 27; m 50, Lois Erwin; c Janet Elizabeth. *Educ:* Mass Inst Technol, BS, 50; Princeton Univ, PhD(physics), 54. *Prof Exp:* Staff mem, Los Alamos Nat Lab, 54-89. *Mem:* AAAS. *Res:* Nuclear weapons; Monte Carlo neutron transport computer code. *Mailing Add:* 156 Tunyo Los Alamos NM 87544

GODFREY, W LYNN, SPENT FUEL REPROCESSING, RADIOACTIVE WASTE MANAGEMENT. *Current Pos:* RETIRED. *Personal Data:* b Washington, DC, Jan 24, 39; m 59; c 5. *Educ:* Brigham Young Univ, BES, 61. *Prof Exp:* Engr, Am Potash & Chem Co, 61-63; sr engr, Atlantic Richfield Hanford Co, 63-73; sr proj engr, Allied-Gen Nuclear Serv, 73-83; pres, BE Inc, 83-95. *Mem:* Am Nuclear Soc. *Res:* Generation, volume reduction, packaging, transportation, storage and disposal of solid, liquid and gaseous radioactive wastes. *Mailing Add:* 2405 Jackson St Barnwell SC 29812

GODFREY, WILLIAM EARL, ORNITHOLOGY. *Current Pos:* cur ornith, Can Mus Nature, 47-76, head, Vert Zool Sect, 68-76, chief, 76-77, EMER CUR ORNITH, CAN MUS NATURE, 77-, RES ASSOC, 93- *Personal Data:* b Wolfville, NS, Mar 18, 10; m 46, Jane Vivian; c Barbara. *Educ:* Acadia Univ, BSc, 34. Hon Degrees: DSc, Acadia Univ, 69. *Honors & Awards:* Doris Heustic Speirs Award, Soc Can Ornithologists, 86. *Prof Exp:* Res assoc ornith, Cleveland Mus Natural Hist, 40-57. *Mem:* Fel Am Ornith Union; corresp mem Brit Ornithologists Union; hon mem Ottawa Field-Naturalists Club. *Res:* Distribution, taxonomy and ecology of North American birds. *Mailing Add:* 4 Sioux Crescent Ottawa ON K2H 7E5 Can

GODHWANI, ARJUN, ELECTRICAL ENGINEERING, CONTROL SYSTEMS. *Current Pos:* asst prof, 72-73, ASSOC PROF ELEC ENG, SOUTHERN ILL UNIV, 73- *Personal Data:* b Sind, India, Dec 29, 41; m 68; c 2. *Educ:* Vikram Univ, India, BS, 63; Roorkee Univ, India, MS, 65; Univ Ark, PhD(elec eng), 71. *Prof Exp:* Lectr elec eng, Pilani Univ, India, 66-68; instr, Univ Ark, 71-72. *Concurrent Pos:* Staff specialist, McDonnell Douglas Astronaut, 77-; Instr Sci Equip Prog Proposal, NSF, 74. *Mem:* Inst Elec & Electronics Engrs; Am Soc Eng Educ. *Res:* Control systems; digital systems including microprocessors. *Mailing Add:* Dept Eng Southern Ill Univ Edwardsville IL 62026

GODICI, NICHOLAS P, ENGINEERING, PATENT MANAGEMENT. *Current Pos:* GROUP DIR, COMMUN DEPT COM PATENTS OFF 95- *Personal Data:* b July 27, 50. *Educ:* Pa State Univ, BA, 72. *Mailing Add:* US Dept Com Patents Off Crystal Park/2-2121 Crystal Dr Arlington VA 22202. *E-Mail:* nicholas.godici@pto.gov

GODIN, CLAUDE, BIOCHEMISTRY. *Current Pos:* RETIRED. *Personal Data:* b Quebec City, Que, Mar 12, 26; m 53; c 5. *Educ:* Laval Univ, BA, 46, BScA, 50, DSc(chem), 53. *Prof Exp:* Res fel, Nat Res Coun, Can & Nat Inst Med Res, Eng, 53-55; from asst prof to assoc prof biol, Ottawa Univ, 56-70; from assoc prof to prof biochem, Laval Univ, Nov 91. *Concurrent Pos:* France-Can exchange fel, Inst Molecular Path, Paris, France, 67-68; Ctr Nat Res Sci, Marseille, France, 78-79. *Mem:* Can Biochem Soc (treas, 72-75); Chem Inst Can. *Res:* Chemistry and biochemistry of proteins and amino acids; membrane proteins; cell differentiation. *Mailing Add:* 1305 Ave de Puiseaux Sillery PQ G1T 2C7 Can

GODINE, JOHN ELLIOTT, ENDOCRINOLOGY. *Current Pos:* Resident, 76-78, fel, 78-81, INSTR, MASS GEN HOSP, MED SCH, HARVARD UNIV, 81- *Personal Data:* b Montreal, Que, Feb 14, 47; m 68; c 2. *Educ:* Princeton Univ, AB, 67; Mass Inst Technol, PhD(physics), 72; Med Sch, Harvard Univ, MD, 76. *Mem:* Am Col Physicians; AAAS. *Res:* Recombinant DNA studies of the biosynthesis of pituitary glycoprotein hormones; neuroendocrinology. *Mailing Add:* Mass Gen Hosp ACC730 Fruit St Boston MA 02114-2620

GODING, JAMES WATSON, CELL MEMBRANE RECEPTORS. *Current Pos:* chmn, Dept Path, 85-95, PROF IMMUNOL, MONASH UNIV, 85-; PRES, AUSTRALIAN SOC IMMUNOL, 97- *Personal Data:* b Melbourne, Australia, July 21, 46; m 80, Emanuela Handman. *Educ:* Monash Univ, MB & BS, 71; Univ Melbourne, BMed Sci, 73, PhD(immunol), 77. *Prof Exp:* C J Martin fel immunol, Dept Genetics, Stanford Univ, 78-79; head, Immunochem Lab Immunol, Walter & Eliza Hall Inst, 80-84. *Concurrent Pos:* Mem, Sci Adv Comt, Anti-Cancer Coun Victoria & Regional Grant Interviewing Comt & Assigner's Panel, Nat Health & Med Res Coun, 85-90, Biotechnol Prod Comt, Commonwealth Dept Health, Australia & Nat Biotechnol Comt, 86-90; assoc dean, Fac Med, Monash Univ, 88-90; vis prof, Ctr Blood Res, Harvard Univ, 91. *Mem:* Am Asn Immunologists; AAAS. *Res:* Structure and function of cell surface receptors, particularly those of the immune system. *Mailing Add:* Monash Med Sch Alfred Hosp Prahran Victoria 3181 Australia. *Fax:* 613529-6484; *E-Mail:* goding@med.monash.edu.au

GODINO, CHARLES F, MATHEMATICS. *Current Pos:* asst prof, 65-74, ASSOC PROF MATH, BROOKLYN COL, 74- *Personal Data:* b Brooklyn, NY, Mar 31, 34; m 56. *Educ:* St Peter's Col, NJ, BA, 55; Univ Notre Dame, MS, 58, PhD(math), 62. *Prof Exp:* Instr math, Univ Notre Dame, 62; Joseph Fels Ritt instr, Columbia Univ, 62-65. *Mem:* Am Math Soc. *Res:* Group theory; group representation theory; number theory. *Mailing Add:* Dept Math 64 Uxbridge St Staten Island NY 10314-5022

GODKE, ROBERT ALAN, REPRODUCTIVE PHYSIOLOGY. *Current Pos:* asst prof reproduction physiol, 73-77, ASSOC PROF REPRODUCTION PHYSIOL, LA STATE UNIV, BATON ROUGE, 77- *Personal Data:* b Kewanee, Ill, Sept 9, 44; m 65; c 3. *Educ:* Southern Ill Univ, BS, 66, MS, 68; Univ Mo-Columbia, PhD(reprod physiol), 74. *Prof Exp:* Br chief preliminary toxicol, US Army Environ Hyg Agency, Edgewood Arsenal, Md, 69-70. *Concurrent Pos:* Teaching fel, Nat Asn Col & Teachers Agr, 80. *Mem:* Am Soc Animal Sci; Int Soc Study Animal Reproduction; Int Embryo Transfer Soc; Soc Study Reproduction. *Res:* Farm and exotic animals; induced behavioral estrus studies; prostaglandins and progestins for estrus synchronization; embryo transfer, cloning and induced twinning in farm animals; ovarian-uterine relationships; luteal function during pregnancy; prostaglandins for inducing parturition. *Mailing Add:* Dept Animal Sci La State Univ Baton Rouge Baton Rouge LA 70803-0001

GODLEY, WILLIE CECIL, GENETICS. *Current Pos:* From instr to asst prof animal husb, 46-47, assoc prof, 52-57, assoc dir, SC Agr Exp Sta, 73-75, PROF ANIMAL SCIENCE, CLEMSON UNIV, 57-, ASSOC DEAN & DIR, SC AGR EXP STA, 75- *Personal Data:* b Miley, SC, Oct 3, 22; m 44; c 3. *Educ:* Clemson Col, BS, 43; NC State Col, MS, 49, PhD, 55. *Concurrent Pos:* Assoc animal husbandman, SC Agr Exp Sta, 54-57, animal husbandman & geneticist, 57-64. *Mem:* Am Soc Animal Sci; Am Genetic Asn; Sigma Xi. *Res:* Animal breeding. *Mailing Add:* 103 Lewis Rd Clemson SC 29631

GODMAN, GABRIEL C, CELL BIOLOGY, PATHOLOGY. *Current Pos:* res assoc surg path, from asst prof to assoc prof microbiol, 54-68, PROF MICROBIOL, COL PHYSICIANS & SURGEONS, COLUMBIA UNIV, 68-, PROF PATH, 69- *Personal Data:* b Albany, NY, Jan 24, 21. *Educ:* NY Univ, AB, 41, MD, 44. *Prof Exp:* House officer med, Bellevue Hosp, NY, 44-45; asst path, Yale Univ, 48-50. *Concurrent Pos:* Fel path, Mt Sinai Hosp Sch Med, 50-52, NIH grant, 64-68; vis investr cell biol, Rockefeller Inst, 57-60; consult study sect, NIH, 64-68. *Mem:* Am Asn Path; Int Acad Path; Am Soc Cell Biol; Harvey Soc; Tissue Cult Asn. *Res:* Cellular pathology. *Mailing Add:* Col Physicians & Surgeons Columbia Univ New York NY 10032

GODOLPHIN, WILLIAM, CLINICAL CHEMISTRY. *Current Pos:* clin chemist, 74-78, DIR RES & DEVELOP, VANCOUVER GEN HOSP, 78-; PROF PATH, UNIV BC, 75-; VPRES RES & DEVELOP, ANDRONIC TECHNOL INC, 86- *Personal Data:* b St Boniface, Man, June 25, 41; m 67; c 2. *Educ:* Univ Man, BSc, 63; Univ Alta, PhD(clin biochem), 74. *Honors & Awards:* MDS Health Group Award, Can Soc Clin Chemists, 86. *Prof Exp:* Prin, Amaranth High Sch, Man, 62-64; sr sci master, Awe Boys High Sch, Nigeria, 64-66; prin & area adminr, Snowdrift Sch, 67-69. *Concurrent Pos:* Mem, Environ Appeal Bd, Govt BC, 83-90 & Assoc Comt Toxicol, Nat Res Coun, 88-91. *Mem:* Can Soc Clin Chemists (secy, 86-89); Can Acad Clin Biochem; Asn Clin Biochemists; Am Asn Clin Chem. *Res:* Investigation of prognostic factors associated with human breast cancer; robotic and other automation for preanalytic specimen handling and preparation in the clinical laboratory. *Mailing Add:* Univ BC 2211 Wesbrook Mall Vancouver BC V6T 2B5 Can. *Fax:* 604-875-4025

GODRICK, JOSEPH ADAM, MECHANICAL BEHAVIOR OF MATERIALS, ELECTRONIC PACKAGING MATERIALS. *Current Pos:* PRIN ENGR, RAYTHEON CO, 82- *Personal Data:* b Rutland, Vt, May 20, 42; m 68; c 2. *Educ:* Univ Vt, BS, 63; Mass Inst Technol, MS, 64, PhD(mech eng), 68. *Prof Exp:* Staff engr, Ledgemont Lab, Kennecott Co, 68-81; sr engr, Foster-Miller Assocs, 81-82. *Mem:* Am Inst Mech Engrs; Am Soc Metals. *Res:* Material systems for electronics, including thick film and thin film techniques, ceramic metalization, ceramics, metals and polymers in electronic packaging, joining methods and materials for electronics. *Mailing Add:* 12 Parker Rd Wellesley MA 02181

GODSAY, MADHU, cellulose chemistry, for more information see previous edition

GODSCHALK, DAVID ROBINSON, GROWTH MANAGEMENT, HAZARD MITIGATION. *Current Pos:* assoc prof, 72-77, PROF PLANNING, UNIV NC, 77-, STEPHEN BAXTER PROF PLANNING & ENDOWED CHAIR, 94- *Personal Data:* b Enid, Okla, May 14, 31; m 59; c 1. *Educ:* Dartmouth Col, BA, 53; Univ Fla, BArch, 59; Univ NC, MRP, 64, PhD(planning), 71. *Honors & Awards:* Serv Medal, Am Inst Planners, 71. *Prof Exp:* Vpres, Milo Smith Assocs, 59-61; planning dir, City Gainesville, Fla, 64-65; asst prof planning, Fla State Univ, 65-67. *Concurrent Pos:* Ed, J Am Inst Planners, 68-71; lectr, Univ NC, 69-71; vis prof, Univ Hawaii, 73; scholar in residence, Southern Growth Policies Bd, 77-78; prin investr, NSF, 75-77, Off Ocean & Coastal Resource Mgt, 83-84, Nat Inst Dispute Resolution & US Dept Housing & Urban Develop, 85, IBM Corp, 89-90, NSF, 94-97. *Mem:* Am Inst Cert Planners; Am Planning Asn. *Res:* Analysis of public policy dealing with growth management, hazard mitigation, dispute resolution, land use planning, and geographic information systems. *Mailing Add:* Dept City & Regional Planning Univ NC Chapel Hill NC 27599-3140

GODSHALK, GORDON LAMAR, AQUATIC ECOLOGY. *Current Pos:* dir environ studies, 87-96, PROF BIOL, ALFRED UNIV, 87- *Personal Data:* b Eugene, Ore, July 19, 48. *Educ:* Univ Calif, Davis, BS, 70; Mich State Univ, MS, 72, PhD(bot), 77. *Prof Exp:* Res assoc aquatic ecol, Dept Environ Eng Sci, Univ Fla, 77-78; adj asst prof bot, 78-79, vis asst prof zool, 79-80; asst prof biol, Univ Southern Miss, 80-85; res ecologist, Waterways Exp Sta, US Army Corps Engrs, 85-87. *Mem:* Am Soc Limnol & Oceanog; Ecol Soc Am; Int Asn Theoret & Appl Limnol; Sigma Xi; Soc Wetlands Scientists; NAm Benthological Soc. *Res:* Heterotrophic metabolism of detritus in aquatic ecosystems; interactions of plants and animals in aquatic ecosystems; physiological ecology of aquatic plants. *Mailing Add:* Environ Studies Alfred Univ Alfred NY 14802-1205. *E-Mail:* godshalk@bigvax.alfred.edu

GODSHALL, FREDRIC ALLEN, METEOROLOGY. *Current Pos:* PHYS SCIENTIST, SCI APPLN INT CORP, 91- *Personal Data:* b Pottstown, Pa, Sept 4, 34; m 59; c 3. *Educ:* Ursinus Col, BS, 56; NY Univ, MS, 58; Univ Md, PhD(civil eng), 73. *Prof Exp:* Meteorologist, Proj Mercury, 61-66 & Argonne Nat Lab, 66; proj scientist, Environ Data Serv, Environ Sci Serv Admin, 66-87; phys scientist, Comput Sci Corp, 88-91. *Res:* Application of satellite data in meteorology. *Mailing Add:* 1661 MacIntosh Way Hummelstown PA 17036

GODSON, GODFREY NIGEL, BIOCHEMISTRY. *Current Pos:* PROF & CHMN, DEPT BIOCHEM, SCH MED, NY UNIV, 80- *Personal Data:* b London, Eng, June 20, 36; US citizen; m 69, Barbara; c Rebecca Charlotte & Vanessa Alexandra. *Educ:* Univ London, Eng, BSc, 57, MSc, 59, PhD(biochem), 62, DSc(biochem/molecular biol), 84. *Prof Exp:* Postdoctoral fel, Div Biol, Calif Inst Technol, Pasadena, 64-66; res assoc, Dept Radiol, Radiobiol Labs, Sch Med, Yale Univ, 66-67; mem sci staff, Dept Phys Chem, Royal Cancer Hosp, Inst Cancer Res, Chester Beatty Res Inst, London, Eng, 61-64; mem sci staff, Biochem Div, Nat Insts Med Res, London, Eng, 67-69; from asst prof to assoc prof radiobiol, Sch Med, Yale Univ, 69-80. *Concurrent Pos:* Vis prof, Dept Physiol Chem, Univ Utrecht, Holland, 76; vis scientist, Med Res Coun, Cambridge, Eng, 76-78; ad hoc mem, Trop Med & Parasitol Study Sect, 84-85, mem, 85-90, chmn, 88-90; mem sci adv comt, Irma T Hirschl Found, 83-87; mem biochem sect, Nat Bds Med Educ Exam Comt, 85-89. *Mem:* Am Soc Biol Chemists; Harvey Soc; Am Soc Microbiol. *Res:* Control of DNA replication in procaryotes and eucaryotes; use of molecular biology to develop anti-parasite strategies. *Mailing Add:* Dept Biochem Med Ctr NY Univ 550 First Ave New York NY 10016-6402

GODSON, WARREN LEHMAN, METEOROLOGY. *Current Pos:* RETIRED. *Personal Data:* b Victoria, BC, May 4, 20; m 77; c 5. *Educ:* Univ BC, BA, 39, MA, 41; Univ Toronto, MA, 44, PhD(phys meteorol), 48. *Honors & Awards:* Darton Prize, Royal Meteorol Soc, 61, Buchan Prize, 64; Patterson Medal, 68; IMO Prize, World Meteorol Orgn, 75. *Prof Exp:* Asst, Meteorol Serv Can, Atmospheric Environ Serv, 42-43, gen res & lectr, 43-51, supvr res unit, 51-54, supt atmospheric res sect, 54-71, dir, Atmospheric Processes Res Br, Atmospheric Environ Serv, 71-73, dir, Gen Atmospheric Res Directorate, 73-84, sr sci adv, 84-93. *Concurrent Pos:* Spec lectr, Univ Toronto, 48-60, hon prof, Inst Environ Studies, 75-80; liaison officer, Int Union Geod & Geophys, World Meteorol Orgn, 60-75, pres, Comn Atmospheric Sci, 73-77. *Mem:* Int Asn Meteorol & Atmospheric Physics (secy, 60-75, vpres, 75-79, pres, 79-83); fel Am Meteorol Soc; Royal Meteorol Soc (pres, Can Br, 57-59); fel Royal Met Can. *Res:* Precipitation physics and induced precipitation; atmospheric infrared radiation; atmospheric ozone; numerical weather prediction; stratospheric fields of wind and temperature in the Arctic; atmospheric thermodynamics; long-period atmospheric oscillations; extreme value statistics. *Mailing Add:* 39 Dove Hawkway Willowdale ON M2R 3M8 Can

GODT, HENRY CHARLES, JR, SYNTHETIC ORGANIC & NATURAL PRODUCTS CHEMISTRY, TECHNICAL MANAGEMENT. *Current Pos:* PVT CONSULT, 87- *Personal Data:* b Ft Smith, Ark, July 26, 25; m 50, Gwendolyn Martin; c Carol A Martin. *Educ:* Univ Mich, BS, 50, MS, 51, PhD(pharmaceut chem), 54. *Prof Exp:* Res chemist, Monsanto Co, 53-58, res group leader, 58-70, technol appraisal mgr, 70-86. *Mem:* Am Chem Soc. *Res:* Organic chemical synthesis and process development; medicinal chemistry; agricultural chemicals; petroleum additives; technology evaluation and appraisal; environmental chemistry. *Mailing Add:* 12410 Ballas Meadows Dr Des Peres MO 63131-3041. *Fax:* 314-694-6858

GODT, ROBERT EUGENE, PHYSIOLOGY, BIOPHYSICS. *Current Pos:* asst prof, 78-81, ASSOC PROF PHYSIOL, MED COL GA, 81- *Personal Data:* b Des Moines, Iowa, Nov 18, 42. *Educ:* Carnegie Inst Technol, BS, 64; Univ Wash, PhD(physiol & biophys), 71. *Prof Exp:* Res asst physiol biochem, Univ Bern, Switz, 71-74; res asst physiol, Lunds Univ, Swed, 74; instr pharmacol, Mayo Found, Rochester, Minn, 74-75, asst prof physiol & biophys, 75-78, asst prof pharmacol, 77-78. *Concurrent Pos:* Res asst, Swiss Nat Fund, 71-74. *Mem:* Biophys Soc; Soc Gen Physiol; AAAS; Am Physiol Soc. *Res:* Muscle physiology, biophysics and biochemistry; physiology and biophysics of excitable membranes. *Mailing Add:* Dept Physiol & Endocrinol Med Col Ga Augusta GA 30912-3000. *Fax:* 706-721-7299

GODWIN, JAMES BASIL, JR, CAUSE & ORIGIN OF PETROLEUM EXPLOSIONS, CRASHWORTHINESS OF AIRCRAFT. *Current Pos:* OWNER & CHIEF EXEC OFFICER FORENSIC ENGR, GODWIN CONSULTS, INC, 80- *Personal Data:* b Beaumont, Tex, Dec 11, 24; m 48; c 4. *Educ:* Univ Tex, Austin, Aero Eng, 49. *Prof Exp:* Dist engr petrol, Mobil Oil Co, Magnolia Petrol Co, 49-60; air staff engr electrostatics in petrol, USAF, 60-85. *Concurrent Pos:* Adv & consult, Am Petrol Inst, 66-91; prin, Static Elec Comt, Nat Fire Protection Asn, 89-91. *Mem:* Fel Nat Acad Forensic Engrs; Am Soc Mech Engrs; Soc Automotive Engrs. *Res:* Electrostatic hazards in petroleum systems and cause/origin of fires and explosions caused by static electricity and/or other defects. *Mailing Add:* 8809 Canyon Crest Boerne TX 78006

GODWIN, JOHN THOMAS, ANATOMIC PATHOLOGY, CLINICAL PATHOLOGY. *Current Pos:* CLIN PROF, MOOREHOUSE SCH MED, 80- *Personal Data:* b Social Circle, Ga, Dec 2, 17; m 48, Sara Moak; c 3. *Educ:* Emory Univ, BS, 38, MD, 41; Am Bd Path, dipl, 49; Am Bd Clin Path, dipl, 61; Am Bd Nuclear Med, dipl, 76. *Honors & Awards:* Silver Medal, Am Soc Clin Path, 52, Gold Medal, 53. *Prof Exp:* Res path, Touro Infirmary, New Orleans, La, 41-41, pathologist & lectr, Ochsner Found Hosp & Sch Med, Tulane Univ, 50-51; head, Div Path & Pathologist, Hosp, Brookhaven Nat Lab, 51-55; clin asst prof path, 55-58, assoc prof, 58-60, PROF DENT PATH, SCH DENT, EMORY UNIV, 60- *Concurrent Pos:* Am Cancer Soc fel, Mem Hosp, 48-50; asst, Radioautographic Div, Physics Dept & preceptor, sr med students, Mem Hosp, Sloan Kettering Inst, New York, 49-50, asst attend pathologist, 51-55; head Biomed Reactor Res Proj & spec res scientist, Ga Inst Technol, 58-83; abstr ed, J Am Cancer Soc, 54-55; asst vis pathologist, James Ewing Hosp, 51-55; pathologist & dir labs, St Joseph's Infirmary, Atlanta, 55-78; res collabr, Brookhaven Nat Lab, 55-58; mem vis staff, Grady Hosp, Atlanta, 58-; consult, Grady Clay Mem Eye Clin, 58-75 & Ministry Health, Saudi Arabia, 80-85; adj clin prof, Allied Health Sci Sch & med dir, Med Technol Prog, Ga State Univ, 71-78; mem, Gov Sci & Technol Comn & Radiation Control Comt, State of Ga; chmn, Dept Path & Lab Med, King Faisal Specialist Hosp & Res Ctr, Riyadh, Saudi Arabia, 80-85; founder, Riyadh Path Group, Saudi Arabia; pathologist, West Paces Ferry Hosp, Atlanta, 86- *Mem:* Fel Col Am Pathologists; Soc Exp Biol & Med; fel Am Soc Clin Path; Am Thyroid Asn; AMA; fel Soc Nuclear Med; Am Asn Pathologists; Soc Head & Neck Surgeons; Soc Surg Oncol. *Res:* Pathology and natural history of human neoplasms; human and animal carcinogenesis, particularly by ionizing radiations; thyroid physiology; radiology; diagnosis and treatment of human cancer; original investigations in thermal neutron; capture therapy and use of short half radioactive isotopes. *Mailing Add:* 4691 Sentinel Post Rd NW Atlanta GA 30327. *Fax:* 404-350-5582

GODWIN, ROBERT O(WEN), LASERS, ELECTRO-OPTICS. *Current Pos:* ENG MGT CONSULT, 90- *Personal Data:* b Dothan, Ala, July 31, 35; m 57; c 2. *Educ:* Ga Inst Technol, BEE, 58; Univ Southern Calif, MS, 60; Calif State Univ, Fullerton, MBA, 73. *Prof Exp:* Mem tech staff, Hughes Aircraft Co, 58-61; sr res engr, Autonetics Div, NAm Rockwell Corp, 62-64, proj engr, 64-66, group scientist, 66-69, mgr, 69-74; proj mgr, Lawrence Livermore Labs, 74-86, assoc dir, 86-90. *Mem:* Inst Elec & Electronics Engrs; Laser Inst Am (treas, 75-77, pres, 79). *Res:* Laser research and development; range finders, illuminators and other applications; optical detection and signal processing; electronic design; design and development of laser fusion facilities. *Mailing Add:* 420 Autumn Chase Dr Venice FL 34292-3181

GODWIN, ROBERT PAUL, PHYSICS, APPLIED PHYSICS. *Current Pos:* STAFF MEM PHYSICS, LOS ALAMOS NAT LAB, 68-,. *Personal Data:* b Harvey, Ill, Apr 4, 37; m 60 Patricia E Zwickel; c Alan R & Susan K. *Educ:* DePauw Univ, AB, 59; Univ Ill, Urbana, MS, 61, PhD(physics), 66. *Prof Exp:* Volkswagen fel physics, Deutsches Elektronen Synchrotron, 66-68. *Concurrent Pos:* Guest scientist & Fulbright grant, Laser Res Proj, Max Planck Inst, Ger, 76-77. *Mem:* Am Phys Soc; Am Asn Physics Teachers; Sigma Xi. *Res:* Laser-plasma interaction experiments and diagnostics basic to laser-fusion studies and laser applications; vacuum ultraviolet and x-ray spectroscopy; surface physics; fluids; medical physics. *Mailing Add:* Los Alamos Nat Lab MS-F664 PO Box 1663 Los Alamos NM 87545

GODYAK, VALERY ANTON, GAS DISCHARGE PHYSICS & TECHNOLOGY. *Current Pos:* SR SCIENTIST, CENT RES, OSRAM SYLVANIA INC, 84- *Personal Data:* b Chernowitz, Ukraine, June 8, 41; US citizen; m 69, Etalina Gorenstein; c Jenya. *Educ:* St Petersburg Tech Univ, Russia, eng-physicist, 64; Moscow State Univ, Russia, PhD(plasma physics), 68. *Prof Exp:* Asst prof gen physics, Ryazan Radiotechnol Univ, Russia, 64; res assoc, State Inst Electro-Phys Apparatus, St Petersburg, 68-72; head RF discharge lab, Physics Dept, Moscow State Univ, Russia, 72-81. *Mem:* Fel Am Phys Soc; sr mem Inst Elec & Electronics Engrs. *Res:* Gas discharge physics, radio-frequency discharges, plasma diagnostics and modeling; probe diagnostics, light source technology. *Mailing Add:* 367 Harvard St No 2 Brookline MA 02146. *Fax:* 978-750-1792; *E-Mail:* godyak@rd.sylvania.com

GODYCKI, LUDWIG EDWARD, PHYSICAL CHEMISTRY. *Current Pos:* CONSULT, SEEC SERV, 67- *Personal Data:* b Bethlehem, Pa, Dec 21, 21; m 46; c 3. *Educ:* Lehigh Univ, BS, 43, MS, 47; Iowa State Col, PhD(chem), 51. *Prof Exp:* Asst Lehigh Univ, 46-48 & Iowa State Col, 48-51; res chemist, Houdry Process Corp, 51-52; asst prof chem, St Louis Univ, 52-56; assoc chemist, Res Lab, Int Bus Mach Corp, NY, 56-64; mgr mat, Bourns, Inc, 64-67. *Mem:* AAAS; Am Chem Soc; Am Phys Soc; Am Crystallog Asn; Sigma Xi. *Res:* X-ray crystallography; surface chemistry and physics; semiconductor chemistry; electrochemistry. *Mailing Add:* 1060 Granada Ave San Marino CA 91108-2429

GODZESKI, CARL WILLIAM, MICROBIOLOGY, BIOCHEMISTRY. *Current Pos:* RETIRED. *Personal Data:* b Champaign Ill, July 17, 26; m 49, 63, 91, Bette Runyan; c Jeffrey M. *Educ:* Univ Ill, BS, 49; Pa State Univ, PhD(bact), 53. *Prof Exp:* Pathogenic bacteriologist, Pitman-Moore Co, 53-54; from res microbiologist to sr res microbiologist, Eli Lilly & Co, 54-65, res assoc, 65-69, chief microbiol immunol serv, 69-74, res assoc bio res div, 74-85. *Mem:* Am Soc Microbiol; Sigma Xi. *Res:* Penicillin-cephalosporin antibiotics; bacterial L-forms and mycoplasma; infectious disease; infection in connective tissue diseases; virology. *Mailing Add:* PO Box 754 Osteen FL 32764

GOE, GERALD LEE, ORGANIC CHEMISTRY. *Current Pos:* assoc dir org res, 77-80, RES CHEMIST, REILLY INDUST INC, 73-, DIR RES, 80- *Personal Data:* b Kansas City, Mo, Aug 17, 42; m 66; c 1. *Educ:* Univ Mo-Columbia, BS, 63; Mass Inst Technol, PhD(org chem), 67. *Prof Exp:* NIH fel, Iowa State Univ, 67-69; asst prof chem, Univ Notre Dame, 69-73. *Mem:* Am Chem Soc. *Res:* Heterogeneous catalysis; synthesis of heterocyclic compounds; organic photochemistry. *Mailing Add:* 4021 W Fairview Rd Greenwood IN 46142

GOEBEL, CARL JEROME, ENVIRONMENTAL SCIENCES, RANGE MANAGEMENT. *Current Pos:* chmn, dept environ sci, 71-73, PROF FORESTRY & RANGE MGT, WASH STATE UNIV, 68- *Personal Data:* b Milwaukee, Wis, Mar 24, 29; m 54; c 5. *Educ:* Univ Idaho, BS, 55; Utah State Univ, PhD(range mgt), 60; Harvard Univ, MPA, 64. *Prof Exp:* Range conservationist, US Forest Serv, 58-59; asst prof forestry, Iowa State Univ, 59-63; range researcher, US Forest Serv, 63-68. *Concurrent Pos:* Fel, Australian Nat Univ, Canberra, 75; Morroco Range Exten, 79-81; Lesotho Res Proj, 83-85; fac, Univ Canterbury, 87-88. *Mem:* Soc Am Foresters; Soc Range Mgt. *Res:* Competition between the native bluebunch wheatgrass; introduced perennials by the annual wheatgrass and other less desirable annuals. *Mailing Add:* 2817 E 35th Ave Spokane WA 99223

GOEBEL, CHARLES GALE, ORGANIC CHEMISTRY. *Current Pos:* Sr chemist, 43-52, mgr lab, 52-59, res dir, 59-66, corp tech dir, 66-69, vpres res & develop, 69-78, VPRES & GEN MGR, EMERY INDUSTS, INC, SUBSID NAT DISTILLERS & CHEM CORP, 78- *Personal Data:* b Indianapolis, Ind, Nov 19, 17; m 45; c 3. *Educ:* Ind Univ, AB, 39; Purdue Univ, MS, 41, PhD(org chem), 44. *Mem:* Am Chem Soc; Am Oil Chemists' Soc. *Res:* Fatty acids and derivatives; plasticizers; synthetic lubricants, resins; plastics and detergents. *Mailing Add:* 543 Larmie Trail Cincinnati OH 45215-2503

GOEBEL, CHARLES JAMES, THEORETICAL PHYSICS. *Current Pos:* assoc prof, 61-64, PROF PHYSICS, UNIV WIS-MADISON, 64- *Personal Data:* b Chicago, Ill, Dec 16, 30; m 51; c 2. *Educ:* Univ Chicago, PhB, 49, PhD(physics), 56. *Prof Exp:* Res assoc, Lawrence Radiation Lab, Univ Calif, 54-56; asst prof, Univ Rochester, 56-59, assoc prof physics & astron, 59-61. *Concurrent Pos:* Alfred E Sloan res fel quantum field theory, 59-61. *Mem:* Fel Am Phys Soc. *Res:* Quantum field theory, especially meson scattering; general relativity. *Mailing Add:* 10 N Ruby Rd Madison WI 53705

GOEBEL, EDWIN DEWAYNE, ENVIRONMENTAL GEOLOGY. *Current Pos:* PROF GEOL, UNIV MO-KANSAS CITY, 71-, CHMN GEOSCI DEPT, 77- *Personal Data:* b Moline Ill, Dec 10, 23; m 50; c 2. *Educ:* Augustana Col, AB, 49; Univ Iowa, MS, 51; Univ Kans, PhD(regional stratig, econ geol), 66. *Prof Exp:* Asst geol, Univ Iowa, 50-51; geologist, State Geol Surv, Kans, 51, div head oil & gas, 51-66, chief admin serv, 66-67, sr geologist, 67-71. *Concurrent Pos:* Tech dir, Nat Gas Surv, Fed Power Comn, 74-76; consult, 71- *Mem:* Geol Soc Am. *Res:* Petroleum geology; subsurface stratigraphy; structural geology; micropaleontology; gas reserves, proved and potential. *Mailing Add:* Dept Geosci Univ Mo 5100 Rockhill Rd Kansas City MO 64110-2446

GOEBEL, JACK BRUCE, COMPUTER SCIENCE. *Current Pos:* RETIRED. *Personal Data:* b Wallowa, Ore, Aug 22, 32; m 83, Janet Gore; c John, Mark, Franz, Joseph & Jacob. *Educ:* Univ Ore, BA, 54, MA, 56; Ore State Univ, PhD(math), 62. *Prof Exp:* Instr math, Ore State Univ, 60-61; from mathematician to sr mathematician, Gen Elec Co, 61-65; res assoc appl math, Pac Northwest Lab, Battelle Mem Inst, 65-67; prof math & head dept, Mont Col Mineral Sci, 67-80, chmn Grad Sch, 69-73, dean, Div Arts & Sci, 73-86, prof math, 86-94. *Mem:* Am Math Soc; Soc Indust & Appl Math; Math Asn Am; Asn Comput Mach; Sigma Xi. *Res:* Abstract algebra; applied mathematics. *Mailing Add:* 69270 Bear Creek Wallowa OR 97885

GOEBEL, MARISTELLA, ABNORMAL PSYCHOLOGY & TEACHING, HEALTH PSYCHOLOGY. *Current Pos:* assoc prof educ, 49, prof, 66-89, EMER PROF PSYCHOL, ROSARY COL, RIVER FOREST, IL, 91-; CONSULT PSYCHOL, SINSINAWA DOMINICAN SISTERS, 66- *Personal Data:* b Racine, WI, Sept 10, 15. *Educ:* Edgewood Col, Madison, BS, 44; Cath Univ Am, MA, 47, PhD(clin psychol), 66. *Honors & Awards:* Cert Distinguished Contrib to Discipline Clin Psychol, Am Psychol Asn, 86. *Prof Exp:* Teacher Eng, Cathedral High Sch Sionx Falls, 46-47, Heart Mary High, Mobile, 47-49; clin psychol, Renal Sect, Hines Vet Admin Hosp, Ill, 70-92. *Concurrent Pos:* Chmn & ed, Southeastern Curric Comt, Teachers guide, 48-51; prin investr, NIMH small res grant, 62-63, 65-66, Hines Vet Admin Hosp, 76-87, Nat Heart Lung & Blood Inst res grant, 82-84, Nat Heart Lung & Blood Inst HIPP proj, 84-86; bd dirs, Am Asn Biofeedback Clinicians, 79-86; bd advocate, Biofeedback Soc Am, 81-83; fel & dipl clin res, Am Asn Biofeedback Clinicians, 83. *Mem:* Am Psychol Asn; fel & dipl Am Asn Biofeedback Clinicians; Biofeedback Soc Am; Soc Clin & Exp Hypn; Soc Behav Med; Am Heart Asn; Int Soc Hypn. *Res:* Biobehavioral treatments in essential hypertension; clinician-friendly model to isolate specific effects; clinical efficacy and cost-effectiveness. *Mailing Add:* 7900 W Division St River Forest IL 60305

GOEBEL, RONALD WILLIAM, ASTROPHYSICS, ASTRONOMY. *Current Pos:* RES ASSOC ASTRON, ALLEGHENY OBSERV, UNIV PITTSBURGH, 78- *Personal Data:* b Cincinnati, Ohio, Dec 23, 47; m 77. *Educ:* Ind Univ, BA, 70; State Univ NY, Albany, MS, 76, PhD(astrophys), 77. *Prof Exp:* Astronomer, US Naval Observ, 70-72; instr physics & astron, Williams Col, 77-78. *Mem:* Am Astron Soc. *Res:* Spectroscopy; development of new astronomical equipment and computer interfacing to such equipment; astrometry. *Mailing Add:* Ten Mayflower Dr Albany NY 12205

GOECKNER, NORBERT ANTHONY, ORGANIC CHEMISTRY. *Current Pos:* from asst prof to prof, 61-92, EMER PROF CHEM, WESTERN ILL UNIV, 92- *Personal Data:* b Chicago, Ill, Sept 30, 30; m 54, Mary Barnard; c 7. *Educ:* Univ Ill, BS, 54; Univ Iowa, MS, 57, PhD(chem), 59. *Prof Exp:* Chemist gas chromatography sect, Stand Oil Co Ind, 59-61. *Mem:* Am Chem Soc. *Res:* Gas chromatography. *Mailing Add:* 340 S Randolph St Macomb IL 61455

GOEDDEL, DAVID V, MOLECULAR BIOLOGY. *Current Pos:* vpres res, 93-96, PRES & CHIEF EXEC OFFICER, TULARIK INC, 96- *Personal Data:* b Pasadena, Calif, May 3, 51. *Educ:* Univ Calif, San Diego, BA, 72; Univ Colo, PhD(biochem), 77. *Honors & Awards:* Eli Lilly Award Biol Chem, 84; Scheele Medal, Swed Acad Pharmaceut Sci, 88. *Prof Exp:* Teaching asst & res asst, Univ Colo, 73-77; postdoctoral fel, Stanford Res Inst, 77-78; sr scientist, Genentech Inc, 78-81, dir, Dept Molecular Biol, 80-93, staff scientist, 81-93. *Mem:* Nat Acad Sci; fel AAAS; fel Am Acad Arts & Sci. *Res:* Enzymology; author of numerous scientific publications. *Mailing Add:* Tularik Inc 2 Corporate Dr South San Francisco CA 94080-4990

GOEDEN, RICHARD DEAN, ENTOMOLOGY, ECOLOGY. *Current Pos:* Asst entomologist & lectr, 65-69, asst prof & asst entomologist, 69-71, assoc prof & assoc entomologist, 71-77, PROF & ENTOMOLOGIST, UNIV CALIF, RIVERSIDE, 77- *Personal Data:* b Neillsville, Wis, May 20, 35; m 62; c 3. *Educ:* Univ Wis, BS, 62, MS, 63, PhD(entom), 65. *Mem:* Entom Soc Am; Entom Soc Wash; Int Orgn Biol Control; Int Weed Sci Soc; Pac Coast Entom Soc. *Res:* Biological control and insect ecology of weeds; phytophagous insect and host-plant relationships; insect life histories; biosystematics of Tephritidae. *Mailing Add:* Dept Entom Univ Calif 900 Univ Ave Riverside CA 92521-0101

GOEDICKE, VICTOR ALFRED, astronomy; deceased, see previous edition for last biography

GOEDKEN, VIRGIL LINUS, inorganic chemistry, for more information see previous edition

GOEHLER, BRIGITTE HANNA, MICROBIOLOGY. *Current Pos:* from asst prof to assoc prof, 67-75, PROF BIOL, CALIF STATE POLYTECH UNIV, 75- *Personal Data:* b Radebeul, Germany, July 24, 26; US citizen. *Educ:* Wayne State Univ, MS, 60, PhD(bact), 64. *Prof Exp:* Biologist, Inst Tobacco Res, Germany, 51-52; biologist, German Acad Agr Sci, Berlin, 52-55; instr biol, Wayne State Univ, 60-62, asst prof, 64-65; NIH fel, 65-67. *Mem:* Am Soc Microbiol; Sigma Xi. *Res:* Bacterial physiology; molecular biology. *Mailing Add:* Dept Biol Sci Calif State Polytech Univ Pomona CA 91768-2557

GOEHRING, JOHN BROWN, INORGANIC CHEMISTRY. *Current Pos:* from asst prof to assoc prof, 63-70, PROF CHEM, WASH & LEE UNIV, 70- *Personal Data:* b Pittsburgh, Pa, Apr 24, 35; m 60, Ouida Reaves; c Dorothy, Patricia & Alexander. *Educ:* Davidson Col, BS, 56; Univ NC, PhD(chem), 62. *Prof Exp:* E I du Pont Co asst chem, Univ NC, 58-59, instr, 60-63. *Concurrent Pos:* NSF sci fac fel, Univ Calif, Los Angeles, 69-70. *Mem:* AAAS; Am Chem Soc; Royal Soc Chem; Hist Sci Soc. *Res:* Properties of inorganic electrolytes; experimentation in educational media; historical development of chemistry. *Mailing Add:* PO Box 1410 Lexington VA 24450

GOEKE, GEORGE LEONARD, ORGANIC & ORGANOMETALLIC CHEMISTRY. *Current Pos:* RES CHEMIST, UNION CARBIDE CORP, 73- *Personal Data:* b Philadelphia, Pa, July 16, 42; m 69; c 1. *Educ:* Pa State Univ, BS, 69; Princeton Univ, MA, 71, PhD(org chem), 73. *Prof Exp:* Indexer jour publ, Inst Sci Info, 67-70. *Mem:* Am Chem Soc; Catalysis Soc; Sigma Xi. *Res:* Synthetic organometallic chemistry; polymerization catalysis; organic synthesis. *Mailing Add:* Hiland Dr Belle Mead NJ 08502

GOEKEN, NANCY ELLEN, INTERNAL MEDICINE. *Current Pos:* res assoc, Dept Med, Univ Iowa, 72-73, res investr, 73-75, asst res scientist, 75-76, res health sci specialist, Vet Admin Med Ctr, 77-78, tech suprv, Tissue Typing Lab, 78-80, dir, Histocompatibility Testing, 80-82, assoc res scientist, Dept Med, Univ Iowa, 80-83, asst prof, 83-86, DIR, TISSUE TYPING LAB, VET ADMIN MED CTR, 82-, ASSOC PROF, DEPT INTERNAL MED & PATH, COL MED, 86- *Educ:* Univ Mo, BA, 68, PhD, 72. *Prof Exp:* NSF res fel, Univ Chicago, 65-67; teaching asst vert histol & gen biol, Univ Mo, 68-72. *Concurrent Pos:* Mem, Nat Task Force Organ Transplantation, 85-86. *Mem:* AAAS; Sigma Xi; Am Soc Histocompatibility & Immunogenetics (vpres, 87-88, pres-elect, 88-89, pres, 89-90); Am Asn Immunologists; Transplantation Soc; Am Soc Transplant Physicians (pres, 86-87). *Res:* Immunobiology; immunoregulation; transplantation immunology; author of numerous scientific publications. *Mailing Add:* Histocompatibility Serv Vet Admin Med Ctr Hwy 6W Rm 10E19 Iowa City IA 52246-2202. *Fax:* 319-339-7171

GOEL, AMRIT LAL, STATISTICS, OPERATIONS RESEARCH. *Current Pos:* from asst prof to assoc prof indust eng, 68-77, PROF INDUST ENG & OPERS RES, SCH COMPUT & INFO SCI, SYRACUSE UNIV, 77- *Personal Data:* b Meerut, India, Mar 4, 38; m 67. *Educ:* Agra Univ, BSc, 57; Univ Roorkee, BEng, 61; Univ Wis, Madison, MS, 63, PhD, 68. *Prof Exp:* Asst mech engr, Dept Atomic Energy, India, 61-62; lectr eng, Univ Wis, Milwaukee, 67-68. *Concurrent Pos:* NSF res grants, 69-71 & 70-71; fel, Rome Air Develop Ctr, Griffiss AFB, 70-71; consult, res grants data mgt systs, USAF, 69-76, reliability & maintainability, 70-76; Air Force grants, 75-78. *Mem:* Am Statist Asn; Opers Res Soc Am; Asn Comput Mach; Am Soc Qual Control; fel Royal Statist Soc; Sigma Xi. *Res:* Reliability theory; software reliability and modelling; sequential analysis; cumulative sum chart procedures; time series analysis. *Mailing Add:* 111 Link Hall Syracuse NY 13244

GOEL, KAILASH C(HANDRA), ENVIRONMENTAL ENGINEERING, ENVIRONMENTAL SCIENCES. *Current Pos:* PRES, G&B ENVIRON, INC, 86- *Personal Data:* b Tasing, India, July 12, 37; m 62; c 2. *Educ:* Banaras Hindu Univ, BS, 59; Univ Roorkee, MEng, 60; Okla State Univ, PhD(water pollution control), 68; Wilmington Col, MBA, 85. *Prof Exp:* Asst engr, Pub Health Eng, State Uttar Pradesh, India, 60-64; sanit engr, Water & Air Resources Comn, State Del, 68, dir labs, 68-69; dir labs, Edward H Richardson Assoc, Inc, 69-77, head, environ sci div & br mgr, 77-86. *Concurrent Pos:* Exten prof, Univ Del, 70-71. *Mem:* Water Pollution Control Fedn; Am Acad Environ Engrs. *Res:* Treatment of waste waters and sludges; wastewater sampling and analysis. *Mailing Add:* 15 Winged Foot Rd Dover DE 19904

GOEL, MAHESH C, PUBLIC HEALTH ADMINISTRATION. *Current Pos:* DIR LABS, DEPT HEALTH, 78- *Personal Data:* b Mathura, India, Aug 1, 35; US citizen; m 70, Chandra; c Neeta, Nisha & Neerja. *Educ:* Agra Univ, DVM, 57; Wis Univ, MS, 67, PhD(microbiol), 70. *Prof Exp:* Fel, Univ Wis, 70-72; clin microbiologist, Hosp Joint Dis, 72-75; head microbiol, Professional Lab, 75-78. *Concurrent Pos:* Nat coordr, Hands to Clin Labs, 87- *Mem:* Am Soc Microbiol; Am Soc Clin Pathologists; Sigma Xi; NYC-ASM. *Res:* Applied research in public health. *Mailing Add:* Dept Health 176 Broadway Paterson NJ 07505. *Fax:* 973-279-7511

GOEL, NARENDRA SWARUP, THEORETICAL BIOCHEMISTRY, RELIABILITY. *Current Pos:* PROF SYST SCI, STATE UNIV NY, BINGHAMTON, 76- *Personal Data:* b Muzaffarnagar, India, June 12, 41; US citizen. *Educ:* Agra Univ, India, BS, 57; Dehi Univ, India, MS, 59 Poona Univ, India, MS, 62; Univ Md, PhD(physics), 65. *Prof Exp:* Res asst, Indian Inst Technol, 59-62; res asst instr physics, Univ Md, 65; asst prof physics & assoc biophysics, Univ Rochester, 66-72; mgr & prin scientist eng & technol, Xerox Corp, 72-76. *Concurrent Pos:* Consult, Inst Defense Analyses, 64-67, Int Bus Mach Corp, 76-81, Gen Elec Corp, 77-78, Xerox Corp, 79- & NASA, 81-; ed, J Theoret Biol, 73-85; Jacobs Scholar, Marine Biol Lab, Univ Md, 66; assoc ed, Bulletin Math Biol, 77-87; pres, Aster Consulting Assoc Inc, 77-; exchange scholar, US-USSR Acad Sci Exchange Prog, 81; vis prof, San Luis Univ, Argentina, 83; regional ed, Remote Sensing Rev, 88- *Mem:* Bioeng Soc; Biophys Soc; Soc Indust & Appl Math; NY Acad Sci; Soc Origin Life; Agron Soc. *Res:* Remote sensing; modeling and analysis of biological and engineering systems; computer simulation of self-organization in biological systems; population biology; failures in digital systems; reliability of complex electro-mechanical machines; continuing education of scientists and engineers; computer graphics; remote sensing of vegetation. *Mailing Add:* Dept Systs Sci State Univ NY PO Box 6000 Detroit MI 48202

GOEL, OM PRAKASH, ORGANIC CHEMISTRY, MEDICINAL CHEMISTRY. *Current Pos:* Assoc res chemist to res chemist, Parke-Davis Co, 66-72, res assoc, 73-80, sr res assoc, 81-89, sect dir, 90-92, DIR, PARKE-DAVIS RES, DIV WARNER-LAMBERT, 93- *Personal Data:* b Delhi, India, Sept 25, 43; nat US; m 68; c 3. *Educ:* Univ Delhi, BSc, 62; Carnegie-Mellon Univ, MS, 65, PhD(org chem), 66. *Concurrent Pos:* Adj assoc prof, Univ Mich, Dearborn, 87. *Mem:* Am Chem Soc; AAAS. *Res:* Fischer indole synthesis mechanism; process research and scaled-up synthesis of new chemotherapeutic agents and chemical intermediates; catalytic hydrogenation and high pressure reactions; radiolabeled drugs; chemical development. *Mailing Add:* Parke-Davis Div Warner-Lambert 2800 Plymouth Rd Ann Arbor MI 48105. *E-Mail:* goelo@aa.wl.com

GOEL, PREM KUMAR, BAYESIAN DECISION ANALYSIS, STATISTICAL MODELING. *Current Pos:* prof statist & dir statist consult serv, 83-88 & 92-93, prof & chmn, Dept Statist, 88-92, PROF STATIST, OHIO STATE UNIV, 93- *Personal Data:* b Bareilly, India, 43; US citizen; m 72, Veena Gupta; c Archna, Anjali & Arun. *Educ:* Agra Univ, India, BSc, 62, MStat, 64; Carnegie-Mellon Univ, MS, 69, PhD(statist), 71. *Prof Exp:* Res fel statist, Inst Social Sci, Agra, 65-67, lectr, 67-68; res asst, Carnegie-Mellon Univ, 68-71; from asst prof to assoc prof statist, Purdue Univ, 71-83. *Concurrent Pos:* Res assoc, Dept Statist, Carnegie-Mellon Univ, 74 & 75, consult, 78, vis assoc prof, 78-79; assoc ed, J Am Statist Asn, 76-82; prin investr, NSF, 80-84 & 89-92, Air Force Off Sci Res, 84-87, Nat Hwy Traffic Safety Admin/VTRC Contracts, 84, 86, 87 & 89-91 & Army Res Off, 85-87; prog dir, Statist & Probability Prog, NSF, 82-83; elect mem, Int Statist Inst, Bharatiya Temple Soc, pres, 87-88; expert witness variety legal cases, 83-; co-prin investr educ grant, Howard Hughes Med Inst, 89-; mem comt, Appl & Theoret Statist, Nat Res Coun, 88-92, panel, Combining Info, 90-92; mem curric index, Statist Mgt Comt, 90-93, chair comt, 93- *Mem:* Fel AAAS; fel Int Statist Inst; fel Inst Math Statist; fel Am Statist Assoc; fel Royal Statist Soc. *Res:* Bayesian decision analysis; probability modeling and statistical inference for applied problems in engineering and social sciences; experimental designs; file merging methodology, combining information. *Mailing Add:* Dept Statist Ohio State Univ 1958 Neil Ave Columbus OH 43210-1247. *Fax:* 614-292-2096

GOEL, RAM PARKASH, PLASTICITY, CONNECTOR MECHANICS. *Current Pos:* PRES/CHIEF EXEC OFFICER, OPTIMA TECHNOL ASSOCS INC, 95- *Personal Data:* b India, Dec 15, 42; m 72, Sarla Gupta; c Shumona, Sujata & Rohit. *Educ:* Punjabi Univ, India, BS, 64; Mich State Univ, MS, 66, PhD(eng), 69. *Prof Exp:* Design Engr, McDowell Wellman Eng Co, Cleveland, 65-67; asst prof teaching, Mich State Univ, 69-70; mem tech staff res, Bell Telephone Labs, Ohio, 70-79; mgr connector mech & res, Amp Inc, 79-85, dir, Eng Assurance, 85-90, dir technol planning, 90-92, gen mgr, 93-95. *Concurrent Pos:* Lectr, M C Polytech, India, 64-65; assoc prof, NC A&T State Univ, 75-76. *Mem:* Am Soc Metals. *Res:* Mechanics of electrical connectors; mathematical modeling; mechanical properties of materials; developing reliability testprograms on electrical connectors; management; strategic planning globalization of technology companies; impact of technology in global markets. *Mailing Add:* 515 Colony Rd Camp Hill PA 17011. *Fax:* 717-932-5878; *E-Mail:* optima1@epix.net

GOEL, VIJAY KUMAR, ORTHOPAEDIC BIOMECHANICS, SPINE BIOMECHANICS. *Current Pos:* from asst prof to assoc prof, Univ Iowa, 82-90, chmn, Dept Biomed Eng, 90-95, actg dir, Iowa Inst Biomed Eng, 92-96, PROF BIOMED ENG, MECH ENG & ORTHOP, UNIV IOWA, 90- *Personal Data:* b Sangrur, Punjab, India, Mar 5, 45; US citizen; m 72, Shashi Rani; c Anuj & Anish. *Educ:* Panjabi Univ, India, BE, 66; Roorkee Univ, India, ME, 71; Univ NSW, Sydney, PhD(mech eng), 77. *Honors & Awards:* Volvo Award, Int Soc Study Lumbar Spine, 81, 90 & 94; AeroMed Award, NAm Spine Soc, 90 & 92. *Prof Exp:* Asst prof mech eng, Thapar Col Eng, India, 66-74; asst prof biomed eng, Indian Inst Technol, India, 78-79; res assoc, Yale Med Sch, 79-82. *Concurrent Pos:* Reviewer, NIH, 86-; mem, Task Force Spinal Implants, Am Soc Testing & Mat, 89-; res Award, Cervical Spine Res Soc, 93; chair, Solids Mech Comt, Biomed Eng Div, Am Soc Mech Engrs, 93- & chair, Coun Dir Bio & Biomed Eng Progs, 95-96. *Mem:* Am Soc Biomech; fel Am Soc Mech Engrs; Int Soc Study Lumbar Spine; Orthop Res Soc; fel Am Inst Med Eng; Am Soc Eng Educ. *Res:* Design and development of spinal implants; basic and applied research in the area of orthopaedic-biomechanics, especially spinal biomechanics. *Mailing Add:* 2912 Meadow Circle NE Iowa City IA 52240. *Fax:* 319-335-5631; *E-Mail:* goel@uiowa.edu

GOELA, JITENDRA SINGH, CHEMICAL VAPOR DEPOSITION, LASER TECHNOLOGY. *Current Pos:* PRIN SCIENTIST, MORTON INT-CVD INC, WOBURN, MASS, 84- *Personal Data:* b New Delhi, India, Apr 20, 51; m 79, Geeta Gupta; c Naveen & Vikas. *Educ:* Indian Inst Technol, BTech, 72; Brown Univ, RI, MSc, 74, PhD(mech eng), 76; Northeastern Univ, MA, MBA, 91. *Honors & Awards:* Arthur L Williston Medal, Am Soc Mech Engrs, 78; Young Scientist Medal, Indian Nat Sci Acad, 82; Eng Excellance Award, Optical Soc Am, 91. *Prof Exp:* Prin scientist, Phys Sci Inc, Andover, Mass, 76-78; from lectr to asst prof mech eng, Indian Inst Technol, Kanpur, India, 78-84. *Concurrent Pos:* Vis scientist, Phys Sci Inc, 79 & 80, CVD Inc, 83; consult, Sanders Assocs, Nashua, NH & Aeromet Inc, Tulsa, Okla, 86-87; pres, Efficient Sys Inc, Andover, Mass, 87-90. *Mem:* Am Soc Mech Engrs; Soc Photo-Optical Instrumentation Engrs; Am Phys Soc; Optical Sco Am; NY Acad Sci; Am Ceramic Soc. *Res:* Development of advanced infrared optical materials, ceramic materials, SIC fiber, superconducting materials and CdZnTe substrates via chemical vapor deposition lasers and applications. *Mailing Add:* 12 Messina Dr Andover MA 01810. *Fax:* 781-933-5473; *E-Mail:* jitgoela@aol.com

GOELL, JAMES E(MANUEL), FIBER OPTICS, ELECTRICAL ENGINEERING. *Current Pos:* DIR, OIMS, OFCD & AMP, 92- *Personal Data:* b New York, NY, Oct 13, 39; m 60; c 2. *Educ:* Cornell Univ, BEE, 62; MS, 63, PhD(elec eng), 65. *Prof Exp:* Mem tech staff, Bell Tel Labs, 65-74; vpres & dir eng, Electro Optical Prod Div, Int Tel & Tel Corp, 74-81; pres, Lightwave Technol, Inc, 81-85; vpres, PCO, 85-92. *Mem:* Fel Inst Elec & Electronics Engrs; Optical Soc Am; Am Phys Soc. *Res:* Ferrites, millimeter waves; periodic structures; communications; microwave tubes and circuits; microwaves; optics; integrated optical circuits; fiber optics. *Mailing Add:* 2416 Schefield Circle Harrisburg PA 17112. *Fax:* 717-986-7535

GOEPEL, CHARLES ALBERT, FIBER OPTICS, FIBER OPTIC SENSORS. *Current Pos:* SR STAFF ENGR, MARTIN MARIETTA, 88- *Personal Data:* b Philadelphia, Pa, June 5, 53; m 73; c 2. *Educ:* Univ Del, BEE, 76. *Prof Exp:* Sr engr, Circuit Prod Div, Gen Tel, 77-81; eng mgr, Optical Info Systs, Exxon Enterprises, 81-83; prin engr, Gould Ocean Systs, 83-88. *Concurrent Pos:* Prin investr fiber optics, Martin Marietta, 88- *Mem:* Inst Elec & Electronics Engrs; Soc Photo-Optical Instrumentation Engrs. *Res:* Fiber optic sensors; interferometric based optical hydrophones; optical communications; lasers; coherent multiplexing; acoustic modeling; loudspeaker design; high strength electro-optic cables; lithium niobate modulators. *Mailing Add:* 181 Berrywood Dr Severna Park MD 21146

GOEPP, ROBERT AUGUST, DENTISTRY, PATHOLOGY. *Current Pos:* Instr dent & path, Univ Hosps & Clins, Univ Chicago, 61-64, asst prof oral path, Zoller Mem Dent Clin & Dept Path, 64-70, assoc prof, Pritzker Sch Med, 70-75, dir, Zoller Dent Clin, 78-87, prof, 75-97, EMER PROF ORAL PATH, PRITZKER SCH MED, UNIV CHICAGO, 97- *Personal Data:* b Chicago, Ill, Nov 3, 30; m 60; c 3. *Educ:* Loyola Univ, Chicago, BS, 54, DDS, 57; Univ Chicago, MS, 61, PhD, 67; Am Bd Oral Path, dipl, 63; Am Bd Oral & Maxillofacial Radiol. *Concurrent Pos:* Consult, Chicago Bd Health, 63-64 & Am Dent Asn, 72-; mem, Nat Coun Radiation Protection & Measurements, 77- & Coun Dent Res, Am Dent Asn, 78-; dir & vpres, Contracap Inc, 81-88. *Mem:* AAAS; Am Dent Asn; fel Am Acad Oral Path; fel Am Acad Dent Radiol (past pres); Am Asn Path & Bact; Sigma Xi; Rad Res Soc; fel Int Col Dentists; fel Am Col Dentists; Odontographic Soc. *Res:* Caries; oral pathology; dental radiology; radiation biology; barrier fertility control. *Mailing Add:* 5841 S Maryland Ave Chicago IL 60637

GOERING, CARROLL EUGENE, AGRICULTURAL ENGINEERING. *Current Pos:* PROF AGR ENG, UNIV ILL-URBANA, 77- *Personal Data:* b Platte Center, Nebr, June 8, 34; m 60; c 3. *Educ:* Univ Nebr, BS, 59; Iowa State Univ, MS, 62, PhD(agr eng, eng mech), 65. *Prof Exp:* Design engr, Int Harvester Co, 59-61; asst agr eng, Iowa State Univ, 61-62, res assoc, 62-65; from asst prof to prof, Univ Mo-Columbia, 65-77. *Mem:* Am Soc Agr Engrs; Am Soc Eng Educ; Am Soc Testing & Mat; Soc Automotive Engrs. *Res:* Biofuels; engine efficiency; author of two books. *Mailing Add:* Dept Agr Eng Univ Ill 1304 W Pennsylvania Urbana IL 61801

GOERING, HARLAN LOWELL, ORGANIC CHEMISTRY. *Current Pos:* from instr to prof, 50-72, SAMUEL M MCELVAIN PROF CHEM, UNIV WIS-MADISON, 72- *Personal Data:* b McPherson, Kans, July 13, 21; m 44; c 1. *Educ:* Bethel Col, AB, 43; Univ Colo, PhD(chem), 48. *Prof Exp:* Res assoc, Univ Calif, Los Angeles, 48-50. *Concurrent Pos:* Vis Prof, Harvard Univ, 63. *Mem:* Am Chem Soc; Royal Soc Chem. *Res:* Mechanisms of organic reactions. *Mailing Add:* 96 Kessel Ct No 32 Madison WI 53711

GOERING, JOHN JAMES, MARINE ECOLOGY. *Current Pos:* From asst prof to assoc prof, 62-68, PROF MARINE SCI, INST MARINE SCI, UNIV ALASKA, 68- *Personal Data:* b Clifton, Kans, June 2, 34; m 56; c 3. *Educ:* Bethel Col, Kans, BS, 56; Univ Wis, MS, 60, PhD(zool), 62. *Concurrent Pos:* NSF res grant, 64-90; coun Agr Sci & Technol. *Mem:* AAAS; Am Soc Limnol & Oceanog; Artic Inst NAm. *Res:* Nitrogen cycle in lakes and the sea; silicon cycle in the sea. *Mailing Add:* PO Box 81478 Fairbanks AK 99708-1478

GOERING, KENNETH JUSTIN, CHEMISTRY. *Current Pos:* CONSULT, 75- *Personal Data:* b San Francisco, Calif, Dec 26, 13; m 36; c 3. *Educ:* Mont State Col, BS, 36; Calif Inst Technol, MS, 38; Iowa State Col, PhD(biophys chem), 41. *Prof Exp:* Asst chemist, Exp Sta, Mont State Col, 36-37; asst org chem, Calif Inst Technol, 37-38 & Iowa State Col, 38-41; res chemist, Anheuser-Busch Inc, Mo, 41-42; instr chem, Iowa State Col, 42-43; chemist, Univ Nebr, 43-44; asst chemist, Farm Crops Processing Corp, Nebr, 44-45; vpres & gen mgr, Mold Bran Co & Enzymes, Inc, 45-49; from asst prof to prof chem, Mont State Univ, 49-75, asst dean Grad Div, 64-67, dean, Col Grad Studies, 67-75. *Concurrent Pos:* Plant mgr, Agr Prods Corp, Iowa, 48-49; lectr, Tech Inst, Rio de Janero, Brazil; consult for several companies; assoc ed, Am Cereal Chemists. *Mem:* Am Chem Soc; Am Asn Cereal Chem; Sigma Xi. *Res:* Concentration and fractionation of enzymes and protein purification; isolation and study of properties of new starch sources. *Mailing Add:* 8383 Saddle Mountain Rd Bozeman MT 59715

GOERINGER, GERALD CONRAD, CELL BIOLOGY, DEVELOPMENTAL BIOLOGY. *Current Pos:* asst prof, 66-70, actg chmn, 80-81, ASSOC PROF ANAT, SCH MED, GEORGETOWN UNIV, 70- *Personal Data:* b Philadelphia, Pa, Jan 2, 33; m 57; c 2. *Educ:* Univ Pa, AB, 55; Northwestern Univ, PhD(embryol), 59. *Prof Exp:* Asst prof biol, San Diego State Col, 63-66. *Concurrent Pos:* Life Ins Med Res Fund fel, 59-62; res fel immunol, Univ Stockholm, 62-63; life sci adv comt, NASA, 83-88. *Mem:* Teratol Soc; Soc Develop Biol; Am Soc Cell Biol; Am Inst Biol Sci; Sigma Xi. *Res:* Developmental biology; lung development; cell hybridization; smoking and health; mechanisms of teratogenesis. *Mailing Add:* Dept Cell Biol Sch Med Georgetown Univ 3900 Reservoir Rd NW Washington DC 20007. *Fax:* 202-687-1823; *E-Mail:* ggoe@erols.com

GOERKE, JON, BIOPHYSICS, SURFACE CHEMISTRY. *Current Pos:* asst res physician & asst clin prof med, 66-67, asst prof med, 67-72, asst prof physiol, 72-74, assoc prof physiol, 74-80, PROF PHYSIOL, UNIV CALIF, SAN FRANCISCO, 80-, SR STAFF, CARDIOVASC RES INST, 74- *Personal Data:* b Newark, NJ, Jan 15, 29; m 54; c 3. *Educ:* Calif Inst Technol, BS, 51; Yale Univ, MD, 55. *Prof Exp:* Intern internal med, Univ Calif, San Francisco, 55-56; resident, Vet Admin Hosp, Boston, 59-60; res fel, Biophys Lab, Harvard Med Sch, 60-62; cardiol trainee, Univ Calif, San Francisco, 62-64; USPHS spec fel, Cardiovasc Res Inst, 64-66. *Concurrent Pos:* Assoc staff, Cardiovasc Res Inst, 67-74; estab investr, Am Heart Asn, 67-72. *Mem:* AAAS; Biophys Soc; Am Physiol Soc. *Res:* Lung surfactant monolayer stability in model systems and excised lung; air-water interface as a model membrane; liposomes as model systems. *Mailing Add:* Dept Physiol Cardiovasc Res Inst Univ Calif Sch Med PO Box 0130 San Francisco CA 94143-0130. *Fax:* 415-476-3586

GOERTEMILLER, CLARENCE C, JR, DEVELOPMENTAL BIOLOGY, CELL BIOLOGY. *Personal Data:* b Big Stone Gap, Va, Feb 19, 28; wid. *Educ:* Univ Md, BS, 51; RI Col, EdB, 59; Brown Univ, ScM, 62, PhD(biol), 64. *Prof Exp:* Res fel biol, Harvard Med Sch, 64-65; from asst prof to prof zool, Univ RI, 65-94. *Mem:* AAAS; Am Soc Zoologists; Am Soc Cell Biol; Sigma Xi. *Res:* Development of secretory competence in salt-secreting epithelia. *Mailing Add:* 115 W Main St North Kingstown RI 02852

GOERTZ, GRAYCE EDITH, FOOD SCIENCE. *Current Pos:* RETIRED. *Personal Data:* b Carnduff, Sask, July 9, 19; US citizen. *Educ:* Kans State Univ, BS, 41, MS, 47, PhD(food sci), 52. *Prof Exp:* Instr pub sch, Kans, 41-44 & pub sch & jr col, 44-46; asst, Kans State Univ, 46-47, 49-52, instr foods, 47-48; instr, Univ Ill, 48-49; asst prof, Ore State Univ, 52-55; prof, Kans State Univ, 55-65; prof & head, Dept Food Sci & Syst Admin, Univ Tenn, Knoxville, 64-74, assoc dean, Col Home Econ, 74-80, emer prof, 80- *Concurrent Pos:* Mem educ comn, Inst Food Technol, 74- *Mem:* Inst Food Technol; Am Dietetic Asn; Am Home Econ Asn. *Res:* Heat effects on proteins including pigments. *Mailing Add:* 923 Portsmouth Circle Maryville TN 37803

GOERTZ, JOHN WILLIAM, VERTEBRATE ZOOLOGY. *Current Pos:* RETIRED. *Personal Data:* b Hackensack, NJ, Aug 25, 29; m 53; c 3. *Educ:* Ore State Univ, BS, 57, MS, 59; Okla State Univ, PhD(zool), 62. *Prof Exp:* From asst prof to prof zool, La Tech Univ, 62-89. *Concurrent Pos:* Environ consult, 89- *Mem:* Am Soc Mammalogists. *Res:* Population dynamics; biology, habitats, parasites, distribution, reproductive; rates in rodent ecology; distribution and biology in mammalogy; nesting behavior in ornithology; wildlife and forest management. *Mailing Add:* 1402 Caddo St Ruston LA 71270

GOERTZEL, GERALD, IMAGE PROCESSING. *Current Pos:* RETIRED. *Personal Data:* b New York, NY, Aug 18, 19; m 41, Marth Bendheim; c 3. *Educ:* Stevens Inst Technol, ME & MS, 40; NY Univ, PhD(physics), 47. *Prof Exp:* Physicist, Oak Ridge Nat Lab, 46-48; assoc prof physics, NY Univ, 48-53; tech dir, Nuclear Develop Corp Am, 53-60; vpres eng, Sage Instruments Inc, 60-64; res staff, IBM, 64-92. *Mem:* Am Phys Soc; Sigma Xi; AAAS; NY Acad Sci. *Res:* Data compression; reactor physics; Fourier analysis; internal conversion; medical electronics; digital halftoning. *Mailing Add:* 7 Sparrow Circle White Plains NY 10605

GOERZ, DAVID JONATHAN, JR, PHYSICS. *Current Pos:* from sr engr to sr supv engr, Bechtel Corp, 63-68, res mgr, 68-71, mgr bus develop, 71-77, mgr coal prog & vpres, Bechtel Nat, Inc, 77-81, mgr new proj develop, Bechtel Civil & Minerals Inc, 81-85, vpres, Bechtel China, Inc, 82, mgr, Strategic Planning & Mkt & vpres, Bechtel Power Corp, 87-89, MGR DIV BUS DEVELOP & MKT, WESTERN PETROL & MINING & METALS DIVS, BECHTEL, INC, 85-; SR VPRES, CITOH & CO (AM) INC; PRES, GOERZ & ASSOCS, INC; PRES, CHINA PARTNERS, INC. *Personal Data:* b Los Angeles, Calif, Sept 25, 34; m 62; c 3. *Educ:* Univ Calif, Los Angeles, AB, 56; Stanford Univ, MS, 57. *Prof Exp:* Res assoc microwave physics, W W Hansen Lab, Stanford Univ, 56 & 58, res assoc, 58-62; pres & tech dir, Vactite, Inc, 62-63. *Concurrent Pos:* Consult, Hughes Aircraft Co, 59 & Phys Electronics Lab, 60; mem, Bd Gov, Int Microwave Power Inst, 68-, chmn, 70-71; gen chmn, Microwave Power Conf, The Hague, 69; alt dir, China Am Int Eng Inc, 84; co-chmn, Comt Scholarly Commun People's Repub China, Nat Acad Sci Nat Acad Eng; mem, Steering Comt, Nat Res Coun. *Mem:* Inst Elec & Electronics Engrs; Sigma Xi. *Res:* Accelerator physics; microwave theory and applications; ultra high vacuum; cryogenics; industrial process development; environmental research; coal technology and regional planning; electric power generation; project financing; petrochemical and refining. *Mailing Add:* 11 Shasta Lane Menlo Park CA 94025

GOETINCK, PAUL FIRMIN, GENETICS. *Current Pos:* from asst prof to assoc prof, 64-72, PROF ANIMAL GENETICS, UNIV CONN, 72- *Personal Data:* b Bruges, Belg, June 17, 33; US citizen; m 58; c 2. *Educ:* Univ Calif, Davis, BS, 56, PhD(genetics), 63. *Prof Exp:* Trainee biochem, Univ Calif, Los Angeles, 62-64. *Concurrent Pos:* NIH res career develop award, 68-73. *Mem:* AAAS; Am Genetic Asn; Soc Develop Biol. *Res:* Developmental genetics; embryology; protein biochemistry. *Mailing Add:* Cutaneous Biol Res Ctr Mass Gen Hosp E Bldg 149 13th St Charleston MA 02129-2060. *Fax:* 617-726-4189

GOETSCH, DENNIS DONALD, VETERINARY PHYSIOLOGY. *Current Pos:* prof & head physiol & pharmacol, 69-89, EMER PROF & HEAD, SCH VET MED, UNIV GA, 89- *Personal Data:* b Brewster, Kans, Dec 6, 24; m 53; c 3. *Educ:* Kans State Univ, BS & DVM, 52, MS, 55; Okla State Univ, PhD, 61. *Prof Exp:* From instr to asst prof physiol, Kans State Univ, 52-56; tech dir, Specified, Inc, Ind, 56-57; from asst prof to prof physiol, Okla State Univ, 57-69. *Concurrent Pos:* NSF fel, 59-60; mem exec coun, Conf of Res Workers in Animal Dis, 72-77, pres, 77; mem coun educ, Am Vet Med Asn, 72-82. *Mem:* Am Soc Vet Physiol & Pharmacol (pres, 77); Am Physiol Soc; Am Vet Med Asn. *Res:* Carbohydrate and energy metabolism, especially of the ruminant; ketosis of the ruminant animal. *Mailing Add:* 25 Trace Way Sanford NC 27330

GOETSCH, GERALD D, ANIMAL PHYSIOLOGY. *Current Pos:* from instr to assoc prof, 52-59, PROF & HEAD DEPT VET PHYSIOL, SCH VET MED, PURDUE UNIV, 59- *Personal Data:* b Colby, Kans, Apr 6, 23; m 47; c 3. *Educ:* Kans State Univ, DVM, 45; Purdue Univ, MS, 55, PhD(animal physiol), 57. *Prof Exp:* Asst state veterinarian, Ill State Dept Agr, 45-46; pvt pract, Ill, 46-47; asst prof vet physiol, Univ Mo, 47 & Okla State Univ, 48-52. *Concurrent Pos:* Mem, NCent Regional Comt Ruminant Bloat, 54-62; mem coun biol & therapeut agents, Am Vet Med Asn, 62- *Mem:* Am Vet Med Asn; Am Soc Vet Physiol & Pharmacol (pres, 64); Conf Res Workers Animal Dis. *Res:* Metabolic diseases of animals; ruminant bloat; ketosis of sheep; gastric ulcers of swine. *Mailing Add:* 328 Fernleaf Dr West Lafayette IN 47906

GOETSCHEL, CHARLES THOMAS, ORGANIC CHEMISTRY, INORGANIC CHEMISTRY. *Current Pos:* INSTR CHEM, CHABOT COL, 72- *Personal Data:* b Chicago, Ill, Sept 21, 35; m 58; c 2. *Educ:* Northwestern Univ, BA, 57; Univ Mich, PhD(org chem), 62. *Prof Exp:* AEC res fel catalysis, Northwestern Univ, 62-64; chemist, Shell Develop Co, 64-70; chemist, Ctr Technol, Kaiser Aluminum & Chem Corp, Pleasanton, 70-72. *Concurrent Pos:* Mem, Int Cong Catalysis. *Mem:* Am Chem Soc. *Res:* Application of organic chemistry to catalysis; inorganic radiation chemistry; inorganic fluorine chemistry; inert gas chemistry and high energy inorganic oxidizers. *Mailing Add:* Dept Chem Chabot Col 25555 Hesperian Blvd Hayward CA 94545-2447

GOETTEL, MARK S, INSECT PATHOLOGY, MICROBIAL PEST CONTROL. *Current Pos:* RES SCIENTIST INSECT PATH, AGR & AGR-FOOD CAN, 88- *Personal Data:* b Cowansville, Que, Jan 23, 54. *Educ:* Concordia Univ, BSc, 75; Univ Ottawa, MSc, 77; Univ Alta, PhD(entom), 87. *Prof Exp:* Res entomologist, Fiji Ministry Health, 78-81; vis scientist, Boyce Thompson Inst, 87-88. *Concurrent Pos:* Adj prof, Dept Biol Sci, Simon Fraser Univ, Burnaby, BC. *Mem:* Soc Invert Path; Int Orgn Biol Control; Entom Soc Can; Am Mycol Soc; Can Forum Biol Control (pres, 93-94). *Res:* Insect pathology, development of pathogens, namely fungi for control of pest insects, namely grasshoppers, aphids and Colorado potato beetle; prevention of disease in beneficial insects, namely chalkbrood in alfalfa leafcutting bees. *Mailing Add:* Res Sta PO Box 3000 Lethbridge AB T1J 4B1 Can. *Fax:* 403-382-3156

GOETTLER, LLOYD ARNOLD, ALLOYS BLENDS & COMPOSITES, RHEOLOGY. *Current Pos:* Sr res engr, Monsanto Co, 66-72, res specialist, 73-76, sr res specialist, 76-85, FEL, MONSANTO CO, 85- *Personal Data:* b Rockville Centre, NY, July 5, 39; m 61, Grace Tynes; c Richard, Donna, Ronald, Dawn & Robert. *Educ:* Cornell Univ, BChE, 62; Univ Del, PhD(chem eng), 67. *Honors & Awards:* Pres Cup, Soc Plastics Engrs, 86. *Concurrent Pos:* Adj prof polymer eng, Univ Akron, 85- *Mem:* Fel Soc Plastics Engrs; Am Chem Soc; Soc Rheology; Am Inst Chem Engrs; Polymer Process Soc (pres, 93-). *Res:* Diffusion with simultaneous chemical reaction; diffusion and growth kinetics in crystallization from the vapor; processing of polymeric materials; short fiber composites; reinforced elastomers; thermoplastic elastomers; adhesion; polymer blends and alloys. *Mailing Add:* Monsanto Chem Co PO Box 97 Gonzalez FL 32560

GOETTLICH RIEMANN, WILHELMINA MARIA ANNA, PROTEIN CHEMISTRY, DAIRY-MEAT SCIENCE & TECHNOLOGY. *Current Pos:* staff res assoc animal sci, Univ Calif, Davis, 66-68, res asst food sci, 68-70, staff res assoc nutrit, 70-82, researcher postgrad food sci, 86-87, EMER RESEARCHER FOOD SCI, UNIV CALIF, DAVIS, 89- *Personal Data:* b Jaworow, Poland, June 25, 34; Polish & US citizen; m 65. *Educ:* Warsaw Agr Univ, BS, 54, MS, 57; Gdansk Polytech, PhD(chem), 77. *Hon Degrees:* LHD, World Univ, Tucson, Ariz, 82. *Prof Exp:* Res asst dairy sci, Warsaw Agr Univ, 54-56 & Warsaw Dairy Res Inst, 57-62; asst prof meat sci, Warsaw Meat Res Inst, 61-65. *Concurrent Pos:* Consult, Polish Eng Asn, 57-65 & Polish Patent Comn, 63-65; coordr, Cameron Meat Res Inst, 62-64. *Mem:* Sigma Xi. *Res:* Protein chemistry; analytical chemistry; dietetics; biochemistry; computer science; nutrition; author of 18 publications. *Mailing Add:* 816 Miller Dr Davis CA 95616-3623

GOETTSCH, ROBERT, PHARMACEUTICS, BIOPHARMACEUTICS. *Current Pos:* assoc prof, 65-68, PROF PHARM, IDAHO STATE UNIV, 68- *Personal Data:* b Atlantic, Iowa, Sept 27, 27; m 58; c 3. *Educ:* Univ Colo, BS, 51; Univ Iowa, MS, 53. *Prof Exp:* Instr pharm, Univ Colo, 53-54; asst prof pharm & pharmaceut chem, Univ Kans, 57-60; asst prof pharmaceut chem, Northeast La State Col, 60-61; assoc prof pharmaceut, Univ Tenn, 61-65. *Concurrent Pos:* Res grant, Burroughs Wellcome & Co, USA, Inc, 62-63; consult, Palmer Chem & Equip Co, Inc, 62-65. *Mem:* AAAS; Am Pharmaceut Asn; Am Chem Soc; Acad Pharmaceut Sci; NY Acad Sci; Sigma Xi. *Res:* Applications of physical-chemical principles to pharmaceutical systems; interaction of drugs with macromolecules; drug degradation and stabilization; analytical methods for drugs and drug mixtures; pharmacy. *Mailing Add:* 540 S 17th Ave Pocatello ID 83201

GOETZ, ABRAHAM, MATHEMATICS. *Current Pos:* vis assoc prof, 62, ASSOC PROF MATH, UNIV NOTRE DAME, 65- *Personal Data:* b Grybow, Poland, Apr 8, 26; nat; m 55, Janina Kupperman; c George S & Victor. *Educ:* Wroclaw Univ, MS, 49; Math Inst, Polish Acad Sci, PhD(math), 57. *Prof Exp:* Asst math, Wroclaw Univ, 48-53, adj, 53-58; lectr, 58-64; lectr math, Math Inst, Polish Acad Sci, 53-62. *Mem:* Am Math Soc; Polish Math Soc; Math Asn Am. *Res:* Topological and Lie groups; differential geometry; universal algebras. *Mailing Add:* Dept Math Univ Notre Dame 1622 E Madison St South Bend IN 46617. *E-Mail:* abraham.goetz.2@nd.edu

GOETZ, ALEXANDER FRANKLIN HERMANN, REMOTE SENSING, RESEARCH ADMINISTRATION. *Current Pos:* PROF GEOL SCI & DIR, CTR STUDY EARTH FROM SPACE, UNIV COLO, BOULDER, 85- *Personal Data:* b Pasadena, Calif, Oct 14, 38; div; c 2. *Educ:* Calif Inst Technol, BS, 61, MS, 62, PhD(planetary sci), 67. *Honors & Awards:* Charles E Ives Award, Soc Photog Scientists & Engrs, 74; Autometrics Award, Soc Photogram 82; William T Pecora Award, 82; Exceptional Sci Achievement Medal, NASA, 82; NASA Space Act Award, 87. *Prof Exp:* Mem tech staff lunar geol, Bell Tel Labs, 67-70; mem tech staff planetology, Calif Inst Technol, 70-73, group supvr earth resources, 73-75, sect mgr planetology & oceanog, 75-77, sr mem tech staff, 77-81, sr res scientist, Jet Propulsion Lab, 81-85. *Concurrent Pos:* Assoc ed, Geophys Res Lett, 74-77, Remote Sensing Environ, 84-; pres, GeoImages Inc, Altadena, Calif, 75-78; vis prof, Univ Calif, Los Angeles, 83; mem, Nat Res Coun Bd Earth Sci, 87-90; trustee, San Juan Capistrano Res Inst, 87-92; distinguished vis scientist, Jet Propulsion Lab, 89-90; pres, Anal Spectral Devices Inc, Boulder, Colo, 90-; assoc ed & geophys ed, 96-. *Mem:* AAAS; Am Geophys Union; Sigma Xi; Am Soc Photogram & Remote Sensing. *Res:* Space and airborne remote sensing in the ultraviolet to microwave spectrum applied to geologic mapping; global change manifestation studies from the standpoint of field observations, field instrument development and hyperspectral image data analysis techniques. *Mailing Add:* 4861 Curie Ct Box 250 Boulder CO 80301. *Fax:* 303-492-5070; *E-Mail:* goetz@cses.colorado.edu

GOETZ, FREDERICK CHARLES, INTERNAL MEDICINE, DIABETES. *Current Pos:* From instr to assoc prof, 55-68, PROF MED, MED SCH, UNIV MINN, MINNEAPOLIS, 68- *Personal Data:* b Fond du Lac, Wis, Nov 60; c 4. *Educ:* Harvard Univ, BS, 43, MD, 46. *Mem:* Endocrine Soc; Am Diabetes Asn. *Res:* Diabetes mellitus in the human being, especially complications of diabetes and mechanisms of insulin secretion; endocrinology. *Mailing Add:* Univ Minn Hosp & Clin 515 Delaware St SE Minneapolis MN 55455-0348

GOETZ, FREDERICK WILLIAM, JR, COMPARATIVE ENDOCRINOLOGY, REPRODUCTIVE BIOLOGY. *Current Pos:* ASST PROF PHYSIOL & ENDOCRINOL, DEPT BIOL, UNIV NOTRE DAME, 77- *Personal Data:* b Philadelphia, Pa, Jan 31, 50; m 72; c 3. *Educ:* Colgate Univ, BA, 72; Univ Wyo, PhD(zool), 76. *Prof Exp:* Fel, Fisheries & Marine Serv, Nat Res Coun Can, 76-77. *Mem:* AAAS; Am Soc Zoologists; Am Fisheries Soc; Soc Study Reproduction. *Res:* Hormonal control of oocyte final maturation and ovulation in piscine vertebrates and the evolution of this control in teleost fish. *Mailing Add:* Dept Biol Sci Univ Notre Dame 148 Galvin Life Sci Notre Dame IN 46556

GOETZ, HAROLD, PLANT ECOLOGY, RANGE ECOLOGY. *Current Pos:* HEAD, RANGE SCI DEPT, COLO STATE UNIV, 85- *Personal Data:* b Halliday, NDak, Dec 20, 32; m 60; c 2. *Educ:* NDak State Univ, BS, 60, MS, 63; Utah State Univ, PhD(range sci), 68. *Prof Exp:* Range conservationist, Bur Indian Affairs, Nebr, 63; from asst prof to assoc prof bot, NDak State Univ, 63-75, dir, Tri-Col Ctr Environ Studies, 70-73, prof bot, 75-85. *Concurrent Pos:* Mem, Great Plains Res Coun Comt, 66- & Great Plains Range & Livestock Adv Comt, 66-; US Govt consult, 67-; sr agr officer, fac renewable natural resources, Univ Tehran, 73-; Fulbright fel. *Mem:* Am Soc Range Mgt (secy-treas, 65-); Am Inst Biol Sci; Am Forestry Asn; Ecol Soc Am. *Res:* Rangeland ecology; effects of nitrogen fertilizer on the botanical composition of range sites as related to water use, phenological development, soil chemical and physical changes and other factors of the individual plant species. *Mailing Add:* Range Sci Dept Col Forestry-Natural Res Colorado State Univ Ft Collins CO 80523

GOETZ, KENNETH LEE, CARDIOVASCULAR PHYSIOLOGY, BODY FLUID HOMEOSTASIS. *Current Pos:* CONSULT, 94- *Personal Data:* b Java, SDak, Jan 7, 32; m 62; c 2. *Educ:* Univ Wis, BS, 58, PhD(physiol), 63; Univ Kans, MD, 67. *Honors & Awards:* Alexander von Humboldt Award, 92. *Prof Exp:* From instr to asst prof physiol, Med Ctr, Univ Kans, 63-68, adj prof, 76-92; med intern, St Lukes Hosp, 69, head exp med, 70-90, dir res, 81-90; vis scientist, Ger Inst Aerospace Med, Cologne, 93-94. *Concurrent Pos:* Vis prof, Univ Kuopio, Finland, 85 & 91, Univ Munich, 92. *Mem:* Am Physiol Soc. *Res:* Cardiovascular physiology; physiologic effects of changes in atrial pressures; regulation of body fluid volume; atrial natriuretic peptides; urodilatin. *Mailing Add:* 4856 Black Swan Dr Shawnee Mission KS 66216-1237. *Fax:* 785-631-7358

GOETZ, RICHARD W, INDUSTRIAL ORGANIC CHEMISTRY. *Current Pos:* RES MGR, QUANTUM CHEM CORP, 87- *Personal Data:* b Cincinnati, Ohio, July 29, 36; m 60; c 4. *Educ:* Univ Cincinnati, ChemE, 59, PhD(org chem), 63. *Prof Exp:* Res chemist, Monsanto Co, 63-64; res chemist, Nat Distillers & Chem Co, 64-73, from res assoc to sr res assoc, 73-81, mgr, US Indust Chem Co Div, Nat Distillers & Chem Co, 81-87. *Mem:* Sigma Xi; Am Chem Soc; AAAS. *Res:* Homogeneous and heterogeneous catalysis of organic reactions by transition metal compounds. *Mailing Add:* Quantum Chem Corp 11530 Northlake Dr Cincinnati OH 45249

GOETZ, WILLIAM H(ARNER), HIGHWAY ENGINEERING, MATERIALS SCIENCE. *Current Pos:* from asst prof to prof hwy eng, 45-85, asst head Sch Civil Eng, 68-85, EMER PROF HWY ENG, PURDUE UNIV, 85- SCH CIVIL ENG, 68- *Personal Data:* b Ann Arbor, Mich, Sept 29, 14; m 38; c 3. *Educ:* Univ Mich, BS, 36; Purdue Univ, MS, 42. *Honors & Awards:* Prevost Hubbard award, Am Soc Testing & Mat, 81. *Prof Exp:* Lab technician, State Hwy Dept, Mich, 36-38. *Concurrent Pos:* consult, Mc Connaughay Assoc, 48-, Corps Engrs, US Army, 52- & Nat Co-op Hwy Res Prog, 62- *Mem:* Am Soc Eng Educ; Nat Soc Prof Engrs; Asn Asphalt Paving Technol (pres, 58); Am Soc Testing & Mat. *Res:* Bituminous materials and pavements; bituminous mixture design; asphalt emulsions. *Mailing Add:* 908 W State St West Lafayette IN 47906-1215

GOETZEL, CLAUS G(UENTER), MATERIALS SCIENCE, METALLURGICAL ENGINEERING. *Current Pos:* RETIRED. *Personal Data:* b Ger, July 14, 13; US citizen; m 38, Lilo G Kallmann; c Rodney G & Vivian L. *Educ:* Tech Hochsch, Berlin, dipl ing, 35; Columbia Univ, PhD(metall), 39. *Honors & Awards:* Alexander von Humboldt Sr US Scientist Award, Fed Repub Ger, 78. *Prof Exp:* Head res lab, Charles Hardy, Inc, 37-39; tech dir & works mgr, Am Electro Metals Corp, 40-47; vpres & dir res, Sintercast Corp Am, 47-57; sr res scientist, NY Univ, 57-60; consult scientist, res lab, Lockheed Aircraft Corp, Palo Alto, 61-78. *Concurrent Pos:* Adj prof, NY Univ, 44-60; chmn prog comt, Int Powder Metall Conf, 60; lectr, Stanford Univ, 61-; vis prof, Univ Karlsruhe, Ger, 78-80. *Mem:* Fel Am Soc Mat; Am Inst Mining, Metall & Petrol Engrs; Am Powder Metall Inst; assoc fel Am Inst Aeronaut & Astronaut; Inst Mat UK. *Res:* Metals technology; high temperature materials; powder metallurgy; dispersion alloys; metal-nonmetal composites; nuclear reactor components; wear and corrosion-resistant parts; tools and dies; graphite composites; rocket propulsion components. *Mailing Add:* 250 Cervantes Rd Portola Valley CA 94028

GOETZINGER, CORNELIUS PETER, AUDIOLOGY, PSYCHOLOGY. *Current Pos:* prof otolaryngol, 53-80, DIR AUDIOL-ELECTRONYSTAGMOGRAPHIC CLIN, SCH MED, UNIV KANS MED CTR, KANSAS CITY, 53-, EMER PROF, 80- *Personal Data:* b Baltimore, Md, Feb 10, 11; m 42; c 2. *Educ:* Washington Univ, BS, 41; Gallaudet Col, MA, 44; Univ Calif, Berkeley, MA, 50; Northwestern Univ, Evanston, PhD(audiol), 55. *Prof Exp:* Teacher deaf & audiologist, Cent Inst Deaf, 41-43; teacher deaf, audiologist & psychologist, Calif Sch for Deaf, Berkeley, 44-51. *Concurrent Pos:* Consult psychol & audiol, Kans State Sch Deaf, 55-; consult audiol, Vet Admin Hosp, 59- & Menninger Found, Childrens Hosp, 64- *Mem:* Fel Am Speech & Hearing Asn. *Res:* Hearing pathology with reference to diagnostic tests and rehabilitation in conjunction with research into the psychological impact of deafness upon intelligence and adjustment; author or co-author of numerous publications and book reviews. *Mailing Add:* 14604 S Chalet Dr Olathe KS 66062

GOFF, CHARLES W, ELECTRON MICROSCOPY, CYTOCHEMISTRY. *Current Pos:* Asst prof, 69-77, ASSOC PROF LIFE SCI, IND STATE UNIV, 78-, DIR, ELECTRON MICROS FAC, 81- *Personal Data:* b Rowlesburg, WVa, July 25, 41; m 74; c 3. *Educ:* Fairmont State Col, BA, 64; Univ Tex, Austin, PhD(bot), 70. *Mem:* AAAS; Am Soc Cell Biol; Am Soc Plant Physiologists; Bot Soc Am; Histochem Soc; Sigma Xi. *Res:* Activities and functions of the cytomembrane system, particularly during mitosis and cytokinesis, as studies by experimental treatment; ultrastructural and cytochemical techniques. *Mailing Add:* Dept Life Sci Ind State Univ Terre Haute IN 47803-0001. *Fax:* 812-237-4480

GOFF, CHRISTOPHER GODFREY, molecular biology, biochemical genetics, for more information see previous edition

GOFF, GERALD K, MATHEMATICS. *Current Pos:* assoc prof, 65-70, PROF MATH, OKLA STATE UNIV, 70- *Personal Data:* b Apache, Okla, June 26, 25; m 51; c 2. *Educ:* Phillips Univ, BA, 50, MEd, 53; Okla State Univ, EdD(math), 62. *Prof Exp:* Instr pub schs, Okla, 50-53, prin, 53-56; from asst prof to assoc prof, Southwestern State Col, Okla, 57-65. *Concurrent Pos:* Consult sch math study group, Stanford Univ, 63-; adj prof, Okla State Univ, 62-64; vis prof, Univ Carabobo, Valencia, Venezuela, 70. *Mem:* Math Asn Am. *Res:* Number theory; prime and composite numbers. *Mailing Add:* 2107 N Frankfurt St Tulsa OK 74106

GOFF, HAROLD MILTON, BIOINORGANIC CHEMISTRY. *Current Pos:* from asst prof to assoc prof, 76-85, PROF CHEM, UNIV IOWA, 85- *Personal Data:* b St Louis, Mo, Sept 24, 47; m 71; c Jason & Justin. *Educ:* Univ Mo, Columbia, BS, 69, MA, 71; Univ Tex, Austin, PhD(chem), 76. *Prof Exp:* Med lab instr, US Army, Ft Sam Houston, Tex, 70-73; fel chem, Univ Calif, Davis, 76. *Mem:* Am Chem Soc. *Res:* Synthesis, ligand binding, redox properties and nuclear magnetic resonance of iron porphyrins as models for hemoproteins; chemistry of peroxidase enzymes. *Mailing Add:* 445 Kimball Rd Iowa City IA 52245

GOFF, JAMES FRANKLIN, SOLID STATE PHYSICS. *Current Pos:* RETIRED. *Personal Data:* b Louisville, Ky, Aug 1, 28; m 59, Barbara Louise Kral; c Sidra Denise & Alexander Kral. *Educ:* Mass Inst Technol, BS, 50; Purdue Univ, MS, 53, PhD(physics), 62. *Prof Exp:* Group leader res, US Naval Surface Weapons Ctr/White Oak Lab, 61-77, ctr coordr nondestructive eval, 77-79, head mat applns, 80-90. *Concurrent Pos:* Tech asst, Naval Sea Systs Command, 75-76. *Mem:* Am Phys Soc; AAAS; Cosmos Club. *Res:* Thermoelectric energy conversion; failure of composite materials; transport properties of semiconductors and transition metals and alloys; thermoelectric energy conversion; failure of composite materials. *Mailing Add:* 3405 34th Pl NW Washington DC 20016

GOFF, JESSE PAUL, VETERINARY MEDICINE. *Current Pos:* biol lab tech, Physiopath Res Unit, 80-84, res assoc, Dept Vet Physiol & Pharmacol, 84-86, VET DUTY OFFICER, MINERAL METAB & MASTITIS RES UNIT, NAT ANIMAL DIS CTR, USDA AGR RES SERV, 85- *Personal Data:* b Nov 12, 55. *Educ:* Cornell Univ, BS, 77; Iowa State Univ, MS, 80, DVM, 84, PhD(nutrit physiol), 86. *Prof Exp:* Microbiologist, Poultry Sci Dept, Cornell Univ, 77-78; teaching asst, Dept Vet Physiol & Pharmacol, Iowa State Univ, 78-80. *Concurrent Pos:* Holco res excellence award, Animal Sci Dept, Iowa State Univ, 86, David R Griffith Res Award, 86; adj asst prof vet physiol & pharmacol, Iowa State Univ, 88. *Mem:* Am Dairy Sci Asn. *Res:* Metabolic diseases in domestic animals; parturient hypocalcemia in dairy cattle; hypomagnesemia of beef cattle; interaction of nutrition with immune competence during the periparturient period; author of numerous scientific publications. *Mailing Add:* Nat Animal Dis Ctr USDA ARS 70 Dayton Rd PO Box 70 Ames IA 50010-0070. *Fax:* 515-239-8458

GOFF, KENNETH W(ADE), ELECTRICAL ENGINEERING. *Current Pos:* VPRES ADVAN TECHNOL, PERFORMANCE CONTROLS INC, 85- *Personal Data:* b Salem, WVa, June 14, 28; m 50; c 3. *Educ:* Univ WVa, BS, 50; Mass Inst Technol, SM, 52, ScD(elec Eng), 54. *Prof Exp:* Consult engr, Bolt Beranek & Newman, Inc, 54-56; proj mgr, Gruen Precision Labs, 56-57; mgt, Leeds & Northrup Co, 57-85. *Mem:* Fel Instrument Soc Am; fel Inst Elec & Electronics Engrs. *Res:* Analysis of control systems; techniques for applying analog and digital computers to the control of industrial processes; hardware and software development for digital computer systems; design of motion control systems. *Mailing Add:* Performance Controls Inc 433 Caredean Dr Horsham PA 19006

GOFF, LYNDA J, ALGAL MOLECULAR BIOLOGY, MOLECULAR SYSTEMATICS. *Current Pos:* from asst prof to assoc prof, 75-81, PROF BIOL, UNIV CALIF, SANTA CRUZ, 81- *Personal Data:* b Oakland, Calif, June 12, 49; m 77. *Educ:* Western Ore State Col, BSc, 71; Univ BC, PhD(bot), 75. *Honors & Awards:* Harold Bold Award, Phycol Soc Am, 75; Darbaker Award, Bot Soc Am, 86; Provasoli Award, Physol Soc, 86 & 90. *Prof Exp:* Teaching asst bot & phycol, Univ BC, 71-75, res assoc phycol, 75. *Concurrent Pos:* Sr res award, Fulbright Found, 83; vis prof marine bot, Univ Wash, 75, 92 & 93, biol, Brown Univ, 82-; assoc ed, J Phycol, Phycol Soc Am, 84- *Mem:* Phycol Soc Am (secy, 89-); Bot Soc Am; Am Inst Biol Sci; fel AAAS. *Res:* Mechanisms by which specific parasites have evolved directly from their hosts; cell biology, evolution and molecular biology approaches; biochemical/molecular aspects of symbiosis. *Mailing Add:* Biol Univ Calif 1156 High St Santa Cruz CA 95064-1077. *Fax:* 408-459-3139; *E-Mail:* goff@orchid.ucsc.edu

GOFF, STEPHEN PAYNE, VIROLOGY, ENZYMOLOGY. *Current Pos:* asst prof biochem, 81-85, assoc prof biochem & molecular biophys, 85-86, PROF BIOCHEM & MOLECULAR BIOPHYS, COL PHYSICIANS & SURGEONS, COLUMBIA UNIV, 86- *Personal Data:* b Providence, RI, Oct 22, 51; m 77; c 2. *Educ:* Amherst Col, AB, 73; Stanford Univ, PhD(biochem), 78. *Honors & Awards:* Harold & Golden Lamport Res Award. *Prof Exp:* Fel biol, Mass Inst Technol, 78-81. *Mem:* Am Soc Microbiol; NY Acad Sci. *Res:* Genetics and molecular biology of two retroviruses (Moloney and Abelson murine leukemia viruses) using in vitro mutagenesis of cloned DNA copies of the viral genomes. *Mailing Add:* Dept Biochem Columbia Univ Col Physicians & Surgeons Columbia Univ 630 W 168th St New York NY 10032-3702. *Fax:* 212-305-8692

GOFFINET, EDWARD P(ETER), JR, CHEMICAL REACTION ENGINEERING, CHEMICAL PROCESS MODELING. *Current Pos:* RETIRED. *Personal Data:* b Louisville, Ky, Nov 15, 30; wid; c Pamela Kay & Terri Ann. *Educ:* Univ Notre Dame, BS, 52. *Prof Exp:* Res engr, 52-62, E I Dupont de Nemours & Co, res div head, Elastomer Chem Dept Exp Sta, 63-72, sr consult, Eng Dept, 72-83, sr res assoc, 83-86, res fel, Polymer Prod Dept, 86-91, sr technol fel, 91-92. *Res:* Applied reaction kinetics; polyester polymerization processes; engineering computer applications; hydrocarbon elastomer processes; definition of new chemical processes. *Mailing Add:* 2403 Annwood Dr Wilmington DE 19803

GOFFMAN, MARTIN, MANAGEMENT CONSULTING, LABORATORY INFORMATION MANAGEMENT SYSTEMS. *Current Pos:* PRIN, MARTIN GOFFMAN ASSOC, 86- *Personal Data:* b Philadelphia, Pa, June 22, 40; m 65; c 3. *Educ:* Temple Univ, AB, 61, MA, 63, PhD(chem), 65. *Prof Exp:* Sr res chemist phys chem & electrochem, Cent Res Lab, Asarco Inc, 65-86, proj leader, 81-85, sect head, 85-86; pres, Dellview USA Med Inc, 90-92. *Concurrent Pos:* Consult, proj dir, Small Bus Innovation Res & course dir, Lab Info Mgt Syst; fel, AEC, 63-65. *Mem:* Am Chem Soc; Asn Consult Chemists & Chem Eng; Asn Independent Info Prof. *Res:* Information management systems and information retrieval; laboratory information management systems, system design and needs assessment; technical management consulting; computer applications and training. *Mailing Add:* Three Dellview Dr Edison NJ 08820-2545. *E-Mail:* mgoffman@goffman.com

GOFMAN, JOHN WILLIAM, CANCER CAUSATION, HEART DISEASE CAUSATION. *Current Pos:* Res assoc chem, Univ Calif, Berkeley, 43-44, intern med, Univ Hosp, 46-47, from asst prof to prof, 47-74, assoc dir, Lawrence Radiation Lab, 63-69, dir biol & med, 63-66, EMER PROF MED PHYSICS, DONNER LAB MED PHYSICS & EMER PROF MOLECULAR & CELLULAR BIOL, UNIV CALIF, BERKELEY, 74- *Personal Data:* b Cleveland, Ohio, Sept 21, 18; m 40; c 1. *Educ:* Oberlin Col, AB, 39; Univ Calif, PhD(chem), 43, MD, 46. *Honors & Awards:* Modern Med Award, 54; Lyman Duff Lectureship Award, Am Heart Asn, 65; Stouffer Prize, 72; Right Livelihood Award, 92. *Concurrent Pos:* Clin instr med, Med Sch, Univ San Francisco, 47-; chmn, Comt Nuclear Responsibility, 71-; vis emer prof, Dept Med, Univ Calif, San Francisco, 75- *Mem:* Fel Am Col Cardiol. *Res:* Manhattan project plutonium chemistry; co-discovery of uranium-233 and its fissionability; separation and identification of lipoproteins and their causal relationships with atherosclerosis; etiology of breast cancer and other cancers; radiation carcinogenesis. *Mailing Add:* PO Box 421993 San Francisco CA 94142

GOFORTH, DERETHA RAINEY, CEREAL CHEMISTRY, FOOD TECHNOLOGY. *Current Pos:* MKT DIR SCHOLARSHIP FOUND SW REGION, 90- *Personal Data:* b San Antonio, Tex, Mar 14, 44; div; c 2. *Educ:* Incarnate Word Col, BA, 65; Okla State Univ, MS, 69; Kans State Univ, PhD(cereal chem), 76. *Prof Exp:* Instr chem, Univ Md Eastern Shore, 69-71; res chemist biochem, USDA Grain Mkt Res Ctr, 71-76; prod develop scientist food chem, Pillsbury Co, 76-89. *Concurrent Pos:* Lectr, Inver Hills Community Col, 84-90. *Mem:* Am Asn Cereal Chem; Inst Food Technol; AAAS. *Res:* Functional properties and biochemistry of wheat proteins and their interaction with each other and other biochemical constituents; semolina and pasta products; starch and its function in food systems; development of refrigerated dough products; development of miscellaneous dessert products in dry mix products. *Mailing Add:* 4909 W 96th St Minneapolis MN 55437

GOFORTH, THOMAS TUCKER, GEOPHYSICS. *Current Pos:* res assoc geophysicist, Southern Methodist Univ, 69-72, sr res assoc geophysicist, 72-74, asst dir, 74-80, DIR DALLAS GEOPHYS LAB, SOUTHERN METHODIST UNIV, 80- *Personal Data:* b Dallas, Tex, June 26, 37; m 72; c 3. *Educ:* Baylor Univ, BS, 59; Univ Tex, MA, 62; Southern Methodist Univ, PhD(geophys), 73. *Prof Exp:* Geophysicist, Teledyne-Geotech, 63-66, sr geophysicist, 66-69. *Concurrent Pos:* Consult, Teledyne-Geotech, 69- *Mem:* Soc Explor Geophysicists; Am Geophys Union. *Res:* Earthquake surface waves; environmental problems associated with exploiting geopressured water reservoirs. *Mailing Add:* Dept Geol Baylor Univ PO Box 97354 Waco TX 76706-9989

GOFORTH, WAYNE REID, BIOLOGY. *Current Pos:* CHIEF, DIV COOP RES, NAT BIOL SERV, 94- *Personal Data:* b Wentzville, Mo, Feb 13, 32; m 63, Prudence Jean Osborn; c Heidi & Paul. *Educ:* Univ Mo, BS, 54, MA, 63, PhD, 68. *Prof Exp:* Prof, Iowa Wesleyan Col, Mt Pleasant, 64-67; prof & unit leader, Univ Mo, Columbia, 68-73; dir, N Prairie Wildlife Res Ctr, Fish & Wildlife Serv, Jamestown, NDak, 73-80, res unit supv, Washington, 83-93; res dir forest environ, Forest Serv, 80-83. *Concurrent Pos:* mem, Gous Coun Wetlands, NDak, 75-76. *Res:* Author of numerous articles. *Mailing Add:* Nat Biol Serv 18th & C Sts NW Washington DC 20240

GOGAN, NIALL JOSEPH, MARINE CHEMISTRY, INORGANIC CHEMISTRY. *Current Pos:* from asst prof to assoc prof, 67-76, PROF CHEM, MEM UNIV NFLD, 76- *Personal Data:* b Dublin, Ireland, Feb 26, 41; m 64; c 3. *Educ:* Nat Univ Ireland, BSc, 62, PhD(inorg chem), 65. *Prof Exp:* Res assoc chem, Univ Chicago, 65-67. *Concurrent Pos:* Assoc vpres res, 83-92. *Mem:* Am Chem Soc; fel Chem Inst Can; Am Soc Limnol & Oceanog. *Res:* Trace metal speciation in seawater; transition element chemistry, organometallics derived from metal carbonyl and mostly group VI and VII; metal chelates; electron spin resonance spectroscopy; water quality and the chemistry of natural water systems; academic administration. *Mailing Add:* Dept Chem Mem Univ Nfld St Johns NF A1B 3X7 Can. *Fax:* 709-737-3702; *E-Mail:* niall@kean.ucs.man.ca

GOGARTY, W(ILLIAM) B(ARNEY), CHEMICAL ENGINEERING, PHYSICAL CHEMISTRY. *Current Pos:* PRES, W BARNEY GOGARTY & ASSOC, INC, 86- *Personal Data:* b Provo, Utah, Apr 23, 30; m 51, Lois G Pritchett; c Laura G (Amerine), Colleen (Madsen), William S, Kathlyn (Baines) & Michael B. *Educ:* Univ Utah, BS, 53, PhD(chem eng), 60. *Honors & Awards:* Muskat Lectr, Univ Utah, 85; Lester C Uren Award, Soc Petrol Engrs, 87, Enhanced Oil Recovery Pioneer Award, 90. *Prof Exp:* Jr engr, Shell Chem Corp, 52; sr res scientist, Marathon Oil Co, 59-67, mgr, Prod Technol Dept, Denver Res Ctr, 67-72, Oil Recovery Dept, 72-73, sr staff engr, 73-75, assoc res dir, 75-86. *Concurrent Pos:* Adj assoc prof, Dept Chem Eng & Metall, Univ Denver, 67-73; distinguished lectr, Soc Petrol Engrs, 82-83; mem, Enhanced Oil Recovery Comt, Nat Petrol Coun Chem Task Group, 82-84; consult, Nat Inst Petrol & Energy Res, Enhanced Oil Recovery Inst, Univ Wyo & Ciba-Geigy Corp; consult, Dept Tech Coop UN, India, 86, Rogaland Res Inst, Norsk Hydro & Statoil, Norway, 87, Petromer Trend Corp, Indonesia, 88 & Petrobas, Brazil, 89; dir, Soc Petrol Engrs, 88-90. *Mem:* Nat Acad Eng; Am Inst Chem Engrs; Sigma Xi; Soc Petrol Engrs. *Res:* Micellar-polymer flooding and polymer flooding of oil as a means of secondary recovery; enhanced oil recovery; fluid flow; 57 United States patents, 80 foreign patents and published 36 technical papers. *Mailing Add:* 2754 E Long Pl Littleton CO 80122. *Fax:* 303-773-6349

GOGEL, GERMAINE E, PROTEIN CHEMISTRY, PHOTOSYNTHESIS GROWTH FACTORS. *Current Pos:* ASST PROF CHEM, COLGATE UNIV, 81- *Personal Data:* b Jasper, Ind, Aug 21, 52; m. *Educ:* Purdue Univ, BS, 74; Northwestern Univ, MS, 76, PhD(biochem), 79. *Concurrent Pos:* Fel biophysics, Cornell Univ, 80-81; vis scientist, Dept Pure & Appl Biol, Imp Col, London, 85; vis prof, Dept Biochem, Univ Col, Cardiff, 88; fel biochem, Med Col Va, 89. *Mem:* NY Acad Sci; AAAS; Am Chem Soc. *Res:* Photosynthesis and proteins involved in photosynthesis; chemical modification of membrane proteins; characterization of growth factors. *Mailing Add:* Chem Colgate Univ 13 Oak Dr Hamilton NY 13346-1338

GOGGANS, JAMES F, FORESTRY, GENETICS. *Current Pos:* RETIRED. *Personal Data:* b Tifton, Ga, Oct 30, 20; m 50; c 2. *Educ:* Univ Ga, BS, 42; Duke Univ, MF, 47; NC State Univ, PhD(forest genetics), 62. *Prof Exp:* From asst prof to assoc prof forestry, Auburn Univ, 47-63, prof forest genetics, 63-84. *Mem:* Soc Am Foresters. *Res:* Tree breeding and genetics of forest trees; variation in anatomy of wood cells. *Mailing Add:* 100 Kuderna Acres Auburn AL 36832

GOGGINS, JEAN A, BIOCHEMISTRY. *Current Pos:* sr res scientist, Vascular Implants Res & Develop, 85-86, MGR, RES & DEVELOP, MEADOX MED, INC, 86- *Personal Data:* b Bronx, NY, July 28, 47. *Educ:* Molloy Col, BS, 69; Fordham Univ, MS, 73; Case Western Reserve Univ, PhD(biomed eng), 85. *Prof Exp:* Instr, dept sci, Dominican Com High Sch, Jamaica, NY, 75-79; res asst, dept anat, mt Sinai Sch Med, NY, 79-80. *Mem:* Am Chem Soc; NY Acad Sci; Sigma Xi; Soc Biomat; Int Soc Artifical Organs. *Res:* Biomaterials; biocompatibility; surface interactions; cellular response; blood-material interactions; vascular grafts. *Mailing Add:* Meadox Med Inc 112 Bauer Dr Oakland NJ 07436

GOGGINS, JOHN FRANCIS, dental research; deceased, see previous edition for last biography

GOGLIA, GENNARO LOUIS, thermodynamics; deceased, see previous edition for last biography

GOGLIA, M(ARIO) J(OSEPH), MECHANICAL ENGINEERING. *Current Pos:* ENG CONSULT, 81- *Personal Data:* b Hoboken, NJ, Mar 30, 16; m 40; c 2. *Educ:* Stevens Inst Technol, ME, 37, MS, 41; Purdue Univ, PhD(thermodyn), 48. *Prof Exp:* Instr mech eng, Stevens Inst Technol, 37-38; asst prof, Univ Ill, 38-46; appln engr, Repub Flowmeters, 46-47; assoc prof mech eng, Purdue Univ, 47-48; prof, Ga Inst Technol, 48-58; dean, Col Eng, Univ Notre Dame, 58-60; regents prof mech eng & assoc dean faculties, Ga Inst Technol, 60-66, dean grad div, 61-66; vchancellor res, Regents, Univ Syst, Ga, 66-81. *Concurrent Pos:* Asst, Munitions Develop Lab, Univ Ill, 45-46; mem adv panel sci & eng, NSF; consult, Nat Acad Sci-Nat Res Coun, NSF, AEC, US Off Educ & Southern Asn Cols & Schs. *Mem:* AAAS; Am Soc Mech Engrs. *Res:* Thermodynamics, heat transfer; fluid mechanics. *Mailing Add:* 3066 Arden Rd NW Atlanta GA 30305-1915

GOGOL, EDWARD PETER, ELECTRON MICROSCOPY, MACROMOLECULAR ASSEMBLIES. *Current Pos:* ASST PROF, PROG MOLECULAR & CELL BIOL, SCH NATURAL SCI & MATH, UNIV TEX, DALLAS, 91- *Personal Data:* b Utica, NY, Oct 18, 53. *Educ:* Cornell Univ, AB, 75; Yale Univ, PhD(molecular biophys & biochem), 81. *Honors & Awards:* US Bioenergetics Award, Bioenergetics Subgroup, Biophys Soc, 90. *Prof Exp:* Fel, Dept Cell Biol, Stanford Univ, 82-86; res assoc, Inst Molecular Biol, Univ Ore, 86-91. *Concurrent Pos:* Fel, Jane Coffin Childs Mem Fund Med Res, 82-85; chair, Gordon Conf Three-Dimensional Electron Micros Macromolecules, 93; mem spec study sect 3, NIH, 93. *Res:* Structural analysis of macromolecular assemblies; electron microscopy and image analysis; numerous publications. *Mailing Add:* Biophys & Cell Biol Univ Mo Kansas City MO 64110-1499. *Fax:* 816-235-5158; *E-Mail:* gogol@utdallas.edu

GOGOLEWSKI, RAYMOND PAUL, THEORETICAL AND APPLIED MECHANICS. *Current Pos:* GROUP LEADER, PHYS SCI DIRECTORATE, LAWRENCE LIVERMORE NAT LAB, 87- *Personal Data:* b Waterbury, Conn, Jan 25, 41; m 64; c 3. *Educ:* Rensselaer Polytech Inst, BS, 62, MS, 64; Cornell Univ, PhD(theoret & appl mech), 70. *Prof Exp:* Staff engr, Tunnel Facil, Arnold Eng Dev Ctr, 64-65; res engr, Systs Div, United Technol Res Ctr, 65-67; fel, Cornell Univ, 67-70; asst prof eng mech, NC State Univ, 70- 73; proj mgr systems eval, Inst Defense Anal, 73-77 & Tactical Warfare, Syst Planning Corp, 77-78; prog mgr tactical technol, Defense Adv Res Proj Agency, 78-83; sr vpres, Aeronaut Res Assocs Princeton, 83-85; pres, Cannonball Consults, 85-87. *Mem:* Am Acad Mech; Soc Ind & Appl Math; Opers Res Soc Am; Sigma Xi. *Res:* Applied research and exploratory development oriented toward military tactical technology; applied mathematics and optimal control theory in dynamical systems theory. *Mailing Add:* 228 Royal Saint Ct Danville CA 94526-5407

GOGOS, COSTAS G, CHEMICAL ENGINEERING. *Current Pos:* From asst prof to assoc prof, 64-74, PROF CHEM ENG, STEVENS INST TECHNOL, 74- *Personal Data:* b Athens, Greece, June 30, 38; m 65. *Educ:* Princeton Univ, BSChE, 61, MS, 62, MA, 64, PhD(mech eng), 66. *Mem:* Am Chem Soc; Soc Plastics Engrs; Soc Rheology. *Res:* Physical properties of high polymers, in particular rheological properties; rheological aspects of polymer processing; kinetics and morphology of deformed polymer crystals. *Mailing Add:* Dept Chem Eng Stevens Inst Tech Castle Point Hoboken NJ 07030

GOGUEN, JOSEPH A, COMPUTER SCIENCE, INFORMATION SCIENCE. *Current Pos:* PROF, UNIV CALIF, SAN DIEGO. *Personal Data:* b Pittsfield, Mass, June 28, 41; c 3. *Educ:* Harvard Col, BA, 63; Univ Calif, Berkeley, MA, 66, PhD(math), 68. *Prof Exp:* From teaching asst to instr math, Univ Calif, Berkeley, 63-68; asst prof info sci, Univ Chicago, 68-73; from asst prof to prof comput sci, Univ Calif, Los Angeles, 72-81; sr staff scientist, SRI WT, Palo Alto, Calif, 79-88, managing dir, struct semantics, 78-, prog mgr, 85-88; prin mem, Ctr Study Lang & Info, Stanford Univ, 83-88; prof comput sci, Oxford Univ, Eng, 88- *Concurrent Pos:* IBM Corp fel, T J Watson Res Lab, NY, 71-72; fac mem, Naropa Inst, Boulder, Colo, 74-; sr vis fel, Univ Edinburgh, 76, 77; co-dir, Software Technol Seminars, Capri, Italy, 80, 81. *Mem:* Math Asn Am; Asn Comput Mach; Inst Elec & Electronics Engrs Comput Soc. *Res:* Software engineering, including specification, correctness, prototyping, requirements; formal methods; theorem proving; algebraic specification; object oriented programming; massively parallel computer architecture; hardware verification; fuzzy sets; sociology; philosophy of computation; linguistics. *Mailing Add:* Dept Comput Sci & Eng Univ Calif 9500 Gilman Dr La Jolla CA 92093-0114

GOH, EDWARD HUA SENG, DRUG METABOLISM, TOXICOLOGY. *Current Pos:* asst prof, 77-82, ASSOC PROF PHARMACOL, IND UNIV, 82- *Personal Data:* b Sarawak, Malaysia, Jan 20, 42; US citizen; m 97, Agatha Wong; c Andrew & Melissa. *Educ:* Berea Col, BA, 68; Vanderbilt Univ, PhD(pharmacol), 74. *Prof Exp:* Fel pharmacol, Univ Mo, Columbia, 74-75, instr, 75-77. *Mem:* Am Soc Pharmacol & Exp Therapeut. *Res:* Metabolism of blood cholesterol; drug metabolism and toxicology; testing of new drugs. *Mailing Add:* Pharmacol Sect Med Sci Prog Sch Med Ind Univ Myers Hall Bloomington IN 47405. *Fax:* 812-855-4436; *E-Mail:* goh@indiana.edu

GOH, KEAN S, ENZYME-LINKED IMMUNOSORBENT ASSAY FOR THE DETECTION OF PESTICIDE RESIDUES IN ENVIRONMENTAL SAMPLES, ENVIRONEMENTAL FATE OF PESTICIDES. *Current Pos:* sr environ res scientist, 88-92, AGR PROG SUPVR IV, DEPT PESTICIDE REGULATION, CALIF ENVIRON PROTECTION AGENCY, 93- *Personal Data:* b Malaysia, Dec 6, 49. *Educ:* Univ Calif, Davis, BS, 74, MS, 76, PhD(entom & environ toxicol), 79. *Prof Exp:* Prod develop rep, DuPont, 80-83; asst prof & dir chem pesticide prog, Cornell Univ, 83-87. *Concurrent Pos:* Consult environ impact assessment, USAID, 92. *Mem:* Am Chem Soc; Entom Soc Am. *Res:* Developing enzyme-linked immunosorbent assay for the detection of trace pesticide residues in environmental samples for research and regulatory purposes. *Mailing Add:* 1020 N St Rm 161 Sacramento CA 95814-5624. *Fax:* 916-654-0539; *E-Mail:* goh@empm3.cdpr.ca.gov.

GOHAGAN, JOHN KENNETH, PREVENTIVE MEDICINE. *Current Pos:* BUR EARLY DETECTION, DIV CANCER PREVENT & CONTROL, NAT CANCER INST, BETHESDA, 90-; CHIEF EARLY DETECTION BR, 92- *Personal Data:* b Barrington, NJ, July 24, 39; m, Dorothy L Childs. *Educ:* Lasalle Col, BS, 64; Temple Univ, MS, 69; Mass Inst Technol, Dr, 73. *Prof Exp:* Mem exec staff proj engr researcher & educr, US Dept Defense Armaments Command/Frankford Arsenal, Philadelphia, 64-74; teacher advan eng, Study Div, Mass Inst Technol, 71-73; actg dir, Div Healthcare Washington Univ, St Louis, prof prevent med, dir prog indust prod mgt, researcher investr schs med & eng, 74-91. *Concurrent Pos:* Prin investr, NASA, 74-76, Am Cancer Soc, 76-82, Rand Grad Inst, 77, US Cong Off Tech Assessment, 79-80, Washington Univ, 79-80 & 81-82, Henry J Kaiser Found, 83-84, Mallinckrodt Inst Radiol, 84, US Dept Health & Human Serv, 84-89, NIH, 89-90, NSF; consult, Fed Hwy Admin, 75, Mo Dept Revenue, 75, Southern Ill Univ, 78, Interagency Inst Fed Healthcare Execs, 80, Pentax Corp, 84; resource prof, Mo Cancer Prog Planning, 78-79, mem biostatist & epidemiol comt, 78-79; thermography, St Louis Health Syst Agency, 78; mem sci working group, Nat Cancer Inst, 82, Div Resource Ctrs & Community Affairs, Bd Sci Coun subcomt screening, 82, breast cancer task force meeting, 83, prog proj site visit team, 87; vis researcher, Div Cancer Prevent & Control, Nat Cancer Inst, 85; vis prof, Div Clin Epidemiol, Dept Med, Univ Pa, 89; sr fel, Dept Finance, Wharton Sch Bus; chmn tech innovative equip task force emission comp; syst anal fel, US Civic Serv. *Mem:* Fel Am Col Epidemiol; Sigma Xi. *Res:* Preventive medicine; cancer prevention and control. *Mailing Add:* 9000 Rockville Pike EPN 305 Bur Early Detection Div Cancer Prevent & Control Nat Cancer Inst Bethesda MD 20892

GOHEEN, AUSTIN CLEMENT, PLANT PATHOLOGY. *Current Pos:* RETIRED. *Personal Data:* b Bellingham, Wash, Apr 22, 17; m 42; c 5. *Educ:* Univ Wash, BS, 47; Wash State Univ, PhD(plant path), 53. *Honors & Awards:* Ruth Allen Award, Am Phytopath Soc, 74. *Prof Exp:* Observer, US Weather Bur, 38-46; asst dept plant path, Wash State Univ, 47-50; agent, NJ Agr Exp sta, 50-53, plant pathologist, Plant Indust Sta, 53-55 & US Hort Field Sta, 55-56, assoc, Univ Calif Exp Sta, USDA, 56-, res plant pathologist, 57-, res leader crops path, agr res serv, 72- *Concurrent Pos:* Asst res specialist, Agr Exp Sta, Rutgers Univ, 50-53. *Mem:* Am Phytopath Soc; Sigma Xi. *Res:* Virus diseases of grapes. *Mailing Add:* 2412 Pine Grove Rd Klamath Falls OR 97603

GOHEEN, DAVID WADE, BOTANY, PLANT BREEDING & GENETICS. *Current Pos:* ABETCO INC, 94- *Personal Data:* b Bellingham, Wash, June 23, 20; m 43, Laura E Smith; c Stephen C & Frank W. *Educ:* Univ Wash, BS, 42, PhD(chem), 51. *Honors & Awards:* Gold Medal, Am Rhododendron Soc, 88. *Prof Exp:* Res chemist org chem, Eng Res Inst, Univ Mich, 51-52; chief, Chem Res Sect, Cent Res Dept, Crown Zellerbach Corp, 52-55, res specialist, Chem Prod Div, 55-67, sr res chemist, 67-78, proj leader pioneering res, Cent Res Div, 78-81; vpres, E M Seidel Assoc, 81-91. *Concurrent Pos:* Vpres, Am Rhododendron Species Found, 80-81, pres, 82-84; mem, Vis Comt, Solar Energy Res Inst, 81-86. *Mem:* Am Chem Soc; Tech Asn Pulp & Paper Indust. *Res:* Natural products; wood extractives; lignin; cellulose; wild plant collectiugand identification; plant breeding. *Mailing Add:* PO Box 826 Camas WA 98607

GOHEEN, LOLA COLEMAN, REQUIREMENTS ANALYSIS. *Current Pos:* Oper analyst, 74-85, SR RES ENGR & SR OPER ANALYST, SRI INT, 85- *Personal Data:* b Los Angeles, Calif; m 69; c 1. *Educ:* Stanford Univ, BS, 70, MS, 72, PhD(opers res), 74. *Mem:* Soc Indust & Appl Math; Am Asn Artificial Intel; Opers Res Soc Am. *Res:* Modeling, analysis, and optimization of systems. *Mailing Add:* 876 Coleman Ave Menlo Park CA 94025

GOHEEN, STEVEN CHARLES, ENVIRONMENTAL CHEMISTRY. *Current Pos:* Res chemist biochem, 77-83, sr res chemist, 83-89, SR RES SCIENTIST, BIO-RAD LABS, MARTINEZ VET ADMIN MED CTR, BATTELLE NORTHWEST, 88- *Personal Data:* b Seattle, Wash, May 14, 51; m 81; c 3. *Educ:* Univ Wash, BS, 73, Northwestern Univ, PhD(mat sci), 78. *Honors & Awards:* R & D 100 Award, 93. *Concurrent Pos:* Tech group mgr, Advan Orgn Anal Methods Group. *Mem:* Am Chem Soc; Am Oil Chemists Soc; NY Acad Sci; Sigma Xi; Am Inst Nutrit; Am Soc Biochem & Molecular Biol. *Res:* Environmental organic chemistry; chromatography; high performance liquid chromotography; development and publication of sampling and analytical methods for mixed waste samples. *Mailing Add:* 2016 Harris Ave Richland WA 99352. *Fax:* 509-373-0169; *E-Mail:* sc_goheen@pnl.gov

GOHR, FRANK AUGUST, ENVIRONMENTAL SCIENCES. *Current Pos:* RETIRED. *Personal Data:* b Boston, Mass, Sept 26, 22; m 49; c 4. *Educ:* Univ Calif, Los Angeles, BA, 48, BS, 49; Univ Calif, Berkeley, MPH, 50, DrPH(sanit sci), 62. *Honors & Awards:* Walter S Mangold Award, Nat Environ Health Asn, 63. *Prof Exp:* Supvr statewide sanit sci, Univ Calif, 50-60; environ health & safety officer, Univ Calif Med Ctr, San Francisco, 60-86. *Concurrent Pos:* Adv, Nat Adv Coun Health Facil, 67-70; consult health serv & ment health admin, USPHS, 67-73. *Mem:* Fel Am Pub Health Asn; Nat Environ Health Asn. *Mailing Add:* 15 Arroyo Dr Orinda CA 94563

GOIHMAN-YAHR, MAURICIO, DERMATOLOGY, CELLULAR IMMUNOLOGY. *Current Pos:* instr dermat, Cent Univ, Venezuela, 69-71, asst prof, 71-72, adj prof, 72-73, assoc prof, 73-79, PROF DERMAT, CENT UNIV, VENEZUELA, 80- *Personal Data:* b Caracas, Venezuela, Apr 8, 38; m 69; c 2. *Educ:* Central Univ, Venezuela, MD, 60; Stanford Univ, PhD(med microbiol), 69. *Honors & Awards:* Cesar Lizardo Prize, Venezuela Soc Dermat, 84; Order of Andres Bello, Venezuelan Govt, 85. *Prof Exp:* Clin lectr dermat, Stanford Univ, 64-68. *Concurrent Pos:* Mem bd dirs, Venezuela Asn Advan Sci, 73-74, Nat Res Coun, 85-89; pres, Comt Clin Med & Res, Asst Res Coun, Venezuela, 74-89; alt mem Super Coun, Nat Res Coun, 90- *Mem:* Soc Investigative Dermat; Am Acad Dermat; Am Soc Microbiol; Soc Exp Biol & Med; Am Asn Immunologists; Int Soc Dermat; Venezuelan Soc Dermat (pres, 74-76); Venezuelan Soc Allergy & Immunol (pres, 81-83). *Res:* Cellular immunology and actions of phagocytes in granulomatous diseases due to live organisms. *Mailing Add:* Jet Int M-154 PO Box 020010 Miami FL 33102

GOINS, TRUMAN, engineering, natural resources, for more information see previous edition

GOINS, WILLIAM C, JR, RESEARCH ADMINISTRATION. *Current Pos:* SR VPRES, O'BRIEN-GOINS-SIMPSON & ASSOC INC, 77- *Honors & Awards:* Lester C Uren Award, Soc Petrol Engrs, 83. *Mem:* Nat Acad Eng; Soc Petrol Engrs. *Mailing Add:* O'Brien-Goins-Simpson & Assoc Inc 6430 Hillcroft Suite 112 Houston TX 77081. *Fax:* 713-270-4105

GOISHI, WATARU, RADIOCHEMISTRY. *Current Pos:* radiochemist, 54-62, group leader, 63-77, ASST DIV LEADER, NUCLEAR WEAPONS DIAG, LAWRENCE LIVERMORE LAB, UNIV CALIF, 77- *Personal Data:* b Florin, Calif, Feb 6, 28; m 52; c 2. *Educ:* Univ Calif, Berkeley, BS, 50; Univ Chicago, PhD(radiochem), 54. *Prof Exp:* Radiochemist, Univ Chicago, 53-54. *Mem:* AAAS; Am Chem Soc. *Res:* Fast neutron reactions and measurements; kinetics and mechanisms of inorganic reactions. *Mailing Add:* 588 Emerald St Livermore CA 94550-5131

GOITEIN, MICHAEL, PROTON THERAPY, BIOLOGICAL MODELING. *Current Pos:* from asst prof to assoc prof, 73-86, PROF RADIATION ONCOL, HARVARD MED SCH, 86- *Personal Data:* b Broadway, Eng, Nov 14, 39; m 68; c 2. *Educ:* Oxford Univ, BA, 61; Harvard Univ, PhD(physics), 68. *Prof Exp:* Res fel physics, Harvard Univ, 68-69; staff physicist, Lawrence Berkeley Lab, 69-72. *Concurrent Pos:* Res career develop award, USPHS, 76- *Mem:* Am Phys Soc; Am Asn Physicists Med; Am Soc Therapeut Radiologists; Radiation Res Soc. *Res:* Radiation therapy, computerized tomography. *Mailing Add:* Dept Radiation Oncol Mass Gen Hosp Boston MA 02114

GOJMERAC, WALTER LOUIS, ENTOMOLOGY. *Current Pos:* assoc prof, 65-73, PROF ENTOM, UNIV WIS-MADISON, 73-, EXTEN ENTOMOLOGIST, 65- *Personal Data:* b Rib Lake, Wis, Apr 8, 25; m 55; c 5. *Educ:* Univ Wis, BS, 49, PhD(entom), 55; Marquette Univ, MS, 53. *Prof Exp:* Teacher, pub sch, 49-51; asst prof entom & asst entomologist, NDak Agr Col, 55-57; res entomologist, Calif Spray Chem Corp, Stand Oil Co Calif, 57-65. *Mem:* Fel AAAS; Entom Soc Am. *Res:* Control of insects affecting man and animals; bees and beekeeping; control of insects in food processing and handling establishments. *Mailing Add:* Dept Entom Univ Wis 237 Russell Lab 1630 Linden Dr Madison WI 53706-1520

GOJNY, FRANK JOSEPH, DEVELOPMENT OF METAL MATRIX COMPOSITES & HYBRID THERMOPLASTIC COMPOSITES. *Current Pos:* VPRES ENG, HYPER INDUSTS, 94- *Personal Data:* b San Francisco, Calif, Jan 24, 52; m 79; c Chris & Steven. *Educ:* Univ Calif, Berkeley, PhD (metall) 75; Fed Studies Bd, PhD (plasma physics), 91. *Prof Exp:* Dep proj engr, Rohr Industs, 86-94; vpres eng, Hypermetallics, 90-94. *Concurrent Pos:* Metallurgist, alloy develop, advan processes & struct develop. *Mem:* Am Soc Metals Int. *Res:* Developed highest fracture toughened granite epoxy composite on record; developed metal matrix composite of highest strength to weight ratio on record. *Mailing Add:* 5388 Dressage Dr Bonita CA 91902-2662

GOKCEN, NEV A(LTAN), THERMODYNAMICS. *Current Pos:* RES SUPVR, THERMODYN LAB, BUR MINES, DEPT INTERIOR, ALBANY, 77- *Personal Data:* b Turkey, Sept 21, 21; nat US; m 46, Emel; c 3. *Educ:* Univ Pittsburgh, BS, 42, MS, 45; Mass Inst Technol, ScD(metall),

51. *Prof Exp:* Instr metall, Lafayette Col, 43-44 & Robert Col, 45-47; asst, Mass Inst Technol, 47-51, res assoc, 51; assoc prof, Mich Technol Univ, 51-56 & Univ Pa, 56-61; head chem thermodyn sect, Aerospace Corp, 61-77. *Concurrent Pos:* Mem, Japan Soc Prom Sci. *Mem:* Am Chem Soc; Am Soc Metals; Metals Minerals Soc. *Res:* Physical chemistry of metals and alloys; high temperature chemistry; thermodynamics of solutions; chemistry; materials science. *Mailing Add:* 440 E Thorton Lake Dr Albany OR 97321-1342. *Fax:* 541-967-5958

GOKEL, GEORGE WILLIAM, ORGANIC CHEMISTRY. *Current Pos:* PROF BIOORG CHEM, DEPT MOLECULAR BIOL & PHARMACOL, SCH MED, WASHINGTON UNIV, 93- *Personal Data:* b New York, NY, June 27, 46; m 78, Kathryn Smiegocki; c Michael R, Matthew G & Mark A. *Educ:* Tulane Univ, BS, 68; Univ Southern Calif, PhD(chem), 71. *Honors & Awards:* Frontiers of Chem lectr, Case Western Res Univ, 81; McElvain lectr, Univ Wis, 93; Izatt-Christensen Int Award Macrocyclic Chem, 96. *Prof Exp:* Fel chem, Univ Southern Calif, 71-72 & Univ Calif, Los Angeles, 72-74; asst prof, Pa State Univ, University Park, 74-78; from assoc prof to prof chem, Univ Md, College Park, 78-85; prof chem, Univ Miami, 85-93. *Concurrent Pos:* Consult, W R Grace Co, 77-87, Lion Corp, Tokyo, 85-, A H Marks Ltd, UK, 88-, Monsanto, 90-92; Japan Soc Prom Sci sr fel, 94. *Mem:* Am Chem Soc; Royal Soc Chem; Sigma Xi; fel AAAS. *Res:* Reactions in mixed phase media; phase transfer chemistry mediated by quaternary salts and heteromacrocycles; novel heteromacrocycles; biologically active and chemically switchable macrocycles lariat ethers and cryptands; synthetic organic models for biological phenomena including molecular receptors, cation channels and membrane formation; novel membrane systems. *Mailing Add:* Dept Molecular Biol & Pharmacol Washington Univ Sch Med 660 S Euclid Campus Box 8103 St Louis MO 63110. *E-Mail:* ggokel@pharmdec.wustl.edu

GOKEN, GAROLD LEE, POLYMER CHEMISTRY, ORGANIC CHEMISTRY. *Current Pos:* RETIRED. *Personal Data:* b Decatur, Ill, Aug 6, 37; m 58, Carol A; c Terry, Tracey & Tricia. *Educ:* Millikin Univ, BA, 59; Univ Utah, PhD(chem, pharmaceut chem), 62. *Prof Exp:* Sr chemist, Tape Res Lab, 3M Co, St Paul, Minn, 62-65, supvr, pioneering res group, 65-69, res supvr, Indust Spec Prod Dept, 69-71, res mgr, 71-72, new prod mgr, 72-74, tech mgr cushioning prod proj, 74-78, tech mgr cushioning & new prod, Indust Specialties Div, 78-79, mgr new bus develop, Indust Specialties Div, 79-80, tech mgr, Europ Tape Labs, 3M Europe, 81-84, tech dir, Adhesives, Coatings & Sealers Div, 84-90, mgr lab & mfg opers, I&E Sector New Prod Dept, 90-96. *Concurrent Pos:* Pres, Minn Acad Sci. *Mem:* Am Chem Soc; Soc Plastics Engrs; AAAS. *Res:* Commercialization of advanced new technologies, particularly materials and product systems for energy and environmental markets. *Mailing Add:* 101 Wildwood Beach Rd Mahtomedi MN 55115. *Fax:* 612-737-4538

GOKHALE, DATTAPRABHAKAR V, STATISTICS. *Current Pos:* from asst prof to assoc prof, 70-79, PROF STATIST, UNIV CALIF, RIVERSIDE, 79-, STATISTICIAN, 70- *Personal Data:* b Poona, India, Mar 18, 36; m 61; c 2. *Educ:* Univ Poona, BSc, 55, MSc, 57; Univ Calif, Berkeley, PhD(statist), 66. *Prof Exp:* Lectr statist, Univ Poona, 59-69, assoc prof, 69-70. *Concurrent Pos:* Asst prof, Univ Calif, Berkeley, 66. *Mem:* Inst Math Statist, Int Statist Inst; Indian Statist Soc; Biomet Soc; Am Statist Asn. *Res:* Distribution theory; nonparametrics; analysis of frequency data; information theoretic approach to statistical problems; statistical ecology. *Mailing Add:* 1250 Nicola Dr Riverside CA 92506

GOKSEL, MEHMET ADNAN, CHEMICAL ENGINEERING, EXTRACTIVE METALLURGY. *Current Pos:* assoc prof chem eng, 65-67, assoc prof extractive metall, 65-76, RES LEADER & ASSOC PROF MINERAL RES, MICH TECHNOL UNIV, 76- *Personal Data:* b Ankara, Turkey, May 27, 24; m 60; c 3. *Educ:* Istanbul Univ, MSc, 49, DSc(chem eng), 51; Karlsruhe Tech Univ, Dr rer nat habil(chem eng), 56. *Prof Exp:* Res asst indust chem, Istanbul Univ, 49-52; sci mil adv, Turkish Gen Staff, 55-57; docent indust chem, Istanbul Univ, 57-60; Fulbright res fel extractive metall, Mich Technol Univ, 60-62; docent indust chem, Istanbul Univ, 62-63, prof, 63-65. *Concurrent Pos:* Consult, Emayetas Co, Turkey, 63-65 & UN, 79 & 81. *Mem:* Sigma Xi; Am Inst Mining, Metall & Petrol Engrs; Inst Briquetting & Agglomeration. *Res:* Agglomeration; pollution; building materials; chemical processes; iron and steel making. *Mailing Add:* 2204 N Oaks Blvd New Brunswick NJ 08902

GOKTEPE, OMER FARUK, NUCLEAR ENGINEERING, ATOMIC PHYSICS. *Current Pos:* ADJ ASSOC PROF, DEPT PHYSICS, GEORGETOWN UNIV, 86-; PROG MGR, DIV HIGH ENERGY PHYSICS, DEPT HIGH ENERGY, 91- *Personal Data:* b Istanbul, Turkey, Aug 7, 39; US citizen; m 73; c Katherine (Emel) & Joy (Saadet). *Educ:* Univ Istanbul, BS, 62; Univ Mich, MS, 69; Univ Md, MS, 72, PhD(nuclear eng), 77. *Honors & Awards:* Alan Berman Award, Naval Res Lab. *Prof Exp:* Res physicist, Inst Nuclear Energy, 62-64; res assoc physics, Gen Technol Corp, 64-66; res asst nuclear, Univ Mich, 66-69; res asst plasma, Univ Md, 69-71; teaching asst kinetic theory, 71-72; res asst exp develop, NASA, Goddard Space Flight Ctr, 72-78; Nuclear Engr, Naval Surface Warfare Ctr, 79-91. *Concurrent Pos:* Res physicist, Plasma Lab, 62-64; res assoc, Inst Phys Sci & Technol, 77-78. *Mem:* AAAS; Am Phys Soc; Am Nuclear Soc. *Res:* Physical phenomena produced by charged particle beams in a solid surface analysis, new material development techniques based on ion bombardment of solid surfaces; radiation transport and shielding; environmental science. *Mailing Add:* PO Box 351 Germantown MD 20875. *Fax:* 301-903-2597; *E-Mail:* omer.goktepe@oer.doe.gov

GOLAB, TOMASZ, AGRICULTURAL BIOCHEMISTRY. *Current Pos:* RETIRED. *Personal Data:* b Dynow, Poland, Oct 18, 22; m 58; c 2. *Educ:* Univ Basel, PhD(org chem), 60. *Prof Exp:* Res assoc, Univ Basel, 60; scientist, Worcester Found Exp Biol, Mass, 60-62; sr agr biochemist, 62-72, res scientist, Lilly Res Labs, Eli Lilly & Co, 72-88. *Mem:* AAAS; Am Chem Soc; NY Acad Sci; Swiss Chem Soc. *Res:* Pesticide metabolism. *Mailing Add:* 1430 Anemone Ct Indianapolis IN 46219

GOLAN, LAWRENCE PETER, GAS-SOLID FLUIDIZATION, MUNICIPAL SOLID WASTE TO ENERGY CONVERSION. *Current Pos:* DIR, RES & DEVELOP CTR, SC ENERGY, 86- *Personal Data:* b Newark, NJ, June 20, 38; m 62, Helen I Hemko; c Lisa M, Wanda M & Lawrence P II. *Educ:* WVa Univ, BS, 61, MS, 64; Lehigh Univ, PhD(mech eng), 68. *Prof Exp:* Mech engr, Picatinny Arsenal, 61-62; instr design, WVa Univ, 62-64; instr thermodyn, Lehigh Univ, 64-68; eng assoc, Exxon Res & Eng, 68-86. *Concurrent Pos:* Prof thermodyn, Clemson Univ, 86-92; prin investr, Plasma Arc Technol, 89, Advan Gas Turbine Prog, US Dept Energy, 92, Waste Technol Prog, 96; chair, Heat Transfer Div, Am Inst Chem Engrs, 91, chmn, Nat Heat Transfer Conf, 96; adv, Strom Thurmond Inst & Mech Eng Dept, WVa Univ. *Mem:* Am Inst Chem Engrs; Am Soc Mech Engrs; Sigma Xi. *Res:* Energy systems research; advanced gas turbines; municipal solid waste conversion to energy; fluidization and plasma. *Mailing Add:* Res & Develop Ctr SC Energy 386-2 College Ave Clemson SC 29634. *Fax:* 864-656-0142; *E-Mail:* glawren@clemson.edu

GOLAND, ALLEN NATHAN, PARTICLE-SOLID INTERACTIONS, LATTICE DEFECTS. *Current Pos:* Res assoc physics, Brookhaven Nat Lab, 56-58, guest scientist, 58-63, assoc physicist, 63-67, physicist, 68-73, assoc chmn, Dept Appl Sci, 82-87, dep chmn, 87-89, sr physicist, 73-96, GUEST SR PHYSICIST, BROOKHAVEN NAT LAB, 96- *Personal Data:* b Chicago, Ill, Apr 26, 30; m 59, Joan Sams; c David & Robert. *Educ:* Roosevelt Univ, BS, 51; Northwestern Univ, PhD(physics), 56. *Concurrent Pos:* Solid state physicist, Ord Mat Res Off, US Army & guest scientist, Brookhaven Nat Lab, 58-63; vis prof, State Univ NY, Stony Brook, 70, adj prof, 74-; dir, NATO Advan Study Inst, 71; vis res consult, Univ Sao Paulo, 71; guest lectr, Enrico Fermi Int Sch Physics, Italy, 74; mem, Tech Adv Panel, Los Alamos Meson Physics Facil, Los Alamos Sci Lab, 75-78, mem, Solid State Physics & Mat Sci Comt, 76-78; secy & mem, Damage Anal & Fundamental Studies Task Group, Off Fusion Energy, Dept Energy, 76-81; consult, Argonne Univ Asn, 76-77; mem ad hoc comt, Use Fission Reactors Div Mag Fusion Energy Alloy Develop Prog, Div Mag Fusion Energy, ERDA, 76-77; mem, Nat Acad Sci-Nat Res Coun panel, Thin Film Microstruct Sci & Technol, 78-; vis prof, State Univ NY, Stony Brook, 78, mem, Exec Comt, Mat Res Sci Energy Ctr, 96-; mem rev panel, Chem & Mat Sci Div, Los Alamos Nat Lab, 80-85, chmn, 81-82; mem panel, Effects Radiation Struct & Properties Mat, US Dept Energy, 81; assoc ed, Phys Rev B, 82-; mem, Res & Rev Comt, NY State Sci & Technol Found, 83-94, Nat Steering Comt Advan Neutron Source, 86-94, Phys Sci Proj Adv Group, Gas Res Inst, 86-, Tech Rev Panel, Dept Energy-HFIR, 87-88 & Radiation Sci Panel, Nat Acad Sci, Nat Res Coun, 88 & 91; US rep, Eval Panel Int Fusion Mat Irradiation Facil, 89; mem, Mat Irradiation Subcomt, Neutron Res & Sources Panel, Dept Energy/BESAC, 92. *Mem:* Fel Am Phys Soc; Am Nuclear Soc; Mat Res Soc; Am Crystallog Asn. *Res:* Defects in solids; radiation effects; x-ray and neutron scattering; applications of particle accelerators to solid-state physics research; positron annihilation in solids. *Mailing Add:* Brookhaven Nat Lab Bldg 815 Upton NY 11973. *Fax:* 516-344-7905; *E-Mail:* goland@bnl.gov

GOLAND, MARTIN, APPLIED MECHANICS, AERONAUTICS. *Current Pos:* PRES, SOUTHWEST INST, 59- *Personal Data:* b New York, NY, July 12, 19; m 48; c 3. *Educ:* Cornell Univ, ME, 40. *Hon Degrees:* LLD, St Mary's Univ, San Antonio, 68. *Honors & Awards:* Spirit of St Louis Jr Award, Am Soc Mech Engrs, 44, Jr Award, 46, Herbert Hoover Medal, 87; Alfred Noble Prize, Am Soc Civil Engrs, 46; Nat Eng Award, Am Acad Eng Sci, 85. *Prof Exp:* Instr mech eng, Cornell Univ, 40-42; sect head appl mech, Res Lab, Curtiss Wright Co, NY, 42-46; chmn, Eng Mech Div, Midwest Res Inst, 46-50, dir eng sci, 50-55; chmn, Comn Eng & Tech Systs, Nat Res Coun, 83-86. *Concurrent Pos:* Mem adv coun, Sch Eng, George Washington Univ, 70; mem, Sci Comt, Gen Motors, 71-81; pres, Southwest Found Biomed Res, 72-82; mem, Naval Res Adv Comt, 74-80, chmn, 77; mem, Comt Int Rels, Nat Acad Sci, 77-79; chmn, Mat & Struct Group, NASA, 79-83; chmn, Bd Army Sci & Technol, Nat Acad Sci, 82-89. *Mem:* Nat Acad Eng; fel AAAS; hon mem Am Soc Mech Engrs; fel Am Inst Aeronaut & Astronaut (pres, 71); Sigma Xi. *Res:* Applied mechanics; applied mathematics and engineering analysis; structures; aerodynamics; fluid flow; aircraft dynamics; vibration and impact problems; engineering analysis; operations research; industrial economics techniques. *Mailing Add:* 306 Country Lane San Antonio TX 78209-2319

GOLANOV, EUGENE V, NEUROPHYSIOLOGY, CIRCULATORY PHYSIOLOGY. *Current Pos:* instr, 92-93, ASST PROF, MED COL, CORNELL UNIV, 94- *Personal Data:* m, Olga V Tcheznyshov; c Dennis, Vladimir, Sergei. *Educ:* First Moscow Med Inst, MD, 77; Inst Normal Physiol, PhD(physiol), 80. *Prof Exp:* Scientist, All-Union Cardiological Res Ctr, 80-85, head, Group Neural Regulation Autonomic Functions Res, 85-91. *Mem:* Am Physiol Soc; Soc Neurosci. *Res:* Neurophysiology of central neural regulation of cerebral blood flow; brain mechanisms of self protection. *Mailing Add:* Dept Neurol Med Col Cornell Univ 411 E 69th St KB410 New York NY 10021. *Fax:* 212-988-3672; *E-Mail:* egolano@mail.med.cornell.edu

GOLARZ-DE BOURNE, MARIA NELLY, MICROSCOPIC ANATOMY, HISTOCHEMISTRY. *Current Pos:* asst anat, Med Sch, Emory Univ, 58-59, res assoc, 60-63, res assoc histochem, 63-66, ASST HISTOCHEMIST, YERKES PRIMATE RES CTR, EMORY UNIV, 66- *Personal Data:* b

Montevideo, Uruguay, Jan 21, 34; nat US; m 64. *Educ:* Univ Repub, Uruguay, 54; Emory Univ, PhD(anat), 63. *Prof Exp:* Res assoc anat micros, Univ Repub, Uruguay, 55-58, asst to prof exp biol, 58. *Concurrent Pos:* Res scientist, Colonial Res Inst, 64-66; co-prin investr, NASA grant, 67-; prof cell biol, histol & neuroscience, St George Univ, Sch Med, Granada, West Indies, 78-, emer dean women & vis prof, St George Univ Sch Med Neurosci. *Mem:* Histochem Soc; Am Asn Anat; Int Primatol Soc; Geront Soc; Sigma Xi; AAAS. *Res:* Golgi apparatus; histochemistry of muscle diseases; space pathology. *Mailing Add:* 849 Lullwater Pkwy NE Atlanta GA 30307

GOLAY, MICHAEL W, NUCLEAR POWER PLANT ENGINEERING, FLUID MECHANICS. *Current Pos:* asst prof, 71-75, assoc prof, 75-86, PROF NUCLEAR ENG, MASS INST TECHNOL, 86- *Personal Data:* US citizen. *Educ:* Univ Fla, BME, 64; Cornell Univ, PhD(nuclear eng), 69. *Prof Exp:* Res assoc nuclear eng, Rensselaer Polytech Inst, 69-71. *Concurrent Pos:* Consult, Stone & Webster Eng Co, 71-, Elec Power Res Inst, 83- & numerous others; mem, Nuclear Safety Res Rev Comt, US Nuclear Reg Comn. *Mem:* Am Nuclear Soc; Am Soc Mech Engrs. *Res:* Reactor engineering; nuclear energy policy; risk management reactor safety. *Mailing Add:* Dept Nuclear Eng Mass Inst Technol Cambridge MA 02139

GOLBECK, AMANDA LORRAINE, EDUCATIONAL ADMINISTRATION. *Current Pos:* VPRES & ACAD DEAN, BETHANY COL, 96- *Personal Data:* b Milwaukee, Wis, May 25, 52; m 79, Craig A Molgaard; c Dan G Molgaard. *Educ:* Grinnell Col, BA, 74; Univ Calif, Berkeley, MA, 77, & 79, PhD(biostatist), 83. *Prof Exp:* From asst prof to prof statist, San Diego State Univ, 83-96, coordr, Div Statist, 87-95, assoc dean undergrad studies, 95-96. *Concurrent Pos:* Programmer, Cancer Ctr Statist, Mayo Clin, 79; res analyst, Inst Pop Res & Anal, Planned Parenthood Minn, St Paul, 80-81, consult, 81; prin investr, Statist Eval Proj, Pac Southwest Forest & Range Exp Sta, USDA, 82-83 & 83-84, Dissertation Res Proj, Sch Pub Health, Univ Calif, Berkeley, 83 & Bootstrapping Life Table Proj, Affirmation Action Fac Develop Prog, San Diego State Univ, 87; consult, Ctr Neurol Study, San Diego, 85, Off City Attorney, San Diego, 87, Dept Prev Med, Univ Western Australia, Perth, 88, Community Psychiat Ctrs, Laguna Beach, 92-94, Sch Med Stroke Ctr, Univ Calif San Diego, 93-94, Southern Indian Health Coun, Alpine, 93-96; co-investr, Epidemiol San Diego Total Waste Recovery Proj, Environ Protection Agency & State Calif, 86-90, Proj Shout, Nat Cancer Inst, 87-92, Epidemiol HTLV-1 Okinawa Proj, Nat Cancer Inst, 88-90 & Nutrit & Low Literacy Proj, Nat Inst Heart, Lung & Blood Dis, 92-96; consult, Gensia Pharmaceut, Inc, 90-92, sr biostatistician, 92-93; dir, Fac Student Mentoring Prog, State Calif, 95-96. *Mem:* Am Asn Higher Educ; Am Statist Asn; Biomet Soc. *Res:* Epidemiological statistics; statistical methods for multicenter clinical trials; computational statistics; applied stochastic processes. *Mailing Add:* 501 S Coronado Ave Lindsborg KS 67456. *Fax:* 785-227-2004; *E-Mail:* golbecka@bethany.bethanylb.edu

GOLBEY, ROBERT (BRUCE), CHEMOTHERAPHY. *Current Pos:* ASSOC PROF CLIN MED, COL MED, CORNELL UNIV, 70- *Personal Data:* b New York, NY, July 15, 22; m 48; c 1. *Educ:* Bethany Col, BS, 43; NY Univ, MD, 49. *Prof Exp:* Res assoc, Sloan Kettering Inst, 55-57, asst, 57-60, assoc mem, Div Clin Chemother, 60- *Concurrent Pos:* Res fel, Div Clin Chemother, Sloan-Kettering Inst, 54; spec fel med, Mem Ctr & James Ewing Hosp, 54-57; from instr to asst prof clin med, Col Med, Cornell Univ, 57-70; clin asst, James Ewing Hosp, 57-59, asst vis physician, 59-62, assoc vis physician, 62-; clin asst physician, Dept Med, Mem Hosp, 57-60, from asst attend physician to assoc attend physician, 60-71, attending physician, 71-; consult, St Joseph's Hosp, 60-, Stamford Hosp, 65-; chief, Solid Tumor Serv, Mem Hosp, 79. *Mem:* AAAS; Am Asn Cancer Res; Am Soc Clin Oncol; Soc Surg Oncol; NY Acad Sci. *Res:* Cancer chemotherapy; biology of malignant tumors and its relationship to clinical course and effective therapy. *Mailing Add:* 34 Wiley Bottom Rd Savannah GA 31411

GOLBUS, MITCHELL S, REPRODUCTIVE GENETICS. *Current Pos:* Res fel med genetics & asst res geneticist, Univ Calif, 71-73, clin instr, Dept Obstet & Gynec, 72-73, asst prof, 73-77, assoc prof, 81-94, EMER PROF OBSTET, GYNEC & PEDIAT, UNIV CALIF, SAN FRANCISCO, 94- *Personal Data:* b Chicago, Ill, Apr 6, 39; m 67; c 3. *Educ:* Ill Inst Technol, BS, 59; Univ Chicago, MD, 63; Am Bd Obstet & Gynec, dipl. *Concurrent Pos:* Clin instr, Dept Obstet & Gynec, Univ Calif, San Francisco, 72-73; mem, Adv Comt Genetics, Calif State Dept Health, 73-, NCalif Tay-Sachs Dis Prev Prog, 73-, Clin Res Grant Review Comt, March of Dimes, 78-, Task Force Predictors Hereditary Dis & Congenital Defects, NIH, 78-79, Med Adv Comt, Nat Genetics Found, 81-; mem, Sci Adv Comt, Nat Tay-Sachs & Allied Dis Asn, 80- *Mem:* Inst Med-Nat Acad Sci; Am Soc Human Genetics; Soc Gynec Invest; AAAS; fel Am Col Obstetricians & Gynecologists. *Res:* Relationship of chromosome heteroploidy to birth defects and reproductive inefficiency; developing techniques for prenatal diagnosis, specifically of defects not demonstrable in amniotic fluid cells. *Mailing Add:* 32 Via San Fernando Tiburon CA 94920. *Fax:* 415-435-3650; *E-Mail:* 102557.315@compuserv.com

GOLCHERT, NORBERT WILLIAM, ENVIRONMENTAL RADIOCHEMISTRY. *Current Pos:* Asst in chem, 58-66, asst chemist, 66-73, chemist, 73-88, ENVIRON SCIENTIST, ARGONNE NAT LAB, 88- *Personal Data:* b Chicago, Ill, July 12, 35; m 58; c 4. *Educ:* Univ Ill, BS, 58; Ill Inst Technol, MS, 65, PhD(chem), 69. *Mem:* Am Chem Soc; Sigma Xi; Am Soc Testing & Mat. *Res:* Measurement of radioactivity in the environment with primary interest in measurement of transuranium nuclides; radioanalytical chemistry of technetium, measurement of nuclear reaction cross-sections, and disposal of low-level radioactive waste. *Mailing Add:* Argonne Nat Lab 9700 S Cass Ave Argonne IL 60439-4804

GOLD, ALBERT, SCIENCE ADMINISTRATION, SOLID STATE PHYSICS. *Current Pos:* ASSOC DEAN ADMIN, DIV ENG & APPL SCIS, HARVARD UNIV, 89- *Personal Data:* b Philadelphia, Pa, July 2, 35; div; c Anthony, Joseph & Josephine. *Educ:* Lehigh Univ, BS, 56; Univ Rochester, PhD(physics), 60. *Prof Exp:* Res assoc physics, Univ Ill, 60-62; from asst prof to assoc prof optics, Univ Rochester, 62-69, assoc dean col eng & appl sci, 67-69; spec asst to pres, Rockefeller Univ, 69-72, dir postdoctoral affairs, 70-72, vpres, 72-78; provost, Polytech Inst New York, 78-81; vpres finance & admin, Desert Res Inst, 81-87; pres, Aurous Assocs, 87-89. *Concurrent Pos:* Consult, Argonne Nat Lab, 60-69, United Aircraft Corp, 63-64 & Eastman Kodak Co, 64-69; dir, Univ Patents, Inc, 79-82. *Mem:* AAAS. *Res:* Theory of optical properties of solids; theory of interaction of intense optical radiation with matter. *Mailing Add:* Div Eng & Appl Sci Harvard Univ 29 Oxford St Cambridge MA 02138

GOLD, ALLEN, MEDICINE, ENDOCRINOLOGY. *Current Pos:* Lectr, 49-70, ASSOC PROF MED, MCGILL UNIV, 70- *Personal Data:* b Montreal, Que, Dec 19, 18; m 42, Bernice Viner; c 5. *Educ:* McGill Univ, BSc, 40, MD, CM, 42, MSc, 48. *Concurrent Pos:* Assoc physician, Montreal Gen Hosp, 51-65, sr physician, 65-; consult endocrinol, Reddy Mem Hosp & Lachine Gen Hosp; hon consult endocrinol, Montreal Gen Hosp. *Mem:* Endocrine Soc; Am Thyroid Asn; Can Soc Clin Invest; Can Med Asn. *Res:* Clinical endocrinology, especially thyroid gland; development of new thyroid diagnostic tests. *Mailing Add:* 360 Victoria Ave Westmount PQ H3Z 2N4 Can

GOLD, ALLEN MORTON, BIOCHEMISTRY, ORGANIC CHEMISTRY. *Current Pos:* asst prof biochem, 62-68, ASSOC PROF BIOCHEM, COLUMBIA UNIV, 68- *Personal Data:* b Chicago, Ill, May 25, 30; m 52; c 2. *Educ:* Univ Chicago, BA, 50, MS, 52; Harvard Univ, PhD(org chem), 55. *Prof Exp:* Staff scientist org chem, Worcester Found Exp Biol, 56-58. *Concurrent Pos:* NIH fel, Swiss Fed Inst Technol, 55-56; spec fel neurochem, Columbia Univ, 58-62; NIH res career develop award, 62-72. *Mem:* AAAS; Am Soc Biol Chem; Am Chem Soc; Harvey Soc. *Res:* Structure and mechanism of enzymes; protein chemistry; biochemistry of parasites. *Mailing Add:* Dept Biochem & Molecular Biophys Columbia Univ New York NY 10032

GOLD, ALVIN HIRSH, BIOCHEMISTRY, PHARMACOLOGY. *Current Pos:* asst prof, 68-71, assoc prof, 71-81, PROF PHARMACOL, ST LOUIS UNIV, 81- *Personal Data:* b Tyler, Tex, May 26, 32; m 59, Jane C; c Paula S. *Educ:* Univ Tex, BA, 58, MA, 61; St Louis Univ, PhD(pharmacol), 65. *Prof Exp:* Res assoc biochem, State Univ NY Buffalo, 64-66; asst prof, Wake Forest Univ, 66-68. *Concurrent Pos:* USPHS res grant, Bowman Gray Sch Med, 66-68; USPHS res grants, St Louis Univ, 68-71 & 75-84; Nat Acad Sci exchange scientist, Univ Zagreb, 71-72. *Mem:* AAAS; Am Soc Biol Chem & Molecular Biol; Am Soc Pharmacol & Exp Therapeut; Am Chem Soc; Brit Biochem Soc; Am Diabetes Asn. *Res:* Enzymology; metabolic control systems; endocrinology. *Mailing Add:* Dept Pharmacol St Louis Univ Med Sch St Louis MO 63104. *Fax:* 314-577-8233; *E-Mail:* goldah@sluvca.slu.edu

GOLD, ANDREW VICK, PHYSICS. *Current Pos:* PROF PHYSICS, UNIV BC, 68- *Personal Data:* b Inveresk, Scotland, Mar 20, 34; m 58; c 3. *Educ:* Univ Edinburgh, BSc, 55; Cambridge Univ, PhD(physics), 58. *Prof Exp:* Fel low-temperature & solid state physics, Nat Res Coun Can, 58-60; res assoc, Iowa State Univ, 60-61, from asst prof to prof, 61-68. *Concurrent Pos:* Sloan res fel, 64-67. *Mem:* Fel Am Phys Soc. *Res:* Electronic and transport properties of metals; de Haas-van Alphen effect; ferromagnetism. *Mailing Add:* Dept Physics Univ BC Vancouver BC V6T 1Z1 Can

GOLD, ARMAND JOEL, MEDICAL PHYSIOLOGY. *Current Pos:* assoc prof, 68-77, PROF PHYSIOL, HOWARD UNIV COL MED, 77- *Personal Data:* b Baltimore, Md, June 7, 26; m 52; c 2. *Educ:* Western Md Col, AB, 49; Univ Md, MS, 51, PhD(physiol), 55. *Prof Exp:* Asst zool, Univ Md, 50-52; physiologist, Chem Corps Med Labs, US Army, 52-55; asst prof physiol res, Sch Med, Univ Md, 56-59; sr develop engr, Goodyear Aircraft Corp, 59-60; physiologist, missile & space vehicle dept, Gen Elec Co, 60-63; staff scientist, res dept, Martin Co, 63-65; head dept environ physiol, Negev Inst Arid Zone Res, Beersheba, Isreal, 65-67. *Mem:* AAAS; Am Physiol Soc; Aerospace Med Asn. *Res:* Heat stress; starvation; hypoxia; cellular metabolism. *Mailing Add:* 1800 Courtyard Circle Baltimore MD 21208

GOLD, BARRY IRA, PHARMACOLOGY, NEUROCHEMISTRY. *Current Pos:* DIR PROJ MGT, WYETH-AYERST RES, 94- *Personal Data:* b Everett, Mass, Apr 30, 46; m 71; c 2. *Educ:* Univ Cincinnati, BS, 68; Boston Univ, PhD(pharmacol), 76. *Honors & Awards:* Sandoz Award, Sandoz Pharmaceut, 75. *Prof Exp:* Res assoc pharmacol, Squibb Inst Med Res, 68-71; fel, Sch Med, Yale Univ, 75-78; asst prof pharmacol, Sch Med, Uniformed Serv Univ, 78-84; res pharmacologist, Anaquest, Div Boc Group, Roberts Pharmaceut Corp, 84-89, dir, Export Mgt Sci, 89-92, assoc dir clin res, 92-93, consult, Genesis Group, 93-94. *Mem:* AAAS; Soc Neurosci; Am Soc Pharmacol & Exp Therapeut. *Res:* Opiate and cholinergic receptors and the effects of centrally acting drugs and neuromuscular blocking drugs. *Mailing Add:* Wyeth-Ayerst Res 145 King of Prussia Rd Radnor PA 19087

GOLD, BARRY IRWIN, BIO-ORGANIC CHEMISTRY, CHEMICAL CARCINOGENESIS. *Current Pos:* res assoc chem carcinogenics, 73-76, asst prof, 76-80, ASSOC PROF BIOMED CHEM, UNIV NEBR MED CTR, 80- *Personal Data:* b Brooklyn, NY, Apr 16, 46; m 71; c 2. *Educ:* Hunter Col, City Univ New York, BA, 66, Univ Nebr-Lincoln, PhD(org chem), 72. *Prof Exp:* Lectr org chem, Univ Toronto, 71-73. *Concurrent Pos:* Prin investr grants,

Nat Cancer Inst, NIH, 77-85. *Mem:* Am Chem Soc; Soc Toxicol; Am Asn Cancer Res. *Res:* Mechanisms by which N-nitroso and chlorinated hydrocarbon compounds initiate the induction of cancer in laboratory animals. *Mailing Add:* Eppley Inst Univ Nebr Med Ctr Omaha NE 68198-6805

GOLD, BERNARD, SPEECH COMMUNICATION, COMPUTER SCIENCE. *Current Pos:* CONSULT, 96- *Personal Data:* b Brooklyn, NY, Mar 31, 23; m 45; c 3. *Educ:* City Col New York, BEE, 44; Polytech Inst Brooklyn, PhD(elec eng), 49. *Honors & Awards:* Soc Award Acoust Speech & Signal Processing, Inst Elec & Electronics Engrs, 86, Jack S Kilby Signal Processing Medal, 97. *Prof Exp:* Mem staff radar, Avion Instrument Corp, 48-50; mem staff noise theory, Hughes Aircraft Co, 50-53; mem staff speech & comput, Lincoln Lab, Mass Inst Technol, 53-69, mem staff, Commun Dept, 69-76, group leader, 76-80, lectr digital processors, 80-96, mem sr staff, 80-96. *Concurrent Pos:* Fulbright fel to Italy, 54-55; vis prof, Mass Inst Technol, 65-66 & 88. *Mem:* Nat Acad Eng; fel Inst Elec & Electronics Engrs; Acoust Soc Am. *Res:* Noise theory; radar; pattern recognition; speech bandwidth compression; theory and design of computers. *Mailing Add:* Lincoln Lab Mass Inst Technol Lexington MA 02173. *E-Mail:* gold@xn.ll.mit.edu

GOLD, DANIEL HOWARD, PHARMACEUTICAL MANUFACTURING. *Current Pos:* PRES D H GOLA ASSOCS, INC, 96- *Personal Data:* b New York, NY, Jan 8, 29; m 52; c 2. *Educ:* Brooklyn Col, BS, 50; Polytech Inst Brooklyn, PhD(chem), 57. *Prof Exp:* Chemist, Jewish Hosp, Brooklyn, 50-51 & Sylvania Elec Prod, Inc, NY, 51-53; sr chemist, Am Cyanamid Co, NJ, 56-62; sr process res specialist, Lummus Co, 62-67; gen supt rubber chem dept, Am Cyanamid Co, Bound Brook, NJ, 67-72, mat mgr, 72-73, mfg mgr, 73-75, res mgr, Stamford, Conn, 75-77, oper mgr pharmaceut, Bound Brook, NJ, 78-83, mgr validation, 84-92, mgr validations, 92-94, dir tech oper, Lederle Labs, Pearl River, NY, 94-96. *Concurrent Pos:* Dir, Parenteral Drug Asn, 84-90; chmn opers, Pharmaceut mfr Asn, 93- *Mem:* Am Chem Soc; NY Acad Sci; Parenteral Drug Asn. *Res:* Organic process development; statistical experimental design and analysis; chromatography; complexation; metal ion-polyelectrolyte interactions; pharmaceutical chemicals. *Mailing Add:* 441 Alpine Terr Ridgewood NJ 07450. *Fax:* 201-612-8216

GOLD, DANIEL P, EXPERIMENTAL BIOLOGY. *Current Pos:* ASST MEM, LA JOLLA INST EXP MED, 90- *Personal Data:* b San Francisco, Calif, July 28, 54. *Educ:* Univ Calif, Los Angeles, BA, 76; Tufts Univ, PhD(immunol), 83. *Prof Exp:* Fel molecular immunol, Ctr Cancer Res, Mass Inst Technol, 83-84, Dana Farber Cancer Ctr, 84-86; asst mem, Div Immunol, Med Biol Inst, 86-90. *Concurrent Pos:* Cancer Res Inst fel, 85-87. *Mem:* Am Asn Immunologists; Am Diabetes Asn. *Res:* Regulation of autoimmune T cell reactivity; identification of auto-antigens in Type I diabetes mellitus; regulation of pathogenic graft versus host disease; author of numerous scientific publications. *Mailing Add:* Sidney Kimmel Cancer Ctr 3099 Science Park Rd San Diego CA 92121

GOLD, DAVID PERCY, GEOLOGY, PETROLOGY. *Current Pos:* res assoc geol & geochem, 64-68, assoc prof, 68-74, PROF GEOL, PA STATE UNIV, 74-, CHMN GEOL GRAD PROG, 77- *Personal Data:* b Durban, Natal, SAfrica, June 22, 33; Can citizen; m 59; c 4. *Educ:* Univ Natal, BSc, 53, Hons, 54, MSc, 58; McGill Univ, PhD(geochem), 63. *Honors & Awards:* Barlow Mem Medal, Can Inst Mining & Metal Eng, 67. *Prof Exp:* Geol asst mineral explor, Union Corp Ltd, SAfrica, 55-56; lectr geol, Loyola Col, Can, 62-64. *Concurrent Pos:* Nat Res Coun Can grant, 63-64; res assoc, Spec Crater Proj, NASA grants, 64-78, NASA earth resources & remote sensing res projs, 72-78; NSF res grants, 65-70; distinguished lectr, Am Geol Inst, 70; mem post-doctoral fel comt, Nat Acad Sci, 71; mem planetology comt, Int Geol Cong, 72; pres, Yellowstone Bighorn Res Asn, 73-75; mem, NASA & Dept Energy tech comt. *Mem:* Geol Soc Am; Mineral Asn Can; Geol Soc SAfrica; Geol Asn Can; Meteoritical Soc; Sigma Xi. *Res:* Geophysical exploration and mining geology in Southern Africa; petrology and geochemistry of carbonatites and alkaline rocks; geological mapping in Northern Quebec; structural analysis in Canadian Appalachians and around volcanic and impact craters; ore deposits; plate tectonics environments and remote sensing; fission track dating and analysis. *Mailing Add:* Geo Sci Penn State Univ University Park PA 16802-1009

GOLD, EDWARD, PHYSICAL METALLURGY. *Current Pos:* PRES, CUSTOM MARBLE INC, 79- *Personal Data:* b New York, NY, Nov 25, 41; m 63, Ilene Levine; c Marci Lyn & Jodi Lauren. *Educ:* Polytech Inst Brooklyn, BS, 63; Columbia Univ, MS, 65. *Hon Degrees:* ScD, Columbia Univ, 67. *Prof Exp:* Sr scientist phys metall, Appl Res Lab, Aeronutronic Div, Philco-Ford Corp, 67-68, prin scientist, Advan Develop Oper, 69-72; chief engr, Resource-Recovery Systs, Barbler Coleman Co, 73-74; vpres eng & mfg, Columbia Yacht Div, Whittaker Corp, 75-76; vpres eng, Chris Craft Corp, 77-79. *Mem:* Am Soc Metall Int. *Res:* Field ion microscope study of short-range order in platinum base alloys; thermomechanical processing of aluminum alloys and superalloy development; physical metallurgy and mechanical properties of beryllium. *Mailing Add:* 20976 Cipres Way Boca Raton FL 33433. *Fax:* 954-979-2674

GOLD, ELI, VIROLOGY, PEDIATRICS. *Current Pos:* RETIRED. *Personal Data:* b New Haven, Conn, July 20, 20; m 43; c 2. *Educ:* Univ Conn, BS, 42; Western Reserve Univ, MD, 50; Am Bd Pediat, dipl. *Prof Exp:* Intern & resident pediat, Boston Children's Med Ctr, 50-53; resident, Cleveland City Hosp, 53-54; from instr to asst prof prev med & pediat, 54-65, from assoc prof to prof pediat, Sch Med, Case Western Reserve Univ, 65-74; chmn dept, Univ Calif, Davis, 74-80, prof pediat, Sch Med, 74-85. *Concurrent Pos:* USPHS spec res fel, Inst Virol, Scotland, 61-62; career develop award, 64-70; clin prof pediat, Univ Wash, Seattle, 85- *Mem:* Soc Pediat Res. *Res:* Synthesis of herpes simplex particle; characteristics of meningococcus; virulence factors, especially immunity. *Mailing Add:* 7216 78th Ave SE Mercer Island WA 98040-5511

GOLD, ELIJAH HERMAN, ORGANIC, MEDICINAL & ANALYTICAL CHEMISTRY. *Current Pos:* PRES, ALLIED INT LABS, 94- *Personal Data:* b New York, NY, May 22, 36; m 62, Lorraine F Berger; c Benjamin Z, Tova M & Aliza S. *Educ:* City Col New York, BS, 57; Yale Univ, MS, 58, PhD(org chem), 63. *Prof Exp:* Fel, Columbia Univ, 62-64; NIH fel, Israel Inst Tech, 64-66; sr res chemist, Schering-Plough Corp, 66-69, prin chemist, 69-70, sect leader, Med Chem Dept, 70-73, mgr, 73-74, assoc dir chem res med, 74-93. *Concurrent Pos:* Mem, Med Res & Develop Comt, US Army, 83; US patent agent, 85. *Mem:* Am Chem Soc; NY Acad Sci; fel Am Inst Chemists. *Res:* Mechanistic and synthetic organic chemistry; organic photochemistry; small ring heterocycles and medicinal chemistry; 49 US patents. *Mailing Add:* 10 Roosevelt Ave West Orange NJ 07052. *Fax:* 973-736-0417

GOLD, GERALD, PHARMACY. *Current Pos:* RETIRED. *Personal Data:* b Pittsburgh, Pa, Aug 8, 27; m 54; c 3. *Educ:* Univ Pittsburgh, BSc, 51, MSc, 58, PhD(pharm), 61. *Prof Exp:* Res pharmacist, Consumer Health Care Div, Miles Home Prod, Miles Labs Inc, 61-80, head, Explor Res Sect, 80- *Concurrent Pos:* Mem staff, Metab Res Univ, Univ Calif, San Francisco. *Mem:* Am Pharmaceut Asn; fel Acad Pharmaceut Sci. *Res:* Emulsions; tableting technology; aerosols. *Mailing Add:* 2309 Kenilworth Dr Elkhart IN 46514

GOLD, HAROLD EUGENE, metallurgical research, quality assurance; deceased, see previous edition for last biography

GOLD, HARRIS, WATER PURIFICATION, SEPARATION SCIENCES. *Current Pos:* MGR, FOSTER-MILLER, INC, WALTHAM, MASS, 83- *Personal Data:* b New York, NY, Mar 20, 36; m 60; c 2. *Educ:* Polytech Inst Brooklyn, BME, 58; Columbia Univ, MS, 59; Calif Inst Technol, PhD(aeronaut), 63. *Prof Exp:* Asst aeronaut, Calif Inst Technol, 59-63; sr staff scientist, Avco Systs Div, 63-66, mgr, Aerophys Dept, 66-68, sr consult scientist, 68-70, prin staff scientist, Avco Systs Div, 70-74; partner, Water Purification Assocs, Cambridge, Mass, 74-82, pres, Water General, 82-83. *Concurrent Pos:* Consult, E H Plesset Assocs, Inc, Calif, 61-62. *Mem:* Am Inst Chem Engrs; Am Water Works Asn; Am Electroplaters Asn; AAAS; Am Chem Soc; Water Pollution Control Fedn. *Res:* Ion exchange; gas separation; membrane separation; protein purification; separation processes; water treatment; molecular sieves; metal complexation. *Mailing Add:* 18 Peachtree Rd Lexington MA 02173-2411

GOLD, HARVEY JOSEPH, decision analysis, system modeling, for more information see previous edition

GOLD, HARVEY SAUL, ANALYTICAL CHEMISTRY, PHYSICAL CHEMISTRY. *Current Pos:* RES CHEMIST, E I DU PONT DE NEMOURS & CO, 85- *Personal Data:* b Neptune, NJ, Feb 23, 52. *Educ:* Cornell Univ, BA, 74; Univ NC, Chapel Hill, PhD(chem), 78. *Prof Exp:* Res asst analytical chem, Univ NC, Chapel Hill, 74-78; asst prof chem, Univ Del, 78-85. *Mem:* Am Chem Soc; Coblentz Soc; Soc Appl Spectros. *Res:* Analytical spectroscopy, vibrational and magnetic resonance; spectroscopy of catalysts and computer treatment of spectroscopic data; inelastic electron tunneling spectroscopy; polymer characterization. *Mailing Add:* 101 Lennie Ct Newark DE 19702-1909

GOLD, JAY JOSEPH, INTERNAL MEDICINE, ENDOCRINOLOGY. *Current Pos:* RETIRED. *Personal Data:* b New York, NY, Feb 17, 23; m 50, Ruea Lane; c Erica & Leah. *Educ:* NY Univ, AB, 46; State Univ NY, MD, 50; Am Bd Internal Med, dipl, 58. *Prof Exp:* Intern, Brooklyn Jewish Hosp, 50-51, resident internal med, 51-52; resident, Bronx Vet Admin Hosp, 54-55; asst prof med, Chicago Med Sch, 56-65; assoc prof med, Med Sch, Northwestern Univ, Chicago, 65-72; clin prof med, Abraham Lincoln Sch Med, Univ Ill Med Ctr, 72-92, adj prof obstet & gynecol, 78-92. *Concurrent Pos:* Fel endocrinol, Col Physicians & Surgeons, Columbia Univ, 52-54; dir, Dept Res Hum Reproduction, Michael Reese Hosp, 55-64; attend endocrinol, Westside Vet Admin Hosp, 59-92, consult endocrinol, 72-92; dir endocrinol & metab sect, St Francis Hosp, Evanston, 65-92; staff consult, Lutheran Gen Hosp, Mercy Hosp; attend, St Francis Hosp, Rush North Shore Hosp; dir, Diab Treat Ctgr, St Francis Hosp. *Mem:* Endocrine Soc; Am Fertil Soc; Am Diabetes Asn; fel Am Col Physicians; Am Soc Intern Med; Am Asn Clin Endocrinol; fel Am Col Endocrinol. *Res:* Chemistry and physiology of pituitary and adrenal glands, gonads, hirsutism and infertility. *Mailing Add:* 251 Princeton Lane Glenview IL 60025

GOLD, JOHN RUSH, GENETICS. *Current Pos:* ASST PROF GENETICS, TEX A&M UNIV, 75- *Personal Data:* b Brownwood, Tex, Dec 14, 46. *Educ:* Knox Col, AB, 68; Univ Calif, Davis, PhD(genetics), 73. *Prof Exp:* Asst res genetics, Dept Animal Sci, Univ Calif, Davis, 73-75. *Mem:* Genetics Soc Am; Am Soc Ichthyologists & Herpetologists; Soc Study Evolution; Soc Syst Zool. *Res:* Genetics, evolution and taxonomy of native North American fish. *Mailing Add:* Biochem & Biophys Tex A&M Univ College Station TX 77843-0100

GOLD, JUDITH HAMMERLING, PSYCHIATRY. *Current Pos:* mem bd regents, Am Col Psychiatrists, 86-89, first vpres, 90-91, pres, 92-93, IMMEDIATE PAST PRES, AM COL PSYCHIATRISTS, 93-; COUN MEM, ROYAL COL PHYSICIANS & SURGEONS CAN, 90- *Personal Data:* b New York, NY, June 24, 41; Can citizen; m 65, Edgar Gold. *Educ:* Dalhousie Univ, MD, 65; FRCP(C), 71. *Honors & Awards:* Order of Can, 94; Howard P Rome Award for Outstanding Leadership in Psychiat, 96. *Prof Exp:* Staff psychiatrist student health, Dalhousie Univ, 71-73; vis colleague psychiat, Welsh Nat Sch Med, Univ Wales, 73-75; from asst prof to assoc prof, Dalhousie Univ, 75-87. *Concurrent Pos:* Lectr psychiat, Dalhousie Univ, 71-75; Med Res Coun fel, Can, 73-75; consult psychiatrist, NS Hosp, Dartmouth, 75-77; health welfare res grant, Can, 77-80; mem, Rev Comt, Nat Health Res & Develop Prog, Can, 78-81; vchmn, Bd Gov, Mt St Vincent Univ, 84-86, chmn, Bd Gov, 86-87; ed, Clin Pract Ser, APPI, 87-; distinguished lectr, Am Psychiat Asn, 93; exec mem, Royal Physicians & Surgeons Can, 92-94. *Mem:* Can Psychiat Asn (pres, 81-82); fel Am Psychiat Asn; Can Med Asn; Royal Col Psychiatrists; NS Med Asn; fel Am Col Psychiatrists (pres, 92-93). *Res:* Crosscultural psychiatry. *Mailing Add:* 5991 Spring Garden Rd Suite 375 Halifax NS B3H 1Y6 Can. *Fax:* 902-425-4170

GOLD, LARRY M, BIOCHEMISTRY, MOLECULAR BIOLOGY. *Current Pos:* from asst prof to assoc prof, 69-78, chmn dept, 88-93, PROF MOLECULAR CELLULAR & DEVELOP BIOL, UNIV COLO, BOULDER, 78-; CHMN BD, FOUNDER & CHIEF SCI OFFICER, NEXSTAR PHARM INC, 91- *Personal Data:* b Schenectady, NY, Aug 16, 41. *Educ:* Yale Univ, BA, 63; Univ Conn, PhD(biochem), 67. *Prof Exp:* NIH postdoctoral fel, Rockefeller Univ, 67-69; researcher, Geneva, 69-70. *Mem:* Nat Acad Sci; AAAS; Am Soc Microbiol. *Res:* Contributed over 125 articles to professional journals. *Mailing Add:* Dept Molecular Cellular & Develop Biol Univ Colo Boulder CO 80309

GOLD, LEWIS PETER, PHYSICAL CHEMISTRY. *Current Pos:* from asst prof to assoc prof, 65-93, PROF CHEM, PA STATE UNIV, 93- *Personal Data:* b Brockton, Mass, May 21, 35; m 65; c 3. *Educ:* Harvard Univ, AB, 57, AM, 59, PhD(chem), 62. *Prof Exp:* Res physicist, Columbia Univ, 61-62, res assoc physics, 62-65. *Mem:* AAAS; Am Chem Soc; Am Phys Soc. *Res:* Molecular spectroscopy and molecular structure; laser-induced fluorescence and optical-optical double resonance spectroscopy of small molecules. *Mailing Add:* Dept Chem Pa State Univ 152 Davey Lab University Park PA 16802. *E-Mail:* lpg@psuvm.psu.edu

GOLD, LORNE W, ENGINEERING PHYSICS, GLACIOLOGY. *Current Pos:* vis scientist, Inst Marine Dynamics, 90-91, EMER RESEARCHER, NAT RES COUN CAN, 87- *Personal Data:* b Saskatoon, Sask, June 7, 28; m 51, Elizabeth Joan L'ami; c Catherine Anne, Patricia Ellen, Judith Sharon & Kenneth Robert. *Educ:* Univ Sask, BSc, 50; McGill Univ, MSc, 52, PhD, 70. *Prof Exp:* Jr res officer snow & ice, Nat Res Coun Can, 50-51, head sect, 52-69, head geotech sect, Div Bldg Res, 69-74, asst dir, 74-79, res mgt chmn & assoc comt geotech res, 76-83, assoc dir, Div Bldg Res, 79-86; sr vis scientist, Ctr Cold Oceans Eng, Mem Univ Nfld, 87-88. *Concurrent Pos:* Can deleg, Int Union Testing & Res Labs Mat & Struct, Can, 82-86. *Mem:* Can Geotech Soc; Int Glaciol Soc (pres, 78-81); Eng Inst Can; fel Royal Soc Can; Can Soc Civil Engrs; fel Can Acad Eng. *Res:* Deformation and failure of ice; ice engineering; ground thermal regime; heat exchange at snow, ice, water and ground surfaces. *Mailing Add:* 1903 Illinois Ave Ottawa ON K1H 6W5 Can

GOLD, MARK STEPHEN, MEDICINE, PSYCHIATRY. *Current Pos:* PROF DEPT NEUROSCI, COL MED, UNIV FLA, GAINESVILLE. *Personal Data:* b New York, NY, May 6, 49; m 71; c 4. *Educ:* Wash Univ, BA, 71; Univ Fla, MD, 75. *Honors & Awards:* Mead Johnson & Roche, Nat Student Res Forum, 75; Seymour F Lustmann, Yale Univ Sch Med & Laughlin Nat Award, Psychiat Endowment Fund, 78; Found Fund Prize, Am Psychiat Asn, 81; Presidential Res Award, Nat Asn Pvt Psychiat Hosps, 82; Silver Anvil Award, 83. *Prof Exp:* Fel neuropsychiat, Yale Univ Sch Med, 75-78; vpres basic res, Psychiat Inst Am, 78-79; lectr psychiat, Yale Univ Sch Med, 78-80; dir res, Fair Oaks Hosp, 78- *Concurrent Pos:* Biol sci training prog fel, Yale Univ Sch Med, 77-78; consult, Addiction Prev & Treatment, 76-78; founder & dir res, Psychiat Diag Labs, 79-84; founder, Nat Cocaine Hotline, 83- *Mem:* Soc Neurosci; Am Psychiat Asn; Int Soc Psychoneuroendocrinol; fel Am Col Clin Pharmacol; Soc Biol Psychiat; Am Acad Psychiatrists Alcoholism & Addiction. *Res:* Neuropsychopharmacology of psychiatric illness and treatment; neuropsychopharmacology and treatment of endogenous and drug-induced euphoric and withdrawal states; development and use of biological measures in psychiatric diagnosis and treatment. *Mailing Add:* Dept Neurosci Univ Fla PO Box 100244 Gainesville FL 32610

GOLD, MARTIN, CLINICAL BIOCHEMISTRY, PHYSIOLOGY. *Current Pos:* RETIRED. *Personal Data:* b Philadelphia, PA, 32. *Educ:* Philadelphia Col Pharm & Sci, BSc, 54; Hahnemann Med Col, MS, 56, PhD(biochem), 59. *Prof Exp:* Res assoc physiol, Hahnemann Med Col, 59-64, res asst prof, 64-67; res assoc, Geront Res Inst, Philadelphia Geriat Ctr, 67-70; dir clin biochem, Dept Lab Med, Nazareth Hosp, 70-78; dir clin chem, Path Dept, Mercer Med Ctr, 78-89, qual assurance coordr, 89-95. *Concurrent Pos:* Nat Inst Arthritis & Metab Dis grant, 64-67; SCent Pa Heart Asn grant, 67-68. *Mem:* AAAS; Am Inst Chem; Am Chem Soc; Am Physiol Soc; Am Asn Clin Chemists. *Res:* Glycolytic enzymes; proteinases; lipid metabolism; specifically free fatty acid and glyceride metabolism. *Mailing Add:* 11000 Greiner Rd Philadelphia PA 19116

GOLD, MARTIN I, MEDICINE, ANESTHESIOLOGY. *Current Pos:* PROF ANESTHESIOL, SCH MED, UNIV MIAMI, 72-; CHIEF ANESTHESIOL SERV, VET ADMIN HOSP, MIAMI, 72- *Personal Data:* b Philadelphia, Pa, Nov 22, 28; m 51; c 3. *Educ:* Univ Pa, BA, 50; State Univ NY, MD, 54. *Prof Exp:* Resident, Grad Hosp, Univ Pa, 54-57; from instr to prof, Sch Med, Univ Md, 59-72, med dir inhalation ther & div acute respiratory care, 68-72. *Concurrent Pos:* NIH fel, 61-67 & spec res fel, 67-68; vis prof, Royal Postgrad Med Sch, London, Eng, 67-68. *Mem:* Am Soc Anesthesiol; Am Soc Pharmacol & Exp Therapeut; Asn Univ Anesthetists; Sigma Xi; Int Anesthesia Res Soc. *Res:* Pulmonary physiology as related to mechanics and gases during anesthesia; respiratory care. *Mailing Add:* Vet Admin Hosp Univ Miami Sch Med 1021 NW 16th St Miami FL 33125-1624

GOLD, MARVIN B, CHEMICAL EDUCATION. *Current Pos:* from asst prof to assoc prof, 63-71, chmn dept chem, 70-73, PROF INORG CHEM, CALIF STATE UNIV, CHICO, 71- *Personal Data:* b New York, NY, June 23, 33; m 62; c 1. *Educ:* Ohio State Univ, BSc, 58; Univ Calif, Berkeley, PhD(chem), 62. *Prof Exp:* Res chemist, Univ Calif, Berkeley, 63. *Mem:* Am Chem Soc; Nat Asn Sci Teachers. *Res:* Computer assisted learning. *Mailing Add:* Dept Chem Calif State Univ Chico CA 95929

GOLD, MARVIN H, BIOCHEMISTRY. *Current Pos:* assoc prof med biophys, 67-69, assoc prof med cell biol, 69-82, PROF MED GENETICS, UNIV TORONTO, 83- *Personal Data:* b Toronto, Ont, Feb 2, 36; m 58; c 5. *Educ:* Univ Toronto, BA, 57, PhD(biophys), 62. *Prof Exp:* Asst prof develop biol, Albert Einstein Col Med, 65-67. *Concurrent Pos:* Jane Coffin Childs fel, 62-63. *Res:* Nucleic acids of bacteria and bacteriophage; genetics; enzymology. *Mailing Add:* Dept Med Genetics Univ Toronto One Kings Col Circle Toronto ON M5S 1A8 Can. *Fax:* 416-978-6885

GOLD, MARVIN HAROLD, POLYMER CHEMISTRY. *Current Pos:* CONSULT, 72- *Personal Data:* b Buffalo, NY, June 23, 15; m 40, Sophye Mendelson; c Judith G (Bloom) & Norman C. *Educ:* Univ Calif, Los Angeles, BA, 37; Univ Ill, PhD(org chem), 40. *Prof Exp:* Fel, Northwestern Univ, 40-42; res chemist, Visking Corp, 42-48; sr scientist, assoc dir chem & mgr, Propellant Chem Div, Aerojet Gen Corp, 48-72. *Mem:* Am Chem Soc; Sigma Xi; Am Inst Aeronaut & Astronaut. *Res:* Polynuclear hydrocarbons; polynitro aliphatic chemistry; polymers; author of more than 30 publications; awarded more than 85 patents. *Mailing Add:* 2601 Latham Dr Sacramento CA 95864

GOLD, MICHAEL HOWARD, LIGNIN BIODEGRADATION, FUNGAL GENETICS & BIOCHEMISTRY. *Current Pos:* from asst prof to assoc prof biochem sci, 76-82, PROF & CHAIR CHEM & BIOL SCI, ORE GRAD INST, 82-, PROF CHEM, BIOCHEM & MOLECULAR BIOL, 92- *Personal Data:* b Paterson, NJ, Jan 16, 41; m 64; c 2. *Educ:* Rutgers Univ, AB, 63; State Univ NY Buffalo, PhD(biochem), 70. *Prof Exp:* Asst prof biochem genetics, Rockefeller Univ, 75-76. *Concurrent Pos:* Fel, Univ Calif, Davis, 70-73; res assoc, Rockefeller Univ, 74-75. *Mem:* Am Soc Microbiol; AAAS; Soc Indust Microbiol; fel Int Acad Wood Sci. *Res:* Biochemistry and genetics of fungi; lignin biodegradation; molecular biology of fungi; oxygen metabolism; gene expression of fungal peroxidases; structure/function; biomass utilization. *Mailing Add:* Dept Chem Biochem & Molecular Biol Ore Grad Inst Sci & Technol PO Box 91000 Portland OR 97291-1000. *Fax:* 503-690-1464; *E-Mail:* mgold@admin.ogi.edu

GOLD, PAUL ERNEST, NEUROBIOLOGY & MEMORY, AGING. *Current Pos:* from asst prof to prof, 76-97, COMMONWEALTH PROF PSYCHOL, UNIV VA, CHARLOTTESVILLE, 97- *Personal Data:* b Detroit, Mich, Jan 7, 45; c 2. *Educ:* Univ Mich, BA, 66; Univ NC, MS, 68, PhD(psychol), 71. *Prof Exp:* Postdoctoral psychobiol, Univ Calif, Irvine, 70-72, lectr, 72-76. *Concurrent Pos:* Postdoctoral fel, NIMH, 72; mem comt, Am Psychol Soc, 90-91, mem, Prog Comt, 91; ed, Psychobiol J, Psychonomic Soc, 90-97; dir neurosci, Univ Va, 91-95. *Mem:* Fel Am Psychol Am; fel Am Psychol Soc; Soc Neurosci. *Res:* Brain mechanisms responsible for the formation of memory, and biological processes which regulate memory function, including meuroendocrine regulation of memory function, contribution of hormonal responses to age-related memory impairments and to memory pathologies. *Mailing Add:* Dept Psychol 102 Gilmer Hall Univ Va Charlottesville VA 22903-2477

GOLD, PHIL, CANCER IMMUNOLOGY. *Current Pos:* from lectr to assoc prof physiol, McGill Univ, 64-74, from teaching fel to assoc prof med & clin med, 65-73, dir, Cancer Ctr, 78-80, chmn, Dept Med, 80-90, PROF MED & CLIN MED, MCGILL UNIV, 73-, PROF PHYSIOL, 74-, DOUGLAS G CAMERON PROF ONCOL, 89-; PHYSICIAN-IN-CHIEF, DEPT MED, MONTREAL GEN HOSP, 80-, EXEC DIR, CLIN RES CTR, 95- *Personal Data:* b Montreal, Que, Sept 17, 36; m 60, Evelyn Katz; c Ian J, Joselyn S & Joel T. *Educ:* McGill Univ, BSc Hons, 57, MSc & MD CM, 61, PhD(physiol), 65; FRCPS(C); Royal Col Physicians & Surgeons, cert internal med, 66. *Hon Degrees:* DSc McMaster Univ, 86. *Honors & Awards:* Medal Med, Royal Col Physicians & Surgeons, Can, 65; E W R Steacie Sci Prize, Nat Res Coun, Can, 73; Can Silver Jubilee Medal, 77, Heath Mem Award, 80; Johann-Georg-Zimmerman Cancer Res Prize, Med Univ, 78; Gairdner Found Award, 78; Terry Fox Inaugural lectr, BC Med Asn, Penticton, 81; Ernest C Manning Found Award, 82; Med Achievement Award, Can Asn Mfrs Med Devices, 83; FNG Starr Award, Can Med Asn, 83; Isaak Walton Killam Award Med, Can Coun, 85; Tower of Hope Award, Israel Cancer Res Fund, 85; Sci Achievement Medal, Italian Govt, 90; Distinguished Serv Award, Can Soc Clin Invest, 92; Distinguished Scientist Award, Can Soc Clin Immunol, 92; RM Taylor Medal, Nat Cancer Inst Can, 92; Ann Res Award, Can Soc Allergy & Clin Immunol, 95. *Prof Exp:* Jr intern, Montreal Gen Hosp, 61-62, jr asst resident med, 62, sr resident, 65-66; fel, Med Res Coun,

Can, 63-65, centennial fel, 67-68. *Concurrent Pos:* Vis scientist, Pub Health Res Inst, New York, 67-68; chmn, Grants Panel, Immunol & Chemother Sect, Am Cancer Soc, 72-73; assoc, Med Res Coun, Can, 68, chmn, Grants Panel Cancer Res, 72-77 & 81-83; sr investr, McGill Univ Med Clin & Montreal Gen Hosp Res Inst, 72-; sr physician, Montreal Gen Hosp, 73-; assoc ed, Cancer Res, 73-80; consult allergy & immunol, Mt Sinai Hosp, Que, 75-; chmn clin immunol, English Exam Bd, Royal Col Physicians & Surgeons, Can, 75-77; mem const comt, Int Res Group Carcinoembryonic Proteins, 76-; dir, Div Clin Immunol & Allergy, Montreal Gen Hosp & McGill Univ Med Ctr, 77-80; pres, Sci Adv Bd, Israel Cancer Res Fund, 77-88; mem cancer grants panel B, Nat Cancer Inst, Can, 77-; mem bd dir, Mt Sinai Inst, Toronto, 78-; patron, Alzheimer Soc Montreal, 86-; hon dir, Can Magen David Adom Inst, 86; mem coun, Med Res Coun Can, 86-, exec comt, 87-, comt ethics & med res, 89-; mem bd dirs, Int Soc Prev Oncol, 89-; counr, Can Inst Acad Med, 90- *Mem:* Am Soc Clin Invest; Am Asn Cancer Res; Am Asn Immunologists; Am Acad Allergy; fel Royal Soc Can; fel Am Col Physicians; Can Fedn Biol Sci; AAAS; Am Fedn Clin Res; Asn Am Physicians; hon mem Can Asn Radiologists. *Res:* Immunologic studies dealing with the presence of specific materials present in cancer cells that are absent from corresponding normal cells, and the use of this information in diagnostic medicine; the study of AIDS in hemophiliacs - disease evolution and immuno-pathology. *Mailing Add:* Montreal Gen Hosp 1650 Cedar Ave Rm D13-173 Montreal PQ H3G 1A4 Can. *Fax:* 416-978-4738

GOLD, PHILIP WILLIAM, NEUROENDOCRINOLOGY. *Current Pos:* clin assoc biol psychiat, 74-76, chief, Neuroendocrinol Unit, 76-81, Neuroendocrinol Sect, 81-88, CHIEF, CLIN NEUROENDOCRINOL BR, INTRAMURAL RES PROG, NIMH, 88- *Personal Data:* b Newport News, Va, Sept 23, 44; m 72; c 3. *Educ:* Duke Univ, BA, 66; Duke Univ Sch Med, MD, 70. *Honors & Awards:* Curt Richter Prize, Int Soc Psychoneuroendocrinol, 85. *Prof Exp:* Intern med, Boston City Hosp, 70-71; resident psychiat, Harvard Med Sch, 71-74. *Concurrent Pos:* Vis prof psychiat, Duke Univ Sch Med, 86-; coun scholars, Library Congress, 88- *Mem:* Endocrine Soc; Am Col Neuropsychopharmacol; Int Soc Psychoneuroendocrinol; Am Soc Clin Res; AAAS; Am Psychiat Asn. *Res:* Physiological and molecular mechanisms of physical and emotional stress and their relevance to major psychiatric and endocrine disorders. *Mailing Add:* NIH Clin Ctr Rm 2D-46 Bldg 10 Clin Neuroendocrinol 9000 Rockville Pike Bethesda MD 20892-0001

GOLD, RAYMOND, EXPERIMENTAL NUCLEAR PHYSICS, REACTOR PHYSICS. *Current Pos:* vpres, 88-90, PRES, METROL CONTROL CORP, 91- *Personal Data:* b New York, NY, Oct 3, 27; m 51, Judith Reiner; c Ilyse Karen, Warren Glen, Mark David & Garry Evan. *Educ:* NY Univ, BA, 51, MS, 54; Ill Inst Technol, PhD, 58. *Prof Exp:* Physicist, Columbia Univ, 52-54; group leader, Gen Elec Co, 54-55; res physicist, Armour Res Found, Ill Inst Technol, 55-58; prof & head, Nuclear Sci & Eng Dept, Lowell Univ, 58-62; sect head, Argonne Nat Lab, 62-72; resident dir, Joint Ctr Grad Study, 72-74; pres, Radiation & Dosimetry Serv, Inc, 75-76; fel scientist, Westinghouse Hanford Co, 76-87. *Concurrent Pos:* Consult, US Naval Radiol Defense Lab, 59-60, Tech Opers Inc, 60-62, Avco Corp, 61-62, Martin Marrietta Co, 71-78 & Westinghouse Hanford Co, 73-75. *Mem:* Am Phys Soc; Am Nuclear Soc; Health Phys Soc. *Res:* Experimental nuclear physics; environmental radiation measurements; reactor physics; nine domestic and foreign patents. *Mailing Add:* 1982 Greenbrook Blvd Richland WA 99352

GOLD, RICHARD HORACE, BREAST CANCER, SKELETAL DISEASES. *Current Pos:* from asst prof to assoc prof, 72-78, PROF RADIOL, UNIV CALIF, LOS ANGELES, 78-, CHIEF, GEN DIAGNOSTIC DIV, DEPT RADIOL, 86-, DIR RESIDENCY TRAINING, 91- *Personal Data:* b New York, NY, Nov 20, 35; m 65, Gittelle Schneider; c Lara & David. *Educ:* NY Univ, BA, 56; Univ Louisville, MD, 60. *Prof Exp:* Fel skeletal radiol, Univ Calif, San Francisco, 67-68, asst prof radiol, 68-72. *Concurrent Pos:* Mem, comt breast imaging, Am Col Radiol, 73-88. *Mem:* Asn Univ Radiologists; Radiol Soc N Am; Am Roentgen Ray Soc; Am Col Radiol; Int Skeletal Soc; Soc Breast Imaging. *Res:* Radiologic diagnosis of diseases of the breast and musculoskeletal systems; breast imaging; breast cancer detection. *Mailing Add:* Dept Radiol Sci Univ Calif Sch Med Los Angeles CA 90024

GOLD, RICHARD MICHAEL, NEUROPSYCHOLOGY. *Current Pos:* RETIRED. *Personal Data:* b New York, NY, Apr 20, 37; c 3. *Educ:* Univ Chicago, PhD(bio-psychol), 66. *Prof Exp:* From asst prof to assoc prof psychol, State Univ NY, Col Cortland, 66-74; prof psychol, Univ Mass, Amherst, 74-92. *Mem:* Soc Neurosci. *Res:* Neuroanatomy of appetite regulation. *Mailing Add:* PO Box 9614 North Amherst MA 01059

GOLD, RICHARD ROBERT, PHYSICS, APPLIED MATHEMATICS. *Current Pos:* PRES, GOLD & ASSOCS, 90- *Personal Data:* b Chicago, Ill, March 27, 30; m 52; c 3. *Educ:* Univ Ill, BS, 51, MS, 55, PhD(gas physics, math), 56. *Prof Exp:* Mem tech staff gas dynamics, McDonnell Aircraft Corp, 51-52 & Inst Math, US Armed Forces Inst, 52-54; mem tech staff aerodyn, Hughes Aircraft Co, 56-59, staff physicist, 59-61; head magnetogas dynamics sect, Lab Div, Aerospace Corp, 61-64; mgr, Aerospace Physics Res Dept, Space Systs Div, Hughes Aircraft Co, 64-68; prof, Calif State Col, Long Beach, 68-75, adj prof math eng, 75-90. *Concurrent Pos:* Lectr, Mech Eng Dept, Univ Southern Calif, 57-58 & phys sci exten, Univ Calif, Los Angeles, 57-62; adj prof mech & struct, Univ Calif, Los Angeles, 81-82. *Mem:* Assoc fel Am Inst Aeronaut & Astronaut; Am Phys Soc; AAAS; Sigma Xi. *Res:* Electromagnetic wave propagation through plasmas; magnetohydrodynamics; fluid dynamics. *Mailing Add:* Gold & Assocs 27520 Hawthorne Blvd Suite 293 Rolling Hills CA 90274

GOLD, ROBERT, NUMBER THEORY. *Current Pos:* from asst prof to assoc prof, 68-86, PROF MATH, OHIO STATE UNIV, 86-, ASSOC DEAN MATH & PHYS SCIS, 91- *Personal Data:* b Philadelphia, Pa, Mar 29, 42; m 68; c 2. *Educ:* Swarthmore Col, BA, 64; Mass Inst Technol, PhD(math), 68. *Prof Exp:* Chief mathematician, S Ross & Co, 68. *Concurrent Pos:* Humboldt fel, 78-79. *Mem:* Am Math Soc. *Res:* Algebraic number theory; Iwasawa theory; structure of ideal class groups; imaginary quadratic fields; cyclotomic fields. *Mailing Add:* Dept Math Ohio State Univ 231 W 18th Ave Columbus OH 43210-1101. *E-Mail:* gold.1@osu.edu

GOLD, ROGER EUGENE, ENTOMOLOGY. *Current Pos:* PROF ENTOM, TEX A&M, 89- *Personal Data:* b Salt Lake City, Utah, Sept 10, 44; m 66; c 3. *Educ:* Univ Utah, BS, 68, MS, 70; Univ Calif, Berkeley, PhD(entom), 74. *Prof Exp:* Res assoc, Vectors Entom Res Group, Univ Calif, Berkeley, 73-74; exten pesticide specialist, asst prof entom & asst prof plant path, Univ Ariz, 74-76, prog dir, Agr Coop Exten Serv, 76-77; assoc prof entom & coordr environ progs, Inst Agr & Natural Resources, Univ Nebr-Lincoln, 77-89. *Mem:* Entom Soc Am; Sigma Xi; Am Coun Sci & Health. *Res:* Insects as vectors of plant pathogens; insect control in the near environment; pesticide assessment in the environment. *Mailing Add:* Entomol Tex A&M Univ College Station TX 77845-0100

GOLD, STEVEN HARVEY, FREE ELECTRON LASERS & CYCLOTRON MASERS. *Current Pos:* Nat Res Coun resident res assoc plasma physics, 78-80, res physicist, 80-87, SUPVRY RES PHYSICIST & SECT HEAD, NAVAL RES LAB, 87- *Personal Data:* b Philadelphia, Pa, Sept 3, 46; m 74; c 2. *Educ:* Haverford Col, BA, 68; Univ Md, MS, 70, PhD(plasma physics), 78. *Concurrent Pos:* Assoc ed, Inst Elec & Electronics Engrs, Transactions on Plasma Sci, 88- *Mem:* Am Phys Soc; Inst Elec & Electronics Engrs. *Res:* High power microwave and millimeter-wave generation using the free-electron laser and cyclotron maser interactions. *Mailing Add:* Code 6793 Naval Res Lab 4555 Overlook Ave SW Washington DC 20375

GOLD, SYDELL PERLMUTTER, GEOMETRY, SYSTEM ANALYSIS. *Current Pos:* SR VPRES & DEP SECTOR MGR, SCI APPLN INT CORP, 92 *Personal Data:* b New York, NY, Jan 3, 41; m 61; c 3. *Educ:* Columbia Univ, AB, 61; Univ NMex, MS, 62; Univ Calif, Berkeley, PhD(math), 73. *Honors & Awards:* David Rist Prize, Mil Opers Res Soc, 80. *Prof Exp:* Staff mem math & tech systs analyst, Sandia Labs, 62-67; mem prof staff & systs analyst, Lawrence Livermore Labs, Univ Calif, 74-80; mem staff, Nat Security Coun, 80-82; off of secy, Air Force, 82-92. *Mem:* Am Math Soc. *Res:* Analysis of United States Air Force weapons systems; scissor congruence of unbounded convex plane subsets. *Mailing Add:* 7301 Westerly Lane McLean VA 22101

GOLD, THOMAS, ASTRONOMY. *Current Pos:* prof, Cornell Univ, 59-71, dir, Ctr Radiophysics & Space Res, 59-81, John L Wetherill prof astron, 71, EMER PROF ASTRON, CORNELL UNIV, 87- *Personal Data:* b Vienna, Austria, May 22, 20; nat US; m 47, 72; c 4. *Educ:* Cambridge Univ, BA, 42, MA, 46, ScD, 69. *Hon Degrees:* MA, Harvard Univ, 57. *Honors & Awards:* Gold Medal, Royal Astron Soc, 85. *Prof Exp:* Exp officer radar res & develop, Brit Admiralty, 42-46; res grant, Cavendish Lab, Cambridge Univ, 46-47, Med Res Coun res grant, Zool Lab, 47-49, fel, Trinity Col, 47-51, demonstr physics, 49-52; sr prin sci officer, Royal Greenwich Observ, 52-56; prof astron, Harvard Univ, 57-58, Robert Wheeler Willson prof appl astron, 58-59. *Concurrent Pos:* Hon fel, Trinity Col, Cambridge, 87. *Mem:* Nat Acad Sci; fel Royal Soc; fel Am Philos Soc; Am Astron Soc; fel Am Geophys Union. *Res:* Cosmology; geophysics; radio astronomy; magnetohydrodynamics. *Mailing Add:* 7 Pleasant Grove Lane Ithaca NY 14850

GOLD, WARREN MAXWELL, PULMONARY PHYSIOLOGY, PULMONARY IMMUNOLOGY. *Current Pos:* CHIEF, CLIN CHEST SECT, MOFFITT HOSP, 69-; PROF, ALTA BASE MED CTR. *Personal Data:* b Chester, Pa, Jan 25, 34; c 4. *Educ:* Harvard Col, BA, 55; Harvard Med Sch, MD, 59. *Prof Exp:* Res fel pulmonary physiol, Cardiovasc Res Inst, Univ Calif, San Francisco, 62-65; dir pulmonary lab & res assoc cardiol, Children's Hosp Med Ctr, 65-69; asst prof med, Univ Calif, San Francisco, 69-72, assoc prof, 72-77, prof, 78-, prof, Cardiovasc Res Inst. *Concurrent Pos:* Assoc pediat & tutor med sci, Harvard Med Sch, 65-69; from assoc mem to sr staff mem, Cardiovasc Res Inst, Univ Calif, San Francisco, 69-; vis scientist, Univ Sydney, Australia, 75; asst dir, Chronic Dis Airways, 76- *Mem:* Am Soc Clin Invest; Am Thoracic Soc; Am Fedn Clin Res; Am Physiol Soc; Am Acad Allergy. *Mailing Add:* Alta Base Med Ctr 2450 Asby Ave San Francisco CA 94705

GOLD, WILLIAM, DENTISTRY. *Current Pos:* RETIRED. *Personal Data:* b Buffalo, NY, Jan 2, 23; m 52, Aida S Frank; c Avram R, Morris S, Rebecca R & Hannah S. *Educ:* Cornell Univ, BS, 43; Univ Wis, MS, 48, PhD(bact), 50. *Prof Exp:* Instr bact & bact physiol, 50; fel, Rutgers Univ, 50-51; res assoc, E R Squibb & Sons, 51-57; microbiologist, Bzura, Inc, 57-63; supvr biol res, Beech Nut Lifesavers, Inc, 63-67; sr scientist oral biol, Cooper Labs, Inc, 73-81; sr microbiologist, Baxter Microscan, 82-93, res fel, 93-94. *Concurrent Pos:* Prin investr, John Hartford Found Grant, 68-73. *Mem:* Am Chem Soc; Am Soc Microbiol; Sigma Xi. *Res:* Biochemistry of microbial processes in oral diseases; control of caries and periodontitis; development of microbiological diagnostics for laboratory use; developing media, equipment and processes to manufacture panels to identify bacteria and the antimicrobials to which they are sensitive. *Mailing Add:* 309 Hillside Rd Elizabeth NJ 07208-1417

GOLDAN, PAUL DAVID, ATMOSPHERIC PHYSICS, ATMOSPHERIC CHEMISTRY. *Current Pos:* PHYSICIST, AERONOMY LAB, NAT OCEANIC & ATMOSPHERIC ADMIN, 66- *Personal Data:* b Reno, Nev, Nov 25, 33; m 59; c 3. *Educ:* Mass Inst Technol, BS, 55; Univ Ill, MS, 58, PhD(plasma physics), 64. *Prof Exp:* Physicist & Nat Res Coun res grant, Boulder Lab, Nat Bur Stand, 64-65; prof physics, Dartmouth Col, 65-66. *Mem:* Am Phys Soc; Am Geophys Union. *Res:* Use of spectroscopic, laser and chromatographic techniques for the measurement of trace atmospheric constituents; characterization of undisturbed atmospheric composition and anthropogenic contributions thereto. *Mailing Add:* Aeronomy Lab Nat Ctr Oceanic & Atmospheric Admin 325 Broadway Boulder CO 80303. *Fax:* 303-497-5126

GOLDANSKII, VITALII IOSIFOVICH, PHYSICS, CHEMISTRY. *Current Pos:* Scientist, 42-52, sr scientist, PN Lebedev Phys Inst, 52-61, DIR, INST CHEM PHYSICS, USSR ACAD SCI, 88-; PROF, INST PHYS ENG, MOSCOW, 51- *Personal Data:* b Vitebsk, USSR, June 18, 23. *Educ:* Moscow Univ, MChem, 47, DSc(physics), 54. *Honors & Awards:* Lenin Order; Order of Oct Revolution; Golden Mendeleev Medal, USSR Acad Sci, 75; Lenin Prize, 80; Karpinsky Prize, Friedrich von Schiller Found, Ger, 83; Boris Pregel Award, NY Acad Sci, 90; Golden Semenov Medal, Russ Acad Sci, 96. *Mem:* Foreign assoc Nat Acad Sci; fel & hon mem Am Chem Soc; fel Am Phys Soc; fel Am Acad Arts & Sci; fel Am Philos Soc; fel Royal Swedish Acad Sci; World Acad Arts & Sci; NY Acad Sci@; Russ Acad Sci. *Mailing Add:* Inst Chem Phys Russ Acad Sci Ulitsa Kosygina 4 Moscow 117334 Russia

GOLDBERG, A JON, DENTAL MATERIALS. *Current Pos:* Asst prof, 75-80, ASSOC PROF RESTORATIVE DENT, SCH DENT MED, UNIV CONN, 81- *Personal Data:* b Baltimore, Md, Feb 18, 47; m 75. *Educ:* Drexel Univ, BS, 70; Univ Mich, MS, 71, PhD(dent mat & metall eng), 77. *Honors & Awards:* Edward H Hatton Award, Int Asn Dent Res, 74. *Mem:* Int Asn Dent Res; Am Soc Metals; Am Soc Testing & Mat. *Res:* Structure-property relationships in polymers and metals of interest in the fields of dentistry and medicine; clinical evaluations of dental restorative materials. *Mailing Add:* Dept Prosthodontics 6100 Univ Conn Health Ctr MC 1615 263 Farmington Ave Farmington CT 06030-1615

GOLDBERG, AARON, TAXONOMIC BOTANY. *Current Pos:* COLLABR, DEPT BOT, SMITHSONIAN INST, 72- *Personal Data:* b Brooklyn, NY, Nov 4, 17. *Educ:* Brooklyn Col, AB, 39; DePaul Univ, MS, 54; George Washington Univ, PhD(bot), 62. *Prof Exp:* Res clerk, Census of Agr, US Bur Census, 40-41; vet parasitologist, Zool Div, Bur Animal Indust, USDA, Md, 47-51, parasitologist in charge, Zool Lab, Ill, 51-53, vet parasitologist, Vet Sci Res Div, Nat Animal Parasite Lab, Agr Res Serv, 53-71, zoologist, 71-72. *Mem:* Soc Syst Biologists; Am Soc Plant Taxon. *Res:* Classification, evolution and phylogeny of angiosperms at family level and above. *Mailing Add:* Dept Bot 166 NHB Smithsonian Inst Washington DC 20560

GOLDBERG, AARON JOSEPH, ELECTRICAL ENGINEERING. *Current Pos:* SR ENG SPECIALIST, GTE SYLVANIA ELECTRONIC SYSTS GROUP, 72- *Personal Data:* b New Haven, Conn, Nov 4, 43; m 69; c 2. *Educ:* Mass Inst Technol, SB & SM, 67, PhD(elec eng), 70. *Prof Exp:* Electronic engr, Defense Commun Agency, 70-72. *Concurrent Pos:* Adj prof, Northeastern Univ, Boston, 75-77; lectr, Univ Lowell, Boston, 78-; adj prof eng, Boston Univ, 79- *Mem:* Inst Elec & Electronics Engrs; Acoust Soc Am. *Res:* Voice, speech processing, digital signal processing, realtime signal processing, microprocessing. *Mailing Add:* Mitre Corp Burlington Rd MS P132 Bedford MA 01730

GOLDBERG, ALAN HERBERT, ANESTHESIOLOGY. *Current Pos:* dir postgrad med educ, Dept Anesthesiol, 84-89, PROF ANESTHESIOL, MED COL WIS, 81- *Personal Data:* b Boston, Mass, Nov 29, 31; m 58, 81; c 3. *Educ:* Brown Univ, AB, 53; Boston Univ, MD, 57; Georgetown Univ, PhD(physiol), 65; Am Bd Anesthesiol, dipl, 63. *Prof Exp:* Intern surg, Univ Hosp, Boston Univ, 57-58; resident anesthesia, Mass Gen Hosp, 58-60; clin instr anesthesia & lectr pharmacol, Georgetown Univ, 63-65; asst prof anesthesiol, Sch Med, Boston Univ & asst anesthesiologist, Univ Hosp, 65-69, assoc prof & assoc anesthesiologist, 69-70, lectr physiol, 70; assoc prof anesthesiol, Harvard Med Sch, 70-75; prof anesthesiol, Sch Med, Boston Univ, 75-81; clin dir, Dept Anesthesiol, Boston City Hosp, 75-81; chief, Dept Anesthesiol, Mt Sinai Med Ctr, Milwaukee, Wis, 81-84. *Concurrent Pos:* NIH career develop award, 66-70; consult, Chelsea Naval Hosp, 69-73; supv physician, Resucitation Serv, Cardiovasc Unit, 70-75, dir anesthesia res & assoc vis physician, Boston City Hosp, 70-75, actg dir, Dept Anesthesiol, 74-75, dir, 75-81; mem, teaching staff, Cardiovasc Block, Harvard Med Sch, 71-72; sr vis anesthesiologist, Univ Hosp, 78-81, actg chmn, Dept Anesthesiol, 80, dir, Anesthesiol Residency Prog, 80-81; assoc ed, Soc for Educ in Anesthesia; sr res assoc, Nuffield Dept Anaesthetics, Radcliffe Infirmary, Univ Oxford, Eng, 89; mem, Educ Meeting Comt, Soc Educ Anesthesia, 87-90, assoc ed, Anesthesia Educ, 88-, prog chmn, 90, treas, 90- *Mem:* Cardiac Muscle Soc; Asn Univ Anesthetists; Am Soc Anesthesiol. *Res:* Myocardial contractility; effects of anesthetics on circulatory system; effects of ischemia and drugs, including anesthetics, on the myocardium; evaluation of myocardial contractility; myocardial preservation. *Mailing Add:* Milwaukee Co Med Ctr 8700 W Wisconsin Ave Milwaukee WI 53226-3512

GOLDBERG, ALAN MARVIN, PHARMACOLOGY, TOXICOLOGY. *Current Pos:* from asst prof to prof environ health sci, Johns Hopkins Univ, 69-78, dir, Div Toxicol, 80-82, assoc dean res, Sch Pub Health, 84-93, DIR, CTR ALTERNATIVES TO ANIMAL TESTING, JOHNS HOPKINS UNIV, 81-, ASSOC DEAN CORP AFFAIRS, 94- *Personal Data:* b New York, NY, Nov 20, 39; m 60, Schoenbach; c Michael D & Naomi J. *Educ:* Long Island Univ, BS, 61; Univ Minn, PhD, 66. *Honors & Awards:* Russel & Busch Award, Humane Soc, 91. *Prof Exp:* Res asst, Univ Wis, 61-62, Univ Minn, 62-66; asst prof pharmacol, Inst Psychiat, Ind Univ, 67-69. *Concurrent Pos:* Res fel, Inst Psychiat, Ind Univ, 66-67; prin res scientist, Chesapeake Bay Instit, 80-83. *Mem:* AAAS; Am Soc Pharmacol & Exp Therapeut; Soc Neurosci; Am Soc Neurochem; Int Soc Neurochem; Soc Toxicol; Am Col Toxicol. *Res:* Acetylcholine metabolism; drug action on the central nervous system; neurotransmitters and environmental toxicology; in vitro toxicology. *Mailing Add:* Assoc Dean for Corp Affairs Sch Hyg Johns Hopkins Univ 111 Market St Baltimore MD 21202-6709. *Fax:* 410-223-1603

GOLDBERG, ALFRED, PHYSICAL METALLURGY, STEEL TECHNOLOGY. *Current Pos:* SR SCIENTIST, LAWRENCE LIVERMORE NAT LAB, 64- *Personal Data:* b Montreal, Que, Oct 2, 23; nat US; m 50, Tanna de la Torre; c John, Teresa, & Edward. *Educ:* McGill Univ, BEng, 46; Carnegie Inst Technol, MS, 47; Univ Calif, Berkeley, PhD(metall eng), 55. *Honors & Awards:* First Metallog Award, Int Metallog Soc. *Prof Exp:* Res engr phys metall, Univ Calif, 47-53; from asst prof to assoc prof metall, US Naval Postgrad Sch, 53-64. *Concurrent Pos:* Metall Consult. *Mem:* Fel Am Soc Metals Int; Sigma Xi. *Res:* Calorimetry of alloys; deformation of metals; phase transformations; corrosion and erosion in energy systems; mechanical properties of elastomers; superplasticity in steels; roll bonding of metals. *Mailing Add:* 1220 Glenwood St Livermore CA 94550. *Fax:* 510-422-2438; *E-Mail:* goldberg3@llnl.gov

GOLDBERG, ALFRED L, PHYSIOLOGY, BIOCHEMISTRY. *Current Pos:* From instr to assoc prof, 68-76, PROF PHYSIOL, HARVARD MED SCH, 77- *Personal Data:* b Providence, RI, Sept 3, 42; m 70; c 2. *Educ:* Harvard Univ, AB, 63, PhD(physiol), 68. *Honors & Awards:* Wise & Helen Burroughs lectr, Univ Iowa, 70. *Prof Exp:* Churchill scholar, Cambridge Univ, 63-64. *Concurrent Pos:* Nat Res Coun fel, 68-69; Med Found Inc fel, 69-71; vis prof, Univ Calif Berkeley, 76; mem, Res Allocations Comn, Am Heart Asn, 76-79; sci bd dirs, Biogen Inc, 82; co-chmn, Fedn Am Soc Exp Biol Conf Protein Degradation, 89; Res Career Dev Award, NIH, 72-74. *Mem:* AAAS; Am Physiol Soc; Soc Biol Chem; Soc Gen Physiol; Biochem Soc. *Res:* Regulation of growth and protein metabolism in mammalian tissues; mechanisms of muscle hypertrophy and atrophy; biochemical mechanisms of protein degradation in animal and bacterial cells; metabolic regulation; amino acid metabolism; hormonal regulation. *Mailing Add:* Dept Cellular & Molecular Physiol Harvard Med Sch 240 Longwood Ave Boston MA 02115-6092. *Fax:* 617-232-0173

GOLDBERG, ALLAN ROY, VIROLOGY. *Current Pos:* res assoc, 71-72, asst prof, 72-78, ASSOC PROF, ROCKEFELLER UNIV, 78- *Personal Data:* b New York, NY, Dec 4, 41; m 65; c 2. *Educ:* Cornell Univ, BA, 63; Princeton Univ, PhD(biochem & biol), 67. *Prof Exp:* Fel, Albert Einstein Col Med, 67-71. *Concurrent Pos:* Asst ed, J Exp Med, 77- *Mem:* Fedn Am Soc Exp Biol; Am Soc Virol; Am Soc Microbiol; Am Soc Cell Biol; NY Acad Sci; Sigma Xi. *Res:* Mechanism of transformation by oncogenic viruses. *Mailing Add:* Innovir Labs Inc 510 E 73rd 2nd Fl New York NY 10021

GOLDBERG, ANDREW PAUL, GERIATRICS. *Current Pos:* adj assoc prof, Dept Food & Nutrit, 84-91, ADJ PROF, COL PHYS EDUC, HEALTH & RECREATION, UNIV MD, COLLEGE PARK, 84-; ASSOC CHIEF STAFF, GERIAT SERV, VET ADMIN MED CTR, BALTIMORE, 90- *Personal Data:* b New York, NY, Mar 12, 45; m; c 2. *Educ:* Clark Univ, BA, 65, State Univ New York, MD, 69; Am Bd Internal Med, cert, 75. *Prof Exp:* Sr res fel, Metab Sect, Vet Admin Hosp, Seattle, 74-76; from instr to asst prof, Dept Med, Univ Wash, 76-83; assoc prof med & head res, Div Geriat Med, Johns Hopkins Univ, 83-90, Francis Scott Key Med Ctr, 88-90. *Concurrent Pos:* Res fel nutrit lipids, Univ Hosp, Seattle, 76-77; asst physician, Barnes Hosp, St Louis, 77-83; chmn, Nutrit Comt, Francis Scott Key Med Ctr, 85-87, prog dir, Gen Clin Res Ctr, 85-90; mem, Nat Comt Sci & Med Progs, Am Diabetes Asn, 89-90, Res Comt, 89-90. *Res:* Effects of obesity on lipid metabolism; effects of exercise training on lipid and carbohydrate metabolism in hemodialysis patients; exercise training in type II diabetes mellitus; exercise, blood pressure and metabolism in the elderly; author of numerous scientific publications. *Mailing Add:* Dept Med Univ Md Sch Med 46 E Lake Ave Baltimore MD 21212. *Fax:* 410-605-7913

GOLDBERG, ARNOLD IRVING, PSYCHOANALYSIS. *Current Pos:* Dir, 90-92, TRAINING & SUPV ANALYST, CHICAGO INST PSYCHOANALYSIS, 70-; PROF PSYCHIAT, RUSH MED COL, CHICAGO, 82- *Personal Data:* b Chicago, Ill, May 21, 29; m, Constance Obenhaus; c Andrew & Sarah. *Educ:* Uiv Ill, BS, 49, MD, 53; Am Bd Psychiat & Neurol, dipl. *Concurrent Pos:* Assoc psychiatrist, Rush Presby St Lukes Hosp, Chicago, 82- *Mem:* Fel Am Psychiat Asn; Am Psychoanal Asn. *Res:* Psychoanalysis; contributed numerous articles to professional journals. *Mailing Add:* Inst Psychoanalysis Chicago Inst 122 S Michigan Ave Chicago IL 60603-6107. *Fax:* 312-922-6748

GOLDBERG, ARTHUR H, physical pharmacy, biopharmaceutics, for more information see previous edition

GOLDBERG, BENJAMIN, physics; deceased, see previous edition for last biography

GOLDBERG, BURTON DAVID, pathology, cell biology, for more information see previous edition

GOLDBERG, CONRAD STEWART, PHYSICS, COMPUTER SCIENCE. *Current Pos:* SYST DIR, TAMBRANDS, INC, 82- *Personal Data:* b New York, NY, June 10, 43; m 67; c 2. *Educ:* City Col New York, BS, 64; Queens Col, MA, 67; City Univ New York, PhD(physics), 74. *Prof Exp:* Prof physics, Queens Col, 65-75; asst dir, Psychol Corp, 76-81; syst mgr, Harcourt, Brace, Jovanovich, 81-82; prof physics, NY Inst Technol, 75- *Concurrent Pos:* Guest physicist, Brookhaven Nat Labs, 65-69 & Lawrence Radiation Lab, 68-69; systs analyst, Control Data Corp, 69-73; coordr educ testing, Harcourt, Brace, Jovanovich, 73-74; sr analyst, Grumman Data Syst, 74-76; consult ed, Faim Inc & Westinghouse Learning Corp, 75. *Res:* Defects in crystals; computer operating systems; education; computer systems design. *Mailing Add:* Six Baylor Circle White Plains NY 10605-3006

GOLDBERG, DAVID, REPRESENTATION THEORY OF REDUCTIVE P-ADIC GROUPS, AUTOMORPHIC FORMS & L-FUNCTIONS. *Current Pos:* res asst prof, 91-94, asst prof, 94-97, ASSOC PROF MATH, PURDUE UNIV, 97- *Personal Data:* b Stoneham, Mass, Nov 7, 61. *Educ:* Reed Col, BA, 84; Univ Md, PhD(math), 91. *Prof Exp:* Actuarial adminr, Fred S James & Co, 84-86. *Concurrent Pos:* NSF postdoctoral fel, 92-95; mem, Math Sci Res Inst, Calif, 94-95; early career develop grant, NSF, 95. *Mem:* Am Math Soc; Math Asn Am. *Res:* Compute reducibility of induced representations and associated number theoretic invariants; determine special values of local Langlands L-functions. *Mailing Add:* Dept Math Purdue Univ West Lafayette IN 47907. *Fax:* 765-494-0508; *E-Mail:* goldberg@math.purdue.edu

GOLDBERG, DAVID C, METALLURGY, MATERIALS SCIENCE. *Current Pos:* supvr metall, Aviation Gas Turbine Div, 51-54, mgr, 54-60, adv engr, 60-61, dir space mat, 61-62, mgr struct mat & processes, Astronuclear Lab, 62-66, mgr mat dept, 66-74, mgr eng dept, 74-76, mgr advan prog, Advan Energy Syst Div, 76-82, PRES CONSULT SERV, WESTINGHOUSE ELEC CORP, 82- *Personal Data:* b Dallas, Tex, June 27, 21; m 43, Barbara Fox; c Marc, Carol (St Onge) & Robert. *Educ:* Antioch Col, BS, 43. *Prof Exp:* Engr, Battelle Mem Inst, 41-44 & Saunders Mach & Tool, 46-47; sr engr, Hamilton Watch Co, 47-51. *Concurrent Pos:* Mem comt toxicity of beryllium, Mat Adv Bd-Nat Acad Sci, 53-54, mem refractory metal sheet rolling panel C, 64-66, chmn tubing comt, 66-67, mem comt tech aspects of strategic mat, 67-71; mem res adv comt, mat, NASA, 67-70; mem, NATO Summer Support Eval Conf Refractory Metals, 67; tech ed, Air Force Struct Mat Handbk, 68-; chmn design panel, Nat Mat Adv Bd, 76-78. *Mem:* Am Inst Aeronaut & Astronaut; Am Soc Metals; Am Soc Testing & Mat; Sci Res Soc Am. *Res:* Development of alternate energy technology; solar, magnetohydrodynamics, wind; hydrogen technologies. *Mailing Add:* 17091 Edgewater Dr Port Charlotte FL 33948

GOLDBERG, DAVID ELLIOTT, INORGANIC CHEMISTRY. *Current Pos:* from instr to assoc prof, Brooklyn Col, 59-70, dep chmn dept, 63-72, chmn dept, 72-78, PROF CHEM, BROOKLYN COL, 78- *Personal Data:* b Scranton, Pa, July 26, 32; wid; c Jeff & Amy. *Educ:* George Washington Univ, BS, 54; Pa State Univ, PhD(inorg chem), 59. *Prof Exp:* Instr chem, Pa State Univ, 58-59. *Concurrent Pos:* F G Cottrell grant, 60-61; City Univ NY grants, 64-65 & 76-77; Nat Inst Gen Med spec fel, Univ Sussex, 66-67. *Mem:* Am Chem Soc; Royal Soc Chem; Sigma Xi. *Res:* Stability and bonding in coordination compounds; solvent extraction of heavy metal ions by coordination; x-ray diffraction of coordination compounds. *Mailing Add:* Dept Chem Brooklyn Col Brooklyn NY 11210

GOLDBERG, DAVID MYER, BIOCHEMISTRY. *Current Pos:* chmn, 77-89, PROF DEPT CLIN BIOCHEM, UNIV TORONTO, 77- *Personal Data:* b Glasgow, UK, Aug 30, 33; m 64; c 2. *Educ:* Univ Glasgow, BSc, 58, PhD(biochem), 65, MD, 74. *Honors & Awards:* Van Slyke Award, Am Asn Clin Chem, 82; Roman Award, Australian Asn Clin Biochemists, 84; Lion of Venice Award for contribs to int med, Ital Ministry Health, 84; Nova Idea Int Prize Lab Med, Ital Asn Clin Pathologists, 85. *Prof Exp:* House surgeon, Stobhill Hosp, Glasgow, 59-60; sr house officer biochem, Western Infirmary, Glasgow, 60-61, registrar, 61-63, sr registrar, 63-67; hon lectr, Univ Sheffield, 67-75; biochemist-in-chief, Hosp Sick Children, Toronto, 75-89. *Concurrent Pos:* House physician, Southern Gen Hosp, Glasgow, 60; consult chem path, United Sheffield Hosps, 67-75; joint ed-in-chief, Clin Biochem. *Mem:* Int Soc Clin Enzymol; Biochem Soc; Am Asn Clin Chem; Can Soc Clin Chemists; Can Biochem Soc. *Res:* Enzymes in diagnosis in liver, pancreatic disease, and heart disease; regulatory aspects of pancreatic enzyme secretion; enzymes in cancer with special emphasis upon regulation of glycolysis; microsomal enzyme induction; biosynthesis and peripheral catabolism of tracylglycerol. *Mailing Add:* 9 Harrison Rd Toronto ON M2L 1V3 Can. *Fax:* 416-975-5650

GOLDBERG, EDWARD B, MOLECULAR GENETICS OF BACTERIOPHAGE & ION TRANSPORT, NEW MATERIALS. *Current Pos:* asst prof microbiol, 65-69, assoc prof, 69-76, PROF MOLECULAR BIOL & MICROBIOL, SCH MED & DENT, TUFTS UNIV, 76-, HEAD, SCI ADV BD APPL MICROBIOL, INC, NY. *Personal Data:* b Bronx, NY, July 19, 35; m 91, Barbara Neufeld; c Donna F & Abigail M. *Educ:* Columbia Univ, BA, 56; Johns Hopkins Univ, PhD(biol), 61. *Prof Exp:* Jr instr biol, Johns Hopkins Univ, 56-57; guest investr bacteriophage genetics, Carnegie Inst, 61-63, fel, Genetics Res Unit, 63-65. *Concurrent Pos:* Fel, Nat Found Med Res, 61-63; NIH career develop awards, 65-75; vis profs, Hadassah Med Sch, Hebrew Univ, Israel, 69-70, Med Res Coun, Lab Molecular Biol, Cambridge, Eng, 76-77 & Dept Microbiol Ecol, Hebrew Univ, 83-84; Guggenheim fel, 83-84. *Mem:* AAAS; Am Soc Biol Chemists; Genetics Soc Am; Am Soc Microbiol; fel Am Acad Microbiol. *Res:* Mechanisms of control of phage attachment and DNA injection, restriction, recombination and transcription of bacteriophage; ion transport in bacteria; design and manufacture of new materials. *Mailing Add:* Dept Molecular Biol & Microbiol Tufts Univ 136 Harrison Ave Boston MA 02111. *E-Mail:* egoldber@pal.turo.edu

GOLDBERG, EDWARD D, MARINE GEOCHEMISTRY. *Current Pos:* From asst prof to prof, 49-94, EMER PROF CHEM, SCRIPPS INST OCEANOG, UNIV CALIF, SAN DIEGO, 94- *Personal Data:* b Sacramento, Calif, Aug 2, 21; m 45, 72, Kathe Bertine; c David W, Wendy J, Kathi K & Beck B. *Educ:* Univ Calif, BS, 42; Univ Chicago, PhD(chem), 49. *Honors & Awards:* Tyler Prize; B H Ketchum Award, Woods Hole Oceanog Inst. *Concurrent Pos:* Guggenheim fel, Univ Bern, 61; NATO fel, Univ Brussels, 70. *Mem:* Nat Acad Sci; Geochem Soc; Am Geophys Union; AAAS. *Res:* Geochemistry of marine waters; marine sedimentation; meteoritics; radiochemistry; atmospheric and marine pollution; coastal zone management. *Mailing Add:* Scripps Inst Oceanog La Jolla CA 92093. *Fax:* 619-534-0784; *E-Mail:* egoldberg@ucsd.edu

GOLDBERG, EDWIN A(LLEN), ELECTRONICS. *Current Pos:* engr, Res Dept, 40-42, mem tech staff, Res Labs, 42-57, mgr missile & weapon systs, Defense Electronic Prods Div, Spec Systs Develop Dept, 57-58, eng & admin, Astro-Electronics Div, 58, design, 58-59, space vehicle systs, 59-62, spacecraft design & testing, 62-64, spacecraft tests, 64-65 & spec projs, 65-75, prof mgr hydrogen clock, RCA Astro Electronics, 75-77, MGR PROD & SYST SAFETY & MISSION ASSURANCE, DYNAMIC EXPLOR PROG, RCA ASTRO ELECTRONICS, RCA CORP, 78- *Personal Data:* b Dallas, Tex, Sept 13, 16; m 42; c 2. *Educ:* Univ Tex, BS, 38, MS, 40. *Prof Exp:* Seismic engr, Magnolia Petrol Co, 38-39; asst elec eng, Univ Tex, 39-40. *Mem:* Inst Elec & Electronics Engrs. *Res:* Electronic analog computer components and systems; color television systems; satellite and space electronics systems; hydrogen maser frequency standard. *Mailing Add:* RCA Corp Astro Electronics PO Box 800 Princeton NJ 08540

GOLDBERG, ERWIN, BIOCHEMISTRY, REPRODUCTIVE BIOLOGY. *Current Pos:* from asst prof to prof biol, 63-74, PROF BIOCHEM, MOLECULAR BIOL & CELL BIOL, NORTHWESTERN UNIV, EVANSTON, 74- *Personal Data:* b Waterbury, Conn, Jan 14, 30; m 51, 85, Pauline Bentley; c Samuel, Larry, Jeffrey, Thomas & Catherine. *Educ:* State Univ NY, BA, 51; Univ Iowa, MS, 53, PhD(zool, biochem), 56. *Prof Exp:* Res assoc zool, Univ Iowa, 56-58; asst prof biol, WVa Univ, 58-61; asst prof zool, NDak State Univ, 61-63. *Mem:* AAAS; Am Soc Biol Chemists; Am Soc Androl; Soc Study Reproduction; Int Soc Immunol Reproduction; Protein Soc. *Res:* Biochemistry and immunology of mammalian male germ cells; reproductive immunology; developmental biology; immunocontraception; regulation of gene expression in the testis. *Mailing Add:* Dept Biochem, Molecular Biol & Cell Biol Northwestern Univ Evanston IL 60208. *E-Mail:* erv@nwu.edu

GOLDBERG, ESTELLE MAXINE, MATHEMATICS. *Current Pos:* RETIRED. *Personal Data:* b Las Vegas, Nev, Apr 19, 34; m 54; c 2. *Educ:* Univ Calif, Los Angeles, BA, 53; Columbia Univ, MA, 59, PhD(math), 65. *Prof Exp:* From asst prof to prof math, San Francisco State Univ, 62-79. *Res:* Algebra; homological algebra. *Mailing Add:* 110 Pine Needle Ln Altamonte Springs FL 32714

GOLDBERG, EUGENE, NUCLEAR PHYSICS. *Current Pos:* sr physicist, Livermore Proj, 53-65, leader, Exp Physics Div, 65-73, assoc leader, B Div, 73-79, STAFF PHYSICIST, LAWRENCE LIVERMORE NAT LAB, UNIV CALIF, 79. *Personal Data:* b Chicago, Ill, May 29, 27; c 2. *Educ:* Ill Inst Technol, BS, 48, MS, 50; Univ Wis, PhD(physics), 53. *Prof Exp:* Asst physics, Ill Inst Technol, 48-50; Alumni Res Found asst, Univ Wis, 50-51. *Mem:* Fel Am Phys Soc; Am Nuclear Soc. *Res:* Experimental nuclear physics; interaction of charged particles with light nuclei, using Van de Graaff generator; nuclear and thermonuclear weapon development; neutronic design of epithermal homogeneous reactors; experimental studies of heavy ion interactions; radiobiological studies involving fast neutrons; radiation dosimetry measurements; foreign energy technology assessment. *Mailing Add:* 5454 Greenridge Rd Castro Valley CA 94552

GOLDBERG, EUGENE P, BIOMATERIALS, BIOPOLYMERS. *Current Pos:* PROF MAT SCI & PHARMACOL & DIR, BIOMED ENG CTR, UNIV FLA, 75- *Personal Data:* b Southampton, NY, Nov 11, 28; m 50; c 3. *Educ:* Univ Miami, BS, 50; Ohio Univ, MS, 51; Brown Univ, PhD(chem), 53. *Prof Exp:* Res & develop chemist, Gen Elec Co, 53-60; assoc dir & head, Chem Res Dept, Res Ctr, Borg-Warner Corp, 60-65; dir, Chem Res Lab, Rochester Res Ctr, Xerox Corp, 66-75. *Concurrent Pos:* Vis prof, Hebrew Univ, 72; mem solid state sci adv panel, Nat Acad Sci-Nat Res Coun, 72-80 & Mat Res Adv Comt, NSF, 80-86; US-USSR sci exchange prog, US Nat Acad Sci, 76; Japan Soc Prom Sci fel, Kyoto Univ, 82. *Mem:* AAAS; Am Chem Soc; Sigma Xi; Am Acad Ophthal; Acad Surg Res; Mat Res Soc; Am Soc Cataract & Refractive Surg. *Res:* Polymer science; biopolymers; biomedical materials and devices; biomaterials; surgical research; biosurfaces; polymer surface modification; hydrophilc polymers; polymer biocompatibility; targeted drug delivery. *Mailing Add:* Dept Mat Sci & Eng Biomed Eng Ctr Univ Fla MAE 317 Gainesville FL 32611-6400

GOLDBERG, GARY STEVEN, PROTEIN SYNTHESIS. *Current Pos:* ASSOC RESEARCHER, UNIV WESTERN ONT, 94- *Personal Data:* b Boston, Mass, Dec 12, 60; m, Junko Hahori. *Educ:* Univ Ga, BS, 83; WVa Univ, PhD(genetics & develop biol), 90. *Prof Exp:* Jr researcher, Univ Hawaii, 90-93. *Res:* Investigate the roles and mechanisms by which gap junctional communication controls the growth of normal and transformed cells. *Mailing Add:* Dept Biol Sci State Univ NY 615 Cooke Hall Box 601300 Buffalo NY 14260-1300. *Fax:* 716-645-2975

GOLDBERG, GERSHON MORTON, PHOTOGRAPHIC CHEMISTRY, MICROLITHOGRAPHY. *Current Pos:* RETIRED. *Personal Data:* b Paterson, NJ, Apr 5, 24; m 51, Marilyn Kosso; c Jay H, Richard & Elise. *Educ:* Pa State Col, BS, 44, MS, 47, PhD(org chem), 49. *Honors & Awards:* Serv Award, Soc Imaging Sci & Technol, 75. *Prof Exp:* Fel, Northeastern Univ, 49-50; res chemist, petrol, Daugherty Refining Div, L Sonnenborn Sons, Inc, 50-54; res chemist, Tech Opers Inc, 54-75; prin scientist, Aerodyne Res, Inc, 75-78; sr scientist, GCA Corp, 81-85; prin scientist, Ionomet Res Corp, 78-87, proj mgr, 87-88; staff scientists, Innovative Imaging Systs, Inc, 88-92, corp scientist chem, 92-96. *Mem:* AAAS; Am Chem Soc; Sigma Xi; Soc Imaging Sci & Technol; Royal Photog Soc Gt Brit. *Res:* Solubility of quaternary ammonium compounds; organosilicon compounds; petroleum sulfonates; sensitizing dyes; thin films; unconventional photographic systems; microencapsulation; microlithography; photoresists; infrared fiber optics. *Mailing Add:* 31 Grand View Rd Arlington MA 02174

GOLDBERG, HAROLD SEYMOUR, ELECTRICAL ENGINEERING. *Current Pos:* assoc dean, Gordon Inst, 88-93, LECTR, TUFTS UNIV, 93- *Personal Data:* b Brooklyn, NY, Jan 22, 25; m 49, Florence Meyerson; c Lawrence & Irene. *Educ:* Cooper Union, BEE, 44; Polytech Inst Brooklyn, MEE, 49. *Honors & Awards:* Award of Distinction, Polytech Inst Brooklyn, 80; John Fluke Sr Pioneer Award, 89; Allen Ploss Award, Electro, 92; Haraden Pratt Award, Inst Elec & Electronics Engrs, 93. *Prof Exp:* eng draftsman, Cole Electric Products Co, 44-45; radio engr, Press Wireless Inc, 45-47; asst proj engr, Radio Receptor Co, 47-48; proj engr, North Radio Co, 48-50; mgr prod test & test equip design sect, Allen B DuMont Labs Inc, 50-56; mgr eng fabrication dept, Emerson Radio & Phonograph Corp, 56-57; chief develop engr, Consolidated Avionics Corp, 57-59; eng mgr data systs, EPSCO Inc, 59-62; vpres res, Lexington Instruments Corp, 62-66; prin res engr, Res Div-Avco, 66-68; opers mgr, Orion Research Inc, 68-70; vpres appln, Analogic Corp, 70-71; opers mgr, Data PRecision Corp, 71-72, pres, 72-82; vpres, Analogic Corp, 79-85; pres, Acrosytems Corp, 85-88. *Concurrent Pos:* US Army, 45-47; int bd dirs, Inst Elec & Electronics Engrs, 71-75, 89-90; consult, Wakefield, 88-92, Analog Corp, 88- *Mem:* Fel Inst Elec & Electronics Engrs (vpres, 75); Instrumentation & Measurement Soc. *Mailing Add:* 10 Alcott Rd Lexington MA 02173-1950

GOLDBERG, HARRY, CARDIOLOGY. *Current Pos:* dir, Cardiovasc Dept, 60-84, EMER CHMN CARDIOVASC DEPT, ALBERT EINSTEIN MED CTR, 84-; PROF MED, SCH MED, TEMPLE UNIV, 69- *Personal Data:* b Philadelphia, Pa, May 19, 18; m 46; c 2. *Educ:* Univ Pa, AB, 39; Long Island Col Med, MD, 44; Am Bd Internal Med, dipl, 53; Am Subspecialty Bd, dipl, 54. *Prof Exp:* Intern, Mt Sinai Hosp, Albert Einstein Med Ctr, 44-45; resident path, Metrop Hosp, NY, 45-46 & 48; resident internal med, Mt Sinai Hosp, Pa, 48-49; asst prof physiol, Hahnemann Med Col, 51-53, asst prof med, 53-60. *Concurrent Pos:* Fel cardiovasc dis, Michael Reese Hosp, Ill, 50; dir cardiopulmonary lab, Hahnemann Med Col, 51-60; dir cardiol dept, Deborah Heart & Lung Ctr, 58-85, vpres-in-chg med affairs, 73-81; assoc prof, Temple Univ, 63-69. *Mem:* AAAS; Am Physiol Soc; Am Heart Asn (pres, 73); fel Am Col Physicians; fel Am Col Chest Physicians; fel Am Col Cardiol; Sigma Xi. *Res:* Clinical cardiovascular research; cardiology. *Mailing Add:* Dept Cardiol Temple Univ Sch Med Albert Einstein Med Ctr 5401 Old York Rd Philadelphia PA 19141-3098. *Fax:* 215-455-1933

GOLDBERG, HERBERT SAM, MICROBIOLOGY, MEDICAL EDUCATION. *Current Pos:* From asst prof to assoc prof microbiol, Sch Med, Univ Mo, Columbia, 53-61, chmn dept, 65-66, asst to dean, 66-67, asst dean, 67-71, dir sch health related prof, 78-83, assoc dean, 71-83, assoc vpres res, 85-86, PROF MICROBIOL, SCH MED, UNIV MO, COLUMBIA, 61-, ASSOC DEAN RES & ACAD AFFAIRS, 87- *Personal Data:* b New York, NY, July 23, 26; m 48; c 2. *Educ:* St Johns Univ, NY, BS, 48; Univ Mo, MA, 50; Ohio State Univ, PhD(bact), 53. *Honors & Awards:* Byler Admin Award, 76. *Concurrent Pos:* Wellcome Trust traveling fel, 60 & 64; NIH grant electron micros, 62; vis scientist, Cambridge Univ, 60; vis prof, Southern Ill Univ, 61, Univ Calif, Los Angeles & Rutgers Univ, 84; consult, WHO, 62-72. *Mem:* AAAS; Am Soc Microbiol; NY Acad Sci; Soc Appl Bact; Brit Soc Gen Microbiol. *Res:* Antibiotic assay techniques; nontherapeutic uses of antibiotics; chemotherapy of Leptospiroses, Bacteroides identification; biomedical research and education administration. *Mailing Add:* Sch Med M-228 Med Sch B-1 Univ Mo Columbia MO 65212-0001

GOLDBERG, HOWARD S, PARTICLE PHYSICS, PULMONOLOGY. *Current Pos:* asst prof, 66-72, assoc prof, 72-80, PROF PHYSICS, UNIV ILL, CHICAGO CIRCLE, 80- *Personal Data:* b Chicago, Ill, Mar 26, 36; m 64; c 2. *Educ:* Univ Mich, Ann Arbor, BSEE, 58; Univ Calif, Berkeley, PhD(physics), 64. *Prof Exp:* Asst prof, Tuskegee Inst, 64-66. *Mem:* Am Phys Soc; Am Asn Physics Teachers. *Res:* Strong and weak interactions in elementary particle high energy physics. *Mailing Add:* Cedar Sinai 8631 W Third St Suite 445E Los Angeles CA 90048

GOLDBERG, HYMAN, PHYSICS. *Current Pos:* from asst prof to assoc prof, 67-75, PROF PHYSICS, NORTHEASTERN UNIV, 75- *Personal Data:* b Montreal, Que, May 21, 39; m 65. *Educ:* McGill Univ, BSc, 59; Mass Inst Technol, PhD(physics), 63. *Prof Exp:* Instr physics, Brandeis Univ, 63-64, res assoc, 64; Nat Res Coun Can overseas fel, Theoret Physics Lab, Orsay, France, 64-65; instr & res assoc, Cornell Univ, 65-67. *Mem:* Am Phys Soc. *Res:* Elementary particle physics. *Mailing Add:* Dept Physics Northeastern Univ 111 Dana Res Ctr Boston MA 02115

GOLDBERG, IRA BARRY, PHYSICAL CHEMISTRY & MICROWAVE MEASUREMENTS, MAGNETIC MATERIALS & SENSORS. *Current Pos:* mgr phys chem, 81-92, mem tech staff, 71-96, PRIN SCIENTIST, MAT SCI, ROCKWELL INT SCI CTR, 96- *Personal Data:* b Brooklyn, NY, Apr 10, 43; m 66, Susan Winterstein; c Elizabeth, Adam & Rachel. *Educ:* Adelphi Univ, AB, 64; Univ Minn, PhD(phys chem), 69. *Prof Exp:* Fel chem, Univ Tex, Austin, 69-71. *Mem:* Am Chem Soc; Am Phys Soc; Microwave Power Inst; sr mem Inst Elec & Electronics Engrs; Electron Paramagnetic Resonance Soc. *Res:* Electron spin resonance; magnetics and magnetic materials; ferromagnetic resonance; electrochemistry; chemical kinetics; radical ions; microwave measurement, materials and instrumentation. *Mailing Add:* 54 Westbury Ct Thousand Oaks CA 91360. *Fax:* 805-373-4775

GOLDBERG, IRVIN H(YMAN), MEDICINE, PHARMACOLOGY & BIOCHEMISTRY. *Current Pos:* assoc prof med, Harvard Med Sch, 64-68, chmn div med sci, 68-70, Gustavus Adolphus Pfeiffer prof pharmacol, 72-83, chmn dept pharmacol, 72-86, PROF MED, HARVARD MED SCH, 68-, OTTO KRAYER PROF, DEPT BIOL CHEM & MOLECULAR PHARMACOL, 83- *Personal Data:* b Hartford, Conn, Sept 2, 26; m 56, Margaret F Ziskin; c Daniel E & Nancy E. *Educ:* Trinity Col, Conn, BS, 49; Yale Univ, MD, 53; Rockefeller Inst, PhD(biochem), 60. *Hon Degrees:* AM, Harvard Univ, 64. *Honors & Awards:* Otto Krayer Award, Am Soc Pharmacol & Exp Therapeut, 94. *Prof Exp:* Intern med, Columbia-Presby Med Ctr, NY, 53-54, asst resident, 54-56, chief resident, 56-57; from asst prof to assoc prof med & biochem, Univ Chicago, 60-64. *Concurrent Pos:* Am Cancer Soc fac res assoc award, 60-71; Guggenheim Mem Found fel, Oxford Univ, 70-71; instr, Col Physicians & Surgeons, Columbia Univ, 56-57; mem, BC Res Coun Can, 59; chief endocrinol metab unit, Beth Israel Hosp, Boston, 64-68, physician, 64-72; mem bd consult med, 72-; mem res comt, Med Found Inc, Boston, 68-; clin consult, Harvard Med Serv, Boston City Hosp, 72-73; consult clin pharmacol, Children's Hosp Med Ctr, 72-91; sr fel, Bd Fels, Trinity Col, 73-76; mem exp therapeut study sect, NIH, 74-77; mem comt proposed legis restruct food & drug admin, Assembly Life Sci, Nat Acad Sci-Nat Res Coun & Inst Med, 76; physician, Div Med Oncol, Sidney Farber Cancer Inst, Boston, 80- *Mem:* Inst Med-Nat Acad Sci; Am Soc Microbiol; Am Soc Pharmacol & Exp Therapeut; Brit Pharmacol Soc; Am Soc Biol Chem; Am Acad Arts & Sci; Am Chem Soc; Am Soc Clin Invest; Asn Am Physicians; AAAS. *Res:* Molecular mechanism of action of antibiotics affecting nucleic acid and protein synthesis and function; DNA damage and repair; biochemistry. *Mailing Add:* Dept Chem & Molecular Pharmacol Harvard Med Sch Boston MA 02115. *Fax:* 617-432-0471; *E-Mail:* vinggold@warren.med.harvard.edu

GOLDBERG, IRVING DAVID, mental health services, for more information see previous edition

GOLDBERG, IVAN D, MICROBIAL GENETICS, MOLECULAR GENETICS. *Current Pos:* assoc prof, 71-77, PROF MICROBIOL, UNIV KANS MED CTR, KANSAS CITY, 77- *Personal Data:* b Philadelphia, Pa, May 13, 34; m 79, Noveta McCracken; c Micki, Judy, Lisa, Nick & Vikki. *Educ:* Univ Pa, AB, 56; Univ Ill, PhD(microbiol), 61. *Prof Exp:* Fel microbial genetics, Inst Microbiol, Rutgers Univ, 61-62, Ore State Univ, 62-63 & Army Biol Labs, Ft Detrick, 63-64, microbial geneticist, 64-71. *Mem:* Am Soc Microbiol; Sigma Xi. *Res:* Microbial genetics, including transformation and transduction; bacteriophages and lysogeny; plasmids; genetics of Neisseria gonorrhoeae; genetic bases of enzyme thermostability. *Mailing Add:* Dept Microbiol Molecular Genetics & Immunol Univ Kans Med Ctr 39th & Rainbow Blvd Kansas City KS 66160-7420. *Fax:* 913-588-7295; *E-Mail:* igoldber@kumc.edu

GOLDBERG, JACOB, computer science, electrical engineering, for more information see previous edition

GOLDBERG, JAY M, NEUROPHYSIOLOGY. *Current Pos:* From asst prof to assoc prof physiol, 63-72, PROF PHYSIOL & NEUROBIOL, UNIV CHICAGO, 72- *Personal Data:* b Chicago, Ill, Nov 9, 35; c 4. *Educ:* Univ Chicago, AB & SB, 56, PhD(psychol), 60. *Honors & Awards:* Javits Neurosci Investr Award. *Concurrent Pos:* NSF fel, 60-62; NIH trainee, 62-63. *Mem:* Fel Acoust Soc Am; Soc Neurosci; AAAS; Barany Soc; Asn Res Otolaryngol; Am Soc Gravitation Space Biol. *Res:* Vestibular neurophysiology. *Mailing Add:* Dept Pharmacol & Physiol Sci Univ Chicago Pritzer Sch Med 947-51 E 58th St Chicago IL 60637

GOLDBERG, JOSEPH, MECHANICAL & AERONAUTICAL ENGINEERING. *Current Pos:* RETIRED. *Personal Data:* b New York, NY, Apr 30, 23; m 45; c 4. *Educ:* NY Univ, BAE, 44; Princeton Univ, MSE, 59. *Prof Exp:* Aerodynamicist, Chance-Vought Aircraft, 44; flight test engr, Wright Field Air Develop Ctr, 44-46; aerodynamicist, Fairchild Aircraft, 46-47; sr aerodynamicist, Glenn L Martin Co, 47-49; aerodyn design specialist, Naval Air Develop Ctr, 49-52; res assoc flight dynamics, Princeton Univ, 52-60; asst prof aeronaut eng, Univ Ill, 60-61; assoc prof mech eng, Drexel Inst, 61-65; assoc prof mech eng, Villanova Univ, 65- *Concurrent Pos:* Consult, Curtiss-Wright Corp, Boeing Vertol Div & Aeronaut Res Assocs, Princeton Univ, 52-60, Thiokol Chem Corp & Piasecki Aircraft, 61- *Mem:* AAAS; Am Inst Aeronaut & Astronaut; Sigma Xi; Am Soc Mech Engrs. *Res:* Flight dynamics of missiles and fixed-wing and rotary wing aircraft; automatic controls; systems dynamics. *Mailing Add:* 327 Vassar Ave Swarthmore PA 19081

GOLDBERG, JOSHUA NORMAN, PHYSICS. *Current Pos:* chmn dept, 76-83, PROF PHYSICS, SYRACUSE UNIV, 63- *Personal Data:* b Rochester, NY, May 30, 25; m 49; c 2. *Educ:* Univ Rochester, AB, 47; Syracuse Univ, MS, 50, PhD(physics), 52. *Prof Exp:* Physicist, Armour Res Found, Ill Inst Technol, 52-56 & Gen Physics Br, Aeronaut Res Lab, US Air Force, 56-63. *Concurrent Pos:* Instr, Grad Ctr, Ohio State Univ, 58-59; NSF sr fel, King's Col, Univ London, 60-61; adj assoc prof, Univ Cincinnati, 62-63; vis prof, Israel Inst Technol, Haifa, 71, Inst Henri Poincar, Paris, 83-84; Int Comt on Gen Relativity & Gravitation, 83-92. *Mem:* AAAS; Am Phys Soc; Sigma Xi; Int Soc Gen Relativity & Gravitation. *Res:* General relativity; cosmology; theoretical physics in general. *Mailing Add:* Dept Physics Syracuse Univ Syracuse NY 13244

GOLDBERG, KENNETH PHILIP, mathematics, statistics, for more information see previous edition

GOLDBERG, LAWRENCE SPENCER, QUANTUM OPTICS, LASERS. *Current Pos:* prog dir quantum electronics, waves & beams, 85-93, actg div dir, 93-94, DIV DIR, NSF, 94- *Personal Data:* b St Louis, Mo, June 11, 40; m 69, Jolande Haas; c Daniel, Elisa & Clarissa. *Educ:* Wash Univ, BS, 61; Cornell Univ, PhD(physics), 66. *Prof Exp:* Res asst solid state physics, Phys Inst, Univ Frankfurt, 66-67; res physicist, Optical Sci Div, Naval Res Lab, 67-85. *Concurrent Pos:* Vis scientist, Dept Physics, Imp Col, Univ London, 76-77; actg head, NSF, London, 89. *Mem:* Optical Soc Am; Sigma Xi; Inst Elec & Electronics Engrs. *Res:* Picosecond spectroscopy; nonlinear optics and laser physics research. *Mailing Add:* NSF Div Elec & Commun Systs 4201 Wilson Blvd Arlington VA 22230. *Fax:* 703-306-0305; *E-Mail:* lgoldber@nsf.gov

GOLDBERG, LEE DRESDEN, ENDOCRINOLOGY. *Current Pos:* co-chief endocrinol, 74-92, CHIEF ENDOCRINOL, MT SINAI HOSP, GREATER MIAMI, 92-; CLIN ASSOC PROF MED, SCH MED, UNIV MIAMI, 80- *Personal Data:* b Pt Pleasant, NJ, July 29, 37; m 67; c 3. *Educ:* Yale Univ, BS, 59; MD, 63. *Prof Exp:* Intern, Mt Sinai Hosp, New York, 63-64; resident internal med, Montefiore Hosp, New York, 64 & 66-68; USPHS fel endocrinol, Albert Einstein Col Med, 68-69; fel, Bellevue Hosp, NY Univ Med Ctr, 69-70; clin instr, Sch Med, Univ Miami, 70-71, clin asst prof, 71-80; chief internal med, S Shore Hosp, 75-79. *Concurrent Pos:* Med officer, US Navy, 64-66; teaching asst med, Sch Med, NY Univ, 69-70; assoc chmn med serv, St Francis Hosp, 77-78; pract endocrinologist, 70- *Mem:* Am Fedn Clin Res; Am Physicians Fel Med Israel; Am Diabetes Asn; Endocrine Soc; Sigma Xi; fel Am Col Physicians; fel Am Col Endocrinol. *Res:* Diabetes mellitus; treatment of type II diabetes; calcium disorders; thyroid problems. *Mailing Add:* 4302 Alton Rd Suite 550 Miami Beach FL 33140

GOLDBERG, LEONARD H, SKIN CANCER, MOHS SURGERY. *Current Pos:* ASSOC PROF DERMAT, BAYLOR COL MED, 81- *Personal Data:* b Pretoria, S Africa, Apr 27, 45; c Guy & Maya. *Educ:* Univ Pretoria, MBCB, 67; Royal Col Physicians, UK, MRCP, 72, FRCP, 88. *Prof Exp:* Res fel dermat, Stanford Univ, 76-79, surg, NY Univ 79-80. *Mem:* Am Acad Dermat; Soc Invest Dermat; Am Soc Dermat Surg; Int Soc Dermat Surg; Am Col Mohs Surg & Cutaneous Oncol. *Res:* Skin cancer, including basal cell cancer, squamous cell cancer and melanoma; effects of sunlight on the skin. *Mailing Add:* Dept Dermat Baylor Col Med One Baylor Plaza Houston TX 77030-3411

GOLDBERG, LOUIS J, NEUROSCIENCE, DENTISTRY. *Current Pos:* DEAN, SCH DENT MED, STATE UNIV NY, BUFFALO, 93- *Personal Data:* b Middletown, NY, July 20, 36; m 63, Carla; c Nathan & Marisa. *Educ:* Brooklyn Col, BA, 56; NY Univ, DDS, 60; Univ Calif, Los Angeles, PhD(anat), 68. *Honors & Awards:* Merit Award, NIH. *Prof Exp:* From asst prof to assoc prof oral biol, Sch Dent, Univ Calif, Los Angeles, 68-72, from asst prof to assoc prof anat, Sch Med, 69-72, dean res, Sch Dent, 72-79, prof oral biol & prof anat, 77-93. *Concurrent Pos:* Nat Inst Dent Res fels, NY Univ, 61-62 & Sch Dent, Univ Calif, Los Angeles, 64-68; NIH career develop award, 68-72. *Mem:* Sigma Xi; Soc Neurosci; Int Asn Dent Res. *Res:* Neurophysiological studies in oral motor control. *Mailing Add:* Sch Dent Med State Univ NY Buffalo NY 14214. *Fax:* 716-833-3517; *E-Mail:* louis_goldberg@sdm.buffalo.edu

GOLDBERG, MARK ARTHUR, PHARMACOLOGY, NEUROLOGY. *Current Pos:* assoc prof neurol & pharmacol, 71-78, CHMN DEPT NEUROL, HARBOR GEN HOSP, 78-; PROF NEUROL & PHARMACOL, UNIV CALIF, LOS ANGELES, 78- *Personal Data:* b New York, NY, Sept 4, 34; wid; c Jonathan L. *Educ:* Columbia Univ, SB, 55; Univ Chicago, PhD(pharmacol), 59, MD, 62. *Prof Exp:* Res assoc & instr pharmacol, Univ Chicago, 59-62; intern, Bronx Munic Hosp, NY, 62-63; resident neurol, Presby Hosp, 63-66; mem staff, US Army Med Res Lab, Md, 66-67; asst prof neurol, Col Physicians & Surgeons, Columbia Univ, 68-71. *Concurrent Pos:* USPHS fel, 64-66. *Mem:* Am Acad Neurol; Am Soc Neurochem; Am Neurol Asn; Soc Neuroscience. *Res:* Neuropharmacology; epilepsy; stroke; aids; neuroscience. *Mailing Add:* Dept Neurol Harbor-UCLA Med Ctr 1124 W Carson St Torrance CA 90502-2006

GOLDBERG, MARTIN, NEPHROLOGY. *Current Pos:* dean, 86-89, prof, 86-96, EMER PROF NEPHROLOGY, SCH MED, TEMPLE UNIV, 97- *Personal Data:* b Philadelphia, Pa, Sept 15, 30; m 51, 78, Marion Lindblad; c Meryl I, Karen L, Dara S & David S. *Educ:* Temple Univ, BA, 51, MD, 55. *Hon Degrees:* MS, Univ Pa, 70. *Honors & Awards:* Res Prize, Philadelphia Gen Hosp, 59; Merck, Sharp & Dohme Hon Lectr, Australasion Soc Nephrol. *Prof Exp:* Rotating intern, Philadelphia Gen Hosp, 55-56; asst resident internal med, Cleveland Clin Hosp, 56-57; resident, Philadelphia Gen Hosp, 57-58, sr resident, 58-59; from asst prof to assoc prof, Chem Sect, Sch Med, Univ Pa, 59-67, assoc prof to prof med, Renal-Electrolyte Sect, 67-79, chief sect, 66-79; prof & chmn, Dept Internal Med, Sch Med, Univ Cincinnati, 79-86. *Concurrent Pos:* NIH res career develop award, 62-70, res grant, 65-90 & training grant, 69-79; Hoechst Found res award, 66-72; Lederle Fund res award, 66-70; John Hartford Found res grant, 70-73; clin investr, Gen Clin Res Ctr, Hosp Univ Pa, 61-79, mem attend staff, 62-79; chmn coun on kidney in cardiovasc dis, Am Heart Asn; mem sci adv bd, Nat Kidney Found, 73-76; chmn nephrology subcomt, Am Bd Internal Med, 77-80; mem gov coun, Int Soc Nephrology, 79-85; prin investr, Gen Clin Res Ctr grant, NIH, Temple Univ Hosp, 86-90; chair, Sci Adv Comt, Gen Clin Res Ctr, Temple Univ Hosp, 93-; asst dean comput-assisted instr, Sch Med, Temple Univ, 97- *Mem:* AAAS; Am Soc Clin Invest; fel Am Col Physicians; Am Soc Nephrology (secy-treas, 75-78); Int Soc Nephrology; Asn Am Physicians. *Res:* Renal physiology and pathophysiology; renal pharmacology; action of diuretics; regulation of sodium excretion; renal regulation of calcium and phosphate transport; action of parathyroid hormone on the kidney; computer-assisted diagnosis and teaching. *Mailing Add:* Parkinson Bldg Fifth Floor Temple Univ Hosp Philadelphia PA 19140. *E-Mail:* v5509e@vmtemple.edu

GOLDBERG, MARTIN A, APPLIED MECHANICS. *Current Pos:* RETIRED. *Personal Data:* b New York, NY, Sept 19, 29; m 51; c 2. *Educ:* NY Univ, BAE, 51; Univ Buffalo, MS, 55; Rensselaer Polytech Inst, PhD(appl mech), 58. *Prof Exp:* Struct engr, Bell Aircraft Corp, 53-55; instr appl mech, Rensselaer Polytech Inst, 55-58; res engr, Grumman Aircraft Corp, 58-62; specialist engr, Repub Aviation Corp, 62-64; assoc prof appl mech, 64-76, assoc prof mech & aerospace eng, Polytech Inst NY, 76-; prof eng, Webb Inst Naval Archit. *Mem:* Assoc Am Soc Mech Eng; Soc Eng Sci; assoc Soc Naval Archit & Marine Eng. *Res:* Solid mechanics; applied elasticity, plates, shells and elastic stability; heat conduction. *Mailing Add:* 14 Chestnut Hill Roslyn NY 11576

GOLDBERG, MARVIN, HIGH ENERGY PHYSICS. *Current Pos:* From res asst to res assoc, Syracuse Univ, 60-66, asst prof, 66-69, assoc prof, 69-74, PROF PHYSICS, SYRACUSE UNIV, 74-, CHAIR, DEPT PHYSICS, 82-; PROG DIR, NSF, 95- *Personal Data:* b New York, NY, Sept 14, 39; m 61; c David & Philip. *Educ:* City Col New York, BS, 60; Syracuse Univ, PhD(physics), 65. *Mem:* Am Phys Soc; Sigma Xi. *Res:* Experimental study of elementary particles and their interactions, especially classification of these particles and measurement of their quantum numbers. *Mailing Add:* Dept Physics Syracuse Univ Syracuse NY 13244

GOLDBERG, MELVIN LEONARD, BIOCHEMISTRY, PATHOLOGY. *Current Pos:* DIR CLIN CHEM, FLA HOSP, 79- *Personal Data:* b Chester, Pa, June 19, 32; m 54, Estelle M Fowler; c 2. *Educ:* Calif Inst Technol, BA, 54; Univ Ill, Urbana, MA, 55; NY Univ, PhD(biochem), 62; Univ Calif, San Francisco, MD, 66; Am Bd Path, cert anat & clin path, 79, cert chem path, 82. *Prof Exp:* Intern, Sch Med, Univ Calif, San Francisco, 66-67, asst res pathologist, 67-69, asst clin prof path, 69-79, resident, 77-78. *Concurrent Pos:* NIH & Univ Calif Cancer Res Coord Comt res grants, 68-78; NIH career develop award, 71-76. *Mem:* Am Asn Pathologists; Col Am Pathologists; Am Soc Clin Pathologists. *Res:* Role of cyclic nucleotides in disease; role of essential fatty acids in atherosclerosis. *Mailing Add:* 110 Pine Needle Lane Altamonte Springs FL 32714-5814

GOLDBERG, MERRILL B, MATHEMATICS, COMPUTER SCIENCES. *Current Pos:* PROF MATH, ROCKHURST COL, MO, 73- *Personal Data:* b Minneapolis, Minn, June 14, 43; m 77; c 5. *Educ:* Univ Minn, Minneapolis, BA, 64; Univ Calif, San Diego, MA, 65, PhD(math), 69. *Prof Exp:* Specialist math, San Diego City Schs, 68-69; asst prof, Univ Colo, Boulder, 69-73. *Concurrent Pos:* Consult, Proj Unified Sci & Math for Elementary Schs, 70-75. *Mem:* Math Asn Am; Asn Comput Math. *Res:* Abstracting Lp spaces; Orlicz spaces; math analysis; math education; math economics; micro-computers and software; co-author Pascal textbook. *Mailing Add:* Dept Math Rockhurst Col 1100 Rockhurst Rd Kansas City MO 64110-2561

GOLDBERG, MICHAEL ELLIS, NEUROLOGY, NEUROPHYSIOLOGY. *Current Pos:* from asst prof to assoc prof, 76-87, PROF NEUROL, GEORGETOWN UNIV, 87- *Personal Data:* b New York, NY, Aug 10, 41; m 66; c 2. *Educ:* Harvard Col, AB, 63, MD, 68. *Honors & Awards:* S Weir Mitchell Award, Am Acad of Neurol, 72. *Prof Exp:* House officer med, Peter Bent Brigham Hosp, Boston, 68-69; staff assoc neurol, NIMH, 69-72; resident, Children's Hosp Med Ctr, Boston, 72-74; res med officer, Armed Forces Radiobiol Res Inst, 74-78. *Concurrent Pos:* Fel neurol, Harvard Univ, 72-75; vis investr, Lab Neurobiol, NIMH, 74-78; res med officer neurol, 78-81, chief, Sect Neuro-ophthal Mechanisms, Lab Sensorimotor Res, Nat Eye Inst, NIH, 81- *Mem:* Soc Neurosci; Am Acad Neurol; Asn Res Vision & Ophthal; Am Neurol Asn. *Res:* Neurophysiology of vision, eye movements, and behavior in the primates; computer methods in neurophysiology. *Mailing Add:* Lab Sensory Motor Res Bldg 49 Rm 2A50 Nat Eye Inst Bethesda MD 20892

GOLDBERG, MICHAEL IAN, TECHNICAL MANAGEMENT, MOLECULAR BIOLOGY. *Current Pos:* EXEC DIR, AM SOC MICROBIOL, 84- *Personal Data:* b New York, NY, Mar 18, 44; c 1. *Educ:* Union Col, BS, 65; Yale Univ, PhD, 70. *Honors & Awards:* Dir Award, NIH. *Prof Exp:* Teaching fel biochem & biophys, Univ Calif, San Francisco, 70-75; health scientist adminr, Nat Inst Gen Med Sci, NIH, 75-78; sr health policy analyst, Off of Secy, Dept Health & Human Serv, 78-79; exec asst to comnr policy coord, Food & Drug Admin, 79-80; br chief, Div Legis Anal, NIH, 80-81; div dir, 81-84, assoc dir, Prog Planning & Eval, 82-84. *Concurrent Pos:* Damon Runyon fel; Gianini Found fel. *Mem:* Sigma Xi; Am Chem Soc; AAAS. *Mailing Add:* 7508 Hampden Lane Bethesda MD 20814-1332

GOLDBERG, MORTON EDWARD, PHARMACOLOGY. *Current Pos:* CONSULT, DRUG DISCOVERY & DEVELOP, 92- *Personal Data:* b Philadelphia, Pa, July 11, 32; m 54, Janet Werlin; c Shellie, Ellen & David. *Educ:* Philadelphia Col Pharm, BS, 54, MS, 55, DSc, 58. *Prof Exp:* Sr res pharmacologist, Abbott Labs, 58-60; res fel, Mellon Inst, 60-63, sr fel, 64; sr pharmacologist, Union Carbide Corp, 65-67, from asst dir to dir pharmacol, 67-69; head, Gen Pharmacol Sect, Warner Lambert Res Inst, 69-71, dir pharmacodynamics, 71-73; dir pharmacol, Squibb Inst Med Res, 73-77; dir, Stuart Pharmaceut, ICI Americas Inc, 77-81, vpres biomed res, 81-84, vpres res, develop & regulatory affairs, 84-92; prof pharmacol, Univ Pa Sch Med, 92-96. *Concurrent Pos:* Adj prof pharmacol, Med Col Pa, 78-; adj prof toxicol, Philadelphia Col Pharm, 82-; adj prof pharmacol, Univ Pa Sch Med, 96- *Mem:* Fel AAAS; fel NY Acad Sci; Am Pharmaceut Asn; Am Soc Pharmacol & Exp Therapeut; Soc Toxicol; Col Int Neuropsychopharmacol. *Res:* Central nervous system and behavioral pharmacology; neuropharmacology; neurochemistry; general drug development activities. *Mailing Add:* 715 Severn Rd Wilmington DE 19803-1725. *Fax:* 302-478-4068

GOLDBERG, MORTON FALK, MEDICINE, OPHTHALMOLOGY. *Current Pos:* WILLIAM HOLLAND WILMER PROF & DIR WILMER EYE INST, JOHNS HOPKINS MED INST & CHMN DEPT OPHTHAL, JOHNS HOPKINS, 89- *Personal Data:* b Lawrence, Mass, June 8, 37; m 68. *Educ:* Harvard Univ, AB, 58, MD, 62; Am Bd Ophthal, dipl, 68. *Honors & Awards:* Sr Hon Award, Am Acad Ophthal, 85; Alcon Res Inst Prize. *Prof Exp:* Intern med, Peter Bent Brigham Hosp, 62-63; resident ophthal, Johns Hopkins Hosp, 63-67; asst prof, Med Sch, Yale Univ, 67-69; pres, Univ Ill Hosp Med Staff, 81-83, prof ophthal & head dept, Col Med, Univ Ill & ophthalmologist-in-chief, Univ Hosp & Eye & Ear Infirmary, 70-89, pres, Univ Ill Hosp Med staff, 81-83. *Concurrent Pos:* Fel ophthal, Johns Hopkins Hosp, 63-67; fel genetics, 69; prog dir, Nat Eye Inst training grants, 70; consult, Vet Admin Hosp, Chicago, 70-; Macy Found Fac Scholar Award, 79-80; vis prof, Pac Med Ctr, San Francisco & Mayo Clin, Rochester, Minn, 79; ed-in-chief, Arch Ophthal, 84-94. *Mem:* Am Ophthal Soc; Asn Res Vision & Ophthal; Am Acad Ophthal & Otolaryngol; Retina Soc; Macula Soc; hon fel Royal Australian Col Ophthal. *Res:* Retinopathies; ocular genetics; diabetes mellitus; sickle cell retinopathy; ocular trauma; laser photocoagulation; retinal and vitreous surgery. *Mailing Add:* Johns Hopkins Med Insts Wilmer Eye Inst 600 N Wolfe St Baltimore MD 21205-2104

GOLDBERG, NELSON D, BIOCHEMISTRY. *Current Pos:* From instr to prof pharmacol, 64-86, PROF PATH, MED SCH, UNIV MINN, MINNEAPOLIS, 73-, PROF BIOCHEM, 87- *Personal Data:* b Cleveland, Ohio, June 22, 31; m 58, Marjorie Vogel; c Daniel & Peter. *Educ:* Univ Toledo, BS, 53; Univ Wis, PhD(pharmacol), 63. *Hon Degrees:* DSc, Univ Toledo, 81. *Concurrent Pos:* NIH fel, Wash Univ, 62-64; Pfizer traveling fel, 78. *Mem:* Am Soc Neurochem; Am Soc Biochem & Molecular Biol; Am Chem Soc; Biophys Soc. *Res:* Regulation of cellular metabolism and function: excitation/contraction coupling, excitation/secretion coupling, phototransduction, adenine and guanine nucleotide metabolism. *Mailing Add:* Univ Minn 435 Delaware St, SE Minneapolis MN 55455. *Fax:* 612-625-2163

GOLDBERG, NORMAN, PHYSICS. *Current Pos:* PHYSICIST, UNIVAC DIV, SPERRY RAND CORP, 59- *Personal Data:* b Philadelphia, Pa, Aug 5, 21; m 63; c 3. *Educ:* Pa State Teachers Col, West Chester, BS, 43; Univ Pa, MS, 48, PhD(physics), 54. *Prof Exp:* Res assoc, Wash Univ, 54-56; asst prof physics, Univ Pa, 56-59. *Mem:* Am Phys Soc; Inst Elec & Electronics Engrs; Optical Soc Am. *Res:* Nuclear physics; magnetism; thin films; magnetooptics; fiber optics. *Mailing Add:* 1580 Tralee Dr Dresher PA 19025

GOLDBERG, PAULA BURSZTYN, CARDIOVASCULAR RESEARCH. *Current Pos:* ASSOC SR INVESTR CLIN RES & DEVELOP, SMITHKLINE FRENCH LABS, 85- *Personal Data:* b Siedlce, Poland, Jan 9, 38. *Educ:* State Univ NY, PhD(pharmacol), 68. *Prof Exp:* From asst prof to assoc prof pharmacol, Med Col Pa, 72-85. *Concurrent Pos:* Vis assoc prof, Med Col Pa, 86- *Mem:* Am Soc Pharmacol & Exp Therapeut; Geront Soc Am; NY Acad Sci; Sigma Xi; Soc Exp Biol & Med. *Mailing Add:* US Regulatory Affairs Smith Kline Beecham Pharmaceut Philadelphia PA 19130-4095. *Fax:* 215-751-4096

GOLDBERG, R J, CARDIOVASCULAR EPIDEMIOLOGY, EPIDEMIOLOGIC METHODOLOGY. *Current Pos:* asst prof, 81-85, ASSOC PROF EPIDEMIOL, UNIV MASS MED SCH, 85- *Personal Data:* b Lowell, Mass, Mar 20, 50; m 78; c 2. *Educ:* Univ Mass, BS, 72; Tufts Univ, MSPH, 73; Johns Hopkins Univ Sch Hyg & Pub Health, PhD(epidemiol), 78. *Prof Exp:* Fel epidemiol, Johns Hopkins Univ Sch Hyg & Pub Health, 78-79; asst prof pub health, Ohio State Univ Sch Med, 79-81. *Mem:* Soc Epidemiol Res; Am Pub Health Asn; Int Epidemiol Asn; Am Heart Asn; Europ Soc Prev Cardiol; Am Col Epidemiol. *Res:* Cardiovascular epidemiology; primary and secondary prevention of coronary heart disease; epidemiologic methodology. *Mailing Add:* Dept Med Univ Mass Med Sch Worcester MA 01655

GOLDBERG, RICHARD ARAN, ATMOSPHERIC PHYSICS. *Current Pos:* Nat Acad Sci-Nat Res Coun resident res assoc, 63-64, physicist, 64-89, prog dir solar terristrial res 89-91, SR SCIENTIST GODDARD SPACE FLIGHT CTR NASA, 91- *Personal Data:* b Boston, Mass, Jan 6, 36; m 65, Paula R Erlick; c Lisa. *Educ:* Rensselaer Polytech Inst, BS, 57; Pa State Univ, PhD(physics), 63. *Concurrent Pos:* Adj prof, Pa State Univ, 95-; chmn middle atmospheric electrodynamics working group, IAGA; regional ed, J Atmospheric & Solar Terrestrial Physics. *Mem:* AAAS; Am Phys Soc; Am Geophys Union; Am Meteorol Soc; Sigma Xi. *Res:* Sounding rocket studies of the upper atmosphere with mass spectrometry, in-situ probes, radio propagation techniques; energentic particles and x-rays mesospheric and stratospheric aeronomy; solar-terrestrial relationships; middle atmospheric electrodynamics and dynamics. *Mailing Add:* 1020 Kathryn Rd Silver Spring MD 20904. *Fax:* 301-286-1648; *E-Mail:* nssdca@gsfc.nasa.gov

GOLDBERG, RICHARD ROBINSON, MATHEMATICS. *Current Pos:* PROF MATH & CHMN DEPT, VANDERBILT UNIV, 76- *Personal Data:* b Chicago, Ill, Sept 6, 31; m 53; c 4. *Educ:* Northwestern Univ, BS, 51; Harvard Univ, AM, 52, PhD(math), 56. *Prof Exp:* From instr to prof, Northwestern Univ, 57-68; prof math, Univ Iowa, 68-76, chmn dept, 70-76. *Concurrent Pos:* Managing ed, Proceedings Am Math Soc. *Mem:* Am Math Soc; Math Asn Am; Soc Indust & Appl Math. *Res:* Fourier analysis; integral transforms. *Mailing Add:* Vanderbilt Univ 1326 Stevenson Ctr Nashville TN 37240-0001

GOLDBERG, ROBERT JACK, ZOOLOGY. *Current Pos:* prof biol, 64-77, vpres acad affairs & dean fac, 64-77, EMER PROF BIOL, NORTHEASTERN ILL UNIV, 77- *Personal Data:* b Denver, Colo, May 22, 14; m 40; c 3. *Educ:* Univ Ill, AB, 37; Ill Inst Technol, PhD(biol), 54. *Prof Exp:* Instr biol, Chicago City Jr Col, 41-54; assoc, Chicago Teachers Col, 54-59, prof, 59-64, dean grad studies, 62-64. *Mem:* Genetics Soc Am; Soc Study Evolution; Soc Syst Zool; Sigma Xi. *Res:* Taxonomy and speciation of Gastrotrichia. *Mailing Add:* 211 Elgin Apt 4C Forest Park IL 60130-1350

GOLDBERG, ROBERT NATHAN, PHYSICAL CHEMISTRY. *Current Pos:* CHEMIST, NAT INST STANDARDS TECHNOL, 69- *Personal Data:* b Stamford, Conn, Dec 11, 43. *Educ:* Johns Hopkins Univ, BA, 65; Carnegie-Mellon Univ, PhD(chem), 68. *Prof Exp:* Asst, Carnegie-Mellon Univ, 65-68, fel electrolyte solutions, Mellon Inst, 68-69. *Concurrent Pos:* Guest mem staff, Univ Newcastle, Tyne, Eng, 80. *Mem:* Am Chem Soc; Am Inst Chemists; Calorimetry Conf; Int Union Pure & Appl Chem. *Res:* Chemical thermodynamics and its applications to biochemistry and electrolyte solutions; microcalorimetry; solution calorimetry; thermodynamic data evaluation. *Mailing Add:* 21404 Davis Mill Rd Germantown MD 20876. *Fax:* 301-975-2128; *E-Mail:* goldber@tiber.nist.gov

GOLDBERG, SABINE RUTH, SOIL CHEMISTRY, ENVIRONMENTAL CHEMISTRY. *Current Pos:* SOIL SCIENTIST, US SALINITY LAB, AGR RES SERV, USDA, RIVERSIDE, CALIF, 83- *Personal Data:* b Erlangen, Ger, Mar 25, 58; US citizen; m 80, Gary; c Daniel & Matthew. *Educ:* Univ Fla, BSA, 77; Univ Calif, Riverside, PhD(soil sci), 83. *Prof Exp:* Res asst, Dept Soil Sci, Univ Calif, Riverside, 78-83, grad regents fel, 80-82. *Mem:* Soil Sci Soc Am; Am Chem Soc; Am Geophys Union; Clay Minerals Soc; Am Soc Agron. *Res:* Inorganic anion adsorption reactions on oxide minerals, clay minerals and soil materials; chemical modeling of anion adsorption reactions using chemical surface complexation models; chemical factors affecting soil structural stability. *Mailing Add:* US Salinity Lab Agr Res Serv USDA 450 W Big Springs Rd Riverside CA 92507

GOLDBERG, SAMUEL, MATHEMATICAL PROBABILITY. *Current Pos:* from asst prof to prof, 53-85, EMER PROF MATH, OBERLIN COL, 85- *Personal Data:* b New York, NY, Mar 14, 25; m 53, Marcia Chinitz; c David. *Educ:* City Col New York, BS, 44; Cornell Univ, PhD(math), 50. *Prof Exp:* From instr to asst prof math, Lehigh Univ, 50-53. *Concurrent Pos:* Vis assoc prof, Grad Sch Bus Admin, Harvard Univ, 59-60; prog officer, Alfred P Sloan Found, 85-91. *Mem:* Math Asn Am; Sigma Xi; Am Math Soc. *Res:* Mathematical theory of probability; mathematical models in the social sciences. *Mailing Add:* 383 Elm St Oberlin OH 44074-1404. *E-Mail:* samuel.goldberg@oberlin.edu

GOLDBERG, SAMUEL I, MATHEMATICS. *Current Pos:* vis assoc prof, 60-61, assoc prof, 61-65, PROF MATH, UNIV ILL, URBANA, 65- *Personal Data:* b Toronto, Ont, Aug 15, 23; nat US; m 53; c 3. *Educ:* Univ Toronto, BA, 48, MA, 49, PhD, 51. *Prof Exp:* Sci officer, Defence Res Bd, Ottawa, 51-52; asst prof math, Lehigh Univ, 52-55; assoc prof, Wayne State Univ, 55-61. *Concurrent Pos:* Res fel, Harvard Univ, 59-60; consult, Avco Corp, 63-66; NSF grant, 64-; on sabbatical, Univ Calif, Berkeley, 66-67 & Israel Inst Technol, 71-72, 79; vis prof, Univ Toronto, 68, Cambridge Univ & Col de France, 79, Queens Univ & Univ Lecce, 87; ed-at-large, Marcel Dekker, Inc, 69- & Tensor J, 74-; Sci Res Coun vis foreign scientist, Univ Liverpool, 73; Lady Davis fel, Israel Inst Technol, 79; adj prof, Queen's Univ, 81- & Queen's Quest Prof, 81; at Ctr Advan Study, Univ Ill, 83-84. *Mem:* Am Math Soc. *Res:* Differential geometry; topology; analysis. *Mailing Add:* Univ Ill 273 A T Geld Hall 1409 W Green Urbana IL 61801-2917

GOLDBERG, SEYMOUR, MATHEMATICS. *Current Pos:* assoc prof, 62-67, PROF MATH, UNIV MD, 67- *Personal Data:* b Brooklyn, NY, Mar 24, 28; m 52; c 2. *Educ:* Hunter Col, AB, 50; Ohio State Univ, MA, 52; Univ Calif, Los Angeles, PhD(math), 58. *Prof Exp:* Asst math, Ohio State Univ, 50-52; math analyst, Lockheed Aircraft Corp, 52-54; asst math, Univ Calif, Los Angeles, 54-58; Brown fel, Hebrew Univ, Israel, 58-59; asst prof math, NMex State Univ, 59-62. *Mem:* Am Math Soc; Math Asn Am. *Res:* Functional analysis, particularly theory of linear operators on a normed linear space. *Mailing Add:* Dept Math Univ Md College Park MD 20742-0001

GOLDBERG, SEYMOUR, electrical engineering, electronics, for more information see previous edition

GOLDBERG, SHELDON SUMNER, otorhinolaryngology, head & neck surgery; deceased, see previous edition for last biography

GOLDBERG, STANLEY, PHYSICS, HISTORY OF PHYSICS. *Current Pos:* STAFF MEM, SMITHSONIAN INST, 85- *Personal Data:* b Cleveland, Ohio, Aug 4, 34; div; c 3. *Educ:* Antioch Col, BS, 60; Harvard Univ, AMT, 61, PhD(educ), 69. *Prof Exp:* Asst prof hist sci, Antioch Col, 65-71; assoc prof, Hampshire Col, 71-79, prof hist sci, 79-85. *Concurrent Pos:* Sr lectr, Sci Educ Ctr, Univ Zambia, 68-70. *Mem:* AAAS; Hist Sci Asn. *Res:* History of physics of the 19th and 20th century, especially electrodynamics; science education for non-scientists in high school and college. *Mailing Add:* 508 Third St SE Washington DC 20003

GOLDBERG, STANLEY IRWIN, BIO-ORGANIC CHEMISTRY, ORGANIC CHEMISTRY. *Current Pos:* PROF CHEM, UNIV NEW ORLEANS, 71- *Personal Data:* b New York, NY, Apr 12, 30; m 83, Irene Prechter; c Andrew S, Beth & Adam A. *Educ:* Univ Md, BS, 53; Ind Univ, PhD, 58. *Honors & Awards:* Matheson, Coleman & Bell Award, 71. *Prof Exp:* Res assoc & instr chem, Univ Ill, 59-60; from asst prof to assoc prof chem, Univ SC, 60-71. *Concurrent Pos:* Vis prof, Univ Bristol, 69-70. *Mem:* Am Chem Soc; Royal Soc Chem; Int Soc Study Orgn Life. *Res:* Origins of the configurationally one-sidedness of life; general organic stereochemistry. *Mailing Add:* Dept Chem Univ New Orleans New Orleans LA 70148. *Fax:* 504-286-6860

GOLDBERG, STEPHEN, NEUROANATOMY, NEUROEMBRYOLOGY. *Current Pos:* asst prof anat & family med, 75-79, ASSOC PROF ANAT, SCH MED, UNIV MIAMI, 80- *Personal Data:* b Brooklyn, NY, Dec 20, 42; m 67; c 4. *Educ:* Yeshiva Col, BA, 63; Albert Einstein Col Med, MD, 67. *Prof Exp:* Intern, Montefiore Hosp, Bronx, NY, 67-68; surgeon neurol, Staten Island USPHS Hosp, 68-70; resident ophthal, NY Med Col, 71-75, asst, 73-75. *Concurrent Pos:* Guest researcher, Nat Eye Inst, NIH, 70-71; dir, Ambulatory Care Unit, Jackson Mem Hosp, 78; prin investr grants, NIH, 79-82. *Mem:* Int Soc Develop Neurosci; Am Asn Anatomists; Asn Res Vision & Ophthal; AAAS; Soc Neurosci. *Res:* Mechanisms of development, regeneration, and degeneration of the nervous system with special emphasis on the visual system. *Mailing Add:* Dept Anat R124 Univ Miami Sch Med 1600 NW 10th Ave Miami FL 33136-1015

GOLDBERG, STEPHEN ROBERT, ZOOLOGY. *Current Pos:* From asst prof to assoc prof, 70-83, PROF BIOL, WHITTIER COL, 83- *Personal Data:* b New York, NY, Mar 4, 41, m; c 1. *Educ:* Boston Univ, BA, 62; Univ Ariz, MS, 65, PhD(zool), 70. *Concurrent Pos:* Res assoc herpet, Los Angeles County Natural Hist Mus, 76- *Mem:* Am Soc Parasitol; Helm Soc Wash; Am Inst Biol Sci; Am Soc Ichthyologists & Herpetologists; Soc Study Amphibians & Reptiles; Wildlife Dis Asn; Herpetologist's League; Entom Soc Am. *Res:* Herpetology; vertebrate reproductive cycles; comparative pathology; parasitology; entomology. *Mailing Add:* Dept Biol Whittier Col Whittier CA 90608

GOLDBERG, STEPHEN Z, INORGANIC CHEMISTRY, STRUCTURAL CHEMISTRY. *Current Pos:* PROF, ADELPHI UNIV, 86- *Personal Data:* b Brooklyn, NY, May 26, 47. *Educ:* Cornell Univ, AB, 68; Univ Calif, Berkeley, PhD(chem), 73. *Prof Exp:* Instr & fel, Univ Rochester, 73-75; asst prof, 75-80, assoc prof chem, Adelphi Univ, 80-86, vis scientist, Weizmann Inst, 82-83. *Concurrent Pos:* Vis scientist, Technion, 89-90. *Mem:* NY Acad Sci; Am Crystallog Asn; Am Chem Soc; AAAS. *Res:* Computer programming, synthetic and structural studies of transition metal compounds and complexes; structural studies of drug compounds. *Mailing Add:* Dept of Chem Adelphi Univ Garden City NY 11530. *Fax:* 516-877-3674; *E-Mail:* goldberg@sable.adelphi.edu

GOLDBERG, STEVEN R, PHARMACOLOGY. *Current Pos:* ASSOC PROF, DEPT PHARMACOL & EXP THERAPEUT, SCH MED, UNIV MD, 81- *Personal Data:* b Boston, Mass, July 5, 41. *Educ:* Northeastern Univ, BA, 64; Univ Mich, DPhil, 69. *Prof Exp:* NIH fel, Dept Psychol & Lab Organismic & Quant & Biol, Univ Miami, Coral Gables, 69; res fel pharmacol & psychobiol, Harvard Med Sch, Boston, 70-73, from instr to asst prof, Dept Psychiat, 73-80; pharmacologist, Lexington, Ky, 79-81, Nat Inst Drug Abuse, Addiction Res Ctr, Baltimore, Md, 81-; chief, Behav Pharmacol & Genetics Lab & Preclin Pharmacol Br, 84- *Concurrent Pos:* Assoc scientist, New Eng Regional Primate Res Ctr, 73-80; actg chief, Neuropsychopharmacol Lab, Nat Inst Drug Abuse, Addiction Res Ctr, 86-87. *Mem:* Am Soc Pharmacol & Exp Therapeut; AAAS; Behav Pharmacol Soc; NY Acad Sci. *Res:* Pharmacology; author of numerous scientific publications. *Mailing Add:* NIDA Addiction Res Ctr PO Box 5180 Baltimore MD 21224-0180. *Fax:* 410-550-1645

GOLDBERG, VLADISLAV V, GEOMETRY. *Current Pos:* prof, 81-85, DISTINGUISHED PROF MATH, NJ INST TECHNOL, 85- *Personal Data:* b Moscow, USSR, Jan 4, 36; US citizen; m 58, Ludmila Pikuleva; c Andrew & ILya. *Educ:* Moscow State Univ, BS, 56, MS, 58, PhD(math), 61. *Honors & Awards:* Harlan J Perlis Award Excellence Res, NJ Inst Technol, 85. *Prof Exp:* Sr sci ed, Pub House MIR, Moscow, 61; Assoc prof math, Yaroslavl' State Pedagogical Inst, USSR, 61-64; prof, Inst Steel & Alloys, Moscow, 64-78; vis prof, Lehigh Univ, 79-81. *Concurrent Pos:* Sr sci consult, Metall Lab, Inst Steel & Alloys, Moscow, 68-78; prin invest geom grant, NSF, 80-82; vis prof, Univ Waterloo, 80, Univ Stuttgart, WGer, 82, Univ Messina, Italy, 86; corresp mem, Academia Peloritana, Messina, Italy, 83-; co-chmn, web geom session, Math Res Inst, Oberwolfach, WGer, 84 & 92; vis mem, Math Sci Res Inst, Berkeley, 85 & Math Res Inst, Oberwolfach, Ger, 91, 92 & 94; sr res fel, Cath Univ, Leuven, Belg, 97. *Mem:* Am Math Soc; Tensor Soc Japan. *Res:* Projective differential geometry, conformal differential geometry and web geometry; linear algebra, tensor calculus and engineering mathematics; mathematical education; author of 11 books and more than 80 science papers. *Mailing Add:* Dept Math NJ Inst Technol Newark NJ 07102. *Fax:* 973-596-6467; *E-Mail:* vlgold@numerics.njit.edu

GOLDBERG, WALTER M, CORAL BIOLOGY, ENVIRONMENTAL IMPACTS. *Current Pos:* from asst prof to assoc prof, 73-88, PROF ZOOL, FLA INT UNIV, 88-, CHAIR BIOL SCI, 88- *Personal Data:* b Mass, Jan 9, 46; m 71; c 2. *Educ:* Am Univ, BS, 68; Fla Atlantic Univ, MS, 70; Univ Miami, PhD(marine biol), 73. *Prof Exp:* Postdoctoral biochem, Papanicolaou Cancer Res Inst, 73. *Mem:* Western Soc Naturalists; AAAS. *Res:* Coelenterate biology; ecology, biochemistry, histology and ultrastructure of corals; community structure, effects of nearshore construction on, effects of beach restoration and sedimentation on reefs. *Mailing Add:* Fla Int Univ 1 FIU South Campus Miami FL 33199-0001

GOLDBERGER, AMY, CHROMATIN BIOCHEMISTRY, HEMATOPOIETIC DIFFERENTIATION. *Current Pos:* INSTR CELL BIOL, UNIV MASS SCH MED, 87- *Personal Data:* b Memphis, Tenn, Aug 15, 57. *Educ:* Univ Tenn, BA, 79; Vanderbilt Univ, PhD(biochem), 83. *Prof Exp:* Fel, dept biochem & molecular biol, Mayo Clin, 84-87. *Mem:* Sigma Xi; Am Soc Cell Biol. *Res:* The role of chromatin proteins in gene expression, using hematopoietic differentiation and steroid hormone action as model systems. *Mailing Add:* Collab Biomed Proc Inc 2 Oak Park Bedford MA 01730-1495. *Fax:* 781-275-0043

GOLDBERGER, MARVIN LEONARD, THEORETICAL HIGH ENERGY PHYSICS. *Current Pos:* PROF PHYSICS, UNIV CALIF, LOS ANGELES, 91-, DEAN, DIV NATURAL SCI, 94- *Personal Data:* b Chicago, Ill, Oct 22, 22; m 45, Mildred Ginsburg; c Samuel & Joel. *Educ:* Carnegie Inst Technol, BS, 43; Univ Chicago, PhD(physics), 48. *Hon Degrees:* DSc, Carnegie-Mellon Univ & Univ Notre Dame, 79, Brandeis Univ, 91; DHL, Hebrew Union Col, 80, & Univ Judaism, 82; LLD, Occidental Col, 80. *Honors & Awards:* Dannie Heineman Prize, 61; Presidential Award, NY Acad Sci, 81; Leonard I Beerman Peace & Justice Award, 87. *Prof Exp:* Physicist, Radiation Lab, Univ Calif, 48-49; res assoc physics, Mass Inst Technol, 49-50; from asst prof to prof, Univ Chicago, 50-57; Higgins prof math physics, Princeton Univ, 57-77, chmn dept, 70-76, Joseph Henry prof physics, 77-78; pres, Calif Inst Tech, 78-87; dir, Inst Advan Studies, Princeton, NJ, 87-91. *Concurrent Pos:* Higgins vis assoc prof, 53-54; mem, President's Sci Adv Comt, 65-69; chmn, Nat Acad Sci Comt Int Security & Arms Control, 80-86, mem, 87-93; Super Collider Site Eval Comt, Nat Acads Sci & Eng, 87; mem, Adv Coun, Plasma Physics Lab, Princeton Univ, 87-; co-chair, Comt Study Res Doctorate Progs US, Nat Acad Sci, 91-95. *Mem:* Nat Acad Sci; fel Am Phys Soc; fel Am Acad Arts & Sci; Am Philos Soc. *Mailing Add:* Dept Physics Univ Calif 9500 Gilman Dr Los Angeles CA 90024

GOLDBERGER, MICHAEL ERIC, experimental neurology; deceased, see previous edition for last biography

GOLDBERGER, ROBERT FRANK, BIOCHEMISTRY. *Current Pos:* vpres health sci, 81-83, provost, 81-89, PROF BIOCHEM & MOLECULAR BIOPHYS, COLUMBIA UNIV, 81- *Personal Data:* b New York, NY, June 2, 33; m 58, Marianne Rudolf; c Malka, Erica & Laura. *Educ:* Harvard Univ, AB, 54; NY Univ, MD, 58. *Prof Exp:* Intern, Mt Sinai Hosp, New York, 58-59; trainee, Inst Enzyme Res, Univ Wis, 59-61; vis scientist, Weizmann Inst, 63; med officer & biochemist, Lab Chem Biol, Nat Inst Arthritis, Metab & Digestive & Kidney Dis, 63-66, chief Biosynthesis & Control Sect, 66-73, actg chief, Lab Chem Biol, 69-70, chief, Lab Biochem, Nat Cancer Inst, 73-79; dep dir sci, NIH, 79-81. *Mem:* Am Fedn Clin; Am Soc Biol Chemists; Am Soc Cell Biol; Am Soc Microbiol; Biophys Soc. *Res:* Protein chemistry; biochemical genetics and evolution; biological regulatory mechanisms; enzyme induction and repression; mechanism of action of steroid hormones; structure of the eukaryotic genome. *Mailing Add:* 4601 Fieldston Rd Riverdale NY 10471-3313

GOLDBERGER, W(ILLIAM) M(ORGAN), CHEMICAL ENGINEERING, METALLURGY. *Current Pos:* sr chem engr, 60-65, chief, Div Minerals & Metall Processing, 65-77, SR RES LEADER, COLUMBUS DIV, BATTELLE MEM INST, 77-, MEM RES COUN, 78-; dir res & develop, 79-89, VPRES RES, SUPER GRAPHITE CO, 89- *Personal Data:* b Perth Amboy, NJ, Dec 26, 28; m 56, Marcia Ginsberg; c Adam, Jesse, Jo & Eli. *Educ:* Ga Inst Technol, BChE, 50; Polytech Inst Brooklyn, MS, 56, PhD(chem eng), 61. *Prof Exp:* Res engr, Appl Res Labs, US Steel Corp, 56-57; instr chem eng, Stevens Inst Technol, 59-60. *Mem:* Am Inst Chem Engrs; Am Inst Mining, Metall & Petrol Engrs; Am Ceramic Soc; Am Carbon Soc. *Res:* High and ultra-high temperature chemical process development; development of new processing for separating and purifying chemical compounds; mineral processing and assessment of mineral resources and methods for recovery; carbon/graphite production technology. *Mailing Add:* 2175 E Broad St Columbus OH 43209

GOLDBLATT, IRWIN LEONARD, TRIBOLOGY, CHEMICAL ENGINEERING. *Current Pos:* CHEMIST TRIBOLOGY & COMBUSTION SCI, CASTROL INC, 87- *Personal Data:* b Bronx, NY, Jan 22, 40; m 62; c 3. *Educ:* City Col New York, BChE, 62; Brandeis Univ, MA, 67, PhD(chem), 73. *Honors & Awards:* W D Hudson Mem Award, Am Soc Lubrication Eng, 74. *Prof Exp:* Chemist, Polaroid Corp, 62-64; chemist tribology & combustion sci, Exxon Corp, 68-86. *Concurrent Pos:* Consult, Sanders Assocs, 64-68. *Mem:* Am Chem Soc; Am Soc Lubrication Eng; Am Soc Mech Engrs; Am Soc Testing & Mat. *Res:* Study of the interactions between lubricant base stock, additives and metal in order to derive an understanding of how to control wear; combustion research in internal combustion engines; polymer grafting; analytical chemistry; mechanical engineering. *Mailing Add:* 8 Celler Rd Edison NJ 08817

GOLDBLATT, PETER, SYSTEMATIC BOTANY. *Current Pos:* res botanist, 72-74, B A KRUKOFF CUR AFRICAN BOT, MO BOT GARDEN, 74- *Personal Data:* b Johannesburg, SAfrica, Oct 8, 43; US citizen. *Educ:* Univ Witwatersrand, BSc, 65, BSc Hons, 66; Univ Cape Town, PhD(bot), 70. *Prof Exp:* Jr lectr bot, Univ Cape Town, 68-72. *Mem:* SAfrican Asn Botanists; Am Soc Plant Taxonomists; Int Asn Plant Taxonomists. *Res:* Systematics and evolution of Iridaceae; cytology of angiosperms in relation to phylogeny; African flora, especially floristics of southern Africa and the Cape region. *Mailing Add:* 7058 Waterman Ave St Louis MO 63130

GOLDBLATT, PETER JEROME, PATHOLOGY. *Current Pos:* PROF & CHMN, DEPT PATH, MED COL OHIO, TOLEDO, 79- *Educ:* Case Western Reserve Univ, AB, 55, MD, 59; Am Bd Path, dipl anat. *Prof Exp:* From instr to asst prof, Dept Path, Sch Med, Univ Pittsburgh, 64-69; assoc prof, Univ Conn, 69-77; prof, Sch Med, Univ Md, 77-79. *Concurrent Pos:* Mem staff, Univ-McCook Hosp, Hartford, Conn, 70-74; mem, Conn Cancer Epidemiol Coun, 73-75; asst med examr, State Conn, 76-77; assoc chmn educ, Dept Path, Sch Med, Univ Md, 77-79; pres, Northwest Ohio Med Mgt, Inc, 84-; consult. *Mem:* Am Soc Clin Pathologists; AAAS; Electron Micros Soc Am; Col Am Pathologists; Am Asn Pathologists; Am Asn Cancer Res; AMA; Am Soc Cytol; Asn Clin Scientists; Soc Toxicol Pathologists. *Res:* Pathology; author of numerous scientific publications. *Mailing Add:* Dept Path Med Col Ohio PO Box 10008 Toledo OH 43699-0008. *Fax:* 419-381-3066

GOLDBLITH, SAMUEL ABRAHAM, FOOD SCIENCE. *Current Pos:* res assoc food sci, Mass Inst Technol, 49-52, asst prof, 52-55, assoc prof & exec officer dept, 55-59, from actg head to assoc head dept nutrit & food sci, 59-74, prof, 59-72, dir indust liaison, 74-78, Underwood-Prescott prof food sci, 72-78, prof food sci & vpres resource develop, 78-86, prof & sr adv to pres, 86-91, EMER PROF, MASS INST TECHNOL, 91- *Personal Data:* b Lawrence, Mass, May 5, 19; wid; c Judith A & Jonathan M. *Educ:* Mass Inst Technol, SB, 40, SM, 47, PhD, 49. *Honors & Awards:* Monsanto Award, Inst Food Technol, 53; Babcock-Hart Award, 69; Nicholas Appert Award, 70; Distinguished Food Scientist Award, 69 & 76. *Prof Exp:* Mem staff, Arthur D Little, Inc, 40-41. *Concurrent Pos:* Tech aide comt radiation preservation food, Nat Acad Sci-Nat Res Coun, 53-56, mem comt radiation preservation food, 59-63 & 71-73, chmn, 63-79, mem ad hoc subcomt high level dosimetry, 56-59, ad hoc subcomt radionuclides in foods, food protection comt, 60-61, comt nutrit, 60-62, gen comt foods, 63-71, US adv comt foot-and-mouth dis, 62-71 & gen comt, Dept Defense Food Prog, 70-, chmn task group feeding study protocol, 70-; mem Am Inst Biol Sci adv comt radiation pasteurization of foods to AEC, 60-62 & 65-70; mem Nat Pub Health Serv comt, Surgeon Gen, US, 61; officer US AEC team to Japan, Conf Radioisotopes, 61, 64, 66 & 67; mem sci adv coun, Refrig Res Found, 70-73; fel, Inst Food Sci & Technol, UK, 74; mem, Order Of Sacred Treasure, Japan, 84. *Mem:* Am Chem Soc; fel Inst Food Technol; fel AAAS; foreign mem Royal Swedish Acad Eng Sci; foreign mem Swiss Acad Eng Sci. *Res:* Radiation preservation of foods; freeze dehydration of foods; microwaves and their application in food processing; food technol. *Mailing Add:* E38-510 Mass Inst Technol Cambridge MA 02139. *Fax:* 781-665-9578

GOLDBLOOM, DAVID ELLIS, NUTRITION, BIOCHEMISTRY. *Current Pos:* asst prof nutrit, 68-74, ASSOC PROF HOME ECON, CALIF STATE UNIV, FRESNO, 74- *Personal Data:* b London, Eng, 1933; US citizen. *Educ:* Cambridge Univ, BA, 55, MA, 61; Univ Calif, Berkeley, PhD(nutrit), 68. *Prof Exp:* Res asst biochem, Unilever Food Res Labs, Eng, 58-60; asst mkt res, F W Berk Chem Co, London, 61; chemist qual control, Watney's Brewery, 61-62. *Res:* Comparative biochemistry of heme proteins. *Mailing Add:* Dept Food Sci Calif State Univ Fresno 5200 N Campus Dr Fresno CA 93740-8017

GOLDBLOOM, RICHARD B, PEDIATRICS. *Current Pos:* physician-in-chief & dept head, Izaak Walton Killam Hosp for Children, 67-85, PROF PEDIAT, DALHOUSIE UNIV, 67- *Personal Data:* b Montreal, Que, Dec 16, 24; m 46, Ruth M Schwartz; c Alan L, Barbara (Hughes) & David S. *Educ:* McGill Univ, BSc, 45, MD, CM, 49; FRCP(C), 55. *Hon Degrees:* DLitt, Univ col Cape Breton. *Prof Exp:* Asst prof pediat, Fac Med, McGill Univ, 62-67. *Concurrent Pos:* Lederle med fac award, 62; assoc physician, Montreal Children's Hosp, 62-67; dir, Atlantic Res Ctr Ment Retardation, 67-75; chmn, Med Adv Bd, Can Cystic Fibrosis Found, 69-71; mem, Med Res Coun Can, 70-73. *Mem:* Soc Pediat Res; Am Acad Pediat; Can Pediat Soc; Am Pediat Soc; Can Soc Clin Invest. *Mailing Add:* Dept Pediat IWK Hosp/Children 5850 University Ave Halifax NS B3J 3G9 Can

GOLDBLUM, DAVID KIVA, MATHEMATICS, CHEMICAL ENGINEERING. *Current Pos:* BIOENVIRON ENGR, KEVRIC CO, INC, 93- *Personal Data:* b Middletown, NY, Apr 13, 53. *Educ:* Carnegie-Mellon Univ, BS, 75; Rice Univ, MS, 81; Univ Mich, PhD(chem eng & environ health sci), 88. *Prof Exp:* Specimen processor, Montefiore Hosp, 77-78; chem engr, PPG Industs Inc, 80-82; teaching asst, Univ Mich, Ann Arbor, 82-88; bioenviron engr, USAF, Ctr Environ Excellence, 88-92; risk assessor, Sverdrup Corp, 92-93. *Concurrent Pos:* Bioenviron engr, USAF Res, 93-; adj prof, Univ Tex, San Antonio, 93-; environ engr, Kelly AFB Environ Mgt Directorate. *Mem:* Am Inst Chem Engrs; Am Pub Health Asn; Nat Soc Prof Engrs; Nat Well Water Asn. *Res:* Mathematical applications in chemical and environmental engineering; biosensor development and chemical risk assessment; chemical oxidation effort; pollution prevention and risk assessment; wastewater treatment. *Mailing Add:* 8 Stonehenge Circle Baltimore MD 21208. *Fax:* 210-925-9972

GOLDBURG, ARNOLD, AEROSPACE ENGINEERING, PETROLEUM ENGINEERING. *Current Pos:* CONSULT, 82- *Personal Data:* b New York, NY, Aug 11, 27; m 58; c 3. *Educ:* Princeton Univ, BSE, 48, PhD(aerospace eng), 60; Mass Inst Technol, MS, 51, Eng, 52. *Prof Exp:* Asst dir Proj SQUID, Princeton Univ-Off Naval Res, 58-60; prin res scientist, Avco-Everett Res Lab, 60-66; head flight sci lab, Boeing Sci Res Labs, 66-70, chief scientist, Supersonic Transport Prog, 70-71, dir sci & technol, Off Corp Bus Develop, Boeing Co, 71-74, dir int technol, Boeing Aerospace Co, 74-75; mgr, Enhanced Oil Recovery, Gary Oil Co, 75-79, vpres, 80-81; Naval Air Systs Command Res Prof, US Naval Acad, 84-85. *Concurrent Pos:* Mem res & tech adv subcomt, fluid mech, NASA, 69-70; mem, Proj Independence Panels, 74; mem res & develop subcomt, Interstate Oil Compact Comn, 79-82. *Mem:* Am Phys Soc; Am Inst Aeronaut & Astronaut. *Res:* Aerothermochemistry of combustion; boundary layer fluid mechanics; reentry heat transfer; flow fields of hypersonic bodies; clear air turbulence; sonic boom; magnetohydrodynamics; stratospheric fluid physics and environmental impact; petroleum reservoir fluid physics; aircraft design. *Mailing Add:* 4 Carriage Lane Littleton CO 80121. *E-Mail:* 71227.3575@compuserve.com

GOLDBURG, WALTER ISAAC, SOLID STATE PHYSICS. *Current Pos:* assoc prof, 63-66, PROF PHYSICS, UNIV PITTSBURGH, 66- *Personal Data:* b New York, NY, Sept 27, 27; m 56; c 2. *Educ:* Cornell Univ, BA, 51; Duke Univ, PhD, 54. *Prof Exp:* Res physicist, Carnegie Inst Technol, 54, 56, instr physics, 56-59; from asst prof to assoc prof, Pa State Univ, 59-63. *Mem:* Fel Am Phys Soc; AAAS. *Res:* Critical phenomena, light scattering, turbulence. *Mailing Add:* Dept Physics Univ Pittsburgh Pittsburgh PA 15260

GOLDE, DAVID WILLIAM, HEMATOLOGY, ONCOLOGY. *Current Pos:* Dir, Aids Ctr, 86-90, PROF MED, SCH MED, UNIV CALIF, LOS ANGELES, 79-, PHYSICIAN & CHIEF, DIV HEMATOL & ONCOL, 81-, DIR, CLIN RES CTR, 87- *Personal Data:* b New York, NY, Oct 23, 40; m; c 2. *Educ:* Fairleigh Dickinson Univ, BS, 62; McGill Univ, MD & CM, 66. *Mem:* Am Col Physicians; Am Soc Clin Invest; Am Soc Hematol; Am Asn Cancer Res; Asn Am Phys. *Res:* Hormonal modulation of normal and neoplastic hematopoiesis and the mechanism of normal and leukemic blood cell function. *Mailing Add:* Sloan/Kettering 1275 York Ave New York NY 10021

GOLDE, HELLMUT, COMPUTER SCIENCE, ELECTRICAL ENGINEERING. *Current Pos:* RETIRED. *Personal Data:* b Berlin, Ger, Feb 6, 30; nat US; m 57; c 3. *Educ:* Munich Tech Univ, Dipl Ing, 53; Stanford Univ, MS, 55, PhD(elec eng), 59. *Prof Exp:* Asst microwave studies, Stanford Univ, 53-55, 55-59, res assoc, 59; from asst prof to assoc prof elec eng, Univ Wash, 60-69, prof elec eng & comput sci, 69-92, vprovost comput, 84-92. *Mem:* Asn Comput Mach. *Res:* Computer languages and language processors. *Mailing Add:* 4407 52nd Ave NE Seattle WA 98105

GOLDEMBERG, ROBERT LEWIS, COSMETIC CHEMISTRY & FORMULATING, DERMATOLOGICAL FORMULATING. *Current Pos:* PRES & OWNER, RAKOMA LABS, INC, 73- *Personal Data:* b Passaic, NJ, Sept 18, 25; div, Sharanne, Kathleen & David; c 3. *Educ:* Princeton Univ, BSE, 48. *Prof Exp:* Textile chemist, United Piece Dye Works, 48-50; sr chemist, Coty Inc, 50-58; res dir, Shulton Inc, 58-64 & Lanvin-Charles Ritz, 64-67; dir tech serv, Van Dyk & Co, 67-73. *Concurrent Pos:* Chmn bd, Soc Cosmetic Chemists, 74; dir, Continuing Educ Ctr Inc, 75-84; pres, Trion Chem Corp, 81-85. *Mem:* Fel Soc Cosmetic Chemists (pres, 73); Am Chem Soc; Dermal Clin Eval Soc; NY Acad Sci. *Res:* Anti-irritants in cosmetic formulating; emulsion technology; sunscreen formulating. *Mailing Add:* Rakoma Licensing Inc PO Box 2083 South Hackensack NJ 07606. *Fax:* 201-847-9142

GOLDEN, ABNER, PATHOLOGY. *Current Pos:* RETIRED. *Personal Data:* b New York, NY, July 22, 18; m 43; c 3. *Educ:* Columbia Univ, AB, 39; Harvard Med Sch, MD, 42. *Prof Exp:* From instr to prof path, Emory Univ, 48-61; prof, Georgetown Univ, 61-76, emer prof, 82-76; prof path & chmn dept, Univ Ky, 76-88. *Mem:* Am Soc Clin Path; Am Asn Path; Col Am Path; Am Fedn Clin Res. *Res:* Endocrine pathology; renal disease. *Mailing Add:* Dept Path Univ Ky Col Med 800 Rose St Lexington KY 40506-0001

GOLDEN, ALFRED, pathology, for more information see previous edition

GOLDEN, ALVA MORGAN, NEMATOLOGY. *Current Pos:* from asst nematologist to nematologist, Calif, 52-59, NEMATOLOGIST, NEMATOL LAB, AGR RES SERV, BELTSVILLE AGR RES STA, USDA, 59- *Personal Data:* b Milledgeville, Ga, July 13, 20; m 57; c 1. *Educ:* Univ Ga, BSA, 50, MSA, 51; Univ Md, PhD(plant path & nematol), 56. *Honors & Awards:* Int Honor Award, USDA, 82. *Prof Exp:* Asst plant path, Univ Ga, 50-51; plant pathologist fungicide develop, Vanderbilt Co, NY, 51. *Mem:* AAAS; fel Soc Nematologists (treas, 63-66, vpres, 66-67, pres, 67-68); fel Am Phytopath Soc; Soc Syst Zool; Am Soc Sugar Beet Technol; Europ Soc Nematologists. *Res:* Plant nematology, with emphasis on taxonomy of plant parasitic nematodes; taxonomy, morphology, life cycle and identification of plant nematodes, hosts, occurence and distribution; curate and expand USDA nematode collection, one of largest in existence; over 165 publications in subject areas. *Mailing Add:* 9110 Drake Pl College Park MD 20740

GOLDEN, ARCHIE SIDNEY, PEDIATRICS. *Current Pos:* assoc prof maternal & child health, 70-76, assoc prof & dir health assoc prog, Sch Health Serv, 73-79, ASSOC PROF INT HEALTH & PEDIAT, SCH HYG & PUB HEALTH & SCH MED, JOHNS HOPKINS UNIV, 79-, CHMN, DEPT

PEDIAT, JOHNS HOPKINS BAYVIEW MED CTR; MED DIR, CHESAPEAKE HEALTH PLAN, 81- *Personal Data:* b Danbury, Conn, Feb 9, 31; m 63, Sylvia Colon; c 3. *Educ:* Univ Conn, BA, 53; Univ Vt, MD, 57; Johns Hopkins Univ, MPH, 66. *Prof Exp:* Dir community health progs, Proj Hope, 62-70. *Concurrent Pos:* Vis prof pediat & pub health, Med Sch, Univ Trujillo, Peru, 62-65 & Sch Med, Univ Cartagena, Colombia, 66-69; chmn interpersonal skills comt, Nat Bd Med Examrs, 72-76; consult, Latin Am Comt Pediat Residencies, 72-79; chmn, Comt Int Child Health, Am Acad Pediat & Comt New Health Practr, Am Pub Health Asn, 76-80; hon prof, Sch Med, Univ Cartagena, Colombia, 69. *Mem:* Am Acad Pediat; Asn Teachers Prev Med; Ambulatory Pediat Asn; Am Pub Health Asn; Asn Physicians Assts Progs (pres, 78-79). *Res:* Utilization of job and task analysis technique in the development of curricula for health professionals; translation of public health needs into curricula for health professionals; content of primary health care practice; education of primary care physicians; doctor-patient relationship. *Mailing Add:* Johns Hopkins Bayview Med Ctr 4940 Eastern Ave Baltimore MD 21224-2735

GOLDEN, BEN ROY, GENETICS. *Current Pos:* asst prof genetics develop, 76-80, ASSOC PROF BIOL, KENNESAW COL, 80- *Personal Data:* b Bainbridge, Ga, Nov 19, 37; m 64; c 4. *Educ:* Mid Tenn State Univ, BS, 58; George Peabody Col, MA, 60; Brown Univ, PhD(genetics), 71. *Prof Exp:* Teacher, High Sch, Ill, 58-66; partic, NSF Acad Year Inst, Brown Univ, 66-67; asst prof genetics develop, Skidmore Col, 70-76. *Mem:* AAAS. *Res:* Analysis of the meiotic behavior of x-ray induced chromosome aberrations in an attempt to determine the mechanisms of pairing and disjunction in the spermatocytes of the Drosophila male. *Mailing Add:* Dept Biol Kennesaw State Col PO Box 444 Marietta GA 30061-0444

GOLDEN, CAROLE ANN, IMMUNOASSAY DEVELOPMENT, IN VITRO DIAGNOSTICS. *Current Pos:* VPRES, RES & DEVELOP, EDITEK, INC, BURLINGTON, NC, 87- *Personal Data:* b Los Angeles, Calif, Sept 23, 42. *Educ:* Okla Col Lib Arts, AB, 63; Miami Univ, MS, 69, PhD(microbiol), 73. *Honors & Awards:* Distinguished Tech Commun Award, Soc Tech Commun. *Prof Exp:* Instr microbiol, Miami Univ, 72-73; res asst prof, Med Sch, Univ Utah, 73-79; sci dir, Microbiol Res Corp, Bountiful, Utah, 78-87. *Concurrent Pos:* Microbial geneticist, Nat Inst Occup Safety & Health, 76; sr consult scientist, Univ Utah Res Inst, 76-82; res & develop mgt comt, Biotech Indust Orgn. *Mem:* AAAS, Sigma Xi; Am Soc Microbiol; Biotech Indust Orgn; NY Acad Sci; Asn Off Anal Chemists. *Res:* Development of immunological-based on-site tests for commercial application in the detection of infectious agents and the detection of toxic substances and drugs of abuse in animals and humans. *Mailing Add:* Editek Inc 1238 Anthony Rd Burlington NC 27215

GOLDEN, DADIGAMUWAGE CHANDRASIRI, CONTROLLED ECOLOGICAL LIFE SUPPORT SYSTEMS RESEARCH, AQUEOUS ALTERATION OF MINERALS IN THE SOLAR NEBULA. *Current Pos:* PRIN SCIENTIST, DUAL INC NASA, 93- *Personal Data:* b Horana, Srilanka, Feb 16, 47; m 81, G H Gunasens; c Shyama. *Educ:* Univ Ceylon, BSc, 70; NC State Univ Raleigh, PhD(soil chem), 78. *Honors & Awards:* Space Act Award, NASA, 92, 93. *Prof Exp:* Agr chemist, Tea Rest Inst Srilanka, 71-80; res assoc, Univ Ill, Urbana-Champagne, 80-81; Tex A&M Univ, 81-88; fel, Massey Univ Palmerston, 88-90; sr res fel, NASA Johnson Space Ctr, 90-93. *Concurrent Pos:* Fulbright scholar, NC State Univ, 74-78; fel, Int Atomic Energy Agency, 79-80; nat res ctr sr res fel, NASA Johnson Space Ctr, 90-93. *Mem:* Soil Sci Soc Am; Clay Minerals Soc; Mineral Soc; Sigma Xi; Int Asn Study Clays; Int Soil Sci Soc. *Res:* Development of a regenerative life support system to regenerate breathable air, potable water, recycle solid wastes and to produce food in planetary outposts; meteorites and their origin. *Mailing Add:* SN-4 NASA Johnson Space Ctr Houston TX 77058. *Fax:* 281-483-2696; *E-Mail:* golden@snmail.jsc.nasa.gov

GOLDEN, DAVID E, ATOMIC PHYSICS, MATERIALS SCIENCE. *Current Pos:* provost & vpres acad affairs, Univ NTex, 85-88, prof, 88-93, dir, Ctr Mat Characterization, 92-95, REGENTS PROF PHYSICS, UNIV NTEX, 93- *Personal Data:* b New York, NY, May 27, 32; m 62, Paula Englander; c Jeffrey B & Leila J. *Educ:* NY Univ, BA, 54, PhD(physics), 61. *Prof Exp:* Asst prof physics, NY Univ, 60-61; asst prof, Adelphi Univ, 61-62; eng specialist, Gen Tel & Electronics Labs, Inc, Calif, 62-63; from res scientist to staff scientist phys electronics, Lockheed Palo Alto Res Labs, 63-67; prof physics, Univ Bari, 67-70; from assoc prof to prof, Univ Nebr, Lincoln, 70-75; George Lynn Cross prof physics & chmn, Dept Physics & Astron, Univ Okla, 75-85. *Concurrent Pos:* Instr physics, City Col New York, 56-58; instr, NY Univ, 58-59, res assoc, 60-61; consult, Autometric Corp, NY, 61-62, Advan Res Instument Systs, Inc, Tex, 70-72, Tracor, Austin, Tex, 72-74, Lawrence Radiation Lab, Livermore, Calif, 75-77 & Minn Mining & Mfg, 84-85; sr scientist, Sylvania Elec Prod, Mass, 69-70; hon lectr, Mid-Am State Univ Asn, 82-83; mem, Comt Atomic & Molecular Sci, Nat Acad Sci, 82-85; bd mem & treas, Say It Straight Found, 84- & Avanta-The Satir Network, 88- *Mem:* Fel Am Phys Soc; Sigma Xi. *Res:* Lasers; atomic collisions; electron scattering from atoms and molecules; electron spectroscopy; resonances in electron scattering; ion-molecule reactions; mass spectroscopy; x-ray photoelectron spectroscopy; Auger spectroscopy; diamond films; field emission micro emitters. *Mailing Add:* Ctr Mat Characterization & Dept Physics Univ NTex Denton TX 76203-5371. *Fax:* 817-565-4824; *E-Mail:* golden@cas1.unt.edu

GOLDEN, DAVID MARK, CHEMICAL KINETICS. *Current Pos:* Phys chemist, SRI Int, 63-70, sr phys chemist, 70-76, dir, Dept Chem Kinetics, 76-88, dir, Chem Lab, 88-91, VPRES PHYS SCI, SRI INT, 91- *Personal Data:* b New York, NY, July 18, 35; m 63, Helen Stenzler; c Rachel E, Erica M & Nodine E. *Educ:* Cornell Univ, AB, 56; Univ Minn, PhD(phys chem), 61. *Honors & Awards:* Award for Creative Advan in Environ Sci & Technol, Am Chem Soc, 90; Newcomb Cleveland Prize, AAAS, 89. *Concurrent Pos:* Consult prof, Stanford Univ, 74-81; ed, Int J Chem Kinetics, 83- *Mem:* Am Chem Soc; fel Am Phys Soc; fel AAAS; Am Geophys Union. *Res:* Chemical kinetics and thermochemistry; molecular spectroscopy; atmospheric chemistry and combustion. *Mailing Add:* SRI Int Menlo Park CA 94025-3346. *Fax:* 650-859-4321; *E-Mail:* golden@mplvax.sri.com

GOLDEN, GERALD SEYMOUR, ANALYTICAL CHEMISTRY, INDUSTRIAL WASTE RECYCLING. *Current Pos:* head, Anal Chem Lab, 62-65, chief, Anal Radioisotope Labs, 65-80, MGR, MAT CHARACTERIZATION & PROCESSING LAB, UNITED TECHNOL RES CTR, 81- *Personal Data:* b Hartford, Conn, June 18, 33; m 55; c 3. *Educ:* Mass Inst Technol, SB, 54; Rensselaer Polytech Inst, PhD(chem), 57. *Prof Exp:* Anal res chemist radiochem, Nuclear Div, Combustion Eng, Inc, 57-61, supvr chem sect, 61-62. *Mem:* Sigma Xi; Am Soc Testing & Mat; Mats Res Soc; Anal Lab Mgrs Asn. *Res:* Analysis of trace elements in materials; general analytical and radiochemistry; resource recovery; industrial chemical processing. *Mailing Add:* United Technol Res Ctr East Hartford CT 06108

GOLDEN, JOHN O(RVILLE), ACADEMIC ADMINISTRATION, CHEMICAL ENGINEERING. *Current Pos:* from asst prof to assoc prof, Colo Sch Mines, 67-70, dir res develop, 75-79, dean grad studies & res, 79-83, vpres acad affairs & dean fac, 83-90, PROF CHEM & PETROL REFINING ENG, COLO SCH MINES, 75- *Personal Data:* b Nashville, Tenn, Jan 8, 37; m 58; c 4. *Educ:* Vanderbilt Univ, BE, 59, MS, 60; Iowa State Univ, PhD(chem eng), 64. *Prof Exp:* Res asst chem eng, Vanderbilt Univ, 59-60 & Iowa State Univ, 60-64; res scientist assoc thermodyn, Huntsville Res & Eng Ctr, Lockheed Missiles & Space Co, 64-67. *Concurrent Pos:* Consult, Samsonite Corp, 68-70, Martin Marietta, 71 & EG&G, 90-; fel, Am Coun Educ Acad Admin, 78-79. *Mem:* Am Chem Soc; Am Inst Chem Engrs; Am Soc Eng Educ. *Res:* Coal liquefaction; coal processing. *Mailing Add:* 2009 Goldenvue Dr Golden CO 80401-1724

GOLDEN, JOHN TERENCE, COLLOID CHEMISTRY, SURFACE CHEMISTRY. *Current Pos:* chemist, 64-75, tech & mfg mgr chem, 75-90, VPRES TECH, RENITE CO, 90- *Personal Data:* b Ft Wayne, Ind, Jan 31, 32. *Educ:* Univ Mich, BSCh, 53; Ohio State Univ, MSc, 58, PhD(phys org chem), 63. *Prof Exp:* Teaching asst, res asst & asst instr chem, Ohio State Univ, 56-62; res chemist, BF Goodrich Res Ctr, 62-63; indexer, Chem Abstracts Serv, 63-64. *Concurrent Pos:* NSF grant, Ohio State Univ, 62. *Mem:* Am Chem Soc; Soc Tribologists & Lubrication Engrs; Am Ceramic Soc. *Res:* Engaged in development and manufacture of high temperature lubricants, coatings, and release agents for the glass and metalworking industries. *Mailing Add:* Renite Co PO Box 30830 Columbus OH 43230. *Fax:* 614-253-1333; *E-Mail:* jgolden@freenet.columbus.oh.us

GOLDEN, KELLY PAUL, IMAGE RECORDING SYSTEMS, COMPUTER SCIENCE & TECHNOLOGY EVALUATION. *Current Pos:* DIR, GOLDEN SYST, INC, 96- *Personal Data:* b Detroit, Mich, Oct 12, 43; m 64, Patricia E Wright; c Edward & Susan. *Educ:* Mich State Univ, BS, 65, & MS, 67, PhD(elec eng), 71. *Prof Exp:* Comput operator, Mich State Univ, 65-66, teaching asst elec eng, 66-67; consult, Okemos Res Lab, Owens-Ill Inc, 67-73; sr res assoc electronic imaging, E I Du Pont de Nemours & Co, Inc, 73-96. *Concurrent Pos:* Consult, Sterling Diag Imaging. *Mem:* Inst Elec & Electronics Engrs; Sigma Xi. *Res:* Electronic circuit design; instrumentation and product development; electric properties of materials and devices; hardware and software; thermal, laser and other electronic imaging systems; technology evaluation. *Mailing Add:* 204 Caravel Dr Suite 1 Bear DE 19701-1629. *Fax:* 302-451-3175; *E-Mail:* goldenkp@goldensys.com

GOLDEN, KENNETH IVAN, PLASMA PHYSICS. *Current Pos:* PROF & CHMN, COMPUT SCI & ELEC ENG, UNIV VT, 86- *Personal Data:* b Chicago, Ill, Oct 24, 32; m 65; c 2. *Educ:* Northwestern Univ, BS, 55; Mass Inst Technol, SM, 56, ME, 57; Inst Henri Poincare, Univ Paris, Dr, 64. *Prof Exp:* Res assoc physics, Brandeis Univ, 65-67, vis asst prof, 67-69; from assoc prof to prof, Northeastern Univ, 69-80, William L Smith prof elec eng, 80-83, George A Snell prof elec eng, 83-86. *Concurrent Pos:* Consult, Lincoln Lab, Mass Inst Technol, 69-72, prin investr, NSF grants, 81-83, Air Force Off Sci Res grants, 76-81 & Air ForceGeophys Lab contract, 73-76; sci collabr, Physics & Plasma Res Ctr, Switz, 76; vis prof, Lab Physics Theoret & High Energy, Univ Paris, 75-76; invited lectr, NATO Advan Inst Strongly Coupled Plasmas, 77; res leader, Int Ctr Theoret Physics, 81; invited lectr, Nanjing & Hoefi Inst Plasma Physics, China, 82; vis prof, Univ NSW, 82, vis prof theoret physics, 84-85; Fulbright sr scholar Australia, 84-85. *Mem:* NY Acad Sci; Sigma Xi; Am Phys Soc. *Res:* Plasma many body theory; statistical mechanics and kinetic theory; strongly coupled plasmas; shock waves in plasmas. *Mailing Add:* Dept Math & Statist Univ Vt 16 Colchester Ave Burlington VT 05405

GOLDEN, LARON E, soil fertility, plant nutrition, for more information see previous edition

GOLDEN, MICHAEL STANLEY, PLANT ECOLOGY, FOREST ECOLOGY. *Current Pos:* asst prof, 75-81, ASSOC PROF FOREST ECOL & SILVICULT, AUBURN UNIV, 81- *Personal Data:* b West Point, Ga, Aug 23, 42; m 72; c 1. *Educ:* Trevecca Col, AB, 64; Auburn Univ, MS, 68; Univ Tenn, PhD(plant ecol), 74. *Prof Exp:* Asst & assoc prof forest ecol, Ala A&M Univ, 72-74. *Mem:* Soc Am Foresters; Ecol Soc Am; Am Inst Biol Sci. *Res:* Descriptive ecology of forested ecosystems; forest site evaluation and classification; factors affecting height growth of loblolly pine and yellow-poplar; silviculture. *Mailing Add:* Sch Forestry Auburn Univ Auburn AL 36849-5418

GOLDEN, OLIVIA A, SCIENCE ADMINISTRATION. *Current Pos:* comnr children, youth & families, 93-96, ACTG ASST SECY CHILDREN & FAMILIES, US DEPT HEALTH & HUMAN SERVS, 96- *Prof Exp:* Budget dir, Mass Exec Off Human Servs, 83-85; dir progs & policy, Children's Defense Fund; lectr pub policy, Harvard Univ, 87-91. *Res:* Child care; Child welfare services; increasing adoptions. *Mailing Add:* Admin Children & Families US Dept Health & Human Servs 370 L'Enfant Promenade SW Washington DC 20447

GOLDEN, SIDNEY, PHYSICAL CHEMISTRY, THEORETICAL CHEMISTRY. *Current Pos:* from asst prof to prof, 51-81, EMER PROF CHEM, BRANDEIS UNIV, 81- *Personal Data:* b Boston, Mass, June 23, 17; m 41, Muriel Nirenberg; c Harriet & Nancy. *Educ:* City Col NY, BS, 38; Harvard Univ, PhD(phys chem), 48. *Honors & Awards:* Presidential Cert Merit, 48. *Prof Exp:* Asst chem, Purdue Univ, 41-42; res assoc, Nat Defense Res Comt, George Washington Univ, 42-46; phys chemist, Hydrocarbon Res, Inc, 48-51. *Concurrent Pos:* Fulbright sr scholar, 59-60; Guggenheim fel, 59-60; lectr, Polytech Inst Brooklyn, 49-50; res assoc, Mass Inst Technol, 52; consult, Nat Bur Stand, 57-64; consult ed, Addison-Wesley Pub Co, 62-67; vis prof, Univ Calif, Berkeley, 63, Hebrew Univ Jerusalem, 67-68 & 74-75 & Ariz State Univ, 92-; consult, Inst Def Anal, 63-65; sr Weizmann fel, Weizmann Inst Sci, 74-75; exchange prof, Univ Paris-Sud, 75. *Mem:* Am Chem Soc; fel Am Phys Soc; fel Am Acad Arts & Sci. *Res:* Theoretical chemical kinetics; quantum mechanics; free radicals; ionic solvation; metal-ammonia solution; quantum statistical inequalities; temporal irreversibility; temporal quantization. *Mailing Add:* 8614 N 84th St Scottsdale AZ 85258

GOLDENBAUM, GEORGE CHARLES, PLASMA PHYSICS, PHYSICS & CHEMISTRY OF LIGHTNING. *Current Pos:* assoc prof, 74-80, actg chmn, Dept Meteorol, 87-89, PROF PHYSICS, UNIV MD, COLLEGE PARK, 80-, ASSOC DEAN, COL COMPUT, MATH & PHYS SCI, 92- *Personal Data:* b New York, NY, Aug 11, 36; c 3. *Educ:* Muhlenberg Col, BS, 57; Univ Md, PhD(physics), 66. *Prof Exp:* Physicist, Nat Bur Standards, 58-61; res assoc plasma physics, Univ Md, 66-69; res physicist, US Naval Res Lab, 69-74. *Concurrent Pos:* Vis scientist, Culham Lab, Eng, 66-67, Lawrence Livermore Nat Lab, Calif, 80-81; TEPCO prof elec eng, Univ Tokyo, 91. *Mem:* Fel Am Phys Soc. *Res:* Dynamics of low density plasmas; collision free shock waves in plasmas; plasma turbulence; interaction of radiation with plasmas; magnetic confinement of plasmas; atmospheric chemistry and dynamics of lightning discharges. *Mailing Add:* Univ Md Col Comput Math Phys Sci 3400 A V Williams College Park MD 20742-3281. *Fax:* 301-405-9377; *E-Mail:* ggoldenb@deans.umd.edu

GOLDENBAUM, PAUL ERNEST, CLINICAL MICROBIOLOGY, MICROBIAL PHYSIOLOGY. *Current Pos:* sr microbiologist, Becton Dickinson Diag Instrument Systs, Md, 81-83, mgr, Clin Microbiol Proj, 83-85, mgr clin microbiol, 85-90, SR MGR CLIN MICROBIOL, BECTON DICKINSON DIAG INSTRUMENT SYSTS, MD, 85- *Personal Data:* b Newport News, Va, Aug 25, 43; m 69; c 2. *Educ:* Lynchburg Col, BS, 66; Western Mich Univ, MA, 68; NC State Univ, PhD(microbiol), 72. *Honors & Awards:* Mary Posten Award, NC Br of Am Soc Microbiol, 68. *Prof Exp:* Asst prof biol, Southern Ill Univ, Edwardsville, 74-78, assoc prof, 78-81. *Concurrent Pos:* Fel res assoc, AB Chandler Med Sch, Dept Biochem, Univ Ky, 72-73; res fel, NIH, Nat Cancer Inst, Pub Health Serv, 73-74; prin investr res grants, Southern Ill Univ, 74-, res scholar, 77-78; vis assoc prof microbiol & immunol, Med Sch, Washington Univ, St Louis, 78-79. *Mem:* Am Soc Microbiol; Sigma Xi; AAAS; fel Am Acad Microbiol; NY Acad Sci; Europ Soc Clin Microbiol & Infectious Dis. *Res:* Microbial physiology; regulation of gene activity in bacteria including catabolite repression; morphogenesis; membrane physiology; automated, rapid detection of bacteria; clinical microbiology: detection and recovery of pathogens. *Mailing Add:* 3931 Brittany Lane Hampstead MD 21074-1633

GOLDENBERG, ANDREW AVI, CONTROL SYSTEMS, ROBOTIC BASED AUTOMATION. *Current Pos:* asst prof elec eng, 81-82, assoc prof mech eng & elec eng, 82-87, PROF MECH ENG & ELEC ENG & BIOMED ENG, UNIV TORONTO, 87- *Personal Data:* b Romania, Aug, 45; Can citizen; m 70; c 2. *Educ:* Israel Inst Technol, BSc, 69, MSc, 72; Univ Toronto, PhD(elec eng), 76. *Prof Exp:* Staff eng, control systs, Spar Aerospace, Ltd, 75-81. *Concurrent Pos:* Consult, Eng Serv, Inc, 80- *Mem:* Inst Elec & Electronics Engrs; Am Soc Mech Engrs; Soc Mech Eng. *Res:* Robots; design; kinematics; control; manufacturing; real-time; sensors. *Mailing Add:* Dept Mech Eng Univ Toronto Five Kings Col Rd Toronto ON M5S 1A4 Can

GOLDENBERG, BARBARA LOU, solid state sensor development, for more information see previous edition

GOLDENBERG, DAVID MILTON, ONCOLOGY, NUCLEAR MEDICINE. *Current Pos:* PRES, CTR MOLECULAR MED & IMMUNOL & ADJ PROF MED & SURG, UNIV MED & DENT NJ, 83- *Personal Data:* b Brooklyn, NY, Aug 2, 38; m 61, Hildegard Gruenbaum; c Eva, Deborah, Marc, Denis, Neil & Lee. *Educ:* Univ Chicago, SB, 58; Univ Erlangen-Nuremburg, ScD(natural sci), 65; Univ Heidelberg, MD, 66. *Honors & Awards:* Outstanding Investr Award, Nat Cancer Inst, NIH, 85. *Prof Exp:* Intern-resident med & path, Univ Hosp, Erlangen, Germany, 66-67, head clin exp oncol, Surg Clin, 67-68; assoc prof path, Sch Med, Univ Pittsburgh, 68-70 & Temple Univ, 70-72; from assoc prof to prof, Univ Ky, 72-73. *Concurrent Pos:* Staff pathologist, Vet Admin Hosp, Pittsburgh, 68-70; Coun Tobacco res grant, 68-71; Nat Cancer Inst grants, 69-; Damon Runyon Fund cancer res grant, 71-75; Am Cancer Soc grant, 73-76; mem & chmn, Vet Admin Merit Rev Bd Oncol, 74-77; consult, Vet Admin Hosp, Lexington, Ky, 74-83 & Brookhaven Nat Labs, 83-87; exec dir, Ephraim McDowell Community Cancer Network, 75-80; mem bd trustees, Assoc Community Cancer Ctr, 77-79; pres, Ephraim McDowell Cancer Res Found, Inc, 78-80; Univ Ky Found res award, 78; ed, J Cancer Res & Clin Oncol, 79-87, Diag Path, 80- & Tumor Diag, 80-; mem exp immunol study sect, NIH, 80-83; mem sci adv bd, German Fund Cancer Res, 80-; assoc ed, Cancer Res, 82- *Mem:* Am Soc Exp Path; Am Asn Path & Bact; Tissue Cult Asn; Am Soc Cell Biol; Am Soc Human Genetics; Am Asn Cancer Res; Am Asn Pathologists; Soc Exp Biol & Med; Soc Nuclear Med; Hon mem Arg Cancer Soc. *Res:* Cancer, improved diagnosis and treatment; immunology; treatment of human tumors with radiolabeled monoclonal antibodies; authored over 875 articles, book chapters and abstracts; granted over 20 patents in field. *Mailing Add:* Ctr Molecular Med & Immunol One Bruce St Newark NJ 07103-2763. *Fax:* 973-982-7047

GOLDENBERG, GERALD J, INTERNAL MEDICINE, ONCOLOGY. *Current Pos:* PROF MED PHARMACOL, UNIV TORONTO, 90-, DIR & ASST DEAN ONCOL, 90- *Personal Data:* b Brandon, Man, Nov 27, 33; m 59; c 4. *Educ:* Univ Man, MD, 57; Univ Minn, PhD(morphol, hemat), 65. *Prof Exp:* Lectr internal med, Univ Man, 64-66, from asst prof to prof internal med, 66-90. *Concurrent Pos:* Res asst, Man Cancer Found, 64-73; clin res assoc, Nat Cancer Inst Can, 67-73; consult, Winnipeg Children's Hosp, 67-70, Princess Margaret Hosp, Toronto, 90-; dir, Man Inst Cell Biol, 73-88. *Mem:* Can Soc Clin Invest; Am Asn Cancer Res; Am Soc Exp Path; fel Am Col Physicians; fel Royal Col Physicians Can. *Res:* Cancer chemotherapy; mechanism of action of alkylating agents; molecular pharmacology of drug resistance; membrane transport; molecular biology of DNA topoisomerase. *Mailing Add:* Dir Oncol Univ Toronto 92 College St Med Sci Bldg Rm 2113 Toronto ON M5S 1A8 Can. *Fax:* 416-971-2462

GOLDENBERG, KIM, DIAGNOSTIC TESTING IN CLINICAL DECISION MAKING, STRUCTURAL TESTING OF ASTRONAUTIC & AERONAUTIC VEHICLES. *Current Pos:* chief, Gen Med Div, Sch Med, Wright State Univ, 83-89, vchair, Med Dept, 88-89, assoc dean acad & students, 89-90, DEAN & PROF MED, SCH MED, WRIGHT STATE UNIV, 90- *Personal Data:* b New York, NY, Jan 1, 47; m 68. *Educ:* State Univ NY, Stony Brook, BSE, 68; Polytech Inst NY, MS, 72; Albany Med Col, MD, 79. *Prof Exp:* Test opers engr, Grumman Aerospace Corp, 68-75; Am Cancer Soc fel, Western Res Care Syst, 79-82, clerkship dir med, 82-83; gen med internist & treas bd, Trumbull Mahoning Med Group, 82-83. *Concurrent Pos:* Dir med pract, Univ Med Servs Asn, 83-90 chmn bd, 90-; consult, Clin Prev Servs, Kellogg Found, 89, Nat Coord Comt Clin Prev Servs, Asn Am Med Col, 92-95, US House Rep, 93, deans mtg Pres Clinton, 94 & Managed Care Conf, AMA, 96-97. *Mem:* AMA; Am Pub Health Asn; fel Am Col Prev Med; Soc Gen Internal Med; Asn Am Med Cols; Fel Am Col Physicians. *Res:* Tested the NASA Lunar Earth Module heat shields and Navy F-14A aircraft; created first artificial intelligence program for aerospace testing; developed models for hormone-receptor interactions in cancer and later performed models of clinical decision making. *Mailing Add:* Wright State Univ Sch Med PO Box 927 Dayton OH 45401-0927

GOLDENBERG, MARTIN IRWIN, MEDICAL BACTERIOLOGY, LABORATORY MEDICINE. *Current Pos:* RETIRED. *Personal Data:* b Jersey City, NJ, May 10, 33; m 54; c 2. *Educ:* Rutgers Univ, BS, 54; Yale Univ, MS, 57, PhD(med microbiol), 60; Univ Md, BA, 82. *Honors & Awards:* Commendation Medal, USPHS, 80. *Prof Exp:* Microbiologist, State Dept Health, Hawaii, 60-61; scientist, Commun Dis Ctr, USPHS, San Francisco, 61-68 & Ft Collins, Colo, 68-70; lab dir, US Med Ctr, 70-75; mem Hq Staff, Div Hosp & Clin, USPHS, 75-81, mem staff grants admin, 81-85, asst dir, spec prog clin ctr, 85-88, chief, Off Med Bd Serv Clin Ctr, NIH, 88-96. *Concurrent Pos:* Assoc mem grad fac, Colo State Univ, 68-70; exec secy, Med Bd, NIH. *Mem:* Fel AAAS; fel Am Pub Health Asn. *Mailing Add:* 21 Cape Jasmine Ct Gaithersburg MD 20879

GOLDENBERG, MARVIN M, PHARMACOLOGY, PHYSIOLOGY. *Current Pos:* INVEST DRUG COORDR, MT SINAI MED INST, 94- *Personal Data:* b New York, NY, July 7, 35; m 57; c Sol Jeffrey & Lisa Shari. *Educ:* Long Island Univ, BS, 57; Temple Univ, MS, 59; Med Col, Pa, PhD(pharmacol), 65. *Prof Exp:* From sr res scientist I to sr res scientist II, Eaton Labs, Norwich-Eaton pharmaceut, 65-73, res assoc, 73-80, Controlled Substances Officer, 75-80; dir immunopharmacol, Merck Sharp & Dohme Res Labs, 80-84, asst dir clin pharmacol, 85-88; dir res & develop ophthal, Am Cyanamid, 88-91; vpres res & develop clin affairs, Block Drug Co, 91-94. *Concurrent Pos:* Ad hoc reviewer, Div Res Grants, NIH; instr pharmacol, State Univ NY Binghamton. *Mem:* Am Soc Pharmacol & Exp Therapeut; Europ Biol Res Asn; Int Inflammation Res Soc; NY Acad Sci; Sigma Xi; Am Gastroenterol Asn; Am Soc Clin Pharmacol; Inflammation Res Asn. *Res:* Autonomic nervous system pharmacology in relation to the gastrointestinal area; toxicology with regard to the antidotal effectiveness of agents against cyanide; anti-inflammatory drug research; clinical protocol monitoring and analysis; immunosuppression and analgesic areas of basic and applied research; clinical monitor for phase I and phase II studies in man in the field of inflammation (rheumatoid arthritis, analgesia), psoriasis, wound healing, ulcerative colitis, hypertension, Alzheimers disease and Parkinsons disease; studies in man on pharmacokinetics and pharmodynamics; bioequivalence in man. *Mailing Add:* 721 Shackamaxon Dr Westfield NJ 07090. *Fax:* 212-348-7927

GOLDENBERG, NEAL, ENVIRONMENT, SAFETY & HEALTH REGULATION. *Current Pos:* tech coordr, Space Nuclear Syst Div, US Dept Energy, 69-72, chief, Isotope Technol Br, 72-76, asst dir advan isotope separation, US Energy Res & Develop Admin, 76-78, dir Advan Nuclear Systs & Projs Div, 78-80, dir Off Plans & Resource Mgt, 80-82, dir div safety,

Qual Assurance & Safeguards, 82-86, dir, Off Qual Assurance &Qual Verification, 86-90, dir, Off Nuclear Safety Policy & Stand, 90-94, ASSOC DEP ASST SECY, US DEPT ENERGY, 95- *Personal Data:* b Brooklyn, NY, Apr 29, 35; m 57, Myrna Gallant; c Elizabeth, David B & Eve L. *Educ:* City Col NY, BS, 56; Univ Ark, MS, 58, PhD(phys chem), 61. *Prof Exp:* Instr chem, Univ Ark, 61; sr res chemist, Mound Lab, Monsanto Res Corp, 61-65, in chg plutonium isotope fuels group, Snap Prog, 65-67; asst prof chem, Fairleigh Dickinson Univ, 67-69. *Concurrent Pos:* Bd dirs, Am Nat Stand Inst. *Mem:* Am Chem Soc. *Res:* Uranium enrichment; advanced and laser isotope separations; photochemistry; plutonium chemistry; reactor fuel reprocessing; nuclear waste management; thermodynamics; plasmas; development and production of nuclear power systems for use in the exploration of space; high temperature gas reactor program; evaluation of advanced nuclear energy system concepts; development of the national fission energy plan for reactor development; strategic analyses; nuclear safety policy; consensus standards; providing oversight to international activities involving government-sponsored research and development. *Mailing Add:* 9328 Garden Ct Potomac MD 20854. *Fax:* 301-903-5492; *E-Mail:* neal.goldenberg@ha.doe.gov

GOLDENBERG, ROBERT L, OBSTETRICS & GYNECOLOGY. *Current Pos:* from asst prof to prof, Sch Med, Univ Ala, Birmingham, 76-88, assoc prof, Sch Pub Health, 81-89, dir, MCH Training Prog, Sch Pub Health, 89-91, DIR, CTR OBSTET RES, UNIV ALA, BIRMINGHAM, 84-, CHARLES E FLOWERS PROF, DEPT OBSTET & GYNEC, 88-, PROF, DEPT PUB HEALTH, 89-, CHMN, DEPT OBSTET & GYNEC, 95- *Personal Data:* b New York, NY, Jan 23, 43. *Educ:* Columbia Univ, BS, 64; Duke Univ Sch Med, MD, 68. *Prof Exp:* Intern, Duke Univ Sch Med, 68, Res Training Prog, 68-69; resident obstet/gynec, Columbia Univ, 69-70; fel, Endocrine-Infertility Sect, Nat Inst Child Health & Human Develop, NIH, 70-72; resident, Yale Univ Sch Med, 72-74, asst prof, 74-76. *Concurrent Pos:* Dir, Yale Infertility Clin, Yale Univ Sch Med, 74-76; dir, Bur Maternal & Child Health, Ala Dept Pub Health, 77-81; fel maternal-fetal med, Dept Obstet/Gynec, Univ Ala, Birmingham, 83-85; mem study sect, Off Maternal & Child Health, Dept Health & Human Serv, 83-86; dir, Obstet Servs, Cooper Green Hosp, 86-87, chmn, Dept Obstet & Gynec, 87-91; mem child health adv panel, Off Technol Assessment, US Cong, 86-88; mem, Maternal & Child Health Res Comt, Nat Inst Child Health & Human Develop, NIH, 90-95, coun mem, 94- *Mem:* Inst Med-Nat Acad Sci; Am Asn Maternal & Neonatal Health; Am Col Obstet & Gynec; Am Gynec & Obstet Soc; Am Pub Health Asn; Nat Perinatal Asn; Soc Perinatal Obstetricians. *Mailing Add:* Dept Obstet & Gynec Univ Ala 618 S 20th St Rm 560 Birmingham AL 35294-7333

GOLDENSOHN, ELI SAMUEL, NEUROLOGY. *Current Pos:* prof, 67-, EMER PROF NEUROL, COL PHYSICIANS & SURGEONS, COLUMBIA UNIV; PROF NEUROL, ALBERT EINSTEIN COL MED, 83- *Personal Data:* b New York, NY, June 25, 15; m 40; c 3. *Educ:* George Washington Univ, AB, 37, MD, 40. *Honors & Awards:* W G Lennox Award, Am Epilepsy Soc, 89. *Prof Exp:* Instr, Med Sch, Univ Colo, 45-48, asst prof physiol, 49-53, attend staff, 51-53, dir epilepsy serv, 53; from asst prof to assoc prof neurol, Col Physicians & Surgeons, Columbia Univ, 53-63; prof, Sch Med, Univ Pa, 63-67. *Concurrent Pos:* Consult, Vet Admin Hosp, Bronx, 59-61. *Mem:* Hon Fel Am Electroencephalog Soc (pres, 71); Am Neurol Asn; Am Epilepsy Soc (pres, 68); Am Acad Neurol; Epilepsy Found Am (pres, 81). *Res:* Brain physiology; electrical activity of the brain; convulsive disorders. *Mailing Add:* Dept Neurol Albert Einstein Col Med 1300 Morris Park Ave Bronx NY 10461

GOLDENSON, JEROME, CHEMISTRY. *Current Pos:* RETIRED. *Personal Data:* b Greensburg, Pa, July 23, 12. *Educ:* Carnegie Inst Technol, BS, 34. *Prof Exp:* Res chemist, Nat Alloy Steel Co, Pa, 35-37, Am Gas & Elec Corp, WVa, 37-38 & Acme Protection Equip Co, Pa, 38-39; design engr, E W Voss Mach Co, 39-40; phys chemist, Chem Ctr, US Army, 40-55, chief colloid br, Physicochem Res Div, Chem Res & Develop Labs, 55-71. *Concurrent Pos:* Mem mining adv bd, Carnegie Inst Technol; chem consult, 71- *Mem:* Am Chem Soc; Coblentz Soc; Sigma Xi; Am Ord Asn. *Res:* Infrared spectroscopy; organic phosphorus compounds; aluminum soaps; aerosols; colloid chemistry; alloy steels; chemical analytical methods of traces of gases in air. *Mailing Add:* 5 Cobbler Court Pikesville MD 21208-1321

GOLDENTHAL, EDWIN IRA, PHARMACOLOGY. *Current Pos:* SR STUDY DIR, MPI RES, 95- *Personal Data:* b Plainfield, NJ, Feb 2, 30; m 70; c 5. *Educ:* George Washington Univ, BS, 52, MS, 53, PhD(pharmacol), 56. *Prof Exp:* Chemist, Geol Surv, US Dept Interior, 51-53; pharmacologist, Food & Drug Admin, HEW, 56-63, chief drug rev br, Div Toxicol Eval, 63-66, dep dir, Off New Drugs, 66-70; dir safety eval, Int Res & Develop Corp, Mattawan, Mich, 70-72, vpres & dir res, 71-92, consult, 92-95. *Mem:* Soc Toxicol; Am Soc Pharmacol & Exp Therapeut. *Res:* Toxicology; drug metabolism; carcinogenesis. *Mailing Add:* MPI Res 54943 N Main Mattawan MI 49071. *Fax:* 616-668-4151

GOLDER, RICHARD HARRY, BIOCHEMISTRY. *Current Pos:* RETIRED. *Personal Data:* b Philadelphia, Pa, July 6, 22; m 57. *Educ:* Univ Wis, BS, 44; Temple Univ, PhD(biochem), 57. *Prof Exp:* Chemist, Barrett Div, Allied Chem & Dye Corp, 44-45; chemist, Philadelphia Rust-Proof Co, 45-46; tech asst, Gen Chem Co, 47-49; asst, Inst Cancer Res, 49-56; assoc prof, Sch Dent, Temple Univ, 64-74, assoc prof biochem, Sch Pharm, 74-87. *Concurrent Pos:* Fel, Johnson Found, Univ Pa, 56-59, Physiol-Chem Inst, Univ Marburg, 59-60; fel chem, Univ Pa, 60-64. *Mem:* AAAS; Am Chem Soc; Sigma Xi. *Res:* Controlling factors in glucose catabolism; nucleic acid changes following drug administration. *Mailing Add:* 2339 Hoffnagle St Philadelphia PA 19152

GOLDER, THOMAS KEITH, CELL BIOLOGY. *Current Pos:* RES SCIENTIST, INT CTR INSECT PHYSIOL & ECOL, 78-, PROD PLANNER, 95- *Personal Data:* b San Francisco, Calif, Nov 3, 42; c 1. *Educ:* Calif State Univ, San Francisco, AB, 66; Univ Calif, Davis, PhD(zool), 75. *Prof Exp:* Instr biol sci, Calif State Univ, San Francisco, 68-69; lectr zool, Univ Calif, Davis, 74-75 & 78, res physiologist, 75-78. *Concurrent Pos:* Consult, NIH grant, 75. *Mem:* AAAS; Am Soc Cell Biol; Sigma Xi; EAfrica Soc Parasitol. *Res:* Localization of acetylcholinesterase in normal and trypanosome infected tsetses; development and cultivation of infective salivarian trypanosomes and relationship to tsetse salivary gland physiology; effect of trypanosome development on tsetse physiology. *Mailing Add:* 2031 Kinsely Santa Cruz CA 95062

GOLDEY, JAMES MEARNS, PHYSICS. *Current Pos:* RETIRED. *Personal Data:* b Wilmington, Del, July 3, 26; m 51, Jeanne Potts; c James P & Kristina C. *Educ:* Univ Del, BS, 50; Mass Inst Technol, PhD(physics), 55. *Prof Exp:* Mem tech staff, Bell Tel Labs, 54-59, engr transistor develop, 59-61, head silicon transistor & integrated circuit dept, 61-66, head device technol dept, 66-69, dir mat & process technol lab, 69-74, dir, Solid State Device & Mat Lab, 74-81, dir, Integrated Circuit Customer Serv Lab, 81-84, dir, Linear & High Voltage Integrated Circuit Lab, AT&T Bell Labs, 84-89. *Mem:* Fel Inst Elec & Electronics Engrs. *Res:* Semiconductor physics; semiconductor device physics. *Mailing Add:* 3930 Azalea Rd Allentown PA 18103

GOLDFARB, DAVID S, EXPERIMENTAL BIOLOGY. *Current Pos:* STAFF PHYSICIAN, DEPT INTERNAL MED, DEPT VET AFFAIRS MED CTR & DIR, RENAL/HYPERTENSION CLIN, 87-; ASST PROF MED, SCH MED, NY UNIV, 91- *Personal Data:* b Mar 14, 56. *Educ:* Yale Col, BA, 77, MD, 81; Am Bd Internal Med, dipl, 85, dipl nephrology, 88. *Prof Exp:* Intern & resident, Dept Internal Med, Dept Vet Affairs Med Ctr & NY Univ Med Ctr, 81-84, res fel, Nephrology Sect, 85-86, clin fel, 86-87, instr, 87-91. *Concurrent Pos:* Attend physician, Adult Emergency Serv, Bellevue Hosp, 85-87, clin asst attend, Dept Med, 87-90, assoc attend, 90-; mem, End Stage Renal Dis Comt, Dept Vet Affairs Med Ctr, 87- *Mem:* Am Col Physicians; Am Fedn Clin Res; assoc mem Am Physiol Soc; Int Soc Nephrology; Am Soc Nephrology. *Res:* Effect of systemic acid-base balance on intestinal absorption and secretion; author of numerous scientific publications. *Mailing Add:* Nephrology Sect/111 Dept Vet Affairs Med Ctr 423 23rd St New York NY 10010-5050. *Fax:* 212-951-5981

GOLDFARB, DONALD, MATHEMATICAL PROGRAMMING. *Current Pos:* PROF INDUST ENG & OPER RES, COLUMBIA UNIV, 82-, CHMN, 84- *Personal Data:* b New York, NY, Aug 14, 41; m 68; c 2. *Educ:* Cornell Univ, BChE, 63; Princeton Univ, MA, 65, PhD(chem eng), 66. *Prof Exp:* Asst res scientist, Courant Inst Math Sci, NY Univ, 66-68; from asst prof to prof comput sci, City Col New York, 71-83, chmn, 78-79. *Concurrent Pos:* NSF fel, 63-66; res assoc, NY Sci Ctr, IBM, 70, T J Watson Res Ctr, 72, 76, 91 & Atomic Energy Res Estab, Harwell, UK, 74-75; assoc ed, Math Comput, Soc Indust & Appl Math, 69-, Opers Res, 83-, Math Prog, 83-; NSF grantee, 73-75 & 80-, Army Res Off, 77-80 & 82-, Off Naval Res, 87-; ed, J Numerical Anal, Soc Indust & Appl Math, 82-84, J Optimization, 89-; mem coun, Mem Am Math Soc, 85-87, Math Prog Soc, 82-85; mem comt, Recommend US Army Basic Sci Res, Nat Res Coun, 83-86. *Mem:* Am Math Soc; Math Prog Soc; Soc Indust & Appl Math; Oper Res Soc Am. *Res:* Mathematical programming/optimization; numerical analysis. *Mailing Add:* Dept Indust Eng Opers Res Columbia Univ 331 Mudd Bldg New York NY 10027-6699

GOLDFARB, JOSEPH, NEUROPHARMACOLOGY, NEUROPHYSIOLOGY. *Current Pos:* From asst prof to assoc prof, 72-89, PROF PHARMACOL, MT SINAI SCH MED, 89- *Personal Data:* b 1943. *Educ:* Mass Inst Technol, BS, 63; Yeshiva Univ, PhD(biomed sci), 69. *Mem:* Soc Neurosci; Am Soc Pharmacol & Exp Therapeut. *Mailing Add:* Dept Pharmacol Box 1215 Mt Sinai Sch Med One Gustave L Levy Pl New York NY 10029-6504. *Fax:* 212-831-0114

GOLDFARB, RONALD B, MAGNETICS, SUPERCONDUCTIVITY. *Current Pos:* SR RES PHYSICIST, NAT INST STAND & TECHNOL. *Educ:* Rice Univ, BA, 73, MS, 75; Colo State Univ, MS, 76, PhD(physics), 79; Univ Colo, MBA, 91. *Concurrent Pos:* Lectr, physics dept, Univ Colo. *Mem:* Inst Elec & Electronics Engrs; Am Phys Soc; Am Soc Testing Mat. *Res:* Magnetism, superconductivity; instrument design. *Mailing Add:* Nat Inst Standards & Technol 325 Broadway Boulder CO 80303-3328. *Fax:* 303-497-5316; *E-Mail:* goldfarb@bldrdoc.gov

GOLDFARB, RONALD H, BIOTECHNOLOGY. *Current Pos:* dir exp therapeut prog, Pittsburgh Cancer Inst, Univ Pittsburgh, 86-89, assoc dir basic res, 89-92, ASSOC PROF PATH, SCH MED, UNIV PITTSBURGH, 86-, DIR CANCER, METASTASIS & CELL BIOL PROG, PITTSBURGH CANCER INST, 89-, DEP DIR BASIC RES, 92-, ASSOC PROF NEUROSURG, SCH MED, 94-, PROF PATH, 96- *Personal Data:* b Brooklyn, NY, July 28, 49; m, Ellen R Feller; c Amy & Andrew. *Educ:* Herbert H Lehman Col, City Univ NY, BA, 70; State Univ NY, PhD(microbiol & immunol), 78. *Prof Exp:* Proj leader cancer metastasis res, Dept Immunol & Infectious Dis, Cent Res Div, Pfizer, Inc, 81-85, mgr cancer metastasis res & develop, 85-86. *Concurrent Pos:* Sr lectr biomed eng prog, Carnegie Mellon Univ, 89-; assoc ed, J Neuro-Oncol, 93-, Nat Immunol, 95- *Mem:* Am Asn Cancer Res; Am Soc Cell Biol; Am Asn Immunologists; Am Asn Pathologists; Am Soc Biochem & Molecular Biol; Soc Nat Immunity. *Res:* Molecular and cellular pathobiology of cancer invasion and metastasis; mechanisms of cell-mediated cytotoxicity of A-NK cells; development of novel drugs and approaches, including biological response modifiers; gene therapy for the control of metastatic cancer; editor of several publications; drug discovery; proteolytic enzymes; tumor immunology, tumor invasion, tumor rescutative. *Mailing Add:* Pittsburgh Cancer Inst Univ Pittsburgh Med Ctr Pittsburgh PA 15213-2582

GOLDFARB, ROY DAVID, CARDIOVASCULAR PHYSIOLOGY. *Current Pos:* asst prof, 75-80, assoc prof, 87-91, PROF PHYSIOL, ALBANY MED COL, 91-, PROF PHYSIOL & MED, RUSH MED COL. *Personal Data:* b New York, NY, Sept 23, 47; m 73; c 2. *Educ:* Colgate Univ, AB, 68; Hahnemann Med Col, MSc, 71, PhD(physiol), 73. *Prof Exp:* NIH fel pharmacol, Col Med, Univ S Ala, 73-74, instr, 74-75. *Concurrent Pos:* Vis scientist, Univ Calif, San Diego, La Jolla, Calif, Heart Res Inst, Sydney, Australia. *Mem:* AAAS; Am Heart Asn; Am Physiol Soc. *Res:* Mechanisms of cardiac injury induced by regional ischemia and septemic sepsis. *Mailing Add:* Dept Med Sect Cardiol Rush-Presby St Luke's Med Ctr 1653 W Congress Pkwy Chicago IL 60612. *Fax:* 312-942-5829

GOLDFARB, STANLEY, CHEMICAL CARCINOGENESIS, HEPATOLOGY. *Current Pos:* PROF PATH, SCH MED, UNIV WIS-MADISON, 69- *Personal Data:* b Mar 20, 31; wid. *Educ:* Univ NY, Buffalo, MD, 55. *Mem:* Am Asn Cancer Res; Am Asn Study Liver Dis; Am Soc Exp Path. *Res:* Histogenesis, growth kinetics and pathobiology of experimental rodent hepatocellular carcinomas with emphasis on factors involved in tumor promotion and progression; histogenesis and pathobiology of estrogen induced and estrogen dependent renal carcinoma in the hamster.. *Mailing Add:* Dept Path Univ Wis Sch Med 470 N Charter St Madison WI 53706-1509. *Fax:* 608-262-2327

GOLDFARB, THEODORE D, ENVIRONMENTAL PHYSICAL CHEMISTRY. *Current Pos:* from asst prof to assoc prof, 59-92, assoc vice provost, 84-88, PROF CHEM, STATE UNIV NY, STONY BROOK, 92- *Personal Data:* b New York, NY, May 6, 35; div; c Glenn E, Brian D, Keith A & Gretchen L. *Educ:* Cornell Univ, AB, 56; Univ Calif, PhD(chem), 59. *Prof Exp:* Asst, Univ Calif, 56-57. *Concurrent Pos:* Consult environ chem effects; prin investr, Sponsored Res Proj. *Mem:* AAAS; Am Chem Soc; Sci for the People. *Res:* Environmental effects of energy production and use, agricultural chemicals and waste disposal technologies; science policy and scientific decision making. *Mailing Add:* Dept Chem State Univ NY Stony Brook NY 11794. *Fax:* 516-632-7960; *E-Mail:* tgoldfarb@ccmail.sunysb.edu

GOLDFELD, DORIAN, MATHEMATICS. *Current Pos:* PROF MATH, COLUMBIA UNIV, 85- *Personal Data:* b Marburg, Ger, Jan 21, 47; US citizen; m 85; c 2. *Educ:* Columbia Univ, BS, 67, PhD, 69. *Honors & Awards:* Vaughn Prize, 85; Cole Prize in Number Theory, 87. *Prof Exp:* Lectr, Tel-Aviv Univ, 72-73; asst prof, Mass Inst Technol, 76-82; assoc prof, Univ Tex, 83-85. *Concurrent Pos:* Sloan fel, NSF, 77-79, prin investr, 83- *Mem:* Am Math Soc; Math Asn Am. *Res:* Analytic number theory; automorphic forms and ecliptic curves. *Mailing Add:* Math Dept Columbia Univ 2990 Broadway New York NY 10027-0029

GOLDFIELD, EDWIN DAVID, DEMOGRAPHY, ECONOMICS. *Current Pos:* study dir, 75-78, exec dir, 78-87, SR ASSOC, COMT NAT STATIST, NAT ACAD SCI, 87- *Personal Data:* b New York, NY, Oct 26, 18. *Educ:* City Univ New York, BS, 39; Columbia Univ, MA, 40. *Prof Exp:* Statist adv, City Court Spec Session, New York, 39; chief, stat reports div, US Bur Census, 55-68, asst dir, 68-71, chief, Int Stat Prog Ctr, 71-75. *Concurrent Pos:* Proj mgr, manpower res, US Econ Coop Admin, 51-52; tech adv, Social Sci Res Coun, 53; staff dir, subcomt Census & Statist, US House Rep, 59-60 & 67; mem bd dirs, Am Statist Asn, 85-89. *Mem:* Fel Am Statist Asn; Pop Asn Am; Int Asn Surv Statisticians; InterAm Statist Inst; Am Econ Asn; Int Statist Inst. *Res:* Federal statistical organization, policy and programs; demography; labor force economics; international development; survey and census procedures; privacy and confidentiality. *Mailing Add:* Nat Acad Sci 2101 Constitution Ave NW Washington DC 20418. *Fax:* 202-334-3751

GOLDFIEN, ALAN, ENDOCRINOLOGY. *Current Pos:* from asst prof to assoc prof, 58-67, RES ASSOC PHSIOL, UNIV CALIF, SAN FRANCISCO, 56-, MEM CARDIOVASC RES INST, 58-, PROF MED, 67-, ASSOC DEAN, SCH MED, 75- *Personal Data:* b Brooklyn, NY, Apr 16, 23; m 50; c Steven, Richard, Robert, Lisa, Jeffrey & Andrea. *Educ:* Univ Calif, AB, 46, MD, 50. *Honors & Awards:* Bennett Prize, 58. *Prof Exp:* Asst meteorol, NY Univ, 43-44; res fel med, Harvard Univ, 53-56. *Concurrent Pos:* Nat Cancer Inst res fel, 53-55, Nat Inst Arthritis & Metab Dis res fel, 56-57; Gianini fel med sci, Univ Calif, 57-58; asst, Peter Bent Brigham Hosp, Mass, 53-56. *Mem:* AAAS; Am Physiol Soc; Endocrine Soc; Am Fedn Clin Res; Am Soc Clin Invest; Sigma Xi; Soc Gynec Invest. *Res:* Adrenal medullary secretion; nervous control of intermediary metabolism; physiology of reproduction; medical complications of pregnancy; signal transmission in smooth muscle. *Mailing Add:* 377 Vista Linda Mill Valley CA 94941

GOLDFINE, HOWARD, BIOCHEMISTRY, MICROBIOLOGY. *Current Pos:* assoc prof, 68-76, PROF MICROBIOL, SCH MED, UNIV PA, 76- *Personal Data:* b Brooklyn, NY, May 29, 32; m 63, Norah C Johnston; c Cynthia A & Sarah C. *Educ:* City Col New York, BS, 53; Univ Chicago, PhD(biochem), 57. *Honors & Awards:* Fel, Am Acad Microbiol. *Prof Exp:* Res fel, Dept Chem, Harvard Univ, 59-63; instr bact & immunol, Harvard Med Sch, 62-63, assoc, 63-66, asst prof, 66-68. *Concurrent Pos:* USPHS res fel, 58-60; Am Cancer Soc scholar, 60-63; tutor biochem sci, Harvard Univ, 60-67; res career develop award, Nat Inst Allergy & Infectious Dis, 65-68; mem, Physiol Chem Study Sect, Div Res Grants, NIH , 69-73; chmn, Lipid Metabolism, Gordon Res Conf, 75; Josiah Macy Jr Found fac scholar, 76-77; assoc ed, J Lipid Res, 83-86; Fogarty sr int fel, 85; exec ed, Anal Biochem. *Mem:* AAAS; Am Soc Biochem & Molecular Biol; Am Soc Microbiol; Soc Gen Microbiol. *Res:* Microbial metabolism; lipid chemistry and metabolism; cell membrane structure and function; bacterial pathogenesis. *Mailing Add:* Dept Microbiol Sch Med Univ Pa Philadelphia PA 19104. *Fax:* 215-573-9068; *E-Mail:* goldfinh@mail.med.upenn.edu

GOLDFINE, IRA D, CELL BIOLOGY. *Current Pos:* from asst prof to assoc prof, Dept Med, Univ Calif, San Francisco, 73-85, dir, Cell Biol Res Lab, Mt Zion Med Ctr, 79-87, PROF, DEPT MED & PHYSIOL, UNIV CALIF, SAN FRANCISCO, 85-, ASSOC CHIEF MED, MT ZION MED CTR, 85-, DIR, DIV DIABETES & ENDOCRINE RES, 87- *Personal Data:* b Chicago, Ill, Aug 10, 43. *Educ:* Univ Ill, MD, 67; Am Bd Internal Med, cert, 72, cert endocrinol & metab, 72. *Honors & Awards:* Mary Jane Kugel Award, Juvenile Diabetes Asn, 88; Rosenthal Award, Am Col Physicians, 89. *Prof Exp:* Intern, Michael Reese Hosp, Chicago, 67-68; resident med, Univ Chicago, 68-70; NIH fel, Nat Inst Arthritis & Metab Dis, Bethesda, Md, 70-71, staff assoc, 71-73. *Concurrent Pos:* Vis scientist, Dept Endocrinol, Karolinska Hosp, Stockholm, Sweden, 70; clin investr, Vet Admin Hosp, San Francisco, 77-78; mem sci rev comt, Juvenile Diabetes Found, 85-89; mem, Metab Study Sect, NIH, 86-87. *Mem:* Fel Am Col Physicians; Am Fedn Clin Res; AAAS; Endocrine Soc; Am Thyroid Asn; Am Diabetes Soc; Am Soc Clin Invest; Am Soc Cell Biol; Am Asn Physicians. *Res:* Diabetes research; author of numerous scientific publications. *Mailing Add:* Diabetes Res Mt Zion Med Ctr Univ Calif 1600 Divisadero St PO Box 1616 San Francisco CA 94143-1616. *Fax:* 415-885-7724

GOLDFINE, LEWIS JOHN, PHYSICAL MEDICINE & REHABILITATION. *Current Pos:* Asst prof, 69-73, ASSOC PROF REHAB MED, SCH MED, UNIV MD, 73- *Personal Data:* b London, Eng. *Educ:* Univ London, MB, BS, 61; Royal Col Physicians & Surgeons, dipl phys med, 67. *Concurrent Pos:* Consult, Vet Admin Hosp, Ft Howard, Md, 85- & Baltimore, Md, 90- *Mem:* Fel Am Acad Phys Med & Rehab; Am Asn Acad Physiatrists. *Res:* Arthritis rehabilitation; undergraduate and postgraduate education in rehabilitation medicine. *Mailing Add:* Univ Md Sch Med 655 W Baltimore St Baltimore MD 21201-1559

GOLDFINGER, ANDREW DAVID, PHYSICS, SYSTEMS ENGINEERING. *Current Pos:* PHYSICIST RES & DEVELOP, APPL PHYSICS LAB, JOHNS HOPKINS UNIV, 72- *Personal Data:* b New York, NY, Mar 12, 45. *Educ:* Rensselaer Polytech Inst, BS, 65; Brandeis Univ, PhD(physics), 72; Johns Hopkins Univ, MS, 80. *Mem:* Am Geophys Union; Inst Elec & Electronics Engrs. *Res:* Remote sensing; atmosphere and ocean physics; orbital mechanics; navigation; image processing; radar; microwave systems; space technology. *Mailing Add:* Johns Hopkins Univ Bldg 24E-198 Johns Hopkins Rd Laurel MD 20723

GOLDFISCHER, SIDNEY L, PATHOLOGY, CYTOCHEMISTRY. *Current Pos:* From asst prof to assoc prof, 65-74, actg chmn path, 84-93, PROF PATH, ALBERT EINSTEIN COL MED, 74- *Personal Data:* b New York, NY, Dec 28, 26; m 90, Cleo M Dana; c Carl, Susan, Michael & Madeline. *Educ:* Columbia Univ, BS, 58; NY Univ, MD, 61. *Concurrent Pos:* attend pathologist, Bronx Munic Hosp Ctr, 71-; dir, Office of Indust Liason, Albert Einstein Col Med, 83-; Burroughs Wellcome Prof, 88; assoc dean, Albert Einstein Col Med, 90- *Mem:* NY Acad Sci; Histochem Soc; Am Soc Cell Biol; Int Acad Path; Am Asn Path. *Res:* Development of cytochemical staining procedures for light and electron microscopy; application of these procedures which permit a synthesis of functional and morphological studies to problems in physiology and pathology at the subcellular level; discovery and elucidation of peroxisomal diseases. *Mailing Add:* Albert Einstein Col Med 1300 Morris Park Ave Bldg B302 Bronx NY 10461-1975. *Fax:* 718-430-8822

GOLDFRANK, LEWIS ROBERT, TOXICOLOGY. *Current Pos:* DIR, EMERGENCY MED SERVS, BELLEVUE HOSP CTR & NY UNIV MED CTR, 79-; ASSOC PROF CLIN MED, NY UNIV MED CTR, 79- *Personal Data:* b Sept 8, 41; m 64, Susan Harrington; c Michelle, Andrew, Jennifer & Rebecca. *Educ:* Clark Univ, BA, 63; Univ Brussels, Belgium, MD, 70; Am Bd Internal Med, cert, 73; Am Bd Med Toxicol, cert, 82. *Hon Degrees:* LHD, Clark Univ, 93. *Prof Exp:* Intern, Mt Sinai Hosp-Univ Conn Health Ctr, 70-71; resident, Montefiore Hosp, 71-73; attending & mem, Dept Med & Ambulatory Servs & dir, Dept Emergency Med, Morrisania City Hosp, 73-76; dir, Emergency Servs, NCent Bronx Hosp, 76-79; dir, Emergency Med Servs, Montefiore Hosp & Med Ctr, 77-79; assoc prof med, Albert Einstein Col Med, 79. *Concurrent Pos:* Assoc attending, Bellevue Hosp Ctr, NY Univ Med Ctr & Manhattan Vet Admin Hosp, 79-; med dir, New York City Poison Control Ctr, 79-; attending, Dept Ambulatory Care, Woodhill Hosp, 84-88; affil clin prof clin pharm, St John's Univ, 85-; mem, Task Force Substance Abuse, Am Col Emergency Physicians; clin assoc fac, Hunter-Bellevue Sch Nursing, 92-93; vis prof, Univ Tex-Houston Med Ctr, 96. *Mem:* Inst Med-Nat Acad Sci; Soc Acad Emergency Med (pres-elect, 94-95, pres, 95-96); fel Am Col Physicians; fel Am Col-Emergency Physicians; Am Asn Poison Control Ctrs; fel Am Acad Clin Toxicol; Am Col Med Toxicol; Am Bd Emergency Med; Am Pub Health Asn; NY Acad Med; fel NY Acad Med. *Mailing Add:* Bellevue Hosp 27th St & First Ave New York NY 10016. *Fax:* 212-562-3001

GOLDFRANK, MAX, chemical engineering; deceased, see previous edition for last biography

GOLDFRIED, MARVIN R, PSYCHOTHERAPY, CLINICAL PSYCHOLOGY. *Current Pos:* PROF PSYCHOL, STATE UNIV NY, STONY BROOK, 64- *Personal Data:* b Brooklyn, NY, Jan 24, 36; m 67, Anita Powers; c Daniel & Michael. *Educ:* Brooklyn Col, BA, 57; State Univ NY, Buffalo, PhD(clin psychol), 61; Am Bd Prof Psychol, dipl, 69. *Hon Degrees:* Dipl, Am Bd Prof Psychol, 69. *Prof Exp:* Instr psychol, State Univ NY, Buffalo, 60-61; asst prof psychol, Univ Rochester, 61-64. *Concurrent Pos:* Vis assoc prof, Bar-Ilan Univ, Ramat Gan, Israel, 70-71; vis scholar, Univ Calif, Berkeley, 77-78; assoc ed, Cognitive Ther & Res, 77-82; prin investr, NIMH grant, 66-68, 67-71, 73-84, 74, 84-88, & 89-; mem adv bd, Soc Explor

Psychother Integration, 83- *Mem:* Am Psychol Asn; Asn Advan Behav Ther; Soc Psychother Res (pres elect, 97); Soc Explor Psychother Integration. *Res:* Delineation of common therapeutic principles of change that can cut across various therapeutic orientations; overall objective is to get beyond the constraints of those language problems that prevent communication across the different orientations; focus on those various activities that effective clinicians use that may be functionally linked to ultimate successful outcome. *Mailing Add:* Dept Psychol State Univ NY-Stony Brook Stony Brook NY 11794. *Fax:* 212-988-4495; *E-Mail:* mgoldfried@ccmail.sunysb.edu

GOLDHABER, ALFRED SCHARFF, THEORETICAL PHYSICS. *Current Pos:* asst prof, 67-72, assoc prof, 72-77, PROF PHYSICS, STATE UNIV NY STONY BROOK, 77- *Personal Data:* b Urbana, Ill, July 4, 40; m 69; c 2. *Educ:* Harvard Univ, AB, 61; Princeton Univ, PhD(physics), 64. *Prof Exp:* Miller fel pysics, Univ Calif, Berkeley, 64-66, lectr, 66-67. *Concurrent Pos:* Vis staff mem, Los Alamos Sci Lab, 64-; US-USSR Acad Sci exchange vis, 70; NSF sr fel, Europ Orgn Nuclear Res, 71; sr vis, Lawrence Berkeley Lab, 77; vis prof, Univ Sussex, 78, Cambridge Univ, 86-87; Coorganizer, Int Sem High Energy Collisions Nuclei, Hakone, Japan, 80. *Mem:* Fel Am Phys Soc. *Res:* High energy theory; weak interactions; optical models; electrodynamics; nuclear physics; classical limits; magnetic monopoles. *Mailing Add:* Inst Theoret Physics State Univ NY at Stony Brook Stony Brook NY 11794

GOLDHABER, GERSON, ELEMENTARY PARTICLE PHYSICS. *Current Pos:* from actg asst prof to assoc prof, 53-64, PROF PHYSICS, GRAD SCH, UNIV CALIF, BERKELEY, 64- *Personal Data:* b Chemnitz, Ger, Feb 20, 24; nat US; m 69; c 3. *Educ:* Hebrew Univ, MSc, 47; Univ Wis, PhD, 50. *Hon Degrees:* PhD, Univ Stockholm, 86. *Honors & Awards:* Pandofsky Prize, Am Phys Soc, 91. *Prof Exp:* Asst physics, Hebrew Univ, 47 & Univ Wis, 48-50; instr, Columbia Univ, 50-53. *Concurrent Pos:* Asst res prof, Miller Inst Basic Res, 57-58; Ford Found fel, Europ Orgn Nuclear Res, 60-61; group leader, Lawrence Berkeley Lab, Berkeley, 62-; Guggenheim fel, Europ Orgn Nuclear Res, 72-73; prof, Miller Inst Basic Res, Univ Calif, 75-76 & 84-85; Morris Loeb lectr, Harvard Univ, 76-77; vis fel, CERN, 86. *Mem:* Nat Acad Sci; fel Am Phys Soc; Swed Royal Acad Sci. *Res:* Experimental meson and antiproton interactions; charmed meson studies in electron-positron annihilation; high energy and elementary particle physics; astro-particle physics. *Mailing Add:* Dept Physics 50-208 Lawrence Berkeley Lab Univ Calif Berkeley CA 94720. *Fax:* 510-486-6738; *E-Mail:* gerson@lbl.gov

GOLDHABER, GERTRUDE SCHARFF, PHYSICS. *Current Pos:* RETIRED. *Personal Data:* b Mannheim, Ger, July 14, 11; nat US; m 39, Maurice; c 2. *Educ:* Univ Munich, PhD(physics), 35. *Prof Exp:* Res assoc physics, Imp Col, Univ London, 35-39; res physicist, Univ Ill, 39-48, spec res asst prof, 48-50; from assoc physicist to sr physicist, Brookhaven Nat Lab, 50-79; adj prof, Cornell Univ, 80-82 & Johns Hopkins Univ, 82-87; adj prof, Johns Hopkins Univ, 82-87. *Concurrent Pos:* Consult, Argonne Nat Lab, 48-50 & Los Alamos Nat Lab, 53-; chmn, Panel Eval Nuclear Data Compilations, Nat Acad Sci-Nat Res Coun, 69-71; mem, Res Adv Comt, NSF, 72-74; mem bd trustees, Fermi Nat Accelerator Lab, 72-77; mem report rev comt, Nat Acad Sci, 73-81, mem forum comt, 74-81; sci consult, Arms Control Disarmament Agency, 74-77; mem nom comt, Presidential Medal of Sci, 77-79; NAm rep, Europhysics J, Inst Physics, Bristol, London, 78-80; mem comt educ & employ women in sci & eng, Nat Res Coun Comn Human Resources, 78-83; mem, Educ Adv Comt, NY Acad Sci, 82-; vis scholar, Nat Adv Comt Sci, Technol & Soc, 83-88; mem, Comt Human Rights, 84-87, Nat Acad Sci, 84-87. *Mem:* Nat Acad Sci; fel Am Phys Soc; fel AAAS; Sigma Xi. *Res:* Spontaneous fission neutrons; identity of beta-rays with atomic electrons; K-forbiddenness; odd-odd nuclei; long-lived isomers; variable moment of inertia law; parity violation in electromagnetic transitions; relation of moment of inertia to quadrupole moment; heavy ion physics; study of band structure in relation to nuclear dynamics, neutron proton interaction in pseudo-magic nuclei; relation of variable moment of inertia law to interacting boson approximation; discovery of heaviest pseudomajor nucleus at major number. *Mailing Add:* Dept Physics Brookhaven Nat Lab Upton NY 11973

GOLDHABER, JACOB KOPEL, ALGEBRA. *Current Pos:* res assoc prof, Univ Md, College Park, 60-61, head dept, 68-77, prof math, 61-93, actg dean grad studies & res, 84-85 & 87-92, actg vpres acad affairs & provost, 92-93, EMER PROF, UNIV MD, COLLEGE PARK, 93- *Personal Data:* b Brooklyn, NY, Apr 12, 24; m 51; c Doreet, David & Aviva. *Educ:* Brooklyn Col, BA, 44; Harvard Univ, MA, 45; Univ Wis, PhD(math), 50. *Prof Exp:* Instr math, Univ Conn, 50-53 & Cornell Univ, 53-55; from asst prof to assoc prof math, Wash Univ, 55-60. *Concurrent Pos:* NSF sci fac fel, 66-67; exec secy, off math sci, Nat Res Coun, 75-82, actg dean grad studies & res, 84-85, 87- *Mem:* AAAS; Am Math Soc; Math Asn Am. *Mailing Add:* 2801 NMex Ave NW Washington DC 20007

GOLDHABER, MAURICE, NUCLEAR PHYSICS, FUNDAMENTAL PARTICLES. *Current Pos:* sr scientist, Brookhaven Nat Lab, Assoc Univs, Inc, 50-60, chmn, Dept Physics, 60-61, dir, 61-73, distinguished scientist, 73-85, EMER DISTINGUISHED SCIENTIST, BROOKHAVEN NAT LAB, ASSOC UNIVS, INC, 85- *Personal Data:* b Lemberg, Austria, Apr 18, 11; nat US; m 39, Gertrude Scharff; c Alfred & Michael. *Educ:* Cambridge Univ, PhD(physics), 36. *Hon Degrees:* PhD, Tel-Aviv Univ, 74; Dr, Univ Louvain-La-Neuve, 82, State Univ NY, Stony Brook, 83; DSc, Univ Notre Dame, 92. *Honors & Awards:* Morris Loeb Lectr, Harvard Univ, 55; Tom W Bonner Prize Nuclear Physics, Am Phys Soc, 71; Pauli Mem Lectr, Zurich, 80; J Robert Oppenheimer Mem Prize, 82; Nat Medal Sci, 83; Leonard Schiff Mem Lectr, Stanford Univ, 84; Henry Newson Mem Lectr, Duke Univ, 84; Brickwedde Lectr, Johns Hopkins Univ, 85; Am Acad Achievement Award, 85; Rutherford Mem Lectr, Royal Soc, Can, 87; Peter Axel Mem Lectr, Univ Ill, 89; Samuel Goudsmit Mem Lectr, Univ Nev, 90; Boris Jacobsen Mem Lectr, Univ Wash, 90; Wolf Prize Physics, Jerusalem, 91. *Prof Exp:* Charles Kingley Bye fel, Magdalene Col, Cambridge, 36-38; from asst prof to prof physics, Univ Ill, 38-50. *Concurrent Pos:* Assoc ed, Phys Rev, 51-53; consult labs, AEC; mem, Nuclear Sci Comt, Nat Res Coun; mem bd gov, Weizmann Inst & Tel-Aviv Univ; adj prof physics, State Univ NY, Stony Brook, 61-; vis fel, Clare Hall, Cambridge, Eng, 67; chmn, Nuclear Phys Div, Am Phys Soc, 68 & Sect B Physics, AAAS, 80; consult, Nat Labs, Nat Res Coun, Adv Panel Physics, NSF & NY State Adv Coun Advan Indust Res & Develop; mem adv bd, Fla State Univ, Univ Ga & Univ Mich; mem sci coun, Ctr Theoret Studies, Univ Miami. *Mem:* Nat Acad Sci; fel Am Philos Soc (pres, 83); Am Acad Arts & Sci; AAAS; fel Am Philos Soc (pres, 83); Sigma Xi. *Res:* Nuclear physics; radioactivity; nuclear isomers; photoelectric effect and models; fundamental particles; electromagnetic transitions in nuclei and their role in elucidating nuclear structure; slow neutrons; nuclear theory; weak interactions; astrophysics. *Mailing Add:* Brookhaven Nat Lab Assoc Univs Inc Upton NY 11973

GOLDHABER, PAUL, DENTISTRY, PERIODONTAL DISEASES. *Current Pos:* res assoc oral path, Harvard Sch Dent Med, 55-56, assoc, 56-59, from asst prof to assoc prof, 59-66, dir postdoctoral studies, 62-68, dean, 68-90, PROF PERIODONT, HARVARD SCH DENT MED, 66-, EMER DEAN, 90- *Personal Data:* b New York, NY, Mar 16, 24; m 49; c 2. *Educ:* NY Univ, DDS, 48; City Col New York, BS, 54; Am Bd Periodont, dipl, 54. *Hon Degrees:* MA, Harvard Univ, 62. *Prof Exp:* Asst ophthal res, Harvard Med Sch, 48-50; asst dent, Sch Dent & Oral Surg, Columbia Univ, 50. *Concurrent Pos:* Vol tissue-cult technician, Sloan-Kettering Inst Cancer Res, 46-48; asst opthal res, Mass Eye & Ear Infirmary, 48-50; res fel dent med, Harvard Sch Dent Med, 54-55; vis res fel, Sloan-Kettering Inst Cancer Res, 54-55, res fel, 55-56; USPHS sr res fel, 56-61 & res career develop award, 61-66; dent consult, Fulbright Med Sci Comt, 65; mem, Periodont Dis Adv Comt, Nat Inst Dent Res, 75-; mem, Nat Adv Dent Res Coun, NIH, 88-; vis prof, Univ Southern Calif, 90-91, Univ Calif, Los Angeles, 90-91, Fac Dent, Louis Pasteur Univ, France, 91. *Mem:* Inst Med-Nat Acad Sci; fel AAAS; Tissue Cult Asn; Int Asn Dent Res (pres, 85-86); Am Soc Cell Biol; fel NY Acad Sci; Am Dent Asn; Am Asn Cancer Res; Am Acad Periodont; Am Asn Dent Res. *Res:* Periodontal disease; oral carcinogenesis; bone transplantation; bone resorption and formation in tissue culture. *Mailing Add:* Harvard Sch Dent Med 188 Longwood Ave Boston MA 02115. *Fax:* 617-432-4262

GOLDHAMMER, PAUL, NUCLEAR PHYSICS. *Current Pos:* RETIRED. *Personal Data:* b Portland, Ore, Nov 10, 29. *Educ:* Reed Col, BA, 52; Wash Univ, PhD(physics), 56. *Prof Exp:* Asst prof physics, Univ Del, 56-57; from asst prof to prof physics, Univ Nebr, 57-64; prof physics, Univ Kans, 64-89. *Mem:* Fel Am Phys Soc. *Res:* Theoretical nuclear physics. *Mailing Add:* 0305 SW Montgomery No 407 Portland OR 97201

GOLDHIRSH, JULIUS, ELECTRICAL ENGINEERING. *Current Pos:* SR ENGR, APPL PHYSICS LAB, JOHNS HOPKINS UNIV, 72-, PRIN STAFF, 79-, GROUP SUPVR, SPACE GEOPHYS GROUP, SPACE DEPT, 79- *Personal Data:* b Philadelphia, Pa, Oct 2, 35; m 71; c 4. *Educ:* Drexel Inst, BS, 58; Rutgers Univ, MS, 60; Univ Pa, PhD(elec eng), 64. *Prof Exp:* Asst instr elec eng, Rutgers Univ, 58-59, res asst plasmas, 59-60; instr elec eng, Univ Pa, 60-65, asst prof, 65-71; assoc prof, Holon Univ Technol, Israel, 71-72. *Concurrent Pos:* Consult, Raytheon Co, Mass, 63-68; mem Int Radio Consult Comt; instr, Johns Hopkins Univ, 85-; vchmn, Int Union Radio Sci, 91- *Mem:* Fel Inst Elec & Electronics Engrs; Int Union Radio Sci; Sigma Xi; Consultative Comt Int Radio. *Res:* Radio wave propagation; remote sensing from ground and satellites; radar meteorology, rain attenuation; mobile satellite system propagation. *Mailing Add:* Appl Physics Lab Johns Hopkins Rd Laurel MD 20707

GOLDHOR, SUSAN, SCIENCE EDUCATION. *Current Pos:* PRES, CTR FOR APPL REGIONAL STUDIES, 81- *Personal Data:* b Brooklyn, NY, Mar 24, 39. *Educ:* Barnard Col, AB, 60; Yale Univ, MS, 62, PhD(biol), 67. *Hon Degrees:* DHL, Wyndham Col, 74. *Prof Exp:* Am Cancer Soc res fel, Dept Biol Sci, Stanford Univ, 67-68, NIH res fel, 68-69; asst prof biol, Hacettepe Univ, Turkey, 69-71; vis fel biol, Yale Univ, 71-73; assoc prof biol & dean natural sci, 73-77, dir New Eng Farm Ctr, Hampshire Col, 78-81. *Concurrent Pos:* Mem, Adv Comt Sci Educ, NSF, 75-78; mem, Biomass Conversion, Advan Study Inst, NATO, 82; leader, Northeastern Regional Aquaculture Ctr Proj, USDA, 90-93. *Mem:* Atlantic Fisheries Technologists; World Aquacult Soc. *Res:* Economic development of natural resources based industries; technology transfer; waste utilization; developing environmentally benign and economically acceptable technologies for utilising animal agriculture and fisheries processing waste and developing products from those wastes; cleaning waste water. *Mailing Add:* 45B Museum St Cambridge MA 02138-1921. *E-Mail:* 70760.742@compuserve.com

GOLDICH, SAMUEL STEPHEN, geology, for more information see previous edition

GOLDIE, JAMES HUGH, MEDICAL ONCOLOGY. *Current Pos:* head oncol, Div Advan Therapeut, 76-95, head med oncol, 84-95, STAFF MED ONCOL, BC CANCER AGENCY, 76-; PROF MED, UNIV BC, 84- *Personal Data:* b Windsor, Ont, Jan 16, 37; m 70; c 1. *Educ:* Univ Toronto, MD, 61; FRCPS(C), 66. *Honors & Awards:* Terry Fox Medal, 82; Camo Lectr, 90. *Prof Exp:* Asst prof med, Univ Toronto, 70-76; from asst prof to assoc prof, Univ BC, 76-84. *Concurrent Pos:* R S McLaughlin Found fel, 69-70; Med Res Coun Can grant, 70-73; Ont Cancer Treatment & Res Found grant, 73-76; chmn invest drugs comt, Nat Cancer Inst Can, 78-82, grant, 80-; mem bd sci counrs, Nat Cancer Inst, 82-85; assoc ed, Cancer Res, 83-86; mem adv coun res, Nat Cancer Inst Can, 86-89; mem, ad hoc drug screening comt,

Nat Cancer Inst US, 86-89. *Mem:* Am Soc Clin Oncol; Am Asn Cancer Res; Can Oncol Soc; Royal Col Physicians Can. *Res:* Clinical and cellular pharmacology of antineoplastic drugs. *Mailing Add:* BC Cancer Agency 600 W Tenth Ave Vancouver BC V5Z 4E6 Can

GOLDIN, ABRAHAM SAMUEL, CHEMISTRY. *Current Pos:* ENVIRON SCIENTIST, US ENVIRON PROTECTION AGENCY, 77- *Personal Data:* b Brooklyn, NY, Apr 22, 17; m 45; c 3. *Educ:* Columbia Univ, AB, 37, AM, 41; Univ Tenn, PhD, 51. *Prof Exp:* Control chemist, Eastern Wine Corp, NY, 41; prod chemist, Mutual Chem Co, NJ, 42; res asst, sam labs, Columbia Univ, 42-45; tech engr & chemist, Carbide & Carbon Chem Corp, 45-50; radiochemist, USPHS, 51-60; chem dir, Nat Lead Co, Inc, 60-61; assoc prof, NY Univ, 61-62; dep officer in charge, Northeastern Radiol Health Lab, 62-68; assoc prof, Sch Pub Health, Harvard Univ, 68-74; dir tech opers, Radiation Mgt Corp, 74-76. *Mem:* AAAS; Am Chem Soc; Health Physics Soc; Am Inst Chemists; Am Pub Health Asn. *Res:* Assessment of envionmental radioactivity and radiation; radio analytical quality assurance; radiation protection standards; measurement of radioactivity and radiation; radioactive waste management and disposal. *Mailing Add:* 6910 Hillmead Rd Bethesda MD 20817-3028

GOLDIN, CLAUDIA DALE, ECONONOMICS. *Current Pos:* PROF, HARVARD UNIV, 90- *Personal Data:* b New York, NY, May 14, 46. *Educ:* Cornell Univ, BA, 67; Univ Chicago, MA, 69, PhD, 72. *Hon Degrees:* MA, Univ Pa, 85 & Harvard Univ, 90; DHL, Univ Nebr, 94. *Prof Exp:* Asst prof econs, Univ Wis, 71-73; asst prof, Princeton Univ, NJ, 73-79; from assoc prof to prof, Univ Pa, Philadelphia, 79-90. *Concurrent Pos:* Vis lectr, Harvard Univ, 75-76; NSF Award, 75-77, 79-81, 81-82, 84-86, 87-89, 92-93 & 96-; res assoc & proj dir, Nat Bur Econ Res, Cambridge, 79-; Guggenheim fel, 87-88; vis fel, Indust Rels Sect, Princeton Univ, NJ, 87-88 & Brookings Inst, 93-94; Spencer Found Res Award, 96- *Mem:* Am Acad Arts & Sci; Am Econ Asn (vpres, 90-91); fel Econometric Soc; Econ Hist Asn (vpres, 88-89). *Mailing Add:* Dept Econs Harvard Univ Cambridge MA 02138

GOLDIN, DANIEL S, SPACE & TECHNOLOGY. *Current Pos:* res scientist, Lewis Res Ctr, Cleveland, 62-67, ADMINR, NASA, WASHINGTON, 92- *Personal Data:* b New York, NY, July 23, 40; M, Judith L Kramer; c Ariel & Laura. *Educ:* City Col New York, BS, 62. *Honors & Awards:* John F Kennedy Astronaut Award, Am Astronaut Soc, 93; Space Pioneer Award, Nat Space Soc, 93. *Prof Exp:* Mem tech staff, TRW Inc, Redondo, 67-86, vpres & gen mgr, Space & Tech Group, 87-92. *Mem:* Fel Am Inst Aeronaut & Astronaut; fel Inst Advan Eng. *Res:* Government agency administrator for space technology. *Mailing Add:* Off Admin 9F44 NASA 300 E St SW Washington DC 20546-0005. *E-Mail:* daniel.goldin@hq.nasa.gov

GOLDIN, EDWIN, QUANTUM OPTICS, COMPUTER EDUCATION. *Current Pos:* asst ed, Div Mgr & Assoc Dir Soc Physics Students, 90-93, MGR, CAREER PLANNING & PLACEMENT, AM INST PHYSICS, 90- *Personal Data:* b Philadelphia, Pa, Oct 12, 38; m 75, Marjorie Bolnardi; c Philip, Matin, Lauren, Amanda & Julia. *Educ:* Temple Univ, BA, 59; Polytech Inst Brooklyn, MA, 61; Polytech Inst NY, PhD(physics), 73. *Prof Exp:* Asst prof physics, Maritime Col, State Univ NY, 66-68; dir, Univ Air, Queens Col, NY, 68-70; asst prof, Fordham Univ NY, 70-76; asst prof math & physics, Ramapo Col NJ, 76-81; proj dir, NSF Cause Comput grant, Bethany Col, WVa, 81-84, dir Acad Comput Ctr & Dual Degree Eng Prog, 81-88, prof physics & head dept, 81-88; prof officer, Fund Improv Post-Sec Educ, US Dept Educ, 88-90. *Concurrent Pos:* Cong scientist fel, Am Phys Soc, 87-88; sci adv & legis asst to US Rep, Edward Markey, 87-88; consult solar design, Hasco, Inc, 80; chnm, Comt Physics Higher Educ, Am Asn Physics Teachers, 84-86; bd mem, comp in educ, Carnegie-Mellon Univ, 86-87; dir, hon Sci Appln Prog, 84-87. *Mem:* Am Asn Physics Teachers; AAAS; Am Phys Soc. *Res:* Coherent states of quantized fields and correlation in quantum optics; computer graphics and animation for instructional quantum theory films; solar design and engineering; computer education; physics education and physics manpower planning, placement and development. *Mailing Add:* 1608 Montmorency Dr Vienna MD 22182. *Fax:* 301-209-0841; *E-Mail:* edg@aip.org

GOLDIN, GERALD ALAN, MATHEMATICAL PHYSICS, MATHEMATICS EDUCATION. *Current Pos:* assoc prof, 84-85, PROF MATH, PHYSICS & COMPUT EDUC, RUTGERS UNIV, 85- *Personal Data:* b Brooklyn, NY, Oct 16, 43; m 68; c 2. *Educ:* Harvard Univ, BA, 64; Princeton Univ, MA, 66, PhD(physics), 69. *Prof Exp:* Res assoc physics, Univ Pa, 68-70, asst prof educ, 71-77; from asst prof to assoc prof math sci, Northern Ill Univ, 77-85. *Concurrent Pos:* US Off Educ fel, Univ Pa, 70-71; vis lectr, Cabrini Col, 74-78 & Beaver Col, 75-78; vis staff mem, Los Alamos Nat Lab, 77-; vis fel, Princeton Univ, 82-83; vis assoc prof, Teachers Col, Columbia Univ, 82-83; guest prof, Tech Univ Clausthal, 86-; vis distinguished prof, Northern Ill Univ, 90-91. *Mem:* Nat Coun Teachers Math; Math Asn Am; Am Educ Res Asn; Am Math Soc; Int Asn Math Physics. *Res:* Group representations in mathematical physics; science and mathematics education; the psychology of mathematical problem solving. *Mailing Add:* Ctr Math Sci & Comput Educ Rutgers Univ SERC Bldg Rm 239 Busch Campus Piscataway NJ 08855-1179

GOLDIN, MILTON, BACTERIOLOGY. *Current Pos:* DIR MICROBIOL DEPT, MT SINAI HOSP MED CTR, 48- *Personal Data:* b New York, NY, July 26, 17; m 51; c 3. *Educ:* Brooklyn Col, BS, 38; Univ Ill, MS, 48; Chicago Med Sch, PhD, 70. *Prof Exp:* Bacteriologist, USPHS, 41-42; chief bacteriologist, Hektoen Inst, Cook Co Hosp, 46-48. *Concurrent Pos:* Assoc prof, Rush Med Sch, 75- *Mem:* Am Soc Microbiol; Sigma Xi. *Res:* Factors determining virulence of infectious organisms; immunological studies in collagen diseases; mycotic infections in humans. *Mailing Add:* 1500 Sheridan Rd Wilmette IL 60091

GOLDIN, STANLEY MICHAEL, BIOCHEMISTRY, NEUROBIOLOGY. *Current Pos:* Harvard Soc Fel biochem, 76-79, from asst prof to assoc prof pharmacol, 79-89, LECTR BIOCHEM, HARVARD MED SCH, 90-; PRES, SPIRATION TECH, 95- *Personal Data:* b New York, NY, 48; m 75; c 2. *Educ:* Mass Inst Technol, SB, SM, 70; Harvard Univ, PhD(biochem), 77. *Honors & Awards:* Chem Commendation, Am Chem Soc, 65; Searle Award, 81. *Prof Exp:* Proj leader membrane develop, Millipore Corp, 70-72. *Concurrent Pos:* Consult, Millipore Corp, 71-75; McKnight scholar, 81 & Rita Allen Scholar, 85; dir pharmacol, Cambridge Neurosci Inc, 95-95. *Mem:* Sigma Xi; AAAS. *Res:* Membrane biochemistry and physiology; biochemistry and organization of nervous system; molecular basis of neuronal electrical activity. *Mailing Add:* Spiration Technol Inc 10 Russell Rd Lexington MA 02173

GOLDING, BRAGE, POLYMER CHEMISTRY, EDUCATION ADMINISTRATION. *Current Pos:* RETIRED. *Personal Data:* b Chicago, Ill, Apr 28, 20; m 41; c 3. *Educ:* Purdue Univ, BS, 41, PhD(chem eng), 48. *Hon Degrees:* LLD, Wright State Univ. *Prof Exp:* Asst dir res, Lilly Varnish Co, 48-57, dir, 57-59; prof chem eng & head sch, Purdue Univ, 59-66, res assoc, 48-57, vis prof, 57-59; vpres, Wright State Campus, Miami Univ, Ohio State Univ, 66; pres, Wright State Univ, 67-72, San Diego State Univ, 72-77, Kent State Univ, 77-82 & Metrop State Col, 84-85; actg pres, Western State Col, 85-92. *Mem:* Fel AAAS; Am Chem Soc; Soc Plastics Engrs; Am Soc Testing & Mat; Am Inst Chem Engrs. *Res:* Surface coatings technology; polymer technology and research; organic technology. *Mailing Add:* 12179 Branicole Lane San Diego CA 92129

GOLDING, BRAGE, JR, EXPERIMENTAL SOLID STATE & ACOUSTICS PHYSICS. *Current Pos:* PROF PHYSICS, MICH STATE UNIV, 91- *Personal Data:* b Ft Bragg, NC, Sept 24, 42; m 64; c 2. *Educ:* Purdue Univ, BMetE, 63; Mass Inst Technol, PhD(mat sci), 66. *Honors & Awards:* Humboldt Prize. *Prof Exp:* Res asst mat sci, Mass Inst Technol, 63-66, res assoc, 66-67; mem tech staff, Bell Labs, 67-81, head, Condensed State Phys Res Dept, 81-84, head, Nonequilibrium Physics Res Dept, 85-91. *Mem:* AAAS; fel Am Phys Soc. *Res:* Experimental research on the behavior of high frequency sound waves propagating in solids undergoing phase transitions; the nature of excitations in amorphous solids at ultra low temperatures; optical properties of glasses; novel superconductors; low temperature physics; resonance; noise in mesoscopic systems. *Mailing Add:* 908 E Geneva Dr Dewitt MI 48824-9569

GOLDING, DOUGLAS LAWRENCE, FOREST HYDROLOGY. *Current Pos:* EMER PROF FOREST HYDROL, UNIV BC, 78- *Personal Data:* b St John, Can, May 5, 31; m 56; c 3. *Educ:* Univ NB, Fredericton, BSc, 53; Purdue Univ, MS, 61; Univ BC, PhD(forest hydrol), 68. *Prof Exp:* From forester mgt to forester inventory, Sask Dept Natural Resources, 54-64; res scientist forest hydrol, Can Forestry Serv, Can Dept Environ, 67-78. *Mem:* Can Inst Forestry; NZ Hydrol Soc; Can Meteorol Soc. *Res:* Snowpack management for water yield and regime through forest cover manipulation; snow ablation during chinook conditions; energy balances in forest and forest openings; erosion and slope stability; water yield and regime changes related to forest management. *Mailing Add:* Fac Forestry MacMillan Bldg Univ BC 2075 Westbrook Mall Vancouver BC V6T 1W5 Can

GOLDING, HANA, VIROLOGY. *Current Pos:* sr staff fel, 87-89, SR INVESTR, DIV VIROL, CBER, FOOD & DRUG ADMIN, 89- *Personal Data:* b Jerusalem, Israel, Dec 26, 49; US citizen; m; c 2. *Educ:* Hebrew Univ, Jerusalem, BSc, 72; Ore Health Sci Univ, PhD(immunol), 81. *Prof Exp:* Res asst, Cell & Clin Immunol Lab, SAfrican Inst Med Res, 73-75. *Concurrent Pos:* Tartar Found res award, 78-80; NIH AIDS res grants, 87-88 & 91. *Mem:* Am Asn Immunologists. *Res:* AIDS; author of numerous scientific publications. *Mailing Add:* Div Virol Prods CBER FDA HFM-457 Bldg 29B Rm 4NN04 Bethesda MD 20892-0001. *Fax:* 301-496-1810

GOLDING, LEONARD S, SATELLITE COMMUNICATIONS, TELEVISION TRANSMISSION. *Current Pos:* founder, Digital Commun, 71-75, vpres & dir, Macon Res Ctr, 82-85, VPRES, RES & DEVELOP, HUGHES AIRCRAFT, 75-, VPRES, ENG NETWORK SYSTS, 87- *Personal Data:* b New York City, NY, June 28, 35; US citizen. *Educ:* Columbia Univ, BA, 57, BS, 58; Yale Univ, MS, 60, DEngr, 66. *Prof Exp:* Res asst, Bell Tel Labs, 60-62; sr tech staff, Raytheon Corp, 62-67; dir, Transmission Systs Lab, 67-75. *Concurrent Pos:* Chmn, US Deleg Working Group, Inter Telecommun Union, 70-75; mem, Fed Commun Comn Advan Tel Inquiry, 88. *Mem:* Sigma Xi; fel Inst Elec & Electronics Engrs. *Mailing Add:* 10007 Bentcross Dr Potomac MD 20854

GOLDINGS, HERBERT JEREMY, PSYCHIATRY. *Current Pos:* SR PHYSICIAN, CHILD PSYCHIAT SERV, MASS MENT HEALTH CTR, 61- *Personal Data:* b Boston, Mass, May 28, 29; m 55; c 3. *Educ:* Harvard Univ, AB, 50, MD, 54; Boston Psychoanal Soc Inst, grad, 65; Am Bd Psychiat & Neurol, dipl, 61, cert child psychiat, 64. *Prof Exp:* Intern med, Boston City Hosp, 54-55; asst psychiat, Harvard Med Sch, 60-65, instr psychiat, 65-69, res psychiat, 55-58, assoc dir child psychiat, 65-77. *Concurrent Pos:* Teaching fel, Harvard Med Sch, 55-57, res fel psychiat, 57-58 & 60-61; consult, Div Legal Med, Mass, 57-58, 5040th USAF Hosp, Alaska, 58-60, & Parents Asn Retarded Children, Alaska, 58-60; asst examr, Am Bd Psychiat & Neurol, 64-; mem fac, Boston Psychoanal Soc & Inst, 68-, training & supv analyst, 73-; asst clin prof psychiat, Harvard Med Sch, 69-77; training & supv analyst, Psychoanal Inst New Eng, 75- *Mem:* Fel Am Psychiat Asn; AMA; fel Am Acad Child Psychiat; Am Psychoanal Asn; Int Psychoanal Asn. *Res:* Child psychiatry; psychoanalysis; medical education. *Mailing Add:* 130 Winding River Rd Needham MA 02192-1025

GOLDISH, DOROTHY MAY (BOWMAN), ORGANIC CHEMISTRY. *Current Pos:* From asst prof to assoc prof, 58-73, PROF CHEM, CALIF STATE UNIV, LONG BEACH, 73- *Personal Data:* b NJ, May 6, 34; m 58; c 2. *Educ:* Stanford Univ, BS, 55; Univ Calif, PhD(chem), 58. *Mem:* Am Chem Soc. *Res:* Heterocyclic chemistry; natural products. *Mailing Add:* Dept Chem Calif State Univ Long Beach CA 90840-3903

GOLDISH, ELIHU, PHYSICAL CHEMISTRY. *Current Pos:* ADJ PROF, DEPT GEOL SCI, CALIF STATE UNIV, LONG BEACH, 86- *Personal Data:* b Marietta, Ohio, Oct 18, 28; m 55; c 2. *Educ:* Marietta Col, BSc, 49; Calif Inst Technol, PhD(chem), 56. *Prof Exp:* Fel, Ohio State Univ, 56-57; res fel chem, Univ Southern Calif, 58-60; res chemist, Res Ctr, Union Oil Co Calif, 60-86. *Concurrent Pos:* Fel, Univ Calif, Los Angeles, 66; fel, Calif Inst Technol, 74. *Mem:* Mineral Soc Am; Clay Minerals Soc; Am Crystallog Asn. *Res:* Materials characterization by x-ray diffraction and x-ray spectrometry. *Mailing Add:* Dept Geol Sci Calif State Univ Long Beach Long Beach CA 90840

GOLDKNOPF, IRA LEONARD, CHEMISTRY. *Current Pos:* FLOGENIX INC, WEBSTER, TX, 94- *Personal Data:* b Mar 13, 46; m; c 4. *Educ:* Hunter Col, BA, 67; Kans State Univ, PhD(biochem), 71. *Prof Exp:* Postdoctoral fel develop therapeut, M D Anderson Hosp, Houston, 71-72; fel pharmacol, Col Med, Baylor Univ, 72-74, Nat Cancer Inst instr, 74-75, asst prof, 75-85; qual assurance supvr, GAF Chem Plant, Calvert City, Ky, 85-88, mgr qual assurance, 88-94. *Res:* Structure and function of proteins of the cell nucleus and their roles in the control of gene expression; management development. *Mailing Add:* 42 Brushwood Ct Woodlands TX 77380

GOLDMACHER, VICTOR S, PHARMACOLOGY, CELL BIOLOGY. *Current Pos:* assoc path, 83-85, asst prof path, 85-88, LECTR PATH, HARVARD MED SCH, 88-; HEAD CELL BIOL DEPT & LECTR PATH, IMMUNOGEN, INC, 88- *Personal Data:* b Chernowitz, USSR, Dec 25, 52; US citizen; m 80; c 2. *Educ:* Moscow Univ, MS, 74, PhD(enzym), 77. *Prof Exp:* Assoc genetic toxicol, Mass Inst Technol, 81-83. *Mem:* Am Soc Cell Biol. *Res:* Cell biology of protein toxins; mechanisms of action of immunotoxins; mechanisms of endocytosis, interaction of monoclonal antibodies and their toxin conjugates with cultured cells. *Mailing Add:* Immunogen Inc 148 Sidney St Cambridge MA 02139-4239

GOLDMAN, AARON SAMPSON, STATISTICS. *Current Pos:* CONSULT STATISTICIAN, 95- *Personal Data:* b Red Lion, Pa, Feb 8, 32. *Educ:* Okla State Univ, PhD, 61. *Prof Exp:* Math statistician, Los Alamos Nat Lab, 60-65; assoc prof, Gonzaga Univ, 65-69; prof math, Univ Nev, Las Vegas, 69-79; mem nuclear safeguards, Los Alamos Nat Labs, 79-88; mem, Int Atomic Energy Agency, 88-91; lab assoc, Los Alamos Nat Labs, 91-93, pvt contract, 93-95. *Mem:* Am Statist Asn; Sigma Xi. *Res:* Nuclear safeguards. *Mailing Add:* 4723 Sandia Los Alamos NM 87544

GOLDMAN, ALAN JOSEPH, MATHEMATICS. *Current Pos:* PROF MATH SCI, JOHNS HOPKINS UNIV, 79- *Personal Data:* b New York, NY, Mar 2, 32; m 55, Cynthia; c Peter. *Educ:* Brooklyn Col, BA, 52; Princeton Univ, MA, 54, PhD(math), 56. *Honors & Awards:* US Dept Com Silver Medal, 67, Gold Medal, 76. *Prof Exp:* Instr math, Princeton Univ, 55-56; mathematician, Nat Bur Stand, 56-61, dep chief, Appl Math Div, 68-78, chief opers res, 61-79. *Concurrent Pos:* Lectr, Am Univ, 56-57 & Cath Univ, 57-63; mathematician, Nat Inst Stand & Technol, 79- *Mem:* Nat Acad Eng; Sigma Xi; Math Asn Am; Inst Opers Res & Mgt Sci. *Res:* Theory of games; linear and non-linear programming; operations research; transport systems; optimal location; ecosystem modelling. *Mailing Add:* Dept Math Sci Johns Hopkins Univ 34th & Charles St Baltimore MD 21218. *Fax:* 410-516-7549; *E-Mail:* goldman@brutus.mts.jhu.edu

GOLDMAN, ALLAN LARRY, PULMONARY DISEASES, CRITICAL CARE MEDICINE. *Current Pos:* PROF MED & DIR, DIV PULMONARY, CRITICAL CARE & OCCUP MED, COL MED, UNIV S FLA, TAMPA, 74- *Personal Data:* b Minneapolis, Minn, June 3, 43; m 69; c 4. *Educ:* Univ Minn, Minneapolis, BA & BS, 64, MD, 68. *Mem:* Am Thoracic Soc; Am Col Physicians; Am Col Chest Physicians. *Res:* Respiratory surveillance; carbon monoxide and smoking; cyclic adenosine monophosphates in lung tissue and drug effects. *Mailing Add:* Univ S Fla Col Med Tampa Vet Admin Hosp 12901 Bruce B Downs Blvd Tampa FL 33612-4742

GOLDMAN, ALLEN MARSHALL, CONDENSED MATTER PHYSICS. *Current Pos:* from asst prof to prof physics, 65-92, INST TECHNOL PROF, UNIV MINN, MINNEAPOLIS, 92-, HEAD, SCH PHYSICS & ASTRON, 96- *Personal Data:* b New York, NY, Oct 18, 37; m 60, Katherine Darnell; c Rachel, Matthew & Benjamin. *Educ:* Harvard Univ, AB, 58; Stanford Univ, PhD(physics), 65. *Prof Exp:* Res assoc, Stanford Univ, 65. *Concurrent Pos:* Alfred P Sloan Found fel, 66-70; co-chmn, Study Advisory Inst, NATO, Les Arcs, France, 83; div coun, Am Phys soc, 93-96; London Medal Comt, 94- *Mem:* Fel Am Phys Soc; fel AAAS; Sigma Xi. *Res:* Experimental condensed matter physics; superconductivity, electron tunneling in superconductors; time dependent effects, fluctuation phenomena, superconducting devices and materials; properties of disordered and dimensionally constrained materials; high temperature superconductors; growth and characterization of thin films. *Mailing Add:* Sch Physics & Astron Univ Minn 116 Church St SE Minneapolis MN 55455. *Fax:* 612-624-4578; *E-Mail:* goldman@physics.spa.umn.edu

GOLDMAN, ALLEN S, TERATOLOGY, PHARMACOLOGY. *Current Pos:* PROF PEDIAT & GENETICS, UNIV ILL, CHICAGO, 86-, DIR CRANIOFACIAL CTR. *Personal Data:* b Providence, RI, Oct 25, 29; m 81, Rachel Bok; c Jonathan, Benjamin A & Adam L. *Educ:* Brown Univ, AB, 51, ScM, 53; State Univ NY, MD, 58. *Hon Degrees:* ScM, Univ Pa, 71. *Prof Exp:* Instr pediat, Univ Pa, 61-64, assoc, 64-66, from asst prof to assoc prof pediat, 66-78, res prof pediat & pediat pharmacol, 78-85. *Concurrent Pos:* Res career develop award, NIH, 66; reviewer, Nat Inst Dent Res, NADRC, 77 & 84 & Toxicol Study Sect, NIH, 85; mem, Res Comt Ment Retardation, Nat Inst Child Health & Human Develop, 79, consult, Five Year Plan For Congenital Defects, 80; mem adv comt, Nat Inst Dent Res, 89-93. *Mem:* Sigma Xi. *Res:* Causes and prevention of birth defects: discovered that some birth defects results from a deficiency of phosphatidylinositol turnover and arachidonic acid leading to prostagladins, the defects can be prevented by supplemental myoinsitol, arachidonic acid or prostaglandins. *Mailing Add:* Dept Pediat Univ Ill Col Med Chicago MC 856 840 S Wood St Chicago IL 60612. *Fax:* 312-413-1157

GOLDMAN, ANNE IPSEN, CLINICAL TRIALS. *Current Pos:* Asst prof, 70-78, assoc prof biomet, 78-84, PROF BIOSTAT, SCH PUB HEALTH, UNIV MINN, MINNEAPOLIS, 84- *Personal Data:* b Copenhagen, Denmark, Apr 13, 35; US citizen; m 67, Jay R; c Elizabeth P (Smith), Alison Pfaelzer & Jonathan. *Educ:* Radcliffe Col, BA, 56; Harvard Univ, PhD(statist), 71. *Mem:* Am Statist Asn; Biomet Soc; Soc Clin Trials. *Res:* Design, management and analysis of research databases, design, management and analysis of clinical trials; multivariate methods of prediction of survival based on risk factors. *Mailing Add:* Sch Public Health Univ Minn Box 303 UMHC Minneapolis MN 55455

GOLDMAN, ARMOND SAMUEL, PEDIATRICS, IMMUNOLOGY. *Current Pos:* From instr to assoc prof pediat, 58-72, DIR, DIV IMMUNOL-ALLERGY, UNIV TEX MED BR, GALVESTON, 59-, PROF, PEDIAT & HUMAN BIOL CHEM & GENETICS, 72-, PROF PATH, 80-, PROF MICROBIOL & IMMUNOL, 90- *Personal Data:* b San Angelo, Tex, May 26, 30; m 50, Barbara Bangert; c Lynn, David, Daniel, Paul & Robert. *Educ:* Univ Tex, MD, 53; Am Bd Pediat, dipl, 60; Am Bd Allergy & Immunol, dipl, 74. *Concurrent Pos:* Prin investr, Nat Inst Child Health & Human Develop, 64-67, 68-71, & 78-81; vis lectr, Univ Olu, Finland, 75; vis prof, Univ Tromso, Norway & Univ Goteborg, Sweden, 75; invited speaker, Nat Inst Child & Human Develop, 76; mem Nat comt, Nat Inst Child Health & Human Develop, 76-77; co-organizer, Int Conf, Maternal-Environ Effects Human Lactation, Oaxaca, Mex, 86, prin organizer, Effects Human Milk on Recipient Infant, Konstanz, Ger, 86; invited speaker, Nutrit Inst, Columbia Univ, 86, Int Cong Mucosal Immunol, Tokyo, Japan, 90, Nat Inst Child Health & Human Develop, 92, Europ Soc Neonatal Haematol Immunol, 92, 95 & 96 & Conf Maternal Fetal & Neonatal Health, 96; hon speaker, Int Cong Neonatal Hemat & Immunol, Siena, Italy, 90; invited partic & speaker, Immunol Milk & Neonate Conf, Miami, Fla, 90; partic, Subcomt Nutrit, Lactation Food & Nutrit Bd, Inst Med-nat Acad Sci, 90-92. *Mem:* Am Asn Immunol; Int Soc Human Milk & Lactation; Soc Pediat Res; Am Pediat Soc; Fedn Am Socs Exp Biol; Clin Immunol Soc; Int Soc Res Human Milk & Lactation (secy-treas, 93-94 & pres-elect, 94-95). *Res:* Characterization of the immune system in human milk; the effects of that system upon the recipient; the molecular genetic basis of immunodeficiencies; the functions of the common gamma chairo upeno cells in the immune system. *Mailing Add:* Dept Pediat Children's Hosp Rm C2 360F Univ Tex Med Br 301 University Blvd Galveston TX 77555-0369. *Fax:* 409-772-5045; *E-Mail:* agoldman@pedi.utmb.edu

GOLDMAN, ARTHUR JOSEPH, ADVANCED NUCLEAR REACTOR DEVELOPMENT, QUALITY MANAGEMENT. *Current Pos:* assoc div dir & sr nuclear eng, 73-92, dir qual mgt, 92-95, DEPUTY CHIEF OPERS OFF, ARGONNE NAT LAB, 95- *Personal Data:* b New York, NY, Aug 14, 34; m 57, Joan Broder; c Jeffrey H & Rona B. *Educ:* City Col NY, BChE, 57; New York Univ, MChE, 61, PhD(chem eng), 66; Univ Chicago, MBA, 80. *Prof Exp:* Consult nuclear eng, United Nuclear Corp, 57-66; proj mgr chem eng, Exxon Corp, 66; vpres & tech dir nuclear eng, Nuclear Technol Corp, 67-70; dir fuel mgt servs, S M Stoller Corp, 71; vpres appl sci, Transfer Systs Inc, 72. *Concurrent Pos:* AEC fel nuclear eng, NY Univ, 64-65, adj assoc prof chem eng, 66-71. *Mem:* Am Nuclear Soc. *Res:* Nuclear reactor safety; nuclear fuel design and performance; engineering of energy production systems. *Mailing Add:* Argonne Nat Lab 9700 S Cass Ave Argonne IL 60439. *Fax:* 630-252-7881; *E-Mail:* agoldman@anl.gov

GOLDMAN, BRUCE DALE, PINEAL GLAND, PHOTOPERIODISM. *Current Pos:* asst prof biobehav sci, 70-80, PROF PHYSIOL & NEUROBIOL, UNIV CONN, 87- *Personal Data:* b Gary, Ind, Dec 11, 40; c 3. *Educ:* Univ Mich, BS, 62; Univ Wis, MS, 66, Med Col Ga, PhD(endocrinol), 68. *Prof Exp:* Postdoctoral fel, Univ Tex Southwestern Med Sch, 68-69, Univ Calif, Los Angeles, 69-70; prof endocrinol, Worcester Found Exp Biol, 81-87. *Mem:* Soc Study Biol Rhythms; Soc Study Reproduction. *Res:* Neuroendocrine basis of photoperiodism in vertebrates, pineal gland, regulation of pituitary gonadotropins and prolactin. *Mailing Add:* Dept Physiol & Neurobiol Univ Conn U-42 75 No Eagleville Storrs Mansfield CT 06269-0002

GOLDMAN, CHARLES REMINGTON, LIMNOLOGY. *Current Pos:* from instr to prof zool, 58-71, dir, Inst Ecol, 66-69, PROF DIV ENVIRON STUDIES, UNIV CALIF, DAVIS, 71-, CHMN, 88- *Personal Data:* b Urbana, Ill, Nov 9, 30; m 74; c 3. *Educ:* Univ Ill, Urbana, BA, 52, MS, 55; Univ Mich, PhD(fisheries & limnol), 58. *Prof Exp:* Asst aquatic biol, State Natural Hist Surv, Ill, 54-55; asst fisheries, Univ Mich, 55-57; biologist fisheries res, US Fish & Wildlife Serv, Alaska, 57-58. *Concurrent Pos:* Consult biologist, Eng Res Inst, Univ Mich, 56-57; consult, Fisheries Res Inst, Univ Wash, 61 & Eng-Sci, Inc, Calif, 62-63; NSF sr fel, 64; Guggenheim fel, 65; consult, Atty Gen, State of Minn, 70 & Environ Protection Agency, 71-; mem sci & technol adv coun, Calif State Assembly, 70-75; mem sci exchange comn to Russia, Food & Agr Orgn & UN Develop Prog, Environ Protection Agency, 73; mem, Calif State Solid Waste Mgt Bd, 73-77; consult to design environ improvement, UN Develop Prog, Papua New Guinea, 74-75, Parana River Flood Control, Argentina, 79, El Cajon Dam & Reservoir studies, Honduras, 79-84, Paute Mazar Dams Ecuador, 81; mem subcomt, US Nat Comt for Man & the Biosphere Prog, UNESCO, 75-, chmn, 88-; Fulbright distinguished prof, Yugoslavia, 85; adv comt, Oak Ridge Nat Lab, 85-87. *Mem:* Am Inst Biol Sci; Int Asn Trop Ecol; Int Soc Theoret & Appl Limnol; Am Soc Limnol & Oceanog (pres); Int Asn Astacology; Orgn Trop Studies. *Res:* Aquatic biology-limnology; biological productivity, eutrophiation and nutrient limiting factors; field work on African, Alaskan, Antarctic, Argentine, Brazil (Amazonia), Ecuadorian, Central American, Philippine, Oregonian, Californian, Swedish, Lapland, Italian, New Guinea, USSR, Lake Baikal and New Zealand; documentary films on Lake Tahoe and Tropics. *Mailing Add:* Div Environ Studies Univ Calif Davis CA 95616-5200

GOLDMAN, DANIEL WARE, PHARMACOLOGY, CELL BIOLOGY. *Current Pos:* ASST PROF IMMUNOL, JOHNS HOPKINS UNIV, 86- *Personal Data:* b Mar 28, 52; m 76; c 2. *Educ:* Harvard Univ, PhD(biochem), 79. *Mem:* Am Asn Immunol; Am Asn Pathol; Am Soc Cell Biol. *Res:* Elucidate the signal transduction mechanisms which mediate the activation of leukocytes by lipid mediators of inflammation; to define the biochemical events which regulate leukocyte activation. *Mailing Add:* Div Hemat 1401 Rockville Pike Rockville MD 20852. *Fax:* 301-402-2780

GOLDMAN, DAVID, BEHAVIORAL GENETICS, POPULATION GENETICS. *Current Pos:* INSTR HUMAN GENETICS, GEORGE UNIV, 84-; CHIEF, SECTION GENETIC STUDIES, LAB CLIN STUDIES, NAT INST ALCOHOL ABUSE & ALCOHOLISM, NIH, BETHESDA, MD, 88-, CHIEF LAB NEUROGENETICS, 91- *Personal Data:* b Galveston, Tex, July 7, 52; m 72; c 3. *Educ:* Yale Univ, BS, 74; Univ Tex, MD, 78. *Concurrent Pos:* Clin assoc, Lab Clin Sci, Nat Inst Ment Health, Bethesda, Md, 80-81, staff physician, 81-84; chief, Unit on Genetic Studies, Lab Clin Studies, Nat Inst Alcohol Abuse & Alcoholism, Bethesda, Md, 84-87; adj prof, Dept Biol Sci, George Washington Univ, 87- *Mem:* Am Soc Human Genetics; Soc Alcoholism; Soc Neurosci. *Res:* Genetic linkage studies for alcoholism and neurobehavioral differences and molecular cloning of alcohol dehydrogenases and genes involved in serotonergic function. *Mailing Add:* 12420 Parklawn Dr Park #5 Bldg Rm 451 Rockville MD 20852. *Fax:* 301-443-8579; *E-Mail:* dgneuro@box-d.nih.gov

GOLDMAN, DAVID ELIOT, BIOPHYSICS, PHYSIOLOGY. *Current Pos:* prof, 67-76, dir grad prog, 70-76, EMER PROF PHYSIOL & BIOPHYS, MED COL PA, 76- *Personal Data:* b Boston, Mass, Aug 11, 10; m 38, Jeanne Loewenstam; c James E. *Educ:* Harvard Univ, AB, 31; Columbia Univ, PhD(physiol), 43. *Honors & Awards:* K S Cole Award, Biophys Soc, 73. *Prof Exp:* Lab asst physiol, Mass Dept Ment Health Comn, Boston, 31-36; instr physiol, Col Physicians & Surgeons, Columbia Univ, 40-41, asst surg, 42-43, res assoc physics, Nat Defense Res Comt, 43-44; mem staff, Naval Med Res Inst, 44-47, head biophys div, 47-55, sci liaison officer, Off Naval Res, London, 55-57, head biophys div, 57-67. *Concurrent Pos:* Mem comt hearing & bioacoust, Nat Res Coun, 53-74, mem comt biol & agr, 68-71, mem coun, 70-74; mem biophys study sect, NIH, 58-64, mem study comt biophys, President's Off Sci & Technol, 64, mem adv coun comt head injury, Nat Inst Neurol Dis & Stroke, 66-70, mem physiol training grant comt, 70-74; mem sect comt bioacoust & vibration, Am Nat Standards Inst, 61-65, mem sect comt microwave hazards, 68-73; mem comt handbook environ biol, Fedn Am Socs Exp Biol, 63-66; adj prof biol, State Univ NY Binghamton, 78-82. *Mem:* Am Phys Soc; Acoust Soc Am; Biophys Soc; Am Physiol Soc; Soc Gen Physiol; fel AAAS. *Res:* Electrical and mechanical phenomena in cells and tissues; theoretical biology; shock-vibration-bioacoustics; physical factors in health and safety. *Mailing Add:* 63 Loop Rd Falmouth MA 02540

GOLDMAN, DAVID TOBIAS, SCIENCE ADMINISTRATION, NUCLEAR PHYSICS. *Current Pos:* mgr, Argome Area Off, Dept Energy, 85-87, asst mgr labs, Chicago Opers Off, 87-90, actg mgr, 90-92, actg dep sci adv civilian res & develop, 92-93, dep mgr, 93-95, SR SCI ADVISOR, SECY ENERGY ADV BD, DEPT ENERGY, 95- *Personal Data:* b Brooklyn, NY, Jan 25, 33; m 57, Elizabeth Ward; c Daniel, Jonathan, Michael, Benjamin & Joshua. *Educ:* Brooklyn Col, BA, 52; Vanderbilt Univ, MS, 54; Univ Md, PhD(physics), 58. *Prof Exp:* Physicist, Evans Signal Lab, 52-53; asst physics, Univ Md, 54-58; res assoc, Univ Pa, 58-59; theoret physicist, Knolls Atomic Power Lab, Atomic Energy Comn, 59-63, supv physicist, 63-65; chief theoret physics, Reactor Radiation Div, Dept Com, 65-69, prog leader, stand nuclear ref data, 65-72, prog analyst, sci & technol prog, 70-72, actg dir, 73-74, dep dir, Inst Basic Stand, 72-77, assoc dir planning, Nat Measurement Lab & metric coordr, Nat Bur Stand, 77-82, exec assoc sci & technol, Dept Com, 82-85. *Concurrent Pos:* Physicist, Naval Res Lab, 56 & Oak Ridge Nat Lab, 57-58; adj assoc prof, Rensselaer Polytech Inst, 60-65; adj prof nuclear eng, Univ Md, 65-77; sci policy analyst, Bur Budget, 69-70; sci fel, Dept Com, 69-70. *Mem:* Fel Am Phys Soc; Am Nuclear Soc; Am Nat Metric Coun; Am Soc Testing & Mat. *Res:* Theoretical nuclear physics; nuclear reactions and structure; reactor physics; effect of chemical binding; technology assessment; measurement of productivity of research performers; principles of research management. *Mailing Add:* Dept Energy 1000 Independence Ave SW Washington DC 20585. *Fax:* 202-586-6279; *E-Mail:* david.goldman@oer.doe.gov

GOLDMAN, DEXTER STANLEY, BIOLOGICAL CHEMISTRY. *Current Pos:* PRES, GOLDMAN ASSOCS INT INC, ROCKVILLE, MD, 88- *Personal Data:* b Boston, Mass, June 17, 25; m 64; c 7. *Educ:* Univ Calif, Los Angeles, BS, 48; Univ Calif, PhD(comp biochem), 51. *Prof Exp:* Asst, Univ Calif, 48-51; trainee, Nat Heart Inst, 51-53, asst prof, Enzyme Inst, 54-59, clin assoc prof, Univ Wis, 59-71; chief biochemist, Vet Admin Hosp, 53-71; prof & dir inst biol, Haifa Univ, 71-73; dir res & develop, Makor Chem Ltd, Israel, 73-80; toxicologist, Prog Operations br, Nat Toxicol Prog, Nat Inst Environ Health, NIH, Bethesda, MD, 80-; sr proj officer, Nat Toxicol Prog/NIEHS NIH, 80-84; dir, Lab Data Integrity Assurance Div, Off Compliance Monitoring, US Environ Protection Agency, Washington, DC, 84-88. *Concurrent Pos:* Vis res prof, Div Biochem, Scripps Clin & Res Found, Univ Calif, La Jolla, 63; vis prof, Hebrew Univ, Israel, 68-69. *Mem:* Am Soc Biol Chem; Am Acad Microbiol; Am Soc Microbiol. *Res:* Physiology and enzyme systems of the tubercle bacillus; enzymatic basis of disease and chemotherapy. *Mailing Add:* PO Box 3374 Gaithersburg MD 20885-3374

GOLDMAN, EMANUEL, PROTEIN SYNTHESIS, REGULATION OF GENE EXPRESSION. *Current Pos:* from asst prof to assoc prof, 79-93, PROF MICROBIOL, UNIV MED & DENT NJ, 93- *Personal Data:* b New York, NY, Feb 19, 45; div. *Educ:* Brandeis Univ, BA, 66; Mass Inst Technol, PhD(biochem), 72. *Prof Exp:* Fel viral oncol, Pub Health Res Inst, New York, 72-73; res fel path, Harvard Med Sch, 73-75; assoc microbiol, Col Med, Univ Calif, Irvine, 75-77, asst res prof, 77-79. *Concurrent Pos:* Contrib ed, New Univ, 75-79; res assoc, Dept Chem, Mass Inst Technol, 75; consult, Dept Path, Harvard Med Sch, 76; res career develop award, NIH, 83-88; vis scientist, Columbia Univ, 90-91; guest assoc scientist, Brookhaven Nat Lab, 91-; vis prof prog biochem, City Univ NY, 96-97. *Mem:* Am Soc Microbiol; Am Soc Biochem Molecular Biol. *Res:* Regulation of protein synthesis in bacteria, particularly transfer RNA decoding properties, mistranslation, efficiency of codon recognition, codon usage transfer RNA isoacceptor utilization, programmed translational frameshifts and ribosomal mutations using in vivo and vitro systems, and also phage MS2 and T7 infected cells. *Mailing Add:* Dept Microbiol NJ Med Sch 185 S Orange Ave Newark NJ 07103. *Fax:* 973-982-3644; *E-Mail:* egoldman@umdnj.edu

GOLDMAN, ERNEST HAROLD, COMPUTER COMMUNICATIONS, INFORMATION SYSTEMS. *Current Pos:* BANNOW-WAHLSTROM PROF COMPUT ENG, UNIV BRIDGEPORT. *Personal Data:* b Lynn, Mass, Oct 4, 22; m 48; c 2. *Educ:* US Coast Guard Acad, BS, 43; Harvard Univ, MS, 49,. *Hon Degrees:* DSc, Harvard UNiv, 52. *Prof Exp:* Instr physics, Univ Bridgeport, 47-48; develop engr, IBM Corp, 51-52, sr engr, 52-55, mgr comput test planning & testing, 55-57, res mgr exp systs, T J Watson Res Ctr, 57-67, res dir, 61-64, mgr, East Fishkill Lab, 64-70, mgr component indust eval, 70-81, tech consult, Corp Hq, 82- *Concurrent Pos:* Adj prof info sci, Pace Univ, 73-82. *Mem:* AAAS; sr mem Inst Elec & Electronics Engrs; Asn Comput Mach; Comput Soc. *Res:* Computer communications; computer technology; computer applications; electronic systems and circuits; business modelling; information retrieval and management systems. *Mailing Add:* 4 Bald Rock Rd West Redding CT 06896

GOLDMAN, HAROLD, NEUROPHARMACOLOGY. *Current Pos:* PROF PHARMACOL, SCH MED, WAYNE STATE UNIV, 74- *Personal Data:* b Chicago, Ill, May 29, 27; m 53; c 2. *Educ:* Univ Chicago, MS, 53; Univ Ill, PhD(physiol), 57. *Prof Exp:* From instr to asst prof psychiat, Col Med, Ohio State Univ, 57-66, asst prof pharmacol, 64-66, from assoc prof to prof psychiat & pharmacol, 66-74. *Concurrent Pos:* Res neuroendocrinologist, Res Div, Columbus Psychiat Inst, 57-62. *Mem:* Biophys Soc; Am Physiol Soc; Endocrine Soc; Am Soc Pharmaceut & Exp Therapeut. *Res:* Interregulation of nervous and endocrine systems; metabolism of nervous tissue; small organ blood flow; neurohumors; regional cerebral blood flow; head injury. *Mailing Add:* Dept Pharmacol Wayne State Univ Sch Med 1750 E Crown Ridge Way Tucson AZ 85737-7103

GOLDMAN, HARVEY, GASTROINTESTINAL PATHOLOGY. *Current Pos:* instr & assoc, 64-67, from asst prof to assoc prof, 67-75, PROF PATH, MED SCH, HARVARD UNIV & DIV HEALTH SCI & TECHNOL, MASS INST TECHNOL, 76-; FAC DEAN, MED EDUC, HARVARD, 88- *Personal Data:* b Philadelphia, Pa, May 25, 32; m 67; c 3. *Educ:* Temple Univ, BA, 53, MD, 57. *Prof Exp:* Intern med, Philadelphia Gen Hosp, 57-58; resident & fel path, Beth Israel Hosp, Boston, 58-62; pathologist, US Naval Base, Great Lakes, Ill, 62-64; asst pathologist, Beth Israel Hosp, Boston, 64-68, assoc pathologist, 68-75, pathologist, 75-84. *Concurrent Pos:* Consult path, Children's Hosp & Brigham & Women's Hosp, Boston, Mass, 74-; sr pathologist, Beth Israel Hosp, Boston, Mass, 85- *Mem:* Gastrointestinal Path Club (pres, 83-84); Am Gastroenterol Asn; Am Asn Pathologists; Int Acad Path. *Res:* General pathology and gastrointestinal pathology. *Mailing Add:* Dept Path New Eng Deaconess Hosp One Deaconess Rd Meissner 123A Boston MA 02215-5399. *Fax:* 617-632-0300

GOLDMAN, ISRAEL DAVID, BIOPHYSICS. *Current Pos:* assoc prof med, 74-75, vchmn dept, 74-80, PROF MED & PHARMACOL, MED COL VA, VA COMMONWEALTH UNIV, 75-, CHMN DEPT, DIV MED ONCOL & BIOCHEM PHARMACOL, DEPT MED & PHARMACOL, 80- *Personal Data:* b Jersey City, NJ, Nov 17, 36; m 64; c 3. *Educ:* NY Univ, BA, 58; Univ Chicago, MD, 62. *Prof Exp:* From asst prof to assoc prof med & pharmacol, Sch Med, Univ NC, Chapel Hill, 69-74. *Concurrent Pos:* Fel, Biophys Lab, Harvard Med Sch, 65-66; Pharmaceut Mfrs Asn Found fac develop award, 71; Nat Cancer Inst res career develop award, 73; prin investr, Nat Cancer Inst res grants, 70-86; prog dir, Membrane Biol Training Grant, 75-85. *Mem:* AAAS; Am Soc Pharmacol & Exp Therapeut; Am Physiol Soc; Am Asn Cancer; fel Am Col Physicians. *Res:* Am Soc Clin Invests. Res: Transport and biochemistry of the folate compounds; mechanisms of membrane transport. *Mailing Add:* 231 Loring Ave Pelham NY 10803-2254

GOLDMAN, JACK LESLIE, HEALTH EDUCATION. *Current Pos:* RETIRED. *Personal Data:* b Chicago, Ill, Nov 20, 35; m 94, Dorothy Reid. *Educ:* Univ Chicago, BA & BS, 58; Loyola Univ, Ill, MS, 61, PhD(chem), 66. *Prof Exp:* Instr chem, Mundelein Col, 63-65; res phys chemist, Velsicol Chem Corp, 66-67; mem fac natural sci & chem, Shimer Col, 67-71; lectr chem, Loyola Univ, Chicago, 72-82, lectr math, 82-87, dir, Post-Baccalaureate Health Sci Prog, 83-95, dir, Pre-Health Prof Prog, 87-95. *Concurrent Pos:* Chmn natural sci, Shimer Col, 67-71. *Mem:* Fel Am Inst Chem; Am Asn Physics Teachers; NY Acad Sci; Am Phys Soc; Nat Asn Adv Health Prof. *Res:* Conceptual development of quantum mechanics; methodology of science, especially the interrelations between biological and physical sciences; integrative principles in the sciences and humanities; health ethics and education. *Mailing Add:* 6629 Rockwell Ave Chicago IL 60645. *Fax:* 773-508-3049

GOLDMAN, JACOB E, PHYSICS, MANAGEMENT OF RESEARCH. *Current Pos:* RETIRED. *Personal Data:* b New York, NY, July 18, 21; c Melvin H, Edith (Hoffman) & Beth (Solomon). *Educ:* Yeshiva Univ, AB, 40; Univ Pa, MA & PhD(physics), 43. *Hon Degrees:* LLD, Yeshiva Univ, 61. *Honors & Awards:* Proctor Award, Res Soc Am. *Prof Exp:* Asst physics, Univ Pa, 41-42, asst instr, 43, res assoc, Nat Defense Res Comt proj, 43; res physicist, Res Labs, Westinghouse Elec Corp, 43-50; lectr, Carnegie Inst Technol, 50, asst prof, 51-55; mgr, Physics Dept, Sci Lab, Ford Motor Co, 55-60, from assoc dir to dir, 60-68; group vpres res & develop, Xerox Corp, 68-74, group vpres, 74-80, chief scientist, 74-83, sr vpres, 80-83. *Concurrent Pos:* Westinghouse lectr, Grad Sch, Univ Pittsburgh, 45-50; group leader, Westinghouse Elec Corp, 46-50; head, Lab Magnetics Res, Carnegie Inst Technol, 53-55; chmn, Sci Adv Comt, Detroit Inst Cancer Res; gen chmn, Nat Conf Magnetism & Magnetic Mat, 56-58; chmn, Panel Mat Res & mem, Solid State Adv Panel, Nat Acad Sci; mem, Adv Panel Select Comt Govt Res, US House Rep; adv comt solid state, Off Sci Res, USAF; Edwin Webster prof, Mass Inst Technol, 59; consult, Oak Ridge Nat Lab, Brookhaven Nat Lab, Naval Ord Lab, US Steel Corp & Allis-Chalmers Mfg Co; chmn, Softstrip Lab, 84-94; chief tech officer, Oxbridge, Inc, 95- *Mem:* Fel Am Phys Soc; Am Asn Physics Teachers; Inst Elec & Electronics Engrs; AAAS (vpres). *Res:* Solid state physics; semiconductors; physics of metals; ferromagnetism; magnetic materials; magnetostriction phenomena; low temperature properties of metals; administration of research. *Mailing Add:* 41 Little Fox Lane Westport CT 06880. *Fax:* 203-226-5846; *E-Mail:* jgonbridge@aol.com

GOLDMAN, JAMES ALLAN, PHILOSOPHY OF SCIENCE, SCIENCE POLICY. *Current Pos:* dir admin, Res & Develop & Higher Educ Officer, 86-90, DEP DEAN, DIV CONTINUING EDUC & DIR, PROG PLANNING & ECON DEVELOP, NEW YORK CITY TECH COL, 90- *Personal Data:* b Chicago, Ill, Nov 20, 35; m 78. *Educ:* Univ Chicago, BS & BA, 58; Northwestern Univ, PhD(chem), 63. *Prof Exp:* Instr chem, Northwestern Univ, 61-62; asst prof, Polytech Inst Brooklyn, 62-71; coordr tech & indust progs, Div Continuing Educ, New York City Community Col, 71-81, coordr & higher educ assoc, 81-86. *Concurrent Pos:* Mem exec bd, ChemTech, 73-77; sci & technol ed, USA Today, 75-86; abstractor, J Col Sci Teaching; Interfaith relation comts & conferences, 88- *Mem:* Sigma Xi; AAAS; Am Chem Soc; Am Asn Physics Teachers; NY Acad Sci. *Res:* Science education; philosophy and contemporary sociology of science; science, technology and society interactions between science and the humanities; theory of titration curves, especially redox titrations; science/religion relationships; Christian/Jewish relations. *Mailing Add:* 300 Jay St M506 New York City Tech Col Brooklyn NY 11201-2902

GOLDMAN, JAMES ELIOT, NEUROBIOLOGY, NEUROPATHOLOGY. *Current Pos:* ASSOC PROF PATH & PSYCHIAT, COLUMBIA UNIV, COL PHYSICIANS & SURGEONS, 87- *Personal Data:* b Washington, DC, Oct 26, 46; m 71; c 2. *Educ:* Amherst Col, BA, 68; NY Univ, MD & PhD(med & neurobiol), 76. *Prof Exp:* Teaching fel neurochem, Albert Einstein Col Med, Bronx, NY, 76-77, resident path, 77-78, resident neuropath, 78-80, asst prof, 80-85, assoc prof neuropath, 85-87. *Concurrent Pos:* Attend neuropathologist, Albert Einstein Col Hosp, Bronx Munic Hosp Ctr & Bronx Lebanon Hosp, 80-87; assoc attend neuropathologist, Presby Hosp, New York; NIH teacher-investr award, 80-85, NIH Jarvits neurosci award, 88-95. *Mem:* Sigma Xi; Am Soc Neurochem; Int Soc Neurochem; Soc Neurosci; Am Asn Neuropathologists; AAAS. *Res:* Molecular mechanisms and pathogenesis of Alzheimer's disease and other neurodegenerative disorders; histogenesis of the central nervous system, especially glial cell development; molecular mechanisms of glial scar formation in neurological diseases. *Mailing Add:* Dept Path Columbia Univ Col Physician & Surgeons 630 W 168th St New York NY 10032-3702

GOLDMAN, JAY, INDUSTRIAL ENGINEERING. *Current Pos:* dean, 84-96, PROF ENG, UNIV ALA BIRMINGHAM, 84- *Personal Data:* b Norfolk, Va, Apr 15, 30; m 59, Renitta Librach. *Educ:* Duke Univ, BSME, 50; Mich State Univ, MSME, 51; Washington Univ, St Louis, DSc(indust eng), 55. *Honors & Awards:* Award, Inst Indust Engrs, 81. *Prof Exp:* Lectr indust mgt, Wash Univ, 52-55, lectr indust eng, 55-56, asst prof, 56-63, actg chmn human & org factor area, 63, dir indust engr, Jewish Hosp St Louis, 60-64; prof indust eng, NC State Univ, 64-68; prof indust eng & chmn dept, Univ Mo, Columbia, 68-84. *Concurrent Pos:* Consult, Off Naval Res, Ill, Artcraft Venetian Blind Mfg Co, Mo, Goffre Carbon Co, Arg, Boeing Airplane Co, Wash, Dr LeGear Med Co, Mo, Shampaine Industs, McDonnell Aircraft Corp, Banner Hardware Co, Beltx Corp, Mead Johnson & Co, Ind, Med Ctr, Duke Univ, DC, Nat Heart, Lung & Blood Inst, Nat Can Inst, Nat Libr Med; mem health care systs study sect, Nat Ctr Health Serv Res & Develop, Dept Health, Educ & Welfare; mem, adv panels grad progs, NC State Univ & Rensselaer Polytech Inst, Safety & Occup Health Study Sect, Ctr Dis Control & Accreditation Bd Eng & Technol. *Mem:* Am Soc Eng Educ; fel Inst Indust Engrs; Coun Indust Eng Acad; Soc Health Systs; Oper Res Soc Am; Ala Soc Prof Engrs. *Res:* Administrative organization and system design for health care delivery; design of man-machine work systems; measurement of human performance; human factors engineering. *Mailing Add:* Sch Eng Univ Ala Birmingham AL 35294. *Fax:* 205-934-8437; *E-Mail:* jgoldman@uab.edu

GOLDMAN, JOEL HARVEY, ELEMENTARY PARTICLE PHYSICS. *Current Pos:* asst prof physics, 79-83, ASSOC RES SCIENTIST, FLA STATE UNIV, 83- *Personal Data:* b Brooklyn, NY, May 26, 43. *Educ:* Mass Inst Technol, BS, 66; Univ Minn, MS, 67; Univ Md, PhD(physics), 72. *Prof Exp:* Res assoc, New York Univ, 72-75; assoc physicist, Brookhaven Nat Lab, 75-78. *Mailing Add:* 1115 Sandhurst Dr Tallahassee FL 32312-2529

GOLDMAN, JOHN ABNER, IMMUNOLOGIC & RHEUMATIC DISEASES. *Current Pos:* from asst prof to assoc prof, 73-82, CLIN PROF MED, EMORY UNIV SCH MED, 82-; PVT PRACT RHEUMATOLOGY & IMMUNOL, 82- *Personal Data:* b Cincinnati, Ohio, Jan 9, 40; m 93, Debbie North; c Joey, Beth & John M. *Educ:* Univ Wis-Madison, BS, 62; Cincinnati Med Ctr, MD, 66. *Prof Exp:* Intern, Med Ctr, Univ Ore, 66-67; resident, Med Ctr, Univ Cincinnati, 67-69, fel immunol & rheumatology, 69-71; mem staff, Med Corps, US Army, 71-73. *Concurrent Pos:* Instr med, Med Col Ga, 72-73; mem, Med Adv Bd, Systemic Lupus Erythematosus Found, Inc, 76-; dir, Med Sects, Am Soc Laser Med & Surg, 81-83. *Mem:* Fel Am Soc Laser Med & Surg; fel Am Col Physicians; Am Acad Allergy; AAAS; Am Med Asn; Am Col Rheumotol. *Res:* Understanding immune mechanisms of immunologic and connective tissue diseases; impact of osteoporosis; pathogenesis of scleroderma and the immunologic aspects of laser on immune response and in the treatment of connective tissue diseases. *Mailing Add:* Med Quarters 5555 Peach Tree Dunwoody Rd Suite 293 Atlanta GA 30342-1711. *Fax:* 404-252-7574; *E-Mail:* jointdoc@mindspring.com

GOLDMAN, JOSEPH L, MESO-METEOROLOGY, AGRO-METEOROLOGY. *Current Pos:* TECH DIR, INT CTR SOLUTION ENVIRON PROB, HOUSTON, 76- *Personal Data:* b San Francisco, Calif, Aug 25, 32; div; c 3. *Educ:* Tex A&M Univ, BS, 58, MS, 60; Univ Okla, PhD, 71. *Prof Exp:* Mathematician, WCoast Res Co, Calif, 56; assoc meteorologist, Gulf Consult, Tex, 56-58; res scientist, Tex A&M Res Found, 58-60; res asst meteorol, Univ Chicago, 60-62, meteorologist, 62-65; tech staff prin investr, Nat Eng Sci Co, Tex, 65, assoc dir, Inst Storm Res, 66-75. *Concurrent Pos:* Assoc prof physics & meterol, Unv St Thomas, Tex, 68-75; gen chmn, Houston Sci & Eng Fair, 75-90, chmn, Disaster Serv, Greater Houston Chap Red Cross, 82-84; pres, TMC Chap, Sigma Xi, 96- *Mem:* AAAS; Am Meteorol Soc; Am Geophys Union; NY Acad Sci; Sigma Xi; Soc Risk Anal. *Res:* Severe weather phenomena; effective forecasting and control through physical-hydrodynamic principles, effects on ocean environment and ecological, sociological and induced behavioristic aspects; urban pollution control; meteorological engineering; urbanization and climate change; mathematical modeling of environmental processes; drift of agricultural herbicide sprays; groundwater contamination by surface released chemicals, through surface ponding and soil seepage; determination of soil temperature and moisture from atmospheric temperature, rainfall and soil type; morphology of soil borne pathogens due to temperature and moisture; wind and water effects on structures. *Mailing Add:* Int Ctr Solution Environ Probs 2616 Commonwealth Ave Houston TX 77006-2609

GOLDMAN, KENNETH M(ARVIN), METALLURGICAL ENGINEERING. *Current Pos:* RETIRED. *Personal Data:* b Pittsburgh, Pa, Dec 8, 22; m 51, Betty Pickholtz; c Howard, Edward & Morton. *Educ:* Carnegie Inst Technol, BS, 43, DSc(metall), 52. *Honors & Awards:* Hunt Award, Am Inst Mining, Metall & Petrol Engrs, 52; Eng Mat Achievement Award, Am Soc Metals, 72. *Prof Exp:* Adv scientist, Bettis Lab, Westinghouse Elec Corp, 80-89. *Concurrent Pos:* Adj prof, Univ Pittsburgh. *Mem:* Fel Am Soc Metals; Am Inst Mining, Metall & Petrol Engrs. *Res:* Physical chemistry of steelmaking; radioactive tracers applied to metallurgy; fissionable materials; metallurgy of zirconium and uranium. *Mailing Add:* 2223 Shady Ave Pittsburgh PA 15217

GOLDMAN, LAWRENCE, MEMBRANE BIOPHYSICS, VOLTAGE-GATED IONIC CHANNELS. *Current Pos:* asst prof zool, 65-67, from asst prof to assoc prof physiol, Sch Med, 67-77, PROF PHYSIOL & BIOPHYS, SCH MED, UNIV MD, BALTIMORE, 77- *Personal Data:* b Boston, Mass, May 6, 36; c 1. *Educ:* Tufts Univ, BS, 58; Univ Calif, Los Angeles, PhD(membrane biophys). *Prof Exp:* NIH fel, Col Physicians & Surgeons, Columbia Univ, 64-65. *Concurrent Pos:* Vis scientist, Lab Biophys, NIH, 66-68; NATO sr fel, Queen Mary Col, London, 70; NIH spec res fel, Univ Cambridge, 73; Fulbright sr prof, I Physiol Inst, Univ Saarlandas, 87-88. *Mem:* Fel AAAS; Soc Gen Physiol; Am Physiol Soc; Soc Neurosci; Biophys Soc. *Res:* Membrane biophysics; theory of excitable membranes; impulse initiation and propagation; membrane transport and selectivity; mathematical modeling. *Mailing Add:* Dept Physiol Univ Md Sch Med Baltimore MD 21201

GOLDMAN, LEE, MEDICINE. *Current Pos:* PROF & CHAIR, DEPT MED & ASSOC DEAN CLIN AFFAIRS, SCH MED, UNIV CALIF, SAN FRANCISCO. *Educ:* Yale Univ, MD; MPH. *Prof Exp:* Prof med & epidemiol, Harvard Med Sch & Sch Pub Health; chief med officer, Brigham Women's Hosp. *Concurrent Pos:* clin training med, Univ Calif, San Francisco & Mass Gen Hosp; clin training cardiol, Yale-New Haven Hosp; assoc ed, New Eng J Med. *Mem:* Inst Med-Nat Acad Sci; Am Soc Clin Invest; Asn Am Physicians; Soc Gen Internal Med. *Res:* Author of more than 315 full-length publications focused on the effectiveness and costs of diagnostic and therapeutic strategies with special emphasis on how the delivery of medical care can be improved based on the results of high quality clinical investigation. *Mailing Add:* Dept Med Univ Calif 505 Parnassus Ave San Francisco CA 94143-0120

GOLDMAN, LEONARD MANUEL, PLASMA PHYSICS. *Current Pos:* CONSULT, 92- *Personal Data:* b New York, NY, Mar 22, 25; m 52, Lee McSwain; c 3. *Educ:* Cornell Univ, AB, 45; McGill Univ, MSc, 48; Univ Rochester, PhD, 52. *Prof Exp:* Asst physics, McGill Univ, 47-48 & Univ Rochester, 48-52; res assoc, Princeton Univ, 52-56 & Res & Develop Ctr, Gen Elec Co, 56-75; prof mech & aerospace sci, Univ Rochester, 75-88; prin scientist, Bechtel Nat Inc, San Francisco, 88-92. *Concurrent Pos:* Vis fel, Culham Lab, UK Atomic Energy Authority, 65-66; actg mgr appl physics, Res & Develop div, Bechtel Inc, San Francisco, 85-86. *Mem:* Fel Am Phys Soc; AAAS. *Res:* High temperature plasma physics; low energy nuclear physics; laser fusion. *Mailing Add:* 2307 Ridgefield Dr Chapel Hill NC 27514

GOLDMAN, LYNN R, PEDIATRICS, EPIDEMIOLOGY. *Current Pos:* ASST ADMINR, OFF PREV PESTICIDES & TOXIC SUBSTANCES, ENVIRON PROTECTION AGENCY, 93- *Educ:* Univ Calif, Berkeley, BS; Johns Hopkins Univ, MPH; Univ Calif, San Francisco, MD. *Prof Exp:* Head, Div Environ & Occup Dis Control, Calif Dept Health Servs. *Concurrent Pos:* Mem, Water Sci & Technol Bd, Nat Res Coun. *Mem:* Fel Am Acad Pediat. *Res:* Advancing pollution prevention, reducing risks of chemicals and pesticides to health and the environment and furthering the public's right to know; ensuring protection of children and addressing emerging issues like endocrine disruptors. *Mailing Add:* Environ Protection Agency 401 M St SW Washington DC 20460

GOLDMAN, MALCOLM, MATHEMATICS. *Current Pos:* assoc prof, 62-75, admin officer, Dept Econ, 75-76, ASSOC PROF MATH, NY UNIV, 76- *Personal Data:* b Brooklyn, NY, July 18, 29; m 66. *Educ:* Univ Minn, BA, 49, MA, 51; Univ Chicago, PhD(math), 55. *Prof Exp:* Mem tech staff, Bell Tel Labs, Inc, 54-55; instr math, Univ Mich, 55-60; vis asst prof math, Reed Col, 60-62. *Mem:* Am Math Soc. *Res:* Probability theory; functional analysis. *Mailing Add:* Dept Math Courant Inst Math Sci 251 Mercer St New York NY 10012

GOLDMAN, MANUEL, MICROBIAL PHYSIOLOGY, METABOLISM. *Current Pos:* ASST PROF BIOL SCI, UNIV ILL, CHICAGO, 67- *Personal Data:* b Montreal, Que, May 19, 32; US citizen; m 69; c 2. *Educ:* Roosevelt Univ, BS, 53; Univ Chicago, SM, 55; Univ Mich, PhD(microbiol), 62. *Prof Exp:* Fel, Inst Sci Technol, Univ Mich, 61-62; asst prof biol & microbiol, Wayne State Univ, 62-64; microbiologist, Stanford Res Inst, 64-67. *Concurrent Pos:* Vis prof microbiol, La State Univ, 85; asst dean, Col Liberal Arts & Sci, Univ Ill, Chicago, 87- *Mem:* Soc Indust Microbiol; Am Soc Microbiol; Am Chem Soc; Mycological Soc Am. *Res:* Metabolism and physiology of sporeforming bacteria; environmental modification of cellular metabolism and development; mode of action of psychopharmacological drugs; regulation of carbohydrate metabolism; metabolism of smut fungi. *Mailing Add:* 723 S Aberdeen Chicago IL 60607

GOLDMAN, MARTIN V, PLASMA & SPACE PHYSICS, NONLINEAR OPTICS. *Current Pos:* from asst prof to assoc prof, 70-95, prof, Dept Astrophys Planetary & Atmospheric Sci & Dept Physics, PROF, DEPT PHYSICS, UNIV COLO, BOULDER, 95- *Personal Data:* b New York, NY, June 9, 38; m 65, Helen C Baroway; c Daniel & Jonathan. *Educ:* Princeton Univ, BA, 60; Harvard Univ, MS, 61, PhD(physics), 65. *Prof Exp:* Woodrow Wilson fel, 60-61, Harvard fel, 61-62, NSF fel, 62- 65, Howard Hughes fel, 64-65, NATO fel, 65-66; res asst, Dept Physics, Univ Calif, Los Angeles, 66-67, asst prof in residence, 67-70. *Concurrent Pos:* Consult, Lawrence Livermore Labs, 62-71 & 87-, Hughes Res Labs, 66-72, Rand Corp, 71-75, Inst Telecommun Sci, 72-74, Jason group, Stanford Res Inst, 79-80, Univ Calif, Irvine, 79-83, Sci Appln Inc, 80-81, Los Alamos Sci Lab, 71-; vis prof, Plasma Physics Res Ctr, Ecote Polytech, Switz, 74, Culham Labs, London, Eng, 77, Dept Physics, Univ Calif, 78, Univ Miami, 81, Dept Theoret Physics, Univ Sydney, Australia, 81; Guggenheim fel, 77-78, fac fel, Univ Colo, 77-78; invited guest, Soviet Acad Sci, Moscow, Telaviv, 80, Kiev, 83; distinguished vis scientist radio physics, Commonwealth Sci & Indust Res Org, Sydney, Australia, 81; assoc fel, LaJolla Inst; vis scientist, CSIRO Radio Physics, 81, Inst Theoret Physics, Univ Calif, Santa Barbara, 82. *Mem:* Sigma Xi; fel Am Phys Soc; Am Geophys Union; Int Astron Union. *Res:* Plasma physics; nonlinear waves; dynamics of dissipative systems; electron beam plasma interaction; nonlinear optics; turbulence; continuum mechanics; classical field theory; stochastic processes; emission of radiation from plasmas; solar radio waves; lasers; radio wave propagation in the ionosphere. *Mailing Add:* Univ Colo Campus Box 390 Boulder CO 80309. *Fax:* 303-492-0642; *E-Mail:* goldman@spot.colorado.edu

GOLDMAN, MARVIN, RADIOBIOLOGY, HEALTH RISK ASSESSMENT. *Current Pos:* assoc res radiation biologist, Sch Med, Univ Calif, Davis, 58-64, res radiation biologist & lectr physiol sci, Sch Vet Med, 64-72, adj prof radiobiol, Sch Med, 69-73, dir, lab energy-related health res, 73-85, PROF RADIOL SCI, SCH VET MED & PROF RADIOL, SCH MED, UNIV CALIF, DAVIS, 73-, CO-DIR, WESTERN REGIONAL CTR, NAT INST GLOBAL ENVIRON CHANGE, UNIV CALIF, DAVIS, 90- *Personal Data:* b New York, NY, May 2, 28; m 53; c 3. *Educ:* Adelphi Col, AB, 49; Univ Md, MS, 51; Univ Rochester, PhD(radiation biol), 57. *Honors & Awards:* E O Lawrence Award, US AEC, 72; Distinguished Sci Award, Health Physics Soc, 88. *Prof Exp:* Asst, Univ Md, 50-51; biologist, Phys Biol Lab, NIH, 51-52; res assoc, Univ Rochester, 53-57, jr scientist, Atomic Energy Proj, Sch Med & Dent, 57-58. *Concurrent Pos:* Consociate mem, Nat Coun Radiation Protection; chmn, Interagency Nuclear Safety, Rev Panel, Biomed and Environ Panel, 73; co-chmn, Nuclear Emergency Procedures, Calif State Senate Task Force, 87-88; chmn, Comt Assessment of Environ & Health Consequences in Exposed Chernobyl Pop, 86; prin investr, Pharm Kenetics New Investigational Drugs, US Army Med Res & Develop Command. *Mem:* AAAS; Soc Risk Anal; Radiation Res Soc; Health Physics Soc. *Res:* Biologic effects of radiation; toxicologic risk assessment; environmental and occupational health; radionuclide toxicity and metabolism; radiation dosimetry; bone and lung physiology and pathology; trace element metabolism; chemical toxicology; health physics; tumor biology; energy related health effects; pharmacokinetics; genotoxicology; cell toxicology. *Mailing Add:* Dept Surg & Radiol Sci/Vet Med Univ Calif Davis CA 95616

GOLDMAN, MAX, ENDOCRINOLOGY, BIOLOGY. *Current Pos:* from assoc prof to prof, 68-91, EMER PROF BIOL, UNIV SDAK, 91- *Personal Data:* b Newtown, Conn, Nov 28, 20; m 58; c 2. *Educ:* NY Univ, BA, 48; Univ Mo, Columbia, MA, 53; Univ Calif, Berkeley, PhD(endocrinol), 64. *Prof Exp:* Asst prof biol, Long Island Univ, 64-68. *Mem:* AAAS; Am Inst Biol Sci; NY Acad Sci. *Res:* Toxicological and behavioral effects of chemical substances, dimethyl sulfoxide, oxalic acid, povidone-iodine, heavy metals, (lead, mercury) sodium acetate, DDT, and acidic amino acids, monosodium glutamate, aspartic acid on endocrine and thyroid function; reviews on chemical agents lewisite, inorgangic arsenic, sulfur mustard. *Mailing Add:* 8232 Niles Center Rd Skokie IL 60077

GOLDMAN, NORMAN L, CHEMISTRY. *Current Pos:* from asst prof to prof, Queens Col, 61-76, chmn dept, 72-77, actg assoc dean & actg dean fac, Div Math & Natural Sci, 77-79, PROF CHEM, QUEENS COL, NY, 76-, DEAN FAC, DIV MATH & NATURAL SCI, 79- *Personal Data:* b New York, NY, Aug 11, 33. *Educ:* City Col New York, BS, 54; Harvard Univ, AM, 56; Columbia Univ, PhD(org chem), 59. *Prof Exp:* NSF fel, Imp Col, Univ London, 59-60; NIH fel, Columbia Univ, 61. *Mem:* Am Chem Soc; Royal Soc Chem. *Res:* Synthetic organic chemistry. *Mailing Add:* Div Math & Natural Sci Remsen Hall 125 Queens Col Flushing NY 11367-1597. *Fax:* 718-997-4103; *E-Mail:* nlg@dfm.qci.qc.edu

GOLDMAN, PETER, PHARMACOLOGY, NUTRITION. *Current Pos:* actg chmn, 84-91, PROF PHARMACOL, HARVARD SCH PUB HEALTH, 72-, PROF HEALTH SCI, DEPT NUTRIT, 82- *Personal Data:* b New York, NY, May 23, 29; m 59; c 2. *Educ:* Cornell Univ, BEngPhys, 52; Harvard Univ, MA, 53; Johns Hopkins Univ, MD, 57. *Prof Exp:* Res assoc biochem, Nat Heart Inst, 59-63; sr investr biochem pharmacol, Nat Inst Arthritis, Metab & Digestive Dis, 63-72. *Concurrent Pos:* NIH fel, 59-60; mem adv comt biotechnol resources, NIH, 77-79. *Mem:* Am Soc Biol Chemists; Am Chem Soc; Am Soc Pharmacol & Exp Therapeut; Am Soc Clin Invests. *Res:* Nutrition; drug metabolism in the intestinal microflora; anaerobic bacteria, nitroimidazoles, laboratory quality control, clinical pharmacology and toxicology. *Mailing Add:* Dept Pharmacol & Nutrit Harvard Univ 665 Huntington Ave Boston MA 02115-6021

GOLDMAN, RALPH FREDERICK, PHYSIOLOGY, PROTECTIVE CLOTHING HUMAN FACTORS. *Current Pos:* SR CONSULT, ARTHUR D LITTLE, 93- *Personal Data:* b Boston, Mass, Mar 3, 28; m 56, Joan Krinsky; c Harry E & Ellen L. *Educ:* Univ Denver, AB, 50; Boston Univ, AM, 51, PhD(physiol), 55; Northeastern Univ, SM, 62. *Honors & Awards:* Holliday Medal, Am Soc Heating, Refrig & Air Conditioning Eng. *Prof Exp:* USPHS res fel, 55; physiologist, US Army Res & Eng Command, 56-62, dir, Mil Ergonomics Lab, US Army Res Inst Environ Med, 62-82; sr vpres, Multi-Tech Corp, Natick, Ma, 82-89; chief scientist, Comfort Technol, 89-93. *Concurrent Pos:* Adj prof, Boston Univ, 69-; lectr, Mass Inst Technol, 73-; adj prof, NC State Univ, 89- *Mem:* Biophys Soc; Am Physiol Soc; Inst Elec & Electronics Engrs; fel Am Soc Heating, Refrig & Air Conditioning Eng; fel Brit Ergonomics Res Soc; Am Soc Testing & Mat; fel Am Col Sports Med. *Res:* Environmental physiology; human heat, cold and work stresses; clothing; heat transfer; body composition; human factors. *Mailing Add:* Arthur D Little Inc Acorn Park Cambridge MA 02140-2390. *Fax:* 508-651-1030; *E-Mail:* 72272.131@compuserve.com

GOLDMAN, RENITTA LEE, LEARNING DISABILITIES, ABUSED CHILDREN & YOUTH. *Current Pos:* ASSOC PROF & PROG COORDR, UNIV ALA, BIRMINGHAM, 85- *Personal Data:* b St Louis, Mo, Aug 15, 38; m 59, Jay Goldman. *Educ:* Wash Univ, BA, 60; NC State Univ, MS, 67; Univ Mo, Columbia, PhD(spec educ), 78. *Prof Exp:* Teacher, Univ City Pub Schs, 60-64; res asst, NC State Univ, 67-68; elem sch counr, Columbia Pub Schs, 68-85. *Concurrent Pos:* Adj asst prof, Univ Mo, Columbia, 78-85; consult, 85-; pres, Ala, Coun Children Behav Dis, 89-90; res assoc, Injury Prev Control Ctr, 92- *Mem:* Int Asn Children Ment Deficiency. *Res:* Published numerous books on abuse of children and youth; adolescent suicide. *Mailing Add:* 213A Educ Bldg Univ Ala Birmingham AL 35294-1250. *Fax:* 205-934-2921; *E-Mail:* rgoldman@uab.edu

GOLDMAN, ROBERT BARNETT, APPLIED PHYSICS. *Current Pos:* RETIRED. *Personal Data:* b Philadelphia, Pa, June 21, 27; m 47; c 3. *Educ:* Temple Univ, BA, 48, MA, 50, PhD, 52. *Prof Exp:* Asst, Villanova Col, 49-50 & Temple Univ, 50-51; physicist, Philco Corp, 51-62, mem corp eng & res staff, 62-68, dir advan technol, Electronics Group, Philco-Ford Corp, 68-69; tech dir, Govt & Indust Div, Urbana Opers, Magnavox Co, 69-71, dir, Res and Develop, Govt Electronics Div, 71-72; assoc dir advan eng resources, Leeds & Northrup Co, 72-74; chief scientist, Systs & Opers Anal Div, Analytics Inc, 75-79, dir, Sci Anal Div, 79-96. *Concurrent Pos:* Lectr, Temple Univ, 54-65. *Mem:* Acoust Soc Am; Inst Elec & Electronics Engrs. *Res:* Acoustics-propagation; transducers; noise control; communications; information theory; control systems; transmission and reception of electromagnetic energy for detection, surveillance and guidance; systems analysis; operations research; applied physics; electronics; electrooptics; military systems. *Mailing Add:* 1360 Woodland Rd Jenkins PA 19046

GOLDMAN, ROBERT DAVID, CELL BIOLOGY, CYTOSKELETON. *Current Pos:* STEPHEN WALTER RANSON, PROF & CHMN, DEPT CELL, MOLECULAR & STRUCT BIOL, MED SCH, NORTHWESTERN UNIV, 81- *Personal Data:* b Port Chester, NY, July 23, 39; m 65; c 2. *Educ:* Univ Vt, BA, 61, MS, 63; Princeton Univ, PhD(biol), 67. *Honors & Awards:* Res Career Develop Award, NIH. *Prof Exp:* Am Cancer Soc fel histochem, Royal Postgrad Med Sch, London & Med Res Coun Gt Brit Exp Virus Res Unit, Glasgow, 67-69; asst prof biol, Case Western Res Univ, 69-74; prof biol, Mellon Inst Sci, Carnegie-Mellon Univ, 74-81. *Concurrent Pos:* Assoc ed, Cell Motility & Cytoskeletal; dir sci writers course, Marine Biol Lab. *Mem:* Biophys Soc; Soc Develop Biol; Am Soc Cell Biol; NY Acad Sci; Soc Invest Dermat. *Res:* Cytoskeletal systems of mammalian cells with special interest in intermediate filament protein structure and function. *Mailing Add:* Dept Cell Molecular & Struct Biol Sch Med Northwestern Univ 303 E Chicago Ave Chicago IL 60611-3072. *Fax:* 312-503-0954

GOLDMAN, RONALD, SPEECH PATHOLOGY, AUDIOLOGY. *Current Pos:* PROF BIOCOMMUN & STAFF PATHOLOGIST SPEECH, CTR DEVELOP & LEARNING DISORDERS, UNIV ALA, BIRMINGHAM, 74-, TRAINING DIR, 81-, PROF EDUC. *Personal Data:* b Brooklyn, NY, Sept 22, 33; m 54; c 3. *Educ:* Birmingham Southern Col, BA, 55; Univ Pittsburgh, MS, 57, PhD(speech path, audiol), 60. *Prof Exp:* Asst prof speech path & audiol, Tulane Univ, 60-64; prof, Sch Med, Vanderbilt Univ, 64-74. *Concurrent Pos:* Assoc prof spec educ, George Peabody Col, 66-71; prof, Ignacio Barraquer Film Award, 67; Am Speech & Hearing Asn fel, 69; res consult, US Off Educ, 70-; consult, NIH, 71; vpres planning Am Speech & Hearing Asn, 78-80. *Mem:* Am Speech & Hearing Asn; Coun Exceptional Children; Am Asn Ment Deficiency. *Res:* Development of new procedures for studying auditory perceptual and processing disorders; development of new therapeutic procedures for articulatory deficits and auditory perceptual disorders. *Mailing Add:* 3416 Mountain Lane Birmingham AL 35213

GOLDMAN, S ROBERT, FLUID PHYSICS, ATMOSPHERIC SCIENCES. *Current Pos:* SR SCIENTIST ENERGY, JAYCOR, 76- *Personal Data:* b New York, NY, Nov 16, 37; m 73; c 2. *Educ:* Harvard Univ, AB, 59; Yale Univ, MS, 61, PhD(physics), 63. *Prof Exp:* Fel plasma physics, Princeton Plasma Lab, 63-64; res assoc fluid physics, Univ Md, 64-66, res asst prof, 66-69; staff scientist field testing, Los Alamos Sci Lab, 69-71; asst prof physics, Hunter Col, 71-74; scientist plasma physics, Sci Applns, Inc, 74-76. *Mem:* Am Phys Soc; Am Geophys Soc. *Res:* Ionospheric physics; plasma physics; fluid physics relating to fossil energy processes. *Mailing Add:* Los Alamos Lab F645 P O Box 1663 Los Alamos NM 87545

GOLDMAN, STANFORD, THEORETICAL PHYSICS, COMMUNICATION THEORY. *Current Pos:* prof, 49-75, EMER PROF ELEC ENG, SYRACUSE UNIV, 75-; RES ASSOC, UNIV CALIF, SAN DIEGO, 77- *Personal Data:* b Cincinnati, Ohio, Nov 14, 07; m 35; c 3. *Educ:* Univ Cincinnati, AB, 26, AM, 28; Harvard Univ, PhD(physics), 33. *Prof Exp:* Sound engr, Photophone, Inc, Radio Corp Am, NY, 30-31; sr engr, Gen Elec Co, Conn, 35-46; res assoc elec eng, Mass Inst Technol, 46-49. *Concurrent Pos:* Consult physicist, Electronics Res Lab, US Air Force, 46-54, Gen Elec Co 54- & Eng & Res Develop Lab, US Army, 58-; vis Makay prof, Univ Calif, Berkeley, 62; vis prof, Univ Calif, San Diego, 70, res assoc, 77- *Mem:* Fel AAAS; Am Phys Soc; Biophys Soc; fel Inst Elec & Electronics Engrs. *Res:* Mathematical biology; theoretical physics and biology; noise and information theory. *Mailing Add:* 7000 N McCormick Blvd Apt 105C Lincolnwood IL 60645-2732

GOLDMAN, STEPHEN ALLEN, PHYSICAL CHEMISTRY, MAGNETIC RESONANCE. *Current Pos:* STAFF SCIENTIST, PROCTER & GAMBLE CO, 72- *Personal Data:* b New York, NY, Apr 2, 46. *Educ:* Brooklyn Col, BS, 67; Cornell Univ, MS, 69, PhD(phys chem), 73. *Mem:* Am Chem Soc; AAAS. *Res:* Magnetic resonance spectroscopy; molecular orientation and motion in liquid crystalline systems; colloid chemistry; physical chemistry of polymer gels, polymer physical chemistry. *Mailing Add:* Winton Hill Tech Ctr 6300 Center Hill Ave Cincinnati OH 45224-1795

GOLDMAN, STEPHEN L, GENETICS. *Current Pos:* PROF BIOL & ADJ PROF MICROBIOL, MED COL OHIO, 80- *Personal Data:* b New York, NY, Sept 18, 42. *Educ:* Brooklyn Col, BS, 63; Univ Mo, Columbia, MS, 67, PhD(genetics), 68. *Prof Exp:* Res asst genetics, Univ Mo, Columbia, 64-68; NIH fel, Univ Tex, Dallas, 69-71; asst prof genetics, Univ Toledo, 71-75; assoc prof, 75-80. *Mem:* AAAS; Genetics Soc Am; Am Inst Biol Sci; Am Soc Microbiol. *Res:* Genetic recombination in maize and gene conversion in Schizosaccharromyces pombe. *Mailing Add:* Dept Biol Univ Toledo 2801 W Bancroft Toledo OH 43606-3328

GOLDMAN, STEPHEN SHEPARD, NEUROSURGERY. *Current Pos:* HEALTH SCI ADMIN, CARDIAC FUNCTIONS BR, NAT HEART & LUNG & BLOOD INST, NIH, 90- *Personal Data:* b Brockton, Mass, Nov 24, 41. *Educ:* Northeastern Univ, BA, 64; Univ Ill, MS, 66, PhD(physiol), 70. *Prof Exp:* Fel neurochem, NIH, 70-72, staff fel, 72-77; asst prof exp nerosurg, Med Ctr, NY Univ, 77-90. *Mem:* Am Physiol Soc; Am Soc Neurochem; NY Acad Sci; AAAS; Sigma Xi. *Res:* Catoin and lipid metabolism in brain with special reference to cerebral ischemia and thyroid hormone. *Mailing Add:* 16601 Bethayres Rd Derwood MD 20855-2043

GOLDMAN, STEVEN, CARDIOLOGY. *Current Pos:* CHIEF CARDIOL, UNIV MED CTR, TUCSON, 86- *Educ:* Univ Med Ctr, Tucson, MD, 86. *Mailing Add:* Dept Internal Med Univ Az Sch Med Cardiol 111C Vet Admin Med Ctr Tucson AZ 85723-0001. *Fax:* 520-629-4636

GOLDMAN, TERRENCE JACK, STRONG INTERACTIONS, GRAVITY & NEUTRINOS. *Current Pos:* staff fel, 75-78, staff mem, 78-91, GROUP LEADER, MEDIUM ENERGY THEORY, LOS ALAMOS NAT LAB, 91- *Personal Data:* b Winnipeg, Man, Can, Feb 20, 47; m 68, Bernadine Zoe Gross; c Oliver, Elizabeth, Leah & Matthew. *Educ:* Univ Man, BSc, 68; Harvard Univ, AM, 69, PhD(theoret physics), 73. *Honors & Awards:* Delphasus Lectr, Univ Calif, Santa Cruz, 88. *Prof Exp:* Fel, Nat Res Coun Can, Stanford Linear Accelerator Ctr, 73-75. *Concurrent Pos:* Sr res fel, Calif Inst Technol, 78-80; panel mem, Solar Neutrino Proj Rev Panel, US Dept Energy, 81; vis assoc prof, Univ Calif, Santa Cruz, 83; distinguished vis scholar, Univ Adelaide, 87. *Mem:* Am Phys Soc. *Res:* Weak radiative corrections to leptonic pseudoscalar meson decay; rare decays of mesons and leptons; neutrino mixing properties; precise proton decay lifetime prediction; grand unified field theories; observable fractional charge hadrons; gravitational properties of anti-matter; quark structure of nuclei. *Mailing Add:* T-5 MS B283 Los Alamos Nat Lab PO Box 1663 Los Alamos NM 87545. *Fax:* 505-667-1931; *E-Mail:* goldman@t5.lanl.gov

GOLDMAN, THEODORE DANIEL, ORGANIC POLYMER CHEMISTRY. *Current Pos:* SCIENTIST POLYMER CHEM, ROHM AND HAAS CO, 75- *Personal Data:* b Washington, DC, Oct 31, 46; m 72. *Educ:* Wash Col, BS, 69; NY Univ, MS, 72, PhD(org chem), 74. *Prof Exp:* NIH fel, 74-75. *Mem:* Am Chem Soc; Sigma Xi. *Res:* Design and synthesis of polymeric modifiers for plastics; organic photochemistry. *Mailing Add:* 1290 Gen Defermoy Rd Washington Crossing PA 18977-1230

GOLDMAN, VLADIMIR J, QUANTUM HALL EFFECT, RESONANT & SINGLE-ELECTRON TUNNELING. *Current Pos:* asst prof, 88-91, ASSOC PROF PHYSICS, STATE UNIV NY, STONY BROOK, 91- *Personal Data:* b Moscow, USSR; US citizen. *Educ:* Moscow State Pedag Inst, dipl physics, 77; Univ Md, PhD(physics), 85. *Prof Exp:* Res assoc physics, Princeton Univ, 85-87; staff mem, 88. *Concurrent Pos:* NSF presidential young investr, 89; Alfred P Sloan Found fel, 89. *Mem:* Am Phys Soc; AAAS; NY Acad Sci. *Res:* Physics of semiconductors; heterostructure devices; fractional quantum Hall effect; Wigner crystallization; single-electron tunneling. *Mailing Add:* Dept Physics State Univ NY Stony Brook NY 11794-3800

GOLDMAN, YALE E, MUSCLE PHYSIOLOGY, BIOPHYSICS. *Current Pos:* ASSOC PROF PHYSIOL, SCH MED, UNIV PA, 85- *Educ:* Univ Pa, MD, 75, PhD(physiol), 76. *Res:* Optics. *Mailing Add:* Dept Physiol Richards Bldg 0701 Univ Pa Sch Med Penn Muscle Inst 37th Hamilton Walk Philadelphia PA 19104-6083. *Fax:* 215-898-2653

GOLDMANN, KURT, MECHANICAL ENGINEERING. *Current Pos:* CONSULT, 87- *Personal Data:* b Eschwege, Ger, Sept 8, 21; nat US; m 55; c 3. *Educ:* Pa State Col, BS, 42; Mass Inst Technol, MS, 46. *Prof Exp:* Chief analyst free piston mach, Lima-Hamilton Corp, 46-49; sr engr nuclear energy aircraft, Fairchild Eng & Aircraft Co, 49-50; res engr, Carrier Corp, 51; mgr, MCR Primary Systs Dept Nuclear Reactors, United Nuclear Corp, 51-71; mgr, Liquid Metal Systs Dept, Gulf United Nuclear Fuels Co, 71-74; chief engr, Transnuclear, Inc, 74-87. *Mem:* Am Soc Mech Engrs; Am Nuclear Soc; Sigma Xi. *Res:* Thermodynamics; fluid flow and heat transfer; liquid metal technology; free piston; gas turbine and nuclear power plants. *Mailing Add:* 62 Holbrooke Rd White Plains NY 10605-4017

GOLDMAN-RAKIC, PATRICIA S(HOER), DEVELOPMENTAL NEUROBIOLOGY, PSYCHOBIOLOGY. *Current Pos:* dir grad studies, Sect Neuroanat, 81-86, actg chmn, 86-87, PROF NEUROSCI, YALE UNIV, SCH MED, 79- *Personal Data:* b Salem, Mass. *Educ:* Vassar Col, AB, 59; Univ Calif, Los Angeles, PhD(psychol), 63. *Hon Degrees:* AM, Yale Univ, 79. *Honors & Awards:* Herbert Birch Mem Lectr, Int Neuropsychobiol Soc, 81; Kendon Smith Mem Lectr, Univ NC, 85; Bernard Sachs Mem Lectr, Child Neurol Soc, 85; Fyssen Found Prize, Neurosci, Paris, 90; Sally Harrington Goldwater Lectr, Barrow Inst, 90; Rushton Lectr, Fla State Univ, 90; Lieber Award, Nat Alliance Res Schizophrenia & Depression, 91; Distinguished Sci Contribution Award, Am Psychol Asn, 91; John P McGovern Award, AAAS, 93; Robert P & Claire Pasarow Found Award, 93; Karl Lashley Award, Am Philos Soc, 96. *Prof Exp:* Staff fel, NIMH, 65-68, res physiologist, 68-78, chief, Sect Develop Neurobiol, Lab Neuropsychol, 78-79. *Concurrent Pos:* Mem, Nat Adv Res Task Force, NIMH, 72-74, pres, Nat Inst Neurol & Commun Disorders & Stroke Assembly Scientists, 74-75; numerous lectrs univs & res ctrs, 72-87; mem, Biol Sci Fel & Training Grants Initial Rev Group, 74-77; mem, Int Res Fel Rev Group, Fogarty Ctr, 76-78; mem, Long-Range Strategy Res Develop Disorders Panel, Adv Panel, Nat Inst Neurol & Commun Disorders & Stroke, 78-79, Develop Neurobiol Adv Panel, 81-84 & 85; sr scientist award, NIMH, 80 & 85; numerous lectrs, Univs & Res Ctrs, 72-87; mem, Third World Cong Comt, Int Brain Res Orgn, 90-91. *Mem:* Nat Acad Sci; Inst Med-Nat Acad Sci; fel AAAS; Am Anat Asn; Int Brain Res Orgn; fel Am Psychol Asn; Am Acad Arts & Sci; Soc Neurosci (pres, 89-90); fel Am Psychopathol Asn; Int Soc Develop Psychobiol; Int Anat Asn; Int Acad Biomed & Drug Res. *Res:* Organization, development and plasticity of primate frontal lobe; neurobiology of memory and cognition. *Mailing Add:* Yale Univ Sch Med Sect Neurobiol 333 Cedar St PO Box 208001 New Haven CT 06510-8001

GOLDNER, ADREAS M, PHYSIOLOGY. *Current Pos:* RETIRED. *Personal Data:* b Zurich, Switz, June 14, 34; US citizen; m 88; c 1. *Educ:* Oberlin Col, BA, 56; Stanford Univ, MA, 57; George Washington Univ, PhD(physiol), 66. *Prof Exp:* Instr physiol sci, Menlo Col, Calif, 59-61; lectr biol, Montgomery Jr Col, Md, 65-66; res assoc, Yale Univ, 69-70; asst prof human physiol, Sch Med, Univ Calif, Davis, 70-75; assoc prof physiol & assoc dean student affairs,

Univ Ariz Col Med, 75-92. *Concurrent Pos:* USPHS fel biophys, Harvard Med Sch, 66-67 & physiol, Sch Med, Yale Univ, 67-69; consult, Biol Commun Proj, George Washington Univ, 66-69; lectr, Southern Conn State Col, 68-69 & SCent Community Col, 69-70; vis scientist, Max Planck Inst Biophys, Frankfurt, 72. *Mem:* AAAS; Am Physiol Soc; Biophys Soc; Biomed Eng Soc. *Res:* Membrane phenomena; intestinal permeability-relationship between nutrients and electrolyte transport; effects of hormones and divalent cations on epithelial permeability. *Mailing Add:* 3607 Cedar Flat Williams OR 97544

GOLDNER, HERMAN, medical microbiology, biohazards control, for more information see previous edition

GOLDNER, JOSEPH LEONARD, ORTHOPEDIC SURGERY. *Current Pos:* Resident orthop, Med Ctr, Duke Univ, 46-50, assoc, 50, from asst prof to assoc prof, 51-56, chmn div orthop surg, 68-77, PROF ORTHOP SURG, MED CTR, DUKE UNIV, 56-, CHIEF ORTHOPAMPUTEE CLINS, 55- *Personal Data:* b Omaha, Nebr, Nov 18, 18; m; c 2. *Educ:* Univ Minn, AB, 39; Univ Nebr, BScMed & MD, 43; Am Bd Orthop Surg, dipl, 52. *Honors & Awards:* Gibson Mem lectr, Winnipeg, Can, 69; Hike-Kite lectr, 71. *Concurrent Pos:* Fel, Amputee Training Sch, Univ Calif, Los Angeles, 55; exchange fel, Am & Brit Orthop Asn, Eng, 55; res, Ga Warm Springs Found, 47-48; mem appl physiol study sect, NIH, 63-67; attend orthop surgeon, Vet Admin Hosp, Durham, NC, Watts Hosp & NC Cerebral Palsy Hosp, consult, McCain Tuberc Sanatorium, NC & Army Hosp, Ft Bragg; mem comt clean air in oper rm, Nat Res Coun; consult, Surgeon Gen, US Navy; vis prof, Children's Hosp, Australia, 66, Univ Calif, Los Angeles, 67, Harvard Univ, 68, Univ NMex, 71 & Crippled Children's Div, Vt State Bd Health, 71. *Mem:* Am Soc Surg of Hand (pres, 69-70); Am Orthop Asn; Can Orthop Asn; Am Acad Orthop Surg; Am Acad Cerebral Palsy; Sigma Xi. *Res:* Tendon healing; hand reconstruction; amputee problems; fat embolism; ultraviolet light in operating room. *Mailing Add:* Dept Surgery Box 3706 Med Ctr Duke Univ Med Ctr Durham NC 27710

GOLDNER, RONALD B, ELECTRICAL ENGINEERING, SOLID STATE PHYSICS. *Current Pos:* from asst prof to assoc prof, 64-77, PROF ELEC ENG, TUFTS UNIV, 77- *Personal Data:* b New York, NY, Mar 24, 35; m 59; c 1. *Educ:* Mass Inst Technol, SB & SM, 57, EE, 59; Purdue Univ, PhD(elec eng), 62. *Prof Exp:* Asst, Mass Inst Technol, 57-59, res assoc, Lab Insulation Res, 59; instr elec eng, Purdue Univ, 59-62; asst prof, Mass Inst Technol, 62-64. *Concurrent Pos:* Ford Found fel eng, 62-64; consult various private industs, 63- *Mem:* Am Phys Soc; Inst Elec & Electronics Engrs; Solar Energy Soc; Electrochem Soc; Optical Soc Am; Sigma Xi. *Res:* Optoelectronic properties of solids; optoelectronic applications. *Mailing Add:* Dept Elec Eng Halligan Hall Tufts Univ Medford MA 02155

GOLDREICH, PETER, ASTROPHYSICS. *Current Pos:* assoc prof, 66-69, PROF ASTRON & PLANETARY SCI, CALIF INST TECHNOL, 69-, LEE A DUBRIDGE PROF ASTROPHYS & PLANETARY PHYSICS, 81- *Personal Data:* b New York, NY, July 14, 39; m 60; c 2. *Educ:* Cornell Univ, BS, 60, PhD(physics), 63. *Honors & Awards:* Henry Norris Russell Lectr, Am Astron Soc, 79, Dirk Brouwer Award, Div Dynamical Astron, 86, Kuiper Prize, Div Planetary Sci, 92; Chapman Medal, Royal Astron Soc, 85, Gold Medal, 93; Amos de Shalit Lectr, Weltzmann Inst, Rehovot, Israel, 86; T Gold Lectr, Cornell Univ, 87 & 88; Nat Medal of Sci, 95. *Prof Exp:* Instr astron, Cornell, 61-63; Nat Acad Sci-Nat Res Coun fel, Cambridge Univ, 63-64; asst prof astron & geophys, Univ Calif, Los Angeles, 64-66. *Concurrent Pos:* Sloan Found fel, 68-70; regents fel, Smithsonian Inst Wash, 88-89 & 89-90; Miller prof, Univ Calif, Berkeley, 90. *Mem:* Nat Acad Sci; Am Acad Arts & Sci. *Res:* Theoretical study of solar system; galactic structure and cosmology. *Mailing Add:* Div Geol & Planetary Sci Calif Inst Technol 1201 E California Blvd Pasadena CA 91125

GOLDRICH, MICHAEL I, ADMINISTRATION. *Current Pos:* Dep dir, Nat Inst Allergy & Infectious Dis, 83-96, DEP DIR & CHIEF OPER OFFICER HOSP, WARREN G MAGNUSON CLIN CTR, NIH, 96- *Personal Data:* b New York, NY, Apr 21, 48. *Educ:* Univ Md, BA, 71; Loyola Univ, MBA, 96. *Mailing Add:* Warren G Magnuson Clin Ctr NIH Bldg 10 Rm 2C146 10 Center Dr MS 1504 Bethesda MD 20892. *Fax:* 301-402-0244; *E-Mail:* mgoldrich@.nih.gov

GOLDRICH, STANLEY GILBERT, PHYSIOLOGICAL PSYCHOLOGY, OPTOMETRIC RESEARCH. *Current Pos:* ASSOC CLIN PROF OPTOM, STATE COL OPTOM, STATE UNIV NY, 74-, ASSOC CLIN PROF, BIOFEEDBACK LAB, 84- *Personal Data:* b New York, NY, Sept 22, 37. *Educ:* Queens Col, NY, BA, 59, MA, 65; City Univ NY, PhD(psychol), 66; Mass Col Optom, OD, 74. *Prof Exp:* Lectr psychol, Queens Col, NY, 64-65; res assoc, Primate Ctr, Univ Wis, 65-67; asst prof, Ohio State Univ, 67-72. *Mem:* Fel Am Acad Optom; Am Psychol Assoc; Am Optom Assoc. *Res:* Biofeedback control of eye movement disorders including nystagmus, strabismus and reading dysfunction; inventor of Orthotone Biofeedback Eye Training System, and Goldrich Contour Rotator for treatment of oculomotor disorders; control of primate visually guided behavior. *Mailing Add:* State Col Optom State Univ NY 100 E 24th St New York NY 10016. *E-Mail:* sgoldrich@sunyopt.edu

GOLDRING, LIONEL SOLOMON, PHYSICAL CHEMISTRY, RESEARCH ADMINISTRATION. *Current Pos:* CONSULT, 92- *Personal Data:* b Los Angeles, Calif, Oct 24, 22; m 49; c 1. *Educ:* Univ Calif, Los Angeles, BA, 43; Mass Inst Technol, PhD(phys chem), 50; NY Univ, MBA, 73. *Prof Exp:* Jr chemist, Oak Ridge Nat Lab, 43-46; res assoc, Mass Inst Technol, 46, asst, 46-49; res chemist, Brookhaven Nat Lab, 50-52; head radiochem group, United Nuclear Corp, 53-57, mem adv proj group, 58-60; sr res chemist, AMF, Inc, 60-64, sr tech specialist, 64-66, sr res specialist, Res Dept, 66-67, lab mgr, 67-70, mgr chem phys res, 70-74, dir chem lab, 74-78; dir appl res, Orion Res, Inc, 78-81; dir Transducer develop, Novametrix Med Systs, Inc, 81-88; sr chemist, Spacelabs, 89-92. *Concurrent Pos:* Consult, Brookhaven Nat Lab, 47-49; adj assoc prof, NY Univ Grad Sch Bus Admin, 74-78. *Mem:* Am Chem Soc; Soc Plastics Engrs. *Res:* Electrochemical sensors; polymer and plastics science and engineering; inorganic chemistry; nuclear science; air and water pollution; polymers and their application; data acquisition and analysis. *Mailing Add:* 1711 N Indian River Dr Cocoa FL 32922-6947

GOLDRING, ROBERTA M, MEDICINE. *Current Pos:* from asst prof to assoc prof, 66-84, PROF MED, SCH MED, NY UNIV, 84- *Personal Data:* b June 18, 29; wid; c 3. *Educ:* Vassar Col, AB, 49; Columbia Univ, MD, 53. *Prof Exp:* Asst med, Col Physicians & Surgeons, 62-66. *Concurrent Pos:* Asst vis physician, Presby Hosp, 56-66, Bellevue Hosp, Univ Hosp, 66-73; dir, Pulmonary Function Lab, Bellevue Hosp, 75-, co-dir, Med Inst Care Unit, 87-; assoc attend physician, Bellevue Hosp, Univ Hosp, 73-84, attend physician, 84- *Mem:* Am Physiol Soc; Am Fedn Clin Res; AAAS; Am Heart Asn; Am Thoracic Soc. *Res:* Medicine. *Mailing Add:* Dept Med NY Univ Sch Med 550 First Ave New York NY 10016-6402

GOLDRING, SIDNEY, NEUROSURGERY. *Current Pos:* head dept, 74-90, PROF NEUROL SURG, SCH MED, WASH UNIV, 66- *Personal Data:* b Kremnitz, Poland, Apr 2, 23; nat US; m 45; c 2. *Educ:* Wash Univ, MD, 47. *Prof Exp:* Instr, Med Unit to Thailand, Univ Wash, 52-53, from instr to assoc prof neurosurg, 56-64; prof & head dept, Univ Pittsburgh, 64-66. *Concurrent Pos:* USPHS div res grants; neurosurgeon-in-chief, Barnes & Allied Hosps, St Louis, 74-90. *Mem:* Am Physiol Soc. *Res:* Electrophysiological studies in animal and human cerebral cortex, employing direct current amplifiers and non-polarizable recording electrodes for correlation of slow electrical changes with various physiological and pathological states; microelectrode and computer techniques in study of experimental epilepsy. *Mailing Add:* Dept Neurol Surg Wash Univ Sch Med 660 S Euclid Ave Campus PO Box 8057 St Louis MO 63110. *Fax:* 314-362-2107

GOLDSACK, DOUGLAS EUGENE, PHYSICAL CHEMISTRY. *Current Pos:* asst prof biophys chem, 68-74, chmn dept chem, 75-80, assoc prof, 74-83, PROF CHEM, LAURENTIAN UNIV, 83-, DEAN SCI & ENG, 81- *Personal Data:* b London, Ont, July 17, 39; m 64; c 2. *Educ:* Univ Western Ont, BSc, 61; Univ Wis, PhD(chem), 66. *Prof Exp:* Res assoc biophys chem, Univ Wis, 66-67; res scientist, Vancouver Lab, Fisheries Res Bd Can, 67-68. *Res:* Physical chemistry of proteins; physical chemistry of solutions. *Mailing Add:* 13 Aspenwood Ct Sudbury ON P3E 5T6 Can

GOLDSBERRY, RONALD E, MARKETING. *Current Pos:* gen mgr, Plastic & Trim Prod Div, Ford Motor Co, 87-90, exec dir sales & serv strategies, 90-91, gen sales & mkt mgr, 91-94, VPRES & GEN MGR, GLOBAL FORD CUSTOMER SERV OPERS, 94- *Personal Data:* b Wilmington, Del, Sept 12, 42. *Educ:* Cent State Univ, BA, 64; Mich State Univ, PhD(inorg chem), 69; Stanford Univ, MBA, 73. *Hon Degrees:* LHD, Central State Univ, 88. *Prof Exp:* Res chemist & asst prof, Univ Calif, 69-72; prod mgr, Hewlett Packard Co, 72-73; mgt consult, Boston Consult Group, 73-75; dir corp planning oper, Gulf Oil Corp, 75-78; vpres bus develop & planning, Occidental Chem Corp, 78-81, vpres & gen mgr, 81-83; pres & chief oper officer, Parker Chem Co, 83-87. *Concurrent Pos:* Bd trustees, Rockefeller Found. *Mem:* Nat Acad Eng. *Res:* Author of numerous publications; granted one patent. *Mailing Add:* Global Ford Customer Serv Opers 300 Renaissance Ctr PO Box 43381 Detroit MI 48243. *Fax:* 313-446-8270

GOLDSBOROUGH, JOHN PAUL, GAS & DYE LASERS, INERT GAS & METAL VAPOR ION. *Current Pos:* ENG MGR, LICONIX, 89-, SR SCIENTIST, 93- *Personal Data:* b Newark, NJ, May 19, 34; m 56; c 2. *Educ:* Lehigh Univ, BS, 56; Stanford Univ, PhD(physics), 61. *Prof Exp:* Res staff mem, IBM Corp, 60-65; dir res, Spectra-Physics Inc, 65-68; sr proj engr, 68-74, mgr, Eng Dept, 74-89. *Mem:* Am Phys Soc. *Res:* Magnetic resonance; photoconductivity; low temperature physics; development of aelium-cadmium, air and water cooled argon ion, and dye lasers as commercial products. *Mailing Add:* Liconix 3281 Scott Blvd Santa Clara CA 95054

GOLDSBY, ARTHUR RAYMOND, ORGANIC CHEMISTRY. *Current Pos:* RETIRED. *Personal Data:* b Flora, Ill, Nov 20, 04; m 34; c 1. *Educ:* Ill Col, AB, 28; Northwestern Univ, MS, 30, PhD(org chem), 32. *Prof Exp:* Asst chem, Northwestern Univ, 28-32; chemist, Nat Aluminate Corp, Ill, 32-33; res chemist, Nat Aniline & Chem Co, NY, 33-36; dir explor res gasoline, Tex Co, 36-40, tech adv, Texaco Develop Corp, 40-55; dir res, Stratford Eng Corp, Mo, 55-57; tech adv, Texaco Inc, 57-69; consult & dir, Stratford-Graham Eng Corp, 69-79. *Mem:* Am Chem Soc; Am Inst Chemists; Am Inst Chem Engrs. *Res:* Reactions of furan and furfural; pyrolysis of olefins and paraffins; synthetic organic detergents; aviation gasoline; alkylation; isomerization; catalytic cracking; fuel composition in relation to engine performance; recovery of sulfuric acid licensing. *Mailing Add:* 2000 Cambridge Ave Apt 329 Wyomissing PA 19610-2714

GOLDSBY, RICHARD ALLEN, BIOCHEMISTRY, IMMUNOLOGY. *Current Pos:* AT DEPT BIOL, AMHERST COL. *Personal Data:* b Kansas City, Mo, Dec 19, 34. *Educ:* Univ Kans, BS, 57; Univ Calif, Berkeley, PhD(chem), 61. *Prof Exp:* Jr org chemist, Monsanto, Inc, 57-58; biochemist-virologist, E I du Pont de Nemours & Co, Inc, 61-66; from asst prof to assoc prof biol, Yale Univ, 66-72; prof chem, Univ Md, College Park, 72- *Concurrent Pos:* Morse fel, Yale Univ, 70-71, master, Pierson Col, 71-72; bd dirs, Carver Found, Tuskegee Inst, 73-; Nat Res Coun Sr fel, Ames Res Ctr, 75- *Mem:* Am Soc Microbiol. *Res:* Somatic cell genetics of thymidine kinase; senescence in cultured somatic cells; immunoglobin synthesis. *Mailing Add:* Dept Biol Univ Mass Amherst Paige Rm 115 Amherst MA 01002

GOLDSCHMID, OTTO, wood chemistry; deceased, see previous edition for last biography

GOLDSCHMIDT, BERNARD MORTON, CANCER. *Current Pos:* NIH res fel, 63-65, res asst, 65-68, asst prof, 68-74, ASSOC PROF ENVIRON MED, MED SCH, NY UNIV, 74- *Personal Data:* b New York, NY, Feb 7, 36; m 65; c 2. *Educ:* City Univ New York, BS, 57; Univ Wis-Madison, PhD(org chem), 62. *Prof Exp:* NIH res fel, State Univ NY Stony Brook, 62-63. *Concurrent Pos:* Adj assoc prof, Adelphi Univ, 68-72; adj asst prof, Manhattan Community Col, 72-73. *Mem:* Am Asn Cancer Res; Am Chem Soc; Royal Soc Chem. *Res:* Chemical carcinogenesis, isolation and identification of chemical carcinogens; mechanism of cancer induction. *Mailing Add:* 411 West End Ave New York NY 10024

GOLDSCHMIDT, ERIC NATHAN, INFORMATION SCIENCE, PHARMACEUTICAL INDUSTRY. *Current Pos:* sr lit scientist, 82-84, SR INFO ASSOC, WARNER LAMBERT CO, 84- *Personal Data:* b Berlin, Ger, Nov 25, 27; nat US; m 54, Helen Warisch; c Daniel J, Howard Z & Judy S. *Educ:* Brooklyn Col, BS, 50; Harvard Univ, AM, 51, PhD(org chem), 55. *Prof Exp:* Lectr chem, Brooklyn Col, 50; scientist, Warner-Chilcott Labs, 56-57; sr scientist, Warner Lambert Res Inst, 57-62, sr lit chemist, 62-67; res specialist, Off Eng Res & lectr, dept chem, Univ Pa, 67-68; asst to dir res, Endo Labs, 68-70, asst to vpres res, 70-72, dir res serv, 72-78, dir sci info, 78-80; mgr prod planning, Mead Data Central, 80-82. *Concurrent Pos:* Lectr, Brooklyn Col, 50 & 69, Univ Pa, 67-68 & Hofstra Univ, 69-79; consult, Ergo Assoc, 82- *Mem:* AAAS; fel Am Inst Chemists; Am Chem Soc; NY Acad Sci; Royal Soc Chem; Drug Info Asn. *Res:* Antimetabolites; biosynthesis inhibitors; nitrogen heterocycles; chemotherapeutic agents; new synthetic methods; information storage and retrieval; research administration. *Mailing Add:* 147-29 68th Rd Kew Gardens Hills Flushing NY 11367-1332. *Fax:* 973-540-4756

GOLDSCHMIDT, MILLICENT, ORAL & MEDICAL MICROBIOLOGY, CLINICAL MICROBIOLOGY, IMMUNOLOGY. *Current Pos:* assoc prof clin microbiol, Prog Infectious Dis & Clin Microbiol, Med Sch, Univ Tex, Houston, 73-76, Nat Inst Dent Res fel microbiol, 77-78, dir grad prog microbiol, 83-90, ASSOC PROF MICROBIOL, DEPT BASIC SCI, DENT BR, GRAD SCH BIOMED SCI, UNIV TEX HEALTH SCI CTR, HOUSTON, 70- *Personal Data:* b Erie, Pa, June 11, 26; wid; c Richard & Carol (Warley). *Educ:* Case Western Reserve Univ, BA, 47; Purdue Univ, MS, 50, PhD(microbiol), 52. *Honors & Awards:* Distinguished Serv Award, Am Soc Microbiol, 80. *Prof Exp:* Asst zool, Purdue Univ, 50-51; Purdue Res Found fel, 51-52; res assoc, Dept Biochem, Sch Med, Case Western Reserve Univ, 53; sr res assoc, Biophys Res Labs, George Washington Univ, 56-59; instr chem, Hood Col, 59-60; asst prof med in bact, Sch Med, Univ Md & US Army Med Unit, Ft Detrick, 60-61; NIH fel microbiol, Univ Tex, 61-63; res instr microbiol, Col Med, Baylor Univ, 63-67; asst prof microbiol & asst microbiologist, Dept Path, Univ Tex M D Anderson Hosp & Tumor Inst, 67-71, assoc microbiologist & actg chief clin microbiol, 70-71; assoc prof, Univ Tex Grad Sch Biomed Sci, 71-73. *Concurrent Pos:* Assoc microbiologist, Dept Med & Dept Lab Med, Univ Tex M D Anderson Cancer Ctr, 70-; dir, Tex Outstanding Biol Teachers Awards Comt, Nat Asn Biol Teachers, 71-80; pres, Tex Br, Am Soc Microbiol, 80-81, Houston Asn Med Microbiologists, 82-84, Rice Univ/Tex Med Ctr Chap Sigma Xi, 85-86 & Gulf Coast Chap, Asn Women in Sci, 87-88; chmn, Prog Comt, Am Acad Microbiol, 81-83 & mem bd gov, 85-88; treas, Southeast Tex Sigma Xi Coun, 84-89; found lectr, Am Soc Microbiol, 87-88; mem eval panel, Biomed Sci Grad Fel Prog, NSF, 90- *Mem:* Sigma Xi; Am Soc Microbiol; fel Am Acad Microbiol; Asn Women Sci; Int Asn Dent Res; Am Asn Dent Res. *Res:* Instrumentation and immunologic methods for rapid detection and characterization of microorganisms; oral, medical, biochemical and biophysical aspects of microbiology, immunology, microbial physiology and nutrition; biochemistry. *Mailing Add:* 3611 Cloverdale St Houston TX 77025. *Fax:* 713-794-1861; *E-Mail:* mgoldsch@bite.db.uth.tmc.edu

GOLDSCHMIDT, PETER GRAHAM, QUALITY MANAGEMENT, HEALTH POLICY. *Current Pos:* PRES, WORLD DEVELOP GROUP, 86- *Personal Data:* b Cardiff, Wales, Feb 18, 45; US citizen. *Educ:* Univ Westminster, London, DMS, 68; Univ Col Hosp Med Sch, MB & BS, 70; John Hopkins Univ, MPH, 71, DrPH, 80. *Prof Exp:* Res assoc, Sch Hyg & Pub Health, Johns Hopkins Univ, 72-75; vpres, Policy Res Inc, 74-81; dir, Health Serv Res & Develop, US Dept Vet Affairs, 81-86; vpres res & develop, Qual Stand Med, 86-90. *Concurrent Pos:* Pres, Health Improv Inst, 90- & Med Care Mgr Coop, 92. *Mem:* AMA; Am Pub Health Asn; Opers Res Soc Am. *Res:* Health care quality management and effectiveness; technology assessment, quality measurement, assurance, and improvement; health information systems. *Mailing Add:* 4340 East West Hwy No 105 Bethesda MD 20814-4411. *Fax:* 301-652-1250; *E-Mail:* pgg@has.cern

GOLDSCHMIDT, RAUL MAX, MICROBIAL GENETICS. *Current Pos:* RETIRED. *Personal Data:* b Santiago, Chile, Sept 23, 41. *Educ:* Univ Chile, Licenciado, 64; Mass Inst Technol, MSc, 67; Columbia Univ, PhD(biol), 70. *Prof Exp:* Assoc prof microbiol, Univ Ala, Birmingham, res assoc, 74, vis prof, 74-82; fac res assoc, Dept Biol, Wash Univ, St Louis, 82-90; res scientist, The Blood Ctr, 90-93. *Mem:* Am Soc Microbiol. *Res:* Elucidation of the molecular mechanisms responsible for bacterial contact, gene transfer and recombination of genetic material during bacterial conjugation and in the in-vivo expression of genes contained on bacterial plasmids; genetical and structural characterization of plasmids responsible for drug-resistance among clinical and animal gram-negative bacterial isolates. *Mailing Add:* 64 Old Colony Hartsdale NY 10530

GOLDSCHMIDT, VICTOR W, FLUID MECHANICS, THERMOSCIENCES. *Current Pos:* from asst prof assoc prof civil eng, 64-68, assoc prof, 68-71, PROF MECH ENG, PURDUE UNIV, 71- *Personal Data:* b Montevideo, Uruguay, Apr 20, 36; US citizen; m 58, Denice Van Liew; c Lisa M, Leanna A & V Matthew. *Educ:* Syracuse Univ, BS, 57, PhD(eng), 65; Univ Pa, MS, 60. *Honors & Awards:* Freeman Fund Award, Am Soc Civil Engrs, 71; Distinguished Serv Award, Am Soc Heating, Refrig & Air- Conditioning Engrs, 84, E K Campbell Award, 87. *Prof Exp:* Appl engr, Control Valve Div, Honeywell, Inc, 57-59, develop engr, 59-60; instr mech eng, Syracuse Univ, 60-64. *Concurrent Pos:* Dir Purdue Fels, Latin Am, 67; UN Indust Develop Orgn consult, Argentina, 79 & 81; Fulbright sr scholar, 79; ambassador, Am Soc Heating, Refrig & Air-Conditioning Engrs, NZ & Australia, 79, Argentina, Brazil, Mexico & Columbia, 82, Mexico, Costa Rica & Columbia, 84, West Indies, Venezuela & Costa Rica, 89, Columbia, 90; vis prof, Univ BC, Vancouver. *Mem:* Am Soc Mech Engrs; Sigma Xi; Am Soc Eng Educ; fel Am Soc Heating, Refrig & Air-Conditioning Engrs; Int Inst Refrig; hon mem Columbian Asn Air-Conditioning & Refrig; hon mem Argentine Asn Cold. *Res:* Fundamental studies in turbulence, particularly related to transport, interaction with acoustics and measurements of properties characterizing turbulence; energy utilization in heating and air conditioning; performance of heating and air conditioning systems. *Mailing Add:* Sch Mech Eng Purdue Univ 1288 Mech Eng Bldg West Lafayette IN 47907-1288. *Fax:* 765-494-0787

GOLDSCHMIDT, YADIN YEHUDA, STATISTICAL MECHANICS, PHASE TRANSITIONS. *Current Pos:* asst prof, 82-86, assoc prof, 86-92, PROF PHYSICS, UNIV PITTSBURGH, 92- *Personal Data:* b Kfar-Saba, Israel, Aug 25, 49; US citizen; m 75, Lidush Youssefi; c Tirtza, Ariel & Margalit. *Educ:* Hebrew Univ, Jerusalem, BSc, 73, PhD(physics), 78; Weizmann Inst Sci, Rehovot, Israel, MSc, 75. *Prof Exp:* Vis scientist physics, Ctr Nuclear Studies, Saclay, France, 78-80; asst prof res, Brown Univ, 80-82. *Concurrent Pos:* Vis scientist, CEA-Saclay, France, 89-90; Erna & Jakob Michael vis prof, Weizmann Inst, 96. *Mem:* Am Physics Soc. *Res:* Phase transitions and critical phenomena; random magnetic systems; random fields; random anisotropies; spin glasses; applications of field theory in statistical mechanics; investigation of two dimensional systems; superconductivity and the vortexglass transition. *Mailing Add:* Dept Physics & Astron Univ Pittsburgh Pittsburgh PA 15260. *Fax:* 412-624-9163; *E-Mail:* yadin@pitt.edu

GOLDSCHNEIDER, IRVING, PATHOLOGY. *Current Pos:* from asst prof to assoc prof, 69-79, PROF, DEPT PATH, SCH MED, UNIV CONN, 79-, DIR, CELL SORTING LAB, 79-, CHMN, DEPT PATH, 82- *Personal Data:* b Philadelphia, Pa, Feb 26, 37; m; c 4. *Educ:* Univ Pa, BA, 58, MD, 62. *Prof Exp:* Res asst, Wistar Inst Anat & Biol, Philadelphia, 58-59; fel, Med Student Res Training Prog, Sch Med, Univ Pa, 59-62; fel, exp path & immunol, Western Res Univ, NIH, 63-66; sr investr, Dept Bact, Walter Reed Army Inst Res, Washington, DC, 66-68; spec res fel develop biol, Nat Cancer Inst, Univ Chicago, 68-69. *Concurrent Pos:* Assoc ed, J Immunol, 74-82. *Mem:* Am Cancer Soc. *Res:* Pathology; numerous publications. *Mailing Add:* Dept Path Univ Conn Health Ctr 263 Farmington Ave Farmington CT 06030-3105. *Fax:* 860-679-2936

GOLDSMITH, CHARLES HARRY, DATA ANALYSIS, APPLIED STATISTICS. *Current Pos:* asst prof biostatist & appl math, 69-73, assoc prof, 73-79, PROF BIOSTATIST, DEPT CLIN EPIDEMIOL & BIOSTATIST, MCMASTER UNIV, 79- *Personal Data:* b Flin Flon, Man, Aug 27, 39; m 66, Lorraine Beauchamp; c Laurie J & Ann E. *Educ:* Univ Man, BSc, 61, MSc, 63; NC State Univ, PhD(exp statist), 69. *Honors & Awards:* Shewell Award, Am Soc Qual Control, 68, Frank J Wilcoxon Award, 70. *Prof Exp:* Lectr statist, Carleton Univ, Ont, 63-65; res assoc biostatist, Univ NC, Chapel Hill, 65-69. *Concurrent Pos:* Consult, Dept Hwys & Educ, Man Prov Govt, 63; abstractor, Exec Sci Inst, 67-71; adv, Med Commun Comt, Mohawk Col, Ont, 70-81; Ont Ministry Health fel & External Affairs Can travel fel, 75; chmn, Demonstration Model Grants Rev Comt, Ont Ministry Health, 79-82; ed consult, J Can Physiother Asn, 80-87; chmn, Rev Comt 53, Epidemiol Chronic Dis & Occup Health, Nat Health Res & Develop Prog, Health & Welfare Can, 83-; chair, Biopharmaceut Sect, Am Statist Asn, 87; mem study sect, Found Chiropractic Educ Res, 87-; Can ed, J Biopharm Statist, 90- *Mem:* Fel Am Statist Asn; Biomet Soc; Royal Statist Soc; Statist Soc Can (secy, 77-81); Int Statist Inst; Soc Clin Trials; Can Rheumatism Asn; Int Soc Pharmacoepidemiol (vpres-elect, 94). *Res:* Design and analysis of health surveys and clinical trials; experimental designs; regression analysis; statistical data analysis; statistical problems in therapeutic compliance; statistical epidemiology and pharmacolepidemiology. *Mailing Add:* Ctr Eval Med St Joseph's Hosp 50 Charlton Ave W Hamilton ON L8P 2C1 Can. *Fax:* 905-574-2838; *E-Mail:* goldsmit@fhs.csu.mcmaster.ca

GOLDSMITH, DALE PRESTON JOEL, BIOCHEMISTRY. *Current Pos:* ASSOC PROF BIOCHEM, COL MED, UNIV NEBR, OMAHA, 64- *Personal Data:* b Catasauqua, Pa, Oct 30, 16. *Educ:* Lehigh Univ, BS, 38; Harvard Univ, MA, 40; Pa State Col, PhD(org chem), 42; Univ Rochester, MS, 57. *Prof Exp:* Chemist, Nat Aniline & Chem Co, NY, 37; chemist, Res Labs, Socony-Vacuum Oil Co, NJ, 38-39; instr org chem, Pa State Col, 40-42, Parke, Davis & Co fel, 42-43; sr res chemist, Merck & Co, Inc, 43-55; from instr to asst prof physiol, Sch Med, Univ Rochester, 57-64. *Mem:* AAAS; Am Chem Soc; Am Physiol Soc; NY Acad Sci; fel Am Inst Chemists; Sigma Xi. *Res:* Mucosal regeneration; atherosclerosis; medicinal chemicals; gastrointestinal biochemistry; lipid metabolism. *Mailing Add:* 11716 Mayberry St Omaha NE 68154-3417

GOLDSMITH, DAVID FREDERIC, SILICA-SILICOSIS, AGRICULTURE HEALTH. *Current Pos:* SR SCIENTIST, PUB HEALTH INST, 91- *Personal Data:* b Portland, Ore, Dec 5, 48; m 75, Susan G Rose. *Educ:* Antioch Col, BA, 72; Univ NC, MSPH, 77, PhD(epidemiol), 83. *Prof Exp:* Res asst health sci, Univ Ore, 74-75; grad res asst, Univ NC, 75-77; staff scientist, Nat Acad Sci, 78; environ epidemiologist, Res Triangle Inst, 79-83; asst prof epidemiol, Univ Calif, San Diego, 83-85 & Univ Calif, Davis, 85-91. *Concurrent Pos:* Monograph mem, Int Agency Res Cancer, 86; Spec asst risk assessment, US Environ Protection Agency, 87-91; reviewer, NIH, 87, 90, 94-95; prin investr, Pub Health Inst, 91-; lectr environ epidemiol, Univ San Francisco, 92- *Mem:* AAAS; Int Soc Environ Epidemiol; Soc Occup & Environ Health; Soc Epidemiol Res. *Res:* Silica, silicosis and cancer; agricultural cancer prevention; risk assessment; epidemiology and toxictorts/Daubert process; pesticides and chronic disease risks. *Mailing Add:* 833 Shattuck Ave Berkeley CA 94707. *Fax:* 510-843-5880; *E-Mail:* davegold@publichealth.org

GOLDSMITH, DAVID JONATHAN, SYNTHETIC ORGANIC CHEMISTRY. *Current Pos:* from asst prof to assoc prof chem, 63-75, chmn, 83-90, PROF CHEM, EMORY UNIV, 75- *Personal Data:* b Flushing, NY, Aug 25, 31; m 59; c 3. *Educ:* Univ Mich, BS, 52, MS, 53; Columbia Univ, PhD(chem), 58. *Prof Exp:* Res fel, Harvard Univ, 57-59; asst prof chem, Wayne State Univ, 59-63. *Concurrent Pos:* Vis prof, Univ Strasbourg, 71-72. *Mem:* Am Chem Soc. *Res:* Synthesis of natural products and synthetic methods. *Mailing Add:* Dept Chem Emory Univ Atlanta GA 30332-0001

GOLDSMITH, DONALD LEON, software development, mathematics, for more information see previous edition

GOLDSMITH, EDWARD, FIRE RETARDANT COATINGS. *Current Pos:* RETIRED. *Personal Data:* b Baltimore, Md, Sept 9, 23; m 50; c 2. *Educ:* Univ Md, BS, 48. *Prof Exp:* Sr chemist, Baltimore Paint & Chem Corp, 58-76; tech dir, Ocean Chem Inc, 76-89. *Concurrent Pos:* Consult plastics, chem & fire retardants, 70- *Mem:* Soc Coatings Technol; Am Soc Testing & Mat. *Res:* Intumescent fire retardant coatings. *Mailing Add:* 117 Todd St Savannah GA 31410

GOLDSMITH, ELI DAVID, DEVELOPMENTAL BIOLOGY, RESEARCH ADMINISTRATION. *Current Pos:* asst prof anat, 45-48, from assoc prof to prof histol, Col Dent, 48-73, from asst prof to prof, Grad Sch Arts & Sci, 45-73, res coordr, 48-69, EMER PROF HISTOL, COL DENT & EMER PROF, GRAD SCH ARTS & SCI, NY UNIV, 73-, SPEC CONSULT RES & TRAINING TO DEAN, COL DENT, 78-, DIR RES TRAINING & PROG DEVELOP, 78- *Personal Data:* b New York, NY, Apr 10, 07; m 40; c 1. *Educ:* City Col NY, BS, 26; Harvard Univ, AM, 28, PhD(biol), 34; NY Univ, MS, 31. *Prof Exp:* Asst zool, Harvard Univ, 28-29; lab instr comp anat, NY Univ, 29-31; asst zool, Harvard Univ, 31-33, Austin teaching fel, 33-34; instr biol & chem, City Col NY, 34-45. *Concurrent Pos:* Harvard grant, Marine Biol Lab, Woods Hole, 32 & Bermuda Biol Sta, 34; Commonwealth Fund grant, 44; Thompson Fund grant, 44, 46; USPHS grant, 47-70; Am Cancer Soc grant, 51-55; biomed res coordr, Off Naval Res, US Dept Navy, NY, 51-53; actg dir, Off Res Serv, NY Univ, 63-64; consult to surgeon gen, USPHS; consult to dir, Nat Inst Dent Res; sci consult, Osborn Labs, Marine Sci; mem corp, Bermuda Biol Sta; mem selection panel sr res fels, NIH; mem dent prog proj comt, Nat Inst Dent Res. *Mem:* AAAS; fel Am Col Dent; fel, NY Acad Med; Int Asn Dent Res; hon mem Acad Gen Dent; Am Chem Soc. *Res:* Regeneration effect of chemicals and endocrines; carcinogenesis; anti-vitamin; vitamin-endocrinology relationship; goitrogenic drugs; radioactive iodine; blood depressors; dental histology; antimetabolites and nucleic acid metabolism in Drosophila; chemosterilants and control of insect populations; teratology. *Mailing Add:* Res Training Prog Develop Ny Univ Col Dent 421 First Ave Rm 1064W New York NY 10010-4001

GOLDSMITH, GEORGE JASON, PHYSICS. *Current Pos:* ASSOC PROF PHYSICS, BOSTON COL, 68- *Personal Data:* b Newburyport, Mass, Mar 29, 23; m 45; c 4. *Educ:* Univ Vt, BS, 44; Purdue Univ, MS, 48, PhD(physics), 55. *Prof Exp:* Instr physics, Purdue Univ, 48-55; physicist, Labs, RCA Corp, 55-68. *Concurrent Pos:* Dir, Boston Col Environ Ctr, 75- *Mem:* AAAS; Am Phys Soc; Sigma Xi. *Res:* Photoconductivity in insulators; solid state and nuclear physics; science and society; energy and environment. *Mailing Add:* Dept Physics Boston Col Chestnut Hill MA 02167

GOLDSMITH, HARRY L, BIOPHYSICS, PHYSICAL CHEMISTRY. *Current Pos:* fel suspension rheology, McGill Univ, 61-64, Med Res Coun Can scholar blood rheology, 64-67, from asst prof to assoc prof exp med, 66-73, PROF EXP MED, MCGILL UNIV, 73-, MED RES COUN CAN CAREER INVESTR BLOOD RHEOLOGY, 67- *Personal Data:* b Nurnberg, Ger, May 11, 28; Can citizen; m 58; c 2. *Educ:* Oxford Univ, BA, 50, BSc, 51; McGill Univ, PhD(chem), 61. *Honors & Awards:* Landis Award, Microcirculatory Soc, Inc, 84. *Prof Exp:* Tech officer phys chem, Dyestuffs Div, Imp Chem Industs, Ltd, Eng, 50-56. *Mem:* Am Physiol Soc; Can Soc Clin Invest; Int Soc Biorheology; European Soc Microcirculation; Microcirculatory Soc; Soc Rheology; NAm Soc Rheology. *Res:* Solution kinetics; lyophopic colloids; flow of suspensions of model rigid and deformable particles through tubes; flow behavior and interactions of human blood cells; measurement of force of adhesion between cells and between cells and the vessel wall. *Mailing Add:* Dept Med McGill Univ Montreal Gen Hosp 1650 Cedar Ave Montreal PQ H3G 1A4 Can. *Fax:* 514-937-6961

GOLDSMITH, HARRY SAWYER, NEUROSURGERY. *Current Pos:* PROF SURG, UNIV NEV, 96- *Personal Data:* b Newton, Mass, Sept 30, 29; m 61, Linda Perry; c John, Robert & Lynne. *Educ:* Dartmouth Col, AB, 52; Boston Univ, MD, 56. *Hon Degrees:* Dr, Shanghai Second Med Univ, 88; Xouzou Med Col, 95. *Prof Exp:* Prof & chmn, Dept Surg, Jefferson Med Col, 70-77; prof surg, Dartmouth Med Sch, 78-83; prof surg & adj prof neurosurg, Boston Univ Sch Med, 83-95. *Concurrent Pos:* Adj prof neurosurg, Boston Univ Sch Med, 83- *Mem:* Am Col Surgeons; Soc Vascular Surg; Int Soc Surg; Soc Surg Oncol. *Res:* Use of the omentum and its effects on the central nervous system. *Mailing Add:* PO Box 493 Glenbrook NV 89413. *Fax:* 702-749-5861

GOLDSMITH, HENRY ARNOLD, PHYSICAL CHEMISTRY. *Current Pos:* RETIRED. *Personal Data:* b Berlin, Ger, Dec 17, 10; nat US; m 41, Emma Stoliar; c Judith A & Nora L (Stander). *Educ:* Univ Berlin, Dipl, 32; Univ Genoa, PhD(chem), 34; Univ Pavia, dipl, 35. *Prof Exp:* From chemist to chief chemist, Glyco Prod Co, Inc, NY, 35-44; coatings chemist, Standard Varnish Works, Inc, 44-46; chief chemist cleaning compounds, Phipps Prod Inc, Mass, 47-48 & org chem, Colgate-Palmolive-Peet 48-50; chief chemist detergents, Theobald Industs, 50-54 & metal cleaners, Solvent or Chem Prod Co, Mich, 54-58; from group leader to mgr surface prep, Turco Prod CDiv, Purex Corp, Calif, 58-64; sr scientist, US Borax Res Corp, Anaheim, 65-67; res chemist, Purex Corp, 68-72, mgr res & develop, 72-81. *Mem:* Am Chem Soc; AAAS. *Res:* Organic chemistry and applications in the fields of fat derivatives, detergents, surfactants, emulsifiers and resins. *Mailing Add:* 421 Via Colusa Torrance CA 90505

GOLDSMITH, JOHN ROTHCHILD, MEDICAL & SCIENCE EDUCATION. *Current Pos:* vis prof, 78-80, PROF, EPIDEMIOL UNIT, FAC HEALTH SCI, BEN GURION UNIV NEGEV, 80- *Personal Data:* b Portland, Ore, Jan 5, 22; m 47; c 4. *Educ:* Reed Col, BA, 42; Harvard Univ, MD, 45, MPH, 57. *Prof Exp:* Res fel prev med, Harvard Med Sch, 55-57; head air pollution med studies, Calif State Dept Pub Health, 57-65; epidemiologist, WHO, Switz, 64-66; Epidemiol Studies Lab, Calif State Dept Health, 66-78. *Concurrent Pos:* Consult, WHO, 63; spec consult, Adv Comt Smoking & Health, Div Air Pollution & Surgeon Gen, USPHS; regents lectr, Univ Calif, Irvine; mem, Int Occup Health; distinguished vis scientist, US Environ Protection Agency, 85-89. *Mem:* AMA; fel Am Pub Health Asn; Int Epidemiol Asn; Int Soc Environ Epidemiol; Int Comt Occup Health. *Res:* Occupational and environmental epidemiology; air quality standard setting; environmental cancer; health effects of energy production; evaluation of health services; epidemiological methods; epidemiology of effects of non-ionizing radiation. *Mailing Add:* Fac Health Sci Ben Gurion Univ Negev PO Box 653 Beer Sheva 84120 Israel

GOLDSMITH, JULIAN ROYCE, MINERALOGY-PETROLOGY, GEOCHEMISTRY. *Current Pos:* asst petrol, Univ Chicago, 46-47, res assoc geochem, 47-51, from asst prof to prof, 51-69, Charles E Merriam distinguished serv prof, 69-88, EMER PROF GEOCHEM, UNIV CHICAGO, 88- *Personal Data:* b Chicago, Ill, Feb 26, 18; m 40, Ethel Frank; c Richard, John & Susan (Woolridge). *Educ:* Univ Chicago, SB, 40, PhD(geol), 47. *Honors & Awards:* Mineral Soc Award, Mineral Soc Am, 55, Roebling Medal, 88; Harry H Hess Medal, Am Geophys Union, 87. *Prof Exp:* Asst petrol, Univ Chicago, 41-42; res chemist, Corning Glass Works, 42-46. *Concurrent Pos:* Co-ed, J Geol, 57-62; mem, Earth Sci Panel, NSF, 58-61, chmn, 60-61, mem, Nat Sci Bd, 64-70; assoc dean phys sci div, Univ Chicago, 60-72, assoc chmn, 61-62, actg dean phys sci div, 62, chmn dept geophys sci, 63-71; consult ed, Encycl Britannica & McGraw-Hill Encycl Sci & Technol; Gov sci adv comt, 89- *Mem:* Fel Am Geophys Union; fel Geol Soc Am (vpres, 73-74, pres, 74-75); Mineral Soc Am (vpres, 68-69, pres, 70-71); Geochem Soc (vpres, 55, pres, 65-66); Am Chem Soc; Sigma Xi. *Res:* Phase equilibria and crystal chemistry of silicates and carbonates. *Mailing Add:* Dept Geophys Sci 5734 Ellis Ave Chicago IL 60637. *Fax:* 773-702-9505

GOLDSMITH, LAURA TOBI, REPRODUCTIVE ENDOCRINOLOGY, CELL BIOLOGY. *Current Pos:* asst prof obstet & gynec, 86-92, ASST PROF BIOCHEM & MOLECULAR BIOL, NJ MED SCH, UMD MED & DENT NJ, 89-, ASSOC PROF OBSTET & GYNEC, 92- *Personal Data:* b New York, NY, June 2, 50. *Educ:* Drexel Univ, BS, 71; NY Univ, MS, 78, PhD(biol), 81. *Prof Exp:* Postdoctoral fel physiol, Med Sch, Univ Pittsburgh, 80-82; res asst prof obstet & gynec, Med Sch, NY Univ, 82-86. *Concurrent Pos:* Vis lectr, Med Sch, NY Univ, 86-88. *Mem:* AAAS; Soc Study Reproduction; Endocrine Soc; Soc Gynec Invest. *Res:* Mechanisms by which ovarian cells recognize extracellular signals enabling proper hormone secretion and the actions of the ovarian hormone relaxin. *Mailing Add:* Dept OB/GYN UMDNJ-NJ Med Sch 185 S Orange Ave Newark NJ 07103-2714. *Fax:* 973-982-4574; *E-Mail:* goldsmit@umdnj.edu

GOLDSMITH, LOWELL ALAN, DERMATOLOGY. *Current Pos:* PROF & CHAIR DERMAT, UNIV ROCHESTER SCH MED, 81- *Personal Data:* b Brooklyn, NY, Mar 29, 38; m 60; c 2. *Educ:* Columbia Col, AB, 59; State Univ NY Downstate Med Ctr, MD, 63. *Honors & Awards:* Res Career Develop Award, NIH. *Prof Exp:* Resident, Harvard-Mass Gen Hosp, 67-69, asst prof, 70-73; from assoc prof to prof, Duke Med Ctr, 73-81. *Concurrent Pos:* Assoc ed, Dialogues in Dermatol, 76-; Res Career & Develop award, NIH, 76 & 81; co-ed, Progress Dermatol, 76-82; Macy Found fel, 78; consult, Roswell Park Mem Inst, 82-; dir, Am Bd Dermat, 93-; mem bd dirs, Am Acad Dermat, 93- *Mem:* Am Soc Biol Chem; Am Dermatol Asn; Am Soc Clin Invest; Am Asn Physicians; Am Bd Dermat; Am Acad Dermat; Asn Professors Dermat. *Res:* Biochemistry of epidermis and epidermal derivatives; mechanism of genetic disorders of human skin; monoclonal antibody probes to human skin; changes in epidermis in neoplasia. *Mailing Add:* Sch Med & Dent Univ Rochester Box 706 Rochester NY 14642-0001. *Fax:* 716-256-1131

GOLDSMITH, MARY HELEN MARTIN, BIOLOGY, PLANT PHYSIOLOGY. *Current Pos:* res assoc, Yale Univ, 61-73, lectr, 63-64 & 66-73, assoc prof, 74-84, PROF BIOL, YALE UNIV, 84-, DIR MARSH BOT GARDEN, 86- *Personal Data:* b Boston, Mass, May 2, 33; m 55; c 2. *Educ:* Cornell Univ, BA, 55; Radcliffe Col, AM, 56, PhD(biol), 60. *Prof Exp:* Nat Cancer Inst fel, Harvard Univ, 59-60; fel, King's Col, Univ London, 60-61. *Concurrent Pos:* Carnegie fel, Carnegie Inst Wash, Dept Plant Biol, Stanford, 78; Guggenheim fel, John Simon Guggenheim Found, 87; master, Silliman Col, Yale Univ, 87-; Brenda Ryman vis fel, Girton Col, Univ Cambridge, 87. *Mem:* Am Soc Plant Physiol; Soc Gen Physiol. *Res:* Plant physiology; polar transport and action of auxin; gravitropic and phototropic responses; role of proton pumps and ion channels in cell growth and plant development; their contribution to electrical properties of plasma membrane and tonoplast. *Mailing Add:* Dept Biol Yale Univ PO Box 208103 New Haven CT 06520-8103

GOLDSMITH, MERRILL E, MOLECULAR BIOLOGY. *Current Pos:* staff fel pharmacol, NIH, 82-86, MICROBIOLOGIST, CLIN PHARMACOL BR, NAT CANCER INST, NIH, 87- *Personal Data:* b Chicago, Ill, Aug 8, 46. *Educ:* Stanford Univ, BA, 68; Yale Univ, MPhil, 71, PhD(biol), 77. *Prof Exp:* USPHS fel, Lab Molecular Biol, Nat Inst Arthritis, Metab & Digestive Dis, NIH, 76-79; staff fel, Clin Hemat Br, Nat Heart Lung & Blood Inst, NIH, 79-81. *Mem:* Am Soc Cell Biol; Am Soc Microbiol. *Res:* Isolation, regulation and expression of genes involved in resistance of tumor cells to chemotherapeutic drugs (dihydrofolate reductase, mdr (P-glycoprotein) glutathione-S- transferases and topoisomerase I and II. *Mailing Add:* Med Br NCI NIH Bldg 10 Rm 12N66 Bethesda MD 20892-0001. Fax: 301-402-0172

GOLDSMITH, MICHAEL ALLEN, MEDICAL ONCOLOGY, PHASE I CLINICAL TRIALS. *Current Pos:* ASST CLIN PROF MED & NEOPLASTIC DIS, MT SINAI SCH MED, 77-; ATTEND PHYSICIAN, ONCOL CONSULT, PC, 77. *Personal Data:* b Bronx, NY, Jan 28, 46; m 71; c 4. *Educ:* Yeshiva Univ, BA, 67; Albert Einstein Col Med, MD, 71. *Prof Exp:* Staff assoc, Nat Cancer Inst, NIH, 72-74. *Mem:* Fel Am Col Physicians; Am Soc Clin Oncol; Am Asn Cancer Res; AAAS; NY Acad Sci. *Res:* Early clinical trials of novel anticancer drugs in evaluation of clinical pharmacology and toxicology in man; animal models as quantitative predictors of human toxicology. *Mailing Add:* 550 N Forest Dr Teaneck NJ 07666-2051. Fax: 212 628-2948

GOLDSMITH, PAUL FELIX, ASTROPHYSICS, ELECTRICAL ENGINEERING. *Current Pos:* PROF ASTRON, CORNELL UNIV, 92- *Personal Data:* b Washington, DC, Nov 5, 48; m 88, Sheryl E Reiss. *Educ:* Univ Calif, Berkeley, AB, 69, PhD(physics), 75. *Prof Exp:* Mem tech staff, AT&T Bell Labs, 75-77; from asst prof to assoc prof, Univ Mass, Amherst, 77-87, prof physics & astron, 87-92. *Concurrent Pos:* Consult, Lincoln Lab, Mass Inst Technol, 77-80; vpres res & develop, Millitech Corp, South Deerfield, Mass, 82- *Mem:* Am Astron Soc; fel Inst Elec & Electronics Engrs; Union Radio Sci Int. *Res:* Structure and composition of interstellar molecular clouds, particularly concerning process of star formation; development of instrumentation for millimeter and submillimeter radio astronomy; developed quasioptical technology for millimeter systems and imaging systems. *Mailing Add:* Cornell Univ 502 Space Sci Bldg Ithaca NY 14853-6801

GOLDSMITH, PAUL KENNETH, COMPARATIVE MARINE BIOCHEMISTRY. *Current Pos:* Biologist, Nat Cancer Inst, 65-71, BIOLOGIST, LAB BIOL MED, NAT INST ARTHRITIS, DIGESTIVE DIS & KIDNEYS, NIH, 71- *Personal Data:* b Washington, DC, Nov 28, 42; m 73. *Educ:* Univ Md, BS, 65, PhD(cytol), 77. *Concurrent Pos:* Investr, Marine Biol Lab, 77-80. *Mem:* AAAS; NY Acad Sci. *Res:* Enzyme activites in hepatocyte endoplasmic reticulum; carbohydrate metabolism in hepatopancreus of marine invertebrates; characterization of immunoglobulin E responses in rheumatic diseases; food allergy and recurrant infections. *Mailing Add:* NIH/NIDDK-MDB BLdg 10 Rm 8C-101 Bethesda MD 20892

GOLDSMITH, RALPH SAMUEL, MEDICINE, ENDOCRINOLOGY. *Current Pos:* assoc dean, 79-89, PROF MED, SCH MED, UNIV CALIF, SAN FRANCISCO, 79- *Personal Data:* b Baltimore, Md, Feb 23, 31; m 53, Mildred Maseritz; c Donna, Lynn & Mark. *Educ:* Franklin & Marshall Col, BS, 50; Univ Md, MD, 54. *Prof Exp:* Intern, Walter Reed Army Hosp, 54-55, resident physician internal med, 55-58, student investr metab, Inst Res, 58-59; chief, Metab Br, US Army Surg Res Unit, 59-63; instr med, Harvard Med Sch, 63-64, assoc, 64-68, asst prof, 68, res assoc, Thorndike Mem Lab, 63-68; from asst prof to prof med, Mayo Grad Sch Med, Univ Minn, 68-74, dir, Clin Study Unit & consult, Div Endocrinol, Mayo Clin & Found, 68-74, from assoc prof to prof med, Mayo Med Sch, 72-74; prof med, Sch Med, Univ Tex, San Antonio, 74-79, dep chmn dept, 74-78; chief med, Audie Murphy Mem Vet Hosp, 74-78. *Concurrent Pos:* Civilian scientist, US Army, 62-63; consult, US Army Res Inst Environ Med, 63-68; asst physician, Second & Fourth Med Serv, Boston City Hosp, 64-68; ed, Bone, 77-86; mem, B Study Sect Gen Med, NIH, 78-82; chief staff, Vet Admin Med Ctr, San Francisco, 79-89. *Mem:* AAAS; Endocrine Soc; Am Fedn Clin Res; Am Soc Clin Invest; Am Soc Bone & Mineral Res; Am Physiol Soc. *Res:* Calcium and phosphorus metabolism; parathyroid hormone; metabolic bone disease; bone diseases; vitamin D. *Mailing Add:* Dept Med Univ Calif San Francisco 80-Q N Cabrillo Hwy Half Moon Bay CA 94019. Fax: 650-726-1339

GOLDSMITH, RICHARD, GEOLOGY. *Current Pos:* RETIRED. *Personal Data:* b Salem, Mass, Sept 30, 18; m 55, June Waterman; c Richard S, Kathryn H & Charles F. *Educ:* Univ Maine, AB, 40; Univ Wash, PhD(geol), 52. *Prof Exp:* Geologist, US Geol Surv, 52-86. *Concurrent Pos:* Consult geologist, 87- *Mem:* AAAS; Geol Soc Am; Am Quaternary Asn. *Res:* Igneous and metamorphic petrology; areal geology; geomorphology and glacial ecology; economic geology. *Mailing Add:* 2 Prince St Marblehead MA 01948

GOLDSMITH, TIMOTHY HENSHAW, VISUAL PHYSIOLOGY. *Current Pos:* from asst prof to assoc prof, 61-70, chmn dept, 71-77, PROF BIOL, YALE UNIV, 70- *Personal Data:* b New York, NY, May 1, 32; m 55; c 2. *Educ:* Cornell Univ, BA, 54; Harvard Univ, PhD(biol), 58. *Prof Exp:* Jr fel, Soc Fels, Harvard Univ, 58-61; instr, Marine Biol Lab, Woods Hole, 59-61. *Concurrent Pos:* Guggenheim fel, 67-68; trustee, Marine Biol Lab, Woods Hole, 72- *Mem:* Fel AAAS; Soc Gen Physiol; Biophys Soc; fel Am Acad Arts & Sci; Asn Res Vision & Ophthal. *Res:* Neurophysiology and biochemistry of light sensitive systems, particularly vision of arthropods and hummingbirds. *Mailing Add:* Dept Biol Yale Univ PO Box 208103 New Haven CT 06520-8103

GOLDSMITH, WERNER, COLLISIONS, BIOMECHANICS. *Current Pos:* from instr to prof, 47-87, emer prof mech eng, 88-97, PROF GRAD SCH, UNIV CALIF, BERKELEY, 55-; CONSULT, 55- *Personal Data:* b Dusseldorf, Ger, May 23, 24; US citizen; m 73, Penelope Alexander; c Stephen M, Andrea J & Remy M. *Educ:* Univ Tex, Austin, BSME, 44, MSME, 45; Univ Calif, Berkeley, PhD(mech eng), 49. *Honors & Awards:* Nat Acad Eng. *Prof Exp:* Engr turbines, Westinghouse Elec Corp, 45-47. *Concurrent Pos:* Mech engr, Detonation Physics Div, US Naval Weapons Ctr, China Lake, Calif, 51-; Guggenheim Mem Found fel, 53-54; consult, numerous gov agencies and priv industs, 53-; prin investr res grants, NIH, NSF, US Army & US Navy, 55-93; chmn head, Injury Model Construct Comt, Nat Inst Neurol Dis & Stroke, NIH, 66-70; Fulbright res fel, US Educ Found, Tech Univ Athens, 74-75, Univ Patras, Greece, 81-82. *Mem:* Fel Am Soc Mech Engrs; fel Am Acad Mech. *Res:* Collisions; wave propagation; dynamic properties of materials; biomechanics; rock mechanics; head and neck injury; experimental mechanics; protective devices for humans. *Mailing Add:* 450 Gravatt Dr Berkeley CA 94705. Fax: 510-486-8050; E-Mail: goldsmith@euler.berkeley.edu, goldsmith@me.berkeley.edu

GOLDSON, ALFRED LLOYD, ONCOLOGY. *Current Pos:* clin instr, 76, from asst prof to prof, 77-84, CHMN DEPT RADIOTHER, HOWARD UNIV, 79- *Educ:* Hampton Inst, BS, 68; Howard Univ, MD, 72; Am Bd Therapeut Radiol, dipl. *Prof Exp:* Res radiation ther, Mem Sloan-Kettering Cancer Ctr, New York, 72-75, fel, 75-76. *Concurrent Pos:* Clin assoc prof radiation oncol, Col Med, Georgetown Univ, Washington, 79; mem comt radiother, res & develop, Am Col Oncol, 82-85; chmn, Howard Univ Cancer Comn, 85-; interim dir, Cancer Ctr, 91. *Mem:* Am Soc Therapeut Radiol; Am Col Radiol; Am Soc Clin Oncol; Nat Med Asn; NY Acad Sci. *Res:* Radiation oncology. *Mailing Add:* Dept Radiother Howard Univ Col Med 520 W St NW Washington DC 20001-2337

GOLDSPIEL, SOLOMON, engineering; deceased, see previous edition for last biography

GOLDSTEIN, ABRAHAM M B, urology, histology; deceased, see previous edition for last biography

GOLDSTEIN, ALBERT, MEDICAL PHYSICS, DIAGNOSTIC ULTRASOUND. *Current Pos:* ASSOC PROF, SCH MED, WAYNE STATE UNIV, 85- *Personal Data:* b New York, NY, May 26, 38; m 68, Anita Mammano; c Jesse & Eva. *Educ:* City Col New York, BS, 60; Mass Inst Technol, PhD(physics), 65. *Prof Exp:* Staff mem physics, Nat Magnet Lab, Mass Inst Technol, 65; res assoc, Ecole Normale Superieure, Paris, 65-67; staff mem, T J Watson Res Ctr, IBM Corp, 67-71; asst prof, Dept Radiol, Univ Kans Med Ctr, 72-76, adj asst prof, Dept Elec Eng, Univ Kans, 73-76; chief, div med physics, Henry Ford Hosp, 76-84. *Concurrent Pos:* Assoc scientist, Mid-Am Cancer Ctr, Kans, 75-76; adj assoc prof radiol, Med Sch, Wayne State Univ, 80-84; adj asst res scientist radiol, Med Sch, Univ Mich, Detroit, 81-82. *Mem:* Fel Am Asn Physicists Med; Inst Elec & Electronics Engrs; fel Am Inst Ultrasound Med; fel Am Col Radiol; Radiol Soc NAm; Acoust Soc Am. *Res:* Physics and quality assurance of diagnostic ultrasound and computed tomography, the information content of medical images; diagnostic ultrasound equipment standardization, tissue characterization and performance calibration. *Mailing Add:* Radiol Detroit Receiving Hosp 4201 St Antoine Detroit MI 48201. Fax: 313-577-8600; E-Mail: agoldst@cms.cc.wayne.edu

GOLDSTEIN, ALBERT, CHEMICAL CONSULTING, HYDROPHILIC RESINS. *Current Pos:* CHEM CONSULT, GOLDSTEIN ASSOCS, 71-; PRES, VENTURE CHEM CO, 72-; PRES HYDROGELIX INC, 87-; PRES/TECH DIR, HYDRO SLIP TECHNOL, INC, 87- *Personal Data:* b Brooklyn, NY, Feb 20, 28; m 52, Barbara; c 4. *Educ:* Rutgers Univ, BSc, 51; Cornell Univ, PhD(org chem), 54. *Prof Exp:* Res chemist, Cent Res Labs, Gen Foods Corp, 54-55 & Catalin Corp Am, 55-59; chief chemist, Chemirad Corp, 59-65; sr scientist, Devro, Johnson & Johnson, 65-69; dir res, Hydron Labs, Nat Patent Develop Corp, NB, 69-71. *Concurrent Pos:* Dir, Vanguard Res, Inc, 87-92. *Mem:* Am Chem Soc; Inst Food Technol; Am Asn Textile Chemists & Colorists; Asn Consult Chemists & Chem Engrs. *Res:* Process and product development, reactive and hydrophilic resins, specialty organics, flame retardants, organic and inorganic coatings, acrylic resins, ink formulation and product formulation; natural and synthetic rubber latex formulation, compounding, dipping. *Mailing Add:* Goldstein Assocs PO Box 88 Adelphia NJ 07710. Fax: 732-462-3644

GOLDSTEIN, ALLAN L, BIOCHEMISTRY, IMMUNOLOGY. *Current Pos:* PROF BIOCHEM & CHMN DEPT, SCH MED & HEALTH SCI, GEORGE WASHINGTON UNIV, 78- *Personal Data:* b Bronx, NY, Nov 8, 37; m 75, Linda Tish; c Dawn, Jennifer & Adam. *Educ:* Wagner Col, BS, 59; Rutgers Univ, MS, 61, PhD(physiol, biochem), 64. *Honors & Awards:*

Copernicus Medal, Univ Krakow, Poland, 74; Gordon Wilson Medal, Am Clin & Climat Soc, 76; Citation for Cancer Res, NIH, 80; Michele Fodera Int Prize Biomed Res, Italy, 90; Chevalier des Palmes Acad Sci Contrib to France, 93. *Prof Exp:* Teaching asst zool, Rutgers Univ, 59-61, from asst instr to instr, 61-64; USPHS res fel biochem, Albert Einstein Col Med, 64-66, from instr to assoc prof, 66-72; prof & dir div, Univ Tex Med Br, Galveston, 72-78. *Concurrent Pos:* Consult, Hoffmann-La Roche Inc, 74-82, Genentech Inc, 79-80 & Battelle Mem Inst, 80; mem, Med Res Serv Merit Rev Bd Oncol, Vet Admin, 77-80; mem, Biol Response Modifier Prog, Div Cancer Treatment, Nat Cancer Inst; assoc ed, Human Lymphocyte Differentiation, 81-; Burroughs Wellcome Van Dyke award, 84-86. *Mem:* AAAS; Am Asn Immunol; Endocrine Soc; Am Soc Biol Chem; Transplantation Soc. *Res:* Isolation, purification, mechanism of action and biological role of thymic humoral factors; lymphoid tissue biochemistry; hormonal control of metabolic processes; co-discoverer of the thymosins, the family of hormones of the thymus gland. *Mailing Add:* 5053 Massachusetts Ave NW Washington DC 20016. *Fax:* 202-994-8974

GOLDSTEIN, ALLEN A, APPLIED MATHEMATICS. *Current Pos:* assoc prof, 64-65, PROF MATH, UNIV WASH, 65- *Personal Data:* b Baltimore, Md, Jan 7, 25; m 49; c 4. *Educ:* St John's Col, Md, BA, 47; Georgetown Univ, MA, 52, PhD, 54. *Prof Exp:* Engr & physicist, Kellex Corp, 48-51; physicist math comput, Appl Math Lab, Nat Bur Stand, 51-54; res assoc astron, Observ, Georgetown Univ, 54-55; design specialist, Convair Div, Gen Dynamics Corp, 55-60; res assoc elec eng, Mass Inst Technol, 60-63; assoc prof math, Univ Tex, 63-64. *Mem:* Am Math Soc. *Res:* Application of functional analysis to numerical analysis and applied mathematics. *Mailing Add:* Dept Math Univ Wash Seattle WA 98195-0001

GOLDSTEIN, ANN L, CARDIOVASCULAR PHARMACOLOGY. *Current Pos:* sr scientist, Dept Pharmacol, 82-88, res investr, Dept Pharmacol & Chemother, 88-96, DIR, EARLY STRATEGIC PLANNING, 96-, HOFFMANN-LA ROCHE INC, 96- *Educ:* Univ Pa, BA, 65; Vassar Col, MS, 68; NY Univ, PhD(biol), 79. *Prof Exp:* Teaching asst, Vassar Col, 67-68; instr biol & bact, Rockland Community Col, 68-69; res assoc, Vassar Col, 76-79, NIH postdoctoral fel, 79-82. *Concurrent Pos:* NIH res grants, 76-79 & 79-; vis asst prof, Vassar Col, 79-82. *Mem:* Sigma Xi; AAAS; NY Acad Sci; Tissue Cult Asn; Am Soc Cell Biol. *Res:* Regulation of cell metabolism including cell proliferation, lipid and protein turnover, and cell-cell interactions; in vitro systems applicable to pharmacological approaches to cardiovascular disease; author of numerous technical publications. *Mailing Add:* Hoffman-La Roche Inc Early Strategic Planning 340 Kingsland St Nutley NJ 07110-1199

GOLDSTEIN, ARTHUR L, CHEMICAL ENGINEERING. *Current Pos:* CHMN & CHIEF EXEC OFFICER, IONICS INC, 90- *Educ:* Rensselaer Polytech Inst, BS; Univ Del, MChE; Harvard Univ, MBA. *Mem:* Nat Acad Eng. *Res:* Granted 8 patents relating to the purification and processing of liquids. *Mailing Add:* Ionics Inc 65 Grove St Watertown MA 02172-2882

GOLDSTEIN, ARTHUR MURRAY, CARBOHYDRATE CHEMISTRY, POLYMER CHEMISTRY. *Current Pos:* tech mgr water soluable polymers, 72-81, mgr Ventures & New Prod Develop, 81-83, MGR MKT OIL FIELD CHEM, CELANESE POLYMER SPECIALITIES CO, 83- *Personal Data:* b New York, NY, Mar 13, 22; m 50; c 3. *Educ:* City Col New York, BS, 43; Ohio State Univ, MS, 47. *Prof Exp:* Chemist natural gum, Stein, Hall & Co, 47-51, chief chemist paper, 51-53, lab mgr gums, paper & resins, 53-57, tech dir, 57-72. *Mem:* Am Chem Soc; Tech Asn Pulp & Paper Indust; Inst Food Technologists; Am Asn Textile Chemists & Colorists; Am Inst Mech Engrs. *Res:* Development of chemically modified guar gum polymers for industrial uses; synthetic water soluble polymers; application of polymers to the oil industry. *Mailing Add:* 9261 Vista Del Lago 19D Boca Raton FL 33428-3131

GOLDSTEIN, AUGUST, JR, PETROLEUM GEOLOGY. *Current Pos:* CONSULT, 85- *Personal Data:* b Shreveport, La, Dec 3, 20; m 45; c 3. *Educ:* La State Univ, BS, 40, MS, 42; Univ Colo, PhD(geol), 48. *Prof Exp:* Geologist, Remvo Superior Vermiculite Co, Colo, 45-46 & Winter-Weiss Co, 46-47; asst geol, Univ Colo, 47-48; res geologist, Stanolind Oil & Gas Co, 48-57; chief geologist, Bell Oil & Gas Co, 57-63, mgr explor, 63-65; gen mgr, Lubell Oil Co, 65-85. *Concurrent Pos:* Instr, Denver exten, Univ Colo, 48. *Mem:* Fel Geol Soc Am (treas, 73-76); Soc Econ Paleont & Mineral; hon mem Am Asn Petrol Geologists (vpres, 73-74). *Res:* Sedimentary petrography; petroleum geology; geology of Ouachita Mountains, Oklahoma and Arkansas. *Mailing Add:* 9 E Fourth St Tulsa OK 74103

GOLDSTEIN, AVRAM, NEUROSCIENCES. *Current Pos:* chmn dept, 55-70, prof, 55-89, EMER PROF PHARMACOL, STANFORD UNIV, 89- *Personal Data:* b New York, NY, July 3, 19; m 47, Dora Benedict; c 4. *Educ:* Harvard Univ, AB, 40, MD, 43. *Honors & Awards:* Franklin Medal, 80; Sollmann Award, Am Soc Pharmacol & Exp Therapeut, 81. *Prof Exp:* Intern, Mt Sinai Hosp, NY, 44; instr pharmacol, Harvard Univ, 47-49, assoc, 49-51, asst prof pharmacol & tutor biochem sci, 52-55. *Concurrent Pos:* Moseley traveling fel, Harvard Univ, 49-50; asst, Univ Bern, 51-52; founder & ed, Molecular Pharmacol, 65-68; dir, Addiction Res Found, 74-87. *Mem:* Nat Acad Sci; Inst Med-Nat Acad Sci; Am Soc Pharmacol & Exp Therapeut; Am Soc Biol Chem; Am Acad Arts & Sci. *Res:* Mechanism of drug action; opiate receptors and opioid peptides; narcotics; narcotic addiction; methadone treatment; national drug policy. *Mailing Add:* 735 Dolores Stanford CA 94305. *E-Mail:* avram.goldstein@stanford.edu

GOLDSTEIN, BERNARD, HUMAN SEXUALITY. *Current Pos:* From asst prof to assoc prof, 68-75, chmn, Dept Physiol & Behav Biol, 73-75, PROF BIOL, SAN FRANCISCO STATE UNIV, 75-, ACTG DIR RES & PROF DEVELOP, 89- *Personal Data:* b San Francisco, Calif, Oct 21, 35; m 61; c 1. *Educ:* San Francisco State Col, BA, 62, MA, 64; Univ Calif, Davis, PhD(functional morphol), 68. *Concurrent Pos:* NSF inst grant, 69, NIH summer grant, 69; chmn, Statewide Acad Senate, Calif State Univ, 84-87. *Mem:* AAAS; Am Soc Zool; Am Asn Sex Educr, Counr & Therapists; Soc Sci Study Sex; Sigma Xi. *Res:* Burrowing mechanisms of fossorial mammals; population dynamics; ecological physiology of vertebrates; biology of man; human sexuality; reproductive physiology. *Mailing Add:* 111 Park Ave San Carlos CA 94070-4734

GOLDSTEIN, BERNARD DAVID, ENVIRONMENTAL MEDICINE, HEMATOLOGY. *Current Pos:* PROF & CHMN ENVIRON MED & PROF MED, UNIV MED & DENT NJ, 80-, DIR, ENVIRON & OCCUP HEALTH SCI INST, ROBERT WOOD JOHNSON MED SCH, 85- *Personal Data:* b Bronx, NY, Feb 28, 39; m 63; c 2. *Educ:* Univ Wis-Madison, BS, 58; NY Univ, MD, 62. *Honors & Awards:* Kehoe Award, Am Col Occup & Environ Med; Ambassador Award, Mid-Atlantic Assoc Toxicol. *Prof Exp:* Intern & resident, Bellevue Hosp, NY, 62-65; teaching asst, Sch Med, NY Univ, 63-66; instr med, Univ Southern Calif, 66-68; from instr to assoc prof, Sch Med, NY Univ, 68-80. *Concurrent Pos:* NIH fel, Med Ctr, NY Univ, 65-66; attend physician, Bellevue & NY Univ Hosps, NY, 68-; chmn, Health Res Coun, Environ Pollution Working Group, New York, NY, 73-75; res collabr, Med Dept, Brookhaven Nat Lab, 73-83; consult, Nat Acad Sci, 74-76, comt mem, 76-80; NIH Fogarty Sr Int fel biochem, Brunel Univ, Eng, 77-78; asst adminr res & develop, US Environ Protection Agency, 83-85; chmn, NAS/NAC Comt Biomarkers Environ Health Res, 86-, NAS/IOM Comt Role Primary Care Practr Environ & Occup Med, 86-89; mem, MH Nat Adv Environ Health Sci Coun, 88-, NAS/NAC bd, Environ Sci & Toxicol; mem, Comn Health & Environ, WHO, chmn, Panel Industrialization; chmn, Panel Risk Assessment Methodology, NAS. *Mem:* Inst Med-Nat Acad Sci; Am Fedn Clin Res; Am Soc Hemat; Soc Toxicol; Am Pub Health Asn; Am Soc Clin Invest. *Res:* Effects of free radicals, peroxides and active states of oxygen on cellular membranes; biochemical toxicity of environmental agents; inhalation toxicology of air pollutants; mechanisms of benzene toxicity. *Mailing Add:* Univ Med & Dent NJ Environ & Occup Health Sci Inst Piscataway NJ 08855-1179. *Fax:* 732-932-0131

GOLDSTEIN, BURTON JACK, PSYCHIATRY, PSYCHOPHARMACOLOGY. *Current Pos:* Instr psychiat, Sch Med, Univ Miami, 64-68, from asst prof to assoc prof, 68-73, assoc prof pharmacol, 71-74, dir, Div Addiction Sci, 75-80, actg chmn, Dept Psychiat, 83-86, PROF PSYCHIAT, SCH MED, UNIV MIAMI, 73-, PROF PHARMACOL, FAC HEALTH SERV RES CTR, 74- *Personal Data:* b Baltimore, Md, Sept 23, 30; m 88, Linda; c Howard, Herb, Brian, Esther, Len & Mark. *Educ:* Univ Md, BS, 53, MD, 60. *Concurrent Pos:* NIMH training fel psychiat, Univ Miami-Jackson Mem Hosp, 61-64; consult psychiat res, Fla State Hosp, 66-, Indust Security Prog, Dept Defense, 67- & Vet Admin Psychiat Serv, Fla, 70-; vchmn, Dept Psychiat, Univ Miami Sch Med, 71-83; examr, Am Bd Psychiat Neurol, 72- *Mem:* Fel Am Col Psychiat; fel Int Col Psychopharmacol; AMA; fel Am Psychiat Asn; Am Col Neuropsychopharmacol; Am Soc Clin Pharmacol; Am Acad Addiction Med. *Res:* Clinical psychopharmacology, especially epidemiology, usage-nature, extent and character of psychotropic drug prescribing; clinical measurement of anxiety and depression and response to pharmacotherapy; development of antidepressant drugs; treatment strategies (inhibitors) Dementia Alzheimer's type. *Mailing Add:* Univ Miami Sch Med 1400 NW Tenth Ave (D93) Suite 1103 Miami FL 33136. *Fax:* 305-243-3353; *E-Mail:* bgoldste@mednet.med.miami.edu

GOLDSTEIN, BYRON BERNARD, BIOPHYSICS. *Current Pos:* STAFF MEM, THEORET BIOL & BIOPHYSICS GROUP, LOS ALAMOS NAT LAB, 77- *Personal Data:* b New York, NY, Nov 24, 39. *Educ:* City Col New York, BS, 61; NY Univ, PhD(plasma physics), 67. *Prof Exp:* Instr physics, NY Univ, 67 & 68; lectr, Queens Col, NY, 68; from assoc prof to prof physics, Farleigh Dickinson Univ, 68-77. *Concurrent Pos:* NIH fel chem, Univ Calif, San Diego, 69-70; vis staff mem, Los Alamos Sci Lab, 75-77. *Mem:* AAAS; Biophys Soc; Am Phys Soc; Am Asn Immunologists. *Res:* Ligand receptor interactions; biophysics of the immune response. *Mailing Add:* Dept Theory Biol & Biophysics Los Alamos Nat Lab PO MS K-710 Los Alamos NM 87545-0001. *Fax:* 505-665-3493

GOLDSTEIN, CHARLES IRWIN, APPLIED MATHEMATICS. *Current Pos:* SR RES SCIENTIST MATH, BROOKHAVEN NAT LAB, 67- *Personal Data:* b New York, NY, Nov 21, 40; m 75, Joyce Kluback; c Andrew & Roger. *Educ:* City Col New York, BS, 62; NY Univ, MS, 64, PhD(math), 67. *Concurrent Pos:* Vis res mathematician, Math Res Ctr, Univ Wis, 72, Inst Comput Appl Sci & Eng, NASA Langley Res Ctr, Hampton, Va, 78, Math Dept, Univ Calif, Berkeley, 79, Naval Res Lab, Washington, DC, 83. *Mem:* Am Math Soc; Soc Indust Appl Math; Sigma Xi. *Res:* Scattering and perturbation theory; microwave physics; the numerical solution of differential equations and mathematical analysis of the finite element method; acoustics and electromagnetic wave propagation; numerical linear algebra; singularly perturbed problems. *Mailing Add:* Brookhaven Nat Lab Bldg 490D DAS PO Box 5000 Upton NY 11973-5000. *Fax:* 516-282-5047; *E-Mail:* goldstei@bnl.gov

GOLDSTEIN, CHARLES M, INFORMATION SCIENCE, COMPUTER TECHNOLOGY. *Current Pos:* RETIRED. *Personal Data:* b Chicago, Ill, Sept 27, 29; m 61; c 3. *Educ:* Purdue Univ, BS, 53, MS, 54. *Honors & Awards:* Brad Rogers Award, Med Libr Asn, 88. *Prof Exp:* Plasma electron physics numerical math, NASA, 55-68; br chief off of computerized info systs info sci

& technol, 68-73; dir data mgt tech info technol, Informatics, 73-74; chief, Info Technol Br, Technol Res & Develop, Info Sci, Lister Hill Nat Ctr Biomed Commun, Nat Libr Med, 74-96. *Concurrent Pos:* Fulbright award, Ger, 54; chief sci comput numerical anal, NASA, 72-73; bd dir, Health Educ Network Inc, 76-78; subcomt technol, Nat Fedn Abstracting & Indexing Socs, 78- *Mem:* Am Soc Info Sci; AAAS; Med Libr Asn. *Res:* Information technology. *Mailing Add:* 3101 NE 145th St Apt 210 Seattle WA 98155

GOLDSTEIN, DAVID, CHEMICAL ENGINEERING, INORGANIC CHEMISTRY. *Current Pos:* RETIRED. *Personal Data:* b New York, NY, Apr 20, 29; m 53; c 4. *Educ:* City Col NY, BChEng, 51; Iowa State Col, MS, 53. *Prof Exp:* Design engr filters, Micro-Metallic Corp, 51-52; res asst thermal res, Eng Exp Sta, Iowa State Col, 52-53; res proj supvr extractive metall, Chem Construct Corp, 53-56; process design engr, Nichols Eng & Res Corp, 56; assoc res chem engr stainless & alloy steels, Crucible Steel Co Am, 56-61; mgr eng develop indust chem, FMC Corp, 61-83, process eng consult, 83-86. *Mem:* Am Inst Chem Engrs. *Res:* Extractive metallurgy; industrial chemicals including soda ash and phosphates; fertilizers; process development; detergents; waste disposal; solvent extraction; alloy steel surface conditioning; corrosion; refractories; magnesia; calcination and heat transfer. *Mailing Add:* 13 Perry Rd East Brunswick NJ 08816

GOLDSTEIN, DAVID BAIRD, SCIENCE POLICY, ENERGY POLICY DEVELOPMENT & IMPLEMENTATION. *Current Pos:* ENERGY PROG DIR, NATURAL RESOURCES DEFENSE COUN, 80. *Personal Data:* m 80, Julia Beth Vetromile; c Elianna L & Abraham M. *Educ:* Univ Calif, Berkeley, BA, 73, PhD(physics), 78. *Prof Exp:* Res asst, Lawrence Berkeley Nat Lab, 75-78, staff scientist, 78-80. *Concurrent Pos:* Bd mem, Calif Home Energy Efficiency Rating Syst, 94-; comt mem, Building Cross Assistance Proj, 94-; bd chair, Inst Market Transformation, 96. *Mem:* Fel Am Phys Soc; Sigma Xi. *Res:* Develop, analyze and implement energy policy initiatives to promote new technologies and methods for increasing energy efficiency and renewable energy. *Mailing Add:* Natural Resources Defense Coun 71 Stevenson St No 1825 San Francisco CA 94105. *Fax:* 415-495-5996; *E-Mail:* dgoldstein@nrdc.org

GOLDSTEIN, DAVID JOEL, MEDICAL GENETICS, CLINICAL PHARMACOLOGY. *Current Pos:* assoc clin res physician, 87-90, clin res physician, 90-95, SR CLIN RES PHYSICIAN, ELI LILLY & CO, 95- *Personal Data:* b New York, NY, June 25, 47; m 92, Lisa J Heid; c Benjamin, Philip & Rachel. *Educ:* Franklin & Marshall Col, BA, 69; Univ Tenn, MD, 73, PhD(biochem), 75. *Honors & Awards:* Quigley Award in Physiol. *Prof Exp:* Residency pediat, Mayo Grad Sch Med, 75-78; fel, Univ Pa, 78-81; asst prof med genetics, Ind Univ, 81-87. *Concurrent Pos:* NIH fel; adj assoc prof pharmacol & toxicol, Ind Univ, 89-; mem, Dept Pediat, Methodist Hosp Ind, 90- *Mem:* Am Soc Human Genetics; NAm Asn Study Obesity; Am Soc Clin Pharmacol Ther; Sigma Xi. *Res:* Clinical pharmacology; medical genetics; analgesia; obesity; eating disorders. *Mailing Add:* Lilly Res Labs Corp Ctr Indianapolis IN 46285-0532. *Fax:* 317-277-2123; *E-Mail:* djgoldstein@lilly.com

GOLDSTEIN, DAVID LOUIS, COMPARATIVE OSMOREGULATORY PHYSIOLOGY, HUMAN ANATOMY & PHYSIOLOGY. *Current Pos:* asst prof, 86-92, ASSOC PROF, DEPT BIOL SCI, WRIGHT STATE UNIV, 92- *Personal Data:* b Providence, RI, Aug 22, 57; m 83, Sarah P; c 3. *Educ:* Univ Pa, BA, 79; Univ Calif, Los Angeles, PhD(biol), 83. *Prof Exp:* Postdoctoral, Dept Physiol, Univ Ariz, 83-86. *Mem:* Am Soc Zool; Am Ornithologists Union; AAAS. *Res:* Research focuses on adaptive and ecological physiology: physiological systems vary in animals from different habitats and how they respond to environmental change; osmoregulation particularly in birds. *Mailing Add:* Dept Biol Sci Wright State Univ Dayton OH 45435. *E-Mail:* dgoldstein@desire.wright.edu

GOLDSTEIN, DAVID STANLEY, HYPERTENSION, DYSAUTONOMIAS. *Current Pos:* clin assoc, Nat Heart, Lung & Blood Inst, NIH, 78-82, med staff fel, 82-83, sr investr, 83-90, SR INVESTR, NAT INST NEUROL DIS & STROKE, NIH, 90-, CHIEF, CLIN NEUROCHEM SECT, CLIN NEUROSCI BR. *Personal Data:* b Newark, NJ, June 23, 48; m 72, Mirka Krasow; c Yakira, Samuel, Zvi, Mona & Joseph. *Educ:* Yale Col, BA, 70; Johns Hopkins Sch Med, MD, PhD(behav sci), 76. *Prof Exp:* Med resident internal med, Univ Wash Affil Hosp, Seattle, 76-78. *Concurrent Pos:* Pvt consultative pract; fel, Coun Circu & Coun High Blood Pressure Res, Am Heart Asn. *Mem:* Fel Am Col Physicians; Am Soc Clin Invest; Am Heart Asn; Am Physiol Soc. *Res:* Sympathetic nervous system activity in cardiovascular diseases; metabolism of catecholamines; pathophysiology of hypertension; neuroendocrinology of stress. *Mailing Add:* 7711 Fontaine St Potomac MD 20854. *Fax:* 301-480-0736; *E-Mail:* davep@box-d.nih.gov

GOLDSTEIN, DORA BENEDICT, PHARMACOLOGY. *Current Pos:* res assoc, Stanford Univ, 55-70, sr scientist, 70-74, adj prof, 74-78, PROF PHARMACOL, SCH MED, STANFORD UNIV, 78-, EMER PROF MOLECULAR PHARMACOL, 92- *Personal Data:* b Milton, Mass, Apr 25, 22; m 47, Avram; c Margaret (Wallace), Daniel, Joshua & Michael. *Educ:* Harvard Med Sch, MD, 49. *Honors & Awards:* Award Sci Excellence, Res Soc Alcoholism, 81; Jellinek Mem Award, Jellinek Mem Fund, 96. *Prof Exp:* Fel bact, Harvard Med Sch, 53-55. *Concurrent Pos:* Co-dir, Fac Mentoring Prog, Stanford Univ. *Mem:* Am Soc Biol Chem; Am Soc Pharmacol & Exp Therapeut; Soc Neurosci; Res Soc Alcoholism (pres, 79-81). *Res:* Induction of cholinesterase synthesis in bacteria; biochemical effects of barbiturates; alcohol; drug dependence; anticonvulsants; effects of drugs on biomembranes. *Mailing Add:* 735 Dolores St Stanford CA 94305

GOLDSTEIN, E BRUCE, PSYCHOPHYSICS. *Current Pos:* asst prof psychol & pharmacol, 69-75, ASSOC PROF PSYCHOL, UNIV PITTSBURGH, 75- *Personal Data:* b Washington, DC, Mar 31, 41; div; c 2. *Educ:* Tufts Univ, BS, 63; Brown Univ, ScM, 65, PhD(psychol), 68. *Prof Exp:* Res asst psychol, Brown Univ, 63-65; USPHS res fel, Harvard Univ, 67-69. *Mem:* Psychonomic Soc; Asn Res Vision & Ophthal. *Res:* Perception of depth in pictures; visual perception; mechanisms of form perception; sensation and perception; introductory psychology; psychology of gender. *Mailing Add:* Dept Psychol Univ Pittsburgh 455 Langley Hall Pittsburgh PA 15260-0001

GOLDSTEIN, EDWARD, TELECOMMUNICATIONS, SYSTEMS ENGINEERING. *Current Pos:* VPRES, MAC GROUP, 85- *Personal Data:* b Stanislawow, Poland, Jan 28, 23. *Educ:* Univ Minn, BS, 49. *Prof Exp:* Dir, Mil Commun Systs & Eng, Bell LabS, 49-66; eng engr, AT&T, 60-70, vpres mkt, NY Tel Co, 70-72, mem staff, 72-83, corp vpres strategy develop, 83-85. *Mem:* Fel Inst Elec & Electronics Engrs. *Mailing Add:* 167 Marborough St Boston MA 02116

GOLDSTEIN, ELISHEVA, MOLECULAR ORBITAL CALCULATIONS, SPECTROSCOPY. *Current Pos:* ASSOC PROF, CALIF POLYTECH UNIV, 81- *Personal Data:* b Bucharest, Rumania, July 12, 47; US citizen; m 68, Damon; c Elon & Danielle. *Educ:* City Col, City Univ New York, BS, 71; Calif Polytech Univ, MS, 76; Univ Southern Calif, PhD(chem), 79. *Prof Exp:* Lectr chem, Calif Polytech Univ, 79-80; asst prof, Claremont Col, 80-81. *Concurrent Pos:* Consult, Chevron Petrol, La Habra. *Mem:* Sigma Xi; Am Chem Soc. *Res:* Molecular orbital calculations, involving fluoro and chloro carbenes and their reactions with substituted olefins; molecular orbital calculations of elctron scattering of small molecules; ab initio calculations on the Diels-Alder reaction of a-pyrone and acetylene; 2 plus 4 and 6 plus 4 cycloaddition calculations using DFT. *Mailing Add:* 19844 E Navilla Pl Covina CA 91724. *E-Mail:* egoldstein@csupomona.edu

GOLDSTEIN, ELLIOT, infectious diseases, for more information see previous edition

GOLDSTEIN, ELLIOTT STUART, DEVELOPMENTAL GENETICS, MOLECULAR BIOLOGY. *Current Pos:* asst prof, 74-78, ASSOC PROF ZOOL, ARIZ STATE UNIV, 78- *Personal Data:* b Brooklyn, NY, July 7, 42; m 63, Suzanne Kussner; c Andrew R & Hyla L. *Educ:* Univ Hartford, BS, 67; Univ Minn, MS, 70, PhD(genetics), 72. *Prof Exp:* Fel molecular biol, Mass Inst Technol, 72-74. *Concurrent Pos:* NIH grant, 76-81; vis assoc prof, Calif Inst Technol, 81; vis scholar, Ind Univ, 88. *Mem:* Sigma Xi; AAAS; Genetics Soc Am; Soc Develop Biol. *Res:* Use of cloned regulated genes to understand the mechanism by which genes control early embryogenesis and by which the genes themselves are regulated; mechanism by which the cancer oncogeneium transforms a normal cell into a tumor cell. *Mailing Add:* Dept Zool Ariz State Univ Tempe AZ 85287-1501. *Fax:* 602-965-2519; *E-Mail:* atesg@asuvm.inre.asu.edu

GOLDSTEIN, FRANZ, GASTROENTEROLOGY, INTERNAL MEDICINE. *Current Pos:* from instr to assoc prof, 57-70, PROF MED, JEFFERSON MED COL, 70- *Personal Data:* b Ger, Feb 23, 22; US citizen; m 49, Beatrice Moore; c Richard E, Jean (Patteson) & Nancy (Shaw). *Educ:* Jefferson Med Col, MD, 53. *Honors & Awards:* Rorer Award, Am Col Gastroenterol, 74 & 81, Weiss Award, 92. *Prof Exp:* From intern to chief med resident & resident gastroenterol, Grad Hosp, Univ Pa, 53-57. *Concurrent Pos:* Am Trudeau Soc fel, Grad Hosp, Univ Pa, 55-56; chief gastroenterol, Lankenau Hosp, 70-87; mem bd trustees & sci adv bd, Nat Found Ileitis & Colitis, 74- *Mem:* Am Gastroenterol Asn; fel Am Col Physicians; master Am Col Gastroenterol (pres, 81-82); Bockus Int Soc Gastroenterol; AMA (pres, 85-87). *Res:* Bacterial flora of gastrointestinal tract in relation to malabsorption; gall bladder kinetics; inflammatory bowel disease. *Mailing Add:* 707 Arlington Rd Narberth PA 19072. *Fax:* 610-896-5207

GOLDSTEIN, FRED BERNARD, biochemistry, for more information see previous edition

GOLDSTEIN, FREDERICK J, NEUROPHARMACOLOGY. *Current Pos:* Asst, Philadelphia Col Pharmacol & Sci, 64-67, from instr to asst prof, 65-72, chmn, Continuing Educ for Pharmacists, 69-76, assoc prof, 72-80, PROF PHARMACOL, PHILADELPHIA COL PHARMACOL & SCI, 80; ASSOC STAFF MEM, DEPT MED, FOX CHASE CANCER CTR, 84- *Personal Data:* b Philadelphia, Pa, Jan 12, 42; c 2. *Educ:* Philadelphia Col Pharm & Sci, BSc, 63, MSc, 65, PhD(pharmacol), 68. *Concurrent Pos:* Reviewer, J Pharm Sci, 71-; lectr, continuing educ, Pa Col Optometry, 72-78; consult, drug abuse legis, Pa State Senate Comt Pub Health & Welfare, 73-76; chmn prog comt, Pharmacol & Toxicol Sect, Acad Pharmaceut Sci, 75; lectr pharmacol, Univ Pa Sch Dent Med, 75-; consult, Franklin Inst Res Labs, 77-79; clin pharmacologist, Walter Reed Army Med Ctr, 83; vis assoc prof pharmacol, Med Col Pa, 84-; chmn prog comt, Pharmacol & Toxicol Sect, Acad Pharmaceut Sci, 75; lectr pharmacol, Univ Pa Sch Dent Med, 75-77; consult, Franklin Inst Res Labs, 77- *Mem:* AAAS; Am Soc Pharmacol & Exp Therapeut; fel Am Col Clin Pharmacol. *Res:* Effects of acute and chronic tricyclic antidepressants on opioid analgesia; mechanisms of narcotic analgesia. *Mailing Add:* Dept Pharmacol & Physiol Philadelphia Col Osteopath Med Philadelphia PA 19131-1694. *Fax:* 215-871-2887

GOLDSTEIN, GERALD, ANALYTICAL CHEMISTRY. *Current Pos:* PHYS SCIENTIST, OFF HEALTH & ENVIRON RES, DEPT ENERGY, 76- *Personal Data:* b New York, NY, Apr 23, 30; m 51, Patricia Sable; c Constance, Leslie, Jonathan & Elizabeth. *Educ:* Brooklyn Col, BA, 51; Univ Tenn, MS, 59, PhD(chem), 65. *Prof Exp:* Anal chemist, Ledoux & Co, 52-53 & Lucius Pitkin, Inc, 53-56; chemist, Oak Ridge Nat Lab, 56-66, group leader anal chem div, 66-72, res staff mem, 72-76. *Mem:* AAAS; Am Chem Soc; Sigma Xi; fel Am Inst Chemists. *Res:* Analytical and environmental chemistry; instrumentation. *Mailing Add:* ER-73 GTN Dept Energy Washington DC 20585. *Fax:* 301-903-7363

GOLDSTEIN, GERALD, MICROBIOLOGY, MEDICINE. *Current Pos:* instr microbiol, Univ Va, 57-59, asst prof microbiol & instr med, 59-63, asst prof med, 63-69, assoc prof microbiol, 63-73, assoc prof internal med, 69-80, PROF MICROBIOL, SCH MED, UNIV VA, 73-, PROF INTERNAL MED, 80- *Personal Data:* b New York, NY, Oct 20, 22; m 53; c 3. *Educ:* Moravian Col, BS, 48; Univ Pa, MD, 52. *Prof Exp:* Intern, Univ Va Hosp, 52-53; resident internal med, Vet Admin Hosp, Dallas, Tex, 53-54 & Martinsburg, WVa, 54-56. *Concurrent Pos:* Damon Runyon cancer res fel, Univ Va, 56-58, USPHS sr res fel, 59- *Res:* Immunology with respect to infectious diseases and tumors. *Mailing Add:* 2709 Magnolia Dr Charlottesville VA 22901

GOLDSTEIN, GIDEON, IMMUNOLOGY, INTERNAL MEDICINE. *Current Pos:* DIR IMMUNOSCI, ORTHO PHARMACEUT CORP, 77- *Personal Data:* b Kaunas, Lithuania, Jan 21, 37; m 65; c 2. *Educ:* Univ Melbourne, MB, BS, 59, MD, 63, PhD(immunopath), 67. *Prof Exp:* Resident med & path, Royal Melbourne Hosp, 61-64; pathologist, Walter & Eliza Hall Inst, 64-66; vis scientist, Lab Immunol, Nat Inst Allergy & Infectious Dis, 67-68; res assoc prof path, Sch Med & Postgrad Med Sch, NY Univ, 68-74; mem, Sloan-Kettering Cancer Res Inst, 74-77. *Concurrent Pos:* Mem med adv bd, Myasthenia Gravis Found, 71. *Mem:* Am Asn Immunologists; Am Soc Exp Path. *Res:* Thymic hormones; immunoregulatory therapy; immunodiagnosis. *Mailing Add:* 30 Dorison Dr Short Hills NJ 07078-1701. *Fax:* 973-467-3891

GOLDSTEIN, HAROLD WILLIAM, AIR POLLUTION. *Current Pos:* RETIRED. *Personal Data:* b Jersey City, NJ, Aug 23, 31; m 59; c 2. *Educ:* Univ Ala, BS, 53, MS, 55; Ohio State Univ, PhD(phys chem), 60. *Prof Exp:* Staff mem, Union Carbide Corp Res Inst, 60-63; sr res scientist, Martin Co, Martin-Marietta Corp, Fla, 63-65; mgr space exp & appln, Space Sci Lab, Gen Elec Co, 65-91. *Mem:* Am Chem Soc; Am Inst Aeronaut & Astronaut. *Res:* High temperature thermodynamics; mass spectrometry; ablation kinetics; material properties; space experiments; spacecraft contamination; design and development of instrumentation for the measurement of trace atmospheric species. *Mailing Add:* 9751 Mainsail Ct Ft Myers FL 33919

GOLDSTEIN, HARRIS SIDNEY, CHILD PSYCHIATRY, PSYCHOSOMATIC DISEASES. *Current Pos:* ASSOC PROF PSYCHIAT, ROBERT WOOD JOHNSON MED SCH, 75- *Personal Data:* b Chicago, Ill, Mar 6, 34; m 61, Brigitte Wolbert; c Marcel, Michael, Nicole & Sharon. *Educ:* Univ Ill, Urbana, BS, 55; Univ Ill, Chicago, MD, 59; Johns Hopkins Univ, MLA, 66; State Univ NY, DMSc, 71. *Prof Exp:* From asst prof to assoc prof psychiat, Downstate Med Ctr, State Univ NY, 68-75. *Mem:* Am Psychiat Asn; Am Psychosomatic Soc; Soc Res Child Develop; Am Acad Child & Adolescent Psychiat; Am Asn Dir Psychiat Residency Training. *Res:* Epidemiological research in child psychopathology; psychophysiological studies of cardiovascular disorders. *Mailing Add:* Robert Wood Johnson Med Sch Univ Med & Dent NJ 675 Hoes Lane Piscataway NJ 08854

GOLDSTEIN, HERBERT, PHYSICS. *Current Pos:* PROF NUCLEAR SCI & ENG, COLUMBIA UNIV, 61- *Personal Data:* b New York, NY, June 26, 22. *Educ:* City Col New York, BS, 40; Mass Inst Technol, PhD(physics), 43. *Prof Exp:* Tutor physics, City Col New York, 40-41; mem staff, Radiation Lab, Mass Inst Technol, 42-46, fel, AEC, 49-50; instr physics, Harvard Univ, 46-49; sr physicist, Nuclear Develop Corp Am, 50-61. *Concurrent Pos:* Vis assoc prof, Brandeis Univ, 52-53. *Mem:* Am Phys Soc; Sigma Xi. *Res:* Electromagnetic theory; radio wave propagation; theory of nuclear forces; neutron cross sections; radiation shielding; nuclear reactors. *Mailing Add:* 144-19 68th Rd Flushing NY 11367

GOLDSTEIN, HERBERT JAY, ORGANIC CHEMISTRY, POLYMER CHEMISTRY. *Current Pos:* RETIRED. *Personal Data:* b New York, NY, Sept 20, 23; m 47; c 4. *Educ:* NY Univ, AB, 46, PhD(chem), 52. *Prof Exp:* Res chemist org, E I du Pont de Nemours Co, Jackson Lab, 52-56; sr res chemist polymer, Synpol Inc, 56-57, sr res scientist, 58-64, mgr org res, 64-69, mgr polymerization res, 69-72, mgr polymer develop, 72-78, mgr res & develop, Tex Res Ctr, 78-82, mem indust res lab, 82-87. *Mem:* Am Chem Soc; Sigma Xi. *Res:* Synthetic elastomers; polymers; polymerization chemistry; olefin chemistry; butadiene chemistry. *Mailing Add:* 17 Dowlen Pl Beaumont TX 77706

GOLDSTEIN, HERMAN BERNARD, TEXTILE CHEMISTRY, PAPER CHEMISTRY. *Current Pos:* RETIRED. *Personal Data:* b Providence, RI, June 19, 17; m 42, Myrtle B Abedon; c Lawrence B & Caila B. *Educ:* Brown Univ, AB, 40. *Honors & Awards:* Olney Award, Am Asn Textile Chemists & Colorists, 73 & Millson Award, 85. *Prof Exp:* Dir res, Providence Textile Chem Co, 40-44; tech mgr, Warwick Chem Div, Sun Chem Corp, 45-52, mgr prod & res, Textile Chem Dept, 53-63, res mgr, Chem Prod Div, 63-67, gen mgr, Chem Div, 68-72, vpres, Chem Div, 72-84; pres, HBG Export Corp, 85-90. *Concurrent Pos:* Adv, USDA, 65-68. *Mem:* Am Asn Textile Chemists & Colorists; Tech Asn Pulp & Paper Industs; Am Chem Soc; Am Soc Testing & Mat; Am Inst Chemists; Sigma Xi. *Res:* Chemical specialties, auxiliaries, and processing aids for related industries including water and oil repellants, soil release agents, permanent press resins, softeners, dyehouse chemicals, paper sizes and coating insolubilizers for United States, Europe and Far East. *Mailing Add:* 138 Park Dr Chester SC 29706. *Fax:* 803-385-2112

GOLDSTEIN, INGE F, EPIDEMIOLOGY, BIOPHYSICS. *Current Pos:* res assoc, 68-78, sr res assoc epidemiol & assoc prof clin pub health, 78-94, SR LECTR EPIDEMIOL, SCH PUB HEALTH, COLUMBIA UNIV, 94- *Personal Data:* b Plauen, Ger, Nov 25, 30; US citizen; m 54, Martin; c Eric, Michael & Aviva. *Educ:* Wellesley Col, BA, 51; Univ Pittsburgh, MA, 56; Columbia Univ, MS, 68, DrPH, 91. *Prof Exp:* Res asst biophys, Univ Mich, 61-64. *Mem:* Soc Environ Geochem & Health; fel Am Col Epidemiol; Soc Epidemiol Res; Sigma Xi; Air Pollution Control Asn. *Res:* Acute and chronic health effects of environmental pollutants; methodological approaches in assessing the physical environment in its effects on human health; asthma; co-author of three books on science for the non-scientist. *Mailing Add:* Columbia Univ Sch Pub Health Div Epidemiol 600 W 168th St New York NY 10032. *Fax:* 212-305-9413

GOLDSTEIN, IRVING SOLOMON, WOOD CHEMISTRY, PAPER CHEMISTRY. *Current Pos:* head dept, 71-78, prof, 71-92, EMER PROF WOOD & PAPER SCI, NC STATE UNIV, 92- *Personal Data:* b Bronx, NY, Aug 20, 21; m 45, Helen Haft; c Ardath, Darra & Jared. *Educ:* Rensselaer Polytech Inst, BS, 41; Ill Inst Technol, MS, 44; Harvard Univ, PhD(org chem), 48. *Honors & Awards:* Alvin Huss Award, Am Paper Inst, 91. *Prof Exp:* Asst chem, Ill Inst Technol, 41-42; teaching fel, Harvard, 46-48; res chemist, NAm Rayon Corp, 48-51; sr chemist, Res Dept, Koppers Co, Inc, 51-53; leader, Wood Preserving Group, 53-55, mgr wood chem, 55-63; sr res chemist, Nalco Chem Co, 63-66; mgr paper res, Corp Res & Develop Dept, Continental Can, 66-68; prof forest sci, Tex A&M Univ, 68-71. *Mem:* AAAS; Am Chem Soc; Forest Prod Soc; Soc Wood Sci & Technol; Tech Asn Pulp & Paper Indust; fel Int Acad Wood Sci. *Res:* Wood, cellulose and lignin chemistry; pulp chemistry; chemical utilization of wood. *Mailing Add:* Dept Wood & Paper Sci Col Forest Res NC State Univ Raleigh NC 27695-8005. *E-Mail:* goldstein@cfr.cfr.ncsu.edu

GOLDSTEIN, IRWIN JOSEPH, BIOCHEMISTRY. *Current Pos:* assoc prof, 65-72, PROF BIOL CHEM, UNIV MICH, ANN ARBOR, 72- *Personal Data:* b Newark, NJ, Sept 8, 29; c 2. *Educ:* Syracuse Univ, BA, 51; Univ Minn, PhD(biochem), 56. *Honors & Awards:* Kaiser Permanente Pre-Clin Teaching Award, 80; Claude S Hudson Carbohydrate Chem Award, Am Chem Soc, 93. *Prof Exp:* Res fel dept agr biochem, Univ Minn, St Paul, 56-59; asst prof biochem, State Univ NY, Buffalo, 61-65. *Concurrent Pos:* Guggenheim fel, 59-60, NIH fel, 60-61; res bd, United Fund, 63-65; consult, Ann Arbor Community, 68-71, Proctor & Gamble, 68-; assoc dean, Res & Grad Studies, Univ Mich, 86-; bd dirs, Guild House, Univ Mich, 75-80; mem res comt, Henry Ford Hosp, 83- *Mem:* Am Heart Asn; Biochem Soc; Chem Soc; Am Soc Biol Chemists; Am Chem Soc; Soc Complex Carbohydrates; Sigma Xi. *Res:* Carboydrate-protein interactions; isolation, purification and characterization of lectins (carbohydrate-binding proteins); use of lectins to study cell-surface phenomena; studies on the structure and biosynthesis of glycoproteins; immunochemistry of carbohydrates. *Mailing Add:* Dept Biol Chem Univ Mich Med Sch 7321 Med Sci Bldg I Ann Arbor MI 48109-0624. *Fax:* 313-763-4936

GOLDSTEIN, JACK, BIOCHEMISTRY. *Current Pos:* ADJ ASSOC PROF BIOCHEM, MED COL, CORNELL UNIV, 65-; MEM, NY BLOOD CTR, 66- *Personal Data:* b Philadelphia, Pa, June 24, 30; m 67; c 3. *Educ:* Brooklyn Col Pharm, BS, 52; Cornell Univ, MNS, 57, PhD(biochem), 59. *Prof Exp:* Asst biochem, Cornell Univ, 55-57; res chemist, US Plant, Soil & Nutrit Lab, 57-59; vis investr biochem, Rockefeller Inst, 59-61, res assoc, 61-64, asst prof, 64-65. *Mem:* Am Soc Biol Chem; Am Chem Soc; Am Soc Cell Biol. *Res:* Ribonucleic acids; protein structure and biosynthesis; Cell surface antigens; structure and function. *Mailing Add:* Dept Cell Biochem 310 E 67th St New York NY 10021-6295

GOLDSTEIN, JACK STANLEY, PHYSICS. *Current Pos:* vis asst prof physics, Brandeis Univ, 56-57, from asst prof to assoc prof, 57-66, chmn, Dept Physics, 67-69, dir, Astrophys Inst, 63-73, sci dir, African Primary Sci Prog, 65-72, dean, Grad Sch, 72-74, dean fac, 74-81, prof, 66-, EMER PROF PHYSICS, BRANDEIS UNIV. *Personal Data:* b New York, NY, May 10, 25; m 48; c 3. *Educ:* City Col New York, BS, 47; Univ Okla, MS, 48; Cornell Univ, PhD(physics), 53. *Prof Exp:* Res physicist, Cornell Aeronaut Lab, 48-50; asst, Cornell Univ, 50-52; mem, Inst Advan Study, 53; res assoc, Mass Inst Technol, 53-54; sr physicist, Baird-Atomic, Inc, Mass, 54-57. *Concurrent Pos:* Fulbright scholar, Israel, 60-61; Fulbright scholar & Guggenheim fel, Univ Rome, 66-67; consult, Div Sci Educ, UNESCO, 67-74; vis scholar, Kyoto Univ, 82. *Mem:* Am Phys Soc; Am Astron Soc; NY Acad Sci. *Res:* Quantum mechanics; field theory; astrophysics; energy; history of science; science policy. *Mailing Add:* Physics Dept Brandeis Univ PO Box 9110 Waltham MA 02154-2700

GOLDSTEIN, JACOB HERMAN, PHYSICAL CHEMISTRY. *Current Pos:* RETIRED. *Personal Data:* b Atlanta, Ga, Dec 18, 15; m 53. *Educ:* Emory Univ, AB, 43, MS, 45; Harvard Univ, MS, 47, PhD(chem), 49. *Honors & Awards:* Charles Herty Medal, Am Chem Soc, 81, Charles H Stone Award, 84. *Prof Exp:* From asst prof to prof, Emory Univ, 49-60, Candler prof chem, 60-85. *Mem:* Am Chem Soc; Am Phys Soc. *Res:* Nuclear magnetic resonance spectroscopy, including biological applications; liquid crystals; computer applications in chemistry. *Mailing Add:* 820 Oakdale Rd NE Atlanta GA 30307-1210

GOLDSTEIN, JEFFREY JAY, PLANETARY ATMOSPHERES, HETERODYNE SPECTROSCOPY. *Current Pos:* DIR, SPACE SCI RES, CHALLENGER CTR, DEPT SPACE SCI, 96- *Personal Data:* b New York, NY, Dec 3, 57; m 93, Kathleen M Benditt. *Educ:* City Univ NY, BA, 80; Univ Pa, MA, 87, PhD(astrophys), 89. *Honors & Awards:* Barry M Goldwater Educ Award, Am Inst Aeronaut & Astronaut, 95. *Prof Exp:* Instr astron & astrophys, Univ Pa, 81-85; grad student researcher, Lab Extraterrestrial Physics, NASA/Goddard Space Flight Ctr, 85-88; astrophysicist, Lab Astrophys, Nat Air & Space Mus, Smithsonian Inst, 88-96. *Concurrent Pos:* Adj lectr, Physics Dept, Queensborough Community Col, City Univ NY, 80, 81 & Queens Col, 82; lectr, Resident Associateship Prog, Smithsonian Inst, 89. *Mem:* Am Astron Soc; AAAS; Am Geophys Union; Nat Sci Teachers Asn. *Res:* Observations of planetary atmospheric circulation using infrared heterodyne and microwave spectroscopy; science education lecturer visiting elementary and secondary classrooms nationwide to foster interest in science through space sciences. *Mailing Add:* Dept Space Sci Res Challenger Ctr 1029 N Royal St Suite 300 Alexandria VA 22314. *Fax:* 703-683-7546; *E-Mail:* jgoldstein@challenger.org

GOLDSTEIN, JEFFREY MARC, PSYCHOPHARMACOLOGY, NEUROPHARMACOLOGY. *Current Pos:* PRIN PHARMACOLOGIST, DEPT PHARMACOL, ZENECA PHARMACEUT GROUP, 76- *Personal Data:* b Bronx, NY, May 9, 47; m 71, Robin; c Kevin & Neal. *Educ:* Colo State Univ, BS, 70; Seton Hall Univ, MS, 73; Univ Del, PhD(neurosci), 80. *Prof Exp:* Assoc scientist, Schering Corp, 70-76. *Mem:* AAAS; NY Acad Sci; Am Soc Pharmacol & Exp Therapeut; Soc Neurosci; Sigma Xi. *Res:* Psychiatric and neurologic drugs, discovery and development. *Mailing Add:* Dept Pharmacol Zeneca Pharmaceut Group 1800 Concord Pike Wilmington DE 19897-0001. *Fax:* 302-886-2766

GOLDSTEIN, JEROME ARTHUR, DIFFERENTIAL EQUATIONS, QUANTUM THEORY. *Current Pos:* PROF MATH, UNIV MEMPHIS, 96- *Personal Data:* b Pittsburgh, Pa, Aug 5, 41; m 92, Gisgle Ruiz; c Maurice Roland. *Educ:* Carnegie-Mellon Univ, BS, 63, MS, 64, PhD(math), 67. *Hon Degrees:* SMD, Loyola Univ, 73. *Prof Exp:* Mem math, Inst Advan Study, 67-68; from asst prof to prof math, Tulane Univ, 68-91; prof, La State Univ, 91-96. *Concurrent Pos:* Prin investr, NSF grants, 68-92; vis prof, Fed Univ Rio de Janiero & Univ Brasilia, 75, Univ Padova, 81, Univ London, 80 81, Univ Graz, 85, 88, 93 & Univ Tubingen, 89; ed, six journals, 82-97. *Mem:* Am Math Soc; Math Asn Am; Soc Indust & Appl Math; Asn Women Math. *Res:* Nonlinear partial differential equations; mathematical quantum theory; operator semi groups; functional analysis; stochastic processes. *Mailing Add:* Dept Math Univ Memphis Memphis TN 38152. *Fax:* 901-678-2480

GOLDSTEIN, JEROME CHARLES, OTOLARYNGOLOGY. *Current Pos:* instr otolaryngol, 71-74, PROF OTOLARYNGOL & HEAD DIV, ALBANY MED COL, 74- *Personal Data:* b Glens Falls, NY, Nov 4, 35; m 65; c 3. *Educ:* Univ Rochester, AB, 57; State Univ NY Upstate Med Ctr, MD, 63. *Prof Exp:* Intern, Philadelphia Gen Hosp, 63-64; resident surg, Bronx Munic Hosp, 64-65; resident otolaryngol, State Univ NY, Syracuse, 65-68; asst prof otolaryngol & maxillofacial surg, Northwestern Univ, 68-71. *Mem:* Fel Am Acad Ophthal & Otolaryngol; fel Am Col Surg; fel Am Soc Head & Neck Surg; fel Am Acad Facial Plastic & Reconstructive Surg; Am Soc Head & Neck Surg (secy, 76-). *Mailing Add:* Am Acad O&O Head Neurosurg One Prince St Alexandria VA 22314-3318

GOLDSTEIN, JOHN CECIL, LASERS. *Current Pos:* fel, 71-73, STAFF MEM PHYSICS, LOS ALAMOS SCI LAB, 73- *Personal Data:* b New York, NY, May 28, 44. *Educ:* Univ Ill, BS, 65; Mass Inst Technol, PhD(physics), 71. *Prof Exp:* Fel physics, Mass Inst Technol, 71. *Mem:* Am Phys Soc. *Res:* High-power short pulse lasers; pulse propagation in amplifiers and attenuators; nonlinear optics; theory of the free-electron laser; theory and numerical simulation of free-electron oscillators and amplifiers, nonlinear phenumena such as sideband generation and refractive index effects; short pulse effects and theory of soft-x-ray free electron lasers. *Mailing Add:* Los Alamos Sci Lab XPA B259 PO Box 1663 Los Alamos NM 87545

GOLDSTEIN, JORGE ALBERTO, ORGANIC CHEMISTRY, ENZYMOLOGY. *Current Pos:* PATENT CHEMIST & CONSULT, OBLON, FISHER, SPIVAK, MCCLELLAND & MAIER, 77- *Personal Data:* b Buenos Aires, Arg, July 17, 49; m 77; c 1. *Educ:* Rensselaer Polytech Inst, BS, 71; Harvard Univ, MS, 73, PhD(chem), 76. *Prof Exp:* Res asst chem, Harvard Univ, 71-76; res assoc chem, Mass Inst Technol, 76-77. *Mem:* Am Chem Soc; AAAS. *Res:* Enzymology; phosphorus chemistry; organic chemical mechanisms; patent law. *Mailing Add:* 6529 Bradley Blvd Bethesda MD 20817

GOLDSTEIN, JOSEPH I, METALLURGY, MATERIALS SCIENCE. *Current Pos:* DEAN ENG, UNIV MASS, AMHERST, 93- *Personal Data:* b Syracuse, NY, Jan, 6, 39; m 63, Barbara Hammond; c Steven & Anne. *Educ:* Mass Inst Technol, BS, 60, MS, 62, ScD(metall), 64. *Prof Exp:* Metallurgist, Smithsonian Astrophys Observ, 63-64; aerospace technologist, Goddard Space Flight Ctr, NASA, 64-68; from asst prof to assoc prof, Lehigh Univ, 68-75, vpres, Grad Studies & Res, Whitaker Lab, 83-90, Theodore L Diamond prof metall & mat sci, 76-93, asst vpres res, 79-93, R D Stout prof mat sci, 90-93. *Concurrent Pos:* Lectr, Univ Md, 66-67. *Mem:* Am Inst Mining, Metall & Petrol Engrs; fel Am Soc Metals Int; Meteoritical Soc (treas, 95-); Microbeam Anal Soc (pres, 77, past pres, 78); Sigma Xi. *Res:* Solid state kinetics; meteorites; phase equilibria; analytical electron microscopy, scanning electron microscopy. *Mailing Add:* Col Eng 125 Marston Hall Univ Mass Amherst MA 01003

GOLDSTEIN, JOSEPH LEONARD, GENETICS & GENETIC ENGINEERING, MEDICINE. *Current Pos:* from asst prof to assoc prof, 72-76, PROF MED, UNIV TEX HEALTH SCI CTR, DALLAS, 76-, PAUL J THOMAS PROF MED & CHMN, DEPT MOLECULAR GENETICS, 77- *Personal Data:* b Sumter, SC, Apr 18, 40. *Educ:* Washington & Lee Univ, BS, 62; Univ Tex, Dallas, MD, 66; Am Bd Internal Med, dipl. *Hon Degrees:* DSc, Univ Chicago, 82, Rensselaer Polytech Inst, 82, Washington & Lee Univ, 86 & Univ Paris-Sud, 88, Univ Buenos Aires, 90, Southern Methodist Univ, 93, Univ Miami, 96. *Honors & Awards:* Nobel Prize in Physiol or Med, 85; Heinrich Wieland Prize, WGer, 74; Pfizer Award, Am Chem Soc, 76; Passano Award, Passano Found, 78; Lounsbery Award, Nat Acad Sci, 79; Biol & Med Sci Award, NY Acad Sci, 81; Int Award, Gairdner Found, 81; Lita Annenberg Hazen Award, 82; Res Achievement Award, Am Heart Asn, 84; Louisa Gross Horwitz Award, 84; Distinguished Res Award, Asn Med Cols, 84; 3M Life Sci Award, Fedn Am Socs Exp Biol, 85; William Allan Award & Albert D Lasker Award, Am Soc Human Genetics, 85; Am Col Physicians Award, 86; Nat Medal Sci, 88. *Prof Exp:* Intern & resident internal med, Mass Gen Hosp, 66-68; clin assoc biochem, NIH, 68-70; spec NIH fel med genetics, Univ Wash, 70-72. *Concurrent Pos:* Mem, Mammalian Cell Lines Nat Adv Comt, NIH, 75-78, Sci Rev Bd, Howard Hughes Med Inst, 78-84 & Adv Bd, 85-; lectr, Harvey Soc, 77; non-resident fel, Salk Inst, 83-93; distinguished res award, Asn Am Med Cols, 84; mem, Sci Adv Bd, Welch Found & Jane Coffin Child Mem Fund Med Res, Prog Adv Comt Human Genome, NIH; bd dirs, Passano Fedn, 85-; bd sci consult, Mem Sloan Kettering Cancer Ctr, 92-; bd trustees, Rockefeller Univ, 94-; bd sci govs, Scripps Res Inst, 96- *Mem:* Nat Acad Sci; Inst Med-Nat Acad Sci; Am Acad Arts & Sci; Am Soc Clin Invest (pres, 85-86); Asn Am Physicians; Am Soc Biol Chemists; Am Fedn Clin Res; Am Col Physicians; Am Soc Human Genetics; Am Philos Soc. *Res:* Human biochemical genetics; regulation of cholesterol and lipoprotein metabolism; membrane receptors. *Mailing Add:* Univ Tex Southwestern Med Ctr 5323 Harry Hines Blvd Dallas TX 75235. *Fax:* 214-648-8804

GOLDSTEIN, JOYCE ALLENE, DRUG-METABOLIZING ENZYMES, HUMAN CYP ENZYMES & GENETIC POLYMORPHISMS. *Current Pos:* PHARMACOLOGIST, NAT INST ENVIRON HEALTH SCI, 77- *Personal Data:* b Whittier, Calif, Mar 8, 41; m 63. *Educ:* Southwest Mo State Univ, BS, 62; Univ Tex Southwestern Med Sch Dallas, PhD(pharmacol), 66. *Prof Exp:* Fel, Emory Univ Med Sch, 67-68; res pharmacologist, Commun Dis Ctr & Food & Drug Admin, 68-72 & Environ Protection Agency, 72-77. *Concurrent Pos:* Adj prof, Dept Toxicol, NC State Univ, 89-; bd dirs, Am Bd toxicol, 95-; counr, Int Soc Study Xenobiotics, 96- *Mem:* Am Soc Pharmacol & Exp Therapeut; Soc Toxicol; Am Soc Biochem & Molecular Biol. *Res:* Cloning and expression of CYP drug-metabolizing enzymes; genetic polymorphisms in CYP enzymes; human CYP enzymes; substrate specificity and structure-activity relationships. *Mailing Add:* Human Metab Sect NIEHS NIH A3-02 PO Box 12233 Research Triangle Park NC 27709-2233

GOLDSTEIN, JULIUS L, ELECTRICAL ENGINEERING, SENSORY PERCEPTION & BIOENGINEERING. *Current Pos:* PROF, DEPT ELEC ENG, WASH UNIV, 96- *Personal Data:* b Brooklyn, NY, July 9, 35; m 62, Batya Abramson; c Hillel, Miriam, Naama & Avi. *Educ:* Cooper Union, BEE, 57; Polytech Inst Brooklyn, MEE, 60; Univ Rochester, PhD(elec eng), 66. *Prof Exp:* Staff engr, Polytech Res & Develop, NY, 57-60; lectr, Univ Rochester, 60-61; fel hearing res, Lab Psychophys, Harvard Univ, 66-68; from asst prof to prof elec eng, Mass Inst Technol, 68-73; chmn bioeng prog, Tel Aviv Univ, 73-76, from assoc prof to prof fac eng, 73-90, chmn, Dept Electronics, 76-78; sr res scientist, Cent Inst Deaf, 88-96. *Concurrent Pos:* Lectr, Polytech Inst Brooklyn, 59-60; NSF fel, Inst Perception Res, Eindhoven, Neth, 65-66; mem, Comt Hearing Bioacoust & Biomed, Nat Res Coun, 77-; vis prof, Johns Hopkins Univ, Baltimore, 86-88; consult models human hearing, Bell Labs (AT&T, Lucent), Murray Hill, NJ, 91-96. *Mem:* Sr mem Inst Elec & Electronics Engrs; fel Acoust Soc Am; Israeli Soc Med & Biol Eng (pres, 75-77); Asn Res Otolaryngol. *Res:* Auditory psychology and physiology; bioengineering; quantitative models of human sensory communication that represent signal processing function, including nonlinear cochlear sound analysis, detection of signal peaks and intervals, and central processing in pitch perception; applications to engineering design. *Mailing Add:* Dept Elec Eng Wash Univ 1 Brookings Dr St Louis MO 63130-4899. *Fax:* 314-935-7500; *E-Mail:* jlg@ee.wustl.edu

GOLDSTEIN, LARRY JOEL, NUMBER THEORY. *Current Pos:* PRES, GOLDSTEIN ED TECHNOL, 91- *Personal Data:* b Philadelphia, Pa, Dec 4, 44; m 67; c Melissa & Jonathan. *Educ:* Univ Pa, BA & MA, 65; Princeton Univ, MA & PhD(math), 67. *Honors & Awards:* Allan C Davis Medal. *Prof Exp:* Josiah Willard Gibbs instr math, Yale Univ, 67-69; assoc prof, Univ Md, College Park, 69-72, prof math, 72-84, distinguished scholar & teacher, 79-90. *Concurrent Pos:* NSF res grants, 69-82; adj prof, Goldstein Software Inc, 84-; US Naval Acad, Secy Navy fel, 89-90. *Mem:* Am Math Soc; Math Asn Am; Asn Comput Mach. *Res:* Algebraic number theory; theory of automorphic functions; computer science-interactive tutorial systems. *Mailing Add:* Bittersweet Dr Doylestown PA 18901. *Fax:* 215-489-4046; *E-Mail:* lgoldst957@aol.com

GOLDSTEIN, LAWRENCE HOWARD, ELECTRICAL ENGINEERING, COMPUTER-AIDED DESIGN. *Current Pos:* AT STANDARD MICROSYSTEMS. *Personal Data:* b New York, NY, Jan 7, 52. *Educ:* Cooper Union, BE, 73; Princeton Univ, MSE, 74, PhD(elec eng), 76. *Honors & Awards:* Browder J Thompson Award, 81. *Prof Exp:* mem tech staff comput-aided design, Sandia Labs, 76-80; mgr sci comput, Inmos Corp, 80- *Mem:* Inst Elec & Electronics Engrs; Asn Comput Mach; Soc Indust & Appl Math. *Res:* Computer-aided design of large scale integrated circuits. *Mailing Add:* Standard Microsyst 35 Marcus Blvd Hauppauge NY 11788-3791

GOLDSTEIN, LAWRENCE S B, CELL & DEVELOPMENTAL BIOLOGY. *Current Pos:* asst prof cell & develop biol, 84-88, John L Loeb assoc prof natural sci, 88-90, PROF CELL & DEVELOP BIOL, HARVARD UNIV, 90- *Personal Data:* b Buffalo, NY, Feb 20, 56. *Educ:* Univ Calif, BA, 76; Univ Wash, PhD(genetics), 80. *Prof Exp:* Postdoctoral fel genetics & biochem, Univ Colo, 80-83; res assoc molecular biol, Harvard Univ & Mass Inst Technol, 83-84. *Concurrent Pos:* Ad hoc mem, Nucleic Acids & Protein Synthesis Adv Comt, Am Cancer Soc, 85 & 88, Cell Biol Study Sect, NIH, 90 & Molecular Cytol Study Sect, 91; NIH grants, 86-91, 88-91 & 88-93; Am Cancer Soc fac res award, 90-95. *Mem:* Genetics Soc Am; Am Soc Cell Biol. *Res:* Molecular, biochemical, and genetic analysis of protein motors, mitotic mechanisms, and cytoskeletal function in Drosophila; author of more than 30 technical publications. *Mailing Add:* Dept Cellular & Molecular Med Univ Calif San Diego 9500 Gilman Dr La Jolla CA 92093-0683. *Fax:* 619-534-9701

GOLDSTEIN, LEON, PHYSIOLOGY. *Current Pos:* assoc prof med sci, 68-72, chmn physiol & biophys, 78-96, PROF MED SCI, BROWN UNIV, 73- *Personal Data:* b Malden, Mass, Feb 6, 33; m 58, Barbara J Goldman; c Pamela B, Jonathan M & Susanne R. *Educ:* Northeastern Univ, BS, 54; Boston Univ, PhD(pharmacol), 58. *Hon Degrees:* MA, Univ Oxford, 83. *Prof Exp:* Res fel zool, Dartmouth Col, 58-59, instr, 59-60; res assoc, Cancer Res Inst, New Eng Deaconess Hosp, 60-62; assoc physiol, Harvard Med Sch, 62-64, asst prof, 64-68. *Concurrent Pos:* Lectr, Harvard Med Sch, 68-69; ed, Physiol & Biochem, J Exp Zool, 78-; dir, Mount Desert Island Biol Lab, 79-83, vpres, 86-92; Res Career Develop Award, NIH, 63; Fogarty Sen Int Fel, 83. *Mem:* Am Chem Soc; Am Soc Zool; Soc Gen Physiol; Am Physiol Soc; fel AAAS. *Res:* Kidney; comparative physiology; membrane transport; metabolic regulation; cell volume regulation. *Mailing Add:* Div Biol & Med Sci Brown Univ Providence RI 02912. *Fax:* 401-863-1222

GOLDSTEIN, LESTER, CELL BIOLOGY. *Current Pos:* VIS SCHOLAR, DEPT GENETICS, UNIV WASH, SEATTLE, 92- *Personal Data:* b Brooklyn, NY, June 28, 24; div; c Natasha & Nina. *Educ:* Brooklyn Col, BA, 48; Univ Pa, PhD, 53. *Prof Exp:* Lectr biol, Queens Col (NY), 50; asst instr zool, Univ Pa, 50-51; USPHS fel, Univ Calif, Berkeley, 53-55, asst res physiologist, Med Ctr, Univ Calif, San Francisco, 55-59; assoc prof zool, Univ Pa, 59-64, prof biol, 64-67; prof, Inst Develop Biol, Univ Colo, Boulder, 67-68, & Dept Molecular, Cellular & Develop Biol, 68-82; prof & dir, T H Morgan Sch Biol Sci, Univ Ky, 82-92,. *Concurrent Pos:* Damon Runyon Mem Fund fel, 55-56; Am Cancer Soc scholar, Univ Wash, Seattle, 77-78. *Mem:* Am Soc Cell Biol; AAAS; Genetics Soc Am. *Res:* Interrelationships of nucleus and cytoplasm; nuclear RNA's and proteins and cell cycle. *Mailing Add:* Dept Genetics Univ Wash Seattle WA 98105. *Fax:* 206-528-1482

GOLDSTEIN, LOUIS, THEORETICAL PHYSICS, LOW TEMPERATURE PHYSICS. *Current Pos:* RETIRED. *Personal Data:* b Dombrad, Hungary, Mar 25, 04; nat US; m 33, Ella Trammer; c John C. *Educ:* Col City Nagyvarad, Testimonium Maturitatis, 22; Univ Paris, lic es S, 26, DSc(theoret physics), 32. *Prof Exp:* Researcher, Inst Henri Poincare, Univ Paris, 28-32, res assoc, 32-39; independent researcher, NY Univ, 39-41; instr physics, City Col, NY, 41-44; mem staff, Wave Propagation Group, Off Sci Res & Develop contract, Columbia Univ, 44-46; physicist, Fed Telecommunications Lab, Int Tel & Tel, NY, 46; mem staff, Los Alamos Nat Lab, 46-71, consult mem staff, 71-96. *Mem:* Fel Am Phys Soc. *Res:* Theory of atoms; atomic nuclei, statistical mechanics; properties of matter at very low temperatures; theory of the helium isotopes. *Mailing Add:* 1300 Canyon Rd Los Alamos NM 87544

GOLDSTEIN, MARCUS SOLOMON, physical anthropology, for more information see previous edition

GOLDSTEIN, MARGARET ANN, CELL BIOLOGY, MUSCULAR PHYSIOLOGY. *Current Pos:* instr cell biol, Baylor Col Med, 70-73, asst prof cell biophys & exp med, 72-77, from asst prof to assoc prof, 77-89, PROF MED & CELL BIOL, BAYLOR COL MED, 89- *Personal Data:* b Sinton, Tex, Mar 13, 39; m 59, Alexander Jr; c David W. *Educ:* Rice Univ, BA, 65, PhD(cell biol), 69. *Prof Exp:* Res asst psychol, Baylor Col Med, 60-61; cardiovasc technician, Vet Admin Hosp, 61-62; head technician pulmonary physiol,Tex Inst Rehab & Res, 63-64; res asst biol & physiol, Rice Univ, 64; instr biol, Univ Tex M D Anderson Hosp & Tumor Inst Houston, 69-70. *Concurrent Pos:* Vis lectr, Rice Univ, 69-74; Am Heart Asn grant, Baylor Col Med, 71-73, Nat Heart, Lung & Blood Inst grants, 71-82 & 74-90; mem, Coun Basic Sci, Am Heart Asn, estab investr; NIH res & career develop award; Rev Comt A, Nat Heart Lung & Blood Inst; panelist, Nat Res Coun; biol dir, Electron Micros Soc Am; mem exec bd coun, Sci Soc Presidents. *Mem:* AAAS; Am Soc Cell Biol; Electron Micros Soc Am (pres elect, 95, pres, 96); Am Heart Asn; Biophys Soc; Sigma Xi; Micros Soc Am. *Res:* Ultrastructure of muscle cells in developing hearts, normal and diseased hearts; optical diffraction analysis of Z lattice in muscle and 3-dimensional reconstructions of Z lattice in relaxed and contracted striated muscle. *Mailing Add:* Dept Med Cardiovasc Sci Baylor Col Med 1 Baylor Plaza Houston TX 77030-3498. *Fax:* 713-790-0681

GOLDSTEIN, MARK KANE, BEHAVIORAL MEDICINE, SENSORY PSYCHOPHYSICS. *Current Pos:* DIR MED SCIENTIST BIOMED RES, CTR AMBULATORY STUDIES, UNIV FLA, 82-; CHMN, MAMMATECH CORP, 82- *Personal Data:* b Allentown, Pa, May 29, 38; m 61; c 3. *Educ:* Muhlenberg Col, AB, 61; Columbia Univ, MA, 62; Cornell Univ PhD, 71. *Prof Exp:* Staff psychologist, exp psychol, US Vet Admn Med Ctr, 71-82. *Res:* Tactile thresholds in breast cancer detection; improved methods for tactile detection of lesions; ambulatory monitoring in chronic physical disease; neurological monitoring and neuro protheses in chronic patents. *Mailing Add:* 1512 NW Seventh Pl Gainesville FL 32603

GOLDSTEIN, MARTIN, PHYSICAL CHEMISTRY. *Current Pos:* RETIRED. *Personal Data:* b New York, NY, Nov 18, 19; m 54, Inge Futter; c Eric, Michael & Aviva. *Educ:* City Col New York, BS, 40; Columbia Univ, PhD(chem), 50. *Honors & Awards:* Forrest & Meyer Award, Am Ceramic Soc, 65. *Prof Exp:* USPHS fel, Polytech Inst Brooklyn, 50-51; fel, Harvard Univ, 51-53 & Mellon Inst, 53-58; vis scientist, Nat Phys Lab Israel, 58-60; staff scientist chem dept, Sci Lab, Ford Motor Co, 60-65; vis assoc prof ceramics, Mass Inst Technol, 64-65; prof chem, Div Natural Sci & Math, Yeshiva Univ, 65-89. *Concurrent Pos:* Chmn, Gordon Res Conf on Glass, 65; vis prof, Univ Ill, 67-68, Israel Inst Technol, 72 & Univ Bristol, 72 & 73; co-chmn workshop conf glassy state, NY Acad Sci, 75, 81, 85. *Mem:* AAAS; fel Am Phys Soc; Sigma Xi. *Res:* Glassy state, thermodynamics and statistical mechanics of glass transition, secondary relaxations in glasses; science for the non-scientist. *Mailing Add:* 299 Riverside Dr New York NY 10025

GOLDSTEIN, MARVIN E, FLUID MECHANICS, APPLIED MATHEMATICS. *Current Pos:* aerospace engr, 67-79, CHIEF SCIENTIST, NASA-LEWIS RES CTR, 80- *Personal Data:* b Cambridge, Mass, Oct 11, 38; m 65; c 2. *Educ:* Northeastern Univ, BS, 61; Mass Inst Technol, MS, 62; Univ Mich, PhD(mech eng), 65. *Honors & Awards:* Except Sci Achievement Award, NASA, 79; Aeoracoustics Award, Am Inst Aeronaut & Astronaut, 83, Pendray Award, 83; Otto Laporte Award Res Fluid Dynamics, Am Phys Soc, 97. *Prof Exp:* Res assoc fluid mech, Mass Inst Technol, 65-67. *Concurrent Pos:* Assoc ed, J Am Inst Aeronaut & Astronaut, 77- *Mem:* Nat Acad Eng; fel Am Inst Aeronaut & Astronaut; fel Am Phys Soc. *Res:* Fluid mechanics, heat transfer, aeroacoustics. *Mailing Add:* NASA-Lewis Res Ctr 21000 Brookpark Rd MS 3-17 Cleveland OH 44135. *Fax:* 216-433-5266; *E-Mail:* marvin.e.goldstein@lerc.nasa.gov

GOLDSTEIN, MARVIN SHERWOOD, PETROLEUM CHEMISTRY, CATALYSIS. *Current Pos:* res chemist, Org Chem Div, Stamford Res Labs, Cytec Indust, 60-69, group leader, Refinishing Catalyst Res, 69-72, proj leader, Chem Res Div, 72-83, dir res, Catalyst Recovery Inc, 83-84, prin res chemist, Am Cyanamid Co, 85-93, PRIN RES CHEMIST, STAMFORD RES LABS, CYTEC INDUST, 94- *Personal Data:* b Newark, NJ, Feb 13, 34; m 66, Harriette Cherdack; c Stephanie, Elaine, Barbara & Jonathan. *Educ:* NY State Col Teachers, Albany, BS, 56; Rensselaer Polytech Inst, PhD(phys chem), 60. *Prof Exp:* Res engr, Allison Div, Gen Motors Corp, 59-60. *Concurrent Pos:* Lectr, Univ Conn, 62-63. *Mem:* Am Chem Soc; Catalysis Soc; Sigma Xi. *Res:* Catalysis; surface chemistry; kinetics and thermodynamics of oxidation and combustion; high energy fuels; boron hydrides; alumina and silica; crystallization. *Mailing Add:* Stamford Res Labs Cytec Indust 1937 W Main St Stamford CT 06904. *Fax:* 203-321

GOLDSTEIN, MAX, mathematics; deceased, see previous edition for last biography

GOLDSTEIN, MELVIN E, PHYCOLOGY. *Current Pos:* RETIRED. *Personal Data:* b Glen Ridge, NJ, July 27, 36. *Educ:* Ind Univ, BA, 58, PhD(bot), 63. *Prof Exp:* Asst prof bot, McGill Univ, 63-74, assoc prof biol, 74-95. *Mem:* Bot Soc Am; Am Phycol Soc; Am Soc Protozool; Int Phycol Soc. *Res:* Speciation, sexuality, cytology and genetics of the colonial green flagellate Eudorina; taxonomy, morphology and ecology of the marine algae of Barbados. *Mailing Add:* 1318 Beach Dr Apt 304 Victoria BC V8S 2N5 Can

GOLDSTEIN, MELVIN JOSEPH, ORGANIC CHEMISTRY. *Current Pos:* CONSULT, CERT CONSULT INT, 95- *Personal Data:* b New York, NY, Dec 28, 33; m 55,90; c Eric J, Deborah E & Daniel J. *Educ:* Columbia Univ, BA, 54; Yale Univ, PhD(chem), 58. *Prof Exp:* NSF fel, Harvard Univ, 58-59; from instr to prof chem, Cornell Univ, 59-85; sr investr, Bromine Compounds Ltd, 84-94. *Concurrent Pos:* NATO sr sci fel, 68; Guggenheim Mem Found fel, 74; Japan Soc Prom Sci prof, 77. *Mem:* Am Chem Soc; Royal Soc Chem; Swiss Chem Soc; Israel Chem Soc. *Res:* Organic reaction mechanisms; organic synthesis, process development and optimization. *Mailing Add:* Sderot Yerushalyayim 33/29 PO Box 180 Beer Sheva 84777 Israel. *E-Mail:* mjgcci@actcom.co.il

GOLDSTEIN, MELVYN L, SPACE PLASMA PHYSICS, ASTROPHYSICS. *Current Pos:* SPACE SCIENTIST SPACE PHYSICS, NASA, GODDARD SPACE FLIGHT CTR, 74- *Personal Data:* b New York, NY, Jan 18, 43; c 1. *Educ:* Columbia Col, AB, 64; Univ Md, PhD(physics), 70. *Prof Exp:* Vis lectr space physics, Tel Aviv Univ, 70-72; res assoc, Nat Res Coun, 72-74. *Concurrent Pos:* Vis scientist astron, Univ Fla, 80. *Mem:* Am Geophys Union; Am Phys Soc. *Res:* Jovian radio science; theory of cosmic ray propagation; magnetohydrodynamic turbulence. *Mailing Add:* NASA Goddard Space Flight Ctr Code 692 Greenbelt MD 20771

GOLDSTEIN, MENEK, BIOCHEMISTRY. *Current Pos:* from instr to assoc prof, 58-69, PROF NEUROCHEM, MED CTR, NY UNIV, 69- *Personal Data:* b Kolmya, Poland, Apr 8, 24. *Educ:* Univ Bern, PhD, 55. *Hon Degrees:* MD, Karolinska Inst, Stockholm, Sweden. *Prof Exp:* Res instr biochem, Univ Bern, 54-56; mem res staff, Worcester Found Exp Biol, 56-57. *Mem:* Am Chem Soc; Am Soc Biol Chem. *Res:* Neuroch- emistry; metabolism and biosynthesis of biogenic amines; role of hormones in the central nervous system; mode of action of hormones and enzymes in vivo; steroid hormones; neurotransmitters and their interaction with specific receptors; purification of neurotransmitter synthesizing enzymes; immunohistochemical mapping of neuronal systems. *Mailing Add:* Dept Neurochem Ny Univ Med Ctr 560 First Ave Rm H544 New York NY 10016-6402. *Fax:* 212-263-8177

GOLDSTEIN, MILTON NORMAN, CELL BIOLOGY. *Current Pos:* RETIRED. *Personal Data:* b Cleveland, Ohio, Jan 15, 25; m 52; c 2. *Educ:* Western Reserve Univ, BS, 46, MS, 47, PhD(zool), 52. *Prof Exp:* USPHS fel path, Western Reserve Univ, 52-54; investr cancer res, Roswell Park Mem Inst, 54-55, sr cancer res scientist, 55-62; sr cancer res scientist, Cell Biol Labs, St Jude Children's Res Hosp, Memphis, Tenn, 62-66; assoc prof anat, Sch Med, Wash Univ, 66-88. *Concurrent Pos:* Grant reviewer oncol, US Vet Admin, 74-76. *Mem:* Tissue Cult Asn; Am Asn Anat; Am Asn Cancer Res; Am Soc Cell Biol. *Res:* Cytology; differentiation of cells in vitro; histochemistry; electron microscopy applied to cell growing in tissue culture. *Mailing Add:* 8145 Amherst University City MO 63130

GOLDSTEIN, MINDY SUE, PROTEIN PURIFICATION. *Current Pos:* SR STAFF SCIENTIST, APPLIED GENETICS INC, 85- *Educ:* NY Univ, PhD(med sci), 83. *Mailing Add:* Lipo Chem Inc 207 19th Ave Paterson NJ 07504. *Fax:* 973-345-8600

GOLDSTEIN, MOISE HERBERT, JR, ELECTRICAL ENGINEERING. *Current Pos:* assoc prof biomed eng, Johns Hopkins Univ, 63-75, Edward J Schaeffer prof elec & biomed eng, 75-90, actg dir, Ctr Speech Processing, 92-93, prof elec eng, 67-95, EMER PROF, JOHNS HOPKINS UNIV, 95- *Personal Data:* b New Orleans, La, Dec 26, 26; m 70, Phyllis Dwonkin; c Claude, Brian, Catherine & Thomas. *Educ:* Tulane Univ, BS, 49; Mass Inst Technol, SM, 51, ScD, 57. *Prof Exp:* Asst elec eng, Mass Inst Technol, 49-51, mem defense staff, 52-55; mem staff, Tex Co, 51-52; instr elec eng, Mass Inst Technol, 55-56, from asst prof to assoc prof, 56-63. *Concurrent Pos:* NSF fel, Univ Pisa, 59-60; vis lectr, Mass Inst Technol, 63-64; Guggenheim Found fel, Jerusalem Inst Technol, 70-71; consult, Fed Drug Admin, NIH, NSF; NIH sr fel, 81-82 & 89-90, Univ Col London, 82, Univ Calif, San Diego, 90. *Mem:* Fel Acoust Soc Am; Inst Elec & Electronics Engrs; Am Auditory Soc; Am Speech Hearing & Lang Soc; Nat Asn Deaf. *Res:* Speech signal processing; prostheses for the deaf; language acquisition in deaf infants. *Mailing Add:* ECE Dept Barton Hall Johns Hopkins Univ Baltimore MD 21218. *Fax:* 410-516-5566; *E-Mail:* moise@olympus.ece.jhu.edu

GOLDSTEIN, MURRAY, RESEARCH ADMINISTRATION, MEDICINE. *Current Pos:* MED DIR, UNITED CEREBRAL PALSY RES & EDUC FOUND, 93- *Personal Data:* b New York, NY, Oct 13, 25; m 57, Sue M Michael; c Patricia & Barbara. *Educ:* NY Univ, PhB, 47; Still Col Osteop & Surg, DO, 50; Univ Calif, MPH, 59. *Hon Degrees:* Var from US & foreign univs, 67-94. *Honors & Awards:* Cert of Merit, Am Neurol Asn; Meritorious Serv Medal, USPHS, Distinguished Serv Medal. *Prof Exp:* Intern, Still Osteop Hosp, Des Moines, Iowa, 50-51, med resident, 51-53; asst chief grants & training br, Nat Heart Inst, 53-58, asst chief res grants rev br, 59-60; neuro res, Mayo Clin, 68-69; dir extramural prog, Nat Inst Neurol Dis & Stroke, 61-76, dir stroke & trauma prog, 76-78, dep dir, 78-81, actg dir, 81-82, dir, 82-93; asst surg gen, USPHS, 80-93. *Concurrent Pos:* Vis scientist, Mayo Grad Sch Med, Univ Minn, 67-68; sr lectr, Uniformed Serv, Univ Health Sci, 83-97. *Mem:* AAAS; Am Osteop Asn; fel Am Public Health Asn; fel Am Acad Neurol; Am Heart Asn; Soc Neurosci; Am Neurol Asn (vpres, 82-83); Am Osteop Col Prev Med (pres, 89-90). *Res:* Nervous system trauma; cerebrovascular diseases; public health; epidemiology; neurodevelopmental disorders. *Mailing Add:* 6210 Swords Way Bethesda MD 20817. *Fax:* 202-776-0414

GOLDSTEIN, MYRON, mathematics, for more information see previous edition

GOLDSTEIN, NORMA ORNSTEIN, CONNECTIVE TISSUE GENES, HUMAN BOVINE & SHEEP ELASTIN. *Current Pos:* RETIRED. *Personal Data:* b Bronx, NY, Dec 13, 21. *Educ:* NY Univ, AB, 42; Columbia Univ, AM, 49; Univ Pa, PhD(molecular biol), 71. *Prof Exp:* Chemist mfg control, Nat Starch Prod, Inc, NJ & NY, 42-44; chemist anal biochem, Food & Drug Res Labs, NY, 44-47; res asst biochem, Montefiore Hosp, Bronx, NY, 49-50, chem embryol, dept zool, Columbia Univ, 50-53 & cytochem, dept zool, Univ Calif, Berkeley, 54-59; res investr exp chemother & biochem, dept chem, Univ Pa, 60-65, trainee molecular biol, Nat Inst Gen Med Sci, USPHS, Grad Sch Arts & Sci, 65-70, res assoc, Cancer Res Unit, dept animal biol, 71; E H Bobst Penn plan scholar, 72-74; res assoc virol, Sloan-Kettering Inst Cancer Res, Walker Lab, Rye, NY, 75-76; res asst prof biochem, dept path, Mt Sinai Sch Med, City Univ New York, 77; res asst prof biochem, dept animal biol, Sch Vet Med, Univ Pa, 78-82, molecular & cell res biologist, Dept Histol & Embryol, Sch Dent Med, 82-89. *Concurrent Pos:* Res fel cancer res, Inst Cancer Res, Columbia Univ, 70; adj res assoc, Sch Dent Med, Univ Pa, 89-92. *Mem:* Am Soc Cell Biol; AAAS; Asn Women Sci. *Res:* Characterization of human elastin genes; i.e., normal vs those from patients with connective tissue pathologies. *Mailing Add:* 2216 Delancey St Philadelphia PA 19103-6502

GOLDSTEIN, NORMAN N, biological science; deceased, see previous edition for last biography

GOLDSTEIN, NORMAN PHILIP, neurology, psychiatry, for more information see previous edition

GOLDSTEIN, NORMAN PHILLIP, NUCLEAR PHYSICS. *Current Pos:* ADV PHYSICIST, ELECTRONICS SYSTS GROUP, NORTHRUP GRUMMAN, 96- *Personal Data:* b Montreal, Que, Aug 11, 40. *Educ:* McGill Univ, BSc, 61, MSc, 63, PhD(nuclear physics), 67. *Prof Exp:* Sr fel physicist, Westinghouse Elec Corp, 67-73, fel physicist, 73-81, adv physicist, Westinghouse Res Labs, 81-88, adv physicist, Electronics Systs Group, 89-96. *Mem:* Am Nuclear Soc; Health Phys Soc. *Res:* Short lifetime measurements with a fast-slow coincidence system; nuclear scattering from low atomic weight nuclei at 100 million electron volts; radiation damage studies; neutron detectors for fast breeder reactors; design of radiation monitors, and new self-powered incore detectors; new core designs for improved fuel utilization in reactors; development of a monitor to measure the burnip of spent fuel. *Mailing Add:* Northrup Grumman Electronics Systs Group PO Box 1521 MS 3D12 Baltimore MD 21203

GOLDSTEIN, PHILIP, APPLIED PHYSICS. *Current Pos:* RETIRED. *Personal Data:* b Bronx, NY, Jan 18, 30. *Educ:* City Col New York, BS, 51; Carnegie-Mellon Univ, MS, 56, PhD(physics), 58. *Prof Exp:* Adminr electronics, Dept Physics, Princeton Univ, 58-60; tech staff mem comput, RCA Lab, 60-68; prof physics, Jersey City State Col, 68-81, prof comput sci, 81-92. *Concurrent Pos:* Mem, Phase III Master Plan Comt Comput & Info Sci, Dept Higher Educ NJ, 72-73. *Mem:* Inst Elec & Electronics Engrs; Int Elec & Electronics Engrs Comput Soc. *Res:* Computer applications in the sciences; development of computer-based educational materials; computer applications in medicine; ada language technology consultant. *Mailing Add:* 7004 Boulevard 37G Guttenberg NJ 07093

GOLDSTEIN, R(ICHARD) J(AY), MECHANICAL ENGINEERING. *Current Pos:* assoc prof mech eng, 61-65, head, 77-97, PROF MECH ENG, UNIV MINN, MINNEAPOLIS, 65-, JAMES J RYAN PROF, 89-, REGENTS PROF, 90- *Personal Data:* b New York, NY, Mar 27, 28; m 63, Barbara; c Arthur S, Jonathan J, Benjamin S & Naomi (Sarith). *Educ:* Cornell Univ, BME, 48; Univ Minn, MS, 50, MS, 51, PhD (mech eng), 59. *Hon Degrees:* DSc, Israel Inst Technol, 94; Dr, Univ Lisbon, 96. *Honors & Awards:* Award for Serv, Am Soc Mech Engrs, 77, Centennial Medallion, 78, Heat Transfer Mem Award, 78, Max Jakob Mem Award, 90; Technical Innovation Award, NASA, 77; Prince Lectr, 83; William Gurley Lectr, 88; AV Lykov Medal, 90; Hawkins Mem Lectr, 91. *Prof Exp:* Instr, Univ Minn, 48-51; develop engr, Oak Ridge Nat Lab, 51-54; sr res engr, Lockheed Aircraft Corp, 56; instr, Univ Minn, 56-58; asst prof eng, Brown Univ, 59-61. *Concurrent Pos:* Consult, 56-; NATO fel, Nat Ctr Sci Res, France, 60-61; NSF sr fel, Univ Cambridge, Eng, 71-72; vis prof, Cambridge Univ, 71-72, Technion Israel, 76, Imp Col, London, Eng, 84; chmn, Coun Eng, Am Soc Mech Eng, Coun Energy, Eng Res, Dept Energy; distinguished lectr, Pa State Univ, 92. *Mem:* Nat Acad Eng; fel Am Soc Mech Engrs (sr vpres, 89-, past pres, 96-97); Am Phys Soc; fel Am Soc Eng Educ; fel AAAS; Sigma Xi; Japan Soc Prom Sci. *Res:* Heat transfer; thermodynamics; fluid mechanics; optical measuring techniques. *Mailing Add:* 520 Janalyn Circle Minneapolis MN 55416-3327

GOLDSTEIN, RAYMOND, SPACE PLASMA, PHYSICS. *Current Pos:* sr scientist, 67-74, MEM TECH STAFF, JET PROPULSION LAB, CALIF INST TECHNOL, 74- *Personal Data:* b Dec 15, 31. *Educ:* City Col New York, BS, 53; Lehigh Univ, MS, 57, PhD(physics), 62. *Prof Exp:* Staff scientist physics, Boeing Sci Res Labs, 62-67. *Concurrent Pos:* Instr phys sci, Art Ctr Col Design, 76-; fel, Japan Soc Prom Sci, Gunma Univ, Japan, 79; detailee, NASA Hq, 80-81; vis prof, Univ Bern, Switz, 83-85. *Mem:* Am Phys Soc; Am Asn Physics Teachers; Sigma Xi. *Res:* Shock waves; condensation; magnetohydrodynamics; gaseous conduction; photoionization; fiber optics; electric propulsion; space plasma physics; mass spectrometry. *Mailing Add:* 169-506 Jet Propulsion Lab 4800 Oak Grove Dr Pasadena CA 91109

GOLDSTEIN, RICHARD, COMPUTER SCIENCE FUNCTION. *Current Pos:* PROF, STATE UNIV NY, ALBANY, 70- *Personal Data:* b Philadelphia, Pa, Mar 18, 39. *Educ:* Univ Pa, PhD(math), 66; Tampa Univ, BA, 69. *Mem:* Am Math Soc; Am Math Asn. *Mailing Add:* State Univ NY Albany Albany NY 12203-3032

GOLDSTEIN, ROBERT, AUDIOLOGY, PSYCHOPHYSIOLOGY. *Current Pos:* RETIRED. *Personal Data:* b Plymouth, Pa, Sept 7, 24; m 48, Gay Swartz; c Mark H & Neal S. *Educ:* Pa State Univ, BS, 48; Wash Univ, PhD(audiol), 52. *Prof Exp:* Res assoc, Cent Inst Deaf, 53-57; dir, Div Audiol & Speech Path, Jewish Hosp, St Louis, 58-67; prof commun dis, Univ Wis-Madison, 67-91. *Concurrent Pos:* From asst prof to assoc prof, Wash Univ, 53-67; mem, Int Elec Response Audiometry Study Group, Sigma Xi. *Mem:* Acoust Soc Am; fel Am Speech-Lang-Hearing Asn (pres, 71-72); Alexander Graham Bell Asn for Deaf; Am EEG Soc; Am Acad Audiol. *Res:* Electrophysiologic tests of hearing; neonatal hearing evaluation; central auditory function; hearing disorders in prison populations; genetic hearing loss. *Mailing Add:* 10332 Villa Ridge Dr Las Vegas NV 89134

GOLDSTEIN, ROBERT, MEDICINE. *Current Pos:* assoc prof, 61-65, chmn dept, 71-77, PROF MED, NY MED COL, 65-, ASSOC DEAN STUDENT AFFAIRS, 76- *Personal Data:* b New York, NY, Aug 6, 12; m 41; c 2. *Educ:* Princeton Univ, AB, 33; Harvard Univ, MD, 37; Am Bd Internal Med, dipl, 49, dipl hemat, 72. *Prof Exp:* Asst med, Harvard Med Sch, 46-51, instr, 51-54, clin assoc, 54-58; asst prof, Med Sch, Tufts Univ, 57-61. *Concurrent Pos:* Asst, Med Sch, Tufts Univ, 46-50, instr, 50-51; estab investr, Am Heart Asn, 58- *Mem:* AAAS; Am Soc Hemat; Am Heart Asn; Am Physiol Soc; Int Soc Hemat. *Res:* Internal medicine, especially hematology; blood coagulation. *Mailing Add:* Prof Med & Physiol Uniformed Serv Univ Health Sci 4301 Jones Bridge Rd Rm A3060 Bethesda MD 20814-4799. *Fax:* 301-295-3557

GOLDSTEIN, ROBERT ARNOLD, ALLERGY & CLINICAL IMMUNOLOGY, INTERNAL MEDICINE. *Current Pos:* resident internal med, Vet Admin Med Ctr, Washington, DC, 67-69, fel pulmonary dis, 69-70, mem staff, 72-76, assoc chief, 77-78, MEM STAFF, PULMONARY DIS,

VET ADMIN MED CTR, WASHINGTON, DC, 78-; DIR, DIV ALLERGY, IMMUNOL & TRANSPLANTATION, NAT INST ALLERGY & INFECTIOUS DIS, NIH. *Personal Data:* b Brooklyn, NY, Dec 1, 41; m 93, Barbara. *Educ:* Brandeis Univ, AB, 62; Jefferson Med Col, MD, 66; George Washington Univ, PhD(micro immunol), 76; NY Univ, MBA, 92. *Prof Exp:* Rotating internship med, Philadelphia Gen Hosp, 66-67; asst chief, Tripler Army Med Ctr, Honolulu, 70-71, chief, 71-72. *Concurrent Pos:* Asst clin prof, Sch Med, Univ Hawaii, 70-72; consult internal med, Queens Hosp, 70-72 & Wash Hosp Ctr, 73-; staff physician, Pulmonary Dis Div, George Washington Univ Med Ctr, 72-74, from asst prof to assoc prof, 72-78, actg dir, 74-76, mem staff, 77-, assoc clin prof, internal medicine, 78-; med care consult, Nat Heart, Lung & Blood Inst, 72-75, extramural prog chief, Nat Inst Allergy & Infectious Dis, NIH, 78-; consult, Children's Nat Med Ctr, 77- *Mem:* Am Thoracic Soc; Am Col Chest Physicians; Am Asn Immunologists; fel Am Col Physicians; Am Acad Allergy & Immunol; Am Fedn Univ Prof. *Res:* Mechanisms of cellular immune responses in infections and non-infectious systemic granulomatous diseases, including sarcoidosis, tuberculosis, aspergillosis and nontuberculous mycobacterial infections. *Mailing Add:* Allergy Immunol & Transplant Nat Inst Allergy & Infectious Diseases NIH SB 4A18 Bethesda MD 20892-0001

GOLDSTEIN, ROBERT HOWELL, SEQUENCE STRATIGRAPHY, DIAGENESIS & FLUID INCLUSIONS. *Current Pos:* From asst prof to assoc prof, 85-96, PROF GEOL, UNIV KANS, 96- *Personal Data:* Baltimore, Md, Nov 22, 57; m 85, Cynthia Keeffe. *Educ:* Juniata Col, BS, 79; Univ Wis-Madison, MS, 81, PhD(geol), 86. *Concurrent Pos:* Co-prin investr, NSF, 88-90, prin investr, 93-95, co-prin investr, 95-, expert panel mem, 96; vis scientist, US Geol Surv, 92; assoc chmn geol, Univ Kans, 93-, actg chmn, 94; lectr fluid inclusions, Soc Sedimentary Geol, 94. *Mem:* Soc Sedimentary Geol; Geol Soc Am; Sigma Xi; Geochem Soc. *Res:* Controls on depositional sequence architecture of the Spanish Miocene; fluid history and diagenesis of the midcontinen; diagenetic significance of brine reflux; Permian paleoclimate; ancient acid fluids; diagenesis in sequence stratigraphy; new fluid inclusion techniques. *Mailing Add:* Dept Geol Univ Kans 120 Lindley Hall Lawrence KS 66045. *Fax:* 785-864-5276; *E-Mail:* gold@kuhub.cc.ukans.edu

GOLDSTEIN, ROBERT LAWRENCE, SOLID STATE LASERS, CRYSTAL GROWTH. *Current Pos:* PRES LASERS & ELECTRO-OPTICS, LASERMETRICS, INC, 65- *Personal Data:* b New York, NY, July 3, 31; m 55; c 2. *Educ:* Newark Col Eng, BSEE, 63; Fla State Univ, PhD, 79. *Prof Exp:* Proj engr stellar invertial navigation, Kearfot Div, Gen Precision, 58-63 & proj engr appolo navigation syst, Barnes Eng, 63-64; dept mgr electronics, Isomet Corp, 64-65. *Concurrent Pos:* Dir & chmn educ comt, Laser Inst Am, 81- *Mem:* Laser Inst Am; Am Asn Crystal Growth; Am Inst Physics; Inst Elec & Electronics Engrs; Optical Soc Am. *Res:* Development of techniques for growth of improved crystals from aqueous solutions; electro-optic crystals and components; development of picosecond optical switching devices. *Mailing Add:* 220 Midland Ave Saddle Brook NJ 07663

GOLDSTEIN, ROBIN SHERYL, INVESTIGATIVE TOXICOLOGY. *Current Pos:* assoc sr investr, 83-88, sr investr, 88-90, ASST DIR INVEST TOXICOL, SMITH KLINE BEECHAM PHARMACEUT, 90- *Personal Data:* b Philadelphia, Pa, Oct 18, 53; m. *Educ:* Mich State Univ, BS, 75, MS, 78, PhD(human nutrit), 82. *Prof Exp:* Res & teaching asst, Dept Food Sci & Human Nutrit, Mich State Univ, 76-78 & 79-82; fel, Dept Gen & Biochem Toxicol, Chem Indust Inst Toxicol, 82-83. *Concurrent Pos:* Lectr, Med Col Pa & Thomas Jefferson Univ, 87-88, Temple Univ, 88 & 89, Tex A&M Univ, 90; mem, Animals Res Comt, Soc Toxicol, 87-90 & In Vitro Toxicol Task Force, Pharmaceut Mfg Asn, 88-; continuing educ comt, Soc Toxicol, 89-91; prog comt, Mid-Atlantic Chap, Soc Toxicol, 91-94; counr mechanisms sect, Soc Toxicol, 93-, Exec Dir Toxicol, Am Soc Pharmacol & Exp Therapeut, 92-94. *Mem:* Soc Toxicol; Am Inst Nutrit; Am Soc Pharmacol & Exp Therapeut; Pharmaceut Mfg Asn; Am Soc Nephrology. *Res:* Mechanisms of nephrotoxicity; age-dependent nephrotoxicity; biochemical mechanisms of cell injury and death; design of chronic toxicity studies; author of more than 70 technical publications; mechanisms of hepatobiliary injury. *Mailing Add:* Dir Exp Toxicol Sandoz Pharmaceut 59 Rte 10 East Hanover NJ 07639. *Fax:* 973-503-6059

GOLDSTEIN, RUBIN, MATHEMATICAL PHYSICS, APPLIED STATISTICS. *Current Pos:* CONSULT SCIENTIST, GOLDSTEIN CONSULT, 87- *Personal Data:* b New York, NY, Mar 29, 33; m 56, Sylvia F Galitzer; c Lori J & Pamela J. *Educ:* Princeton Univ, AB, 55; Harvard Univ, AM, 56, PhD(physics), 60. *Prof Exp:* Res assoc appl physics & instr appl math, Harvard Univ, 60; asst prof nuclear eng, Univ Calif, Berkeley, 60-65; physicist, Dept Appl Sci, Brookhaven Nat Lab, 65-71; consult staff physicist, Dept Physics, Combustion Eng, Inc, 71-73, sr consult physicist, 73-76, sr consult physicist & area mgr, Dept Performance Anal, 77-79, prin consult scientist, nuclear power systs & mgr statist margin develop, 80-82, sr prin consult scientist, Nuclear Power Systs, 83-86. *Concurrent Pos:* Consult, Gen Elec Co, 62-65; adj prof, Columbia Univ, 70, Dept Math Sci, Cent Conn State Univ, 90-, Dept Math, Physics & Comput Sci, Univ Hartford, 90- & Dept Physics, Univ Conn, 93-; consult, Div Reactor Safety Res, US Nuclear Regulatory Comn, Washington, DC, 76-, Combustion Eng, Inc, 87-89, Asea Brown Boveri, 90- & Northeast Utilities, 90-; adj prof, Eng & Comput Info Sci Divs, Hartford Grad Ctr, 77- *Mem:* Am Phys Soc; Am Nuclear Soc. *Res:* Theoretical reactor physics; resonance absorption theory; analytic approximation techniques; transport theory; variational and iterative methods; statistical design of experiments; statistical analysis of scientific and engineering problems; market forecasting, strategic planning; quality control methods and procedures; nuclear material safeguards and accountability; statistical process control. *Mailing Add:* 8 E Normandy Dr West Hartford CT 06107-1405. *Fax:* 860-285-9004

GOLDSTEIN, SAMUEL JOSEPH, (JR), RADIO ASTRONOMY. *Current Pos:* RETIRED. *Personal Data:* b Indianapolis, Ind, June 23, 25; m 56; c 3. *Educ:* Purdue Univ, BS, 48; Stanford Univ, MS, 54, PhD(elec eng), 58. *Prof Exp:* Res engr, Jet Propulsion Lab, Calif Inst Technol, 51-53; actg instr elec eng, Stanford Univ, 55; res asst astron, Harvard Univ, 55-58, res assoc, 58-61, lectr, 61-65; assoc prof astron, Univ Va, 65- *Concurrent Pos:* Consult, Jet Propulsion Lab, Calif Inst Technol, 60-62; vis res off, Astrophys Br, Nat Res Coun Can, 70-71. *Mem:* Inst Elec & Electronics Engrs; Am Astron Soc; Int Astron Union. *Res:* Galactic structure. *Mailing Add:* 117 Cameron Lane Charlottesville VA 22903-3199

GOLDSTEIN, SANDU M, BIOTECHNOLOGY, BIOANALYTICAL CHEMISTRY. *Current Pos:* DIR BIOPROCESS SECTOR, BIOTECHNOL RES INST, MONTREAL, 94- *Personal Data:* b Iasi, Romania, May 22, 36; m 66, Sylvia Weinstein; c Miron. *Educ:* Polytech Inst Iasi, MSc, 58, PhD(anal chem), 75. *Prof Exp:* Chem engr, process eng res & develop, Antibiotics & Vitamines Lab, Iasi, Romania, 58-75; chemist res & develop anal chem, ICN Pharmaceut, Can, 76-77, assoc dir quality control, 77-79, quality control & regulatory affairs, 79-80, dir regulatory affairs, 80-81, dir sci & regulatory affairs, 81-86; dir res, admin & planning, Merck Frosst Ctr Therapeut Res, Can, 86-92, dir, Indust Acad & Govt Affairs, 92-93. *Concurrent Pos:* Nominee, Comt Rev, US Pharmacopeia, 80-85 & 85-90; mem bd dirs, Can Inst Sci & Tech Info, 92-94, Can Mgt Res Asn, 93-, Can Chem Olympiad, 92-94 & Can Soc Chem, 96- *Mem:* Chem Inst Can; Am Chem Soc; Can Soc Chem Eng; fel Royal Soc Chem UK. *Res:* Applied analytical chemistry in fermentation, separation and purification of biological products; isolation and purification of cobalt corrinoids (vitamin B12 group substances); biotechnology; bioprocess engineering biosynthesis: manufacturing of pharmaceutical products. *Mailing Add:* Biotechnol Res Inst Nat Res Coun Can 6100 Royalmount Ave Montreal PQ H4P 2R2 Can. *Fax:* 514-496-7251; *E-Mail:* sander.goldstein@nrc.ca

GOLDSTEIN, SELMA, HYDRODYNAMICS, SOLID STATE PHYSICS. *Current Pos:* MEM STAFF DETONATION PHYSICS, LOS ALAMOS SCI LAB, 77- *Personal Data:* b New York, NY, Feb 28, 49. *Educ:* NY Univ, AB, 69; Yale Univ, MPhil, 71, PhD(appl physics), 74. *Prof Exp:* Battelle Inst fel solid state physics, Battelle Columbus Labs, 74-76. *Mem:* Am Phys Soc. *Res:* Properties of materials at high pressure; physics of detonations; properties of explosives. *Mailing Add:* 28932 Kommers Lane Silverado CA 92676

GOLDSTEIN, SETH RICHARD, BIOMEDICAL INSTRUMENTATION, DYNAMIC SYSTEMS & CONTROL. *Current Pos:* mech engr, 71-80, CHIEF, MECH ENG SECT, BIOMED ENG & INSTRUMENTATION BR, DIV RES SERV, NIH, 80- *Personal Data:* b New York, NY Dec 10, 39; c 1. *Educ:* Mass Inst Technol, BS, 61, MS, 62, MS, 63, ScD(mech eng), 65. *Honors & Awards:* IR 100 Award, 84. *Prof Exp:* Eng scientist, Aerospace Systs Div, RCA, 65-67; proj engr, Foster Miller Assocs, Consult Engrs, 67-71. *Concurrent Pos:* Assoc ed, Transaction J Dynamic Systs Measurement & Control, Am Soc Mech Engrs, 74-77 & J Biomed Eng, 77-83. *Mem:* Fel Am Soc Mech Engrs. *Res:* Conception, analysis, design, development and usage of novel, complex biomedical instrumentation and clinical systems; miniaturized and minimally invasive techniques and sensors. *Mailing Add:* Biomed Eng & Instrumentation Br NIH Bldg 13 Rm 3W13 Bethesda MD 20892

GOLDSTEIN, SHELDON, FOUNDATIONS OF QUANTUM MECHANICS, BOHMIAN MECHANICS. *Current Pos:* PROF MATH, RUTGERS UNIV, 77- *Personal Data:* b Augusta, Ga, Oct 24, 47; m 69, Rebecca Newberger; c Yael & Danielle. *Educ:* Yeshiva Univ, BA, 69, BS, 71, PhD(physics),73. *Mem:* AAAS. *Res:* Finding a coherent account of quantum phenomena. *Mailing Add:* Math Dept Rutgers Univ New Brunswick NJ 08903. *Fax:* 732-445-5530; *E-Mail:* oldstein@math.rutgers.edu

GOLDSTEIN, SIDNEY, CARDIOLOGY. *Current Pos:* EMER HEAD, CARDIOVASC UNIT, HENRY FORD HOSP, DETROIT, 74-; PROF CLIN MED, UNIV MICH, 75-; PROF MED, CASE WESTERN RESERVE UNIV, 96- *Personal Data:* b Utica, NY, Oct 18, 30; m 56; c 2. *Educ:* Cornell Univ, BA, 52, MD, 56. *Prof Exp:* Intern, NY Hosp-Cornell Med Ctr, 56-57, resident, 59-61, NY Heart Asn res fel, 61-62; chief cardiol, Rochester Gen Hosp, 62-74; from asst prof to assoc prof med, Univ Rochester, 66-74. *Concurrent Pos:* Mem coun clin cardiol, Am Heart Asn. *Mem:* Am Fedn Clin Res; fel Am Col Physicians; fel Am Col Cardiol. *Res:* Cardiac physiology. *Mailing Add:* Henry Ford Hosp 2799 W Grand Blvd Detroit MI 48202

GOLDSTEIN, SIDNEY, PHARMACOLOGY. *Current Pos:* VPRES SCI & TECHNOL, DURAMED PHARMACEUT, 95- *Personal Data:* b Philadelphia, Pa, Mar 27, 32; m 55; c 3. *Educ:* Philadelphia Col Pharm, BSc, 54, MSc, 55, DSc, 58. *Prof Exp:* Sr res pharmacologist, Eaton Labs, Norwich Pharmacal Co, 58-59 & Lederle Labs, Am Cyanamid Co, 59-61; sr res pharmacologist, Nat Drug Co, 61-64, dir pharmacol, 64-67, dir prod develop, 67-70; sect head anti-inflammatory & respiratory sects & clin monitor, Med Res Dept, Merrell Dow Pharmaceut Inc, 70-72, assoc group dir, Dept Clin Pharmacol, 72-73, exec asst to vpres res, Merrell-Nat Labs, 74-76, dir pharmaceut sci, 77-93, vpres, 93-94; pres & consult, Pharmaceut Develop Resources, 94-95. *Concurrent Pos:* Lectr, Philadelphia Col Pharm, 67-70; adj assoc prof pharmaceut, Univ Cincinnati, 84- *Mem:* Acad Pharmaceut Sci; Am Soc Clin Pharmacol & Therapeut; Am Pharmaceut Asn; Am Soc Pharmacol & Exp Therapeut; Soc Exp Biol & Med. *Res:* Respiratory research; topical steroids; anti-inflammatory, central nervous system, cardiovascular and biopharmaceutics drugs; pharmaceutics. *Mailing Add:* 1125 Ft View Pl Cincinnati OH 45202

GOLDSTEIN, SOLOMON, MYCOLOGY. *Current Pos:* RETIRED. *Personal Data:* b New York, NY, May 2, 29; m 54. *Educ:* City Col New York, BA, 52; Univ Mich, MS, 53, PhD(bot), 59. *Prof Exp:* Instr bot, Univ Mich, 58-59; asst prof biol, State Univ NY Stony Brook, 59-60; res assoc microbiol, Yale Univ, 60-64; dep chmn, Grad Div, 64-69, actg dean, Sch Sci, 76-77, PROF BIOL, BROOKLYN COL, 69-; dean res, Grad Ctr, City Univ NY, 79-92. *Mem:* Bot Soc Am; Mycol Soc Am; Am Soc Microbiol; Am Soc Protozool; Brit Soc Gen Microbiol. *Res:* Physiology and morphology of marine phycomycetes. *Mailing Add:* 1200 Fifth Ave Apt 9C New York NY 10029

GOLDSTEIN, STANLEY P(HILIP), ASTRONAUTICAL ENGINEERING. *Current Pos:* prof, Hofstra Univ, 54-84, chmn dept, 57-69, 71-73 & 80-83, dir acad comput ctr, 71-74, assoc provost, 74-76, assoc dean, 77-79, dir, C Step Prog, 87-89, EMER PROF ENG, HOFSTRA UNIV, 84-; PRES, TECHMARK ENTERPRISES, 84- *Personal Data:* b Brooklyn, NY, Feb 3, 23; m 49, Wanda Rouse; c Bruce & Richard. *Educ:* Univ Okla, BS, 49; NY Univ, MS, 56; Polytech Inst Brooklyn, PhD(astronaut), 69. *Prof Exp:* Develop engr, Vapor Recovery Systs, Co, 50-52; proj engr, Aldison Res Labs, 52-54. *Concurrent Pos:* Dir domestic opers, Hofstra Int Trade & Develop Corp, 85-87. *Mem:* Sigma Xi. *Res:* Compressible flow; free convection heat transfer; computer science. *Mailing Add:* 18 Millers Lane Kingston NY 12401

GOLDSTEIN, STEVEN ALAN, MECHANICAL ENGINEERING & APPLIED MECHANICS. *Current Pos:* Res investr surg, 81-83, from asst prof to assoc prof surg, 83-92, PROF SURG, UNIV MICH, ANN ARBOR, 92-, PROF, MECH ENG & APPLI MECH, 92-; RES SCIENTIST, INST GERONT, UNIV MICH MED SCH, 93-. ASST DEAN RES & GRAD STUDIES, 93- *Personal Data:* b Reading, Pa Sept 15, 54; M 76, Nancy E Gehr; c Aaron M & Jonathan D. *Educ:* Tufts Univ, BS, 76; Univ Mich, MS, 77, PhD(bioeng), 81. *Honors & Awards:* Young Res Investr Award, 3m Corp, 84-; Nicolas Andre Award, Asn Bone & Joint Surgeons, 87-88; Y C Fung Young Investr Award, 87. *Concurrent Pos:* Res asst, Bioeng Ctr, Tufts, New Eng Med Ctr, 74-76; co-dir, orthop biomechanics lab, Univ Mich, 81-82, dir, Orthop Res Labs, 82-, adj asst prof mech eng & appl mech, 85-88, adj assoc prof mech eng & appl mech, 88-92; res dir, adv, Univ Mich Med Ctr, 81-, mem fac bioeng prog, 82-, interim chmn, 85-89; consult, Libbey-Owens, Ill, Gen Tire & Rubber, Upjohn, Ethyl Corp, Norwich Eaton, KMS Fusion, Whitby Pharmaceut, Norian Corp, Genetics Inst, Ann Arbor Vet Admin Med Ctr, 84-87; mem calcium homeostasis adv group, NASA, 87-89; mem bd assoc ed, J Bone & Joint Surg, 89-; assoc ed, J Biomech Eng, 92- *Mem:* Am Soc Mech Eng; Am Soc Biomechanics; Am Acad Orthop Surgeons; Orthop Res Soc; Biomed Eng Soc; Knee Soc. *Res:* Intracone reamer, instacone prosthetic surface, flexible connecting shaft for intramedullary reamer, tissue pressure measurement transducer system, continuous flow tissue pressure measurement transducer system, prosthesis interface surface and method of implanting. *Mailing Add:* Univ Mich Surg/Orthop 400 N Ingalls Bldg Rm G-0161 Ann Arbor MI 48109-0486

GOLDSTEIN, STUART FREDERICK, CELL PHYSIOLOGY. *Current Pos:* ASSOC PROF GENETICS & CELL BIOL, UNIV MINN, ST PAUL, 77- *Personal Data:* b Beloit, Wis, Sept 11, 39; m 78, Mary Martini; c Sarah & Laura. *Educ:* Univ Minn, BA, 62; Calif Inst Technol, PhD(cell biol), 68. *Prof Exp:* Med Res Coun Gt Brit grant, Queen Elizabeth Col, London, 68-69; USPHS grant, Univ Calif, Berkeley, 69-71; asst prof zool, Univ Minn, Minneapolis, 71-77. *Concurrent Pos:* NSF grant, Univ Poitiers, France, 77-78. *Mem:* Am Soc Cell Biol; AAAS; Sigma Xi. *Res:* Flagellar and bacterial motility. *Mailing Add:* Dept Genetics & Cell Biol Univ Minn St Paul MN 55108. *Fax:* 612-625-5754; *E-Mail:* golds004@staff.tc.umn.edu

GOLDSTEIN, SUSAN T, MICROPALEONTOLOGY, PALEOECOLOGY. *Current Pos:* from asst prof to assoc prof, 84-92, ASSOC PROF GEOL & MARINE SCI, UNIV GA, 92- *Personal Data:* b Wooster, Ohio, June 24, 52. *Educ:* Bowling Green State Univ, BS, 74; Univ Fla, MS, 76; Univ Calif, Berkeley, PhD(paleont), 84. *Concurrent Pos:* Prin investr, NSF, 89-91. *Mem:* Cushman Found Foraminiferal Res; Paleont Soc; Soc Sedimentary Geol; Sigma Xi; AAAS. *Res:* Biology, paleobiology and paleoecology of benthic foraminifera; their roles in modern and ancient oceans. *Mailing Add:* Dept Geol Univ Ga Athens GA 30602

GOLDSTEIN, THEODORE PHILIP, ORGANIC CHEMISTRY, GEOCHEMISTRY. *Current Pos:* CONSULT, WORLDWIDE GEOSCI, INC, 94- *Personal Data:* b Baltimore, Md, Feb 23, 28; m 68. *Educ:* Johns Hopkins Univ, BA, 51, MA, 58, PhD(chem), 61. *Prof Exp:* Chemist, US Army Chem Corps, 52-55 & Sinai Hosp, Baltimore, 55-56; res chemist, Cent Res Lab, Mobil Oil Co, Inc, 61-63; sr res chemist, Mobil Res & Develop Corp, 63-75, assoc, 75-93. *Concurrent Pos:* Assoc ed, Org Geochem, 77-82. *Mem:* AAAS; Sigma Xi; Am Chem Soc; NY Acad Sci; Catalysis Soc; Am Inst Chem. *Res:* Histochemistry; catalysis; organic geochemistry; origin of oil; low temperature catalytic reactions; enzyme models. *Mailing Add:* 16 Springtree Yardley PA 19067-1830

GOLDSTEIN, WALTER ELLIOTT, FERMENTATION & CELL CULTURE, PHARMACEUTICALS. *Current Pos:* PRES & FOUNDER, GOLDSTEIN CONSULTING CO, 94- *Personal Data:* b Chicago, Ill, Nov 28, 40; m 62, Paula Copen; c Susan & Marc. *Educ:* Ill Inst Technol, BS, 61; Mich State Univ, MBA, 68; Univ Notre Dame, MS, 71, PhD(chem eng), 73. *Prof Exp:* Develop engr cryogenics, Linde Div, Union Carbide Corp, 61-64; assoc proj engr pharmaceut & chem, Corp Eng Div, Miles Labs Inc, 64-67, assoc res scientist clin diag tests, Ames Div, 67-72, res scientist, 72-74, res supvr, 74-76, mgr chem eng res & pilot serv, Marschall Div, 76-78, dir chem eng res & pilot serv, biotechnol group res & develop, 78-82, vpres res & develop, biotechnol group, 82-87; vpres & dir res, ESCA Genetics Corp, 87-94. *Concurrent Pos:* Adj prof chem eng, Univ Notre Dame, 74-75, San Jose State Univ, 95-96; advisor mat, biotech, energy, Nat Acad Sci, 86-87, biotechnol, Nat Inst Stand & Technol, 87-91; indust eng consult, 87. *Mem:* Sigma Xi; AAAS; Am Inst Chem Engrs; NY Acad Sci; Inst Food Technologists; Am Asn Pharmacognosy. *Res:* Technology and business analysis; chemical engineering and biotechnology; fermentation and cell culture; process development and bioprocesses; phytochemicals; clinical diagnostics; business development; research management; agricultural development; plant cell culture; pharmaceuticals from plants. *Mailing Add:* 4 E Court Lane Foster City CA 94404-2133. *Fax:* 650-638-1906; *E-Mail:* goldconsul@aol.com

GOLDSTICK, THOMAS KARL, PHYSIOLOGICAL OXYGEN TRANSPORT. *Current Pos:* from asst prof to assoc prof chem eng & biol sci, 67-81, PROF CHEM ENG, BIOMED ENG, NEUROBIOL & PHYSIOL, NORTHWESTERN UNIV, 81- *Personal Data:* b Toronto, Ont, Aug 21, 34; m 82, Marcia A. *Educ:* Mass Inst Technol, BS, 57, MS, 59; Univ Calif, Berkeley, PhD(eng sci), 66. *Prof Exp:* Res engr iron ore, Jones & Laughlin Steel Corp, 59-61; asst res engr mech eng & surg, Univ Calif, Berkeley & San Francisco, 66-67. *Concurrent Pos:* NIH spec res fel, Univ Calif, San Diego, 71-73; assoc staff mem, Evanston Hosp, 71-; mem bd dir, Biomed Eng Soc, 83-86; chmn, Publ Bd, 85-87. *Mem:* Biomed Eng Soc; Int Soc Oxygen Transp Tissue (secy, 81-86); Am Inst Chem Engrs; Microcirc Soc; Asn Res Vision & Opthal. *Res:* Mass transport in biological and medical systems, applying traditional engineering techniques to living systems; oxygen transport in the cornea, retina and choroid of the eye; diabetes mellitus; oxygen transport to and in tissue, retinal vascular disease and impaired oxygen transport; perfluorocarbon artificial blood; whole blood coagulation parameters by thrombelastography in diabetes; correlated with retinal microvascular disease. *Mailing Add:* 2025 Sherman Ave No 504 Evanston IL 60201. *Fax:* 847-491-3728; *E-Mail:* goldstick@hwu.edu

GOLDSTINE, HERMAN HEINE, NUMERICAL ANALYSIS. *Current Pos:* assoc proj dir, Electronic Comput Proj, 46-55, actg proj dir, 54-57, MEM, INST ADVAN STUDY, 52-; EXEC OFFICER, AM PHILOS SOC, 84. *Personal Data:* b Chicago, Ill, Sept 13, 13; m 41, 66, Ellen Watson; c Jonthan & Madien. *Educ:* Univ Chicago, BS, 33, MS, 34, PhD(math), 36. *Hon Degrees:* PhD, Lund Univ, Sweden, 74; DSc, Adelphi Univ, 78, Anherst Col, 78, Rutgers Univ, 94,. *Honors & Awards:* Harry Goode Award, 79; Charter Pioneer Award, 82; Nat Medal Sci, 83. *Prof Exp:* Assoc & instr math, Univ Chicago, 36-39; instr, Univ Mich, 39-42, asst prof, 42-50; IBM fel, Thomas J Watson Res Ctr, IBM Corp, 69. *Concurrent Pos:* Dir sci develop, math sci, IBM Corp, 60-65 & Data Processing Div, 65-67, consult to dir res, 67-69; mem adv coun, Phys Sci Div, Univ Chicago. *Mem:* Nat Acad Sci; Am Math Soc; Math Asn Am; Am Philos Soc; AAAS. *Res:* Applied mathmatics; electronic computers; history of computers and mathematics. *Mailing Add:* Am Philos Soc 150 S Independence Mall E Philadelphia PA 19106-3387. *Fax:* 215-440-3430

GOLDSTON, ROBERT J, PLASMA PHYSICS. *Current Pos:* res asst, Plasma Physics Lab, Princeton Univ, 72-77, res staff, 77-81, res physicist, 81-84, prin res physicist, 84-92, PROF ASTROPHYS SCI, PLASMA PHYSICS LAB, PRINCETON UNIV, 92- *Personal Data:* b May 6, 50; c 2. *Educ:* Harvard Col, BA, 72; Princeton Univ, PhD(astro phys), 77. *Honors & Awards:* Prize for Excellence in Plasma Physics, Am Phys Soc, 86. *Prof Exp:* Res aide, Francis Bitter Nat Magnet Lab, Mass Inst Technol, 71-72. *Concurrent Pos:* Prog comt invited papers, Div Plasma Physics, Am Phys Soc, 84 & 94, prog comt contributed papers, 84, prog comt, 86, select comt for prize in excellence in plasma physics, 90, fel comt, 91; prog comt, Conf Plasma Physics & Controlled Fusion, Int Atomic Energy Asn, 88 & 94; energy resources strategic planning group, Dept Energy, 93- *Mem:* Fel Am Phys Soc. *Res:* Plasma physics; author of over 200 publications. *Mailing Add:* Plasma Physics Lab Princeton Univ Princeton NJ 08543

GOLDSTONE, ALFRED D, MECHANISM OF HORMONE ACTION, BIOCHEMISTRY. *Current Pos:* ASSOC PROF NEUROL & BIOCHEM, NORTHWESTERN MED SCH, 80- *Educ:* St Louis Univ, PhD(pharmacol), 64. *Mailing Add:* Dept Neurol Molelcular Biol NW Univ Med Sch 303 E Chicago Ave Chicago IL 60611-3008

GOLDSTONE, JEFFREY, THEORETICAL PHYSICS, ELEMENTARY PARTICLE PHYSICS. *Current Pos:* PROF PHYSICS, MASS INST TECHNOL, 77- *Personal Data:* b Manchester, Eng, Sept 3, 33; m 80, Roberta Gordon; c Andrew. *Educ:* Cambridge Univ, BA, 54, PhD(theoret physics), 58. *Honors & Awards:* Heineman Prize, Am Phys Soc, 81; Guthrie Medal, Inst Physics, London, 83; Dirac Medal, Int Ctr Theoret Physics, 91. *Prof Exp:* Res fel, Trinity Col, Cambridge, 56-60; lectr appl math & theoret physics, Cambridge Univ, 61-76, reader math physics, 76. *Concurrent Pos:* Staff fel, Trinity Col, Cambridge, 62-81; dir, Ctr Theoret Physics, Mass Inst Technol, 83-89. *Mem:* Am Acad Arts & Sci; fel Am Phys Soc; Royal Soc London. *Res:* Theoretical particle physics and quantum field theory. *Mailing Add:* 6-313 Mass Inst Technol Cambridge MA 02139. *Fax:* 617-253-8674; *E-Mail:* goldstone@mitlns.mit.edu

GOLDSTONE, PHILIP DAVID, PHYSICS. *Current Pos:* Appointee nuclear physics, Los Alamos Nat Lab, Univ Calif, 76-77, mem staff laser & plasma physics, 77-81, group leader, laser matter interaction exp, 81-89, prog mgr inertial confinement fusion exp, 87-89, MEM STAFF, WEAPONS TECHNOL PROG, LOS ALAMOS NAT LAB, UNIV CALIF, 89- *Personal Data:* b Brooklyn, NY, Mar 5, 50; m 72, 90. *Educ:* Polytech Inst Brooklyn,

BS, 71, MS, 72; State Univ NY, Stony Brook, PhD(physics), 75. *Mem:* Am Phys Soc; Sigma Xi; Optical Soc Am. *Res:* Study of interactions of matter with intense laser beams; physics of inertial confinement fusion including physics of dense plasmas. *Mailing Add:* 2723 Caballero Del Sur Sante Fe NM 87505-6532

GOLDTHWAIT, DAVID ATWATER, BIOCHEMISTRY, MOLECULAR BIOLOGY. *Current Pos:* From asst prof to assoc prof biochem & med, 51-68, PROF BIOCHEM, SCH MED, CASE WESTERN RES UNIV, 68-, PROF MED, 78. *Personal Data:* b Providence, RI, Nov 7, 21; m 49; c 4. *Educ:* Columbia Univ, MD, 45. *Mem:* Am Soc Biol Chemists; Am Soc Clin Invest; Sigma Xi. *Res:* Nucleic acids; metabolism; cancer. *Mailing Add:* Dept Biochem Case Western Reserve Univ Sch Med Cleveland OH 44106

GOLDTHWAIT, R(ICHARD) G(RAHAM), CHEMICAL ENGINEERING. *Current Pos:* RETIRED. *Personal Data:* b Duluth, Minn, Feb 9, 19; wid; c Richard G Jr & Allen T. *Educ:* Pa State Univ, BS, 40. *Prof Exp:* Asst, Pa State Univ, 40-41; buyer, Westinghouse Elec Corp, 41-43; proj leader & chem engr, Gulf Res & Develop Co, 43-49, asst group leader, 49-53, group leader, 53-56, asst sect head, 56-60, sect supvr, 60-65, staff engr, 65-66, tech consult, 66-72, Gulf Res Lab, Neth, 69-72, dir planning & coord, refinery dept, Gulf Oil-Eastern Hemisphere, London, 72-75, safety adv, 75-76, sr staff engr, Gulf Sci & Technol Co, 76-82. *Mem:* Am Chem Soc; Am Inst Chem Engrs. *Res:* Pilot plant work in petroleum refining and related fields; catalytic reforming; thermal and catalytic cracking; isomerization; distillation; hydrogenative processes; correlation development; process control; coal liquefaction. *Mailing Add:* 114 Kinvara Ct Pittsburgh PA 15237-3922

GOLDTHWAITE, DUNCAN, PETROLEUM GEOLOGY, EXPLORATION. *Current Pos:* CONSULT GEOLOGIST, 85- *Personal Data:* b New York, NY, Mar 31, 27; m 56, Margaret Temple; c Madelyn (Hamilton), Virginia (Clark), Mary (Pollard) & Martha. *Educ:* Oberlin Col, BA, 50; Harvard Univ, MA, 52. *Honors & Awards:* Distinguished Serv Award, Gulf Coast Asn Geol Soc, 95. *Prof Exp:* Geologist, Chevron Oil Co, NDak & SDak, 52-54, geophysicist, Miss & NLa, 54-57, dist geologist, NLa, 57-58, Mich & Appalachians, 58-64, sr geologist, SLa & Atlantic Coast Phosphates & Appalachians, 64-77, sr geologist, Tex Coast, 78-85; teacher subsurface geol mapping, Atwater Consult, New Orleans, 86-; petrol res estimates. *Mem:* Fel Geol Soc Am; Am Asn Petrol Geol; Soc Indust Prof Earth Scientists. *Res:* Structure and stratigraphy as related to petroleum in Michigan, Appalachians, and Gulf Coast; phosphate investigations; subsurface mapping. *Mailing Add:* 4608 James Dr Metairie LA 70003

GOLDWASSER, EDWIN LEO, PHYSICS. *Current Pos:* res assoc, Univ, Ill, Urbana, 51-53, from asst prof to prof,. *Personal Data:* b New York, NY, Mar 9, 19; m 40; c 5. *Educ:* Harvard Univ, BA, 40; Univ Calif, Berkeley, PhD(physics), 50. *Prof Exp:* Physicist, Degaussing Ships, Bur Ord, Dept Navy, 41-43, sr physicist, Navy Yard, Mare Island, 43-45; asst physics, Univ Calif, Berkeley, 46-49, res assoc, 50-51; dep dir, Fermi Lab, 67-78; assoc dir, Cent Design Group, Superconducting Super-Collider, 86-88. *Concurrent Pos:* Consult, Phys Sci Study Comt, 56-61; Fulbright & Guggenheim fels, Univ Rome, 57-58; vchmn div phys sci, Nat Res Coun, 61-66, chmn, 66-68; mem panel high energy accelerator physics, Gen Adv Comt, AEC & President's Sci Adv Comt, 62-63; mem physics surv comt, Nat Acad Sci, 63-65, site selection comt, 65-66; mem sci adv comn, State of Ill, 67-70; mem comn on particles & fields, Int Union Pure & Appl Physics, 72-81, secy, 75-78, chmn, 78-81; mem, US-USSR Joint Coord Comt Fundamental Properties of Matter, 75-78 & Int Comn Future Accelerators, 78-81; chmn, Sci & Educ Adv comt, Univ Calif, 86- *Mem:* Fel Am Phys Soc; Fedn Am Sci; Sigma Xi. *Res:* Elementary particle physics; cosmic rays; electron and photon interactions; ion physics. *Mailing Add:* 612 W Delaware Urbana IL 61801

GOLDWASSER, EUGENE, BIOCHEMISTRY. *Current Pos:* Res assoc, Univ Chicago, 52-56, from asst prof to assoc prof, 56-63, chmn, Comt Develop Biol, 76-88, chmn, Dept Biochem & Molecular Biol, 84-85; PROF BIOCHEM, UNIV CHICAGO, 63-, CHMN, DEPT BIOCHEM & MOLECULAR BIOL, 94- *Personal Data:* b New York, NY, Oct 14, 22; m 49, 86, Deone Jackman; c Thomas A, Matthew L & James H. *Educ:* Univ Chicago, SB, 43, PhD(biochem), 50. *Hon Degrees:* ScD, NY Med Col. *Honors & Awards:* Ann Langer Award, Cancer Res, 87; Annual Prize of Int Soc Blood Purification, 88; William Simpson Award, Wayne State Univ, 91; Karl Lansteiner Award, Am Asn Blood Banks, 96. *Concurrent Pos:* Am Cancer Soc fel, Copenhagen Univ, 50-52; Guggenheim fel, Dept Biochem, Oxford Univ, 66-67. *Mem:* Fel AAAS; Am Soc Biol Chem; Biochem Soc; Endocrine Soc; Int Soc Exp Hemat; Am Soc Hemat; fel Am Acad Arts & Sci. *Res:* Biochemistry of differentiation; biochemistry of erythropoiesis and erythropoietin. *Mailing Add:* Dept Biochem & Molecular Biol Univ Chicago 920 E 58th St Chicago IL 60637. *Fax:* 773-702-0439

GOLDWASSER, SAMUEL M, IMAGE PROCESSING & DISPLAY, COMPUTER ARCHITECTURE. *Current Pos:* TECH DIR VISUALIZATION CT DIV, PICKER INC, 92- *Personal Data:* b Philadelphia, Pa. *Educ:* Drexel Univ, BS, 74; Mass Inst Technol, MS, 76, PhD(elec eng), 79. *Prof Exp:* Asst prof, Comput Sci & Elec Eng, Univ Pa, 80-86, co-dir, Gen Robotics & Active Sensory Processing Lab & dir, Digital Systs Lab, 85-92. *Concurrent Pos:* IBM fel, 78; consult, Assoc Press, Providence Gravure Inc, Psychol Dept, Mass Inst Technol, OCR Syst, E I du Pont, Glassboro State Col & RCA. *Mem:* Sigma Xi; Inst Elec & Electronics Engrs. *Res:* Special purpose computer architecture and digital hardware design for image processing, graphics, machine perception and robotics; real-time interactive display and manipulation of 3-D medical objects. *Mailing Add:* Picker Int Suite 100-G 130 Radnor-Chester Rd St Davids PA 19087

GOLDWATER, WILLIAM HENRY, RESEARCH CONTRACT & GRANT PROJECT MANAGEMENT. *Current Pos:* PVT CONSULT, 93- *Personal Data:* b Plattsburgh, NY, Apr 4, 21; m 48, Marilyn Rubin; c Charles A & Diane L. *Educ:* Columbia Univ, AB, 41, PhD(biochem), 47. *Honors & Awards:* Dir Award, NIH, 78; Super Serv Award, Pub Health Serv, 89. *Prof Exp:* Res technician, Mt Sinai Hosp, NY, 41-42; asst, Columbia Univ, 42-43, div war res, 43-45, med sch, 46-47; res chemist, Mt Sinai Hosp, 47-48; res assoc, Sch Med, Tulane Univ, 48-49, assoc, 49-51, asst prof biochem & med, 51; radiol biochemist, US Naval Radiol Defense Lab, 52-59; exec secy, Metab Study Sect, Div Res Grants, NIH, 59-62, chief, Spec Res Projs, Nat Heart Inst, 62-69, assoc dir extramural Progs, Nat Inst Environ Health Sci, 69-70, spec asst to assoc dir extramural res & training & to dir, Extramural Progs Mgt Off dir, 70-93. *Concurrent Pos:* Mem res & develop & grants study groups, Comn Govt Procurement, 71-72. *Mem:* Fel AAAS; Am Chem Soc; fel Am Heart Asn (secy, 84-85); NY Acad Sci; Soc Res Adminr; Nat Grants Mgt Asn (secy, 84-85). *Res:* Biomedical research administration and policy; peer review; statutory, regulation and legal issues in research and development contract and grant policies and procedures; statutory and regulation bases for peer review advisory functions; freedom, privacy and confidentiality of information; standards of conduct, conflicts of interest human subjects. *Mailing Add:* 5508 Durbin Rd Bethesda MD 20814. *Fax:* 301-652-2199; *E-Mail:* depmobg@aol.com

GOLDWEIN, MANFRED ISAAC, INTERNAL MEDICINE, HEMATOLOGY. *Current Pos:* From asst instr to asst prof, 55-75, ASSOC PROF MED, UNIV PA, 75- *Personal Data:* b Bochum, Ger, Apr 19, 24; US citizen; m 49; c 3. *Educ:* Univ Del, BS, 50; Univ Vt, MD, 54. *Mem:* Am Col Physicians; Am Soc Hemat. *Res:* Clinical hematology; vitamin B12 metabolism; ineffective erythropoiesis. *Mailing Add:* Univ Pa Col Med Philadelphia PA 19104

GOLDWHITE, HAROLD, INORGANIC CHEMISTRY. *Current Pos:* from asst prof to assoc prof, 62-67, PROF CHEM, CALIF STATE UNIV, LOS ANGELES, 67- *Personal Data:* b London, Eng, Dec 25, 31; m 58; c 4. *Educ:* Univ Cambridge, BA, 53, PhD(chem), 56. *Prof Exp:* Res assoc chem, Cornell Univ, 56-58; lectr, Univ Manchester, 58-62. *Mem:* Am Chem Soc; Royal Chem Soc; Sigma Xi; AAAS. *Res:* Chemistry of compounds containing phosphorus; fluorine chemistry; organometallic chemistry. *Mailing Add:* Dept Chem Calif State Univ Los Angeles CA 90032

GOLDWIRE, HENRY C, JR, THERMAL & NUCLEAR PHYSICS. *Current Pos:* TEST DIR & RELEASE SOURCE PHYSICIST, REMOTE SENSOR TEST RANGE, US DEPT ENERGY NEV TEST SITE, LAWRENCE LIVERMORE NAT LAB, 80-, CONTAINMENT PHYSICIST, EARTH SCI DEPT, 80- *Educ:* Rice Univ, BA, 63, PhD(space physics & astron), 67. *Prof Exp:* Res fel, Kellogg Radiation Lab, Calif Inst Technol, 67-68; asst prof, Space Sci Dept, Rice Univ, 68-75; hydrodyn physicist, Nuclear Testing Prog, Los Alamos Nat Lab, 75-80. *Concurrent Pos:* Partic, US Deleg Nuclear Testing Talks, Geneva, 88; measurement scientist, Joint Verification Exp, NTS & Semipalatinsk, USSR, 88. *Mem:* Int Astron Union; Am Phys Soc. *Res:* Containment of underground nuclear explosions; hydrodynamic yield analysis; author of numerous scientific publications. *Mailing Add:* Lawrence Livermore Nat Lab L-221 PO Box 808 Livermore CA 94551

GOLDWYN, ROBERT MALCOLM, PLASTIC & RECONSTRUCTIVE SURGERY OF THE BREAST. *Current Pos:* CLIN PROF SURG, HARVARD MED SCH, 72-; DIR, DIV PLASTIC SURG, BETH ISRAEL HOSP, 72- *Personal Data:* b Worcester, Mass, Sept 17, 30; m 58, Roberta Mildender; c Linda (Isaacs) & Laura A (Brissot). *Educ:* Harvard Univ, AB, 56, MD, 56. *Honors & Awards:* Dieffenbach Medal, Charite Hosp & Humboldt Univ, 92; Spec Achievement Award, Am Soc Plastic & Reconstructive Surgeons, 92. *Concurrent Pos:* John B Erich vis prof plastic surg, Mayo Med Sch, 91; Kazanjian vis prof, NY Univ Med Ctr, 93. *Mem:* Am Asn Plastic Surgeons (pres). *Res:* Unfavorable results in plastic surgery; clinical problems in plastic surgery; experimental limb transplantation. *Mailing Add:* 1101 Beacon St Brookline MA 02146-5502. *Fax:* 617-720-5525

GOLDWYN, ROGER M(ARTIN), COMPUTER SCIENCE, APPLIED MATHEMATICS. *Current Pos:* PRODUCER & DEVELOP MGR, SPEECH DICTATION RECOGNITION POWER PERSONAL SYSTS DIV, BOCA RATON, FLA, 92- *Personal Data:* b Tulsa, Okla, Dec 18, 36; m 64, Carol; c Jodi & Andrew. *Educ:* Rice Univ, BA, 58, BS, 59, MS, 60; Harvard Univ, AM, 61, PhD(appl math), 64. *Prof Exp:* Asst prof eng, Rice Univ, 64-66; mem res staff, Thomas J Watson Res Ctr, IBM Mach Corp, 67-70, mgr, Comput Sci Dept, 71-77, sr mgr prototype systs, Thomas J Watson Res Ctr, IBM Corp, 77-84, mgr adv systs prod, IBM, 84-87, prog mng, IBM Entry Systs Div, Boca Raton, Fla, 88-92. *Concurrent Pos:* NSF grant, 64-66; consult, Guid & Control Div, Manned Spacecraft Ctr, NASA, Vet Admin Hosp, Houston & Esso Prod Res Lab, 64-66; asst clin prof, Albert Einstein Col Med & lectr, Dept Elec Eng, Univ Conn, 69-71. *Mem:* Sigma Xi; Inst Elec & Electronics Engrs. *Res:* Computer sciences; speech; communications; multivariate; biomedical data analysis; stability problems in control theory. *Mailing Add:* 5428 NW 20th Ave Boca Raton FL 33496-3441

GOLDYNE, MARC E, DERMATOLOGY, PROSTAGLANDINS. *Current Pos:* ASSOC PROF MED, UNIV CALIF, SAN FRANCISCO, 84-; ASST CHIEF DERMAT, SAN FRANCISCO VET ADMIN MED CTR, 85- *Personal Data:* b San Francisco, Calif, Oct 15, 44. *Educ:* Univ Calif, San Francisco, MD, 70; Univ Minn, PhD(dermat), 80. *Mailing Add:* Dept Med & Dermat Vet Admin Med Ctr MS190 Univ Calif 4150 Clement St San Francisco CA 94121-1598. *Fax:* 415-751-3927

GOLE, JAMES LESLIE, HIGH TEMPERATURE CHEMICAL PHYSICS. *Current Pos:* from assoc prof to prof chem, 77-83, PROF PHYSICS, GA INST TECHNOL, 83- *Personal Data:* b Chicago, Ill, Sept 17, 45; m 70. *Educ:* Univ Calif, Santa Barbara, BS, 67; Rice Univ, PhD(chem), 71. *Honors & Awards:* Sustained Res Award, Sigma Xi. *Prof Exp:* Asst prof chem, Mass Inst Technol, 73-77. *Concurrent Pos:* NSF fel, 71-73; mem, Nat Res Coun, 85-; consult, Sanders Assocs, 85- *Mem:* Am Chem Soc; Am Physical Soc; AAAS; Sigma Xi. *Res:* Laser induced fluorescence applied to the study of small metal clusters and the products of their oxidation; chemiluminescent techniques applied as a probe of metal cluster and surface oxidation; molecular electronic structure, ultrafast energy transfer and molecular dynamics; chemical lasers; quantum chemistry. *Mailing Add:* Dept Physics Ga Inst Technol Atlanta GA 30332

GOLEMAN, D(ENZIL), ECONOMIC ENTOMOLOGY. *Current Pos:* RETIRED. *Personal Data:* b Coles Co, Ill, Jan 3, 24; m 52; c 3. *Educ:* Eastern Ill State Univ, BS, 49; Iowa State Univ, MS, 51, PhD(entom), 54. *Prof Exp:* Assoc, Agr Exp Sta & Agr Exten Serv, Iowa State Univ, 51-54; from asst exten entomologist to exten entomologist, Ohio State Univ, 54-59; entomologist, Am Cyanamid Co, 59-65; exten specialist agr chem, Ohio State Univ, 65-68, chmn, Dept Entom, 68-83, prof, 83-89. *Mem:* AAAS; Entom Soc Am. *Res:* Management of insect pests; use of insecticides including benefits and risks. *Mailing Add:* 2261 Pinebrook Rd Columbus OH 43220

GOLEMBA, FRANK JOHN, POLYMER CHEMISTRY, REINFORCED PLASTICS. *Current Pos:* MGR TECH SERV ORGN, OWENS CORNING, 94- *Personal Data:* b Hamilton, Ont, Dec 3, 43; m 67; c 2. *Educ:* Univ Toronto, BSc, 65, MSc, 67, PhD(polymer chem), 70. *Prof Exp:* Res scientist & mgr anal, polyester chem & res & develop, Indust Mat Group, 70-89, gen mgr mia chem & mgr textiles & reinforcements mkt, 89-94. *Mem:* Soc Plastics Engrs; Am Chem Soc; fel Chem Inst Can. *Res:* Polymer synthesis, structure and properties; reinforced polymers; polymer photochemistry; chemistry of the matrix reinforcement interface; rheology and cure behavior of thermosetting resins; unsaturated polyesters; analytical research characterizing glass bonding thermoset resin behavior; cure and high temperature behavior; industrial hygiene. *Mailing Add:* Owens Corning 165 York Rd Guelph ON N1E 3G1 Can

GOLENBERG, EDWARD MICHAEL, MOLECULAR EVOLUTION, ANCIENT DNA. *Current Pos:* ASST PROF, WAYNE STATE UNIV, 90- *Personal Data:* b Cleveland, Ohio, Feb 13, 52. *Educ:* Johns Hopkins Univ, BA, 74; State Univ NY, Stony Brook, PhD(ecol & evolution), 86. *Prof Exp:* Instr, Haifa Univ, 82-86; fel, Univ Calif-Riverside, 86-90. *Res:* Analysis of the evolution of the chloroplast genome; recovery and analysis of ancient and fossil DNA. *Mailing Add:* Dept Biol Sci Wayne State Univ 210 Sci Hall Detroit MI 48202-3940

GOLES, GORDON GEORGE, TECTONICS, ARCHAEOLOGY. *Current Pos:* assoc prof, 67-72, dir, Ctr Volcanology, 71-74, PROF CHEM & GEOL, UNIV ORE, 72- *Personal Data:* b Chicago, Ill, Mar 6, 34; m 63; c 2. *Educ:* Harvard Univ, AB, 56; Univ Chicago, PhD(chem), 61. *Prof Exp:* Asst res chemist, Univ Calif, San Diego, 61-62, asst prof chem, 62-67. *Mem:* AAAS; Sigma Xi; Geol Soc NZ. *Res:* Volcanism and Tectonics; trace element geochemistry; activation analysis; archaeology. *Mailing Add:* Dept Geol Sci 1272 Univ Ore Eugene OR 97403-1272

GOLET, FRANCIS CHARLES, WILDLIFE ECOLOGY, WETLAND ECOLOGY. *Current Pos:* ASSOC PROF NATURAL RESOURCES SCI, UNIV RI, 72- *Personal Data:* b Middletown, Conn, Nov 20, 45; m 72; c 1. *Educ:* Brown Univ, BA, 67; Cornell Univ, MS, 69; Univ Mass, PhD(wildlife biol), 73. *Mem:* Wildlife Soc; Wilson Ornithol Soc; Ecol Soc Am. *Res:* Wetland classification and evaluation; wetland plant ecology and wetland wildlife ecology; wetland habitat management. *Mailing Add:* Nat Res Univ RI Kingston RI 02881

GOLIBER, EDWARD WILLIAM, INORGANIC CHEMISTRY, METALLURGY. *Current Pos:* CONSULT, 83- *Personal Data:* b Buffalo, NY, Nov 21, 20; m 52; c 4. *Educ:* Canisius Col, BS, 43; Mass Inst Technol, PhD(chem), 48. *Prof Exp:* Lab technician, Nat Aniline Div, Allied Chem & Dye Corp, NY, 41-42; res chemist, Linde Air Prod Co, NY, 43-46; sr res chemist, Carboloy Dept, Gen Elec Co, 48-58, consult engr, Carboloy Syst Dept, 58-60, mgr mat res, 60-83. *Mem:* Am Chem Soc; Am Ceramic Soc. *Res:* Cemented carbides; powder metallurgy; oxides; refractory materials; inorganic chemistry. *Mailing Add:* 1722 Green Leaf Dr Royal Oak MI 48067

GOLIBERSUCH, DAVID CLARENCE, KNOWLEDGE BASED SYSTEMS, TECHNICAL MANAGEMENT. *Current Pos:* physicist, Gen Elec Res & Develop Ctr, 70-74, mgr tech relations, 74-75, Energy Sci Br, 75-77, Signal Lab, 77-83, consult strategic anal & planning, 83-84, INFO SCIENTIST, GEN ELEC CORP RES & DEVELOP, 85- *Personal Data:* b Buffalo, NY, Jan 20, 42; m 68; c 2. *Educ:* Rensselaer Polytech Inst, BS, 63; Univ Pa, MS, 65, PhD(physics), 69. *Prof Exp:* NSF fel physics, Imp Col Sci & Technol, Univ London, 69-70. *Mem:* Inst Elec & Electronics Engrs; Am Asn Artificial Intel; Asn Comput Mach. *Res:* Information systems; knowledge based systems; artificial intelligence; expert systems; physics. *Mailing Add:* 828 Londonderry Rd Schenectady NY 12309

GOLIK, WOJCIECH L, NUMERICAL ANALYSIS, COMPUTATIONAL MATHEMATICS. *Current Pos:* Asst prof, 88-97, RES FEL, DEPT MATH & COMPUT SCI, UNIV MO, 97- *Personal Data:* b Poznan, Poland, Aug 26, 59; US citizen. *Educ:* Poznan Tech Univ, MSc, 82; NMex State Univ, MSc, 85, PhD(math), 89. *Concurrent Pos:* Vis asst prof, Univ Mo, 88-90; vis res fel, Univ NMex, 93. *Mem:* Soc Indust & Appl Math. *Res:* Computational electromagnetics; numerical linear algebra. *Mailing Add:* Dept Math & Comput Sci Univ Mo St Louis MO 63121. *Fax:* 314-516-5400; *E-Mail:* golik@arch.umsl.edu

GOLIN, JOHN EUSTER, BIOLOGY. *Current Pos:* PROF BIOL, CATH UNIV AM, 85- *Personal Data:* b Wilmington, Del, Aug 24, 51; m 80, Patricia A Weisman; c Seth, Karey & Hannah. *Educ:* Haverford Col, BA, 73; Univ Chicago, PhD(genetics), 79. *Prof Exp:* Fel, Univ Ore, 79-83; vis scientist, E I Du Pont Co, 83-85. *Mem:* Genetics Soc Am; Sigma Xi. *Res:* Analysis of genes mediating multiple drug resistance in yeast; molecular mechanism of genetic exchange in mitotic cells. *Mailing Add:* Dept Biol Cath Univ Am Washington DC 20064. *Fax:* 202-319-5721

GOLIN, STUART, IMAGE COMPRESSION, VIDEO ANALYSIS. *Current Pos:* MEM TECH STAFF, DAVID SARNOFF RES CTR, 70-88 & 96- *Personal Data:* b Chicago, Ill, Jan 15, 38; m 70, Michaela. *Educ:* Univ Chicago, MSc, 59, PhD(physics), 63. *Prof Exp:* Res assoc physics, Univ Chicago, 63-64; NSF fel, Nuclear Res Ctr, Saclay, France, 64-65; asst prof metall eng, Univ Ill, 65-66; asst prof physics, Univ Pittsburgh, 66-69; mem tech staff, David Sarnoff Res Ctr, 70-88; sr software engr, Intel, 88-95. *Mem:* Asn Comput Mach; Inst Elec & Electronics Engrs Comput Soc; Int Soc Optical Eng. *Res:* Video analysis; motion estimation; computer systems. *Mailing Add:* David Sarnoff Res Ctr Princeton NJ 08543-5300. *E-Mail:* sgolin@sarnoff.com

GOLINKIN, HERBERT SHELDON, PHYSICAL ORGANIC CHEMISTRY, POLYMER CHEMISTRY. *Current Pos:* RES ASSOC, ITW TECHNOL INC, 92- *Personal Data:* b Chicago, Ill, May 24, 40; m 61; c 2. *Educ:* Johns Hopkins Univ, AB, 61; Univ Alta, Calgary, PhD(phys org chem), 66. *Prof Exp:* Fel phys org chem, Div Pure Chem, Nat Res Coun Can, 66-68; asst prof chem, Univ Minn, 68-70; res chemist, Res & Develop Dept, Amoco Chem Corp, 70-83, staff res chemist, Res & Develop Dept, Amoco Petrol Additives Co, 83-92. *Concurrent Pos:* Petrol Res Fund grant, 68-70; counr, Am Chem Soc, 82- *Mem:* Am Chem Soc; Chem Inst Can; Soc Petrol Engrs; Can Soc Chem. *Res:* Aqueous solutions; reaction kinetics; reaction mechanisms; piezochemistry; effects of external fields on chemical reactions; condensation polymers; oil production chemicals; petroleum additives; addition polymers; lubricants. *Mailing Add:* 1157 George Lane Naperville IL 60540-5614

GOLL, DARREL EUGENE, MOLECULAR BIOLOGY, BIOCHEMISTRY. *Current Pos:* PROF BIOCHEM, UNIV ARIZ, 76- *Personal Data:* b Garner, Iowa, Apr 19, 36; c Laura E, Jeffrey E & Kathleen K. *Educ:* Iowa State Univ, BS, 57, MS, 59; Univ Wis, PhD(biochem), 62. *Honors & Awards:* Samuel Cate Prescott Res Award, Inst Food Technol, 71; Distinguished Res Award, Am Meat Sci Asn, 72; Meats Res Award, Am Soc Animal Sci, 73; Animal Growth & Develop Award, Am Soc Animal Sci, 92. *Prof Exp:* From asst prof to prof biochem, Iowa State Univ, 62-76. *Concurrent Pos:* USPHS res grant, 64-67 & 69-; NIH spec fel, Univ Calif, Los Angeles, 66-67 & Univ Oxford, Eng, 72. *Mem:* AAAS; Am Chem Soc; Biophys Soc; Am Soc Biochem & Molecular Biol; Protein Soc. *Res:* Chemistry of muscle proteins; muscle contraction; protein turnover and intracellular proteases; cell motility; connective tissue protein; protein structure; nucleic acid and protein biosynthesis. *Mailing Add:* Muscle Biol Group Univ Ariz 624 Shantz Tucson AZ 85721-0001. *Fax:* 520-621-1396; *E-Mail:* darrelg@ag.arizona.edu

GOLL, ROBERT JOHN, PHYSICAL CHEMISTRY. *Current Pos:* chmn dept, 70-75, PROF PHYSICS, MIAMI-DADE JR COL, 69- *Personal Data:* b Milwaukee, Wis, Jan 14, 26. *Educ:* Beloit Col, BS, 47; Northwestern Univ, BS, 48; Univ Wis, PhD(chem), 60. *Prof Exp:* Res chemist cent res dept, E I du Pont de Nemours & Co, Inc, Del, 59-69. *Mem:* AAAS. *Res:* Molecular structure; science education. *Mailing Add:* 1287 NE 100 St Miami Shores FL 33138

GOLLAHALLI, SUBRAMANYAM RAMAPPA, MECHANICAL ENGINEERING, PROPULSION ENGINEERING. *Current Pos:* from asst prof to prof, 76-92, LESCH CENTENNIAL PROF MECH ENG, UNIV OKLA, 92- *Personal Data:* b Sadali, India, Nov 26, 42; m 67, Rangamani Nadig; c Suma & Anil. *Educ:* Univ Mysore, BE, 63; Indian Inst Sci, ME, 65; Univ Waterloo, MASc, 70, PhD(mech eng), 73. *Honors & Awards:* Robert Angus Medal, Can Soc Mech Eng, 78; Ralph Teetor Award, Soc Automotive Engrs, 78; Haliburton Distinguished Lectr, 84; Ralph James Award, Am Soc Mech Engrs, 93. *Prof Exp:* Lectr internal combustion eng, Indian Inst Sci, 65-68; res & develop engr mech eng, John Fowlers Ltd, India, 68; res asst prof, Univ Waterloo, 73-75, asst prof, 75-76. *Concurrent Pos:* Fel Univ Waterloo, 73; Nat Res Coun Can res grant, 75-76; Nat Sci Found grant, 84-87, Dept Energy, 87-89, NASA, 94-98. *Mem:* Fel Am Soc Mech Engrs; Soc Automotive Engrs; Int Combustion Inst; Soc Eng Educr; assoc fel Am Soc Aeronaut Engrs. *Res:* Combustion; fires; internal combustion engines; gas turbines. *Mailing Add:* Sch Aerospace Mech & Nuclear Eng Univ Okla Norman OK 73019. *Fax:* 405-325-1088; *E-Mail:* gollahal@ou.edu

GOLLAMUDI, RAMACHANDER, ANTITHROMBOTIC DRUGS, DRUG-ENZYME INTERACTIONS. *Current Pos:* sect head biotransformation & anal chem, 75-76, assoc prof, 76-90, PROF MED CHEM, CTR HEALTH SCI, UNIV TENN, 91- *Personal Data:* b India, June 27, 34; m 60; c 2. *Educ:* Osmania Univ, India, PhD(chem), 60; Fairleigh Dickinson Univ, MBA, 76. *Prof Exp:* Group leader drug metab, USV Pharmaceut Corp, 65-71; sr scientist drug disposition, Warner-Lambert Co, 71-75. *Concurrent Pos:* Res assoc biochem & Fulbright scholar, Northwestern Univ Sch Med, 62-65. *Mem:* Am Soc Pharmacol & Exp Therapeut; Am Chem Soc; Sigma Xi. *Res:* Drug metabolism; mechanism of drug action; chemical constitution and biological activity. *Mailing Add:* Dept Pharm Sci Univ Tenn Ctr Health Sci Memphis TN 38163-0001. *Fax:* 901-528-6517

GOLLER, EDWIN JOHN, ORGANIC CHEMISTRY. *Current Pos:* from asst prof to assoc prof, 69-78, PROF CHEM, VA MIL INST, 78-, HEAD, CHEM DEPT, 89- *Personal Data:* b Lawrence, Mass, Jan 28, 40; m 84; c 1. *Educ:* Merrimack Col, BS, 61; Northeastern Univ, MS, 64; Univ NH, PhD(org chem), 69. *Prof Exp:* Instr chem, Merrimack Col, 63-66. *Mem:* Sigma Xi; Am Chem Soc. *Res:* Mechanistic organometallic chemistry; stereochemistry; organic synthesis. *Mailing Add:* RR 5 Box 217 Lexington VA 24450-8836

GOLLEY, FRANK BENJAMIN, ECOLOGY. *Current Pos:* instr zool, Univ Ga, 59-62, asst prof, 62-64, assoc prof zool & dir Savannah River Ecol Lab, 64-68, prof zool & exec dir Inst Ecol, 68-81, dir, Inst Ecol, 84-87, RES PROF ECOL, UNIV GA, 81- *Personal Data:* b Chicago, Ill, Sept 24, 30; m 53, Priscilla McKinzie; c 3. *Educ:* Purdue Univ, BS, 52; Wash State Univ, MS, 54; Mich State Univ, PhD(zool), 58. *Prof Exp:* Asst prof zool, Univ NC, 59; prof biol, NC Col, 59. *Concurrent Pos:* Pres, Intecol. *Mem:* AAAS; Ecol Soc Am; Int Soc Trop Ecol; Int Asn Ecol; Int Asn Landscape Ecol. *Res:* Ecosystem and tropical ecology; energy flow; mineral cycling; ecological succession; landscape ecology. *Mailing Add:* Inst Ecol Univ Ga Athens GA 30609-4066. *E-Mail:* fgolley@uga.cc.uga.edu

GOLLIN, SUSANNE MERLE, CYTOGENETICS, CELL BIOLOGY. *Current Pos:* ASST PROF PATH & PEDIAT & DIR, CYTOGENETICS LAB, ARK CHILDREN'S MED CTR, UNIV ARK MED SCI, LITTLE ROCK, 84- *Educ:* Northwestern Univ, PhD(biol sci), 80. *Mailing Add:* Dept Human Genetics Univ Pittsburgh 130 De Soto St Pittsburgh PA 15261-0001. *Fax:* 412-624-3020

GOLLMAR, DOROTHY MAY, MATHEMATICS. *Current Pos:* ASSOC PROF MATH, WIS STATE UNIV-WHITEWATER, 62- *Personal Data:* b Big Bend, Wis, May 4, 27; m 62. *Educ:* Univ Wis, BS, 49, MA, 51. *Prof Exp:* Teacher pub sch, Wis, 49-50 & Ill, 50-51; instr math, Monticello Col, 51-54; from asst prof to assoc prof, State Univ NY Col Cortland, 54-62. *Mem:* AAAS; Am Math Soc; Math Asn Am; Nat Coun Teachers Math; Am Asn Univ Professor. *Mailing Add:* Box 337 Rochester WI 53167-0337

GOLLOB, FRED, PHYSICAL CHEMISTRY. *Current Pos:* dir, 62-74, pres, 74-76, DIR, GOLLOB ANAL SERV, INC, 76- *Personal Data:* b New York, NY, Oct 7, 27; m 51; c 3. *Educ:* Columbia Univ, BA, 50, MA, 51, PhD, 54. *Prof Exp:* Res chemist, Marshall & Newburgh Labs, E I du Pont de Nemours & Co, 53-58; group leader cent res lab, Air Reduction Co Inc, 58-62. *Mem:* AAAS; Instrument Soc; Am Asn Consult Chemists & Chem Engrs; Am Chem Soc; Soc Appl Spectros; Sigma Xi. *Res:* Gas analysis. *Mailing Add:* 31 Pine Ridge Saratoga Springs NY 12866

GOLLOB, LAWRENCE, RESEARCH & DEVELOPMENT PROJECT EVALUATION & SELECTION, NEW PRODUCT DEVELOPMENT & COMMERCIALIZATION. *Current Pos:* sr develop chemist, 82-86, res & develop group leader, 86-94, BUS MGR, GA-PAC RESINS, INC, 94- *Personal Data:* b Yonkers, NY; m 76, Sherry; c 2. *Educ:* State Univ NY, Stony Brook, BS, 74; Duke Univ, MS, 76; Ore State Univ, PhD(wood technol & polymer chem), 82. *Prof Exp:* Staff res asst, Ore State Univ, 76-82. *Concurrent Pos:* Competitive grant reviewer prod; efficiency team; variation reduction team; customer value anal. *Mem:* Am Chem Soc; Soc Wood Sci & Technol. *Res:* Interaction of chemical structure with performance of wood adhesive systems; technical management; marketing and product technical support; business development. *Mailing Add:* Ga Pac Resins Inc 55 Park Pl 19th Floorr Rd Atlanta GA 30303-2529

GOLLON, PETER J, PARTICLE PHYSICS, HEALTH PHYSICS. *Current Pos:* physicist, Isabelle Proj, 79-82, PHYSICIST, SAFETY & ENVIRON PROTECTION DIV, BROOKHAVEN NAT LAB, 82- *Personal Data:* b New York, NY. *Educ:* Columbia Univ, BA, 63, MA, 65, PhD(physics), 69. *Prof Exp:* Physicist, 68-74, group leader and sr radiation safety officer, 74-77, liason physicist, Proton Dept, Fermi Nat Accelerator Lab, 78-79. *Concurrent Pos:* Lectr, Sch High Energy Radiation Dosimetry & Protection, Erice, Italy, 75. *Mem:* Am Phys Soc; Sigma Xi. *Res:* Accelerator shielding, personnel dosimetry, neutron spectroscopy; accelerator radiation dosimetry. *Mailing Add:* 15 Eleanor Pl Huntington NY 11743

GOLLUB, ERICA L, PUBLIC HEALTH & EPIDEMIOLOGY, WOMENS HEALTH. *Current Pos:* ADJ ASST PROF CLIN PUB HEALTH, COLUMBIA UNIV, 94-; DIR EPIDEMIOL UNIT, AIDS ACTIVITIES COORD OFF, PHILADELPHIA DEPT PUB HEALTH, 94- *Personal Data:* b Philadelphia, Pa, July 26, 56. *Educ:* Stanford Univ, BS, 79; Columbia Univ, MPH, 82, PhD(epidemiol), 91. *Prof Exp:* Res technician, City Hope Nat Med Ctr, Duarte, Calif, 80-81; instr, Sch Optometry, State Univ NY, 81-83; consult, Dept Int Econ & Soc Affairs, UN, 83-85; res fel, HIV Ctr Clin & Behav Studies, NY State Psychiat Inst, 91-94. *Concurrent Pos:* Founder, Womancap, NY, 86-; Fulbright scholar, Regional Observ de la Sante, Marseille, France, 97. *Res:* Author of numerous publications in field. *Mailing Add:* AIDS Activities Coord Off City Philadelphia Dept Pub Health 500 S Broad St 2nd Floor Philadelphia PA 19146

GOLLUB, JERRY PAUL, NONLINEAR DYNAMICS & TURBULENCE. *Current Pos:* Kenan prof, 87-92, PROF PHYSICS, HAVERFORD COL, 79-, JOHN & BARBARA BUSH PROF NATURAL SCI, 96- *Personal Data:* b St Louis, Mo, Sept 9, 44; m 84, Diane B Nissen; c Nikki Ruth & Aaron Nissen. *Educ:* Oberlin Col, AB, 66; Harvard Univ, AM, 67, PhD(physics), 71. *Honors & Awards:* Am Phys Soc Award Res Undergrad Inst, 85. *Concurrent Pos:* Adj prof physics, Univ Pa, 81-; Sigma Xi nat lectr, 83-85; Guggenheim fel, 84-85; secy-treas, Div Fluid Dynamics, Am Phys Soc, 85-88, counr, 92-; vis prof, Ecole Normale, Paris, 85 & 91; mem, Mat Res Adv Comt, NSF, 86-87; provost, Haverford Col, 88-90; dir, Mid Atlantic Pew Sci Prog, 88-91. *Mem:* Nat Acad Sci; Fedn Am Scientists; AAAS; Sigma Xi; fel Am Acad Arts & Sci; fel Am Phys Soc. *Res:* Non-equilibrium condensed matter physics, especially pattern formation, hydrodynamic instabilities and turbulence; nonlinear dynamics, granular materials and instrumentation for research and education; instrumentation for research and education. *Mailing Add:* Physics Dept Haverford Col Haverford PA 19041. *E-Mail:* jgollub@haverford.edu

GOLLUB, SEYMOUR, NUCLEAR MEDICINE. *Current Pos:* PVT PRACT. *Personal Data:* b Philadelphia, Pa, Feb 21, 25; m 50; c 2. *Educ:* Univ Pa, BA, 47; Jefferson Med Col, PhD(physiol), 54; Hahnemann Med Col, MD, 58; Am Bd Nuclear Med, cert, 73. *Prof Exp:* Res asst path, Mt Sinai Hosp, Philadelphia, 49-50; res assoc, Albert Einstein Med Ctr, 50-53, assoc dir res surg, Southern Div, 55-63, dir, Mandell Lab, 56-63; dir hemat, St Barnabas Hosp, 63-73, dir nuclear med, 73- *Concurrent Pos:* Pvt & govt res grants physiol & hemat, 55-; dir coagulation lab, Hahnemann Hosp, 56-63, assoc res surg, Med Col, 58-60; consult, Roswell Park Mem Hosp, Buffalo, NY, 57-59; dir res lab, Hillman Med Ctr, 57-63; mem, Comn Plasma, Nat Res Coun, 68-71. *Mem:* Am Soc Hemat; Am Soc Hemat; Microcirculatory Soc; Am Soc Exp Path. *Res:* Hematology, coagulation, surgery circulation; enzymology. *Mailing Add:* 3235 Grand Concourse Bronx NY 10468-1108

GOLOD, WILLIAM HERSH, PHARMACY. *Current Pos:* From asst prof to assoc prof, 58-66, dir pharm serv, 59-63, asst dean, 63-65, DEAN COL PHARM, MED UNIV SC, 65-, PROF PHARM, 66- *Personal Data:* b New York, NY, June 28, 33; m 61; c 3. *Educ:* Fordham Univ, BS, 54; St Louis Col Pharm, MS, 55; Purdue Univ, PhD(phys pharm), 58. *Mailing Add:* 14 Nuffield Rd Charleston SC 29407

GOLOMB, FREDERICK M, SURGICAL ONCOLOGY. *Current Pos:* From asst prof to assoc prof, 56-77, dir tumor serv, Univ Hosp, 70-86, DIR SURG CHEMOIMMUNOTHER DIV, TUMOR SERV, MED CTR, NY UNIV, 67-, PROF CLIN SURG, SCH MED, 77- *Personal Data:* b New York, NY, Dec 18, 24; m 54, Joan Schneider; c 2. *Educ:* Yale Univ, BS, 45; Rochester Univ, MD, 49; Am Bd Surg, dipl. *Mem:* Am Soc Clin Oncol; Am Asn Cancer Res; Soc Surg Oncol; Soc Head & Neck Surg; Soc Surg Alimentary Tract; Sigma Xi. *Res:* Cancer surgery, immunotherapy and chemotherapy; regional techniques for administration of cancer chemotherapeutic agents; techniques of reconstructive surgery following radical exenterations; tumor immunology. *Mailing Add:* NYU Sch Medicine 530 First Ave New York NY 10016-6402

GOLOMB, HARVEY MORRIS, HEMATOLOGY, ONCOLOGY. *Current Pos:* fel hemat & oncol, 73-75, asst prof, 75-79, ASSOC PROF, UNIV CHICAGO HOSP, 79-, CHIEF HEMAT & ONCOL, 81- *Personal Data:* b Pittsburgh, Pa, Feb 13, 43; m 65; c 2. *Educ:* Univ Chicago, BA, 64; Univ Pittsburgh, MD, 68; Am Bd Internal Med, dipl, 75. *Prof Exp:* Intern internal med, Boston City Hosp, 68-69; resident internal med, Baltimore City Hosp, 71-72; fel med genetics, Johns Hopkins Univ Hosp, 72-73. *Mem:* Am Soc Human Genetics; AAAS; Electron Micros Soc Am; Am Soc Hemat; Am Fedn Clin Res. *Res:* Hairy cell leukemia; acute leukemia and malignant lymphomas; surface characteristics of malignant cells; cells; staging and chemotherapy of lung cancer. *Mailing Add:* Univ Chicago Hosps Box 420 5841 S Maryland Ave Chicago IL 60637

GOLOMB, MICHAEL, MATHEMATICS. *Current Pos:* assoc prof, 46-50, prof, 50-76, EMER PROF MATH, PURDUE UNIV, 76- *Personal Data:* b Munich, Ger, May 3, 09; nat US; m 39, Dagmar Racic; c Miriam & Deborah (Sedgwick). *Educ:* Univ Berlin, PhD(math), 33. *Prof Exp:* Res assoc elec eng, Cornell Univ, 39-42, instr math, 40-42; instr, Purdue Univ, 42-44; res engr & chief anal sect, Franklin Inst, 44-46. *Concurrent Pos:* Vis prof, Math Res Ctr, Univ Wis, 56-57, 58, 67 & 78, Brown Univ, 75; distinguished vis prof, San Diego State Univ, 84-85; mem, Coun Am Math Soc, 73-75; consult, Appl Math Div, Argonne Nat Lab, 61-70. *Mem:* Am Math Soc; Math Asn Am; Soc Indust & Appl Math; fel AAAS; Sigma Xi. *Res:* Approximation theory; differential and integral equations; applied mathematics. *Mailing Add:* Dept Math Purdue Univ West Lafayette IN 47907

GOLOMB, SOLOMON WOLF, DISCRETE MATHEMATICS, INFORMATION THEORY & CODING. *Current Pos:* prof elec eng & math, Univ Southern Calif, 63-93, vprovost res, 86-89, dir technol, Annenberg Ctr Commun, UNIV PROF, UNIV SOUTHERN CALIF, 93- *Personal Data:* b Baltimore, Md, May 31, 32; m 56; c 2. *Educ:* Johns Hopkins Univ, AB, 51; Harvard Univ, AM, 53, PhD(math), 57. *Hon Degrees:* DSc, Dubna Int Univ, 95; LHD, Hebrew Union Col, 96. *Honors & Awards:* Shannon Lectr, Int Symp Info Theory, Brighton, Eng, 85; Lomonosov Medal,

Russ Acad Sci, 94, Kapitsa Medal, 95; Shannon Award, Inst Elec & Electronics Engrs, 95. *Prof Exp:* Fulbright fel, Univ Oslo, 55-56; sr res engr, Jet Propulsion Lab, 56-58, leader, Info Processing Group, 58-60, asst chief, Telecommun Res Sect, 60-63. *Concurrent Pos:* Consult, aerospace & electronics indust, 54-; res fel, Inst Commun Sci, Mass Inst Technol, 59; mem, Comn C, Int Sci Radio Union, 60-, US deleg gen assembly; vis prof, Calif Inst Technol, 71-72; fel, Sackler Inst Advan Study, Tel Aviv Univ, 90. *Mem:* Nat Acad Eng; Am Math Soc; Math Asn Am; Soc Indust & Appl Math; fel Inst Elec & Electronics Engrs; Int Union Radio Sci; fel AAAS; Am Asn Univ Prof; foreign mem Russ Acad Natural Sci. *Res:* Applications of mathematical techniques to problems involving the storage, transfer, communication of information and computer technology; social implications of developments in science and technology; technology forecasting, particularly with reference to communications and computer technology; probability; prime number theory; combinatorial analysis, mathematical games and modelling; author of 5 books; author of over 250 technical articles. *Mailing Add:* EEB-504A Univ Southern Calif Los Angeles CA 90089-2565. *Fax:* 213-740-8729

GOLOMSKI, WILLIAM ARTHUR, APPLIED MATHEMATICS, STATISTICS. *Current Pos:* PRES, W A GOLOMSKI & ASSOC, 70- *Educ:* Milwaukee Sch Eng, MSEM, 69; Univ Chicago, MBA, 72; Columbia Col, BA, 87. *Honors & Awards:* Testimonial Award, Am Soc Qual Control, 70; Edwards Medal, 76; W A Golomski Medal, Am Soc Qual Control, 86. *Concurrent Pos:* Mgt consult, 49-70; lectr, Univ Wis, 58, mem adv coun, Sch Educ, 58-64; consult, US Bur Census, 60; mem, Comn on Prod Qual, 67-70; sr lectr bus policy, Univ Chi, 89- *Mem:* Nat Acad Eng; fel Am Soc Qual Control (vpres, 64-66, pres, 66-67); fel NY Acad Sci; Fel AAAS; fel Am Statist Asn; Int Acad for Quality (vpres, 91-). *Res:* Marketing; management science; research and development management; applied mathematics and statistics in quality, nutrition, sociology, public health. *Mailing Add:* W A Golomski & Assoc N9690 County Trunk U Algoma WI 54201-9528

GOLOSKIE, RAYMOND, NUCLEAR PHYSICS. *Current Pos:* asst prof, 62-74, ASSOC PROF PHYSICS, WORCESTER POLYTECH INST, 74- *Personal Data:* b Providence, RI, Oct 30, 30; m 54; c 2. *Educ:* Brown Univ, ScB, 53; Harvard Univ, MA, 55, PhD(physics), 61. *Prof Exp:* Instr physics, Colgate Univ, 59-62. *Mem:* Am Phys Soc. *Res:* Experiments in electron and photon interactions with nuclei at intermediate energies; ion micro probes. *Mailing Add:* Dept Physics Worcester Polytech Inst 100 Institute Rd Worcester MA 01609-2247

GOLOVCHENKO, JENE ANDREW, PHYSICS & APPLIED PHYSICS. *Current Pos:* PROF PHYSICS & GORDON MCKAY PROF APPL PHYSICS, DIV APPL SCI, HARVARD UNIV, 87- *Personal Data:* b New York, NY, July 14, 46; m, Elizabeth M Catricala; c Peter, Eric & Katya. *Educ:* Rensselaer Polytech Inst, BEE, 67, MEE, 68, PhD, 72. *Hon Degrees:* MA, Harvard Univ, 87. *Prof Exp:* Lectr, Inst Physics, Aarhus Univ, Denmark, 74-76; mem tech staff, Bell Labs, Murray Hill, NJ, 76-87, distinguished mem staff, 84. *Concurrent Pos:* Mem, Rowland Inst Sci, 89- *Mailing Add:* Physics Dept Harvard Univ Lyman 228 Cambridge MA 02138. *Fax:* 617-496-5144

GOLOVIN, MICHAEL N, ENGINEERING PHYSICS. *Current Pos:* prin physicist aeronaut sci, 53-54, eng physicist aerospace sci, 58-78, RES SCIENTIST, BATTELLE COLUMBUS DIV, OHIO, 78- *Personal Data:* b Harbin, China, June 30, 23; US citizen; m 56; c 3. *Educ:* Univ Calif, Berkeley, BS, 52. *Prof Exp:* Physicist rocket propulsion, Naval Weapons Ctr, China Lake, Calif, 52-53; thermodynamicyst, McDonnell Aircraft Corp, St Louis, 54-55. *Res:* Pulsed power supplies for advanced weapons systems; advanced armor and anti-armor technologies; ball lightning phenomena; directed energy technologies, aerosol science, electromagnetic launchers and power supplies; geophysical electromagnetic phenomena. *Mailing Add:* 774 Stanley Ave Columbus OH 43206

GOLOWICH, EUGENE, PHYSICS. *Current Pos:* asst prof, 67-70, assoc prof, 70-76, PROF PHYSICS, UNIV MASS, AMHERST, 76- *Personal Data:* b Mt Vernon, NY, July 21, 39; m 61; c 2. *Educ:* Rensselaer Polytech Inst, BS, 61; Cornell Univ, PhD(physics), 65. *Prof Exp:* Instr physics, Cornell Univ, 65; res assoc, Carnegie-Mellon Univ, 65-67. *Concurrent Pos:* Vis assoc prof, Cornell Univ, 73-74; vis res scientist, Stanford Linear Accelerator Ctr, 74; vis res scientist, Inst Theoret Physics, Univ Calif, Santa Barbara, 81; vis prof, Univ Hawaii, 87, Univ Paris-sud, 88. *Mem:* AAAS; Am Phys Soc. *Res:* Theoretical physics; high energy physics. *Mailing Add:* Dept Physics LGRT-C Univ Mass Amherst MA 01003

GOLTON, WILLIAM CHARLES, ANALYTICAL CHEMISTRY. *Current Pos:* Res chemist, 62-68, staff chemist, 68-73, res supvr, 73-80, qual mgr, fabrics & finishes dept, 81-85, SR RES ASSOC, MARSHALL LAB, E I DU PONT DE NEMOURS & CO, INC, 85- *Personal Data:* b Chicago, Ill, Mar 27, 36; m 64; c 3. *Educ:* Univ Ky, BS; Univ Iowa, MS, 59, PhD(anal chem), 62. *Mem:* Am Chem Soc; Sigma Xi; Am Soc Testing & Mat; Am Soc Qual Control. *Res:* General analytical chemistry; physical measurements of paint and related materials; quality assurance; organic finishes, polymers, consumer products. *Mailing Add:* 509 Beatty Rd Springfield PA 19064-1509

GOLTZ, MARK NEIL, HAZARDOUS WASTE MANAGEMENT, PHYSICAL-CHEMICAL PROCESSES. *Current Pos:* ASSOC PROF ENG & ENVIRON MGT, USAF INST TECHNOL, 96- *Personal Data:* b Brooklyn, NY, July 1, 51; m 77, Misuk So; c Hugh & Eric. *Educ:* Cornell Univ, BS, 72; Univ Calif, Berkeley, MS, 73; Stanford Univ, PhD(environ eng), 86. *Prof Exp:* Civil eng officer, USAF, 73-86, assoc prof environ eng, USAF Inst Technol, 86-93, actg assoc prof environ eng, Stanford Univ, 93-96. *Mem:* Asn Environ Eng Professors; Am Geophys Union; Water Environ Fedn; Soc Am Mil Engrs. *Res:* Fate and transport of organic contaminants in ground water; hazardous waste site remediation; mathematical modeling of contaminant transport. *Mailing Add:* Dept Eng & Environ Mgt Airforce Inst Technol 2950 P St Bldg 640 Wright Patterson AFB OH 43433-7765. *Fax:* 650-725-8662; *E-Mail:* mgoltz@afit.aft.at.mil

GOLTZ, ROBERT W, DERMATOLOGY, DERMATOPATHOLOGY. *Current Pos:* RETIRED. *Personal Data:* b St Paul, Minn, Sept 21, 23; m 45; c 2. *Educ:* Univ Minn, Minneapolis, BS, 43, MB, 44, MD, 45. *Prof Exp:* From clin instr to clin assoc prof dermat, Univ Minn, Minneapolis, 51-65; prof & dir div, Med Ctr, Univ Colo, Denver, 65-71; prof & chmn dept, Med Sch, Univ Minn, Minneapolis, 71-85. *Concurrent Pos:* Am Cancer Soc res grant, 58-59; USPHS res grant, 59-66; res grant, Grad Sch, Univ Minn, Minneapolis, 62-64. *Mem:* Am Dermat Asn; hon mem Am Acad Dermat; Soc Invest Dermat; Histochem Soc; Am Soc Dermatopath; Pac Dermatol Soc; Brit Asn Dermatol; Columbian Dermat Soc; SAfrican Dermat Soc; Can Dermat Soc. *Res:* Venereology; dermatopathology; histochemistry. *Mailing Add:* Univ Calif San Diego Med Ctr 200 W Arbor Dr No 8420 San Diego CA 92103-8420

GOLTZMAN, DAVID, ENDOCRINOLOGY & METABOLISM, HUMORAL CONTROL OF SKELETAL & CALCIUM HOMEOSTASIS. *Current Pos:* intern, 68-69, from asst physician to assoc physician, 78-87, SR PHYSICIAN, ROYAL VICTORIA HOSP, MONTREAL, 87-, PHYSICIAN-IN-CHIEF, 94-; PROF MED, MCGILL UNIV, 83-, PROF PHYSIOL, 88-, MASSABKI PROF MED, 94- *Personal Data:* b Montreal, Que, Sept 22, 44; m 68, Naomi Lyon; c Jonathan, Rebecca & Daniel. *Educ:* McGill Univ, BSc, 66, MD, 68. *Honors & Awards:* Andre Lichtwitz Prize for Res in Calcium, Nat Inst Health & Med Res, Inserm, France, 87. *Prof Exp:* Resident, Columbia-Presby Med Ctr, NY, 69-71; clin & res fel endocrinol, Mass Gen Hosp, 71-75; instr med, Med Sch, Harvard Univ, 74-75; from asst prof to assoc prof, McGill Univ, 75-83, chmn, Dept Physiol, 88-93. *Concurrent Pos:* Chmn, comt for exp med, Med Res Coun Can, 84-88, mem exec comt, 93-96; scientist award, Med Res Coun Can, 83-88; mem, Gen Med B Study Sect, NIH, 88-92; assoc ed, Bone, 89-; chmn prog comt, Am Soc Bone & Mineral Res, 90-91, assoc ed, Bone & Mineral Res, 94. *Mem:* Am Soc Clin Invest; Am Asn Physicians; Am Soc Bone & Mineral Res; Endocrine Soc; Can Soc Endocrinol & Metab (secy-treas, 81-84, pres, 90-92); Can Soc Clin Invest (vpres 96-97). *Res:* Examination of the humoral control of calcium and skeletal homeostasis; exploration of the chemical structure, molecular biology, metabolism and mechanism of action of hormones and of other humoral factors involved in calcium and bone homeostasis; co-author of numerous research articles. *Mailing Add:* Calcium Res Lab Royal Victoria Hosp Rm H4-67 687 Pine Montreal PQ H3A 1A1 Can. *Fax:* 514-843-8182; *E-Mail:* gdgoltzma@rvhmed.lan.mcgill.ca

GOLUB, ABRAHAM, OPERATIONS RESEARCH, SCIENCE ADMINISTRATION. *Current Pos:* PRES, ABRAHAM GOLUB INC, CONSULT SERV, 76- Instr, Univ Del, 50-51. *Personal Data:* b Brooklyn, NY, May 16, 21; m 50; c 2. *Educ:* Brooklyn Col, BA, 41; Univ Del, MA, 49. *Honors & Awards:* Army Res & Develop Tech Achievement Award, 62. *Prof Exp:* Sect chief, Surveillance Br, Ballistic Res Labs, Aberdeen Proving Ground, 46-50, asst chief, 50-55, chief, Artillery Weapon Systs Br, 55-62, assoc tech dir, Ballistic Res Labs, 62-64; dep spec asst opers res, Off Asst Secy Army, 64-67, asst dep undersecy army, 67-69, sci adv to asst chief of staff for force develop, Dept Army, Washington, DC, 69-73, tech adv to dep chief of staff for opers & plans, Hq, 73-76. *Mem:* Opers Res Soc Am; Am Math Soc; Inst Math Statist; Am Ord Asn. *Res:* Weapons systems analysis; ordnance; statistical estimation; acceptance sampling; experimental design; analysis of variance; force analysis and design; cost and operational effectiveness analysis. *Mailing Add:* 203 S Yoakum Pky Alexandria VA 22304

GOLUB, EDWARD S, IMMUNOLOGY, CELL BIOLOGY. *Current Pos:* PRES, PAC CTR FOR STUDY APPL BIOL, 92-; PRES, LYKEION CORP, 94- *Personal Data:* b Chicago, Ill, Oct 6, 34; m 59; c 2. *Educ:* Roosevelt Univ, BS, 56; Miami Univ, MS, 59; Univ NC, PhD(bact), 64. *Prof Exp:* Res fel immunol, Duke Univ, 64-65 & Scripps Clin & Res Found, 65-68; from asst prof to prof biol sci, Purdue Univ, 68-88; dir res, Ortho Pharmaceut, 88-90; dir, J&J Labs, Scripps, 90-92. *Concurrent Pos:* USPHS career develop award, 68; Merck Found fac develop award, 69; assoc ed, J Immunol Methods & Modern Methods in Immunol; mem study sect, USPHS, 77-81; mem rev group, NSF, 82-86; mem study sect, Nat Cancer Inst, 87- *Mem:* AAAS; Am Asn Immunol; Hist Sci Soc; Am Asn Hist Med. *Res:* Induction of immunological tolerance; cell interactions in the immune response; history of science. *Mailing Add:* Pacific Ctr Study of Appl Biol 450 Lirio St Solana Beach CA 92075. *Fax:* 619-793-3632

GOLUB, EFIM I, MOLECULAR BIOLOGY, VIROLOGY. *Current Pos:* RES SCIENTIST, YALE UNIV, 90- *Personal Data:* b Minsk, USSR, July 15, 34; m 68; c Olga & Ilya. *Educ:* State Univ, USSR, BS, 57; Inst Gen Genetics, USSR, PhD(biophys), 65, SciD, 75. *Prof Exp:* Res microbiologist, Inst Gen Genetics, Moscow, 63-70; assoc prof genetics, Pedagogical Inst, USSR, 70-71; sr res microbiologist, All-Union Res Inst Antiobiotics, USSR, 71-79; res asst prof, Col Med, Northeastern Ohio Univ, 80-81; res scientist microbiol, Sch Med, Yale Univ, 81-85; res scientist, Columbia Univ, 88-90. *Res:* Physical-chemical properties of nucleic acids; genetics of temperate phages of E coli; R-factors and other plasmid of E coli; transposable elements of bacteria; mechanism of genetical recombination. *Mailing Add:* One Campbell Ave No 2 New Haven CT 06511

GOLUB, ELLIS ECKSTEIN, BIOCHEMISTRY. *Current Pos:* from asst prof to assoc prof, 77-90, PROF BIOCHEM, SCH DENT MED, UNIV PA, 90-, CHAIR BIOCHEM, 96- *Personal Data:* b New York, NY, Nov 1, 42; m 64, Linda Bender; c Michael, Daniel & Karen. *Educ:* Brandeis Univ, BA, 63; Tufts Univ, PhD(biochem), 69. *Prof Exp:* NIH res fel biol, Calif Inst Technol, 69-71, res fel, Jet Propulsion Lab, 71-72; mem fac oral biol, Health Ctr, Univ Conn, 72-77. *Concurrent Pos:* Consult, Merck, Sharp & Dohme Res Labs, 87-; mem, oral biol & med study sect, NIH. *Mem:* AAAS; Am Chem Soc; Am Soc Bone & Mineral Res; Protein Soc; Am Soc Biochem & Molecular Biol. *Res:* Calcification of bone and cartilage; computer analysis of protein structure. *Mailing Add:* Dept Biochem Univ Pa Sch Dent Med 4001 Spruce St Philadelphia PA 19104-6003. *Fax:* 215-898-3695; *E-Mail:* ellis@biochem.dental.upenn.edu

GOLUB, GENE H, MATHEMATICS. *Current Pos:* vis asst prof, Stanford Univ, 62-64, from asst prof to assoc prof, 64-70, from asst prof, 81-84, PROF COMPUT SCI, STANFORD UNIV, 70- *Personal Data:* b Chicago, Ill, Feb 29, 32. *Educ:* Univ Ill, BS, 53, MA, 54, PhD(math), 59. *Hon Degrees:* DrTech, Linkoping Univ, Sweden, 84; Dr, Technol & Med Univ Grenoble, 86, Univ Louvana, Belg, 92, Univ Umea, 95, Australian Nat Univ, 96; LLD, Univ Dundee, 87; DSc, Univ Ill, 91. *Honors & Awards:* Forsythe Lectr, 78; A R Mitchell Lectr, 91; Bolzano Medal, Czech Repub Acad Sci, 94. *Prof Exp:* NSF fel, Math Lab, Univ Cambridge, 59-60; mem staff, Lawrence Radiation Lab, Univ Calif, 60-61; mem tech staff, Space Tech Labs, Inc, TRW, Inc, 61-62. *Concurrent Pos:* Adj asst prof, Courant Inst Math Sci, NY Univ, 65-66; assoc ed, Linear Algebra & Its Appln, 72-, Appl Math & Optimization, 74-85, Soc Indust & Appl Math Rev, 74-80, J Am Statist Asn, 76-79; mem coun, Soc Indust & Appl Math, 75-78, gov bd, Ger Soc Appl Math & Mech & Adv Comt Comput Sci, NSF, 82-85, US Nat Comt Math, 84-86 & Adv Comt Eng & Math Div, Oak Ridge Nat Lab, 84-87; Guggenheim fel, 87-88. *Mem:* Nat Acad Sci; Nat Acad Eng; hon mem Inst Elec & Electronics Engrs; Soc Indust & Appl Math (pres, 85-87); Math Asn Am; fel AAAS; Am Acad Sci. *Res:* Numerical analysis; derivation of numerical algorithms for solving problems arising in linear algebra; statistical application and the solution of sparse linear systems arising in approximations to elliptic partial differential equations. *Mailing Add:* Dept Comput Sci MC 9025 Stanford Univ Gates Bldg 22203 Rm 280 Stanford CA 94305-9025

GOLUB, LORNE MALCOLM, PERIODONTOLOGY, ORAL BIOLOGY. *Current Pos:* assoc prof, 73-77, PROF ORAL BIOL & PATH, SCH DENT MED, STATE UNIV NY, STONY BROOK, 77- *Personal Data:* b Winnipeg, Man, Jan 13, 41; m 64; c 2. *Educ:* Univ Man, DMD, 63, MSc, 65; Harvard Univ, Cert Periodont, 68. *Honors & Awards:* Merit Award Res, NIH, 87. *Prof Exp:* Res fel periodont, Harvard Sch Dent Med, 65-68; assoc prof, Fac Dent, Univ Man, 68-73. *Concurrent Pos:* Prin investr, Nat Inst Dent Res, NIH, 76-, Kroc Found, New York Diabetes Asn, 77-79 & 81-83; consult, Periodont Dis Prog, Nat Inst Dent Res, NIH, 77, 78 & 80. *Mem:* Int Asn Dent Res; Am Acad Periodont; AAAS; Int Group Peridont Res; Am Asn Oral Biologists. *Res:* Periodontitis; diabetes and collagen metabolism; anti-collagenases. *Mailing Add:* 29 Whitney Gate Smithtown NY 11787

GOLUB, MORTON ALLAN, POLYMER CHEMISTRY, PLASMA CHEMISTRY. *Current Pos:* Nat Res Coun-NASA sr resident res assoc, 68-70, RES SCIENTIST, AMES RES CTR, NASA, 70- *Personal Data:* b Montreal, Que, June 11, 25; nat US; div; c 2. *Educ:* McGill Univ, BSc, 44; Univ NB, MSc, 47; Univ Mo, PhD(chem), 51. *Prof Exp:* Chemist, Defense Indust, Ltd, Que, 44-45; teacher pvt sch, Montreal, 45-46; demonstr physics, Univ NB, 46-47; asst chem, Univ Mo, 47-48, instr math, 49-51; res chemist, B F Goodrich Chem Co, 51-54 & Res Ctr, 54-60; sr polymer chemist, Stanford Res Inst, 60-68. *Concurrent Pos:* Instr, Foothill Col, 63-68. *Mem:* Am Chem Soc. *Res:* Chemical reactions and microstructural characterization of polymers; plasma chemistry; elastomers. *Mailing Add:* Ames Res Ctr Mail Stop 239-23 NASA Moffett Field CA 94035-1000. *Fax:* 650-604-1092

GOLUB, SAMUEL J(OSEPH), textile technology, biology; deceased, see previous edition for last biography

GOLUB, SHARON BRAMSON, HEALTH PSYCHOLOGY, PSYCHOLOGY OF WOMEN. *Current Pos:* from asst prof to assoc prof, 74-86, PROF PYSCHOL, COL NEW ROCHELLE, 86- *Personal Data:* b New York, NY, Mar 25, 37; m 58, Leon M; c 2. *Educ:* Columbia Univ, BS, 59, MA, 66; Fordham Univ, PhD(psychol), 74. *Honors & Awards:* Distinguished Publ Award, Asn Women Psychol, 84. *Prof Exp:* Head nurse psychiat, Mt Sinai Hosp, 57-59; ed, RN Mag, 67-74. *Concurrent Pos:* Dir women's studies, Col New Rochelle, 78-79, chmn, 79-82; pvt pract, 76-; adj prof psychiat, NY Med Col, 80-; dir, Soc Menstrual Cycle Res, 81- *Mem:* Fel Am Psychol Asn; Soc Menstrual Cycle Res (pres, 81-83); Asn Women Psychol; fel Am Psychol Soc; Am Asn Appl & Prev Psychol. *Res:* The menstrual cycle, health psychology and the psychology of women. *Mailing Add:* Dept Psychol Col New Rochelle 29 Castle Pl New Rochelle NY 10805-2338

GOLUB, SIDNEY HARRIS, IMMUNOLOGY. *Current Pos:* from asst prof to assoc prof surg & microbiol & immunol, 71-83, PROF SURG, DIV ONCOL & PROF MICROBIOL & IMMUNOL, SCH MED, UNIV CALIF, LOS ANGELES, 83- *Personal Data:* b Hartford, Conn, July 28, 43; m 66. *Educ:* Brandeis Univ, BA, 65; Temple Univ, PhD(microbiol), 70. *Prof Exp:* Damon Runyon Mem Fund fel cancer res, Karolinska Inst, Sweden, 69-71. *Concurrent Pos:* NIH career develop award, 74; mem, Nat Breast Cancer Task Force, 75-; vis investr, Sloan-Kettering Inst, 78-79; assoc dean career develop, Sch Med, Univ Calif, Los Angeles, 86- *Mem:* Am Soc Microbiol; Am Asn Cancer Res; Am Asn Immunol; Reticuloendothelial Soc; Sigma Xi. *Res:* Tumor immunology; cellular immunology; tumor biology; viral oncology; functioning of the reticuloendothelial system. *Mailing Add:* Dean Med Univ Calif 509 Admin Irvine CA 92717-1000

GOLUBA, RAYMOND WILLIAM, MECHANICAL ENGINEERING. *Current Pos:* engr, Lawrence Livermore Nat Lab, 68-85, dep div leader, 85-90, proj mgr, Dept Mech Eng, 90-91, ASSURANCE MGR ENG, LAWRENCE LIVERMORE NAT LAB, 91- *Personal Data:* b Streator, Ill, Oct 5, 39; m 61; c 3. *Educ:* Univ Ill, BS, 61, MS, 62; Univ Wis, PhD(mech eng), 68. *Prof Exp:* Engr, ARO, Inc, Arnold Air Force Sta, Tenn, 62-63; instr thermodyn, Univ Wis-Madison, 63-64. *Mem:* Am Soc Mech Engrs. *Res:* Heat transfer in oscillating flows; heat transfer from capillary wetted surfaces with applications toward heat pipes; computerized data bases. *Mailing Add:* 2527 Corte Bella Pleasanton CA 94566

GOLUBIC, STEPHAN, ECOLOGY, PHYCOLOGY. *Current Pos:* assoc prof, 70-80, PROF BIOL, BOSTON UNIV, 80- *Personal Data:* b Zagreb, Yugoslavia, May 4, 34. *Educ:* Univ Zagreb, dipl biol, 56, PhD(biol sci), 63. *Prof Exp:* Res asst inst exp biol, Yugoslavia Acad Sci, Univ Zagreb, 56-59; res asst, Inst Marine Biol, Rovinj, 59-63; Alexander von Humboldt Found fel, Inst Limnol, Univ Freiburg, 63-65; res assoc geol, Princeton Univ, 65-66; from instr to asst prof biol, Yale Univ, 66-69; assoc prof, Peterson State Col, 69-70. *Concurrent Pos:* NSF res grant, 67-69 & 70-71, 71-75, 74-76, 76-79; res grant, NASA, 79 & 81. *Mem:* Brit Phycol Soc; Phycol Soc Am; Int Phycol Soc; Int Asn Theoret & Appl Limnol; Sigma Xi. *Res:* Phycology, ecology and taxonomy of Cyanophyta; limnology; marine biology; ecology of carbonate deposition and dissolution; precambrian microfossils and stromatolites; water pollution. *Mailing Add:* Dept Biol Boston Univ Five Cummington St Boston MA 02215

GOLUBITSKY, MARTIN AARON, BIFURCATION THEORY, SINGULARITY THEORY. *Current Pos:* PROF MATH, UNIV HOUSTON, 83- *Personal Data:* b Philadelphia, Pa, Apr 5, 45; m 76, Barbara L Keyfitz; c Elizabeth & Alexander. *Educ:* Univ Pa, AB & AM, 66; Mass Inst Technol, PhD(math), 70. *Prof Exp:* From asst prof to assoc prof math, Queens Col, NY, 74-79; prof math, Ariz State Univ, 79-83. *Concurrent Pos:* Vis mem, Courant Inst, New York Univ, 77-78, Inst Advan Study, 78; assoc prof, Univ Nice, 80; vis prof, Duke Univ, 81; vis sr scientist, Univ Calif, Berkeley, 82. *Mem:* Fel AAAS; Am Math Soc; Soc Indust & Appl Math; Soc Natural Philos. *Res:* Application of singularity theory & group theory techniques to bifurcation theory & their application to physical problems, such as pattern formation in fluid systems. *Mailing Add:* Dept Math Univ Houston Houston TX 77204. *Fax:* 713-743-3505; *E-Mail:* mg@uh.edu

GOLUBJATNIKOV, RJURIK, MICROBIOLOGY, EPIDEMIOLOGY. *Current Pos:* ASST PROF PREV MED & CHIEF, IMMUNOL SECT, STATE LAB HYG, UNIV WIS-MADISON, 67- *Personal Data:* b Kuressaare, Estonia, June 19, 31; US citizen. *Educ:* Millikin Univ, BA, 54; Univ Mich, MPH, 58, PhD(epidemiol sci), 64. *Prof Exp:* Asst prof prev med & dir, Vaccine Eval Prog Lab, State Univ NY, Buffalo, 64-67. *Concurrent Pos:* Assoc investr, USPHS res grant, 64-68; prin investr, Huixquilucan Serum Surv grant, 67-68; Ecol Studies Mycoplasma grant, 68-69; adv, Inst Nutrit Cent Am & Panama, 68; Alpha-Fetoprotein Maternal Serum Screening Proj grant, 77-; partic, Int Schoolchildren Study Serum Cholesterol Levels, 78; AIDS Studies, 84-; effects of aldicarb contaminated well water on immunity, 86-; specialist microbiologist, Pub Health & Med Lab Microbiol, Am Acad Microbiol. *Mem:* AAAS; Am Pub Health Asn; Am Soc Microbiol; Asn Teachers Prev Med; Am Venereal Dis Asn; Soc Epidemiol Res. *Res:* Immunology, including primary and secondary antibody responses and immunologic memory; infectious disease epidemiology; serological epidemiology; vaccine sxudies; perinatal health; childhood antecendents of coronary heart disease, epidemiology of AIDS; effects of aldicarb contaminated well water on immunity; clinical trials of immunodiagnostic devices; hepatitis C serodiagnosis; hepatitis E seroepidemiology. *Mailing Add:* 2920 Harvard Dr Madison WI 53705

GOLUBOVIC, ALEKSANDAR, CHEMISTRY. *Current Pos:* RES SCIENTIST CHEM, ROME LAB, HANSCOM AFB, BEDFORD, MASS, 64- *Personal Data:* b Maribor, Yugoslavia, Feb 19, 20; US citizen; m 60; c 1. *Educ:* Univ Zagreb, dipl, 43, PhD(chem), 60. *Prof Exp:* Res chemist, Inst Indust Res, Univ Zagreb, 45-56; res assoc chem, Mass Inst Technol, 56-62; sr scientist, Tyco Labs, Mass, 62-64. *Mem:* Am Chem Soc; Am Vacuum Soc. *Res:* Semiconductors and photoconductors; thin film technology and phenomena. *Mailing Add:* 31 Heath St Brookline MA 02146-5909

GOLUBOW, JULIUS, biochemistry, for more information see previous edition

GOLUEKE, CLARENCE GEORGE, ENVIRONMENTAL SCIENCES. *Current Pos:* dir res & develop, 78-92, VPRES, CAL RECOVERY SYSTS, INC, 92- *Personal Data:* b Menominee, Mich, Sept 28, 11; m 48; c 1. *Educ:* St Louis Univ, BA, 39; Univ Ill, MA, 41; Univ Calif, PhD(mycol), 53. *Honors & Awards:* Arthur M Wellington Prize, Am Soc Civil Engrs, 66. *Prof Exp:* Instr gen sci, Nazareth Col, 45-46; asst bot, Univ Ill, 48; asst bot, Sanit Eng Res Lab, Univ Calif, Berkeley, 48-51, lectr & res biologist, 51-78. *Concurrent Pos:* Consult, Erco, Inc, Cambridge, Mass, Calif State Depts Water Resources & Pub Health, US Environ Protection Agency & UN Indust Develop Orgn, Vienna, Austria; sr ed, Biocycle, Emmaus, Pa. *Mem:* Sigma Xi; Am Pub Health Asn; AAAS. *Res:* Environmental health sciences; waste treatment and resource recovery; closed environmental systems; on-site waste disposal. *Mailing Add:* Cal Recovery 725-C Alfred Noble Dr Hercules CA 94547

GOLUMBIC, CALVIN, BIOCHEMISTRY. *Current Pos:* RETIRED. *Personal Data:* b Lock Haven, Pa, Nov 8, 12; m 46, Norma Richman; c Jennifer. *Educ:* Pa State Col, BS, 34; Rutgers Univ, MS, 35, PhD(org chem), 37. *Honors & Awards:* Cert Merit, USDA, 63 & 69. *Prof Exp:* Res assoc antioxygens, Univ Iowa, 37-42; chemist, Rockefeller Inst, 42-45; asst res prof chem, Univ Pittsburgh, 45-47; chemist, Bur Mines, 47-53; chemist, Naval Stores Res Sect, Agr Res Serv, USDA, 53-54, head, Qual Eval Sect, Biol Sci Br, Mkt Res Div, 54-60, chief field crops & animal prod br, 60-67, asst dir, Mkt Qual Div, 67-68, asst dep adminr, 68-72, staff officer, 72-82. *Concurrent Pos:* Consult, 82- *Mem:* Am Chem Soc; NY Acad Sci; Inst Food Technol; Am Asn Cereal Chemists. *Res:* Antioxidants and autooxidation of fats; vitamin E; nitrogen mustards; countercurrent distribution; coal, food and agricultural chemistry; synthetic liquid fuels; terpenes. *Mailing Add:* 6000 Highboro Dr Bethesda MD 20817-6008

GOLUMBIC, MARTIN CHARLES, COMPUTER SCIENCE & MATHEMATICS. *Current Pos:* RES STAFF MEM, IBM ISRAEL SCI CTR, HAIFA, ISRAEL, 83- *Personal Data:* b Erie Pa, Sept 30, 48; c 4. *Educ:* Pa State Univ, BS, 70, MA (Math), 70; Columbia Univ, Ma, 71; PhD, 75. *Honors & Awards:* Rensselaer Medal for Excellence in Math, 66; Hon Mention, NSF, 70. *Prof Exp:* Jr mathematician, U S Army Comput Syst Command, 70; vis scientist, IBM Watson Res Ctr, Yorktown Heights, NY, 74 & 89-90; mem tech staff, Bell Tel Lab, Murray Hill, NJ, 80-82. *Concurrent Pos:* Asst prof Comput Sci, New York Univ, Courant Instit Math, 75-80; vis prof, Universite de Paris VI, Istutut de Programmation, 76-77; res grants, NSF, 78-81; adj prof, Bar-Ilan Univ, Ramat Gan, Israel, 85-; mem adv bd, Int J Expert Syst: Res & Appln, 86-90; ed-in-chief, J Annals Math & Artificial Intel, 88-; Found fel, Inst Combinatorics & Appln, 91. *Res:* Computer science and mathematics; patents; author of book and numerous publications. *Mailing Add:* 318 E 37th St Erie PA 16504

GOLUMBIC, NORMA, CANCER. *Current Pos:* FREE LANCE MEDICAL WRITER, 79- *Personal Data:* b Brooklyn, NY, Apr 30, 16; m 46, Calvin; c Jennifer. *Educ:* Brooklyn Col, BA, 36; Univ Iowa, MS, 38. *Prof Exp:* Chemist, Bur Mines, 42-50; sci writer, Agr Res Serv, USDA, 55; sci writer, Nat Cancer Inst, 56-58, head, Res & Prog Reports Sec, 58-69, asst chief, Res Info Br, 65-69; info officer, Div Nursing, NIH, 69-74, sr sci ed, Nat Cancer Inst, 74-79. *Mem:* AAAS; Am Chem Soc; fel Am Inst Chemists; Nat Asn Sci Writers. *Res:* Synthetic liquid fuels; coal chemistry; catalysis; cancer research literature; medical writing. *Mailing Add:* 6000 Highboro Dr Bethesda MD 20817-6008

GOLWAY, PETER L, animal care research; deceased, see previous edition for last biography

GOMATOS, PETER JOHN, BIOCHEMISTRY, VIROLOGY. *Current Pos:* AT LETTERMN ARMY MED CTR. *Personal Data:* b Cambridge, Mass, Feb 13, 29. *Educ:* Mass Inst Technol, SB, 50; Johns Hopkins Univ, MD, 54; Rockefeller Inst, PhD(virol), 63. *Prof Exp:* Med asst resident, Boston City Hosp, 57-58; sr med resident, Mass Gen Hosp, 58-59; guest investr, Rockefeller Inst, 63-64; mem, Sloan-Kettering Inst, 64- *Concurrent Pos:* Vis investr, Max Planck Inst Virus Res, 64 & Inst Virol, Univ Glasgow, 64-65. *Mem:* Am Chem Soc; Harvey Soc; Am Asn Immunologists; Am Col Physicians. *Res:* Study of physical-chemical characteristics of viruses; effects of viruses on cells; neoplastic potential of various viruses. *Mailing Add:* Ctr Spec Immunol 1625 SE Third Ave Ft Lauderdale FL 33316

GOMBAR, CHARLES T, experimental biology, for more information see previous edition

GOMBERG, HENRY J(ACOB), nuclear engineering; deceased, see previous edition for last biography

GOMBERG, JOAN SUSAN, REGIONAL NETWORK SEISMOLOGY, SEISMIC HAZARD ASSESSMENT. *Current Pos:* CTR EARTHQUAKE RES & INFO, MEMPHIS STATE UNIV, 94- *Personal Data:* b Chicago, Ill, Nov 1, 57; m 89. *Educ:* Mass Inst Technol, BS, 79; Univ Calif, San Diego, PhD(geophys), 86. *Prof Exp:* Postdoctoral, Univ Nev, Reno, 87-88; geophysicist, US Geol Surv, 88-94. *Mem:* Am Geophys Union; Seismol Soc Am. *Res:* Seismic network operations; analysis of seismicity data; assessing regional seismic hazard. *Mailing Add:* 300 Hawthorne St Memphis State Univ Memphis TN 38112

GOMBOS, ANDREW MICHAEL, JR, MICROPALEONTOLOGY, MARINE GEOLOGY. *Current Pos:* RES SPECIALIST, EXXON PROD RES CO, 78-, EXPLOR GEOPHYSICIST, 95- *Personal Data:* b Beaver Falls, Pa, June 10, 48. *Educ:* Washington & Lee Univ, BS, 70; Univ Ill, MS, 73; Fla State Univ, PhD(geol), 76. *Prof Exp:* Develop geologist, Chevron USA, Inc, 76-78. *Concurrent Pos:* Penrose grant, Geol Soc Am, 74; res assoc, Carnegie Mus Natural Hist, 81- *Mem:* Soc Economic Paleontologists & Mineralogists; Sigma Xi; Geol Soc Am; Gulf Coast Asn Geol Sci; Am Asn Petrol Geologists. *Res:* Stratigraphical distribution and evolution of diatoms; antarctic marine geology and paleohistory; seismic stratigraphy of fluvial facies. *Mailing Add:* Exxon Explor Co PO Box 146 Houston TX 77001-0146. *E-Mail:* airburst@neosoft.com

GOMER, RICHARD HANS, CELL BIOLOGY, DICTYOSTELIUM. *Current Pos:* ASST PROF, RICE UNIV, 88- *Personal Data:* b Chicago, Ill, Oct 11, 56; m 86, Maureen Price; c Katie. *Educ:* Pomona Col, BA, 77; Calif Inst Technol, PhD(biol), 83. *Honors & Awards:* Tileston Physics Prize. *Prof Exp:* Fel, Dept Biol, Univ Calif, San Diego, 83-88. *Concurrent Pos:* Vis scientist, Mt Wilson & Las Campanas Observ, Carnegie Inst Wash, 83; asst investr, HHMI, 90-; adj asst prof, Baylor Col Med, 90- *Mem:* Am Soc Cell Biol. *Res:* Using physics, cell and molecular biology techniques to study cell density sensing and cell fate determination in Dictyostelium discoideum. *Mailing Add:* Dept Biochem & Cell Biol Howard Hughes Med Inst Rice Univ Houston TX 77251-1892. *Fax:* 713-285-5154

GOMER, ROBERT, PHYSICAL CHEMISTRY. *Current Pos:* from instr to prof, James Frank Inst, Univ Chicago, 50-77, dir, James Franck Inst, 77-83, C W Eisendrath distinguished prof, 84-96, EMER PROF CHEM, JAMES FRANCK INST, UNIV CHICAGO, 96- *Personal Data:* b Vienna, Austria, Mar 24, 24; nat US; m 55; c 2. *Educ:* Pomona Col, BA, 44; Univ Rochester, PhD(chem), 49. *Honors & Awards:* Bourke Lectr, Eng, 59; Kendall Award, Am Chem Soc, 75, Arthur W Adamson Award, 96; Humboldt Sr US Scientist Award, 78; Davisson-Germer Prize, Am Phys Soc, 81; M W Welch Award, Am Vacuum Soc, 89. *Prof Exp:* AEC fel chem, Harvard Univ, 49-50. *Concurrent Pos:* Sloan fel, 58-61; Guggenheim fel, 69-70; Fulbright prof, Austria, 81. *Mem:* Nat Acad Sci; Am Chem Soc; Am Acad Arts & Sci; Lepoldina Akademie. *Res:* Surface chemistry and physics; field and ion emission; surface diffusion; electron stimulated desorption; metal overlayers. *Mailing Add:* 4824 S Kimbark Ave Chicago IL 60615-1916

GOMES, WAYNE REGINALD, REPRODUCTIVE BIOLOGY, ANIMAL SCIENCES. *Current Pos:* prof & head dairy sci, 81-85, prof & head animal sci, 85-89, DEAN, COL AGR, UNIV ILL, 89- *Personal Data:* b Modesto, Calif, Nov 15, 38; m 64, Carol L Gerlach; c John & Regina. *Educ:* Calif Polytech State Univ, BS, 60; Wash State Univ, MS, 62; Purdue Univ, PhD(endocrine physiol), 65. *Prof Exp:* From asst prof to prof dairy sci, Animal Reproduction Ctr, Ohio State Univ, 65-81. *Concurrent Pos:* Res award, Ohio Sigma Xi, 70; Fulbright-Hays traveling fel, 74. *Mem:* Am Dairy Sci Asn; Am Soc Animal Sci; Am Physiol Soc; Soc Study Reproduction; fel Japan Soc Prom Sci; Endocrine Soc. *Res:* Biochemistry and endocrinology of testis function. *Mailing Add:* 2402 Provine Circle Urbana IL 61801. *Fax:* 217-244-2911; *E-Mail:* w_gomes@uiuc.edu

GOMEZ, ARTURO, CARDIOPULMONARY INTERACTIONS IN SECONDARY PULMONARY HYPERTENSION. *Current Pos:* ASSOC PROF MED, PROF MED CARDIOL & SR SCIENTIST, NAT HEART INST, MEX, 89-, ASSOC PROF MED, NURSING SCH, 90- *Personal Data:* b Monterrey, NL, Sept 27, 51; m 82; c 3. *Educ:* Univ Nuevo Leon, Bachelor, 69, MD, 76; Univ Man, PhD(physiol), 86. *Honors & Awards:* St Boniface Res Found Inc Award, 88. *Concurrent Pos:* Sr clin fel crit care med, ABC Hosp, Mex, 80-82, chest med, Univ Man, 86-87; sr res fel cardiorespiratory serv, Nat Heart Inst, 83-84, Univ Man, 87-89; sr scientist, Nat Res Syst, Mex, 89-, Nat Health Care Syst, Mex, 90- *Mem:* Am Thoracic Soc; Fedn Am Socs Exp Biol. *Res:* Heart and lung interactions in patients; experimental studies in animals with pulmonary hypertension, especially the right ventricle; teaching cardiopulmonary interactions. *Mailing Add:* Nat Inst Cardiol Dept Cardioneumolog Juan Badiano I Tlalpan Mexico City DF 14080 Mexico

GOMEZ, ILDEFONSO LUIS, ORGANIC CHEMISTRY, POLYMER CHEMISTRY. *Current Pos:* INT CONSULT, 91- *Personal Data:* b Cardenas, Cuba, Jan 23, 28; div; c 6. *Educ:* Univ Havana, DSc(chem), 52. *Prof Exp:* Anal chemist, Cia Rayonera Cuba, 51-52, res chemist, 52-56; tech supvr, Plinex SA, 56-58, tech supt, 58-61; sr res chemist, Monsanto Co, Mass, 61-67, res specialist, 67-68, specialist, Tech Dept, Plastic Prod & Resins Div, 68-70, specialist, Packaging Div, 70-74, group leader, New Prod Develop, Bloomfield, 74-79, sr technol specialist, 79-82, sci fel, Indust Res Div, 82-91. *Concurrent Pos:* Consult, Ministry Com, Cuba, 58-60; vis lectr, Univ Havana, 59-60; ed-at-large, Marcel Dekker, Inc, 84- *Mem:* Am Chem Soc; Soc Plastics Engrs; NY Acad Sci. *Res:* Rheology and melt processing of high nitrile and polyester polymers for carbonated beverage and food containers fabrication; coloring and recycle of polymers; prototype equipment development for processing polymers into containers; phenolic resins for glass fiber bonding applications; polyvinylbutyral interlayers for architectural applications. *Mailing Add:* 223 Franklin Rd Longmeadow MA 01106

GOMEZ, VERNON R, METAL & NONMETAL MINE SAFETY & HEALTH. *Current Pos:* metal & nonmetal mine inspector, SDak Field Off, Mine Safety & Health Agency, 74-81, sub-dist mgr metal & nonmetal, Phoenix, Ariz Subdist Off, 81-87, dist mgr, Rocky Mountain Dist Off, Colo, 87-91, dist mgr, Western Dist Off, Calif, 91-92, ADMIN METAL & NONMETAL MINE SAFETY & HEALTH, HQ OFF, MINE SAFETY & HEALTH AGENCY, 92- *Personal Data:* b Woodsboro, Tex. *Prof Exp:* Miner, San Manuel Div, Magma Copper Co. *Mailing Add:* Mine Safety & Health Agency Metal/Non Metal 4015 Wilson Blvd Arlington VA 22203

GOMEZ-CAMBRONERO, JULIAN, SIGNAL TRANSDUCTION, CELL BIOLOGY. *Current Pos:* Fel cell biol, 86-90, instr physiol, 91-92, ASST PROF, DEPT PHYSIOL, SCH MED, UNIV CONN HEALTH CTR, 92- *Personal Data:* b Manzanares, Spain, Sept 29, 59; m 82, Teresa Madrid; c David. *Educ:* Univ Complutense, Madrid, BS, 82, MS, 83, PhD(biochem), 86. *Concurrent Pos:* Fel, Am Heart Asn, 87-88; young investr award, Soc Leukocyte Biol, 92; appointee, Farmington, Conn Pub Sch Syst K-12 Sci Curric Eval Comt, 93-94. *Mem:* Am Soc Cell Biol; Soc Leukocyte Biol; Am Soc Biochem & Molecular Biol. *Res:* Molecular mechanisms of cell activation and signal transduction in leukocytes; intracellular changes by cytokines and colony-stimulating factors; tyrosine phosphorylation induced by several cell agonists; inflammatory mediators of lipidic nature and mechanisms of actuation; enzyme purification and characterization; tyrosine phosphorylation. *Mailing Add:* Dept Physiol & Biophys Wright State Univ Sch Med 064 Med Sci Bldg 3640 Colonel Glenn Hwy Dayton OH 45435-0002. *Fax:* 937-873-3769

GOMEZPLATA, ALBERT, CHEMICAL ENGINEERING. *Current Pos:* after 58-68, prof chem eng, 68-82, assoc dean, 82-85, EMER PROF, UNIV MD BALTIMORE COUNTY, 85- *Personal Data:* b Colombia, SAm, July 2, 30; nat US; c 3. *Educ:* Polytech Inst Brooklyn, BSc, 52; Rensselaer Polytech Inst, MSc, 54, PhD(chem eng), 59. *Prof Exp:* Process engr, Gen Chem Div, Del Works, 52-53. *Concurrent Pos:* Year in indust prof, E I du Pont de Nemours & Co, Inc, 65-66; vis prof, Univ PR, 70-71; consult, Naval Ship Res Develop Ctr, Anapolis Md. *Mem:* Fel Am Inst Chem; Am Inst Chem Engrs; Am Soc Eng Educ; NY Acad Sci; Sigma Xi. *Res:* Kinetics; heterogeneous flow systems; fluidized beds. *Mailing Add:* Dept Chem Eng Univ Md Baltimore County Baltimore MD 21228

GOMEZ-RODRIGUEZ, MANUEL, THEORETICAL PHYSICS, SOLID STATE PHYSICS. *Current Pos:* asst prof physics, 69-71, chmn dept, 71-75, dean, Col Nat Sci, 75-86, PROF PHYSICS, UNIV PR, 75-, DIR RESOURCE CTR SCI & ENG, 86- *Personal Data:* b Ponce, PR, Oct 15, 40; US citizen; m 65; c 2. *Educ:* Univ PR, BSc, 62; Cornell Univ, PhD(theoret physics), 68. *Prof Exp:* Fel solid state physics, Naval Res Lab, Washington, DC, 67-69; scientist, PR Nuclear Ctr, 70-74. *Concurrent Pos:* Fel Nat Res Coun-Nat Acad Sci, 67-69; NSF grant, Off Naval Res, 74 & Army Res Off, 81-; proj dir comput in teaching sci, NSF, 76-, minority ctr grad educ sci, 77-79 & dir, Resource Ctr Sci & Eng, PR, 80-, dir, Exp Prog Stimulate Competitive Res, 86. *Mem:* Am Phys Soc; Sigma Xi; Sci Teachers Asn PR (pres, 74). *Res:* Theoretical solid state physics; optical properties of solids; optical properties of CERMET materials utilized in thermal solar collectors; phase transitions of ferroelectrics materials. *Mailing Add:* Univ PR Resource Ctr Sci & Eng PO Box 23334 Rio Piedras PR 00931

GOMMEL, WILLIAM RAYMOND, METEOROLOGY. *Current Pos:* asst prof math, 65-69, assoc prof math & earth sci, 69-75, PROF MATH & EARTH SCI, IND CENT UNIV, 76-, CHMN DEPT EARTH SCI, 66- *Personal Data:* b Indianapolis, Ind, Aug 16, 24; m 43; c 3. *Educ:* Univ Calif, Los Angeles, AB, 51, MA, 52; Purdue Univ, PhD(atmospheric sci), 73. *Prof Exp:* Weather cent anal supvr, USAF, Ger, 52-53, chief, Tech Info & Ed, Hqs 2nd Weather Wing, 53-55, Tech Pubs Br, Sci Servs, Hqs Air Weather Serv, 55-56, asst to dir, Sci Serv, 56-58, staff meteorologist, Ballistic Missile Div, 60-61, Space Systs Div, 62-63, staff scientist, Directorate Sci & Tech, Hqs, 64-65. *Concurrent Pos:* Meteorologist, Channel 13, Video Ind, Inc, Indianapolis, 75; cooperator, NOAA Weather Radio Broadcast Facil, Indianapolis, 77- *Mem:* AAAS; Am Geophys Union; Am Meteorol Soc; Sigma Xi. *Res:* Interaction between sea and atmosphere; climatic change; synoptic meteorology; cloud physics; upper atmosphere; satellites; instrumentation; tropical storms; hurricanes; eclipse meteorology. *Mailing Add:* 2301 Lawrence Ave Indianapolis IN 46227-8635

GOMOLL, ALLEN W, PHARMACOLOGY. *Current Pos:* res fel, 84-90, SR RES FEL, BRISTOL-MYERS SQUIBB PRI, 90- *Personal Data:* b Chicago, Ill, July 10, 33; m 55, Elaine Kirkpatrick; c Gary A & Lisa E. *Educ:* Univ Ill, BS, 55, MS, 58, PhD(pharmacol), 61. *Honors & Awards:* Grad Res Award, Sigma Xi, 61. *Prof Exp:* From instr to asst prof pharmacol, Col Med, Univ Ill, 61-66; sr scientist, Mead Johnson Pharmaceut, 66-67, group leader cardiovasc pharmacol, 67-69, sect leader, 69-70, prin investr cardiovasc pharmacol, 70-76, prin res assoc, 76-80, prin mgr, 80- 81, prin res scientist, Biol Res, 81-84. *Concurrent Pos:* Mem, Basic Sci Coun & fel Coun Circulation, Am Heart Asn. *Mem:* AAAS; NY Acad Sci; Am Heart Asn; Am Soc Pharmacol & Exp Therapeut; Soc Exp Biol & Med; Sigma Xi; fel Am Col Cardiol; Int Soc Heart Res. *Res:* Cardiovascular pharmacology; renal pharmacology; myocardial ischamia. *Mailing Add:* Dept Cardiovasc Pharmacol PO Box 4000 Bldg Fl 4514 Princeton NJ 08543-4000

GOMORY, RALPH E, APPLIED MATHEMATICS. *Current Pos:* PRES, ALFRED P SLOAN FOUND, 89- *Personal Data:* b New York, NY, May 7, 29; div; c 3. *Educ:* Williams Col, BA, 50; Princeton Univ, PhD(math), 54. *Hon Degrees:* DSc, Williams Col, 73, Polytech Univ, 86, Syracuse Univ, 89, Carnegie Mellon Univ, 89, Worcester Polytech Univ, 89; LHD, Pace Univ. *Honors & Awards:* Lanchester Prize, Opers Res Soc Am, 63; John von Neumann Theory Prize, Opers Res Soc & Inst Mgt Sci, 84; Harry Goode Mem Award, Am Fedn Info Processing Soc, 84; Indust Res Inst Medal, 85; nat Medal of Sci, 88; Leadership Recognition Award, Inst Elec & Electronics Engrs, 88; Pres Award, NY Acad Sci, 92; Arthur M Bueche Award, Nat Acad Eng, 93. *Prof Exp:* Asst prof math & Higgins lectr, Princeton Univ, 57-59; mgr mgt sci & combinatorial studies, T J Watson Res Ctr, IBM Corp, 59-64, dir, Math Sci Dept, 65-70, mem, Corp Tech Comt, 70, dir res, 70-86, vpres, 73-84, sr vpres, 85-86, sr vpres sci & technol, 86-89. *Concurrent Pos:* Mem, Adv Panel Appl Math Div, Nat Bur Stand, 64-68; mem, Mayor's Opers Res Coun NY, 66-70, vchmn, 69-70; consult, NSF, 67-69; mem, Comt Appln Math, Div Math Sci, Nat Res Coun, 67-70, chmn, 69-70, mem-at-large, 69-72; adj prof, Courant Inst, NY Univ, 70-71; Andrew D White prof-at-large, Cornell Univ, 70-76; mem, Vis Comt, Sloan Sch Mgt, Mass Inst Technol, 71-77; mem, Coun Grad Sch Bus, Univ Chicago, 71-80; bd trustees, Conf Bd Math Sci, 72-74; bd trustees, T A Edison Found, 73-77 & Hampshire Col, 77-86; chmn, Nat Acad Sci Sci Adv Comt, Int Inst Appl Systs Res, 73-75; mem, Comt Soc Sci, Yale Univ Coun, 74-77; mem adv coun, Sch Eng, Stanford Univ, 78-85; dir, Bank NY, 81-, Wash Post Co, Ashland Oil, Inc & Lexmark Int, Inc; mem adv coun, Dept Math, Princeton Univ, 82-85, chmn, 84-85; mem, Pres Coun Adv Sci & Technol, 90- *Mem:* Nat Acad Sci; Nat Acad Eng; Am Acad Arts & Sci;

fel Economet Soc; Am Math Soc; Am Philos Soc; Sigma Xi; hon mem Inst Elec & Electronics Engrs; Oper Res Soc Am. *Res:* Linear and integer programming; network flow theory; nonlinear differential equations; computers; nature of technology and product development; research in industry; industrial competitiveness. *Mailing Add:* Alfred P Sloan Found 630 Fifth Ave Suite 2550 New York NY 10111

GOMPERTZ, MICHAEL L, INTERNAL MEDICINE, GASTROENTEROLOGY. *Current Pos:* from instr to assoc prof, 55-68, prof, 68-87, EMER PROF MED GASTROENTEROL, COL MED, UNIV TENN, MEMPHIS, 87- *Personal Data:* b New Haven, Conn, Dec 10, 12; m 41; c 2. *Educ:* Yale Univ, BA, 33; Columbia Univ, MD, 37. *Prof Exp:* Asst chief gastroenterol, Vet Admin Hosp, Memphis, 53-55, chief, 55-83. *Mem:* Fel Am Col Physicians; Am Gastroenterol Asn. *Res:* Clinical research in liver disease and peptic ulcer disease. *Mailing Add:* Univ Tenn 951 Court Ave Memphis TN 38163

GONA, AMOS G, ENDOCRINOLOGY, DEVELOPMENTAL NEUROBIOLOGY. *Current Pos:* from asst prof to assoc prof, 68-77, PROF ANAT, UNIV MED & DENT NJ, 77- *Personal Data:* b Nandyal, India, July 16, 33; US citizen; m 62; c 2. *Educ:* Andhra Univ, India, BSc, 54; City Col New York, MA, 65; Albert Einstein Col Med, PhD(anat), 67. *Prof Exp:* Lectr demonstr zool, Andhra Christian Col, India, 54-55 & Univ Rangoon, 55-57; sci master, Anglo-Chinese Sch, Malaysia, 57-60; sr biol master, Opoku Ware Sch, Ghana, 60-63; NIH fel anat, Albert Einstein Col Med, 68. *Mem:* Am Asn Anat; Soc Neurosci; Bioelectromagnetics Soc; Int Soc Bioelec. *Res:* Electron microscopy; endocrines and neuroendocrines in amphibian metamorphosis; normal and thyroid-induced maturation of cerebellum; biological effects of low frequency electromagnetic fields. *Mailing Add:* Dept Anat UMDJ-NJMS 185 S Orange Ave Newark NJ 07103-2757. *Fax:* 973-982-7489

GONA, OPHELIA DELAINE, OPHTHALMIC RESEARCH, ENDOCRINOLOGY. *Current Pos:* asst prof, 77-86, ASSOC PROF ANAT, NJ MED SCH, UNIV MED & DENT NJ, 86- *Personal Data:* b Columbia, SC; m 62; c 2. *Educ:* Johnson C Smith Univ, BS, 57; Yeshiva Univ, MS, 64; City Col New York, MA, 69; City Univ New York, PhD(biol), 71. *Prof Exp:* Lab technician, New York Univ, 57-58; high sch instr biol, New York City Public Schs, 58-61; vol, US Peace Corps, 61-63; instr, City Col New York, 69-71; asst prof, Montclair State Col, 71-77. *Mem:* Am Asn Anatomists; AAAS; NY Acad Sci; Nat Asn Res Sci Teachers; Am Asn Univ Women; Asn Advan Health Educ. *Res:* Educational methodology for effective teaching of science to educationally deprived pre-college students. *Mailing Add:* Dept Anat Univ Med & Dent NJ NJ Med Sch 185 S Orange Ave Newark NJ 07103

GONANO, JOHN ROLAND, RESEARCH & DEVELOPMENT MANAGEMENT, COMMERCIALIZATION OF US GOVERNMENT DEVELOPED TECHNOLOGY. *Current Pos:* CONSULT, COMMERCIALIZATION US GOVT TECHNOL & RES & DEVELOP MGT, 96- *Personal Data:* b Winchester, Va, Jan 21, 39; m 59, Joyce Dove; c Gina (Bickish), Dawn & John. *Educ:* Univ WVa, BS, 60; Duke Univ, PhD(physics), 67. *Prof Exp:* Fel, Univ Fla, 66-68; res physicist, Nat Bur Stand, 68-71; res physicist, US Army Mobility Equip Res & Develop Command, 71-82; res & develop mgr, US Army Mat Command, 82-86; mgr & chair, US Army Adv Concepts & Technol Comt, US Army Res Lab, 86-92, technol transfer mgr, 92-95. *Mem:* Am Phys Soc; Sigma Xi. *Res:* Research and development management and measures of effectiveness for research and development investment; commercialization of technology; defense research and technology. *Mailing Add:* 10401 Regina Ct Clarksburg MD 20871

GONDA, MATTHEW ALLEN, AIDS VIROLOGY, AIDS ANIMAL MODELS. *Current Pos:* HEAD, LAB CELL & MOLECULAR STRUCT, NCI-FREDERICK CANCER RES FACIL, 88- *Personal Data:* b Cheverly, Md, Aug 13, 49; m 83; c 2. *Educ:* Univ Va, BS, 71; George Mason Univ, MS, 76; Johns Hopkins Univ, PhD(virol), 82. *Prof Exp:* Res asst electron micros, Meloy Labs, 71-73; head electron micros, Litton Bionetics, Frederick Cancer Res Facil, 73-87. *Concurrent Pos:* Lectr, Grad Prog, Hood Col, 79 & Sch Hyg & Pub Health, Johns Hopkins Univ, 88-91; consult, Kirkegard & Perry Labs, Inc & Bethesda Res Labs, 81-82, Johns Hopkins Univ, 85-86, Oncor, 84-85, Serano Labs, 87, Centocor, 88 & NY State Inst Basic Res, 90. *Mem:* AAAS; Sigma Xi; Am Soc Microbiol. *Res:* To understand the molecular mechanisms of pathogenesis and persistence of lentiviruses by using animal retroviruses (lentiviruses) related to AIDS; develop animal models for AIDS to test vaccines and therapeutic agents; retrovirus biology; gene expression; gene regulation. *Mailing Add:* 3517 Runneymeade Dr Newton Square PA 19073

GONDER, ERIC CHARLES, POULTRY, POULTRY PRODUCTION. *Current Pos:* VET POULTRY, GOLDSBORO MILLING CO, 86- *Personal Data:* b Jefferson, Iowa, July 7, 50; m 87. *Educ:* Iowa State Univ, DVM, 74; Univ Minn, MS, 76; NC State Univ, PhD(vet path), 91. *Prof Exp:* Vet med asst I&II, Dept Path, Col Vet Med, Univ Minn, 74-76; vet virol, USAMRIID, US Army, 76-78; net poultry, ASL/Schering Plough, 78-83; vet med asst I&II, FAE, Col Vet Med, NC State Univ, 83-86. *Mem:* Am Asn Avian Pathologists; Poultry Sci Asn; US Animal Health Asn; Asn Vet Turkey Prod; World Poultry Sci Asn; Am Asn Indust Veteuinaricing. *Res:* Focal ulcerative dermatitis of turkeys; enteric disease of turkeys. *Mailing Add:* Goldsboro Milling Co PO Drawer 10009 Goldsboro NC 27532

GONDOS, BERNARD, EXPERIMENTAL BIOLOGY. *Current Pos:* SR SCIENTIST, SANSUM MED RES FOUND, SANTA BARBARA, CALIF, 86-, DIR PATH, 86- *Personal Data:* b New York, NY, Jan 6, 35. *Educ:* Yale Univ, BS, 56; George Washington Univ, MD, 59. *Prof Exp:* Asst prof path,

Sch Med, Univ Calif, Los Angeles, 67-73; assoc clin prof path, Sch Med, Univ Calif, San Francisco, 73-75, assoc prof path, 75-78; dir anat path, Health Ctr Univ Conn, 78-86. *Concurrent Pos:* Chief cytol & gynec path, Harbor Gen Hosp, Torrance, Calif, 67-73; fac mem, prog reproductive biol, Harbor Gen Hosp & Sch Med, Univ Calif, Los Angeles, 68-70; dir, Sch Cytotechnol, Harbor Gen Hosp, 69-73; chief cytol serv & gynec path, San Francisco Med Ctr, Univ Calif, 73-78; fac mem & dir, ultrastruct studies fac, Reproductive Endocrinol Ctr, Univ Calif, San Francisco, 74-78. *Res:* Experimental biology; numerous publications. *Mailing Add:* 637 Avenida Pequena Santa Barbara CA 93111

GONG, PENG, remote sensing, geographic information systems, for more information see previous edition

GONG, WILLIAM C, CLINICAL PHARMACY, PRIMARY CARE PHARMACY PRACTICE. *Current Pos:* Lectr, 74-75, asst prof, 75-82, ASSOC PROF CLIN PHARM, UNIV SOUTHERN CALIF, 82- *Personal Data:* b San Francisco, Calif, Aug 22, 48; m 84, Li-In Chen; c Cynthia L, Jennifer S, Elizabeth C, Daniel W & Carole Ann. *Educ:* San Jose State Univ, BA, 70; Univ Southern Calif, PharmD(pharm), 74. *Honors & Awards:* Outstanding Serv Award, Am Diabetes Asn, 89. *Concurrent Pos:* Residency in clin pharm, Los Angeles Co, Univ Southern Calif Med Ctr, Los Angeles, 74-75, coordr, Residency Prog, Sch Pharm, 78-90, sect leader, Ambulatory Care Progs, 78-85; course coordr ambulatory care & skill nursing, 85-; dir, Residency & Fel Training Progs, 90-; vchair primary care, Am Soc Hosp Pharmacists, 90, chmn, 91. *Mem:* Am Col Clin Pharmacol; fel Am Soc Hosp Pharmacists; Am Asn Col Pharm; Am Pharmaceut Asn. *Res:* Investigation of the utilization of pharmacists as an active member of the health care team in providing direct patient care services, especially in the ambulatory care settings; developing residency training programs for pharmacists so that they may become proficient educators, researchers, and health care practitioners in the area of pharmacy practice; training programs for family practice residents; identifying predictors for control of diabetes; developing primary care pharmacy services. *Mailing Add:* Sch Pharm Univ Southern Calif 1985 Zonal Ave Los Angeles CA 90033. *Fax:* 213-342-1395; *E-Mail:* wgong@hsc.usc.edu

GONG, YU, CANCER IMMUNOLOGY DIAGNOSIS & TREATMENT, HUMAN IMMUNODEFICIENCY VIRUS DIAGNOSTIC STUDY & TREATMENT TRIAL. *Current Pos:* SCIENTIST, LAB MOLECULAR BIOL, HRI RES INC, 90- *Personal Data:* b Shanghai, China, Oct 6, 39; m 67, Shu L Hu; c Qin. *Educ:* Fu Dan Univ, BS, 62; First Med Col, PhD(immunol & virol), 67. *Prof Exp:* Res fel, Immunol Dept, Shanghai Cancer Inst, 67-82; vis fel, Lab Molecular Hemat, Nat Heart, Lung & Blood Inst, NIH, 83-85, Lab Chem Biol, Nat Inst Diabetes, Digestive & Kidney Dis, 85-86, vis assoc, Lab Oral Med, Nat Inst Dent Res, 86-88; scientist, Lab Molecular Biol, Pan-Date Syst, Inc, 89-90. *Mem:* Am Soc Microbiol; Soc Oncol Chinese Med Asn; Soc Immunol China. *Res:* Diagnostic study for human immunodeficiency virus infection, quantitative analysis of human immunodeficiency virus, DNA and RNA and for the assessment of efficacy of antivirus therapy including for vaccine trial; cancer immunodiagnosis and immunotherapy. *Mailing Add:* 11484 Brundidge Terr Germantown MD 20876. *Fax:* 301-916-1469; *E-Mail:* yugong@erals.com

GONGLEWSKI, JOHN D, PHYSICS, OPTICS. *Current Pos:* RES PHYSICIST, PHILLIPS LAB, USAF, ALBUQUERQUE. *Honors & Awards:* Eng Excellence Award, Optical Soc Am, 95. *Mailing Add:* PL/LIMI 3550 Aberdeen Ave SE Kirtland AFB NM 87117

GONICK, ELY, INORGANIC CHEMISTRY. *Current Pos:* RETIRED. *Personal Data:* b Detroit, Mich, May 24, 25; m 52; c 2. *Educ:* Drew Univ, AB, 48; Pa State Col, PhD(inorg chem), 51. *Prof Exp:* Res chemist, E I du Pont de Nemours & Co, Inc, 51-55, tech supvr, 55-58, asst lab dir, 58-62, tech sect mgr, 62-64, asst dir res, 65-70, mgr, Inorg Fibers Div, Pigments Dept, 70-72, dir int develop, 73-74, dir res, Pigments Dept & asst dir, Finishes Div, Fabrics & Finishes Dept, 78-79, dir res, Finishes Dept, 80-81; vpres technol, Int Paper Co, NY, 81-89. *Mem:* Am Chem Soc; Sigma Xi. *Res:* Coordination compounds; polymers; pigments; surface chemistry; fiber reinforcement of plastics; light absorption and scattering; high temperature reactions. *Mailing Add:* 611 Millersville Lancaster PA 17603-6025

GONICK, HARVEY C, NEPHROLOGY. *Current Pos:* dir, Trace Element Lab, 79-94, COORD NEPHOL TRAINING, CEDARS-SINAI MED CTR, 96- *Personal Data:* b Apr 10, 30; US citizen; m 67; c 2. *Educ:* Univ Calif, Los Angeles, BS, 51; Univ Calif, San Francisco, MD, 55. *Prof Exp:* Intern internal med, Peter Bent Brigham Hosp, Boston, Mass, 55-56; asst med, Sch Med, Boston Univ, 56-57; resident internal med, Wadsworth Vet Admin Hosp, 59-61, clin investr, 61-64, sect chief, Metab Balance Ward, 64-67; from instr to assoc prof, Univ Calif, Los Angeles, 64-76, adj prof med, 76-79. *Concurrent Pos:* Nat Heart Inst fel nephrol, Mass Mem Hosp, Boston, 56-57; fel nephrol, Wadsworth Vet Admin Hosp, Los Angeles, 59-61; Nat Kidney Found traveling fel, 63; mem, Nat Kidney Found, 63-, chmn, Res Comt, 67, actg secy, Nat Med Adv Coun, 69-70, regional rep, 70-73; mem, Coun Circulation, Am Heart Asn, 64-; chmn, Sci Adv Coun, SCalif Kidney Found, 68-70, mem bd dirs, 74-83; mem, Renal Dialysis & Transplantation Adv Comt, Calif State Dept Pub Health, 69-71; mem, Ad Hoc Steering Comt, Kidney Dis Planning Proj, Calif Regional Med Prog, 70, area rep, 71; clin chief nephrol, Cedars-Sinai Med Ctr, 83-85. *Mem:* AAAS; fel Am Col Physicians; Am Fedn Clin Res; AMA; Am Soc Nephrol; Western Soc Clin Res. *Res:* Renal pathophysiology; trace element metabolism; effects of transport inhibitors on renal tubular function; circulating inhibitors of active trasnsport, also lead-induced hypertension. *Mailing Add:* Cedars-Sinai Med Ctr 8700 Beverly Blvd Los Angeles CA 90048

GONNELLA, PATRICIA ANNE, CELL BIOLOGY. *Current Pos:* fel, 82-85, instr, 86, ASST PROF, HARVARD MED SCH, HARVARD UNIV, 87- *Personal Data:* b Philadelphia, Pa, Nov 25, 49. *Educ:* Temple Univ, AB, 71, MA, 76, PhD(biol), 79. *Prof Exp:* Fel, Sch Med, Univ Pa, 78-81. *Mem:* AAAS; Am Soc Cell Biologists. *Res:* Barrier function in the developing intestine and immune function in response to trauma and sepsis. *Mailing Add:* Brigham & Women's Hospital 75 Francis St Boston MA 02115

GONOR, JEFFERSON JOHN, INVERTEBRATE ZOOLOGY, MARINE BIOLOGY. *Current Pos:* asst prof biol oceanog, 65-74, assoc prof oceanog & zool, 74-82, PROF BIOL OCEANOG, ORE STATE UNIV, 82-, HEAD ADV, COL OCEANOG, 87-, DIR, MARINE RESOURCE MGT GRAD PROG, 87- *Personal Data:* b Lafayette, La, Nov 8, 32; m 69; c 2. *Educ:* Univ Southwestern La, BS, 53; Univ Wash, PhD(invert zool), 64. *Prof Exp:* Actg instr zool, Univ Wash, 59 & 60; vis asst prof biol, Univ of the Pac, 60 & 62; asst prof marine sci, Univ Alaska, 62-64. *Concurrent Pos:* Res partic, Orgn Trop Studies, 64; resident staff, OSU Marine Sci Ctr, Newprot, Ore, 65-; consult mitigation methods estuarine land use planning & develop, 77-; regional ed, Marine Biol, Int J Life Oceans & Coastal Waters, 76-77. *Mem:* AAAS; Soc Syst Zool; Ecol Soc Am. *Res:* Systematics of opisthobranch gastropods; molluscan functional anatomy; neurosecretion in barnacles; marine invertebrate reproduction and larval biology; biological oceanography; population biology of introduced marine wood boring isopods. *Mailing Add:* 33267 SE White Oak Rd Corvallis OR 97333-2506

GONSALVES, DENNIS, PLANT VIROLOGY. *Current Pos:* assoc prof, 77-86, PROF PLANT PATH, CORNELL UNIV, 86- *Personal Data:* b Kohala, Hawaii, Apr 2, 43; m 65; c 2. *Educ:* Univ Hawaii, BS, 65, MS, 68; Univ Calif, Davis, PhD(plant path), 72. *Prof Exp:* Asst plant path, Univ Hawaii, 65-66; asst prof, Univ Fla, 72-77. *Mem:* Am Phytopath Soc; Soc Gen Microbiol. *Res:* Characterization of fruit tree viruses; genetics of plant viruses; cross protection. *Mailing Add:* 595 Castle St Geneva NY 14456

GONSALVES, LENINE M, ELECTRICAL ENGINEERING. *Current Pos:* instr elec eng, 53-56, assoc prof, 56-57, chmn elec eng dept, 57-69 & 77-78, PROF ELEC ENG, SOUTHEASTERN MASS UNIV, 57-, CHMN ELEC ENG TECHNOL DEPT, 87- *Personal Data:* b New Bedford, Mass, Nov 23, 27; m 52; c 4. *Educ:* US Naval Acad, BS, 52; Northeastern Univ, MSEE, 60. *Prof Exp:* Proj engr, Res Dept, Aerovox Corp, 52-53. *Concurrent Pos:* Consult, Eng & Res Sect, Aerovox Corp, 57, 61-62; prof & chmn dept elec eng, Col Petrol & Mineral, Univ Dharan, Saudi Arabia, 69-71; acad adv eng technol, Nat Inst Elec & Electronics Engrs, 78-79. *Mem:* Nat Soc Prof Engrs; Am Soc Eng Educ; Inst Elec & Electronics Engrs. *Res:* Circuit theory; electrical power systems. *Mailing Add:* 1850 Homewood Blvd 309 Delray Beach FL 33445

GONSALVES, NEIL IGNATIUS, GENETICS. *Current Pos:* asst prof genetics, 69-73, assoc prof biol, 73-78, PROF BIOL, RI COL, 78-, CHMN DEPT, 81- *Personal Data:* b Georgetown, Brit Guiana, Feb 1, 38; US citizen; m 61; c 2. *Educ:* Georgetown Univ, BS, 59; Brown Univ, PhD(biol), 69. *Prof Exp:* Asst prof genetics, Lowell State Col, 68-69. *Concurrent Pos:* Vis prof, Brown Univ, 76- *Mem:* Am Soc Zool; Genetics Soc Am; Am Soc Cell Biol; Am Genetics Asn; Soc Invest Dermat; Sigma Xi. *Res:* Radiation biology of mammalian skin; mechanisms of wound healing in mammalian skin; developmental biology and genetics of anophthalmia in the mouse. *Mailing Add:* Dept Biol RI Col 600 Mt Pleasant Ave Providence RI 02908-1991. *Fax:* 401-456-8379

GONSALVES, ROBERT ARTHUR, ELECTRICAL ENGINEERING. *Current Pos:* dir, Electro-Optics Technol Ctr, 85-94, prof, 85-, CHMN, DEPT ELEC ENG & COMPUT SCI, TUFTS UNIV, MEDFORD, MASS, 96- *Personal Data:* b Woburn, Mass, Apr 17, 35; m 62, Patricia Liberge; c Maria, Robert, Richard, Joanna & Paul. *Educ:* Tufts Univ, BS, 56; Northeastern Univ, MS, 61, PhD, 65. *Prof Exp:* Mem staff, RCA, Burlington, Mass, 59-62; res assoc, Northeastern Univ, Boston, 62-65, prof, 65-85. *Concurrent Pos:* Consult numerous cos. *Mem:* Fel Int Soc Optical Eng; AAAS; Inst Elec & Electronics Engrs; Sigma Xi. *Res:* Wavefront sensing by phase retrieval; achromatic volume holography apparatus. *Mailing Add:* Dept Elec Eng & Comput Sci Tufts Univ 161 College Ave Medford MA 02155

GONSER, BRUCE WINFRED, METALLURGY. *Current Pos:* RETIRED. *Personal Data:* b Hudson, Ind, Sept 9, 99; wid; c Gretchem (Cumming) & Diana (Witter). *Educ:* Purdue Univ, BS, 23; Univ Utah, MS, 24; Harvard Univ, SD(metall), 33. *Hon Degrees:* DrEng, Purdue Univ, 67. *Honors & Awards:* James Douglas Gold Medal, Am Inst Mining, Metall & Petrol Engrs, 71; Award Merit, Am Soc Testing & Mat. *Prof Exp:* Res engr, Am Smelting & Refining Co, 24-31; metall engr, Nat Radiator Corp, 33-34; res chief, Battelle Mem Inst, 34-50, asst dir metall, 50-53, tech dir, 53-64; consult, 64-84. *Mem:* Am Inst Mining, Metall & Petrol Engrs; Am Soc Metals; Am Soc Testing & Mat; Wire Asn; Electrochem Soc. *Res:* Nonferrous metallurgy; uncommon metals; extractive metallurgy. *Mailing Add:* 1800 Riverside Dr Apt 440 Columbus OH 43212

GONTIER, JEAN ROGER, PHYSIOLOGY OF RESPIRATION, RESPIRATION & DIVING. *Current Pos:* CONSULT INTERNAL MED, 79- *Personal Data:* b Lens Pas de Calais, France, Mar 8, 27; m 68, Sylviane Prevost; c Sylviane, Yannick, Jean-Yves & Yann. *Educ:* Col d'Etampes France, BA, 45; Col Sci Paris, MS, 48; Sch Med Paris, MD, 65. *Honors & Awards:* Silver Medal, Sch Med, Paris, 66. *Prof Exp:* Prof physiol, UGSEL, Paris, 57-62; instr med, Sch Med Paris, 60-65; dir physiol, Sch Med Reims, 66-68; prof physiol, Sch Med, Univ Montreal, 70-78. *Concurrent Pos:* Consult

& ed, var publ, New York, 79- *Mem:* Am Physiol Soc; Can Physiol Soc; NY Acad Sci; AAAS. *Res:* physiology of respiration in man; respiratory adaptions to diving in man; mechanical factors in breathing; cardiovasc physiol. *Mailing Add:* 133 rue Michel-Ange Paris F-75016 France

GONYEA, WILLIAM JOSEPH, ANATOMY, EXERCISE BIOLOGY. *Current Pos:* From asst prof to assoc prof, 72-80, PROF ANAT, UNIV TEX HEALTH SCI CTR, 80-, CHMN DIV ANAT, 85- *Personal Data:* b Springfield, Mass, Aug 18, 42; m 66; c 2. *Educ:* Univ Miami, BEd, 68, MA, 69; Univ Chicago, PhD(anat), 73. *Mem:* Am Asn Anatomists; Am Col Sports Med; Am Soc Zoologists; Nat Strength & Conditioning Asn. *Res:* Structure and function of skeletal muscle and the cardiovascular system; evolutionary biology of vertebrates especially mammaliam carnivores. *Mailing Add:* Dept Cell Biol & Neurosci Univ Tex Southwestern Health Met Ctr 5323 Harry Hines Blvd Dallas TX 75235-9039. *Fax:* 214-648-8950

GONZALES, CIRIACO Q, COMPARATIVE PHYSIOLOGY. *Current Pos:* DIR, MINORITY BIOMED RES SUPPORT PROG, NIH, 75- *Personal Data:* b Socorro, NMex, Oct 22, 33; m 58; c 4. *Educ:* NMex State Univ, BS, 54; Univ Ariz, MS, 58; Univ Calif, Berkeley, PhD(entomol & physiol), 62. *Prof Exp:* Asst res entomologist, Univ Calif, Berkeley, 61-63; from asst prof to assoc prof biol, Col Santa Fe, NMex, 63-72; health scientist adminr, NIH, 72-75. *Concurrent Pos:* Mem, Nat Acad Sci Panel, Peru, 75. *Mem:* AAAS; Am Soc Microbiol. *Res:* Pesticide toxicology; physiological effects on humans and animals and effects on the environment; transmission of viruses by insect vectors to fruit trees. *Mailing Add:* 1508 Aintree Dr Rockville MD 20850

GONZALES, ELWOOD JOHN, CELLULOSE CHEMISTRY. *Current Pos:* RETIRED. *Personal Data:* b New Orleans, La, Oct 19, 27; m 63; c Lisa, Elwood III, Guy & Eric. *Educ:* Loyola Univ, La, BS, 53; Tulane Univ, MS, 55, PhD(chem), 58. *Prof Exp:* Res chemist cellulose chem, USDA, New Orleans, 57-63, res chemist chem invests, 63-72, res chemist, Polymer Finishes Res Unit, Southern Reg Res Ctr, 72-78, res chemist, Cellulose Polymer Res Div, Agr Res Serv, 78-84, res chem ist textile finishing chem, 85-87. *Mem:* AAAS; Am Chem Soc; Sigma Xi; Am Asn Textile Chemists & Colorists; Am Inst Chemists. *Res:* Kinetics and mechanisms of cellulose recactions; modification of cotton cellulose; flame retardant and cellulose chemistry; application of statistics for cellulose reactions; dyeing modified cotton celluloses. *Mailing Add:* 2137 Graham Dr Gretna LA 70056

GONZALES, FEDERICO, CELL BIOLOGY. *Current Pos:* ASSOC PROF ANAT, SCHS DENT & MED, NORTHWESTERN UNIV, CHICAGO, 63- *Personal Data:* b San Antonio, Tex, July 16, 21; m 45; c 7. *Educ:* St Louis Univ, BS, 48, MS, 51, PhD(biophys), 54. *Prof Exp:* Sr res fel biol, Univ Tex M D Anderson Hosp & Tumor Inst, 53-54, res assoc, 54-55; from instr to asst prof anat, Dent Br, Univ Tex, 55-61; asst prof anat, Col Med, Baylor Univ, 57-63, asst prof exp biol, 61-63. *Concurrent Pos:* USPHS sr res fel, 58-62 & career develop award, 62-63. *Mem:* Am Soc Cell Biol; Am Physiol Soc; Am Asn Anat; Tissue Cult Asn; Soc Develop Biol; Sigma Xi. *Res:* Differentiation in tissue culture; structure and function of the nucleolus; survival of frozen tissues; ultrastructure of bone and other hard tissues; ultrastructure of heart. *Mailing Add:* Dept Neurobiol & Physiol OT Hogan Bldg 2153 Sheridan Rd Evanston IL 60208-3520. *Fax:* 847-491-5211

GONZALES, SERGE, stratigraphy-sedimentation, for more information see previous edition

GONZALEZ, EDGAR, MECHANICAL ENGINEERING. *Current Pos:* CONSULT ENGR, E GONZALEZ ENGRS, PROF CONSULTS, 80- *Personal Data:* b San Juan, PR, Nov 29, 24; US citizen; m 53; c 1. *Educ:* Univ Wis-Madison, BSEE, 47. *Prof Exp:* Elec engr, US Steel Corp, 47-50; proj engr, Skidmore, Owings & Merrill A/E, 50-53; proj engr, Fay, Spofford & Thorndike Engrs, 54-56; proj engr, Guy B Panero Engrs, 56-68; contract engr, E Gonzalez Consult, 58-64; sr proj engr, Am Can Co, 64-80. *Concurrent Pos:* Consult engr, E Gonzalez Prof Engrs-Consult Engrs, 87- *Mem:* Inst Elec & Electronics Engrs; Am Soc Mech Eng; Soc Am Mil Engrs. *Mailing Add:* 11218 86th Ave Jamaica NY 11418

GONZALEZ, ELMA, CELL BIOLOGY, PLANT PHYSIOLOGY. *Current Pos:* asst prof cell biol, 74-81, assoc prof biol, 81-93, PROF BIOL, UNIV CALIF, LOS ANGELES, 93- *Personal Data:* b June 6, 42; US citizen. *Educ:* Tex Woman's Univ, BS, 65; Rutgers Univ, PhD(cell biol), 72. *Prof Exp:* NIH fel plant physiol, Univ Calif, Santa Cruz, 72-74. *Concurrent Pos:* Fel, Nat Chicano Coun Higher Educ Ford Found, 78. *Mem:* Am Soc Plant Physiologists; AAAS; Am Soc Cell Biol; Soc Advan Chicanos & Native Am in Sci; Phycol Soc Am. *Res:* Mechanisms and regulation of the formation of microbodies and other metabolic compartments; intracellular protein traffic and sorting; calcification and golgi apparatus in marine micro algae. *Mailing Add:* Dept Biol Univ Calif Los Angeles CA 90024-1606. *E-Mail:* gonzalez@biology.lifesci.ucla.edu

GONZALEZ, EULOGIO RAPHAEL, neuroendocrinology, for more information see previous edition

GONZALEZ, FRANCISCO MANUEL, NEPHROLOGY. *Current Pos:* from asst prof to assoc prof med, 66-74, PROF MED & PHARMACOL, MED CTR, LA STATE UNIV, NEW ORLEANS, 74-; DIR DEPT NEPHROLOGY, CHARITY HOSP, 66- *Personal Data:* b San Juan, PR, Sept 28, 33; c 5. *Educ:* Va Mil Inst, BA, 53; Med Col Va, MD, 57. *Prof Exp:* Intern, Georgetown Univ Hosp, 57-58, resident internal med, 58-61; dir, Renal Div, US Naval Hosp, Oakland, Calif, 63-65. *Concurrent Pos:* Clin & res fel nephrology, Georgetown Univ Hosp, 61-63; vis physician, Hotel Dieu Hosp, New Orleans, 66-, E Jefferson Hosp, 66- & Charity Hosp, 66-; consult nephrology, East LA Long Hosp, Baton Rouge, 66-, Lake Charles Charity Hosp, 66- & Lafayette Charity Hosp, 66-; mem, Nat Kidney Found, 66- *Mem:* Am Soc Nephrology; Am Fedn Clin Res; Am Soc Artificial Internal Organs; Am Heart Asn; fel Am Col Physicians. *Res:* Renal disease; physiology and pharmacology; artificial kidney and transplantation. *Mailing Add:* 2000 Tulane Ave New Orleans LA 70112-2250

GONZALEZ, FRANK J, MOLECULAR CARINOGENETICS. *Current Pos:* staf fel, Lab Develop Pharmacol, Nat Inst Child Health & Human Develop, NIH, Bethesda, 82-84, sr staff fel, Lab Molecular Carcinogenesis, Nat Cancer Inst, 84-88, actg chief, Nucleic Acids Sect, 86-89, SUPVRY RES CHEMIST, LAB MOLECULAR CARCINOGENESIS, NAT CANCER INST, NIH, BETHESDA, 88-, CHIEF, NUCLEIC ACIDS SECT, 89- *Personal Data:* b Tampa, Fla, Nov 30, 53. *Educ:* Univ SFla, Tampa, BA, 75, MA, 77; Univ Wis-Madison, PhD(oncol), 81. *Honors & Awards:* Rawls-Palmer Progress Med Award, Am Soc Clin Pharmacol & Therapeut, 91. *Prof Exp:* Fel, McArdle Lab Cancer Res, Univ Wis-Madison, 81-82. *Concurrent Pos:* Ad hoc mem, Phys Biochem Study Sect, NIH, 86 & 88, Nat Inst Drug Abuse, 89, Prom Rev Comt, Nat Inst Environ Health Serv, 89, ad hoc reviewer, Chem Path Study Sect, 89, adv comt, Pharmacol Res Assoc Training Prog, 90-94; ad hoc mem, Carcinogenesis & Nutrit Study Sect, Am Cancer Soc, 91. *Mem:* Am Soc Biochem & Molecular Biol; Int Soc Study Xenobiotics; Am Fedn Clin Res. *Res:* Molecular carinogenetics; numerous publications. *Mailing Add:* Nucleic Acids Sect Lab Molecular Carcinogen NCI NIH Bldg 37 Rm 3E24 Bethesda MD 20892-0001. *Fax:* 301-496-8419

GONZALEZ, GLADYS, LAND RESOURCE ECONOMICS, AGRICULTURAL PRODUCTION ECONOMICS. *Current Pos:* res asst, 77-79, asst prof, 84-87, PROF & CHAIR AGR ECON, UNIV PR, MAYAQUEZ, 87- *Personal Data:* b San German, PR, Oct 11, 55; US citizen; m 77; c 2. *Educ:* Univ PR, BA, 76, MS, 81; Univ Mo, PhD(agr econ), 84. *Prof Exp:* Res asst agr econ, Univ Mo, Columbia, 79-83. *Concurrent Pos:* Dept chairperson, Dept Agr Econ, Univ PR, Mayaquez, 84-, actg assoc dean for resident instr, Fac Agr, 91- *Mem:* Am Agr Econ Asn; Asn Economist PR. *Res:* Tropical agriculture and food consumption in Puerto Rico; three years of research experience in US agricultural land use problems. *Mailing Add:* Dept Agr Econ PO Box 5000 Mayaguez PR 00681

GONZALEZ, GUILLERMO, ELECTRICAL ENGINEERING. *Current Pos:* from asst prof to assoc prof, 69-79, PROF ELEC ENG, UNIV MIAMI, 79- *Personal Data:* b Havana, Cuba, June 25, 44; US citizen; m, Patricia Smith; c Alex & Donna. *Educ:* Univ Miami, BSEE, 65, MSEE, 66; Univ Ariz, PhD(elec eng), 69. *Prof Exp:* Sr engr elec eng, Bell Aerosyst Co, 67-69. *Concurrent Pos:* Prin investr, Univ Miami Inst grant, 69-70, NSF grant, 71-72, 73-75, 76-77 & Ryder Prog Transp grant, 78. *Mem:* Sigma Xi. *Res:* Microwave electronics and electromagnetics. *Mailing Add:* Dept Elec Eng Univ Miami PO Box 248294 Coral Gables FL 33124

GONZALEZ, HECTOR JULIAN, RHEOLOGY OF SURFACTANTS IN EMULSION POLYMERIZATION, COATINGS FORMULATION. *Current Pos:* VPRES & DIR RES, ESSENTIAL INDUSTS, 85- *Personal Data:* m 42, Myrtha C; c Pedro J & Margarita R. *Educ:* Havana Univ, BS, 48, PhD(physics-chem), 52, BS, 52. *Prof Exp:* Res chemist, Sinclair Petrochem Res, 62-65; supvr polymers, Richardson Co, 65-74, mgr tech group, 74-78, dir res, 78-82; group mgr urethanes-acrylics, Witco Chem Co, 82-85. *Mem:* Am Chem Soc; Tech Asn Pulp & Paper Indust; NY Acad Sci; Am Soc Testing & Mat; Am Asn Textiles & Colorists. *Res:* Technical service, product development and research and development on water based products in the specialty coatings application industry. *Mailing Add:* 28391 Essential Rd Merton WI 53056. *Fax:* 414-538-1354

GONZALEZ, LUIS L, surgery, for more information see previous edition

GONZALEZ, MARIO J, hardware systems, software systems, for more information see previous edition

GONZALEZ, NORBERTO CARLOS, MEDICAL PHYSIOLOGY. *Current Pos:* from asst prof to assoc prof, 70-78, PROF PHYSIOL, COL HEALTH SCI & HOSP, UNIV KANS MED CTR, 78- *Personal Data:* b La Plata, Arg, Aug 1, 37; m 71; c 2. *Educ:* Nat Univ La Plata, MD, 62. *Prof Exp:* Instr physiol, Nat Univ La Plata, 62-65; fel, Univ Kans Med Ctr, 65-67; asst prof, Nat Univ La Plata, 67-70. *Concurrent Pos:* Fel, Nat Coun Invests, Arg, 65-66; USPHS fel, 66-67; fel, Alexander von Humboldt Found, Bonn, WGer, 77-78 & 80. *Mem:* Sigma Xi; Am Physiol Soc. *Res:* Intra- and extracellular acid-base regulation; tissue and lung gas exchange; acid-base effects on cardiovascular system; myocardiol hypertrophy; adaption to hypoxia, systemic oxygen transport. *Mailing Add:* Dept Physiol Col Health Sci Univ Kans Med Ctr 3901 Rainbow Blvd Kansas City KS 66160-7401. *Fax:* 913-588-7430

GONZALEZ, PAULA, PUBLIC EDUCATION OF ENVIRONMENTAL SCIENCE, RENEWABLE ENERGY. *Current Pos:* from asst prof to prof, Col Mt St Joseph, 65-82, chmn, Dept Biol, 68-73, adj prof biol, 82-86, EDUC BIOLOGIST, COL MT ST JOSEPH, 86- *Personal Data:* b Albuquerque, NMex, Oct 25, 32. *Educ:* Col Mt St Joseph, AB, 52; Cath Univ Am, MS, 62, PhD(cell physiol), 66. *Prof Exp:* Instr anat, physiol & chem, Regina Sch Nursing, NMex, 52-54; biol teacher, Seton High Sch, Ohio, 55-60.

Concurrent Pos: Freelance futurist, lectr & consult, 86-; founding dir, Earth Connection, Environ Learning Ctr. *Mem:* Union Concerned Scientists; Am Solar Energy Asn; Sigma Xi. *Res:* Nucleolar changes during the cell cycle; course development; energy and environment; biomedical advances and their human implications; science, technology and human values; global ecology; development of personalized learning system for human anatomy and physiology, (including use of audio-visual components); planetary consciousness, hope through alternatives, passive solar design. *Mailing Add:* 5820 Bender Rd Cincinnati OH 45233

GONZALEZ, RAFAEL C, DIGITAL IMAGE PROCESSING, PATTERN RECOGNITION. *Current Pos:* DEPT CHMN ELEC & COMPUT ENG, UNIV TENN, KNOXVILLE, 94- *Personal Data:* b Havana, Cuba, Aug 26, 42; US citizen; m 65; c 2. *Educ:* Univ Miami, Coral Gables, Fla, BSEE, 65; Univ Fla, Gainesville, ME, 67, PhD(elec eng), 70. *Prof Exp:* Design engr, Gen Tel & Electronics, 66-67; grad asst, Univ Fla, Gainesville, 67-70; from asst prof to prof, 70-81, IBM PROF, UNIV TENN, KNOXVILLE, 81-; pres, Perceptics Corp, Knoxville, Tenn, 80- *Concurrent Pos:* Consult, Oak Ridge Nat Lab, Tenn, 72-82, Lockheed Corp, Sunnyvale, Calif, 81-84 & Tex Instruments, Inc, Dallas, 84-87; chmn bd, Perceptics Corp, Knoxville, Tenn, 80-; prof eng, Magnavox, 80; M E Brooks distinguished prof, Univ Tenn, Knoxville, 81 & distinguished serv prof, 84-; prof, IBM, 81. *Mem:* Fel Inst Elec & Electronics Engrs; Pattern Recognition Soc. *Res:* Image processing; pattern recognition; machine learning. *Mailing Add:* Dept Chmn Elec & Comput Eng Univ Tenn Knoxville TN 37996

GONZALEZ, RAMON RAFAEL, JR, BIOENGINEERING & BIOMEDICAL ENGINEERING. *Current Pos:* asst prof, 73-85, ASSOC PROF PHYSIOL, SCH MED, LOMA LINDA UNIV, 85- *Personal Data:* b Los Angeles, Calif, May 25, 40; m 64; c 1. *Educ:* Walla Walla Col, BS, 62, MA, 65; Wake Forest Univ, PhD(physiol), 73. *Prof Exp:* Teaching asst, Dept Biol, Walla Walla Col, 62-64; physiologist, Virginia Mason Res Ctr, Seattle, Wash, 66-68. *Concurrent Pos:* Res fel, Dept Neurosurg, Univ Basel, 73-75; consult cardiovasc pharmacol & biomed electronics, Delalande Int, Paris, France, 74-75; assoc res, Univ Calif Irvine, 88-89. *Mem:* Am Physiol Soc; Am Heart Asn; Sigma Xi; Am Inst Ultrasound Med. *Res:* Autonomic control of the circulation of blood in mammals, especially the neurovascular smooth muscle interface in skeletal muscle; human brain blood flow as studied with ultrasound. *Mailing Add:* Dept Physiol Loma Linda Univ Sch Med Loma Linda CA 92350-0001. *Fax:* 909-478-4119; *E-Mail:* rgonzalez@ccmail.llu.edu

GONZALEZ, RAUL A(LBERTO), CHEMICAL ENGINEERING. *Current Pos:* RETIRED. *Personal Data:* b Talca, Chile, Feb 8, 33; US citizen; m 58, Iris Laudien; c Iris, Ralph & David. *Educ:* Santa Maria Univ, Chile, BS, 57; Univ Va, MSc, 60, DSc(chem eng), 62. *Prof Exp:* Res engr, Santa Maria Univ, Chile, 57-58; prof chem eng, Cath Univ, Chile, 62; eng fel, Jackson Lab, E I Dupont De Nemours & Co, Inc, NJ, 62-96. *Res:* Reaction kinetics; reverse osmosis; process evaluation and design; high temperature reactions. *Mailing Add:* 206 Dallas Ave Newark DE 19711

GONZALEZ, RICHARD DONALD, PHYSICAL CHEMISTRY. *Current Pos:* AT DEPT CHEM ENG, UNIV ILL. *Personal Data:* b New York, NY, Apr 11, 32; m 62; c 1. *Educ:* Rensselaer Polytech Inst, BChE, 61; Johns Hopkins Univ, MA, 63, PhD(chem), 65. *Prof Exp:* From asst prof to assoc prof chem, 65-77, prof chem, Univ RI, 77- *Mem:* Am Chem Soc. *Res:* Surface chemistry; heterogeneous catalysis. *Mailing Add:* Dept Chem Eng Tulane Univ New Orleans LA 70118-5674

GONZALEZ, RICHARD RAFAEL, PHYSIOLOGY & BIOPHYSICS, THERMOPHYSIOLOGY. *Current Pos:* sr res phys, 83-90, chief biophys, 84-89, DIR, BIOPHYS & BIOMED MODELING DIV, US ARMY RES INST, 90- *Personal Data:* b El Paso, Tex, Sept 15, 42; m 65, M Yvonne Bromley; c 4. *Educ:* Univ Tex, BS, 62; Univ San Francisco, MS, 66; Univ Calif, Davis, PhD(physiol, biophys), 70. *Honors & Awards:* Ralph Nevins Award, Am Soc Heating Refrig & Air Conditioning Engrs, 83. *Prof Exp:* Vis asst fel physiol, John B Pierce Found, 70-72, asst fel, 72-75, assoc fel bioeng, 75-83; asst prof, Sch Med, Yale Univ, 72-76, assoc prof environ physiol, 76-83. *Concurrent Pos:* USPHS fel physiol, Sch Med, Yale Univ, 70-72; fel, Branford Col, Yale Univ, 72-77; assoc prof, Dept Kinesiology, Univ Calif, Los Angeles, 73-75; vis prof, Harvard Sch Pub Health, 83-89. *Mem:* Am Physiol Soc; fel Am Soc Heating Refrig & Air Conditioning Engrs. *Res:* Thermal physiology; peripheral circulation; environmental physiology; temperature regulation. *Mailing Add:* Dept Biophys & Biomed US Army Res Inst Environ Med 5 Kansas St Bldg 42 Natick MA 01760-5007. *Fax:* 508-651-5298

GONZALEZ, ROBERT ANTHONY, NUCLEAR PHYSICS, COMPUTER SCIENCE. *Current Pos:* Nuclear analyst radiation, 71-75, nuclear engr, 75-80, LEAD ENGR RADIATION ANAL & MGR, SHIELDING METHODS DEVELOP, KNOLLS ATOMIC POWER LAB, 80-, MGR SERV ENG, 85- *Personal Data:* b Victoria de las Tunas, Cuba, Jan 17, 45; US citizen; m 66; c 3. *Educ:* Fla Southern Univ, BS, 71; State Univ NY, MS, 79. *Res:* Radiation analysis, specifically the shielding of all radiation, ie gamma, neutron, emanating from fission reactors; large scientific computers. *Mailing Add:* Knolls Atomic Power Lab PO Box 1072 Schenectady NY 12301-1072

GONZALEZ-ANGULO, AMADOR, neuropathology, for more information see previous edition

GONZALEZ DE ALVAREZ, GENOVEVA, organic chemistry, pharmaceutical chemistry, for more information see previous edition

GONZALEZ-FERNANDEZ, JOSE MARIA, MATHEMATICS, PHYSIOLOGY. *Current Pos:* RES MATHEMATICIAN, NAT INSTS HEALTH, 62- *Personal Data:* b Buenos Aires, Arg, Nov 10, 22; US citizen; m 57; c 2. *Educ:* Univ Buenos Aires, MD, 47; Northwestern Univ, MSc, 54, PhD(math), 58. *Prof Exp:* Instr math, Univ Wash, 57-58; res assoc physiol, Mayo Clin, 58-59; temp mem staff math, Courant Inst Math Sci, NY Univ, 59-60; mem staff math res ctr, Univ Wis, 60-62. *Mem:* Am Math Soc. *Res:* Integrability theorems in trigonometric series; tauberian theorems; integral equations; transport and consumption of oxygen in blood capillary-tissue systems. *Mailing Add:* NIDDK Math Res Br 9190 Wisconsin Ave Suite 350 Bethesda MD 20814

GONZALEZ-LAGOA, JUAN GERARDO, PLANKTON BIOLOGY, SCIENCE ADMINISTRATION. *Current Pos:* Assoc prof marine sci, Univ PR, Mayaguez, 64-68, sr scientist, Ctr Energy & Environ Res, 76-81, assoc prof, 81-88, assoc dir, Marine Sci Dept, 85-87, assoc dean arts & sci, 87-90, assoc dean acad affairs, 90-93, PROF MARINE SCI, UNIV PR, MAYAGUEZ, 81-, ASSOC DIR, RESOURCE CTR SCI & ENG, 93- *Personal Data:* b Mayaguez, PR, Jan 19, 33; m 67, Carmen Rosado; c Maria, Barbara, Ivan, Marie, Adelissa & Mara. *Educ:* Univ PR, BS, 55; Tex A&M Univ, MS, 57; Univ RI, PhD(oceanog), 73. *Prof Exp:* Aquatic biologist, US Environ Protection Agency, 68-76. *Concurrent Pos:* Dir, Minority Res Ctrs Excellence, NSF, Univ PR, 93-95. *Res:* Extensive study of bioluminescent bays; identifying causes of the phenomenon and the factors that nurture or diminish its occurrence. *Mailing Add:* Dept Marine Sci Univ PR Mayaguez Contract Sta Mayaguez PR 00681. *Fax:* 787-832-4680; *E-Mail:* ju_gonsalez@rumac.upr.clu.edu

GONZALEZ-LIMA, FRANCISCO, FUNCTIONAL NEUROANATOMY. *Current Pos:* assoc prof, 91-97, PROF PSYCHOL & NEUROSCI, UNIV TEX, AUSTIN, 97- *Personal Data:* b Havana, Cuba, Dec 7, 55; US citizen; m 81, Erika Musiol; c Francisco Musiol & Marcos Musiol. *Educ:* Tulane Univ, BS, 76, BA, 77; Univ PR, PhD(anat), 80. *Honors & Awards:* Int Soc Neuroethology Prize, 87. *Prof Exp:* Res fel neurophysiol, Sch Med, Univ PR, 80-81; from asst prof to assoc prof neuroanat, Ponce Sch Med, 80-85; asst prof med neuroanat, Col Med, Tex A&M Univ, 85-90. *Concurrent Pos:* Prin investr, NSF, 81-83 & 93-97, Resource Ctr Sci & Eng, PR, 82-83, NIH, 82-86, NATO, 87-88 & 91-93 & NIMH, 88-; consult, Dept Radiol, PR Med Ctr, 81-85; Humboldt res fel, Alexander Von Humboldt Found, WGer, 82-83; vis prof, Ger Sci Found, Inst Zool, Tech Univ Darmstadt, WGer, 84-85; pres, Tex A&M Chap, Soc Neurosci, 89-90; mem, Grant Rev Comt, NIMH, 90-93. *Mem:* Soc Neurosci; Europ Neurosci Asn; Int Soc Neuroethology; Int Behav Neurosci Soc; Int Brain Res Orgn. *Res:* Neuroanatomical bases of integrative processes, such as arousal, motivation, learning and memory; application of 2-deoxyglucose method and histochemistry for functional brain mapping of behavioral activities. *Mailing Add:* Dept Psychol & Inst Neurosci Univ Tex Austin TX 78712

GOO, EDWARD KWOCK WAI, CERAMICS ENGINEERING, METALLURGY & PHYSICAL METALLURGICAL ENGINEERING. *Current Pos:* asst prof, 85-90, ASSOC PROF MAT SCI, UNIV SOUTHERN CALIF, 90- *Personal Data:* b Honolulu, Hawaii, Nov 25, 56; m 86; c William, Elizabeth & James. *Educ:* Cornell Univ, BS, 78; Univ Calif, Berkeley, MS, 80; Stanford Univ, PhD(mat sci), 85. *Honors & Awards:* Hardy Gold Medal, Metall Soc, 86. *Prof Exp:* staff scientist, Lawrence Berkeley Lab, 85. *Concurrent Pos:* NSF presidential young investr, 88; Off Naval Res young investr, 90. *Mem:* Am Phys Soc; Am Ceramic Soc; Am Soc Metals; Metall Soc; Electron Micros Soc Am. *Res:* Transmission electron micrscopy of materials; structure-property relationship. *Mailing Add:* 53 Via Malona Palos Verdes Peninsula CA 90275. *Fax:* 213-740-7797; *E-Mail:* ekgoo@m1zar.usc.edu

GOOCH, EDGAR EUGENE, III, MOLECULAR MODELING OF ORGANIC COMPOUNDS, ORGANOBORANE CHEMISTRY. *Current Pos:* asst prof, 88-92, ASSOC PROF & CHAIR, CHEM DEPT, ELON COL, 92- *Personal Data:* b Knoxville, Tenn, Dec 14, 51; m 76, Marcia Lee Thomas. *Educ:* Carson-Newman Col, BS, 73; Univ Tenn, PhD(org chem), 81. *Prof Exp:* Res assoc, Chem Dept, Brookhaven Nat Labs, 81-82, Univ Ga, 82-83; asst prof chem, Chem Dept, Union Univ, 83-88. *Mem:* Am Chem Soc; Sigma Xi. *Res:* Molecular modeling of small organic molecules; synthesis of biologically active molecules via organoborane technology; correlation of structure with biological activity; incorporation of selected isotopes into organic molecules; isolation and identification of natural products. *Mailing Add:* Chem Dept Elon Col 2220 Campus Box Elon College NC 27244

GOOCH, VAN DOUGLAS, CELL PHYSIOLOGY. *Current Pos:* ASST PROF BIOL, UNIV MINN, MORRIS, 78- *Personal Data:* b Oakland, Calif, July 23, 45; m 73. *Educ:* Calif State Univ, Hayward, BS, 67; Univ Calif, Berkeley, PhD(biophys), 73. *Prof Exp:* Fel circadian rhythm, Harvard Univ, 73-76; asst prof biol, Univ Minn, 76-77; asst prof, Hiram Col, 78. *Concurrent Pos:* Fel, NIH, 74-76. *Mem:* Biophys Soc; Int Soc Chronobiol. *Res:* Circadian rhythms; biological oscillators; bioluminescence; membrane biology. *Mailing Add:* Univ Minn Univ Minn Morris MN 56267-2134

GOOCHEE, HERMAN FRANCIS, INORGANIC CHEMISTRY. *Current Pos:* RETIRED. *Personal Data:* b Emporium, Pa, Oct 13, 21; m 49; c 3. *Educ:* St Vincent Col, BS, 43; Univ Tenn, MS, 57. *Prof Exp:* Lab engr, Stupakoff Ceramic & Mfg Co, 43-45; engr, Speer Carbon Co, 46-52; supvr process eng, Union Carbide Nuclear Co, Tenn, 52-57; consult & supvr cent eng, Speer Carbon Co Div, Air Reduction Co, Inc, 57-60, dir process eng, 60-61, dir develop & tech serv, 61-67, dir mfg carbon & graphite, 67-70, vpres mfg, 70-76, vpres tech opers, Carbon-Graphite, Airco Carbon Div, 76-88. *Mem:*

AAAS; Am Ceramic Soc; Am Chem Soc; Am Inst Mech Engr. *Res:* Technical management; ceramic research; carbon and graphite development; utilities operations; nuclear engineering and operations; combustion engineering and furnace design; technical supervision and planning. *Mailing Add:* 301 Russ Lane St Mary's PA 15857

GOOD, A L, VETERINARY PHYSIOLOGY. *Current Pos:* RETIRED. *Personal Data:* b Marysville, Pa, Jan 8, 21; m 43; c 4. *Educ:* Univ Pa, VMD, 43; Kans State Univ, MS, 50; Univ Minn, PhD(vet physiol), 56. *Prof Exp:* Asst prof physiol, Col Vet Med, Kans State Univ, 46-51; from instr to prof physiol, Col Vet Med, Univ Minn, St Paul, 51-87. *Mem:* AAAS; Am Vet Med Asn; Am Physiol Soc. *Res:* Cardiovascular physiology of domestic animals; temperature regulation in animals; effects of cold environmental temperatures on new-born calves. *Mailing Add:* Univ Minn Col Vet Med St Paul MN 55108

GOOD, ANNE HAINES, IMMUNOCHEMISTRY, EDUCATION. *Current Pos:* Fel immunol, Dept Biol, Univ Calif, San Diego, 63-66, from lectr to sr lectr, Dept Microbiol & Immunol, Berkeley, 66-89, SR LECTR IMMUNOL, DEPT MOLECULAR & CELL BIOL, UNIV CALIF, BERKELEY, 89- *Personal Data:* b Everett, Wash, June 25, 31; m 64, Robert H; c Howard, Joseph & Samuel. *Educ:* Wellesley Col, BA, 52; Yale Univ, MD, 57; Western Reserve Univ, PhD(immunol & exp path), 63. *Mem:* NY Acad Sci; Am Asn Immunologists; AAAS. *Res:* Immunochemistry. *Mailing Add:* Dept Molecular & Cell Biol Rm 142 LSA Box 4 Univ Calif Berkeley CA 94720. *E-Mail:* good@violet.berkeley.edu

GOOD, CARL M, III, BIOCHEMISTRY, GENETICS. *Current Pos:* technol mgr, Millipore Corp, 72-74, res group leader, 74-76, tech dir, 76-80, ASSOC TECH DIR, MILLIPORE CORP, 76-, VPRES DEVELOP, 80-; PRES, ICSC, DEVELOPMENT CAMBRIDGE BIOTECH, 91- *Personal Data:* b Akron, Ohio, Mar 7, 44; m 69. *Educ:* Ohio Wesleyan Univ, BS, 66; Iowa State Univ, PhD(biochem genetics), 70. *Prof Exp:* Fel bact genetics, Univ Wis Sch Med, 70-71; fel biochem, Univ Mass Sch Med, 71-72. *Mem:* Am Soc Microbiol; Am Asn Clin Chem; Sigma Xi. *Res:* Molecular genetics; clinical biochemistry; retrovirology. *Mailing Add:* 560 Longley Rd Groton MA 01450-1025

GOOD, DON L, ANIMAL SCIENCE. *Current Pos:* From instr to assoc prof, 47-61, PROF ANIMAL SCI, KANS STATE UNIV, 61-, HEAD DEPT ANIMAL SCI & INDUST, 66- *Personal Data:* b Van Wert, Ohio, Oct 8, 21; m 47; c 3. *Educ:* Ohio State Univ, BS, 47; Kans State Univ, MS, 50; Univ Minn, PhD(animal sci), 56. *Concurrent Pos:* Mem res comt, Am Hereford Asn, 63-; USAID consult, Ahmadu Bello Univ, Zaria, Nigeria, 68 & 69; consult, Govt Turkey, 71. *Mem:* Am Soc Animal Sci. *Res:* Production and relationship of live animal evaluation to carcass characteristics and economical production traits in beef cattle. *Mailing Add:* Animal Sci-Ind Dept Kansas State Univ Manhattan KS 66502

GOOD, ERNEST EUGENE, WILDLIFE MANAGEMENT. *Current Pos:* instr, Ohio State Univ, 48-53, from asst prof to assoc prof, 53-70, chmn, Div Fisheries & Wildlife Mgt, 69-80, prof zool, 70-80, EMER PROG NATURAL RESOURCES, OHIO STATE UNIV, 80- *Personal Data:* b Van Wert, Ohio, Jan 7, 13; m 40; c 3. *Educ:* Ohio State Univ, BSc, 40, MSc, 47, PhD(zool), 52. *Prof Exp:* Proj biologist, Soil Conserv Serv, USDA, 35-40, asst agr aide, 40-41; proj leader, Ind Dept Conserv, 41-42; farmer, 42-48. *Concurrent Pos:* Collabr, US Fish & Wildlife Serv, Dept Interior, 49- *Mem:* Wildlife Soc; Am Soc Mammal; Wilson Ornith Soc; Am Ornith Union; Sigma Xi. *Res:* Animal ecology and behavior; ecology. *Mailing Add:* 7085 Linworth Rd Worthington OH 43235

GOOD, HAROLD MARQUIS, PLANT PATHOLOGY. *Current Pos:* RETIRED. *Personal Data:* b Brantford, Ont, Jan 16, 20; m 45; c 4. *Educ:* Univ Toronto, BA, 43, PhD, 47. *Prof Exp:* Lectr bot, Univ Toronto, 47-49; from asst prof to prof biol, Queen's Univ, Ont, 49-83, assoc head dept, 70-73. *Concurrent Pos:* Dir, Ont Univ Prog Instr Develop, 73- *Mailing Add:* Centreville ON K0K 1N0 Can

GOOD, IRVING JOHN, MATHEMATICS, STATISTICS. *Current Pos:* res prof, 67-69, distinguished prof, 69-93, PROF STATIST, VA POLYTECH INST & STATE UNIV, 93- *Personal Data:* b London, Eng, Dec 9, 16. *Educ:* Cambridge Univ, BA, 38, PhD(math), 41, MA, 43, ScD(math, statist), 63; Oxford Univ, DSc, 64. *Prof Exp:* Civil servant, Foreign Off, 41-45; lectr math & electronic comput, Univ Manchester, 45-48; civil servant, Govt Commun HQ, 48-59; spec merit dep chief sci officer, Admiralty Res Lab, 59-62; consult math, statist & electronic comput, Commun Res Div, Inst Defense Anal, 62-64; sr res fel, Trinity Col, Oxford & Atlas Comput Lab, Sci Res Coun, 64-67. *Concurrent Pos:* Mem commun theory comt, Ministry Supply, Gt Brit, 53-59; vis res assoc prof, Princeton Univ, 55; distinguished mem, Crypto-Math Inst, 67; mem adv bd, Ctr Study Pub Choice, Va; adj prof philos, Va Polytech Inst & State Univ. *Mem:* Am Math Soc; Math Asn Am; hon mem Int Statist Inst; fel Inst Math Statist; fel Am Statist Asn; fel Am Acad Arts & Sci. *Res:* Mathematical analysis; cryptology; computers; foundations of statistical and scientific inference; machine intelligence; scientific speculation; probabilistic casuality; self-consistency of the special theory of relativity. *Mailing Add:* Dept Statist Va Polytech Inst & State Univ Blacksburg VA 24061-0439. *Fax:* 540-231-3863

GOOD, MARY LOWE, INORGANIC CHEMISTRY, RADIOCHEMISTRY. *Current Pos:* UNDER SECY FOR TECHNOL, US DEPT COM, 93- *Personal Data:* b Grapevine, Tex, June 20, 31; m 52; c 2. *Educ:* Ark State Teachers Col, BS, 50; Univ Ark, MS, 53, PhD(inorg chem, radiochem), 55. *Hon Degrees:* Various from US Cols & Univs, 79-95. *Honors & Awards:* Garvan Medal, Am Chem Soc, 73; Priestley Medal, 97; Gold Medal, Am Inst Chemists, 83; Delmer S Fahrney Medal, Franklin Inst, 88; Charles Lathrop Parsons Award, Am Chem Soc, 91; Roe Medal, Am Soc Mech Engrs, 93. *Prof Exp:* From instr to asst prof chem, La State Univ, Baton Rouge, 54-58; from assoc prof to prof, Univ New Orleans, 58-74, Boyd prof, 74-80; vpres & dir res, UOP, Inc, 80-85; dir res, Signal Res Ctr, 85-86, pres, Eng Mat Res, Allied Signal Inc, 86-88, sr vpres technol, Allied Signal Res & Technol Lab, 88-93. *Concurrent Pos:* Mem bd dirs, Oak Ridge Assoc Univ, 71-76, Am Chem Soc, 71-80, Indust Res Inst, 82-87, Nat Inst Petrol & Energy Res; mem, NSF Chem Adv Panel, 72-76; mem & chmn med chem B study sect, NIH, 72-76; chmn bd dirs, Am Chem Soc, 78 & 80; pres, Inorganic Div, Int Union Pure & Appl Chem; mem, res coord coun, Gas Res Inst; Nat Acad Sci Panel Sci Communs & Nat Security, 83, Nat Res Coun/Nat Acad Sci Panel Impact Nat Security Controls Int Technol Transfer, 83-86; vchmn, Nat Sci Bd, 84-86, chmn, 88-92; mem, Joint High Level Adv Panel, US-Japan agreement Res & Develop in Sci & Technol. *Mem:* Nat Acad Eng; Int Union Pure & Appl Chem; Am Chem Soc (pres, 87); fel AAAS. *Res:* Radiochemistry, especially tracer technology; spectroscopy and structure of inorganic materials; catalytic chemistry and catalytic materials; materials chemistry and materials engineering, especially polymer-based materials; research management and research and development policy issues. *Mailing Add:* 3321 O St NW Washington DC 20007

GOOD, MYRON LINDSAY, PHYSICS. *Current Pos:* PROF PHYSICS, STATE UNIV NY STONY BROOK, 67- *Personal Data:* b Buffalo, NY, Oct 25, 23; m 50; c 3. *Educ:* Univ Buffalo, BA, 43; Duke Univ, PhD(physics), 51. *Prof Exp:* Physicist, Radiation Lab, Univ Calif, 51-59; from assoc prof to prof physics, Univ Wis, 60-67. *Mem:* Am Phys Soc. *Res:* Beta decay; high energy physics. *Mailing Add:* Dept Physics Grad Physics Bldg/Rm D137 State Univ NY Stony Brook NY 11794

GOOD, NORMA FRAUENDORF, PLANT ECOLOGY. *Current Pos:* ED, BIOL ABSTRACTS, 68- *Personal Data:* b Elizabeth, NJ, Aug 24, 39; m 62; c 1. *Educ:* Rutgers Univ, BA, 61, PhD(plant ecol), 65. *Prof Exp:* Teaching asst biol, Rutgers Univ, 61-65; asst prof, Wagner Col, 65-67. *Mem:* Ecol Soc Am; Torrey Bot Club; Sigma Xi. *Res:* Forest ecology; population dynamics; productivity. *Mailing Add:* c/o Judy Personnel Dept Bio Sci Info Serv 2100 Arch St Philadelphia PA 19103

GOOD, NORMAN EVERETT, plant physiology; deceased, see previous edition for last biography

GOOD, RICHARD ALBERT, ALGEBRA. *Current Pos:* from asst prof to prof, 45-88, EMER PROF MATH, UNIV MD, 89- *Personal Data:* b Ashland, Ohio, Sept 24, 17; m 46; c 3. *Educ:* Ashland Col, AB, 39; Univ Wis, MA, 40, PhD(algebra), 45. *Prof Exp:* Asst math, Univ Wis, 41-43, actg instr, 43-45. *Mem:* AAAS; Soc Indust & Appl Math; Am Math Soc; Math Asn Am. *Res:* Semigroups; matrices; games; linear programing. *Mailing Add:* Dept Math Univ Md College Park MD 20742-4015

GOOD, ROBERT ALAN, PEDIATRICS. *Current Pos:* chmn, Dept Pediat, 85-91, PROF PEDIAT, MICROBIOL IMMUNOL & MED, UNIV SFLA, ST PETERSBURG, 85-, HEAD ALLERGY & CLIN IMMUNOL, 85-, GRAD RES PROF, 89-; PHYSICIAN-IN-CHIEF, ALL CHILDREN'S HOSP, ST PETERSBURG, 85- *Personal Data:* b Crosby, Minn, May 21, 22; m 46, 86, Nourbibi Day; c Robert, Mark, Alan, Margaret & Mary. *Educ:* Univ Minn, BA, 44, MB, 46, MD & PhD(anat), 47. *Hon Degrees:* Dr Med, Univ Uppsala, 66; DSc, NY Med Col, 73, Med Col Ohio, 73, Col Med & Dent NJ, Hahnemann Med Col & Univ Chicago, 74, St John's Univ NY, 77, Univ Health Sci Chicago Med Sch, 78 & Univ Minn, 89. *Honors & Awards:* E Mead Johnson First Award, 55; Theobald Smith Award, AAAS, 55; Parke-Davis Award, Soc Exp Path, 62; Pemberton Lectr, 66; RE Dyer Lectr, 67; Cooke Medal, Am Acad Allergy, 68; Squibb Award, Infectious Dis Soc Am, 68; Borden Award, Asn Am Med Cols, 70; Gairdner Found Award, 70; Albert Lasker Clin & Med Res Award, 70; Am Col Physicians Award, 72; Swed Med Soc Silver Medal, 72; David A Karnofsky Medal, Am Soc Clin Oncol, 73; Col Medalist, Am Col Chest Physicians, 74; Lila Gruber Mem Award Cancer Res, Am Acad Dermat, 74. *Prof Exp:* Asst anat, Med Sch, Univ Minn, Minneapolis, 44-45; from instr to assoc prof pediat, 50-54, Am Legion Mem res prof 54-73, prof microbiol, 62-72, regents prof pediat & microbiol, 69-73, prof path & chmn dept, 70-72; pres & dir, Sloan-Kettering Inst Cancer Res, 73-80, vpres, 80-82; dir & prof path, Sloan-Kettering Div, Grad Sch Med Sci, Cornell Univ, 73-82, prof med & pediat, Med Col, 73-82; res prof med, prof microbiol & head clin immunol, Dept Pediat, Univ Okla, 82-85. *Concurrent Pos:* Res fel poliomyelitis, Med Sch Univ Minn, Minneapolis, 47-48, Whitney fel rheumatic fever, 48-49; vis investr, Rockefeller Inst, 49-50, asst physician, Hosp, 49-50, adj prof & vis physician, Rockefeller Univ, 73-; Markle Found scholar med sci, 50-55; mem, President's Cancer Panel, 72-73; dir res & attend physician, Mem Hosp Cancer & Allied Dis, 73- attend pediat, NY Hosp, 73-; chmn, Int Bone Marrow Registry, 77-79, mem, 80-, chmn, Gov Task Force Acquired Immune Deficiency Syndrome, 85-87, mem, 88-; emer prof, Cath Med Col, Seoul, SKorea, 77-; first foreign, Chinese Acad Med Sci, People's Repub China, 80-; head, Cancer Res Prog, Okla Med Res Found, Oklahoma City, 82-85; mem, WHO Sci Group Immunodeficiency, 82-; dir, Children's Res Inst, All Children's Hosp, St Petersburg, 85-; hon mem med staff, Miami Children's Hosp, 86; Wellcome vis prof, Fedn Am Scientists Exp Biol, 86; Theodore & Venette Askounes-Ashford distinguished scholar award, Univ SFla, 90. *Mem:*

Nat Acad Sci; Inst Med-Nat Acad Sci; AAAS; Am Soc Exp Path (pres, 74-75); Am Asn Immunol (pres, 75-76); Am Soc Clin Invest (pres, 66); Cent Soc Clin Res (pres, 66); Reticuloendothelial Soc (pres, 75); hon mem Am Soc Transplant Surgeons; Am Pediat Soc; Soc Exp Biol & Med; Soc Pediat Res; Int Soc Blood Transfusion; Infectious Dis Soc Am; Asn Am Physicians; hon fel Am Acad Pediat; Am Acad Arts & Sci; NY Acad Sci; Am Soc Microbiol; Harvey Soc. *Res:* Natural and acquired resistance to gram-negative endotoxins, primary and secondary immunodeficiencies, agammaglobulinemias and hypergammaglobulinemias; rheumatic, rheumatoid and autoimmune diseases; acute-phase reactions, immunology and hypersensitivity reactions; cellular basis of immunity; development of lymphoid systems; bone marrow transplantation; thymus function; immunologic tolerance; biology of retroviruses. *Mailing Add:* 801 Sixth St S Box 753 St Petersburg FL 33701

GOOD, ROBERT CAMPBELL, MEDICAL MICROBIOLOGY, MYCOBACTERIOLOGY. *Current Pos:* COLLAB SCIENTIST, YERKES PRIMATE RES CTR, EMORY UNIV, 96- *Personal Data:* b Erwin, Tenn, Aug 23, 26; m 51, Loraine Sparling; c Heather (Gruber) & Holly (Mitchell). *Educ:* Univ Tenn, BA, 49, MS, 50; Northwestern Univ, PhD(med microbiol), 54. *Honors & Awards:* Pub Health Lab Excellence Award, Asn State & Territorial Pub Health Lab Dirs, 95. *Prof Exp:* Res bacteriologist, Bauer & Black Div, Kendall Co, 50-51; sr res microbiologist, Int Minerals & Chem Corp, 54-59; sr res asst exp tuberc, Christ Hosp Inst Med Res, 59-60, res assoc, 60-63; assoc res bacteriologist, Nat Ctr Primate Biol, Univ Calif, Davis, 63-69; mem staff microbiol, Life Sci Ctr, 69-71, sr proj mgr, Hazleton Labs Am, 71-76, dir microbiol-virol dept, 72-76; chief, Mycobact Br, Ctr Infectious Dis, Ctr Dis Control, 76-82, chief respiratory spec pathogens lab br, 82-85, chief, Respiratory Dis Br, 85-92, chief tuberc & other mycobacterioses lab sect, 93-95, guest researcher, Tuberc/Mycobacteriology Br, 96-97. *Concurrent Pos:* Chmn, Sci Assembly Microbiol & Immunol, 71-72; rep, Comt on Guidance of Tuberc/Respiratory Dis Prog, Am Lung Asn, 72-73; chmn, Mycobaterial Div, Am Soc Microbiol, 83-84; adj assoc prof, dept parasitol lab pract, Sch Pub Health, Univ NC, 83-; adj fac, Dept Pathol Lab Med, Emory Univ Sch Med, 85- f; div univ lectr, Am Soc Microbiol, 93. *Mem:* Am Soc Microbiol; fel Am Acad Microbiol. *Res:* Mycobacteria; chemotherapy; virulence; bacterial respiratory diseases, epidemiology. *Mailing Add:* 8095 Habersham Waters Rd Dunwoody GA 30350. *E-Mail:* rcgood@worldnet.att.net

GOOD, ROBERT HOWARD, HIGH ENERGY PHYSICS. *Current Pos:* PROF PHYSICS, CALIF STATE COL, HAYWARD, 66- *Personal Data:* b Ann Arbor, Mich, Aug 26, 31; m 64; c 3. *Educ:* Univ Mich, AB, 53; Univ Calif, Berkeley, PhD(physics), 61. *Prof Exp:* Physicist, Saclay Nuclear Res Ctr, France, 61-62 & Univ Calif, San Diego, 62-66. *Res:* Experimental high energy nuclear physics. *Mailing Add:* Dept Physics Calif State Univ 25800 Carlos Bee Blvd Hayward CA 94542

GOOD, ROBERT JAMES, SURFACE CHEMISTRY, CHEMICAL ENGINEERING. *Current Pos:* PROF CHEM ENG, STATE UNIV NY BUFFALO, 64- *Personal Data:* b Lincoln, Nebr, Aug 13, 20; m 64; c 3. *Educ:* Amherst Col, BA, 42; Univ Calif, MS, 43; Univ Mich, PhD(chem), 50. *Honors & Awards:* Kendall Award, Am Chem Soc, 76; Schoellkopf Award, 79. *Prof Exp:* Asst chem, Univ Calif, 42-43; teaching fel, Univ Mich, 46-48; chemist, Dow Chem Co, Calif, 43-44 & Am Cyanamid & Chem Co, Calif, 44-46; res chemist, Monsanto Chem Co, Ala, 49-53; asst prof appl sci, Univ Cincinnati, 53-56; sr staff scientist, Convair Sci Res Lab, Gen Dynamics Corp, 57-64. *Concurrent Pos:* Vis prof, Univ Bristol, Eng, 70-71, City Univ, London, 71 & Univ Col London, 80; vis scientist, NIH, Bethesda, Md, 79-80. *Mem:* Am Chem Soc; The Chem Soc; Nat Asn Corrosion Engrs. *Res:* Surface chemistry; interfacial tension; adhesion; wetting; porosity and pore penetration; thermodynamics; intermolecular forces; solubility of nonelectolytes; polymer solvent-swelling, biophysics; electron diffraction of solids; fracture; emulsions; corrosion; materials science, coal. *Mailing Add:* Chem Eng Dept State Univ NY Buffalo NY 14260-0001

GOOD, ROLAND HAMILTON, JR, LIQUID CRYSTALS, MASS SPECTRA. *Current Pos:* RETIRED. *Personal Data:* b Toronto, Ont, Can, Oct 22, 23; US citizen; m 44, Ferol Hendrickson; c Roland H, Patricia G & Sue M. *Educ:* Lawrence Inst Technol, BME, 44; Chrysler Inst Eng, MAE, 46; Univ Mich, MS, 48, PhD(physics), 51. *Prof Exp:* Engr, Chrysler Corp, 42-47; instr physics, Univ Calif, 51-53; asst prof, Pa State Univ, 53- 56; from assoc prof to prof, Iowa State Univ, 56-70, distinguished prof, 70-72; head, Physics Dept, Pa State Univ, 72-81, prof physics, 72-88. *Concurrent Pos:* Vis lectr, Univ Colo, 58; mem, Inst Advan Study, 60-61; NSF sr fel, 60-61; vis prof, Inst Math Sci, Madras, India, 68; guest, Stanford Linear Accelerator Ctr, 68-69; vis prof, Seoul Nat Univ, Korea, 79. *Mem:* Fel Am Phys Soc. *Res:* Author of about 100 papers on various aspects of theoretical physics. *Mailing Add:* 653D Avenida Sevilla Laguna Hills CA 92653

GOOD, WILFRED MANLY, RESEARCH ADMINISTRATION. *Current Pos:* RETIRED. *Personal Data:* b Hope, Kans, Oct 13, 13; m 40; c 3. *Educ:* Univ Kans, AB, 36 & MS, 38; Mass Inst Tech, PhD(physics), 44. *Prof Exp:* Res asst nuclear physics, Oak Ridge Nat Lab, 46-48, dir, High Voltage Acceleration Lab, 48-66; head, Nuclear Data Sect, Int Atomic Energy Agency, 66-70; sr physicist, Oak Ridge Nat Lab, 70-78. *Mem:* Sigma Xi; AAAS; NY Acad Sci. *Res:* Properties of beta-decay including angular correlations of emitted radiation; particle reaction with light nuclei; neutron reactions; nuclear structure. *Mailing Add:* 13 Essex Circle Sherwood Forest Brevard NC 28712

GOOD, WILLIAM BRENEMAN, physics; deceased, see previous edition for last biography

GOOD, WILLIAM E, COLOR TELEVISION PROJECTION SYSTEMS. *Current Pos:* PRES, GOOD ELECTRONICS, INC, 77- *Personal Data:* b Hillsdale, Mich, Apr 25, 16; m 41; c 6. *Educ:* Kalamazoo Col, AB, 37; Univ Ill, MS, 39; Univ Pittsburgh, PhD(physics), 46. *Prof Exp:* Engr, Westinghouse Res Labs, 41-50; engr, Gen Elec Co, 50-65; mgr, Advan Develop, TV Receiver Dept, 65-77; consult, Gen Elec Co, 77-87. *Mem:* Fel Inst Elec & Electronics Engrs; Soc Info Display; Am Radio Relay League. *Res:* Color television large screen projection using diffraction grating written on a fluid control layer to determine the hue and brightness of each picture element in real time; radio controlled model airplanes. *Mailing Add:* Good Electronics Inc 700 Tulip St Liverpool NY 13088

GOODACRE, ROBERT LESLIE, GASTROENTEROLOGY. *Current Pos:* Res fel gastroenterol, 74-77, assoc prof, 78-84, ASSOC PROF MED, MCMASTER UNIV, 84- *Personal Data:* b Grantham, Eng, Feb 3, 47; m 72; c 3. *Educ:* London Univ, MB, BS, 70; FRCP(C), 75. *Mem:* Am Gastroenterol Asn; Can Asn Gastroenterol; Royal Col Physicians. *Res:* Gastroenterology; inflammatory bowel disease; mucosal immunology. *Mailing Add:* 14 Ravine Dr Dundas ON L9H 6K6 Can. *Fax:* 905-521-6068

GOODAIRE, EDGAR GEORGE, NONASSOCIATIVE RING THEORY & LOOP THEORY. *Current Pos:* Head, Dept Math & Statist, 91-94, PROF, DEPT MATH & STATIST, MEM UNIV NFLD, 73- *Personal Data:* b Toronto, Ont, Mar 31, 47; m, Linda R Hensman; c 2. *Educ:* Univ Toronto, BSc, 69; Univ BC, PhD(math), 73. *Concurrent Pos:* Co-ed-chief, Can Math Bull, 80-85. *Mem:* Can Math Soc; Am Math Soc; Math Asn Am. *Res:* Nonassociative rings especially alternative rings and alternative loop rings; loop theory. *Mailing Add:* Dept Math & Statist Memorial Univ St John's NF A1C 5S7 Can. *Fax:* 709-737-3010; *E-Mail:* edgar@math.mun.ca

GOODALE, DOUGLAS M, FORAGE CROPS, SOIL SCIENCE. *Current Pos:* PROF AGRON & CHAIR, DEPT PLANT SCI, STATE UNIV NY, COBLESKILL, 74- *Personal Data:* b Cortland, NY, Oct 22, 47; m, Sandra Pond; c Brian & Eric. *Educ:* Univ Del, BS, 69; State Univ NY, Albany, MS, 78; Pa State Univ, PhD(agr educ & agron), 83. *Mem:* Am Soc Agron; Nat Asn Col Teachers Agr. *Res:* Solid waste management, crop production and the efficacy of crop protectants (herbicides). *Mailing Add:* Plant Sci A&T Coil Coblesk State Univ NY Cobleskill NY 12043-1701. *Fax:* 518-234-5333

GOODALE, FAIRFIELD, ANATOMIC PATHOLOGY, CLINICAL PATHOLOGY. *Current Pos:* DEAN & MED DIR, MED COL GA, 76-, PROF PATH, 76- *Personal Data:* b Framingham, Mass, May 4, 23; m 45; c 5. *Educ:* Western Reserve Univ, MD, 50. *Prof Exp:* Asst in path, Harvard Med Sch, 57-58; asst prof, Dartmouth Med Sch, 58-60; assoc prof, Albany Med Col, 60-63; prof path & chmn dept, Med Col Va, Commonwealth Univ, 63-76, asst dean curriculum, 72-76. *Concurrent Pos:* Teaching fel, Harvard Med Sch, 54-55; Am Cancer Soc res fel, Mass Gen Hosp, Boston, 54-55; USPHS res fels, St Mary's Hosp, London, 55-56, Oxford Univ, 56-57 & Mass Gen Hosp, Boston, 57-58; assoc dir labs, Mary Hitchcock Mem Hosp & Clin, Hanover, NH, 58-60; Nat Bd Med Examr; chmn path test comt, Int Path Coun, 78-81, vpres, 74-77, pres, 77-79. *Mem:* Int Acad Path; Am Soc Clin Path; Am Asn Path & Bact; fel Col Am Path; Am Soc Exp Path. *Res:* Pathogenesis of fever. *Mailing Add:* Black Hawk 100 North Brooklin ME 04661-9999

GOODALL, JANE, ZOOLOGY. *Current Pos:* RESEARCHER ANIMAL BEHAV & SCI DIR, GOMBE STREAM RES CTR, TANZANIA, 60- *Personal Data:* b London, Eng, Apr 3, 34; wid; c Hugo E. *Educ:* Cambridge Univ, Eng, PhD, 65. *Honors & Awards:* Conserv Award, Nat Geog Soc, Centennial Award, 88. *Prof Exp:* Asst & secy, Dr Louis S B Leakey Coryndon Mem Mus Natural Hist, Tanzania. *Concurrent Pos:* Vis prof psychiat & human biol, Stanford Univ, 70-75; hon vis prof zool, Univ Dar Es Salaam, Tanzania; lectr, Yale Univ, 73. *Mem:* Hon foreign mem Am Acad Arts & Sci. *Res:* Primate behavior and ethology. *Mailing Add:* Jane Goodall Inst PO Box 599 Ridgefield CT 06877

GOODARZI, FARIBORZ, ORGANIC PETROLOGY, SCIENCE EDUCATION. *Current Pos:* PRIN RES SCIENTIST, COAL & PETROL, INST SEDIMENTARY & PETROL GEOL, 82-, CO-COORDR, GLOBAL CHANGE, 88- *Personal Data:* b Tehran, Iran, Feb 20, 40; Can citizen; m 74, Margaret E Bailey; c Aaron, Nina & Zahra. *Educ:* Univ Tehran, BS, 63; Univ Newcastle-Upon-Tyne, MS, 71, PhD(geol), 75. *Prof Exp:* Geologist, ASK Coal Co, 63-64; sect head, geol, Ministry Water & Power; asst prof geol, Univ Technol, Iran, 75-80; dir, coal & petrol, FG consul, 80-82. *Concurrent Pos:* Adj prof Univ Regina, Sask, 85-, Univ Waterloo, 87-, Univ Western Ont, 89-; adv, Geol Surv Greece, 86- *Mem:* Royal Micros Soc; Int Comt Coal Petrol; Am Soc Org Petrol; Can Mineral Asn; Can Soc Coal Sci & Org Petrol (pres, 92-). *Res:* Investigation of inorganic and organic compositional characteristics of carbonaceous material, for example coal, bitumen, and kerogen; results of research relevant to understanding utilization behavior of coal; geological interpretation of burial and thermal histories with reference to oil exploration; global change and environmental impact of elements. *Mailing Add:* 3303 33rd St NW Calgary AB T2L 2A7 Can. *Fax:* 403-292-5377

GOODCHILD, MICHAEL, PHYSICAL GEOGRAPHY. *Current Pos:* PROF GEOG, UNIV CALIF, SANTA BARBARA. *Honors & Awards:* Scholarly Distinction Geog Award, Can Asn Geogr, 90. *Mailing Add:* Nat Ctr Geog Info & Analysis Univ Calif Santa Barbara CA 93106-4060

GOODDING, JOHN ALAN, AGRONOMY. *Current Pos:* asst dir resident instr, 61-770, from assoc prof to prof agron, 61-89, asst dean, Col Agr, 70-73, actg dean, 73-76, EMER PROF AGRON, DEPT AGRON & PLANT GENETICS, UNIV MINN, ST PAUL, 89- *Personal Data:* b Lincoln, Nebr, Mar 11, 22; m 45; c 2. *Educ:* Univ Nebr, BS, 47; Kans State Univ, MS, 50; Wash State Univ, PhD, 57. *Prof Exp:* Instr, Kans State Univ, 48-51 & Wash State Univ, 53-55; asst prof agron & asst agronomist, Univ Nebr, 55-61. *Mem:* Am Soc Agron; Nat Asn Col & Teachers Agr. *Res:* Range management; seed technology; miscellaneous legumes. *Mailing Add:* 3180 W Owasso Blvd St Paul MN 55113

GOODE, HARRY DONALD, GEOLOGY. *Current Pos:* RETIRED. *Personal Data:* b Newark, NJ, May 31, 12; m 46. *Educ:* Univ Ariz, BS, 51; Univ Colo, PhD(geol), 59. *Prof Exp:* Field asst geol, US Geol Surv, 49-52, geologist, 52-59, asst dist geologist, 59-62; from assoc prof to prof, Univ Utah, 62-77; consult, 77-85. *Mem:* Fel AAAS; fel Geol Soc Am. *Res:* Ground water geology, especially springs in bedrock; geomorphology; Quaternary geology, especially deposits of Lake Bonneville; study of thermal waters of Utah. *Mailing Add:* 680 E 100 South No 101 Salt Lake City UT 84102-1128

GOODE, JULIA PRATT, ANALYTICAL CHEMISTRY. *Current Pos:* RETIRED. *Personal Data:* b Carnesville, Ga, Feb 26, 29. *Educ:* Agnes Scott Col, BA, 50; Emory Univ, MS, 52. *Prof Exp:* Chemist, Ga Dept Pub Health, 52-53; asst to dir agr res, Tenn Corp, 53-56; chmn dept sci, Fulton County Bd Ed, 56-66; assoc prof chem, Baptist Col, Charleston, 66-69; asst prof, Med Univ SC, 69-73, assoc prof med technol & assoc dean, Col Allied Health Sci, 73-83, registr & dir admis, 83-90. *Mem:* Am Chem Soc. *Res:* Quantitative techniques in paper chromatography. *Mailing Add:* 5490 Stonoview Dr John's Island SC 29455

GOODE, LEMUEL, PHYSIOLOGY, ANIMAL PHYSIOLOGY. *Current Pos:* RETIRED. *Personal Data:* b Saulsville, WVa, Jan 2, 21; m 47; c 2. *Educ:* WVa Univ, BS, 42, MS, 46; Univ Fla, PhD, 61. *Prof Exp:* Asst county agent, NC State Univ, 46-47, from instr to assoc prof, 47-65, prof animal sci, 65-86. *Concurrent Pos:* Southern Fels Fund fac fel. *Mem:* Fel Am Soc Animal Sci. *Res:* Physiology of reproduction; effects of nutrition and environment on ovarian activity, reproductive rate and milk production; roughage and pasture utilization. *Mailing Add:* 3336 Thomas Rd Raleigh NC 27607

GOODE, MELVYN DENNIS, CELL BIOLOGY, BIOPHYSICS. *Current Pos:* asst prof, 68-73, ASSOC PROF ZOOL, UNIV MD, COLLEGE PARK, 73- *Personal Data:* b New Albany, Ind, Feb 18, 40; m 68. *Educ:* Univ Kans, BS, 63; Iowa State Univ, PhD(cell biol), 67. *Honors & Awards:* Nikon Award, 79. *Prof Exp:* Asst biomed res, Argonne Nat Labs, 63; res assoc anat, Univ Pa, 67-68. *Concurrent Pos:* Vis investr, Univ Tex MD Anderson Hosp & Tumor Inst, 69, Kings Col, London, 75, Sta Zool, Villefranche-sur-mer, 83; res grants, Univ Md Gen Res Bd, 69-70, biomed sci comt, 70-71 & 84-85, Am Cancer Soc, 70-73 & 87-88, Am Heart Asn, 74-75, NIH, 76-78, NSF, 78-83, Juv Diabetes Found, 89-91. *Mem:* Am Soc Cell Biol; Electron Micros Soc Am; Int Soc Evolution Protistology (pres, 85-87). *Res:* Mechanism of kinesin-based movement of secretory granules; Mechanism and evolution of mitosis; relationship between differentiation and DNA synthesis in cultured cells. *Mailing Add:* Dept Zool Univ Md College Park MD 20742. *Fax:* 301-314-9358; *E-Mail:* goode@zool.umd.edu

GOODE, PHILIP RANSON, SYSTEMS ENGINEERING. *Current Pos:* PROF & CHMN PHYSICS, NJ INST TECHNOL, 84- *Personal Data:* b San Francisco, Calif, Jan 4, 43. *Educ:* Univ Calif, Berkeley, AB, 64; Rutgers Univ, PhD(physics), 69. *Prof Exp:* Res assoc physics, Rutgers Univ, 69; res assoc, Univ Rochester, 69-71; asst prof, Rutgers Univ, 71-77, mem tech staff, Bell Tel Labs, 77--80; assoc prof, Univ Ariz, 80-84. *Mem:* Am Phys Soc; Sigma Xi; Am Astron Soc; AAAS; Inst Am Univ. *Res:* Astrophysics. *Mailing Add:* 116 Jefferson Ave Westfield NJ 07090-1911

GOODE, ROBERT J, FRACTURE MECHANICS. *Current Pos:* RETIRED. *Personal Data:* b McDonald, Pa, Dec 21, 32. *Educ:* Carnegie Inst Technol, BS, 56. *Honors & Awards:* Award of Merit, Am Soc Testing & Mat, 83. *Prof Exp:* Assoc supt mat sci technol, Naval Res Lab, Washington, DC, 80-87. *Mem:* Fel Am Soc Metals; fel Am Soc Testing & Mat. *Mailing Add:* 2402 Kegwood Lane Bowie MD 20715

GOODE, ROBERT P, BIOLOGY, EMBRYOLOGY. *Current Pos:* from asst prof to assoc prof, 64-82, PROF EMBRYOL, CITY COL NEW YORK, 82-, DIR, PROG IN PREMED STUDIES, 80- *Personal Data:* b New York, NY, Sept 12, 36. *Educ:* NY Univ, BS, 57; Columbia Univ, MA, 60, PhD(exp embryol), 64. *Prof Exp:* asst prof embryol & histol, Otterbein Col, 63-64. *Mem:* Am Soc Zool; Soc Develop Biol. *Res:* Regeneration of limbs in amphibia, particularly of adults in several species of Anurans under natural conditions; induction of regeneration in amphibians and mammals. *Mailing Add:* Dept Biol CUNY City Col NY 160 Convent Ave New York NY 10031-9101

GOODE, SCOTT ROY, ANALYTICAL CHEMISTRY. *Current Pos:* asst prof, 74-80, ASSOC PROF CHEM, UNIV SC, 80- *Personal Data:* b Chicago, Ill, July 9, 48; m 75. *Educ:* Univ Ill, Urbana, BS, 69; Mich State Univ, PhD(chem), 74. *Prof Exp:* Res asst chem, Mich State Univ, 69-74. *Mem:* Am Chem Soc; Soc Appl Spectros; Optical Soc Am. *Res:* Atomic flame and furnace spectrometry; analytical instrumentation and interactive computer control of experimentation. *Mailing Add:* Dept Chem Univ SC Columbia SC 29208-0001

GOODEARL, KENNETH RALPH, ALGEBRA. *Current Pos:* PROF MATH, UNIV CALIF, SANTA BARBARA, 91- *Personal Data:* b Weymouth, Mass, Sept 4, 45; m 86. *Educ:* Amherst Col, BA, 67; Univ Wash, MS, 69, PhD(math), 71. *Prof Exp:* Instr math, Univ Chicago, 71-72; instr math, Univ Utah, 72-75, from asst prof to assoc prof, 75-84, prof, 84-92. *Concurrent Pos:* Sr vis fel, Univ Leeds, Eng, 77; prin investr res grants, Nat Sci Found, 74-; Humboldt res fel, Univ Passau, Ger, 84-85. *Mem:* Am Math Soc. *Res:* Noncommutative ring theory; nonsingular rings; von Neumann regular rings; differential operator rings; C*-algebras; ordered K-theory; noetherian rings. *Mailing Add:* Dept Math Univ Calif Santa Barbara CA 93106

GOODELL, HORACE GRANT, GEOLOGY, HYDROGEOLOGY. *Current Pos:* chmn dept, 71-79, PROF ENVIRON SCI, UNIV VA, CHARLOTTESVILLE, 70-, CHMN MARINE AFFAIRS, 80- *Personal Data:* b Decatur, Ill, Oct 12, 25; m 56; c 3. *Educ:* Southern Methodist Univ, BS, 54; Northwestern Univ, PhD(geol), 58. *Prof Exp:* From asst prof to prof geol, Fla State Univ, 57-70, chmn, Dept Oceanog, 67-70. *Mem:* Oceanog Soc; Am Inst Prof Geologists; Natural Hazards Soc; Am Asn Petrol Geologists; fel Geol Soc Am; Am Groundwater Asn. *Res:* Sedimentary petrology; lithostratigraphy; geochemistry; marine geology; hydrogeology. *Mailing Add:* Dept Environ Sci Clark Hall Univ Va Charlottesville VA 22903. *Fax:* 804-982-2137; *E-Mail:* hgg@virginia.edu

GOODENOUGH, DANIEL ADINO, MOLECULAR BIOLOGY. *Current Pos:* from instr to prof anat, 71-93, PROF CELL BIOL, HARVARD MED SCH, 93- *Personal Data:* b New Haven, Conn, July 6, 44; m 68, Carol; c Sophia & Abigail. *Educ:* Harvard Univ, BA, 66, PhD(anat), 70. *Prof Exp:* NSF grant, Cardiovasc Res Inst, Univ Calif, San Francisco, 70-71. *Concurrent Pos:* Takeda Prof, 89. *Mem:* Am Soc Cell Biol; Biophys Soc. *Res:* Structure and function of intercellular junctions, particularly the gap junction; electron microscopy; protein and lipid chemistry; x-ray diffraction; subcellular isolation; molecular biology. *Mailing Add:* Dept Cell Biol Harvard Med Sch 420 Longwood Ave Boston MA 02115-6092. *Fax:* 617-432-2955

GOODENOUGH, DAVID GEORGE, REMOTE SENSING. *Current Pos:* CHIEF RES SCI & HEAD, ADVAN FOREST TECHNOL PROG, PAC FORESTRY CTR, 91- *Personal Data:* b Victoria, BC, Nov 12, 42; m 65, 88; c 2. *Educ:* Univ BC, BSc, 64; Univ Toronto, MSc, 67, PhD(astron), 69. *Prof Exp:* Fel, Univ Victoria, BC, 69-70; asst prof astron, Wheaton Col, Mass, 70-73; res scientist, Can Ctr Remote Sensing, Ottawa, Can, 73-74, res scientist head, Methodology Sect, 74-91, sr res scientist & head, 78-85, chief res scientist & head, 85-90, chief res scientsit & head knowledge-based methods & systs sect, 90-91. *Concurrent Pos:* Consult, 75-; assoc ed, J Can Aeronaut & Space Inst, 75-78; adj prof, Physics Dept, York Univ, 76-86; adj prof, Dept Elec Eng, Univ Ottawa, 79-; mem adv comt, Inst Elec & Electronics Engrs Geosci & Remote Sensing Soc, 87- *Mem:* Am Astron Soc; Royal Astron Soc Can; Can Aeronaut & Space Inst; Pattern Recognition Soc; sr mem Inst Elec & Electronics Engrs; Geosci & Remote Sensing Soc (vpres, 87-); Asn Artificial Intel; AAAS. *Res:* Multiple expert systems for integrating remote sensing data, geographic information systems, domain knowledge for resource management and environmental monitoring; physical and mathematical bases for microwave, visible and infrared remote sensing systems. *Mailing Add:* Pac Forestry Ctr 506 W Burnside Rd Victoria BC V8Z 1M5 Can

GOODENOUGH, DAVID JOHN, MEDICAL PHYSICS, RADIOLOGICAL PHYSICS. *Current Pos:* assoc prof & dir div radiol physics, Dept Radiol, 75-84, PROF RADIOL, GEORGE WASHINGTON UNIV, 85-;CO-DIR, INST MED IMAGING & IMAGE ANALYSIS, 90- *Personal Data:* b Reading, Eng, Oct 3, 44; m 63, Marjorie; c Jennifer & Meredith. *Educ:* Univ Chicago, BS, 67, PhD(med physics), 72. *Honors & Awards:* Serv Citation, Soc Photo-Optical Instrument Engr, 77; Medal Award, Int Cong Radiol, 89. *Prof Exp:* Instr radiol, Ctr Radiologic Image Res, Univ Chicago, 72-73; vis assoc, Bur Radiol Health, 73; asst prof radiol, Sch Med, Johns Hopkins Univ, 74-75. *Concurrent Pos:* Adj asst prof, Hood Col, Md, 73-75; pres, Inst Radiol Image Sci, 75-; mem, Nat Adv Comt Diag Radiol, nat Cancer Inst, 77-81; IAEA expert, 89- *Mem:* NY Acad Sci; Asn Univ Radiologists; Soc Photo-Optical Instrumentation Engrs; Soc Magnetic Resonance Med; Soc Nuclear Med. *Res:* Image analysis and signal detection theory applied to diagnostic procedures; application of information and communication theory to analysis of radiologic system performance; computed tomography; magnetic resonance imaging; granted patents in radiological imaging. *Mailing Add:* Div Radiol George Washington Univ Hosp 901 23rd St NW Washington DC 20037-2377

GOODENOUGH, EUGENE ROSS, FOOD SCIENCE. *Current Pos:* food scientist res & develop, 75-82, dir prod develop, 82-88, DIR OPERS SUPPORT, BEST FOODS RES CTR, UNION, NJ, 89- *Personal Data:* b Neptune, NJ, Jan 8, 46; m 66; c 1. *Educ:* Rutgers Univ, BS, 69, MS, 71, PhD(food sci), 75. *Prof Exp:* Res food technologist, Merck Chem Corp, 66; res asst, Rutgers Univ, 70-75. *Mem:* Sigma Xi; Inst Food Technologists; Am Dairy Sci Asn. *Res:* Shelf stable food products; packaging technology and quality assurance management. *Mailing Add:* 645 State Rd 523 Whitehouse Station NJ 08889

GOODENOUGH, JOHN, COMPUTER PROGRAMMING LANGUAGES. *Current Pos:* CHIEF TECH OFFICER, SOFTWARE ENG INST, CARNEGIE-MELLON UNIV. *Educ:* Harvard Univ, MA, PhD(appl math). *Prof Exp:* Mgr, Res Develop Dept, SofTech Inc. *Concurrent Pos:* Vis scholar, Wang Inst Grad Studies. *Mem:* Fel Asn Comput Mach; Inst Elec & Electronics Engrs Comput Soc. *Mailing Add:* Software Eng Inst Carnegie-Mellon Univ 4500 Fifth Ave Rm 5102 Pittsburgh PA 15213

GOODENOUGH, JOHN BANNISTER, PHYSICS, CHEMISTRY OF SOLIDS. *Current Pos:* CENTENNIAL PROF, UNIV TEX, 86- *Personal Data:* b Jena, Ger, July 25, 22; US citizen; m 51, Irene Johnston Wiseman. *Educ:* Yale Univ, AB, 43; Univ Chicago, MS, 51, PhD(physics), 52. *Hon Degrees:* Dr, Univ Bordeaux, 67; MA, Univ Oxford, Eng, 76. *Honors & Awards:* Cenntenary Lectr, Royal Soc Chem, 76, Solid State Chem Prize, 80; Von Hippel Award, Mat Res Soc, 89; Sr Res Award, Am Soc Eng Educ, 90; John Bordeaux Award, Minerals, Metals & Mat Soc, 97. *Prof Exp:* Res engr, Westinghouse Elec Corp, 51-52; group leader & res physicist, Lincoln Lab, Mass Inst Technol, 52-76; prof & head inorg chem lab, Univ Oxford, Eng, 76-86. *Concurrent Pos:* Fel, Neurosci Res Prog, 62-76, mem exec comt, Div Solid State Physics, 65-68; assoc ed, Mat Res Bull, 66-, J Solid State Chem, 68-, Struct & Bonding, 77-, Nouveau J de Chimie, J Solid State Ionics, 80-, Superconductor Sci & Technol, 87, J Mats Chem, 91- & Chem Mats, 89-92; mem bd, Univ Without Walls, Roxbury, Mass, 71-73; mem, Solid State Sci Panel & Comt, 74-76 & Nat Mat Adv Bd, 75-77; gen ed, Int Ser Monogrs Chem, 78-86; vis Raman prof, Indian Inst Sci, 83; assoc prof, Northwestern Univ, 96, Slenyang & Jilin Univ, China, 96. *Mem:* Nat Acad Eng; AAAS; Phys Soc Japan; fel Am Phys Soc; Am Chem Soc; Royal Soc Chem; foreign assoc Indian Acad Sci; Sigma Xi; hon mem Mat Res Soc. *Res:* Theory of solids; transition metal compounds; magnetism; superconductivity; materials for energy conversion and storage; author of numerous articles to professional journals. *Mailing Add:* Ctr Mat Sci & Eng ETC 9-102 Univ Tex Austin TX 78712-1063. *Fax:* 512-471-7681

GOODENOUGH, JUDITH ELIZABETH, ANIMAL BEHAVIOR, BIOLOGICAL RHYTHMS & PHYSIOLOGY. *Current Pos:* lectr-staff asst, 75-83, LECT-STAFF ASSOC, UNIV MASS, 83- *Personal Data:* b Geneva, NY, 1948; m 71, Stephen M; c Aimee E & Heather M. *Educ:* Wagner Col, NY, BS, 70; NY Univ, PhD(biol), 77. *Prof Exp:* Instr biol, NY Univ, 74. *Concurrent Pos:* Fac res grant, 80 & 82; consult, Saunders Col Publ, Benjamin Cummings/Addison Wesley Publ, Prentice Hall Publ, W C Brown Publ, Times Mirror & Harper Collins Worth, McGraw Hill/Random House. *Mem:* Sigma Xi; AAAS; Animal Behav Soc. *Res:* Circadian and monthly biological rhythms. *Mailing Add:* Dept Biol Univ Mass Amherst MA 01003. *Fax:* 413-545-1696; *E-Mail:* jegebio.umass.edu

GOODENOUGH, URSULA WILTSHIRE, CELL BIOLOGY, GENETICS. *Current Pos:* assoc prof, 78-82, PROF BIOL, WASHINGTON UNIV, 82- *Personal Data:* b Queens Village, NY, Mar 16, 43; m 80, John Heuser; c Jason, Mathea, Jessica, Thomas & James. *Educ:* Barnard Col, BA, 63, Columbia Univ, MA, 65; Harvard Univ, PhD(biol), 69. *Prof Exp:* NIH fel, Biol Lab, Harvard Univ, 69-71, from asst prof to assoc prof biol, 71-78. *Concurrent Pos:* Ed, J Cell Biol, Cell Motifily Cytoskeleton & J Phycol; mem, NIH & NSF Study Sects; mem, Comn Life Sci, Nat Res Coun. *Mem:* Am Soc Cell Biol (pres); Phycol Soc Am. *Res:* Cell biology and genetics of gametic differentiation in Chlamydomonas reinhardi; structure and function of cilia; hydroxyproline-rich glycoproteins. *Mailing Add:* Dept Biol Washington Univ Campus Box 1229 St Louis MO 63130. *Fax:* 314-935-5125

GOODER, HARRY, MICROBIAL STRUCTURE, MICROBIAL PHYSIOLOGY. *Current Pos:* from asst prof to assoc prof, 61-68, actg chair, 79-81 & 89-91, PROF MICROBIOL & IMMUNOL, SCH MED, UNIV NC, CHAPEL HILL, 68- *Personal Data:* b Castleford, Eng, May 7, 28; nat US; m 54, 79, Sally C Vilas; c Patricia & Caroline. *Educ:* Univ Leeds, BSc, 49, PhD(biochem), 52; FRSC. *Prof Exp:* Res fel bact, Harvard Med Sch, 52-54, teaching fel, 54-55; mem sci staff, Cent Pub Health Lab, Med Res Coun, Eng, 55-61. *Concurrent Pos:* Mem coun policy comt, Am Soc Microbiol, 78-88, chmn bd meetings, 78-88; chmn fac, Univ NC, 88-91. *Mem:* Am Soc Microbiol; Brit Soc Gen Microbiol; Brit Soc Immunol; fel Am Acad Microbiol. *Res:* Bacterial structure and chemistry, specifically cell walls and L forms; bacterial physiology in relation to pathogenicity; bacterial genetics; medical bacteriology. *Mailing Add:* Dept Microbiol & Immunol CB 7290 622 FLOB 231H Univ NC Chapel Hill NC 27514

GOODEVE, ALLAN MCCOY, PHARMACOGNOSY. *Current Pos:* RETIRED. *Personal Data:* b Toronto, Ont, Aug 12, 23; wid. *Educ:* Univ Toronto, PhB, 48, MSc, 56; Univ Sask, BSP, 50; Purdue Univ, PhD(pharmacog), 60. *Prof Exp:* Asst prof pharmacog, Univ NC, 59-60; asst prof pharmacog, Univ BC, 60-86, emer prof, 86. *Mem:* AAAS; Am Soc Pharmacog; Am Chem Soc; Can Pharmaceut Asn. *Res:* Alkaloid biosynthesis; solanaceous alkaloids. *Mailing Add:* 4055 W 29th Ave Vancouver BC V6S 1V4 Can

GOODEY, PAUL RONALD, CONVEX SETS THEORY. *Current Pos:* PROF PATH, OKLA UNIV, 83- *Personal Data:* b Hull, Eng, Oct 16, 46; m 70; c 2. *Educ:* London Univ, BSc, 68, PhD(math), 70. *Prof Exp:* Lectr math, Royal Holloway Col, London Univ, 70-83. *Concurrent Pos:* Vis prof, Okla Univ, 79-80, Siegen Univ, WGer, 82-83. *Mem:* London Math Soc; Am Math Soc. *Res:* Geometric analysis; convexity; geometric probability and stochastic geometry. *Mailing Add:* Univ Okla Univ Okla Norman OK 73019-0315

GOODFRIEND, LAWRENCE, PROTEIN CHEMISTRY, ALLERGIES. *Current Pos:* assoc prof, Dept Immunol, 63-88, EMER PROF, MCGILL UNIV, 88- *Educ:* McGill Univ, PhD(biochem), 61. *Res:* Human immuno-genetics. *Mailing Add:* 4895 Haulkner Chomedey Laval PQ H7W 1H9 Can

GOODFRIEND, LEWIS S(TONE), ACOUSTICS. *Current Pos:* PRES, L S GOODFRIEND & ASSOCS, 72- *Personal Data:* b New York, NY, May 21, 23; m 50, 61, 85; c 4. *Educ:* Stevens Inst Technol, ME, 47; Polytech Inst Brooklyn, MEE, 52. *Prof Exp:* Staff engr, Stevens Inst Technol, 47-49; chief elec engr acoust instruments, Audio Instruments Co, 50-53; vpres noise control eng, Zurn Environ Engrs, 69-72. *Concurrent Pos:* Ed, Noise Control, 55-58 & Sound & Vibration, 67-71; mem bd dir, Inst Noise Control Eng, 72-75 & 82-85; mem bd of trustees, Stevens Inst Technol, 78-93. *Mem:* Fel Acoust Soc Am; Am Indust Hyg Asn; Inst Elec & Electronics Engrs; Inst Noise Control Eng, (pres, 83); fel Audio Eng Soc. *Res:* Noise control by design of products and systems; environmental noise impact on people and societal goals; architectural acoustics. *Mailing Add:* L S Goodfriend & Assocs 760 Route 10 Whippany NJ 07981. *Fax:* 973-540-0391

GOODFRIEND, PAUL LOUIS, physical chemistry; deceased, see previous edition for last biography

GOODFRIEND, THEODORE L, INTERNAL MEDICINE, BIOCHEMISTRY. *Current Pos:* from asst prof to assoc prof med & pharmacol, 65-74, PROF MED & PHARMACOL, UNIV WIS-MADISON, 74-, HEAD SECT CLIN PHARMACOL, 73-; ASSOC CHIEF STAFF RES, VET ADMIN HOSP, MADISON, 75- *Personal Data:* b Philadelphia, Pa, Sept 30, 31; div; c 2. *Educ:* Swarthmore Col, AB, 53; Univ Pa, MD, 57. *Prof Exp:* Intern, Univ Hosps Cleveland, 57-58; asst resident med, Barnes Hosp, Wash Univ, 60-62. *Concurrent Pos:* Helen Hay Whitney res fel biochem, Brandeis Univ, 62-65; NIH res career develop award, 68-73; mem med adv bd coun high blood pressure res, Am Heart Asn, 69-, mem res study comt, Cardiovascular A, 73-; mem endocrinol & metab adv comt, Food & Drug Admin, 72- *Mem:* Am Soc Pharmacol & Exp Therapeut; Am Soc Clin Pharmacol & Therapeut; NY Acad Sci; Soc Exp Biol & Med; Sigma Xi. *Res:* Receptors for polypeptide hormones; angiotensin; pharmacology; antibodies to small polypeptides; kinins. *Mailing Add:* Dept Med & Pharmacol Vet Admin Hosp 2500 Overlook Terr Madison WI 53705-2254. *Fax:* 608-262-7644

GOODGAL, SOL HOWARD, MOLECULAR BIOLOGY, GENETICS. *Current Pos:* assoc prof, 61-66, PROF MICROBIOL, SCH MED, UNIV PA, 66- *Personal Data:* b Baltimore, Md, July 25, 21; div; c 2. *Educ:* Univ Md, BS, 42; Johns Hopkins Univ, PhD(biol), 50. *Prof Exp:* Res assoc, Inst Coop Res, Johns Hopkins Univ, 50-52, res assoc biochem, 52-58, asst prof sch hyg & pub health, 58-61. *Concurrent Pos:* Fel, Pasteur Inst, 59-60; vis prof, L'Institut de Biolgie Physico-Chemique, 68-69; mem, Johns Hopkins Soc Scholars, 70. *Mem:* AAAS; Genetics Soc Am; Am Soc Microbiol; Am Soc Nat; Am Soc Biol Chem. *Res:* Transformation of bacteria; bacteriophage; role of nucleic acid in genetic determination; radiation effects on genetics of microorganisms; biochemistry. *Mailing Add:* Dept Microbiol Med Univ Pa Sch Med 346 Johnson/G2 36th St & Hamilton Philadelphia PA 19104-6076. *Fax:* 215-573-9068

GOODGAME, THOMAS H, ENVIRONMENTAL ENGINEERING, CHEMICAL ENGINEERING. *Current Pos:* RETIRED. *Personal Data:* b Camden, Ark, May 23, 21; m 46; c 1. *Educ:* La Tech Univ, BS, 42; La State Univ, Baton Rouge, MS, 47; Mass Inst Technol, ScD(chem eng), 53; Am Acad Environ Engrs, dipl, 70. *Honors & Awards:* Environ Award, Am Inst Chem Engrs, 78; President's Award, Porcelain Enamel Inst, 84. *Prof Exp:* Engr, Jones Mills Works, Aluminum Co Am, 42-43; asst prof mech & chem eng, La Tech Univ, 47-49; group leader res & develop & sr chem engr, Cabot Corp, 53-55; head res & develop, Tex Butadiene & Chem Corp, 55-57; assoc prof chem eng, Ga Inst Technol, 57-59; sr proj engr, Cabot Corp, 59-62, gen mgr, Chem Plant, Cabot Titania Corp, 63-64; sr res engr, Whirlpool Corp, 64-67, mgr eng res, 67-70, dir environ control, 70-84; pres, Environ & Chem Consult Engrs Inc, 84-96. *Concurrent Pos:* Consult engr, 47-49 & 57-59; prof, Mich State Univ, 65- *Mem:* Sigma Xi; fel Am Inst Chem Engrs; Am Acad Environ Engrs; AAAS; Am Chem Soc; Rog Prof Engr NMex. *Res:* Air and water pollution control; solid waste management; resource recovery, membrane separation processes; process and equipment design and evaluation; engineering economy; transport phenomena, hydrocarbon emission control; leaching of solid waste. *Mailing Add:* 10801 Lagrima De Oro Rd NE No 804 Albuquerque NM 87111-8502

GOODGE, WILLIAM RUSSELL, HUMAN ANATOMY, VERTEBRATE MORPHOLOGY. *Current Pos:* asst prof, 64-70, interim dept chmn, 70-80, ASSOC PROF ANAT, SCH MED, UNIV MO-COLUMBIA, 70- *Personal Data:* b Seattle, Wash, Apr 26, 28; m 57; c 2. *Educ:* Univ Wash, BS, 49, PhD(zool), 57; Univ Mich, MA, 50. *Prof Exp:* Asst zool, Univ Wash, 53-55, actg instr, 55-57; instr gross & neurol anat, Sch Med, WVa Univ, 57-61, asst prof, 61-64. *Mem:* AAAS; Am Asn Anat; Cooper Ornith Soc; Am Ornith Union. *Res:* Vertebrate functional anatomy, musculature, sense organs and glands; histology and histochemistry. *Mailing Add:* Dept Path & Anat Sci Univ Mo Sch Med M304 Med Sci Bldg Columbia MO 65212. *Fax:* 572-884-4123

GOODGOLD, JOSEPH, MEDICINE. *Current Pos:* lectr rehab med, Sch Educ, 56, assoc prof phys med & rehab, Sch Med, 58-63, prof rehab med, 63-75, DIR ELECTRODIAG DEPT, INST REHAB MED, MED CTR, NY UNIV, 56-, HOWARD A RUSK PROF REHAB MED, 75-, CHMN DEPT, 81- *Personal Data:* b New York, NY, Mar 21, 20; m 42; c 2. *Educ:* Brooklyn Col, BA, 41; Middlesex Univ, MD, 45. *Honors & Awards:* Krusen Award, 85. *Prof Exp:* Chief dept phys med & rehab, Ft Campbell Hosp, Ky, 52-53. *Concurrent Pos:* Consult, Div Voc Rehab, State Educ Dept, 59, Brookdale Hosp Ctr, Brooklyn, 64- & Manhattan Vet Admin Hosp, 69; attend, Bellevue Hosp, 65; dir rehab med serv, Sch Med, NY Univ, 81- *Mem:* AMA; Am Asn Electromyog & Electrodiag; Am Rheumatism Asn; Am Cong Rehab Med; NY Acad Sci. *Res:* Electrophysiology. *Mailing Add:* Inst Rehab Med NY Univ Sch Med 550 First Ave New York NY 10016-6481

GOODHEART, CLARENCE F(RANCIS), ELECTRICAL ENGINEERING, ENGINEERING EDUCATION. *Current Pos:* prof, 47-81, chmn, Dept Elec Eng, 55-65 & 74-77, EMER PROF ELEC ENG, UNION COL, NY, 82- *Personal Data:* b Porterville, Calif, Jan 24, 16; m 41, 61, Carolyn Petroski; c Lawrence & Carol. *Educ:* Calif Inst Technol, BS, 36; Ohio State Univ, MS, 38. *Prof Exp:* Asst elec eng, Ohio State Univ, 36-38; instr, Agr & Mech Col, Tex, 38-42; proj engr & sect head, Naval Ord Lab, 42-47. *Concurrent Pos:* Consult, Gen Elec Co, 47-92. *Mem:* Fel Inst Elec & Electronics Engrs. *Res:* Electrical engineering education; underwater ordnance, particularly in magnetic devices and torpedics. *Mailing Add:* Dept Elec Eng & Comput Sci Union Col Schenectady NY 12308

GOODHEART, CLYDE RAYMOND, BIOPHARMACEUTICALS. *Current Pos:* PRES, BIOLABS, INC, 70- *Personal Data:* b Erie, Pa, June 9, 31; m 53, Barbara J Peterson; c Kenneth, Diane & Karen. *Educ:* Northwestern Univ, BS, 53, MS & MD, 57, MM, 87. *Prof Exp:* Res fel animal virol & cell biol, Calif Inst Technol, 58-61; asst prof pediat, Sch Med, Univ Southern Calif, 61-64, assoc prof, 65; assoc mem staff, Inst Biomed Res, AMA-Educ & Res Found, Ill, 65-69, mem staff, 69-70; sr microbiologist & vis prof, Rush-Presby-St Luke's Med Ctr, Chicago, 70-80. *Mem:* AAAS; Tissue Cult Asn; Sigma Xi. *Res:* Experimental embryology; respiratory physiology; tissue culture; autoradiography; animal virology and viral oncology. *Mailing Add:* BioLabs Inc 15 Sheffield Ct Lincolnshire IL 60069-3161

GOODHUE, CHARLES THOMAS, BIOCONVERSIONS, ENZYMOLOGY. *Current Pos:* res microbiologist, Eastman Kodak Co, 65-74, res assoc, 74-80, mem sci bd, 88-90, SR RES ASSOC, EASTMAN KODAK CO, 80-, MEM, GENENCOR INT, 90- *Personal Data:* b Ames, Iowa, Apr 30, 32; m 77; c Andrew, Thomas, Steven, Sara, Dean & Dawn. *Educ:* Univ Ill, BS, 54; Univ Calif, PhD(biochem), 61. *Prof Exp:* Res biochemist, Distillation Prod Indust, 61-65. *Mem:* Am Chem Soc; Am Soc Microbiol; Sigma Xi; Soc Indust Microbiol. *Res:* Biochemistry of microorganisms; bioconversions, enzymology; microbiol sources for enzymes useful for analytical systems; bioconversion processes useful for combined organic and biological syntheses of natural products and photographic chemicals; fermentation processes for production of enzymes and bioconversion products; chemistry and biochemistry of vitamin E; chemistry and biochemistry of nucleosides/nucleotides. *Mailing Add:* 4 Sorrell Place Dr San Antonio TX 78248-1691. *Fax:* 210-479-0361

GOODIN, JOE RAY, plant physiology; deceased, see previous edition for last biography

GOODING, GRETCHEN ANN WAGNER, ULTRASONOGRAPHY. *Current Pos:* PROF RADIOL, UNIV CALIF, SAN FRANCISCO, 86-, VCHMN DEPT, 87- *Personal Data:* b Columbus, Ohio, July 2, 35; m 61; c 3. *Educ:* Col St Mary of Springs, Ohio, BA, 57; Col Med, Ohio State Univ, MD, 61. *Prof Exp:* Asst chief, Vet Admin Med Ctr, San Francisco, 78-87, CHIEF, ULTRASONOGRAPHY, 75-, CHIEF, DEPT RADIOL, 87- *Mem:* Fel Am Col Radiol; fel Am Inst Ultrasound in Med; Am Asn Wome Radiologists (pres, 84-85); World Fedn Ultrasound in Med; Asn Univ Radiologists; Radiol Soc NAm. *Res:* Ultrasonography; diagnostic radiology. *Mailing Add:* Dept Vet Affairs Med Ctr Rad 114 4150 Clement St San Francisco CA 94121

GOODING, GUY V, JR, phytopathology, for more information see previous edition

GOODING, JAMES LESLIE, GEOCHEMISTRY. *Current Pos:* Investr, NASA/Caltech Jet Propulsion Lab, 79-81, space scientist, Johnson Space Ctr, 81-92, SR SCIENTIST, NASA-JOHNSON SPACE CTR, 92- *Personal Data:* b Tehachapi, Calif, Sept 13, 50; div; c 3. *Educ:* Calif Polytech State Univ, San Luis Obispo, BS, 72; Univ Hawaii, Manoa, MS, 75; Univ NMex, PhD(geol), 79. *Honors & Awards:* Arthur S Plemming Award, Pub Serv, 89. *Concurrent Pos:* Adj prof, Univ Houston, Clear Lake. *Mem:* NAm Thermal Anal Soc; Meteoritical Soc; Geochem Soc. *Res:* Chemical-mineralogical analysis of extraterrestrial materials; environmental geochemistry. *Mailing Add:* NASA Johnson Space Ctr SN21 Houston TX 77058

GOODING, LINDA R, IMMUNOLOGY, VIROLOGY. *Current Pos:* assoc prof, 81-84, PROF MICROBIOL, SCH MED, EMORY UNIV, 84- *Personal Data:* b Portland, Maine, Nov 23, 45. *Educ:* Bowling Green State Univ, BS, 67; Cornell Univ, PhD(biochem), 72. *Prof Exp:* Fel immunol, Johns Hopkins Univ, 72-74; assoc, Duke Univ Med Ctr, 74-75, asst prof immunol, 76-80. *Mem:* Am Asn Immunol; Am Soc Microbiol; AAAS. *Res:* Immune recognition and response to DNA tumor viruses. *Mailing Add:* Dept Microbiol & Immunol Emory Univ 1510 Clifton Rd NE Atlanta GA 30322. *Fax:* 404-727-0293; *E-Mail:* gooding@microbio.emory.edu

GOODING, ROBERT C, NAVAL ARCHITECTURE, ENGINEERING ADMINISTRATION. *Current Pos:* CHMN, COLUMBIA RES CORP, 80- *Personal Data:* b New Orleans, La, June 27, 18. *Educ:* US Naval Acad, BSc, 41; Mass Inst Technol, MSc, 46. *Honors & Awards:* Gold Medal, Am Soc Naval Eng, 88; Saunders Award, Am Soc Mech Engrs, 89. *Prof Exp:* VAdm, USN, 40-76; consult, 76- *Concurrent Pos:* Instr calculus, Pratt Inst, Brooklyn, NY, 58-62. *Mem:* Nat Acad Eng; Sigma Xi. *Mailing Add:* 3440 S Jefferson St Falls Church VA 22041. *Fax:* 703-418-1139; *E-Mail:* rgooding@columbiaresearch.com

GOODING, RONALD HARRY, ENTOMOLOGY, BIOCHEMISTRY. *Current Pos:* from asst prof to assoc prof, 66-76, chair, 89-94 PROF ENTOM, UNIV ALTA, 76-, PROF BIOL SCI, 94- *Personal Data:* b Edmonton, Alta, Oct 18, 36; m 59, Sheila Stewart; c Richard A. *Educ:* Univ Alta, BSc, 57; Rice Inst, MA, 60; Johns Hopkins Univ, ScD(pathobiol), 64. *Prof Exp:* Res assoc biochem, Vanderbilt Univ, 64-66. *Concurrent Pos:* Oper grants, Univ Alta Gen Res Fund, 67-71 & 93-94, Nat Res Coun Can, 67-. Can Dept Agr, 67-71 & 76-79, Alta Agr Res Trust, 67-71 & 74-76, Defense Res Bd Can, 69-74 & WHO, 75-77. *Mem:* Entom Soc Can; Can Soc Zool; Genetics Soc Can; Entom Soc Am; Soc Study Evolution. *Res:* Insect biochemistry; medical entomology; tsetse fly genetics; genetics of hybrid sterility. *Mailing Add:* Dept Biol Sci Univ Alta Edmonton AB T6G 2E9 Can. *Fax:* 403-492-9234; *E-Mail:* ron.gooding@ualberta.ca

GOODINGS, DAVID AMBERY, CONDENSED MATTER PHYSICS, NONLINEAR DYNAMICS. *Current Pos:* assoc prof, 69-74, prof, 74-96, EMER PROF PHYSICS, MCMASTER UNIV, 96- *Personal Data:* b Toronto, Ont, July 8, 35; m 60, 80, Judith M Fenn; c Sarah, Matthew & Joseph. *Educ:* Univ Toronto, BA, 57; Cambridge Univ, PhD(physics), 61. *Prof Exp:* Res assoc theoret physics, Atomic Energy Res Establish, Harwell, 60-61; res assoc physics, Univ Pittsburgh, 61-64; lectr, Univ Sussex, 64-68; asst prof, Am Univ Beirut, 68-69. *Concurrent Pos:* Vis lectr, Univ Ife, Nigeria, 66; vis prof, KFA Julich, Fed Repub Ger, 76. *Mem:* Can Asn Physicists. *Res:* Nonlinear dynamics and chaos in physical systems; condensed matter theory. *Mailing Add:* Dept Physics & Astron McMaster Univ Hamilton ON L8S 4M1 Can. *E-Mail:* goodings@physun.physics.mcmaster.ca

GOODINGS, JOHN MARTIN, PHYSICAL CHEMISTRY, FLAME CHEMISTRY. *Current Pos:* assoc prof, 65-72, chmn dept, 79-82, PROF CHEM, YORK UNIV, ONT, 72- *Personal Data:* b Toronto, Ont, Feb 18, 37; Can citizen; m 61, Sally A Maxwell; c Kimberley A & Peter J. *Educ:* Univ Toronto, BA, 58; Univ Cambridge, PhD(phys chem), 61. *Prof Exp:* Asst prof chem, McGill Univ, 62-65. *Concurrent Pos:* Thornton res fel, Thornton Res Ctr, Eng, 71-72; vis prof, Dept Chem Eng & Fuel Technol, Univ Sheffield, Eng, 78-79; vis fel, Dept Chem Eng, Univ Cambridge, Eng, 87. *Mem:* Fel Chem Inst Can; Combustion Inst. *Res:* Flame ionization; combustion; flame-ion mass spectrometry; ion chemistry in hydrocarbon flames and hydrogen flames with additives; involving nitrogen and sulphur pollutants, soot formation, metallic ions, and negative ions formed by electron scavenging. *Mailing Add:* Dept Chem York Univ 4700 Keele St North York ON M3J 1P3 Can. *Fax:* 416-736-5936; *E-Mail:* goodingsd@turing.sci.yorku.ca

GOODISMAN, JERRY, CHEMICAL PHYSICS. *Current Pos:* assoc prof, 69-75, PROF CHEM, SYRACUSE UNIV, 75- *Personal Data:* b Brooklyn, NY, Mar 22, 39; m 63; c 2. *Educ:* Columbia Col AB, 59; Harvard Univ, AM, 60, PhD(chem), 63. *Prof Exp:* Instr phys chem, Univ Ill, Urbana, 63-65, asst prof chem, 65-69. *Mem:* Am Phys Soc. *Res:* Theoretical description of the ideally polarisable interface; kinetics of DNA and RNA cleavage; statistical mechanics of electrode interfaces; scattering from noncrystalline systems. *Mailing Add:* Dept Chem Syracuse Univ Syracuse NY 13210

GOODJOHN, ALBERT J, REACTOR PHYSICS. *Current Pos:* RETIRED. *Personal Data:* b Calgary, Alta, Feb 18, 28; m 51, Rhea M Deibert; c Susan, Jennifer, Christine, Andrew, James & Michael. *Educ:* Univ Alta, BSc, 50, MSc, 51; Queen's Univ, Ont, PhD(physics), 56. *Prof Exp:* Design specialist, Canadair Div, Gen Dynamics Corp, 56-59; mem staff theoret physics, Gen Atomics, 59-61, div head, 61-63, proj mgr advan concepts, 63-66, asst dept chmn reactor physics, 64-66, assoc div mgr, 66-70, gen mgr mkt, 70-75, dir reactor progs, 76-86. *Concurrent Pos:* Energy consult, 86- *Mem:* Fel Am Nuclear Soc. *Res:* Experimental and theoretical reactor and nuclear physics. *Mailing Add:* PO Box 1767 Rancho Santa Fe CA 92067

GOODKIN, JEROME, PHYSICAL CHEMISTRY, ELECTROCHEMISTRY. *Current Pos:* PROF CHEM, TRENTON STATE COL, 68- *Personal Data:* b New York, NY, Mar 22, 29; m 52; c 2. *Educ:* NY Univ, BA, 52, MS, 54; Rensselaer Polytech Inst, PhD(phys chem), 59. *Prof Exp:* Res asst phys chem, NY Univ, 52-54; asst, Rensselaer Polytech Inst, 54, 56-58; sect coordr, Catalyst Res Corp, 58-61; res chem, Res Div, FMC Corp, 62-63; sr res scientist, Yardney Elec Corp, 63-68. *Concurrent Pos:* Adj prof, Mercer County Community Col, 63-68. *Mem:* Am Chem Soc; Electrochem Soc. *Res:* Molten salt chemistry; constitution of solution and electrochemical phenomena; corrosion of steel; electrode processes; batteries. *Mailing Add:* 22 Camelia Ct Lawrenceville NJ 08648-3202

GOODKIND, JOHN M, PHYSICS. *Current Pos:* from asst prof to assoc prof, 62-74, PROF PHYSICS, UNIV CALIF, SAN DIEGO, 74- *Personal Data:* b New York, NY, Aug 27, 34; m 63; c 2. *Educ:* Amherst Col, AB, 56; Duke Univ, PhD(physics), 60. *Prof Exp:* Res asst physics, Stanford Univ, 60-62. *Concurrent Pos:* Sloan Found fel, 62-66; NSF res grant, 62- *Mem:* Am Phys Soc; Am Geophys Union; Sigma Xi. *Res:* Low temperature physics; liquid and solid helium three; nuclear adiabatic demagnetization; superconductivity; geophysics; gravimetry. *Mailing Add:* Physics Dept 0319 Univ Calif San Diego 9500 Gilman Dr La Jolla CA 92093-0319

GOODKIND, MORTON JAY, INTERNAL MEDICINE. *Current Pos:* RETIRED. *Personal Data:* b New York, NY, Apr 29, 28; div; c 2. *Educ:* Princeton Univ, AB, 49; Columbia Univ, MD, 53. *Prof Exp:* Instr internal med, Sch Med, Yale Univ, 58-62, asst prof, 62-64; from asst prof to assoc prof, Sch Med, Univ Pa, 64-74, clin assoc prof med, 74-93. *Concurrent Pos:* Am Heart Asn advan fel, 59-61, grants-in-aid, 59-61 & 61-67; USPHS grant-in-aid, Nat Heart Inst, 61-67; consult, Vet Admin Hosp, Philadelphia & Walson Army Hosp, Ft Dix, NJ; dir, Coronary Care Unit, Philadelphia Gen Hosp, 71-74; attend assoc, Mercer Med Ctr, Trenton, NJ. *Mem:* Am Fedn Clin Res; Am Physiol Soc; Am Col Physicians. *Res:* Effects of thyroid hormone on myocardial metabolism of norepinephrine and on myocardial contractility and hemodynamics; cardiovascular hemodynamics; renal function in congestive heart failure; cardiology; effects of alcohol on heart. *Mailing Add:* 1711 River Rd New Hope PA 18938

GOODKIND, RICHARD JERRY, PROSTHODONTICS. *Current Pos:* RETIRED. *Personal Data:* b Brooklyn, NY, Oct 5, 37; m 60, Sondra; c Risa & Ian. *Educ:* Columbia Univ, 55-58; Tufts Univ, DMD, 62; Univ Mich, MS, 64; Am Bd Prosthodont, dipl, 67. *Prof Exp:* Dir grad combined prosthodontics, Univ Minn, Minneapolis, 66-77, prof dent, Sch Dent, 77-. *Concurrent Pos:* Consult & mem prosthodontic staff, Univ Minn Hosp, 68-; consult, Am Dent Asn & Vet Admin. *Mem:* Midwest Prosthodont Soc; Am Col Prosthodontists; Am Dent Asn. *Res:* Fixed and removable prosthodontics; color of natural dentition. *Mailing Add:* 4123 Sunset Blvd Minneapolis MN 55416

GOODLAND, ROBERT JAMES A, ECOLOGY, ENVIRONMENTAL MANAGEMENT. *Current Pos:* ecologist, Off Environ & Health Affairs, 78-87, chief, Environ Div, 86-90, ADV, ENVIRON ASSESSMENT, WORLD BANK, 90-. *Personal Data:* b Sept 26, 45; Can citizen; m 86; c 1. *Educ:* McGill Univ, BSc, 64, MSc, 65, PhD(trop ecol), 69. *Honors & Awards:* Logan Prize; Penhallow Prize; Rose-Hulman Prize. *Prof Exp:* Prof ecol, Univ Brasilia, 69-71; prof environ studies, McGill Univ, 71-72; ecologist, Cary Arboretum, NY Bot Garden, 72-75, chmn & asst dir, Environ Assessment Dept, 75-78. *Concurrent Pos:* Ecologist, Amazonian ecosysts course, Nat Inst Amazonian Res, Manaus, 73; World Bank Environ Missions, Indonesia & Malaysia, 74 & 75; Environ Mission, El Salvador & Guatemala, Pan Am Health Orgn, 75, Bangladesh, 76. *Mem:* Ecol Soc NAm (pres, 88); Int Asn Impact Assessment (pres); Am Soc Ecol; Int Soc Ecol Econs. *Res:* Environmental assessment of development projects, especially tropical; biodiversity and ecosystem conservation. *Mailing Add:* Environ Dept World Bank Washington DC 20433. *E-Mail:* reoodland@worldbank.org

GOODMAN, A(LVIN) M(ALCOLM), ELECTRICAL ENGINEERING, SOLID STATE PHYSICS. *Current Pos:* RETIRED. *Personal Data:* b Philadelphia, Pa, July 8, 30; m 66, Constance Moench; c Bruce & Kimberly. *Educ:* Drexel Inst Technol, BS, 52; Princeton Univ, MA, 55, PhD(elec eng), 58. *Honors & Awards:* Charles Ira Young Medal, 58. *Prof Exp:* Asst elec eng, Princeton Univ, 56-57; asst prof, Case Inst Technol, 57-59; mem tech staff, Solid State Devices Res Lab, David Sarnoff Res Ctr, RCA Corp, 59-82, sr mem tech staff, 82-87; sci officer, Electronics Div, Off Naval Res, 87-96. *Concurrent Pos:* Lectr, Ariz State Univ, 84-89. *Mem:* Am Phys Soc; Inst Elec & Electronics Engrs; Sigma Xi; Mat Res Soc; Electrochem Soc. *Res:* Metal-semiconductor physics and devices; insulator physics and chemistry; physical measurements and instrumentation; semiconductor device processing and fabrication; author of various scientific articles and 57 publications; granted 24 patents. *Mailing Add:* Off Naval Res-Code 312 800 N Quincy St Arlington VA 22217-5660

GOODMAN, ADOLPH WINKLER, MATHEMATICS, GEOMETRIC FUNCTION THEORY. *Current Pos:* PROF MATH, UNIV SFLA, 64-. *Personal Data:* b San Antonio, Tex, July 20, 15; m 49, Betty Posman; c Dianne E, William L, Sheila L & Glenn. *Educ:* Univ Cincinnati, BSc, 39, MA, 41; Columbia Univ, PhD(math), 47. *Prof Exp:* Prin eng draftsman, US Navy Yard, Pa, 41-43; instr math, Syracuse Univ, 43-44; sr stress engr, Repub Aviation Corp, NY, 44-46; instr math, Rutgers Univ, 47-49; from assoc prof to prof, Univ Ky, 49-64. *Concurrent Pos:* Mem, Inst Advan Study, 56-57. *Mem:* Am Math Soc; Math Asn Am. *Res:* Theory of functions of a complex variable; conformal mapping; polynomials; graph theory; number theory. *Mailing Add:* Dept Math Univ SFla Tampa FL 33620. *E-Mail:* al.goodman@pchelp.com

GOODMAN, ALAN LAWRENCE, QUALITY MANAGEMENT & TECHNOLOGY, PRODUCT QUALITY MANAGEMENT SYSTEMS. *Current Pos:* DIR QUAL IMPROV, INT SPECIALTY PRODS, 94-. *Personal Data:* b Miami Beach, Fla, July 27, 38; m 64, Devara Felson; c 2. *Educ:* Univ Del, BS, 59; Stanford Univ PhD(org chem), 64. *Prof Exp:* Res fel, Brandeis Univ, 63-64; sr res chemist, Plastics Div, Allied Chem Corp, 64-66; res chemist, Elastomer Chem Dept, E I du Pont de Nemours & Co, Inc, 66-80, sr res chemist, Polymer Prod Dept, 80-83, sr consult, eng dept, 83-93. *Concurrent Pos:* Regional dir, Am Soc Qual Control, 93-94. *Mem:* Am Chem Soc; fel Am Soc Qual Control. *Res:* Statistical quality control; management of change; quality function deployment; process reengineering; organization change. *Mailing Add:* One Eagles Circle Raven Crest Chadds Ford PA 19317-9193

GOODMAN, ALAN LEONARD, MEAN FIELD THEORIES, PHASE TRANSITIONS. *Current Pos:* from asst prof to assoc prof, 76-81, PROF PHYSICS, TULANE UNIV, 81-. *Personal Data:* b Newark, NJ, July 28, 41. *Educ:* Cornell Univ, BS, 64; Univ Calif, Berkeley, MS, 66, PhD(nuclear sci), 69. *Prof Exp:* Fel physics, Argonne Nat Lab, 69-71 & Carnegie-Mellon Univ, 73-76. *Concurrent Pos:* Prin investr, NSF grants theoret nuclear physics, 77-98; consult, Oak Ridge Nat Lab, 77-; ed, Proceedings Int Conf Band Structure & Nuclear Dynamics, 80; vis prof, Mich State Univ, 77, Niels Bohr Inst, Copenhagen, 79. *Mem:* Fel Am Phys Soc; Sigma Xi. *Res:* Quantum-mechanical many-body theories are applied to the nucleus; phase transitions in excited nuclear energy levels. *Mailing Add:* Physics Dept Tulane Univ New Orleans LA 70118. *E-Mail:* alan.goodman@tulane.edu

GOODMAN, ALBERT, POLYMER CHEMISTRY. *Current Pos:* RETIRED. *Personal Data:* b New York, NY, Jan 22, 27; m 48, Ruth Fisher; c Connie A & Nancy L. *Educ:* City Col, BS, 46; NY Univ, MS, 51; Polytech Inst Brooklyn, PhD(chem), 56. *Prof Exp:* Instr biol, City Col, 47-51; res chemist, Dextran Corp, 51-55; res chemist, E I Du Pont de Nemours & Co, Inc, 55-66, res supvr, 66-69, supvr plant technol, Nylon Div, 69-73, supvr textile res, 73-85, sr res assoc, 85-90. *Concurrent Pos:* Consult, 91-. *Mem:* AAAS; Am Chem Soc; Sigma Xi. *Res:* Structure-property relationships in fibers; polymer physics and rheology; polymer chemistry; enzymatic polymerizations; ionic and stereoregular polymerizations; kinetics of polymerizations; fiber-fabric structural relationships; electrical properties of fibers and fabrics; textile processability of fibers; dye stability; UV stability of polymers. *Mailing Add:* 2806 Bodine Dr Wilmington DE 19810

GOODMAN, BARBARA EASON, RESPIRATORY PHYSIOLOGY IN MEMBRANE TRANSPORT. *Current Pos:* asst prof, 86-91, ASSOC PROF PHYSIOL, SCH MED, UNIV SDAK, 91-. *Personal Data:* b Hanover, NH, Nov 17, 49; m 72, Douglas Robert; c Corey & Timothy. *Educ:* Duke Univ, BA, 72; Univ Minn, PhD(physiol), 81. *Prof Exp:* Asst res prof med, Univ Calif, Los Angeles, 84-86. *Concurrent Pos:* Prin investr, 88 & 89; vis lectr, 90-; mem, Cardiopulmonary Coun, Am Heart Asn; educ comt, Am Physiol Soc, 96-. *Mem:* Am Physiol Soc; Am Thoracic Soc; Sigma Xi; Am Heart Asn. *Res:* Characteristics and regulation of active transport across the pulmonary alveolar epithelium which may be important for physiological and pathological lung fluid balance. *Mailing Add:* Dept Physiol Sch Med Univ SDak Vermillion SD 57069-2390. *E-Mail:* bgoodman@charlie.usd.edu

GOODMAN, BERNARD, THEORETICAL SOLID STATE PHYSICS. *Current Pos:* prof, 65-93, EMER PROF PHYSICS, UNIV CINCINNATI, 93-. *Personal Data:* b Philadelphia, Pa, June 14, 23; m 51, Joyce J Willonghby; c David N, Jonathan B & Mark W. *Educ:* Univ Pa, AB, 43, PhD(physics), 55. *Prof Exp:* Res stress analyst, Int Harvester Co, 47-52; res assoc physics, Univ Mo, 52-54, from asst prof to prof, 54-64. *Concurrent Pos:* Consult, Argonne Nat Lab, 61-70; Guggenheim fel, 62; guest prof, Inst Theoret Physics, Univ Uppsala, 62 & Gothenberg Univ, 71 & 85; Fulbright scholar & guest prof, Inst Theoret Physics, Trieste, 79; Gordon Godfrey fel, Univ New South Wales, 90. *Mem:* Fel Am Phys Soc. *Res:* Lattice dynamics; quantum liquids; electron correlations and many-body theory; disordered systems; semi-conductors. *Mailing Add:* Dept Physics Univ Cincinnati ML11 Cincinnati OH 45221. *Fax:* 513-556-2884; *E-Mail:* bernard.goodman@uc.edu

GOODMAN, BILLY LEE, POULTRY SCIENCE. *Current Pos:* PROF ANIMAL INDUST, SOUTHERN ILL UNIV, CARBONDALE, 58-. *Personal Data:* b Pauls Valley, Okla, Jan 21, 30; m 51; c 5. *Educ:* Okla State Univ, BS, 51, MS, 53; Ohio State Univ, PhD, 59. *Prof Exp:* Asst poultry, Okla State Univ, 51-52, instr, 52-55; instr, Ohio State Univ, 55-58. *Mem:* Poultry Sci Asn. *Res:* Poultry genetics and breeding. *Mailing Add:* RR 1 Box 166 Makanda IL 62958

GOODMAN, CHARLES DAVID, EXPERIMENTAL NUCLEAR PHYSICS. *Current Pos:* PROF, IND UNIV, 80-. *Personal Data:* b New York, NY, May 9, 28; m 52, Joan L Wright; c Henry N & Diana R. *Educ:* Clark Univ, AB, 49; Univ Rochester, PhD, 55. *Honors & Awards:* Tom W Bonner Prize, Am Phys Soc, 83; Humboldt Res Award, 91. *Prof Exp:* From physicist to sr physicist, Oak Ridge Nat Lab, 55-80. *Concurrent Pos:* Vis scientist, Weizmann Inst Sci, 66; vis prof, Univ Colo, Boulder, 72-73. *Mem:* Fel Am Phys Soc; AAAS; Inst Elec & Electronics Engrs. *Res:* Experimental nuclear physics; nuclear charge exchange to study nuclear models; Gamow-Teller transitions; neutrino detection; neutron spectroscopy 50-800 MeV meson production near threshold. *Mailing Add:* Ind Univ 2401 Milo Sampson Lane Bloomington IN 47408-0768. *E-Mail:* goodman@iucf.indiana.edu

GOODMAN, COREY SCOTT, DEVELOPMENTAL NEUROBIOLOGY, DEVELOPMENTAL BIOLOGY. *Current Pos:* prof biochem, 87-89, PROF NEUROBIOL, DEPT MOLECULAR & CELL BIOL, UNIV CALIF, BERKELEY, 89-, PROF & HEAD DIV NEUROBIOL, 92-; INVESTR, HOWARD HUGHES MED INST, 88-. *Personal Data:* b Chicago, Ill, June 29, 51; m 84, Marcia Barinaga. *Educ:* Stanford Univ, BS, 72; Univ Calif, Berkeley, PhD(neurobiology), 77. *Honors & Awards:* Charles Judson Herrick Award, 82; Alan T Waterman Award, Nat Sci Bd, 83; Javits Neurosci Investr Award, 85 & 92; Merit Award, NIH, 86; Alden Spencer Award, 93; J Allyn Taylor Int Award Med, 96. *Prof Exp:* From asst prof to assoc develop neuobiology, Dept Biol Sci, Stanford Univ, 79-87. *Concurrent Pos:* Fel, H H Whitney Found, 77-79; McKnight Found Scholar; Sloan Found Fel; McKnight scholars award rev comt, 84-, chmn, 89-; ed bd reviewing, Sci, 86-96, ed, Develop Neurobiol sect, J Neurosci, 89-93; Searle scholars adv comt, 88-92; assoc ed, develop, 93-. *Mem:* Nat Acad Sci; Soc Develop Biol; fel Am Acad Arts & Sci; AAAS; Neurosci Soc. *Res:* Developmental neurobiology; cell recognition during neuronal development; growth cone guidance; target recognition; formation of specific synaptic connections; neurogenetics; synaptic growth and plasticity. *Mailing Add:* 140 Panoramic Way Berkeley CA 94704. *Fax:* 510-643-5548; *E-Mail:* goodman@uclink4.berkeley.edu

GOODMAN, DAVID BARRY POLIAKOFF, CLINICAL CHEMISTRY, TUMOR MARKERS. *Current Pos:* assoc prof & dir, Div Lab Med, 80-83, PROF, DEPT PATH & LAB MED, SCH MED, UNIV PA, 84-; DIR, ENDOCRINE ONCOL LAB, HOSP UNIV PA. *Personal Data:* b Lynn, Mass, June 1, 42; m 94, J K Greenacre; c Derek & Alex. *Educ:* Harvard Univ, AB, 64; Univ Pa, MD, 68, PhD(biochem), 72. *Honors & Awards:* Lamport Award, NY Acad Sci, 81. *Prof Exp:* Assoc biochem, Univ Pa, 72-73, assoc pediat, 72-73, res asst prof, 73-76; asst prof med, Sch Med, Yale Univ, 76-79, assoc prof, 79-80. *Concurrent Pos:* Consult neurobiol & biol, NSF, 73- & consult endocrinol, Vet Admin, 79-; ed, Bone & Related Res; vis scientist, Minority Inst, Fedn Am Socs Exp Biol, 90. *Mem:* AAAS; Soc Neurosci; Soc Develop Biol; Am Fedn Clin Res; Am Asn Path; Am Physiol Soc. *Res:* Biochemistry of hormone action and glyoxylcte cycle, ion transport, cell activation and oxygen toxicity; laboratory medicine; clinical pathology. *Mailing Add:* Dept Path & Lab Med Hosp Univ Pa Founders 7102 3400 Spruce St Philadelphia PA 19104. *Fax:* 215-662-7529; *E-Mail:* david__goodman@pathia.med.upenn.edu

GOODMAN, DAVID JOEL, ELECTRICAL & COMPUTER ENGINEERING. *Current Pos:* PROF & CHAIR ELEC & COMPUTER ENG, RUTGERS UNIV, 88- *Personal Data:* b Brooklyn, NY, June 9, 39; m 80; c 2. *Educ:* Rensselaer Polytech Inst, BEE, 60; NY Univ, MEE, 62; Univ London, PhD(elec eng), 67. *Prof Exp:* Dept head, AT&T Bell Lab, 67-88. *Concurrent Pos:* Vis prof, Imp Col, Univ London, 83-88 & Southampton, 87-89; dir, Rutgers Wireless Info Network Lab, 89. *Mem:* Fel Inst Elec & Electronics Engrs; fel Inst Elec Engrs; Radio Club Am. *Res:* Wireless access to information networks; communication network architecture; digital signal processing; speech communication. *Mailing Add:* Dept Elec & Computer Eng Rutgers Univ PO Box 909 Piscataway NJ 08855

GOODMAN, DAVID WAYNE, SURFACE CHEMISTRY, MOLECULAR SPECTROSCOPY. *Current Pos:* head, Phys Chem Div, 91-93, PROF, 88-95, ROBERT A WELCH PROF CHEM, TEX A&M UNIV, COLLEGE STATION, TX, 95- *Personal Data:* b Glen Allen, Miss, Dec 14, 45; m 67; c 1. *Educ:* Miss Col, BS, 68; Univ Tex-Austin, PhD(phys chem), 74. *Hon Degrees:* DSc, Miss Col, 91. *Honors & Awards:* Ipatieff Prize, Am Chem Soc, 83, Colloid & Surface Chem Award, 93; Proctor & Gamble lectr, Univ Cincinnati, 90; Langmuir lectr, Am Chem Soc, 90; Ipateff lectr, Northwestern Univ, 93. *Prof Exp:* NATO fel chem, Tech Univ, Parmstadt, Ger, 74-76; Nat Res Coun fel, Nat Bur Stand, Washington, DC, 76-78, res scientist, 78-80; mem tech staff, Sandia Nat Labs, Albuquerque, NMex, 80-85, head, Surface Sci Div, 85-88. *Concurrent Pos:* Distinguished lectr, Univ Tex, Austin, 82, adj prof, 85-86; chair, Div Colloid & Surface Sci, Am Chem Soc, 85; frontiers chem lectr, Tex A&M Univ, 87. *Mem:* Am Chem Soc; Am Phys Soc; Am Vacuum Soc; Mat Res Soc; AAAS; Catalysis Soc. *Res:* Studies of chemisorption & catalytic reactions on atomically clean & chemically modified metal single crystal surfaces using modern surface science techniques. *Mailing Add:* Dept Chem Tex A&M Univ College Sta TX 77843

GOODMAN, DONALD, POLYMER CHEMISTRY. *Current Pos:* MGR TECH PROJS, OCCIDENTAL CHEM CORP, 86- *Personal Data:* b Boston, Mass, Apr 7, 33; m 61; c 2. *Educ:* Harvard Univ, AB, 54. *Prof Exp:* Res assoc res & develop polymer chem, W R Grace & Co, Dewey & Almy Chem Div, 56-65; group leader res & develop polymer chem, Continental Oil Co, Thompson Apex Div, 65-68; mgr res res & develop polymer chem, Olin Corp, Olin Plastics Div, 68-72; mgr polymers res & develop, Tenneco Inc, Tenneco Chem Div, 72-86. *Mem:* Am Chem Soc; AAAS; Soc Plastics Engrs. *Res:* Polymer science and technology, especially polymer structure versus properties relationships; polymer kinetics and mechanisms of polymerization; emulsion polymerization; polymer characterization; environmental science, industry and regulatory affairs; issues management. *Mailing Add:* 19 Valley Beech Lane Malvern PA 19355

GOODMAN, DONALD CHARLES, NEUROANATOMY, COMPARATIVE NEUROLOGY. *Current Pos:* dean med sci & vpres acad affairs, State Univ NY Upstate Med Ctr, 75-76, prof & chmn dept, 68-82, dean, Col Grad Studies, 73-82, vpres res & acad affairs, 76-82, DEAN & CHMN DEPT, STATE UNIV NY UPSTATE MED CTR, 83-, PROVOST, 85-, INTERIM PRES, 92- *Personal Data:* b Chicago, Ill, Nov 24, 27; m 68; c 6. *Educ:* Univ Ill, BS, 49, MS, 50, PhD(zool), 54. *Honors & Awards:* Res Award, Sigma Xi, 62. *Prof Exp:* Instr anat, Sch Med, Univ Pa, 54-56; instr, Univ Mich, 56; from asst prof to prof, Univ Fla, 56-68, chmn dept, 65-68. *Concurrent Pos:* Fel, Inst Neurol Sci, Univ Pa, 54-55; Nat Inst Neurol Dis & Stroke res grant, 58-; mem study sect neurol B, NIH, 69-71, mem anat training prog, 71-75; adj prof neurosci, State Univ NY, Binghamton. *Mem:* Nat Coun Univ Res Admin; AAAS; Am Asn Anat; fel Am Soc Allied Health Prof. *Res:* Neuromorphological plasticity of central nervous system and its relationship to recovery of brain function; comparative neurology of cerebellum and basal ganglia and of brain structure of reptiles. *Mailing Add:* State Univ NY Upstate Med Ctr 750 E Adams St Syracuse NY 13210. *Fax:* 315-464-6914

GOODMAN, ELI I, nuclear engineering, chemical engineering, for more information see previous edition

GOODMAN, ERIK DAVID, GENETIC ALGORITHMS, MANUFACTURING PROCESS SIMULATION & SCHEDULING. *Current Pos:* From asst prof to assoc prof, Mich State Univ, 72-84, dir, Case Ctr Comput Aided Eng & Mfg, 83-, prof elec eng, 84- , PROF MECH ENG, MICH STATE UNIV, 92-; DIR, MFG RES CONSORTIUM, & CO-DIR GENETIC ALGORITHMS RES & APPLNS GROUP, 93- *Personal Data:* b Palo Alto, Calif, Feb 14, 44; m 68, 78, Cheryl D Barris; c David R. *Educ:* Mich State Univ, BS, 66, MS, 68, PhD(comput commun), 72. *Concurrent Pos:* Gen co-chmn, Int Comput Graphics Conf, Detroit, 86; pres, Tech Gateway Inc, East Lansing; consult, Chinese Comput Comn Inc, Lansing, 88; chair res & future dir subcomt CAD/CAM Tech Comt, Am Inst Aeronaut & Astronaut, 87-89. *Mem:* Am Inst Aeronaut & Astronaut; Inst Elec & Electronics Engrs Comput Soc; sr mem Soc Mfg Engrs; Int Acad Informatics. *Res:* Theory and application of genetic algorithms for problems in manufacturing; simulation of manufacturing processes; liaison with Russian and Chinese researchers in genetic algorithms and in manufacturing technology. *Mailing Add:* Col Eng 2325 Eng Bldg Mich State Univ East Lansing MI 48824. *Fax:* 517-355-7516; *E-Mail:* goodman@egr.msu.edu

GOODMAN, EUGENE MARVIN, CELL BIOLOGY. *Current Pos:* Fel cell biol, McArdle Lab Cancer Res, 66-69, from asst prof to assoc prof, 69-79, PROF CELL BIOL, UNIV WIS, PARKSIDE, 80, DIR, BIOMED RES INST, 81- *Personal Data:* b Buffalo, NY, June 26, 37; m 57; c 4. *Educ:* State Univ NY Buffalo, BA, 63, PhD(biol), 67. *Mem:* AAAS; Bioelectromagnetics Soc. *Res:* Molecular effects of extremely low frequency electromagnetic fields on growth; cell cycle controls. *Mailing Add:* Biol Sci Univ Wis-Parkside PO Box 2000 Kenosha WI 53141-2000

GOODMAN, FRANK R, PHARMACOLOGY. *Current Pos:* mgr, Dept Cardiopulmonary Res, 83-86, dir, Portfolio Mgt, 86-89, DIR, STRATEGY & BUS DEVELOP, CIBA-GEIGY CORP, 89- *Personal Data:* b Norfolk, Va, Dec 26, 43; m 67; c 2. *Educ:* Univ Richmond, BA, 66; Med Col Va, PhD(pharmacol), 70; Fairleigh Dickenson Univ, MBA, 85. *Prof Exp:* Instr pharmacol, Univ Tex Health Sci Ctr, Dallas, 72-73, asst prof, 73-77; pharmacologist, Dow Chem Co, 77-83. *Concurrent Pos:* Adj assoc prof, Med Sch, Ind Univ, Indianapolis, 78-83; adj prof, Sch Pharm, Univ Ky, 84-86. *Mem:* Physiol Soc; Am Soc Bone & Mineral Res; Am Soc Pharmacol & Exp Therapeut; NY Acad Sci; Am Heart Asn. *Res:* Cellular pharmacology; mechanisms of drug interactions in smooth and lung muscle; action of drugs in asthma and diabetes; lipid metabolism. *Mailing Add:* Strategy Bus & Develop Dept Ciba-Geigy Corp 556 Morris Ave Summit NJ 07901-1398. *Fax:* 908-277-7629

GOODMAN, FRED, molecular genetics, for more information see previous edition

GOODMAN, GERALD JOSEPH, INFORMATION SCIENCE. *Current Pos:* CONSULT, 91- *Personal Data:* b Winthrop, Mass, Oct 24, 42. *Educ:* Rutgers Univ, BA, 64; Johns Hopkins Univ, PhD, (physics), 69. *Prof Exp:* Res assoc physics, Johns Hopkins Univ, 69-70; mgr, Am Inst Physics, 70-91. *Mem:* Am Phys Soc. *Mailing Add:* 1350 15th St Apt 6B Ft Lee NJ 07024. *E-Mail:* redouble@webtv.net

GOODMAN, GORDON LOUIS, ELECTRONIC STRUCTURE OF ATOMS, MOLECULES & SOLID-STATE SYSTEMS. *Current Pos:* HEAD, COMMUNAISSANCE, 70- *Personal Data:* b Chicago, Ill, Aug 19, 33; m 62; c 2. *Educ:* Harvard Univ, AB, 55, PhD, 59. *Prof Exp:* Chemist, Argonne Nat Lab, 59-71 & 83-90. *Concurrent Pos:* Vis prof, Cornell Univ, 64, Univ Leuven, Belgium, 87; prof, Southern Ill Univ, 70; sci assoc, CEA, Saclay, France, 74. *Mem:* AAAS; Asn Comput Mach; fel Am Phys Soc; Sigma Xi. *Res:* Modeling electronic structure of solid-state systems, such as actinide compounds and ceramic copper oxides; interpretation of photoionization and high resolution spectra of open-shell atoms and molecules. *Mailing Add:* PO Box 422 Downers Grove IL 60515

GOODMAN, HAROLD ORBECK, GENETICS. *Current Pos:* RETIRED. *Personal Data:* b Minneapolis, Minn, Sept 8, 24; m 43; c 4. *Educ:* Univ Minn, BA, 48, MA, 50, PhD, 53. *Prof Exp:* Fel med genetics, Bowman Gray Sch Med, 53-54; from instr to asst prof zool, Mich State Col, 54-58; from asst prof to assoc prof, Bowman Gray Sch Med, 58-70, prof & head, Sect Med Genetics & assoc dean, Biomed Grad Studies, 70- *Mem:* Am Soc Human Genetics; Am Genetic Asn; Brit Eugenics Soc; Sigma Xi. *Res:* Genetics of dental caries; salivary components; atherosclerosis; mongolism. *Mailing Add:* 311 Wake Dr Winston-Salem NC 27106

GOODMAN, HENRY MAURICE, PHYSIOLOGY, ENDOCRINOLOGY. *Current Pos:* PROF PHYSIOL & CHMN DEPT, MED SCH, UNIV MASS, 70- *Personal Data:* b Glen Cove, NY, May 4, 34; m 61; c 3. *Educ:* Brandeis Univ, AB, 56; Harvard Univ, AM, 57, PhD(physiol), 60. *Prof Exp:* From instr to assoc prof physiol, Harvard Med Sch, 62-70. *Concurrent Pos:* Jr fel, Harvard Univ, 60-62; teaching fel med, Tufts Univ, 61-62; USPHS career develop award, 66-70; assoc dean sci affairs, Med Sch, Univ Mass, 79- 81, assoc dean, 81- *Mem:* Am Physiol Soc; Endocrine Soc. *Res:* Physiological actions of growth hormone; endocrine regulation of metabolism; physiology of adipose tissue. *Mailing Add:* Dept Physiol Univ Mass Med Sch 55 Lake Ave N Worcester MA 01605-0127. *Fax:* 508-856-5997

GOODMAN, HOWARD CHARLES, IMMUNOLOGY. *Current Pos:* dir trop dis res & training & res prom & develop, 75-77, dir, Trop Med Ctr, 77-86, EMER PROF, DEPT IMMUNOL & INFECTIOUS DIS, JOHNS HOPKINS UNIV, 86- *Personal Data:* b Rochester, NY, July 18, 20; m 42; c 3. *Educ:* Harvard Univ, AB, 41; Johns Hopkins Univ, MD, 44. *Prof Exp:* Intern & asst resident med serv, Peter Bent Brigham Hosp, Boston, 44-45, 47-48; resident med serv, Sawtelle Vet Admin Hosp, Los Angeles, 48-49; res assoc, Inst Med Res, Cedars of Lebanon Hosp, 49-53; res assoc, Nat Heart Inst, 53-60, head clin immunol sect, Nat Inst Allergy & Infectious Dis, 60-63; chief immunol unit, WHO, 63-75; prof path, Fac Med, Univ Geneva, 72-75. *Concurrent Pos:* Howard Hughes med res fel, 51-53; asst med unit, St Mary's Hosp, London, 51-52; clin assoc prof, Med Sch, Univ Southern Calif, 52-53. *Mem:* AAAS; Am Fedn Clin Res; Am Asn Immunol. *Res:* Internal medicine; basic and clinical immunology. *Mailing Add:* 615 N Wolfe St Baltimore MD 21205-2103

GOODMAN, HOWARD MICHAEL, BIOCHEMISTRY. *Current Pos:* from asst prof to assoc prof, 70-76, PROF BIOCHEM, UNIV CALIF, SAN FRANCISCO, 76- *Personal Data:* b Brooklyn, NY, Nov 29, 38; m 69; c 1. *Educ:* Williams Col, BA, 60; Mass Inst Technol, PhD(biophys), 64. *Prof Exp:* Lab teaching asst genetics, Mass Inst Technol, 62; Helen Hay Whitney fel, 64-67, Am Cancer Soc fel, 67-69; asst prof, Univ Geneva, 69-70. *Concurrent*

Pos: Investr, Howard Hughes Med Inst, 78- *Mem:* Am Soc Biol Chemists. *Res:* Mechanisms of specific recognition of DNA by restriction endonucleases; study of eucaryotic gene organization using molecular cloning techniques; regulation of transcription and control. *Mailing Add:* Dept Molecular Biol Mass Gen Hosp Wellman II Needham Boston MA 02114. *Fax:* 617-726-3535

GOODMAN, JACOB ELI, DISCRETE GEOMETRY, CONFIGURATIONS. *Current Pos:* from asst prof to assoc prof, 67-80, PROF MATH, CITY COL, CITY UNIV NEW YORK, 81- *Personal Data:* b Lynn, Mass, Nov 15, 33; m 73, Josephine Fox; c Rachel & Naomi. *Educ:* New York Univ, BA, 53; Columbia Univ, MA, 55, PhD(math), 67. *Honors & Awards:* Lester R Ford Award, Math Asn Am, 90. *Prof Exp:* From inst to asst prof math, NY Univ, 60-67. *Concurrent Pos:* NSF res grants, 67-; co-ed-in-chief, Discrete & Computational Geom, 86-; Fulbright Scholar, 91-92. *Mem:* Am Math Soc. *Res:* Classification of configurations of points in the plane and higher-dimensional space, and of topological generalizations; combinatorial and computational questions relating to configurations. *Mailing Add:* Dept Math City Col CUNY New York NY 10031. *E-Mail:* jegcc@cunyvm.cuny.edu

GOODMAN, JAMES R, STRUCTURAL & CIVIL ENGINEERING. *Current Pos:* head, Civil Eng, 92-93, VPRES, SDAK SCH MINES & TECHNOL, 93- *Personal Data:* b Riverton, Wyo, May 23, 33; m 53, 88, Evalynn R Pier; c David A & J Edward. *Educ:* Univ Wyo, BS, 55; Colo State Univ, MS, 61; Univ Calif, Berkeley, 63, PhD(struct eng), 67. *Honors & Awards:* L J Markwardt Award, Am Soc Testing & Mat, 74. *Prof Exp:* Bridge designer, Wyo State Hwy Dept, 55-57; from instr to prof civil eng, Colo State Univ, 57-87; pvt consult, 87-92. *Concurrent Pos:* Field tech, US geol Surv, 51 & 52. *Mem:* Am Soc Civil Engrs; Am Soc Eng Educ; Forest Prod Res Soc. *Res:* Properties of wood and wood engineering; application of computers to engineered structures. *Mailing Add:* 4140 Red Rd Dr Rapid City SD 57702

GOODMAN, JAY IRWIN, PHARMACOLOGY, TOXICOLOGY & CHEMICAL CARCINOGENESIS. *Current Pos:* from asst prof to assoc prof, 71-82, PROF PHARMACOL & TOXICOL, MICH STATE UNIV, 82- *Personal Data:* b Brooklyn, NY, Apr 4, 43; m 65; c 2. *Educ:* Brooklyn Col Pharm, BS, 65; Univ Mich, PhD(pharmacol), 69; Am Bd Toxicol, dipl. *Prof Exp:* Nat Cancer Inst res fel, McArdle Lab Cancer Res, Univ Wis, 69-71. *Concurrent Pos:* Fel, Nat Cancer Inst, NIH, 69-71. *Mem:* AAAS; Am Soc Pharmacol & Exp Therapeut; Am Asn Cancer Res; Soc Toxicol. *Res:* Chemical carcinogenesis; genetic toxicology. *Mailing Add:* Dept Pharmacol & Toxicol Mich State Univ East Lansing MI 48824-1317. *Fax:* 517-353-8915

GOODMAN, JEROME, RESEARCH ADMINISTRATION, WRITING. *Current Pos:* grants adminr, 74-92, CHMN, ETHICAL REV COMT, AM HEALTH FOUND, 75- *Personal Data:* b Brooklyn, NY, Apr 2, 26; m 67, Helen Geyh; c Johanna & Ethan. *Educ:* Polytech Inst Brooklyn, BS, 49, PhD(chem), 61. *Prof Exp:* Dir res, Radiation Res Corp, 55-57, 59; sr scientist, Radiation Appln Inc, 59-60; dir chem res, Nuclear Res Assocs, Inc, 60-71; sr analyst, Edwards & Hanly, 71-74. *Concurrent Pos:* Fulbright grant, Lab de Chim Phys, Paris, 58-59; sr instr, Polytech Inst Brooklyn, 64-65, chmn human subjs, Inst Rev Bd, 75- *Mem:* AAAS; Am Chem Soc; Sigma Xi. *Res:* Research administration in preventive medicine; grant writer. *Mailing Add:* 26 Patterson Rd Pound Ridge NY 10576-1520

GOODMAN, JOAN WRIGHT (MRS CHARLES D), PHYSIOLOGY. *Current Pos:* RETIRED. *Personal Data:* b El Paso, Tex, May 14, 25; m 52, Charles D; c Henry N & Diana R. *Educ:* Barnard Col, Columbia Univ, BA, 45; Univ Rochester, PhD(physiol), 52; Univ San Francisco, JD, 89. *Prof Exp:* Chemist, Tidewater Assoc Oil Co, 45; asst chem, Manhattan proj, Univ Rochester, 45-46, technician electromyog, Dept Orthop, 46-47, jr scientist cell physiol, Div Radiation Biol, Univ Atomic Energy Proj, 53-54; res assoc biol, Mass Inst Technol, 56; sr res biologist, Div Biol, Oak Ridge Nat Lab, 57-78; prof, Grad Sch Biomed Sci, Univ Tenn, 69-78; staff sr scientist, Univ Calif, Berkeley, 78-85, mem group immunol, Lawrence Berkeley Lab, 80-85. *Concurrent Pos:* mem, Calif Bar, 96. *Mem:* Am Physiol Soc; Radiation Res Soc; Soc Exp Biol & Med; Fedn Am Socs Exp Biol; Int Soc Exp Hemat. *Res:* Transplantation; immunogenetics; hemopoiesis; cellular immunology. *Mailing Add:* 1885 Grand View Dr Oakland CA 94618-2339

GOODMAN, JOEL MITCHELL, PROTEIN SORTING, ORGANELLE ASSEMBLY. *Current Pos:* fr asst prof, 82-88, ASSOC PROF PHARMACOL, UNIV TEX SOUTHWESTERN MED SCH, 88- *Personal Data:* b New York, NY, Oct 13, 48; m 77; c 1. *Educ:* Univ Calif San Diego, BA, 71; Univ Southern Calif, PhD(pharmacol), 80. *Prof Exp:* fel molecular biol, Univ Calif Los Angeles Molecular Biol Inst, 79-82. *Concurrent Pos:* Prin investr, Nat Inst Health, 84-; fac researcher, Am Cancer Soc, 87- *Mem:* Sigma Xi; Am Soc Biochemists & Molec Biologists; Am Soc Cell Biologists. *Res:* Assembly of mitracellular organelles, particularly the mechanism of translocation of proteins across organellar membranes. *Mailing Add:* Dept Pharmacol Univ Tex Southwestern Med Ctr 5323 Harry Hines Blvd Dallas TX 75235-9041. *Fax:* 214-648-2994

GOODMAN, JOEL WARREN, IMMUNOLOGY. *Current Pos:* from asst prof to assoc prof, 60-70, PROF MICROBIOL, SCH MED, UNIV CALIF, SAN FRANCISCO, 70- *Personal Data:* b New York, NY, Feb 2, 33; div; c Mark & Clifford. *Educ:* Brooklyn Col, BA, 53; Columbia Univ, PhD(microbiol), 59. *Prof Exp:* Fel, Nat Inst Med Res, London, 59-60. *Concurrent Pos:* Mem, Study Sect, NIH, 72-76; fel Rev Panel, Am Cancer Soc, 78-81; consult, Space Prog, NASA, 74; NIH study sect, 90- *Mem:* AAAS; Am Asn Immunol; The Planetary Soc. *Res:* Chemical substructure of antigens; mechanisms of lymphocyte activation; mechanism of immune induction; tumor immunology. *Mailing Add:* Dept Microbiol & Immunol Univ Calif Box 0414 San Francisco CA 94143-0414. *Fax:* 415-476-0939

GOODMAN, JOSEPH WILFRED, OPTICS, ELECTRICAL ENGINEERING. *Current Pos:* res assoc, Stanford Univ, 63-67, from asst prof to assoc prof, 67-88, dir, Info Syst Lab, 81-82, chmn dept, 88-96, WILLIAM E AYER PROF ELEC ENG, STANFORD UNIV, 88-, SR ASSOC DEAN ENG, 96- *Personal Data:* b Boston, Mass, Feb 8, 36; m 62; c 1. *Educ:* Harvard Univ, AB, 58; Stanford Univ, MS, 60, PhD(elec eng), 63. *Hon Degrees:* DSc, Univ Ala, 96. *Honors & Awards:* F E Terman Award, Am Asn Eng Educ, 71; Max Born Award, Optical Soc Am, 83, Frederik Ives Medal, 90, Esther Hoffman Beller Medal, 95; Dennis Gabor Award, Int Optical Eng Soc, 87; Education Medal, Inst Elec & Electronics Engrs, 87. *Prof Exp:* Res asst elec eng, Stanford Univ, 58-62; fel, Norweg Defense Res Estab, 62-63. *Concurrent Pos:* Ed adv, Optics Commun, 72-; vis prof, Univ Paris XI, 73-74; assoc ed, Optical Eng, 76-79; ed, J Optical Soc Am, 78-83; vpres, Int Comn Optics, 85-87, pres, 87-90. *Mem:* Nat Acad Eng; fel Soc Photo-Optical Engrs; fel Optical Soc Am (pres elect, 91, pres, 92); fel Inst Elec & Electronics Engrs; fel, AAAS. *Res:* Optical computing; fourier optics; holography; statistical optics. *Mailing Add:* Terman 214 Stanford Univ Stanford CA 94305

GOODMAN, L(AWRENCE) E(UGENE), APPLIED MECHANICS, STRUCTURAL ENGINEERING. *Current Pos:* RETIRED. *Personal Data:* b New York, NY, Mar 12, 20; m 51, Katherine Lewis; c Jennifer, Jeanne & Alice. *Educ:* Columbia Univ, AB, 39, BS, 40, PhD(appl mech), 49; Univ Ill, MS, 42, MA, Cambridge Univ, 62. *Honors & Awards:* Newmark Gold Medal, Am Soc Civil Engrs, 90. *Prof Exp:* Electro-mech engr, Appl Physics Lab, Johns Hopkins Univ, 43-44, 46; instr civil eng, Sch Eng, Columbia Univ, 47-48; from res asst prof to res assoc prof, Univ Ill, 49-53; prof mech, Univ Minn, Minneapolis, 54-65, head, Dept Civil Eng, 65-72, prof civil eng, 65-80, James L Record prof civil eng, 80-88; vis prof, Tex A&M Univ, 90-92. *Concurrent Pos:* NSF sr fel, 62-63; mem sci comt, Conf Mech of Contact, Int Union Theoret & Appl Mech, 73-75. *Mem:* Fel Am Soc Civil Engrs; fel Am Soc Mech Engrs. *Res:* Stress analysis; vibration of structures; material damping; structural analysis; contact stresses. *Mailing Add:* 1589 Vincent St St Paul MN 55108

GOODMAN, LEON, ORGANIC CHEMISTRY. *Current Pos:* RETIRED. *Personal Data:* b Livingston, Mont, Dec 16, 20; m 56, Marilyn Shear; c Laura & Andrew. *Educ:* Univ Calif, Berkeley, BS, 41; Univ Calif, Los Angeles, PhD(chem), 50. *Prof Exp:* Res asst explosive chem, Off Sci Univ & Develop, 42-45; res chemist, Los Alamos Sci Lab, 50-55; chemist, Stanford Res Inst, 55-61, chmn, Dept Bioorg Chem, 61-70; prof chem & chmn dept, Univ RI, 70-76, prof chem, 76-89. *Concurrent Pos:* Res assoc, Univ Southern Calif, 53-54; mem, Med Chem Study Sect, NIH, 70-73; Eleanor Roosevelt Int Cancer Fel, 77-78; mem bd sci counr, Div Cancer Treat, Nat Cancer Inst, 82-86. *Mem:* Am Chem Soc; fel AAAS. *Res:* Cancer chemotherapy; nucleoside chemistry; carbohydrate chemistry; nitrogen heterocyclic chemistry; silicon chemistry; organic chemistry of high explosives; organic sulfur chemistry. *Mailing Add:* 211 Woodruff Ave Wakefield RI 02879-3596

GOODMAN, LIONEL, CHEMICAL PHYSICS, PHOTOBIOLOGY. *Current Pos:* PROF CHEM, RUTGERS UNIV, 66- *Personal Data:* b Brooklyn, NY, Apr 23, 27; m 50; c 2. *Educ:* Iowa State Univ, PhD, 54. *Honors & Awards:* Frontiers Chem Lectr, Wayne State Univ, 88. *Prof Exp:* Fel, Fla State Univ, 54-55; from asst prof to assoc prof chem, Pa State Univ, 56-66. *Concurrent Pos:* Vis prof, Sorbonne, 64; vis prof molecular biophysics, Stockholm Univ, 68; NSF Sr Fel, 61-62; Guggenheim fel, 65-66. *Mem:* Am Chem Soc. *Res:* Laser spectroscopy, especially involving multiphoton excitation in supersonic jets; coupling of vibrational and electronic motions in molecules; molecular potential surfaces; theoretical simulation of molecular spectra. *Mailing Add:* Dept Chem Rutgers Univ New Brunswick NJ 08903

GOODMAN, LOUIS SANFORD, PHARMACOLOGY. *Current Pos:* RETIRED. *Personal Data:* b Portland, Ore, Aug 27, 06; m 33; c 2. *Educ:* Reed Col, BA, 28; Univ Ore, MD & MA, 32. *Hon Degrees:* DSc, Univ Man, 65, Univ Utah, 69 & Med Col Wis, 73. *Prof Exp:* Asst psychol, Reed Col, 27-29; asst neurol & pharmacol, Sch Med, Univ Ore, 29-32; house officer med, Johns Hopkins Hosp, 32-33; Nat Res Coun fel, Sch Med, Yale Univ, 34, instr pharmacol & toxicol, 35-37, asst prof, 37-43; prof pharmacol & physiol & chmn dept, Col Med, Univ Vt, 43-44; prof pharmacol & chmn dept, Col Med, Univ Utah, 44-72, distinguished prof pharmacol, 72- *Concurrent Pos:* Mem, Pharmacol Study Sect, USPHS, 48-52, Pharmacol & Exp Therapeut Study Sect, 54; ed-in-chief, Pharmacol Rev, Am Soc Pharmacol & Exp Therapeut, 49-53; mem, Res Comt Sci Coun, Am Heart Asn, 53-55; mem med bd, Myasthenia Gravis Found, 53-58; mem, Nat Adv Neurol Dis & Blindness Coun, 54-58; mem, Pharmacol Test Comt, Nat Bd Med Exam, 55-59; mem adv coun, Life Inst Med Res Fund, 56-59; mem sci bd, Nat Neurol Res Found, 57-64; chmn, Pharmacol Training Comt, NIH, 58-61, mem, Comt Res Career Awards, Div Gen Med Sci, mem, Nat Adv Ment Health Coun, 62-66 & Nat Adv Coun, Health Res Facil, 66-70; mem, Adv Comt Psychopharmacol, Serv Ctr, NIMH, 58-62 & Panel Neuropharmacol, Int Brain Res Orgn, 60; mem, Depts State & Health, Educ & Welfare Neurol Sci Mission to USSR, 58; US rep, Int Union Physiol Sci, 63-66. *Mem:* Nat Acad Sci; AAAS; Am Soc Pharmacol & Exp Therapeut (pres, 59-60); fel Am Col Neuropsychopharmacol; fel NY Acad Sci. *Res:* Anticonvulsant and autonomic drugs; pharmacodynamics. *Mailing Add:* Dept Pharmacol Univ Utah Col Med Salt Lake City UT 84132

GOODMAN, MADELEINE JOYCE, human biology, biophilosophy-bioethics; deceased, see previous edition for last biography

GOODMAN, MAJOR M, GENETICS. *Current Pos:* vis asst prof statist, 67-68, from asst prof to prof, 68-88, WILLIAM NEAL REYNOLDS DISTINGUISHED UNIV PROF CROP SCI, BOT, STATIST & GENETICS, NC STATE UNIV, 88- *Personal Data:* b Des Moines, Iowa, Sept 13, 38; m 70, Sheila Dail; c 2. *Educ:* Iowa State Univ, BS, 60; NC State Univ, MS, 63, PhD(genetics), 65. *Prof Exp:* NSF fel, Inst Genetics, Advan Sch Agr, Univ Sao Paulo, 65-67. *Concurrent Pos:* Del, Int Genetics Cong, Tokyo, 67; mem, Maize Germ Plasm Resources Comt, Rockefeller Found, 69-72; chmn, Maize Coop Adv Comt, 81-86; panel dir, Competitive Grants Panel Plant Genetics & Molecular Biol, USDA, 87-88. *Mem:* Nat Acad Sci; Genetics Soc Am; Soc Econ Bot; Soc Syst Bot; Crop Sci Soc Am. *Res:* Evolution of cultivated plants; numerical taxonomy; history and evolution of maize; applied multivariate statistics; plant breeding. *Mailing Add:* PO Box 7620 Raleigh NC 27695

GOODMAN, MICHAEL GORDON, IMMUNOLOGY, IMMUNOMODULATION. *Current Pos:* res fel, 75-78, asst mem, 78-83, ASSOC MEM IMMUNOL, SCRIPPS CLIN & RES FOUND, 83- *Personal Data:* b Denver, Colo, July 4, 46. *Educ:* Yale Univ, BA, 68; Univ Calif, San Francisco, MD, 72; dipl, Am Bd Internal Med, 75. *Prof Exp:* Intern, Univ Miami Affil Hosps, 73; med resident internal med, Jefferson Univ Hosp, 74; med res II internal med, Univ Calif, Los Angeles & Wadsworth Hosp, 75; consult, Ortho Pharmaceut Corp, 82-92. *Concurrent Pos:* US Pub Health Serv Nat Res Serv Award, Scripps Clin & Res Found, 75-78, prin investr, 78-, arthritis found fel, 78-80, US Pub Health Serv Career Develop Award, 80-85; vis physician, Univ Calif, San Diego, 80-83; ad hoc mem, Med Biochem Study Sect, NIH, 87-88. *Mem:* NY Acad Sci; fel Am Col Physicians; Am Asn Immunologists; Am Asn Pathologist. *Res:* Biochemistry of B lymphocyte activation to proliferation and immunoglobulin production; post-transduction events and consequences of intracellular receptor-ligand interactions; purine nucleoside biochemistry. *Mailing Add:* Dept Immunol PO Box 9218 Rancho Santa Fe CA 92067. *Fax:* 619-554-6705

GOODMAN, MORRIS, IMMUNOLOGY. *Current Pos:* res assoc & assoc, Lafayette Clin, 58-60, res assoc prof, 60-66, PROF ANAT, COL MED, WAYNE STATE UNIV, 66- *Personal Data:* b Milwaukee, Wis, Jan 12, 25; m 46, Selma Kessler; c Louise, Julia & David. *Educ:* Univ Wis, BS, 48, MS, 49, PhD(zool), 51. *Honors & Awards:* Lady Margaret Lectr, Christ's Col, Cambridge Univ, Eng, 84; von Hofsten Mem Lectr, Univ Uppsala, 87; Lawrence M Weiner Res Award, 95. *Prof Exp:* USPHS res fel, Calif Inst Technol, 51-52; res assoc, Med Col, Univ Ill, 52-54; res assoc, Detroit Inst Cancer Res, 54-58. *Concurrent Pos:* Dir res, Plymouth State Home & Training Sch, 66-72; mem adv panel syst biol, Div Biol & Med Sci, NSF, 69-72; co-ed, J Human Evolution, 72-77; ed-in-chief, Molecular Phylogenetics & Evolution, 91- *Mem:* Am Asn Immunol; Am Soc Zool; Am Asn Phys Anthrop; Am Soc Naturalists; Soc Study Evolution; Sigma Xi; fel Am Acad Arts & Sci. *Res:* Molecular evolution and systematics of primates, other mammals and vertebrates; analysis of the evolution of genes for globins and other protein families; analysis of the evolution of elements for globins and other protein families. *Mailing Add:* 24211 Oneida St Oak Park MI 48237. *Fax:* 313-577-1080; *E-Mail:* mg@tree.roc.wayne.edu

GOODMAN, MURRAY, ORGANIC CHEMISTRY. *Current Pos:* chmn, Chem Dept, 76-81, PROF CHEM, UNIV CALIF, SAN DIEGO, 71- *Personal Data:* b New York, NY, July 6, 28; m 51; c 3. *Educ:* Brooklyn Col, BS, 49; Univ Calif, PhD(org chem), 52. *Hon Degrees:* DSc, City Univ NY, 95 & Univ Ioannina, Grece, 95. *Honors & Awards:* Scoffone Medal, Biopolymer Res Ctr, Univ Padova, 80; Alberta Heritage Vis Prof Award, Med Res, Univ Alta, 81; William H Rauscher Lectr, Rensselaer Polytech Inst, 82; Humboldt Award, 86-87; Pierce Award, Peptide Chem, 89; Max-Bergmann Medal, Peptide Chem, 91; Givaudan Roure Award, Asn Chemoreception Scis, 91; Ralph Hirschmann Award Peptide Chem, 97. *Prof Exp:* Res assoc org chem, Mass Inst Technol, 53-55; fel, Am Cancer Soc Nat Res Coun, Cambridge Univ, 55-56; from asst prof to prof chem, Polytech Inst Brooklyn, 56-71, dir, Polymer Res Inst, 67-71. *Concurrent Pos:* Ed, Biopolymers, 63-; mem, steering comt human reproduction, WHO, 74-79 & US Nat Comt Int Union Pure & Appl Chem, 80-86; Goldberg Chair, Bio-Med Eng, Technion, Israel Inst Technol, 82; vis prof, Hong Kong Univ Sci & Technol, 94. *Mem:* AAAS; Am Chem Soc; Am Soc Biol Chemists; The Chem Soc; Sigma Xi; Biophys Soc. *Res:* Peptide synthesis; biopolymers; conformational analyses; nuclear magnetic resonance and computer; spectroscopy; biologically-active peptides peptidomimetics and their analogs; simulations, structure based drug design. *Mailing Add:* 9760 Blackgold Rd La Jolla CA 92037. *Fax:* 619-534-0202

GOODMAN, MYRON F, BIOCHEMISTRY. *Current Pos:* PROF MOLECULAR BIOL, UNIV SOUTHERN CALIF, 80- *Personal Data:* b New York, NY, Dec 31, 39. *Educ:* Johns Hopkins Univ, PhD(elec eng), 68. *Mailing Add:* Molecular Biol Sec Dept Biol Sci SHS Rm 560 Univ Southern Calif University Park CA 90089-1340. *Fax:* 213-740-8631

GOODMAN, NELSON, INDUSTRIAL MICROBIOLOGY. *Current Pos:* res leader, 86-95, RES MICROBIOLOGIST, AGR RES SERV, USDA, 95- *Personal Data:* b Brooklyn, NY, Aug 16, 32; m 56; c 3. *Educ:* Brooklyn Col, BS, 56; Brandeis Univ, PhD(biol), 62. *Prof Exp:* NIH fel, 62-64; microbiologist, Bioferm, Int Minerals & Chem Co, 64-67; microbiologist, Midwest Res Inst, 67; microbiologist, Accent Int & Supvr Indust Microbiol, San Jose Res Lab, Stauffer Chem Co, 68-79, supvr food & biotechnol, Western Res Labs, 79-85. *Mem:* Sigma Xi; Am Soc Microbiol; Soc Indust Microbiol; Soc Invert Path. *Res:* Monosodium glutamate fermentation; microbial insecticides; functionalized food fermentations. *Mailing Add:* USDA/ARS/WRRC 800 Buchanan St Albany CA 94710

GOODMAN, NICOLAS DANIELS, PROOF THEORY, INTUITIONISM. *Current Pos:* from asst prof to assoc prof, 69-89, interim vprovost undergrad educ, 93-94, PROF MATH, STATE UNIV NY, BUFFALO, 89-, VPROVOST UNDERGRAD EDUC, 94- *Personal Data:* b Berlin, Ger, June 23, 40; US citizen; div; c Charles & Eleanor. *Educ:* Harvard Univ, AB, 61; Stanford Univ, MS, 63, PhD(math), 68. *Prof Exp:* Instr math, Univ Ill, Chicago Circle, 65-66; asst prof, Univ Santa Clara, 68-69. *Mem:* Am Math Soc; Asn Symbolic Logic; Math Asn Am. *Res:* Constructive and numerical analysis, with an emphasis on their metamathematical and philosophical aspects; recursion-theoretic and proof-theoretic techniques; modal logic. *Mailing Add:* Dept Math State Univ NY Buffalo NY 14214

GOODMAN, NORMAN L, CLINICAL MICROBIOLOGY, MEDICAL MYCOLOGY. *Current Pos:* assoc prof, 70-78, prof community med, med mycol prog, 78-80, DIR, CLINICAL MICROBIOL LABS, 79-, PROF PATH & MED MICROBIOL & IMMUNOL, COL MED, UNIV KY, 80- *Personal Data:* b Milburn, Okla, Sept 29, 31; m 57, Markita Staton; c James M & Cathryn J. *Educ:* Southeast State Col, BS, 54; Univ Okla, MS, 60, PhD(microbiol), 65; Am Bd Med Microbiol, dipl. *Honors & Awards:* Meridian Award, Med Mycrological Soc Am, 89; Rhoda Benham Award, Med Mycological Soc Am, 96. *Prof Exp:* Teacher pub sch, Okla, 56-57; microbiologist, Oper Res, Tuberc Br, Commun Dis Ctr, USPHS, 63-68; asst prof microbiol & dir diag bact labs, Med Univ SC, 68-70. *Concurrent Pos:* Chmn comt continuing educ, Am Soc Microbiol, 73-79, mem bd educ & training, 76-79, chmn, Div Med Mycol, 76-77 & Comt Undergrad & Grad Educ, 81-84; mem stand & exam comt, Am Bd Med Microbiol, 78-84; mem comt postdoctoral educ progs, Am Acad Microbiol, 79-82, bd gov; mem US nat comt, Int Union Microbiol Socs, 82-86; mem exec comt & chmn, Mycol Div, Int Union Microbiol Soc, 71-90 & 82-86; assoc ed, Diag Microbiol & Infectious Dis, 82-88; counr, Am Soc Microbiol, 90-97, mem, Subcomt Lab Regulations, Pub & Sci Affairs Bd, 92-96; chmn, Stand & Exam Comt Mycol, Am Bd Med & Microbiol, 91-97; ed, Mycopathologica, 94- *Mem:* AAAS; Am Soc Microbiol; Mycological Soc Am (pres, 82); fel Am Acad Microbiol; Int Soc for Human & Animal Mycoses; Soc for Exp Biol & Med. *Res:* Pathogenesis of systemic mycoses and epidemiology of histoplasmosis; clinical microbiology. *Mailing Add:* Dept Path Univ Ky Col Med Lexington KY 40536-0840. *Fax:* 606-257-1399; *E-Mail:* nlgoodol@pop.uky.edu

GOODMAN, RICHARD E, CIVIL & GEOLOGICAL ENGINEERING. *Current Pos:* From asst prof to assoc prof, 62-77, CAHILL PROF GEOL ENG, UNIV CALIF, BERKELEY, 77- *Personal Data:* b New York, NY, Dec 25, 35; m 57, Lillian Gates; c Paula, Holly & Lilly. *Educ:* Cornell Univ, BA, 55, MS, 58; Univ Calif, PhD(geol eng), 63. *Honors & Awards:* Rock Mech Award, Assoc Inst Mining & Metal Engrs, 76; Burwell Award, Geol Soc Am, 77; Basic Res Award, US Nat Comn Rock Mech, 84. *Concurrent Pos:* Grants, NSF & others; Gugenheim fel; pres, Geol Eng Found; consult, Defense Nuclear Agency, Corps Engrs, Colombian govt, Codelco Mines, Chile, US Bur Reclamation & Pac Gas & Elec Co. *Mem:* Nat Acad Eng; Asn Eng Geologists; Am Soc Civil Engrs. *Res:* Applications of geological data in civil engineering design, dams and underground works; block theory; physical and mathematical model studies of jointed rock masses; author of 4 books and 180 publications; researching life of Karl Torzaghi. *Mailing Add:* Dept Civil Eng 434B Davis Hall Univ Calif Berkeley CA 94720. *Fax:* 510-642-7476

GOODMAN, RICHARD E, MICROBIAL PHYSIOLOGY, GENERAL BIOLOGY. *Current Pos:* DIR LABS, DEPT BIOL SCI, UNIV SOUTHERN CALIF, 78- *Personal Data:* b Los Angeles, Calif, Jan 28, 38; div; c 1. *Educ:* Univ Calif, Los Angeles, BA, 60, PhD(microbiol), 65. *Prof Exp:* USPHS fel microbiol, Sch Med, Univ Wash, 65-67; from asst prof to assoc prof biol, Calif State Col, San Bernardino, 67-77. *Res:* Delayed lactose fermentation by Enterobacteriaceae; physiology of streptomycin-dependent and thermophilic bacteria. *Mailing Add:* Med Ctr Dept IM Pulmonary Div 3916 Taubman Ctr Ann Arbor MI 48109-0360

GOODMAN, RICHARD HENRY, NUMERICAL ANALYSIS, COMPUTER SCIENCE. *Current Pos:* DIR, VOLLUM INST, ORE HEALTH SCI UNIV. *Personal Data:* b Brooklyn, NY. *Educ:* Harvard Univ, AB, 63, AM, 64, PhD(math), 71. *Prof Exp:* Asst prof math, Univ Maimi, 70-78, assoc prof, 78- *Concurrent Pos:* Vis scientist, Argonne Nat Lab, 78-79; NSF fel; Woodrow Wilson Nat fel. *Mem:* Sigma Xi; Soc Indust & Appl Math; Asn Comput Mach. *Res:* Numerical solution of differential equations; theory of computer arithmetic, with applications to computer design. *Mailing Add:* Dir Vollum Inst 1474 Ore Health Sci Univ 3181 SW Sam Jackson Park Rd Portland OR 97201-3098. *Fax:* 503-494-4353

GOODMAN, RICHARD S, MEDICINE, LAW. *Current Pos:* ATTEND PHYSICIAN, ST JOHNS HOSP, SMITHTOWN, NY, 67- *Personal Data:* b Brooklyn, NY, Aug 4, 34; m 86; c 5. *Educ:* Alfred Univ, BA, 55; NY Univ, MD, 60; Am Bd Orthop Surg, cert, 69; Touro Col, JD, 87. *Prof Exp:* Intern surg, Ind Univ Med Ctr, 60-61; asst resident, Bronx Munic Hosp Ctr, 61-62; resident orthop, NY Univ Med Ctr & Bellevue Hosp, 64-67; attend physician, Community Hosp Western Suffolk, 67-96. *Concurrent Pos:* Solo practr lectr; asst prof, Dept Anat, State Univ NY, Stonybrook, 71-88; mem, bd trustees, Alfred Univ, 78-84; pres med staff, Community Hosp Western Suffolk, 78, chmn, Disaster Comt, 78-96, Ethics Comt, 90-, Med StaffAffairs Comt, 90-; pres, Marine Sci Res Ctr, Stonybrook Found, 80-84; policy adv, Inst Advan Health Care Mgt, State Univ NY, Albany, 92- *Mem:* Fel Am Acad Orthop Surgeons; Am Col Sports Med; fel Am Col Legal Med; Am Rheumatism Asn; Am Soc Law & Med; Int Col Surgeons; Arthritis Found; Int Health Lawyers Asn; AMA; Nat Health Lawyers Asn. *Res:* Author of numerous technical articles & publications, lecturers and writes on medical-legal issues such as risk management, malpractice and insurance. *Mailing Add:* 285 E Main St Smithtown NY 11787

GOODMAN, ROBERT M(ENDEL), electrical engineering; deceased, see previous edition for last biography

GOODMAN, ROBERT MERWIN, MOLECULAR MICROBIOLOGY ECOLOGY, ENVIRONMENTAL MICROBIOLOGY. *Current Pos:* vis prof, 90-91, PROF, UNIV WIS, MADISON, 91- *Personal Data:* b Ithaca, NY, Dec 30, 45; c Nathan M. *Educ:* Cornell Univ, BSc, 67, PhD(plant virol), 73. *Prof Exp:* From asst prof to prof plant pathol, Univ Ill, Urbana-Champaign, 74-82; exec vpres res & develop, Calgene Inc, 82-90; sr scholar in residence, Nat Res Coun, 90-91. *Concurrent Pos:* Mem, Nat Acad Sci-Nat Res Coun Bd Agr, 86-; adj prof, Univ Calif, Berkeley, 86-89; panel mem, Nat Res Coun, Biosci Res Agr, 84-85, Alt Farming Methods in Prod Agr, 86-89; chmn, Comt Exam Plant Sci Res Prog US, 90-92; bd dirs, Cornell Res Found, 90-; chair, Oversight Comt, McKnight Found Collab Coops Res Prog, 92- *Mem:* AAAS; Soc Gen Microbiol; Am Chem Soc; Am Soc Virol; Int Soc Plant Molecular Biol; Am Soc Microbiol. *Res:* Discovery of the plant viruses, geminiviruses which contain as their genetic material single-stranded DNA; replication of DNA plant viruses; plant molecular biology & genetics; microbial community ecology; genetic basis and interactions between plants and rhizosphere microbes; microbiology diversity in terrestrial environments; soil microbiol ecology. *Mailing Add:* Russell Labs Rm 687A Univ Wis 1630 Linden Dr Madison WI 53706. *Fax:* 608-262-8643; *E-Mail:* rgoodman@facstaff.wisc.edu

GOODMAN, ROBERT NORMAN, PLANT PATHOLOGY. *Current Pos:* RETIRED. *Personal Data:* b Yonkers, NY, Dec 15, 21; m 49; c 3. *Educ:* Univ NH, BS, 48, MS, 50; Univ Mo, PhD(plant path), 52. *Honors & Awards:* Lalor Found Award, 59. *Prof Exp:* Asst hort, Univ NH, 48-50; from asst to assoc prof, Univ Mo-Columbia, 50-61, chmn dept, 68-79, prof plant path, 68-93. *Concurrent Pos:* Guggenheim fel, Swiss Fed Inst Technol, 58-59; NIH spec fel, Astbury Dept Biophys, Univ Leeds, 65-66; vis scientist, Volcanic Res Ctr, Israel Ministry Agr, 72-73, Weizmann Inst Sci, Israel, 79-80. *Mem:* Fel Am Phytopath Soc; Soc Am Microbiol. *Res:* Control of bacterial pathogens with antibiotics and antibacterial substances; adsorption and translocation of organic antimicrobial substances by foliage; bacterial toxins; ultrastructural changes in plants caused by bacteria; induced resistance in plants to bacterial pathogens. *Mailing Add:* 605 Crestland Columbia MO 65203

GOODMAN, ROE WILLIAM, MATHEMATICAL ANALYSIS. *Current Pos:* assoc prof, 71-75, PROF MATH, RUTGERS UNIV, 75- *Personal Data:* b Pasadena, Calif, Jan 9, 38; c 1. *Educ:* Fla Southern Col, BS, 58; Mass Inst Technol, PhD(math), 63. *Prof Exp:* Instr math, Mass Inst Technol, 62-63; Nat Acad Sci-Nat Res Coun fel, Harvard Univ, 63-64; lectr, Mass Inst Technol, 64-66, asst prof, 66-71. *Concurrent Pos:* Vis mem, Inst Advan Study, 68-69 & Inst Advan Study Sci, 75-76. *Mem:* Am Math Soc; Math Asn Am; Math Soc France. *Res:* Functional analysis and operator theory; representations of Lie groups and harmonic analysis; quantum field theory. *Mailing Add:* Dept Math Rutgers Univ New Brunswick NJ 08903-2101

GOODMAN, RONALD KEITH, PLASMA PHYSICS, THOMSON SCATTERING. *Current Pos:* res operator, 61-66, PHYSICIST, LAWRENCE LIVERMORE NAT LAB, UNIV CALIF, 66- *Personal Data:* b Yuma, Ariz, Oct 31, 29; m 59; c 4. *Educ:* Wheaton Col, BS, 53; San Jose State Col, MS, 67. *Prof Exp:* Engr, Fargo Co, Calif, 57-58, chief engr, 58-61. *Mem:* Am Phys Soc; Am Vacuum Soc. *Res:* Ultra-high vacuum and related surface physics; plasma physics in controlled thermonuclear research. *Mailing Add:* 3923 Fordham Way Livermore CA 94550

GOODMAN, SEYMOUR, COMPUTER SCIENCE, PHYSICAL CHEMISTRY. *Current Pos:* From instr to assoc prof, 62-70, chmn, Dept Comput Sci, 70-76, DIR, ACAD COMPUT CTR, QUEENS COL NY, 65-, PROF COMPUT SCI, 70- *Personal Data:* b New York, NY, Nov 12, 33. *Educ:* City Col New York, BS, 54; Univ Chicago, MS, 54; Columbia Univ, PhD(chem), 62. *Concurrent Pos:* NSF grant, 65-67. *Mem:* AAAS; Am Chem Soc; Am Phys Soc; Asn Comput Mach; Pattern Recognition Soc; Sigma Xi. *Res:* Data acquisition and signal processing; computer architecture. *Mailing Add:* 6744 171st St Flushing NY 11365-3312

GOODMAN, SHERRI, ENVIRONMENTAL SCIENCE. *Current Pos:* DEP UNDER SECY ENVIRON SECURITY, US DEPT DEFENSE, 93- *Personal Data:* b Apr 9, 59. *Educ:* Amherst Col, BA; Harvard Univ, MA & JD. *Mailing Add:* US Dept Defense 3400 Defense Pentagon Arlington VA 20301-3400

GOODMAN, STEVEN RICHARD, BIOCHEMISTRY. *Current Pos:* AT DEPT PHYSIOL, PA STATE UNIV MED SCH. *Personal Data:* b New York, NY, Dec 29, 49; c 1. *Educ:* State Univ NY, Stony Brook, BS, 71; St Louis Univ, PhD(biochem), 76. *Prof Exp:* Res fel biochem, Sidney Farber Cancer Inst, Harvard Univ, 76-77, res fel cell biol, 77- *Concurrent Pos:* Nat Heart, Lung & Blood Inst fel, 77- *Res:* Membrane biochemistry, especially the association of peripheral cytoskeletal proteins with the membrane surface and the role of peripheral proteins in regulating the mobility of integral membrane proteins and hence cell surface topography. *Mailing Add:* Dept Struct & Cellular Biol Univ SAla Rm 2042 Mobile AL 36688-0001. *Fax:* 334-460-6771

GOODMAN, SUE ELLEN, MATHEMATICS. *Current Pos:* ASST PROF MATH, UNIV NC, 74- *Personal Data:* b East St Louis, Ill, Nov 26, 46. *Educ:* St Louis Univ, AB, 68, MA, 71, PhD(math), 74. *Prof Exp:* Pvt br tel exchange engr, Southwestern Bell, 68-69; res asst math, Wash Univ, 73-74. *Concurrent Pos:* NSF res grant, 74-; vis mem, Inst Advan Study, 76-77. *Mem:* Am Math Soc. *Res:* Foliations and dynamical systems. *Mailing Add:* Dept Math Univ NC Chapel Hill NC 27599-3902

GOODMAN, THEODORE R(OBERT), FLUID DYNAMICS, APPLIED MATHEMATICS. *Current Pos:* RETIRED. *Personal Data:* b Brooklyn, NY, Mar 21, 25. *Educ:* Rensselaer Polytech Inst, BAE, 45; Calif Inst Technol, MAE, 46; Cornell Univ, PhD(aeronaut eng), 54. *Prof Exp:* From jr aerodynamicist to assoc aerodynamicist, Cornell Aeronaut Lab, 46-51, prin engr, 53-55; prin engr, Allied Res Assocs, Inc, 56-61; vpres, Oceanics, Inc, 62-76; sr res scientist, 76-80, assoc res prof, 78-82, chief, Fluid Mech Div, Davidson Lab, Stevens Inst Technol, 80-82. *Mem:* Assoc fel Am Inst Aeronaut & Astronaut; Am Soc Mech Engrs; Sigma Xi. *Res:* Hydrodynamics; theoretical aerodynamics; fluid mechanics; boundary layer and wing theory; heat transfer; aeroelasticity; ballistics; system identification. *Mailing Add:* 21 Chapel Pl Great Neck NY 11021

GOODMAN, VICTOR HERKE, plant anatomy, for more information see previous edition

GOODMAN, VICTOR WAYNE, PURE MATHEMATICS. *Current Pos:* asst prof, 72-80, ASSOC PROF MATH, IND UNIV, 80- *Personal Data:* b Wellington, Kans, Oct 1, 43. *Educ:* Univ Kans, BA, 65; Cornell Univ, PhD(math), 70. *Prof Exp:* Fel math, Univ NMex, 70-72. *Concurrent Pos:* NSF res grant, 72. *Mem:* Am Math Soc; Sigma Xi. *Res:* Investigation of mathematical models of brownian motion and deriving such models as asymptotic limits of certain sampling situations in the theory of statistics. *Mailing Add:* Dept Math Ind Univ Bloomington IN 47405-4301

GOODNER, DWIGHT BENJAMIN, pure mathematics; deceased, see previous edition for last biography

GOODNEY, DAVID EDGAR, INSTRUMENTAL ANALYSIS. *Current Pos:* from asst prof to assoc prof, 77-88, PROF CHEM, WILLAMETTE UNIV, 88 - *Personal Data:* b Wilmington, Del, Dec 2, 49; m 71; c 2. *Educ:* Austin Col, BA, 71; Univ Hawaii, PhD(chem), 77. *Prof Exp:* Res asst chem, Univ Hawaii, 77. *Concurrent Pos:* Vis prof chem, Ore Grad Ctr, 86. *Mem:* Am Chem Soc; AAAS. *Res:* Solving analytical problems related to environmental concerns, such as the composition of carbonaceous aerosols, trace metals in natural waters and trace chemicals in foods. *Mailing Add:* Willamette Univ 900 State St Salem OR 97301. *Fax:* 503-375-5425; *E-Mail:* dgoodney@willamette.edu

GOODNICK, PAUL JOEL, MOOD DISORDERS, PSYCHOPHARMACOLOGY. *Current Pos:* clin asst prof, 88-90, from asst prof to assoc prof, 90-93, PROF CLIN PSYCHIAT, UNIV MIAMI, 93-, DIR, MOOD DIS PROG, 90- *Personal Data:* b Philadelphia, Pa, Sept 29, 50; m 78, Malriam Rabinowitz; c Sarah & Chana. *Educ:* Univ Pa, BA, 72; State Univ NY, Downstate, MD, 76. *Prof Exp:* Resident psychiat, Washington Univ, St Louis, 77, Columbia Univ, 78; asst prof psychiat, Wayne State Univ, 80-81; asst res prof psychiat, Univ Chicago, 81-84; asst prof clin psychiat, Columbia Univ, 84-87. *Concurrent Pos:* Dir, Spec Studies Unit, Vet Admin Med Ctr, Allen Park, 80-81; dir clin, Ill State Psychiat Inst, 81-84; asst dir lithium, NY State Psychiat Inst, 84-87; asst ed, Lithium, 90-94. *Mem:* Fel Am Psychiat Asn; fel Am Psychopath Asn; Soc Biol Psychiat; AAAS; NY Acad Sci. *Res:* Improved clinical treatment of mood disorders (manic depression and depression) as well as chronic fatigue syndrome based on biological markers and followup parameters. *Mailing Add:* 1400 NW Tenth Ave No 304A Miami FL 33136. *Fax:* 305-243-4061; *E-Mail:* pgoodnick@aol.com

GOODNO, BARRY JOHN, SOLID MECHANICS, CIVIL ENGINEERING. *Current Pos:* Asst prof, 74-79, ASSOC PROF CIVIL ENG, GA INST TECHNOL, 79- *Personal Data:* b Madison, Wis, July 19, 47. *Educ:* Univ Wis-Madison, BS, 70; Stanford Univ, MS, 71, PhD(civil eng), 75. *Concurrent Pos:* Res grant, NSF, 75; consult, US Army Corps Engrs, 76; mem Comt Electronic Comput, Struct Div & Dynamics Comt, Eng Mech Div, Am Soc Civil Engrs, 76- *Mem:* Am Soc Civil Engrs; Earthquake Eng Res Inst, Seismol Soc Am; Sigma Xi. *Res:* Analysis of structural dynamics of buildings with applications to wind and earthquake engineering; finite element methods in structural engineering; matrix methods of structural analysis; analysis of cladding on buildings. *Mailing Add:* Sch Civil Eng Ga Inst Technol 225 North Ave NW Atlanta GA 30332-0355

GOODPASTURE, JESSIE CARROL, reproduction, endocrinology, for more information see previous edition

GOODRICH, CECILIE ANN, DEVELOPMENT. *Current Pos:* from asst prof to assoc prof, 71-84, dean, Col Arts & Sci, 91-95, PROF BIOL, CLEVELAND STATE UNIV, 84- *Personal Data:* b Denver, Colo, Apr 27, 41; m, Peter C Baker. *Educ:* Univ Mich, BS, 62; Harvard Univ, PhD(physiol), 67. *Prof Exp:* Fel physiol, Lab Neuropharmacol, Nat Inst Med Res, Eng, 67-68; res fel anat, Harvard Med Sch, 68-71. *Concurrent Pos:* NIH fels, 67-71, res grant, 69-72, 73-76 & 83-87. *Mem:* Am Physiol Soc; AAAS; Soc Integrative Comp Biol. *Res:* Maturation of serotonin system and its functions; temperature regulation; cerebrospinal fluid; neonatal maturation of behaviors. *Mailing Add:* Dept Biol Cleveland State Univ Cleveland OH 44115

GOODRICH, JUDSON EARL, ORGANIC CHEMISTRY. *Current Pos:* RETIRED. *Personal Data:* b Seneca, Kans, Aug 14, 22; m 51, Leslie Whitney; c Whitney, Allen & Joan. *Educ:* Univ Kans, AB, 47, MA, 48; Univ Calif, PhD(chem), 51. *Prof Exp:* Asst instr, Univ Kans, 47-48 & Univ Calif, 48-51; assoc res chemist, Calif Res Corp, Standard Oil Co Calif, 51-54, res chemist, 54-60, sr res chemist, 60-64, sr res assoc, Chevron Res Co, 64-85. *Mem:* Am

Chem Soc. *Res:* Positive halogen salts; desulfurization of thioamides; cyclic ketals of diketones; fuel oil stability; lubricating grease gelling agents; cationic polymerization; stabilization of polyolefins; polyurethanes; asphalt emulsions; industrial asphalt chemistry. *Mailing Add:* 6396 Stone Bridge Rd Santa Rosa CA 95409-5824. *Fax:* 707-538-8911; *E-Mail:* judrich@aol.com, judgood@metro.net

GOODRICH, MAX, EXPERIMENTAL PHYSICS. *Current Pos:* from instr to prof & dean Grad Sch, 36-73, EMER PROF PHYSICS & EMER DEAN GRAD SCH, LA STATE UNIV, 73- *Personal Data:* b Calhoun, Mo, Dec 11, 05; m 29; c 2. *Educ:* Westminster Col, Mo, BA, 27; Univ Minn, PhD(physics), 36. *Prof Exp:* Instr math, Salt Lake Collegiate Inst, 27-29; asst instr physics, Univ Minn, 29-36. *Concurrent Pos:* Physicist, War Res Lab, Univ Tex, 45; sr physicist, Oak Ridge Nat Lab, 49-50; chief, Grad Acad Prog Br, US Off Educ, 68-69; mem comput comt, Southern Regional Educ Bd, 68-72; mem coun, Oak Ridge Assoc Univs, 69-72 & mem bd dir, 72-78. *Mem:* Fel AAAS; fel Am Phys Soc; Am Asn Physics Teachers. *Res:* Electron impact phenomena; electron diffraction; electron scattering in helium; spectrometry of beta- and gamma-rays. *Mailing Add:* 4702 Woodcraft Rd Okemos MI 48864

GOODRICH, MICHAEL ALAN, SYSTEMATICS, ECOLOGY. *Current Pos:* from assoc prof to prof, 64-95, chmn dept, 82-88, EMER PROF ZOOL, EASTERN ILL UNIV, 95- *Personal Data:* b New York, NY, Apr 24, 33; m 55, Suzanne Huelle; c Michael, Thomas & Monica. *Educ:* Bucknell Univ, BS, 55; Pa State Univ, MEd, 61, PhD(entom), 64. *Prof Exp:* Asst zool & entom, Pa State Univ, 61-64, instr entom, 63. *Mem:* Entom Soc Am; Entom Soc Can; Animal Behav Soc; Coleopterists Soc; Am Entom Soc; Sigma Xi. *Res:* Taxonomy ecology and evolution of Coleoptera; evolution of behavior; systematics of Coleoptera, especially Byturidae, Biphyllidae, Erotylidae Staphglinidae (Oxyporinae) and Scarabaeidae of the world. *Mailing Add:* Dept Zool Eastern Ill Univ Charleston IL 61920. *E-Mail:* cfmag@eiu.edu

GOODRICH, RICHARD DOUGLAS, ANIMAL NUTRITION. *Current Pos:* PROF ANIMAL SCI, UNIV MINN, ST PAUL, 65- *Personal Data:* b New Richmond, Wis, July 2, 36; m 56; c 2. *Educ:* Wis State Univ, River Falls, BS, 58; SDak State Univ, MS, 62; Okla State Univ, PhD(animal nutrit), 65. *Mem:* Am Soc Animal Sci; Am Inst Nutrit. *Res:* Ruminant and mineral nutrition; forage evaluation; characterization of silage fermentation; adaptation to and utilization of nonprotein nitrogen by ruminants; feedlot nutrition and management; beef cow nutrition; feedlot housing systems. *Mailing Add:* Dept Animal Sci 122 Peters Hall Univ Minn 1404 Gortner Ave St Paul MN 55108-6160

GOODRICH, ROBERT KENT, MATHEMATICS. *Current Pos:* PROF MATH, UNIV COLO, BOULDER, 66- *Personal Data:* b Lapoint, Utah, July 5, 41; m 65; c 2. *Educ:* Univ Utah, BA, 63, PhD(math), 66. *Mem:* Am Math Soc. *Res:* Functional analysis. *Mailing Add:* Dept Math Univ Colo PO Box 395 Boulder CO 80309-0426

GOODRICH, ROY GORDON, SOLID STATE PHYSICS. *Current Pos:* from asst prof to assoc prof, 65-72, chmn, Dept Physics & Astron, 73-76, PROF PHYSICS, LA STATE UNIV, BATON ROUGE, 72- *Personal Data:* b Dallas, Tex, Sept 17, 38; m 59; c 3. *Educ:* La Polytech Inst, BS, 60; Univ Calif, Riverside, MA, 63, PhD(physics), 65. *Prof Exp:* Instr physics, Univ Southern Miss, 60-61. *Mem:* Am Phys Soc. *Res:* Thermal and magnetic properties of solids at low temperatures. *Mailing Add:* Dept Physics & Astron La State Univ Baton Rouge LA 70803-4001

GOODRICK, RICHARD EDWARD, MATHEMATICS. *Current Pos:* from asst prof to prof, 69-91, EMER PROF MATH, CALIF STATE UNIV, HAYWARD, 91-; PROF MATH, UNIV WASH, 92- *Personal Data:* b Verdun, Que, Feb 19, 41; US citizen; m 77, Sanday; c 1. *Educ:* Univ Wash, BS, 62; Univ Wis, MS, 64, PhD(math), 66. *Prof Exp:* Asst prof math, Univ Utah, 66-69. *Concurrent Pos:* Vis fel, Univ Warwick, 68-69; vis prof, Cambridge Univ, 76. *Mem:* Am Math Soc. *Res:* Piece wise linear topology. *Mailing Add:* 13211 Frazier Pl NW Seattle WA 98177-4132. *E-Mail:* goodrick@math.washington.edu

GOODRIDGE, ALAN G, METABOLIC REGULATION, GENE EXPRESSION. *Current Pos:* PROF & HEAD, DEPT BIOCHEM, UNIV IOWA, 87- *Personal Data:* b Peabody, Mass, Apr 2, 37; m 60, Ann Funderburk; c Bryant C & Alan G Jr. *Educ:* Tufts Univ, BS, 58; Univ Mich, MS, 63, PhD(zool), 64. *Prof Exp:* Asst prof physiol, Med Ctr, Univ Kans, 66-68; assoc prof med sci, Univ Toronto, 68-76, prof, 76-77; prof pharmacol, Case Western Res Univ, 77-87, prof biochem, 80-87. *Concurrent Pos:* Nat Inst Arthritis & Metab Dis res fel, Harvard Med Sch, 64-66; Josiah Macy Jr fac scholar, 75-76; assoc ed, J Biol Chem, 90- *Mem:* AAAS; Asn Med & Grad Dept Biochem (treas, 90-92, pres, 94); Am Soc Biochem & Molecular Biol; Am Thyroid Asn. *Res:* Regulation of metabolism; nutritional and hormonal regulation of gene expression; hormone action. *Mailing Add:* Dept Biochem Col Biol Sci Ohio State Univ 105 Biol Sci Bldg 484 W 12th Ave Columbus OH 43210-1292. *Fax:* 614-292-1538

GOODROAD, LEWIS LEONARD, SOIL BIOLOGY & BIOCHEMISTRY, SOIL CHEMISTRY. *Current Pos:* SCIENTIST, RUST REMEDIAL SERV, CLEMSON TECH CTR, 93- *Personal Data:* b Watertown, SDak, Feb 2, 48. *Educ:* Univ Minn, BS, 71, MS, 78; Univ Wis, PhD(soil sci), 83. *Prof Exp:* Res assoc, Univ Minn, 72-77, jr scientist, 77-78; res assoc soil sci, Univ Wis, 78-83; asst prof agron, Univ Ga, 83-90; assoc prof chem & chair natural sci div Northland Col, 90-93. *Concurrent Pos:* Assoc prof chem, Luc Courte Oreilles Community Col, 90-93; adj assoc prof environ systs eng, Clemson Univ, 93. *Mem:* Am Chem Soc; Soil Sci Soc Am; Soc Environ Toxicol & Chem; Sigma Xi; Environ Indust Asn; Nat Solid Waste Mgt Asn. *Res:* Development and demonstration of innovative technologies for remediation of contaminated soils and groundwater. *Mailing Add:* 109 Houston St Clemson SC 29631. *Fax:* 864-646-5311

GOODSON, ALAN LESLIE, INFORMATION SCIENCE, ORGANIC CHEMISTRY & FULLERENES. *Current Pos:* ed, 64-69, mem ed develop, 69-83, NOMENCLATOR, CHEM ABSTRACTS SERV, 83- *Personal Data:* b London, Eng, Apr 11, 33; US citizen; m 76, Christel Wickardt. *Educ:* Univ London, BSc, 57, PhD(chem), 61; ARIC, 58; Woolwich Polytech, AWP, 61; Royal Soc Chem, Cert Chem, 77. *Prof Exp:* Control chemist, Prince Regent Tar Co, 55-57; res chemist, Shell Chem Co, 60-63, info officer, 63-64. *Concurrent Pos:* Rep Am Chem Soc, Am Nat Standards Inst, 84- *Mem:* Am Chem Soc; fel Royal Soc Chem; AAAS; Soc Chem Indust. *Res:* Chemical nomenclature; chemical literature; allenes; acetylenes; aluminum alkyls; polyalkylene glycols. *Mailing Add:* 1060 Woodmere Rd Columbus OH 43220

GOODSON, JAMES BROWN, JR, sanitary engineering, for more information see previous edition

GOODSON, LOUIE AUBREY, JR, TEXTILE CHEMISTRY. *Current Pos:* RETIRED. *Personal Data:* b Providence, NC, Dec 20, 22; m 45; c 4. *Educ:* NC State Col, BS, 43; Georgetown Univ, JD, 51. *Prof Exp:* Res chemist, Dan River Mills, Inc, 46-48, asst dir res, 51-53; patent searcher, Fisher & Christen, 48-51, patent lawyer & partner, Fisher, Christen & Goodson, 53-59; vpres & dir res, Dan River Inc, 59-80, sr vpres develop & govt regulations & pres, Chem Prod Div, 80-89. *Concurrent Pos:* Mem nat adv comt, Flammable Fabrics Act, Consumer Prod Safety Comn, 75-77; hon fel, Textile Res Inst, 80. *Mem:* Am Chem Soc; Am Asn Textile Chem & Colorists; Am Asn Textile Technol. *Mailing Add:* 101 Mowbray Arch Danville VA 24541

GOODSON, RAYMOND EUGENE, SYSTEMS & CONTROL ENGINEERING. *Current Pos:* GROUP VPRES, AUTOMOTIVE PROD GROUP, HOOVER UNIV, INC, SALINE, MICH, 81- *Personal Data:* b Canton, NC, Apr 22, 35; m 57; c 2. *Educ:* Duke Univ, AB, 57, BSME, 59; Purdue Univ, MSME, 61, PhD(fluids, automatic control), 63. *Prof Exp:* From asst prof to assoc prof, Purdue Univ, 63-70, prof mech eng, 70-81, dir, Energy Policy Res & Info Ctr & Energy Policy Prog, 77-81. *Concurrent Pos:* Consult various industs & govt, 63-; res grants, NSF, NASA & Off Naval Res; vis prof, Weizmann Inst Sci, Rehovot, Israel, 72; Japanese Soc Prom Sci traveling scholar, 72; chief scientist, US Dept Transp, 73-75, mem Fed Interagency Task Force Motor Vehicle Goals Beyond 1980, 75-76; mem NASA Adv Comt Guid & Control, 73-74; chmn transp subcomt, Energy Storage Comt, Nat Acad Sci, 75; dir, Inst Interdisciplinary Eng Studies, Purdue Univ, 76-, dir, Opportunity Risk Anal Proj, Energy Res & Develop Admin, 77- & assoc dir, Eng & Exp Sta, 78-; rep US/USSR Environ Agreement, Transp Source Air Pollution Control Technol, USSR, 76; mem Comt Advan Energy Storage Systs, Nat Res Coun, Nat Acad Eng, 76; tech rep, UN Motor Vehicle Conf, Int Metalworkers Fedn, Paris, 76; mem, Comt on Nuclear & Alternative Energy Systs Study, Nat Acad Sci/Nat Acad Eng & chmn, Transp Resource Group, Demand-Conserv Panel, 76-77; mem energy eng bd, Nat Res Coun Assembly Engrs; chmn, Off Tech Assessment, Automobile Adv Panel. *Mem:* Am Soc Mech Engrs; Instrument Soc Am; Inst Elec & Electronics Engrs; Sigma Xi. *Res:* Energy systems and energy conservation; transportation systems; particularly motor vehicles and urban transportation, glass industry research, and distributed systems. *Mailing Add:* 1545 Arboretum Dr No 415 Oshkosh WI 54901-2795

GOODSPEED, ROBERT MARSHALL, ENVIRONMENTAL SCIENCES. *Current Pos:* From asst prof to assoc prof geol, Susquehanna Univ, 66-83, chmn, Dept Geol Sci, 69-81 & 85-88, chmn, Sci Div, 70-74, PROF GEOL, SUSQUEHANNA UNIV, 83- *Personal Data:* b Somerville, Mass, Feb 11, 38; div; c 2. *Educ:* Tufts Univ, BS, 60; Univ Maine, MS, 62; Rutgers Univ, PhD(geol & geochem), 68. *Concurrent Pos:* Air pollution researcher & consult, 90- *Mem:* AAAS; Mineral Soc Am; Geol Soc Am; Nat Asn Geol Teachers. *Res:* Concentrations of radon in air and water associated with lithologic units; concentrations of outdoor-indoor air pollutants in industrial and rural areas. *Mailing Add:* RR 1 Selinsgrove PA 17870-0001

GOODSTEIN, DAVID LOUIS, CONDENSED MATTER PHYSICS, SCIENTIFIC ETHICS. *Current Pos:* res fel, 66-67, from asst prof to assoc prof, 68-75, PROF PHYSICS, CALIF INST TECHNOL, 75-, VPROVOST, 87-, FRANK J GILLOON DISTINGUISHED TEACHING & SERV PROF, 95- *Personal Data:* b New York, NY, Apr 5, 39; m 60, Judith Koral; c Marcia & Mark. *Educ:* Brooklyn Col, BS, 60; Univ Wash, Seattle, PhD(physics), 65. *Honors & Awards:* Japan Prize for Television, Mech Universe, 87. *Prof Exp:* Asst physics, Univ Wash, Seattle, 60-61, res instr, 65-66; res fel, Calif Inst Technol, 66-67; NSF fel, Univ Rome, 67-68. *Concurrent Pos:* Sloan fel, Calif Inst Technol, 69-71; NATO vis prof, Frascati Nat Lab, Italy, 72 & res collabr, 73-; creator & host, The Mech Universe & Beyond, PBS Educ Ser, 82-87; bd dir, Calif Coun Sci & Technol, 88- *Mem:* Fel AAAS; Sigma Xi. *Res:* Thermal properties of helium and other gases in thin films; two dimensional matter; surfaces; interfaces; phase transtitions. *Mailing Add:* Calif Inst Technol Pasadena CA 91125. *Fax:* 626-796-7820; *E-Mail:* dg@cco.caltech.edu

GOODSTEIN, MADELINE P, SCIENCE EDUCATION, CHEMISTRY. *Current Pos:* CONSULT, 87- *Personal Data:* b New York, NY, Oct 23, 20; m 47, Julian; c Elaine (Alexander), Barbara & Ronald. *Educ:* Brooklyn Col, BA, 41; Polytech Inst Brooklyn, MS, 48; Columbia Univ, EdD(chem), 68. *Prof Exp:* Chemist, Trubek Labs, 41-47, consult, 48; asst prof chem, Cent Conn State Univ, 68-71, assoc prof, 71-77, prof, 78-83; dir, US Dept Educ, Nat Diffusion Network, Sci-Math Proj, 83-87; dir, Proj Ramps, 92-96. *Concurrent Pos:* Dir, NSF Teacher Inst, 72-73 & NSF Curric Proj, 77-79 & 79-82; ed, Conn J Sci Educ, 76-79; ed, NEACT J, 90-92. *Mem:* Am Chem Soc; Nat Sci Teachers Asn. *Res:* Oxidation-reduction concept; science education for non-scientist; art chemistry. *Mailing Add:* 6 Woodland Dr Woodbridge CT 06525. *E-Mail:* mgoodste@inet.ed.gov, goodstein@scsud. ctstateu.edu

GOODWILL, ROBERT, QUANTITATIVE GENETICS, POPULATION GENETICS. *Current Pos:* asst prof, 69-75, ASSOC PROF ANIMAL SCI, UNIV KY; 75- *Personal Data:* b Ridgeway, Pa, Dec 13, 36; m 65; c 2. *Educ:* State Univ NY, Col Fredonia, BS, 63; Univ Minn, PhD(genetics), 69. *Prof Exp:* Asst prof biol, Bemidji State Col, 68-69. *Mem:* AAAS; Genetics Soc Am; Am Genetic Asn; Am Inst Biol Scientists; Am Soc Animal Sci. *Res:* Experimental evaluation of population and quantitative genetic theory using Tribolium castaneum and computer simulation. *Mailing Add:* 92102 Bayou Dr Tampa FL 33635

GOODWIN, ARTHUR VANKLEEK, SOLENOID DESIGN, VALVE DESIGN. *Current Pos:* CONSULT, 90- *Personal Data:* b Hartford, Conn, Feb 1, 40; m 64; c 2. *Educ:* Bates Col, BS, 63. *Prof Exp:* Engr, Chandler-Evans, Div of Colt Indust, 63-68, Hamilton Stand, Div of United Technol, 68-72; engr, Wright Components Inc, 72-74, chief engr, 74-77, chief engr & dir, 77-83, chief engr, EG&G Wright Components, 83-86, vpres eng, 86-90. *Mem:* Am Inst Aeronaut & Astronaut. *Res:* Magnetic circuit design and solenoid equations. *Mailing Add:* 28 Charter Oaks Dr Pittsford NY 14534

GOODWIN, BRUCE K, GEOLOGY. *Current Pos:* from asst prof to assoc prof, 63-71, chmn dept, 70-76 & 83-88, PROF GEOL, COL WILLIAM & MARY, 71-, CHMN DEPT, 92- *Personal Data:* b Providence, RI, Oct 14, 31; m 56, c 3. *Educ:* Univ Pa, AB, 53; Lehigh Univ, MS, 57, PhD(geol), 59. *Prof Exp:* Instr geol, Univ Pa, 59-63. *Mem:* AAAS; fel Geol Soc Am; Nat Asn Geol Teachers; Sigma Xi; Am Inst Prof Geologists; Coun Undergrad Res. *Res:* Geology of the eastern piedmont of North America; Triassic Richmond basin and other Triassic-Jurassic basins; structural geology. *Mailing Add:* Dept Geol Col William & Mary Williamsburg VA 23187-8795. *Fax:* 804-221-3540; *E-Mail:* bkgood@mail.wm.edu

GOODWIN, CHARLES ARTHUR, SOLID STATE ELECTRONICS, CERAMICS. *Current Pos:* mem tech staff, 73-80, PRIN TECH STAFF, BELL LABS, 80- *Personal Data:* b Oneida, NY, Sept 6, 47; m 69; c 2. *Educ:* Alfred Univ, BS, 69; Mass Inst Technol, PhD(ceramics), 73. *Mem:* Am Ceramic Soc; Electrochem Soc. *Res:* Electronic devices including metal-oxide-silicon integrated circuits. *Mailing Add:* AT&T Bell Labs 2525 N 12th St Wyomissing PA 19610

GOODWIN, FRANK ERIK, NONFERROUS METALLURGY, CORROSION OF METALS. *Current Pos:* VPRES, INT LEAD ZINC RES ORGN, 86- *Personal Data:* b Bethlehem, Pa, Jan 6, 54; m 87, Rosalind Volpe; c Adrian E & Marianna R. *Educ:* Cornell Univ, BS, 75; Mass Inst Tech, SM, 76, ScD(mat eng), 79. *Prof Exp:* Metallurgist, Chambersburg Eng Co, 79-81; asst dir prod & process develop, Chromalloy Am Corp, 81-82; mgr develop, Int Lead Zinc Res Orgn, 82-83; mgr metall, 83-86. *Concurrent Pos:* Postdoctoral fel, Mass Inst Technol, 79. *Mem:* Am Soc Mats Int; Iron & Steel Soc; Am Inst Metall Engrs; Am Foundrymen's Soc; Am Soc Testing & Mat; NY Acad Sci. *Res:* Development of new uses and improvement of existing uses of lead and zinc metals; areas of specialization are die casting, steel coatings, nuclear waste containment, composite structures and resistance welding; processing and properties of high strength galvanized steels; creep resistant casting alloys; high voltage cable sheathing alloys; earthquake dampers. *Mailing Add:* PO Box 12036 Res Triangle Park NC 27709-2036

GOODWIN, FREDERICK KING, NEUROLOGY. *Current Pos:* PROF PSYCHIAT & DIR, CTR NEUROSCI, MED PROGRESS & SOC, GEORGE WASHINGTON UNIV, 94- *Personal Data:* b Cincinnati, Ohio, Apr 21, 36; m 63, Rose Mary P; c 3. *Educ:* Georgetown Univ, BS, 58; St Louis Univ, MD, 63. *Honors & Awards:* A E Bennett Award for Clin Res, Soc Biol Psychiat, 70; Psychopharmacol Res Prize, Am Psychol Asn, 70; Hofheimer Prize, Am Psychiat Asn, 71; Int Anna-Monika Prize, 71; Taylor Manor Award, 76; Edward A Strecker Award, 83; George C Ham Mem Lectr, Univ NC, Chapel Hill, 84; David C Wilson Lectr, Univ Va, Charlottesville, 85; Theodore L Dehne MD Mem Lect, Friends Hosp Clin Conf, 87; John P McGovern Award Lect, Asn Acad Health Ctrs, 90; Herbert S Ripley Lect, Univ Wash, 91; Mathilde Soloway Award Lect in Neurosci, Found Advan Educ Sci, NIH, 94; Distinguishe Serv Award, Nat Alliance Ment Ill, 94; Richard Simpson Mem Award, Icurably Ill for Animal Res, 94. *Prof Exp:* Fel philos, St Louis Univ, 58-59, Wash Sch Psychiat, 69-71; res asst, Lab Clin Biochem, Nat Heart Inst, NIH, 60, 61 & 62, spec res fel, 67-68; chief, Clin Res Unit, Sect Psychiat, Lab Clin Sci, NIMH, NIH, 68-73; chief, Sect Psychiat, 73-77, chief, Clin Psychol Br, 77-81, dir, Intramural Res Prog, 82-88, adminr, Alcohol Drug Abuse & Ment Health Admin, 88-92, dir, 92-94. *Concurrent Pos:* Res psychiatrist, Univ NC, Chapel Hill, 64-65; clin assoc, Adult Psychiat Br, NIMH, 65-67; vis prof, Univ Wis, 76, Boston Univ, 76, Univ Calif, 77, Univ Southern Calif, 79, Duke Univ, 79- & Univ Tenn, 86; consult, Coun Res, Am Psychiat Asn, 83-88; assoc ed, J Neuropsychiat & Clin Neurosci, 88-; sr sci adv to dir, NIMH, 94- *Mem:* Inst Med-Nat Acad Sci; AAAS; Am Philos Asn; fel Am Psychiat Soc; Am Psychosomatic Soc; Soc Biol Psychiat; Am Acad Psychoanal; Soc Neurosci; Am Psychopath Asn; Psychiat Res Soc; Am Soc Clin Psychopharmacol; Ger Psychiat Soc; Soc Light Treatment & Biol Rhythm. *Res:* Psychiatry and psychopharmacology; major depression and manic-depressive illness; author of 7 books and over 368 publications. *Mailing Add:* Ctr Neurosci Med Progress & Soc 2300 1 St NW Ross Hall 514 Washington DC 20037. *Fax:* 301-443-2578

GOODWIN, GENE M, joining, for more information see previous edition

GOODWIN, JAMES CRAWFORD, ORGANIC & CARBOHYDRATE CHEMISTRY, SPECIFICALLY IN NONENZYMATIC BROWNING REACTIONS. *Current Pos:* CHEM PROF, PHILANDER SMITH COL, LITTLE ROCK, ARK, 89- *Personal Data:* b Camden, Ark, Mar 21, 26; wid, Bobbie J Hawkins; c Dennis M, Danny K, Phillip L, Vicki L & Carter M. *Educ:* Philander Smith Col, Ark, BS, 49; Ore State Univ, MS, 59. *Prof Exp:* Teacher chem, Hempstead County Sch Dist, Ark, 49-54, Little Rock Sch Dist, 57-58 & Grambling State Univ, La, 59-60; res chemist org chem, USDA Northern Regional Res Ctr, Peoria, Ill, 61-89. *Concurrent Pos:* Fel, NSF, 58-59; teacher chem, Ill Cent Col, East Peoria, 80-81. *Mem:* Nat Orgn Prof Advan Black Chemists & Chem Engrs; Am Chem Soc; Nat Inst Sci; Am Asn Univ Profs. *Res:* Organic-carbohydrate chemistry; correlation of stereochemical structure of simple sugars and sugar analogs with their sweet and bitter tastes; carbohydrate chemistry, specifically in nonenzymatic browning reactions and organic reactions and structure of carbohydrates; food science and technology; author or co-author of 34 publications. *Mailing Add:* 5 Peachtree Pl Little Rock AR 72204-8516

GOODWIN, JAMES GORDON, JR, HETEROGENEOUS CATALYSIS, KINETICS. *Current Pos:* from asst prof to assoc prof, 79-87, PROF CHEM ENG, UNIV PITTSBURGH, 87-, WILLIAM DEPLER WHITEFORD PROF CHEM ENGR, 90- *Personal Data:* b Walterboro, SC, Dec 14, 45; m 94, Carol Shoemaker. *Educ:* Clemson Univ, BS, 67; Ga Inst Technol, MS, 69; Univ Mich, PhD(chem eng), 76. *Prof Exp:* Instr math, Nasson Col, 68-69, Middle East Tech Univ, 69-70 & Univ Liberia, 70-71; res asst catalysis, Univ Mich, 73-76; exchange scientist, French Inst Catalysis, 77-78; asst prof chem eng, Univ SC, 78-79. *Concurrent Pos:* Consult, Altamira Instruments, 84-, Gas-to-Oil, 86-89, Energy Int, 91-; guest prof, Tech Univ, Vienna, 87- *Mem:* Am Inst Chem Engrs; Am Chem Soc; NAm Catalysis Soc. *Res:* Analysis of catalytically active surfaces; synthesis of chemicals and fuels from natural gas and coal; catalyst modification; zeolite-based catalysts; metal catalysts. *Mailing Add:* Dept Chem & Petrol Eng 1249 Benedum Hall Univ Pittsburgh Pittsburgh PA 15261-2212. *Fax:* 412-624-9639

GOODWIN, JAMES SIMEON, GERIATRICS. *Current Pos:* PROF MED & CHIEF GERIAT, UNIV WIS, MILWAUKEE, 88- *Personal Data:* b Cleveland, Ohio, May 19, 45; m; c 4. *Educ:* Amherst Col, BA, 67; Harvard Univ, MD, 71; Am Bd Internal Med, cert, 76, cert rheumatology, 78. *Prof Exp:* Intern, Harbor Gen Hosp, 71-72; staff assoc, Nat Heart & Lung Inst, NIH, 72-74; resident internal med, Sch Med, Univ NMex, 74-76, fel rheumatology, 76-78, from asst prof to res prof, Dept Med, 78-87, chief, Div Geront, 80-85; prof & vchmn, Dept Med, Med Col Wis, 88- *Concurrent Pos:* Nat Inst Allergy & Infectious Dis young investr award, 78-81; Nat Inst Aging res grants, 79-96; mem, Ad Hoc Study Sect Immunol Sci, NIH, 79, Subcomt Nutrit & Rheumatic Dis, Nat Inst Aging Res Planning Panel, 82, Fel Selection Comt, Nat Arthritis Found, 85-89, Arthritis Ctr Rev, NIH, 85, Nat Prog Comt, Am Rheumatologic Asn, 87, Clin Liaison Team, Nat Res Agenda Aging, Nat Acad Sci, Inst Med, 88-89 & Prog Comt, Am Asn Immunologists, 88-91; assoc ed, J Immunol, 85-89; chmn, Inflammation-Immunopharmacol Block, Am Asn Immunologists, 88-91; dir, Div Geriat Med, Univ Tex Med Br, Galveston, Tex, dir, Ctr Aging, George & Cynthia Mitchell distinguished prof; med dir, Sinai Samaritan Geriat Inst. *Mem:* Am soc Clin Invest; Am Rheumatologic Asn; Am Fedn Clin Res; Am Asn Immunologists; Am Geront Asn; Am Geriat Soc. *Res:* Immunobiology of aging; role of arachidonic acid metabolites in modulation of the immune response; effects of subclinical malnutrition in the elderly; patterns of cancer care in the elderly; author of more than 180 technical publications. *Mailing Add:* 2619 Christopher Dr Galveston TX 77551

GOODWIN, JESSE FRANCIS, CLINICAL BIOCHEMISTRY, ANALYTICAL CHEMISTRY. *Current Pos:* RETIRED. *Personal Data:* b Greenville, SC, Feb 7, 29; div; c Gordon F, Jesse Stephen & Paula (Hammond). *Educ:* Xavier Univ, La, BS, 51; Wayne State Univ, MS, 53, PhD(chem), 57. *Prof Exp:* Res assoc, Col Med & spec instr, Col Pharm, Wayne State Univ, 58-59; clin biochemist, Wayne Co Gen Hosp, Eloise, Mich, 58-62; instr pediat, Col Med, Wayne State Univ, 64-66, asst prof biochem, 66-70, dir, Core Lab, Gen Clin Res Ctr Childrens Hosp & Sch Med, 63-73, asst prof pediat, Col Med, 70-73; dir labs, Detroit Health Dept, 73-97. *Concurrent Pos:* Biochemist, Dept Labs, Children's Hosp, Detroit; bd trustees, Horizon Health Systs, Southfield, Mich, 82-, Marygrove Col, Detroit, Mich, 77-83, 85-93; bd dirs, Am Asn Clin Chem, 87-89, Nat Acad Clin Biochem, 86 & Loyola High Sch, Detroit, Mich; bd, Archdioces Detroit Educ Advan Comt. *Mem:* AAAS; Am Chem Soc; Am Pub Health Asn; fel Am Inst Chemists; Am Asn Clin Chem; fel Nat Acad Clin Biochem. *Res:* Methodology in clinical chemistry procedures; metabolism of muco-polysaccharides, chelates and gold; clinical chemistry methodology, trace metal estimation, amino acid estimation and carbohydrate interaction with various amines; methodology in carbohydrate, protein, drug and trace metal estimation analysis; seroprevalence studies; AIDS. *Mailing Add:* 8447 Mangrove Dr Detroit MI 48221-2942

GOODWIN, JOHN THOMAS, JR, ORGANIC CHEMISTRY. *Current Pos:* CONSULT, 79- *Personal Data:* b San Diego, Calif, May 28, 14; m 38, Olla G Whitelock; c John III, Nancy, Sharon, Heidi & Tanya. *Educ:* Okla Agr & Mech Col, BS, 36; Univ Pittsburgh, PhD(org chem), 48. *Prof Exp:* Chemist, Mid-Continent Petrol Corp, 36-39; asst org chem, Univ Pittsburgh, 39-40; res chemist, Gulf Res & Develop Co, Pa, 40-41; fel, Mellon Inst, 41-43, indust fel, 46, sr fel, 46-49; group leader, Dow Corning Corp, 49-51; chemist, Gen Elec Co, 51-54; mgr chem res, Midwest Res Inst, 54-57; vpres, Corn Industs Res Found Inc, DC, 57-65; vpres chem & chem eng, Southwest Res Inst, 65-79. *Mem:* AAAS; Am Chem Soc; fel NY Acad Sci. *Res:* Microencapsulation; membrane technology; radiation polymerization; organosilicon chemistry; carbohydrates. *Mailing Add:* PO Box 28510 San Antonio TX 78228

GOODWIN, KENNETH, GENETICS. *Current Pos:* prof poultry sci & head dept, 66-84, EMER PROF, PA STATE UNIV, 84- *Personal Data:* b New York, NY, Sept 30, 20; m 47; c 1. *Educ:* Cornell Univ, BS, 48, MS, 50, PhD(animal genetics), 52. *Prof Exp:* Asst animal genetics, Cornell Univ, 48-52; geneticist, Kimber Farms, Inc, Calif, 52-64 & Heisdorf & Nelson Farms, Inc, 64-66. *Mem:* Fel AAAS; Genetics Soc Am; Am Genetic Asn; fel Poultry Sci Asn. *Res:* Genetics of poultry; improvement of economic characters; genetics and disease resistance. *Mailing Add:* Dept Poultry Sci Pa State Univ 222 Henning Bldg University Park PA 16802. *Fax:* 814-865-5691

GOODWIN, LESTER KEPNER, NUCLEAR SCIENCE. *Current Pos:* PHYSICIST, AERONUTRONIC-FORD, 73- *Personal Data:* b Casper, Wyo, July 2, 28; m 58; c 1. *Educ:* Calif Inst Technol, BS, 50; Univ Calif, Berkeley, MA, 57, PhD(physics), 60. *Prof Exp:* Physicist, Los Alamos Sci Lab, 51-53 & 56 & Lawrence Radiation Lab, Univ Calif, 60; physicist, Aeronutronic Div, Ford Motor Co, 60-63, sect supvr, Aeronutronic Div, Philco Corp, 63-69; sr scientist, KMS Technol Ctr, 69-73. *Mem:* AAAS; Am Phys Soc; Sigma Xi. *Res:* Laser effects; nuclear weapons effects; neutron, gamma and meson cross-section measurements; aerosol research; nuclear weapon testing; rfion-source development; application of gamma rays to reentry erosion measurements. *Mailing Add:* 303 Esperanza Newport Beach CA 92660-3923

GOODWIN, MELVIN HARRIS, JR, EPIDEMIOLOGY, PARASITOLOGY. *Current Pos:* prof family & community med & sr epidemiologist, 77-87, SR CLIN LECTR, UNIV ARIZ, COL MED, 88- *Personal Data:* b Thomasville, Ga, Jan 9, 17; m 42, Virginia Peacock; c Siana & Melvin H. *Educ:* Univ Ga, BS, 41, MS, 51; Emory Univ, PhD(parasitol), 55. *Prof Exp:* Asst, Rabies Lab, State Dept Health, Ga, 38-39, malaria control biologist, 42-43; mem staff, Entom Div, Commun Dis Ctr, USPHS, 44-46, chief lib & reports div, 47-48, chief malaria invests sect, 49-53, asst chief invests, Tech Br, 53-57, chief, Phoenix Field Sta, 57-66; dir, Div Prev Med Serv, Ariz State Health Dept, 66-69; dir, Ariz Health Planning Authority, 69-74; consult, health & environ sci, 74-75; dir health studies, Copley Int Corp, 76-77. *Concurrent Pos:* Biologist-in-chg malaria res sta, Emory Univ, 39-42, dir, 44-57, assoc, Sch Med, 48-57. *Mem:* AAAS; Am Pub Health Asn; Sigma Xi; Am Soc Trop Med & Hyg. *Res:* Epidemiology; ecology of enteric diseases, malaria and other infectious diseases. *Mailing Add:* 327 W Orchid Lane Phoenix AZ 85021

GOODWIN, PAUL NEWCOMB, RADIOLOGICAL PHYSICS. *Current Pos:* RETIRED. *Personal Data:* b Evanston, Ill, Nov 3, 26; m 51, EmmaLeigh Lambeth; c Thomas & Margaret. *Educ:* Harvard Univ, BS, 48; Johns Hopkins Univ, MA, 56; Univ London, PhD(med physics), 59; Am Bd Radiol & Am Bd Health Physics, dipl, 61. *Prof Exp:* Physicist, USPHS Hosp, Baltimore, 49-56; USPHS fel, Royal Cancer Hosp, London, Eng, 56-59, Radiol Dept, Johns Hopkins Hosp, 59-66; asst prof radiol, Sch Med & Sch Hyg & Pub Health, Johns Hopkins Univ, 62-66; asst prof, Col Physicians & Surgeons, Columbia-Presby Med Ctr, Columbia Univ, 66-71; assoc prof radio, Albert Einstein Col Med, Yeshiva Univ, 71-94, assoc prof nuclear med, 87-94. *Mem:* Health Physics Soc; Am Asn Physicists Med; Soc Nuclear Med; fel Am Col Med Physics; Am Col Radiol. *Res:* Radiological physics; medical application of radiation and radioactive isotopes; radiation dosimetry and protection; calorimetric measurement of x-rays; computed tomography; bone mineral measurement. *Mailing Add:* 122 Locust Dr Nyack NY 10960

GOODWIN, PETER WARREN, STRATIGRAPHY. *Current Pos:* From instr to assoc prof, 63-83, PROF GEOL, TEMPLE UNIV, 83- *Personal Data:* b Wilmington, Del, Apr 12, 36; m 84; c 2. *Educ:* Dartmouth Col, AB, 58; Univ Iowa, MS, 61, PhD(geol), 64. *Concurrent Pos:* Chmn geol dept, Temple Univ, 76-87. *Mem:* Geol Soc Am; Soc Econ Palentologists & Mineralogists; Int Asn Sedimentologists. *Res:* Paleozoic stratigraphy of Appalachian Basin; paleoenvironments and paleogeography; punctuated aggradational cycles (PACs); general model of episodic stratigraphic accumulation. *Mailing Add:* Dept Geol Temple Univ 1701 N Broad St Philadelphia PA 19122-2504

GOODWIN, RICHARD HALE, BOTANY, MANAGEMENT OF NATURAL AREAS. *Current Pos:* dir arboretum, 44-65, prof, 44-76, EMER PROF BOT, CONN COL, 76- *Personal Data:* b Brookline, Mass, Dec 14, 10; m 36, Esther Bemis; c Mary G (Wetzel) & Richard H Jr. *Educ:* Harvard Univ, AB, 33, MA, 34, PhD(biol), 37. *Honors & Awards:* Environ Merit Award, Environ Protection Agency, 90. *Prof Exp:* Am-Scand Found fel, Copenhagen, 37-38; instr bot, Univ Rochester, 38-41, asst prof, 41-44. *Concurrent Pos:* Comnr, Conn Geol & Natural Hist Surv, 45-72; pres, Conserv & Res Found, 53-94 & Nature Conservancy, 56-58 & 64-66; mem biol coun, Nat Res Coun, 53-57; bd dirs, Am Inst Biol Sci, 62-71. *Mem:* AAAS; Bot Soc Am; Soc Study Develop & Growth (secy, 49-53); fel Am Acad Arts & Sci; Inst Ecol (treas, 75-77). *Res:* Effect of light on growth of plants; physiology of growth; plant hormones; fluorescent substances in plants; morphogenesis of roots; bioecology of natural areas. *Mailing Add:* Dept Bot Conn Col New London CT 06320

GOODWIN, ROBERT ARCHER, JR, INTERNAL MEDICINE. *Current Pos:* RETIRED. *Personal Data:* b Kuling, China, Aug 3, 14; US citizen; m 44; c 3. *Educ:* Univ Va, BS, 36; Johns Hopkins Univ, MD, 40. *Prof Exp:* Asst res physician, Thorndike Mem Lab, Boston City Hosp, 41-42; from asst resident to resident physician, Hosp, Vanderbilt Univ, 46-47, from instr to asst prof, Univ, 46-56, assoc prof clin med, 56-74, prof, 74-81, emer prof med, 81- *Concurrent Pos:* Chief pulmonary dis serv, Vet Admin Hosp, 47-81. *Mem:* Am Thoracic Soc; fel Am Col Physicians. *Res:* Infectious diseases; pulmonary diseases. *Mailing Add:* 3720 Benham Ave Nashville TN 37215

GOODWIN, ROBERT EARL, VERTEBRATE ECOLOGY & SYSTEMATICS. *Current Pos:* Instr comp anat, Colgate Univ, 59-67, assoc prof, 67-70, chmn, Dept Biol, 81-84, PROF ZOOL, COLGATE UNIV, 70- *Personal Data:* b Rensselaer, NY, May 16, 26; m 54; c 2. *Educ:* Hartwick Col, BS, 51; Cornell Univ, MS, 53, PhD(vert zool), 60. *Mem:* Am Soc Mammal; Am Ornith Union. *Res:* Ecology, behavior and systematics of vertebrates, particularly bats. *Mailing Add:* Dept Biol Colgate Univ Hamilton NY 13346-1383

GOODWIN, RONALD HAYSE, INSECT PATHOLOGY, CELL BIOLOGY. *Current Pos:* RETIRED. *Personal Data:* b Los Angeles, Calif, Oct 15, 33; m 66, Edna A Unger; c 2. *Educ:* Univ Calif, Berkeley, BS, 56, MS, 61, PhD(insect path), 66. *Prof Exp:* Res scientist insect path, Commonwealth Sci & Indust Res Org, Div Entom, Australia, 66-69; res entomologist insect virol & tissue cult, Insect Path Lab, Agr Res Serv, USDA, 69-92; consult, Am Cynamid, 92-94. *Concurrent Pos:* Res fel entomol, Nat Res Coun, Agr Res Serv, 69-71; adv, Subcomt Invert Viruses, Int Comt Nomenclature Viruses, 68-75. *Mem:* Soc Invert Path; Tissue Cult Asn; Entom Soc Am. *Res:* Insect cell biology and cell culture for the study of insect pathogens, primarily arthropod specific viruses of the baculovirus and entomopoxvirus groups. *Mailing Add:* PO Box 6039 Bozeman MT 59771

GOODWIN, SIDNEY S, MINING GEOLOGY. *Current Pos:* RETIRED. *Personal Data:* b Corbin, Ky, May 3, 06. *Educ:* Univ Ky, BS, 28. *Prof Exp:* From mining geologist to vpres explor & mining, NJ Zinc Co, 30-71; consult, 71-73. *Mem:* Fel Geol Soc Am; Soc Econ Geologists; Geochem Soc; Am Inst Mining & Metall Engrs; Mining & Metall Soc Am. *Mailing Add:* 1902 Huntington Chase Atlanta GA 30350

GOODWIN, STEPHEN BRUCE, POPULATION GENETICS, EVOLUTION OF HOST-PATHOGEN INTERACTIONS. *Current Pos:* RES ASSOC, CORNELL UNIV, 87- *Personal Data:* b Bethlehem, Pa, Oct 27, 58. *Educ:* Duke Univ, BS, 81; Univ Calif, Davis, PhD(genetics), 88. *Concurrent Pos:* Vis prof, Univ Campinas, Brazil, 92. *Mem:* Genetics Soc Am; Soc Study Evolution; Am Phytopath Soc. *Res:* Genetics, population genetics and evolution of plant pathogenic fungi and of plant-pathogen co-evolution; genetics of the speciation process in plant pathogenic fungi; migration of fungi. *Mailing Add:* Botany & Plant Path Purdue Univ 1155 Lily Hall West Lafayette IN 47907-1155. *Fax:* 607-255-4471; *E-Mail:* sbg2@rsrch1.cit.cornell.edu

GOODWIN, THOMAS ELTON, ORGANIC CHEMISTRY. *Current Pos:* ASST PROF ORG CHEM, HENDRIX COL, 78- *Personal Data:* b Nashville, Ark, Aug 8, 47; m 70; c 2. *Educ:* Ouachita Baptist Univ, BS, 69; Univ Ark, PhD(chem), 74. *Prof Exp:* Robert A Welch fel org chem, Rice Univ, 74-75; res scientist, Continental Oil Co, 75-76; lectr & res assoc, Tex A&M Univ, 76-78. *Mem:* Am Chem Soc. *Res:* Organic synthesis; natural products synthesis; the synthesis of therapeutically active organic chemicals. *Mailing Add:* Dept Chem Hendrix Col Conway AR 72032-3099

GOODWIN, TOMMY LEE, FOOD SCIENCE. *Current Pos:* PRES, GOODWIN & ASSOCS, 91- *Personal Data:* b Little Rock, Ark, Apr 6, 36; m 59, Alice Featherston; c Greg & Kelli (Peters). *Educ:* Univ Ark, BSA, 58, MS, 60; Purdue Univ, PhD(food technol), 62. *Honors & Awards:* Res Award, Poultry & Egg Inst Am, 75. *Prof Exp:* From asst prof to prof poultry prod technol, Univ Ark, Fayetteville, 64-86; sr vpres, Pilgrim's Pride Corp, 86-91. *Mem:* Inst Food Technol; Poultry Sci Asn; World's Poultry Sci. *Res:* Factors affecting nutrition, quality and tenderness of poultry meat and improving quality of eggs; meat yields. *Mailing Add:* Rte 1 Box 71 Pittsburg TX 75686. *Fax:* 903-856-6433

GOODWIN, WILLIAM JENNINGS, medical entomology, for more information see previous edition

GOODWINE, JAMES K, JR, MECHANICAL & AUTOMOTIVE ENGINEERING, TECHNICAL MANAGEMENT. *Current Pos:* RETIRED. *Personal Data:* b Evanston, Ill, Mar 9, 30; m 59, Helen Murray; c 2. *Educ:* Purdue Univ, BS, 52, MS, 56, PhD(mech eng), 60. *Prof Exp:* Res asst mech eng, Purdue Univ, 56-57, instr, 57-59; res engr petrol prod, Chevron Res Co, 59-67; staff engr, Eng Dept, United Airlines, 67-70, mgr, power plant eng, 70-79, new aircraft & oper eng, 79-82, dir, engine tech serv, 82-87, mgr new technol eng, 87-89. *Mem:* Soc Automotive Engrs; Sigma Xi. *Res:* Petroleum products, especially jet fuels and gasolines; fundamentals of combustion, including computer simulation of engine cycles; turbine engine maintenance; aircraft performance; aircraft maintenance systems and facilities. *Mailing Add:* 1423 Enchanted Way San Mateo CA 94402

GOODWYN, JACK RAY, POLYMER CHEMISTRY. *Current Pos:* RETIRED. *Personal Data:* b Center, Tex, June 28, 34; m 55; c 3. *Educ:* Baylor Univ, BA, 56, PhD(phys chem), 60. *Prof Exp:* Chemist, Tex Eastman Co, 60-65, sr chemist, Plastics Lab, 65-73, asst to mgr, 73-76, mem, Staff Prod Dept, 76-77, coordr, Clean Environ Prog, 77-97. *Mem:* Am Chem Soc; Soc Plastics Engrs; Air Pollution Control Fedn. *Res:* Molecular structure of high polymers. *Mailing Add:* 1113 Windsong Lane Longview TX 75604-2816

GOODY, RICHARD (MEAD), ATMOSPHERIC PHYSICS. *Current Pos:* RETIRED. *Personal Data:* b Eng, June 19, 21; nat US; m; c 1. *Educ:* Univ Cambridge, BA, 42, PhD, 49. *Hon Degrees:* AM, Harvard Univ, 58. *Honors & Awards:* Buchan Prize, Royal Meteorol Soc, 58; 50th Anniversary Medal, Am Meteorol Soc, 70 & Cleveland Abbe Award, 77; Pub Serv Medal, NASA, 80. *Prof Exp:* Sci officer, Ministry Aircraft Prod, Eng, 42-46; fel, St John's Col, Univ Cambridge, 50-53; reader, Imp Col, Univ London, 53-58; Abbott Lawrence Rotch prof dynamic meteorol & dir, Blue Hill Meteorol Observ, Harvard Univ, 58-68, Mallinckrodt prof planetary physics, 70-91, dir, Ctr Earth & Planetary Physics, 71-74, Gordon McKay prof appl physics, 80-91. *Mem:* Nat Acad Sci; Am Meteorol Soc; Am Acad Arts & Sci; Royal Meteorol Soc. *Res:* Physics and dynamics of the atmospheres of the earth and other planets; infrared spectroscopy. *Mailing Add:* 101 Cumloden Dr PO Box 430 Falmouth MA 02541-0430

GOODYEAR, WILLIAM FREDERICK, JR, wood and technology; deceased, see previous edition for last biography

GOODYER, ALLAN VICTOR, cardiovascular diseases, for more information see previous edition

GOODZEIT, CARL LEONARD, MECHANICAL ENGINEERING. *Current Pos:* MECH ENGR, BROOKHAVEN NAT LAB, 59- *Personal Data:* b Newark, NJ, Mar 19, 28; m 64; c 4. *Educ:* Rutgers Univ, BSc, 50; Brown Univ, ScM, 59. *Prof Exp:* Res engr, Gen Motors Res Labs, 50-59. *Res:* Structural mechanics; computer methods in mechanical design; high energy physics. *Mailing Add:* 1409 Yardley Pl DeSoto TX 75115

GOON, DAVID JAMES WONG, MEDICINAL CHEMISTRY. *Current Pos:* PRIN SYNTHETIC CHEMIST, LECTEC CORP, MINNOTONKA, MINN, 94- *Personal Data:* b LaCrosse, Wis, Jan 15, 42. *Educ:* Univ Minn, Minneapolis, BCh, 64; Univ Ill, Urbana, MS, 66, PhD(org chem), 68. *Prof Exp:* Fel chem, Univ Ill, Chicago Circle, 68-69, instr, 68-70; teaching fel, Univ Guelph, 70-71; sr res chemist, Gen Mills, Inc, Minneapolis, 72; instr, Normandale Community Col, Bloomington, Minn, 76-84; asst prof, Univ Wisc, Eau Claire, 85-87; asst scientist, Gen Clin Res Ctr, Univ Minn, Minneapolis, 72-73, res fel, Dept Med Chem, 74-76, assoc, 89-93, res assoc, Dept Med Chem, 93-94; consult chemist, Bloomington Minn, 87-93. *Mem:* AAAS; Am Chem Soc. *Res:* Smoking cessation; transdermal drug delivery; medicinal chemistry; ethanol metabolism; kinetics and mechanism. *Mailing Add:* 8624 Columbus Ave S Bloomington MN 55420. *Fax:* 612-725-2255

GOONEWARDENE, HILARY FELIX, PLANT RESISTANCE, PLANT BREEDING. *Current Pos:* RETIRED. *Personal Data:* b Colombo, Sri Lanka, Apr 9, 25; US citizen; m 55; c Julie K (Wallin), Howard M & David R. *Educ:* Univ Sydney, BSc, 53; Univ NZ, BAgrSc, 57; Rutgers Univ, MS, 60, PhD(entom, plant path), 61. *Prof Exp:* Res officer, Comn Sci & Indust Res Org, Australia, 52-53; crop protection officer, Coconut Res Inst, Sri Lanka, 56-58; res asst entom, Rutgers Univ, 58-61, agr chem, 61; tech dir pesticides, Corona Chem Div, Pittsburgh Plate Glass Co, 61-63; head pesticides res & develop, Smith Kline & French Labs, Inc, 63-64; res entomologist, Agr Res Serv, USDA, 65-88, collabr, 88-90; emer prof entom, Dept Entom, Purdue Univ, 90-93. *Concurrent Pos:* Agr res grants adminstr for several cols, univs & industs, 61-64; consult, Pittsburgh Plate Glass, 63, Sandoz Ag Chem, 66, Marriott Facilities Mgt, 88-91, Morrisson Crolhall, 92, Unicco Serv, 93-95, Gardens Alive, 95; adj assoc prof, Col Biol Sci, Ohio State Univ & Dept Entom, Ohio Agr Res & Develop Ctr, 71-74; adj assoc prof, Purdue Univ, 74-; mem Crop Adv Comt, Malus, 87-88; vpres, Strategic Systs Inc, 93- *Mem:* Emer mem AAAS; Am Pomol Soc; emer mem Entom Soc Am; emer mem Sigma Xi; emer mem Am Soc Hort Sci. *Res:* Fruit tree breeding; insect and/or mite resistance to high quality disease-resistant cultivars and development of new cultivars with these characteristics; pest management of resistant germ plasm. *Mailing Add:* 630 Eden St West Lafayette IN 47906. *Fax:* 765-463-5031

GOOR, RONALD STEPHEN, BIOCHEMISTRY, NUTRITION. *Current Pos:* DIR, HEALTH PROSPECT ASSOCS, 86- *Personal Data:* b Washington, DC, May 31, 40; m 67; c 2. *Educ:* Swarthmore Col, BA, 62; Harvard Univ, PhD(biochem), 67, MPH, 76. *Prof Exp:* NIH fel, 67-69; staff fel biol viruses, Nat Inst Allergy & Infectious Dis, 69-70; spec asst to dir, Nat Mus Natural Hist, Smithsonian Inst, 70-72; prog mgr, Environ Aspects Trace Contaminants, Res Appl to Nat Needs, NSF, 72-76; int coordr, coronary primary prev trial, Nat Heart, Lung & Blood Inst, NIH, 76-83, coordr, Nat Cholesterol Educ Prod, 83-85. *Mem:* AAAS; Am Chem Soc; Am Soc Biol Chemists; NY Acad Sci; Am Dietetic Asn. *Res:* Environmental contamination; public health; nutrition. *Mailing Add:* 9301 Cedarcrest Dr Bethesda MD 20814

GOOREY, NANCY REYNOLDS, DENTISTRY. *Current Pos:* From instr to prof dent, Col Dent, Ohio State Univ, 55-86, dir & chmn, Div Dent Hyg, 69-86, asst dean, 76-86, EMER PROF DENT & ASST DEAN AUXILIARY PROGS, COL DENT, OHIO STATE UNIV, 86- *Personal Data:* b Davenport, Iowa; m; c 4. *Educ:* Wooster Col, BS, 40; Ohio State Univ, DDS, 55. *Concurrent Pos:* Pvt pract, Gen Dent & Gen Anesthesiol, 56-74; consult. *Mem:* Am Dent Asn; Int Asn Dent Res; Am Asn Dent Schs. *Res:* Dental hygiene. *Mailing Add:* 2201 Castle Crest Dr Worthington OH 43085

GOORVITCH, DAVID, ASTROPHYSICS. *Current Pos:* PHYSICIST, AMES RES CTR, 67- *Personal Data:* b San Pedro, Calif, July 16, 41; m 66. *Educ:* Univ Calif, Berkeley, BA, 63, PhD(physics), 67. *Mem:* Am Phys Soc; Optical Soc Am; Sigma Xi; Am Astron Soc. *Res:* Isotope shift and hyperfine structure of radioactive elements; spectroscopy of highly stripped elements; accurate wavelength determinations of thorium transitions; airborne infrared astronomy; astrophysics; infrared Fourier spectroscopy; infrared astronomy of the planets, cool stars, H-II regions and our galactic center from high altitudes. *Mailing Add:* N245-6 Ames Res Ctr Moffett Field CA 94035

GOOS, ROGER DELMON, MICROBIOLOGY. *Current Pos:* from assoc prof to prof, 70-72, chmn dept, 71-95, EMER PROF BOT, UNIV RI, 95- *Personal Data:* b Beaman, Iowa, Oct 29, 24; m 46, Mary L Engel; c Marinda L & Suzanne M. *Educ:* Univ Iowa, BA, 50, MS, 55, PhD, 58. *Prof Exp:* Teacher pub sch, Iowa, 51-53; asst bot, Univ Iowa, 53-58; mycologist, Cent Res Labs, United Fruit Co, Mass, 58-62; scientist, NIH, 62-64; cur fungi, Am Type Cult Collection, 64-68; assoc researcher bot, Univ Hawaii, 68-69, vis assoc prof, 69-70. *Concurrent Pos:* Vis res assoc, Dept Bot, Univ BC, 77 & Dept Bot, Univ Hawaii, 77, Univ Exeter, Eng, 84; vis Indo-Am fel, Univ Madras, 81; vis res, Bishop Mus, Honolulu, 90; Fulbright fel, Univ Lisbon, Port, 93. *Mem:* Mycol Soc Am (secy-treas, 80-83, vpres, 83-84, pres-elect, 84-85, pres, 85-86); Am Phytopath Soc; Brit Mycol Soc; Am Soc Microbiol; Mycol Soc Japan; AAAS. *Res:* Classification and life histories of the fungi imperfecti and ascomycetes; tropical fungi; helicosporous hyphomycetes; meliolaceous fungi. *Mailing Add:* Dept Biol Sci Univ RI Kingston RI 02881-0812. *E-Mail:* rgoos@uriacc.uri.edu

GOOSMAN, DAVID R, RADIOGRAPHY, ELECTRO-OPTICS. *Current Pos:* Physicist, 74-80, GROUP LEADER, LAWRENCE LIVERMORE LABS, 80- *Personal Data:* b Portland, Ore, Feb 6, 41. *Educ:* Reed Col, BA, 62; Calif Inst Technol, PhD(physics), 67. *Mem:* Am Phys Soc. *Mailing Add:* Lawrence Livermore Lab L-368 PO Box 808 Livermore CA 94550

GOOSSENS, JOHN CHARLES, ORGANIC POLYMER CHEMISTRY. *Current Pos:* RETIRED. *Personal Data:* b Chicago, Ill, Aug 19, 28; m 56, LaVerne Charleston; c Paul, Theresa & Joan. *Educ:* Univ Notre Dame, BS, 50; Univ Md, PhD(org chem), 57. *Prof Exp:* Asst, Wayne State Univ, 50-51; chemist, Stand Oil Co, Ind, 55-60; res chemist, Silicone Prod Dept, Gen Elec Co, Pittsfield, 60-71, res chemist, Plastics Dept, 71-77; coatings res chemist, Structured Prod Dept, Gen Elec Plastics Group, Mt Vernon, Ind, 77-88. *Mem:* Am Chem Soc. *Res:* Polymers; lubrication; organometallics. *Mailing Add:* 1612 Magnolia Ct Mt Vernon IN 47620-9304

GOOTENBERG, JOSEPH ERIC, PEDIATRIC HEMATOLOGY & ONCOLOGY. *Current Pos:* asst prof pediat, 83-89, MEM, VINCENT T LOMBARDI CANCER RES CTR, SCH MED, GEORGETOWN UNIV, 83-, CHIEF, DIV PEDIAT HEMAT-ONCOL, 88-, ASSOC PROF PEDIAT, 90- *Personal Data:* b Boston, Mass, Aug 9, 49; m. *Educ:* Harvard Col, AB, 71; Albert Einstein Col Med, MD, 75. *Prof Exp:* Pediat resident, Children's Hosp Med Ctr, Boston, 75-78; clin assoc, Pediat Oncol Br, Nat Cancer Inst, NIH, 78-80 & Lab Tumor Cell Biol, 80-82, cancer expert, 82-83. *Concurrent Pos:* Guest worker, Metab Br, Nat Cancer Inst, NIH, 75, prin investr, 83-85 & 84-88; prin investr, Div Res Resources, NIH, 83-84, Naval Med Res Inst, 86-87, Nat Inst Dent Res, 85-89, Lombardi Cancer Ctr Develop Funds, 88-89 & Hoechst-Roussel Pharmaceut, Inc, 88-90; Leukemia Soc Am spec fel, 84-86; Am Cancer Soc jr fac clin fel, 84-86; med adv, Asn Retarded Citizens, 85-; vis res assoc, Naval Med Res Inst, 86-; mem, Med Adv Bd, Ronald McDonald House, 88- *Mem:* Am Soc Hemat; Am Soc Clin Oncol; Int Asn Comp Res Leukemia & Related Dis; Am Asn Cancer Res; Am Asn Immunologists; Am Soc Pediat Hemat-Oncol; Am Acad Pediat. *Res:* Pediatric hematology-oncology; author of numerous technical publications. *Mailing Add:* Div Pediat Hemat-Oncol Vincent T Lombardi Cancer Res Ctr Georgetown Univ Hosp 3800 Reservoir Rd NW Washington DC 20007-2197. *Fax:* 202-687-6402

GOOTMAN, NORMAN, CARDIOVASCULAR DISEASES & PHYSIOLOGY. *Current Pos:* from assoc prof to prof pediat, Stony Brook, 72-89, EMER PROF PEDIAT CARDIOL, HEALTH SCI CTR, STATE UNIV NY, BROOKLYN, 94-; CLIN PROF PEDIAT, ALBERT EINSTEIN COL MED, 94- *Personal Data:* b Philadelphia, Pa, Feb 6, 33; m 58, Phyllis Madler; c Sharon H (Rosen) & Craig S. *Educ:* Univ Vt, BS, 54, MD, 58; Am Bd Pediat, dipl, 64. *Prof Exp:* Clin assoc prof pediat, Downstate Med Ctr, 65-72; assoc prof 72-75, PROF PEDIAT, SCH MED, HEALTH SCI CTR, STATE UNIV NY, STONY BROOK, 75- *Concurrent Pos:* Chief pediat cardiol, Schneider Children's Hosp, Long Island Jewish-Hillside Med Ctr, 65-90, assoc chmn pediat, 77-90, consult, 91-; consult, Queens Hosp Ctr, 65-, St Johns Episcopal, 77-, Peninsula Hosp Ctr, 77-, Jamaica Hosp, 78-, Huntington Hosp, 78-, Cent Gen Hosp, 81- & Winthrop Univ Hosp, 83-93; prof pediat, Albert Einstein Col Med, 89-94; vis prof physiol, State Univ NY Health Sci Ctr, Brooklyn, 91-, physiol & biophys, Sch Grad Studies, 93- *Mem:* Am Heart Asn; Soc Pediat Res; fel Am Col Cardiol; fel Am Acad Pediat; Am Pediat Soc; Am Physiol soc; NY Acad Sci. *Res:* Developmental aspects of neural control circulation; postnatal development of cardiovascular system; development of animal model of sudden infant death syndrome. *Mailing Add:* Dept Physiol Box 31 State Univ NY Health Ctr 450 Clarkson Ave Brooklyn NY 11203. *Fax:* 718-270-3103; *E-Mail:* gootman@hscbklyn.edu

GOOTMAN, PHYLLIS MYRNA ADLER, NEUROPHYSIOLOGY, PHYSIOLOGY. *Current Pos:* from asst prof to assoc prof, 73-81, PROF PHYSIOL, HEALTH SCI CTR, STATE UNIV NY, BROOKLYN, 81- *Personal Data:* b New York, NY, June 8, 38; m 58, Norman; c Craig S & Sharon H (Rosen). *Educ:* Columbia Univ, BA, 59; Albert Einstein Col Med, PhD(physiol), 67. *Prof Exp:* Res assoc physiol, Sch Med, Univ Wash, 63; from instr to asst prof, Albert Einstein Col Med, 68-73. *Concurrent Pos:* NIH fels, 68-69, 70-71, prin investr, 74-77, 78-81, 82-94 & 92-, mem, Study Sect Cardiovasc Renal B, 81-85; John Miles Davidson fel physiol, Albert Einstein Col Med, 73-76, vis prof, 89-; staff app pediat & consult pediat cardiol, Schneider Children's Hosp, Long Island Jewish Med Ctr, 76- *Mem:* AAAS; Am Physiol Soc; Biophys Soc; Soc Neurosci; Am Assoc Lab Animal Sci; Am Inst Biol Sci; Soc Exp Biol & Med; Int Soc Develop Neurosci; Sigma Xi; Am Autonomic Soc; fel Royal Soc Med. *Res:* Central nervous system regulation of cardiovascular function; interrelations between sympathetic vasomotor and central respiratory rhythm generators; postnatal maturation of central nervous system regulation of cardiovascular function; postnatal development of the respiratory pattern generator; electrophysiological and neuroanatomical studies of the autonomic nervous system; development of an animal model for Sudden Infant Death Syndrome. *Mailing Add:* Dept Physiol State Univ NY Health Sci Ctr Brooklyn Brooklyn NY 11203. *Fax:* 718-270-3103; *E-Mail:* gootman@hscbklyn.edu

GOPAL, RAJ, ENERGY SYSTEMS, DEMAND SIDE MANAGEMENT-TECHNICAL. *Current Pos:* PRIN ENGR, TRI/WIS ELEC, 93- *Personal Data:* b Bangalore, India, Feb 1, 42; US citizen; m 67, Parvathi Bhaskar; c Mira & Neil. *Educ:* Univ Mysore, India, BS, 63; Indian Inst Tech, Madras, India, MTech, 65; Univ Akron, PhD(mech eng), 73. *Prof Exp:* Prod mgr, Hin Dustan Ferobo Ltd, Bombay, India, 65-69; res scientist, Johnson Controls Inc, 73-84; pres, Eng Consult Serv, 84-87; res & develop mgr, Anco Consult Group, 87-93. *Concurrent Pos:* Lectr, Milwaukee Sch Eng, 85-86, Univ Wis, 86-87. *Mem:* Am Soc Mech Eng; Am Soc Heating, Refrig & Air Conditioning Engrs; Sigma Xi; Asn Energy Eng. *Res:* Technology-analysis; assessment and promotion of technologies; demand side management to electric utilities; thermal energy storage; energy management control system; HVAC and knowledge based technology evaluation and technology impact evaluation for electric utilities; improving energy efficiency of supermarket refrigeration; improving energy efficiency of plant air compressors; supermarket desiccant systems. *Mailing Add:* 6267 W Silverbrook Lane Brown Deer WI 53223-2246

GOPALAKRISHNA, K V, INFECTIOUS DISEASES, INTERNAL MEDICINE. *Current Pos:* CHIEF, INFECTIOUS DIS SECT, FAIRVIEW GEN HOSP, 76-; ASSOC CLIN PROF MED, CASE WESTERN UNIV, 77- *Personal Data:* b Mysore, India, Jan 11, 44; m 71; c 4. *Educ:* Mysore Univ, MBBS, 65. *Prof Exp:* Chief, Gen Med Sect, Vet Admin Hosp, 72-74, chief infectious dis sect, 73-76. *Concurrent Pos:* Consult, Lutheran Med Ctr, 72-, St Johns Hosp, 72-, Lakewood Hosp, 72-, Parma Community Hosp, 72- & Southwest Gen Hosp, 75- *Mem:* Am Soc Microbiol; Asn Practicioners Infection Control; Infectious Dis Soc; fel Am Col Physicians. *Res:* Pathogenesis of endocarditis; antimicrobial agents and mode of action. *Mailing Add:* 1139 Richmar Dr Westlake OH 44145

GOPALAKRISHNAN, BHASKARAN, EXPERT SYSTEMS DEVELOPMENT, MANUFACTURING SYSTEMS ENGINEERING. *Current Pos:* ASSOC PROF INDUST & MGT SYSTS ENG, WVA UNIV, 88- *Personal Data:* b Tiruchendurai, Tamilnadu, India, Aug 27, 60; m 86, Uma Gururajan; c Kamala. *Educ:* Univ Madras, BE, 83; Southern Methodist Univ, MS, 85; Va Inst Technol, PhD(indust eng), 88. *Concurrent Pos:* Prin investr, USDA Forest Serv Projs, 91-, Indust Assessment Ctr, 92- & Dept Energy/Nat Res Coun, 94- *Mem:* Sigma Xi; Soc Mfg Engrs; Inst Indust Engrs. *Res:* Manufacturing engineering artificial intelligence applications, concurrent engineering, mechatronics and energy/waste/productivity management. *Mailing Add:* 110 William St Morgantown WV 26505. *E-Mail:* gopal@cemr.wvu.edu

GOPALAKRISHNAN, KAKKALA, BIOLOGICAL OCEANOGRAPHY, INVERTEBRATE ZOOLOGY. *Current Pos:* INSTR OCEANOG, HONOLULU COMMUNITY COL, UNIV HAWAII, 75- *Personal Data:* b Kundoor, India, Mar, 42; m 71, Vijaya; c Raj. *Educ:* Univ Kerala, India, BSc, 63, MSc, 65; Scripps Inst Oceanog, Univ Calif, PhD(biol oceanog), 73. *Prof Exp:* Jr sci asst, Nat Inst Marine Biol, Indian Ocean Biol Ctr, India, 65-67; fel, Inst Marine Biol, Univ Hawaii, 71-75. *Mem:* Ecol Soc Am. *Res:* Krill (euphausid) biology, ecology and zoogeography; aquaculture, particularly crustaceans. *Mailing Add:* Dept Nat Sci Honolulu Community Col 874 Dillingham Blvd Honolulu HI 96817

GOPIKANTH, M L, ELECTROCHEMICAL ENGINEERING, ELECTROCHEMISTRY. *Current Pos:* VPRES, CSI, 86- *Personal Data:* b Mysore, India, Aug 9, 54; US citizen; m, Prathima G. *Educ:* Univ Mysore, India, BS, 72; Birla Inst Technol & Sci, Pilani, India, MS, 74; Indian Inst Sci, PhD(electrochem), 78; Northeastern Univ, Boston, Mass, MBA, 85. *Prof Exp:* Res asst, Indian Inst Sci, 78 & I Dept Chem Eng, Ill Inst Technol, Chicago, 80; sr res scientist, Cardiac Pacemakers, Inc Minn, 79-81; prin scientist, Duracell Inc, Needham, Mass, 81-85; prin engr, Life Systs, Inc, Cleveland, Ohio, 85-86. *Mem:* Sigma Xi; Am Chem Soc; Electrochem Soc. *Res:* Batteries and chemical sensors. *Mailing Add:* CSI PO Box 1067 Burlington MA 01803. *E-Mail:* mlg@msg.tl.com

GOPLEN, BERNARD PETER, GENETICS, PLANT BREEDING. *Current Pos:* RETIRED. *Personal Data:* b Griffin, Sask, March 6, 30; m 56; c 4. *Educ:* Univ Sask, BSA, 52, MSc, 55; Univ Calif, PhD(genetics), 58. *Honors & Awards:* Merit Cert, Am Forage & Grassland Coun, 86. *Prof Exp:* Asst agron, Univ Calif, 55-57; prin res scientist & head forage sect, Res Sta, Can Dept Agr, 58-93. *Concurrent Pos:* Adj prof crop sci, Univ Sask, 79-; Pres, NAm Alfalfa Improv Conf, 84-86. *Mem:* Fel Agr Inst Can (vpres, 83-84); Genetics Soc Can; Am Soc Agron; Crop Sci Soc Am; Can Soc Agron; hon life, mem, Can Seed Growers Assoc, 82. *Res:* Bloat research in legumes; developing bloat-safe alfalfa; developing low-coumarin sweetclover. *Mailing Add:* 17 Kirk Crescent Saskatoon SK S7H 3B1 Can

GOPLERUD, CLIFFORD P, OBSTETRICS & GYNECOLOGY. *Current Pos:* from asst prof to assoc prof, 58-66, PROF OBSTET & GYNEC, UNIV IOWA HOSPS, 66- *Personal Data:* b Osage, Iowa, Dec 6, 24; m 47; c 4. *Educ:* Carlton Col, 42-43; Washington & Lee Univ, 43-44; Univ Iowa, MD, 48. *Prof Exp:* Intern med, Cincinnati Gen Hosp, Ohio, 48-49; asst resident obstet & gynec, Grady Mem Hosp, 49-50, 51-52, resident, 52-53. *Mem:* AMA; Am Col Obstet & Gynec; Am Gynec Soc; Am Asn Obstet & Gynec; Asn Profs Gynec & Obstet. *Res:* Erythroblastosis; amniocentesis; diabetes in pregnancy; infectious problems in obstetric patients. *Mailing Add:* State Univ Iowa Hosps Obstet & Gynec Univ Iowa Hosp Univ Iowa Col Med Iowa City IA 52240

GORA, EDWIN KARL, THEORETICAL PHYSICS. *Current Pos:* from asst prof to prof, 49-82, chmn physics dept, 68-72, EMER PROF PHYSICS, PROVIDENCE COL, 82- *Personal Data:* b Bielsko, Poland, Oct 22, 11; nat US; m 45; c 5. *Educ:* Jagellonian Univ, Poland, PhM, 34; Univ Leipzig, Ger, ScD, 43. *Prof Exp:* Lectr physics, St Xaviers Col, India, 35-37; asst theoret physics, Univ Lwow, Poland, 37-38 & Univ Warsaw, 38-39; asst physics, Univ Munich, 44-45, lectr, 45-47, asst theoret physics, 47-48; asst prof physics, Col Steubenville, 48-49. *Concurrent Pos:* Vis prof, Univ RI, 62-63; consult, US Army Missile Command, 63-70; vis scientist, Max Planck Inst for Physics & Astrophys, 72. *Mem:* Am Phys Soc; Europ Phys Soc. *Res:* Classical and quantum theory of radiation; molecular spectroscopy; cosmology. *Mailing Add:* 86 Sandringham Ave Providence RI 02908

GORA, PAWEL, DYNAMICAL SYSTEMS, ERGODIC THEORY. *Current Pos:* asst prof, 90-93, ASSOC PROF, DEPT MATH & STATIST, CONCORDIA UNIV, 93- *Personal Data:* b Warsaw, Poland, Mar 27, 51; m 75, Ewa Duma; c Jan & Maria. *Educ:* Warsaw Univ, Master in Math, 74, PhD(math), 81, doktor habil, 91. *Prof Exp:* Asst, Warsaw Univ, 74-82, asst prof, 82-90. *Concurrent Pos:* Vis prof, Concordia Univ, 87-89. *Mem:* Polish Math Soc; Can Math Soc; Am Math Soc. *Res:* Problems of the existence and properties of absolutely continuous invariant measures for piecewise expanding transformations in one and higher dimensions. *Mailing Add:* Dept Math & Statist Concordia Univ Loyola 7141 Sherbrooke St W Montreal PQ H4B 1R6 Can. *Fax:* 514-848-2831; *E-Mail:* pgora@vax2.concordia.ca

GORA, THADDEUS F, JR, ELECTROMAGNETIC LAUNCH. *Current Pos:* Physicist, 68-88, chief, Elec Armaments Div, 89-90, SR RES SCIENTIST, ELECTROMECH, HYPERVELOCITY & PULSE POWER, US ARMY RES & DEVELOP CTR, PICTANNY ARSENAL, US ARMY, 91- *Personal Data:* b Elizabeth, NJ, Nov 16, 41; m 95, Josephine Sippie; c 1. *Educ:* Rensselaer Polytech Inst, BS, 63; Univ Del, PhD(solid state physics), 68. *Honors & Awards:* Army Res & Develop Award, US Army, 70. *Mem:* Am Phys Soc. *Res:* Band structure of psuedo-stable solids; x-ray photoelectron spectroscopy; graded band structure in heterogeneous materials; field effects in reactive solids; physics of perception; physics of electromagnetic and electrothermal launchers; pulse power physics. *Mailing Add:* 4 Dogwood Trail Kinnelon NJ 07405. *E-Mail:* tgora@pica.army.mil

GORADIA, CHANDRA P, ELECTRICAL ENGINEERING, PHYSICS. *Current Pos:* asst prof, 67-71, ASSOC PROF ELEC ENG, CLEVELAND STATE UNIV, 71- *Personal Data:* b Rajula, India, Aug 6, 39; m 69. *Educ:* Univ Bombay, BSc, 60, MSc, 62; Univ Okla, MEE, 64; PhD(elec eng), 68. *Prof Exp:* Asst res scientist, Biophys Res Lab, Tulsa Div, Avco Corp, 64-65. *Mem:* AAAS; Inst Elec & Electronics Engrs; Sigma Xi. *Res:* Semiconductor surfaces; surface barrier nuclear radiation detectors. *Mailing Add:* 12550 Lake Ave Lakewood OH 44107

GORAN, MICHAEL I, MEDICINE. *Current Pos:* RES ASST PROF, DEPT MED, DIV ENDOCRINOL, METAB & NUTRIT, UNIV VT, BURLINGTON, 89- *Personal Data:* b Glasgow, Scotland, June 19, 61. *Educ:* Univ Manchester, UK, BSc Hons, 82, PhD, 86. *Prof Exp:* Res asst, Dept Pharmacol, Hebrew Univ, Israel, 82-83; res fel, Dept Biochem, Univ Bath, UK, 86-87 & Metab Unit, Shriners Burn Inst, Tex, 87-89. *Concurrent Pos:* Prod biochemist, Makor Chemicals, Jerusalem, Israel, 82-83; reserve instr chem, Galveston Community Col, Tex, 88-89; instr, Div Human Nutrit, Med Br, Univ Tex, Galveston, 88-89; clin nutrit fel award, Am Soc Clin Nutrit, 90. *Mem:* Am Soc Clin Nutrit; Am Inst Nutrit. *Mailing Add:* Univ Ala Webb Bldg 1675 University Blvd Birmingham AL 35294. *Fax:* 205-975-7823

GORAN, MORRIS, CHEMISTRY. *Current Pos:* assoc prof chem, 46-58, PROF PHYS SCI, ROOSEVELT UNIV, 58-, CHMN DEPT, 46- *Personal Data:* b Chicago, Ill, Sept 4, 16; m 51; c 2. *Educ:* Univ Chicago, BS, 36, MS, 39, PhD(sci educ), 57. *Prof Exp:* Chemist, Dearborn Chem Co, Ill, 41-43; instr physics, Ind Univ, 43-44. *Concurrent Pos:* Lectr, George Williams Col, 51-53; res chemist, Manhattan Proj, Oak Ridge, Tenn; sr consult, Ctr Sci Anomaly Res. *Mem:* AAAS; Am Chem Soc; Am Phys Soc; Hist Sci Soc; Am Inst Chemists; Am Asn Physics Teachers. *Res:* Natural science history and methods; science education. *Mailing Add:* 7330 N Kilbourne Ave Chicago IL 60646

GORANSON, EDWIN ALEXANDER, EXPLORATION GEOLOGY, SOLID MINERALS. *Current Pos:* RETIRED. *Personal Data:* b New Westminster, BC, Nov 12, 04; m 35; c 3. *Educ:* Univ BC, BASc, 28; Harvard Univ, AM, 30, PhD(geol), 33. *Prof Exp:* From asst prof to prof, E S Larsen, Harvard Univ, 29, instr mining geol, 30-33; geologist, Labrador Explor Co, 33; geologist & engr, Base Metals Mining Corp, 33-37; geologist, E Malartic Mines, Ltd, Can, 37-43 & J P Norrie, Ltd, 43-45; consult geologist, 45-49; geologist, NJ Zinc Explor, Ltd, 49-50 & NJ Zinc Explor Co Can Ltd, 50-70, consult, 70-80. *Mem:* Fel Soc Econ Geologists; Am Inst Mining, Metall & Petrol Engrs; fel Geol Soc Can; Can Inst Mining & Metall. *Mailing Add:* 2201 Riverside Dr Apt 303 Ottawa ON K1H 5K7 Can

GORANSON, H T, UNIFIED MODELS, OPEN SYSTEMS. *Current Pos:* SR SCIENTIST, SIRIUS-BETA INC, 88- *Personal Data:* b Annapolis, Md, Apr 3, 47; m 70, Susan Loughlin; c Jesse. *Educ:* Mass Inst Technol, BSEE, 69, BS, 70, BSAD, 71. *Prof Exp:* Sr scientist, Arcturus, Inc, 69-81 & Sirius Inc, 81-88. *Concurrent Pos:* Govt tech adv, Sematech; engr, Enterprise Integration; US agent, Esprit Collab, Dept Defense. *Mem:* Am Asn Artificial Intel; Asn Comput Mach; Computer Professionals for Social Responsibility; Inst Elec & Electronics Engrs Comput Soc; Int Soc Interdisciplinary Study Symmetry. *Res:* National government and industry program in models and integrated model services; morphology of perception. *Mailing Add:* 1976 Munden Point Rd Virginia Beach VA 23457-1227. *Fax:* 757-721-0781; *E-Mail:* tedg@infi.net

GORBACH, SHERWOOD LESLIE, INFECTIOUS DISEASES, INTERNAL MEDICINE. *Current Pos:* CHIEF, INFECTIOUS DIS SECT, NEW ENG MED CTR HOSP & PROF MED, SCH MED, TUFTS UNIV, 75- *Personal Data:* b Hartford, Conn, Oct 25, 34; m; c 3. *Educ:* Brandeis Univ, BA, 55; Tufts Univ, MD, 62; London Sch Hyg & Trop Med, dipl appl parasitol & entom, 67; Am Bd Internal Med, dipl, 72. *Prof Exp:* Intern, Cornell Univ 2nd Med Div, Bellevue Hosp, 63, asst resident med, 64; vis scientist bact & gastroenterol, Postgrad Med Sch, Hammersmith Hosp, London, 66-67; instr med & pathobiol, Sch Med, Johns Hopkins Univ, 67-69; assoc prof med & microbiol, Univ Ill Col Med & dir, Dept Parasitol, Univ Ill Hosp, 69-72; prof med, Sch Med, Univ Calif, Los Angeles, 72-75; prof microbiol & immunol, 73-75. *Concurrent Pos:* Vis staff mem, Infectious Dis Hosp & Sch Trop Med, Calcutta, India, 66-67; chief, Dept Infectious Dis, Cook Co Hosp, Chicago, 70-72; chief, Infectious Dis Sect, Vet Admin Hosp, Sepulveda, Calif, 72-75. *Mem:* Am Soc Microbiol; Am Gastroenterol Asn; Am Soc Clin Invest; Am Fedn Clin Res; Infectious Dis Soc Am. *Res:* Anaerobes in intraabdominal sepsis; enterotoxin of Escherichia coli in diarrhea; cholera-like toxigenic coliform diarrhea in children; intestinal bacteria in acute diarrhea; Escherichia coli isolated from food; mucosal bacteria in colonic cancer. *Mailing Add:* Cmty Med Tufts Univ Sch Med 136 Harrison Ave Boston MA 02111-1800

GORBATKIN, STEVEN M, MATERIALS SCIENCE ENGINEERING, METALLURGY. *Personal Data:* b Chicago, Ill, July 13, 60. *Educ:* Univ Ill, BS, 81, PhD(mat sci), 87. *Prof Exp:* Res asst, Coord Sci Lab, Univ Ill, 81-87, instr thermodyn, 84-85; Eugene Wigner fel, Oak Ridge Nat Lab, 87-89, res staff, 89-96. *Concurrent Pos:* Res asst, IBM T J Watson Res Ctr, 81; prin investr, Sematech, Joint Advan Etch Prog, Oak Ridge Nat Lab, 89-91; secy, Plasma Sci & Technol Div, Am Vacuum Soc, 91-95; consult, Tegal Corp, 93. *Mem:* Am Vacuum Soc; Mat Res Soc; AMA. *Res:* Thin film plasma processing, including deposition and etching using electron cyclotron resonance microwave plasmas. *Mailing Add:* 108 Kirk Crossing Decatur GA 30030

GORBATSEVICH, SERGE N, pulp & paper technology; deceased, see previous edition for last biography

GORBATY, MARTIN LEO, COAL SCIENCE, PETROLEUM CHEMISTRY. *Current Pos:* res chemist org synthesis, Exxon, 69-72, sr res chemist, polymer sci, 72-75, group head, coal sci, 75-78, lab dir heavy hydrocarbons, 78-84, sci coordr, 84-87, SR RES ASSOC, EXXON, 87- *Personal Data:* b Brooklyn, NY, Nov 17, 42; m 68, Dianne Morse; c Howard, Matthew & Lisa. *Educ:* City Col New York, BS, 64; Purdue Univ, PhD(org chem), 69. *Honors & Awards:* RA Glenn Award in Bituminous Coal Res, Am Chem Soc, 90, Henry H Storch Award in Fuel Chem, 93. *Concurrent Pos:* Chmn petrol chem div, Am Chem Soc, 83-84, coun petrol chem div, 88-; chmn, Gordon Conf Fuel Sci, 88. *Mem:* AAAS; Sigma Xi; NY Acad Sci; Am Chem Soc. *Res:* Fundamental chemical and physical structures of refractory hydrocarbons including heavy oils, shale and coal; the relationships between structure and reactivity, and their conversion to clean usable fuels and chemicals. *Mailing Add:* Exxon Res & Eng Co Clinton Twp Rte 22 E Annadale NJ 08801-0998. *E-Mail:* mlgorba@erenj.com

GORBET, DANIEL WAYNE, AGRONOMY, PLANT BREEDING. *Current Pos:* From asst prof to assoc prof, 70-84, PROF AGRON AGR RES & EDUC CTR, UNIV FLA, 84- *Personal Data:* b Corpus Christi, Tex, Oct 16, 42; m 62, Mary F Gurka; c Daniel K & Mitchel W. *Educ:* Tex A&I Univ, BS, 65; Okla State Univ, MS, 68, PhD(crop sci), 71. *Concurrent Pos:* NSF fel. *Mem:* Fel Am Soc Agron; Crop Sci Soc Am; Am Peanut Res & Educ Soc (pres, 87-88); Am Genetic Asn; Coun Agri Sci & Technol. *Res:* Sorghum breeding and genetics; breeding, genetics, management and variety development of peanuts. *Mailing Add:* N Fla Res & Educ Ctr 3925 Hwy 71 Marianna FL 32446-8091

GORBMAN, AUBREY, ZOOLOGY. *Current Pos:* RETIRED. *Personal Data:* b Detroit, Mich, Dec 13, 14; m 38; c 4. *Educ:* Wayne Univ, AB, 35, MS, 36; Univ Calif, PhD(zool), 40. *Prof Exp:* Asst zool, Univ Calif, 36-40, res assoc Inst Exp Biol, 40-41; instr biol, Wayne Univ, 41-44; Childs fel, Univ Calif, 44-46; from asst prof to prof zool, Barnard Col, Columbia Univ, 46-63, exec officer dept univ, 52-55, col, 57-60; prof & chmn, Dept Zool, Univ Wash, 63-66. *Concurrent Pos:* Fulbright scholar, Col of France, 51-52; res collabr, Brookhaven Nat Lab, 52-60; Guggenheim fel, Univ Hawaii, 55-56; vis prof, Nagoya Univ, 56; USPHS fel & vis prof, Univ Tokyo, 60; ed-in-chief, Gen & Comp Endocrinol, 60-; mem, Endocrinol Study Sect, NIH, 68-72 & Regulatory Biol Panel, NSF, 74-77; vis prof biol, Tokyo Univ & Toho Univ, Japan, 84; James chmn, Biol Dept, St Francis Xavier Univ, Nova Scotia, Can, 85; vis prof zool, Univ Alberta, 86. *Mem:* Am Soc Naturalists; Soc Exp Biol & Med; Am Soc Ichthyologists & Herpetologists; Am Soc Zoologists (pres, 77); fel NY Acad Sci. *Res:* Comparative endocrinology; actions of hormones on nervous system. *Mailing Add:* 4218 55th Ave NE Seattle WA 98105

GORBSKY, GARY JAMES, CELL BIOLOGY, MITOSIS. *Current Pos:* ASST PROF, DEPT ANAT & CELL BIOL, UNIV VA, 88-, STAFF INVESTR, UNIV VA CANCER CTR, 88- *Personal Data:* b Jan 2, 55; m, Marie H Hanigan; c Michael & Paul. *Educ:* Col William & Mary, BS, 76; Princeton Univ, MS, 78, PhD(biol), 82. *Prof Exp:* Res assoc molecular biol, Univ Wis, 83-88. *Mem:* Am Soc Cell Biol; Am Asn Cancer Res. *Res:* Cell cycle regulation of chromosome assembly and movement. *Mailing Add:* Box 439 Health Sci Ctr Univ Va Charlottesville VA 22908-0439. *Fax:* 804-982-3912

GORBUNOFF, MARINA J, ORGANIC CHEMISTRY. *Current Pos:* SR RES ASSOC BIOCHEM, BRANDEIS UNIV, 67- *Personal Data:* b Moscow, Russia, May 25, 27; US citizen; m 53; c 1. *Educ:* Syracuse Univ, BS, 51; Yale Univ, MS, 54, PhD(chem), 56. *Prof Exp:* Res fel org chem, Bryn Mawr Col, 56-57 & Univ Pa, 58-59; fel, Nat Renderes Asn, USDA, 61-64; res chemist, Eastern Regional Res Lab, Agr Res Serv, USDA, 64-67. *Concurrent Pos:* Res fel, Inst Molecular Biol, Paris, 72-73; vis scientist, Inst Chem Natural Substances, Gif-sur-Yvette, France, 82-83 & Univ Orsay, France, 86-87. *Mem:* Am Chem Soc; Am Soc Biol Chemists; Sigma Xi. *Res:* Structure of proteins; chemical modification of active groups on proteins; synthetic organic chemistry. *Mailing Add:* Grad Dept Biochem Brandeis Univ Waltham MA 02254-9110. *Fax:* 781-736-2349

GORCHOV, DAVID LOUIS, PLANT ECOLOGY, SEED DISPERSAL. *Current Pos:* asst prof, 90-95, ASSOC PROF BOT, MIAMI UNIV, 95- *Personal Data:* b Philadelphia, Pa, July 12, 58; m 93, Vivian Negron; c Alan. *Educ:* Princeton Univ, AB, 80; Univ Mich, MS, 81, PhD(biol), 87. *Prof Exp:* Vis asst prof biol, Rutgers Univ, 87-88; res assoc, Princeton Univ, 88-89. *Mem:* Ecol Soc Am; Bot Soc Am; Asn Trop Biol; Am Soc Naturalists; Soc Conserv Biol. *Res:* Natural regeneration of tropical rain forest; seed dispersal; ecology of invasive plants; population biology of rare and economic plants. *Mailing Add:* Dept Bot Miami Univ Oxford OH 45056. *E-Mail:* gorchodl@muohio.edu

GORCZYNSKI, REGINALD MEICZYSLAW, IMMUNOLOGY, CELL BIOLOGY. *Current Pos:* MEM RES STAFF IMMUNOL & CELL BIOL, ONT CANCER INST, 74- *Personal Data:* b Plymouth, Eng, Oct 23, 47; m 70; c 2. *Educ:* Oxford Univ, BA, 69; Toronto Univ, PhD(immunol), 72. *Prof Exp:* Fel immunol & virol, Imperial Cancer Res Fund, London, 72-74. *Concurrent Pos:* Can Med Res Coun res grant, 74-80, Can Nat Cancer Inst, 74-79; consult, Cedarlove Labs, London, Ont, 76- *Mem:* Europ Asn Cancer Res; Can Soc Immunol; Am Soc Immunol. *Res:* Self-non-self discrimination or tolerace as studied in neonates; role of response to fetal antigens in neoplasia; regulation of immune responses by antigen presenting cells. *Mailing Add:* 429 Drewry Ave Willowdale ON M2R 2K6 Can

GORDAN, GILBERT SAUL, ENDOCRINOLOGY. *Current Pos:* intern, Univ Hosp, Univ Calif, 40-41, asst resident med, Med Sch, 41-42, clin instr, 45-47, from instr to asst prof med & pharmacol, 48-54, from assoc prof to prof, 54-85, EMER PROF MED, MED SCH, UNIV CALIF, sAN fRANCISCO, 85- *Personal Data:* b San Francisco, Calif, July 8, 16; m 78, Cynthia Vaughan. *Educ:* Univ Calif, AB, 37, MD, 41, PhD(endocrinol), 47. *Honors & Awards:* Arnold O Beckman lectr, 79. *Prof Exp:* US Army, 42-45. *Concurrent Pos:* Commonwealth fel, Harvard Med Sch, 47-48; ed, Yr Bk Endocrinol, 51-63; consult, Cancer Chemother Nat Serv Ctr, USPHS, 57-59, chmn coop breast cancer group, 56-59, mem & spec consult hormone evaluation joint comt clin & endocrinol panels, 57-69; Commonwealth Fund fel, Col Physicians & Surgeons, Columbia Univ, 62-63 & Strangeways Lab, Cambridge Univ; consult, Manned Orbiting Lab Proj, USAF, Aerospace Corp, 64-; Guggenheim fel & vis prof, Makerere Univ, Univ Athens & Hebrew Univ Jerusalem, 67-68; William Beaumont vis prof, Sch Med, Wash Univ, 70; Lady Davis vis prof, Hebrew Univ, 78; assoc chief staff educ, VAMC, Martinez, Calif, 85-88. *Mem:* Fel AAAS; Am Soc Clin Invest; Endocrine Soc; hon mem Royal Soc Med; fel Am Col Physicians; Asn Am Physicians. *Res:* Clinical and experimental endocrinology; calcium metabolism; bone physiology; parathyroid function; establish method for growth stimulating activity of steroids, growth hormone, thyroxine; demonstrate safety, efficacy of hormonal replacement in menopausal women; prevention and treatment of postmenopausal osteoporosis. *Mailing Add:* 1100 West K St Benicia CA 94510

GORDEE, ROBERT STOUFFER, MICROBIOLOGY, CHEMOTHERAPY. *Current Pos:* RETIRED. *Personal Data:* b Chicago, Ill, June 12, 32; m 61; c 2. *Educ:* Mich State Univ, BS, 54; Purdue Univ, MS, 59, PhD(mycol, biochem), 61. *Prof Exp:* Fisheries biologist, Great Lakes Fishery

Invest, US Fish & Wildlife Serv, 54; res scientist, Biophys-Res Div, Lockheed-Calif Co, 61-64; sr microbiologist, Biol-Pharmacol Res Div, Eli Lilly & Co, 64-68, res scientist, Biol Res Div, 69-71, head exp chemother, Res Labs, 71-76, head, Microbiol & Fermentation Prods Res, 76-79, res assoc, 79-93. *Concurrent Pos:* Vis scholar, Univ Mich, 62. *Mem:* AAAS; Am Soc Microbiol; NY Acad Sci. *Res:* Antimicrobial agents; chemotherapy of infectious diseases. *Mailing Add:* 27701 Kings Kew Ct Bonita Springs FL 34134-3808

GORDEN, BERNER J, ORGANIC CHEMISTRY. *Current Pos:* chmn dept chem, 67-74, from asst prof to assoc prof, 67-75, PROF CHEM, SAGINAW VALLEY STATE UNIV, 75- *Personal Data:* b Detroit, Mich, Jan 22, 39; m 62, Annette Orke; c Steven & Kathy. *Educ:* Luther Col, Iowa, BA, 61; Wayne State Univ, MS, 64, PhD(org chem), 65. *Prof Exp:* Asst prof chem, Muskingum Col, 65-67. *Concurrent Pos:* Instr, Dow Forman's Acad, 74-76; Univ Hawaii res grant, 75; sabbaticals, Mich State Univ, 80 & Univ Ga, 81, Saginaw Valley State Univ, 92 & 93. *Mem:* Am Chem Soc; Sigma Xi. *Res:* Conformational analysis; organic synthesis; mechanisms and reagents in organic reactions; heats of hydrogenation. *Mailing Add:* Dept Chem Saginaw Valley State Univ University Center MI 48710

GORDEN, PHILLIP, ENDOCRINOLOGY & METABOLISM, INTERNAL MEDICINE. *Current Pos:* clin dir, 80-89, chief, Diabetes Br, 83-89, CHIEF, SECT CLIN & CELLULAR BIOL, DIABETES BR, NAT INST ARTHRITIS, DIABETES & DIGESTIVE & KIDNEY DIS, NIH, 78-, DIR, 86- *Personal Data:* b Baldwyn, Miss, Dec 22, 34; m 59; c 2. *Educ:* Vanderbilt Univ, BA, 57, MD, 61; Am Bd Internal Med, dipl; Am Bd Endocrinol & Metab, dipl. *Hon Degrees:* DMed, Univ Geneva, 86. *Honors & Awards:* Distinguished Serv Medal, USPHS, 86 & Commendation Medal, 88; Nesbitt lectr, Univ Minn Sch Med, Minneapolis, 83; James Grant Thompson Mem lectr, Am Diabetes Asn, Chicago, 88; Alexander Marble lectr, Joslin Diabetes Ctr, Boston, 90. *Prof Exp:* Intern, Yale Univ, 61-62, asst resident, 62-64, USPHS clin fel metab, 64-65, USPHS res fel metab, 65-66; sr investr, Clin Endocrinol Br, NIAMDD, NIH, 66-74, Diabetes Br, NIADDK, 74-78, clin dir, Nat Inst Arthritis, Metab & Digestive Dis, 74-76; vis prof, Sch Med, Univ Geneva, 76-78. *Concurrent Pos:* Vis prof, Univ Geneva, 78-, Nat Univ La Plata, Arg, 80, Univ Mich Sch Med, 87, Sch Med, Univ Calif-Los Angeles, 89 & Univ Tenn Col Med, 90; attend physician, Howard Univ Sch Med, Wash, DC, 70-76, clin assoc prof, 78-; clin prof med, Uniformed Serv Med Sch, Bethesda, Md, 78-; plenary lectr, 78-89; Thomas Amatruda vis prof, Yale affil Waterbury Hosp, 90; chmn, Med Bd Clin Ctr, NIH, 75-76, dir, Endocrine-Metab Student Elective Prog, 72-76; attend physician, Nat Naval Med Ctr, 79-; mem, Nat Comt Res, Am Diabetes Asn, 80-83, Nat Comn Orphan Dis, 87-89. *Mem:* Fel Am Col Physicians; Am Soc Clin Invest; Endocrine Soc; Asn Am Physicians; Am Soc Biochem & Molecular Biol; Am Diabetes Asn; Am Fedn Clin Res; Am Soc Cell Biol. *Res:* Clinical studies of diabetes and related endocrine disorders; biochemical and cell biological approaches to the study of the insulin receptor and insulin action in normal and pathologic states. *Mailing Add:* NIDDK NIH Bldg 31 Rm 9A-52 31 Center Dr Bethesda MD 20892-3100. *Fax:* 301-402-2125

GORDEN, ROBERT WAYNE, microbiology, ecology, for more information see previous edition

GORDH, GEORGE RUDOLPH, JR, GENERAL MATHEMATICS, CONTINUUM THEORY. *Current Pos:* from asst prof to assoc prof, 74-86, PROF MATH, GUILFORD COL, 86- *Personal Data:* b Macon, Ga, May 12, 44; m 79, Betty J Griffel. *Educ:* Guilford Col, BA, 66; Univ Calif, Riverside, PhD(topology), 71. *Prof Exp:* Asst, Univ Calif, Riverside, 71; fel math, Univ Ky, 71-72, vis asst prof, 72-73; exchange scientist, Nat Acad Sci, Yugoslavia, 73-74. *Mem:* Math Asn Am; Am Math Soc; Sigma Xi. *Res:* Continua; ordered spaces; upper semicontinuous decompositions; inverse limits; shape theory. *Mailing Add:* Dept Math Guilford Col Greensboro NC 27410

GORDH, GORDON, ENTOMOLOGY, SYSTEMATICS. *Current Pos:* from asst prof to assoc prof, 77-85, PROF ENTOM, UNIV CALIF, RIVERSIDE, 85- *Personal Data:* b Augusta, Ga, Jan 7, 45. *Educ:* Univ Colo, BA, 67; Univ Kans, MA, 72; Univ Calif, Riverside, PhD(entom), 74. *Prof Exp:* Res entomologist, Syst Entom Lab, US Nat Mus, 74-77. *Concurrent Pos:* Asst adj prof entom, NC State Univ, 75-76; res assoc, Georgetown Univ, 75-76; adj asst prof, Univ Md, 74-77. *Mem:* Royal Entom Soc London; Entom Soc Can; Sigma Xi; Entom Soc SAfrica; Soc Study Evolution. *Res:* Systematics, biology, behavior and evolution of the parasitic Hymenoptera belonging to the super-family Chalcidoidea. *Mailing Add:* 7 Garnet Ct Kenmore Qld 4069 Australia

GORDIS, ENOCH, ALCOHOL ABUSE. *Current Pos:* DIR, NAT INST ALCOHOL ABUSE & ALCOHOLISM, 87- *Personal Data:* b Feb 21, 31. *Educ:* Columbia Univ, BA, 50, MD, 54. *Prof Exp:* From asst prof to assoc prof med, Rockefeller Univ, 63-71; assoc prof clin med, Mt Sinai Hosp, 71-85, asst physician & dir, Alcoholism Prog, 86-87. *Concurrent Pos:* Adj prof & vis physician, Rockefeller Univ, NY, 71-; prog chmn, Nat Meeting Alcoholism, Am Med Soc, New Orleans, 81, Washington, DC, 82, Houston, Tex, 83; mem, Treatment & Prev Study Sect, Nat Inst Alcohol Abuse & Alcoholism, 85-86; corresp, Comt Human Rights, Inst Med-Nat Acad Sci, 88-89. *Mem:* Inst Med-Nat Acad Sci; Am Col Neuropsychopharmacol; Am Fedn Clin Res; Am Gastroenterol Asn; Am Soc Addiction Med; Am Physiol Soc; fel Am Col Physicians; Int Soc Biomed Res Alcoholism; Sigma Xi. *Res:* Author or co-author of over 40 publications. *Mailing Add:* Nat Inst Alcohol Abuse & Alcoholism Wilko Bldg Suite 400 6000 Executive Blvd MSC No 7003 Bethesda MD 20892-7003. *Fax:* 301-443-7043

GORDIS, LEON, PEDIATRICS, EPIDEMIOLOGY. *Current Pos:* assoc prof, Johns Hopkins Univ, 72-92, chmn dept, Sch Hyg & Pub Health, 73-93, prof epidemiol, 93, PROF PEDIAT, SCH MED, JOHNS HOPKINS UNIV, 92- *Personal Data:* b New York, NY, July 19, 34; m 55, Hadassah Cohen; c 3. *Educ:* Columbia Col, BA, 54; State Univ NY Downstate Med Ctr, MD, 58; Johns Hopkins Univ, MPH, 66, DrPH, 68. *Honors & Awards:* T Dukette Jones lectr, Am Heart Asn, 84. *Prof Exp:* Chief, Dept Community Med, Sinai Hosp, Baltimore, 68-; vis prof med ecol, Hebrew Univ Jerusalem, 69-71. *Mem:* Fel Am Acad Pediat; Am Heart Asn; Soc Epidemiol Res (pres, 79-80); Am Epidemiol Soc; Soc Pediat Res. *Res:* Epidemiology of chronic diseases; evaluation of health care. *Mailing Add:* Dept Epidemiol Sch Hyg & Pub Health Johns Hopkins Univ Baltimore MD 21205

GORDON, ADRIENNE SUE, NEUROBIOLOGY, MEMBRANE BIOCHEMISTRY. *Current Pos:* ADJ PROF PHARMACOL & NEUROL, MED SCH, UNIV CALIF, SAN FRANCISCO, 74- *Educ:* Mass Inst Technol, PhD(chem), 66. *Mailing Add:* Gallo Ctr Univ Calif San Francisco CA 94110. *Fax:* 415-648-7116

GORDON, ALBERT MCCAGUE, MUSCULAR PHYSIOLOGY, BIOPHYSICS. *Current Pos:* fel biophys, 62-64, from instr to assoc prof, 64-75, PROF PHYSIOL & BIOPHYS, UNIV WASH, 75- *Personal Data:* b Tanta, Egypt, Sept 23, 34; US citizen; m 78, Della L Guier; c Sarah, Andrew & Dana. *Educ:* Univ Rochester, BS, 56; Cornell Univ, PhD(solid state physics), 61. *Honors & Awards:* Jacob Javits Neurosci Investr Award. *Prof Exp:* Nat Found fel, Univ Col, Univ London, 60-62. *Mem:* AAAS; Biophys Soc; Am Physiol Soc; Soc Gen Physiologists. *Res:* Mechanical properties of muscle and the contractile mechanism; muscle pathophysiology; control of contraction in muscle. *Mailing Add:* Dept Physiol & Biophys Univ Wash Box 357290 Seattle WA 98195-7290. *Fax:* 206-685-0619; *E-Mail:* amg@u.washington.edu

GORDON, ALBERT RAYE, CELL BIOLOGY, ELECTRON MICROSCOPY. *Current Pos:* from asst prof to assoc prof, 69-78, PROF LIFE SCI, SOUTHWEST MO STATE UNIV, 78- *Personal Data:* b McKeesport, Pa, Sept 22, 39; m 65; c 2. *Educ:* Western Res Univ, BA, 61, MA, 67, Case Western Res Univ, PhD(biol), 68. *Prof Exp:* Fel biol, Case Western Res Univ, 67-68; asst prof, Knox Col, Ill, 68-69. *Mem:* AAAS; Am Soc Cell Biol; Electron Micros Soc Am; Am Soc Plant Physiol; Am Inst Biol Sci; Sigma Xi. *Res:* Significance and functions of multiple enzyme systems; cellular and ultrastructural localization of peroxidase isoenzymes and their relationship to plant tissue differentiation and function. *Mailing Add:* Biomed Sci Dept Southwest Mo State Univ Springfield MO 65804. *Fax:* 417-836-6905

GORDON, ALVIN S, PHYSICAL CHEMISTRY. *Current Pos:* RETIRED. *Personal Data:* b New York, NY, Oct 25, 14; m 42. *Educ:* Polytech Inst Brooklyn, BS, 37; NY Univ, PhD(phys chem), 41. *Prof Exp:* Asst phys chemist, Boyce Thompson Inst, 41-42; res assoc, Nat Defense Res Comt, Carnegie Inst Technol, 42-45; phys chemist, US Bur Mines, 45-51; phys chemist, Naval Weapons Ctr, 51-75, sci liaison officer, Off Naval Res, London, Eng, 57-59; adj prof eng chem, Univ Calif San Diego, 76-82. *Concurrent Pos:* Vis sr res scientist, Princeton Univ, 64-65; mem Calif Air Resources Bd, 76-82. *Mem:* Am Chem Soc; fel Am Phys Soc. *Res:* Kinetics and mechanism of reactions. *Mailing Add:* 1412 Ivyglen Dr Encinitas CA 92024

GORDON, ANNETTE WATERS, ORGANIC CHEMISTRY, BIOCHEMISTRY. *Current Pos:* PROF CHEM, SW MO STATE UNIV, 93- *Personal Data:* b Sylvania, Ga, Aug 9, 37; m 62; c 1. *Educ:* Duke Univ, BS, 59; Vanderbilt Univ, PhD(org chem), 68. *Prof Exp:* From asst prof to prof chem, Murray State Univ, 62-79. *Mem:* Am Chem Soc. *Res:* Stereochemistry. *Mailing Add:* PO Box 3691 Springfield MO 65808

GORDON, ARNOLD J, PUBLIC HEALTH & EPIDEMIOLOGY. *Current Pos:* group assoc dir, Sci Affairs, Pfizer Pharmaceut, 71-75, dir sci affairs, 75-86, exec dir sci affairs & safety assurance, Pfizer Int, 86-92, sr dir, Clin Data Opers, Pharmaceut, 92-96, SR DIR WORLDWIDE HARMONIZATION, PFIZER INC, 96- *Personal Data:* b Boston, Mass, Dec 13, 37; m 64, Francesca Yablonsky; c Shira & Ian. *Educ:* Northeastern Univ, BSc, 60; NY Univ, MS, 62, PhD(org chem), 64. *Prof Exp:* Instr gen & org chem, NY Univ, 64; res chemist, Capt, US Army, Edgewood Arsenal, 65-66; asst prof chem, Cath Univ Am, 66-71. *Concurrent Pos:* Res grants, Cath Univ, 67 & Res Corp, Am Chem Soc Petrol Res Fund & NSF, 67-71; manuscript referee, J Org Chem, 67- & Chem Rev, 68; Am Chem Soc-Du Pont small grants award, 68; topic leader, Int Conf Harmonization New Drug Develop, 92-; chair, Int Issues, Clin Safety Surveillance, Pharmaceut Mfrs Asn. *Mem:* Am Chem Soc; AAAS; NY Acad Sci; Am Inst Chemists; Sigma Xi (pres, 70-71); Drug Info Asn; Asn Res Dirs (vpres, 86-87, pres, 87-88). *Res:* Chemistry and biochemistry of drugs; stereochemistry of di-coordinated oxygen; synthesis and properties of imides and other nitrogen compounds; chemical education; new drug development and research; practical data, techniques and references for chemists; clinical research on new drugs; clinical data storage and analysis; clinical drug safety and pharmacoepidemiology; research policy (medicines). *Mailing Add:* Pfizer Inc 235 E 42nd St New York NY 10017. *Fax:* 212-573-1976; *E-Mail:* gordoa@pfizer.com

GORDON, ARNOLD L, PHYSICAL OCEANOGRAPHY. *Current Pos:* Res asst, 61-65, assoc prof, 71-77, RES ASSOC OCEANOG, LAMONT-DOHERTY GEOL OBSERV, COLUMBIA UNIV, 65-, PROF, 77- *Personal Data:* b New York, NY, Feb 4, 40; m 70; c 4. *Educ:* Hunter Col, BA, 61; Columbia Univ, PhD(oceanog), 65. *Honors & Awards:* Henry Bigelow Medal, Woods Hole Oceanog Inst, 84. *Concurrent Pos:* Ford Found fel, 61-65, NSF res grant, 65-; asst prof oceanog, Columbia Univ, 66-71. *Mem:* AAAS; Am Geophys Union; Sigma Xi. *Res:* Circulation of the Caribbean Sea; physical oceanographic investigations in the Southern Hemisphere oceans. *Mailing Add:* Lamont-Doherty Geol Observ Columbia Univ Palisades NY 10964

GORDON, BARRY MAXWELL, PHYSICAL CHEMISTRY, NUCLEAR CHEMISTRY. *Current Pos:* from assoc chemist to chemist, 63-92, CONSULT, BROOKHAVEN NAT LAB, 92- *Personal Data:* b Chicago, Ill, Jan 26, 30; m 58, Edith L Oppenheimer; c Daniel L & Elizabeth. *Educ:* Univ Calif, Los Angeles, BS, 51; Wash Univ, PhD(chem), 55. *Prof Exp:* Res assoc chem, Brookhaven Nat Lab, 55-57; asst prof, State Univ NY, Stony Brook, 57-63. *Mem:* Am Chem Soc; Sigma Xi. *Res:* Kinetic studies of oxidation-reduction reactions; nuclear reactions; radiochemistry; trace-elemental analysis in medicine; applications of synchrotron radiation to chemical analysis. *Mailing Add:* 8 Park St PO Box 2938 Setauket NY 11733

GORDON, BARRY MONROE, CORROSION ENGINEERING. *Current Pos:* prog mgr, Mat Corrosion Prog, 75-88, LEAD ENGR, CORROSION PERFORMANCE, GEN NUCLEAR ENERGY, 92-, PROJ MGR CORROSION TECHNOL, 93- *Personal Data:* b New York, NY, July 15, 47; m 81, Aldene E Stoner; c Haley S (Robertson). *Educ:* Carnegie-Mellon Univ, BS, 69, MS, 71; Nat Asn Corrosion Engrs, cert. *Honors & Awards:* Waldemar Cancer Res Award, Waldemar Cancer Res Inst, 65. *Prof Exp:* Assoc engr, Westinghouse Elec Corp, 69-70, engr corrosion, 71-75; teaching asst thermodynamics, Carnegie-Mellon Univ, 70-71. *Mem:* Nat Asn Corrosion Engrs; Am Soc Metals. *Res:* Mitigation of environmental assisted cracking of structural alloys in high temperature aqueous environments; corrosion control in nuclear power systems; granted four patents. *Mailing Add:* GE Nuclear Energy MC785 175 Curtner Ave San Jose CA 95125. *Fax:* 408-925-4175; *E-Mail:* gordonb@sjcpo5.ne.ge.com

GORDON, BENJAMIN EDWARD, ANALYTICAL CHEMISTRY, RADIOCHEMISTRY. *Current Pos:* SUPVR RADIOCHEM, LAWRENCE RADIATION LAB, UNIV CALIF, BERKELEY, 74- *Personal Data:* b New York, NY, May 8, 16; m 40; c 3. *Educ:* Univ Ill, BS, 40, MS, 42. *Prof Exp:* Res chemist, Shell Oil Co, 42-54, sr technologist radiochem, 54-57, group leader radiochem & radiation chem, 57-61, supvr radiochem, Shell Develop Co, 61-71 & Koninklijke Shell Labs, 71-74. *Concurrent Pos:* Mgr, Nat Tritium Labeling Facil. *Mem:* Am Chem Soc. *Res:* Novel methods of labeling with tritium; gas chromatography; product and process research; reaction mechanism; kinetics; activation analysis; instrumentation; applying nuclear techniques to problems in environmental conservation; hot atom chemistry of Carbon-14; excitation labeling with tritium. *Mailing Add:* 1330 Brewster Dr El Cerrito CA 94530-2506

GORDON, BERNARD LUDWIG, MARINE BIOLOGY, MARINE RESOURCES. *Current Pos:* instr natural sci, 61-65, asst prof, 65-68, ASSOC PROF EARTH SCI, NORTHEASTERN UNIV, 69- *Personal Data:* b Westerly, RI, Nov 6, 31; m 59, Esther Saranga; c Jocelyn & Zimra. *Educ:* Univ RI, BSc, 55, MSc, 58. *Prof Exp:* Instr biol, RI Col, 56-60; teaching fel, Boston Univ, 60-61. *Concurrent Pos:* Consult, Mass State Dept Educ, 63 & Quincy Marine Sci Prog, Mass, 65-; mem bd dirs, Southern New Eng Marine Sci Asn, 65- Littauer Found grant, 66; consult, Wally Sea Prod Co, 67- & Oceanog Educ Ctr, Woods Hole Oceanog Inst, Bur Com Fisheries & Marine Biol Lab, 68-; pres of fels, Mystic Seaport Libr, 90-91. *Mem:* AAAS; Nat Asn Biol Teachers; Am Soc Limnol & Oceanog; Marine Technol Soc; Am Fisheries Soc; Explorers Club. *Res:* Marine ichthyology; parasitology; oceanography; marine sciences; fish surveys; life history studies; history of sciences; author of 16 science books; New England Fisheries. *Mailing Add:* Geol Dept Northeastern Univ Boston MA 02115

GORDON, BERNARD M, ANALOG-DIGITAL INTERFACE. *Current Pos:* PRES, CHIEF EXEC OFFICER & CHMN, ANALOGIC CORP, 67- *Personal Data:* b 1927. *Honors & Awards:* Nat Medal of Technol, 86; Leadership Recognition Award, Inst Elec & Electronics Engrs, 92; John Fulke Sr Mem Award, 93. *Mem:* Nat Acad Eng; fel Inst Elec & Electronics Engrs. *Mailing Add:* Analogic Corp 8 Centennial Dr B-1 Peabody MA 01960

GORDON, BURTON LEROY, BIOGEOGRAPHY. *Current Pos:* RETIRED. *Personal Data:* b Asotin, Wash, Feb 13, 20; m 41; c 4. *Educ:* San Francisco State Col, AB, 42; Univ Calif, PhD(geog), 54. *Prof Exp:* Asst prof geog, Univ NMex, 55-60, assoc prof & chmn dept, 60-65; prof geog, Calif State Univ, San Francisco, 65-87. *Concurrent Pos:* Collabr, US Forest Serv, 49-54; consult, Jicarilla Apache Indian Tribe, 59-65; exchange lectr geog, Queen Mary Col, Univ London, 62-63. *Mem:* AAAS; Am Asn Univ Prof; NY Acad Sci. *Res:* Biogeography of central California coast and Western Europe. *Mailing Add:* 113 David Way Santa Cruz CA 95060

GORDON, CAROLYN SUE, RIEMANNIAN GEOMETRY, LIE GROUPS. *Current Pos:* PROF, DARTMOUTH COL, 92- *Personal Data:* b Charleston, WVa, Dec 26, 50; m 89, David Webb. *Educ:* Purdue Univ, BS, 71, MS, 72; Wash Univ, PhD(math), 79. *Prof Exp:* Lady Davis fel, Technion-Israel Inst Technol, 79-80; asst prof math, Lehigh Univ, 80-84; from asst prof to prof, Wash Univ, 84-92. *Concurrent Pos:* Vis asst prof, Univ Pa, 86-87; mem, Math Sci Res Inst, 93-94. *Mem:* Am Math Soc; Math Asn Am; Asn Women Math. *Mailing Add:* Dartmouth Col Hanover NH 03755. *E-Mail:* carolyn.s.gordon@dartmouth.edu

GORDON, CARROLL K, FLUID DYNAMICS. *Current Pos:* CONSULT, 89- *Personal Data:* b Chicago, Ill, 1924. *Educ:* Loyola Univ, BS, 50; Fordham Univ, PhD(physics), 51. *Mem:* Am Phys Soc; Sigma Xi; NY Acad Sci. *Mailing Add:* 120 Carroll Ave Bay St Louis MS 39520

GORDON, CHESTER DUNCAN, ORGANIC CHEMISTRY, ADDITIVES FOR PETROLEUM PRODUCTS. *Current Pos:* RETIRED. *Personal Data:* b Ankerton, Alta, Oct 13, 20; nat US; m 50, Sybil M MacLeod; c Robert, John & Susan. *Educ:* Univ Alta, BSc, 49; Univ Notre Dame, PhD(org chem), 52. *Prof Exp:* Res chemist, Calif Res Corp Div, Stand Oil Co Calif, 52-60, sr res chemist, 60-66, sr res assoc, Chevron Res Co, 66-84. *Concurrent Pos:* Consult; expert witness. *Mem:* Am Chem Soc; Sigma Xi. *Res:* Organic synthesis; vinyl polymerizations; nitrogen chemistry; process development; additives for petroleum products. *Mailing Add:* 2579 Patra Dr El Sobrante CA 94803-3627. *Fax:* 510-223-0574

GORDON, CHESTER MURRAY, MATHEMATICS, STATISTICS. *Current Pos:* RETIRED. *Personal Data:* b Brooklyn, NY, Mar 31, 18; m 42; c 2. *Educ:* City Col NY, BS, 38, MSEd, 43. *Prof Exp:* Indust specialist, AEC, 48-51, defense coordr & procurement asst, 53-71, chief, Property Mgt Br & relocation officer, 71-72, chief logistics staff, 73; mobilization specialist, Off Defense Mobilization, Exec Off of Pres, 51-53; consult, Dept Energy, 74. *Concurrent Pos:* Asst opers chief, Bur Census, 40-42; statist analyst, War Prod Bd, 42-48; mgt analyst, Dept Navy, 48. *Res:* Industrial mobilization; priorities; civil defense. *Mailing Add:* 3330 N Leisure World Blvd No 609 Silver Spring MD 20906

GORDON, CHRISTOPHER JOHN, THERMAL PHYSIOLOGY, TOXICOLOGY. *Current Pos:* RES PHYSIOLOGIST, US ENVIRON PROTECTION AGENCY, 80- *Personal Data:* b Ventura, Calif, Mar 24, 53; m 77, Susan; c Kevin G & Karen L. *Educ:* Univ Idaho, BS, 75, MS, 77; Univ Ill, Urbana, PhD(physiol), 80. *Concurrent Pos:* Trainee physiol, NIH, 78; consult, Gen Elec. *Mem:* AAAS; Am Physiol Soc. *Res:* Mechanisms for the central neural control of body temperature; physiological effects of exposure to microwave radiation; pharmacology and toxicology of thermoregulation. *Mailing Add:* Neurotoxicol Div US Environ Protection Agency Mail Drop 74B Research Triangle Park NC 27711-0001. *Fax:* 919-541-4849

GORDON, CLAIRE CATHERINE, ANTHROPOMETRY, HUMAN ENGINEERING. *Current Pos:* res anthropologist, US Army Natick Res, Develop & Eng Ctr, 83-87, group leader, 88-90, sr anthropologist, 90-93, chief, Behav Sci Div, 93-95, SR ANTHROPOLOGIST, US ARMY NATICK RES, DEVELOP & ENG CTR, 95- *Personal Data:* b New Orleans, La, June 12, 54; m 79, Douglas B Hanson; c Katherin T. *Educ:* Univ Notre Dame, BS, 76; Northwestern Univ, MA, 77, PhD(bioanthrop), 82; Harvard Univ, MS, 90. *Prof Exp:* Res assoc phys anthrop & archaeol, Pac Studies Inst, 80; res coordr human genetics, Northwestern Univ Med Sch, 82-83. *Concurrent Pos:* Rep, Air Stand Coord Comt, US Army, 85- *Mem:* Am Asn Phys Anthropologists; Sigma Xi; Human Factors & Ergonomics Soc; Human Biol Coun. *Res:* Anthropometric instrumentation and methodology; age-sex-racial components of human physical variation; dimensional relationships between body parts; statistics of human engineering design, sizing and tariffing; human factors. *Mailing Add:* Attn SATNC-YB US Army Natick Res Develop & Eng Ctr Natick MA 01760-5020. *Fax:* 508-233-5104; *E-Mail:* cgordon@natick_emh1.army.mil, cgordon@natick_amed02.army.mil

GORDON, DANIEL ISRAEL, ELECTROMAGNETISM, COMPUTER SCIENCES. *Current Pos:* CONSULT, 91- *Personal Data:* b Norwich, Conn, Aug 12, 20; m 43, Clara Siegel; c 3. *Educ:* Yale Univ, BE, 42, MEng, 47. *Honors & Awards:* Centennial Medal, Inst Elec & Electronics Engrs, 84. *Prof Exp:* Elec engr, Naval Surface Weapons Ctr, 42-64, res physicist, Naval Surface Weapons Ctr, 64-80; prog mgr, Naval Sea Systs Command, 80-84; consult, Vela Assocs, 84-90. *Concurrent Pos:* Guest scientist, Israel Inst Technol, 68-69 & Weizmann Inst Sci, 68-69. *Mem:* Am Phys Soc; sr mem Inst Elec & Electronics Engrs; Am Soc Testing & Mat; Magnetics Soc (secy-treas, 75-76, vpres, 77-78, pres, 79-80); Sigma Xi. *Res:* Magnetism and magnetic materials; measurements; thin films; magnetic device research including magnetometers, amplifiers, transducers, and memory elements; electron devices and hardware systems; very high speed integrated circuits for computers. *Mailing Add:* 2711 Colston Dr Chevy Chase MD 20815-3033

GORDON, DAVID BUDDY, PHYSIOLOGY. *Current Pos:* RETIRED. *Personal Data:* b Chicago, Ill, Dec 17, 18; m 48; c 3. *Educ:* Univ Chicago, BS, 45; Univ Southern Calif, MS, 49, PhD(physiol), 51. *Prof Exp:* Instr physiol, Univ Southern Calif, 51-55; asst prof, Univ Miami, 57-72; from asst chief to chief physiol res lab, Vet Admin Hosp, San Francisco, 64-71; res physiologist, 71-72, Vet Admin Hosp, Livermore, 72-82, dir res lab, 72-82. *Concurrent Pos:* Am Heart Asn fel, 55-56, adv fel, 62-64; lectr physiol, Univ Calif, Berkeley, 75-76. *Mem:* AAAS; Am Physiol Soc; Am Heart Asn; Int Soc Hypertension; Am Soc Hypertension. *Res:* Cardiovascular physiology; hypertension; endocrine function of kidneys. *Mailing Add:* Res Lab Vet Admin Hosp Livermore CA 94550

GORDON, DAVID STEWART, BONE MARROW TRANSPLANTATION, HEMATOLOGY. *Current Pos:* PROF MED HEMAT & ONCOL, SCH MED, EMORY UNIV, 82-; SR VPRES MED AFFAIRS, ARONEX PHARM, INC, TEX, 97- *Educ:* Univ Colo, MD, 67. *Mem:* Am Soc Hemat; Am Asn Immunol. *Res:* Immunology. *Mailing Add:* Aronex 3400 Research Forest Dr The Woodlands TX 77387

GORDON, DENNIS T, FOOD SCIENCE & NUTRITION. *Current Pos:* asst prof, 79-82, ASSOC PROF, DEPT FOOD SCI & NUTRIT, UNIV MO-COLUMBIA, 82- *Personal Data:* b Chicago, Ill, Nov 13, 41. *Educ:* Univ Ill, Champaign, BS, 63; Univ Conn, MS, 69, PhD(nutrit biochem), 74. *Prof Exp:* Lt, US Army, Quartermaster Corps, Ger, 63-66, Capt, Vietnam, 66-67; grad asst, Dept Animal Indust, Univ Conn, 67-69, res asst, Dept Nutrit Sci, 70-73; res assoc, Dept Food Sci & Technol, 74-77, asst prof, 77-79. *Concurrent Pos:* Adj prof, Food Sci & Human Nutrit Dept, Univ Fla, 86. *Mailing Add:* Dept Cereal Sci Harris Hall NDak State Univ PO Box 5728 Fargo ND 58105-5728. *Fax:* 701-237-7723

GORDON, DONALD, PLANT TAXONOMY. *Current Pos:* from asst prof to assoc prof, 58-74, PROF BIOL, MANKATO STATE COL, 74- *Personal Data:* b Indianapolis, Ind, June 5, 39; m 62; c 1. *Educ:* Hanover Col, BA, 61; Ind Univ, MA, 64, PhD(bot), 66. *Prof Exp:* Asst prof biol, NMex State Univ, 66-68. *Concurrent Pos:* NSF res grant, 68-70. *Mem:* AAAS; Bot Soc Am; Am Soc Plant Taxon; Int Soc Plant Taxon. *Res:* A revision of the genus Gleditsia; biosystematics of Maurandya and related genera. *Mailing Add:* Dept Biol Scis Mankato State Univ 515 Malin St Mankato MN 56001-6001

GORDON, DONALD THEILE, PLANT PATHOLOGY, VIROLOGY. *Current Pos:* Assoc prof, 66-80, PROF PLANT PATH, OHIO STATE UNIV & OHIO AGR RES & DEVELOP CTR, WOOSTER, 80- *Personal Data:* b Cincinnati, Ohio, June 10, 35; m 61; c 3. *Educ:* Univ Cincinnati, BS, 60; Univ Wis, PhD(plant path), 66. *Mem:* AAAS; Am Phytopath Soc. *Res:* Isolation, characterization and identification of plant viruses, especially those of corn. *Mailing Add:* Dept Plant Path Ohio Agr Res & Develop Ctr Ohio State Univ 1680 Madison Ave Wooster OH 44691

GORDON, DONOVAN, VETERINARY MEDICINE, VETERINARY PATHOLOGY. *Current Pos:* CONSULT VET PATH, 85-; DIR PATH, BAXTER HEALTHCARE CORP, ROUNDLAKE IL, 91- *Personal Data:* b Beloit, Wis, Aug 15, 34; m 63; c 2. *Educ:* Iowa State Univ, DVM, 59; Univ Wis, MS & PhD(vet path), 67; Am Col Vet Path, dipl. *Prof Exp:* Vet, Pines Meadow Vet Clin, 61-63; pathologist, Abbott Labs, 68-71, head path sect, Indust Bio-Test Labs, 71-84. *Concurrent Pos:* Mem, Ill State Bd Vet Examr, 74-78; consult, vet path, 85- *Mem:* Am Vet Med Asn; Soc Toxicol Pathologists; Am Col Vet Pathologists. *Res:* Viral oncology; chemical carcinogens; diagnostic and toxicologic pathology. *Mailing Add:* 833 Kimball Rd Highland Park IL 60035

GORDON, DOUGLAS LITTLETON, MEDICINE, ENDOCRINOLOGY. *Current Pos:* from clin asst prof to clin assoc prof, 57-67, CLIN PROF MED, SCH MED, LA STATE UNIV MED CTR, NEW ORLEANS, 67- *Personal Data:* b Baton Rouge, La, Mar 15, 24; m 47, 61, Florence Vine; c Douglas, Pamela (Graham), Stephen & Stewart. *Educ:* Tulane Univ, MD, 46; Am Bd Internal Med, dipl, 53. *Prof Exp:* Intern, Charity Hosp, New Orleans, La, 46-47; fel internal med, Ochsner Clin, 47-49; instr med, Sch Med, Tulane Univ, 49-51, 53-57. *Concurrent Pos:* Clin assoc, Endocrinol Res Lab, mem staff, Sect Endocrinol, clin & mem vis staff, Hosp, Alton Oschner Med Found, 49-51, 53-57; asst vis physician, Tulane Univ, Charity Hosp, 51, vis physician, 53-57; mem vis staff, Baton Rouge Gen & Our Lady of the Lake Hosps, 54-; pvt pract, 54-; dep coroner, East Baton Rouge Parish, 55-71; vis physician, La State Univ, 57-61, sr vis prof, Charity Hosp, 61-; mem staff, Sect Med, Baton Rouge Clin, 59-92; med dir, Diabetes Ctr, Baton Rouge Gen Med Ctr, 92-; vis prof, Pennington Biomed Res Ctr, 92- *Mem:* AAAS; AMA; fel Am Col Physicians; Am Diabetes Asn; Endocrine Soc; Am Asn Clin Endocrinologists. *Res:* Internal medicine and endocrinology; effects of new antiappetite medication in obesity; assessment of diabetic status and complications of diabetic mellitus in a Native American people living in southwest Louisiana. *Mailing Add:* Diabetes Ctr 3910 Convention St Baton Rouge LA 70806-3805

GORDON, ELLIS DAVIS, HYDROLOGY, HYDROGEOLOGY. *Current Pos:* RETIRED. *Personal Data:* b Johnson Co, Kans, Aug 6, 13; m 37; c 3. *Educ:* Univ Kans, AB, 43; Univ Nebr, MSc, 49. *Prof Exp:* Chief party, test drill unit, Kans Geol Surv, 39-42; geologist, Kans State Hwy Comn, 42-44; geologist & ground water hydrologist, Nebr Geol Surv, 44-49; geologist, Ground Water, Br, US Geol Surv, NDak, 49-51, Mineral Deposits Br, Colo, 51-52, Ground Water Br, Washington DC, 52-54 & NMex, 54-58, dist geologist, Water Resources Div, Wyo, 58-67, staff hydrologist, regional staff Hq, Water Resources Div, US Geol Surv, Cent Region, 67-79. *Concurrent Pos:* Consult, USAID, Tanzania, 72. *Mem:* Am Geophys Union; Asn Prof Geol Scientists; fel Geol Soc Am. *Res:* Ground water hydrology; subsurface research in ground water; stratigraphy. *Mailing Add:* 514 S Church St Waynoka OK 73860-1308

GORDON, ERIC MICHAEL, ENZYME INHIBITORS, AMINO ACIDS & PEPTIDES. *Current Pos:* PRES & CHIEF EXEC OFFICER, VERSICOR INC, 96- *Personal Data:* b New York, NY, Feb 10, 46; m 71; c 2. *Educ:* Beloit Col, BS, 67; Univ Wis, MS, 69, PhD(med chem), 73. *Prof Exp:* Res chemist org chem, Hoffmann-LaRoche Inc, 69-70; assoc nat prod chem, Yale Univ, 73-74; assoc, Squibb Inst Med Res, 74-75, res investr, 75-79, sr res investr, 79-80, res group leader, cardiovasc chem, 80-86, sect head mem chem, 86-87, dir med chem; vpres res, Affymark, 92-96. *Concurrent Pos:* NIH fel, 67-69; Henry S Wellcome Mem fel, Am Found Pharmaceut Educ, 72. *Mem:* Am Chem Soc; Sigma Xi; AAAS. *Res:* Rational design of enzyme inhibitors of medicinal importance; amino acids and peptide chemistry; chemistry and biology of naturally occurring materials; combinational chemistry. *Mailing Add:* Versicor Inc 270 E Grand Ave South San Francisco CA 94080

GORDON, EUGENE IRVING, PHYSICS, OPHTHAMOLOGY & OPTOELECTRONS. *Current Pos:* PRES, MEDJET INC, 93; PROF, DEPT OPHTHAL, UNIV MED & DENT, NJ, 94- *Personal Data:* b New York, NY, Sept 14, 30; m 56; c 2. *Educ:* City Col New York, BS, 52; Mass Inst Technol, PhD(physics), 57. *Honors & Awards:* Vladimir K Zworykin Award, Inst Elec & Electronics Engrs, 75, Edison Medal & Centennial Medal, 84. *Prof Exp:* Mem staff, Mass Inst Technol, 57; tech staff, Bell Tel Labs, Inc, 57-64, head optical device dept, 64-68, dir electrooptical device lab, 68-73, dir pattern generation technol lab, 73-75, dir, Integrated Circuit Support Lab, 75-79, dir optical devices lab, 80-83; chmn & pres, Lytel Inc, 84-87; vpres & dir res labs, Hughes Aircraft Co, 87-88; founder, chief exec officer & pres, Photon Imaging Corp, 88-89; distinguished prof elec eng & dep exec dir, Ctr Mfg Systs, NJ Inst Technol, 89-93. *Concurrent Pos:* Chmn, Adv Group Electron Devices, Dir Defense, 71-84; consult, 83-84. *Mem:* Hon mem Nat Acad Eng; Electron Devices Soc; fel Inst Elec & Electronics Engrs. *Res:* Properties of ionized media; microwave tubes; lasers; coherent light techniques; image and display devices; pattern generation tools and techniques for the manufacture of semiconductors devices and packaging of silicon integrated circuits; manufacturing systems; waterjet surgery. *Mailing Add:* 1535 Coles Ave Mountainside NJ 07092-1311. *Fax:* 732-738-3984

GORDON, FLORENCE S, MATHEMATICAL STATISTICS, STATISTICAL & MATHEMATICAL EDUCATION. *Current Pos:* PROF MATH, NY INST TECHNOL, 83- *Personal Data:* b Montreal, Que; m 65, Sheldon; c Craig & Kenneth. *Educ:* McGill Univ, BSc, 63, MSc, 64, PhD(math), 68. *Prof Exp:* Asst prof, CW Post Col, Long Island Univ, 68-72, assoc prof math, 75-77; adj prof math, Adelphi Univ, 77-82, asst prof statist & electronic data processing, 82-83. *Mem:* Math Asn Am; Am Stat Asn; Am Math Soc. *Res:* Characterization problems for both univariate and multivariate statistical distributions using regression properties of one statistic on another; computer usage in statistical education; author of three books and 35 publication. *Mailing Add:* 61 Cedar Rd East Northport NY 11731

GORDON, GARY DONALD, SPACECRAFT TECHNOLOGY, SPACE PHYSICS. *Current Pos:* AEROSPACE CONSULT, 84- *Personal Data:* b Elkins, WVa, May 28, 28; m 56, Doris Estelle Nichols; c Donald, Peter, Alan, Norman & Carol. *Educ:* Wesleyan Univ, BA, 50, Harvard Univ, MA, 51, PhD(physics), 54. *Prof Exp:* Instr physics, Harvard Univ, 54; res physicist, Biol Warfare Labs, US Army, 55-56; mem staff, Opers Res, Inc, 57-58; sr engr astro-electronics div, RCA Corp, NJ, 59-64, adminstr course develop, Current Concepts Sci & Eng Prog, Prod Eng, 65-68; sr staff scientist, Comsat Clarksburg, 69-83. *Concurrent Pos:* Mem, Tech Comt Space Systs, Am Inst Aeronaut & Astronaut, 74-75. *Mem:* Am Inst Aeronaut & Astronaut. *Res:* Spacecraft technology; geostationary orbit; spacecraft thermal design; satellite reliability; spacecraft attitude; spacecraft bearings; in-orbit servicing; space and plasma physics; Fortran and Speakeasy programming; operations research; cosmic rays; piezoelectricity. *Mailing Add:* 400 Center St Box 125 Washington Grove MD 20880-0125

GORDON, GEOFFREY ARTHUR, CLIMATOLOGY, COMPUTER APPLICATIONS. *Personal Data:* b St Louis, Mo, Feb 5, 48; m 70. *Educ:* Univ Mo, BS, 71, MS, 73, PhD(atmospheric sci), 79. *Prof Exp:* Res assoc, Lab Tree-Ring Res, Univ Ariz, 77-81; fac assot, Inst Quaternary Studies, Univ Maine, 81-89. *Concurrent Pos:* Consult, Lab Tree-Ring Res, Univ Ariz, 81; fel, Nat Oceanic & Atmospheric Admin, 81-82. *Mem:* Am Meteorol Soc; Am Quaternary Asn; AAAS; Asn Am Geographers; Tree-Ring Soc. *Res:* Exploitation of proxy records of climate variation including tree rings and historical documents and the development of statistical methodology for interpreting those records. *Mailing Add:* 22 Hamlin St Orono ME 04473

GORDON, GERALD ARTHUR, POLYMER SCIENCE. *Current Pos:* res consult, 80-89, REG COMPLIANCE SPECIALIST, SONOCO FIBRE DRUM, 89- *Personal Data:* b Chicago, Ill, Mar 5, 34; m 67, Sandra LaVine; c Jacob & Eva. *Educ:* Purdue Univ, BS, 56; Mass Inst Technol. MS, 57, ScD(chem eng), 61. *Prof Exp:* Res chemist, Munising Div, Kimberly-Clark Corp, 61-63; sr res chemist, Continental Can Co, 63-70, sr res scientist, 70-74, adv scientist, 74-80. *Concurrent Pos:* Lectr, Dept Chem, Roosevelt Univ, Ill Inst Technol & Univ Ill, Chicago Circle, 71-81. *Mem:* AAAS; Am Soc Testing & Mat; Am Chem Soc; Fedn Am Scientists; Tech Asn Pulp & Paper Indust; Nat Fire Protection Asn. *Res:* Permeability of polymers; structure of highly cross-linked polymers; polymer morphology; product development in regard to fibre drums; plastic drums and IBC's. *Mailing Add:* Sonoco Prod Co Indust Container Div 245 Eisenhower Lane Lombard IL 60148-5412. *Fax:* 630-620-3427

GORDON, GERALD BERNARD, PATHOLOGY. *Current Pos:* assoc prof, 70-77, PROF PATH, STATE UNIV NY UPSTATE MED CTR, 77- *Personal Data:* b Harrisburg, Pa, June 4, 34; m 56, Lois N Klein; c Robin, Marilyn, Lisa & Jeffrey. *Educ:* Franklin & Marshall Col, BS, 56; Yale Univ, MD, 59. *Prof Exp:* Rotating intern, Univ Hosps, Cleveland, Ohio, 59-60; resident path, Yale-New Haven Med Ctr, 60-63; instr, Yale Univ, 63-64; asst pathologist, Armed Forces Inst Pathol, Washington, DC, 64-66; from asst prof to assoc prof, Rutgers Med Sch, 66-70. *Concurrent Pos:* USPHS trainee & fel, 61-64, grant, 67-; res fel, Sch Med, Yale Univ, 63-64; consult, Vet Admin Hosp, Lyons, NJ & Muhlenberg Hosp, Plainfield, 66-70; assoc attending pathologist, State Univ Hosp, Syracuse, NY, 70-77; attend pathologist, State Univ Hosp, Syracuse, NY, 77- & Vet Admin Hosp, 71- *Mem:* US & Can Acad Pathol; Col Am Pathologists. *Res:* Experimental cellular pathology utilizing electron microscopy, tissue culture, histochemistry and biochemistry; studies in phagocytosis, intracellular digestion, lipid metabolism and accumulation; muscular diseases. *Mailing Add:* Dept Path State Univ Ny Health Sci Ctr Syracuse 766 Irving Ave Syracuse NY 13210-1605. *Fax:* 315-464-7130; *E-Mail:* gordong@vax.cs.hscsyr.edu

GORDON, GERALD M, METALLURGICAL ENGINEERING, CORROSION. *Current Pos:* CONSULT MAT & CORROSION PERFORMANCE, 95- *Personal Data:* b Detroit, Mich, May 24, 31; m 79, Priscilla M Caston; c 5. *Educ:* Wayne State Univ, BS, 56; Ohio State Univ, PhD(metall), 59. *Prof Exp:* Sr metallurgist, Stanford Res Inst, 59-63; sr metallurgist, Vallecitos Nuclear Ctr, Gen Elec Co, 63-69, mgr metall develop, 69-73, mgr zircaloy performance, Nuclear Energy Div, 73-75, mgr plant mat eng, Nuclear Energy Div, 76-95, mgr, Plant Component Behav Anal, mgr mats technol, 79-85, mgr fuel & plant mats technol, 86-92, chief technologist mat & corrosion, 93-95. *Mem:* Am Inst Mining, Metall & Petrol Engrs; fel Am Soc Metals; Nat Asn Corrosion Engrs. *Res:* Physical metallurgy of nuclear reactor materials; stress corrosion and electrochemistry of stainless steels and zirconium alloys; oxidation mechanism in high temperature alloys; materials engineering management. *Mailing Add:* 10916 Grand Haven Ave Las Vegas NV 89134. *Fax:* 702-242-6377

GORDON, GILBERT, INORGANIC CHEMISTRY. *Current Pos:* prof chem, 73-84, VOLWILER DISTINGUISHED RES PROF, MIAMI UNIV, 84- *Personal Data:* b Ill, Nov 11, 33; m 57, Joyce Elaine; c Thomas & Lyndi. *Educ:* Bradley Univ, BS, 55; Mich State Univ, PhD(inorg chem), 59. *Honors & Awards:* Benjamin Harrison Award, Miami Univ, 93. *Prof Exp:* Asst, Mich State Univ, 55-59; res assoc, Univ Chicago, 59-60; from asst prof to prof, Univ Md, 60-67; prof, Univ Iowa, 67-73. *Concurrent Pos:* Chem abstr sect ed, Catalysis & Reaction Kinetics Sect, Am Chem Soc, 71-; consult, Environ Protection Agency & Am Water Works Asn. *Mem:* Am Chem Soc; Chem Soc London; Int Union Pure Appl Chem. *Res:* Electron transfer processes; coordination chemistry; equilibria in aqueous solutions; mechanisms of inorganic reactions; water purification processes; reactions and interactions of chlorine-containing oxidizing agents. *Mailing Add:* Dept Chem Miami Univ Oxford OH 45056

GORDON, GLEN EVERETT, trace element analysis, receptor modeling; deceased, see previous edition for last biography

GORDON, HAROLD THOMAS, BIOCHEMISTRY. *Current Pos:* asst insect toxicologist, Univ Calif, Berkeley, 47-50, assoc insect toxicologist, 50-58, insect toxicologist, 58-63, insect biochemist, 63-77, LECTR ENTOM, UNIV CALIF, BERKELEY, 77- *Personal Data:* b Holyoke, Mass, Nov 21, 18; m 55; c 3. *Educ:* Mass State Col, BS, 39; Harvard Univ, MA, 40, PhD(biol), 47. *Prof Exp:* Asst, Off Sci Res & Develop Proj, Harvard Med Sch, 42-45, res assoc insecticides univ, 45-46. *Mem:* Entom Soc Am; NY Acad Sci; Brit Biochem Soc. *Res:* Insect growth, nutrition, reproduction and toxicology; ultramicroanalysis. *Mailing Add:* Dept Entom Univ Calif 201 Wellman Hall Berkeley CA 94720

GORDON, HARRY WILLIAM, BIOCHEMISTRY, PHARMACOLOGY. *Current Pos:* PRES, GORDON ASSOC CONSULT, 91- *Personal Data:* b New York, NY, Mar 31, 24; m 50, Rosalind Weinberg; c Bebe G. *Educ:* Long Island Univ, BS, 48; Georgetown Univ, MS, 51, PhD(biochem & pharmacol), 52. *Prof Exp:* Instr indust med, NY Univ-Bellevue Med Ctr, 52-55; res assoc enzym, Colgate-Palmolive Co, 55-57; asst dir res & develop, Block Drug Co, 57-59; dir exp res lab, St Barnabas Med Ctr, 59-62; vpres res & develop, Julius Schmid Labs, Inc, 62-76, Cosmetic & Drugs, DEL Labs, Inc, 76-91. *Concurrent Pos:* Mem Clin Res Comt, St Barnabas Med Ctr, 62-65; res consult, Interboro Gen Hosp, 65-70. *Mem:* Fel AAAS; Am Chem Soc; Electron Micros Soc Am; NY Acad Sci; Am Pharmaceut Asn. *Res:* Pharmacology-toxicology; clinical studies; international as well as domestic regulatory affairs; transplantation and teratology. *Mailing Add:* 1832 Cornelius Ave Wantagh NY 11793-3207. *Fax:* 516-781-6966

GORDON, HOWARD ALLAN, EXPERIMENTAL ELEMENTARY PARTICLE PHYSICS. *Current Pos:* Res assoc, 70-71, from assoc physicist to physicist, 71-82, SR PHYSICIST, BROOKHAVEN NAT LAB, 82- *Personal Data:* b Chicago, Ill, Oct 1, 43; m 68, Lynne Myers; c Michael J & Bethe H. *Educ:* Univ Ill-Urbana, BS, 64, MS, 66, PhD(physics), 70. *Concurrent Pos:* Mem, high energy adv comt, Brookhaven Nat Lab, 82-84, elem physics panel, Nat Res Coun, 83-85, Lawrence Berkeley Lab, 84-87, Fermilab Prog, 84-88 & high energy physics adv; vpres, Div Particles & Fields, Am Phys Soc, 97 panel, Dept Energy, 85-90. *Mem:* Fel Am Physical Soc; AAAS. *Res:* Experimental study of elementary particle physics; large transverse momentum phenomena; rare K decays; search for objects beyond the standard model. *Mailing Add:* Physics Dept 510 A Brookhaven Nat Lab Upton NY 11973. *Fax:* 516-344-5568; *E-Mail:* gordon1@dbnl.gov

GORDON, HOWARD R, OPTICS, OCEANOGRAPHY. *Current Pos:* asst prof physics & marine sci, 67-70, assoc prof, 70-76, PROF PHYSICS & MARINE SCI, UNIV MIAMI, 76- *Personal Data:* b Plattsburg, NY, May 21, 40; m 76. *Educ:* Clarkson Col Technol, BS, 61; Pa State Univ, MS, 63, PhD(physics), 65. *Prof Exp:* Asst prof physics, Col William & Mary, 65-67. *Mem:* Fel Optical Soc Am; Am Geophys Union. *Res:* Oceanography; light scattering; underwater optics; radiation transfer; ocean remote sensing; atmospheric optics; digital simulations. *Mailing Add:* Dept Physics Univ Miami Box 248046 Coral Gables FL 33124-8106

GORDON, HUGH, MATHEMATICAL ANALYSIS. *Current Pos:* from assoc prof to prof, 66-96, EMER PROF MATH, STATE UNIV NY ALBANY, 96- *Personal Data:* b New York, NY, Nov 23, 30. *Educ:* Columbia Univ, AB, 51, AM, 52, PhD(math), 58. *Prof Exp:* Asst math, Columbia Univ, 52-53, lectr, 53-58; Peirce instr, Harvard Univ, 58-61; asst prof, Univ Pa, 61-66. *Mem:* Am Math Soc. *Res:* Abstract analysis. *Mailing Add:* Dept Math State Univ NY Albany NY 12222

GORDON, HYMIE, medical genetics, internal medicine; deceased, see previous edition for last biography

GORDON, IRVING, MEDICAL MICROBIOLOGY. *Current Pos:* PROF MICROBIOL, SCH MED, UNIV SOUTHERN CALIF, 55-; SR ATTEND PHYSICIAN, LOS ANGELES CO GEN HOSP, 56- *Personal Data:* b Cleveland, Ohio, June 20, 14; m 39; c 3. *Educ:* Univ Mich, MD, 37; Am Bd Path, Am Bd Microbiol & Nat Bd Med Examrs, dipl. *Prof Exp:* Intern & resident, State Univ NY Down State, 37-39; jr med bacteriologist, NY State Dept Health, 39-40; fel, Rockefeller Found, 41; from instr to assoc path & bact, Albany Med Col, 42-43 & 46-48, assoc prof med & bact, 48-55. *Concurrent Pos:* Vol asst, Trudeau Sanitorium, NY, 42; from sr med bacteriologist to prin med bacteriologist, Div Lab & Res, NY State Dept Health, 46-53, asst dir, 53-55; bacteriologist & immunologist comn acute respiratory dis, Epidemiol Bd, US Army, 43-46, assoc mem, comn liver dis, 50-55, comn enteric infections, 53-59, mem comn viral infections, 53-71; consult, USPHS, 51-55, 56-57 & 66-71, Chem Corps, US Army, 56-62 & Virus Lab, Calif State Dept Pub Health, 56-64; sr lectr, Univ Sheffield, Eng & Holme lectr, Univ Col Hosp Sch Med, Univ London, 54; mem bact test comt, Nat Bd Med Exam, 56-59; mem allergy & infectious dis training grant comt, NIH, 62-66, Spec Study Sect, 76-, mem, Comt Etiology of Cancer, Am Cancer Soc, 60-63 & Personnel in Res, 64-69; Coun Res & Invest Awards, 70-75; mem spec adv comt prophylaxis of poliomyelitis, Calif State Dept Pub Health, 60-63; assoc dean, Univ Southern Calif, 63-66. *Mem:* AAAS; Am Soc Clin Invest; Am Soc Microbiol; Soc Exp Biol & Med; Am Asn Immunol. *Res:* Virology; immunology; host-parasite relationships. *Mailing Add:* Dept Microbiol Univ Southern Calif Sch Med 2025 Zonal Ave HMR 401 Los Angeles CA 90033-1054

GORDON, JAMES POWER, LASERS, OPTICS. *Current Pos:* mem tech staff electronics res, 55-59, head, Quantum Electronics Res Dept, 59-80, AT&T BELL LABS, 80-96, SR TECH STAFF CONSULT, LUCENT TECHNOL, 96- *Personal Data:* b New York, NY, Mar 20, 28. *Educ:* Mass Inst Technol, BS, 49; Columbia Univ, MA, 51, PhD(physics), 55. *Honors & Awards:* Charles Hard Towas Award, Optical Soc Am 81, Max Born Award, 91. *Prof Exp:* Asst physics, Columbia Univ, 53-55. *Mem:* Nat Acad Sci; Nat Acad Eng; fel Am Phys Soc; sr mem Inst Elec & Electronics Engrs. *Res:* Quantum electronics; interaction of electromagnetic waves with matter; communication theory. *Mailing Add:* Lucent Technol Rm 4E-410 101 Crawfords Corner Rd PO Box 3030 Holmdel NJ 07733-3030. *E-Mail:* jamespgordon@worldnet.att.net

GORDON, JAMES SAMUEL, PSYCHOSOMATIC MEDICINE, HOLISTIC MEDICINE. *Current Pos:* CLIN PROF, DEPTS PSYCHIAT, COMMUNITY FAMILY MED, GEORGETOWN UNIV SCH MED, 80- *Personal Data:* b New York, NY, Oct 12, 41. *Educ:* Harvard Univ, AB, 62, MD, 67. *Prof Exp:* Resident & chief resident psychiat, Albert Einstein Col Med, 68-71; res psychiatrist, NIMH, 71-82. *Concurrent Pos:* Teaching fel gen educ, Harvard Col, 63-67; vol physician, Haight-Ashbury Free Clin, 67-68; vis lectr, Grad Sch Psychol, Cath Univ Am, 74-75, Community Ther Training Ctr, 75-76; dir spec study & alternative servs, Presidents Comn Ment Health, 78-79; Blanche Ittleson consult, Group Advan Psychiat, 79-80; chief adolescent servs br, St Elizabeths Hosp, 80-82. *Mem:* Am Psychiat Asn; Am Holistic Med Asn; Physicians Social Responsibility. *Res:* Author of one book. *Mailing Add:* 5225 Connecticut Ave NW Washington DC 20015-2531

GORDON, JAMES WYLIE, PHYSICS. *Current Pos:* mem physics staff, 74-85, group leader, Thermonuclear Applications, 85-88, LAB FEL, LOS ALAMOS NAT LAB, 88- *Personal Data:* b Topeka, Kans, Jan 21, 34; m 63; c 3. *Educ:* Univ Kans, BS, 61, PhD(physics), 68. *Honors & Awards:* Ernest Orlando Lawrence Award, Dept Energy, 87. *Prof Exp:* Res scientist physics, Kaman Sci Corp, 68-74. *Mem:* Am Phys Soc; Sigma Xi. *Res:* Nuclear weapon development. *Mailing Add:* 149 Piedra Loop Los Alamos NM 87544-3838

GORDON, JANICE TAYLOR, THYROID HORMONE ACTIONS IN BRAIN, THYROID HORMONE METABOLITES. *Current Pos:* fel endocrinol, Med Col Pa, 78-79, res instr, 79-83, res asst prof, 83-89, RES ASSOC PROF, MED ENDOCRINOL, MED COL PA, 89- *Personal Data:* b Yonkers, NY, July 28, 30; m 51, Kenneth H; c Deirdre (Jacques), Pamela (Washington) & Sheila (Ulrich). *Educ:* Bryn Mawr Col, AB, 51, MA, 58, PhD(org chem), 61. *Prof Exp:* Org chemist, Merck-Sharp & Dohme Labs, 51-55; fel, Bryn Mawr Col, 61-62, res assoc org chem, 62-65; fel x-ray crystallog, Villanova Univ, Pa, 65-68; head, Dept Sci, Shipley Sch, Pa, 68-78. *Concurrent Pos:* Res chemist, Vet Admin Med Ctr, Pa, 83-86, mgr, Endocrinol Res Lab, 89-; staff scientist, Dept Psychiat, Univ Pa, Hosp & Sch Med, 89- *Mem:* Am Thyroid Asn; Am Chem Soc; fel Am Inst Chemists; Sigma Xi; AAAS. *Res:* Elucidation of the mechanism of action of thyroid hormone in neural (as opposed to nuclear) tissue of brain using the laboratory rat as model; emphasis has been on in vivo rates routes and products of metabolism using, as analytical tools, isotopic labeling, HPLC, autoradiography and recently immunohistochemistry; author of over 50 publications. *Mailing Add:* 1250 Upper Gulph Rd 1250 Upper Gulph Rd Radnor PA 19087. *Fax:* 215-823-5171

GORDON, JEFFREY I, INTESTINAL DEVELOPMENT, STEM CELL BIOLOGY. *Current Pos:* asst prof med, Div Gastroenterol, Sch Med, Washington Univ, St Louis, Mo, 81-84, asst prof biol chem, 82-84, assoc prof med & biol chem, 85-87, prof med & biochem & molecular biophys, 87-90, ALUMNI PROF & HEAD, DEPT MOLECULAR BIOL & PHARMACOL, SCH MED, WASHINGTON UNIV, ST LOUIS, MO, 91- *Personal Data:* b Oct 4; m 71, Deborah Gratz; c Brian & Alison. *Educ:* Univ Chicago, MD, 73. *Honors & Awards:* Young Investr Award, Am Fed Clin Res, 90; Young Scientist Award, Nat Inst Diabetes & Digestive & Kidney Diseases, 90; Distinguished Acheievement Award, Am Gastroenterol Asn, 92; Marion Merrell Dow Distinguished Prize Gastrointestinal Physiol, Am Physiol Soc, 94. *Concurrent Pos:* Estab invest, Am Heart Asn, 85-90. *Mem:*

Am Soc Biochem & Molecular Biol; Am Soc Cell Biol; Am Soc Clin Invest; fel AAAS; Am Gastroeuterol Asn; Am Asn Pathologists. *Res:* Gut development; gut epithelial biology; protein N-myristoylation. *Mailing Add:* Dept Molecular Biol & Pharmacol Washington Univ Sch Med 660 S Euclid Ave Box 8103 St Louis MO 63110-1093. *Fax:* 314-362-7047; *E-Mail:* jgordon@pharmdec.wustl.edu

GORDON, JEFFREY MILES, SOLAR ENERGY, APPLIED OPTICS. *Current Pos:* lectr, Inst Desert Res, Ben-Gurion Univ, 78-82, sr lectr, 82-87, assoc prof, 87-90, PROF, DEPT MECH ENG, INST DESERT RES, BEN-GURION UNIV, ISRAEL, 90- *Personal Data:* b Brooklyn, NY, June 10, 49; m 77, Yocheved Shadmon; c Shere, Nirit & Rona. *Educ:* Columbia Col, BA & MA, 70; Brown Univ, PhD(chem), 76. *Honors & Awards:* Ben-Gurion Prize, Israel, 80. *Prof Exp:* Fel polymer sci, Weizmann Inst Sci, 76-78. *Concurrent Pos:* Vis assoc prof, Univ Colo, Boulder, 85-86; vis prof, Nat Univ Singapore, 93-94. *Mem:* Int Solar Energy Soc. *Res:* Solar thermal energy systems; irreversible thermodynamics; heat engines and heat pumps; nonimaging optics; illumination optics; high-flux solar; medical optics. *Mailing Add:* Inst Desert Res Bur-Gurion Univ Sede Boqer Campus Sede Boqer 84990 Israel. *Fax:* 972-7-6555-058; *E-Mail:* jeff@menix.bgu.ac.il

GORDON, JOAN, FOOD SCIENCE, NUTRITION. *Current Pos:* chmn dept, 72-74, PROF FOOD SCI & NUTRIT, UNIV MINN, ST PAUL, 67- *Personal Data:* b Pine Island, Minn, Feb 8, 23. *Educ:* Univ Minn, BS, 45, MS, 47, PhD(home econ), 53. *Prof Exp:* Asst home econ, Univ Minn, 45-47, instr, 47-53; asst prof, Iowa State Col, 53-54; from asst prof to assoc prof, Univ Minn, 54-60; prof foods & nutrit, Pa State Univ, 60-67. *Mem:* AAAS; Am Home Econ Asn; Am Dietetic Asn; Inst Food Technol; Am Chem Soc; Sigma Xi. *Res:* Vitamins; food quality. *Mailing Add:* Dept Food Sci & Nutrit Univ Minn St Paul MN 55108

GORDON, JOEL ETHAN, PHYSICS. *Current Pos:* From asst prof to prof physics, 57-81, prof physics, 68-81, William R Kenan Jr prof, 83-87, STONE PROF NATURAL SCI, AMHERST COL, 81- *Personal Data:* b Denver, Colo, May 9, 30; m 56; c 2. *Educ:* Harvard Univ, AB, 52; Univ Calif, Berkeley, PhD(physics), 58. *Concurrent Pos:* Attached staff, Atomic Energy Res Estab, Harwell, Eng, 64-65; spec attached staff mem, Rockefeller Found, 68-69; vis prof, Univ Valle, Colombia, 68-69; book rev ed, Am J Physics, 74-; vis Scientist, Ceng Grenoble, France, 82; vis Scholar, Univ Calif, Berkeley & Lawrence Berkeley Lab, 87. *Mem:* Am Phys Soc; Am Asn Physics Teachers. *Res:* Low temperature and solid state physics. *Mailing Add:* Dept Physics Amherst Col Amherst MA 01002

GORDON, JOHN C, PLANT PHYSIOLOGY, SILVICULTURE. *Current Pos:* dean, 83-92, prof forestry & environ studies, 83-91, PINCHOT PROF, SCH FORESTRY, YALE UNIV, 91- *Personal Data:* b Nampa, Idaho, June 10, 39; m 64, Helka Lema Lehtinen; c Sean Nicholas. *Educ:* Iowa State Univ, BS, 61, PhD(plant physiol, silviculture), 66. *Hon Degrees:* MA, Yale Univ, 84. *Honors & Awards:* Green Lectr, Univ BC, 85; Distinguished Serv Award, Soc Am Forresters, 96. *Prof Exp:* Instr forestry, Iowa State Univ, 65-66; res plant physiologist pioneering res proj, NCent Forest Exp Sta, US Forest Serv, 66-70; assoc prof forestry, Iowa State Univ, 70-73, prof forestry, 73-77; prof forest sci & head dept, Ore State Univ, 77-83. *Concurrent Pos:* Act dir, Yale Inst Biospheric Studies, 94-96. *Mem:* AAAS; Soc Am Foresters; Sigma Xi. *Res:* Photosynthesis and translocation in trees; closyslem productivity and management; nitrogen fixation. *Mailing Add:* Sch Forestry Yale Univ New Haven CT 06511. *Fax:* 203-624-4505; *E-Mail:* john.gordon@yale.edu

GORDON, JOHN EDWARD, ORGANIC CHEMISTRY, PHYSICAL CHEMISTRY. *Current Pos:* RETIRED. *Personal Data:* b Columbus, Ohio, Aug 5, 31; m 56; c 2. *Educ:* Ohio State Univ, BSc, 53; Univ Calif, PhD(chem), 56. *Prof Exp:* Instr chem, Brown Univ, 56-58; fel, Mellon Inst, 58-65; from asst to assoc scientist, Woods Hole Oceanog Inst, 65-68; assoc prof, Kent State Univ, 68-70, chmn dept, 78-81, prof chem, 70-91. *Mem:* Am Chem Soc. *Res:* Organic electrolytes; chemical information science. *Mailing Add:* 69 Oviatt St Hudson OH 44236

GORDON, JOHN P(ETERSEN), electrical engineering, for more information see previous edition

GORDON, JOHN S(TEVENS), CHEMICAL ENGINEERING, INDUSTRIAL ENGINEERING. *Current Pos:* SUPPORT COORDR, CLEAN COAL TECHNOL, EG&G INC, 90- *Personal Data:* b Mt Kisco, NY, Sept 7, 31; m 67, Rowena O Francis; c Heather O & Grant P. *Educ:* Cornell Univ, BChE, 53; Ohio State Univ, MS, 56. *Prof Exp:* Process develop technologist, Socony-Mobil Labs, 53-54; proj engr liquid rocket fuels, Wright-Patterson AFB, 54-57; unit supvr propellant liaison & thermochem, Reaction Motors Div, Thiokol Chem Corp, NJ, 57-62; mgr phys chem technol, Astrosyst Int, Inc, 62-67; prin res scientist, Atlantic Res Corp, 67-70; prog mgr, Pope, Evans & Robbins, 70-72; staff engr, Res Cottrell Inc, 72-73; prin investr, TRW Inc, 73-74; group leader, Mitre Corp, 74-77; chem engr, TRW Inc, 77-81; chem engr, Engr Soc Comn Energy, 81-85; chem engr, Nat Syst Mgt Corp, 86-89, Versar Inc, 89-90. *Mem:* Am Chem Soc; Am Inst Aeronaut & Astronaut; Am Inst Chem Engrs; Combustion Inst. *Res:* Thermochemical calculations and propellant properties; high temperature thermodynamic, radiative and electromagnetic properties of gases; synthetic fuels; integrated combustion gasification environmental control systems; ordnance technology; hazardous waste technology. *Mailing Add:* 2364 Gallant Fox Ct Reston VA 20191-2611

GORDON, JON W, DEVELOPMENTAL BIOLOGY. *Current Pos:* MEM STAFF, DEPT OBSTET & GYNEC, MT SINAI SCH MED, NY, 82-, MATHERS PROF GERIATRIC & ADULT DEVELOP, 87- *Personal Data:* b Pasadena, Calif, Jan 12, 49; m 78. *Educ:* Columbia Univ, BA, 71; Yale Univ, PhD(biol), 78, MD, 80. *Prof Exp:* Hudson Brown fel obstet & gynec, Sch Med, Yale Univ, 79-80, fel, Dept Biol, 80-82. *Concurrent Pos:* Fel reviewer, NSF. *Mem:* AAAS; Soc Develop Biol. *Res:* Production of allophenic mice; study of mammalian sex determination and gainetogenesis; transfer of cloned genes into developing mice. *Mailing Add:* Dept Obstet & Gynec Mt Sinai Sch Med 1 Gustave Levy Plaza New York NY 10029-6504

GORDON, JOSEPH GROVER, II, ELECTROCHEMISTRY, SPECTROSCOPY. *Current Pos:* mem res staff, Almaden Res Ctr, IBM, 75-78, mgr interfacial electrochem, 78-84, mgr interfacial sci, 84-87, tech asst to dir res, 86-87, mgr mat sci & anal, 90-94, BATTERIES & DISPLAYS MGR, ALMADEN RES CTR, IBM, SAN JOSE, 94- *Personal Data:* b Nashville, Tenn, Dec 25, 45; m 72, Ruth M Gordon; c Perry M. *Educ:* Harvard Col, AB, 66; Mass Inst Technol, PhD(inorg chem), 70. *Honors & Awards:* Percy Julian Award, Nat Orgn Black Chemists & Chem Engrs, 93. *Prof Exp:* Asst prof chem, Calif Inst Technol, 70-75. *Concurrent Pos:* Chmn grad fel evaluation panels, NSF, 79-81; chmn, Gordon Conf Electrochem, 87; mem bd dir, Soc Electroanal Chem, 92-94, treas, 94-; bd mem, Chem Sci & Technol, Nat Res Coun, 93- *Mem:* Am Chem Soc; Royal Chem Soc; Nat Orgn Black Chemists & Chem Engrs; AAAS; Electrochem Soc; Am Phys Soc. *Res:* Structure of electrode-solution interface and adsorbed layers using synchnotron radiation, x-ray diffraction and absorption; novel, display technology, liquid crystals, organic light; emitting diodes, and others. *Mailing Add:* IBM Res Div Dept 650 Harry Rd San Jose CA 95120-6099. *Fax:* 408-927-2100; *E-Mail:* gordon@almaden.ibm.com

GORDON, JOSEPH R, ORGANIC CHEMISTRY, POLYMER CHEMISTRY. *Current Pos:* dir develop res, 64-70, admin asst res & develop, 70-77, DIR ENVIRON AFFAIRS, LUBRIZOL CORP, 77- *Personal Data:* b Boston, Mass, May 17, 24; m 47; c 3. *Educ:* Amherst Col, BA, 44; Univ Ill, PhD(chem), 49. *Prof Exp:* Res chemist, Johnson & Johnson, NJ, 49-51 & Kolker Chem, 51-52; res chemist, Gen Chem Div, Allied Chem Corp, 52-59, res supvr, 59-63, mgr polymer res, 63-64. *Mem:* Am Chem Soc. *Mailing Add:* 3170 Bayou Sound Longboat Key FL 34228-4096

GORDON, JULIUS, IMMUNOLOGY. *Current Pos:* from asst prof to assoc prof, 65-80, PROF, DEPT SURG, MCGILL UNIV, 81- *Personal Data:* b Budapest, Hungary, Nov 22, 32; Can citizen; m 54; c 2. *Educ:* Sir George Williams Col, BS, 54; McGill Univ, PhD(biochem), 58. *Prof Exp:* Fel immunol, Chester Beatty Res Inst, London, 58-60; res assoc, Montreal Cancer Inst, 61-64. *Concurrent Pos:* Res assoc, Med Res Coun Can, 66. *Mem:* Transplantation Soc; Am Asn Immunologists; Can Soc Immunol. *Res:* Cell-mediated immunity as applied to transplantation and tumor immunology. *Mailing Add:* 4130 Trafalgar Rd Montreal PQ H3Y 1R2 Can

GORDON, KENNETH RICHARD, VERTEBRATE FUNCTIONAL MORPHOLOGY. *Current Pos:* asst prof, 82-87, ASSOC PROF, DEPT BIOL SCI, FLA INT UNIV, MIAMI, 87- *Personal Data:* b Oakland, Calif, Feb 15, 45; m 88, Susan R Reese; c Bret R & Anne M. *Educ:* San Jose State Univ, BS, 72, MA, 74; Univ Calif, Davis, PhD(zool), 79. *Prof Exp:* Fel & res assoc, Univ Ill Med Ctr, 79-82. *Mem:* Am Soc Zoologists; Union Concerned Scientists; Sigma Xi; Am Soc Gravitational & Space Biol. *Res:* Analysis of the development and regeneration of bone in response to loading; mechanics of locomotion and feeding of mammals; evolution of feeding and locomotion, especially in marine mammals. *Mailing Add:* 14465 NE Third Ct Miami FL 33161. *Fax:* 305-348-1986

GORDON, KURTISS JAY, COMPUTER SCIENCE. *Current Pos:* sr res assoc comput sci, 85-87, sci image appln coordr, 87-95, SR INFO APPLN DESIGN & DEVELOP, OIT COMPUT SERV, UNIV MASS, 95- *Personal Data:* b New York, NY, July 20, 40; m 64, Courtney Parks; c 3. *Educ:* Antioch Col, BS, 64; Univ Mich, MA, 66, PhD(astron), 69; Univ Mass, MSECE, 85. *Prof Exp:* Jr res assoc, Nat Radio Astron Observ, Va, 67-69, res assoc, 69-70; from asst prof to assoc prof astron, Hampshire Col, 70-85. *Concurrent Pos:* Danforth assoc, 81-86. *Mem:* Am Astron Soc; Asn Comput Mach; Inst Elec & Electronics Engrs; Sigma Xi. *Res:* Information systems and applications design; computer graphics and image processing. *Mailing Add:* OIT Comput Serv Univ Mass Lederle GRC Amherst MA 01003-4640. *E-Mail:* gordon@oit.umass.edu

GORDON, LANCE KENNETH, HUMAN VACCINE, CLINICAL TRIALS MANAGEMENT. *Current Pos:* PRES & CHIEF EXEC OFFICER MUCOSAL IMMUNITY, ORAVAX, INC, 90- *Personal Data:* b Chicago, Ill, Dec 11, 47; m 69; c 2. *Educ:* Univ Calif, Humboldt, BS, 73; Univ Conn, Farmington, PhD(biomed sci), 77. *Prof Exp:* Postdoctoral immunol, Wash Univ Med Sch, 77-79; sect head immunol, Connaught Labs, Inc Pa, 80-83; res dir vaccines, Connaught Labs Ltd, Toronto, Can, 83-87; assoc med dir infectious dis, E R Squibb & Sons, 87-88; chief exec officer admin, Selcore Labs, Inc, 88-89; sr vpres res & develop vaccines, NAm Vaccines, 89-90. *Mem:* Am Asn Immunologists; Am Soc Microbiol. *Res:* First successful carrier-hapten vaccine; haemophilus influenzae b vaccine licensed; new pertussis vaccine through phase II clinical trials; awarded three US patents. *Mailing Add:* Oravax Inc 38 Sidney St 4th Floor Cambridge MA 02139-4169

GORDON, LOUIS, MATHEMATICAL STATISTICS. *Current Pos:* assoc prof, 83-88, PROF MATH, UNIV SOUTHERN CALIF, 88- *Personal Data:* b Philadelphia, Pa, Dec 13, 46. *Educ:* Mich State Univ, BS, 68, MS, 68; Stanford Univ, MS, 69, PhD(statist), 71. *Prof Exp:* Asst prof statist, Stanford Univ, 71-73; statistician, Alza Corp, 73-78 & US Dept Energy, 78-83. *Concurrent Pos:* Mem, Comt Nat Statist, 87-93; fel, John S Guggenheim Found, 89-90; scholar, Fulbright-Hays Scholar, 89-90. *Mem:* Am Math Soc; fel Inst Math Statist; Am Statist Asn; Soc Indust & Appl Math. *Res:* Nonparametric inference in high dimensional parameter spaces. *Mailing Add:* Math Dept DRB-155 Univ Southern Calif 1042 W 36th Pl Los Angeles CA 90089-0001. *E-Mail:* gordon@mtha.usc.edu

GORDON, LOUIS IRWIN, CHEMICAL OCEANOGRAPHY. *Current Pos:* instr oceanog, 69-72, asst prof, 72-77, ASSOC PROF OCEANOG, ORE STATE UNIV, 77- *Personal Data:* b Los Angeles, Calif, Aug 17, 28; m 51; c 3. *Educ:* Univ Calif, Los Angeles, BS, 51, San Diego, MS, 53; Ore State Univ, PhD(chem oceanog), 73. *Prof Exp:* Asst geochem, Scripps Inst Oceanog, Univ Calif, 58, res chemist, 58-62, asst specialist marine chem, San Diego, 62-64, assoc specialist, 64-66. *Mem:* Am Geophys Union; Am Soc Limnol & Oceanog; Sigma Xi. *Res:* Chemical oceanography; dissolved gases; nutrients; carbon; analytical chemistry; stable isotopes in oceanography; atmospheric and biological exchange processes, coastal processes. *Mailing Add:* 2941 Ashwood Dr Corvallis OR 97330-1255. *E-Mail:* lgordon@occ.orst.edu

GORDON, MALCOLM STEPHEN, COMPARATIVE ECOLOGICAL PHYSIOLOGY, MARINE BIOLOGY. *Current Pos:* from instr to assoc prof, 58-68, dir, Inst Evolutionary Environ Biol, 70-76, PROF BIOL, UNIV CALIF, LOS ANGELES, 68- *Personal Data:* b Brooklyn, NY, Nov 13, 33; m 92, Carol Rogasner; c Dana M Gordon. *Educ:* Cornell Univ, BA, 54; Yale Univ, PhD(zool), 58. *Prof Exp:* Asst oceanog, Cornell Univ, 51-53. *Concurrent Pos:* Guggenheim fel, 61-62; Nat Acad Sci exchange vis, USSR, 65; asst dir res, Nat Fisheries Ctr & Aquarium Dept Interior, DC, 68-69; vis prof, Chinese Univ, Hong Kong, 71-72; sr Queen's fel marine sci, Dept Sci Govt Australia, 76; chair, Div Comp Physiol Biochem, Am Soc Zoologists, 88-89; chair, Int Comt Comp Physiol, Int Union Physiol Sci, 94- *Mem:* AAAS; Am Soc Ichthyol & Herpetol; Soc Integrative Comp Biol; Soc Exp Biol; Am Physiol Soc. *Res:* Comparative vertebrate ecological physiology with emphasis on fishes and amphibians; activity metabolism; amphibious fishes; mechanisms of osmoregulation and salinity adaptation; adaptation to low temperatures and high hydrostatic pressures; ecological physiology; nutrient recycling from wastewater; fish aquaculture. *Mailing Add:* Dept Biol Univ Calif Box 951606 Los Angeles CA 90095-1606. *Fax:* 310-206-3987; *E-Mail:* msgordon@ucla.edu

GORDON, MALCOLM WOFSY, biochemistry, for more information see previous edition

GORDON, MANUEL JOE, GENETICS, CELL BIOLOGY. *Current Pos:* MGR APPLN, RES DEPT, SPINCO DIV, BECKMAN INSTRUMENTS, INC, 61- *Personal Data:* b Cleveland, Ohio, July 3, 22; m 43; c 2. *Educ:* Ohio State Univ, BSc, 49; Univ Calif, MA, 52, PhD(zool), 55. *Prof Exp:* Res fel zool, Univ Calif, 55-57; asst prof res, Dairy Dept, Mich State Univ, 57-61. *Mem:* NY Acad Sci; Am Soc Human Genetics; AAAS; Am Inst Biol Sci; Soc Sci Study Sex; Sigma Xi. *Res:* Molecular structure of proteins, methods for characterization of human serum lipoproteins; physico-chemical biology; reproductive physiology, genetics. *Mailing Add:* 3640 Evergreen Dr Palo Alto CA 94303-4427

GORDON, MARK A, RADIO ASTRONOMY. *Current Pos:* asst scientist, Nat Radio Astron Observ, 69-72, assoc scientist, 72-77, asst dir, Ariz Opers, 73-84, SCIENTIST, NAT RADIO ASTRON OBSERV, 77- *Personal Data:* b Springfield, Mass, Oct 13, 37; m 80; c 2. *Educ:* Yale Univ, BA, 59; Univ Colo, PhD(astrophysics-geophys), 66. *Prof Exp:* Scientist, Arctic Inst NAm, 59-61; staff, Lincoln Lab, Mass Inst Technol, 66-69. *Mem:* Am Astron Soc; Int Union Radio Sci; Int Astron Union. *Res:* Interstellar medium, galactic structure. *Mailing Add:* Nat Radio Astron Observ 949 N Cherry Ave Campus Bldg 65 Tucson AZ 85721

GORDON, MARK STEPHEN, QUANTUM CHEMISTRY. *Current Pos:* from asst prof to assoc prof, 70-78, PROF CHEM, NDAK STATE UNIV, 78-, CHMN DEPT, 81- *Personal Data:* b New York, NY, Jan 18, 42; m 65; c 1. *Educ:* Rensselaer Polytech Inst, BS, 63; Carnegie-Mellon Univ, PhD(chem), 68. *Prof Exp:* Assoc, Iowa State Univ, 67-70. *Mem:* Am Chem Soc; Sigma Xi; Am Phys Soc. *Res:* Molecular structure and chemical bonding in ground and excited states; calculations on excited states, intramolecular hydrogen bonding; internal rotation; localized orbital calculations. *Mailing Add:* Dept Chem Iowa State Univ Ames IA 50010

GORDON, MAXWELL, MEDICINAL CHEMISTRY. *Current Pos:* RETIRED. *Personal Data:* b USSR, Feb 13, 21; nat US; wid; c 2. *Educ:* Philadelphia Col Pharm, AB & BS, 41; Univ Pa, MS, 46, PhD(org chem), 48; Imp Col, London, dipl, 51. *Prof Exp:* Anal chemist, US Naval Med Supply Depot, NY, 41-42; instr org chem, Philadelphia Col Pharm, 46-47; res fel, Radiation Lab, Univ Calif, 49-50, Swiss Tech Inst, Zurich, 48-49 & Imp Col, London, 50-51; res assoc, Radio-Isotope Lab, Squibb Inst Med Res, 51-55; sr scientist, Smith Kline & French Labs, 55-57, head phys sci sect, 57-68, assoc dir res activ, 68-70; dir res planning, Bristol Labs, 70-74, vpres, 74-82, sr vpres, Sci & Technol Group, 82-86. *Mem:* Am Chem Soc; Royal Soc Chem; Swiss Chem Soc; Soc Ger Chem; Austrian Chem Soc. *Res:* Chemical kinetics; azulenes; heterocycles; cancer; radioactive tracers; antibiotic biosynthesis; medicinal chemistry; scientific documentation; research planning; bio-electronics; analgetics and antagonists; central nervous system drugs; recombinant DNA, interferon, antiviral drugs. *Mailing Add:* 60 E End Ave Apt 22A New York NY 10028-7907

GORDON, MICHAEL ANDREW, MEMBRANE BIOPHYSICS, MOLECULAR GRAPHICS. *Current Pos:* ASSOC PROF PHARMACOL, MED CTR, KANS UNIV, 82- *Educ:* Univ Calif, PhD(pharmacol), 76. *Mailing Add:* Dept Pharm Kans Univ Med Ctr Kansas City KS 66103

GORDON, MICHAEL DAVID, INFORMATION RETRIEVAL. *Current Pos:* asst prof, 84-91, ASSOC PROF, SCH BUSINESS, UNIV MICH, 91-, CHAIR, 95- *Personal Data:* b Evanston, Ill, Jan 10, 51; m 82, Candace White; c 2. *Educ:* Univ Mich, PhD(comput sci), 84. *Prof Exp:* Asst prof, Wayne State Univ, 83-84. *Concurrent Pos:* Assoc ed, J Info Technol Mgt, 88- *Res:* Improving the storage and retrieval of textual information in computers. *Mailing Add:* Sch Bus Univ Mich Ann Arbor MI 48109. *E-Mail:* mdgordon@umich.edu

GORDON, MILLARD F(REEMAN), ELECTRICAL ENGINEERING. *Current Pos:* RETIRED. *Personal Data:* b Eastvale, Pa, Sept 3, 21; m 43; c 2. *Educ:* Carnegie Inst Technol, BS, 42, MS, 47, DSc, 48. *Prof Exp:* Assoc prof eng, Brown Univ, 50-54; head, Penetrations Systs Dept, Thompson-Ramo-Wooldridge, Inc, 54-60; sr staff adv, Bissett-Berman Corp, 60-67; chief scientist radar, Hughes Aircraft Co, Culver City, 67-82. *Mem:* Inst Elec & Electronics Engrs. *Res:* Research, development and management. *Mailing Add:* 2826 Scarlet Circle Pharr TX 78577

GORDON, MILTON, MICROBIOLOGY. *Current Pos:* RETIRED. *Personal Data:* b New York, NY, May 28, 29; m 52, Joyce Justman; c Marc Richard Esq, Bruce Earl & Jacqueline Ann (Haynes). *Educ:* Univ Calif, Los Angeles, AB, 50; George Washington Univ, MS, 55, PhD, 62. *Prof Exp:* Microbiologist, US Army Biol Labs, 51-70; health scientist adminr, Div Res Grants, NIH, 70-86. *Mem:* AAAS; Am Soc Microbiol; Sigma Xi. *Res:* Immunology; medical bacteriology. *Mailing Add:* 1409 Pinewood Dr Frederick MD 21701-4263

GORDON, MILTON ANDREW, MATHEMATICAL STATISTICS. *Current Pos:* PRES, CALIF STATE UNIV, FULLERTON, 90- *Personal Data:* b Chicago, Ill, May 25, 35; m 88, Margaret Faulwell; c Vincent, Patrick & Michael. *Educ:* Xavier Univ La, BS, 57; Univ Detroit, MA, 60; Ill Inst Technol, PhD(math), 68. *Prof Exp:* Mathematician, Labs Appl Sci, Univ Chicago, 59-62; from instr to asst prof math, Loyola Univ Chicago 66-71, dir Afro-Am studies prog, 71-78; dean, Col Arts & Sci, Chicago State Univ, 78-86; vpres acad affairs, Sonoma State Univ, 86-90. *Mem:* Math Asn Am; Am Math Soc. *Res:* General algebraic systems and statistics, especially as they relate to the social and behavioral sciences; curriculum for Afro-American Studies Program. *Mailing Add:* 800 N State College Blvd Fullerton CA 92634

GORDON, MILTON PAUL, BIOCHEMISTRY & GENETIC ENGINEERING OF PLANTS, PHYTOREMEDIATION. *Current Pos:* from asst prof to assoc prof, 59-66, assoc chmn, 84-85, PROF BIOCHEM, UNIV WASH, 66- *Personal Data:* b St Paul, Minn, Feb 8, 30; m 55, Elaine Travis; c David, Karen, Nancy & Peter. *Educ:* Univ Minn, BA, 50; Univ Ill, PhD(biochem), 53. *Prof Exp:* Res fel, Univ Ill, 52-53; res fel, Nat Cancer Inst, Sloan-Kettering Inst, 53-55, asst, 55-57; asst res biochemist virus lab, Univ Calif, 57-59. *Concurrent Pos:* Ed, Biochem, Am Chem Soc, 61-93; vis res chemist, Princeton Univ, 66-67; adv, Ctr Molecular Biol, Liahore, Pakistan. *Mem:* AAAS; Am Chem Soc; Am Soc Biol Chemists. *Res:* Molecular basis of crown gall tumorigenesis of plants and biological engineering of plants; plant physiology; remediation of toxic waste sites with plants. *Mailing Add:* Dept Biochem SJ70 Univ Wash Box 357350 Seattle WA 98195. *Fax:* 206-685-8279; *E-Mail:* miltong@u.washington.edu

GORDON, MORRIS AARON, MEDICAL MYCOLOGY, MICROBIOLOGY. *Current Pos:* RETIRED. *Personal Data:* b Waterbury, Conn, Apr 3, 20; m 45,70, Ruth Kathryn McKee; c Barbara J, David S & Sarah E. *Educ:* City Col New York, BS, 40; Univ Chicago, MS, 42; Duke Univ, PhD(bot, mycol), 49; Am Bd Microbiol, dipl. *Honors & Awards:* Benham Award, Med Mycol Soc Am, 88; Georg Award, Int Soc Human & Animal Mycol, 91. *Prof Exp:* Lab officer, Region Hosp, US Army, 45-46; mycologist, Commun Dis Ctr, USPHS, 49-53, head, Airborne Pathogens Lab, 53-54; res specialist, Chem Corps Training Command, Ft McClellan, Ala, 54-55; asst prof microbiol & mycol, Med Col, SC, 55-57, assoc prof, 57-59; from sr res scientist to prin res scientist & dir, Mycol Lab, NY State Dept Health, Albany, 59-87, dir, Clin Microbiol Labs, 83-87, emer dir clin microbiol & mycol, 87-96. *Concurrent Pos:* Instr med sch, Emory Univ, 49-54; La State Univ Inter-Am fel, Cent Am, 59; consult, Albany Vet Admin Hosp, 59-96; res prof microbiol, Albany Med Col, 64-93; mem bact & mycol study sect, NIH, 71-75; mem adv comt, Brown-Hazen Prog of Res Corp, 74-78; Fulbright prof, Uruguay, 78; prof, Grad Sch Pub Health Scis, State Univ NY, Albany, 85-89; prin investr, NIH res grants. *Mem:* Fel Am Acad Microbiol; Am Soc Microbiol; Sigma Xi; Int Soc Human & Animal Mycol (vpres, 82-85); Med Mycol Soc Am (pres, 78-79). *Res:* Fungal serology; cryptococcosis; invented latex antigen test; dermatophilus first human cases; antifungal antibiotics; fluorescent antibody first to apply to fungal diagnosis; lipophilic yeasts culture. *Mailing Add:* 501 Penneross Dr Raleigh NC 27610-2176

GORDON, MORTON MAURICE, ACCELERATOR THEORY, CYCLOTRON DESIGN. *Current Pos:* assoc prof, 59-62, PROF PHYSICS, MICH STATE UNIV, 62- *Personal Data:* b Atlantic City, NJ, Nov 8, 24; m 50; c 2. *Educ:* Univ Chicago, BS, 46; Wash Univ, PhD(physics), 50. *Prof Exp:* From instr to prof physics, Univ Fla, 50-59. *Concurrent Pos:* Physicist, Oak Ridge Nat Lab, 57-58; vis prof & consult, Ind Univ, 72-73 & TRUME Cyclotron, 83; consult, TRIUMF Cyclotron, 83. *Mem:* Am Phys Soc; Am Asn Physics Teachers. *Res:* Atomic and nuclear scattering theory; accelerator theory; migma fusion theory; super conducting cyclotron design. *Mailing Add:* Cyclotron Labs Mich State Univ East Lansing MI 48824

GORDON, MYRA, ORGANIC CHEMISTRY, ANALYTICAL CHEMISTRY. *Current Pos:* PRIN, MG ASSOC, 90- *Personal Data:* b Mt Vernon, NY, Dec 12, 39. *Educ:* Mt Holyoke Col, AB, 60; Univ Pittsburgh, PhD(chem), 65. *Prof Exp:* Asst prof chem, Tulane Univ, 66-70 & Univ Western Ont, 70-74; Isotopes Div, Merck, Sharp & Dohme Can Ltd, 74-87; Isotec Inc, 87-90. *Mem:* Am Chem Soc; Chem Inst Can. *Res:* Intermolecular interactions; molecular spectroscopy, particularly nuclear magnetic resonance spectroscopy; applications of stable isotopes in chemistry and medicine; applications of nmr in process analysis and control. *Mailing Add:* MG Assoc 612-1209 Richmond St London ON N6A 3L7 Can. *Fax:* 519-439-4820

GORDON, NANCY ROWAN, INORGANIC CHEMISTRY. *Current Pos:* ASST PROF CHEM, UNIV SOUTHERN MAINE. *Personal Data:* b Plainfield, NJ, Apr 6, 46; wid; c 2. *Educ:* Mt Holyoke Col, AB, 68; Boston Univ, PhD(inorg chem), 74. *Prof Exp:* Vis asst prof chem, Carnegie-Mellon Univ, 73-74; from asst prof to assoc prof chem, Am Univ, 78- *Mem:* Am Chem Soc. *Res:* Kinetics of transition metal reactions; models for metal binding sites in proteins. *Mailing Add:* Chem Dept Univ Southern Main Portland ME 04104-9300

GORDON, NATHAN, biochemistry, for more information see previous edition

GORDON, P(AUL), physical metallurgy, for more information see previous edition

GORDON, PHILIP N, FORESTRY, ECOLOGY. *Current Pos:* RES ASSOC, INST ECON BOT, NY BOT GARDEN, 88-, CONN FOREST & PARK ASN, 90- *Personal Data:* b Boston, Mass, Apr 21, 19; m 44; c 4. *Educ:* Polytech Inst Brooklyn, BS, 42; Univ Minn, MS, 50. *Prof Exp:* Jr anal chemist, Tenn Valley Authority, 42-43; res org chemist, Pfizer, Inc, 50-67; residue chemist, 67-73, sr res scientist, 73-82; res assoc, Dept Biol, Yale Univ, 82-90. *Mem:* AAAS; Am Chem Soc; Soc Econ Bot; Int Asn Plant Tissue Cult; Am Inst Biol Sci; Am Soc Plant Physiol; Sigma Xi. *Res:* Forest ecology; plant genetics; antibiotics; trace analysis; plant tissue culture. *Mailing Add:* 16 Landing Rd Old Lyme CT 06631-1446

GORDON, PHILIP RAY, CUTANEOUS GERONTOLOGY, NUTRITION. *Current Pos:* scientist III, USDA Human Nutrit Res Ctr Aging, Tufts Univ, 84-87, instr, Dept Biochem & Pharmacol, Sch Med, 85-88, ASST PROF, SCH NUTRIT, TUFTS UNIV, BOSTON, MASS, 86-, SCIENTIST II, USDA HUMAN NUTRIT RES CTR AGING, 87-, ASST PROF, DEPT BIOCHEM, SCH MED, 88- *Personal Data:* b Sacramento, Calif, Mar 4, 55. *Educ:* Univ Calif, Davis, BS, 77; Univ Mo-Columbia, MS, 80, PhD(biochem nutrit), 82. *Honors & Awards:* Ruth L Pike Frontiers Nutrit lectr, Pa State Univ, 89. *Prof Exp:* Res fel, Ctr Biochem & Biophys Sci & Med, Harvard Med Sch, 81-84. *Concurrent Pos:* Reviewer, J Nutrit, 86- & J Invest Dermat, 87-; mem, Spec Rev Comt, Nat Inst Arthritis & Musculoskeletal & Skin Dis, 88, Nat Cancer Inst, 89; reviewer, Vet Health Serv & Res Admin, 90. *Mem:* Soc Invest Dermat; Fedn Am Socs Exp Biol; Am Inst Nutrit; AAAS. *Mailing Add:* Asst Prof Biochem Off Med Educ Med Col Pa Allegheny Univ Health Sci 2900 Queens Lane Philadelphia PA 19129. *Fax:* 215-843-5495

GORDON, PORTIA BEVERLY, BIOCHEMISTRY. *Current Pos:* Fel, Albert Einstein Col Med, 79-83, res assoc biochem, 83-85, ASST PROF MED, MONTEFIORE MED CTR, ALBERT EINSTEIN COL MED, 85- *Personal Data:* b Brooklyn, NY, May 7, 52. *Educ:* Smith Col, BA, 74; Albert Einstein Col Med, MSc, 77, PhD(molecular pharmacol), 80. *Mem:* AAAS; Am Women Sci; NY Acad Sci; Am Soc Cell Biol; Fedn Am Soc Cell Biol. *Res:* Author of numerous publications. *Mailing Add:* 459 E 19th St Brooklyn NY 11226-0001

GORDON, RANDOLPH LEE, PUBLIC HEALTH & EPIDEMIOLOGY. *Current Pos:* COMNR HEALTH, VA DEPT HEALTH, 95- *Personal Data:* b Richmond, Va, Apr 23, 58; m 83, Kimberly J Ball; c Matthew, Michelle & Anna. *Educ:* Univ Va, BA, 80; Med Col Va, MD, 84; Johns Hopkins Univ, MPH, 88. *Prof Exp:* Resident family pract, Roanoke Mem Hosp, 84-87, chief resident, 86-87; prev med resident, Johns Hopkins Univ, 87-89; physician, Johns Hopkins Health Syst, Wyman Park Hosp, 87-88; dir, Weld Co Health Dept & asst dir, NColo Family Med Residency Training Prog, Greeley, Colo, 88-93; assoc dir managed care, Pub Health Pract Prog Off & actg/asst dir, Div Pub Health Systs, Ctr Dis Control, 93-95. *Concurrent Pos:* Clin asst prof, Dept Prev Med & Biometrics, Univ Colo Health Sci Ctr, 91 & Family & Prev Med, Emory Univ Sch Med, 95; bd dir, Nat Asn Co Health Officers, 91-93. *Mem:* Am Acad Family Physicians; fel Am Col Prev Med; Christian Med Dent Soc; Nat Asn Co Health Officers. *Mailing Add:* Va Dept Health 1500 E Main St Suite 214 Richmond VA 23219

GORDON, RICHARD, MORPHOGENESIS, MEDICAL IMAGING. *Current Pos:* prof bot, 84-94, PROF RADIOL, UNIV MAN, 78- *Personal Data:* b New York, NY, Nov 6, 43; m 93, Natalie K Bjorklund; c Leland, Bryson, Justin, Chason, Alan & Lana. *Educ:* Univ Chicago, BSc, 63; Univ Ore, PhD(chem physics), 67. *Prof Exp:* Res assoc theoret biol, Ctr Theoret Biol, State Univ NY, Buffalo, 69-72; fel, Math Res Br, NIH, 72-75, expert, Image Processing Unit, 75-78. *Concurrent Pos:* Assoc res prof, Dept Radiol, George Washington Univ, 74-78; adj prof, Dept Elec Eng, Univ Man, 82-; vis prof, Solid Mech Div, Univ Waterloo, 86-88; adj prof physics & elec & comput eng, Univ Man. *Mem:* Can Asn Theoret Biologists (pres); Int Soc Diatomic Res. *Res:* Morphogenesis, differentiation waves, developmental control of genetics and differentration; neural tube defects; molecular basis of diatom shell patterns, diatom gliding motility; medical imaging; theory of computed tomography; detection of early breast cancer. *Mailing Add:* Dept Radiol Univ Man Winnepeg MB R3A 1R9 Can. *Fax:* 204-787-2080; *E-Mail:* gordonr@cc.umanitoba.ca

GORDON, RICHARD G, GEOPHYSICS. *Current Pos:* W M KECK PROF GEOPHYSICS, RICE UNIV, 95- *Personal Data:* b Oceanside, Calif, Nov 20, 53. *Educ:* Univ Calif, Santa Cruz, AB, 75; Stanford Univ, MS, 77, PhD(geophys), 79. *Honors & Awards:* James B Macelwane Medal, Am Geophys Union, 89. *Prof Exp:* From asst prof to prof, NWestern Univ, 80-95, dept chair, 93-95. *Concurrent Pos:* Fac fel, Shell Found, 82; Alfred P Sloan Found Res Fel, 84; vis scholar, Univ Cambridge, 85-86; assoc ed, J Geophys Res, 87-90, tech tonophysics ed, 90-92; mem, Space Explor Initiative Panel, Am Geophys Union, 92; vis researcher, Geody Submarine Lab, Nat Ctr Sci Res, 92-93; vis distinguished scientist, Jet Propulsion Lab, Calif Inst Technol, 94- *Mem:* Fel Am Geophys Union; fel Geol Soc Am; AAAS. *Res:* Tectonics and Kinematics of the crust and lithosphere; applications of marine magnetic, paleomagnetic, marine geophysical, seismological and space geodetic data; author numerous publications. *Mailing Add:* Dept Geol & Geophys Rice Univ 6100 Main St MS 126 Houston TX 77005-1892. *Fax:* 713-285-5214; *E-Mail:* rgg@geophysics.rice.edu

GORDON, RICHARD K, ENZYMOLOGY, SPECTROSCOPY. *Current Pos:* RES SCIENTIST, DIV BIOCHEM, WALTER REED ARMY INST, 81- *Personal Data:* b Boston, Mass. *Educ:* Boston Univ, BA, 74, MA, 78, PhD(microbiol, immunol), 81. *Mem:* Am Soc Pharmacol & Exp Therapeut; Am Soc Biochem & Molecular Biol. *Res:* Biochemical actions of chemical agents, toxins and peptides on enzymes and cellular receptors. *Mailing Add:* Div Biochem Walter Reed Army Inst Res Washington DC 20307-5100. *E-Mail:* dr._richard_gordon@wrsmtp_ccmail.army.mil

GORDON, RICHARD LEE, PHYSICS. *Current Pos:* sr res scientist Solid State Physics, Pac Northwest Labs, EMER PROF, BATELLE MEM INST, 96- *Personal Data:* b Lewiston, Idaho, Nov 6, 35; m 59; c 3. *Educ:* Wash State Univ, BS, 58, PhD(physics), 66. *Prof Exp:* Physicist, Lawrence Radiation Lab, Univ Calif, 58-61. *Concurrent Pos:* Lectr physics, Joint Ctr Grad Study, 68- *Res:* Shock hydrodynamics; surface physics; stimulated Brillouin scattering; solid state physics. *Mailing Add:* 429 Kemnerer Rd State University PA 16802-5010

GORDON, RICHARD SEYMOUR, AQUACULTURE, DEVELOPMENT OF NEW FOODS. *Current Pos:* dir, Newcast Ctr, 81-90, PROF AGRIBUS, SCH AGRIBUS & ENVIRON RESOURCES, ARIZ STATE UNIV 80-; PRES, GORDON GROUP, 77- *Personal Data:* b New York, NY, June 28, 25; m 51, Emily C Evarts; c Richard E, Elizabeth J (Lang), Jacquis N, Helen E (Seblitz) & Charlotte C. *Educ:* Univ Rochester, BS, 47; Harvard Univ, Med Sci, 54; Mass Inst Technol, PhD(biochem & biophys), 54. *Prof Exp:* Chief scientist, Monsanto Co, 51-71; sr adv, Food & Drug Admin, 71-73; pres, Inst Urban Develop, 72-76; proj dir & vis prof, Harvard Univ, 77-79. *Concurrent Pos:* Vchmn, Bd Agr, Nat Acad Sci & Nat Res Coun, 63-69; vis prof, Wash Univ, Princeton Univ & Calif Inst Technol; panel chair, White House Conf Food, Health & Nutrit, 67-70. *Mem:* Am Chem Soc; Am Soc Microbiol; AAAS; Soc Chem Indust; Poultry Sci Asn. *Res:* Mulitple use of natural resource; physiological and environmental control of growth and development in plants and animals; novel approaches to organizing and managing technically driven ventures particularly in agribusiness and technology; economic incentives for environmental restoration. *Mailing Add:* Sch Agribus & Environ Resources Ariz State Univ Tempe AZ 85287-3306. *Fax:* 520-727-1961; *E-Mail:* aarsg@asu.edu

GORDON, ROBERT BOYD, geophysics, engineering, for more information see previous edition

GORDON, ROBERT DIXON, PHYSICAL CHEMISTRY. *Current Pos:* from asst prof to prof, 66-97, EMER PROF CHEM, QUEEN'S UNIV, ONT, 97- *Personal Data:* b Toronto, Ont, Dec 15, 36; m 60; c 2. *Educ:* McMaster Univ, BSc, 59, MSc, 61; Univ London, PhD(phys chem), 64. *Prof Exp:* Lectr chem, Univ Ibadan, 64-66. *Res:* Electronic spectroscopy; large-amplitude molecular motion. *Mailing Add:* Dept Chem Queen's Univ Kingston ON K7L 3N6 Can

GORDON, ROBERT EDWARD, zoology, herpetology; deceased, see previous edition for last biography

GORDON, ROBERT JAY, PHYSICAL CHEMISTRY, CHEMICAL PHYSICS. *Current Pos:* from asst prof to assoc prof, 73-80, PROF CHEM, UNIV ILL, CHICAGO, 80- *Personal Data:* b Brooklyn, NY, Feb 29, 44; m 69, Evelyn Rabinowitz; c Ilana (Goldhaber), Tamar & Dov. *Educ:* Harvard

Univ, AB, 65, AM, 66, PhD(chem physics), 70. *Prof Exp:* Res assoc chem physics, Calif Inst Technol, 70-72; res assoc chem, Naval Res Lab, 72-73. *Concurrent Pos:* NSF grant, 75-; Dept Energy grant, 77-; vis scholar, Stanford Univ, 80-81, Bav Ilan, 85; Petrol Res Fund grant, 82-91; vis prof, Hokkaido Univ, 92. *Mem:* Am Chem Soc; Am Phys Soc. *Res:* Experimental studies in chemical kinetics, laser-induced chemical reactions. *Mailing Add:* Dept Chem MCD 111 Univ Ill Chicago Chicago IL 60607. *E-Mail:* robert.j.gordon@.uic.edu

GORDON, ROBERT JULIAN, ENVIRONMENTAL CHEMISTRY. *Current Pos:* INDEPENDENT CONSULT, 88- *Personal Data:* b Seattle, Wash, July 31, 23; m 48; c 2. *Educ:* Univ Calif, Los Angeles, BS, 47, PhD(chem), 52. *Prof Exp:* Technologist petrol res, Shell Oil Co, 52-58, sr technologist, 58-59, group leader, 59-61, res supvr, Shell Develop Co, 61-64; supvry physicist, Vehicle Pollution Lab, Calif State Dept Health, 64-68; asst prof path, Sch Med, Univ Southern Cailf, 68-77, assoc clin prof, 77-78; lab mgr, Pac Environ Serv, 78-80; div mgr, Global Geochem Corp, 80-88. *Concurrent Pos:* Prin, Sage Resources Inc, 86-93. *Mem:* AAAS; Am Chem Soc. *Res:* Reaction mechanisms in Grignard alkylations, aromatic sulfonation, preflame combustion reactions and photochemical air pollution; mass spectrometry; infrared spectrophotometry; chromatography; environmental carcinogens; toxic pollutants. *Mailing Add:* 335 Montecito Ave Pismo Beach CA 93449-1924

GORDON, RONALD E, lung pathology, for more information see previous edition

GORDON, RONALD STANTON, MATERIALS SCIENCE, ENGINEERING. *Current Pos:* PROF MAT SCI & ENG, UNIV UTAH, 74-; CHMN, CERAMATEC, INC, 84- *Personal Data:* b Oakland, Calif, Sept 29, 37; m 63. *Educ:* Univ Calif, Berkeley, BS, 59, MS, 61; Mass Inst Technol, ScD(ceramics), 64. *Prof Exp:* Res asst cement chem, Univ Calif, Berkeley, 56-61; res asst ceramics, Mass Inst Technol, 61-64; asst prof ceramic eng, Univ Utah, 64-69, assoc prof mat sci & eng, 69-74; pres, Ceramatec, Inc, 77-84. *Concurrent Pos:* Res initiation grant, NSF, 65-67; res grant, Dept Energy, 66-81; mem, staff lighting res lab, Gen Elec Co, Ohio, 71-73; NSF, Dept Energy contracts, 73-85. *Mem:* Fel Am Ceramic Soc; Nat Inst Ceramic Engrs; Electrochem Soc; Mat Res Soc. *Res:* Properties of ceramic materials; thermodynamics of solids; mechanical behavior of ceramics at elevated temperatures; solid state electrochemistry; processing and characterization of solid electrolytes and advanced ceramics. *Mailing Add:* Dept Mat Eng Va Polytech Inst & State Univ 205 Holden Hall Blackburg VA 24061

GORDON, ROY GERALD, PHYSICAL CHEMISTRY, SOLID STATE PHYSICS. *Current Pos:* Jr fel, Harvard Univ, 64-66, from asst prof to prof, 66-82, chmn, Dept Chem, 92-95, THOMAS D CABOT PROF CHEM, HARVARD UNIV, 82- *Personal Data:* b Akron, Ohio, Jan 11, 40; m 61, Myra Miller; c Avra, Emily & Steven. *Educ:* Harvard Univ, BA, 61, MA, 62, PhD(chem physics), 64. *Honors & Awards:* Pure Chem Award, Am Chem Soc, 72, Baekeland Award, 79, Esselen Award, 96; Bourke Award, Faraday Soc, 77; R&D 100 Award, 91. *Concurrent Pos:* Assoc ed, J Chem Physics & Chem Physics Lett; lectr, Univ Calif, Berkeley, 69, Univ Wis-Madison, 70, Yale Univ, 73, Oxford Univ, 77, Univ Paris, 80, Weizmann Inst, 84; chmn, Div Chem Physics, Am Phys Soc, 76; Einstein fel, Israel, 84. *Mem:* Nat Acad Sci; fel Am Phys Soc; fel Am Chem Soc; Am Acad Arts & Sci; Union Concerned Scientists; fel Europ Acad Sci; fel AAAS. *Res:* Theory of intermolecular forces; bonding in molecules and solids; crystal structures and phase transitions; dynamics of chemical reactions; mechanisms of chemical vapor deposition; materials for solar energy and energy conservation. *Mailing Add:* Dept Chem Harvard Univ 12 Oxford St Cambridge MA 02138. *Fax:* 617-495-4723; *E-Mail:* gordon@chemistry.harvard.edu

GORDON, RUTH VIDA, STRUCTURAL ENGINEERING. *Current Pos:* PRES, PEGASUS ENG, INC, 84- *Personal Data:* b Seattle, Wash, Sept 19, 26; m 49, Michael H Schnapp; c Madeline R, Marcia L & Michael G. *Educ:* Stanford Univ, BS, 48, MS, 49. *Honors & Awards:* Outstanding Serv Award, Golden Gate Sect Soc, Woman Engrs, 79 & 84. *Prof Exp:* Struct designer, Isadore Thompson, Consult engr, San Francisco, Calif, 50-51, K P Norrie, Consult Engr, Spokane, Wash, 51 & Bechtel Corp, San Francisco, Calif, 51-53; civil engr, Caltrans, San Francisco, Calif, 53-54; struct designer, Russell Fuller, Consult Engr, San Francisco, Calif, 54 & Western Knapp Eng Corp, San Francisco, Calif, 54-55; struct eng assoc, State Calif, Off State Architect, Struct Safety Sect, San Francisco, Calif, 56-57, sr struct designer, 57-59, sr struct engr, 59-76 & dist struct engr, 76-84. *Concurrent Pos:* Mem, Adv Comt Master Plan Use Educ Facil, San Francisco Unified Sch Dist, 71-72; vpres, Golden Gate Sect, Soc Women Engrs, 76-77, pres, 78-79, vchair & actg chair, Nat Conv, 79, chair, Affirmative Action, 79-80, 84-; dir, San Francisco Bay Area Eng Coun, 77-79, co-chair prof, 77-87, treas, 79-80, secy, 80-81, vpres, 81-82, pres, 82-83; chair, Legis Comt, Struct Engrs Asn Northern Calif, 78-79, deleg, Calif Legis Coun Prof Engrs, 78-79, chair, Prof Policies Comt, 82-83, dir, 84-86, deleg, San Francisco Bay Area Eng Coun, 85-87; affirmative action coordr, Nat Soc Women Engrs, 79-80; mem, Adv Panel Calif Bd Archit Examr Exam Rev Proj, 79-81; deleg, San Francisco Bay Area Eng Coun, Am Soc Civil Engrs, 81-85; dir, Struct Engrs Asn Northern Calif, 84-86. *Mem:* Am Soc Civil Engrs; Earthquake Eng Res Inst; Asn Women Sci; Struct Engrs Asn. *Res:* Author of one publication. *Mailing Add:* 726 23rd Ave San Francisco CA 94121-3710

GORDON, SAMUEL ROBERT, MATHEMATICS. *Current Pos:* SR COMPUT SCIENTIST, MEGADINE INFO SYSTS, 94- *Personal Data:* b Alton, Ill, Feb 19, 43. *Educ:* Calif Inst Technol, BS, 64; Yale Univ, MA, 66, PhD(math), 69. *Prof Exp:* Actg instr math, Yale Univ, 68-69; asst prof in residence, Univ Calif, Los Angeles, 69-70; asst prof, Univ Calif, Riverside, 70-77; mem tech staff, Aerospace Corp, 77-94. *Concurrent Pos:* Vis asst prof, Univ Va, 73. *Mem:* Math Asn Am; Am Math Soc. *Res:* Jordan algebras and Lie algebras and the connections between them, especially the use of techniques from algebraic groups to study the automorphism groups and Lie algebras of Jordan algebras. *Mailing Add:* Megadine Info Systs 12635 Burnside Ave Los Angeles CA 90019-2609

GORDON, SAUL, SCIENCE EDUCATION. *Current Pos:* RETIRED. *Personal Data:* b Bronx, NY, Nov 29, 25; m 46, 74, 82; c 7. *Educ:* Ohio State Univ, BA, 46; Univ Ky, MS, 49, PhD(chem), 51. *Prof Exp:* Chemist, Picatinny Arsenal, 51-52, group leader, 52-55, chief, Basic Chem Res Unit, 55-59, staff chemist specialist, Pyrotech Lab, 59-61; from asst prof to prof chem, Florham-Madison Campus, Fairleigh Dickinson Univ, 60-67, chmn dept, 63-67, dir annual thermoanal insts, 62-67; pres, Ctr Prof Advan, Div Technol Advan Ctrs, Inc, 67-94. *Concurrent Pos:* Govt & indust consult; chmn bd trustees, Inst Advan through Educ. *Mem:* AAAS; Am Chem Soc; fel Am Inst Chem; Am Soc Eng Educ; Sigma Xi. *Res:* Continuing professional education for scientists, engineers and technical managers. *Mailing Add:* 6481 Via Rosa Boca Raton FL 33433-6420

GORDON, SHEFFIELD, RADIATION CHEMISTRY. *Current Pos:* RETIRED. *Personal Data:* b Chicago, Ill, Feb 10, 16; m 64, Marceline Dzurus. *Educ:* Univ Chicago, SB, 37; Univ Notre Dame, PhD(phys chem), 53. *Prof Exp:* Chemist, Alton RR Co, 38-41; asst, Univ Chicago, 41-42; res assoc, Metall Lab, 42-46 & Univ Notre Dame, 46-49; chemist, Argonne Nat Lab, 50-84. *Concurrent Pos:* Foreign collabr, Saclay Nuclear Res Ctr, France, 65. *Mem:* Am Phys Soc; Am Chem Soc; Radiation Res Soc. *Res:* Photochemistry; chemical dynamics using fast reaction techniques. *Mailing Add:* 5000 S East End Ave Chicago IL 60615. *E-Mail:* shefg@aol.com

GORDON, SHELDON P, APPLIED MATHEMATICS, STATISTICS. *Current Pos:* PROF MATH, SUFFOLK CO COMMUNITY COL, 74-, ADJ PROF APPL MATH & STATIST, STATE UNIV NY, STONY BROOK, 93- *Personal Data:* b New York, NY, July 11, 42; m 65, Florence Shenfield; c Craig & Kenneth. *Educ:* Polytech Inst Brooklyn, BS, 63; McGill Univ, MSc, 65, PhD(math), 69. *Prof Exp:* Lectr math, McGill Univ, 63-68; asst prof, Queens Col, NY, 68-74. *Concurrent Pos:* State Univ NY fac res fel & improv undergrad instr res award, 75, 78, 81, 85, 87 & 89; proj dir, NSF, Sci Educ proj & Course Improv proj, Suffolk Co Community Col, 77-80; pres, Mathegraphics Software, 86-; Harvard Univ Calculus Reform Proj, 89-, prog dir, Math Modeling PreCalculus Reform Proj, 91-; adj prof appl math & statist, State Univ NY, Stony Brook. *Mem:* Am Math Asn Two Year Col; Math Asn Am. *Res:* Stability theory of both differential equations and difference equations; characterizations of multivariate statistical distributions using regression properties; applications of discrete mathematics to undergraduate calculus; uses of computers in mathematics and science education; computers in statistics education; author eight books, 90 articles. *Mailing Add:* 61 Cedar Rd East Northport NY 11731. *E-Mail:* sgordon@ccmail.sunysb.edu

GORDON, SHELDON ROBERT, HISTOCHEMISTRY, CYTOCHEMISTRY. *Current Pos:* asst prof, 83-89, ASSOC PROF, OAKLAND UNIV, 89- *Personal Data:* b Detroit, Mich, Sept 13, 49; m 78; c 4. *Educ:* Oakland Univ, Mich, BA, 72; Univ Vt, PhD(zool), 80. *Prof Exp:* Res asst, Kresge Eye Inst, Wayne State Univ, 78-80, res assoc, 80-83. *Mem:* Am Soc Cell Biol; Asn Res Vision & Ophthal; Sigma Xi; Histochem Soc. *Res:* Cell biology of corneal endothelial cell regeneration; role of cytoskeleton and extracellular matrixin cell movement. *Mailing Add:* Dept Biol Scis Oakland Univ Rochester MI 48309-4401. *Fax:* 248-370-2286

GORDON, STEPHEN L, musculoskeletal diseases, orthopedics, for more information see previous edition

GORDON, SYDNEY MICHAEL, MASS SPECTROMETRY, EXPOSURE ASSESSMENT. *Current Pos:* RES LEADER, BATTELLE COLUMBUS, 91- *Personal Data:* b Pretoria, SAfrica, Apr 18, 39; m 64, 84, Maria Hawryluk; c Danielle, Anna, Stephanie & Andrew. *Educ:* Univ Pretoria, BS, 59, MS, 62, PhD(phys chem), 65. *Prof Exp:* Chief scientist & head kinetics subdivision, Atomic Energy Bd, SAfrica, 63-77; head, Mass Spectrometry, IIT Res Inst, Chicago, 77-91, sci advy, 82-91. *Concurrent Pos:* Mem, Sr Tech Comt, Nat Inst Petrol Energy Res, Bartlesville, Okla, 85-86; chmn, Peer Rev Panel, US Environ Protection Agency, 85 & 87; prin investr, various govt & indust progs, 85- *Mem:* Am Soc Mass Spectrometry; Am Chem Soc; Int Soc Exposure Anal. *Res:* Multi-media, multi-pathway human exposure assessment research; analytical methods development; mass spectrometric applications. *Mailing Add:* Battelle 505 King Ave Columbus OH 43201. *Fax:* 614-424-4185; *E-Mail:* gordonsm@bclcl1.im.battelle.org

GORDON, TAVIA, ANALYTICAL STATISTICS. *Current Pos:* RES PROF, GEORGE WASHINGTON UNIV, 81- *Personal Data:* b Chicago, Ill, Dec 14, 17; m 48; c 4. *Educ:* Univ Calif, Berkeley, BA, 38. *Prof Exp:* Statistician, USPHS, 52-77; sr scientist, Gen Elec Corp, 80-82. *Concurrent Pos:* Statistician, Nat Heart, Lung & Blood Inst. *Mem:* Fel Am Statist Asn; fel Am Heart Asn. *Res:* Biomedical statistics; health and vital statistics. *Mailing Add:* 14800 Pennfield Circle No 104 Silver Spring MD 20906

GORDON, TERENCE MICHAEL, THEORETICAL & COMPUTATIONAL GEOLOGY. *Current Pos:* PROF, DEPT GEOL & GEOPHYSICS, UNIV CALGARY, 89- *Personal Data:* b South Porcupine, Ont, Jan 10, 41; c 2. *Educ:* Univ BC, BASc, 64; Princeton Univ, PhD(geol), 69. *Prof Exp:* Res scientist, Geol Surv Can, 70-89. *Concurrent Pos:* Assoc ed, Can Mineralogist, 89-91; mem, Sci Comt, Lithoprobe, 95- *Mem:* Fel Geol Asn Can; Mineral Asn Can; Int Asn Math Geologists; Asn Comput Mach; Soc Indust & Appl Math; Mineral Soc Am. *Res:* Development of theory and numerical methods for analysis of dynamics of geochemical systems; field studies and application of the theory. *Mailing Add:* Dept Geol & Geophysics Univ Calgary Calgary AB T2N 1N4 Can. *Fax:* 403-284-0074

GORDON, WAYNE ALAN, PSYCHOLOGY, REHABILITATION MEDICINE. *Current Pos:* assoc prof rehab med & psychiat, 86-90, ASSOC DIR REHAB MED, MT SINAI SCH MED, 86-, PROF, REHAB MED, 91-; ASST PROF CLIN REHAB MED, SCH MED, NY UNIV, 77- *Personal Data:* b New York, NY, Feb 2, 46; m 79; c 1. *Educ:* NY Univ, BA, 66; Yeshiva Uinv, PhD(educ psychol), 72; Am Bd Prof Psychol, dipl, 85; Am Bd Clin Neuropsychol, dipl, 85. *Honors & Awards:* Licht Award, Am Cong Rehab Med, 86; Roger Burker, Res Award, Am Psychol Asn. *Prof Exp:* Sr psychologist, Sch Med, NY Univ, 72-77. *Concurrent Pos:* Consult, United Cerebral Palsy, NY State, 79- & Rehab Sect, Pa Cancer Control Prog, 82-; prin investr, NIH, NIDRR & RSA grants. *Mem:* Am Psychol Asn; Am Cong Rehab Med; Acad Behav Med Res; Soc Behav Med; Int Neuropsychol Soc. *Res:* Neuropsychological rehabilitation following traumatic brain damage; diagnosis and treatment of post-stroke depression; rehabilitation of persons with disabilities. *Mailing Add:* Dept Rehab Med Mt Sinai Med Ctr Box 1240 1 Gustave Pl New York NY 10029

GORDON, WAYNE LECKY, OVARIAN POLYPEPTIDES. *Current Pos:* SR SCIENTIST, TANOX BIOSYSTS, 87. *Personal Data:* b Stamford, Conn, Jan 15, 52; m 76; c 2. *Educ:* Westminster Col, BS, 73; Univ Ill, MS, 77, PhD(physiol), 82. *Prof Exp:* Fel, Syst Cancer Ctr, Univ Tex, 81-83, res assoc, M D Anderson Hosp & Tumor Inst, 83-87. *Mem:* Soc Study Reproduction; Endocrine Soc; AAAS; NY Acad Sci; Sigma Xi; Am Chem Soc. *Res:* Purification and biochemical characterization of the ovarian polypeptide inhibitors inhibin-F and luteinizing hormone-receptor binding inhibitor; antibody purification and chemical modification. *Mailing Add:* 2843 E Pebble Beach Dr Missouri City TX 77459-2528

GORDON, WILLIAM BERNARD, GLOBAL ANALYSIS, RADAR SYSTEMS. *Current Pos:* SFA INC, 96- *Personal Data:* b Washington, DC, Nov 16, 35; m 61, Eve Bronstein; c Robert & David. *Educ:* George Washington Univ, BS, 59, MS, 60; Johns Hopkins Univ, PhD(math), 68. *Prof Exp:* Mathematician, Naval Res Lab, 60-62; asst prof math, Towson State Col, 66-68; instr, Johns Hopkins Univ, 68-69; res mathematician, Math Res Ctr, Naval Res Lab, 69-72, res mathematician, Radar Div, 72-96. *Mem:* Am Math Soc; Inst Elec & Electronics Engrs; Sigma Xi. *Res:* Global analysis; analysis on manifolds; Riemannian geometry; dynamical systems; optics. *Mailing Add:* SFA Inc 14013 Manorvale Rd Rockville MD 20853

GORDON, WILLIAM E(DWIN), RADIO SCATTERING. *Current Pos:* prof elec eng, space physics & astron, Rice Univ, 66-86, dean sci & eng, 66-75, dean, Sch Natural Sci, 75-80, provost & vpres, 80-86, DISTINGUISHED EMER PROF SPACE SCI, RICE UNIV, 86- *Personal Data:* b Paterson, NJ, Jan 8, 18; m 41, Elva Freile; c Larry S & Nancy L. *Educ:* Montclair State Col, BA, 39, MA, 42; NY Univ, MS, 46; Cornell Univ, PhD(elec eng), 53. *Hon Degrees:* PhD, Austin Col. *Honors & Awards:* Balth van der Pol Award, 66; Artowski Medal, Nat Acad Sci, 84; Medal Geophys, USSR, 85. *Prof Exp:* Assoc dir elec eng, Res Lab, Univ Tex, 46-48; res assoc, Cornell Univ, 48-53, from assoc prof to prof elec eng, 53-65; dir, Arecibo Ionospheric Observ, PR, 60-65. *Concurrent Pos:* Chmn bd trustees, Upper Atmosphere Res Corp, 71-78; vpres to pres, Int Sci Radio Union, 75-84; trustee, Cornell Univ. 76-80; mem, Arecibo Observ Adv Bd, 77-80 & 90-; mem bd trustees, Univ Corp Atmospheric Res, 77-86 & 91-; vpres, Int Coun Sci Unions, 88-93. *Mem:* Nat Acad Sci (foreign secy, 86-90); Nat Acad Eng; fel Inst Elec & Electronics Engrs; Am Meteorol Soc; fel Am Geophys Union; Am Acad Arts & Sci. *Res:* Radio physics, meteorology and waves; concept design and construction of world's largest antenna reflector. *Mailing Add:* Rice Univ Space Sci PO Box 1892 Houston TX 77251-1892. *Fax:* 713-285-5143; *E-Mail:* bgordon@spacsun.rice.edu

GORDON, WILLIAM JOHN, APPLIED MATHEMATICS. *Current Pos:* MEM STAFF, OFF NAVAL RES, LONDON, 76- *Personal Data:* b East McKeesport, Pa, Dec 4, 39; m 65. *Educ:* Univ Pittsburgh, BS, 61; Brown Univ, PhD(appl math), 65. *Prof Exp:* Reactor analyst, Westinghouse Elec Corp, 60-61; res mathematician, Res Labs, Boeing Co, 62; res asst appl math, Brown Univ, 62-65; sr res mathematician, Res Labs, Gen Motors Corp, 65-71, asst head, Dept Math, 71-76. *Mem:* Am Math Soc; Soc Indust & Appl Math; Asn Comput Mach. *Res:* Numerical analysis; optimization techniques; approximation theory. *Mailing Add:* PO Box 52 Palmerton PA 18071

GORDON, WILLIAM LIVINGSTON, CONDENSED MATTER PHYSICS. *Current Pos:* from instr to prof, 55-95, EMER PROF PHYSICS, CASE WESTERN RES UNIV, 95- *Personal Data:* b Tanta, Egypt, Jan 17, 27; US citizen; m 49, Jean Crea; c David W, Amy J (Erbskorn) & Timothy L. *Educ:* Muskingum Col, BSc, 48; Ohio State Univ, MSc, 50, PhD, 54. *Prof Exp:* Instr physics, Ohio State Univ, 54-55. *Mem:* Am Phys Soc. *Res:* Cryogenics; structure of liquid helium; fermi surfaces in metals; transport properties in metals; electrical properties of polymers. *Mailing Add:* Dept Physics Case Western Res Univ Cleveland OH 44106

GORDON, WILLIAM RANSOME, PLANT PHYSIOLOGY, DEVELOPMENTAL BOTANY. *Current Pos:* ASST PROF BOT & PLANT PHYSIOL, HOWARD UNIV, 78- *Personal Data:* b Richmond, Va, June 1, 43; m 67; c 1. *Educ:* Tuskegee Univ, BS, 65, MS, 71; Univ Minn, PhD(plant physiol), 77. *Prof Exp:* Res assoc biol, Brookhaven Nat Lab, 77-78. *Concurrent Pos:* Mem ecol comt, Sci Adv Bd, Environ Protection Agency, 79-81. *Mem:* Am Soc Plant Physiologists; Bot Soc Am; Int Soc Chronobiol; Scandinavian Soc Plant Physiol; Sigma Xi. *Res:* Physiology of plant growth and development; influence of heavy metals on nitrogen metabolism; secondary metabolism and allelopathy; phytochrome physiology; circadian rhythmicity. *Mailing Add:* Dept Biol Howard Univ 415 College St Washington DC 20059-0001

GORDUS, ADON ALDEN, ANALYTICAL CHEMISTRY. *Current Pos:* Asst, Univ Mich, 56-57, from instr to assoc prof, 57-70, assoc dir honors prog, 64-80, PROF CHEM, UNIV MICH, ANN ARBOR, 70- *Personal Data:* b Chicago, Ill, Mar 23, 32; wid. *Educ:* Ill Inst Technol, BS, 52; Univ Wis, PhD, 56. *Concurrent Pos:* John Simon Guggenheim Mem Found fel, 74. *Mem:* AAAS; Am Chem Soc; Sigma Xi. *Res:* Neutron activation analysis of archaeological artifacts, ancient and medieval coins; environmental and forensic chemistry; trace element analysis of environmental, clinical, archaeological, historical and forensic samples; synthetic fuel production by nuclear radiation. *Mailing Add:* Dept Chem Univ Mich Ann Arbor MI 48109. *Fax:* 313-747-4865; *E-Mail:* adon.gordus@um.cc.umich.edu

GORDY, EDWIN, BIOMEDICAL ENGINEERING. *Current Pos:* CONSULT, BIOMED INSTRUMENTATION, 71- *Personal Data:* b Philadelphia, Pa, May 17, 25; c 3. *Educ:* Jefferson Med Col, MD, 48; Univ Pa, DSc(physiol chem), 52. *Prof Exp:* Intern, Jewish Hosp, Philadelphia, 48-49; head, Instrument Design & Develop Dept, Roswell Park Mem Inst, 54-65; sr scientist, Instrument Design & Develop Lab, Worcester Found Exp Biol, 65-67; dir res, Lexington Instruments Corp, 67-73; vpres res & develop, Kalvex Inc, 73-80. *Concurrent Pos:* Consult, Biomed Instrumentation, 71- *Mem:* Biophys Soc; assoc Inst Elec & Electronics Engrs. *Res:* Development of new research tools for use in biological research. *Mailing Add:* 17 Otis St Newtonville MA 02160

GORDZIEL, STEVEN A, ANALYTICAL CHEMISTRY, PHARMACEUTICAL PRODUCT DEVELOPMENT. *Current Pos:* mgr pharmaceut develop, Carter-Wallace Inc, 79-81, dept head, 81-84, dir develop res, pharmaceut prod develop, 84-92, VPRES DEVELOP RES, CARTER-WALLACE INC, 93- *Personal Data:* b Santa Monica, Calif, Nov 19, 46; m 70; c 3. *Educ:* Philadelphia Col Pharm & Sci, BS, 70; Univ Conn, PhD(pharmaceut chem), 76. *Prof Exp:* Sr res scientist pharmaceut prod develop, Wyeth Labs Inc, 74-77; scientist, Ortho Pharmaceut Inc, 77-79. *Mem:* Am Asn Pharmaceut Scientists; Acad Pharmaceut Sci; Am Pharmaceut Asn; Parenteral Drug Asn; Controlled Release Soc. *Res:* Direct pharmaceutical scientists and analytical chemists in the physical-chemical characterization of drug substances; the development of pharmaceutical products and analytical methods and specifications. *Mailing Add:* 32 Cheston Ct Belle Mead NJ 08502

GORE, BRYAN FRANK, REACTOR OPERATIONS, RISK AND SAFETY ANALYSIS. *Current Pos:* STAFF SCIENTIST, PAC NORTHWEST LABS, BATTELLE MEM INST, 72- *Personal Data:* b Berwyn, Ill, Dec 3, 38; m 63, Barbara Boynton; c Marcy, Russell & David. *Educ:* Cornell Univ, BEngPhys, 61; Univ Mich, MS, 64, PhD(physics), 67. *Prof Exp:* Asst prof physics, Univ Idaho, 67-68 & Cent Wash Univ, 68-72. *Concurrent Pos:* Consult, Bunker Hill Co, Kellogg, Idaho, 67-68; vis scientist, Ctr Theoret Physics, Univ Md, College Park, 69-70; fac researcher, Northwest Col & Univ Asn Sci (NORCUS), 72-73; mem fac, Tri Cities Br, Wash State Univ, 75-90; reactor operator licensing examr, Nuclear Regulatory Comn, 81-89; power plant inspections proj mgr, 84-; lead instr, Probabilistic Risk Assessment Methods & Applns Courses, US Dept Energy & US Nuclear Regulatory Comn, 88-90. *Mem:* Am Nuclear Soc; Am Asn Univ Prof; Am Phys Soc; Am Asn Physics Teachers. *Res:* Nuclear reactor risk and safety analysis; nuclear reactor operations, staffing, training and qualifications; probabilistic risk assessment applications to power plant inspections; generic probabilistic risk assessment applications; nuclear waste management; environmental analysis; nuclear criticality; neutron interactions and transport; blanket design and environmental effects of controlled nuclear fusion and hybrid fusion-fission reactors. *Mailing Add:* 1641 Alder Ave Richland WA 99352. *Fax:* 509-372-4411

GORE, DOROTHY J, geology & geography, environmental science; deceased, see previous edition for last biography

GORE, ERNEST STANLEY, INORGANIC CHEMISTRY, PHYSICAL CHEMISTRY. *Current Pos:* GROUP LEADER INORG CHEM, JOHNSON MATTHEY, INC, 81- *Personal Data:* b Toronto, Can, May 8, 42; m 71. *Educ:* Univ Toronto, BS, 64; Univ Ill, Urbana, MS, 66, PhD(phys chem), 68. *Prof Exp:* Res chemist phys chem, E I Du Pont de Nemours & Co, Inc, 73-77; res chemist inorg chem, Matthey Bishop, Inc, 77-81. *Concurrent Pos:* Lectr chem, Widener Col, 77- *Mem:* Am Chem Soc. *Res:* Transition metal chemistry; organometallic compounds; homogeneous and heterogeneous catalysis. *Mailing Add:* Johnson Matthey Inc 2001 Nolte Dr West Deptford NJ 08066-1727

GORE, IRA, PATHOLOGY. *Current Pos:* RETIRED. *Personal Data:* b New York, NY, Sept 10, 13; m 54; c 2. *Educ:* Cornell Univ, AB, 34, MD, 37. *Prof Exp:* From intern to resident, 37-41; pathologist, Armed Forces Inst Path, 46-50; pathologist, Col Med, Baylor Univ, 50-51; pathologist, Henry Ford Hosp, 51-52; pathologist, Col Med, Univ Utah, 52-53; pathologist, Mt Sinai Hosp, Ill, 53-54; from asst clin prof to assoc clin prof path, Sch Med & assoc nutrit, Sch Pub Health, Harvard Univ, 54-62; prof path, Sch Med, Boston Univ, 62-68; prof path, Sch Med, Univ Ala, Birmingham, 68-74; dir path, Park Ridge Hosp, 74-79; clin prof path, obstet & gynec, Med Sch, Univ Ala, 82-84. *Concurrent Pos:* Pathologist, Vet Admin Hosp, 54-62; lectr, Harvard Med Sch, 62-68; clin prof path, Sch Med, Rochester Univ, 74-80. *Mem:* Am Soc Clin Path; AMA; Am Asn Path & Bact; Col Am Path. *Res:* Hemopoietic and cardiovascular diseases. *Mailing Add:* 5101 Kirkwall Lane Birmingham AL 35242-4120

GORE, PAMELA J(EANNE) W(HEELESS), DISTANCE LEARNING USING THE WORLD WIDE WEB & COMPRESSED VIDEO, EARTHQUAKE INTENSITY STUDIES. *Current Pos:* asst prof, 89-91, ASSOC PROF GEOL, DEKALB COL, 91- *Personal Data:* b Washington, DC, Oct 10, 55; m 77, Thomas J III; c Miranda J. *Educ:* Univ Md, Col Park, BS, 77; George Washington Univ, MS, 81, MPhil, 83, PhD(geol), 83. *Prof Exp:* Res asst geol, Univ Md, 76-77; res asst, George Washington Univ, 77-78, teaching asst, 77-79 & 80-83; asst prof geol, Emory Univ, 83-89. *Concurrent Pos:* Consult, Texaco, 85-89; chmn, US working group, Int Geol Correlation Prog, Working Group 219, 85-90; prin investr, Nat Geog Soc grant, Triassic Deep River Basin, NC, 85-86; Texaco grant, Sedimentary Struct & Textures of Petrol Source Rocks, 86-88; campus rep DeKalb Col, Geol Soc Am; adj prof geosci, Emory Univ, 89- *Mem:* Geol Soc Am; Nat Asn Geol Teachers; Sigma Xi. *Res:* Distance learning and applications of World Wide Web in teaching geology; intensity studies of Norris Lake, Ga (1993) and Dacula, Ga (1995-96) earthquake swarm; paleoecology of Solnhofen sponge mounds; sedimentology, stratigraphy and invertebrate paleontology of Triassic-Jurassic eastern North America; lacustrine sequences. *Mailing Add:* Dept Geol DeKalb Col 555 N Indian Creek Dr Clarkston GA 30021. *E-Mail:* pgore@dekalb.dc.peachnet.edu

GORE, ROBERT W, ENGINEERING. *Current Pos:* RES ENGR, W L GORE & ASSOCS, 64-, PRES & CHIEF EXEC OFFICER. *Educ:* Univ Minn, PhD, 64. *Mem:* Nat Acad Eng. *Mailing Add:* W L Gore & Assocs PO Box 9329 Newark DE 19714

GORE, WILBERT LEE, PHYSICAL CHEMISTRY. *Current Pos:* pres, 59-76, CHMN, W L GORE & ASSOC, INC, 76- *Personal Data:* b Meridian, Idaho, Jan 25, 12; m 35; c 5. *Educ:* Univ Utah, BS, 33, MS, 35. *Hon Degrees:* HHD, Westminster Col, Salt Lake City, 71. *Prof Exp:* Analyst & chem engr, Am Smelting & Refining Co, 35-41; eng supvr, Remington Arms Co, 41-45; res supvr, E I Du Pont de Nemours & Co, Inc, Del, 45-57. *Concurrent Pos:* Tech consult, UN Tech Mission India, 62. *Mem:* Am Chem Soc; Inst Elec & Electronics Engrs. *Res:* Polytetrafluoroethylene structure, processing and application; rheology of thermoplastics; applications of statistical methods; sociology of enterprise; medical prosthetics; filtration membranes; transmission of electronic signals. *Mailing Add:* 487 Paper Mill Rd Newark DE 19711

GORE, WILLIS C(ARROLL), ELECTRICAL ENGINEERING. *Current Pos:* From jr instr to assoc prof, 47-73, chmn dept, 74-80 & 86-87, PROF ELEC ENG, JOHNS HOPKINS UNIV, 73- *Personal Data:* b Baltimore, Md, May 20, 26; m 50, E Sue Lohn; c 3. *Educ:* Johns Hopkins Univ, BE, 48, DrEng, 52. *Mem:* Sr mem Inst Elec & Electronics Engrs; Sigma Xi. *Res:* Digital computers; information theory; algebraic coding theory. *Mailing Add:* Dept Elec & Comput Eng Johns Hopkins Baltimore MD 21218

GOREE, JAMES GLEASON, COMPOSITE MATERIALS, STRESS ANALYSIS & FRACTURE MECHANICS. *Current Pos:* from asst prof to prof, 66-89, Univ Centennial Prof, 89-96, EMER CENTENNIAL PROF, CLEMSON UNIV, 96- *Personal Data:* b Birmingham, Ala, June 21, 35; m 61, Katherine Norman; c 2. *Educ:* Univ Fla, BSME, 60; Univ Wash, Seattle, MSAE, 62; Univ Ala, PhD(eng mech), 66. *Prof Exp:* Res engr, Redstone Arsenal Res Div, Rohm & Haas Co, 61-62; asst prof eng mech, Univ Ky, 62-63. *Mem:* Am Soc Mech Engrs; Am Soc Composites; Am Soc Testing & Mat; Am Acad Mech; Russ Acad Sci. *Res:* Elasticity; mathematical analysis of composite materials; fracture mechanics. *Mailing Add:* 174 Laurel Ridge Rd Clemson Univ Six Mile SC 29682

GORELICK, JERRY LEE, RADIATION EFFECTS, RADIATION HARDNESS. *Current Pos:* Sr staff scientist, 85-88, SCIENTIST, HUGHES AIRCRAFT CO, 88- *Personal Data:* b Los Angeles, Calif, Oct 21, 46. *Educ:* Univ Calif Los Angeles, BS, 68; Pa State Univ, PhD(physics), 76. *Mem:* Am Phys Soc; Inst Elec & Electronics Engrs. *Mailing Add:* MS B364/Bldg 541 Hughes Aircraft Co S & CG PO Box 92919 Los Angeles CA 90009

GORELICK, KENNETH J, CRITICAL CARE MEDICINE, PULMONARY DISEASE. *Current Pos:* DIR, CRITICAL CARE & INFECTIOUS DIS, XOMA CORP, 87- *Personal Data:* b New York, NY, Dec 14, 52; m 84; c 1. *Educ:* State Univ NY, Buffalo, BS, 73; Cornell Univ, MD, 78. *Prof Exp:* Asst dir, Pulmonary Div, Palo Alto Vet Admin Med Ctr, 83-84; med dir, Intensive Care Unit, Community Hosp, Sacramento, 84-85; assoc med dir, Fisons Corp, 85-87. *Concurrent Pos:* Clin instr, Stanford Univ, 84-86. *Mem:* Fel Am Col Chest Physicians; Soc Critical Care Med; Am Thoracic Soc. *Res:* Development of monoclonal antibodies for the prevention and treatment of gram negative sepsis and septic shock. *Mailing Add:* Fisons Corp 2 Preston Ct Bedford MA 01730-2334

GORELL, THOMAS ANDREW, ENDOCRINOLOGY, DEVELOPMENTAL BIOLOGY. *Current Pos:* from asst prof to assoc prof zool & entomol, 75-81, asst dean, Col Nat Sci, 84-86, PROF BIOL & ASSOC DEAN, COL NAT SCI, COLO STATE UNIV, 86- *Personal Data:* b Chicago, Ill, Oct 9, 40; m 65; c 2. *Educ:* Quincy Col, BS, 63; Univ Ark, MS, 66; Northwestern Univ, PhD(biol sci). 70. *Prof Exp:* Teaching asst biol sci, Northwestern Univ, 66-67, res assoc, 70; res fel biochem, Ben May Lab Cancer Res, Univ Chicago, 70-72, res assoc & asst prof, 72-75. *Mem:* AAAS; Am Soc Zoologists; Sigma Xi; Soc Study Reproduction; Endocrine Soc. *Res:* Relationship of steroid hormones and their receptor proteins during the growth, development and functioning of hormonal target tissues; enzyme induction and regulation by steroids. *Mailing Add:* 4313 Picadilly Dr Ft Collins CO 80526

GOREN, ALAN CHARLES, PHYSICAL CHEMISTRY, ENVIRONMENTAL CHEMISTRY. *Current Pos:* ASSOC PROF CHEM, TRANSYLVANIA UNIV, 85- *Personal Data:* b Brookline, Mass, Dec 8, 46. *Educ:* Univ Mass, BA, 68; Univ Del, PhD(chem), 75. *Prof Exp:* Res engr polyester fibers, Fiber Industs, Inc, 74-78; asst prof chem, Hollins Col, 78-79; vis prof chem, Va Polytech Inst & State Univ, 79-81; assoc prof environ chem, New England Col, 81-85. *Concurrent Pos:* Assoc prof chem, Johnson C Smith Univ, 76-77. *Mem:* Am Chem Soc; Am Soc Agron. *Res:* Synthetic polymer research, flame retardant polyester fibers; surface chemistry of polyester tire cord adhesion to rubber; thermochemistry of ion-molecule reactions; soil chemistry associated with surface mine reclamation; enviromental chemistry. *Mailing Add:* Chem Dept Transylvania Univ Lexington KY 40508

GOREN, HOWARD JOSEPH, BIOCHEMISTRY, ENDOCRINOLOGY. *Current Pos:* From asst prof to assoc prof, 70-82, PROF MED BIOCHEM, UNIV CALGARY, 82- *Personal Data:* b Bialocerkwe, Ukraine, Apr 9, 41; Can citizen; m 65, Fran Moran; c Robyn & Jeff. *Educ:* Univ Toronto, BS, 64; State Univ NY Buffalo, PhD(biochem, pharmacol), 69. *Concurrent Pos:* Nat Res Coun Can fel, Weizmann Inst Sci, 68-70; Med Res Coun Can operating grants, 71-92; Can Diabetes Asn grant, 79-84; asst ed, Molecular Pharmacol, 74-77; vis scientist, NIH, 77-78, Med Res Coun Can, 84-85; vis prof, Harvard Med Sch, 84-85, Hormone Res Inst, Univ Calif San Francisco, 92-93. *Mem:* Am Diabetes Asn, Am Soc Biochem & Molecular Biol, Can Biochem Soc; Am Soc Pharmacol & Exp Therapeut. *Res:* Insulin signaling; early post-receptor events. *Mailing Add:* 3248 Breen Crescent NW Calgary AB T2L 1S7 Can. *Fax:* 403-270-0737; *E-Mail:* goren@acs.ucalgary.ca

GOREN, MAYER BEAR, ORGANIC CHEMISTRY, LIPID CHEMISTRY & CELL BIOLOGY. *Current Pos:* RETIRED. *Personal Data:* b Tomaszow, Poland, Mar 19, 21; US citizen; m 43, Ethel Levy; c Rise (Koben). *Educ:* Rice Univ, AB, 42, AM, 43; Harvard Univ, PhD(org chem), 49. *Prof Exp:* Jr chemist, Shell Develop Co, 43-44; asst prof chem, Northeastern Univ, 50-52; chief res chemist, Kerr-McGee Corp, 52-60, chief, Microbiol Div, 60-63; sr res scientist, Nat Jewish Ctr Immunol & Respiratory Med, 63-75 & Margaret Regan investr chem path, 75-90; from asst prof to prof microbiol & immunol, Sch Med, Univ Colo, Denver, 78-90. *Concurrent Pos:* Prin investr grants, NIH, 65-90 & mem, Bact & Mycol Study Sect, 77-81, US Tuberculosis Panel, US-Japan Coop Med Sci Prog, 77-86, chmn, 80-86; vis scientist, Nat Cancer Inst, 74, Nat Inst Med Res, Mill Hill, London, 74 & Weizmann Inst Sci, 86. *Mem:* AAAS; Am Chem Soc; Am Soc Microbiol. *Res:* Chemistry of lipids from tubercle bacilli-mechanisms in virulence and biological activities; anti-tumor activities; macrophage function; synthesis of glycolipids. *Mailing Add:* 125 Locust St Denver CO 80220. *Fax:* 303-398-1806

GOREN, SIMON L, CHEMICAL ENGINEERING. *Current Pos:* from asst prof to assoc prof, 62-71, PROF CHEM ENG, UNIV CALIF, BERKELEY, 71- *Personal Data:* b Baltimore, Md, Aug 31, 36; m 62; c 1. *Educ:* Johns Hopkins Univ, BES, 58, DEng(chem eng), 62. *Prof Exp:* Eng, Esso Res & Eng Co, Stand Oil Co NJ, 61-62. *Concurrent Pos:* Prog dir, Particulate & Multiphase Processes Prog, NSF, 77-78. *Res:* Formation, hydrodynamic behavior and separation of particulates systems. *Mailing Add:* Dept Chem Eng Univ Calif Berkeley CA 94720-0001

GORENSTEIN, DAVID GEORGE, BIO-ORGANIC CHEMISTRY. *Current Pos:* PROF CHEM & DIR BIOL & MED RES LAB, PURDUE UNIV, 85- *Personal Data:* b Chicago, Ill, Oct 6, 45; m 67. *Educ:* Mass Inst Technol, SB, 66, AM, 67; Harvard Univ, PhD(chem), 69. *Honors & Awards:* AP Sloan Found Fel, 75; Guggenheim Fel, 86. *Prof Exp:* From asst prof to prof chem, Univ Ill, Chicago, 69-73. *Concurrent Pos:* Nat Inst Gen Med Sci grant, 76-; NSF grant, 76-; Fulbright sr res fel, Oxford Univ, 77- *Mem:* Soc Biol Chemists; Int Soc Magnetic Resonance; Am Chem Soc; Sigma Xi. *Res:* Application of nuclear magnetic resonance spectroscopy to enzymology and molecular biology; physical organic and bioorganic studies of biologically important phosphate esters. *Mailing Add:* Struct Biol Univ Tex Med Br Sealy Ctr Galveston TX 77555-1157. *Fax:* 409-747-6850

GORENSTEIN, MARC VICTOR, ASTROPHYSICS. *Current Pos:* ASSOC ASTROPHYS, MASS INST TECHNOL, 78- *Personal Data:* b Boston, Mass, Sept 21, 50. *Educ:* Mass Inst Technol, BS, 72; Univ Calif, Berkeley, PhD(physics), 78. *Mem:* Am Phys Soc; Am Astron Soc. *Res:* Cosmology; anisotropy of cosmic microwave background radiation; radio astronomy; quasars; conduct observations of compact radio sources using Very Long Baseline Interferometry technique; observations and understanding of gravitationally produced quasar images. *Mailing Add:* Chromatography Div RDE Waters Corp 34 Maple St Milford MA 01757-3604. *Fax:* 508-634-9629

GORENSTEIN, PAUL, ASTROPHYSICS, NUCLEAR PHYSICS. *Current Pos:* ASTROPHYSICIST, CTR ASTROPHYS, 73- *Personal Data:* b New York, NY, Aug 15, 34; c Caroline (Cooke). *Educ:* Cornell Univ, BEng Phys, 57; Mass Inst Technol, PhD(physics), 62. *Honors & Awards:* Excpt Sci Achievement Medal, NASA, 73. *Prof Exp:* Instr physics, Mass Inst Technol, 62-63; Fulbright fel & spec consult, Nat Comt Nuclear Energy, Italy, 63-65; sr scientist, Am Sci & Eng, Inc, 65-70, sr staff scientist, 70-73. *Concurrent Pos:* Lectr astron, Harvard Univ, 73- *Mem:* Am Phys Soc; Am Astron Soc. *Res:* X-ray astronomy and planetology, especially using nuclear techniques; nuclear instrumentation and high energy nuclear physics. *Mailing Add:* 100 Memorial Dr Cambridge MA 02142

GORENSTEIN, SHIRLEY SLOTKIN, MATERIAL CULTURE, ANTHROPOLOGY. *Current Pos:* assoc prof anthrop, Rensselaer Polytech Inst, 75-78, assoc dean, H&SS, 82-89, chair, dept sci & technol studies, 82-85, PROF SCI & TECHNOL STUDIES, RENSSELAER POLYTECH INST, 78- *Personal Data:* b NY, Mar 4, 28; m 48, Samuel; c Ethan E & Gabriel W. *Educ:* Queens Col, BA, 49; Columbia Univ, MA, 53, PhD(anthrop), 63. *Prof Exp:* Lectr anthrop, Columbia Univ, 63-71, from asst prof to assoc prof, 71-75. *Concurrent Pos:* Prin investr, NSF & NEH, 65-67 & 76-79 & Grad Ctr, New Sch Social Res, 75-76; bd mem, NY State Bd Hist Preserv, 76-84; mem stand bd, Soc Prof Archaeol, 82-85; co-prin investr, Fund Improvement Postsecondary Educ, 90-93. *Mem:* Am Anthrop Asn; Soc Social Studies Sci; Hist Sci Soc; Soc Hist Technol. *Res:* Science and technology studies; cultural and social contexts of science and technology; material culture research evaluates these contexts for scientific instrumentation and for technology. *Mailing Add:* Rensselaer Polytech Inst 5508 Sage Lab Troy NY 12180-3590. *E-Mail:* userec8c@rpi.edu

GORES, GREGORY J, GASTROENTEROLOGY. *Current Pos:* Resident, Dept Med, 80-83, fel, Div Gastroenterol, 83-86, ASSOC PROF MED, MAYO MED SCH, MAYO CLIN, 86-, SR ASSOC CONSULT, DIV GASTROENTEROL, DEPT INTERNAL MED, 88- *Personal Data:* b Devils Lake, NDak, May 22, 55; m 80, Amy Haakenstad; c 2. *Educ:* Univ NDak, Williston Br, AA, 74; Univ NDak, Grand Forks, BS, 76, BS, 78, MD, 80; Am Bd Internal Med, dipl, 83. *Concurrent Pos:* Assoc ed, Gastroenterol. *Mem:* Fel Am Col Physicians; Am Gastroenterol Asn; Am Asn Study Liver Dis; Am Soc Cell Biol; Gastroenterol Res Group; Am Fedn Clin Res; Sigma Xi; AMA; AAAS; Am Physiol Soc. *Res:* Gastroenterology; numerous publications. *Mailing Add:* Div Gastroenterol Mayo Clin Rochester MN 55905. *Fax:* 507-284-0762

GORESKY, CARL A, internal medicine; deceased, see previous edition for last biography

GORETTA, LOUIS ALEXANDER, organic chemistry; deceased, see previous edition for last biography

GORFIEN, HAROLD, PLANT PHYSIOLOGY, FOOD PROCESSING & PRESERVATION. *Current Pos:* RETIRED. *Personal Data:* b New York, NY, Aug 29, 24; m 51; c 2. *Educ:* City Col New York, BS, 48; Univ Mass, MS, 51. *Prof Exp:* Processed food inspector, Prod & Mkt Admin, USDA, 50-51; res assoc, Univ Mass, 51-53; food spec supvr, USN Res & Develop Facil, 53-56; food technologist, DCA Food Industs, Inc, 56-62 & USN Res & Develop Facil, 62-66; food technologist, US Army Natick Res & Develop Ctr, 66-92. *Concurrent Pos:* Teacher, NY Inst Dietetics, 63-66, Essex Agr & Tech Inst, 71-73. *Mem:* Am Chem Soc; Inst Food Technologists; fel AAAS. *Res:* Post harvest physiology and biochemistry; enzyme and controlled atmosphere studies; development of cereal, hydrocolloid, nutritional and dairy products; development of processes for adhesion and coating. *Mailing Add:* 19 Heather Dr Framingham MA 01701

GORFIEN, STEPHEN FRANK, CELL CULTURE. *Current Pos:* res scientist, 89-90, SR SCIENTIST, GIBCO LAB, CELL CULT RES & DEVELOP, GRAND ISLAND, 90- *Personal Data:* b Staten Island, NY, Feb 4, 58; m 85; c 2. *Educ:* State Univ NY, BS, 80, PhD(exp path), 85. *Prof Exp:* Res assoc, Connective Tissue Res Inst, Philadelphia, 85-88, Am Heart Asn spec investr, 88-89. *Mem:* Am Soc Cell Biol; NY Acad Sci; Soc In Vitro Biol; Europ Soc Animal Cell Technol; Soc Invertebrate Path. *Res:* Cell culture; numerous publications. *Mailing Add:* Media Develop Dept Cell Cult Res & Develop Life Technologies Inc Grand Island NY 14072-0068. *Fax:* 716-774-6996; *E-Mail:* sgorfien@lifetech.com

GORGES, HEINZ A(UGUST), MECHANICAL ENGINEERING. *Current Pos:* PRES, VINETA INC, 75- *Personal Data:* b Stettin, Ger, July 22, 13; US citizen; m 57, Sapienza T Coco. *Educ:* Dresden Tech Univ, ME, 38; Hanover Tech Univ, PhD(mech eng), 46. *Prof Exp:* Group leader supersonics, Aero Res Estab, Ger, 40-45; scientist, Royal Aircraft Estab, Eng, 46-49; prin sci officer, Weapons Res Estab, SAustralia, 49-59; sci asst aeroballistics, Marshall Space Flight Ctr, NASA, Ala, 59-61; dir adv projs, Cook Technol Ctr, Ill, 61-62; sci adv, IIT Res Inst, 62-66; asst vpres, Environ & Phys Sic Div, Tracor, Inc, 66-72, vpres & chief engr, Tracor-Jitco, Inc, 72-75. *Concurrent Pos:* Prof, Redstone Exten, Univ Ala, 60-61. *Mem:* Assoc fel Am Inst Aeronaut & Astronaut; Am Soc Mech Engrs; Acoust Soc Am. *Res:* Supersonics and hypersonics; aerodynamics of propulsion; energy management; energy systems; life cycle economics. *Mailing Add:* 3705 Sleepy Hollow Rd Falls Church VA 22041

GORGONE, JOHN T, COMPUTER INFORMATION SYSTEMS. *Current Pos:* Chmn dept, 77-85, PROF COMPUT INFO, BENTLEY COL, 77- *Personal Data:* b Johnstown, Pa, Dec 23, 41. *Educ:* Univ Southern Colo, BA, 66; Univ Northern Colo, MA, 66; Southern Ill Univ, PhD(comput info systs), 74. *Concurrent Pos:* Actg dean, Grad Sch, Bentley Col, 89-90. *Mem:* Asn Comput Mach; Inst Elec & Electronics Engrs; Soc Info Mgt. *Mailing Add:* 319 Pleasant St Belmont MA 02178

GORHAM, ELAINE DEBORAH, GEOPHYSICS. *Current Pos:* Fel, Sandia Labs, 74-76, staff physicist, 76-79, mem tech staff, 81-87, TECH SUPVR, SANDIA LABS, 87- *Personal Data:* b Brattleboro, Vt, July 19, 45. *Educ:* Brown Univ, ScB, 67; Northeastern Univ, PhD(physics), 71. *Concurrent Pos:* Foreign sci attache, Nuclear Regulatory Comn, Caderache, France. *Mem:* Am Phys Soc. *Res:* Blasting technology for oil shale mining; hydrogen diffusion in metals; electrical conductivity in semiconductors and low temperature metals; reactor safety core debris coolability; equations of state and other materials properties of reactor fuel. *Mailing Add:* Sandia Nat Labs Dept 9104 MS 0828 PO Box 5800 Albuquerque NM 87185

GORHAM, EVILLE, LIMNOLOGY, BIOGEOCHEMISTRY & WETLAND ECOLOGY. *Current Pos:* head dept bot, Univ Minn, St Paul, 67-71, prof bot, 66-75, prof ecol, 75-84, REGENTS' PROF ECOL & BOT, UNIV MINN, ST PAUL, 84- *Personal Data:* b Halifax, NS, Oct 15, 25; m 48, Ada V MacLeod; c Kerstin, Vivien, Jocelyn & James. *Educ:* Dalhousie Univ, BSc, 45, MSc, 47; Univ London, PhD(plant ecol), 51. *Hon Degrees:* LLD, Dalhousie Univ, Halifax, Can, 91; DSc, McGill Univ, Montreal, Can, 93. *Honors & Awards:* George C Wheeler Distinguished lectr, Univ NDak, 70; C P Snow lectr, Ithaca Col, 80 & 89; Moore lectr, Univ Va, 81; Oosting Mem lectr, Duke Univ, 83; G Evelyn Hutchinson Medal, Am Soc Limnol & Oceanog, 86; Sigurd Olson Award, Sierra Club, 86; Jack R Hargis Mem lectr, Univ Minn, Duluth, 91. *Prof Exp:* Lectr bot, Univ Col, Univ London, 50-54; ecologist, Brit Freshwater Biol Asn, 54-58; lectr bot, Univ Toronto, 58-59, asst prof, 59-62; assoc prof, Univ Minn, 62-65; prof biol & head dept, Univ Alta, Calgary, 65-66. *Concurrent Pos:* Mem vis comt to rev progs in toxicol, Nat Acad Sci-Nat Res Coun, 74-75; mem coord comt sci & tech assessment environ pollutants, Environ Studies Bd, Nat Acad Sci, Nat Res Coun, 75-78, mem comt med & biologic effects environ pollutants, Assembly Life Sci, Nat Acad Sci-Nat Res Coun, 76-77; mem NATO, Adv Res Inst Acid Precipitation, Can, 78 & Adv Res Wkshp Acid Deposition, Can, 85; mem comt atmosphere & biosphere, Bd Agr & Renewable Resources, Nat Acad Sci, Nat Res Coun, 79-81; mem, diesel impact study comt, Nat Res Coun-Nat Acad Eng, 80-81; mem, US, Can, Mex Tri-Acad Comt, Acid Precipitation, Environ Studies Bd, Nat Acad Sci, Nat Res Coun, Royal Soc Can, Mex Acad Sci, 81-84; mem panel to rev final reports for US/Can Memorandum Intent Transboundary Air Pollution, Royal Soc Can, 82-83 & rev panel Can fed govt progs on long-range transport air pollution, 84; environ consult for var US & Can govt agencies; mem workshops on global change, Royal Soc Can, 85, 90 & 92; co-ed, Environ Encycl, Gale Res, Inc, 94; mem, Comt Inland Aquatic Ecosyst Water Sci & Technol Bd, Nat Acad Sci-Nat Res Coun, 93-96, Water Sci & Technol Bd, 96- & Comt Eval Indicators for Monitoring Aquatic & Terrestrial Environs, 97-; mem, Coun Sci Advisors, Marine Biol Lab, Woods Hole, Mass, 96- *Mem:* Nat Acad Sci; fel Am Acad Arts & Scis; Am Asn Univ Prof (vpres, 67-68, pres, 68-69); fel AAAS; hon mem Swed Phytogeog Soc; fel Royal Soc Can. *Res:* Biogeochemical aspects of ecology, limnology and soil science; wetland/peatland ecology; chemistry of atmospheric precipitation with special attention to acid deposition; history of ecology and biogeochemistry; ecosystem acidification. *Mailing Add:* Dept Ecol Evolution & Behav Univ Minn 1987 Upper Buford Circle St Paul MN 55108. *Fax:* 612-624-6777; *E-Mail:* gorha001@maroon.tc.umn.edu

GORHAM, JOHN FRANCIS, CHEMICAL ENGINEERING. *Current Pos:* from instr to assoc prof, 62-86, chmn dept, 81-86, EMER PROF CHEM ENG, UNIV MAINE, 86- *Personal Data:* b Medford, Mass, Sept 24, 21; m 48; c 2. *Educ:* Univ Maine, BS, 50, MS, 52. *Prof Exp:* Jr engr, Stamford Lab, Am Cyanamid Co, 52-53. *Mem:* Am Inst Chem Engrs; Tech Asn Pulp & Paper Indust. *Res:* Process dynamics and control; pulp and paper technology; electronic computer specialties. *Mailing Add:* 5 Maplewood St Orono ME 04473

GORHAM, JOHN RICHARD, VETERINARY MEDICINE. *Current Pos:* vet-in-chg, Fur Animal Dis Sta, 53-66, DIR, ANIMAL DIS UNIT, AGR RES SERV, WASH STATE UNIV, USDA, 66- *Personal Data:* b Puyallup, Wash, Dec 19, 22; m 44; c 2. *Educ:* State Col Wash, BS & DVM, 46, MS, 47; Univ Wis, PhD, 54. *Prof Exp:* Asst prof path, State Col Wash, 47-51; asst virol, Univ Wis, 51-53. *Concurrent Pos:* Assoc prof path, Wash State Univ, 53-57, prof, 57-79. *Mem:* Am Soc Exp Path; Am Vet Med Asn. *Res:* Virology and epizootiology; virus and rickettsial diseases of carnivores; slow virus diseases. *Mailing Add:* Dept Vet Microbiol & Pathol Col Vet Med Wash State Univ 237 Bustad Hall Pullman WA 99164-7030. *Fax:* 509-335-8328

GORHAM, JOHN RICHARD, MEDICAL ENTOMOLOGY, DISASTER MANAGEMENT. *Current Pos:* res entomologist, 73-95, DIR, COORD CTR DISASTER PREV MED, FOOD & DRUG ADMIN, 95- *Personal Data:* b Montgomery Co, Ohio, July 27, 31; m 52, June Curry; c Susan D (Mason), Sharon L (Leivestad), Lynda D (Marquardt), John F, Daniel P, Anna M (Chatman-Warner) & Joseph M. *Educ:* Miami Univ, AB, 53, MS, 56; Ohio State Univ, PhD(entom), 60; Malaria Eradication Training Ctr, Jamaica, dipl, 61. *Honors & Awards:* Distinguished Entomologist Award, Am Registry Prof Entomologists, 91; Pub Health Serv Citation, Pub Health Serv, 91; Outstanding Serv Medal, 92, Surgeon Gen's Exemplary Serv Medal, 93, Surgeon Gen's Medallion, 93, Distinguished Serv Medal, 93; Gorgas Medal, Asn Mil Surgeons US, 92. *Prof Exp:* Res asst invert zool, Univ NMex, 53; prev med technician, Army Health Nursing Serv, Walter Reed Army Med

Ctr, 54-55; grad asst zool, Miami Univ, 55-56, instr, 56-57; grad asst, Ohio State Univ, 57, asst instr, 58-60; consult entomologist malaria eradication, Pan Am Health Orgn, Paraguay, 61-63; res assoc, Inst Int Med, Univ Md, 63-64; res assoc, Pakistan Med Res Ctr, 64-65; sr scientist, Vector Borne Dis Training Sect, Ctr Dis Control, Ga, 66-69, res entomologist, Arctic Health Res Ctr, Alaska, 69-73. *Concurrent Pos:* USPHS trainee, Sch Trop Med, Univ PR, 60-61; res assoc, Conserv Found, NY, 58-59; aquatic entomologist, Maine Forest Serv, 58-59; vis lectr, Atlanta Baptist Col, 68-69; consult entomologist, Alaska Air Command, 70-73; lectr, Univ Alaska, 71-73; Food & Drug Admin liaison rep, Armed Forces Pest Mgt Bd, 74-95; scientist dir, USPHS, 76-95; adj prof prev med, Uniformed Serv Univ Health Sci, 90- *Mem:* Entom Soc Am; Am Acad Sanitarians; Am Mosquito Control Asn; Soc Vector Ecol; Nat Environ Health Asn; Disaster Emergency Response Asn. *Res:* Ecology and systematics of mosquitoes; ecology of Paraguay; arctic ecology; pest management; terrestrial and aquatic ecology; zoonoses; ecology of vector-borne diseases; malariology; arbovirology; disaster preventive medicine; myrmecology; venomous arthropods; food pests. *Mailing Add:* 2537 Ridge Rd Xenia OH 45385-7503. *Fax:* 937-372-4781; *E-Mail:* jgorham@lx.netcom.com

GORHAM, PAUL RAYMOND, PLANT PHYSIOLOGY, PHYCOLOGY. *Current Pos:* prof bot, Univ Alta, 69-83, chmn dept, 71-79, assoc dir, Bot Garden, 76-83, EMER PROF BOT, UNIV ALTA, 83- *Personal Data:* b Fredericton, NB, Apr 16, 18; m 43, Evelyn R Woods; c John H, Arthur R & Harriet R. *Educ:* Univ NB, BA, 38; Univ Maine, MS, 40; Calif Inst Technol, PhD(plant physiol), 43. *Hon Degrees:* DSc, Univ NB, 73. *Honors & Awards:* Centennial Medal, 67; Silver Jubilee Medal, 78; Mary E Elliot Award, Can Bot Soc, 79, George Lawson Medal, 88; Gold Medal, Can Soc Plant Physiol, 87. *Prof Exp:* Agr asst plant physiol, Div Bot & Plant Path, Dom Dept Agr, Ottawa, 43-45; jr res officer, Div Biosci, Nat Res Coun Can, 45-46, asst res officer plant sci invests, 46-51, from assoc res officer prin res officer, Plant Physiol Sect, 51-69. *Concurrent Pos:* Head, Plant Physiol Sect, Nat Res Coun Can, 52-69; mem, Can Comt, Int Biol Prog, 67-74, secy, 68-69; mem adv comt, Alta Oil Sands Environ Res Prog, 75-76. *Mem:* Can Soc Plant Physiol (pres, 58-59); Am Soc Plant Physiologists; Can Bot Asn (pres, 77-78); fel Royal Soc Can; fel Rawson Acad Aquatic Sci. *Res:* Phloem translocation; physiology of submerged aquatic macrophytes; toxic cyanobacteria (blue-green algae); hydrobiology. *Mailing Add:* 12408 49th Ave Edmonton AB T6H 0H2 Can

GORHAM, WILLIAM FRANKLIN, ORGANIC CHEMISTRY, POLYMER CHEMISTRY. *Current Pos:* group leader, Plastics Div, 56-65, asst dir res, 65-72, ASSOC DIR RES & DEVELOP, CHEM & PLASTICS, UNION CARBIDE CORP, 72-; MGR RES & DEVELOP, ENG POLYMER, 81- *Personal Data:* b Brandon, Vt, Aug 13, 26; m 53; c 4. *Educ:* Univ Miami, Ohio, AB, 48; Mass Inst Technol, PhD(chem), 51. *Prof Exp:* Sr res chemist, Bakelite Corp, 51-56. *Mem:* Am Chem Soc. *Res:* Synthetic organic chemistry; management of research and development on thermoplastic polymers, new product invention and market development, parylene vapor deposition technology, applications for parylene, analytical chemistry and the combustibility properties of plastics; product safety. *Mailing Add:* 64 Baxter Rd PO Box 478 Hollis NH 03049-5944

GORI, GIO BATTA, TOXICOLOGY, EPIDEMIOLOGY. *Current Pos:* DIR, HEALTH POLICY CTR, 88- *Personal Data:* b Tarcento, Italy, Feb 23, 31; US citizen; m 58, Anna Gobessi; c Caterina & Aurelius. *Educ:* Univ Camerino, ScD, 56; Harvard Univ, SMG cert, 76; Johns Hopkins Univ, MPH, 78; Acad Toxicol Sci, dipl, 82. *Honors & Awards:* Super Serv Award, USPHS, 76. *Prof Exp:* Assoc microbiol, Ist Superiore Sanita, Italy, 56-58; assoc virol, Univ Pittsburgh, 58-59; assoc dir, Ist Sclavo, Italy, 59-60; assoc virol, Wistar Inst, Univ Pa, 60-62; dir qual control & asst to pres, Microbiol Assocs Inc, 62-63, dir prod, 63-65; head virol, Toxicol & Immunol Dept, Melpar Inc, 65-67; dir biol res lab, Litton Systs Inc, 67-68; assoc sci dir prog etiology, Nat Cancer Inst, 68-73, dep dir, Div Cancer Causes & Prev, 73-80; dir, Policy Anal Ctr, Franklin Inst, 80-88. *Concurrent Pos:* Ed, Nutrit & Cancer, 78- *Mem:* AAAS; Am Pub Health Asn; Soc Toxicol; Int Soc Regulatory Toxicol & Pharmacol. *Res:* Algae; halophilic bacteria; virus epidemiology; production and control of polio vaccines; cell physiology and transformation; continuous cultivation of cells and viruses; environmental analysis and toxicology; chemical carcinogenesis; tobacco smoking and health; nutrition and cancer epidemiology; ultraviolet radiation and cancer; health economics management; policy analysis of health and safety regulation. *Mailing Add:* 6503 Pyle Rd Bethesda MD 20817. *Fax:* 301-229-4278

GORIN, GEORGE, PHYSICAL BIOCHEMISTRY, CHEMICAL INFORMATION. *Current Pos:* from asst prof to prof, 55-90, EMER PROF CHEM, OKLA STATE UNIV, 62- *Personal Data:* b Como, Italy, Aug 19, 25; m 52, Helen Surber; c Sarah & Victor. *Educ:* Brooklyn Col, AB, 44; Princeton Univ, MA, 47, PhD(chem), 49. *Prof Exp:* Asst, Princeton Univ, 44; chemist, Heyden Chem Corp, 45; res assoc, Rutgers Univ, 49-50; fel, Purdue Univ, 51; asst prof chem, Univ Ore, 52-55. *Concurrent Pos:* NIH career develop award, 63-73. *Mem:* Am Chem Soc; Am Soc Biol Chemists. *Res:* Enzymes; kinetics and thermodynamics of biochemical reactions; radiation damage; sulfur compounds; chemical information. *Mailing Add:* Dept Chem Okla State Univ Stillwater OK 74078. *Fax:* 405-744-6007; *E-Mail:* gochem@vm1.ucc.okstate.edu

GORIN, MICHAEL BRUCE, OPHTHALMIC GENETICS, MEDICAL & GENETIC RETINAL DISORDERS. *Current Pos:* ASSOC PROF, OPHTHAL & HUMAN GENETICS, UNIV PITTSBURGH, 90- *Personal Data:* b Baltimore, Md, Nov 11, 53; m 82, Jane R Leinwohl; c Joshua & Alexander. *Educ:* Pomona Col, BA, 74; Univ Pa, MD, 80, PhD(biochem), 80. *Prof Exp:* Fel med retina, Moorfields Eye Hosp, 86-87; med officer, Nat Eye Inst, NIH, 87-90. *Mem:* Asn Res Vision & Ophthal; Am Soc Human Genetics. *Res:* Molecular genetics of inherited retinal disorders especially animal models of retinal degenerations and the molecular genetics of human macular and retinal degenerations; intraocular gene therapy. *Mailing Add:* Dept Ophthal 203 Lothrop St Pittsburgh PA 15213. *Fax:* 412-647-5880

GORING, DAVID ARTHUR INGHAM, WOOD CHEMISTRY. *Current Pos:* PROF CHEM ENG, UNIV TORONTO, 86- *Personal Data:* b Toronto, Ont, Nov 26, 20; m 48, Elizabeth D Haswell; c James, Rosemary & Christopher. *Educ:* Univ Col, London, BSc, 42; McGill Univ, PhD(phys chem), 49; Cambridge Univ, PhD(colloid chem), 53. *Honors & Awards:* Anselme Payen Award, Cellulose, Wood & Fiber Chem Div, Am Chem Soc, 73; Gunnar Nicholson Tappi Gold Medal, Tech Asn Pulp & Paper Indust, 86; John Bates Mem Gold Medal, Can Pulp & Paper Asn, 95. *Prof Exp:* Asst res officer phys chem, Atlantic Regional Lab, Nat Res Coun Can, 51-55; scientist II, Pulp & Paper Res Inst, 55-60, res group leader, 60-71, prin scientist, 69-85, dir res, 71-76, vpres sci, 76-83, vpres acad, 83-85. *Concurrent Pos:* Res assoc, McGill Univ, 56-68, sr res assoc, 68-86. *Mem:* Fel Chem Inst Can; Can Pulp & Paper Asn; fel Royal Soc Can; fel Int Acad Wood Sci; fel Tech Asn Pulp & Paper Indust. *Res:* Chemistry of wood and wood pulp. *Mailing Add:* Dept Chem Eng & Appl Chem Univ Toronto Toronto ON M5S 3E5 Can. *Fax:* 416-971-2106

GORING, GEOFFREY E(DWARD), CHEMICAL ENGINEERING, PHYSICS. *Current Pos:* assoc prof 63-67, PROF ENG SCI, TRINITY UNIV, 67- *Personal Data:* b New York, NY, Nov 8, 20; m 55; c 3. *Educ:* Yale Univ, BE, 42; Mass Inst Technol, ScD(chem eng), 49; Fairleigh Dickinson Univ, MS, 62. *Prof Exp:* Proj leader, Pittsburgh Consol Coal Co, Pa, 49-52; proj scientist, Stand Oil Co Ind, 52-54; proj dir, Am Messer Corp, NY, 54-56; tech liaison, Argonne Nat Lab, Ill, Union Carbide Corp, 56-69, sr scientist, NY, 59-62; asst div dir, Atlantic Res Corp, Va, 62-63. *Mem:* Am Phys Soc. *Res:* Thermodynamics; applied mathematics; environmental science; materials science. *Mailing Add:* 224 Gardenview San Antonio TX 78213

GORLA, RAMA S R, HEAT TRANSFER, FLUID MECHANICS. *Current Pos:* PROF MECH ENG, CLEVELAND STATE UNIV, 77- *Personal Data:* b India; US citizen. *Educ:* S V Univ, BS, 63; Indian Inst Technol, MS, 65; Univ Toledo, PhD(mech eng), 72. *Honors & Awards:* Outstanding Am Soc Mech Engrs Awward, 77. *Prof Exp:* Lectr mech eng, S V Univ, 65-66; asst prof space eng & rocketry, Birla Inst Technol, 66-68; res asst mech eng, Univ Toledo, 68-72; res engr, Teledyne CAE, 72-73 & Chrysler Corp, 73-74; asst prof mech eng, Gannon Univ, 74-77. *Concurrent Pos:* Prin investr, Lewis Res Ctr, NASA, 79-; consult, USAF. *Mem:* Am Soc Mech Engrs; Am Soc Eng Educ. *Res:* Computational and experimental aspects of heat transfer, fluid flow, rheology, finite elements and numerical analysis. *Mailing Add:* 8041 Oxford Dr Strongsville OH 44136

GORLAND, SOL H, PROPULSION SYSTEMS, COMBUSTION ENGINE CONDITION MONITORING. *Current Pos:* Aerospace engr, Power Syst Div, NASA, 62-75, prog mgr, Off Energy Prog, Hq, 75-76, head, Power Syst Sect, 77-80, mgr syst anal off, Lewis Res Ctr, 81-84, chief, Launch Vehicle Technol Br, 84-96, CHIEF COMBUSTION BR, NASA, 96- *Personal Data:* b Brooklyn, NY, Sept 14, 41; m 66, Harriet Mortach; c Rachelle & Robyn. *Educ:* Cooper Union, BS, 62; Univ Toledo, MS, 70. *Concurrent Pos:* Mem, Energy Res & Develop Admin, Dept Energy Geothermal Adv Panel, 75-78, Space Syst Technol Adv Comt, NASA, 78-80 & Aerospace Power Systs Tech Comt, Am Inst Aeronaut & Astronaut, 78-81; assoc ed, J Energy, 80-84; mem, Engine Condition Monitoring Comt, Soc Automotive Eng, 94- *Mem:* Assoc fel Am Inst Aeronaut & Astronaut. *Res:* Systems analysis for space power and propulsion; technology for primary propulsion systems for space; aircraft combustors and emissions. *Mailing Add:* Lewis Res Ctr NASA 21000 Brookpark Rd MS 60-4 Cleveland OH 44135. *Fax:* 216-977-7500; *E-Mail:* sol.h.gorland@lerc.nasa.gov

GORLIN, RICHARD, MEDICINE. *Current Pos:* ROSENBERG PROF MED & CHMN DEPT, MT SINAI SCH MED, 74-, PHYSICIAN-IN-CHIEF, MT SINAI HOSP, 74- *Personal Data:* b Jersey City, NJ, June 30, 26. *Educ:* Harvard Med Sch, MD, 48; Am Bd Internal Med, dipl. *Prof Exp:* Intern & med house officer, Peter Bent Brigham Hosp, 48-49, asst, 49-51, sr asst res, 51-52, chief resident physician, 53-54, from assoc to sr assoc, 57-66, physician, 66-69, chief cardiol, 69-74. *Concurrent Pos:* Res fel med, Harvard Med Sch, 49-51, teaching fel, 51-52; Moseley traveling fel, St Thomas' Hosp, London, 52-53; Brower traveling scholar, Am Col Physicians, 60; instr med, Harvard Med Sch, 56-58, assoc, 58-61, from asst prof to assoc prof, 61-74; attend physician, US Vet Hosp, Rutland, 58-; lectr, US Naval Hosp, Chelsea, 59-; clin asst, St Thomas' Hosp, London, 60; consult, Nat Heart & Lung Inst. *Mem:* Am Physiol Soc; Am Soc Clin Invest; Am Heart Asn; Am Fedn Clin Res; fel Am Col Cardiol. *Res:* Academic medicine; cardiac physiology. *Mailing Add:* Mt Sinai Sch Med Mt Sinai Med Ctr 1 Gustave Levy Pl Box 1018 New York NY 10029-6574

GORLIN, ROBERT JAMES, ORAL PATHOLOGY, CLINICAL GENETICS. *Current Pos:* from assoc prof to prof oral path, chmn div, Univ Minn, 58-91, chmn, Dept Oral Path, 79-91, regents prof, 78-93, EMER REGENTS PROF, UNIV MINN, 93- *Personal Data:* b Hudson, NY, Jan 11, 23; m 52, Marilyn Alpern; c Cathy & Jed. *Educ:* Columbia Univ, AB, 43; Wash Univ, DDS, 47; Univ Iowa, MS, 56; Am Bd Oral Path, dipl, 56; Am Bd Med Genetic, dipl, 84. *Hon Degrees:* DSc, Univ Athens, 82, Univ Thesalonika, 92. *Honors & Awards:* Howard Fox lectr, NY Acad Med, 68; Carl M Lingamfelter lectr, Univ Va, 71; Frank Hoopes lectr, Wilmington Del, 77; Wincompleck lectr, Univ Okla, 82; Chase Mem lectr, Univ Minn, 83; Samuel Charles Miller Award, Am Acad Oral Med, 85; Frederick Birnberg

Res Award, Columbia Univ, 87; Col Harland Sanders Award, March of Dimes, 89; Second Edward Sheridan lectr, Dublin, Ireland, 89; Windermere lectr, British Pediat Asn, 90; Am Cleft Palate Asn Award, 93; Norton Ross Prize, Am Dent Asn, 95; Int Asn Dent Res, 97. *Prof Exp:* Instr dent, Columbia Univ, 50-51. *Concurrent Pos:* Fulbright exchange prof & Guggenheim fel, Royal Dent Sch, Copenhagen, 61; consult, Univ Minn Hosps, 60-, dir human genetics clin, 71-; consult, US Vet Admin Hosp, Minneapolis, Nat Fedn Birth Defects, Glenwood Hills Med Ctr, Mt Sinai Hosp, Hennepin County Gen Hosp, Ramsey County Gen Hosp, Minneapolis Children's Hosp, St Paul Children's Hosp, WHO, NIH & coun dent educ, Am Dent Asn & Armed Forces Inst Path; assoc ed, Am J Human Genetics, 70-73, J Oral Path, 72-, J Maxillo-Facial Surg, 73-, Cleft Palate J, 76-, Embryol & Pathogenesis & Prenatal Diag, 77, Am J Med Genetics, 77-, J Craniofacial Genetic Develop Biol, 80-, J Clin Dysmorphol, 82-85, J Gerodontics, 84-89, Dysmorph Clin Genet, 86- & Birth Defects Encycl, 86-; mem, Minn Human Genetics League; consult dent study sect, NIH; dir, Am Bd Oral Path, 70-75; mem adv comt, Nat Found Clin Res, 74-90; mem bd dirs, Group Health, Inc; prof path, prof derm & prof pediat, Sch Med, Univ Minn, 71-, prof obstet & gynec & prof otolaryngol, 73-; vis prof, Sch Med, Tel-Aviv Univ, 81, Sch Dent, Jerusalem, 81, Univ Mo, 84, Univ Ill, 84 & Univ Pittsburgh, 87; Robert J Gorlin vis prof dysmorphol, Royal Soc Med, London, 89, Burroughs Wellcome vis prof, 90-91; Spinoza chair, Univ Amsterdam, 95. *Mem:* Sr mem Inst Med-Nat Acad Sci; fel Am Acad Oral Path (secy-treas, 58-64, vpres, 64-65, pres, 66-67); Am Acad Dermat; Int Asn Dent Res; Int Soc Craniofacial Biol (pres, 69-70); Am Soc Human Genetics; Birth Defects & Clin Genetics Soc; fel Royal Col Surgeons Eng; fel Royal Col Surgeons Ireland; Am Dent Asn. *Res:* Pediatrics; relationships between oral and systemic disease; oral syndromes; human genetics. *Mailing Add:* Depts Oral Path & Genetics Univ Minn Health Sci Ctr Minneapolis MN 55455. *Fax:* 612-626-2327; *E-Mail:* gorli002@maroon.tc.umn.edu

GORMAN, ARTHUR DANIEL, ASYMPTOTICS, CAUSTICS. *Current Pos:* ASST PROF, LAFAYETTE COL, 82-, CHMN DEPT, 88- *Personal Data:* b Chicago, Ill, Oct 31, 46; m 68, 85; c 2. *Educ:* Univ Ill, BS, 68; Pa State Univ, PhD(physics), 80. *Prof Exp:* Syst engr develop, Univac, 68-69; prog engr, Gen Elec, 69-71; res asst, Wash Univ, 71-74; res asst develop, Appl Res Lab, Pa State Univ, 74-82. *Mem:* Am Math Soc; Sigma Xi. *Res:* Asymptotic solution of differential equations near caustics. *Mailing Add:* Lafayette Col Easton PA 18042

GORMAN, COLUM A, ENDOCRINOLOGY, INTERNAL MEDICINE. *Current Pos:* consult internal med, Mayo Clin, 66, from instr to asst prof med, Mayo Grad Sch, 66-73, from asst prof to assoc prof, 73-81, chmn, div endocrinol, 85, PROF MED, MAYO MED SCH, 81- *Personal Data:* b Mayobridge, N Ireland, June 27, 36; m 61, Una Elizabeth O'Neill; c Kevin, Paul, Fiona & Michael. *Educ:* Queens Univ, MB & BCh, 59; Univ Minn, PhD(med, biochem), 68. *Honors & Awards:* Hamburger Medal, Technion-Israel Inst Technol, 85; Distinguished Serv Award, Am Thyroid Asn, 90; Ruitinga van Swieten Medal, Univ Amersterdan, 92; Robert Campbell Mem Medal, 96. *Prof Exp:* NIH fel, 64-65. *Concurrent Pos:* Bd govs, Mayo Clin, Rochester, 97- *Mem:* Am Fedn Clin Res; Am Thyroid Asn (secy, 84-89, pres, 95-96); Endocrine Soc; fel Am Col Physicians; hom mem Europe Thyroid Asn. *Res:* Thyroxine and triiodothyronine; ophthalmopathy of Graves' disease; thyroid carcinoma; thyroid radiation dosimetry. *Mailing Add:* Mayo Clin Grad Sch Med 200 First St SW Rochester MN 55905-0001. *Fax:* 507-284-0728; *E-Mail:* gorman.colum@mayo.edu

GORMAN, CORNELIA M, BIOCHEMICAL GENETICS. *Current Pos:* AM CANCER SOC FEL, NAT CANCER INST, 81- *Personal Data:* b El Paso, Tex, Dec 16, 51. *Educ:* Univ Tex, El Paso, BS, 74; Wash State Univ, MS, 76, PhD(genetics), 81. *Prof Exp:* Teaching asst biol & zool, Wash State Univ, 74-77, res asst biochem, 78-80. *Mem:* AAAS; Asn Women Sci; Am Soc Cell Biol. *Res:* Construction of eucaryotic vectors which will allow for increased efficiency in modifying mammalian cells, involving development of new cloning vehicles. *Mailing Add:* 124 Belvedere St San Francisco CA 94117

GORMAN, EUGENE FRANCIS, welding technology, roll formed metal shapes, for more information see previous edition

GORMAN, GEORGE CHARLES, HERPETOLOGY. *Current Pos:* assoc prof, 73-80, PROF BIOL, UNIV CALIF, LOS ANGELES, 80- *Personal Data:* b Brooklyn, NY, July 9, 41; m 69; c 1. *Educ:* Cornell Univ, BA, 62; Harvard Univ, PhD(biol), 68. *Prof Exp:* Miller fel, Univ Calif, Berkeley, 68-70; res assoc herpet, Mus Comp Zool, Harvard Univ, 71-72. *Concurrent Pos:* NATO fel, Hebrew Univ Jerusalem, Israel, 70. *Mem:* Am Soc Ichthyol & Herpet; Herpet League; Soc Study Amphibians & Reptiles; Soc Syst Zool; Ecol Soc Am. *Res:* Evolutionary genetics; ecology of lizards; cytotaxonomy. *Mailing Add:* 952 The Alameda Berkeley CA 94707

GORMAN, JOHN RICHARD, mathematics, for more information see previous edition

GORMAN, MARVIN, BIO-ORGANIC CHEMISTRY, DRUG DEVELOPMENT & CLINICAL TRIALS MANAGEMENT. *Current Pos:* VPRES SCI DEVELOP, VERSICOR INC, 96- *Personal Data:* b Detroit, Mich, Sept 24, 28; m 76, Lura; c 3. *Educ:* Univ Mich, BS, 50; Wayne State Univ, PhD(org chem), 55. *Prof Exp:* Res fel, Israel Inst Technol, 54-55 & Wayne State Univ, 56; org chemist, Eli Lilly & Co, 56-69, res assoc, 64-69, res adv res labs, 69-82; exec vpres, Oncogen Div, Bristol-Myers Co, 82-91; vpes develop, Pathogenesis Corp, 91-94. *Concurrent Pos:* Consult, Pharmaceut Co, 92- *Mem:* Am Soc Microbiol; AAAS; Am Chem Soc. *Res:* Natural products; isolation, characterization and structure determination, primarily of alkaloids and antibiotics; chemistry of beta-lactam antibiotics; ionophoretic substances; antiviral agents immunoregulators; pharmaceutical development of antibiotics and proteins; anticancer agents. *Mailing Add:* 3724 Sunrise Lane Key West FL 33040-4540

GORMAN, MELVILLE, inorganic chemistry, history of science; deceased, see previous edition for last biography

GORMAN, ROBERT ROLAND, BIOCHEMISTRY. *Current Pos:* sr res scientist biochem, Upjohn Co, 72-82, from assoc dir to dir cell biol, 82-88, exec dir, Discovery Res, 88-90, VPRES DISCOVERY RES, UPJOHN CO, 90- *Personal Data:* b Mojave, Calif, Aug 19, 44; m 66, Paula Spence; c Robert R III & Stephanie C. *Educ:* Univ Idaho, BS, 66, MS, 68; Colo State Univ, PhD(biochem), 70. *Prof Exp:* Fel pharmacol, State Univ NY Upstate Med Ctr, 70-72. *Mem:* AAAS; Am Soc Biol Chemists. *Res:* Mechanism of action of prostaglandins and the role of cyclic nucleotides in this area. *Mailing Add:* Pharmacia Upjohn Knyvett House Causeway Staines Middlesex KW183BA England. *Fax:* 616-385-5268

GORMAN, WILLIAM ALAN, QUATERNARY GEOLOGY, ENVIRONMENTAL ENGINEERING. *Current Pos:* from asst prof to assoc prof, 55-71, prof geol sci, 71-91, ADJ PROF, QUEEN'S UNIV, ONT, 91- *Personal Data:* b Montreal, Que, Oct 18, 25; m 50, Luella Anderson; c Ian, Barbara & Judy. *Educ:* McGill Univ, BSc, 49, MSc, 52, PhD(geol), 56. *Prof Exp:* Field geologist, Que Dept Mines, 51-56. *Concurrent Pos:* Geologist, Steep Rock Iron Mines, 57-59; spec lectr, Royal Mil Col, Can, 59-64 & 68-77; photogeologist, Neilson Assoc, 79-80; geologist, Mobil Oil, 80-81. *Mem:* Fel Geol Asn Can. *Res:* Late quaternary geology of eastern Ontario; problems in environmental engineering, eastern Ontario. *Mailing Add:* Dept Geol Queen's Univ Kingston ON K7L 3N6 Can

GORMICAN, ANNETTE, NUTRITION. *Current Pos:* AT DEPT FOOD SCI & NUTRIT, UNIV MINNEAPOLIS. *Personal Data:* b Fond du Lac, Wis, Apr 26, 24. *Educ:* Col St Catherine, BS, 46; Univ Iowa, MS, 47, PhD(nutrit), 65. *Prof Exp:* Chief dietitian, Mercy Hosp, Jackson, Mich, 48-50; instr sch home econ, Univ Minn, St Paul, 52-54; asst prof nutrit, 55-60; educ dir dietetics, Sch Med, Univ Wis-Madison, 61-62; therapeut dietitian, Univ Iowa, 62-64; asst prof nutrit, Col Med, Univ Nebr, 65-66; assoc prof dept nutrit sci & dir dietetic internship, 67-68; dir dietetic internship & residency prog, Univ Wis-Madison, 68-, assoc prof nutrit sci, 80- *Mem:* Am Soc Clin Nutrit; Am Inst Nutrit; Am Inst Chemists; NY Acad Sci; AAAS. *Res:* Trace elements in foods, mineral absorption, computer applications in nutrition, clinical dietetics. *Mailing Add:* 2240 Midland Grove Rd No 206 Roseville MN 55113-3864

GORMLEY, WILLIAM THOMAS, ORGANIC CHEMISTRY. *Current Pos:* RES CHEMIST, KOPPERS CO, INC, MONROEVILLE, 61- *Personal Data:* b Versailles, Ky, May 24, 15; m 47; c 5. *Educ:* Univ Ky, BS, 37, MS, 45; NY Univ, PhD(chem), 52. *Prof Exp:* Chemist, State Testing Labs, Ky, 37-42; Cincinnati Ord Dist, 42-43; instr chem, Army Student Training Prog, Univ Ky, 43-44; chemist, Wm S Merrell Co, 44-46; instr chem, Hunter Col, 46-52; res chemist, E I Du Pont de Nemours & Co, 52-53; fel, Mellon Inst, 53-60. *Mem:* Am Chem Soc. *Res:* Mannich reaction; organic peroxides; synthetic lubricants; high polymers. *Mailing Add:* 406 W Swissvale Ave Pittsburgh PA 15218-1637

GORMUS, BOBBY JOE, INFECTIOUS DISEASES, BIOLOGY OF CELL MEMBRANES. *Current Pos:* RES SCIENTIST, DELTA REGIONAL PRIMATE RES CTR, TULANE UNIV, COVINGTON, LA, 79- *Personal Data:* b Buckingham Co, Va, Nov 7, 41; m 60; c 1. *Educ:* Univ Richmond, BS, 64; Duke Univ, PhD(biochem), 71. *Prof Exp:* Fel, Univ Fla, Gainesville, 71-74; res chemist, Vet Admin Hosp, Minneapolis, 74-79. *Concurrent Pos:* Prin investr, NIH grant, 82- *Mem:* Am Asn Immunologists; Am Leprosy Asn; Am Soc Trop Med & Hyg. *Res:* Immunology and pathology of experimental leprosy in monkeys; immunology of AIDS in monkeys (Simian AIDS or SAIDS). *Mailing Add:* Dept Microbiol Delta Primate Res Ctr Tulane Univ 18703 Three Rivers Rd Covington LA 70433-8907. *Fax:* 504-893-1352

GORNALL, ALLAN GODFREY, BIOCHEMISTRY. *Current Pos:* lectr path chem, Univ Toronto, 46, from asst prof to prof, 46-63, chem dept, 66-76, prof, 63-80, EMER PROF CLIN BIOCHEM, UNIV TORONTO, 80- *Personal Data:* b River Hebert, NS, Aug 28, 14; m 41, Sheila Stewart; c William S, Douglas A, Thomas H & Catherine A. *Educ:* Mt Allison Univ, BA, 36; Univ Toronto, PhD(path chem), 41. *Hon Degrees:* DSc, Mt Allison Univ, 78. *Honors & Awards:* Reeve Prize, 41; Nuffield Fel, 49; Ames Award, Can Soc Clin Chemists, 77, Beckman Award for Outstanding Contribution to Educ, 89. *Prof Exp:* Clin chemist, Can Naval Med Serv, 42-46. *Mem:* Can Soc Clin Chemists; Can Physiol Soc (treas, 54-57); Can Soc Endocrinol & Metab; Can Fedn Biol Soc (hon treas, 57-62); fel Royal Soc Can; fel Can Acad Clin Biochem. *Res:* Urea synthesis; liver function; protein and steroid methodology; metabolic effects of hormones; aldosterone; electrolytes; hypertension; pregnancy toxemia; active site of carbonic anhydrase; histamine receptor proteins. *Mailing Add:* Dept Clin Biochem Univ Toronto 100 Col St Toronto ON M5G 1L5 Can

GORNEY, RODERIC, INTERPERSONAL CONFLICTS, PSYCHOANALYSIS. *Current Pos:* From asst prof to assoc prof psychiat, 71-73, assoc dir, Outpatient Dept, 71-76, DIR, PROG PSYCHOSOCIAL ADAPTATION & THE FUTURE, DEPT PSYCHIAT, UNIV CALIF, LOS

ANGELES, 71-, PROF PSYCHIAT, NEUROPSYCHIAT INST, 80- *Personal Data:* b Grand Rapids, Mich, Aug 13, 24; m 86, Carol Sobel. *Educ:* Stanford Univ, BS, 48, MD, 49; Southern Calif Psychoanal Inst, PhD(psychoanal), 77. *Concurrent Pos:* Lectr psychiat, Sch Social Welfare, Univ Calif, Los Angeles, 72-73, mem, Div Biobehav Res, 75-; mem, Comt Social Issues, Group Advan Psychiat. *Mem:* Fel Am Acad Psychoanal; fel AAAS; fel Am Psychiat Asn. *Res:* Effects of television and motion picture drama on adults; cultural determinants of achievement, aggression and psychological distress; past and future evolution of values and behavior; marital-relationship problems; neurotic character disorders. *Mailing Add:* Neuropsychiat Inst Univ Calif 760 Westwood Plaza Los Angeles CA 90024-1759. *Fax:* 310-825-3002

GORNIAK, GERARD CHARLES, ANATOMICAL SCIENCES, FUNTIONAL MORPHOLOGY. *Current Pos:* assoc prof, 93-97, PROF, UNIV ST AUGUSTINE HEALTH SCI, 97- *Personal Data:* b Erie, Pa, Apr 23, 49; m 71, Jo Ellen Kierzek; c Michelle & Brian. *Educ:* State Univ NY, Buffalo, BS, 71, PhD(anat), 76. *Prof Exp:* Asst clin res, Rehab Med Eng Lab, E J Meyer Mem Hosp, Buffalo, 71-72; chief phys ther & treat, Columbus Hosp, Buffalo, 72-73; NIH fel, Univ Mich, 76-80; asst prof, Dept Biol Sci, Fla State Univ, 80-86, assoc dir, Prog Med Sci, 86-91; asst prof, Div Phys Therapy, Fla A&M Univ, 91-94. *Concurrent Pos:* Assoc ed, J Morphol, 78- *Mem:* Am Phys Ther Asn. *Res:* The functional morphology of the musculoskeletal system; the morphology, physiology and function of growing and stressed muscle; comparative muscle morphology and physiology. *Mailing Add:* 850A1A Beach Blvd Unit 119 St Augustine FL 32084

GORNICK, FRED, PHYSICAL CHEMISTRY. *Current Pos:* CONSULT, NAT BUR STAND, 65- *Personal Data:* b New York, NY, Mar 12, 29; m 50; c 2. *Educ:* City Col New York, BS, 51; Univ Pa, PhD(phys chem), 59. *Prof Exp:* Chemist, Allied Chem & Dye Corp, 51-52 & Rohm & Haas Co, 52-53; asst instr chem, Univ Pa, 53-54, asst, 56-59; phys chemist, Nat Bur Stand, 59-65; assoc prof mat sci, Univ Va, 65-67; assoc prof chem, Univ Md, Baltimore County, 67-69, prof & chmn dept, 69-75. *Concurrent Pos:* Nat Res Coun fel, 59-60; lectr, Georgetown Univ, 64-65; prog mgr, Chem & Hydrogen Energy Systs, Dept Energy, 80-81; vis scientist, Appl Physics Lab, Johns Hopkins Univ, 89-90. *Mem:* AAAS; Am Chem Soc; Am Phys Soc. *Res:* Physical chemistry of macromolecules; thermodynamics and kinetics of crystallization in high polymers; investigations of synthetic polypeptides; sol-gel chemistry. *Mailing Add:* Dept Phys Univ Md Baltimore Co 5401 Wilkens Ave Baltimore MD 21228. *Fax:* 410-455-2608; *E-Mail:* gornick@umbc.edu

GORODETZKY, CHARLES W, clinical pharmacology, drug development, for more information see previous edition

GORODY, ANTHONY WAGNER, exploration, natural gas geochemistry, for more information see previous edition

GOROFF, DIANA K, BIOTECHNOLOGY. *Current Pos:* RES ASSOC DIAG PROD RES, ORGANON TECKNIKA CORP. *Mem:* Am Asn Immunologists; Am Soc Microbiologists. *Res:* Mechanism of IgA blockage of immune lysis and its role in disease caused by Neisseria meningitides; immunochemical studies of the Group B Streptococcal antigen. *Mailing Add:* Dir Mfg Per Immune Inc Organon Tecknika Biotech Res Inst 1330 Piccard Dr Rockville MD 20850-4396. *Fax:* 301-840-2161

GOROG, ISTVAN, ELECTRICAL ENGINEERING, PHYSICS. *Current Pos:* MGR, CRT ENG, THOMSON CONSUMER ELECTRONICS, 92- *Personal Data:* b Budapest, Hungary, Mar 13, 38; US citizen. *Educ:* Univ Calif, Berkeley, BSc, 61, MSc, 62, PhD(elec eng), 64. *Prof Exp:* Asst, Univ Calif, Berkeley, 61-64; mem tech staff, RCA Labs, 64-70, head optical electronics, 70-78, head, Mfg Res Group, 78-82, dir, Mfg Technol Res Lab, 82-87; at David Scronoff Res Ctr, SRI Int, 87-92. *Concurrent Pos:* NSF fel, Italy, 68- *Mem:* Am Phys Soc. *Res:* Lasers and quantum electronics; electro-optics; plasmas; video systems; psycho-physics and visual perception; video discs; manufacturing technology. *Mailing Add:* 1275 Wheatland Ave Lancaster PA 17603

GOROVSKY, MARTIN A, BIOLOGY, CELL BIOLOGY. *Current Pos:* from asst prof to assoc prof, 70-80, PROF BIOL, UNIV ROCHESTER, 80-, CHMN DEPT, 81-, RUSH RHEES PROF, 90- *Personal Data:* b Chicago, Ill, Apr 26, 41; m 67; c 2. *Educ:* Univ Chicago, AB, 63, PhD(cell biol), 68. *Prof Exp:* NSF fel, 68-70. *Mem:* AAAS; Am Soc Cell Biol. *Res:* Molecular biology; study of structure and function of eukaryotic nuclei; regulation of gene expression and organelle biogenesis in tetrahymena. *Mailing Add:* Dept Biol Univ Rochester Rochester NY 14627. *Fax:* 716-275-2070

GOROZDOS, RICHARD E(MMERICH), ELECTRICAL ENGINEERING. *Current Pos:* RETIRED. *Personal Data:* b Chicago, Ill, May 20, 28; m 54; c 6. *Educ:* Univ Ill, BS, 50, MS, 51; Univ Md, PhD(elec eng), 60. *Prof Exp:* Elec engr, Naval Res Lab, 51-54 & Ballistic Res Lab, 54-56; elec engr, Appl Physics Lab, Johns Hopkins Univ, 56-94. *Res:* Tactical missile guidance and control systems; nonlinear control systems; precision tracking; network synthesis. *Mailing Add:* 16309 Dustin Ct Burtonsville MD 20866

GORRAFA, ADLY ABDEL-MONIEM, TEXTILE SCIENCE & TECHNOLOGY. *Current Pos:* MGR, INT TEXTILE TECHNOL LICENSING, 88- *Personal Data:* b Alexandria, Egypt, Sept 5, 35; m 63. *Educ:* Alexandria Univ, Egypt, BSc Hons, 56; Manchester Univ, Eng, PhD(textile technol), 61. *Prof Exp:* Instr eng design, Alexandria Univ, Egypt, 56-58; from res engr to sr res engr, E I Du Pont de Nemours & Co, Inc, 62-72, from res assoc to sr res assoc textile technol, 72-88. *Concurrent Pos:* Mgr, Worldwide Licensing Taslan, Air Jet Bulking Technol, 86- *Mem:* Fel Textile Inst Eng; Licensing Execs Soc. *Res:* Textile technology process and product development leading to diversified uses of synthetic fibers in apparel, carpets, upholstry and industrial fabrics. *Mailing Add:* Lancaster Pike & Loveville Rd Wilmington DE 19899. *Fax:* 302-999-5300

GORRELL, THOMAS EARL, BIOCHEMICAL PARASITOLOGY & CYTOLOGY. *Current Pos:* DIR RES, EPCO INC, 85- *Personal Data:* b Ft Wayne, Ind, Aug 7, 50; m 74. *Educ:* Purdue Univ, BS, 72; Mich State Univ, PhD(microbiol), 78. *Prof Exp:* Fel, Dept Microbiol, Univ Iowa, 77-79; res assoc, Rockefeller Univ, 79-80, fel, Dept Biochem & Cytol, 80-85. *Mem:* Soc Protozool; Am Soc Microbiol. *Res:* Physiology and biochemistry of anaerobic microorganisms; hydrogenosomes; pyruvate catabolism; activation of nitroheterocyclic drugs. *Mailing Add:* 2 N Washington Sq Apt 16 Larchmont NY 10538

GORRILL, WILLIAM R, civil engineering; deceased, see previous edition for last biography

GORRY, G ANTHONY, MEDICAL INFORMATICS. *Current Pos:* assoc prof community med, Baylor Col Med, 75-78, dir, Eval Res Group, Nat Heart & Blood Vessel Res & Demonstration Ctr, 75-82, dir, Health Mgt Res, 78-80, prof health mgt, 78-85, assoc dean, 79-83, vpres, 80-83, vpres instnl develop, 83-86, PROF MED INFORMATICS, DEPT COMMUNITY MED, BAYLOR COL MED, 78-, PROF, DIV NEUROSCI & VPRES INFO TECHNOL, 86- *Educ:* Yale Univ, BSE, 62; Univ Calif, Berkeley, MS, 62; Mass Inst Technol, PhD(comput sci), 67. *Prof Exp:* Asst prof, Sloan Sch Mgt, Mass Inst Technol, 67-70, assoc prof, 70-73, assoc prof comput sci, 73-75. *Concurrent Pos:* Assoc fac mem, Opers Res Ctr, Mass Inst Technol, 71-75, lectr, Dept Med, Tufts Univ Sch Med, 71-75; adj assoc prof math sci, Rice Univ, 75-78, adj prof, 78-85, adj prof, Dept Comput Sci, 85-; adj prof bus & econ, Tex Woman's Univ, 78-79; mem, Biomed Libr Rev Comt, Nat Libr Med, 84-88; prin fac mem, Prog Info Technol, Asn Am Med Cols; dir, W M Keck Ctr Comput Biol, Baylor Col Med & Rice Univ. *Mem:* Inst Med-Nat Acad Sci; fel Am Col Med Informatics. *Res:* Information technology; computational biology; community medicine. *Mailing Add:* Rice Univ 6100 S Main St MS 4 Houston TX 77005. *Fax:* 713-798-3729

GORSE, JOSEPH, CAPILLARY ELECTROPHORESIS, HIGH PERFORMANCE LIQUID CHROMATOGRAPHY. *Current Pos:* ASSOC PROF CHEM, BALDWIN-WALLACE COL, 88- *Personal Data:* b Warren, Ohio, Sept 13, 45; m 82; c 4. *Educ:* Ohio State Univ, BS, 67; Cleveland State Univ, MS, 70; Univ Ariz, PhD(chem), 85. *Prof Exp:* Teacher math & chem, J F Kennedy High Sch & Walsh High Sch, 67-71; chemist, Morgan Adhesives, 72-73 & Firestone Tire & Rubber, 73-76; asst prof chem, Knox Col, 85-88. *Concurrent Pos:* Res assoc, Dept Chem, Univ Tenn, 86, 87 & 90 & NASA Lewis, 91; co-prin, Dept Chem, Knox Col, 87 & 88. *Mem:* Am Chem Soc; Soc Appl Spectros. *Res:* Solid-liquid interface responsible for retention and selectivity in bonded-phase liquid chromatography; solid-liquid interface responsible for electroosmotic flow in capillary electrophoresis. *Mailing Add:* Dept Chem Baldwin-Wallace Col Berea OH 44017. *E-Mail:* jgorse@rs6000.baldwinw.edu

GORSE, ROBERT AUGUST, JR, ATMOSPHERIC CHEMISTRY & PROCESSES, VEHICLE EMISSIONS. *Current Pos:* sr res scientist, 78-80, prin res scientist chem, Sci Res Lab, 81-90, PRIN RES ENGR, AUTOMOTIVE EMISSIONS OFF, FORD MOTOR CO, 91- *Personal Data:* b San Diego, Calif, Apr 7, 42; m 77; c 2. *Educ:* San Diego State Univ, BS, 64, MS, 67; Univ Calif, Davis, PhD(chem), 72. *Prof Exp:* Teaching & res asst chem, San Diego State Univ, 66-67 & Univ Calif, Davis, 67-72; res assoc, Univ Tex, 72-75 & Argonne Nat Lab, Univ Chicago, 75-78. *Concurrent Pos:* Fel, Off Sci Res, US Air Force, 72-73 & Robert A Welch Foun, 73-75; chmn, Coord Res Coun Comt Acid Rain, 80-; mem comt pyrenes, Nat Acad Sci, 81-83; chmn comt Heterogeneous Drobiet, 84-; chmn comt Cloud Chem, 83-84; chmn comt Mobile Emissions, 86- *Mem:* Am Chem Soc; AAAS; Sigma Xi. *Res:* Characterization and environmental importance of mobile source emissions; formation and reactions of atmospheric particulates; atmospheric chemistry and gas phase kinetics; reactions of free radicals; modeling of atmospheric process; analysis of field measurements; auto/oil air quality improvement; research program analysis and reporting. *Mailing Add:* 5714 Blue Grass Lane Saline MI 48176

GORSIC, JOSEPH, PLANT GENETICS. *Current Pos:* assoc prof, 59-78, prof, 78-91, EMER PROF BIOL, ELMHURST COL, 91- *Personal Data:* b Ponova vas, Slovenia, Jan 6, 24; nat US; m 66, Franciska Mavec; c Milena, Daniel, Gregor, Olga, Helena & Lidija. *Educ:* Univ Ill, BS, 52; Univ Chicago, PhD, 57; State Univ Agr & Forestry, Austria, Dipl Ing, 65. *Prof Exp:* Instr biol, Marquette Univ, 57-59. *Mem:* AAAS; Am Genetic Asn; Sigma Xi. *Res:* Comparative genetics in plants. *Mailing Add:* 442 Ida Lane Elmhurst IL 60126

GORSKI, ANDRZEJ, TRANSPLANTATION IMMUNOLOGY, IMMUNOMODULATION. *Current Pos:* HEAD, DEPT IMMUNOL, WARSAW MED SCH, POLAND, 84-, PROF MED & IMMUNOL, 89- *Personal Data:* b Wroclaw, Poland, Aug 11, 46; m 88; c 2. *Educ:* Warsaw Med Sch, MD, 70, PhD(immunol), 73, bd cert, 80; Educ Coun For Med Graduates, ECFMG cert, 75. *Honors & Awards:* Meller Award for Excellence in Cancer Res, Sloan-Kettering Inst Cancer Res, 76; J Sniadecki Mem Award, Polish Acad Sci, 88. *Prof Exp:* Assoc scientist, Sloan-Kettering Inst Cancer Res, New York, NY, 76. *Concurrent Pos:* Vis prof, Weizmann Inst Sci, Rehovot, Israel, 88; Guy's Hosp, Univ London, UK, 90; head, Senate Comn Sci, Warsaw Med Sch, Poland, 90- & vpres, Sci Affairs; head, Nat Comt Coop, Int Union Immunol Socs, 91-; pres, immunol comt, Polish Acad Sci, 91-; prin investr res projs. *Mem:* Polish Acad Sci; Int Union Immunol Socs; Am Asn Immunologists; Transplantation Soc; Int Soc Exp Hemat; NY Acad Sci. *Res:* Immunobiology of graft rejection and the development of novel modalities to control this process; immunomodulating action of heparin and the perspectives for its application in clinical immunosuppressive therapy; role of cell adhesion molecules in the immune response. *Mailing Add:* Nowogrodzka 59 Warsaw 02066 Poland. *Fax:* 48-2-6256264

GORSKI, JACK, BIOCHEMISTRY, ENDOCRINOLOGY. *Current Pos:* PROF BIOCHEM, UNIV WIS-MADISON, 73- *Personal Data:* b Green Bay, Wis, Mar 14, 31; m 55; c 2. *Educ:* Univ Wis, BS, 53; Wash State Univ, MS, 56, PhD(animal sci), 58. *Honors & Awards:* Oppenheimer Award, Endocrine Soc, 71; Wellcome lectr, 81. *Prof Exp:* USPHS fel, Univ Wis, 58-61; from asst prof to assoc prof physiol & biophys, Univ Ill, Urbana, 61-69, prof physiol & biochem, 69-73. *Concurrent Pos:* NSF sr fel, Princeton Univ, 66-67; mem, Endocrinol Study Sect, NIH, 67-71; mem biochem & chem carcinogenesis, Adv Comt, Am Cancer Soc, 73-76, Adv Comt, Dept Exp Therapeut, Roswell Park Inst, 73-75 & Molecular Biol Study Sect, NIH, 77-81; adv comt, Am Cancer Soc, 84- *Mem:* Nat Acad Sci; Am Soc Biol Chemists; Endocrine Soc. *Res:* Molecular mechanisms of hormone action; estrogen control of the uterus; regulation of protein synthesis; mechanisms of estrogenic hormone action, biosynthesis of pituitary hormones. *Mailing Add:* Dept Biochem Univ Wis 420 Henry Mall Madison WI 53706-1569

GORSKI, JEFFREY PAUL, EXTRACELLULAR MATRIX, CELL BIOLOGY. *Current Pos:* ASSOC PROF, UNIV MO, KANSAS CITY, 87- *Personal Data:* b May 17, 47; m 71, Mary C; c Andrew & Anna. *Educ:* Univ Wis-Madison, PhD(biochem), 75. *Honors & Awards:* Charnley Award, 86; Zimmer Award, 84. *Prof Exp:* Asst prof biochem, Mayo Clin & Med Sch, 79-87. *Concurrent Pos:* Vis asst prof, Univ Minn, 81-82. *Mem:* Am Soc Biochem & Molecular Biol; Orthop Res Soc; Am Chem Soc; Am Soc Bone Mineral Res. *Res:* Bone matrix biochemistry and bone cell biology. *Mailing Add:* Div Biochem & Molecular Biol Sch Basic Life Sci Univ Mo-KC 5007 Rockhill Rd Kansas City MO 64110

GORSKI, LEON JOHN, ECOLOGY, BIOLOGY. *Current Pos:* From asst prof to assoc prof ecol & biol, 65-77, asst to dean arts & sci, 74-77, PROF BIOL & COORDR GRANTS, CENT CONN STATE COL, 77- *Personal Data:* b New Britain, Conn, Sept 29, 38; m 62; c 2. *Educ:* Cent Conn State Col, BS, 61; Univ Conn, MS, 63, PhD, 69. *Mem:* Am Ornith Union; Am Inst Biol Sci; Soc Syst Zool; Sigma Xi. *Res:* Systematics and ecology of sibling species of the Traill's flycatchers; significance of vocalizations as reproductive isolating mechanisms; tropical overwintering behavior of the two song forms of the Traill's flycatcher in Panama and Peru; multidisciplinary environmental education programs at college and state levels. *Mailing Add:* 6107 Mirada Circle St Petersburg FL 33715

GORSKI, ROBERT ALEXANDER, PHYSICAL ORGANIC CHEMISTRY. *Current Pos:* RETIRED. *Personal Data:* b Passaic, NJ, Nov 24, 22; m 44, Helen M; c Robert J, Mary AB, Mark G, Stephen T & Paul F. *Educ:* La Salle Col, BA, 47; Univ Pa, MS, 49, PhD(phys chem), 51. *Prof Exp:* Instr algebra, trigonom & calculus, La Salle Col, 46-48, instr phys chem, 48-49; res asst Thermodynam Res Lab, Univ Pa, 49-51; res chemist org phys chem, Jackson Labs, E I Du Pont de Nemours & Co, Inc, 51-54, res chemist, Freon Prods Lab, 54-90, tech assoc, 67-71, sr res chemist, 71-85, res assoc, 85-87, consult, Freon Prods Lab, 87-90. *Concurrent Pos:* Mem, Am Stand & Testing Mat Comt Vapor Degreasing & Solvent Anal, & reviewer, Fire Res, Nat Acad Sci-Nat Res Coun, 58-78, mem, 71. *Mem:* Am Chem Soc; Sigma Xi. *Res:* Interaction coefficients of binary gas mixtures; organic physical chemistry; development of technical and material compatibility data for fluorinated compounds for sales promotion. *Mailing Add:* 735 Harvard Lane Newark DE 19711-3134

GORSKI, ROGER ANTHONY, NEUROENDOCRINOLOGY. *Current Pos:* Vchmn grad affairs, Univ Calif, Los Angeles, 67-74, from asst prof to assoc prof, 62-70, chmn dept, 80-92, PROF ANAT, SCH MED, UNIV CALIF, LOS ANGELES, 70-, DIR, LAB NEUROENDOCRINOL BRAIN RES INST, 81- *Personal Data:* b Chicago, Ill, Dec 30, 35; wid, Bentley; c Denise M (MacFarlane), Kevin B & Brian M. *Educ:* Univ Ill, BS, 57, MS, 59; Univ Calif, Los Angeles, PhD(anat), 62. *Honors & Awards:* Ernst Oppenheimer Mem Award, Endocrine Soc, 76; Res Award, Soc Study Reproduction. *Mem:* Int Brain Res Orgn; Int Soc Neuroendocrinol; Soc Exp Biol Med; AAAS; Am Asn Anatomists; Sigma Xi; Am Acad Arts Sci. *Res:* Sexual differentiation of hypothalamic control of reproduction; effect of steroids on brain; electrical activity of hypothalamus; regulation of sexual behavior. *Mailing Add:* Dept Neurobiol Univ Calif Sch Med Los Angeles CA 90095-1763. *Fax:* 310-825-2224

GORSLINE, DONN SHERRIN, MARINE GEOLOGY. *Current Pos:* assoc prof, 62-66, PROF GEOL, UNIV SOUTHERN CALIF, 66- *Personal Data:* b Los Angeles, Calif, Dec 15, 26. *Educ:* Mont Sch Mines, BS, 50; Univ Southern Calif, MS, 54, PhD(geol, oceanog), 58. *Prof Exp:* Asst oceanog, Allan Hancock Found, Univ Southern Calif, 54-56, res assoc geol, 53-57; asst prof marine geol, Oceanog Inst, Fla State Univ, 58-61, assoc prof & actg dir, 61-62. *Concurrent Pos:* Mem adv panel coastal geog, Nat Acad Sci-Nat Res Coun, 61 & chmn adv panel on ocean waste disposal, 74-76; gen chmn & ed, Nat Shallow Water & Coastal Res Inst, 61-62 & 71; ed Marine Geol, 67-70; mem adv panel on oceanog, NSF, 72-74; mem adv panel geol & geophys continental margins, 77-78, adv comn ocean resources, Calif, 65-69. *Mem:* Fel AAAS; fel Geol Soc Am; Am Soc Limnol & Oceanog; Soc Econ Paleont & Mineral(pres, 77-78); Coastal Res Soc; Sigma Xi. *Res:* Sedimentology; marine geology; coastal studies; shallow water oceanography; continental margin. *Mailing Add:* Dept Geol Sci Sci Hall Rm 117 Univ Southern Calif Los Angeles CA 90089-0740

GORSON, ROBERT O, RADIOLOGY, MEDICAL PHYSICS. *Current Pos:* assoc prof radiol, Thomas Jefferson Univ, 59-65, chief, Div Med Physics, Col Hosp 59-89, prof, 65-89, EMER MED PHYSICS, THOMAS JEFFERSON UNIV, 89- *Personal Data:* b Philadelphia, Pa, July 16, 23; m 46. *Educ:* Univ Pa, BA, 49, MS, 52; Am Bd Radiol, dipl, 54, Am Bd Health Physics, dipl, 60. *Prof Exp:* Univ health physicist, Univ Pa, 49-51, instr radiol physics, 52-53, assoc, 53-59, assoc grad sch med, 55-59. *Concurrent Pos:* Vis lectr, Grad Sch Med, Univ Pa, 59-71; consult, Philadelphia Dept Pub Health, 57- & div radiation health, USPHS, 63-; chmn subcomt 3, Nat Comt Radiation Protection, 61-77, mem, 77-, mem subcomt 16 & sci comt 9, 63- & sci comt 44, 73-; mem comn units, stand and protection, Am Col Radiol, 59-; mem, Nat Coun Radiation Protection & Measurements, 64-; mem adv comt med x-ray protection, USPHS, 64-66; mem, Am Bd Health Physics, 64-65, chmn, 65-67; deleg, coun Alliance for Eng in Med & Biol, 70-; mem diag res adv group, Nat Cancer Inst, 75-; asst ed, Med Physics, 77-; consult, IAEA, Pan Am Health Orgn & World Health. *Mem:* Radiol Soc NAm; Am Asn Physicists in Med; Radiation Res Soc; Health Physics Soc; fel Am Col Radiol; Sigma Xi. *Res:* Radiation and health physics. *Mailing Add:* 5152 Sugarloaf Rd Boulder CO 80302-9216

GORTATOWSKI, MELVIN JEROME, INHERITED METABOLIC DISORDERS, ORGANIC BIOCHEMISTRY & HEALTH SCIENCES. *Current Pos:* RETIRED. *Personal Data:* b Chicago, Ill, Oct 30, 25. *Educ:* Univ Ill, BS, 50, PhD(chem), 55; Wash State Col, MS, 52. *Prof Exp:* Asst chem res, Div Fluorine Chem, Ill State Geol Surv, 52-53; res instr & fel, Lab for Study Hereditary & Metab Disorders, Col Med, Univ Utah, 56-58, res assoc, Dept Psychiat, 58-59, res instr biochem, 59-65; asst prof pediat, Univ Southern Calif, 65-71; chief clin chem sect, Utah State Health Dept Lab, 71-87. *Concurrent Pos:* Biochemist, Vet Admin Hosp, Salt Lake City, 59-65; assoc investr, Clin Res Ctr, Childrens Hosp, Los Angeles, 65-71. *Mem:* Am Chem Soc; Sigma Xi. *Res:* Metabolic disease associated with mental retardation including inherited disorders of amino acid, carbohydrate and fat metabolism; environmental chemistry, especially health hazards from drugs, pesticides, pollutants in air, water and food; screening for metabolic diseases in newborn population. *Mailing Add:* 4045 Foubert Ave Salt Lake City UT 84124

GORTHY, WILLIS CHARLES, CYTOPATHOLOGY, HISTOLOGY. *Current Pos:* from asst prof to assoc prof, 66-96, EMER PROF ANAT, COLO STATE UNIV, 96- *Personal Data:* b Buffalo, NY, Dec 4, 34; m 59, Carol I Lawton; c Willis III, Brent & Scott. *Educ:* Columbia Univ, AB, 56; NY Univ, MS, 61; Princeton Univ, MA, 63, PhD(biol), 65. *Prof Exp:* Res aide, Sloan-Kettering Cancer Res, 57-60; Nat Acad Sci-Nat Res Coun res assoc, Human Nutrit Res Div, USDA, 64-66. *Concurrent Pos:* Res grants, Nat Inst Neurol Dis & Blindness, 68-70 & Nat Eye Inst, 71-74, 74-77, 77-81 & 87-90, HEW. *Res:* Light and electron microscopical studies of mammalian eye; morphological and histochemical studies of the lens; studies involve morphological and histochemical changes in mammalian lenses during development of hereditary and senescent cataracts; histochemical experiments are aimed at exploration of transport and digestive properties of the lens. *Mailing Add:* Dept Anat & Neurobiol Colo State Univ Ft Collins CO 80523

GORTLER, LEON BERNARD, ORGANIC CHEMISTRY, HISTORY OF SCIENCE. *Current Pos:* from instr to assoc prof, 62-74, chmn, 84-87, PROF CHEM, BROOKLYN COL, 74- *Personal Data:* b Des Moines, Iowa, Jan 30, 35; m 60, Selma Bass; c Jan, Andrew & Jocelyn. *Educ:* Univ Chicago, AB, BS & MS, 57; Harvard Univ, PhD(chem), 62. *Prof Exp:* Fel, Univ Calif, Berkeley, 61-62. *Concurrent Pos:* Chmn, Div Hist Chem, Am Chem Soc, 82-83. *Mem:* Am Chem Soc; Sigma Xi; Hist Sci Soc. *Res:* Synthesis and decomposition of peresters; study of reaction mechanisms; history of chemistry. *Mailing Add:* 1009 E 22nd St Brooklyn NY 11210

GORTNER, SUSAN REICHERT, CARDIAC RECOVERY. *Current Pos:* PROF FAMILY HEALTH CARE, SCH NURSING, UNIV CALIF, SAN FRANCISCO, 78-, ADJ PROF, INTERNAL MED, 89- *Personal Data:* b San Francisco, Calif, Dec 23, 32; m 60; c 2. *Educ:* Stanford Univ, Palo Alto, AB, 53; Western Res Univ, MN, 57; Univ Calif, Berkeley, PhD(higher educ), 64. *Honors & Awards:* Helen Nahm Res lectr, Sch Nursing, Univ Calif San Francisco, 87; Fulbright lectr, Inst Nursing Sci, Univ Oslo, 88. *Prof Exp:* Asst supvr & instr surg, Johns Hopkins Hosp & Sch Nursing, 57-58; instr nursing, Col Nursing, Univ Hawaii, 58-63, asst prof nursing & chmn, Unit Med Surg Nursing, 63-64; spec consult, Nursing Educ & Training Br, Div Nursing, Pub Health Serv, Dept Health, Educ & Welfare, 66-67, exec secy res nursing patient care review, Nursing Res Br, 67-72, chief, Res Grants Sect, Nursing Res Br & actg br chief, 71-73, chief, 73-78 & chief, Nursing Pract Br, 75-76.

Concurrent Pos: Mem cabinet nursing res, Am Nurses' Asn, 84-86; assoc dean res, Sch Nursing, Univ Calif, San Francisco, 78-86; clin assoc cardiovasc surg, Dept Nursing Serv, Moffitt-Long Hosp, San Francisco, 81-; mem Coun Cardiovasc Nursing, Am Heart Asn, 87-91. *Mem:* Fel Am Acad Nursing; Am Nurses Asn; Am Heart Asn; Soc Behav Med. *Res:* Heart surgery patients and families treatment beliefs and outcomes and recovery processes; protocols for assisting recovery; study of elders undergoing heart surgery; history of nursing science; philosophy of health science. *Mailing Add:* Box 1056 Soda Springs CA 95728

GORTON, ROBERT LESTER, MECHANICAL ENGINEERING. *Current Pos:* from instr to assoc prof, 60-74, asst head dept, 66-69, PROF MECH ENG, KANS STATE UNIV, 74- *Personal Data:* b Houston, Tex, Oct 19, 31; m 60, Rosalind Davis; c Elaine, Catherine, Christine & Robert J. *Educ:* La Polytech Inst, BS, 53; La State Univ, MS, 60; Kans State Univ, PhD(mech eng), 66. *Honors & Awards:* Centennial Medallion, Am Soc Mech Engrs; Distinguished Serv Award, Am Soc Heating, Refrig & Air Conditioning Engrs. *Prof Exp:* Engr, Schlumberger Well Surv Corp, 55-58; assoc mech eng, La State Univ, 59-60. *Concurrent Pos:* NASA fac fel, 70; tech consult, Black & Veach Consult Engrs, 74-, Oak Ridge Nat Lab, 80-82, Wilson Co Consult Engrs & Meritek Eng Corp; Halliburton prof mech eng, 82-85. *Mem:* Fel Am Soc Mech Engrs; fel Am Soc Heating, Refrig & Air Conditioning Engrs. *Res:* Environmental engineering; energy systems, heat transfer, fluid mechanics; industrial air conditioning. *Mailing Add:* 3106 Amherst Ave Manhattan KS 66503

GORTSEMA, FRANK PETER, INORGANIC CHEMISTRY. *Current Pos:* CHEM FEL TECH OPERS, MERCK & CO, RAHWAY, NJ, 90- *Personal Data:* b Grand Rapids, Mich, Dec 25, 33; m 59, Janet Phillips; c Susan & Grant. *Educ:* Calvin Col, AB, 55; Purdue Univ, PhD(phys chem), 60. *Prof Exp:* Sr res chemist, Parma Res Ctr, Union Carbide Corp, Ohio, 59-63, sr res chemist, Res Inst, 63-79, develop assoc, Linde Div, Molecular Sieve, NY, 79-89. *Mem:* Am Chem Soc; Mat Res Soc. *Res:* Chemistry of ruthenium in solution; thermoelectric properties of rare earth nitrides and monosulfides; preparation and properties of reduced valency transition metal fluorides; platinum hexafluoride chemistry; solar energy conversion; preparation of fine powders, fibrous ceramics; catalysis, molecular sieves; hydrocracking; catalytic preparation of drug intermediates. *Mailing Add:* 7 Brairwood Lane Pleasantville NY 10570-3507

GORZ, HERMAN JACOB, PLANT GENETICS, PLANT BREEDING. *Current Pos:* RETIRED. *Personal Data:* b Eagle River, Wis, Nov 22, 20; m 51, Jeanette M Gundlach; c Marily & Jean. *Educ:* Univ Wis, BS, 42, MS, 48, PhD(agron, genetics), 51. *Honors & Awards:* Distinguished Grasslander Award, Am Forage & Grassland Coun, 89. *Prof Exp:* Assoc prof agron & assoc agronomist, NDak State Univ, 51-54; supvry res geneticist & res leader, Wheat & Sorghum Res Unit, Agr Res Serv, USDA & prof agron, Univ Nebr, 54-88. *Mem:* Fel Am Soc Agron; Genetics Soc; Soc Agron; fel Crop Sci Soc Am. *Res:* Genetic, breeding and biochemical studies in Sorghum, Melilotus, Trifolium and other forage species; insect resistance and quality factors in forages. *Mailing Add:* 6126 Leighton Ave Lincoln NE 68507-2456

GORZYNSKI, EUGENE ARTHUR, IMMUNOLOGY. *Current Pos:* PROF MICROBIOL, SCH MED, STATE UNIV NY, BUFFALO, 69-, PROF PATH, 89- *Personal Data:* b Buffalo, NY, Oct 8, 19; m 46, Ruth Repa (deceased); c David, Timothy & Kathleen. *Educ:* State Univ NY Buffalo, BA, 49, MA, 53, PhD(microbiol), 68. *Prof Exp:* Assoc res bacteriologist, Children's Hosp, 47-68; sr cancer res scientist, Springville Labs, Roswell Park Mem Inst, 68-69; asst dir, Pub Health Div, Erie County Lab, 69-75. *Concurrent Pos:* Mem, Ctr Immunol, State Univ NY, Buffalo, 74-; Microbiologist & clin lab coordr, Vet Admin Med Ctr, 75-80; chief, microbiol sect, Vet Affairs Med Ctr, Buffalo, 80- *Mem:* Fel AAAS; Am Soc Microbiol; Asn Mil Surg US; Am Asn Immunologists; fel Am Acad Microbiol; Sigma Xi; fel Infectious Dis Soc Am. *Res:* Enterobacterial antigens and immunity; host defense mechanisms; infectious diseases. *Mailing Add:* Microbiol 203 Sherman SUNY Buffalo Sch Med 3435 Main St Buffalo NY 14214-3001

GORZYNSKI, JANUSZ GREGORY, PSYCHIATRY. *Current Pos:* CLIN ASST PROF, COL PHYSICIANS & SURGEONS, COLUMBIA UNIV, 84- *Personal Data:* b Warsaw, Poland, Aug 6, 40; US citizen. *Educ:* Acad Med, Warsaw, MD, 63. *Prof Exp:* Resident psychiat, Montefiore Hosp Med Ctr, Bronx, 71-74; instr, Albert Einstein Col Med, 74-77; asst clin prof psychiat, Cornell Univ Med Col, 77-84. *Concurrent Pos:* Sci dir, Barbara P Johnson Found, New York, 76-; J J Johnson & B P Johnson Found res grant, 76-78; asst attend, St Luke's Roosevelt Med Ctr, 84-; coordr res, Mem-Sloan Kettering Cancer Ctr, 78-84. *Mem:* Am Psychiat Asn; Am Psychosom Soc; AAAS; NY Acad Sci. *Res:* Psychological adjustment in cancer patients; endocrinology of anorexia nervosa; psychosexual findings in polycystic ovary syndrome. *Mailing Add:* 108 E 91st St New York NY 10128-1657

GORZYNSKI, TIMOTHY JAMES, IMMUNOLOGY. *Current Pos:* res immunologist, 85-89, SR RES IMMUNOLOGIST, E I DU PONT DE NEMOURS, GLASGOW, 89- *Personal Data:* b March 19, 50; m; c 3. *Educ:* State Univ NY, BA, 76, MA, 78, PhD(microbiol), 80. *Honors & Awards:* McGrath Biol Award. *Prof Exp:* Lab technologist, Vet Admin Med Ctr, 73-81; res fel, Mayo Clin, 81-84, res assoc, 85. *Concurrent Pos:* Fel, State Univ NY, 76-80; res grants, Minn Arthritis Found, 85-86, DuPont Seed Grant, 86-87. *Res:* Immunology; numerous publications; enhancement of antibody response in mice; T-cells-B-cell epitope peptides as immunogens; identification of high affinity monoclonal antibodies during primary screeing; enchancing ascites yield in mice; mouse model for testing anti-arthritic drugs. *Mailing Add:* Immunol Dept E I Du Pont de Nemours & Co Glasgow Site 709 PO Box 6101 Newark DE 19714-6101. *Fax:* 302-451-3039

GOSE, EARL E(UGENE), ENGINEERING. *Current Pos:* assoc prof, 65-77, PROF INFO ENG, UNIV ILL, CHICAGO CIRCLE, 77- *Personal Data:* b Aberdeen, Wash, Mar 14, 34; m 62. *Educ:* Carnegie Inst Technol, BS, 56; Univ Calif, PhD(chem eng), 60. *Prof Exp:* NSF fel, Sorbonne, 60-61; fel, Mass Inst Technol, 61-62; asst prof eng, Case Inst Technol, 62-65. *Concurrent Pos:* Assoc prof physiol, Univ Ill Med Ctr; staff mem, Presby St Luke's Hosp, Chicago; prof, Rush Med Col. *Mem:* AAAS; Am Soc Cybernet; Asn Comput Mach; Inst Elec & Electronics Engrs; Instrument Soc Am. *Res:* Pattern recognition; natural and artificial intelligence; neurophysiology; biomedical engineering. *Mailing Add:* 812 Lathrop Ave Univ Ill Box 4348 River Forest IL 60305

GOSFIELD, EDWARD, JR, INTERNAL MEDICINE, CARDIOLOGY. *Current Pos:* from asst instr to assoc prof internal med, Univ Pa, 50-92, chmn med bd, Grad Hosp, 75-77, actg chmn, Dept Med, 79-80 & 90-92, ASSOC CHMN, GRAD HOSP, UNIV PA, 80-, EMER ASSOC PROF MED, 92- *Personal Data:* b New York, NY, Aug 17, 18; m 41, 85, Thelma Bradburd; c Edward III, Alice & Gregory. *Educ:* Univ Pa, AB, 39, MS, 40, MD, 44; Am Bd Internal Med, dipl, 52, recert, 77. *Concurrent Pos:* Consult, Wills Eye Hosp, 50-77; chief hypertension clin, Grad Hosp, Univ Pa, 57-79, assoc physician, Hosp, 59-; assoc physician, Presby-Univ Pa Med Ctr, 71-87. *Mem:* Am Heart Asn; fel Am Col Physicians; fel Am Col Cardiol. *Res:* Cardiovascular disease. *Mailing Add:* 2113 Spruce St Philadelphia PA 19103

GOSHAW, ALFRED THOMAS, EXPERIMENTAL HIGH ENERGY PHYSICS. *Current Pos:* from asst prof to assoc prof, 73-84, PROF PHYSICS, DUKE UNIV, 84- *Personal Data:* b West Bend, Wis, Aug 26, 37; m 66; c 2. *Educ:* Univ Wis-Madison, BS, 59, MS, 61, PhD(physics), 66. *Prof Exp:* Instr physics, Princeton Univ, 66-69; vis scientist, Nuclear Physics Apparatus Div, Europ Orgn Nuclear Res, 69-70; mem staff, 70-73. *Concurrent Pos:* Alfred P Sloan Found fel, 57-58; NSF fel, 59-61; Swiss Am Fedn Sci Exchange fel, 69. *Mem:* Am Phys Soc; Am Asn Univ Prof. *Res:* Hyperon resonance studies; inclusive pion and photon production in pion proton and pion nucleus collisions; high energy electromagnetic processes; heavy quark photo and hadro production. *Mailing Add:* Dept Physics Duke Univ Durham NC 27706-8001

GOSHTASBY, A ARDESHIR, ELECTRONICS ENGINEERING. *Current Pos:* ASSOC PROF, DEPT COMPUT SCI & ENG, WRIGHT STATE UNIV, 95- *Educ:* Univ Tokyo, BE, 74; Univ Ky, MS, 75; Mich State Univ, PhD(comput sci), 83. *Mem:* Inst Elec & Electronics Engrs Comput Soc; Pattern Recognition Soc; sr mem Inst Elec & Electronics Engrs. *Mailing Add:* Dept Comput Sci & Eng Wright State Univ 303 Russ Eng Ctr Dayton OH 45435. *Fax:* 937-873-5133; *E-Mail:* grdeshir@cs.wright.edu

GOSINK, JOAN P, ARCTIC HYDROLOGY. *Current Pos:* DIR ENG, COLO SCH MINES, 91- *Personal Data:* b Jamaica, NY, Mar 26, 41; m 61; c 4. *Educ:* Mass Inst Technol, BS, 62; Old Dominion Univ, MS, 73; Univ Calif, Berkeley, PhD(mech eng), 79. *Prof Exp:* Teaching asst thermodyn & fluid dynamics, Univ Calif, Berkeley, 75-76, res asst, 76-78; fel, Geophys Inst, Univ Alaska, 79-81, asst prof geophys, 81-91. *Concurrent Pos:* Res fel, NASA, 72-73 & Fulbright-Hayes Found, 74-75; mem, Glaciol Comt, Nat Res Coun, 81- & Polar Res Bd, 81- *Mem:* Am Soc Civil Engrs; Am Soc Mech Engrs; Am Meteorol Soc; Int Glaciol Soc. *Res:* Mass, heat and momentum transport in ice and water systems. *Mailing Add:* Div Eng Colo State Sch Mines Golden CO 80401

GOSLINE, JOHN M, BIOMECHANICS. *Current Pos:* from asst prof to assoc prof 73-86, PROF ZOOL, UNIV BC, 86- *Personal Data:* b Oakland, Calif, Dec 14, 43; m 69; c 2. *Educ:* Univ Calif, Berkeley, BA, 66; Duke Univ, PhD(zool), 70. *Prof Exp:* Res fel zool, Cambridge Univ, 70-73. *Concurrent Pos:* Sr Killam scholar, Univ BC Killam Found, 83. *Mem:* Fel AAAS; Am Soc Biomech; Am Soc Zoologists; Biophys Soc Can. *Res:* Molecular biomechanics of structural biomaterials, including elastin and other rubber-like proteins, invertebrate connective tissues, silks and related fibrous proteins; mechanics of jet-propelled swimming in animals. *Mailing Add:* Dept Zool Univ BC 6270 University Blvd Vancouver BC V6T 1Z4 Can

GOSLING, JOHN THOMAS, SPACE PLASMA PHYSICS. *Current Pos:* mem staff, 75-92, LAB FEL, LOS ALAMOS NAT LAB, 92- *Personal Data:* b Akron, Ohio, July 10, 38; m 94, Margaret J Stanley; c Mark & Steve. *Educ:* Ohio Univ, BS, 60; Univ Calif, Berkeley, PhD(physics), 65. *Prof Exp:* Fel, Los Alamos Sci Lab, 65-67; staff mem, High Altitude Observ, Nat Ctr Atmospheric Res, 67-75. *Mem:* fel Am Geophys Union; Int Astron Union. *Res:* Solar wind physics; space plasma physics; collisionless shocks, reconnection, solar-terrestrial physics. *Mailing Add:* MS D466 Los Alamos Nat Lab Los Alamos NM 87545. *Fax:* 505-665-7395; *E-Mail:* jgosling@lanl.gov

GOSLOW, GEORGE E, JR, VERTEBRATE MORPHOLOGY. *Current Pos:* CO-CHMN, DEPT ECOL & EVOLUTIONARY BIOL & PROF BIOL & MED, BROWN UNIV, - *Personal Data:* b Tacoma, Wash, May 16, 39; m 60; c 3. *Educ:* Univ Calif, Los Angeles, AB, 62, PhD(zool), 67; Humboldt State Col, MA, 65. *Prof Exp:* Assoc zool, Univ Calif, Davis, 65-66; from asst prof to prof biol, Northern Ariz Univ, 67-89. *Mem:* Am Soc Zoologists; Soc Neurosci; Sigma Xi. *Res:* Functional vertebrate morphology, especially bone-muscle systems as they relate to the control of locomotion; motor units and muscle proprioceptors. *Mailing Add:* Biomed Div Brown Univ Box G-BMC Providence RI 02971

GOSMAN, ALBERT LOUIS, THERMODYNAMICS, HEAT TRANSFER. *Current Pos:* head, Dept Mech Eng, Wichita State Univ, 67-71, assoc dean col eng & assoc dir eng res, 71-80, prof, 67-93, EMER PROF MECH ENG, WICHITA STATE UNIV, 93- *Personal Data:* b Detroit, Mich, May 27, 23; m 48, Marguerite E Lemieux; c Erica J & Stephanie F (Snyder). *Educ:* Univ Mich, BS, 50; Univ Colo, Boulder, MS, 55; Univ Iowa, PhD(thermodyn), 65. *Prof Exp:* Asst prof mech eng, Colo Sch Mines, 50-56; sr res engr, Northrop Aircraft, Inc, Calif, 56-58; asst prof mech eng, Colo Sch Mines, 58-62; instr, Univ Iowa, 62-65; assoc prof, Wayne State Univ, 65-67. *Concurrent Pos:* Res found, Colo Sch Mines, 58-60; res engr, Colo Sch Mines, 52-56, Cryogenics Div, Nat Bur Stand, Colo, 61-72; panel deleg, Nat Res Coun & Nat Bur Stand Conf Thermodyn, 69; mem, Nat Res Admin, Am Soc Eng Educ, 74-76; bd dirs, Am Soc Eng Educ res coun, 79-83. *Mem:* Am Soc Mech Engrs; Am Soc Eng Educ; AAAS; Sigma Xi. *Res:* Determination of thermodynamic properties of liquids and gases; equation of state for liquid and gaseous argon from triple point to 1000 atmospheres and 1000 degrees Kelvin. *Mailing Add:* 224 Bonnie Brae Wichita KS 67207

GOSNELL, AUBREY BREWER, DRUG MATOBLISM, POLYMER MODIFIED ASPHALTS. *Current Pos:* RETIRED. *Personal Data:* b Provo, Ark, Sept 1, 29; m 48, Tammy S Parsons; c Charles T, Steven K & Paul A. *Educ:* Henderson State Univ, BS, 51; Univ Ark, MS, 62; NC State Univ, PhD(org chem), 67. *Honors & Awards:* Harry W Wiley Medal. *Prof Exp:* Teacher high sch, Mansfield, Ark, 49-51; tester refinery lab, El Dorado Refinery, Am Oil Co, Ark, 51-58, refinery operator, 58-60; res chemist, Camile Dreyfus Lab, Res Triangle Inst, 62-67; from assoc prof to prof chem, Henderson State Univ, 67-86; plant mgr, Siplast Roofing Mfg, 86-89; Dept Defense Eng Technol Transfer Div, PBA, 89-92. *Concurrent Pos:* Pres, Go Chem, Inc, 73-93; chemist, Dept Health & Human Servs, Food & Drug Admin & Nat Ctr Toxicol Res, Jefferson, Ark, 80-86. *Mem:* Am Chem Soc; Sigma Xi. *Res:* Gas chromatographic analysis of chlorinated fatty acids; synthesis and characterization of branched polystyrenes; solution properties of polymers; synthesis and properties of well defined graft copolymers; anionic polymerization; drug analysis; pesticide toxicology; metabolism of antihistamines; analysis of doxylamine and metabolites in rats. *Mailing Add:* 2075 Elaine Circle Arkadelphia AR 71923

GOSS, CHARLES RAPP, JR, ELECTRICAL ENGINEERING. *Current Pos:* Develop engr electronic warfare, 75-76, actg dep chief electronic warfare div, 76-77, actg dept chief, Syst Avionics Div, 77-78, DEP CHIEF ELECTRONIC TECHNOL DIV, AIR FORCE AVIONICS LAB, 78-; AT ARNOLD ENG DEVELOP CTR. *Personal Data:* b Bridgeton, NJ, Apr 15, 37; m 62; c 1. *Educ:* NMex State Univ, BS, 73, MS, 74. *Mem:* Inst Elec & Electronics Engrs. *Res:* Microwave and microelectronics technology. *Mailing Add:* Bldg 260 Teas Group Sverdrup Technol PO Box 1935 Eglin AFB FL 32542

GOSS, DAVID, THEORETICAL PHYSICS, GEOPHYSICS. *Current Pos:* From asst prof to assoc prof, 64-75, PROF PHYSICS, NEBR WESLEYAN UNIV, 75- *Personal Data:* b July 20, 37; m 90, Lois M Loder. *Educ:* Southwestern Univ, Tex, BS, 59; Mich State Univ, MS, 61; Univ Tex, PhD(nuclear physics), 64; Univ Nebr-Lincoln, BS, 82. *Concurrent Pos:* Consult & vis scientist, SSC/CDG (URA), 85-89, SSC Lab, 89-94. *Mem:* AAAS; Am Phys Soc; Am Asn Physics Teachers; Fedn Am Sci; Am Geophys Union. *Res:* Accelerator geophysics; radon as a probe of geol structure; general geophysics and geology related to accelerator construction and operation; health physics. *Mailing Add:* Dept Physics Nebr Wesleyan Univ 5000 St Paul St Lincoln NE 68504-2796. *Fax:* 402-465-2179; *E-Mail:* goss@nebrwesleyan.edu

GOSS, DAVID A, PHYSIOLOGICAL OPTICS. *Current Pos:* PROF OPTOM, IND UNIV, 92- *Personal Data:* b Joliet, Ill, July 22, 48; m 74. *Educ:* Ill Wesleyan Univ, BA, 70; Pac Univ, BS, 72, OD, 74; Ind Univ, PhD(physiol optics), 80. *Prof Exp:* Optometrist, Storm Lake, Iowa, 74-75; assoc instr optom, Ind Univ, 76-78, res assoc, 78-80; from asst prof to prof physiol optics & optom, Northeastern State Univ, 80-92. *Concurrent Pos:* Mem, working group on myopia, Nat Acad Sci, 84-87; mem jour rev bd, J Am Optom Asn, 88-94; consult ed, J Am Optom Assoc, 95- *Mem:* Am Acad Optom; Asn Res Vision & Ophthal; Optical Soc Am; Am Optom Asn; Optometric Hist Soc; Asn Optometric Educators; AAAS. *Res:* Ocular refractive errors; myopia; ocular optics; clinical accommodative convergence data. *Mailing Add:* Sch Optom Ind Univ Bloomington IN 47405. *Fax:* 812-855-8664; *E-Mail:* dgoss@indiana.edu

GOSS, GARY JACK, BIOLOGY, ENTOMOLOGY. *Current Pos:* From asst prof to assoc prof, 76-84, PROF BIOL, PALM BEACH ATLANTIC COL, 84-, CHAIR, DIV NATURAL SCI, MATH, 85- *Personal Data:* b South Bend, Ind, Apr 8, 46. *Educ:* Fla Atlantic Univ, BS, 69, MS, 73; Univ Miami, PhD(biol), 77. *Concurrent Pos:* Adj asst prof biol, Fla Atlantic Univ, 80-; consult, Palm Beach Co Sch Bd, 84-87. *Mem:* Am Inst Biol Sci. *Res:* Plant and animal interaction including pollination biology and association between Lepidoptera and pyrrolizidine plants; spermatophore nutrient transfer in insects and parental investment; marine biology; botany. *Mailing Add:* Palm Beach Atlantic Col PO Box 24708 West Palm Beach FL 33416-4708

GOSS, GEORGE ROBERT, CHEMISTRY. *Current Pos:* chief chemist, 84-87, TECH DIR, OIL DRI CORP, 87- *Personal Data:* b Kewanee, Ill, Dec 16, 52; m 75; c Robert J, Thomas P & Phillip M. *Educ:* Western Ill Univ, BS, 74, MS(chem), 78, MS(bot), 82, PhD (chem), 94. *Prof Exp:* Technician, Ill Environ Protection Agency, 77-78; res assoc, Kalo Inc, 78-81; res mgr, Kalo Agr Chems Inc, 81-84. *Mem:* Am Chem Soc; Am Oil & Chemists Soc; Am Soc Testing & Mat. *Res:* Clay minerals for industrial use; pet box absorbents; agricultural chemical carriers; vegetable oil purification; fertilizer production. *Mailing Add:* Oil Dri Corp 777 Forest Edge Dr Vernon Hills IL 60061-3106. *Fax:* 847-634-4595; *E-Mail:* 102070,3065@compuserve.com

GOSS, JOHN DOUGLAS, EXPERIMENTAL NUCLEAR PHYSICS. *Current Pos:* DEVELOP PHYSICIST SENSOR GROUP, MEASUREX CORP, 75- *Personal Data:* b Columbus, Ohio, June 14, 42. *Educ:* Ohio State Univ, BSc. 65, MS, 67, PhD(physics), 70. *Prof Exp:* Fel physics, Univ Notre Dame, 70-73,from staff fac fel to asst fac fel, 73-75. *Mem:* Am Phys Soc. *Res:* Measurements of reaction Q-values, excitation energies, angular distributions and study of heavy-ion reactions using broad-range magnetic spectrography; application of these techniques in nuclear gauging development. *Mailing Add:* 6151 Hancock Ave San Jose CA 95123

GOSS, JOHN R(AY), MACHINERY ENGINEERING, GASIFICATION OF BIOMASS. *Current Pos:* Asst specialist agr eng, Univ Calif, Davis, 53-57, assoc specialist, 57-58, asst prof eng & asst agr engr, 58-62, assoc prof eng & assoc agr engr, 62-67, acad asst to chancellor, 63-66, chmn dept agr eng, 68-74, PROF ENG & AGR ENGR, UNIV CALIF, DAVIS, 67- *Personal Data:* b Winona, Minn, May 30, 23; m 47; c 4. *Educ:* Univ Calif, Los Angeles, BS, 52; Univ Calif, Davis, MS, 55. *Concurrent Pos:* Consult, US Dept Energy, USAID, Calif Energy Comm & pvt firms on gasification biomass. *Mem:* Fel Am Soc Agr Engrs; Am Soc Eng Educ; fel AAAS; Soc Am Foresters; NY Acad Sci; Nat Soc Prof Engrs. *Res:* Combine harvester performance in legume, cereal and dry bean crops for seed and food; pneumatic conveying and forage harvesting machinery research; microclimatic factors; gasification of agricultural and forest residues and utilization of producer gas in boilers, heated air burners; gasoline, natural gas and dual fuel diesel engines. *Mailing Add:* 754 Plum Lane Davis CA 95616-3237

GOSS, RICHARD JOHNSON, developmental anatomy; deceased, see previous edition for last biography

GOSS, ROBERT CHARLES, MICROBIOLOGY. *Current Pos:* from assoc prof to prof microbiol, 64-77, PROF BIOL, UNIV NORTHERN IOWA, 77- *Personal Data:* b Huntington, Ind, Mar 31, 29; m 50; c 3. *Educ:* Huntington Col, BS, 51; Purdue Univ, MS, 53, PhD(plant sci), 57. *Prof Exp:* Asst biol & plant path, Purdue Univ, 51-55, instr zool & chem exten, 55-56; plant pathologist, United Fruit Co, Costa Rica, 56; instr gen sci & math, Woodworth Sch, Mich, 57-58; asst prof microbiol, Loyola Univ, La, 58-64. *Mem:* Soc Indust Microbiol; Am Phytopath Soc; Nat Asn Biol Teachers. *Res:* Soil microbiology; plant pathogens, control and cancer. *Mailing Add:* 1416 Laurel Circle Cedar Falls IA 50613

GOSS, ROBERT NICHOLS, mathematics; deceased, see previous edition for last biography

GOSS, WILBUR HUMMON, PHYSICS. *Current Pos:* CONSULT, 67- *Personal Data:* b Tacoma, Wash, June 16, 11; m 38, Mildred Wallin; c Barry D, Barbara (Levi) & Carolyn (Willis). *Educ:* Univ Puget Sound, BS, 32; Univ Wash, PhD(physics), 39. *Honors & Awards:* Presidential Cert Merit; Potts Medal, Franklin Inst; Distinguished Pub Serv Award, USN. *Prof Exp:* Lectr physics, Univ BC, 39-40; asst prof, NMex State Univ, 40-42; res physicist, Appl Physics Lab, Johns Hopkins Univ, 42-61, asst dir, 61-67. *Concurrent Pos:* Vpres, Seatek Corp, 76-87. *Mem:* Fel Am Phys Soc. *Res:* Electron physics; combustion; ordnance development. *Mailing Add:* 1050 Monte Dr Santa Barbara CA 93110

GOSS, WILLIAM PAUL, HEAT TRANSFER, THERMAL INSULATION. *Current Pos:* assoc prof, 70-77, PROF MECH ENG, UNIV MASS, AMHERST, 78- *Personal Data:* b Milford, Conn, May 23, 38; c Lee. *Educ:* Univ Conn, BSE, 61, MS, 62, PhD(thermal sci), 67. *Honors & Awards:* Centenial Medal, Am Soc Mech Engr. *Prof Exp:* Res asst heat transfer, Univ Conn, 61-62; sr anal engr, Pratt & Whitney Div, United Aircraft Corp, 62-64; instr mech eng, Univ Conn, 64-67; asst prof, Va Polytech Inst, 67-70. *Concurrent Pos:* Consult, Mitre Corp, 67-71, Pratt & Whitney Commerical Div, United Technol Corp & Alfa-Thermal Systs Div, Alfa-Laval Thermal Inc, 78-81, Owens-Corning Fiberglass, 81-86, Cold Regions Res & Eng Lab, 82-87, Nat Bur Stand, 83-88, Ctr Appl Eng, 85-, US Dept Energy, 88-, Fed Trade Comn, 92- & Nat Fenistration Rating Coun, 93-95. *Mem:* Am Soc Testing & Mat; Am Soc Eng Educ; Am Soc Mech Engrs; Am Soc Heat, Refrig & Air-Conditioning Engrs. *Res:* Window thermal performance; thermal insulation; thermal measurements and modeling. *Mailing Add:* Dept Mech & Indust Eng Univ Mass Amherst MA 01003. *Fax:* 413-545-1027; *E-Mail:* goss@ecs.umass.edu

GOSSAGE, THOMAS LAYTON, CHEMICALS. *Current Pos:* pres, Hercules Specialty Chem Co, 88-89, pres & chief exec officer, Aqualon Group, Unit Hercules, 89-91, CHMN & CHIEF EXEC OFFICER, HERCULES INC, 91- *Personal Data:* b Nashville, Tenn, May 7, 34; m 57, Virginia Eastman; c Laura Eastman & Virginia (Lowry). *Educ:* Ga Inst Technol, BS, 56, MS, 57. *Prof Exp:* Process engr, Humble Oil Co, 57; asst dir govt rel, Monsanto Res Corp, Dayton, Ohio, 61-66, dir res & develop mkt, 66-68, group mkt dir, New Enterprises Div, St Louis, 68-70, mkt dir, Specialty Prod, 70-75, dir results mgt, Monsanto Chem Co, 75-77, asst gen mgr, Plasticizers Div, 77, gen mgr, 77-79, gen mgr detergents & phosphates, 79-80, asst managing dir, 80-81, vpres managing dir, 81-83, group vpres managing dir, Monsanto Int, 83-86, group vpres & sr vpres, Monsanto Chem Co, 86-88. *Mem:* Chem Mfrs Asn. *Res:* Product development and manufacturing. *Mailing Add:* 8 Wood Rd Wilmington DE 19806

GOSSAIN, VED VYAS, INTERNAL MEDICINE, ENDOCRINOLOGY & METABOLISM. *Current Pos:* from asst prof to assoc prof, 73-82, assoc chmn, dept Med, 88-95, PROF MED, COL HUMAN MED, MICH STATE UNIV, 82-, CHIEF, DIV ENDOCRINOL & METAB, 96- *Personal Data:* b Jhang, India, Mar 25, 41; c 3. *Educ:* DAV Col, India, BSc, 58; Med Col Amritsar, MBBS, 63; All India Inst Med Sci, New Delhi, MD, 67. *Prof Exp:* Asst prof, St Louis Univ Sch Med, 73-75. *Concurrent Pos:* Asst res officer, Indian Coun Med Res, 65-67; clin fel endocrinol, Univ Cincinnati Med Ctr, res fel, 71-72; res fel Med Col Wis, 72-73; fel, All India Inst Diabetes. *Mem:* Fel Am Col Physicians; fel Royal Col Physicians Can; Endocrine Soc; Am Fedn Clin Res; Am Diabetes Asn; Int Diabetes Fedn. *Res:* Diabetes mellitus; insulin; obesity; very-low-calorie diets in the treatment of obesity; bone mineral density in obesity. *Mailing Add:* Dept Med CHM Mich State Univ East Lansing MI 48824

GOSSARD, ARTHUR CHARLES, PHYSICS. *Current Pos:* PROF MATS, ELEC & COMPUT ENG, UNIV CALIF, SANTA BARBARA, 87- *Personal Data:* b Ottawa, Ill, June 18, 35. *Educ:* Harvard Univ, BA, 56; Univ Calif, Berkeley, PhD(physics), 60. *Honors & Awards:* Oliver Buckley Condensed Matter Physics Prize, Am Physics Soc, 84; Page Prize lectr, Physics Dept, Yale Univ, 86. *Prof Exp:* Mem tech staff, AT&T Bell Labs, 60-87. *Concurrent Pos:* NSF fel, Saclay Nuclear Res Ctr, France, 62-63; Humboldt fel, Univ Erlangen, Ger, 96. *Mem:* Nat Acad Eng; fel Am Phys Soc; Inst Elec & Electronics Engrs; Mat Res Soc. *Res:* Solid state physics, nuclear magnetic resonance; ferromagnetism; transition metals; superconductivity; semiconductor films; heterostructures; interfaces; superlattices; molecular beam epitaxy. *Mailing Add:* Mat Dept Univ Calif Santa Barbara Santa Barbara CA 93106

GOSSARD, EARL EVERETT, PHYSICAL OCEANOGRAPHY, RADIO METEOROLOGY. *Current Pos:* SR RES ASSOC, UNIV COLO, 82- *Personal Data:* b Eureka, Calif, Jan 8, 23; m 48; c 3. *Educ:* Univ Calif, Los Angeles, BA, 48; Univ Calif, San Diego, MS, 51, PhD, (oceanog), 56. *Honors & Awards:* Dept Com Silver Medal, 77; Excellence in Refereeing Award, Am Geophys Union. *Prof Exp:* From physicist to head, Radio Physics Div, USN Electronics Lab, San Diego, 48-71; chief geoacoust res prof, Wave Propagation Lab, Environ Res Lab, Nat Oceanic & Atmospheric Admin, Boulder, Colo, 71-73, chief, Lab Meteorol Radar Prog, 73-82. *Concurrent Pos:* Chmn, US Nat Comn F, Int Radio Sci Union; consult, Interunion Comt Radio Meteorol; assoc ed, J Appl Meteorol & Radio Sci. *Mem:* Nat Acad Eng; Am Geophys Union; Int Radio Sci Union; fel Am Meteorol Soc. *Res:* Micrometeorology; lower ionosphere physics; internal gravity waves; radar meteorology; published over 100 articles and 2 books; holds 1 patent. *Mailing Add:* CIRES Campus Box 449 Univ Colo Boulder CO 80309. *Fax:* 303-497-6574; *E-Mail:* egossard@etl.noaa.gov

GOSSEL, THOMAS ALVIN, PHARMACOLOGY. *Current Pos:* PROF PHARMACOL & TOXICOL, OHIO NORTHERN UNIV, 72-, CHMN DEPT PHARMACOL & BIOMED SCI, 77- *Personal Data:* b Lancaster, Ohio, Oct 20, 41; m 62; c 3. *Educ:* Ohio Northern Univ, BS, 63; Purdue Univ, MS, 70, PhD(pharmacol), 72. *Concurrent Pos:* Consult, Nat Asn Bd Pharm, 73- *Mem:* AAAS; Sigma Xi; Soc Exp Biol & Med; Am Pharmaceut Asn. *Res:* Adult continuing education. *Mailing Add:* Ohio Northern Univ 525 S Main St Ada OH 45810-1555

GOSSELIN, ARTHUR JOSEPH, electrophysiology, interventional medicine, for more information see previous edition

GOSSELIN, EDWARD ALBERIC, HISTORY OF SCIENCE, SCIENCE EDUCATION. *Current Pos:* From asst prof to assoc prof, 69-79, PROF HIST, CALIF STATE UNIV, LONG BEACH, 79-, CHAIR, DEPT HIST, 86- *Personal Data:* b Rutland, Vt, Feb 12, 43; m 70; c 2. *Educ:* Yale Univ, BA, 65; Columbia Univ, MA, 66, PhD(early mod hist), 73. *Concurrent Pos:* Co-dir hist & sci proj, Calif State Univ, Long Beach, 73-74, dir, Modernization Global Perspective Proj, 80-81; ed, Hist Teacher, 85- *Mem:* Hist Sci Soc; Renaissance Soc Am. *Res:* Giordano Bruno; Bruno's and Galileo's trials; Hermetism and scientific revolution; French scientific and mathematical reform, 1495-1540. *Mailing Add:* 2502 Vuelta Grande Ave Long Beach CA 90815

GOSSELIN, RICHARD PETTENGILL, MATHEMATICAL ANALYSIS. *Current Pos:* from assoc prof to prof, 55-88, EMER PROF MATH, UNIV CONN, 88- *Personal Data:* b Springfield, Mass, June 29, 21; m 44; c 2. *Educ:* Univ Chicago, BS, 44, PhD, 51; Univ Rochester, MA, 48. *Prof Exp:* Sr mathematician, Inst Air Weapons Res, Univ Chicago, 51-52; prof math & head dept, Youngstown Col, 52-55. *Concurrent Pos:* Res contract, USAF, 59-60; consult, Inst Air Weapons Res, Univ Chicago. *Mem:* Am Math Soc; Math Asn Am. *Res:* Trigonometric series; trigonometric interpolating polynomials; localization theory and LP Fourier series. *Mailing Add:* Univ Conn Storrs CT 06269-0001

GOSSELIN, ROBERT EDMOND, PHARMACOLOGY, TOXICOLOGY. *Current Pos:* chmn dept, 56-75, prof, 56-89, EMER PROF PHARMACOL, DARTMOUTH MED SCH, 89- *Personal Data:* b Springfield, Mass, Sept 2, 19; m 48, 81, Patricia Stopkie; c Peter G & Andrea G (Haraldsson). *Educ:* Brown Univ, AB, 41; Univ Rochester, PhD(mammalian physiol), 45, MD, 47. *Prof Exp:* Asst, Off Sci Res & Develop contract, Univ Rochester, 42-44; med intern, Grace-New Haven Community Hosp, Conn, 47-48; from instr to asst prof pharmacol, Sch Med, Univ Rochester, 48-56. *Concurrent Pos:* Researcher, Atomic Energy Proj, 48-52 & 54-56; mem toxicol study sect, USPHS, 64-68; consult, Food & Drug Admin, 66-69, Consumer Prod Safety Comn, 79-85. *Mem:* Am Physiol Soc; Soc Pharmacol & Exp Therapeut; Soc Toxicol. *Res:* Atropine metabolism; ultraphagocytosis of radiocolloids; physiology and pharmacology of cilia; drug receptor kinetics; microcirculatory function; clinical toxicology; coronary blood flow. *Mailing Add:* Dept Pharmacol & Toxicol Dartmouth Med Sch Hanover NH 03756

GOSSELINK, EUGENE PAUL, POLYMER CHEMISTRY. *Current Pos:* res staff chemist org chem, 66-92, RES FEL, PROCTER & GAMBLE, 92- *Personal Data:* b Pella, Iowa, Jan 13, 37; m 64; c 3. *Educ:* Cent Col, Iowa, BA, 59; Univ Wis, PhD(org chem), 64. *Prof Exp:* Fel org chem, Univ Toronto, 64-65; fel, Yale Univ, 65-66. *Mem:* Am Chem Soc. *Res:* Synthesis of new organic compounds; study of their effects at interfaces. *Mailing Add:* Miami Valley Lab PO Box 398707 Cincinnati OH 45061-8707

GOSSELINK, JAMES G, PLANT, WETLAND & LANDSCAPE ECOLOGY. *Current Pos:* asst prof plant physiol, La State Univ, 64-66, asst prof bot & dir, Sci Training Progs, 66-68, assoc prof bot & marine sci, 68-73, chmn, Dept Marine Sci, 74-79 & 79-85, dir, Coastal Ecol Lab, Ctr Wetland Resources, 77-79, prof, Marine Sci & Coastal Ecol Lab, 73-90, EMER PROF, MARINE SCI, LA STATE UNIV, BATON ROUGE, 90- *Personal Data:* b Kodaikanal, India, Sept 14, 31; US citizen; m 55, Jean Vining; c Jena, Leila & Patrick G. *Educ:* Oberlin Col, AB, 53; Rutgers Univ, MS, 58, PhD(hort), 59. *Prof Exp:* Res horticulturist, New Crops Res Br, USDA, 59-61; asst prof biol, State Univ NY, Binghamton, 61-64. *Mem:* Fel AAAS; Am Inst Biol Sci; Soc Wetland Scientists; Estuarine Res Fedn. *Res:* Physiological systems and landscape ecology, especially of wetlands. *Mailing Add:* 7133 Sevenoaks Ave Baton Rouge LA 70806

GOSSER, LAWRENCE WAYNE, PHYSICAL ORGANIC & ORGANOMETALLIC CHEMISTRY. *Current Pos:* CHEMIST, CENT RES DEPT, 65-, DIR CORP AFFIL, E I DU PONT DE NEMOURS & CO, INC, 80- *Personal Data:* b Seattle, Wash, Aug 21, 38. *Educ:* Univ Wash, BS, 60; Univ Calif, Los Angeles, PhD(chem), 64. *Prof Exp:* Instr chem, Cent Ore Col, 64-65. *Mem:* Am Chem Soc. *Res:* Organic reactions involving carbanions; homogeneous catalysis; chemistry of organo-transition metal complexes. *Mailing Add:* 4627 Talley Hill Lane Wilmington DE 19803

GOSSETT, BILLY JOE, WEED SCIENCE. *Current Pos:* From asst prof to assoc prof, 62-72, PROF AGRON, AGRON & SOILS DEPT, CLEMSON UNIV, 72- *Personal Data:* b Holladay, Tenn, Dec 13, 35; m 63; c 2. *Educ:* Univ Tenn, BS, 57; Univ Ill, MS, 59, PhD(agron), 62. *Mem:* Weed Sci Soc Am; Am Soc Agron. *Res:* Weed biology and control in agronomic cropping systems. *Mailing Add:* Dept Agron Clemson Univ Clemson SC 29632-0001

GOSSETT, CHARLES ROBERT, NUCLEAR PHYSICS. *Current Pos:* RETIRED. *Personal Data:* b Manila, PI, Sept 29, 29; m 52; c 4. *Educ:* Duke Univ, BS, 51; Rice Univ, MA, 53, PhD(physics), 55. *Prof Exp:* Physicist Nucleonics Div, Naval Res Lab, 55-58, supvry physicist Radiation Div, 58-66, res physicist, Condensed Mat & Radiation Sci Div, 66-89; res physicist, SFA Inc, 89-95. *Mem:* Am Phys Soc; Sigma Xi. *Res:* Application of nuclear techniques to surface and near-surface materials analysis. *Mailing Add:* 5402 Woodland Ct Oxen Hill MD 20745

GOSSETT, DORSEY MCPEAKE, AGRONOMY. *Current Pos:* asst prof agron, Univ Tenn, 65-70, supt, WTenn Exp Sta, 70-72, asst dean, 72-76, DEAN, AGR EXP STA, UNIV TENN, 76- *Personal Data:* b Benton Co, Tenn, Dec 10, 31; m 57; c 1. *Educ:* Univ Tenn, Martin, BS, 55; Univ Ill, MS, 57; NC State Univ, PhD(crop physiol), 61. *Prof Exp:* Ext asst prof agron, NC State Univ, 61-65. *Res:* Administering the Tennessee Agricultural Experiment Station program; weed science. *Mailing Add:* 9400 Turf Rd Knoxville TN 37923

GOSSETT, JAMES MICHAEL, WASTEWATER TREATMENT. *Current Pos:* Asst prof, 76-82, ASSOC PROF ENVIRON ENG, CORNELL UNIV, 82- *Personal Data:* b San Rafael, Calif, May 3, 50; m 81; c 2. *Educ:* Stanford Univ, BS, 73, MS, 73, PhD(civil eng), 77. *Concurrent Pos:* Fel, US Air Force Fac Res Prog, 80; vis prof, Univ Resident Res Prog, USAF Systs Command, 84-85. *Mem:* Am Soc Microbiol; Water Pollution Control Fedn; Int Asn Water Pollution Res; Asn Environ Eng Professors. *Res:* Anaerobic biological processes; biological wastewater treatment; methane production from biomass; biomass energy conversion; treatment and restoration of contaminated groundwaters. *Mailing Add:* 107 Horizon Dr Ithaca NY 14850

GOSSLEE, DAVID GILBERT, BIOMETRICS. *Current Pos:* RETIRED. *Personal Data:* b Fargo, NDak, June 22, 22; m 47; c 3. *Educ:* Moorhead State Col, BS, 47; Iowa State Univ, MS, 50; NC State Col, PhD, 56. *Prof Exp:* Instr math, NDak State Univ, 50-54, statistician, 54-58; assoc prof biomet, Univ Conn, 58-61; statist sect head, Comput Sci Div, Union Carbide Corp, 61-87. *Concurrent Pos:* Instr, Univ Tenn, Oak Ridge Biomed Grad Sch, 68- *Mem:* Fel Am Statist Asn; Sigma Xi; Biomet Soc; fel AAAS. *Res:* Consulting and collaboration; statistical analysis of toxicological assays. *Mailing Add:* 106 Indian Lane Oak Ridge TN 37830

GOSSLING, JENNIFER, INDIGENOUS BACTERIA, PATHOGENIC BACTERIA. *Current Pos:* CLIN MICROBIOLOGIST, BARNES-JEWISH HOSP, ST LOUIS, 80- *Personal Data:* b Eng, July 25, 34; m 56, William F. *Educ:* Cambridge Univ, BA, 55; WVa Univ, PhD(microbiol), 73. *Prof Exp:* Clin microbiologist, Ottawa Civic Hosp, 57-59; vet microbiologist, Ont Vet Col, 59-61; asst vet microbiol, Univ Ill, 62-66; bacteriologist, Univ

Manchester, 66-69; asst instr med microbiol, WVa Univ, 69-73; biochemist, Med Col Ohio, 75; fel, Dent Res Inst, Univ Mich, 78-79; clin microbiologist, Ind Hosp, 79-80. *Concurrent Pos:* Asst prof dent microbiol, Sch Dent Med, Washington Univ, 81-91; asst prof biol, St Louis Col Pharm, 93-95. *Mem:* Am Soc Microbiol; AAAS; NY Acad Sci; Am Soc Clinical Path. *Res:* Investigation of oral and intestinal bacteria of man and other animals; the predominant anaerobes and some potential pathogens, analyzed by serology, culture and serial studies. *Mailing Add:* 8401 University Dr St Louis MO 63105-3641

GOSSMANN, HANS JOACHIM, SURFACE SCIENCE, ION SCATTERING. *Current Pos:* Fel, 84-85, MEM TECH STAFF, AT&T BELL LABS, 85- *Personal Data:* b Schwandorf, Fed Rep Ger, Sept 15, 55; m 87. *Educ:* Univ Wurzburg, Ger, Vordipl, 77, dipl, 81; State Univ NY, Albany, MS, 79, PhD, 84. *Honors & Awards:* Morton H Traum Award, Am Vacuum Soc, 84. *Mem:* Am Vacuum Soc; Mat Res Soc; Am Phys Soc. *Res:* Fundamental aspects of epitaxial growth and strained layer hetero structures; investigation of phenomena and processes occurring during initial stage of interface formation; silicon molecular beam epitaxy. *Mailing Add:* AT&T Bell Labs 600 Mountain Ave Murray Hill NJ 07974

GOSWAMI, AMIT, THEORETICAL PHYSICS, SCIENCE OF CONSCIOUSNESS. *Current Pos:* assoc prof, 68-74, PROF PHYSICS, UNIV ORE, 74- *Personal Data:* b Faridpur, India, Nov 4, 36; M 74, Maggie Burnett; c 2. *Educ:* Presidency Col, Univ Calcutta, India, BSc, 55, MSc, 60, DPhil(physics), 64. *Prof Exp:* Instr physics, Case Western Res Univ, 63-65, asst prof, 65-67. *Concurrent Pos:* Res assoc, Inst Theoret Sci, Univ Ore, 68- *Mem:* Am Phys Soc. *Res:* Generalized pairing in light nuclei; bootstrap theory of vibrations; use of surface-delta-interaction in nuclear structure calculations; theory of fine structure of giant dipole resonance; gapless superconductivity in nuclei; pion condensation in nuclear matter; quantum theory of consciousness. *Mailing Add:* 5405 Donald St Eugene OR 97405. *Fax:* 541-346-5217

GOSWAMI, BHUVENESII C, TEXTILE PHYSICS, TEXTILE TECHNOLOGY. *Current Pos:* PROF TEXTILE TECH, CLEMSON UNIV, 84- *Personal Data:* b Bannu, Pakistan, Oct 13, 37; US citizen; m 69, Dixie Reed. *Educ:* Delhi Univ, BS, 59; Univ Bombay, MSc, 63; Univ Manchester, PhD(textile physics), 66. *Hon Degrees:* FTI, Textile Inst, Eng, 72. *Prof Exp:* Spinning supvr spinning mills, Arvind Mills, India, 59-61; res engr prod develop, Calico Chem & Plastics, Bombay, 66-67; vis lectr textile sci, Clemson Univ, 67-68; staff scientist textile physics, Textile Res Inst, Princeton, 69-75; from assoc prof to prof textile physics, Univ Tenn, Knoxville, 80-84. *Concurrent Pos:* Fel, Textile Res Inst, 69; res fel, Inst Sci & Technol, Univ Manchester, 72-73. *Mem:* Textile Inst; Fiber Soc; Am Asn Textile Tech; fel Am Soc Mech Eng; Soc Adv Mat Process Engrs. *Res:* Structural mechanics of fibers, yarns and fabrics; thermal behavior of textile structures; dynamics of processing of yarns; non-wovens; textile structures for composites; geotetiles. *Mailing Add:* 200 Strawberry Lane Clemson SC 29631. *Fax:* 864-656-5973; *E-Mail:* gbhuven@clemson.clemson.edu

GOSWAMI, MEETA J, SLEEP DISORDERS, NARCOLEPSY. *Current Pos:* dent res asst, Columbia Univ, 64-65, res asst, 66-67, grad US Pub Health trainee, 71-75, trainee, 76-78, ADMIN & PLANNING ASST, COLUMBIA UNIV, 79-; DIR, NARCOLEPSY INST, MONTEFIORE MED CTR, 85-, ASST PROF PSYCHOSOCIAL MGT NARCOLEPSY, 93- *Personal Data:* b Bombay, India; c Anup & Mihir. *Educ:* Gov Dental Col Bombay, Bachelor Dent Surg, 59; Columbia Univ, MPH, 66, PhD(sociomed sci, sociol), 78. *Prof Exp:* Pedodontist, Govt Dent Col, Bombay, India, 60-62. *Concurrent Pos:* Asst clin prof psychosocial basis pract mgt, Columbia Univ, 82-93; prin investr & chief exec officer, Narcolepsy Inst, Ctr Montefiore Med; consult, Cephalon, Inc, 94. *Mem:* Asn Prof Sleep Socs; Am Pub Health Asn; Am Sociol Asn; Found Thanatol. *Res:* Psychosocial management of narcolepsy epidemiology, quality of life and evaluation research; doctor-patient relationship, patient compliance, women and the professions, women and health and the spiritual dimension of health. *Mailing Add:* 111 E 210th St Bronx NY 10467

GOSWITZ, FRANCIS ANDREW, NUCLEAR MEDICINE, HEMATOLOGY. *Current Pos:* clinician internal med & coordr med radioisotope courses, Spec Training Div, 65-68 & Med Div, 68-75, SR CLINICIAN INTERNAL MED, MED DIV, OAK RIDGE MED CLIN, 75- *Personal Data:* b St Paul, Minn, Sept 8, 31; m 56; c 3. *Educ:* Marquette Univ, BS, 53, MD, 56. *Prof Exp:* Intern, Univ Iowa Hosps, 56-57, resident internal med, 57-58, 60 & 61-63; fel nuclear med, Oak Ridge Inst Nuclear Studies, 60-61; fel Hemat, Med Ctr, Univ Utah, 63-65. *Mem:* Soc Nuclear Med; Am Med Asn; Am Soc Hemat; NY Acad Sci; Am Inst Ultrasound Med. *Res:* Internal medicine; effects of irradiation on hematopiesis; radioprotective cytologic agents; diagnostic applications of radioisotopes in medicine; biochemical and physiological characteristics of the erythrocyte and lymphocyte; cancer chemotherapy. *Mailing Add:* 170 W Tennessee Ave Oak Ridge TN 37830

GOSWITZ, HELEN VODOPICK, HEMATOLOGY & ONCOLOGY, NUCLEAR MEDICINE. *Current Pos:* INTERNIST, OAK RIDGE MED CLIN, 74- *Personal Data:* b Milwaukee, Wis, Apr 29, 31; m 56; c 3. *Educ:* Marquette Univ, BS, 53, MD, 56. *Prof Exp:* Intern, Univ Iowa Hosp, 56-57, resident internal med, 57-60, instr internal med, Hosp, 61-63; clinician internal med, Oak Ridge Assoc Univs, 65-74. *Concurrent Pos:* Fel nuclear med, Oak Ridge Inst Nuclear Studies, 60-61; fel hemat, Univ Utah, 63-65. *Mem:* Fel Am Col Physicians; Soc Nuclear Med; AMA; Am Soc Hemat; Am Soc Clin Oncol. *Res:* Internal medicine; granulocytokinetics; histocompatibility testing; oncology. *Mailing Add:* Oak Ridge Med Clin 170 W Tenn Ave Oak Ridge TN 37830-6500

GOSZ, JAMES ROMAN, ECOLOGY. *Current Pos:* from asst prof to assoc prof, 70-78, dir, Ecosysts Studies Prog, 84-86, PROF ECOL, UNIV NMEX, 78-, PROF, DEPT BIOL. *Personal Data:* b Menasha, Wis, May 4, 40. *Educ:* Mich Technol Univ, BS, 63; Univ Idaho, PhD(forest sci), 68. *Prof Exp:* Res assoc ecol, Dartmouth Col, 68-69 & Cornell Univ, 69-70. *Concurrent Pos:* Univ Founder Rep, Inst Ecol, 73- *Mem:* Ecol Soc Am; Int Asn Ecol. *Res:* Ecosystem analysis through mineral cycling and energy flow dynamics; physiological plant ecology. *Mailing Add:* Dept Biol Univ NMex Main Campus 1 University Campus Albuquerque NM 87131-0001

GOTCHER, JACK EVERETT, ORAL & MAXILLOFACIAL SURGERY, BONE HISTOMORPHOMETRY. *Current Pos:* clin instr, 78-82, ASSOC PROF ORAL-MAXILLOFACIAL SURG, CTR HEALTH SCI, UNIV TENN, 83- *Personal Data:* b Wichita Falls, Tex, May 11, 49; m 72; c 2. *Educ:* Midwestern Univ, BS, 71; Harvard Sch Dent Med, DMD, 75; Univ Utah, PhD(anat), 79. *Honors & Awards:* Res Travel Award, Johnson & Johnson Co, 75. *Prof Exp:* Teaching asst anat, Col Med, Univ Utah, 75-77, lectr histol, 77; asst prof oral-maxillofacial surg, Sch Dent, Emory Univ, 82-83. *Concurrent Pos:* Prin investr, Nat Inst Dent Res, Univ Utah, 75-78 & Upjohn Co Clin Trial Alveolar Atrophy, 84-; vis prof oral surg, Sch Dent Loyola Univ, 85; guest lectr, III Int Sem Maxillofacial Surg, Guadalajaha, 86; chmn, Accredited Dent Educ, Tenn Dent Asn, treas, 2nd Dist, Tenn Dent Soc, 88. *Mem:* Int Asn Dent Res; Am Bd Oral & Maxillofacial Surg; Am Asn Oral & Maxillofacial Surgeons; Am Col Oral & Maxillofacial Surgeons; Am Dent Asn; Am Asn Dent Schs. *Res:* Hard and soft tissue histomorphometry in areas of interest to oral and maxillofacial surgeons; temporomandibular joint pathology; alveolar atrophy. *Mailing Add:* 1928 Alcoa Hwy Knoxville TN 37920

GOTELLI, DAVID M, BOTANY, MYCOLOGY. *Personal Data:* b Stockton, Calif, Jan 1, 43; m 65; c 1. *Educ:* Univ Calif, Berkeley, BA, 64; Univ Wash, PhD(bot), 69. *Prof Exp:* From asst prof to assoc prof biol, Calif State Col, Stanislaus, 70-80, prof bot, 72-89. *Mem:* Mycol Soc Am; Bot Soc Am. *Res:* Ultrastructure and development of biflagellate fungi; culture and development of higher basidiomycetes. *Mailing Add:* 18911 SE 44th Way Issaquah WA 98027-9761

GOTH, JOHN W, METALLURGY & PHYSICAL METALLURGICAL ENGINEERING. *Current Pos:* DIR DEVELOP, MINERAL INFO INST, 86- & EXEC DIR, DENVER GOLD GROUP, 91- *Personal Data:* b Ree Heights, SDak, Apr 22, 27; m 52, Ree M; c Jax, Patrick & William. *Educ:* SDak Sch Mines, BS, 50; McGill Univ, MS, 51. *Hon Degrees:* PhD, SDak Sch Mines, 81. *Prof Exp:* Sr exec vpres, Amax Corp, 85. *Concurrent Pos:* Dir, var mining co; mem, Nat Strategic Mat & Minerals Prog Adv Comt. *Mem:* Fel Am Soc Metals; Am Inst Mech Engrs. *Res:* Molybdenum market development. *Mailing Add:* 15140 Foothill Rd Golden CO 80401

GOTH, ROBERT W, PLANT PATHOLOGY, VIROLOGY, MYCOLOGY & MICROBIOLOGY. *Current Pos:* plant pathologist, 61-68, res plant pathologist potato invest, 68-72, RES PLANT PATHOLOGIST, VEG LAB, USDA, 72- *Personal Data:* b Phillips, Wis, May 10, 27; m 54, Joyce Nelson; c Valerie, Robert W Sr & Stephen. *Educ:* Wis State Univ, Superior, BS, 54; Univ Minn, MS, 57, PhD(plant path), 61. *Honors & Awards:* Seed Research of the Year, Nat Potato Coun, 93. *Prof Exp:* Instr, Univ Minn, 60. *Concurrent Pos:* Vpres, Potmac Div, Am Phytopath Soc, 84-85, pres, 85-86. *Mem:* Am Phytopath Soc (secy-treas, 81-83); Am Potato; Mycol Soc; hon mem Potato Asn Am. *Res:* Nature of resistance, mode of infection, physical and chemical nature of the causal organisms of virus, fungal and bacterial diseases of potatoes, beans, peas and related legumes. *Mailing Add:* Bldg 010A Rm 226 Vega Lab Agr Res Serv USDA Beltsville MD 20705. *Fax:* 301-504-5555

GOTHELF, BERNARD, PHARMACOLOGY, TOXICOLOGY. *Current Pos:* CONSULT & DIR, 5-STAR TOXICOL ANALYSIS & CONSULT, DALLAS, 77- *Personal Data:* b Chicago, Ill, May 8, 28; m 58, Judith D Meisler; c 5. *Educ:* Univ Ill, BS, 50; Univ Iowa, MS, 52; Loyola Univ Chicago, PhD(pharmacol), 65. *Prof Exp:* Asst prof pharmacol, Loyola Univ, La, 63-64; instr, Sch Med, Marquette Univ, 64-66; asst prof, Dent Br, Univ Tex, Houston, 66-69; res assoc, Univ Tex Med Br, Galveston, 70-73 & assoc prof pharmacol, Tex Col Osteopath Med, 73; asst prof pharmacol, Baylor Col Dent, 73-77; vis prof, Univ de Caribe, Escuela de Medicina de Cayey, Inc, Cayey, PR, 77-78. *Concurrent Pos:* Fel, Marquette Univ; dir, Asbestos Anal & Consult, Inc, 86- *Mem:* Am Col Toxicol; Am Indust Hyg Asn. *Res:* Neuropharmacology; neurochemistry; analysis and distribution of chlorpromazine in tissues. *Mailing Add:* 6406 Dykes Way Dallas TX 75230

GOTLIEB, AVRUM I, PATHOLOGY. *Current Pos:* from asst prof to assoc prof, 78-88, PROF PATH, UNIV TORONTO, 88- *Personal Data:* b Montreal, Que, Jan 17, 46. *Educ:* McGill Univ, BSc, 67, MD, 71; Am Bd Path, cert, 76; FRCPS(C). *Prof Exp:* Staff pathologists, St Michael's Hosp, 78-89. *Concurrent Pos:* Assoc pathologist, Toronto Hosp, 80-82, consult staff pathologist, 82-88; dir, Vascular Res Lab, Dept Path & Banting & Best Diabetes Ctr, 83- *Mem:* Soc Cardivasc Path (secy, 86); Am Asn Pathologists; fel Am Heart Asn; Am Soc Cell Biol; Sigma Xi; NY Acad Sci. *Res:* Pathology; vascular cell and molecular biology; atherosclerosis. *Mailing Add:* Dept Path Toronto Gen Hosp Res Ctr CCRW 1-857 Univ Toronto Fac Med 200 Elizabeth St Toronto ON M5G 2C4 Can. *Fax:* 416-971-2130

GOTLIEB, C(ALVIN) C(ARL), COMPUTER SCIENCE, SOFTWARE SYSTEMS & INFORMATION SCIENCE & SYSTEMS. *Current Pos:* from asst prof to prof physics, Univ Toronto, 48-64, dir, Inst Comput Sci, 62-70, head, Dept Comput Sci, 64-67, prof, 64-88, EMER PROF COMPUT SCI,

UNIV TORONTO, 88- *Personal Data:* b Toronto, Ont, Mar 27, 21; m 49; c Leo, Margaret & Jane. *Educ:* Univ Toronto, BA, 42, MA, 46, PhD(physics), 47. *Hon Degrees:* DrMath, Univ Waterloo, 68; DEng, NS Tech Univ, 85; LLD, Univ Toronto, 96. *Honors & Awards:* Order of Can, 96; Auerbach Medal, Int Fedn Info Processing Soc, 97. *Prof Exp:* Asst, Nat Res Coun Can, Toronto, 42-47. *Concurrent Pos:* Civilian sci officer, Nat Res Coun Can, 42-47; mem, Admiralty Sig Estab & Ministry Supply, Eng, 43-44; consult, Defense Res Med Labs, Royal Can Air Force, 46-56; Can deleg, Int Fedn Info Process Socs, 59-65, vchmn prog comt, Int Fedn Info Processing Cong, 71; ed-in-chief, J Asn Comput Mach, 66-68, ed, 69-; chmn tech comt, Int Fedn Info Processing, 76-85; consult, UN & Can. *Mem:* Fel Royal Soc Can; fel Asn Comput Mach; hon mem Can Info Processing Soc (vpres, 58-59, pres, 59-60); fel Brit Comput Soc. *Res:* Computer systems and applications; business data processing; social implications of computers; economics of computers; author of over one hundred publications-research papers, books and articles. *Mailing Add:* Dept Comput Sci Sandford Fleming Bldg Univ Toronto Toronto ON M5S 1A4 Can. *Fax:* 416-978-2986; *E-Mail:* ccg@cs.toronto.edu

GOTOFF, SAMUEL P, IMMUNOLOGY. *Current Pos:* PROF PEDIAT, RUSH MED COL & CHMN, DEPT PEDIAT, RUSH-PRESBY-ST LUKE'S MED CTR, 86- *Personal Data:* b New York, NY, Mar 22, 33; m 56; c 3. *Educ:* Amherst Col, BA, 54; Univ Rochester, MD, 58. *Prof Exp:* Instr, Sch Med, Yale Univ, 60-61; clin instr pediat, Abraham Lincoln, Sch Med, Univ Ill Col, 61-63, from asst to assoc prof, 65-71, assoc prof microbiol, 68-71, prof pediat & microbiol, Abraham Lincoln Sch Med, Univ Ill Col Med, 71-73; prof pediat, Univ Chicago & chmn dept pediat, Michael Reese Med Ctr, 73-86. *Concurrent Pos:* Attend physician, Munic Contagious Dis Hosp, 67-73. *Mem:* AAAS; Am Acad Pediat; Soc Pediat Res; Am Asn Immunol; Am Soc Microbiol. *Res:* Neonatal infections; neonatal immunity; group b streptococci. *Mailing Add:* Rush Presby St Luke's Med Ctr 1653 W Congress Pkwy Chicago IL 60612-3833. *Fax:* 312-942-2243

GOTOLSKI, WILLIAM H(ENRY), CIVIL ENGINEERING. *Current Pos:* instr, Pa State Univ, 52-60, assoc prof, 60-65, asst dean & res instr, 74-84, spec asst to dean, 84-85, assoc dean & undergrad instr, 87-88, PROF CIVIL ENG, PA STATE UNIV, UNIVERSITY PARK, 65- DIR, ENG ADVAN CTR, 85- *Personal Data:* b Newark, NJ, Sept 6, 26; m 51; c 2. *Educ:* Columbia Univ, BS, 46, MS, 47; Pa State Univ, PhD(civil eng), 59. *Prof Exp:* Instr civil eng, Ohio Univ, 47-52. *Concurrent Pos:* Mem, Transp Res Bd, Nat Acad Sci-Nat Res Coun; consult civil engr, 50- *Mem:* Am Soc Civil Engrs; Am Soc Testing & Mat. *Res:* Soil mechanics, foundations and earth structures; bituminous concrete. *Mailing Add:* 623 W Hillcrest Ave State College PA 16803-3422

GOTOW, KAZUO, NUCLEAR PHYSICS. *Current Pos:* assoc prof, 64-69, PROF, PHYSICS DEPT, VA POLYTECH INST & STATE UNIV, 69- *Educ:* Univ Tokyo, BS, 54, MS, 55; Univ Rochester, PhD, 59. *Prof Exp:* Res assoc, Physics Dept, Univ Rochester, 59-64. *Concurrent Pos:* Assoc dir, Space Radiation Effects Lab & adj prof, Physics Dept, Col William & Mary, 68-69; vis scientist, Inst Nuclear Study, Univ Tokyo, 71-72 & Japanese Nat Lab High Energy Physics, 85-86. *Mem:* Fel Am Phys Soc; Sigma Xi. *Res:* Experimental particle physics; electroweak and hadronic interactions; author of over 70 scientific publications. *Mailing Add:* Col Arts & Sci Va Polytech Inst & State Univ Blacksburg VA 24060-0435

GOTS, JOSEPH SIMON, MICROBIOLOGY, BIOCHEMICAL GENETICS. *Current Pos:* from instr to assoc bact, 48-51, from asst prof to assoc prof, 51-63, PROF MICROBIOL, SCH MED, UNIV PA, 63- *Personal Data:* b Phila, Pa, Oct 12, 17; m 42; c 2. *Educ:* Temple Univ, AB, 39; Univ Pa, MS, 41, PhD(med bact), 48; Am Bd Microbiol, dipl. *Prof Exp:* Bact lab aide, Univ Pa, 39-41; spec field agent Bang's dis res, USDA, 41-42. *Concurrent Pos:* Vis investr, Inst Radium, Paris, 65-66; consult, Parke Davis & Co, Mich; vis prof, Peking Union Med Col, Beijing, China, 85 & Univ Hawaii, 90. *Mem:* AAAS; Am Soc Microbiol; Soc Exp Biol & Med; Genetics Soc Am; Am Soc Biol Chem; Am Asn Cancer Res; Sigma Xi; Am Acad Microbiol; NY Acad Sci. *Res:* Mechanism of action and resistance to chemotherapeutics; bacterial metabolism; biochemical mutations in bacteria; regulation of gene expression; biosynthesis of purines and amino acids. *Mailing Add:* Dept Microbiol Univ Pa Sch Med Philadelphia PA 19104-6076. *Fax:* 215-898-9557

GOTSCH, AUDREY ROSE, PROFESSIONAL TRAINING, COMMUNICATION STRATEGIES. *Current Pos:* actg dir, Off Consumer Health Educ, Univ Med & Dent NJ, 76-78, adj asst prof, Dept Community Med, 78-80, from asst prof to assoc prof, 80-93, CHIEF, DEPT ENVIRON & COMMUNITY MED, DIV COMMUNITY HEALTH EDUC, UNIV MED & DENT NJ, 78-, PROF, 93- *Personal Data:* b Milwaukee, Wis, May 30, 39; m 59, Thomas; c Allison L & Christine A. *Educ:* Ind Univ, BS, 63; Univ Mich, MPH, 66; Columbia Univ, DrPH, 76. *Honors & Awards:* Secy Award Outstanding Community Health Prom, US Dept Health & Human Servs, 88, Secy Community Health Prom Award, 94; Distinguished Career Award, Am Pub Health Asn, 96. *Prof Exp:* Dent hygienist, pvt pract, 62-65; pub dent health educr, Div Dent Health, Ill Dept Pub Health, 66-67; health educr, Cancer Control Prog, NJ State Dept Health, 68. *Concurrent Pos:* Consult, Hunterdon Med Ctr, 77-78, Univ Ill, 78, Perth Amboy Gen Hosp, 78-80, Health Care Financing Admin & Robert Wood Johnson Found, 80, Hospice Cent NY, 80, Nat Cancer Inst, 81-, Fox Chase Cancer Ctr, 83, Medcom Inc, 85, Off Prevention Educ & Control NIH, 85-, Nat Inst Occup Safety & Health, 90-, Thomas Jefferson Univ, 93, Nat Eye Health Educ Prog, 94, Nat Res Coun, 96; dep dir, NJ Grad Prog Pub Health, Univ Med & Dent NJ, 83-, chair, Environ Issues Policy Comt, 90-91; mem, Outreach Task Force, Cancer Inst NJ, 91- *Mem:* Am Asn Health Educ; Am Pub Health Asn; Asn Social Sci Health; Asn Teachers Prev Med; Int Union Health Promotion & Educ; Nat Ctr Health Educ; Nat Hospice Orgn; NY Acad Sci; Soc Pub Health Educ; Soc Risk Anal; Soc Toxicol. *Res:* Design, implementation and replication of an environmental and occupational health information program that includes environmental health sciences curriculum to provide critical thinking skills for youth; directed a training program that enhanced the skills of over 170,000 workers in environmental and occupational health areas. *Mailing Add:* 681 Frelinghuysen Rd Piscataway NJ 08855-1179. *Fax:* 732-445-0122; *E-Mail:* perc@eohsi.rutgers.edu

GOTSCHLICH, EMIL C, IMMUNOLOGY. *Current Pos:* From asst prof to assoc prof, 68-78, PROF & SR PHYSICIAN, ROCKEFELLER UNIV, 78-, HEAD, LAB BACT/IMMUNOL, 81-, VPRES MED SCI, 96- *Personal Data:* b Bangkok, Thailand, Jan 17, 35. *Educ:* NY Univ, AB, 55; NY Univ Sch Med, MD, 59. *Honors & Awards:* Albert Lasker Award, 78. *Concurrent Pos:* Staff, Med Corp, US Army, Walter Reed Army Inst Res, Washington, DC, 66-68. *Mem:* Inst Med-Nat Acad Sci; Sigma Xi; Am Asn Immunol. *Res:* Published numerous articles in various journals. *Mailing Add:* Dept Immunol Lab Bact Pathogenesise Immunol Rockefeller Univ 1230 York Ave New York NY 10021-6399. *Fax:* 212-327-8960; *E-Mail:* ecg@rockvax.rockefeller.edu

GOTSHALL, DANIEL WARREN, MARINE ECOLOGY. *Current Pos:* RETIRED. *Personal Data:* b Springfield, Ill, Dec 20, 29; m 52, Cordie A Moreland. *Educ:* Humboldt State Col, BS, 57, MS, 70. *Honors & Awards:* Fel, Explorers Club, 80. *Prof Exp:* Fisheries biologist, Marine Resources Opers, 57-59, from marine biologist to sr marine biologist, Marine Resources Region, Long Beach, 60-72, sr marine biologist, Marine Res Br, Calif Dept Fish & Game, Avila Beach, 72-83, Monterey, 84-87. *Concurrent Pos:* Mem adv bd underwater parks & reserves, Calif Dept Parks & Recreation, 71, vice chmn, 74-; assoc invert zool, Calif Acad Sci, San Francisco, 87-88. *Mem:* Am Fisheries Soc; fel Am Inst Fishery Res Biologists; Western Soc Naturalists. *Res:* Life history of blue rockfish; marine sport fishing; population dynamics of the ocean shrimp, Pandalus jordani and the Dungeness crab, Cancer magister; benthic ecology using scuba and underwater photography; conducting baseline marine ecological surveys around nuclear power plants to determine effects of construction and operation of plants. *Mailing Add:* 4 Somerset Rise Skyline Forest Monterey CA 93940-4112. *Fax:* 408-373-6306

GOTSHALL, ROBERT WILLIAM, PHYSIOLOGY. *Current Pos:* asst prof physiol, 75-77, ASSOC PROF PHYSIOL & BIOPHYSICS, SCH MED, WRIGHT STATE UNIV, 78- *Personal Data:* b Carrollton, Ohio, Apr 28, 45. *Educ:* Mt Union Col, BS, 67; Ohio State Univ, MS, 69, PhD(physiol), 71. *Prof Exp:* Fel physiol, Sch Med, Univ Mo, 71-73; asst prof, Med Col Wis, 73-75. *Mem:* Am Physiol Soc; Am Heart Asn; Soc Exp Biol & Med. *Res:* Cardiac function and control in adults and newborns. *Mailing Add:* Dept Exer & Sport Sci Colorado State Univ Ft Collins CO 80523. *Fax:* 970-491-0445

GOTT, EUYEN, ELECTRICAL ENGINEERING, SOFTWARE DESIGN. *Current Pos:* RETIRED. *Personal Data:* b Kweilin, China, Jan 2, 15; US citizen; m 48, Wanda Lee; c Sherwin & Sheldon. *Educ:* Nat Kwangsi Univ, China, BS, 38; Stanford Univ, AM, 45; Johns Hopkins Univ, DrEng, 59. *Prof Exp:* Instr elec eng, Nat Kwangsi Univ, China, 38-41; head design engr, Yee-Chong Mfg Co, 41-44; develop engr, Radio Corp Am, 45-49; proj engr, Sierra Electronics Corp, 50-53; res assoc radiation lab, Johns Hopkins Univ, 53-59; assoc prof elec eng, Univ Hawaii, 59-63, prof, 63-65; mem tech staff, Hughes Aircraft Co, 65-66, staff engr, 66-67; sr tech specialist, Autonetics Div, NAm Rockwell Corp, 67-69; sr res scientist, Norden Div, United Aircraft Corp, 71-72; staff scientist, Lockheed Missiles & Space Co, 72-86. *Concurrent Pos:* Vis prof, Calif State Col, Fullerton, 70-71. *Mem:* Inst Elec & Electronics Engrs; Am Soc Eng Educ. *Res:* Detection of signal in noise; information processing systems; circuit theory; computer-aided active network analysis and synthesis; software design and development; emulation, automatic fault isolation, automatic flowcharting. *Mailing Add:* 1221 Eichler Ct Mountain View CA 94040

GOTT, J RICHARD, III, COSMOLOGY, GALAXY FORMATION. *Current Pos:* from asst prof to assoc prof, 76-87, PROF, PRINCETON UNIV, 87- *Personal Data:* b Louisville, Ky, Feb 8, 47; m 78, Lucy Pollard; c Elizabeth. *Educ:* Harvard Univ, AB, 69; Princeton Univ, PhD(astrophys), 72. *Honors & Awards:* Trumpler Award, Astron Soc Pac, 75. *Prof Exp:* Fel, Calif Inst Technol, 73-74; vis fel, Cambridge Univ, 75. *Concurrent Pos:* Alfred P Sloan Found res fel, 77; chmn judges, Westinghouse Sci Talent Search, 86- *Mem:* Int Astron Union; Am Astron Soc. *Res:* Cosmology, galaxy formation and galaxy clustering; theory that the universe is open and will continue expanding forever; solution to Einstein's field equations for the gravitational field around cosmic strings. *Mailing Add:* Dept Astrophys Sci Princeton Univ Princeton NJ 08544

GOTT, PRESTON FRAZIER, ASTRONOMY, DIRECTOR OBSERVATORY. *Current Pos:* from asst prof to assoc prof, 49-89, EMER ASSOC PROF PHYSICS & DIR, TEX TECH OBSERV, TEX TECH UNIV, 89- *Personal Data:* b Waxahachie, Tex, Nov 21, 19; m 42, 90, Orene Whitcomb; c Eugene & Suzanne. *Educ:* Univ Tex, BS, 44, MA, 47. *Prof Exp:* Tutor, Univ Tex, 44-46; from instr to asst prof, Hardin Col, 47-49. *Concurrent Pos:* Engr II, Arnold Eng Develop Ctr, Tullahoma, Tenn, 57; prin investr res contract, Tex Tech Univ, 59-60; physicist, Land-Air Div, Dynalectron Corp, White Sands Missile Range & Holloman AFB, NMex, 61-64 & consult, 63 & 65; sr scientist space instruments sect, Jet Propulsion Lab, Calif Inst Technol, 65, 66, 67, 70; co-ed proc, Southwest Regional Conf Astron & Astrophys, 75-84, mem bd, 76-78. *Mem:* Fel AAAS; Soc Photo-Optical Instrument Eng; Optical Soc Am; Am Astron Soc; Sigma Xi. *Res:* Photography; atmospheric optics; space physics; experimental optical design. *Mailing Add:* 2410 W 24th St Odessa TX 79763

GOTT, VINCENT LYNN, CARDIOVASCULAR SURGERY. *Current Pos:* chief cardiac surg, 65-82, assoc prof, 65-68, PROF SURG, SCH MED, JOHNS HOPKINS UNIV, 68- *Personal Data:* b Wichita, Kans, Apr 14, 27; m 54; c 3. *Educ:* Univ Wichita, BS, 51; Yale Univ, MD, 53. *Honors & Awards:* Holstoen Gold Medal, Am Med Asn, 57. *Prof Exp:* Instr surg, Med Sch, Univ Minn, 59-60; from asst prof to assoc prof, Sch Med, Univ Wis, 60-65. *Concurrent Pos:* Markle scholar acad med, 62-67. *Mem:* Soc Univ Surg; fel Am Col Surg; Am Soc Artificial Internal Organs; Am Asn Thoracic Surg. *Res:* Cardiovascular research, including myocardial metabolism, artificial heart valves; artificial pacemakers; coronary artery disease; intravascular clotting problems; clinical problems; clinical surgery of the heart and blood vessels. *Mailing Add:* Johns Hopkins Hosp 614 Blalock Bldg Baltimore MD 21205

GOTTERER, GERALD S, MEDICAL EDUCATION. *Current Pos:* ASSOC DEAN & PROF MED ADMIN, VANDERBILT SCH MED, 86-, DIR, DIV CONTINUING MED EDUC, 92- *Personal Data:* b New York, NY, Oct 17, 33; m 78, Shelley McCullough; c 4. *Educ:* Harvard Univ, AB, 55; Univ Chicago, MD, 58; Johns Hopkins Univ, PhD(biochem), 64. *Prof Exp:* Intern internal med, Grace-New Haven Community Hosp, 58-59; asst dean student affairs, Sch Med, Johns Hopkins Univ, 70-72, from instr to asst prof physiol chem, 65-78, dean predoctoral progs, 72-78; assoc prof biochem & assoc dean med student progs, Rush Med Col, 78-86. *Concurrent Pos:* USPHS fels, 59-64. *Mem:* Am Chem Soc; Am Soc Biol Chem; Sigma Xi. *Res:* Medical education. *Mailing Add:* Vanderbilt Univ Sch Med 21st Ave S & Garland Nashville TN 37232-0001. *Fax:* 615-343-8397; *E-Mail:* gottergs@ctrvax.vanderbilt.edu

GOTTERER, MALCOLM HAROLD, INFORMATION SCIENCE, COMPUTER SCIENCE. *Current Pos:* dir info systs, Fla Int Univ, 77-78, prof comput sci, 73-86, dir, Grad Studies Comput Sci, 79-86, EMER PROF, FLA INT UNIV, 86-; COMPUT CONSULT, 70- *Personal Data:* b New York, NY, Mar 11, 24; m 57, Shirley Lasher; c David A. *Educ:* Suffolk Univ, BS, 55, MS, 56; Harvard Univ, DBA, 60. *Prof Exp:* Instr bus, Grad Sch Bus, Harvard Univ, 56-57; asst prof, Univ Calif, Berkeley, 59-62; assoc prof indust mgt, Ga Inst Technol, 62-64; prof bus admin & comput sci, Pa State Univ, University Park, 65-74. *Concurrent Pos:* Int Bus Mach Systs Res Inst fel, NY, 64; Soc Sci Res Coun res grant, Info Processing Div, Syst Develop Corp, Calif, 65; consult, Ctr Comput Sci & Technol, Nat Bur Stand, 66-68 & Human Resources Res Orgn, George Washington Univ, 67; prin sect comt comput & info processing & comt credit card stand, US Am Stand Inst, 68-70; mem UN tech asst mission to Jamaica, 69; mem US comt admin data processing group, Int Fedn Info Processing; fel comput sci, Johns Hopkins Univ, 71-72; mem comt professionalism, Am Fedn Info Processing Socs; nat lectr, Asn Comput Mach, 70-73. *Mem:* Asn Comput Mach; Inst Elec & Electronics Engrs. *Res:* Computer system evaluation; performance improvement, and configuration administration; data structures. *Mailing Add:* 12208 Staunton Ct Raleigh NC 27613. *E-Mail:* mgottererm64318@worldnet.att.net

GOTTESFELD, ZEHAVA, NEUROBIOLOGY, NEUROCHEMISTRY. *Current Pos:* ASSOC PROF NEUROBIOL, UNIV TEX MED SCH, HOUSTON, 78- *Personal Data:* b Tel Aviv, Israel. *Educ:* Hebrew Univ, Jerusalem, MSc, 60; Univ NC, Chapel Hill, PhD(physiol), 67. *Prof Exp:* Fel neurochem, McGill Univ, 68-70; investr neurobiol, Weizmann Inst Sci, 71-74, sr scientist, 75-76; vis scientist histopharmacol, NIH, Bethesda, Md, 76-78. *Concurrent Pos:* Assoc prof biomed res grant, Univ Tex, 78-79; vis scientist, NIH. *Mem:* Int Soc Neurochem; Soc Neurosci; Am Soc Neurochem. *Res:* Neurocytology; neuroanatomy; histochemistry; neurochemistry; neuroendocrinology. *Mailing Add:* Dept Neurobiol & Anat Univ Tex Med Sch Houston 6431 Fannin St Houston TX 77030-1501

GOTTESMAN, ELIHU, PHARMACEUTICAL CHEMISTRY, SAFETY. *Current Pos:* RETIRED. *Personal Data:* b Brooklyn, NY, June 6, 19; m 49, Muriel Schifrin; c Pamela (Freedman), Suzette (Martin) & Margo (Bycer). *Educ:* Johns Hopkins Univ, BA, 39; Fordham Univ, MS, 40. *Prof Exp:* Chemist, Food & Drug Res Labs, Inc, 41-42; supvr, Vitamin Lab, Endo Labs, Inc, 46-52, mgr, Parenteral Prod Div, 52-73; safety supvr, E I Du Pont de Nemours & Co, Garden City, 73-85. *Concurrent Pos:* Ed, Int Blue Book, 47-52. *Mem:* Am Chem Soc; Am Soc Safety Engrs. *Res:* Development of pharmaceutical equipment and procedures and of pharmaceutical dosage forms; equipment and special building construction for pharmaceutical industry. *Mailing Add:* 148 Mead Ct Wantagh NY 11793

GOTTESMAN, IRVING ISADORE, PSYCHOLOGY, BEHAVIOR GENETICS. *Current Pos:* commonwealth prof, 85-94, SHERRELL J ASTON PROF PSYCHOL, UNIV VA, 94- *Personal Data:* b Cleveland, Ohio, Dec 29, 30; m 70, Carol Applen; c Adam M & David B. *Educ:* Ill Inst Technol, BS, 53; Univ Minn, PhD, 60. *Honors & Awards:* R Thornton Wilson Prize, Eastern Psychiat Res Asn, 65; Hofheimer Prize, 72; Stanley Dean Award, Am Col Psychiatrists, 88; T Dobzhansky Award, Behavior Genetics Asn, 90; Eric Stromgren Medal, Danish Psychiat Soc, 91; Kurt Schneider Prize, Bonn, Ger, 92; Alexander Gralnick Prize, Am Asn Suicidology, 92; Distinguished Scientist Award, Am Psychiat Asn Soc Sci Clinical Psychol. *Prof Exp:* Intern clin psychol, Vet Admin Hosp, Minneapolis, 59-60; lectr, Dept Social Rel, Harvard Univ, 60-63; fel psychiat genetics, Inst Psychiat, London, 63-64; assoc prof psychiat genetics, Dept Psychiat, Univ NC, 64-66; prof, Dept Psychol, Univ Minn, 66-80, dept psychiat, Wash Univ, St Louis, 80-85. *Concurrent Pos:* Training consult, Vet Admin, Wash, 68-85; Guggenheim fel, Univ Copenhagen, 72; consult, NIMH, Wash, 75-79, 92-, Nat Plan for Schizophrenia, 88-89; fel, Ctr Advan Studies in the Behav Sci, 87-88; inst med comt consult, Vietnam War Experience Study, 87-88; consult, mental illness & genetics, Off Technol, 93-94. *Mem:* Fel Am Psychiat Asn; fel Am Psychopath Asn; fel Royal Col Psychiatrists; fel Am Psychol Soc; Soc Study Social Biol (vpres, 76-80); Behavior Genetics Asn (pres, 76-77); Am Soc Human Genetics; Soc Res Psychopath (pres, 93); fel AAAS. *Res:* Genetic aspects of human normal and abnormal behavior using twins, families, and adoptees. *Mailing Add:* Gilmer Hall Univ Va Charlottesville VA 22903. *Fax:* 804-982-4766; *E-Mail:* iig@atvirginia.edu

GOTTESMAN, MICHAEL, CELL BIOLOGY. *Current Pos:* CHIEF LAB CELL BIOL, NAT CANCER INST, 80- *Personal Data:* b Jersey City, NJ, Oct 7, 46; m 66; c 2. *Educ:* Harvard Univ, MD, 70. *Honors & Awards:* Soma Weiss, 70; James Tolbert Shipley Prize, 70; Milken Award, 90. *Mem:* Am Soc Cell Biologist; AAAS; Genetics Soc Am; Am Asn Cancer Res; Am Soc Biochem & Molecular Biol. *Res:* Molecular basis of drug resistance, growth regulation, invasiveness and metastasis in cancer. *Mailing Add:* NIH Bldg 37 Rm 1B22 37 Convent Dr Bethesda MD 20892-4255. *Fax:* 301-402-0450

GOTTESMAN, ROY TULLY, ORGANIC & POLYMER CHEMISTRY. *Current Pos:* EXEC DIR, VINYL INST, 83- *Personal Data:* b Bayonne, NJ, March 6, 28; m 54; c 2. *Educ:* Rutgers Univ, BS, 47, MS, 50, PhD(chem), 51. *Prof Exp:* Asst chem, Univ Minn, 47-48; asst, Rutgers Univ, 48-51; chemist res & develop, Heyden Chem Corp, 51-56, group leader, Res & Develop Dept, Heyden Div, Heyden Newport Chem Corp, 56-61, supvr org res, 61-65; mgr, Tenneco Chem, Inc, 65-70, mgr, tech develop intermediates div, 70-71, mgr res & develop, org & polymers div, 71-76, dir, chem develop, 76-77, dir, 77-80, vpres, environ & regulatory affairs, 80-83. *Mem:* Am Chem Soc; NY Acad Sci; Sigma Xi. *Res:* Synthetic organic chemistry; preparation and reactions of polyols; chemistry of salicylic acid; process development and improvement; agricultural chemicals; research administration; biocides, paint and plastics additives; polymers; environmental regulations; occupational health and safety; product safety; hazardous waste disposal; vinyl polymers. *Mailing Add:* 1619 Lacebark Rd Toms River NJ 08755-1811

GOTTESMAN, STEPHEN T, RADIO ASTRONOMY. *Current Pos:* from asst prof to assoc prof, 72-81, chmn, Dept Astron, 88-93, PROF ASTRON, UNIV FLA, 81- *Personal Data:* b New York, NY, Feb 23, 39; m 68, 90, Mariou Barr; c 5. *Educ:* Colgate Univ, BA, 60; Manchester Univ, PhD(radio astron), 67. *Prof Exp:* Lectr physics, Univ Keele, 68-69; res assoc radio astron, Nat Radio Astron Observ, 69-71; res fel, Calif Inst Technol, 71. *Concurrent Pos:* Chmn, Int Astron Union Working Group Internal Motion Galaxies, 79-85; Fulbright Scholar, 60-61; Leverhulme fel, 61-64; guest prof, Onjala Space Observ, Sweden, 83; vacation consult, Royal Observ, Edinburgh, 83; fac fel, Goddard Space Flight Inst, 95; vis prof, Inst de Astrofisica de Conanai, 95-96. *Mem:* Am Astron Soc; Int Astron Union; Comn V, Int Union Radio Sci. *Res:* Neutral hydrogen and other radio spectral line observations of the interstellar medium and of the structure, kinematics and dynamics of the galaxy and of extragalactic nebulae; the mass of galaxies; dark helos. *Mailing Add:* Dept Astron Univ Fla-211 SSRB Gainesville FL 32611-2002. *Fax:* 352-392-5089; *E-Mail:* gott@astro.ufl.edu

GOTTFRIED, BRADLEY M, BEHAVIORAL ECOLOGY, ORNITHOLOGY. *Current Pos:* DEAN, ACAD AFFAIRS, MONTGOMERY, CO COMMUNITY COL, BLUEBELL, PA. *Personal Data:* b Philadephia, Pa, Mar 1, 50; c 1. *Educ:* W Chester State Col, BA, 71; Western Ill Univ, MS, 73; Miami Univ, PhD(zool), 76. *Prof Exp:* Instr biol, Mt Mercy Col, 76-78; assoc prof biol, Col St Catherine, 78-81, prof & chmn dept, 81-; at Dept Biol, Armstrong State Col, Ga. *Concurrent Pos:* Student res zool, Miami Univ, 76. *Mem:* AAAS; Am Ornithologists' Union; Am Soc Zool; Ecol Soc Am; Sigma Xi. *Res:* Ecological aspects of nest predation; factors influencing the size of avian territories; winter ecology of birds; biogeography of small mammals; feeding ecology of birds. *Mailing Add:* Off Dean Acad Affairs Montgomery Co Community Col 340 DeKalb Pike PO box 400 Bluebell PA 19422

GOTTFRIED, BYRON S(TUART), COMPUTER APPLICATIONS, COAL TECHNOLOGY. *Current Pos:* assoc prof, 70-75, dir energy resources prog, 75-76, PROF INDUST ENG, ENG MGT OPERS RES, UNIV PITTSBURGH, 75- *Personal Data:* b Detroit, Mich, May 24, 34; m 59; c 3. *Educ:* Purdue Univ, BS, 56; Univ Mich, MS, 58; Case Inst Technol, PhD(chem eng), 62. *Prof Exp:* Assoc engr, Lewis Res Ctr, NASA, 59-62; assoc engr, Gulf Res & Develop Co, 62-65; asst prof mech eng, Carnegie-Mellon Univ, 65-68; sect supvr, Econ & Comput Sci Div, Gulf Res & Develop Co, 68-70. *Concurrent Pos:* Consult, Lord Corp, 65-68, Westinghouse Elec Corp, 66-, US Dept Energy, 75- & US Civil Serv Comn, 75-, Syst Modeling Corp, 89- *Mem:* Am Inst Indust Engrs; Soc Comput Simulation; Soc Mfg Engrs. *Res:* Applied operations research; computer simulation; optimization; applications to manufacturing and coal utilization. *Mailing Add:* 129 Old Suffolk Dr Monroeville PA 15146

GOTTFRIED, EUGENE LESLIE, HEMATOLOGY, LABORATORY MEDICINE. *Current Pos:* clin prof lab med, 81-93, VCHMN, DEPT LAB MED, UNIV CALIF, SAN FRANCISCO, 81-, PROF CLIN LAB MEC, 93- *Personal Data:* b Passaic, NJ, Feb 26, 29; m 57, Phyllis Swain. *Educ:* Columbia Univ, AB, 50, MD, 54; Am Bd Internal Med, dipl, 63 & cert hemat, 72. *Prof Exp:* Intern, Presby Hosp, NY, 54-55, asst resident, 57-58; resident, Bronx Munic Hosp Ctr, 58-59; from asst instr to instr med, Albert Einstein Col Med, 59-61, assoc, 61-65, asst prof, 65-69; assoc prof med, Med Col, Cornell Univ, 69-81, assoc prof path, 75-81. *Concurrent Pos:* Fel med, Bronx Munic Hosp Ctr, 59-60; asst vis physician, Bronx Munic Hosp Ctr, 60-66, assoc attend physician, 66-69; asst vis physician, Lincoln Hosp, 63-69; Health Res Coun NY, career scientist, 64-72; assoc attend physician & dir lab clin hemat, NY Hosp, 69-81, assoc attending pathologist, 75-81; attending physician, Burke Rehab Ctr, White Plains, NY, 75-81; dir clin labs, San Francisco Gen Hosp Med Ctr, 81-; chief, Lab Med Serv, San Francisco Gen Hosp, 81- *Mem:* Am Soc Hemat; Acad Clin Lab Physicians & Scientists; fel

Am Col Physicians; fel Int Soc Hemat; Nat Comt Clin Lab Stand. *Res:* Laboratory medicine; plasmalogens; lipids of blood cells; hemolytic phosphatides; quality assurance and clinical utility of diagnostic tests. *Mailing Add:* San Francisco Gen Hosp Med Ctr 1001 Potrero Ave San Francisco CA 94110. *Fax:* 415-206-3045; *E-Mail:* eugeneg@pangloss.ucsf.edu

GOTTFRIED, KURT, THEORETICAL PHYSICS. *Current Pos:* assoc prof, dept chair, 91-94, PROF PHYSICS, CORNELL UNIV, 64- *Personal Data:* b Vienna, Austria, May 17, 29; m 55; c 2. *Educ:* McGill Univ, BEng, 51, MSc, 53; Mass Inst Technol, PhD(theoret physics), 55. *Prof Exp:* Jr fel, Soc of Fels, Harvard Univ, 55-58; res fel, Inst Theoret Physics, Copenhagen, 58-59; res fel physics, Harvard Univ, 59-60, asst prof, 60-64. *Concurrent Pos:* Guggenheim fel, European Orgn Nuclear Res, Geneva, 63-64, mem staff, 70-73; mem bd dirs, Union Concerned Scientists; chmn, div particles & fields, Am Phys Soc, 81, coun-at-large, 90-94. *Mem:* Fel Am Phys Soc; fel Am Acad Arts & Sci; fel AAAS. *Res:* Theory of nuclear structure; quantum-mechanical many body problems; elementary particles; arms control & international security. *Mailing Add:* Newman Lab Cornell Univ Clark Hall Ithaca NY 14853. *E-Mail:* kg13@cornell.edu

GOTTFRIED, PAUL, RELIABILITY, SYSTEM SAFETY. *Current Pos:* SELF-EMPLOYED, 71- *Personal Data:* b Vienna, Austria, Nov 7, 27; US citizen; m 51, Kitty T Nakada; c 2. *Educ:* Rose-Hulman Inst Technol, BS, 49. *Honors & Awards:* Centennial Medal, Inst Elec & Electronics Engrs, 84. *Prof Exp:* Design engr, Charles N Debes & Assocs, 49-50; specialty engr, Chambers Corp, 50-53; sr engr, Inland Testing Labs, Cook Elec Co, 53-54, proj dir, 56-59; components engr, Chicago Aerial Industs, Inc, 54-55; partner, Reliability Eng Assocs, 59-61; prin scientist, Booz, Allen & Hamilton, Inc, 61-71. *Concurrent Pos:* Newslett ed, Inst Elec & Electronics Engrs Reliability Soc, 68-74; trans assoc ed, 86. *Mem:* Fel AAAS; Am Statist Asn; sr mem Inst Elec & Electronics Engrs (treas, 75-78, vpres, 89-91; 96-97); Inst Opers Res & Mgmt Sci. *Res:* Methodology for prediction of reliability and safety in systems involving new technology. *Mailing Add:* 9251 3 Oaks Dr Silver Spring MD 20901-3366

GOTTHEIL, EDWARD, PSYCHIATRY, PSYCHOLOGY. *Current Pos:* assoc prof, 64-69, PROF PSYCHIAT, JEFFERSON MED COL, 69- *Personal Data:* b Montreal, Que, Aug 6, 24; US citizen; m 51, Ruth I Ranville; c Ellen F & Gerald L. *Educ:* Queen's Univ, Ont, BA, 46; McGill Univ, MA, 48; Univ Tex, PhD(psychol), 51, MD, 55. *Honors & Awards:* C Nelson Davis Award, 93. *Prof Exp:* Chief psychologist, Austin State Hosp, Tex, 49-51; intern, Roanoke Mem Hosp, Va, 55-56; resident psychiat, Letterman Gen Hosp, San Francisco, Calif, 56-59; post psychiatrist, Ft Riley, Kans, 60-62; chief med res proj, West Point, NY, 62-64. *Concurrent Pos:* Consult, Friend's Hosp, Philadelphia, 64-68, East Pa Psychiat Inst, 66-69, Del State Hosp, 65-90, Coatesville Vet Admin Hosp, 67-90. *Mem:* AAAS; Am Psychol Asn; Am Psychiat Asn; Sigma Xi; Am Col Psychiatrists; Am Acad Psychiatrists Alcoholism & Addiction. *Res:* Small group interactions; psychiatric decision making; diagnosis; preventive social psychiatry; behavioral recording and data reduction; alcoholism; schizophrenia; medical education; emotional communication; sexual beliefs and behavior; addiction medicine. *Mailing Add:* 1201 Chestnut St 15th Floor Philadelphia PA 19107-4192. *Fax:* 215-568-3596

GOTTLIEB, A ARTHUR, IMMUNOLOGY, MOLECULAR BIOLOGY. *Current Pos:* PROF MICROBIOL & IMMUNOL & CHMN DEPT, SCH MED, TULANE UNIV, 75-, PROF MED, 76- *Personal Data:* b Dec 14, 37; US citizen; m 58, Marise S; c Mindy & Joanne. *Educ:* Columbia Univ, AB, 57; NY Univ, MD, 61. *Honors & Awards:* F S Burns Award, Mass Div, Am Cancer Soc, 68. *Prof Exp:* Med house officer, Peter Bent Brigham Hosp, 61-62, asst resident physician, 62-63, from asst-in-med to assoc-in-med, 65-68; comn director, USPHS Clin Assoc, Nat Heart Inst, NIH, 63-65; chem res fel, Harvard Univ, 65-67, assoc-in-med, 68, asst prof med, 69; from assoc prof to prof microbiol, Inst Microbiol, Rutgers Univ, New Brunswick, 69-75. *Concurrent Pos:* Nat Inst Gen Med Sci spec fel, Harvard Univ, 65-67 & career develop award, Harvard Med Sch, 67-69; consult, Squibb Inst Med Res, 69- & Vet Admin Hosp, East Orange, NJ, 73-75; mem ed adv bd, Immunol Commun; ed-in-chief, Unisci Ser Immunol, CRC Press, Cleveland; mem breast cancer task force, Nat Cancer Inst, 76-80; consult, Nat Ctr Toxicol Res, Jefferson, Ark, 76-78; vis prof, Walker & Elizabeth Hall Inst, Melbourne, 79 & Wakayama Med Col & Gunma Med Col, Japan, 80; chmn, Publ Comt, Reticuloendothelial Soc, 77-78; keynote lectr, 33rd Ann Meeting, Japan Hemat Soc, 80; pres & chief exec officer, Imreg Inc, 85-96; vis prof med & pharmacol, Shanghai Med Univ, 91. *Mem:* Sigma Xi; fel Am Col Physicians; fel Am Acad Microbiol; Am Chem Soc; AAAS; NY Acad Sci; Am Asn Cancer Res; Am Asn Immunologists; Am Soc Biol Chemists; Am Soc Clin Invest. *Res:* Structure and function of immunoregulatory molecules in man; development of new approaches to immunotherapy; studies of unique DNA sequences in malignant human and murine lymphoid cells; eukaryotic DNA polymerases, especially those associated with murine nyeloma; macrophage function, particularly in regard to antigen presentation; author of 90 publications. *Mailing Add:* Dept Microbiol & Immunol Tulane Univ Sch Med 1430 Tulane Ave New Orleans LA 70112. *Fax:* 504-588-5144; *E-Mail:* agottli@timepop.turc.tulane.edu

GOTTLIEB, ABRAHAM MITCHELL, MEDICINE, CARDIOLOGY. *Current Pos:* prof, 68-75, EMER PROF CLIN MED, STANFORD UNIV, 75-; CONSULT, VET ADMIN HOSP, PALO ALTO, 75- *Personal Data:* b Chicago, Ill, Feb 22, 09; m 34; c 2. *Educ:* Univ Ill, BS, 30, MD, 33; Am Bd Internal Med, dipl, 48. *Honors & Awards:* Dist Serv Medal, Vet Admin, 75. *Prof Exp:* Ward physician, Med Serv, Vet Admin Hosp, Tuscaloosa, Ala, 38-39, Milwaukee, Wis, 39-40, sect chief cardiol, 40-42; sect chief cardiol, Vet Admin Hosp, Dearborn, 46; asst prof med, Col Med, Wayne State Univ, 48-60; from assoc prof to prof, Univ Wis Madison, 60-68. *Concurrent Pos:* Chief prof serv, Vet Admin Hosp, Dearborn, 46-60, attend consult, 48-60, hosp dir, Madison, Wis, 60-68; dir, Vet Admin Hosp, Palo Alto, 68-75. *Mem:* AMA; Am Heart Asn; fel Am Col Physicians. *Res:* Cardiovascular; pulmonary; sarcoidosis. *Mailing Add:* 10150 Torre Ave Apt 222 Cupertino CA 95014

GOTTLIEB, ALICE BENDIX, PSORIASIS, IMMUNODERMATOLOGY. *Current Pos:* ASSOC MED DIR DERMAT, HOFFMAN-LA ROUCHE, INC, 93- *Personal Data:* b New York, NY, July 24, 522. *Educ:* Brandeis Univ, BA, 73; Rockefeller Univ-Cornell Univ, PhD, 79, Med Col, MD, 80; Am Bd Internal Med, cert, 82, rheumatology, 84; Am Bd Dermat cert, 93. *Honors & Awards:* Sarah O-Laughlin Foley Prize Clin Med, 80; Physicians Recognition Award, AMA, 83-86. *Prof Exp:* Med resident, NY Hosp, 80-82; rheumatic dis fel, Hosp Spec Surg, NY, 82-84; asst prof, Rockefeller Univ, 82-89, assoc prof, 89-93. *Concurrent Pos:* Assoc physician, Rockefeller Univ Hosp, 82-89, physician, 89-; fel biomed res, Hartford Found, 82-85; prin investr, NIH, 82-85 & 85-88, Arthritis Found, 85-86, Squibb Corp, 87-91, Sandoz Corp, 88, 90 & 92, Nat Psoriasis Found, 89, Skin Dis Soc, 90, Roche, 91, Carl J Herzog Found, 91, Amgen, 92 & Harold & Beatrice Renfield Found, 92; adj asst prof dermat, Cornell Univ Med Col, 85-; vis prof, Dept Dermat, New Eng Med Ctr & Johns Hopkins Univ, 92; geriat leadership acad award lectr, Albert Einstein Col Med, 92. *Mem:* Soc Invest Dermat; Am Col Rheumatology; Am Asn Immunologists; Am Acad Dermat. *Res:* Rheumatology; immunology; internal medicine; dermatology. *Mailing Add:* 45 Athens Rd Short Hills NJ 07078

GOTTLIEB, ALLAN, HIGHLY PARALLEL COMPUTERS, SHARED MEMORY COMPUTERS. *Current Pos:* assoc res prof, Courant Inst, 81-85, assoc prof comput sci, 85-90, assoc dir, Ultracomput Res Lab, 86-89, DIR, ULTRA COMPUT RES LAB, COURANT INST, 89-; PROF COMPUT SCI, NY UNIV, 90- *Personal Data:* b Queen's NY, Aug 2, 45; m 72; c 2. *Educ:* Mass Inst Technol, BS, 67; Branders Univ, MA, 68, PhD(math), 73. *Prof Exp:* Instr math, State Col Mass, North Adams, 72-73; from asst prof to assoc prof math, York Col, City Univ New York 73-81. *Concurrent Pos:* Ed, Technol Rev, 71; vis mem, Courant Inst Math Sci, NY Univ, 79-81; sci adv bd mem, NCR, 88-, Parallel Processing Adv Comt, 90- *Mem:* Am Math Soc; Asn Comput Mach; Inst Elec & Electronics Engrs Comput Soc; NY Acad Sci. *Res:* Large-scale parallel processing emphasizing shared-memory designs; fetch-and-add and combining memory references to avoid hot-spot slowdowns; prototype hardware; parallel operating systems; full-custom very large scale integration switches. *Mailing Add:* NY Univ Dept Comput Sci NY Univ 715 Broadway Tenth Floor New York NY 10003-6607

GOTTLIEB, ARLAN J, hematology, oncology, for more information see previous edition

GOTTLIEB, CHARLES F, CANCER RESEARCH, RADIOBIOLOGY. *Current Pos:* from asst prof to assoc prof radiol, 76-86, ASSOC PROF RADIATION ONCOL, UNIV MIAMI, 86-, DIR ENVIRON HEALTH & SAFETY, 89- *Personal Data:* b Paris, Tex, Jan 17, 44; m 64; c 1. *Educ:* Univ Tenn, Knoxville, PhD(radiobiol), 70. *Prof Exp:* Instr, Univ Tenn, 70-76, mem Shadd Fac, 73-76. *Mem:* Radiation Res Soc; Am Soc Therapeut Radiol & Oncol; Bioelectromagnetics Soc; Am Soc Safety Engrs. *Mailing Add:* 8385 SW 90 St Miami FL 33156

GOTTLIEB, DANIEL HENRY, TOPOLOGY, MATHEMATICAL PHYSICS. *Current Pos:* PROF MATH, PURDUE UNIV, 67- *Personal Data:* b Hollywood, Calif, Dec 7, 37; div; c 2. *Educ:* Univ Calif, Los Angeles, BA, 59, MA, 61, PhD(math), 62. *Prof Exp:* Instr math, Univ Ill, 62-64; res mathematician, Inst Defense Anal, NJ, 64-67. *Mem:* Am Math Soc; Math Asn Am. *Res:* Algebraic topology; study of fibre bundles; mathematical physics. *Mailing Add:* 1160 Camelback Blvd West Lafayette IN 47906

GOTTLIEB, FREDERICK JAY, GENETICS, DEVELOPMENTAL BIOLOGY. *Current Pos:* instr zool, 62-63, asst prof, 64-67, ASSOC PROF BIOL, UNIV PITTSBURGH, 67-, ASSOC PROF BIOL & BIOSTATIST, GRAD SCH PUB HEALTH, 71. *Personal Data:* b New York, NY, June 17, 35; m 58; c 3. *Educ:* Hofstra Col, BA, 56; Wesleyan Univ, MA, 58; Univ Calif, Berkeley, PhD(genetics), 62; Univ Pittsburgh, MS. *Prof Exp:* NIH trainee entom, Univ Calif, Berkeley, 60-61 & NIH trainee genetics, 60-62. *Concurrent Pos:* Consult, Proj Solo; Am Cancer Soc instnl res grants, 63-66; USPHS res grant, 63-67; mem exec comt, Comput Ctr, Univ Pittsburgh, 69-73; Alexander von Humboldt Found sr scientist award & sr res scholar, Fulbright-Hays Prog, W Germany, 73-74. *Mem:* AAAS; Soc Develop Biol; Genetics Soc Am. *Res:* Genetic control of behavior in Drosophila; genetic control of host-symbiont recognition in Drosophila paulistorum and Ephestia kuehniella; genetic control of development of eye structure and pigmentation mutants in Ephestia kuehniella and Drosophila melanogaster; genetic and developmental effects of environmental pollutants. *Mailing Add:* Biol & Life Sci Univ Pittsburgh A-234 Langley Hall Pittsburgh PA 15260-0001

GOTTLIEB, GERALD LANE, ELECTRICAL ENGINEERING, PHYSIOLOGY. *Current Pos:* asst prof biomed eng, 70-73, assoc prof physiol & biomed eng, 73-80, PROF PHYSIOL, RUSH MED COL, 80-, PROF NEUROL SCI, 90- *Personal Data:* b New York, NY, Feb 6, 41; m 68; c Benjamine & Rachel. *Educ:* Mass Inst Technol, BS, 62, MS, 64; Univ Ill Med Ctr, PhD(physiol), 70. *Prof Exp:* Res & develop engr, Aeronutronics Div, Philco-Ford Corp, 64-66; instr bioeng, Univ Ill, Chicago Circle, 67-73. *Concurrent Pos:* Adj assoc prof biomed eng, Univ Ill, Chicago Circle, 73- *Mem:* AAAS; Soc Neurosci; fel Inst Elec & Electronics Engrs; Sigma Xi. *Res:*

Nervous control of human motor system; computer applications for research and clinical testing in a medical scientific environment. *Mailing Add:* Neuro Muscular Res Ctr Boston Univ 44 Cummington St Boston MA 02215. *Fax:* 312-633-1564; *E-Mail:* glg@neuro.rpslmc.edu

GOTTLIEB, GILBERT, PSYCHOBIOLOGY. *Current Pos:* head, 82-86, EXCELLENCE PROF, PSYCHOL DEPT, UNIV NC, GREENSBORO, 82- *Personal Data:* b Brooklyn, NY, Oct 22, 29; m 61, Nora L Willis; c Jonathan B, David H, Aaron L & Marc S. *Educ:* Univ Miami, AB, 55, MS, 56; Duke Univ, PhD(psychol), 60. *Prof Exp:* Res assoc med psychol, Med Ctr, Duke Univ, 58-59; mem staff clin psychol, Dorothea Dix Hosp, Raleigh, 59-61; res scientist biopsychol, Psychol Lab, Res Sect, NC Div Ment Health, 61-82. *Concurrent Pos:* Res award, Nat Inst Child Health & Human Develop, 62-85, NSF, 85-88 & NIMH, 89-92 & 93-98; contrib ed, NC J Ment Health, 65-72 & 77-80; res prof psychol, Univ NC Chapel Hill, 73-82; assoc ed, J Comp & Physiol Psychol, 74-80; US del, Int Ethological Cong Comt, 77-83. *Mem:* Fel AAAS; Int Soc Develop Psychobiol (pres, 87-88); fel Animal Behav Soc; Int Ethological Cong; fel Am Psychol Asn; Sigma Xi; Int Conf Infant Studies. *Res:* Developmental comparative psychology; behavioral embryology. *Mailing Add:* Ctr Develop Sci CB8115 Univ NC 100 E Franklin St Chapel Hill NC 27599-8115

GOTTLIEB, IRVIN M, INORGANIC CHEMISTRY, ANALYTICAL CHEMISTRY. *Current Pos:* head dept, 67-70, prof, 61-91, EMER PROF CHEM, WIDENER COL, 91- *Personal Data:* b Philadelphia, Pa, July 15, 21. *Educ:* Univ Pa, BS, 43, MS, 47, PhD, 53. *Prof Exp:* Dep chief, Textile Finishes Lab, Qm Res & Develop Lab, Pa, 51-54; group leader, Textile Res Inst, NJ, 55-58; prof chem, Trenton State Col, 58-61. *Mem:* Fiber Soc; Chem Soc; fel Am Inst Chem; fel Royal Inst Chem; Sigma Xi. *Res:* Flame and thermal protection; functional finishes for textiles; science education; communication. *Mailing Add:* Apt 342 Fairmount Terr 3601 Conshohocken Ave Philadelphia PA 19131-5343

GOTTLIEB, LEONARD SOLOMON, PATHOLOGY. *Current Pos:* assoc dir, 66-72, DIR, MALLORY INST PATH, BOSTON CITY HOSP, 72-; PROF PATH, SCH MED, BOSTON UNIV, 71-, CHIEF PATH, UNIV HOSP, BOSTON UNIV MED CTR, 73-, CHMN DEPT, 80- *Personal Data:* b Boston, Mass, May 26, 27; c 3. *Educ:* Bowdoin Col, AB, 46; Tufts Univ, MD, 50; Harvard Sch Pub Health, MPH, 69. *Prof Exp:* From instr to prof path, Tufts Univ, 53-71. *Concurrent Pos:* Instr, Med Sch, Boston Univ, 53-61; lectr path, 67-71; consult & lectr, US Naval Hosp, Chelsea, Mass, 57-58; from asst pathologist to assoc pathologist, Mallory Inst Path, Boston City Hosp, 57-66; lectr, Harvard Med Sch, 63-; hon mem, Fac Med, Hebrew Univ, Jerusalem, 87. *Mem:* Am Soc Clin Path; Am Soc Cell Biol; Int Acad Path; Am Soc Exp Path; Am Asn Study Liver Dis. *Res:* Gastrointestinal and liver diseases; nutritional pathology. *Mailing Add:* Chmn Mallory Inst Pathol 784 Massachusetts Ave Rm 323 Boston MA 02118-2383. *Fax:* 617-534-5315

GOTTLIEB, MARISE SUSS, preventive medicine, epidemiology, for more information see previous edition

GOTTLIEB, MELVIN BURT, PHYSICS. *Current Pos:* assoc dir, Proj Matterhorn, 54-61, assoc chmn astrophys sci, 74-80, DIR, PLASMA PHYSICS LAB & PROF ASTROPHYS SCI, PRINCETON UNIV, 61- *Personal Data:* b Chicago, Ill, May 25, 17; m 48; c 2. *Educ:* Univ Chicago, BS, 40, PhD, 50. *Prof Exp:* Res assoc, Harvard Univ, 43-45; instr phys sci, Univ Chicago, 45-46, asst physics, 46-50; asst prof, Univ Iowa, 50-54. *Mem:* Sigma Xi; Am Phys Soc. *Res:* Cloud chamber studies of penetrating showers; rocket and balloon-borne studies of primary cosmic ray intensities; low momentum cut off in intensity of heavy nuclei in cosmic rays; plasma physics; controlled thermonuclear reactors. *Mailing Add:* 14 Mershon Dr Princeton NJ 08540

GOTTLIEB, MELVIN HARVEY, BIOPHYSICS. *Current Pos:* res scientist, 65-87, HEALTH SCI ADMIN, NAT INST ARTHRITIS & METAB DIS, NIH, 87- *Personal Data:* b New York, NY, May 2, 29; m 60; c 3. *Educ:* Brooklyn Col, BS, 49; Polytech Inst Brooklyn, PhD(chem), 54. *Prof Exp:* Chemist textile finishes, United Merchants & Mfrs, 49-50; scientist, Nat Heart Inst, NIH, 54-56; chemist, Interchem Corp, 56-59; mem tech staff, Bell Tel Labs, 59-65. *Mem:* Am Chem Soc. *Res:* Ion exchange; ion exchange membranes; surface chemistry; electrochemistry; lipid physical chemistry; biological membranes. *Mailing Add:* Nat Inst Arthritis & Musculo Dis NIH Bethesda MD 20892

GOTTLIEB, MICHAEL STUART, IMMUNE DEFICIENCY, HUMAN IMMUNOLOGY. *Current Pos:* ASST PROF MED, SCH MED, UNIV CALIF, LOS ANGELES, 80- *Personal Data:* b New Brunswick, NJ, Dec 26, 47. *Educ:* Rutgers Univ, AB, 69; Univ Rochester, MD, 73. *Prof Exp:* Intern med & surg, Strong Mem Hosp, 73-74; resident internal med, 74-77; fel immunol, Sch Med, Stanford Univ, 77-79 & Howard Hughes Med Inst, 79-80. *Mem:* AAAS; Am Fedn Clin Res. *Res:* Human immunology and immune deficiency; experimental transplantation; advanced immune deficiency syndrome. *Mailing Add:* Univ Calif Los Angeles Santa Monica Hosp 4955 Van Nuys Blvd Suite 715 Sherman Oaks CA 91403-1819

GOTTLIEB, MILTON, PHYSICS, OPTICS. *Current Pos:* SR SCIENTIST, CARNEGIE MELLON RES INST, 95- *Personal Data:* b New York, NY, July 2, 33; m 57, Joan Eiger; c Erik & Sara. *Educ:* City Col New York, BS, 54; Univ Pa, MS, 56, PhD(physics), 59. *Prof Exp:* Res assoc physics, Gen Atomic Div, Gen Dynamics Corp, 56-59; consult scientist, Res Labs, Westinghouse Elec Corp, 59-93; sr scientist, Rosemount Anal Inc, 93-95. *Mem:* Optical Soc Am; Am Phys Soc; Int Soc Optical Eng. *Res:* Solid state physics superconductivity; interactions of light with acoustic waves; materials and techniques for optical signal processing, fiber optic sensors; acoustics. *Mailing Add:* 2310 Marbury Rd Pittsburgh PA 15221. *E-Mail:* mg6b@andrew.cmu

GOTTLIEB, OTTO RICHARD, SYSTEMATICS, ECOLOGY. *Current Pos:* RETIRED. *Personal Data:* b Brno, Czech, Aug 31, 20; Brazilian citizen; m 47, Franca Cohen; c Hugo E, Paul C & Marcel B. *Educ:* Univ Brazil Indust Chem, Rio de Janeiro, 45; Univ Fed Rural Rio Jan, Liore Docente, 66, DSc, 66. *Hon Degrees:* Dr, Univ Fed Alagoas, 81, Univ Fed Pariba & Univ Hamburg, 88, Univ Fed Minas Gerais, 92, Univ Fed Rural do Riol de Janeiro, 97. *Honors & Awards:* Feigl Prize Chem, 77; Sci Medal Amazonia, 78; Golden Retort Chem Syndicate, 80; Alvaro Alberto Prize Sci Technol, 90; Chem Award, Third World Acad Sci; Pergamon Phytochem Prize, 92; Nat Order Scientific Merit, 96. *Prof Exp:* Prod chemist, Ornstein & Cia, Brazil, 46-54; from res assoc to res head natural prod chem inst agr chem, Ministry Agr & Nat Res Coun, 55-63; prof org chem & coordr cent inst chem, Univ Brasilia, 64-65; prof org chem, Fed Rural Univ, Rio de Janeiro, 66-73; prof, Univ Sao Paulo, 74-90. *Concurrent Pos:* Res fel org chem, Weizmann Inst Sci, 60; prof & adv grad org chem, Univ Minas Gerais, 62-75; vis prof, Univ Sheffield, 64; prof & coordr grad org chem, Fed Univ Pernambuco, 66-67; vis prof, Univ Sao Paulo, 68-73; coordr phytochem, Nat Res Inst Amazonia, 67-73; vis prof, Inst Oswaldo Cruz, Rio de Janeiro, 91- *Mem:* Brazil Acad Sci; Latin Am Acad Sci; Int Acad Wood Sci. *Res:* Analytical chemistry; gasometric titrations; natural products chemistry; chemistry of Brazilian Lauraceae, Leguminosae, Guttiferae, Myristicaceae and Gnetaceae; micromolecular evolution, systematics and ecology; chemical variability of plants with environmental pressure; medicinal plants; basic principles and methodology for the application of secondary plant metabolites as markers; chemical nomenclature; basic principles and methodology for the application of secondary plant metabolites as systematic markers; replacement-nodal-subtractive nomenclature and codes of chemical compounds; biodiversity via metabolism, morphology, ecogeography, mechanisms of nature; author or co-author of over 46 articles and three books. *Mailing Add:* Rua Cinco de Julho 323 Apt 1001 Rio de Janeiro 22051030 Brazil. *Fax:* 55-21-2571807

GOTTLIEB, PAUL DAVID, IMMUNOLOGY, MOLECULAR BIOLOGY. *Current Pos:* PROF MICROBIOL, UNIV TEX, AUSTIN, 80-, DIR CENT HYBRIDOMA FACIL, 81- *Personal Data:* b New Brunswick, NJ, Dec 4, 43; m 69, Nell Harrell; c Erin. *Educ:* Princeton Univ, BA, 65; Rockefeller Univ, PhD(life sci), 71. *Prof Exp:* Fel immunol, Rockefeller Univ, 71; spec fel biochem, Stanford Univ Sch Med, 71-73; asst prof immunol, Mass Inst Technol, 73-77, assoc prof immunol, 77-80. *Mem:* Sigma Xi; Am Asn Immunol; fel AAAS; NY Acad Sci. *Res:* Function and regulation of expression of mouse CD8 alpha and CD8 beta chains; study of Bop gene and its expression in T lymphocytes and in muscle. *Mailing Add:* 104 W 32nd St Austin TX 78705

GOTTLIEB, PETER, statistics, physics, for more information see previous edition

GOTTLIEB, SHELDON F, PHYSIOLOGY, MICROBIOLOGY. *Current Pos:* dean grad sch & dir res, 80-85, PROF BIOL SCI, UNIV SALA, MOBILE, 85- *Personal Data:* b New York, NY, Dec 22, 32; m 56, Eda J R Held; c Stephen, Pamela, Glenn & William. *Educ:* Brooklyn Col, BA, 53; Univ Mass, MS, 56; Univ Tex, PhD(physiol), 59. *Honors & Awards:* Edgar End Mem Award, Gulf Coast Chap Undersea Hyperbaric Med Soc; Jefferson Davis Award. *Prof Exp:* Res physiologist, Res Labs, Linde Div, Union Carbide Corp, 59-64; asst prof physiol & anesthesiol, Jefferson Med Col, 64-68; assoc prof to prof dept biol sci, Purdue Univ, 68-80. *Concurrent Pos:* Consult, Comt High Oxygen Pressure Equip, Am Soc Anesthesiol, 64 & US Air Force Sch Aviation Med, 75; res dir Baromed Res Inst, New Orleans, La, 84. *Mem:* AAAS; Am Soc Microbiol; Am Physiol Soc; Undersea Hyperbaric Med Soc; Aerospace Med Asn; Am Col Hyperbaric Med. *Res:* Physiological and biochemical effects of gaseous environments on living systems; pharmacology; hyperbaric medicine. *Mailing Add:* 2532 Tahoe Dr Mobile AL 36695. *E-Mail:* sgottlie@jaguar1.usouthal.edu

GOTTLIEB, STEVEN ARTHUR, LATTICE GAUGE THEORY, QUANTUM CHROMODYNAMICS. *Current Pos:* from asst prof to assoc prof, 85-92, PROF, IND UNIV, 92- *Personal Data:* b Brooklyn, NY, Jan 28, 52; m 82, Laura B; c Robert J. *Educ:* Cornell Univ, AB, 73; Princeton Univ, MA, 75, PhD(physics), 78. *Prof Exp:* Appointee, Argonne Nat Lab, 78-80; res assoc, Fermi Nat Lab, 80-82 & Univ Calif, San Diego, 82-85. *Concurrent Pos:* Vis physicist, Brookhaven Nat Lab, 92-93; vis scientist, Mass Inst Technol, 93-95. *Mem:* Am Phys Soc; Sigma Xi. *Res:* Field theory models of the strong interactions; lattice gauge theory; finite temperature quantum chromodynamics; quark-gluon plasma. *Mailing Add:* Dept Physics Ind Univ Bloomington IN 47405. *Fax:* 812-855-5533; *E-Mail:* sg@fuji.physics.indiana.edu

GOTTLING, JAMES GOE, SOLID STATE ELECTRONICS. *Current Pos:* RETIRED. *Personal Data:* b Baltimore, Md, Dec 11, 32; m 56; c 3. *Educ:* Lehigh Univ, BS, 53 & 54; Mass Inst Technol, SM, 56, ScD(elec eng), 60. *Prof Exp:* Res asst elec eng, Mass Inst Technol, 54-56 & 57-60, div sponsored res, 60, asst prof, 60-65; assoc prof, Ohio State Univ, 65-70, prof elec eng, 70-95. *Concurrent Pos:* Ford Found fel, 61-63. *Mem:* Inst Elec & Electronics Engrs. *Res:* Computer analysis of electronic circuits; modeling and analysis of electronic devices. *Mailing Add:* 173 Lake Ave Sunapee NH 03782

GOTTO, ANTONIO MARION, JR, BIOCHEMISTRY, METABOLISM. *Current Pos:* DEAN, MED COL, CORNELL UNIV, 97- *Personal Data:* b Nashville, Tenn, Oct 10, 35; m 59; c 3. *Educ:* Vanderbilt Univ, BA, 57, MD, 65; Oxford Univ, DPhil(biochem), 61. *Hon Degrees:* LLD, Abilene Christian Univ, 79; LHD, Univ Bologna, 82. *Honors & Awards:* Albert Weinstein Award for Proficiency in Internal Med, 65; Serv Award, Am Heart Asn, 75, Outstanding Leadership Award, 80, Gold Heart Award, 89, Distinguished Serv Award, Coun Arteriosclerosis, 92; Matteu-Sandoz Lect, Rutgers Univ, 80; Citation for Distinguished Serv, Am Diabetes Asn, 82; Achievement & Sci Award, Alexander Humboldt Found, 82. *Prof Exp:* Res assoc biochem, Vanderbilt Univ, 61-64, res assoc molecular biol, 64-65; intern, Mass Gen Hosp, 65-66, med resident, 66-67; staff assoc, Nat Heart Inst, 67-69, head, Sect Molecular Struct, Molecular Dis Br, Nat Heart & Lung Inst, 69-71; prof med & biochem & chief, Div Arteriosclerosis & Lipoprotein Res, Baylor Col Med & Methodist Hosp, Houston, 71-96, chmn, Dept Internal Med, 77-96, chief, Internal Med Serv, 77-96, sci dir, Michael E Debalcey Heart Ctr, 85-96. *Concurrent Pos:* Fel, Coun Arteriosclerosis, Am Heart Asn; dir, Specialized Ctr Res Arteriosclerosis & Lipid Res Clin, NIH, Houston; mem, Metab Study Sect, NIH, 72-; sci dir & co-prin investr, Nat Heart & Blood Vessel Res & Demonstration Ctr, 74-96; mem, Nat Diabetes Adv Bd, 77-80, 81-; pres, Int Atherosclerosis Soc, 79-; ed, Atherosclerosis Reviews; co-ed, J Cardiovasc Risk, 93-, Milestones in Med. *Mem:* Inst Med-Nat Acad Sci; Am Col Cardiol; Am Soc Clin Invest (vpres, 81-82); Asn Am Physicians; Asn Prof Med; Am Heart Asn (pres, 83-84); Int Soc Atherosclerosis (pres, 85-). *Res:* Lipid metabolism; structure and function of the plasma lipoproteins; cardiovascular risk factors. *Mailing Add:* Off Dean Med Col Cornell Univ 1300 York Ave Rm F105 New York NY 10021

GOTTSCHALK, ALEXANDER, RADIOLOGY, NUCLEAR MEDICINE. *Current Pos:* PROF RADIOL, MICH STATE UNIV, 92- *Personal Data:* b Chicago, Ill, Mar 23, 32; m 60; c 3. *Educ:* Harvard Univ, BA, 54; Wash Univ, MD, 58. *Honors & Awards:* Gold Medal, Asn Univ Radiologists. *Prof Exp:* Res assoc radiol, Donner Lab, Lawrence Radiation Lab, Univ Calif, Berkeley, 62-64; from asst prof to prof radiol, Univ Chicago Hosps, 64-74, chief, Nuclear Med Sect, 64-74; dir nuclear med, Sch Med, Yale Univ, 74-77, prof diag radiol, 74-77, vchmn diag radiol, 77-90. *Concurrent Pos:* Fac res assoc, Am Cancer Soc, 65-; dir, Argonne Cancer Res Hosp, 67-74. *Mem:* Fel Am Col Radiol; Radiol Soc NAm; Asn Univ Radiol (secy-treas, 68-69, pres elect, 69-70, pres, 70-71); Soc Nuclear Med (pres, 74-75), Am Roentgen Ray Soc; fel Am Col Clin Physicians. *Res:* Isotope development and clinical applications; instrumentation in nuclear medicine; image processing; diagnosis pulmonary embolism. *Mailing Add:* Dept Radiol B-220 Clinical Ctr Mich State Univ East Lansing MI 48824

GOTTSCHALK, BERNARD, MEDICAL PHYSICS, ACCELERATOR PHYSICS. *Current Pos:* SR RES FEL, HARVARD UNIV, 81- *Personal Data:* b Frankfurt, Ger, Jan 6, 35; US citizen; m 62; c 3. *Educ:* Rensselaer Polytech Inst, BS, 55; Harvard Univ, AM, 57, PhD, 62. *Prof Exp:* Res fel physics, Harvard Univ, 62-65; from asst prof to assoc prof physics, Northeastern Univ, 65-73, prof, 73-81. *Concurrent Pos:* Vis scientist, Stanford Linear Accelerator Ctr, 71-72, Max Planck Inst, Munich, 74-75 & Stanford Linear Accelerator Ctr, 79-81. *Mem:* Am Phys Soc. *Res:* Medium-energy nuclear physics; experimental high energy physics; particle accelerator design. *Mailing Add:* Harvard Cyclotron Lab 44 Oxford St Cambridge MA 02138

GOTTSCHALK, CARL WILLIAM, PHYSIOLOGY, NEPHROLOGY. *Current Pos:* from instr to prof med, Univ NC Chapel Hill. 53-61, from assoc prof to prof physiol, 59-61, Kenan prof med & physiol, 69-92, actg chair, Dept Physiol, 90-92, DISTINGUISHED RES PROF MED & PHYSIOL, UNIV NC CHAPEL HILL, 92- *Personal Data:* b Salem, Va, Apr 28, 22; wid; c Carl S, Walter P & Karen E. *Educ:* Roanoke Col, BS, 42; Univ Va, MD, 45. *Hon Degrees:* DSc, Roanoke Col, 66; Dr, Univ Mons-Hainaut, Belgium, 92. *Honors & Awards:* Horsley Mem Prize, Univ Va, 56; NC Award, 67; Homer W Smith Award, NY Heart Asn, 70; David M Hume Award, Nat Kidney Found, 76; O Max Gardner Award, Univ NC, 78; Hon Mem, Hungarian Physiol Soc, 88; A N Richards Award, Int Soc Nephrology, 90; Robert W Berliner Award, Am Physiol Soc, 93. *Prof Exp:* Intern med, Mass Gen Hosp, 45-46, asst resident & resident med, 50-52. *Concurrent Pos:* Res fel physiol, Harvard Med Sch, 48-50; fel cardiol, NC Mem Hosp, Univ NC, Chapel Hill, 52-53; consult to Surgeon Gen, 51; estab investr, Am Heart Asn, 57-61, career investr, 61-92; mem, Physiol Study Sect, NIH, 61-65; Harvey lectr, 62; mem, Res Career Awards Comt, 65-69, Physiol Training Comt, 69-73, Nat Adv Coun, Nat Inst Gen Med Sci, 77-81 & Nat Inst Arthritis, Diabetes, Digestive & Kidney Dis, 82-86, Physiol Test Comt, Nat Bd Med Exam, 66-70; biol & med sci adv comt, NSF, 67-69, vchmn, 68 & chmn, 69; Burroughs-Wellcome Fund Adv Comt Clin Pharmacol, 80-93. *Mem:* Nat Acad Sci; Inst Med; Am Soc Nephrology (pres, 75-76); Am Soc Clin Invest; Am Clin & Climat Asn; Am Acad Arts & Sci; Asn Am Physicians. *Res:* Renal physiology, utilizing micropuncture techniques. *Mailing Add:* Dept Med CB No 7155 Univ NC Sch Med Chapel Hill NC 27599-7155. *Fax:* 919-966-6927

GOTTSCHALK, CHARLES M, INTERNATIONAL RELATIONS. *Current Pos:* CONSULT EXPERT, CMG INT ENERGY CONSULTANCY, PARIS & WASHINGTON, 94- *Personal Data:* b Bochum, Ger, Feb 2, 28; nat US; m 48, Marianne Ida Besser; c Diane L & Leslie A. *Educ:* Cleveland State Univ, BS, 50; Pa State Univ, MA, 51; Cath Univ, MLS, 66. *Prof Exp:* Res analyst, Libr Cong, 51-54, phys sci adminr, head, Ref Sect, Sci & Technol Div, 56-62, chief, Stock & Reader Div, 62, head, Systs Identification & Anal Sect, 62-63; instrumentation physicist, Nat Bur Stand, 54-56; info systs specialist, Atomic Energy Comn, 63-66, dir libr, 66-69; sr officer, Int Atomic Energy Agency, Austria, 69-73, Energy Res & Develop Admin, Wash, 73-77, Dept Energy, 77-79; sr officer, UNESCO, Paris, 79-88, consult expert, 88-94. *Concurrent Pos:* Consult, Arctic Inst NAm, 54-59; NSF grantee, 61-62; lectr, Dept Agr Grad Sch, 64-66; exec secy, Opers Comt, Fed Coun Sci & Technol Comt Sci & Technol Info, 65, Panel Educ & Teaching, 65-66, mem, Panel Info Sci & Technol, 66-68; liaison officer/registr, Int Technol Univ, London & Paris, 89-93; liaison officer, World Fedn Eng Opers, London & Paris, 95- *Mem:* World Energy Coun. *Mailing Add:* 9619 Bexhill Dr Kensington MD 20895

GOTTSCHALK, JOHN SIMISON, CONSERVATION. *Current Pos:* RETIRED. *Personal Data:* b Berne, Ind, Sept 27, 12; m 37; c 2. *Educ:* Earlham Col, AB, 34; Ind Univ, MA, 43; Earlham Col, LLD, 66. *Honors & Awards:* Seth Gordon Award, Int Asn Game Fish & Conserv Comnrs, 75; Leopold Award, Wildlife Soc, 76. *Prof Exp:* Naturalist, Ind State Dept Conserv, 34-38, supt fisheries, 38-41; sr bacteriologist, Schenley Labs, 44-45; aquatic biologist, US Fish & Wildlife Serv, 45-51, asst chief br fed aid, 51-57, chief div sport fisheries, 58-59, regional dir, 59-64, dir, Bur Sport Fisheries & Wildlife, 64-70, asst to dir, Nat Marine Fisheries Serv, 70-73; exec vpres, Int Asn Game, Fish & Conserv Comnrs, 73-78, coun, 78-81. *Mem:* Wildlife Soc (vpres, 55); Am Fisheries Soc (vpres, 41, 63, pres, 64). *Res:* Limnology; fish population dynamics; wildlife management. *Mailing Add:* 900 N Taylor St No 1117 Arlington VA 22203-1158

GOTTSCHALK, LOUIS AUGUST, PSYCHIATRY, NEUROLOGY. *Current Pos:* chmn, Dept Psychiat & Human Behav, Col Med, Univ Calif, 67-77, dir clin psychiat, Irvine Med Ctr, 71-77, dir, Psychiat Consult & Liaison Div, Irvine Med Ctr, Orange, 77-86, PROF PSYCHIAT & HUMAN BEHAV, COL MED, UNIV CALIF, IRVINE, 67- *Personal Data:* b St Louis, Mo, Aug 26, 16; m 44, Helen Reller; c Guy H, Claire (Weaver), Louise (Clickner) & Susan (Smith). *Educ:* Wash Univ, AB, 40, MD, 43; S Calif Psychoanal Inst, PhD, 77. *Honors & Awards:* Hofheimer Award, Am Psychiat Asn, 55; Franz Alexander Essay Prize, Southern Calif Psychoanal Inst, 73; Found Fund Prize Res Psychiat, Am Psychiat Asn, 78; Ripley lectr, Univ Wash, Seattle, 81; Daniel Aldrich Distinguished Serv Award, 92. *Prof Exp:* Asst neuropsychiat, Sch Med, Wash Univ, 44-46; clin psychiatrist, chmn & dir EEG lab, USPHS Hosp, Fort Worth, Tex, 46-48; res assoc & instr EEG & clin neurophysiol, Inst Psychosom & Psychiat Res, Michael Reese Hosp, Chicago, Ill, 48-51; res psychiatrist, NIMH, 51-53; from assoc prof to res prof psychiat & coordr res, Med Col, Univ Cincinnati, 53-67. *Concurrent Pos:* Asst chief child psychiat clin, Michael Reese Hosp, 50-51; attend physician clin psychiat, Cent Psychiat Clin, Cincinnati Gen Hosp, 53-67; supv & training analyst, Chicago Inst Psychoanal, 57-67 & Southern Calif Psychoanal Inst & Soc, 74-; NIMH USPHS res career award, 61-67; mem clin psychopharmacol res rev comt, NIMH, 68-71; mem res adv comt, Calif State Dept Ment Hyg, 68-71 & 84-; physician consult, Fairview State Hosp, Costa Mesa, Calif, 68-76; consult psychiat, Vet Admin Hosp, Long Beach, Calif, 68-; consult res, Metrop State Hosp, Norwalk, Calif, 70-77; prin investr, Nat Inst Drug Abuse, 72-77, chmn psychosocial panel & mem extramural res rev comt, 73-74; sci co-dir, Alcohol Res Ctr, Nat Inst Alcohol Abuse & Alcoholism, 78-84; res scholar, Rockefeller Study & Conf Ctr, Bellagio, Italy, 85. *Mem:* AAAS; Am Psychosom Soc; fel Am Col Neuropsychopharmacol; Am Psychoanal Asn; life fel Am Psychiat Asn; Nat Acad Med Pract. *Res:* Improving the quality of measurement in psychiatry and the medical sciences; from the form and content of verbal behavior, developing a method of objective assessment of psychological states and traits, validated independently by clinical, physiological and biochemical data, including the effects of psychopharmacological agents; development of artificial intelligence software to computerize the content analysis of natural language; neuropsychopharmacology. *Mailing Add:* Dept Psychiat & Human Behav Univ Calif Irvine CA 92697. *Fax:* 714-824-7012; *E-Mail:* lgottsch@uci.edu

GOTTSCHALK, ROBERT NEAL, PROJECT MANAGEMENT, MANUFACTURING MANAGEMENT. *Current Pos:* CERT ASBESTOS INSPECTOR & MGMT PLANNER, AHERA INSPECTIONS, 88- *Personal Data:* b Milwaukee, Wis, Apr 24, 28; m 52, Phyllis Moe; c Laurie (Rhude), Linda (Matthews), Jill & Rob T. *Educ:* Univ Wis, BSChE, 52. *Prof Exp:* Pilot plant engr, Chem Prod Div, Ansul Co, 53-60, sr proj engr, 60-65, eng mgr, 65-69, mgr chem mfg eng, 69-70, mgr chem environ eng, 70-74, int proj mgr, 74-75, mfg mgr, 76-77, sr proj mgr, 78-79; gen mgr, Wormald US Inc, 79-82, facil mgr, 83-87. *Concurrent Pos:* Mgr design, construct & start-up of herbicide plants, Malaysia, 68-70, 74-75 & 91. *Res:* Design, development and production; process for nitrogen heterocyclics; glycol ethers; organic arsenic compounds; plant start-ups. *Mailing Add:* 628 Carney Blvd Marinette WI 54143

GOTTSCHALK, WALTER HELBIG, MATHEMATICS, TOPOLOGICAL DYNAMICS. *Current Pos:* prof, 63-82, chmn dept, 64-69 & 70-71, EMER PROF MATH, WESLEYAN UNIV, 82- *Personal Data:* b Lynchburg, Va, Nov 3, 18; m 52, Margaret Hemsworth; c Heather & Steven. *Educ:* Univ Va, BS, 39, MA, 42, PhD(math), 44. *Hon Degrees:* MA, Wesleyan Univ, 64. *Prof Exp:* From instr to prof math, Univ Pa, 44-63, chmn dept, 55-58. *Concurrent Pos:* Mem, Inst Advan Study, Princeton, 47-48; res assoc, Yale Univ, 60-61. *Mem:* Am Math Soc; Math Asn Am; Indust & Appl Math; Sigma Xi. *Res:* Topological dynamics. *Mailing Add:* 500 Angell St Apt 414 Providence RI 02906-4455

GOTTSCHALL, ROBERT JAMES, RESEARCH & SCIENCE ADMINISTRATION, MATERIALS, METAL & CERAMIC SCIENCES. *Current Pos:* ceramist, Div Mat Sci, US Dept Energy, 77-88, br chief, Metall & Ceramics Br, 88-93, actg dir, Div Mat Sci, 93-95, TEAM LEADER METAL & CERAMIC SCI, US DEPT ENERGY, 95- *Personal Data:* b Mt Vernon, NY, Apr 28, 35; m 96, Yukiko Tani; c 1. *Educ:* Rensselaer Polytech Inst, BS, 57; Polytech Inst Brooklyn, MS, 62; Columbia Univ, PhD(mat sci), 75. *Prof Exp:* Metallurgist, Lycoming Div, Avco Corp, 57-59, Nuclear Develop Corp, 59-60; staff scientist, T J Watson Res Ctr, IBM, 60-61, Philips

Labs, 62-65; res assoc, Univ Ill, 75-77. *Mem:* Fel Am Ceramic Soc; Nat Inst Ceramic Engrs; Am Inst Mining, Metall & Petrol Engrs Metall Soc; Am Phys Soc; Mat Res Soc; AAAS. *Res:* Superconductors; electron beam microcharacterization; surface and interface behavior; corrosion; powder metallurgy and ceramics; coating processes; thin films; metallic glasses; semiconductors; Metal and ceramic sciences; creep, fatigue; fracture mechanics; internal friction; metal and ceramic sciences. *Mailing Add:* 19901 Germantown Rd Germantown MD 20874-1290. *Fax:* 301-903-9513

GOTTSCHALL, W CARL, RADIATION CHEMISTRY, HEALTH & SAFETY. *Current Pos:* CHEMIST, EG&G, RFP, 91- *Personal Data:* b Pittsburgh, Pa, Nov 15, 38; m 62, Eileen A Moore; c 3. *Educ:* Calif Inst Technol, BS, 60; Univ Colo, PhD(inorg chem), 64. *Prof Exp:* Res assoc radiation chem, Argonne Nat Lab, 64-66; from asst prof to prof chem, Univ Denver, 66-86; training coordr pub serv, Colo, 86-91. *Concurrent Pos:* Vis scholar, Linus Pauling Inst Sci & Med, 74; fel, Princeton Univ, Nuclear Regulatory Comn, 83-85; chmn chem safety comt, Nat Am Chem Soc. *Mem:* Am Chem Soc; Radiation Res Soc; Sigma Xi. *Res:* Radiation chemistry of chelates and salts; radiation damage and protection in biochemical compounds and in vivo; chemical health safety. *Mailing Add:* 17 Bradbury Lane Littleton CO 80120-4162

GOTTSCHANG, JACK LOUIS, MAMMALOGY, HERPETOLOGY. *Current Pos:* from asst prof to assoc prof, 50-70, head, Dept Biol Sci, 75-83, PROF ZOOL, UNIV CINCINNATI, 70- *Personal Data:* b Woodland, Calif, Feb 16, 23; m 42; c 4. *Educ:* San Jose State Col, BA, 47; Cornell Univ, PhD(zool), 50. *Prof Exp:* Asst zool, Cornell Univ, 47-50. *Mem:* AAAS; Am Soc Mammal; Am Soc Zool. *Res:* Taxonomy; ecology; life history studies; small mammals. *Mailing Add:* 3636 Middleton Ave Cincinnati OH 45220

GOTTSCHLICH, CHAD F, CHEMICAL ENGINEERING. *Current Pos:* RETIRED. *Personal Data:* b Laura, Ohio, Feb 26, 29; m 50; c 4. *Educ:* Univ Cincinnati, ChE, 51, Phd(chem eng), 61; Princeton Univ, MSE, 53. *Prof Exp:* Engr petrol refining, Stand Oil Co, Ohio, 52-54; instr chem eng, Univ Cincinnati, 54-60; res assoc mech eng, Northwestern Univ, 60-61, asst prof, 61-63; asst prof, Univ Pa, 63-66; sect mgr res, Selas Corp Am, 66-81, dir res, 81- *Mem:* Am Inst Chem Engrs; Am Chem Soc. *Res:* Measurements of the properties of high temperature gases; industrial heating. *Mailing Add:* 4616 Hazel Ave Philadelphia PA 19143-2104

GOTTSCHLING, DANIEL E, MOLECULAR BIOLOGY. *Current Pos:* RES BIOLOGIST, UNIV CHICAGO. *Honors & Awards:* Molecular Biol Award, Nat Acad Sci, 95. *Mailing Add:* Dept Molecular Genetics Univ Chicago 920 E 58th St Chicago IL 60637-1432

GOTTSCHO, ALFRED M(ORTON), TOBACCO SCIENCE, SHEET MANUFACTURING. *Current Pos:* RETIRED. *Personal Data:* b Brooklyn, NY, Apr 29, 19; m 41; c 3. *Educ:* City Col New York, BChE, 40; Franklin & Marshall Col, MS, 54. *Honors & Awards:* Res Award Cigar Res Coun, 73. *Prof Exp:* Tech serv engr rubber & plastic printing plates, Mosstype Corp, NJ, 40-41; engr fuel consumption study, US Corps Engrs, 41-42; prod supvr explosives, Plumbrook Ord Works, Ohio, 42-44; chem engr tobacco processing, Res Lab, Gen Cigar Co, Div of Culbro Corp, 46-57, asst dir develop, 57-68, dir res & develop & asst vpres, 68-75, vpres, 75-86; vpres, Helme Tobacco Co, Div Am Maize-Prods Co, 86-89. *Mem:* AAAS; Am Chem Soc; Am Inst Chem Engrs; Soc Chem Indust. *Res:* Alkaloids of tobacco and their changes during industrial processing; changes in nitrogenous constituents in cigar tobaccos; development of tobacco sheets and smokeless tobacco products; tobacco fermentation. *Mailing Add:* 223 Suncrest Rd Lancaster PA 17601-4800

GOTTSCHO, RICHARD ALAN, PLASMA PROCESSING, DISPLAY TECHNOLOGY. *Current Pos:* dir res, DIR PLASMA, CHEMICAL VAPOR DEPOSITION, LAM RESEARCH, 96- *Personal Data:* b Lancaster, Pa, May 19, 52. *Educ:* Pa State Univ, BS, 74; Mass Inst Technol, PhD(phys chem), 79. *Honors & Awards:* Peter Mark Mem Award, Am Vacuum Soc; Tegal Thinker Award. *Prof Exp:* Chaim S Weizmann fel, Dept Physics, Mass Inst Technol, 79-80; mem tech staff, AT&T Bell Labs, 80-88, head, electronics packaging res, 88-93, head, Display Res Dept, 93-96. *Concurrent Pos:* Co-chair, Comt Plasma Sci, Nat Res Coun, 94-95. *Mem:* Fel Am Phys Soc; Am Vacuum Soc; Sigma Xi; Mat Res Soc; Soc Info Display. *Res:* Plasma chemistry; mechanisms for plasma etching; deposition in microelectronic fabrication; display technology. *Mailing Add:* 4990 Lapis Lane Pleasanton CA 94566

GOTTSEGEN, ROBERT, DENTISTRY. *Current Pos:* From asst clin prof to assoc clin prof dent, Columbia Univ 49-69, prof dent, chmn dept periodont & postdoctoral periodont, 69-89, EMER PROF DENT, COLUMBIA UNIV, 89- *Personal Data:* b New York, NY, June 21, 19; m 52; c 3. *Educ:* Univ Mich, AB, 39; Columbia Univ, DDS, 43, cert, 47. *Honors & Awards:* Isadore Hirschfeld Medal, NE Soc Periodontists, 84; Gold Medal, Am Acad Periodont, 88. *Concurrent Pos:* USPHS res fel, NIH, 48-50; attend dent, Presby Hosp. *Mem:* AAAS; hon fel Am Acad Periodont (pres, 70-71); Int Asn Dent Res; fel Am Col Dent. *Res:* Metabolic influences on periodontal diseases; diabetes and periodontal diseases. *Mailing Add:* Sch Dent & Oral Surg Columbia Univ 630 W 168th St New York NY 10032

GOTTSTEIN, WILLIAM J, PHARMACEUTICAL CHEMISTRY. *Current Pos:* SR RES SCIENTIST, LE MOYNE COL, SYRACUSE, NY, 86- *Personal Data:* b Syracuse, NY, July 15, 29; m 55, Mary J Lisson; c Thomas, Robert & Barbara. *Educ:* Le Moyne Col, NY, BS, 51. *Hon Degrees:* LHD, LeMoyne Col, 92. *Prof Exp:* Sr res scientist, Bristol-Myers Inc, Syracuse, 52-86. *Mem:* Am Chem Soc. *Res:* Chemical alteration of natural products; beta-lactam and quinolines. *Mailing Add:* 116 Woodmancy Lane Fayetteville NY 13066. *E-Mail:* gottstwj@maple.lemoyne.com

GOTTWALD, JIMMY THORNE, ACOUSTICS. *Current Pos:* RETIRED. *Personal Data:* b San Antonio, Tex, May 29, 38; m 60; c 3. *Educ:* Baylor Univ, BS, 61, MS, 62. *Prof Exp:* Asst prof physics, Southwestern Univ, 62-65; engr scientist, Tracor Inc, 65-72, dept dir ocean sci, 73-86. *Mem:* Am Inst Physics; Acoust Soc Am. *Res:* Underwater acoustic propagation, background noise and signal coherence; underwater sound generation by optical means. *Mailing Add:* 3600 River Rd W Goochland VA 23063

GOTTWALD, TIMOTHY R, MYCOLOGY, EPIPHYTOLOGY, TREE PATHOLOGY. *Current Pos:* PLANT PATHOLOGIST, AGR RES SERV, US DEPT AGR, 79- *Personal Data:* b Lynnwood, Calif, Feb 14, 53; m 79. *Educ:* Long Beach State Univ, BS, 75; Ore State Univ, PhD(plant path), 80. *Prof Exp:* Res asst plant path, Dept Bot & Plant Path, Ore State Univ, 75-79, res assoc dis diag, 79. *Mem:* Am Phytopath Soc; Mycological Soc Am; Int Orgn Citrus Virologists. *Res:* Diseases of pecan especially those caused by fungi; basic biology of host-parasite interaction; epiphytology of disease, especially spore release and dispersal; mycology and physiology. *Mailing Add:* 3913 Bibb La Orlando FL 32817

GOTWALD, WILLIAM HARRISON, JR, SYSTEMATIC ENTOMOLOGY. *Current Pos:* from asst prof to assoc prof, 68-78, PROF BIOL, UTICA COL, SYRACUSE UNIV, 78- *Personal Data:* b Trenton, NJ, May 6, 39; div; c Kymry & Glynis. *Educ:* Millersville State Col, BS, 61; Pa State Univ, MS, 64; Cornell Univ, PhD(entom), 68. *Prof Exp:* Instr zool, Pa State Univ, Altoona, 63-65. *Concurrent Pos:* NSF grants, 70-73, 73-76, 76-79, 79-81, 82-84 & 84-86; consult, sex & aging; vis prof biol, Xiamen Univ, Xiamen, China, 89 & 91. *Mem:* Int Union Study Social Insects; Am Asn Univ Profs. *Res:* Phylogeny and systematics of the ants, especially the morphology and behavior of tropical ants commonly known as army ants (aenictinae, dorylinae and ecitoninae). *Mailing Add:* Dept Biol Utica Col Burrstone Rd Utica NY 13502. *E-Mail:* wgotwald@utica.ucsu.edu

GOUBAU, WOLFGANG M, PLASMA PROCESSING, PROCESS CONTROL & STATISTICS. *Current Pos:* PROCESS ENGR MAGNETIC RECORDING, IBM SAN JOSE, 86- *Personal Data:* b Jena, EGer, Oct 17, 44; US citizen. *Educ:* Rutgers Univ, AB, 66. *Prof Exp:* Teaching asst physics, Cornell Univ, 66-68, res asst solid state physics, 68-74; IBM fel physics, Univ Calif, Berkeley, 74-76; staff physicist geophys, Earth Sci Div, Lawrence Berkeley Lab, 76-83; res staff mem packaging technol, Yorktown, NY, 83-86,. *Mem:* Am Phys Soc. *Res:* Thermaland acoustic properties of solids with pulsed phonons; design of the first thin film direct current superconducting quantum interference device (SQUID) with Nb-oxide-PB tunnel junctions; superconducting quantum interference device magnetometers and gradiometers for geophysics; magnetotelurics removal of bias and error analysis; packaging technology for computer circuits. *Mailing Add:* 315/015 IBM Adstar 5600 Cottle Rd San Jose CA 95193

GOUD, PAUL A, TELECOMMUNICATIONS. *Current Pos:* from asst prof to assoc prof, 66-72, PROF ELEC ENG, UNIV ALTA, 72- *Personal Data:* b The Hague, Neth, Sept 2, 37; Can citizen; m 61, Miriam H Haahti; c Daphne L, Paul A & Corneil J. *Educ:* Univ Alta, BSc, 59; Univ BC, MASc, 61, PhD(elec eng), 64. *Prof Exp:* Mem sci staff, Res & Develop Labs, Bell Northern Res, Ont, 65-66. *Concurrent Pos:* Natural Sci & Eng Res Coun Can res grants, 66-; vis mem tech staff, Bell Labs, 69; vis mem sci staff, Philips Res Labs, 73-74; CIDA expert, Brazil, 76-77; adj prof, Telecommun Res Labs, Edmonton, 86-, assoc dean, 89-91; sr indust fel, Nat Sci & Eng Res Coun Can, 87-88. *Mem:* Sr mem Inst Elec & Electronics Engrs; Am Soc Eng Educ. *Res:* Wireless communications-coded modulation; adaptive equalisation; amplifier distortion reduction; distributed systematic program implementation; computer-aided system simulation. *Mailing Add:* Dept Elec Eng Univ Alta Edmonton AB T6G 2G7 Can. *Fax:* 403-492-1811; *E-Mail:* goud@eigen.ee.ualberta.ca

GOUDARZI, GUS (HOSSEIN), mining & geological engineering; deceased, see previous edition for last biography

GOUDSMIT, ESTHER MARIANNE, MOLLUSCAN NEUROENDOCRINOLOGY, BIOCHEMISTRY. *Current Pos:* from asst to prof, 72-95, EMER PROF BIOL, OAKLAND UNIV, ROCHESTER, MICH, 95- *Personal Data:* b Ann Arbor, Mich, July 29, 33. *Educ:* Univ Mich, Ann Arbor, BA, 55, MS, 59, PhD(zool), 64. *Prof Exp:* Res asst marine ecol, Woods Hole Oceanog Inst, 59; USPHS trainee, Univ London, 60-61; USPHS fel biochem, Nat Inst Arthritis & Metab Dis, Bethesda, MD, 64-66; res assoc pathobiol, Sch Pub Health, Johns Hopkins Univ, 67-69; asst prof biol, Brooklyn Col, 69-72. *Concurrent Pos:* NIH res grant, 75-80, NSF res grant, 87-93. *Mem:* Soc Develop Biol; Soc Cell Biologists. *Res:* Carbohydrate metabolism in snails; neurohormonal regulation of galactogen and glycogen synthesis. *Mailing Add:* Dept Biol Oakland Univ Rochester MI 48309-4401

GOUGE, EDWARD MAX, INORGANIC CHEMISTRY. *Current Pos:* From asst prof to assoc prof, 76-88, PROF CHEM, PRESBY COL, 89- *Personal Data:* b Marion, NC, Aug 30, 47; m 70, Diane Burnette; c Jennifer D. *Educ:* Western Carolina Univ, 69; Clemson Univ, PhD(inorg chem), 76. *Mem:* Am Chem Soc. *Res:* Coordination chemistry-preparation, characterization and properties of polydentate ligands and their coordination compounds. *Mailing Add:* Dept Chem Presby Col Clinton SC 29325-2998

GOUGE, SUSAN CORNELIA JONES, MEDICAL MICROBIOLOGY, PUBLIC HEALTH. *Current Pos:* MICROBIOLOGIST, DIV OPHTHAL DEVICES, OFF DEVICE EVAL, FOOD & DRUG ADMIN, 79- *Personal Data:* b Chicago, Ill, Apr 18, 24; m 43, John O; c John R, Richard M (deceased) & Claudia R (Carr). *Educ:* George Washington Univ, BS, 48; Norwich Univ, MA, 84. *Prof Exp:* Med technician, Children's Hosp, Washington, DC, 48-49; bacteriologist, George Washington Univ Res Lab, DC Gen Hosp, 50-53; med microbiologist, Walter Reed Army Inst Res, 53-61, res asst, 61-62; microbiologist, Antibiotics Div, HEW, Food & Drug Admin, 62-63; supvr qual control, John D Copanos Co, Baltimore, Md, 63-64; res teaching asst, Howard Univ, Med Sch, 64-65; res assoc & chief technologist, Georgetown Univ Lab Infectious Dis, DC Gen Hosp, 66-69; mycologist, Georgetown Univ Hosp, 69-70; microbiologist, Res Found, Wash Hosp, Ctr, 71-73, dir qual control, Bio-Medium Corp, 73-76; staff microbiologist, Alcolac Inc, Baltimore, Md, 76-77; microbiologist, div labs, Dept Human Resources, Community Health & Hosps Admin, Washington, DC, 78-79. *Concurrent Pos:* Tech consult, Volunteers Int Tech Asst Proj, 70-71 & Wesley-Jessen Inc, 74; Zacchaeus Free Clin, 79-84. *Mem:* Am Soc Microbiol; AAAS; Am Chem Soc; Am Pub Health Asn; NY Acad Sci; Sigma Xi. *Res:* Antibiotic sensitivity; reversal of resistance; methodology for antibiotic assays; rapid diagnostic methods; microbial ecology; sterilization and disinfection of contact lenses. *Mailing Add:* 724 Old Baltimore Rd Winchester VA 22603

GOUGEON, REJEANNE, DIABETES, PROTEIN METABOLISM. *Current Pos:* fac lectr, MacDonald Col, 84-86, ASST PROF NUTRIT, MCGILL UNIV, 86- *Personal Data:* b Montreal, Que, Oct 6, 43; div; c Stefan, Katya, Michael & Erika. *Educ:* Univ Laval, Que, BSc, 63; Columbia Univ, NY, MSc, 67; Univ Montreal, Can, PhD(exp med), 79. *Prof Exp:* Dietitian, Douglas Hosp Verdun, Que, 64-66; instr nutrit, Marianopolis Col, 67-68, Univ BC, 68-71; fac lectr nutrit, Univ Montreal, 74-78, asst prof, 79-81. *Concurrent Pos:* Med scientist, Dept Med, Royal Victoria Hosp, 88-, group leader behav modification, 84-; assoc mem, Sch Dietetics & Human Nutrit, MacDonald Col, McGill Univ. *Mem:* Am Inst Nutrit; Am Soc Clin Nutrit; Can Soc Nutrit Sci; Can Diabetes Found; Can Asn Advan Sci; Am Diabetes Asn; Nat Asn Acad Sci. *Res:* Studies of the kinetics of protein metabolism using 15N-glycine in obese subjects with or without type 2 diabetes in settings of uncontrolled diabetes with hyperglycemia and of normoglycemia with insulin therapy, with oral hypoglycemic agents and with energy restricted diets; studies of effect of diabetes control on thermogenesis; studies of norepinephrine turnover during starvation. *Mailing Add:* McGill Nutrit & Food Sci Ctr Royal Victoria Hosp 687 Pine Ave W Montreal PQ H3A 1A1 Can. *Fax:* 514-982-0893; *E-Mail:* rgougeon@ruhmed.lan.mcgill.ca

GOUGH, DAVID ARTHUR, BIOMEDICAL ENGINEERING, PHYSIOLOGY. *Current Pos:* vchair, Dept Appl Mech & Eng Sci, 89-93, PROF BIOENG, UNIV CALIF, SAN DIEGO, 76-; NIH STUDY SECT, 89-; SCI REV BD, JUV DIABETES FOUND, 93- *Personal Data:* b Salt Lake City, Utah, Aug 16, 46; m 70, Carol; c Monica, Andrea, Daniel & James. *Educ:* Univ Utah, BS, 70, BA, 71, PhD(mat sci, eng), 74. *Prof Exp:* Res asst mat sci & eng, Univ Utah, 71-74; res assoc med, Harvard Med Sch, 74-76. *Concurrent Pos:* Res assoc, E P Joslin Res Lab, Joslin Diabetes Found, Inc, Boston, 74-76; assoc, Peter Bent Brigham Hosp, Boston; NIH fel, Harvard Med Sch, 74-76. *Mem:* AAAS; Am Soc Artificial Internal Organs; Juv Diabetes Found; Biomed Eng Soc. *Res:* Biochemical specific sensors; mass transfer in physiologic systems; correction of metabolic disturbances in diabetes; artificial internal organs; biomaterials; immobilized catalysts. *Mailing Add:* Dept Bioeng Univ Calif San Diego La Jolla CA 92093-0412

GOUGH, DENIS IAN, GEOPHYSICS. *Current Pos:* dir, Inst Earth & Planetary Physics, 75-80, PROF PHYSICS, UNIV ALTA, 66- *Personal Data:* b Port Elizabeth, SAfrica, June 20, 22; m 45; c 2. *Educ:* Rhodes Univ Col, SAfrica, BSc, 43, MSc, 47; Univ Witwatersrand, PhD(geophys), 53. *Prof Exp:* Res officer geophys, SAfrican Nat Phys Res Lab, 47-55; sr res officer, 55-58; lectr physics, Univ Col Rhodesia & Nyasaland, 58-60, sr lectr, 61-63; assoc prof geophys, Southwest Ctr for Advan Studies, Dallas, 64-66. *Concurrent Pos:* Mem, Nat Comt Geod & Geophys, Cent African Fedn, 60-63; mem subcomt gravity, adv comt geophys & geod, Nat Res Coun Can, 67-, mem subcomt geomag & aeronomy, 67-; mem, Can Nat Comt Develop & Evolution Lithosphere. *Mem:* Am Geophys Union; fel Royal Soc Can; fel Royal Astron Soc; fel Geol Asn Can; chmn Int Asn Geomagnetism. *Res:* Studies of crustal structure through gravity and magnetic anomalies; studies of paleomagnetism, especially in relation to continental drift; study of crustal structure and upper mantle temperature distribution through electromagnetic induction; study of induced earthquakes and of stress in the lithosphere. *Mailing Add:* Dept Physics Univ Alta Edmonton AB T6G 2J1 Can. *Fax:* 403-492-4256

GOUGH, FRANCIS JACOB, PLANT PATHOLOGY. *Current Pos:* RETIRED. *Personal Data:* b Grafton, WVa, Apr 9, 28; m 50; c 2. *Educ:* Univ WVa, BS, 52, MS, 54, PhD(plant path), 57. *Prof Exp:* Asst plant path, Univ WVa, 52-57; plant pathologist cereal rusts, USDA, NDak State Univ, 57-67; res plant pathologist, USDA, Tex A&M Univ, 67-74; res plant pathologist, USDA, Okla State Univ, 74-92. *Concurrent Pos:* Dir, Plant Sci & Water Conserv Lab, USDA-Agr Res Serv. *Mem:* Am Phytopath Soc; Sigma Xi; Int Phytopath Soc; NY Acad Sci. *Res:* Genetics of host-parasite relationships. *Mailing Add:* 764 Willow Springs Rd Wetumpka AL 36093

GOUGH, LARRY PHILLIPS, PLANT ECOLOGY, BIOGEOCHEMISTRY. *Current Pos:* botanist, 74-87, SUPVRY BOTANIST, US GEOL SURV, 87- *Personal Data:* b New Castle, Ind, Dec 28, 44; c 2. *Educ:* Carroll Col, BS, 67; Univ Louisville, MS, 68; Univ Colo, PhD(bot), 73. *Prof Exp:* Asst prof biol, Oakland City Col, 73-74. *Concurrent Pos:* Assoc ed, Reclamation & Revegetation Res. *Mem:* Am Bryological & Lichenological Soc; Am Soc Agron; Sigma Xi. *Res:* Geochemical survey of the Western coal regions; impact of industrial emissions on the element content of plants and soils; availability measures and soil-plant element transfer processes. *Mailing Add:* 7224 Terry St Arvada CO 80403

GOUGH, LILLIAN, MATHEMATICS. *Current Pos:* from assoc prof to prof, 55-83, chmn dept, 56-80, EMER PROF MATH, UNIV WIS-RIVER FALLS, 83- *Personal Data:* b Detroit, Mich, May 15, 18. *Educ:* Univ Buffalo, BA, 39, MA, 49, PhD(math), 53. *Prof Exp:* Instr math, Univ Buffalo, 46-53; asst prof, Oswego State Teachers Col, 53-55. *Mem:* Math Asn Am; Nat Coun Teachers Math. *Res:* Topology. *Mailing Add:* 1105 Wasson Circle River Falls WI 54022-2542

GOUGH, MICHAEL, SCIENCE POLICY. *Current Pos:* DIR SCI & RISK STUDIES, CATO INST, WASHINGTON, DC, 96- *Personal Data:* b Springfield, Mo, Feb 4, 39; m 64; c 2. *Educ:* Grinnell Col, BA, 61; Brown Univ, PhD(biol), 66. *Prof Exp:* Fel microbial genetics, Dept Human Genetics, Univ Mich, 65-68; asst prof microbiol, Baylor Col Med, 68-72; from asst to assoc prof microbiol, State Univ NY, Stony Brook, 72-76; health scientist adminr, NIH, Bethesda, 76-78; sr analyst, Off Technol Assessment, US Cong, Washington, DC, 78-85,mgr biol appln prog, 91-95; dir, Risk Sci Inst, Washington, DC, 85; sr fel, Ctr Risk Mgt, Resources for the Future, 87-90, dir, 90; vis fel, Ctr Technol Assessment, Stuttgart, Ger, 95. *Concurrent Pos:* Fulbright lectr, Peru, 71 & India, 75; mem adv panel, Health Prog, Off Technol Assessment, 85-90, Assessment Agt Orange, 85-90; chmn, Adv Comt Health Effects Herbicides, Dept Vet Affairs, 87-90 & Comt Oper Ranch Hand Studies, Dept Health & Human Serv; fel, Soc Risk Anal. *Mem:* Soc Risk Anal (secy, 85-86). *Res:* Interrelationships among science, technology and public policy. *Mailing Add:* CATO Inst 1000 Massachusetts Ave NW Washington DC 20001. *Fax:* 202-842-3490

GOUGH, ROBERT EDWARD, POMOLOGY, DEVELOPMENTAL ANATOMY. *Current Pos:* ASSOC PROF, MONT STATE UNIV, 95- *Personal Data:* b Wakefield, RI, Jan 31, 49; m 85, Patricia M Albro; c Jonathan, Robert, Amy & Andrew. *Educ:* Univ RI, BA, 70, MS, 73, PhD(bot), 77. *Prof Exp:* Co agt, Va Polytech Inst & State Univ, 73-74, instr, 76-77, asst prof, 77-81; assoc prof plant & soil sci, Univ RI, 81-88; asst publ, Hayworth Press, 92-95. *Concurrent Pos:* Fel, Lilly Endowment, 78-79. *Mem:* Am Soc Hort Sci; Sigma Xi; Bot Soc Am. *Res:* Small fruit production; developmental anatomy of fruit crops; tissue culture; somatic embryogenesis. *Mailing Add:* 8003 Indian Paintbrush Bozeman MT 59718. *Fax:* 406-994-3933; *E-Mail:* ussgr@nsu.edu

GOUGH, ROBERT GEORGE, ORGANIC CHEMISTRY. *Current Pos:* AT ERVIN, VARN, JACOBS, ODOM & KITCHEN. *Personal Data:* b Kitchener, Ont, May 20, 39; US citizen; m 67. *Educ:* Univ Waterloo, BSc, 62; Pa State Univ, PhD(chem), 67. *Prof Exp:* Res assoc chem, Cincinnati Milacron Inc, 67-77, mgr regulatory affairs, 77- *Mem:* Am Chem Soc. *Res:* Polymer rheology; polymer extrusion lubricants and processing aids; heat stabilizers; light stabilizers and fire retardants. *Mailing Add:* Environ Protection Agency 2 Twin Towers MS 35 2600 Blairstone Rd Tallahassee FL 32399-2400

GOUGH, SIDNEY ROGER, PHYSICAL CHEMISTRY, SCIENTIFIC NUMERIC DATA BASES. *Current Pos:* RETIRED. *Personal Data:* b Staffordshire, Eng, Oct 30, 38; m 62, Doreen M Moseley; c Allister C, Imogen B & Ingrid E. *Educ:* Univ Wales, BSc, 61, PhD(phys chem), 64. *Prof Exp:* Fel, Nat Res Coun Can, 64-66, from asst res officer to sr res officer, 66-85, serv coordr, Sci Numeric Database Serv, 85-96. *Res:* Dielectric properties of solids and liquids; molecular motions and structure; clathrate hydrates; scientific numeric databases; database systems; information science and systems. *Mailing Add:* 1289 Turner Crescent Orleans ON K1E 2Y5 Can

GOUGH, STEPHEN BRADFORD, PHYCOLOGY, SOFTWARE AND SYSTEMS ENGINEERING. *Current Pos:* RES ASSOC ENVIRON RES, ENVIRON SCI DIV, OAK RIDGE NAT LAB, 76-; ASST PROF BIOL SCIS, MARY WASHINGTON COL, 93- *Personal Data:* b New Castle, Ind, Sept 13, 50; m 71, Cynthia Jordan; c Christopher, Jennifer & Lisa. *Educ:* Carroll Col, Wis, BS, 72; Univ Wis-Madison, PhD(bot), 76. *Prof Exp:* Res asst bot, Univ Wis-Madison, 72-75, teaching asst, 75-76; comput systs specialist, Syst Develop Corp, Fredericksburg, Va, 82-86; sr software engr, Int Comput Equip, Inc, Fredericksburg, Va, 86-87; prod develop mgr, TRW Inc, 87-93. *Concurrent Pos:* Adj fac mem, Dept Biol Sci, Mary Washington Col, Fredericksburg, Va, 90-93. *Mem:* Phycol Soc Am; Sigma Xi; Am Soc Limnol & Oceanog; AAAS; Soc Ecol Restoration; Ecol Soc Am. *Res:* Rapid assessment of environmental quality; biology of legionnaires disease bacterium; restoration and enhancement of natural and artificial ecosystems; bacterial ecology and physiology; ecological toxicology; algal ecology, systematics and physiology; software and systems engineering. *Mailing Add:* 8 Norman Ct Fredericksburg VA 22407. *Fax:* 540-654-1081; *E-Mail:* sgough@s850.mwc.edu

GOUIN, FRANCIS R, PLANT PHYSIOLOGY. *Current Pos:* Exten specialist, 65-69, from asst prof to prof, 69-95, EMER PROF HORT, UNIV MD, COLLEGE PARK, 95-, CHMN DEPT, 90- *Personal Data:* b Laconia, NH, June 3, 38; m 62, Clara Olesniewicz; c Cristina & Bonnie. *Educ:* Thompson Sch Agr, cert, 58; Univ NH, BS, 62; Univ Md, College Park, MS, 65, PhD(hort, bot), 69. *Honors & Awards:* Nursery Exten Award, Am Asn Nutrit & Am Soc Hort Sci, 82; Norman J Coleman Res Award, Am Asn Nurseryman, 87; L C Chadwick Award, Am Nurserymen Asn; Rufus Chaney Composting Sci Award, Composting Coun; Francis R Gouin Award Excellence, Land Contractors Asn. *Concurrent Pos:* Consult organic waste recycling & ornamental hort landscape architects & landscape contractors. *Mem:* Fel Am Soc Hort Sci; Int Plant Propagators; Sigma Xi. *Res:* Mineral nutrition of woody ornamental plants; winter hardiness of roots of container grown woody ornamental plants; chemical weed control in and around woody ornamental plants; composted sewage sludge on non-food crops; composted municipal solid waste. *Mailing Add:* 420 E Bay Front Rd Deal MD 20751. *Fax:* 301-394-9308; *E-Mail:* fgouin@umpil.umd.edu

GOULARD, BERNARD, THEORETICAL PHYSICS, NUCLEAR PHYSICS. *Current Pos:* assoc prof, 73-75, PROF PHYSICS, UNIV MONTREAL, 75- *Personal Data:* b Paris, France, May 9, 33; m 59; c 1. *Educ:* Univ Nancy, lic, 57; Univ Grenoble, Dr(nuclear physics), 60; Univ Pa, PhD(physics), 64. *Prof Exp:* Fel theoret physics, Bartol Res Found, 64-65; from asst prof to assoc prof, 65-73. *Mem:* Am Phys Soc. *Res:* Weak interaction of muons and neutrinos with nuclei; electron scattering and isobaric properties of nuclei. *Mailing Add:* Lab Nuclear Physics Univ Montreal Montreal PQ H3C 3J7 Can

GOULD, A LAWRENCE, BIOMETRICS. *Current Pos:* sect head, Merck Sharp & Dohme Res Labs, 69-73, mgr clin biostatist, Div Med Affairs, 73-77, dir invest res, Clin Biostatist & Res Data Syst, 76-83, SR STATIST SCIENTIST, MERCK RES LABS, 83- *Personal Data:* b Feb 6, 41; US citizen; m 73; c 2. *Educ:* Case Western Res Univ, AB, 62, PhD(biomet, statist), 67. *Prof Exp:* Statistician, Res Triangle Inst, 67-69. *Concurrent Pos:* Assoc bus admin, Wharton Sch, Univ Pa, 75; adj assoc prof, Biomet Dept, Temple Univ, 75-; secy, Biopharmaceut Subsect, Am Statist Asn, 75-76. *Mem:* Fel Am Statist Asn; Biomet Soc. *Res:* Statistical methodology pertinent to problems arising in reality, especially in the biological and medical sciences. *Mailing Add:* Biostatist & Res Data Syst Merck Res Labs West Point PA 19486

GOULD, ADAIR BRASTED, GENETICS. *Current Pos:* RETIRED. *Personal Data:* b New York, NY, Feb 18, 16; m 40, Charles W; c Ann, Mary E & Alison. *Educ:* Barnard Col, AB, 36; Univ Rochester, AM, 38, PhD(genetics), 40. *Prof Exp:* Res assoc genetics, Univ Del, 64-69, lab tech biol, 70-72, from instr to assoc prof, 72-81. *Mem:* AAAS; Genetics Soc Am; Sigma Xi. *Res:* Developmental genetics, especially as related to the genetic control of longevity. *Mailing Add:* 106 Hoiland Dr Wilmington DE 19803-3228

GOULD, ANNE BRAMLEE, BIOCHEMISTRY, BIOLOGY. *Current Pos:* asst prof med, 73-81, RES ASSOC PROF MED, HAHNEMANN UNIV, 80- *Personal Data:* b Bangor, Maine, Jan 30, 28. *Educ:* Univ Maine, BS, 50; Rutgers Univ, MS, 54; Brown Univ, PhD(biol), 61. *Prof Exp:* Res biochemist, Vet Admin Hosp, Cleveland, 62-66, Mt Sinai Hosp, Cleveland, 66-73. *Concurrent Pos:* Fel, Coun High Blood Pressure, Am Heart Asn. *Mem:* Am Heart Asn; Int Soc Hypertension. *Res:* Biochemistry and physiology of high blood pressure; the question of whether or not high blood pressure is the result of a blood vessel adaptation to a renal energy deficiency caused by disease, poor nutrition or heredity. *Mailing Add:* 945 Ginger Way Melbourne FL 32940

GOULD, CHARLES JAY, PLANT PATHOLOGY. *Current Pos:* from asst plant pathologist to plant pathologist, 41-77, EMER PLANT PATHOLOGIST, WESTERN WASH RES & EXTEN CTR, WASH STATE UNIV, 77- *Personal Data:* b Eaton, Ohio, Feb 28, 12; m 40, Dorothy F Ebersole; c James F & Carl David. *Educ:* Marshall Col, AB, 34; Iowa State Col, MS, 37, PhD(plant path), 42. *Honors & Awards:* Res Award, Soc Am Florists, 50. *Prof Exp:* Instr bot, Iowa State Col, 37-41; asst prof, Okla Agr & Mech Col, 40. *Concurrent Pos:* Collabr, USDA, 47-77; Fulbright scholar, Neth, 51; sabbatical leave, Europe, 67. *Mem:* Fel Am Phytopath Soc; Sigma Xi. *Res:* Diseases of turf grasses, iris, tulips, narcissus, pyracantha and syringa; history of the flower bulb industry in Washington State. *Mailing Add:* 12316 123rd Street Ct E Puyallup WA 98374

GOULD, CHRISTOPHER M, ULTRALOW TEMPERATURE, SUPERFLUID HELIUM THREE. *Current Pos:* res asst prof, 78-81, from asst prof to assoc prof, 81-93, PROF PHYSICS & ASTRON, UNIV SOUTHERN CALIF, 93- *Personal Data:* b Oakland, Calif, Nov 24, 51. *Educ:* Stanford Univ, BS, 73; Cornell Univ, MS & PhD(physics), 79. *Concurrent Pos:* Res fel, Alfred P Sloan Found, 83. *Mem:* Am Phys Soc. *Res:* Ultralow temperature condensed matter physics, especially superfluid helium 3; electronic transport at ultralow temperatures, especially thermalization problems. *Mailing Add:* Dept Physics & Astron Seaver Sci Ctr Univ Southern Calif Los Angeles CA 90089-0484. *Fax:* 213-740-6653; *E-Mail:* gould@usc.edu

GOULD, CHRISTOPHER ROBERT, POLARIZED NEUTRON PHYSICS, POLARIZED TARGET PHYSICS. *Current Pos:* from asst prof to assoc prof, 71-83, PROF PHYSICS, NC STATE UNIV, 83-, DEPT HEAD, 95- *Personal Data:* b Newbury, Eng, Mar 11, 44. *Educ:* Imp Col, London, BS, 65; Univ Pa, MS, 66, PhD(physics), 69. *Prof Exp:* Res assoc, Dept Physics, Duke Univ, Durham, NC, 69-71. *Concurrent Pos:* Alexander von Humboldt Award, Univ Frankfurt, 76-77; guest lectr, Inst Atomic Energy, Beijing, People's Repub China, 84, Univ Petrol & Minerals, Dhahran, Saudi Arabia, 86; mem, Panel Basic Nuclear Data Needs, Nat Res Coun, 87-90, Tech Comt Comput Appln in Nuclear & Plasma Sci, Inst Elec & Electronics Engrs, 87- & Instrumentation Subcomt, Nuclear Sci Adv Comt, 88-89; Assoc Western Univs sabbatical fel, Los Alamos Meson Physics Facil, Los Alamos Nat Lab, 90-91. *Mem:* Fel Am Phys Soc; Am Asn Univ Profs; Am Asn Physics Teachers; Sigma Xi; Inst Elec & Electronics Engrs. *Res:* Experimental nuclear physics; accelerators; scattering of polarized and unpolarized fast neutron beams; cryogenic polarized target development; parity and time reversal violation in nuclear physics. *Mailing Add:* Dept Physics NC State Univ Box 8202 Raleigh NC 27695-8202. *Fax:* 919-515-6538; *E-Mail:* chris_gould@ncsu.edu

GOULD, DAVID HUNTINGTON, TOXICOLOGY, STRUCTURE-ACTIVITY RELATIONSHIPS. *Current Pos:* RETIRED. *Personal Data:* b New York, NY, Nov 23, 21; m 45, 82; c 3. *Educ:* Yale Univ, BS, 42, MS, 44, PhD(org chem), 45. *Honors & Awards:* Bronze Medal, US Environ Protection Agency. *Prof Exp:* Lab asst, Yale Univ, 42-44; res chemist, Nopco Chem Co, 44-48; res assoc, Hickrill Chem Res Found, 48-49; sr res chemist, Schering Corp, 49-57, adminr extramural sci res, 57-59; grant res, Colgate-Palmolive Co, 59-68, head tech info serv, 68-70; clin res assoc, Merck Sharpe & Dohme Res Labs, 70-72; sr scientist, Off Toxic Substances, US Environ Protection Agency, 77-88. *Concurrent Pos:* Dir, NValley Consumers Coop, 54-58; exec secy, Schering Found, 58-59; mem, Chem Select Working Group, Nat Cancer Inst-Nat Tox Prog, 77-88. *Mem:* Soc Toxicol; Am Chem Soc; fel AAAS; Am Col Toxicol; Soc Risk Anal; Asn Govt Toxicologists; Int Soc Study Xenobiotics. *Res:* Natural products; cortical and sex hormones; chemotherapeutics; chemical structure retrieval; mechanisms of toxicity; metabolism; chemical carcinogenicity; risk assessment; xenobiotic toxicity; structure activity relationships; toxicology. *Mailing Add:* Swan's Way Rte 2 Box 436 Scottsville VA 24590-9507

GOULD, DOUGLAS JAY, MEDICAL ENTOMOLOGY. *Current Pos:* RETIRED. *Personal Data:* b San Francisco, Calif, May 29, 23; wid; c 3. *Educ:* Univ Calif, BA, 44, PhD(parasitol), 53. *Prof Exp:* Parasitologist, State Dept Pub Health, 48-50; asst parasitol, Univ Calif, 50-51; entomologist, Walter Reed Army Inst Res, 51-64; chief, Dept Entom, Southeast Asia Treaty Orgn Med Res Lab, 64-77; chief, Dept Entom, Walter Reed Army Inst Res, 77-79. *Concurrent Pos:* Collabr, US Nat Mus, 53-55. *Mem:* Am Soc Trop Med & Hyg; Am Mosquito Control Asn; Sigma Xi; Soc Vector Ecologists. *Res:* Arthropod transmission of infectious diseases; ecology of arthropod borne diseases. *Mailing Add:* PO Box 519 Plymouth CA 95669-0519

GOULD, EDWIN, ecology, animal behavior, for more information see previous edition

GOULD, EDWIN SHELDON, INORGANIC CHEMISTRY, ORGANIC CHEMISTRY. *Current Pos:* PROF CHEM, KENT STATE UNIV, 67- *Personal Data:* b Los Angeles, Calif, Aug 19, 26; m 52, Marjorie McFarlin; c Richard F & Kirk B. *Educ:* Calif Inst Technol, BS, 46; Univ Calif, Los Angeles, PhD(chem), 50. *Prof Exp:* Instr chem, Polytech Inst Brooklyn, 50, from asst prof to assoc prof, 52-59; sr inorg chemist, Stanford Res Inst, 59-66; prof chem, San Francisco State Univ, 66-67. *Concurrent Pos:* NSF sci fac fel, 57-58, sr fel, Stanford Univ, 62-63; NIH spec fel, Univ Calif, 63-64. *Mem:* Am Chem Soc; Royal Soc. *Res:* Chelating agents; electron transfer reactions in solution; metalloaromatics; catalysis of oxidation by transition metals. *Mailing Add:* Chem Dept Kent State Univ Kent OH 44242-0002. *Fax:* 330-672-3816

GOULD, G(ERALD) G(EZA), ELECTRICAL ENGINEERING. *Current Pos:* ENGR CONSULT, GERALD GOULD ASSOC, INC, 81- *Personal Data:* b Budapest, Hungary, Nov 17, 13; m 41; c 3. *Educ:* City Col, BS, 35; Purdue Univ, MS, 36. *Prof Exp:* Elec engr develop high voltage equip, Porcelain Prods, Inc, 36-40 & signal syst, New York Subways, 40-42; proj engr frequency control, Acoustics, US Naval Ord Lab, 46-51; chief engr torpedo res & develop, US Navy Bur Ord, 51-55, tech dir, US Naval Underwater Weapons Res & Engr Sta, 55-70, dep tech dir, US Naval Underwater Systs Ctr, 70-72, tech dir, Naval Coastal Systs Ctr, 72-81. *Concurrent Pos:* Chmn, Undersea Warfare Res & Develop Planning Coun, 65-66 & US Navy Lab Dirs Coun, 67-69. *Mem:* Fel, Inst Elec & Electronics Engrs; Nat Soc Prof Engrs; Acoust Soc Am. *Res:* Management of research and development; underwater weapons systems; electrical generation; high voltage engineering. *Mailing Add:* Gerald Gould Assocs, Inc 2329 Magnolia Dr Panama City FL 32408

GOULD, GEORGE EDWIN, entomology; deceased, see previous edition for last biography

GOULD, GORDON, OPTOELECTRONICS, RESEARCH ADMINISTRATION. *Current Pos:* RETIRED. *Personal Data:* b New York, NY, July 17, 20; m 93, Marilyn Appel. *Educ:* Union Col, BS, 41, DSc, 78; Yale Univ, MS, 43; Columbia Univ, MS, 52. *Hon Degrees:* DSc, Union Col, 78, Polytech Univ, 92. *Honors & Awards:* John Scott Medal, 83. *Prof Exp:* Instr, Yale Univ, 41-43; physicist, Manhattan Proj, 43-45; engr, Semon Bache Co, 45-50; instr, City Col New York, 47-54; res asst, Columbia Univ, 54-57; res dir, TRG Inc, Control Data Corp, NY, 58-67; prof electrophys, Brooklyn Polytech Inst, 67-74; vpres eng & mkt, Optelecom, Inc, Gaithersburg, 74-85, dir, 74-85. *Concurrent Pos:* Bd dirs, Polygon Inc, Colo, Integram Inc, Va & Am Fluoroseal Inc, Md. *Mem:* Am Inst Physics; Optical Soc Am; Inst Elec & Electronics Engrs; AAAS; Fiber Optics Commun Soc; Laser Inst Am (pres, 71-72); Sigma Xi. *Res:* Physics; optical; electrophysics; fiber optics; lasers. *Mailing Add:* PO Box 4359 Breckenridge CO 80424-4359

GOULD, HARRY J, III, COMPARATIVE NEUROLOGY, PAIN MANAGEMENT. *Current Pos:* from asst to assoc prof anat, 80-90, RESIDENT NEUROL, LA STATE MED CTR, 90- *Personal Data:* b Columbus, Ohio, Mar 1, 47; m 71, Anne Thompson; c Trevor N & Laura N. *Educ:* State Univ NY Stony Brook, BS, 69; Brown Univ, PhD(biol), 74; La State Univ Med Sch, MD, 90. *Prof Exp:* Instr anat, Col Med, Univ Cincinnati, 74-76, asst prof, 76-80. *Concurrent Pos:* Vis scientist, Vanderbilt Univ 82 & 85. *Mem:* Cajal Club; Sigma Xi; Am Asn Anatomists; Am Acad Neurol; Int Asn Study Pain; Soc Neurosci. *Res:* Neuroanatomical and physiological analysis of the intrinsic circuitry of the motor and somatosensory cerebral cortex. *Mailing Add:* Dept Neurol Med Ctr La State Univ 1542 Tulane Ave New Orleans LA 70112. *Fax:* 504-568-7130; *E-Mail:* hgouldmd3@aol.com

GOULD, HARVEY A, STATISTICAL MECHANICS. *Current Pos:* assoc prof, 71-81, PROF PHYSICS, CLARK UNIV, 81- *Personal Data:* b Oakland, Calif, Sept 4, 38; m 74, Patti Orbuch; c Joshua, Emily & Evan. *Educ:* Univ Calif, Berkeley, BA, 60, PhD(physics), 66. *Prof Exp:* Nat Res Coun-Nat Acad Sci res fel, Nat Bur Stand, DC, 66-67; asst prof physics, Univ Mich, Ann Arbor, 67-71. *Concurrent Pos:* Vis assoc prof physics, Bar-Ilan Univ, Israel, 74-75; vis scientist, Univ Chicago, 78-79; vis res prof, Boston Univ, 80-86, vis prof, 86-87. *Mem:* Fel Am Phys Soc; Am Asn Physics Teachers. *Res:* Computer simulation and dynamics of first-order phase transitions. *Mailing Add:* Dept Physics Clark Univ Worcester MA 01610-1477. *E-Mail:* hgould@clarku.edu

GOULD, HARVEY ALLEN, FEW-ELECTRON VERY-HEAVY IONS, RELATIVISTIC ATOMIC COLLISIONS. *Current Pos:* fel, 71-76, staff physicist, 76-88, SR PHYSICIST, LAWRENCE BERKELEY LAB, UNIV CALIF, BERKELEY, 88- *Personal Data:* b Brooklyn, NY, Feb 28, 45; m 87, Lynette Levy; c Benjamin. *Educ:* Stevens Inst Technol, BS, 65; Brandeis Univ, MS, 67, PhD(physics), 70. *Prof Exp:* Fel, Brandeis Univ, 70-71. *Mem:* Fel Am Phys Soc; fel AAAS. *Res:* Experimental atomic physics; relativistic atomic collisions; capture from pair production; electron electric dipole moment as a test of CP violation; few electron very heavy ions. *Mailing Add:* Lawrence Berkeley Lab Bldg 71 Berkeley CA 94720. *Fax:* 510-486-7981; *E-Mail:* gould@lbl.gov

GOULD, HENRY WADSWORTH, MATHEMATICS, COMBINATORICS. *Current Pos:* From instr to assoc prof, 58-69, PROF MATH, WVA UNIV, 69- *Personal Data:* b Portsmouth, Va, Aug 26, 28; m 69, 96, Virginia J West. *Educ:* Univ Va, BA, 54, MA, 56. *Concurrent Pos:* Consult Sci Serv, DC, 59-60; NSF res grant, 60-67; assoc ed, Fibonacci Quart, 62-; lectr, Math Asn Am, 67-70 & Soc Indust & Appl Math, 74-76; ed-in-chief, Proc WVa Acad Sci, 74-79; dep ed-in-chief, J Math Res & Expos, Hefei, People's Repub China. *Mem:* Fel AAAS; Am Math Soc; Math Asn Am; Soc Indust & Appl Math; Fibonacci Asn; Sigma Xi; fel Inst Combinatrics & Appln. *Res:* Theory of combinatorial identities; combinatorial analysis; special functions; number theory; theory of binomial coefficient summations; history of mathematics; about 150 journal publications and one book. *Mailing Add:* Dept Math WVa Univ PO Box 6310 Morgantown WV 26506-6310. *E-Mail:* gould@math.wvu.edu

GOULD, HOWARD ROSS, GEOLOGY. *Current Pos:* INDEPENDENT GEOLOGIST, 86- *Personal Data:* b Adrian, WVa, Nov 10, 21; m 48, Marilyn B; c Brad & Suzanne. *Educ:* Univ Minn, BA, 43; Univ Southern Calif, PhD(geol), 53. *Prof Exp:* Training assoc, Div War Res, Univ Calif, 43-45, assoc marine geologist, 46; asst geol, Scripps Inst, Calif, 46-47, geologist, US Geol Surv, DC, 47-54; asst prof oceanog, Univ Wash, 53-56, sr geologist, Geol Res Sect, Humble Oil & Ref Co, 56-63, staff geologist, 63-64, chief, 64; mgr stratig & struct geol div, Exxon Prod Res Co, 64-66, mgr stratig geol div, 66-67, res scientist, 67-86. *Concurrent Pos:* Spec consult, US Navy. *Mem:* Fel AAAS; fel Geol Soc Am (vpres, 80, pres, 81); hon mem Soc Econ Paleontologists & Mineralogists (vpres, 68); hon mem Am Asn Petrol Geol; Am Geophys Union; Am Geol Inst (vpres, 83, pres, 84). *Res:* Sedimentation, especially in marine and lake environments; general geology of the sea floor; petroleum geology. *Mailing Add:* 5231 Piping Rock Lane Houston TX 77056

GOULD, JACK RICHARD, ENVIRONMENTAL SCIENCE & TECHNOLOGY. *Current Pos:* RETIRED. *Personal Data:* b Brooklyn, NY, Feb 28, 22; m 45; c 2. *Educ:* Brooklyn Col, BA, 43; Pa State Univ, MS, 47, PhD(org chem), 49. *Prof Exp:* Chemist res & develop, Montrose Chem Co, 43-45; asst chem, Pa State Univ, 45-48; res chemist petrochems, Houdry Process Corp, 49-51; proj leader, Reaction Motors, Inc, Olin Mathieson Chem Corp, 51-53, sect head, Chem Dept, 54-56; head, Org Chems Sect, Eastern Res Ctr, Stauffer Chem Co, 56-63; dir res, Metalsalts Corp, 63-64; sr staff contract res, Eng Res & Develop Dept, M W Kellogg Co, 64-69; sr environ coordr, Am Petrol Inst, 69-80, sr environ scientist, Environ Affairs Dept, 80-85, Health & Environ Sci Dept, 85-91. *Concurrent Pos:* Pres greater Washington chap, Nat Retinitis Pigmentosa Found Fighting Blindness, 71-85, mem bd trustees, 79-81; managing ed, Div Petrol Chem, Am Chem Soc, 77-79; mem adv bd, Vol Visually Handicapped, 78-83. *Mem:* Am Chem Soc; NY Acad Sci; Sigma Xi; AAAS; Marine Tech Soc. *Res:* Organic and organometallic chemistry and industrial applications; high energy liquid rocket propellants; water pollution control technology and regulations related to the petroleum industry; prevention, control and effects of oil spills; alternate fuels; fate and environmental effects of petroleum and related substances in marine environment and human health implications; natural resource damage assessment. *Mailing Add:* 6021 Neilwood Dr Rockville MD 20852-3703

GOULD, JAMES L, ETHOLOGY. *Current Pos:* asst prof animal behav, 75-80, assoc prof, 80-83, PROF BIOL, PRINCETON UNIV, 83- *Personal Data:* b Tulsa, Okla, July 31, 45; m 70, Carol Grant; c Grant F & Clare H. *Educ:* Calif Inst Technol, BS, 70; Rockefeller Univ, PhD(ethology), 75. *Concurrent Pos:* NSF fel; Guggenheim Found fel. *Mem:* Fel AAAS; fel Animal Behav Soc. *Res:* Communication, learning, and orientation behavior of animals; animal cognition; female-choice sexual selection. *Mailing Add:* 11 Herrontown Circle Princeton NJ 08540. *Fax:* 609-258-1712; *E-Mail:* gould@pucc.princeton.edu

GOULD, JAMES P, ENGINEERING ADMINISTRATION. *Current Pos:* CONSULT. *Educ:* Univ Wash, BSCE, 44; Mass Inst Technol, MSCE, 46; Harvard Univ, MS, 48, ScD, 49. *Honors & Awards:* Kapp Mem Lectr, Am Soc Civil Engrs, 74 & 82; Crom Lectr, Univ Fla, 78; Haley Mem Lectr, 85. *Prof Exp:* US Army Engrs, 44-45; eng asst, Harvard Univ, 48-49; US Bur Reclamation, Earth Dams Sect, 50-53; staff, Mueser Rutledge Consult Engrs, 53-55, assoc, 55-73, partner, 73- *Concurrent Pos:* Transp Res Bd, 62-66; mem, Underground Technol Res Coun; adj prof, Purdue Univ, 69; fel, Am Consult Engrs Coun; consult var subway projs. *Mem:* Nat Acad Eng; hon mem Am Soc Civil Engrs. *Res:* Author of about three dozen technical articles or publications. *Mailing Add:* Mueser Rutledge Consult Engrs 708 Third Ave 5th Floor New York NY 10017

GOULD, JOHN MICHAEL, MICROBIAL BIOTECHNOLOGY, PLANT BIOCHEMISTRY. *Current Pos:* VPRES & DIR RES, US SUGAR CORP, 96- *Personal Data:* b Dayton, Ohio, Dec 15, 49; m 74; c 2. *Educ:* Univ Cincinnati, BS, 71, MS, 72; Mich State Univ, PhD(plant biochem), 74. *Honors & Awards:* Fed Lab Consortium Award, 87; R & D 100 Award, 89. *Prof Exp:* Res assoc, Dept Biochem, Cell & Molecular Biol, Cornell Univ, 74-75; NIH fel, Dept Biol Sci, Purdue Univ, 75-77; asst prof biochem, Dept Chem, Univ Notre Dame, 77-81; res biochemist, USDA, 81-83, res leader, Northern Regional Res Ctr, 83-86, dir res, Biotechnol Res & Develop Corp, 90-96. *Concurrent Pos:* Consult, US Fed Trade Comn (biodegradation), 90- *Mem:* Biophys Soc; Am Soc Microbiol. *Res:* Biodegradation of plastics and polymer composites; properties of plant cell walls; modification of starch and cellulose to produce novel products; photoacoustic spectrometry; polymer biochemistry; microbial biotechnology. *Mailing Add:* US Sugar Corp PO Drawer 1207 Clewiston FL 33440-1207

GOULD, K LANCE, CARDIOVASCULAR MEDICINE. *Current Pos:* PROF & DIR, CTR CARDIOVASC & IMAGING RES, UNIV TEX HEALTH SCI CTR, HOUSTON, 80- *Personal Data:* b Wilsonville, Ala, Oct 28, 38. *Educ:* Western Res Med Sch, MD, 64. *Concurrent Pos:* Mem bd trustees, Am Col Cardiol. *Mem:* Asn Am Physicians; Am Asn Univ Cardiologists; Am Soc Clin Invest. *Mailing Add:* Div Cardiol Univ Tex Med Sch Box 20708 Houston TX 77225-0708

GOULD, KENNETH G, REPRODUCTIVE BIOLOGY, CONTRACEPTIVE DEVELOPMENT. *Current Pos:* RES PROF & CHIEF, DIV REPRODUCTIVE BIOL, YERKES CTR, EMORY UNIV, 89- *Personal Data:* b Woodford, Eng, Aug 18, 43; m 71, Janet Paisey; c Sandra, Jeff, Debby, Doug & Lisa. *Educ:* London Univ, Eng, DVM, 66, PhD, 73. *Mem:* Am Fertil Soc; Am Physiol Soc; Brit Vet Asn; Int Primate Soc. *Res:* In vitro fertilization/artificial breeding in endangered primates; intergeneric pregnancy. *Mailing Add:* Dept Molecular Med Yerkes Regional Primate Res Ctr Emory Univ Atlanta GA 30322. *Fax:* 404-727-2958

GOULD, LAWRENCE A, INTERNAL MEDICINE, CARDIOLOGY. *Current Pos:* clin assoc prof, 75-81, CLIN PROF MED, DOWNSTATE MED CTR, STATE UNIV NY, 81-; CHIEF CARDIOL SERV, METHODIST HOSP, 74- *Personal Data:* b Brooklyn, NY, Dec 15, 30; m 57; c 2. *Educ:* Brooklyn Col, BA, 52; NY Univ, MD, 56; Am Bd Internal Med, dipl & Am Bd Cardiovasc Dis, dipl. *Prof Exp:* Clin instr med, NY Med Col, 62-65; from asst chief to chief cardiol serv, Bronx Vet Admin Hosp, NY, 65-69; chief cardiac catheterization lab, Misericordia-Fordham Hosp, 69-74; assoc prof med, NY Med Col, 72-75. *Mem:* Am Heart Asn; fel Am Col Physicians; fel Am Col Cardiol; Am Fedn Clin Res. *Res:* Clinical research of the cardiovascular system; cardiac hemodynamic studies. *Mailing Add:* Methodist Hosp 506 6th St Brooklyn NY 11215-3609

GOULD, LEONARD A(BRAHAM), ELECTRICAL ENGINEERING. *Current Pos:* Asst, 48-50, from instr to assoc prof, 50-68, PROF ELEC ENG, MASS INST TECHNOL, 68- *Personal Data:* b Brooklyn, NY, Nov 20, 27; m 59. *Educ:* Mass Inst Technol, SB, 48, ScD(elec eng), 53. *Concurrent Pos:* Fulbright res fel, Tech Univ Denmark, 57; vis prof, Dept Appl Physics, Michelson Inst, Bergen, Norway, 68-69. *Mem:* Fel Inst Elec & Electronics Engrs. *Res:* Control and estimation. *Mailing Add:* Dept Elec Eng Mass Inst Tech 77 Massachusetts Ave Cambridge MA 02139-4307

GOULD, MARK D, BENTHIC ECOLOGY, TROPICAL MARINE BIOLOGY. *Current Pos:* biol area, 76-79, PROF MARINE BIOL & ZOOL, COORDR DIV NATURAL SCI & DEAN, SCI & MATH, ROGER WILLIAMS UNIV, 72-, DEAN, ARTS & SCI. *Personal Data:* b Washington, DC, Feb 1, 46; m 72, Lisa Lofland; c Hannah & Meggan. *Educ:* Univ RI, BS, 67, MS, 70, PhD(biol sci), 73. *Honors & Awards:* Chautauqua Award, NSF, Univ Hartford, 79 & Hampshire Col, 81. *Prof Exp:* Lectr aquatic ecol, Univ RI, 70-72, asst prof, 74-78. *Concurrent Pos:* Sr biologist, Grumman Ecosysts Corp, 74-75; res biologist, Environ Protection Agency, 81-; lectr, Mystic Aquarium, 85. *Mem:* Sigma Xi; AAAS; Ecol Soc Am; Soc Nematologists. *Res:* Interrelationships between the micro, meio and macrofauna and the effect of various pollutants; taxonomy of tropical marine organisms; indicator organisms in fresh water. *Mailing Add:* Dean Arts & Sci Roger Williams Univ Old Ferry Rd Bristol RI 02809. *Fax:* 401-254-3286; *E-Mail:* mdg@alpha.rnu.edu

GOULD, MICHAEL NATHAN, RADIATION BIOLOGY, EXPERIMENTAL ONCOLOGY. *Current Pos:* INSTR HUMAN ONCOL RADIOL, UNIV WIS-MADISON, 78- *Personal Data:* b New York, NY, Sept 9, 47. *Educ:* Univ Wis-Madison, BS, 69, MS, 73, PhD(radiation biol), 77. *Prof Exp:* Fel cell biol, Argonne Nat Lab, 77-78. *Concurrent Pos:* Fel, Am Cancer Soc, 77-78. *Mem:* Radiation Res Soc; Tissue Cult Asn. *Res:* Normal tissue response to radiation; chemical and radiation carcinogenesis; biology of the mammary gland. *Mailing Add:* Hum Orcol Univ Wis Clin Sci Ctr 600 Highland Ave Madison WI 53792-0001

GOULD, PHILLIP, MECHANICAL ENGINEERING. *Current Pos:* ASST DIR, SYSTS EVAL DIV, INST FOR DEFENSE ANAL, 85-, MEM, 67- *Personal Data:* b New York, NY, Feb 19, 40; m 64, 80; c 2. *Educ:* City Col New York, BME, 61; Mass Inst Technol, SM, 63, ScD(mech eng), 65. *Prof Exp:* Asst prof mech eng, Mass Inst Technol, 65-67. *Concurrent Pos:* Fel eng, Mass Inst Tech, 65-67. *Mem:* NY Acad Sci; Am Inst Aeronaut & Astronaut; Am Soc Mech Engrs; fel AAAS; Opers Res Soc Am. *Res:* Continuum mechanics; operations analysis. *Mailing Add:* 4590 Indian Rock Terr Washington DC 20007-2567. *Fax:* 703-845-6722; *E-Mail:* pgould@ida.org

GOULD, PHILLIP L, STRUCTURAL ENGINEERING, SOLID MECHANICS. *Current Pos:* from asst prof to assoc prof, 66-74, chmn dept, 74-81, PROF CIVIL ENG, WASH UNIV, ST LOUIS, 75-, HAROLD D JOLLEY CHAIR CIVIL ENG, 81- *Personal Data:* b Chicago, Ill, May 24, 37; m 61, Deborah Rothholtz; c Elizabeth, Nathan, Rebecca & Joshua. *Educ:* Univ Ill, Urbana, BS, 59, MS, 60; Northwestern Univ, PhD(civil eng), 66. *Honors & Awards:* Sr Scientist Award, Alexander von Humboldt Found, 74-75. *Prof Exp:* Struct designer, Skidmore, Owings & Merrill, Ill, 60-63; prin struct engr, Westenhoff & Novick, 63-64. *Concurrent Pos:* Consult design of shell roof struct, 66-; vis prof, Univ Sydney, Australia, 81; adv prof, Dept Civil Eng, Shaghai Inst Technol, China, 86. *Mem:* Am Soc Civil Engrs; Am Soc Eng Educ; Am Acad Mech; Int Asn Shell Struct; Earth Engr Res Inst. *Res:* Analysis and design of multistory building frames, highway bridges, shell roof structures, and pressure vessels; development of computer-based numerical techniques for the analysis of thin shells and human hearts; earthquake engineering. *Mailing Add:* Sch Eng & Appl Sci Wash Univ St Louis MO 63130

GOULD, ROBERT GEORGE, MEDICAL RADIOLOGIC PHYSICS. *Current Pos:* ASST PROF RADIOL, UNIV CALIF, SAN FRANCISCO, 77- *Personal Data:* b Plattsburg, NY, June 12, 47; m 77. *Educ:* Col Wooster, BA, 69; Univ Pa, MS, 71; Harvard Univ, ScD, 78. *Prof Exp:* Hosp physicist, Beth Israel Hosp, Boston, 72-77. *Concurrent Pos:* Prin investr, NIH grants, 80-81 & 82-84. *Mem:* Am Asn Physicists Med; Soc Photo-Optical Instrumentation Engrs. *Res:* Medical x-ray imaging instrumentation; digital radiography; fluoroscopy; computed tomography. *Mailing Add:* Dept Radiol Univ Calif San Francisco Med Sch 513 Parnassus Ave San Francisco CA 94122-2722

GOULD, ROBERT JAMES, ANTITHROMBOTICS, PLATELETS. *Current Pos:* sr res pharmacologist, Merck, Sharp & Dohme Res Labs, 84-87, res fel, 87-90, assoc dir, 90-91, dir Thrombosis Res, 92-93, sr dir thrombosis res, 93-95, EXEC DIR PHARMACOL, MERCK RES LABS, 95- *Personal Data:* b Hong Kong, Dec 9, 54; Can citizen; m 78, Sherry L Roe; c John & Ryan. *Educ:* Spring Arbor Col, BA, 76; Univ Iowa, PhD (biochem), 81. *Prof Exp:* Res fel, Dept Neurosci, Johns Hopkins Univ, 81-84. *Mem:* Am Soc Biochem & Molecular Biol; Am Soc Pharmacol & Exp Therapeut; Soc Neurosci; Thrombosis Coun Am Heart Asn. *Res:* Membrane receptors, platelets and antithrombotics. *Mailing Add:* Merck Sharp & Dohme Res Labs W26-265 West Point PA 19486. *Fax:* 215-652-0800; *E-Mail:* robert_gould@merck.com

GOULD, ROBERT JOSEPH, THEORETICAL PHYSICS, ASTROPHYSICS. *Current Pos:* From res physicist to asst res physicist, 63-65, from asst prof to assoc prof, 65-76, PROF PHYSICS, UNIV CALIF, SAN DIEGO, 76- *Personal Data:* b Providence, RI, May 31, 35. *Educ:* Providence Col, BS, 57; Cornell Univ, PhD(theoret physics), 63. *Concurrent Pos:* Sr lectr, Univ Sydney, 68-69; vis scholar, Stanford Univ, 75-76. *Mem:* Am Phys Soc; Am Astron Soc. *Res:* Theoretical astrophysics; atomic processes in low-density plasmas; high-energy phenomena in astrophysics. *Mailing Add:* Dept Physics 0319 Univ Calif La Jolla CA 92093

GOULD, ROBERT K, ACOUSTICS. *Current Pos:* RETIRED. *Personal Data:* b Gloucester, Mass, Jan 4, 29; div; c 3. *Educ:* Univ Maine, BS, 51; Brown Univ, MS, 56, PhD(physics), 61. *Prof Exp:* Asst prof physics, Muskingum Col, 57-59; from asst prof to assoc prof, Lafayette Col, 60-68; chmn dept, Middlebury Col, 68-80, prof physics, 80- *Mem:* Acoust Soc Am; Am Asn Physics Teachers. *Res:* High intensity sound. *Mailing Add:* 650 W Harrison Ave Claremont CA 91711

GOULD, ROBERT KINKADE, CHEMICAL PHYSICS, FLUID MECHANICS. *Current Pos:* SR RES SCIENTIST, STAND OIL ENG MATS CO, 86- *Personal Data:* b Lawrenceville, Ill, Sept 6, 40; m 65; c 2. *Educ:* Wash Univ, AB, 62; Univ Wis, PhD(physics), 69. *Prof Exp:* Staff scientist, Aerochem Res Labs, 69-78, head, Appl Physics Group, 78-81; res dir, Universal Silicon Inc, 81-86. *Mem:* Am Phys Soc; Mat Res Soc; Fire Particle Soc; AAAS. *Res:* Turbulence; two-phase flows; combustion and high temperature chemistry; aerosol science. *Mailing Add:* 9835 Hollingson Rd Clarence NY 14031

GOULD, ROBERT WILLIAM, MATERIALS FAILURE ANALYSIS. *Current Pos:* from instr to prof metall, 59-80, prof mat sci & eng, 80-89, EMER PROF MAT SCI & ENG, UNIV FLA, 89-; ADJ PROF, HOLLAND LAW CENTER. *Personal Data:* b Shanghai, China, Feb 5, 34; US citizen; m 55, Marcia Rodes; c 4. *Educ:* Univ Fla, BS, 55, MS, 62, PhD(metall), 64. *Prof Exp:* Field engr, Am Cyanamid Co, 57; res engr, Kaiser Aluminum & Chem Corp, 57-59. *Concurrent Pos:* Pres PLC Inc; consult engr, Gould Lewis & Proctor. *Mem:* Am Soc Testing & Mat; Am Soc Metals; Soc Automotive Engrs; Soc Plastics Engrs; Am Inst Mining & Metall Engrs; Am Soc Mech Engrs; Am Ceramic Soc; Sigma Xi. *Res:* Characterization of materials, especially x-ray diffraction and electron spectroscopy; failure analysis of materials; product liability and engineering. *Mailing Add:* Gould Lewis & Proctor 6712 NW 18th Dr Gainesville FL 32653. *Fax:* 352-375-7689; *E-Mail:* plcinc@vectornet.com

GOULD, ROY W(ALTER), PHYSICS, ELECTRICAL ENGINEERING. *Current Pos:* asst prof elec eng, Calif Inst Technol, 55-58, from assoc prof to prof elec eng & physics, 58-73, prof appl physics, 74-79, exec officer appl physics, 73-79, chmn, Div Eng & Appl Sci, 79-85, Simon Ramo Prof, 79-96, EMER PROF ENG, CALIF INST TECHNOL, 96- *Personal Data:* b Los Angeles, Calif, Apr 25, 27; m 52, Ethel Stratton; c 2. *Educ:* Calif Inst Technol, BS, 49, PhD(physics), 56; Stanford Univ, MS, 50. *Honors & Awards:* James Clerk Maxwell Prize Plasma Physics, Am Phys Soc, 94. *Prof Exp:* Res engr missile guid, Jet Propulsion Lab, Calif Inst Technol, 51-52; res engr electron tubes, Hughes Aircraft Co, 53-55. *Concurrent Pos:* NSF sr fel, 63-64; asst dir res, US AEC, DC, 70-72. *Mem:* Nat Acad Sci; Nat Acad Eng; fel Am Phys Soc; fel Inst Elec & Electronics Engrs; fel Am Acad Arts & Sci. *Res:* Electron and ion dynamics; plasma oscillation and wave phenomena; physics of ionized gases; electromagnetism; microwaves; plasma physics; fusion energy. *Mailing Add:* Calif Inst Technol Mail Sta 128-95 Pasadena CA 91125. *E-Mail:* rwgould@caltech.edu

GOULD, STEPHEN JAY, PALEONTOLOGY. *Current Pos:* from asst prof to assoc prof, 67-73, from asst cur to assoc cur invert paleont, 67-73, PROF GEOL, HARVARD UNIV, 73-, ALEXANDER AGASSIZ PROF ZOOL, 82- *Personal Data:* b New York, NY, Sept 10, 41; m 65; c 2. *Educ:* Antioch Col, AB, 63; Columbia Univ, PhD(paleont), 67. *Hon Degrees:* Many from US Cols & Univs, 82-95. *Honors & Awards:* Schuchert Award, Paleont Soc, 75; Distinguished Serv Award, Am Humanists' Asn, 84 & Am Geol Inst, 86; Meritorious Serv Award, Am Asn Systs Collections; Silver Medal, Zool Soc London, 84; Tanner Lectr, Cambridge Univ, Eng, 84; Terry Lectr, Yale Univ, 86; Glenn T Seaborg Award, Int Platform Asn, 86; Anthrop Media Award, Am Anthrop Asn, 87; Hist Geol Award, Geol Soc Am, 88; Distinguished Serv Award, Am Inst Prof Geologists, 89; Brittanica Award & Gold Medal, 90; Inaugural Lectr for Isaiah Berlin Ann Lect, Wolfson Col, Oxford Univ, 91; Lilly Lectr, Royal Col Physicians, London, 93. *Prof Exp:* Instr geol, Antioch Col, 66. *Concurrent Pos:* Prin investr var grants, NSF, 69-; assoc ed, Evolution, 70-72; assoc cur invert paleont, Mus Comp Zool, Harvard Univ, 71-73, cur invert paleont, 73-, adj mem, Dept Hist Sci, 73-; counr, Paleont Soc, 73-75; mem coun, AAAS, 74-76 Nat Portrait Gallery, 89- & Space Explor Coun, NASA, 89-91; bd dirs, Biol Sci Curric Study, 76-79, Brit Mus Natural Hist Int Found, 92-; mem, Smithsonian Coun, 76-88, adv bd, Children's TV Workshop, 78-81 & adv bd, NOVA, 80-; McArthur Prize fel, 81-86; int bd dirs, Gallery Evolution, Mus Natural Hist, Paris, 89; mem bd, Brit Mus Natural Hist Int Found, 92-; mem, Comn Future, Smithsonian Inst, 92-94; mem bd trustees, Rockefeller Found, 94- *Mem:* Nat Acad Sci; Paleont Soc (pres, 85-86); Soc Study Evolution (vpres, 75-76, pres, 90-91); Soc Syst Zool; Am Soc Naturalists (pres, 79-80); fel Am Acad Arts & Sci; hon foreign fel Europ Union Geosci; Sigma Xi; Hist Sci Soc; fel AAAS. *Res:* Evolutionary paleontology; quantitative studies of form, function and ontogeny in relation to phylogeny; evolution and speciation in land snails; systematic zoology; history and philosophy of geology and evolutionary biology; author of 18 books. *Mailing Add:* Mus Comp Zool Harvard Univ Cambridge MA 02138

GOULD, STEVEN JAMES, NATURAL PRODUCT CHEMISTRY. *Current Pos:* EXEC DIR, NATURAL PROD DRUG DISCOVERY, MERCK RES LABS. *Personal Data:* b New York, NY, Feb 18, 46; m 88, Mary Marshall. *Educ:* Univ Calif, Los Angeles, BS, 66; Mass Inst Technol, PhD(org chem), 70. *Prof Exp:* Fel, Swiss Fed Inst Technol, 70-72; sr res chemist org chem, Syva Res Inst, Palo Alto, 72-74; asst prof, Sch Pharm, Univ Conn, 74-80, assoc prof pharmacog, 80-82; assoc prof chem, Ore State Univ, 82-86, prof chem, 86- *Concurrent Pos:* Res career develop award, Nat Cancer Inst, NIH, 79-84; Fulbright fel, 89-90; Am Cancer Soc, 89-90. *Mem:* Am Chem Soc; Am Soc Pharmacog; AAAS; Sigma Xi. *Res:* Biosynthesis of natural products; enzyme reaction mechanisms as studied with isotopically-labeled substrates; synthesis of natural products; steptomyces molecular genetics; isolation and sructures of natural products. *Mailing Add:* 4 Nottingham Way Warren NJ 07059. *Fax:* 732-594-1300; *E-Mail:* steve.gould@merck.com

GOULD, WALTER LEONARD, WEED SCIENCE, NATURAL RESOURCES. *Current Pos:* instr, 57-60, asst prof, 66-69, ASSOC PROF AGRON, N MEX STATE UNIV, 69- *Personal Data:* b Burlington, Wyo, Apr 5, 23; m 47; c 3. *Educ:* Univ Wyo, BS, 48, MS, 57; Oregon State Univ, PhD(field crops), 64. *Prof Exp:* Conservationist, Soil Conserv Serv, USDA, 48-56, agronomist, Agr Res Serv, 64-66. *Mem:* Weed Sci Soc Am; Soc Range Mgt. *Res:* Weed control in field and vegetable crops and on rangeland; control of brush on rangeland; reclamation of surface-mine spoils. *Mailing Add:* 1812 Imperial Ridge St Las Cruces NM 88011

GOULD, WALTER PHILLIP, FORESTRY, WILDLIFE MANAGEMENT. *Current Pos:* assoc prof forest & wildlife mgt & chmn dept, 54-87, EMER PROF, UNIV RI, 87- *Personal Data:* b North Adams, Mass, July 14, 25; m 54; c 2. *Educ:* Univ Mass, BS, 50; Yale Univ, MF, 51; Syracuse Univ,

PhD(forest shrub ecol), 66. *Prof Exp:* Forester, Brown Co, 51-54. *Concurrent Pos:* Fel, Mem Univ Nfld, 67-68. *Mem:* Soc Am Foresters; Wildlife Soc. *Res:* Effects of silvicultural practices on the ecology of forest wildlife species. *Mailing Add:* 6 Johnny Cake Trail S Narragansett RI 02879

GOULD, WILBUR ALPHONSO, FOOD SCIENCE, HORTICULTURE. *Current Pos:* RETIRED. *Personal Data:* b Colebrook, NH, Aug 7, 20; m 44; c 3. *Educ:* Univ NH, BS, 42; Ohio State Univ, MS, 47, PhD(hort, food technol), 49. *Prof Exp:* Plant breeder, Ferry-Morse Seed Co, 42; food inspector, USDA, 43-44; from instr to prof hort, Ohio State Univ, 47-85, head div food processing, 56-85. *Concurrent Pos:* Exec dir, Mid Am Food Processors Asn, 56-; food consult annual fine food expos, Ger, USDA, 59. *Mem:* Fel AAAS; Am Soc Hort Sci; fel Inst Food Technologists. *Res:* Quality evaluation and control in food processing, especially plant efficiencies; new product development; food regulations and standards. *Mailing Add:* PO Box 312 Worthington OH 43085

GOULD, WILLIAM ALLEN, MATHEMATICS, COMPUTER SCIENCE. *Current Pos:* From instr to assoc prof math, 66-70, prof & asst dir comput ctr, 70-82, DIR COMPUT CTR, SHIPPENSBURG UNIV, 82- *Personal Data:* b Clearfield, Pa, Dec 3, 41; m 65; c 5. *Educ:* Elizabethtown Col, BS, 63; Pa State Univ, MA, 66, EdD(math), 71. *Mem:* Math Asn Am. *Res:* Solution preserving operators for three-dimensional second order partial differential equations; computer simulation of the academic course loadings. *Mailing Add:* Comput Ctr Shippensburg Univ Shippensburg PA 17257

GOULD, WILLIAM DOUGLAS, MICROBIOLOGY. *Current Pos:* RES MICROBIOLOGIST, ENERGY MINES & RESOURCES, CAN, 86- *Personal Data:* Orillia, Ont, Apr 13, 44. *Educ:* Univ Manitoba, BSc, 65; Univ Alta, MSc, 70, PhD(soil microbiol), 76. *Prof Exp:* Chemist, Kalium Chem, Ltd, 66-67; fel, Colo State Univ, 76-79; environ microbiologist, Agr Can, 79-82; res microbiologist, Allied Corp, 82-86. *Concurrent Pos:* Adj asst prof, State Univ NY, Syracuse, 83-; adj res prof, Carleton Univ, Ottawa, 91- *Mem:* Sigma Xi; Am Soc Microbiol; Can Soc Microbiol; Am Soc Agron; Int Soc Soil Sci. *Res:* Metabolism of thiobacilli; treatment of wastes produced by the mining industry. *Mailing Add:* Energy Mines & Resource Co 555 Booth St Ottawa ON K1G 0G1 Can

GOULD, WILLIAM E, MATHEMATICS. *Current Pos:* assoc prof, 69-74, PROF MATH, CALIF STATE UNIV, DOMINGUEZ HILLS, 74- *Personal Data:* b Orange, NJ, May 7, 34. *Educ:* Rutgers Univ, BA, 56, MS, 58; Princeton Univ, MA, 64, PhD(math), 66. *Prof Exp:* Instr math, Rutgers Univ, 61-62 & Wash Col, 62-66; assoc prof, Bradley Univ, 66-69. *Mem:* Math Asn Am. *Res:* Logic. *Mailing Add:* 12529 Sleepyhollow Lane Cerritos CA 90701-2083

GOULD, WILLIAM RICHARD, MECHANICAL ENGINEERING, ELECTRICAL ENGINEERING. *Current Pos:* Mech engr, Southern Calif Edison Co, 48-49, asst supt, 49-54, supt, 54-58, gen supt, 58-59, from asst mgr to mgr, Eng Dept, 59-63, vpres, 63-67, sr vpres, 67-73, exec vpres, 73-78, pres, 78-80, chief exec officer & chmn bd, 80-84, EMER CHMN BD, SOUTHERN CALIF EDISON CO, 84- *Personal Data:* b Provo, Utah, Oct 31, 19; c 4. *Educ:* Univ Utah, BS, 42; USN, dipl naval archit, 47. *Honors & Awards:* Power-Life Award, Inst Elec & Electronics Engrs, 78, Centennial Medal, 84; George Westinghouse Gold Medal, Am Soc Mech Engrs, 79, Centennial Award for Serv, 79; Achievement Award, Nat Energy Found, 81; Distinguished Contrib Award, Inst Advan Eng, 82. *Concurrent Pos:* Fel, Inst Advan Eng, 71-, chmn bd, 76-; US comt pres, Int Conf Large High Voltage Elec Syts, 73; gen adv comt, US Dept Energy, 75; trustee, Calif Inst Technol, 78-; dir, Mono Power Co, Environ & Energy Serv Co, Joy Technol Inc, dir & consult, Southern Calif Edison Co. *Mem:* Nat Acad Eng; fel Am Soc Mech Engrs; Elec Power Res Inst. *Res:* Electric power generation, transmission and distribution. *Mailing Add:* Southern Calif Edison Co 2244 Walnut Grove Ave Rosemead CA 91770

GOULD, WILLIAM ROBERT, III, ICHTHYOLOGY. *Current Pos:* RETIRED. *Personal Data:* b Cincinnati, Ohio, Nov 16, 31; m 62; c 2. *Educ:* Colo State Univ, BS, 54; Okla State Univ, MS, 60, PhD(zool), 62. *Prof Exp:* NIH fel, 62-63; prog leader, Bur Com Fisheries, US Fish & Wildlife Serv, 63; asst leader, Mont Coop Fishery Res Unit, Mont State Univ, 64-91. *Mem:* Am Fisheries Soc. *Res:* Biology and ecology of fishes. *Mailing Add:* 323 N 20th Ave Bozeman MT 59718

GOULDEN, CLYDE EDWARD, ECOLOGY, LIMNOLOGY. *Current Pos:* assoc cur, Dept Limnol, Acad Natural Sci, Philadelphia, 66-72, vpres res, 72-73, dir, Div Environ Res, 73-77, CUR, ACAD NATURAL SCI, PHILADELPHIA, 81-, DIR, INST MONGOLIAN BIO-DIVERSITY & ECOL STUDIES. *Personal Data:* b Kansas City, Kans, Nov 30, 36; m 57; c 2. *Educ:* Kans State Teachers Col, BS, 58, MS, 59; Ind Univ, PhD(zool), 62. *Prof Exp:* Res assoc limnol, Yale Univ, 62-64, lectr biol, 63-64, assoc prof, 64-66. *Concurrent Pos:* Res grants, Am Philos Soc Penrose Fund & Soc Sigma Xi, 64; exchange scientist, Cult Exchange Prog, Acad Sci USSR-Nat Acad Sci, 66 & NSF, 67-; adj assoc prof biol, Univ Pa, 70-71, ed, Aquatics & Ecol & Ecol Soc dir, Div Limnol & Ecol, Acad Natural Sci Philadelphia, 73-77; NSF grant, 76-78, 79 & 84-85; EPA grant, 81-82. *Mem:* Fel AAAS; Am Soc Naturalists; Soc Study Evolution; Ecol Soc Am; Int Asn Theoret & Appl Limnol. *Res:* Ecology and systematics of the Cladocera; paleolimnology; ecology of the zooplankton; evolution of the aquatic community. *Mailing Add:* Inst Mongolian Bio-Diversity & Ecol Studies 1900 Benjamin Franklin Pkwy Philadelphia PA 19103

GOULDIN, FREDERICK CASKEY, COMBUSTION, FLUID MECHANICS. *Current Pos:* from asst prof to assoc prof, 70-85, PROF MECH & AEROSPACE ENG, CORNELL UNIV, 85- *Personal Data:* b Washington, DC, July 4, 43. *Educ:* Princeton Univ, BSE, 65, PhD(aerospace eng), 70. *Concurrent Pos:* Vis staff, Sandia Nat Lab, Livermore, Calif, 76-77; vis fel, Cambridge Univ, 85-86; researcher, Nat Ctr Sci Res, Orleans, France, 93. *Mem:* Am Inst Aeronaut & Astronaut; Am Soc Mech Engrs; Soc Automotive Engrs; AAAS; Combustion Inst. *Res:* Fluid mechanics of combustion; combustion control with smart sensors; waste incineration problems; new fire suppressants to replace ozone depleting halogens. *Mailing Add:* Cornell Univ Upson Hall Ithaca NY 14853. *Fax:* 607-255-9410; *E-Mail:* fcg2@cornell.edu

GOULDING, CHARLES EDWIN, JR, bioelectronics, biomagnetics; deceased, see previous edition for last biography

GOULDING, MERRILL KEITH, FINITE ELEMENT ANALYSIS, DOME DESIGN. *Current Pos:* PRES, M K GOULDING & ASSOC, INC, 73- *Personal Data:* b Eric, Pa, Jan 21, 33; m 96, Ellen De Guzman; c Dan, Robert, Nida & Aristana. *Educ:* Univ Calif, Los Angeles, BA, 67, PhD(eng), 80. *Prof Exp:* Chief mech engr, Electronic Resources, 63-69 & Whittaker Electronics, 69-74. *Concurrent Pos:* Pres & consult, Fed Aviation Admin, 76-79, Dept Transp, 76-79, Defense Nuclear Agency, 80-81; assoc prof, Northrup Univ, 86-89. *Res:* Designed asde-3 rotodome; navy's satellite ships antenna; designed-silver legacy dome in Remo-world's largest composite structure; designed Seattle I-max dome; worked on Wai-Pau-Tau-Pam-Thailand; designed Lantau airpost asde antenna. *Mailing Add:* Merrill K Goulding & Assoc Inc 8616 La Tijera Blvd Suite 511 Los Angeles CA 90045-3945. *E-Mail:* merrill1@juno.com

GOULD-SOMERO, MEREDITH, developmental biology, for more information see previous edition

GOULET, JACQUES, FOOD SCIENCE, FOOD MICROBIOLOGY. *Current Pos:* from asst prof to assoc prof, 74-86, head dept, 80-82, PROF FOOD SCI, LAVAL UNIV, 86-; RES DIR, LALLEMAND, INC, 82- *Personal Data:* b Quebec, Can, June 22, 46; m 70; c 4. *Educ:* Laval Univ, BA, 66, BSA, 70; McGill Univ, PhD(microbiol), 74. *Prof Exp:* Res coordr, Vermette & Fils Dairy, 73-74. *Concurrent Pos:* Consult, dairy & fermentation industs. *Mem:* Am Soc Microbiol; Am Dairy Sci Asn; Inst Food Technol. *Res:* Fermented dairy products; biological treatment of industrial effluents for biomass and fermentation products recovery; probiotics. *Mailing Add:* Dept Food Sci Laval Univ Quebec PQ G1K 7P4 Can. *Fax:* 418-656-3353

GOULIAN, DICRAN, PLASTIC SURGERY. *Current Pos:* instr, Cornell Univ, 60-61, from clin asst prof to clin assoc prof surg, 61-71, assoc prof to prof, 71-94, EMER PROF SURG, MED COL, CORNELL UNIV, 95- *Personal Data:* b Weehawken, NJ, Mar 31, 27; m 54, 89, Nancy Kessler; c Linda Susan (Dastefano), Dicran III, Beverly Ann (Sherin) & Elizabeth Vera (kahle). *Educ:* Columbia Col, AB, 48; Columbia Univ, DDS, 51; Yale Univ, MD, 55; Am Bd Plastic Surg, dipl, 62. *Honors & Awards:* Ella Marie Ewell Medal Outstanding Proficiency Dent, Sch Dent & Oral Surg, Columbia Univ. *Prof Exp:* Intern gen surg, Grace-New Haven Community Hosp, 55-56, resident, 56-58; resident plastic surg, NY Hosp, 58-60. *Concurrent Pos:* NSF fel surg res, Yale Univ, 56-57; USPHS fel, Cornell Univ, 60-61; attend surgeon-in-chg plastic surg, NY Hosp-Cornell Univ Med Ctr; adj surgeon, Lenox Hill Hosp, NY; consult plastic surgeon, Bronx Vet Admin Hosp; clin abstr ed, Transplantation Bull, 61 & Transplantation, 62-66; pvt pract, 64-; treas, NY Regional Soc Plastic Surgeons, 69-72; pres sect plastic surg, NY State Med Soc, 71-72; secy sect plastic surg, NY Acad Med, 71- *Mem:* AAAS; Am Asn Cleft Palate Rehab; Am Soc Plastic & Reconstruct Surg; Am Soc Maxillofacial Surg (secy-treas, 67-71); fel NY Acad Med. *Mailing Add:* 245 E 24th St Apt 5G New York NY 10010

GOULIAN, MEHRAN, HEMATOLOGY. *Current Pos:* PROF MED, UNIV CALIF, SAN DIEGO, 70- *Personal Data:* b Weehawken, NJ, Dec 31, 29; m 61; c 3. *Educ:* Columbia Univ, AB, 50, MD, 54. *Prof Exp:* Intern, Barnes Hosp, St Louis, Mo, 54-55; resident med, Mass Gen Hosp, Boston, 58-59 & 61; instr, Harvard Univ, 63-65; assoc prof med & biochem, Univ Chicago, 67-70. *Concurrent Pos:* Fel hemat, Sch Med, Yale Univ, 59-60; res fel, Harvard Univ & Mass Gen Hosp, 60 & 62-63; fel biochem, Sch Med, Stanford Univ, 65-67. *Mem:* Am Soc Biol Chem; Am Soc Clin Invest; Am Soc Hemat; Asn Am Physicians. *Res:* Biochemistry of nucleic acids. *Mailing Add:* Dept Med Univ Calif San Diego 0613G La Jolla CA 92092-0613. *Fax:* 619-534-3946

GOULIANOS, KONSTANTIN, HIGH ENERGY PHYSICS. *Current Pos:* assoc prof, 71-81, PROF PHYSICS, ROCKEFELLER UNIV, 81- *Personal Data:* b Salonica, Greece, Nov 9, 35; m 90, Karen Grahn. *Educ:* Columbia Univ, MA, 60, PhD(physics), 63. *Prof Exp:* Res assoc physics, Columbia Univ, 63-64; instr, Princeton Univ, 64-67, asst prof, 67-71. *Concurrent Pos:* Fulbright scholar, 58-59. *Mem:* Fel Am Phys Soc. *Res:* High energy neutrino interactions; time reversal invariance; elastic scattering and diffraction dissociation; hadron collider experiments. *Mailing Add:* 11 W 69th St Apt 4A New York NY 10023-4742. *Fax:* 212-362-3840

GOULSON, HILTON THOMAS, PARASITOLOGY. *Current Pos:* Instr, Univ NC, Chapel Hill, 54-57, res assoc, 57-59, from asst prof to assoc prof, 59-69, PROF PARASITOL & LAB PRACT, SCH PUB HEALTH, UNIV NC, CHAPEL HILL, 69- *Personal Data:* b Montevideo, Minn, May 4, 30;

wid; c 2. *Educ:* Luther Col, AB, 52; Univ NC, MSPH, 53, PhD(parasitol), 57. *Mem:* Am Soc Trop Med & Hyg; Am Soc Parasitol; fel Am Pub Health Asn. *Res:* Medical parasitology; immunity studies and host-parasite relationships of nematode parasites. *Mailing Add:* 52 Oakwood Dr Chapel Hill NC 27514. *Fax:* 919-966-7141

GOUNARIS, ANNE DEMETRA, BIOCHEMISTRY, PROTEINASES. *Current Pos:* from asst prof to prof, 66-90, EMER PROF BIOCHEM, VASSAR COL, 90- *Personal Data:* b Boston, Mass, Oct 27, 24. *Educ:* Boston Univ, AB, 55; Radcliffe Col, PhD(chem), 60. *Prof Exp:* NIH res fel, Brookhaven Nat Lab, 60-62; NIH fel, Carlsberg Lab, Denmark, 62-63; Rast-Osted Found fel, 63-64; res assoc enzyme action & protein structure, Rockefeller Inst, 64-66. *Concurrent Pos:* NIH grant, 68-71 & A&M Inst, 72-76; vis scientist, Rockefeller Univ, 72-73, Dept Chem, Harvard Univ, 76-77 & Strangeways Lab, Cambridge, UK, 80-81 & 83-85; fel med, Mass Gen Hosp, 78-83; Ann Horton fel, Newnham Col, Cambridge Univ, UK, 80-81. *Mem:* AAAS; Am Chem Soc; Am Soc Biochem & Molecular Biol; Sigma Xi. *Res:* Thiamine pyrophosphate requiring enzymes; alpha-keto decarboxylase; cathepsin B; cysteine proteinase inhibitor; protein sequence analysis. *Mailing Add:* 144 Marble St No 501 Stoneham MA 02180

GOURARY, BARRY SHOLOM, MICROCOMPUTER APPLICATIONS SOFTWARE. *Current Pos:* PRES, GOURARY ASSOC INC, 73- *Personal Data:* b Rostov, Russia, Feb 10, 23; nat US; m 53, Mina Haskind; c Sonia R & Nora S (Friedman). *Educ:* Columbia Univ, AM, 50. *Prof Exp:* Asst radiation lab, Columbia Univ, 47-50, lectr math, 50-51; physicist, Sound Sect, Nat Bur Stand, 51; mem sr staff, Appl Physics Lab, Johns Hopkins Univ, 51-59, prin staff, 59-60; fel physicist, Res Labs, Westinghouse Elec Corp, 60, supvry physicist, 61, mgr luminescence sect, 61-62; sr staff scientist, Res Labs, United Aircraft Corp, 62-68; dir electronic & optical technol, Defense-Space Group, Int Tel & Tel Corp, 68-70, tech dir, Electron Tube Div, 70, dir technol, Defense-Space Group, 70-71. *Concurrent Pos:* Consult, Inst Defense Anal, 72-87. *Mgt:* Fel Am Phys Soc; Inst Elec & Electronics Engrs; Inst Mgt Sci; Am Defense Prep Asn. *Res:* Operations research; microcomputer applications software; technology assessments; planning studies; technical management; solid state physics; quantum theory; cost studies. *Mailing Add:* Gourary Assocs Inc 187 Gates Ave Montclair NJ 07042

GOURAS, PETER, PHYSIOLOGY, OPHTHALMOLOGY & RETINA. *Current Pos:* PROF OPHTHAL, COL PHYSICIANS & SURGEONS, COLUMBIA UNIV, 81- *Personal Data:* b Brooklyn, NY, Apr 15, 30; m 59; c 3. *Educ:* Johns Hopkins Univ, AB, 51, MD, 55. *Honors & Awards:* Award, Res to Prevent Blindness Inc; Alcon Res Award, 83, 91. *Prof Exp:* Intern surg, Johns Hopkins Univ, 55-56; res assoc physiol, NIH, 56-57; assoc physiol, Med Sch, Univ Pa, 59-60; res assoc ophthal & physiol, NIH, 60-68, chief, Sect Ophthal Physiol, Nat Inst Neurol Dis & Stroke, 68-71, head, Sect Physiol, Lab Vision Res, Nat Eye Inst, 71-76; head, Lab Neurobiol, Edward S Harkness Eye Inst, 76-81. *Concurrent Pos:* Nat Found fel, Cambridge Univ, 58-59; mem, Comt Vision Res & Training, Nat Eye Inst, 70-74; mem, Comt Sensory Prosthesis, Nat Inst Neurol Dis & Stroke, 70-74; mem, Sci Coun, Nat Retinitis Pigmentosa Soc, 72-78; vis prof, Neurol Inst, Univ Freiburg, 74-75; mem, Am Comt Optics & Visual Physiol, Sect Opthal, AMA, 75-78; mem, NIH Visual Sci Study Sect B, 78-82. *Mem:* AAAS; fel Optical Soc Am; Am Physiol Soc; Int Soc Clin Electroretinography; Asn Res Vision & Ophthal. *Res:* Neurophysiology; retina; visual pathways; vision. *Mailing Add:* Dept Ophthal Columbia Univ 630 W 168th St New York NY 10032-3702. *E-Mail:* pg10@columbia.edu

GOURDINE, MEREDITH CHARLES, DIRECT ENERGY CONVERSION, MAGNETOHYDRODYNAMICS. *Current Pos:* PRES ENERGY, ENERGY INNOVATIONS, INC, 74- *Personal Data:* b Newark, NJ, Sept 26, 29. *Educ:* Cornell Univ, BS, 53; Calif Inst Technol, PhD(eng), 60. *Prof Exp:* Res scientist aerospace, Jet Propulsion Lab, 59-60; lab dir aerospace, Plasmadyne Corp, 60-62; chief scientist aeronaut, Curtiss Wright Corp, 62-64; pres energy conversion res & develop, Gourdine Systs, Inc, 64-73. *Mem:* Nat Acad Eng; NY Acad Eng; Am Inst Aeronaut & Astronaut; Sigma Xi. *Res:* Direct energy conversion; electrogasdynamic which is related to interaction between an electric field and charged particles in gases; applications include: airport fog clearing, air pollution control systems, coating systems etc; thermovoltaic batteries and vortadynamic energy conversion systems; 70 US/foreign patents; author and co-author of over 20 publications. *Mailing Add:* Energy Innovations Inc 8709 Knight Rd Houston TX 77054

GOURISHANKAR, V (GOURI), ELECTRICAL ENGINEERING, CONTROL SYSTEMS. *Current Pos:* from assoc prof to prof, 65-94, EMER PROF ELEC ENG, UNIV ALTA, 94- *Personal Data:* b Simla, Punjab, India, Jan 22, 29; m 66, Radha; c Arvind & Sita. *Educ:* Univ Madras, BE, 50; Univ Ill, MS, 58, PhD, 61. *Prof Exp:* Asst prof elec eng, Univ Ill, Urbana-Champaign, 61-65. *Mem:* Inst Elec & Electronics Engrs. *Res:* Process control systems; identification; adaptive control; robotics. *Mailing Add:* Dept Elec Eng Univ Alta Edmonton AB T6G 2G7 Can. *Fax:* 403-492-1811; *E-Mail:* gour@eigen.ee.ualberta.ca

GOURLEY, DESMOND ROBERT HUGH, PHARMACOLOGY. *Current Pos:* prof, 73-86, EMER PROF PHARMACOL, EASTERN VA MED SCH, 86- *Personal Data:* b Thunder Bay, Ont, Nov 2, 22; US citizen; m 46, Marjorie E Curl; c Robin C, David W, Alan W, Bruce D & Donald R. *Educ:* Univ Toronto, BA, 45, PhD(cellular physiol), 49. *Honors & Awards:* Horsley Prize for Res, 52. *Prof Exp:* Lab instr comp anat, Univ Toronto, 45-46, asst cellular physiol, 46-47, demonstr, 47-49; res asst, Sch Med, Univ Va, 49-51, from asst prof to prof pharmacol, 51-73, actg chmn dept, 65, chmn dept, 67-68. *Concurrent Pos:* Fedn Am Soc Exp Biol travel grant, Brussels, 56 & Int Union Physiol Soc travel grant, Buenos Aires, 59; mem, US Pharmacopeial Conv, 60-65 & 80-86; Humboldt Found fel, Univ Freiburg, 68-69; adj instr, Sch Continuing Educ, Univ Va, 70-91; adj prof chem, Old Dom Univ, 75-86. *Mem:* Am Soc Pharmacol & Exp Therapeut; Am Physiol Soc; Soc Exp Biol & Med; Pharmacol Soc Can. *Res:* Effects of insulin on isolated muscle tissue; active transport and phosphate metabolism in erythrocytes; effects of drugs at cell membranes; molecular mechanism of drug tolerance and dependence. *Mailing Add:* Rte 1 Box 572 Roseland VA 22967-9204

GOURLEY, EUGENE VINCENT, ZOOLOGY. *Current Pos:* assoc prof, 69-79, PROF BIOL, RADFORD COL, 79- *Personal Data:* b Detroit, Mich, Nov 15, 40; m 62; c 2. *Educ:* Eastern Mich Univ, BA, 62, MS, 64; Univ Fla, PhD(turtle behav), 69. *Prof Exp:* Interim instr zool, Univ Fla, 68-69. *Mem:* AAAS; Am Soc Zoologists; Animal Behav Soc; Sigma Xi. *Mailing Add:* 1009 Ninth St Radford VA 24141-2803

GOURLEY, FRANK ARNETT, JR, ENGINEERING TECHNOLOGY ADMINISTRATION. *Current Pos:* DIV DIR ENG TECHNOL/INDUST TECHNOL, WVA UNIV INST TECHNOL, 90- *Personal Data:* div; c Elizabeth G (Read) & Frank A. *Educ:* Va Polytech Inst, BS, 62; NC State Univ, MS, 70, PhD(occup educ), 84. *Prof Exp:* Instr eng, Danville Br, Va Polytech Inst, 62-65; dir eng tech progs, NC Dept Community Cols, 66-80; coordr craft & tech develop, Carolina Power & Light Co, 80-87, sr engr, Safety Sect, 87-90. *Concurrent Pos:* Dir, Eng Tech Coun, Am Soc Eng Educ; comnr, Technol Accreditation Comn, Accreditation Bd Eng & Technol, 95-. *Mem:* Am Soc Mech Engrs; Am Soc Eng Educ. *Res:* Extensive curriculum development activities in engineering technology and industrial technology programs at the state community college and university level; coordinated development of industrial training materials and programs at the corporate level. *Mailing Add:* PO Box 241 Montgomery WV 25136

GOURLEY, LLOYD EUGENE, JR, PHYSICS. *Current Pos:* from assoc prof to prof, Austin Col, 59-88, assoc dean & chmn sci area, 74-77, dean sci, 77-80, EMER PROF PHYSICS, AUSTIN COL, 88- *Personal Data:* b Bergheim, Tex, Apr 22, 23; m 48, 76, Martha Tarry; c Martha Terry. *Educ:* Univ Tex, BS, 46, MA, 48, PhD, 59. *Prof Exp:* Asst physicist, Atlantic Refining Co, 48-51; res physicist, NMex Inst Mining & Technol, 51-56. *Res:* Properties of solids under high pressures. *Mailing Add:* 3731 Jefferson Dr Denison TX 75020

GOURLEY, PAUL LEE, EXPERIMENTAL CELL BIOPHYSICS, PHYSICS OF SEMICONDUCTORS. *Current Pos:* mem tech staff, 80-87, div supvr, 87-92, sr staff/prog coordr, sandia nat lab, 92-, DISTINGUISHED MEM STAFF, 95- *Personal Data:* b Fargo, ND, Mar 15, 52; m 81, Gail Goforth; c Cheryl R & Brett A. *Educ:* Univ NDak, BS, 74; Univ Ill, MS, 76, PhD(physics), 80. *Honors & Awards:* Dept Energy Award Outstanding Semiconductor Res, 85 & 93. *Prof Exp:* Res asst, Univ NDak, 72-73, US Bur Mines, 73-74; teaching asst & res asst, Univ Ill, 76-79. *Concurrent Pos:* Bd chmn, Soc Photo Optical Instrumentation Engr. *Mem:* Fel Am Phys Soc; Optical Soc Am; Mat Res Soc; Sigma Xi; Soc Photo-Instrumentation Engrs. *Res:* Artifically structured materials, semiconductors, surface-emitting and strained-layer lasers; optical switching phenomenon and devices; semiconductor optical interference structure devices; lattice mismatched semiconductor epitaxy, excitonic phenomenon, electronic transport and recombination; defects in semiconductors; experimental cell biophysics; biological microcavity laser; semiconductor handstructures; laser spectroscopy. *Mailing Add:* 12508 Loyola Ave NE Albuquerque NM 87112. *Fax:* 505-844-1197; *E-Mail:* plgourl@sandia.gov

GOURSE, JEROME ALLEN, ORGANIC CHEMISTRY. *Personal Data:* b Bristol, Va, June 15, 29; m; c 2. *Educ:* Va Polytech Inst, BS, 50; Univ Del, MS, 51; Univ Ill, PhD(chem), 59. *Prof Exp:* Res chemist & group leader, Velsicol Chem, Corp, 58-82. *Mem:* Am Chem Soc; fel Am Inst Chem; Sigma Xi. *Res:* Agricultural chemistry. *Mailing Add:* 16606 Calico Pl Tampa FL 33618

GOURSE, RICHARD LAWRENCE, MOLECULAR BIOLOGY, GENETICS. *Current Pos:* FEL, UNIV WIS, 82- *Personal Data:* b Fall River, Mass, Apr 5, 49; m 76. *Educ:* Brown Univ, AB, 71, MAT, 73, PhD(molecular biol), 80. *Prof Exp:* Fel, Brown Univ, 80-82. *Res:* Methods for introducing and analyzing site-directed mutations in ribosomal RNA in order to examine ribosome structure and function; control of gene expression; ribosome structure and function. *Mailing Add:* Dept Bact Univ Wis 1550 Linden Dr Madison WI 53706-1567. *Fax:* 608-262-9865

GOURZIS, JAMES THEOPHILE, CLINICAL PHARMACOLOGY, RESEARCH ADMINISTRATION. *Current Pos:* VPRES, MTRA. *Personal Data:* b Boston, Mass, Mar 30, 28; m 62; c 2. *Educ:* Harvard Univ, AB, 49; Boston Univ, AM, 51; Univ Man, PhD, 62, MD, 63. *Prof Exp:* Jr pharmacologist, Ciba Pharm Prod Inc, 51-52; sr pharmacologist, Riker Lab, Inc, 52-57; res assoc pharmacol & therapeut, Univ Man, 57-62, lectr, 62-63; lectr, Col Med, Univ Cincinnati, 63-66; asst dir clin invest, McNeil Labs Inc, 66-68, dir clin pharmacol, 68-70; dir clin pharmacol, Schering Corp, 70-73, sr dir clin res, 73-77; dir clin pharmacol, Merrell Res Ctr, 77-80, exec dir med serv, 80-81; vpres med affairs, Gensia Pharmaceut, 88-89; pres, Medrand, Inc, 81- *Concurrent Pos:* Assoc dir, Bethesda Med Res Ctr, 64-66; mem bd dirs, Sperti Drug Prod Inc, 81-83, Itesco, Inc 85-87; gen mgr & dir, Hill Top Pharmatest, 86-88. *Mem:* Am Soc Pharmacol & Exp Therapeut; Drug Info Asn; Can Pharmacol Soc; Am Soc Clin Pharmacol & Therapeut; Asn Clin Pharmacol. *Res:* Cardiovascular physiology and pharmacology; drug development; consultation. *Mailing Add:* Parexel Int Corp 195 West St Waltham MA 02154. *Fax:* 781-487-0525

GOUSE, S WILLIAM, JR, SYSTEM DESIGN & MECHANICAL ENGINEERING, ENERGY SYSTEMS & TECHNOLOGY. *Current Pos:* ASSOC ED, ENERGY SOURCES, 94- *Personal Data:* b Utica, NY, Dec 15, 31; m 55, Jacqueline McLaughlin; c Linda E & S William III. *Educ:* Mass Inst Technol, SB & SM, 54, ScD(mech eng), 58. *Honors & Awards:* Sir AL Mudslior Endowment Lectr Technol, Univ Madras, India, 69; Meritorious Serv, Energy Res & Develop Admin, 76; Lord Melchatt Medal & Lectr, Inst of Energy, London 94. *Prof Exp:* From instr to assoc prof mech eng, Mass Inst Technol, 56-67; prof, Carnegie-Mellon Univ, 67-69; tech asst for civilian technol to dir, Off Sci & Technol, Off to Pres, 69-70; assoc dean Carnegie Inst Technol & Sch of Urban & Pub Affairs, Carnegie-Mellon Univ, 71-73; dir, Off Res & Develop & Sci Adv to Secy, US Dept Interior, 73-75, actg dir, Off Coal Res, 74-75; dep asst adminr fossil energy, Energy Res & Develop Admin, 75-77; chief sci, Mitre Corp, Va, 77-79, vpres Metrek Div, 79-80, vpres & gen mgr, Metrek Div, 80-84, sr vpres & gen mgr, Civil Systs Div, 84-92, sr vpres, 92-94. *Concurrent Pos:* Mem fluid mech comt, Am Soc Mech Engrs, 65-73, Energy Conversion Comt, Am Soc Eng Educ, 69-72, Panel Eval US Nat Heart & Lung Inst Artificial Heart Prog, 70, Int Comt Coal Res, 74-, Nat Energy Outlook Comt, US Energy Asn, 87-; distinguished lectr, mech eng, Pa State Univ, 80; adj prof eng & pub policy, Carregie-Mellon Univ, 80-90; managing dir, Energy Sys & Techno, 94. *Mem:* Explorers Club, US Energy Asn; fel Am Soc Mech Engrs; Soc Automotive Engrs; assoc fel Am Inst Aeronaut & Astronaut; Sigma Xi. *Res:* Energy; transportation; housing; environment; heat transfer; engineering education; automotive propulsion; information systems. *Mailing Add:* 22518 Curtis Mill Lane Richardsville VA 22736-1815. *Fax:* 540-392-1540

GOUST, JEAN MICHEL, NEUROIMMUNOLOGY, CLINICAL IMMUNOLOGY. *Current Pos:* asst prof immunol, 75-80, med, 76-80, PROF IMMUNOL, MED UNIV SC, 85-, ASSOC PROF NEUROL, 81- *Personal Data:* b Paris, France, Jan 21, 41; m 63; c 2. *Educ:* Facul Med, Univ Paris, BA, 58, Dr, 71, Am Bd Med Lab Immunol, dipl, 80. *Prof Exp:* Resident med, Univ Paris VI, 68-72, instr exp path, 69-72, asst prof med, 72-74, asst prof immunol, 72-74. *Concurrent Pos:* Prin investr, Nat Inst Neurol Commun Disorders & Stroke, 80-83 & Nat Multiple Sclerosis Soc, 78-85. *Mem:* Am Asn Immunologists; Am Soc Microbiol; Soc Exp Biol & Med; Am Fedn Clin Res. *Res:* Clinical immunology: investigation of abnormal immunoregulation in various neurological disorders, primarily multiple sclerosis. *Mailing Add:* Dept BCIM Med Univ SC 171 Ashley Ave Charleston SC 29425-0001

GOUSTIN, ANTON SCOTT, DNA CLONING, SITE-DIRECTED MUTAGENESIS. *Current Pos:* INVESTR, CTR BLOOD RES, BOSTON, 86-; INSTR PEDIAT, HARVARD MED SCH, 87- *Personal Data:* b Minneapolis, Minn, July 8, 53; m 83; c 2. *Educ:* Univ Minn, BA, 74; Univ Calif, Berkeley, PhD(zool), 79. *Prof Exp:* Res asst biochem, Univ Minn, St Paul, 81-82; asst appl cell & molecular biol, Univ Umea, Sweden, 82-85; res assoc biochem & molecular biol, Mayo Clin & Found, Rochester, Minn, 85-86. *Concurrent Pos:* Prin investr award, Soc Develop Biol, 79. *Mem:* Am Soc Cell Biol; Soc Develop Biol; AAAS. *Res:* Peptide growth factors, their mechanism of action and role in embryonic development and in neoplasia; transforming growth factors alpha and beta, and their platelet derived growth factor; structural-functional analysis of platelet-derived growth factor-like proteins. *Mailing Add:* Ctr Molecular Biol Wayne State Univ 5047 Gullen Mall Detroit MI 48202-3917. *Fax:* 313-577-6200

GOUTERMAN, MARTIN (PAUL), CHEMICAL PHYSICS. *Current Pos:* assoc prof, 66-68, PROF CHEM, UNIV WASH, 68- *Personal Data:* b Philadelphia, Pa, Dec 26, 31; c Mikaelin Bluespruce. *Educ:* Univ Chicago, BA, 51, MS, 55, PhD(physics), 58. *Prof Exp:* Res fel chem, Harvard Univ, 58-59, instr, 59-61, asst prof, 61-66. *Mem:* Fel Am Phys Soc; Am Chem Soc. *Res:* Electronic spectra of porphyrins; electronic phenomena porphyrin solids; porphyrin luminesence sensors; pressure sensitive paint for aerodynamic research. *Mailing Add:* Univ Wash Box 351700 Seattle WA 98195-1700. *Fax:* 206-685-8665; *E-Mail:* goutermn@chem.washington.edu

GOUTMANN, MICHEL MARCEL, COMMUNICATION SYSTEMS, INFORMATION THEORY. *Current Pos:* mem res & develop staff, Magnavox/Gen Atronics Corp, 67-73, dept mgr, 73-81, tech dir, 81-85, DIR ENG, MAGNAVOX/GEN ATRONICS CORP, 85- *Personal Data:* b Lyon, France, Jan 2, 39; US citizen; m 68; c 2. *Educ:* Mass Inst Technol, BS & MS, 61; Cornell Univ, PhD (elec eng), 65. *Prof Exp:* Ford fel & asst prof elec eng, Mass Inst Technol, 65-67. *Concurrent Pos:* Adj prof, Univ Pa, 80-86. *Mem:* Fel Inst Elec & Electronics Engrs. *Res:* Design and implementation of digital communication systems and networks operating in the presence of distortion, noise and electronic counter measures. *Mailing Add:* Vpres Gen Atronics Corp 1200 E Mermaid Lane Philadelphia PA 19118

GOUW, T(AN) H(OK), ANALYTICAL CHEMISTRY, CHEMICAL ENGINEERING. *Current Pos:* res chemist, Chevron Res Co, 63-68, sr res engr, 68-76, sr engr assoc, 76-88, sr staff scientist, 88-92, TECH CONSULT, CHEVRON RES CO, 92- *Personal Data:* b Jakarta, Indonesia, Jan 17, 33; US citizen; m 60; c 2. *Educ:* Delft Technol Univ, ChemIng, 58, DSc, 62. *Prof Exp:* Asst chem eng, Delft Technol Univ, 58-62; assoc res chemist, Calif Res Corp, 62-63. *Concurrent Pos:* Mem staff, letters & sci exten, Univ Calif, Berkeley, 64-72. *Mem:* Am Chem Soc; Neth Royal Inst Eng; Am Soc Testing & Mat. *Res:* Chromatography; analytical physico-chemical separation methods; instrumental methods of analysis; petroleum chemistry. *Mailing Add:* 7783 Duke Ct El Cerrito CA 94530-2544. *Fax:* 510-527-2640; *E-Mail:* flavoral@aol.com

GOVAN, DUNCAN EBEN, UROLOGY. *Current Pos:* from asst prof to assoc prof, 61-70, PROF SURG, SCH MED, STANFORD UNIV, 70- *Personal Data:* b Winnipeg, Man, Aug 23, 23; m 50; c 6. *Educ:* Univ Man, MD, 48; FRCP(C), 56; Univ Chicago, PhD(surg), 57. *Prof Exp:* Instr urol, Sch Med, Univ Chicago, 53-54; pvt pract, Can, 54-61. *Concurrent Pos:* Surg consult, Vet Admin Hosp, Palo Alto, Calif, 61-67 & Santa Clara County Hosp, San Jose, 65-67. *Mem:* Fel Am Col Surg. *Res:* Neurophysiology of the urinary tract; pediatric urology; hydronephrosis and urinary infection. *Mailing Add:* Dept Urol S287 Stanford Univ Med Ctr Stanford CA 94305

GOVE, HARRY EDMUND, PHYSICS. *Current Pos:* chmn dept physics, 77-80, PROF PHYSICS & DIR, NUCLEAR STRUCT RES LAB, UNIV ROCHESTER, 63- *Personal Data:* b Niagara Falls, Ont, Can, May 22, 22; nat US; m 45; c 2. *Educ:* Queen's Univ, BSc, 44; Mass Inst Technol, PhD(physics), 50. *Prof Exp:* Res assoc, Mass Inst Technol, 50-52; assoc res officer, Atomic Energy Can, Ltd, 52-58, br head nuclear physics, 56-63, sr res officer, 58-63. *Mem:* Fel Am Phys Soc; Can Asn Physicists. *Res:* Structure of nuclei and mechanisms of nuclear reactions principally employing particle accelerators; ultrasensitive atom spectrometry with electrostatic accelerators. *Mailing Add:* Univ Rochester River Campus Sta Rochester NY 14627

GOVE, NORWOOD BABCOCK, NUCLEAR PHYSICS. *Current Pos:* COMPUT ANALYST, OAK RIDGE NAT LAB, 58- *Personal Data:* b New York, NY, Oct 23, 32; m 59; c 3. *Educ:* Harvard Univ, BA, 53; Univ Ill, PhD(physics), 58. *Mem:* Am Phys Soc; Am Soc Info Sci; Sigma Xi. *Res:* Decay schemes of radioactive nuclei; information science. *Mailing Add:* 120 Dana Dr Oak Ridge TN 37830

GOVER, JAMES E, RADIATION EFFECTS IN MICROELECTRONICS. *Current Pos:* Staff mem, 63-73, DIV SUPVR, SANDIA NAT LABS, 73- *Personal Data:* b Bronston, Ky, Dec 30, 40; m 64; c 2. *Educ:* Univ Ky, BS, 63; Univ NMex, MS, 65, PhD(nuclear eng), 71. *Concurrent Pos:* Lectr, Inst Elec & Electronics Engrs, 80, 81, 83, 84, 86 & 87; gen chem, Inst Elec & Electronics Engrs, 83, steering comt, 81-84, Nuclear & Spec Radiation Effects Conf, cong fel, 88 & 91, vchmn, 91; gen chmn, Heart Conf, 83, tech prog chmn, 86, invited speaker 89; US House Reps, 88. *Mem:* Fel Inst Elec & Electronics Engrs; Heart Soc; AAAS. *Res:* Radiation effects and radiation effects phenomena; pulsed power technology; thermomechanical shocks; energy systems technology; electromagnetic pulse phenomena; competitiveness of American technology and industry. *Mailing Add:* 3701 Big Sky Dr NE Albuquerque NM 87111

GOVETT, GERALD JAMES S, GEOCHEMISTRY. *Current Pos:* head, Sch Appl Geol, 79-84, PROF GEOL, UNIV NSW, 78-, DEAN, FAC APPL SCI, 84- *Personal Data:* b Barry, South Wales, July 30, 32; m 68, 90, Idelies M Louwers. *Educ:* Univ Wales, BSc, 55; Univ London, DIC & PhD(geol), 58; Univ Wales, DSc, 73. *Prof Exp:* Assoc res off & geochemist, Res Coun Alta, 58-65; UN tech expert & vis prof, Univ Philippines, 65-66; vis prof, Univ NB, 66-67; UN consult, Cyprus, 67-68; from assoc prof to prof geol, Univ NB, 68-77. *Concurrent Pos:* Dir, Delta Gold NL, 83- *Mem:* Asn Explor Geochemists; Australian Inst Mining & Metall. *Res:* Exploration geochemistry, primary and secondary dispersion; geochemistry and genesis of mineral deposits, especially sulfides; availability and supply of world mineral resources. *Mailing Add:* Dept Appl Geol Univ NSW Sydney NSW 2052 Australia. *Fax:* 61-2-9546-1240

GOVIER, G(EORGE) W(HEELER), CHEMICAL ENGINEERING. *Current Pos:* PRES, GOVIER CONSULT SERV LTD, 78- *Personal Data:* b Nanton, Alta, June 15, 17; m 40; c 3. *Educ:* Univ BC, BASc, 39; Univ Alta, MSc, 45; Univ Mich, ScD(chem eng), 49. *Hon Degrees:* LLD, Univ Calgary. *Honors & Awards:* R S Jane Mem Award, Chem Inst Can, 66, Selwyn G Blaylock Medal, 71; Anthony F Lucas Gold Medal, Soc Petrol Engrs, Am Inst Mech Engrs, 89. *Prof Exp:* Plant operator, Stan Oil Co, BC, 39-40; from lectr to asst prof chem eng, Univ Alta, 40-48; prof chem eng & head, Dept Chem & Petrol Eng, Univ Alta, 48-59, dean, Fac Eng, 59-63; chmn, Energy Resources Conserv Bd, 62-78. *Concurrent Pos:* Consult, 40-62; mem permanent coun, World Petrol Cong, 60-; part-time prof, Univ Alta & Univ Calgary, 63-; vpres & mem bd dirs, Petrol Recovery Res Inst, 66-; chmn, Sci Prog Comt, World Petrol Cong, 75-83; dir, Can Foremost Ltd & Texaco, Inc, Can, 79-, Can-Mont Gas Co Ltd, Can-Mont Pipe Line Co, Roan Resources Ltd, C-E Combustion Eng Ltd & Stoned Webster Ltd, Can, 80-, Bow Valley Resources Ltd, 81-, Coop Energy Develop Corp, 82- *Mem:* Nat Acad Eng; Am Inst Chem Engrs; fel Chem Inst Can. *Res:* Pipeline flow of complex mixtures, especially non-Newtonians, gas-liquid, liquid-liquid and solid-liquid mixtures. *Mailing Add:* Govier Consult Serv Ltd 1507 Cavanaugh NW Calgary AB T2L 0M8 Can. *Fax:* 403-282-2964

GOVIER, WILLIAM CHARLES, RESEARCH ADMINISTRATION. *Current Pos:* DIR PHARMACEUT RES & DEVELOP, E I DU PONT DE NEMOURS & CO. *Personal Data:* b Nashville, Tenn, Apr 6, 36; m 59; c 2. *Educ:* Kalamazoo Col, BA, 57; McGill Univ, MD, 61; Univ Miss, PhD(pharmacol), 65. *Prof Exp:* From instr to asst prof pharmacol, Univ Miss, 63-66; asst prof, Univ Tex Southwestern Med Sch, 66-68; sr surgeon, Exp Therapeut Br, Nat Heart Inst, 68-70; dir res systs develop, Worley & Ringe, Inc, 70-71; mem staff, Clin Pharmacol Div, Ciba-Geigy Corp, 71-73, exec dir biol res, Pharmaceut Div, 73-75; dir, pharmaceut res, Lederle Labs, 75-77, dir, med res, 77-80; mem staff, med res, Am Cyanamid Co, 80- *Concurrent Pos:* Fel pharmacol, Med Ctr, Univ Miss, 62-63; fel, Oxford Univ, 65-66. *Mem:* AAAS; NY Acad Sci; Am Soc Pharmacol & Exp Therapeut; Soc Exp Biol & Med; Am Soc Clin Pharmacol & Therapeut. *Res:* Cardiovascular; autonomic; peptides; tissue regeneration. *Mailing Add:* 2001 Commonwealth Blvd Ann Arbor MI 48108

GOVIL, NARENDRA KUMAR, COMPLEX ANALYSIS, APPROXIMATION THEORY. *Current Pos:* assoc prof, 85-86, PROF MATH, AUBURN UNIV, 86- *Personal Data:* b Aligarh, UP India, Jan 05, 40; m 64, Urmila Agrawal; c Sanjay & Sandeep. *Educ:* Agra Univ, India, BSc, 57; Aligarh Univ, India, MSc, 59; Univ Montreal, PhD(math), 68. *Prof Exp:* Lectr math, Concordia Univ Montreal, 67-68, asst prof math, 68-70; from asst prof to prof math, Indian Inst Technol, New Delhi, India, 70-85. *Concurrent Pos:* Fel, Univ Montreal, Can, 72-73; vis scientist, Dalhousie Univ, Halifax, Can, 80; vis prof, Univ Alta, Edmonton, Can, 81 & Auburn Univ, 83-85. *Mem:* Fel Nat Acad Sci; Indian Math Soc; Am Math Soc; fel Nat Acad Sci India. *Res:* Published papers in extremal problems for polynomials and related entire functions of exponential type; location of the zeros of a polynomial; lie theory of hypergeometric functions, harmonic analysis. *Mailing Add:* Dept Math Auburn Univ Auburn AL 36849-5310. *Fax:* 334-844-6555; *E-Mail:* nkgovil@ducvax.auburn.edu

GOVIN, CHARLES THOMAS, JR, GEOLOGY, HYDROLOGY. *Current Pos:* DIR ADMIN SERV DEPT, WIS NATURAL GAS, 89- *Personal Data:* b Evanston, Ill, May 6, 46; m 68; c 4. *Educ:* Univ Wis-Madison, BS, 68; Univ Tex, Austin, MA, 73. *Prof Exp:* Asst geologist, Dames & Moore, 73-74, staff geologist, 74-75, proj geologist, 75-77; sr geologist, Wis Elec & Power Co, 77-89. *Concurrent Pos:* Rep utility solid waste act group, Edison Elec Inst, 77-78. *Mem:* Am Water Resources Asn; Geol Soc Am. *Res:* Ground water flow in the surficial saturated zone as relates to land disposal of industrial waste; behavior of industrial waste materials in land disposal situations; methodology for siting of industrial waste disposal facilities. *Mailing Add:* 601 Cheyenne Dr Waukesha WI 53188

GOVIND, CHOONILAL KESHAV, NEUROBIOLOGY DEVELOPMENT. *Current Pos:* from asst prof to assoc prof, 72-81, PROF ZOOL, SCARBOROUGH COL, UNIV TORONTO, 82- *Personal Data:* b Durban, SAfrica, Oct 14, 38; Can citizen; m 67, Preshiela; c Karuna & Nisha. *Educ:* Rhodes Univ, BSc, 61; Natal Univ, MSc, 65; Univ Man, PhD(zool), 71. *Prof Exp:* Asst prof biol, Med Sch, Natal Univ, 63-67. *Concurrent Pos:* Vis res assoc, Marine Prog, Boston Univ, 73-78, adj assoc prof, 79; mem & chmn, grant selection comt, NSERC, 83-85 & 90-92. *Mem:* Soc Neurosci; Am Soc Zoologists; Can Soc Zoologists. *Res:* Electrophysiological and ultrastructural analysis of the mechanisms governing the development, growth and aging of specific neurons, muscle fibers and neuromuscular synapses in the lobster, crayfish and fruit-fly where they are easily identified and manipulated. *Mailing Add:* Scarborough Col 1265 Military Trail Scarborough ON M1C 1A4 Can. *Fax:* 416-287-7642; *E-Mail:* govind@macpost.scar.utoronto.ca

GOVINDARAJULU, ZAKKULA, MATHEMATICS, STATISTICS. *Current Pos:* PROF STATIST, UNIV KY, 68- *Personal Data:* b Atmakur, India, May 15, 33; US citizen; m 61, Gayatri; c Sushma, Sadhna & Usha. *Educ:* Univ Madras, BA, 52, MA, 53; Univ Minn, PhD(math, statist), 61. *Prof Exp:* Lectr asst math, Madras Christian Col, Univ Madras, 52-54, res asst statist, Univ, 53-56; asst biostatist, Univ Minn, 56-57, asst math, 57-60, instr, 60-61; from asst prof to assoc prof, Case Inst Technol, 61-68. *Concurrent Pos:* Lectr asst math & statist, Govt Arts Col, Madras Christian Col, 52-54; NSF grants, 62-64, 68-69; USAF grant & vis assoc prof, Univ Calif, Berkeley, 64-65; USPHS Nat Ctr Health Statist res grant, 70-71; vis prof, Univ Mich, Ann Arbor, 72; res contracts, Off Naval Res, 73-75, 80-81, Water Resources Inst, 74-76; Univ Ky Found res award, 75; NSF grant, Northwestern Univ, 76; vis prof, Indian Statist Inst, 76; Ger Res Asn grant award, 77; Brit fel Royal Statist Soc; Bernoulli Soc Math Statist & Off Naval Res, 83-84; vis prof, Stanford Univ, 84, Columbia Univ, 88-89, Univ Calif, Davis, 94; distinguished summer fac fel, Naval Auxiliary Aircraft Carrier Develop Ctr, Warminster, Pa, 88, 89, 90; res contract, Naval Air Develop Ctr, 89-90; res fel, Stanford Univ, 94; consult, Case Western Res Univ, Several Res Prog, Hosp Cleveland. *Mem:* Nat Acad Sci; fel Inst Math Statist; Int Statist Inst; fel Am Statist Asn; fel AAAS; Allahabad Math Soc; Indian Soc Probability & Statist; Sigma Xi; Royal Statist Soc; Indian Statist Inst. *Res:* Large sample theory; nonparametric inference; sequential procedures; authored several publications. *Mailing Add:* Dept Statist Univ Ky S Limestone St Lexington KY 40506-0027. *Fax:* 606-258-1973

GOVINDJEE, M, BIOPHYSICS, PLANT PHYSIOLOGY. *Current Pos:* fel physico-chem biol, Univ Ill, Urbana, 56-59, res asst bot, 59-60, USPHS fel biophys, 60-61, asst prof bot, 61-65, assoc prof bot & biophys, 65-69, assoc head dept, 73-74, actg head, Dept Bot, 74-75, chmn, Biophys Div, 77, PROF PLANT BIOL & BIOPHYS, UNIV ILL, URBANA, 69- *Personal Data:* b Allahabad, India, Oct 24, 33; US citizen; m 57, Rajni Varma; c Anita & Sanjay. *Educ:* Univ Allahabad, BSc, 52, MSc, 54, Univ Ill, PhD(biophys), 60. *Prof Exp:* Lectr bot, Univ Allahabad, 54-56. *Concurrent Pos:* Distinguished lectr, Sch Life Sci, 78; vis prof, Ariz State Univ, Temple, 90, Univ Geneva, Switz, 92; fulbright scholar, 96-97. *Mem:* Fel AAAS; Am Soc Plant Physiol; Biophys Soc; Am Soc Photobiol (pres, 81-82); Sigma Xi. *Res:* Photosynthetic mechanisms of green plants and the relation of chlorophyll fluorescence to photosynthesis; mechanisms of excitation energy transfer and electron transfer in photosynthesis, particularly, the role of anions (bicarbonate and chloride) in the oxygen evolving system; use of chlorophyll flourescence in monitoring the effect of stress during photosynthesis. *Mailing Add:* Dept Plant Biol 265 Morrill Hall Univ Ill 505 S Goodwin Ave Urbana IL 61801-3707. *Fax:* 217-244-7246, 217-337-6196; *E-Mail:* gov@uiuc.edu

GOVONI, JOHN JEFFREY, ICHTHYOLOGY, EARLY LIFE HISTORY OF FISHES. *Current Pos:* fisheries biologist, 84-87, ECOLOGIST, NAT OCEANIC & ATMOSPHERIC ADMIN-NAT MARINE FISHERIES SERV, BEAUFORT LAB, 87- *Personal Data:* m 73, Mary J Morrissey; c Daniel M. *Educ:* St Anselm Col, AB, 70; Univ Mass, Dartmouth, MS, 73; Col William & Mary, PhD(marine sci), 80. *Prof Exp:* Assc prof marine sci, Va Inst Marine Sci, 79-83. *Concurrent Pos:* Assoc prof marine sci, Col William & Mary, 84- *Mem:* Am Soc Ichthyologists & Herpetologists. *Res:* Ontogeny of functional organ systems in fishes and the relationship of these to their survival potential in early life history; physical processes that shape the spatial distribution of planktonic organisms. *Mailing Add:* 104 Grayson Ct Beaufort NC 28516

GOW, K V, PHYSICAL METALLURGY, CERAMICS. *Current Pos:* from assoc prof to prof, 64-84, EMER PROF PHYS METALL, TECH UNIV NOVA SCOTIA, 85- *Personal Data:* b Ottawa, Ont, Aug 29, 19; m 61, Joy Dowling; c Philip, Nina & Stephanie. *Educ:* Univ Toronto, BASc, 43, PhD(phys metall), 51; Rutgers Univ, MSc, 49; Univ Birmingham, MSc, 53. *Prof Exp:* Sr sci officer phys metall, Can Dept Energy & Mines, 55-62. *Concurrent Pos:* Consult metall failure Anal. *Res:* Fracture mechanics, transformations in alloy steels. *Mailing Add:* 5850 Chain Rock Rd Halifax NS B3H 1A1 Can

GOW, WILLIAM ALEXANDER, metallurgical engineering; deceased, see previous edition for last biography

GOWANS, CHARLES SHIELDS, GENETICS, PHYCOLOGY. *Current Pos:* from asst prof to prof, 68-90, EMER PROF BOT, UNIV MO-COLUMBIA, 90- *Personal Data:* b Salt Lake City, Utah, Sept 17, 23; m 50; c 3. *Educ:* Univ Utah, AB, 49; Stanford Univ, PhD(biol), 57; Indiana Univ, NIH fel, 56-57. *Honors & Awards:* Lalor Found Award, Harvard Univ, 58. *Prof Exp:* Asst biol, Stanford Univ, 52-55. *Concurrent Pos:* Vis prof, Dept Bot, Nat Taiwan Univ, 65-66; spec chair, Inst Bot, Acad Sinica, Nankang, Taiwan, 65-66; Fulbright-Hays Res fel, Inst Microbiol, Gottingen Univ, 72-73. *Mem:* Genetics Soc Am; Phycol Soc Am; Am Soc Microbiol. *Res:* Genetics of algae, specifically biochemical genetics of Chlamydomonas. *Mailing Add:* 701 Redbud Lane Columbia MO 65203

GOWANS, JAMES L, CELLULAR IMMUNOLOGY, LYMPHOCYTES. *Current Pos:* RETIRED. *Personal Data:* b Sheffield, Eng, May 7, 24; m 56, Moya Leatham; c William, Jenny & Lucy. *Educ:* London Univ, MB & BS, 47; Oxford Univ, BA, 48, DPhil(path), 53; FRCP. *Hon Degrees:* ScD, Yale Univ, 66; DSc, Univ Chicago, 71, Univ Birmingham, UK, 78, Univ Rochester, 87; MD, Univ Edinburgh, 79; DM, Univ Southampton, UK, 87; LLD, Univ Glasgow, 88. *Honors & Awards:* Gairdner Found Int Award, Can, 68; Paul Ehrlich Prize, Ger, 74; Feldberg Found Award, 79; Wolf Prize in Med, Israel, 80; Medawar Prize, Int Transplantation Soc, 90. *Prof Exp:* Dir, Cellular Immunol Univ, UK Med Res Coun London, Sch Path, Oxford Univ, 63-77, secy & chief exec, 77-87; secy-gen, Human Frontier Sci Prog, Strasbourg, France, 89-93. *Concurrent Pos:* Res prof, Royal Soc, 62-77; mem, Gov Coun, Int Agency Res Cancer, 80-87, Res Progs Adv Comt, Nat Mult Sclerosis Soc, NY, 88-90 & Awards Comt, Gen Motors Cancer Res Found, 88-90; chmn, Europ Med Res Coun, 85-87; consult, Global Prog Acquired Immune Deficiency Syndrome, WHO, Geneva, 87-88. *Mem:* Foreign assoc Nat Acad Sci; hon mem Am Asn Immunologists; hon mem Am Asn Anatomists; fel Royal Soc London. *Res:* Discovered the recirculation of small lymphocytes from blood to lymph by way of the lymph nodes and their interaction with antigens to initiate immune response. *Mailing Add:* 75 Cumnor Hill Oxford 0X2 9HX England. *Fax:* 44-1865-865548

GOWDEY, CHARLES WILLIS, PHARMACOLOGY. *Current Pos:* lectr, Univ Western, Ont, 48-49, from asst prof to assoc prof, 50-60, prof & head dept, 60-81, EMER PROF PHARMACOL, MED SCH, UNIV WESTERN ONT, 81- *Personal Data:* b St Thomas, Ont, Sept 3, 20; m 46, Madelon Gilmour; c David, Katherine, Kevin & Sheila. *Educ:* Univ Western Ont, BA, 44, MSc, 46; Oxford Univ, DPhil(pharmacol), 48. *Prof Exp:* Demonstr pharmacol, Oxford Univ, 46-48. *Mem:* Am Soc Pharmacol & Exp Therapeut; Can Pharmacol Soc; Brit Pharmacol Soc. *Res:* Decompression sickness; narcotic dependence; cardiovascular pharmacology; adverse drug reactions. *Mailing Add:* 428 Wortley Rd London ON N6C 3S8 Can

GOWDY, JOHN NORMAN, DIGITAL SIGNAL PROCESSING, SPEECH SIGNAL PROCESSING. *Current Pos:* PROF ELEC ENG, CLEMSON UNIV, 71- *Personal Data:* b Elk City, Okla, Feb 7, 45; m 70; c 3. *Educ:* Mass Inst Technol, BS, 67; Univ Mo-Columbia, MS, 68, PhD(elec eng), 70. *Concurrent Pos:* Interim dept head, Elec Eng, Comput Sci Dept, Clemson Univ, 88-90. *Mem:* Inst Elec & Electronics Engrs; Inst Elec & Electronics Engrs Signal Processing Soc; Inst Elec & Electronics Engrs Comput Soc; Inst Elec & Electronics Engrs Commun Soc. *Res:* Digital signal processing; speech recognition; speaker recognition; speech synthesis. *Mailing Add:* Elec Eng & Comput Sci Dept Clemson Univ Clemson SC 29634

GOWDY, KENNETH KING, MECHANICAL ENGINEERING. *Current Pos:* PROF & ASSOC DEAN ENG, KANS STATE UNIV, MANHATTAN, 84- *Personal Data:* b Memphis, Tenn, June 25, 32; m 52, Dolores; c 4. *Educ:* Kans State Univ, BS, 55, MS, 61; Okla State Univ, PhD(mech eng), 65. *Honors & Awards:* Outstanding Serv Award, Am Soc Eng Educ. *Prof Exp:* Engr trainee, Continental Pipeline, 55; instr & asst to dean, Kans State Univ, 57-62, from asst prof to assoc prof mech eng, 62-79, asst dean eng, 65-75, head Dept Eng Technol, 75-79; prof & head Dept Eng Technol, Tex A&M Univ, Col Station, Tex, 79-84. *Mem:* Am Soc Eng Educ; Am Soc Mech Engrs; Sigma Xi. *Res:* Automatic controls; systems analysis. *Mailing Add:* Col Eng Kans State Univ Manhattan KS 66506

GOWDY, ROBERT HENRY, GENERAL RELATIVITY, COSMOLOGY. *Current Pos:* asst prof, 78-82, chmn dept, 82-92, ASSOC PROF PHYSICS, VA COMMONWEALTH UNIV, 82- *Personal Data:* b Putnam, Conn, Apr 7, 41; m 66, Cellissa Norcross; c Jay W, Cellissa B & William H. *Educ:* Worcester Polytech Inst, BS, 63; Yale Univ, MS, 64, PhD(physics), 68. *Prof Exp:* AEC fel physics res, Yale Univ, 68-70; sr fel, Dept Physics & Astron, Univ Md, 70-72, asst prof, 72-78. *Mem:* Am Inst Physics; Am Phys Soc; Am Astron Soc; AAAS; Sigma Xi. *Res:* General relativity and cosmology with a particular emphasis on the application of geometrical methods. *Mailing Add:* Va Commonwealth Univ Dept Physics PO Box 2000 Richmond VA 23284-2000. *E-Mail:* rgowdy@cabell.vcu.edu

GOWDY, SPENSER O, MATHEMATICS. *Current Pos:* from instr to asst prof, 65-74, ASSOC PROF MATH, ST JOSEPH'S COL, 74- *Personal Data:* b Philadelphia, Pa, July 6, 41. *Educ:* West Chester State Col, BS, 63; Villanova Univ, MA, 65; Temple Univ, PhD(math), 71. *Prof Exp:* Asst math, Villanova Univ, 63-65. *Mem:* Math Asn Am. *Res:* Group theory; small cancellation groups. *Mailing Add:* 216 E Manoa Rd Havertown PA 19083-3933

GOWE, ROBB SHELTON, POULTRY BREEDING, ANIMAL BREEDING. *Current Pos:* ADJ PROF, UNIV GUELPH, 90- *Personal Data:* b St Boniface, Man, Oct 9, 21; m 46, Christa B Olsen; c Thomas, Beverly & Margaret. *Educ:* Univ Toronto, BSA, 45; Cornell Univ, MS, 47, PhD(genetics & physiol), 49. *Honors & Awards:* Tom Newman Mem Int Award; Sir John Hammond Mem Lect Award, Sir John Hammond Mem Fund, 74; Merit Award, Can Soc Animal Sci, 84; Int Hall of Fame, World's Poultry Sci Asn, 88. *Prof Exp:* Asst genetics, Dept Poultry, Cornell Univ, 45-49; head poultry breeding, Poultry Div, Exp Farms Serv, 49-59, chief genetics sect, 59-65, dir Animal Res Ctr, Can Dept Agr, 65-86; dir res, Shaver Poultry Breeding Farm Ltd, 87-90. *Concurrent Pos:* Chmn Ottawa Regional Hosp Planning Bd, 74, Queensway Carleton Hosp Bd, 78- *Mem:* Fel Poultry Sci Asn; Am Genetic Asn; Genetics Soc Am; World Poultry Sci Asn; Genetics Soc Can; Can Soc Animal Sci. *Res:* Poultry genetics. *Mailing Add:* 14 Fernbank Pl Guelph ON N1C 1A7 Can. *Fax:* 519-763-3999; *E-Mail:* rgowe@uoguelph.ca

GOWEN, RICHARD J, ELECTRICAL & BIOMEDICAL ENGINEERING. *Current Pos:* vpres & dean eng, 77-84, prof elec eng, 80-84, PRES, SDAK SCH MINES & TECHNOL, 87- *Personal Data:* b New Brunswick, NJ, July 6, 35; m 55; c 5. *Educ:* Rutgers Univ, BS, 57; Iowa State Univ, MS, 61, PhD(elec eng), 62. *Honors & Awards:* Centennial Medal, Inst Elec & Electronics Engrs, 84. *Prof Exp:* USAF, 57-77, ground electronics officer, 57-59, asst prof elec eng, USAF Acad, 62-63, res assoc bioeng, 63-64, from asst prof to prof elec eng, 64-77, dep head dept, 69-77; pres Dak State Univ, 77-84. *Concurrent Pos:* Consult numerous cos, 63-; dir, Joint Air Force-NASA Med Instrumentation Lab, 65-77, Mgt Eval, Dept Defense Mil Health Care Syst Spec Study Group, Off Asst Secy Defense, 75-76; mem numerous comts, Inst Elec & Electronics Engrs, 69-; dir & prin investr, SDak Sch Mines & Technol Res Proj Support Space Cardiovasc Studies, 77-80; prin investr, Effects Electromagnetic Energy Biol Tissue, SDak Sch Mines & Technol, 78-; co-chmn, Joint Nuclear Regulatory Comt & Inst Elec & Electronics Conf Identify Applns Adv Electrotechnol Nuclear Power Plants, 79-80, Joint Indust Probabilistic Risk Assessments Guidelines Nuclear Power Plants Proj, 80-83; co-chmn, Nat Eng Leadership Forum, Nat Acad Eng, 88; pres, Tech Assistance Prog, 88- *Mem:* Fel Inst Elec & Electronics Engrs; Nat Soc Prof Engrs; Inst Elec & Electronics Engrs Eng Med & Biol Soc (vpres, 74, pres-elect, 75, pres, 76); Am Asn Eng Soc (secy-treas, 86). *Res:* Physiological monitoring; biological simulation; computer design; semiconductor circuits; health care systems; author of numerous publications. *Mailing Add:* 1609 Palo Verde Rapid City SD 57701-4461

GOWGIEL, JOSEPH MICHAEL, DENTISTRY, ANATOMY. *Current Pos:* ASSOC PROF ANAT, SCH DENT, LOYOLA UNIV CHICAGO, 64-, CHMN DEPT, 69- *Personal Data:* b Summit, Ill, May 19, 26; c 1. *Educ:* Loyola Univ Chicago, DDS, 50; Univ Chicago, PhD, 58. *Prof Exp:* Intern, Zoller Dent Clin, Univ Chicago, 50-51, from instr to asst prof, 58-63. *Mem:* Fel AAAS; Am Asn Anat; Int Asn Dent Res; Sigma Xi; Am Asn Dent Sch. *Res:* Normal histophysiology of the oral tissues, especially of tooth development and the adult periodontal ligament. *Mailing Add:* 5719 Ridgewood Dr Western Springs IL 60558

GOY, ROBERT WILLIAM, PSYCHOPHYSIOLOGY. *Current Pos:* RETIRED. *Personal Data:* b Detroit, Mich, Jan 25, 24; m 48; c 3. *Educ:* Univ Mich, BS, 47; Univ Chicago, PhD, 53. *Prof Exp:* USPHS fel anat & psychol, Univ Kans, 54-56, from instr to assoc prof anat, 56-63; assoc scientist, Ore Regional Primate Res Ctr, 63-65, chmn dept reproductive physiol & behav, 65-71, sr scientist, 67-71; dir, Wis Regional Primate Res Ctr, 71-91. *Concurrent Pos:* Vis scientist, Wis Regional Primate Res Ctr, 61-63; from assoc prof to prof, Med Sch, Univ Ore, 65-71; prof psychol, Univ Wis-Madison, 71- *Mem:* Am Asn Anatomists; Endocrine Soc; Animal Behav Soc; Brit Soc Study Fertil; Int Soc Psychoneuroendocrinol. *Res:* Comparative endocrinology of reproduction and reproductive behavior. *Mailing Add:* 50 Millstone Rd Madison WI 53717

GOYAL, MEGH R, IRRIGATION, DRIP-TRICKLE IRRIGATION. *Current Pos:* asst agr eng, 79-83, assoc agr engr irrig, 83-88, PROF UNIV PR, MAYAGUEZ, 88- *Personal Data:* b Sangrur, India, Aug 1, 49; m 70, Subhadra; c Vijay, Vinay & Neena. *Educ:* Punjab Agr Univ, India, BSc, 71; Ohio State Univ, MSc, 77, PhD(agr eng), 79. *Honors & Awards:* Blue Ribbon Award, Am Soc Agr Engrs, 83 & 86, Eng Achievement Award, 87. *Prof Exp:* Lectr irrig, Haryana Agr Univ, India, 72-75. *Concurrent Pos:* Consult, Col Engrs & Survrs, PR, 82-; mem, US Comt Irrig & Drainage, Pan Am Fedn Eng Socs (UPADI), 84-,. *Mem:* Am Soc Agr Engrs; Int Soc Soil Sci. *Res:* Drip irrigation in vegetables; small farm mechanization; soil crusting. *Mailing Add:* PO Box 5984 Mayaguez PR 00681-5984. *Fax:* 787-265-0280; *E-Mail:* m_goyal@rumac.upr.clu.edu

GOYAL, RAJ K, DISEASES OF THE ESOPHAGUS. *Current Pos:* CHIEF GASTROENTEROL, BETH ISRAEL HOSP, BOSTON, 81- *Educ:* Maulana Azad Med Col, New Delhi, India, MD, 65. *Concurrent Pos:* Ed-in-chief, Gastroenterol. *Mailing Add:* Res & Develop Vet Admin Med Ctr 1400 VFW Pkwy West Roxbury MA 02132-4927. *Fax:* 617-469-4081

GOYAL, SURESH, MATHEMATICAL MODELING & APPLIED MECHANICS, SOFTWARE DEVELOPMENT. *Current Pos:* mem tech staff, Interactive Systs Res, 89-92, MEM TECH STAFF, ELECTRONIC PACKAGING RES DEPT, AT&T BELL LABS, MURRAY HILL, NJ, 92- *Personal Data:* b India, Dec 6, 60; m, Shefali Agrawal. *Educ:* Indian Inst Technol, Kharagpur, B Tech, 82; Univ Iowa, Iowa City, MS, 84; Cornell Univ, Ithaca, NY, PhD(mech eng), 88. *Prof Exp:* Trainee engr, Int Tractor, Bombay, 81; res & training asst mech, Univ Ky, Lexington, 82-83; res asst bio-mech, Univ Iowa, Iowa City, 83-84; res & teaching asst mech & mech eng, Cornell Univ, Ithaca, NY, 84-88, sci, 88-89. *Mem:* Inst Elec & Electronics Engrs; Am Soc Mech Engrs. *Res:* Software development for simulation of multi body dynamics with friction for product design and development, automation, interactive technologies and virtual reality applications; material characterization, impact testing, friction modelling; analysis and geometry in mechanics; algorithms and complexity theory; experimental spinal biomechanics. *Mailing Add:* 34 Sycamore Way Warren NJ 07059. *Fax:* 908-582-2783; *E-Mail:* goyal@allwise.att.com

GOYAN, JERE EDWIN, PHARMACEUTICAL CHEMISTRY. *Current Pos:* PRES & CHIEF EXEC OFFICER, ALTEON INC, 94- *Personal Data:* b Oakland, Calif, Aug 3, 30; div; c 3. *Educ:* Univ Calif, San Francisco, BS, 52; Univ Calif, Berkeley, PhD(pharmaceut chem), 57. *Hon Degrees:* DSc, Albany Col Pharm, Union Univ, 79, Philadelphia Col Pharm & Sci, 80; LLD, Mass Col Pharm & Allied Health Prof, 80. *Honors & Awards:* T Edward Hicks Lectr, State Univ NY, 72; Hugo H Schaefer Med, Am Pharmaceut Asn, 80; Herman Lubin Lectr, Univ Tenn, 81; Kremer's Mem Lectr, Univ Wis, 81; Samuel W Melendy Mem Lectr, Univ Minn, 82; Albertson's Mem Lectr, Idaho State Univ, 88. *Prof Exp:* From asst prof to assoc prof pharm, Univ Mich, 56-63; assoc prof, Univ Calif, San Francisco, 63-65, chmn dept, 65-67, prof pharm & pharmaceut chem, 65-94, assoc dean, Sch Pharm, 66-67, dean, 67-94. *Concurrent Pos:* Mem, Div Physician Manpower, Bur Health Manpower, Dept Health, Educ & Welfare, 67-69; Am Pharmaceut Asn rep on US Adopted Names Rev Bd, 70-79; consult, Alaska Health Manpower Corp, Univ Alaska, 74-75; comnr, Food & Drug Admin, Dept Health, Educ & Welfare, Pub Health Serv, 79-81; mem, Pew Health Professions Comn, 90. *Mem:* Inst Med-Nat Acad Sci; NY Acad Sci; fel AAAS; fel Acad Pharmaceut Sci; Am Asn Col Pharm (pres, 78-79); Am Asn Pharmaceut Soc. *Res:* Kinetics of drug degradation, properties of drugs in solution. *Mailing Add:* Alteon Inc 170 Williams Dr Ramsey NJ 07446. *Fax:* 201-934-8880

GOYER, ROBERT ANDREW, PATHOLOGY. *Current Pos:* RETIRED. *Personal Data:* b Hartford, Conn, June 2, 27; m 55; c 4. *Educ:* Col of Holy Cross, BS, 50; St Louis Univ, MD, 55; Am Bd Path, dipl, 64. *Prof Exp:* Instr path, St Louis Univ, 60-62, asst prof, 62-65; from asst prof to prof path, Sch Med, Univ NC, Chapel Hill, 71-74; dep dir, Nat Inst Environ Health Sci, 79-87; prof path & chmn dept, Health Sci Ctr, Univ Western Ont, 74-79 & 87-92. *Concurrent Pos:* Nat Found fel, Sch Med, St Louis Univ, 59-60; res fel, Metab Unit, Univ Col Hosp, Med Sch, Univ London, 61-62; clin pathologist, Cardinal Glennon Mem Hosp Children, St Louis, 62-63, dir labs, 63-65; chmn, World Health Orgn Task Group on Environ Health Criteria for Lead, 75, Task Group on Health Criteria for Cadmium, 84 & 89; mem, Int Regist Potentially Toxic Chemicals, UN Environ Prog Expert Group Meeting, Geneva, 86 & 91, Metals Subcomt Sci Adv Bd, US Environ Protection Agency, 85-, Res Grants Comt, Med Res Coun Can, 87-; pres, Metals Specialty Sect, Soc Toxicol, 90-91. *Mem:* Fel Col Am Path; Soc Exp Biol & Med; Soc Toxicol. *Res:* Environmental pathology; metal toxicology; nephrotoxicity. *Mailing Add:* 6405 Huntingridge Rd Chapel Hill NC 27514

GOYER, ROBERT G, PHARMACOLOGY. *Current Pos:* prof fac pharm, 65-94, DEAN FAC PHARM, UNIV MONTREAL, 94- *Personal Data:* b Montreal, Que, May 13, 38; m 60; c 2. *Educ:* Univ Montreal, BA, 58, BSc, 62; Univ Sorbonne, PhD(pharmacol), 65. *Concurrent Pos:* Grants, Med Res Coun Can, Med Res Coun Que & Can Found Advan Pharm, 66-; consult, Desbergers & Nadeau Pharmaceut Labs, sci dir, 71-77; pres, Clinipharm Inc, 77-87; vpres, Can Med Rev Bd, 87- *Mem:* AAAS; NY Acad Sci; Fr-Can Asn Advan Sci; Fr Soc Therapeut & Pharmacodyn; Pharm Soc Can. *Res:* Clinical evaluation of new drugs. *Mailing Add:* Fac Pharm Univ Montreal PO Box 6128 Sta Succursale Downtown Montreal PQ H3C 3J7 Can

GOYERT, SANNA MATHER, MOLECULAR BIOLOGY PROTEIN STRUCTURE. *Current Pos:* SR SCIENTIST, DEPT RHEUMATOL, DIV CELLULAR & MOLECULAR BIOL, HOSP FOR JOINT DIS, 85- *Educ:* NY Univ, PhD, 83. *Mailing Add:* Dept Med Northshore Univ Hosp Cornell Univ Med Col 350 Community Dr Manhasset NY 11030-3816. *Fax:* 516-562-2866

GOYINGS, LLOYD SAMUEL, PATHOLOGY, BIOCHEMISTRY. *Current Pos:* RETIRED. *Personal Data:* b White Cloud, Mich, Dec 26, 33; m 54; c 5. *Educ:* Mich State Univ, BS, 58, DVM, 60, MS, 61, PhD(path), 65. *Prof Exp:* Instr path, Mich State Univ, 61-65, asst prof path, surg & med, 65-66;

res assoc, UpJohn Co, 66-70, ras head plant & animal path, 70- *Concurrent Pos:* Consult. *Mem:* Am Vet Med Asn; Conf Res Workers Animal Dis; Am Asn Lab Animal Sci. *Res:* Canine dermatology; atypical mycobacteniosis in cattle, dogs, cats and chickens; canine hypothyroidism; causation of canine leukemia; canine cancer registry. *Mailing Add:* 9491 Milo Rd Plainwell MI 49080

GOZ, BARRY, PHARMACOLOGY, BIOCHEMISTRY. *Current Pos:* PROF PHARMACOL, SCH MED, UNIV NC, CHAPEL HILL, 74- *Personal Data:* b Brooklyn, NY, Oct 21, 37; m 61, Rebecca Greenberg; c Martha Libbie & Emily Lisa. *Educ:* Columbia Univ, BA, 58; State Univ NY, PhD(pharmacol), 65. *Prof Exp:* Asst prof pharmacol, Sch Med, Yale Univ, 67-74. *Concurrent Pos:* USPHS fel pharmacol, Yale Univ, 65-67. *Mem:* Am Soc Pharmacol & Exp Therapeut; Am Soc Biol Chem; Am Asn Cancer Res. *Res:* Cellular and viral replication and control mechanisms; pyrimidine analogues and nucleic acid metabolism; cancer chemotherapy; antiviral agents. *Mailing Add:* Dept Pharmacol Univ NC Sch Med CB 7365 Mary Ellen Jones Bldg Chapel Hill NC 27599

GOZZO, JAMES J, MEDICAL SCIENCE. *Current Pos:* lectr, Northeastern Univ, 70-73, from asst prof to assoc prof health sci, 72-80, dir, Med Lab Sci Grad Prog, 76-88, assoc dean, 85-88, actg dean, 88-89, ELEANOR W BLACK PROF HEALTH SCI, NORTHEASTERN UNIV, 80-, DEAN, COL PHARM & ALLIED HEALTH PROFESSIONS, 89- *Personal Data:* b Hartford, Conn, May 30, 43; m; c 3. *Educ:* Univ Conn, BS, 65; Boston Col, PhD, 69. *Prof Exp:* Teaching asst, Boston Col, 65-66, teaching fel, 66-67, instr, 67-68, NSF fel, 67-69. *Concurrent Pos:* Sr res assoc, Cancer Res Inst, New Eng Deaconess Hosp, 75-82, vis asst lab med, 75-80, assoc mem, 83- *Mem:* Transplantation Soc; Am Asn Immunologists; Am Soc Microbiol; Am Diabetes Asn; AAAS; Fedn Am Soc Exp Biologists. *Res:* Immunodiagnostic assay of bladder carcinoma. *Mailing Add:* Dept Health Sci Northeastern Univ Bouve Pharmaceut & Health Sci Boston MA 02115

GRAAE, JOHAN E A, mechanical & chemical engineering; deceased, see previous edition for last biography

GRAB, EUGENE GRANVILLE, JR, food science; deceased, see previous edition for last biography

GRABEL, ARVIN, ELECTRONICS. *Current Pos:* from asst prof to assoc prof, 64-78, PROF ELEC ENG, NORTHEASTERN UNIV, 78- *Personal Data:* b New York, NY, Mar 8, 35; m 69. *Educ:* NY Univ, BEE, 56, MEE, 57, ScD(elec eng), 64. *Prof Exp:* Instr elec eng, NY Univ, 57-63. *Concurrent Pos:* Ed, Circuit Theory Newslett, Inst Elec & Electronics Engrs, 59-61. *Mem:* AAAS; Inst Elec & Electronics Engrs; Am Soc Eng Educ; Sigma Xi. *Res:* Solid state circuits; active network synthesis. *Mailing Add:* 259 Otis St Newton MA 02165

GRABEN, HENRY WILLINGHAM, THEORETICAL PHYSICS. *Current Pos:* RETIRED. *Personal Data:* b Talladega, Ala, Nov 9, 34; m 61; c 2. *Educ:* Birmingham-Southern Col, BS, 57; Univ Tenn, MS, 61, PhD(physics), 62. *Prof Exp:* Physicist plasma physics, Oak Ridge Nat Lab, 62-63; from asst prof to prof physics, Clemson Univ, 63-93. *Mem:* Am Phys Soc; Am Asn Physics Teachers. *Res:* Theoretical study of intermolecular forces; statistical mechanics. *Mailing Add:* PO Box 848 Clemson SC 29633

GRABENSTETTER, JAMES EMMETT, OIL RESERVOIR SIMULATION. *Current Pos:* RES SCIENTIST, COMPUT MODELLING GROUP, 89- *Personal Data:* b Cincinnati, Ohio, Sept 18, 46; Can citizen. *Educ:* Reed Col, BA, 68; McGill Univ, PhD(chem), 74; Univ Calgary, MSc, 88. *Prof Exp:* Fel quantum chem, Univ NB, 73-75; res assoc theoret chem, Univ Waterloo, 75-79; res chemist corrosion chem, 79-82, atmospheric chem, Ont Hydro, 82-84. *Mem:* Soc Indust & Appl Math; Soc Petrol Engrs. *Res:* Numerical methods for oil reservoir simulation. *Mailing Add:* Comput Modeling Group 3512-33 St NW Calgary AB T2L 2A6 Can

GRABER, CHARLES DAVID, BACTERIOLOGY, IMMUNOLOGY. *Current Pos:* from assoc prof to prof, 66-84, EMER PROF MICROBIOL, MED UNIV SC, 85- *Personal Data:* b Pomeroy, Ohio, Dec 19, 17; m 44, Agnes T Teachey; c C Scott, David R & Ellen R. *Educ:* Ohio State Univ, BS, 39, PhD(bact, immunol), 57; Univ Colo, MS, 54. *Prof Exp:* Bacteriologist & immunologist, Surg Res Unit, Brooke Army Med Ctr, 57-62; asst prof microbiol, Col Med, Baylor Univ, 62-66. *Concurrent Pos:* Fel, Am Bd Microbiol; adj prof, Clemson Univ, 89- *Mem:* Am Acad Microbiol; Fr Soc Immunol; Soc Exp Biol & Med; Am Asn Immunol; Sigma Xi. *Res:* Burn infection immunology; effect of intestinal microflora on bile acid metabolism in atherosclerosis; the role of ureaplasma and chlamydia in infertility and nongonococcal urethritis. *Mailing Add:* 436 Trapier Dr Charleston SC 29412

GRABER, GEORGE, ANIMAL NUTRITION. *Current Pos:* ANIMAL HUSBANDMAN, DIV DRUGS SWINE & MINOR SPECIES, METAB PROD BR, BUR VET MED, FOOD & DRUG ADMIN, 71- *Personal Data:* b New York, NY, Nov 24, 40; m 65. *Educ:* Rutgers Univ, BS, 63, MS, 67; Univ Ill, Urbana, PhD(animal sci), 71. *Mem:* Am Inst Nutrit. *Res:* Amino acid metabolism in chick and pig; vitamin-amino acid interrelation; swine metabolism studies; grain source-antimicrobial agent interrelationship in chick. *Mailing Add:* Ctr Vet Med 7500 Standish Pl Rockville MD 20855. *Fax:* 301-295-8812

GRABER, HARLAN DUANE, NUCLEAR PHYSICS. *Current Pos:* From asst prof to assoc prof, 62-76, PROF PHYSICS, CORNELL COL, 76- *Personal Data:* b Newton, Kans, July 19, 35; m 58; c 3. *Educ:* Bethel Col, BS, 57; Univ Kans, PhD(physics), 64. *Mem:* Am Phys Soc; Am Asn Physics Teachers. *Res:* Low energy nuclear physics; gamma ray spectroscopy. *Mailing Add:* Dept Physics Cornell College Mt Vernon IA 52314-1098

GRABER, JAMES STANLEY, DIGITIZING. *Current Pos:* Chief tech assessment, 86-90, TECH ASSESSMENT MGR, LIBR CONG, 90- *Personal Data:* b Newton, Kans, 1941. *Educ:* Harvard Univ, BA, 62. *Mem:* Am Math Soc; Am Phys Soc. *Mailing Add:* 407 Seward Sq SE Washington DC 20003

GRABER, LELAND D, MATHEMATICS. *Current Pos:* ASSOC PROF MATH, CENT COL, IOWA, 70- *Personal Data:* b Marion, SDak, Nov 5, 24; m 55; c 3. *Educ:* Wheaton Col, Ill, BS, 48; Univ Minn, MA, 50; Iowa State Univ, PhD(math), 64. *Prof Exp:* Res engr, Aeronaut Res Dept, Minneapolis-Honeywell Regulator Co, 51-53; instr math, Am Univ Beirut, 53-59 & Iowa State Univ, 59-64; asst prof, Fla Presby Col, 64-70. *Mem:* Math Asn Am; Am Math Soc. *Res:* Functional analysis, linear operators in banach spaces. *Mailing Add:* 803 E Second St Pella IA 50219

GRABER, RICHARD REX, ZOOLOGY, WILDLIFE. *Current Pos:* RETIRED. *Personal Data:* b Kingman Co, Kans, Aug 25, 24; m 45, Jean Weber. *Educ:* Washburn Univ, BS, 48; Univ Mich, MA, 49; Univ Okla, PhD, 55. *Prof Exp:* Asst zool, Univ Mich, 48-50; mus field collector, La State Univ, 51-52; asst, Biol Surv, Univ Okla, 52-55; instr biol, Southwestern Tex State Teachers Col, 55-56; wildlife specialist, Ill Natural Hist Surv, 56-83, emer prin scientist, 84- *Mem:* Cooper Ornith Soc; Wilson Ornith Soc; Am Ornith Union. *Res:* Evolution, migration and ecology of birds. *Mailing Add:* RR 1 Box 216 A Golconda IL 62938-9729

GRABER, ROBERT PHILIP, STEROIDS, FERMENTATIONS. *Current Pos:* RETIRED. *Personal Data:* b Glen Ullin, NDak, Oct 4, 18; m 59, Graciela Pesquera; c Jessica & Jennifer. *Educ:* Univ Minn, BChem, 41; Univ Wis, PhD(chem), 49. *Prof Exp:* Jr chemist, Merck & Co Inc, 41-46, sr chemist, 49-56; proj leader, Res Labs, Gen Mills Inc, 57-58, sect leader, 58-63; mem res staff, Searle Chem Inc, 63, sci dir, Searle Mex, SA CV, 64-77, G D Searle & Co, Ltd, 77-80, sci dir, Compania Espanola Sintesis Quimica, SA, 81-91. *Mem:* Am Chem Soc; AAAS. *Res:* Antibiotics; synthetic estrogens; steroids; natural products; fermentations; enzymes. *Mailing Add:* Las Planas 12 Sant Pere De Ribes Barcelona 08810 Spain. *Fax:* 93-896-3442

GRABER, T(OURO) M(OR), ORTHODONTICS. *Current Pos:* RETIRED. *Personal Data:* b St Louis, Mo, May 27, 17; m 41, Doris Appel; c 5. *Educ:* Wash Univ, DDS, 40; Northwestern Univ, MSD, 46, PhD, 50; Am Bd Orthod, dipl, 54. *Hon Degrees:* Dr(odontol), Univ Gothenburg, Sweden, 89; DSc, Wash Univ, 91. *Honors & Awards:* Distinguished Serv Award, Am Asn Orthod,70; Ketcham Award, 75; Benno Lischer Award, 88; Strang Mem lectr, 88; Mershon Award, 89; Northcroft lectr, 89; Wylie Mem Award, 89; Salzmann lectr, 91. *Prof Exp:* From instr to assoc prof orthod, Northwestern Univ, 45-58, dir res cleft lip & palate inst, 49-58; assoc attend orthodontist, Childrens Mem Hosp, 58-62; spec lectr, Univ Mich, 58-67; prof orthod, Univ Chicago, 69-80, chmn dept orthod, 69-80, prof biol sci, pediat & anthrop, 74-80, res assooc prof plastic & reconstruction surg, 80-83; adj prof, Univ Mich, 84-88. *Concurrent Pos:* Dir, Kenilworth Res Found, 68; Australian Res Found lectr, 71; mem lectr, Univ Witwatersrand, 71; vis scientist, Am Dent Asn, 79-90; ed, Am J Orthod, 85- *Mem:* AAAS; Am Asn Orthod; Am Dent Asn; Europ Orthod Soc. *Res:* Maxillo-facial deformities; diagnosis of orthodontic therapy; craniofacial growth and development; use of orthopedic appliances in orthodontic therapy; temporomandibular joint dysfunction. *Mailing Add:* 2895 Sheridan Pl Evanston IL 60201

GRABIEL, CHARLES EDWARD, ORGANIC CHEMISTRY. *Current Pos:* RETIRED. *Personal Data:* b Alliance, Ohio, July 31, 27; m 49; c 4. *Educ:* Col Wooster, AB, 50; Brown Univ, PhD(chem), 54. *Prof Exp:* Asst, Brown Univ, 50-53; chemist, Dow Chem Co, 54-65, mgr chem mkt res, 65-92. *Mem:* Chem Mkt Res Asn; Am Chem Soc. *Res:* Vapor-liquid equilibrium; polynitroparaffins; polyelectrolytes. *Mailing Add:* 505 W Main St Midland MI 48640

GRABINER, JUDITH VICTOR, HISTORY OF SCIENCE, MATHEMATICS. *Current Pos:* PROF MATH, PITZER COL, CLAREMONT, CALIF, 85- *Personal Data:* b Los Angeles, Calif, Oct 12, 38; m 64, Sandy Grabiner; c David & Rebecca. *Educ:* Univ Chicago, BS, 60; Harvard Univ, MA, 62, PhD(hist sci), 66. *Prof Exp:* Instr hist sci, Harvard Univ, 66-69; lectr hist, Univ Calif, Santa Barbara, 69-70; lectr hist & math, Calif State Univ, Los Angeles, 70-71; from asst prof to prof hist sci, 72-75, Small Col, Calif State Univ, Dominguez Hills, 72-85. *Concurrent Pos:* Fel, Am Coun Learned Soc, 71-72; mem comns hist math, Div Hist Sci, Int Union Hist & Philos Sci, 74- *Mem:* Sigma Xi; Hist Sci Soc; Math Asn Am; Am Math Soc. *Res:* History of mathematics, especially analysis in 18th and 19th centuries; Scopes trial; mathematics in America. *Mailing Add:* Dept Math Pitzer Col Claremont CA 91711-4204. *Fax:* 909-621-8521; *E-Mail:* jgrabiner@pitzer.claremont.edu

GRABINER, SANDY, BANACH ALGEBRAS, OPERATOR THEORY. *Current Pos:* assoc prof, 74-82, PROF MATH, POMONA COL, 82- *Personal Data:* b New York, NY, Dec 15, 39; m 64, Judith Victor; c David & Rebecca. *Educ:* Rice Univ, BA, 60; Harvard Univ, AM, 61, PhD(math), 67. *Prof Exp:* Instr math, Mass Inst Technol, 67-69; asst prof, Claremont Grad Sch, 69-74.

Concurrent Pos: Vis assoc prof math, Ind Univ, 81-82; chmn, Prog Comt, Math Asn Am, 84-85. *Mem:* AAAS; Am Math Soc; Math Asn Am; London Math Soc. *Res:* Banach algebras and operators on Banach spaces. *Mailing Add:* Dept Math Pomona Col Claremont CA 91711. *E-Mail:* sgrabiner@pomona.edu

GRABLE, ALBERT E, SYSTEMATIC BOTANY, INSECT ECOLOGY. *Current Pos:* FOUNDER & PRES, AGREEABLE PEST CONTROL, 91- *Personal Data:* b San Bernardino, Calif, Mar 10, 39; m 62; c 3. *Educ:* La Sierra Col, BA, 59; Univ Minn, MS, 62, PhD(entom), 65. *Prof Exp:* From instr to assoc prof biol, Walla Walla Col, 63-91. *Concurrent Pos:* Consult, US Bur Reclamation, 74, Trop Insects, Dominican Repub, 87. *Mem:* Entom Soc Am; Am Registry Prof Entomologists. *Res:* Biology of social hymenoptera; taxonomy of flowering plants. *Mailing Add:* 630 SW Third St College Place WA 99324

GRABNER, ELISE M, COVERING PROPERTIES OF TOPOLOGICAL SPACES, BASE OF COUNTABLE ORDER THEORY. *Current Pos:* Asst prof, 84-92, ASSOC PROF MATH, SLIPPERY ROCK UNIV, 92- *Personal Data:* m 75, Gary C; c Sarah. *Educ:* Ohio Univ, BS, 73, MS, 75, PhD(math), 84. *Concurrent Pos:* Vis lectr math, Pa State Univ, 80-82. *Mem:* Am Math Soc; Math Asn Am; Asn Women Sci; Asn Women Math; Asn Comput Mach. *Res:* Point-set topology with most concern in covering and base properties. *Mailing Add:* Dept Math Slippery Rock Univ Slippery Rock PA 16057-8599

GRABOIS, NEIL, ALGEBRA, NUMBER THEORY. *Current Pos:* PRES, COLGATE COL, 88- *Personal Data:* b New York, NY, Dec 11, 35; m 56; c 2. *Educ:* Swarthmore Col, BA, 57; Univ Pa, MA, 59, PhD(math), 63. *Prof Exp:* Asst instr math, Univ Pa, 57-61; instr, Lafayette Col, 61-63; from asst prof to assoc prof, William Col, 63-73, dean fac, 75-77, provost, 77-80, prof math, 73-88, chmn dept math sci, 81-88. *Mem:* NY Acad Sci; Am Math Soc; Math Asn Am. *Res:* Algebraic number theory; graph theory and combinatorial mathematics with a particular interest in matchings and matroids. *Mailing Add:* Watson House 13 Oak Dr Colgate Col Watson House 13 Oak Dr Hamilton NY 13346

GRABOW, BARRY EDWARD, SUPER CONDUCTING DETECTORS OF MICROWAVE ENERGY, BIOMEDICAL APPLICATIONS OF OPTOELECTRONICS & LASERS. *Current Pos:* Instr digital design, 89, eng & appl sci, Electronics Lab, 91-92, INSTR INTEGRATED ELECTRONICS/MICRO-ELECTRONICS, JOHNS HOPKINS UNIV, 92-, RESEARCHER, APPL PHYSICS LAB, 93- *Personal Data:* m 94, Cynthia R Himes. *Educ:* Milwaukee Sch Eng, BS, 87; Johns Hopkins Univ, MS, 90, PhD(elec eng), 92. *Mem:* Int Soc Optical Eng. *Res:* Development of optical and microwave detectors using high temperature superconducting thin films. *Mailing Add:* 9872 Softwater Way Columbia MD 21046. *E-Mail:* barry.grabow@jhuapl.edu

GRABOWSKI, CASIMER THADDEUS, EMBRYOLOGY, ZOOLOGY. *Current Pos:* assoc prof, 60-67, chmn, 87-90, PROF BIOL, UNIV MIAMI, 67- *Personal Data:* b Cleveland, Ohio, Aug 16, 27; m 80; c 1. *Educ:* Case Western Res Univ, BS, 50; Johns Hopkins Univ, PhD(zool), 54. *Prof Exp:* Jr instr biol, Johns Hopkins Univ, 50-52; from instr to asst prof anat, Univ Pittsburgh, 54-60. *Mem:* Am Soc Zoologists; Teratol Soc (pres, 87-88); Soc Develop Biol; Int Soc Develop Biol. *Res:* Experimental embryology; teratology and embryonic physiology, as related to normal and abnormal morphogenesis; effects of teratogenic agents on cardiovascular physiology of mammalian embryos; teratogenic effects of atmospheric pollutants and pesticides. *Mailing Add:* Dept Biol Univ Miami PO Box 248106 Miami FL 33124-8106

GRABOWSKI, EDWARD JOSEPH JOHN, PROCESS RESEARCH. *Current Pos:* Sr chemist, Merck, Sharp & Dohme Res Labs, Merck & Co Inc, 65-72, from res fel to sr res fel, 72-79, sr investr, 79-86, dir, 86-88, SR DIR, PROCESS RES, MERCK, SHARP & DOHME RES LABS, MERCK & CO INC, 88- *Personal Data:* b Jamaica, NY, Apr, 23, 40; m 61; c 1. *Educ:* Mass Inst Technol, SB, 61; Univ Rochester, PhD(chem), 65. *Mem:* Am Chem Soc; Royal Soc Chem; Eur Photochem; Int Soc Heterocyclic Chem. *Res:* Design and development of synthesis for new drug candidates; development of processes for drug manufacture with emphasis on beta-lactam, heterocyclic, amino acid, aromatic and natural product chemistry; reaction mechanisms; physical organic chemistry. *Mailing Add:* 741 Marcellus Dr Westfield NJ 07090-2012

GRABOWSKI, JOSEPH J, GAS-PHASE ION CHEMISTRY, PHOTOACOUSTIC CALORIMETRY. *Current Pos:* ASSOC PROF CHEM, UNIV PITTSBURGH, 92- *Personal Data:* b Elkridge, Md, Nov 4, 56; m 77. *Educ:* Univ Md, Baltimore County, BA, 78; Univ Colo, PhD(org chem), 83. *Honors & Awards:* VG Instruments Res Award, Am Soc Mass Spectrometry, 86. *Prof Exp:* Teaching asst chem, Univ Colo, 78-79, res asst, 79-83; fel, Harvard Univ, 83-84, asst prof org chem, 84-88, assoc prof, 88-92. *Concurrent Pos:* NSF presidential young investr award, 86-91; chmn, Dept Teaching Fel Training Prog, 88-91. *Mem:* Fel AAAS; Am Chem Soc; Am Soc Mass Spectrometry. *Res:* Investigations to elucidate the intrinsic factors that control organic reactions; utilization of the flowing afterglow technique to analyze ionic organic reactions; development and exploitation of photoacoustic calorimetry for bioorganic problems. *Mailing Add:* Dept Chem Univ Pittsburgh Pittsburgh PA 15267

GRABOWSKI, KENNETH S, SURFACE MODIFICATION ACCELERATOR MASS SPECTROMETRY. *Current Pos:* res physicist, 81-94, PROJ LEADER, NAVAL RES LAB, 94- *Personal Data:* b Detroit, Mich, Aug 15, 52; m 76; c 2. *Educ:* Univ Mich, BSE, 74, MSE, 75, PhD(nuclear eng), 80. *Prof Exp:* Mem lab staff, Argonne Nat Lab, 76-79, res assoc, 79-80. *Mem:* Am Vacuum Soc; AAAS; Mat Res Soc. *Res:* Application of accelerator mass spectrometry to state of the art characterizations of trace elements and isotope ratios in materials; thin film growth and surface modification using ion and laser beams; ion-beam and x-ray characterization of materials. *Mailing Add:* Naval Res Lab Code 6670 Washington DC 20375-5345. *Fax:* 202-767-5301; *E-Mail:* grabowsk@nrlfs1.nrl.navy.mil

GRABOWSKI, SANDRA REYNOLDS, NEUROBIOLOGY, HUMAN PHYSIOLOGY. *Current Pos:* NIH fel & res fel neurobiol, 73-77, INSTR BIOL SCI, PURDUE UNIV, WEST LAFAYETTE, IND, 77- *Personal Data:* b Chicago, Ill, Mar 3, 43; m 65. *Educ:* Purdue Univ, BS, 65, PhD(biol), 73. *Mem:* AAAS; Asn Women Sci; Human Anat & Physiol Soc (pres, 93-94); Asn Biol Lab Educ. *Res:* Visual electrophysiology. *Mailing Add:* Dept Biol Sci Purdue Univ West Lafayette IN 47907-1392

GRABOWSKI, THOMAS J, SAMPLE PREP TECHNIQUES. *Current Pos:* PRES, COMPUT WIZARD INC, 89- *Personal Data:* b New Brunswick, NJ, Aug 21, 50; m 70; c 3. *Educ:* Southwestern Univ, BSME, 82. *Concurrent Pos:* Sr tech, NL Industs Corp Labs, 69-79; engr, Revere Co, Revere Res inc, 79-82; mgr metall eng, Exide Corp, 82-89. *Mem:* Am Soc Metals. *Res:* Metallographic laboratory techniques. *Mailing Add:* 990 N Westend Blvd Quakertown PA 18951

GRABOWSKI, WALTER JOHN, FLUID DYNAMICS, PHYSICAL OCEANOGRAPHY. *Current Pos:* PROJ MGR, AT&T BELL LABS, 89- *Personal Data:* b Philadelphia, Pa, May 19, 49; m 70; c 1. *Educ:* Univ Pa, BS, 71; Univ Calif, Berkeley, MS, 72, PhD(mech eng), 74. *Prof Exp:* Scientist fluid dynamics, Sci Appln Inc, 74-75; scientist, Flow Res Inc, 75-76; physicist, David Taylor Naval Ship Res & Develop Ctr, 76-77; scientist phys oceanog, Sci Applns Inc, 77-81, proj mgr, 81-89. *Mem:* Am Geophys Union. *Res:* Theoretical analysis and numerical modeling of fluid dynamic phenomena; emphasis on oceanic phenomena such as internal waves. *Mailing Add:* 9718 Laurel St Fairfax VA 22032

GRABOWSKI, ZBIGNIEW WOJCIECH, NUCLEAR PHYSICS. *Current Pos:* res assoc, 63-65, from asst prof to assoc prof, 65-75, PROF PHYSICS, PURDUE UNIV, 75- *Personal Data:* b Plock, Poland, June 22, 31; US citizen; m 65, Sandra Reynolds. *Educ:* Jagiellonian Univ, MS, 54; Univ Uppsala, Fil lic, 61, PhD(physics), 62. *Prof Exp:* Teaching asst, Tech Univ Gliwice, Poland, 54-55; res asst nuclear physics, Nuclear Res Inst, Poland, 55-58; Univ Uppsala, 58-62; proj mgr physics of Aurora, Kiruna Geophys Observ, Sweden, 62-63. *Mem:* Am Phys Soc; Sigma Xi; Am Asn Physics Teachers. *Res:* Nuclear spectroscopy; angular correlation of nuclear radiation; internal conversion; magnetic moments of excited nuclear states; hyperfine fields; nuclei at high angular momentum. *Mailing Add:* Dept Physics Purdue Univ 1396 Physics Bldg West Lafayette IN 47907-1396. *Fax:* 765-494-0706; *E-Mail:* grabz@physics.purdue.edu

GRACE, DONALD J, RESEARCH ADMINISTRATION. *Current Pos:* dir, Eng Exp Sta, 76-, EMER VPRES & EMER DIR, GA TECH RES INST, GA INST TECHNOL, 93- *Personal Data:* b Oklahoma City, Okla, Feb 21, 26; m 49; c 2. *Educ:* Ohio State Univ, BSEE, 48, MSEE, 49; Stanford Univ, PhD, 62. *Prof Exp:* Lectr, Ohio State Univ, 48-49; res engr, Airborne Instruments Lab, 59-61; res assoc, Stanford Univ, 62-63, sr res assoc, Systs & Techniques Lab, 63-66, assoc prof elec eng, 63-67, dir, 66-67, assoc dean eng, 67-69; dir res, Kentron Hawaii, Ltd, 69-73; dir, Ctr Eng Res, Univ Hawaii, 73-76. *Concurrent Pos:* Mem, FORECAST Panel, USAF, 63, mem reconnaissance adv bd, 64-65; tech adv, US Army Security Agency, 65-66; dir, Stanford Univ Instruct TV Network, 67-69; asst secy, Ga Tech Res Inst & rep, Pub Serv Satellite Consortium, 77-; univ adv panel, Nat Solar Energy Res Inst, 78-79; mem forum, Nat Security Affairs, Pentagon, 80. *Mem:* Inst Elec & Electronics Engrs; Sigma Xi; AAAS. *Res:* Microwave components and subsystems; defense electronics; alternate energy; instructional television; research administration, management and planning. *Mailing Add:* 4836 Fairforest Dr Stone Mountain GA 30088

GRACE, EDWARD EVERETT, POINT SET TOPOLOGY. *Current Pos:* PROF MATH, ARIZ STATE UNIV, 63- *Personal Data:* b Gulfport, Miss, Apr 15, 27; m 54, Joan Combs; c Geoffrey, Elizabeth & David. *Educ:* Univ NC, BS, 51, PhD(math), 56. *Prof Exp:* Instr math, Univ NC, 55-56; asst prof, Emory Univ, 56-62; vis assoc prof, Univ Ga, 62-63. *Concurrent Pos:* NSF fac fel, Univ Wis, 61-62, res assoc, 62; vis prof, Univ Wis, 69-70 & Univ Houston, 77. *Mem:* Am Math Soc; Math Asn Am; Sigma Xi; Am Asn Univ Profs. *Res:* Point set topology, particularly continuum theory. *Mailing Add:* Dept Math Ariz State Univ Box 871804 Tempe AZ 85287-1804. *E-Mail:* grace@math.la.asu.edu

GRACE, HAROLD P(ADGET), CHEMICAL ENGINEERING, COLLON CHEMISTRY. *Current Pos:* RETIRED. *Personal Data:* b Parsons, Kans, Apr 19, 19; m 42, Edith Hultman; c Peter & Cynthia. *Educ:* Univ Pa, BS, 41. *Honors & Awards:* Colburn Award, Franklin Inst, 56. *Prof Exp:* Field engr, Eng Dept, E I Du Pont de Nemours & Co, Inc, 41-44, res engr, Eng Res Lab, 46-52, res proj engr, 52-56, res assoc, 56-71, res fel, Eng Res Lab, 71-79; consult, 80-93. *Mem:* Am Chem Soc; Am Inst Chem Engrs. *Res:* Chemical engineering research and development involving particulate solids, particle mechanics, mechanical separations, particle size analysis, size reduction and flocculation; dispersion, mixing in polymer melts. *Mailing Add:* 108 N Concord Ave Havertown PA 19083. *E-Mail:* 104346.2711compuserve.com

GRACE, JOHN ROSS, MULTIPHASE SYSTEMS, FLUIDIZATION. *Current Pos:* head dept, 79-87, dean grad studies, 90-96, PROF CHEM ENG DEPT, UNIV BC, 79- *Personal Data:* b London, Ont, June 8, 43; m 64, Sherrill Elizabeth Perley; c Elizabeth & Malcolm. *Educ:* Univ Western Ont, BESc, 65; Cambridge Univ, PhD(chem eng), 68. *Honors & Awards:* Erco Award; L S Lauchland Medal; Killam Res Prize; R S Jane Award. *Prof Exp:* From asst prof to prof chem eng, McGill Univ, 68-79. *Concurrent Pos:* Sr proj engr, Survr, Nenniger & Chenevert Inc, 74-75; Nat Res Coun Can sr indust fel, 74-75; ed, Chem Eng Sci, 84-90. *Mem:* Chem Inst Can (pres, 95-96); Brit Inst Chem Engrs; Can Soc Chem Eng (pres, 89-90); Asn Prof Engrs BC. *Res:* Fluidization; circulating fluidized beds; dynamics of bubbles, drops and particles; reactor design; energy technology; spouted beds; multiphase flow; combustion; gasification; sedimentation; occupational exposures; air pollution control. *Mailing Add:* Dept Chem Eng Univ BC 2216 Main Mall Vancouver BC V6T 1Z4 Can. *E-Mail:* jgrace@chml.ubc.ca

GRACE, MARCELLUS, PHARMACY ADMINISTRATION. *Current Pos:* asst prof clin pharm, 76-78, DEAN & PROF ADMIN, XAVIER UNIV, LA, 83- *Personal Data:* b Selma, Ala, Oct 17, 47; m 73; c 3. *Educ:* Xavier Univ, La, BS, 71; Univ Minn, MS, 75, PhD(pharm admin), 76. *Prof Exp:* Hosp pharm resident, USPHS Hosp, Md, 71-72, staff pharmacist, Mass, 72-73; staff pharmacist, Thrifty Drug Stores, Los Angeles, 73 & Methodist Hosp, St Louis Park, Minn, 74; asst dir pharm, Bethesda Hosps, Cincinnati, 75; dir pharm serv, Tulane Univ Med Ctr, Nola, 76-77; asst dean & assoc prof pharm, Howard Univ, Wash, DC, 79-82. *Concurrent Pos:* Chmn bd, Minority Health Prof Found, 89-91; mem, Adv Coun, Nat Heart, Lung & Blood Inst, NIH, Inst Rev Bd, Clin Res Ctr, New Orleans & bd dirs, St Thomas Clin, 90-; pharm consult, United Teachers New Orleans Health & Welfare, 90- *Mem:* Am Asn Cols Pharm (secy, 83-86); Asn Minority Health Prof Schs (secy, 85-87, pres, 87-89). *Res:* Management with emphasis on motivation; patient education; hypertension with emphasis on patient compliance; pharmacist communication skills; author of 35 technical publications. *Mailing Add:* Xavier Univ La 7325 Palmetto St New Orleans LA 70125-1056

GRACE, NORMAN DAVID, GASTROENTEROLOGY, INTERNAL MEDICINE. *Current Pos:* from instr to assoc prof, 65-88, asst dean hosp affairs, 71-85, PROF MED, SCH MED, TUFTS UNIV, 88-; CHIEF GASTROENTEROL, FAULKNER HOSP, 71- *Personal Data:* b Worcester, Mass, Sept 23, 36; m 60, Judith Saslow; c 2. *Educ:* Brown Univ, AB, 58; Tufts Univ, MD, 62. *Prof Exp:* Asst clin instr med, Albany Med Col, 63-65. *Concurrent Pos:* Clin fel gastroenterol, Albany Med Col, 64-65; Nat Inst Arthritis & Metab Dis res fel, Sch Med, Tufts Univ, 65-67; chief gastroenterol, Lemuel Shattuck Hosp, 72-93. *Mem:* AAAS; Am Gastroenterol Asn; Am Asn Study Liver Dis; Am Fedn Clin Res; Am Soc Gastrointestinal Endoscopy; Int Asn Study of Liver Dis; fel Am Col Physicians; fel Am Col Gastroenterol; Europ Asn Study Liver; Int Asn Study Disorder iron Metab (pres, 93-95). *Res:* Liver disease; portal hypertension; iron metabolism; hemochromatosis. *Mailing Add:* Faulkner Hosp 1153 Centre St Boston MA 02130. *Fax:* 617-524-6599

GRACE, O DONN, SYSTEM SCIENCE, ACOUSTICS. *Current Pos:* INDEPENDENT CONSULT, 87- *Personal Data:* b Kansas City, Mo, Feb 10, 36. *Educ:* Portland State Col, BS, 63; Colo State Univ, MS, 66; Univ Calif, San Diego, PhD(appl physics), 75. *Prof Exp:* Assoc res scientist acoust, Appl Res Lab, Univ Tex, Austin, 65-69; physicist acoust, Naval Ocean Syst Ctr, San Diego, 69-80; sr prin engr, Orincon Corp, 80-83; staff scientist, Phys Dynamics, La Jolla, Calif, 83-87. *Concurrent Pos:* Lectr, Univ Calif, San Diego & San Diego State Univ. *Res:* System analysis, data processing signal physics, random processes. *Mailing Add:* 20503 Fortuna Del Sur Escondido CA 92029. *Fax:* 760-744-5541; *E-Mail:* graceod@concentric.net

GRACE, OLIVER DAVIES, VETERINARY PATHOLOGY. *Current Pos:* RETIRED. *Personal Data:* b Washington, DC, Dec 21, 14; m 48, Vera Hanawalt; c Kerstin E (Lanser) & Edward O. *Educ:* Colo Agr & Mech Col, DVM, 40; Univ Ill, MS, 51; Am Col Vet Microbiol, dipl. *Prof Exp:* Field vet, Bur Animal Indust, USDA, 40-42, vet-in-charge, Serol Lab, NH, 42-46; food & drug admin, Dept Health, Educ & Welfare, Ill, 46-53; head dept vet med, Baxter Labs, Inc, 53-55; from assoc prof to prof vet sci, Univ Nebr-Lincoln, 55-82, interim head, 76-77. *Concurrent Pos:* Asst prof animal hyg, Ill, 46-53. *Mem:* Am Vet Med Asn; Am Asn Avian Path; Conf Res Workers Animal Dis. *Res:* Etiology, pathogenesis and pathology of the infectious diseases of large animals and poultry. *Mailing Add:* 1720 Donald Circle Lincoln NE 68505

GRACE, RICHARD E(DWARD), ENGINEERING EDUCATION, STUDENT SERVICES. *Current Pos:* From asst prof to prof metall eng, Purdue Univ, 54-62, head sch, 64-72, head div interdisciplinary eng studies, 70-82, head dept freshman eng & asst dean eng, 81-87, vpres student serv, 87-95, PROF METALL ENG, PURDUE UNIV, 62-, DIR, UNDERGRAD STUDIES PROG, 95- *Personal Data:* b Chicago, Ill, June 26, 30; m 55, Connie Fotos; c Virginia & Richard (deceased). *Educ:* Purdue Univ, BSMetE, 51; Carnegie Inst Technol, PhD, 54. *Honors & Awards:* Bradley Stoughton Award, Am Soc Metals, 62; Grinter Award, Accreditation Bd Eng & Technol, 89; Centennial Medallion, Am Soc Eng Educ, 93. *Mem:* Fel Am Soc Metals; fel Am Soc Eng Educ; Am Inst Mining, Metall & Petrol Engrs. *Res:* Diffusion and mass transport; corrosion and oxidation; Undergraduate Student Life, The Undecided Freshman. *Mailing Add:* 2175 Tecumseh Park Lane West Lafayette IN 47906

GRACE, ROBERT ARCHIBALD, OCEAN ENGINEERING. *Current Pos:* from asst prof to assoc prof, 66-76, PROF CIVIL ENG, UNIV HAWAII, 76- *Personal Data:* b London, Ont, Jan 1, 38; m 82; c 4. *Educ:* Univ Western Ont, BESc, 60; Mass Inst Technol, SM, 62, PhD(hydrodyn & water resources), 66. *Prof Exp:* Assoc res scientist, Hydronautics, Inc, Md, 61-63; engr, Electricite de France, Chatou, 63, 68. *Concurrent Pos:* Vis prof, Ore State Univ, 77, 79-81; vis lectr, Univ Cape Town, 83. *Res:* Coastal engineering; ocean wave forces on structures; marine disposal of wastes; artificial reefs. *Mailing Add:* Dept Civil Eng Univ Hawaii Manoa Honolulu HI 96822

GRACE, THOM P, COMPUTER GRAPHICS, PROGRAMMING LANGUAGES. *Current Pos:* asst prof, 82-86, ASSOC PROF COMPUT SCI DEPT, ILL INST TECHNOL, 86- *Personal Data:* b Evergreen Park, Ill, Jan 30, 55; m 90; c 1. *Educ:* Univ Ill, BS, 76, MS, 79, PhD(math), 82. *Prof Exp:* Res & teaching asst, Math Dept, Univ Ill, Chicago, 76-82. *Concurrent Pos:* Consult, Dewar Info Systs Corp, 90-91; expert witness, 91. *Mem:* Asn Comput Mach; Math Asn Am; Am Math Soc; Inst Elec & Electronics Engrs Comput Soc. *Res:* Realistic computer-generated imagery using approximations of physically correct behavior; programming languages, programming environments and novel programming paradigms; numerical and nonnumerical computation; discrete mathematics: graph theory, algebra, error-correcting codes. *Mailing Add:* Dept Comput Sci Ill Inst Technol Chicago IL 60616-3730

GRACE, THOMAS MICHAEL, CHEMICAL ENGINEERING. *Current Pos:* PRES, T M GRACE CO, INC, 89- *Personal Data:* b Beaver Dam, Wis, Oct 3, 38; m 63, 80, Mary; c Misty (Goss), Michelle (Jensen) & Mara. *Educ:* Univ Wis-Madison, BS, 60; Univ Minn, Minneapolis, PhD, 63. *Honors & Awards:* Forest Prod Div Award, Am Inst Chem Eng, 84; Eng Div Award, Tech Asn Pulp & Paper Indust, 91. *Prof Exp:* Aerospace technologist, Lewis Res Ctr, NASA, 63-65; from assoc prof chem eng & res assoc to prof chem eng & sr assoc, Inst Paper Chem, 66-89, chmn dept, 70-76. *Mem:* Fel Tech Asn Pulp & Paper Ind; Am Inst Chem Engrs. *Res:* Chemical recovery technology; heat and mass transfer. *Mailing Add:* 2517 S Harmon St Appleton WI 54915

GRACH, ELLA, PHARMACOLOGY. *Current Pos:* DIR CLIN RES, WAKE RES ASSOCS, 93- *Personal Data:* b Kiev, Ukraine, June 28, 59; US citizen. *Educ:* Uzgorod Univ, Ukraine, MD, 83. *Prof Exp:* Res fel, Nat Inst Health Fellows, 87-89. *Res:* Clinical investigations and research in phase I, II and III clinical research trials in a variety of therapeutic areas: gastroenterology, pulmonology and immunology. *Mailing Add:* 3100 Blue Ridge Rd Raleigh NC 27612

GRACIE, G(ORDON), PHOTOGRAMMETRY. *Current Pos:* prof, 71-96, DIR, CTR SURV SCI, UNIV TORONTO, 88-, EMER PROF SURV SCI, 96- *Personal Data:* b Toronto, Ont, Sept 11, 30; m 58, Jansje von Donselaar; c 2. *Educ:* Univ Toronto, BASc, 52; Univ Ill, PhD(civil eng), 63. *Prof Exp:* Proj engr aerial surv, Photog Surv Corp, 52-55; from instr to asst prof civil eng, Univ Ill, 57-65; sr scientist photogram autometric opers, Raytheon Co, 65-71. *Mem:* Am Soc Civil Engrs; Am Soc Photogram; Am Cong Surv & Mapping; Can Inst Geomatics. *Res:* Aerial surveying; survey analysis; analytical photogrammetry; non-topographic photogrammetry; statistics. *Mailing Add:* Erindale Campus Univ Toronto Mississauga ON L5L 1C6 Can

GRACY, ROBERT WAYNE, ENZYMOLOGY, AGING. *Current Pos:* from asst prof to assoc prof, 70-75, chmn, Dept Biochem & Molecular Biol, 76-93, PROF BIOCHEM & MOLECULAR BIOL, HEALTH SCI CTR, UNIV NTEX, FT WORTH, 76-, ASSOC DEAN RES & BIOTECHNOL, 93- *Personal Data:* b McKinney, Tex, Dec 30, 41; m 63, Peggy Vroman. *Educ:* Calif State Polytech Col, BS, 64; Univ Calif, Riverside, PhD(biochem), 68. *Honors & Awards:* Wilfred T Doherty Award, Am Chem Soc, 95. *Prof Exp:* Chemist, Space Gen, El Monte, Calif, 63-64; Damon Runyon Fel molecular biol, Albert Einstein Col Med, 68-70; prof & chmn, Dept Biochem & Molecular Biol, Tex Col Osteop Med, 76-93, actg chmn, Dept Microbiol & Immunol, 86-88. *Concurrent Pos:* Lectr, Calif State Polytech Col, 63-64; res career develop award, NIH, 72-77, SPEC STUDY SECTS PHYSIOL CHEM, 82-88, merit award for res aging, 87-97; fel, Alexander von Humboldt Found, 76-77 & 90-91; Gutensohn-Denslow Res Award, Admin on Aging, 89; vis prof, Dept Physiol, Univ Wurzburg, 75-76 & 90-91, Peoples Repub China, 88; Fedn Am Socs Exp Biol vis prof, Univ Virgin Islands, 84, Univ PR, 86, Univ Sacred Heart, 86, Fla A&M Univ, 88, Inst Geront, 88 & Barry Univ, 89. *Mem:* AAAS; Am Chem Soc; Am Asn Biol Chem; Am Soc Biochem & Molecular Biol; Am Asn Univ Professors; Am Osteop Asn; Asn Geront Higher Educ; Sigma Xi; Protein Soc. *Res:* Protein chemistry and enzymology; structure and function of enzymes and relation to catalytic mechanisms; physical, chemical and catalytic properties of enzymes, especially metalloproteins and metabolic diseases; molecular basis of altered enzymes during aging; aging and the failure of the immune system. *Mailing Add:* Tex Health Sci Ctr, Univ NTex Res Biotechnol 3500 Camp Bowie Blvd Ft Worth TX 76107-2699. *Fax:* 817-735-5485; *E-Mail:* rgracy@hsc.unt.edu

GRAD, ARTHUR, MATHEMATICS. *Current Pos:* RETIRED. *Personal Data:* b Stryj, Austria, Jan 31, 18; nat US; m 46; c 2. *Educ:* City Col New York, BS, 38; Columbia Univ, AM, 39; Stanford Univ, PhD(math), 48. *Prof Exp:* Mathematician, US Coast & Geod Surv, 41-46; res assoc & actg instr math, Stanford Univ, 46-48; mathematician, Off Naval Res, 48-53 & Courant Inst, NY Univ, 53-54; head math br, Off Naval Res, 54-59; prog dir math sci & head math sci sect, NSF, 59-63; assoc dean grad div, Stanford Univ, 63-64; prof math & dean grad sch, Ill Inst Technol, 64-71; pres, Polytech Inst Brooklyn, 71-73; prof, City Col, NY, 74- *Concurrent Pos:* Lectr, Univ Md, 49-53; mem Comt Expert Examiners, US Civil Serv Comn, 51-53; liaison rep, Div Math, Nat Acad Sci-Nat Res Coun, 59-63, mem comt on travel grants, 60-63, liaison rep, Comt on Use of Electronic Comput, 62-63, mem comt on sources & forms of support, Div Math, 69-, chmn, 70-; adv coun automatic data processing, US Bur Budget, 62-63; rep, Coun Grad Schs, 64-71, Argonne

Univs Asn, 67-71; consult, Dept Sci Develop Sect, NSF, 67-68; chmn, Div Math, Nat Acad Sci-Nat Res Coun, 69-72; vchmn & mem exec comt, Brooklyn Instnl Coun, 71-73; vis prof, City Univ NY, 73-76, spec asst to dep chancellor, 76-85. *Mem:* Math Asn Am. *Res:* Functions of a complex variable, conformal mapping; schlicht functions. *Mailing Add:* 19 Mountain View Ave Ardsley NY 10502

GRAD, BERNARD RAYMOND, EXPERIMENTAL BIOLOGY. *Current Pos:* CONSULT, 86- *Personal Data:* b Montreal, Que, Feb 4, 20; m 48, Lottie Dainoff; c Roland M & Willis B. *Educ:* McGill Univ, BSc, 44, PhD(exp morphol), 49. *Honors & Awards:* Ciba Found Award, 55. *Prof Exp:* Asst endocrinol, geront & cancer, McGill Univ, 49-55, lectr, 55-61, asst prof, 61-65, assoc prof biol; assoc prof, Inst Armand Frappier, Univ Que, Montreal, 85-93. *Mem:* Am Asn Cancer Res. *Res:* Variables effecting quantitative changes in coronal images; stress and aging; placebo effect; bioenergetics; biomagnetics; anti-cancer compounds; biopoiesis. *Mailing Add:* 5317 Snowdon Montreal PQ H3X 1Y3 Can

GRADIE, JONATHAN CAREY, PLANETARY SCIENCES, ASTRONOMY. *Current Pos:* ASSOC RESEARCHER PLANETARY GEOSCI, UNIV HAWAII, 84-, ADJ FAC, DEPT GEOL & GEOPHYS; PRES & SR SCIENTIST, TERRA SYSTS, INC, 92- *Personal Data:* b Putnam, Conn, June 20, 51; m 77; c 2. *Educ:* Univ Ariz, BS, 73, PhD(planetary sci), 78. *Honors & Awards:* Asteroid named in hon, 3253 Gradie. *Prof Exp:* Res assoc planetary sci, Lab Planetary Studies, Cornell Univ, 78-84. *Mem:* AAAS; Am Astron Soc; Int Astron Union; Am Geophys Union. *Res:* Planetary surfaces; asteroids, comets and natural satellites; optical design visible and infrared spectrometers; geophysics; terrestrial remote sensing. *Mailing Add:* 169 Kuukama St Kailua HI 96734. *E-Mail:* jgradie@terrasys.com

GRADSTEIN, FELIX MARCEL, MICROPALEONTOLOGY, MARINE GEOLOGY. *Current Pos:* res scientist, 74-95, EMER SCIENTIST BIOSTRATIG, GEOL SURV CAN, 95- *Personal Data:* b Nov 8, 41; Canadian citizen; m 68; c 2. *Educ:* Utrecht State Univ, PhD(micropaleont, biostratig), 72. *Prof Exp:* Asst paleont, Utrecht State Univ, 64-72; res scientist, Imp Oil Ltd, Calgary, 72-74. *Concurrent Pos:* Consult, Arps Consult Ltd, 70-72; vis fel, Woods Hole Oceanog Inst, 78; chief scientist, ocean drilling expeds, 81 & 88. *Mem:* Koninklijk Nederlands Geologisch Mijnbouwkundig; Can Soc Petrol Geologists; Comt Quantitative Stratigraphy. *Res:* Foraminiferal biostratigraphy; paleo-oceanography; agglutinated benthonic foraminifera, particularly as applied in stratigraphic/paleoecologic evolutions of petroleum basins such as North Sea and Labrador Sea; quantitative biostratigraphy; development of new stratigraphic correlation methods; Canadian quantitative stratigraphy. *Mailing Add:* Atlantic Geosci Ctr Geol Surv Can Bedford Inst Dartmouth NS B2Y 4A2 Can

GRADY, CECIL PAUL LESLIE, JR, BIOLOGICAL WASTEWATER TREATMENT, BIOGRADATION. *Current Pos:* prof environ eng, 81-83, R A BOWEN PROF ENVIRON ENG, CLEMSON UNIV, 83- *Personal Data:* b Des Arc, Ark, June 25, 38; m 61; c 2. *Educ:* Rice Inst, BA, 60; Rice Univ, BSCE, 61, MS, 63; Okla State Univ, PhD(environ eng), 69. *Prof Exp:* Res asst environ eng, Rice Univ, 60-61, res fel, 61-63; design engr, Charles R Haile Assoc Consult Engrs, 63; environ engr, US Army Environ Hyg Agency, 63-65; res fel environ eng, Okla State Univ, 65-68; from asst prof to prof, Purdue Univ, 68-81. *Concurrent Pos:* Career develop award, Merck Found, 71; vis scholar, Dept Chem Eng, Univ Tex, 75-76. *Mem:* Water Pollution Control Fedn; Am Inst Chem Eng; Am Soc Microbiol; Am Chem Soc; Int Asn Water Pollution Res & Control. *Res:* Microbial kinetics; application of biochemical engineering principles to wastewater treatment; microbial ecology; biodegradation of toxic organic pollutants. *Mailing Add:* Clemson Univ 342 Computer Ct Clemson Univ 501 Rhodes Clemson SC 29625

GRADY, HAROLD JAMES, CLINICAL BIOCHEMISTRY. *Current Pos:* RETIRED. *Personal Data:* b Excelsior Springs, Mo, May 3, 20; m 44; c 5. *Educ:* St Louis Univ, PhD(biochem), 51. *Prof Exp:* Asst prof biochem & med, Univ Kans Med Ctr, Kansas City, 50-55, from assoc prof to prof biochem path, 55-70; clin biochemist, Baptist Mem Hosp, Kansas City, 70-92. *Concurrent Pos:* Consult, Vet Admin & Independence Hosps, Kansas City. *Mem:* AAAS; Am Soc Clin Path; Am Chem Soc; Am Asn Clin Chemists. *Res:* Steroid metabolism and clinical chemistry. *Mailing Add:* 3510 W 73rd St Prairie Village KS 66208-2901

GRADY, HAROLD ROY, PHYSICAL CHEMISTRY. *Current Pos:* mgr vanadium chem res, Foote Mineral Co, 67-71, vpres & gen mgr, Lithium Battery Dept, 71-88, VPRES RES, CYPRUS FOOTE MINERAL CO, 88- *Personal Data:* b Wooster, Ohio, Aug 8, 22; m 45; c 3. *Educ:* Wooster Col, AB, 43; Brown Univ, PhD(chem), 49. *Prof Exp:* Res chemist, Manhattan Proj, Oak Ridge, Tenn, 44-46; prof chem & head dept, Muskingum Col, 49-53, 54-55; cryog engr, H L Johnston, Inc, 53-54; dir chem res, Vanadium Corp Am, Ohio, 55-67. *Mem:* Am Chem Soc; Electrochem Soc. *Res:* Infrared spectroscopy; vanadium compounds; analytical chemistry; metallurgy. *Mailing Add:* 725 Fox Lane Chester Springs PA 19425

GRADY, JOSEPH EDWARD, MICROBIOLOGY, BIOCHEMISTRY. *Current Pos:* RETIRED. *Personal Data:* b Plains, Pa, Apr 1, 27; m 54; c 4. *Educ:* Univ Scranton, BS, 48; Purdue Univ, MS, 51, PhD, 58. *Prof Exp:* Microbiologist, Lederle Labs Div, Am Cyanamid Co, 51-54; microbiologist, Upjohn Co, 58-78, mgr infectious dis res, 78-88. *Mem:* AAAS; Am Soc Microbiol; NY Acad Sci. *Res:* Antibiotics, screening, in vitro and in vivo evaluation. *Mailing Add:* 3825 Greenleaf Circle Kalamazoo MI 49008

GRADY, LEE TIMOTHY, ANALYTICAL CHEMISTRY, PHARMACEUTICAL CHEMISTRY. *Current Pos:* dir, Drug Res & Testing Lab, 75-78, dir, Drug Stand Div, 79-95, VPRES & DIR, US PHARMACOPEIA, 95- *Personal Data:* b Chicago, Ill, Mar 21, 37; m 64; c Meghan & Patricia. *Educ:* Univ Ill, BS, 59, PhD(org chem), 63. *Honors & Awards:* Res Award, Am Soc Hosp Pharmacists, 82; Justin Powers Award, 90. *Prof Exp:* Sr res pharmacologist, Merck Inst Therapeut Res, 65-68; sr supvr, Drug Stand Lab, Am Pharmaceut Asn Found, 68-71, dir, 71-74. *Concurrent Pos:* Mem adj fac, Sch Pharm, Univ Md, Baltimore, 72-; expert adv, WHO, 79-87 & Pan-Am Health Orgn, 84-85. *Mem:* Fel AAAS; Am Chem Soc; fel Acad Pharmaceut Sci; Fed Int Pharm; fel Am Asn Pharm Sci. *Res:* Physical organic chemistry; drug metabolism; chromatography; analytical chemistry; drug assay; chemical purity and methods; analysis of packaging materials; drug bioequivalence; standards setting. *Mailing Add:* USP Drug Stand Div 12601 Twinbrook Pkwy Rockville MD 20852. *Fax:* 301-816-8373; *E-Mail:* hg@usp.org

GRADY, MICHAEL D, PROBABILITY. *Current Pos:* PROF, DEPT MATH, LOYOLA MARYMOUNT UNIV, 75- *Personal Data:* b St Louis, Mo, Aug 3, 46. *Educ:* Univ Mo, BS, 68; Southern Ill Univ, MS, 70; Univ Utah, PhD(probability). *Mem:* Math Asn Am. *Res:* Probability. *Mailing Add:* Dept Math Loyola Marymount Univ 7900 Loyola Blvd Los Angeles CA 90045

GRADY, PERRY LINWOOD, POLYMER SCIENCE, ELECTRICAL ENGINEERING. *Current Pos:* Res asst, NC State Univ, 62-67, res instr, 67-73, from asst prof to assoc prof, 73-82, PROF & ASSOC DEAN, COL TEXTILES, NC STATE UNIV, 82- *Personal Data:* b Mt Olive, NC, Sept 10, 40; m 62, Patricia Whitman; c Patricia L (Moore) & Julie A. *Educ:* NC State Univ, BS, 62, MS, 67, PhD(fiber & polymer sci), 73. *Honors & Awards:* Fiber Soc Award, Inst Soc Am Award, Exten Award; Cates-Rutherford Award. *Mem:* Fel Instrument Soc Am; Fiber Soc; Inst Elec & Electronics Engrs; Am Phys Soc; Am Asn Textile Chemists & Colorists. *Res:* Instrument design and development; physical properties of fibers; electrostatic and charge transport properties of fibers; open end spinning; computer applications in textiles; ballistic testing of textile materials; energy utilization and conservation. *Mailing Add:* Col Textiles NC State Univ PO Box 8301 Raleigh NC 27695-8301. *Fax:* 919-515-3057; *E-Mail:* perry-grady@ncsu.edu

GRAEBEL, WILLIAM P(AUL), ENGINEERING MECHANICS, APPLIED MATHEMATICS. *Current Pos:* from instr to assoc prof eng mech, 56-67, prof appl mech, 67-91, EMER PROF, UNIV MICH, 91-; OWNER, NEV ENG R&D SYSTS, 91- *Personal Data:* b Manitowoc, Wis, July 15, 32; m 54, June Ness; c Jeffrey & Susan. *Educ:* Univ Wis, BS, 54, MS, 55; Univ Mich, PhD(eng mech), 59. *Prof Exp:* Mem tech staff, Bell Labs, Inc, 55-56. *Concurrent Pos:* Adj prof, Dept Mech Eng, Univ Las Vegas, 91-; consult. *Mem:* Am Phys Soc; Am Soc Mech Eng; fel Am Inst Aeronaut & Astronaut; Sigma Xi. *Res:* Fluid mechanics. *Mailing Add:* 6452 Viewpoint Dr Las Vegas NV 89115-7052

GRAEBER, EDWARD JOHN, X-RAY CRYSTALLOGRAPHY. *Current Pos:* STAFF MEM CRYSTALLOG, SANDIA LABS, 56- *Personal Data:* b Denver, Colo, May 14, 34; m 56; c 4. *Educ:* Colo Sch Mines, BS, 56; Univ NMex, PhD(geol), 70. *Mem:* Am Inst Physics; Am Crystallog Asn. *Res:* X-ray diffraction; organic, inorganic and mineral structures; solid state. *Mailing Add:* 9720 Mesa Arriba Ave NE Albuquerque NM 87111

GRAEBERT, ERIC W, TOXICOLOGY MANAGEMENT. *Current Pos:* PRES, GRAEBERT ASSOCS, 82- *Personal Data:* b Laren, Holland, Jan 20, 24; US citizen; m 46; c 3. *Educ:* Univ Pittsburgh, BSCheE, 49. *Prof Exp:* Mgt positions detergent & food prod & paper fields, Procter & Gamble Co, Eng & US, 49-78; vpres opers, Bio/Dynamics, Inc, 78-80, sr vpres, 80-82. *Res:* Industrial food product development; development of raw material sources in Europe; reorganization and formalization programs for carrying out safety (toxicology) evaluations of product materials prior to marketing; contract research in the life sciences. *Mailing Add:* Solitude Rd St Michaels MD 21663

GRAEDEL, THOMAS ELDON, ATMOSPHERIC CHEMISTRY, CORROSION OF METALS. *Current Pos:* PROF INDUST ECOL, YALE UNIV, 97- *Personal Data:* b Portland, Ore, Aug 23, 38; m 66, Susannah Ketchum; c Laura & Martha. *Educ:* Wash State Univ, BS, 60; Kent State Univ, MS, 64; Univ Mich, MA, 67, PhD(astrophys), 69. *Honors & Awards:* Louis Batten Prize, Am Meteorol Soc. *Prof Exp:* Res assoc space physics, Radio Astron Observ, Univ Mich, 68-69; mem tech staff, Bell Labs, 69-83, distinguished mem tech staff atmospheric chem, 84-96. *Concurrent Pos:* Atmospheric Sci Rev Comt, Langley Res Ctr, NASA, 79; oxidant panel, Nat Comn on Air Quality, 79-80; Air Quality Div Rev Panel, Nat Ctr for Atmospheric Res, 80 & 86; Publ Comt, Am Geophys Union, 80-82, chmn, 82-84, Budget & Finance Comt, 86-88, assoc ed, J Atmospheric Environ, 79-82; invitee & rapporteur, Dahlem Conf Atmospheric Chem, Berlin, 82 & Chemrawn 4, Keystone, Colo, 87; mem tech adv group, Nat Acid Deposition Modeling Proj, 84-87; Gov Panel Acid Deposition NJ, 84-85; corrosion consult, Statue Liberty Restoration Proj, 84-86; mem, Comt Conserv Hist & Artistic Works, Nat Asn Corrosion Engrs, 86-92; bd atmospheric sci & climate, Nat Res Coun, 87-93; convener, Global Emissions Inventory Activ, 90-; chmn, Nat Res Coun Panel on Atmospheric Effects of Stratospheric Aircraft, 93; mem, Comn Geosci, Environ & Resources, Nat Res Coun, 97- *Mem:* AAAS; Am Chem Soc; fel Am Geophys Union; Am Meteorol Soc. *Res:* Chemistry and physics of atmospheric gases and aerosols; effects of atmospheric contaminants on materials and electrical and mechanical equipment; environmentally-responsible industrial product and process design. *Mailing Add:* Sch Forestry & Environ Studies Yale Univ 205 Prospect St New Haven CT 06511. *E-Mail:* thomas.graedel@yale.edu

GRAEF, PHILIP EDWIN, BIOLOGY. *Current Pos:* RETIRED. *Personal Data:* b New York, NY, Oct 29, 23; m 49; c 1. *Educ:* Emory & Henry Col, AB, 47; George Peabody Col, MA, 48; Univ Va, PhD(biol), 55. *Prof Exp:* Asst prof chem, Bridgewater Col, 48-50; asst prof biol, ECarolina Col, 55-57; prof biol, Columbia Col, Sc, 57-90, chmn, Dept Biol, 71-90. *Mem:* Nat Asn Biol Teachers; Am Inst Biol Sci; Nat Sci Teachers Asn. *Res:* Megasporogenesis, ovule development and megagametogenesis of flowering plants. *Mailing Add:* 820 Stebondale Rd Columbia SC 29203

GRAEF, WALTER L, ORGANIC CHEMISTRY, PHARMACEUTICAL CHEMISTRY. *Current Pos:* asst ed, Chem Abstr Serv, 66-67, dept head, Org Index Ed Dept, 67-69, mgr, 69-71, mgr, Org Index Dept, 71-72, mgr, Phys Inorg Anal Chem Dept, 72-73, mgr, Chem Substance Handling Dept, 73-77, MGR, CHEM TECHNOL DEPT, CHEM ABSTR SERV, 77- *Personal Data:* b Staten Island, NY, Jan 17, 38; m 65; c 1. *Educ:* Albany Col Pharm, NY, BS, 59; Univ Wis, MS, 61, PhD(pharmaceut chem), 63. *Prof Exp:* Res chemist org chem, Dyes Div, E I Du Pont de Nemours & Co, 63-64; asst prof pharmaceut chem, Fordham Univ, 64-66. *Mem:* Am Chem Soc. *Res:* Stereochemical requirements for ganglionic blockade; synthesis of short chain mono- and bis-quaternary ammonium compounds. *Mailing Add:* 164 S Stanwood Rd Columbus OH 43209

GRAESSLEY, WILLIAM W(ALTER), POLYMER SCIENCE, RHEOLOGY. *Current Pos:* PROF CHEM ENG, PRINCETON UNIV, 87- *Personal Data:* b Muskegon, Mich, Sept 10, 33; m 53, Helen Carlsen; c Kathryn, William & Laurie. *Educ:* Univ Mich, BS & BSE, 56, MSE, 57, PhD(chem eng), 60. *Honors & Awards:* Bingham Medal, Soc Rheol; Whitby Lectr, Akron, 86; Physics Prize, Am Phys Soc, 90. *Prof Exp:* Sr chemist, Air Reduction Co, NJ, 59-63; from asst prof to prof, Northwestern Univ, 63-81, Walter Murphy prof chem eng & mat sci, 81-83; sr sci adv, Corp Res Lab, Exxon Res & Eng Co, 82-88. *Concurrent Pos:* Sr vis fel, Cambridge Univ, 79-80. *Mem:* Nat Acad Eng; Am Inst Chem Engrs; fel Am Phys Soc; Soc Rheol; Am Phys Soc. *Res:* Relationship between molecular structure and properties of polymer solutions, melts and networks. *Mailing Add:* Dept Chem Eng Princeton Univ Princeton NJ 08544. *E-Mail:* graessle@princeton.edu

GRAETZ, DONALD ALVIN, SOIL CHEMISTRY, WATER CHEMISTRY. *Current Pos:* asst prof soils, 71-77, ASSOC PROF SOIL SCI, UNIV FLA, 77- *Personal Data:* b Pound, Wis, Nov 19, 42. *Educ:* Univ Wis, BS, 64, MS, 67, PhD(soils), 70. *Prof Exp:* Proj assoc soils, Univ Wis, 70-71. *Mem:* Am Soc Agron; Soil Sci Soc Am; Sigma Xi. *Res:* Soil and water pollution; nitrogen transformations and transport in soils; nutrient cycles in aquatic systems. *Mailing Add:* Dept Soil Sci Univ Fla PO Box 110510 Gainesville FL 32611-0510

GRAETZER, HANS GUNTHER, PHYSICS, SCIENCE COMMUNICATIONS. *Current Pos:* From asst prof to prof, 56-92, chmn dept, 76-80, EMER PROF PHYSICS, SDAK STATE UNIV, 92- *Personal Data:* b Ger, Feb 13, 30; US citizen; m 57, Miriam Michel; c Michael, Daniel, David & Martha (Henze). *Educ:* Oberlin Col, BA, 52; Yale Univ, MS, 53, PhD(physics), 56. *Concurrent Pos:* NSF fel, Univ Colo, 63-64; Fulbright teacher exchange, Switz, 87. *Mem:* Am Asn Physics Teachers; Am Phys Soc; Sigma Xi. *Res:* Nuclear reactions; gamma ray spectroscopy; history of science and technology; neutron activation analysis of biological and soil samples; author of articles on science topics for the general public. *Mailing Add:* PO Box 339 Estes Park CO 80517-0339

GRAETZER, REINHARD, DNA REPAIR MECHANISMS. *Current Pos:* asst prof, 65-73, ASSOC PROF PHYSICS, PA STATE UNIV, 73-, ASST DEPT HEAD, 93- *Personal Data:* b Ger, Sept 28, 33; US citizen; m 62, Maryalice Carroll; c Catherine & Laura. *Educ:* Oberlin Col, AB, 55; Univ Wis, MA, 57, PhD(physics), 62. *Prof Exp:* Ford Found fel, Niels Bohr Inst, Denmark, 62-64; res assoc & instr physics, Univ Wis, 64-65. *Concurrent Pos:* Sabbatical, Univ Colo, Boulder, 71-72; fac res partic, Oak Ridge Nat Lab, 73, 85, Argonne Nat Lab, 82, & USAF Sch Aerospace Med, 90; sabbatical, Nat Inst Environ Health Sci, Research Triangle Park, NC, 87. *Mem:* Am Phys Soc; Am Asn Physics Teachers. *Res:* Radiation and-chemically induced DNA damage and repair in microorganisms. *Mailing Add:* Dept Physics 104 Davey Lab Pa State Univ University Park PA 16802-6300. *Fax:* 814-865-3604

GRAF, DONALD LEE, GEOCHEMISTRY. *Current Pos:* prof, 69-82, EMER PROF GEOL, UNIV ILL, URBANA, 82- *Personal Data:* b Howard Co, Iowa, Jan 24, 25; m. *Educ:* Colo Sch Mines, Geol E, 45; Columbia Univ, AM, 47, PhD(mineral), 50. *Honors & Awards:* Mineral Soc Am Award, 60. *Prof Exp:* Geologist, Indust Minerals Div, Ill State Geol Surv, 48-63, geochemist, Chem Group, 63-65; prof geol & geophys, Univ Minn, Minneapolis, 65-69. *Concurrent Pos:* Res fel geophys, Harvard Univ, 61-63. *Mem:* Fel Am Geophys Union; fel Mineral Soc Am. *Res:* Sedimentary mineralogy and geochemistry. *Mailing Add:* 2836 E First St Tucson AZ 85716

GRAF, E(DWARD) R(AYMOND), ELECTRICAL ENGINEERING. *Current Pos:* assoc prof, 63-69, PROF ELEC ENG, AUBURN UNIV, 69- *Personal Data:* b Cullman, Ala, Sept 26, 31; m 61; c 1. *Educ:* Auburn Univ, BSc, 57, MSc, 58; Stuttgart Tech Univ, PhD(elec eng), 63. *Prof Exp:* Asst prof elec eng, Auburn Univ, 58-59; asst, Ger Res Found, 60-63. *Concurrent Pos:* Consult, US Army Missile Command, Redstone Arsenal & George C Marshall Space Flight Ctr, 65- *Mem:* Asn Ger Engrs. *Res:* Electromagnetic field theory; antennas and propagation; laser. *Mailing Add:* Epos Corp 391 Industry Dr PO Box 3140 Auburn AL 36830

GRAF, ERLEND HAAKON, LOW TEMPERATURE PHYSICS. *Current Pos:* Asst prof, 67-74, ASSOC PROF PHYSICS, STATE UNIV NY, STONY BROOK, 74- *Personal Data:* b Oslo, Norway, Oct 21, 39; US citizen; m 68. *Educ:* Mass Inst Technol, BS, 61; Cornell Univ, PhD(physics), 68. *Mem:* Am Phys Soc. *Res:* Liquid and solid helium; solid hydrogen; nuclear magnetic resonance. *Mailing Add:* Dept Physics State Univ NY Stony Brook Main Campus Stony Brook NY 11794-1400

GRAF, GEORGE, PROTEIN DYNAMICS, NUCLEAR SPECTROSCOPY. *Current Pos:* RETIRED. *Educ:* Univ Budapest, PhD(biochem), 44. *Prof Exp:* Prof biochem, NDak State Univ, 68-88. *Mailing Add:* 3131 E Alameda Ave No 207 Denver CO 80209-3410

GRAF, HANS PETER, ARTIFICIAL NEURAL NETWORKS, PATTERN RECOGNITION. *Current Pos:* MEM TECH STAFF RES, AT&T BELL LABS, 83- *Personal Data:* b Rebstein, Switz, Jan 28, 52; m 80; c 3. *Educ:* Swiss Fed Inst Technol, dipl physics, 76, Dr ScNat, 81. *Prof Exp:* Res asst, Swiss Fed Inst Technol, 76-81; mem tech staff res, Spreches & Schuh, Aarau, Switz, 81-83. *Concurrent Pos:* Mem, Darpa Panel on Neural Networks, 87-88; lectr, Summer Sch on Neural Networks, NATO, 89 & Course Analog, Mos Intergrated Circuits, 90 & 91. *Mem:* Am Phys Soc; Inst Elec & Electronics Engrs; Am Phys Soc. *Res:* Design of microelectronic circuits implementing artificial neural networks; applications of artificial neural networks to pattern recognition, in particular to machine vision. *Mailing Add:* Crawford Corners Rd Rm 4G320 Holmdel NJ 07733

GRAF, LLOYD HERBERT, BIOCHEMISTRY. *Current Pos:* Biochemist, 48-53, SUPVRY BIOCHEMIST, PHYS DEFENSE DIV, US ARMY BIOL LABS, 53- *Personal Data:* b Madison, Wis, Sept 14, 19; m 43; c 6. *Educ:* Univ Wis, BS, 41, MS, 43, PhD(biochem), 48. *Mem:* Sigma Xi. *Res:* Microbial nutrition and physiology; analytical biochemistry. *Mailing Add:* 618 Wilson Pl Frederick MD 21702-4168

GRAF, PETER EMIL, PHYSICAL CHEMISTRY. *Current Pos:* SR RES CHEMIST, CHEVRON RES CORP, 66- *Personal Data:* b Baltimore, Md, Mar 31, 30; m 58, Susan Ward; c Michael, David & Peter. *Educ:* Univ Rochester, BS, 51; Univ Wis, PhD(phys chem), 56; Golden Gate Univ, JD, 75. *Prof Exp:* Res chemist, Calif Res Corp, 56-66. *Mem:* Am Chem Soc. *Res:* Chemical kinetics; photochemistry; non-electrolyte solutions; colloid chemistry; emulsion theory and technology. *Mailing Add:* 339 Clay St Nevada City CA 95959

GRAF, WILLIAM L, PHYSICAL GEOGRAPHY & FLUVIAL GEOMORPHOLOGY, POLICY FOR PUBLIC LAND AND WATER. *Current Pos:* REGENTS PROF GEOG, ARIZ STATE UNIV, TEMPE, 78- *Personal Data:* b Zanesville, Ohio, Feb 7, 47; m 83, Patricia A Gober; c Kelly Ryan. *Educ:* Univ Wis, BA, 69, MS, 71, PhD(geog & water resources), 74. *Honors & Awards:* G K Gilbert Award, Asn Am Geographers, 84; Cole Mem Award, Geol Soc Am, 85; Honrs Award, Asn Am Geogr, 90. *Prof Exp:* Intel officer, US Air Force, 71-74; from asst prof to assoc prof geog, Univ Iowa, 74-78. *Concurrent Pos:* Consult geomorphologist, 79-; Guggenheim fel, 94. *Mem:* Geol Soc Am; Asn Am Geographers; Brit Geomorphol Group. *Res:* River mechanics; flooding; river channel changes; heavy metals and radionuclides in river systems; downstream impacts of dams. *Mailing Add:* Dept Geog Ariz State Univ PO Box 870104 Tempe AZ 85287-0101. *Fax:* 602-965-8313; *E-Mail:* graf@asu.edu

GRAFF, DARRELL JAY, PHYSIOLOGY, NUTRITION. *Current Pos:* from asst prof to assoc prof, 65-72, PROF PHYSIOL, WEBER STATE COL, 72- *Personal Data:* b Cedar City, Utah, Sept 8, 36; m 62; c 4. *Educ:* Utah State Univ, BS, 58, MS, 60; Univ Calif, Los Angeles, PhD(parasitol), 63. *Prof Exp:* Asst, Zool, Physiol & Parasitol Labs, Utah State Univ, 57-60 & Univ Calif, Los Angeles, 60-62; NSF fel, Rice Univ, 63-64, NIH fel, 64-65. *Concurrent Pos:* Res asst, Commun Dis Ctr, USPHS, 57-58; partic, Int Cong Parasitol, Washington, DC, 70 & Conf on Aging, NIH, Univ Calif, Riverside, 70; tech writer, Allied Health Prof Projs, Univ Calif, Los Angeles, 70; co-dir, NSF Undergrad Res Proj Grant to Weber State Col, 70, partic, NSF Col Sci Improv Proj Grant, 71-; consult, Albion Labs, Clearfield, Utah. *Mem:* Am Soc Parasitologists. *Res:* Carbohydrate and protein metabolism of parasites; active absorption of amino acids and minerals by animals and plants (foliar sprays); behavioral effects of abnormal trace metals mercury and lead. *Mailing Add:* Dept Zool Weber State Univ 3750 Harrison Blvd Ogden UT 84408-0001

GRAFF, GEORGE STEPHEN, AERODYNAMICS. *Current Pos:* RETIRED. *Personal Data:* b New York, NY, Mar 16, 17; m 42, 87, Marjory V Kassabaum; c Mary A, George S Jr, James R, Thomas G & Maureen R. *Educ:* DeSales Col, BA, 39; Univ Detroit, BS, 42. *Hon Degrees:* Dr Eng, Rose Hulman Inst Technol, 82. *Prof Exp:* Draftsman, Continental Aviation & Eng Corp, 40-42; aerodynamicist, McDonnell Aircraft Corp, 42-45, proj aerodynamicist, 45-50, chief aerodynamicist, 50-54, chief aerodyn tech, 54-57, mgr aeromech, 57-60, asst chief engr, 60-61, dir syst tech, 61-64, vpres eng technol, 64-68, vpres eng, 68-70, exec vpres, 70-71, pres, 71-82, vpres & dir, McDonnell Douglas Corp, 71-86. *Concurrent Pos:* Mem subcomt stability & control, Nat Adv Comt Aeronaut, 51-56, mem subcomt aerodyn stability & control, NASA, 56-58 & missile & spacecraft aerodyn, 59-61, chmn res & technol adv subcomt aircraft aerodyn, 67-68, mem res & technol adv comt aeronaut, 67-; vpres, McDonnell Douglas Corp, 71, dir, 73, mem exec comt, 74, mem subcomt, 74- *Mem:* Nat Acad Eng; Am Inst Aeronaut & Astronaut. *Res:* Stability and control. *Mailing Add:* 761 Kent Rd St Louis MO 63124

GRAFF, GUSTAV, ENZYMOLOGY, PROSTAGLADINS CHEMISTRY. *Current Pos:* SR RESEARCHER, A H ROBINS CO, 83- *Educ:* Univ Ill, PhD(biochem), 74. *Mailing Add:* Dept Res Alcon Labs Inc 6201 S Freeway Ft Worth TX 76134-2099. *Fax:* 817-551-4584

GRAFF, MORRIS MORSE, ENDOCRINOLOGY. *Current Pos:* RETIRED. *Personal Data:* b Lafayette, Ind, Mar 3, 10; m 39; c 3. *Educ:* NY Univ, BA, 39; Tulane Univ, MSc, 46. *Prof Exp:* Asst biochem, Columbia Univ, 29-42; from asst chemist to assoc chemist, USDA, La, 42-47; chemist, US Army Chem Ctr, Md, 47-49; resident, Med Br, Endocrinol Serv, NIH, 49-56, resident, Endocrinol Sect Cancer Chemother, Nat Serv Ctr, Nat Cancer Inst, 56-59, exec secy, Endocrinol Study Sect, Div Res Grants, NIH, 59- 85. *Mem:* Am Chem Soc; Endocrine Soc. *Res:* Fats and sterols; food chemistry; rosin acids; naval stores; chromatography; rubber chemistry; cancer chemotherapy; biochemistry. *Mailing Add:* 10023 Raynor Rd Silver Spring MD 20901

GRAFF, ROBERT A, COAL CONVERSION TECHNOLOGY, MUNICIPAL WASTE. *Current Pos:* from lectr to prof chem eng, City Univ NY, 56-80, dir, Clean Fuels Inst, 76-90, act dir, Inst Munic Waste Res, 90-94, MICHAEL POPE PROF ENERGY RES, CITY UNIV NY, 80-, CHAIR, DEPT CHEM ENG, 89-, DEP DIR, CTR APPL STUDIES ENVIRON, 93- *Personal Data:* b 1933; US citizen; m 56; c 3. *Educ:* NY Univ, BE, 55; Columbia Univ, MS, 57, DSc, 63. *Prof Exp:* Vis prof, Imp Col Sci & Technol, London, 70-71; assoc ed, Fuel Processing Technol, 76-92; dir, NY State Consortium Advan Coal Res, 79-81. *Mem:* Sigma Xi; Am Inst Chem Engrs; Am Chem Soc; Am Soc Eng Educ. *Res:* Coal conversion technology; pyrolysis; liquification; hot gas cleaning; sewage sludge treatment; hazardous waste remediation. *Mailing Add:* Dept Chem Eng City Col NY New York NY 10031

GRAFF, SAMUEL M, APPLIED MATHEMATICS. *Current Pos:* From asst to assoc prof math, 71-80, chmn, Math Dept, 84-90, PROF MATH, JOHN JAY COL CRIMINAL JUSTICE, CITY UNIV NEW YORK, 81- *Personal Data:* b New York, NY, May 22, 45. *Educ:* Rensselaer Polytech Inst, BS, 66; NY Univ, MS, 68, PhD(math), 71. *Mem:* Am Math Soc; Math Asn Am; Soc Indust & Appl Math; Sigma Xi *Res:* Application of stochastic processes to the modelling of criminal justice and the computer simulation of rail transportation networks; a text on differential equalieres and stability has been completed. *Mailing Add:* John Jay Col Criminal Justice Dept Math 445 W 59 St New York NY 10019

GRAFF, THOMAS D, ANESTHESIOLOGY. *Current Pos:* RETIRED. *Personal Data:* b Paoli, Pa, Feb 10, 26; m 49; c 2. *Educ:* Haverford Col, AB, 49; Temple Univ, MD, 53. *Prof Exp:* Intern, USPHS Hosp, 53-54; resident anesthesia, Detroit Receiving Hosp, 54-56; instr, Sch Med, Univ Md, 56; anesthesiologist, Hosp Women of Md, Baltimore, 57; jr asst resident pediat, Baltimore City Hosps, 61-62; from asst prof to assoc prof anesthesia, Sch Med, Johns Hopkins Univ, 62-86. *Mem:* AMA; Am Soc Anesthesiol. *Mailing Add:* 600 Memorial Ave Cumberland MD 21502

GRAFF, WILLIAM (ARTHUR), CERAMICS. *Current Pos:* RETIRED. *Personal Data:* b Highland, Ill, Dec 25, 23; m 45, Roberta Partridge; c A Steven & Trudy G (Bailey). *Educ:* Univ Ill, BS, 46, MS, 47, PhD(ceramics), 49. *Prof Exp:* Asst ceramics, Univ Ill, 46-47; res glass technologist, Glass Tech Lab, Gen Elec Co, 49-53, res supvr, 53-66, mgr glass res lab, Lamp Glass Dept, 66-74, mgr, Mat Lab, Lamp Glass Prod Dept, 74-80, mgr eng support, Lamp Glass & Components Dept, 80-85, mgr, Glass Sci Projs, Glass & Metall Prods Dept, 85-86. *Concurrent Pos:* Glass consult, 86- *Mem:* Am Chem Soc; Am Ceramic Soc; Brit Soc Glass Technol. *Res:* Formation, properties, structure, reactions and uses of glasses and semi-vitreous materials. *Mailing Add:* 1089 Seven Lakes N West End NC 27376

GRAFF, WILLIAM J(OHN), JR, STRUCTURAL & MECHANICAL ENGINEERING. *Current Pos:* PROF CIVIL ENG, UNIV HOUSTON, 66- *Personal Data:* b Marshall, Tex, May 10, 23; m 44, 77; c 3. *Educ:* Tex A&M Univ, BS, 47, MS, 48; Purdue Univ, PhD(mech eng), 51. *Prof Exp:* Instr mech, Tex A&M Univ, 46-48; instr mech design, Purdue Univ, 48-51; sr propulsion engr, Gen Dynamics-Convair, 51-54, nuclear group engr, 54-56; prof mech eng & chmn dept, Southern Methodist Univ, 56-61; dean instr, Tex A&M Univ, 61-65, dean acad admin, 65-66. *Concurrent Pos:* Conviar, grant, Oak Ridge Sch Reactor Technol, 52-53; consult, Gen Dynamics-Conair, 56-57 & Tex Instruments, Inc, 58-61; partic, Scand & Russian comp educ field study, 63; vis prof, Aalborg Univ Ctr, Denmark, 77-78; Fulbright scholar, Comn Educ Exchange, Denmark & US, 77-78; invited lectr, offshore structs, Tokyo Japan, 81. *Mem:* Am Soc Mech Engrs; Am Soc Eng Educ; Am Soc Civil Engrs. *Res:* Structures; vibrations; properties of materials; offshore structures; welded tubular joints; dynamics; heat transfer. *Mailing Add:* 7815 Wind Swept Lane Houston TX 77063

GRAFFEO, ANTHONY PHILIP, TOXICOLOGY, ANALYTICAL CHEMISTRY. *Current Pos:* VPRES PROD REGIST, BIODEVELOP LABS INC, 94- *Personal Data:* b Boston, Mass, Oct 26, 47; m 73, Marilyn Long; c Micheal & Andrea. *Educ:* Northeastern Univ, BA, 70, PhD(analytical chem), 75. *Prof Exp:* Dir analytical & marine chem, Battelle New Eng Marine Lab, 75-86; vpres, chem life sci, Arthur D Little Inc, 87-93. *Concurrent Pos:* Dir, Mass Ctr Excellence, Marine Sci Bd. *Mem:* Am Chem Soc; Sigma Xi; AAAS; Soc Toxicol. *Res:* Isolating and separating organic and biochemical compounds from complex mixtures using high performance separation techniques; environmental and marine science; preclinical toxicology and analytical chemistry on biopharmaceuticals; registration studies on agrichemicals. *Mailing Add:* PO Box 2220 Duxbury MA 02332-2220

GRAFFIS, DON WARREN, FORAGE CROP MANAGEMENT. *Current Pos:* EXTEN & RES AGRONOMIST, DEPT AGRON, UNIV ILL, URBANA, 66- *Personal Data:* b Royal Center, Ind, Feb 17, 28; m 56, Nancy Newman; c 3. *Educ:* Purdue Univ, BS, 50, MA, 56; Univ Ill, PhD(agron), 60. *Honors & Awards:* Merit Cert, Am Forage & Grassland Coun, 84. *Prof Exp:* Voc agr instr, Van Buren Twp Schs, Ind, 50; field rep, Plant Food Div, Swift & Co, 52-53; voc agr instr, Noble Twp Schs, Ind, 53-55; res assoc forage crops, Univ Ill, 58-60; exten agronomist, Rutgers Univ, 60-63; exten agronomist, Ohio State Univ, 63-66. *Concurrent Pos:* Pvt consult, 88-; Exec Soc, Ill Forage & Grassland Coun, 77- *Mem:* Fel Am Soc Agron; fel Crop Sci Soc Am; Am Forage & Grassland Coun. *Res:* Production management of forage crops in humid regions. *Mailing Add:* Dept Crop Sci Univ Ill 1102 S Goodwin Ave Urbana IL 61801. *Fax:* 217-333-5299; *E-Mail:* graffisd@idea.ag.uiuc.edu

GRAFFIUS, JAMES HERBERT, BOTANY. *Current Pos:* asst prof, 62-68, ASSOC PROF BOT, OHIO UNIV, 68- *Personal Data:* b Pitcairn, Pa, June 8, 28; m 67. *Educ:* Univ Pittsburgh, BS, 54, MS, 58; Mich State Univ, PhD(bot), 63. *Prof Exp:* Asst biol, Univ Pittsburgh, 54-58; asst bot, Mich State Univ, 58-62. *Mem:* Phycol Soc Am; Int Phycol Soc; Am Micros Soc; Bot Soc Am; Sigma Xi. *Res:* Phycology; taxonomy and ecology of fresh-water algae; bog algae; aquatic biology. *Mailing Add:* Dept Bot Ohio Univ Athens OH 45701-2979

GRAFIUS, EDWARD JOHN, ENTOMOLOGY, INSECT POPULATIONS MANAGEMENT RESEARCH. *Current Pos:* asst prof, Dept Entom, 77-82, assoc prof, 82-90, ENTOM EXTEN PROJ LEADER, MICH STATE UNIV, 89-, PROF, 90- *Personal Data:* b Brookings, SDak, Oct 16, 48; m 70, Ellen K Baumgartner; c 2. *Educ:* Mich State Univ, BS, 70; Ore State Univ, MS, 73, PhD(entom), 77. *Prof Exp:* Grad res asst, Dept Entom, Ore State Univ, 70-77, res assoc, USDA-Agr Res Sta, 77. *Mem:* Entom Soc Am; AAAS; Sigma Xi. *Res:* Insect populations management research; population dynamics; economic thresholds; insecticide resistance management; biological control. *Mailing Add:* Dept Entom Mich State Univ East Lansing MI 48824. *Fax:* 517-353-4354

GRAFSTEIN, BERNICE, REGENERATION, DEVELOPMENT. *Current Pos:* assoc prof, 69-73, PROF PHYSIOL, MED COL, CORNELL UNIV, 73-, VINCENT & BROOKE ASTOR DISTINGUISHED PROF NEUROSCI, 84- *Personal Data:* b Toronto, Ont, Sept 17, 29; m 63, Howard S Shanet; c Laurence P. *Educ:* Univ Toronto, BA, 51; McGill Univ, PhD(physiol), 54. *Prof Exp:* Asst physiol, McGill Univ, 51-54, lectr, 54-55; hon res asst anat, Univ Col London, 55-57; asst prof physiol, McGill Univ, 57-62; asst prof, Rockefeller Univ, 62-69. *Concurrent Pos:* Nat Res Coun Can fel, Univ Col London, 55-56; Grass Found fel, Woods Hole Marine Biol Lab, 61; trustee, Grass Found, 65-; adj prof, Rockefeller Univ, 69-90; chmn comt brain sci, Nat Res Coun-Nat Acad Sci, 75-78; nat adv coun, Nat Inst Neurol & Commun Dis & Stroke, 83-87; sci adv bd, Pew Found, 87-90. *Mem:* AAAS; Am Physiol Soc; Int Brain Res Orgn; Soc Neurosci (treas, 77-80, pres, 85-86). *Res:* Intracellular movement in neurons; growth and regeneration of nervous tissue; extracellular milieu of the nervous system. *Mailing Add:* Dept Physiol Cornell Univ Med Col 1300 York Ave New York NY 10021. *Fax:* 212-746-8690

GRAFSTEIN, DANIEL, CHEMISTRY. *Current Pos:* RETIRED. *Personal Data:* b New York, NY, Dec 24, 27; m 47; c 1. *Educ:* City Col NY, BS, 48; Purdue Univ, MS, 49, PhD(chem), 51. *Prof Exp:* Res chemist, Westinghouse Elec Corp, 51-56; res chemist, Reaction Motors Div, Thiokol Chem Corp, 56-57, group leader, 57-58, unit supvr, Adv Res Group, 59-61; sr staff scientist, Aerospace Res Ctr, Gen Precision, Inc, 62-63, prin staff scientist & mgr chem dept, 63-66, mgr, Mat Dept, 66-69; mgr, Chem Res Prog, Govt Res Lab, Exxon Res & Eng Co, 69-75, mgr laser fusion, 75-77, mgr biomass fuels proj, 77-79, sr res assoc, Corp Res Sci Labs, 79-82; H H Seedoffs Straede, Denmark; mgr dir, London Corp, Senetek DLC, 82-85. *Mem:* AAAS; Am Chem Soc; Am Phys Soc; NY Acad Sci. *Res:* Fluorine, boron and structural chemistry; organometallics; carboranes; photochemistry; lasers; fluorescence; laser fusion. *Mailing Add:* 4100 N Ocean Dr Singer Island FL 33404-2855

GRAFTON, ROBERT BRUCE, APPLIED MATHEMATICS, NUCLEAR ENGINEERING. *Current Pos:* PROG DIR, NSF, 86- *Personal Data:* b Rochester, NY, May 15, 35; m 67; c 2. *Educ:* Brown Univ, ScB, 58, PhD(appl math), 67. *Prof Exp:* Engr, Bur Ships, AEC, 58-62; asst prof math, Univ Mo, Columbia, 67-71, asst prof math, Trinity Col, 71-75; mathematician, Off Naval Res, 75-78, comput scientist, 78-86. *Mem:* Math Asn Am; Inst Elec & Electronics Engrs; Sigma Xi. *Res:* Differential equations; periodic solutions. *Mailing Add:* MIRS Div NSF 4201 Wilson Blvd Arlington VA 22230

GRAFTON, THURMAN STANFORD, LABORATORY ANIMAL MEDICINE. *Current Pos:* CONSULT, MED RES MGT, 81- *Personal Data:* b Chicago, Ill, Dec 20, 23; m 46; c Scott, Michael, Donald & Glynis. *Educ:* Mich State Univ, DVM, 47; Am Col Lab Animal Med, dipl, 66. *Prof Exp:* Instr surg & med, Vet Col, Mich State Univ, 47-48; vet lab officer, Walter Reed Army Inst Res, 48-50; asst chief, Dept Virus & Rickettsial Dis, 406th Med Gen Lab, Japan, 50-52; assoc prof virol, Univ Md, 52-53; course supvr vet serv, USAF Sch Aviation Med, 53-56; exec officer clin lab, 7520th Med Clin Lab, Eng, 56-60; chief vivarium br, 6571st Aeromed Res Lab, Holloman AFB, NMex, 60-64; asst chief nutrit br, Food Div, US Army Natick Labs, Mass, 64-66; prof lab animal sci & chmn dept, Sch Health Rel Professions & res assoc prof microbiol, Sch Med & dir lab animal facil, State Univ NY, Buffalo, 66-76; exec dir, Nat Soc Med Res, 76-80. *Concurrent Pos:* USAF Rep, Int Conf Vet Educ, London, 59; consult, univs, hosps & med res insts; distinguished vis prof, State Univ NY, Buffalo, 76- *Mem:* Am Vet Med Asn; Asn Gnotobiotics; Conf Pub Health Vets; Am Soc Lab Animal Practitioners (pres, 71-72); Am Asn Zoo Vets. *Res:* Improved support of the use of animals in biomedical research; diseases and treatment of aquatic animals; medical research management; education and utilization of animal technicians. *Mailing Add:* 4939 Floramar Terr Apt 907 New Port Richey FL 34652-3314

GRAGE, THEODOR B, SURGERY. *Current Pos:* RETIRED. *Personal Data:* b Munster, Ger, Mar 24, 27; US citizen; m 53; c 8. *Educ:* Creighton Univ, MD, 55; Univ Minn, MS & PhD(surg), 63. *Prof Exp:* Intern med, Creighton Mem St Joseph's Hosp, 55-56; from instr to assoc prof surg, Univ Minn Hosps, 61-92. *Concurrent Pos:* Fel surg, Univ Minn Hosps, 56-61; Am Cancer Soc adv clin fel, 62-65. *Mem:* Soc Head & Neck Surg; Am Col Surg; Am Asn Clin Oncol; Am Asn Cancer Res. *Res:* Surgical treatment of malignant diseases and chemotherapy of solid tumors. *Mailing Add:* Univ Surg Oncol Pa Harvard St E River Rd Minneapolis MN 55455

GRAGG, WILLIAM BRYANT, JR, MATHEMATICS. *Current Pos:* PROF MATH, UNIV KY, 80- *Personal Data:* b Bakersfield, Calif, Nov 2, 36; m 58, 78; c 3. *Educ:* Univ Denver, BS, 57; Stanford Univ, MS, 59; Univ Calif, Los Angeles, PhD(math), 64. *Prof Exp:* Mathematician numerical analysis, Bell-Comm, Inc, 63-64; mathematician, Oak Ridge Nat Lab, 64-67; from asst prof to assoc prof math, Univ Calif, San Diego, 67-75, prof, 75-80. *Concurrent Pos:* Vis asst prof, Univ Tenn, 65-67; vis prof math, Univ Colo, 74-75; vis scientist, Inst Comput Appln Sci & Eng, Langley Res Ctr, NASA, 75-76. *Mem:* Soc Indust & Appl Math; Am Math Soc. *Res:* Numerical analysis, especially ordinary value problems, Pade table, continued fractions and matrices. *Mailing Add:* Dept Math Naval Postgrad Sch Code 53 Gr Monterey CA 93943-5100

GRAHAM, A RICHARD, ADVANCED MANUFACTURING SYSTEMS, INSTRUMENTATION. *Current Pos:* from asst prof to prof, Wichita State Univ, 65-79, chmn dept, 78-84, assoc dir, 84-86, PROF, MECH ENG, WICHITA STATE UNIV, 84-, DIR, CTR TECHNOL APPLN, 86- *Personal Data:* b Wichita, Kans, Aug 5, 34; m 62; c Evan T & Cara L. *Educ:* Kans State Univ, BSME, 57, MS, 60; Univ Iowa, PhD(mech eng), 66. *Prof Exp:* Struct engr, Cessna Aircraft Co, 57-58; instr mech eng, Kans State Univ, 58-60, Univ Mo, Rolla, 60-63, & Univ Iowa, 63-64. *Concurrent Pos:* Prin investr, City Wichita Energy Off, 76-80 & Energy Planning Proj, US Off Educ, 77-80; dir, Am Soc Eng Educ, 87-89; dir, Wichita Regional Off, Nat Inst Sci & Technol, Mid-Am Mfg Technol Ctr. *Mem:* Am Soc Mech Engrs; Soc Mfg Engrs; Am Soc Eng Educ; Am Soc Qual Control. *Res:* Application of advanced manufacturing systems in small and medium size companies. *Mailing Add:* 5722 E Tenth St N Wichita KS 67208. *Fax:* 316-689-3175

GRAHAM, A(LBERT) RONALD, MINERALOGY, MINING ENGINEERING. *Current Pos:* RETIRED. *Personal Data:* b Red Deer, Can, Feb 15, 17; m 42; c 1. *Educ:* Univ Alberta, BA, 37; Queen's Univ, Ont, BSc, 40, MSc, 47; Univ Toronto, PhD(mineral), 50. *Honors & Awards:* Berry Medal, Mineral Asn of Can, 87. *Prof Exp:* Asst engr, MacKenzie Red Lake Gold Mines Ltd, 40, shift boss, 41-42; mines scientist, Mines Br, Govt of Can, 49-52; res mineralogist, geol explor, Dominion Gulf Co, 52-55; sect head, Metall Labs, Falconbridge Nickel Mines Ltd, 55-70, asst mgr, 70-77, consult, 77-82. *Concurrent Pos:* Consult, 77-82. *Mem:* Mineral Asn Can (pres, 70-72); Can Geosci Coun (secy-treas, 72-75); Can Inst Mining & Metall; fel Mineral Soc Am; fel Geol Asn Can. *Res:* Instrumentation for mineral exploration; applications for use in deposit evaluations of X-ray diffraction and fluorescence, neutron activation analysis, microscopy (optical and electron). *Mailing Add:* 515 St George St E Fergus ON N1M 1L1 Can

GRAHAM, ALAN KEITH, PLANT MORPHOLOGY, PALEOBOTANY. *Current Pos:* from asst prof to assoc prof, 64-72, PROF BOT, KENT STATE UNIV, 72- *Personal Data:* b Houston, Tex, May 5, 34; m 60. *Educ:* Univ Tex, BA, 56, MA, 58; Univ Mich, PhD(bot), 62. *Prof Exp:* Instr bot, Univ Mich, 62-63; fel, Evolutionary Biol Prog, Harvard Univ, 63-64. *Concurrent Pos:* NSF res grants, 66-68, 69-71, 79-81, 82-84, 85-87 & 87-89; vis res scientist, Univ Amsterdam, 69-70 & Univ Tex, 79-80. *Mem:* AAAS; Bot Soc Am; Int Asn Plant Taxon. *Res:* Tertiary history of Latin American vegetation; palynology and taxonomy. *Mailing Add:* Biol Sci Kent State Univ Main Campus PO Box 5190 Kent OH 44242-0001

GRAHAM, ANGUS FREDERICK, MOLECULAR BIOLOGY, GENETICS. *Current Pos:* chmn dept, 70-80, Gilman Cheyney prof, Dept Biochem, 70-86, EMER PROF BIOCHEM, MED SCH, MCGILL UNIV, 86- *Personal Data:* b Toronto, Ont, Mar 28, 16; nat US; m 54, Jacqueline Poirier; c Robert J, Andrew D & Paul F (deceased). *Educ:* Univ Toronto, BASc, 38, MASc, 39; Univ Edinburgh, PhD(biochem), 42, DSc(microbiol), 52. *Prof Exp:* Lectr biochem, Univ Edinburgh, 40-47; res assoc microbiol, Connaught Med Res Labs, Univ Toronto, 47-58, assoc prof, 53-58; prof, Univ Pa, 58-70; mem, Wistar Inst, 58-70. *Concurrent Pos:* Eleanor Roosevelt Int Cancer fel, 64; mem, Study Sect on Virol & Rickettsiology, NIH, 65-69; ed-in-chief, J Cellular Physiol, 65-70; mem, Comt Recombinant DNA, Med Res Coun Can, 71-83; mem, Comt Recombinant DNA, Med Res Coun Can, 71-83; Josiah Macy, Jr Found fac scholar award, 77-78; mem bd dir, W Alton Jones Cell Sci Ctr, 80- *Mem:* Am Soc Microbiol; Royal Soc Can. *Res:* Replication of mammalian viruses; bacterial bioluminescence. *Mailing Add:* 4300 De Maisonneuve O Westmount PQ H3G 3C7 Can

GRAHAM, ARTHUR H(UGHES), METALLURGY, ELECTROCHEMISTRY. *Current Pos:* CONSULT, 92- *Personal Data:* b Philadelphia, Pa, Nov 18, 33; m 60; c 1. *Educ:* Pa State Univ, BS, 58, MS, 60, PhD(metall), 63. *Prof Exp:* Res metallurgist, EI DuPont de Nemours & Co, Inc, 63-66, sr res metallurgist, 66-70, sr res specialist, 70-74, res assoc, 74-75, sr res assoc, 75-83, res fel, Eng Technol Lab, 83-90, sr res fel, 90-92. *Mem:* Am Soc Metals; Electrochem Soc; Am Electroplaters Soc. *Mailing Add:* 24 Dogwood Hill Lane Chadds Ford PA 19317

GRAHAM, ARTHUR RENFREE, ANIMAL PHYSIOLOGY. *Current Pos:* RETIRED. *Personal Data:* b London, Ont, Nov 2, 19; m 50; c 4. *Educ:* Univ Western Ont, BSc, 48, MSc, 51, PhD(physiol), 54. *Prof Exp:* Assoc prof zool, Mem Univ, 54-57; from assoc prof to prof physiol sci, Ont Vet Col, Univ Guelph, 71-84. *Mem:* AAAS; NY Acad Sci; Can Physiol Soc. *Res:* Physiology of central nervous system; ruminant digestive system. *Mailing Add:* 15 Lockyer Rd Guelph ON N1G 1J9 Can

GRAHAM, BEARDSLEY, SCIENCE COMMUNICATIONS. *Current Pos:* CONSULT, MGT, 67- *Personal Data:* b Berkeley, Calif, Apr 24, 14; m 76, Lorraine J Shaw; c M Sherry & Heather. *Educ:* Univ Calif, Berkeley, BS, 35. *Prof Exp:* Asst dir, Stanford Res Inst, 53-57; staff mem, Lockheed Missile & Space Co, 57-61; pres, Spindletop Res Inc, Lexington, Ky, 61-67. *Concurrent Pos:* Vchmn, Eng Technol Adv Comt, Cent Ore Community Col; incorporator & mem bd, app by Pres Kennedy, Commun Satellite Corp; vchmn, Eng Technol Adv Comt, Cent Ore Community Col; mem, Cent Ore Coun Higher Educ. *Mem:* Fel Inst Elec & Electronics Engrs; assoc fel Am Inst Aeronaut & Astronaut. *Res:* Instrumental in the creation of Communication Satellite Corp; broad-band communication systems and television; video programming; satellite systems and applications; nuclear weapons and power; hydro-electric policy and its implementation; solar energy, applications and implementation; electronic devices. *Mailing Add:* 214 Hillcrest Pl Baker City OR 97814

GRAHAM, BENJAMIN FRANKLIN, BOTANY, PLANT ECOLOGY. *Current Pos:* from assoc prof to prof, 59-91, EMER PROF BIOL, GRINNELL COL, 91- *Personal Data:* b East Milton, Mass, Sept 24, 20; m 47, Susanne Mallard; c 4. *Educ:* Univ Maine, BS, 43, MS, 48; Duke Univ, PhD(bot), 59. *Prof Exp:* Instr bot, Univ Maine, 48-51; instr, Miami Univ, 54-56; res fel, Dartmouth Col, 57-59. *Concurrent Pos:* Vis biologist, Brookhaven Nat Lab, 65-66; consult land restoration, 65-; dir, Conard Environ Res Area, 70-86. *Mem:* Fel AAAS; Am Inst Biol Sci; Ecol Soc Am. *Res:* Forest ecology; natural root grafts; palynology; radiation ecology. *Mailing Add:* 1514 West St Grinnell IA 50112-1443

GRAHAM, BETTIE JEAN, MOLECULAR GENOMICS, BIOMEDICAL RESEARCH. *Current Pos:* STAFF FEL, NIH, 74- *Personal Data:* b Beaumont, TX, July 11, 41. *Educ:* Texas Southern Univ, BS, 62; Baylor Col Med, PhD(virol), 71. *Prof Exp:* Fel, Albert Einstein Col Med, 71-74. *Mem:* Am Soc Microbiol; AAAS. *Res:* Defining gaps in biomedical research areas; genomic research. *Mailing Add:* Rm 610 Bldg 38A Nat Human Genome Res Inst NIH Bethesda MD 20892

GRAHAM, BRUCE ALLAN, ORGANIC CHEMISTRY. *Current Pos:* from res & develop chemist agr chem to sect mgr pollution control, 67-76, sect mgr org & anal chem, 76-81, DIR RES & DEVELOP, UNIROYAL CHEM LTD, RES LAB, GUELPH, ONT, 81- *Personal Data:* b Menzies, Western Australia, Aug 27, 38; m 65, Karin Wallis; c Christina. *Educ:* Univ Western Australia, BSc, 59; Univ Alta, PhD(chem), 68. *Prof Exp:* Develop chemist, Assoc Pulp & Paper Mfrs, 60-61. *Mem:* Chem Inst Can. *Res:* Synthesis of organic chemicals for evaluation as agricultural and rubber chemicals. *Mailing Add:* Uniroyal Chem Res Lab 120 Huron St Guelph ON N1E 5L7 Can

GRAHAM, BRUCE DOUGLAS, PEDIATRICS. *Current Pos:* RETIRED. *Personal Data:* b Roberts, Wis, Dec 15, 15; m 46; c 3. *Educ:* Univ Ala, AB, 39; Vanderbilt Univ, MD, 42. *Prof Exp:* From asst prof to prof pediat, Univ Mich Hosp, 51-59, dir pediat labs, 54-59; prof & head dept, Fac Med, Univ BC, 59-64; chief staff, Children's Hosp, 64-70, med dir, 70-74, dir ambulatory serv, 74-82; prof pediat, Col Med, Ohio State Univ, 64-82. *Concurrent Pos:* Pediatrician-in-chief, Health Ctr Children, Vancouver, BC, 59-64; chief pediat, Children's Hosp, 61-64; head dept pediat, Ohio State Univ, 64-76. *Mem:* AAAS; Soc Pediat Res; Am Acad Pediat(exec bd, 70-78, vpres, 78-79, pres, 79-80); Am Pediat Soc; AMA. *Res:* Acid base metabolism of premature infants, full term and sick children; oxygen tension study of newborn infants and sick children. *Mailing Add:* 6470 Post Rd Suite 108 Dublin OH 43017-3263

GRAHAM, C BENJAMIN, RADIOLOGY, PEDIATRIC RADIOLOGY. *Current Pos:* From asst to assoc radiol, Univ Wash, 59-63, from instr to assoc prof radiol & pediat, 63-74, dir, Children's Hosp & Med Ctr Radiol, 78-90, PROF RADIOL & PEDIAT, SCH MED, UNIV WASH, 74- *Personal Data:* b Hannibal, Mo, Jan 15, 31; m 56, Pearl Relling; c Leslie E. *Educ:* Univ Ill, Urbana, BA, 54; Univ Wash, MD, 58; Am Bd Radiol, dipl, 66. *Concurrent Pos:* Am Cancer Soc clin fel, 60; James Picker Found adv fel acad radiol, 62-64 & scholar radiol res, 64-66. *Mem:* Am Roentgen Ray Soc; Soc Pediat Radiol; fel Am Col Radiol; Radiol Soc NAm; fel Am Acad Pediat; Asn Univ Radiologists. *Res:* Bone development; neonatal diagnostic imaging. *Mailing Add:* Dept Radiol CH-69 Children's Hosp & Med Ctr PO Box 5371 Seattle WA 98105-0371. *Fax:* 206-528-2730

GRAHAM, C ROBIN, PARTIAL DIFFERENTIAL EQUIATION. *Current Pos:* PROF, DEPT MATH, UNIV WASH, 84- *Personal Data:* b Ger, Sept 17, 54. *Educ:* Rice Univ, BA, 76, MA, 76; Princeton Univ, PhD(math), 81. *Res:* Partial defferential equation. *Mailing Add:* Dept Math Univ Wash Seattle WA 98195-0001

GRAHAM, CHARLES, COGNITIVE SCIENCES, PSYCHOPHYSIOLOGY. *Current Pos:* sr exp psychologist, 74-79, prin exp psychologist, 79-93, SR ADV BIOBEHAV SCI, MIDWEST RES INST, 94-, SR ADV LIFE SCI, 95- *Personal Data:* b Atlantic City, NJ, Nov 21, 37; m

96, Mary Cook; c Ronna, Glenn & Christopher. *Educ:* Univ Md, BS, 66; Pa State Univ, MS, 68, PhD(psychol), 70. *Prof Exp:* Res assoc psychol & fac mem, Inst Pa Hosp, 70-74; instr psychiat, Sch Med, Univ Pa, 70-74. *Concurrent Pos:* Lectr psychol, Univ Pa, 70-74; prin investr, Nat Inst Drug Abuse, 74-76, Nat Cancer Inst, 77-79, Nat Inst Gen Med Sci, 79-82, US Army Med Res & Develop Comn, 79-82, NY Dept Health, 82-84 & Dept Energy, 84-; reviewer, 4 sci journals; prin investr, Nat Inst Environ & Health Scis, 94-98. *Mem:* Sigma Xi; Am Psychol Asn; Bioelectromagnetics Soc; Soc Psychophysiol Res. *Res:* Neurobehavioral studies of human health, behavior and productivity under stress. *Mailing Add:* Midwest Res Inst 425 Volker Blvd Kansas City MO 64110. *Fax:* 816-753-7380

GRAHAM, CHARLES D(ANNE), JR, PHYSICAL METALLURGY, MAGNETIC MATERIALS. *Current Pos:* chmn, 79-84, PROF MAT SCI & ENG, UNIV PA, 69- *Personal Data:* b Philadelphia, Pa, Oct 15, 29; m 52, Alison Bliss; c 3. *Educ:* Cornell Univ, BMetE, 52; Univ Birmingham, Eng, PhD(metall), 54. *Prof Exp:* Res metallurgist, Res & Develop Ctr, Gen Elec Co, NY, 54-69. *Concurrent Pos:* Guggenheim fel, Inst Solid State Physics, Univ Tokyo, 61-62; UK Sci Res Coun sr fel, Wolfson Ctr, Univ Col, Cardiff, 78; coop res, Res Develop Corp, Japan, 85; vis prof, Univ Bath, UK, 92-93. *Mem:* Am Phys Soc; Metall Soc; Inst Elec & Electronics Engrs; Am Soc Metal Int; Mat Res Soc. *Res:* Magnetic materials; magnetic measurements. *Mailing Add:* Dept Mat Sci & Eng Univ Pa 3231 Walnut St Philadelphia PA 19104-6272. *Fax:* 215-573-2128; *E-Mail:* cgraham@sol1.lrsm.upenn.edu

GRAHAM, CHARLES EDWARD, GEOLOGY. *Current Pos:* from instr to prof geol, 53-81, EMER PROF GEOL, DENISON UNIV, 81- *Personal Data:* b St Paul, Minn, Nov 22, 19; m 43; c 3. *Educ:* State Col Wash, BS, 47, MS, 49; Univ Iowa, PhD(geol), 54. *Prof Exp:* Asst geologist, State Bur Mines & Geol, Mont, 49-50; asst instr geol, Univ Iowa, 51-53. *Mem:* Geol Soc Am; Am Geophys Union. *Res:* Structural and urban geology. *Mailing Add:* 166 Hermosa Dr Durango CO 81301-3706

GRAHAM, CHARLES LEE, ENTOMOLOGY, PARASITOLOGY. *Current Pos:* STAFF ENTOMOLOGIST, FED PEST CONTROL, WASHINGTON, 84- *Personal Data:* b White Lake, SDak, Aug 12, 31; m 58; c 3. *Educ:* Northern State Col, BS, 59; Utah State Univ, MS, 62, PhD(entom, parasitol), 64. *Prof Exp:* Res entomologist, Plant Dis Res Lab, Sci & Educ Admin, USDA, 63-84. *Concurrent Pos:* Instr, Frederick Community Col. *Mem:* Entom Soc Am; Am Mosqui; Sigma Xi. *Res:* Insect flight and aging as related to the epidemiology of insect borne diseases; current authority on the biology and taxonomy of the bot fly genus Cuterebra. *Mailing Add:* 416 Megan Ct Frederick MD 21701

GRAHAM, CHARLES RAYMOND, JR, ICHTHYOLOGY, PHYSIOLOGY. *Current Pos:* from instr to assoc prof, 66-80, chmn dept, 75-79, PROF BIOL, LOYOLA COL, MD, 80- *Personal Data:* b Baltimore, Md, June 17, 40; m 62, Patricia Cole; c Charles, Kelly, Michael & Kerri. *Educ:* Loyola Col, BS, 62; Univ Del, MS, 64, PhD(ichthyol, cytol), 67. *Prof Exp:* Lab dir, Med Eye Bank Md, 74-84; sci consult, Tissue Banks Int, 84-87. *Concurrent Pos:* Res assoc, Univ Md, Marquette Univ, 69 & 70. *Mem:* Am Soc Zool; Am Asn Tissue Banks (secy, 81-86); Nat Asn Adv Health Professions; Am Elasmobr Soc. *Res:* Morphology and physiology of chondrichthian reproductive systems; morphology and physiology of cellular membranes; corneal physiology; preservation of corneal tissue. *Mailing Add:* 2 Deer Pass Ct Cockeysville MD 21030-2605

GRAHAM, COLIN C, mathematics, for more information see previous edition

GRAHAM, DALE ELLIOTT, COMPUTATIONAL MOLECULAR BIOLOGY. *Current Pos:* mem staff, Cancer Expert Lab Molecular Biol, Nat Cancer Inst, 80-84, mem staff, Spec Expert, Molecular, Cellular & Nutrit Endocrinol Br, Nat Inst Diabetes & Digestive & Kidney Dis, 84-91, MEM STAFF & COMPUTATIONAL BIOLOGIST, SCI COMPUT RESOURCE CTR, DISTRIB SYSTS BR, RES & TECHNOL, NIH, 91- *Personal Data:* b Newark, NJ, Aug 15, 44; m 80. *Educ:* Univ Tenn, Knoxville, BS, 66; Univ Tenn, Oak Ridge, PhD(biomed sci), 71. *Prof Exp:* Res fel molecular biol, Calif Inst Technol, 71-74; asst prof molecular biol, Purdue Univ, West Lafayette, 74-80. *Concurrent Pos:* Damon Runyon Mem Found Cancer Res fel, 71-73; Carnegie Inst Wash fel, 73-74. *Res:* Mechanisms of molecular evolution; evolving DNA sequences as related to genome structure and function; nucleic acid reassociation; gene expression; nucleic acid technology; computational sequence analysis. *Mailing Add:* DCRT NIH Bldg 12A Rm 3043 Bethesda MD 20892

GRAHAM, DAVID LEE, VETERINARY PATHOLOGY, WILDLIFE DISEASES. *Current Pos:* DIR, SCHUBOT EXOTIC BIRD HEALTH CTR & PROF VET PATHOBIOL, COL VET MED, TEX A&M UNIV, 87- *Personal Data:* b New York, NY, Dec 5, 39; m 73; c 2. *Educ:* Pa State Univ, BSc, 61; Cornell Univ, 65; Iowa State Univ, PhD(vet path), 73. *Prof Exp:* Intern, Animal Med Ctr, 65-66, resident, 66-67; from instr to prof vet path, Iowa State Univ, 67-81; prof vet path, Cornell Univ, 81-87. *Mem:* Am Vet Med Asn; Wildlife Dis Asn; Am Col Vet Pathologists; Am Asn Zoo Vets. *Res:* Diseases of wildlife, avian herpesvirus infections, pseudorabies; diseases of zoo animals; diseases of birds of prey and cage and aviary birds. *Mailing Add:* 5120 Stagecoach Rd College Station TX 77845

GRAHAM, DAVID TREDWAY, INTERNAL MEDICINE. *Current Pos:* ADJ PROF PSYCHOL, UNIV DEL, 86- *Personal Data:* b Mason City, Iowa, June 20, 17; m 41; c 3. *Educ:* Princeton Univ, BA, 38; Yale Univ, MA, 41; Wash Univ, MD, 43. *Prof Exp:* Asst prof med, Wash Univ, 51-57; assoc prof, 57-63, chmn dept, 71-80, prof med, Sch Med, Univ Wis-Madison, 63-85. *Concurrent Pos:* Commonwealth fel med, Med Col, Cornell Univ, 48-51; ed, Proc, Am Fedn Clin Res, 54-59. *Mem:* Am Psychosom Soc (pres, 78-79); AMA; Am Fedn Clin Res; Soc Psychophysiol Res (pres, 69-70); Am Soc Internal Med. *Res:* Psychosomatic medicine. *Mailing Add:* Dept Psychol Univ Del Wolf Hall Newark DE 19716

GRAHAM, DEE MCDONALD, FOOD SCIENCE, FOOD TECHNOLOGY. *Current Pos:* asst dir sci res, Del Monte Corp, 75-80, dir cent res, 80-84, dir technol develop, 84-86, dir technol servs & int prod develop, 86-90, sr consult, 91-93, PRES, RES & DEVELOP ENTERPRISES, DEL MONTE CORP, 91- *Personal Data:* b Dixon, Miss, Oct 11, 27; m 87, Ruth; c 7. *Educ:* Miss State Col, BSc, 50; Iowa State Col, MSc, 51, PhD(dairy bact), 54. *Prof Exp:* Res assoc dairy bact, Iowa Agr Exp Sta, 51-52; from asst prof to assoc prof dairy mfg, Clemson Col, 53-58; div chief evaporated milk res, Pet Milk Co, 58-60, mgr milk prod develop, 61-65, assoc dir res, 65-68, tech dir, Grocery Prod Div, 68-69; chmn dept food sci & nutrit, Univ Mo, Columbia, 69-75. *Concurrent Pos:* Mem food protect comt & comt on rev of food additives, Nat Acad Sci-Nat Res Coun; dir, Res & Develop Assoc; dir, Coun Agr Sci & Technol; exec comt, Calif Inst Food & Age Res; bd dir, Food Technol Ctr, Environ Prot Res Inst. *Mem:* Am Dairy Sci Asn; fel Inst Food Technologists; Soc Nutrit Educ. *Res:* Product and process development; flavor chemistry; milk manufacturing technology; human nutrition; fruits and vegetable technology; process water management. *Mailing Add:* Res & Develop Enterprises 2747 Hutchinson Ct Walnut Creek CA 94598. *Fax:* 510-938-0928; *E-Mail:* deeg213050@aol.com

GRAHAM, DONALD C W, FOOD SCIENCE, MICROBIOLOGY. *Current Pos:* res technician nutrit, 65-68, asst prof, 71-77, ASSOC PROF FOOD SCI, CORNELL UNIV, 77-, MEM FAC, 71- *Personal Data:* b Thomasville, Ga, Jan 11, 32; m 53; c 4. *Educ:* Ft Valley State Col, BS, 54; Tuskegee Univ, MS, 58; Cornell Univ, PhD(food sci), 71. *Prof Exp:* Clerk, Off Registrar, Ft Valley State Col, 54-56; res asst physiol, Tuskegee Univ, 58-61, instr nutrit, 59-61; instr nutrit & gen sci, Ala State Univ, 61-65. *Concurrent Pos:* Mem, Grad Fac Food Sci & Technol & Fac Inst Food Sci, Cornell Univ, 71-; asst dir off instr, Col Agr & Life Sci, Cornell Univ, 76-82. *Mem:* AAAS; Inst Food Technol; NY Acad Sci; Sigma Xi; Am Soc Microbiol. *Res:* Characterization of Plasmid DNA and bacteriophages from Pediococci; use of Pediococci in the manufacture of fermented dairy products; unusual food fermentations, their characterization and nutritional evaluation. *Mailing Add:* Dept Food Sci Cornell Univ 114 Stocking Ithaca NY 14853-7201

GRAHAM, DOYLE GENE, NEUROTOXICOLOGY, NEUROPATHOLOGY. *Current Pos:* Lectr, Duke Univ, 70-71, asst prof, 71-78, assoc clin prof, 78-81, assoc prof, 81-86, dean med educ, 87-92, PROF PATH & DIR INTEGRATED TOXICOL PROG, DUKE UNIV, 86-, DIR NEUROPATH, 93- *Personal Data:* b Coeur D'Alene, Idaho, Aug 18, 42; m 84, Lea O'Quinn Nikides; c Camilla, Brevick, Mariah & Will. *Educ:* Duke Univ, MD, 66, PhD(exp path), 71. *Honors & Awards:* Merit Award, NIH. *Concurrent Pos:* Vis asst prof path, Sch Med, Temple Univ, 71-72; asst prof, Sch Med, Emory Univ, 72-73; vis prof path, Univ Edinburgh, 80-81; mem, NIH Toxicol Study Sect, 84-88, chmn, 87-88, EPA Sci Rev Panel Health Res, 85-87, Nat Adv Environ Health Sci Coun, 93-96, Burroughs Welcome Fund Scholars Toxicol Adv Cmte, 93-96; dir, Integrated Toxicol Prog, 86-; vchmn, Comt Neurotoxicol & Risk Assessment, Comn Life Sci, Bd Environ Studies & Toxicol, Nat Res Coun, 88-91. *Mem:* Am Soc Investigative Path; AAAS; Soc Toxicol; Am Asn Neuropathologists; Sigma Xi. *Res:* Development of anti-cancer agents; Parkinson's disease; neurotoxicity of hexane, carbon disulfide and other toxicants; mechanisms of metabolic and degenerative nervous system disease. *Mailing Add:* Dept Path Vanderbilt Univ Med Ctr C3322 McN Nashville TN 37232-2561. *Fax:* 919-684-3324

GRAHAM, EDWARD UNDERWOOD, ENVIRONMENTAL SYSTEMS, INFORMATION SCIENCE. *Current Pos:* SR PROJ MGR, PARSON ENG SCI, 95- *Personal Data:* b Washington, DC, Sept 27, 43; div. *Educ:* Mass Inst Technol, BS, 64; Carnegie-Mellon Univ, MS, 65, PhD(systs & commun sci), 69. *Prof Exp:* Consult systs eng & info processing, Auerbach Corp, Arlington, Va, 68-72; environ planner, Off Environ Planning, Montgomery Co, Md, 72-76, asst dir, 76-79; head, Sewer Syst Planning Sect, Washington Suburban Sanit Comn, Hyattsville, Md, 79-83, head, Water Resources Planning Sect, 83-84, asst to gen mgr, 84-90; dir, Dept Environ Protection, 90-95. *Concurrent Pos:* Dir, Off Technol Resource Mgt, Washington Suburban Sanit Comn, Laurel, Md, 86- *Mem:* Simulation Coun; Inst Elec & Electronics Engrs; Water Pollution Control Fedn; Am Water Works Asn. *Res:* Environmental systems engineering and modeling; information systems; optimization theory. *Mailing Add:* Parson Eng Sci 10521 Rosehaven St Fairfax VA 22038

GRAHAM, FRANCES KEESLER, PSYCHOPHYSIOLOGY. *Current Pos:* res prof, 86-89, EMER PROF PSYCHOL, UNIV DEL, 89- *Personal Data:* b USA, Aug 1, 18; m 41; c 3. *Educ:* Pa State Univ, BA, 38; Yale Univ, PhD(psychol), 42. *Hon Degrees:* DSc, Univ Wis-Madison, 96. *Honors & Awards:* Distinguished Contrib Award, Soc Psychophysiol Res, 81; G Stanley Hall Medal, Am Psychol Asn, 82, Award Distinguished Sci Contrib, 90; Distinguished Sci Contrib Award, Soc Res Child Develop, 91; Wilbur L Cross Medal, Yale Univ, 92; Gold Medal, Am Psychol Found, 97. *Prof Exp:* Asst & instr med psychol, Wash Univ, 42-48, instr & res assoc, 53-57; instr psychol, Barnard Col, Columbia Univ, 48-51; res assoc, Univ Wis-Madison, 57-64, from assoc prof to prof pediat, 64-80, prof psychol, 69-80, Hillsdale res prof,

80-86. *Concurrent Pos:* Psychologist & actg dir, St Louis Psychiat Clin, 42-44; res scientist award, NIMH, 64-89, mem, Exp Psychol Study Sect, 70-74, mem, Bd Sci Counr, 77-81, chair, 79-81; Am Psychol Asn rep, Nat Res Coun, 71-74; spec consult, Nat Inst Neurol Dis & Blindness; mem, Study Ethics in Med & Biomed & Behav Res, Pres' Comn, 80-82; William James fel, Am Psychol Soc, 90. *Mem:* Nat Acad Sci; AAAS; Soc Psychophysiol Res (pres, 73-74); Soc Res Child Develop (pres, 75-77); Am Psychol Asn; Soc Exp Psychol; Soc Neuroscience; Am Psychol Soc; Psychonomic Soc. *Res:* Psychophysiology and developmental psychophysiology with special interest in attentional processes, reflex modifiability and brain-behavior relations. *Mailing Add:* Dept Psychol Univ Del Newark DE 19716. *Fax:* 302-831-3645; *E-Mail:* fkgraham@strauss.udel.edu

GRAHAM, FRANK LAWSON, VIROLOGY, MOLECULAR BIOLOGY. *Current Pos:* from asst prof to assoc prof, 75-83, PROF VIROL, MCMASTER UNIV, 83- *Personal Data:* b Preeceville, Sask, Mar 23, 42; m 68. *Educ:* Univ Man, BS, 64; Univ Toronto, MA, 65, PhD(biophys), 70. *Prof Exp:* Res assoc virol, State Univ Leiden, 70-74. *Concurrent Pos:* Fel, Nat Cancer Inst Can, 70-72, res scholar, 75-81, res assoc, 81- *Mem:* NY Acad Sci; Am Asn Microbiol; Cancer Soc Cell Biol. *Res:* Transformation of mammalian cells by oncogenic DNA viruses; adenovirus DNA structure and replication; adenovirus based expression vectors and recombinant vaccines. *Mailing Add:* Dept Biol McMaster Univ 1280 Main St W Hamilton ON L8S 4K1 Can

GRAHAM, GEORGE ALFRED CECIL, APPLIED MATHEMATICS, MECHANICS. *Current Pos:* from asst prof to assoc prof, 67-80, dept chmn, 81-86, PROF MATH, SIMON FRASER UNIV, 80- *Personal Data:* b Ireland, Feb 25, 39; m 68. *Educ:* Univ Dublin, BA, 61; Brown Univ, MS, 64; Glasgow Univ, PhD(math), 66. *Prof Exp:* Asst prof math, NC State Univ, 66-67. *Res:* Mathematical theories of elasticity and viscoelasticity. *Mailing Add:* Dept Math & Statist Simon Fraser Univ Burnaby BC V5A 1S6 Can

GRAHAM, GEORGE G, PEDIATRICS, NUTRITION. *Current Pos:* dir Nutrit Prog, 76-85, ASSOC PROF PEDIAT, SCH MED, JOHNS HOPKINS UNIV, 65-, PROF INT HEALTH, SCH HYG & PUB HEALTH, 68- *Personal Data:* b Hackensack, NJ, Oct 4, 23; m 49, Simone Custer; c Marianne (Moxon), Alec, Monica (Gurney) & Carol (Mann). *Educ:* Univ Pa, AB, 41, MD, 45. *Honors & Awards:* Goldberger Award, AMA, 72; Borden Award, Am Acad Pediat, 77. *Prof Exp:* Mem staff pediat, Brit Am Hosp, Lima, Peru, 47-50, chief, 52-55; res resident, Hosp Univ Pa, 51; resident, Baltimore City Hosps, Md, 55-57; mem staff, Cleveland Clin, 57-59; dir res, Brit Am Hosp, 60-71. *Concurrent Pos:* Lectr, Mass Inst Technol, 62-65; vis prof, Agrarian Univ, Peru, 62-65; assoc chief pediat, Baltimore City Hosps, 65-68; mem comt amino acids, Food & Nutrit Bd, Nat Res Coun, 66-71, mem, US Nat Comt, 77-84, mem, Comt Int Nutrit Progs, 78-80, mem, Food & Nutrit Bd, 81-84; consult nutrit, NIH, 66-71, mem nutrit study sect, 71-75, chmn, 73-75; consult nutrit, US AID, 69-; dir res, Inst Invest Nutrit, Lima, Peru, 71- *Mem:* Am Inst Nutrit; Am Soc Clin Nutrit; Soc Pediat Res; Am Pediat Soc. *Mailing Add:* Dept Int Health Johns Hopkins Univ Sch Hyg & Pub Health PO Box 205 Skippers Row Gibson Island MD 21056-0205. *Fax:* 410-435-1367

GRAHAM, GEORGE WADE, SURFACE SCIENCE, CATALYSIS. *Current Pos:* res scientist, 81-88, PRIN RES SCIENTIST, FORD RES LAB, FORD MOTOR CO, 88- *Personal Data:* b Galesburg, Ill, Dec 25, 49; m 79; c 1. *Educ:* Univ Ill, Champaign, BS, 72; Cornell Univ, MS, 75, PhD(solid state physics), 78. *Prof Exp:* Res assoc, Cornell Univ, 78-80; mem res staff, Western Elec Co, 80-81. *Mem:* Am Phys Soc; Am Vacuum Soc; Catalysis Soc. *Res:* Electronic structure, chemisorption and oxidation of alloy surfaces; thin film growth; surface-reaction mechanisms and kinetics; catalyst characterization. *Mailing Add:* 2424 Placid Way Ann Arbor MI 48105

GRAHAM, HAROLD L(AVERNE), chemical engineering, for more information see previous edition

GRAHAM, HAROLD NATHANIEL, ORGANIC CHEMISTRY, BIOCHEMISTRY. *Current Pos:* RETIRED. *Personal Data:* b New York, NY, July 27, 21; m 44, Alaine Krim; c Peter, Margaret, Vicki, Robert & Emily. *Educ:* Cornell Univ, BA, 41; Univ Chicago, PhD(org chem), 46. *Honors & Awards:* Distinguished Food Scientist Award, 87. *Prof Exp:* Res chemist, Thomas J Lipton, Inc, 52-60, mgr food res, 60-62, asst dir res, 62-67, dir food res & nutrit, 67-77, vpres res & prod develop, 77-87. *Concurrent Pos:* Dir, Ceytea Ltd, Colombo, Ceylon, 66; consult food indust, 87- *Mem:* AAAS; Am Chem Soc; fel Am Inst Chem; Inst Food Tech; Sigma Xi. *Res:* Free radical chemistry; chemistry of natural products; biochemistry of plants and microorganisms; petroleum and synthetic rubber research; flavor chemistry; gas-liquid chromatography; food chemistry; food product development; plant proteins. *Mailing Add:* 251 Central Park W New York NY 10024. *Fax:* 201-567-0048

GRAHAM, HARRY MORGAN, ENTOMOLOGY. *Current Pos:* RETIRED. *Personal Data:* b Whittier, Calif, June 18, 29. *Educ:* Univ Calif, BS, 51, MS, 53, PhD(entom), 59. *Prof Exp:* Entomologist, Agr Res Serv, USDA, 58-71, location-res leader, Cotton Insects Lab, Brownsville, Tex, 71-77, res leader, Biol Control Insects Lab, 77-87. *Concurrent Pos:* Vis prof entom, Univ Ariz, 75-76, adj prof, 77-87. *Mem:* AAAS; Entom Soc Am; Int Orgn Biol Control; Sigma Xi. *Res:* Insect ecology and economic entomology; ecology of insect pests of cotton. *Mailing Add:* 5655 E Towner St Tucson AZ 85712

GRAHAM, HENRY COLLINS, CERAMIC ENGINEERING. *Current Pos:* RETIRED. *Personal Data:* b Pittsburgh, Pa, Aug 16, 34; m 57; c 3. *Educ:* Alfred Univ, BS, 56, MS, 58; Ohio State Univ, PhD(ceramic eng), 65. *Prof Exp:* Mem staff crystalizable glasses, Res Lab, Pittsburgh Plate Glass, Pa, 57-60; res physicist, Aerospace Res Labs, Wright Patterson AFB, 60-77, mem staff, Air Force Mat Lab, 77-97. *Mem:* Am Ceramic Soc. *Res:* Determining the defect structure of both metals and metal oxides by making measurements such as electrical conductivity and continuous weight change under various ambient conditions; behavior of materials in reactive atmospheres including the determination of the reaction mechanisms and the influence of the defect structure and the microstructural features on these mechanisms. *Mailing Add:* 1148 Ludlow Rd Xenia OH 45385

GRAHAM, JACK BENNETT, PHYSICAL GEOLOGY. *Current Pos:* RETIRED. *Personal Data:* b Superior, Nebr, Oct 16, 13; m 41; c 6. *Educ:* York Col, AB, 35; Univ Nebr, BS, 37; Univ Iowa, MS, 40, PhD(geol), 42. *Prof Exp:* Asst geol, Univ Iowa, 38-42; jr geologist, Water Br, US Geol Surv, 42-43, from asst geologist to assoc geologist, 43-48, dist geologist, 48-52, chief, Water Utilization Sect, Tech Coord Br, 52-54; ground water geologist, Leggette & Brashears, 54-55, partner, 55-76, pres, Leggette, Brashears & Graham, Inc, 76-79. *Concurrent Pos:* Mem adv bd, Am Inst Hydrol. *Mem:* AAAS; Am Inst Prof Geol (vpres, 67); Geol Soc Am; Am Inst Mining, Metall & Petrol Eng; Am Inst Hydrol. *Res:* Ground water geology and hydrology; hydrogeology. *Mailing Add:* 1 Detmer Rd East Setauket NY 11733

GRAHAM, JACK RAYMOND, organic chemistry, for more information see previous edition

GRAHAM, JAMES CARL, AGRONOMY, BOTANY. *Current Pos:* sr res chemist, Monsanto Co, 66-69, res specialist, 69-75, develop assoc, 75-77, regional mgr prod develop, 77-79, dir, 79-89, dir herbicide technol, 89-91, dir plant protection, improv & licensing, 91-92, DIR NEW PROD EUROP/AFRICA, MONSANTO CO, 93- *Personal Data:* b Clarendon, Tex, May 20, 41; m 64; c 2. *Educ:* Tex Tech Col, BS, 63; Univ Wis, MS, 64, PhD(agron), 66. *Prof Exp:* Res asst, Univ Wis, 63-66. *Mem:* Am Soc Agron; Crop Sci Soc Am; Weed Sci Soc. *Res:* Crop physiology, physiological aspects of yield of major field crops; practical aspects of stress physiology and plant growth regulation. *Mailing Add:* Monsanto Europe SA Avenue de Tervuren 270-272 PO Box 1 B-1150 St Louis Belgium

GRAHAM, JAMES W, MATHEMATICS, COMPUTER SCIENCE. *Current Pos:* PRES, WATFAC, 97- *Personal Data:* b Copper Cliff, Ont, Jan 17, 32; m 55; c 3. *Educ:* Univ Toronto, BA, 54, MA, 55. *Prof Exp:* Appl sci rep, Int Bus Mach Corp, 55-59; from asst prof to prof math, Waterloo Univ, 59-97, dir comput ctr, 61-97. *Mem:* Asn Comput Mach; Am Math Soc; Math Asn Am; Comput Soc Can (pres, 65-66). *Res:* Non-numeric computing including sorting; specialized computer languages; information retrieval. *Mailing Add:* 158 University Ave W Waterloo ON N2L 3E9 Can

GRAHAM, JOHN, catalysis, low temperature reactions; deceased, see previous edition for last biography

GRAHAM, JOHN, GENERAL PHYSIOLOGY. *Current Pos:* VPRES, BNFL INC, 91- *Personal Data:* b Windsor, Eng, Jan 25, 33; Brit & US citizen; m 58, 96, Emmy Roos; c Paul & Jennifer. *Educ:* Univ Wales, BSc, 54. *Prof Exp:* Sr sci officer, UK Atomic Energy Authority, 58-68; fel scientist, Westinghouse Elec Corp, 68-71, mgr, 71-84; mgr, Rockwell Hanford Opers, 84-87; mgr, Westinghouse Hanford Opers, 87-88; dir, Atomic Energy Can, Ltd, 88-91. *Concurrent Pos:* Assoc prof nuclear safety, Carnegie-Mellon Univ, Pittsburgh, 75-74; mem bd, Am Nuclear Soc, 77-80 & 86-92; consult, Nat Acad Sci, 82. *Mem:* Fel Am Nuclear Soc (pres, 94-96); Am Col Sports Med. *Res:* Nuclear energy applied to raise the standard of our life and our environment; innovative and safe licensing of large and small nuclear plants. *Mailing Add:* 8899 E Prentice Ave No 4-102 Greenwood Village CO 80111-3353. *Fax:* 303-694-1816; *E-Mail:* jgraham@ans.org

GRAHAM, JOHN ALAN, INFRARED SPECTROSCOPY, RAMAN SPECTROSCOPY. *Current Pos:* From res chemist to sr res chemist, 84-90, res supvr, 90-93, SR RES SCIENTIST, HERCULES INC, 93- *Personal Data:* b Ft Scott, Kans, Jan 22, 58; m 80, Carol S Davis; c Christopher J & Timothy A. *Educ:* Pittsburg State Univ, BS, 80, MS, 81; Kans State Univ, PhD(analytical chem), 85. *Concurrent Pos:* Prog/chair, Fed Anal Chem & Spectros Socs, 96. *Mem:* Soc Appl Spectros; Coblentz Soc. *Res:* Analytical applications of Fourier transfer infrared and Raman to selected industrial problems including ATR, kinetic studies, surface characterization, reaction mechanisms, degree of polymerization, orientation and problem solving. *Mailing Add:* 500 Hercules Rd Wilmington DE 19808. *E-Mail:* jgraham@herc.com

GRAHAM, JOHN BORDEN, PATHOLOGY. *Current Pos:* from instr to prof, Univ NC, Chapel Hill, 46-66, chmn bd pop ctr, 64-67, mem, 72-76 & 76-80, assoc dean med sch, 68-70, dir genetics training prog, 61-85, chmn curric in genetics, 63-85, coodr interdepartmental grad progs biol, 68-85, ALUMNI DISTINGUISHED PROF PATH, UNIV NC, CHAPEL HILL, 66- *Personal Data:* b Goldsboro, NC, Jan 26, 18; m 43, Ruby Barrett; c Barrett, Virginia & Thomas. *Educ:* Davidson Col, BS, 38; Cornell Univ, MD, 42; Am Bd Path, dipl, 61. *Hon Degrees:* DSc, Davidson Col, 84. *Honors & Awards:* O Max Gardner Award, Univ NC, 68. *Prof Exp:* Intern path, NY Hosp, 42-43; asst, Cornell Univ, 43-44. *Concurrent Pos:* Markle scholar,

49-54; mem res career award comt, USPHS, 59-62, mem genetics training comt, 62-66, chmn, 67-71, mem genetic basis disease comt, 77-80; mem path test comt, Nat Bd Med Exam, 63-67; Int Comt Hemostasis & Thrombosis, 63-67; mem med & sci adv comt, Nat Hemophilia Found, 75-78. *Mem:* AAAS; Am Soc Exp Path; Soc Exp Biol & Med; Am Soc Human Genetics (secy, 64-67, pres, 72); AMA. *Res:* Physiology of blood coagulation; hemorrhagic diseases; human genetics; human population dynamics. *Mailing Add:* PO Box 607 Chapel Hill NC 27514-0607. *Fax:* 919-966-3548

GRAHAM, JOHN D, SCIENCE POLICY. *Current Pos:* From asst prof to assoc prof, 85-91, PROF POLICY & DECISION SCI, HARVARD UNIV, 91- *Personal Data:* b Pittsburgh, Pa, Oct 3, 56; m 78, Susan Woerner; c Jennifer & Kathryn. *Educ:* Wake Forest Univ, BA, 78; Duke Univ, MA, 80; Carnegie Mellon Univ, PhD(pub policy), 83. *Honors & Awards:* Outstanding Serv Develop & Support Nat Agenda Injury Control, US Surgeon Gen. *Concurrent Pos:* Dir, Harvard Ctr Risk Analysis, 89-, Injury Control Ctr, 91-, dep chmn, Dept Health Policy & Mgt, Harvard Sch Pub Health; mem, Comt Transp Safety Mgt, Transp Res Bd, 93- *Mem:* Am Asn Arts & Sci. *Res:* Methods of risk analysis and cost-benefit analysis; societal responses to health, safety and environmental hazards; vehicle safety. *Mailing Add:* Health Sci Harvard Sch Pub Health 677 Huntington Ave Boston MA 02115-6023

GRAHAM, JOHN ELWOOD, STATISTICS, MATHEMATICS. *Current Pos:* from asst prof to assoc prof math, 65-82, PROF STATIST, CARLTON UNIV, ONT, 83- *Personal Data:* b Kingston, Ont, Jan 30, 33; div; c 1. *Educ:* Carleton Univ, BSc, 55; Queen's Univ, Ont, MA, 57; Iowa State Univ, MS, 60, PhD(statist), 63. *Prof Exp:* Statistician, Dominion Bur Statist, 57-58; asst, Statist Lab, Iowa State Univ, 58-63; statistician, Dominion Bur Statist, 63-65. *Concurrent Pos:* Vis assoc prof, NC State Univ, 78-79. *Mem:* Am Statist Asn. *Res:* Sample survey methods and theory. *Mailing Add:* Dept Math & Statist Carleton Univ Ottawa ON K1S 5B6 Can

GRAHAM, JOHN W, metallic & ceramic processing; deceased, see previous edition for last biography

GRAHAM, JOSEPH H, ORGANIC CHEMISTRY *Current Pos:* Res chemist, Div Drug Chem, Food & Drug Admin, 59-78, referee drugs, steroids & terpinoids, Asn Off Anal Chemists, 60-81, dir, Nat Ctr Antibiotics Anal, 78-82, CHIEF, ANTIMICROBIAL DRUGS BR, FOOD & DRUG ADMIN, 82- *Personal Data:* b Richmond, Va, Sept 23, 33; m 58, Vanette Ray; c Kevin. *Educ:* Va Union Univ, BS, 53; Howard Univ, MS, 56, PhD(org chem), 59. *Mem:* Am Chem Soc; Sigma Xi. *Res:* Preparation and properties of benzyl-o-nitrophenylglyoxals; development of analytical procedures for equine conjugated estrogens, synthetic estrogens and iodoamino acids in pharmaceuticals; gel filtration. *Mailing Add:* 7516 Greer Dr Ft Washington MD 20744-3319

GRAHAM, JOSEPH HARRY, PHYTOPATHOLOGY. *Current Pos:* RETIRED. *Personal Data:* b Anderson, SC, Sept 11, 21; m 46; c 2. *Educ:* Clemson Univ, BS, 42; NC State Col, PhD(plant path), 50. *Prof Exp:* Plant pathologist, US Regional Pasture Res Lab, 50-66; asst br chief, Veg & Ornamentals Res Br, Agr Res Ctr, USDA, 66-72, Plant Stress Lab, Beltsville Md, 72-77; plant pathologist, Waterman-Loomis Co, 77-80 & Waterman-Loomis Res, Inc, 80-88. *Mem:* Am Phytopath Soc. *Res:* Diseases of forage grasses, legumes and field crops; research administration; production of vegetables and ornamentals; plant stress-pathogen relationships. *Mailing Add:* 900 Balmoral Dr Silver Spring MD 20903

GRAHAM, KENNETH JUDSON, ENERGETIC MATERIALS CHEMISTRY, DETONATION PHYSICS. *Current Pos:* PRIN SCIENTIST, ATLANTIC RES CORP, 89- *Personal Data:* b Modesto, Calif, Jan 17, 47; m 71, Betty J Bushell; c Kenneth J Jr & Jonathan J. *Educ:* Univ Calif, Berkeley, AB, 68; Naval Postgrad Sch, MS, 79. *Prof Exp:* Chemist, Naval Postgrad Sch, 70-78; res chemist, Naval Weapons Ctr, China Lake, 78-88. *Concurrent Pos:* Instr chem, Monterey Peninsula Col, 74-78; adj res prof aeronaut eng, Naval Postgrad Sch, 83-84; lectr & course coordr, Computational Mech Assocs, 86-93; mem var subcomts, Joint-Army-Navy-NASA-Air Force Interagency Propulsion Comt. *Mem:* Sigma Xi. *Res:* Propellants and explosives performance and sensitivity tailoring; insensitive munitions; detonation physics & chemistry; internal and external blast; explosives testing; detonation modeling; co-author of book on explosive shock in air and one patent. *Mailing Add:* 6462 Appomattox Dr Warrenton VA 20187. *Fax:* 703-754-5346; *E-Mail:* graham@arceng.com

GRAHAM, LE ROY CULLEN, SYNTHETIC APERTURE RADAR APPLICATIONS, APPLIED MATHEMATICS. *Current Pos:* CONSULT, 89- *Personal Data:* b Meeker, Colo, Dec 14, 26; m 92, Joan Tweedy; c Patricia, James, Constance & Robert. *Educ:* Univ Colo, BS, 50; Stevens Inst Technol, MS, 56. *Prof Exp:* Mem tech staff, Bell Tel Labs, 50-56; sr develop engr, Loral Defense Systs-Ariz, 56-57, eng specialist, 57-60, sr eng specialist, 60-76, dir recon systs, 76-89. *Mem:* Inst Elec & Electronics Engrs. *Res:* Coherent radar system; synthesis of new systems and image analysis; radar elevation measurement; interferometry and stereo. *Mailing Add:* 5 E Butler Dr Phoenix AZ 85020

GRAHAM, LINDA KAY EDWARDS, BOTANY, CTYOLOGY. *Current Pos:* Asst prof, 76-82, ASSOC PROF BOT, UNIV WIS-MADISON, 82- *Personal Data:* b Springfield, Mo, Mar 4, 46; m 69; c 1. *Educ:* Wash Univ, BA, 67; Univ Tex, Austin, MA, 69; Univ Mich, Ann Arbor, PhD(bot), 75. *Concurrent Pos:* Lectr electronmicros, Eastern Mich Univ, 76. *Mem:* Am Inst Biol Sci; Phycol Soc Am; Bot Soc Am. *Res:* Origin of lang plants (embryophytes) from ancestral green algae; elctronmicroscopy, cell biology, chemical systematics of advanced green algae as compared to that of lower plants; evolutionary origins of plant reproduction. *Mailing Add:* Dept Bot 139 Birge Hall Univ Wis 430 Lincoln Dr Madison WI 53706

GRAHAM, LOREN R, HISTORY OF SCIENCE, SCIENCE POLICY. *Current Pos:* PROF HIST SCI, MASS INST TECHNOL, 78-; PROF HIST SCI, HARVARD UNIV, 85- *Personal Data:* b Hymera, Ind, June 29, 33; m 55, Patricia Albjerg; c Marguerite. *Educ:* Purdue Univ, BS, 55; Columbia Univ, MA, 60, PhD(hist), 64. *Hon Degrees:* DHL, Purdue Univ, 86. *Honors & Awards:* George Sartou Medal, Hist Sci Soc, 96. *Prof Exp:* Asst prof hist sci, Ind Univ, 63-66; from assoc prof to prof hist, Columbia Univ, 66-78. *Concurrent Pos:* Guggenheim Found fel, 69-70; mem Inst Advan Study, Princeton Univ, 69-70; Rockefeller Found fel, 76-77; Prog Sci Int Affairs res fel, Harvard Univ, 76-77; consult, Nat Acad Sci, 76-78, Nat Endowment Humanities, 76-77 & NSF, 76. *Mem:* AAAS; Hist Sci Soc; Am Asn Advan Slavic Studies (treas, 66-67); Am Hist Asn; Soc Hist Technol; foreign mem Acad Nat Sci; Am Philos Soc; fel Am Acad Arts & Sci. *Res:* History of science especially in Russia; science and values. *Mailing Add:* 7 Francis Ave Cambridge MA 02138. *Fax:* 617-298-8118; *E-Mail:* lrg@mit.edu

GRAHAM, LOUIS ATKINS, TEXTILES, COLOR SCIENCE. *Current Pos:* PRES, LOU GRAHAM & ASSOCS, INC, 87- *Personal Data:* b Kenbridge, Va, Mar 27, 25; m 55; c 1. *Educ:* Univ Va, BCh Eng, 49; Univ Louisville, MChEng, 50. *Honors & Awards:* Forrest L Dimicic Award, Color Mkt Group, 81. *Prof Exp:* Chem engr, fibers, Am Viscose Div, FMC Corp, 50-52, mgr qual control, 52-54, color specialist, 53-56, corp color specialist, 56-63, div color specialist, 63-66, sect leader fibers res & develop, 66-67; res & develop mgr textiles, Burlington Industs, 67-87. *Concurrent Pos:* Assoc adj prof textile chem, NC State Univ, Raleigh, 70-79; co-founder, Color Mkt Group. *Mem:* Am Asn Textile Chemists & Colorists; Optical Soc Am; Color Mkt Group (pres, 62-65); Inter-Soc Color Coun (pres, 82-84); Sigma Xi. *Res:* Textiles and color science (dyeing, color technology). *Mailing Add:* 1207 Colonial Ave Greensboro NC 27408-4901

GRAHAM, MALCOLM, MATHEMATICS. *Current Pos:* from asst prof to prof math, Univ Nev, Las Vegas, 56-85, chmn, Div Sci, math & appl sci, 59-64, chmn, Dept Math, 65-66, EMER PROF, UNIV NEV, LAS VEGAS. *Personal Data:* b Pa, Nov 26, 23; m 52; c 2. *Educ:* NJ State Col, Trenton, BS, 46; Univ Mass, MS, 48; Columbia Univ, EdD(math, educ), 54. *Prof Exp:* Instr math, Marion Inst, 48-49; assoc prof, Longwood Col, 51-55; instr, E Carolina Col, 55-56. *Mem:* Math Asn Am; Am Math Soc. *Res:* Applied science. *Mailing Add:* 9636 Sundial Dr Las Vegas NV 89134

GRAHAM, MARGARET HELEN, INFORMATION SCIENCE. *Current Pos:* VPRES, JANDEC CORP, 86- *Personal Data:* b Dallas, Tex; m 50, Ronald; c 3. *Educ:* Univ Va, BS, 47. *Prof Exp:* Info chemist, Sharples Chem Co, 47-50; supvr lit searching, Ethyl Corp, 50-56; consult tech lit, 56-63; info scientist, Gen Motors Res Labs, 63-66; mgr info serv, Exxon Res & Eng Co, 66-85, sr staff adv, 85-86. *Concurrent Pos:* Mem bd dirs & secy, Eng Info, 82-; int consult. *Mem:* Am Chem Soc; Am Soc Info Sci; fel Am Inst Chemists; Am Petrol Inst. *Res:* Computer technology in the handling of documented information for building of knowledge information data bases for online access; application of information resources to support scientific and engineering efforts. *Mailing Add:* 92 Pine Way New Providence NJ 07974-1821

GRAHAM, MARTIN H(AROLD), INSTRUMENTATION, COMPUTER SCIENCE. *Current Pos:* assoc dir comput ctr, 66-69, PROF COMPUT SCI, UNIV CALIF, BERKELEY, 66- *Personal Data:* b Jamaica, NY, July 12, 26; m 49; c 2. *Educ:* Polytech Inst Brooklyn, BEE, 47, DEE(electronics), 52; Harvard Univ, MSc, 48. *Prof Exp:* Instr, Polytech Inst Brooklyn, 47-50; res assoc, Brookhaven Nat Lab, 50-52, electronic engr, 52-57; from assoc prof to prof elec eng, Rice Univ, 57-66. *Concurrent Pos:* Consult, Brookhaven Nat Lab, 57-61, US Atomic Energy Comn, 60-63, Manned Spacecraft Ctr, NASA, 63-64 & Lawrence Berkeley Lab, 74-77; vis prof, Univ Calif, Berkeley, 64-65. *Mem:* Fel Inst Elec & Electronics Engrs. *Res:* Electronic instrumentation; medical electronics; digital computers. *Mailing Add:* Elec Eng Dept Univ Calif Cory Hall Berkeley CA 94720

GRAHAM, MICHAEL JOHN, PHYSICAL CHEMISTRY, SEMICONDUCTOR DEVICES. *Current Pos:* res officer chem, 69-77, head metallic corrosion & oxidation, 77-93, HEAD CHEM CHARACTERIZATION, NAT RES COUN CAN, 93-, HEAD SURFACES & INTERFACES. *Personal Data:* b Carlisle, Eng, Mar 21, 40; Can citizen; c Karen, John & Andrew. *Educ:* Liverpool Univ, BSc, 61, Hons, 62, PhD(surface chem), 65. *Honors & Awards:* T P Hoar Prize, Inst Corrosion Sci & Technol, 83, U R Evans Award, 93. *Prof Exp:* Fel chem, Nat Res Coun Can 65-67; res officer mat, Cent Elec Generating Bd, UK, 67-69. *Mem:* Nat Asn Corrosion Engrs; Royal Soc Chem; Royal Inst Chem; Inst Corrosion Sci & Technol; Am Soc Metals; Chem Inst Can; Electrochem Soc. *Res:* Kinetics and mechanism of metallic corrosion and oxidation; application of surface-analytical techniques to oxidation and corrosion research and microelectronics degradation; surface passivation of semiconductors. *Mailing Add:* Inst Microstruct Sci Nat Res Coun Can Ottawa ON K1A 0R6 Can

GRAHAM, PAUL WHITENER LINK, CERAMICS ENGINEERING. *Current Pos:* Sr technologist, Corp Res, 65-69, sr scientist, Glass Container Div, 69-75, SECT CHIEF PROD & PROCESS PERFORMANCE, GLASS CONTAINER DIV, OWENS ILL, INC, 75- *Personal Data:* b Elmira, NY,

Sep 19, 39; m 60; c 2. *Educ:* Pa State Univ, BS, 61, MS, 62, PhD(ceramic technol), 65. *Mem:* Am Ceramic Soc; AAAS; Soc Glass Technol; Am Soc Testing & Mat. *Res:* New product development; glass container design; surface treatments; chemical properties; quality control; glass strength; computer aided design; computer simulation. *Mailing Add:* 3105 Pelham Rd Toledo OH 43606

GRAHAM, RAY LOGAN, MATHEMATICS. *Current Pos:* PROF MATH, APPALACHIAN STATE UNIV, 74- *Personal Data:* b Tex, July 1, 34. *Educ:* WTex State Univ, BS, 56; NMex State Univ, MAT, 60, PhD(math), 68. *Prof Exp:* Mathematician, White Sands Missile Range, 56-58; teacher math, Las Cruces High Sch, 59; asst prof, Hardin-Simmons Univ, 59-62 & Appalachian State Univ, 63-65; res assoc, Ctr Res Sci & Math, 67-68; prof, Appalachian State Univ, 69-70, chmn math dept, 70-73; dir instrnl syst, Drexel Univ, 73-74. *Mem:* Math Asn Am; Nat Coun Teachers Math; Nat Educ Asn. *Res:* Effects of computer usage upon elementary analysis courses. *Mailing Add:* 144 Logan Lane Blowing Rock NC 28605

GRAHAM, RAYMOND, PHYSICAL CHEMISTRY, MOLECULAR SPECTROSCOPY. *Current Pos:* ASST PROF CHEM, ROCKY MOUNTAIN COL, 70- *Personal Data:* b Clinton, Ind, July 1, 35. *Educ:* Ind State Univ, Terre Haute, BS, 62; Mont State Univ, PhD(chem), 70. *Mem:* Am Chem Soc. *Res:* Absorption spectroscopy of forbidden transitions in organic molecules; luminescence spectra of transition metal complexes; polarized luminescence of aromatic molecules. *Mailing Add:* Rocky Mountain Col Eaton Hall #2 Billings MT 59102-1796

GRAHAM, RICHARD CHARLES BURWELL, PHARMACOLOGY. *Current Pos:* PRES, PHARMACEUT CONSULT CO, 91- *Personal Data:* b Miami Beach, Fla, Apr 17, 26; Can citizen; m 80, Elizabeth Montreuil; c 4. *Educ:* Univ Western Ont, BSc, 49, MSc, 51, PhD(endocrinol, pharmacol), 55. *Honors & Awards:* Cairncross & Lawrence Prize, Ont, 55. *Prof Exp:* Pharmacologist, Food & Drug Labs, Dept Nat Health & Welfare, Can, 55-60; investr med sci, Inst Exp Med, Caracas, Venezuela, 60-62; pharmacologist, Food & Drug Labs, Dept Nat Health & Welfare, Can, 62-66, asst chief div med & pharmacol, 66-70, asst dir Bur Drugs, 70-87, actg dir Bur Human Prescription Drugs, 87-88, special adv, Bur Human Prescription Drugs, Health Protection Br, 88-91. *Res:* Toxicology of pesticides and drugs; biological activity of plant products; endocrinology; pharmacology. *Mailing Add:* 2117 Kingsley Rd Ottawa ON K2C 2X6 Can. *Fax:* 613-721-8520; *E-Mail:* rcbgcon@compuserve.com

GRAHAM, ROBERT (KLARK), optics; deceased, see previous edition for last biography

GRAHAM, ROBERT, MEDICINE. *Current Pos:* EXEC VPRES, AM ACAD FAMILY PHYSICIANS, 85- *Personal Data:* b Pueblo, Colo, Feb 17, 43; m. *Educ:* Earlham Col, AB, 65; Univ Kans, MD, 70. *Prof Exp:* Asst adminr agency goals, Health Serv & Ment Health Admin, HEW, Washington, DC, 70-73; asst dir, Div Educ, Am Acad Family Physicians, Kansas City, Mo, 73-76; dep dir, Bur Health Manpower, Health Resources Admin, HEW, 76-78, dep adminr, 78-79; prof staff mem, Subcomt Health & Sci Res, Comt Labor & Human Resources, US Senate, 79-80; actg adminr, Health Resources Admin, Dept Health & Human Serv, 81-82, adminr, 82-85. *Concurrent Pos:* Consult, Off Dir, Nat Health Serv Corps, 73-74, Social Security Studies, Inst Med-Nat Acad Sci, 74-76; resident family pract, Baptist Mem Hosp, 74-75; staff, Prog Health Mgt, Baylor Col Med, 76; exec secy, Grad Med Educ Nat Adv Comt, 78-79; mem, Am Asn Med Soc Execs Adv Comt Exec Vpres, AMA, 86-; mem, Rural Health Adv Comt, Off Technol Assessment, Washington, DC, 88-; mem, Bd Dirs, Sun Valley Forum Nat Health, 89- *Mem:* Inst Med-Nat Acad Sci; Asn Am Med Cols; AMA; Am Acad Family Physicians; Am Acad Med Dirs; Am Asn Med Soc Execs; Am Soc Asn Execs. *Res:* Family medicine. *Mailing Add:* Am Acad Family Physicians 8880 Ward Pkwy Kansas City MO 64114

GRAHAM, ROBERT ALBERT, PHYSICS. *Current Pos:* DIR RES, THE TOME GROUP, 96- *Personal Data:* b Dallas, Tex, Feb 11, 31; m 51, 96, Nell Heard Griffin; c Stephanie A (Farrow), Mark L & Stuart R. *Educ:* Univ Tex, BS, 54, MS, 58; Tokyo Inst Technol, DSc, 90. *Honors & Awards:* Excellence Award, Dept Energy, 83; C B Sawyer Award, 84; Shock Compression Sci Award, Am Phys Soc, 93; ISL Medal, Inst Franco-Allemand Res, St Louis, France. *Prof Exp:* Res engr, Southwest Res Inst, 56-57; mem res staff, Sandia Labs, 58-83, distinguished mem tech staff, 83-96. *Concurrent Pos:* Managing ed, Shock Waves Int J. *Mem:* Fel AAAS; fel Am Phys Soc; Inst Elec & Electronics Engrs; Mat Res Soc; Am Chem Soc. *Res:* Mechanical and physical properties of solids under shock wave loading conditions; shock compression science; high pressure physics. *Mailing Add:* 383 La Entrada Rd Tome Los Lunas NM 87031

GRAHAM, ROBERT LESLIE, INORGANIC CHEMISTRY, PHYSICAL CHEMISTRY. *Current Pos:* RETIRED. *Personal Data:* b Saratoga, Iowa, Jan 9, 26; m 57; c 1. *Educ:* Mankato State Col, BA, 52; Univ Minn, MS, 54; Univ Va, PhD(inorg chem), 58. *Prof Exp:* Res chemist, Orlon Res Dept, E I DuPont de Nemours & Co, 58-59; assoc prof chem, Va Polytech Inst, 59-63; assoc prof, Mankato State Col, 63-70, chmn dept 64-80, prof chem, 70-77, mem fac, Dept Chem & Geol, 77-92. *Mem:* Am Chem Soc; Sigma Xi. *Res:* Thermochemistry of inorganic compounds by solution calorimetry. *Mailing Add:* 211 Floral Ave Mankato MN 56001

GRAHAM, ROBERT LOCKHART, PHYSICS. *Current Pos:* RETIRED. *Personal Data:* b Peterborough, Ont, Feb 17, 21; m 44; c 3. *Educ:* McMaster Univ, BA, 43, MA, 45; Univ London, PhD(physics), 49; Imp Col, Univ London, Dipl, 49. *Prof Exp:* Res physicist, Nat Res Coun Can, Atomic Energy Can, Ltd, 43-46, asst res officer, 49-54, assoc res officer, 54-61, sr res officer, Nuclear Labs, 62-85; adj prof, Univ Guelph, 85-90. *Concurrent Pos:* Vis physicist, Lawrence Radiation Lab, Univ Calif, 62-63. *Mem:* Fel Am Phys Soc; Can Asn Physicists. *Res:* Low energy nuclear physics, chiefly beta and gamma ray spectroscopy and associated techniques; positron annihilation in liquids and solids; computer control system for superconducting cyclotron. *Mailing Add:* 4 Tweedsmuir Rd Deep River ON K0J 1P0 Can

GRAHAM, ROBERT M, HYPERTENSION. *Current Pos:* PROF, DEPT PHYSIOL & BIOPHYS, CASE WESTERN RES UNIV, 89-; ROBERT C TARAZI CHMN, DEPT HEART & HYPERTENSION RES, RES INST, CLEVELAND CLIN FOUND, 89- *Personal Data:* b Sydney, Australia, Apr 2, 48. *Educ:* Univ NSW, Sydney, BS & MB, 72, MD, 80, FRCP(A), 79. *Honors & Awards:* Pfizer Lectr. *Prof Exp:* Intern med, St Vincent's Hosp, Sydney, Australia, 72-73, resident, 73-74, registrar, 74-75; postdoctoral fel, Dept Pharmacol, Health Sci Ctr, Univ Tex, Dallas, 77-78, asst prof pharmacol & internal med, 78-82, fac mem, Grad Sch Biomed Sci, 81-82; assoc prof med, Harvard Med Sch, Boston, 82-89. *Concurrent Pos:* Physician, Parkland Mem Hosp, Dallas, 78-82; asst med, Mass Gen Hosp, Boston, 82-86, dir, Cardiac Immunodiagnostic Lab, 84-87, consult, 87-89; staff physician, Dept Hypertension & Nephrology, Cleveland Clin Found, 89-; consult. *Mem:* Brit Med Asn; Int Soc Nephrology; Am Fedn Clin Res; Am Soc Pharmacol & Exp Therapeut; AAAS; Am Soc Clin Invest. *Res:* Antihypertensive drug pharmacology; role of the sympathetic nervous system in circulatory homeostasis; molecular characterization of adrenergic receptors; adrenergic mechanisms and lipoprotein metabolism; molecular and cellular biology of atrial natriuretic factor; author of numerous scientific publications. *Mailing Add:* Victor Chang Cardiac Res Inst 384 Victoria St Darlinghurst Sydney NSW 2010 Australia. *Fax:* 61-2-9295-8501

GRAHAM, ROBERT MONTROSE, SOFTWARE DEVELOPMENT METHODS, OPERATING SYSTEMS & OTHER SYSTEMS SOFTWARE. *Current Pos:* prof, 75-96, EMER PROF COMPUT SCI, UNIV MASS, 96- *Personal Data:* b St Johns, Mich, Sept 26, 29. *Educ:* Univ Mich, BA, 56, MA, 57. *Prof Exp:* Mem staff, Univ Mich, 57-61, res assoc, 61-63; prog coordr, Proj Mac, Mass Inst Technol, 63-66, staff mem, Elec Eng Dept, 65-67, assoc prof comput sci, 67-72; assoc prof, City Col NY, 72-75. *Concurrent Pos:* Vis assoc prof, Univ Calif, Berkeley, 70-72; chmn, Dept Comput & Info Sci, Univ Mass, 75-81; mem, Comput Sci Bd, 80-83; consult, Gen Motors Tech Ctr, 61-63 & 68, Honeywell Info Syst, 72-74 & 77 & Bell Telephone Labs, 74-75; vis scholar, Stanford Univ, 81. *Mem:* Fel Asn Comput Mach. *Res:* Programming languages and compiler building systems; operating systems; software development methods and environments; computer science education. *Mailing Add:* Commput Sci Dept LGRC Univ Mass Box 34610 Amherst MA 01003-4610. *Fax:* 413-545-1249; *E-Mail:* bob@cs.umass.edu

GRAHAM, ROBERT REAVIS, ELECTRICAL ENGINEERING. *Current Pos:* RETIRED. *Personal Data:* b Hiawatha, Kans, Jan 8, 25; m 50; c 3. *Educ:* Univ Kans, BS, 49. *Prof Exp:* Dept head microwave eng, McDonnell Douglas Electronics Co, 61-64, dir foliage progs, 64-65, vpres foliage progs, 65-66, vpres & group exec, Mil Radar Div, Mich, 66-68, vpres & gen mgr, Ann Arbor Div, 68-71, div vpres, Mo, 71-75, prog mgr, F-15 Avionics Automatic Test Equip Div, McDonnell Douglas Corp, 75-85, dir aircraft support eng, McDonnell Aircraft Co, 85-89. *Mem:* Sigma Xi. *Mailing Add:* 25 Arrowhead Chesterfield MO 63017

GRAHAM, ROBERT WILLIAM, HEAT TRANSFER. *Current Pos:* RETIRED. *Personal Data:* b Cleveland, Ohio, Oct 10, 22; m 51; c 3. *Educ:* Case Inst Technol, BS, 48; Purdue Univ, MS, 50, PhD(mech eng), 52. *Honors & Awards:* Centennial Medal, Am Soc Mech Engrs, 80; Except Eng Achievement Medal, NASA, 82. *Prof Exp:* Instr mech eng, Purdue Univ, 48-52; aero res scientist, Lewis Res Ctr, NASA, 53-57, res supvr, 57-80, sr staff scientist, 81-84, chief, Off Technol Aassessment, 84-90. *Concurrent Pos:* Adj prof, NC State Univ, 65-72; consult, 90- *Mem:* Fel Am Soc Mech Engrs; Sigma Xi; assoc fel Am Inst Aeronaut & Astronaut. *Res:* Rotating stall of axial flow compressors; liquid rocket heat transfer; cryogenic fluid heat transfer; boiling and two phase flow; turbulent boundary layers; curvature effects on heat transfer; alternate fuels and gas; turbine heat transfer. *Mailing Add:* 22895 Haber Dr Fairview Park OH 44126-2931

GRAHAM, ROGER NEILL, COMPUTER SCIENCE. *Current Pos:* WRITER, 78- *Personal Data:* b Augusta, Ga, Feb 21, 41. *Educ:* Valdosta State Col, BS, 63; Univ NC, PhD(physics), 71. *Prof Exp:* Asst prof physics, Concord Col, 68-76, assoc prof, 76-78. *Mem:* Asn Comput Mach; Sigma Xi. *Res:* Computer science. *Mailing Add:* 913 Papaya Street Augusta GA 30904

GRAHAM, RONALD A(RTHUR), CHEMICAL ENGINEERING. *Current Pos:* PRES, GRAHAM ASSOCS INC, 73- *Personal Data:* b College Point, NY, Jan 6, 24; m 50; c 3. *Educ:* Columbia Univ, BS, 44. *Prof Exp:* Glass technol engr, Corning Glass Works, 44-47; res proj engr, Wyandotte Chem Corp, 47-50, sect head eng, 50-53, asst to dir contract res, 53, mgr dept, 54-57, dir, 57-61, asst to vpres engr, 61-64 & mfg, 64-66; mgr lab facil, Celanese Res Co, 66-68, dir admin & tech support, 68-73. *Mem:* Am Chem Soc; Am Inst Chem Engrs; fel Am Inst Chemists; Soc Chem Indust. *Res:* Rocket propellant technology; glass technology; silicates; high temperature reactions; heat transfer; chemical process development; management of research and industrial chemicals manufacturing. *Mailing Add:* 92 Pine Way New Providence NJ 07974-1821

GRAHAM, RONALD LEWIS, MATHEMATICS. *Current Pos:* Dir, Math Sci Res Ctr, 62-88, ADJ DIR, INFO SCI DIV, AT&T BELL LABS, 88-, VPRES, INFO SCI RES, AT&T LABS, 96-; UNIV PROF, RUTGERS UNIV, 87- *Personal Data:* b Taft, Calif, Oct 31, 35; m 83, Fan Chung; c 2. *Educ:* Univ Alaska, BS, 58; Univ Calif, Berkeley, MA & PhD(math), 62. *Hon Degrees:* LLD, Western Mich Univ, 84; DSc, St Olaf Col, 85, Univ Alaska, 88. *Honors & Awards:* Polya Prize in Combinatorics, 72. *Concurrent Pos:* Regents prof math, Univ Calif, Los Angeles, 74; vis prof comput sci, Stanford Univ, 79 & 81; Fairchild distinguished scholar, Calif Inst Technol, 82; vis prof comput sci, Princeton Univ, 87 & 89. *Mem:* Nat Acad Sci; Math Asn Am; Sigma Xi; Soc Indust & Appl Math; Asn Comp Mach; Am Math Soc; fel Am Acad Arts & Sci. *Res:* Combinatorics; graph theory; algorithms; number theory; combinatorial geometry. *Mailing Add:* AT&T Labs 2T-102 Murray Hill NJ 07974

GRAHAM, RONALD POWELL, analytical chemistry; deceased, see previous edition for last biography

GRAHAM, SHIRLEY ANN, BOTANY, TAXONOMY. *Current Pos:* res assoc, 67-74, ADJ PROF BIOL SCI, KENT STATE UNIV, 84-, ASSOC PROF, 93- *Personal Data:* b Flint, Mich, Mar 20, 35; m 60, Alan; c 3. *Educ:* Mich State Univ, BS, 57; Univ Mich, PhD(bot), 63. *Prof Exp:* Botanist, Harvard Univ, 63-64; asst prof bot, Univ Akron, 65-66. *Mem:* Bot Soc Am; Am Soc Plant Taxon (treas, 82-85); Asn Trop Biol; Int Asn Plant Taxon. *Res:* Taxonomic studies in family Lythraceae, especially genus Cuphea. *Mailing Add:* Dept Biol Sci Kent State Univ Main Campus PO Box 5190 Kent OH 44242-0001

GRAHAM, STEPHAN ALAN, SEDIMENTARY TECTONICS, PETROLEUM GEOLOGY. *Current Pos:* assoc prof, 80-88, PROF APPL EARTH SCI & GEOL, STANFORD UNIV, CALIF, 88- *Personal Data:* b Evansville, Ind, Apr 25, 50; div; c 2. *Educ:* Ind Univ, AB, 72; Stanford Univ, MS, 74, PhD(geol), 76. *Honors & Awards:* Sproule Award, Am Asn Petrol Geologists. *Prof Exp:* Instr field geol, Ind Univ Geol Field Sta, 72 & Stanford Univ Geol Surv, 74; res geologist plate tectonics, Exxon Prod Res Co, 76; explor geologist petrol, Chevron USA, Inc, 76-80. *Concurrent Pos:* Petrol geologist consult, 80- *Mem:* Fel Geol Soc Am; Soc Econ Paleontologists & Mineralogists; Sigma Xi; Am Asn Petrol Geologist; Am Geophys Union. *Res:* Interplay of sedimentation and tectonics, particularly sedimentary response to plate tectonic processes; application of sedimentary tectonics to exploration for energy resources. *Mailing Add:* Dept Appl Earth Sci Stanford Univ 138 Mitchell Stanford CA 94305-2115

GRAHAM, SUSAN LOIS, COMPUTER SCIENCE. *Current Pos:* from asst prof to assoc prof, 71-81, PROF COMPUT SCI, UNIV CALIF, BERKELEY, 81- *Personal Data:* b Cleveland, Ohio, Nov 16, 42; m 71. *Educ:* Harvard Univ, AB, 64; Stanford Univ, MS, 66, PhD(comput sci), 71. *Honors & Awards:* Forsythe Lectr, Stanford Univ, 93. *Prof Exp:* Assoc res scientist & adj asst prof comput sci, Courant Inst Math Sci, NY Univ, 69-71. *Concurrent Pos:* NSF res grant, 74-; ed, Commun, Asn Comput Mach, 75-79, ed-in-chief, Trans Prog Lang & Systs, 78-92; vis prof, Comput Systs Lab, Stanford Univ, 81; lectr, IBM Can Lab, Toronto, 88-92. *Mem:* Nat Acad Eng; fel AAAS; Inst Elec & Electronics Engrs; fel Asn Comput Mach; Am Acad Arts & Sci. *Res:* Programming language design and implementation; syntax error recovery, parsing, code generation and optimization. *Mailing Add:* Univ Calif Comput Sci Div 771 Soda Hall Berkeley CA 94720. *Fax:* 510-642-3962; *E-Mail:* graham@cs.berkeley.edu

GRAHAM, TERRY EDWARD, PHYSIOLOGICAL ECOLOGY. *Current Pos:* Instr, 70-73, from asst prof to assoc prof, 73-83, PROF BIOL, WORCESTER STATE COL, 83- *Personal Data:* b Grand Rapids, Mich, Sept 19, 40; m 64; c 2. *Educ:* Suffolk Univ, AB, 65; Univ NH, MS, 67; Univ RI, PhD(zool), 72. *Concurrent Pos:* Prin investr, US Fish & Wildlife Serv, 79-81, Mass Div Fisheries & Wildlife, 81-88 & NY Zool Soc Conserv grant, 81-82. *Mem:* Am Soc Ichthyologists and Herpetologists; Soc Study Reptiles & Amphibians; Herpetologists' League. *Res:* Turtle ecology; determination of the effects of temperature and photoperiod on acclimatization of temperature preference and locomotor activity patterns in reptiles and amphibians; analysis of growth, morphometric variation and population structure in freshwater turtles; zoogeography of New England amphibians and reptiles. *Mailing Add:* Dept Human Biol Univ Guelph Guelph ON N1G 2W1 Can. *Fax:* 519-763-5902

GRAHAM, TOM MANESS, BIOLOGY. *Current Pos:* from asst prof to assoc prof, 72-83, PROF BIOL, UNIV ALA, 83- *Personal Data:* b Paducah, Ky, Mar 16, 37; m 76. *Educ:* Florence State Univ, BS, 59; Univ Ala, MS, 66, PhD(zool, physiol), 70. *Prof Exp:* Asst prof physiol, Tex Col Osteop Med, 70-71 & Chicago Col Osteop Med, 71-72. *Res:* Physiology and morphogenesis of Hydra. *Mailing Add:* Biol Univ Ala Box 870344 Tuscaloosa AL 35487

GRAHAM, W(ALTER) DONALD, BIOCHEMISTRY. *Current Pos:* RETIRED. *Personal Data:* b Ottawa, Ont, June 2, 19; m 42; c 2. *Educ:* Ont Agr Col, BSA, 40; McGill Univ, MSc, 42; Univ Toronto, PhD(biochem), 45. *Prof Exp:* Ont Res Found res fel pharmaceut, Toronto, 45-47; biochemist nutrit res, Wash State Col, 48-49; chemist pharmacol res, Food & Drug Lab, Can Dept Nat Health & Welfare, 49-58; dir res, Midwest Med Res Found, 58-64; dir prod & process res, Farmland Indust, Inc, 64-78, exec dir res & develop, 78-82. *Concurrent Pos:* Mem shock & plasma expander panel, Defence Res Bd Can, 56-58. *Mem:* Am Chem Soc; Am Soc Pharmacol & Exp Therapeut. *Res:* Feeds; fertilizers; petroleum; chemical engineering; agricultural engineering; pesticides; plant sciences; pollution control; waste utilization; small scale fuel alcohol production. *Mailing Add:* 645 Coquina Ct Ft Myers FL 33908-1621

GRAHAM, WALTER WAVERLY, III, NUCLEAR ENGINEERING, TECHNICAL MANAGEMENT. *Personal Data:* b Nashville, Tenn, Apr 30, 33; m 55; c 2. *Educ:* US Naval Acad, BS, 55; Vanderbilt Univ, MS, 60; Ga Inst Technol, PhD(nuclear eng), 65. *Prof Exp:* Res & develop staff assoc, Gen Atomic Div, Gen Dynamics Corp, 60-62; asst prof nuclear eng, Ga Inst Technol, 65-68, assoc prof, 68-70, res scientist, Nuclear Res Ctr, 65-70; pres, Tech Analysis Corp, 70-83, exec vpres, Digital Commun Asn, 83-85. *Concurrent Pos:* Consult comput systs. *Mem:* Sigma Xi. *Res:* Computer-aided experimentation; minicomputer, microcomputer and time-sharing project management. *Mailing Add:* 13505 Freemanville Rd Alpharetta GA 30201-3510

GRAHAM, WILLIAM ARTHUR GROVER, METAL CARBONYLS, HYDROCARBON ACTIVATION. *Current Pos:* from assoc prof to prof, 62-95, EMER PROF CHEM, UNIV ALTA, 95-, ASSOC DEAN SCI, 95- *Personal Data:* b Rosetown, Sask, Aug 23, 30; m 51, Sydna Cantelon; c 5. *Educ:* Univ Sask, BA, 52, MA, 53; Harvard Univ, PhD(chem), 56. *Honors & Awards:* Noranda Award, Chem Inst Can, 70; Centenary Lectr, Royal Soc Chem, 87-88; E W R Steacie Award, Can Soc Chem, 91; CIC Medal, Chem Inst Can, 94. *Prof Exp:* Lectr & res assoc chem, Univ Southern Calif, 56-57; res chemist & consult, Arthur D Little, Inc, 57-62. *Mem:* Am Chem Soc; Chem Inst Can; Royal Soc Chem; fel Royal Soc Can. *Res:* Synthesis, reactions and structure of organometallic and coordination compounds; transition metal hydrides and carbonyls; activation of carbon-hydrogen bonds under mild conditions. *Mailing Add:* Dept Chem Univ Alta Edmonton AB T6G 2G2 Can

GRAHAM, WILLIAM DOYCE, JR, PLANT GENETICS, PLANT BREEDING. *Current Pos:* CONSULT, 88-; DEPT CHAIR, DEPT AGRON, CLEMSON UNIV, 95- *Personal Data:* b Clarendon, Tex, Feb 22, 39; m 62; c 2. *Educ:* Purdue Univ, MS, 65, PhD(genetics), 67. *Prof Exp:* From asst prof to prof plant genetics & breeding, Clemson Univ, 66-88. *Mem:* Am Soc Agron; Crop Sci Soc Am. *Res:* Small grain genetics, including disease resistance; genetics of yield and variety development. *Mailing Add:* Dept Agron Clemson Univ PO Box 340359 Clemson SC 29634-0359. *Fax:* 864-656-3443; *E-Mail:* dgraham@clnstl.clemson.edu

GRAHAM, WILLIAM JOSEPH, BEHAVIORAL ECOLOGY. *Current Pos:* asst prof, 75-85, ASSOC PROF BIOL & CHMN, MONROE COMMUNITY COL, ROCHESTER, NY, 85- *Personal Data:* b Cle Elum, Wash, Jan 6, 32; m 75, Margaret C Orbison; c James S Lungu. *Educ:* Whitman Col, BA, 54; Univ Mich, MS, 62, PhD(zool), 68. *Prof Exp:* Teacher pub schs, 56-58 & 59-60; teaching asst, Univ Mich, 65-67; from lectr to asst prof biol, City Col New York, 67-71; asst prof biol, State Univ NY Col Geneseo, 71-75. *Mem:* Am Soc Zool; Ecol Soc Am; Am Soc Mammal. *Res:* Daily activity patterns and social interactions in small mammals; effects of behavior on numbers and densities of animals. *Mailing Add:* Dept Biol Monroe Community Col 1000 E Henrietta Rd Rochester NY 14623

GRAHAM, WILLIAM RENDALL, PHYSICS, MATERIALS SCIENCE. *Current Pos:* assoc prof, 74-85, PROF MAT SCI & ENG, UNIV PA, PHILADELPHIA, 86- *Personal Data:* b Melbourne, Australia, Nov 22, 38; m 84; c 2. *Educ:* Univ Melbourne, BSc, 59, MSc, 61; Oxford Unit, PhD(exp nuclear physics), 65. *Prof Exp:* Res staff molecular biophysicist, Yale Univ, 65-68, asst prof molecular biophys, 68-72; vis asst prof metall, Univ Ill, Urbana, 72-74. *Mem:* Am Vacuum Soc; Sigma Xi. *Res:* Surfaces and interfaces; materials science; ion scattering, electron spectroscopics, auger, leed, ups, field ion microscopy. *Mailing Add:* Dept Metall Mat Sci Univ Pa Philadelphia PA 19104

GRAHAM, WILLIAM RICHARD MONTGOMERY, MOLECULAR SPECTROSCOPY, LABORATORY ASTROPHYSICS. *Current Pos:* asst prof, Tex Christian Univ, 77-81, assoc prof, 81-87, chmn, Dept Physics, 84-86, PROF PHYSICS, TEX CHRISTIAN UNIV, 87- *Personal Data:* b New Westminster, BC, Jan 22, 44; US Citizen; m 92, H Mei Wu; c Timothy. *Educ:* Univ Western Ont, BSc, 66, MSc, 68; York Univ, PhD(physics), 71. *Prof Exp:* Nat Res Coun Can fel, Dept Chem, Univ Fla, 71-75; res assoc molecular spectros, Herzberg Inst Astrophys, Nat Res Coun Can, 75-77. *Mem:* Am Phys Soc; Am Chem Soc; Am Astron Soc; Sigma Xi. *Res:* Molecular spectroscopy; spectroscopic studies of molecules of astrophysical interest; solid state electron paramagnetic resonance studies; characterization and utilization of fossil fuels. *Mailing Add:* Dept Physics Box 32915 Tex Christian Univ Ft Worth TX 76129. *Fax:* 817-921-7742; *E-Mail:* w.graham@tcu.edu

GRAHN, DOUGLAS, GENETICS, RADIOBIOLOGY. *Current Pos:* assoc scientist, Argonne Nat Lab, 53-58, assoc biologist, 61-62, assoc dir, 62-66, sr biologist, 66-78, div dir, 78-81, sr biologist, Div Biol & Med Res, 66-87, SCIENTIST, SPEC TERM APPOINTEE, CTR MECH BIOL & BIOTECHNOL, ARGONNE NAT LAB, 87- *Personal Data:* b Newark, NJ, Apr 25, 23; m 46, 73, Ann Wagoner; c Frederick S, Catherine L & Alice A. *Educ:* Rutgers Univ, BS, 48; Iowa State Univ, MS, 50, PhD(genetics), 52. *Prof Exp:* Asst zool, Rutgers Univ, 48; asst genetics, Iowa State Col, 48-51; geneticist, US AEC, 58-61. *Concurrent Pos:* Mem radiation control adv bd, Md State Dept Health, 60-61; mem radiobiol adv panel, Space Sci Bd, Nat Acad Sci-Nat Res Coun, 62-71, chmn, 71-74; consult, McDonnell Aircraft Corp, Mo, 63-65 & Off Manned Space Flight, NASA, 64-70; sci prog coordr foreign exhibit prog, US AEC, 66-69, sr analyst, Div Biomed & Environ Res, 73-74; mem comt biol sci, Ill Bd Higher Educ, 69-70; mem sci comt biol aspects radiation protection criteria, Nat Coun Radiation Protection, 72-90, coun mem, 78-84; chmn working group life sci, Comt Space Res, Int Coun Sci Unions, 74-78; mem, comt Biol Effects Ionizing Rad, Nat Acad Sci & Nat

Res Coun, 87-89 & Bd Radiation Effects Res, 91-94. *Mem:* Radiation Res Soc; Environ Mutagen Soc. *Res:* Mammalian radiation genetics; genetic effects of transuranic elements; external radiation toxicology; neutron radiobiology. *Mailing Add:* Ctr Mech Biol & Biotechnol Argonne Nat Lab Argonne IL 60439

GRAHN, EDGAR HOWARD, inorganic chemistry; deceased, see previous edition for last biography

GRAIFF, LEONARD B(ALDINE), MECHANICAL ENGINEERING. *Current Pos:* Res engr fuels res, Shell Oil Co, Ill, 59-62, res engr, Thornton Res Ctr, Shell Res Ltd, Eng, 62-64, res group leader, Shell Oil Co, Ill, 64-69, res group leader, Tex, 69-70, staff engr fuels res, 70-79, sr staff engr, 79-84, sr prin scientist, Thornton Res Centre, Shell Res Ltd, Eng, 84-87, RES ADV, SHELL DEVELOP CO, 87- *Personal Data:* b Litchfield, Ill, Dec 16, 33; m 63, Arlene Walsh; c Lisa, Philip & Laura. *Educ:* Univ Ill, BSc, 55, MSc, 56; Purdue Univ, PhD(combustion eng), 59. *Honors & Awards:* Henry Ford Mem Award, Soc Automotive Engrs, 67, Colwell Award, 67 & 80, McFarland Award, 94. *Mem:* Soc Automotive Engrs; Combustion Inst. *Res:* Combustion phenomena; petroleum fuels; gasoline additives; automotive exhaust emissions. *Mailing Add:* 13727 Hambleton Circle Houston TX 77069

GRAIKOSKI, JOHN T, ENVIRONMENTAL MICROBIOLOGY. *Current Pos:* SUPVRY RES MICROBIOL ECOL, NAT MARINE FISHERIES SERV, MILFORD, CONN, 70- *Personal Data:* b Wakefield, Mich, June 7, 24; m 58; c 4. *Educ:* Univ Mich, BS, 49, MS, 52, PhD(bact), 61. *Prof Exp:* Res asst botulium studies, Univ Mich, Ann Arbor, 52-55, res assoc, 55-64; supvry res microbiol, Bur Com Fisheries, Ann Arbor, 64-70. *Concurrent Pos:* Lectr radiation biol, Univ Mich, 56-58 & fisheries, 65-67; consult, Bur Com Fisheries, 63-64 & Governor's Comt Botulism Control, 63-66; mem, Toxic Microorganism Panel, US-Japan, 64-75, Comt Compendium Food Microbiol Methods, 71- *Mem:* Am Soc Microbiol; Wildlife Dis Asn; Int Asn Great Lakes Res. *Res:* Botulism; radiation sterilization; radiation biology; microbial ecology, especially marine; anaerobic bacteria; heat sterilization of foods. *Mailing Add:* 379 W River Rd Orange CT 06477

GRAINGER, CEDRIC ANTHONY, CLOUD PHYSICS, WEATHER MODIFICATION. *Current Pos:* DIR ATMOSPHERIC RES, CTR AEROSPACE SCI, UNIV NDAK, 79- *Personal Data:* b Juneau, Alaska, Mar 1, 41; m 65; c 4. *Educ:* Mont State Univ, BS, 66, MS, 68; State Univ NY, Albany, PhD(atmospheric sci), 73. *Prof Exp:* Res assoc, Mont State Univ, 72-73; asst prof meteorol, State Univ NY, Oswego, 73-76; res scientist meteorol, Environ Res & Technol, 77-79. *Mem:* Am Meteorol Soc; Royal Meteorol Soc; Am Geophys Union; Weather Modification Asn. *Res:* Atmospheric sciences; cloud physics, employing research aircraft and radar; formation of precipitation and the potential of clouds for precipitation augmentation; wind shear and turbulence measurements in cloud and aircraft icing. *Mailing Add:* Dept Atmos Sci Univ NDak PO Box 8216 Grand Forks ND 58202-8216

GRAINGER, JOHN JOSEPH, ENERGY ENGINEERING, ELECTRICAL ENGINEERING. *Current Pos:* assoc prof, 77-81, PROF ELEC ENG, NC STATE UNIV, 81- *Personal Data:* b Dublin, Ireland, Jan 29, 34; US citizen; m 63; c 4. *Educ:* Nat Univ Ireland, BE, 61; Univ Wis, Madison, MSEE, 64, PhD(elec eng), 68. *Prof Exp:* Asst prof elec eng, Ill Inst Technol, 68-70; prin engr, Wis Elec Power Co, Milwaukee, 70-77. *Concurrent Pos:* Consult, Ill Res Inst Technol, 68, Commonwealth Edison Co, Chicago, 69; Res Triangle Inst, Raleigh, 77-, NC Power & Light Co, 78- *Mem:* Inst Elec & Electronics Engrs; Nat Soc Prof Engrs; Am Soc Eng Educ; Sigma Xi. *Res:* Electric power engineering; electrical machinery; transmission and distribution engineering; solar energy systems; switching overvoltages. *Mailing Add:* 6100 Battleford Dr Raleigh NC 27612

GRAINGER, ROBERT BALL, NUTRITION, BIOCHEMISTRY. *Current Pos:* RETIRED. *Personal Data:* b Centerview, Mo, Mar 3, 23; m 47; c 2. *Educ:* Cent Mo State Col, BS, 47; Univ Mo, MA, 49, PhD(physiol chem), 54. *Prof Exp:* Asst, Univ Mo, 47-52, instr, 52-53; from asst prof to assoc prof animal nutrit, Univ Ky, 53-60; res chemist, Monsanto Co, St Louis, 60-61, prod develop, 61-63, res group leader, 63-68; dir res, Diamond A Cattle Industs, 68-70; vpres, Agr Technol Inc, 70-80; researcher, Great Plains Consult Inc, 80-87. *Mem:* Am Soc Animal Sci; Poultry Sci Asn Am; Am Dairy Sci Asn; Sigma Xi; Fedn Am Socs Exp Biol. *Res:* Monogastric and ruminant intermediary metabolism. *Mailing Add:* 2850 E Serendipity Circle Colorado Springs CO 80917-3059

GRAINGER, ROBERT MICHAEL, DEVELOPMENTAL BIOLOGY. *Current Pos:* from asst prof to assoc prof, 76-89, PROF BIOL, UNIV VA, 89- *Personal Data:* b San Francisco, Calif, Sept 10, 48. *Educ:* Stanford Univ, AB, 70; Univ Calif, Berkeley, PhD(zool), 74. *Prof Exp:* Fel biol, Yale Univ, 74-76. *Concurrent Pos:* Fel USPHS, 70-74; fel, J C Childs Mem Fund for Med Res, 74-76; NIH grant, 78-94. *Mem:* Am Soc Cell Biol; Am Soc Zoologists; Soc Develop Biol; AAAS. *Res:* Molecular basis of early development; determination of the eye, lens and other anterior structures. *Mailing Add:* Dept Biol 229 Gilmer Hall Univ Charlottesville VA 22903

GRAINGER, THOMAS HUTCHESON, JR, MEDICAL BACTERIOLOGY. *Current Pos:* BACTERIOLOGIST, MONROE PATH ASN, 71- *Personal Data:* b Bethlehem, Pa, Dec 14, 13; m 41; c 1. *Educ:* Lehigh Univ, BA, 36, MS, 38, PhD(bact), 46. *Prof Exp:* Asst, Sharp & Dohme, Pa, 36-38; asst instr, Med Sch, Univ Pa, 39-41; from instr to assoc prof bact, Lehigh Univ, 46-59; asst dir biol labs, Nat Drug Co, Swiftwater, Pa, 59-70, mgr biol serv, 70-71. *Concurrent Pos:* Lectr, Inst Microbiol, Univ Colo, 64. *Mem:* Fel Am Pub Health Asn; Hist Sci Soc; NY Acad Sci; Am Med Writers' Asn; Sigma Xi. *Res:* General bacteriology; history of bacteriology. *Mailing Add:* PO Box 26 Swiftwater PA 18370-0026

GRALLA, EDWARD JOSEPH, EXPERIMENTAL TOXICOLOGY. *Current Pos:* RETIRED. *Personal Data:* b Wyoming Co, Pa, Mar 14, 32; m 59; c 3. *Educ:* Univ Pa, VMD, 61. *Prof Exp:* Vet pract, 61-62; toxicologist, Med Res Lab, Chas Pfizer & Co, Inc, 62-69; assoc prof comp med & pharmacol, Sch Med, Yale Univ, 69-75; dir pharmacol & toxicol, Mason Res Inst, 75-76; chief toxicol & mem staff, Chem Indust Inst Toxicol, 77-82; pres, Toxicoconsult, Inc, 82-87. *Concurrent Pos:* Consult, 82-87. *Mem:* AAAS; Am Col Vet Comp Toxicol; Am Vet Med Asn; Am Asn Lab Animal Sci; Soc Toxicol. *Res:* Experimental toxicology; improving animal models for predicting adverse chemical effects in man; toxicology of anti-cancer agents. *Mailing Add:* 169 Springmoor Dr Raleigh NC 27607

GRALLA, JAY DOUGLAS, BIOCHEMISTRY. *Current Pos:* from asst prof to assoc prof, 75-85, PROF CHEM & MOLECULAR BIOL, UNIV CALIF, LOS ANGELES, 85- *Personal Data:* b Brooklyn, NY, Jan 28, 48. *Educ:* Clarkson Col, BS, 69; Yale Univ, PhD(chem), 73. *Prof Exp:* Jane Coffin Childs fel, Harvard Univ, 73-75. *Res:* Regulation of gene expression; protein-nucleic acid interactions. *Mailing Add:* Dept Chem Univ Calif Los Angeles 405 Hilgard Ave Los Angeles CA 90095

GRALNICK, SAMUEL LOUIS, plasma physics, fusion engineering, for more information see previous edition

GRAM, THEODORE EDWARD, PHARMACOLOGY, BIOCHEMISTRY. *Current Pos:* supvry pharmacologist & head drug interactions sect, Lab Med Chem & Biol, 72-84, DEP CHIEF, TOXICOL BR, NAT CANCER INST, 84- *Personal Data:* b Minneapolis, Minn, Sept 26, 34; m 59; c 3. *Educ:* Univ Minn, MS, 62, PhD(pharmacol, biochem), 64. *Prof Exp:* Asst pharmacol, Univ Minn, 58-64; res assoc chem pharmacol, Nat Inst Gen Med Sci, Nat Heart Inst, Md, 67-70; supvry pharmacologist & head sect enzyme-chem interaction, Pharmacol-Toxicol Br, Nat Inst Environ Health Sci, 70-72. *Concurrent Pos:* USPHS fel, Univ Iowa, 65-67; NIH fel, Lab Chem Pharmacol, Nat Heart & Lung Inst, 67-70; counr, Am Soc Pharmacol & Exp Therapeut, 84- *Mem:* AAAS; Soc Exp Biol & Med; Am Soc Biol Chemists; Sigma Xi; Soc Toxicol; Am Soc Pharmacol & Exp Therapeut; Biochem Soc; NY Acad Sci; Int Soc Study Xenobiotics. *Res:* Hepatic microsomal structure and function; biochemistry and enzymology of microsomal drug metabolism and electron transport; cell biology; biochemistry; toxicology. *Mailing Add:* 1036 Welsh Dr Rockville MD 20852-1202

GRAMBLING, JEFFREY A, metamorphic petrology, precambrian geology; deceased, see previous edition for last biography

GRAMERA, ROBERT EUGENE, BIOCHEMISTRY, ORGANIC CHEMISTRY. *Current Pos:* PRES, BARLEY PROD INT, INC, 80- *Personal Data:* b Joliet, Ill, Feb 6, 36; m 57; c 2. *Educ:* Lewis Col, BS, 57; Purdue Univ, MS, 61, PhD(biochem), 63. *Prof Exp:* State analytical control chemist, Purdue Univ, 57-63; res scientist, Moffett Tech Ctr, Corn Prod Co, 63-65, res sect head polymer res & develop, 65-69; tech supvr appl packaging, Crown Zellerbach Corp, Calif, 69-70, supvr plant & customer trials, packaging res & develop lab, 70-71; dir tech develop & serv, Great Western Sugar Co, 71-75, exec dir mfg res & develop, 75-76; tech consult & pres, World Future, Inc, 76-80. *Concurrent Pos:* Tech consult & vpres, Agribus Blackstone Group Ltd, Consults, Denver, Colo, 82- *Mem:* Am Chem Soc. *Res:* Isolation, purification and structural investigation of polysaccharides; synthesis of polymerizable monosaccharide monomers; organic reaction mechanisms of carbohydrates; chemistry of urethane foams from carbohydrate based polyols. *Mailing Add:* 704 County Rd 220 Durango CO 81301-8018

GRAMIAK, RAYMOND, MEDICINE, RADIOLOGY. *Current Pos:* RETIRED. *Personal Data:* b Philadelphia, Pa, Mar 23, 24; m 49; c 4. *Educ:* Univ Rochester, MD, 49. *Prof Exp:* Resident radiol, Univ Rochester, 53-56, instr, 56-57; pvt pract, NY, 57-65; from assoc prof to emer prof radiol, Univ Rochester, 65-94. *Concurrent Pos:* Fel cinefluorography, Univ Rochester, 52-53. *Mem:* Am Col Radiol; Radiol Soc NAm. *Res:* Diagnostic radiology; cardiac ultrasonics. *Mailing Add:* Dept Radiol Univ Rochester Strong Mem Hosp 601 Elmwood Ave PO Box 648 Rochester NY 14642-0001

GRAMICK, JEANNINE, MATHEMATICS. *Current Pos:* CONSULT, 84- *Personal Data:* b Philadelphia, Pa, Aug 8, 42. *Educ:* Col Notre Dame, Md, BA, 65; Univ Notre Dame, MS, 69; Univ Pa, PhD(educ), 75. *Prof Exp:* Teacher sr high sch math, Notre Dame Prep Sch, 65-68; asst prof math, Col Notre Dame, Md, 72-76; co-dir, New Ways Ministry, Mt Rainier, Md, 76-84. *Res:* Whether arithmetic algorithms should be taught to conform to observed behaviors. *Mailing Add:* 4012 29th St Mt Rainier MD 20712

GRAMINSKI, EDMOND LEONARD, PHYSICAL ORGANIC CHEMISTRY, RHEOLOGY. *Current Pos:* CHIEF, OFF RES, BUR ENGRAVING & PRINTING, 80- *Personal Data:* b Dunkirk, NY, Oct 14, 29; m 56, Marla Reynolds; c Jeanne, Jerry, Mary, Marla, Susan, John, Deborah & Michael. *Educ:* Univ Buffalo, BS, 52, PhD(chem), 56. *Prof Exp:* Sr res chemist, Olin Mathieson Chem Co, 55-60 & Harris Res Labs Div, Gillette Razor Co, 60-64; proj leader rheology of paper, Nat Bur Stand, 64-80.

Mem: Tech Asn Pulp & Paper Indust; Tech Asn Graphic Arts; Am Chem Soc. *Res:* Counterfeit deterrence materials, inks, graphic arts. *Mailing Add:* Bur Engraving & Printing 14th & C Sts SW Washington DC 20228. *Fax:* 202-874-3689

GRAMLICH, JAMES VANDLE, plant physiology, for more information see previous edition

GRAMS, ANNE P, MATHEMATICS. *Personal Data:* b Albany, Ga, May 28, 47; m 68. *Educ:* Fla State Univ, BA, 68, PhD(math), 72; Cath Univ Am, MA, 70. *Prof Exp:* From asst prof to assoc prof math, Univ Tenn, Nashville, 77-80, coordr pub serv activ, Div Arts & Sci, 75-77, assoc prof math, Embry-Riddle Aero Univ, Daytona Beach, Fla, 80-82. *Mem:* Am Math Soc; Math Asn Am; Sigma Xi. *Res:* Commutative rings, problems relating to factorization, Dedekind domains, power series rings. *Mailing Add:* 3909 Cardinal Blvd Daytona Beach FL 32127

GRAMS, GARY WALLACE, ORGANIC CHEMISTRY, INORGANIC CHEMISTRY. *Current Pos:* mgr res & develop, Pearsall Chem Corp, 76-79, vpres res & develop, 79-80, vpres, Argus Div, Pearsall Prods, 80- 92, DIR, QUAL MGT, WITCO CORP, 92- *Personal Data:* b Moline, Ill, June 13, 42; m 64, Sharon; c Jeffery & Joel. *Educ:* Valparaiso Univ, BS, 64; Northwestern Univ, PhD(org chem), 68. *Prof Exp:* Chemist, Cereal Properties Lab, Northern Mkt & Nutrit Res Div, Agr Res Serv, USDA, 68-72; dir res & develop, Benz Oil Inc, 72-76. *Mem:* Am Chem Soc; Am Inst Chemists; Am Soc Testing & Mat; AAAS; Am Soc Qual Control. *Res:* Organochemical approaches to the synthesis of ribonucleotides; processing effects on cereal nutrients; photoxidation of vitamin E; lubricant formulation and synthesis; flame retardent and plastic additives; aluminum chloride catalysis. *Mailing Add:* Witco Chem Corp One American Ln 3rd Fl E Greenwich CT 06831-2559. *Fax:* 201-337-3753

GRAMS, GERALD WILLIAM, METEOROLOGY, LASERS. *Current Pos:* PRES, GRAMS ENVIRON LABS, 90- *Personal Data:* b Mankato, Minn, Dec 7, 38; m 88, c 3. *Educ:* Mankato State Col, BS, 60; Mass Inst Technol, PhD(meteorol), 66. *Prof Exp:* Teacher high sch, Minn, 60-61; res assoc meteor & laser applns, Mass Inst Technol, 66-67; aerospace technologist, Electronics Res Ctr, NASA, Cambridge, 67-70; scientist meteor & laser applns, Nat Ctr Atmospheric Res, 70-77; prof geophys sci, Ga Inst Technol, 77-90. *Concurrent Pos:* Lectr, Northeastern Univ, 67-70; res affil, Res Lab Electronics, Mass Inst Technol, 67-70; mem various comts, Nat Acad Sci & NASA. *Mem:* Am Meteorol Soc; Am Geophys Union; fel Optical Soc Am; AAAS; Soc Photo-Optical Instrumentation Engrs. *Res:* Meteorology and physics of the upper atmosphere; laser atmospheric probing techniques; stratospheric aerosols; noctilucent clouds; optical properties of atmospheric particulates; satellite observations of atmospheric constituents; atmospheric optics and radiation transfer. *Mailing Add:* 5064 Mink Livsey Rd Lithonia GA 30058

GRAMZA, ANTHONY FRANCIS, ZOOLOGY, ETHOLOGY. *Current Pos:* ASSOC PROF, DEPT NAT SCI, LOYOLA UNIV, CHICAGO, 91- *Personal Data:* b Milwaukee, Wis, June 26, 36; m 77; c 1. *Educ:* Marquette Univ, BS, 62; Univ Wis, MS, 65, PhD(zool), 69. *Prof Exp:* Asst prof psychobiol, Children's Res Ctr, Univ Ill, 68-74; fac psychobiol, Nat Col Educ, 74-76; from asst prof to assoc prof biol, Mundelein Col, 76-91, chmn dept, 82-90. *Mem:* AAAS; Am Inst Biol Sci; Animal Behav Soc; Sigma Xi. *Res:* Evolution and adaptive significance of behavioral systems; human ethology; social behavior; communication; ontogeny of behavior. *Mailing Add:* Dept Nat Sci Loyola Univ Lake Shore Campus 6525 N Sheridan Rd Chicago IL 60626-5311

GRAN, RICHARD J, CONTROL THEORY, IMAGE & SIGNAL PROCESSING. *Current Pos:* VPRES & CHIEF TECH OFFICER, MAGLEV USA, 89- *Personal Data:* b Brooklyn, NY, Apr 16, 40; m 84; c 1. *Educ:* Polytech Inst Brooklyn, BS, 61, MS, 65, PhD(systs sci), 69. *Prof Exp:* Design engr, Grumman Aerospace Corp, 62-70, sr res scientist, Corp Res Ctr, 70-75, lab head, 75-88, dir advan concepts, 88-95. *Concurrent Pos:* Adj prof, Polytech Univ, 65-85, State Univ NY, Stony Brook, 75-; consult, Math Analysis Co, Legal Consult & Pension & Annuity Analysis, 85-; mem, Maglev Technol Adv Comt, US Senate, 88-89. *Mem:* Inst Elec & Electronics Engrs. *Res:* Control systems design methods; image processing; multidimensional signal processing; tracking filters. *Mailing Add:* 5 Smith Rd Northborough MA 01532-1051

GRANATEK, ALPHONSE PETER, PHARMACEUTICAL CHEMISTRY. *Current Pos:* RETIRED. *Personal Data:* b Hartford, Conn, Feb 13, 20; m 43; c 2. *Educ:* Trinity Col, Conn, BS, 42; Syracuse Univ, MS, 53. *Prof Exp:* Chemist, US Indust Chem, Md, 42-44; chemist, Ernest Bischoff Pharmaceut Co, Conn, 44-46; dir prod develop labs, Bristol-Myers Co, 46-67, dir prod develop res, 67-80; vpres, IMS Ltd, 80-85. *Concurrent Pos:* Consult, 85-. *Mem:* Am Chem Soc; Am Pharmaceut Asn. *Res:* Insecticides; resins; antacid resins; antibiotics; pharmacy; development of pharmaceuticals; medical biochemistry; physics; electronics. *Mailing Add:* 13449 N 82nd St Scottsdale AZ 85260-3500

GRANATH, JAMES WILTON, STRUCTURAL GEOLOGY, REMOTE SENSING. *Current Pos:* sr res geologist, 81-84, sr res scientist, Explor Res Div, 84-87, GEOL ADV, INT EXPLOR, CONOCO, INC, 87- *Personal Data:* b Chicago, Ill, Oct 3, 49; M 95, Kay Scott Goss. *Educ:* Univ Ill, Urbana, BS, 71, MS, 73; Monash Univ, Australia, PhD(struct geol), 77. *Prof Exp:* Asst prof geol, State Univ NY, Stony Brook, 76-81. *Concurrent Pos:* Vis prof, Field Camp Wyo, Univ Mo, Columbia, 80 & Univ Ill, 81. *Mem:* Geol Soc Am; Am Geophys Union; AAAS; Sigma Xi; Am Asn Petrol Geol. *Res:* Evolution of structural geometries; geotectonics. *Mailing Add:* Conoco Inc Advan Explor Orgn 600 N Dairy Ashford Houston TX 77079. *Fax:* 281-558-1256; *E-Mail:* granath@ibm.net

GRANATO, ANDREW VINCENT, PHYSICS, DISLOCATIONS & INTERSTITIALS. *Current Pos:* res asst prof, 57-59, assoc prof, 61-64, PROF PHYSICS, UNIV ILL, URBANA, 64- *Personal Data:* b Cleveland, Ohio, May 9, 26; m 56, Pauline Brassard; c Sam, Andrea, Sarah & Ann. *Educ:* Rensselaer Polytech Inst, BS, 48, MS, 50; Brown Univ, PhD(appl math), 55. *Honors & Awards:* Alexander von Humboldt US Sr Scientist Award, 76. *Prof Exp:* Res assoc appl math, Brown Univ, 53-57. *Concurrent Pos:* Guggenheim Found fel, Ger, 59-60; vis prof, Aachen Tech Univ, 60-61; Berndit Matthiar Scholar, Los Alamos Nat Lab, 87-88. *Mem:* Fel Am Phys Soc; Acoust Soc Am; Mat Res Soc; Inst Elec & Electronics Engrs; Am Inst Mech Engrs. *Res:* Ultrasonic wave propagation; dislocations in crystals; radiation damage; liquid and amorphous states. *Mailing Add:* Physics Dept Univ Ill 1110 W Green St Urbana IL 61801. *Fax:* 217-333-9819; *E-Mail:* chancesa@uxl.cso.uiuc.edu

GRANATSTEIN, VICTOR LAWRENCE, PLASMA PHYSICS, MICROWAVE PHYSICS. *Current Pos:* PROF ELEC ENG, 83-, DIR, INST FOR PLASMA RES, UNIV MD, 88- *Personal Data:* b Toronto, Ont, Feb 8, 35; m 55; c 3. *Educ:* Columbia Univ, BS, 60, MS, 61, PhD(eng, plasma physics), 63. *Honors & Awards:* E O Hulburt Award, 80; R D Conrad Gold Medal Award Sci Achievement, 81; Plasma Sci & Applications Award, Inst Elec & Electronics Engrs, 91. *Prof Exp:* Res assoc plasma waves, Columbia Univ, 63-64; mem tech staff, Bell Tel Labs, Inc, 64-72; head high power electromagnetic radiation br, Plasma Physics Div, Naval Res Lab, 72-83. *Concurrent Pos:* Vis sr lect, Dept Physics, Hebrew Univ, Jerusalem, 69-70; Vis prof, Dept Elec Eng, Tel Aviv Univ, 94. *Mem:* Fel Inst Elec & Electronics Engr; fel Am Phys Soc. *Res:* Microwave generation with intense relativistic electron beams; millimeter and submillimeter wave generation; radiofrequency plasma heating; turbulence of fluids and plasmas; electromagnetic propagation through random media; plasma waves; free electron lasers; gyrotrons; radiofrequency sources for TeV linear colliders. *Mailing Add:* Lab Plasma Res Univ Md College Park MD 20742

GRANBERG, CHARLES BOYD, PHARMACY, PHARMACOLOGY. *Current Pos:* RETIRED. *Personal Data:* b Wessington, SDak, May 6, 21; m 55; c 3. *Educ:* SDak State Col, BS, 42; Univ Ill, MS, 47; PhD(pharmacol), 50. *Prof Exp:* Instr pharm, Univ Ill, 47-49; prof pharm, Drake Univ, 50-84, dean, col Pharm, 77-84. *Concurrent Pos:* Ed, Am J Pharmaceut Educ, 61-74. *Res:* Gastrointestinal x-ray contrast media; pharmacodynamics. *Mailing Add:* 4105 Plumwood Dr West Des Moines IA 50265

GRANBERRY, DARBIE MERWIN, PLANT BREEDING. *Current Pos:* asst prof exten hort, Attapulgus Exten-Res Ctr, 76-, PROF HORT, UNIV GA. *Personal Data:* b Dothan, Ala, Jan 23, 43; m 62; c 2. *Educ:* Auburn Univ, BS, 68, ME, 69, PhD(plant breeding), 75. *Prof Exp:* Teaching asst, Dept Voc & Adult Educ, Auburn Univ, 68-69, res asst, Dept Hort, 69-72; res assoc hort, Dept Plant & Soil Sci, Tuskegee Inst, 72-75; asst prof, Edisto Br Res Sta, Clemson Univ, 75-76. *Mem:* Am Soc Hort Sci; Am Phytopath Soc; AAAS. *Res:* Increase efficiency of existing vegetable production and determine the potential of other vegetable crops not presently commercially produced in Georgia. *Mailing Add:* Rural Dev Ctr PO Box 1209 Tifton GA 31793

GRANBORG, BERTIL SVANTE MIKAEL, ELECTRICAL ENGINEERING. *Current Pos:* ASSOC PROF ELEC ENG, UNIV HAWAII, 64- *Personal Data:* b Stockholm, Sweden, Aug 9, 23; US citizen; m 63; c 1. *Educ:* Royal Inst Technol, Sweden, MS, 53; Univ Wis, PhD(elec eng, math), 61. *Prof Exp:* Invest engr, Swed State Power Bd, 53-56; instr elec eng, Univ Wis, 56-60; res engr, Gen Elec Co, 61-63. *Concurrent Pos:* Mem staff, high tension lab, Royal Inst Technol, Sweden, 51-52 & high tension & short circuit labs, Electricite de France, 52; vis teacher, Trade Sch Math, Sweden, 54-55; Nat Res Coun sr resident res assoc with vis scientist, Manned Spacecraft Ctr, NASA, 70-71. *Mem:* Inst Elec & Electronics Engrs; Swed Asn Eng & Architects. *Res:* Automatic feedback control; industrial process control; steel mill and steam station automation; power production, distribution and control; magnetic materials. *Mailing Add:* Dept Elec Eng Univ Hawaii Honolulu HI 96822

GRANCHELLI, FELIX EDWARD, MEDICINAL CHEMISTRY. *Current Pos:* SUPVR & SR STAFF MEM, NEW ENG NUCLEAR, 77- *Personal Data:* b Cambridge, Mass, Oct 22, 23; m 48; c 4. *Educ:* Northeastern Univ, BS, 48, PhD(med chem), 72; Boston Univ, MA, 50. *Prof Exp:* Sr staff res & develop chem, Arthur D Little Inc, 51-75; sr scientist med chem, Col Pharm, Northeastern Univ, 75-77. *Concurrent Pos:* Consult, Arthur D Little Inc, 75-. *Mem:* Am Chem Soc; Sigma Xi. *Res:* Synthesis of heterocyclics, chiefly alkaloids, as potential antitumor agents, central nervous system drugs and antifertility compounds; dopaminergic, anti-Parkinsonian and analgesic activities; radiochemical synthesis utilizing 14C and 3H isotopes. *Mailing Add:* 120 Spring St Arlington MA 02174-7949

GRANCHI, MICHAEL PATRICK, MICROCHEMICAL ANALYSIS, CHROMATOGRAPHY. *Current Pos:* ASSOC CHEMIST, MOBIL RES & DEVELOP CORP, 77- *Personal Data:* b Uniontown, Pa, June 6, 46; m 72; c 1. *Educ:* Waynesburg Col, BS, 68; Univ Pittsburgh, PhD(inorg chem), 77. *Mem:* Am Chem Soc. *Res:* Chromatography, microchemical analysis, laboratory automation. *Mailing Add:* 636 Howard Ave Pitman NJ 08071-1833

GRAND, RICHARD JOSEPH, PEDIATRICS. *Current Pos:* res fel med, 69-70, asst prof, 70-76, ASSOC PROF PEDIAT, HARVARD MED SCH, 76-; CHIEF, DIV GASTROENTEROL, CHILDREN'S HOSP MED CTR, BOSTON, 75-, SR ASSOC MED, 76- *Personal Data:* b New York, NY, Feb 1, 37; c 3. *Educ:* Harvard Univ, BA, 58; NY Univ, MD, 62. *Prof Exp:* Intern, Bellevue Hosp, New York, 62-63; jr asst resident, Children's Hosp Med Ctr, Boston, 63-64, teaching fel pediat, 66-67, fel med, 67-70. *Concurrent Pos:* Med Found Res Award, NIH, 70, Nat Res Serv Award, 70-71; Acad Career Develop Award, Nat Inst Arthritis, Metab & Digestive Dis, 72-76; assoc med, Children's Hosp Med Ctr, Boston, 70-76; asst pediat, Beth Israel Hosp, Boston, 72-; asst pediatrician, 72, consult pediatrician, Boston Hosp Women, 76- *Mem:* Am Acad Pediat; Am Fedn Clin Res; NY Acad Sci; Soc Pediat Res; Am Gastroenterol Asn. *Mailing Add:* Div GI Nutr Dept Pediat New England Med Ctr 750 Washington St Box 213 Boston MA 02111. *Fax:* 617-350-8388

GRAND, STANLEY, BIOCHEMISTRY. *Current Pos:* CONSULT CLIN CHEM, STANLEY GRAND INC, 74- *Personal Data:* b Paterson, NJ, Jan 5, 27; m 47; c 2. *Educ:* NY Univ, BS, 48; Polytech Inst Brooklyn, PhD(phys chem), 51. *Prof Exp:* Sect leader analytical chem, Mineral Benefits Lab, Columbia Univ, 54-57; dir res & develop, Radiation Res Corp, 57-60; head dept chem & physics, W Orange Lab, Vitro Labs, 60-66; vpres, Nuclear Res Assocs, Inc, 66-71; dir labs, Brooklyn-Cumberland Med Ctr, 71-73. *Mem:* Am Chem Soc; Am Asn Clin Chem; Clin Ligand Assay Soc. *Res:* High temperature materials and coatings; nuclear weapons effects, arcs and plasmas; clinical chemistry methods. *Mailing Add:* 2040 Wellington Ct Westbury NY 11590

GRAND, STEPHEN P, SEISMOLOGY, EARTH STRUCTURE. *Current Pos:* asst prof, 88-93, ASSOC PROF GEOPHYS, UNIV TEX, 93- *Personal Data:* b Montreal, Que, Mar 21, 57. *Educ:* McGill Univ, Can, BS, 78; Calif Inst Technol, PhD(geophys), 86. *Prof Exp:* Asst prof geophys, Univ Ill, Urbana, 86-88. *Mem:* Am Geophys Union. *Mailing Add:* Dept Geophys Univ Tex Austin TX 78712. *Fax:* 512-471-9425; *E-Mail:* steveq@maestvo.geo.utexas.edu

GRAND, THEODORE I, GROSS ANATOMY. *Current Pos:* RES ASSOC, DEPT ZOOL RES, NAT ZOO, SMITHSONIAN INST, 83- *Personal Data:* b Newark, NJ, Feb 10, 38. *Educ:* Brown Univ, BA, 59; Univ Calif, Berkeley, PhD(anthrop), 64. *Prof Exp:* Asst scientist phys anthrop, Ore Regional Primate Res Ctr, 63-66, assoc scientist, 67-78, scientist, 78-83. *Concurrent Pos:* Vis asst prof, Univ Ore, 65, vis lectr, 74; vis lectr, Univ Western Australia, 69; res assoc, Smithsonian Inst, 76 & 80-81; vis fel, Cornell Univ, 78; vis prof, Univ Colo, 79, NECOM, 84-88; adj assoc prof anat, Uniformed Serv Univ Health Sci, 91- *Res:* Comparative anatomy of musculo-skeletal system; primate anatomy and evolution; history of anatomy; growth and development of mammals. *Mailing Add:* Dept Zool Res Nat Zoo Washington DC 20008. *Fax:* 202-673-4748

GRANDA, ALLEN MANUEL, VISION, SENSORY PROCESSES. *Current Pos:* assoc prof, 65-71, dir, Inst Neurosci, 75-84, PROF NEUROSCI, UNIV DEL, 71- *Personal Data:* b Belvedere, Calif, Feb 20, 29; div; c 3. *Educ:* Univ Calif, Los Angeles, AB, 50; Brown Univ, PhD, 59. *Honors & Awards:* Humboldt Prize. *Prof Exp:* Res physiologist, Walter Reed Army Inst Res, 58-65. *Concurrent Pos:* Vis prof, Sch Med, Keio Univ, Japan, 71-72; vis prof, Physiol Inst, Free Univ Berlin, 78-79; lectr, Taniguchi Found Int; vis prof, Nat Res Coun, Pisa, Italy. *Mem:* Sigma Xi; Asn Res Vision & Ophthal; Soc Neurosci. *Res:* Vision; sensory processes. *Mailing Add:* Sch Life Sci Univ Del Newark DE 19716-0001

GRANDAGE, ARNOLD HERBERT EDWARD, EXPERIMENTAL STATISTICS. *Current Pos:* RETIRED. *Personal Data:* b Springfield, Mass, Nov 12, 18; m 45; c 2. *Educ:* Lehigh Univ, BA, 42; NC State Col, PhD(statist), 54. *Prof Exp:* From assoc prof to prof statist, NC State Univ, 55-81. *Concurrent Pos:* Consult var industs & govt agencies. *Mem:* Biomet Soc; Sigma Xi. *Res:* Industrial, physical science, behavioral science and highway construction applications of statistics; use of computers in statistics. *Mailing Add:* 2600 Barracks Rd Charlottesville VA 22901

GRANDEL, EUGENE ROBERT, DENTISTRY. *Current Pos:* PVT PRACT, 93- *Personal Data:* b Chicago, Ill, Jan 16, 33; m 62; c 2. *Educ:* Univ Ill, BS, 56, DDS, 58, MS, 62. *Prof Exp:* Instr oral path, Univ Ill, 61-63; asst prof, Sch Dent, Loyola Univ Chicago, 63-68, assoc prof oral path, 68-80, assoc prof pedodont, 70-80, prof, 80-93. *Mem:* Am Acad Oral Path; Int Asn Dent Res; Sigma Xi. *Res:* Cytology; histochemistry; enzymatic cytology. *Mailing Add:* 475 W 55th Countryside IL 60525

GRANDHI, RAJA RATNAM, ANIMAL NUTRITION. *Current Pos:* RES SCIENTIST SWINE NUTRIT, AGR CAN RES STA, BRANDON, MAN, 77- *Personal Data:* b Kullur, India, July 1, 38; Can citizen; m 61, Anna; c Rajendra & Sumathi. *Educ:* Venkateswara Univ, India, BVSc, 60; Univ Guelph, Ont, MSc, 70, PhD(animal nutrit), 73. *Prof Exp:* Vet asst surg & animal husb exten officer, Dept Animal Husb, Ministry Agr & Food, India, 61-68; dir animal nutrit, Agron Consult Ltd, Ont, 73-74; res assoc, Dept Animal Sci, Univ Guelph, 74-77. *Mem:* Can Soc Animal Sci; Agr Inst Can; Am Soc Animal Sci; Am Registry Prof Animal Scientists. *Res:* Nutrition and physiology; study of nutritional and metabolic factors and interrelationships affecting the nutrition and reproduction of domestic animals (swine). *Mailing Add:* Agr Can Res Sta PO Box 1000A Brandon MB R7A 5Y3 Can. *Fax:* 204-728-3858; *E-Mail:* rgrandhi@im.agr.ca

GRANDI, STEVEN ALDRIDGE, ASTRONOMY. *Current Pos:* AT NAT OPTICAL ASTRON OBSERV, ARIZ. *Personal Data:* b Santa Monica, Calif, Nov 9, 50. *Educ:* Calif Inst Technol, BS, 72; Univ Ariz, PhD(astron), 75. *Prof Exp:* Res astronr, Lick Observ, Univ Calif, Santa Cruz, 76-78; asst prof astron, Univ Calif, Los Angeles, 78- *Mem:* Am Astron Asn. *Res:* Observational and theoretical studies of QSOs, Seyfert galaxies, H II regions, planetary nebulae and other emission line objects. *Mailing Add:* KPNO PO Box 26732 Tucson AZ 85726

GRANDJEAN, CARTER JULES, BIOCHEMISTRY, PHARMACOLOGY. *Current Pos:* ASSOC PROF PEDIAT & BIOCHEM, UNIV NEBR MED CTR, OMAHA. *Personal Data:* b Socorro, NMex, Sept 10, 41; m 70; c 2. *Educ:* NMex Inst Mining & Technol, BS, 65; Tex Tech Univ, MS, 68, PhD(biochem), 70. *Prof Exp:* Trainee, Eppley Cancer Inst & Col Pharm, Univ Nebr Med Ctr, from asst prof to assoc prof cancer res, 71-79; mem staff, Midwest Res Inst, 79- *Concurrent Pos:* NIH res grant, 73. *Mem:* Am Chem Soc; Am Soc Pharmacol & Exp Therapeut; Am Inst Chemists; AAAS; Am Asn Cancer Res. *Res:* Basic biochemical studies concerning the mechanisms of biological activation of probable environmental chemical carcinogens such as polycyclic aromatic hydrocarbons and N-nitrosamines; pharmacokinetics of xenobiotics and carcinogens and their metabolism in rodents. *Mailing Add:* 3908 N 110th Plaza Omaha NE 68164

GRANDOLFO, MARIAN CARMELA, PETROLEUM ENGINEERING. *Current Pos:* COMPUT CONSULT & TEACHER, DATA DETECHTIVE, 84- *Personal Data:* b Chicago, Ill, May 27, 43; m 78; c 1. *Educ:* Marquette Univ, BS, 65; Univ Notre Dame, MS, 72, PhD(inorg chem), 74. *Prof Exp:* Technician chem, Mt Sinai Hosp, 65; sci asst, Argonne Nat Lab, 65-69; sr chemist anal chem, Anal & Info Div, Exxon Res & Eng Co, 74-82. *Mem:* Soc Appl Spectros; Am Chem Soc. *Res:* Vibrational analysis of carbonates and transition metal and lanthanide trifluorides; chromatography of naturally occurring substances and investigation of their structure; analysis of petroleum, its fractions; inorganic, organic and polymeric materials; method development to aid in functional group analysis. *Mailing Add:* 15 King St Fanwood NJ 07023

GRANDTNER, MIROSLAV MARIAN, FOREST ECOLOGY, DENDROLOGY. *Current Pos:* asst forest ecol, Laval Univ, 57-58, from asst prof to assoc prof bot, 58-67, prof 67-93, EMER PROF ECOL, LAVAL UNIV, 93- *Personal Data:* b Liptovska-Teplicka, Slovak, Aug 23, 28; Can citizen; div; c Anne-Marie. *Educ:* Univ Louvain, Ing E & F, 55, Dr Sc(agron), 62; Laval Univ, MSc, 59. *Prof Exp:* Chief cartographer, Ctr Phytosociol Mapping, Belg, 56-57. *Concurrent Pos:* Consult, Eastern Que Mgt Off, 63-66; asst ed, Le Naturaliste Can, 68-79; lectr, Univ Montreal & Univ Que Rimuski, 71-93; chmn, Port-au-Saumon Ecol Ctr, 73-87; coed, Phytocoenologia, 74-; ed, World Dict Trees, Laval Univ, 89- & Etudes Ecol, Dossiers Foresteri Int, 90- *Mem:* Int Asn Veg Sci. *Res:* Forest ecology, Dendrology and phytosociology; vegetation mapping; contributor of numerous articles to research and professional journals. *Mailing Add:* Wood & Forest Sci Laval Univ Quebec PQ G1K 7P4 Can

GRANDY, CHARLES CREED, MATHEMATICS, PHYSICS. *Current Pos:* PRES, MC GROUP INC, 90- *Personal Data:* b Alamosa, Colo, Dec 6, 28; m 51, 83; c 6. *Educ:* Colo State Univ, BS, 52; Northeastern Univ, MS, 62; Am Univ, MS, 84. *Prof Exp:* Mem tech staff digital comput applns, Lincoln Lab, Mass Inst Technol, 52-58, assoc group leader air defense systs, 58; head, Dept Systs Testing & Eval, Mitre Corp, 58-60 & Dept Command & Control Systs, 60-62, assoc tech dir systs eng, 62-65, systs planning, 65-67, tech dir, Nat Command & Control Systs Div, 67-71, asst vpres, Washington Opers, 71-72, vpres, Civil Systs Div, 72-90. *Mem:* AAAS; Math Asn Am; Soc Indust & Appl Math; Am Inst Aeronaut & Astronaut. *Res:* Applications of digital computers to real time control problems; systems engineering in military command and control systems; operations research; statistical inference and experimental design. *Mailing Add:* HC 75 PO Box 626B Locust Grove VA 22508

GRANDY, WALTER THOMAS, JR, THEORETICAL PHYSICS. *Current Pos:* from asst prof to assoc prof, 63-69, chmn dept, 71-78, PROF PHYSICS, UNIV WYO, 69- *Personal Data:* b Philadelphia, Pa, June 1, 33; m 58, Patricia Langan; c Christopher, Neal, Susan & Jeanne. *Educ:* Univ Colo, BS, 60, PhD(physics), 64. *Prof Exp:* Phys sci aide, Nat Bur Stand, Colo, 58-60, mathematician, 60-61, physicist, 61-63. *Concurrent Pos:* Fulbright scholar, Brazil, 66-67; vis prof, Univ Sao Paulo, Brazil, 82, Univ Tubingen, Ger, 78-79 & Univ Sydney, Australia, 88. *Mem:* Am Asn Physics Teachers; Am Phys Soc; AAAS. *Res:* Electrodynamics; nonequilibrium statistical mechanics. *Mailing Add:* Dept Physics & Astron Univ Wyo Laramie WY 82071. *E-Mail:* wtg@uwyo.edu

GRANEAU, PETER, ELECTRICAL ENGINEERING, PHYSICS. *Current Pos:* PRES RES & DEVELOP, UNDERGROUND POWER CORP, 70- *Personal Data:* b Mar 13, 21; Brit citizen; m 55, Brigitte Weil; c Neal. *Educ:* Univ Nottingham, BScEE, 55, PhD(elec eng), 62. *Prof Exp:* Dept head instr & control, BICC Res Lab, Eng, 55-62, asst res mgr elec eng & physics, 62-67; tech dir cable res, Simplex Wire & Cable Co, Mass, 67-70. *Concurrent Pos:* Consult, A D Little Inc, 71-76, Lincoln Lab, Mass Inst Technol, 73-75; vis scientist, Nat Magnetic Lab, Mass Inst Technol, 72-; vis prof, Northeastern Univ, 84-90, res fel, 90- *Mem:* Fel Brit Inst Physics; Inst Elec & Electronics Engrs. *Res:* Underground power transmission; conductor metal; dielectrics for high voltage cables; electromagnetism; superconductors; inertia; Newtonian physics; electrodynamics. *Mailing Add:* 205 Holden Wood Rd Concord MA 01742. *Fax:* 978-369-7936

GRANET, IRVING, MECHANICAL & NUCLEAR ENGINEERING. *Current Pos:* from asst prof to assoc prof, 77-82, PROF MECH ENG TECHNOL, QUEENSBOROUGH COMMUNITY COL, CITY UNIV NEW YORK, 82- *Personal Data:* b New York, NY, July 2, 24; m 51; c 3. *Educ:* Cooper Union, BME, 44; Polytech Inst Brooklyn, MME, 48. *Prof Exp:* Proj engr, Res Dept, Foster Wheeler Corp, 47-53, sr engr, Nuclear Energy Dept, 53-55, dir staff eng, 55-59; assoc scientist plasma propulsion proj, Repub Aviation Corp, 59-64 & Power Conversion Div, 64-70, proj mgr, Repub Aviation Div, Fairchild-Hiller Corp, 70-73; vpres & chief engr, EMS Develop Corp, NY, 73-76; assoc prof mech eng, NY Inst Technol, 76-77. *Concurrent Pos:* Instr, Polytech Inst Brooklyn, 51-52; adj asst prof, C W Post Col, Long Island, 59-; adj assoc prof, NY Inst Technol, 68- *Mem:* Am Soc Mech Engrs; Nat Soc Prof Engrs; NY Acad Sci; Am Soc Naval Engrs; Am Soc Eng Educ. *Res:* Physics; heat transfer and fluid mechanics; applied magnetohydrodynamics and space propulsion; thermodynamics. *Mailing Add:* 1375 Anchor Dr Wantagh NY 11793

GRANEY, DANIEL O, ANATOMY. *Current Pos:* From instr to asst prof, 66-74, ASSOC PROF BIOL STRUCT, SCH MED, UNIV WASH, 74- *Personal Data:* b Los Angeles, Calif, Oct 29, 36; m 60; c 2. *Educ:* Univ Calif, Berkeley, AB, 58, Univ Calif, San Francisco, MA, 62, PhD(anat), 65. *Mem:* Am Asn Anat; Am Soc Cell Biol. *Res:* Fine structure of gastrointestinal absorption and secretion; transport by capillary endothelia; clinical anatomy. *Mailing Add:* Dept Biol Structure Univ Wash Sch Med Seattle WA 98195-0001

GRANGE, RAYMOND A, THERMOMECHANICAL TREATMENT. *Current Pos:* RETIRED. *Personal Data:* b Darlington, Wis, Aug 14, 10. *Educ:* Univ Wis-Madison, BS, 35. *Prof Exp:* Scientist, US Steel, 38-74, sr scientist, 69-74. *Mem:* Am Soc Metals Int. *Mailing Add:* 4733 Flournoy Valley Roseburg OR 97470

GRANGER, CARL V, PHYSICAL MEDICINE & REHABILITATION. *Current Pos:* HEAD, REHAB MED, BUFFALO GEN HOSP, 83-, PROF REHAB, STATE UNIV NY, BUFFALO, 83- *Personal Data:* b Brooklyn, NY, Nov 26, 28, m 95, Eloise Morrow; c Glenn & Marilyn. *Educ:* Dartmouth Col, AB, 48; NY Univ, MD, 52. *Hon Degrees:* MA, Brown Univ. *Honors & Awards:* Krusen Award, Am Acad Phys Med & Rehab, 94. *Prof Exp:* Asst chief phys med, Letterman Gen Hosp, 58-61; from instr to asst prof, Sch Med, Yale Univ, 61-67, assoc clin prof, 67-68; assoc dir dept phys med, New Haven Hosp, 61-66, actg chief, 66-67; prof phys & rehab med & chmn dept, Sch Med, Tufts Univ, 68-77; dir phys med & rehab, Mem Hosp, Pawtucket, 78-83; prof community health, phys med & rehab, Brown Univ, 78-83. *Concurrent Pos:* Survey consult, Comn Accreditation of Rehab Facil, 68; mem expert med comt, Am Rehab Found, 68; physiatrist in chief, New Eng Med Ctr Hosp, 68-77; mem adv bd, Nat Multiple Sclerosis Soc, 69-75. *Mem:* Am Asn Electromyog & Electrodiag (pres, 68-69); Am Cong Rehab Med; Am Acad Phys Med & Rehab (pres, 75-76); Asn Acad Physiatrists. *Res:* Electrodiagnosis; peripheral nerve disorders; patient care outcome measures; braces and splints. *Mailing Add:* Erie Co Med Ctr 462 Grider St Buffalo NY 14215-3021. *Fax:* 716-829-2080; *E-Mail:* granger@acsu.buffalo.edu

GRANGER, D NIEL, OXYGEN RADICALS, MICROCIRCULATION. *Current Pos:* PROF PHYSIOL, UNIV S ALA, 78- *Educ:* Univ Miss, PhD(physiol), 77. *Mailing Add:* Dept Physiol LSU Med Ctr 15011 Kings Hwy PO Box 33932 Shreveport LA 71130-3932. *Fax:* 318-675-6005

GRANGER, DONALD LEE, infectious diseases, for more information see previous edition

GRANGER, GALE A, MICROBIOLOGY. *Current Pos:* From asst prof to assoc prof, 67-73, PROF IMMUNOL & MICROBIOL, UNIV CALIF, IRVINE, 73- *Personal Data:* b San Pedro, Calif, June 18, 37; m 60; c 2. *Educ:* Univ Wash, BS, 62, MS, 63, PhD(microbiol), 65. *Prof Exp:* NIH res grants & career develop award, 67- *Mem:* Am Asn Cancer Res; Am Asn Immunol; NY Acad Sci. *Res:* Immunology; cell biology especially in vitro studies of immune cell induced graft cell destruction; cellular and sub cellular mechanisms. *Mailing Add:* Dept Molecular Biol & Biochem Univ Calif Irvine CA 92717-3900. *Fax:* 714-856-5048

GRANGER, HARRIS JOSEPH, MICROCIRCULATION. *Current Pos:* assoc prof, 76-78, PROF PHYSIOL, TEX A&M UNIV, 78-, HEAD DEPT, 82- *Personal Data:* b Erath, La, Aug 26, 44; M, Ramona A Vice; c Ashley, Jarrod & Brent. *Educ:* Univ Southwestern La, BS, 66; Univ Miss, PhD(physiol), 70. *Honors & Awards:* Harold Lamport Award, Am Physiol Soc, 78; Merit Award, Nat Heart Lung & Blood Inst, 87. *Prof Exp:* From asst prof to assoc prof physiol, Univ Miss Med Ctr, 70-76. *Concurrent Pos:* Vis assoc prof, Univ Calif, San Diego, La Jolla, 75-76; Res Career Develop Award, Nat Heart Lung & Blood Inst, 78-83; dir, Microcirculation Res Inst, Tex A&M Univ, 81; mem study sect, NIH Exp Cardiovasc Sci Study Sect, 82-86 & 88-; assoc ed, Am J Physiol, 87-93, ed 93- *Mem:* Microcirculatory Soc; Am Physiol Soc. *Res:* Contributed articles to professional journals. *Mailing Add:* Microcirculation Res Inst Col Med Tex A&M Univ College Station TX 77843-4114. *Fax:* 409-847-8635

GRANGER, JOEY PAUL, CARDIOVASCULAR & RENAL PHYSIOLOGY. *Current Pos:* ASSOC PROF PHYSIOL, EASTERN VA MED SCH, 88- *Educ:* Univ Miss, PhD(physiol), 83. *Prof Exp:* Asst prof physiol, Mayo Med Sch, 83-88. *Mailing Add:* Dept Physiol & Biophys Univ Miss Med Sch 2500 N State St Jackson MS 39216-4505. *Fax:* 601-984-1817

GRANGER, JOHN VAN NUYS, ELECTRONICS ENGINEERING. *Current Pos:* RETIRED. *Personal Data:* b Cedar Rapids, Iowa, Sept 14, 18; m 45, 83; c 3. *Educ:* Cornell Col, AB, 41; Harvard Univ, MS, 42, PhD(physics), 48. *Prof Exp:* Instr math, Cornell Col, 41; res assoc, Harvard Univ, 42-47; head, Radio Systs Lab, Stanford Res Inst, 49-53, asst dir, Eng Div, 53-56; pres, Granger Assocs, 56-70; dep dir, Bur Int Sci & Technol Affairs, US Dept State, 71-74; dep asst dir, NSF, 74-77; counr sci & technol, US Embassy, London, 77-81; sci attache, US Permanent Deleg, UNESCO, 81-83. *Mem:* Nat Acad Eng; Sigma Xi; fel Inst Elec & Electronics Engrs (pres, 71). *Res:* Antennas and propagation; communications systems; science policy; technical management. *Mailing Add:* No 6 Roberts Close Stratton Cirencester 072RP England

GRANGER, ROBERT A, II, MATHEMATICAL PHYSICS, FLUID DYNAMICS. *Current Pos:* PROF ENG, US NAVAL ACAD, 60- *Personal Data:* b Evanston, Ill, Aug 7, 28; m 51, Ruth Nickerson; c Erin & Alyson. *Educ:* Pomona Col, BA, 55; Drexel Inst Technol, MS, 59; Univ Md, PhD(physics), 70. *Prof Exp:* Res scientist aeroelasticity, Martin Co, Md, 55-60. *Concurrent Pos:* Consult, US Naval Reserve Officer Candidate Sch, Md, 64-, Trident Eng Assoc, Md, 65-, Bay-Tech Eng, Md, 69-70 & Cadcom Inc, Md, 70-; guest lectr, Royal Aircraft Estab, Eng, & Munich Tech Univ, 68-69 & Eugenides Found, 70-71; prin engr & consult, Boeing Com Airplane Co, Wash, 75; vis prof, Univ Petrol & Minerals, Dhahran, Saudi Arabia, 77-79; organizer & dir, lect ser vortex dynamics, Von Karman Fluid Dynamics Inst, 86; vis prof mech eng, Yale Univ, 90. *Mem:* Hon mem Inst Mod Physics Greece; Am Inst Aeronaut & Astronaut. *Res:* Applied and theoretical mathematical physics; boundary layer research; vortex dynamics; solutions of Navier-Stokes equations; experimental fluid dynamics; turbulence; author of 15 books and over 400 technical papers. *Mailing Add:* Dept Mech Eng US Naval Acad Annapolis MD 21402. *E-Mail:* granger@arctic.hadn.navy.mil

GRANICK, STEVE, POLYMER SURFACES, TRIBOLOGY. *Current Pos:* from asst prof to assoc prof, 85-96, PROF, DEPT MAT SCI, UNIV ILL, URBANA-CHAMPAIGN, 96- *Personal Data:* b Hanover, NH, July 10, 53; m 78, Helen Lau; c Bruce & Martin. *Educ:* Princeton Univ, BA, 78; Univ Wis-Madison, PhD(chem), 82. *Honors & Awards:* Spec Creativity Award, NSF, 93. *Prof Exp:* Researcher, Col France, 82-83 & Univ Minn, 83-84. *Concurrent Pos:* Sabbatical scholar, Kyoto Univ, 94. *Mem:* Am Chem Soc; fel Am Phys Soc; Mat Res Soc; Soc Rheology. *Res:* Macromolecules, especially at interfaces; surface and colloid chemistry; diffusion, surface forces and tribology. *Mailing Add:* Dept Mat Sci Univ Ill Urbana IL 61801. *E-Mail:* sgranick@uiuc.edu

GRANIK, ALEX T, RELATIVISTIC HYDRODYNAMICS, QUANTUM MECHANICS. *Current Pos:* ASSOC PROF PHYSICS, UNIV PAC, 82- *Personal Data:* m, Rita Vizitei. *Educ:* Odessa Inst Technol, USSR, MSc, 61; Odessa Univ, USSR, PhD(theoret & math physics), 68. *Prof Exp:* Res scientist, Odessa Inst Technol, USSR, 70-77; appln programmer, PBL Assocs, 78-79; assoc prof physics, Ky State Univ, 79-82. *Concurrent Pos:* Vis scientist, Lawrence Livermore Nat Lab, 84, consult, 84-90; vis fel, Ames Res Ctr, NASA, Mt View, Calif, 87. *Mem:* Soc Photo-Instrumentation Engrs. *Res:* Relativistic flows related to astrophysical phenomena; Clifford algebra and its application in quantum mechanics; fuzzy logic to quantum mechanics; foundations of quantum mechanics. *Mailing Add:* 1905 Iron Peak Ct Antioch CA 94509

GRANIRER, EDMOND, MATHEMATICS. *Current Pos:* PROF MATH, UNIV BC, 65- *Personal Data:* b Constantsa, Romania, Feb 19, 35. *Educ:* Hebrew Univ, MSc, 59, PhD(math), 62. *Prof Exp:* Prof math, Univ Ill, 62-63 & Cornell Univ, 64-65. *Concurrent Pos:* Sr mem, Killiam fel, 86-87. *Mem:* Fel Royal Soc Can; Acad Sci Can; Can Math Soc; Am Math Soc. *Res:* Harmonic analysis and functional analysis. *Mailing Add:* Dept Math Univ BC 1984 Math Rd Vancouver BC V6T 1Z2 Can

GRANITO, CHARLES EDWARD, CHEMISTRY, INFORMATION SCIENCE. *Current Pos:* PRES & CHIEF RES EXEC, INT PROD CORP, 81- *Personal Data:* b Brooklyn, NY, Nov 14, 37; m 59; c 3. *Educ:* Univ Miami, BS, 60, MS, 62. *Prof Exp:* Chemist, Indust Liaison Off, US Army Res Labs, Edgewood Arsenal, Md, 62-66; from chemist to sr res chemist T R Evans Res Ctr, Diamond Shamrock Corp, 66-69; mgr info serv, Inst Sci Info, 69-70, dir chem info serv, 70-72; consult, C G Assocs, 73-75; pres, Chem Info Mgt, Inc, 75-80. *Mem:* AAAS; Am Chem Soc; Chem Notation Asn (vpres, 68, pres, 69); Sigma Xi; Soap & Detergent Asn; President's Asn. *Res:* Organic chemistry; physical chemistry. *Mailing Add:* 1948 Cardinal Lake Dr Cherry Hill NJ 08003-2598

GRANNAN, RALPH T, PHYSICS. *Current Pos:* PROF, DEPT PHYSICS, COL OF THE DESERT, PALM DESERT, CALIF, 71- *Personal Data:* b Cincinnati, Ohio, Nov 2, 33. *Educ:* Univ Calif, Riverside, BS, 68, MS, 69. *Mem:* Math Asn Am; Am Phy Soc. *Res:* Physics. *Mailing Add:* 558 Bruin Dr Riverside CA 92507

GRANNEMANN, W(AYNE) W(ILLIS), SOLID STATE PHYSICS, ELECTRICAL ENGINEERING. *Current Pos:* RETIRED. *Personal Data:* b New Haven, Mo, Oct 11, 23; m 47; c 3. *Educ:* Univ Tex, BS, 47, MA, 49, PhD(physics), 53. *Prof Exp:* Asst prof physics, Ark Polytech Col, 49-51; res physicist, Defense Res Lab, Tex, 52-53; res physicist, Calif Res Corp, Standard Oil Co, Calif, 53-56; assoc prof elec eng, Univ NMex, 56-63, Dir, Eng Exp Sta, 58-63, dir, Bur Eng Res, 60-71, prof, 63-87. *Concurrent Pos:* Consult, McAllister & Assocs, Inc & Sandia Corp. *Mem:* Inst Elec & Electronics Engrs. *Res:* Semiconductors; solid state devices; waves in solids; physical electronics; seismic instrumentation; radiation effects on electronics. *Mailing Add:* Star Rte PO Box 762A Sandia Park NM 87111

GRANNER, DARYL KITLEY, ENDOCRINOLOGY. *Current Pos:* asst prof, Univ Iowa, 70-72, assoc prof, 72-75, PROF MED & BIOCHEM & DIR, DIV ENDOCRINOL & METAB, UNIV IOWA, 75-, DIR, DIABETES & ENDOCRINOL RES CTR, 79-; PROF PHYSIOL, VANDERBILT UNIV. *Personal Data:* b Algona, Iowa, Dec 12, 36; m 58; c 2. *Educ:* Univ Iowa, BA, 58, MS & MD, 62. *Prof Exp:* Asst prof med, Univ Wis, 69-70. *Mem:* Endocrine Soc; Am Soc Biol Chemists; Am Fedn Clin Res; Am Soc Clin Invest; Asn Am Physicians. *Res:* Action of hormones such as insulin, glucocorticoids and cyclic nucleotides at the molecular level; pathophysiology of non-insulin dependent diabetes mellitus. *Mailing Add:* Dept Molecular Physiol & Biophys Vanderbilt Univ Med 707 Light Hall Nashville TN 37232-0615

GRANNIS, PAUL DUTTON, HADRONIC INTERACTIONS. *Current Pos:* from asst prof to assoc prof, 69-74, PROF PHYSICS, STATE UNIV NY, STONY BROOK, 74. *Personal Data:* b Dayton, Ohio, June 26, 38; m 72; c 4. *Educ:* Cornell Univ, BEng, 61; Univ Calif, Berkeley, PhD(physics), 65. *Prof Exp:* Res assoc, Lawrence Radiation Lab, Univ Calif, Berkeley, 65-66. *Concurrent Pos:* Vis scientist, Europ Ctr Nuclear Res, Geneva, 73; mem, High Energy Adv Comt, Brookhaven Nat Lab, 74-76; sr res fel, Sci Res Coun, UK, 76. *Mem:* Am Phys Soc. *Res:* Experimental high energy physics. *Mailing Add:* Dept Physics 3800 State Univ NY Stony Brook NY 11794

GRANOFF, ALLAN, VIROLOGY. *Current Pos:* chmn virol lab, St Jude Children's Res Hosp, 62-69, chmn biol, 65-69, chmn virol & immunol labs, 69-75, assoc dir, Basic Sci, 79-83, dep dir, 84-92, dir, 92-93, CHMN DEPT VIROL & MOLECULAR BIOL, ST JUDE CHILDREN'S RES HOSP, DEP DIR, 93- *Personal Data:* b New Haven, Conn, June 26, 23; c 4. *Educ:* Univ Conn, BS, 48; Univ Pa, MS, 49, PhD(virol), 52; Am Bd Med Microbiol, dipl. *Honors & Awards:* Stuart Mudd lectr, 87. *Prof Exp:* From asst to assoc, Div Infectious Dis, Pub Health Res Inst NY, 52-62. *Concurrent Pos:* From assoc prof to prof microbiol, Univ Tenn, Memphis, 62-85; mem, Virol Study Sect, NIH, 69-73, chmn, Small Bus Grants Study Sect, 85-90; assoc ed, Virol, 70-88, Intervirol, 73-90; mem, Virol & Cell Biol Study Sect, Am Cancer Soc, 76-79, Inst Grant Study Sect, 86-89. *Mem:* AAAS; Am Soc Microbiol; Soc Exp Biol & Med; Am Asn Cancer Res; Am Asn Immunol; Am Soc Virol. *Res:* Molecular biology of virus replication. *Mailing Add:* PO Box 318 Memphis TN 38101-0318. *Fax:* 901-523-2622

GRANOFF, BARRY, APPLIED MATHEMATICS. *Current Pos:* asst prof, 66-70, ASSOC PROF MATH, BOSTON UNIV, 70- *Personal Data:* b Jersey City, NJ, June 30, 38; m 89. *Educ:* Fairleigh Dickinson Univ, BS, 60; NY Univ, MS, 62, PhD(math), 65. *Prof Exp:* Assoc res scientist, Courant Inst Math Sci, NY Univ, 65-66. *Concurrent Pos:* Assoc prof math, Harvard Univ Summer Sch, 84-97. *Mem:* Soc Indust & Appl Math; Math Asn Am. *Res:* Applied mathematics and analysis, partial and ordinary differential equations, asymptotic methods, methods of mathematical physics; singular perturbation techniques. *Mailing Add:* Dept Math Boston Univ 111 Cummington St Boston MA 02215. *E-Mail:* bg@math.bu.edu

GRANOFF, BARRY, FUEL SCIENCE, CHEMICAL KINETICS. *Current Pos:* MEM TECH STAFF, SANDIA LABS, 69- *Personal Data:* b Brooklyn, NY, Sept 7, 40; m 65; c 2. *Educ:* City Col New York, BS, 62; Princeton Univ, MA, 64, PhD(x-ray crystallog), 66. *Prof Exp:* Res chemist, E I DuPont de Nemours & Co, Inc, 66-69. *Mem:* Am Chem Soc; Inst Elec & Electronics Engrs; Am Crystallog Asn; Sigma Xi. *Res:* Structure of carbon and graphite; oil shale conversion; pyrolysis kinetics; coal liquefaction; hydrodesulfurization; structure and reactivity of coal; hydrogenation. *Mailing Add:* 2219 Camino de los Artesanos NW Albuquerque NM 87107

GRANOFF, DAN MARTIN, IMMUNOGENETICS, HAEMOPHILUS INFLUENZAE. *Current Pos:* assoc prof, 80-85, PROF PEDIAT & ASSOC PROF MICROBIOL, WASH UNIV MED SCH, ST LOUIS, 85- *Personal Data:* b New York, NY, Jan 22, 44. *Educ:* Johns Hopkins Univ, AB, 65, MD, 68. *Prof Exp:* Intern, pediat, Children's Hosp, Philadelphia, 68-69; res pediat, Johns Hopkins Hosp, 69-71; fel infectious dis, Case Western Res Univ, 73-75; from instr to asst clin prof, pediat, Univ Calif, San Francisco, 76-79. *Concurrent Pos:* Dir, infectious dis, St Louis Children's Hosp, 80-; consult, Nat Acad Sci, 84-; assoc ed, Pediat Res, 89-; prin investr, NIH, 79- *Mem:* Am Soc Clin Invest; Infectious Dis Soc Am; Soc Pediat Res; Am Pediat Soc; Am Soc Microbiol; Am Acad Pediat. *Res:* Haemophilius influenzae, bacterial meningitis in children, the molecular epidemiology of disease. *Mailing Add:* 400 S Kingshighway Blvd St Louis MO 63110

GRANSTROM, MARVIN L(E ROY), SANITARY ENGINEERING, CIVIL ENGINEERING. *Current Pos:* RETIRED. *Personal Data:* b Anaconda, Mont, Sept 25, 20; m 44, Ruth M Olson; c David M, Kay R & Chris C. *Educ:* Morningside Col, BS, 42; Iowa State Col, BS, 43; Harvard Univ, MS, 47, PhD(sanit eng), 55. *Prof Exp:* Instr sanit eng, Case Inst Technol, 47-49; assoc prof, Univ NC, 49-58; prof civil & environ eng, Rutgers Univ, 58-83. *Concurrent Pos:* Consult, Univ Peru, 55-57 & WHO, Peru, Chile, Arg & Brazil, 66-; mem, sanit eng subcomt, Nat Acad Sci-Nat Res Coun, 63- *Mem:* Am Soc Civil Engrs Environ Engrs; Sigma Xi. *Res:* Ecology; water resources planning and design. *Mailing Add:* 931 Oakwood Pl Plainfield NJ 07060

GRANT, ALAN LESLIE, GROWTH BIOLOGY. *Current Pos:* asst prof, 90-95, ASSOC PROF GROWTH BIOL, PURDUE UNIV, 95- *Personal Data:* b Watertown, NY, May 8, 62; m 85, Brenda M Murdie. *Educ:* Cornell Univ, BS, 84; Mich State Univ, MS, 87, PhD(animal sci), 90. *Prof Exp:* Grad res asst dairy nutrit, Mich State Univ, 84-87, growth biol, 87-90. *Mem:* Am Soc Animal Sci; AAAS; Am Meat Sci Asn; Sigma Xi; Endocrine Soc. *Res:* Identification and characterization of cellular and molecular mechanisms that regulate skeletal muscle growth and development in food-producing animals. *Mailing Add:* Dept Animal Sci Purdue Univ West Lafayette IN 47907. *Fax:* 765-494-6816; *E-Mail:* agrant@www.ansc.purdue.edu

GRANT, ARTHUR E, PHYSICAL MEDICINE & REHABILITATION. *Current Pos:* prof phys med & rehab & chmn dept, 67-89, EMER PROF, UNIV TEX MED SCH, SAN ANTONIO, 90- *Personal Data:* b Freeport, Ill, Oct 27, 23; m 47; c 3. *Educ:* Case Western Reserve Univ, MD, 50. *Prof Exp:* Intern, Fitzsimons Gen Hosp, 50-51, resident phys med & rehab, Letterman Gen Hosp, 51-54, staff physician, Phys Med Serv, 54-55; staff physician, Brooke Gen Hosp, 55-57; chief, Outpatient Serv, 5th Gen Hosp, Ger, 58-59 & div surgeon, 24th Inf Div, Ger, 59-60; chief, Phys Med Serv, Brooke Gen Hosp, 60-66 & Letterman Gen Hosp, 66-67. *Mem:* Am Cong Rehab Med; Am Acad Phys Med & Rehab; Am Asn Electrodiag Med. *Res:* Clinical and research electromyography and electrodiagnosis; rehabilitation of neurologic disorders. *Mailing Add:* 13147 N Hunters Circle San Antonio TX 78230

GRANT, B ROSEMARY, EVOLUTION, ECOLOGY. *Current Pos:* RES SCHOLAR, PRINCETON UNIV, 86- *Personal Data:* b Arnside, Eng, Oct 8, 36; m 62, Peter R; c Nicola & Kristina T. *Educ:* Edinburgh Univ, BSc, 60; Upsala Univ, PhD(zool), 86. *Prof Exp:* Res assoc, Univ BC, Can, 60-64, Yale Univ, 64-65, McGill Univ, 73-77, Univ Mich, 77-85. *Res:* Extent to which genetic, ecological and behavioral factors are responsible for morphological variation among individuals within a population, how natural selection acts on this variation; evolutionary responses to natural selection; bearing on the process of speciation and the maintenance of genetic variation in small populations of endangered species. *Mailing Add:* Dept Ecol & Evolutionary Biol Princeton Univ Princeton NJ 08544

GRANT, BARBARA DIANNE, synthetic organic chemistry, for more information see previous edition

GRANT, BRUCE S, GENETICS. *Current Pos:* From asst prof to assoc prof, 68-82, PROF BIOL, COL WILLIAM & MARY, 82- *Personal Data:* b New York, NY, Apr 17, 42; m 64; c 2. *Educ:* Bloomsburg State Col, BS, 64; NC State Univ, MS, 66, PhD(genetics), 68. *Mem:* Am Genetics Asn; Soc Study Evolution. *Res:* Behavioral genetics as it pertains to questions of population genetics and evolution. *Mailing Add:* Dept Biol Col William & Mary PO Box 8795 Williamsburg VA 23185

GRANT, CLARENCE LEWIS, MUNITIONS RESIDUES, STATISTICAL ANALYSIS & ENVIRONMENTAL SAMPLING DESIGN. *Current Pos:* res assoc prof, Chem Eng Exp Sta, Univ NH, 61-64, res prof, Ctr Indust & Instnl Develop, 64-76, assoc dir, 73-81, chmn dept, 76-79, prof chem, 76-89, EMER PROF CHEM, UNIV NH, 89- *Personal Data:* b Dover, NH, July 8, 30; m 52, Helen M Garland; c David A, Philip W & Stephen R. *Educ:* Univ NH, BS, 51, MS, 56; Rutgers Univ, PhD(soils, chem), 60. *Honors & Awards:* Distinguished Serv Award, Soc Appl Spectros, 87. *Prof Exp:* Instr, Pub Sch, NJ, 51-52; res asst chem, Univ NH, 52-53, instr, 53-55, res assoc, 55-57, asst prof, 57-58; asst instr soils & chem, Rutgers Univ, 58-60, assoc prof soils, 60-61. *Concurrent Pos:* Consult, US Army & industs on environ & qual control problems. *Mem:* Am Chem Soc; Soc Appl Spectros (pres, 69); Am Soc Testing & Mat. *Res:* Development of analytical methods for trace pollutants; distribution of trace metals and organics in aquatic systems; spectrochemistry; radio tracers; statistics in chemistry. *Mailing Add:* 5634 Sam Snead Dr Harlingen TX 78552

GRANT, CONRAD JOSEPH, APPLIED PHYSICS, COMMAND DISPLAY SYSTEMS. *Current Pos:* Sr physicist, Appl Physics Lab, 78-89, PRIN PROF STAFF PHYSICIST, JOHNS HOPKINS UNIV, 90- *Personal Data:* b Corpus Christi, Tex, Apr 2, 56; m 78, Monica L Vekeman; c Michael, Stephen, Brendan & Matthew. *Educ:* Univ Md, College Park, BS, 78; Johns Hopkins Univ, MS, 82 & 84. *Concurrent Pos:* Instr, Appl Technol Inst. *Mem:* Inst Elec & Electronics Engrs; Am Soc Naval Engrs; Naval Inst. *Res:* Combat system design; display system engineering; command, control and communications applications; cooperative engagement capability. *Mailing Add:* Appl Physics Lab Johns Hopkins Rd Laurel MD 20723-6099

GRANT, CYNTHIA ANN, SOIL CHEMISTRY & FERTILITY, SOIL MANAGEMENT. *Current Pos:* Info officer, 82-83, RES SCIENTIST, BRANDON RES STA, AGR CAN, 86- *Personal Data:* b Minnedosa, Man, Mar 24, 58; m 80, Gregory; c Robin & Laurel. *Educ:* Univ Man, BSA, 80, MSc, 82, PhD(soil chem), 86. *Concurrent Pos:* Adj prof, Dept Soil Sci, Univ Man, 92- *Mem:* Agr Inst Can; Can Soil Sci; Can Soc Agron. *Res:* Effects of fertilization and tillage management on crop yield and quality; heavy metal accumulation in crops; soil quality and potential for nitrate movement into groundwater. *Mailing Add:* Brandon Res Sta Agr Can Box 1000A RR No 3 Brandon MB R7A 5Y3 Can. *Fax:* 204-728-3858; *E-Mail:* grant@mbrsbr.agr.ca

GRANT, DALE WALTER, MICROBIOLOGY. *Current Pos:* RETIRED. *Personal Data:* b Woodland, Maine, Dec 22, 23; m 48; c 3. *Educ:* Colo State Univ, BS, 52, MS, 53; Purdue Univ, PhD, 65. *Prof Exp:* Res microbiologist, Bioferm Corp, Calif, 53-57, head, Microbiol Res Unit, 57-61; res asst microbiol, Purdue Univ, 61-65; from prof to assoc prof microbiol, Colo State Univ, 65-86. *Mem:* AAAS; Am Soc Microbiol; Sigma Xi. *Res:* Polypeptide biosynthesis; antibiotic biosynthesis; mycotoxins; microbial decomposition of agricultural wastes. *Mailing Add:* 608 Birky Pl Ft Collins CO 80526

GRANT, DAVID EVANS, polymer science, physical chemistry, for more information see previous edition

GRANT, DAVID GRAHAM, RADIATION PHYSICS. *Current Pos:* Prin prof staff, Appl Physics Lab, 59-75, assoc prof radiation oncol, 75-76, DIR PHYSICS, SCH MED, JOHNS HOPKINS UNIV, 75-, ASST PROF BIOMED ENG, ONCOL & RADIOL, 76-, DIGITAL IMAGE ANALYST, 80-, PROF MGR SATELITES, 85- *Personal Data:* b Fall River, Mass, May 14, 37; m 59; c 5. *Educ:* Southeastern Mass Univ, BS, 59; Univ Md, MA, 66. *Mem:* Sigma Xi; Am Asn Physicists Med; AAAS. *Res:* 3-D radiotherapy treatment planning; 3-D radiographic imaging techniques; optical image and signal processing techniques. *Mailing Add:* 14865 Triadelphia Rd Glenelg MD 21737

GRANT, DAVID JAMES WILLIAM, PHARMACEUTICS, PHYSICAL CHEMISTRY OF SOLIDS & SOLUTIONS. *Current Pos:* PROF & PETERS ENDOWED CHAIR PHARMACEUT, COL PHARM, UNIV MINN, 88- *Personal Data:* b Walsall, Eng, Mar 26, 37. *Educ:* Oxford Univ, Eng, BA, 61, MA & DPhil(phys chem), 63, DSc, 90. *Honors & Awards:* Res Award, Leverhulme Found, 69. *Prof Exp:* Lectr pharm, Univ Col Sierra Leone, 63-65; lectr pharmaceut chem, Univ Nottingham, Eng, 65-74; sr lectr, 74-81; prof phys pharm, Univ Toronto, 81-88. *Concurrent Pos:* Vis prof pharmaceut chem, Univ Kans, 80, Pharmaceut Mfr Asn Can, 84 & Med Res Coun Can, 87; mem, Grants Comt Pharmaceut Sci, Med Res Coun Can, 83-87; mem, Ont Univ Comt Health Res, 85-87; assoc ed, J Pharmaceut Sci, 94-; consult several co. *Mem:* Fel Royal Soc Chem; Am Pharmaceut Asn; Am Asn Col Pharm; fel Am Asn Pharmaceut Scientists; Am Chem Soc; Am Inst Chem Eng. *Res:* Improving drug delivery; fundamental science of the preparation of solid dosage forms; interactions of drug molecules in the solid state and in solution. *Mailing Add:* Dept Pharmaceut Col Pharm Univ Minn Weaver-Densford Hall 308 Harvard St SE Minneapolis MN 55455. *E-Mail:* grant001@maroon.tc.umn.edu

GRANT, DAVID MILLER, molecular genetics, for more information see previous edition

GRANT, DAVID MORRIS, PHYSICAL CHEMISTRY. *Current Pos:* from asst prof to prof, Utah State Univ, 58-85, chmn dept, 62-73, dean sci, 76-85, assoc vpres, acad & res comput, 88-92, DISTINGUISHED PROF CHEM, UTAH STATE UNIV, 85- *Personal Data:* b Salt Lake City, Utah, Mar 24, 31; m 53, Reva Carlow; c David J, Linda (Halling), Heidi (Cox), Karen (Lindstrom) & John C. *Educ:* Univ Utah, BS, 54, PhD(chem), 57. *Honors & Awards:* Am Chem Soc Award in Petrol Chem, 91; Gov Medal Sci & Technol, 92. *Prof Exp:* Instr chem, Univ Ill, 57-58. *Concurrent Pos:* Sherman Fairchild distinguished scholar, Calif Inst Technol, 73-74; adj prof fuels eng, Univ Utah, 85-, chmn comput task force, 85-92. *Mem:* Fel AAAS; Am Chem Soc; Am Phys Soc; Sigma Xi. *Res:* High resolution nuclear magnetic resonance; carbon-13 magnetic resonance; molecular and electronic structure. *Mailing Add:* Dept Chem Univ Utah 1320 HEB Salt Lake City UT 84112. *Fax:* 801-581-8433; *E-Mail:* Grant@Chemistry.Chem.Utah.edu

GRANT, DONALD LLOYD, TOXICOLOGY. *Current Pos:* DIR, HEALTH EVAL DIV, TEST MGT REGULATORY AGENCY, 95- *Personal Data:* b Pictou, NS, Dec 31, 38; m 59, Emilie Ritcey; c Alexander D & Jeffrey A. *Educ:* McGill Univ, BSc, 60, MSc, 62, PhD(biochem), 66. *Prof Exp:* Res scientist, Bur Chem Safety, Can, 65-74, toxicologist, Health Protection Br, 74-86, div chief, 86-95. *Mem:* Soc Toxicol; Soc Toxicol Can. *Res:* Pesticides, particularly toxicity, metabolism and analysis; polychlorinated biphenyls, dioxin. *Mailing Add:* Health Eval Div Test Mgt Regulatory Agency Sir Charles Tupper Bldg 2250 Riverside Dr Ottawa ON K1A 0K9 Can

GRANT, DONALD R, BIOCHEMISTRY, ORGANIC CHEMISTRY. *Current Pos:* from asst prof to prof, Univ Sask, 63-93, head, Dept Chem Eng, 81-82, head, Dept Chem, 81-84, EMER PROF ORG & CEREAL CHEM, UNIV SASK, 93- *Personal Data:* b Cut Knife, Sask, Aug 4, 32; m 55, Melba Brick; c Keith, Paul, Marvin (deceased), Dale, Barbara & Robert. *Educ:* Univ Sask, BSA, 55; Wash State Univ, PhD, 64. *Prof Exp:* Chemist, Maple Leaf Milling Co, Toronto, 55-58; jr chemist, Wash State Univ, 58-63. *Mem:* Fel Chem Inst Can; Am Asn Cereal Chemists; Can Inst Food Sci & Technol. *Res:* Separation and properties of seed proteins of agricultural crops, particularly wheat and peas; functions of additives in bread flour; enzymes in cereal crops. *Mailing Add:* Dept Chem Univ Sask Saskatoon SK S7N 0W0 Can

GRANT, DOUGLAS HOPE, CHEMISTRY. *Current Pos:* from asst prof to assoc prof, 64-83, PROF CHEM, MT ALLISON UNIV, 83- *Personal Data:* b Glasgow, Scotland, Apr 29, 34; m 95, Shirley Austin; c 8. *Educ:* Glasgow Univ, BSc, 56, PhD(polymer chem), 62. *Prof Exp:* Res fel polymer chem, Appl Chem Div, Nat Res Coun Can, 59-61; NATO-Dept Sci & Indust Res fel & res asst phys chem, Bristol Univ, 61-62, Imp Chem Indust res fel, 62-64. *Concurrent Pos:* Vis lectr, Loughborough Univ Technol, 71-72; vis prof, NM State Univ, 96-97. *Mem:* Chem Inst Can; Can Asn Univ Teachers. *Res:* Kinetics and mechanism of thermal decomposition reactions of synthetic polymers in solid state and in solution, by appropriate techniques; analytical chemistry, especially electrochemical methods. *Mailing Add:* Dept Chem Mt Allison Univ Sackville NB E0A 3C0 Can. *Fax:* 506-364-2313; *E-Mail:* dgrant@mta.ca

GRANT, DOUGLAS RODERICK, ENVIRONMENTAL GEOLOGY. *Current Pos:* CONSULT, 96- *Personal Data:* b Toronto, Ont, Mar 4, 39; m 64; c 2. *Educ:* Dalhousie Univ, BSc, 60, MSc, 63; Cornell Univ, PhD(sea level changes), 70. *Prof Exp:* Sci officer, Geol Surv Can, 68-69, res scientist, 70-96. *Concurrent Pos:* Secy, Can Quaternary Asn, 79- & Can Nat Comt Int Union Quaternary Res, 82-; assoc ed, J Coastal Res. *Mem:* Fel Geol Asn Can. *Res:* Quaternary, surficial and applied geology; glacial history; environmental change; crustal, eustatic, isostatic and geodetic movements. *Mailing Add:* 5 Birchview Ct Nepean ON K2G 3M7 Can

GRANT, DOUGLASS LLOYD, topological groups & semigroups, biomathematics, for more information see previous edition

GRANT, EDWARD R, CHEMISTRY. *Current Pos:* PROF CHEM, PURDUE UNIV, 86- *Personal Data:* b Tacoma, Wash, Sept 23, 47; m 80; c Alexander E & Janine C. *Educ:* Occidental Col, BS, 69; Univ Calif, Davis, PhD, 74. *Honors & Awards:* Nobel Laureate Signature Award, 86. *Prof Exp:* Fel, Univ Calif, Irvine, 74-76 & Berkeley, 76-77; from asst prof to assoc prof, Cornell Univ, 77-86. *Concurrent Pos:* Vis prof physics, Dept Physics & Res Ctr, Univ Crete, 88; vis prof chem, Univ Paris, 91, Tech Univ, Munich, 92-93. *Mem:* Am Chem Soc; fel Am Phys Soc. *Res:* Experimental and theoretical studies of the dynamics of elementary chemical rate processes especially the unimolecular relaxation and fragmentation of highly excited states; multiresonant multiphoton spectroscopy; vibronic coupling; gas-phase kinetics of organometallic reactions. *Mailing Add:* Dept Chem Purdue Univ West Lafayette IN 47907. *Fax:* 765-496-2512; *E-Mail:* egrant@chem.purdue.edu

GRANT, ERNEST WALTER, PHARMACEUTICAL CHEMISTRY. *Current Pos:* RETIRED. *Personal Data:* b Brockton, Mass, July 17, 18; m 45; c 2. *Educ:* Mass Col Pharm, BS, 39, MS, 48; Purdue Univ, PhD(pharmaceut chem), 51. *Prof Exp:* Chemist, Eli Lilly & Co, 51-83. *Mem:* Am Chem Soc. *Res:* Analytical chemistry; alkaloids. *Mailing Add:* 8810 Colby Blvd Apt 242 Indianapolis IN 46268-1387

GRANT, EUGENE F(REDRICK), ELECTRICAL ENGINEERING. *Current Pos:* Consult, 86- *Personal Data:* b Baker, Ore, June 15, 17; wid; c 2. *Educ:* Ore State Col, BS, 41, MS, 42. *Prof Exp:* Res engr res lab, Westinghouse Elec Corp, Pa, 42-45; proj engr, Sperry Gyroscope Co, NY, 45-46; chief appl math br, electronic res lab, Air Force, US Army, 46-51; sect mgr electronics, W L Maxson Corp, NY, 51-54; vpres eng, Nat Co Inc, Mass, 54-62; chief scientist, Space Systs Div, Hughes Aircraft Co, El Segundo, 62-78, Space & Commun Group, Systs Labs, 71-88. *Concurrent Pos:* Consult, Hughes Aircraft Co. *Mem:* Sr mem Inst Elec & Electronics Engrs; NY Acad Sci. *Res:* Space systems and technology; communication systems; atomic frequency standards. *Mailing Add:* 1304 Marinette Rd Pacific Palisades CA 90272-2625

GRANT, EUGENE LODEWICK, engineering economy, statistical quality control; deceased, see previous edition for last biography

GRANT, FREDERICK CYRIL, PHYSICS. *Current Pos:* PHYSICIST, NASA, 58- *Personal Data:* b Boston, Mass, July 18, 25; m 53, 76. *Educ:* Mass Inst Technol, BS, 47; Col William & Mary, MA, 62; Va Polytech Inst, PhD(physics), 67. *Prof Exp:* Scientist, Nat Adv Comt Aeronaut, 48-58. *Concurrent Pos:* Adj prof physics, Christofer Newport Col, 80- *Mem:* Am Phys Soc; Sigma Xi. *Res:* Theoretical and experimental supersonic aerodynamics; flight mechanics of entry into planetary atmospheres; plasma physics, especially Vlasov equations; tornado structure, dynamics. *Mailing Add:* 399 Stanton Rd Newport News VA 23606-2926

GRANT, GEORGE C, BIOLOGICAL OCEANOGRAPHY, ZOOPLANKTON. *Current Pos:* from asst prof to prof, 68-92, EMER PROF MARINE SCI, COL WILLIAM & MARY, 93- *Personal Data:* b Medford, Mass, Aug 13, 29; m 52, Eileen M O'Connor; c Shelley A (Damian) & George C. *Educ:* Univ Mass, BS, 56; Col William & Mary, MA, 62; Univ RI, PhD(biol oceanog), 67. *Prof Exp:* Fishery res biologist, Bur Com Fisheries, US Fish & Wildlife Serv, NC, 56-60. *Concurrent Pos:* From assoc marine scientist to sr marine scientist, Va Inst Marine Sci, 67-81, actg asst dir, 81-82, asst dir, 82-86; asst prof marine sci, Univ Va, 67-77. *Mem:* Am Soc Limnol & Oceanog; Sigma Xi; Atlantic Estuarine Res Soc; fel Am Inst Fishery Biologists. *Res:* Distribution, ecology and morphometrics of North Atlantic Chaetognatha; marine zooplankton; population dynamics and ecology of commercially important fisheries; early life history and population dynamics of marine fishes. *Mailing Add:* PO Box 709 Gloucester Point VA 23062

GRANT, GREGORY ALAN, PROTEIN CHEMISTRY, ENZYMOLOGY. *Current Pos:* Res assoc, Sch Med, Wash Univ, 75-78, res asst prof, 78-82, from asst prof to prof biochem, 82-95, PRIN INVESTR, WASH UNIV, 81-, DIR PROTEIN CHEM LAB, SCH MED, 82-, PROF MED, MOLECULAR BIOL & PHARMACOL, 95- *Personal Data:* b Decorah, Iowa, Oct, 18, 49; m 71. *Educ:* Iowa State Univ, BS, 71; Univ Wis-Madison, PhD(biochem), 75. *Concurrent Pos:* Mem, Biochem Study Sect, NIH, 92-96; chmn, Protein Sequence Comt, Asn Biomolecular Resource Facil, 90-91, mem, exec bd, 92-96, pres, 93-94. *Mem:* AAAS; Am Chem Soc; Am Soc Biochemists & Molecular Biologists; Protein Soc; Am Peptide Soc; Asn Biomolecular Resource Facil (pres, 93-94). *Res:* Structure-function relationships in proteins; collagenases, dehydrogenases, neurotoxins; protein sequencing, site-directed mutagenesis; peptide chemistry. *Mailing Add:* Dept Molecular Biol & Pharmacol Sch Med Wash Univ Box 8103 St Louis MO 63110. *Fax:* 314-362-4698; *E-Mail:* ggrant@pharmdec.wustl.edu

GRANT, IAN S, TRANSMISSION DESIGN, LIGHTNING & TRANSIENT ANALYSIS. *Current Pos:* staff mem, Power Technol Inc, 72-74, sr engr, 74-84, mgr, 84-86, DEPT MGR SOFTWARE PROD, POWER TECHNOL INC, 86-, COMPANY VPRES, 89- *Personal Data:* b Auckland, NZ, 1940; US citizen; m 62, 74; c 5. *Educ:* Univ Nz, Auckland, BE, 62; Univ New SW, ME, 67. *Prof Exp:* Elec Comn NSW, 62-67, head, Transmission Line Elec Design Group, 67-69; staff mem, Lightning & Transient Group & Proj UHV, Elec High Voltage Lab, 69-72. *Concurrent*

Pos: US mem & convener, Lightning Work Group, Int Conf Large High Voltage Elec Systs & Co; vchmn, T & D Comt, Inst Elec & Electronics Engrs. *Mem:* Fel Inst Elec & Electronics Engrs. *Res:* Applications of compact lines; electrical and structural uprating; advanced insulator; structure applications; high phase order; line optimization; development of advanced computer hardware application; author of over 40 technical publications; computer and software applications. *Mailing Add:* 1482 Erie Blvd Schenectady NY 12308

GRANT, JAMES ALEXANDER, PETROLOGY. *Current Pos:* assoc prof, 69-74, PROF GEOL, UNIV MINN, DULUTH, 74- *Personal Data:* b Inverness, Scotland, Oct 3, 35; m 64; c 2. *Educ:* Aberdeen Univ, BSc, 57; Queen's Univ, Ont, MSc, 59; Calif Inst Technol, PhD(geol), 64. *Prof Exp:* Asst prof geol, Univ Minn, Minneapolis, 64-69. *Concurrent Pos:* Geologist, Ont Dept Mines, 56-62 & Minn Geol Surv, 64-71; NSF grants, 66-68, 76-78, 82-86 & 88-90; dir, Wasatch-Uinta Geol Field Camp, 72-79 & Study in Eng Prog, Univ Minn, Duluth, 80-81. *Mem:* Geol Soc Am; Mineral Soc Am; Sigma Xi. *Res:* Metamorphic petrology; field, petrologic and isotopic studies of the Grenville front and the Precambrian of southwestern Minnesota; phase equilibria in high-grade metamorphism and partial melting; petrology of the aureole of the Laramie anorthosite complex. *Mailing Add:* Dept Geol Univ Minn Duluth MN 55812

GRANT, JAMES J, JR, THEORETICAL PHYSICS. *Current Pos:* From instr to assoc prof, St Peter's Col, NJ, 58-74, chmn dept, 63-81, acad dean, 81-85, acad vpres, 85-91, PROF PHYSICS, ST PETER'S COL, NJ, 74-, DEPT CHAIR, 91- *Personal Data:* b Teaneck, NJ, May 24, 35; m 57, Edythe Hammond; c 4. *Educ:* Manhattan Col, BS, 56; Rensselaer Polytech Inst, MS, 58; Fordham Univ, PhD(physics), 64. *Mem:* NY Acad Sci. *Res:* Atomic scattering theory; theoretical astrophysics, optics. *Mailing Add:* Physics Dept St Peter's Col 2641 Kennedy Blvd Jersey City NJ 07306

GRANT, JAMES WILLIAM ANGUS, TERRITORIALITY, FISH BEHAVIOR. *Current Pos:* asst prof, 89-95, ASSOC PROF ECOL, CONCORDIA UNIV, 95- *Personal Data:* b London, Ont, Jan 23, 55; m 81; c 1. *Educ:* Univ Western Ont, BSc, 77; Queen's Univ, MSc, 80; Univ Guelph, PhD(zool), 87. *Prof Exp:* Fel, McGill Univ, 87-89. *Mem:* Animal Behav Soc; Can Soc Zoologists; Int Soc Behav Ecol. *Res:* Behavioral ecology of aggression in animals; effect of resource distribution on defence behavior; consequences of aggression on population regulation. *Mailing Add:* Biol Dept Concordia Univ 1455 de Maisonneuve W Montreal PQ H3G 1M8 Can

GRANT, JOHN ANDREW, JR, ALLERGY & IMMUNOLOGY, INTERNAL MEDICINE. *Current Pos:* asst prof internal med, 73-77, assoc prof internal med & genetics, 77-83, PROF INTERNAL MED & MICROBIOL, UNIV TEX MED BR, GALVESTON, 83-, DIR ALLERGY & IMMUNOL SECT, 73-, VCHMN RES, 90- *Personal Data:* b Tallahassee, Fla, Jan 2, 41; m 62; c 3. *Educ:* Harvard Univ, AB, 62; Duke Univ, MD, 66; Am Bd Internal Med, dipl, 72; Am Bd Allergy & Immunol, dipl, 74; Diag Lab Immunol, dipl, 90. *Prof Exp:* Intern & resident, NY Hosp & Cornell Med Ctr, 66-68; clin assoc immunol, NIH, 68-71; fel, Johns Hopkins Univ, 71-73. *Concurrent Pos:* NIH fel, 71-73; career develop award, Nat Inst Allergy & Infectious Dis, 75-80, prin investr, 75-93; prin investr, Merrell Ddow, Janssen, Fisons, Merck, Smith-Kline; consult immunol, Vet Admin, 77-80 & Food & Drug Admin, 81-84. *Mem:* Fel Am Acad Allergy; Am Asn Immunol, fel Am Col Physicians; Sigma Xi. *Res:* Mechanisms of hypersensitivity reactions, especially the role of the basophil; activation of basophils by complement fragments and by lymphokines; diagnosis and treatment of rhinitis, asthma and urticaria. *Mailing Add:* Univ Tex Med Br Div Allergy & Immunol Clin Sci Bldg 409-0762 301 University Blvd Galveston TX 77555-0762. *Fax:* 409-772-5841

GRANT, JOHN WALLACE, BIOMECHANICS, VESTIBULAR MECHANICS. *Current Pos:* ASSOC PROF, MECH & BIOMED ENG, ENG SCI & MECH DEPT, VA POLYTECH INST & STATE UNIV, 80- *Personal Data:* b Weston, WVa, May 12, 46; m 69; c 3. *Educ:* WVa Inst Technol, BS, 65; Tulane Univ, MS, 70, PhD(mech eng), 74. *Prof Exp:* Proj engr, Chem Plastics Div, Union Carbide Corp, 65-69; sr res engr, instrument prod, DuPont Co, 74-80. *Concurrent Pos:* Fel, Naval Acceleration Physiol Res Lab, 85 & Naval Aerospace Med Res Lab, 90; mem bd dirs, Biomed Eng Soc, 85-87. *Mem:* Biomed Eng Soc; Am Soc Mech Eng; Am Soc Eng Educ; Am Aerospace Med Soc; Asn Res Otolaryngol. *Res:* Development of mathematic descriptions which quatify how the inner ear measure linear and rotational motion of the skull. *Mailing Add:* 4469 Pearman Rd Blacksburg VA 24060

GRANT, LELAND F(AUNTLEROY), geological engineering; deceased, see previous edition for last biography

GRANT, LOUIS RUSSELL, JR, synthetic inorganic & organometallic chemistry, for more information see previous edition

GRANT, MARTIN, NONEQUILIBRIUM STATISTICAL PHYSICS, COMPUTATIONAL PHYSICS. *Current Pos:* asst prof, 86-90, ASSOC PROF, PHYSICS DEPT, MCGILL UNIV, 90- *Personal Data:* b St John, NB, Nov 30, 56; m 83. *Educ:* Univ PEI, BSc, 78; Univ Toronto, MSc, 80, PhD(physics), 82. *Prof Exp:* Res assoc, Physics Dept, Temple Univ, 83-86. *Mem:* Can Asn Physicists; Am Phys Soc. *Res:* Kinetics of ordering systems: domain growth during first-order transitions, interface dynamics and crystal growth; analytic theory and large-scale numerical modelling. *Mailing Add:* Physics Dept Rutherford Bldg McGill Univ 3600 University St Montreal PQ H3A 2T8 Can

GRANT, MICHAEL CLARENCE, POPULATION BIOLOGY, BOTANY. *Current Pos:* Dir, Mountain Res Sta, Univ Colo, Boulder, 74-76, from asst prof to assoc prof, 74-84, chmn, 82-85, PROF, DEPT ENVIRON POP & ORG BIOL, UNIV COLO, BOULDER, 84- *Personal Data:* b Louisville, Ky, Oct 20, 42; m 61, Karen; c Shane. *Educ:* Tex Tech Univ, BA, 69, MS, 70; Duke Univ, PhD(bot), 74. *Concurrent Pos:* Statist consult. *Mem:* Phycol Soc Am; Bot Soc Am; Ecol Soc Am; Soc Study Evolution; Soc Syst Zool. *Res:* Genetic and ecological structure of natural plant populations, life history adaptations, evolutionary mechanisms. *Mailing Add:* Dept Environ Pop Org Biol Univ Colo Boulder Box 334 Boulder CO 80309-0334. *Fax:* 303-492-8699; *E-Mail:* grant_m@cubldr.colorado.edu

GRANT, MICHAEL P(ETER), ELECTRICAL ENGINEERING. *Current Pos:* VPRES, SYNGENICS CORP, 87- *Personal Data:* b Oshkosh, Wis, Feb 26, 36; m 61, Susan Corcoran; c James, Steven & Laura. *Educ:* Purdue Univ, BS, 57, MS, 58, PhD(elec eng), 64. *Prof Exp:* Engr, Westinghouse Res Labs, 53-57; instr elec eng, Purdue Univ, 58-64; mem tech staff, Aerospace Corp, 61; sr engr, Accuray Corp, 64-66, mgr systs & control, 66-74, asst gen mgr, 74-76, mgr systs design, 76-87. *Concurrent Pos:* Dir comput integrated opers, Nat Ctr Mfg Sci, Ann Arbor, Mich, 88-95. *Mem:* Inst Elec & Electronics Engrs; Sigma Xi. *Res:* Control of industrial processes in real time employing digital computer systems; management of collaborative research and development programs in consortia. *Mailing Add:* 4461 Sussex Dr Columbus OH 43220. *E-Mail:* 103605.3405@compuserve.com

GRANT, NEIL GEORGE, PLANT PHYSIOLOGY. *Current Pos:* assoc prof, 77-93, PROF BIOL SCI, WILLIAM PATERSON COL, NJ, 93- *Personal Data:* b Chicago, Ill, Dec 7, 37. *Educ:* Univ Ill, Urbana, BS, 60; Univ NC, Chapel Hill, PhD(bot), 72. *Prof Exp:* Asst prof biol, City Col NY, 71-77. *Concurrent Pos:* Plant quarantine inspector, USDA, 60-64. *Mem:* Am Soc Plant Physiologists; NY Acad Sci; Biophys Soc; AAAS; Phycol Soc Am. *Res:* Investigation of the roles of respiration and photosynthesis in the energy economy of algal cells. *Mailing Add:* Dept Biol William Paterson Col Wayne NJ 07470. *Fax:* 973-595-2338; *E-Mail:* ngrant@frontier.wilpatevsoni.edu

GRANT, NICHOLAS J(OHN), METALLURGY, MATERIALS SCIENCE. *Current Pos:* Abex prof, 75-85, EMER PROF & SR LECTR, MASS INST TECHNOL, 85- *Personal Data:* b South River, NJ, Oct 21, 15; m 63; c 5. *Educ:* Carnegie Inst Technol, BS, 38; Mass Inst Technol, ScD(metall), 44. *Honors & Awards:* J Wallenberg Award, Royal Swed Acad Engr Sci; Krumb Lectr, Am Inst Mining, Metall & Petrol Engrs, 78. *Prof Exp:* Metall engr, Bethlehem Steel Co, 38-40; instr steel making, Mass Inst Technol, 42-43, from asst prof to prof metall, 44-57, dir, Ctr Mat Sci & Eng, 68-77; chmn US Side of US-USSR Sci Technol Agreement, Electrometall & Mat, State Dept, 77-82. *Concurrent Pos:* Chmn mat adv comt, Nat Adv Comt Aeronaut & NASA, 48-67; tech dir, Invest Casting Inst, 56; tech dir, Titanium Adv Bd; pres, New Eng Mat Lab, Inc, 56-67; lectr, Am Powder Metall Inst & Metal Powder Indust Fedn, 60; lectr, Japanese Advan Mat & Processes Comt, 86; Nicholas J Grant Ann Grad Res Fel, Mass Inst Technol, 87. *Mem:* Nat Acad Eng; fel Am Inst Mining, Metall & Petrol Engrs; Metal Powder Indust Fedn; Am Soc Testing & Mat; fel Am Soc Metals; Am Acad Arts & Sci; hon mem Japan Inst Metals; Mat Res Soc. *Res:* Heat resistant materials; powder metallurgy; deformation and fracture; structure-property control; rapid solidification; author of numerous technical publications. *Mailing Add:* Mass Inst Technol Rm 8-413 Cambridge MA 02139. *Fax:* 617-258-8836

GRANT, NORMAN HOWARD, BIOCHEMISTRY. *Current Pos:* sr res scientist biochem, Wyeth Labs, 56-57, asst mgr, 68-74, mgr biochem, 74-78 assoc dir res, 78-82, DIR RES & DEVELOP ADMIN, WYETH LABS, 83- *Personal Data:* b Chicago, Ill, July 21, 27; m 50; c 2. *Educ:* Univ Chicago, SB, 47; Univ Ill, MS, 48, PhD(chem), 50. *Prof Exp:* Sr res biochemist, Labs, Armour & Co, 50-56. *Mem:* Soc Tech Commun; Am Soc Biol Chemists. *Res:* Chemotherapy; low temperature biochemistry; hormonal peptides; anti-infectious agents; inflammation; connective tissue proteins. *Mailing Add:* 2 Downes Circle Wynnewood PA 19096

GRANT, PATRICK MICHAEL, RADIOCHEMISTRY, ANALYTICAL CHEMISTRY. *Current Pos:* radiochemist, Nuclear Chem Div, 83-92, DEP DIR, FORENSIC SCI CTR, LAWRENCE LIVERMORE NAT LAB, 92- *Personal Data:* b Oakland, Calif, Sept 20, 44; m 69; c 2. *Educ:* Univ Calif, Santa Barbara, BS, 67; Univ Calif, Irvine, PhD(chem), 73. *Honors & Awards:* Award of Excellence, US Dept Energy, 86. *Prof Exp:* Teaching & res asst chem, Univ Calif, Irvine, 67-73; res radiochemist nuclear med, Sch Med, Univ NMex, 73-74; staff mem nuclear & radiochem, Los Alamos Sci Lab, 74-80, assoc group leader med radioisotopes, 80-81; res chemist, Anal Res & Serv, Chevron Res Co, 81-83. *Concurrent Pos:* Adj asst prof chem, Univ NMex, 77-81; consult, Los Alamos Nat Lab, 81-83. *Mem:* Am Chem Soc; Am Nuclear Soc; Am Phys Soc; AAAS; Am Acad Forensic Sci. *Res:* Radiochemistry; nuclear chemistry; nuclear medicine; analytical chemistry; inorganic chemistry; forensic science. *Mailing Add:* Forensic Sci Ctr L-371 Lawrence Livermore Nat Lab Livermore CA 94550

GRANT, PAUL MICHAEL, SOLID STATE PHYSICS. *Current Pos:* EXEC SCIENTIST, OFF EXPLOR & APPL RES, ELEC POWER RES INST, 93- *Personal Data:* b Poughkeepsie, NY, May 9, 35; m 58; c 4. *Educ:* Clarkson Col Technol, BS, 60; Harvard Univ, AM, 61, PhD(physics), 65. *Prof Exp:* Staff mem solid state physics, Res Lab, IBM Corp, 65-93. *Mem:* Am Phys Soc. *Res:* Solid state physics of high temperature superconductors. *Mailing Add:* Elec Power Res Inst Office of Explor Res 3412 Hillview Ave PO Box 10412 Palo Alto CA 94303

GRANT, PETER MALCOLM, SCIENCE POLICY, POLYMER CHEMISTRY. *Current Pos:* res chemist, Distillation Prod Industs Div, Eastman Kodak Co, 61-62, head, Chem Use Lab, 62-69, sr res chemist, Eastman Chem, 69-73, res assoc, 73-81, tech info assoc, 81-88, SR TECH INFO ASSOC, EASTMAN CHEM, 88- *Personal Data:* b Cleethorpes, Eng, Sept 30, 33; m 58. *Educ:* Univ Birmingham, BSc, 54, PhD(org chem), 57. *Prof Exp:* UK Atomic Energy Res Estab fel, Univ Birmingham, 57-58; plant mgr, Gen Chem Div, Imp Chem Industs, Ltd, 58-59; res chemist, Textile Fibers Div, Du Pont Can, Ltd, 59-61. *Mem:* Am Chem Soc. *Res:* Opportunity analysis; business analysis; strategy analysis; international technical liaison; polymers; coatings. *Mailing Add:* 3632 Hemlock Park Dr Kingsport TN 37663

GRANT, PETER RAYMOND, ZOOLOGY. *Current Pos:* PROF, PRINCETON UNIV, 85- *Personal Data:* b London, Eng, Oct 26, 36; m 62; c 2. *Educ:* Cambridge Univ, BA, 60; Univ BC, PhD(zool), 64. *Honors & Awards:* Brewster Award, Am Ornith Union, 83. *Prof Exp:* Fel zool, Yale Univ, 64-65; from asst prof to prof, McGill Univ, 65-77; prof zool, Univ Mich, Ann Arbor, 77-85. *Mem:* AAAS; Soc Study Evolution; Am Ornith Union; Ecol Soc Am; Soc Am Naturalists; fel Royal Soc. *Res:* Evolutionary significance of interactions among animal species, approached through ecology, behavior, systematics and genetics. *Mailing Add:* Dept Biol Princeton Univ Thomas Lewis Lab Princeton NJ 08544-1099

GRANT, PHILIP, DEVELOPMENTAL BIOLOGY, NEUROEMBRYOLOGY. *Current Pos:* EMER PROF BIOL, NIH, 92- *Personal Data:* b New York, NY, Sept 22, 24; m 46; c 4. *Educ:* Columbia Univ, AM, 49, PhD(zool), 52. *Prof Exp:* Tutor & instr biol, City Col New York, 47-54; res assoc embryol, Inst Cancer Res, 54-57; asst prof pathobiol, Sch Hyg & Pub Health, Johns Hopkins Univ, 57-62; prog dir develop biol, NSF, 62-66; prof, Univ Ore, 66-91, emer prof biol, 91-92. *Concurrent Pos:* USPHS fel, Columbia Univ, 52-54, sr res fel, 58; trustee, Marine Biol Lab, 76-79 & 80-84 & Biosis, 80-86; ed, J Exp Zool, 78-; spec expert, NIH, 88-91. *Mem:* AAAS; Am Soc Zool; Soc Develop Biol; Marine Biol Asn; Am Soc Cell Biol; Soc Neurosci. *Res:* Ontogeny of fiber patterns between eye and brain in amphibia; growth and guidance of optic fibers in vitro and in vivo; neurofilament development and regulation of cytoskeletal protein phosphorylation. *Mailing Add:* Lab Neurochem NINDS Bldg 36 Rm 4D20 NIH Bethesda MD 20892. *Fax:* 301-496-1339; *E-Mail:* grant@codon.nih.gov

GRANT, PHILIP R, JR, GEOLOGY. *Current Pos:* CONSULT GEOLOGIST & PRES, ENERGY RESOURCES EXPLOR INC, 65-;. *Educ:* Univ NMex, BSc, 51. *Prof Exp:* From jr petrol geologist to regional explor geologist, Sinclair Oil & Gas Co, 51-65. *Concurrent Pos:* Mem bd dirs, Albuquerque Bd Realtors, 69-71; Realtor's Asn NMex, 70-81 & vpres, 70, acad adv comt, Am Asn Petrol Geologists, 72-, sci & technol comt, Nat Conf States Legislatures, 75-78, Albuquerque Indust Develop Serv Inc, 75-81; Realtor's Asn NMex, 70-81; vpres, Am Asn Petrol Geologists, 70, acad adv comt, 72-; sci & technol comt, Nat Conf States Legislatures, 75-78; Albuquerque Indust Develop Serv Inc, 75-81. *Mem:* Fel Geol Soc Am; Am Asn Petrol Geologists. *Res:* Author of over 30 publications. *Mailing Add:* 1101 Rocky Point Ct NE Albuquerque NM 87123

GRANT, RHODA, gastric cancer, gastric mucosa in health and disease; deceased, see previous edition for last biography

GRANT, RICHARD EVANS, INVERTEBRATE PALEONTOLOGY. *Current Pos:* chmn dept paleobiol, 72-77, cur paleobiol, 72-83, SR GEOLOGIST, NAT MUS NATURAL HIST, SMITHSONIAN INST, 83- *Personal Data:* b St Paul, Minn, June 18, 27; m 58; c 3. *Educ:* Univ Minn, MS, 53; Univ Tex, PhD(geol), 58. *Honors & Awards:* Daniel Giraud Elliot Medal, Nat Acad Sci, 79. *Prof Exp:* Instr geol, Univ Tex, 53-54; res asst invert paleont, Smithsonian Inst, 57-61; geologist, US Geol Surv, 61-72. *Mem:* AAAS; Geol Soc Am; Paleont Soc (pres, 79); Int Paleont Asn (treas, 80-89). *Res:* Permian Brachiopods; their biostratraphy, functional morphology and biogeography. *Mailing Add:* 6007 Sumner Rd Alexandria VA 22310

GRANT, RICHARD J, physical chemistry; deceased, see previous edition for last biography

GRANT, RODERICK M, JR, MEDICAL PHYSICS, EDUCATION. *Current Pos:* from asst prof to assoc prof, Denison Univ, 65-77, chmn dept, 70-74 & 76, prof & Henry Chisholm chair, 77-94, EMER PROF PHYSICS, DENISON UNIV, 94- *Personal Data:* b Chicago, Ill, July 9, 35; m 57, Susan Fisher; c 3. *Educ:* Denison Univ, BS, 57; Univ Wis, MS, 59, PhD(physics), 65. *Prof Exp:* Teaching asst physics, Univ Wis, 57-59, instr, Marathon Co Ctr, 59-61, res asst, Univ, 61-65. *Mem:* AAAS; Am Asn Physics Teachers (secy, 77-83); Am Asn Physicists Med; Am Phys Soc; Am Inst Physics (secy, 82-). *Res:* Problems of medical physics; problems of computer-assisted instruction in physics and astronomy. *Mailing Add:* Dept Physics Denison Univ Granville OH 43023. *E-Mail:* rmg@aip.org

GRANT, RONALD W(ARREN), SEMICONDUCTOR INTERFACE, EPITAXIAL GROWTH OF III-V SEMICONDUCTORS. *Current Pos:* Mem tech staff, Rockwell Int, 63-76, group leader solid state physics, Sci Ctr, 76-79, mgr, Mat Properties Sect, Microelectronics Res & Develop Ctr, 79-87, mgr, Epitaxial Mat Dept, 87-91, PROJ LEADER, SCI CTR, ROCKWELL INT, 91- *Personal Data:* b Cleveland, Ohio, Nov 4, 37; m 59, Patricia Farmer; c Karen, Susan & Cynthia. *Educ:* Case Inst Technol, BS, 59; Univ Calif, Berkeley, PhD(nuclear chem), 63. *Concurrent Pos:* Mem ad hoc comt, Nat Res Coun, 70-74; chmm, 18th Ann Physics & Chem Semiconductor Interface Conf, 91; vis assoc, Appl Physics Dept, Calif Inst Technol, 92- *Mem:* Am Phys Soc; Sigma Xi; Am Vacuum Soc. *Res:* Semiconductor surface and interface characterization by using X-ray photoelectron spectroscopy; epitaxial growth of III-V semiconductor materials. *Mailing Add:* 948 Chalet Circle Thousand Oaks CA 91362

GRANT, SHELDON KERRY, MINERALOGY, PETROLOGY. *Current Pos:* Asst prof geol eng, 65-70, assoc prof, 70-83, PROF GEOL, UNIV MO, ROLLA, 83- *Personal Data:* b Cedar City, Utah, Apr 29, 39; m 60; c 3. *Educ:* Univ Utah, BS, 61, PhD(geol eng), 66. *Mem:* Am Inst Mining, Metall & Petrol Eng; Mineral Soc Am; Geol Soc Am; Sigma Xi. *Res:* Stratigraphy, mineralogy, alteration, relation to ore deposits and tectonic evolution of ash-flow tuffs; petrology and chemistry of igneous rocks; field tectonics in the Cordillera. *Mailing Add:* Dept Geol & Geophys Univ Mo Rolla MO 65401

GRANT, STANLEY BAUGH, ENVIRONMENTAL MICROBIOLOGY, COLLOID SCIENCE. *Current Pos:* ASST PROF ENVIRON ENG, UNIV CALIF, IRVINE, 91- *Personal Data:* b Everett, Wash, Apr 25, 62; m 84, Lisa; c Erika & Kevin. *Educ:* Stanford Univ, BS, 85; Calif Inst Technol, MS, 90, PhD(environ eng sci), 92. *Honors & Awards:* Career Award, NSF, 95. *Prof Exp:* Seismic analyst, Unocal Corp, 85-87. *Mem:* Am Chem Soc; AAAS; Am Soc Civil Engrs. *Res:* Application of colloid science, environmental microbiology, and environmental engineering to the removal of microbial contaminants (specifically viruses) from water by coagulation and/or physicochemical filtration. *Mailing Add:* Dept Civil & Environ Eng Univ Calif Irvine CA 92697

GRANT, STANLEY CAMERON, GEO-TECHNICAL MANAGEMENT, ENVIRONMENTAL ADMINISTRATION. *Current Pos:* ASSOC DIR, GREAT PLAINS-ROCKY MOUNTAIN HAZARDOUS SUBSTANCE RES CTR, KANS STATE UNIV, MANHATTAN, 91-, PROG DIR, PUB ENVIRON INFO SERV & ADJ PROF CIVIL ENG & GEOL, 92- *Personal Data:* b Cedar Rapids, Iowa, Apr 21, 31; m 54, 84, Norine A Kruse; c Laura L, Stuart C & Douglas S. *Educ:* Coe Col, BA, 53; Univ Wyo, MA, 55; Univ Idaho, PhD(geol), 71. *Prof Exp:* Petrol geologist, Calif Co, Stand Oil Calif, 55; chief geologist, Gas Hills Uranium Co, Am Nuclear, 55-56; instr, Howard Co Jr Col, Big Spring, Tex, 61-62; asst prof aerospace study, Univ Idaho, 66-69; assoc prof geol, Univ Northern Iowa, 70-75; state geologist & dir, Iowa Geol Surv, 75-80; vpres oper, Bishop Oil & Refining Co, 80-81; partner, Grant Geol Serv, 81-87; secy health & environ, State Kans, 87-91. *Concurrent Pos:* Sci adv to Gov of State of Iowa, Iowa Interagency Resources Coun, 75-80; Kans Water Authority, 88-91; Kans Geog Info Syst Policy bd, 89-91; Environ Protection Agency/State Opers coun, 90-91; sr scientist & partner, Grant Environ Consult, 91- *Mem:* Geol Soc Am; Am Inst Mining, Metall & Petrol Engrs; Asn Eng Geologists; Am Inst Prof Geologists; Sigma Xi; Am Asn Petrol Geologists (vpres, 95-96). *Res:* Environmental risk analysis; photographic remote sensing of the physical environment; remote sensing applications to petroleum geology; environmental remediation in the Midwest and Western US; environmental technology deployment, public environment information transfer technology. *Mailing Add:* 8251 SW 61st St Topeka KS 66610-9042. *Fax:* 785-532-5985; *E-Mail:* scgrant@aol.com, scgrant@juno.com

GRANT, VERNE (EDWIN), BOTANY, EVOLUTION. *Current Pos:* prof, 70-87, EMER PROF BOT, UNIV TEX, AUSTIN, 87- *Personal Data:* b San Francisco, Calif, Oct 17, 17; m 46, 60, Karen Alt; c Joyce, Brian & Brenda. *Educ:* Univ Calif, AB, 40, PhD(bot), 49. *Honors & Awards:* Cert Merit, Bot Soc Am, 71. *Prof Exp:* Asst bot, Univ Calif, 46-49; vis investr, Carnegie Inst Wash, Stanford, Calif, 49-50; geneticist & exp taxonomist, Rancho Santa Ana Bot Garden, Claremont, Calif, 50-67; prof biol, Inst Life Sci, Tex A&M Univ, 67-68; prof biol sci & dir Boyce Thompson Southwest Arboretum, Univ Ariz, Superior, 68-70. *Concurrent Pos:* Nat Res Coun fel, 49-50; from asst prof to prof bot, Claremont Col, 51-67. *Mem:* Nat Acad Sci; fel Am Acad Arts & Sci; Genetics Am; Soc Study Evolution (vpres, 66, pres, 68); Bot Soc Am; Am Soc Naturalists; Int Soc Plant Taxonomists; Am Soc Plant Taxonomists. *Res:* Cytotaxonomy and phylogeny of Polemoniaceae; fertility relationships in annual Gilias; effects of pollinating animals on flower evolution; evolutionary theory; speciation in higher plants; population biology of cacti (opuntia); systematics of the Ipomopsis aggregata group and the alpine Polemoniums (Polemoniaceae). *Mailing Add:* Dept Bot Univ Tex Austin TX 78713. *Fax:* 512-471-3878

GRANT, WALTER MORTON, ophthalmology, for more information see previous edition

GRANT, WARREN HERBERT, PHYSICAL CHEMISTRY, POLYMER CHEMISTRY. *Current Pos:* RES CHEMIST, NAT BUR STAND, 62-, PROJ LEADER, 68- *Personal Data:* b New Orleans, La, Oct 16, 33; m 59; c 3. *Educ:* Talladega Col, BS, 55; Howard Univ, MS, 62, PhD(chem), 68. *Concurrent Pos:* Sci adv, Nat Acad Sci-Nat Res Coun, 73- *Mem:* Am Chem Soc; Soc Biomat. *Res:* Polymers; polymer adsorption, flocculation and fractionation; surface properties; interfaces; biomaterials; conformation of polymers. *Mailing Add:* 4917 Morning Glory Ct Rockville MD 20853-1638

GRANT, WILLARD H, GEOLOGY. *Current Pos:* Assoc prof, 52-69, PROF GEOL, EMORY UNIV, 69- *Personal Data:* b Springfield, Mass, Jan 19, 23; m 50; c 4. *Educ:* Emory Univ, AB, 48, MS, 49; Johns Hopkins Univ, PhD(geol), 55. *Mem:* AAAS; Geochem Soc; Clay Minerals Soc. *Res:* Chemistry and mineralogy of the weathering environment; structural petrology. *Mailing Add:* 3971 Ashleywood Ct Tucker GA 30084-4305

GRANT, WILLIAM B, LIDAR SYSTEMS. *Current Pos:* SR RES SCIENTIST, ATMOSPHERIC SCI DIV, LANGLEY RES CTR, NASA, 89- *Personal Data:* b Fresno, Calif, Feb 4, 42; div. *Educ:* Univ Calif, Berkeley, BA, 64, PhD(physics), 71. *Prof Exp:* Res assoc, Inst Physics, Free Univ Berlin, 71-73; sr physicist, SRI Int, 73-79; mem tech staff, Jet Propulsion Lab, Calif Inst Technol, 79-89. *Mem:* AAAS; fel Optical Soc Am; Am Meteorol Soc; Am Geophys Union; AAAS. *Res:* Development and demonstration of laser systems for the remote measurement of atmospheric gases and aerosols; effects of ozone and acid deposition on forests of the eastern US; author of several publications. *Mailing Add:* Atmospheric Sci Div Langley Res Ctr NASA MS 401A Hampton VA 23681

GRANT, WILLIAM CHASE, JR, zoology, for more information see previous edition

GRANT, WILLIAM FREDERICK, CYTOGENETICS, HIGHER PLANT NUTAGENESIS. *Current Pos:* from asst prof to prof, 55-90, EMER PROF GENETICS, MCGILL UNIV, MACDONALD CAMPUS, 90- *Personal Data:* b Hamilton, Ont, Oct 20, 24; m 49, Phyllis K Harshaw; c William T. *Educ:* McMaster Univ, BA, 47, MA, 49; Univ Va, PhD(biol), 53. *Honors & Awards:* Andrew Fleming Award, 53; Gov Gen Silver Medal, 77; George Lawson Medal, Can Bot Asn, 89; Presidential Citation, Genetic Soc Can, 91. *Prof Exp:* Botanist, Colombo Plan, Dept Agr, Malaya, 53-55. *Concurrent Pos:* Ed, Lotus Newslett, 70-84 & Can J Genetics & Cytol, 74-82; treas, Biol Coun Can, 74-78; mem, Environ Contaminants Adv Comt, Ministers Environ & Nat Health & Welfare, Ottawa, 78-; adj prof biol, York Univ, 83-; adv, Int Prog Chem Safety Collab Study Short-term Tests Genotoxicity & Carcinogenicity, WHO, 84-; archivist, Gen Soc Can; sr res fel, Japan Soc Prom Sci, 89; hon ed-in-chief, Plant Species Biol, 93. *Mem:* Fel AAAS; fel Linnean Soc; Genetics Soc Can (pres, 74-75); Int Orgn Plant Biosyst (pres, 81-87); Soc Study Evolution (vpres, 72); Sigma Xi; Can Bot Asn; Am Bot Asn; Am Soc Plant Taxonomists; fel Royal Soc Can. *Res:* Lotus cytogenetics; cytogenetic effects of environmental agents; biosystematics. *Mailing Add:* Dept Plant Sci Box 4000 McGill Univ Macdonald Campus Ste-Anne-de-Bellevue PQ H9X 3V9 Can. *Fax:* 514-398-7897; *E-Mail:* ef16@musica.mcgill.ca

GRANTHAM, DONALD JAMES, CHEMISTRY, ELECTRICAL ENGINEERING. *Current Pos:* RETIRED. *Personal Data:* b Grantham, NC, Aug 1, 16; c David S & Philip L. *Educ:* Univ NC, BA, 39. *Prof Exp:* Founder, Pres, Grantham Col Eng, 51-90. *Mem:* Inst Elec & Electronics Engrs; Am Soc Elec Engrs. *Mailing Add:* 34641 Grantham College Rd Slidell LA 70460-6815

GRANTHAM, JARED JAMES, MEDICINE, NEPHROLOGY. *Current Pos:* Assoc prof, 69-76, PROF MED, SCH MED, UNIV KANS, 76-, HEAD, NEPHROL SECT, 70- *Personal Data:* b Dodge City, Kans, May 19, 36; m 58; c 4. *Educ:* Baker Univ, AB, 58; Univ Kans, MD, 62. *Concurrent Pos:* Fel nephrology, NIH, 64-66; Kaw Valley Heart Asn grant, 69-70; Nat Inst Arthritis & Metab Dis grant, 69-83. *Mem:* Am Soc Nephrology; Am Soc Clin Invest; Am Physiol Soc; Am Fedn Clin Res; Asn Am Phys. *Res:* Fluid and electrolyte metabolism; electrolyte transport; mechanism of action of antidiuretic hormone; polycystic kidney disease. *Mailing Add:* Nephrology Div Univ Kans Med Ctr 39th & Rainbow Blvd Kansas City KS 66160-7382. *Fax:* 913-588-3867

GRANTHAM, LEROY FRANCIS, INORGANIC CHEMISTRY, PHYSICAL CHEMISTRY. *Current Pos:* sr chemist, 59-63, res specialist, 63-67, SR SCIENTIST, ATOMICS INT, ROCKWELL INT CORP, 67- *Personal Data:* b Chadron, Nebr, Nov 23, 29; m 52; c 5. *Educ:* Chadron State Col, BS, 51; Iowa State Univ, MS, 54; Kans State Univ, PhD(chem), 59. *Prof Exp:* Jr chemist, Ames Lab, Iowa State Univ, 54; chemist, Phosphate Develop Works, 54-56. *Mem:* Am Chem Soc; Sigma Xi; Am Nuclear Soc. *Res:* Isotopic and electron exchange; corrosion; fused salts; metal-salt melts; high temperature chemistry; mass spectrometry; radioactive waste handling, volume reduction and insolubilization; pollution control; hazardous waste management; nuclear fuel cycle. *Mailing Add:* 26117 Hatmor Calabasas CA 91302

GRANTMYRE, EDWARD BARTLETT, radiology, for more information see previous edition

GRANTZ, ARTHUR, MARINE GEOLOGY, GEOLOGY OF THE ARCTIC OCEAN. *Current Pos:* CONSULT PROF, DEPT GEOL & ENVIRON SCI, STANFORD UNIV, 95- *Personal Data:* b New York, NY, Nov 9, 27; m 51, Marcha Ruth Burns; c David A, Eric, Carol (Bohan) & Sarah (Plafker). *Educ:* Cornell Univ, AB, 49; Stanford Univ, MS, 61, PhD(geol), 66. *Honors & Awards:* Distinguished Serv Award, US Dept Interior, 96. *Prof Exp:* Asst, Cornell Univ, 49; geologist, Br Alaska Geol, US Geol Serv, 49-66, chief, Br Pac Environ Geol, 66-71, geologist, Br Alaskan Geol & Br Pac-Arctic Marine Geol, 71-95. *Concurrent Pos:* Mem & vchmn, Calif State Mining & Geol Bd, 76-79; group adv, US Arctic Res Commn, 86-; sr scientist, Dept Geol & Geophysics, Univ Wis, 96- *Mem:* Fel Geol Soc Am; Am Asn Petrol Geol; Am Geophys Union. *Res:* Structural geology and stratigraphy of Alaska; geologic structure and petroleum resources of northern Alaska's continental shelves, geology of the Arctic Ocean. *Mailing Add:* 930 Van Auken Circle Palo Alto CA 94303. *Fax:* 650-329-5134; *E-Mail:* agrantz@aol.com

GRANTZ, DAVID ARTHUR, STOMATAL PHYSIOLOGY, AIR POLLUTION. *Current Pos:* ASSOC RES PLANT PHYSIOLOGIST, STATEWIDE AIR POLLUTION RES CTR & ASSOC EXTEN AGR, DEPT BOT & PLANT SCI, UNIV CALIF, RIVERSIDE, 90- *Personal Data:* b Nashville, Tenn, Dec 29, 51; m 80; c 2. *Educ:* Univ Calif, Santa Cruz, AB, 73, Riverside, MS, 79; Univ Ill, Urbana, PhD(plant physiol), 83. *Prof Exp:* Res assoc, Dept Biol Sci, Stanford Univ, 83-85; plant physiologist, Agr Res Serv, USDA, 85-90. *Concurrent Pos:* Golda Meier fel, Hebrew Univ, Israel, 85; res fel, Hebrew Univ Jerusalem, 86. *Mem:* Am Soc Plant Physiologists; Am Soc Agron; AAAS; Crop Sci Soc Am; Air & Waste Mgt Asn; Soc Environ Toxicol & Chem. *Res:* Plant responses to environmental stress including water deficit and air pollution; regulation of leaf gas exchange, stomatal physiology and biomass allocation. *Mailing Add:* Kearney Agr Ctr Univ Calif Riverside 9240 S Riverbend Ave Parlier CA 93648. *E-Mail:* david@uckac.edu

GRANVILLE, ANDREW JAM, MATHEMATICS, STATISTICS. *Current Pos:* ASST PROF, UNIV GA, ATHENS, 89- *Personal Data:* b London, Eng, Sept 7, 62. *Educ:* Cambridge Univ, Eng, BA, 83, CASM, 84; Queen's Univ, Kingston, Ont, PhD, 87. *Honors & Awards:* Merten Hasse Prize, Math Asn Am, 95. *Prof Exp:* Asst prof, Univ Toronto, 87-89; mem, Inst Advan Study, 89-91. *Concurrent Pos:* Grantee, NSF, 90- & Nat Security Agency, 90- *Mem:* Am Math Soc; Can Math Soc; Can Number Theory Asn. *Res:* Unexpected limitations on the equi-distribution of primes and discovery of criteria for the first case of Fermat's last theorem; disproof of Kummer's conjecture for the size of the class number; fine multiplicative structure of integers in binomial coefficients and cellular automata with many states; contributed over 50 articles to journals. *Mailing Add:* Dept Math Univ Ga Athens GA 30602

GRANZOW, KENNETH DONALD, PHYSICS, ELECTRICAL ENGINEERING. *Current Pos:* SCI CONSULT, 87- *Personal Data:* b Oak Park, Ill, Mar 26, 33; m 52, Elinor Parsons; c Mark, Barbara (Erickson), Glen & Lee A (Nevius). *Educ:* Univ Ill, BS, 58, MS, 59. *Prof Exp:* Staff mem, Sandia Corp, 59-63; from res physicist to sr res physicist, The Dikewood Corp, 63-68, leading scientist, 68-80, prin scientist & dir, 80-85; sci asst div mgr, Mission Res Corp, 85-87. *Concurrent Pos:* Consult, Logicon RDA, 87-96, tech staff, 96-97. *Res:* Nuclear weapon effects; nuclear safeguards; electromagnetism; quantum field theory; atmospheric physics; gas discharges; digital transmission lines. *Mailing Add:* 1079 Haverhill Pl Colorado Springs CO 80919

GRAPER, EDWARD BOWEN, THIN FILMS, HIGH VACUUM FOR SCIENCE & TECHNOLOGY. *Current Pos:* PRES, LEBOW CORP, GOLETA, CALIF, 73. *Personal Data:* b Los Angeles, Calif, June 1, 47; m 68. *Educ:* Univ Calif, Berkeley, BSME, 65. *Honors & Awards:* I-R 100 Award, 77 & 79. *Prof Exp:* Engr, Unified Sci Inc, Pasadena, Calif, 65-67; proj engr, Sloan Technol, Santa Barbara, Calif, 67-73. *Concurrent Pos:* Expert thin films, UN Indust Develop Orgn, Vienna, 86- *Mem:* Am Vacuum Soc; Am Optical Soc; Soc Photo-Optical Instrumentation Engrs. *Res:* Deposition of thin films by evaporating and sputtering; vacuum technology; application of thin films and vacuum to industrial and laboratory products and processes. *Mailing Add:* Las Varas Cyn Goleta CA 93117

GRASSE, PETER BRUNNER, CHEMISTRY. *Current Pos:* Sr prod develop chemist, indust tape div lab, 83-89, PROD ENG SUPVR, AUTOMOTIVE DESIGN SYSTS, 3M CO, 89- *Personal Data:* b Chicago, Ill, Feb 3, 56. *Educ:* Carleton Col, BA, 78; Univ Ill, PhD(org chem), 83. *Mem:* Sigma Xi; Am Chem Soc. *Res:* Pressure sensitive adhesive development; products for electronics market. *Mailing Add:* 3M Co 3M Ctr Bldg 218-1-05 St Paul MN 55144-1000

GRASSELLI, JEANETTE GECSY, SPECTROSCOPY. *Personal Data:* b Cleveland, Ohio, Aug 4, 28; m 87, Glenn R Brown. *Educ:* Ohio Univ, BS, 50; Western Res Univ, MS, 58. *Hon Degrees:* DSc, Ohio Univ, 78, & Clarkson Univ, 86, Wilson Col, 94, Notre Dame Col, 95, Kenyon Col, 95, Mat Union Col, 96; DEng, Mich Technol Univ, 89. *Honors & Awards:* Anachem Award, 78; Williams-Wright Award, 80; Harry Hallan Mem lectr, Swansea, UK, 80; Lucy Pickett Mem lectr, Mt Holyoke Col, 80; Garvan Medal, Am Chem Soc, 86. *Prof Exp:* Chemist infrared spectros, BP Am Res & Develop, 50-56, proj leader, Absorption Spectros Group, 56-70, supvr molecular spectros, 70-81, dir, Analytical Sci Lab, 81-83, dir; Tech Support Dept, Ohio Univ, 83-85, dir, Corp, Res & Anal Sci 85-89, dir, res enhancement & distinguished vis prof, 90-95. *Concurrent Pos:* vpres, NE Ohio Sci & Eng Fair, 77-; bd dirs, Nic Instr Co, 82-92; chmn bd trustees, Ohio Univ, 85-94; mem bd, Ohio Sci & Technol, Nat Res Coun, 86-92 & Edison Biotech Ctr, 88-95; adv bd, US Dept Energy, 87-89; adv comt chem, NSF, 94; vis comt, Nat Inst Stand Technol, 88-91; chmn, Anal Div, Am Chem Soc, 90-91; exhibition adv bd, Smithsonian, 90-94; bd dirs, BF Goodrich, 91-, AGA Gas, Inc, 93-, USX Corp, 93-, Diatrac Holdings, 94-, McDonald & Co Investments, 96-; chmn, Analytical Div, Am Chem Soc, 90-91; mem, Ohio Bd Regents, 95- *Mem:* Am Chem Soc; Soc Appl Spectros (pres, 70); Coblentz Soc; Fedn Analytical Chem & Spectros Socs (secy, 76-80); AAAS. *Res:* Molecular spectroscopy; infrared; raman. *Mailing Add:* 150 Greentree Rd Chagrin Falls OH 44022-2424

GRASSELLI, ROBERT KARL, PHYSICAL CHEMISTRY & CATALYSIS. *Current Pos:* ADJ PROF, UNIV DEL, 95-; VIS GUEST PROF, UNIV MUNICH, 95- *Personal Data:* b Celje, Slovenia, June 7, 30; nat US; m 89, Eva-Maria Hauck. *Educ:* Harvard Univ, AB, 52; Case Western Res Univ, MS, 55, PhD(phys chem), 59. *Honors & Awards:* Charles D Hurd Lectr, Northwestern Univ, 82; E V Murphree Award, Am Chem Soc, 84 & Petrol Chem Award, 90; Humboldt Prize, Alexander von Humboldt Found, 95. *Prof Exp:* Chemist, Stand Oil Co, Ohio, 52-55, sr chemist & proj dir, 55-59, sr res chemist & group leader, 60-65, res assoc, 65-69, sr res assoc, 69-74, res supvr explor & fundamental catalysis, 74-78, sr scientist, 78-80, sci fel & dir, Catalysis & Solid State Sci Lab, 81-85; dir, Chem Div, Off Naval Res, 86-89; res scientist, Mobil Res & Develop Corp, Princeton, 89-95. *Concurrent Pos:* Adj prof chem, Case Western Res Univ, 83-89; guest prof indust chem, Univ Bologna, Italy, 87-95; assoc ed, Catalysis Today, 87-96; chmn & bd trustees, Gordon Res Conf, 88-89; adj res prof chem, Georgetown Univ, 88-90; dir, Phil Catalysts Soc, 90-92. *Mem:* Nat Acad Eng; Catalysis Soc; fel AAAS; Sigma Xi; Am Chem Soc. *Res:* Heterogeneous catalysis; selective oxidation catalysis, kinetics of solid state and surface dynamics; reaction mechanisms; petrochemicals; surface reactions; controlled sequencing of catalytic sites; synthesis of inorganic solids; alternate fuels. *Mailing Add:* Dept Chem Eng Ctr Catalytic Sci & Technol Univ Del Newark DE 19716-3119. *Fax:* 302-831-2085 or 49 89 5902 602; *E-Mail:* rkrasse@lise.phys.chemie.uni—muenchen.de

GRASSER, BRUCE HOWARD, CHEMICAL ENGINEERING. *Current Pos:* group leader chem processing res & develop, 70-77, group leader maintenance & eng, 72-77, asst dept head, 77-78, DEPT HEAD PILOT PLANT CHEM PROCESS ENG RES & DEVELOP, LUBRIZOL CORP, 78- *Personal Data:* b Cleveland, Ohio, Mar 8, 41; m 61; c 3. *Educ:* Iowa State Univ, BSChE, 64; Case Western Reserve Univ, MBA, 71. *Prof Exp:* Process engr chem process develop, Goodrich-Gulf Chem, Inc, 64-68. *Mem:* Am Chem Soc; Am Inst Chem Engrs. *Res:* Chemical process research and development relative to lubricant and fuel additive chemistry. *Mailing Add:* 10055 Woodview Dr Chardon OH 44024-9105

GRASSETTI, DAVIDE RICCARDO, BIOPHARMACEUTICS, PHARMACOLOGY. *Current Pos:* RETIRED. *Personal Data:* b Padua, Italy, Aug 24, 20; US citizen; m 52, Mine Simons; c Daniel, Richard, Silvia & Elizabeth. *Educ:* Univ Lausanne, BS, 41, PhD(chem), 45, ChE, 45. *Prof Exp:* Instr pharmaceut chem, Univ Padua, 48-50; res assoc org chem, Mass Inst Technol, 50-52; res assoc, Yale Univ, 52-54; res chemist, Nopco Chem Co, 54-56; assoc res chemist, Sch Med, Univ Calif, San Francisco, 57-62; proj dir cancer chemother, Inst Chem Biol, Univ San Francisco, 62-66; dir res, Arequipa Found, San Francisco, 67-74; pres, Newcell Biochem, Berkeley, 75-80; prof chem, Univ Pac, Stockton, Calif, 84-86. *Concurrent Pos:* Lectr, Med Ctr, Univ Calif, San Francisco, 60-64; clin assoc prof biochem, Sch Dent, Univ of the Pac, 73-; vis prof pharmacol, Univ Padua Med Sch, Italy, 79-82. *Mem:* Am Chem Soc. *Res:* Sulfhydryl groups on cell surfaces; modification of cell surfaces by heterocyclic disulfides; prevention of cancer metastases; cancer therapy. *Mailing Add:* 19810 Peppermint Falls Rd Jamestown CA 95327

GRASSHOFF, JURGEN MICHAEL, POLYMER CHEMISTRY, ORGANIC CHEMISTRY. *Current Pos:* CONSULT, 95- *Personal Data:* b Berlin, Ger, May 7, 36; US citizen; m 89, Toyet Pham; c Sibylle, David & Michaela. *Educ:* Hannover Tech Univ, MS, 61; Swiss Fed Inst Technol, PhD(org chem), 65. *Prof Exp:* Head, Prod Develop Lab, Steding & Co, WGer, 61-62; sci co-worker, Swiss Fed Inst Technol, 65; res chemist, Pennsalt Chem Corp, Pa, 65-67; scientist, Polaroid Corp, Cambridge, 67-77, sr scientist, 79-95. *Concurrent Pos:* Abstractor, Chem Abstr Serv, 69- *Mem:* Am Chem Soc. *Res:* Aromatic diepoxides and diglycols; radical copolymerization of highly fluorinated monomers; swelling of water-soluble polymers; grafting of cellulose derivatives; release of photographic reagents; synthesis of polymeric mercaptides; emulsion polymers; photoacid generation; associative thickeners; biominetic polymers; liquid crystalline thermosets. *Mailing Add:* Seven John Robinson Rd Hudson MA 01749-2821. *E-Mail:* grasshoff@aspensystems.com

GRASSI, RAYMOND CHARLES, MECHANICAL ENGINEERING. *Current Pos:* instr mech eng, 42-44, 45-46, asst prof, 46-52, assoc prof indust eng, 52-60, PROF INDUST ENG, UNIV CALIF, BERKELEY, 60-, PROF OPER RES, 70- *Personal Data:* b Highland Park, Mich, Nov 27, 18; m 42. *Educ:* Univ Calif, BS, 40, MS, 44. *Prof Exp:* Inspector, Nordstrom Valve Co, 40-41; tool design engr, 41-42. *Concurrent Pos:* Ed supvr, Bur Ships Contract, 43-44, 46, res engr, 48-49; engr, Boeing Aircraft Co, Wash, 46; res engr, Off Sci Res & Develop contract, 44-46, Off Naval Res contract, 49-50, Atomic Energy Comn, Oak Ridge, 50-52 & Off Ord Res, US Army, 54- *Mem:* Am Soc Mech Engrs; Am Soc Metals; Am Soc Eng Educ; Sigma Xi. *Res:* Welding; residual stresses; structure; copper brazing of steel; effect of combined stresses on materials; production processes involving metal working or forming; stress rupture tests of various metals subjected to liquid-metal environment. *Mailing Add:* 4185 Etcheverry Hall Univ Calif Berkeley CA 94720-1777

GRASSI, VINCENT G, CHEMICAL PROCESS CONTROL, CHEMICAL PROCESS DEVELOPMENT & DESIGN. *Current Pos:* Comp control analyst, MIS, Air Prod & Chem Inc, 78-80, process engr, chem group engr, 80-83, sr process engr, process syst, 83-86, prin process engr process technol, 86-94, GROUP LEADER, PROCESS TECHNOL MODELING & PROCESS DYNAMICS, AIR PROD & CHEM INC, 95-, MGR PROCESS MODELING & CONTROL, 95- *Personal Data:* b Geneva, NY, Feb 21, 56; m 86, Kimberly Schroeder; c Christine. *Educ:* Univ Rochester, BS, 78; Lehigh Univ, MS, 84, PhD(chem eng), 91. *Concurrent Pos:* Lectr, distillation dynamics & control short course, Lehigh Univ, 86-; sem lectr, Chem Process Modeling & Control Ctr. *Res:* Development of computer models and analysis methods of chemical process dynamics and control; distillation processes including the process design and control of extraction distillation; plantwide control; process modeling distillation and collaborative computing information systems. *Mailing Add:* Air Prod & Chem Inc 7201 Hamilton Blvd Allentown PA 18195-1501. *E-Mail:* grassivg@apci.com

GRASSINO, ALEJANDRO E, RESPIRATORY MEDICINE. *Current Pos:* PROF MED, UNIV MONTREAL & MCGILL UNIV, 85- *Educ:* Univ Rosario, Arg, MD, 64. *Res:* Respiratory muscle physiology; chest wall mechanics. *Mailing Add:* Dept Med Univ Montreal & McGill Univ 3626 St Urbain St Montreal PQ H2X 2P2 Can. *Fax:* 514-398-7483

GRASSL, STEVEN MILLER, PHARMACOLOGY, PHYSIOLOGY. *Current Pos:* INSTR PHARMACOL, HEALTH SCI CTR, STATE UNIV NY, SYRACUSE, 83- *Personal Data:* b East Lansing, Mich, Mar 3, 52; m 75; c 3. *Educ:* Dickinson Col, BS, 74; Rutgers Univ, MS, 79; Cornell Univ, PhD(physiol), 83. *Prof Exp:* Fel physiol, Yale Sch Med, 80-83. *Mem:* Am Physiol Soc. *Res:* Membrane transport physiology. *Mailing Add:* Dept Pharmacol State Univ Ny Health Sci Ctr Syracuse 766 Irving Ave Syracuse NY 13210-1605

GRASSLE, JOHN FREDERICK, ECOLOGY, BIOLOGICAL OCEANOGRAPHY. *Current Pos:* DIR, INST MARINE & COASTAL SCI, 89- *Personal Data:* b Cleveland, Ohio, July 14, 39; m 64, Judith Payne; c J Thomas. *Educ:* Yale Univ, BS, 61; Duke Univ, PhD(zool), 67. *Prof Exp:* Fulbright-Hays grant, Univ Queensland, 67-69; from asst scientist to sr scientist, Woods Hole Oceanog Inst, 69-89. *Mem:* Am Soc Limnol & Oceanog; Soc Study Evolution; Ecol Soc Am; Oceanog Soc; Soc Am Naturalists. *Res:* Population biology of marine benthic organisms; coastal, deep-sea and coral reef communities. *Mailing Add:* Inst Marine & Coastal Sci Rutgers Univ PO Box 231 New Brunswick NJ 08903. *E-Mail:* grassle@ahab.rutgers.edu

GRASSLE, JUDITH PAYNE, POPULATION GENETICS. *Current Pos:* PROF, RUTGERS UNIV, 89- *Personal Data:* b Brisbane, Australia, Dec 4, 36; m 64, J Frederick Grassle; c Tom. *Educ:* Univ Queensland, BSc, 58, Hons, 60; Duke Univ, PhD(zool), 68. *Prof Exp:* Res asst physiol larval crustacea, Marine Lab, Duke Univ, 60-61; teaching asst zool, 61-62, res asst hemocyanin, 62-67; res assoc coelenterate toxins, Univ Queensland, 68-69; res assoc marine invert, Marine Biol Lab, Woods Hole, 70, independent investr pop genetics, 72-86, sr scientist, 86-89. *Mem:* AAAS; Sigma Xi; Soc Integrative & Comp Biol; Estuarine Res Fedn; Am Soc Leinol & Oceanog; Am Geophys Union. *Res:* Population genetics, dispersal and recruitment of marine invertebrates. *Mailing Add:* Inst Marine & Coastal Sci Rutgers Univ PO Box 231 New Brunswick NJ 08903-0231. *Fax:* 732-932-8959; *E-Mail:* jgrassle@imcs.rutgers.edu

GRASSMICK, ROBERT ALAN, PROTOZOOLOGY, PARASITOLOGY. *Current Pos:* asst prof, 71-75, ASSOC PROF ZOOL, MIAMI UNIV, 75- *Personal Data:* b Gering, Nebr, Aug 25, 36; m 62; c 2. *Educ:* Univ Nebr, BS, 58; Univ Mich, Ann Arbor, MA, 64; Iowa State Univ, PhD(zool), 71. *Prof Exp:* Instr life sci, Sutherland High Sch, Sutherland, Nebr, 58-59; instr, Deuel County High Sch, Chappell, Nebr, 61-63; instr life sci, Dept Biol, Mankato State Col, 64-67; from grad teaching asst zool to instr, Iowa State Univ, 67-71. *Concurrent Pos:* NSF fel, 75. *Mem:* Soc Protozoologists; Am Inst Biol Sci; AAAS; Soc Invert Pathologists; Sigma Xi. *Res:* Potential of ciliated protozoa as possible biological control agents for medically important mosquitoes; isolation of new strains of parasitic ciliates, host specificity and mode of infection. *Mailing Add:* 7 Mckee Ave Oxford OH 45056

GRASSO, JOSEPH ANTHONY, ANATOMY, CYTOLOGY. *Current Pos:* assoc prof, 75-78, PROF ANAT, UNIV CONN HEALTH CTR, 78- *Personal Data:* b Cambridge, Mass, Sept 17, 35; m 63; c 1. *Educ:* Tufts Univ, BS, 57; Ohio State Univ, PhD(anat), 61. *Prof Exp:* From instr to asst prof anat, Ohio State Univ, 59-61; from sr instr to asst prof, Sch Med, Case Western Res Univ, 63-70; assoc prof anat, Sch Med, Boston Univ, 70-75. *Concurrent Pos:* USPHS fel, Univ Chicago, 61-64; USPHS Career Develop Award, 65-73. *Mem:* NY Acad Sci; Am Soc Hematol; Soc Develop Biol; Am Soc Cell Biol; AAAS. *Res:* Biochemistry and ultrastructure of red blood cell development; iron metabolism; receptor mediated iron delivery. *Mailing Add:* Anat Univ Conn Sch Med 263 Farmington Ave Farmington CT 06030-0001

GRATCH, SERGE, THERMODYNAMICS. *Current Pos:* CONSULT. *Personal Data:* b Monte San Pietro, Italy, May 2, 21; nat US; m 51, Rosemary DeLay; c Susan, Mary, Lucia, Karen, Elizabeth, Ann, Barbara, Amy, Ellen & Thomas. *Educ:* Univ Pa, BS, 43, MS, 45, PhD(mech eng), 50. *Honors & Awards:* John Fritz Medal, 92. *Prof Exp:* Asst instr mech eng, Univ Pa, 43-44, instr, 44-47, assoc, 47-49, asst prof, 49-51; sr scientist res, Rohm & Haas Co, 51-59; assoc prof, Tech Inst, Northwestern Univ, 59-61; supvr appl sci, Ford Motor Co, 61-62, mgr, Chem Process & Develop Appl Res Off, 62-69, asst dir eng sci, sci res staff, 69-72, dir, Chem Sci Lab, 72-83 & Mat Sci Lab, 84-85, dir vehicle, power train & component res, 85-86; prof mech eng, GMI Eng & Mgt Inst, 86-96. *Concurrent Pos:* Regional ed, Int S Fracture, 65-91; mem, Air Pollution Res Adv Comt Coord Res Coun, Inc, 67-86 & chmn, 83-85; mem, Bd Lubricant Rev, Inst Soc Automotive Engrs, 78-85 & chmn, 83-84; presidential app, Nat Alcohol Fuels Comn, 79-81. *Mem:* Nat Acad Eng; AAAS; Am Chem Soc; hon mem Am Soc Mech Engrs (pres-elect, 81-82, pres, 82-83); fel Soc Automotive Engrs; Am Soc Eng Educ. *Res:* Thermodynamic properties of moist air; intermolecular forces in gas mixtures; zero-pressure thermodynamic properties of gases from spectroscopic data; chemical kinetics; polymerization kinetics; viscoelasticity; pollution control. *Mailing Add:* 32475 Bingham Rd Bingham Farms MI 48025-2427. *Fax:* 248-646-1264; *E-Mail:* sgratch124@aol.com

GRATIAN, J(OSEPH) WARREN, ACOUSTICS, MAGNETICS. *Current Pos:* RETIRED. *Personal Data:* b Hartford, Conn, Sept 5, 18; m 43, Anne Campbell; c Richard, Alexander & Elizabeth. *Educ:* Univ Ill, BS, 41; Univ Rochester, MS, 63. *Prof Exp:* From jr engr to asst elec engr, Naval Ord Lab, DC, 41-43; from res asst to res assoc physics, Univ Mich, 43-45; elec engr, Res Div, Stromberg Carlson Co, 45-50, sr engr, 50-56, asst sect head, Electroacoust Lab, Res & Develop Dept, Stromberg Carlson Div, Gen Dynamics Corp, 56-58, sect head info storage sect, Appl Physics Lab, 58-61, prin engr, Electronics Div, 62, eng staff specialist, 63-71; consult, 71-80. *Mem:* Acoust Soc Am; Audio Eng Soc; Inst Elec & Electronics Engrs; Sigma Xi; Nat Elec Eng Hon Soc. *Res:* Analog and digital magnetic recording; electronic circuits; electroacoustics; signal analysis; solid-state devices and digital information storage techniques; 32 US patents awarded and author of 10 publications and papers. *Mailing Add:* 156 Willowbend Rd Rochester NY 14618

GRATTAN, JAMES ALEX, IMMUNODIAGNOSTICS, BIO-ORGANIC CHEMISTRY. *Current Pos:* sr res scientist diagnostics, Bristol Labs, 79-82, dir, diagnostics res & develop, 82-83, assoc dir, Immunol, 83-90, sr med writer, 90-93, PRIN MED WRITER, BRISTOL-MYERS PHARMACEUT RES & DEVELOP DIV, 94- *Personal Data:* b New Brunswick, NJ, Feb 17, 48; div; c Noelle & Lauren. *Educ:* Col of the Holy Cross, AB, 70; Mass Inst Technol, PhD(org chem), 74. *Prof Exp:* Res scientist bio-org chem, Union Carbide Corp, 74-76, proj leader chem/immunochem, 76-78, group leader immunochem, 78-79. *Mem:* Am Chem Soc; Sigma Xi; AAAS. *Res:* Cancer diagnosis; immunoassay; immunochemistry; immunology; product development; protein conjugation; antibody targeted therapy; monoclonal antibodies; regulatory documentation of clinical trials in infectious disease, cancer, CNS. *Mailing Add:* 15-17 Forest Glen Circle Middletown CT 06457

GRATTON, ENRICO, BIOPHYSICS, BIOCHEMISTRY. *Current Pos:* res assoc biochem, 77-78, ASST PROF PHYSICS, UNIV ILL, URBANA, 78- *Personal Data:* b Merate, Italy, May 23, 46; m 70; c 2. *Educ:* Univ Rome, DPhys, 69. *Prof Exp:* Fel biophys, Inst Advan Health, Rome, 69-70; researcher, Snam Prog, Rome, 70-77. *Res:* Enzyme mechanism; fluorescence life time; enzyme dynamics. *Mailing Add:* Dept Physics Univ Ill 1110 W Green St Urbana IL 61801-3080. *Fax:* 217-244-7187

GRATTO-TREVOR, CHERI LYNN, SHOREBIRDS, WILDLIFE BIOLOGY. *Current Pos:* RES SCIENTIST, WILDLIFE RES SECT, ECOL RES, CAN WILDLIFE SERV, ENVIRON CAN, 89- *Personal Data:* b Halifax, NS, Dec 9, 56; m, John T Trevor. *Educ:* Acadia Univ, Wolfville, NS, BS, Hons, 78; Queen's Univ, Kingston, Ont, MS, 83, Univ NDak, PhD(biol), 89. *Mem:* Am Ornithologists Union; Prof Inst Pub Serv Can; Can Soc Ornithologists. *Res:* Shorebirds-breeding biology, population dynamics, migratory strategies; wildlife biology and conservation. *Mailing Add:* Can Wildlife Serv 115 Perimeter Rd Saskatoon SK S7N 0X4 Can. *Fax:* 306-975-4089

GRATZ, NORMAN G, MEDICAL ENTOMOLOGY. *Current Pos:* CONSULT, USAID & INDUST, 87- *Personal Data:* b Minneapolis, Minn, May 16, 25; m 58, Catherine Thosni; c 1. *Educ:* Univ Calif, Berkeley, BSc, 48, MSc, 50; Univ Geneva, DSc(zool), 66. *Honors & Awards:* Medal of Honor, Am Mosquito Control Asn, 85. *Prof Exp:* Dir vector control, Ministry Health, Israel, 53-58; proj leader, Res Unit, WHO, Liberia, 58-61 & Nigeria, 61-62, chief ecol & control vectors, 62-81, dir, Div Vector Biol & Control, Switz, 81-86. *Concurrent Pos:* Guest lectr, Hebrew Univ, Israel, 55-58, vis prof, Dept Med Ecol, Med Sch, 70; consult, WHO, 87- *Mem:* Am Mosquito Control Asn; Am Soc Trop Med & Hyg; Soc Vector Ecol. *Res:* Biology and control of arthropod vectors and rodent reservoirs of human disease. *Mailing Add:* 4 Chemin du Ruisseau Commugny 1291 Switzerland. *E-Mail:* gratz@lbm.net

GRATZ, RONALD KARL, VERTEBRATE PHYSIOLOGY, HERPETOLOGY. *Current Pos:* asst prof, 78-83, ASSOC PROF BIOL SCI, MICH TECHNOL UNIV, 83- *Personal Data:* b Northfield, NJ, June 1, 46. *Educ:* Univ Notre Dame, BS, 68, MS, 72; Univ Okla, PhD(zool), 76. *Prof Exp:* Sci asst physiol div, Max Planck Inst Exp Med, 76-78. *Mem:* Am Soc Zoologists; Am Physiol Soc; Sigma Xi; Nat Asn Adv Health Professions. *Res:* Comparative vertebrate physiology/physiological ecology. *Mailing Add:* Dept Biol Sci Mich Technol Univ Houghton MI 49931. *Fax:* 906-487-3167

GRATZ, ROY FRED, ORGANIC CHEMISTRY, POLYMER CHEMISTRY. *Current Pos:* from asst prof to assoc prof, 75-86, dept chmn, 83-91, PROF CHEM, MARY WASHINGTON COL, 86- *Personal Data:* b Pittsburgh, Pa, Nov 6, 42; m 69, Mary M Womeldorf; c Margaret K. *Educ:* Univ Pittsburgh, BS, 64; Duke Univ, MA, 68, PhD(org chem), 70. *Prof Exp:* Assoc pharmaceut chem, Med Univ SC, 70-71; asst prof chem, Salem Col, 71-75. *Concurrent Pos:* Fac fel, NASA Lewis Res Ctr, Cleveland, 83, 84, NASA Langley Res Ctr, Hampton, Va, 93; fac res prog, Naval Res Lab, Washington, DC, 85, 86, Naval Air Warfare Ctr, China Lake, Calif, 96. *Mem:* Am Chem Soc. *Mailing Add:* Dept Chem Mary Washington Col Fredericksburg VA 22401-5358

GRATZEK, JOHN B, VIROLOGY. *Current Pos:* PROF MICROBIOL & PREV MED & HEAD DEPT, UNIV GA, 66-, MEM FAC MICROBIOL, 76- *Personal Data:* b St Paul, Minn, Jan 23, 31; m 57; c 4. *Educ:* St Mary's Col, Minn, BS, 52; Univ Minn, DVM, 56; Univ Wis, MS, 59, PhD(virol), 61. *Prof Exp:* Instr vet sci, Univ Wis, 56-61; assoc prof virol, Iowa State Univ, 61-66. *Mem:* Am Vet Med Asn; Sigma Xi. *Res:* Bovine virus diarrhea; infectious bovine rhinotracheitis; infectious enteritis of turkeys; fish diseases. *Mailing Add:* 102 Colonial Dr Athens GA 30606

GRATZER, GEORGE, MATHEMATICS. *Current Pos:* prof, 67-85, DISTINGUISHED PROF MATH, UNIV MAN, 85- *Personal Data:* b Budapest, Hungary, Aug 2, 36; m 61, Catherine Zahomy; c Thomas & David. *Educ:* Eotvos Lorand Univ, Budapest, PhD, 60; Hungarian Acad Sci, DSc, 63. *Honors & Awards:* Grunwald Mem Prize, 60; Steacie Prize, Nat Res Coun Can, 71; Zubek Res Award, Univ Man, 74. *Prof Exp:* Researcher algebra, Math Inst, Hungarian Acad Sci, 59-63; vis asst prof math, Pa State Univ, 63-64, from assoc prof to prof, 64-67. *Concurrent Pos:* Can Res Coun Can fels, 61, grant, 67-; NSF grant, 65-67; vis prof math, Univ Man, 66-67; ed-in-chief, Algebra Universalis; mem math grant comt, Nat Res Coun; Killam fel, 86-88. *Mem:* Am Math Soc; Can Math Cong; fel Royal Soc Can. *Res:* Lattice theory; universal algebra; applications of logic to lattices and algebras. *Mailing Add:* Dept Math & Astron Univ Man Winnipeg MB R3T 2N2 Can. *E-Mail:* gratzer@cc.umanitoba.ca

GRATZL, MIKLOS, ELECTROANALYTICAL CHEMISTRY. *Current Pos:* ASST PROF, DEPT BIOMED ENG, CASE WESTERN RES UNIV, 90- *Personal Data:* b Veszprem, Hungary, June 18, 50; US citizen. *Educ:* Univ Veszprem, Hungary, MS, 73; Tech Univ Budapest & Hungarian Acad Sci, PhD(electroanal chem), 86. *Prof Exp:* Res assoc, Dept Gen & Anal Chem, Tech Univ Budapest, 76-81, 81-84, res assoc, Lab Solution Chem, 81-82, sr res assoc, Dept Gen & Anal Chem, 85-87; vis asst prof, Dept Mats Sci & Eng, Univ Utah, 87-90. *Concurrent Pos:* Scholarship Int Sci Exchange Prog, USA, Zurch, 79-80; exchange res assoc, Lab Solution Chem, Univ Fla, Gainesville, 81-82, Dept Chem, Univ NC, Chapel Hill, 84-85. *Mem:* Biomed Eng Soc. *Res:* Contributed numerous articles to publications and professional journals worldwide; diffusional microtitration for analyzing biomedical specimens including ultramicro amounts of enzymes and single cells. *Mailing Add:* 15805 Hemlock Rd Chagrin Falls OH 44022. *Fax:* 216-368-4969; *E-Mail:* mxgl3@po.cwru.edu

GRATZNER, HOWARD G, GENETICS, GENETIC TOXICOLOGY. *Personal Data:* b Philadelphia, Pa, July 21, 34; m 60. *Educ:* Pa State Univ, BS, 56; Temple Univ, AM, 60; Fla State Univ, PhD(genetics), 64. *Prof Exp:* Res asst biochem, Albert Einstein Med Ctr, 56-58; asst prof zool, Univ SFla, 64-67; asst prof, Univ Miami, 68-71; res scientist, Papanicolaou Cancer Res Inst, 71-; asst prof path, Sch Med, Univ Miami, 75-, asst prof surg, 80- *Concurrent Pos:* NIH spec res fel, Calif Inst Technol, 67-68. *Mem:* AAAS; Genetics Soc Am; Tissue Cult Asn; Soc Analytical Cytol. *Res:* Genetic control of DNA and protein synthesis; mutagenesis/carcinogenesis; chromosome structure; monoclonal antibodies; flow cytometry. *Mailing Add:* 14455 SW 85th St Miami FL 33183

GRAU, CHARLES RICHARD, POULTRY NUTRITION. *Current Pos:* From instr to assoc prof, Univ Calif, Davis, 46-58, chmn dept, 69-76, prof avian sci, 58-89, nutritionist, Exp Sta, 58-89, EMER PROF AVIAN SCI, UNIV CALIF, DAVIS, 89- *Personal Data:* b National City, Calif, Nov 5, 20; m 41; c 4. *Educ:* Univ Calif, BS, 42, PhD(animal nutrit), 46. *Mem:* Soc Develop Biol; Teratol Soc; Am Soc Cell Biol; Soc Exp Biol & Med; Poultry Sci Asn. *Res:* Amino acid requirements and metabolism in the chick; protein concentrates as amino acid sources; metabolism of phenylalanine and tyrosine in the chick and mouse; metabolism of gossypol in laying hens; energy needs and food intake; nutrition of chick embryos; egg formation; seabird reproductive ecology; silt pollution and seabird reproduction. *Mailing Add:* Dept Avian Sci Univ Calif Davis CA 95616

GRAU, CRAIG ROBERT, PHYTOPATHOLOGY. *Current Pos:* ASST PROF PLANT PATH, UNIV WIS, 76- *Personal Data:* b Manning, Iowa, Dec 5, 46; m 69; c 2. *Educ:* Iowa State Univ, BS, 69, MS, 71; Univ Minn, PhD(plant path), 75. *Prof Exp:* Res assoc plant path, NC State Univ, 75-76. *Concurrent Pos:* NDEA Title IV fel, Univ Minn. *Mem:* Am Phytopath Soc; Am Inst Biol Sci; Sigma Xi. *Res:* Biology and control of soil-borne plant pathogens and the mechanism and use of host resistance to this group of plant pathogens. *Mailing Add:* Dept Plant Path Univ Wis 284 Russell Lab Madison WI 53706-1520

GRAU, EDWARD GORDON, COMPARATIVE ENDOCRINOLOGY, NEUROENDOCRINOLOGY. *Current Pos:* from asst prof to assoc prof, 82-87, PROF ZOOL, UNIV HAWAII, 87- *Personal Data:* b Baltimore, Md, May 3, 46; m 69; c 1. *Educ:* Loyola Col, BS, 68; Morgan State Univ, MS, 73; Univ Del, PhD(biol sci), 78. *Prof Exp:* NIH fel, Univ Calif, Berkeley, 79-82. *Concurrent Pos:* NIH fel, 78; mem, US-Japan Collab Study Salmon Biol, NSF, 80-81. *Mem:* Am Soc Zoologists; AAAS. *Res:* Comparative endocrinology of reproduction, growth and development: special interest in pituitary control of thyroid function and in the mechanisms by which hypothalamic neurosecretory factors regulate the secretion of thyrotropin, prolactin, growth hormone. *Mailing Add:* Dept Zool Univ Hawaii Honolulu HI 96822

GRAUE, DENNIS JEROME, CHEMICAL ENGINEERING, PETROLEUM. *Current Pos:* PARTNER, NITEC, 95- *Personal Data:* b Minot, NDak, Sept 12, 39; m 59; c 2. *Educ:* Univ Colo, BS, 61; Calif Inst Technol, MS, 62, PhD(chem eng), 65. *Prof Exp:* Res engr, Chevron Oil Field Res Co, 65-69, engr, Chevron Standard Ltd, Alta, Can, 69-72, sr res engr, Chevron Oil Field Res Co, 72-76, sr staff engr, Chevron USA, Inc, 76-78; mgr, Sci Software Co, 78-81, div vpres, Sci Software Intercomp, 81-95. *Concurrent Pos:* NSF fel, 61-65; distinguished lectr, Enhanced Oil Recovery, Soc Petrol Engrs, 83-84. *Mem:* Am Inst Chem Engrs; Soc Petrol Engrs. *Res:* Fluid flow through porous media; oil reservoir behavior; diffusion; transport phenomena. *Mailing Add:* NITEC 475 17th St Suite 850 Denver CO 80202

GRAUE, LOUIS CHARLES, MATHEMATICS. *Current Pos:* assoc prof, 59-70, chmn dept, 65-74, PROF MATH, BOWLING GREEN STATE UNIV, 70- *Personal Data:* b Louisiana, Mo, Dec 23, 23; m 49; c 2. *Educ:* Univ Chicago, BS, 47, MS, 48; Ind Univ, PhD(math), 50. *Prof Exp:* Asst prof math, Sacramento State Col, 50-56; assoc prof, Coe Col, 56-59. *Mem:* Math Asn Am. *Res:* Mathematics, algebra and differential geometry and computers. *Mailing Add:* 624 Campbell Hill Rd Bowling Green OH 43402

GRAUER, ALBERT D, ASTRONOMY. *Current Pos:* ASSOC PROF ASTRON, UNIV ARK, LITTLE ROCK, 77- *Personal Data:* b Chicago, Ill, May 21, 42; c 2. *Educ:* Concordia Col, Seward, Nebr, BS, 64; NC State Univ, PhD(physics), 71. *Prof Exp:* Woodrow Wilson fel, 68, assoc prof physics, North Ga Col, 71-77. *Concurrent Pos:* Assoc vis prof astron, La State Univ, 77- *Mem:* Am Astron Soc; Royal Astron Soc; Am Asn Variable Star Observers. *Res:* Astronomical photoelectric photometry of variable stars; development of instrumentation for astronomical measurements. *Mailing Add:* 7001 Archwood Dr Little Rock AR 72204

GRAUERT, JOHANNES (HANS), MATHEMATICS. *Current Pos:* PROF MATH, UNIV GOTTINGEN, 59- *Personal Data:* b Haren, Ger, Feb 8, 30; m 56, Marie-Luise Meyer; c 2. *Hon Degrees:* Numerous from Ger univs. *Concurrent Pos:* Pres, Gottingen Acad Sci, 92-96. *Res:* Contributed articles to professional journals. *Mailing Add:* Bunsenstr 3-5 37073 Goettingen Germany

GRAUL, WALTER DALE, BEHAVIORAL BIOLOGY, VERTEBRATE ECOLOGY. *Current Pos:* nongame bird specialist, Colo Div Wildlife, 75-79, nongame res leader, 79-82, NE regional mgr, Wildlife Mgt, 83-95, ADMINR, WILDLIFE PROGS, COLO DIV WILDLIFE, 96- *Personal Data:* b Wichita, Kans, Jan 5, 44; m, Cynthia Feldman; c Julianne Leppert. *Educ:* Emporia Kans State Col, BS, 66, MS, 68; Univ Minn, PhD(ecol), 73. *Prof Exp:* High sch teacher biol, Bear Creek High Sch, 67-68 & Hastings High Sch, 70-71; asst prof, Univ NC, Charlotte, 73-75; assoc fac mem, Colo State Univ, 75-95. *Mem:* Sigma Xi; Am Ornithologists Union; Wildlife Soc; Wilson Ornith Soc; Cooper Ornith Soc. *Res:* Behavioral adaptations in birds with an emphasis on social behavior of shorebirds; applied research regarding endangered avian species and ecosystem management. *Mailing Add:* 6060 Broadway Denver CO 80216. *Fax:* 303-294-0874

GRAULTY, ROBERT THOMAS, QUALITY ASSURANCE, DEVELOPMENT OF EMPLOYEE INVOLVEMENT MANAGEMENT METHODS. *Current Pos:* CONSULT, 93- *Personal Data:* b Troy, NY, July 22, 28; m 50, Jacqueline Shields; c Kevin, James, Mark, Karen, Dianne, Daniel & John. *Educ:* US Merchant Marine Acad, BS, 49. *Prof Exp:* Proj engr, Am Locomotive Co, 49-55; engr, Westinghouse Bettis Atomic Power Lab, 55-69, mgr, Submarine Reactor Design, 69-77, mgr mfg, 77-82, plant mgr mfg, Fuel Div, 82-86; pvt consult, 86-91; consult, Westinghouse Savannah River Co, 91-93. *Mem:* Nat Soc Prof Engrs; Soc Mfg Engrs. *Res:* Design and development of nuclear reactor cores, vessels, components and systems; development of unique manufacturing processes; design of highly automated manufacturing plants; quality assurance in design and manufacturing. *Mailing Add:* 109 Miles Rd Columbia SC 29223-3110

GRAUMAN, JOSEPH URI, TOTAL QUALITY MANAGEMENT. *Current Pos:* DISTINGUISHED MEM TECH STAFF, AT&T BELL LABS, 80- *Personal Data:* b Hadera, Israel, Oct 1, 41; US citizen; m 69, Elaine K Morgan; c Ronnie L & Tracy L. *Educ:* Stevens Inst Technol, BS, 63, MS, 65, PhD(physics), 69; Rutgers Univ, MBA, 80. *Prof Exp:* Vis asst prof physics, Stevens Inst Technol, 69-70; asst prof physics, Jersey City State Col, 70-77; intermediate engr, Singer-Kearfott, 77-78; sr scientist, Xybion Corp, 78-80. *Concurrent Pos:* Res assoc, Stevens Inst Technol, 70-77. *Mem:* Am Phys Soc; NY Acad Sci; Sigma Xi; Am Soc Qual Control. *Res:* Implementation of total quality management in research and development environment; development of metrics for measurement of performance on research and development projects; development of business and financial reports, proposals and cost estimates on research and development projects; digital signal processing in connection with passive surveillance ASW program; communications systems engineering. *Mailing Add:* 2244 Copper Hill Dr Union NJ 07083-5145. *Fax:* 973 386-6633

GRAUPE, DANIEL, CONTROL SYSTEMS, SYSTEMS & BIOMEDICAL ENGINEERING. *Current Pos:* PROF ELECT ENG, COMPUTER SCI & BIOMED, UNIV ILL, CHICAGO, 85-, PROF PHYS MED & REHAB, 90-; VPRES, SIGMEDICS INC, NORTHBROOK. *Personal Data:* b Jerusalem, Israel, July 31, 34; m 68; c 3. *Educ:* Israel Inst Technol, BSME, 58, BSEE, 59, Dipl Eng, 60; Univ Liverpool, PhD(elec eng), 63. *Prof Exp:* Engr automatic control, Israel Govt Industs, Tel Aviv, 59-60; lectr elec eng, Univ Liverpool, 63-67; sr lectr mech eng, Israel Inst Technol, 67-70; from assoc prof to prof elec eng, Colo State Univ, 70-78; Bodine chair & distinguished prof elec & comput eng, Ill Inst Technol, 78-85. *Concurrent Pos:* Vis prof elec eng, Univ Notre Dame, 76; Russell Springer vis chair & prof mech eng, Univ Calif, Berkeley, 77; mem med staff res, Michael Reese Hosp & Med Ctr, Chicago. *Mem:* Fel Inst Elec & Electronics Engrs; NY Acad Sci. *Res:* Problems of automatic control, specifically adaptive control and artificial intelligence applications; methods of identification and estimation of processes and signals; applications of same to industrial and medical systems; systems theory; biomedical engineering; time series analysis; artificial limbs and powered braces for high-level amputees and hemiplegics; self-adaptive filter of noise from speech; EMG control of electrical stimulation to enable paraplegics to ambulate independently. *Mailing Add:* 496 Hillside Dr Highland Park Chicago IL 60035

GRAVA, JANIS (JOHN), SOIL SCIENCE. *Current Pos:* res fel, 54-57, from asst prof to prof, 57-85, EMER PROF SOIL SCI, UNIV MINN, ST PAUL, 85- *Personal Data:* b Vecgulbene, Latvia, Jan 24, 20; US citizen; m 42, 68; c 2. *Educ:* Univ Gottingen, MS, 48, PhD(agron), 50. *Prof Exp:* Res asst soil sci, Kans State Univ, 52-53, instr, 53-54. *Concurrent Pos:* Mem, Regional Soil Test Comt, 55-, chmn, 58. *Mem:* Am Soc Agron; Soil Sci Soc Am; Int Soc Soil Sci. *Res:* Crop production; soil fertility, chemical analyses and testing; grass seed and wild rice production. *Mailing Add:* 1255 NE Lincoln Terr Minneapolis MN 55421

GRAVANI, ROBERT BERNARD, FOOD SAFETY & SANITATION, EDUCATION & TRAINING. *Current Pos:* from asst prof to assoc prof, 78-90, PROF FOOD SCI, CORNELL UNIV, 91- *Personal Data:* b Jersey City, NJ, Aug 11, 45; m 80; c 2. *Educ:* Rutgers Univ, BS, 67; Cornell Univ, MS, 69, PhD(food sci), 75. *Honors & Awards:* William V Hickey Award, Asn Milk & Food Sanitarians, 84; Norbert F Sherman Award, Nat Restaurant Asn Educ Found, 89. *Prof Exp:* Asst dir, Inst Food Sci & Mkt, Cornell Univ, 73-75; sci dir Cereal Inst, Inc, 75-78; dir, Empire State Food & Agr Leadership Inst, 87-89. *Concurrent Pos:* Continuing educ comt, Inst Food Technologists, 82-86, vchmn, 83-84, chmn, 84-85 & past chmn, 85-86; comt, Inter Am Conf Food Protection, NAS & Food & Nutrit Bd, 84-86; tuna processing & stand rev comt, Can Dept Fisheries & Oceans, 86; vis prof, dept food sci, Univ Minn, 86; vis scholar, Dept Food Sci, Univ Nebr, 87; chmn, Educ Award Subcomt, Int Asn Milk, Food & Environ Sanitarians, 84-88, prog chmn, 88; mem bd trustees, Food Processors Inst, 88-; leadership develop fel, Nat Ctr Food & Agr Policy Resources for the Future, Wash, DC, 90; mem, Nat Adv Comt Microbiol Criteria for Foods, 90-; mem, Nat Food Safety & Qual Implementation Team, USDA, 91- *Mem:* Inst Food Technologists; Int Asn Milk, Food & Environ Sanitarians (secy, 84-86, vpres, 87, pres elect, 88, pres, 89); Am Soc Microbiol; Nat Restaurant Asn; Asn Food & Drug Officials. *Res:* Microbiological safety and qualtiy of foods; publics knowledge of selected food safety topics. *Mailing Add:* Dept Food Sci 114 Stocking Cornell Univ Ithaca NY 14853-7201. *E-Mail:* rbg2@cornell.edu

GRAVANIS, MICHAEL BASIL, PATHOLOGY. *Current Pos:* From asst to assoc prof, 65-70, prof & chmn dept, 70-85, PROF PATH, EMORY UNIV, 85- *Personal Data:* b Krokylion Doridos, Greece, Jan 27, 29; US citizen; m 77; c 2. *Educ:* Univ Thessaloniki, MD, 52. *Mem:* Col Am Path; Int Acad Path; Am Asn Path & Bact; AMA. *Res:* Cardiovascular pathology. *Mailing Add:* Dept Path Rm 701 WMB Emory Univ 1639 Pierce Dr Atlanta GA 30322-1100

GRAVATT, CLAUDE CARRINGTON, JR, MANAGEMENT OF TECHNOLOGY. *Current Pos:* res chem physicist, Nat Bur Stand, 69-73, asst to dir, 73-75, dep chief, Ctr Analytical Chem, 75-77, dir, Off Environ Measures, 77-79, dep dir, Nat Measurement Lab, Nat Inst Stand & Technol, Dept Com, 80-83, dir, Landsat Transition Group, 83-86, dep dir, Off Space Com, 86-88, assoc dir planning, 89-90, dir, Technol Analysis Group, 90-92, sr asst to under secy tecchnol, 90-95, sr asst to dir, 95-96, ASSOC DIR, MICROELECTRONICS PROGS, NAT INST STAND TECHNOL, 96- *Personal Data:* b Washington, DC, Dec 12, 39; m 64, Ann Lee Sullivan; c Lee G (Wilke) & Ann E. *Educ:* Univ Richmond, BS, 62; Duke Univ, PhD(phys chem), 66. *Prof Exp:* Res grant chem physics, Cornell Univ, 65-67; mem tech staff, Bell Tel Labs, NJ, 67-69. *Concurrent Pos:* vis prof eng & mgr, Ga Inst Technol, 95-96. *Mem:* Am Phys Soc; AAAS; Optical Soc Am; Soc Automotive Engrs; Am Soc Photogram & Remote Sensing. *Res:* Management of technology and innovation; science and technology policy; electromagnetic scattering studies of particulates, critical phenomena, liquid crystals and solutions; satellite remote sensing and image analysis. *Mailing Add:* Nat Inst Stand & Technol Tech A-323 Gaithersburg MD 20899-0001. *Fax:* 301-948-0978; *E-Mail:* cary.gravatt@nist.gov

GRAVE, GILMAN DREW, ENDOCRINOLOGY. *Current Pos:* res assoc, Lab Cerebral Metab, Div Biol & Biochem Res, Intramural Res Prog, NIMH, NIH, 68-70; staff fel, Lab, 70-72, med officer, Growth & Develop Br, Nat Inst Child Health & Human Develop, 72-76, Develop Biol & Nutrit Br, 76-77, actg chief, 77-79, chief, Sect Nutrit & Endocrinol, Clin Nutrit & Early Develop Br, 79-85, CHIEF ENDOCRINOL, NUTRIT & GROWTH BR, NAT INST CHILD HEALTH & HUMAN DEVELOP, NIH, BETHESDA, 85- *Personal Data:* b Rhineback, NY, Jan 3, 41; m; c 1. *Educ:* Harvard Univ, AB, 62, MD, 66; Am Bd Internal Med, dipl, 72. *Prof Exp:* Hemat technician, Mass Gen Hosp, Boston, 61-66, intern internal med, 66-67, resident, 67-68; instr med, Harvard Univ, 67-68. *Concurrent Pos:* Res assoc, Huntington Mem Labs, 63; med staff, Alexandria Gen Hosp, Va, 68-75, Doctor's Hosp, Washington, DC, 75-79 & Shady Grove Adventist Hosp, Md, 79-82; inst dir rep, Nat Diabetes Adv Bd, 78-; asst ed, Am J Clin Nutrit, 80-81; chmn, Subcomt Med Appln Diabetes Res, 81 & Clin Rev Subpanel, Nat Inst Child Health & Human Develop, 88-; mem, Sci Adv Comt, Nat Diabetes Res Interchange, 82- *Mem:* Am Diabetes Asn; Am Fedn Clin Res; Am Soc Neurochem. *Mailing Add:* NIH Nat Inst Child Health & Human Develop 9000 Rockville Pike Bethesda MD 20892

GRAVEEL, JOHN GERARD, SOIL MICROBIOLOGY, SOIL BIOCHEMISTRY. *Current Pos:* PROF AGRON & DIR, NAT RES & ENVIRON SCI PROG, PURDUE UNIV. *Personal Data:* b Mishawaka, Ind, Dec 8, 53; m 79; c 3. *Educ:* Purdue Univ, BS, 77, MS, 79, PhD(soil microbiol), 84. *Prof Exp:* Soil scientist, Ind Dept Natural Resources, 76; lab technician bionucleonics, Purdue Univ, 76, res asst soil microbiol, 77-84, teaching asst soil sci, 79-84; asst prof soil mgt, Univ Tenn, 83- *Concurrent Pos:* Instr, Ind Univ & Purdue Univ, 81. *Mem:* Am Soc Agron; Am Chem Soc; Soil Conserv Soc Am; Nat Asn Col Teachers Agr; Sigma Xi. *Res:* Decomposition of anthropogenic substances in the environment; effect of no-tillage farming practices on the physical, chemical and biological properties of soil. *Mailing Add:* Dept Agron Purdue Univ 1150 Lilly Hill West Lafayette IN 47907

GRAVEL, DENIS FERNAND, PHOTOCHEMISTRY. *Current Pos:* from asst prof to assoc prof, 64-73, PROF ORG CHEM, UNIV MONTREAL, 73- *Personal Data:* b St Lambert, Que, Nov 24, 35; m 66; c 2. *Educ:* Univ Montreal, BSc, 58, MS, 59, PhD(org chem), 62. *Prof Exp:* Nat Res Coun Can fel org chem, Swiss Fed Inst Technol, 62-64. *Mem:* Am Chem Soc; Chem Inst Can; Brit Chem Soc. *Res:* Synthetic organic chemistry; organic photochemistry. *Mailing Add:* Dept Chem Univ Montreal Succ Centreville PO Box 6128 Montreal PQ H3C 3J7 Can

GRAVELL, MANETH, VIROLOGY. *Current Pos:* res microbiologist, Viral Biol Br, Div Cancer Cause & Prev, Nat Cancer Inst, 74-75, CHIEF SECT NEUROVIROL, INFECTIOUS DIS BR, NAT INST NEUROL & COMMUN DIS & STROKE, NIH, BETHESDA, MD, 76- *Personal Data:* b Tamagua, Pa, Aug 15, 32; m 63; c 3. *Educ:* Muhlenberg Col, BS, 59; Lehigh Univ, MS, 65, PhD(biol), 66. *Prof Exp:* Res assoc virus & tissue cult, Merck Inst Ther Res, 59-61; spec technologist, St Jude's Children's Res Hosp, 65-66; instr microbiol, Hahnemann Med Col, 66-67; res assoc, St Jude Children's Res Hosp, 67-68, asst mem virol, 68-72; virologist, Microbiol Assocs Inc, Bethesda, Md, 72-73; dir, biol develop & exp oncol & prin investr, Nat Cancer Inst contract, Litton Bionetics, Inc, Kensington, Md, 73-74. *Concurrent Pos:* From instr to asst prof, Col Med, Univ Tenn, 67-72. *Mem:* AAAS; Am Soc Microbiol; Sigma Xi. *Res:* Cell and virus interactions. *Mailing Add:* 14901 Plainfield Lane Germantown MD 20878

GRAVEN, STANLEY N, PEDIATRICS & CHILD DEVELOPMENT, BIOCHEMISTRY. *Current Pos:* prof & chair, Dept Community & Family Health, Col Pub Health, 84-93, PROF & HEAD, DIV CHILD DEVELOP & NEUROL, UNIV SFLA, 93- *Personal Data:* b Greene, Iowa, May 20, 32; m 54, Maria N Johnson; c Nadine, Michael, Kendall & Douglas. *Educ:* Wartburg Col, BS, 55; Univ Iowa, MD, 56; Am Bd Pediat, dipl, 61, dipl, neonatal-perinatal med, 75. *Prof Exp:* Intern med, Madigan Army Hosp, Tacoma, Wash, 56-57; resident pediat, Cincinnati Children's Hosp, Ohio, 57-58 & Univ Iowa Hosps, 58-60; chief pediat serv, USAF Hosp, Fairchild AFB, Wash, 60-62, dir newborn & premature serv, Wilford Hall, Lackland AFB, Tex, 62-64; from asst prof to prof pediat, 66-76; co-dir, Wis Perinatal Ctr, 66-76; prof, Dept Pediat & Obstet/Gynec, Univ SDak, 76-80; prof, dept child health, Univ Mo, 80-84. *Concurrent Pos:* USPHS fel biochem & pediat, Univ Wis-Madison, 64-66; consult, Lakeland Village, Wash, 60-62; sr prog consult, Robert Wood Johnson Found, 79-, consult, Mo Div Health, 80-; med dir, Off Maternal-Child Health, SDak Dept Health, 76-79. *Mem:* Am Acad Pediat; Soc Pediat Res; Am Pediat Soc; Am Pub Health Asn; Sigma Xi. *Res:* Neonatology; newborn and premature physiology and biochemistry; high risk infant development. *Mailing Add:* Col Pub Health Univ SFla 13301 N Bruce B Downs Blvd Tampa FL 33612-3807

GRAVENSTEIN, JOACHIM STEFAN, MEDICINE, ANESTHESIOLOGY. *Current Pos:* GRAD RES PROF, COL MED, UNIV FLA, GAINESVILLE, 79- *Personal Data:* b Berlin, Ger, Jan 25, 25; nat US; m 49; c 8. *Educ:* Univ Bonn, Dr med, 51; Harvard Univ, MD, 58; Am Bd Anesthesiol, dipl. *Hon Degrees:* Dr, Univ Graz, 88. *Prof Exp:* Intern, Surg Univ Hosp, Switz, 51; assoc anesthetist, Mass Gen Hosp, 54-58; res assoc anesthesia, Harvard Univ, 55-56; prof surg & chief anesthesia, Col Med, Univ Fla, 58-65, prof anesthesiol & chmn dept, 65-69; prof anesthesiol & chmn dept, Sch Med, Case Western Res Univ, 69-79. *Concurrent Pos:* Clin fel anesthesia, Mass Gen Hosp, 52-54; fel, Mass Gen Hosp, 54-58. *Mem:* Am Soc Anesthesiol; Am Soc Pharmacol & Exp Therapeut; World Fedn Socs Anaesthesiologists. *Res:* Anesthetics and cardiovascular pharmacology; monitoring. *Mailing Add:* Dept Anesthesiol Col Med Univ Fla Box J-254 Gainesville FL 32610-0001. *Fax:* 352-392-7029

GRAVER, JACK EDWARD, MATHEMATICS. *Current Pos:* from asst prof to assoc prof, 66-75, chmn dept, 79-82, PROF MATH, SYRACUSE UNIV, 75- *Personal Data:* b Cincinnati, Ohio, Apr 13, 35; m 61, Yana R Hanus; c Juliet R, Yana-Maria & Paul C. *Educ:* Miami Univ, BA, 58; Ind Univ, MA, 61, PhD(math), 64. *Prof Exp:* Lectr math, Ind Univ, 64; res instr, Dartmouth Col, 64-66. *Concurrent Pos:* Vis prof math, Univ Nottingham, Eng, 71-72. *Mem:* AAAS; Am Math Soc; Math Asn Am; Soc Indust & Appl Math; Am Asn Univ Professors; Nat Coun Teachers Math; fel Inst Combinatorics & Applications. *Res:* Combinatorics; graph theory; systems of subsets of a finite set; integer programming. *Mailing Add:* Dept Math Syracuse Univ Syracuse NY 13244-0001. *Fax:* 315-443-1475; *E-Mail:* jegraver@mailbox.syr.edu

GRAVER, RICHARD BYRD, ORGANIC POLYMER CHEMISTRY. *Current Pos:* RETIRED. *Personal Data:* b Cambridge City, Ind, Apr 5, 32; m 52; c 5. *Educ:* Purdue Univ, BSChE, 54; Univ Mich, MSE, 55, PhD(chem eng), 58. *Prof Exp:* Res chemist resins, Archer Daniels Midland Co, 57-59, proj leader, 59-61, group leader, 61-67; mgr polymer res, Celanese Polymer Specialties Co, 67-73, tech mgr powder coatings, 73-76, tech mgr res, 76-78, tech mgr specialty resins, 78-92. *Concurrent Pos:* Prod safety specialist, Rhone-Paulenc. *Mem:* Am Chem Soc; Fedn Paint Soc; Sigma Xi; Am Soc Testing & Mat. *Res:* Polymers for coatings; water soluble polymers. *Mailing Add:* 9802 Calamar Ct Louisville KY 40241-3127

GRAVER, WILLIAM ROBERT, ELECTRO-OPTICS, LASERS. *Current Pos:* SR SCIENTIST, BALL CORP, 85- *Personal Data:* b Allentown, Pa, Apr 24, 47. *Educ:* Muhlenberg Col, BS, 49; Am Univ, MS, 74; Georgetown Univ, PhD(physics), 78. *Prof Exp:* Res physicist, Riverside Res Inst, 78-83; sr engr, W J Schafer Assoc, 83-85. *Mem:* Am Phys Soc; Optical Soc Am; Acoust Soc Am. *Mailing Add:* 6137 Ninth Rd N Arlington VA 22205

GRAVES, ANNE CAROL FINGER, PLANT CELL CULTURE, PLANT CELL TRANSFORMATION. *Current Pos:* RETIRED. *Personal Data:* b Ludlow, Miss, Nov 29, 33; m 56, Robert C; c Robert W, Anita E & Charles L. *Educ:* Millsaps Col, BS, 55; Northwestern Univ, MS, 56; Bowling Green State Univ, PhD(biol sci), 82. *Prof Exp:* From instr to assoc prof biol, Flint Community Col, 57-65; from instr to asst prof, Bowling Green State Univ, 67-90. *Concurrent Pos:* Asst prof, Univ Toledo, 83-89. *Mem:* Am Soc Microbiol; AAAS; Sigma Xi; Electron Micros Soc Am; Int Soc Molecular Genetics Plant-Microbe Interactions. *Res:* Ecology of fungus-inhabiting insects; transformation of monocotyledonous plants by Agrobacterium tumefaciens; bacterial attachement to plant cells; bacteria-plant cell interactions, plant cell culture. *Mailing Add:* 627 Crestview Dr Bowling Green OH 43402

GRAVES, BRUCE BANNISTER, ELECTROCHEMISTRY, PHYSICS. *Current Pos:* from asst prof to assoc prof, 68-74, PROF CHEM, EASTERN MICH UNIV, 74- *Personal Data:* b Lafayette, Ind, Dec 7, 28; m 53; c 3. *Educ:* Swarthmore Col, BA, 51; Univ Louisville, MS, 64, PhD(chem), 67. *Prof Exp:* Sci glassworker, Purdue Univ, 52-59; chemist, Radiochem, Inc, Ky, 60-62, chief chemist, 62-65, lab mgr, 64-65; from asst prof to assoc prof chem, Ky Southern Col, 66-68, actg head dept, 67-68. *Concurrent Pos:* Prin investr, NSF Grant, 69-73. *Mem:* AAAS; Electrochem Soc; Sigma Xi. *Res:* Differential thermal analysis; differential scanning calorimetry; catalysis and transient processes in electrochemistry; glass surface chemistry; history of glassworking and science; carbon 14 and tritium dating; isotope substitutions in spectrophotometry; photosensitivity; thermodyanmics. *Mailing Add:* 1209 Roosevelt Ypsilanti MI 48197-2119

GRAVES, CARL N, periodontal disease, root caries, for more information see previous edition

GRAVES, CHARLES NORMAN, PHYSIOLOGY, BIOCHEMISTRY. *Current Pos:* Res assoc, 61-64, asst prof, 64-68, ASSOC PROF REPRODUCTION PHYSIOL, UNIV ILL, URBANA, 68 *Personal Data:* b Fitchburg, Mass, Feb 6, 30; m 63, Charois Turner; c Cara, Carl, Christa & Colin. *Educ:* Okla State Univ, BS, 58; Univ Ill, Urbana, MS, 59, PhD(dairy sci), 62. *Concurrent Pos:* Res fel, Johns Hopkins Univ, 68-69; res scientist, Beltsville Res Ctr, USDA, 94. *Mem:* AAAS; Am Dairy Sci Asn; Am Soc Animal Sci; Soc Study Reprod. *Res:* Oogenesis; fertilization; early embryonic development; alterations in spermatozoa during storage. *Mailing Add:* Dept Animal Sci Univ Ill 330 Animal Sci Lab 1207 W Gregory St Urbana IL 61801. *Fax:* 217-333-8286

GRAVES, CLINTON HANNIBAL, JR, PLANT PATHOLOGY. *Current Pos:* PROF PLANT PATH, MISS STATE UNIV, 66- *Personal Data:* b Ackerman, Miss, July 22, 27; m 64; c 1. *Educ:* Miss State Univ, BS, 50; Univ Wis, PhD(phytopath), 54. *Prof Exp:* From asst plant pathologist to assoc plant pathologist, Miss Agr Exp Sta, 53-66. *Concurrent Pos:* Gen Educ Bd scholar; bd dir, Assoc Southern Agr Scientists, 71-72, exec comt, 72-; counr, Am Phytopath Soc, 72-77. *Mem:* Am Phytopath Soc Southern Div; Am Phytopath Soc. *Res:* Diseases of fruits and nuts; chemical control; breeding for disease resistance; interspecific crosses; molecular and cellular genetics; etiology. *Mailing Add:* 817 Pine Circle Starkville MS 39759

GRAVES, DAVID E, BIOCHEMISTRY, BIOPHYSICAL CHEMISTRY. *Current Pos:* asst prof, 85-90, ASSOC PROF CHEM, UNIV MISS, 90- *Personal Data:* b Cullman, Ala, Dec 12, 50; m 78, Janet Whitlow; c Clinton & Andrew. *Educ:* Univ Ala, Birmingham, BS, 74, PhD(biochem), 79. *Prof Exp:* NIH fel biophys, Univ Rochester, 80-84. *Mem:* Am Chem Soc; AAAS; Biophys Soc; Sigma Xi; Am Asn Chem Res. *Res:* Structural and functional properties of nucleic acids; interactions of antitumor agents with DNA; characterization of ligand-DNA interactions by design and development of topoisomerase inhibitors high resolution nuclear magnetic resonance techniques. *Mailing Add:* Dept Chem Univ Miss University MS 38677. *Fax:* 601-232-7300; *E-Mail:* graves@graves.chem.olemiss.edu

GRAVES, DAVID J(AMES), CHEMICAL & BIOMEDICAL ENGINEERING. *Current Pos:* Asst prof, 69-74, ASSOC PROF CHEM ENG, UNIV PA, 74- *Personal Data:* b Niagara Falls, NY, Feb 25, 41; m 66; c 2. *Educ:* Carnegie-Mellon Univ, BS, 63; Mass Inst Technol, MS, 65, DSc(chem eng), 67. *Hon Degrees:* MA, Univ Pa, 74. *Concurrent Pos:* Consult legal & indust concerns, 70-; NSF, NIH & Dept Energy Grants; Humboldt Found fel, 76-77; Fulbright-Hays award, Coun Int Exchange Scholars, Sweden, 76-77. *Mem:* AAAS; Am Chem Soc; Am Inst Chem Engrs. *Res:* Applied chemistry, particularly polymer, surface and enzyme chemistry; biomedical applications of chemical engineering; enzyme technology; ultrasound; gas diffusion through the skin. *Mailing Add:* Univ Pa 311 A Towne Bldg Philadelphia PA 19104

GRAVES, DONALD C, MEDICAL VIROLOGY, MOLECULAR PARASITOLOGY. *Current Pos:* from asst prof to assoc prof, 77-90, PROF MICROBIOL, UNIV OKLA HEALTH SCI CTR, 91- *Personal Data:* b Detroit Lakes, Minn, Jan 4, 42; m 64, Cheryl Bunkowski; c Timothy & Todd. *Educ:* St John's Univ, BS, 64; NDak State Univ, MS, 68; Mich State Univ, PhD(microbiol), 73. *Prof Exp:* Res assoc virol, Univ Pa, 74-76 & Southern Ill Univ, 76-77. *Concurrent Pos:* Prin investr, Nat Inst Allergy & Infectious Dis, 78-; mem, Bd Educ & Training, Nat Am Soc Microbiol, 80-85; mem, NIH Study Sect, 94- *Mem:* Am Soc Microbiol; Sigma Xi; AAAS; Soc Gen Microbiol; Am Soc Virol. *Res:* Studies on the basic biology of Pneumocystis carinii; immunological studies using antibodies and molecular biology studies using Pc/DNA probes are being conducted to demonstrate strain variation in this organism. *Mailing Add:* Dept Microbiol & Immunol Univ Okla Health Sci Ctr PO Box 26901 Oklahoma City OK 73190. *Fax:* 405-271-3117

GRAVES, DONALD J, BIOCHEMISTRY. *Current Pos:* from asst prof to assoc prof, 61-68, PROF BIOCHEM, IOWA STATE UNIV, 68- *Personal Data:* b Evanston, Ill, Oct 15, 33; m 58; c 5. *Educ:* Univ Ill, BS, 55; Univ Wash, PhD(biochem), 59. *Prof Exp:* NIH fel enzymol, Univ Minn, 59-61. *Concurrent Pos:* NIH career develop award, 65-69 & 70- *Mem:* Am Soc Biol Chemists; Am Chem Soc. *Res:* Mechanism of enzyme action; protein chemistry. *Mailing Add:* Dept Biochem & Biophys Iowa State Univ 4216 Molecular Biol Bldg Ames IA 50011-0001. *Fax:* 515-294-0453

GRAVES, GLEN ATKINS, NUCLEAR PHYSICS. *Current Pos:* MEM STAFF, LOS ALAMOS SCI LAB, 77- *Personal Data:* b Monroe Co, Ind, Nov 11, 27; m 51; c 3. *Educ:* Ind Univ, AB, 48, MS, 50, PhD(physics), 53. *Prof Exp:* Res assoc, Los Alamos Sci Lab, 49, mem staff, 52-67, asst group leader, 67-74; at off energy res & develop policy, NSF, 74-77. *Concurrent Pos:* Prof, Univ NMex, 54-74; head physics sect, Int Atomic Energy Agency, Austria, 69-70. *Mem:* Am Phys Soc; Am Inst Aeronaut & Astronaut; Am Nuclear Soc. *Res:* Nuclear spectroscopy; beta and gamma emission; nuclear reactor physics; radiation problems of propulsion reactors. *Mailing Add:* 80 Barranca Rd Los Alamos NM 87544

GRAVES, GLENN WILLIAM, MATHEMATICS. *Current Pos:* assoc prof bus admin, 65-71, assoc prof, 71-74, PROF QUANT METHODS, UNIV CALIF, LOS ANGELES, 74- *Personal Data:* b Detroit, Mich, June 22, 29; m 55. *Educ:* Western Mich Col Educ, BA, 51; Mich State Col, MA, 52; Univ Mich, PhD(math), 63. *Prof Exp:* Asst, Willow Run Res Ctr, Univ Mich, 52-54, asst, Statist Res Lab, 54-62; mem staff, Aerospace Corp, Calif, 62-64 & Rand Corp, 64-65. *Mem:* Am Math Soc; Asn Comput Mach. *Res:* Linear programming; numerical analysis; large scale digital computers; statistics. *Mailing Add:* 3642 Seahorn Dr Malibu CA 90265-5601

GRAVES, HANNON B, ethology, for more information see previous edition

GRAVES, HAROLD E(DWARD), CHEMICAL ENGINEERING. *Current Pos:* RETIRED. *Personal Data:* b Beardsley, Minn, Feb 20, 09; m 35; c 2. *Educ:* Univ Minn, BS & MS, 32, PhD(chem eng), 35. *Prof Exp:* Res chemist, Calco Chem Div, Am Cyanamid Co, 35-36; assoc prof chem eng, Miss State Col, 36-38; instr, Yale Univ, 38-40; asst prof, Worcester Polytech Inst, 40-41, prof, 41-48; prof & head dept, RI State Col, 48-52; chief chem engr, Jackson & Church Co, 52-56; supvr process eng sect, Dow Chem Co, 56-64, chief process engr, 64-67, staff asst, Midland Div, 67-74. *Mem:* Am Chem Soc; Am Inst Chem Engrs. *Res:* Process design. *Mailing Add:* 4305 Berkshire Ct Midland MI 48640-3319

GRAVES, HARVEY W(ILBUR), JR, NUCLEAR ENGINEERING. *Current Pos:* PRES, ENERGY ANALYSIS SOFTWARE SERV, INC, 79- *Personal Data:* b Rochester, NY, June 18, 27; m 60; c 3. *Educ:* Dartmouth Col, BA, 50, MS, 51; Univ Mich, PhD, 73. *Prof Exp:* Engr, Westinghouse Elec Corp, 51-53, nuclear engr, 53-55, supvry engr, 55-56, mgr nuclear eng, 56-66, mgr advan reactor develop, 66-68; consult engr, 68-79. *Concurrent Pos:* Lectr, Dept Nuclear Eng, Univ Mich, 68-73; adj prof, Dept Chem & Nuclear Eng, Univ Md, 81-84, 88- *Mem:* Fel Am Nuclear Soc. *Res:* Development of interactive software and expert systems software for engineering applications; nuclear reactor physics and engineering; nuclear fuel management. *Mailing Add:* 7723 Curtis St Chevy Chase MD 20815

GRAVES, JERRY BROOK, ENTOMOLOGY. *Current Pos:* Res assoc, Ls State Univ, 61-63, from asst prof to assoc prof, 63-71, head dept, 77-85, PROF ENTOM, LA STATE UNIV, BATON ROUGE, 77- *Personal Data:* b Tylertown, Miss, Feb 28, 35; m 60, Ellen Brumfield; c Shannon. *Educ:* Miss State Univ, BS, 55, MS, 58; La State Univ, PhD(entom), 62. *Honors & Awards:* Mobay Cotton Res Recognition Award, Nat Cotton Coun, 90. *Mem:* Entom Soc Am; Sigma Xi. *Res:* Control of cotton insects; insecticide resistance; insect toxicology. *Mailing Add:* Dept Entom La State Univ Baton Rouge LA 70803. *Fax:* 504-388-1643

GRAVES, JOSEPH L, biology of aging, for more information see previous edition

GRAVES, LEROY D, CIVIL ENGINEERING. *Current Pos:* from asst prof to assoc prof civil eng, Univ Notre Dame, 46-77, acting head dept, 60-61, asst chmn dept, 68-77, EMER PROF CIVIL ENG, UNIV NOTRE DAME, 77- *Personal Data:* b Kokomo, Ind, Mar 12, 12; m 34; c 2. *Educ:* Purdue Univ, BS, 33, MS, 41. *Prof Exp:* Field engr, State Dept Conserv, Ind, 33-37; res engr, joint hwy res proj, Purdue Univ, 37-41; soils engr, Ohio River Div Labs, Corps Engrs, 41-46. *Concurrent Pos:* Assoc, Hwy Res Bd, Nat Acad Sci-Nat Res Coun, 38-; soil mech consult, 46-; mem, Int Coun Soil Mech & Found Eng, 48-; secy-treas, Shilts, Graves & Assocs, Inc, 77- *Mem:* Fel Am Soc Civil Engrs; Nat Soc Prof Engrs; Am Soc Eng Educ. *Res:* Soil mechanics and foundation engineering; highways and airports. *Mailing Add:* 19681 Brick Rd South Bend IN 46637

GRAVES, ROBERT CHARLES, ENTOMOLOGY. *Current Pos:* from assoc prof to prof, 66-93, EMER PROF BIOL, BOWLING GREEN STATE UNIV, 93- *Personal Data:* b Evanston, Ill, Oct 24, 30; m 56, Anne C Finger; c Robert W, Anita E & Charles L. *Educ:* Northwestern Univ, BS, 52, MS, 53, PhD(biol sci), 56. *Prof Exp:* Asst biol, Northwestern Univ, 52-56; instr, Lake Forest Col, 56-57; prof, Flint Community Col, 57-66. *Concurrent Pos:* Ed, Cicindela, 69- *Mem:* Am Entom Soc; Entom Soc Can; Coleopterists Soc; Sigma Xi. *Res:* Ecology, systematics and distribution of Cicindelidae and Carabidae; fungus-inhabiting insects; Coleoptera. *Mailing Add:* Dept Biol Sci Bowling Green State Univ Bowling Green OH 43403-0212

GRAVES, ROBERT EARL, PHYSICAL CHEMISTRY, ORGANIC CHEMISTRY. *Current Pos:* PROF CHEM, E TEX BAPTIST COL, 77- *Personal Data:* b Haynesville, La, Oct 25, 38. *Educ:* Ouachita Baptist Univ, BS, 60; Baylor Univ, PhD(chem), 72. *Prof Exp:* Asst prof, Moody Col, Tex A&M Univ, 71-77. *Mem:* Am Chem Soc. *Res:* Environmental quality; nitrogen fixation. *Mailing Add:* Rte 7 Box 93 Marshall TX 75670-9109

GRAVES, ROBERT GAGE, EXPERIMENTAL NUCLEAR PHYSICS. *Current Pos:* PHYSICIST, RADIO THER UPSTATE NY, 88- *Personal Data:* b Gilroy, Calif, May 16, 42; m 62; c 3. *Educ:* Bucknell Univ, BS, 65; State Univ NY, Stony Brook, MA, 69, PhD(physics), 71. *Prof Exp:* Jr res assoc nuclear physics, Brookhaven Nat Lab, 69-71; res scientist nuclear physics, Cyclotron Inst, Tex A&M Univ, 71-80; mem fac, Univ Rochester Cancer Ctr, 80-88. *Mem:* Am Phys Soc. *Res:* Measurements of polarization transfer, analyzing power and neutron cross section in three nucleon systems and in proton-neutron reactions using light nuclei; production of polarized and unpolarized monoenergetic neutron beams. *Mailing Add:* Radio Ther Upstate NY 815 James St Syracuse NY 13203

GRAVES, ROBERT JOHN, INDUSTRIAL ENGINEERING, OPERATIONS RESEARCH. *Current Pos:* PROF DECISION SCIS & ENG SYSTS, RENSSELAER POLYTECH INST, 91- *Personal Data:* b Buffalo, NY, Sept 25, 45; m 68, Virginia; c Peter, Anna & Christopher. *Educ:* Syracuse Univ, BS, 67; State Univ NY, Buffalo, MS, 69, PhD(opers res), 74. *Honors & Awards:* Outstanding Res Contribution Award, Sigma Xi, 78; Spec Citation Award, Inst Indust Engrs, 85. *Prof Exp:* Dir Scheduling & Inventory Div, State Univ NY, Buffalo, 68-71, asst vpres facil planning, 71-73; instr indust eng, Sch Indust & Syst Eng, Ga Inst Technol, 73-74, asst prof, 74-79; from assoc prof to prof indust eng, Univ Mass, 88-91; prof decision sci eng syst, Rensselaer Poltech Inst, 91- *Concurrent Pos:* Consult engr, Clorox Corp, Bath Iron Works Shipyard, Draper Labs & Peterson Builders Shipyard, Digital Equip Corp, 77-91; dir, Rensselaer's Electronics Agile Mfg Res Inst. *Mem:* Inst Indust Engrs; Sigma Xi; fel Inst Indust Engrs. *Res:* Location theory and facilities planning, production planning and control, computerized layout, project planning and control; flexible assembly systems; information systems; design for assembly and manufacturability; electronics manufacturing. *Mailing Add:* 179 N Valley Rd RR 4 Pelham MA 01002-9719. *Fax:* 518-276-2120; *E-Mail:* graver@rpi.edu

GRAVES, ROBERT JOSEPH, ANALYTICAL CHEMISTRY. *Current Pos:* DIR, GC/MS LAB, UNIV ALA, 83- *Personal Data:* b Hammond, Ind, Aug 2, 52. *Educ:* Univ Ala Birmingham, BS, 78, MS, 81. *Prof Exp:* Mass spectrometrist & lectr chem, Univ Ala Birmingham, 80-82; prod develop scientist, Craven Labs, Austin, Tex, 82-83. *Concurrent Pos:* Consult, IBM Corp, Dionex Corp, Sunnyvale, Calif, P E LaMoureaux & Assocs, Tuscaloosa, Ala, Tuscaloosa Testing Lab, Jim Walter Resources Corp, Merichem Chem Co, Tex, Koppers Corp Pittsburgh & South Eastern Analytical Serv, Huntsville, Ala. *Mem:* Am Chem Soc; AAAS; Asn Off Analytical Chemists. *Res:* Development of new and superior analytical instrumentation and methodologies in the fields of biomass energy conversion; alternate fuel and chemical feedstock sources and environmental investigations. *Mailing Add:* 701 S Friendswood Dr Apt 402 Friendswood TX 77546

GRAVES, ROBERT LAWRENCE, MATHEMATICS. *Current Pos:* from asst prof to assoc prof, 58-65, assoc dean, Grad Sch Bus, 72-73 & 75-81, PROF APPL MATH, UNIV CHICAGO, 65-, DEP DEAN, 81- *Personal Data:* b Chicago, Ill, Sept 1, 26; m 51; c 4. *Educ:* Oberlin Col, BA, 47; Harvard Univ, MA, 48, PhD(math), 52. *Prof Exp:* Sr proj supvr, Stand Oil Co, Ind, 51-58. *Mem:* Am Math Soc; Opers Res Soc Am; Math Asn Am; Asn Comput Mach; Inst Mgt Sci. *Res:* Operations research, especially linear programming; digital computers. *Mailing Add:* Grad Sch Bus Univ Chicago Chicago IL 60637-1511

GRAVES, ROY WILLIAM, JR, GEOLOGY. *Current Pos:* RETIRED. *Personal Data:* b Ada, Okla, Dec 29, 15; m 42, Kathleen M Wasmuth; c Sandra, Michael & Terrill. *Educ:* Agr & Mech Col, Tex, BS, 39; Mo Sch Mines, MS, 41; Univ Tex, PhD(geol), 49. *Prof Exp:* Lab asst mineral, Mo Sch Mines, 39-41; instr geol, Univ Tex, 46-48; res geologist, Calif Res Corp, Stand Oil Co, Calif, 49-55; div stratigrapher, Calif Co, 55-57, area geologist, 57-61; sr geologist, Monsanto Chem Co, 61-63; adj assoc prof geol & geophys ed, Info Serv Div, Univ Tulsa, 63-83, adj prof & actg dir, Info Serv, 80-82. *Mem:* Fel Geol Soc Am; Am Asn Petrol Geol; Geosci Info Soc; Sigma Xi; Asn Earth Sci Ed. *Res:* Sedimentary petrology and paleoecology. *Mailing Add:* 9760 Capilano Rd Desert Hot Springs CA 92240-1101

GRAVES, SCOTT STOLL, CELLULAR & MOLECULAR IMMUNOLOGY, CELL BIOLOGY. *Current Pos:* SR SCIENTIST, NEORX CORP, 87-, SECT HEAD, DEPT MOLECULAR & CELL BIOL. *Personal Data:* b Oxnard, Calif, Sept 11, 51; m 78, Janet L Spear; c Sean M. *Educ:* Univ Calif, Davis, BS, 74; San Diego State Univ, MS, 79; Univ Ga, PhD(microbiol & immunol), 84. *Honors & Awards:* Dale A Porter Award Parasitol, 84. *Prof Exp:* Res asst marine biol, Scripps Inst Oceanog, La Jolla, 75-76 & immunol, Salk Inst, 79-81; lab technician & teaching asst, Dept Med Microbiol, Univ Ga, 81-84; fel, Dept Microbiol & Immunol, Univ Calif, 84-87. *Mem:* Am Asn Immunologists; AAAS. *Res:* Monoclonal antibody based cancer therapy; novel cytokine; bacterial toxins as cancer therapeutics; new technologies for cancer therapy; humanizing marine monoclonal antibodies; unique fusion proteins. *Mailing Add:* NEO Rx Corp 410 W Harrison St Seattle WA 98119. *Fax:* 206-298-9442

GRAVES, TOBY ROBERT, POLYMER CHEMISTRY. *Current Pos:* Develop engr, Petrolite Corp, 72-74, develop mgr, 75-80, tech mgr, 80-88, VPRES & GEN MGR, PETROLITE SPECIALTY POLYMERS GROUP, PETROLITE CORP, 88- *Personal Data:* b Stillwater, Okla, Jan 25, 46; m 66, Donna Brown; c Kimberly & Thomas. *Educ:* Okla State Univ, BS, 67, MS, 70, PhD(chem eng), 72. *Mem:* Am Inst Chem Engrs; Nat Soc Prof Eng. *Res:* Development of new polymers, derivations and applications for such products. *Mailing Add:* 10814 S Erie Ave Tulsa OK 74137. *Fax:* 918-831-6641

GRAVES, VICTORIA, ORGANOMETALLIC CHEMISTRY, INORGANIC CHEMISTRY. *Current Pos:* SR RESIN DEVELOP ENGR, PLASTICS TECH CTR, PHILLIPS 66 CO, 89- *Personal Data:* b Houston, Tex, Feb 14, 41. *Educ:* Incarnate Word Col, BA, 67; Univ Tex, Austin, MA, 69, PhD(inorg chem), 75. *Prof Exp:* Instr chem, Incarnate Word Col, 69-71; teaching asst, Univ Tex, Austin, 71-74; asst prof, Incarnate Word Col, 74-75; res assoc, Mass Inst Technol, 75-76; teaching fel, Latin Am Found, Technol Inst Monterrey, Mex, 76-77; res chemist plastics res & develop, Gulf Oil Chem Co, 78-79; res chemist, Plastics Technol Div, Exxon Chem Co, 79-89. *Mem:* Am Chem Soc; Soc Plastics Engrs. *Res:* Synthetic reactions of transition metal atoms; electronic structure and chemical reactions of transition metal pi-complexes; use of organometallic compounds in homogeneous and heterogeneous catalysis. *Mailing Add:* 1414 Walter St Longview TX 75605

GRAVES, WAYNE H(AIGH), PHYSICS, ELECTRICAL ENGINEERING. *Current Pos:* tech rep, 74-80, CONSULT, AM MED SYSTS, INC, 80- *Personal Data:* b Des Moines, Iowa, Dec 6, 25. *Educ:* Iowa State Univ, BS, 50; Univ Iowa, MS, 58, PhD(elec eng), 61. *Prof Exp:* Physicist, Eng Res Assoc, Minn, 50-51; staff engr commun, Collins Radio Co, Iowa, 52-63; staff engr electronics, Viron Div, Geophys Corp Am, 64-66; electronics res engr, N Star Res & Develop Inst, Minneapolis, 66-71; consult, 72-74. *Mem:* Inst Elec & Electronics Engrs; NY Acad Sci; Sigma Xi. *Res:* Nonlinear circuit theory and electromagnetic propagation; neurology and urology instrumentation. *Mailing Add:* 11511 Lakeview Lane Minnetonka MN 55305

GRAVES, WILLARD L, MATHEMATICAL MODELLING, MEDICAL IMAGE QUANTIFICATION. *Current Pos:* ASSOC PROF ENG, JOHNS HOPKINS UNIV, 62-, DIR C DISC, 80- *Personal Data:* b Springfield, Mo, Nov, 40; m 62, Carol Gevecker; c Karen G (Richardson) & Paul W. *Educ:* Drory Col, BA & BS, 62; Johns Hopkins Univ, BES, 65, MS, 67, PhD(environ eng), 72. *Concurrent Pos:* Owner & pres, Comput Coun Serv Inc, 64-; prof & chmn, Towson State Univ, 71-78; assoc prof epidemiol, Univ Md, 78-80. *Mem:* Nat Soc Prof Engrs; Am Radio Relay League; Asn Comput Mach. *Res:* Mathematical modelling of cardiac function through image evaluation, beat to beat; system design and integration. *Mailing Add:* 220 Chancery Rd Baltimore MD 21218-2501. *Fax:* 410-366-7123; *E-Mail:* Wlg@jhunix.hcf.jhu.edu

GRAVES, WILLIAM EARL, ENDOCRINOLOGY, PHYSIOLOGY. *Current Pos:* EXTEN PROF, UNIV MASS, 89- *Personal Data:* b Conway, Mass, June 1, 41; m 60; c 3. *Educ:* Univ Mass, Amherst, BS, 63; Univ Wis-Madison, MS, 65, PhD(endocrinol, reprod physiol), 67. *Prof Exp:* From asst prof to assoc prof vert physiol, State Univ NY, Col Environ Sci & Forestry, 67-76; asst vpres, Graves Farms Inc, 73-76, PRES, 76- *Res:* Agriculture; dairy management. *Mailing Add:* 915 Bardswell Ferry Rd Conway MA 01341

GRAVES, WILLIAM EWING, reactor physics, for more information see previous edition

GRAVES, WILLIAM HOWARD, VECTOR-VALUED MEASURES. *Current Pos:* from asst prof to assoc prof, 67-79, assoc dean, 81-87, PROF MATH, UNIV NC CHAPEL HILL, 79-, SPEC ASST TO PROVOST, 87- *Personal Data:* b Lebanon, Ky, July 4, 40; m 62. *Educ:* Ind Univ, AB, 62, MS, 65, PhD(math), 66. *Prof Exp:* Res assoc programming, Jet Propulsion Lab, Calif Inst Technol, 62-63. *Concurrent Pos:* NSF res grant, 69-70; consult scholar, IBM, 87-88. *Mem:* Am Math Soc; Math Asn Am; Asn Develop Comput-Based Instrs Systs. *Res:* Theory of vector-valued measures. *Mailing Add:* Univ NC Chapel Hill NC 27599-3250

GRAVETT, HOWARD L, GENETICS. *Current Pos:* from asst prof to prof, 46-76, EMER PROF BIOL, TEX A&M UNIV, 76- *Personal Data:* b Normal, Ill, Sept 21, 11; m 37, Loretta V Mehl. *Educ:* James Millikin Univ, AB, 33; Univ Ill, MA, 34, PhD(genetics), 39. *Prof Exp:* Asst biol, Univ Ill, 33-35, asst genetics, 35-37; from asst prof to prof biol, Elon Col, 37-46, head dept, 46. *Mem:* AAAS; Am Inst Biol Sci; Am Soc Zool; Nat Asn Biol Teachers. *Res:* Genetics of Drosophila; embryology. *Mailing Add:* 204 W Exchange Danvers IL 61732

GRAVITZ, SIDNEY I, SYSTEMS ENGINEER, PROGRAM DEVELOPMENT. *Current Pos:* CONSULT ENGR, 90- *Personal Data:* b Baltimore, Md, June 28, 32; m 64; c 2. *Educ:* Mass Inst Technol, BS, 53, MS, 54. *Prof Exp:* Dynamics group engr, NAm Aviation, 57-60; syst & prog eng mgr, Boeing Co, 60-90. *Concurrent Pos:* Res engr aeroelasticity, Aerospace Eng Dept, Mass Inst Technol, 52-57; mem, NASA-Indust Space Shuttle Design Criteria Working Group, 70, Radio Tech Comn for Aeronaut Panel, 80-81 & Naval Res Adv Comt Panel, 90; adj lectr, Cogswell Col, 90. *Mem:* AAAS; Am Soc Mech Eng; Am Inst Aeronaut & Astronaut; Sigma Xi. *Res:* Author, supervisor and consultant of papers and studies concerned with concept formulation and program development. *Mailing Add:* 8428 SE 62nd St Mercer Island WA 98040-4923

GRAY, A(UGUSTINE) H(EARD), JR, ENGINEERING, MATHEMATICS. *Current Pos:* PRES, A H GRAY ASSOCS, 93- *Personal Data:* b Long Beach, Calif, Aug 18, 36; m 59; c 1. *Educ:* Mass Inst Technol, SM & SB, 59; Calif Inst Technol, PhD(eng sci), 64. *Prof Exp:* Instr physics, San Diego State Col, 59-60; instr eng sci, Calif Inst Technol, 64; from asst prof to prof elec eng, Unif Calif, Santa Barbara, 68-80; sr scientist, Signal Technol Inc, 80-93. *Concurrent Pos:* Consult, Delco Electronics, Gen Motors Corp & Culler Harrison Labs. *Mem:* Inst Elec & Electronics Engrs; Soc Indust & Appl Math; Acoust Soc Am; Am Soc Mech Engrs. *Res:* Applied mathematics; stochastic processes; applied mechanics; numerical analysis; signal processing. *Mailing Add:* 88039 Leeward Dr Florence OR 97439

GRAY, ALAN, VIROLOGY. *Current Pos:* RETIRED. *Personal Data:* b Brooklyn, NY, Oct 11, 26; m 51; c 2. *Educ:* Pa State Univ, BA, 48, MS, 50; Univ Pa, PhD(pub health, prev med), 53; Am Bd Microbiol, dipl. *Prof Exp:* Asst, Pa State Univ, 49-50; fel, USPHS Univ Pa, 53-55; chief, Virus Dept, Microbiol Assocs, Washington, DC, 55-60; mgr biol develop, 60-63, mgr bact & viral vaccine prod, 63-70, dir biol prod, 70-74, sr dir biologics, Merck Sharp & Dohme, 74-88; pvt consult, 88-90. *Concurrent Pos:* Res assoc, Children's Hosp, Philadelphia, 53-55; instr, Univ Md, 58; mem rev comt, US Pharmacopeia, 70-80. *Mem:* AAAS; Am Soc Microbiol; Tissue Cult Asn; NY Acad Sci; Int Asn Biol Stand; Sigma Xi. *Res:* Viral diagnosis; veterinary and human vaccines; viral tumors; blood products. *Mailing Add:* 9 Pastern Lane Blue Bell PA 19422

GRAY, ALFRED, GEOMETRY. *Current Pos:* assoc prof, 68-70, PROF MATH, UNIV MD, COLLEGE PARK, 70- *Personal Data:* b Dallas, Tex, Oct 22, 39; m 64. *Educ:* Univ Kans, BA, 60, MA, 61; Univ Calif, Los Angeles, PhD(math), 64. *Prof Exp:* From instr to asst prof math, Univ Calif, Berkeley, 64-68. *Concurrent Pos:* NSF fel, Univ Calif, Berkeley, 65-66; Univ Md fac develop fel, 69; partic, Int Cong Mathematicians, Moscow, 66 & Nice, 70; partic, Oberwolfach Conf, 67 & 69. *Mem:* AAAS; Am Math Soc; Math Asn Am. *Res:* Differential geometry; complex analysis. *Mailing Add:* Dept Math Univ Md College Park MD 20742-0001

GRAY, ALLAN, JR, MATHEMATICS. *Current Pos:* from assoc prof to prof, 61-91, EMER PROF MATH, NORTHERN ARIZ UNIV, 91- *Personal Data:* b San Angelo, Tex, Aug 27, 30; m 54; c 2. *Educ:* NMex State Univ, BS, 52, MS, 55, PhD(math), 60. *Prof Exp:* Instr math, NMex State Univ, 55-58; mathematician, White Sands Missile Range, 58-61. *Mem:* Am Math Soc; Math Asn Am. *Res:* Monomial and permutation groups. *Mailing Add:* 503 W Apache Rd Flagstaff AZ 86001

GRAY, ALLAN P, ENVIRONMENTAL SCIENCES, TOXICOLOGY. *Current Pos:* ENVIRON & HEALTH CONSULT, A P GRAY ASSOCS, 90- *Personal Data:* b New York, NY, May 14, 22; wid; c Stefanie. *Educ:* Cornell Univ, AB, 43; Columbia Univ, AM, 47, PhD(org chem), 50. *Prof Exp:* Jr chemist, Cent Labs, Gen Foods Corp, 43-44; asst, Columbia Univ, 47-50; fel, Univ Chicago, 50-51; res chemist, Neisler Labs, Inc, 51-56, dir chem res, 56-66, sect head, Neisler Labs, Subsid Union Carbide, 66-69; assoc prof pharmacol, Col Med, Univ Vt, 69-73; proj mgr & sci adv, ITT Res Inst, 73-79; dept mgr, Environ Sci, Dynamac Corp, 79-84, dir environ & health sci, 84-90. *Concurrent Pos:* Reviewer, NIH, NIDA, NIEHS contracts & grant appls; chmn, Decatur-Springfield Subsect, Am Chem Soc, 55, vchmn, Div Med Chem, 74 & 75, chmn div, 76; mem, Develop Therapeut Contract Rev Comt, Nat Cancer Inst, 85-88; adj Prof, Dept Pharmacol, Sch Med, Georgetown Univ, 87- *Mem:* Fel AAAS; NY Acad Sci; Am Chem Soc. *Res:* Synthesis and properties of nitrogen heterocycles; hypotensive agents; muscle relaxants; analgesics; central agents; narcotic antagonists; toxic environmental contaminants; cancer chemotherapy; environmental health and environmental effects of industrial chemicals; risk assessment; design, synthesis and evaluation of potential medicinal agents. *Mailing Add:* A P Gray Assoc Health & Environ Consults 11905 Renwood Lane Rockville MD 20852. *Fax:* 301-417-9801

GRAY, ALLEN G(IBBS), physical chemistry, metallurgy & critical & strategic materials; deceased, see previous edition for last biography

GRAY, ANDREW P, VETERINARY MEDICINE, PATHOLOGY. *Current Pos:* assoc prof & vet pathologist, 66-86, EMER PROF VET PATH, KANS STATE UNIV, 86- *Personal Data:* b Bonner Springs, Kans, July 20, 16; wid; c 1. *Educ:* Kans State Univ, BS & DVM, 53, MS, 63, PhD(path), 66. *Prof Exp:* Pvt pract vet med, Ind, 53-61. *Mem:* Am Vet Med Asn. *Res:* Lungs, upper respiratory tract, eye and adnexa of domesticated animals. *Mailing Add:* 3011 Wayne Dr Manhattan KS 66502

GRAY, BRAYTON, ALGEBRAIC TOPOLOGY & HOMOTOPY THEORY. *Current Pos:* from asst prof to assoc prof, 66-90, PROF MATH, UNIV ILL, CHICAGO CIRCLE, 90- *Personal Data:* b Chicago, Ill, Dec 19, 40; div; c Lucas. *Educ:* Univ Chicago, BS & MS, 62, PhD(math), 65. *Prof Exp:* Lectr math, Manchester Univ, 64-66. *Concurrent Pos:* Lectr, Aarhus Univ, Denmark, 69-71; vis prof, Univ Heidelberg, Ger, 77-78; researcher, Max Plank Inst, Bonn, Ger, 86; adj prof, Northwestern Univ, 91- *Mem:* Am Math Soc. *Res:* Algebraic topology; homotopy groups of spheres; homotopy theory; cobordism theory. *Mailing Add:* Dept Math Univ Ill 851 S Morgan St M/C 249 Chicago IL 60607-7045. *Fax:* 312-996-1491; *E-Mail:* brayton@math.nwu.edu

GRAY, BRUCE WILLIAM, CYTOLOGY. *Current Pos:* from asst prof to assoc prof, 72-89, PROF VET HIST, AUBURN UNIV, 89- *Personal Data:* b Ithaca, NY, May 27, 37; m 58; c 3. *Educ:* Cornell Univ, DVM, 61, PhD(vet anat), 70. *Prof Exp:* Asst prof, Okla State Univ, 69-72. *Mem:* Am Asn Vet Anatomists; World Asn Vet Anatomists; Am Asn Anatomists; Int Embryo Transfer Soc. *Res:* Adenosine triphosphatase activity in bovine rumen; clinical sensory innervation of the equine metacarpophalangeal joint; fine structure of the excurrent duct system of the male goat. *Mailing Add:* 1374 Peachtree Lane Auburn AL 36830

GRAY, CHARLES A(UGUSTUS), chemical engineering, for more information see previous edition

GRAY, CLARKE THOMAS, MICROBIOLOGY, BIOCHEMISTRY. *Current Pos:* from assoc prof to prof, 60-84, chmn dept, 66-80, EMER PROF MICROBIOL, DARTMOUTH MED SCH, 84- *Personal Data:* b Norwood, Ohio, May 7, 19; m 42, Mary Finneran; c Charles & Eileen (Cater). *Educ:* Eastern Ky Univ, BS, 41; Ohio State Univ, PhD(bact), 49. *Hon Degrees:* MA, Dartmouth Col, 64; DSc, Eastern Ky State Univ, 89. *Prof Exp:* Instr bact, Ohio State Univ, 48-49; res assoc, Harvard Med Sch, 49-59. *Concurrent Pos:* Biochemist, Leonard Wood Mem Found, Harvard Med Sch, 4-59; Guggenheim fel, Oxford Univ, 59-60; adj prof biol, Dartmouth Col, 71-84. *Mem:* AAAS; Am Soc Biol Chem. *Res:* Physiology of mycobacteria; oxidative-phosphorylation; biological formation of hydrogen; nitrate reduction; cytochromes; aerobic and anaerobic electron transport. *Mailing Add:* Dept Microbiol Dartmouth Med Sch Hanover NH 03755

GRAY, CLIFFTON HERSCHEL, JR, GEOLOGY. *Current Pos:* RETIRED. *Personal Data:* b Riverside, Calif, Dec 27, 25; m 55; c 1. *Educ:* Univ Calif, Los Angeles, BA, 49; Claremont Grad Sch, MA, 53. *Prof Exp:* Asst geol sci, Pomona Col, 50-51; geologist, Mineral Deposits Br, US Geol Surv, 51-54; jr mining geologist, State Div Mines & Geol, Calif, 54-55, asst mining geologist, 55-58, assoc mining geologist, 58-70, sr geologist, 70-74, supv dist geologist, 70-88. *Mem:* Fel AAAS; fel Geol Soc Am; Mineral Soc Am; Am Asn Petrol Geologists; Soc Econ Geologists; Am Inst Pro Geologists; Am Inst Mining, Metall, Petrol Engrs. *Res:* Economic geology; nonmetallic industrial minerals, especially limestone and dolomite in California; engineering geology. *Mailing Add:* 4464 Edgewood Pl Riverside CA 92506

GRAY, CONSTANCE HELEN, ANATOMY. *Current Pos:* RETIRED. *Personal Data:* b Medway, Mass, Feb 27, 26; c 2. *Educ:* Univ Mass, BS, 47; Univ Hawaii, MS, 51; Univ Calif, Berkeley, PhD(anat), 74. *Prof Exp:* Lectr anat, Univ Calif, Berkeley, 74-76; lectr, Calif Polytech State Univ, 76-78, from asst prof to prof biol, 85-88. *Mem:* Soc Neurosci; AAAS; Am Pub Health Asn. *Res:* Neuropathology; cancer education. *Mailing Add:* 2630 Bonifacio Dr Tracy CA 95376

GRAY, D ANTHONY, ENVIRONMENTAL CHEMISTRY & MODELING. *Current Pos:* Res assoc, 79-84, fel, 84-88, CTR DIR, SYRACUSE RES CORP, 88- *Personal Data:* b Los Angeles, Calif, May 17, 50; m 74; c 3. *Educ:* Drexel Univ, BS, 73; Syracuse Univ, PhD(org chem), 81. *Mem:* Am Chem Soc; Soc Environ Toxicol & Chem. *Res:* Development of documentation to support the Environmental Protection Agency's regulatory actions; determination of environmental testing needs for commercial chemicals, modeling the fate and transport of chemicals in the environment; development of information systems. *Mailing Add:* Syracuse Res Corp Merrill Lane Syracuse NY 13210-4080. *Fax:* 315-426-3429; *E-Mail:* gray@syrres.com

GRAY, DAVID BERTSCH, EXPERIMENTAL ANALYSIS OF BEHAVIOR. *Current Pos:* ASSOC DIR RES, PROG OCCUP THER, WASHINGTON UNIV, 95- *Personal Data:* b Grand Rapids, Mich, Feb 7, 44; m 67; c 3. *Educ:* Lawrence Univ, BA, 66; Western Mich Univ, MA, 70; Univ Minn, PhD(psychol), 74. *Prof Exp:* Instr psychol, Seton Hill Col, 68-70; prog dir admin, Rochester State Hosp, 75-79, res dir, 80-81; health scientist adminr, Nat Inst Rehab Res, HSA, NIH, 82-86, dir, 87-95. *Mem:* Am Psychol Asn; AAAS; Nat Spinal Cord Injury Asn; Behav Genetics Asn. *Res:* Applied behavioral fields; mental retardation and developmental disabilities language development, behavior genetics, developmental behavioral pharmacology and learning disabilities. *Mailing Add:* Washington Univ Sch Med Prog Occup Ther 4444 Forest Park Rd St Louis MO 63108-2292

GRAY, DAVID ROBERT, MAMMALOGY, ARCTIC RESEARCH. *Current Pos:* RES SCI & WRITER, GRAYHOUND INFO SERVS, 94- *Personal Data:* b Victoria, BC, Oct 4, 45; m 78; c 4. *Educ:* Univ Victoria, BSc, 67; Univ Alta, PhD(zool), 73. *Prof Exp:* From asst cur to assoc cur, Nat Mus Natural Sci, Can, 73-88; cur vet ethol, Can Mus Nature, 88-94. *Concurrent Pos:* Comt mem, Tundra Panel, Can Comt Int Biol Prog, 73-75; prin investr, Nat Mus Natural Sci, High Arctic Res Sta, Can, 73-79, dir, 88-; mem, comt Polar Bear Pass, Nat Wildlife Area. *Mem:* Arctic Inst NAm. *Res:* Long-term ethological research on arctic mammals, particularly social behavior of muskoxen, arctic hare; collection of visual and sound documentation of avian and mammalian behavior patterns. *Mailing Add:* 3107 Eighth Line Rd Metcalfe ON K0A 2P0 Can

GRAY, DENNIS JOHN, CELL CULTURE, PLANT DEVELOPMENTAL BIOLOGY. *Current Pos:* asst prof, 84-89, ASSOC PROF DEVELOP BIOL, UNIV FLA, 89- *Personal Data:* b Juneau, Alaska, Nov 17, 53; m 83. *Educ:* Calif State Col, Stanislaus, BA, 76; Auburn Univ, MS, 79; NC State Univ, PhD(bot), 82. *Prof Exp:* Res asst mycol, Auburn Univ, 77-79; res asst bot & path, NC State Univ, 79-82; res assoc cell cult, Univ Tenn, 82-84. *Concurrent Pos:* Chmn, Tissue Cult Working Group, Am Soc Hort Sci, 88; consult, Inst Paper Sci & Technol, 88-, Goodyear Tire & Rubber Co, 88-89; assoc ed, Plant Cell Tissue & Organ Cult, 88-; prin investr, USDA & Int Bd Plant Genetic Resources, 89- & USAID, 90- *Mem:* AAAS; Am Inst Biol Sci; Am Soc Hort Sci; Bot Soc Am; Tissue Cult Asn; Coun Agr Sci & Technol. *Res:* Nonconventional methods of crop germ plasm improvement; conservation and propagation using cell, tissue and organ culture; synthetic seed technology; genetic transformation; grape, watermelon, canteloupe, squash, corn, mango and coniferous trees. *Mailing Add:* 5336 University Ave Leesburg FL 34748

GRAY, DEREK GEOFFREY, PHYSICAL CHEMISTRY, POLYMER SCIENCE. *Current Pos:* res scientist, 72-84, dir, Appl Chem Div, 84-89, PRIN SCIENTIST, PULP & PAPER RES INST CAN, 89- *Personal Data:* b Belfast, Ireland, Feb 9, 41; Can citizen; m 67; c 2. *Educ:* Queen's Univ, Belfast, BSc, 63; Univ Man, MSc, 65, PhD(chem), 68. *Honors & Awards:* Anselme Payer Award for Cellulose Chem, Am Chem Soc, 94. *Prof Exp:* Fel electrochem, Univ Newcastle, Eng, 68-69; fel polymer chem, Univ Toronto, 69-71. *Concurrent Pos:* Paprican adj prof, Dept Chem, McGill Univ, 75-; mem bd dirs, Can Soc Chem, 85-88. *Mem:* Tech Asn Pulp & Paper Indust; Am Chem Soc; Can Pulp & Paper Asn; Chem Inst Can. *Res:* Surface chemistry of paper and cellulose; properties of wood fibres; liquid crystalline derivatives of cellulose. *Mailing Add:* Pulp & Paper Ctr McGill Univ 3420 University St Montreal PQ H3A 2A7 Can

GRAY, DON NORMAN, ORGANIC POLYMER CHEMISTRY. *Current Pos:* PRES, ANATRACE INC, 85-; ADJ PROF PATH, MED COL OHIO, 85- *Personal Data:* b Carlyle, Ill, July 28, 31; m 59; c 3. *Educ:* Colo State Univ, BS, 53; Univ Colo, PhD(org chem), 56. *Prof Exp:* Res chemist, Denver Res Inst, Univ Denver, 57-64, asst prof chem, 60-64; mem staff, Martin Marietta Corp, Md, 64-66; sr res scientist, Owens-Ill Res Lab, Owens-Ill Tech Ctr, Mich, 66-68, sect head, 68-70, mgr biotechnol & toxicol, 70-85. *Concurrent Pos:* Instr, Univ Colo Exten, 57-64. *Mem:* AAAS; Am Chem Soc; Am Soc Artificial Internal Orgn; Int Soc Artificial Orgn. *Res:* Fluorine and polymer chemistry; membrane chemistry; biopolymers; high temperature polymers. *Mailing Add:* Anatrace Inc 1280 Dussel Dr Maumee OH 43537-1640

GRAY, DONALD HARFORD, SOIL MECHANICS, GEOLOGICAL ENGINEERING. *Current Pos:* from asst prof to assoc prof, 66-75, PROF CIVIL ENG, UNIV MICH, ANN ARBOR, 75- *Personal Data:* b San Salvador, El Salvador, Dec 14, 36; US citizen; m 60; c 2. *Educ:* Univ Calif, Berkeley, BS, 59, MS, 61, PhD(civil eng), 66. *Prof Exp:* Res engr petrol, Chevron Res Corp, 61-63. *Concurrent Pos:* Proj dir res grants, NSF, 68-73, Alcoa Found, 73-75 & Rockefeller Found, 75-76; actg dir Inst Environ Qual, Univ Mich, 71-72; consult, State Mich Atty Gen Off, 73-74. *Mem:* Am Soc Civil Engrs. *Res:* Soil reinforcement and slope stabilization by woody vegetation; engineering properties and utilization of residuals; creep behavior and rheological properties of soils. *Mailing Add:* Dept Civil Eng Univ Mich Main Campus Herbert Ave Ann Arbor MI 48109-2125

GRAY, DONALD MELVIN, BIOPHYSICAL CHEMISTRY. *Current Pos:* from asst prof to assoc prof, 70-83, head molecular & cell biol, 89-95, PROF MOLECULAR BIOL, UNIV TEX, DALLAS, 83- *Personal Data:* b Milton, Pa, Apr 4, 38; m 70, Carla Winlund. *Educ:* Susquehanna Univ, BA, 60; Yale Univ, MS, 63, PhD(molecular biophys), 67. *Prof Exp:* Nat Inst Gen Med Serv fel, Univ Calif, Berkeley, 67-69. *Concurrent Pos:* Fogarty Sr Int fel, Europ Molecular Biol Lab, 77-78. *Mem:* Fel AAAS; Biophys Soc; Am Chem Soc; Am Asn Univ Profs. *Res:* The circular dichroism of polynucleotides; the relationship of polynucleotide sequence to secondary and tertiary conformations; the structure of DNA-binding proteins. *Mailing Add:* Prog Molecular & Cell Biol Univ Tex-Dallas Mail Sta F031 Box 830688 Richardson TX 75083-0688

GRAY, DOUGLAS CARMON, INDUSTRIAL TOXICOLOGY, GOVERNMENTAL RELATIONS. *Current Pos:* mgr, Corp Indust Hyg, 84-95, CONSULT INDUST HYG, CABOT CORP, 95- *Personal Data:* b Poplar Bluff, Mo, Dec 19, 38; m 60; c 2. *Educ:* Univ Calif, Davis, BS, 60; Univ Cincinnati, MS, 70, PhD(environ health), 74. *Prof Exp:* Comdr, 33rd Chem Detachment, US Army, 61-62; indust hyg, Aerojet Gen Corp, 63-67; assoc prof community health, Northwestern Univ Med Sch, 72-74; indust hygienist, Los Alamos Sci Lab, 74-81; mgr environ hyg, Olin Corp, 81-82; dir occup safety & health, Univ New Haven, 82-83. *Concurrent Pos:* Chmn, Aeresol Technol Comt, Am Indust Hyg Asn, 85, Comt E34.18, Am Soc Testing & Mat, 85- & Synthetic Amorphous Silicas & Silicates Indust Asn, 86-88. *Mem:* Air Pollution Control Asn; Am Asn Aerosol Res; Am Indust Hyg Asn; Am Soc Testing & Mat; Am Conf Govt Indust Hygenists; Synthetic Amorphous Silica & Silicate Indust Asn. *Res:* Collection characteristics of aerosol inertial size analyzers (cascade impactors and cyclones), prediction of fluid evaporation and diffusion, and respiratory protection devices. *Mailing Add:* 267 Pine Hill Rd Chelmsford MA 01824

GRAY, EARL E, ELECTRICAL ENGINEERING. *Current Pos:* asst prof, Univ Idaho, 62-65, NSF sci fac fel, 69-70, assoc prof, 66-80, PROF ELEC ENG, UNIV IDAHO, 80- *Personal Data:* b Milliken, Colo, Jan 30, 29; m 49; c 2. *Educ:* Colo State Univ, BSEE, 55, MEE, 60. *Prof Exp:* Specialist elec eng, Gen Elec Co, 55-56; instr, Mich Col Mining & Technol, 56-57; asst prof, Colo State Univ, 57-62. *Concurrent Pos:* Elec engr, Nat Bur Stand, 61. *Mem:* Inst Elec & Electronics Engrs; Am Soc Eng Educ. *Res:* Electronics; logic design; information theory. *Mailing Add:* Dept Elec Eng Univ ID Moscow ID 83843-4199

GRAY, EDWARD RAY, EXPERIMENTAL NUCLEAR PHYSICS, PARTICLE ACCELERATOR PHYSICS. *Current Pos:* PHYSICIST, LOS ALAMOS NAT LABS, 84- *Personal Data:* b Ava, Ill, Nov 20, 38; m 60; c 2. *Educ:* Univ Ill, BS, 60, MS, 62, PhD(physics), 67. *Prof Exp:* Physicist, Aeronaut Div, Philco-Ford Corp, 66-67; physicist, Fermi Nat Accelerator Lab, Energy Res Develop Admin, 68-81; physicist, Technicare Corp, 81-84. *Mem:* Am Phys Soc; Sigma Xi. *Res:* Design and development of particle accelerator components. *Mailing Add:* 295 Donna Ave Los Alamos NM 87544

GRAY, EDWARD THEODORE, JR, INORGANIC CHEMISTRY. *Current Pos:* ASSOC PROF CHEM, UNIV HARTFORD, 77-, CHAIR, DEPT CHEM, 90- *Personal Data:* b Little Falls, NY, June 25, 50; m 73; c 1. *Educ:* Union Col, Schenectady, NY, BS, 72; Purdue Univ, PhD(analytical chem), 77. *Mem:* Am Chem Soc; Sigma Xi. *Res:* Bio-inorganic analytical chemistry; analytical measurement and/or separation of chloramines and chloramino acids to nanomolar concentrations; redox properties of metal-peptide complexes. *Mailing Add:* Dept Chem Univ Hartford 200 Bloomfield Ave West Hartford CT 06117

GRAY, ELMER, PLANT BREEDING. *Current Pos:* assoc prof, 68-71, PROF AGRON & DEAN GRAD COL, WESTERN KY UNIV, 71- *Personal Data:* b Gray Hawk, Ky, Mar 29, 34; m 57; c 1. *Educ:* Berea Col, BS, 56; Univ Ky, MS, 58; Cornell Univ, PhD(plant breeding), 62. *Prof Exp:* From asst prof to assoc prof agron, Univ Tenn, 62-68. *Mem:* Am Soc Agron; Crop Sci Soc Am; Am Genetic Asn; World Pop Soc. *Res:* Plant science; genetics; statistics. *Mailing Add:* Dept Agr Western Ky Univ 1 Big Red Way St Bowling Green KY 42101-3576

GRAY, ERNEST DAVID, BIOCHEMISTRY, IMMUNOLOGY. *Current Pos:* asst prof, 62-68, ASSOC PROF PEDIAT & BIOCHEM, UNIV MINN, MINNEAPOLIS, 68- *Personal Data:* b Winnipeg, Man, Oct 3, 30, m 57; c 2. *Educ:* Univ Man, BSc, 52; Univ Minn, PhD(physiol chem), 58. *Prof Exp:* From asst to instr physiol chem, Univ Minn, 52-58; asst lectr biochem, Glasgow Univ, 58-59; res assoc, Col Physicians & Surgeons, Columbia Univ, 60-62. *Concurrent Pos:* Res fel, Imp Chem Industs, 59-60. *Mem:* AAAS; Brit Biochem Soc; Am Soc Biol Chem; Am Chem Soc; Am Soc Microbiol. *Res:* Nucleic acid; metabolism, nuclease action; streptococcal products; purification and characterization of biological and chemical properties; analysis of cellular immune response to these products and its relationship to the pathogenesis of rheumatic heart disease. *Mailing Add:* Dept Biochem Pediat 420 Delaware SE PO Box 296 UMHC Minneapolis MN 55455. *Fax:* 612-624-8927

GRAY, ERNEST PAUL, ELECTROMAGNETIC SCATTERING, FLUID SURFACE & INTERNAL WAVES. *Current Pos:* sr staff mem & physicist, Johns Hopkins Univ, 51-58, chief, Theoret Plasma Physics Staff, 66-73, mem staff, Res Ctr, 73-83, mem, Staff Space Dept, 84-90, prin staff mem, Appl Physics Lab, 58-95, ADJ PROF, JOHNS HOPKINS UNIV, 59- *Personal Data:* b Vienna, Austria, Mar 12, 26; nat US; m 54; c 2. *Educ:* Cornell Univ, AB, 47, PhD(theoret physics), 52. *Prof Exp:* Asst physics, Cornell Univ, 49-52. *Concurrent Pos:* Parsons fel, 57-58; Parsons vis prof, Johns Hopkins Univ, 68-69 & 84-85, mem staff, Submarine Technol Dept, 91-; consult, Argonne Nat Lab, 75-77. *Mem:* AAAS; Am Phys Soc. *Res:* Problems in the propagation and scattering of microwaves; atomic excitation, ionization and recombination; highly ionized plasmas; charged particle trajectories; fluid dynamics; internal waves and surface waves in fluids. *Mailing Add:* 412 Kimblewick Dr Silver Spring MD 20904

GRAY, F(ESTUS) GAIL, COMPUTER DESIGN. *Current Pos:* from asst prof to assoc prof, 71-84, PROF ELEC ENG, VA POLYTECH INST & STATE UNIV, 84- *Personal Data:* b Moundsville, WVa, Aug 16, 43; m 68, Caryl e Anderson; c David, Andrew & Daniel. *Educ:* WVa Univ, BSEE, 65, MSEE, 67; Univ Mich, PhD(comput info control eng), 71. *Prof Exp:* Instr, elec eng, WVa Univ, 66-67; teaching fel, comput eng, Univ Mich, 67-70. *Concurrent Pos:* Trainee, US Aviation Mat Lab, 62, 63 & 64; res asst, Argonne Nat Lab, 67 & Univ Mich, 69-70; fac fel, NASA-Am Soc Elec Eng, Langley Res Ctr, 75; prin investr, NSF, 72-79 & 90-93, Rome Air Develop Ctr, 80-81, NASA Langley Res Ctr, 81-82, Naval Surface Weapons Ctr, 73-74, Dahlgren, 82-84, Off Naval Res, 80-83, Army Res Off, 82-85 & Adv Res Proj Agency, 93-; vis scientist, Res Triangle Inst, 84-85, consult, 86- *Mem:* Inst Elec & Electronics Engrs; Sigma Xi. *Res:* Fault tolerant computer architectures reconfigurable structures; digital design using hardware description languages modeling systems at a high level of abstraction; parallel computer architectures; algebraic coding theory for data storage and retrieval. *Mailing Add:* Dept Elec Eng Va Polytech Inst & State Univ Blacksburg VA 24061-0111. *Fax:* 540-231-3362; *E-Mail:* fggray@vt.edu

GRAY, FAITH HARRIET, ZOOLOGY. *Current Pos:* ASSOC PROF BIOL, HOLLINS COL, 74- *Personal Data:* b Mt Vernon, NY, Jan 15, 40. *Educ:* Chatham Col, BS, 62; Mt Holyoke Col, MA, 64; Ohio State Univ, PhD(entom), 68. *Prof Exp:* Fel physiol, Univ Miami, 68-70; fel entom, Ohio State Univ, 70-71; asst prof biol, Washington & Lee Univ, 71-73; asst prof, Wellesley Col, 73-74. *Mem:* AAAS; Am Inst Biol Sci; Am Entom Soc; Am Soc Zool; Tissue Cult Asn; Sigma Xi. *Res:* Insect physiology; comparative endocrinology; mechanisms of cellular aging. *Mailing Add:* Dept Biol Hollins Col PO Box 9616 Roanoke VA 24020

GRAY, FENTON, SOIL SCIENCE. *Current Pos:* RETIRED. *Personal Data:* b Santa Clara, Utah, Aug 12, 16; m 38; c 5. *Educ:* Univ Utah, BS, 38; Ohio State Univ, PhD(soils), 51. *Honors & Awards:* Ed Award, Soil Conserv Soc Am, 69. *Prof Exp:* Soil surveyor, Utah Agr Exp Sta, 39-41 & Soil Conserv Serv, USDA, 41-48; asst soils, Ohio State Univ, 48-51; from asst prof to prof soils, Okla State Univ, 51-82. *Concurrent Pos:* Sr soil scientist & proj leader, Food & Agr Admin, UN, Brazil, 61-62; travel grant to NZ, Australia & Orient, 68. *Mem:* Fel AAAS; Am Soc Agron; Soil Sci Soc Am; Soil Conserv Soc Am; Clay Minerals Soc. *Res:* Basic chemical, physical and mineralogical properties of Oklahoma soils with relationships to morphology, genesis, classification, soil and water conservation, productivity and good land use. *Mailing Add:* 1017 S Orchard Lane Stillwater OK 74074

GRAY, FRANK DAVIS, JR, INTERNAL MEDICINE. *Current Pos:* RETIRED. *Personal Data:* b Marshall, Minn, Aug 24, 16; m 41. *Educ:* Northwestern Univ, BS, 38; Columbia Univ, MD, 43. *Prof Exp:* Intern & asst resident med, Bellevue Hosp, 43-44; asst surg, Johns Hopkins Univ, 46-47; asst resident med, Yale Univ, 47-48, res fel, 48-49, from instr to assoc prof, 49-68; dir, Div Med, Lankenau Hosp, 68-76; prof med, Jefferson Med Col, 68-76, Magee prof med & chmn dept, 76-81, interim dean, 81-82. *Concurrent Pos:* Fel med, Yale Univ, 48-49; physician-in-chief, Thomas Jefferson Univ Hosp, 76-81. *Mem:* Am Soc Clin Invest; AMA; fel Am Col Physicians; fel Am Col Chest Physicians; Am Fedn Clin Res; Sigma Xi. *Res:* Clinical physiology of heart and lungs. *Mailing Add:* 5 Pond Lane Bryn Mawr PA 19010

GRAY, FREDERICK WILLIAM, ORGANIC CHEMISTRY. *Current Pos:* RETIRED. *Personal Data:* b Wakefield, Mass, Oct 4, 18; m 49, Ella Mae Watters; c William F & Patricia A. *Educ:* Tufts Col, BS, 41, MS, 43; Pa State Col, PhD(chem), 49. *Prof Exp:* Asst, Tufts Col, 41-43; res chemist, Cent Res Lab, Gen Aniline & Film Co, 43-46; asst, Pa State Univ, 46-49; res chemist, Colgate-Palmolive Co, Piscataway, 49-63, res assoc, 63-68, sr res assoc, 68-78, sr scientist, 78-83. *Mem:* Am Chem Soc; fel Am Inst Chem; Am Oil Chemists Soc. *Res:* Organic synthesis; dye intermediates; vinyl polymers; synthetic detergents; optical brighteners; chlorine and oxygen bleaches; development of household specialty product. *Mailing Add:* 14 Stockton Rd Summit NJ 07901

GRAY, FRIEDA GERSH, INTERNAL MEDICINE. *Current Pos:* prof community med & environ health, 77-79, PROF MED, HAHNEMANN UNIV SCH MED, 77- *Personal Data:* b Hartford, Conn, Nov 30, 17; m 41. *Educ:* Hunter Col, AB, 39; NY Med Col, MD, 44. *Prof Exp:* Asst bact, Col Physicians & Surgeons, Columbia Univ, 39-41; intern & asst resident med, Bellevue Hosp, 44-46; asst path, Johns Hopkins Univ & Hosp, 46-47; instr med, Sch Med, Yale Univ, 49-53, from asst clin prof to assoc clin prof, 53-60, from asst prof to assoc prof, 60-68; assoc prof, Jefferson Med Col, 68-73; assoc prof med, Sch Med, Univ Pa, 73-77. *Concurrent Pos:* Res fel med, Sch Med, Yale Univ, 47-49; supt & chief med, Woodruff Hosp, 53-60; attend physician & dir, Med Clins, Yale-New Haven Hosp, 60-68; dir div ambulatory care, Lankenau Hosp, 68-73; chief ambulatory serv & sr attend physician, Philadelphia Gen Hosp, 73-77; assoc vpres health affairs, Hahnemann Univ Hosp, 77-82, hon staff, 88- *Mem:* AAAS; AMA; Am Heart Asn; Am Rheumatism Asn; Am Fedn Clin Res; Sigma Xi. *Res:* Quality assurance and utilization review. *Mailing Add:* 5 Pond Lane Bryn Mawr PA 19010

GRAY, GARY D, BIOCHEMISTRY, IMMUNOLOGY. *Current Pos:* RETIRED. *Personal Data:* b St Louis, Mo, Aug 6, 36; m 59; c 2. *Educ:* Cent Methodist Col, AB, 59; Univ Mo, MS, 63, PhD(biochem), 64. *Prof Exp:* Res scientist, Upjohn Co, Kalamazoo, 64-67, sr res scientist, 67-91. *Res:* Enzymology; immunosuppression; transplantation; infectious diseases; immunopotentiation; hypersensitivity diseases. *Mailing Add:* 2015 Central Ave NE No 401 Minneapolis MN 55418

GRAY, GARY M, GASTROENTEROLOGY, BIOCHEMISTRY. *Current Pos:* from asst prof to assoc prof, Sch Med, Stanford Univ, 66-78, actg dir, Gen Clin Res Ctr, 68-71, head div gastroenterol, 71-88, PROF MED, STANFORD UNIV, SCH MED, 78-, DIR, DIGESTIVE DIS CTR, 87- *Personal Data:* b Seattle, Wash, June 4, 33; m 57; c 5. *Educ:* Seattle Univ, BS, 55; Univ Wash, MD, 59. *Prof Exp:* Fel gastroenterol, Univ Hosp, Boston, 62-64; gastroenterologist, US Army Trop Res Med Lab, 64-65, chief, Med Div, 65-66. *Concurrent Pos:* NIH grants, 67-, 72- & 84-86; prog dir, NIH training grant gastroenterol, 72-85, 86-88, Digestive Dis Ctr, 87-; mem, NIH Gen Med A Study Sect, 72-76, Vet Admin Merit Rev Bd, Gastroenterol, 72-76, Cellular Molecular Dis Rev Group, Nat Inst Gen Med Sci, 81-85, res career develop award, 70-75; counr, Am Gastroenterol Asn, 80-84; vis prof & lectr, Ohio State Univ, 69, Univ Wash, 70, Univ Pittsburgh, 72, Univ Pa, 74, Univ Fla, 74-87, Wayne State Univ, 77, Univ Tex, San Antonio, 77, Duke Univ, 77, Harvard Univ, 77, Univ Calif, Davis, 79, Univ Kans, 80, Mex Asn Gastroenterol, 81, Univ Calif, San Diego, 82, Univ Southern Calif, 82 & 86, Cent Am Cong Gastroenterol, 82, Univ Mich, 85, Univ Chicago, 87, Univ Hawaii, 87 & Yale Univ, 89; chmn, Digestive Dis Ctr, Rev Comt, NIH, NIDDK, 90; mem, NIH Panel Technol Assessment Conf Bovine Somatotropin, 90. *Mem:* Am Fedn Clin Res; Am Soc Clin Invest; Am Chem Soc; Am Soc Biol Chem & Molecular Biol; Am Gastroenterol Asn; Asn Am Physicians; Am Clin & Climatol Soc; Am Inst Nutrit. *Res:* Regulation of expression of intestinal membrane glycoproteins and definition of their role in nutrition. *Mailing Add:* Digestive Dis Ctr Div Gastroenterol Stanford Univ Sch Med Lab Surge Bldg Rm P 304 Stanford CA 94305-5487. *Fax:* 650-723-5488

GRAY, GARY RONALD, CARBOHYDRATE CHEMISTRY. *Current Pos:* from asst prof to assoc prof, 72-83, PROF CHEM, UNIV MINN, MINNEAPOLIS, 83- *Personal Data:* b Coushatta, La, Dec 4, 42; m 80, Linda; c Kathi, Lauren & Kevin. *Educ:* Ouachita Baptist Univ, BS, 64; Univ Iowa, MS, 67, PhD(biochem), 69. *Prof Exp:* Fel biochem, Univ Iowa, 69; NIH fel, Univ Calif, Berkeley, 69-71. *Mem:* Am Chem Soc. *Res:* Structural studies of polysaccharides and lipopolysaccharides; carbohydrate chemistry and reaction mechanisms; chemical immunology of bacterial infections. *Mailing Add:* Dept Chem Univ Minn 207 Pleasant St SE Minneapolis MN 55455. *Fax:* 612-626-7541; *E-Mail:* gray@chem.umn.edu

GRAY, GEORGE A(LEXANDER), CIVIL ENGINEERING, ENGINEERING EDUCATION. *Current Pos:* RETIRED. *Personal Data:* b Armagh, Ireland, Apr 16, 21; nat US; m 44, 90, Ann Gardner; c Robert & Margaret (Kellogg). *Educ:* Tech Univ, BCE, 43; Yale Univ, MEng, 48, DEng, 59. *Prof Exp:* Instr math, Clarkson Tech Univ, 46-47, asst prof civil eng, 48-51; asst prof, Yale Univ, 53-59; prof civil eng, Va Polytech Inst & State Univ, 59-84, assoc dean eng acad affairs, 77-84. *Mem:* Am Soc Civil Engrs; Am Soc Eng Educ; Nat Soc Prof Engrs. *Res:* Structural engineering; structural mechanics. *Mailing Add:* PO Box 56 Shawsville VA 24162-0056

GRAY, GRACE WARNER, PHARMACOLOGY. *Current Pos:* RETIRED. *Personal Data:* b Chicago, Ill, Nov 20, 24. *Educ:* Mt Holyoke Col, BA, 45; Univ Mich, PhD(pharmacol), 51. *Prof Exp:* Sr res pharmacologist, Bristol Labs, 51-54; from instr to asst prof pharmacol, Sch Med, Marquette Univ, 54-63; USPHS trainee lipid metab, Col Med, Univ Tenn, 63-64; asst prof pharmacol, Woman's Med Col Pa, 64-67; assoc prof pharmacol, Col Vet Med, Univ Minn, St Paul, 67-83. *Concurrent Pos:* Jr res pharmacologist, Wm S Merrell Co, 45-47; res assoc, Univ Pa Med Sch, 66. *Mem:* AAAS; Am Chem Soc; Am Soc Pharmacol & Exp Therapeut. *Res:* Autonomic and gastrointestinal pharmacology. *Mailing Add:* 5719 Donegal Dr Shoreview MN 55126

GRAY, GREGORY EDWARD, ADMINISTRATIVE & ORGANIZATIONAL PSYCHIATRY, CLINICAL EPIDEMIOLOGY. *Current Pos:* PROF, DEPT PSYCHIAT, CHARLES R DREW UNIV MED & SCI, 96-, CHMN, 96-; DIR, AUGUSTUS HAWKINS COMMUNITY MENT HEALTH CTR, 96- *Personal Data:* b Los Angeles, Calif, Sept 27, 54; m 77, Lorraine Kulhanek; c Thomas. *Educ:* Univ Calif, Davis, BS, 75, MS, 76; Univ Southern Calif, PhD(biomet), 80, MD, 83. *Prof Exp:* Teaching asst biol, Univ Southern Calif, 76-77, nutritionist, Dept Family & Prev Med, 77-79, Dept Prev Med, 83, physician, Dept Psychiat, 83-87, asst prof, Dept Psychiat & Dept Prev Med, 87-91, assoc prof, Dept Psychiat, 91-96, chmn, 93-96. *Concurrent Pos:* Instr, Azusa Pac Col, 80; lectr, Med Sch, Univ Southern Calif, 84-86; mem, Nat Coun Against Health Fraud; dir, Pac Geriat Educ Ctr, 88-92; asst dir, Los Angeles Co, Univ Southern Calif Psychiat Hosp, 89-91, dir Adult Inpatient Psychiat, 91-93, chief psychiat, 93-96; chief psychiat, King-Drew Med Ctr, 96- *Mem:* AMA; Am Pub Health Asn; Asn Acad Psychiat; Am Asn Chmn Depts Psychiat; Acad Orgn & Occup Psychiat; Asn Dept Psychiat. *Res:* Nutritional assessment; diet and cancer; diet and behavior; clinical epidemiology; geriatric psychiatry and nutrition; psychopharmacology; organizational development; community psychiatry. *Mailing Add:* Augustus Hawkins Community Ment Health Ctr 1720 E 120th St Los Angeles CA 90059. *Fax:* 213-224-7721

GRAY, H(ARRY) J(OSHUA), ELECTRICAL ENGINEERING, ELECTRONICS ENGINEERING. *Current Pos:* from assoc prof to prof, 57-89, EMER PROF ELEC ENG, MOORE SCH ELEC ENG, UNIV PA, 89- *Personal Data:* b St Louis, Mo, June 24, 24; m 49, Cecilia McNulty; c Margaret, Cecilia, Kathleen & Mary E. *Educ:* Univ Pa, BS, 44, MS, 47, PhD, 53. *Prof Exp:* Staff mem elec eng, Moore Sch, Univ Pa, 47-53, asst prof, 53-54; proj engr, Remington Rand Corp & Univac, 54-55, staff engr, 55-57. *Concurrent Pos:* Consult, Philco Corp, 58-63, Int Tel & Tel Corp, 59, Curtiss-Wright Electronics Div, 60, Xerox Corp, 66-67 & Burroughs Corp, 67-70. *Mem:* Inst Elec & Electronics Engrs. *Res:* Digital, analog, and interface circuits and their associated electromagnetic circuit problems. *Mailing Add:* 412 Colonial Park Dr Springfield PA 19064-3405

GRAY, HARRY B, INORGANIC CHEMISTRY. *Current Pos:* ARNOLD O BECKMAN PROF CHEM & DIR, BECKMAN INST, 66- *Personal Data:* b Woodburn, Ky, Nov 14, 35; m 57; c 3. *Educ:* Western Ky Univ, BS, 57; Northwestern Univ, PhD(chem), 60. *Hon Degrees:* DSc, Northwestern Univ, 84, Univ Rochester, 87, Univ Chicago, 87, Greem State Univ, 94, Columbia Univ, 94, Univ Pa, 95, Oberlin Col, 96 & Univ Ariz, 97; Dr, Univ Paul Sabatier, Toulouse, 91. *Honors & Awards:* E C Franklin Mem Award, 67; Fresenius Award & Shoemaker Award, 70; Award Pure Chem, Am Chem Soc, 70 & Award Inorg Chem, 78, Distinguished Serv in Advan Inorg Chem, 84; Harrison Howe Award, 72; Remsen Award, 79; Edgar Fahs Smith Award, 84; Centenary Medal, Royal Soc Chem, 85; Nat Medal of Sci, 86; Dickinson-Priestly Award, 91; Madison Marshall Award, 91; Gibbs Medal, 92; Basolo Medal, 94. *Prof Exp:* NSF fel chem, Copenhagen Univ, 60-61; from asst prof to prof, Columbia Univ, 61-66. *Concurrent Pos:* Mem, Adv Bd, Oak Ridge Nat Lab, 84-; vis comt, Los Alamos Nat Lab, 84-; mem coun, Nat Acad Sci, 86. *Mem:* Nat Acad Sci; foreign mem Royal Danish Acad Sci & Lett; Am Chem Soc; Am Acad Arts & Sci; Swedish Royal Acad; hon mem Hal Chem Soc; fel Am Inst Chemists. *Res:* Electronic structure of metal complexes; inorganic reaction mechanisms. *Mailing Add:* Beckman Inst Calif Inst Technol Pasadena CA 91125

GRAY, HARRY EDWARD, polymers used as cell culture substrates, for more information see previous edition

GRAY, HENRY HAMILTON, GEOLOGY. *Current Pos:* coal geologist, Ind Geol Surv, 54-60, map ed, 55-61, head stratigrapher, 60-87, EMER HEAD STRATIGRAPHER, IND GEOL SURV, 87- *Personal Data:* b Terre Haute, Ind, Mar 18, 22; m 44, Alice V King; c David L & Bonnie H (Boulding). *Educ:* Haverford Col, BS, 43; Univ Mich, MS, 46, Ohio State Univ, PhD(geol), 54. *Honors & Awards:* John C Frye Mem Award, 92. *Prof Exp:* Geologist, US Geol Surv, 43-45; from instr to asst prof geol, Kent State Univ, 48-53. *Mem:* Soc Econ Paleontologists & Mineralogists; Am Asn Petrol Geologists. *Res:* Stratigraphy; sedimentary petrology; geomorphology; geologic mapping. *Mailing Add:* 5431 E King Rd Bloomington IN 47408

GRAY, HORACE BENTON, JR, PHYSICAL BIOCHEMISTRY. *Current Pos:* from asst prof to assoc prof biophysics, 69-81, PROF, DEPT BIOCHEM & BIOPHYS SCI, UNIV HOUSTON, 81- *Personal Data:* b DeLand, Fla, Oct 29, 41; m 72, Rosemary Johnston; c Thomas & David. *Educ:* Fla State Univ, BS, 63; Univ Calif, Berkeley, PhD(chem), 67. *Prof Exp:* Nat Cancer Inst fel, Calif Inst Technol, 67-69. *Mem:* Sigma Xi; Am Soc Biol Chemists; Biophys Soc; AAAS. *Res:* Interaction of nucleic acids with nucleases and other enzymes of nucleic acid metabolism. *Mailing Add:* Dept Biochem & Biophys Sci Univ Houston Houston TX 77204-5934. *Fax:* 713-743-8351; *E-Mail:* hgray@uh.edu

GRAY, IAN, FOOD CHEMISTRY. *Current Pos:* res assoc, 72-74, ASSOC DIR, AGR EXP STA, MICH STATE UNIV, 78- *Personal Data:* b Cookstown, NIreland, Dec 26, 44. *Educ:* Queens Univ, Valfast, BS, 68, PhD(food sci), 71. *Prof Exp:* Res assoc agr, Univ Guelph, Ont, 74-78. *Mem:* Am Oil Chemists Soc; Inst Food Technol. *Res:* Liquid oxidation; food safety; food packaging. *Mailing Add:* Agr Exp Sta Mich State Univ 109 Agr Hall East Lansing MI 48824

GRAY, IRVING, biochemistry, biophysics, for more information see previous edition

GRAY, JAMES EDWARD, ELECTRONICS ENGINEERING, PHYSICS. *Current Pos:* ENGR INSTRUMENTATION, NAT INST STANDARDS & TECHNOL, 73- *Personal Data:* b Santa Barbara, Calif, June 3, 32; m 76. *Educ:* Univ Calif, BA, 54, MA, 60. *Prof Exp:* Physicist dielec, Nat Bur Standards, 60-66, physicist atomic time, 66-73,. *Mem:* Sigma Xi. *Res:* Time and frequency metrology. *Mailing Add:* 942 Seventh St Boulder CO 80302

GRAY, JAMES N, DATA BASE SYSTEMS. *Current Pos:* CONSULT ENGR, MICROSOFT CORP. *Mem:* Nat Acad Eng. *Mailing Add:* Microsoft Corp 950 Tower Lane Suite 900 Foster City CA 94404

GRAY, JAMES P, DATA COMMUNICATIONS, SYSTEMS NETWORK ARCHITECTURE. *Current Pos:* Res staff mem, IBM Res Div, 70-72, adv engr, Systs Commun Div, 72-79, sr engr, Commun Prods Div, 79-82, sr tech staff, 82-84, IBM FEL, IBM NETWORKING SOFTWARE DIV, 84- *Personal Data:* b Los Angeles, Calif. *Educ:* Yale Univ, BE, 65, PhD(elec eng), 70. *Mem:* Fel Inst Elec & Electronics Engrs; Asn Comput Mach. *Res:* Research and advanced technology on distributed operating systems and networking, especially as applied to SNA and transmission control protocol and internet protocol; software development practice, defect reduction and productivity. *Mailing Add:* IBM Corp Cpd-F92/673 PO Box 12195 Research Triangle Park NC 27709

GRAY, JAMES S, ELECTRICAL ENGINEERING. *Current Pos:* PRIN ENGR, SATELLITE COMMUN DIV, SCIENTIFIC-ATLANTA, INC, 77- *Personal Data:* US citizen. *Educ:* Southwestern Univ, Memphis, BS, 62; Ga Inst Technol, MS, 65, PhD(elec eng), 67. *Honors & Awards:* Harris Corp Eng Award, 76. *Prof Exp:* From assoc prin engr to prin engr, Electron Systs Div, Harris Corp, 67-77. *Mem:* Inst Elec & Electronics Engrs; Sigma Xi. *Res:* Statistical communications; circuit theory; digital processing; filtering. *Mailing Add:* 4718 Pine Acres Ct Dunwoody GA 30338-4932

GRAY, JANE, PALEOECOLOGY, EVOLUTION PALEOBIOLOGY. *Current Pos:* PROF BIOL, UNIV ORE, 66- *Personal Data:* b Omaha, Nebr, Apr 19, 31. *Educ:* Harvard Univ, BA, 51; Univ Calif, PhD(paleont), 58. *Prof Exp:* Ed asst, J Sedimentary Petrol, Univ Ill, 51-52; instr geol, Univ Tex, 56-58; res assoc palynology, Univ Ariz, 58-61. *Concurrent Pos:* New world secy, Proj Ecostratigraphy, IUGS & IGCP, UNESCO, 74- *Mem:* Bot Soc Am; Soc Study Evolution; Int Soc Taxon. *Res:* Ecosystem evolution; evolution of early land plants; nonmarine paleoecology; Silurian biostratigraphy; late Cenozoic pollen analysis. *Mailing Add:* Dept Biol Univ Ore Eugene OR 97403-1210

GRAY, JOE WILLIAM, CANCER GENETICS, MOLECULAR CYTOGENETICS. *Current Pos:* Biomed scientist, 72-91, SR SCIENTIST, LAWRENCE LIVERMORE LAB, 92-; PROF LAB MED, UNIV CALIF, SAN FRANCISCO, 91- *Personal Data:* b Hobbs, NMex, Apr 26, 46; m 67, Jane E Madison; c Gerald. *Educ:* Kans State Univ, PhD(physics), 72. *Honors & Awards:* Res Award, Radiation Res Soc, 85; E O Lawrence Award, Dept Energy, 86. *Concurrent Pos:* Adj asst prof radiol, Univ Calif, Davis, 76-; adj prof lab med, Univ Calif, San Francisco, 84-; NIH Genome coun, 90; prin investr, NIH & DOE grants. *Mem:* Am Asn Cancer Res; Int Soc Analytical Cytol (pres, 96); Cell Kinetics Soc (pres, 83); Soc Analytical Cytol; fel AAAS; Radiation Res Soc; Am Soc Human Genetics. *Res:* Molecular cytogenics; analytical cytology; genetic disease diagnosis; prenatal diagnosis; tumor cytogenetics; biological dosimetry; genetic progression in breast and ovarian cancer. *Mailing Add:* Univ Calif Dept Lab Med MCB230 PO Box 080 San Francisco CA 94143. *Fax:* 415-476-8218; *E-Mail:* gray@ee.ucsf.edu

GRAY, JOEL EDWARD, DIAGNOSTIC RADIOLOGY. *Current Pos:* from asst prof to assoc prof, 77-87, PROF RADIOL PHYSICS, MAYO MED SCH, 87- *Personal Data:* b Carlisle, Pa, Aug 14, 43; m 82, Judith Tervo; c Adam H & Kirsten E. *Educ:* Rochester Inst Technol, BS, 70; Univ Ariz, MS, 72; Univ Toronto, PhD(radiol sci), 77. *Prof Exp:* Res asst, Optical Sci Ctr, Univ Ariz, 71-73, res fel, diag radiol & optical sci, Dept Radiol, 73-74; res fel radiol sci, Inst Med Sci, Univ Toronto, 74-77. *Concurrent Pos:* Ed, J Appl Photog Eng, 75-79; review ed, Med Physics, Am Asn Physicists Med, 76-81; consult, diag radiol, Mayo Clin, 77-; adj asst prof, Dept Med Physics, Univ Wis-Madison, 82-; mem bd dir, Am Asn Physicists Med, 83-85; prog comt, Radiol Soc NAm, 85-89, chmn, physics prog subcomt, 89-92; mem, Int Comn Radiol Protection, 85-, Nat Coun Radiation Protection & Measurements, 87- *Mem:* Radiol Soc NAm (vpres, 93); fel Am Asn Physicists Med; Am Col Radiol; fel Soc Photog Scientists & Engrs; Asn Univ Radiologists; Am Roentgen Ray Soc; Sigma Xi; Soc Motion Picture & TV Engrs. *Res:* Medical imaging; application of optical image evaluation techniques in diagnostic radiology; application of psychophysical techniques in the evaluation of radiological imaging systems; radiation effects and risks; epidemiology of radiation carcinogenesis; public perception of chemical and radiation risks. *Mailing Add:* 2804 Second St SW Rochester MN 55902-4121. *Fax:* 507-284-8996; *E-Mail:* joel_gray@msgw.mayo.edu

GRAY, JOHN AUGUSTUS, III, PHYSICAL CHEMISTRY, DENTISTRY. *Personal Data:* b Waterbury, Conn, Aug 13, 24; m 52, Margaret Jean Holman; c David Randolph, Timothy Holman & Joanna (Banta). *Educ:* Yale Univ, BS, 45, PhD(chem), 49. *Prof Exp:* Res chemist, Miami Valley Labs, Procter & Gamble Co, 48-80; exec dir, Int Assoc Dent Res, 80-90. *Concurrent Pos:* Trustee, Children's Dent Care Found, 66-; mem, Bd Sci Counrs, Nat Inst Dental Res, 74-78; trustee, Children's Hosp Med Ctr, 74-80. *Mem:* Fel AAAS; Am Chem Soc; Int Asn Dent Res (pres, 80); Am Asn Dent Res (secy-treas, 73-76); hon fel Am Col Dentists. *Res:* Physical chemical studies of detergents, solutions, dentifrices, tooth structure and caries mechanism. *Mailing Add:* 9300 Meadow Ridge Dr Cincinnati OH 45241

GRAY, JOHN EDWARD, MOLECULAR BIOLOGY, MICROBIOLOGY. *Current Pos:* sr res scientist, 89-96, SR REGULATORY AFFAIRS ASSOC, E I DUPONT DE NEMOURS & CO, 96- *Personal Data:* b Syracuse, NY, May 24, 49. *Educ:* Ursinus Col, BS, 71; Univ Del, PhD(biol), 79. *Prof Exp:* Fel genetics, Microbiol Dept, Mt Sinai Sch Med, 78-81; staff scientist, Genetics Div, Bethesda Res Labs, Gaithersburg, Md, 81-89. *Mem:* Sigma Xi; AAAS; Am Soc Microbiol. *Res:* Modification of bacteria for industrial production of amino acids; genetic regulation of metabolism in bacteria; translational processes in cyanobacteria. *Mailing Add:* DuPont Merck Pharmaceut Co Dupont Merck Plaza Maple Run Rm 2122 PO Box 80721 Wilmington DE 19880-0721

GRAY, JOHN MALCOLM, WELDING METALLURGY, CORROSION OF PIPELINE MATERIALS. *Current Pos:* PRES, MICROALLOYING INT, 76- *Personal Data:* b Thurnscoe, UK, Mar 28, 40; m 63; c 3. *Educ:* Univ Sheffield, Eng, AMet, 61, MMet, 62, PhD(metall), 65. *Prof Exp:* Metallurgist, Brit Steel, Rotherham, UK, 56-65; sr researcher, US Steel Res, Monroeville, Pa, 66-70; vpres, Molycorp Div, Union Oil Calif, 71-76. *Mem:* Fel Am Soc Metals; fel Metals Soc; Nat Asn Corrosion Engrs; Metall Soc; Am Welding Soc; fel Mat Soc. *Res:* Physical metallurgy of low carbon microalloyed steels; corrosion in wet H2S environment. *Mailing Add:* 9025 Briar Forest Dr Houston TX 77024. *Fax:* 713-776-9634

GRAY, JOHN WALKER, MATHEMATICS. *Current Pos:* from asst prof to assoc prof, 61-66, PROF MATH, UNIV ILL, URBANA, 66- *Personal Data:* b St Paul, Minn, Oct 3, 31; m 57; c 2. *Educ:* Swarthmore Col, BA, 53; Stanford Univ, PhD(math), 57. *Prof Exp:* Mem, Inst Advan Study, 57-59; Ritt instr math, Columbia Univ, 59-62. *Concurrent Pos:* NSF sr fel, 66-67; Fulbright-Hays sr scholar, Australian-Am Educ Found, 75-76. *Mem:* AAAS; Am Math Soc; Asn Comput Mach. *Res:* Category theory; sheaf theory and its geometrical applications; categorical semantics of programming languages. *Mailing Add:* Dept Math Univ Ill Urbana IL 61801. *E-Mail:* gray@math.uiuc.edu

GRAY, JOSEPH B(URNHAM), CHEMICAL ENGINEERING. *Current Pos:* RETIRED. *Personal Data:* b Annapolis, Md, Aug 8, 15; m 41; c 3. *Educ:* St John's Col, Md, BA, 36; Johns Hopkins Univ, BE, 38, PhD(chem eng), 41. *Prof Exp:* Chem engr, process design div, res lab, Standard Oil Co, Ind, 41-43, group leader, 43-47; from asst prof to assoc prof chem eng, Syracuse Univ, 47-51; res engr, E I DuPont de Nemours & Co, Inc, 51-60, consult, 61-81; mixing consult, Beechwood Consults, Inc, 81-88. *Mem:* Am Chem Soc; fel Am Inst Chem Engrs. *Res:* Fluid mechanics; agitation and mixing. *Mailing Add:* 1909 Beechwood Dr Westwood Manor Wilmington DE 19810

GRAY, KENNETH EUGENE, PETROLEUM ENGINEERING. *Current Pos:* from asst prof to assoc prof petrol eng, 62-68, chmn dept, 66-74, HALLIBURTON PROF PETROL ENG, UNIV TEX, AUSTIN, 68-, DIR CTR EARTH SCI, 68- *Personal Data:* b Herrin, Ill, Jan 11, 30; m 55; c 3. *Educ:* Univ Tulsa, BS, 56, MS, 57; Univ Tex, PhD(petrol eng), 63. *Prof Exp:* Drilling engr, Calif Co, 57-59; reservoir engr, Sohio Petrol Co, 59-60. *Concurrent Pos:* Res grants, Petrol Res Fund, Am Chem Soc, 63-, Tex Petrol Res Comt, 63-, Am Petrol Inst, 64- & Gulf Res & Develop Co, 64-; consult, Res Dept, Continental Oil Co, 63-; mem, US Nat Comt Rock Mech. *Mem:* Fel Am Inst Chemists; NY Acad Sci; Am Acad Mech. *Res:* Rock mechanics; properties and behavior of rocks under conditions of elevated temperature and pressure; reservoir transients; unsteady state reservoir pressure analysis. *Mailing Add:* Dept Petrol Eng CPE 2 502 Univ Tex 26th & Speedway Austin TX 78712-1061

GRAY, KENNETH STEWART, SPECIAL PURPOSE MEMORY DESIGN, LOGIC DESIGN. *Current Pos:* Adv engr electronics eng, 67-92, ELECTRONIC ENG, IBM CORP, 92- *Personal Data:* b Teaneck, NJ, June 28, 45; m 67; c 2. *Educ:* Norwich Univ, BS, 67; Univ Vt, MS, 78. *Mem:* Nat Soc Prof Engrs; Inst Elec & Electronics Engrs. *Res:* Two patents and forty publications in the areas of NMOS, CMOS, BICMOS circuit, memory and chip design. *Mailing Add:* 288 Griswold Jericho VT 05465

GRAY, KENNETH W, corrosion resistant coatings, coating application equipment, for more information see previous edition

GRAY, LAWRENCE FIRMAN, PROBABILITY. *Current Pos:* Asst prof, 77-97, PROF MATH, UNIV MINN, 97- *Personal Data:* b Santa Monica, Calif, May 25, 49; m 72; c 4. *Educ:* Univ Calif, San Diego, BA, 73; Cornell Univ, PhD(math), 77. *Mem:* Inst Math Statist. *Res:* Analysis of Markov processes which model systems of large numbers of interacting components; percolation theory; statistical mechanics. *Mailing Add:* Sch Math Univ Minn 127 Vincent Hall 206 Church St SE Minneapolis MN 55455

GRAY, LEWIS RICHARD, PLANT MORPHOLOGY. *Current Pos:* From instr to assoc prof biol, Mayfair Col, 65-76, PROF BIOL, CITY COLS CHICAGO, TRUMAN COL, 76- *Personal Data:* b Madison, Wis, Feb 14, 36; m 58, Carmen Brunsell; c Thomas, Barbara & Marjorie. *Educ:* Univ Miami, BS, 59; Univ Cincinnati, MS, 61; Univ Ill, PhD(bot), 65. *Mem:* Am Asn Stratigraphic Palynologists. *Res:* Paleozoic palynology. *Mailing Add:* Biol Truman Col 1145 W Wilson Ave Chicago IL 60640-5616

GRAY, LINSLEY SHEPARD, JR, SPECTROSCOPY, PHYSICAL PROPERTIES. *Current Pos:* GEN MGR, ALPHA CONSULT LABS, INC, 92- *Personal Data:* b Sandwich, Ill, Oct 11, 29; m 51; c 4. *Educ:* Beloit Col, BS, 51; Iowa State Univ, PhD(chem), 58. *Prof Exp:* Jr chemist, Ames Lab, Iowa State Univ, 51-52, asst, 52-58; chemist, E I DuPont de Nemours & Co, 58-59; chemist, Armour & Co, 59-60, sr res chemist, Akzo Chem Inc, 60-66, sect head phys chem res, 66-91; prod mgr, Diosynth, Inc, 91-92. *Mem:* Am Chem Soc; Am Geophys Union; Coblentz Soc; Soc Appl Spectros; Am Oil Chemists' Soc. *Res:* Spectroscopy; surface chemistry; material characterization; product deformation. *Mailing Add:* 3948 Forest Ave Downers Grove IL 60515. *Fax:* 630-620-0845; *E-Mail:* 70524.1015@compuserve.com

GRAY, MARY JANE, MEDICINE. *Current Pos:* prof obstet & gynec, 77-90, asst dean, 86-90, EMER PROF OBSTET & GYNEC, UNIV NC, 90- *Personal Data:* b Columbus, Ohio, June 13, 24; div; c 4. *Educ:* Swarthmore Col, BA, 49; Wash Univ, MD, 49; Am Bd Obstet & Gynec, dipl, 59. *Hon Degrees:* ScD, Columbia Univ, 53. *Prof Exp:* Intern, Barnes Hosp, 49-50; asst resident obstet & gynec, Presby Hosp, 50-53, chief resident, 56; instr, Col Physicians & Surgeons, Columbia Univ, 56-59, assoc, 59-60; from asst prof to prof obstet & gynec, Col Med, Univ Vt, 60-77. *Concurrent Pos:* Barnes Foster res fel, Columbia Univ, 53-54 & Karolinska Inst, Sweden, 55; attend physician, Med Ctr Hosp Vt; trainee, Marriage Coun Philadelphia, dept psychiat, Univ Pa, 70-71. *Mem:* AAAS; Am Med Asn; Soc Gynec Invest; Am Col Obstet & Gynec; Am Obstet & Gynec Soc. *Res:* Toxemia of pregnancy; electrolyte changes of menstrual cycle; gynecologic cancer; sex education; marriage counseling. *Mailing Add:* 1622 NW Riber Pl Univ NC Corvallis OR 97330

GRAY, MARY WHEAT, MATHEMATICAL STATISTICS. *Current Pos:* assoc prof, 68-71, PROF MATH, AM UNIV, 71-, CHAIR, 77- *Personal Data:* b Hastings, Nebr, Apr 8, 39; m 64, Alfred. *Educ:* Hastings Col, AB, 59; Univ Kans, MA, 62, PhD(math), 64; Am Univ, JD, 79. *Hon Degrees:* LLD, Univ Nebr, 93; DHL, Hastings Col, 96. *Prof Exp:* Instr, Univ Calif, Berkeley, 65; from asst prof to assoc prof math, Calif State Col, Hayward, 65-68. *Concurrent Pos:* Translator, Am Math Soc, 64-66; consult statist, comput sci, law, 79- *Mem:* Fel AAAS; Am Math Soc; Math Asn Am; NY Acad Sci; Asn Women Math; Sigma Xi; Am Statist Asn; Asn Comput Mach; Am Asn Univ Prof. *Res:* Mathematics education; computers and the law; applied statistics. *Mailing Add:* Dept Math Statist & Comput Sci Am Univ Washington DC 20016-8050. *Fax:* 202-885-3155; *E-Mail:* mgray@american.edu

GRAY, MICHAEL WILLIAM, ORGANELLE MOLECULAR BIOLOGY, GENEOME EVOLUTION & RIBOSOMAL RNA. *Current Pos:* From asst prof to assoc prof, 70-83, PROF BIOCHEM, DALHOUSIE UNIV, 83- *Personal Data:* b Medicine Hat, Alta, July 18, 43; m 68, Jean D Gillis; c Jennifer L & Meghan E. *Educ:* Univ Alta, BSc, 64, PhD(biochem), 68. *Honors & Awards:* Fraser Medal, Atlantic Prov Coun Sci, 82; Max Forman Res Prize, Dalhousie Med Res Found, 86; Boehringer Mannheim Can Prize, Can Biochem Soc, 87; Merit Award, Can Soc Plant Molecular Biol, 93. *Concurrent Pos:* Nat Res Coun Can fel, Stanford Univ, 68-70; Med Res Coun Can grant, Dalhousie Univ, 70- & Med Res Coun Can scholar, 73-78; Natural Sci & Eng Res Coun Can grant, 82-91; vis scientist, Med Res Coun Can, Stanford Univ, 84-85; counr, Can Soc Biochem & Molecular Biol, 91-94. *Mem:* Am Soc Biochem & Molecular Biol; Int Soc Plant Molecular Biol; Can Soc Plant Molecular Biol (vpres, 86, pres, 87); fel Can Inst Advan Res; Can Soc Biochem, Cell & Molecular Biol; fel Royal Soc Can. *Res:* Structure, function and evolution of mitochondrial DNA, especially in plants and protists; evolution of ribosomal RNA structure; complete sequencing of organellar genomes; transfer RNA editing. *Mailing Add:* Dept Biochem Dalhousie Univ Halifax NS B3H 4H7 Can. *Fax:* 902-494-1355; *E-Mail:* m.w.gray@dal.ca

GRAY, NANCY M, medicinal chemistry, pharmacology, for more information see previous edition

GRAY, PATRICK WILLIAM, MOLECULAR IMMUNOLOGY, CLONING OF RECOMBINANT PHARMACEUTICALS. *Current Pos:* SR DIR SCI, ICOS CORP, 90- *Personal Data:* b Fukuoka, Japan, May 26, 51; US citizen; m 94, Debra Torgeson; c Justin & Benton. *Educ:* Univ Ore, BS, 74; Univ Colo, PhD(chem), 78. *Prof Exp:* Damon-Runyon fel, Univ Calif, San Francisco, 79-80; sr scientist, Genentech, Inc, 80-89; res fel, Charing Cross Sunley Res Ctr, 89-90. *Mem:* Am Asn Immunologists; Am Soc Biochem & Molecular Biol; Brit Soc Immunol; Int Soc Interferon Res. *Res:* Cloning and expressing novel recombinant products for medicinal use; characterization of hepatitis B virus surface antigen, interferon-gamma, lymphotoxin, and bactericidal/permeability increasing protein. *Mailing Add:* ICOS Corp 22021 20th Ave SE Bothell WA 98021-4406. Fax: 425-485-0885

GRAY, PAUL, INFORMATION SYSTEMS, MANAGEMENT SCIENCE. *Current Pos:* PROF & CHMN, INFO SCI, CLAREMONT GRAD SCH, 83- *Personal Data:* b Vienna, Austria, Dec 8, 30; US citizen; m 52, Muriel Blynn; c T A Childs. *Educ:* NY Univ, BA, 50; Univ Mich, MA, 54; Purdue Univ, MS, 62; Stanford Univ, PhD(opers res), 68. *Honors & Awards:* Syst Sci Prize, NATO, 78. *Prof Exp:* Asst systs eng, Willow Run Labs, Univ Mich, 51-52; asst tech ed, 52-55; nuclear engr, Convair/Gen Dynamics, 55-58; proposal engr, Solar Aircraft Co, 58-60; instr elec eng, Purdue Univ, 60-62; res engr, Systs Eng, SRI Inst, 62-64, sr res engr, 65-69, prog dir transp, 69-70; prof, Ga Inst Technol, 71-72; prof, Univ Southern Calif, 72-79; prof & chmn mgt sci & comput, Southern Methodist Univ, 79-83. *Concurrent Pos:* Lectr, Stanford Univ, 68-69, consult assoc prof, 69-70, assoc prof, 70-71; vis scholar, Mass Inst Technol, 86; mem coun, Opers Res Soc Am, 88-91. *Mem:* Inst Mgt Sci (secy, 75-79, vpres, 83-86, pres-elect, 91-92, pres, 92-93, past pres, 93-94); Opers Res Soc Am; Asn Comput Mach; Soc Info Mgt. *Res:* Decision support systems; technology assessment; modeling and simulation; urban systems; transportation; public safety; air traffic control; mixed integer programming; site location; information and decision processes; numerical analysis and digital computation. *Mailing Add:* Claremont Grad Sch Claremont CA 91711. Fax: 909-621-8564; E-Mail: grayp@cgsvax.claremont.edu

GRAY, PAUL EDWARD, ELECTRICAL ENGINEERING. *Current Pos:* from instr to prof elec eng, Mass Inst Technol, 57-71, assoc dean student affairs, 65-67, asst provost, 67-69, Class 1922 prof, 68-71, assoc provost, 69-70, dean, Sch Eng, 70-71, chancellor, 71-80, pres, 80-90, chmn corp, 90-97, PROF ELEC ENG, MASS INST TECHNOL, 97- *Personal Data:* b Newark, NJ, Feb 7, 32; m 55; c 4. *Educ:* Mass Inst Technol, SB, 54, SM, 55, ScD(elec eng), 60. *Hon Degrees:* LHD, Wheaton Col, 80; DEng, Northeastern Univ, 81 & Tech Univ NS, 84; PhD, Cairo Univ, 85; ScD, Rensselaer Polytech Inst, 88. *Concurrent Pos:* Ford Found fel, 61-63; mem, White House Sci Coun, 82-86. *Mem:* Nat Acad Eng; fel Am Acad Arts & Sci; AAAS; corresp mem Mex Nat Acad Eng; fel Inst Elec & Electronics Engrs. *Res:* Physical electronics and circuit characterization of semiconductor devices; electric and magnetic properties of high-field superconductors; solid-state energy conversion; author of numerous technical publications. *Mailing Add:* Dept Elec Eng Mass Inst Technol Cambridge MA 02139

GRAY, PAUL EUGENE, electrical engineering, for more information see previous edition

GRAY, PAUL R, INTEGRATED CIRCUITS. *Current Pos:* dir, Electronics Res Lab, 85-86, vchmn, Dept Comput Resources, 88-90, ASSOC PROF, DEPT ELEC & ELECTRONICS ENG, UNIV CALIF, BERKELEY, 71-, DEAN COL ENG, 93-, ROY W CARLSON PROF ENG, 93- *Personal Data:* b Jonesboro, Ariz, Dec 8, 42; c 2. *Educ:* Univ Ariz, Tucson, BS, 63, MS, 65, PhD, 69. *Honors & Awards:* Baker Prize, Inst Elec & Electronics Engrs, 80, Morris N Liebmann Mem Award, 83, Solid State Circuit Award, 94; Achievement Award, Inst Elec & Electronics Engrs Circuits & Syst Soc, 87. *Prof Exp:* Mem tech staff, Res & Develop Lab, Fairchild Semiconductor, 69-71. *Concurrent Pos:* Proj mgr, Telecommun Filters, Intel Corp, 77-78; ed, J Solid State Circuits, Inst Elec & Electronics Engrs, 77-79; prog chmn, Int Solid; dir, CMOS Design Eng Microlinear Corp, 84-85; pres, Solid State Circuits Coun, Inst Elec & Electronics Engrs, 88-90. *Mem:* Nat Acad Eng; fel Inst Elec & Electronics Engrs. *Mailing Add:* Univ Calif 320 McLaughlin Hall Berkeley CA 94720-1700

GRAY, PAULETTE S, CELL & DEVELOPMENTAL BIOLOGY, CYTOGENETICS. *Current Pos:* exec secy, Nat Cancer Inst, NIH, 83-84, spec rev officer & health adminr, Off of Dir, 84-87, CHIEF, REV LOGISTICS BR, NAT CANCER INST, NIH, 88- *Personal Data:* b Chattanooga, Tenn, Feb 21, 43; m 64, Walter L Sr; c 2. *Educ:* Tuskegee Inst, BS, 66; Atlanta Univ, MS, 76, PhD(cell & develop biol), 78. *Honors & Awards:* H E Finley Mem Award, 78. *Prof Exp:* Asst prof & dir, Electron Micros Lab, Atlanta Univ, 78-79; res assoc, Univ Kaiserslautern, Fed Repub Ger, 79-81; instr biol, Europ Div, Univ Md, 80-82; supvr, Clin Microbiol Sect, Landstuhl Army Med Ctr, Fed Repub Ger, 81-82. *Concurrent Pos:* Mem, Adv Comt Women, NIH, 85-90, chmn, Organizing Subcomt, 86-87; mem, Sci Educ Comt, Am Asn Cancer Res, 91-92; mem, Inter-Agency Cancer Working Group Breats & Cynec Cancer, Nat Cancer Inst, 94-, Long Island Breast Cancer Study Proj, 94- Am Asn Cancer Res; Women Cancer Res; Fed Exec Inst; Am Asn Cell Biol. *Mailing Add:* Exec Plaza N Rm 600 6130 Executive Blvd Bethesda MD 20892-0001. Fax: 301-402-0956; E-Mail: grayp@dea.ngi.nih.gov

GRAY, PETER NORMAN, biomedical sciences, human biochemical genetics, for more information see previous edition

GRAY, RALPH DONALD, JR, CHEMICAL ENGINEERING, THERMODYNAMICS. *Current Pos:* Engr, Exxon Res & Eng Co, 64-67, res engr, 67-71, sr res engr, 71-77, staff engr, 77-80, SR STAFF ENGR, HYDROCARBON THERMODYNAMICS, EXXON RES & ENG CO, 80- *Personal Data:* b Akron, Ohio, May 15, 38; m 68; c 2. *Educ:* Case Inst Technol, BSChE, 60; Univ Del, MChE, 63, PhD(chem eng), 65. *Concurrent Pos:* Adj assoc prof, Manhattan Col, 81- *Mem:* Am Inst Chem Engrs; Am Chem Soc. *Res:* Chemical engineering thermodynamics with emphasis on hydrocarbon thermodynamics, equation of state methods and computer calculation techniques. *Mailing Add:* 20 Colonial Rd Morristown NJ 07960

GRAY, RALPH J, COAL & COKE PETROGRAPHY, GEOLOGY. *Current Pos:* INDEPENDENT CONSULT, RALPH GRAY SERVS, 83- *Personal Data:* b Wheeling, WVa, Oct 28, 23; m 49, Anna Holly; c Glenn, Dan, Susan & Cathy. *Educ:* WVa Univ, BS, 51, MS, 52. *Honors & Awards:* Joseph Becker Award, Iron & Steel Soc, 84; Gilbert H Cady Award, Geol Soc Am, 88. *Prof Exp:* Geol asst, WVa Geol & Econ Surv, 50-51; cartog photogram aide, Photogram Div, Army Map Serv, 51-52; geologist, Fuels Br, US Geol Surv, 52-57; sr res consult, Appl Res Lab, US Steel Corp, 57-83. *Concurrent Pos:* Tech adv, Dept Energy, Coal Characterization Evaluation Int Coal Classification, 83- *Mem:* Geol Soc Am; Am Asn Petrol Geologists; Mineral Soc Am; Am Asn Stratig Palynologists; Asn Inst Mining Engrs; Am Soc Testing & Mat. *Res:* Use of palynology in coal correlation; application of coal petrographic techniques to the prediction of coking properties of coal; use of microscopic techniques in coke evatuation; raw materials utilization; development of automatic microscope techniques for coal and coke analysis; Petrography of coal-tar pitch solids and electrode carbons. *Mailing Add:* Ralph Gray Serv 303 Drexel Dr Monroeville PA 15416. Fax: 412-798-2302

GRAY, REED ALDEN, BIOCHEMISTRY, WEED SCIENCE. *Current Pos:* CONSULT, 86- *Personal Data:* b Santa Clara, Utah, Jan 12, 21; m 51, 77, Hazel I Cramer; c Arlene J (Smith) & Linda J (Stiborek). *Educ:* Univ Utah, BS, 43, MS, 44; Calif Inst Technol, PhD(biochem & plant physiol), 48. *Honors & Awards:* Glycerine Res Award, 55; Outstanding Indust Mem Award, Weed Sci Soc Am, 89. *Prof Exp:* Assoc biochemist, Pineapple Res Inst, Hawaii, 48-53; plant physiologist, Merck & Co, NJ, 53-60; plant physiologist & mgr herbicide res & biochem, Stauffer Chem Co, 60-74, sr scientist, Agr Res Ctr, 74-86. *Mem:* Am Chem Soc; Weed Sci Soc Am. *Res:* Plant biochemistry; study of plant growth regulators; antibiotics and plant diseases; metabolism and mode of action of herbicides and herbicide antidotes; behavior and persistence of herbicides in soils; herbicide soil extenders. *Mailing Add:* 19327 Portos Ct Saratoga CA 95070-5119

GRAY, ROBERT DEE, BIOCHEMISTRY. *Current Pos:* from asst prof to assoc prof, 71-84, PROF BIOCHEM, SCH MED, UNIV LOUISVILLE, 84- *Personal Data:* b Evansville, Ind, May 7, 41; m; c 2. *Educ:* DePauw Univ, BA, 63; Fla State Univ, PhD(chem), 68. *Prof Exp:* Res assoc biochem, Cornell Univ, 68-70. *Mem:* Am Soc Biol Chemists; AAAS. *Res:* Reaction kinetics of hemoproteins; biochemistry of collagenases. *Mailing Add:* Dept Biochem Univ Louisville Sch Med Louisville KY 40292-0001. Fax: 502-852-6222; E-Mail: rdgray01@ulkyvm.edu

GRAY, ROBERT H, ECOLOGY, FISH & WILDLIFE SCIENCE. *Current Pos:* prog mgr, Environ Health & Safety Res, 79-87, PROG MGR, OFF HANFORD ENVIRON & MGR, OFF HEALTH & ENVIRON, PAC NW LABS, BATTELLE MEM INST, 87- *Personal Data:* b Beacon, NY, Feb 15, 40; m 65; c 2. *Educ:* Winona State Col, BA, 64; Univ Ore, MA, 67; Ill State Univ, PhD(zool, biol), 71. *Prof Exp:* Med technician gastroenterol, Mayo Clinic, 64-65; teaching asst biol, Univ Ore, 65-67 & Ill State Univ, 67-71; NSF traineeship, 68-71; asst prof, Lake Erie Col, 71-73. *Concurrent Pos:* Lectr biol, Joint Ctr Grad Study & Wash State Univ, 78-; fel, Am Inst Fisheries Res Biologists, 83 & mem, People to People Fisheries Res Deleg, Citizen Ambassador Prog to East Asia, 85; chmn, Richland Ecol Comn. *Mem:* Am Fisheries Soc (pres, Water Qual Sect); Am Inst Fisheries Res Biologist; Ecol Soc Am; Nat Wildlife Fedn. *Res:* Environmental effects of nuclear and nonnuclear power production and hazardous materials release; environmental, health and engineering aspects of energy technology development; environmental monitoring and assesesment; toxicol behavior-ethology. *Mailing Add:* PO Box 999 Mail Stop K1-33 Richland WA 99352. Fax: 509-373-6603

GRAY, ROBERT HOWARD, SUB-CELLULAR TOXICOLOGY, CELL BIOLOGY. *Current Pos:* chair, Environ & Indust Health, Univ Mich, Ann Arbor, 86-91, asst dean curric & stud affairs, 91-92, assoc dean, 92-93, asst prof, Univ Mich, Ann Arbor, 69-75, actg asst dean curric, 78-79, assoc prof, 75-79, RES ASSOC, INST ENVIRON & INDUST HEALTH, UNIV MICH, ANN ARBOR, 69-, PROF ENVIRON & INDUST HEALTH, 79-, RES SCIENTIST, 79-, ASSOC DEAN RES & STUD AFFAIRS, 94- *Personal Data:* b Meadville, Pa, Sept 14, 37; m 61, Judy Kerresz; c Jenine, Kathleen & Heidi. *Educ:* Ohio Univ, BSEd, 60, MS, 62; Univ Ill, PhD(bot), 67. *Prof Exp:* NIH fel, Univ Wis, 67-69. *Concurrent Pos:* Vis sr scientist, Lovelace Inhalation Toxicol Res Inst, 79-80; consult, Lovelace Inhalation Toxicol Res Inst, 80 & Warner-Lambert/Parke-Davis, 81. *Mem:* AAAS; Microbeam Analysis Soc; Am Soc Cell Biol; Electron Micros Soc Am. *Res:* Biochemical and ultrastructural studies on cellular accommodation to environmental stress; sterological studies on hepatic subcellular responses to hypolipidemic compounds; development of an animal model for Reye's Syndrome. *Mailing Add:* Sch Pub Health Univ Mich 109 Observatory St Ann Arbor MI 48109-2029. Fax: 313-763-5455; E-Mail: rhgray@sph.umich.edu

GRAY, ROBERT J, METALLURGY. *Current Pos:* CONSULT & MEM STAFF, AM SOC METALS INT, 85- *Personal Data:* b Sterling, Kans, Nov 15, 18. *Educ:* Sterling Col, BS, 41. *Prof Exp:* Sr staff mem, Metallog Div, Oak Ridge Nat Lab, 48-85. *Concurrent Pos:* Mem bd dirs, Int Metallog Soc, 73-89. *Mem:* Am Soc Metals; Int Metallog Soc (pres, 77-79). *Mailing Add:* 137 Orchard Lane Oak Ridge TN 37830

GRAY, ROBERT MOLTEN, DATA COMPRESSION, INFORMATION THEORY. *Current Pos:* From asst prof to assoc prof, 69-80, PROF ELEC ENG, STANFORD UNIV, 80-, VCHMN, 93- *Personal Data:* b San Diego, Calif, Nov 1, 43; m 73, Arlene Ericson; c Timothy & Lori. *Educ:* Mass Inst Technol, BS, 66, MS, 66; Univ Southern Calif, PhD(elec eng), 69. *Honors & Awards:* Sr Award, Inst Elec & Electronics Engrs ASSP, 83, Centennial Medal, 84; Soc Award, Signal Processing Soc, 93. *Concurrent Pos:* Assoc ed & ed-in-chief, Trans Info Theory, Inst Elec & Electronics Engrs, 77-80, ed, 80-; Guggenheim fel, 81-82; dir, Info Systs Lab, Stanford Univ, 84-87; assoc ed, Math Control & Systs Sci. *Mem:* Fel Inst Elec & Electronics Engrs; fel Inst Math Statist; Am Math Soc; AAAS; fel Soc Sci Engrs France; Sigma Xi. *Res:* Image compression and enhancement; classification trees; information theory, the mathematical theory of communication including coding theorems for probabilistic sources and channels and applications of ergodic theory to information theory; computer aided design of data compression systems; quantization and analog-to-digital conversion theory; author of six books and editor of two collections. *Mailing Add:* Elec Eng Dept 127 Durand Bldg Stanford Univ Stanford CA 94305-4055. *Fax:* 650-723-8473

GRAY, ROBIN B(RYANT), aerospace engineering, for more information see previous edition

GRAY, RUSSELL HOUSTON, COLOR-SPECTROPHOTOMETRIC SCIENCE, IMAGING SCIENCES. *Current Pos:* RETIRED. *Personal Data:* b Akron, Ohio, May 30, 18; m 42, Edith M Pullam; c Linda, Barrett, Eric & Douglas. *Educ:* Univ Akron, BSc, 40. *Honors & Awards:* Serv Award, Soc Photog Scientists & Engrs, 65; IR100 Award, 74. *Prof Exp:* Chemist, Quaker Oats Co, 40-41; photo chemist, Wright Field Aerial Photo Lab, 41-42; officer, US Army Air Corps, 42-46; res assoc, Photo Prod Dept, E I DuPont de Nemours, 46-80. *Concurrent Pos:* Consult, Appl Color Systs, 80-81, Mead Paper Co, 83- & various other indust cos, 80-89. *Mem:* Soc Photog Scientists & Engrs; Sigma Xi; Inter-Soc Color Coun; Tech Asn Graphic Arts; Am Chem Soc. *Res:* Colorants and color reproduction, particularly for graphic arts applications; color proofing systems; photographic and color sciences research and development; color imaging. *Mailing Add:* 9 Circle Dr Rumson NJ 07760

GRAY, SAMUEL HUTCHISON, mathematics, for more information see previous edition

GRAY, SARAH DELCENIA, CARDIOVASCULAR PHYSIOLOGY. *Current Pos:* from asst prof to assoc prof, 72-83, PROF PHYSIOL, SCH, MED, UNIV CALIF, DAVIS, 83-, LECTR, LAW SCH, 77- *Personal Data:* b Newark, NJ, Aug 1, 34. *Educ:* Barnard Col, BA, 56; NY Univ, MS, 60; Univ Calif, San Francisco, PhD(physiol), 66. *Honors & Awards:* Nat Res Coun travel award, Int Union Physiol Sci, India, 74. *Prof Exp:* Res assoc physiol, Univ Calif Med Ctr, San Francisco, 66; assoc, Mt Sinai Sch Med, 68-71, asst prof, 71-72. *Concurrent Pos:* NIH fel, 66-67, consult, minority biomed support prog, 76-, ischemic heart dis, Spec Ctr Res, 78-79 & study sect, 82-86; sr investr, NY Heart Asn, 69-72; assoc ed, Microvascular Res, 77-84 & Blood Vessels, 85- *Mem:* Sigma Xi; Microcirculatory Soc; Europ Soc Microcirculation; Am Physiol Soc; Am Heart Asn; Int Soc Hypertension. *Res:* Mechanisms governing microvascular behavior, especially reactivity to neural and hormonal stimuli which influence patterns of pressure and flow in skeletal muscle during neonatal development, exercise, and the development of genetic hypertension. *Mailing Add:* Dept Human Physiol Univ Calif Sch Med Davis CA 95616. *Fax:* 530-752-5423

GRAY, STEPHEN WOOD, ANATOMY, EMBRYOLOGY. *Current Pos:* ASSOC DIR, THALIA & MICHAEL CARLOS CTR SURG ANAT & TECHNIQUE, 83- *Personal Data:* b Oakland, Calif, Apr 27, 15; m 38, 73. *Educ:* Lake Forest Col, AB, 36; Univ Ill, AM, 37, PhD(zool), 39. *Hon Degrees:* DSc, Lake Forest Col, 90. *Prof Exp:* Instr physiol, Univ Ill, 39-42; prof anat, Sch Med, Emory Univ, 46-83. *Concurrent Pos:* Mem working group room space res, Int Coun Sci Unions. *Mem:* Am Soc Zool; Am Physiol Soc; Am Asn Anat; Am Asn Clin Anat. *Res:* Biological effects of gravity; dynamics of growth; embryological defects; surgical anatomy. *Mailing Add:* Ctr Surg & Anat Technol Emory Univ Sch Med 1462 Clifton Rd NE Ste 307 Atlanta GA 30322

GRAY, THEODORE FLINT, JR, polymer chemistry, for more information see previous edition

GRAY, THOMAS JAMES, PHYSICAL CHEMISTRY, CERAMIC & MATERIALS SCIENCE ENGINEERING. *Current Pos:* CONSULT, 81- *Personal Data:* b Atherstone, Eng, July 28, 17; nat US; m 41; c 3. *Educ:* Bristol Univ, BSc & PhD(chem), 38. *Prof Exp:* Lectr chem, Bristol Univ, 46-53; from assoc prof to prof phys chem, State Univ NY Col Ceramics, Alfred Univ, 53-68, adminr, Off Res, 64-68; dir, Atlantic Indust Res Inst, NS Tech Col, 68-76; chief phys chemist, Metals Res Lab, Olin Corp, 76-80. *Concurrent Pos:* Consult scientist, 48- *Mem:* Am Chem Soc; fel Am Soc Metals; Nat Inst Ceramic Engrs. *Res:* Catalysis; semiconductors; dielectric and magnetic properties of materials; high temperature materials; fuel cells; strontium containing ceramics; tidal power; unconventional energy systems. *Mailing Add:* 971 Hoop Pole Rd Guilford CT 06437

GRAY, THOMAS MERRILL, entomology, ecology, for more information see previous edition

GRAY, TIMOTHY KENNEY, INTERNAL MEDICINE, ENDOCRINOLOGY. *Current Pos:* PVT PRACT, 91- *Personal Data:* b Baltimore, Md, Oct 4, 39; m 63; c 3. *Educ:* Loyola Col, BS, 61; Univ Md, MD, 65. *Honors & Awards:* Jefferson Pilot Award, Sch Med, Univ NC, 73. *Prof Exp:* Resident, Sch Med, Univ Md, 65-68, chief resident & instr, 70-71; from asst prof to prof med, Univ NC, 71-91, dir, Clin Res Ctr, 76-79, vchmn, Dept Med, 77-80. *Concurrent Pos:* Spec USPHS res fel, Dept Pharmacol, 68-70; investr NIAMDD res grant award, 74-80, NSF clin res award, 75-79, & NSF basic res award, 78-80. *Mem:* Am Fedn Clin Res; Endocrine Soc; AAAS; fel Am Col Physicians. *Res:* Mineral metabolism and its hormonal regulation; mineral metabolism of pregnancy and fetal development; vitamin D metabolism and fetal skeletal development. *Mailing Add:* 9279 A Medical Plaza Dr North Charleston SC 29406

GRAY, TOM J, PHYSICS. *Current Pos:* vis prof, 75-77, PROF PHYSICS, KANS STATE UNIV, 77- *Personal Data:* b Newton, Kans, Dec 2, 37; m, Martha Shosa Caughron; c 2. *Educ:* NTex State Univ, BS, 60, MS, 62; Fla State Univ, PhD(physics), 67. *Prof Exp:* From asst prof to prof, NTex State Univ, 67-75. *Concurrent Pos:* Consult, Tex Instruments Inc, 73-75. *Mem:* Fel Am Phys Soc. *Res:* Cryogenics, superconducting linear accelerator design and fabrication; experimental ion/atom and ion molecule collisions studies; molecular ion production and cluster ion production studies. *Mailing Add:* Dept Physics Cardwell Hall Kans State Univ Manhattan KS 66506. *Fax:* 785-532-6806; *E-Mail:* tgray@phys.ksu.edu

GRAY, WALTER C(LARKE), chemical engineering; deceased, see previous edition for last biography

GRAY, WALTER STEVEN, NUCLEAR PHYSICS. *Current Pos:* Res assoc nuclear physics, 64-66, asst prof physics, 66-74, ASSOC PROF PHYSICS, UNIV MICH, 74- *Personal Data:* b Ponca City, Okla, Feb 21, 38. *Educ:* Okla State Univ, BS, 58, MS, 60; Univ Colo, PhD(physics), 64. *Mem:* Am Phys Soc. *Res:* Nuclear spectroscopy and accelerator-induced nuclear reactions. *Mailing Add:* Dept Physics Univ Mich Ann Arbor MI 48109

GRAY, WILLIAM DAVID, PHARMACOLOGY. *Current Pos:* RETIRED. *Personal Data:* b Gilford, Northern Ireland, May 12, 16; nat US; m 44, Marianne C Cannon; c Geoffrey I & Kevin S. *Educ:* Clark Univ, BA, 38; Univ Toronto, MA, 40; Yale Univ, PhD(pharm), 50. *Prof Exp:* Res assoc, Ciba Pharmaceut Prods, Inc, NJ, 40-52; res assoc, Merck Inst Therapeut Res, 46-47; pharmacologist, Lederle Labs Div, Am Cyanamid Co, 50-54, group leader pharmacol, 54-56, head dept exp pharmacol, 56-71, dir cent nerv syst dis ther res, 71-73; mgr toxicol, Schering Corp, 73-75, assoc dir, 75-77, assoc dir lab compliance, 77-80; dir res, Biosphere Res Ctr, Inc, 80-81, consult, 81-82. *Mem:* Am Soc Pharmacol & Exp Therapeut; Soc Neurosci; Soc Toxicol; Sigma Xi. *Res:* Neuropharmacology; general pharmacodynamic and behavioral actions of CNS agents; biochemical pharmacology of CNS agents; biogenic amines and anticonvulsant action of carbonic anhydrase inhibitors. *Mailing Add:* 31 Diane Dr New City NY 10956

GRAY, WILLIAM GUERIN, CIVIL ENGINEERING, HYDROLOGY. *Current Pos:* PROF & CHMN, CIVIL ENG, UNIV NOTRE DAME, 84- *Personal Data:* b San Francisco, Calif, Jan 9, 48; m 70; c 5. *Educ:* Univ Calif, Davis, BS, 69; Princeton Univ, PhD(chem eng), 74. *Prof Exp:* Res hydrol, US Geol Surv, 73-74; lectr, Princeton Univ, 74-75, from asst prof to assoc prof civil eng, 75-84. *Concurrent Pos:* Hydrologist, US Geol Surv, 74-75. *Mem:* Inst Assoc Hydraul Res; Sigma Xi; Am Inst Chem Engrs; Am Geophys Union. *Res:* Numerical solution of differential equations; finite element method; surface flow modeling; physics of porous media flow. *Mailing Add:* Civil Eng & Geol Scis Dept Univ Notre Dame Notre Dame IN 46556-0767

GRAY, WILLIAM HARVEY, SUPERCONDUCTING MAGNETS, COMPUTER GRAPHICS. *Current Pos:* DEVELOP ENGR, OAK RIDGE NAT LAB, 74- *Personal Data:* b Nashville, Tenn, Dec 15, 48; m 70; c 2. *Educ:* Vanderbilt Univ, BE, 70, MS, 73, PhD(mech eng), 75. *Prof Exp:* Grad res asst, Los Alamos Nat Lab, 73-74. *Mem:* Inst Elec & Electronics Engrs. *Res:* Structural analysis problems associated with toroidal and polidal superconducting and normal magnets for fusion and physics research. *Mailing Add:* Martin Marietta Energy Systs PO Box Y Bldg 9103 MS 4 Oak Ridge TN 37831

GRAY, WILLIAM MASON, METEOROLOGY. *Current Pos:* asst meteorologist, 61-64, from asst prof to assoc prof, 64-74, PROF ATMOSPHERIC SCI, COLO STATE UNIV, 74- *Personal Data:* b Detroit, Mich, Oct 9, 29; m 54; c 3. *Educ:* George Washington Univ, BA, 52; Univ Chicago, MS, 59, PhD(geophys sci), 64. *Prof Exp:* Res asst meteorol, Univ Chicago, 57-61. *Concurrent Pos:* NSF res grant, Japan, 65-66, England 70-71. *Mem:* Am Meteorol Soc. *Res:* Atmospheric science; tropical meteorology and hurricanes; cumulus convection; meteorological observations; tornadoes. *Mailing Add:* Dept Atmospheric Sci Colo State Univ Ft Collins CO 80523-0001

GRAYBEAL, JACK DANIEL, MICROWAVE SPECTROSCOPY, NUCLEAR QUADRUPOLE RESONANCE. *Current Pos:* assoc prof, Va Polytech Inst & State Univ, 68-69, asst head dept, 74-75, PROF CHEM, VA POLYTECH INST & STATE UNIV, 69-, ASSOC HEAD DEPT, 75-

Personal Data: b Detroit, Mich, May 16, 30; m 54, Evelyn A Nicolai; c Daniel L, David E & Dale K. *Educ:* WVa Univ, BS, 51; Univ Wis, MS, 53, PhD(phys chem), 55. *Prof Exp:* Mem tech staff, Bell Tel Labs, 55-57; from asst prof to assoc prof chem, WVa Univ, 57-68. *Mem:* Am Chem Soc; Am Phys Soc; Sigma Xi. *Res:* Microwave spectroscopy; nuclear quadrupole resonance spectroscopy; molecular structure; dielectric behavior. *Mailing Add:* Dept Chem Va Polytech Inst & State Univ Blacksburg VA 24061-0212. *Fax:* 540-231-3255; *E-Mail:* jgraybeal@chemserver.chem.vt.edu

GRAYBIEL, ANN M, NEUROANATOMY. *Current Pos:* Res assoc, 71-73, from asst prof to assoc prof psychol, 73-80, PROF NEUROANAT, DEPT BRAIN & COGNITIVE SCI, MASS INST TECHNOL, 83- *Honors & Awards:* Williams & Wilkins Award, Am Asn Anatomists, 70, Charles Judson Herrick Award, 78; McKnight Award, 85. *Concurrent Pos:* Javits neurosci investr, 88. *Mem:* Nat Acad Sci; Inst Med-Nat Acad Sci; hon mem Royal Acad Med; assoc Neurosci Res Prog. *Res:* Co-author of numerous publications. *Mailing Add:* Dept Brain & Cognitive Sci Mass Inst Technol 45 Carlton St Cambridge MA 02139

GRAYBIEL, ASHTON, medicine; deceased, see previous edition for last biography

GRAYBILL, BRUCE MYRON, PHYSICAL ORGANIC CHEMISTRY. *Current Pos:* RETIRED. *Personal Data:* b Council Bluffs, Iowa, Oct 2, 31; m 52; c David, Steve & Diana G (McAlister). *Educ:* Iowa State Univ, BS, 55; Fla State Univ, PhD(chem), 59. *Prof Exp:* Res chemist, Rohm and Haas Co, 59-61; from asst prof to distinguished prof chem, Graceland Col, 61-94, chmn, Div Sci & Math 66-74, actg dean fac, 74-75, chmn Div Sci & Math, 81-94. *Concurrent Pos:* AEC comn fac fel, PR Nuclear Ctr, 70. *Mem:* Am Chem Soc; Am Inst Chem; Sigma Xi. *Res:* Organic reaction mechanisms. *Mailing Add:* 208 N Elm St Lamoni IA 50140

GRAYBILL, DONALD LEE, RESOURCE MANAGEMENT, INSTITUTIONAL STRENGTHENING. *Current Pos:* PRES, GCP INT, INC, 93- *Personal Data:* b Harrisburg, Pa, Feb 25, 43; m 65; c 3. *Educ:* Bucknell Univ, BA, 65; Univ Pittsburgh, ME, 66, PhD(ecol), 70. *Prof Exp:* Asst prof biol, Alliance Col, Cambridge Springs, Pa, 70-73; res assoc ecol, Univ Mass, 73-74; ecologist, sr mgr consult & suprv, Environ Sci Sect, Gilbert/Commonwealth, 74-85; sr mgt consult, mgr & vpres, Int Opers, Mgt Resources Int, Inc, 85-93. *Concurrent Pos:* Res assoc, Dept Biol, Univ Pittsburgh, 71-73; fel, E-W Ctr Environ & Policy Inst, Honolulu, Hawaii, 85-86; mem, US Comt Large Dams, Environ Effects Subcomt, 86-95. *Mem:* Ecol Soc Am; Nat Asn Environ Professionals; Int Asn Impact Assessment; Int Water Res Asn; Am Soc Testing & Mat. *Res:* Ecology. *Mailing Add:* 25 W 34th St Reading PA 19606-2908. *Fax:* 610-779-5963

GRAYBILL, FRANKLIN A, MATHEMATICAL STATISTICS. *Current Pos:* dir statist lab, 60-88, PROF MATH STATIST, COLO STATE UNIV, 88- *Personal Data:* b Carson, Iowa, Sept 23, 21; m 47; c 2. *Educ:* William Penn Col, BS, 47; Okla State Univ, MS, 49; Iowa State Univ, PhD(math statist), 52. *Prof Exp:* Prof math & sta statistician, Agr Exp Sta, Okla State Univ, 52-60. *Concurrent Pos:* Consult, Standard Oil Co, NJ, 54-; mem adv panel, Am Inst Biol Sci, NASA, 71-74; ed, Biometrics, J Biometric Soc, 71-75. *Mem:* Fel Am Statist Asn (pres, 76-); fel Inst Math Statist; fel AAAS; Int Statist Inst; Biomet Soc. *Res:* Variance component analysis. *Mailing Add:* 415 S Howes Ft Collins CO 80521

GRAYBILL, HOWARD W, high-power electrical equipment, for more information see previous edition

GRAYDON, WILLIAM FREDERICK, PHYSICAL CHEMISTRY. *Personal Data:* b Toronto, Ont, June 27, 19; m 45; c 5. *Educ:* Univ Toronto, BASc, 42, MASc, 45; Univ Minn, PhD(chem), 49. *Prof Exp:* Asst prof chem eng, 49-59, prof, 59-84, assoc dean fac appl sci, 66-77, chmn dept chem eng & appl chem, 70-77, emer prof, Univ Toronto, 84-93. *Mem:* Am Chem Soc; Royal Soc Chem; Chem Inst Can. *Res:* Ion exchange; corrosion; process dynamics; applied physical chemistry. *Mailing Add:* 3 Mossom Pl Toronto ON M6S 1G4 Can

GRAYHACK, JOHN THOMAS, UROLOGY. *Current Pos:* from asst prof to assoc prof, 56-63, PROF UROL & CHMN DEPT, MED SCH, NORTHWESTERN UNIV, CHICAGO, 63- *Personal Data:* b Kankakee, Ill, Aug 21, 23; m 50; c 5. *Educ:* Univ Chicago, BS, 45, MD, 47. *Prof Exp:* Instr urol, Sch Med, Johns Hopkins Univ, 52-54. *Concurrent Pos:* Am Cancer Soc fel, 50-51; Runyon fel, 52-54. *Mem:* AAAS; AMA; Am Asn Genito-Urinary Surg; Am Surg Asn; Endocrine Soc. *Res:* Factors in normal and abnormal prostatic growth; evaluation and treatment of diseases of genito-urinary tract. *Mailing Add:* Urol Northwestern Univ Med Sch 303 E Chicago Ave Chicago IL 60611-3008

GRAYSON, HERBERT G, CHEMICAL ENGINEERING. *Current Pos:* Sr develop engr, Eng Dept, Socony Mobil Oil Co Inc, 47-64, prod planner, Prod Dept, 64-74, environ assoc, 74-79, MGR INDUST/ENERGY PROG, MOBIL OIL CORP, 79- *Personal Data:* b New York, NY, Jan 5, 26; m 47; c 3. *Educ:* City Col New York, BS, 46; Polytech Inst Brooklyn, MS, 52. *Mem:* Am Inst Chem Engrs; Sigma Xi; Air Pollution Control Asn; Am Petrol Inst. *Res:* Properties of petroleum; vapor-liquid equilibria and enthalpy; unit operations; fluid flow; heat transfer; tray efficiency; properties of granular solids; air pollution; energy and technological forecasting; automobile emissions reduction. *Mailing Add:* 325 Laurel Ln Syosset NY 11791

GRAYSON, JOHN, PHYSIOLOGY. *Current Pos:* prof, 68-84, EMER PROF PHYSIOL, UNIV TORONTO, 84- *Personal Data:* b Huddersfield, Eng, Jan 4, 19; m 61. *Educ:* Victoria Univ Manchester, BSc, 40, MSc, 41, MB & ChB, 43, MD, 49, DsC(physiol), 66. *Prof Exp:* Res asst surg, Royal Victoria Infirmary, Eng, 47-49; lectr physiol, Univ Bristol, 49-55; prof & chmn dept, Univ Ibadan, 55-67; vis prof, Univ Alta, 67-68. *Mem:* Can Physiol Soc; Brit Physiol Soc; Europ Soc Microcirc; Can Soc Microcirc (vpres, 71). *Res:* Human skin blood vessels, environmental change, cold and frostbite; gastrointestinal and liver blood vessels in general and glucose homeostasis; autoregulation and brain blood flow; heart blood vessels, nutritional role of anastomotic network, effect of acute occlusion and atheroma. *Mailing Add:* 33 Anderson Toronto ON M5P 1H5 Can

GRAYSON, JOHN FRANCIS, PALYNOLOGY, GEOCHEMISTRY. *Current Pos:* CONSULT, 83- *Personal Data:* b Bay City, Mich, Mar 23, 28; m 51, Louise Moore; c Kathleen Marie (Young), Susan (Moore), Nancy (Gruenau) & David John. *Educ:* Univ Mich, BS, 51, MS, 52, PhD(bot), 56. *Honors & Awards:* John F Grayson Palynology Libr, Nat Museums Can, Ottawa, Can. *Prof Exp:* Sr res palynologist, Res Labs, Socony Mobil Oil Co, Tex, 54-62; res group suprv, Res Ctr, Pan Am Petrol Corp, 61-68, res assoc, 68-71, res assoc, Res Ctr, Amoco Prod Co, 71-83. *Mem:* Am Asn Petrol Geol; Am Geol Inst; Am Asn Stratig Palynologists; Geol Soc Am. *Res:* Plant geography and ecology; stratigraphic geology; paleontology; paleobotany; microspectrofluorescence; organic matter present in rocks as it pertains to petroleum exploration. *Mailing Add:* 561 Sage Brush Trail Durango CO 81301

GRAYSON, LAWRENCE P(ETER), ELECTRICAL ENGINEERING. *Current Pos:* dep dir, 87-90, DIR POSTSEC RELS STAFF, US DEPT EDUC, 90- *Personal Data:* b Brooklyn, NY, May 16, 37; m 64; c Mary L, Catherine, Lawrence, Elizabeth, Maureen & Therese. *Educ:* Polytech Inst Brooklyn, BEE, 58, MEE, 59, PhD(elec eng), 62. *Hon Degrees:* DEng, Milwaukee Sch Eng, 88. *Honors & Awards:* William Elgin Wickenden Award, Am Soc Eng Educ, 79; Centennial Medal, Inst Elec & Electronics Engrs, 84, Roland J Schmidt Award, 85; Distinguished Serv Citation, Am Soc Eng Educ, 81 & Centennial Medal, 93; Herbert Hoover Medal, 87; George Washington Medal, Freedom Found, 89 & 91; Distinguished Contrib to Eng Professionalism Award, Inst Elec & Electronics Engrs, 91. *Prof Exp:* Asst prof elec eng, Johns Hopkins Univ, 62-67; Ford Found researcher eng pract, Thomas J J Watson Res Ctr, IBM Corp, 67-68; assoc prof elec eng, Manhattan Col, 68-69; specialist comput in educ, Bur Res, US Off Educ, 69-70, dep dir, Div Educ Technol, Bur Libr & Educ Technol, 70-72, dir, Div Technol, 72-73; mem, task force productivity & technol, Nat Inst Educ, 73-75, dir div technol develop, 75-78, head info technol, media & pub commun, 78-81, asst dir regional progs, 81-82, inst advan math, 82-86; Inst Elec & Electronics Engrs Cong fel, Off Congressman Jack Kemp, 86-87; vis prof, Elec & Eng, Cath Univ Am, 88-89. *Concurrent Pos:* Consult, Math Br, Frankford Arsenal, 62-66, Johns Hopkins Hosp, 67, UNESCO, 73-82, Gen Elec Co & Lawrence Livermore Nat Labs; mem educ systs comt, Nat Acad Eng Comn on Educ, 68-73; mem, Nat Comt Full Develop Instrnl TV Fixed Serv, 69-73; mem educ comt, World Fedn Eng Orgn, 76-81; adj prof libr & info sci, Cath Univ Am, 79-87, mem vis bd, 80- *Mem:* Fel Inst Elec & Electronics Engrs; fel Am Soc Eng Educ (vpres, 72-74, pres, 88-); fel AAAS; Sigma Xi; Am Asn Eng Soc. *Res:* Nonlinear oscillations; nonlinear and adaptive control systems; engineering education; educational technology; computers, satellites; societal implications of technology. *Mailing Add:* Off Postsec Educ US Dept Educ Washington DC 20202

GRAYSON, MARTIN, CHEMISTRY. *Current Pos:* RETIRED. *Personal Data:* b New York, NY; m 70, Virginia Suggs; c Michael. *Educ:* NY Univ, BS; Purdue Univ, PhD(chem). *Prof Exp:* Chemist, Nitrogen Div, Allied Corp, 52-56; sr res chemist, Am Cyanamid Co, 56-60, group leader, 60-71, prin res scientist, 72-75; exec ed, John Wiley & Sons, 75-81, publisher, 81-87; pres, VCH Publs, 87-91, bd dirs, 91-93. *Concurrent Pos:* Adj prof, Univ Bridgeport, 65-72; ed, Topics Phosphorus Chem, 60-; ed-in-chief, Phosphorus & Sulfur, 70-87, ed emer, 87- *Mem:* Fel NY Acad Sci; fel AAAS; Am Chem Soc. *Res:* Organophosphorus chemistry; chemical technology. *Mailing Add:* 82 Valleywood Rd Cos Cob CT 06807-2319

GRAYSON, MERRILL, ophthalmology, corneal surgery, for more information see previous edition

GRAYSON, MICHAEL A, ENVIRONMENTAL AGING OF POLYMERIC MATERIALS, MASS SPECTROMETRY INSTRUMENTS. *Current Pos:* Res scientist, 66-70, scientist, 70-85, SR SCIENTIST, MCDONNELL DOUGLAS RES LABS, 85- *Personal Data:* b Wichita, Kans, July 18, 41; m 64; c 4. *Educ:* St Louis Univ, BA, 63; Univ Mo, Rolla, MA, 65. *Concurrent Pos:* Lectr, Wash Univ Sch Continuing Educ, 69-71. *Mem:* Am Soc Mass Spectrometry; NY Acad Sci; Sigma Xi; Am Chem Soc; AAAS. *Res:* Development and application of mass spectrometric techniques to the characterization and study of environmental aging in polymeric and composite material systems. *Mailing Add:* 3433 Bluff View Dr St Charles MO 63303-6608

GRAYSON, WILLIAM CURTIS, JR, NUCLEAR WEAPONS PHYSICS. *Current Pos:* SR SCIENTIST, DYNMERIDIAN CORP, 90- *Personal Data:* b Decatur, Miss, Nov 17, 29; m 51, 76, Antionette Joseph; c William O, John C, Robert A, William J & Katherine A. *Educ:* Univ Chicago, SB, 50; Duke Univ, PhD(physics), 55. *Prof Exp:* Physicist, Lawrence Livermore Nat Lab, Univ Calif, 54-56, group leader, 66-68, div, leader, 68-71, dept div leader, 71-76, dept assoc dir, 76-78; tech adv to asst secy defense progs, US Dept Energy, 78-81; sr scientist, R&D Assoc, 81-90. *Mem:* Am Phys Soc; Am Nuclear Soc. *Res:* Nuclear physics; physics of nuclear explosives; computational physics; technical management; arms control. *Mailing Add:* 5644 Bent Branch Rd Bethesda MD 20816

GRAYSTON, J THOMAS, EPIDEMIOLOGY. *Current Pos:* prof prev med & chmn dept, Sch Med, Univ Wash, 60-70, founding dean, Sch Pub Health & Community Med, 70-71, vpres health sci, 71-83, PROF EPIDEMIOL, UNIV WASH, 70- *Personal Data:* b Wichita, Kans, Sept 6, 24; m 47, 80; c 3. *Educ:* Univ Chicago, BS, 47, MD, 48, MS, 52; Am Bd Internal Med, dipl, 57; Am Bd Prev Med, dipl, 68. *Honors & Awards:* Joseph E Smadel Award & Medal, Infectious Dis Soc Am, 89. *Prof Exp:* Epidemiologist, Commun Dis Ctr, USPHS, 51-53; from instr to assoc prof med, Univ Chicago, 53-60. *Concurrent Pos:* Chief, Div Microbiol & Epidemiol, Naval Med Res Unit, Taiwan, 57-60; assoc mem, Comn Acute Respiratory Dis, 61-65, mem, 65-74; mem, Panel Biol & Med, Dept Defense, 62-66, Virol & Rickettsiology Study Sect, NIH, 63-67, Int Ctrs Comt, 67-71; mem, Wxpert Comt Trachoma, WHO, 71- *Mem:* Inst Med-Nat Acad Sci; fel Am Pub Health Asn; Am Epidemiol Soc; Am Asn Physicians; fel Infectious Dis Soc Am. *Res:* Epidemiology and prevention of infectious diseases; international health. *Mailing Add:* Dept Epidemiol F262 Univ Wash Box 3572-36 Seattle WA 98195. *Fax:* 206-543-8525; *E-Mail:* grayston@uwashington.edu

GRAYZEL, ARTHUR I, MEDICINE. *Current Pos:* PROF MED, ALBERT EINSTEIN COL MED, 77- *Personal Data:* b New York, NY, Mar 8, 32; m 57; c 3. *Educ:* Harvard Col, AB, 53; Harvard Med Sch, MD, 57. *Concurrent Pos:* Head, Div Rheumatol, Montefiore Med Ctr, 69-89. *Mem:* Am Asn Immunologists; fel Am Rheumatism Asn; fel Am Col Physicians; Brit Soc Rheumatologists. *Res:* Pathogenesis and immunologic basic and treatment of rheumatic diseases including rheumatoid arthritis and systemic lupus erythematosus. *Mailing Add:* 1401 Fairway Green Mamaroneck NY 10543

GRAZIADEI, WILLIAM DANIEL, III, BIOLOGY. *Current Pos:* from asst prof to assoc prof, 73-80, PROF BIOL, STATE UNIV NY, PLATTSBURGH, 80-, DIR-IN-VITRO CELL BIOL & BIOTECHNOL, MINER INST, 82- *Personal Data:* b Hartford, Conn, Mar 12, 43; c William D IV, Mark C, Michael J, Keith N & Kevin M. *Educ:* Fairfield Univ, BS, 65; Boston Col, MS, 67, PhD(microbiol & molecular biol), 70. *Prof Exp:* NIH fel, Yale Univ, Conn, 70-73. *Concurrent Pos:* Prin investr, NIH, 72 & 74, Am Cancer Soc, 77, Fitzpatrick Oncol Ctr, 89; coordr-in-vitro cell biol, W Alton Jones Cell Ctr, 80-83. *Mem:* Tissue Cult Asn; AAAS; Sigma Xi. *Res:* Microbiology; biotechnology; molecular biology; cell biology. *Mailing Add:* 6 Laurel Ct Plattsburgh NY 12901

GRAZIANO, FRANK M, MEDICINE, ALLERGY. *Current Pos:* assoc prof, 78-, PROF MED & IMMUNOL, DEPT MED, UNIV WIS HOSP. *Educ:* Univ Va, MD & PhD(microbiol), 73. *Res:* Rheumatology. *Mailing Add:* Univ Wis Hosp & Clin Rm H6/367 600 Highland Ave Madison WI 53792-3244. *Fax:* 608-623-3104

GRDINA, DAVID JOHN, RADIATION BIOLOGY, CHEMOPREVENTION. *Current Pos:* scientist, 83-87, SR SCIENTIST RADIATION CARCINOGENESIS, ARGONNE NAT LAB, 87-; PROF RADIATION ONCOL, UNIV CHICAGO, ILL, 87- *Personal Data:* b Hammond, Ind, Oct 26, 44; m 67, Judith A Moothart; c Joseph, Karen, Wendy & John. *Educ:* St Mary's Col, Winona, Minn, BA, 66; Univ Kans, Lawrence, MS, 69, PhD(radiation biophys), 71; Univ Houston, Tex, MBA, 80. *Honors & Awards:* Japanese Govt Res Awards, Foreign Specialists, 88. *Prof Exp:* Res fel DNA repair, M D Anderson Hosp & Tumor Inst, Houston, Tex, 71-72, res assoc tumor radiobiol, 72-75, from asst prof to assoc prof exp radiother, 75-83. *Concurrent Pos:* Vis lectr nuclear med, Baylor Col Med, Houston, Tex, 76-83; vis assoc prof therapeut radiol, Rush Med Col, Rush-Presbyterian-St Lukes Med Ctr, Chicago, Ill, 84-85; assoc prof radiation oncol, Univ Chicago, 85-87; mem radiation study sect, NIH, 90-94; mem Ill Div study sect, Am Cancer Soc, 91-95. *Mem:* Am Asn Cancer Res; Radiation Res Soc; Am Soc Therapeut Radiol & Oncol. *Res:* Chemical radiation modifying agents to study mechanisms involved in radiation carcinogenesis; tumor heterogeneity and the associated factors involved in the prevention treatment, and control of tumors in experimental systems. *Mailing Add:* 94 N Stauffer Dr Naperville IL 60540

GREAGER, OSWALD HERMAN, physical chemistry; deceased, see previous edition for last biography

GREASER, MARION LEWIS, MUSCLE BIOLOGY, MEAT SCIENCE. *Current Pos:* from asst prof to assoc prof, 71-77, PROF, UNIV WIS-MADISON, 77- *Personal Data:* b Vinton, Iowa, Feb 10, 42; m 65, Marilyn Pfister; c Suzanne & Scott. *Educ:* Iowa State Univ, BS, 64; Univ Wis, MS, 67, PhD(biochem-muscle biol), 69. *Honors & Awards:* Distinguished Res Award, Am Meat Sci Asn, 81; Outstanding Researcher Award, Am Heart Asn Wis, 85. *Prof Exp:* Fel, Boston Biomed Res Found, 68-71. *Concurrent Pos:* NIH fel, Boston Biomed Res Found, 68-70. *Mem:* Am Soc Biochem & Molecular Biol; Biophys Soc; Am Soc Cell Biol; Am Meat Sci Asn; Inst Food Technologists. *Res:* Mechanism of muscle contraction and its control; mechanisms of muscle growth and assembly. *Mailing Add:* Muscle Biol Lab Univ Wis 1805 Linden Dr Madison WI 53706

GREASHAM, RANDOLPH LOUIS, MICROBIAL BIOCHEMISTRY. *Current Pos:* RES MICROBIOLOGIST INDUST MICROBIOL, INT MINERALS & CHEM CORP, 72-; AT MERCK & CO. *Personal Data:* b Evansville, Ind, Apr 7, 42; m 65. *Educ:* Univ Evansville, BA, 64; Villanova Univ, MS, 67; Hahnemann Med Col, PhD(microbiol), 70. *Prof Exp:* Res assoc indust microbiol, Mass Inst Technol, 70-72. *Mem:* Am Chem Soc; Am Soc Microbiol. *Res:* Fermentation biochemistry; microbial genetics. *Mailing Add:* Merck & Co PO Box 2000 Rahway NJ 07065-4687

GREATBATCH, WILSON, BIOMEDICAL ENGINEERING. *Current Pos:* PRES, GREATBATCH GEN-AID LTD, 86- *Personal Data:* b Buffalo, NY, Sept 6, 19; m 45; c Warren, John, Kenneth, Anne & Peter. *Educ:* Cornell Univ, BEE, 50; Univ Buffalo, MSEE, 57. *Hon Degrees:* ScD, Houghton Col, 71, State Univ NY, Buffalo, 84, Clarkson Univ, 86 & Roberts Wesleyan Col, 87,. *Honors & Awards:* William Morlock Award, Inst Elec & Electronic Engrs, 68, Centennial Medal, 84; Laufman Award, Asn Advan Med Instrumentation, 85; Holley Award, Am Soc Mech Engr, 87; Nat Technol Medal, Pres Bush, 90; Nat Inventors Hall of Fame; US Aerospace Hall of Fame; Prince Ranier Pacemaker Award. *Prof Exp:* Proj engr, Cornell Aeronaut Lab, Inc, 50-52; asst prof elec eng, Univ Buffalo, 52-57; mgr, Electronics Div, Taber Instrument Corp, 57-60; vpres, Mennen Greatbatch Electronics, Inc, 62-78, pres, Wilson Greatbatch, Ltd, 70-86. *Concurrent Pos:* Adj prof phys sci, Houghton Col, 70-; adj prof elec eng, State Univ NY, Buffalo, 81-; adj prof eng, Cornell Univ, 87- *Mem:* Nat Acad Engrs; fel Am Col Cardiol; fel Royal Soc Health; fel Am Inst Biol & Med Engrs; fel NY Acad Sci; Sigma Xi; fel AAAS; fel Am Soc Angiol; fel Inst Elec & Electronics Engrs. *Res:* Invention of implantable cardiac pacemaker; implantable power supplied for medical uses; molecular biology; anti AIDS vaccines. *Mailing Add:* Greatbatch Gen-Aid LTD 5935 Davison Rd Akron NY 14001

GREATHOUSE, TERRENCE RAY, ANIMAL NUTRITION. *Current Pos:* assoc dean agr, Col Agr, Tex A&M Univ, 77-78, assoc vpres agr & renewable resources & coordr int affairs, 78-79, vpres int affairs, 79-82, assoc dean admin, 82-89, PROF ANIMAL SCI, COL AGR, TEX A&M UNIV. *Personal Data:* b Hindsboro, Ill, Nov 7, 32; m 61, Barbara Moore; c Scott & Lance. *Educ:* Univ Ill, Urbana, BS, 55, MS, 58; Univ Ky, PhD(animal nutrit), 64. *Prof Exp:* Asst prof beef cattle res & animal scientist, Univ Ill, Urbana, 58-67; from asst prof to prof beef cattle res, Mich State Univ, 67-73; head dept animal sci, Colo State Univ, 73-77. *Mem:* Fel Am Soc Animal Sci; Am Dairy Sci Asn; Am Poultry Sci Asn; AAAS; Sigma Xi. *Res:* Beef cattle feeding, breeding and management. *Mailing Add:* Dept Animal Sci Col Agr Tex A&M Univ College Station TX 77843-0100

GREATRIX, DAVID ROBERT, PROPULSION, FLIGHT VEHICLE PERFORMANCE. *Current Pos:* ASST PROF AEROSPACE ENG, RYERSON POLYTECH UNIV, 93- *Personal Data:* b Portage la Prairie, Man, Oct 3, 58. *Educ:* Univ Man, BSc, 81; Univ Toronto, MASc 82, PhD(aerospace eng), 87. *Prof Exp:* Defense scientist, Defense Res Estab Valcartier, 82-84; aerospace engr, Boeing Winnipeg, 87-89; aerospace systs engr, Bombardier Canadari, 89-91. *Mem:* Am Inst Aeronaut & Astronaut. *Res:* Internal flow and combustion processes in various propulsion systems; flight vehicle performance and design. *Mailing Add:* Dept Mech Eng Ryerson Polytech Univ Toronto ON M5B 2K3 Can. *Fax:* 416-979-5265; *E-Mail:* greatrix@acs.ryerson.ca

GREAVES, BETTINA BIEN, HISTORY OF WORLD WAR II, HISTORY OF ECONOMIC THOUGHT. *Current Pos:* SR STAFF MEM, FOUND ECON EDUC, 51-, PROF ECON, NY INST CREDIT, 86- *Personal Data:* b Washington, DC, July 21, 17; m 71. *Educ:* Wheaton Col, Norton Mass, BA, 38; Columbia Univ, MLS, 67. *Hon Degrees:* Dr Soc Sci, Univ Francisco Marroquin, Guatemala, 83. *Prof Exp:* Secretarial, Bd Econ Warfare, Foreign Econ Admin, 44-46; ed asst, Found Freedom, 46-47. *Res:* Economic theory, Austrian School of Economics, background and revelation concerning the Japanese attack on Pearl Harbor, Dec 7, 1941. *Mailing Add:* 19 Pines Lane Irvington NY 10533

GREAVES, WALTER STALKER, VERTEBRATE PALEONTOLOGY. *Current Pos:* asst prof, 75-80, ASSOC PROF ORAL ANAT, UNIV ILL, CHICAGO, 80- *Personal Data:* b New York, NY, Feb 7, 37; m 67; c 1. *Educ:* State Univ NY, Oswego, BS, 66; Ohio Univ, MS, 67; Univ Chicago, PhD(evolutionary biol), 71. *Prof Exp:* Asst prof biol, Indiana Univ, Pa, 71-75, assoc prof, 75. *Concurrent Pos:* Res assoc, Sect Vert Fossils, Carnegie Mus Nat Hist, 74- *Mem:* Sigma Xi; Soc Study Evolution; Soc Vert Paleont; AAAS; Am Soc Zoologists; Am Soc Phys Anthropologists. *Res:* Functional morphology of fossil and recent mammalian jaw mechanisms. *Mailing Add:* 5340 Lyman Ave Downers Grove IL 60515

GREBE, JANICE DURR, GENETICS, ANATOMY. *Current Pos:* CONSULT, 85- *Personal Data:* b Alton, Ill, Nov 24, 40; m 79. *Educ:* Univ Tex, Austin, BA, 62, MA, 63, PhD(zool), 65. *Prof Exp:* Vis asst prof biol, Univ Kans, 67-68; asst prof, Avila Col, 69-71; instr & chmn biol, Pa Valley Commun Col, 72-79; asst prof, Rock Hurst Col, Kans Univ, 79-81; asst prof, Univ Health Sci, Kans City, Mo, 81-85. *Concurrent Pos:* NSF fel, Univ Wash, 65-67; NSF sci fac prof develop grant, Univ Kans Med Ctr, Kansas City, 78-79. *Mem:* Am Asn Anat; Sigma Xi; Am Soc Law & Med. *Res:* Developmental genetics; cytogenetics. *Mailing Add:* 4820 W 57th St Shawnee Mission KS 66205

GREBENAU, MARK DAVID, EXPERIMENTAL IMMUNOLOGY. *Current Pos:* asst dir, 83-86, assoc dir, 86-90, ASSOC MED DIR, SANDOZ MED OPERS, 90- *Personal Data:* b Newport News, Va, Mar 26, 51; m; c 2. *Educ:* Yeshiva Col, BA, 72, NY Univ, MS, 76, MD, 78, PhD(immunol), 79. *Prof Exp:* Residency internal med, King's Co Hosp Ctr/Downstate Univ Med Ctr/Brooklyn Vet Admin Hosp Ctr, 78-81; Lita Annenberg Hazen fel clin res & assoc physician, Rockefeller Univ Hosp, 81-83. *Concurrent Pos:* Assoc med staff, Dept Pediat, United Hosps Med Ctr, Newark, NJ, 85-87, courtesy staff, 87- *Mem:* Am Col Physicians; NY Acad Sci; Am Asn Immunologists; Am Asn Clin Immunol & Allergy; Am Soc Clin Pharmacol & Therapeut; Am Col Allergists. *Res:* Immunoglobulin therapy; development of immunological products. *Mailing Add:* 46 Porter Rd West Orange NJ 07052-2021

GREBENE, ALAN B, ELECTRONICS. *Current Pos:* SR VPRES & FOUNDER, EXAR INTEGRATED SYSTS, INC, 71-; PRES, MICRO-LINEAR CORP. *Personal Data:* b Istanbul, Turkey, Mar 13, 39; m 67; c 1. *Educ:* Robert Col, Istanbul, BSc, 61; Univ Calif, Berkeley, MSc, 63; Rensselaer Polytech Inst, PhD(elec eng), 68. *Prof Exp:* Mem tech staff, Fairchild Semiconductor, 63-64 & Sprague Elec Co, 64-65; lectr elec eng, Rensselaer Polytech Inst, 65-68; mgr circuit res, Signetics Corp, 68-71. *Concurrent Pos:* Lectr, Univ Santa Clara, 68-71. *Mem:* AAAS; Inst Elec & Electronics Engrs; Am Soc Eng Educ. *Res:* Integrated circuits research and development. *Mailing Add:* 15479 Belnap Dr Saratoga CA 95070

GREBER, ISAAC, MECHANICAL ENGINEERING, BIOENGINEERING & BIOMEDICAL ENGINEERING. *Current Pos:* assoc prof eng, 59-70, chmn, Dept Mech & Aerospace Eng, 79-84, PROF ENG, CASE WESTERN RES UNIV, 70- *Personal Data:* b Poland, Sept 20, 28; US citizen; m 53; c 2. *Educ:* City Col New York, BME, 50; Univ Mich, MSAE, 52; Mass Inst Technol, PhD(aerodyn), 59. *Honors & Awards:* Distinguished Res Award, NASA, 72. *Prof Exp:* Group leader theoret aerodyn, United Aircraft Res Labs, 52-54; sr aerodyn engr, Chance Vought Aircraft Corp, 54-55. *Concurrent Pos:* Fulbright prof, Appl Math Dept, Univ Tel-Aviv, 66-67; vis prof, Dept Aeronaut & Astronaut, Mass Inst Technol, 84-85 & 96. *Mem:* AAAS; Am Inst Aeronaut & Astronaut; Am Soc Eng Educ; Am Phys Soc; Sigma Xi. *Res:* Viscous flows; viscid-inviscid interactions; molecular dynamics. *Mailing Add:* 17937 Sherrington Rd Shaker Heights OH 44122

GREBNER, EUGENE ERNEST, BIOCHEMISTRY, BIOCHEMICAL GENETICS. *Current Pos:* RETIRED. *Personal Data:* b Pittsburgh, Pa, Feb 6, 31; m 55; c 2. *Educ:* Hiram Col, AB, 52; Univ Pittsburgh, MS, 60, PhD(biochem), 64. *Prof Exp:* Res biochemist, Albert Einstein Med Ctr, 67-74; res assoc prof, Thomas Jefferson Univ, 74-96. *Concurrent Pos:* USPHS fel biochem, NIH, Md, 64-67. *Mem:* Soc Complex Carbohydrates; Sigma Xi; AAAS. *Res:* Lysosomal storage diseases. *Mailing Add:* 228 Cowbell Rd Willow Grove PA 19090

GREBOGI, CELSO, CHAOTIC DYNAMICS, SYMPLECTIC GEOMETRY. *Current Pos:* res assoc physics, 81-85, res scientist physics & math, 85-90, ASSOC PROF MATH, UNIV MD, 90- *Personal Data:* b Curitiba, Parana, Brazil, May 29, 47; nat US; m 80. *Educ:* Fed Univ Parana, BS, 70; Univ Md, MS, 75, PhD(physics), 78. *Prof Exp:* Instr physics, Pontificia Catolica Univ, 71-74; staff scientist physics, Lawrence Berkeley Lab, 78-81. *Concurrent Pos:* Consult, Naval Surface Warfare Ctr, 83-; Lawrence Livermore Lab, 84-85, Science Applications Intern, Corp, 86-89; vis scientist, Univ Calif, Santa Barbara, 85; comt mem, US Dept Energy, 84-85; panel, Office Naval Technol, 87-90; prin invest, US Dept Energy, 84-. *Mem:* Am Math Soc; Soc Indust & Appl Math; AAAS. *Mailing Add:* Inst Plasma Res Univ Md College Park MD 20742

GREBOW, PETER ERIC, BIOPHARMACEUTICS. *Current Pos:* DIR, DRUG DEVELOP, CEPHALON, INC, 91- *Personal Data:* b New York, NY, Nov 25, 46; m 69; c 2. *Educ:* Cornell Univ, AB, 67; Rutgers Univ, MS, 69; Univ Calif, Santa Barbara, PhD(chem), 73. *Prof Exp:* Res fel pharmacol, Col Physicians & Surgeons, Columbia Univ, 73-75; group leader drug metab biopharmaceut, USV Pharmaceut Corp, 75-81, from assoc dept dir to dept dir drug disposition, Revlon Health Care Group, 81-88; vpres, New Drug Develop, Rorer, 88-90. *Mem:* Am Chem Soc; AAAS. *Res:* Drug and product development. *Mailing Add:* 704 Buckley Dr Penllyn PA 19422-1147

GRECCO, WILLIAM L, CIVIL ENGINEERING, URBAN PLANNING. *Current Pos:* prof civil eng & head dept, 72-86, ASSOC DEAN, UNIV TENN, KNOXVILLE, 86- *Personal Data:* b Brockway, Pa, Aug 28, 24; m 47; c 9. *Educ:* Univ Pittsburgh, BS, 47, MS, 51; Mich State Univ, PhD(transp), 62. *Prof Exp:* From instr to assoc prof civil eng, Univ Pittsburgh, 47-61; res asst, Mich State Univ, 61-62; from assoc prof to prof urban planning & eng, Purdue Univ, 62-72. *Concurrent Pos:* Consult, Dines & Grecco, 50-52, Found Assocs, 52 & Donald M McNeil, 53-58; mem info syst storage & retrieval comt, Hwy Res Bd, Nat Acad Sci-Nat Res Coun, 64; mem bd dirs, Purdue Calument Found, 67-71; ed, Am Soc Civil Engrs J, 68-71; eng accreditation comt, Accreditation Bd Eng & Technol, 80-85. *Mem:* Am Soc Civil Engrs; Am Soc Eng Educ; Inst Traffic Engrs; Am Planning Asn; Am Inst Cert Planners. *Res:* Urban traffic forecasting by system engineering; recreational travel; synthetic travel patterns. *Mailing Add:* 7935 Corteland Dr Knoxville TN 37909

GRECO, CLAUDE VINCENT, ORGANIC CHEMISTRY. *Current Pos:* RETIRED. *Personal Data:* b Bronx, NY, Sept 13, 30. *Educ:* Manhattan Col, BS, 52; NMex Highlands Univ, MS, 55; Fordham Univ, PhD(chem), 60. *Prof Exp:* Asst chem, Wellcome Res Labs, 52-53 & Fordham Univ, 56-57; assoc chemist, Midwest Res Inst, 59-61; fel, State Univ NY, 61-62; from asst prof to assoc prof, St John's Univ, 62-73, prof org chem, 73-94. *Concurrent Pos:* Adj prof, St John's Univ, 95 & 96. *Mem:* Am Chem Soc; Sigma Xi. *Res:* Synthetic organic chemistry; substitution reactions; mesoionic compounds; condensed heterocyclic systems; chemotherapy. *Mailing Add:* Dept Chem St John's Univ Jamaica NY 11432

GRECO, EDWARD CARL, CORROSION CHEMISTRY, CORROSION ENGINEERING. *Current Pos:* VPRES & SR CORROSION ENGR, F W CORROSION CONTROL, INC, 74- *Personal Data:* b Marsala, Italy, Nov 2, 11; US citizen; m 38; c Carl & Scotti (Rodgers). *Educ:* Northwestern State Univ, La, BS, 34. *Hon Degrees:* DSc, Centenary Col, La, 63. *Honors & Awards:* Prof Engrs Award, Eng & Sci Coun, 68; Edward C Greco Award, Int Corrosion Coun. *Prof Exp:* State dir, Fed Surplus Commodities Corp, 35-38; analytical chemist, United Gas Pipeline Co, 38-43; develop chemist, E I Du Pont de Nemours, 43-45; res chemist, United Gas Corp, 45-55, sr res assoc, 55-68; dir chem res, Northwestern State Univ, 68-74. *Concurrent Pos:* Dir, La State Sci Fairs, 56-65; pres, 2nd Int Cong, Metallic Corrosion, 62; head team, Scientists & Engrs Reciprocal Exchange, USSR, 62; chmn, Permanent Int Corrosion Coun, 63-68; ed, J, Mat Protection, 63-74. *Mem:* Emer mem Am Chem Soc; emer mem Am Inst Chemists; fel Nat Assn Corrosion Engrs (pres, 62-63). *Res:* Effect of hydrogen sulfide in aqueous solutions and various concentrations on high strength steels. *Mailing Add:* 1406 Captain Shreve Dr Shreveport LA 71105

GRECO, SALVATORE JOSEPH, PHARMACY. *Current Pos:* assoc prof & asst to dean, Sch Pharm, 56-58, Creighton Univ, dean, 58-71, prof pharm, 58-92, EMER DEAN, CREIGHTON UNIV, 92- *Personal Data:* b Richmond, Calif, Jan 25, 21; m 46, Betty Hicks; c Thomas, Janet, Amy, Sheryl, Robert & Marianne. *Educ:* Duquesne Univ, BS, 42; Univ Md, PhD(pharm), 48. *Prof Exp:* Asst prof chem, Temple Univ, 48-49; from asst prof to assoc prof pharm, George Washington Univ, 49-56. *Mem:* Am Pharmaceut Asn; Am Asn Cols Pharm. *Res:* Product development of pharmaceuticals. *Mailing Add:* 4004 Maple St Omaha NE 68111

GRECO, WILLIAM ROBERT, PHARMACO-MATHEMATICS, DATA ANALYSIS. *Current Pos:* RES SCIENTIST CANCER DATA ANALYSIS, DEPT BIOMATH & DEPT EXP THERAPEUT, ROSWELL PARK MEM INST, 80-; PROF BIOMET, NIAGRA UNIV, 81- *Personal Data:* b Detroit, Mich, Oct 14, 51; m 71; c 2. *Educ:* Rensselaer Polytech Inst, BS, 73; State Univ NY Buffalo, PhD(pharmacol), 79. *Prof Exp:* Fel pharmacol, State Univ NY Buffalo, 79. *Concurrent Pos:* Assoc prof biomet, State Univ NY, Buffalo, 80- *Mem:* Asn Comput Mach; Am Statist Asn; AAAS; Am Asn Cancer Res; Am Soc Biol Chemists. *Res:* Biomathematics in pharmacology; biostatistics; modelling of cancer growth; assessment of synergism for drug interactions; physiological pharmacokinetic modelling. *Mailing Add:* Dept Biomath Roswell Park Cancer Elm Carlton Sts Buffalo NY 14263-0001

GREDEN, JOHN F, PSYCHIATRICS. *Current Pos:* asst prof psychiat, Med Sch, Univ Mich, 74-77, dir, Clin Studies Unit Affective Disorders Inpatient Prog, 77-80, assoc prof psychiat, 77-81, dir, Clin Studies Unit Affective Disorders, 80-85, PROF PSYCHIAT, MED SCH, UNIV MICH, 81-, CHMN, 85- *Personal Data:* b Winona, Minn, July 24, 42. *Educ:* Univ Minn, BS, 65; Univ Minn Med Sch, 67. *Honors & Awards:* A E Bennett Award, A E Bennet Cent Neuropsychiat Found, 74; Ralph Patterson Mem Award, Ohio State Univ, 80; Nolan D C Lewis Vis Scholar Award, Carrier Found, Belle Meade, 82. *Prof Exp:* Asst chief, Psychiat Outpatient Clin, Ft Lee, US Army, 69-70; assoc dir, Walter Reed Army Med Ctr, 72-73, dir psychiat res, 73-74. *Concurrent Pos:* Mem, Am Psychiat Assoc Task Force to Eval Melancholia in Diag & Stat Manual, 83-86; mem, Samuel G Hibbs Bd, Am Psychiat Assoc; mem, NIMH Health Psychopharmacol, Biol & Physician Treatments Subcomt, 86-89; prin invest, NIAAA Ctr Grant, 88-, NIMH Grant, 85-88. *Mem:* Fel Am Psychiat Asn; Biol Psychiat; Am Col Neuropsychopharmacol; AAAS; Asn Med Educ & Res Substance Abuse; Psychiat Res Soc (counr, 88-89, pres elect, 89-90). *Res:* Neuroendocrine regulation in patients with affective disorders; cholinergic function in depression; pharmacological manifestations of catteinism; interaction between aging and alcoholism in the production of central nervous system abnormalities. *Mailing Add:* Dept Psychiat B4950 Univ Hosp Univ Mich Med Sch Ctr Ann Arbor MI 48109-0999

GREDING, EDWARD J, JR, HERPETOLOGY. *Current Pos:* PROF BIOL, DEL MAR COL, 73- *Personal Data:* b Mar 30, 40; US citizen; m 61, Marcia Clack; c Lisa & Laura. *Educ:* Univ Tex, Arlington, BS, 61; ETex State Univ, MS, 62; Univ Tex, Austin, PhD(zool), 68. *Prof Exp:* Instr biol, Tarleton State Col, 62-65; asst prof, Pan Am Col, 68-71; prof, Univ El Salvador, 71-73. *Mem:* Herpetologists League; Soc Study Amphibians & Reptiles; Am Soc Ichthyologists & Herpetologists. *Res:* Ecology and evolution of frogs of the American tropics. *Mailing Add:* Dept Biol Del Mar Col Corpus Christi TX 78404

GREEAR, PHILIP FRENCH-CARSON, ECOLOGY, GEOENVIRONMENTAL SCIENCE. *Current Pos:* From asst prof to assoc prof, Shorter Col, 61-63, from actg head to head, Dept Biol & Earth Sci, 64-86, prof, 71-86, EMER PROF BIOL, SHORTER COL, 86- *Personal Data:* b Troutdale, Va, Aug 25, 18; m 43; c 5. *Educ:* Univ Ga, BSA, 49, MS, 59, PhD(bot-ecol), 67. *Honors & Awards:* Nat Conservationist, Am Motors Corp, 73. *Concurrent Pos:* NSF res partic, 64; mem, Ga Natural Areas Coun & Ga Environ Educ Coun; mem bd & exec comt, Ga Conservancy; chmn, Coosa Basin Water & Resources Group; trustee, Ga Chap, Nature Conservancy, Ossahaw Island Found. *Mem:* AAAS. *Res:* Effect of Hydroperiod on plant zonation. *Mailing Add:* 330 Mt Alto Rd Rome GA 30165

GREECHIE, RICHARD JOSEPH, MATHEMATICS. *Current Pos:* PROF, HEAD & DIR SCH SCI, LA STATE UNIV, 91- *Personal Data:* b Boston, Mass, Apr 12, 41. *Educ:* Boston Col, BA, 62; Univ Fla, PhD(math), 66. *Prof Exp:* Asst prof math, Univ Mass, Boston, 65-67; from asst prof to prof math, Kans State Univ, 67-91, dir, Asn Math Found Empirical Studies, 70-91. *Concurrent Pos:* NSF grant, 70-73; vis prof, Inst Phys Theory, Univ Geneva, 73-74, Tech Hochschule Darmstadt, WGer, 80, McMaster Univ, 80, Univ Denver, 81, Univ Genova, Italy, 81. *Mem:* AAAS; Am Math Soc; Math Asn Am; Soc Indust & Appl Math. *Res:* Orthomodular lattice theory; empirical logics ranging from the classical logics to the non-classical quantum-mechanical logics, especially the way in which the classical sub-logics interrelate in the non-classical logic. *Mailing Add:* 1307 Bienville Ave Ruston LA 71270-0001

GREEDAN, JOHN EDWARD, SOLID STATE CHEMISTRY & MATERIALS CHEMISTRY. *Current Pos:* assoc prof, 74-83, PROF CHEM, MCMASTER UNIV, 83- *Personal Data:* b Beaver, Pa, June 4, 42. *Educ:* Bucknell Univ, BA, 64; Tufts Univ, PhD(chem), 69. *Prof Exp:* Fel chem, Univ Pittsburgh, 69-71; res asst prof, 71-72; asst prof, Dalhousie Univ, 72-74. *Mem:* Can Inst Chem. *Res:* Synthesis, crystal growth and solid state properties of inorganic materials; emphasis on rare earth and transition metal oxides and intermetallics; x-ray and neutron diffraction; magnetic, transport and optical properties. *Mailing Add:* Dept Chem McMaster Univ Hamilton ON L8S 4M1 Can

GREELEY, FREDERICK, BIOLOGY, WILDLIFE MANAGEMENT. *Current Pos:* assoc prof, 60-81, EMER PROF, WILDLIFE BIOL, UNIV MASS, AMHERST, 81- *Personal Data:* b Winnetka, Ill, Aug 26, 19; m 44; c 4. *Educ:* Kenyon Col, BA, 41; Univ Wis, MS, 49, PhD(zool, wildlife mgt), 54. *Prof Exp:* Res assoc endocrine studies of pheasants, Univ Wis, 54-55; res assoc deer nutrit, Univ NH, 55-56; proj leader pheasant range analysis & nutrit, Ill Natural Hist Surv, 56-60. *Mem:* Wildlife Soc; Wilson Ornith Soc; Am Ornithologists Union; Am Soc Mammalogists. *Res:* Avian ecology; forest wildlife ecology and management. *Mailing Add:* 11 Teawaddle Hill Rd Leverett MA 01054. *E-Mail:* fgreeley@forwild.umass.edu

GREELEY, GEORGE H, JR, GASTROINTESTINAL ENDOCRINOLOGY. *Current Pos:* ASSOC PROF SURG, UNIV TEX MED BR, GALVESTON, 83- *Personal Data:* b Detroit, Mich, Oct 15, 47. *Educ:* Med Col Ga, PhD(endocrinol), 74. *Mailing Add:* Dept Surg Univ Tex Med Br 301 University Blvd McCullough 6118 Rte G25 Galveston TX 77555-0725. *Fax:* 409-772-6368

GREELEY, RICHARD STILES, PHYSICAL CHEMISTRY. *Current Pos:* RETIRED. *Personal Data:* b Framingham, Mass, Dec 25, 27; m 51, Loretta Betke; c Richard Stiles Jr & Benjamin Betke. *Educ:* Harvard Univ, BS, 49; Northwestern Univ, MS, 51; Univ Tenn, PhD, 59. *Prof Exp:* Develop engr, Oak Ridge Nat Lab, 54-60; engr advan design, Mitre Corp, Bedford, Mass, 60-63, assoc dept head strategic systs, 63-68, dept head spec projs, 68-70, assoc tech dir systs develop, 70-75; tech dir energy, resources & environ, Metrek Div, Mitre Corp, McLean, Va, 76-80; vpres, Econenvironics Div, Roy F Weston, Inc, West Chester, Pa, 80-82; pres, Greeley-Polhemns Group, Inc, St Davids, Pa, 82-92. *Concurrent Pos:* Prof lectr chem, West Chester Univ, Pa, 83-84. *Mem:* Am Chem Soc. *Res:* Energy and environmental systems engineering; high temperature aqueous electrochemistry. *Mailing Add:* 418 Roundhill St Davids PA 19087

GREELEY, RONALD, GEOLOGY, PLANETARY SCIENCE. *Current Pos:* chmn geol, 86-90, PROF GEOL, ARIZ STATE UNIV, 77- *Personal Data:* b Columbus, Ohio, Aug 25, 39; m 60, Cynthia Moody; c Randall. *Educ:* Miss State Univ, BS, 62, MS, 63; Univ Mo, Rolla, PhD(geol), 66. *Honors & Awards:* Pub Serv Medal Mars-Viking, NASA, 77. *Prof Exp:* Instr geol, Univ Mo, Rolla, 65-66; geologist, Stand Oil Co Calif, 66-67; US Army res scientist, Ames Res Ctr, NASA, 67-69, Nat Res Coun geologist, 69-71, Univ Santa Clara res prof, 71-77. *Concurrent Pos:* Prof geol, Foothill Col, 70-77; consult, Jet Propulsion Lab, Pasadena, Calif & Lunar Planetary Inst, Houston, Tex, 72-75; hon res fel, Univ London, 75; vis assoc prof planetary sci, Calif Inst Technol, 77; adj prof geol, State Univ NY, Buffalo, 78; consult, Kuwait Inst Sci Res, 85-88; vis prof, Cambridge Univ, 84. *Mem:* Fel Geol Soc Am; Am Geophys Union; AAAS; Meteoritical Soc; Sigma Xi. *Res:* Fundamental research on the geology of the planets through the analysis of spacecraft data coupled with laboratory simulation and geological field work of terrestrial analogs to planetary surface features; emphasis on volcanology and windblown sand. *Mailing Add:* Dept Geol Ariz State Univ Tempe AZ 85287-1404

GREEN, ALBERT WISE, PHYSICAL OCEANOGRAPHY. *Current Pos:* br head phys oceanog, 77-84, HEAD OCEANOG DIV, NAVAL OCEAN & ATMOSPHERIC RES LAB, 84- *Personal Data:* b Jackson, Miss, Dec 15, 38; m 67; c 2. *Educ:* Vanderbilt Univ, BA, 60; Mass Inst Technol, PhD(phys oceanog), 69. *Prof Exp:* Mem staff, Inst Geophys, Univ Oslo, Norway, 69-70; asst prof oceanog & meteorol, Dept Atmospheric & Oceanic Sci, Univ Mich, 70-77. *Concurrent Pos:* Prin Investr, Circulation Modelling Proj, Sea Grant, Univ Mich, 70-76; consult, Aeromatrix, Inc & Environ Eng Co, 75-76 & Environ Studio & Argonne Nat Lab, 76; mem steering comt, Nat Marine Bd, 80-81. *Mem:* Am Geophys Union; Am Meteorol Soc; Sigma Xi. *Res:* Turbulent oceanic boundary layer processes; experimental study of non-linear wave interactions; experimental and theoretical research in mesoscale ocean hydrodynamics; design, testing and modelling of physical oceanographic measuring instruments. *Mailing Add:* Oceanog Div Naval Ocean & Atmospheric Res Lab Bldg 1105 Stennis Space Ctr MS 39529

GREEN, ALEX EDWARD SAMUEL, PHYSICS. *Current Pos:* GRAD RES PROF PHYSICS, NUCLEAR ENG SCI, ELEC ENG & ENG SCI, UNIV FLA, 63-, DIR, CTR AERONOMY & OTHER ATMOSPHERIC SCI, 74- *Personal Data:* b New York, NY, June 2, 19; m 46; c 5. *Educ:* City Col New York, BS, 41; Calif Inst Technol, MS, 41; Univ Cincinnati, PhD(physics), 48. *Honors & Awards:* Medal of Freedom Award, 47. *Prof Exp:* Physicist & instr, Calif Inst Technol, 40-44; instr physics & math, Newark Col Eng, 45-46; asst prof physics, Univ Cincinnati, 46-53; from assoc prof to prof & actg head dept, Fla State Univ, 53-59, sci dir, Tandem Van de Graaff Lab, 58-59; chief physics, Convair Div, Gen Dynamics & mgr space sci lab, Astronaut Div, 59-63. *Concurrent Pos:* Consult, Jet Propulsion Lab, Marshall Space Flight Ctr & Inst Defense Anal; consult & group leader theoret div, Los Alamos Sci Lab, 57-58; lectr exten div, Univ Calif, 60-63. *Mem:* Fel Am Phys Soc; Am Asn Physics Teachers; fel Optical Soc Am; Am Geophys Union; Am Soc Photobiol. *Res:* Theoretical nuclear, atomic, radiation and atmospheric physics and ultraviolet photoclimatology. *Mailing Add:* 2900 NW 14th Pl Gainesville FL 32605

GREEN, ALLEN T, NONDESTRUCTIVE TESTING, ACOUST EMISSION. *Current Pos:* PRES, ACOUST TECHNOL GROUP, 91- *Personal Data:* b Chicago, Ill, Mar 30, 34; m 93, Carolyn Reuben; c Keri, Leah, Brady & Natanya. *Educ:* Univ Ill, Urbana, BS, 56. *Prof Exp:* Test engr, Convair, 56-61; prog engr, Aerojet Gen Corp, 61-70; vpres, Dunegan Res Corp, 70-71; pres, Acoust Emission Tech Corps, 71-88; pres, HSB Inspection Technol, 88-91. *Concurrent Pos:* Founder, Acoust Emission Working Group, 67- *Mem:* Am Soc Testing & Mat; fel Am Soc Nondestructive Testing; Soc Exp Mech; Am Soc Mech Engrs. *Res:* Development of acoustic emission for uses in material science; structural testing; nondestructive testing. *Mailing Add:* 2644 La Via Way Sacramento CA 95825. *Fax:* 916-483-2124; *E-Mail:* green24@asme.org

GREEN, ALWIN CLARK, MATHEMATICS. *Personal Data:* b Meadville, Pa, Dec 19, 30; m; c 3. *Educ:* Hiram Col, BA, 56; Syracuse Univ, MA, 68, PhD(math), 72. *Prof Exp:* Design engr mercury vapor arcs, Large Lamp Div, Gen Elec Co, 56-64; asst prof math, State Univ NY, Buffalo, 72-78, prof math & chmn Math Dept, 78-81. *Concurrent Pos:* Panel vis lectrs, Math Asn Am, 78-90, 92-94. *Mem:* Math Asn Am. *Res:* Theoretical research in connectedness of networks; applications, networks and finite mathematics in the social sciences, tiling and geometry. *Mailing Add:* 13851 Whitney Rd Holland NY 14080

GREEN, ARTHUR R, GEOLOGY, TECTONICS & STRUCTURAL ANALYSIS. *Current Pos:* sr scientist oceanog, Exxon Prod Res Co, 69-72, global geol studies mgr, 72-82, res scientist, 82-92, RES SCIENTIST, EXXON EXPLOR CO, 92- *Personal Data:* b Loma Linda, Calif, May 21, 34; div. *Educ:* Wash State Univ, BS, 57; Univ Ore, MS, 62. *Prof Exp:* Explor & prod, Humble Co, 62-69. *Concurrent Pos:* Sr adv comt, Inc Res Inst Semisol; adv comt, US Geol Surv & Fr Petrol Inst; chmn, Nat Sci Found Adv Comt, 88-; mem adv bd, Int Union Geol Sci; mem, Ocean Drilling Prog Safety & Pollution Prev Comt, Deep Observ & Sampling of the Earth's Continental Crust, NSF; mem, Marine Geol Comt, Am Asn Petrol Geologists. *Mem:* Fel AAAS; Am Geophys Union; Sigma Xi; fel Geol Soc Am. *Res:* Evolution of the Arctic & its hydrocarbon potential; integrated basin analysis methods; regional tectonic analysis. *Mailing Add:* Exxon Explor Co PO Box 4778 Houston TX 77210-4778

GREEN, BARRY A, THEORETICAL SOLID STATE PHYSICS. *Current Pos:* TECH STAFF, ELECTRONIC SYSTS GROUP, ROCKWELL INT, 78- *Personal Data:* b Los Angeles, Calif, Mar 17, 40; m 70; c 3. *Educ:* Pomona Col, BA, 62; Northwestern Univ, MS, 64; Univ Ariz, PhD(nuclear eng), 72. *Prof Exp:* Res engr compact reactor res & develop, Atomics Int, 64-65; sr physicist, Gulf Radiation Technol, Div Gen Atomic, 72-73; sr physicist theoret solid state physics, IRT Corp, 73-76; sr physicist, Air Force Mat Lab, Wright-Patterson AFB, 77-78. *Concurrent Pos:* Vis theorist, Air Force Mat Lab, Wright-Patterson AFB, 78- *Mem:* Am Phys Soc. *Res:* Solid state studies of metal oxide insulators and ternary alloy semiconductors, including radiation effects, electrical transport, photon absorption, lifetime and defect studies; hole mobility and Hall resistance factor in silicon; infrared detector development. *Mailing Add:* 11710 N Skywire Way Tucson AZ 85737

GREEN, BARRY GEORGE, PSYCHOPHYSICS. *Current Pos:* SCIENTIST, JOHN P PIERCE LAB, 96- *Personal Data:* b Gloucester, Mass, Mar 17, 49. *Educ:* Univ Calif, Riverside, AB, 71; Ind Univ, PhD(psychol), 75. *Prof Exp:* NIH fel psychol, John B Pierce Found Lab, 75-78; res assoc psychol, Princeton Univ, 78-80; res assoc psychol, Ind Univ, 80-83; mem staff, Monell Chem Senses Ctr, Philadelphia, 83-96. *Concurrent Pos:* Lectr, South Conn State Col, 77; vis asst prof epidemiol & pub health, Yale Univ, 75-78. *Mem:* AAAS; Sigma Xi; Psychonomic Soc. *Res:* Psychophysics of the skin senses, including the interactions among vibrotactile, tactile and thermal stimuli; cutaneous communication of speech. *Mailing Add:* 440 White Birch Dr Guilford CT 06437-2144

GREEN, BEVERLEY R, BIOCHEMISTRY, PLANT PHYSIOLOGY & PHOTOSYNTHESIS. *Current Pos:* from asst prof to assoc prof, 67-84, PROF BOT, UNIV BC, 84- *Personal Data:* b Vancouver, BC, Apr 17, 38. *Educ:* Univ BC, BSc, 60; Univ Wash, PhD(biochem), 65. *Prof Exp:* NATO fel, Free Univ Brussels, 66-67. *Concurrent Pos:* Res fel, Biol Labs, Harvard Univ, 75; vis res scientist, Lawrence Berkeley Labs, 82-83; Killam Fac Res Fel, 87-88. *Mem:* AAAS; Can Soc Plant Physiologists; Am Soc Plant Physiologists; Int Soc Plant Molecular Biol. *Res:* Evaluation of lights harvesting systems, orgin of the chloroplast; chlorophyll-protein complexes; synthesis and assembly of photosynthetic membranes. *Mailing Add:* Dept Bot Univ BC 3529-6270 Univ Blvd Vancouver BC V6T 1Z4 Can. *Fax:* 604-822-6089; *E-Mail:* beverly.green@mtsg.ubc.ca

GREEN, BRIAN, ORGANIC CHEMISTRY. *Current Pos:* from asst prof to prof, 65-87, DISTINGUISHED MAINE PROF CHEM, UNIV MAINE, 87- *Personal Data:* b Liverpool, Eng, Feb 21, 35; m 62, Karen I Boucias; c Christopher & Johathan. *Educ:* Univ Liverpool, BSc, 56, PhD(org chem), 59. *Prof Exp:* Res asst org chem, Univ Maine, 59-61, res assoc, 61-64; Alexander von Humboldt fel, Max Planck Inst Biochem, Munich, Ger, 64-65. *Concurrent Pos:* Alexander von Humboldt fel org chem, Univ Bonn, 71-72; coop prof oceanog, Univ Maine, 77- *Mem:* Am Chem Soc; The Chem Soc. *Res:* Chemistry of natural products, especially terpenoids and steroids with emphasis on both synthetic and degradative aspects of the field. *Mailing Add:* 387 Aubert Hall Univ Maine Orono ME 04469. *Fax:* 207-581-1191; *E-Mail:* bgreen@maine.maine.edu

GREEN, BYRON DAVID, CHEMICAL PHYSICS. *Current Pos:* PRIN SCIENTIST RES, PHYS SCI INC, 76- *Personal Data:* b Philadelphia, Pa, June 25, 50. *Educ:* Univ Pa, BA, 71; Mass Inst Technol, PhD(phys chem), 76. *Honors & Awards:* Marcus O'Day Award, Air Force Geophys Lab. *Mem:* Optical Soc Am; Sigma Xi; Am Geophys Union. *Res:* Molecular spectroscopy; energy transfer; chemiluminescence, kinetics; radiative transfer; atmospheric modeling; optical detection of trace species; laser development; electron irradiation of gases. *Mailing Add:* 20 New Eng Bus Ctr Andover MA 01810-1077

GREEN, CECIL HOWARD, GEOPHYSICS, EARTH SCIENCES. *Current Pos:* FOUNDER & DIR, TEX INSTRUMENTS INC. *Personal Data:* b Manchester, Eng, Aug 6, 1900; m 26, Ida M Flansburgh. *Educ:* Mass Inst Technol, BSEE, 23, SM, 24; Colo Sch Mines, DEng, 53. *Hon Degrees:* Various from US & foreign univs. *Honors & Awards:* Kaufman Medal, Soc Explor Geophysicists, 66, Maurice Ewing Medal, 78; Human Needs Medal, Am Asn Petrol Geologists, 74; Int Educ & Res Tribute, Nat Acad Sci, 78, Pub Welfare Medal, 79; Hon Lay Award Distinguishing Serv, AMA, 84; Gold Plate Award, Am Acad Achievement, 84; Waldo E Smith Medal, Am Geophys Union, 95. *Prof Exp:* Res engr, AC Eng Dept, GE, Schenectady, 24-26, Raytheon Mfg Co, Cambridge, Mass, 26-28, Fed Tel Co Palo Alto & Newark, 28-30; party chief, Geophys Serv Inc, Dallas, 30-36, suprv, 36-41, vpres, 41-50, pres, 50-56, chmn bd, 56-59. *Concurrent Pos:* Hon lectr, Mass Inst Technol, 73-, Stanford Univ, 83, Univ BC, 84; consult prof earth sci, Stanford Univ, 83; founder, Green Col, Oxford Univ, 79, Green Ctr Study Sci & Soc, Univ Tex, Dallas, 92. *Mem:* Hon mem Nat Acad Sci; hon mem Inst Elec & Electronics Engrs; hon mem Am Asn Petrol Geologists; fel Am Acad Arts & Sci; Europ Asn Explor Geophysicists; Mex Asn Petrol Geophlogists; hon mem Am Geophys Union; hon mem Soc Explor Geophysicists. *Mailing Add:* 3525 Turtle Creek Blvd Apt 20A Dallas TX 75219-5514

GREEN, CHARLES E, underwater acoustics, electroacoustics; deceased, see previous edition for last biography

GREEN, CHARLES RAYMOND, ANALYTICAL CHEMISTRY, TOBACCO CHEMISTRY. *Current Pos:* sr res chemist, 68-80, MASTER SCIENTIST, R J REYNOLDS TOBACCO CO, 80- *Personal Data:* b Fredericksburg, Va, Aug 15, 42; m 64; c 2. *Educ:* Univ Va, BS, 64, PhD(chem), 68. *Mem:* Am Chem Soc; Sigma Xi. *Res:* Tobacco smoke chemistry; gas chromatography; gas chromatography-mass spectrometry; glass capillary gas chromatography. *Mailing Add:* 430 Burkeridge Ct Winston-Salem NC 27104-2602

GREEN, CLAUDE CORDELL, COMPUTER SCIENCE. *Current Pos:* DIR, KESTREL INST, 81- *Personal Data:* b Ft Worth, Tex, Dec 26, 41. *Educ:* Rice Univ, BA & BS, 64; Stanford Univ, MS, 65, PhD(elec eng), 69. *Honors & Awards:* Grace Hopper Award, Asn Comput Mach. *Prof Exp:* Res mathematician artificial intel, Stanford Res Inst, 66-69; res & develop prog mgr & info processing tech officer, Advan Res Projs Agency, 70-71; asst prof comput sci, Stanford Univ, 72-78; chief scientist comput sci, Systs Control Inc, 78-81. *Concurrent Pos:* Consult, Stanford Res Inst, 71-73, Xerox Corp, 71-78 & Systs Control Inc, 75-76; ed artificial intel area, J Asn Comput Mach, 72- *Mem:* Asn Comput Mach. *Res:* Artificial intelligence, especially automatic programming, problem solving and answering. *Mailing Add:* Kestrel Inst 3260 Hillview Ave Palo Alto CA 94304

GREEN, DANIEL G, PHYSIOLOGICAL OPTICS. *Current Pos:* asst prof physiol optics, 66-70, assoc prof, 71-76, PROF PHYSIOL OPTICS, PSYCHOL & ELEC ENG, UNIV MICH, ANN ARBOR, 76- *Personal Data:* b New York, NY, Sept 3, 37; m 57, Norma Anderson; c Peter & Rebecca. *Educ:* Univ Ill, BSEE, 59; Northwestern Univ, MS & PhD(elec eng), 64. *Prof Exp:* Asst elec eng & bioeng, Northwestern Univ, 59-64; NSF fel, Physiol Lab, Cambridge Univ, 64-65; USPHS fel, Nobel Insts Neurophysiol, Stockholm, Sweden, 65-66. *Concurrent Pos:* Vis scientist, Biol Labs, Harvard Univ, 72-73; vis prof ophthal, Univ Calif, San Francisco, 80-81; vis scientist, Physiol Lab, Cambridge Univ, 81. *Mem:* AAAS; Am Physiol Soc; Asn Res Vision & Ophthal; fel Optical Soc Am; Soc Neurosci; fel Inst Elec & Electronics Engrs. *Res:* Biomedical engineering and physiology of vision; synaptic mechanisms and functional interactions used by the vertebrate retina to process visual information; neural basis for the desensitizing effects of light adaptation. *Mailing Add:* Univ Mich Neurosci Bldg 1103 E Huron Ann Arbor MI 48109. *Fax:* 313-936-2690; *E-Mail:* dgg@umich.edu

GREEN, DANIEL R, HAORON COLLIDER PHYSICS, HEAVY FLAVOR SPECTROSCOPY. *Current Pos:* SCIENTIST III, FERMI NAT ACCELERATOR LAB, 91- *Personal Data:* b South Haven, Mich, Mar 30, 43; m 69, Anorea Tinlot; c Michael. *Educ:* Univ Rochester, BS, 64, PhD(physics), 69. *Prof Exp:* Postdoctoral fel, State Univ NY, Stony Brook, 70-73; asst prof, Carnegie-Mellon Univ, 73-78. *Mem:* Am Phys Soc; AAAS. *Res:* Haoron colliders beginning with the CERN ISR, following to the Fermilab Teratron to the SSC SDC experiment, and to the CERN CMS experiment. *Mailing Add:* CMS Dept MS205 Fermilab PO Box 500 Batavia IL 60510. *Fax:* 630-840-2194; *E-Mail:* dgreen@fnal.gov

GREEN, DAVID, HEMATOLOGY. *Current Pos:* ATTEND PHYSICIAN, REHAB INST CHICAGO & NORTHWESTERN UNIV, CHICAGO, 67-, PROF INTERNAL MED, MED SCH, 67- *Personal Data:* b Philadelphia, Pa, Oct 1, 34; m 58; c 3. *Educ:* Univ Pa, AB, 56; Jefferson Med Col, MD, 60; Am Bd Internal Med, dipl, 67, cert hemat, 72; Northwestern Univ, PhD(biochem), 74. *Res:* Hemostasis with particular emphasis on relation to atherosclerosis. *Mailing Add:* Rehab Inst Chicago 345 E Superior St Rm 1407 Chicago IL 60611-4496

GREEN, DAVID CLAUDE, ORGANIC CHEMISTRY. *Current Pos:* Res chemist, 74-81, SR RES ASSOC, PROCESS RES DEPT, CHEVRON RES CO, CALIF, 81- *Personal Data:* b Ft Wayne, Ind, June 7, 45; m 67; c 3. *Educ:* DePauw Univ, BA, 67; Univ Wash, MS, 69, PhD(org chem), 74. *Mem:* Am Chem Soc. *Res:* Petroleum hydroprocessing; residuum processing; fluid catalytic cracking technology. *Mailing Add:* 486 Blackstone Dr San Rafael CA 94903-1302

GREEN, DAVID J, BIOTECHNOLOGY. *Current Pos:* PRES & SCI DIR, BIOTECHNOL MGT ASN INC, 88- *Personal Data:* b Reading, Eng, Jan 7, 40. *Mem:* Am Asn Clin Chem; Am Biol Asn. *Mailing Add:* Biotechnol Mgt Asn Inc 25 S Olympia Ave Woburn MA 01801. *Fax:* 781-932-8705

GREEN, DAVID M(ARTIN), HERPETOLOGY. *Current Pos:* ASST PROF BIOL, REDPATH MUS, MCGILL UNIV, 86- *Personal Data:* b Vancouver, BC, Jan 20, 53. *Educ:* Univ BC, BSc, 76; Univ Guelph, MSc, 79, PhD(zool), 82. *Prof Exp:* Fel zool, Mus Vert Zool, Univ Calif, Berkeley, 81-83; lectr biol, McMaster Univ, 83-84; asst prof, 84-85; asst prof biol, Univ Windsor, 85-86. *Concurrent Pos:* Res assoc, Herpet Sect, Can Mus Nature, 84-, mem, Collections Comt, 90-; affil prof, Dept Biol, McGill Univ, 86-; ed, Can Asn Herpetologists Bull, 86- *Mem:* Am Soc Ichthyologists & Herpetologists; Herpetologists League; Soc Study Amphibians & Reptiles; Soc Study Evolution; Sigma Xi. *Res:* Biosystematics and evolution; interspecific hybridization, geographic variation and chromosome evolution in frogs; evolution of sex determination in tetrapods; evolution of supernumerary chromosomes; dynamical systems and fractals as models of evolution; functional morphology of adhesive organs in vertebrates. *Mailing Add:* Redpath Mus McGill Univ 859 Sherbrooke St W Montreal PQ H3A 2K6 Can

GREEN, DAVID MARVIN, PSYCHOACOUSTICS, SIGNAL DETECTION & MAXIMUM LIKELIHOOD. *Current Pos:* prof, 85-95, EMER GRAD RES PROF, UNIV FLA, 95- *Personal Data:* b Jackson, Mich, June 7, 32; m, Marian Heinzmann; c Allan, Phillip, Katherine & George. *Educ:* Univ Chicago, BA, 52; Univ Mich, MA, 55, PhD, 58; Univ Cambridge & Harvard Univ, MA, 73. *Honors & Awards:* Co-recipient, Warren Medal, Soc Exp Psychologist, 85, Silver Medal Psychol & Physiol Acoust, Acoust Soc Am, 90, Gold Medal, 94. *Prof Exp:* Res assoc, Electronics Defense Group, Univ Mich, 54-56; asst prof psychol, Mass Inst Technol, 58-63; assoc prof & vchmn psychol, Univ Pa, 63-66; prof psychol, Univ Calif, San Diego, 66-73; prof psychophys & chmn, Dept Psychol & Soc Relations, Harvard Univ, 73-85. *Concurrent Pos:* Consult, Bolt, Beranek & Newman Inc, 58-; chmn, Comt Hearing, Bioacoust & Biomech, Nat Res Coun, 70-71, 78-79 & 85-88, Comt Low-Frequency Sound & Marine Mammals, 92-; ed, J Acoust Soc Am, 70-73; mem, Commun Sci Study Sect, NIH, 70-74; William James fel, Am Psychol Asn, 89. *Mem:* Nat Acad Sci; fel AAAS; Soc Exp Psychologists; Psychonomic Soc; Psychomet Soc; Am Asn Univ Professors; fel Am Acad Arts & Sci; fel Acoust Soc Am (pres, 81); fel Am Psychol Asn. *Res:* Acoustics. *Mailing Add:* 399 Federal Point Rd East Palatka FL 32131. *Fax:* 904-392-5173; *E-Mail:* green@psych.ufl.edu

GREEN, DAVID WILLIAM, PHYSICAL CHEMISTRY. *Current Pos:* chemist, Chem Eng Div, 82, MGR, ANALYTICAL CHEMLAB, ARGONNE NAT LAB, 82-, ASSOC DIR, CHEM TECH DIV, 88- *Personal Data:* b Hudson, Mich, Nov 19, 42; m 67, Mary S McCullough; c Laura, Brenda, Mark, Brian & William. *Educ:* Albion Col, BA, 64; Univ Calif, Berkeley, PhD(chem), 68; Univ Chicago, MBA, 85. *Prof Exp:* Lectr chem, Univ Calif, Berkeley, 68; res assoc physics, Lab Molecular Struct & Spectra, Univ Chicago, 68-71; asst prof chem, Albion Col, 71-74. *Concurrent Pos:* Fel, Lawrence Radiation Lab, Univ Calif, Berkeley, 68; instr, Col DuPage, 91-93; ed Managing the Mod Lab, 95- *Mem:* AAAS; Am Chem Soc; Analytical Lab Mgrs Asn (treas, pres). *Res:* Molecular electronic spectroscopy and structure; high resolution optical spectroscopy; high temperature chemistry; molecular hyperfine structure; matrix isolation spectroscopy; infrared spectroscopy; analytical chemistry methods and devices. *Mailing Add:* Chem Technol Div Argonne Nat Lab Argonne IL 60439. *Fax:* 630-252-5655; *E-Mail:* green@cmt.aue.gov

GREEN, DETROY EDWARD, AGRONOMY. *Current Pos:* from asst prof to assoc prof, Iowa State Univ, 64-70, prof argon, 70-89, interim dean, 89-90, ASSOC DEAN, IOWA STATE UNIV, 90- *Personal Data:* b Zalma, Mo, Mar 26, 30; m 51; c 5. *Educ:* Univ Mo, BS, 54, MS, 61, PhD(field crops), 65. *Honors & Awards:* Agron Resident Educ Award, Am Soc Agron, 80; Fel Award, Am Soc Agron, 81; Fel Award, Crop Sci Soc Am, 85. *Prof Exp:* High sch instr voc agr, Mo, 54-59; instr field crops, Univ Mo, 61-64. *Mem:* Am Soc Agron; Crop Sci Soc Am; Nat Asn Col & Teachers Agr; Am Soybean Asn. *Res:* Genetics, breeding, and physiology related to soybean improvement. *Mailing Add:* RR 3 Ames IA 50014

GREEN, DON WESLEY, CHEMICAL & PETROLEUM ENGINEERING. *Current Pos:* from asst prof to assoc prof chem & petrol eng, Univ Kans, 64-71, actg chmn dept, 67-68, chmn dept, 70-74, PROF CHEM & PETROL ENG, UNIV KANS, 71- *Personal Data:* b Tulsa, Okla, July 8, 32; m 54, Patricia L Polston; c 3. *Educ:* Univ Tulsa, BS, 55; Univ Okla, MS, 59, PhD(chem eng), 63. *Honors & Awards:* Distinguished Fac Achievement Award, Soc Petrol Engrs. *Prof Exp:* Res reservoir engr, Continental Oil Co, 62-64. *Concurrent Pos:* Co-dir, Tertiary Oil Recovery Proj, 74- *Mem:* Am Soc Eng Educ; fel Am Inst Chem Engrs; Soc Petrol Engrs. *Res:* Fluid flow through porous media; dispersion of heat and mass in porous media; mathematical modeling of natural resource systems; enhanced oil recovery. *Mailing Add:* 1020 Sunset Dr Lawrence KS 66044

GREEN, DONALD EUGENE, BIOCHEMICAL PHARMACOLOGY, ANALYTICAL CHEMISTRY. *Current Pos:* RETIRED. *Personal Data:* b Napa, Calif, Nov 25, 26; m 51; c 5. *Educ:* Univ Calif, Berkeley, BS, 48; Univ Calif, San Francisco, MS, 52, BS, 55; Wash State Univ, PhD(med chem), 62. *Prof Exp:* Instr pharmaceut chem, Idaho State Univ, 55-57; instr, Wash State Univ, 57-58 & Idaho State Univ, 58-60; res chemist, Varian Assocs, 62-64, mgr, Dept Biophys, 64-66; sr res chemist, Syva Res Inst, 66-67 & Anal Instrument Res, Varian Assocs, 67-70; res biochemist, Drug Res Lab, Vet Admin Hosp, 70-74, res scientist, Biochem Res Lab, 71-80 & Drug Metab Res Lab, 80-85; sr scientist, Bioorg Chem Dept, Appl Immune Sci, 85-90. *Concurrent Pos:* Res fel, Sch Pharm, Univ Calif, San Francisco, 62; biochemist, Biochem Res Lab, Vet Admin Hosp, 62-64; res assoc, Sch Med, Stanford Univ, 71-74; consult, Universal Monitor Corp, Pasadena, 71-76; sr res scientist, Inst Chem Biol, Univ San Francisco, 74-82. *Mem:* Am Chem Soc; Am Pharmaceut Asn; Western Pharmacol Soc; Am Soc Pharmacol & Exp Therapeut; Int Asn Forensic Toxicol. *Res:* Chemical structure-pharmacological activity relationships of central nervous system drugs; mechanisms of drug actions; metabolism of cannabinoids and phenothiazine tranquilizers; development of gas chromatography/mass spectrometry interfaces and automated mass fragmentography instrumentation; immobilization of DNA or proteins on polymer surfaces for use in medical therapy devices. *Mailing Add:* 765 Harvard Ave Sunnyvale CA 94087-1207

GREEN, DONALD MACDONALD, GENETICS. *Current Pos:* PROF BIOCHEM & GENETICS, UNIV NH, 67-, CHMN BIOCHEM, 85- *Personal Data:* b Poughkeepsie, NY, Apr 6, 30; m 57; c 3. *Educ:* Oberlin Col, AB, 54; Univ Rochester, PhD, 58. *Prof Exp:* Res assoc, Biol Div, Oak Ridge Nat Lab, 58-60; res fel chem & tutor biochem sci, Harvard Univ, 60-64; assoc prof biol, Univ Pittsburgh, 64-67. *Concurrent Pos:* Prog dir biochem, NSF, 79-80; chmn genetics, Univ NH, 70-72, 85-88. *Res:* Microbial genetics; genetic structure of bacteria and viruses; bacterial transformation and transfection. *Mailing Add:* Dept Biochem Univ NH Durham NH 03824

GREEN, DONALD WAYNE, PHYSICS. *Current Pos:* Assoc prof, 54-70, PROF PHYSICS, KNOX COL, ILL, 70- *Personal Data:* b Coldwater, Mich, June 19, 24; c 2. *Educ:* Kalamazoo Col, BA, 49; Ohio State Univ, PhD(physics), 54. *Mem:* Am Asn Physics Teachers. *Res:* Low energy particle accelerators; stopping power of various materials for protons. *Mailing Add:* Dept Physics Knox Col Galesburg IL 61401

GREEN, DOUGLAS R, IMMUNOLOGY. *Current Pos:* asst prof, 85-87, ASSOC PROF, DEPT IMMUNOL, UNIV ALTA, 87-; MEM & HEAD, DIV CELLULAR IMMUNOL, LA JOLLA INST ALLERGY & IMMUNOL, 90- *Personal Data:* b New York, NY, Feb 15, 55. *Educ:* Yale Univ, BS, 77, PhD(biol), 81. *Prof Exp:* Fel, Dept Path, Yale Univ, 81-83, res assoc, 83-84, assoc res biologist, 84-85. *Concurrent Pos:* Assoc ed, Cytokines & J Exp Zool, 89- *Mem:* Am Asn Immunologists; Sigma Xi. *Res:* Thermal trauma and immunity; bacterial sepsis and immunity; inhibitory lymphokines in thermal trauma; antigen specific T cell factors; antigen-specific regulatory factors; author of numerous scientific publications. *Mailing Add:* 4153 Tynbourne Circle San Diego CA 92130

GREEN, EDWARD JEWETT, chemical oceanography, for more information see previous edition

GREEN, EDWARD LEWIS, ALGEBRA. *Current Pos:* asst prof, 77-79, assoc prof, 80-82, PROF MATH, VA POLYTECH INST & STATE UNIV, 83- *Personal Data:* b Brooklyn, NY, Apr 4, 46; m 66; c 2. *Educ:* Cornell Univ, AB, 67; Brandeis Univ, MA, 68, PhD(math), 73. *Prof Exp:* Instr math, Univ Pa, 73-75; vis lectr, Univ Ill, Urbana, 75-77. *Mem:* Am Math Soc. *Res:* Representation theory of rings and algebras, particularly the study of what internal structural properties of a module make it direct sum indecomposable. *Mailing Add:* Dept Math Va Polytech Inst & State Univ PO Box 0123 Blacksburg VA 24063-0123

GREEN, EDWIN JAMES, FOREST BIOMETRICS. *Current Pos:* ASST PROF FORESTRY, RUTGERS UNIV, 81-, PROF FOREST BIOMETRICS. *Personal Data:* b Oceanside, NY, Nov 11, 54; m 76; c 2. *Educ:* State Univ NY, Col Environ Sci & Forestry, 76, MS, 78; Va Polytech Inst & State Univ, PhD(forest biometrics), 81. *Mem:* Soc Am Foresters; Am Statist Asn; Biometric Soc. *Res:* Developing growth and yield systems; applying modern quantitative methods to forestry research. *Mailing Add:* Ecol Evol & Natural Resources Cook Col Rutgers Univ College Farm Rd New Brunswick NJ 08903

GREEN, ERIC DOUGLAS, HUMAN GENETICS, CLINICAL PATHOLOGY. *Current Pos:* RESIDENT LAB MED, WASHINGTON UNIV SCH MED, 87-, FEL, DEPT GENETICS, 88- *Personal Data:* b St Louis, 1959; m 84. *Educ:* Univ Wis, Madison, BS, 81; Washington Univ, MD, 87, PhD(cell biol), 87. *Res:* Structure, synthesis and function of protein-bound oligosaccharides; development and application of recombinant DNA technologies for studying human diseases. *Mailing Add:* 30 Lymbrook Rd St Louis MO 63131

GREEN, ERIKA ANA, MEDICAL MICROBIOLOGY, SCIENCE WRITING. *Current Pos:* RETIRED. *Personal Data:* b Lucenec, Czech, May 27, 28; US citizen; m 61, James W; c Philip & Stephen. *Educ:* Cent Univ Ecuador, BS, 55; Hunter Col, MA, 59; Rutgers Univ, PhD(microbiol), 71. *Prof Exp:* Res technician org chem, Sloan Kettering Inst Cancer & Allied Dis, 55-59; res assoc biochem, Rutgers Univ, 59-62; lit scientist, Coun Tobacco Res, 71-72 & Carter-Wallace, Inc, 72-73; lit scientist, 73-81, clin res scientist, Hoffmann-La Roche Inc, 81-85; med writer, Theradex Systs Inc, Du Pont Med Prod, Sandoz Pharmaceut, 85-93. *Mem:* Am Soc Microbiol; NY Acad Sci; Sigma Xi. *Res:* Literature research in health sciences, especially immunology, medical microbiology and biomedical pharmacology; clinical development of new drugs, especially antibiotics. *Mailing Add:* 409 Grant Ave Highland Park NJ 08904

GREEN, EUGENE L, PHYSICS, OPTICS. *Current Pos:* RETIRED. *Personal Data:* b Minneapolis, Minn, Oct 15, 27; m 51, 69, Lillian Young; c Bruce A, Nancy R, Janet M (Zucker), Rita S & Michelle K (Zahalsky). *Educ:* Carnegie Inst Technol, BS, 47, MS, 49; Temple Univ, PhD(physics), 65. *Prof Exp:* Physicist, US Army, Frankford Arsenal, Pa, 49-65; res physicist, Naval Underwater Systs Ctr, New London Lab, 65-87; consult, Sarasota, Fla, 90- *Mem:* AAAS; Optical Soc Am. *Res:* Optical information processing, properties of alloys, image analysis and instrumentation; laser development; holography; acoustic array signal processing; optical hydrophones; fiber optics; granted seven patents. *Mailing Add:* 1627 Waldemere St Sarasota FL 34239

GREEN, FLOYD J, ORGANIC & ANALYTICAL CHEMISTRY. *Current Pos:* RETIRED. *Personal Data:* b Sharonville, Ohio, Dec 11, 17; m 41; c 3. *Educ:* Maryville Col, Tenn, AB, 41; Univ Cincinnati, MS, 50; St Thomas Inst, PhD, 69. *Prof Exp:* Res chemist bldg mat, Phillip Carey Mfg, 41-46; chemist reagent chem, Matheson, Coleman & Bell Div, Matheson Co Inc, 46-50, chief chemist, 50-54; tech dir, MC&B Mfg Chemists, Will Ross Co, Inc, 54-73, vpres, 68-73; partner, vpres & treas, Aristo Custom Chem Inc, 73-77; vpres, Aldrich Chem Co, 77-86. *Concurrent Pos:* Adj asst prof, St Thomas Inst. *Mem:* AAAS; fel Am Inst Chemists; Am Chem Soc; Am Soc Testing & Mat. *Res:* Dyes, particularly oxazones; high purity organic reagents. *Mailing Add:* 40 Tokumto St Franklin NC 28734-8979

GREEN, FRANK ORVILLE, CHEMISTRY. *Current Pos:* from asst prof to prof, 45-82, EMER PROF CHEM, WHEATON COL, 82- *Personal Data:* b Toledo, Iowa, Nov 2, 08; m 35; c 3. *Educ:* Greenville Col, BS, 31; Northwestern Univ, MS, 37, PhD(org chem), 39. *Prof Exp:* Pub sch teacher, Ohio, 31-35; asst instr, Northwestern Univ, 37-39; prof & dir dept, Greenville Col, 39-41; res chemist, Bauer & Black Co, Ill, 41-42 & Swift & Co, 42-45. *Concurrent Pos:* Fulbright vis lectr, Univ Cairo & Ibrahim Univ, Egypt, 52-53; res assoc, Radiobiol Unit, Mt Vernon Hosp, Eng, 57-58; chem consult, Daubert Chem Co, 60-66; reader, Advan Placement Exam Chem, Educ Testing Serv, NJ, 61, 63, 64, 66, 67 & 68; instr, Sch Nursing, W Suburban Hosp, 75-82; Childs Mem Fund award, 57. *Mem:* Am Chem Soc. *Res:* Acylals; phenoxthins; biochemistry; organic chemistry. *Mailing Add:* 1006 Cherry St Wheaton IL 60187-4308

GREEN, G W, microscopy, for more information see previous edition

GREEN, GARY MILLER, NUTRITION, PHYSIOLOGY. *Current Pos:* asst prof med, 79-84, asst prof, 84-88, ASSOC PROF PHYSIOL, UNIV TEX HEALTH SCI CTR, SAN ANTONIO, 88- *Personal Data:* b Bakersfield, Calif, Dec 28, 40; m 67; c 2. *Educ:* Univ Calif, Berkeley, BS, 66, PhD(nutrit), 71. *Prof Exp:* Fel nutrit & digestion res, Univ Calif, Berkeley, 71-72; asst res physiol, B Lyon Mem Res Lab, Children's Hosp Med Ctr, Oakland, Calif, 72-79. *Concurrent Pos:* NIH fel, dept nutrit sci, Univ Calif, Berkeley, 71-72; NIH grant, B Lyon Mem Res Lab, Children's Hosp Med Ctr, 74-80, cystic fibrosis found grant, 78-80. *Mem:* Am Inst Nutrit; Am Physiol Soc. *Res:* Physiology of digestion and absorption in non-ruminants; regulation of exocrine pancreatic secretion; bile acid metabolism; nutrition and gastrointestinal function in digestive diseases, particularly cystic fibrosis. *Mailing Add:* Dept Physiol Univ Tex Health Sci Ctr 7703 Floyd Curl Dr San Antonio TX 78284-7756. *Fax:* 210-567-4410

GREEN, GEORGE G, animal science, animal nutrition, for more information see previous edition

GREEN, HAROLD D, mechanism of action & control of heart circulation, for more information see previous edition

GREEN, HAROLD RUGBY, number theory, for more information see previous edition

GREEN, HARRY, BIOCHEMISTRY. *Current Pos:* RETIRED. *Personal Data:* b Philadelphia, Pa, Sept 7, 17; m 45; c 2. *Educ:* Univ Pa, AB, 38, MS, 39, PhD(org chem), 42. *Prof Exp:* Sr res chemist, Lion Oil Refining Co, Ark, 41-44 & Whitemarsh Res Labs, Pennsalt Mfg Co, 44-47; res assoc physiol chem, Univ Pa, 47-52; chief biochem res, Wills Eye Hosp, 52-58; sr res scientist, Smithkline Corp, 58-64, head neurobiochem, 64-67, dir biochem, 67-75, dir sci liaison, 75-80, vpres sci liaison, 80-83. *Concurrent Pos:* Harrison fel chem, 40-41; asst prof biochem, Grad Sch Med, Univ Pa, 54-68. *Mem:* AAAS; Am Chem Soc; Am Soc Biol Chem; Asn Res Nerv & Ment Dis; Am Soc Pharmacol & Exp Therapeut. *Res:* Intermediary metabolism; ocular biochemistry and physiology; enzymology; corticosteroids; neurobiochemistry; drug metabolism; biochemistry of respiratory glycoproteins; diabetes. *Mailing Add:* 5771 Fairway Park Ct Boynton Beach FL 33437

GREEN, HARRY J(AMES), JR, CHEMICAL ENGINEERING. *Current Pos:* SCIENTIST RES DEPT, XEROX CORP, 70- *Personal Data:* b St Louis, Mo, Dec 7, 11; m 39; c 2. *Educ:* Ohio State Univ, BChE, 32; PhD(chem eng), 43; Mass Inst Technol, MS, 38. *Prof Exp:* Instr chem, Agr & Tech Col, NC, 34-37, asst prof, 38-41, prof, 43-44; sr engr, Mat Eng Dept, Stromberg-Carlson Co, 44-59, supvr mfg res & develop, Prod Eng Dept, 59-67, prin engr microelectronics, Electronics Div, Gen Dynamics, 67-70. *Mem:* Am Chem Soc; Am Soc Metals. *Res:* Materials engineering; metals; polymer applications; wire and insulation; telephone transmitter materials; electrical properties of plastics; microelectronic packaging of thick and thin film hybrid circuits; xerographic materials development. *Mailing Add:* 307 Greeley St Rochester NY 14609-4850

GREEN, HARRY WESTERN, II, GEOPHYSICS, STRUCTURAL GEOLOGY. *Current Pos:* from asst prof to assoc prof, 70-80, chmn dept, 84-88, PROF GEOL, UNIV CALIF, DAVIS, 80-; PROF GEO & GEOPHYSICS, CHANCELLOR RES, UNIV CALIF, RIVERSIDE. *Personal Data:* b Orange, NJ, Mar 13, 40; m 75; c 7. *Educ:* Univ Calif, Los Angeles, AB, 63, MS, 67, PhD(geol), 68. *Prof Exp:* Res assoc geol & metall, Case Western Res Univ, 68-70. *Concurrent Pos:* NSF res grants, 69-; US-France exchange scientist, 73; vis prof, Univ Nantes, France, 78-79 & Monash Univ, Australia, 84; spec adv, China Univ Geosci, 88; DOE res grants, 88-; adj sr researcher, Lamont-Doherty Geol Observ, Columbia Univ, 89- *Mem:* Am Geophys Union; fel Mineral Soc Am. *Res:* Experimental rock deformation at high temperature and pressure; elucidation of deformation mechanisms utilizing high voltage transmission electron microscopy; theoretical studies of deformation in the earth's interior; solid earth geophysics; role of volatiles in the dynamics of the earths mantle; mechanism of deep focus earthquakes; effect of stress on phase transformations. *Mailing Add:* Dept Earth Sci 1432 Geol Bldg Riverside CA 92521

GREEN, HOWARD, CELLULAR PHYSIOLOGY, MOLECULAR BIOLOGY. *Current Pos:* George Higginson prof cellular physiol & chmn, Dept Cellular & Molecular Physiol, 80-94, GEORGE HIGGINSON PROF CELL BIOL, HARVARD MED SCH, 94- *Personal Data:* b Toronto, Ont, Sept 10, 25; nat US; m 54. *Educ:* Univ Toronto, MD, 47; Northwestern Univ, MS, 50. *Hon Degrees:* DSc, Univ Conn, 85 State Univ NY, Stony Brook, 93, MD, Univ Goteborg, 89. *Honors & Awards:* J Howard Mueller Mem Lectr, Harvard Univ, 69; J N Taub Int Mem Award, 77; Selman A Waksman Award, 78; Lewis S Rosenstiel Award, 80; Lila Gruber Res Award, Am Acad Dermat, 80; Howard Fox Mem Lectr, NY Univ, 78; Harvey Lectr, 79; Marchon Lectr, Newcastle, Eng, 82; Unilever Lectr, Eng, 84; Ravdin Lectr, Am Col Surgeons, 85; Passano Award, 85; H M Evans Mem Lectr, Univ Calif, San Francisco, 88; Nobel Found Res Recognition Award, 92. *Prof Exp:* Instr biochem, Univ Chicago, 51-53; instr, Dept Pharmacol, Sch Med, NY Univ, 54, asst prof chem path, 56-59, from assoc prof to prof path, 59-68, prof & chmn, Dept Cell Biol, 68-70; capt, Immunol Div, Walter Reed Army Inst Res, USAR, 55-56; prof cell biol, Dept Biol, Mass Inst Technol, 70-80. *Concurrent Pos:* NIH vis scientist, Cornell Univ, 54. *Mem:* Nat Acad Sci; Am Soc Cellular Biol; Am Acad Arts & Sci. *Res:* Differentiation; genetics; cancer; epidermal drafts in burn treatments. *Mailing Add:* Dept Cellular & Molecular Biol Harvard Med Sch 240 Longwood Ave Boston MA 02115

GREEN, HUBERT GORDON, PUBLIC HEALTH, PEDIATRICS. *Current Pos:* DEAN, SOUTHWESTERN ALLIED HEALTH SCI SCH, UNIV TEX, SOUTHWESTERN MED CTR, 91- *Personal Data:* b Dallas, Tex, Oct 31, 38; m 69, Jean An Hunter; c Elaine, David, Whitney & Emily. *Educ:* Rice Univ, BA, 62; Univ Tex Southwestern Med Sch, MD, 68; Univ Calif, MPH, 72. *Prof Exp:* Assoc prof pediat, Col Med, Univ Ark, Little Rock, 72-77, assoc prof biomet, 75-77; med dir, Ark Children's Hosp, 73-77; dir Handicapped Children's Ctr, Ark Dept Health, 75-76; dep dir, Div Health Serv, US Pub Health Serv, Dallas, Tex, 77-83; dir, Dallas Co Health Dept, 83-90. *Mem:* Am Pub Health Asn; Am Col Prevent Med; Am Acad Pediat; AMA. *Res:* Teratogenic effects, drugs and chemicals; organization of health services; handicapped children. *Mailing Add:* 5323 Harry Hines Blvd Dallas TX 75235-9082. *Fax:* 214-648-1505; *E-Mail:* ggreen@mednet.swmed.edu

GREEN, IRA, TUMOR IMMUNOLOGY, CLINICAL IMMUNOLOGY. *Current Pos:* SR INVESTR IMMUNOL, NAT INST ALLERGY & INFECTIOUS DIS, NIH, 68- *Educ:* State Univ NY, Brooklyn, MD, 53. *Mailing Add:* Agency Health Care Policy 6207 Hollins Dr Bethesda MD 20817

GREEN, JACK PETER, PHARMACOLOGY. *Current Pos:* PROF PHARMACOL & CHMN DEPT, MT SINAI SCH MED, 68- *Personal Data:* b New York, NY, Oct 4, 25; m 58. *Educ:* Pa State Univ, BS, 47, MS, 49; Yale Univ, PhD(pharmacol), 51, MD, 57. *Honors & Awards:* Claude Bernard Award, 66. *Prof Exp:* From asst prof to assoc prof pharmacol, Yale Univ, 57-66; assoc prof, Med Sch, Cornell Univ, 66-68. *Concurrent Pos:* Res fel, Polytech Inst, Denmark, 53-55; USPHS res career prog award, 58-66; Eleanor Roosevelt fel, 64-66; vis scientist, Inst Phys Chem Biol, Univ Paris, 64-66; consult, chem/biol info handling rev comt, Div Res Facil & Resources, NIH, 66-68, mem, 68-70, mem preclin psychopharmacol res rev comt, NIMH, 69-73; mem steering comt, exec comt, Biochem Pharmacol Discussion Group, 66-70; mem prog comt, Gordon Res Conf on Med Chem, 67-68, vchmn, 73, chmn, 74; mem res coun, Pub Health Res Inst New York, 72-75; consult, Health Res Coun New York, 72-75, chmn, 75; mem med adv bd, Dysautonomia Found, 74-77; mem sci adv comt, Irma T Hirschl Trust, 77-; sci counr, Nat Inst Environ Health Serv, 81-84. *Mem:* NY Acad Sci; Soc Drug Res; Int Soc Quantum Biol; fel Am Col Neuropsychopharmacol; Asn Med Sch Pharmacol (treas, 73-75); Am Soc Neurochem. *Res:* Mechanism of action of drugs. *Mailing Add:* Dept Pharmacol Mt Sinai Sch Med New York NY 10029-6507. *Fax:* 212-241-7014

GREEN, JAMES WESTON, physiology; deceased, see previous edition for last biography

GREEN, JEFFREY DAVID, CELL BIOLOGY, FERTILIZATION & EARLY DEVELOPMENT. *Current Pos:* asst prof, 83-88, ASSOC PROF ANAT, MED CTR, LA STATE UNIV, NEW ORLEANS, 88- *Personal Data:* b Worcester, Mass, Feb 22, 47; m 89, Linda Carnegie. *Educ:* Clark Univ, Worcester, Mass, AB, 69; Univ NC, Chapel Hill, MA, 76; State Univ NY, Buffalo, PhD(anat), 81. *Prof Exp:* NIH fel, Univ Wash, Seattle, 81-83. *Concurrent Pos:* Vis scientist, Bodega Marine Lab, Unif Calif, Davis, 90. *Mem:* Am Asn Anatomists; Am Soc Cell Biol; AAAS; Am Soc Zoologists. *Res:* Cell biology of fertilization; role of proteolytic enzymes during sperm-egg interaction and early development; pesticide effects on development. *Mailing Add:* Dept Anat La State Univ Med Ctr 1901 Perdido St New Orleans LA 70112-1393. *E-Mail:* jgreen@lsumc.edu

GREEN, JEFFREY SCOTT, PREDATOR RESEARCH, WILDLIFE RESEARCH. *Current Pos:* res wildlife biologist, Agr Res Serv, 79-88, wildlife biologist, Animal & Plant Health Inspection Serv, Animal Damage Control, 88-95, ASST REGIONAL DIR, US DEPT AGR, 95- *Personal Data:* b Colorado Springs, Colo, Oct 22, 47; m 75, Lisa Herran; c Joshua, Jacob, Jeffrey, Sarah & Laura. *Educ:* Brigham Young Univ, BS, 71, MS, 76, PhD(wildlife & range resources), 78. *Prof Exp:* Res assoc, Brigham Young Univ, 78-79. *Mem:* Wildlife Soc. *Res:* Methodology for reducing predation of sheep by coyotes: livestock guarding dogs, coyote attractants and antifertility agents. *Mailing Add:* US Dept Agr Animal Damage Control Div 12345 W Alameda Pkwy Suite 204 Lakewood CO 80228. *Fax:* 303-969-6578

GREEN, JEROME, PLANT PHYSIOLOGY. *Current Pos:* Res biologist, 79-91, RES ASSOC, E I DUPONT DE NEMOURS & CO, INC, 91- *Personal Data:* b Cameron, Mo, June 3, 53; m 76; c 4. *Educ:* Univ Iowa, BA, 75, MS, 77, PhD(bot), 79. *Mem:* Am Soc Plant Physiol; Plant Growth Regulator Soc Am; Weed Sci Soc Am. *Res:* Plant growth regulators; herbicides. *Mailing Add:* Stine-Haskell Res Ctr Bldg 210 DuPont Agr Prod PO Box 30 Elkton Rd Newark DE 19714

GREEN, JEROME GEORGE, medicine, for more information see previous edition

GREEN, JEROME JOSEPH, MAGNETISM. *Current Pos:* CONSULT, 94 *Personal Data:* b Chicago, Ill, Oct 10, 32; m 58; c 4. *Educ:* Northwestern Univ, BS, 54; Harvard Univ, AM, 55, PhD(appl physics), 59. *Prof Exp:* Asst, Harvard Univ, 57-59; mem staff, Raytheon, Inc, 59-62, mgr magnetic group, 70-84, prin res scientist, Res Div, 62-94. *Mem:* Sr mem Inst Elec & Electronics Engrs. *Res:* Microwave physics; ferromagnetic resonance; magnetic circuits; phase shifters; magnetic memories. *Mailing Add:* 28 Winchester Dr Lexington MA 02173

GREEN, JOHN ARTHUR SAVAGE, electrochemistry, materials science, for more information see previous edition

GREEN, JOHN CHANDLER, VOLCANOLOGY, GEOCHEMISTRY. *Current Pos:* From asst prof to assoc prof, 58-68, head dept, 74-77, PROF GEOL, UNIV MINN, DULUTH, 68- *Personal Data:* b West Hartford, Conn, Feb 7, 32; m 58, Janet Curtis; c Martha (Nielsen) & Sarah (Osgood). *Educ:* Dartmouth Col, AB, 53; Harvard Univ, MA, 56, PhD, 60. *Concurrent Pos:* Geologist, Minn Geol Survey, 62-78 & 85 & Minn Dept Natural Resources, 72 & 84. *Mem:* AAAS; Geol Soc Am; Mineral Soc Am; Norweg Geol Soc; Am Geophys Union; Nat Asn Geol Teachers. *Res:* Petrology of igneous rocks; origin of large, high-T rhyolites; Pre-Cambrian geology of Minnesota; Keweenawan lavas and dikes; evolution of Midcontinent Rift System. *Mailing Add:* 1754 Old North Shore Rd Duluth MN 55804. *Fax:* 218-726-8275

GREEN, JOHN H, FOOD MICROBIOLOGY, FERMENTATION BIOCHEMISTRY. *Current Pos:* RETIRED. *Personal Data:* b Pittsburgh, Pa, Jan 23, 29. *Educ:* Univ Rochester, BA, 51; State Univ NY Col Teachers, Albany, 55; Mich State Univ, PhD(microbiol), 63; Univ Md, MSc, 76. *Prof Exp:* Instr chem & bact, State Univ NY Agr & Tech Inst, Alfred Univ, 56-58; fel, Dept Environ Sci, Univ Mass, 63-64, NIH res assoc, 64-66; res microbiologists, US Nat Marine Fisheries Serv, Nat Oceanic & Atmospheric Agency, 66-76; sr res assoc, Dept Food Sci, Cornell Univ, 76-77; auth & consult food waste mgt, 77-79; environ & energy specialist, Animal & Plant Health Inspection Serv, 79-81; microbiologist, Food Microbiol Br, Food Safety & Inspection Serv, USDA, 81-93. *Concurrent Pos:* Instr food microbiol & food processing waste mgt, Univ Md, College Park. *Mem:* Am Soc Microbiol; Inst Food Technol; Soc Indust Microbiol; Brit Soc Appl Microbiol; Sigma Xi. *Res:* Microbial physiology; food science; industrial (food) waste management; author of over 40 publications; author of one book. *Mailing Add:* 1660 Jennings Mill Rd Apt 408 Bogart GA 30622

GREEN, JOHN IRVING, ECOLOGY, BOTANY. *Current Pos:* RETIRED. *Personal Data:* b Cedarhurst, NY, Mar 25, 24; m 60; c 2. *Educ:* State Univ NY, BS, 49; Syracuse Univ, MS, 51; Cornell Univ, PhD(sci educ), 61. *Prof Exp:* High sch teacher, NY, 51-53; asst prof biol, bot & zool, State Univ NY, Col Brockport, 55-56; exten biologist wildlife educ, Wildlife Div, Mines & Resources Dept, Prov Nfld, 58-60; asst prof, NJ State Sch Conserv, 61-62; asst prof conserv, Exten Div, Cornell Univ, 62-65; from asst prof to assoc prof ecol & bot, St Lawrence Univ, 65-77, chmn dept, 77-80, prof biol, 77-90. *Concurrent Pos:* Guest lectr, Mem Univ Nfld, 59-60; mem, Temp State Comn Youth Educ Conserv, 70-73. *Mem:* Wildlife Soc; Ecol Soc Am; Am Nature Study Soc (pres, 73). *Res:* Wildlife and sociological impact; development of techniques and methods for teaching conservation; wildlife ecology; waterfowl; wildlife-plant ecology. *Mailing Add:* One Hillside Circle Canton NY 13617

GREEN, JOHN M, MARINE SCIENCES GENERAL. *Current Pos:* Asst prof marine biol, 68-73, assoc prof biol, 74-78, PROF BIOL, MEM UNIV, 79- *Personal Data:* b Carlisle, Pa, Jan 10, 40; m 66, Jane Scholefield; c 3. *Educ:* Univ Mich, BSc, 61; Univ Miami, MSc , 64; Univ BC, PhD(ichthyol), 68. *Concurrent Pos:* Consult, marine biol; instr, Bamfield Marine Sta; vis prof, Simon Fraser Univ, 80-, Univ BC, 81, Univ Mauritius, 89 & 92-, Pattamura Univ, 91- & MOI Univ, 93. *Mem:* Am Soc Ichthyol & Herpet; Can Soc Zool; Sigma Xi. *Res:* Behavioral ecology of fishes, particularly with respect to reproductive behavior, social behavior and mechanisms of orientation and homing; ecology of arctic fishes. *Mailing Add:* Dept Biol Mem Univ Nfld St John's NF A1B 3X9 Can. *Fax:* 709-737-4000; *E-Mail:* jmgreen@morgan.ucs.mun.ca

GREEN, JOHN ROOT, PHYSICS. *Current Pos:* From asst prof to prof, 50-81, EMER PROF PHYSICS, UNIV NMEX, 81- *Personal Data:* b Alameda, Calif, Sept 19, 20; m 51, Anna Vallevik; c John V, Mary A & Jane K. *Educ:* Univ Calif, BS, 41, PhD(physics), 50. *Concurrent Pos:* Fulbright fel, Univ Aleppo, 66-67; Fulbright lectr physics, Univ Jordan, 73-74. *Mem:* Am Phys Soc. *Res:* Cosmic radiation; design of cloud chambers; plastic crystals; phase transformations; dielectric properties. *Mailing Add:* 249 Old Church Rd Corrales NM 87048

GREEN, JOHN WILLIE, MATHEMATICS. *Current Pos:* from asst prof to prof, 45-84, EMER PROF MATH, UNIV CALIF, LOS ANGELES, 84- *Personal Data:* b Hearne, Tex, Mar 8, 14; m 38; c 2. *Educ:* Rice Inst, BA, 35, MA, 36; Univ Calif, PhD(math), 38. *Prof Exp:* Asst math, Rice Inst, 35-36; asst, Pierce Inst, Harvard Univ, 38-39; from instr to asst prof, Univ Rochester, 39-43; mathematician, Ballistic Res Lab, Aberdeen Proving Grounds, 43-45. *Concurrent Pos:* Mem, Inst Adv Study, 51; chmn, Conf Bd Math Sci, 71-72. *Mem:* Am Math Soc (assoc secy, 47-55, secy, 57-67); Math Asn Am. *Res:* Potential theory; theory of functions; convex bodies; harmonic functions. *Mailing Add:* Univ Calif Los Angeles Los Angeles CA 90095-1555

GREEN, JONATHAN P, ZOOLOGY, PHYSIOLOGY. *Current Pos:* CHMN & PROF BIOL, ROOSEVELT UNIV, 79- *Personal Data:* b New York, NY, June 16, 35; m 59; c 2. *Educ:* Pa State Univ, BS, 57; Univ Minn, PhD(zool), 63. *Prof Exp:* NIH training grant pathobiol, Johns Hopkins Univ, 63, fel, 63-64; asst prof biol, Brown Univ, 64-72; lectr physiol, Lab Comp Physiol, Dept Zool, Univ Malaya, 71-78; assoc prof biol, Reed Col, 78-79. *Concurrent Pos:* Mem, Marine Biol Lab, Woods Hole, Mass, instr invertebrate zool, 66-70; fel, Thailand Nat Acad Sci, 84-86 & 88-90. *Mem:* AAAS; Am Soc Zool; Malaysian Nature Soc; Am Inst Biol Sci. *Res:* physiology and ultrastructure of the crustacean epidermis; physiological and morphological color changes in Crustacea. *Mailing Add:* Roosevelt Univ Sch Sci & Math 430 S Michigan Ave Chicago IL 60605-1301

GREEN, JOSEPH, FLAME RETARDANTS, PLASTICS. *Current Pos:* mgr polymer additives res & develop, 80-88, prin scientist, 88-93, RES FEL, FMC CORP, PRINCETON, NJ, 93- *Personal Data:* b Brooklyn, NY, Oct 5, 28; m 51; c Howard, Mitchell & Robert. *Educ:* City Col New York, BS, 50; Univ Kans, MS, 52. *Prof Exp:* Chemist, US Rubber Reclaiming Co, Inc, 51-55 & Food Mach & Mfg Corp, Inc, 55-56; supvr, Appl Chem Res Sect, Reaction Motors Div, Thiokol Chem Corp, 56-66, mgr, Synthesis & Polymer Chem Dept, 66-67; mgr polymerization res, Petrochem Res Group, Cities Serv Res Ctr, Cranbury, 67-78; vpres mkt & technol, Saytech, Inc, Cranbury, 78-80. *Concurrent Pos:* Sem fac, Soc Plastics Eng; mem bd dirs, Fire Retardant Chem Asn. *Mem:* Fel Am Inst Chemists; Am Chem Soc; fel Soc Plastics Engrs; Fire Retardant Chem Asn (pres, 89-91). *Res:* Polymer chemistry, synthesis and evaluation and organic chemistry; flame retardancy; thermoplastics, thermosets, polymer additives, rubber chemistry and formulation; thermal stability and chemical resistance; propellant chemistry; boron and nitroso polymers; carboranes; fluorocarbons; polyurethanes; polyesters; polypropylene; polyethylene; acrylonitrile butadiene styrene; polystyrene, PVC, engineering plastics and polymer alloys; organobromine chemistry; organophosphorus chemistry and polymer additives; over 175 technical publications. *Mailing Add:* 94 Chichester Rd Jamesburg NJ 08831. *Fax:* 609-951-3399

GREEN, JOSEPH BARNET, NEUROLOGY. *Current Pos:* DIR REHAB RES, HINES VET ADMIN MED CTR, 94-; PROF NEUROL, LOYOLA UNIV, STRITCH SCH MED, 94- *Personal Data:* b Philadelphia, Pa, Aug 2, 28; m; c Charna A (Evans). *Educ:* St Joseph's Col, Philadelphia, BS, 50; Jefferson Med Col, Philadelphia, MD, 54. *Prof Exp:* Intern, Wilkes-Barre Gen Hosp, Pa, 54-55; resident neurol, Georgetown Univ Med Ctr, 55-58; asst neurologist, Pa Hosp, 60-64; from asst prof to prof, Ind Univ, Med Col, 64-72, prof neurol & pediat & chmn, Dept Neurol, Med Col Ga, Augusta, 72-82; prof & chmn, Dept Psychiat & Neurol, Tulane Univ, Sch Med, New Orleans, 82-87, prof neurol & clin prof pediat, 86-87; dir neurol, Vet Admin Cent Off, Wash, 87-88; chmn, Dept Med & Surg Neurol, Tex Technol Univ, Health Sci Ctr, Lubbock, 88-94. *Concurrent Pos:* Fogarty int res fel, Israel, 81. *Mem:* AMA; Am Acad Neurol; Child Neurol Soc; Am Neurol Asn; Am Epilepsy Soc (secy, 72); Asn Univ Profs Neurol (vpres, 81). *Res:* Neurology. *Mailing Add:* Hines Vet Admin Med Ctr 151 L Bldg 1 Rm 1A202B Fifth & Roosevelt Rd Hines IL 60141

GREEN, JOSEPH MATTHEW, THEORETICAL PHYSICS. *Current Pos:* RETIRED. *Personal Data:* b New York, NY, Nov 29, 26; m 64, Marion Mohr; c Katherine, David, Leeta & Judith. *Educ:* Calif Inst Technol, BS, 49, PhD(physics), 57. *Prof Exp:* Asst physics, Univ Chicago, 49-50; asst math, Calif Inst Technol, 52-54, asst hydrodyn, Hydrodyn Lab, 50-57; physicist, Rand Corp, 57-71; physicist, res & develop assocs, 71-90; consult physics, Lawrence Livermore Nat Labs, 90-93. *Mem:* Am Phys Soc; Sigma Xi. *Res:* Interaction of radiation with matter; equation of state; plasma physics. *Mailing Add:* 24617 Eilat St Woodland Hills CA 91367

GREEN, JUDY, HISTORY OF MATHEMATICS. *Current Pos:* PROF MATH, MARYMOUNT UNIV, 90- *Personal Data:* b Brooklyn, NY, Sept 6, 43; m 64, Paul S; c Joanna (DePorter) & Seth. *Educ:* Cornell Univ, BA, 64; Yale Univ, MA, 66; Univ Md, PhD(math), 72. *Prof Exp:* Instr math, Howard Univ, 66-67; from asst prof to assoc prof math, Rutgers Univ, Camden, 72-90, chair, Dept Math Sci, 83-86. *Concurrent Pos:* Vis asst prof, Howard Univ, 75; hon res fel, div math, Nat Mus Am Hist, Smithsonian Inst, 79- *Mem:* Am Math Soc; Asn Women Math (secy, 71-72, vpres, 77-78, treas, 92-96); Am Asn Univ Professors (1st vpres, 88-90); Asn Symbolic Logic; Math Asn Am. *Res:* History of women in American mathematics; history of the algebra of logic. *Mailing Add:* 10106 Leder Rd Silver Spring MD 20902

GREEN, KEITH, PHYSIOLOGY, BIOPHYSICS. *Current Pos:* from assoc prof to prof, 74-78, REGENTS PROF OPHTHAL, SCH MED, MED COL GA, AUGUSTA, 78-, DIR OPHTHAL RES, 74-, PROF PHYSIOL, 80- *Personal Data:* b Nuneaton, Eng, Aug 16, 40; US citizen; m 64, Mary A Vallance; c Kathryn A & John P. *Educ:* Univ Leicester, BSc, 61; Univ St Andrews, PhD(pharmacol), 64, DSc, 84. *Honors & Awards:* Manpower Award, Res Prev Blindness Inc, 80. *Prof Exp:* From instr to assoc prof ophthal, Sch Med, Johns Hopkins Univ, 66-74. *Concurrent Pos:* NIH res fel ophthal, Sch Med, Johns Hopkins Univ, 64-66; Nat Eye Inst res career develop award, 70-74; lectr physiol, Med Col Ga, 74-80; vis A study sect, NIH, 78-82, Fogarty sr int fel, 82-83; vis prof, Univ Edinburgh, 82-83. *Mem:* Am Physiol Soc; Asn Res Vision & Ophthal; Sigma Xi. *Res:* Solute and solvent transfer across biological membranes; mechanisms underlying control of corneal thickness; mechanism of aqueous humor formation; hormonal effects on membrane transport; mechanisms of fluid dynamics in the eye; ocular toxicology; marijuana effects on eye. *Mailing Add:* Dept Ophthal Med Col Ga Augusta GA 30912-3400. *Fax:* 706-721-7913; *E-Mail:* kgreen@mail.mcg.edu

GREEN, LARRY A, MEDICINE. *Current Pos:* from asst prof to assoc prof, 77-85, PROF & CHMN FAMILY MED, UNIV COLO HEALTH SCI CTR, 85-, WOODWARD-CHISHOLM CHMN FAMILY MED, 89- *Personal Data:* b Ardmore, Okla, Mar 27, 48; m, Margie; c Nathan & Kate. *Educ:* BA, Univ Okla, 69; MD, Baylor, Houston, Tex, 73; Am Bd Family Pract, cert, 76. *Prof Exp:* Resident family med, Univ Rochester & Highland Hosp, NY, 73-76; family physicion, Nat Health Serv Corp, 76-77. *Concurrent Pos:* Residency dir, Dept Family Med, Univ Colo, 78-80; dir, Family Med Residency, Mercy Med Ctr, 80-85; med bd, Univ Hosp, 85- *Mem:* Inst Med-Nat Acad Sci; Am Acad Family Physicians. *Mailing Add:* Univ Colo Health Sci Ctr 1180 Clermont St Denver CO 80220. *Fax:* 303-315-9748; *E-Mail:* larry.green@uchse.edu

GREEN, LARRY J, ORTHODONTICS. *Current Pos:* from asst prof to assoc prof, 65-71, PROF ORTHOD, SCH DENT, STATE UNIV NY, BUFFALO, 71- *Personal Data:* b Memphis, Tenn, Jan 1, 31; m 58; c 3. *Educ:* Univ Pittsburgh, BS, 53, DDS, 56, MS, 60; Univ Iowa, PhD(anat growth), 65; Am Bd Orthod, dipl. *Prof Exp:* Asst prof orthod, Univ Pittsburgh, 60-62. *Concurrent Pos:* Clin pract, 60-62, 65-; consult, NY State Dent Rehab Prog, 84-; pres, Erie Co Dent Soc, 85. *Mem:* Am Dent Asn; Am Asn Orthod; Int Asn Dent Res; fel Int Col Dent; fel Am Col Dent; Nat Adv Dent Res Coun; Nat Inst Dent Res. *Res:* Anatomic growth, especially facial. *Mailing Add:* Dept Orthodont Sch Dent Med 140 C Squire Hall State Univ NY Buffalo NY 14214

GREEN, LAWRENCE, FUSION TECHNOLOGY. *Current Pos:* Sr scientist, Bettis Atomic Power Lab, Westinghouse Elec Corp, 64-73, fel scientist, 73-78, fel scientist, Fusion Power Systs Div, 78-84, fel scientist, Nuclear Fuels Div, 84-93, PROG MGR, THERMONUCLEAR FUSION, SCI & TECHNOL CTR, WESTINGHOUSE ELEC CORP, 93- *Personal Data:* b Gelenes, Hungary, May 3, 37; US citizen; m 63; c 2. *Educ:* City Col New York, BS, 59; Pa State Univ, PhD(nuclear physics), 63. *Concurrent Pos:* Vis prof, Ben Gurion Univ, Israel, 77-78; vis scientist, Swiss Fed Inst Technol, Lausanne, 83-84. *Mem:* AAAS; Am Nuclear Soc; Am Phys Soc. *Res:* Low energy nuclear physics; reactors; fusion technology. *Mailing Add:* 151 Dutch Lane Pittsburgh PA 15236. *E-Mail:* lgreen@cis.wec.com

GREEN, LAWRENCE WINTER, PUBLIC HEALTH EDUCATION. *Current Pos:* PROF & DIR, INST HEALTH PROM RES, 91- *Personal Data:* b Bell, Calif, Sept 16, 40; m 62, Judith M Ottoson; c Beth & Jennifer. *Educ:* Univ Calif, Berkeley, BS, 62, MPH, 66, DrPH, 68. *Honors & Awards:* Award for Advan Fertil Control, Excerpta Medica Found & Syntex Labs, 70; Beryl J Roberts Mem Award for Res, Soc Pub Health Educ, 72; Distinguished Career Award, Am Public Health Asn, 78, Award Excellence, 94. *Prof Exp:* USPHS trainee pub health educ, Calif State Dept Pub Health, 62-63; training assoc family planning, Ford Found, Dacca & Karachi, Pakistan, 63-65; lectr pub health educ, Sch Pub Health, Univ Calif, Berkeley, 68-70; from asst prof to prof pub health admin, pop dynamics & behav sci, Sch Hyg & Pub Health, Johns Hopkins Univ, 70-81, asst dean continuing educ, 72-76; prof & head, Health Educ Div, Health Serv Res & Develop Ctr, Johns Hopkins Med Insts, 76-81, dir health educ studies, 75-81; dir, US Off Health Info & Health Prom, Dept Health & Human Serv, 79-81; prof community med & dir, Ctr Health Prom Res & Develop, & co-dir, Southwest Center for Prev Res, Health Sci Ctr, Univ Tex, Houston, 81-88; vpres, Henry J Kaiser Family Found, Menlo Park, Calif, 88-91; policy scholar, Inst Health Policy Studies, Univ Calif, San Francisco, 91. *Concurrent Pos:* Res specialist, Family Res Ctr, Langley Porter Neuropsychiat Inst, 68-70; ed, Soc Pub Health Educ, 72-75; consult, WHO & AID, 73-74, 81-84, Vet Admin, Am Heart Asn, Kellogg Found & Dept Health, Educ & Welfare, 74-76 & Nat Ctr Health Serv Res, 75-; mem, Nat Policy Comt, Nat Ctr Health Educ, Nat Health Coun, 74-75; counr, Coun Educ for Pub Health, 74-78; consult & task force mem, Nat Heart & Lung Inst, 75-76; mem, Expert Panel Consumer Health Educ, Am Col Prev Med

& NIH, 76; vis lectr, Div Health Policy Res & Educ, Harvard Univ, 81-82; mem, Nat Adv Comt Vital & Health Statist, 85-87; chmn, Comt on Drug Abuse Prev Res, Nat Res Coun, Nat Acad Sci, 89-91; Alliance Scholar, Am Alliance Health, Phys Educ & Recreation. *Mem:* Fel Am Pub Health Asn; distinguished fel Soc Pub Health Educ (pres, 83-84); Acad Behav Med Res; Soc Behav Med; Can Pub Health Asn; assoc fel Acad Phys Ed; hon fel Am Sch Health Asn. *Res:* Cardiovascular disease prevention; secondary prevention of stroke and cancer; diffusion of health and family planning innovations in the public; health attitudes and behavior; economic and administrative analyses of health education; health promotion. *Mailing Add:* Inst Health Prom Res Univ BC 2206 East Mall Vancouver BC V6T 1Z4 Can. *Fax:* 604-822-9210

GREEN, LEON WILLIAM, MATHEMATICS. *Current Pos:* from instr to asst prof, 53-63, PROF MATH, UNIV MINN, MINNEAPOLIS, 63- *Personal Data:* b Passaic, NJ, Dec 12, 25; m 56, 83; c 2. *Educ:* Harvard Univ, AB, 48; Yale Univ, MA, 49, PhD(math), 52. *Prof Exp:* Instr math, Princeton Univ, 52-53. *Mem:* Am Math Soc; Math Asn Am. *Res:* Differential geometry; topological dynamics. *Mailing Add:* Dept Math/127 Vincent Hall Univ Minn Inst Technol Minneapolis MN 55455-0488

GREEN, LISLE ROYAL, RANGE MANAGEMENT. *Current Pos:* CONSULT, 83- *Personal Data:* b Ogden, Utah, Nov 18, 18; m 46; c 4. *Educ:* Utah State Univ, BS, 41, MS, 48. *Prof Exp:* Ranch planner, Soil Conserv Serv, USDA, 46-47, range conservationist, US Forest Serv, 48-54; asst prof range mgt, Calif State Polytech Col, 55-60; fuel-break proj leader & supvry range scientist, US Forest Serv, 60-77, range scientist forest fire res, 77-82. *Concurrent Pos:* Assoc, Agr Exp Sta, Univ Calif, Riverside, 64- *Mem:* Soil Conserv Soc Am; Soc Range Mgt; Soc Am Foresters. *Res:* Ecology and management of annual plant and chaparral covered land, including revegetation, use of prescribed fire, goats and herbicides, irrigation of chaparral with sewage effluent, and effects of these practices. *Mailing Add:* 22586 Main St Grand Terrace CA 92313

GREEN, LOUIS CRAIG, ASTROPHYSICS. *Current Pos:* from instr to prof astron, Haverford Col, 41-76, chmn, Dept Astron, 42-76, chmn, Dept Physics, 63-65, provost, 65-68, prof physics, 79-80, prof astron, 80-85, EMER PROF ASTRON, HAVERFORD COL, 76- *Personal Data:* b Macon, Ga, Feb 2, 11; m 40. *Educ:* Princeton Univ, AB, 32, MA, 33, PhD(astron), 37. *Hon Degrees:* DSc, Haverford Col, 83. *Prof Exp:* From instr to asst prof math & astron, Allegheny Col, 37-41. *Concurrent Pos:* Vis asst prof, Swarthmore Col, 44; lectr, Bryn Mawr Col, 44-46; Guggenheim fel, 55-56; vis prof, Max Planck Inst Munich, 59; mem, Inst Advan Study, 62-63 & 68-69. *Mem:* Fel Am Phys Soc; Am Astron Soc; Sigma Xi. *Res:* Far ultraviolet spectroscopy; rapidly rotating single stars and close binaries; atomic wave functions; solar and stellar pulsations. *Mailing Add:* 3300 Darby Rd Apt 1208 Haverford PA 19041

GREEN, LOUIS DOUGLAS, PATHOLOGY. *Current Pos:* RETIRED. *Personal Data:* b Birmingham, Ala, July 4, 16; m 39; c 2. *Educ:* Tuskegee Inst, BS, 37; Fisk Univ, MA, 40; Meharry Med Col, MD, 48. *Prof Exp:* Teacher gen sci, Bd Educ, Birmingham, 37-38; instr chem, Fisk Univ, 38-40; instr org chem, Iowa State Col, 40-42; prof chem, Tenn State Univ, 42-44; intern med, Homer G Phillips Hosp, St Louis, Mo, 48-49; pvt pract, Birmingham, Ala & Cleveland, Ohio, 49-61; resident path, Marymount Hosp, Cleveland, 61-64; resident, Cleveland Clin & Hosp, 64-67; dir path, Hillcrest Hosp, 67-73; prof path & chmn dept, Meharry Med Col, 73-81; pathologist, George W Hubbard Hosp, 73-81. *Concurrent Pos:* Consult lab serv, Riverside Hosp, Nashville, 73-81; pathologist, Cloverbottom Develop Ctr, 73-81. *Mem:* Fel Col Am Path; fel Am Soc Clin Path; Int Acad Path. *Mailing Add:* 5467 Granny White Pike Brentwood TN 37027

GREEN, MARGARET, microbiology, for more information see previous edition

GREEN, MARIE RODER, HISTOCHEMISTRY, ATHEROSCLEROSIS. *Current Pos:* NIH fel, Nat Inst Arthritis, Metab & Digestive Dis, 67-69, res chemist, Molecular Carcinogenesis Lab, Nat Cancer Inst, Bethesda, MD, 70-88, HEALTH SCIENTIST ADMINR, DIV HEART & VASCULAR DIS, NIH, 88- *Personal Data:* b Vienna, Austria, March 19, 29; US citizen; m 52, Jerome G; c 2. *Educ:* Brooklyn Col, NY, BS, 50; Univ Wis-Madison, MS, 52; Albany Med Col, NY, PhD(exp path), 56. *Prof Exp:* Res biochemist, NY State Dept Health, Albany, 52-55, Nat Inst Health, 56-57, Mt Zion Hosp, San Francisco, 57-58, Case-Western Res Univ, Cleveland, 62-66; res assoc, Armed Forces Inst Path, 66-67. *Concurrent Pos:* NIH fel, Nat Inst Arthritis, Metab & Digestive Dis, 67-69. *Mem:* Soc Develop Biol; Histochem Soc; Am Dairy Sci Asn; Am Heart Asn; Am Soc Cell Biol. *Res:* Differentiation and development of mammary gland; hormonal, chemical and viral factors in mammary gland carcinogenesis; altered expression of macromolecules in neoplasia; histochemistry of metachromatic dyes. *Mailing Add:* NHLBI NIH RKL 2 6701 Rockledge Dr Bethesda MD 20892

GREEN, MARK ALAN, RADIOPHARMACEUTICAL CHEMISTRY, NUCLEAR PHARMACY. *Current Pos:* asst prof, 87-90, assoc prof, 90-94, PROF MED CHEM, SCH PHARM, PURDUE UNIV, 94- *Personal Data:* b Sidney, Ohio, Sept 10, 56; m 90. *Educ:* Rose-Hulman Inst Technol, BS, 78; Ind Univ, PhD(inorg chem), 82. *Honors & Awards:* Twelfth Tetalman Mem Award, Soc Nuclear Med. *Prof Exp:* Assoc radiol, Sch Med, Washington Univ, 82-85; asst prof radiol, Univ Minn, 85-87. *Concurrent Pos:* Prin investr, Nat Heart, Lung & Blood Inst Res Career Develop Award, 86-91, grant, Nat Cancer Inst, 87-, res grant, US Dept Energy, 89-92; adj prof, Sch Med, Ind Univ, 90- *Mem:* Am Chem Soc; Soc Nuclear Med; Int Soc Cerebral Blood Flow & Metab. *Res:* Radiopharmaceuticals labeled with metal radionuclides; diagnostic imaging by positron emission tomography; design and synthesis of radiotracers for use in diagnostic nuclear medicine and biomedical research. *Mailing Add:* Dept Med Chem Purdue Univ West Lafayette IN 47907. *Fax:* 765-494-6790

GREEN, MARK LEE, MATHEMATICS. *Current Pos:* from asst prof to assoc prof, 75-82, PROF, UNIV CALIF, LOS ANGELES, 82- *Personal Data:* b Minneapolis, Minn, Oct 1, 47; m c 3. *Educ:* Mass Inst Technol, BS, 68; Princeton Univ, MA, 70, PhD(math), 72. *Prof Exp:* Lectr, Univ Calif, Berkeley, 72-74, Mass Inst Technol, 74-75. *Concurrent Pos:* Fel, NSF, 68-72, Woodrow Wilson Found, 68-72, Procter fel, Princeton Univ, 70-71 & Alfred P Sloan Found, 76-80. *Mem:* Am Math Soc. *Res:* Several complex variables; differential geometry; algebraic geometry. *Mailing Add:* Univ Calif Los Angeles CA 90024-7009

GREEN, MARK M, STEREOCHEMISTRY. *Current Pos:* assoc prof, 80-86, PROF CHEM, POLYTECH INST NEW YORK, 86- *Personal Data:* b New York, NY, Apr 6, 37; m 85; c 4. *Educ:* City Univ New York, BSc, 58; Princeton Univ, PhD(chem), 66. *Prof Exp:* Asst prof chem, Univ Mich, 67-74 & Mich State Univ, 74-76; assoc prof, Clarkson Col, 76-79. *Concurrent Pos:* NIH fel, 66-67; vis prof, Technion Haifa, Israel, 71-72, Chem Inst, Barcelona, 71 & Indian Inst Exp Med, Calcutta, 78; Fulbright fel, India, 78; US-Japan NSF fel, 89-90. *Mem:* Am Chem Soc; AAAS. *Res:* Stereochemistry of macromolecules; physical organic chemistry. *Mailing Add:* Dept Chem Polytech Univ 6 Metro Tech Ctr Brooklyn NY 11201-3840

GREEN, MARTIN DAVID, EXPERIMENTAL DESIGN, COMPUTER MODELING. *Current Pos:* Prin investr, USA Med Mat Develop Activity, 80-81, chief, appl pharmacol, 81-84, chief, drug assessment div, 84-86, PROD MGR, USA MED MAT DEVELOP ACTIVITY, 86- *Personal Data:* b Detroit, Mich, Aug 29, 47; m 75; c 2. *Educ:* Univ Calif, Los Angeles, BA, 70, PhD(pharmacol), 75. *Mem:* Am Soc Pharmacol & Exp Therapeut; Am Chem Soc; Sigma Xi; NY Acad Sci. *Res:* Drug extrapolates; utilization of pharmacological data. *Mailing Add:* 5699 Glenrock Dr Frederick MD 21701-7046. *Fax:* 301-443-9292

GREEN, MARTIN LAURENCE, ELECTRONIC MATERIALS, MATERIALS SCIENCE. *Current Pos:* Assoc mem tech staff, 70-74, MEM TECH STAFF, BELL LABS, 77- *Personal Data:* b New York, NY, Jan 24, 49; m 70, Sharon Alperin; c David & Susanna. *Educ:* Polytech Inst, Brooklyn, BS, 70, MS, 72; Mass Inst Technol, PhD(mat sci), 78. *Mem:* Am Inst Mining, Metall & Petrol Eng; Electrochem Soc; Mat Res Soc. *Res:* Metallurgy; thin films; electronic materials; phase transformations; materials science. *Mailing Add:* Bell Labs Rm 2D-316B Murray Hill NJ 07974. *Fax:* 908-582-2699; *E-Mail:* mlg@physics.att.com

GREEN, MARY ELOISE, NUTRITION, FOOD MANAGEMENT. *Current Pos:* from instr to prof, 39-72, EMER PROF FOODS & NUTRIT, OHIO STATE UNIV, 72- *Personal Data:* b East Liberty, Ohio, June 10, 03. *Educ:* Ohio State Univ, BS, 28, MS, 33; Iowa State Univ, PhD(foods, nutrit), 49. *Prof Exp:* Pub sch teacher, Ohio, 28-37; instr educ, Ohio Wesleyan Univ, 37-39. *Mem:* Fel AAAS; Am Asn Family Consumer Sci; Am Dietetic Asn; Inst Food Technol. *Res:* Physical properties of meats, flour mixtures and starchy foods; food preservation. *Mailing Add:* 116 W Como Ave Columbus OH 43202-1028

GREEN, MAURICE, BIOCHEMISTRY. *Current Pos:* from asst prof to assoc prof, 56-63, PROF MICROBIOL, SCH MED, ST LOUIS UNIV, 63-, CHMN, INST MOLECULAR VIROL, 64- *Personal Data:* b New York, NY, May 5, 26; m 50; c 3. *Educ:* Univ Mich, BS, 49; Univ Wis, MS, 52, PhD(biochem), 54. *Honors & Awards:* Dyer Award, 72; Howard Taylor Ricketts Award, 76. *Prof Exp:* Instr biochem, Univ Pa, 55-56. *Concurrent Pos:* Nat Found Infantile Paralysis res fel, Univ Pa, 54-55, Lalor fel, 55-56; sr fel, USPHS, 58-62; lifetime res career award, Nat Inst Allergy & Infectious Dis, 63-; Burroughs-Wellcome fel, 87. *Mem:* AAAS; Am Soc Biol Chem; Am Chem Soc; Am Soc Microbiol. *Res:* Molecular biology of eucaryotic cells and tumor viruses; virus-cell transformation; oncology; cell regulation. *Mailing Add:* Inst Molecular Virol St Louis Univ Sch Med 3681 Park Ave St Louis MO 63110-2511. *Fax:* 314-577-8419

GREEN, MELVIN HOWARD, BIOCHEMISTRY, VIROLOGY. *Current Pos:* asst prof, 63-67, assoc prof, 67-77, PROF BIOL, UNIV CALIF, SAN DIEGO, 77- *Personal Data:* b Pittsburgh, Pa, Feb 21, 37; m 65; c 4. *Educ:* Univ Pittsburgh, BS, 58; Univ Ill, PhD(biochem), 62. *Prof Exp:* NIH fel virol, Calif Inst Technol, 62-63. *Concurrent Pos:* Am Cancer Soc res scholar, Imp Cancer Res Fund, London, Eng, 70-71. *Mem:* Am Soc Cell Biol. *Res:* Regulation of genetic expression of lytic and temperate bacteriophages; development of DNA tumor viruses; chromatin structure and function; cancer cell biology; wound repair. *Mailing Add:* Dept Biol Univ Calif San Diego 9500 Gilman Dr La Jolla CA 92093-0322

GREEN, MELVIN MARTIN, GENETICS. *Current Pos:* from asst prof to prof, 50-82, geneticist, Exp Sta, 69-82, EMER PROF GENETICS & EMER GENETICIST, UNIV CALIF, DAVIS, 82- *Personal Data:* b Minneapolis, Minn, Aug 24, 16; m 46. *Educ:* Univ Minn, BA, 38, MA, 40, PhD(zool), 42. *Hon Degrees:* Dr, Univ Umea, Sweden, 72. *Prof Exp:* Asst prof zool, Univ Mo, 46-50. *Mem:* Nat Acad Sci; Genetics Soc Am (pres, 73); Am Soc Naturalists. *Res:* Drosophila genetics; mutation; pseudoallelism. *Mailing Add:* Dept Genetics Univ Calif Davis CA 95616

GREEN, MICHAEL, MEMBRANE BIO-GENESIS, PROTEIN SORTING. *Current Pos:* PROF MICROBIOL, SCH MED, ST LOUIS UNIV, 81- *Personal Data:* c 2. *Educ:* Univ Wis, PhD(molecular biol), 72. *Mem:* Am Soc Biochem & Molecular Biol. *Res:* Synthesis and assembly of biological membranes and protein sorting. *Mailing Add:* Dept Molecular Microbiol St Louis Univ Sch Med 1402 S Grand Blvd St Louis MO 63104-1080. Fax: 314-773-3403

GREEN, MICHAEL ENOCH, PHYSICAL CHEMISTRY, LABORATORY SAFETY. *Current Pos:* from asst prof to assoc prof, 66-83, PROF PHYS CHEM, CITY COL NEW YORK, 84-, CHMN, DEPT CHEM, 90- *Personal Data:* b New York, NY, Nov 5, 38; m 74; c Omar. *Educ:* Cornell Univ, BA, 59; Yale Univ, MS, 61, PhD(phys chem), 64. *Prof Exp:* Res assoc exciton transport, Calif Inst Technol, 63-64; Peace Corps vis lectr chem, Mid ETech Univ, Ankara, 64-66. *Concurrent Pos:* Vchmn, Biophys Sect, NY Acad Sci, 85-86, chmn, 87-88. *Mem:* AAAS; Am Chem Soc; Am Phys Soc; NY Acad Sci; Biophys Soc. *Res:* Electrical noise generated during ion transport across membranes; membrane transport; mechanisms of ion channel gating. *Mailing Add:* Dept Chem City Col City Univ New York NY 10031-9137

GREEN, MICHAEL H(ENRY), NUTRITION, BIOLOGY. *Current Pos:* prof in charge, 77-79, ASSOC PROF NUTRIT SCI, PA STATE UNIV, NUTRIT DEPT, 85- *Personal Data:* b Fresno, Calif, Feb 9, 44; m; c 1. *Educ:* Univ Calif, Berkeley, BA, 67, PhD(nutrit sci), 73. *Prof Exp:* Lab asst, Lawrence Radiation Lab, Berkeley, 65-67, fel, Dept Nutrit Sci, Univ Calif, 73; assoc, Div Nutrit Sci, Cornell Univ, 73-75, asst prof nutrit Sci, 75-84. *Concurrent Pos:* Physiol fac, Pa State Univ, 76-; vis scientist, NIH, Lab Math Biol, 82; Fulbright res scholar, Eon Found Norway & Ctr Int Exchange Scholars, 85; vis researcher, Inst Nutrit Res, Univ Oslo, Norway, 85-86; vis scientist, Univ Pa, Sch Vet Med, 86; Mead Johnson Award Comt, 87-90. *Mem:* Am Inst Nutrit; Am Soc Clin Nutrit; Soc Math Biol; Am Heart Asn; Soc Exp Biol & Med. *Res:* Application of model-based compartmental analysis to biological systems, for example, metabolism of retinol, triglyceride-rich lipoproteins, copper, receptor mediated endocytosis; lipid absorption. *Mailing Add:* Nutrit Dept S-126 Henderson Bldg S Pa State Univ University Park PA 16802-0001. Fax: 814-863-6103

GREEN, MICHAEL JOHN, MEDICINAL CHEMISTRY. *Current Pos:* DIR ALLERGY & INFLAMMATION, SCHERING-PLOUGH RES, 71- *Personal Data:* b Slough, Eng, Nov 30, 42; m 68; c 2. *Educ:* Sheffield Univ, BS, 64, PhD(org chem), 67. *Prof Exp:* Res assoc org chem, Ben May Lab Cancer Res, Univ Chicago, 67-69 & Brookhaven Nat Lab, 69-71. *Mem:* Am Chem Soc; The Chem Soc. *Res:* Steroid chemistry; synthesis and structure-activity relationships of biologically active organic compounds. *Mailing Add:* 43 Meadow Run Dr Skillman NJ 08558

GREEN, MICHAEL PHILIP, ELECTROCHEMISTRY, ATOMIC SURFACE STRUCTURE. *Current Pos:* hardware develop mgr, 92-97, DIR ENG, TOPOMETRICS, 97- *Personal Data:* b London, Eng, Feb 1, 61. *Educ:* Yale Univ, BS, 83; Stanford Univ, MS, 87, PhD(appl physics), 90. *Prof Exp:* Mem tech staff, AT&T Bell Labs, 90-92. *Mem:* Am Phys Soc. *Res:* Application of scanning tunneling microscopy to electrochemical reactions; atomic resolution investigation of metal plating and stripping. *Mailing Add:* Topometrics 5403 Betsy Ross Dr Santa Clara CA 95054

GREEN, MILTON, APPLIED PHYSICS. *Current Pos:* RETIRED. *Personal Data:* b Pueblo, Colo, Jan 13, 12; m 44; c 2. *Educ:* Univ Wyo, BS, 35; Univ Calif, MA, 37, PhD(physics), 41. *Prof Exp:* Asst physics, Univ Calif, 36-39; jr physicist, Nat Bur Stand, 42-45, asst physicist, 43-45; physicist, Res & Develop Labs, US Army Signal Corps, Ft Monmouth, 45-54, phys scientist & group leader, 54-60; sr staff scientist, Res Labs, Burroughs Corp, Pa, 60-64; res physicist, US Navy Underwater Sound Lab, 64-70; res assoc, Naval Underwater Systs Ctr, 70-90. *Mem:* Am Phys Soc; Optical Soc Am. *Res:* Electrical conduction in solids, mainly semiconductors; transport phenomena; thermoelectricity; photoelectricity; photographic photometry; underwater optics; instrumentation; signal processing. *Mailing Add:* 201 Gardner Ave New London CT 06320

GREEN, MILTON, PHOTOGRAPHIC CHEMISTRY. *Current Pos:* RETIRED. *Personal Data:* b Boston, Mass, Apr 30, 20; m 54; c 4. *Educ:* Mass Inst Technol, BS, 40; Columbia Univ, PhD(chem), 51. *Prof Exp:* Chemist, Atlantic Gelatin Co, 40-41; res chemist biochem & proteins, Burroughs-Wellcome Co, 41-42; res chemist sulfa drugs, Hoffmann-La Roche Inc, 42-43; res chemist pharmaceut & amino acids, Wyeth Inst, 43-44; res chemist textile finishing, US Finishing Corp, 46-47; sr chemist & group leader photog & org chem, Polaroid Corp, 51-59, asst mgr, Org Res Div, 59-65, mgr photog chem res, 65-68, asst dir chem res & develop, 68-82. *Concurrent Pos:* Consult, toxicol, 82- *Mem:* Am Chem Soc; fel Soc Photog Scientists & Engrs. *Res:* Chemistry of the photographic process; pharmaceuticals; proteins; amino acids; dyes; chemistry of diffusion transfer photography. *Mailing Add:* 38 Winston Rd Newton Centre Boston MA 02159-3062

GREEN, MORRIS, RADIATION BIOLOGY. *Current Pos:* DIR, SECT BEHAV & DEVELOP PEDIAT, IND UNIV-PURDUE UNIV, 89- *Personal Data:* b Brooklyn, NY, Apr 27, 31. *Educ:* Brooklyn Col, BA, 52; Univ Rochester, PhD(radiation biol), 58. *Prof Exp:* Coffin res fel radiation biol, Univ Rochester, 58-64; from asst prof to assoc prof biol, Hunter Col, 64-70, Perry W Lash prof pediat, 70-89, physician-in-chief & chmn, Dept Pediat, 89. *Concurrent Pos:* Vis radiation biologist, Am Inst Biol Sci-AEC, 73- *Mem:* Inst Med-Nat Acad Sci; Am Chem Soc. *Res:* Biological effects of radiation; blood and liver proteins and their functions; tracer chemistry; diabetes, action of insulin; amino acid and protein metabolism in normal, aging and cataractous rat lenses. *Mailing Add:* Dept Pediat Riley Hosp Children 702 Barnhill Dr Indianapolis IN 46202

GREEN, MORTON, PALEONTOLOGY. *Current Pos:* RES ASSOC, MUS NATURAL HIST, UNIV KANS, 80- *Personal Data:* b Brooklyn, NY, Oct 25, 17; m 46; c 3. *Educ:* Univ Kans, AB, 40, MA, 42; Univ Calif, PhD(paleont), 54. *Prof Exp:* Res assoc, SDak Sch Mines & Technol, 50-61, chmn dept biol, 50-80, assoc dir, Mus Geol, 68-75, cur vert paleont, 62-80. *Mem:* Soc Vert Paleont; Sigma Xi; Paleont Soc. *Res:* Mammals. *Mailing Add:* 1933 Hillview Rd Lawrence KS 66046-2653

GREEN, NANCY R, NUTRITION & FOOD SCIENCE. *Current Pos:* From asst prof to assoc prof, 74-87, asst dean, 89-90, PROF, DEPT NUTRIT & FOOD SCI, FLA STATE UNIV, 88-, ASSOC DEAN GRAD STUDIES & RES, COL HUMAN SCI, 90- *Educ:* Univ Tenn, BS, 71, DPhil(nutrit), 74. *Concurrent Pos:* Mem, Educ comt, Inst Food Technologist, 80-83, secy-treas, Nutrit Div, 91-93; actg dept head, Dept Nutrit & Food Sci, Fla State Univ, 88, grad prog adminr, 88-89. *Mem:* Inst Food Technologist; Am Inst Nutrit; Am Coun Sci & Health; Environ Mutagen Soc; AAAS; Sigma Xi. *Res:* Sodium reduction in hypertensive elderly; influence of dietary fats on mutagenicity; author of numerous scientific publications. *Mailing Add:* Dept Nutrit Food Sci Tropicana Prod 1001 13th Ave E Bradenton FL 34208

GREEN, NORMAN EDWARD, PLANT PATHOLOGY. *Current Pos:* ASSOC PROF SOIL MICROBIOL & RANGE MGT, HUMBOLDT STATE UNIV, 76- *Personal Data:* b Electric City, Wash, Aug 22, 38; m 85; c 2. *Educ:* Wash State Univ, BS, 67, PhD(plant path), 74; Colo State Univ, MS, 69. *Prof Exp:* Res asst range sci, Colo State Univ, 67-69; res technician plant path, Wash State Univ, 69-74. *Concurrent Pos:* Fel libr, Dept Environ Sci, Wash State Univ, 74-75. *Mem:* Soc Range Mgt. *Res:* Influence of endomycorrhizal fungi on growth and development of selected range grasses and subclover. *Mailing Add:* Dept Range Mgt Humboldt State Univ 1 Harps St Arcata CA 95521-8299

GREEN, PAUL BARNETT, BOTANY. *Current Pos:* PROF BIOL, STANFORD UNIV, 70- *Personal Data:* b Philadelphia, Pa, Feb 15, 31; m 57. *Educ:* Univ Pa, BA, 52; Princeton Univ, PhD, 57. *Honors & Awards:* Darbaker Prize, Botanical Soc of Am, Pelton Award. *Prof Exp:* From asst prof to prof bot, Univ Pa, 58-70. *Mem:* Soc Develop Biol(pres, 82); Bot Soc Am; Am Soc Plant Physiologists; foreign mem Royal Belg Acad Arts & Sci. *Res:* Plant development; growth of cell walls. *Mailing Add:* Dept Biol Stanford Univ Gilbert Hall Stanford CA 94305-9991

GREEN, PAUL E(LIOT), JR, ELECTRONICS. *Current Pos:* DIR, TELL LABS OPTICAL NETWORKING, 97- *Personal Data:* b Durham, NC, Jan 14, 24; m 48, Dorrit Gegan; c Dorrit G (Rodemeyer), Nancy E, Judith J (Godin), Paul M & Gordon M. *Educ:* Univ NC, AB, 44; NC State Col, MS, 48; Mass Inst Technol, ScD, 53. *Honors & Awards:* Aerospace Electronics Pioneer Award, Inst Elec & Electronics Engrs, 80, Simon Rano Medal, 91. *Prof Exp:* Staff mem, Lincoln Lab, 53-58, group leader, 58-69; sr mgr, Comput Sci Dept, IBM Res, 69-74 & 77-81, mem, Corp Tech Comt, 75-76 & 81-83, staff mem, 83-96. *Mem:* Nat Acad Eng; fel Am Inst Elec & Electronics Engrs. *Res:* Communication theory applied to radar astronomy, seismology, computer network architecture, optical fiber networking. *Mailing Add:* 35 Roseholm Pl RFD 3 Mt Kisco NY 10549

GREEN, PHILIP PALMER, mathematical & computer methods for genome analysis, for more information see previous edition

GREEN, PHILIP S, ULTRASOUND, ELECTRONICS. *Current Pos:* PRES, TELESURGICAL CORP, 93- *Personal Data:* b Youngstown, Ohio, Aug 4, 36; m 60; c 3. *Educ:* Johns Hopkins Univ, BESc, 58; Stanford Univ, MS, 67. *Prof Exp:* Assoc engr, Johns Hopkins Appl Physics Lab, 58-60; sr res engr, Lockheed Res Labs, 60-68; mgr, Ultrasonics Prog, SRI Int, 68-78, dir, Bioeng Res Lab, 78-93. *Concurrent Pos:* Consult & prin investr grants, NIH, 72-; lectr, Med Schs, US & Europe, 75-; chmn, 5th Int Symp Acoust Holography & Imaging, 73; mem, Task Group Med Ultrasound, NSF, 75. *Mem:* Am Inst Ultrasound Med. *Res:* Ultrasonic imaging methods for medical diagnosis; holography and optical imaging. *Mailing Add:* 820 Miranda Green Palo Alto CA 94306

GREEN, R(ALPH) V(ERNON), CHEMICAL ENGINEERING. *Current Pos:* CONSULT, 77- *Personal Data:* b Litchfield, Ill, Feb 11, 13; m 39; c 2. *Educ:* Univ Ill, BS, 35, MS, 36. *Prof Exp:* Tech asst, Exp Sta, Univ Ill, 33-34, instr chem, 35-36; chem engr, Indust & Biol Chem Dept, E I DuPont de Nemours & Co, Inc, Del, 36-39, & WVa, 40-43, group leader, 43-45, asst tech supt, 45-52, tech supt, 52-54, tech specialist, 54-58, staff engr, 58-77. *Mem:* Am Chem Soc; Am Inst Chem Engrs; fel Am Inst Chem. *Res:* Synthesis gas generation and processing. *Mailing Add:* 210 Sheller Dr Charleston WV 25314-1060

GREEN, RALPH, HEMATOLOGY, NUTRITION. *Current Pos:* CHMN, DEPT LAB HEMAT, CLEVELAND CLIN FOUND. *Personal Data:* b Johannesburg, SAfrica, Sept 18, 40; m 64; c 5. *Educ:* Univ Witwatersrand, MB, BCh, 63, MD, 76. *Prof Exp:* Inter med & surg, Johannesburg Gen Hosp, 64; NIH res fel, Univ Witwatersrand, 65-66; Wellcome res fel lab hemat, St Bartholomew's Hosp, London, Eng, 67-69; resident hemat, SAfrican Inst Med Res, 70-71; lectr & sr lectr, Sch Path, Univ Witwatersrand, 72-74; assoc hemat, Scripps Clin & Res Found, 75-80, asst mem, 80- *Concurrent Pos:* Adj assoc prof path, Univ Cal, San Diego, 75-; mem nat comt clin lab standards, iron sect, Nat Inst Arthritis & Metabolic Dis, NIH. *Mem:* Am Soc Hemat; Am Fedn Clin Res; Am Inst Nutrit; Soc Exp Biol & Med. *Res:* Nutritional anemias; iron cobalamin and folate metabolism; iron ferritin and vitamin assays; drug targeting with erythrocyte ghosts; iron and metal storage diseases; neurobiology of cobalamin, other vitamins and trace minerals; fruit bat animal model for cobalamin deficiency; drug-nutrient interactions. *Mailing Add:* Sect Lab Hematol Cleveland Clin Found 9500 Euclide Ave L30 Cleveland OH 44195-5139. *Fax:* 216-444-2806

GREEN, RALPH J, JR, PLANT PATHOLOGY. *Current Pos:* RETIRED. *Personal Data:* b Naylor, Mo, Aug 17, 23; m 44; c 3. *Educ:* Ind State Univ, BS, 48; Purdue Univ, MS, 50, PhD, 54. *Prof Exp:* Instr plant path, Purdue Univ, 51-53; instr, Univ Chicago, 53-55; from asst prof to prof Purdue Univ, 55-88, emer prof plant path, 88- *Mem:* Fel Am Phytopath Soc (pres, 74-75); Coun Agr Sci Technol. *Res:* Soilborne plant pathogens and soil microbiology. *Mailing Add:* 680 Vine St West Lafayette IN 47906

GREEN, RAY CHARLES, chemical engineering, for more information see previous edition

GREEN, RAYNA DIANE, ETHNOSCIENCE, THIRD WORLD SCIENTIFIC DEVELOPMENT. *Current Pos:* ASSOC AM HIST, DIV SCI & TECHNOL, SMITHSONIAN INST, 83-; DIR, AM INDIA PROG, NAT MUS AM HIST, 86- *Personal Data:* b Dallas, Tex, July 18, 42. *Educ:* Southern Methodist Univ, BA, 63, MA, 66; Ind Univ, PhD(Am studies), 73. *Prof Exp:* Prof folklore, Univ Ark, 71-72 & Univ Mass, 72-75; dir, Proj Native Am Sci, AAAS, 75-79; prof native Am studies & dir, Native Am Sci Resource Ctr, Dartmouth Col, 79-83, prof, 80-84. *Concurrent Pos:* Res fel, Smithsonian Inst, 70-71; planner, US Dept Energy, 76-80 & NIH & NSF, 77-79; res fel, Fund Improv Post-Sec Educ, 77-81; res fel, Ford Found-NRC, 83-84; mem bd, Indian Law Resource Ctr, 84- *Mem:* Am Indian Sci & Eng Soc; Soc Advan Chicano & Native Am Scientists; AAAS; Soc Ethnobot; Am Folklore Soc (pres, 86); Am Anthrop Asn. *Res:* Native American scientific and technical traditions, including ethnoscience, ethnobotany, ethnomedicine; native American scientific and technical development, energy, agriculture, medicine; philosophy of non-Western scientific traditions. *Mailing Add:* 814 G St SE Washington DC 20003

GREEN, RICHARD, PSYCHIATRY, LAW. *Current Pos:* from asst prof to assoc prof, 68-74, PROF PSYCHIAT, STATE UNIV NY, STONY BROOK, 74- *Personal Data:* b Brooklyn, NY, June 6, 36; m 94, Melissa Hines; c Adam H. *Educ:* Syracuse Univ, AB, 57; Johns Hopkins Univ, MD, 61. *Prof Exp:* Resident, Univ Calif, Los Angeles, 62-64; clin assoc, NIMH, 64-66; fel, Maudsley Hosp, 66-67; prof psychiat, State Univ NY, Stony Brook, 74-86. *Concurrent Pos:* Prin investr, NIMH res grants, 68-81, mem, study sect appl res, 74-78; res scientist develop award, NIMH, 68-73; psychiat sabbatical fel, Cambridge Univ, 80-81; fel, Ctr Adv Study Behav Sci, Stanford, 82-83; Fulbright scholar, 92. *Mem:* Am Psychiat Asn; Soc Sci Study Sex (pres, 76-78); Int Acad Sex Res (pres, 75); Psychiat Res Soc; World Asn Sexology (secy, 78). *Res:* Psychosexual development in children; environmental and biological influences; legal aspects of sexual behavior. *Mailing Add:* Charing Cross Hosp London W68RF England

GREEN, RICHARD D, PHARMACOLOGY. *Current Pos:* PROF PHARMACOL, DEPT PHARMACOL, SCH MED, UNIV ILL, 86- *Personal Data:* b Trenton, NY, Mar 1, 40. *Educ:* Philadelphia Col, BS, 61; Univ Minn, PhD(pharmacol), 65. *Mem:* Pharmacol Soc. *Mailing Add:* Dept Pharmacol Univ Ill Sch 835 S Wolcott Ave M/C 868 Chicago IL 60680

GREEN, RICHARD E, SOIL PHYSICS. *Current Pos:* asst agronomist, Maui Br, 62-65, assoc prof, 65-73, PROF SOIL SCI, MANOA CAMPUS, UNIV HAWAII, 73- *Personal Data:* b Seward, Nebr, Mar 23, 31; m 55; c 4. *Educ:* Colo State Univ, BS, 53; Univ Nebr, MS, 57; Iowa State Univ, PhD(soil mgt), 62. *Prof Exp:* Instr soil sci, Univ Nebr, 57-58. *Mem:* Am Soc Agron; Soil Sci Soc Am. *Res:* Behavior of pesticides in soils and water; water quality. *Mailing Add:* Dept Agron Univ Hawaii Manoa 1910 E West Rd Sherman Lab Rm 101 Honolulu HI 96822

GREEN, RICHARD H, microbiology, for more information see previous edition

GREEN, RICHARD JAMES, RESEARCH & DEVELOPMENT MANAGEMENT, SCIENCE POLICY. *Current Pos:* RETIRED. *Personal Data:* b Newark, NJ, Apr 15, 28; m 57, Patricia Higgins; c John A, Alice E, Richard J & Patricia T. *Educ:* Col Holy Cross, BS, 49; Fordham Univ, MS, 55; Harvard Bus Sch, AMP, 77. *Honors & Awards:* Excep Sci Achievement Award, NASA, 69; Commendation award, AEC, 70; Meritorious Serv award, NSF, 77; President's Meritorious Serv Achievement Award, US Govt, 87. *Prof Exp:* Eng positions, Pratt & Whitney Aircraft & Socony Mobil Oil Co, 55-61; tech asst to assoc adminr & mgr, Apollo Lunar Surface Exp Prog, NASA, 61-70; exec asst, NSF, 70-72, dep asst dir appl res, 72-79; assoc dir res, Presidential Appointee, Fed Emergency Mgt Agency, 79-81; asst dir, Sci Technol & Int Affairs, NSF, 82-89, dir, Res Facil Prog, 89-91; res prof & dir spec proj, Colo Sch Mines & Univ Wyo, 92-95; consult, 96- *Mem:* AAAS. *Res:* Aerospace engineering; general management; international science and technology; solar and geothermal energy; advanced high temperature lubricants; lunar and planetary exploration; nuclear systems. *Mailing Add:* 3304 Carpenter St SE Washington DC 20020. *Fax:* 202-584-7605; *E-Mail:* rjgreensr@aol.com

GREEN, RICHARD STEDMAN, SANITARY ENGINEERING. *Current Pos:* CONSULT ENGR, 73- *Personal Data:* b Somerville, Mass, Mar 2, 14; wid; c 3. *Educ:* Harvard Univ, SB, 36, SM, 37; Am Acad Environ Engrs, dipl. *Honors & Awards:* William B Hatfield Award, Water Pollution Control Fedn, 70. *Prof Exp:* Sr sanit eng aide, Mass Dept Pub Health, 37-38; supt water purification, Panama Canal, 38-40; res assoc, Sch Med, Univ Pa, 40-41; sanit engr, USPHS, Md , Wash & Maine, 41-42; dir div pub health eng, Dept Health, Alaska, 42-46; sanit engr dir, hq, Washington, DC, 46-67; dir, Off Environ Health, Indian Health Serv, Md, 67-71; asst surg gen & chief eng officer, Washington, DC, 71-73. *Mem:* Fel Am Soc Civil Engrs; fel Am Pub Health Asn; Am Water Works Asn; Am Acad Environ Engrs (pres, 76, treas, 81-83); Water Pollution Control Fedn. *Res:* Water quality control. *Mailing Add:* 9209 E Parkhill Dr Bethesda MD 20814

GREEN, ROBERT A, INTERNAL MEDICINE. *Current Pos:* RETIRED. *Personal Data:* b Brooklyn, NY, May 13, 25; m 51; c 5. *Educ:* Univ Ill, BS, 46, MD, 48. *Prof Exp:* Chief tuberc sect, Talihina Med Ctr, Okla, 52-54; asst chief pulmonary dis sect, Vet Admin Hosp, Bronx, NY, 54-58; assoc prof, Med Sch, Univ Mich, Ann Arbor, 63-70, assoc dean student affairs, 68-74, assoc dean, 74-77, prof internal med, 70-95. *Concurrent Pos:* Chief, Pulmonary Dis Sect, Vet Admin Hosp, Ann Arbor, 58-72, staff physician, 78- *Mem:* Am Thoracic Soc. *Res:* Pulmonary diseases; tuberculosis; unclassified mycobacterial disease; lung cancer. *Mailing Add:* 2125 Nature Cove Ct Ann Arbor MI 48104

GREEN, ROBERT BENNETT, LASER SPECTROSCOPY. *Current Pos:* asst prof, 79-81, ASSOC PROF ANALYTICAL CHEM, DEPT CHEM, UNIV ARK, 81- *Personal Data:* b Coffeyville, Kans, Dec 22, 43; m 76. *Educ:* Okla State Univ, BS, 66; Ohio Univ, PhD(analytical chem), 74. *Prof Exp:* Process chemist, Monsanto Co, 66-68; analytical chemist, Jefferson Chem Co, Inc, 68-70; res assoc, Nat Bur Stand, 74-76; asst prof analytical chem, Dept Chem, WVa Univ, 76-79. *Concurrent Pos:* Prin investr, Laser Intra-Cavity Detection for Gas Chromatography, Dept Interior, 80-82 & Laser Enhanced Ionization Spectrometry, NSF, 81-84. *Mem:* Sigma Xi; Soc Appl Spectros; Am Chem Soc. *Res:* Applications of lasers to analytical chemistry: laser enchanced ionization, optogalvanic, intra-cavity absorption, atomic and molecular fluorescence. *Mailing Add:* Asn Western Univ 723 The Pkwy Suite 100 Richland WA 99352-4234

GREEN, ROBERT CASTLEMAN, BEHAVIORAL NEUROLOGY. *Current Pos:* PROF, COL HEALTH SCI, GA STATE UNIV, 96- *Personal Data:* m, Sally E McNagny; c Nathaniel, Courtney & Lachlan. *Educ:* Amherst Col, BA, 76; Univ Va Med Sch, MD, 80. *Prof Exp:* Res fel neurol, Harvard Med Sch, 85-87, instr neurol, 87-88; asst/assoc prof neurol, Emory Univ Sch Med, 88-96. *Concurrent Pos:* Chief neurol, Wesley Woods Ctr, 91-96; co-prin investr, Nat Intel Authority, 91-94, prin investr, 92-95. *Mem:* Am Acad Neurol; Soc Neurosci; Am Epilepsy Soc; Behav Neurol Soc; Am Neuropsychiat Asn. *Res:* Clinical features and neurobiologic mechanisms of neurobehavioral disorders. *Mailing Add:* 1 Park Pl Eighth Floor Atlanta GA 30303. *Fax:* 404-651-0320; *E-Mail:* rcgreen@gsu.edu

GREEN, ROBERT E(DWARD), JR, MATERIALS SCIENCE, NONDESTRUCTIVE EVALUATION. *Current Pos:* from asst prof to assoc prof, Mech Dept, Johns Hopkins Univ, 60-70, prof mech & mat sci & chmn dept, 70-73, chmn dept, 80-85, & 91-93, PROF MAT SCI & ENG, JOHNS HOPKINS UNIV, 70-, DIR CTR NONDESTRUCTIVE EVAL, 85- *Personal Data:* b Clifton Forge, Va, Jan 17, 32; m 62, Sydney Truitt; c Kirsten (Adair) & Heather (Scott). *Educ:* Col William & Mary, BS, 53; Brown Univ, ScM, 56, PhD(metal physics), 59. *Honors & Awards:* Mehl Honor Lectr Award, Am Soc Nondestructive Testing, Lester Honor Lect Award, Gold Medal. *Prof Exp:* Physicist, Underwater Explosions Res Div, Norfolk Naval Shipyard, 59; Fulbright grant metal physics, Aachen Tech Univ, 59-60. *Concurrent Pos:* Ford Found residency as sr engr, Radio Corp Am, Pa, 66-67; consult, Orn Army Ballistic Res Labs, 73-74 & Johns Hopkins Appl Physics Lab, 77-79; physicist, Nat Bur Stand, 74-80; prog mgr, Defense Advan Res Off, 80-81. *Mem:* Acoust Soc Am; Am Phys Soc; fel Am Soc Metals Int; fel Am Soc Nondestructive Testing; Nat Mat Adv Bd; Am Inst Mining Metall Petrol Engrs. *Res:* Elasticity; plasticity; crystal growth and orientation; x-ray diffraction; electrooptical systems; linear and non-linear elastic waves; light-sound interactions; ultrasonic attenuation; fatigue; acoustic emission; nondestructive testing; residual stress; high-power ultrasonics composites; polymers; biomaterials. *Mailing Add:* Dept Mat Sci & Eng Johns Hopkins Univ Baltimore MD 21218. *Fax:* 410-516-5293; *E-Mail:* robert.green@jhu.edu

GREEN, ROBERT I, UNIT OPERATIONS IN PARTICULATE SOLIDS PROCESSING & HANDLING. *Current Pos:* PRES MKT, ROBERT I GREEN ASSOCS, 83- *Personal Data:* b New York, NY, May 7, 29; m 57; c 2. *Educ:* Clarkson Univ, BChE, 50; Pa State Univ, MS, 52. *Prof Exp:* Process/proj engr, Singmaster & Breyer, 55-59; tech eng salesman, Vibro Dynamics Co, 59-73; pres, E-V Systs, Inc, 73-83. *Concurrent Pos:* Lectr, NJ Ctr Prof Advan, 82-85. *Mem:* Com Develop Asn; NY Acad Sci; Asn Consult Chemists & Chem Engrs; Am Chem Soc; Am Inst Chem Engrs; AAAS. *Res:* International marketing of chemical processes and process equipment; project management. *Mailing Add:* 168 E 74th St New York NY 10021. *Fax:* 201-438-6102

GREEN, ROBERT LAMAR, agricultural engineering; deceased, see previous edition for last biography

GREEN, ROBERT LEE, JR, PSYCHIATRY. *Current Pos:* RETIRED. *Personal Data:* b Fairfield, Ala, Aug 17, 21; div; c 2. *Educ:* Univ Ala, BS, 43; Hahnemann Med Col, MD, 46. *Prof Exp:* Intern, Jeff-Hillman Hosp, Birmingham, Ala, 46-47; resident obstet & gynec, Carraway Methodist, De Paul & St Vincent's Hosp, 49-52; pvt pract, Ala, 52-53; staff psychiatrist, Kennedy Vet Admin Hosp, Memphis, Tenn, 53, staff psychiatrist, Phys Med & Rehab Serv, 54-55, actg chief serv, 55-56; chief, Dept Psychiat, Vet Admin Hosp, Durham, 61-74, chief of staff, 72-80; resident psychiatrist, Med Ctr, Duke Univ, 56-59, from instr to prof psychiat, 59-86. *Concurrent Pos:* Clin investr, Vet Admin, 59-60, mem, Cent Off Res Comt, 63-65; lectr serv training prog, Cherry State Hosp, Goldsboro, 64-66; from resident psychiatrist to staff psychiatrist, Vet Admin Hosp, Durham, 56-61; med dir, Holly Hills Hosp, 80-90. *Mem:* AMA; Am Psychiat Asn; Acad Psychosom Med; Am Electroencephalographic Soc; Am Col Psychiat. *Res:* Electroencephalography; psychophysiology; neurophysiology. *Mailing Add:* 4100 Chapel Hill Rd Durham NC 27707

GREEN, ROBERT PATRICK, PULP & PAPER TECHNOLOGY. *Current Pos:* process sales engr, 73-78, mkt mgr, 78-83, SR ASSOC, MEAD CHEM SYSTS, 83- *Personal Data:* b New York, NY, Mar 17, 25; m 47; c 4. *Educ:* Syracuse Univ, BS, 49; Miami Univ, MBA, 59. *Prof Exp:* Res chemist pulp res & develop, Champion Papers, Inc, 49-54, pilot plant engr, 54-58, group leader, 58-59, mgr, 59-61; res chemist, Kimberly-Clark Corp, 61-62, mgr pulp process controls, 62-71, sr develop engr, 71-73. *Mem:* Fel Tech Asn Pulp & Paper Indust; Can Pulp & Paper Asn. *Res:* Pulping and bleaching, including wood and agricultural fibers; end use of pulp fibers; research management. *Mailing Add:* 259 Constitution Dr Chillicothe OH 45601

GREEN, ROBERT WOOD, cryogenics, optics; deceased, see previous edition for last biography

GREEN, ROGER HARRISON, ECOLOGY. *Current Pos:* assoc prof zool, 77-85, PROF ZOOL, UNIV WESTERN ONT, 85- *Personal Data:* b New York, NY, June 22, 39; c 3. *Educ:* Col William & Mary, BS, 61; Cornell Univ, PhD(zool), 65. *Prof Exp:* Fulbright fel, Dept Zool, Univ Queensland, 65-66; resident ecologist, Syst-Ecol Prog, Marine Biol Lab, Woods Hole, 66-68; asst prof zool, Univ Man, 68-71, assoc prof, 71-76; adj prof biol, City Col New York, & vis prof biol, Upsala Col, 76-77. *Concurrent Pos:* Consult, Can Dept Environ, Can Dept Indian & Northern Affairs, Acad Natural Sci Philadelphia, Ont Govt Ministries, Sask Res Coun, US Environ Protection Serv, US Minerals Mgt Serv, Battelle Marine Res, Du Pont de Nemours, Smithsonian Tropical Res Inst, Seakem Oceanog, Booth Aquatic Res Inc & Gartner-Lee Ltd; vis prof, City Col, New York, 76, Upsala Col, NJ, 76-77 & Nat Univ Singapore, 82-83; comt mem, US Nat Res Coun, US Nat Oceanic & Atmospheric Admin; workshops organizer, UNESCO, Singapore, 85 & Philippines, 87 & Univ Auckland, NZ, 85 & 87; ed, Can J Fisheries & Aquatic Sci, 86- *Mem:* Can Soc Zool; Ecol Soc Am; Biometric Soc. *Res:* Ecology of marine and fresh-water populations and communities; statistical methods in ecological research. *Mailing Add:* Dept Zool Univ Western Ont B&G Bldg London ON N6A 5B7 Can

GREEN, RONALD W, VETERINARY MEDICINE, RADIOLOGY. *Current Pos:* asst prof, 80-86, ASSOC PROF RADIOL, TEX A&M UNIV, 86- *Personal Data:* b Mexia, Tex, Nov 15, 48; m 70; c 2. *Educ:* Abilene Christian Univ, BS, 71; Tex A&M Univ, DVM, 74, MS, 77; Am Col Vet Radiol, dipl, 78. *Prof Exp:* Res assoc radiol, Tex A&M Univ, 74-75, vet clin assoc, 75-77; asst prof biol, Ohio State Univ, 77-80, staff radiologist, Vet Teaching Hosp, 77-80. *Concurrent Pos:* Consult radiologist, Acres North Animal Hosp, San Antonio, Tex, 75-, Med Col, Ohio State Univ, 77-, Oak Hills Vet Hosp, San Antonio, Tex & Animal Med Clin, Columbus, Ohio, 78- *Mem:* Am Vet Med Asn; Am Col Vet Radiol; Am Animal Hosp Asn; Am Asn Vet Clinicians. *Res:* Radiation therapy and oncology; nuclear medicine, tumor scanning and clinical imaging; diagnostic radiology. *Mailing Add:* Tex A&M Col Vet Med College Station TX 77843-4475

GREEN, SAUL, BIOCHEMISTRY, IMMUNOLOGY. *Current Pos:* RETIRED. *Personal Data:* b New York, NY, Jan 8, 25. *Educ:* City Col New York, BS, 48; Univ Iowa, MS, 50, PhD(biochem), 52. *Prof Exp:* Instr biochem, Univ Va, 52-54; res assoc, Dept Med, Med Col, Cornell Univ, 54-59; from asst mem to assoc mem, Sloan-Kettering Inst, 59-61, assoc, 61-67; asst prof biochem, Sloan-Kettering Div Grad Sch Med Sci, Cornell Univ, 62-67, assoc prof, 67-; assoc mem, Sloan-Kettering Inst, 67-; dir res & develop, US Bio Prod, Inc, 82-85; sci dir, Philadelphia Biologics, 85-88; pres, Zol Consult, Sci Dir, Emprise, Inc, 88-91. *Concurrent Pos:* NIH res career develop award, 63; dir clin chem lab, Univ Va Hosp, 52-54; lectr, City Col NY, 56-59; vis prof, dept surg, Univ Va Hosp, 84-86. *Mem:* Am Soc Biol Chem; Am Asn Cancer Res; AAAS. *Res:* Isolation, characterization and mechanism of action of naturally occurring antitumor agents (TNF) (NHG) in serum and tissues of bacillus Calmette-Guerin vaccine or c parvum primed, endotoxin treated mice; science education in medical quackery. *Mailing Add:* ZOL Consults Inc 340 W 57th St Suite 85 New York NY 10019-3755

GREEN, SIDNEY, TOXICOLOGY. *Current Pos:* PHARMACOLOGIST, FOOD & DRUG ADMIN, 80- *Personal Data:* b New Orleans, La, Dec 12, 39; m 63; c 3. *Educ:* Dillard Univ, BA, 61; Howard Univ, PhD(pharmacol), 72. *Prof Exp:* Lab technician cancer chemother, Microbiol Assocs, Inc, 61-65; pharmacologist, Food & Drug Admin, 65-78; assoc prof pharmacol, Med Sch, Howard Univ, 78-79; pharmacologist, Environ Protection Agency, 79-80. *Concurrent Pos:* Adj assoc prof pharmacol, Howard Univ, 79- *Mem:* Soc Toxicol; Tissue Cult Asn; Environ Mutagen Soc; Soc Risk Analysis. *Res:* Mutagenic assay systems; toxicology of food additives; cancer chemotherapy; genetic effects of chemicals in mammals and cells in culture. *Mailing Add:* 5753 Desert View Dr La Jolla CA 92037-7241

GREEN, SIDNEY J, MECHANICAL ENGINEERING, MATERIALS SCIENCE. *Current Pos:* PRES, CHMN & CHIEF EXEC OFFICER, TERRA TEK, INC, SALT LAKE CITY, 70- *Personal Data:* b Rolla, Mo, Nov 17, 37; m 62; c 4. *Educ:* Univ Mo, Rolla, BS, 59; Univ Pittsburgh, MS, 60. *Honors & Awards:* Gold Medallion Award, Am Soc Mech Engrs, 80; Lazan Award, Soc Exp Mech, 83. *Prof Exp:* Instr, Univ Mo, 58-59; sr engr, Westinghouse, Pa, 59-62 & Gen Motors Defense Res Lab, Calif, 64-67; head develop staff, Dept Mfg, Gen Motors Tech Ctr, Mich, 67-70. *Concurrent Pos:* Mem, Geol Mt Property Comt, 72-74; chmn, NSF Thermal-mech Fragmentation Rock Prog Rev Comt & Rock Mech Subcomt, Petrol Div, Am Soc Mech Engrs, 74-75; vchmn, Paper Comt, Exp Mech, 74-76; adj prof mech eng, Univ Utah, 74-; consult, Drilling Technol Comt, Nat Acad Eng, 75-76; chmn, Int Comt Rock Mech, Nat Acad Sci, 75-; chmn, Panel Limitations Imposed by Rock Mech on Energy Resource Recovery, Nat Acad Sci, 76 & Gordon Res Conf, 76-78; US alt & deleg, Int Soc Rock Mech, Stockholm, Rio de Janeiro & Montreux, Switz, 77-79; dir, Native Plants, Inc, Utah, 77- & Plant Resources Inst, Inc, Utah, 78-; guest lectr, Oxford Univ & Imp Col, London, 78; mem, Drilling, Offshore & Arctic Workshop, Dept Energy, 81. *Mem:* Nat Acad Eng; Soc Exp Stress Analysis; Geothermal Resources Coun; Am Underground Space Asn; Am Soc Mech Engrs. *Res:* Materials science, geoscience; technological innovation, technology based business start-up and development, and the management and financing of such businesses; international business development, marketing and foreign trade; author or coauthor of over 40 papers and numerous reports; granted several patents. *Mailing Add:* 400 Wakara Way Salt Lake City UT 84108. *Fax:* 801-584-2406; *E-Mail:* terratek@terratek.com

GREEN, STANLEY J(OSEPH), CHEMICAL ENGINEERING. *Current Pos:* RETIRED. *Personal Data:* b New York, NY, Mar 11, 20; m 51, Alice Denenholz; c David, Douglas & Ron. *Educ:* City Col New York, BChE, 40; Drexel Inst, MS, 53; Univ Pittsburgh, PhD(chem eng), 68. *Honors & Awards:* Centennial Medallion, Am Soc Mech Engrs, 80; Donald Q Kern Award, Am Inst Chem Engrs, 85. *Prof Exp:* Inspector, US CEngr, NY, 41; concrete engr, Sci Concrete Serv Corp, 41-42; from jr chem engr to assoc chem engr, US Bur Mines, Md, 42-45; chem engr, Fercleve Corp, Oak Ridge, 45 & Acme Coppersmithing & Mach Co, 45-54; mgr thermal & hydraul eng sect, Bettis Atomic Power Lab, Westinghouse Elec Corp, 55-74, mgr, reactor develop & analysis, 74-77; sr prog mgr, Elec Power Res Inst, 77-79, dir, Steam Generator Proj Off, 79-91. *Mem:* Fel Am Soc Mech Engrs; Am Inst Chem Engrs. *Res:* Phase rule chemistry applied to separation of compounds from solution by evaporation and crystallization; heterogeneous kinetics; production of alcohol from potatoes; batch solvent extraction of oil seeds; design chemical process equipment; liquid-vapor equilibrium; heat transfer and fluid flow research and design; single phase and two phase heat transfer and pressure drop; thermal, hydraulics, chemistry and materials of pressurized water nuclear steam generators. *Mailing Add:* 3348 Middlefield Rd Palo Alto CA 94306

GREEN, TERRY C, ELECTRICAL ENGINEERING, APPLIED PHYSICS. *Current Pos:* res engr, Dept Electronics & Elec Eng, Southwest Res Inst, 62-65, sr res engr, Dept Appl Electromagnetics, 65-71, mgr intercept & direction finding res, 71-74, asst dir, Electromagnetics Div, 74-75, DIR, DEPT ELECTROMAGNETIC ENG, ELECTROMAGNETICS DIV, SOUTHWEST RES INST, 75- *Personal Data:* b Abilene, Tex, Nov 4, 35; m 63; c 2. *Educ:* Univ Tex, BSEE, 58; Trinity Univ, Tex, MS, 69. *Prof Exp:* Design engr, Chance Vought Aircraft Co, Tex, 58; capt, Electronic Warfare, USAF, 58-62. *Mem:* Inst Elec & Electronics Engrs; Sigma Xi. *Res:* Design and development of low frequency through ultra high frequency direction finding antennas and associated electronics subsystems, including ferrite core and air core quadrupole and dipole mode antennas, interferometer antenna arrays, ring goniometers, low-noise preamplifiers and antenna control circuits; electromagnetic polarization measurements and analysis in the high frequency and very high frequency range including measurements on the non-thermal high frequency radiation from the planet Jupiter. *Mailing Add:* Automation & Data Syst Southwest Res Inst 8500 Culebra Drawer 28510 San Antonio TX 78284

GREEN, THEODORE, III, PHYSICAL OCEANOGRAPHY, FLUID MECHANICS. *Current Pos:* PROF, VA INST MARINE SCI, 96- *Personal Data:* b Buffalo, NY, Mar 7, 38; m 65, 96, Margann Frautzen; c Theodore & Wendelin. *Educ:* Amherst Col, AB, 59; Stanford Univ, MS, 61, PhD(eng mech), 65. *Prof Exp:* Asst prof oceanog, Naval Postgrad Sch, 65-69; assoc prof meteorol & civil eng, Univ Wis-Madison, 69-72, prof atmospheric & oceanic sci & civil & environ eng, 72-96. *Mem:* AAAS; Am Geophys Union; Int Asn Great Lakes Res. *Res:* Convection; coastal engineering; small-scale air-sea interaction; lake and estuary circulations; remote sensing; water waves; groundwater; benthic boundary layers. *Mailing Add:* Va Inst Marine Sci PO Box 1346 Gloucester Point VA 23062

GREEN, THEODORE JAMES, MICROBIOLOGY. *Current Pos:* ASSOC PROF VET MICROBIOL, UNIV MO, COLUMBIA, 80- *Personal Data:* b North Adams, Mass, Oct 29, 35. *Educ:* Cornell Univ, BS, 57; Ohio State Univ, MS, 75, PhD(microbiol), 77. *Prof Exp:* Res asst pharmacol, Sterling Winthrop Res Inst, 57-66, res assoc, 66-68; head animal care & res pharm, Warren-Teed Pharmaceut, Div Rohm & Haas Chem, 68-74; sr res scientist immunol, Parke-Davis Co, Div Warner-Lambert, 77-80. *Concurrent Pos:* Prin investr, Malaria Proj, Agency Int Develop, 78-87. *Mem:* Am Soc Trop Med & Hyg; Am Soc Parasitologists; NY Acad Sci; AAAS; Am Soc Microbiol. *Res:* Immunoparasitology of protozoa and helminthis including isolation and characterization of antigens, immune mechanisms, serology and vaccination studies; diagnosis. *Mailing Add:* Dept Microbiol Univ Mo Columbia Med Sch 1 Hospital Dr Columbia MO 65201-5276

GREEN, THOM HENNING, PETROLEUM GEOLOGY. *Current Pos:* CONSULT & PETROL EXPLOR RES, 87- *Personal Data:* b Steamboat Springs, Colo, Sept 1, 15; m 42, 60; c 3. *Educ:* Univ Colo, BA, 39; Univ Calif, Los Angeles, cert, 43. *Prof Exp:* Geophysicist, Shell Oil Co, 39-43, geologist, 46-48; from dist geologist to div geologist, Sunray Oil Corp, 48-52; chief geologist, Fargo Oils, Ltd, 52-56; consult geologist, 56-60; explor mgr, Wilcox Explor Co, 60-87. *Mem:* Am Asn Petrol Geol. *Res:* Structural geology; petroleum reservoir fluid mechanics as related to migration and accumulation. *Mailing Add:* 2749 S Elder Broken Arrow OK 74012

GREEN, THOMAS ALLEN, ALKALI HALIDES, AUGER THEORY. *Current Pos:* mem staff, Lab, 63-69, supvr div 5261 atomic & molecular processes theory, 69-76, MEM STAFF LAB, SANDIA CORP, 76- *Personal Data:* b Cleveland, Ohio, Mar 21, 25; m 49, 73; c 4. *Educ:* Case Inst Technol, BS, 47; Univ Geneva, ScD(physics), 51. *Prof Exp:* Asst, Univ Geneva, 49-50; mem theoret staff, Radiation Lab, Univ Calif, 51; assoc physics, Columbia Univ, 51-53; from asst prof to assoc prof, Wesleyan Univ, 53-64. *Mem:* Fel Am Phys Soc; Sigma Xi. *Res:* Solid state theory. *Mailing Add:* 5063 Arroyo Chamisa Rd NE Albuqueque NM 87111-3723

GREEN, THOMAS L, FORESTRY. *Current Pos:* URBAN FORESTRY PROF, WESTERN ILL UNIV, 93- *Personal Data:* b Burlington, Iowa, Jan 7, 47; m 69, Diana L George; c Mark & Benjamin. *Educ:* Western Ill Univ, BS, 69, MS, 71; Iowa State Univ, PhD(plant path), 79. *Prof Exp:* Teacher sci, Iowa Sch Dist, Burlington, 71-72; teaching grad asst, plant path, Iowa State Univ, Ames, 76-78; arborist, City Burlington, Iowa, 79-80; res plant pathologist, Morton Arboretum, Lisle, Ill, 80-93. *Concurrent Pos:* Second lt, chem officer, Chem, Biol & Radiol Defense, 49th ADA Unit, Ft Lawton, Wash, 72-74; exten grad asst, plant path coop exten, Iowa State Univ, Ames, 74-76; consult, tree assessment & inventory, 81- *Mem:* Int Soc Arboricult; Int Ornamental Crabapple Soc; Am Phylopath Soc. *Res:* National crabapple evaluation program; studying the effects of mulch on the growth of woody plants. *Mailing Add:* Dept Agr Western Ill Univ 900 W Adams St Macomb IL 61455-1396. *Fax:* 309-298-2280

GREEN, VERNON ALBERT, BIOCHEMICAL PHARMACOLOGY. *Current Pos:* RETIRED. *Personal Data:* b McClain County, Okla, Apr 13, 21; m 49; c 2. *Educ:* Univ Okla, BS, 49, MS, 50; Univ Tex, PhD(pharmacol), 60. *Prof Exp:* Instr pharm, Univ Okla, 49-50; from instr to asst prof pharmacol, Univ Tex, 50-62; prof pharmacol, Univ Mo, Kansas City, 62-88; toxicologist, Children's Mercy Hosp, 68-88. *Mem:* AAAS; Am Pharmaceut Asn; Am Soc Pharmacol & Therapeut; Am Acad Clin Toxicol; Soc Toxicol. *Res:* Pharmacodynamics; mechanisms of drug absorption and activity; cholinesterase activity in cellular permeability. *Mailing Add:* 18303 E 231st St Harrisonville MO 64701

GREEN, VICTOR EUGENE, JR, FIELD CROPS. *Current Pos:* from asst agronomist to assoc agronomist, Everglades Exp Sta, 51-65, agronomist, 65-, EMER PROF AGRON, UNIV FLA, 87- *Personal Data:* b De Ridder, La, Sept 3, 22; m 45; c 2. *Educ:* La State Univ, BS, 47, MS, 48; Purdue Univ, PhD(soil sci), 51. *Prof Exp:* Asst agronomist, Agr Exp Sta, La, 47-49; emer prof, Agron, 87. *Concurrent Pos:* Adv, AID-Univ Fla Contract, Costa Rican Govt, 65-68; curric adv, Sch Agr, Jamaica, WI, 70; chief agr officer, Transp Feasibility Surv for Panama, Int Bank for Reconstruction & Develop, 74, Cape Verde, 79 & Bahamas, 82. *Mem:* Am Soc Agron; Soil Sci Soc Am; Int Soc Soil Sci; Latin Am Railways Asn; Am Soc Hort Sci. *Res:* Organic soils; tropical crops including rice, aloe, dioscorea, sugarcane and coffee; corn; sorghum; millets; sunflower; rural development and crop campaigns in tropical areas. *Mailing Add:* 3915 SW Third Ave Gainesville FL 32607-2709

GREEN, WALTER L(UTHER), ELECTRICAL & SYSTEMS ENGINEERING. *Current Pos:* prof, 68-83, head, Dept Elec Eng, 83-88, PROF ELEC ENG, UNIV TENN, KNOXVILLE, 88- *Personal Data:* b Roanoke Rapids, NC, Mar 13, 34; m 56; c David & Derrick. *Educ:* Auburn Univ, BS, 57, MS, 60; Tex A&M Univ, PhD(elec eng), 65. *Prof Exp:* Instr elec eng, Auburn Univ, 58-61; staff engr, Missile Systs Proj Eng, Sandia Corp, NMex, 61-62; instr elec eng, Tex A&M Univ, 62-65; assoc prof, Miss State Univ, 65-66; adv engr, Fed Systs Div, IBM Corp, Ala, 66-68. *Concurrent Pos:* Consult, Nuclear Div, Union Carbide Corp, Oak Ridge, Tenn, 69- & IBM, 74- *Mem:* Sr mem Inst Elec & Electronics Engrs; Am Soc Eng Educ; Instrument Soc Am. *Res:* Control system theory and application, including guidance and control of space vehicles, multivariable and machine-tooling control systems; process control; system simulation; discret signal processing. *Mailing Add:* Dept Elec Eng Univ Tenn Knoxville TN 37996

GREEN, WILLIAM LOHR, MATHEMATICAL ANALYSIS. *Current Pos:* from asst prof to assoc prof, 77-91, coordr Undergrad Math Progs, 86-88, COORDR GRAD MATH PROGS, GA INST TECHNOL, 91-, PROF MATH, 91- *Personal Data:* b Harrisonburg, Va, May 1, 45; m 84, Antoinette J Early. *Educ:* Yale Univ, BA, 67; Univ Pa, MA, 70, PhD(math), 73. *Prof Exp:* Vis lectr math, Inst Math, Univ Oslo, 72-74; asst prof, Ga Inst Technol, 74-75; asst prof, Williams Col, 75-77. *Concurrent Pos:* Vis assoc prof, Tulane Univ, 81. *Mem:* Am Mat Soc; Mat Asn Am; Soc Lit & Sci. *Res:* Automorphisms of operator algebras and their relations to topological dynamics and to ergodic theory; applications of Banach algebras to problems in Banach spaces, systems theory and circuits; operator means. *Mailing Add:* Sch Math Ga Inst Technol Atlanta GA 30332-0160. *Fax:* 404-894-4409; *E-Mail:* william.green@math.gatech.edu

GREEN, WILLIAM ROBERT, IMMUNOLOGY, MICROBIOLOGY. *Current Pos:* asst prof, 83-85, assoc prof microbiol, 85-90, PROF, DARTMOUTH MED SCH, 90- *Personal Data:* b Toledo, Ohio, Jan 25, 50; m 71, Kathy Hutchinson; c Andrea & Matthew. *Educ:* Univ Mich, BS, 72; Case Western Reserve Univ, PhD(microbiol), 77. *Prof Exp:* Fel, Med Sch, Johns Hopkins Univ, 77-78; fel immunol, Fred Hutchinson Cancer Res Ctr, 78-79, assoc basic immunol, 79-80, asst mem basic immunol, 80-83; res asst prof microbiol, Univ Wash, 81-83. *Concurrent Pos:* Fel, Nat Cancer Inst, 77-79. *Mem:* Am Asn Immunologists; Am Soc Microbiol. *Res:* Characterization of the generation, regulation, and specificity of cytolytic murine T lymphocytes, especially those that arise in response to retrovirus induced tumors and as related to mouse AIDS (MAIDS); mechanism of enhancement of histocompatibility antigen expression by interferon. *Mailing Add:* Dept Microbiol Dartmouth Med Sch 1 Medical Center Dr Lebanon NH 03756. *Fax:* 603-650-6223

GREEN, WILLIAM WARDEN, AUDIOLOGY. *Current Pos:* assoc prof pediat, 73, assoc prof spec educ, 73-79, DIR CLIN COMMUN DIS, UNIV KY, 73-, PROF NEUROL, PEDIAT & SPEC EDUC, 79- *Personal Data:* b Akron, Ohio, Mar 12, 39; m 63; c 3. *Educ:* Kent State Univ, BS, 62, MA, 64; Case Western Res Univ, PhD(audiol), 70. *Prof Exp:* From instr to asst prof audiol, Kent State Univ, 64-70. *Concurrent Pos:* Consult, Vet Admin Hosp, 70- & Ky Dept Labor & Educ, 72-; consult, Cardinal Hill Hosp, 81- *Mem:* Am Speech & Hearing Asn; fel Am Speech Lang & Hearing Asn; Am Auditory Soc. *Res:* Clinical audiology; pediatric audiology; noise induced hearing loss. *Mailing Add:* 543 Laketower Dr Lexington KY 40502

GREENAWAY, FREDERICK THOMAS, BIOINORGANIC CHEMISTRY, MAGNETIC RESONANCE. *Current Pos:* from asst prof to assoc prof, Clark Univ, 80-93, chair, 90-94, assoc provost, 95-97, PROF CHEM, CLARK UNIV, 93-, PROVOST, 97- *Personal Data:* b Rakaia, NZ, Aug 18, 47. *Educ:* Univ Canterbury, NZ, BSc, 69, PhD(chem), 73. *Prof Exp:* Res assoc chem, Mich State Univ, 73-74; res assoc, Syracuse Univ, 74-77, vis asst prof, 77-80. *Concurrent Pos:* Vis scientist, Boston Univ Sch Med, 87-88. *Mem:* Am Chem Soc; Int Elec Pressure Regulator Soc; Int Soc Magnetic Resonance. *Res:* Bioinorganic chemistry with special emphasis on metal-drug interactions; structural studies of metalloenzymes; magnetic resonance spectroscopy of transition metal compounds. *Mailing Add:* Dept Chem Clark Univ Worcester MA 01610-1477. *Fax:* 508-793-8861; *E-Mail:* fgrenaway@clarku.edu

GREENAWAY, KEITH R(OGERS), ELECTRONICS. *Current Pos:* CONSULT, 94- *Personal Data:* b Woodville, Ont, Apr 8, 16; m 44; c 2. *Hon Degrees:* DMilS, Royal Rds Mil Col, Victoria, BC, 78. *Honors & Awards:* Pres Prize, Royal Meteorol Soc, 50; Thurlow Award, Inst Navig, 51; Can Trophy, McKee Trans-Can, 52; Massey Medal, Royal Can Geog Soc, 60. *Prof Exp:* Instr electronics & navig, Royal Can Air Force, 40-45, researcher, Navig Projs, US Navy, 45-46, USAF, 46-48, researcher arctic res, Defencee Res Bd, 48-54, lectr navig, Strategic Air Command, USAF, 54-56, adminstr, hqs, 56-59, commanding officer, Cent Navig Sch, Royal Can Air Force, 59-63, Royal Can Air Force Sta Clinton, 63-67, air adv to chief of air staff, Royal Malasian Air Force, 67-70; consult, Dept Indian Affairs & Northern Develop, 70-75 & 78-93, sr sci adv, 75-78. *Concurrent Pos:* Chmn, Comt Navig Res, Defense Res Bd, 52; chmn bd, Land-Sea Resources Can, 80-84; fel, Lady Eaton Col, Trent Univ, 83. *Mem:* Inst Navig; fel Arctic Inst; fel Can Aeronaut & Space Inst (pres, 77-78); assoc fel Can Meteorol & Oceanog Soc; fel Brit Inst Navig. *Res:* Aerial navigation, especially polar navigation; arctic research; seven publications. *Mailing Add:* 3099 Carling Ave Apt 402 Nepean ON K2H 5A6 Can

GREENBANK, MICK, SURFACE CHEMISTRY, ACTIVATED CARBON TECHNOLOGY. *Current Pos:* SURFACE CHEMIST, CALGON CARBON CORP, 80- *Personal Data:* b Wadsworth, Ohio, June 9, 56; m 92, Jeanine Dadey. *Educ:* Kent State Univ, BS, 77, PhD(phys chem), 80. *Mem:* Am Chem Soc; Sigma Xi. *Res:* Characterization of activated carbons and the effects of the activation process on those characteristics; theory and practice of performance predictions of adsorption on activated carbons. *Mailing Add:* 5010 Park Dr Monaca PA 15061. *Fax:* 412-787-4541; *E-Mail:* greenbank@calconcarbon.com

GREENBAUM, ELIAS, BIOLOGICAL ENERGY PRODUCTION, BIOELECTRONIC COMPOSITE MATERIALS. *Current Pos:* staff scientist, 79-81, GROUP LEADER, OAK RIDGE NAT LAB, 81- *Personal Data:* b Brooklyn, NY, May 12, 44; m 73; c 3. *Educ:* Brooklyn Col, BS, 65; Columbia Univ, MS, 67, PhD(physics), 70. *Prof Exp:* Res assoc, Univ Ill, Urbana-Champaign, 70-72; asst prof quantum mech, Rockefeller Univ, 72-77; staff scientist, Corp Res Lab, Union Carbide Corp, 77-79. *Concurrent Pos:* Adj assoc prof, Rockefeller Univ, 77-79; prin investr, Dept Energy, Washington, DC, 79-, Gas Res Inst, Chicago, 82- & Solar Energy Res Inst, Golden, Colo, 82-84; deleg, Int Solar Energy Soc, UN Conf on New & Renewable Sources Energy, Nairobi, Kenya, 81; Watkins vis prof, Wichita State Univ, 91; assoc ed, Biophys J, 89-; ed-in-chief, Int Series Basic & Appl Biol Physics, Am Inst Physics, 93-; vis scholar, Exchange Prog People Repub China, Nat Acad Scis. *Mem:* Fel Am Phys Soc; Am Chem Soc; Biophys Soc; fel AAAS; Sigma Xi. *Res:* Production of fuels and chemical feedstocks from renewable inorganic resources; fundamental studies of the physics and chemistry of photosynthesis; development of composite photocatalytic bioelectronic materials. *Mailing Add:* Chem Technol Div Oak Ridge Nat Lab PO Box 2008 Oak Ridge TN 37831-6194. *Fax:* 423-574-6843

GREENBAUM, IRA FRED, EVOLUTIONARY ZOOLOGY, CYTOGENETICS. *Current Pos:* From asst prof to assoc prof biol, 78-88, PROF BIOL & GENETICS, TEX A&M UNIV, 88- *Personal Data:* b Brooklyn, NY, Feb 27, 51; m 71; c 1. *Educ:* Hofstra Univ, BA, 73; Tex Tech Univ, MS, 75, PhD(zool), 78. *Concurrent Pos:* NSF grant, 76-78, 82-85 & 87-90; NIH grant, 80-85 & 87-90. *Mem:* Am Soc Mammalogists; Sigma Xi; Soc Syst Zoologists; AAAS; Soc Study Evolution. *Res:* Biochemical genetics; cytogenetics; evolutionary and systematic genetics; vertebrate speciation. *Mailing Add:* Biol Tex A&M Univ College Station TX 77843-0100

GREENBAUM, LOWELL MARVIN, PHARMACOLOGY, BIOCHEMISTRY. *Current Pos:* prof & chmn pharmacol, 79-85, VPRES RES & DEAN SCH GRAD STUDIES, MED COL GA, 85- *Personal Data:* b Brooklyn, NY, June 13, 28; m 50; c 3. *Educ:* City Col New York, BS, 49; Tufts Col, PhD(physiol), 53. *Prof Exp:* From instr to asst prof pharmacol, Col Med, State Univ NY Downstate Med Ctr, 56-64; from asst prof to prof pharmacol, Col Physicians & Surgeons, Columbia Univ, 64-79. *Concurrent Pos:* Am Cancer Soc res fel biochem, Sch Med, Yale Univ, 54-56; vis prof, Osaka Univ, 70; chmn pub affairs comt, Am Soc Pharmacol & Exp Therapeut, 71-78. *Mem:* AAAS; Am Soc Biol Chem; Am Soc Pharmacol & Exp Therapeut; Am Chem Soc; Am Col Clin Pharmacol; Sigma Xi; Asn Med Sch Pharmacologists (pres, 84-86). *Res:* Intracellular proteinases; pharmacologically active polypeptides; protein precursors of pharmacologically active polypeptides; inflammation and injury; ascites fluid; T-kinin and T-kininogen. *Mailing Add:* Sch Grad Studies Med Col Ga Augusta GA 30912. *E-Mail:* lowellg@uscn.uscn.edu.uga

GREENBAUM, SHELDON BORIS, ORGANIC CHEMISTRY. *Current Pos:* RETIRED. *Personal Data:* b Brooklyn, NY, Apr 15, 23; m 48; c 3. *Educ:* City Col NY, BS, 44; Univ Tenn, MS, 46; Univ Md, PhD(chem), 52. *Prof Exp:* Res chemist, Gordon-Lacey Chem Prod Co, 43-44; res chemist, Pyridium Corp, 44; asst, Univ Md, 46-50; res assoc & instr med chem, Dept Pharmacol, Sch Med, Western Res Univ, 52-53; asst, Yale Univ, 53-56; res chemist, Hooker Chem Corp, 56-66; group mgr, Org & Fermentation Labs, Diamond Shamrock Chem Co, 66-76; mgr biosci technol, New Technol & Licensing Div, Diamond Shamrock Corp, 76-83; vpres spec serv, Howsafe Corp, 84-88; lectr chem, Baldwin-Wallace Col, Cuyahoga Community Col, 88-95. *Concurrent Pos:* Vis assoc prof, Univ Tenn. *Mem:* Am Chem Soc; Licensing Execs Soc; Pac Indust Properties Asn. *Res:* Chemistry of vitamin D; vitamin E; riboflavin; calcium pantothenate; animal health products; antibiotics; pesticides; pyrimidines; chemical patents; technology transfer; licensing. *Mailing Add:* 15302 W Tranquility Lake Dr Delray Beach FL 33446

GREENBAUM, STEVEN GARRY, MAGNETIC RESONANCE, STRUCTURAL PROBES OF DISORDERED SOLIDS. *Current Pos:* from asst prof to assoc prof, 83-91, PROF PHYSICS, GRAD CTR, HUNTER COL, CITY UNIV NEW YORK, 92-, DEPT CHMN PHYSICS, 88- *Personal Data:* b New York, NY, Oct 17, 54; m 83; c 2. *Educ:* Clark Univ, BA, 76; Brown Univ, SM, 78, PhD(physics), 81. *Prof Exp:* Grad teaching asst physics, Brown Univ, 76-77, grad res asst, 77-81; Naval Res Coun fel, Naval Res Lab, 81-83. *Concurrent Pos:* Fulbright scholar vis scientist, Dept Chem Physics, Weitmann Inst Sci, 90-91. *Mem:* Am Phys Soc; Electrochem Soc; Mat Res Soc. *Res:* Structural studies of disordered solids (inorganic glasses, polymers); ion transport in solids for electrochemical applications; magnetic resonance (nuclear magnetic resonance, nuclear quadrupole resonance, electron spin resonance) spectroscopy of solids. *Mailing Add:* Physics Dept Hunter Col City Univ New York 695 Park Ave New York NY 10021

GREENBERG, ALLAN S, LOW TEMPERATURE PHYSICS. *Current Pos:* CONSULT, 85- *Personal Data:* b Brooklyn, NY, Oct 14, 43. *Educ:* Rensselaer Polytech Inst, BS, 65; Cornell Univ, MS, 68, PhD(physics), 71. *Prof Exp:* Teaching asst physics, Cornell Univ, 65-66, NDEA fel, 66-69; res assoc & instr, Univ Fla, 71-72, vis asst prof, 72-74; asst prof physics, Colo State Univ, 74-78; scientist, Nat Ctr Sci Res, France, 78-85. *Concurrent Pos:* Vis assoc prof, Northwestern Univ, 85; consult, 86- *Mem:* Am Phys Soc; Sigma Xi. *Res:* Low temperature research with specific interests in the nuclear and thermodynamic properties of solid 3He, solid isotopic mixtures, polarized liquid 3He and spin polarized atomic hydrogen. *Mailing Add:* 825 Washington Ave No 12 Santa Monica CA 90403-4041

GREENBERG, ARNOLD HARVEY, CANCER, IMMUNOLOGY. *Current Pos:* Asst prof pediat, Univ Man, 74-80, asst prof immunol, 74-80, assoc prof pediat & immunol, 80-85, PROF PEDIAT, UNIV MAN, 86-; DIR, MAN INST CELL BIOL, 88- *Personal Data:* b Winnipeg, Man, Sept 29, 41. *Educ:* Univ Man, BS & MD, 65; Univ London, PhD(immunol), 74. *Concurrent Pos:* Terry Fox cancer res scholar. *Mem:* Can Soc Immunol; Am Asn Immunologists; Am Asn Cancer Res. *Res:* Molecular mechanisms of cytotoxicity; TGF-B in inflammation; genetic basis of metastasis formation. *Mailing Add:* Man Inst Cell Biol Univ Man 100 Olivia St Winnipeg MB R3E 0V9 Can. *Fax:* 204-787-2190

GREENBERG, ARTHUR, ORGANIC CHEMISTRY, ENVIRONMENTAL CHEMISTRY. *Current Pos:* PROF & DEPT CHAIR, DEPT CHEM, UNIV NC, CHARLOTTE, 94- *Personal Data:* b Brooklyn, NY, Sept 27, 46; m 68, Susan Joan Covici; c David & Rachel. *Educ:* Fairleigh Dickinson Univ, BS, 67; Princeton Univ, MA, 70, PhD (chem), 71. *Honors & Awards:* Harlan J Perlis Res Award, 86; Joseph B Hyman Award, 90; Morris Katz Mem Lectr Environ Res, York Univ, 96. *Prof Exp:* Vis asst prof, Fairleigh Dickinson Univ, 71-72; chmn sci dept, Englewood Cliffs Col, 71-72; from asst prof to assoc prof, Frostburg State Col, 72-77; from asst prof to prof chem, NJ Inst Technol, 77-89; prof, Rutgers Univ, 89-94. *Concurrent Pos:* Ed, J Struct Chem; ed book ser, Struct, Energy & Reactivity Chem. *Mem:* Am Chem Soc. *Res:* Stereochemistry; strained organic molecules; theoretical chemistry; thermochemistry; organic substituent effects; organic pollutants on airborne particulates. *Mailing Add:* Dept Chem UNC Charlotte Charlotte NC 28223. *Fax:* 704-547-3151; *E-Mail:* agreenbe@unccvm.uncc.edu

GREENBERG, ARTHUR BERNARD, energy systems, systems engineering, for more information see previous edition

GREENBERG, BARRY H, MEDICINE. *Current Pos:* from asst prof to assoc prof, 77-86, PROF MED, DIV CARDIOL, ORE HEALTH SCI UNIV, 87-, COLLAB SCIENTIST, 88- *Personal Data:* b Brooklyn, NY, June 24, 44. *Educ:* Brooklyn Col, BA, 66; Upstate Med Ctr, MD, 70; Am Bd Internal Med, 75 & 77. *Prof Exp:* Staff assoc, Nat Inst Heart, Lung & Blood, Lipid Metab Br, NIH, 71-73; resident med, Yale-New Haven Hosp, 73-75; fel cardiol, Univ Calif, 75-77; asst res physician I, Cardiovasc Res Inst, 76-77. *Concurrent Pos:* Dir, Coronary Care Unit, Ore Health Sci Univ, 77-; vis colleague, Respiratory Unit, Royal Postgrad Med Sch, Hammersmith Hosp, 84-85. *Mem:* Fel Am Col Cardiol; Am Fedn Clin Res; Am Heart Asn; Int Soc Heart Res; Am Soc Pharmacol & Exp Therapeut. *Res:* Long term vasodilator therapy of mitral regurgitation; long term vasodilator therapy inaortic insufficiency; left ventricular dysfunction; expression of vasoactive genes in heart failure; author of numerous scientific publications. *Mailing Add:* Div Cardiol Ore Health Sci Univ 3181 SW Sam Jackson Park Rd Portland OR 97201-3098. *Fax:* 503-494-8550

GREENBERG, BERNARD, systems analysis, for more information see previous edition

GREENBERG, BERNARD, FORENSIC ENTOMOLOGY, FLY BIOLOGY. *Current Pos:* From instr to prof, 54-90, EMER PROF BIOL SCI, UNIV ILL, CHICAGO, 90- *Personal Data:* b New York, NY, Apr 24, 22; m 49, Barbara Dickler; c Gary, Daniel, Linda (Hanessian) & Deborah (Irwin). *Educ:* Brooklyn Col, BA, 44; Univ Kans, MA, 51, PhD, 54. *Concurrent Pos:* NSF grant, 59-60, 79-83; NIH grant, 60-63, 63-67; vis scientist, Istituto Superiore Sanita, Rome, 60-61; Fulbright res fel, 67-68, Inst Pub Health & Trop Dis, Mex, 62-63; USA Med Res Develop Command grant, 66-68, 69-72, 84 & 85; Fulbright-Hays sr res fel, 67-68; consult, Ill Inst Technol & US Navy, 71-76; Metrop Sanit Dist of Gtr Chicago, 73-75, Elec Power Res Inst, 75-83, forensic entomol, enforcement & expert witness, 76-, forensic entomol, Sci Gov, Chicago Acad Sci, 81-; ONR grant, 77-78. *Mem:* Fel AAAS; Entom Soc Am; Sigma Xi. *Res:* Fly biology; insect transmission of disease; biological impact of electromagnetic fields; forensic entomology. *Mailing Add:* Dept Biol Sci M/C 066 Univ Ill Chicago IL 60607-7060. *Fax:* 312-996-2435

GREENBERG, BRUCE MATTHEW, PHOTOBIOLOGY, PHOTOINDUCED TOXICOLOGY. *Current Pos:* asst prof, 88-93, ASSOC PROF BIOL, UNIV WATERLOO, 93- *Personal Data:* m 84, Lorelei F Zeiler; c Sean, Johanna & Isaac. *Educ:* Univ Calif, Berkeley, BS, 80; Univ Colo, PhD(chem), 85. *Prof Exp:* Res assoc, plant genetics, Weizmann Inst Sci, 85-88. *Mem:* Am Soc Plant Physiol; Am Soc Testing & Mat; Soc Environ Toxicologists & Chemists; Am Soc Photobiologists; Can Soc Plant Physiol; Int Soc Plant Molecular Biol. *Res:* Interaction of light with plant, focusing on adaption of plants to ultraviolet irradiation, photoinduced phytotoxicity of pollutants and chloroplast development. *Mailing Add:* Dept Biol Univ Waterloo Waterloo ON N2L 3G1 Can. *Fax:* 519-746-0614; *E-Mail:* greenber@biology.watstar.uwaterloo.ca

GREENBERG, CHARLES BERNARD, THIN FILMS, SWITCHABLE FILMS. *Current Pos:* Sr res ceramist, Glass Res Ctr, PPG Industs, 65-69, res assoc, 69-71, sr res assoc, 71-77, staff scientist, 77-91, SR SCIENTIST, GLASS TECHNOL CTR, PPG INDUSTS, 91- *Personal Data:* b Elizabeth, NJ, Dec 20, 39; m 67; c 3. *Educ:* Rutgers Univ, BS, 61; Univ Ill, MS, 62, PhD(ceramics), 65. *Concurrent Pos:* Pres, PPG Collegium, 82-84. *Mem:* Electrochem Soc; Am Ceramic Soc. *Res:* Thin transparent films on flat glass deposited by chemical and physical means; passive solar control in buildings and variable transmission; product and process development and life projections in use. *Mailing Add:* 3268 Wingdate Dr Murrysville PA 15668. *Fax:* 412-820-8515

GREENBERG, DANIEL, PHYSICAL CHEMISTRY. *Current Pos:* RETIRED. *Personal Data:* b New York, NY, Dec 31, 27; m 53; c 3. *Educ:* Yale Univ, BS, 48; Univ Chicago, MS, 49; Columbia Univ, PhD(chem), 54. *Prof Exp:* Res assoc radiochem, Columbia Univ, 54-55; res scientist nuclear physics, Armour Res Found, 55-57; proj leader radiation chem res, Indust Reactor Labs, US Indust Chems Co, 58-68, sr res assoc, Polymer Serv Lab, 68-71, group leader, Pilot Plant, 71-73, asst mgr, Polymer Compounds Res Dept, 73-74, mgr, 74-75, asst dir res, 75- *Mem:* AAAS; Am Chem Soc; Am Phys Soc. *Mailing Add:* 6244 Caribou Ct Cincinnati OH 45243-2947

GREENBERG, DANIELLE, INGESTIVE BEHAVIOR, BEHAVIORAL NEUROSCIENCE. *Current Pos:* fel, 84-86, instr, 86-89, ASST PROF PSYCHIAT, MED COL, CORNELL UNIV, 89- *Personal Data:* b Paris, France, Dec 18, 48; m 80; c 2. *Educ:* Columbia Univ, BS, 75; City Univ New York, MPhil, 83, PhD(physiol psychol), 84. *Prof Exp:* Adj prof psychol, Hunter Col, City Univ New York, 81-82; res asst psychiat, Montefiore Med Ctr, 81-83. *Concurrent Pos:* Nat res serv award, NIH, 85-86. *Mem:* AAAS; Am Physiol Soc; Am Psychol Soc; Soc Neurosci; NAm Soc Study Obesity. *Res:* Physiological controls of ingestion of nutritional fats; mechanism for the action of peptides such as cholecystokinin or bombesin on feeding behavior; ingestive behavior of genetically obese rodents; developmental nutrition; adequate stimulus for fat-induced satiety. *Mailing Add:* Dept Psychol Bourne Lab Cornell Univ Med Col 21 Bloomingdale Rd White Plains NY 10605. *Fax:* 914-682-3793

GREENBERG, DAVID B(ERNARD), BIOTECHNOLOGY. *Current Pos:* RETIRED. *Personal Data:* b Norfolk, Va, Nov 2, 28; div; c Lisa (Akchin), Jan (Evans) & Jill. *Educ:* Carnegie Inst Technol, BS, 52; Johns Hopkins Univ, MS, 59; La State Univ, PhD, 64. *Prof Exp:* Res engr, Victor Div, Radio Corp Am, 52-53, Nat Distillers Prods Corp, 53-55 & Food Mach & Chem Corp, 55-56; asst, Johns Hopkins Univ, 56-58; asst prof chem, US Naval Acad, 58-61; from instr to prof chem eng, La State Univ, 61-74, res fel, 64-65; prof chem & nuclear eng & head dept, Univ Cincinnati, 74-81, prof chem eng & dir grad studies, 81-86. *Concurrent Pos:* Prog dir eng div, NSF, 72-73; sr scientist, US Army Chem Res, Develop & Eng Ctr, Aberdeen PG, MD, 81-86; prog dir, Eng Div, NSF, 89-90. *Mem:* Am Chem Soc; Am Inst Chem Engrs; Am Soc Eng Educ; fel Am Soc Laser Med & Surg; Sigma Xi. *Res:* Heat, mass, momentum transfer; reaction kinetics; laser research; water treatment; biotechnology; biomedical engineering. *Mailing Add:* Dept Chem Eng Univ Cincinnati Cincinnati OH 45221-0171. *Fax:* 513-556-3473

GREENBERG, DONALD P, COMPUTER GRAPHICS. *Current Pos:* JACOB GOULD SCHURMAN PROF COMPUT GRAPHICS, CORNELL UNIV, 68-, DIR, PROG COMPUT GRAPHICS, 68- *Educ:* Cornell Univ, BCS, 58, PhD(struct eng), 68. *Honors & Awards:* Steven A Coons Award, Asn Comput Mach, 87; NCSA Educr Award, Nat Acad Eng. *Prof Exp:* Consult engr, Severud Assocs, 60-65. *Concurrent Pos:* Guest prof, ETH, Zurich, Switz, 70-71; vis prof, Yale Univ; dir, Nat Sci & Technol Ctr Comput Graphics & Sci Visualization. *Mem:* Nat Acad Eng; Asn Comput Mach; Inst Elec & Electronics Engrs; Int Asn Med & Biol Environ. *Res:* Advancement of state-of-the-art computer graphics; hidden surface algorithms; geometric modeling; color science; realistic image generation. *Mailing Add:* Rhodes Hall Cornell Univ Ithaca NY 14853-0258

GREENBERG, ELLIOTT, PHYSICAL CHEMISTRY, INORGANIC CHEMISTRY. *Current Pos:* RETIRED. *Personal Data:* b New York, NY, Mar 14, 27; m 51, Roslyn Sherman; c Daniel M, Kenneth E & Ronald I. *Educ:* City Col New York, BS, 47; Univ Mich, MS, 48, PhD(chem), 55. *Prof Exp:* Instr, Univ Mich, 51-54; assoc chemist, Argonne Nat Lab, Ill, 54-69; prof chem, Prairie State Col, 69-88. *Concurrent Pos:* Chmn, Indust Sponsors, Two-Yr Col Chem Conf, 78-87, 90 & Div Chem Educ, Am Chem Soc. *Mem:* Am Chem Soc. *Res:* Fluorine bomb calorimetry; general chemistry. *Mailing Add:* 203 Berry St Park Forest IL 60466

GREENBERG, EVERETT PETER, MICROBIOLOGY. *Current Pos:* resident instr microbiol ecol, 79-83, CO-DIR, MARINE BIOL LABS, WOODS HOLE, 85-; PROF MICROBIOL, UNIV IOWA, 90- *Personal Data:* b Hempsted, NY, Nov 7, 48. *Educ:* Western Wash Univ, BA, 70; Univ Iowa, MS, 72; Univ Mass, PhD(microbiol), 77. *Prof Exp:* Fel biol, Biol Labs, Harvard Univ, 77-78; from asst prof microbiol to assoc prof microbiol, Cornell Univ, 78-88. *Concurrent Pos:* Prin investr, NSF, 80-, NIH, 86-90 & ONR, 88-; assoc prof microbiol, Cornell Univ, 84-88, assoc prof, 88-90. *Mem:* Am Soc Microbiol; fel AAAS; NY Acad Sci; Marine Biol Labs; Am Acad Microbiol. *Res:* Mechanisms of bacterial behavior, particularly studies of chemosensory transduction in bacteria and studies of chemical communication between bacterial cells. *Mailing Add:* 4020 Stewart Rd NE Iowa City IA 52240

GREENBERG, FRANK, MEDICAL GENETICS, DYSMORPHOLOGY & TERATOLOGY. *Current Pos:* CLIN CONSULT, MED GENETICS BR, NIH, 96- *Personal Data:* b Perth Amboy, NJ, Aug 24, 48. *Educ:* Univ Mich, BA, 70, Rutgers Med Sch, MMS, 72, Univ Pa, MD, 74. *Prof Exp:* Pediat Resident, Childrens Hosp Pittsburgh, 74-76; pediat resident, St Christophers Children Hosp, 76-77, genetics fel, 77-79; EIS off, Ctr Dis Control, 79-81; dir birth defects, Tex Childrens Hosp, 81-96; assoc prof, Baylor Col Med, 87-96. *Concurrent Pos:* Adj asst prof, Sch Pub Health, Univ Tex, 85-94; mem, Social Issues Comt, Am Soc Human Genetics, 85-88; co-chair, Tex Genetics Network Adv Comt, 86-94; secy Planning Coun, Regional Networks, Genetics Servs, 89-95. *Mem:* AAAS; Am Fedr Clin Res; Am Acad Pediat; Am Soc Human Genetics; Teratol Soc. *Res:* Birth defects with a particular interest in microdeletion syndromes including Williams syndrome, Prader-Willi syndrome, Digeorge anomaly and lissencephaly; Smith-Magenis Syndrome. *Mailing Add:* Nat Human Genonze Res Inst NIH Bldg 10 Rm 3053 10 Center Dr MSC 1267 Bethesda MD 20892-1267. *Fax:* 202-319-7301; *E-Mail:* frankg@nhgri.nih.gov

GREENBERG, G(OODWIN) ROBERT, BIOCHEMISTRY, MOLECULAR BIOLOGY. *Current Pos:* prof, 57-88, EMER PROF BIOL CHEM, UNIV MICH, ANN ARBOR, 88- *Personal Data:* b Danube, Minn, June 23, 18; m 65, Susan Jiga; c James B, Paula (Marshall), Bettie J, Alice (Vorbach), Ela & Efraim. *Educ:* Univ Minn, BA, 41, MS, 42, PhD, 44. *Honors & Awards:* Paul Lewis Lab Award in Enzyme Chem, Am Chem Soc, 57. *Prof Exp:* Asst physiol chem, Univ Minn, 42-44; res fel med, Univ Utah, 44-46; sr instr biochem, Western Res Univ, Cleveland, 46-48, from asst prof to assoc prof, 48-57. *Concurrent Pos:* NSF sr fel, Univ Durham, Eng, 56-57; vis scientist, Univ Geneva, Switz, 66; Josiah Macy Jr found scholar & vis prof, Mass Inst Technol, 74-75; Am Cancer Soc Scholar & vis prof, Dept Microbiol, Univ BC, 82-83. *Mem:* Am Soc Microbiol; Am Soc Biol Chemists. *Res:* Nucleic acid and bacteriophage metabolism; microbial and molecular genetics; nucleotide biosynthesis and metabolism. *Mailing Add:* Dept Biol Chem Univ Mich Rm 5443 Med Sci I Ann Arbor MI 48109-0606. *E-Mail:* grog@umich.edu

GREENBERG, HERBERT JULIUS, APPLIED MATHEMATICS. *Current Pos:* chmn, Dept Math, 65-74, prof, 65-89, EMER PROF MATH, UNIV DENVER, 89- *Personal Data:* b Chicago, Ill, Nov 28, 21; m 46; c 3. *Educ:* Northwestern Univ, BS, 40, MS, 41; Brown Univ, PhD(appl math), 46. *Prof Exp:* Asst, Brown Univ, 43-45, res assoc, 45-47, asst prof math, 47-49; from asst prof to assoc prof, Carnegie Inst Technol, 49-56; assoc dir, AEC Comput & Appl Math Ctr & assoc prof, Inst Math Sci, NY Univ, 56-58; mem staff, Res Div, IBM Corp, 58-65, asst dir math sci, 60-65, dir, 65. *Concurrent Pos:* Mem appl math group, Off Sci Res & Develop, Brown Univ, 43-45; assoc prof, Inst Math Sci, NY Univ, 56-68; head math sci div, Denver Res Inst, 66-74. *Mem:* AAAS; Soc Indust & Appl Math; Math Asn Am. *Res:* Applied mechanics; numeric analysis; computing; mathematical education. *Mailing Add:* 2280 S St Paul St Denver CO 80210

GREENBERG, HERMAN SAMUEL, SCIENCE EDUCATION, ORGANIC CHEMISTRY. *Current Pos:* TEACHER SCI, SCH DIST PHILADELPHIA, 73- *Personal Data:* b Philadelphia, Pa, Jan 13, 39; m 70, Helen Meiner; c Aaron, Michael & Rachel. *Educ:* Temple Univ, AB, 60, AM, 64; Univ Pa, PhD(org chem), 69. *Prof Exp:* Jr medicinal chemist, Smith Kline & French Labs, 60-63; chemist, Polysci Inc, 69-70; fel pharmacol, Sch Med, Univ Pa, 70-72; res assoc, Inst Cancer Res, 72-73. *Mem:* Am Chem Soc; Royal Soc Chem; Nat Sci Teachers Asn; Am Asn Physics Teachers. *Res:* General chemistry; chemical education; organic chemistry. *Mailing Add:* 1701 Fox Chase Rd Philadelphia PA 19152. *E-Mail:* hgreenbe@mail.sas.upenn.edu

GREENBERG, IRWIN, OPERATIONS RESEARCH, STATISTICS. *Current Pos:* assoc prof, 79-85, PROF OPERS RES, GEORGE MASON UNIV, 85- *Personal Data:* b New York, NY, Sept, 18, 35; m 56, Anita Burland; c Cheryl L & Madelyn S. *Educ:* NY Univ, BIE, 56, EngScD, 64; Northeastern Univ, MS, 60. *Prof Exp:* Opers analyst, Avco Res & Adv Develop Div, 56-60; from instr to assoc prof indust eng, NY Univ, 61-73; adj prof math, Pace Univ, 73-77; dir, Statist Res Ctr, Mathtech Div Mathematica, Inc, 77-79. *Concurrent Pos:* Res analyst, Port NY Authority, 60-66; Fulbright travel grant & vis res scientist, Delft Univ, 66-67; assoc prof mgt sci, Univ New Haven, 76-77, Rand Corp, 88- *Mem:* Opers Res Soc Am; Inst Mgt Sci; Sigma Xi; Decision Sci Inst. *Res:* Stochastic processes; queuing; applied probability; weapon systems analysis; applied statistics. *Mailing Add:* George Mason Univ 4400 University Dr Fairfax VA 22030-4444. *Fax:* 703-993-1521; *E-Mail:* igreenbe@gmuvax

GREENBERG, JACK SAM, NUCLEAR SPECTROSCOPY. *Current Pos:* from instr to asst prof, Yale Univ, 56-64, dir grad studies, 67-69, assoc prof, 64-75, PROF PHYSICS, YALE UNIV, 75- *Personal Data:* b Warsaw, Poland, May 23, 27; m 52; c 2. *Educ:* McGill Univ, BEng, 50, MSc, 51; Mass Inst Technol, PhD(physics), 55. *Honors & Awards:* Alexander von Humbolt US Sr Scientist Award, 76-77. *Prof Exp:* Rutherford mem fel, 55-56. *Concurrent Pos:* NSF grant, 61-64; vis scientist, Weizmann Inst Sci, 69-70; vis prof, Gesellschaft fur Schwerionenforschung, Darmstadt, 76-77. *Mem:* Fel Am Phys Soc; Sigma Xi; AAAS. *Res:* Weak interactions; quantum electrodynamics; nuclear structure physics; kaon and hyperon physics; inner-shell vacancy formation; electronic quasimolecules; electrodynamics of strong fields; vacuum decay in over critical fields. *Mailing Add:* Dept Physics Yale Univ PO Box 6666 New Haven CT 06511

GREENBERG, JAMES M, NONLINEAR CONSERVATION LAWS. *Current Pos:* PROF & CHMN, DEPT MATH SCI, CARNEGIE MELLON UNIV, 95- *Personal Data:* b Chicago, Ill, July 30, 40; m 90. *Educ:* Cornell Univ, BCE, 63; Brown Univ, PhD, 66. *Prof Exp:* Vis mem, Courant Inst Math Sci, 73-74; assoc chmn math, State Univ NY, Buffalo, 75-76, prof, 76-82; prof, Ohio State Univ, 82-85; consult, Dept Energy, 85-86; prof & chmn, Math Dept, Univ Md, Baltimore Co, 86-95. *Concurrent Pos:* Prog dir, NSF, 78-79 & 80-81; mem, Adv Comt Super Comput Computations Res Inst, Fla State Univ & Comt Appln Math, Nat Res Coun, 86-88. *Mem:* Am Math Soc; Soc Indust & Appl Math. *Res:* Nonlinear conservation laws; continuum mechanics; transport theory; discrete particle systems. *Mailing Add:* Dept Math Sci Carnegie Mellon Univ Pittsburgh PA 15213. *Fax:* 412-268-6380; *E-Mail:* greenber@andrew.cmu.edu

GREENBERG, JAY R, CELL BIOLOGY, MOLECULAR BIOLOGY. *Current Pos:* SR RES ASSOC, DEPT BIOL, UNIV ROCHESTER, 91- *Personal Data:* b Davenport, Iowa, Aug 23, 43. *Educ:* Univ Chicago, BS, 64, PhD(cell biol), 68. *Prof Exp:* Res assoc molecular biol, Inst Cancer Res, 70-73; staff scientist, Worchester Found Exp Biol, 73-83, sr scientist, 83-86; assoc res scientist, Dept Molecular Biophys & Biochem, Yale Univ, 86-90. *Concurrent Pos:* NIH fel molecular biol, Inst Cancer Res, 68-70; cancer res scholar, Am Cancer Soc, 74-77; res grants, Nat Cancer Inst, 74-77, NSF, 78 & 81, Nat Inst Gen Med Sci, NIH, 81-; mem biomed sci study sect, NIH, 81- *Mem:* Am Soc Cell Biol; Am Soc Microbiol; AAAS; Am Soc Biol Chemists. *Res:* Messenger RNA production and function in eukaryotes; protein-nucleic acid interactions. *Mailing Add:* Dept Biol Univ Rochester Hutchison Hall Rochester NY 14627

GREENBERG, JEROME HERBERT, PREVENTIVE MEDICINE. *Current Pos:* RETIRED. *Personal Data:* b Trenton, NJ, Sept 1, 23; m 45; c 3. *Educ:* Georgetown Univ, MD, 49; Am Bd Prev Med, dipl, 58. *Prof Exp:* Chief dept epidemiol, Walter Reed Army Inst Res, 57-58, asst chief, Commun Dis Br, Prev Med Div, Off Surgeon Gen, 58-60, prev med adv, Korean Mil Adv Group, 60-62, chief prev med br, Hq Fourth US Army, Tex, 64-65, dir dept prev med, Med Field Serv Sch, Brooke Army Med Ctr, 65-69, assoc commandant, Walter Reed Army Inst Res, Med Ctr, Washington, DC, 69-70, chief, Prev Med Div, Off Surgeon Gen, 70-71, dir health environ, Off Surgeon Gen, Dept Army, 71-73; dir pub health, Indianapolis-Marion Co Health Dept, 73-75; chief, Bur Tuberc Servs, Tex Dept Health Resources, 76, assoc comnr preventable dis, 76-86. *Concurrent Pos:* Fel trop med, Sch Trop Med, Univ Calcutta, 59; partic interam trop med prog, La State Univ, 64. *Mem:* AMA; Am Pub Health Asn; Am Col Prev Med; Soc Med Consult Armed Forces. *Res:* Epidemiology; immunology. *Mailing Add:* 124 Glendobbin Lane Winchester VA 22603

GREENBERG, JEROME MAYO, ASTROPHYSICS. *Current Pos:* PROF LAB ASTROPHYSICS, UNIV LEIDEN, 75- *Personal Data:* b Baltimore, Md, Jan 14, 22; m 47; c 4. *Educ:* Johns Hopkins Univ, PhD(physics), 48. *Prof Exp:* Physicist, Nat Adv Comt Aeronaut, 44-46; instr physics, Exten Div, Univ Va, 45-46; asst prof, Univ Del, 48-51; res assoc, Inst Fluid Dynamics & Appl Math, Univ Md, 51-52; from asst prof to prof physics, Rensselaer Polytech Inst, 52-70; prof astrophys, State Univ NY Albany, 70-75, chmn dept astron & space sci, 71-74, res prof astrophysics, Res Div, 75. *Concurrent Pos:* Orgn Europ Econ Coop sr vis fel, Univ Leiden, 61; mem Sch Math, Inst Advan Study, Princeton Univ, 65-66; dir astron, Rensselaer Polytech Inst, 67-70; prof lab astrophys, Univ Leiden, 68-69; mem comn interstellar matter & planetary nebulae, Int Astron Union; mem comn six, Int Radio & Sci Union; sr res assoc, Dudley Observatory, 70-75; adj prof, Rensselaer Polytech Inst, 81-; distinguished res prof, Univ Fla, 81- *Mem:* AAAS; Am Astron Soc; fel Am Phys Soc; Int Astron Union. *Res:* Theory of particle scattering and wave scattering; photochemistry of low temperature solids; photochemistry; interstellar matter; comets; origin of life. *Mailing Add:* Huygens Astrophys Lab Univ Leiden Nielsbohrweg 2 PO Box 9504 Leiden 2300 RA Netherlands

GREENBERG, JERROLD, biochemistry, molecular biology, for more information see previous edition

GREENBERG, JOEL S, ECONOMIC ANALYSIS, POLICY ANALYSIS. *Current Pos:* PRES, PRINCETON SYNERGETICS INC, 84- *Personal Data:* b Brooklyn, NY, May 21, 31; m 52, Roslynn Ginberg; c Robert, Marian & Judith. *Educ:* Polytech Inst Brooklyn, BEE, 52; Syracuse Univ, MEE, 60. *Prof Exp:* Br chief & mem, Advan Studies Off, Rome Air Develop Ctr, USAF, 52-61; mem corp staff, RCA, 61-69; vpres, Ventures Res & Develop Group, 69-71; res scientist, Aerospace & Mech Sci Dept, Princeton Univ, 71-75; vpres, Econ Inc, 73-84. *Concurrent Pos:* Chmn, Econ Space Oper Comt, Int Acad Astronaut, 83-; mem, Com Develop Space Working Group, Ctr Strategic & Int Studies, 88-89; mem, Pub Policy Comt, Am Inst Aeronaut & Astronaut, 88-; prin investr, Dept Transp, 89-, Battelle Pac NW Labs, Dept Energy, 93-, Marshall Space Flight Ctr, NASA, 95-97. *Mem:* Fel Am Inst Aeronaut & Astronaut; Int Acad Astronaut. *Res:* Economic, policy and decision analyses relating to the commercial development of space, energy conservation and casino gaming operations; public and private sector interactions; role of government in affecting private sector investment decisions. *Mailing Add:* Princeton Synergetics Inc 900 State Rd Princeton NJ 08540-1425

GREENBERG, JOSEPH H, ANTHROPOLOGY, LINGUISTICS. *Current Pos:* RETIRED. *Personal Data:* b Brooklyn, NY, May 28, 15; m 40, Selma Berkowitz. *Educ:* Columbia Univ, AB, 36; Northwestern Univ, PhD(anthrop), 40. *Hon Degrees:* DSc, Northwestern Univ, 82. *Honors & Awards:* Haile Selassie Award African Res, 67; Behav Sci Award, NY Acad Sci, 80. *Prof Exp:* Signal Intel Corps, US Army, 40-45; fac, Univ Minn, 46-48; from asst prof to prof anthrop, Columbia Univ, 48-62; prof, Stanford Univ, 62-85, Ray Lyman Wilbur prof soc sci anthrop, 71. *Concurrent Pos:* Soc Sci Res Coun fel, Northwestern Univ, 40; grant, Ford Found, 52, 57-62; Guggenheim Award, 54-55, 58-59 & 82-83; vis prof, Ling Inst, Mich Univ, 57, Univ Minn, 60, Summer Inst, Univ Colo, 61; Stanford humanities fel, 58-59 & 82-83; mem panel anthrop, philos & hist sci, NSF, 59-61; dir, WAfrican Langs Serv, 59-66, Nat Defense Educ Act African Lang & Area Ctr, 67-78; Ling Soc Am prof, Summer Inst, Oswego, NY, 76; Collitz prof, Summer Ling Inst, Stanford, 87, coordr, Stanford Proj Lang Universals. *Mem:* Am Anthrop Asn; Ling Soc; NY Acad Sci; Am Acad Arts & Sci; Am Philos Soc. *Mailing Add:* 860 Mayfield Ave Stanford CA 94305-1051

GREENBERG, JUDITH HOROVITZ, DEVELOPMENTAL GENETICS & BIOLOGY. *Current Pos:* DIR DIV GENETICS & DEVELOP BIOL, NAT INST GEN MED SCI, NIH, 88- *Personal Data:* b Philadelphia, Pa, Apr 2, 47; m 69, Warren Greenberg; c Elyssa. *Educ:* Univ Pittsburgh, BS, 67; Boston Univ, MA, 70; Bryn Mawr Col, PhD(biol), 72. *Honors & Awards:* Spec Recognition Award, Pub Health Serv. *Mem:* Am Soc Human Genetics; Soc Develop Biol. *Mailing Add:* Bldg 45 R 2AS25 45 Ctr Dr Nat Inst Gen Med Sci Bethesda MD 20892-6200. *E-Mail:* greenbej@gm1.nigms.nih.gov

GREENBERG, LEONARD JASON, BIOCHEMISTRY, IMMUNOLOGY. *Current Pos:* assoc prof, 72-77, PROF PATH, UNIV MINN, MINNEAPOLIS, 77-, PROF LAB MED, 80- *Personal Data:* b Roxbury, Mass, July 8, 26; m 72. *Educ:* Northeastern Univ, BS, 52; Univ Rochester, MS, 54; Univ Minn, PhD(biochem), 58. *Prof Exp:* Asst prof biochem, Univ Minn, 60-61; asst prof path, Stanford Univ, 61-62; sr investr exp path, Naval Radiol Defense Lab, San Francisco, 62-65; asst prof path, NY Univ Med Ctr, 65-67; group leader biochem, Union Carbide Res Inst, NY, 67-69, dir virus res, 69-72. *Concurrent Pos:* Assoc prof path, NY Univ Med Ctr, 67-72. *Mem:* AAAS; Am Chem Soc; Am Soc Microbiol; Histochem Soc; Sigma Xi. *Res:* Immunogenetic aspects of susceptibility or resistance to disease. *Mailing Add:* Dept Path Univ Med Sch Minn 420 Delaware St SE Box 198 Mayo Minneapolis MN 55455-0374

GREENBERG, LES PAUL, SOCIAL INSECT BEHAVIOR, URBAN ENTOMOLOGY. *Current Pos:* POSTGRAD RES, UNIV CALIF, RIVERSIDE, 96- *Personal Data:* b Brooklyn, NY, July 13, 46. *Educ:* Brooklyn Col, City Univ NY, BS, 67, MA, 75; Univ Kans, PhD(entom), 81. *Prof Exp:* Postdoctoral res assoc, Tex A&M, 81-96. *Mem:* Entom Soc Am; Animal Behavior Soc; AAAS; Int Union Study Social Insects; Sigma Xi. *Res:* Social behavior of insectsCling Argentine ants; low toxic baits for controlling Argentine Ants. *Mailing Add:* 600 Central Ave No 248 Riverside CA 92507. *E-Mail:* lesgreen@ucrac1.ucr.edu

GREENBERG, MARK SHIEL, analytical chemistry, for more information see previous edition

GREENBERG, MARVIN JAY, MATHEMATICS. *Current Pos:* RETIRED. *Personal Data:* b New York, NY, Dec 22, 35; div; c 1. *Educ:* Columbia Univ, AB, 55; Princeton Univ, PhD, 59. *Prof Exp:* Asst math, Princeton Univ, 55-57 & Univ Chicago, 58; instr, Rutgers Univ, 58-59; asst prof, Univ Calif, Berkeley, 59-64; NSF res fel, Harvard Univ, 64-65; assoc prof, Northeastern Univ, 65-67; from assoc prof to prof math, Univ Calif, Santa Cruz, 67-92. *Concurrent Pos:* NSF res fel, Harvard Univ, 61 & Univ Paris, 62; res asst, Erhard Sem Training, 75-76, cert in hypn, 88. *Res:* Algebraic geometry; algebraic number theory; algebraic topology; non-Euclidean geometry; mathematical logic. *Mailing Add:* 66 Poppy Lane Berkeley CA 94706

GREENBERG, MICHAEL D(AVID), APPLIED MATHEMATICS TEXTBOOKS. *Current Pos:* from asst prof to assoc prof, 69-79, PROF MECH & AEROSPACE ENG, UNIV DEL, 79- *Personal Data:* b Brooklyn, NY, Nov 15, 35; m 95, Yisraela Myers; c Ellen, Kenneth, Daniel & Alitzah. *Educ:* Cornell Univ, BME, 58, MS, 60, PhD(theoret mech), 64. *Prof Exp:* Staff scientist, Therm Advan Res, Inc, 63-69. *Concurrent Pos:* Adj asst prof, Cornell Univ, 64-66, vis asst prof, 68-69. *Mem:* Sigma Xi. *Res:* Hydromechanics; modelling of aesthetics. *Mailing Add:* Dept Mech Eng Univ Del Newark DE 19716. *Fax:* 302-831-3619; *E-Mail:* greenberg@me.udel.edu

GREENBERG, MICHAEL JOHN, COMPARATIVE PHYSIOLOGY & PHARMACOLOGY. *Current Pos:* DIR, WHITNEY LAB & PROF PHARMACOL & THERAPEUT, COL MED, UNIV FLA, 81- *Personal Data:* b Brooklyn, NY, Sept 28, 31; m 54; c 3. *Educ:* Cornell Univ, AB, 53; Fla State Univ, MA, 55; Harvard Univ, PhD(biol), 58. *Honors & Awards:* Merit Award, Nat Heart Lung Blood Inst, NIH, 87. *Prof Exp:* From instr to asst prof invert zool, Univ Ill, 58-64; from assoc prof to prof biol, Fla State Univ, 64-81, sci dir, Marine Lab, 78-81. *Concurrent Pos:* NSF sr fel, Melbourne & Misaki Marine Labs, Japan, 64-65; dir exp invert zool course, Marine Biol Lab, Woods Hole, 75-77; vis prof, Dept Physiol, Med Sch, Hiroshima Univ, 78, Dept Zool, Univ Hong Kong, 82; mem, Regulatory Biol Panel, NSF, 83-85; ed-in-chief, Biol Bull, 89- *Mem:* Fel AAAS; Soc Neuro; Soc Gen Physiol; Am Soc Pharmacol & Exp Therapeut; Am Soc Zool; Tallahassee, Sopchoppy & Gulf Coast Marine Biol Asn (pres, 69-). *Res:* Comparative physiology and pharmacology of invertebrate muscle; invertebrate neuropeptides; intracellular volume regulation. *Mailing Add:* Whitney Lab 9505 Ocean Shore Blvd St Augustine FL 32086-8623. *Fax:* 904-461-4008

GREENBERG, MICHAEL RICHARD, ENVIRONMENTAL HEALTH POLICY, ENVIRONMENTAL EPIDEMIOLOGY. *Current Pos:* PROF PUB HEALTH, EDWARD BLOUSTEIN SCH PLANNING & POLICY, RUTGERS UNIV, 71- *Personal Data:* b New York, NY, Aug 22, 43; m, Gwendolyn Barker; c Alexandria, Joshua Suggs, Heather Suggs & Seana Suggs. *Educ:* City Univ NY, BA, 65; Columbia Univ, MA, 66, PhD(med geog), 69. *Honors & Awards:* Distinguished Scholar, Asn Am Geographers, 97. *Prof Exp:* Asst prof geog, Columbia Univ, 69-71. *Concurrent Pos:* Dir environ policy, Hazardous Substance Mgt Res Ctr, 84-; mem, Hazardous Waste Remediation Priorities, Nat Acad Sci, 92-93. *Mem:* AAAS; Soc Epidemiol Res; Asn Am Geographers; Soc Risk Analysis; Am Planning Asn. *Res:* Formation and implementation of environmental health policy; environmental risk, neighborhood quality and quality of life. *Mailing Add:* Dept Urban Studies & Commun Health Rutgers State Univ New Brunswick NJ 08090. *Fax:* 732-932-0934

GREENBERG, MILTON, ATMOSPHERIC SCIENCES. *Current Pos:* RETIRED. *Personal Data:* b Carteret, NJ, April 21, 18; m 48, Maxine; c Eve, David & Alan. *Educ:* City Col New York & NY Univ, BA, 43; Harvard Univ, MPA, 54. *Hon Degrees:* ScD, Canaan Col, New Hampshire, 61 & Merrimack Col, Mass, 81, DHL, Univ Lowell, Mass, 85. *Prof Exp:* Dep dir, USAF Geophysics Res Directorate, 50-54, dir, 54-58; pres & chmn, GCA Corp, 58-86. *Concurrent Pos:* Consult, Nat Acad Sci Spec Study Group Geophysics, 57-58; ed in chief, Planetar & Space Sci, 57-62; mem & chmn, Physics Atmosphere & Space Comt, Am Rocket Soc, 58-59; Govt Affairs Comt, Sci Apparatus Makers Asn, 65-75; mem, State Indust Adv Coun, Mass Inst Technol Sea Grant Prog, 73-74. *Mem:* Sigma Xi; fel AAAS; assoc fel Am Inst Aeronaut & Astronaut. *Mailing Add:* 4941 Mission Hill Pl Tucson AZ 85718-1818

GREENBERG, NEIL, ETHOLOGY. *Current Pos:* PROF, DEPT ECOL & EVOLUTIONARY BIOL, UNIV TENN, KNOXVILLE, 93- *Personal Data:* b Newark, NJ, Oct 30, 41; m 88, Katherine Harris; c Haley Jessica Elise. *Educ:* Drew Univ, BA, 63; Rutgers Univ, MS, 67, PhD(zool), 73. *Honors & Awards:* Stokely Inst lectr. *Prof Exp:* Res scientist ethology, Lab Brain Evolution & Behav, NIMH, 73-78. *Concurrent Pos:* NIMH Grant Found fel, 73-75; res assoc, Mus Comp Zool, Harvard Univ, 77-83; Danforth assoc, 81-86. *Mem:* Animal Behav Soc; Am Soc Zoologists; Soc Neurosci; Int Soc Neuroethology; fel AAAS. *Res:* Neural and endocrine aspects of social behavior, behavioral and physiological ecology and the evolution of behavior; interactions of physiological stress, aggression, and reproductive behavior. *Mailing Add:* Dept Zool Univ Tenn Knoxville TN 37996-0810. *Fax:* 423-974-4057; *E-Mail:* ngreenbe@utk.edu

GREENBERG, NEWTON ISAAC, THEORETICAL PHYSICS. *Current Pos:* from asst prof to assoc prof, 63-75, PROF PHYSICS, STATE UNIV NY BINGHAMTON, 75- *Personal Data:* b Brooklyn, NY, Feb 26, 36; m 60; c 2. *Educ:* Brooklyn Col, BS, 57; Univ Md, PhD(physics), 61. *Prof Exp:* Asst physics, Univ Md, 57-61; fel, Bartol Res Found, 61-63. *Mem:* Am Phys Soc; Am Asn Physics Teachers. *Res:* Many body problem; nuclear structure theory. *Mailing Add:* Dept Physics & Astron State Univ NY Binghamton PO Box 6000 Binghamton NY 13902-6000

GREENBERG, OSCAR WALLACE, ELEMENTARY PARTICLE PHYSICS, HIGH ENERGY PHYSICS. *Current Pos:* from asst prof to assoc prof, 61-67, PROF PHYSICS, UNIV MD, COLLEGE PARK, 67- *Personal Data:* b New York, NY, Feb 18, 32; m 69, Yael Shapiro; c Joshua D, Jeremy H & Benjamin G. *Educ:* Rutgers Univ, BS, 52; Princeton Univ, PhD(physics), 57. *Honors & Awards:* Phys Sci Award, Wash Acad Sci, 71. *Prof Exp:* Instr physics, Brandeis Univ, 56-57; NSF fel, Mass Inst Technol, 59-61. *Concurrent Pos:* Mem, Inst Advan Study, 64; Sloan Found fel, 64-66; vis assoc prof, Rockefeller Univ, 65-66; vis prof, Tel-Aviv Univ, 68-69 & Johns Hopkins Univ, 77; Guggenheim fel, 68-69; assoc ed, Phys Rev Lett, 76-78; vis scientist, NASA/Goddard Space Flight Ctr, 78 & Fermi Nat Accelerator Lab, 84-85; vis scholar, Univ Chicago, 84-85. *Mem:* Am Phys Soc; Int Asn Math Phys. *Res:* Quantum field theory; elementary particle and high energy physics; introduction of color degree of freedom in elementary particle physics and the symmetric quark model of baryons; study of subquark models of quarks and leptons; study of small violations of Pauli exclusion principle. *Mailing Add:* Dept Physics Univ Md College Park MD 20742-4111. *Fax:* 301-314-9525; *E-Mail:* greenberg@umdhep.umd.edu

GREENBERG, PHILIP D, MICROBIOLOGY, IMMUNOLOGY. *Current Pos:* sr fel, Div Oncol, Univ Wash & Fred Hutchinson Cancer Res Ctr, Seattle, 76-78, from asst prof to prof, 78-88, PROF MED, DIV ONCOL, SCH MED, UNIV WASH, 88- & PROF IMMUNOL, 89- *Personal Data:* b Brooklyn, NY, Nov 26, 46. *Educ:* Wash Univ, St Louis, BA, 67; State Univ NY, MD, 71; Am Bd Internal Med, cert, 74. *Prof Exp:* Intern & resident med, Univ Calif, San Diego, 71-74, res fel immunol, 74-76. *Concurrent Pos:* Asst mem, Fred Hutchinson Cancer Res Ctr, 78-82, assoc mem, 82-88, mem, 88-; assoc ed, J Immunol, 82-85; mem, US-Japan Cancer Res Coop Prog Comt Tumor Immunol, 85-89; NIH merit award, 91-01. *Mem:* Am Asn Cancer Res; Am Asn Immunologists; Am Soc Clin Invest. *Res:* Bone marrow transplantation. *Mailing Add:* Univ Wash Health Sci Bldg Box 356527 Seattle WA 98195-6527. *Fax:* 206-685-3128

GREENBERG, RALPH, MATHEMATICS. *Current Pos:* from asst prof to prof, 78-83, PROF MATH, UNIV WASH, 83- *Personal Data:* b Chester, Pa, Sept 2, 44. *Educ:* Univ Pa, BA, 66; Princeton Univ, PhD(math), 71. *Prof Exp:* Asst prof, Univ Md, 70-74, Brandeis Univ, 74-78. *Mem:* Am Math Soc. *Res:* Algebraic number theory; theory of cyclotomic fields, p-adic L-functions. *Mailing Add:* Dept Math Univ Wash Box 354350 Seattle WA 98195-4350. *E-Mail:* greenber@math.washington.edu

GREENBERG, RAYMOND SETH, MEDICINE. *Current Pos:* VPRES ACAD AFFAIRS & PROVOST, MED UNIV SC, 95- *Personal Data:* b Chapel Hill, NC, Aug 10, 55; m 88, Leah D Dacus. *Educ:* Univ NC, BA, 76, PhD, 83; Duke Univ, MD, 79; Harvard Univ, MPH, 80. *Prof Exp:* From asst prof to assoc prof, Sch Med, Emory Univ, 83-90, dep dir, Winship Cancer Ctr, 85-90, chair epidemiol & biostatist, 88-90, dean pub health, 90-95. *Concurrent Pos:* Chair prev med, Nat Bd Med Exams, 91-93; chair, Epidemiol Study Sect, NIH, Md, 92- *Mem:* Fel Am Col Epidemiol (pres, 90-91); Am Pub Health Asn; Am Statist Asn; Am Epidemiol Soc; Soc Epidemiol Res. *Res:* Epidemiology; biostatistics; medicine. *Mailing Add:* Med Univ SC 171 Ashley Ave 200 H Administration Charleston SC 29425. *Fax:* 803-792-5110; *E-Mail:* greenber@musc.edu

GREENBERG, RICHARD AARON, bacteriology, for more information see previous edition

GREENBERG, RICHARD ALVIN, BIOSTATISTICS, EPIDEMIOLOGY. *Current Pos:* RETIRED. *Personal Data:* b Hartford, Conn, Oct 28, 27; m 50, Marjorie Hurwitz; c Joan (Drumond) & Merle White. *Educ:* Univ Conn, BA, 50; Yale Univ, MPH, 59, PhD(biometry), 63. *Prof Exp:* From instr to assoc prof pub health, Yale Univ, 69-75; prof epidemiol & biostatist, Univ Louisville, 75-89. *Concurrent Pos:* Vis prof epidemiol, Tel Aviv Univ, 71-72. *Mem:* Am Pub Health Asn; Am Statist Asn. *Res:* Biometric aspects of epidemiological research; cancer epidemiology; chronic disease epidemiology. *Mailing Add:* 7360 S Oriole Blvd Apt 402 Delray Beach FL 33446

GREENBERG, RICHARD JOSEPH, PLANETARY SCIENCES, CELESTIAL MECHANICS. *Current Pos:* res assoc, Univ Ariz, 72-75, asst prof planetary sci, 75-76, sr res scientist, Lunar & Planetary Lab, 86-88, assoc dean sci, 88-89, PROF PLANETARY SCI & TEACHING & TEACHER EDUC & DIR, SCI & MATH EDUC CTR, UNIV ARIZ, 89- *Personal Data:* b New York, NY, June 19, 47; m 68; c 3. *Educ:* Mass Inst Technol, BS, 68, PhD(planetary sci), 72. *Prof Exp:* Res asst geophys, Mass Inst Technol, 68-70, teaching asst planetary sci, 70-72; res scientist, Planetary Sci Inst, Sci Applns Inc, 76-86. *Mem:* Am Astron Soc. *Res:* Celestial mechanics and planetary dynamics with emphasis on processes of long-term evolution of the solar systems, resonant coupling between motions of planetary bodies and dynamics of the formation of the solar system; educational technology and science education. *Mailing Add:* Lunar & Planetary Lab Univ Ariz Space Sci Bldg Tucson AZ 85721

GREENBERG, ROLAND, pharmacology, for more information see previous edition

GREENBERG, RUVEN, PHYSIOLOGY. *Current Pos:* asst prof, 53-59, assoc prof, 59-69, PROF PHYSIOL, UNIV ILL COL MED, 69- *Personal Data:* b Columbus, Ohio, Mar 15, 18; m 48; c 3. *Educ:* Ohio State Univ, BS, 38, PhD(physiol), 48; Northwestern Univ, MSc, 40. *Prof Exp:* Instr physiol, Med Sch, Ohio State Univ, 48-49; asst prof, Univ Tex Med Br, 49-53. *Concurrent Pos:* Fulbright lectr, Univ Madrid, 63. *Mem:* Am Physiol Soc; Am Soc Pharmacol & Exp Therapeut; Soc Neurosci; Soc Exp Biol & Med; Am Soc Cell Biol. *Res:* Neuro-mediators; histo-physiology; blood-brain barrier; psychopharmacology. *Mailing Add:* 351 Ferndale Ave Elmhurst IL 60126-2101

GREENBERG, SANFORD DAVID, ESOTERIC TESTING. *Current Pos:* CHMN & CHIEF EXEC OFFICER, TEI INDUSTRIES, INC, 83- *Personal Data:* b Buffalo, NY, Dec 13, 40; m 62, Susan Roseno; c Paul, James & Kathryn. *Educ:* Columbia Col, AB, 62; Oxford Univ, Marshall Scholar, 64-65, Harvard Univ, MA, 65, PhD, 65; Columbia Univ, MBA, 66. *Prof Exp:* Asst prof, Dept Pub Law & Govt, Columbia Univ, 65; res assoc, Ctr Internal Affairs, Harvard Univ, 66; asst, Presidential Sci Adv Staff, White House, 66-67. *Concurrent Pos:* Dir, Nat Comt US-China Rels, 70-75; mem, Coun Foreign Rels, 74-; fel, Brandeis Univ, 86; founding dir, Am Agenda, 88-89; mem, Nat Sci Bd, NSF, 96- *Mem:* NSF. *Res:* Techniques used by American Presidents to obtain policy advice on managing the federal government; granted one US patent. *Mailing Add:* TEI Industs Inc 600 New Hampshire Ave NW Suite 1250 Washington DC 20037

GREENBERG, SEYMOUR SAMUEL, GEOLOGY. *Current Pos:* assoc prof sci, 64-69, prof geol, 69-81, PROF EARTH SCI, WEST CHESTER STATE COL, 80- *Personal Data:* b Brooklyn, NY, Feb 20, 30; m 64. *Educ:* Brooklyn Col, BS; Ind Univ, AM & PhD, 59. *Prof Exp:* Petrogr, Ind Geol Surv, 52-62; geologist, Va Div Mineral Resources, 62-64. *Mem:* Geol Soc Am; Am Mineral Soc; Soc Econ Paleontologists & Mineralogists; Geochem Soc; Mineral Asn Can; Sigma Xi. *Res:* Petrology and mineralogy. *Mailing Add:* 317 W Virginia Ave West Chester PA 19380

GREENBERG, SIDNEY ABRAHAM, PHYSICAL CHEMISTRY. *Current Pos:* CONSULT, MACROMEASURE, FAIRFAX, CALIF, 73- *Personal Data:* b New York, NY, Nov 26, 18; m 46; c 2. *Educ:* Wash Univ, BA, 39; Polytech Inst Brooklyn, MS, 47, PhD(phys chem), 50. *Prof Exp:* Chemist indust res, 41-43; res assoc, Polytech Inst Brooklyn, 46-50; res chemist, Sylvania Elec Co, 50-51 & Johns Manville Res Ctr, 52-55; res assoc, Univ Leiden, 55-56; assoc prof chem, Seton Hall Univ, 56-58; sr res chemist, Portland Cement Asn, 58-62; mgr appl res & adv develop, Ampex Corp, 62-64; res mgr, Mechrolab Div, Hewlett-Packard, 64-66; assoc prof phys sci, Dominican Col, Calif, 66-72; vis res prof, Zagreb Univ, Yugoslavia, 72-73. *Mem:* Fel AAAS; Am Chem Soc. *Res:* Kinetics of chemical reactions and crystallization; properties of luminescent solids; structure and properties of inorganic materials; colloid chemistry of silicates; magnetic materials; chemical research and analytical instruments. *Mailing Add:* 187 Bothin Rd Fairfax CA 94930

GREENBERG, STANLEY SHIMEN, CELL BIOLOGY, PHARMACOLOGY. *Current Pos:* PROF MED, LA STATE UNIV, 91-, PROF PHYSIOL, 91-, PROF PHARMACOL, 92-, MEM GRAD FAC, 92- *Personal Data:* b Brooklyn, NY, Sept 14, 48; m 68; c Johnathan M. *Educ:* Long Island Univ, BS, 68; Univ Iowa, MS, 70, PhD(pharmacol), 72. *Prof Exp:* Med intern clin pharmacol, Univ Iowa Col Med, 72-73; NIH fel, Univ Mich, 73-74; instr physiol & cell biophys, Baylor Col Med, 74-75, instr pharmacol, 74-75; asst prof, Ohio State Univ Col Med, 75-77; assoc prof, Univ Southern Ala Col Med, 77-79, tenured assoc prof, 80-83; sect head vascular/gen pharmacol, Berlex Labs Inc, 83-86, investr pharmacol, 86-87, sr investr & corp consult, 87-88; adj prof physiol, Univ Med & Dent NJ, 88-91. *Concurrent Pos:* Res career develop award, Nat Heart Lung & Blood Inst, NIH, 76-80; fel, High Blood Pressure Coun, Am Heart Asn, 80; adj prof physiol, Univ Med & Dent NJ, 83-88, Fairleigh Dickinson Col Dent, 84-87; consult, Genentech Corp, 89-90, Am Cyanamid, 89-91; sr pharmacologist, Block Drug, 90- *Mem:* Am Soc Pharmacol & Exp Therapeut; Am Physiol Soc; Am Fedn Clin Invest; fel Am Col Nutrit; Am Heart Asn; Am Thoracic Soc. *Res:* Study of the role of cytokines and celluar mediators in cardiopulmonary host defense mechanisms, including cell signaling, receptor transduction mechanisms and gene expression and regulation in phagocytes, endothelium and smooth muscle. *Mailing Add:* Div Pulmonary & Critical Care Med Dept Med La State Univ 1542 Tulane Ave New Orleans LA 70112-1393. *Fax:* 504-568-7864

GREENBERG, STANLY DONALD, CYTOPATHOLOGY, RESPIRATORY PATHOLOGY. *Current Pos:* instr path, Baylor Col Med, 62-63, from asst prof to assoc prof path & otolaryngol, 63-74, prof, 75-94, EMER PROF PATH, MED & OTOLARYNGOL, BAYLOR COL MED, 94- *Personal Data:* b Beaumont, Tex, July 27, 30; m 53; c 3. *Educ:* Univ Tex, BA, 54; Baylor Univ, MD, 54; Univ Iowa, MS, 58. *Prof Exp:* Surg pathologist, Jefferson Davis Hosp, Houston, Tex, 62, dir path labs, Tuberc Div, 62-63. *Concurrent Pos:* Attend, Ben Taub Gen Hosp, 63-, Vet Admin Hosp, 64-, Methodist Hosp, 65-; dir cytopath, Harris Co Hosp Dist, 73-78. *Mem:* AMA; Am Soc Clin Path; Col Am Path; Am Soc Exp Path; Am Thoracic Soc. *Mailing Add:* 5106 Braesheather Dr Houston TX 77096

GREENBERG, STEPHEN B, MEDICINE. *Current Pos:* INTERNAL MED, SUB-INFECTIOUS DIS, BAYLOR COL MED, 72- *Mailing Add:* Dept Med Baylor Col Med One Baylor Plaza Rm 559E Houston TX 77030-3498

GREENBERG, STEPHEN ROBERT, PATHOLOGY, MEDICAL EDUCATION. *Current Pos:* instr, Chicago Med Sch, 55-57, assoc, 57-62, asst prof, 62-69, ASSOC PROF PATH, CHICAGO MED SCH, 69- *Personal Data:* b Omaha, Nebr, May 5, 27; m 52; c 2. *Educ:* St Louis Univ, BS, 51, MS, 52, PhD(path), 54. *Prof Exp:* Asst path, Clarkson Hosp, Omaha, Nebr, 54-55.

Concurrent Pos: Grantee, Forensic Sci Found. *Mem:* Fel Asn Clin Scientists; Int Acad Path; Am Geriat Soc; fel AAAS; Sigma Xi; Am Soc Clin Path; Am Acad Forensic Sci; Am Asn Pathologists. *Res:* Anatomic and clinical pathology; environmental pathology; experimental pulmonary disease; pathology of retained metals; tissue effects of metals implanted experimentally in animals and retained for long periods, simulating retained bullets in man. *Mailing Add:* 418 Huron St Park Forest IL 60466-2206

GREENBERG, WILLIAM, MATHEMATICAL PHYSICS. *Current Pos:* from asst prof to assoc prof, 73-80, PROF MATH, VA POLYTECH INST & STATE UNIV, 80- *Personal Data:* b Lakewood, NJ, Aug 4, 41; m 68; c 3. *Educ:* Princeton Univ, BA, 63; Harvard Univ, MA, 65, PhD(physics), 70. *Prof Exp:* Vaclav Hlavaty asst prof math, Ind Univ, 70-73. *Concurrent Pos:* Fel, Nat Sci Res Ctr, Marseille, France, 70; vis res assoc, Physics Theory Lab, Fed Polytech Sch, Lausanne, Switz, 72; vis prof, Univ Firenze, Italy, 82-83. *Mem:* Am Math Soc; Am Phys Soc. *Res:* Mathematical foundations of physics; rigorous statistical mechanics and solution of transport equations. *Mailing Add:* 1111 Highland Circle Blacksburg VA 24060

GREENBERG, WILLIAM MICHAEL, APPLIED PHYSICS. *Current Pos:* RES PHYSICIST THIN FILMS, LIBBEY-OWENS-FORD CO, 67- *Personal Data:* b Toledo, Ohio, Nov 6, 38; m 74. *Educ:* Univ Toledo, BS, 60; Univ Mich, MS, 61, PhD(physics), 67. *Mem:* Am Vacuum Soc. *Res:* Applied research on the physics of large-scale production of thin film optical coatings. *Mailing Add:* Oregon Res 3250 Dogwood Dr Oregon OH 43616

GREENBERGER, DANIEL MORDECAI, THEORETICAL PHYSICS, QUANTUM THEORY. *Current Pos:* from asst prof to assoc prof, 63-78, PROF PHYSICS, CITY COL NEW YORK, 79- *Personal Data:* b Bronx, NY, Sept 29, 33; m 87, Suzanne Dohm. *Educ:* Mass Inst Technol, BS, 54; Univ Ill, Urbana, MS, 56, PhD(physics), 58. *Honors & Awards:* A V Humboldt Prize, 88. *Prof Exp:* Asst prof physics, Ohio State Univ, 60-61; NSF vis fel, Univ Calif, Berkeley, 61-62, asst prof, 62-63. *Concurrent Pos:* Vis scientist, Oxford Univ, 71 & Mass Inst Technol, 80-90; vis prof, Mass Inst Technol, 79-80; Fulbright guest prof, Atom Inst Austrian Univ, 86, Humboldt prof, Max Planck Inst Quantum Optics, 88; adj prof, Hampshire Col, Amherst, Mass, 90- *Mem:* AAAS; Am Phys Soc; Am Asn Physics Teachers; Sigma Xi. *Res:* Foundations of quantum theory; relativity and gravitation; neutron diffraction. *Mailing Add:* Dept Physics City Col New York New York NY 10031. *Fax:* 212-650-6940

GREENBERGER, JOEL S, RADIATION ONCOLOGY. *Current Pos:* PROF & CHMN, DEPT RADIATION ONCOL, UNIV PITTSBURGH. *Personal Data:* b Pittsburgh, Pa, Dec 10, 46; m 82, Catherine Guyton; c Rodd, Emily, Josh & Ben. *Educ:* Columbia Univ, BA, 67; Harvard Med Sch, MD, 71. *Prof Exp:* Staff assoc, Viral Carcinogenesis Br, Nat Cancer Inst, 72-74; resident, Joint Ctr Radiation Ther, Harvard Med Sch, 74-76; instr radiation ther, Sidney Farber Cancer Inst, 76-79; from asst prof to assoc prof radiation ther, Harvard Med Sch, 79-84, assoc dir res, Joint Ctr Radiation Ther, Dept Radiation Ther, 82-84; prof & chmn, Dept Radiation Oncol, Med Ctr, Univ Mass, 84- *Concurrent Pos:* Chmn, Comt Selection Fuller Jr Res Fel, Am Cancer Soc, 79-82, res grant sci adv comt, 83-88. *Mem:* AMA; AAAS; Soc Microbiol; Am Fedn Clin Res; Tissue Cult Asn; Am Soc Hemat; Int Asn Comp Res Leukemia & Related Dis; Radiation Res Soc; Int Asn Exp Hemat; Am Soc Clin Oncol. *Res:* Radiation oncology; numerous publications. *Mailing Add:* Dept Radiation Oncol Univ Pittsburgh Presby Univ Hosp DeSoto O'Hara Sts Pittsburgh PA 15213-2582

GREENBERGER, LEE M, BIOCHEMISTRY. *Current Pos:* sr scientist, 90-91, GROUP LEADER CANCER PHARMACOL, LEDERLE LABS, NY, 91- *Personal Data:* b Brooklyn, NY, June 5, 55; m 77. *Educ:* Univ Rochester, BA, 77; Emory Univ, PhD(anat), 84. *Prof Exp:* Res asst neurosci, Rochelle Univ, 77-79; postdoctorate neurosci, Columbia Univ, 84-86; postdoctorate molecular pharmacol, Albert Einstein Col Med, NY, 86-88, instr, 88-90. *Concurrent Pos:* Vis asst prof med pharmacol, Albert Einstein Col Med, NY, 90- *Mem:* AAAS; Am Asn Cancer Res; Am Soc Biochem & Molecular Biol. *Res:* Identify and understand mechanisms and drug resistance in tumor cells; develop novel chemotherapeutic agents for the treatment of cancer. *Mailing Add:* Lederle Labs Bldg 200 Rm 4608 401 N Middletown Rd Pearl River NY 10965-1299. *Fax:* 914-732-5557

GREENBERGER, MARTIN, POLICY ANALYSIS, FUTURE STUDIES. *Current Pos:* IBM PROF COMPUT & INFO SYSTS & DIR, CTR DIGITAL MEDIA, GRAD SCH MGT, UNIV CALIF, LOS ANGELES, 82- *Personal Data:* b Elizabeth, NJ, Nov 30, 31; m 82, Liz Attardo; c Kari (Edwards), David, Beth (Jonit), Jonah & Jilly. *Educ:* Harvard Univ, AB, 55, AM, 56, PhD(appl math), 58. *Prof Exp:* Mgr appl sci, Int Bus Mach Corp, 57-58; from asst prof to assoc prof indust mgt, Mass Inst Technol, 58-67; prof comput sci, chmn & dir info processing, Johns Hopkins Univ, 67-72, prof math sci, 72-82. *Concurrent Pos:* Guggenheim fel, Univ Calif, Berkeley, 65-66; mem bd trustees, EDUCOM, 68-73, chmn coun, 68-69; mem comput sci & eng bd, Nat Acad Sci, 70-72; adv, Off of Technol Assessment, US Cong, 74-75 & consult, Gen Acct Off, 75; chmn sect T on info, comput & commun, AAAS, 74-76; mem, Harvard Bd Overseers Vis Comt on Off for Info Technol, 75-81; mgr systs prog, Elec Power Res Inst, 76-77; chmn adv comt, Nat Ctr Analytical Energy Systs, Brookhaven Nat Lab, 78; Isaac Taylor vis prof energy, Technion-Israel Inst Technol, 78-79 & Stanford, 80; mem rev comt, Appl Sci Div, Lawrence Berkeley Lab, 84-87; pres, Coun Technol & Individual, 84- *Mem:* Fel AAAS. *Res:* Strategy studies multimedia; future technology; computer systems; digital communications. *Mailing Add:* Anderson Grad Sch Mgt Univ Calif 110 Westwood Plaza Los Angeles CA 90095-1481. *Fax:* 310-393-9120; *E-Mail:* mg@ucla.edu

GREENBERGER, NORTON JERALD, INTERNAL MEDICINE, GASTROENTEROLOGY. *Current Pos:* PROF MED & CHMN DEPT, UNIV KANS MED CTR, KANSAS CITY, 72- *Personal Data:* b Cleveland, Ohio, Sept 13, 33; m 64, Joan E Narcus; c Sharon, Rachel & Wendy. *Educ:* Yale Univ, AB, 55; Western Res Univ, MD, 59. *Prof Exp:* From asst prof to prof med, Col Med, Ohio State Univ, 65-72, dir div gastroenterol, 67-72. *Concurrent Pos:* Attend physician, Ohio State Univ Hosp, 65-; consult, Vet Admin Hosp & Wright Patterson AFB Hosp, Dayton, Ohio; ed, J Lab Clin Med, 82-86. *Mem:* Am Gastroenterol Asn (pres, 84-85); Asn Am Physicians; Am Soc Clin Invest; Am Col Physicians (pres, 90-91); Cent Soc Clin Res (pres, 80-81); Asn Prof Med (pres, 86-87). *Res:* Intestinal absorption of lipids and iron; intestinal transport of digitalis glycosides; acute and chronic pancreatic disease. *Mailing Add:* Dept Med Univ Kans Med Ctr 39th St & Rainbow Blvd Kansas City KS 66103. *Fax:* 913-588-3995; *E-Mail:* ngreenbe@kvmc.edu

GREENBLATT, CHARLES LEONARD, microbiology, parasitology, for more information see previous edition

GREENBLATT, DAVID J, PHARMACOLOGY. *Current Pos:* CHIEF, DIV CLIN PHARMACOL, NEW ENG MED CTR & PROF PSYCHIAT, MED, ANESTHESIA & PHARMACOL, TUFTS UNIV SCH MED, 79- *Personal Data:* b Boston, Mass, Apr 8, 45; m 91, Lisa-Lynn Graefin von Moltke; c Heinrich-Karl v. *Educ:* Amherst Col, BA, 66; Harvard Med Sch, MD, 70. *Honors & Awards:* Rawls-Palmer Award, Am Soc Clin Pharmacol Therapeut; McKeen-Cattell Award, Am Col Clin Pharmacol. *Prof Exp:* Asst prof med, Harvard Med Sch, 74-79; chief, clin pharmacol unit, Mass Gen Hosp, 75-79. *Concurrent Pos:* Prog dir, Gen Clin Res Ctr, New Eng Med Ctr, 79-; chmn, Dept Pharmacol & Exp Therapeut, Tufts Univ Sch Med, 79- *Mem:* Am Soc Clin Invest; Am Col Neuopsychopharmacol; Am Soc Pharmacol & Exp Therapeut; Am Soc Clin Pharmacol Therapeut; Am Col Clin Pharmacol. *Res:* Investigating the mechanisms of altered drug sensitivity in the elderly; neuropharmacology of the benzodiazedine receptor; chemistry of the cytochrome enzymes. *Mailing Add:* 136 Harrison Ave Boston MA 02111

GREENBLATT, GERALD A, PLANT PHYSIOLOGY. *Current Pos:* sr res fel, Inst Life Sci, 70-74, asst prof plant sci, 74-82, ASST PROF VET PHYSIOL & PHARMACOL, TEX A&M UNIV, 82- *Personal Data:* b Los Angeles, Calif, May 19, 32; m 61; c 1. *Educ:* Los Angeles State Col, BA, 55; Univ Calif, Davis, PhD(plant physiol), 65. *Prof Exp:* Instr biol, Princeton Univ, 65-66; asst prof, Tex Tech Univ, 66-70. *Mem:* AAAS; Am Soc Plant Physiologists. *Res:* Abscission and senescence; growth hormones; secondary material products of plants; byssenosis; physiology host and pothogen interactions. *Mailing Add:* 625 NW Saginaw Ave Bend OR 97701

GREENBLATT, HELLEN CHAYA, RESOURCE MANAGEMENT, START-UPS. *Current Pos:* sr develop virol, E I DuPont, 88-90, managing dir, M-Cap Technol, 90-93, BTR SEPARATIONS, DIR TECH AFFAIRS, DUPONT CHEM, 93- *Personal Data:* US citizen. *Educ:* City Univ New York, BA, 68; Univ Okla, MS, 71; State Univ Ny, Brooklyn, PhD(microbiol & immunol), 77. *Prof Exp:* Resident res assoc, Walter Reed Army Inst Res, Washington, DC, 78-80; sr res immunoparisitologist, Merck, Sharp & Dohme, 80-81; assoc, Dept Med, Albert Einstein Col Med, 81-84; dir res develop, Clin Sci, Inc, 84-86, dir sci & new bus develop, 86-87. *Res:* Facilitate laboratory and quality control needs of business. *Mailing Add:* BTR/DuPont Quillen Bldg Rm 1K03 Concord Plaza 3411 Silverside Rd Wilmington DE 19810. *Fax:* 302-998-9651

GREENBLATT, IRWIN M, GENETICS, BOTANY. *Current Pos:* assoc prof, 68-84, prof, 84-91, EMER PROF GENETICS, UNIV CONN, 91- *Personal Data:* b Brooklyn, NY, June 4, 30; m 55, 83; c 3. *Educ:* Ohio State Univ, BS, 53; Univ Wis, MS, 55, PhD(genetics), 59. *Prof Exp:* Res assoc genetics, Univ Wis, 59-60; asst prof biol, Marquette Univ, 60-66 & Northwestern Univ, 66-68. *Concurrent Pos:* NSF & NIH grants, 61-; consult, Teweles Seed Co, Wis, 64-68. *Mem:* Fel AAAS; Genetics Soc Am; Am Genetic Asn; Bot Soc Am. *Res:* Genetics of regulatory mechanisms as seen in higher plant material; cytogenetics of maize and alfalfa; root tissue culture of maize callus; alfalfa; tissue culture of maize and tobacco; transposons in maize. *Mailing Add:* 27 Deer Ridge Rd Killingworth CT 06417

GREENBLATT, JACK FRED, TRANSCRIPTION, REGULATION OF GENE EXPRESSION. *Current Pos:* from asst prof to assoc prof, 77-84, PROF MOLECULAR BIOL, BANTING & BEST DEPT MED RES, UNIV TORONTO, 84-, PROF, DEPT MOLECULAR & MED GENETICS, 84- *Personal Data:* b Montreal, Que, June 6, 46; m 69, Anna Lou; c Jordan & Joshua. *Educ:* McGill Univ, BSc, 67; Harvard Univ, PhD(biophys), 73. *Honors & Awards:* Ayerst Award, Can Biochem Soc, 83. *Prof Exp:* Fel molecular biol, Dept Molecular Biol, Univ Geneva, 72-74; sr researcher, 74-76. *Concurrent Pos:* Embo fel, Pasteur Inst, 77; prin investr, Med Res Coun Can, 77- & Nat Cancer Inst Can, 81-; int res scholar, Howard Hughes Med Inst, 91-; distinguished scientist, Med Res Coun Can, 95- *Mem:* Fel Royal Soc Can. *Res:* Regulation of the termination of transcription in eubacteria; regulation of transcription by human RNA polymerase II. *Mailing Add:* Banting & Best Dept Med Res C H Best Inst Univ Toronto 112 College St Toronto ON M5G 1L6 Can

GREENBLATT, JAYSON HERSCHEL, EARTH SCIENCES. *Current Pos:* RETIRED. *Personal Data:* b Montreal, Que, Mar 5, 22; m 44; c 2. *Educ:* Dalhousie Univ, BSc, 42, MSc, 43; McGill Univ, PhD, 48. *Prof Exp:* From res chemist to head chem sect, Naval Res Estab, 48-62, head, Dockyard Lab, 63-64, supt eng physics wing, 64-68; dir physics div, Defense Res Estab

Ottowa, 68-70, dir earth sci div, 70-75; counr defense res & develop, Can Defence Liaison Staff, Can Embassy, Washington, DC, 75-81; sr scientist to chief, Res & Develop Br, Dept Nat Defense, Can, 81-82. *Concurrent Pos:* Adj prof, Dalhousie Polytech, 81- *Mem:* Fel Chem Inst Can. *Res:* Physical properties of explosives and propellants; homogeneous gas phase reactions; physical electrochemistry as applied to the protection of metals in a marine environment; oceanography; arctic geophysics, especially water-air-ice interactions, properties of arctic terrain and remote sensing; studies of the combustion of cool liquid slurries, wood and other non oil fuels. *Mailing Add:* 6095 Coburg Rd Apt 101 Halifax NS B3H 4K1 Can

GREENBLATT, MARSHAL, RADIATION DEVICES. *Current Pos:* MGR CONSULT, GREENBLATT ASSOC, 79- *Personal Data:* b Philadelphia, Pa, Dec 11, 39; wid; c Drew, Robert & Mark. *Educ:* Columbia Univ, BA, 61; Princeton Univ, PhD(aerodyn eng), 71. *Prof Exp:* Vpres, Fusion Systs, 74-78; vpres mkt, Isomet Corp, Springfield, Va, 78-79; pres, Mat Eng Assocs Inc, 81-93, Buffalo Mat Res Inc, 85-93. *Res:* Radiation and photochemistry; materials testing. *Mailing Add:* Greenblatt Assoc 10830 Spring Knoll Dr Potomac MD 20854. *Fax:* 301-983-3255

GREENBLATT, MARTHA, SOLID STATE CHEMISTRY, CRYSTALLOGRAPHY. *Current Pos:* from asst prof to assoc prof, 74-85, PROF CHEM, RUTGERS UNIV, 85- *Personal Data:* b Hungary, Jan 1, 41; US citizen; m 59, Martin; c 2. *Educ:* Brooklyn Col, BSc, 62; Polytech Inst Brooklyn, PhD(inorg chem), 67. *Prof Exp:* Asst prof chem, Polytech Inst Brooklyn, 67-70, res assoc, 70-72; vis scientist, Weizmann Inst Sci, 72-73; vis asst prof, Polytech Inst Brooklyn, 73-74. *Mem:* Am Chem Soc; Am Crystallog Asn. *Res:* Preparation of solid materials; crystal growth, study relationship between structural and physical properties by electrical resistivity, magnetic susceptibility; optical spectroscopy; x-ray diffraction. *Mailing Add:* Chem Dept Rutgers Univ PO Box 939 Piscataway NJ 08854-0939

GREENBLATT, MILTON, psychiatry; deceased, see previous edition for last biography

GREENBLATT, RICHARD ELIOT, BIOELECTRO MAGNETISM. *Current Pos:* PRES, SOURCE SIGNAL IMAGING, 90- *Personal Data:* b New York, NY, July 14, 45. *Educ:* Cornell Univ, BS, 66; Mass Inst Technol, PhD(biol), 74. *Prof Exp:* Sr scientist, Biomagnetic Technol, 85-90. *Res:* Source estimation; inverse problems in bioelectromagnetism. *Mailing Add:* 2323 Broadway Suite 102 San Diego CA 92102

GREENBLATT, SAMUEL HAROLD, ALEXIA, NEUROHISTORY. *Current Pos:* ASSOC PROF NEUROSURG, BROWN UNIV, 89-, CHIEF NEUROSURG, MEM HOSP RI, PAWTUCKET, 89- *Personal Data:* b Potsdam, NY, May 16, 39; m 63; Judith Shapiro; c Rachel, Daniel & Miriam. *Educ:* Cornell Univ, BA, 61, MD, 66; Johns Hopkins Univ, MA, 64; Brown Univ, MA, 91. *Prof Exp:* Intern surg, Boston City Hosp, 66-67; resident neurol, Boston Vet Admin Hosp, 67-68; neurologist, Walson Army Hosp, Ft Dix, NJ, 68-70; resident neurol surg, Dartmouth Affil Hosps, 70-74; instr, Albert Einstein Med Col, 74-77; from asst prof to assoc prof neurosurg, Med Col Ohio, Toledo, 80-89. *Concurrent Pos:* Hon sr registr, Neurosurg Unit Guy's, Maudsley & Kings Col Hosps, London, 72; Tiffany Blake fel, Hitchcock Found, 72-73. *Mem:* Int Soc Hist Neurosci; Cong Neurol Surgeons; Am Asn Neurol Surgeons; fel Am Col Surgeons. *Res:* Anatomical basis of reading disorders; history and conceptual foundations of the neurosciences; medical education. *Mailing Add:* Brown Univ Prog Neurosurg Mem Hosp Pawtucket RI 02860. *Fax:* 401-729-2781; *E-Mail:* samuel_greenblatt@brown.edu

GREENBLATT, SETH ALAN, WAVELET ANALYSIS, COMPUTATIONAL LOGIC. *Current Pos:* CHIEF SCIENTIST, BETAL INT CORP, 97- *Personal Data:* b Bath, Maine, Mar 26, 60; m 81, Lynn V Signenza; c Alexander N & Adrienne A. *Educ:* Barry Univ, BPS, 85; George Washington Univ, MPhil, 89, PhD(econ), 93. *Prof Exp:* Consult, 74-81; proj mgr, Martin Marietta Corp, 81-82; mgr, Realtron Corp, 82-83; proj mgr, Viewdata Corp Am, Knight-Ridder, 83-86; mgr, Entre Computer Centers, Inc, 86-87; sr consult, Systemhouse, Ltd, 87-89; vpres economet, Sorites Group, Inc, 89-91; prof economet, Univ Reading, 91-99. *Concurrent Pos:* Lectr, var prof conferences, 84-; res consult, George Washington Univ, 88-89; vpres, Wash-Baltimore Sect, Soc Indust & Appl Math, 89-91, pres, 90-; vis scholar, Univ Indonesia, 91; vis lectr, Thomas Valley Univ, 94-95, City Univ, 96; vis prof, Univ London, 96-97. *Mem:* Soc Indust & Appl Math; fel Royal Statist Soc; Soc Comput Econ; Sigma Xi; Am Math Soc. *Res:* Wavelet analysis of images and signals; pattern recognition; atomic decompostion of signals; data mining; automated reasing and automated theorem proving. *Mailing Add:* Betac Int Corp 2001 N Beauregard St Alexandria VA 22311

GREENE, ALAN CAMPBELL, SOLID STATE SCIENCE. *Current Pos:* assoc prof, 71-74, PROF PHYSICS, CALIF STATE COL, 74- *Personal Data:* b Boston, Mass, Mar 31, 35; m 63; c 3. *Educ:* Northeastern Univ, BS, 58; Brown Univ, PhD(physics), 64. *Prof Exp:* Asst prof physics, Rensselaer Polytech Inst, 64-70; staff physicist, Comn Col Physics, 70-71. *Mem:* Am Asn Physics Teachers. *Res:* Defect interactions in ionic solids; production of defects by radiation; magnetic properties of crystalline defects. *Mailing Add:* Dept Physics & Geol Calif State Univ 9001 Stockdale Hwy Bakersfield CA 93311-1022

GREENE, ARTHUR E, CELL BIOLOGY. *Current Pos:* VPRES, RES & SCI AFFAIRS, CORNELL INST MED RES, 85- *Personal Data:* b Philadelphia, Pa, Aug 8, 23; m 53; c 2. *Educ:* Univ Pa, AB, 47; Phila Col Pharm, BSc, 49, MSc, 50, DSc(bact), 52; Am Bd Microbiol, dipl, 65. *Prof Exp:* Res fel virol, Children's Hosp of Philadelphia, 52-53, res assoc, Polio Res Lab, 53-56, res assoc, S Jersey Med Res Found, 56-57; res virologist, Nat Drug Co, Philadelphia, 57-59; virologist, Smith, Kline & French Labs, 59-60; assoc dir, Nat Inst Gen Med Sci, 72-83, dir, human genetic mutant cell repository, 83-88; head, Dept Cell Biol, Nat Inst Aging, 61-88, dir aging cell cult respository, 80-88. *Concurrent Pos:* Thomas H Powers scholar, Philadelphia Col Pharm & Sci, 49, lectr virol, 56-85, vis asst res prof vet virol, 62-64; res assoc surg, Pa Med Sch, 64-; vis assoc prof microbiol, Jefferson Med Col, 68-73; assoc virol, Philadelphia Col Osteopath Med, 61-76; adj prof biol, Rowan Col, 94-97. *Mem:* AAAS; Am Soc Microbiol; Tissue Cult Asn; Soc Cryobiol; NY Acad Sci. *Res:* Preservation and characterization of cell cult; cryobiology of cells and organs; techniques for the species identification of insect and animal cell lines; studies on genetic and biochemical cell cultures; virus chemotherapy and vaccines; aging syndrome cell cultures. *Mailing Add:* 37 S Syracuse Dr Cherry Hill NJ 08034

GREENE, ARTHUR EDWARD, computational physics, laser physics; deceased, see previous edition for last biography

GREENE, ARTHUR FRANKLIN, ELEMENTARY PARTICLE PHYSICS. *Current Pos:* PHYSICIST, BROOKHAVEN NAT LAB, 79- *Personal Data:* b Hartford, Conn, Dec 18, 39; m 63; c 2. *Educ:* Worcester Polytech Inst, BS, 61, MS, 63; Tufts Univ, PhD(exp elem particle physics), 67. *Prof Exp:* Asst, Worcester Polytech Inst, 61-63 & Tufts Univ, 63-67; physicist, div res, AEC, 67-69; res assoc high energy physics, Argonne Nat Lab, Ill, 69-72; physicist, Fermi Nat Accelerator Lab, 72-79, asst dir prog planning, 76-79. *Mem:* Am Phys Soc. *Res:* Experimental high energy physics; elementary particle research using bubble chambers and electronic techniques; administration, with emphasis on planning for experiments related to high energy physics research; development of superconducting magnets for a high energy particle accelerator. *Mailing Add:* RHIC Proj Bldg 902A Brookhaven Nat Lab Upton NY 11973

GREENE, ARTHUR FREDERICK, JR, ANALYTICAL CHEMISTRY, INORGANIC CHEMISTRY. *Current Pos:* analyst, 62-64, RES ANALYTICAL CHEMIST, ENGELHARD CORP, 64- *Personal Data:* b Cleveland, Ohio, Sept 28, 27; m 57. *Educ:* Ohio State Univ, BSc, 51; Case Western Res Univ, MSc, 61. *Honors & Awards:* George B Hogaboom Mem Award, 69. *Prof Exp:* Tech serv, R O Hull & Co, Inc, 55-61. *Mem:* Am Chem Soc; Royal Soc Chem; NAm Thermal Analysis Soc; Int Confederation Thermal Analysis; Int Union Pure & Appl Chem. *Res:* Development of new analytical methods; thermal analysis techniques for synthesis and characterization of inorganic materials. *Mailing Add:* 1056 Lakeland Ave Lakewood OH 44107-1228

GREENE, BETTYE WASHINGTON, PHYSICAL CHEMISTRY, COLLOID CHEMISTRY. *Current Pos:* RETIRED. *Personal Data:* b Palestine, Tex, Mar 20, 35; m 55; c 3. *Educ:* Tuskegee Inst, BS, 55; Wayne State Univ, PhD(phys chem), 65. *Prof Exp:* Res chemist, Dow Chem Co, 65-70, sr res chemist, 70-75, res assoc, 75-81, assoc scientist, 81-86. *Mem:* AAAS; Am Chem Soc; Sigma Xi. *Res:* Light scattering method for determining size distributions in colloid systems; determination of electrokinetic properties of pigment dispersions used for paper coatings; rheology of paper coating dispersions; design of composites for building products. characterization of polymers and latexes; repeptization in hydrophobic colloids; latex fiber interactions; heterofloeculation studies. *Mailing Add:* 5213 Cortland St Midland MI 46642

GREENE, BRUCE EDGAR, plastics, automotive engineering, for more information see previous edition

GREENE, CHARLES EDWIN, organic chemistry; deceased, see previous edition for last biography

GREENE, CHARLES RICHARD, PHYSICAL CHEMISTRY, CHEMICAL ENGINEERING. *Current Pos:* DIR, ENERGY INDUST PROG, SRI INT, 80- *Personal Data:* b Chicago, Ill, Oct 3, 23; m 47; c 2. *Educ:* Univ Chicago, BS, 48, SM, 49, PhD(phys & org chem), 52. *Honors & Awards:* Norton Prize. *Prof Exp:* Res chemist dermat cancers, Chicago Med Sch, 51; prof chem, George Williams Col, 51-52; res chemist, Stand Oil Co Ind, 52-54; res chemist, Shell Develop Co, 54-64, res supvr, 64-67, mgr prod, Shell Chem Co, NY, 67-68, mgr exp opers, Shell Develop Co, 68-69, mgr prod, 69-72, mgr surface projs, 72-80. *Concurrent Pos:* Consult, res appl nat needs, NSF, 73- *Mem:* Am Chem Soc; fel Am Inst Chem Engrs; Sigma Xi; AAAS; fel Am Inst Chemists. *Res:* Petrochemicals; research in coal as source of chemicals; project management in development of new processes for manufacture of chemical intermediates; energy consulting. *Mailing Add:* Greeneridge Sci Inc 4512 Via Huerto Santa Barbara CA 93110-2324

GREENE, CHARLOTTE HELEN, PHYSIOLOGY, HISTOLOGY. *Current Pos:* Instr, 75-77, from asst prof to assoc prof, 81-88, PROF PHYSIOL, PHILADELPHIA COL OSTEOP MED, 88- *Personal Data:* b Philadelphia, Pa, Mar 10, 43; m 71. *Educ:* West Chester State Col, BS, 65; Thomas Jefferson Univ, PhD(physiol), 74. *Concurrent Pos:* Investr, Am Heart Asn, 77-79, dir electron micros, 88- *Mem:* Am Zool Soc; Am Physiol Soc; Sigma Xi. *Res:* Cardiovascular, endocrine physiology; lasers in medicine. *Mailing Add:* Dept Physiol & Pharmacol Philadelphia Col Osteop Med 4170 City Ave Philadelphia PA 19131

GREENE, CHRISTOPHER HENRY, THEORETICAL ATOMIC PHYSICS. *Current Pos:* Asst prof, 81-84, ASSOC PROF PHYSICS, LA STATE UNIV, 84- *Personal Data:* b Lincoln, Nebr, Aug 1, 54; m 77. *Educ:* Univ Nebr, Lincoln, BS, 76; Univ Chicago, MS, 77, PHD(physics), 80. *Concurrent Pos:* Alfred P Sloan Found fel. *Mem:* Am Phys Soc; Sigma Xi. *Res:* Electron correlations in atoms and small molecules; threshold laws in photoabsorption and electron scattering. *Mailing Add:* Joint Inst Lab Astrophys Univ Colo CB 440 Boulder CO 80309-0440

GREENE, CHRISTOPHER STORM, AERONAUTICAL ENGINEERING. *Current Pos:* PROD MGR, HORTON, INC, 91- *Personal Data:* b Aurora, Ill; c 2. *Educ:* Univ Colo, Boulder, BS(elec eng) & BS(bus), 73; Mass Inst Technol, PhD(elec eng), 78. *Prof Exp:* Res engr, Honeywell Mil Avionics, 78-81, sect chief, Honeywell Syst & Res Ctr, 81-83, sr prog mgr, 83-91. *Mem:* Am Inst Aeronaut & Astronaut; Inst Elec & Electronics Engrs; Sigma Xi. *Res:* Guidance, navigation and control. *Mailing Add:* 2701 NW 13th Terr New Brighton MN 55112

GREENE, CURTIS, MATHEMATICS, ALGEBRA. *Current Pos:* assoc prof, 78-81, PROF MATH & CHMN DEPT, HAVERFORD COL, 81- *Personal Data:* b Philadelphia, Pa, Nov 10, 44. *Educ:* Harvard Col, AB, 66; Calif Inst Technol, PhD(math), 69. *Prof Exp:* C L E Moore instr, Mass Inst Technol, 69-71, asst prof math, 71-76; assoc prof math, State Univ NY Buffalo, 75-78. *Mem:* Am Math Soc; Math Asn Am; Soc Indust & Appl Math. *Res:* Algebraic combinatorics. *Mailing Add:* Haverford Col Haverford PA 19041-1392. *Fax:* 215-896-1224; *E-Mail:* cgreene@haverford.edu

GREENE, DARYLE E, NUTRITION, BIOCHEMISTRY. *Current Pos:* RETIRED. *Personal Data:* b Garfield, Ark, June 27, 32; m 54; c 4. *Educ:* Univ Ark, BS, 54, MS, 55; Univ Ill, PhD(animal sci), 60. *Prof Exp:* Asst mgr turkey res div, Ralston Purina Co, 60-62, mgr, 62-64; assoc prof poultry nutrit, Univ Ark, 64-65; dir poultry res, 66-75, dir chow res & develop, 75-83, vpres & dir res, Purina Mills Inc, 83-88. *Mem:* AAAS; Poultry Sci Asn; Animal Nutrit Res Coun; Am Soc Animal Sci; Am Registry Cert Prof Animal Scientists. *Res:* Amino acid nutrition; unidentified growth factors; mineral metabolism; biological availability of nutrients in feed ingredients. *Mailing Add:* 514 Webster Forest Dr St Louis MO 63119

GREENE, DAVID C, PHYSICS, ACOUSTICS. *Current Pos:* RETIRED. *Personal Data:* b Elyria, Ohio, Nov 24, 22; m 49; c 4. *Educ:* Oberlin Col, BA, 49; Pa State Univ, MS, 59. *Prof Exp:* Physicist, US Naval Ord Lab, Md, 50-53; sr engr, Cook Res Labs, Ill, 53-55; physicist & res assoc, Ord Res Lab, Pa State Univ, 55-62; physicist & head acoust & electronics sect, Torpedo Supporting Res Br, Antisubmarine Warfare Off, US Bur Naval Weapons, 62-66, actg head, Acoust Br, Acoust & Electromagnetics Div, Res & Technol Directorate, Naval Ord Systs, Command Hq, Washington, DC, 66-67; sr res scientist, Pac Northwest Labs, Battelle Mem Inst, 67-69; sr staff engr, Sensor Systs Dept, Electronic Systs Lab, Trw Inc, Wash, 69-87; systs analyst, Fairfax Co, Va, 87. *Mem:* Acoust Soc Am. *Mailing Add:* 382 Elm St Oberlin OH 44074

GREENE, DAVID LEE, INORGANIC CHEMISTRY. *Current Pos:* chmn dept phys sci, 76-80, dean arts & sci, 80-89, FAC MEM CHEM, RI COL, 72- *Personal Data:* b Louisville, Ky, Dec 19, 44; m 68; c 1. *Educ:* Univ Notre Dame, 67; Univ Ky, PhD(chem), 71. *Prof Exp:* Fel inorg chem, WVa Univ, 71-72. *Concurrent Pos:* fel, WVA Univ, 71-72; Student Sci Training Prog grantee, NSF, 77; vis scientist, Oxford Univ, 89-90. *Mem:* Am Chem Soc; Sigma Xi. *Res:* Synthesis and characterization of coordination compounds; utilization of microwave heating in synthesis. *Mailing Add:* Dept Phys Sci RI Col Providence RI 02908

GREENE, DAVID LEE, PHYSICAL ANTHROPOLOGY, DENTAL ANTHROPOLOGY. *Current Pos:* assoc prof, 67-71, PROF ANTHROP, UNIV COLO, BOULDER, 71- *Personal Data:* b Denver, Colo, Aug 23, 38; m 62, Kathleen Kerger; c Andrew D. *Educ:* Univ Colo, BA, 60, MA, 62, PhD(anthrop), 65. *Prof Exp:* Asst prof anthrop & orthod, State Univ NY Buffalo, 64-65; asst prof anthrop & head dept, Univ Wyo, 65-67. *Concurrent Pos:* Chmn, Dept Anthrop, Univ Colo, Boulder, 75-77, 81-83 & 90-91. *Mem:* Am Asn Phys Anthrop. *Res:* Human evolution; primatology; population genetics; nubian prehistory. *Mailing Add:* Dept Anthrop Univ Colo Boulder CO 80303

GREENE, DONALD MILLER, AGRICULTURAL CLIMATOLOGY, AGRICULTURAL STATISTICS. *Current Pos:* Lectr, 79-81, asst prof, 81-88, ASSOC PROF EARTH SCI, BAYLOR UNIV, 88- *Personal Data:* b Dallas, Tex, Jan 9, 49; m 72; c 3. *Educ:* ETex State Univ, BS, 73; Univ Okla, MA, 77, PhD(geog), 79. *Concurrent Pos:* Asst ed, Baylor Geol Studies Bull, 80- *Mem:* Asn Am Geographers. *Res:* Relationship between agricultural productivity and weather; statistical models that predict yield based upon the climate experienced during the growing season. *Mailing Add:* Dept Geol Baylor Univ Main Campus PO Box 97354 Waco TX 76706-9989

GREENE, DOUGLAS A, MEDICINE. *Current Pos:* PROF INTERNAL MED & DIR, MICH DIABETES RES & TRAINING CTR, UNIV MICH, ANN ARBOR, 86-, MEM FAC NEUROSCI, 88-, CHIEF DIV ENDOCRINOL & METAB, 91- *Educ:* Princeton Univ, AB, 66; Johns Hopkins Univ, MD, 70. *Prof Exp:* Intern, Johns Hopkins Univ Hosp, Baltimore, 70-71, asst resident, 71-72; res fel, George S Cox Med Res Inst, Univ Pa Hosp, 72-75; asst prof med, Univ Pa, 75-80; assoc prof med & dir, Clin Res Unit & Diabetes Res Labs, Univ Pittsburgh, 80-86. *Res:* Medicine; diabetes; endocrinology; metabolism. *Mailing Add:* Univ Mich Hosp Diabetes Res & Training Inst 3920 Taurman Ctr Box 0354 1331 E Medical Ctr Dr Ann Arbor MI 48109-0580

GREENE, EDWARD FORBES, PHYSICAL CHEMISTRY. *Current Pos:* res assoc, Brown Univ, 49-51, from instr to prof chem, 51-92, Jesse H & Louisa D Sharpe Metcalf, prof, 85-92, EMER PROF CHEM, BROWN UNIV, 93- *Personal Data:* b New York, NY, Dec 29, 22; m 49, Hildegarde Forbes; c Susan, Judith, David & Roger. *Educ:* Harvard Univ, AB, 43, AM, 47, PhD(chem), 49. *Prof Exp:* Chemist, Shell Oil Co, 43-44; mem staff, Los Alamos Sci Lab, 49. *Concurrent Pos:* NSF sr fel, Univ Bonn, 59-60 & Calif Inst Technol, 66-67; vis prof, Tougaloo Col, 65; res vis, Bell Labs, Murray Hill, 76-77; chmn, Chem Dept, Brown Univ, 80-84. *Mem:* Am Chem Soc; Am Phys Soc. *Res:* Chemical kinetics; scattering in molecular beams; molecule surface interactions scattering, energy transfer, electron transfer, reactions. *Mailing Add:* Dept Chem Box H Brown Univ Providence RI 02912. *Fax:* 401-863-2594; *E-Mail:* efgreene@brownvm.brown.edu

GREENE, ELIAS LOUIS, IMMUNOLOGY, VIROLOGY. *Current Pos:* asst dir med oper, 77-80, MGR REGULATORY AFFAIRS INT, MILES INC, BERKELEY, 80-, DIR, 85- *Personal Data:* b New York, NY, Jan 7, 32; m 54, Lena Sykes; c Summer J & Francesca. *Educ:* Brooklyn Col, BS, 53; Cornell Univ, PhD(virol immunol), 64. *Prof Exp:* Res asst virol, Sloan Kettering Inst Cancer Res, 55-64; virologist-immunologist, Res Inst, Henry Putnam Mem Hosp, Bennington, Vt, 64-65; res immunologist pediat, Long Island Jewish Hosp, NY, 65-67; from instr to asst prof pediat, Sch Med, Univ Miami, 67-73; asst dir diag eval, Behring Diag, Am Hoechst Corp, 73-77. *Concurrent Pos:* Nat Cystic Fibrosis Res Found fel, 68; lab technologist, Mercy Hosp, Rockville Centre, NY, 60-67; lectr, New York Community Col, 67; lab technologist, clin lab, Miami Heart Inst, 67-68, consult immunologist, Organ Transplant Prog, 68-73; dir qual control & responsible head biol prog, NAm Biol, Inc, Fla, 70-73; consult immunologist, United Labs, NY, 74- *Mem:* Am Acad Cosmetic Surg; Am Soc Microbiol; Int Asn Biol Standardization; Am Asn Immunol. *Res:* Immunologic and histochemical identification and enumeration of tissue antigens in normal and diseased states, especially in cystic fibrosis and liver diseases; properties of arthropod-borne and H-group viruses. *Mailing Add:* Regulatory Affairs Int 800 Dwight Way PO Box 1986 Berkeley CA 94716-1986. *Fax:* 510-420-5553

GREENE, FRANK CLEMSON, BIOCHEMISTRY. *Current Pos:* RES CHEMIST, WESTERN REGIONAL RES CTR, USDA, BERKELEY, 69- *Personal Data:* b Memphis, Tenn, Sept 2, 39; div; c 2. *Educ:* Morehouse Col, BS, 58; Atlanta Univ, MS, 65; Univ Calif, Davis, PhD(biochem), 69. *Prof Exp:* Chemist, Western Regional Res Lab, USDA, Albany, 61-65; chemist, USDA & Univ Calif, Davis, 65-69. *Mem:* Am Chem Soc; AAAS; Sigma Xi; Am Soc Plant Physiol. *Res:* Physical chemistry of proteins; fluorescent probe mechanisms; biosynthesis of proteins; gene expression. *Mailing Add:* Russell Res Ctr Box 5677 950 College Station Rd Athens GA 30613. *Fax:* 706-546-3367

GREENE, FRANK EUGENE, DEVELOPMENTAL PHARMACOLOGY, DRUG METABOLISM. *Current Pos:* RETIRED. *Educ:* Univ Fla, PhD(pharmacol), 62. *Prof Exp:* Assoc prof pharmacol, Milton S Hershey Med Ctr Pa State, 71-97. *Mailing Add:* 12 Holly Dr Palmyra PA 17033-0850

GREENE, FRANK SULLIVAN, JR, ELECTRICAL ENGINEERING. *Current Pos:* bd dirs, 86, pres, 89-91, CHMN, NETWORKED PICTURE SYSTS, INC, 91- *Personal Data:* b Washington, DC, Oct, 19, 38; c Angela, Frank & Ronald. *Educ:* Washington Univ, St Louis, BS, 61; Purdue Univ, MS, 62; Univ Santa Clara, Calif, PhD(elec eng), 70. *Prof Exp:* Electronic eng officer, USAF, 61-65; mem tech staff & dir labs, Fairchild Res, 65-71; pres, Technol Develop Corp, 72-85, dir, 85-92; pres, Zero One SYsts, Inc, Calif, 85-87, Zero One Systs Groups, 87-89. *Concurrent Pos:* Lectr elec eng, Howard Univ, 62-65, Am Univ, 64-65 & Santa Clara Univ, 72-74; asst chmn & lectr, Stanford Univ, 72-74; gov bd, Inst Elec & Electronics Engrs, 73-75; bd dirs, Bay Area Purchasing Coun, 78-84. *Mem:* Inst Elec & Electronics Engrs; Asn Black Mfrs; Am Elec Asn; Security Affairs Support Asn; Sigma Xi. *Res:* Cross field switching properties of magnetic thin films, magnetic thin film computer memory components and bipolar semiconductor memory components design; illiac IV computer memory. *Mailing Add:* 96 La Mesa Terr Suite F Sunnyvale CA 94086

GREENE, FRANK T, CHEMICAL PHYSICS. *Current Pos:* assoc physicist, 62-63, sr physicist, 63-68, PRIN CHEMIST, MIDWEST RES INST, 68- *Personal Data:* b Saginaw, Mich, Nov 26, 32; m 59; c 3. *Educ:* Univ Mich, BS, 55; Univ Calif, MS, 57; Univ Wis, PhD(phys chem), 61. *Prof Exp:* Res assoc chem, Univ Kans, 61-62. *Mem:* Am Chem Soc; Combustion Inst; Am Soc Mass Spectrometry. *Res:* High temperature chemistry and thermodynamics; mass and optical spectroscopy; boron chemistry; molecular beams; combustion; radiation-material interaction. *Mailing Add:* 169 Terrace Trail West Lake Quivira Kansas City KS 66106-9504

GREENE, FREDERICK DAVIS, II, ORGANIC CHEMISTRY. *Current Pos:* from instr to assoc prof, 53-62, PROF ORG CHEM, MASS INST TECHNOL, 62- *Personal Data:* b Glen Ridge, NJ, July 9, 27; m 53, Theodora Whatmough; c Alan, Carol, Elizabeth & Phillips. *Educ:* Amherst Col, AB, 49; Harvard Univ, AM, 51, PhD(chem), 53. *Hon Degrees:* ScD, Amherst Col, 69. *Prof Exp:* Res assoc chem, Univ Calif, Los Angeles, 52-53. *Concurrent Pos:* Ed, J Org Chem, 62-88. *Mem:* Am Chem Soc; The Chem Soc; Am Acad Arts & Sci; AAAS; Fed Am Scientist. *Res:* Mechanisms of organic reactions. *Mailing Add:* Dept Chem Mass Inst Technol Cambridge MA 02139

GREENE, FREDERICK LESLIE, SURGICAL ONCOLOGY, GENERAL SURGERY. *Current Pos:* assoc prof, 80-85, PROF SURG, SCH MED, UNIV SC, 85- *Personal Data:* b Norfolk, Va, Dec 18, 44; m 70, Donna Weingart; c 2. *Educ:* Univ Va, BA, 66, MD, 70. *Honors & Awards:* Distinguished Serv Award, Columbia Med Soc. *Prof Exp:* Instr surg, Sch Med, Yale Univ, 75-76; attend surgeon, Portsmouth Naval Hosp, 77-78; clin instr, Univ Md, 78-80; chief surg, William J Bryan Dorn Vet Admin Hosp, 80-85 & Richland Mem Hosp, Columbia, SC, 88-92. *Concurrent Pos:* Dir surg oncol & surg endoscopy, Sch Med, Univ SC. *Mem:* Am Col Surgeons; Asn Acad Surg; Am Soc Clin Oncol; Am Asn Cancer Educ; Soc Am Gastrointestinal Endoscopic Surgeons; hon mem Endoscopic & Laparascopic Surgeons Asia. *Res:* Effects of nutrition and trace metals on production of colon cancer in animal models; methods of breast-sparing for breast cancer; screening for breast cancer. *Mailing Add:* Dept Surg Univ SC Two Med Park Rd Suite 402 Columbia SC 29203

GREENE, GEORGE C, III, ENVIRONMENTAL CONSULTING. *Current Pos:* VPRES ENVIRON CONSULT, GEN ENG LABS, CHARLESTON, SC, 81- *Educ:* Univ Fla, BS, 67; Columbia Univ, MS, 69; Tulane Univ, PhD(chem eng), 73. *Prof Exp:* Engr, Lurgi Mineraloetechnik, Frankfurt, WGer, 73-77; sr engr, Exxon Res & Eng, Florham Park, NJ, 77-81. *Mem:* Am Inst Chem Engrs; Am Soc Testing & Mats; Am Chem Soc; Am Waterwell Asn. *Res:* Environmental consulting: waste characterization and site evaluation for impact to soils, surface water and groundwater; groundwater studies, metals, inorganic and organic analyses at trace levels; development and design of contaminant removal processes. *Mailing Add:* Gen Eng Labs PO Box 30712 Charleston SC 29417-0172

GREENE, GEORGE W, JR, ORAL PATHOLOGY. *Current Pos:* RETIRED. *Personal Data:* b Brooklyn, NY, Aug 5, 19; c 2. *Educ:* Univ Notre Dame, BS, 41; Columbia Univ, DDS, 44; Am Bd Oral Path, dipl. *Honors & Awards:* Am Cancer Soc Nat Award, 70. *Prof Exp:* Assoc prof oral path, Sch Dent, Georgetown Univ, 50-62; prof & chmn dept, Sch Dent, State Univ NY, Buffalo, 63-85, dir, Oral Diag Serv, 73-85. *Concurrent Pos:* Sr oral pathologist, Cent Lab Path Analysis & Res, Armed Forces Inst Path, 53-60, chief, Environ Oral Path Br, 54-60; secy res prog comt oral dis, Vet Admin, 58-62; asst dir dent prof serv, 60-62; chmn bd examr, Am Bd Oral Path, 63-65, pres, 65-, secy treas, 71-73; USPHS cancer coordr, dir continuing educ & dir diag serv, State Univ NY Buffalo, 63-68, dir grad & postgrad educ, 66-67; consult oral tumors, AMA, oral cytol reproducibility study, Cancer Control Prog, Nat Ctr Chronic Dis Control, 67-, path dept, Roswell Park Mem Inst & res & develop div, Off Surgeon Gen, US Army. *Mem:* Am Dent Asn; fel Am Col Dent; fel Am Acad Oral Path (pres, 64). *Res:* Bone physiology; cryogenics; oral diseases; oral cancer; enosseous implantology. *Mailing Add:* 544 Flotilla Rd North Palm Beach FL 33408

GREENE, GERALD L, ENTOMOLOGY. *Current Pos:* head Garden City Exp Sta, 76-82, PROF LIVESTOCK ENTOM, KANS STATE UNIV, 82- *Personal Data:* b Jewell, Kans, July 7, 37; m 60, Phyllis A Rutledge; c 2. *Educ:* Kans State Univ, BS, 59, MS, 61; Ore State Univ, PhD(entom, bot), 66. *Prof Exp:* Res asst entom, Kans State Univ, 59-61 & Ore State Univ, 61-64; asst entomologist, Univ Ky, 64-66 & Cent Fla Exp Sta, 66-70; asst prof entom, agr res & educ ctr, Univ Fla, 70-76. *Mem:* Entom Soc Am. *Res:* Insect ecology and life tables; field crop insect, biological control; university administration; livestock entomology; confined livestock fly biocontrol. *Mailing Add:* SWKS Res-Ext Ctr 4500 E Mary Garden City KS 67846. *Fax:* 316-276-6028

GREENE, GORDON WILLIAM, GEOPHYSICS. *Current Pos:* RETIRED. *Personal Data:* b San Francisco, Calif, Feb 8, 21; m 42, Phyllis Coulam; c Stephen C, Bruce W, Robert A, David A, Kenneth E, James R, Elizabeth A & Janet R. *Educ:* Fresno State Col, AB, 54; Stanford Univ, MS, 57. *Prof Exp:* Technician, Pac Cement & Aggregates, Inc, 46-47, dist engr, 47-55, geologist, US Geol Surv, 56-57, geophysicist, 57-70; geophysicist, Off Earthquake Studies, 70-81. *Mem:* AAAS; Am Geophys Union; Geol Soc Am; Seismol Soc Am. *Res:* Seismology; tectonics; heat flow; permafrost; remote sensing. *Mailing Add:* 303 W 220 S Orem UT 84058-5475

GREENE, HARRY LEE, GENETIC LIVER DISEASES, INTESTINAL TRANSPORT OF NUTRIENTS. *Current Pos:* PROF PEDIAT & BIOCHEM, MED CTR, VANDERBILT UNIV, 79- *Educ:* Emory Univ, MD, 64. *Mailing Add:* Dir Nutrit Sci Mead Johnson Nutrit Group PO Box 120342 Nashville TN 37212

GREENE, HOKE SMITH, physical chemistry, organic chemistry; deceased, see previous edition for last biography

GREENE, HOWARD LYMAN, CHEMICAL ENGINEERING. *Current Pos:* from asst prof to assoc prof chem eng, 65-74, PROF CHEM ENG, UNIV AKRON, 74-, HEAD DEPT, 77- *Personal Data:* b Hackensack, NJ, Apr 3, 35; m 58; c 3. *Educ:* Cornell Univ, BChemE, 59, MChemE, 63, PhD(chem eng), 66. *Prof Exp:* Asst prof chem tech, Broome Tech Community Col, 59-63; consult, Int Bus Mach Corp, NY, 63-64. *Concurrent Pos:* HEW grant biomed polymers, 69-75; consult, Chemstress Consult Co, 72- *Mem:* Am Inst Chem Engrs; Sigma Xi. *Res:* Reaction engineering; mixing; chemical kinetics; direction of graduate study in these areas; biomedical engineering. *Mailing Add:* 2238 Randolph Rd Mogadore OH 44260-9345

GREENE, JACK BRUCE, PHYSICS. *Current Pos:* RETIRED. *Personal Data:* b Bloomington, Ind, June 9, 15; m 40; c 2. *Educ:* Ind Univ, AB, 37; Univ Pittsburgh, MS, 40, PhD(physics), 42. *Prof Exp:* Asst physics, Univ Pittsburgh, 37-41; instr, Univ Ill, 41-43; from instr to assoc prof physics, Marquette Univ, 45-80, assoc chmn dept, 70-76. *Mem:* Am Phys Soc; Am Asn Physics Teachers. *Res:* Electronic structure of metals; cyclotron assembly and operation; electronic energy bands in the face-centered iron. *Mailing Add:* 542 N 66th St Wauwatosa WI 53213

GREENE, JAMES H, INDUSTRIAL & MANUFACTURING ENGINEERING. *Current Pos:* PROF INDUST ENG, PURDUE UNIV, 48- *Personal Data:* b Elmwood, Nebr, Mar 12, 15; m 43, Barbara Holt; c Robin E (Tower) & Timothy J. *Educ:* Univ Iowa, BS, 47, MS, 48, PhD, 57. *Honors & Awards:* Pres Award, Am Prod & Inventory Control Soc. *Concurrent Pos:* Vis prof & Fulbright scholar, Finland Sch Technol; consult, Europ Productivity Coun & var co; ed, Am Product & Inventory Control Handbook. *Mem:* Fel Am Prod & Inventory Control RNC; Soc Mfg ENgrs; Am Soc Eng Educ. *Res:* Industrial engineering; author of four industrial engineering books, some translated in Japanese, Spanish and Italian. *Mailing Add:* Sch Indust Eng Purdue Univ West Lafayette IN 47905

GREENE, JANICE L, ORGANIC CHEMISTRY. *Current Pos:* RETIRED. *Personal Data:* b Adams, NY, Mar 12, 30. *Educ:* Alfred Univ, BA, 51; Pa State Univ, PhD(org chem), 58. *Prof Exp:* From asst prof to assoc prof chem, Univ NC, Greensboro, 55-60; sr res chemist, Standard Oil Co, Ohio, 60-66, res assoc, 66-79, sr res assoc, 79-81, sr scientist, 81-88. *Mem:* AAAS; Am Chem Soc; Soc Plastics Engrs. *Res:* Organic reactions; mechanisms and processes; small ring compounds; nitrile chemistry. *Mailing Add:* 28649 Jackson Rd Chagrin Falls OH 44022

GREENE, JANICE SCHNAKE, TEACHER PREPARATION, ENVIRONMENTAL EDUCATION. *Current Pos:* ASST PROF BIOL, SOUTHWEST MO STATE UNIV, 93- *Personal Data:* b Carthage, Mo, Apr 12, 61; m 89, Brian D; c Amy D & Stephanie E. *Educ:* SW Mo State Univ, BSEd, 83, MS, 87; Tex A&M Univ, PhD(wildlife & fisheries sci), 92. *Prof Exp:* Teacher sci, La Monte High Sch, 83-85; teacher biol, Lebanon Jr High, 87-88; conserv educr, Rob & Bessie Welder Wildlife Found, 92-93. *Mem:* Nat Asn Biol Teachers; Nat Sci Teachers Asn; Southwestern Asn Naturalists; Human Dimensions Wildlife Study Group; NAm Asn Environ Asn. *Res:* Evaluation of environmental education materials, teaching methods and environmental attitudes and knowledge of individuals; human dimensions of natural resource management. *Mailing Add:* 901 S National Ave Springfield MO 65804. *Fax:* 417-836-4204; *E-Mail:* jsg326f@vmg.smsu.edu

GREENE, JOHN CLIFFORD, DENTISTRY. *Current Pos:* dean, Sch Dent & prof, 81-94, EMER PROF, DEPT DENT PUB HEALTH & HYG & EMER DEAN, SCH DENT, UNIV CALIF, SAN FRANCISCO, 94- *Personal Data:* b Ashland, Ky, July 19, 26; c 3. *Educ:* Univ Louisville, DMD, 52; Univ Calif, Berkeley, MPH, 61. *Hon Degrees:* DSc, Univ Ky, 72, Boston Univ, 75 & Univ Louisville, 80. *Prof Exp:* Intern, USPHS, Chicago, 52-53, staff, Pub Health Serv Hosp, 53-54, asst regional dent consult, Region 9, San Francisco, 54-56; epidemic intel, Ctr Dis Control, 56-57; res staff, Epidemiol & Biomet Br, Nat Inst Dent Res, NIH, 57-58; asst to chief dent officer, Pub Health Serv, 58-60; chief, Epidemiol Prog, Dent Health Ctr, San Francisco, 61-66; dep dir, Div Dent Health Care, Bethesda, 66-73; actg dir, Bur Health Resources Develop & chief dent officer, Pub Health Serv, 73-75; spec asst dent affairs, Off Asst Secy Health & chief dent officer, 75-78, dep surgeon gen, 78-81. *Concurrent Pos:* Spec consult, WHO, India, 57-; nutrit surv team mem, Ecuador, 59; vis lectr, Sch Dent, Univ Calif, 65-72; lectr, Sch Dent, Univ Pa & Sch Pub Health, Univ Mich, 72-75; chmn, Comn Dent Pub Health, Fed Dent Int; panel experts dent health, WHO, 76-; mem comt, Inst Med, Nat Acad Sci, 82-, sect leader, 83-87, Gov Coun, 85-; dean, Search Comt, Sch Med, Univ Calif, San Francisco, 82-83, bd adv, Off Res, Sch Nursing, 86- & dean, Search Comt, 87-; chmn, Syst Health Sci Comt, Univ Calif, 82-86 & 83-85, Acad Planning & Prog Rev Bd, 83-84; mem, Nat Affairs Comt, Am Asn Dent Res, 83-, Prog Comt, 84-; vpres, Western Conf Dent Examr & Dent Sch Deans, 84-85, pres, 85-86; mem, US Prev Serv Task Force, 85- *Mem:* Inst Med-Nat Acad Sci; Am Asn Dent Res (vpres, 84-85, pres-elect, 85-86 & pres, 86-87); Inst Asn Dent Res (pres-elect, 86); fel Am Col Dentists; Am Asn Pub Health Dentists; Inst Health Policy Studies; Am Pub Health Asn; Nat Acad Pract; fel Int Col Dentists; fel AAAS. *Res:* Author of over 70 publications. *Mailing Add:* Sch Dent Univ Calif San Francisco CA 94143

GREENE, JOHN M, PLASMA PHYSICS. *Current Pos:* SR TECH ADV, GEN ATOMIC CO, 82- *Personal Data:* b Pittsburgh, Pa, Sept 22, 28; m 57; c 1. *Educ:* Calif Inst Technol, BS, 50; Univ Rochester, PhD(physics), 56. *Honors & Awards:* Maxwell Prize, Am Phys Soc, 92. *Prof Exp:* Res physicist, Plasma Physics Lab, Princeton Univ, 56-82. *Mem:* Fel Am Phys Soc. *Res:* Magnetohydrodynamics; nonlinear equations. *Mailing Add:* Gen Atomic Co PO Box 85608 San Diego CA 92186-9784

GREENE, JOHN PHILIP, THIN FILM PHYSICS, METALLURGY. *Current Pos:* SCI ASSOC, ARGONNE NAT LAB, 82- *Personal Data:* b Chicago, Ill, Oct 13, 55; m 85; c 2. *Educ:* Univ Ill, Chicago, BA, 78; DePaul Univ, MS, 82. *Prof Exp:* Proj chemist, DeSoto Inc, 78-82. *Mem:* Am Chem Soc; Am Phys Soc; Soc Appl Spectros; Sigma Xi; Int Nuclear Target Develop Soc. *Res:* Nuclear target development; heavy-ion research. *Mailing Add:* 1200 Andover Circle Aurora IL 60504-5995

GREENE, JOHN W, JR, OBSTETRICS & GYNECOLOGY. *Current Pos:* PROF OBSTET & GYNEC & CHMN DEPT, MED CTR, UNIV KY, 63- *Personal Data:* b East Orange, NJ, July 25, 26; m 54; c 3. *Educ:* Univ Pittsburgh, BS, 48; Univ Pa, MD, 52. *Prof Exp:* From intern to resident obstet & gynec, Hosp Univ Pa, 52-56; res assoc, Sch Med, Univ Pa, 57-59, asst prof, 59-63. *Concurrent Pos:* Res fel, Sch Med, Univ Pa, 56-57. *Mailing Add:* Univ Ky Med Ctr Lexington KY 40536

GREENE, KINGSLEY L, ECOLOGY. *Current Pos:* RETIRED. *Personal Data:* b New York, NY, Nov 26, 26; m 48; c 3. *Educ:* Cornell Univ, BS, 60, MS, 61. *Prof Exp:* High sch teacher, NY, 49-51 & 56-58; prof biol, Eastern Baptist Col, 61-66; dir outdoor educ, Rose Tree Media Sch Dist, Media, Pa, 66-67; prof natural resources, State Univ NY Agr & Tech Col Morrisville, 67-85. *Mem:* AAAS; Am Nature Study Soc. *Res:* Prey-predator relationships in aquatic communities. *Mailing Add:* Rte 51 Hannacroix NY 12087

GREENE, LAURA H, CONDENSED MATTER PHYSICS, MATERIALS PHYSICS. *Current Pos:* PROF PHYSICS, UNIV ILL, 92- *Personal Data:* b Cleveland, Ohio, June 12, 52; m 89, Russell W Giannetta; c Max Greene Giannetta & Leo Greene Giannetta. *Educ:* Ohio State Univ, BS, 74, MS, 77; Cornell Univ, MS, 80, PhD(physics), 84. *Honors & Awards:* Maria Goeppert-Mayer Award, Am Phys Soc, 94. *Prof Exp:* Mem tech staff, Hughes Aircraft Co, 74-75; teaching assoc, Ohio State Univ, 75-76, res assoc, 76-77; teaching assoc, Cornell Univ, 77-79, res assoc, 79-83; fel, Bellcore, 83-85, mem tech staff, 85-92. *Concurrent Pos:* Gen counr, Am Phys Soc, 93-96; Ctr Advan Study prof, Beckman Assoc, Univ Ill, 96-97. *Mem:* Fel Am Phys Soc; Mat Res Soc; fel AAAS; Am Asn Physics Teachers; Int Union Pure & Appl Physics; Mat Res Soc. *Res:* Physics of novel superconducting materials; thin film, multilayer and bulk growth, materials analysis and physical measurements including tunneling, electronic transport and nonlinear optics; author of numerous publications. *Mailing Add:* Univ Ill Loomis Lab Physics 1110 W Green St Urbana IL 61801-3080. *Fax:* 217-244-7187; *E-Mail:* lhg@uiuc.edu

GREENE, LEWIS JOEL, PROTEIN CHEMISTRY, ENZYMOLOGY. *Current Pos:* prof biochem, 74-85, prof pharmacol, 85-91, PROF OBSTET & GYNEC, FAC MED, UNIV SAO PAULO, RIBEIRAO, 91- *Personal Data:* b New York, NY, Aug 10, 34; m 58, Eletka Cardinali; c Mark & Elena. *Educ:* Amherst Col, BA, 55; Rockefeller Inst, PhD(biochem), 62. *Prof Exp:* From asst to assoc biochemist, Brookhaven Nat Lab, 62-68, biochemist, 68-76. *Concurrent Pos:* Affil, Rockefeller Univ, 68-72; adj staff, Cleveland Clin, 87-91. *Mem:* Am Chem Soc; Am Soc Cell Biol; Am Soc Biol Chemists; Nat Acad Sci Brazil; Brazilian Soc Biol Chemists; Brazilian Soc Pharm & Exp Theory. *Res:* Protein chemistry; amino acids sequence determination of biologically active peptides and proteins; metabolism of peptide hormones; characterization of protein and peptide drugs; prepared by conventional on modern method of biotechnology. *Mailing Add:* Dept Obstet & Gynec Univ Sao Paulo 14049-900 Ribeirao Preto Sao Paulo Brazil. *Fax:* 55-16-633-2119; *E-Mail:* ljgreene@fmrp.usp.br

GREENE, LLOYD A, NEUROBIOLOGY, NEUROCHEMISTRY. *Current Pos:* PROF PATH, COLUMBIA UNIV COL, PHYSICIANS & SURGEONS. *Personal Data:* b Chicago, Ill, Aug 28, 44; m 74; c 1. *Educ:* Univ Chicago, ScB, 65; Univ Calif, San Diego, PhD(chem), 70. *Prof Exp:* Asst prof neuropath, Harvard Med Sch, 74-77, assoc prof, 77-79; from assoc prof to prof pharmacol, Sch Med, NY Univ, 82-87. *Res:* Neurochemical and cell biological studies on development of the nervous system. *Mailing Add:* Columbia Univ Col P & S 630 W 168th St New York NY 10032

GREENE, MARK IRWIN, IMMUNOLOGY. *Current Pos:* DIR, DIV IMMUNOL, DEPT PATH & PROF, SCH MED, UNIV PA, 86-, ASSOC HEAD FUNDAMENTAL RES, CANCER CTR, 87-, FAC SENATE, 88- *Personal Data:* b Winnipeg, Man, Aug 3, 48; c 3. *Educ:* Univ Man, MD, 72, PhD(immunol), 77; FRCP(C), 76. *Honors & Awards:* Math Asn Prize, 66; Lotte Strauss Award, 86. *Prof Exp:* Intern internal med, Health Sci Ctr, Winnipeg, 72-73, resident, 73-76; res fel path, Harvard Med Sch, Boston, 76-77, from instr to assoc prof, 77-85, assoc prof immunol, Dept Cancer Biol, 82-85; prof med & chief div rheumatol/immunol, Sch Med, Tufts Univ, 84-85. *Concurrent Pos:* Med Res Coun fel, Can, 73-75, Boston, 76-78; consult med, Dana Farber Cancer Ctr, 80-86, Hosp Univ Pa, 85-; chmn rev comt, Struct & Molecular Biol, Univ Pa, 88-89, mem, Howard Hughes Adv Comt, 89; ed, DNA & Cell Biol & Pathobiol, 90. *Mem:* Am Soc Clin Invest; Brit Soc Immunol; Am Asn Immunologists; Am Asn Pathologists. *Mailing Add:* Div Immunol Dept Path & Lab Med Univ Pa Sch Med 252 John Morgan Bldg 36th & Hamilton Walk Philadelphia PA 19104-6082. *Fax:* 215-898-2401

GREENE, MICHAEL P, SOLID STATE PHYSICS, SCIENCE POLICY. *Current Pos:* ASSOC DIR, BD SCI & TECHNOL IN INT DEVELOP, NAT ACAD SCI, 81- *Personal Data:* b New York, NY, June 20, 38; m 63, Anne Sargent; c Lesley & Diana. *Educ:* Cornell Univ, BEngPhys, 60; Univ Calif, San Diego, MS, 62, PhD(physics), 65. *Prof Exp:* Asst prof physics, Univ Calif, Davis, 65; res assoc, Brown Univ, 65-67; asst prof, Univ Md, College Park, 67-74, assoc chmn dept physics & astron, 71-74; tech dir, Vol In Tech Assistance, 74-76; dep dir sci & technol, Org Am States, 76-80. *Concurrent Pos:* Fulbright-Orgn Am States lectr, Nat Univ Eng, Peru, 70-71; resident dir, Indonesia Prog, Nat Acad Sci, 90-93. *Mem:* Fel AAAS; Am Phys Soc; Soc Int Develop. *Res:* Science and technology policy for developing countries; technology transfer; project management. *Mailing Add:* Nat Res Coun FO 2060 Washington DC 20418. *Fax:* 202-334-2660; *E-Mail:* mgreene@nas.edu

GREENE, NATHAN DOYLE, IMMUNOLOGY, IMMUNOTOXICOLOGY. *Current Pos:* RETIRED. b Steele, Ala, Mar 2, 38; m 60; c 2. *Educ:* Berea Col, BA, 60; NC State Univ, MS, 62; Emory Univ, PhD(biol), 65. *Prof Exp:* Med microbiologist, Nat Commun Dis Ctr, USPHS, Ga, 65-68; assoc found scientist, Southwest Found Res & Educ, 68- *Concurrent Pos:* Adj asst prof microbiol, Health Sci Ctr, Univ Tex, San Antonio; adj assoc prof, Univ Tex, San Antonio. *Mem:* AAAS; Am Inst Biol Sci; Am Soc Parasitol; fel Royal Soc Trop Med & Hyg; Am Asn Immunologists. *Res:* Immunology of non-human primates; immunological aspects of pulmonary defense systems; inhalation toxicology; immunotoxicology related to environmental agents; mechanisms of immunomodulation by toxic agents. *Mailing Add:* 1015 Kearny St Manhattan KS 66502

GREENE, NEIL E(DWARD), heat transfer, thermodynamics, for more information see previous edition

GREENE, NICHOLAS MISPLEE, ANESTHESIOLOGY. *Current Pos:* prof, 55-87, EMER PROF ANESTHESIOL, YALE UNIV, 87- *Personal Data:* b Milford, Conn, July 11, 22; m 46; c 3. *Educ:* Yale Univ, BS, 44; Columbia Univ, MD, 46; Am Bd Anesthesiol, dipl. *Hon Degrees:* MA, Yale Univ, 55;. *Prof Exp:* Surg intern, Presby Hosp, 46-47; instr anesthesia, Harvard Med Sch, 51-53; from assoc prof to asst prof pharmacol, Sch Med, Univ Rochester, 53-55. *Concurrent Pos:* Resident, Mass Gen Hosp, 49-51, asst, 51-53; vis fel, Royal Infirmary of Edinburgh, 51; anesthetist in chief, Strong Mem Hosp, Rochester, 53-55; dir anesthesiol, Yale-New Haven Hosp, 55-73; ed, Anesthesiology, 65-73, ed-in-chief, 73-76; ed-in-chief, Anesthesia & Analgesia, 77- *Mem:* Asn Univ Anesthetists; Am Soc Anesthesiol; Int Anesthesia Res Soc; Sigma Xi. *Res:* Academic anesthesiology. *Mailing Add:* 333 Cedar St New Haven CT 06510-3289

GREENE, PETER RICHARD, MECHANICAL ENGINEERING, APPLIED PHYSICS. *Current Pos:* DIR RES ENGR, BGKT CONSULT, LTD, 83- *Personal Data:* b Huntington, NY, Mar 23, 51. *Educ:* Cornell Univ, BS, 73; Harvard Univ, MS, 75, PhD, 78. *Res:* Applied mechanics/bioengineering. *Mailing Add:* BGKT Consult Ltd 153 Main St Huntington NY 11743. *Fax:* 516-427-1873

GREENE, REGINALD, RADIOLOGY. *Current Pos:* from instr to assoc prof, 71-85, PROF RADIOL, HARVARD MED SCH, 85- *Personal Data:* b Mar 27, 34. *Educ:* Harvard Col, AB, 56; NY Med Col, MD, 60; Am Bd Radiol, dipl nuclear med, 68. *Honors & Awards:* Silver Medal, Am Roentgen Ray Soc; Fleischner Medal Lectr, Interlaken, Switz. *Prof Exp:* Intern, US Naval Hosp, Philadelphia, 60-61, resident, Oakland, 61-62, Mass Gen Hosp, Boston, 65-68; advan fel acad radiol, James Picker Found, Nat Acad Sci-Nat Res Coun, 68-71. *Concurrent Pos:* Clin asst radiol, Mass Gen Hosp, 70-71, asst radiologist, 71-75, dir thoracic radiol, 71-82, assoc radiologist, 75-77, radiologist, Mass Gen Hosp, 78-, dir, Wang Ambulatory Care Ctr & assoc radiologist-in-chief, 82- *Mem:* Radiol Soc NAm; Fleischner Soc (pres, 87); Am Physiol Soc; Am Thoracic Soc; Royal Col Radiologists; Am Roentgen Ray Soc; Am Col Radiol; Am Col Chest Physicians; AMA; Soc Computer Appln Radiol. *Res:* Diffuse lung damage, functional and anatomic consequences; radiologic screening methodology for the pneumoconioses; digital radiography; author of numerous scientific publications. *Mailing Add:* Dept Radiol ACC 219 Mass Gen Hosp Fruit St Boston MA 02114

GREENE, RICHARD LORENTZ, SOLID STATE PHYSICS. *Current Pos:* PROF & DIR, DEPT PHYSICS, SUPERCONDUCTIVITY CTR, UNIV MD, 89- *Personal Data:* b Bridgeport, Conn, Aug 26, 38. *Educ:* Mass Inst Technol, BS, 60; Stanford Univ, PhD(physics), 67. *Prof Exp:* Res assoc physics, Stanford Univ, 67-70; res scientist & mgr, IBM Res Lab, 70-89. *Mem:* Fel Am Phys Soc. *Res:* Physical properties of one-dimensional organic and inorganic conductors; superconductivity; thin films. *Mailing Add:* Dept Physics Univ Md College Park MD 20742

GREENE, RICHARD WALLACE, INVERTEBRATE BIOLOGY, ALGAL PHYSIOLOGY. *Current Pos:* COORD, ENVIRONMENT & SAFETY, PETROLITE CORP, 84- *Personal Data:* b San Francisco, Calif, Oct 29, 41; m 65; c 2. *Educ:* Univ Calif, Berkeley, BA, 64; Univ Calif, Los Angeles, MA, 66, PhD(zool), 69. *Prof Exp:* USPHS training grant, Univ Calif, Los Angeles, 69-70; from asst prof to assoc prof biol, Univ Notre Dame, 70-84, assoc dir, Environ Res Ctr, 75-84. *Concurrent Pos:* Mem exec comt, Am Midland Naturalist, 72- *Mem:* AAAS; Am Soc Zool; NAm Benthological Soc; Sigma Xi. *Res:* Symbiosis between algae and chloroplasts with invertebrates; biology of heavy metals; environmental biology. *Mailing Add:* 209 Haggin St Bakersfield CA 93309-1973

GREENE, ROBERT CARL, GEOLOGY, INDUSTRIAL MINERALS. *Current Pos:* GEOLOGIST, US GEOL SURV, 61- *Personal Data:* b Bridgeport, Conn, Aug 14, 32; m 55, Edith Blancy; c David, Barbara (Aston), Walter, Judith (Jause) & Benjamin. *Educ:* Cornell Univ, AB, 55; Univ Tenn, MS, 59; Harvard Univ, PhD(geol), 64. *Prof Exp:* Explor geologist, NJ Zinc Co, 55-57. *Mem:* Geol Soc Am. *Res:* Talc commodity geologist; structure and petrology of volcanic rocks in Death Valley region. *Mailing Add:* 31 Seaview Dr Daly City CA 94015

GREENE, ROBERT EVERIST, geometry, for more information see previous edition

GREENE, ROBERT MORRIS, DEVELOPMENTAL BIOLOGY, ANATOMY. *Current Pos:* ASST PROF ANAT, JEFFERSON MED COL, 78- *Personal Data:* b Dorpen, Ger, Dec 15, 45; US citizen; m 67; c 2. *Educ:* Utica Col Syracuse Univ, BA, 67; Univ Va, PhD(anat), 74. *Prof Exp:* Staff fel biochem, Nat Inst Dent Res, NIH, 76-78. *Concurrent Pos:* Fel, Nat Inst Dent Res, NIH, 74-76. *Mem:* Soc Develop Biol; Am Soc Cell Biol; Teratology Soc; Int Asn Dent Res; Sigma Xi. *Res:* Developmental biology; craniofacial development; teratology; cleft palate. *Mailing Add:* Dept Anat Thomas Jefferson Med Col 1020 Locust St Philadelphia PA 19107-6799. *Fax:* 215-955-3808

GREENE, RONALD C, BIOCHEMISTRY. *Current Pos:* ASSOC PROF BIOCHEM, SCH MED, DUKE UNIV, 71- *Personal Data:* b Los Angeles, Calif, June 7, 28; m 50; c 2. *Educ:* Calif Inst Technol, BS, 49, PhD(biochem), 54. *Prof Exp:* Asst scientist biochem, NIH, 54-55, sr asst scientist, 55-57; instr biochem, Sch Med, Duke Univ, 57-58, assoc, 58-62, asst prof, 62-71; biochemist radioisotope serv, 57-69, CHIEF BASIC SCI LAB, VET ADMIN HOSP, 69- *Mem:* AAAS; Am Chem Soc; Am Soc Biol Chem; Am Soc Microbiol; Sigma Xi. *Res:* Biochemistry of sulfonium compounds; regulation of methionine biosynthesis; metabolism of methionine and related compounds. *Mailing Add:* Basic Sci Vet Admin Med Ctr 508 Fulton St Durham NC 27705

GREENE, TERRY R, COGNITION, COGNITIVE DEVELOPMENT. *Current Pos:* asst prof, 89-93, ASSOC PROF PSYCHOL, FRANKLIN & MARSHALL COL, 93- *Personal Data:* b Bryn Mawr, Pa, June 23, 46; c David. *Educ:* Goucher Col, BA, 68; Univ Pittsburgh, MS, 84, PhD(psychol), 86. *Prof Exp:* Asst prof psychol, Murray State Univ, 87-89. *Mem:* Soc Res Child Develop; Psychonomics Soc; Am Asn Univ Profs. *Res:* Investigations of reasoning abilities, categorization skills and understanding of the relations expressed in class inclusion hierarchies of young children; effects of schema (perspective) on perception, comprehension and memory in adults. *Mailing Add:* Dept Psychol Franklin & Marshall Col PO Box 3003 Lancaster PA 17604-3003. *E-Mail:* t_greene@acad.fandm.edu

GREENE, THOMAS FREDERICK, astrophysics, for more information see previous edition

GREENE, TIMOTHY J, PRODUCTION MANAGEMENT, COMPUTER INTEGRATED MANUFACTURING. *Current Pos:* prof & head, Sch Indust Eng & Mgt, 91-96, ASSOC DEAN RES, COL ENG ARCH & TECHNOL, OKLA STATE UNIV, 95- *Personal Data:* b Lafayette, Ind, Oct 18, 52; m 96, Nancy E VanKuren. *Educ:* Purdue Univ, BS, 75, MS, 77, PhD(indust eng), 80. *Prof Exp:* From asst prof to assoc prof prod control, Sch Indust Eng & Opers Res, Va Polytech Inst & State Univ, 80-86, assoc prof & asst dept head, Sch Indust Systs Eng, 86-91. *Concurrent Pos:* Consult, Greene Assocs, 80-; vpres indust, Inst Indust Engrs, 91-92, sr vpres prof enhancement, 92-94, sr vpres tech opers, 94-96. *Mem:* Inst Indust Engrs (pres elect, 96-97, pres, 97-98); Am Prod & Inventory Control Soc; Soc Mfg Eng; Am Soc Eng Educ. *Res:* Research and design of production and inventory management systems including the implementation and integration of information and control systems in manufacturing environments. *Mailing Add:* Off Res Admin 110 Eng North Stillwater OK 74078. *Fax:* 405-744-7545; *E-Mail:* tgreene@master.ceat.okstate.edu

GREENE, VELVL WILLIAM, noscomial infections, medical ethics, for more information see previous edition

GREENE, VIRGINIA CARVEL, TOXICOLOGY. *Current Pos:* CHEMIST, US ARMY FOREIGN SCI & TECHNOL CTR, 79- *Personal Data:* b Warrenton, Va, Jan 8, 34; m 77. *Educ:* Sweet Briar Col, AB, 55; Tulane Univ, MS, 57; Univ Va, PhD(chem), 63. *Prof Exp:* Instr chem, Tulane Univ, 57-59; res assoc mat sci, Univ Va, 63-64, res assoc clin chem, univ hosp, 65-67; assoc prof chem, Longwood Col, 67-69; res chemist, Fed Bur Invest, 69-77; res asst, Univ Va, 77-78. *Mem:* Am Chem Soc. *Res:* Analytical spectrophotometry and chromatography; toxicology and drug analysis; gas chromatography/mass spectrometry; clinical chemistry; geomagnetism and aeronomy. *Mailing Add:* 540 E Rio Rd Charlottesville VA 22901-3706

GREENE, WILLIAM ALLAN, PSYCHOSOMATIC MEDICINE. *Current Pos:* RETIRED. *Personal Data:* b Worcester, Mass, June 15, 15; m 45; c 2. *Educ:* Harvard Col, BA, 36; Harvard Med Sch, MD, 40; Am Bd Internal Med, cert, 49. *Prof Exp:* Rotating intern, Mary Imogene Bassett Hosp, Cooperstown, NY, 40-42; asst med res, Strong Mem Hosp, Rochester, NY, 46-48; from instr to prof med & psychiat, Sch Med, Univ Rochester, 50-90; physician & psychiatrist, Strong-Mem Hosp, 76-90. *Concurrent Pos:* Commonwealth Fund fel med & psychiat, Sch Med, Univ Rochester, 48-50. *Mem:* Fel Am Col Physicians; Am Psychosom Soc (secy-treas, 64-68, pres, 68). *Res:* Psychological factors in the development and course of organic disease; neoplasias, coronary artery disease, hemodialysis and renal transplantation. *Mailing Add:* Univ Rohester Hosp Rochester NY 14618

GREENEBAUM, BEN, BIOLOGICAL EFFECTS OF ELECTROMAGNETIC FIELDS. *Current Pos:* from asst prof to assoc prof, Univ Wis-Parkside, 70-80, actg vchancellor, 82-83 & 84-85, assoc dean fac, 79-89, head, Sci Div, 87-89, dean, Sch Sci & Technol, 89-96, PROF PHYSICS, UNIV WIS-PARKSIDE, 80- *Personal Data:* b Chicago, Ill, Nov 30, 37; m 63, Nancy Jung; c 3. *Educ:* Oberlin Col, AB, 59; Harvard Univ, AM, 61, PhD(physics), 65. *Prof Exp:* Res assoc & instr physics, Harvard Univ, 65-66 & Princeton Univ, 66-70. *Concurrent Pos:* Fac res prog mem, Argonne Nat Lab, 70-76; assoc ed, Bioelectromagnetics, 90-92. *Mem:* Am Phys Soc; Am Asn Physics Teachers; Bioelectromagnetics Soc. *Res:* Biological effects of weak, low frequency electromagnetic radiation. *Mailing Add:* Univ Wis-Parkside PO Box 2000 Kenosha WI 53141. *Fax:* 414-595-2056; *E-Mail:* greeneba@cs.uwp.edu

GREENEBAUM, MICHAEL, OPTICAL PHYSICS, ATMOSPHERIC PHYSICS. *Current Pos:* PRIN SCIENTIST, ELECTRO-OPTICAL SCI INC, IRVINGTON, NY, 91- *Personal Data:* b Brooklyn, NY, Aug 10, 40; m 68; c 5. *Educ:* Yeshiva Univ, NY, BA, 61; Mass Inst Technol, Cambridge, PhD(physics), 67. *Prof Exp:* Gen physicist, Naval Appl Sci Lab, Brooklyn, NY, 67-69; prin mem res staff, Riverside Res Inst, NY, 69-91. *Concurrent Pos:* Lectr physics, Sch Gen Studies, Brooklyn Col, City Univ New York, 70-71, adj asst prof physics, 71-75; consult, Columbus Labs, Battelle Mem Inst, 77-78 & 80; adj prof physics, Long Island Univ, Brooklyn, 94- & Cooper Union, NY, 95- *Mem:* Optical Soc Am; Sigma Xi. *Res:* Effects of environmental (eg, atmospheric) attenuation, scattering, and dispersion on various aspects of the design of both coherent and non-coherent optical systems in the region between the ultraviolet and microwave wavelengths; thermal effects on ultrasonic light modulators; analysis of medical ultrasonic spectral analysis systems; applications of cizean interferometry to remote sensing; multispectral imaging of biological tissue. *Mailing Add:* 1177 E 19th St Brooklyn NY 11230. *Fax:* 718-252-6493

GREENER, EVAN H, DENTAL MATERIALS. *Current Pos:* assoc prof, Northwestern Univ, 64-69, chmn dept, 64-96, prof biol mat, 69-96, EMER PROF, NORTHWESTERN UNIV, 96- *Personal Data:* b Brooklyn, NY, Sept 8, 34; m 57; c 2. *Educ:* Polytech Inst Brooklyn, BMetE, 55; Northwestern Univ, MS, 57, PhD(mat sci), 60. *Prof Exp:* Lab instr, Polytech Inst Brooklyn, 55; Aitcheson fel metall, Northwestern Univ, 55-58, res fel, 58-59, prin investr, 59-60; from asst prof to assoc prof mat sci, Marquette Univ, 60-64. *Concurrent Pos:* Sr Fogarty Int fel, Turner Dent Sch, Univ Manchester, 77-78. *Mem:* Fel AAAS; NY Acad Sci; Am Soc Metals; Am Inst Mining, Metall & Petrol Engrs; Int Asn Dent Res. *Res:* Materials science. *Mailing Add:* 8865 E Baseline Rd Mesa AZ 85208

GREENEWALT, DAVID, GEOPHYSICS. *Current Pos:* RETIRED. *Personal Data:* b Wilmington, Del, Mar 26, 31; m 60; c 6. *Educ:* Williams Col, BA, 53; Mass Inst Technol, PhD(geophys), 60. *Prof Exp:* Instr geophys, Mass Inst Technol, 60-64, lectr, 64-66; geophysicist, US Naval Res Lab, 66-96. *Mem:* Am Geophys Union. *Res:* Rock magnetism; electrical prospecting methods; gravity interpretation; sea floor magnetic field; physical oceanography. *Mailing Add:* 2509 Foxhall Rd NW Washington DC 20007

GREENFELD, SIDNEY H(OWARD), SCIENCE ADMINISTRATION, CHEMICAL ENGINEERING. *Current Pos:* RETIRED. *Personal Data:* b Baltimore, Md, Apr 25, 23; m 48; c 4. *Educ:* Univ Del, BChE, 44; Mass Inst Technol, SM, 45. *Prof Exp:* Res assoc colloid chem, Mass Inst Technol, 45-48; res chemist soap chem, Fels & Co, 48; res assoc phys & org chem, Asphalt Roofing Indust Bur, Nat Bur Stand, 49-57; res engr, Calif Res Corp, 57-59; res assoc, Asphalt Roofing Indust Bur, Nat Bur Stand, 59-68, mat engr bur, 68-69, spec asst to chief, Off Flammable Fabrics, 69-73; tech asst to dir, Off Stand Coord & Appraisal, 73-76, tech asst to assoc exec dir eng & sci, Consumer Prod Safety Comn, 76-85. *Mem:* Am Chem Soc. *Res:* Surface chemistry of limestone, chalk, lime and related materials; colloid chemistry of Portland cement, soaps and detergents; asphalts and related substances; fabric flammability; product safety; residential building construction. *Mailing Add:* 6613 Belle Chase Ct Gaithersburg MD 20882-1257

GREENFIELD, DAVID WAYNE, ICHTHYOLOGY. *Current Pos:* DEAN, GRAD DIV, UNIV HAWAII, MANOA, 87- *Personal Data:* b Carmel, Calif, Apr 21, 40; m 71; c 1. *Educ:* Humboldt State Univ, AB, 62; Univ Wash, PhD(fisheries), 66. *Prof Exp:* Asst prof zool, Calif State Univ, Fullerton, 66-70; assoc prof, Northern Ill Univ, 70-77, prof biol sci, 77-84; assoc vchancellor, Univ Colo, Denver, 84-87. *Concurrent Pos:* Res assoc, Field Mus Natural Hist, Chicago. *Mem:* Am Soc Ichthyologists & Herpetologists; Soc Study Evolution; Soc Syst Zool. *Res:* Zoogeography; systematics of coral-reef fishes; zoogeography of marine and freshwater fishes; systematics of fishes of Belize; systematics of mosquitofishes (Gambusia). *Mailing Add:* Dean-Grad Div Univ Hawaii-Manoa 2540 Maile Way Honolulu HI 96822

GREENFIELD, EUGENE W(ILLIS), PHYSICS, ELECTRICAL ENGINEERING. *Current Pos:* RETIRED. *Personal Data:* b Baltimore, Md, Nov 27, 07; m 29; c 2. *Educ:* Johns Hopkins Univ, BE, 29, DE, 34. *Honors & Awards:* Distinguished Engr, Inst Elec & Electronics Engrs, 65, Centennial Medal, 84. *Prof Exp:* Asst, Nat Elec Light Asn, Johns Hopkins Univ, 29-33, res assoc, 33-34; transmission engr, Pa RR, 34-35; res engr, Anaconda Wire & Cable Co, 35-41, supvr elec lab, 41-49; asst tech dir, Kaiser Aluminum & Chem Corp, 50-51, asst plant mgr, 51-52, head elec eng res, 52-57, res supvr, 57-58; prof elec eng & dir div indust res, Wash State Univ, 58-73, chmn elec power res & develop ctr, 64-73, asst dean col eng, 70-73. *Concurrent Pos:* Mem comt elec insulation, Nat Res Coun, 32-, exec comt, 48-, vchmn, 48-49; consult power transmission, 73- *Mem:* Am Phys Soc; Am Soc Eng Educ; Am Soc Testing & Mat; Acoust Soc Am; fel Inst Elec & Electronics Engrs (vpres, 62-64). *Res:* Electrical insulation; electrical measuring instruments; application of insulation in the fields of power and communication; research and development of underground cables and conductors; research administration; electrical accident analyses. *Mailing Add:* 4747 Oakcrest Rd Fallbrook CA 92028-9084

GREENFIELD, GEORGE B, RADIOLOGY, MEDICINE. *Current Pos:* PROF RADIOL, UNIV SFLA, TAMPA. *Personal Data:* b Brooklyn, NY, May 4, 28; m 56, Barbara Anne O'Driscoll; c Edward J & Stellagh A. *Educ:* NY Univ, BA, 49; State Univ Utrecht, MedDs, 56. *Prof Exp:* Attend radiologist, Cook Co Hosp, Ill, 61-69; asst dir diag radiol, 66-69; prof radiol & chmn dept, Chicago Med Sch & Mt Sinai Hosp, 69-; prof, Cook Co Gard Sch Med, 66-; Dept Radiol, Rush Univ. *Concurrent Pos:* Consult radiologist, Vet Admin Hosp, Dwight, Ill, 63-65; attend radiologist, Res & Educ Hosp, Chicago, 63-69; clin assoc prof, Col Med, Univ Ill, 67-69. *Mem:* Am Col Radiol; Asn Univ Radiol; Int Skeletal Soc; Int Soc Magnetic Resonance; Radiologic Soc NAm. *Res:* Imaging of bone and soft tissue tumors. *Mailing Add:* 12438 First St W Treasure Island FL 33706-5044

GREENFIELD, HAROLD, CATALYSIS, HYDROGENATION. *Current Pos:* RETIRED. *Personal Data:* b New York, NY, May 6, 23; m 92, Carmela Costello; c Lynn, Kenneth & Scott. *Educ:* City Col New York, BS, 43; Polytech Inst Brooklyn, MS, 48; Univ Pittsburgh, PhD(chem), 55. *Honors & Awards:* Chamberland Award, Am Chem Soc, 91; Paul N Rylander Award, Org Reactions Catalysis Soc, 92. *Prof Exp:* Org chemist, Biochem Res Corp, NY, 48; phys chemist, Explosives Res Sect, US Bur Mines, Pa, 48-50, org chemist, Org Chem Sect, 50-55 & Coal Hydrogenation Sect, 55-58; sr res scientist, Uniroyal Inc, 58-80, res assoc Chem Div, 80-86; sr assoc chemist, First Chem Corp, 87-92. *Concurrent Pos:* Pres, HGV Consult Co. *Mem:* AAAS; Am Chem Soc; Catalysis Soc. *Res:* Heterogeneous and homogeneous catalysis; hydrogenation and reduction; nitration oxo reaction; metal carbonyl chemistry; organic synthesis; high pressure reactions; amine chemistry. *Mailing Add:* 373 W Rio Santa Cruz Green Valley AZ 85614-3933

GREENFIELD, HARVEY STANLEY, medical biophysics; deceased, see previous edition for last biography

GREENFIELD, IRWIN G, SURFACE PROPERTIES, METAL MATRIX COMPOSITES. *Current Pos:* RETIRED. *Personal Data:* b Philadelphia, Pa, Nov 30, 29; m 51; c 3. *Educ:* Temple Univ, BA, 51; Univ Pa, MS, 54, PhD(metall eng), 62. *Prof Exp:* Metallurgist, Naval Air Exp Sta, Philadelphia, 51-53; sr scientist, Franklin Inst Labs Res & Develop, Philadelphia, 53-63; from asst prof to prof metall, mech & aerospace, Univ Del 63-, dean, Col Eng, 75-84, asst to pres, 84-86, prof metall sci, 84- *Concurrent Pos:* Grants, Univ Del, 63-64, NSF, 64-69, 70-74, 77-83, 78-79, NASA, 69-70, Air Force Off Sci Res, 70-74 & Argonne Nat Lab, 81-83; vis lectr, Univs Sendai, Tokyo, Osaka, Nagoya & Kyoto, Japan, 65; NSF travel grant, 65-73; vis prof, Stanford Univ, 69-, Oxford Univ, 70 & Eindhoven Tech Univ, 78; chmn exec comt, Del Prog Minority Engrs, 74-77; mem, Sen Roth's Energy Adv Comt, 75-79, Del Energy Resources Comn, 75-76. *Mem:* Am Inst Mining, Metall & Petrol Engrs; Electron Micros Soc Am; Sigma Xi; Am Soc Metals; Am Soc Eng Educ. *Res:* Surfaces; electron microscopy; mechanical properties; fatigue; erosion; processing and properties of metal matrix composites; interfaces; extrusion. *Mailing Add:* 155 Cooper Hawk Lane Landenberg PA 19350

GREENFIELD, JOHN CHARLES, BIO-ORGANIC CHEMISTRY. *Current Pos:* res chemist infectious dis res, Upjohn Co, Kalamazoo, 76-82, sr res scientist drug metab res, 82-93, sr proj mgr, 93-96, SR TECHNOL ASSESSMENT SPECIALIST, PHARMACIA & UPJOHN, INC, 96- *Personal Data:* b Dayton, Ohio, 1945; m 80, Liga Miervaldis; c John H & Mark R. *Educ:* Ohio Univ, BS, 67; Univ Ill, PhD, 74. *Prof Exp:* Res fel, Swiss Fed Inst Technol, Zurich, 75-76. *Concurrent Pos:* Am Swiss Found Sci Exchange fel, 75; NSF-NATO fel, 75-76; chmn, Kalamazoo Sec, Am Chem Soc, 94. *Mem:* Am Chem Soc; AAAS; NY Acad Sci; Am Asn Pharm Scientists; Sigma Xi. *Res:* Identification, evaluation and management of worldwide research and development projects for new pharmaceutical agents. *Mailing Add:* Pharmacia & Upjohn Inc 301 Henrietta St Kalamazoo MI 49007. *Fax:* 616-833-9507; *E-Mail:* john.c.greenfield@am.pnu.com

GREENFIELD, JOSEPH C, JR, CARDIOVASCULAR PHYSIOLOGY. *Current Pos:* assoc med, Med Ctr, Duke Univ, 62-63, from asst prof to prof, 63-75, chief, Cardiol Sect, Sect, 81-88, DIR HEART STA, MED CTR, DUKE UNIV, 75-, JAMES B DUKE PROF MED, 81- *Personal Data:* b Atlanta, Ga, July 20, 31; m 55; c 3. *Educ:* Emory Univ, BA, 54, MD, 56; Am Bd Internal Med, dipl; Am Bd Cardiovasc Dis, dipl. *Honors & Awards:* Distinguished Scientist Award, Am Col Cardiol, 85. *Prof Exp:* From intern to sr asst resident med, Duke Univ Hosp, 56-59; clin assoc, Sect Clin Biophys, Cardiol Br, Nat Heart Inst, 59-62. *Concurrent Pos:* Clin investr, 62-63, asst chief med serv, Vet Admin Hosp, 63-75; career develop award, Nat Heart Inst, 66-75; mem cardiovasc & pulmonary study sect, NIH, 74-78, chmn, 75-78; consult, IBM, 71-84, Hewlett Packard Corp, 85-89 & Spacelabs Corp, 88-; mem, Coun Clin Cardiol, Am Heart Ass, 72-74, Coun Basic Sci, 74-80 & Coun Circulation, 77-80; mem bd gov, Am Bd Internal Med, 88-; res prog specialist cardiol, Vet Admin, 89- *Mem:* Inst Med-Nat Acad Sci; Am Physiol Soc; fel Am Heart Asn; fel Am Col Physicians; Am Soc Clin Invest; AAAS; Am Fedn Clin Res; fel Am Col Cardiol; Asn Am Physicians; Asn Profs Med. *Res:* Coronary blood flow. *Mailing Add:* Box 3246 Duke Univ Med Ctr Durham NC 27710

GREENFIELD, LAZAR JOHN, VASCULAR SURGERY. *Current Pos:* PROF & CHMN, DEPT SURG, UNIV MICH, 87- *Personal Data:* b Houston, Tex, Dec 14, 34; m 56; c 3. *Educ:* Baylor Univ, MD, 58; Am Bd Surg, dipl, 67; Am Bd Thoracic Surg, dipl, 67; Am Bd Gen Vascular Surg, dipl, 82. *Prof Exp:* Intern surg, Johns Hopkins Hosp, 58-59, from asst resident to resident, 61-66; sr asst surgeon, Nat Heart Inst, Md, 59-61; chief surg serv, Vet Admin Hosp, Oklahoma City, 66-74; prof surg & chmn dept, Med Col Va, Va Commonwealth Univ, 74-87. *Concurrent Pos:* Prof surg, Med Ctr, Univ Okla, 66-74; John & Mary R Markle scholar, 68- *Mem:* Inst Med-Nat Acad Sci; Am Physiol Soc; Am Thoracic Soc; Soc Univ Surg. *Res:* Pulmonary embolism; shock; cardiac function. *Mailing Add:* Dept Surg Univ Mich Hosp 2101 Taubman Ctr 1500 E Medical Center Dr Ann Arbor MI 48109-0346. *Fax:* 313-763-5615; *E-Mail:* lazavg@umich.edu

GREENFIELD, LEONARD JULIAN, BIOCHEMISTRY. *Current Pos:* from res asst prof to assoc prof, 59-74, assoc dean grad sch, 66-76, PROF BIOCHEM & ECOL PHYSIOL, MARINE LAB, UNIV MIAMI, 74-, CHMN, DEPT BIOL, 70-; PRES, MEGALINE SCI CORP, 82- *Personal Data:* b New York, NY, May 18, 26. *Educ:* City Col New York, BS, 49; Univ Miami, MS, 51; Stanford Univ, PhD, 59. *Prof Exp:* Asst biochem marine wood borers, Marine Lab, Univ Miami, 51-54; asst productivity of Gulf Stream, 54-55; asst biochem marine invert, Hopkins Marine Sta, Stanford Univ, 55-59. *Concurrent Pos:* Consult, 77-; mem sci adv bd, US Environ Protection Agency, 79-82. *Mem:* AAAS. *Res:* Ecological physiology and ecological biochemistry of marine organisms; biological and chemical ecology of south Florida wetlands. *Mailing Add:* 6721 SW 69th Terr South Miami FL 33143-3134

GREENFIELD, MICHAEL DENNIS, ANIMAL COMMUNICATION, BIOACOUSTICS. *Current Pos:* assoc prof, 91-94, PROF ENTOM, UNIV KANS, 94- *Personal Data:* b New York, NY, Mar 2, 52; m 82, Valery J Terwilliger. *Educ:* NY Univ, BA, 73; Univ Wis-Madison, MS, 75, PhD(entom), 78. *Prof Exp:* Fel, Smithsonian Trop Res Inst, 78-79; postdoctoral researcher, Univ Fla-USDA, 79-81; from asst prof to assoc prof biol, Univ Calif, Los Angeles, 81-91. *Concurrent Pos:* Vis lectr zool, Hebrew Univ, Jerusalem, 89. *Mem:* Animal Behav Soc; Am Soc Naturalists; Ecol Soc Am; Soc Study Evolution; Orthopterists' Soc. *Res:* Sexual selection and animal communication; evolution of acoustic signaling and signal interactions (chorusing) in insects and the mechanisms of female choice in mating systems of insects; behavioral ecology. *Mailing Add:* Dept Entom Univ Kans Lawrence KS 66045. *Fax:* 785-864-5321; *E-Mail:* greenfie@kuhub.cc.ukans.edu

GREENFIELD, RICHARD SHERMAN, METEOROLOGY. *Current Pos:* prog dir global atmospheric res prog, 74-80, head, Grant Prog Sect, 80-93, DIR, DIV ATMOSPHERIC SCI, NSF, 93- *Personal Data:* b New York, NY, May 29, 33; m 66; c 3. *Educ:* New York Univ, BS, 55, MS, 62, PhD(meteorol), 66. *Prof Exp:* Asst res scientist meteorol, Res Div, Col Eng, NY Univ, 55-57; chief forecaster, Kirtland AFB, USAF, 57-58, asst staff meteorologist, Air Force Ballistic Missiles Div, 58-59; asst res scientist, Geophys Sci Lab, NY Univ, 59-66; sr res scientist, Travelers Res Ctr, 66-69, Ctr Environ & Man, 70-74. *Concurrent Pos:* Consult, Res Found, State Univ NY Albany; lectr, Hartford Grad Ctr, Rensselaer Polytech Inst, 72-74; sr exec fel, Harvard Univ, 82. *Mem:* AAAS; fel Am Meteorol Soc. *Res:* Numerical modeling of atmospheric phenomena; dynamic meteorology; computer programming techniques; scientific administration; science policy. *Mailing Add:* Div Atmospheric Sci Geosci Directorate 4201 Wilson Blvd Arlington VA 22230

GREENFIELD, ROY JAY, GEOPHYSICS. *Current Pos:* from asst prof to assoc prof, 68-78, PROF GEOPHYS, PA STATE UNIV, 78- *Personal Data:* b New York, NY, Apr 8, 36; m 61, Steinman; c Leon, David & John. *Educ:* Mass Inst Technol, BS, 58, MS, 62, PhD(geophys), 65. *Prof Exp:* Assoc engr, IBM Corp, 60-61, staff engr, 61-62; staff mem seismol, Lincoln Lab, Mass Inst Technol, 65-68. *Mem:* Am Geophys Union; Soc Explor Geophys; Seismol Soc Am. *Res:* Seismology; ground probing radar. *Mailing Add:* Pa State Univ 441 Deike University Park PA 16802. *Fax:* 814-863-7823; *E-Mail:* roy@geosc.psu.edu

GREENFIELD, SEYMOUR, neurochemistry, for more information see previous edition

GREENFIELD, SHELDON, MEDICINE. *Current Pos:* sr scientist, Health Inst, 88-93, DIR, PRIMARY CARE OUTCOMES RES INST, NEW ENG MED CTR HOSPS, 93- *Personal Data:* b Cincinnati, Ohio, Apr 22, 38. *Educ:* Harvard Univ, AB, 60; Univ Cincinnati, MD, 64. *Honors & Awards:* Blanchard Lectr, Soc Teachers Family Med, 93; Yules Lectr, Dept Med, Tufts Univ Med, 93; George Silver Lectr, Univ Miami, 94; Primary Care Lifetime Achievement Award, Pew Health Professions Comn, 94; Ann Evans Day Distinguished Clin Lectr, Boston Univ, 94; Glaser Award, Soc Gen Internal Med, 97. *Prof Exp:* Intern Boston City Hosp, Boston Univ, 64-66; epidemic intel serv officer, USPHS & fel, Dept Prev Med, State Univ NY, 66-68; sr asst resident med, Beth Israel Hosp, Harvard Med Sch, 68-69, training fel infectious dis, 69-71; chief resident, 71-72 & staff mem, Ambulatory Care Proj, 71-76; co-prin investr, Univ Calif, Los Angeles, 74-76, from asst prof to prof med & pub health, 72-88, dir, Master Sci Pub Health Track, 80-88, co-dir res & develop, 82-88, dir 86-88. *Concurrent Pos:* Mem, First Pub Health Deleg, Cuba, 74, Nat Comt Qual Assurance, 96-; vis prof, Ben Gurion Univ Negev, Israel, 81, Mario Negri Inst, Milan, 93; med dir, Nat Study Med Outcomes, 84-; prof med & chief, Div Health Servs Res, Dept Med, Tufts Univ Sch Med, 88-; adj prof, Harvard Sch Pub Health, 88; prin investr, Diabetes Patient Outcome Res Team, 90-; Spinoza-chair vis prof, Univ Amsterdam, 92; Anglo-Am vis prof, Royal Soc Med, Eng, 94; acad dir, Tufts Managed Care Inst, 95-; comt mem, Robert Wood Johnson Found Patient-Provider Relationship Under Managed Care Initiative, 96. *Mem:* Inst Med-Nat Acad Sci; fel Am Col Physicians; Am Fedn Clin Res; Soc Res & Educ Primary Care Internal Med (pres-elect, 83-84, pres, 84-85). *Mailing Add:* Primary Care Outcomes Res Inst New Eng Med Ctr Hosps 750 Washington St Box 345 Boston MA 02111. *Fax:* 617-636-7988

GREENFIELD, STANLEY MARSHALL, environmental science, environmental management, for more information see previous edition

GREENFIELD, SYDNEY STANLEY, BOTANY, PLANT PHYSIOLOGY. *Current Pos:* from asst prof to assoc prof biol, Rutgers Univ, 46-59, prof bot, 59-84, chmn, Bot Dept, 61-72, EMER PROF BOT, RUTGERS UNIV, NEWARK, 84- *Personal Data:* b Brooklyn, NY, Nov 28, 15. *Educ:* Brooklyn Col, BA, 36; Columbia Univ, MA, 37, PhD(bot), 41. *Prof Exp:* Res assoc plant physiol, Columbia Univ, 41-45, instr bot, 43. *Concurrent Pos:* Pub sch teacher, NY, 37-45; chmn, Sci Dept, Harlem Eve High Schs, 43-45; ed, Plant Sci Bull, 59-62. *Mem:* AAAS; Bot Soc Am. *Res:* Photosynthesis in Chlorella; mineral toxicity in plants; plant-growth substances; selenium poisoning and effects on plants; physiology of plant cells; economic botany. *Mailing Add:* 10 Huron Ave 11A Jersey City NJ 07306-3625

GREENFIELD, WILBERT, PHYSIOLOGY. *Current Pos:* PRES, JOHNSON C SMITH UNIV, 73-; PRES VA STATE UNIV, 83-; NAT ASN EQUAL OPPORTUNITY & HIGHER EDUC, WASHINGTON, DC. *Personal Data:* b Seven Springs, NC, July 18, 33; m 59; c 2. *Educ:* A&T State Univ NC, BS, 56; Univ Iowa, MS, 58, PhD(physiol), 60. *Prof Exp:* Res asst physiol, Univ Iowa, 57-60; head, Dept Biol, 60-67, assoc dean Sch Liberal Studies, 67, prof biol, Jackson State Univ, 60-73, dean acad affairs, 70-73. *Concurrent Pos:* Consult, Paper Co Found grant, High Sch, Miss, 63-67; acad dean's inst, Am Coun Educ, Univ Chicago, 67; mentor, Acad Admin Internship Prog, 68-69. *Res:* Cardiovascular and respiratory physiology dealing with cross circulation and peripheral blood flow; sickle cell anemia. *Mailing Add:* 1205 Sharon Dr Titusville FL 32796

GREENGARD, OLGA, BIOCHEMISTRY. *Current Pos:* RES PROF PEDIAT & PROF PHARMACOL, MT SINAI SCH MED, 78- *Personal Data:* b Arad, Hungary, Jan 13, 26; US citizen; m 54; c 2. *Prof Exp:* Univ London, BSc, 51, PhD(biochem), 55. Prof Exp: Res asst biochem, Inst Psychiat, Maudsley Hosp, Univ London, 55-56; biochemist, Courtauld Inst Biochem, Middlesex Hosp, London, 56-58; res assoc, Col Physicians & Surgeons, Columbia Univ, 62-65; res assoc, 65-69, prin assoc biochem, sr res assoc, Harvard Med Sch, 69-78; sr res assoc, mem cancer res inst, New Eng Deaconess Hosp, Boston, 65-78. *Mem:* Am Asn Cancer Res; Am Soc Biol Chemists; Am Soc Cell Biol; Brit Biochem Soc; Harvey Soc. *Res:* Regulation of enzyme synthesis in mammalian liver, in neoplastic tissues and in normal, developing organs during various stages of differentiation. *Mailing Add:* Dept Pediat Mt Sinai Sch Med PO Box 1198 One Gustave Levy Pl New York NY 10029-6504

GREENGARD, PAUL, BIOCHEMISTRY. *Current Pos:* prof, 83-91, HEAD, LAB MOLECULAR & CELLULAR NEUROSCI, ROCKEFELLER UNIV, 83-, VINCENT ASTOR PROF, 91- *Personal Data:* b New York, NY, Dec 11, 25; m 54; c 2. *Educ:* Hamilton Col, AB, 48; Johns Hopkins Univ, PhD(neurophysiol), 53. *Hon Degrees:* MD, Karolinska Inst, 87. *Honors & Awards:* Mayor's Gold Medallion, City of Milan; Lamson Mem Lectr, Vanderbilt Univ, 74; Louis B Flexner Lectr, Univ Pa, 76; Ciba-Geigy Drew Award, 79; Harvey Soc Lectr, 80; Biol & Med Sci Award, NY Acad Sci, 80; Oscar Bodansky Basic Sci Award & Lectr, Mem Sloan-Kettering Cancer Ctr, 82; Schueler Lectr, Tulane Univ, 86; 3M Life Sci Award, Fedn Am Socs Exp Biol, 87; Oliver H Lowry Lectr, Wash Univ, 87; William R McAlpin, Jr Ment Health Res Achievement Award, Nat Ment Health Asn, 87; Hughlings Jackson Mem Lectr, Montreal Neurol Inst, 87; Nat Acad Sci Award in Neurosci, 91; Ralph W Gerard Prize Neurosci, Soc Neurosci, 94; Thudichum Medal, Biochem Soc, 96. *Prof Exp:* Dir, Dept Biochem, Geigy Res Labs, NY, 59-67; dir, Dept Neuropharmacol, Inst Basic Res Ment Retardation, NY State Dept Ment Hyg, 67-68; prof pharmacol & psychiat, Sch Med, Yale Univ, 68-83; Andrew D White prof-at-large, Cornell Univ, 81-87. *Concurrent Pos:* NSF fel neurochem, Inst Psychiat, Univ London, 53-54; Nat Found Infantile Paralysis fel enzymol, Molteno Inst, Cambridge Univ, 54-55; Paraplegia Found fel neurochem, Nat Inst Med Res, Eng, 55-56, Nat Inst Neurol Dis & Blindness fel, 56-58; vis scientist, Nat Heart Inst, 58-59; vis assoc prof, Albert Einstein Col Med, 61-68, vis prof, 68-; vis prof, Vanderbilt Univ, 67-68; founder & ser ed, Advances Biochem Psychopharmacol, 68- & Advances Cyclic Nucleotide & Protein Phosphorylation Res, 71-; assoc ed, J Cyclic Nucleotide Res, 74-84; first distinguished lectr, Soc Gen Physiologists, Int Cong Physiol Sci, Paris, 77; assoc, Neurosci Res Prog; mem, Med Adv Bd, Am Parkinson Dis Asn, 84-, Extramural Sci Adv Bd, NIMH, 86- & Bd Sci Counselors, Nat Inst Alcohol Abuse & Alcoholism, 86-88. *Mem:* Nat Acad Sci; Am Acad Arts & Sci; fel Am Col Neuropsychopharmacol; Soc Neurosci; Soc Gen Physiologists; Int Brain Res Orgn; Am Soc Biol Chemists; Am Soc Pharmacol & Exp Therapeut; Biochem Soc; Res Soc Alcoholism; Am Philos Soc; hon mem Am Neurol Asn. *Res:* Neurochemistry; cyclic nucleotides; protein phosphorylation; chemical neurophysiology; microchemistry; enzymology; biochemical pharmacology. *Mailing Add:* Lab Molecular & Cellular Neurosci Rockefeller Univ 1230 York Ave New York NY 10021

GREENHALGH, ROY, PESTICIDE, MYCOTOXIN & ANALYTICAL CHEMISTRY. *Current Pos:* CONSULT, XENOS LABS, 91- *Personal Data:* b Stockport, Eng, May 25, 26; Can citizen; m 54; c 1. *Educ:* Univ Manchester, Eng, BSc(hons), 51; Univ Queensland, Australia, PhD(chem), 54. *Honors & Awards:* Caledon Award, 83. *Prof Exp:* Fel natural prod, Nat Res Coun Can, 55-57; res chemist, Defense Res Bd Can, 57-67; vis prof organophosphorus chem, Univ Kent, Eng, 67-68; res chemist pesticide chem, Agr Can Chem & Biol Res Inst, 69-80; res chemist, mycotoxin prog, Plant Res Ctr, 81-91. *Concurrent Pos:* Mem, Can Adv Comt Common Names for Pesticides, 71; chmn tech comt, Int Standards Orgn, 73-; secy comn terminal pesticide residues, Int Union Pure & Appl Chem, 74-; Int Cong Pesticide Chem, Ottawa, 86; FAO expert, JMPR, 86, 87, 88, 89 & 90; adj prof, Ottawa Univ, 83-, Carleton Univ, 84-; secy, Int Union Pure & Appl Chem Appl Chem Div, exec comt, 87; consult, IARC, 90. *Mem:* Royal Soc Chem; Chem Inst Can; Am Chem Soc. *Res:* Development of new analytical procedures for pesticides and herbicide residues in animal, plant tissues and soil; metabolism and chemistry of pesticides; biosynthesis of mycotoxins; new analytical procedures for the toxins and metabolites; NMR of trichothecenes; characterization of fungal secondary metabolites. *Mailing Add:* 321 Cloverdale Ottawa ON K1M 0Y3 Can

GREENHALL, ARTHUR MERWIN, MAMMALOGY, CHIROPTERA, BAT RABIES. *Current Pos:* RETIRED. *Personal Data:* b New York, NY, Aug 6, 11; m 42, Elizabeth Rusk Jones; c Paul Rusk & Alice Rusk. *Educ:* Univ Mich, BA, 34, MS, 35. *Prof Exp:* Dir, Portland Zool Park, Ore, 42-47; gen cur animal div, Detroit Zool Park, Mich, 47-53; cur mus, Royal Victoria Inst, Trinidad, WI, 53-63; res assoc Am Mus Nat Hist, 57-67; chief mammal sect, Bird & Mammal Labs, US Sport Fisheries & Wildlife, 63-68; bat ecologist, Food & Agr Orgn UN, 68-72; staff mem, Div Wildlife Res, US Sport Fisheries & Wildlife, US Fish & Wildlife Serv, 63-88, zoologist, Nat Fish & Wildlife Lab & Off Sci Auth, 85-88; res assoc, US Nat Mus, Smithsonian Inst, 67-88; res assoc, Am Mus Nat Hist, 88. *Concurrent Pos:* Dir, Emperor Valley Zoo, Trinidad, 54-56; zoologist, Ministry Agr, Govt Trinidad & Tobago, 54-63; expert rabies investr, Govt Grenada, 55; lectr, Univ Col West Indies, 55-56; Rockefeller Found travel grant, 56; mammalogist, Trinidad Regional Virus Lab, 56-63; WHO fel, 57; expert rabies investr, Govt British Guiana, 59; mem Food & Agr Orgn-WHO Mission assess vampire bat rabies prob in Arg, Brazil, Venezuela, Trinidad & Mex, 66; staff specialist bat res, 77-81; staff specialist zoologist, Conv Int Trade Endangered Species Wild Fauna & Flora, 81-; consult, Pan Am Health Orgn/WHO, 89- *Mem:* Am Soc Icthyol & Herpet; Am Soc Mammal; fel Linnean Soc London; hon life mem, Zool Soc Trinidad & Tobago. *Res:* Life history and ecology of bats, including bat associated diseases affecting man and animals; control and management of bats which enter buildings, damage fruit crops, and vampire bats which attack livestock and humans, bat rabies, bat conservation, flying fox fruit bats. *Mailing Add:* 171 W 12th St New York NY 10011. *Fax:* 212-929-4353

GREENHALL, CHARLES AUGUST, MATHEMATICAL STATISTICS, TIME & FREQUENCY. *Current Pos:* consult, 73-77, MEM TECH STAFF, JET PROPULSION LAB, 77- *Personal Data:* b New York, NY, May 5, 39. *Educ:* Pomona Col, BA, 61; Calif Inst Technol, PhD(fourier series), 66. *Prof Exp:* Physicist, US Naval Ord Testing Sta, Calif, 62; Nat Res Coun resident res assoc, Jet Propulsion Lab, 66-68; asst prof math, Univ Southern Calif, 68-73. *Mem:* Am Math Soc; Soc Indust & Appl Math; Math Asn Am; Inst Elec & Electronics Engrs. *Res:* Statistics and measurement of precise time and frequency; NASA award for patent (frequency stability measurement). *Mailing Add:* Jet Propulsion Lab 298 4800 Oak Grove Dr Pasadena CA 91109

GREENHOUSE, GERALD ALAN, CYTOLOGY. *Current Pos:* EXEC SECY, CELL BIOL STUDY SECT, NIH, 77-, REFERRAL OFFICER, DIV RES GRANTS, 83- *Personal Data:* b New York, NY, Oct 18, 42; m 68; c 2. *Educ:* Queens Col, City Univ New York, BA, 64; City Univ NY, PhD(biol), 69. *Prof Exp:* Fel molecular biol, Mass Inst Technol, 69-71; fel, Univ Geneva, Switz, 71-72; asst prof anat, cell & develop biol, Univ Calif, Irvine, 72-76; grants assoc, NIH, 76-77. *Mem:* Teratology Soc; Am Soc Cell Biol. *Mailing Add:* Div Res Grants NIH Westwood Bldg 1AO6 6701 Rockledge Dr Bethesda MD 20892-7840. *Fax:* 301-480-2065

GREENHOUSE, HAROLD MITCHELL, PHYSICAL INORGANIC CHEMISTRY, HYBRID MICROELECTRONICS. *Current Pos:* dir microelectronics lab, Benidix Commun Div, Allied Bendix Aerospace Co, 59-71, sr staff engr, 71-91, prin engr, 91-97, EMER SCIENTIST MATS, COMMUN SYSTS, ALLIED SIGNAL AEROSPACE, 97- *Personal Data:* b Chicago, Ill, Nov 20, 24; m 48; c 3. *Educ:* Ohio State Univ, BS, 48, MS, 51. *Prof Exp:* Res assoc, Res Found, Ohio State Univ, 50-53; res chemist, Ferroxcube Corp, 53-55; dir semiconductor res & magnetics, Aladdin Electronics Co, 55-59. *Mem:* Int Soc Hybrid Microelectronics; Inst Elec & Electronics Eng; Sigma Xi. *Res:* Materials research; solid state physical chemistry; x-ray diffraction; emission and adsorption spectroscopy; high temperature materials; ferrites; magnetic materials and devices; thin films; microelectronics; thick film hybrid microcircuits; precision crystal oscillators; hereticity. *Mailing Add:* One Mica Ct Baltimore MD 21209

GREENHOUSE, N ANTHONY, HEALTH PHYSICS, ENVIRONMENTAL SCIENCE. *Current Pos:* SR HEALTH PHYSICIST, STAFF SCIENTIST, LAWRENCE BERKELEY LAB, 80- *Personal Data:* b Washington, DC, June 20, 40; m 90, Ella A Liggins. *Educ:* Catholic Univ Am, BA, 61; Univ Rochester, MS, 66; Univ Calif, Berkeley, MPH, 82, PhD, 94. *Prof Exp:* Health physicist, Lawrence Livermore Lab, Univ Calif, 66-71; sr health physicist, Brookhaven Nat Lab, 71-80. *Concurrent Pos:* Consult, Dames & Moore, 75-; mem, Am Bd Health Physics, 78-80; chair, Am Bd Health Physics, 81-83; mem, Nat Acad Sci comt, film badge dosimetry in atmospheric nuclear tests, 87-88. *Mem:* Health Physics Soc; Sigma Xi. *Res:* Transport of man-made environmental radioactive materials to man; modeling of radionuclide exposure pathways; internal and external radiation dosimetry. *Mailing Add:* Univ Calif LBL Bldg 90-0026 Berkeley CA 94720. *Fax:* 510-486-6939; *E-Mail:* tonyg@csa.lu.gov

GREENHOUSE, SAMUEL WILLIAM, STATISTICS. *Current Pos:* prof, George Washington Univ, 74-88, chmn, 76-79, EMER PROF STATIST, GEORGE WASHINGTON UNIV, 88-, ASSOC DIR RES DEVELOP, BIOSTATIST CTR, 93-; CONSULT, 88- *Personal Data:* b New York, NY, Jan 13, 18; m 44, Selma Simon; c Joan (Goldstein), Richard, Joel & Robin (Shapiro). *Educ:* City Col New York, BS, 38; George Washington Univ, MA, 54, PhD(math statist), 59. *Prof Exp:* Jr statistician, US Census Bur, 40-42; statistical analyst, UNRRA, 45-48; math statistician, Nat Cancer Inst, NIH, 48-54, chief, Statist & Appl Math Sect, NIMH, 54-66, assoc dir epidemiol &

biomet, Nat Inst Child Health & Human Develop, 66-74, actg assoc dir planning & eval, 69-74. *Concurrent Pos:* Mem psychopharmacol adv comt, NIH, 57-59, mem accident prev study sect, 58-62, mem statist & math res review panel, 63-70; med res adv coun, Fed Aviation Asn, 59-64; vis prof, Stanford Univ, 60-61; NSF vis lectr, 66-68; mem biomet & epidemiol methodol adv comt, Food & Drug Admin, 67-73, chmn, 71-73; appointed mem study sect, Comput Sci, Biomath & Statist, NIH, 75-77; vis prof, Dept Biostatist, Sch Pub Health, Harvard Univ, 81-82; mem Clin Trials Rev Comt, Nat Heart, Lung & Blood Inst, NIH, 83-86. *Mem:* Fel AAAS; Am Math Asn; fel Am Statist Asn; fel Inst Math Statist; Royal Statist Sec; Int Statist Inst; Biomet Soc. *Res:* Statistical methods and theory; application of statistical methods and mathematical models to the medical, biological and behavioral sciences; design, conduct and interpretation of clinical trials; methods for epidemiological research. *Mailing Add:* 1724 Ladd St Silver Spring MD 20902-3523. *Fax:* 301-881-3742

GREENHOUSE, STEVEN HOWARD, MASS SPECTROMETRY, SURFACE ANALYSIS. *Current Pos:* chemist, 74-77, res chemist, 77-88, SR RES CHEMIST, AM CYANAMID CO, 88- *Personal Data:* b Rockville Center, NY, Oct 10, 47. *Educ:* Adelphi Univ, Garden City, NY, BA, 69. *Prof Exp:* Chemist, Grumman Aerospace, 69-74. *Mem:* Am Soc Mass Spectrometry; Am Vacuum Soc. *Res:* Spectroscopic characterization of inorganic, organic and polymeric substances including combinations with chromatographic separation techniques; nuclear magnetic resonance spectroscopy. *Mailing Add:* Cytec Industs Inc 1937 W Main St PO Box 60 Stamford CT 06904-0060

GREENHUT, SAUL EPHRAIM, IMPLANTABLE MEDICAL DEVICES, ELECTROPHYSIOLOGY. *Current Pos:* scientist, 91-94, staff scientist, 94-95, MGR APPL RES, TELECTRONICS, 96- *Personal Data:* b Detroit, Mich, May 27, 61; m 85, Nancy J Cronk; c Adam, Jonathan & Jordan. *Educ:* Univ Mich, BSE, 83, MS, 84, PhD(eng), 91. *Honors & Awards:* Young Investr Award, Int Soc Computerized Electrocardiol, 90. *Prof Exp:* Res engr, Newark Beth Israel Med Ctr, 84-85; comput coordr, William Beaumont Hosp, 85-88. *Mem:* Inst Elec & Electronics Engrs; NAm Soc Pacing & Electrophysiol. *Res:* Algorithms for implantable cardiac electronic devices; signal processing; pattern recognition; modeling of electrophysiologic processes. *Mailing Add:* 3586 S Waco St Aurora CO 80013. *E-Mail:* saulg@tps.com

GREENKORN, ROBERT A(LBERT), CHEMICAL ENGINEERING. *Current Pos:* assoc prof chem eng, Purdue Univ, 65-67, head dept, 67-72, prof chem eng, 67-95, asst dean, Schs Eng, 72-76, assoc dean, Schs Eng & Dir, Eng Exp Sta, 76-80, vpres & assoc provost, 80-86, vpres res, 86-93, vpres res & dean, Grad Sch, 93-94, VPRES, PURDUE RES FOUND, 80-, R GAMES SLAYTER DISTINGUISHED PROF CHEM ENG, 95- *Personal Data:* b Oshkosh, Wis, Oct 12, 28; m 52, Rosemary Drexler; c David, Eileen, Susan & Nancy. *Educ:* Univ Wis, BS, 54, MS, 55, PhD(chem eng), 57. *Prof Exp:* Asst chem eng & math, Univ Wis, 56-57; NSF fel, Norway's Tech Univ, Trondheim, 57-58; res engr sec recovery, Jersey Prod Res Co, 58-63; assoc prof eng, Marquette Univ, 63-65. *Concurrent Pos:* Lectr, Univ Tulsa, 59-63; consult, Jersey Prod Res Co, 63-65, Esso Prod Res Co, 65-73, Occidental Petrol Corp, 83-84 & World Bank, 84; mem bd, Bemis Co Inc, 84-; vpres & mem bd, Inventure, Inc, 85-; dir tech assistance prog, Purdue Univ, 96- *Mem:* Fel Am Inst Chem Engrs; Soc Petrol Engrs; fel Am Soc Eng Educ; Am Geophys Union; Am Chem Soc; AAAS. *Res:* Flow in porous media; thermodynamic properties. *Mailing Add:* Sch Chem Eng Purdue Univ West Lafayette IN 47907

GREENLAW, JON STANLEY, ornithology, population ecology, for more information see previous edition

GREENLAW, RAYMOND, COMPUTER SCIENCE. *Current Pos:* ASSOC PROF COMPUT SCI, UNIV NH, 89- *Personal Data:* b Providence, RI, July 27, 61. *Educ:* Pomona Col, BA, 83; Univ Wash, MS, 86, PhD(comput sci), 88. *Honors & Awards:* Asn Comput Mach; Europ Asn Theoret Comp Sci. *Concurrent Pos:* Humbolt fel, 95; Spanish fel sci & tech, 96; vis fel, Univ Rome, 96; Fulbright scholar, Polytech Univ, Catalonia, Barcelona, 95-96. *Mailing Add:* Dept Comput Sci Univ NH Durham NH 03824. *Fax:* 603-862-3493; *E-Mail:* greenlaw@cs.unh.edu

GREENLEAF, FREDERICK P, GROUP REPRESENTATONS & NONCOMMUTATIVE HARMONIC ANALYSIS, SCIENCE EDUCATION REFORM. *Current Pos:* asst prof, 68-69, assoc prof, 69-79, PROF MATH, NY UNIV, 79- *Personal Data:* b Allentown, Pa, Jan 8, 38; m 64, 89, Marjorie Raskin; c 2. *Educ:* Pa State Univ, BS, 59; Yale Univ, MA, 62, PhD(math), 64. *Prof Exp:* Instr math, Yale Univ, 63-64; from instr to asst prof, Univ Calif, Berkeley, 64-68. *Concurrent Pos:* Prin investr, NSF Res Contract Math Anal, 71-84, 85-96; vis prof math, Univ Calif, Los Angeles, 79-80, 81-82 & Univ Calif, Berkeley, 85; NSF curric develop grants, 93-95 & 95-97. *Mem:* AAAS; Am Math Soc. *Res:* Analysis and integration theory, with special emphasis on noncommutative harmonic analysis; fourier analysis on nilpotent groups, solvability of differential operators on nilpotent groups, structure of invariant differential operators on Lie; curriculum reform: math/science undergraduate; curriculum reform: math/science undergraduate. *Mailing Add:* Dept Math NY Univ 251 Mercer St New York NY 10012. *E-Mail:* greenlea@acf2.nyu.edu

GREENLEAF, JAMES FOWLER, BIOMEDICAL IMAGING, ULTRASONIC IMAGING. *Current Pos:* STAFF CONSULT, MAYO FOUND, 76- *Educ:* Purdue Univ, PhD(eng sci), 70. *Res:* Ultrasound tissue characterization. *Mailing Add:* Dept Physiol & Biophysiol Med Sci Bldg Mayo Clin Rochester MN 55905-0001

GREENLEAF, JOHN EDWARD, EXERCISE PHYSIOLOGY, ENVIRONMENTAL & SPACE PHYSIOLOGY. *Current Pos:* RES PHYSIOLOGIST, LAB HUMAN ENVIRON PHYSIOL, LIFE SCI DIV, AMES RES CTR, NASA, 63-, PRIN INVESTR. *Personal Data:* b Joliet, Ill, Sept 18, 32; m 60, Carol Johnson. *Educ:* Univ Ill, Urbana, BS, 55, MS, 62, PhD(physiol), 63; NMex Highlands Univ, MA, 56. *Honors & Awards:* Ellingson Award, Aerospace Med Asn, 83, 84, Eric Liljencrantz Award, 90. *Concurrent Pos:* Swed Med Res Coun fel, Stockholm, 66-67; Nat Acad Sci exchange fel, Warsaw, Poland, 73, 74, 77, 89; NIH fel, Warsaw, Poland, 80; ed bd, J Appl Physiol; consult, Shaklee US Inc, San Francisco, 82-; adj prof, San Francisco State Univ, 88- & Univ Calif, Davis, 96; vis prof, Univ Occup Environ Health, Kitakyushu, Japan, 89. *Mem:* Fel Am Physiol Soc; Am Physiol Soc; fel Aerospace Med Asn; Int Soc Exercise & Immunol; Int Soc Gravitational Physiol. *Res:* Thirst and drinking; heat acclimatization; exercise temperature regulation; body water metabolism; dehydration; space physiology, deconditioning. *Mailing Add:* 12391 Farr Ranch Ct Saratoga CA 95070-6527. *Fax:* 650-604-3954; *E-Mail:* jgreenleaf@mail.arc.nasa.gov

GREENLEAF, ROBERT DALE, CELL CULTURE. *Current Pos:* MED TECH, UNILAB, 86- *Personal Data:* b Salt Lake City, Utah, Apr 10, 48; m 78; c 1. *Educ:* Utah State Univ, BS, 71; Univ Utah, PhD(anat), 75. *Prof Exp:* Fel, Cardiovasc Res Inst, Univ Calif, San Francisco, 76-78; asst prof anat, Tufts Univ, 78-86. *Concurrent Pos:* Guest ed, Am Rev Respiratory Dis, 81; guest reviewer, Am Thoracic Soc, 82. *Mem:* Am Thoracic Soc; Tissue Cult Asn; AAAS. *Res:* Regulation of metabolism of the lung. *Mailing Add:* 6019 Bear Creek Ct Elk Grove CA 94524

GREENLEAF, WALTER HELMUTH, PLANT BREEDING. *Current Pos:* prof, Exp Sta, 47-82, EMER PROF HORT, AUBURN UNIV, 82- *Personal Data:* b Stuttgart, Ger, Apr 3, 12; nat US; m 39, Vida M Goheen; c 3. *Educ:* Univ Calif, BS, 36, PhD(genetics), 40. *Prof Exp:* Plant breeder, Vaughan Seed Store, Ill, 41-42; assoc horticulturist, Exp Sta, Univ Ga, 44-47. *Mem:* Fel AAAS; Am Soc Hort Sci. *Res:* Plant breeding; virology; cytology; horticulture; Nicotiana polyploids from auxin-induced callus; inheritance of resistance to tobacco etch virus in Capsicum; breeding multiple disease resistant quality tomatoes and peppers; Atkinson tomato, Bighart pimento, Greenleaf Tabasco and Auburn 76 FMN tomato. *Mailing Add:* Dept Hort Auburn Univ Auburn AL 36849-5408

GREENLEE, HERBERT BRECKENRIDGE, SURGERY. *Current Pos:* assoc prof, 67-72, PROF SURG, STRITCH SCH MED, LOYOLA UNIV CHICAGO, 72- *Personal Data:* b Rockford, Ill, Sept 6, 27; m 55; c 4. *Educ:* Beloit Col, AB, 51; Univ Chicago, MD, 55. *Prof Exp:* From intern to resident, Univ Chicago Hosps, 56-62; pvt pract, Chicago, Hosps, 56-62; pvt pract, Chicago, Ill, 64-66; asst prof surg, Univ Wis-Madison, 66-67; chief surg serv, Vet Admin Hosp, Hines, 72-89. *Concurrent Pos:* Am Cancer Soc fel, Univ Chicago clins, 60-61; staff surgeon, Vet Admin Hosp, Madison, Wis, 66-67; asst chief surg serv, Vet Admin Hosp, Hines, 67-72; consult, Henrotin Hosp, Chicago, 73-79. *Mem:* Fel Am Col Surgeons; Am Gastroenterol Asn; Soc Surg Alimentary Tract; Asn Acad Surg; Int Col Digestive Surg; Am Surg Asn. *Res:* Gastro-intestinal physiology; bacterial flora of gastrointestinal tract; complications of chronic pancreatitis. *Mailing Add:* 1635 Leytonstone Dr Wheaton IL 60187

GREENLEE, JOHN EDWARD, NEUROLOGY, NEUROVIROLOGY. *Current Pos:* ASST PROF NEUROL, UNIV VA HOSP, 76- *Personal Data:* b Mercedes, Tex, Sept 24, 40; m 65; c 3. *Educ:* Hamilton Col, BA, 62; Univ Rochester, MD, 69. *Honors & Awards:* USPHS Teacher-Investr Award, NIH-NINCDS, 77. *Prof Exp:* Fel path, Sch Med, Univ Rochester, 67-68; intern med, Univ Va Hosp, 67-70, asst resident med, 70-71, resident neurol, 71-74; fel neurovirol, Johns Hopkins Univ Hosp, 74-76. *Concurrent Pos:* Attend neurologist, Baltimore City Hosp, 75-76; consult neurologist, Vet Admin Hosp, Salem, Va, 77- *Mem:* Am Acad Neurol; Am Soc Microbiol. *Res:* Central nervous system infections; papovaviruses and progressive multifocal leukoencephalopathy. *Mailing Add:* Va Med Ctr Univ Hosp 500 Foothill Dr Salt Lake City UT 84148

GREENLEE, KENNETH WILLIAM, liquid ammonia reactions, pheromones synthesis, for more information see previous edition

GREENLEE, THEODORE K, ORTHOPEDIC ONCOLOGY. *Current Pos:* ASSOC PROF ORTHOP SURG, UNIV WASH, SEATTLE, 71- *Personal Data:* b Rockford, Ill, May 14, 34. *Educ:* Northwestern Univ, MD, 59. *Mailing Add:* Dept Orthoped Univ Wash 1959 NE Pacific St Box 356500 Seattle WA 98195-6500. *Fax:* 206-685-3139

GREENLEE, THOMAS RUSSELL, ATOMIC PHYSICS. *Current Pos:* MEM FAC, BETHEL COL, 80- *Personal Data:* b Lakewood, Ohio, Oct 25, 48. *Educ:* Mich Technol Univ, BS, 70; Calif Inst Technol, MS, 73, PhD(physics), 78. *Prof Exp:* Teaching & res asst physics dept, Calif Inst Technol, 71-78; lectr physics, Univ Wis, 78-80. *Concurrent Pos:* NSF fel, physics dept, Calif Inst Technol, 71-74. *Mem:* Am Phys Soc; Am Asn Physics Teachers; Am Sci Affil. *Res:* Beam-foil spectroscopy; solar abundances of elements; oscillator strengths. *Mailing Add:* 864 Sherwood Ave St Paul MN 55106

GREENLER, ROBERT GEORGE, SURFACE PHYSICS, METEOROLOGICAL OPTICS. *Current Pos:* from assoc prof to prof, 62-91, chmn lab surface studies, 66-71, ADJ PROF PHYSICS, UNIV WIS, MILWAUKEE, 91- *Personal Data:* b Kenton, Ohio, Oct 24, 29; m 54,

Barbara Stacy; c Leland, Karen & Robin. *Educ:* Univ Rochester, BS, 51; Johns Hopkins Univ, PhD(physics), 57. *Honors & Awards:* Glover Award, 75; Millikan Lectr Award, Am Asn Physics Teachers, 88; Beller Award, Optical Soc Am, 93. *Prof Exp:* Res assoc, Radiation Lab, Johns Hopkins Univ, 57; res physicist, Allis-Chalmers Mfg Co, 57-62. *Concurrent Pos:* Sci Res Coun sr vis fel, Sch Chem Sci, Univ EAnglia, 71-72; traveling lectr, Optical Soc Am, 73-74; sr Fulbright scholar, Fritz Haber Inst Max Planck Soc, WBerlin, 83; physics teacher, Midwest Univs Consortium Int Activities, Malaysia, 90-91. *Mem:* Am Asn Physics Teachers; fel AAAS; fel Optical Soc Am (vpres, 85, pres, 87). *Res:* Infrared interferometry; gas adsorption by infrared spectroscopy; physics and chemistry of solid surfaces; optical phenomena of the sky; structural colors in nature; iridescence in biological systems. *Mailing Add:* Dept Physics Univ Wis Milwaukee WI 53201. *Fax:* 414-229-5589; *E-Mail:* greenler@csd.uwm.edu

GREENLEY, ROBERT Z, BIOLOGICAL APPLICATIONS OF POLYMERS. *Current Pos:* sr res chemist, 60-70, sr res specialist & group leader, 70- 79, FEL, MONSANTO CO, 80- *Personal Data:* b Chicago, Ill, Jan 25, 34; m 56; c 3. *Educ:* John Carroll Univ, BS, 56; Univ Ill, PhD(org chem), 60. *Prof Exp:* Chemist, Lewis Labs, Nat Adv Comt Aeronaut, 56-57. *Mem:* Am Chem Soc. *Res:* Vinyl copolymers; ring opening polymerizations; thermally stable polymers and monomer synthesis; bioactive polymers. *Mailing Add:* 544 Oak Valley Dr St Louis MO 63131-4730

GREENLICK, MERWYN RONALD, PUBLIC HEALTH. *Current Pos:* dir, Ctr Health Res, Kaiser Permanente, Northwest Region, 64-95, vpres res, Kaiser Found Hosps, 81-95; SR INVESTR, CTR HEALTH RES, KAISER PERMANENTE, NORTHWEST REGION, 64-; PROF & CHAIR, DEPT PUB HEALTH & PREV MED, ORE HEALTH SCI UNIV, 90-; DIR, ORE HEALTH POLICY INST, 93- *Personal Data:* b Detroit, Mich, Mar 12, 35; m 56; c 3. *Educ:* Wayne State Univ, BS, 57, MS, 61; Univ Mich, PhD(med care orgn), 67. *Honors & Awards:* Pres Award, Asn Health Serv Res, 94. *Prof Exp:* From spec instr to instr pharm admin, Col Pharm, Wayne State Univ, 58-62. *Concurrent Pos:* Adj prof, Portland State Univ, 64-; assoc clin prof prev med & pub health, Ore Health Sci Univ, 72-84, clin prof, 84-90, prof & actg chair, 90-93; consult, Israel Ministry Health, Jerusalem, 72, WHO, Colombia, 76 & 78; vis fac, Belgrade Fac Med, Yugoslavia, 72, Ben Gurion Univ, 73; mem, Inter-Soc Comn Heart Dis Res, 80-; adj prof, Sch Pub Health, Univ Hawaii, 80-; mem, Comt Opportunities Res Prev & Treatment Alcohol Related Probs, Inst Med-Nat Acad Sci, 87-89, Steering Comt Study Treatment Alcohol Probs, 87-89, Nat Res Agenda Aging, 88-89; dir & fac mem, Training Inst Res Mgt, 87-; sr fel, Ctr Advan Study Behav Sci, Stanford, 95-96. *Mem:* Inst Med-Nat Acad Sci; AAAS; Am Pub Health Asn; Am Heart Asn; Am Sociol Asn; Am Statist Asn; Am Soc Aging; Asn Health Serv Res. *Res:* Medical care organization, especially investigation of the relationship between the organization of the medical care system and individuals' utilization of medical care services; health behavior, cardiovascular and epidemiology. *Mailing Add:* Dept Pub Health & Prev Med Sch Med CB669 Ore Health Sci Univ 3181 SW Sam Jackson Park Rd Portland OR 97201-3098. *E-Mail:* mitchg@ohsu.edu

GREENLIEF, CHARLES M, SURFACE CHEMISTRY. *Current Pos:* asst prof, 72-80, ASSOC PROF CHEM, EMPORIA STATE UNIV, 80-, CHAIR DEPT, 85- *Personal Data:* b Perkins, WVa, July 27, 37; m 60; c 3. *Educ:* Univ Calif, Berkeley, BS, 65; Univ Wash, PhD(phys chem), 70. *Prof Exp:* Welch fel, Univ Tex, Austin, 70-72. *Concurrent Pos:* Consult reviewer, Oceana Publ, Inc, 71-; vis prof, Univ Wash, 82-83 & Univ Colo, 85. *Mem:* AAAS; Am Chem Soc; Am Phys Soc; Sigma Xi. *Res:* Thermodynamics and statistical mechanics of physical adsorption; thermodynamics and transport properties of electrolytes in pure and mixed solvents. *Mailing Add:* Dept Chem Emporia State Univ Box 4030 Emporia KS 66801

GREENLIEF, CHARLES MICHAEL, SURFACE CHEMISTRY, MATERIALS CHEMISTRY. *Current Pos:* asst prof, 89-94, ASSOC PROF, UNIV MO, COLUMBIA, 94- *Personal Data:* b Oakland, Calif, June 8, 61; m 82, Jana Godderz; c Marysa R, Allen M & Monica E. *Educ:* Emporia State Univ, Kans, BS, 83; Univ Tex, Austin, PhD(chem), 87. *Honors & Awards:* Grad Student Award, Mat Res Soc, 86; Young Investr Award, NSF, 93. *Prof Exp:* Res asst, Univ Tex Austin, 83-87; res assoc, IBM TJ Watson Res Ctr, 87-89. *Mem:* Am Chem Soc; Am Vacuum Soc; Mat Res Soc; Sigma Xi; Soc Advance Chicanos & Native Am Sci. *Res:* Surface chemistry; electronic materials; deposition of thin films; electronic structure and morphology of surfaces; catalysis. *Mailing Add:* Dept Chem Univ Mo Columbia MO 65211. *Fax:* 573-882-2751; *E-Mail:* chemcmg@showme.missouri.edu

GREENMAN, DAVID LEWIS, CANCER, ENDOCRINOLOGY. *Current Pos:* RETIRED. *Personal Data:* b Williamston, Mich, Jan 19, 34; m 56, Jessie Blackman; c Karen & Martha. *Educ:* Asbury Col, AB, 56; Purdue Univ, MS, 59, PhD(endocrinol), 62. *Prof Exp:* Res assoc enzym, Oak Ridge Nat Lab, 62-63, USPHS fel, 63-64; asst prof & res assoc biol, Johns Hopkins Univ, 64-70; pharmacologist, Food & Drug Admin, 70; pharmacologist, Environ Protection Agency, 70-71, actg chief pharmacologist, Pesticides Regulation Div, 71-72; pharmacologist, Nat Ctr Toxicol Res, 72-76, actg chief chronic studies, 74-75, res physiologist, 76-84. *Concurrent Pos:* Prin investr res grant, Nat Inst Arthritis Metab Dis, Pub Health Serv, 65-70; chmn, Precautionary Labeling Comt, Asn Am Pest Control Oper, 71-72; consult, Nigerian Food & Drug Admin, 82; lectr, Intro Oncol, Univ Ark Med Sch, 86, 89, 91 & 92; chmn, Ins Animal Care & Use Comt, 90-92. *Res:* Hormonal influences on nucleic acid metabolism of estrogen target tissues; effect of age, genetic, nutritional and environmental factors on chemical carcinogenesis; mechanism and nutritional modulation of estrogen carcinogenesis, risk assessment. *Mailing Add:* 4204 Dunkeld Dr North Little Rock AR 72116

GREENMAN, NORMAN, LUNAR & PLANETARY GEOLOGY, ECONOMIC & TAX EVALUATION OF PETROLEUM PROPERTIES. *Current Pos:* RETIRED. *Personal Data:* b Chicago, Ill, Nov 5, 20; m 49, Marion Shapiro; c Edward, Ellen, Todd & Laurel. *Educ:* Univ Chicago, BA, 41, MS, 48, PhD(geol), 51. *Prof Exp:* Geologist, Shell Oil Co, 51-61 & McDonnell Douglas Astronaut Co, 61-73; consult geologist, 73-76; geologist, Santa Fe Energy Co, 76-85. *Mem:* AAAS; Am Geophys Union; Geol Soc Am; emer mem Soc Sedimentary Geol; Sigma Xi. *Res:* Lunar and planetary geology; cosmic dust; mineral and Apollo lunar sample luminescence; sedimentary petrology. *Mailing Add:* 1437 Ninth St Manhattan Beach CA 90266

GREENOUGH, RALPH CLIVE, ANALYTICAL CHEMISTRY. *Current Pos:* TECH DIR, CRYODYNE TECHNOLOGIES, AIRGAS, 85- *Personal Data:* b Medford, Mass, June 1, 32; m 61, Dorothy Cotton; c Virginia. *Educ:* Mass Inst Technol, SB, 53; Calif Inst Technol, PhD(chem), 62. *Prof Exp:* Sr res engr, Rocketdyne Div, NAm Aviation, Inc, 61-66; sr scientist, Warner-Lambert Co, 66-77; res scientist, Uniroyal, Inc, 77-85. *Mem:* Am Chem Soc; Am Soc Mass Spectrometry; Sigma Xi. *Res:* Infrared, ultraviolet, nuclear magnetic resonance and mass spectrometry of drugs, metabolites and fluorine compounds; infrared and chromatographic analysis of rubbers, plastics, gases and solvents; ultrapurification of gases and solvents. *Mailing Add:* 29 Lynwood Dr PO Box 19 Milldale CT 06467-0019. *Fax:* 860-526-3199

GREENOUGH, WILLIAM B, III, GERIATRICS, INFECTIOUS DISEASES. *Current Pos:* MEM, DIV GERIAT MED, JOHNS HOPKINS UNIV, JOHNS HOPKINS BAYVIEW MED CTR, 85- *Personal Data:* b Providence, RI, Jan 3, 32; m 54, 65, Quaneta Ahmed; c William B, Kate, Thomas C, Elisabeth (Bates) & Zarin FarahNaz. *Educ:* Amherst Col, BA, 53; Harvard Med Sch, MD, 57. *Honors & Awards:* UNICEF Gold Medal, 83, Maurice Pate Prize, 84; King Faisal Int Prize in Med, 84; Daniel V Kimberg Mem lectr, 86; Fourth James Bordley III Mem lectr, 92. *Prof Exp:* Intern & asst resident med, Columbia-Presby Med Ctr, 57-59; resident med, Peter Bent Brigham Hosp, 61-62; res assoc, Cholera Res Lab, Dacca, 62-64, chief clin res, 64-65; assoc metab, Nat Heart Inst, 65-67; asst prof med, Johns Hopkins Univ, 67-69, assoc prof med & microbiol, 69-83, Chief, Infectious Dis Div, 70-76, prof, 83, prof int health, 85; dir, Int Ctr Diarrheal Dis Res, Bangladesh, 79-85. *Concurrent Pos:* Fel hemat, Mary Imogene Bassett Hosp, Cooperstown, NY, 59-61; dir Robert Wood Johns Found clin scholar prog, Johns Hopkins Univ, 74-77; chmn, Bacteriol & Mycol Study Sect, Nat Inst Allergy & Infectious Dis, 74-76; assoc ed, Infection & Immunity, 75-78; ed-in-chief, J Diarrhoel Dis Res, 83-85; exec vpres & founding trustee, Int Child Health Found 85-88, pres, 88-94, chmn bd trustees, 94-95; chmn endowment fund comt, int ctr diarrheal dis res, Bangladesh. *Mem:* Infectious Dis Soc Am; Am Soc Clin Invest; Am Soc Microbiol; Int Epidemiol Asn; Bangladesh Med Soc; Asn Am Physicians. *Res:* Treatment and complications of diarrhea/malnutrition particularly food-based oral rehydration solutions and bismuth subsalicylate; demonstrated mode of action of cholera and E. coli enterotoxins; clinical and laboratory research in infectious diseases, metabolism and transport processes; numerous articles and publications. *Mailing Add:* Dept Med Div Geriat Johns Hopkins Bayview Med Ctr 5505 Hopkins Bayview Circle Baltimore MD 21224. *Fax:* 410-550-2513

GREENOUGH, WILLIAM TALLANT, PHYSIOLOGICAL PSYCHOLOGY, NEUROANATOMY. *Current Pos:* From instr to assoc prof, 68-78, PROF PSYCHOL, PSYCHIAT & CELL STRUCT BIOL, UNIV ILL, URBANA-CHAMPAIGN, 78- *Personal Data:* b Seattle, Wash, Oct 11, 44; m 86; c Jennifer. *Educ:* Univ Ore, BA, 64; Univ Calif, Los Angeles, MA, 66, PhD(psychol), 69. *Honors & Awards:* Merit Award, NIMH, 90; Schizophrenic Depression Established Investr Award, Nat Ans Res, 96. *Concurrent Pos:* NIMH grants, Univ Ill, 83-, ONR grant, 85-91; vis asst prof psychobiol, Univ Calif, Irvine, 72; NSF grant, 74-82 & 89-94; vis assoc prof, Univ Wash, 75-76; J McKeen Cattell Found fel, Ctr Adv Study, Univ Ill, 75-76; chair, Univ Ill Neurol & Behav Biol Prog, 76-87, assoc dir, Beckman Inst Advan Sci & Technol, 86-90; prog chair, Winter Conf Brain Res, 84-85; ed, Behav & Neurol Biol J; NSF Integrative Neurol Systs Panel, 86-90; Nat Inst Mental Health prog eval panel, 83-84; forum res mgt, Fedn Behav, Psychol & Cognitive Sci, 88-90; vpres & exec coun, Fedn Behav & Cognitive Sci, 91-93; mem, Biol Sci Direct Adv Comt, NSF, 91-; William James fel, Am Psychol Soc, 96. *Mem:* Nat Acad Sci; Soc Neurosci; Soc Develop Psychobiol; fel AAAS; fel Soc Exp Psychologists; fel Am Psychol Soc; fel Am Psychol Asn. *Res:* Role of experience and other extra-nervous influences in the development of brain and behavior, with particular interest in changes in neuronal organization brought about by long-term behavioral treatment; molecular and quantitative neuroanatomical methods in biology; neural bases of learning and memory. *Mailing Add:* Beckman Inst Univ Ill 405 N Mathews Urbana IL 61801-2325. *Fax:* 217-244-8371; *E-Mail:* wgreenou@psych.uiuc.edu

GREENSHIELDS, JOHN BRYCE, PHYSICAL CHEMISTRY. *Current Pos:* Asst prof, 56-61, ASSOC PROF CHEM, DUQUESNE UNIV, 61- *Personal Data:* b Bridgeport, Ill, June 19, 26. *Educ:* Carnegie-Mellon Univ, BS, 50, MS, 53, PhD(chem), 56. *Concurrent Pos:* Res fel, Univ Chicago, 62-64. *Mem:* AAAS; Am Chem Soc; Am Phys Soc; Sigma Xi. *Res:* Molecular quantum mechanics; statistical mechanics. *Mailing Add:* 5620 Fifth Ave Apt A6 Pittsburgh PA 15232-2634

GREENSLADE, FORREST C, PHARMACOLOGY. *Current Pos:* PRES, IPAS, 90- *Personal Data:* b Endicott, NY, Sept 23, 39; m 63; c 1. *Educ:* State Univ NY, BA, 63; Tulane Univ, MS, 65, PhD(develop biol), 66. *Prof Exp:* Harpur Col Alumni asst biol & NSF asst, Tulane Univ, 63-65; Argonne Nat Lab fel, 66-67; sr scientist & group leader reprod biol, Ortho Res Found,

67-73, dir pharmacol, 73-75, prin scientist biochem pharmacol, asst dir med res, Ortho Pharmaceut Corp, 75-78; sr assoc dir, Pfizer Pharmaceut, 78-82; sr assoc, Int Prog, Pop Coun, 82-84; pres, Hunterdon Biomed Res Ctr Inc, 84-90. *Concurrent Pos:* Sr assoc, Molecular Technol Mgt Assocs. *Mem:* AAAS; Am Soc Pharmacol & Exp Therapeut. *Res:* Technology and the quality of health care; policy and programmatic research. *Mailing Add:* Pres IPAS 303 E Main St Carrboro NC 27510

GREENSLADE, THOMAS BOARDMAN, JR, PHYSICS, HISTORY OF PHYSICS. *Current Pos:* From instr to assoc prof, 64-88, PROF PHYSICS, KENYON COL, 88- *Personal Data:* b Staten Island, NY, Dec 23, 37; m 59, Sonia Burggraf; c Thomas & Russell. *Educ:* Amherst Col, BA, 59; Rutgers Univ, MS, 61, PhD(physics), 65. *Honors & Awards:* Distinguished Serv Citation, Am Asn Physics Teachers. *Concurrent Pos:* Lectr, Univ WI, 72-73; vis assoc prof, Kans State Univ, 85-86. *Mem:* Am Asn Physics Teachers; Sigma Xi. *Res:* Nineteenth century physics teaching and apparatus. *Mailing Add:* Dept Physics Kenyon Col Gambier OH 43022. *E-Mail:* greenslade@kenyon.edu

GREENSPAN, BERNARD, MATHEMATICS EDUCATION. *Current Pos:* instr, Drew Univ, 44-47, asst prof math & physics, 47-58, chmn, Dept Math, 59-75, from assoc prof to prof, 58-81, EMER PROF MATH, DREW UNIV, 81- *Personal Data:* b New York, NY, Dec 17, 14; m 39, Beatrice Meltzer; c Valerie (Levy) & Ellen (Delaney). *Educ:* Brooklyn Col, BS, 35, MA, 36; Rutgers Univ, PhD(math), 58. *Prof Exp:* Instr math, Brooklyn Col, 35-44 and Polytech Inst Brooklyn, 43-44. *Concurrent Pos:* Consult & lectr, Bell Tel Labs, Whippany, NJ, 53-58; dir & prof, NSF Math Inst, Drew Univ, 61-75, NSF Math Summer Inst, 62-74; vis prof, Univ Santa Clara, 61 & Rutgers Univ, 71; reader math advan placement exams, EONL Testing Serv, Princeton, NJ, 66-71, table leader, 72. *Mem:* Am Math Soc; Math Asn Am. *Res:* Differential algebra; theory of numbers and mathematics education for secondary school teachers; review mathematics texts. *Mailing Add:* 24441 Calle Sonora Apt 126 Laguna Hills CA 92653-7702

GREENSPAN, DANIEL S, MOLECULAR BIOLOGY, BIOCHEMISTRY. *Current Pos:* from asst prof to assoc prof, 86-97, PROF, DEPT PATH & LAB MED, UNIV WIS SCH MED, 97-, MEM, UNIV WIS COMPREHENSIVE CANCER CTR, 96- *Personal Data:* b Jersey City, NJ, Aug 31, 51. *Educ:* NY Univ, BA, 74; NY Univ Sch Med, MS, 78, PhD(med sci), 81. *Prof Exp:* Fel dept human genetics, Yale Univ Sch Med, 81-84, assoc res scientist, 84-86. *Concurrent Pos:* Fel trainee, USPHS, 81-84; fel, Arthritis Found, 84-87; prin investr, Nat Inst Health, 87- *Mem:* Sigma Xi; Am Soc Biochem & Molecular Biol; Am Soc Microbiol; Am Soc Human Genetics. *Res:* Study of genes important to mammalian development and mutations in such genes leading to diseases in people. *Mailing Add:* Dept Path Univ Wisc 1300 University Ave Madison WI 53706-1509

GREENSPAN, DONALD, mathematics, for more information see previous edition

GREENSPAN, FRANK PHILIP, ORGANIC CHEMISTRY. *Current Pos:* VPRES RES & DEVELOP, REEVES BROS, INC, 67- *Personal Data:* b New York, NY, May 7, 17; m 43; c 1. *Educ:* City Col New York, BS, 38; Polytech Inst Brooklyn, MS, 41; Univ Buffalo, PhD(org chem), 51. *Prof Exp:* Chief chemist, Lane Bryant, Inc, 37-41; chemist, Hart Prod Corp, 41 & Chem Warfare Serv, 42-45; res chemist, Buffalo Electro-Chem Co, 45, group leader, 47-52, mgr org res & develop, Becco Chem Div, FMC Corp, 53-56, dir develop, Chem & Plastics Div, 56-58, tech dir, Epoxy Dept, 58-61, dir res & develop, Plastics Dept, Org Chem Div, 61-64, mgr new prod develop, Chem Div, 65-66; vpres res & develop, Dexter Chem Corp, 66-67. *Concurrent Pos:* Instr, Univ Buffalo, 52-56. *Mem:* AAAS; Am Chem Soc; Am Inst Chemists; Am Oil Chemists Soc; Com Develop Asn. *Res:* Chemistry, reactions and applications of hydrogen peroxides and peracids; organic peroxides; organic oxidative reactions; epoxidation-hydroxylation reactions; fats, oils and derivatives; plasticizers; epoxy, vinyl and allylic resins; polymers and polymerization; polyurethane foam; textiles; coated fabrics. *Mailing Add:* 2525 Lynbridge Dr Charlotte NC 28226

GREENSPAN, HARVEY PHILIP, APPLIED MATHEMATICS. *Current Pos:* assoc prof, 60-64, PROF APPL MATH, MASS INST TECHNOL, 64- *Personal Data:* b New York, NY, Feb 22, 33; m 53; c 2. *Educ:* City Col, BS, 53; Harvard Univ, MS, 54, PhD(appl math), 56. *Hon Degrees:* Dr Technol, Royal Inst Technol, Stockholm, Sweden, 91. *Prof Exp:* Asst prof appl math, Harvard Univ, 57-60. *Mem:* Am Acad Arts & Sci. *Res:* Fluid dynamics. *Mailing Add:* Dept Math Mass Inst Technol Cambridge MA 02139

GREENSPAN, JOEL R, PUBLIC HEALTH. *Current Pos:* MED EPIDEMIOLOGIST, CTR DIS CONTROL, 75-, ASST DIR, DIV STAND PREV, NAT CTR HEALTH STATIST, 95- *Personal Data:* b Ottawa, Ill, Apr 21, 48. *Educ:* St Louis Univ, MD, 74; Columbia Univ, MPH, 79; Am Bd Prev Med, dipl & cert. *Mem:* Am Pub Health Asn; Am Soc Trop Med. *Mailing Add:* NCHSTP Ctr Dis Control MSE02 1600 Clifton Rd Atlanta GA 30333. *Fax:* 404-639-8608

GREENSPAN, JOHN SIMON, ORAL PATHOLOGY. *Current Pos:* dir, Grad Prog Oral Biol, 76-90, chmn div, 81-89, PROF ORAL BIOL & PATH, SCH MED, 76-, DIR, AIDS SPECIMEN BANK, 82-, DIR, ORAL AIDS CTR, SCH DENT, 87-, CHMN, DEPT STOMATOL, 89-, DIR, AIDS CLIN RES CTR, SCH MED, 92- *Personal Data:* b London, Eng, Jan 7, 38; m 62; c 2. *Educ:* Univ London, BSc, 59, BDS, 62, PhD(exp path), 67; MRCPath, 71; FRCPath, 83. *Hon Degrees:* ScD, Georgetown Univ, 90. *Honors & Awards:* Gurley lectr, Univ Calif, San Francisco, 80; Pindborg lectr, Scand Soc Oral Path & Oral Med, 85; Ship Mem Lectr, World Dent Cong, Jerusalem, 86; Seymour J Kreshover Lect Award, Nat Inst Dent Res, NIH, 89; Oral Biol Res Award, Int Asn Dental Res, 92. *Prof Exp:* Asst lectr oral path, Royal Dent Hosp, London, Sch Dent Surg, Univ London, 63-65, lectr, 65-68, sr lectr, 68-76. *Concurrent Pos:* Fel path, Royal Postgrad Med Sch, 63-64, Med Sch, St George's Hosp, 68-71; consult & dent surgeon, St George's Hosp, London, 72-76; consult oral path, St John's Hosp & Inst Dermat, London, 73-76; chmn, Oral Soft Tissue Dis Panel, Nat Inst Dent Res, 80-; assoc ed, J Oral Path, 80-92; counr, Am Asn Dent Res, 81-83, prog chair, 87-88; vis scholar, Univ Wash, Seattle, 83 & Univ Iowa, Iowa City, 84; prin investr, numerous insts, 64-; consult, Coun Dent Therapeut, Am Dent Asn, 88-; vis assoc prof oral path, Sch Dent & Sch Med, Univ Calif, San Francisco, 72-73, assoc dir, Dent Clin Epidemiol Prog, 87-91; ed, Oral Dis, 94- *Mem:* Foreign assoc Inst Med-Nat Acad Sci; Int Asn Dent Res (vpres, 94-95, pres-elect, 95-96, pres, 96-97); Am Acad Oral Path; Histochem Soc; Path Soc UK; fel Am Col Dentists; fel AAAS; Int Acad Oral Path; Int Asn Dent Asn; Am Asn Pathologists; Am Asn Dent Res (vpres, 94-95, pres-elect, 95-96, pres, 96-97). *Res:* Pathogenesis of oral soft tissue diseases notably AIDS, oral cancer, aphthous ulceration, periodontal disease and Sjogren's syndrome; immunological mechanisms as indicated by the mononuclear cells within the lesions; in site evidence of viral etiology; author of numerous publications. *Mailing Add:* Dept Stomatol Rm S-612 Univ Calif San Francisco Sch Dent 513 Parnassus Ave San Francisco CA 94143-0422. *Fax:* 415-476-4204; *E-Mail:* stom%johng@ccmail.ucsf.edu

GREENSPAN, JOSEPH, instrumentation, physical chemistry; deceased, see previous edition for last biography

GREENSPAN, KALMAN, ELECTROPHYSIOLOGY, PHARMACODYNAMICS. *Current Pos:* RETIRED. *Personal Data:* b Bariez, Poland, Apr 27, 25; US citizen; m 50; c 3. *Educ:* Long Island Univ, BS, 48; Boston Univ, MA, 50; Columbia Univ, MA, 53; State Univ NY Brooklyn, PhD(physiol), 60. *Prof Exp:* Teaching asst biol, Boston Univ, 49-50; instr, Long Island Univ, 50; teaching asst physiol, State Univ NY Downstate Med Ctr, 57-60, instr, 60-62; from asst prof med to prof med & physiol, Sch Med, Ind Univ, Indianapolis, 62-90, prof physiol & med, Terre Haute Ctr Med Educ, 74-90. *Concurrent Pos:* Mem coun basic sci, Am Heart Asn; sr res assoc, Krannert Inst Cardiol, 62-65, head sect physiol, 65-74, dir instrumentation lab, 68-74. *Mem:* Fel Am Col Clin Pharmacol; fel Am Col Cardiol; Am Soc Pharmacol & Exp Therapeut; Am Physiol Soc; Am Heart Asn. *Res:* Cardiac research in the determination of the basic mechanisms for cardiac dysrhythmias and possible modes of therapy. *Mailing Add:* 660 Holliday Lane Indianapolis IN 46260-3519

GREENSPAN, MARSHALL, AIRBORNE RADAR, SIGNAL PROCESSING. *Current Pos:* DIR TECHNOL, NORTHROP GRUMMAN NORDEN SYSTS, 85- *Personal Data:* b Hartford, Conn, Apr 5, 39; m 62, Shiela Ruth Waldman; c Emmanuel, Howard & Shelley. *Educ:* Mass Inst Technol, SB & SM, 61; Univ Conn, PhD(elec eng), 69. *Honors & Awards:* George Mead Gold Medal, United Technol Corp, 73. *Prof Exp:* Radar systs engr, Norden Systs Inc, 62-75, mgr, 75-85. *Concurrent Pos:* Mem Air Force Studies Bd, Nat Acad Sci, 83-84; mem, Radar Systs Panel, Aerospace Electronics Systs Soc, Inst Elec & Electronics Engrs, 97- *Mem:* Inst Elec & Electronics Engrs; sr mem Aerospace Electronics Systs Soc; Am Defense Preparedness Asn. *Res:* Design and development of advanced air to surface radar systems; surface moving target detection and identification. *Mailing Add:* 137 Pheasant Lane Fairfield CT 06430. *Fax:* 203-852-7423; *E-Mail:* greenspan@juno.com

GREENSPAN, NEIL SANFORD, MOLECULAR IMMUNOLOGY, IMMUNOLOGY OF INFECTIOUS AGENTS. *Current Pos:* DIR, CLIN HISTOCOMPATABILITY LAB, UNIV HOSP, CLEVELAND, 86- *Personal Data:* b Chicago, Ill, Nov 15, 53; m 80, Judith Keene; c Aaron J & Simon K. *Educ:* Harvard Univ, AB, 75; Univ Pa, MD & PhD(immunol), 81. *Concurrent Pos:* From assoc prof to asst prof path, Case Western Res Univ, 86-93; tech staff expert, Teltech Resource Network, Teltech Inc, 91-; mem, Immunol, Virol & Path Study Sect, NIH, 92-96. *Mem:* Am Asn Immunologists; Am Soc Investigative Path; Clin Immunol Soc; AAAS; Am Soc Histocompatibility & Immunogenetics. *Res:* Molecular basis for antigen recognition and specificity by antibodies and other proteins of the immune system; clarifying key concepts related to molecular recognition; molecular aspects of bacterial immunity and vaccines. *Mailing Add:* Biomed Res Bldg Rm 927 Case Western Res Univ 10900 Euclid Ave Cleveland OH 44106-4943. *Fax:* 216-368-1300; *E-Mail:* nsg@po.cwru.edu

GREENSPAN, RICHARD H, RADIOLOGY. *Current Pos:* prof diag radiol & chmn dept, ASSOC DEAN CLIN AFFAIRS, SCH MED, YALE UNIV, 86- *Personal Data:* b New York, NY, Apr 25, 25; m 52; c 3. *Educ:* Columbia Univ, AB, 45; Syracuse Univ, MD, 48. *Prof Exp:* From instr to asst prof radiol, Univ Minn, 57-60; asst prof, Sch Med, Yale Univ, 60, attend radiologist, 60-61, from assoc prof to prof radiol & actg chmn dept, 61-68; prof, Univ Calif, San Francisco, 68-73. *Mem:* Am Roentgen Ray Soc; Asn Univ Radiol; Fed Am Socs Exp Biol; Sigma Xi. *Res:* Vascular radiologic studies and the application of isotopes to cardiovascular disease. *Mailing Add:* Dept Radiol Yale Univ Sch Med PO Box 208042 New Haven CT 06520-8042

GREENSPAN, STANLEY IRA, PSYCHIATRY, PSYCHOANALYSIS. *Current Pos:* PSYCHIATRIST, SUPV CHILD PSYCHOANALYST & CLIN PROF CHILD HEALTH DEVELOP PSYCHIAT, GEORGE WASHINGTON UNIV MED SCH, 86- *Personal Data:* b New York, NY, June 1, 41; m 75; c 3. *Educ:* Harvard Univ, BA, 62; Yale Univ, MD, 66. *Honors & Awards:* Lucie Jessner Prize in Child Psychoanal, 74; Blanche F Ittleson Award, Am Psychiat Asn, 81- *Prof Exp:* Resident psychiat, Psychiat Inst, Columbia Presby Med Ctr, New York, 67-69; res psychiatrist, Lab Psychol, 70-72, Ment Health Study Ctr, 72-74, asst chief, 74, acting chief, 74-75, chief, ment health study ctr, NIMH, 75-84, chief, Clin Infant-Child Develop Ctr, Health Resources & Serv Admin & NIMH, 84-86. *Concurrent Pos:* Fel, Hillcrest Children's Ctr, Children's Hosp Nat Med, 69-71; clin assoc prof psychiat, behav sci & child health & develop, Med Sch, George Washington Univ, 71-; acad fac, Children's Hosp Nat Med Ctr, 71-; pres & mem bd dir, Nat Ctr Clin Infant Progs, 77- *Mem:* Am Psychiat Asn; Am Psychoanal Asn; Am Acad Child Psychiat. *Res:* Personality development, particularly its roots in the first three years of life and the development of clinical approaches for infants and toddlers; integrating different theories of personality development, especially learning theory and psychoanalytic theory; change in the therapeutic process. *Mailing Add:* 7201 Glenbrook Rd Bethesda MD 20814

GREENSPON, JOSHUA EARL, ACOUSTICS, APPLIED MECHANICS. *Current Pos:* OWNER, J G GREEN RES ASSOC, 58- *Personal Data:* b Baltimore, Md, Sept 3, 28; m 54; c 3. *Educ:* Johns Hopkins Univ, BE, 49, MS, 51, DEng, 56. *Honors & Awards:* Silver Medal in Eng Acoust, Acoust Soc Am, 89. *Prof Exp:* From jr instr to instr mech eng, Johns Hopkins Univ, 49-53; physicist vibrations, David Taylor Model Basin, 53-56; res engr aeroelasticity, Martin Co, 56-58. *Concurrent Pos:* Assoc Ed, J Acoust Soc. *Mem:* Inst Aerospace Sci; Soc Naval Archit & Marine Engrs; Am Soc Mech Engrs; fel Acoust Soc Am. *Res:* Underwater acoustics, statics and dynamics of structures. *Mailing Add:* 6211 Benhurst Rd Baltimore MD 21209

GREENSTADT, MELVIN, INORGANIC CHEMISTRY, SCIENCE EDUCATION. *Current Pos:* RETIRED. *Personal Data:* b New York, NY, Jan 18, 18; m 41, Helen Levy; c Laurie (Brown), Kenneth & Olivia (Jones). *Educ:* City Col New York, BS, 38; Univ Southern Calif, BA, 48, MA, 49, PhD(sci ed), 56. *Honors & Awards:* Western Regional Award, Am Chem Soc, 72, James Bryant Conant Award, 73; Western Regional Award, Chem Mfg Asn, 78. *Prof Exp:* Chemist, Littauer Fund, Sch Med, NY Univ, 38-40 & War Dept, 41-42; teacher high schs, Calif, 50-66; assoc prof chem, Calif State Col Long Beach, 66-69; teacher high schs, Calif, 69-80. *Res:* Sulfa drugs; photolytic reactions; chemical education. *Mailing Add:* 344 S Sycamore Ave Los Angeles CA 90036

GREENSTEIN, BENJAMIN JOEL, EVOLUTIONARY PALEOBIOLOGY, TROPICAL MARINE ECOSYSTEMS. *Current Pos:* PROF GEOL, STATE UNIV NY, CORTLAND. *Personal Data:* b Rochester, NY, Feb 28, 59; m 86; c 2. *Educ:* Univ Rochester, BA, 83; Univ Cincinnati, MS, 86, PhD(geol), 90. *Prof Exp:* asst prof geol, Smith Col, 90- *Mem:* Sigma Xi; Paleont Soc; Soc Econ Paleontologists & Mineralogists; Geol Soc Am. *Res:* Processes affecting the preservation potential of marine invertebrates, primarily echinoderms and corals; quantitative assessment of these processes and their effects on the evolutionary histories of several echinoid groups. *Mailing Add:* Dept Geol State Univ NY Cortland NY 13045. *Fax:* 413-585-3786; *E-Mail:* bgreenst@science.smith.edu

GREENSTEIN, DAVID SNELLENBURG, MATHEMATICS. *Current Pos:* RETIRED. *Personal Data:* b Wilmington, Del, Mar 26, 28; m 52; c 6. *Educ:* Univ Del, BS, 49; Univ Pa, AM, 53, PhD(math), 57. *Prof Exp:* Res student biophys, Univ Pa, 50-52; eng physicist, Philco Corp, 52-53; from asst instr to instr elec eng, Univ Pa, 53-56; prof engr, Radio Corp Am, 56-57; from instr to asst prof math, Univ Mich, 57-60; asst prof math, Northeastern Ill Univ, 60-63, assoc prof, 63-68, prof, 68- *Mem:* Am Math Soc; Math Asn Am. *Res:* Approximation theory; moment problems; complex variables; real variables. *Mailing Add:* 5500 N St Louis Chicago IL 60625

GREENSTEIN, GEORGE, ASTRONOMY, PHYSICS. *Current Pos:* from asst prof to prof, 71-83, PROF ASTRON, AMHERST COL, 83- *Personal Data:* b Williams Bay, Wis, Sept 28, 40. *Educ:* Stanford Univ, BS, 62; Yale Univ, PhD(physics), 68. *Prof Exp:* Res assoc, Yeshiva Univ, 68-70 & Princeton Univ, 70-71. *Mem:* Am Astron Soc; Int Astron Union. *Res:* Cosmology; neutron star structure and pulsar physics; x-ray astronomy; foundations of quantum theory. *Mailing Add:* Dept Astron Amherst Col Amherst MA 01002

GREENSTEIN, JEFFREY IAN, NEUROIMMUNOLOGY. *Current Pos:* from asst prof to assoc prof neurol, 83-89, actg chmn dept, 87-89, DIR MULTIPLE SCLEROSIS CTR, TEMPLE UNIV SCH MED, 86-, PROF & CHMN, DEPT NEUROL, 89- *Personal Data:* b Durban, SAfrica, July 27, 47; US citizen; m 74. *Educ:* Univ Cape Town, MBChB. *Prof Exp:* Resident neurol, Cleveland Metrop Gen Hosp, Case Western Res Univ, 76-79; staff fel neuroimmunol, Neuroimmunol Br, Nat Inst Neurol & Commun Dis & Stroke, NIH, 79-82, sr staff fel, 82-83. *Mem:* Am Acad Neurol; Am Asn Immunologists; Am Soc Microbiol; NY Acad Sci; Am Soc Advan Sci. *Res:* Study of immune regulation in multiple sclerosis; involved in experimental immunotherapy for multiple sclerosis. *Mailing Add:* Dept Neurol Temple Univ Sch Med 3401 N Broad St Philadelphia PA 19140-5104. *Fax:* 215-707-8235

GREENSTEIN, JESSE LEONARD, ASTROPHYSICS. *Current Pos:* staff mem, Hale Observ, 48-80, prof astrophys, 48-70, Lee A Dubridge prof, 70-79, LEE A DUBRIDGE EMER PROF ASTROPHYS, CALIF INST TECHNOL, 80- *Personal Data:* b New York, NY, Oct 15, 09; m 34, Naomi Mitoy; c George & Peter. *Educ:* Harvard Univ, AB, 29, AM, 30, PhD(astron), 37. *Hon Degrees:* DSc, Univ Ariz, 87. *Honors & Awards:* Bruce Medal, Astron Soc Pac, 71; Distinguished Pub Serv Med, NASA, 74; Gold Medal, Royal Astron Soc, 75. *Prof Exp:* Nat Res Coun fel, Yerkes Observ, Univ Chicago, 37-39, from instr to assoc prof astrophys, 39-47; res assoc, McDonald Observ, Chicago & Tex, 39-48. *Concurrent Pos:* Chmn panel astron, NSF, 52-57, mem, Div Comt Math, Phys & Eng Sci, 57-60; pres comn stellar spectra, Int Astron Union, 52-58; foreign ed, Annales d' Astrophysiques, 53-59; mem bd overseers, Harvard Univ, 65-71; mem coun, Nat Acad Sci, 66-69, chmn astron surv, 69-71; vis prof, Princeton Univ, 54, Inst Advan Studies, 68-69, Nordita, 72, Bohr Inst, Copenhagen, 79 & Univ Hawaii, 79, Univ Del, 81; Russell Lectr, Am Astron Soc; ed, Stellar Atmospheres; corres ed, Astrophys Lett, Comments on Astrophys & Space Sci; mem sci adv bd, Itek Corp, 72-76; chmn bd, Assoc Univ Res Astron, 74-77. *Mem:* Nat Acad Sci; Am Astron Soc (vpres, 55-57); Am Philos Soc; assoc Royal Astron Soc; fel Royal Belgian Acad Sci, Liege. *Res:* Interstellar matter; quantitative analysis of stellar atmospheres; the origin of elements; spectra, colors, compositions, magnetic fields and rotations of white dwarfs; the nature of the quasi-stellar objects; evolution of stars; faint stars; ultraviolet spectra of stars; brown dwarfs. *Mailing Add:* 1763 Royal Oaks Dr B5 Duarte CA 91010. *E-Mail:* jlg@deimos.caltech.edu

GREENSTEIN, JULIA L, IMMUNOREGULATION, DIFFERENTIATION. *Current Pos:* sr scientist, 87-91, dir immunol, 91-92, VPRES, DISCOVERY RES, IMMUNOLOGIC PHARMACEUT CORP, 92- *Personal Data:* b Nov 6, 56; m 77; c 2. *Educ:* Univ Rochester, PhD(microbiol & immunol), 81. *Prof Exp:* Asst prof, Dana-Farber Cancer Inst, Sch Med, Harvard Univ, 84-87. *Mem:* Am Asn Immunol; Am Asn Allergy Immunol. *Res:* Cellular immunology. *Mailing Add:* Dept Res Biol Transplant Inc Bldg 75 Third Ave C Navy Yard Charlestown MA 02129. *Fax:* 617-241-8780

GREENSTEIN, JULIUS S, ZOOLOGY, ACADEMIC ADMINISTRATION. *Current Pos:* PRES, CENT OHIO TECH COL & DEAN & DIR, OHIO STATE UNIV, NEWARK, 80- *Personal Data:* b Boston, Mass, July 13, 27; m 54; c 5. *Educ:* Clark Univ, AB, 48; Univ Ill, MS, 51, PhD(zool), 55. *Prof Exp:* Asst zool, Univ Ill, 50-54; from asst res prof to assoc res prof animal sci, Univ Mass, 54-59; from assoc prof to prof biol, Duquesne Univ, 59-70, chmn dept, 61-70; prof & chmn dept, State Univ NY Col, Fredonia, 70-74, actg dean arts & sci, 73-74; dean, Sch Math & Nat Sci, Shippensburg State Col, 74-80, dir, Ctr Sci & Citizen, 75-80. *Concurrent Pos:* NIH grant, 61-64; NSF grant, 64-65; fel, Sch Med, Harvard Univ, 66; Am Inst Biol Sci vis lectr, 66-; ed, Int J Fertil & Proc Pa Acad Sci; consult, Human Life Found; grant evaluator, Basic Sci, NSF & NATO. *Mem:* Am Pub Health Asn. *Res:* Embryology and histochemistry of female reproductive organs and related endocrine glands; semen biochemistry and male accessory gland physiology; placental physiology; endocrinology; information science; mammalian reproduction particularly fertility and sterility. *Mailing Add:* Sci Ohio State Univ Newark Campus 1179 Univesity Dr Newark OH 43055-1797

GREENSTEIN, TEDDY, BIOCHEMICAL ENGINEERING, LOW REYNOLDS NUMBER HYDRODYNAMICS. *Current Pos:* from asst prof to assoc prof, 67-84, PROF CHEM ENG, NJ INST TECHNOL, 84- *Personal Data:* b Czech, Mar 16, 37; US citizen; m 82, Judith Lefkowich; c Joshua A & Leah. *Educ:* City Col New York, BChE, 60; NY Univ, MChE, 62, PhD(chem eng), 67. *Prof Exp:* Rating engr, Davis Eng, 60; high sch teacher, 63-64; res asst chem eng, NY Univ, 64-67. *Concurrent Pos:* Found Advan Grad Study Eng res grant, 67-69. *Mem:* Am Soc Microbiol; Am Soc Eng Educ; Am Asn Univ Professors; Am Inst Chem Engrs; Sigma Xi. *Res:* Low Reynolds number hydrodynamics; biochemical engineering; fermentation; enzymes; antibiotics; bioelectrochemical fuel cells. *Mailing Add:* Dept Chem Eng Chem & Environ Sci NJ Inst Technol 323 M L King Blvd Newark NJ 07102

GREENSTOCK, CLIVE LEWIS, MEDICAL BIOPHYSICS, RADIATION PROTECTION. *Current Pos:* res officer, Med Biophys Br, Pinawa, 70-88, sr res officer, Radiation Biol & Health Physics Br, 88-96, SR SCIENTIST, RADIATION PROTECTION BR, AECL, CHALK RIVER, 96- *Personal Data:* b High Wycombe, UK, Aug 14, 39; m 65, Gwen D Johns; c Erica J & Andrea G. *Educ:* Univ Leeds, BSc, 60; Univ London, MSc, 63; Univ Toronto, PhD(med biophys), 68. *Honors & Awards:* Royal Soc Commonwealth Res Award, 83; Heineman Award, 84; Nat Sci & Engine Res Coun Indust Award, 86; Int Union Against Cancer Technol Transfer Award, 87. *Prof Exp:* Med physicist, Cardiff Radiother Ctr, UK, 60-61, Ont Cancer Inst, 63; radiol physics, Nat Phys Lab, UK, 63-64. *Concurrent Pos:* Fel, Nat Cancer Inst Can, Gray Lab, Mt Vernon Hosp, UK, 68-70; lectr, Atomic Energy Can Ltd, 70-; consult, Radiation Chem Data Ctr, Notre Dame, 75-, Nat Cancer Inst, 77-, Med Res Coun, 80- & Can Cancer Soc, 83-; adj prof, Univ Man, 75-90, Ottawa Univ, 89-, Carleton Univ, 92-; vis scientist, Nat Res Coun Can, 82; appointee radiosensitize-protector, Radiation Oncol Coord Comt, Nat Cancer Inst, 82-; sabbatical fel, Heineman Found, Royal Soc, Patterson Labs, Christie Hosp, UK, 83-84; deleg, People to People Inst Cancer Res & Treat, SAfrica, 85; vis prof, Wallac Oy, Finland, 87; exchange scientist, USSR, 87; hon prof, Man Cancer Ctr, Winnipeg, 87-90; vis lectr, Int Atomic Energy Agency, 91; Atomic Energy adv SAm, 91, India, 93 & Korea, 95; counr, Oxygen Soc, 92-, Int Risk Res; consult, King Faisal Hosp Res Ctr, Riyadh, Saudi Arabia, 93. *Mem:* Radiation Res Soc; Biophys Soc Can; Am Asn Cancer Res; fel Inst Physics; Health Phys Soc; Can Radiation Protection Asn; Inst Risk Res; fel oxygen soc. *Res:* Radiation damage and biological effects; risk assessment and cancer markers; free radical mechanisms of carcinogenesis and its prevention; immune system, stress and adaptation; spectroscopic studies of cancer diagnosis and treatment; molecular radiobiology; kinetic probes of macromolecule conformation; inducible response; radiosensitivity and antioxidant defense; biological dosimetry; health effects; radiation protection. *Mailing Add:* Radiation Protection Br AECL Chalk River ON K0J 1J0 Can. *Fax:* 613-584-1713; *E-Mail:* greenstockc@aecl.ca

GREENSTONE, REYNOLD, METEOROLOGY, PHYSICS. *Current Pos:* sr scientist, 60-72, PRIN SCIENTIST ATMOSPHERIC SCI, ORI INC, 72- *Personal Data:* b New York, NY, Sept 30, 24; m 52; c 5. *Educ:* NY Univ, BS, 47; Univ Md, MS, 58. *Prof Exp:* Atmospheric scientist, Nat Bur Stand, 49-55; res scientist opers res, Tech Opers Inc, 55-59, Booz Allen Appl Res Inc, 59-60. *Mem:* Am Meteorol Soc; Am Phys Soc; Am Geophys Union; Am Inst Aeronaut & Astronaut. *Res:* Upper atmospheric physics; air pollution analysis. *Mailing Add:* 1720 Brighton Dam Rd Brookeville MD 20833

GREENSTREET, WILLIAM (B) LAVON, MECHANICAL ENGINEERING, SOLID MECHANICS. *Current Pos:* RETIRED. *Personal Data:* b Cora, Mo, Feb 22, 25; m 50, Elizabeth L Chadsey; c Timothy A, Cynthia A (Wiley), Teresa A & Carl W. *Educ:* Colo State Univ, BS, 50; Univ Tenn, MS, 58; Yale Univ, PhD(solid mech), 68. *Prof Exp:* Design engr, Boeing Airplane Co, Wash, 50-51; engr, Oak Ridge Nat Lab, 51-58, head appl mech sect, Reactor Div, 58-74, dir res progs, Eng Technol Div, 74-90. *Concurrent Pos:* Mem pressure vessel res coun, 63-90; policy comt, Southeastern Conf on Theoret & Appl Mech, 68-; Am Soc Mech Engrs comt on Oper & Maintenance of Nuclear Power Plants, 85-90. *Mem:* Fel Am Soc Mech Engrs; Sigma Xi. *Res:* Applied solid mechanics; plasticity and creep. *Mailing Add:* 106 Westlook Circle Oak Ridge TN 37830

GREENWALD, EDWARD S, MEDICAL ONCOLOGY. *Current Pos:* From asst clin prof to prof, 71-90, PROF, DEPT MED, ALBERT EINSTEIN COL, 90- *Personal Data:* b New Rochelle, NY, May 13, 28; m 49, Edith D Aaronson; c David, Daniel, Joel & Joshua. *Educ:* Amherst Col, BA, 48; NY Univ, MD, 52. *Concurrent Pos:* Actg chief, Dept Oncol, Montefiore Med Ctr, 76-82, attend physician, 78- *Mem:* Fel Am Col Physicians; Am Asn Cancer Res; Am Soc Clin Oncol; Am Radium Soc. *Res:* Cancer chemotheraphy. *Mailing Add:* Dept Oncol Montefiore Med Ctr 111 E 210th ST Bronx NY 10467. *Fax:* 718-798-7474

GREENWALD, GILBERT SAUL, PHYSIOLOGY, REPRODUCTIVE PHYSIOLOGY. *Current Pos:* from assoc prof to prof anat, obstet & gynec, Univ Kans Med Ctr, 61-67, distinguished prof anat, 73, res prof human reproduction, 61-77, prof gynec & obstet, 77-90, chmn, 77-93, distinguished prof, Dept Physiol, 77-96, EMER DISTINGUISHED PROF, UNIV KANS MED CTR, KANSAS CITY, 96- *Personal Data:* b New York, NY, June 24, 27; m 50; c Susan (Waxman), Beth (Jordan) & Douglas. *Educ:* Univ Calif, AB, 49, MA, 51, PhD, 54. *Honors & Awards:* Higuchi Res Award, Univ Kans, 84; Distinguished Serv Award, Soc Study Reproduction, 88, Hartman Award, 93. *Prof Exp:* Assoc zool, Univ Calif, 54; from instr to asst prof anat, Univ Wash, 56-61. *Concurrent Pos:* Fel, Carnegie Inst, 54-56; mem reproductive biol study sect, NIH, 66-70, population res adv comt, 67-71, consult, Ctr Population Res, 68-72; assoc ed, Anat Rec, 68-74; referee ed, Soc Exp Biol Med, 73-76; ed-in-chief, Biol of Reproduction, 74-76; hon lectr, Mid-Am State Univ Asn, 78-79; mem, Regulatory Biol Panel, NSF, 83-86. *Mem:* AAAS; Am Physiol Soc; Brit Soc Study Fertil; Soc Study Reproduction (vpres, 70-71, pres, 71-72); Endocrine Soc. *Res:* Reproductive physiology; endocrinology; embryology; ovarian function; fertility control; pituitary-ovarian relationships. *Mailing Add:* Dept Physiol Univ Kans Med Ctr Kansas City KS 66103. *Fax:* 913-588-7430; *E-Mail:* ggreenwa.kumc.edu

GREENWALD, HAROLD LEOPOLD, hydrology & water resources, technical management; deceased, see previous edition for last biography

GREENWALD, LEWIS, comparative physiology, for more information see previous edition

GREENWALD, PETER, CANCER PREVENTION & CONTROL, CANCER EPIDEMIOLOGY. *Current Pos:* DIR, DIV CANCER PREV & CONTROL, NAT CANCER INST, NIH, 81- *Personal Data:* b Newburgh, NY, Nov 7, 36; m Harriet; c Rebecca, Laura & Daniel. *Educ:* Colgate Univ, BA, 57; State Univ NY, Syracuse, MD, 61; Harvard Univ, MPH, 67, PhD(cancer epidemiol), 74. *Honors & Awards:* Redway Medal, NY State J Med, 78; Meritorious Serv, Commendation & Distinguished Serv Medals, USPHS. *Prof Exp:* Asst med, Peter Bent Brigham Hosp, 67-68; dir, Cancer Control Bur, NY State Dept Health, 68-78, Div Epidemiol, 77-81. *Concurrent Pos:* Bd dirs, Am Col Epidemiol, 81-83; ed-in-chief, J Nat Cancer Inst, 81-87. *Mem:* Fel Am Col Epidemiol; fel Am Col Physicians; fel Am Col Prev Med; Am Asn Cancer Res; Am Epidemiol Soc. *Res:* Human cancer prevention trials; cancer epidemiology; cancer control. *Mailing Add:* Div Cancer Prev & Control NCI NIH 9000 Rockville Pike Bldg 31 Rm 10A52 Bethesda MD 20892-3100. *Fax:* 301-496-9931

GREENWALT, TIBOR JACK, TRANSFUSION MEDICINE, HEMATOLOGY. *Current Pos:* dir, 79-87, DIR RES, HOXWORTH BLOOD CTR, 87- *Personal Data:* b Budapest, Hungary, Jan 23, 14; nat US; wid; c Peter. *Educ:* NY Univ, BA, 34, MD, 37; Am Bd Internal Med, dipl, 46. *Honors & Awards:* John Elliot, Morten Grove-Rasmussen & Bernard Fantus Awards, Am Asn Blood Banks, 66. *Prof Exp:* Intern path & bact, Mt Sinai Hosp, NY, 37-38; intern med, Kings County Hosp, 38-40; med resident, Montefiore Hosp, 40-41; hemat fel, New England Med Ctr & instr med, Med Col, Tufts Univ, 41-42; med dir, Milwaukee Blood Ctr, 47-66; clin instr med, Sch Med, Marquette Univ, 48-51, from asst clin prof to assoc clin prof, 51-60, from assoc prof to prof, 60-66; nat med dir, Am Red Cross Blood Serv, 66-78, sr sci adv, 78-79. *Concurrent Pos:* Res asst, New Eng Med Ctr, 41-42; consult, Vet Admin Hosp, Wood, Wis, 46-66 & Milwaukee County Gen Hosp, 46-66; ed, Vox Sanguinis, 56-77; mem, hemat study sect, NIH, 60-63, chmn, 70-72, consult clin ctr, 67-, mem adv coun, Nat Heart, Lung & Blood Inst, 86-91; founding ed, Transfusion, 60-; chmn, Comt Blood & Transfusion Probs, Nat Acad Sci-Nat Res Coun, 63-66; clin prof med, Sch Med, George Washington Univ, 67-79; ed, Gen Principles of Blood Transfusion; emer prof med & path, Univ Cincinnati, Col Med; historian, Int Soc Blood Transfusion, 75-96. *Mem:* Inst Med-Nat Acad Sci; fel Am Col Physicians; Int Soc Blood Transfusion (pres, 66-72); Am Soc Hemat (treas, 63-67); fel AAAS; fel NY Acad Sci. *Res:* Immunohematology; blood banking; blood group genetics; 19 books, 172 papers and articles related to blood transfusion. *Mailing Add:* Hoxworth Blood Ctr 3130 Highland Ave, PO Box 670055 Cincinnati OH 45267-0055. *Fax:* 513-558-1522; *E-Mail:* tibor.greenwalt@uc.edu

GREENWAY, CLIVE VICTOR, CARDIOVASCULAR, LIVER. *Current Pos:* assoc prof, 68-79, PROF PHARMACOL, UNIV MAN, 79- *Personal Data:* b Gloucester, Eng, Mar 6, 37; m 69, Anne E Lawson; c 3. *Educ:* Cambridge Univ, BA, 58, PhD(pharmacol), 61. *Prof Exp:* Demonstr pharmacol, Cambridge Univ, 60-63; lectr physiol, Aberdeen Univ, 63-67; asst prof, Univ Alta, 67-68. *Mem:* Am Physiol Soc; Am Soc Pharmacol & Exp Therapeut; Can Physiol Soc; Pharmacol Soc Can. *Res:* Vascular beds of the liver, intestine and spleen; control of blood flow, volume and fluid exchange; hepatic drug metabolism; control of cardiac output and its modification by drugs. *Mailing Add:* Dept Pharmacol Fac Med Univ Man 770 Bannatyne Ave Winnipeg MB R3E 0W3 Can. *Fax:* 204-783-6915

GREENWOOD, ALLAN NUNNS, ELECTRICAL ENGINEERING. *Current Pos:* prof elec eng, 72-80, dir, Ctr Elec Power Eng, 72-87, PHILIP SPORN PROF ENG, RENSSELAER POLYTECH INST, 80- *Personal Data:* b Cambridge Univ, BA, 43, MA, 48; Univ Leeds, PhD(elec eng), 52. *Honors & Awards:* Attwood Award, Int Conf Large High Voltage Elec Systs. *Prof Exp:* Develop engr high voltage, Steatite & Porcelain Prod, Stourport, UK, 46-48; lectr elec engr, Leeds Univ, 48-54; vis prof, Univ Toronto, 54-55; sr res engr & consult, Gen Elec Co, 55-72. *Concurrent Pos:* Consult elec power res inst, state & fed govt labs & numerous pvt co, 72-; vis fel, Churchill Col, Cambridge, 88; vpres, US Nat Comt, Int Conf Large High Voltage Elec Systs. *Mem:* Fel Inst Elec & Electronics Engrs; Sigma Xi. *Res:* Power switching technology. *Mailing Add:* Rensselaer Polytech Inst 110 Eighth St Troy NY 12180

GREENWOOD, BRIAN, GEOMORPHOLOGY, SEDIMENTOLOGY. *Current Pos:* From lectr to asst prof, 67-72, assoc prof geog, 72-79, PROF GEOG, SCARBOROUGH COL, UNIV TORONTO, 79-, PROF GEOL, 81- *Personal Data:* b Berkeley, UK, Jan 1, 43; m 67. *Educ:* Univ Bristol, BSc, 64, PhD(geog/geol), 70. *Hon Degrees:* PhD, Fac Math & Natural Sci, Uppsala Univ, Sweden, 93. *Concurrent Pos:* Vis fel, Univ Bristol, 75-76; vis prof, Univ Uppsala, 82 & Univ Sydney, 83; vis scientist, US Geol Surv, 83; mem, Assoc Comt for Res on Shoreline Erosion & Sedimentation, Nat Res Cound Can, Int Geogr Union Comn Coastal Syst. *Mem:* Int Asn Great Lakes Res; Can Asn Geogrs; Soc Econ Paleontologists & Mineralogists; Int Asn Sedimentology; Brit Geomorphol Res Group; Am Geophys Union; Can Coastal Sci & Eng Asn; Can Geomorphol Res Group. *Res:* Coastal geomorphology and sedimentology; nearshore hydrodynamics and process-response modelling in modern coastal environments; use of modern analogues in the reconstruction of paleoenvironments; assessment of environmental impact in the coastal zone. *Mailing Add:* Dept Environ Sci Univ Toronto 1265 Military Trail Scarborough ON M1C 1A4 Can. *Fax:* 416-287-7204; *E-Mail:* greenw@scar.utoronto.ca

GREENWOOD, D(ONALD) T(HEODORE), ENGINEERING. *Current Pos:* from asst prof to prof, 56-94, EMER PROF AERONAUT ENG, UNIV MICH, ANN ARBOR, 94- *Personal Data:* b Clarkdale, Ariz, Dec 8, 23; m 51, Esther Harju; c Brian. *Educ:* Calif Inst Technol, BS, 44, MS, 48, PhD(elec eng), 51. *Prof Exp:* Lectr elec eng, Univ Southern Calif, 54-55. *Concurrent Pos:* Group engr, Lockheed Aircraft Corp, 51-56. *Mem:* Am Soc Mech Engrs; Am Inst Aeronaut & Astronaut; AAAS; Sigma Xi. *Res:* Dynamical theory and dynamical simulation. *Mailing Add:* 1630 Hanover Rd Ann Arbor MI 48103

GREENWOOD, DONALD DEAN, PSYCHOACOUSTICS. *Current Pos:* assoc prof psychol, 66-71, res assoc prof, 71-86, prof audiol & speech sci, 87-96, EMER PROF AUDIOL & SPEECH SCI, UNIV BC, 96- *Personal Data:* b Milwaukee, Wis, Apr 22, 31; m 60, 87; c 2. *Educ:* Univ Wis, BA, 51; Harvard Univ, PhD(exp psychol), 60. *Prof Exp:* Fel neurophysiol, Univ Wis, 60-63, proj assoc, 63-64; asst prof physiol, Duke Univ, 64-66. *Mem:* Soc Neurosci; fel Acoust Soc Am; Asn Res Otolaryngol. *Res:* Hearing; sensory systems; research in audition. *Mailing Add:* Sch Audiol/Speech Sci Univ BC 5804 Fairview Ave Vancouver BC V6T 1Z3 Can

GREENWOOD, FREDERICK C, BIOCHEMISTRY, ENDOCRINOLOGY. *Current Pos:* PROF BIOCHEM, UNIV HAWAII, 73-, DIR, PAC BIOMED RES CTR. *Personal Data:* b Portsmouth, Eng, July 5, 27; m 50; c 2. *Educ:* Univ London, BSc, 50, MSc, 51, PhD(biochem), 53, DSc(endocrinol), 67. *Prof Exp:* Mem acad staff steroid biochem, Imp Cancer Res Fund, 53-58, head, Protein Chem Sect, 58-68. *Concurrent Pos:* Rockefeller fel protein chem, Univ Wis, 58-59; consult, Med Sch, St Mary's Hosp, 66-68; mem, Coord Comt Human Tumor Invests, 65-67; secy, Sub-Comt Polypeptide

Hormones, Med Res Coun, 67-68. *Mem:* AAAS; Brit Soc Endocrinol; Brit Biochem Soc. *Res:* Steroid biochemistry and its application to clinical research; peptide hormones; chemistry and measurements in biological fluids. *Mailing Add:* Dept Biochem & Biophys Univ Hawaii Burns Med Sch 1960 East-West Rd Honolulu HI 96822-2319

GREENWOOD, GEORGE W(ATKINS), CIVIL ENGINEERING. *Current Pos:* RETIRED. *Personal Data:* b North New Portland, Maine, Nov 28, 29; m 51; c 3. *Educ:* Univ Maine, BS, 51; Univ Ill, MS, 60, PhD(traffic eng), 63. *Prof Exp:* Eng aide, Bridge Div, Maine State Hwy Comn, 51 & 53-54; instr eng graphics, Univ Maine, 54-56; instr eng, Univ Ill, 56-58, res assoc civil eng, 58-62; assoc prof civil eng, Univ Maine, Orono, 63-94. *Res:* Highway and traffic engineering; intercommunity traffic estimation models. *Mailing Add:* 1104 Chase Rd Vezie ME 04401

GREENWOOD, GIL JAY, ANALYTICAL & ORGANIC CHEMISTRY. *Current Pos:* Sr res chemist mass spectrometry, Phillips Petrol Co, 77-84, sr res chemist hydrotreating catalyst, 84-86, sr res chemist incineration, 86-88, bus develop mgr, Incinatrol, 88-89, SR LICENSING SPECIALIST, PHILLIPS PETROL CO, 89- *Personal Data:* b Lincoln, Nebr, Jan 10, 49; m 71, Meg; c Kris, Gina & Elise. *Educ:* Okla State Univ, BS, 71, PhD(chem), 77. *Mem:* Am Chem Soc; Am Soc Mass Spectrometry; Licensing Exec Soc. *Res:* Mass spectrometry as applied to the analysis of alternate fuels, petroleum and petrochemicals; emphasis on FI/MS, FD/MS, LV/MS and GC/MS; chemistry of HDM/HDS; HDM/HDS catalysis; foster and develop technology based business opportunities. *Mailing Add:* Phillips Petrol Co 252 PLB Bartlesville OK 74004. Fax: 918-662-2007

GREENWOOD, HUGH J, geology, petrology, for more information see previous edition

GREENWOOD, JAMES ROBERT, PLASMA PHYSICS, COMPUTER SCIENCE. *Current Pos:* PHYSICIST FUSION, LAWRENCE LIVERMORE NAT LAB, 75- *Personal Data:* b Jersey City, NJ, Mar 27, 43. *Educ:* Rutgers Univ, New Brunswick, BA, 69; Univ Wis-Madison, PhD(plasma physics), 75. *Prof Exp:* Systs programmer, Bell Tel Labs, Murray Hill, 70. *Mem:* Am Phys Soc. *Res:* Laser fusion; systems programming; control systems; programming language development. *Mailing Add:* Lawrence Livermore Nat Lab PO Box 808 Livermore CA 94551

GREENWOOD, JANET KAE DALY, PSYCHOLOGY, EDUCATIONAL ADMINISTRATION. *Current Pos:* CONSULT, PARTNER, HEIDRICK & STRUGGLES, WASHINGTON DC, 92- *Personal Data:* b Goldsboro, NC, Dec 9, 43; c Gerald Thompson. *Educ:* E Carolina Univ, BS, 65, MEd, 67; Fla State Univ PhD(coun & higher educ admin), 72. *Honors & Awards:* Meritorious Serv Award, Am Asn State Cols & Univs. *Prof Exp:* Teacher Eng, Kinston NC City Schs, 65-66, Goldsboro City Schs, 66-67; counr & psychometrist, Primary & Sec Schs, Co Wake, NC, 67-69; counr, Fla State Univ, 69-72; asst dir coun, Rutgers Univ, 72-73, consult to vpres student servs, 73-74; coordr & assoc prof coun educ, Univ Cincinnati, 74-77, adv grad stud, 74-77, vprovost student affairs, 77-81; pres, Longwood Col, Farmville, Va, 81-87, Univ Bridgeport Conn, 87-92. *Concurrent Pos:* coordr Am Inst Foreign Study, 69; suprv, student tours, Eng, France, Switzerland, Italy & Capri, 69; lectr coun psychol, Ruthers Univ, 72-74; consult guid, So Plainfield Pub Schs, 73-76. *Mem:* Am Col Pers Asn; Am Pers & Guid Asn; Am Sch Counr Asn; Am Asn Univ Prof. *Res:* Contributed numerous articles to journals. *Mailing Add:* Heidrick & Struggles 1301 K St NW Suite 500E Washington DC 20005-3317

GREENWOOD, JOSEPH ALBERT, mathematics, for more information see previous edition

GREENWOOD, MARY RITA COOKE, PHYSIOLOGY, NUTRITION. *Current Pos:* CHANCELLOR, UNIV CALIF, SANTA CRUZ, 96- *Personal Data:* b Gainesville, Fla, Apr 11, 43; div; c 1. *Educ:* Vassar Col, AB, 68; Rockefeller Univ, PhD(physiol develop biol & neurosci), 73. *Honors & Awards:* Award in Exp Nutrit, Am Inst Nutrit, 82; John Guy Vassar Chair, 86. *Prof Exp:* Fel, Rockefeller Univ, 68-73; fel, Columbia Univ, 73-74; res assoc, 74-75; asst prof genetics & develop, Inst Human Nutrit, 75-78; assoc prof biol, Vassar Col, 78-81, prof, 81-96, chmn dept, 85. *Concurrent Pos:* Res asst, Rutgers Univ, 62-65 & Vassar Col, 65-68; adj instr, Pratt Inst, 74; adj res assoc, Rockefeller Univ, 74-; adj assoc prof, Inst Human Nutrit, Columbia Univ; career develop award, NIH, 78-83; dir, Animal Model Core Lab, Obesity Res Ctr; mem, Nutrit Study Sect, NIH; mem, Food & Nutrit Bd, Nat Acad Sci; pres, NAm Asn Study Obesity; prin investr, NIH grants, Am Heart Asn grant & prof dir, NIH Core Grant. *Mem:* Inst Med-Nat Acad Sci; Am Inst Nutrit; AAAS; Am Asn Diabetes; Soc Exp Biol Med; NAm Asn Study Obesity; Am Physiol Soc. *Res:* Determination of the effect of environmental, nutritional and genetic influences on the development of obesity and of adipose tissue; behavioral correlates; pregnancy, lactation and sexual dimorphism in obesity. *Mailing Add:* Univ Calif 296 McHenry Libr Santa Cruz CA 95064. Fax: 408-459-2098; E-Mail: mrcgrnwd@cats.ucsu.edu

GREENWOOD, PAUL GENE, CELL PHYSIOLOGY. *Current Pos:* ASST PROF CELL BIOL, COLBY COL, 87- *Personal Data:* b Peoria, Ill, Aug 1, 58; m 88. *Educ:* Knox Col, BA, 80; Fla State Univ, MS, 83, PhD(biol sci), 87. *Mem:* Am Soc Cell Biol; Am Soc Zoologists; AAAS; Sigma Xi; NY Acad Sci; Western Soc Naturalists. *Res:* Physiology and biochemistry of nematocysts; stinging structures characteristic of the Cnidaria; organisms that feed on Cnidarians incorporate nematocysts into their own cells for use later. *Mailing Add:* Dept Biol Colby Col 150 Mayflower Hill Dr Waterville ME 04901-4799

GREENWOOD, REGINALD CHARLES, nuclear physics, for more information see previous edition

GREENWOOD, ROBERT EWING, mathematics; deceased, see previous edition for last biography

GREENWOOD, WILLIAM R, GEOLOGY. *Current Pos:* geologist, US Geol Surv, 70-81, dep chief, Off Mineral Resources, 81-84, assoc chief, Off Int Geol, 84-88, ASSOC CHIEF GEOLOGIST, US GEOL SURV, 88- *Personal Data:* b St Louis, Mo, Sept 15, 38; m 61; c 2. *Educ:* Univ Idaho, BS, 61, MS, 66, PhD(geol), 68. *Prof Exp:* Proj chief, Idaho Bur Mines & Geol, 66-68; geologist, Manned Spacecraft Ctr, NASA, 68-70. *Mem:* Geol Soc Am; Sigma Xi; Am Geog Union; Nat Asn Biol Teachers; Nat Earth Sci Teachers Asn; Nat Sci Teachers Asn. *Res:* Metamorphic petrology and structural geology; lunar geology; Saudi Arabian geology; wilderness resource assessment. *Mailing Add:* 1402 Earnshaw Ct Reston VA 22090

GREENWOOOD, MICHAEL E, MATHEMATICS. *Current Pos:* instr, 66-95, PROF, DEPT MATH, CLARK COL, VANCOUVER, WASH, 96- *Personal Data:* b Vancouver, Wash, May 8, 41. *Educ:* Ore State Univ, BS, 63, MS, 66; Univ Ill, PhD(math educ), 76. *Prof Exp:* Teacher math, Ridgefield High Sch, Wash, 63-65. *Concurrent Pos:* Field supvr math & biol sci, Univ Ill, 74-75, res asst, Dept Sec Educ, 76; chmn, Math Dept, Clark Col, 78-80; Fulbright grantee, 96-97. *Mem:* Nat Educ Asn; Math Asn Am; Nat Coun Teachers Math. *Res:* Effects of small group help session on an individualized program in community college mathematics. *Mailing Add:* Math & Comput Sci Div Clark Col 1800 E McLoughlin Blvd Vancouver WA 98663

GREEP, ROY ORVAL, ANATOMY. *Current Pos:* RETIRED. *Personal Data:* b Longford, Kans, Oct 8, 05; m 31, Eunice Hauserman; c Ann L, Marjorie & Nancy. *Educ:* Kans State Col, BS, 30; Univ Wis, MS, 32, PhD(zool), 34. *Hon Degrees:* MA, Harvard Univ, 46; DSc, Univ Buffalo, 60; ScD, Kans State Univ, 68, Univ Sheffield, 71. *Honors & Awards:* Henry Dale Medal, 67; Fred Conrad Koch Award, 71; Marshall Medal, Fel Inst Health Serv Admin, 86. *Prof Exp:* Asst zool, Univ Wis, 30-35; asst, Harvard Univ, 35-37, instr, 38; res assoc, Squibb Inst Med Res, 38-44; asst prof dent sci, Sch Dent Med, Harvard Univ, 44-46, lectr endocrinol, Dept Physiol, 46-47, from assoc prof to prof dent sci, 46-55, prof anat, 55-67, 72-74, dean, 52-67, actg chmn dept anat, 56-59, John Rock Prof Pop Studies, Sch Pub Health, 67-72, dir, Human & Reproductive Biol, 67-74. *Concurrent Pos:* Teaching fel anat, Harvard Med Sch, 44-46; Schering scholar, 57; consult, Opers Res Off, with Off Sci Res & Develop, 44; ed, Endocrinol, 52-62, chmn comt dent, Nat Res Coun, 56-61; mem endocrinol study sect, NIH, 56-59, 63-67; mem med adv bd, Nat Pituitary Agency, 63-67; expert adv panel biol of human reprod, WHO, 65-82; mem basic sci comt, Int Planned Parenthood Fedn, 71-; hon pres, Int Cong Endocrinol, 72-76, pres, Laurentian Hormone Conf, 72-85; proj specialist, Ford Found, 74-76. *Mem:* Soc Exp Biol & Med (pres, 69-71); Endocrine Soc (pres, 65-66); fel Am Acad Arts & Sci; NY Acad Sci; Int Soc Endocrinol (pres, 65-66); Am Physiol Soc. *Res:* Endocrinology; adrenal cortex; gonadotropins; parathyroids; growth hormone; mineral metabolism; hermaphroditism; genetics; dental education. *Mailing Add:* 5369 Algarrobo Unit 2A Laguna Hills CA 92653-2577. E-Mail: roygreep@aol.com

GREER, ALBERT H, ORGANIC CHEMISTRY. *Current Pos:* res group leader ion exchange & org res, Ionac Chem Co, 49-59, res assoc. 49-92, sr res chemist, 59-65, mgr adv res, 65-69, chief res chemist, 69-75, SR SCIENTIST, SYBRON CHEM CO, 93- *Personal Data:* b New York, NY, Jan 30, 20; m 46; c Adriane. *Educ:* City Col, BS, 41; Polytech Inst Brooklyn, MS, 45, PhD(chem), 49. *Prof Exp:* Chemist biol chem, State Hosp, Brooklyn, NY, 42-43; res chemist fungicides, Centro Res Co, 43-44; res chemist pharmaceuts, Day Chem Co, 44-45; res chemist textile chems, Commonwealth Color & Chem, 45-49. *Mem:* Am Chem Soc; Sigma Xi. *Res:* Synthetic ion exchangers; organic monomers and polymers; pyridines; guanidines; detergents; fungicides. *Mailing Add:* 228 Warwick Rd Haddonfield NJ 08033

GREER, DAVID STEVEN, INTERNAL MEDICINE. *Current Pos:* assoc dean med, Brown Univ, 74-81, dir, Family Pract Residency Prog, 75-78, chmn, Sect Commun Health, 78-81, dean med, 81-92, PROF COMMUN HEALTH, PROG MED, BROWN UNIV, 75- *Personal Data:* b Brooklyn, NY, Oct 12, 25; m 50; c 2. *Educ:* Univ Notre Dame, BS, 48; Univ Chicago Sch Med, MD, 53. *Hon Degrees:* Brown Univ, MS, 75; Southeastern Mass Univ, DHL, 81. *Prof Exp:* Fel med, Univ Chicago, USPHS, 55-56, instr endocrinol & med, 57; pract internal med, Truesdale Clin, 57-74. *Concurrent Pos:* Sr clin instr med, Tufts Univ Col Med, 69-71, asst clin prof med, 71-78; chief staff, Dept Med, Fall River Gen Hosp, 59-62; med dir, Earle E Hussey Hosp, 62-75; chief of staff, Dept Med, Truesdale Clin & Truesdale Hosp, 71-74; chmn, bd trustees, Southeastern Mass Univ, 73-74, mem, bd trustees, 70-81; clin assoc prof commun health, Prog Med, Brown Univ, 73-75; delegate, White House Conf Aging, 71 & 81. *Mem:* Inst Med-Nat Acad Sci; Am Col Physicians; Am Cong Rehab Med; Int Soc Rehab Med. *Res:* Study of long-term care, including the impact of housing and community based services; rehabilitation medicine, including functional assessment; health care evaluation. *Mailing Add:* Brown Univ PO Box G Providence RI 02912

GREER, DONALD LEE, MEDICAL MYCOLOGY. *Current Pos:* assoc prof mycol, 81-88, PROF MYCOL, LA STATE UNIV, 89-; DIR, TUBERC & MYCOL DIAG LAB, CHND, 81- *Personal Data:* b Silver City, NMex, June 14, 36. *Educ:* Col Idaho, BS, 58; Univ Wash, MS, 61; Tulane Univ, PhD(microbiol), 65. *Prof Exp:* Sr asst scientist mycol, Ctr Dis Control, USPHS, 65-68; prof microbiol, Univ Valle, 68-71; assoc prof mycol, Univ Valle, 71-77; actg asst dir, Int Ctr Med Res & Training, 73-74, scientist mycol, 68-81; prof mycol, Univ Valle, 77-81. *Concurrent Pos:* Consult, Ochsner Hosp, ND & Vet Admin Hosp, ND; adj prof, Med Technol Dept & Microbiol Dept. *Mem:* Am Soc Microbiol; Int Soc Human & Animal Mycol; Med

Mycol Soc of the Americas; Sigma Xi; fel Am Acad Microbiol; Am Acad Dermat; Am Infectious Dis Soc. *Res:* Epidemiology of paracoccidioidomycosis and dermatophytosis in tropical America. *Mailing Add:* Dept Dermat La State Univ Sch Med 1542 Tulane Ave New Orleans LA 70112-2825. *Fax:* 504-568-2170

GREER, GEORGE GORDON, MICROBIOLOGY. *Current Pos:* RES SCIENTIST MICROBIOL, AGR CAN, 78-, HEAD MEAT RES, 95- *Personal Data:* b Toronto, Ont, Apr 16, 46. *Educ:* Univ Guelph, BSc, 70, MSc, 72; Queen's Univ, Ont, PhD(microbiol), 75. *Mem:* Int Soc Milk, Food & Environ Sanitarians. *Res:* Bacterial spoilage and safety of meats with emphasis on the contribution of meat processing procedures to the microbial load and shelf life of retail meat cuts. *Mailing Add:* Agr & Agri Food Can Lacombe Res Ctr 6000 Cand E Trail Lacombe AB T4L 1W1 Can. *Fax:* 403-782-6120

GREER, HOWARD A L, WEED SCIENCE. *Current Pos:* RETIRED. *Personal Data:* b Warrensville, NC, Feb 7, 36; m 58; c 2. *Educ:* Berea Col, BS, 58; Univ Ky, MS, 61; Iowa State Univ, PhD(agron, plant physiol), 64. *Honors & Awards:* Geigy Award Agron, 70. *Prof Exp:* Instr agron, Iowa State Univ, 60-63; instr biol, Appalachian State Teachers Col, 64-65; asst prof exten agron, Okla State Univ, 65-74, prof agron, 74-92, emer prof, 92- *Mem:* Am Soc Agron; Crop Sci Soc Am; Weed Sci Soc Am. *Res:* Effects of herbicides on plant growth and development. *Mailing Add:* 2614 Ivy Ct Stillwater OK 74075

GREER, MONTE ARNOLD, ENDOCRINOLOGY. *Current Pos:* assoc prof, Ore Health Sci Univ, 56-62, head div endocrinol, 56-80, head div endocrinol metab & clin nutrit, 80-84, head sect endocrinol, 84-90, PROF MED, ORE HEALTH SCI UNIV, 62-, PROF PHYSIOL, 92- *Personal Data:* b Portland, Ore, Oct 26, 22; m 43, Peggy Johnson; c Susan & Richard. *Educ:* Stanford Univ, AB, 44, MD, 47. *Honors & Awards:* Oppenheimer Award, Endocrine Soc, 58; Discovery Award, Med Res Found Ore, 85. *Prof Exp:* Asst med, Tufts Univ, 47-49, instr, 50-51, sr asst surgeon, NIH, 51-55; asst clin prof med, Univ Calif, Los Angeles, 55-56. *Concurrent Pos:* NIH res career award, 62-81; asst, Boston Univ, 49-50; assoc, George Washington Univ, 51-55; dir radioisotope serv, Long Beach Vet Hosp, 55-56; mem pharmacol & endocrinol fel comt, NIH, 68-72; dir, Am Thyroid Asn, 73-77, mem, Endocrinol Study Sect, NIH, & Thyroid Task Force, NIH Comt Eval Endocrinol & Metab Dis, 77-80, dir. *Mem:* Endocrine Soc (vpres, 76-77); Am Soc Clin Invest; Am Thyroid Asn (2nd vpres, 68-69, 1st vpres, dir, 73-77, pres, 80); Am Fedn Clin Res; AAAS; hon mem Endocrine Soc Japan; hon mem Czech Endocrine Soc; Europ Thyroid Asn; Int Brain Res Orgn; Asn Am Physicians; Soc Exp Biol & Med. *Res:* Normal and abnormal thyroid physiology; neural control of pituitary function; cell volume regulation of secretion. *Mailing Add:* Dept Med Ore Health Sci Univ Portland OR 97201. *E-Mail:* greerm@ohsu.edu

GREER, RAYMOND T(HOMAS), SOLID STATE & MATERIALS SCIENCE. *Current Pos:* from asst prof to assoc prof eng, 70-73, PROF AEROSPACE ENG & ENG MECH, IOWA STATE UNIV, 77- *Personal Data:* b East Orange, NJ, Apr 26, 40; m 65, Mary H Tunks; c Franklin. *Educ:* Rensselaer Polytech Inst, BS, 63; Pa State Univ, PhD(solid state sci), 68. *Prof Exp:* Res asst atomic develop, NY State Off Atomic & Space Develop, 62-63; res asst mat sci, Mat Res Lab, Pa State Univ, 63-68, res assoc, 68-69; resident res assoc, Jet Propulsion Lab, Calif Inst Technol, 69-70. *Concurrent Pos:* Nat Res Coun fel, 69. *Mem:* Sigma Xi; AAAS. *Res:* Biomaterials. *Mailing Add:* 3611 Woodland Ames IA 50014. *E-Mail:* rtgreer@iastate.edu

GREER, SANDRA CHARLENE, PHYSICAL CHEMISTRY, POLYMER SCIENCE. *Current Pos:* assoc prof, 78-83, dept chair, 90-93, PROF CHEM, UNIV MD, COLLEGE PARK, 83-, PROF CHEM ENG, 95- *Personal Data:* b Greenville, SC, Jan 7, 45; m 68; c 2. *Educ:* Furman Univ, BS, 66; Univ Chicago, MS, 68, PhD(chem), 69. *Prof Exp:* Res chemist, Nat Bur Stand, 69-78. *Mem:* Am Chem Soc; fel Am Phys Soc; fel AAAS; Asn Women Sci; Am Inst Chem Eng. *Res:* Experimental thermodynamics of phase transitions and critical phenomena of fluid mixtures, especially polymer solutions. *Mailing Add:* Dept Chem Eng Univ Md College Park MD 20742. *E-Mail:* sg28@umail.umd.edu

GREER, SHELDON, MOLECULAR GENETICS. *Current Pos:* assoc prof microbiol, 61-74, PROF MICROBIOL & BIOCHEM, SCH MED, UNIV MIAMI, 74-, PROF IMMUNOL, MOLECULAR BIOL & RADIATION ONCOL, 86- *Personal Data:* b Brooklyn, NY, July 11, 28; m 57; c 2. *Educ:* Brooklyn Col, BA, 50; Columbia Univ, MA, 52, PhD(zool), 57. *Prof Exp:* Asst, Columbia Univ, 52-56; res assoc biochem, Col Physicians & Surgeons, Columbia Univ, 58-61. *Mem:* Sigma Xi. *Res:* Ultra-violet light effects on unnatural deoxyribonucleic acid; regulatory mechanisms; sensitization of tumors to x-ray; pyrimidine metabolism-catabolism-transformation in Bacillus subtilis; lysogenic conversion in Streptococcus mutans; curing cells of their proviruses; mutagenesis and repair; selective chemotherapy of tumors and of herpes viruses by pyrimidine analogs. *Mailing Add:* Microbiol R138 Univ Miami Sch Med 1600 NW Tenth Ave Miami FL 33136-1015

GREER, WILLIAM LOUIS, CHEMICAL PHYSICS, DEFENSE ANALYSIS. *Current Pos:* DEFENSE ANALYST, INST DEFENSE ANALYSIS, 86- *Personal Data:* b Bardstown, Ky, Apr 7, 43; m 68; c 2. *Educ:* Vanderbilt Univ, AB, 65; Univ Chicago, PhD(chem), 69. *Prof Exp:* Nat Res Coun-Nat Bur Stand res assoc & res chemist, Nat Bur Stand, 69-71; lectr chem, Georgetown Univ, 71; res assoc, Inst Molecular Physics, Univ Md, 72; asst prof, Dept Chem, George Mason Univ, 72-76, assoc prof, 76-78; defense analyst, Ctr Naval Anal, 78-84; defense analyst, Off Secy Defense, 84-86. *Concurrent Pos:* Chem lectr, George Mason Univ, 80-85. *Mem:* Am Phys Soc; Am Chem Soc. *Res:* Theoretical research on the nature of electronic states in organic solids and fluids; naval defense issues; strategic defense analysis, command and control analysis; strategic lift. *Mailing Add:* 714 Queen St Alexandria VA 22314

GREESON, PHILLIP EDWARD, LIMNOLOGY. *Current Pos:* LIMNOLOGIST, WATER RESOURCES DIV, US GEOL SURV, 67- *Personal Data:* b Lexington, Ky, Aug 11, 40; m 64, Bonnie Dortan; c Jeffrey M & Matthew H. *Educ:* Univ Ky, BS, 62, MS, 63; Univ Louisville, PhD(limnol), 67. *Mem:* Sigma Xi; Int Asn Theoret & Appl Limnol; Am Water Resources Asn; NAm Lake Mgt Soc. *Res:* Aquatic ecology; lake productivity and eutrophication; algal ecology. *Mailing Add:* US Geol Surv WRD/SR Spalding Woods Off Park Suite 160 3850 Holcomb Bridge Rd Norcross GA 30092-2202. *E-Mail:* pgreeson@usgs.gov

GREEVER, JOE CARROLL, ORGANIC CHEMISTRY, ENVIRONMENTAL CHEMISTRY. *Current Pos:* assoc prof, 75-80, PROF CHEM, DELTA STATE UNIV, 80- *Personal Data:* b Kansas City, Mo, Nov 5, 44; m 65; c 1. *Educ:* Northeastern State Univ, Okla, BS, 65; Univ Ark, PhD(chem), 70. *Prof Exp:* From asst prof to assoc prof, Drury Col, Mo, 69-74; environ chemist, City Springfield, Mo, 74, asst supvr wastewater treatment, 74-75. *Mem:* Sigma Xi; Am Chem Soc. *Res:* Acid rain-alkalinity; improving the quality of the undergraduate laboratory experience in organic chemistry. *Mailing Add:* Dept Phys Sci Delta State Univ Cleveland MS 38733

GREEVER, JOHN, MATHEMATICAL MODELLING, GENERALIZATIONS OF COMPACTNESS PROPERTIES. *Current Pos:* from asst prof to prof, Harvey Mudd Col, 61-95, chmn dept, 72-75, dir math clin, 73-75, dir, Freshman Div, 81-83, EMER PROF MATH, HARVEY MUDD COL, 95- *Personal Data:* b Pulaski, Va, Jan 30, 34; m 53, Margaret L Quarles; c Catherine P, Richard G & Cynthia D. *Educ:* Univ Richmond, BS, 53; Univ Va, MA, 56, PhD(math), 58. *Prof Exp:* Asst prof math, Fla State Univ, 58-61. *Concurrent Pos:* Instr, Univ Va, 53-58; vis prof, Res Inst Math Sci, Kyoto Univ, Japan, 67-68 & Inst Animal Resource Ecol, Univ BC, 84-85; res assoc, Dept Biol, Univ Calif, Riverside, 75-78, vis res mathematician, Dept Entom, 78; vchmn, Math 2nd Comput Sci Sect, Coun Undergrad Res, 91-92, chmn, 92-94. *Mem:* Am Math Soc; Math Asn Am; Coun Undergrad Res. *Res:* Mathematical modelling of insect populations, with consideration of control strategies; modelling of the effect of migration on the size of ungulate populations. *Mailing Add:* Grey Havens Loop Orcas WA 98280. *E-Mail:* greever@.hmc.edu

GREFSRUD, GARY W, MATHEMATICS. *Current Pos:* PROF MATH, FT LEWIS COL, 71- *Personal Data:* b Great Falls, Mont, 38. *Educ:* Mont State Univ, PhD(math), 71. *Mem:* Math Asn Am. *Res:* Mathematics. *Mailing Add:* 31417 Highway 160 Durango CO 81301

GREGER, JANET L, HUMAN NUTRITION, MINERAL METABOLISM. *Current Pos:* from asst prof to assoc prof, 78-83, assoc dean, Grad Sch, 90-96, PROF NUTRIT, UNIV WIS-MADISON, 83-, ASSOC DEAN MED SCH, 96- *Personal Data:* b Joliet, Ill, Feb 18, 48. *Educ:* Univ Ill, Urbana, BS, 70; Cornell Univ, MS, 71, PhD(human nutrit), 73. *Prof Exp:* Asst prof nutrit, Purdue Univ, 73-78. *Concurrent Pos:* Prin investr grants, NIH, USDA & W K Kellogg Found, 75-95; mem, Nutrit Study sect, NIH, 85-89; mem, Nat Nutrit Adv Comt, Pew Found, 86-91; assoc ed, Proceedings Soc Exp Biol & Med, 94-97; bd dir, Am Asn Accreditation Lab Animal Care, 91-97; bd mgt, Coun Govt Rels, 93- *Mem:* Am Inst Nutrit; Am Soc Clin Nutrit; Inst Food Technologists; AAAS; Am Dietetics Asn; Soc Exp Biol Med. *Res:* Mineral metabolism from a nutritional and toxicological point of view; minerals studied include aluminum, calcium, zinc, tin and manganese. *Mailing Add:* Dept Nutrit Sci Univ Wis 1415 Lin Dr Madison WI 53706. *Fax:* 608-262-9972

GREGERMAN, ROBERT ISAAC, ENDOCRINOLOGY, GERONTOLOGY. *Current Pos:* PROF MED, HEALTH SCI CTR, UNIV TEX, SAN ANTONIO, 93- *Personal Data:* b Boston, Mass, Apr 18, 30; m 57, Marjorie Libby Bender; c 2. *Educ:* Harvard Univ, AB, 51; Tufts Univ, MD, 55. *Honors & Awards:* Clin Res Award, Am Aging Asn, 90. *Prof Exp:* Intern med, New Eng Med Ctr, Tufts Univ, 55-56; clin assoc, Geront Res Ctr, NIH, 56-58; resident med, Vet Admin Hosp, Washington, DC, 58-59; resident, Univ Mich Hosp, 59-60, instr, 60-61; asst, Johns Hopkins Univ, 63-64, from instr to assoc prof, 64-88, prof, 88-93. *Concurrent Pos:* Fel endocrinol, Univ Mich Hosp, 60-61; chief, Endocrinol Sect, Geront Res Ctr, Nat Inst Aging, 63-88; head, Div Endocrinol, Hopkins Bayview Med Ctr, 65-70 & 75-93. *Mem:* Am Soc Biochem & Molecular Biol; Am Soc Clin Invest; Am Thyroid Asn; Endocrine Soc; Geront Soc. *Res:* Clinical endocrinology; gerontology; geriatrics; isolation of cytokine that induces fat cell differentiation and may be involved in the relationship of obesity to diabetes. *Mailing Add:* Audie L Murphy Vet Admin Hosp GRECC 182 San Antonio TX 78284. *Fax:* 210-617-5312; *E-Mail:* gregerman@uthscsa.edu

GREGERSEN, HANS MILLER, FOREST ECONOMICS, RESOURCE MANAGEMENT. *Current Pos:* asst prof, 70-72, assoc prof forestry, 72-77, PROF FOREST SERVS, UNIV MINN, 78- *Personal Data:* b Pasadena, Calif, Dec 9, 38; m 61; c 2. *Educ:* Pa State Univ, BS, 61; Univ Wash, MS, 63; Univ Mich, MA, 69, PhD(forest resource econ), 69. *Prof Exp:* Res forester, Forest Serv, USDA, 61-63, forestry officer planning, Food & Agr Orgn UN, 65-67; res assoc forestry, Univ Mich, 67-69. *Concurrent Pos:* Consult, World Bank, 69- & Food & Agr Orgn UN, 72-, Inter Am Bank, 74- *Mem:* Soc Am

Foresters; Am Agr Econ Asn; Soc Int Develop; Sigma Xi. *Res:* Forest economics, benefit-cost analysis and project analysis, economic development; economic policy; research evaluation. *Mailing Add:* Sch Forestry Univ Minn St Paul MN 55108

GREGERS-HANSEN, VILHELM, RADAR SYSTEM ENGINEERING. *Current Pos:* CONSULT SCIENTIST, EQUIP DIV, RAYTHEON CO, 68-. *Personal Data:* b Odense, Denmark, Sept 30, 34; US citizen; m 59; c 2. *Educ:* Tech Univ Denmark, MSc, 59. *Prof Exp:* Scientist, SHAPE Tech Ctr, Hague, Neth, 60-66; asst prof common theory, Tech Univ Denmark, 66-69. *Concurrent Pos:* Lectr, Northeastern Univ, Mass, 71-80 & George Washington Univ, 78-86. *Mem:* Fel Inst Elec & Electronics Engrs. *Res:* Analysis & design of modern radar systems for military & civilian applications. *Mailing Add:* 7709 Maid Marian Ct Alexandria VA 22306-2718

GREGG, CHARLES THORNTON, BIOCHEMISTRY, TECHNICAL MANGEMENT. *Current Pos:* PRES, BETHCO INC, 72-; PRES, INNOVATIVE SURG TECHNOL, INC, 92- *Personal Data:* b Billings, Mont, July 27, 27; m 47, Elizabeth Whitaker; c Paul, Diane, Brian & Elaine. *Educ:* Ore State Univ, BS, 52, MS, 55, PhD(biochem), 59. *Prof Exp:* Instr, Ore State Univ, 55-59; USPHS res fel physiol chem, Sch Med, Johns Hopkins Univ, 59-63; staff mem biochem, Los Alamos Sci Lab, 63-85, dir res, Mesa Diagnostics, 85, vpres res, Los Alamos Diag, 86-90. *Concurrent Pos:* Vis prof, Free Univ Berlin, 74-75. *Mem:* Fel AAAS; Am Soc Microbiol; Am Soc Biol Chemists. *Res:* Energy metabolism of mammalian cells; biological applications of stable isotopes; biosynthesis of stable isotope labeled compounds; mammalian toxicology; biological luminescence; author of three books. *Mailing Add:* PO Box 148 Los Alamos NM 87544

GREGG, CHRISTINE M, ENDOCRINE PHYSIOLOGY, RENAL PHYSIOLOGY. *Current Pos:* asst prof, 80-87, SR RES ASSOC, PA STATE UNIV, UNIV PARK, 87- *Personal Data:* b Rochester, NY, Nov 4, 38; m 70. *Educ:* Case Western Res Univ, BS, 62; Univ Mich, MS, 68, PhD(physiol), 73. *Prof Exp:* Fel, Univ Rochester, NY, 73-77, asst prof, 77-80. *Mem:* Am Physiol Soc; AAAS; Sigma Xi; NY Acad Sci. *Res:* Regulation of vasopressin release using in vivo and in vitro techniques. *Mailing Add:* 433 Glenn Rd State College PA 16803-3471

GREGG, DAVID HENRY, PHARMACEUTICAL CHEMISTRY, ORGANIC CHEMISTRY. *Current Pos:* RETIRED. *Personal Data:* b Minneapolis, Minn, Oct 19, 26; m 50; c 1. *Educ:* Univ Minn, BS, 49, PhD(pharmaceut chem), 53. *Prof Exp:* Asst pharm, Univ Minn, 49-51; res scientist pharmaceut chem & develop, Upjohn Co, 53-57, head fine chems dept, 57-61, head chem sales, 61-63, mgr Europ agency dist, Upjohn Int, 63-67, mgr eng, distrib & prod, 67-72, group mgr, 72-74, dir, 74-78; dir pharmaceut mfg technol & dir prod mfg opers admin, Upjohn Co, 78-85, exec dir pharmaceut mfg technol, 85-87. *Mem:* AAAS; Am Hemat Soc; Am Pharmaceut Asn. *Res:* Cardiac glycosides and phytochemistry; steroid synthesis. *Mailing Add:* 1917 Argyle Ave Kalamazoo MI 49008-2213

GREGG, JAMES HENDERSON, DEVELOPMENTAL BIOLOGY. *Current Pos:* RETIRED. *Personal Data:* b Mobile, Ala, Mar 17, 20; m 45; c 2. *Educ:* Univ Ala, BS, 43; Princeton Univ, MS, 48, PhD(biol), 49. *Prof Exp:* Res assoc zool, Univ Chicago, 49-50; interim asst prof biol, Vanderbilt Univ, 50-51; from asst prof to assoc prof, Univ Fla, 51-63, prof biol & zool, 64-76, prof microbiol & cell sci, 76- *Concurrent Pos:* Mem corp, Marine Biol Lab, 54; NIH career develop award, 62-72. *Mem:* Soc Develop Biol. *Res:* Developmental biology of cellular slime molds. *Mailing Add:* 1502 NW 36th Way Gainesville FL 32605

GREGG, JAMES R, OPTOMETRY. *Current Pos:* prof optom & dir, Tech Prog, 75-76, GRANTS ADMINR, SOUTHERN CALIF COL OPTOM, 72-, INTERIM DEAN, 76-, EMER PROF, 84- *Personal Data:* b Napoleon, Ohio, Oct 26, 14; m 38; c 2. *Educ:* Ohio State Univ, BS, 37 & 42; Los Angeles Col Optom, DO, 48, D Ocular Sci, 53. *Prof Exp:* From assoc to prof optom, Los Angeles Col Optom, 47-72. *Mem:* Fel Am Acad Optom. *Res:* Physiological optics; practice management; author of over 500 articles. *Mailing Add:* 412 S Rolling Hills Pl Anaheim CA 92807

GREGG, JAY MASON, CARBONATE PETROLOGY, SEDIMENTARY GEOCHEMISTRY. *Current Pos:* from asst prof to assoc prof, 88-95, PROF GEOL, UNIV MO, ROLLA, 95- *Personal Data:* b Pittsburgh, Pa, Jan 24, 51; m 77, Elizabeth M Prudot; c Patricia M, Nicholas M & Jay W. *Educ:* Bowling Green State Univ, BS, 74; Okla State Univ, MS, 76; Mich State Univ, PhD(geol), 82. *Prof Exp:* Assoc geologist, Sun Oil Co, 76-78; sr res geologist, St Joe Minerals Corp, 82-87; prin scientist, Westinghouse Hanford Corp, 87-88. *Concurrent Pos:* Fulbright scholar & vis prof geol, Univ Col Dublin, Ireland, 95-96; vis lectr, Queen Univ Belfast, NIreland, 95-96. *Mem:* Geol Soc Am; Soc Sedimentary Geol; Int Asn Sedimentologists; Irish Asn Econ Geol; Sigma Xi; AAAS. *Res:* Origin of textures in dolomite applied to understanding the diagnetic history of these rocks; regional diagnetic patterns in sedimentary basins with respect to genesis and distribution of base metal and petroleum deposits. *Mailing Add:* Dept Geol & Geophys Univ Mo Rolla MO 65409-0001. *Fax:* 573-341-6935; *E-Mail:* greggjay@umr.edu

GREGG, JOHN BAILEY, OTOLARYNGOLOGY, PHYSICAL ANTHROPOLOGY. *Current Pos:* RETIRED. *Personal Data:* b Sioux Falls, SDak, June 5, 22; m 46, Pauline Benfer Snyder; c Michele L, John B, Steward D & Rebecca J (Anderson). *Educ:* Univ Iowa, BA, 43, MD, 46, Am Bd Otolaryngol & Maxillo-Facial Surg, dipl, 67. *Hon Degrees:* DSc, Univ SDak, 89. *Prof Exp:* Extern anesthesia, Univ Iowa Hosps, 45-46; intern, Univ Md Hosp, 46-47; resident gen surg, Univ Iowa Hosps, 49-51, resident otolaryngol, 51-53, instr, 53-54; assoc prof, Univ SDak, 55-59; asst prof, Med Sch, Univ Iowa, 59-60; assoc prof, 60-62, dir anesthesia, internship & residency proj, McKennan Hosp, 61-63, prof otolaryngol, 62-78, pres med staff & mem surg sect, 63-65, chmn dept, 71-77, prof surg, Sch Med, Univ SDak, 78-. *Concurrent Pos:* Chief otolaryngol, Vet Admin Hosp, Iowa City, 53-54; designated examr com pilots, Fed Aviation Agency, 54-78 & airline transport pilots, 61-78; consult, 54-59 & 60-77, mem staff, Vet Admin Hosp, Sioux Falls, SDak, 80-, Crippled Children's Field Clins, SDak, 54-56 & 60-72, Crippled Children's Hosp & Pub Sch Syst, Sioux Falls, 54-59 & 60, Indian Div, USPHS, 56-59 & 60-78 & Speech & Hearing Clin, Univ SDak, 61-; mem intern com, McKennan Hosp, 57-58; mem intern & extern comt, Sioux Valley Hosp, 58-59; mem preceptorship comt, Col Med, Univ Iowa, 59-60; dir broncho-esophagol clin, Univ Iowa Hosps, 59-60; chmn Deafness Res Found & Temporal Bone Bank, N & SDak, 63-69; assoc prof otolaryngol, Sch Med, Univ Nebr, 71-81; prof anthrop, Univ Tenn, Knoxville, 72-; coordr, Surg Spec, Sch Med, Univ SDak, 80; vchmn Surg Dept, Univ SDak, 85; fel, otolaryngic path, Armed Forces Inst Path, 67. *Mem:* AMA; Am Acad Otolaryngol-Head & Neck Surg; fel Am Col Surgeons; Deafness Res Found; Soc Univ Otolaryngologists; AAAS; Am Asn Phys Anthropologists. *Res:* Bronchoesophagology; facial plastic surgery; otorhinolaryngology; ancient osteopathology, paleopathology; epidemiology; biomedical research. *Mailing Add:* 2807 S Phillips Ave Sioux Falls SD 57105-4829. *E-Mail:* jbgregg@imst.augie.edu

GREGG, JOHN RICHARD, ZOOLOGY. *Current Pos:* assoc prof, 57-60, PROF, 60-, EMER PROF ZOOL, DUKE UNIV. *Personal Data:* b Mobile, Ala, Dec 23, 16; m 42. *Educ:* Univ Ala, BS, 42; Princeton Univ, PhD(biol), 45. *Prof Exp:* Lab asst biol, Univ Ala, 40-42 & histol, 41-42; asst, Off Sci Res & Develop Contract, Princeton Univ, 42-45 & Columbia Univ, 45-46; instr biol, Johns Hopkins Univ, 46-47; from asst prof to assoc prof zool, Columbia Univ, 47-57. *Concurrent Pos:* Mem corp, Marine Biol Lab, Woods Hole Oceanog Inst, 47-72; Killough fel, 49; Rockefeller fel, Carlsberg Labs, Denmark, 49 & Middlesex Hosp, London, 53-54. *Mem:* Harvey Soc; Am Soc Nat; Asn Symbolic Logic; Int Soc Develop Biol. *Res:* Chemical embryology of amphibia; mathematical and philosophical biology. *Mailing Add:* 3702 Randolph Rd Durham NC 27705

GREGG, MICHAEL CHARLES, PHYSICAL OCEANOGRAPHY. *Current Pos:* asst res prof, Dept Oceanog & Sr Oceanog, 74-77, assoc res prof, 77-80, RES PROF & PRIN, DEPT OCEANOG, APPL PHYSICS LAB, UNIV WASH, 80-, PROF, 89- *Personal Data:* b Knoxville, Tenn, May 13, 39; m 63; c 3. *Educ:* Yale Univ, BS, 61; Univ Calif, San Diego, PhD(oceanog), 71. *Prof Exp:* Asst res oceanogr, Scripps Inst Oceanog, Univ Calif, San Diego, 71-74. *Mem:* Fel Am Geophys Union; Am Meteorol Soc. *Res:* Small scale mixing processes in the ocean; instrumentation; signal processing; internal waves; equatorial dynamics. *Mailing Add:* Appl Physics Lab 1013 NE 40th St Univ Wash Seattle WA 98105

GREGG, ROBERT VINCENT, anatomy, for more information see previous edition

GREGG, ROGER ALLEN, PHYSICAL METALLURGY, RESEARCH ADMINISTRATION. *Current Pos:* res engr, E I Du Pont de Nemours & Co, Inc, 68-69, sr engr, 69-70, sr res supvr reactor fuel & target elements, 70-75, chief supvr, 75-77, Dept Supt Raw Mat Technol, 77-78, Dept Supt Fuel Reprocessing, Savannah River Plant, 78-79, sect dir solid waste technol, 79, supt employee rels, 80, mgr DMT Plant, Old Hickory, Tenn, 81-83, tech mgr polymer intermediates, 83-86, dir res & develop, Petrochem Dept, 86-89, dir mfg comput syts, DuPont Info Systs, 89-91, dir, Global Opers, DuPont Agr Prods, 91-93, DIR, SOURCING-MATS & EQUIP, E I DU PONT DE NEMOURS, INC, WILMINGTON, DEL, 93- *Personal Data:* b Lenoir, NC, July 19, 38; m 61, Susan Davis; c Cynthia & Helen. *Educ:* NC State Univ, BS, 60, MS, 62; Univ Fla, PhD(metall eng), 68. *Prof Exp:* Res asst alloy develop, Advan Mat Res & Develop Lab, Pratt & Whitney Aircraft Co, 62-63. *Mem:* Am Inst Mining, Metall & Petrol Engrs; Sigma Xi. *Res:* Alloy development of nickel and cobalt base superalloys; sintering phenomena and surface tension of metals; irradiation stability of actinide oxide-aluminum systems; powder metallurgy; reprocessing of irradiated reactor fuel; polymer intermediates. *Mailing Add:* 435 Fox Meadow Lane West Chester PA 19382

GREGG, THOMAS G, GENETICS. *Current Pos:* from asst prof to assoc prof, 60-71, PROF ZOOL, MIAMI UNIV, 71- *Personal Data:* US citizen, Dec 3, 31; m 56; c 4. *Educ:* Col Wooster, BA, 54; Univ Tex, MA, 56, PhD(genetics), 58. *Prof Exp:* NIH fel genetics, Univ Wis, 58-60. *Concurrent Pos:* NSF grant, 60-62; NIH grants, 63-65 & 71-73, spec fel, Univ Tex, 67-68. *Mem:* Genetics Soc Am; Sigma Xi. *Res:* Drosophila genetics. *Mailing Add:* Dept Zool Miami Univ Oxford OH 45056

GREGO, NICHOLAS JOHN, PHYSIOLOGY, PHARMACOLOGY. *Current Pos:* CLIN ASST PROF PHYSIOL & PHARMACOL, PHILADELPHIA COL OSTEOP MED, 72- *Personal Data:* b New York, NY, Feb 10, 45. *Educ:* Fairfield Univ, BS, 66; Adelphi Univ, MS, 68; Thomas Jefferson Univ, PhD(physiol), 74. *Mem:* AAAS; Sigma Xi; Am Osteop Asn. *Res:* Gastric secretion in cats; peripheral blood flow and osteopathic manipulative therapy. *Mailing Add:* 350 Meadow Wood Lane Souderton PA 18964

GREGOR, CLUNIE BRYAN, GEOLOGY. *Current Pos:* PROF GEOL, WRIGHT STATE UNIV, 72- *Personal Data:* b Edinburgh, Scotland, Mar 5, 29; m 55, 93, Anna Bramanti; c Andrew J, Thomas J & Matthew J. *Educ:* Cambridge Univ, BA, 51, MA, 54; State Univ Utrecht, DSc(earth sci), 67. *Prof Exp:* From instr to assoc prof geol, 59-68, chmn dept, Am Univ Beirut, 67-68; res asst crystallog 64-65, head dept, Technol Univ Delft, 65-67; vis prof, Case Western Reserve Univ, 68-69; from assoc prof to prof, WGa Col, 69-72. *Concurrent Pos:* Mem, Comt Natural Resources, Nat Coun Sci Lebanon, 67-68; Neth deleg, Comn Non-Metallic Minerals, Orgn Econ Coop & Develop, 68-69; consult, Food & Agr Orgn, UN, 69-; chmn, USA Work Group Geochemical Cycles, 72-; ed, Geochem News, 80-; vchmn panel Geochem Cycles, Nat Res Coun, Nat Acad Sci, 87- 90. *Mem:* Geol Soc Am; Am Geophys Union; Geochem Soc (secy, 83-89); Geol Soc London. *Res:* Geochem cycles of the elements; models of sedimentary cycle. *Mailing Add:* 136 W North College St Yellow Springs OH 45387

GREGOR, HARRY PAUL, applied chemistry, for more information see previous edition

GREGORICH, DAVID TONY, INFRARED ASTRONOMY. *Current Pos:* assoc prof, 68-77, PROF PHYSICS & ASTRON, CALIF STATE UNIV, LOS ANGELES, 77- *Personal Data:* b Crawford, Nebr, Feb 11, 37; div; c Tamara, David, Mary & John. *Educ:* Univ Calif, Los Angeles, BA, 62; Los Angeles State, MA & MS, 64; Univ Calif, Riverside, PhD(physics), 68. *Honors & Awards:* NASA Group Achievement Award, 86 & 92. *Prof Exp:* Jr engr, Consolidated Systs Corp, 60-62; assoc res physicist, Bell & Howell Res Labs, 62-64; res asst physics, Univ Calif, Riverside, 64-68. *Concurrent Pos:* Consult, Bell & Howell Res Labs, 68-72; IRAS Sci Opers Team, Jet Propulsion Labs, 82-85; sci support staff, IPAC, Calif Inst Technol, 85-92. *Mem:* Am Phys Soc; Am Astron Soc; Sigma Xi; Am Geophys Union. *Res:* Far-infrared astronomy; galaxy evolution. *Mailing Add:* 945 Swiss Trails Rd Duarte CA 91010-2181. *Fax:* 213-343-2497; *E-Mail:* dtg@calstatela.edu

GREGORY, A(LVIN) R(AY), RESERVOIR ENGINEERING, ROCK PHYSICS. *Current Pos:* res scientist assoc, 73-80, RES SCIENTIST & ENGR, UNIV TEX, AUSTIN, 80- *Personal Data:* b Gainesville, Tex, Nov 26, 15; div; c 5. *Educ:* Univ Tex, BS, 38. *Prof Exp:* Res engr prod eng & geophys, Phillips Petrol Co, 45-51; sr res engr petrophys, Gulf Res & Develop Co, 51-68, res assoc, Explor Dept, 68-73. *Concurrent Pos:* Radar proj officer, Radiation Lab, Mass Inst Technol, 44-45. *Mem:* Am Inst Mining, Metall & Petrol Engrs; Soc Explor Geophys. *Res:* Sonic and electrical well logging, propagation of acoustic energy in rocks; physical properties of rocks; fluid flow in porous media; geothermal energy from geopressured reservoirs on the Texas Gulf Coast. *Mailing Add:* 11515 Fast Horse Dr Austin TX 78759

GREGORY, ARTHUR ROBERT, INHALATION TOXICOLOGY, ONCOLOGY. *Current Pos:* PRES, TECHTO ENTERPRISES, 87- *Personal Data:* b Binghamton, NY, Oct 19, 25; m 75; c 15. *Educ:* Cornell Univ, AB, 45; Univ NC, MSPH, 63, PhD(pub health), 65; Am Bd Tocixol, dipl, 84. *Prof Exp:* Asst toxicol, Med Ctr, Univ Calif, 65-66; physicist, Cutter Labs, 66-67; res prof physiol, Univ Calif, 67-69; lab mgr toxicol, NASA Labs, Houston, Tex, 69-72; sr scientist, Roswell Park Mem Inst, 72-73; dir biostatist, Erie Co Health Dept, 73-76; pharmacologist, Nat Inst Occup Health, 77-80; pharmacologist, Consumer Prod Safety Comn, 80-87. *Concurrent Pos:* Indust epidemiol, Buffalo Med Sch, 72-77; adv, Chem Selection Working Group, Nat Cancer Inst, NIH, 77-86; toxicologist, Interagency Testing Comt, Toxic Substances Control Act, 80-84; state adv, US Cong Adv Bd, 82-86. *Mem:* Fel Am Inst Chemists; fel NY Acad Sci; Soc Toxicol; Asn Govt Toxicologists; Am Col Toxicologists; Int Soc Philos Inquiry; Am Indust Hyg Asn; Am Asn Cancer Res; Int Soc Regulatory Toxicol; Sigma Xi. *Res:* Toxicology of dyes; oncogenicity of benzidine and its dyes; lung edema-producing toxicant gases; effects of neonatal thymectomy on blood parameters; aerospace toxicology research on food additives and food colorants and maintenance of toxicology data base for the Food and Drug Administration. *Mailing Add:* 1 Gregory Lane Luray VA 22835. *Fax:* 540-743-2601

GREGORY, BOB LEE, electrical engineering; deceased, see previous edition for last biography

GREGORY, BRIAN CHARLES, PLASMA PHYSICS, ELECTRONIC PHYSICS. *Current Pos:* RES DIR, CENTRE CANADIEN DE FUSION MAGNETIQUE, 88- *Personal Data:* b Toronto, Ont, July 9, 38; m 84; c 2. *Educ:* Univ Toronto, BASc, 60; Cambridge Univ, PhD(elec eng), 63. *Prof Exp:* Res engr, Compagnie Generale de Telegraphie sans Fil, France, 63-66; from asst prof to assoc prof physics, Trent Univ, 66-70; dir, 70-78, scientist, Ctr Nuclear Studies, Grenoble, 78-79, prof, Inst Nat Res Sci, Univ Que, 79- *Mem:* Fel Am Phys Soc; assoc Can Asn Physicists; Inst Elec & Electronics Engrs; Nuclear & Plasma Sci Soc. *Res:* Electron beams and guns; microwave interaction with plasmas; plasmas and electron beams; physics of ionized gases; vacuum ultraviolet spectroscopy of tokamak plasmas; engineering physics; tokamak and fusion physics. *Mailing Add:* Ctr Energie Inst Nat Res Sci Univ Que CP 1020 Varennes PQ J3X 1S2 Can

GREGORY, BROOKE, LOW TEMPERATURE PHYSICS, ASTRONOMICAL INSTRUMENTATION. *Current Pos:* ASSOC SUPPORT SCIENTIST, CERRO TOLOLO INT-AM OBSERV, 80- *Personal Data:* b Boston, Mass, Apr 27, 41. *Educ:* Amherst Col, BA, 63; Brown Univ, PhD(physics), 73. *Prof Exp:* Asst prof physics, Trinity Col, Conn, 71-80. *Concurrent Pos:* Fulbright scholar & vis researcher, Bariloche Atomic Ctr, Nat Comn Atomic Energy, San Carlos de Bariloche, Arg, 75. *Mem:* Am Phys Soc. *Res:* Superconducting semiconductors; superconducting metrology with Josephson devices. *Mailing Add:* 950 N Clerry Ave Cerro Tololo Int-Am Observ Tucson AZ 85719

GREGORY, BRUCE NICHOLAS, ASTROPHYSICS, SCIENCE EDUCATION. *Current Pos:* ASSOC DIR, HARVARD-SMITHSONIAN CTR ASTROPHYS, CAMBRIDGE, MASS, 83- *Personal Data:* b New York, NY, July 12, 38; m 83, Jane G Jacobik; c David, Christopher, James & Christianne. *Educ:* Univ Mass, AB, 60, MS, 63. *Prof Exp:* Astronr, US Naval Res Lab, Washington, 63-65; staff dir, Nat Acad Sci, Washington, 66-82. *Res:* Astronomy; astrophysics; author and co-author. *Mailing Add:* Harvard-Smithsonian Ctr Astrophys 60 Garden St Cambridge MA 02138. *Fax:* 617-495-7105; *E-Mail:* bgregory@cfa.harvard.edu

GREGORY, CLARENCE LESLIE, JR, CHEMICAL ENGINEERING. *Personal Data:* b Stamford, Conn, Mar 14, 30. *Educ:* Mass Inst Technol, BS, 51, ScD(chem eng), 57. *Prof Exp:* Res asst, Mass Inst Technol, 54-55; engr, Knolls Atomic Power Lab, Gen Elec Co, 57-61, engr supv eng, 61-65, proj engr, 65-80. *Mem:* Am Chem Soc. *Res:* Mass transfer; nucleate and film boiling, two-phase pressure drop, vapor fractions, and flow oscillations; thermal and hydraulic design of nuclear reactors; chemistry of high pressure, high temperature water. *Mailing Add:* 2112 Baker Ave E Schenectady NY 12309-2336

GREGORY, CONSTANTINE J, ENVIRONMENTAL SCIENCES, AIR POLLUTION. *Current Pos:* From asst prof to assoc prof environ sci, 67-76, assoc prof, 76-80, PROF CIVIL ENG, NORTHEASTERN UNIV, 80- *Personal Data:* b Brockton, Mass, June 17, 39; m 62; c 3. *Educ:* Northeastern Univ, BA, 62; Rutgers Univ, MS, 64, PhD(environ sci), 68. *Concurrent Pos:* Mem bd dirs, New Eng Consortium on Air Pollution, 70- *Mem:* AAAS; Am Chem Soc; Air Pollution Control Asn. *Res:* Fate and effects of atmospheric pollutants. *Mailing Add:* Dept Civil Eng Northeastern Univ 360 Huntington Ave Boston MA 02115-5096

GREGORY, DALE R(OGERS), CHEMICAL ENGINEERING. *Current Pos:* chem engr, Tenn Eastman Co, 65-66, sr chem engr, 66-67, sr res chem engr, 67-74, res assoc, 74-87, sr res assoc, 87-88, sr tech assoc, 88-90, SR DEVELOP ASSOC, TENN EASTMAN CO, 90- *Personal Data:* b Lake Village, Ark, Aug 1, 34; m 56; c 3. *Educ:* Va Polytech Inst, BS, 56, PhD(chem eng), 66. *Prof Exp:* Prod supvr, Carbide & Carbon Chem Co, WVa, 56-57, 59-60; develop engr, E I du Pont de Nemours & Co, Inc, Va, 60-62. *Concurrent Pos:* Instr, Dept Chem & Metall Eng, Univ Tenn, 71- *Mem:* Am Inst Chem Engrs; Am Chem Soc; Am Soc Qual Control; Am Asn Textile Technol. *Res:* Fibers research and development; organic chemicals production; polymers engineering; melt spinning research. *Mailing Add:* 3308 Grimes Circle Kingsport TN 37663

GREGORY, DANIEL HAYES, internal medicine, gastroenterology, for more information see previous edition

GREGORY, DONALD CLIFFORD, HEALTH PHYSICS, INSTRUMENTATION. *Current Pos:* res assoc, 80-83, staff scientist physics, 83-91, HEALTH PHYSICIST, OAK RIDGE NAT LAB, 91- *Personal Data:* b Tyler, Tex, Sept 12, 49; m 71, Jean Wheat; c Eric & Lauren. *Educ:* Univ Tex, Austin, BS, 71, MA, 73, PhD(physics), 76. *Prof Exp:* Exchange scientist chem, Ctr Study Molecular Struct, NSF & Hungarian Acad Sci, Budapest, 74-75; researcher physics & chem, Univ Tex, Austin, 75-76; res assoc physics, Joint Inst Lab Astrophys, Nat Bur Stand & Univ Colo, Boulder, 76-78; asst scientist physics, Brookhaven Nat Lab, 78-80. *Concurrent Pos:* Fel Welch Found, Ctr Struct Studies & Physics Dept, Univ Tex, Austin, 75-76; vis worker, Oak Ridge Nat Lab, 76-78. *Mem:* Am Phys Soc; Health Physics Soc. *Res:* Instrumentation; experimental atomic physics (electron scattering from ions). *Mailing Add:* Oak Ridge Nat Lab Bldg 5505 MS6375 PO Box 2008 Oak Ridge TN 37831-6375

GREGORY, ERIC, METALLURGY, RESEARCH ADMINISTRATION. *Current Pos:* tech dir, Sintercast Corp Am, 56-61, phys res, 61-68, dir metals res, Cent Res Labs, 68-72, dir corp res & develop, Cent Res & Develop Labs, 72-79, GEN MGR, AIRCO, INC, 79- *Personal Data:* b Golborne, Eng, Jan 5, 28; US citizen; m 56; c 1. *Educ:* Cambridge Univ, BA, 48, MA, 52, PhD(metall), 54. *Prof Exp:* Res engr, Manganese Bronze Co, Eng, 54-56. *Mem:* Am Soc Metals; Am Inst Mining, Metall & Petrol Engrs; Am Ceramic Soc; Am Iron & Steel Inst; Brit Inst Metals. *Res:* High temperature alloys; powder metallurgy; high pressure, superconducting alloys; corrosion of stainless steels; materials produced by high vacuum electron beam processing. *Mailing Add:* 336 Sterling Rd Jefferson MA 01522-1304

GREGORY, EUGENE MICHAEL, ENZYMOLOGY. *Current Pos:* asst prof, 75-80, ASSOC PROF BIOCHEM, VA POLYTECH INST & STATE UNIV, 80- *Personal Data:* b Thirsk, Gt Brit, Mar 1, 45; US citizen. *Educ:* Appalachian State Univ, BA, 67; Univ NC, Chapel Hill, PhD(biochem), 71. *Prof Exp:* Res assoc biochem, Med Ctr, Duke Univ, 72-74; asst prof, Ohio Univ, 74-75. *Mem:* Am Chem Soc; Am Soc Biol Chemists. *Res:* Mechanism of action of antioxidant enzymes and their physiological roles. *Mailing Add:* Dept Biochem & Nutrit Va Polytech Inst & State Univ Rm 101A Engel Hall Blacksburg VA 24061. *Fax:* 540-231-9070

GREGORY, FRANCIS JOSEPH, MICROBIOLOGY, BIOCHEMISTRY. *Current Pos:* RETIRED. *Personal Data:* b Brooklyn, NY, June 21, 21; c 2. *Educ:* Brooklyn Col, BA, 42; Rutgers Univ, PhD(microbiol), 54. *Prof Exp:* Res scientist, 55-81, mgr, Microbiol Dept, Wyeth Labs, Inc, 81-87. *Concurrent Pos:* Fel microbiol, Rutgers Univ, 54-55; dir res, Mushroom Growers Asn of Pa, 87- *Mem:* Am Asn Cancer Res; Tissue Cult Asn; Am Soc Parasitol; Am Soc Microbiol. *Res:* Cancer research; screening for antineoplastic agents; biological response modifiers; anti-metastatic spread; drugs that restore immune competence; cancer and immunity; in vivo assays for anaerobic infections; athymic mice; effect of drugs on experimental systemic lupus erythematosus; monobeta-lactams; quinolone anti-infectives; reverse transcriptase; cephalosporin antibiotics; enzyme inhibitors; basidiomycete strain development; mushroom supplements; FIV research (feline AIDS). *Mailing Add:* 228 Rock Lake Dr Zelienople PA 16063

GREGORY, GAROLD FAY, PHYTOPATHOLOGY. *Current Pos:* RETIRED. *Personal Data:* b Arkansas City, Kans, Aug 15, 26; m 53, Flossy J Lewman; c CheryLynn G (O'dell) & Andrew F. *Educ:* Kans State Univ, BS, 51; Iowa State Univ, MS, 56; Cornell Univ, PhD(plant path), 62. *Prof Exp:* Plant pathologist, Northeastern Forest Exp Sta, US Forest Serv, 62-69, prin plant pathologist, 69-81, supvry plant pathologist, 81-87. *Mem:* Am Phytopath Soc; Int Soc Arboricult. *Res:* Research on chemical and biological control of tree diseases, particularly Dutch Elm disease; insect and disease problems of urban trees; microbiology and genetic manipulation to produce enhanced amounts of antibiotics by antigonistic organisms. *Mailing Add:* 11604 Mackel Dr Oklahoma City OK 73170

GREGORY, GARRY ALLEN, CHEMICAL ENGINEERING. *Current Pos:* vpres, 76-82, PRES, NEOTECHNOL CONSULTS LTD, 82- *Personal Data:* b London, Ont, July 27, 41; m 63, Janice M Marshall; c Jill, Lori, Ian & Carla. *Educ:* Univ Waterloo, BASc, 64, MASc, 65, PhD(chem eng), 69. *Prof Exp:* From asst prof to prof chem eng, Univ Calgary, 68-83. *Concurrent Pos:* Pres, Gregory Eng Ltd, 73- *Mem:* Can Soc Chem Eng; mem Am Inst Chem Engrs; Soc Petrol Engrs; Petrol Soc Can; fel Chem Inst Can. *Res:* Multiphase gas-liquid flow in pipelines and producing wells. *Mailing Add:* Neotechnol Consult Ltd 510 1701 Centre St Nw Calgary AB T2E 8A4 Can. *Fax:* 403-277-6687; *E-Mail:* gregory@neotec.com

GREGORY, IAN (WALTER DE GRAVE), PSYCHIATRY. *Current Pos:* RETIRED. *Personal Data:* b London, Eng, July 14, 26; US citizen; m 50; c 4. *Educ:* Cambridge Univ, BA, 46, MBCh, 48, MA, 51; Univ Toronto, DPsych, 54; Cambridge Univ, MD, 56; Univ Mich, MPH, 59; FRCP(C). *Prof Exp:* Intern & res, Verdun Protestant Hosp, Montreal, 48-50; asst supt, Hollywood Sanitarium, BC, 50-52; instr psychiat, Univ Western Ont, 55-58; from asst prof to assoc prof, Univ Minn, 59-65; prof psychiat & chmn dept, Col Med, Ohio State Univ, 65-87. *Concurrent Pos:* Psychiatrist, Ont Hosp, London, 54-58; consult psychiatrist, Carleton Col, 59-65; consult, Div Res Grants, NIH, 63-67, Vet Admin, 64- *Mem:* Fel Am Psychiat Asn; Can Psychiat Asn; fel Royal Col Psychiat. *Res:* Etiological research in psychiatry and abnormal psychology. *Mailing Add:* 4828 Tete Ct Columbus OH 43220

GREGORY, JESSE FORREST, III, FOOD CHEMISTRY, NUTRITION. *Current Pos:* from asst prof to assoc prof, 77-86, PROF FOOD CHEM, UNIV FLA, 86- *Personal Data:* b Columbus, Ohio, Aug 12, 50; m 76; c 2. *Educ:* Cornell Univ, BS, 72, MS, 75; Mich State Univ, PhD(food sci & human nutrit), 78. *Honors & Awards:* Prescott Award Res, Inst Food Technologists, 83. *Prof Exp:* Asst, Cornell Univ, 72-74, Mich State Univ, 74-77. *Mem:* Inst Food Technologists; Am Chem Soc; AAAS; Am Inst Nutrit; Soc Exp Biol & Med. *Res:* Nutritional quality and safety of foods; food chemistry and analysis; isotopic methods of vitamin research; stability, bioavailability, analysis of nutrients. *Mailing Add:* Dept Food Sci & Human Nutrit Univ Fla Gainesville FL 32611. *Fax:* 352-392-9467

GREGORY, JOHN DELAFIELD, BIOCHEMISTRY. *Current Pos:* RETIRED. *Personal Data:* b New York, NY, May 18, 23; m 58; c 2. *Educ:* Yale Univ, BS, 44, PhD(org chem), 47. *Prof Exp:* Asst, Rockefeller Inst, 47-49; from asst biochemist to assoc biochemist, Mass Gen Hosp, 49-57; assoc prof biochem, Rockefeller Univ, 57-91. *Mem:* AAAS; Am Soc Biol Chem; Soc Complex Carbohydrates (pres, 76); Harvey Soc; Biochem Soc. *Res:* Sulfate metabolism; enzyme chemistry; glycosaminoglycans; connective tissues; structure of proteoglycans. *Mailing Add:* 2400 Monkton Rd Monkton MD 21111

GREGORY, JOSEPH TRACY, VERTEBRATE PALEONTOLOGY. *Current Pos:* cur amphibians & reptiles Mus Paleont, Univ Calif, Berkeley, 60-79, dir, 71-75, prof, 60-79, EMER PROF PALEONT, UNIV CALIF, BERKELEY, 79- *Personal Data:* b Eureka, Calif, July 28, 14; m 49, Jane Everest; c Carl D & Sarah J. *Educ:* Univ Calif, AB, 35, PhD(vert paleont), 38. *Prof Exp:* Lectr zool, Columbia Univ, 39; technician, Paleont Lab, Bur Econ Geol, Univ Tex, 39-41; instr geol, Univ Mich, 41-46; asst prof geol, Yale Univ, 46-52, cur vert paleont, Peabody Mus Natural Hist, 46-60, assoc prof vert paleont, 52-60. *Concurrent Pos:* Cur, Mus Paleont, Univ Mich, 41-46; asst ed, Am J Sci, 54-60; mem, US Nat Comt Hist Geol, 77-83; vis prof, Paleont Inst, Johannes-Gutenberg Univ Mainz, FRG, 67-68; ed, Bibliog Fossil Vert, 69-89. *Mem:* Fel Paleont Soc; Soc Vert Paleont (pres, 58); fel Geol Soc Am; Am Soc Mammal; Soc Study Evolution; Am Soc Zoologists; Hist Earth Sci Soc; Nat Asn Geol Teachers. *Res:* Fossil reptiles and amphibians; history of paleontology. *Mailing Add:* Mus Paleont Univ Calif Berkeley CA 94720-4780. *Fax:* 510-642-1822; *E-Mail:* jtg@ucmp1.berkeley.edu

GREGORY, KEITH EDWARD, ANIMAL BREEDING. *Current Pos:* animal geneticist & regional coordr, Beef Cattle Breeding Res, Agr Res Serv, USDA 55-66, dir, US Meat Animal Res Ctr, 66-77, dir, Kans-Nebr area, Agr Res Serv, 72-77, res geneticist, US Meat Animal Res Ctr, 77-84, supv res geneticist & res leader prod syts, 84-87, RES GENETICIST, AGR RES SERV, USDA, 87- *Personal Data:* b Franklin, NC, Oct 27, 24; m 51, Wanda Eldredge; c Mark & Greta. *Educ:* NC State Univ, BS, 47; Univ Nebr, MS, 49; Univ Mo, PhD(animal breeding), 51. *Honors & Awards:* Animal Breeding & Genetics Award, Am Soc Animal Sci, 67; Res Award, Polled Hereford Asn, 71; Pioneer Award, Beef Improv Fedn, 75; Res Award, Nat Cattlemens Asn, 85; Morrison Award, Am Soc Animal Sci, 92. *Prof Exp:* res asst, Univ Mo, 49-51; assoc prof, Auburn Univ, 51-55. *Concurrent Pos:* Res asst animal husb, 47-49, prof animal sci, 78, res geneticist, prof animal sci, Univ Nebr, 87-; vis prof, Tex A&M Univ, 77-78. *Mem:* Fel AAAS; fel Am Soc Animal Sci; Am Genetic Asn; Sigma Xi. *Res:* Beef cattle breeding research--heterosis, selection, heterosis retention, maternal effects, breed characterization, twinning, composite populations. *Mailing Add:* US Meat Animal Res Ctr Clay Center NE 68933. *Fax:* 402-762-4173

GREGORY, KENNETH FOWLER, MICROBIOLOGY. *Current Pos:* RETIRED. *Personal Data:* b Calgary, Alta, May 12, 26; m 53; c Carolyn, Richard & Mark. *Educ:* Univ BC, BSA, 47; Univ Wis, MSc, 49, PhD(bact), 51. *Prof Exp:* Asst bact, Univ Wis, 47-51, res assoc, 51-52; asst prof, Dalhousie Univ, 52-54; asst prof, Ont Agr Col, 54-56, assoc prof microbiol, 56-67; prof microbiol, Univ Guelph, 67-87, chmn, 81-86. *Mem:* Can Soc Microbiol. *Res:* Bacterial genetics; the genetic improvement of microorganisms for use as single-cell protein and the use of thermotolerant fungi as food and feed. *Mailing Add:* 156 Maple St Guelph ON N1G 2G7 Can

GREGORY, M DUANE, PHYSICAL CHEMISTRY. *Current Pos:* SCIENTIST, RES & DEVELOP DEPT, CONTINENTAL OIL CO, 68- *Personal Data:* b Weatherford, Okla, June 24, 42; m 63; c 2. *Educ:* Southwestern State Col, Okla, BS, 64; Univ Okla, PhD(phys chem), 68. *Mem:* Am Chem Soc; Soc Petrol Eng. *Res:* Hydration of organic amines in nonaqueous solvents; surfactant waterflooding; resolution of oil in water dispersions. *Mailing Add:* 115 Orchard Lane Ponca City OK 74604

GREGORY, MAX EDWIN, FOOD SCIENCE. *Current Pos:* RETIRED. *Personal Data:* b Yorkville, Tenn, Jan 14, 31; m 54; c 3. *Educ:* Univ Tenn, BS, 53; NC State Col, MS, 56, PhD(dairy mfg), 59. *Prof Exp:* Dairy prod specialist, Ohio State Univ, 59-62; dairy prod specialist, NC State Univ, 62-80, exten prof food sci, 80-93. *Res:* Dairy products. *Mailing Add:* 1127 Alpine Dr Blowing Rock NC 28605

GREGORY, MICHAEL BAIRD, MATHEMATICAL ANALYSIS. *Current Pos:* PROF MATH, UNIV NDAK, 71- *Personal Data:* b Sacramento, Calif, Apr 15, 44; div; c 2. *Educ:* Univ Conn, BA, 66, MS, 67, PhD(math), 71. *Concurrent Pos:* Vis prof math, Mich State Univ, 87-88. *Mem:* Am Math Soc; Math Asn Am. *Res:* Classical analysis, including real functions, measure and integration; complex analysis. *Mailing Add:* Univ NDak PO Box 8376 Grand Forks ND 58202-8376

GREGORY, MICHAEL VLADIMIR, PROCESS SIMULATION, THERMAL-HYDRAULIC METHODS. *Current Pos:* SR ADV ENGR, WESTINGHOUSE SAVANNAH RIVER CO, 90- *Personal Data:* b Shanghai, China, Jan 31, 45; US citizen; m 68, Lois Korolevich; c Tania E & Alex M. *Educ:* Columbia Univ, AB, 66, BS, 67; Mass Inst Technol, PhD(nuclear eng), 73. *Prof Exp:* Res asst nuclear eng, Brookhaven Nat Lab, 67; nuclear engr, US Army Engrs Reactor Group, 69-71; res asst reactor physics, Mass Inst Technol, 72-73; staff analyst reactor physics, Savannah River Lab, E I Du Pont De Nemours & Co, 73-84, res assoc nuclear eng, 84-89. *Concurrent Pos:* Vis scientist, Risoe Nat Lab, Denmark, 79; chmn math & comp div, Am Nuclear Soc, 84-85. *Mem:* Am Nuclear Soc; Soc Computer Simulation. *Res:* Development of digital computation methods for reactor physics, thermal-hydraulic and safety analyses; applications of neutron diffusion theory; large scale data handling techniques; reactor simulator software; chemical process simulation. *Mailing Add:* Savannah River Technol Ctr Westinghouse Savannah River Co Aiken SC 29808-0001

GREGORY, NORMAN WAYNE, PHYSICAL CHEMISTRY, THERMODYNAMICS & METAL HALIDES. *Current Pos:* from instr to prof, 46-89, chmn, Dept Chem, 70-75, EMER PROF CHEM, UNIV WASH, 89- *Personal Data:* b Albany, Ore, June 23, 20; m 43, Lillian V Larson; c Norman W Jr, Martha J & Brian N. *Educ:* Univ Wash, Seattle, BS, 40, MS, 41; Ohio State Univ, PhD(chem), 43. *Prof Exp:* Chemist, Radiation Lab, Univ Calif, 44-46. *Mem:* Am Chem Soc; Sigma Xi. *Res:* Molecular composition of vapors; thermodynamics of metal halide systems; crystal structure; vaporization reactions. *Mailing Add:* Dept Chem 8610 Box 351700 Univ Wash Seattle WA 98195. *Fax:* 206-685-8665; *E-Mail:* gregory@chem.washington.edu

GREGORY, PETER, plant biochemistry, agriculture, for more information see previous edition

GREGORY, R(OBERT) LEE, control systems, for more information see previous edition

GREGORY, RICHARD ALAN, JR, SEPARATION SCIENCE. *Current Pos:* Sr engr, Union Carbide Corp, 80-74, proj scientists, 74-76, group leader, 76-79, sr group leader, 79-81, ASSOC DIR, UNION CARBIDE CORP, 81- *Personal Data:* b Ayer, Mass, June 2, 43; m 68; c Linda Manerchia; c Alan, Melissa & Emma. *Educ:* Drexel Univ, BS, 66; Princeton Univ, MA, 68, PhD(chem eng), 70. *Mem:* Am Inst Chem Engrs; Sigmi Xi. *Res:* Separation systems including cyclicial absorption processes and gas-liquid and liquid-liquid absorption with emphasis on acid gas removal. *Mailing Add:* Union Carbide Corp PO Box 670 Bound Brook NJ 08805. *Fax:* 732-563-5840

GREGORY, RICHARD LEE, MUCOSAL IMMUNOBIOLOGY, MEDICAL MICROBIOLOGY. *Current Pos:* ASSOC PROF ORAL BIOL & PATH & LAB MED, IND UNIV, 91- *Personal Data:* b Elmhurst, Ill, Oct 31, 54; m 81, Rebecca J Brown; c Amanda, Emily & Eric. *Educ:* Eastern Ill Univ, BS, 76; Southern Ill Univ, PhD(microbiol), 82. *Prof Exp:* Fel, Univ Ala, Birmingham, 81-84; from asst prof to assoc prof, Emory Univ, 84-91. *Concurrent Pos:* Prin investr, NIH, 82-, Smokeless Tobacco Res Coun, 86-; vis instr, Univ Ala, Tuscaloosa, 84; pres, Ind Br, Am Soc Microbiol, 94-96 & Ind Sect Am Asn Dent Res. *Mem:* Am Soc Microbiol; Am Soc Clin Path; Am Soc Med Technol; Am Asn Immunologists; Int Asn Dent Res; Soc Mucosal Immunol. *Res:* Host-parasite relationships with emphasis on infectious diseases, mucosal immunity and molecular, biology of microbiol pathogenesis; investigation of dental anti-microbiol products and evaluation. *Mailing Add:* Ind Univ 1121 W Michigan St Indianapolis IN 46202. *Fax:* 317-278-1411; *E-Mail:* rgregory@iusd.iupui.edu

GREGORY, RICHARD WALLACE, FISHERIES. *Current Pos:* CHIEF, WILDLIFE & FISH ADMIN, OFF INFO TRANSFER, NAT BIOL SURVEY, 89- *Personal Data:* b Chicago, Ill, Sept 28, 36; m 57; c 2. *Educ:* Colo State Univ, BS, 58, PhD(fish mgt), 69; Univ Wash, MS, 62. *Prof Exp:* Fish biologist, Colo Game, Fish & Parks Dept, 63; wildlife researcher cand, 63-64, asst wildlife researcher, 64-66, wildlife researcher, 66-69; asst prof zool & asst leader Coop Fisheries Unit, Univ Maine, Orono, 69-74; assoc prof biol & leader Coop Fish Res Unit, Mont State Univ, 74-79; prof wildlife ecol & leader Coop Fish & Wildlife Res Unit, Univ Fla, 79-84, chief Info Transfer Section, 84-87, deputy chief, Off Info Transfer, 87-88, chief, 88-89. *Concurrent Pos:* Prin investr, Decker Coal Co, US Forest Serv, US Fish & Wildlife Serv. *Mem:* Am Fisheries Soc (pres elect, 90-91, pres, 91-92); Am Inst Fishery Res Biol. *Res:* Biological and economic value of wetlands; limnology of Florida lakes; wetland habitat requirements of gallinules and river otters; impacts of rock mining on fish and wildlife; impacts of exotic fishes on native fishes; cryo preservation of fish sperm; habitat use by bass in heavily vegetated Florida lakes. *Mailing Add:* 1600 Quail Hollow Dr Ft Collins CO 80525-5589

GREGORY, ROBERT AARON, PLANT PHYSIOLOGY, BOTANY. *Current Pos:* RETIRED. *Personal Data:* b Hudson Falls, NY. *Educ:* Cornell Univ, BS, 52; Yale Univ, MF, 54; Ore State Univ, PhD(bot), 68. *Prof Exp:* Res forester, Pac Northwest Forest & Range Exp Sta, Southeast Alaska, 54-58, proj leader, 58-68, res plant physiologist, Northeastern Forest Exp Sta, Forest Physiol Lab, Beltsville, Md, 68-74, res plant physiologist, Northeastern Forest Exp Sta, USDA, Burlington, Vt, 74-88, proj leader, 82-88. *Concurrent Pos:* Adj assoc prof, George D Aiken Sch Natural Resources, Univ Vt, 81- *Mem:* AAAS; Int Asn Wood Anatomists. *Res:* Xylem translocation; circulation, storage and mobilization of assimilates; effects of stress on growth, development and physiological processes in trees. *Mailing Add:* Ferry Rd Charlotte VT 05445

GREGORY, STEPHEN ALBERT, astrophysics, for more information see previous edition

GREGORY, THOMAS BRADFORD, LIE ALGEBRAS. *Current Pos:* lectr math & comput sci, 77-78, asst prof math, 78-84, ASSOC PROF MATH, OHIO STATE UNIV, MANSFIELD, 84- *Personal Data:* b Traverse City, Mich, Dec 13, 44; m 95, Deirdre D Mason. *Educ:* Oberlin Col, AB, 67; Yale Univ, MA, 69, MPhil, 75, PhD(math), 77. *Prof Exp:* Head, Systs Design Br, Mgt Info Ctr, US Naval Commun Command, 69-72. *Concurrent Pos:* Translator, Am Math Soc, 74-82; exec officer, commanding officer & eng duty officer, US Naval Res, 79-96. *Mem:* Am Math Soc; Am Soc Naval Engrs. *Res:* Classification of the simple finite-dimensional Lie algebras over algebraically closed fields of prime characteristic, focusing on graded lie algebras. *Mailing Add:* 411 Overlook Rd Mansfield OH 44907-1533. *Fax:* 419-755-4367, 755-4241; *E-Mail:* tgregory@magnus.acs.ohio_state.edu, tgregory@math.ohio-state.edu

GREGORY, WESLEY WRIGHT, JR, ECONOMIC ENTOMOLOGY. *Personal Data:* b Camden, SC, Sept 9, 42; m 65, Anne Rogers; c Wesley W III & Juliana B. *Educ:* Wofford Col, BS, 64; Clemson Univ, MS, 66, PhD(entom, environ health & bot), 69. *Prof Exp:* Res asst invert zool, Clemson Univ, 65-66; asst prof entom, Univ Ky, 69-72, assoc prof, 72-80. *Mem:* AAAS; Entom Soc Am. *Res:* Bioaccumulation and transferal of pesticide residues in biological systems; development of insect management systems for soil and foliar pests of corn and vegetable crops, arthropod ecology. *Mailing Add:* 2018 Sheldon Dr Anderson SC 29621-3930

GREIBACH, SHEILA ADELE, COMPUTER SCIENCE. *Current Pos:* RETIRED. *Personal Data:* b New York, NY, Oct 6, 39; m 70, Jack W Carlyle; c Jay. *Educ:* Radcliffe Col, AB, 60, AM, 62; Harvard Univ, PhD(appl math), 63. *Prof Exp:* Lectr appl math, Harvard Univ, 63-65, asst prof, 65-69; from assoc prof to prof, Univ Calif, Los Angeles, 69-63, vchmn comput sci, 85-88. *Concurrent Pos:* Consult, Systs Develop Corp, 64-70. *Mem:* Am Math Soc; Asn Comput Math; Inst Elec & Electronics Engrs Comput Soc; Soc Indust & Appl Math. *Res:* Theoretical computer science in general with emphasis on formal languages, algorithms and computational complexity. *Mailing Add:* Dept Comput 3731 Boelter Hall Univ Calif Los Angeles CA 90024. *E-Mail:* greibach@cs.ucla.edu

GREIDER, MARIE HELEN, CYTOLOGY. *Current Pos:* asst prof, 68-70, ASSOC PROF PATH, WASH UNIV, 70- *Personal Data:* b Newark, Ohio, Jan 15, 22. *Educ:* Ohio State Univ, BSc, 49, MSc, 55, PhD(zool), 60. *Prof Exp:* Asst prof, Ohio State Univ, 51-60, res assoc, 60-64, asst prof, 66-68. *Mem:* AAAS; Am Soc Cell Biol; Am Asn Anat; NY Acad Sci; Electron Micros Soc Am. *Res:* Electron microscopy; cytochemistry; endocrinology. *Mailing Add:* 5516 Lancaster Rd Hebron OH 43025

GREIF, KAREN FAYE, DEVELOPMENTAL NEUROSCIENCE. *Current Pos:* from asst prof to assoc prof biol, 82-94, chair, Dept Biol, 93-96, PROF BIOL, BRYN MAWR COL, 94- *Personal Data:* b New York, NY, Feb 11, 52. *Educ:* Brown Univ, AB, 73; Calif Inst Technol, PhD(psychobiol & biochem), 78. *Prof Exp:* Fel neurosci, Univ Calif, San Francisco, 78-82. *Concurrent Pos:* Vis asst prof anat, Med Col Pa, 83-84; vis assoc prof biol, Univ Calif, Los Angeles, 89-90; prog officer, Nat Res Coun, 96-97. *Mem:* AAAS; Soc Neurosci; Soc Develop Biol; Asn Women Sci. *Res:* Regulation of expression of synaptic vesicle proteins in the developing rodent nervous system, using immunological and molecular biological methods. *Mailing Add:* Dept Biol Bryn Mawr Col Bryn Mawr PA 19010-2899

GREIF, MORTIMER, SURFACE CHEMISTRY, POLYMER CHEMISTRY. *Current Pos:* tech dir, 63-78, ASST GEN MGR, STAHL FINISH CO, 78- *Personal Data:* b New York, NY, Aug 13, 26; m 48; c 2. *Educ:* City Col New York, BS, 47; Univ Ky, MS, 49; Polytech Inst Brooklyn, PhD(phys chem), 53. *Prof Exp:* Staff chemist phys res, Fabrics & Finishes Div, E I du Pont de Nemours & Co, 52-63. *Mem:* Am Chem Soc; AAAS; Am Leather Chemists Asn. *Res:* Alternating current polarography; film formation; emulsion paints; pigment dispersions; leather finishes. *Mailing Add:* 20 Ocean Ave Unit 4 Marblehead MA 01945-3614

GREIF, RALPH, MECHANICAL ENGINEERING, HEAT & MASS TRANSFER. *Current Pos:* from asst prof to assoc prof, 63-73, vchmn dept, 74-76, PROF MECH ENG, UNIV CALIF, BERKELEY, 73- *Personal Data:* b New York, NY, Nov 28, 35; m 58; c 3. *Educ:* NY Univ, BS, 56; Univ Calif, Los Angeles, MS, 58; Harvard Univ, MA & PhD(eng), 62. *Honors & Awards:* Heat Transfer Mem Award, Am Soc Mech Engrs, 85. *Prof Exp:* Mem tech staff, Hughes Res & Develop Labs, 56-58, Raytheon Res Labs, 58; res fel gas dynamics, Harvard Univ, 62-63. *Concurrent Pos:* Consult var industs, 61-; Guggenheim fel, John Simon Guggenheim Mem Found, 69-70; vis scholar, Imp Col Sci & Technol, London, 69-70; vis prof & Lady Davis fel, Technion, Israel Inst Technol, 77; chmn Heat Transfer Div, Am Soc Mech Engrs, 70-73, comput technol policy comt, 75-79, assoc tech ed, J Heat Transfer, 83- 89, tech comt aerospace heat transfer, 67- *Mem:* Am Inst Aeronaut & Astronaut; fel Am Soc Mech Engrs. *Res:* Mass transfer; thermal radiation; natural convection; combustion; unsteady heat transfer; two phase flow; solar collection; rotating flows; chemical vapor deposition. *Mailing Add:* Dept Mech Eng Etcheverry Hall Univ Calif Berkeley Berkeley CA 94720

GREIF, ROBERT, APPLIED MECHANICS, MECHANICAL ENGINEERING. *Current Pos:* from asst prof to assoc prof, 67-78, chmn dept, 81-89, PROF MECH ENG, TUFTS UNIV, 78- *Personal Data:* b New York, NY, Jan 17, 38; m 63, Joyce Ambrose; c 2. *Educ:* NY Univ, BME, 58; Harvard Univ, SM, 59, PhD(appl mech), 63. *Prof Exp:* Staff scientist, Missile Systs Div, Avco Corp, 63-65, sr staff scientist, 65-67. *Concurrent Pos:* Consult, Beverly Res Lab, USM Corp, 67-68, Stone & Webster Eng Corp, 71-78 & Transp Systs Ctr, US Dept Transp, 77-; vis res fel, Univ Sussex, 74; vis scholar, Harvard Univ, 81; NRC sr res assoc, NASA, Langley, 88. *Mem:* Fel Am Soc Mech Engrs; assoc fel Am Inst Aeronaut & Astronaut; Am Soc Eng Educ; Am Asn Univ Professors chanics. *Res:* Vibration and dynamics; stress analysis; applied mechanics; fracture mechanics; rail mechanics. *Mailing Add:* Dept Mech Eng Tufts Univ Medford MA 02155. *E-Mail:* rgreif@tufts.edu

GREIF, ROGER LOUIS, ANIMAL PHYSIOLOGY, ENDOCRINOLOGY. *Current Pos:* prof, 65-82, EMER PROF PHYSIOL, MED COL, CORNELL UNIV, 82- *Personal Data:* b Baltimore, Md, Aug 23, 16; m 50, 73, Alice Falvey; c Peter C & Matthew P. *Educ:* Haverford Col, BS, 37; Johns Hopkins Univ, MD, 41. *Prof Exp:* Intern med, Johns Hopkins Hosp, 41-42; asst resident, Lakeside Hosp, 42-43; asst physician, Rockefeller Inst Hosp, 47-53; from asst prof to assoc prof physiol, 53-65. *Concurrent Pos:* Fel, Johns Hopkins Hosp, 46-47; asst physician outpatients, NY Hosp, 53-60; consult, Metab Sect, Health Res Coun & NY, 84; vis investr, Univ Aix-Marseille, France, 65-66 & 76; vis prof, Nat Defense Med Ctr & Med Sch, Nat Taiwan Univ, 82; mem bd dirs, Am Mem Hosp, Reims, France, 84. *Mem:* Soc Exp Biol & Med; Am Physiol Soc; Endocrine Soc; Am Thyroid Asn; Soc Gen Physiol. *Res:* Thyroid and endocrine physiology; hormone-enzyme relationships. *Mailing Add:* Dept Physiol Cornell Univ Med Col New York NY 10021-4885. *Fax:* 212-746-8690

GREIFER, AARON PHILIP, PHYSICAL INORGANIC CHEMISTRY, MAGNETIC MATERIALS. *Current Pos:* RETIRED. *Personal Data:* b Passaic, NJ, Sept 29, 19; m 43, Rita Weiss; c Roberta O & Margaret J. *Educ:* Ohio State Univ, BA, 42; Columbia Univ, MA, 48; Am Inst Chem, cert, 71. *Honors & Awards:* Cert Appreciation, Corps Engrs, Manhattan Dist, War Dept, 45. *Prof Exp:* Chemist, Elwood Ord Plant, Ill, 42-44; res assoc cryogenics, Res Found, Ohio State Univ, 44-45; chemist, Kellex Corp, NY, 48-49 & Fed Tel & Radio Corp, 51; scientist, Gen Elec Co, 51-56; sr scientist, Radio Corp Am, 56-61; proj chemist, Clevite Corp, 61-64; staff chemist, Univac Div, Sperry Rand Corp, 64-67; mgr ferrite core res, 67-71; staff scientist, 71-81. *Concurrent Pos:* Jr scientist, Los Alamos Sci Lab, Calif; lectr chem, Villanova Univ, 84- *Mem:* Am Chem Soc; Am Phys Soc; fel Am Inst Chem. *Res:* Magnetic materials; crystal growth; piezomagnetic ferrites; low loss ferrites; memory cores; bubble memory development; LPE growth of garnet films; glass gapped recording heads; magnetic coatings. *Mailing Add:* 51 E Golf View Rd Ardmore PA 19003

GREIFF, DONALD, CRYOBIOLOGY. *Current Pos:* PROF PATH, MED COL WIS, 57-, ASSOC DEAN GRAD AFFAIRS, 68- *Personal Data:* b Toronto, Ont, Aug 20, 15; nat US; m 42; c 2. *Educ:* Marquette Univ, BS, 38; Johns Hopkins Univ, ScD(genetics), 42. *Prof Exp:* From instr to prof biol, St

Louis Univ, 42-57. *Concurrent Pos:* Mem, Comn C1, Int Inst Refrig. *Mem:* Asn Am Med Cols; affil Royal Soc Med; Soc Cryobiol (pres, 67). *Res:* Effects of enzyme inhibitors and activators on the multiplication of viruses and Rickettsiae; freezing and freeze-drying of biologic materials; studies on freeze-dried biologic materials. *Mailing Add:* 33857 Shady Palms Circle Thousand Palms CA 92276

GREIFINGER, CARL, THEORETICAL PHYSICS. *Current Pos:* RETIRED. *Personal Data:* b Poland, Apr 19, 26; nat US; m 47, Phyllis Stoliar; c Lynne, David & Richard. *Educ:* Cornell Univ, AB, 48, PhD(physics), 54. *Prof Exp:* Instr physics, Univ Pa, 53-55; asst prof, Univ Southern Calif, 55-58; physicist, Rand Corp, 58-71; physicist, R&D Assocs, 71-91. *Concurrent Pos:* Consult, Hughes Aircraft Co, 55-58. *Mem:* Am Geophys Union. *Res:* Theoretical nuclear physics; magneto-hydrodynamics; ionospheric physics; low frequency electromagnetics; e-m propagation ocean electromagnetics and magnetic surveillance. *Mailing Add:* 16948 Dulce Ynez Lane Pacific Palisades CA 90272

GREIG, DOUGLAS RICHARD, ANALYTICAL CHEMISTRY, COMPUTER SCIENCE. *Current Pos:* AT NELSON ANALYTICAL. *Personal Data:* b Oakland, Calif, Oct 26, 50; m 77. *Educ:* Univ Calif, Berkeley, BS, 72; Northwestern Univ, PhD(chem), 76. *Prof Exp:* asst prof chem, Lake Forest Col, 77-80; mem staff, Varian Assoc, 80- *Concurrent Pos:* Consult, Northwestern Univ, 77- *Mem:* Am Chem Soc; Sigma Xi. *Res:* Computer control of chemical instrumentation; Raman spectroscopy. *Mailing Add:* 3833 N First St San Jose CA 95134

GREIG, JAMES KIBLER, JR, horticulture; deceased, see previous edition for last biography

GREIG, JOSEPH ROBERT, PLASMA PHYSICS, INTERIOR BALLISTICS. *Current Pos:* PHYSICIST, RADIATION ONCOL BR, NAT CANCER INST/NIH, BETHESDA, MD, 94- *Personal Data:* b Maidenhead, Eng, Apr 12, 38; m 64; c 3. *Educ:* Univ London, BSc & ARCS, 59, PhD(physics) & DIC, 65. *Prof Exp:* Res officer, Cent Electricity Res Lab, Eng, 62-65; asst prof physics, Univ Md, 65-70; res physicist, Imp Chem Industs, Ltd, Eng, 70-73; Naval Res Lab, Washington, Dc, 73-86; sr scientist, GT-Devices, Alexandria, Va, 86-94. *Concurrent Pos:* Adj assoc prof radiol, George Washington Univ, Washington, DC, 95-; sr scientist, UTRON Inc, Manassas, Va, 94- *Mem:* Am Phys Soc; Am Asn Phys Med. *Res:* Plasma spectroscopy and diagnostic methods used in plasma physics; laser produced plasmas and intense relativistic electron beams; electrothermal guns and interior ballistics; physics and dosimetry of radiation oncology. *Mailing Add:* 103 Northway Rd Greenbelt MD 20770. *E-Mail:* jrgreig@box-j.nih.gov

GREIM, BARBARA ANN, COMPUTER SCIENCE EDUCATION. *Current Pos:* ASSOC PROF MATH SCI, UNIV NC, WILMINGTON, 69-, ASST CHAIR, DEPT MATH SCI, 94- *Personal Data:* b Philadelphia, Pa. *Educ:* Ursinus Col, BS, 64; Univ NC, Chapel Hill, PhD(math), 70. *Mailing Add:* Dept Math Univ NC PO 601 S College Rd Wilmington NC 28403-3297

GREIMANN, LOWELL F, CIVIL & CONSTRUCTION ENGINEERING. *Current Pos:* PROF CIVIL & CONSTRUCT ENG, IOWA STATE UNIV, 73-, CHAIR, 90- *Educ:* Iowa State Univ, BS, 64; Univ Colo, MS, 66, PhD(struct eng), 68. *Prof Exp:* Staff, Southwest Res Inst, 68-73. *Mem:* Fel Am Soc Civil Engrs; Nat Soc Prof Engrs; Am Soc Eng Educ. *Res:* Reliability of nuclear containment vessels; maintenance management systems; bridge management systems; foundation design for standpipes and water towers; integral abutment bridges; lightning effects on concrete; tornado structural damage documentation. *Mailing Add:* Dept Civil Eng Iowa State Univ Ames IA 50011-9012

GREIN, FRIEDRICH, QUANTUM CHEMISTRY. *Current Pos:* asst prof physics, Univ NB, 62-63, from asst prof to assoc prof chem, 63-72, chmn, Chem Dept, 77-82 & 92-93, PROF CHEM, UNIV NB, 72- *Personal Data:* b Freudenberg am Main, Ger, Dec 22, 29; m 59, Hedemaria H Dinkela; c Rosalinde H, Christoph H & Andreas F. *Educ:* Univ Gottingen, 54, MSc, 58; Univ Frankfurt, PhD(chem physics), 60. *Prof Exp:* Fel quantum chem, Univ NB, 60-61 & Nat Res Coun Can, 61-62. *Concurrent Pos:* Vis prof, Uppsala Univ, 68-69, Univ Fla, 76 & Univ Bonn, 83-96. *Mem:* Can Asn Physicists; fel Chem Inst Can. *Res:* Quantum theoretical studies on electronic structure and spectra of diatomic and polyatomic molecules; development of MR-CI methods for hyperfine coupling constants and molecular g-factors; chemical reactions and stereoelectronic effects. *Mailing Add:* Dept Chem Univ NB Bag Serv No 45222 Fredericton NB E3B 6E2 Can. *Fax:* 506-453-4981; *E-Mail:* fritz@unb.ca

GREINER, DALE L, CELLULAR IMMUNOLOGY, AUTOIMMUNITY. *Current Pos:* PROF, DEPT MED, UNIV MASS, 91- *Educ:* Univ Iowa, PhD(microbiol), 78. *Prof Exp:* Asst prof immunol, Univ Conn Health Ctr, 79-91. *Mailing Add:* Univ Mass Dept Med 373 Plantation St Worcester MA 01605-2377

GREINER, DOUGLAS EARL, EXPERIMENTAL NUCLEAR PHYSICS, COSMIC RAY PHYSICS. *Current Pos:* Physicist space physics, Space Sci Lab, 64-74, PHYSICIST EXP NUCLEAR PHYSICS, LAWRENCE BERKELEY LAB, UNIV CALIF, 74- *Personal Data:* b Los Angeles, Calif, Jan 29, 39; m 61; c 3. *Educ:* Univ Calif, BA, 61, PhD(physics), 64. *Mem:* Am Phys Soc; Am Geophys Union; Sigma Xi. *Res:* Study of relativistic heavy ion reactions; fragmentation cross sections; search for abnormal matter; multiparticle inclusive reactions; isotopic abundances of the cosmic rays. *Mailing Add:* Lawrence Berkeley Lab One Cyclotron Rd Berkeley CA 94720

GREINER, NORMAN ROY, CHEMICAL KINETICS, LASERS. *Current Pos:* Sect leader chem, 64-74, alt group leader laser chem, 76-77, ASST GROUP LEADER CHEM LASERS, LOS ALAMOS SCI LAB, 74- *Personal Data:* b Muskegon, Mich, Aug 30, 38; m 64; c 2. *Educ:* St Mary's Univ, Tex, BS, 60; Univ Tex, Austin, PhD(phys chem), 64. *Mem:* AAAS; Am Chem Soc. *Res:* Gas kinetics; photochemistry; air pollution control; reactions of internally excited molecules; reactions initiated by flash photolysis; reactions of excited noble gas atoms; chemistry of planetary atmospheres; chemical lasers; laser isotope separation; environmental chemistry of natural radioisotopes. *Mailing Add:* 9 Loma Vista Los Alamos NM 87544-3066

GREINER, PETER CHARLES, MATHEMATICS. *Current Pos:* asst prof, 65-70, assoc prof, 70-77, PROF MATH, UNIV TORONTO, 77- *Personal Data:* b Budapest, Hungary, Nov 1, 38; Can citizen; m 65, 89, Inge Geilich; c Michael & Melissa. *Educ:* Univ BC, BSc, 60; Yale Univ, MA, 62, PhD(math), 64. *Honors & Awards:* Steacie Prize in Natural Sci, Can, 77. *Prof Exp:* Instr math, Princeton Univ, 64-65. *Concurrent Pos:* Mem, Inst Advan Study, 73-74; vis prof, Univ Paris, 80-81; mem, Max-Planck Inst, Bonn Ger, 87-88. *Mem:* Am Math Soc; Can Math Soc; Fel Royal Soc Can. *Res:* Partial differential equations; functional analysis. *Mailing Add:* Dept Math Univ Toronto Toronto ON M5S 1A1 Can

GREINER, RICHARD A(NTON), ELECTRICAL ENGINEERING. *Current Pos:* From asst prof to assoc prof, 57-63, prof, 63-, EMER PROF ELEC ENG, UNIV WIS-MADISON. *Personal Data:* b Milwaukee, Wis, Feb 13, 31. *Educ:* Univ Wis, BS, 54, MS, 55, PhD(elec eng), 57. *Mem:* Audio Eng Soc; Inst Elec & Electronics Engrs. *Res:* Solid state devices, circuits and electroacoustics. *Mailing Add:* Dept Elec & Comput Eng Univ Wis 1415 Johnson Dr Madison WI 53706-1607

GREINER, RICHARD WILLIAM, PHYSICAL CHEMISTRY, POLYMER CHEMISTRY. *Current Pos:* RETIRED. *Personal Data:* b New York, NY, Feb 24, 32; m 49, June; c Robert & Catherine. *Educ:* Bucknell Univ, BS, 53; Univ Wis, PhD(org chem), 57. *Prof Exp:* Res chemist, Hercules Powder Co, 57-69, sr res chemist, 69-76, res scientist, 76-83, res assoc, res ctr, Hercules Inc, 83-94; adj prof, Univ Minn, 90-94. *Mem:* Am Chem Soc; Sigma Xi. *Res:* Colloid and surface chemistry; organic polymer chemistry; chemistry of free radicals; physical organic chemistry. *Mailing Add:* 48 Clifton Dr Kennett Square PA 19348. *E-Mail:* dickgreinr@aol.com

GREINKE, EVERETT D, SPACE ELECTRONICS. *Current Pos:* Asst br head res & develop, Photo Div Bur Naval Weapons, Navy Dept, 56-61, tech adv data proc, Tech Anal & Adv Group, Dep Chief Naval Opers, 56-65, asst dir command control, 65-67, staff specialist, 67-75, asst dir combat support, 75-77, dir combat support, 77-80, dir NATO/Europ affairs, defense res & eng, 80-82, actg dep undersecy defense, Int Progs, 82, sci adv Sageur Shape/NATO, 82-86, dep undersevy defense, int progs, 86-88, vpres interpar, 90-94, IPAC, 94-96, GMD SOLUTIONS, INT PROGY, 96- *Personal Data:* b Elmhurst, Ill, Oct 31, 29; m 51; c 3. *Educ:* Northern Ill Univ, BS, 51, MS, 56. *Mem:* Am Inst Chem. *Res:* Development, testing, evaluation and engineering programs in the fields of command and control, navigation, electronic warfare, reconnaissance and intelligence; armaments cooperation, international scientific cooperation. *Mailing Add:* 8315 Toll House Rd Annandale VA 22003

GREINKE, RONALD ALFRED, ANALYTICAL CHEMISTRY. *Current Pos:* analytical chemist, Chem & Plastics Div, Union Carbide Corp, 67-69, res scientist, Carbon Prod Div, 69-70, head analytical res & develop, 71-75, res assoc, Carbon Prod Div, 75-95, SR RES ASSOC, UCAR CARBON CO, 96- *Personal Data:* b Mt Prospect, Ill, Aug 20, 35; m 67; c 2. *Educ:* Univ Ill, BS, 63; Univ Mich, MS, 65; PhD(analytical chem), 67. *Honors & Awards:* Pergamon Press Prize, J Carbon, 87. *Mem:* Am Chem Soc. *Res:* Kinetics in analytical chemistry; gas chromatography; thermal analysis; carbon chemistry; environmental polycyclic hydrocarbon analysis; mesophase chemistry; carbonization kinetics and mechanisms; graphite intercalation chemistry. *Mailing Add:* 4431 Pine Lake Dr Medina OH 44256-9031. *Fax:* 216-676-2423

GREISEN, ERIC WINSLOW, RADIO ASTRONOMY. *Current Pos:* Res assoc radio astron, 72-74, asst scientist, 74-76, ASSOC STAFF SCIENTIST RADIO ASTRON, NAT RADIO ASTRON OBSERV, ASSOC UNIVS INC, 76- *Personal Data:* b Los Alamos, NMex, Apr 14, 44; m 67. *Educ:* Cornell Univ, AB, 66; Calif Inst Technol, PhD(astron), 73. *Mem:* Am Astron Soc. *Res:* Radio spectral-line interferometry of interstellar neutral hydrogen including galactic structure, interstellar medium, HII region, and high velocity cloud questions. *Mailing Add:* 208 Georgetown Rd Charlottesville VA 22901

GREISEN, KENNETH I, COSMIC RAYS. *Current Pos:* asst physics, Cornell Univ, 38-42, instr, 42-43, from asst prof to prof physics, 46-84, prof astron, 75-79, chmn, Astron Dept, 76-79, dean fac, 78-83, EMER PROF PHYSICS, CORNELL UNIV, 84- *Personal Data:* b Perth Amboy, NJ, Jan 24, 18; wid; c Eric & Kathryn. *Educ:* Franklin & Marshall Col, BS, 38; Cornell Univ, PhD(physics), 42. *Prof Exp:* Mem staff, Manhattan Proj, AEC, Los Alamos Sci Lab, 43-45, group leader, 45-46. *Concurrent Pos:* Adj prof physics, Univ Utah, 75-81. *Mem:* Nat Acad Sci; Am Phys Soc; Am Astron Soc; Int Astron Union. *Res:* Cosmic rays; nuclear physics; high energy astrophysics. *Mailing Add:* 379 Savage Farm Dr Ithaca NY 14850

GREISMAN, SHELDON EDWARD, physiology, medicine, for more information see previous edition

GREISS, FRANK C, JR, OBSTETRICS & GYNECOLOGY. *Current Pos:* From instr to prof, 60-89, chmn dept, 72-89, EMER PROF OBSTET & GYNEC, BOWMAN GRAY SCH MED, WAKE FOREST UNIV, 89- *Personal Data:* b Philadelphia, Pa, July 13, 28; m 53, Barbara Diebel; c Linda (Gray), Virginia G (Mitchell), Barbara C (Welsh) & Frank C III. *Educ:* Univ Pa, BA, 49, MD, 53. *Honors & Awards:* Found Prize Thesis, Am Asn Obstet & Gynec, 68. *Mem:* Fel Am Col Obstet & Gynec; AMA; Am Gynec Soc; Am Asn Obstetricians & Gynecologists; Soc Gynec Invest; Sigma Xi. *Res:* Obstetric and fetal physiology; uterine blood flow. *Mailing Add:* 518 Stonemarker Rd Mooresville NC 28115

GREIST, JOHN HOWARD, psychiatry; deceased, see previous edition for last biography

GREITZER, EDWARD MARC, AERONAUTICAL ENGINEERING, MECHANICAL ENGINEERING. *Current Pos:* from asst prof to assoc prof, 77-84, prof & dir, Gas Turbine Lab, 84-96, H N SLATER PROF AERONAUT/ASTRONAUT, MASS INST TECHNOL, 88-, ASSOC DEPT HEAD, 96-; DIR AEROCHEM, CHEM & FLUID SYSTS, UNITED TECHNOLS RES CTR, 96- *Personal Data:* b New York, NY, May 8, 41; m 66; c 2. *Educ:* Harvard Col, BA, 62; Harvard Univ, MS, 64, PhD(eng), 70. *Honors & Awards:* Gas Turbine Power Award, Am Soc Mech Engrs, 77, 79 & 96, Freeman Scholar Award, 80; T Bernard Hall Prize, Inst Mech Engrs, 78; Aircraft Engine Technol Award, Int Gas Turbine Inst. *Prof Exp:* Res asst, Div Eng & Appl Physics, Harvard Univ, 66-69; res engr, Pratt & Whitney Aircraft, 69-76; indust fel commoner, Cambridge Univ, 75; sr res engr, United Technol Res Ctr, 76-77. *Concurrent Pos:* Consult, United Technol Res Ctr, 77-, Cummins Engine Co, 78- & Sundstrand Corp, 81-; guest fel, Royal Soc; overseas fel, Churchill Col, Cambridge Univ, 83-84; vis fel, Peterhouse, Cambridge Univ, 90-91 & Japan Soc Prom Sci, 87-; mem, Aeronaut Adv Comt, NASA, 90-94; mem bd dirs, Int Gas Turbine Inst, Am Soc Mech Engrs, 93- *Mem:* Nat Acad Eng; fel Am Soc Mech Engrs; Sigma Xi; fel Am Inst Aeronaut & Astronaut. *Res:* Internal fluid dynamics; fluid mechanics and thermodynamics of gas turbine engines; propulsion; flow control. *Mailing Add:* 31-264 Dept Aeronaut & Astronaut Mass Inst Technol 77 Massachusetts Ave Cambridge MA 02139. Fax: 617-258-6093

GREIZERSTEIN, HEBE BEATRIZ, POLYMER COATINGS, TOXICOLOGY PHARMACOLOGY. *Current Pos:* PRES, E B ASSOC LABS, INC, 83-; DIR ANALYTICAL LAB, TOXICOL RES CTR, STATE UNIV NY, BUFFALO, 88- *Personal Data:* b Buenos Aires, Arg; US citizen. *Educ:* Univ Buenos Aires, Lic, 58, PhD(org chem), 61. *Prof Exp:* Res assoc pharmacol, State Univ NY Buffalo, 69-70; sr res scientist, 70-73, assoc res scientist pharmacol, Res Inst Alcoholism, NY State Dept Ment Hyg, 73-75, res scientist V, 75-79, actg dir, 79-80, res scientist VII, 80-83. *Concurrent Pos:* Res instr pharmacol, State Univ NY Buffalo, 73-75, res asst prof, 75-; consult, Inst Child Health & Human Develop, 74-75; res grant, Nat Inst Alcohol Abuse & Alcoholism, 74-76 & Am Heart Asn, 81-84. *Mem:* AAAS; Am Chem Soc. *Res:* Research administration; adaptions of state-of-the-art instrumentation to the analysis of industrial products; management information systems, data bases and computer communications; analytical toxicology. *Mailing Add:* 72 Brandywine Dr Williamsville NY 14221. Fax: 716-631-3234

GREIZERSTEIN, WALTER, ORGANIC CHEMISTRY. *Current Pos:* VPRES RES & DEVELOP, EB ASSOC LABS, 93- *Personal Data:* b Buenos Aires, Arg, Sept 30, 35; US citizen; m 60; c 3. *Educ:* Univ Buenos Aires, PhD(org chem), 60; State Univ NY, MBA, 75. *Prof Exp:* Res fel org chem, Univ Buenos Aires, 60-61; Petrol Res Fund fel, Brown Univ, 61-62; res chemist, Rohm and Haas Co, 62-68, lab mgr indust finishes, 68-75, dir int develop, 75-78, tech dir, Pierce & Stevens Chem Corp, 78-85; dir, Int Div, Pratt & Lambert, 85-88, tech dir specialty prods, 89-92. *Mem:* Am Chem Soc. *Res:* Electronic and steric effects in nucleophilic substitutions; London Forces; correlations of structure and properties in polymers; reactions of ligands in organometallic complexes. *Mailing Add:* 90 Earhart Dr Suite 6 EB Assoclab Ins Williamsville NY 14221-7802. *E-Mail:* waltergreiz@juno.com

GREK, BORIS, LASER DEVELOPMENT, VERY LOW LIGHT LEVEL DETECTION. *Current Pos:* RES PHYSICIST, PRINCETON PLASMA PHYSICS, PRINCETON UNIV, 80- *Personal Data:* b Vinperk, Czechoslovakia, Feb 2, 46; US citizen; m 69; c 3. *Educ:* Royal Mil Col Can, BSc, 69; Princeton Univ, PhD(physics). *Prof Exp:* Res physicist laser development, Defense Res Estab, 72-75; prof plasma physics, Inst Nat Res Sci Can, 75-80. *Concurrent Pos:* Vis prof, Princeton Plasma Physics Lab, PRinceton Univ, 78-80; invited prof, Univ Quebec, Montreal, 82- *Mem:* Am Phys Soc. *Res:* Laser development; plasma physics and tokamak transport; non-linear plasma physics; Thomson scattering. *Mailing Add:* 421 S Main St Pennington NJ 08534

GRELECKI, CHESTER, PHYSICAL CHEMISTRY, CHEMICAL ENGINEERING. *Current Pos:* PRES & CHIEF SCIENTIST CHEM, HAZARDS RES CORP, 69- *Personal Data:* b Newton Twp, Pa, June 22, 27; m 50; c 7. *Educ:* King's Col, Pa, BS, 50; Duquesne Univ, MS, 52; Catholic Univ Am, PhD(chem), 57. *Prof Exp:* Res chem, Reaction Motors Div, Olin Matheson Corp, 56-59, sr supvr, Reaction Motors Div, Thiokol Chem Corp, 59-67, res dir, 67-69. *Mem:* Am Chem Soc; Am Soc Testing & Mat. *Res:* Combustion and explosion phenomena; fire and explosion hazards evaluation; shock waves and blast effects. *Mailing Add:* 38 Birch Terr Mt Arlington NJ 07856-1327

GRELEN, HAROLD EUGENE, RANGE SCIENCE. *Current Pos:* RETIRED. *Personal Data:* b Bryan, Tex, Nov 13, 29; m 53; c 3. *Educ:* Agr & Mech Col Tex, BS, 52, MS, 56. *Prof Exp:* Range conservationist, US Soil Conserv Serv, 54-55; range scientist, US Forest Serv, 56-85. *Mem:* Soc Range Mgt. *Res:* Range ecology; plant taxonomy; effects of prescribed burning and grazing on southern pine range. *Mailing Add:* 607 Edgewood Dr Pineville LA 71360

GRELLER, ANDREW M, BIOCLIMATOLOGY, CONSERVATION. *Current Pos:* From asst prof to assoc prof, 67-86, PROF BOT, QUEENS COL, NY, 86- *Personal Data:* b New York City, NY, Mar 18, 41; m 64; c 2. *Educ:* City Col, New York, 62; Columbia Univ, MA, 64, PhD(bot), 67. *Concurrent Pos:* Collabr, Rocky Mt Nat Park, US Nat Park Serv, 70-72; vis asst prof, Univ Colo, 71, Univ Calif, Davis, 74; vis scientist, Am Mus Natural Hist, 76-80; Fulbright sr lectr, Dept Bot, Univ Peradeniya, Sri Lanka, 80-81; vis assoc prof, Univ Peradiniya, 85. *Mem:* Torrey Bot Club (pres, 88); Bot Soc Am; Int Soc Plant Morphologists; Sigma Xi. *Res:* Cape ecology, classification, climatology and conservation of tropical Asian forests and eastern North American forests. *Mailing Add:* Dept Biol Queens Col CUNY 65-30 Kissena Blvd Flushing NY 11367-1597

GREMINGER, GEORGE KING, JR, PULP CHEMISTRY, PAPER CHEMISTRY. *Current Pos:* RETIRED. *Personal Data:* b Syracuse, NY, Feb 4, 16; m 46, 85, Nancy Sian; c 8. *Educ:* State Univ NY, BS, 38. *Prof Exp:* With Mead Corp, Ohio, 37-38; Dow chem group leader, Dow Chem Co, 38-57, sect head tech serv & develop, 57-65, chem develop & serv specialist, 65-66 & Switz, 66-68, develop assoc, Designed Prod Dept, 68-72, assoc develop scientist, 72-86. *Concurrent Pos:* Sr consult scientist, Omni Tech Int Ltd, Midland, Mich. *Mem:* Am Chem Soc; Tech Asn Pulp & Paper Indust; AAAS. *Res:* Water soluble gums, especially cellulose ethers. *Mailing Add:* 802 W Larkin Midland MI 48640-4236

GRENANDER, ULF, APPLIED MATHEMATICS, PATTERN THEORY. *Current Pos:* prof, 57-58 & 66-69, L HERBERT BALLOU UNIV PROF APPL MATH, BROWN UNIV, 69- *Personal Data:* b Vastervik, Sweden, July 23, 23; US citizen; m 46; c Sven, Angela & Charlotte. *Educ:* Univ Stockholm, Fil Dr, 50. *Hon Degrees:* DSc, Univ Chicago, 94. *Prof Exp:* Docent math statist, Univ Stockholm, 50-51 & 54-57, prof, 59-66; asst prof statist, Univ Chicago, 51-52; assoc prof, Univ Calif, 53. *Mem:* Nat Acad Sci; Royal Swed Acad Sci; Int Statist Inst; hon fel Royal Statist Soc (London); Am Acad Sci; Fel Inst Math Statist. *Res:* Probability; theoretical statistics; operations research and insurance mathematics; pattern theory and applications to anatomy and target recognition. *Mailing Add:* 26 Barberry Hill Providence RI 02906

GRENCHIK, RAYMOND THOMAS, ASTROPHYSICS. *Current Pos:* RETIRED. *Personal Data:* b Whiting, Ind, Aug 24, 22; m 57, Jeanne Ford; c Mary, Stephen, Robert & Ruth. *Educ:* St Procopius Col, BA, 43; Univ NMex, MS, 49; Ind Univ, PhD(astrophys), 56. *Prof Exp:* Lab instr elec & electronics, Signal Corps Sch, Chicago, 43; jr physicist, Instrument Sect, Metall Lab, 43-46; instr physics, Univ NMex, 46-50, Sault Br, Mich Tech Univ, 50-52 & Vanderbilt Univ, 55-57; asst prof, La State Univ, Baton Rouge, 57-61, assoc prof physics & astron, 61-88. *Concurrent Pos:* Mem comt educ astron, 66-72; consult, La Arts & Sci Ctr, 73-75. *Mem:* Am Astron Soc; AAAS. *Res:* Stellar atmospheres; radiative and convective transport; solar system physics. *Mailing Add:* 5960 Menlo Dr Baton Rouge LA 70808-5049

GRENDA, STANLEY C, INORGANIC CHEMISTRY. *Current Pos:* chmn dept chem, 72-73, asst prof, 67-70, ASSOC PROF CHEM, UNIV NEV, LAS VEGAS, 70- *Personal Data:* b Chicago, Ill, Aug 12, 34. *Educ:* DePaul Univ, BS, 58; Univ Ariz, MS, 62; Lehigh Univ, PhD(chem), 64. *Prof Exp:* Asst prof chem, Wis State Univ, Superior, 64-65, Whitewater, 65-67. *Concurrent Pos:* Treas, Boulder Dam Sect, Am Chem Soc, 84. *Mem:* Am Chem Soc. *Res:* Educational research in qualitative inorganic chemistry; organometallic chemistry closely related to Grignard reagents; molybdenum chemistry. *Mailing Add:* Dept Chem Univ Nev 4505 S Maryland Pkwy Las Vegas NV 89154-9900

GRENDA, VICTOR J, ORGANIC CHEMISTRY. *Current Pos:* RETIRED. *Personal Data:* b Boston, Mass, May 18, 33. *Educ:* Northeastern Univ, BS, 55; Mass Inst Technol, PhD(org chem), 60. *Prof Exp:* Sr res chemist, Merck Sharp & Dohme Res Labs, 60-66, sect leader, 66-72, sr proj coordr, proj planning & mgt, 72-77, dir process res, 77-84, sr dir, 84-90. *Mem:* Am Chem Soc; Chem Soc London. *Res:* Research and development of chemical processes; project management and planning. *Mailing Add:* 15 Loriann Rd Warren NJ 07059

GRENFELL, RAYMOND FREDERIC, INTERNAL MEDICINE. *Current Pos:* RETIRED. *Personal Data:* b West Bridgewater, Pa, Nov 23, 17; m 44; c 4. *Educ:* Univ Pittsburgh, BS, 39, MD, 41. *Honors & Awards:* Bronze Medal, Am Heart Asn, 63, Silver Medal, 65. *Prof Exp:* Intern, Western Pa Hosp, 41-42; clin instr, Sch Med, Univ Miss, 55-59, head, Hypertension Clin, 56-79, clin asst prof med, 59-97, vis prof, 77-97. *Concurrent Pos:* Mem staff, Hinds Gen Hosp, Riverside Hosp, St Dominic-Jackson Mem Hosp, Miss Baptist Hosp & Doctor's Hosp; pvt pract, 46- *Mem:* Fel Am Col Angiol; fel Int Col Angiol; fel Am Col Chest Physicians; Am Soc Clin Pharmacol & Therapeut (vpres, 76); Am Fedn Clin Res. *Res:* Investigation of antihypertensive drugs. *Mailing Add:* 1151 N State St Jackson MS 39202

GRENGA, HELEN E(VA), PHYSICAL CHEMISTRY & METALLURGY. *Current Pos:* Fel, 67, from asst prof to assoc prof, 68-77, PROF METALL, SCH CHEM ENG, GA INST TECHNOL, 77-, PROF CHEM ENG & ACTG ASSOC DEAN, GRAD DIV, 80- *Personal Data:* b Newnan, Ga, Apr 11, 38. *Educ:* Shorter Col, Ga, BA, 60; Univ Va, PhD(phys chem), 67. *Concurrent Pos:* NSF res grants, 69-70 & 71- *Mem:* Am Soc Metals; Am Inst Mining, Metall & Petrol Engrs; Sigma Xi. *Res:* Chemistry and physics of solid surfaces; structure-property correlations of gas-solid and solid-solid interfaces; oxidation; corrosion; catalysis; extractive metallurgy; field-ion and emission microscopy. *Mailing Add:* 6139 Hickory Dr Forest Park GA 30050

GRENIER, CLAUDE GEORGES, SOLID STATE PHYSICS. *Current Pos:* RETIRED. *Personal Data:* b Les Rousses, France, Feb 24, 23; m 53, Helen Peterson; c Catherine & Christopher. *Educ:* Sorbonne, DSc, 56. *Prof Exp:* Res assoc, La State Univ, 56-57, from asst prof physics to assoc prof physics, 57-65, prof physics & astron, 65-90. *Res:* Low temperature physics; electron transport phenomena. *Mailing Add:* Dept Physics La State Univ Baton Rouge LA 70803

GRENIER, FERNAND, GEOGRAPHY, ENVIRONMENTAL SCIENCE. *Current Pos:* RETIRED. *Personal Data:* b East Broughton, Que, Mar 30, 27; m 84, Nilma St-Gelais; c Mira & Chloe. *Educ:* Laval Univ, Que, BA & BPh, 48, MA, 50; Univ Paris, DES, 55. *Hon Degrees:* Dr, Athabasca Univ, Can, 79. *Honors & Awards:* Serv to Profession Award, Can Asn Geogrs, 93. *Prof Exp:* Prof geog, Laval Univ, 55-73, dean, Fac Letters, 67-73; dir gen, Univ Quebec, 73-81, sr admin, 83-88. *Mem:* Can Asn Geogrs (pres, 64); Can Asn Study Names. *Res:* Evaluation of books and manuscripts; Ruman geography; study of place names; tourism as cultural and economic activity. *Mailing Add:* 1035 Rte Laurier Ste Croix PQ G0S 2H0 Can

GRENNEY, WILLIAM JAMES, CIVIL ENGINEERING. *Current Pos:* WATER QUALITY SYSTS DIR, US FISH & WILDLIFE SERV, 78- *Personal Data:* b Saginaw, Mich, Aug 10, 37; m 59; c 3. *Educ:* Mich Technol Univ, BS, 60; Ore State Univ, MS, 69, PhD(civil eng), 72. *Honors & Awards:* Outstanding Res Award, Col Eng, Utah State Univ, 76. *Prof Exp:* Proj engr civil eng, Bethlehem Steel Corp, 60-62; consult engr, Consult Engrs, 67-68; asst prof, Calif State Polytech Univ, 71-72; res engr water res, Utah Water Res Lab, 72-74; assoc prof civil eng, 74-76, div head, environ eng, 76-77, prof & dept head civil & environ eng, Utah State Univ, 77- *Concurrent Pos:* Pres, Intermountain Consult & Planners, 74-79; water quality systs dir, US Fish & Wildlife Serv, 78-79. *Mem:* AAAS; Am Soc Civil Engrs; Am Water Res Asn; Water Pollution Control Fedn; Asn Environ Eng Profs; Sigma Xi. *Res:* Mathematical simulation and stochastic modeling of the chemical and biological responses of aquatic systems. *Mailing Add:* 1716 E 1600 N Logan UT 84341

GRENVIK, AKE N A, CRITICAL CARE MEDICINE. *Current Pos:* vis assoc prof, 68-70, assoc prof, 70-74, PROF ANESTHESIOL, SCH MED, UNIV PITTSBURGH, 74-, PROF SURG, 81-, PROF MED, 90- *Personal Data:* b Sunne, Sweden, July 10, 29; m 52; c 4. *Educ:* Karolinska Inst, Sweden, MD, 56; Univ Uppsala, Sweden, PhD, 66. *Prof Exp:* Asst prof surg, Univ Uppsala, Sweden, 66-68. *Concurrent Pos:* Prin investr grants, Swed Asn Against Heart & Lung Dis, 64-66 & NIH; med dir, Intensive Care Unit, Presby-Univ Hosp & Critical Care Med Training Prog, Univ Pittsburgh Med Ctr, 73-; ed, Clins Critical Care Med, 77-89, co-ed Textbk Critical Care, 85-; co-ed, Contemp Mgt Critical Care, 89- *Mem:* Soc Critical Care Med (secy, 75-76, pres, 77-78); World Fedn Soc Intensive Critical Care Med (treas, 81-85); Am Col Chest Physicians; Am Soc Anesthesiologists; AMA. *Res:* Pathophysiology and management of cardiac, respiratory and brain failure; intensive care unit design and organization; critical care medicine education and certification; brain death, foregoing life sustaining therapy, ethical problems in organ donation and transplantation; author or coauthor of over 300 publications. *Mailing Add:* 2629 Thorntree Dr Pittsburgh PA 15241. *Fax:* 412-835-6083; *E-Mail:* grenvik@smtp.anes.upmc.edu

GRESHAM, ROBERT MARION, MATERIALS SCIENCE ENGINEERING. *Current Pos:* lab mgr res & develop, 81-82, tech dir, 82-84, VPRES TECHNOL RES & DEVELOP, E M CORP, 84- *Personal Data:* b Akron, Ohio, Aug 7, 43; m 66; c 2. *Educ:* Emory Univ, BS, 65, PhD(chem), 69. *Prof Exp:* Sr res chemist res & develop, DuPont Co, 80-81. *Concurrent Pos:* Indust coun coordr, Soc Tribologists & Lubrication Engrs, 88-, chmn solid lubricants tech comt, 84-88, chmn aerospace indust coun, 84-88; mem Asn Finishing Processes, Soc Mfg Engrs, 88- *Mem:* Am Soc Testing & Mat; Armed Forces Commun & Electronics Asn; Soc Advan Mat & Process Engrs; Nat Lubricating Grease Inst; Soc Mfg Engrs; Soc Tribologists & Lubrication Engrs. *Res:* Design and development of solid lubrication materials primarily used in the aerospace industry; materials for shielding electromagnetic radiation. *Mailing Add:* 3828 N 800 W West Lafayette IN 47906

GRESHAN, GLEN EDWARD, ADMINISTRATION, RESEARCH. *Current Pos:* PROF & CHMN, DEPT REHAB MED, STATE UNIV NY, BUFFALO, 78- *Personal Data:* b Ft Worth, Tex, Dec 1, 31. *Educ:* Harvard Col, AB, 53; Columbia Univ, MD, 58. *Res:* Stroke and osteoarthritis and functional assessment. *Mailing Add:* 462 Grider St Buffalo NY 14215

GRESIK, EDWARD WILLIAM, ANATOMY. *Current Pos:* PROF CELL BIOL & ANAT, MED SCH, CITY UNIV NY, 90- *Personal Data:* b Chicago, Ill, Oct 14, 39. *Educ:* Xavier Univ, Ohio, BA, 61; Univ Ill, MS, 66, PhD(anat), 68. *Prof Exp:* Instr anat, State Univ NY Downstate Med Ctr, 67-74; assoc, Mt Sinai Sch Med, 74-76, from asst prof to assoc prof anat, 76-90. *Mem:* Histochem Soc; Am Asn Anatomists; Sigma Xi; AAAS. *Res:* Cell fine structure; histochemistry; developmental biology; influence of drugs and hormones on the fine structure of the developing and mature salivary glands; growth factors. *Mailing Add:* City Univ NY Med Sch 138th St & Convent Ave New York NY 10031

GRESKOVICH, CHARLES DAVID, TECHNICAL CERAMICS. *Current Pos:* STAFF SCIENTIST CERAMICS, CORP RES & DEVELOP, GEN ELEC CO, 69- *Personal Data:* b Fredericktown, Pa, June 13, 42; m 66, Maria; c 3. *Educ:* Pa State Univ, BS, 64, MS, 66, PhD(ceramic sci), 68. *Honors & Awards:* Ross Coffin Purdy Award Ceramic Lit, Am Ceramic Soc, 78; Richard M Fulrath Award, 83; Dushman Award, 86. *Concurrent Pos:* NSF fel, 68; Coolidge fel, 91; Pa State Centennial fel, 96. *Mem:* Am Ceramic Soc; Electrochem Soc; Nat Inst Ceramic Engrs. *Res:* Preparation and processing of ionic and covalent polycrystalline ceramics, and the effect of these on microstructural development and optical, magnetic and mechanical properties; ceramic optical elements, microwave ferrites, ceramics for turbine engines and cores/molds for casting alloys; x-ray scintillators for modern x-ray detectors are of major interest. *Mailing Add:* 1229 Viewmont Dr Niskayuna NY 12309

GRESS, MARY EDITH, RESEARCH ADMINISTRATION, PHYSICAL CHEMISTRY. *Current Pos:* STAFF MEM, DIV CHEM SCI, OFF BASIC ENERGY SCI, US DEPT ENERGY, 80-, PROG MGR, PHOTOCHEM & RADIATION SCI, 82- *Personal Data:* b Pensacola, Fla, July 11, 46. *Educ:* Sweet Briar Col, AB, 68; Iowa State Univ, PhD(phys chem), 73. *Prof Exp:* Res chemist, E I du Pont de Nemours & Co, 73-74; res assoc, Brookhaven Nat Lab, 74-77; vis asst prof phys chem, Univ Vt, 77-79; asst chemist, Ames Lab, Iowa State Univ, 79-82. *Mem:* Am Chem Soc; Am Crystallog Asn; AAAS. *Res:* Crystal structure determination by x-ray and neutron diffraction. *Mailing Add:* Div Chem Sci ER 141 US Dept Energy Germantown MD 20874

GRESS, RONALD E, CELLULAR IMMUNOLOGY. *Current Pos:* SR INVESTR, IMMUNOL BR, NIH, 83- *Personal Data:* b Genoa, Nebr, Dec 5, 49; m 80, Janet Salisbury; c 2. *Educ:* Baylor Univ, MD, 75. *Mem:* Am Asn Immunologists; Transplantation Soc. *Mailing Add:* Exp Immunol Br Bldg 10 Rm 4B17 Nat Cancer Inst NIH Bethesda MD 20892-0001. *Fax:* 301-496-0887

GRESSEL, JONATHAN BEN, developmental biology, biochemistry, for more information see previous edition

GRESSER, MICHAEL JOSEPH, BIOENERGETICS, PHYSICAL ORGANIC CHEMISTRY. *Current Pos:* asst prof, 80-84, assoc prof biochem, Simon Fraser Univ, 84-88, DIR BIOCHEM, MERCK FROSST CTR THERAPEUT RES, 88- *Personal Data:* b Booneville, Mo, May 6, 45; m 68. *Educ:* Univ Kans, BA, 67; Brandeis Univ, PhD(biochem), 76. *Prof Exp:* Fel, Univ Calif, Los Angeles, 76-80. *Mem:* Am Chem Soc; Am Soc Biochemists; Can Biochem Soc; Can Soc Chem. *Res:* Energy transducing mechanisms in biological systems; enzymic and nonenzymic acyl and phosphoryl transfer reaction mechanisms; regulatory mechanisms; biochemistry of vanadium. *Mailing Add:* Dept Biochem & Molecular Merck Frosst Canada Inc PO Box 1005 Pointe Claire-Dorval PQ H9R 4P8 Can. *Fax:* 514-695-0693

GRESSHOFF, PETER MICHAEL, NODULATION-NITROGEN FIXATION, GENOME ANALYSIS & DNA FINGERPRINTING. *Current Pos:* PROF & RACHEFF CHAIR PLANT MOLECULAR GENETICS, UNIV TENN, 88- *Personal Data:* b Berlin, Ger, Nov 26, 48; Australian citizen; m 73, Rosalyn Marie; c Michael & Nikolas. *Educ:* Univ Alta, Edmonton, BS, 70; Australia Nat Univ, PhD(plant genetics), 73. *Hon Degrees:* DSc, Australian Nat Univ, Canberra, 89. *Prof Exp:* Dr Alexander Von Humboldt fel, Hohenheim Univ, Stuttgart, 73-75; res fel genetics, Australia Nat Univ, 75-79, sr lectr, 79-87. *Concurrent Pos:* Asst dir, Ctr Legume Res; Alexander von Humboldt fel, 72 & 85. *Mem:* Sigma Xi; NY Acad Sci; Int Soc Plant Molecular Biol; Int Soc Molecular Plant Microbe Interactions; fel AAAS; fel Russian Acad Agr Sci; Int Soc Plant Molecular Biol; hon fel SAfrican Soc Genetics. *Res:* Plant genes, which are expressed in development of new growth; developed and patented new soybean mutants as well as a new DNA fingerprinting method used in plant genome analysis. *Mailing Add:* Plant Molecular Genetics Univ Tenn Knoxville TN 37901-1071. *Fax:* 423-974-2765; *E-Mail:* jcrocket@utk.edu

GREST, GARY STEPHEN, CONDENSED MATTER PHYSICS. *Current Pos:* staff physicist, 81-84 SR STAFF PHYSICIST, EXXON, 84- *Personal Data:* b New Orleans, La, Nov 22, 49; m 70; c 4. *Educ:* La State Univ, BS, 71, MS, 73, PhD(physics), 74. *Prof Exp:* Res asst, Rutgers Univ, 74-77; Chaim Weizmann fel & res asst, James Franck Inst, Univ Chicago, 77-78; asst prof physics, Purdue Univ, 79-81. *Concurrent Pos:* Alfred P Sloan Found fel, 81. *Mem:* Am Phys Soc. *Res:* Problems in condensed matter and many-body physics including spin-glasses, complex fluids and polymers, structural and dynamical properties of glasses; molecular dynamics and Monte Carlo simulation techniques. *Mailing Add:* Exxon Res & Eng Co Rte 22 E Annandale NJ 08801

GRETHE, GUENTER, COMPUTER APPLICATIONS IN SYNTHESIS, DATA BASE MANAGEMENT SYSTEMS IN CHEMISTRY. *Current Pos:* DIR, SCI APPLNS, MDL INFO SYSTS, INC, 85- *Personal Data:* b Hannover, Ger, Oct 13, 33; US citizen; m 60, Inge Warwel; c Jeffrey S & Nadine I. *Educ:* Braunschweig Tech Univ, Dipl chem, 60, PhD(org chem), 61. *Prof Exp:* Fel chem, Univ Wis, 62-63; sr res chemist, Chem Res Div,

Hoffman-La Roche, Inc, 63-71, res fel, 72-80, res group chief, 80-85. *Concurrent Pos:* Adv, NY Univ, 74-77. *Mem:* Am Chem Soc; Ger Chem Soc. *Res:* Synthetic work in the fields of tetracyclines, alkaloids and heterocyclic compounds; drug design, SAR; computer assisted synthesis; computers in chemistry; reaction indexing. *Mailing Add:* 352 Channing Way Alameda CA 94501-7409. *Fax:* 510-483-4738; *E-Mail:* guenter@mdli.com

GRETSKY, NEIL E, MATHEMATICAL ECONOMICS. *Current Pos:* Asst prof, 67-74, ASSOC PROF MATH, UNIV CALIF, RIVERSIDE, 74- *Personal Data:* b Boston, Mass, Mar 17, 41; m 86, Teresa A Maushake; c Aaron & Miles. *Educ:* Calif Inst Technol, BS, 62; Carnegie Inst Technol, MS, 64, PhD(math), 67. *Concurrent Pos:* Vis, Dept Math, Univ Calif, Los Angeles, 70-71, Univ Calif, Berkeley, 75-76, Univ Ill, Urbana, 78-79 & Univ Calif, Los Angeles, 92-93; consult, Mathematica, Inc, 74-75; consult, 75- *Mem:* Am Math Soc; Math Asn Am. *Res:* Functional analysis; vector measures; mathematical economics; game theory. *Mailing Add:* Univ Calif Riverside CA 92521. *E-Mail:* neg@math.ucr.edu

GREUB, LOUIS JOHN, AGRONOMY. *Current Pos:* assoc prof plant sci, 68-77, PROF AGRON, UNIV WIS-RIVER FALLS, 77- *Personal Data:* b Humbird, Wis, Feb 18, 33; m 65, Barbara Freie; c Cherie S Becca. *Educ:* Wis State Univ, River Falls, BS, 63; Iowa State Univ, MS, 66, PhD(crop prod, plant physiol), 68. *Prof Exp:* Res asst agron, Iowa State Univ, 63-66, assoc, 66-68. *Mem:* Am Soc Agron; Coun Agr Sci & Technol. *Res:* Crop physiology, especially forage physiology and management; leaf area, yield, carbohydrate reserves and photosynthesis of forage legumes; forage quality. *Mailing Add:* Dept Plant & Earth Sci Univ Wis River Falls WI 54022-5099

GREUER, RUDOLF E A, MINING ENGINEERING. *Current Pos:* PROF MINING ENG, MICH TECHNOL UNIV, 67-, CHMN DEPT, 79- *Personal Data:* b Guetzlaffshagen, Ger, Apr 6, 27; m 63; c 2. *Educ:* Clausthal Tech Univ, Dipl Ing, 53, Dr Ing, 55. *Prof Exp:* Res student mine ventilation, Univ Witwatersrand, 56; lectr mining eng, Tech Univ Istanbul, 57; res engr, Mining Res Estab, WGer, 57-67. *Concurrent Pos:* Mem subcomts fires in mineshafts & mine ventilation, Europ Community Coal & Steel, 60-67. *Mem:* Am Inst Mining, Metall & Petrol Engrs. *Res:* Thermodynamics of mine ventilation; computer simulation of ventilation systems. *Mailing Add:* Dept Mining Eng & Petrol Mich Technol Univ 1400 Townsend Dr Houghton MI 49931-1295

GREULICH, RICHARD CURTICE, ANATOMY, GERONTOLOGY. *Current Pos:* RETIRED. *Personal Data:* b Denver, Colo, Mar 22, 28; m 58; c 4. *Educ:* Stanford Univ, AB, 49; McGill Univ, PhD(anat), 53. *Honors & Awards:* Res Award, Int Asn Dent Res, 63; Super Serv Award, Dept Health, Educ & Welfare, 71. *Prof Exp:* From instr to prof anat, Sch Med, Univ Calif, Los Angeles, 53-66, from assoc prof to prof oral biol, Sch Dent, 61-66; sci dir intramural res, Nat Inst Dent Res, 66-74; staff dir, Pres Biomed Res Panel, Nat Inst Aging, NIH, 74-75, actg dir, 75-76, dir, Geront Res Ctr, 76-88. *Concurrent Pos:* Bank Am-Giannini Found fel, 55-57; USPHS spec fel, 62-63; res assoc, Karolinska Inst, Sweden, 55-57; vis investr, Univ London, 62 & McGill Univ, 63; consult, Nat Inst Dent Res, 64-66 & Procter & Gamble Co, 64-66. *Mem:* AAAS; Am Soc Cell Biol; Am Inst Biol Sci; Am Asn Anat; Geront Soc. *Res:* Physiology of growth, differentiation and aging; autoradiography; microradiography; histochemistry; physiology of mineralization. *Mailing Add:* 137 St Andrews Rd Severna Park MD 21146. *Fax:* 410-987-8576

GREVE, JOHN HENRY, VETERINARY PARASITOLOGY, VETERINARY PATHOLOGY. *Current Pos:* from asst prof to assoc prof, 63-68, PROF VET PARASITOL, IOWA STATE UNIV, 68- *Personal Data:* b Pittsburgh, Pa, Aug 11, 34; m 56, Sally Doane; c John Haven, Suzanne Carol & Pamela Jean. *Educ:* Mich State Univ, BS, 56, DVM, 58, MS, 59; Purdue Univ, PhD(vet parasitol), 63. *Prof Exp:* Res assoc vet path, Mich State Univ, 58-59; instr vet parasitol, Purdue Univ, 59-62. *Concurrent Pos:* Secy-treas, Ann Midwestern Conf Parasitologists, 67-75, pres, 75-76. *Mem:* Am Vet Med Asn; Am Asn Vet Parasitol (pres, 68-70); Am Soc Parasitol; World Asn Advan Vet Parasitol; Asn Am Vet Med Cols. *Res:* Pathological response and host-parasite relationships in arthropods and nematodes of veterinary medical importance. *Mailing Add:* 334 24th St Ames IA 50010. *Fax:* 515-294-5423

GREVILLE, THOMAS NALL EDEN, MATHEMATICS. *Current Pos:* RETIRED. *Personal Data:* b New York, NY, Dec 27, 10; m 34, 51, Florence Nusim; c Alice (Parra) & Edgar. *Educ:* Univ of the South, BA, 30; Univ Mich, AM, 32, PhD(math), 33. *Prof Exp:* Actuarial asst, Acacia Mutual Life Ins Co, DC, 33-37; instr math, Univ Mich, 37-40; actuarial mathematician, US Bur Census, 40-46; USPHS, 46-52; statist consult, Int Coop Admin, 52-54; asst chief actuary, US Social Security Admin, 54-58; dep chief mathematician, US Army Qm Corps, 58-60, chief mathematician, 60-61; vpres, S A Miller Co, DC, 61-62; prof, Math Res Ctr, Univ Wis-Madison, 63-81, prof, 64-81, emer prof, Sch Bus, 81. *Concurrent Pos:* Statist ed, J Parapsychol, 44-67; vis prof, Univ Mich, 62-63; ed, J Appl Math, Soc Indust Appl Math, 68-77 & J Math Anal, 77-81; actuarial adv, Nat Ctr Health Statist, 73-76. *Mem:* Fel Soc Actuaries; Am Math Soc; fel Am Statist Asn; Soc Sci Explor. *Res:* Matrices, approximation and interpolation; actuarial mathematics. *Mailing Add:* 2600 Barracks Rd Apt 249 Charlottesville VA 22901-2192

GREW, EDWARD STURGIS, HIGH-GRADE METAMORPHISM. *Current Pos:* res assoc prof, 84-93, RES PROF, UNIV MAINE, ORONO, 93- *Personal Data:* b Boston, Mass, May 29, 44; m 75, Priscilla C Perkins. *Educ:* Dartmouth Col, BA, 65; Harvard Univ, PhD(geol), 71. *Honors & Awards:* Bellingshausen Medal; US Antarctic Serv Medal. *Prof Exp:* Field asst geol, US Geol Surv, Denver, 65, Boston, 66, res assoc, Washington, DC, 71-72; proj assoc, Geophys & Polar Res Ctr, Univ Wis, 72-75; asst res geologist, Univ Calif, Los Angeles, 75-83; Humboldt fel, Ruhr-Univ Bochum, Fed Repub Ger, 83-84. *Concurrent Pos:* US exchange scientist, Soviet Antarctic Exped, Molodezhnaya Sta, 72-74; Fulbright scholar, Australia, 78; Indo-Am Fel Prog, 80-81; US exchange scientist, Japan Antarctic Res Exped, 87-88; mem, interacad exchange, USSR, 87 & 90; res scientist, Nat Inst Polar Res, Tokyo, 88-89. *Mem:* Geol Soc Am; Am Geophys Union; Mineral Soc Am; Sigma Xi; AAAS; Mineral Soc Gt Brit. *Res:* Petrology and mineralogy of granulite-facies rocks in Antarctica, US and Russia; petrologic significance of the light elements (lithium, beryllium, boron and fluorine) in rock-forming minerals; petrology of highly magnesian metamorphic rocks, so-called whiteschists. *Mailing Add:* Dept Geol Univ Maine Orono ME 04469

GREW, JOHN C, CELL BIOLOGY OF ORTHOPEDIC DISEASE, SKELETAL BIOLOGY. *Current Pos:* ASST PROF BIOL, ST FRANCIS COL, 91- *Personal Data:* b Methuen, Mass, Dec 29, 61. *Educ:* Univ Lowell, BS, 83, MS, 84; NY Univ, PhD(basic med sci), 91. *Res:* Investigation of the growth kinetics, mediator response, attachment properties and matrix production by marrow-derived bone cells in vitro. *Mailing Add:* 222 Edgewood Terr South Orange NJ 07079

GREW, PRISCILLA CROSWELL PERKINS, GEOLOGY, EARTH SCIENCES. *Current Pos:* VCHANCELLOR RES, UNIV NEBR, LINCOLN, 93-, PROF GEOL, 93-, PROF, CONSERV & SURV DIV, 93- *Personal Data:* b Glens Falls, NY, Oct 26, 40; m 75, Edward S. *Educ:* Bryn Mawr Col, BA, 62; Univ Calif, Berkeley, PhD(geol), 67. *Prof Exp:* Instr geol, Boston Col, 67-68, asst prof, 68-72; asst res geologist, Inst Geophys, Univ Calif, Los Angeles, 72-77; dir, Calif Dept Conserv, 77-81; comnr, Calif Pub Utilities Comn, 81-86; dir, Minn Geol Surv, 86-93. *Concurrent Pos:* Secy, Geosci Adv Panel, Los Alamos Sci Lab, Univ Calif, 72-75, vis staff mem, 72-77; mem, Comt Minority Partic Earth Sci & Mineral Eng, US Dept Interior, 72-75; exec secy & co-ed, Bull Lake Powell Res Proj, 72-77; vis asst prof geol, Univ Calif, Davis, 73-74; adj asst prof environ sci & eng, Univ Calif, Los Angeles, 75-76; chmn, Calif State Mining & Geol Bd, 76-77, Calif Geothermal Resources Task Force, 77 & Calif Resources Bd, 77-81; chmn, Calif Oil Shale Task Force, Geol Soc Am, 77, Comt Pub Policy, 81-84, counr, 87-90; mem, US Geol Surv Earthquake Studies Eval Panel, 79-83, Comt Eng, Nat Asn Regulatory Utility Comn, 81-82, Comt Mineral Resource Eval, Nat Res Coun, 81-82, Comt Gas, 82-86, Exec Comt, 84-86, Comt Energy Conserv, 83-84; trustee, Nat Parks & Conserv Asn; mem, Adv Coun, Gas Res Inst, 82-86, Bd Mineral & Energy Resources, Nat Res Coun, 82-88, Comt Adv, US Geol Surv, 82-86 & Subcomt Earthquake Res, 84-88, Comt Equal Opportunities Sci & Technol, NSF, 85-86 & US Nat Comt Geol, 85-93; chmn, Comt Pub Affairs, Am Geophys Union, 84-89; mem, Bd Earth Sci & Resources, Nat Res Coun, 88-90, Bd Global Chg, 91-; mem, Minn Minerals Coord Comt, 86-93; prof geol, Univ Minn, 86-93; mem, Res Coord Coun, Gas Res Inst, 86-, chmn, 96-; mem, Adv Comt, Sci & Technol Ctr, NSF, 87-90, 96; mem bd trustees, Am Sci Inst Found, 88-; mem, Fed Coun Continental Sci Drilling, 92-96; chair geog, AAAS, 95-96. *Mem:* Fel AAAS; fel Geol Soc Am; Am Geophys Union; fel Mineral Soc Am; fel Geol Asn Can. *Res:* Environmental geology; policy analysis for natural resource management; oil, gas, geothermal and coal resource development; geothermal and other alternative energy development; water resources management. *Mailing Add:* Univ Nebr VChancellor Res 302 Admin Bldg PO Box 880433 Lincoln NE 68588-0433

GREWAR, DAVID, medicine, pediatrics, for more information see previous edition

GREWE, ALFRED H, JR, ZOOLOGY, BOTANY. *Current Pos:* asst prof, 65-71, PROF BIOL, ST CLOUD STATE COL, 71- *Personal Data:* b St Cloud, Minn, Mar 21, 26. *Educ:* St Cloud State Col, BA, 50; Univ Minn, MA, 54; Univ SDak, PhD(zool), 66. *Prof Exp:* Mus scientist & teaching asst zool, Univ Minn, 51-56; instr biol, St Cloud State Col, 58-59; instr, Itasca Jr Col, 59-62. *Mem:* AAAS; Am Ornith Union; Sigma Xi. *Res:* Natural history of the bald eagle. *Mailing Add:* Dept Biol/Col Sci & Technol St Cloud State Univ 720 4th Ave S St Cloud MN 56301-4498. *Fax:* 320-255-4166

GREWE, JOHN MITCHELL, ORTHODONTICS, ANATOMY. *Current Pos:* STAFF ORTHODONTIST, JOHNS HOPKINS HOSP, 79- *Personal Data:* b Eau Claire, Wis, Feb 6, 38; m 59; c Sarah, Martha, George & Janet. *Educ:* Univ Minn, Minneapolis, BS, 60, DDS, 62, MSD, 64, PhD(anat), 66. *Prof Exp:* USPHS nonserv fel dent & anat, Univ Minn, 62-66, asst prof pediat & dent, acting chmn dept, Sch Dent & Med Sch, 66-67; asst prof orthod & anat, Cols Dent & Med, Univ Iowa, 67-69; assoc prof, Sch Dent, Univ Md, Baltimore, 69-75, chmn dept, 69-79, prof orthod, 75-84. *Concurrent Pos:* Consult, Univ Minn, 67, Fedn Dentaire Int, 73-, WHO, 75 & Nat Inst Dent Res, NIH, 75-; bd, Md Soc Orthod, 72-79, pres, 75-76; pres, Md Soc Dent Children, 73-74, bd dir, 75-; bd dirs, Mid Atlantic Soc Orthodontists, 88-93, pres, 93-94; mem, Coun Educ, Am Asn Orthodontist, 95- *Mem:* Fel Am Col Dentists; fel Int Col Dentists; Am Asn Orthod; Am Dent Asn; Am Soc Dent for Children. *Res:* Genetic and environmental influences on the growth of the craniofacial complex; dental development; malocclusion indices; bone development; orthogathic surgery. *Mailing Add:* 2601 Merrymans Mill Rd Phoenix MD 21131

GREY, ALAN HOPWOOD, HISTORICAL GEOGRAPHY. *Current Pos:* RETIRED. *Personal Data:* b Auckland, NZ, Oct 8, 32; US citizen; m 57, Patricia Barney; c Anthony & Eve. *Educ:* Brigham Young Univ, BA, 59; Univ Wis, MA, 60, PhD(geog), 63. *Prof Exp:* Asst prof geog & geol, Western Ill Univ, 63-64; from asst prof to prof geog, Brigham Young Univ, 64-97. *Concurrent Pos:* Vis lectr geog, Univ Canterbury, 71. *Mem:* NZ Geog Soc. *Res:* Climatology; historical geography of the Western United States; regional and historical geography of Australasia; book author. *Mailing Add:* Dept Geog Brigham Young Univ 690 SWKT Provo UT 84602

GREY, CLARE PHILOMENA, SOLID STATE CHEMISTRY, SOLID STATE NUCLEAR MAGNETIC RESONANCE. *Current Pos:* ASST PROF CHEM, STATE UNIV NY, STONY BROOK, 94- *Personal Data:* b Middlesbrough, UK, Mar 17, 65. *Educ:* Oxford Univ, BA, 87, DPhil(chem), 91. *Prof Exp:* Royal Soc postdoctoral fel, Univ Nijmegen, 91; vis scientist, DuPont, 92-93. *Concurrent Pos:* Prin investr, NSF, 95- *Mem:* Am Chem Soc. *Res:* Nuclear magnetic resonance and diffraction studies of zeolite hydrofluorocarbon binding and hydrofluorocarbon reactions; development of new nuclear magnetic resonance methods for studying acid and basic catalysts; disordered materials study of ionic motion and structure in fast-ion conductors and electrode materials. *Mailing Add:* Dept Chem State Univ NY Stony Brook NY 11794-3400. *Fax:* 516-632-5731; *E-Mail:* cgrey@ccmail.sunysb.edu

GREY, GOTHARD C, SCIENCE EDUCATION. *Current Pos:* ASST PROF PHYSICS, WESTMINSTER COL, SALT LAKE CITY, 89- *Personal Data:* b Sheridan, Wyo, Oct 9, 57; m 80, Susan Serna; c Christian H, Donald S & Benjamin S. *Educ:* Univ Utah, BS(math), BS(chem) & BS(physics), 80; Calif Inst Technol, MS, 82; Univ Wis-Madison, PhD(chem), 87. *Prof Exp:* Fac intern phys chem, Dept Chem, Univ Utah, 87-88; teacher chem, Alta High Sch, 88-89. *Mem:* Am Phys Soc; Am Chem Soc; Am Asn Physics Teachers; Nat Sci Teachers Asn. *Res:* Science education and curriculum development at all levels, kindergarten through undergraduate; new laboratory exercises; strong experimentally motivated curricula; coupled relaxation in nuclear magnetic resonance. *Mailing Add:* Westminster Col 1840 S 1300 E Salt Lake City UT 84105-3697. *E-Mail:* g_grey@whitewater.wcslc.edu

GREY, HOWARD M, EXPERIMENTAL BIOLOGY. *Current Pos:* VPRES RES & DEVELOP, CYTEL, LA JOLLA, 88- *Personal Data:* b New York, NY, Aug 16, 32. *Educ:* Univ Pa, BA, 53, NY Univ, MD, 57. *Honors & Awards:* William B Coley Award, Cancer Res Inst, 89. *Prof Exp:* Med intern, Johns Hopkins Hosp, Baltimore, 57-58; res fel, Dept Med & Path, Univ Pittsburgh, 58-61; Dept Exp Path, Scripps Clin & Res Found, La Jolla, 61-63; guest investr, Rockefeller Univ, New York, 63-64, asst prof, 64-65; assoc prof, Dept Exp Path, Scripps Clin & Res Found, 65-67, assoc mem, 67-70; from assoc prof to prof path, Med Ctr, Univ Colo, Denver, 70-88. *Concurrent Pos:* Mem, Dept Med, Nat Jewish Ctr Immunol & Respiratory Med, Denver, 70-88, actg dir, 77-78, head, Basic Immunol Div, 78-88; mem, Bd Sci Counr, NIH, 88-91. *Mem:* Am Soc Exp Path; Am Asn Immunologists; Am Soc Clin Invest. *Res:* Molecular and cellular mechanisms of antigen recognition by T cells; structure-function relationships of immunoglobulins; author of numerous scientific publications. *Mailing Add:* Res Dept La Jolla Inst Allergy & Immunol 11149 N Torrey Pines Rd La Jolla CA 92037. *Fax:* 619-558-3525

GREY, JAMES TRACY, JR, INORGANIC CHEMISTRY, RESEARCH MANAGEMENT. *Current Pos:* RETIRED. *Personal Data:* b Newstead Twp, NY, May 27, 14; m 41; c 3. *Educ:* Univ Buffalo, BA, 36, PhD(chem), 40. *Prof Exp:* Asst chem, Univ Buffalo, 36-39; res chemist, Durez Plastics & Chem, Inc, NY, 39-43; plastics res engr, Res Lab, Aeroplane Div, Curtiss-Wright Corp, 42-46; sr res chemist, Cornell Aeronaut Lab, Inc, 46-47, head, Chem & Fuels Sects, 47-57; sci adv to dir res & develop, Hqs, US Air Force, Wash, DC, 57-59; dir res planning staff, Rocket Div, Thiokol Chem Corp, 57-64, dir res opers, 64-65, asst to pres res & develop, 65-81, corp dir res & develop, 81-82. *Mem:* Am Chem Soc; Am Inst Aeronaut & Astronaut; Combustion Inst. *Res:* Resins and plastics; catalytic oxidation and reduction; chlorination of hydrocarbons; fundamentals of combustion; catalytic combustion; heat transfer at extreme conditions; fuels; magnetic susceptibility measurements. *Mailing Add:* Pennswood Village C-212 Newton PA 18940-2403

GREY, JERRY, AEROSPACE SCIENCE & ENGINEERING. *Current Pos:* adminr pub policy, 71-82, publ, Aerospace Am, 82-87, DIR, SCI & TECHNOL POLICY, AM INST AERONAUT & ASTRONAUT, 87- *Personal Data:* b New York, NY, Oct 25, 26; m 74, Florence Maier; c Leslie & Jacquelyn (deceased). *Educ:* Cornell Univ, BME, 47, MS, 49; Calif Inst Technol, PhD(aeronaut eng), 52. *Prof Exp:* Mem tech staff, Engine Div, Fairchild Engine & Airplane Corp, 49-50; hypersonic aerodynamicist, Calif Inst Technol, 50-52; res assoc aerospace eng, Princeton Univ, 52-56, from asst prof to assoc prof, 56-67; pres, Greyrad Corp, 67-71; pres, Calprobe Corp, 72-80, chmn, 80-83. *Concurrent Pos:* Sr engr, Marquardt Aircraft Co, 51-52; consult var univs, pvt industs & govt agencies; vpres publ, Am Inst Aeronaut & Astronaut, 66-71; chmn, Solar Adv Panel, Off Technol Assessment, US Cong, 74-79; adj prof, Long Island Univ, Southampton, 76-81; dir, Scientists Inst Pub Info, 77-89 & Appl Solar Energy Corp, 79-92; chmn coord comt energy, Asn Coop Eng, 78; dir, Am Astronaut Soc, 78-82; vis prof, Princeton Univ, 90- *Mem:* AAAS; Int Solar Energy Soc; Int Astron Fedn (vpres, 78-84, pres, 84-86); Int Acad Astronaut (vpres, 79-84); Am Astronaut Soc. *Res:* Aerospace propulsion systems; heat transfer; combustion, nuclear power generation, instrumentation; solar energy; conservation technology; plasma dynamics. *Mailing Add:* 881 Ocean Dr 22-A Key Biscayne FL 33149

GREY, MARGARET, NURSING. *Current Pos:* vis prof, 92-94, ASSOC DEAN RES & DOCTORAL STUDIES & INDEPENDENCE FOUND PROF NURSING, SCH NURSING, YALE UNIV, 94- *Personal Data:* b Easton, Pa, Sept 25, 49. *Educ:* Univ Pittsburgh, BSN, 70; Yale Univ, MSN, 76; Columbia Univ, DrPH(sociomed sci), 85. *Prof Exp:* Staff nurse, Infant Referral Ctr, Magee-Women's Hosp Pa, 70-72; staff nurse, Children's Clin Res Ctr, Yale New Haven Hosp, Conn, 72-74, nurse clinician pediat endocrinol, 76-78; clin instr, Columbia Univ, 76-78, instr, 78-80, assoc nursing, 80-84, asst prof clin nursing, 84; asst prof & coordnr, Young Family Track, Primary Care Family Nurse Clin Prog, Univ Pa, 85-88, asst prof & dir, Primary Care Div, 88-91, assoc prof & dir, Primary Care Grad Prog, 91-93. *Concurrent Pos:* Pediat nurse practr, Diabetes Serv, Presby Hosp, NY, 78-95, ABCs Diabetes Proj Yale Sch Nursing & Med, 96-; consult practr, Children's Aid Soc, 80-82. *Mem:* Fel Am Acad Nursing; distinguished fel Nat Asn Pediat Nurse Assocs & Nurse Practitioners; Am Diabetes Asn; Nat Inst Nursing Res; Am Asn Col Nursing. *Res:* Natural history of adaptation to chronic illness in childhood; intervention project designed to help adolescents implementing intensive insulin regimens to cope with such care. *Mailing Add:* Yale Sch Nursing 100 Church St S New Haven CT 06519

GREY, PETER, ANALYTICAL CHEMISTRY. *Current Pos:* Res chemist, Mobil Res & Develop Corp, 66-68, sr res chemist, 68-70, supvry chemist, Tech Serv Div, 70-81, res assoc, 81-89, SR RES ASSOC, MOBIL RES & DEVELOP CORP, PAULSBOROUGH, 89-, SR SUPV CHEMIST, ANALYTICAL CHEM, RES SERV DIV, 81- *Personal Data:* b Karachi, Pakistan, May 1, 38; m 61; c 3. *Educ:* McGill Univ, BS, 61, PhD(analytical chem), 67. *Concurrent Pos:* Adj prof, Temple Univ. *Mem:* Am Chem Soc; Am Soc Qual Control. *Res:* Chemistry of metal chelates in nonaqueous solvents; total quality management. *Mailing Add:* 15757 N 90th Pl Apt 2008 Scottsdale AZ 85260

GREY, ROBERT DEAN, CELL BIOLOGY, DEVELOPMENTAL BIOLOGY. *Current Pos:* from asst prof to assoc prof, Univ Calif, 67-78, from vchmn dept to chmn, 74-83, dean biol sci, 85-93, PROF ZOOL, UNIV CALIF, 78-, SCI, 85-, EXEC VCHANCELLOR, 93- *Personal Data:* b Liberal, Kans, Sept 5, 39; m 61; c 2. Kathleen Archer; c Erin K & Joel M. *Educ:* Phillips Univ, BA, 61; Wash Univ, St Louis, PhD(biol), 66. *Prof Exp:* Res asst, Washington Univ, St Louis, 65-66, asst prof biol, 66-67. *Mem:* AAAS; Am Soc Cell Biol; Am Soc Zool; Soc Develop Biol. *Res:* Fertilization; gamete interactuous; egg activation mechanisms. *Mailing Add:* Chancellor Off Univ Calif Davis CA 95616-8501. *Fax:* 530-752-2400; *E-Mail:* rdgrey@ucdavis.edu

GREY, ROGER ALLEN, ORGANOTRANSITION METAL CHEMISTRY. *Current Pos:* Sr res chemist, Oxirane Int, 80-81, sr res chemist, 81-84, res adv, 84-88, SR RES ADV, ARCO CHEM CO, 88- *Personal Data:* b Pittsburgh, Pa, Nov 12, 47; m 72; c 2. *Educ:* Grove City Col, BS, 69; Mich State Univ, PhD(chem), 73. *Prof Exp:* Teaching fel, Univ Calif, Los Angeles, 73-75; res chemist, Allied Chem Corp, 75-80. *Mem:* Am Chem Soc. *Res:* Synthesis, reactions and mechanistic studies of organometallic complexes; hydrogenation of organic compounds using homogeneous and heterogeneous catalysts; synthesis of surfactants for enhanced oil recovery; polymer synthesis; oxidation reactions. *Mailing Add:* 111 Piedmont Rd West Chester PA 19382-7257

GREYSON, JEROME, PHYSICAL CHEMISTRY, CLINICAL CHEMISTRY. *Current Pos:* OWNER, J & J G ASSOC, PROD DEVELOP CONSULT, 85- *Personal Data:* b New York, NY, Nov 7, 27; m 57; c 3. *Educ:* Hunter Col, AB, 50; Pa State Univ, PhD, 56. *Prof Exp:* Chemist, Sylvania Elec Corp, 51-53; mem tech staff, Bell Tel Labs, 56-57; staff chemist, Int Bus Mach Corp, NY, 57-62; group leader phys chem, Stauffer Chem Co, 62-64; res specialist, Atomics Int Div, NAm Aviation, Inc, 64-67, prin scientist, Rocketdyne Div, NAm Rockwell Corp, 67-70; sect head phys sci, Ames Res Lab, 70-76, dir, Blood Chem Res & Develop Lab, Ames Co Div, 76-81, dir res & develop, Lab Tech Div, Miles Labs, 81-82; tech dir, Precision Scientific, 82-85. *Mem:* Am Chem Soc. *Res:* Physical chemistry of surfaces and membranes, biosensors. *Mailing Add:* 10742 Timothys Rd Conifer CO 80433-8210

GREYSON, RICHARD IRVING, PLANT MORPHOLOGY. *Current Pos:* lectr, 64-65, from asst prof to prof, 65-92, EMER PROF PLANT SCI, UNIV WESTERN ONT, 92- *Personal Data:* b Nelson, BC, May 26, 32; m 56; c 5. *Educ:* Univ BC, BA, 54; Univ Ore, MS, 60, PhD(biol), 65. *Prof Exp:* Instr biol, Univ Notre Dame, BC, 55-58, 59-61. *Mem:* Am Bot Soc; Can Bot Asn. *Res:* Growth in intercalary meristems; initiation of floral primordia; plant organ culture; hormonal interaction between plant organs; description and analysis of plant organs of genetic strains of Lycopersicon, Zea and Nigella; experimental plant morphology; ears and tassels of zea. *Mailing Add:* 2475 York Ave Apt 209 Vancouver BC V6K 1C9 Can

GREYTAK, THOMAS JOHN, LIGHT SCATTERING, LOW TEMPERATURE PHYSICS. *Current Pos:* From instr to assoc prof, 67-77, PROF PHYSICS, MASS INST TECHNOL, 77-, HEAD DIV ATOMIC & CONDENSED MATTER PHYSICS, 88- *Personal Data:* b Annapolis, Md, Mar 24, 40; m 66, Elizabeth Bardeen; c Andrew & Matthew. *Educ:* Mass Inst Technol, BS & MS, 63, PhD(physics), 67. *Concurrent Pos:* Alfred P Sloan res fel, 71-73,. *Mem:* Fel Am Phys Soc. *Res:* Light scattering from thermal fluctuations in matter; low temperature physics; spin-polarized atomic hydrogen. *Mailing Add:* Dept Physics Mass Inst Technol Cambridge MA 02139

GREYWALL, DENNIS STANLEY, LOW TEMPERATURE PHYSICS. *Current Pos:* MEM STAFF LOW TEMPERATURE PHYSICS, BELL LABS, 71- *Personal Data:* b Detroit, Mich, Nov 16, 43; m 67, Doris A Iotis; c Rebecca, Sarah, Rachel & Gretchen. *Educ:* Univ Detroit, BS, 65; Ind Univ, MS, 67, PhD(physics), 70. *Honors & Awards:* Iritz London Mem Award, 93. *Mem:* Fel Am Phys Soc. *Res:* Properties of liquid and solid helium; physics of small mechanical systems. *Mailing Add:* ID 261 AT&T Bell Lab 600 Mountain Ave Murray Hill NJ 07974

GREYWALL, MAHESH S, FLUID MECHANICS. *Current Pos:* assoc prof, 69-81, PROF, DEPT MECH ENG, WICHITA STATE UNIV, 81- *Personal Data:* b Patiala, India, Oct 15, 34; US citizen; m 60; c 2. *Educ:* Univ Calif, Berkeley, BS, 57, MS, 59, PhD, 62. *Prof Exp:* Vis prof eng, Univ Wash, Seattle, 62-63; mem tech staff, Aerospace Corp, Calif, 63-65; theoret physicist, Lawrence Radiation Lab, Univ Calif, Livermore, 65-69. *Mem:* Am Soc Mech Engrs. *Res:* Fluid dynamics; computational methods; kinetic theory. *Mailing Add:* Dept Mech Eng Wichita State Univ Wichita KS 67208

GREZLAK, JOHN HENRY, ORGANIC CHEMISTRY, POLYMER CHEMISTRY. *Current Pos:* PROF CHEM, SHIPPENSBURG UNIV, 78- *Personal Data:* b Englewood, NJ, June 13, 45. *Educ:* Pa State Univ, BS, 67; Princeton Univ, MA, 72, PhD(chem), 74. *Prof Exp:* Res chemist, Rohm and Haas Co, 69-71 & 74-77; asst prof, Mansfield State Col, 77-78. *Concurrent Pos:* Asst instr, Princeton Univ, 67-68, asst res, 68-69, Am Can fel, 71-72 & 72-73; consult, A D Little, Inc, 73; instr, Pa State Univ, 74-75. *Mem:* Sigma Xi; Am Chem Soc; AAAS. *Res:* Polymer synthesis; organometallics; block and graft copolymers; application of macromolecules to organic synthesis and organic reaction mechanisms. *Mailing Add:* 403 Springfield Rd Shippensburg PA 17257

GRGURIC, GORDAN, SEAWATER AQUARIUM CHEMISTRY, OZONATION BY-PRODUCTS IN SEAWATER. *Current Pos:* ASST PROF MARINE SCI, RICHARD STOCKTON COL, 95- *Personal Data:* b Zagreb Croatia, Mar 22, 65. *Educ:* Lehigh Univ, BA(chem) & BA(comput sci), 88; Fla Inst Technol, MS, 90, PhD(oceanog), 93. *Prof Exp:* Postdoctoral fel, Fla Inst Technol, 93-94. *Mem:* Sigma Xi; Int Ozone Asn. *Res:* Seawater aquarium chemistry; major ion maintenance; ph/alkalinity; influence of ozone on chemical speciation; denitrification systems. *Mailing Add:* Richard Stockton Col Pomona NJ 08240

GRIBBLE, DAVID HAROLD, VETERINARY PATHOLOGY. *Current Pos:* Asst prof, 66-74, ASSOC PROF PATH, SCH VET MED, UNIV CALIF, DAVIS, 74- *Personal Data:* b Seattle, Wash, Dec 26, 32; m 55; c 4. *Educ:* Wash State Univ, DVM, 62; Univ Calif, Davis, PhD(comp path), 70. *Mem:* Am Vet Med Asn; Am Col Vet Path; Int Acad Path. *Res:* Infectious diseases; nervous system; endocrine and primate pathology. *Mailing Add:* 1563 Hwy 9 Mt Vernon WA 98274

GRIBBLE, GORDON W, ORGANIC CHEMISTRY. *Current Pos:* from asst prof to assoc prof, 68-80, chmn, 88-91, PROF ORG CHEM, DARTMOUTH COL, 80- *Personal Data:* b San Francisco, Calif, July 28, 41; c Julie & Jon. *Educ:* Univ Calif, Berkeley, BS, 63; Univ Ore, PhD(chem), 67. *Hon Degrees:* AM, Dartmouth Col, 81. *Honors & Awards:* Am Cyanamid Acad Achievement Award, 88. *Prof Exp:* Nat Cancer Inst fel org chem, Univ Calif, Los Angeles, 67-68. *Concurrent Pos:* Res Corp grant, 68; Petrol Res Fund grant, 68-70; Eli Lilly grant, 69-71; NSF grant, 69-71; NIH career develop award, 71-76; consult, Merck, Sharp & Dohme, 72-74; NSF fac develop award, 77-78, NIH grants, 73-89, Petrol Res Fund grant, 75-77, 83-86, 87-90 & 93-97; vis prof, Calif Inst Technol, 77-78, Hawaii, 91-92; assoc mem, Norris Cotton Cancer Ctr, 93-; sci adv, Am Coun Sci & Health, 94- *Mem:* Am Chem Soc; Chem Soc; Int Soc Heterocyclic Chem; Sigma Xi; Am Soc Pharmacog; Am Soc Enol & Viticulture. *Res:* Synthetic organic chemistry; indole alkaloids; nuclear magnetic resonance spectroscopy; reaction mechanisms; chemical carcinogenesis; anticancer drug synthesis; marine natural products; organochlorines; natural halogen compounds. *Mailing Add:* Dept Chem Dartmouth Col Hanover NH 03755-1894. *Fax:* 603-646-3946; *E-Mail:* grib@dartmouth.edu

GRIBOV, VLADIMIR N, PHYSICS. *Current Pos:* SR SCIENTIST, LANDAU INST THEORET PHYSICS, MOSCOW. *Honors & Awards:* JJ Sakvrai Prize, Am Phys Soc, 91. *Mailing Add:* Landau Inst Theoret Physics UL A N Kosyeina 2 Moscow 117940 V-234 Russia

GRIBOVAL, PAUL, electron optics; deceased, see previous edition for last biography

GRICE, GEORGE DANIEL, JR, MARINE FOOD CHAINS, ENVIRONMENTAL QUALITY. *Current Pos:* chief res planning & coord, 92-96, DEP DIR, NE FISHERIES SCI CTR, NAT MARINE FISHERIES SERV, WOODS HOLE, MASS, 96- *Personal Data:* b Charleston, SC, Oct 9, 29; div; c George D & Dorothy E. *Educ:* Clemson Col, BS, 50; Fla State Univ, MA, 53, PhD(biol oceanog), 57. *Prof Exp:* Fishery res biologist, US Fish & Wildlife Serv, 57-58; fel, Guggenheim Mem Found, 58-59; assoc scientist, Woods Hole Oceanog Inst, 59-73, chmn, Dept Biol, 74-81, sr scientist, 73-92, assoc dir sci opers, 81-92. *Mem:* Ecol Soc Am. *Res:* Food chain dynamics, experimental ecosystems; zooplankton ecology, particularly the taxonomy and zoogeography of marine calanoid copepods. *Mailing Add:* Nat Marine Fisheries Serv NE Fisheries Sci Ctr 166 Water St Woods Hole MA 02543-1097

GRIDER, JOHN RAYMOND, GASTROINTESTINAL PHYSIOLOGY, SMOOTH MUSCLE PHYSIOLOGY. *Current Pos:* NIH fel gastroenterol, 81-83, from instr to asst prof, 84-90, ASSOC PROF PHYSIOL, MED COL VA, 91- *Personal Data:* b Chester, Pa, Oct 12, 52; m 79, Linda S D'Andrea; c Amanda L. *Educ:* Univ Pa, BA, 73; Hahnemann Univ, PhD(physiol & biophysics), 81. *Prof Exp:* Res assoc gastroenterol, Philadelphia Gen Hosp, Univ Pa, 73-74; teaching fel physiol, Hahnemann Univ, 75-81. *Concurrent Pos:* NSF fel, Albert Einstein Med Ctr, Div Reprod Endocrine, Philadelphia, 69; microbiologist, Div Labs, Pa State Health Dept, 73; prin investr NIH grants, 83-; chmn, Abstract Selection Comt, Am Gastroenterol Asn, 87, 88, 93 & 94; Vet Admin Merit Rev Bd for Gastroenterol, 91-94. *Mem:* Am Physiol Soc; Am Gastroenterol Asn; Am Motility Soc; Gastroenterol Res Group; Soc for Neurosci. *Res:* Elucidating the regulation of contraction of gastrointestinal smooth muscle by neuropeptides of the myenteric plexus; studies have been conducted on the regulation of the release of neuropeptides, on the neural pathways which coordinate peristalsis and on the intracellular mechanisms responsible for smooth muscle contraction; enteric neurophysiology. *Mailing Add:* Box 980551 Va Commonwealth Univ Richmond VA 23298-0551

GRIEB, MERLAND WILLIAM, INORGANIC CHEMISTRY. *Current Pos:* RETIRED. *Personal Data:* b Carey, Idaho, Jan 26, 20. *Educ:* Univ Idaho, BS, 42, MS, 49; Univ Ill, PhD(chem), 53. *Prof Exp:* Instr chem, Univ Idaho, 48-49; asst, Univ Ill, 49-53; asst prof, Wayne State Univ, 53-56; from asst prof to assoc prof chem, Univ Idaho, 56-84. *Mem:* Am Chem Soc. *Mailing Add:* 1532 35th Ave S Seattle WA 98144-4005

GRIECO, MICHAEL H, INFECTIOUS DISEASES, ALLERGY. *Current Pos:* CHIEF, DIV ALLERGY CLIN IMMUNOL & INFECTIOUS DIS, ST LUKE'S ROOSEVELT HOSP CTR, 73-, DIR, DEPT MED, 91-; PROF CLIN MED, COLUMBIA UNIV, 84- *Personal Data:* b Aug 10, 32; m 19, Dorothea P Reggiero; c Michael, Angela & Susan. *Educ:* State Univ NY, MD, 59. *Mem:* Am Acad Allergy, Asthma & Immunol; Infectious Dis Soc Am; Am Soc Microbiol; Am Asn Immunol; Clin Immunol Soc Am; Soc Trop Med & Hyg. *Res:* Clinical trials program for treatment of HIV and opportunistic infections in HIV infected subjects. *Mailing Add:* Div Allergy Dept Clin Immunol St Lukes Roosevelt Hosp Ctr 1000 Tuth Ave New York NY 10019. *Fax:* 212-523-8605; *E-Mail:* 74563.167@compuserve.com

GRIECO, PAUL ANTHONY, SYNTHETIC ORGANIC CHEMISTRY. *Current Pos:* prof, 80-85, EARL BLOUGH PROF CHEM, IND UNIV, 85-, CHMN, DEPT CHEM, 88- *Personal Data:* b Framingham, Mass, Oct 27, 44; m 71; c 4. *Educ:* Boston Univ, BA, 66; Columbia Univ, MA, 67, PhD(org chem), 70. *Honors & Awards:* William P Timmie lectr, Emory Univ; Ernet Guenther Award Chem Essential Oils & Related Prod, 82. *Prof Exp:* NSF fel, Harvard Univ, 70-71; from asst prof to prof chem, Univ Pittsburgh, 71-80. *Concurrent Pos:* Fel, Alfred P Sloan, 74-76 & Japan Soc Prom Sci, 78-79; mem, Med Chem A Study Sect, NIH, 78-82, Rev Panel Nat Res Coun Associateship Prog, 87- *Mem:* Am Chem Soc; Royal Soc Chem; Chem Soc Japan; Swiss Chem Soc. *Res:* Development of new synthetic methods for construction of complex natural products. *Mailing Add:* Dept Chem AO53 Ind Univ 1410-3000 Bloomington IN 47405

GRIEGO, RICHARD JEROME, PROBABILITY. *Current Pos:* CHAIR, DEPT MATH, NORTHERN ARIZ UNIV, 92- *Personal Data:* b Albuquerque, NMex, June 11, 39; m 60, Genara Gallegos; c 2. *Educ:* Univ NMex, BS, 61; Univ Ill, PhD(math), 65. *Prof Exp:* Lectr math, Univ Calif, Riverside, 65-66; from asst prof to prof, Univ NMex, 66-85, coordr, Chicano Studies Prog, 70-71, dir, Minority Access Res Careers Prog, 75-85, chmn, math dept, 77-80, dir, Resource Ctr, Sci & Eng, 79-85, dean grad studies, 88-91, presidential prof math, 85-92. *Mem:* Am Math Soc. *Res:* Markov processes; potential theory; probability theory. *Mailing Add:* Dept Math Northern Ariz Univ Flagstaff AZ 86011-5717

GRIEM, HANS RUDOLF, PHYSICS. *Current Pos:* res asst prof plasma physics, 57-61, assoc prof, 61-63, PROF PHYSICS, UNIV MD, COLLEGE PARK, 63- *Personal Data:* b Kiel, Ger, Oct 7, 28; nat US; m 57; c 4. *Educ:* Univ Kiel, PhD(physics), 54. *Hon Degrees:* PhD, Ruhr Univ, 89. *Honors & Awards:* Meggers Award, Optical Soc Am, 87. *Prof Exp:* Asst upper atmospheric physics, Univ Md, 54-55; asst high temperature physics, Univ Kiel, 55-57. *Concurrent Pos:* Consult, US Naval Res Lab, 57-, Los Alamos Nat Lab, 76- & Lawrence Livermore Nat Lab, 76- *Mem:* Fel Am Phys Soc. *Res:* High temperature and plasma physics; spectroscopy; line broadening theory. *Mailing Add:* Lab Plasma Res Univ Md Col Park MD 20742

GRIEM, MELVIN LUTHER, RADIOLOGY, PHYSICS. *Current Pos:* from instr to prof, 57-96, EMER PROF RADIOL, SCH MED, UNIV CHICAGO, 96- *Personal Data:* b Milwaukee, Wis, May 22, 25; m 51; c 3. *Educ:* Univ Wis, BS, 48, MS, 50, MD, 53. *Prof Exp:* Dir, Chicago Tumor Inst, 66-82. *Concurrent Pos:* Am Cancer Soc clin fel, 58-60, career res develop award, 63-65; mem, Med Adv Bd, Nuclear Regulatory Comn, 80-; mem, Radiation Study Sect, HEW, 84-88. *Mem:* Am Asn Cancer Res; Am Roentgen Ray Soc; Am Soc Therapeut Radiol; Radiation Res Soc; Radiol Soc NAm. *Res:* Radiobiology; radiation therapy; radiologic physics; radioactive isotopes; micro vascular imaging of radiation and drug induced vascular injury; radiation carcinogenesis. *Mailing Add:* 44 Sunset Trail Ogden Dunes IN 46368

GRIEM, SYLVIA F, MEDICINE, DERMATOLOGY. *Current Pos:* RETIRED. *Personal Data:* b West Allis, Wis, Feb 24, 29; m 51, Melvin L; c Katherine, Robert & Melanie. *Educ:* Univ Wis, BS, 50, MD, 53. *Prof Exp:* Asst prof, Univ Chicago, 61-80, assoc prof med, 80-96. *Mem:* Am Acad Dermat. *Res:* Hypersensitivity to physical agents, especially cold; microangiography of skin; diagnosis and treatment of mycosis fungoides. *Mailing Add:* 44 Sunset Trail Ogden Dunes IN 46368

GRIEMAN, FREDERICK JOSEPH, LASER SPECTROSCOPY. *Current Pos:* PROF, CHEM DEPT, POMONA COL, 82-, ASSOC DEAN, 97- *Personal Data:* b Long Beach, Calif, May 19, 52; m 76, Janet Bloom; c Zachary & Mackenze. *Educ:* Univ Calif, Irvine, AB, 74, Berkeley, MS, 76, PhD(chem), 79. *Prof Exp:* Res fel, Phys Dept, Univ Ore, 79-81, res assoc, 81-82. *Concurrent Pos:* Vis scientist, Lab des Collinions Atomiques et Moleculaires, Univ Paris, 80-81 & Phys Chem Lab, Univ Oxford, 88-89; Chem Dept, Ariz State Univ, 95-96. *Mem:* Am Chem Soc. *Res:* Laser induced fluorescence and electron impact emission spectra of molecular radicals supersonically expanded in a nozzle; spectra of molecular ions by laser induced fluorescence of ions confined in a three dimensional ion trap. *Mailing Add:* Chem Dept Pomona Col Claremont CA 91711. *E-Mail:* fgrieman@pomona.edu

GRIENINGER, GERD, BIOCHEMISTRY. *Current Pos:* HEAD LAB PLASMA PROTEIN REGULATION, NY BLOOD CTR, 81- *Educ:* Univ Tubingen, Ger, PhD(biochem), 70. *Mailing Add:* L F Kimball Res Inst NY Blood Ctr 310 E 67th St New York NY 10021-6264. *Fax:* 212-737-4506

GRIER, CHARLES CROCKER, ECOLOGY, FOREST SOILS. *Current Pos:* PROF & HEAD, DEPT FOREST SCI, COLO STATE UNIV, 93- *Personal Data:* b Pasadena, Calif, Sept 1, 38; m 60; c 1. *Educ:* Univ Wash, BS, 68, PhD(forest soils), 72. *Honors & Awards:* Antarctic Serv Medal, NSF, 72. *Prof Exp:* Res assoc ecol, Sch Forestry, Ore State Univ, 72-76; res asst prof ecol, Col Forest Res, Univ Wash, 76-78, from assoc prof to prof, 78-85; prof, Sch Forestry, Northern Ariz Univ, 85-91; prof & head, Dept Forest Resources, Utah State Univ, 91-93. *Concurrent Pos:* Affil asst prof, Univ Idaho, 78-84; adj prof, Northern Ariz Univ, 91-93 & Utah State Univ, 94- *Mem:* Ecol Soc Am; Soil Sci Soc Am; Soc Am Foresters; Sigma Xi. *Res:* Productivity of wildland ecosystems as related to their physical environment, soils and mineral nutrition. *Mailing Add:* Dept Forest Sci Colo State Univ Ft Collins CO 80623

GRIER, HERBERT E, TECHNICAL MANAGEMENT. *Current Pos:* RETIRED. *Educ:* Mass Inst Technol, BS & MS, 34. *Hon Degrees:* DSc, Univ Nev, 67. *Honors & Awards:* Commendation of the President, 48; Presidential Cert Appreciation, 71; Nat Medal Sci, 89. *Prof Exp:* Pres, EG&G, 47-76; pres, CER Geonuclear Co, 65-83; pres & chmn bd, Reynolds Elec & Eng Co, Inc, 69-71; dir, Cer Corp, 83-94; consult, EG&G, 83-94. *Concurrent Pos:* Mem, Res Group Electronic Flash Photog, Night Aerial Reconnaissance, Mass Inst Technol; atomic weapons res, Manhattan Eng Dist & AEC; dir, CER Geonuclear Corp, AUX Corp; consult, Aerospace Safety Adv Panel, NASA; mem STS-1 Readiness Adv Team, 81, Shuttle Oper Strategic Planning Group, NASA, 84. *Mem:* Nat Acad Eng. *Res:* Stroboscopic and flash lighting techniques; ultra high speed photography; atomic weapons research; development and implementation of methods of using the power of nuclear explosives in commercial applications with primary emphasis on improving methods for the extraction of underground natural resources; numerous patents and publications. *Mailing Add:* 9648 Blackgold Rd La Jolla CA 92037

GRIER, JAMES WILLIAM, ZOOLOGY. *Current Pos:* Asst prof, 73-77, assoc prof, 77-83, PROF ZOOL, NDAK STATE UNIV, 83- *Personal Data:* b Waterloo, Iowa, Sept 15, 43; m 65; c 2. *Educ:* Univ Northern Iowa, BA, 65; Univ Wis-Madison, MS, 68; Cornell Univ, PhD(ecol, evolutionary biol), 75. *Mem:* AAAS; Wildlife Soc. *Res:* Ecology, population dynamics, reproduction and behavior of birds of prey, particularly bald and golden eagles, snakes, paleontology. *Mailing Add:* Dept Zool NDak State Univ Fargo ND 58105-5517. *Fax:* 701-237-8444; *E-Mail:* grier@vm1.nodak.edu

GRIER, NATHANIEL, MEDICINAL CHEMISTRY. *Current Pos:* RETIRED. *Personal Data:* b Brooklyn, NY, Mar 27, 18; m 41, Roslyn Levine; c Paul Carl, Eli & Dianne Esther. *Educ:* Long Island Univ, BS, 37; Univ Mich, MS, 38, PhD(chem), 43. *Prof Exp:* Res chemist, Dept Eng Res, Univ Mich, 40-41; sr res chemist, Hoffmann-La Roche, Inc, 42-46; chief res chemist, Dar-Syn Lab, Inc, 46-57; vpres & dir res, Metalsalts Corp, 57-66; sr investr, Merck Sharp & Dohme Res Lab Div, Merck & Co, Inc, Rahway, 66-80. *Mem:* Fel AAAS; Am Chem Soc; NY Acad Sci; Soc Indust Microbiol. *Res:* Isolation of antibiotics; synthetic organic chemistry; process development. *Mailing Add:* 153 Morse Pl Englewood NJ 07631

GRIER, RONALD LEE, VETERINARY SURGERY. *Current Pos:* asst prof, 70-72, ASSOC PROF VET CLIN SCI, IOWA STATE UNIV & CHMN, SMALL ANIMAL TEACHING HOSP, 72- *Personal Data:* b Cedar Rapids, Iowa, May 9, 41; m 66; c 2. *Educ:* Iowa State Univ, DVM, 65; Colo State Univ, PhD(surg), 70; Am Col Vet Surgeons, dipl, 72. *Prof Exp:* Chief exp surg, Res & Develop Lab & Vivarium, Madigan Gen Hosp, US Army, 65-67; NIH fel res, Colo State Univ, 67-70. *Mem:* Am Col Vet Surgeons; Am Asn Vet Clinicians; Am Vet Med Asn; Comp Gastroenterol Soc; Sigma Xi. *Res:* Study of comparative oncology and alimentary tract diseases in the canine. *Mailing Add:* RR 1 Ames IA 50010

GRIERSON, DONALD, CIVIL ENGINEERING. *Current Pos:* PROF CIVIL ENG, UNIV WATERLOO, ONT, 68- *Educ:* Univ Waterloo, PhD, 68. *Honors & Awards:* Dr E Whitman Wright Award, Can Soc Civil Eng, 95. *Mem:* Can Soc Civil Eng. *Res:* Strysy and Soda software; contributed numerous articles to professional journals. *Mailing Add:* Dept Civil Eng Univ Waterloo 200 University Ave W Waterloo ON N2L 3G1 Can

GRIES, DAVID, COMPUTER SCIENCE. *Current Pos:* from assoc prof to prof comput sci, 69-92, chmn dept, 82-87, WILLIAM L LEWIS PROF ENG, CORNELL UNIV, 92- *Personal Data:* b Flushing, NY, Apr 26, 39; m 61; c 2. *Educ:* Queens Col, NY, BS, 60; Univ Ill, Urbana, MS, 63; Munich Tech Univ, Dr rer nat(math), 66. *Honors & Awards:* Spec Interest Group Comput Sci Educ Award Outstanding Contributions Comput Sci Educ, Asn Comput Math, 91. *Prof Exp:* Mathematician, US Naval Weapons Lab, 60-62; res asst, Univ Ill, Urbana, 62-63; res asst math, Munich Tech Univ, 63-66; asst prof comput sci, Stanford Univ, 66-69, res assoc, Linear Acceierator, Ctr, 66-69. *Concurrent Pos:* Guggenheim fel, 83-84; chmn, Comput Res Bd, 87-; ed, Info Processing Lett, Acta Informatica & Springer Verlag. *Mem:* Fel Asn Comput Mach; fel AAAS. *Res:* Programming methodology, programming languages, compiler construction. *Mailing Add:* Dept Comput Sci Upson Hall Cornell Univ Ithaca NY 14853

GRIES, GEORGE ALEXANDER, PLANT PATHOLOGY, BOTANY. *Current Pos:* RETIRED. *Personal Data:* b Cambridge, Mass, May 2, 17; m 39, Mary L Carpenter; c James C & Judy L. *Educ:* Miami Univ, AB, 38; Kans State Univ, MS, 40; Univ Wis, PhD(plant physiol), 42. *Prof Exp:* Asst plant pathologist, Conn Agr Exp Sta, 42-45; assoc prof bot & assoc plant physiologist, Agr Exp Sta, Purdue Univ, 45-53, prof plant physiol & plant physiologist, 53-60; plant pathologist, prof plant path & head dept, Univ Ariz, 60-66, actg head dept bot, 63-65, prof biol sci & head dept & biologist, Agr Exp Sta, 66-68; dean, Col Arts & Sci, Okla State Univ, 68-80, prof biol, 80-82. *Concurrent Pos:* Res demonstr, Univ Col, Swansea, Wales, 57-58; mem, Comn Educ & Natural Resources, 62-68; mem exec comt & mem, Comn Undergrad Educ Biol Sci, 68-71; consult-evaluator, NCent Asn Cols & Sec Schs; consult, Coord Coun Higher Educ, State Calif, 69-71; mem, Gov Bd, Am Inst Biol Sci, 70-78; vol diagnostician, Univ Ariz Coop Ext, 85-96; consult, Ark Dept Higher Educ, 87. *Mem:* Am Inst Biol Sci (pres, 77); Am Phytopath Soc. *Res:* Physiology of parasitic fungi; soil-borne diseases; diagnostics. *Mailing Add:* 501 W Ocotillo Green Valley AZ 85614

GRIES, JOHN CHARLES, STRUCTURAL GEOLOGY. *Current Pos:* asst prof, 71-79, ASSOC PROF GEOL, WICHITA STATE UNIV, 80-, CHMN, 87- *Personal Data:* b Rapid City, SDak, May 17, 40; m 68; c 1. *Educ:* Univ Wyo, BS, 62; MS, 65; Univ Tex, Austin, PhD(geol), 70. *Prof Exp:* Instr geol, Univ Tex, Austin, 70-71. *Concurrent Pos:* Res assoc, Bur Econ Geol, Univ Tex, Austin, 71-72; mem seismicity task force, City of Wichita, Kans, 72-; consult, Tex, 78. *Mem:* Geol Soc Am; Am Asn Petrol Geologists; Sigma Xi; Am Inst Prof Geologists. *Res:* Structural relationship between the Rio Grande Rift in New Mexico, Colorado and the evaporite tectonic region of Northern Chihuahua, Mexico; stress distribution about southern Rocky Mountain foreland thrusting. *Mailing Add:* Dept Geol Wichita State Univ Wichita KS 67260-0027

GRIES, JOHN PAUL, GEOLOGY. *Current Pos:* assoc prof geol & mineral, SDak Sch Mines, 46-49, prof geol eng, 49-76, dean grad div, 64-76, dir grad studies, 50-76, EMER PROF GEOL ENG, SDAK SCH MINES & TECHNOL, 76-, GEOL CONSULT, 76- *Personal Data:* b Washington, DC, June 7, 11; m 33; c 2. *Educ:* Miami Univ, Ohio, AB, 32; Univ Chicago, MS, 33, PhD(geol, paleont), 35. *Hon Degrees:* Dr, SDak Sch Mines & Technol, 94. *Prof Exp:* Asst geologist, State Geol Surv, Ill, 35-36; from instr to assoc prof geol & mineral, SDak Sch Mines & Technol, 36-44; geologist, Magnolia Petrol Co, 44-46. *Mem:* Geol Soc Am; Paleont Soc; Am Asn Petrol Geol; Am Inst Mining, Metall & Petrol Eng; AAAS. *Res:* Stratigraphy of northern Great Plains and Rocky Mountain area as applied to development of coal, oil and ground water. *Mailing Add:* 238 St Charles St Rapid City SD 57701. *Fax:* 605-394-6703

GRIESBACH, ROBERT JAMES, PLANT TISSUE CULTURE, SOMATIC CELL GENETICS. *Current Pos:* RES GENETICIST GENETICS ENG, USDA, 81- *Personal Data:* b Chicago, Ill, June 21, 55; m 84, Pamela D Bateman; c Robert M & Jennifer L. *Educ:* De Paul Univ, BS, 77; Mich State Univ, PhD(genetics), 80. *Prof Exp:* Res assoc hort, Mich State Univ, 80-81. *Mem:* Am Genetics Asn; Am Soc Hort Sci; Plant Molecular Biol Asn. *Res:* Current techniques in somatic cell genetics to plant improvement. *Mailing Add:* Floral & Nursery Plant Res US Nat Arboretum USDA Agr Res Serv BARC-W Beltsville MD 20705

GRIESEMER, RICHARD ALLEN, veterinary pathology, for more information see previous edition

GRIESER, DANIEL R, OPTICAL PHYSICS. *Current Pos:* OPTICAL ENGR, COLUMBUS LABS, BATTELLE, 53- *Personal Data:* b Newark, Ohio, May 5, 26; m 69. *Educ:* Ohio State Univ, BS, 53. *Mem:* Nat Soc Prof Engrs; Soc Photo-Optical Instrumentation Engrs; Optical Soc Am. *Res:* Instrumentation for environmental extremes; optical meteorology; holography and coherent optical signal processing; spectroscopy of optical transitions; laser plasma diagnostics; on-line graphical analysis by microcomputer. *Mailing Add:* 4326 Kenny Rd Columbus OH 43220

GRIESHABER, CHARLES K, TOXICOLOGY, DRUG DEVELOPMENT. *Current Pos:* br chief, Drug Develop Br, 90, DIR, DIV RES & TESTING, CTR DRUG EVAL & RES, FOOD & DRUG ADMIN, 90- *Personal Data:* b Erie, Pa, Dec 1, 41. *Educ:* Gannon Univ, BA, 64; Pa State Univ, MS, 66, PhD(physiol), 69. *Honors & Awards:* Tagnon lectr, 87. *Prof Exp:* Chief, Toxicol Br, Develop Therapeut Prog, Nat Cancer Inst, NIH, 83-90. *Mem:* Am Asn Cancer Res; AAAS; Am Asn Clin Chem; Sigma Xi. *Mailing Add:* Food & Drug Admin Ctr Drug Eval & Res 5600 Fishers Lane HFD 900 Rm 13BO6 Rockville MD 20857

GRIESHAMMER, LAWRENCE LOUIS, ANALYTICAL CHEMISTRY, PHYSICAL CHEMISTRY. *Current Pos:* RETIRED. *Personal Data:* b Jefferson City, Mo, Aug 28, 22; m 45, Mary L Meador; c Mary Lynn (Morek), Brian K Struhammer, David L, Jane E (Terry), Charles R, Patrick N & Sue A (Harrington). *Educ:* Univ Calif, Los Angeles, BS, 49; Univ Mo, MA, 51. *Prof Exp:* Asst, Univ Mo, 49-51; anal res chemist, Lubrizol Corp, 51-53, res supvr, Spectros Lab, 53-61, sect leader, 61-70, supvr, Anal & Instrumental Labs, 70-84. *Mem:* Am Chem Soc; Soc Appl Spectros; Am Soc Testing & Mat. *Res:* Emission spectroscopy; ultraviolet and infrared absorption spectroscopy; instrumental methods of analysis and analytical organic chemistry, particularly on lubricating oil additives. *Mailing Add:* 1982 Idlehurst Dr Euclid OH 44117-1852

GRIESINGER, DAVID HADLEY, AUDIO ENGINEERING, NUCLEAR PHYSICS. *Current Pos:* REC ENGR MUSIC, DAVID GREISINGER REC, 66- *Personal Data:* b Cleveland, Ohio, Mar 22, 44; m 69; c 1. *Educ:* Harvard Univ, BA, 66, MA, 69, PhD(physics), 76. *Honors & Awards:* Silver Medal, Audio Eng Soc. *Prof Exp:* Gov, Audio Eng Soc. *Concurrent Pos:* Musician, Boston Comerota Inc, 75-80; design consult, Lexicon Inc, Waltham, 77-; instr, Elec Dept Physics, Harvard Univ, 79-81. *Mem:* Fel Audio Eng Soc; Acoust Soc Am. *Res:* Sound recording; microphone design, acoustics, electronics and music; digital electronics; high speed digital audio equipment and microprocessors; Mossbauer effect; nuclear magnetic resonance; concert hall acoustics; surround sound. *Mailing Add:* 23 Bellevue Ave Cambridge MA 02140

GRIESMER, JAMES HUGO, EXPERT SYSTEMS. *Current Pos:* RETIRED. *Personal Data:* b Cleveland, Ohio, Dec 18, 29; m 56, 84; c 4. *Educ:* Univ Notre Dame, BS, 51; Princeton Univ, PhD(math), 58. *Prof Exp:* Asst math, Princeton Univ, 54-57; assoc mathematician, IBM Corp, 57-58, staff mathematician, 58-60, res staff mem, 60-65, mgr, Res Comput Ctr, 64-65, mgr symbol manipulation proj, 65-76, mgr educ & develop, 76-81, res staff mem, T J Watson Res Ctr, 81-92. *Concurrent Pos:* Vis Mackay lectr, Univ Calif, Berkeley, 70-71; adj prof, Polytech Univ, 87-88. *Mem:* Asn Comput Mach; Am Asn Artificial Intel; Math Asn Am; Inst Elec & Electronics Engrs. *Res:* Expert systems. *Mailing Add:* 308 Inman Dr Decatur GA 30030

GRIESS, JOHN CHRISTIAN, JR, CORROSION, ELECTROCHEMISTRY. *Current Pos:* RETIRED. *Personal Data:* b Mt Vernon, Ind, July 13, 22; m 47; c 7. *Educ:* Ind Univ, BS, 43, AM, 47. *Honors & Awards:* Young Authors Award, Electrochem Soc, 50. *Prof Exp:* res assoc corrosion, Oak Ridge Nat lab, Union Carbide Corp, 47-84; res assoc corrosion, Martin Marietta Corp, 84-86. *Mem:* Nat Asn Corrosion Engrs; Sigma Xi. *Res:* Corrosion phenomena in nuclear reactor and associated technologies. *Mailing Add:* 10803 Fox Park Rd Knoxville TN 37931

GRIESS, ROBERT LOUIS, JR, ALGEBRA. *Current Pos:* from asst prof to assoc prof, 75-81, PROF MATH, UNIV MICH, ANN ARBOR, 81- *Personal Data:* b Savannah, Ga, Oct 10, 45. *Educ:* Univ Chicago, BS, 67, MS, 68, PhD(math), 71. *Prof Exp:* Hildebrandt res instr math, Univ Mich, 71-73, asst prof, 73-74; vis instr math, Rutgers Univ, 74-75. *Concurrent Pos:* Vis prof, Yale Univ, 83-84; CNRS prof, Ecole Normale Superieure, Paris, 86-87. *Mem:* Am Math Soc. *Res:* Classification of finite simple groups; properties of finite simple groups; group extensions and cohomology; lie algebras. *Mailing Add:* Dept Math Univ Mich Ann Arbor MI 48109-1003

GRIEST, KIM, PHYSICS. *Current Pos:* asst prof, 92-94, ASSOC PROF, UNIV CALIF, SAN DIEGO, 94- *Personal Data:* b Mar 7, 55; c 2. *Educ:* Univ Calif, Irvine, BA, 76; Univ Calif, Santa Cruz, MS, 84, PhD(physics), 87. *Honors & Awards:* R&D 100 Award, 93; Outstanding Jr Investr Award, Dept Energy, 93. *Prof Exp:* Process engr, Fairchild Semiconductors, Mountain View, Calif, 77-78; team leader & programmer, Stand Tel & Cables, London, Eng, 79-81; sr software engr, Avera Corp, Scotts Valley, Calif, 81-82; teaching asst & res asst, Univ Calif, Santa Cruz, 83-87; postdoctoral fel, Univ Chicago, 87-89; postdoctoral fel, Univ Calif Berkeley, 89-92, instr physics, 91. *Concurrent Pos:* Alfred P Sloan fel, 94; Cottrell scholar, 95. *Mem:* Am Phys Soc; Am Astron Soc. *Res:* Dark matter; theoretical astrophysics; particle astrophysics. *Mailing Add:* Physics Dept Univ Calif San Diego La Jolla CA 92093-0319

GRIEVE, CATHERINE MACY, PLANT PHYSIOLOGY. *Current Pos:* PLANT PHYSIOLOGIST, US SALINITY LAB, RIVERSIDE, CALIF, 79- *Personal Data:* b Watertown, NY, Nov 24, 26; m 61; c 2. *Educ:* St Lawrence Univ, BS, 48; Univ Calif, Riverside, PhD(bot), 78. *Prof Exp:* Res librn, Mathieson Chem Corp, Niagara Falls, NY, 48-51; res chemist, US Naval Ordnance Lab, Corona, Calif, 54-71. *Mem:* Sigma Xi. *Res:* Biosystematics of Aurantioideae (rutacae); effects of salinity on plant metabolism; synthesis of substituted phosphonitriles; polymerization kinetics of phosphonitriles. *Mailing Add:* US Salinity Labs 450 W Big Springs Rd Riverside CA 92507

GRIEVE, RICHARD ANDREW, METEORITE IMPACT, CRUSTAL EVOLUTION. *Current Pos:* RES SCIENTIST V GEOPHYS, GEOL SURV, ENERGY MINES & NATURAL RESOURCES, CAN, 90- *Personal Data:* b Aberdeen, Scotland, Sept 15, 43. *Educ:* Univ Aberdeen, Scotland, BSc, 65; Univ Toronto, MSc, 67, PhD(geol), 70. *Hon Degrees:* MA, Brown Univ, 83; DSc, Univ Aberdeen, 85. *Honors & Awards:* Barringer Medal, Meteoritical Soc, 90. *Prof Exp:* From res scientist I to res scientist IV geophys, Earth Physics, Energy, Mines & Resources, Can, 74-84; assoc prof geol, Brown Univ, 82-84. *Concurrent Pos:* Vis prof, Brown Univ, 80-81 & Univ Munster 93-94; secy, Adv Comt Comp Planetology, Int Union Geol Sci, 80-84, Comn Comp Planetology, 84-92; assoc ed, Proc Conf Multi Ring Basins & Proc 12th Lunar & Planetary Sci Conf, 81, Meteoritics, 88-; assoc ed, J Geophys Res, 82-84; vchmn, Comt Comp Planetology, Int Union Geol Sci, 92- *Mem:* Geol Asn Can; Can Geophys Union; Am Geophys Union; fel Meteoritical Soc; Sigma Xi; AAAS; fel Royal Soc Can. *Res:* Impact phenomena and their relation to crustal evolution and the terrestrial biosphere; early crustal evolution of the terrestrial planets; use of large spatial geophysical data bases for the interpretation of crustal structure. *Mailing Add:* Continental Geophys Div Geol Surv Can One Observ Crescent Ottawa ON K1A 0Y3 Can. *Fax:* 613-952-8987; *E-Mail:* impacr@gsc.ca

GRIEVE, ROBERT B, IMMUNOPARASITOLOGY. *Current Pos:* VPRES RES & DEVELOP & VCHMN, PARAVAX INC, 92- *Personal Data:* b Torrington, Wyo, Oct 27, 51; m 82, Marcia Mika; c Jonahton R, Megan M & Madeline R. *Educ:* Univ Wyo, BS, 73, MS, 75; Univ Fla, PhD(parasitol), 78. *Honors & Awards:* Henry Baldwin Ward Medal, Am Soc Parasitologists. *Prof Exp:* Res immunoparasitol, Cornell Univ, 78-79, res assoc, 79-81; asst prof parasitol, Univ Pa, 81-84; assoc prof, Univ Wis, 84-87; assoc prof parasitol, Colo State Univ, 87-90, prof parasitol, 90-94. *Concurrent Pos:* Assoc investr, USAF, 79-84; adv, WHO, 84; consult, NIH, 85 & 93; head, Lab Parasitol, Univ Pa, 82-84; reviewer, Competitive Grants Prog, USDA, 85 & Spec Constraints Grants Prog, AID-CSRS, 88; mem coun, Am Soc Parasitologists, 89-92; bd sci reviewers, Am J Vet Res, 88-90; pres, Rocky Mountain Conf Parasitologists, 92-93. *Mem:* AAAS; Am Asn Immunologists; Am Asn Vet Parasitologists; Am Soc Parasitologists; Am Soc Trop Med & Hyg; Conf Res Workers Animal Dis. *Res:* The immunology and biology of host and parasite interactions in the course of parasitic nematode infections. *Mailing Add:* Heska Corp 1825 Sharp Point Dr Ft Collins CO 80525. *Fax:* 970-493-7333

GRIEVES, ROBERT BELANGER, CHEMICAL ENGINEERING, SANITARY ENGINEERING. *Current Pos:* RETIRED. *Personal Data:* b Evanston, Ill, Oct 15, 35; m 66; c 2. *Educ:* Northwestern Univ, BA, 56, MS, 59, PhD(chem eng), 62. *Prof Exp:* Asst prof civil eng, Northwestern Univ, 61-63; from asst prof to assoc prof environ eng, Ill Inst Technol, 63-67; chmn dept,Univ Ky, 67-69, prof chem eng, 67-93, dir, Ky Water Resources Res Inst, 74-93, assoc dean admin & grad prog & res, Col Eng, 76-93. *Concurrent Pos:* Dean eng, Univ Tex, El Paso. *Mem:* Am Inst Chem Engrs; Water Pollution Control Fedn. *Res:* Critical point of multicomponent hydrocarbon mixtures; foam fractionation for industrial water and waste treatment; biological waste treatment; chemical separations; membrane processes. *Mailing Add:* Univ Tex El Paso TX 79968-0001

GRIFFEL, MAURICE, PHYSICAL CHEMISTRY. *Current Pos:* CONSULT, 73- *Personal Data:* b Brooklyn, NY, Mar 10, 19; m 64, Margaret Dealy. *Educ:* City Col New York, BS, 39; Univ Mich, MS, 40; Univ Chicago, PhD(chem), 49; Yale Univ, MPH, 75. *Prof Exp:* Asst prof chem, Iowa State Col, 49-55; adv chemist, Westinghouse Elec Corp, 55-57; vis scientist, Saclay Nuclear Res Ctr, France, 57-58; prof chem, US Naval Postgrad Sch, 59-62; mem staff, Inst Defense Analysis, 62-65; vis res assoc chem, Univ Pa, 65-67; dir div prof educ, NY State Educ Dept, 67-71; dean instr, Piedmont Va Community Col, 72-73. *Concurrent Pos:* Consult, Nat Bur Stand, 51 & Lawrence Radiation Lab, Univ Calif, Berkeley, 59-75. *Mem:* AAAS; Am Chem Soc; Am Phys Soc. *Res:* Thermodynamics; biochemistry; kinetics of fast reactions; epidemiology; occupational health. *Mailing Add:* 10 Sage Hill Lane Albany NY 12204

GRIFFEN, DANA THOMAS, CRYSTAL CHEMISTRY. *Current Pos:* res assoc geol, 75-77, from asst prof assoc prof, 79-88, PROF GEOL, BRIGHAM YOUNG UNIV, 88-, CHAIR DEPT, 90- *Personal Data:* b Washington, DC, Sept 29, 43; m 67; c 5. *Educ:* US Naval Acad, BS, 65; Va Polytech Inst & State Univ, MS, 73, PhD(mineral), 75. *Prof Exp:* Res geologist, Phillips Petrol Co, 77-79. *Concurrent Pos:* Assoc ed, Am Mineralogist, 86- *Mem:* Mineral Soc Am; Am Crystallog Asn; Sigma Xi. *Res:* Crystallography and crystal chemistry of silicate minerals. *Mailing Add:* Dept Geol Brigham Young Univ 258 Esc Provo UT 84602-1022

GRIFFEN, WARD O, JR, SURGERY. *Current Pos:* assoc prof surg, physiol & biophys, 65-66, chmn dept, 67-87, PROF SURG, SCH MED, UNIV KY, 67- *Personal Data:* b New Orleans, La, July 21, 28; m 52; c 7. *Educ:* Princeton Univ, AB, 48; Cornell Univ, MD, 53; Univ Minn, PhD(surg), 63. *Prof Exp:* From instr to asst prof surg, Med Col, Univ Minn, Minneapolis, 62-65. *Concurrent Pos:* USPHS fel, 61-63; Markle scholar acad med, 62-67. *Mem:* Soc Exp Biol & Med; Sigma Xi. *Res:* Gastrointestinal and hepatic physiology and surgery. *Mailing Add:* Dept Surg Sch Med Univ Ky 800 Rose St Lexington KY 40536

GRIFFENHAGEN, GEORGE BERNARD, PHARMACY. *Current Pos:* consult cur & archivist, Am Pharmaceut Asn, 53-59, managing ed, J, 59-62, dir div commun, 59-69, ed, J, 62-76, exec dir commun, 69-86, dir int affairs, 86-89, CONSULT, AM PHARMACEUT ASN, 90- *Personal Data:* b Portland, Ore, June 9, 24; m 46; c 3. *Educ:* Univ Southern Calif, BS, 49, MS, 50. *Honors & Awards:* Squibb Pan-Am Pharmaceut & Biochem Award, 63; Am Red Cross Meritorious Serv Citation, 64; Edward Kremers Award, 69; Nat Coord Coun on Drug Educ Award, 70; Distinguished Serv Award, Am Wholesalers Asn, 71; Hugo H Schaefer Award, 84; Distinguished Serv Award, Pharm Guild of Australia, 88; Remington Honor Medal, 91. *Prof Exp:* Dir pharmaceut res & asst gen mgr, Nion Corp, Calif, 50-52; cur div med sci, US Nat Mus, Smithsonian Inst, 52-59. *Concurrent Pos:* Lectr, Univ Southern Calif, 50-52; del, Int Pharmaceut Fedn, London Assembly, 55, Brussels Assembly, 58, Copenhagen Assembly, 60, Vienna Assembly, 62, Amsterdam Assembly, 64, Hamburg Assembly, 68, Geneva Assembly, 70, Lisbon Assembly, 72, Rome Assembly, 74, Warsaw Assembly, 76, The Hague, 77,

Montreal, 85, Helsinki, 86, Amsterdam, 87, Sydney, 88, Munich, 89, Istanbul, 90; secy gen, Pan-Am Cong Pharm & Biochem, Washington, DC, 57, vpres, Pan-Am Pharm Fedn, 63-; proj adminr, USPHS, secy organizing comn, Int Cong Pharmaceut Sci, Washington, DC, 71, secy gen, Int Cong Hist Pharmaceut, 83, secy gen, Japan-US Cong Pharmaceut Sci, Honolulu, HI, 87, secy, Pharm World Cong, Washington, DC, 91. *Mem:* Am Inst Hist Pharm (pres, 60-61); hon mem, Mex, Arg & Gt Brit Pharmaceut Asn; Int Hist Pharm (treas, 70-81, pres 71-); Int Acad Hist Pharm (treas, 70-81). *Res:* History of pharmacy and medical science; pharmaceutical journalism; pharmaceutical philately. *Mailing Add:* 2501 Drexel St Vienna VA 22180

GRIFFIN, ALLAN, CONDENSED MATTER PHYSICS. *Current Pos:* from asst prof to assoc prof theoret physics, 67-76, PROF PHYSICS, UNIV TORONTO, 76- *Personal Data:* b Vancouver, BC, Feb 10, 39; m 78, Christine Johnston. *Educ:* Univ BC, BSc, 60, MSc, 61; Cornell Univ, PhD(theoret physics), 65. *Prof Exp:* Fel, Dept Physics, Univ Calif, San Diego, La Jolla, 65-67. *Mem:* Am Phys Soc; Can Asn Physicists. *Res:* Many-body problems in condensed matter physics; superfluid 4 helium; high temperature superconductivity; bose condensation in trapped atomic gases. *Mailing Add:* Dept Physics Univ Toronto Toronto ON M5S 1A7 Can. *Fax:* 416-978-2537; *E-Mail:* griffin@physics.utoronto.ca

GRIFFIN, ANSELM CLYDE, III, PHYSICAL ORGANIC CHEMISTRY. *Current Pos:* from asst prof to assoc prof, 75-83, PROF CHEM & POLYSCI, UNIV SOUTHERN MISS, 83- *Personal Data:* b Greenville, Miss, Dec 19, 46; m 69; c 3. *Educ:* Miss Col, BS, 69; Univ Tex, Austin, PhD(chem), 75. *Mem:* Am Chem Soc; North Am Thermal Anal Soc; Royal Soc Chem. *Res:* Structure-property relationships in liquid crystals; solid state chemistry; liquid crystalline polymers; synthetic polymer chemistry. *Mailing Add:* Chem Dept Univ SMiss Box 5043 Southern Sta Hattiesburg MS 39406

GRIFFIN, CHARLES CAMPBELL, BIOCHEMISTRY. *Current Pos:* asst prof biochem, 68-74, actg chmn dept chem, 84-86, ASSOC PROF BIOCHEM, MIAMI UNIV, 74- *Personal Data:* b Philadelphia, Pa, July 23, 38; m 60; c 2. *Educ:* Cath Univ, AB, 60; Johns Hopkins Univ, PhD(biochem), 69. *Prof Exp:* Res assoc biochem, Armed Forces Inst Path, 60-64. *Mem:* Am Soc Biochem & Molecular Biol; Am Chem Soc. *Res:* Mechanisms of enzyme action; membrane transport; heparin derivatives. *Mailing Add:* Hughes Labs Miami Univ Oxford OH 45056

GRIFFIN, CHARLES FRANK, PHYSICS. *Current Pos:* from asst prof to assoc prof, 67-76, PROF PHYSICS, UNIV AKRON, 76- *Personal Data:* b Slaton, Tex, Nov 2, 35; m 58; c 3. *Educ:* Tex Tech Col, BS, 59, MS, 61; Ohio State Univ, PhD(physics), 64. *Prof Exp:* Asst physics, Tex Tech Col, 59-61 & Ohio State Univ, 61-64; assoc prof, Sam Houston State Col, 64-67. *Mem:* Am Phys Soc; Am Asn Physics Teachers. *Res:* Nuclear magnetic resonance; computer aided instruction. *Mailing Add:* Dept Physics Univ Akron Akron OH 44325-4001

GRIFFIN, CLAIBOURNE EUGENE, JR, ORGANIC CHEMISTRY. *Current Pos:* RETIRED. *Personal Data:* b Rocky Mount, NC, Oct 15, 29; m 72; c 2. *Educ:* Princeton Univ, BA, 51; Univ Va, MS, 53, PhD(chem), 55. *Prof Exp:* Instr chem, Univ Va, 53-55, res assoc biochem, Sch Med, 55; USPHS res fel chem, Cambridge Univ, 55-57; from instr to prof, Univ Pittsburgh, 57-69; prof & chmn dept, Univ Toledo, 69-74; dean grad studies & res, Univ Akron, 74-77, prof chem, 74-, dean, Col Arts & Sci, 77- *Concurrent Pos:* Consult, Stauffer Chem Co, 62-82; adj prof chem, Bowling Green State Univ, 73-74. *Res:* Synthesis and reactions of organophosphorus compounds; nuclear magnetic resonance spectroscopy. *Mailing Add:* 4169 Tomahawk Trace Akron OH 44321

GRIFFIN, CLAUDE LANE, pharmacology; deceased, see previous edition for last biography

GRIFFIN, CLAYTON HOUSTOUN, TRANSMISSION & DISTRIBUTION SYSTEMS. *Current Pos:* RETIRED. *Personal Data:* b Atlanta, Ga, June 14, 25; m 53, Lela Lofgren; c George Duncan, Bryan G & Phillips Lounsbery G. *Educ:* Ga Inst Technol, BEE, 45, MS, 50. *Honors & Awards:* Charles Proteus Steinmetz Award, Inst Elec & Electronics Engrs, 94. *Prof Exp:* Elec officer, USN, 51-53; tester, Ga Power Co, 49-51, test engr, 53-62, protection engr, 62-67, chief protection engr, 67-79, mgr, Syst Protection & Control Dept, 79-89; consult, elec engr, 89-95. *Concurrent Pos:* Mem, Comn Protective Relays & High Voltage Fuses, Am Nat Stand Inst, 73-88; vis prof, Sch Elec Eng, GA Inst Technol, 75-89; chmn, Stand Comn Dispersed Generation, Inst Elec & Electronics Engrs, 82-88, Power Systs Relaying Comn, 87-88. *Mem:* Fel Inst Elec & Electronics Engrs. *Res:* High impedance faults on distribution systems; ground fault protection of AC turbine generators; interface protection of cogeneration installations; coordination of transmission line directional ground relays. *Mailing Add:* 221 S Chace Atlanta GA 30328

GRIFFIN, DANA GOVE, III, BRYOLOGY. *Current Pos:* from asst prof to assoc prof, 67-79, PROF BOT, UNIV FLA, 79- *Personal Data:* b Fort Worth, Tex, Nov 9, 38; m 64. *Educ:* Tex Tech Col, BS, 61, MS, 62; Univ Tenn, PhD(bot), 65. *Prof Exp:* Res asst bot, Tex Tech Col, 60-62; from instr to asst prof, Univ Tenn, 65-67. *Concurrent Pos:* Fulbright lectr, Peru, 65-66; invited lectr, Inst Nat de Pesquisas da Amazonia, Manaus, Brazil, 74. *Mem:* Bot Soc Am; Am Soc Plant Taxon; Int Asn Plant Taxon; Brit Bryol Soc; Nordic Bryol Soc; Sigma Xi. *Res:* Taxonomy and ecology of the lower plants; taxonomy of bryophytes, especially of tropical mosses; migration of floras, plant geography. *Mailing Add:* Dept Bot Univ Fla 220 Bartram Hall Gainesville FL 32611-2009

GRIFFIN, DAVID H, MYCOLOGY, FUNGAL PHYSIOLOGY. *Current Pos:* from asst prof to assoc prof, 68-80, PROF, COL ENVIRON SCI & FORESTRY, STATE UNIV NY, 80- *Personal Data:* b Buffalo, NY, Mar 13, 37; m 60, Barbara Nelson; c 3. *Educ:* State Univ NY, BS, 59; Univ Calif, Berkeley, MA, 60, PhD(bot), 63. *Prof Exp:* Res fel biol, Calif Inst Technol, 63-64; asst prof bot, Univ Iowa, 64-68. *Concurrent Pos:* Air Force Off Sci Res fel, 63-64; res fel DGRST, Univ Louis Pasteur, Strasbourg, France, 74-75; ed-in-chief, Mycologia, 95- *Mem:* Soc Indust Microbiol; Mycol Soc Am; Am Phytopath Soc. *Res:* Physiology and biochemistry of development in fungi; mechanisms of fungal parasitism. *Mailing Add:* Col Environ Sci & Forestry State Univ NY Syracuse NY 13210-2788. *E-Mail:* griffin@mailbox.syr.edu

GRIFFIN, DAVID WILLIAM, ENVIRONMENTAL PHYSIOLOGY. *Current Pos:* PVT SURG PRACT; STAFF SURGEON, SACRAMENTO VET SURG SERV, 89- *Educ:* Univ Calif, Davis, BS, 79 & 83, MS, 84, DVM, 85. *Prof Exp:* Physiologist, Rasor Assoc Inc, 80-81; intern med & surg, Sacramento Animal Med Group, 85-86; resident surg, Vet Med Teaching Hosp, Univ Calif, Davis, 86-89, assoc vet, Sect Neurobiol, Physiol & Behav, 89-94. *Mem:* Am Vet Med Asn; Am Col Vet Surgeons; Am Animal Hosp Asn; Int Soc Gravitational Physiol. *Res:* Environmental physiology-effects of altered environments (light, temperature, gravity) on physiological processes. *Mailing Add:* 9700 Bus Park Dr Suite 404 Sacramento Davis CA 95827. *Fax:* 530-752-5851

GRIFFIN, DIANE EDMUND, IMMUNOLOGY, VIROLOGY. *Current Pos:* fel virol, 70-73, from asst prof to assoc prof, 73-86, PROF MED & NEUROL, SCH MED, JOHNS HOPKINS UNIV, 86-, PROF & CHAIR, MOLECULAR MICROBIOL & IMMUNOL, 94- *Personal Data:* b Iowa City, Iowa, May 12, 40; m 65, John W; c Todd & Erik. *Educ:* Augustana Col, BA, 62; Stanford Univ, MD, 68, PhD(med microbiol), 71. *Prof Exp:* Intern med, Stanford Univ Hosp, 68-69, resident, 69-70. *Concurrent Pos:* Investr, Howard Hughes Med Inst, 75-82. *Mem:* Am Asn Immunologists; Am Soc Microbiol; AAAS; Am Fedn Clin Res; Infectious Dis Soc Am; Am Soc Clin Invest. *Res:* Pathogenesis of viral infection; role of the immune response in recovery from or production of viral disease; neurovirulence of alphaviruses. *Mailing Add:* Dept Molecular Microbiol & Immunol E5132 Johns Hopkins Univ Sch Pub Health 615 N Wolfe St Baltimore MD 21205. *Fax:* 410-955-0105; *E-Mail:* dgriffin@welchlink.welch.jhu.edu

GRIFFIN, DONALD R(EDFIELD), COGNITIVE ETHOLOGY, COMPARATIVE PHYSIOLOGY. *Current Pos:* ASSOC, MUS COMP ZOOL, HARVARD UNIV, 89- *Personal Data:* b Southampton, NY, Aug 3, 15; m 41, 65, Jocelyn Crane; c Nancy (Jackson), Janet (Abbott), John & Margaret. *Educ:* Harvard Col, BS, 38; Harvard Univ, MA, 40, PhD(biol), 42. *Hon Degrees:* DSc, Ripon Col, Wis, 66, Eberhard-Karls Univ, Tubingen, Ger, 88. *Honors & Awards:* Eliot Medal, Nat Acad Sci, 61. *Prof Exp:* Teaching asst biol, Harvard Univ, 38-40, jr fel, 40-41 & 46, res assoc, 42-45; from asst prof to prof zool, Cornell Univ, 46-53; prof zool, Harvard Univ, 53-65, chmn, Dept Biol, 62-65; prof, Rockefeller Univ, 65-86; vis lectr, Dept Biol, Princeton Univ, 87-89. *Concurrent Pos:* Dir, Inst Res Animal Behav, Rockefeller Univ & NY Zool Soc, 65-69; mem bd trustees, Rockefeller Univ, 73-76; pres, Harry Frank Guggenheim Found, 79-83. *Mem:* Nat Acad Sci; Am Philos Soc; Am Acad Arts & Sci; Animal Behav Soc; Am Soc Zoologists; Am Physiol Soc; Ecol Soc Am. *Res:* Animal orientation; echolocation of bats, especially their use of sonar to capture flying insects; cognitive ethology; evidence of animal cognition and consciousness, especially the use of animal communication as a window on animal minds. *Mailing Add:* Concord Field Sta Harvard Univ Old Causeway Rd Bedford MA 01730. *Fax:* 781-275-9613; *E-Mail:* efs@oeb.harvard.edu

GRIFFIN, DONALD SPRAY, MECHANICAL ENGINEERING. *Current Pos:* from sr engr to mgr struct mech, Bettis Atomic Lab, 59-72, consult, 72-74, staff, Adv Energy Systs Div, 74-91, CONSULT, WESTINGHOUSE, PITTSBURGH, 91- *Educ:* Cornell Univ, BME, 52; Standford Univ, MS, 53, PhD(eng mech), 59. *Honors & Awards:* Pressure Vessel & Piping Award, Am Soc Mech Engrs, 92. *Concurrent Pos:* Assoc ed, J Appl Mech, 73-80. *Mem:* Fel Am Soc Mech Engrs; Nat Res Coun. *Res:* Design criteria and software for structural analysis and computer operations for design of advanced energy systems; contributed articles to journals. *Mailing Add:* 208 Oakcrest Lane Pittsburgh PA 15236-4208

GRIFFIN, EDMOND EUGENE, PHYSIOLOGY, RADIOBIOLOGY. *Current Pos:* PROF & CHMN, BIOL DEPT, UNIV CENT ARK, 86- *Personal Data:* b Marshall, Ark, June 5, 30; m 54; c 2. *Educ:* Univ Ark, BSEd, 62; Univ Tenn, MS, 64, PhD(radiation biol), 69. *Prof Exp:* Fel Med Sch, Univ Tex, San Antonio, 69 & Sch Med, Univ Rochester, 69-73; asst prof physiol, Southwestern Med Sch, Univ Tex Health Sci Ctr Dallas, 73-77; prof biol & chmn dept, Univ Cent Ark, 77-78; assoc dir environ health, Univ Tex Health Sci Ctr, Dallas, 78-82; sci adminr, Am Heart Asn, 82-84. *Mem:* AAAS; Radiation Res Soc; Am Soc Zoologists; Sigma Xi. *Res:* Actions of hormones and effects of radiation on metabolism. *Mailing Add:* Dept Biol Univ Cent Ark Conway AR 72035

GRIFFIN, EDWARD L(AWRENCE), JR, CHEMICAL ENGINEERING. *Current Pos:* RETIRED. *Personal Data:* b Washington, DC, Jan 9, 19; m 41; c 2. *Educ:* Cornell Univ, BCh, 40, ChE, 41. *Prof Exp:* Chem engr, James Lees & Sons, Pa, 41-42; chem engr, Eastern Regional Res Lab, Bur Agr & Indust Chem, USDA, 42-57, chief, Eng & Develop Lab, Northern Regional Res Ctr, 57-75. *Mem:* Am Inst Chem Engrs; Am Chem Soc; Am Oil Chem Soc; Am Asn Cereal Chemists; Inst Food Technol. *Res:* Chemical engineering pilot plant studies; rubber from guayule and Kok-Saghyz; volatile flavor from fruit juices; acrylic ester polymerization; production of allyl-sucrose; tanning material from canaigre; extraction of rutin from dried plants; cereal crop and oilseed utilization research. *Mailing Add:* 4206 Keeland Ave Peoria IL 61614-6804

GRIFFIN, ERNEST LYLE, MATHEMATICS. *Current Pos:* PROF MATH, LA STATE UNIV, BATON ROUGE, 67- *Personal Data:* b Tampa, Fla, May 25, 21. *Educ:* Emory Univ, BA, 43; Univ Chicago, MS, 47, PhD(math), 52. *Prof Exp:* From instr to asst prof math, Univ Mich, 52-62; assoc ed, Math Rev, 62-63; vis assoc prof math, Univ Pa, 63-66, assoc prof, 66-67. *Concurrent Pos:* Vis asst prof, Columbia Univ, 57-58. *Mem:* Am Math Soc. *Res:* Theory of algebras of operators on Hilbert spaces and applications to representations of locally compact groups and quantum physics; classification and properties of von-Neumann algebras. *Mailing Add:* 940 Sanford Ave Apt 404 Baton Rouge LA 70808

GRIFFIN, FRANK M, JR, INTERNAL MEDICINE, INFECTIOUS DISEASES. *Current Pos:* Asst prof med, 75-83, assoc prof microbiol, 79-85, PROF MED, UNIV ALA, BIRMINGHAM, 83-, PROF MICROBIOL, 85- *Personal Data:* b Orangeburg, SC, May 17, 41. *Educ:* Col Charleston, BS, 62; Univ SC, MD, 66. *Mem:* Am Fedn Clin Res; Infectious Dis Soc Am; AAAS; Am Bd Internal Med; Am Soc Microbiol. *Mailing Add:* Dept Med Univ Ala Birmingham UAB Sta Birmingham AL 35294-0001

GRIFFIN, GARY J, BIOLOGY. *Current Pos:* asst prof plant path & physiol, 67-70, assoc prof, 70-76, PROF PLANT PATH, VA POLYTECH INST & STATE UNIV, 76- *Personal Data:* b Glen Cove, NY, Dec 23, 37; m 59; c 3. *Educ:* Colo State Univ, BS, 59, MS, 61, PhD(plant path), 62. *Prof Exp:* Plant pathologist, Agr Res Serv, USDA, 62-63; from asst prof to assoc prof biol, Morehead State Col, 63-67. *Mem:* Am Phytopath Soc. *Res:* Soil microbiology; root diseases. *Mailing Add:* Dept Plant Path Va Poolytech Inst & State Univ PO Box 0331 Blacksburg VA 24061-0001

GRIFFIN, GARY WALTER, organic chemistry; deceased, see previous edition for last biography

GRIFFIN, GEORGE MELVIN, JR, MARINE GEOLOGY, SEDIMENTOLOGY. *Current Pos:* PROF GEOL, UNIV FLA, 70- *Personal Data:* b Baltimore, Md, Apr 14, 28; m 50; c 2. *Educ:* Univ NC, BA, 52, MS, 54; Rice Univ, PhD(geol), 60. *Prof Exp:* Res geologist clay petrol, Explor & Prod Res Div, Shell Develop Co, 54-65; assoc prof & head dept geol, Dayton Campus, Miami-Ohio State Univ, 65-66; proj leader, World Wide Tech Serv Ctr, Gulf Oil Corp, 66-67; assoc prof geol, 67-70. *Concurrent Pos:* Proj dir & chief scientist, Key Largo Lab, Harbor Br Found, 72-74; vpres explor & prod, Campbell Oil Co, 77-78; consult, minerals, oil & gas, environ probs, 70-, mem Coun Gulf Univ Res Consortium, 75- *Mem:* Am Asn Petrol Geol; Soc Econ Paleontologists & Mineralogists. *Res:* Geologic significance of mineral assemblages in sedimentary rocks, especially clay minerals; geothermal gradients; turbidity in coastal waters; and environmental effects of dredging and offshore petroleum production; sedimentation processes and products. *Mailing Add:* PO Box 58004 St Petersburg FL 33715

GRIFFIN, GERALD D, plant nematology, plant pathology, for more information see previous edition

GRIFFIN, GREGORY LEE, HETEROGENEOUS CATALYSIS. *Current Pos:* ASSOC PROF CHEM ENG, LA STATE UNIV, 87- *Personal Data:* b Montebello, Calif. *Educ:* Calif Tech, BS, 75; Princeton Univ, PhD(chem eng), 79. *Prof Exp:* Fel Nat Bur Stand, 79-80, asst prof chem eng, Univ Minn, 80-87. *Mem:* Am Inst Chem Engrs; Am Chem Soc; Am Vacuum Soc; Am Ceramics Soc. *Res:* Heterogeneous catalysis; chemical vapor deposition of ceramic coatings. *Mailing Add:* Dept Chem Eng La State Univ Baton Rouge LA 70803-0100

GRIFFIN, GUY DAVID, CHEMICAL CARCINOGENESIS, CELL CULTURE. *Current Pos:* investr cancer res, 72-76, staff scientist, Biol Div, 76-78, STAFF SCIENTIST HEALTH EFFECTS RES ADVAN MONITOR DEVELOP, LIFE SCI DIV, OAK RIDGE NAT LAB, 78- *Personal Data:* b Omaha, Nebr, Aug 27, 42; m 97, Doris Elaine Henegar; c 1. *Educ:* Univ Nebr, Omaha, BA, 64, MS, 69, PhD(biochem), 71. *Honors & Awards:* IR-100 Award, 87. *Prof Exp:* Supv cystic fibrosis res, Pediat Lab, Med Ctr, Univ Nebr, 65-71, res instr, 71-72. *Concurrent Pos:* Res fel, Nat Cystic Fibrosis Res Found, 71-72; fel, Am Cancer Soc 72-74 & Nat Cancer Inst, USPHS, 74-76; instr org chem & biochem, Bryan Col, 86-87, 89- *Mem:* Am Chem Soc; Sigma Xi; Am Soc Biochem & Molecular Biol. *Res:* Molecular basis for the toxicity of environmental pollutants; biological indicators of extent of human exposure to chemicals; in vitro toxicology; cellular regulation by transfer RNA; mechanisms of carcinogenesis; membrane structure and function; liposomes. *Mailing Add:* 109 Euclid Circle Oak Ridge TN 37830. *E-Mail:* gfu@ornl.gov

GRIFFIN, HAROLD LEE, STARCH, CELLULOSE. *Current Pos:* CONSULT, 92- *Personal Data:* b Canton, Ill, Nov 23, 28; m 54, Janet Michalek; c Michael L, Cynthia S & Diana E. *Educ:* Univ Ill, Urbana, BS, 54. *Prof Exp:* Chemist dextran, Agr Res Serv, Midwest Area, USDA, 54-56, chemist starch, 56-59, chemist starch & enzymes, 59-63, res chemist starch enzymes & feedlot waste, 63-75, res chemist fungal cellulase, 75-85, res chemist bact cellulase & proteases, Nat Ctr Agr Res, 85-92. *Mem:* AAAS. *Res:* Molecular parameters and dilute solution properties of native and modified macromolecular carbohydrates; isolation and characterization of enzymes of starch biosynthesis in various corn varieties; pollution control particularly feedlot waste; cellulase enzymology; isolation and physical and chemical characterization of fungal bacterial enzyme systems; fungal and bacterial cellulases and proteases. *Mailing Add:* 2702 W Scenic Dr Peoria IL 61615

GRIFFIN, HENRY CLAUDE, NUCLEAR SPECTROSCOPY, RADIOCHEMISTRY. *Current Pos:* from asst prof to assoc prof, 64-89, dir freshman studies, Dept Chem, 74-82, PROF NUCLEAR CHEM & RADIOCHEM, UNIV MICH, ANN ARBOR, 89- *Personal Data:* b Greenville, SC, Feb 14, 37; m 60; c 2. *Educ:* Davidson Col, BS, 58; Mass Inst Technol, PhD(nuclear chem), 62. *Prof Exp:* Resident res assoc nuclear chem, Argonne Nat Lab, 62-64. *Concurrent Pos:* Guest scientist, Swiss Fed Inst for Reactor Res, 71-72; res partic Nuclear Chem Div, Lawrence Livermore Lab & vis res engr Dept Nuclear Eng, Univ Calif, Berkeley, 78-79; consult, Environ Res Group Inc, Energy Data Systs Inc. *Mem:* AAAS; Am Phys Soc; Am Chem Soc. *Res:* Nuclear fission; nuclear spectroscopy; nuclear reactions; radiochemistry. *Mailing Add:* Dept Chem 1055 Univ Mich Ann Arbor MI 48109-1055

GRIFFIN, JAMES EDWARD, ELEMENTARY PARTICLE PHYSICS. *Current Pos:* RETIRED. *Personal Data:* b Sioux City, Iowa, Oct 11, 25; m 53, Marilyn; c Margaret, Jeanne, Rosemary, Ellen & Michael. *Educ:* Iowa State Univ, BS, 51, PhD(physics), 63. *Prof Exp:* Asst prof & assoc physicist, Iowa State Univ & Ames Lab, 63-69; physicist, Fermi Nat Accelerator Lab, 69-91. *Mem:* Fel Am Phys Soc; AAAS. *Res:* Properties of fundamental particles and design considerations of high energy particle accelerators. *Mailing Add:* PO Box 261 Wayne IL 60184. *E-Mail:* jgriffin@fnal.gov

GRIFFIN, JAMES EMMETT, ENDOCRINOLOGY. *Current Pos:* fel endocrinol, 74-76, from instr to prof internal med, 75-89, assoc dean med educ, 83- 86, ASSOC DEAN ACAD PLANNING, UNIV TEX SOUTHWESTERN MED SCH, 86- *Personal Data:* b Kansas City, Mo, Dec 10, 44; c 3. *Educ:* Rockhurst Col, BA, 66; Univ Kans, MD, 70. *Prof Exp:* Intern internal med, Univ Kans Med Ctr, 70-71, resident, 71-72. *Mem:* Am Col Physicians; Am Fedn Clin Res; Am Soc Clin Invest. *Res:* Disorders of sexual differentiation; androgen resistance syndromes. *Mailing Add:* Univ Tex Southwestern Med Ctr 5323 Harry Hines Blvd Dallas TX 75235-8857. *Fax:* 214-648-8917

GRIFFIN, JAMES J, THEORETICAL PHYSICS. *Current Pos:* from asst prof to assoc prof physics & astron, 66-74, assoc chmn dept, 68-69, PROF PHYSICS, UNIV MD, COLLEGE PARK, 74- *Personal Data:* b Philadelphia, Pa, Oct 20, 30; m; m 55, Mary Cornely; c Kevin, Michael, Sean, Terence & Sheilagh. *Educ:* Villanova Col, BS, 52; Princeton Univ, MA, 54, PhD(physics), 56. *Prof Exp:* Theoret physicist, Los Alamos Sci Lab, 56-66. *Concurrent Pos:* Fulbright scolar, N Bohr Inst, Copenhagen, 55-56; NSF fel, 59-60; vis lectr, Univ Wis-Madison, 65-66; Guggenheim fel, Univ Berkeley, 72-73; Alexander von Humboldt sr vis US scientist, WGer, 75-76; vis scientist, Los Alamos Nat Lab, Oak Ridge Nat Lab, Lawrence Berkeley Nat Lab, Brookhaven Nat Lab, ISN (Grenoble), GSI (Darmstadt) & CENBG (Bordeaux). *Mem:* Am Phys Soc; Union Concerned Scientist; Comt Concerned Scientists; Am Civil Liberties Union; Amnesty Int. *Res:* Nuclear physics; nuclear collective model via generator coordinates; pre-equilibrium nuclear reactions; dynamical nuclear many body problem; heavy ion reactions; fission and nuclear structure; nonlinear and quantal/classical connections; hypothetical quadronium (e plus e plus e minus e minus) leptonic atom. *Mailing Add:* Dept Physics Univ Md College Park MD 20742. *Fax:* 301-405-6114; *E-Mail:* griffin@quark.umd.edu

GRIFFIN, JANE FLANIGEN, PHYSICAL CHEMISTRY, BIOPHYSICS. *Current Pos:* Fel, 74-77, res scientist, 77-88, HEAD, MOLECULAR BIOPHYS DEPT, MED FEDN BUFFALO, 88- *Personal Data:* b Mar 26, 33; US citizen; m 54; c 4. *Educ:* D'Youville Col, BA, 54; State Univ NY, Buffalo, PhD(chem), 74. *Concurrent Pos:* Co-prin investr, NIH grant, 77-79, prin investr, 80-82. *Mem:* Am Chem Soc; Am Crystallog Asn; Royal Soc Chem; NY Acad Sci; AAAS. *Res:* Structure of steroid hormones; oproid peptides; cardioactive drugs. *Mailing Add:* 64 Tudor Pl Buffalo NY 14222-1616

GRIFFIN, JERRY HOWARD, VIBRATIONS, FRACTURE MECHANICS. *Current Pos:* from asst prof to assoc prof, 80-87, PROF MECH ENG, CARNEGIE MELLON UNIV, 87- *Personal Data:* b Miami, Fla, July 14, 45; m 67; c 2. *Educ:* Univ SFla, BS & MS, 69; Calif Inst Technol, PhD(eng), 73. *Prof Exp:* Sr engr vibrations, Pratt & Whitney Aircraft, 73-74; lectr appl mech, Univ Auckland, NZ, 74-76; sr engr vibrations, Pratt & Whitney Aircraft, 76-77, tech specialist fatigue, 77-79, mgr fan struct group, 79-80. *Concurrent Pos:* Vis sr scientist, Air Force Wright Aeronaut Labs, 81; consult, USN, 84-85, NASA, 86-87, Rocketdyne Div, Rockwell Int, 86-, Pratt & Whitney Aircraft & AVCO Lycoming, 88-; sr partner, Griffin Consult, 83- *Mem:* Am Soc Mech Engrs; Am Inst Aeronaut & Astronaut. *Res:* Structural dynamics which include vibration of jet engines, boat drive-trains, friction effects, space structures and random response of nonlinear systems; fracture mechanics which include path independent integrals, thermo-mechanical fatigue. *Mailing Add:* Dept Mech Engr Carnegie Mellon Univ Pittsburgh PA 15213

GRIFFIN, JOE LEE, CELL BIOLOGY. *Current Pos:* res biologist, Armed Forces Inst Path, 64-74, chief, Div Exp Neuropath, 74-83, res neuromyologist, Div Neuromuscular Path, 83- 90, RES BIOLOGIST, DIV CELLULAR PATH, ARMED FORCES INST PATH, 90- *Personal Data:* b Bass, Ark, Sept 8, 35; m 58; c 2. *Educ:* Univ of the South, BS, 56; Princeton Univ, PhD(biol), 59. *Prof Exp:* From instr to asst prof biol, Brown Univ, 59-62; NIH spec fel anat, Harvard Univ, Med Sch, 62-64. *Res:* Flow cytometry; cell cycles; neuromuscular reeducation, adult learning, stress and pain release. *Mailing Add:* 10211 Lorain Ave Silver Spring MD 20901

GRIFFIN, JOHN HENRY, BIOCHEMISTRY, EXPERIMENTAL PATHOLOGY. *Current Pos:* asst, 74-75, assoc, 75-80, ASSOC MEM IMMUNOPATH, MOLECULAR IMMUNOL, SCRIPPS CLIN RES FOUND, 80- *Personal Data:* b Seattle, Wash, June 26, 43; m 65; c 3. *Educ:* Univ Santa Clara, BS, 65; Univ Calif, Davis, PhD(biophys), 69. *Prof Exp:* Guest worker, NIH, 71-73; mem staff biochem, Ctr Nuclear Studies, Saclay, France, 73-74. *Concurrent Pos:* Helen Hay Whitney Found res fel biol chem, Harvard Med Sch, 69-71. *Mem:* Am Soc Biol Chemists; Am Asn Immunol; Am Asn Path; Am Chem Soc; Sigma Xi. *Res:* Basic biochemical and clinical research on the regulation of thrombosis and hemostasis based on studies of purified blood coagulation proteins. *Mailing Add:* Dept Molecular & Exp Med Scripps Res Inst 10550 N Torrey Pines Rd SBR-5 La Jolla CA 92037-1092. *Fax:* 619-784-2243

GRIFFIN, JOHN LEANDER, PHYSICAL CHEMISTRY. *Current Pos:* RETIRED. *Personal Data:* b Toledo, Ohio, Nov 9, 23; m 47; c 2. *Educ:* Univ Toledo, BEng, 45, MS, 53; Univ Mich, PhD(chem), 62. *Prof Exp:* Jr chemist, Chase Bag Co Lab, 45-46; teaching fel chem, Univ Toledo, 46-47, instr, 47-48, 49-50; asst anal chemist, Res Lab, Owens-Ill Glass Co, 48-49; plant chemist, Kaylo Div, 50-51; lectr chem, Univ Toledo, 51-52; sr res chemist, Gen Motors Corp, 57-69, supvry res chemist, 69-77, dept res scientist, 77-81, sr staff res scientist, electrochem dept, Res Labs, 81-84. *Mem:* AAAS; Am Chem Soc; Electrochem Soc (treas, 76-82); hon mem Electrochem Soc. *Res:* Electrochemistry, especially electrodeposition, secondary batteries and corrosion; industrial analytical chemistry. *Mailing Add:* 26177 Lepley Rd Howard OH 43028-9783

GRIFFIN, JOHN R(OBERT), CHEMICAL ENGINEERING, PLASTICS TECHNOLOGY. *Current Pos:* Res chem engr process develop, Humble Oil & Refining Co, 63-65, res chem engr, Esso Res & Eng Co, 65, supvr polymerization process develop, 65-71, supvr low density polyethylene & new prod, 71-72, mgr high performance plastics technol, 72-78, SR RES ASSOC, EXXON CHEM CO, 78- *Personal Data:* b Du Quoin, Ill, Apr 21, 36; m 68, Becky Bush; c Paul, Julia, Ann & John. *Educ:* Univ Ill, BS, 59; Purdue Univ, PhD(chem eng), 63. *Honors & Awards:* A M White Award, Am Inst Chem Engrs, 59. *Mem:* Am Inst Chem Engrs. *Res:* Plastic process and product research and development. *Mailing Add:* 225 Pin Oak Dr Baytown TX 77520

GRIFFIN, KATHLEEN (MARY), speech pathology, audiology, for more information see previous edition

GRIFFIN, MARTIN JOHN, BIOCHEMISTRY. *Current Pos:* RETIRED. *Personal Data:* b Chicago, Ill, Oct 1, 33; wid; c Will, Rachel, Hope & Joe. *Educ:* Loyola Univ, Ill, SB, 55; Univ Chicago, SM, 57, PhD(org chem), 60. *Prof Exp:* Chemist, E I du Pont de Nemours & Co, Del, 60-61; from asst prof to prof biochem, Sch Med, Univ Okla, 65-85; Travenol Labs, 85-87; res scientist, G D Searle, 88-95. *Concurrent Pos:* NIH fel biochem, Mass Inst Technol, 61-63; NIH fel genetics & med, NY Univ, 63-65; mem staff, Cancer Sect, Okla Med Res Found, 65-85; career develop award, 69-75. *Mem:* AAAS; Am Asn Cancer Res; Am Soc Biol Chemists; Am Asn Pharmaceut Sci. *Res:* Enzymology and mammalian regulatory mechanisms; membrane biochemistry and oncology; drug metabolism and drug delivery. *Mailing Add:* 4821 Grain St Skokie IL 60077. *Fax:* 847-982-4900

GRIFFIN, PATRICK J, NUCLEAR THEORY DEFINITION, RADIATION TRANSPORT COUPLING. *Current Pos:* SCIENTIST, SANDIA NAT LAB, 89- *Personal Data:* b Warren, Ohio, Oct 26, 51; m 74, 87. *Educ:* Ohio Univ, BS, 73, PhD(physics), 79. *Prof Exp:* Res scientist, Kaman Sci Corp, 79-85, prog mgr, 85-88. *Mem:* Am Phys Soc; Inst Elec & Electronics Engrs. *Res:* Reactor simulation fidelity, neutron damage to materials and radiation transport. *Mailing Add:* 2872 Tramway Circle NE Albuquerque NM 87122

GRIFFIN, PAUL JOSEPH, DIELECTRIC FLUIDS. *Current Pos:* lab mgr, 78-96, VPRES, DOBLE ENG CO, 96- *Personal Data:* b Westfield, Mass, Dec 31, 54; m 83; c 1. *Educ:* Am Int Col, BS, 76; Univ RI, MS, 80. *Mem:* Am Soc Testing & Mat. *Res:* Physical, chemical and electric properties of dielectric fluids; gassing characteristics of various liquids under electrical stresses; static electrification of flowing liquids; long term stability of dielectric liquids in-service. *Mailing Add:* 9 Anis Rd Belmont MA 02178

GRIFFIN, RICHARD B, AQUEOUS CORROSION, ENVIRONMENTAL DEGRADATION. *Current Pos:* from asst prof to assoc prof mat sci & corrosion, 77-90, ASST DEPT HEAD, UNDERGRAD PROG, MECH ENG DEPT, TEX A&M UNIV, 90- *Personal Data:* b Buffalo, NY, Aug 31, 42; m 65; c 2. *Educ:* Pa State Univ, BS, 64; Iowa State Univ, PhD(metall), 69. *Prof Exp:* Mat res engr, Watervliet Arsenal, NY, 69-74; mat engr, US FSTC, Charlottesville, Va, 74-77. *Mem:* Nat Asn Corrosion Engrs; Am Soc Metals; Am Soc Eng Educ. *Res:* Aqueous corrosion; cathodic protection of offshore structures and corrosion of coatings. *Mailing Add:* Mech Eng Dept Tex A&M Univ College Station TX 77843-3123

GRIFFIN, RICHARD NORMAN, PLASTICS ENGINEERING. *Current Pos:* RETIRED. *Personal Data:* b Winchester, Mass, Nov 2, 29; m 55; c 3. *Educ:* Columbia Univ, AB, 51; Mass Inst Technol, PhD(org chem), 58. *Prof Exp:* Res chemist, E I du Pont de Nemours & Co, 57-61; res chemist, Space Div, GE Elec Co, 61-77, mgr solar progs, Energy Syst Prog Dept, 78-83, mgr advan composites, GE Aircraft Engrs, 83-91. *Mem:* Am Chem Soc; Soc Advan Mat & Process Eng. *Res:* Kinetics and mechanisms of organic reactions; photochemistry; energy transfer; radiation chemistry; electrophoretic purification of biologicals; plastics and composites. *Mailing Add:* 18 Rollingwood Rd Eliot ME 03903

GRIFFIN, ROBERT ALFRED, GEOCHEMISTRY, SOIL CHEMISTRY. *Current Pos:* DIR ENVIRON INST, CUDWORTH PROF ENVIRON ENG, UNIV ALA, 90- *Personal Data:* b Long Beach, Calif, June 7, 44; m 64; c 2. *Educ:* Univ Calif, Davis, 66, MS, 68; Utah State Univ, PhD(soil chem), 73. *Prof Exp:* Res assoc, 73-74; from asst geochemist to assoc geochemist, Ill State Geol Surv, 74-78, geochemist & head sect geochem, 78-90. *Mem:* Am Soc Agron; Soil Sci Soc Am; Am Chem Soc; Sigma Xi. *Res:* Solid and hazardous waste disposal; geochemistry of ground waters; soil physical chemistry; solution thermodynamics; adsorption by earth materials; global climate change. *Mailing Add:* Eng Dept Univ Ala Box 870200 Tuscaloosa AL 35487

GRIFFIN, SUMNER ALBERT, ANIMAL HUSBANDRY. *Current Pos:* CONSULT, 88- *Personal Data:* b Ashland, NY, May 11, 22; m 51; c 3. *Educ:* Cornell Univ, BS, 49; Univ Ky, MS, 50; Mich State Univ, PhD(animal husb), 55. *Prof Exp:* Instr animal husb, Mich State Univ, 52-55; mgr animal health & nutrit, Mallinckrodt Chem Works, 55-57; assoc prof animal husb & vet sci, Univ Tenn, Knoxville, 57-70; dean & prof, Sch Agr & Home Econ, Tenn Technol Univ, 70-87. *Concurrent Pos:* Consult, Oak Ridge Nat Lab. *Mem:* Am Soc Animal Sci; Animal Nutrit Res Coun. *Res:* Swine nutrition and physiology management. *Mailing Add:* 987 Georgetown Rd Cookville TN 38501

GRIFFIN, TRAVIS BARTON, BIOCHEMISTRY. *Current Pos:* EXEC VPRES, COULSTON FOUND, INC, 80- *Personal Data:* b Trinidad, Tex, Apr 30, 34; m 56; c 4. *Educ:* Tex A&M Univ, BS, 57, MS, 61, PhD(biochem), 66. *Prof Exp:* Asst prof biochem, Tex A&M Univ, 65-69; asst prof, Inst Comp & Human Toxicol, Albany Med Col, 69-73, res assoc prof toxicol, 73-80. *Mem:* AAAS; Am Chem Soc; Sigma Xi; NY Acad Sci. *Res:* Enzymology; protein chemistry; toxicology of environmental chemicals. *Mailing Add:* 1841 Corte Del Sol Alamogordo NM 88310

GRIFFIN, VILLARD STUART, JR, geology, for more information see previous edition

GRIFFIN, WILLIAM DALLAS, ACADEMIC ADMINISTRATION, ORGANIC CHEMISTRY. *Current Pos:* sci lab coordr, 73-90, ADJ ASSOC PROF CHEM, COUNTY COL MORRIS, 90- *Personal Data:* b Plainfield, NJ, Jan 1, 25; m 47, Margaret Rutledge; c William, Richard, Lawrence, Robert, John & Jeffrey. *Educ:* Rutgers Univ, BSc, 48. *Prof Exp:* Assoc chemist, Cent Res Lab, Allied Chem & Dye Corp, 48-52, res chemist, 52-58, res chemist, Allied Chem Corp, 58-59, group leader, 59-71; sr chemist, Pavelle Corp, 72-73. *Concurrent Pos:* granted 11 US patents. *Res:* Process development; organic synthesis; hydrocarbon hydroperoxidation. *Mailing Add:* 35 Terry Dr Morristown NJ 07960

GRIFFIN, WILLIAM G, TECHNICAL MANAGEMENT. *Current Pos:* mgr, 76-80, assoc dir, 80-82, LAB DIR, GTE LABS, 82- *Personal Data:* b Binghamton, NY, Feb 22, 44; m 82; c 2. *Educ:* Clarkson Col Technol, BS, 66; Stevens Inst Technol, MS, 68. *Prof Exp:* Mem tech staff, Mitre Corp, 68-75; mgr technol planning, Gillette Corp, 75. *Mem:* Am Asn Artificial Intel; Inst Elec & Electronics Engrs Comput Soc; Asn Comput Mach; Sigma Xi. *Res:* Computer science, information science and systems and software systems. *Mailing Add:* GTE Labs 40 Sylvan Rd Waltham MA 02254. *E-Mail:* griffin@gte.com

GRIFFIN, WILLIAM THOMAS, OBSTETRICS & GYNECOLOGY. *Current Pos:* resident physician, Sch Med, 60-63, from instr to assoc prof, 63-74, prof, 74-92, EMER PROF OBSTET & GYNEC, UNIV MO-COLUMBIA, 92-, ATTEND OBSTETRICIAN & GYNECOLOGIST, MED CTR, 63- *Personal Data:* b Thompson, Mo, May 13, 32; m 52; c 3. *Educ:* Univ Mo-Columbia, MD, 59; Am Bd Obstet & Gynec, dipl, 67, recert, 81. *Prof Exp:* Comdr 451st Surg Team, KA, USAR & 5503rd, USAR Hosp; chief surg, Ft Leonard Wood Hosp. *Concurrent Pos:* Consult gynecologist, Fifth Army, Ft Leonard Wood, Mo, 69- *Mem:* Am Col Obstet & Gynec; AMA; Asn Profs Gynec & Obstet; Am Fertil Soc; Am Col Surgeons. *Res:* Urinary incontinence; cancer control. *Mailing Add:* Univ Mo Health Sci Ctr 807 Stadium Rd Columbia MO 65201-5276

GRIFFING, DAVID FRANCIS, PHYSICS & SPORTS, PHYSICS EDUCATION. *Current Pos:* PROF PHYSICS, MIAMI UNIV, 56- *Personal Data:* b Nanking, China, Feb 23, 26; US citizen; m 49; c 2. *Educ:* Miami Univ, AB, 49, MA, 50; Univ Ill, Urbana, PhD(physics), 56. *Mem:* Am Phys Soc; Am Inst Physics; Am Asn Physics Teachers; Sigma Xi. *Res:* Low temperature physics; nuclear orientation; radioactivity and nuclear spectroscopy; ultrasonic studies in metals. *Mailing Add:* 4 Oakhill Dr Oxford OH 45056

GRIFFING, GEORGE WARREN, theoretical physics, for more information see previous edition

GRIFFING, J BRUCE, genetics, for more information see previous edition

GRIFFING, LAWRENCE RANDOLPH, CELL BIOLOGY. *Current Pos:* asst prof, 86-91, ASSOC PROF BIOL, TEX A&M UNIV, 86- *Personal Data:* b Kansas City, Kans, Feb 9, 53; m 83; c 3. *Educ:* Univ Utah, BS, 76; Stanford Univ, PhD(biol), 81. *Prof Exp:* Res assoc, Ore State Univ, 81-82, Univ Sask, 82-84, Plant Biotechnol Inst, Nat Res Coun, Can, 84-86. *Concurrent Pos:* Prog dir, molecular & cell biol, NSF, 94- *Mem:* Am Soc Plant Physiologists;

Am Soc Cell Biol. *Res:* Plant endocytosis and intracellular trafficking of proteins, polysaccharides, and secondary metabolites. *Mailing Add:* Biol Dept Tex A&M Univ College Station TX 77843-0100. *Fax:* 409-845-2891; *E-Mail:* larry@bio.tamu.edu

GRIFFING, WILLIAM JAMES, COMPARATIVE PATHOLOGY, VETERINARY TOXICOLOGY. *Current Pos:* RETIRED. *Personal Data:* b Manhattan, Kans, July 18, 22; m 45, Ann Moore; c Jack, Beverly (Gardner), William Jr & Jean (Madden). *Educ:* Kans State Univ, DVM, 44, MS, 60, PhD(vet path), 63. *Prof Exp:* Pvt pract, Bremen, Ind, 44-59; Nat Defense fel, Kans State Univ, 59-62, NIH fel, 62-63; sr pathologist, Eli Lilly & Co, 63-65, electron microscopist, 65-85, res pathologist, 72-74, res assoc, 74-85. *Mem:* Emer mem Electron Micros Soc Am; Am Vet Med Asn; fel Am Col Vet Toxicol; emer mem Int Acad Path; Sigma Xi. *Res:* Electron microscopic examination of the tissues of laboratory animals subjected to agriculture chemical compounds. *Mailing Add:* 1174 Cricket Reel Greenfield IN 46140

GRIFFIOEN, ROGER DUANE, NUCLEAR PHYSICS, CHEMISTRY. *Current Pos:* acad dean, 85-92, from instr to PROF PHYSICS & CHMN DEPT, CALVIN COL, 61- *Personal Data:* b Grand Rapids, Mich, Sept 7, 34; m 56, 88, Susan Kingma; c Keith, Pamela, Kevin & Denise. *Educ:* Calvin Col, AB, 56; Purdue Univ, PhD(nuclear chem), 60. *Prof Exp:* Univ fel, Lawrence Radiation Lab, Univ Calif, 60-61. *Concurrent Pos:* Consult, Argonne Nat Lab, 63-67 & Lawrence Radiation Lab, 67-69; NSF sci fac fel, Fla State Univ, 70-71, sr res assoc, 71-72; prog officer, Res Corp, Tucson, Ariz, 92-93. *Mem:* Am Phys Soc; Am Asn Physics Teachers. *Res:* Nuclear structure; spectroscopy; radioactivity. *Mailing Add:* Physics Dept Calvin Col Grand Rapids MI 49546. *E-Mail:* grif@calvin.edu

GRIFFISS, JOHN MCLEOD, MEDICINE. *Current Pos:* assoc prof lab med & med, 83-85, PROF LAB MED & MED, UNIV CALIF, SAN FRANCISCO, 85- *Personal Data:* b Chattanooga, Tenn, July 9, 40. *Educ:* Univ NC, BA, 62; Yale Univ, MD, 66; Am Bd Internal Med, cert, 72, cert infectious dis, 74. *Prof Exp:* Intern med, King Co Hosp, Seattle, 66-67; asst res med, Univ Wash Affil Hosps, 67-68; prev med officer, Stuttgard Med Serv Area, Bad Cannstatt, WGer, 68-71; fel infectious dis, Walter Reed Army Inst Res, 71-73, med res officer, 73-75, actg chief, Dept Bact Dis, 76, sr med res officer, 77-79; asst prof med, Harvard Med Sch, 79-83, lectr, 83-84. *Concurrent Pos:* Staff physician, Infectious Dis Serv, Walter Reed Army Med Ctr, 71-79; consult, Sch Med, George Washington Univ, 71-74; USPHS Hosp, Brighton, Mass, 80-81, Nat Acad Sci, 84-86; assoc med, Brigham & Women's Hosp, 79-82, physician, 82-83; assoc med, Dana Farber Cancer Inst, 82-83; chief microbiol, Clin Path Serv, Vet Admin Med Ctr, San Francisco & staff infectious dis, 83-; expert consult, Meningitis Trust, 87-, Wellcome Trust, 88-, WHO, 89- *Mem:* AMA; Am Soc Microbiol; Am Fedn Clin Res; Am Asn Immunologists; fel Infectious Dis Soc Am; Int Endotoxin Soc. *Res:* Immunologic function of the IgA system; epidemiology and immunochemistry of Neisseria meningitidis; immunochemistry of Neisseria gonorrhoeae; immunology of bacterial vaccines; epidemiology and immunochemistry of Gram negative sepis; bacterial outer membrane glycolipids; immunochemistry of Pneumocystis carinii; author of numerous publications. *Mailing Add:* Dept Lab Med Univ Calif San Francisco Vet Admin Med Ctr 4150 Clement St San Francisco CA 94121-1598. *Fax:* 415-221-7542

GRIFFITH, B HEROLD, PLASTIC & RECONSTRUCTIVE SURGERY. *Current Pos:* RETIRED. *Personal Data:* b New York, NY, Aug 24, 25; m 48, Jeanne Lethbridge; c Susan & Tristan. *Educ:* Yale Univ, MD, 48; Am Bd Plastic Surg, dipl, 59; Johns Hopkins Univ, BA, 92. *Prof Exp:* Intern, Grace-New Haven Hosp, Conn, 48-49; resident surg, Vet Admin Hosps, Newington, Conn, 49-50, plastic surg, Bronx, NY, 53-55; asst resident, sec surg div, Bellevue Hosp, 52-53; asst surgeon inpatients, NY Hosp-Cornell Med Ctr, 55, sr registr, Glasgow Royal Infirmary, Scotland, 55; resident plastic surg, NY Hosp-Cornell Med Ctr, 56; assoc surg, Northwestern Univ, 59-62, from asst prof to assoc prof, 61-70, chief, Div Plastic Surg, Sch Med, 70-91, prof, 71-95, EMER PROF SURG, NORTHWESTERN UNIV, 96. *Concurrent Pos:* Res fel, Med Sch, Cornell Univ, 56-57; pvt pract, 57-96; mem med adv comt, Nat Paraplegia Found, 67-79; chmn, Plastic Surg Res Coun, 68-69; dir, Am Bd Plastic Surg, 74-82, chmn, 81-82. *Mem:* AAAS; fel Am Asn Plastic Surg; Am Soc Plastic & Reconstruct Surg; fel Am Col Surgeons; NY Acad Sci; fel Royal Soc Med; Sigma Xi; Soc Head & Neck Surgeons; Am Burn Asn; Asn Mil Surgeons US. *Res:* Experimental embryology; transplantation; cancer chemotherapy; physiology of flaps and grafts; wound-healing; decubitus ulcers; cleft lip and palate; tumors of the skin, head and neck. *Mailing Add:* 320 Greenwood St Evanston IL 60201-4716

GRIFFITH, CECIL BAKER, PHYSICAL CHEMISTRY, PROCESS METALLURGY. *Current Pos:* CONSULT, 84- *Personal Data:* b New Lexington, Ohio, Nov 9, 23; m 46. *Educ:* Ohio Univ, BS, 47. *Prof Exp:* Supvr gas metals, Battelle Mem Inst, 47-55; res engr phys chem, Cramet Inc, 55-58; div head, Res Ctr, Repub Steel Corp, 58-84. *Res:* Process metallurgy of ironmaking, steelmaking and refractories. *Mailing Add:* 17856 Bennett Rd Cleveland OH 44133-6032

GRIFFITH, DANIEL ALVA, SPATIAL STATISTICS, APPLIED STATISTCS. *Current Pos:* chair, Geol Dept, 95-97, PROF GEOG, SYRACUSE UNIV, 88- *Personal Data:* b Nov 5, 48; m 70, Diane E Swartz; c Darren L & Michele R. *Educ:* Indiana Univ Pa, BS, 70, MA, 72; Pa State Univ, MS, 85; Univ Toronto, PhD(geog), 78. *Honors & Awards:* Nystrom Dissertation Award, Am Asn Geographers, 80, First Prize Best Software, 93, 2nd Prize Best Software, 96. *Prof Exp:* Instr geog, Ryerson Polytech Univ, 75-78; from asst prof to prof, State Univ NY, Buffalo, 78-88. *Concurrent Pos:* Dir, NATO Advan Studies Inst, 79-80, 81-82 & 85, Interdisciplinary Statist Prog, Syracuse Univ, 91-92 & 93-; chair, Math Models & Quant Methods Specialty Group, Asn Am Geographers, 87-88; Fulbright res fel, Coun Int Exchange Scholars, 92; vis res prof, Erasmus Univ, Rotterdam, 92 & Univ Rome, 95; adj prof, Col Environ Sci & Forestry, State Univ NY, 92-; pres, NAm Reg Sci Asn Coun, 96-97. *Mem:* Am Statist Asn; Asn Am Geographers; Fulbright Asn; Regional Sci Asn; Sigma Xi. *Res:* Spatial and applied statistics; quantative-urban-economic geography; mathematical spatial theory; geographic information systems. *Mailing Add:* Geog Dept Syracuse Univ 144 Eggers Hall Syracuse NY 13244-1090. *Fax:* 315-443-4227; *E-Mail:* dgriffith@maxwell.sry.edu

GRIFFITH, DONAL LOUIS, cell physiology, for more information see previous edition

GRIFFITH, EDWARD JACKSON, PHYSICAL CHEMISTRY. *Current Pos:* Scientist, 51-67, adv scientist, 67-72, SR FEL, MONSANTO CO, 72- *Personal Data:* b Atlanta, Ga, Apr 4, 25; wid; c 2. *Educ:* Howard Col, BS, 47; Univ Ky, MS, 48, PhD(chem), 51. *Honors & Awards:* Du Boise Award. *Concurrent Pos:* Lectr, Int Union Pure & Appl Chem, Chem Indust Basle Found. *Mem:* AAAS; Am Chem Soc; Sigma Xi; Am Inst Chemists. *Res:* Inorganic chemistry; phosphates; nitrates; tailings and mining waste disposal. *Mailing Add:* 310 Coventry Lane Manchester MO 63021-5123

GRIFFITH, ELIZABETH ANN HALL, ORGANOMETALLIC CHEMISTRY, PHYSICAL CHEMISTRY. *Current Pos:* res fel, 73-82, asst prof, 82-92, ASSOC PROF RES, DEPT CHEM & BIOCHEM, UNIV SC, 92-, ASST CHAIR, 91- *Personal Data:* b Washington, DC, Feb 3, 35; wid. *Educ:* Pfeiffer Col, AB, 60; Duke Univ, MA, 63; Univ SC, PhD(phys chem), 70. *Prof Exp:* Asst prof chem, Jacksonville State Univ, 62-63; instr, Pfeiffer Col, 63-64; asst prof, Campbell Col, NC, 64-65; res fel, Univ Sask, Regina, 70-73. *Mem:* AAAS; Am Chem Soc; Am Crystallog Asn; Sigma Xi. *Res:* Structure determination by x-ray diffraction of single crystals; synthesis and structure of organometallic compounds which are models for biologically significant systems; structure of enzyme substrate model systems; cadium nuclear magnetic resonance as a structural probe. *Mailing Add:* Dept Chem Univ SC Columbia SC 29208. *Fax:* 803-777-9521; *E-Mail:* griffith@psc.sc.edu

GRIFFITH, GORDON LAMAR, PHYSICS. *Current Pos:* RETIRED. *Personal Data:* b Bogue, Kans, Oct 12, 21; m 41; c 2. *Educ:* Kans State Col, BS, 43; Univ Ill, PhD(physics), 50. *Prof Exp:* Physicist, Tenn Eastman Corp Div, Eastman Kodak Co, 44-45; res physicist, Res Lab, Westinghouse Elec Corp, Pa, 49-62; from assoc prof to prof physics, 62-85, chmn dept, Muskingum Col, 67-76, 80-85. *Concurrent Pos:* Consult, Stanford Res Inst, 55 & Lawrence Radiation Lab, Calif, 58; res assoc, Sci Res Coun, Daresbury Lab, Eng, 69, 77. *Mem:* Am Phys Soc; Am Asn Physics Teachers; Sigma Xi. *Res:* Elastic and inelastic scattering of neutrons; x-ray scintillation spectrometry; plasma physics; surface ion mass spectroscopy. *Mailing Add:* 1928 Adriel Ct Ft Collins CO 80524

GRIFFITH, IRWIN J, allergy, autoimmunity, for more information see previous edition

GRIFFITH, JACK DEE, PREVENTIVE MEDICINE. *Current Pos:* BR CHIEF EPIDEMIOL, HUMAN EFFECTS MONITORING BR, TECH SERV DIV, ENVIRON PROTECTION AGENCY, ROCKVILLE, 74-; PROF MICROBIOL & IMMUNOL, SCH MED, UNIV NC. *Personal Data:* b Knox City, Tex, Aug 13, 36; m 69. *Educ:* ECent State Univ, BS, 59; Okla Univ, PhD(prev med), 69. *Prof Exp:* Demonstration coordr community control epidemiol, Commun Dis Ctr, USPHS, 64-69, dep dir epidemiol, Nat Ctr Health Serv Res & Develop, 69-71, assoc dir data & eval, Off Exp Health Serv Delivery Syst, 71; asst prof epidemiol, Univ Okla, 72-73; prog dir data & eval, Div Cancer Control & Rehab, Nat Cancer Inst, NIH, 73-74. *Concurrent Pos:* Consult, Nat Ctr Health Serv Res & Develop, Off Exp Health Serv Delivery Syst, 72-74. *Mem:* Soc Epidemiol Res. *Res:* Application of epidemiologic principles to the development of an index of community and personal health status, quantifiable by aggregate indicators of community and individual health symptomatology. *Mailing Add:* Dept Microbiol & Immunol Lineberger Cancer Res Ctr Univ NC Sch Med Chapel Hill Chapel Hill NC 27514

GRIFFITH, JERRY DICE, NUCLEAR ENGINEERING. *Current Pos:* CONSULT, 94- *Personal Data:* b Sturgis, Mich, Sept 8, 33; m 65, Gloria L Hessie; c Jennifer L & Bradley J. *Educ:* Mich State Univ, BS, 55, MS, 57; Calif Inst Technol, ME, 59; Princeton Univ, PFPA, 67. *Prof Exp:* Dir nuclear safety, CEngrs, US Army, Wash, 67-72; chief, Res & Develop Br, AEC & ERDA, Wash, 72-76; asst dir reactor safety, Dept Energy, Wash, 76-79, dir, Div Nuclear Power Develop, 79-80, dir, Off Light Water Reactors, 80-85, actg asst secy nuclear energy, 89, actg prin & asst secy, 90-92, assoc & asst secy reactors systs develop & technol, 85-94. *Concurrent Pos:* US rep, Orgn Europ Coop & Develop, Nuclear Energy Agency, Paris, 76-86, 89- *Mem:* Am Nuclear Soc. *Res:* Nuclear engineering. *Mailing Add:* 14711 Bauer Dr Rockville MD 20853

GRIFFITH, JOHN E(DWARD), engineering mechanics, for more information see previous edition

GRIFFITH, JOHN RANDALL, HOSPITAL ADMINISTRATION. *Current Pos:* asst prof, Univ Mich, Ann Arbor, 60-64, assoc dir, 63-70, assoc prof, 64-68, dir hosp admin, 70-82, PROF HEALTH MGT, UNIV MICH, ANN ARBOR, 68-, ANDREW PATTULLO COL PROF, 85- *Personal Data:* b Baltimore, Md, Mar 22, 34; m 55, Helen Klenner; c Julie, Alison & Richard. *Educ:* Johns Hopkins Univ, BEng, 55; Univ Chicago, MBA, 57. *Prof Exp:* Admitting officer hosp admin, Johns Hopkins Hosp, 55; asst, Univ Rochester, 56-60. *Concurrent Pos:* Admin asst hosp admin, Strong Mem Hosp, 56-60; mem hosp mgt syts soc, Am Hosp Asn, 56-; assoc mem health applns sect, Opers Res Soc Am, 66-; vis assoc prof, Yale Univ, 67; consult, Health Ins Benefits Adv Coun, Social Security Admin, 68-69; chmn med care sect, Am Pub Health Asn, 70-71; mem exec comt, Asn Univ Progs in Health Admin, 72-76, pres, 74-75; dir, Medicus Systs Corp, 73-78, chmn, 74-78; dir, Allegiance Corp, 93- *Mem:* Fel Am Pub Health Asn; Am Hosp Asn; fel Am Col Hosp Adminr. *Res:* Management of health care systems; health facilities planning; measurement of health care costs and utilization. *Mailing Add:* Dept Pub Health Univ Mich Main Campus 109 Observatory St Ann Arbor MI 48109-2029. *E-Mail:* jrg@umich.edu

GRIFFITH, JOHN SIDNEY, ASTRONOMY, MATHEMATICS. *Current Pos:* chair, Dept Math Sci, 93-95, PROF MATH, LAKEHEAD UNIV, 68-, DIR, SCH MATH SCI, 95- *Personal Data:* b Hull, Eng, Dec 30, 35; Can citizen; m 63, Anne; c Richard, Catherine A & Joanna. *Educ:* Univ London, BSc, 57, PhD(astrophys), 62. *Prof Exp:* Asst lectr math, Univ London, 57-58; asst lectr astron, Univ Glasgow, 58-61; sci officer math, Atomic Weapons Res Estab, 61-62; lectr, Royal Mil Col Sci, 62-64; sr sci officer astron, Royal Greenwich Observ, 64-68. *Concurrent Pos:* Consult, US Ephemeris Working Group, 71-73; prof, World Open Univ, 72-; mem, Ont Math Comn, 72-74; ed, Ont Math Gazette, 72-74; past pres, Lakehead Univ Fac Asn; past dir, Ont Confederational Univ Fac Asn; past mem exec, Confederation Ont Univs & Coun Ont Univs. *Mem:* Fel Royal Astron Soc; fel Brit Interplanetary Soc. *Res:* Analysis; celestial mechanics; mathematics education; education in astronomy. *Mailing Add:* Dept Math Sci Lakehead Univ Thunder Bay ON P7B 5E1 Can. *E-Mail:* john.griffith@lakeheadu.ca

GRIFFITH, JOHN SPENCER, FISHERY BIOLOGY, ECOLOGY. *Current Pos:* asst prof, 77-81, ASSOC PROF BIOL, IDAHO STATE UNIV, 81- *Personal Data:* b Utica, NY, July 18, 44. *Educ:* Cornell Univ, BS, 66, MS, 67; Univ Idaho, PhD(fisheries), 71. *Prof Exp:* Fisheries res officer, Govt Repub Zambia, 71-74; res assoc, Environ Sci Div, Oak Ridge Nat Lab, 74-77. *Concurrent Pos:* Assoc ed, Trans Am Fisheries Soc, 76-77. *Mem:* Am Fisheries Soc; Ecol Soc Am; AAAS; Sigma Xi. *Res:* Behavior of salmonid fishes; African fishery development; fish ecology and population dynamics. *Mailing Add:* Box 8007 Idaho State Univ Pocatello ID 83209-0009

GRIFFITH, LINDA M(AE), HEMATOPATHOLOGY, PATHOLOGY. *Current Pos:* FEL HEMATOPATH, LAB PATH, NAT CANCER INST, NIH, 92- *Personal Data:* b Edwards, Calif, Feb 16, 52. *Educ:* Tulane Univ, BS, 73; Univ Calif, Los Angeles, MA, 75; Harvard Univ, PhD(anat & cellular biol), 79; Univ Miami, MD, 87. *Prof Exp:* Fel cell biol & anat, Sch Med, Johns Hopkins Univ, 79-80; fel cell biol, Sch Med, Stanford Univ, 81-84; resident physician path, Sch Med, Yale Univ, 87-90, resident physician lab med, 90-92. *Concurrent Pos:* Am Soc Cell Biol travel award, Second Int Cong Cell Biol, Berlin, 80; Muscular Dystrophy Asn fel, 80-81; NIH fel, Dept Cell Biol, Sch Med, Stanford Univ, 81-84. *Mem:* Int Acad Path; Am Soc Clin Pathologists; Am Soc Cell Biol; Am Soc Hemat; Soc Hematopath. *Res:* Hematopathology; applications of cell biology to diagnostic surgical pathology; cell motility and the cytoskeleton. *Mailing Add:* Dept Hemolymphatic Path Armed Forces Inst Path Washington DC 20306-6000. *Fax:* 301-402-2415

GRIFFITH, M S, ELECTRICAL ENGINEERING. *Current Pos:* TECH LECTR & AUTHOR. *Personal Data:* b Dec 25, 40; c 2. *Educ:* Univ Mich, BSSE. *Honors & Awards:* Achievement Award, Inst Elec & Electronics Engrs/I & CPS. *Mem:* Fel Inst Elec & Electronics Engrs. *Mailing Add:* Brown & Root USA Inc 03-626 PO Box 3 Houston TX 77001

GRIFFITH, MARTIN G, LUBRICATION CHEMISTRY. *Current Pos:* RES ASSOC, EXXON RES & ENG CO, 67- *Personal Data:* b Philadelphia, Pa, Dec 4, 39; m 70, Rosemary; c Lisa, Christopher & David. *Educ:* Haverford Col, BS, 61; Pa State Univ, PhD(chem), 67. *Mem:* Am Chem Soc; Am Soc Testing & Mat. *Res:* Physical and chemical properties, solution thermodynamics of petroleum and synthetic fuel fractions; petroleum lubricant and gasoline development. *Mailing Add:* Exxon Res & Eng Co PO Box 51 Linden NJ 07036

GRIFFITH, MICHAEL GREY, TECHNICAL MANAGEMENT, ORGANIC CHEMISTRY. *Current Pos:* dir explor res, 77-80, dir insulation technol, 80-81, dir res & develop, 81-83, VPRES RES & DEVELOP, TECH CTR, OWENS-CORNING FIBERGLAS CORP, OHIO, 83- *Personal Data:* b Mansfield, La, Sept 30, 41; m 64; c 2. *Educ:* Northwestern Univ, BS, 63; La State Univ, Baton Rouge, PhD(chem), 67. *Prof Exp:* Res fel chem, Univ Minn, Minneapolis, 67-68; res chemist, Carothers Res Lab, Exp Sta, E I du Pont de Nemours & Co, Inc, 68-70, res chemist, Textile Res Lab, Chestnut Run, 71-73, res & develop supvr, Chattanooga Qiana Tech Lab, 73-75, res & develop supvr, Old Hickory Spunbonded Res Lab, 76-77. *Mem:* Am Chem Soc. *Res:* Fiber chemistry; free radical chemistry; nuclear magnetic resonance spectroscopy; chemical engineering. *Mailing Add:* Arco Chem Co 3801 W Chester Pike Newtown Square PA 19073

GRIFFITH, MICHAEL JAMES, ENZYMOLOGY, THROMBOSIS. *Current Pos:* Fel, Dept Path, Univ NC, Chapel Hill, 77-80, RES ASST PROF, DEPT MED, DIV HEMAT, 80-; VPRES SCI AFFAIRS, HYLAND DIV, BAXTER HEALTH CORP. *Personal Data:* b Kalamazoo, Mich, Dec 1, 48; m 69; c 2. *Educ:* Western Mich Univ, BS, 70; Univ Tex Health Sci Ctr, San Antonio, PhD(biochem), 77. *Concurrent Pos:* Mem, Coun Thrombosis, Am Heart Asn, 80- *Mem:* Am Soc Biol Chemists; Am Chem Soc. *Res:* Thrombosis and hemostasis involving the anticoagulant, heparin and plasma protease inhibitors; the role of blood coagulation factor IX in hemostasisis. *Mailing Add:* Prod Develop Dept Baxter Immunotherapy Div 9 Parker Irvine CA 92718. *Fax:* 714-470-6644

GRIFFITH, O HAYES, BIOPHYSICAL CHEMISTRY. *Current Pos:* from asst prof to assoc prof, 66-71, PROF CHEM & RES ASSOC, INST MOLECULAR BIOL, UNIV ORE, 71- *Personal Data:* b Torrance, Calif, Sept 14, 38; m 85, Karen Hedberg; c Daniel & Austin. *Educ:* Univ Calif, Riverside, BA, 60; Calif Inst Technol, PhD(chem), 64. *Honors & Awards:* Camille & Henry Dreyfus Found Teacher - Scholar Award, 70. *Prof Exp:* Nat Acad Sci-Nat Res Coun fel chem, Stanford Univ, 65-66. *Concurrent Pos:* Woodrow Wilson fel, 60-61, NSF fel, Calif Inst Technol, 61-64; fel, Nat Acad Sci, Nat Res Coun, Stanford Univ, 65, Sloan Found fel, 67-69, Guggenheim Found fel, 77-78; career develop award, Nat Cancer Inst, 72-76. *Mem:* Am Chem Soc; Biophys Soc; Electron Micros Soc Am; Am Soc Cell Biol; Am Asn Cancer Res. *Res:* Biophysical chemistry; electron and nuclear magnetic spectroscopy; photoelectron microscopy; lipid-protein interactions; cell surfaces. *Mailing Add:* Dept Chem Univ Ore Eugene OR 97403-1253. *Fax:* 541-346-4643; *E-Mail:* hayes@imagel.uoregon.edu

GRIFFITH, OWEN MALCOLM, biochemistry, biophysics, for more information see previous edition

GRIFFITH, OWEN W, ENZYMOLOGY, METABOLIC REGULATION. *Current Pos:* PROF & CHMN BIOCHEM, MED COL WIS, 92- *Personal Data:* b Oakland, Calif, June 19, 46. *Educ:* Univ Calif, Berkeley, BA, 68; Rockefeller Univ, PhD(biochem), 74. *Prof Exp:* Fel, NIII, 75-77; from asst prof to prof biochem, Cornell Univ Med Col, 78-92. *Concurrent Pos:* Prin investr var NIH, March of Dimes & Juv Diabetes Found grants, 81-; career scientist, Irma Hirschl Found, 81-85; exec ed, Analytical Biochem, 84-; ed-in-chief, Protein Expression & Purification, 90. *Mem:* Am Soc Biochem & Molecular Biol; Am Soc Pharmacol & Exp Therapeut; Am Chem Soc; AAAS. *Res:* Synthesis and function of glutathione and on its role with ascorbate in controlling oxidative stress; enzymology, physiology and pharmacology of nitric oxide as it relates to septic shock. *Mailing Add:* 8701 Watertown Plank Rd Milwaukee WI 53226. *Fax:* 414-266-8497

GRIFFITH, PETER, MECHANICAL ENGINEERING. *Current Pos:* asst, 52-56, from asst prof to assoc prof, 56-70, PROF MECH ENG, MASS INST TECHNOL, 70- *Personal Data:* b London, Eng, Sept 23, 27; m 83; c 2. *Educ:* NY Univ, BS, 50; Univ Mich, MSE, 52; Mass Inst Technol, ScD, 56. *Prof Exp:* Asst, Univ Mich, 50-52. *Mem:* Am Soc Mech Engrs; Am Nuclear Soc; Am Inst Chem Engrs. *Res:* Heat transfer with phase change and two phase flow; nuclear reactor thermal-hydraulics; reactor safety. *Mailing Add:* Rm 7-044 Mass Inst Technol 77 Mass Ave Cambridge MA 02139-4307

GRIFFITH, PHILLIP A, MATHEMATICS. *Current Pos:* from asst prof to assoc prof, 70-77, PROF MATH, UNIV ILL, URBANA, 77- *Personal Data:* b Danville, Ill, Dec 29, 40; m 60; c 2. *Educ:* Northern Mich Univ, BS, 63; Univ Mo, MA, 65; Univ Houston, PhD(math), 68. *Prof Exp:* Instr math, Univ Houston, 67-68; instr, Univ Chicago, 68-70. *Concurrent Pos:* Alfred P Sloan fel, 71-73. *Mem:* Am Math Soc. *Res:* Infinite Abelian groups; homological algebra of locally compact Abelian groups; ring theory. *Mailing Add:* Dept Math Univ Ill 1409 W Green St Urbana IL 61801-2917

GRIFFITH, ROBERT W, research administration, for more information see previous edition

GRIFFITH, THOMAS, BIOCHEMISTRY. *Current Pos:* assoc prof, Northern Mich Univ, 62-65, head dept, 65-66, assoc dean, Sch Arts & Sci, 66-67, dean, 67-72, PROF CHEM, NORTHERN MICH UNIV, 72- *Personal Data:* b Minneola, Kans, June 22, 30; m 58; c 3. *Educ:* Kans State Univ, BS, 52, MS, 54; Mich State Univ, PhD(chem), 58. *Prof Exp:* Asst cereal chem, Kans State Univ, 52-54; asst chem, Mich State Univ, 54-58, instr, 58-62. *Mem:* Am Chem Soc; Sigma Xi. *Res:* Plant metabolism; alkaloid biosynthesis; transmethylation; cereal chemistry; fermentation. *Mailing Add:* 806 W Kaye Ave Marquette MI 49855-2615

GRIFFITH, VIRGIL VERNON, COMPUTER SCIENCE. *Current Pos:* chief eng-electronics, 67-83, STAFF DIR, MCDONNEL AIRCRAFT CORP, 83- *Personal Data:* b Cicero, Ill, Dec 30, 28; m 48; c 5. *Educ:* Wash Univ, AB, 56, BS, 56, MS, 58; Case Inst Technol, PhD(systems), 67. *Prof Exp:* Sr group engr, McDonnel Aircraft Corp, St Louis, Mo, 52-61; sr tech specialist, Goodyear Aerospace, 61-67. *Concurrent Pos:* Instr, Washington Univ, 58-59; lectr, St Louis Community Col, Flo Valley, 70-74. *Mem:* Am Inst Aeronaut & Astronaut; Inst Elec & Electronics Engrs. *Res:* Applicability of new digital system techniques to avionic systems for advanced fighter aircraft. *Mailing Add:* 2750 Redman Ave St Louis MO 63136

GRIFFITH, W(ILLIAM) A(LEXANDER), EXTRACTIVE METALLURGY. *Current Pos:* RETIRED. *Personal Data:* b Sioux Falls, SDak, Mar 28, 22; m 49; c 3. *Educ:* SDak Sch Mines & Technol, BS, 47, DBA, 86; Mass Inst Technol, SM, 50. *Hon Degrees:* DBA, SDak Sch Mines & Technol, 86; DSc, Univ Idaho, 90. *Honors & Awards:* A M Gaudin Award, Am Inst Mining, Metall & Petrol Engrs, Robert A Richards Award, 81. *Prof Exp:* Metallurgist, Santiago-Alaska Mines, Inc, 47; investr mineral dressing, Res Dept, NJ Zinc Co, 49-52, group leader, 52-55, chief milling & maintenance, 55-57; chief metallurgist, Rare Metals Corp Am, Ariz, 57-58; head res dept, Morenci Br, Phelps Dodge Corp, 58-68; dir res, Hecla Mining Co, 68-73, vpres metall, 73-77, sr vpres, 77-78, exec vpres, 78-79, pres & chief exec officer, 79-85, chmn, 86-87, dir, 79-96. *Mem:* Hon mem Am Inst Mining, Metall & Petrol Engrs. *Res:* Unit operations of mineral benefication, extractive metallurgy. *Mailing Add:* 630 S 14th St Coeur D Alene ID 83814

GRIFFITH, WALTER M, JR, RAPID SOLIDIFICATION-POWER METALLURGY OF ALUMINUM & TITANTIUM ALLOYS, LIGHT ALLOYS FOR AEROSPACE STRUCTURES. *Current Pos:* res scientist struct metals, Mat Directorate, Wright Lab, 73-85, sr res scientist, 85-88, tech area mgr metals, Mfg Technol Directorate, 88-89, br chief, 89-91, br chief, Mat Process Design Mat Directorate, 91-94, CHIEF, METALS & CERAMICS DIV, MAT DIRECTORATE, WRIGHT LAB, 94- *Personal Data:* m 70, DuBois; c Catherine, Scott & Brian. *Educ:* Univ Cincinnati, BS, 72, MS, 73, PhD(eng), 84. *Concurrent Pos:* Air Force liaison, Expert Systs Mat Selection, Nat Mat Adv Bd, 91-, Sensors Comt, 92-; tech dir, Mfg Sci Prog, Man Tech Directorate, Wright Lab, 91-; mem, Aerospace Div Coun, Am Soc Mats Int, 91- *Mem:* Am Soc Mats Int. *Res:* Development and understanding of high strength and elevated temperature aerospace quality powder metallurgy aluminum alloys. *Mailing Add:* WL/MLL 2230 Tenth St Suite 1 Wright-Patterson AFB OH 45433-7817. *Fax:* 937-476-9792; *E-Mail:* griffiwm@mlgate.ml.wpafb.af.mil

GRIFFITH, WAYLAND C(OLEMAN), FLUID MECHANICS, ENERGY MANAGEMENT. *Current Pos:* RETIRED. *Personal Data:* b Champaign, Ill, June 26, 25; m 61; c 2. *Educ:* Harvard Univ, AB, 45, MS, 46, PhD(appl sci), 49. *Prof Exp:* Fel physics, Atomic Energy Comn, Princeton Univ, 49-50, from instr to asst prof, 50-57; mgr, Flight Sci Div, Missiles & Space Div, Lockheed Aircraft Corp, 57-58, assoc dir res, 58-59, asst dir res, 59-62, dir res, 62-66, vpres & asst gen mgr res & technol, Lockheed Missiles & Space Co, 66-71, asst dir new bus, 71-73; prof mech eng, NC State Univ, 73-97. *Concurrent Pos:* NSF fel, Univ Col, London, 55-56; vis prof, NC State Univ, 70-71; mem, Adv Comt Fluid Mech, NASA; mem, Div Comt Math & Phys Sci, NSF; mem, Bd Human Resources, Nat Acad Sci; mem panels 213 & 274, Nat Bur Stand. *Mem:* Am Phys Soc; Royal Aeronaut Soc; Am Inst Aeronaut & Astronaut; Sigma Xi. *Res:* Shock waves; supersonic flow; shock tube; turbocompressors; design engineering. *Mailing Add:* 809 Rosemont Ave Raleigh NC 27607

GRIFFITH, WILLIAM KIRK, AGRONOMY. *Current Pos:* eastern agronomist, 60-66, asst to pres, 66-68, EASTERN DIR, POTASH & PHOSPHATE INST, 68- *Personal Data:* b Henry, Ill, May 25, 29; m 51; c 2. *Educ:* Western Ill Univ, BS, 51; Univ Ill, MS, 52; Purdue Univ, PhD(agron), 60. *Honors & Awards:* Agron Serv Award, Am Soc Agron, 74. *Prof Exp:* Asst county agt, Univ Ariz Coop Exten Serv, 56-58. *Mem:* Am Soc Agron; Soil Sci Soc Am; Crop Sci Soc Am; Am Forage & Grassland Coun. *Res:* Stimulation and development of sound soil fertility research in the Northeastern United States. *Mailing Add:* 865 Seneca Rd Great Falls VA 22066

GRIFFITH, WILLIAM SCHULER, RELIABILITY THEORY, APPLIED PROBABILITY. *Current Pos:* asst prof, 79-85, ASSOC PROF STATIST, UNIV KY, 85- *Personal Data:* b Bradford, Pa, Oct 10, 49; m 72, Deborah A Fragale; c Mark & Lisa. *Educ:* Grove City Col, BS, 71; Univ Pittsburgh MA, 73, PhD(math statist), 79. *Prof Exp:* Teaching asst & fel, Dept Math & Statist, Univ Pittsburgh, 71-76; lectr math, Dept Exact Sci, Carlow Col, 77; casual mathematician, Systs Sci, Westinghouse Res & Develop Ctr, 77-79. *Mem:* Inst Math Statist; Am Statist Asn; Oper Res Soc Am; Soc Indust & Appl Math; Biometric Soc. *Res:* Mathematical theory of reliability with particular emphasis on multistate reliability models, shock models, minimal repair models; applied probability models in engineering and biology. *Mailing Add:* Dept Statist Univ Ky Lexington KY 40506-0027. *Fax:* 606-323-1973; *E-Mail:* griffith@ms.uky.edu

GRIFFITH, WILLIAM THOMAS, CRYSTAL GROWTH, HOLOGRAPHY. *Current Pos:* from asst prof to assoc prof, Pac Univ, 67-81, chmn, Dept Physics, 71-76 & 85-88, chmn, Div Sci & Math, 76-82, chmn, Dept Physics, 90-95, PROF PHYSICS, PAC UNIV, 81- *Personal Data:* b Palmerton, Pa, Aug 15, 40; m 67, Adelia Sasaki; c Lewis T, W Clark & Mark O. *Educ:* Johns Hopkins Univ, BA, 62; Univ NM, MS, 64, PhD(physics) 68. *Prof Exp:* NASA trainee, Univ NM, 65-67. *Concurrent Pos:* Consult, Energy Resources, Holographic Toy Design. *Mem:* Am Phys Soc; Am Asn Physics Teachers; Am Asn Crystal Growth; Sigma Xi. *Res:* Kinetics of phase transformations; plastic crystals; thermodynamics of solids; crystal growth; solar energy; science teaching, research, holography. *Mailing Add:* Dept Physics Pac Univ Forest Grove OR 97116. *E-Mail:* griffitt@pacificu.edu

GRIFFITHS, ANTHONY J F, GENETICS, MOLECULAR BIOLOGY. *Current Pos:* teaching fel, 70-71, from asst prof to assoc prof, 77-82, PROF BOT, UNIV BC, 82- *Personal Data:* b Bristol, Gr Brit, Oct 24, 40; m 63; c 4. *Educ:* Univ Keele, BA, 63; McMaster Univ, PhD(molecular biol), 67. *Prof Exp:* Res assoc biol, Kans State Univ, 67-68; NIH fel, Oak Ridge Nat Lab, 68-70. *Mem:* Environ Mutagen Soc; Genetics Soc Am; Genetics Soc Can. *Res:* Senescence plasmids in Neurospora. *Mailing Add:* Dept Bot Univ BC Suite 3529 6270 University Blvd Vancouver BC V6T 1Z4 Can

GRIFFITHS, CLIFFORD H, SOLID STATE & POLYMER PHYSICS. *Current Pos:* prin scientist, 72-91, MGR, NEW DEVICE MAT, MAT RES LAB, WEBSTER RES CTR, XEROX CORP, 92- *Personal Data:* b Chester, Eng, Jan 28, 36; m 57; c 2. *Educ:* Nottingham Univ, Eng, BSc, 57; London Univ, MSc, 64, PhD(phys chem), 73. *Prof Exp:* Scientist chem, Noranda Mines Ltd, Que, 57-61; res fel physics, London Univ, 61-63; group leader, Noranda Res Ctr, Noranda Mines Ltd, 63-67; assoc scientist, Rochester Corp Res Ctr, Xerox Corp, 67-70; group leader, Multi-State Devices, Montreal, 70-72. *Mem:* Mat Res Soc; Soc Imaging Sci & Technol. *Res:* Morphology structure and structure-electronic property relationships in organic and inorganic polymers; thin film structure and properties. *Mailing Add:* Xerox Corp Webster Res Ctr W114 800 Philips Rd Webster NY 14580. *Fax:* 716-422-2126; *E-Mail:* griffiths.wbst128@xerox.com

GRIFFITHS, DAVID, PHYSICS. *Current Pos:* RETIRED. *Personal Data:* b Neath, Wales, May 2, 38; m 76, 84; c 4. *Educ:* Univ Wales, BSc, 60, PhD(physics), 64. *Prof Exp:* Asst lectr physics, Univ Col Swansea, Wales, 64-65; res physicist, Eng Physics Lab, E I du Pont de Nemours & Co, 65-69, supvr, Electronics Group, 69-70, res supvr, Appl Physics Sect, 70-72, sr supvr, 72-74, field supvr & sr supvr, Tech Serv Sect, Chamber Works Chem Plant, NJ, 74-76, mgr instruments & control, Eng Physics Lab, Exp Sta, 76-79, mgr mat & mach dynamics, Eng Technol Lab, 79-87, mgr bioeng, 87-91. *Mem:* Brit Inst Physics; Am Inst Physics. *Res:* Electrical breakdown and gaseous ionization; surface physics, especially conductivity, friction, static properties, polymer adhesion and highpower laser technology; color, computer technology, textile fiber technology; catalysis, coatings, wear, microscopy, metallurgy, electrochemistry; vibrational analysis, computer monitoring, robotics, micro and mini computers. *Mailing Add:* 12 Jarrell Farm Dr Newark DE 19711

GRIFFITHS, DAVID JEFFERY, THEORETICAL PHYSICS. *Current Pos:* from asst prof to assoc prof, 78-88, PROF PHYSICS, REED COL, 88- *Personal Data:* b Washington, DC, Dec 5, 42; m 70, Terry Marshall; c Jennifer & Timothy. *Educ:* Harvard Univ, BA, 64, MA, 66, PhD(physics), 70. *Prof Exp:* Res assoc & assoc instr physics, Univ Utah, 70-72; res assoc & assoc instr, Univ Mass, 72-74; asst prof, Mt Holyoke Col, 74-77, Trinity Col, 77-78. *Concurrent Pos:* Visitor, Theory Group, Stanford Linear Accelerator Ctr, 84-85, Lawrence Berkeley Lab, 91. *Mem:* Am Asn Physics Teachers; Am Phys Soc. *Res:* Classical and quantum theory of fields. *Mailing Add:* Dept Physics Reed Col Portland OR 97202. *Fax:* 503-777-7770; *E-Mail:* griffith@reed.edu

GRIFFITHS, DAVID JOHN, PHYSICS. *Current Pos:* asst prof, 67-71, assoc prof, 71-86, PROF PHYSICS, ORE STATE UNIV, 86. *Personal Data:* b Vancouver, BC, June 15, 38; m 62; c 3. *Educ:* Univ BC, BA, 59, MSc, 60, PhD(low temperature physics), 65. *Prof Exp:* Teaching asst, Univ BC, 62-64; res assoc superconductivity & lectr, Univ Southern Calif, 65-67. *Concurrent Pos:* Mem tech staffs, Oak Ridge Nat Lab, 74-75, Cen Saclay, 82-83. *Mem:* Am Phys Soc. *Res:* Magnetic properties of amorphous alloys and shock-wave physics. *Mailing Add:* Dept Physics Ore State Univ Corvallis OR 97331

GRIFFITHS, DAVID WARREN, PHYSICAL ORGANIC CHEMISTRY, BIO-ORGANIC & ENVIRONMENTAL CHEMISTRY. *Current Pos:* PRES, OLVER LAB, INC, 89- *Personal Data:* b St Louis, Mo, Oct 23, 44; m 65; c Sarah & Benjamin. *Educ:* Wilmington Col, AB, 65; Washington Univ, St Louis, PhD(chem), 70. *Prof Exp:* Fel, Northwestern Univ, 70-73; res chemist, Petrolite Corp, 73-77, mgr water res, tretolite div, 77-83; dir res & technol, Olin Water Serv, Kans, 83-89. *Mem:* Am Chem Soc; Sigma Xi; AAAS; Water Environ Fedn; Air & Waste Mgt Asn. *Res:* Efficient management of water resources; water and waste water treatment technologies; remediation of contaminated soils and ground water; risk assessments, environmental policy. *Mailing Add:* Olver Inc 1116 S Main St Blacksburg VA 24060. *Fax:* 540-552-5577; *E-Mail:* labs@olver.com

GRIFFITHS, GEORGE MOTLEY, NUCLEAR PHYSICS, RESOURCE MANAGEMENT. *Current Pos:* from asst prof to assoc prof, 55-63, PROF PHYSICS, UNIV BC, 63- *Personal Data:* b Thorold, Ont, Dec 12, 23; m 48; c 5. *Educ:* Univ Toronto, BSc, 49; Univ BC, MA, 50, PhD(physics), 53. *Prof Exp:* Asst physics, Nat Res Coun Can, Chalk River, 48-49; Rutherford Mem fel, Cavendish Lab, Cambridge Univ, 53-55. *Concurrent Pos:* Sr res fel, Calif Inst Technol, 62-63; energy adv, Ministry of State, Sci & Technol, Govt Can, 73-75. *Mem:* Am Phys Soc; Can Asn Physicists. *Res:* Low energy nuclear physics, direct radiative capture reactions; technical, economic and political factors in Canadian energy policy. *Mailing Add:* 1975 W 15th Ave Vancouver BC V6J 2L2 Can

GRIFFITHS, JAMES EDWARD, INORGANIC CHEMISTRY, SPECTROSCOPY. *Current Pos:* DISTINGUISHED CONSULT IN RESIDENCE, ARMSTRONG STATE COL, 87- *Personal Data:* b Ft Frances, Ont, June 1, 31; m 54; c 1. *Educ:* Univ Man, BSc, 55, MSc, 56; McGill Univ, PhD(inorg chem), 59. *Prof Exp:* Res assoc phys chem, Univ Southern Calif, 58-60; mem tech staff, AT&T Bell Labs, 60-86; DIR/CONSULT, INSTRUMENTS SA INC, 85- *Concurrent Pos:* Vis prof physics, Univ Paris VI, 78-79. *Mem:* AAAS; Am Phys Soc; Soc Appl Spectros; fel Optical Soc Am. *Res:* Synthesis, properties, molecular structure of volatile compounds; molecular structure and interactions in gases and liquids; arc phenomena in ultraviolet and vacuum ultraviolet; Raman scattering, absolute scattering cross-sections and molecular dynamics in the liquid state; structure of glasses; thin films; semiconductor-oxide interfacial reactions; surface physics; solid state physics. *Mailing Add:* 6 Lampwick Lane Savannah GA 31411

GRIFFITHS, JOAN MARTHA, BIOCHEMISTRY, CHEMISTRY. *Current Pos:* ASST PROF CHEM & BIOCHEM, KEUKA COL, 76-; LECTR, CORNELL UNIV, 79- *Personal Data:* b Rutherford, NJ, Apr 23, 35. *Educ:* Univ Rochester, BS, 57; Cornell Univ, PhD(biochem), 67. *Prof Exp:* Lab technician, Sloan-Kettering Inst, 57-58; teacher sci, North Babylon Pub Sch, 58-62; res assoc biochem, Cornell Univ, 67-69, lectr, 70-76. *Mem:* Am Chem Soc; Sigma Xi; AAAS. *Res:* Methylation reactions. *Mailing Add:* Dept Molecular Biol Cornell Univ Biotechnol Bldg Ithaca NY 14853-0001

GRIFFITHS, JOHN CEDRIC, petrology, geology statistics; deceased, see previous edition for last biography

GRIFFITHS, JOHN FREDERICK, METEOROLOGY. *Current Pos:* from asst prof to assoc prof, 62-70, PROF METEOROL, TEX A&M UNIV, 70-, PROF GEOG, 86- *Personal Data:* b London, Eng, Feb 8, 26; m 62. *Educ:* Univ London, BS, 47, MS, 49, dipl, Imp Col, 48. *Prof Exp:* Bioclimatologist, Brit, Colonial Sci Res Serv, 50-57; chief res, EAfrican Meteorol Dept, 57-62. *Concurrent Pos:* Mem comts instruments, agr meteorol & climat, World Meteorol Orgn, 58-63; Rockefeller & Munitalp Found travel grants, 60; pres, Appl Trop Res; chief consult, World Meteorol Orgn, 74 & 78-; prin investr climatic res, NSF, NIH & Nat Weather Serv; Key consult, Food Agr Orgn; state climatologist, Tex, 73- *Mem:* Am Meteorol Soc; World Acad Art & Sci; fel Royal Meteorol Soc; fel Royal Geog Soc. *Res:* All aspects of biometeorology, especially statistical analysis, instrumentation and agricultural climatology. *Mailing Add:* Dept Meteorol Tex A&M Univ College Station TX 77843-0100

GRIFFITHS, LLOYD JOSEPH, ELECTRICAL ENGINEERING, APPLIED MATHEMATICS. *Current Pos:* prof elec eng, 84-86, ASSOC DEAN ENG, UNIV SOUTHERN CALIF, 86- *Personal Data:* b Edmonton, Alta, Sept 30, 41; m 61, 84; c 3. *Educ:* Univ Alta, BSc, 63; Stanford Univ, MSc, 65, PhD(elec eng), 68. *Honors & Awards:* B J Thompson Award, Inst Elec & Electronics Engrs, 71. *Prof Exp:* Res engr, Defence Res Bd, Ottawa, 63; res asst radiosci, Stanford Univ, 63-65; circuit engr, Hewlett Packard Co, 65; res asst, Stanford Univ, 65-68; staff scientist commun, Barry Res Corp, 69 70; prof, Univ Colo, 68-69, prof elec eng, 70-84. *Concurrent Pos:* Res scientist, Nat Ctr Atmospheric Res, 71; consult, Marathon Oil Co, 71-77, IBM Corp, 73-79, Nat Oceanic & Atmospheric Admin, 76-78, SRI Int, 76-, MIT Lincoln Lab, 79-80, Ball Bros Aerospace Corp, 80-84, NCR Corp, 81-84, MRO Assoc, 81, Ford Aerospace Corp, 81-84, TRW, 84- *Mem:* Inst Elec & Electronics Engrs; Soc Explor Geophysicists; Sigma Xi. *Res:* Adaptive antenna arrays; baseband high density recording and equalization; seismic processing; adaptive noise cancelling; short term spectral estimation techniques; communication systems; direction finding systems; neural networks. *Mailing Add:* Univ Southern Calif University Park Los Angeles CA 90089

GRIFFITHS, PETER ROUGHLEY, FOURIER TRANSFORM INFRARED SPECTROMETRY, RAMAN SPECTROMETRY. *Current Pos:* PROF & CHAIR, DEPT CHEM, UNIV IDAHO, 89- *Personal Data:* b Cheam, Surrey, Eng, Jan 20, 42; m 71, Marie F Burns; c Sian B & Megan C. *Educ:* Oxford Univ, BA, 64, DPhil, 67. *Honors & Awards:* Coblentz Award, Coblentz Soc, 75. *Prof Exp:* Assoc, Univ Md, 67-69; prod specialist, Digilab Inc, 69-70; anal servs mgr, Sadtler Res Labs Inc, 70-72; from asst prof to prof chem, Ohio Univ, 72-82; prof, Univ Calif, Riverside, 82-89. *Mem:* Soc Appl Spectros, (pres-elect, 93, pres, 94); Am Chem Soc; Am Soc Testing & Mat; Coblentz Soc (pres, 77). *Res:* Analytical chemistry with special emphasis on vibrational spectrometry; fourier transform infrared spectroscopy and applications in hyphenated techniques, diffuse reflection and photoacoustic spectrometry; instrument developments in step-scanning interferometry and near infrared raman spectrometry. *Mailing Add:* Chem Dept Univ Idaho 375 S Line St Moscow ID 83843-4140. *Fax:* 208-885-6173; *E-Mail:* chemoff@idui1

GRIFFITHS, PHILLIP A, ALGEBRAIC GEOMETRY. *Current Pos:* DIR, INST ADVAN STUDY, 91- *Personal Data:* b Raleigh, NC, Oct 18, 38. *Educ:* Wake Forest Univ, BS, 59; Princeton Univ, PhD(math), 63. *Hon Degrees:* Dr, Wake Forest Univ, 73, Angers Univ, France, 79, Univ Peking, 83. *Honors & Awards:* LeRoy P Steele Prize, Am Math Soc, 71; Dannie-Heineman Prize, Acad Sci, Gottingen, 79. *Prof Exp:* Miller fel, Univ Calif, Berkeley, 62-64, mem fac, 64-67 & 75-76; prof math, Princeton Univ, 68-72; prof, Harvard Univ, 72-83, Dwight Robinson Parker prof, 82; James B Duke prof & provost, Duke Univ, 83-91. *Concurrent Pos:* Vis prof, Princeton Univ, 67-68; Guggenheim fel, 80-82; Guggenheim fel, Peking Univ & Nanking; ed, J Differential Geom, 80-90, Composito Mathematica, 80-92 & Duke Math J; mem exec off, US Nat Comt Mathematicians; treas, Comn Develop & Exchange, Int Math Union; mem, Comn Phys Sci, Math & Resources; mem bd trustees, NC Sch Sci & Math; mem bd trustees, Woodward Acad; guest prof, Univ Peking, 83; mem, Bd Gov, Res Triangle Inst, bd dirs, 83-91; bd dirs, Bankers Trust NY Corp, 94- *Mem:* Nat Acad Sci; Am Philos Soc; Am Acad Arts & Sci. *Mailing Add:* Inst Advan Study Princeton NJ 08540

GRIFFITHS, RAYMOND BERT, BIOLOGY, MEDICINE. *Current Pos:* RETIRED. *Personal Data:* b Worcester, Mass, June 16, 15; m 51; c 1. *Educ:* Univ Rochester, 37; Princeton Univ, AM, 39, PhD(biol), 40; Northwestern Univ, MD, 46. *Prof Exp:* Instr zool, Univ Ariz, 40-42; resident physician, Cushing Vet Admin Hosp, Framingham, Mass, 48-49; instr anat, Yale Univ, 52-54; consult, Med Serv Div, Ciba Pharmaceut Prods, Inc, NJ, 54-58; ed dir, med affairs dept, Am Cancer Soc, Inc, 58-60; exec ed, J Cell Biol, Rockefeller Univ, 60- *Concurrent Pos:* Res fel pediat & anat, Sch Med, Yale Univ, 49-52. *Mem:* AAAS; Coun Biol Ed; Am Asn Anat. *Res:* Cytology of amphibia; human anatomy; biological and medical editing and writing. *Mailing Add:* 1700 York Ave New York NY 10128

GRIFFITHS, ROBERT BUDINGTON, STATISTICAL MECHANICS, QUANTUM MECHANICS. *Current Pos:* from asst prof to assoc prof, 64-69, PROF PHYSICS, CARNEGIE-MELLON UNIV, 69- *Personal Data:* b Etah, India, Feb 25, 37; US citizen. *Educ:* Princeton Univ, AB, 57; Stanford Univ, MS, 58, PhD(physics), 62. *Honors & Awards:* US Sr Scientist Award, Alexander von Humboldt Found, 73; A Cressy Morrison Award, NY Acad Sci, 81; Dannie Heineman Prize, 84. *Prof Exp:* NSF fel, Univ Calif, San Diego, 62-64. *Concurrent Pos:* Alfred P Sloan res fel, 66-68; vis assoc prof, State Univ NY Stony Brook, 69; Guggenheim Found fel, 73; Otto Stern prof physics, Carnegie-Mellon, 79. *Mem:* Nat Acad Sci; Am Sci Affil; Am Phys Soc. *Res:* Interpretation of quantum mechanics; quantum computation; incommensurate phases; relation of physical science and Christian theology. *Mailing Add:* Dept Physics Carnegie-Mellon Univ Pittsburgh PA 15213. *Fax:* 412-681-0648; *E-Mail:* rgrif@cmu.edu

GRIFFITHS, ROLAND REDMOND, BEHAVIORAL PHARMACOLOGY. *Current Pos:* From asst prof to assoc prof, 72-86, PROF BEHAV BIOL & NEUROSCI, JOHNS HOPKINS UNIV SCH MED, 86- *Personal Data:* b Glen Cove, NY, July 19, 46; c Sylvie, Jennie & Morgan. *Educ:* Occidental Col, BA, 68; Univ Minn, PhD(psychopharmacol), 72. *Mem:* Behav Pharmacol Soc; Am Psychol Asn; Am Col Neuropsychopharmacol; Col Probs Drug Dependence. *Res:* Behavioral and pharmacological analysis of human and infrahuman drug self-administration with special emphasis on benzodiazepines and caffeine. *Mailing Add:* Dept Psychiat Behav Biol Res Ctr Johns Hopkins Bayview Res Campus 5510 Nathan Shock Dr Baltimore MD 21224. *Fax:* 410-550-0030; *E-Mail:* griffiths@bpru.uucp.jhu.edu

GRIFFITHS, THOMAS ALAN, COMPARATIVE ANATOMY, SYSTEMATICS. *Current Pos:* from asst prof to assoc prof, 81-90, PROF BIOL, ILL WESLEYAN UNIV, 90- *Personal Data:* b Lewiston, Maine, Sept 16, 51; m 73, 91, Margaret Darner; c Jennifer & Anne. *Educ:* Bates Col, BS, 73; Univ Vt, MS, 76; Univ Mass, PhD(zool), 81. *Prof Exp:* Instr biol, State Univ NY, Col Plattsburgh, 77-78. *Concurrent Pos:* Res assoc, Dept Mammal, Am Mus Nat Hist, NY, 84- *Mem:* Am Soc Mammalogists; Soc Syst Zool; Soc Study Evolution; Soc Vert Paleont; Sigma Xi; Asn Trop Biol. *Res:* Dissection and histological examination of the musculo skeletal system of bats; evolution and biogeography of bats; functional anatomy of the larynx. *Mailing Add:* Dept Biol Ill Wesleyan Univ PO Box 2900 Bloomington IL 61702-2900. *Fax:* 309-556-3411; *E-Mail:* griffith@vmd.cso.uiuc.edu

GRIFFITHS, VERNON, FAILURE ANALYSIS, MATERIALS ENGINEERING. *Current Pos:* assoc prof metall, Mont Col Mineral Sci & Technol, 59-64, dir res, 76-84, exec dir, Mont Tech Found, 76-80, dir grad sch, 77-85, PROF METALL, MONT COL MINERAL SCI & TECHNOL, 64-, HEAD DEPT, 59- *Personal Data:* b Treorchy, Wales, May 4, 29; US citizen; m 54; c 5. *Educ:* Univ Wales, BSc, 49, MSc, 51; Mass Inst Technol, ScD(metall), 55. *Prof Exp:* Res assoc, Univ BC, 55-59. *Concurrent Pos:* Res metallurgist, Sherritt Gordon Mines, Ltd, 55-57. *Mem:* Am Soc Metals; Metall Soc Am Inst Mech Engrs; Am Powder Metall Inst; Inst Metals; Am Ceramic Soc; Mat Res Soc. *Res:* Corrosion of muffle tube alloys; ceramics. *Mailing Add:* Dept Metall Mont Col Mineral Sci & Technol 1470 W Park St Butte MT 59701

GRIFFITHS, WILLIAM C, CLINICAL CHEMISTRY. *Current Pos:* asst prof, Dept Biomed Sci, 74-85, ASSOC PROF, DEPT CLIN SCI, BROWN UNIV, 85-; CLIN BIOCHEMIST, ROGER WILLIAMS HOSP, 71- *Personal Data:* b Fall River, Mass, Nov 23, 39; m 68; c 2. *Educ:* Providence Col, BS, 62, PhD(org chem), 67; Am Bd Clin Chem, dipl. *Prof Exp:* Fel, Ohio State Univ, 67-68; org chemist, RI Hosp, 68-71. *Mem:* AAAS; Am Chem Soc; Am Asn Clin Chemists; Asn Clin Scientists. *Res:* Analytical methodology in endocrinology and toxicology; protein binding of small molecules. *Mailing Add:* Chalkstone Ave Providence RI 02908-4728

GRIFFITTS, JAMES JOHN, medicine; deceased, see previous edition for last biography

GRIFFITTS, WALLACE RUSH, ECONOMIC GEOLOGY. *Current Pos:* geologist, 46-91, EMER GEOLOGIST, US GEOL SURV, 91- *Personal Data:* b Ann Arbor, Mich, Oct 28, 19; m 46; c 4. *Educ:* Univ Mich, BS, 42, MS, 49, PhD(geol), 58. *Mem:* Mineral Soc Am; Geochem Soc; Am Soc Econ Geologists; Am Geophys Union; Soc Geol Appl Mineral Deposits. *Res:* Exploration geochemistry; geology of pegmatites; nonmetallic mineral deposits; geology of beryllium deposits; rock weathering. *Mailing Add:* 810 14th St Boulder CO 80302

GRIFFO, JAMES VINCENT, JR, NATURAL HISTORY, PARASITOLOGY. *Current Pos:* RETIRED. *Personal Data:* b Brooklyn, NY, Sept 17, 28; m 54; c 3. *Educ:* Univ Ky, BS, 52, MS, 53; Univ Fla, PhD(biol), 60. *Prof Exp:* Asst zool, Univ Ky, 52-53; asst parasitol, Univ Tenn, 55-56; asst biol, Univ Fla, 56-60; instr, Farleigh Dickinson Univ, 60-61; res biologist, Patuxent Wildlife Res Ctr, 61-62; from asst prof to assoc prof, Farleigh Dickinson Univ, 62-69, chmn, Biol Dept, 62-69, dean campus, 67-71, prof biol, 69-89, provost campus, 71-89. *Mem:* Am Soc Mammalogists; Wildlife Soc; Wilderness Soc. *Res:* Experimental natural history; mammals and insects; comparative parasitology; small mammal behavior. *Mailing Add:* 33 Sherbrooke Dr Florham Park NJ 07932

GRIFFO, JOSEPH SALVATORE, PHYSICAL CHEMISTRY, INORGANIC CHEMISTRY. *Current Pos:* RETIRED. *Personal Data:* b Mt Morris, NY, Oct 13, 27; m 54, Zora Jasincuk; c 2. *Educ:* Col St Bonaventure, BS, 51, MS, 54; St Louis Univ, PhD(inorg chem), 61. *Prof Exp:* Teacher high sch, NY, 51-52; res chemist, Olin Mathieson Chem Corp, 55-57; res asst boron hydrides, St Louis Univ, 57-61; sr res chemist, Mound Lab, Monsanto Res Corp, 61-66; isotopic fuels specialist, US AEC Hq, Germantown, 66-75; systs engr, Energy Res & Develop Admin, 75-77; systs engr, US Dept Energy, 77-88. *Mem:* AAAS; Am Chem Soc; Am Inst Physics; Sigma Xi. *Res:* Plutonium chemistry; systems analysis; chemistry of boron hydrides; high energy fuels; chemistry of rare earths; salts of barbituric acid. *Mailing Add:* 12330 Old Canal Rd Potomac MD 20854-6238

GRIFFO, ZORA JASINCUK, PHYSIOLOGY. *Current Pos:* RETIRED. *Personal Data:* b Prague, Czech, Nov 24, 28; US citizen; m 54, Joseph S; c 2. *Educ:* St Bonaventure Univ, BS, 52; Buffalo Univ, PhD(physiol), 59. *Prof Exp:* Asst anesthesiol, Sch Med, Wash Univ, 58-61; grants assoc, Div Res Grants, NIH, 68-69, prog officer, Craniofacial Anomalies Prog, Nat Inst Dent Res, 69-70 & prog chief, 70-73, health sci adminr, Off of Dir, 73-75, spec progs officer, 75-85, appeals officer, 85-89. *Res:* Cardiovascular and pulmonary physiology. *Mailing Add:* 12330 Old Canal Rd Potomac MD 20854

GRIFFY, THOMAS ALAN, THEORETICAL PHYSICS. *Current Pos:* assoc prof, 65-68, assoc dean grad sch, 70-73, chmn dept, 74-84, PROF PHYSICS, UNIV TEX, 68- *Personal Data:* b Oklahoma City, Okla, Dec 16, 36; m 58; c 3. *Educ:* Rice Univ, BA, 59, MA, 60, PhD(physics), 61. *Prof Exp:* Asst prof physics, Duke Univ, 61-62; res assoc Stanford Univ, 62-65. *Mem:* Am Phys Soc; Acoust Soc Am. *Res:* Theoretical physics. *Mailing Add:* Dept Phys Univ Tex-Austin 6806 Pioneer Pl Austin TX 78732

GRIGAL, DAVID F, SOIL SCIENCE, FOREST ECOLOGY. *Current Pos:* from asst prof to assoc prof, 70-80, PROF SOIL SCI, UNIV MINN, ST PAUL, 80- *Personal Data:* b Orr, Minn, Sept 21, 41; m 64; c 2. *Educ:* Univ Minn, St Paul, BS, 63, MS, 65, PhD(soil sci), 68. *Prof Exp:* AEC fel, 68-70; res assoc, Ecol Sci Div, Oak Ridge Nat Lab, 70. *Mem:* AAAS; Ecol Soc Am; Am Soc Agron; Soc Wetland Scientists. *Res:* Nutrient cycling; water quality; air pollution impacts; forest management impacts. *Mailing Add:* Dept Soil Water & Climate Univ Minn St Paul MN 55108. *E-Mail:* dave.grigal@soils.umn.edu

GRIGARICK, ALBERT ANTHONY, JR, ENTOMOLOGY. *Current Pos:* Lectr & asst entomologist to assoc prof & assoc entomologist, 57-70, PROF ENTOM & ENTOMOLOGIST, UNIV CALIF, DAVIS, 70- *Personal Data:* b Redding, Calif, Dec 22, 27; m 46; c 3. *Educ:* Univ Calif, BS, 53, PhD(entom) 57. *Mem:* Entom Soc Am; Sigma Xi. *Res:* Economic entomology; biology and control of pests in field crops; systematics; Pselaphidae; Megachilidae; Tardigrada. *Mailing Add:* 1001 Plum Lane Davis CA 95616

GRIGG, PETER, BIOMECHANICS, MECHANORECEPTORS. *Current Pos:* PROF PHYSIOL, MED SCH, UNIV MASS, 72- *Educ:* NY State Univ, PhD(physiol), 69. *Mailing Add:* Dept Physiol Univ Mass Med Sch 55 Lake Ave N Worcester MA 01655. *Fax:* 508-856-5997

GRIGG, RICHARD WYMAN, OCEANOGRAPHY, CORAL REEF ECOLOGY & PALEOECOLOGY. *Current Pos:* from asst prof to assoc prof, 70-81, PROF OCEANOG, UNIV HAWAII, 82- *Personal Data:* b Los Angeles, Calif, Apr 12, 37; m 94; c Romy, Raina & Carol. *Educ:* Stanford Univ, BS, 58; Univ Hawaii, MS, 64; Univ Calif, San Diego, PhD(oceanog), 70. *Prof Exp:* Res asst oceanog, Univ Calif, San Diego, 64-70. *Concurrent Pos:* Assoc prog dir, Nat Sea Grant Prog, 75-77; mem, WPac Fisheries Mgt Coun, 77-79; consult UNESCO & UN Develop Prog, 79-81. *Mem:* Am Soc Limnol & Oceanog; Am Inst Biol Sci; Ecol Soc Am; Sigma Xi; AAAS; Int Soc Reef Studies. *Res:* Coral reef ecology, patterns of response of marine temperate and tropical shallow water communities to stress; ecology and fishery dynamics of precious corals; paleoceanography; marine accident reconstruction. *Mailing Add:* Dept Oceanog Univ Hawaii 1000 Pope Rd Honolulu HI 96822. *E-Mail:* rgrigg@soest.hawaii.edu

GRIGGER, DAVID JOHN, ELECTROCHEMICAL PROCESSES, SEMICONDUCTOR PROCESSES. *Current Pos:* CHEM ENGR, LIFE SYSTS INC, 87- *Personal Data:* b Cleveland, May 5, 60. *Educ:* Cleveland State Univ, BS, 82; Ohio State Univ, MS, 83; John Carroll Univ, MBA, 93. *Prof Exp:* Intern, Stand Oil Co, 82; assoc mem tech staff, RCA Corp, 84-87. *Mem:* Am Inst Chem Engrs; Soc Automotive Engrs; Int Asn Hydrogen Energy. *Res:* Development and mathematical modeling of chemical and electrochemical processes for regenerative life support systems used in space applications. *Mailing Add:* 6507 Marsol Rd No 122 Cleveland OH 44124

GRIGGS, ALLAN BINGHAM, GEOLOGY. *Current Pos:* RETIRED. *Personal Data:* b Cottage Grove, Ore, June 10, 09; m 40; c 1. *Educ:* Univ Ore, BS, 32; Stanford Univ, PhD(geol), 52. *Prof Exp:* Geol field asst, US Engrs, Ore, 35-38; lab asst geol, Stanford Univ, 39-40; geologist, US Geol Surv, 40-74. *Concurrent Pos:* Mem staff, Inst Int Mining Res, Japan, 74-76; courtesy prof, Univ Ore, 77- *Mem:* Soc Econ Geologists; fel Geol Soc Am. *Res:* Economic geology, particularly chromite and lead-zinc deposits; areal geology of Coeur d'Alene district, Idaho. *Mailing Add:* 1121 Spyglass Dr Eugene OR 97401

GRIGGS, DOUGLAS M, JR, PHYSIOLOGY, MEDICINE. *Current Pos:* assoc prof, 67-70, PROF PHYSIOL & MED, SCH MED, UNIV MO-COLUMBIA, 70- *Personal Data:* b Aug 14, 28; US citizen; m 56; c 2. *Educ:* Harvard Univ, AB, 49; Univ Va, MD, 53; Am Bd Internal Med, dipl. *Prof Exp:* From intern to asst resident, St Lukes Hosp, New York, 53-58; clin biophys, Nat Heart Inst, 61-62; from asst med to assoc prof, Hahnemann Med Col & Hosp, 62-67. *Concurrent Pos:* NY Heart Asn fel, St Lukes Hosp, 58-60; fel, Univ Pittsburgh, 60-61; USPHS fel, 60-62, res career develop awards, 63-67 & 68-73. *Mem:* Am Fedn Clin Res; Am Physiol Soc; Soc Exp Biol & Med. *Res:* Cardiovascular physiology particularly myocardial metabolism and coronary physiology. *Mailing Add:* Dept Physiol Univ Mo Sch Med MA-415 Med Sci Bldg Columbia MO 65211-0001. *Fax:* 573-884-4232

GRIGGS, GARY B, COASTAL GEOLOGY & PROCESSES. *Current Pos:* From asst prof to assoc prof, Univ Calif, Santa Cruz, 69-79, chmn dept, 81-84, assoc dean, Div Natural Sci, 91-94, PROF EARTH SCI, UNIV CALIF, SANTA CRUZ, 79-, DIR, INST MARINE SCI, 91- *Personal Data:* b Pasadena, Calif, Sept 25, 43; m 80, Veneta Bradfield; c Joel, Amy, Shannon, Callie & Cody. *Educ:* Univ Calif, Santa Barbara, BA, 65; Ore State Univ, PhD(oceanog), 68. *Concurrent Pos:* Fulbright scholar, Greece, 74-75; vis prof, Semester at Sea, 84 & 96. *Mem:* Geol Soc Am; Am Geophys Union; Am Shore & Beach Preserv Asn; Coastal Res Found. *Res:* Coastal geology and engineering; environmental geology; geomorphology; author or coauthor of over 100 publications. *Mailing Add:* Long Marine Lab Univ Calif 100 Shaffer Rd Santa Cruz CA 95060

GRIGGS, ROBERT C, MEDICINE. *Current Pos:* RETIRED. *Personal Data:* b Rochester, NY, July 11, 25; m 53; c 3. *Educ:* Harvard Univ, MD, 49. *Prof Exp:* From instr to prof med, Sch Med, Case Western Res Univ, 56-76. *Concurrent Pos:* Webster-Underhill fel, Case Western Reserve Univ, 58-60; from asst vis physician to physician, Metrop Gen Hosp, Cleveland, 56-; consult, Marymount Hosp, 58-; attend hemat, Vet Admin Hosp, 61- *Mem:* Am Fedn Clin Res; Am Soc Hemat; Soc Exp Biol & Med. *Res:* Internal medicine; hematology; medical education. *Mailing Add:* 3170 Chadburne Rd Cleveland OH 44120

GRIGGS, THOMAS RUSSELL, MEDICINE, PATHOLOGY. *Current Pos:* instr path, 73-75, asst prof, 75-78, ASSOC PROF MED & PATH, SCH MED, UNIV NC, 78- *Personal Data:* b Lexington, NC, July 26, 43; m 66; c 1. *Educ:* Univ NC, AB, 65, MD, 69. *Prof Exp:* Med officer, Environ Protection Agency, 73-75. *Concurrent Pos:* Dir, Cornary Care Unit, NC Mem Hosp, 75; consult, Off Chief Med Examr, 76-; Jefferson-Pilot fel acad med, 78-82. *Mem:* Am Asn Pathologists; Int Soc Thrombosis & Haemostasis; Am Fedn Clin Res; Am Heart Asn. *Res:* Use of animal models to study hemostasis, thrombosis and atherosclerosis; study of atherogenesis in pigs with Von Willebrand's disease. *Mailing Add:* 2736 Dairyland Rd Hillsborough NC 27278-9315

GRIGGS, WILLIAM HOLLAND, POMOLOGY. *Current Pos:* from asst prof to prof, 47-77, EMER PROF POMOL, UNIV CALIF, DAVIS, 77- *Personal Data:* b Novelty, Mo, May 31, 16; m 44, Ruth Buchanan; c David B, Holly R (Coles) & Paula G (Lenz). *Educ:* Mo State Teachers Col, BS, 37; Univ Mo, MA, 39; Univ Md, PhD(pomol), 43. *Honors & Awards:* Stark Award, Am Soc Hort Sci, 64. *Prof Exp:* Asst pomol, Univ Mo, 37-39 & Univ Md, 39-42; asst prof, Univ Conn, 46-47. *Mem:* Am Soc Hort Sci. *Res:* Pollination requirements of fruits and nuts; physiological problems in pear production; pear breeding. *Mailing Add:* 633 A St Davis CA 95616

GRIGORIEV, DIMA YU, MATHEMATICS. *Current Pos:* jr researcher, 78-84, sr researcher, 84-88, LAB HEAD ALGORITHMICAL METHODS, INST ACAD SCIS, ST PETERSBURG, 88- *Personal Data:* b St Petersburg, Russia, May 10, 54; m 75, Alla N Sokolova; c Andrei D. *Educ:* Univ St Petersburg, Russia, MS, 76; Math Inst Acad Sci, PhD(math), 79, DSci, 85. *Honors & Awards:* Alexander von Humboldt-Found Award & Max Planck Res Prize, 94. *Prof Exp:* Tested researcher, Math VA Steklov, 76-78. *Concurrent Pos:* Vis prof, Comput Sci Dept, Univ Bonn, Ger, 91-92. *Res:* Contributed numerous articles to professional journals. *Mailing Add:* Comput Sci Dept Univ Bonn Roemerstr 164 53117 Bonn Germany

GRIGORIU, MIRCEA DAN, CIVIL ENGINEERING. *Current Pos:* ASSOC PROF STRUCT RELIABILITY, CORNELL UNIV, 80- *Personal Data:* b Bucharest, Romania, Mar 2, 43; m 69; c 1. *Educ:* Bucharest Inst Civil Eng, dipl ing, 67; Univ Bucharest, dipl math, 72; Mass Inst Technol, PhD(civil eng), 76. *Prof Exp:* Asst prof struct analysis, Bucharest Inst Civil Eng, 67-73; res asst struct reliability, Mass Inst Technol, 73-76; assoc prof eng, Univ Simon Bolivan, Caracas, 76-77; vis prof, McGill Univ & Univ Waterloo, 77-80. *Mem:* Am Soc Civil Engrs; Am Acad Mech. *Res:* Structural reliability analysis, especially reliability of structural systems, probabilistic models for loads and load combinations, random vibration and structural analysis. *Mailing Add:* 30 Eagleshead Rd Ithaca NY 14850

GRIGOROPOULOS, SOTIRIOS G(REGORY), environmental & engineering, for more information see previous edition

GRIGSBY, JOHN LYNN, ELECTRICAL ENGINEERING. *Current Pos:* RETIRED. *Personal Data:* b Tulsa, Okla, Apr 28, 24; m 50, Virgina R Eck; c David A, Sharon L, Susan E & Gloria J. *Educ:* Univ Colo, BS, 49; Stanford Univ, MS, 55, PhD(elec eng), 59. *Prof Exp:* Radio operator, Fed Commun Comn, 42-43; instr elec eng, Iowa State Col, 49; engr, Gen Elec Co, 49-52; res assoc elec eng, Stanford Univ, 52-59; chief engr, Appl Technol Div, ITEK

Corp, 60-61, vpres eng, 61-71, exec vpres, 71-75, pres, 75-84, corp vpres, Defense Electronics Opers, 80-84; chief exec officer, Saxpy Comput Corp, 84-86; pres, Advent Systs, Inc 87-93. *Concurrent Pos:* Mem, Rientjes Comt, Dept Army, 59. *Mem:* Sr mem Inst Elec & Electronics Engrs; Sigma Xi. *Res:* Electronic countermeasures systems; reconnaissance and surveillance receiving systems; broadband low-noise amplifiers. *Mailing Add:* 729 Viola Pl Los Altos CA 94022

GRIGSBY, LEONARD LEE, ELECTRICAL ENGINEERING. *Current Pos:* G A POWER DISTINGUISHED PROF, AUBURN UNIV. *Personal Data:* b Floydada, Tex, Dec 31, 29; m 55; c 3. *Educ:* Tex Technol Col, BSEE, 61, MSEE, 62; Okla State Univ, PhD(eng), 65. *Prof Exp:* Instr elec eng, Tex Technol Col, 57-60, asst prof, 60-61; from instr to asst prof, Okla State Univ, 61-66; assoc prof, Va Polytech Inst & State Univ, 66-72, prof elec eng, 72-. *Concurrent Pos:* NASA grant, 69-71; consult, Nuclear Develop Ctr, Babcock & Wilcox, Va, 69-72; dir, Energy Res Group, 72-. *Mem:* Inst Elec & Electronics Engrs; Am Soc Eng Educ. *Res:* Network and system modeling, simulation and design; control and power systems. *Mailing Add:* Dept Elec Eng Auburn Univ Auburn AL 36849

GRIGSBY, MARGARET ELIZABETH, MEDICINE. *Current Pos:* RETIRED. *Personal Data:* b Prairie View, Tex, Jan 16, 23. *Educ:* Prairie View State Col, BS, 43; Univ Mich, MD, 48; Univ London, DTM&H, 63. *Prof Exp:* From intern to asst resident, H G Phillips Hosp, St Louis, Mo, 48-50; asst resident, Freedmen's Hosp, Washington, DC, 50-51; from instr to assoc prof, Col Med, Howard Univ, 52-66, prof med, 66. *Concurrent Pos:* Rockefeller Found res fel, Harvard Med Sch, 51-52; China Med Bd fel, Sch Trop Med, Univ PR, 56; attend physician, Freedmen's Hosp, 52- & DC Gen Hosp, 58-; med epidemiologist, USPHS, Ibadan, Nigeria, 66; consult, US AID, 70-71; mem anti-infective agents adv comt, Food & Drug Admin, 70-71. *Mem:* Fel Am Col Physicians; AMA; Nat Med Asn. *Res:* Internal medicine; infectious diseases antibiotic research; electrophoresis of proteins. *Mailing Add:* Howard Univ Col Med Washington DC 20059

GRIGSBY, RONALD DAVIS, MASS SPECTROMETRY, PETROLEUM ANALYSIS. *Current Pos:* SR CHEMIST, BDM PETRO TECHNOL, BARTLESVILLE, OKLA, 97- *Personal Data:* b Tulsa, Okla, Feb 28, 36; m 62, Nancy J Hampton; c Lynn E, Brian P, Debra C, David R, Steven A, Jonathan C & Sara J. *Educ:* Univ Okla, BS, 58 & 59, PhD(phys chem), 66. *Prof Exp:* Asst chem, Univ Okla, 59-64, teaching asst Russ, 62; res chemist, Continental Oil Co, Okla, 64-68; from asst prof to assoc prof biochem & biophys, Tex A&M Univ, 68-80; vis prof chem, Univ Okla, 82-84; res fel, Assoc Western Univ, 84-86; sr chemist, Nat Inst Petrol & Energy Res, Niper, Okla, 86-96. *Concurrent Pos:* Adj prof chem, Okla State Univ, 65-66; proprietor, Mass Spectrometer Accessories, 72-77; vis scientist, Nat Res Coun Can, NS, 73-74; pres, Masspec, Inc, 77-92; adj prof chem, Univ Okla, 84-86, adj prof physics & astron, 89-92; chmn, Comt E-14 Mass Spectrometry, Am Soc Testing & Mat, 88-89, vchmn, 86-87. *Mem:* Am Soc Mass Spectrometry; Am Chem Soc; Sigma Xi; Am Soc Testing & Mat. *Res:* Analysis of mixtures from petroleum by mass spectrometry; development of mass spectrometric instrumentation and computer techniques. *Mailing Add:* 275 Turkey Creek Rd Bartlesville OK 74006-8034

GRIGSBY, WILLIAM REDMAN, PERIODONTICS. *Current Pos:* PROF PERIODONT, COL DENT, UNIV IOWA, 73- *Personal Data:* b Denver, Colo, Oct 15, 34; m 58; c 2. *Educ:* Dartmouth Col, BA, 56; Univ Mo, Kansas City, DDS, 60; Med Col Va, Va Commonwealth Univ, PhD(biochem), 70; Univ Iowa, Periodont cert, 75. *Prof Exp:* Asst prof oper dent & biochem, Med Col Va, Va Commonwealth Univ, 68-73. *Mem:* AAAS; Am Dent Asn; Int Asn Dent Res; Am Acad Periodont. *Res:* Prevention of bacterial colonization of teeth. *Mailing Add:* Dept Periodont Univ Iowa Col Dent Iowa City IA 52242-1001

GRILIONE, PATRICIA LOUISE, MICROBIOLOGY. *Current Pos:* From asst prof to assoc prof, 66-76, PROF MICROBIOL, SAN JOSE STATE UNIV, 76- *Personal Data:* b Fresno, Calif, Apr 15, 35. *Educ:* Fresno State Col, BA, 57, MA, 59; Univ Calif, Davis, PhD(microbiol), 66. *Mem:* Am Soc Microbiol; Inst Food Technologists; Soc Indust Microbiologists. *Res:* General microbiology; ecology. *Mailing Add:* Dept Biol San Jose State Univ San Jose CA 95192

GRILL, HERMAN, JR, DAIRY SCIENCE, BIOCHEMISTRY. *Current Pos:* Mgr flavor res, Carnation Res Lab, Van Nuys, Calif, 66-73, mgr fundamental res, 73-75, dir tech serv, 75-85, DIR TECH SERV & QUAL ASSURANCE, BASIC VEG PROD, VACAVILLE, CALIF, 81- *Personal Data:* b New York, NY, June 30, 36; m 59. *Educ:* Mich State Univ, BS, 59; Univ Minn, MS, 62; Pa State Univ, PhD(dairy sci, biochem), 66. *Mem:* Am Chem Soc; Inst Food Technologists; Sigma Xi; Am Soc Qual Control. *Res:* Flavor chemistry of foods, both the chemical and sensory aspects; research and development of dehydrated vegetables, primarily onions and garlic. *Mailing Add:* PO Box 3659 Modesto CA 95358-3659

GRILLO, RAMON S, BIOLOGY. *Current Pos:* assoc prof, 64-69, PROF BIOL, ADELPHI UNIV, 69- *Personal Data:* b New York, NY, May 28, 31; m 56; c 1. *Educ:* NY Univ, BA, 53; Fordham Univ, MS, 57, PhD(cytol), 60. *Prof Exp:* Instr biol, Marymount Col NY, 59-60 & Bronx Community Col, 60; from asst prof to assoc prof, Seton Hall Univ, 60-64. *Concurrent Pos:* USPHS res grant, 63-65; US Atomic Energy Contract, 67-69. *Mem:* AAAS; Am Soc Zoologists; Am Soc Cell Biol. *Res:* Study of the dynamics of cell proliferation in normal and regenerating tissues of the newt, Triturus viridescens, using tritiated thymidine and autoradiography. *Mailing Add:* 22 St Pauls Crescent Garden City NY 11530

GRILLOS, STEVE JOHN, BOTANY, PLANT ANATOMY. *Current Pos:* PROF BOT, CALIF STATE UNIV, STANISLAUS, 65- *Personal Data:* b Rock Springs, Wyo, Jan 15, 28; m 61; c 3. *Educ:* Univ Denver, BS, 51; Univ Wyo, MS, 52; Ore State Col, PhD(bot), 56. *Prof Exp:* Asst bot, Univ Wyo, 51-52; asst, Ore State Col, 52-53, instr, 53-56; instr biol sci, Modesto Jr Col, 56-60; assoc prof bot, Univ Pac, Stockton, 60-62; prof biol, Calif State Col, Hayward, 62-65. *Concurrent Pos:* Vis prof, Stephen F Austin State Col, 60. *Res:* Tissue structure and development; systematics of fern and fern allies and weeds. *Mailing Add:* Dept Biol Sci Calif State Univ Stanislaus 801 W Monte Vista Ave Turlock CA 95382-0299

GRILLOT, GERALD FRANCIS, ORGANIC CHEMISTRY. *Current Pos:* RETIRED. *Personal Data:* b Versailles, Ohio, Jan 24, 14; m 41; c 2. *Educ:* Ohio State Univ, BA, 36; Univ Ill, PhD(org chem), 40. *Prof Exp:* Asst chem, Univ Ill, 36-40; head dept, Blue Ridge Col, 40-41; from instr to asst prof, Univ Ky, 41-46; asst prof chem, Syracuse Univ, 46-53, assoc prof, 53-80, emer assoc prof, 80. *Mem:* Am Chem Soc. *Res:* Mannich reaction; stereochemistry; synthesis of organic pharmaceuticals; preparation and properties of aminomethyl sulfides; Hofmann-Martius rearrangement. *Mailing Add:* 119 W Drunker St Dunmore PA 18502

GRILLY, EDWARD ROGERS, THERMODYNAMICS. *Current Pos:* mem staff, 47-80, CONSULT, LOS ALAMOS NAT LAB, UNIV CALIF, 80- *Personal Data:* b Cleveland, Ohio, Dec 30, 17; m 73, Juliamarie Andreen; c David & Janice. *Educ:* Ohio State Univ, BS, 40, PhD(phys chem), 44. *Prof Exp:* Asst chem, Univ Wis, 40-41 & Ohio State Univ, 41-44; chemist, Carbide & Carbon Chem Co, Oak Ridge, 44-46; asst prof chem, Univ NH, 46-47. *Concurrent Pos:* Mem, Los Alamos County Coun, 76-78 & NMex Legis, 67-70. *Mem:* Am Phys Soc; Sigma Xi. *Res:* Gaseous kinetic theory; cryogenics; thermodynamics; transport properties of gases; pressure-volume-temperature at low temperatures and high pressure; cryogenic laser and magnetic confinement fusion targets; helium & hydrogen isotopes. *Mailing Add:* 705 43rd St Los Alamos NM 87544

GRIM, EUGENE, PHYSIOLOGY. *Current Pos:* From instr to prof physiol, 52-89, head dept, 68-86, EMER PROF PHYSIOL, UNIV MINN, MINNEAPOLIS, 89- *Personal Data:* b Stillwater, Okla, July 19, 22; m 46; c 1. *Educ:* Kans State Univ, BS, 45, MS, 46; Univ Minn, PhD(physiol chem), 50. *Concurrent Pos:* Lederle med fac award, 54; USPHS sr res fel, Univ Minn, Minneapolis, 58-63, USPHS career develop award, 63-68; sect ed, J Physiol, 66-68; mem physiol study sect, NIH, 67-69, chmn sect, 69-71. *Mem:* Fel AAAS; Am Physiol Soc; Am Chem Soc; Am Gastroenterol Soc; Biophys Soc. *Res:* Membrane transport phenomena; intestinal absorption; visceral circulation; regional blood flow. *Mailing Add:* 6-255 Millard H-Physiol Univ Minn 435 Delaware St SE Minneapolis MN 55455-0347

GRIM, J(OHN) NORMAN, CELL BIOLOGY, PROTOZOOLOGY. *Current Pos:* from assoc prof to prof, 67-94, EMER PROF BIOL, NORTHERN ARIZ UNIV, 94- *Personal Data:* b Santa Barbara, Calif, Sept 8, 33; m 54, Carole A Werly; c Stephen J & Kristine L (Weisskopf). *Educ:* Univ Calif, Santa Barbara, BA, 56; Univ Calif, Los Angeles, MA, 60; Univ Calif, Davis, PhD(zool), 67. *Prof Exp:* Lab technician, Univ Calif, Davis, 60-67. *Mem:* Soc Protozoologists; Am Micros Soc. *Res:* Ultrastructure and function of ciliated protozoan organelles; species identification; ciliate-fish gut symbioses; food selection; endocytobionts of the ciliates. *Mailing Add:* Dept Biol Sci Box 5640 Northern Ariz Univ Flagstaff AZ 86011. *Fax:* 520-523-7500; *E-Mail:* jng@nauvax.ucc.nau.edu

GRIM, LARRY B, IMAGE COMPRESSION & PROCESSING. *Current Pos:* VPRES, MESH INC, 83- *Personal Data:* b Philadelphia, Pa, Aug 20, 45; m 69; c 2. *Educ:* Univ Del, BEE, 67; Univ Mass, MSEE, 69; Univ Pa, PhD(comput sci), 80. *Prof Exp:* res engr, E I Du Pont De Nemours Inc, 68-83. *Mem:* Inst Elec & Electronics Engrs. *Res:* Pattern recognition as applied to medical images and reversible image compression. *Mailing Add:* 802 Bethel Rd Oxford PA 19363

GRIM, SAMUEL ORAM, ORGANOPHOSPHORUS, CHEMISTRY. *Current Pos:* from asst prof to assoc prof, 62-65, chmn, Inorg Chem Div, 70-77, 80-87 & 95-96, PROF CHEM, UNIV MD, 68-, ASSOC CHAIR, DEPT CHEM & BIOCHEM, 96- *Personal Data:* b Landisburg, Pa, Mar 11, 35; m 57, 83; c Stephen, Amy, Lucy & Christina. *Educ:* Franklin & Marshall Col, BS, 56; Mass Inst Technol, PhD(inorg chem), 60. *Honors & Awards:* Sci Achievement Award, Sigma Xi, 83. *Prof Exp:* Asst prof chem, Univ Md, 60-61; res fel, Imp Col, Univ London, 61-62. *Concurrent Pos:* Res grants, NSF, 62-81, Air Force Off Sci Res, 64-68 & NATO, 80-82; Sir John Cass's Found sr res fel, City London Polytechnic, 79-80; prof officer rotator, inorg & organometallic chem, NSF, 88-90. *Mem:* AAAS; Am Chem Soc; Royal Soc Chem; NY Acad Sci; Am Inst Chemists; Sigma Xi. *Res:* Organometallic and organophosphorus chemistry; coordination compounds; phosphorus nuclear magnetic resonance studies. *Mailing Add:* Dept Chem Univ Md College Park MD 20742-2021. *Fax:* 301-314-9121; *E-Mail:* sg31@umail.umd.edu

GRIM, WAYNE MARTIN, PHARMACEUTICAL CHEMISTRY. *Current Pos:* CONSULT, 88- *Personal Data:* b York, Pa, Apr 12, 30; m 52; c 4. *Educ:* Philadelphia Col Pharm, BSc, 52, MSc, 54; Univ Mich, PhD(pharmaceut chem), 59. *Prof Exp:* Res assoc pharmaceut res, Merck & Co, Inc, 54-56, Res Labs, 59-61, unit head, 61-62, sect head, 62-64, mgr pharmaceut develop, 64-68, dir, 68-69, dir pharmaceut res, Merck, Sharp & Dohme Res Labs, 69-75, sr dir, 75-78; dir, New Prods Develop, William H Rorer Inc, 78-86, vpres, New Prods Develop, Rorer Cent Res, 86-88. *Concurrent Pos:* Fel, Am Found Pharm Educ, 56-59. *Mem:* AAAS; Am Pharmaceut Asn; Am Asn

Prom Sci; NY Acad Sci. *Res:* Rheology and the physical stabilization of suspensions; topical and inhalation aerosol development; oral and topical liquid, semisolid and solid dosage form development; particle size reduction and measurement; biopharmaceutics and bioavailability research. *Mailing Add:* 2290 Yorkshire Doylestown PA 18901

GRIMALDI, JOHN VINCENT, CHEMICAL & SAFETY ENGINEERING. *Current Pos:* actg exec dir, Inst Safety & Systs Mgt, 77-80, dir degree progs, 77-82, EXEC DIR DEGREE PROGS, UNIV SOUTHERN CALIF, 82- *Personal Data:* b New York, NY, Sept 6, 16; m 42; c 2. *Educ:* NY Univ, BS, 39, MA, 41, PhD(acoust), 56; Polytech Inst Brooklyn, BChE, 51. *Honors & Awards:* Medal of the Assoiacado National de Medicina de Trabalho, Brazil; Centennial Medal, Am Soc Mech Engrs. *Prof Exp:* Apprentice, Grumman Aircraft Eng Corp, 41-42, dir safety, 42-45; res engr, Nat Conserv Bur, 45-46, dir res div, 46-47, dir indust div & asst mgr safety, 47-56; consult safety & plant protection, Gen Elec Co, 56-62, consult health, safety & plant protection, 62-67; dir, Ctr for Safety, NY Univ, 67-77. *Concurrent Pos:* Mem, President's Comt Employ of Physically Handicapped, 47-56, NY State Gov Comt Occup Safety, 58-63, US Secy Labor's Nat Adv Comt Occup Safety & Health, 69-73, Nat Inst Occup Safety & Health Study Sect, 70-74, 78-, Harvard Bd Overseers Health Serv Comt, 76-81 & Bd Gov, Flight Safety Found, 78-80; consult, Creole Petrol Co, 57 & 63 & Tenn Valley Authority, 68-70. *Mem:* Fel Am Inst Chemists; Am Soc Mech Engrs; fel Am Soc Safety Engrs (pres, 61-62); Am Chem Soc; fel Am Acad Safety Educ. *Res:* Management performance measurement methods; employment of the physically handicapped; executive health examinations and their relative value; effect of noise on human performance. *Mailing Add:* Grimaldi General Indust 13044 Mindanao Way Marina Del Rey CA 90292-6463

GRIMES, CAROL JANE GALLES, BIOINORGANIC CHEMISTRY. *Current Pos:* VIS ASST PROF CHEM, GOLDEN WEST COL, 77- *Personal Data:* b Long Beach, Calif, Sept 30, 46; m 69. *Educ:* Immaculate Heart Col, BA, 69; Northwestern Univ, Evanston, PhD(chem), 73. *Prof Exp:* Fel, Univ Calif, Irvine, 72-73, lectr chem, 73-75; vis asst prof chem, Univ Southern Calif, 75-77. *Mem:* Am Chem Soc. *Res:* Electro-transfer processes in biological and bioinorganic model systems. *Mailing Add:* 3212 Tigertail Dr Los Alamitos CA 90720-4836

GRIMES, CAROLYN E, EYE RESEARCH. *Current Pos:* Grants mgt specialist, Grants Mgt Sect, 80-85, chief, 85-87, GRANTS MGT OFFICER, EXTRAMURAL SERV BR, NAT EYE INST, NIH, 87- *Personal Data:* b Kansas City, Mo, Oct 21, 43. *Mailing Add:* Nat Eye Inst Exec Plaza S Suite 350 MSC 6120 Exec Blvd Bethesda MD 20892

GRIMES, CHARLES CULLEN, SOLID STATE & LOW TEMPERATURE PHYSICS. *Current Pos:* RETIRED. *Personal Data:* b Norman, Okla, June 11, 31; m 57, Anne Maher; c Susan, Andrew & Anne. *Educ:* Univ Okla, BS, 53; Stanford Univ, MS, 54; Univ Calif, Berkeley, PhD(physics), 62. *Prof Exp:* Electronics physicist, US Naval Air Missile Test Ctr, 54-55; mem tech staff, Bell Labs, 62-68 & 85-91, head, Solid State & Low Temperature Physics Res Dept, 68-84; consult, 91-92. *Mem:* Fel Am Phys Soc. *Res:* Experimental studies of electrons in surface states outside liquid helium and electron bubbles in liquid helium. *Mailing Add:* Box 84 West Southport ME 04576

GRIMES, CHURCHILL BRAGAW, FISH BIOLOGY, MARINE ECOLOGY. *Current Pos:* RES ECOLOGIST, FISHERIES SERV, 84-93, LAB DIR, NAT MARINE FISHERIES SERV, 93- *Personal Data:* b Washington, NC, Apr 29, 45; m 65; c 2. *Educ:* ECarolina Univ, BS, 67, MS, 71; Univ NC, PhD(marine sci), 76. *Honors & Awards:* Southern Div, Am Fisheries Soc, 91; Bronze Medal Award, Nat Oceanic & Atmospheric Admin, 96. *Prof Exp:* Marine biologist, Fla State Dept Natural Resources, 69-72; fishery biologist, Nat Marine Fisheries Serv, 75-76; dir, NC Marine Resources Ctr, 76-77; from asst to assoc prof marine fisheries, Rutgers Univ, 77-84. *Concurrent Pos:* Mem, Menhaden Pop Dynamics Comt, Atlantic State Fish Comn, 77-80, Spec Sci & Stratist Comn, Mid Atlantic Fishery Coun, 79-84, Manned Undersea Res Prog, Fisheries Planning Coun, Nat Oceanic & Atmospheric Admin, 80, Spec Sci & Statist Comn, Gulf Mex Fishery Mgt Coun, 86-94, Gulf Mex Prog, Nutrient Enrichment Comn, Environ Protection Agency, 90-96; ecol, behavior & fisheries biol of tilefish, 78-85, ecol & fishery biol of weakfish in US Middle Atlantic waters, 79-84 & stock identity, growth & recruitment processes of coastal pelagic fishes in US S Atlantic & Gulf of Mex waters, 85-; mem, Northeastern Rep, Marine Fisheries Sect, Am Fisheries Soc, 82-84, Outstanding Publ Selection Comt, 87-88, Marine & Estaurine Resource Comt, Southern Div, 88-90; assoc ed, Trans Am Fishery Soc, Am Fisheries Soc, 84-86; chmn, Marine & Estuarine Resource Comt, Southern Div, Am Fisheries Soc, 84-86; pres-elect, Marine Fishery Sect, Am Fisheries Soc, Am Fisheries Soc, 90-92. *Mem:* Am Fisheries Soc; Am Soc Ichthyologists & Herpetologists; Ecol Soc Am; Am Soc Limnol & Oceanog; Estuarine Res Fedn; Sigma Xi; Am Inst Fishery Res Biologists. *Res:* Life history, population dynamics, community ecology, recruitment processes and management of marine fishes. *Mailing Add:* Nat Marine Fisheries Serv Southeast Fisheries Sci Ctr 3500 Delwood Beach Rd Panama City FL 32408-7499. *Fax:* 850-235-3559; *E-Mail:* churchill.grimes@hoaa.gov

GRIMES, CRAIG ALAN, ELECTRICAL & COMPUTER ENGINEERING. *Current Pos:* ASST PROF, DEPT ELEC ENG, UNIV KY, 94- *Personal Data:* b Ann Arbor, Mich, Nov 6, 56. *Educ:* Penn State Univ, BSEE & BS(physics), 84; Univ Tex, Austin, MS, 86, PhD(elec & comput eng), 90. *Prof Exp:* Res asst elec & comput eng, Univ Tex, Austin, 85-87, lectr, 87-90; res scientist & sr mem, Lockheed Res Labs, 90-92; dir, Advan Mat Lab, Southwall Technologies, 92-94. *Concurrent Pos:* Pres, Crale Inc, Austin, 85- *Mem:* AAAS; Inst Elec & Electronics Engrs; Am Phys Soc. *Res:* Analysis of wave propagation in materials; calculating the effective electromagnetic properties of granular media; radio frequency instrumentation and antennas. *Mailing Add:* Dept Elec Eng Univ Ky 453 Anderson Hall Lexington KY 40506. *Fax:* 650-967-8713

GRIMES, DALE M(ILLS), ELECTROMAGNETIC THEORY, ANTENNAS. *Current Pos:* head dept, 79-86, prof, 79-91, EMER PROF ELEC ENG, PA STATE UNIV, 92- *Personal Data:* b Marshall Co, Iowa, Sept 7, 26; m 47, Janet L; c Prudence R & Craig A. *Educ:* Iowa State Univ, BS, 50, MS, 51; Univ Mich, PhD(elec eng), 56. *Prof Exp:* Lab asst physics, Iowa State Univ, 48; asst, Ames Lab, Atomic Energy Comn, 49-51; asst, Univ Mich, 51-52, res assoc, 52-54, assoc res physicist, 54-56, prof elec eng, 56-76; prof elec eng & chmn dept, Univ Tex, El Paso, 76-79. *Concurrent Pos:* Consult, Boulder Labs, Nat Bur Stand, 57-68 & Gen Motors Tech Ctr, 68-91; chief scientist, Conductron Corp, 60-63; chief scientist, Crale Inc, 86- *Mem:* AAAS; Inst Elec & Electronics Engrs; Am Phys Soc. *Res:* Electromagnetic theory; electromagnetic properties of solids; antenna theory; quantum electronics. *Mailing Add:* Dept Elec & Comput Eng Pa State Univ University Park PA 16802. *Fax:* 814-865-7065

GRIMES, DAVID, SMOOTH MUSCLE RECEPTOR PHARMACOLOGY, ALLERGY IMMUNOLOGY. *Current Pos:* sr scientist, Ayerst Labs, Montreal, 77-81, res assoc, 81-82, coordr, Isolated Tissue Sect, 82-84, SECT HEAD, ISOLATED TISSUE RECEPTOR, PHARMACOL SECT, AYERST RES, PRINCETON, NJ, 84-, SECT HEAD PULMONARY SECT, 87- *Personal Data:* b Hull, Eng, Apr 7, 48; Brit & Can citizen; c 2. *Educ:* Univ Bath, BSc, 74, PhD(pharmacol), 77. *Prof Exp:* Lab instr, Dept Pharmacol, Univ Bath, Eng, 74-77. *Concurrent Pos:* Mem, Res & Develop Info Syst Steering Comt, Wyeth-Ayerst Res, 88-89, co-chair, Immunopharmacol Div Subcomt, 88-90, mem, Bradykinin Discovery Team, 90- *Mem:* Am Soc Pharmacol & Exp Therapeut; Am Thoracic Soc; AAAS. *Res:* In vivo evaluation of pulmonary effects of load compounds; in vitro screening evaluation receptor profiling and mechanism studies on new compounds. *Mailing Add:* 84 Pennington-Hopewell Rd Hopewell NJ 08525. *Fax:* 609-466-8790

GRIMES, DONALD WILBURN, WATER-SOIL-PLANT RELATIONS, AGRICULTURAL ECONOMICS. *Current Pos:* from asst water scientist to water scientist, 66-92, EMER WATER SCIENTIST, UNIV CALIF, DAVIS, 92- *Personal Data:* b Maysville, Okla, July 28, 32; m 57, Julia A Rupp; c Janette, Sandra & Debra. *Educ:* Okla State Univ, BS, 54, MS, 56; Iowa State Univ, PhD(soil fertil), 66. *Prof Exp:* Soil scientist, Soil Conserv Serv, USDA, 55-56; asst agronomist, Kans State Univ, 56-61; assoc agron, Iowa State Univ, 61-66. *Concurrent Pos:* USAID, Sudan, 83; consult, Dominican Repub, 86-89, Irrigation Dist, 92-, water specialist, Mex, 93. *Mem:* Am Soc Agron; Soil Sci Soc Am; Int Soc Soil Sci; Crop Sci Soc Am; Sigma Xi. *Res:* Soil, plant and water relations; shallow water table use by growing crops to meet ET demands; crop water-yield production functions. *Mailing Add:* Kearney Agr Ctr Univ Calif 9240 S Riverbend Ave Parlier CA 93648. *Fax:* 209-646-6593; *E-Mail:* dwgrimes@uckac.edu

GRIMES, GARY WAYNE, DEVELOPMENTAL GENETICS. *Current Pos:* PROF BIOL, HOFSTRA UNIV, 73- *Personal Data:* b Henderson, Ky, Oct 28, 46; m 67; c 2. *Educ:* Ind Univ, BA, 68, MA, 72, PhD(genetics), 72. *Prof Exp:* Res assoc genetics, Ind Univ, 68-69, NIH trainee, 72-73. *Mem:* Sigma Xi; Soc Protozoologists; Soc Develop Biol; Am Soc Zoologists. *Res:* Morphogenesis and cortical inheritance in ciliated protozoa; comparative structure and function of mammalian tissues; pattern formation. *Mailing Add:* Dept Biol Hofstra Univ 1000 Fulton Ave Hempstead NY 11550-1090

GRIMES, HUBERT HENRY, SOLID STATE PHYSICS. *Current Pos:* RES PHYSICIST, NASA, 56-, HEAD SOLID STATE PHYSICS SECT, LEWIS RES CTR, 61- *Personal Data:* b Cleveland, Ohio, Mar 11, 29; m 55; c 2. *Educ:* Western Reserve Univ, BS, 52, MS, 53, PhD(phys chem), 56. *Mem:* Am Phys Soc; Am Inst Mining, Metall & Petrol Engrs; Am Soc Metals. *Res:* Imperfections in solids, diffusion; radiation damage; composite materials; ceramics. *Mailing Add:* 31308 Aldrich Dr Bay Village OH 44140

GRIMES, L NICHOLS, regeneration, wound healing, for more information see previous edition

GRIMES, ORVILLE FRANK, THORACIC SURGERY. *Current Pos:* from asst resident to chief resident, 42-49, assoc prof, 49-80, vchmn dept, 64-71, PROF SURG, SCH MED, UNIV CALIF, SAN FRANCISCO, 80- *Personal Data:* b San Bernardino, Calif, Jan 13, 16; m 41; c 4. *Educ:* Univ Calif, AB, 37; Northwestern Univ, MD, 41. *Prof Exp:* Intern, Passavant Mem Hosp, Northwestern Univ, 41-42. *Concurrent Pos:* In chg teaching surg, mem attend staff, chief thoracic surg serv, dir & chief surg consult, Outpatient Dept, San Francisco Gen Hosp, 49; consult, Hamilton AFB Hosp, 50-64. *Mem:* AMA; Am Surg Asn; Am Asn Thoracic Surg; Am Col Surg. *Res:* Management of various esophageal lesions including carcinoma, strictures, acquired and short esophagus and hiatal hernias; tissue transplantation as it reflects pulmonary changes. *Mailing Add:* Dept Surg Univ Calif San Francisco CA 94143

GRIMES, RUSSELL NEWELL, BORON CHEMISTRY, CLUSTER CHEMISTRY. *Current Pos:* from asst prof to assoc prof, 63-73, chmn dept, 81-84, PROF CHEM, UNIV VA, 73- *Personal Data:* b Meridian, Miss, Dec 10, 35; m 62, Nancy Hall; c Susan & David. *Educ:* Lafayette Col, BS, 57; Univ Minn, PhD(chem), 62. *Honors & Awards:* Boron USA Award, 90; Humboldt

Award, Ger, 97. *Prof Exp:* Fel, Harvard Univ, 62 & Univ Calif, Riverside, 62-63. *Concurrent Pos:* Fulbright res scholarship, US State Dept, NZ-US Educ Found, 74-75; pres, Va Chap Sigma Xi, 90; mem bd dirs, Inorg Syntheses, Inc, 91-; ed-in-chief, Inorg Syntheses, Vol 29, 92; prin investr, NSF & Army Res Off Grants, 76- *Mem:* Fel AAAS; Am Chem Soc (secy-treas, Inorg Div, 81-84); Sigma Xi; Corp Inorg Syntheses. *Res:* Organometallic and boron chemistry, especially carboranes, multi-decker sandwich complexes, metallacarboranes and carborane-metal complexes; synthesis and structural studies of electron-delocalized cage compounds; reaction mechanisms of carborane formation and cage rearrangements. *Mailing Add:* Dept Chem Univ Va Charlottesville VA 22901. *Fax:* 804-924-3710; *E-Mail:* rng@virginia.edu

GRIMES, SIDNEY RAY, JR, BIOCHEMISTRY, MOLECULAR BIOLOGY. *Current Pos:* asst prof biochem, 76-89, res assoc prof, 89-96, RES PROF, LA STATE UNIV MED CTR, SHREVEPORT, 97-; RES CHEMIST, VET ADMIN MED CTR, SHREVEPORT, 76- *Personal Data:* b Washington, DC, July 31, 47; m 69, Judith Watts; c Natalie, Gregory & Nathan. *Educ:* Univ NC, BS, 69, PhD(biochem), 73. *Prof Exp:* Res asst biochem, Univ NC, 69-73; proj investr, M D Anderson Hosp & Tumor Inst, Univ Tex Syst Cancer Ctr, 73-74, res assoc, 74-75; res assoc, Vanderbilt Univ, 75-76. *Concurrent Pos:* Merit rev grant, Vet Admin Med Ctr, 77-80, 80-82, 84-86, 86-90, 90-93, 96-99; prin investr, NIH grant, 78-81 & 93-96. *Mem:* Sigma Xi; Am Soc Cell Biol; Am Soc Microbiol. *Res:* Regulation of gene activity in eucaryotes; the role of nuclear and chromosomal proteins in cellular differentiation and development; regulation of transcription of histone genes; gene therapy to treat prostate cancer. *Mailing Add:* Med Res Serv Vet Admin Med Ctr 510 E Stoner Ave Shreveport LA 71101-4295. *Fax:* 318-429-5733; *E-Mail:* sgrime@nomvs.lsumc.edu, srgrimes@prysm.net

GRIMES, STEVEN MUNROE, NUCLEAR PHYSICS, APPLIED PHYSICS. *Current Pos:* vis prof, 78-79, dir, Edwards Accelerator Lab, 85-91, PROF PHYSICS, OHIO UNIV, 81- *Personal Data:* b St Louis, Mo, Aug 20, 41; m 67, Betty J Stephenson; c 2. *Educ:* Stanford Univ, BS, 63; Univ Wis-Madison, MS, 64, PhD(physics), 68. *Prof Exp:* Fel, Univ Basel, Switz, 68-69; fel, Lawrence Livermore Lab, 69-71, physicist, 71-81. *Concurrent Pos:* Vis prof, Univ Ky, 91-92. *Mem:* Sigma Xi; fel Am Phys Soc. *Res:* Neutron-induced and neutron-producing reactions, nuclear level density calculation and experiment; light exotic nuclei. *Mailing Add:* Dept Physics Ohio Univ Athens OH 45701-2979. *Fax:* 614-593-1496

GRIMINGER, PAUL, VITAMIN NUTRITION, GERIATRIC NUTRITION. *Current Pos:* asst prof, Rutgers Univ, 57-62, assoc prof, 62-67, chmn biol sci, 77-81, PROF NUTRIT, GRAD SCH, RUTGERS UNIV, 67-, DIR, GRAD PROG NUTRIT, 81-, SCI ADV, 87- *Personal Data:* b Vienna, Austria, Aug 29, 20; US citizen; m 54, Olga Maria Egger; c 4. *Educ:* Univ Ill, BS, 52, MS, 53, PhD(nutrit), 55. *Honors & Awards:* Nutrit Res Award, Am Feed Mfr Asn, 73. *Prof Exp:* Asst prof nutrit, Univ Nebr, 55-57. *Concurrent Pos:* Guggenheim Found fel, 64. *Mem:* Am Inst Nutrit; Soc Exp Biol & Med; Poultry Sci Asn; fel NY Acad Sci; fel AAAS. *Res:* Nutrition and aging; nutritional factors in atherosclerosis and osteoporosis; various aspects of avian nutrition; requirements and metabolism of vitamins in man and vertebrate animals. *Mailing Add:* Dept Nutrit Sci 131 Thompson Hall Cook Col Rutgers Univ New Brunswick NJ 08903. *Fax:* 732-932-6837; *E-Mail:* pomgrim@aol.com

GRIMLEY, EUGENE BURHANS, III, INORGANIC CHEMISTRY. *Current Pos:* ASSOC PROF CHEM, MISS STATE UNIV, 71- *Personal Data:* b Passaic, NJ, Oct 28, 41; m 64; c 3. *Educ:* Olivet Col, BA, 63; Univ Iowa, PhD(chem), 71. *Mem:* Am Chem Soc; Sigma Xi. *Res:* Studies on stoichiometry; rates and mechanisms of ligand substitution and electron transfer reactions in solution; synthesis and characterization of transition metal complexes; chlorine oxidation reduction studies; environmental studies on pollution; nuclear magnetic resonance spectroscopy. *Mailing Add:* Campus Box 2267 Elon College NC 27244-2010

GRIMLEY, PHILIP M, MEDICINE, PATHOLOGY. *Current Pos:* PROF PATH, HEBERT MED SCH, UNIFORMED SERV UNIV HEALTH SCI, 82- *Personal Data:* b New York, NY, Mar 10, 35; m 62, Judith Lee Rosenblum; c 3. *Educ:* City Col New York, BS, 56; Albany Med Col, MD, 61; Am Bd Path, dipl, 67, 80. *Prof Exp:* Intern, Cornell Div, Bellevue Hosp, 61-62; resident path, Univ Calif, San Francisco, 62-63; resident, Nat Cancer Inst, 63-65, staff pathologist, 65-70, head ultrastructural path, 70-73; dir, Clin Path Lab, NY State Dept Health, 73-77; prof path, Univ Md, 78-81. *Concurrent Pos:* Nat Heart Found res fel, NY State Dept Health, 58-60; assoc ed, J Nat Cancer Inst, 70-73, J Exp Path, 84-93; adj assoc prof path, Albany Med Col, 74-77; adj prof path, Univ Md, 82- *Mem:* Am Asn Cancer Res; Col Am Path; Am Asn Invest Path. *Res:* Cellular effects of interferon; cytokine signal transduction; macrophage differentiation. *Mailing Add:* Dept Path Uniformed Serv Univ Health Sci 4301 Jones Bridge Rd Bethesda MD 20814-4799. *Fax:* 301-295-1640; *E-Mail:* grimley@usuhsb.usuhs.mil

GRIMLEY, ROBERT THOMAS, HIGH TEMPERATURE CHEMISTRY, MASS SPECTROMETRY. *Current Pos:* from asst prof to prof, 61-95, EMER PROF CHEM, PURDUE UNIV, 96- *Personal Data:* b North Attleboro, Mass, Jan 3, 30; m 52, Margaret Rockwood; c Mark, Maureen, Kevin, Terrence & Peter. *Educ:* Univ Mass, BS, 51; Univ Wis, PhD(phys chem), 58. *Prof Exp:* Res chemist, Corning Glass Works, 57-59; res assoc physics, Univ Chicago, 59-61. *Concurrent Pos:* Vis asst, Calif Inst Technol, 92-96. *Mem:* Am Chem Soc; Am Phys Soc; Sigma Xi. *Res:* High temperature mass spectrometry; kinetics of vaporization; high temperature chemistry. *Mailing Add:* Dept Chem Purdue Univ 1393 Brwn Bldg West Lafayette IN 47907-1393. *Fax:* 765-494-0239; *E-Mail:* grimley@vm.cc.purdue.edu

GRIMM, ARTHUR F, PHYSIOLOGY, HISTOLOGY. *Current Pos:* Instr, Cols Med & Dent, Univ Ill, 58-62, asst prof, Col Med, 62-66, assoc prof, Cols Dent & Med, 66-69, PROF PHYSIOL & HISTOL, COLS DENT & MED, UNIV ILL, 69- *Personal Data:* b Berwyn, Ill, June 16, 31; m 54; c 2. *Educ:* Northwestern Univ, BS, 53; Univ Ill, DDS & MS, 56, PhD(physiol), 62. *Concurrent Pos:* Career develop awards, 64-69 & 70-74. *Mem:* Am Physiol Soc; Am Dent Asn; Sigma Xi. *Res:* Growth and development of striated muscles. *Mailing Add:* Dept Histol Rm 437-A Univ Ill Col Dent 801 S Paulina St Chicago IL 60612

GRIMM, CARL ALBERT, MATHEMATICS. *Current Pos:* From instr to assoc prof, 52-64, PROF MATH, SDAK SCH MINES & TECHNOL, 64- *Personal Data:* b Cincinnati, Ohio, Apr 1, 26; m 48; c 3. *Educ:* Univ Cincinnati, MA, 52. *Mem:* Math Asn Am; Sigma Xi. *Res:* Differential equations. *Mailing Add:* 5231 Pine Tree Dr Rapid City SD 57702-9210

GRIMM, CHARLES HENRY, ORGANIC CHEMISTRY, FLAVOR CREATION RESEARCH. *Current Pos:* dir flavor develop, 53-66, vpres, Flavor Creation Res, 66-76, DIR, INT FLAVORS & FRAGANCES, 67-, SR VPRES, FLAVOR CREATION RES, 76- *Personal Data:* b New York, NY, Oct 28, 11; m 38; c 1. *Educ:* NY Univ, BSc, 34, MSc, 38. *Honors & Awards:* Merit Award for Sci Contrib, Essential Oil Asn, 53. *Prof Exp:* Res chemist, Fritzsche Bros Inc, 34-43; chief chemist & dir lab, Felton Chem Co, Inc, 43-53. *Concurrent Pos:* Mem food liaison panel, Nat Acad Sci-Nat Res Coun; tech consult, Navy, Army, Air Force Inst Gt Brit, Toronto, Ont, Can, 43-45; res comt, Essence Oil Assoc, Inst Food Technologists. *Mem:* AAAS; Am Chem Soc; Inst Food Technol; Am Soc Enologists; Essential Oil Asn; Am Inst Chemists; chanter mem Soc Flavor Chemists. *Res:* Essential oil and flavor; development of research on flavor creation; new aroma chemicals; flavor creation. *Mailing Add:* 3589 S Ocean Blvd Apt 804 Palm Beach FL 33480-5734

GRIMM, ELIZABETH ANN, CELLULAR IMMUNOLOGY, LYMPHOCYTE ACTIVATION. *Current Pos:* assoc prof, 86-93, PROF TUMOR BIOL & SURG, M D ANDERSON HOSP & TUMOR INST, 93- *Personal Data:* b Charleston, WVa, Nov 29, 49. *Educ:* Randolph-Macon Woman's Col, AB, 71; Univ Calif Sch Med, Los Angeles, PhD(microbiol), 79. *Prof Exp:* Cancer res, Surg Br, Nat Cancer Inst, NIH, 80-84; sr staff fel, 84-85, sr investr immunol, Surg Neurol Br, Nat Inst of Neurol & Commun Disorders, NIH, 85-86. *Concurrent Pos:* Young Investr Travel Award, Am Asn Immunologists, 83; consult, Hoffman-LaRoche, NJ, 83 & 87-89, Bristol Lab, Rochester, 84, E I DuPont Res Facil, 84-85, Cetus Corp, Emeryville, Calif, 84, Eli Lily, Indianapolis, 83-84, Amgen Corp, Calif, 85, Div Life Sci, NASA, 93-; vis prof, Dept Microbiol, Howard Univ, 84-85, Dept Neurosurg, Harvard Med Sch, 90, Mt Sinai Med Ctr, 92, Univ Colo, 93; assoc ed, J Immunol, 85-89. *Mem:* Am Asn Immunologists; Am Asn Cancer Res; Am Asn Univ Women; AAAS; Am Brain Tumor Res; Clin Immunol Soc; Women Cancer Res Soc. *Res:* Investigation of ways to utilize cytotoxic lymphocytes for cancer therapy; studies in vitro lymphocyte activation. *Mailing Add:* Univ Tex M D Anderson Cancer Ctr Dept Tumor Biol 1515 Holcombe Blvd Rm AC7-021 Box 79 Houston TX 77030. *Fax:* 713-794-4784

GRIMM, JAMES K, ENTOMOLOGY, HUMAN ANATOMY. *Current Pos:* PROF ENTOM, JAMES MADISON UNIV, VA, 58- *Personal Data:* b St Paul, Va, Jan 17, 30; m 48, 75; c 4. *Educ:* Concord Col, BSEd, 56; Univ Tenn, Knoxville, MS, 58, PhD(entom), 63. *Mem:* Entom Soc Am; Am Soc Baxiatrics. *Res:* Microenvironmental studies relating to insects; gypsy moth surveys, biological control; arthropods found in birdnests and their interrelationship to certain species of birds. *Mailing Add:* Dept Biol James Madison Univ 800 S Main St Harrisonburg VA 22807-0001

GRIMM, LOUIS JOHN, MATHEMATICS. *Current Pos:* assoc prof, 69-74, chmn math & statist, 81-87, dir, Inst Appl Math, 83-87, PROF MATH, UNIV MO-ROLLA, 74- *Personal Data:* b St Louis, Mo, Nov 30, 33; m 67; c 2. *Educ:* St Louis Univ, BS, 54; Ga Inst Technol, MS, 60; Univ Minn, PhD(math), 65. *Prof Exp:* Chemist, Walter Reed Army Inst Res, 56-58; asst prof math, Univ Utah, 65-69. *Concurrent Pos:* Chemist, Tech Develop Labs, USPHS, 58-61; instr, Armstrong State Col, 61; vis asst prof, Univ Minn, 66; NSF res grants, 69-73 & 76-79; vis prof, Univ Nebr, Lincoln, 78-79; Nat Acad Sci exchange scientist, Polish Acad Sci, 81; vis prof, Univ Gdansk, 85, Univ Southern Calif, 87-88. *Mem:* Soc Indust & Appl Math; Ger Soc Appl Math & Mech; Polish Math Soc. *Res:* Difference and functional equations; delay-differential equations; numerical analysis; boundary value problems; singular point theory. *Mailing Add:* Dept Math & Statist Univ Mo Rolla MO 65401

GRIMM, ROBERT ARTHUR, ORGANIC CHEMISTRY. *Current Pos:* SECT MGR, PLASTICS & BONDING, EDISON WELDING INST, 87- *Personal Data:* b Two Rivers, Wis, July 25, 37; m 65; c 3. *Educ:* Univ Wis, BS, 59; Stanford Univ, PhD(org chem), 63. *Prof Exp:* Res chemist, Archer Daniels Midland Co, 63-67; sr res chemist, Ashland Oil Inc, 67-73, mgr, 73, sect mgr org chem, 73-80, res mgr, 80-87. *Mem:* Am Chem Soc; Sigma Xi; AAAS; Soc Plastics Engrs. *Res:* Fatty acid chemistry, fatty amines and salts; malonitrile; high-temperature radical reactions; catalysis; catalytic oxidation; hydroformylation; aminimides; reductive alkylation; unsym-dimethylhydrazine synthesis; chlorination; carbon suboxide; hydrometallurgy; petrochemical process discovery and development; composites; polymers joining; adhesives. *Mailing Add:* 1810 Ivanhoe Ct Upper Arlington OH 43220-3006

GRIMM, ROBERT BLAIR, PLANT PATHOLOGY. *Current Pos:* asst prof, 64-77, ASSOC PROF BOT, FLA ATLANTIC UNIV, 77- *Personal Data:* b New York, NY, Nov 26, 30. *Educ:* Univ Miami, BS, 55, MS, 57; La State Univ, PhD(bot), 60. *Prof Exp:* Asst, Univ Miami, 56-57, La State Univ, 57-59 & Nicholls State Col, 60-62; res assoc bot, Univ Miami, 62-64. *Mem:* AAAS; Phycol Soc Am; Am Inst Biol Sci; Bot Soc Am; Sigma Xi. *Res:* Cryptogamic botany; effects of environmental factors on growth and development of algae. *Mailing Add:* Dept Biol Sci Fla Atlantic Univ Boca Raton FL 33431

GRIMM, ROBERT JOHN, NEUROLOGY, NEUROPHYSIOLOGY. *Current Pos:* PVT PRACT NEUROL, 77- *Personal Data:* b Detroit, Mich, May 24, 33; m 59; c 2. *Educ:* Antioch Col, BS, 57; Univ Mich, Ann Arbor, MS, 59, MD, 61. *Prof Exp:* Intern med, Univ Mich Hosp, Ann Arbor, 61-62; Nat Inst Neurol Dis & Blindness fel physiol & biophys, Univ Wash, 62-64; Nat Inst Neurol Dis & Blindness fel, Lab Neurophysiol, 64-65, neurol residency, 65-77, assoc scientist, Neurol Sci Inst, Med Ctr, Good Samaritan Hosp, 68- *Concurrent Pos:* Dir, Electromyography Lab, Med Ctr, Good Samaritan Hosp, 69-71; dir neurol teaching & res, 70-73, asst dir neurol, 74-76, dir, Myasthenia Gravis Clin, 76-; asst prof neurol, Health Sci Ctr, Univ Ore, 69-74, assoc prof, 75-86, prof, 87. *Mem:* Soc Neurosci; Cooper Soc. *Res:* Disorders of movement; head injuries & labyrinth injury, bioethical issues having to do with neurological, psychiatric disorders. *Mailing Add:* Good Samaritan Hosp Med Ctr 2455 NW Marshall Suite 14 Portland OR 97210-2949

GRIMMELL, WILLIAM C, MATHEMATICAL ANALYSIS, ELECTRONICS ENGINEERING. *Current Pos:* RETIRED. *Personal Data:* b Brooklyn, NY, Mar 16, 41; m 66; c 1. *Educ:* Mass Inst Technol, BS, 61; Univ Mich, Ann Arbor, MS, 62 & 64, PhD(elec eng), 65. *Prof Exp:* Mem tech staff control systs res, Bell Tel Labs, 66-68; sr mathematician, Hoffman-La Roche, 68-74, group leader, Appl Sci Sect, 74-77, group leader, Tech Div, 77- *Mem:* Inst Elec & Electronics Engrs; AAAS; Sigma Xi. *Res:* Computer applications of industrial processes, pattern recognition and feature analysis, on line quality control. *Mailing Add:* 38 E Hawthorne Ave Valley Stream NY 11580

GRIMMER, RONALD CALVIN, INTEGRODIFFERENTIAL EQUATIONS. *Current Pos:* from asst prof to assoc prof, 67-76, PROF MATH, SOUTHERN ILL UNIV, 76- *Personal Data:* b Minneapolis, Minn, Aug 16, 41; m 63; c 3. *Educ:* Carthage Col, BA, 63; Univ Iowa, MS, 65, PhD(math), 67. *Concurrent Pos:* Vis assoc prof, Iowa State Univ, 73-74, vis prof Univ Warwick, 80-81. *Mem:* Am Math Soc; Soc Rheology; Soc Natural Philos. *Res:* Integrodifferential equations in the Banach spaces; application to various questions in linear viscoelasticity. *Mailing Add:* Southern Ill Univ Carbondale IL 62901-4408

GRIMM-JORGENSEN, YVONNE, COMPARATIVE ENDOCRINOLOGY, NEUROENDOCRINOLOGY. *Current Pos:* ASST PROF ANAT, UNIV CONN HEALTH CTR, 76-, MEM FAC, DEPT PHYSIOL. *Personal Data:* b Zurich, Switz, Apr 19, 42; m 70; c 1. *Educ:* Portland State Univ, BA, 69; Univ Conn, PhD(med sci), 74. *Mem:* Soc Neurosci; Am Physiol Soc; Am Soc Anatomists; AAAS; Am Soc Zoologists. *Res:* Various aspects of neurosecretion; mechanism of synthesis and release of neuropeptides and the mechanism of action of neurohormones; evolution of the neurohormones and their targets; molluscan model systems. *Mailing Add:* Dept Physiol Univ Conn Health Ctr 263 Farmington Ave Farmington CT 06030-3505. *Fax:* 860-679-1269

GRIMSAL, EDWARD GEORGE, FLUIDS, ACOUSTICS. *Current Pos:* ASSOC PROF PHYSICS, UNIV SOUTHWESTERN LA, 65- *Personal Data:* b Detroit, Mich, Sept, 15, 27; div; c 2. *Educ:* Western Mich Univ, AB, 48; Iowa State Univ, MS, 50; La State Univ, Baton Rouge, PhD(physics), 55. *Prof Exp:* Instr physics, Western Mich Univ, 50-51; instr, La State Univ, 53-54; asst prof, Canisius Col, 54-56; res physicist acoustics, Armour Res Found, 56-62; chief physicist, Universal Oil Prod Inc, 62-65. *Mem:* Am Phys Soc; Acoust Soc Am; Am Asn Physics Teachers. *Res:* Physical acoustics; non-linear acoustics and noise control. *Mailing Add:* 214 Longview Dr Lafayette LA 70506

GRIMSBY, F(RANK) NORMAN, CHEMICAL ENGINEERING. *Current Pos:* engr process develop, design & eval, Shell Develop Co, 53-54, 56-69, head, Chem Eng Div, Carrington Plastics Lab, Shell Res Ltd, Eng, 69-71, SR ENGR, POLYMERS DIV, SHELL CHEM CO, 71- *Personal Data:* b Seattle, Wash, Sept 15, 27; m 55; c 3. *Educ:* Univ Wash, Seattle, BS, 48, MS, 49; Mass Inst Technol, ScD, 54. *Prof Exp:* Engr, Calif Res Corp, 48; instr indust chem, Mass Inst Technol, 51-52. *Concurrent Pos:* Engr, Process Design, Chem Ctr, Md, 54-55, Phosphate Develop Works, Ala, 55 & Westvaco Res Detachment, WVa, 55-56. *Mem:* Am Chem Soc; Am Inst Chem Engrs. *Res:* Design and economics of chemical processes; epoxy resins; high-pressure polyethylene; Ziegler polyethylene and polypropylene; polymerization catalysis and kinetics. *Mailing Add:* 819 Thornvine Lane Houston TX 77079

GRIMSHAW, PAUL R, AGRICULTURAL ECONOMICS. *Current Pos:* RETIRED. *Personal Data:* b Cedar City, Utah, Mar 17, 22; m 46; c 4. *Educ:* Utah State Univ, BS, 48, MS, 49; Ore State Univ, PhD(agr econ & mkt), 71. *Prof Exp:* Vet farm training farm mgt, Iron Co Sch Dist, 49-50; co exten agt, Utah State Univ Exten, 52-54, better farming agt farm mgt, 54-60, co agt, 60-63, mkt specialist, 63-68 & 70-72; grad asst, Ore State Univ, 68-70; mkt specialist, Utah State Univ, 72-81, assoc dean resident instr, Col Agr, 72-81. *Concurrent Pos:* Chief of Party, USU-Somalia Contract, 81-83; consult, USAID Proj, Pragma Corp, Yemen, 83-84. *Res:* Interregional linear programming computer model to analyze competition in markets facing farmers in Utah and the United States; agricultural marketing. *Mailing Add:* 21238 Cass St Farmington MI 48335

GRIMSON, BAIRD SANFORD, OPHTHALMOLOGY. *Current Pos:* ASST PROF, DEPT OPHTHAL, UNIV NC SCH MED, 77- *Personal Data:* b Durham, NC, June 23, 43. *Educ:* Washington & Lee Univ, BA, 65; Duke Univ, MD, 69; Am Bd Ophthal, dipl, 76. *Prof Exp:* Intern, Dept Internal Med, Iowa Univ, 69-70; flight surgeon, US Army Marine Corp, Vietnam and Pa, 70-72; resident, Dept Ophthal, Univ Iowa, 73-75, assoc, 76; fel, Bascom Palmer Eye Inst, Univ Miami, 76-77. *Res:* Effects of serotonin and norepinephrine on carotid artery blood flow in primates; effects of head-down position during hypotension; drug testing in Horner's Syndrome; Raeder's Syndrome; fourth cranial nerve palsies following Herpes Zoster. *Mailing Add:* 617 Clin Sci Bldg CB No 7040 Univ NC Chapel Hill Chapel Hill NC 27599-7040

GRIMSRUD, DAVID T, LOW TEMPERATURE PHYSICS. *Current Pos:* DIR, MINN BLDG RES CTR, GRAD SCH, UNIV MINN, 89- *Personal Data:* b Minot, NDak, Aug 14, 38; m 60. *Educ:* Concordia Col, Minn, BA, 60; Univ Minn, MS, 63, PhD(physics), 65. *Prof Exp:* Fulbright grant, Rome, 65-66; from asst prof to assoc prof physics, Muhlenberg Col, 66-71; assoc prof physics, St Olaf Col, 71-77; staff scientist, Lawrence Berkeley Lab, Berkeley, Calif, 77-88. *Mem:* Am Phys Soc; Am Asn Physics Teachers. *Res:* Liquid helium temperature scale; transport phenomena near critical point. *Mailing Add:* Minnesota Bldg Res Ctr Rm 220 1425 University Ave SE Minneapolis MN 55455

GRIMSTAD, PAUL ROBERT, ARBOVIROLOGY, MEDICAL ENTOMOLOGY. *Current Pos:* res fel biol, Univ Notre Dame, 74-76, asst fac fel, 76-80, asst prof, 80-86, DIR, LAB ARBOVIRUS RES & SURVEILLANCE, UNIV NOTRE DAME, 76-, ASSOC PROF, 86- *Personal Data:* b Dallas, Tex, Feb 24, 45; m 70, Roberta Cooper; c Barri & Joel. *Educ:* Concordia Col, BA, 67; Univ Wis, Madison, MS, 72, PhD(entom), 73. *Prof Exp:* Prev med specialist entom, Med Serv Corps, US Army, 68-70; proj assoc entom & virol, Univ Wis, Madison, 73-74. *Mem:* Entom Soc Am; Am Mosquito Control Asn; Sigma Xi; Am Soc Trop Med & Hyg; Am Soc Microbiol. *Res:* Epidemiology and ecology of Jamestown Canyon and Cache Valley viruses, their vectors & vertebrate hosts; the ecology and causes of outbreaks of LaCrosse virus encephalitis in nature. *Mailing Add:* Dept Biol Sci Univ Notre Dame Notre Dame IN 46556-5645. *Fax:* 219-631-7413; *E-Mail:* paul.r.grimstad.1@nd.edu

GRIMWOOD, BRIAN GENE, BIOCHEMICAL GENETICS. *Current Pos:* RES SCIENTIST, DIV LABS & RES, DEPT HEALTH, STATE NY, 75- *Personal Data:* b Yorkville, Ill, Aug 2, 40; m 65; c 1. *Educ:* Aurora Col, BS, 64; Northern Ill Univ, MS, 67; Univ Ariz, PhD(genetics), 72. *Prof Exp:* Res assoc, Univ Ariz, 70-72; NIH fel, Univ Tex, Austin, 72-74. *Mem:* AAAS; Am Soc Microbiol. *Res:* Biochemistry and physiology of mitochondria, microbial antibiotic susceptibility testing; bacterial DNA replication; biochemistry and metabolism of parasitic protozoan cultures. *Mailing Add:* Ten Crestwood Lane Delmar NY 12054

GRINA, LARRY DALE, ORGANIC CHEMISTRY, POLYMER CHEMISTRY. *Current Pos:* Sr chemist, 70, res chemist, 70-78, GROUP LEADER, POLYMER RES GROUP, TEXACO INC, BEACON, 78- *Personal Data:* b Seattle, Wash, June 12, 43; m 64; c 2. *Educ:* Univ NDak, BS, 65; Univ Wash, PhD(org chem), 70. *Mem:* Am Chem Soc. *Res:* Synthetic and physical organic chemistry. *Mailing Add:* 8801 Waterfowl Flyway Chesterfield VA 23838

GRINBERG, ERIC L, GEOMETRIC ANALYSIS. *Current Pos:* PROF MATH, TEMPLE UNIV, 87- *Personal Data:* b Galati, Romania. *Educ:* Cornell Univ, BA, 78; Cambridge Univ, 79; Harvard Univ, PhD(math), 83. *Prof Exp:* Hildebrandt A Prof Math, Univ Pa, 83-87; fel math, Inst des Hautes Etudes Sci, 85-86. *Concurrent Pos:* Reviewer Math Rev, 83- & Nat Sci Found, 83- *Mem:* Am Math Soc. *Res:* Integral geometry; geometric analysis on homogeneous spaces; isoperimetric inequalities; several complex variables. *Mailing Add:* Dept Math Temple Univ Philadelphia PA 19122-2585

GRINBERG, JAN, PHYSICS, ELECTRICAL ENGINEERING. *Current Pos:* sect head device physics, 72-80, MGR, EXPLORATORY STUDIES DEPT, HUGHES RES LABS, 80- *Personal Data:* b Krakow, Poland, Nov 30, 33; US citizen; m 60; c 3. *Educ:* Technion-Israel Inst Technol, BS, 60, MS, 64; Weizman Inst Sci, Israel, PhD(physics), 70. *Prof Exp:* Res & develop engr elec eng, Soreq Nuclear Res Ctr, Israel, 60-65; asst prof, Tel-Aviv Univ, 65-72. *Concurrent Pos:* Consult, Elscient, Electronic Indust, Israel, 67-72 & Soreq Nuclear Res Ctr, Israel, 70-72. *Mem:* Sigma Xi. *Res:* Solid state physics; ferroelectric phase transitions; solid state devices; liquid crystals; electrooptic devices; image processing devices; thin film technology; array computers. *Mailing Add:* 1141 Carmelina Ave Los Angeles CA 90049-5811

GRINBERG-FUNES, RICARDO A, CLINICAL NUTRITION & VITAMINS, HEALTH ECONOMICS. *Current Pos:* Assoc info scientist, Hoffmann-La Roche, Inc, 81-85, info scientist, 86-94, res scientist, 94-96, PRIN SCIENTIST, HOFFMANN-LA ROCHE, INC, 96- *Personal Data:* b Buenos Aires, Arg, Aug 10, 52; US citizen. *Educ:* C W Post Col, BA, 74; Univ Mass, MSPH, 80; Columbia Univ, DrPH, 93. *Mem:* Am Pub Health Asn; Nat Environ Health Asn; Am Indust Hyg Asn; Am Asn Cancer Res; NY Acad Sci; AAAS. *Res:* Molecular epidemiology to determine whether vitamins A, E, C and beta-carotene are inversely associated with the binding of polycyclic aromatic hydrocarbons to DNA of mononucleated cells of heavy cigarette smokers. *Mailing Add:* 110 Palisade Ave Leonia NJ 07605-1924. *Fax:* 973-235-7292

GRINDEL, JOSEPH MICHAEL, DRUG METABOLISM, PROJECT MANAGEMENT & SCIENCE ADMINISTRATION. *Current Pos:* VPRES PROJ PLANNING & MGT, R W JOHNSON PHARMACEUT RES INST, 90- *Personal Data:* b Kansas City, Mo, Dec 18, 46; m 70; c 3. *Educ:* St Benedict's Col, Kans, BSc, 69; Univ Kans, PhD(med chem), 73. *Prof Exp:* Staff officer pharmacol, Walter Reed Army Inst Res, 74-75; chief, Clin Drug Metab Lab, 75-76; res scientist, 76-77, group leader, 77-78, sect head biochem, 78-80, dir, dept drug metab, 80-82, exec dir proj planning, 82-85, exec dir qual improv, McNeil Pharmaceut, 85-88; exec dir proj mgt, Johnson & Johnson, 88-89. *Mem:* Am Chem Soc; Am Soc Pharmacol & Exp Therapeut; AAAS; Drug Info Asn; Proj Mgt Inst. *Res:* Project management process in new product development; management of human resources in pharmaceutical research and development; disposition and pharmacokinetics of drugs in man. *Mailing Add:* 213 Willowgate Rise Holliston MA 01746. *Fax:* 908-704-9486

GRINDELAND, RICHARD EDWARD, PHYSIOLOGY. *Current Pos:* RES SCIENTIST SPACE PHYSIOL, AMES RES CTR, NASA, 62- *Personal Data:* b Decorah, Iowa, Mar 11, 29; m 52; c 5. *Educ:* Luther Col, Iowa, BA, 53; Univ Iowa, PhD(physiol), 58. *Prof Exp:* Asst prof, Univ Sask, 58-61; NIH fel, 60 & 61-62; vis asst prof physiol, Howard Univ, 62-63. *Mem:* Endocrine Soc; Am Physiol Soc. *Res:* Physiology of growth hormone. *Mailing Add:* Life Sci Div NASA Ames Res Ctr 239-11 Moffett Field CA 94035. *Fax:* 650-604-3954

GRINDLAY, JOHN, NON-LINEAR MECHANICS. *Current Pos:* chmn dept, 82-88, prof physics, 69-96, ADJ PROF, UNIV WATERLOO, 96- *Personal Data:* b Glasgow, Scotland, June 24, 33; Can citizen; m 60; c 1. *Educ:* Glasgow Univ, BSc, 55; Oxford Univ, DPhil, 58. *Prof Exp:* Proj assoc theoret chem, Univ Wis, 58-59; from instr to asst prof theoret physics, Univ BC, 59-64; asst res officer pure chem, Nat Res Coun Can, 64-65, assoc prof, 65-69. *Res:* Non-linear mechanics and chaos. *Mailing Add:* Dept Physics Univ Waterloo Waterloo ON N2L 3G1 Can. *Fax:* 519-746-8115; *E-Mail:* grindlay@sciborg.uwaterloo.ca

GRINDLAY, JONATHAN ELLIS, ASTROPHYSICS & ASTRONOMY, SEMI-CONDUCTOR DEVICES. *Current Pos:* Jr fel astrophys, Harvard Univ, 71-74, lectr, 74-76, asst prof, 76-81, chmn dept, 85-90, PROF ASTRON, HARVARD UNIV, 81- *Personal Data:* b Richmond, Va, Nov 9, 44; m 70, Sandra K Smyrski; c Graham C & Kathryn J. *Educ:* Dartmouth Col, BA, 66; Harvard Univ, MA, 69, PhD(astrophys), 71. *Honors & Awards:* Bok Prize, 76. *Concurrent Pos:* Astrophysicist, Smithsonian Astrophys Observ, 74-76; Sloan fel, 78; Guggenheim fel, 91. *Mem:* Fel Am Physics Soc; Sigma Xi; Am Astron Soc (secy-treas, 81-84); Int Astron Union; fel AAAS. *Res:* Studies of galactic and extragalactic x-ray sources; models for x-ray and gamma ray sources; optical identification and studies of x-ray sources; studies of hard x-ray and gamma ray sources; development of imaging hard x-ray and optical gamma-ray detectors. *Mailing Add:* Ctr Astrophys Harvard Univ 60 Garden St Cambridge MA 02138. *Fax:* 617-495-7356; *E-Mail:* grindlay@cfa.harvard.edu

GRINDLEY, NIGEL DAVID FORSTER, DNA TRANSPOSITION, SITE-SPECIFIC RECOMBINATION. *Current Pos:* fel molecular biol, 75-78, from asst prof to assoc prof, 80-86, PROF, DEPT MOLECULAR BIOPHYS & BIOCHEM, YALE UNIV, 86- *Personal Data:* b Leeds, UK, Nov 24, 45; m, Catherine Joyce; c Alexander & Christina. *Educ:* Cambridge Univ, UK, BA, 67; London Univ, UK, PhD(bact genetics), 74. *Prof Exp:* Sci staff bact genetics, Cent Pub Health Lab, London, UK, 67-73; fel molecular biol, Carnegie Mellon Univ, Pittsburgh, 73-75; asst prof, Univ Pittsburgh, 78-80. *Concurrent Pos:* Mem, Microbiol Physiol & Genetics NIH Study Sect, 88-92 & Immunol of Leprosy Steering Comt, WHO, 90-96; mem, Steering Comt, Immunol Mycobact Dis, WHO, 93-96. *Mem:* Am Soc Microbiol; AAAS; Am Soc Biochem & Molecular Biol. *Res:* DNA transposition and site-specific recombination; DNA polymerase I structure and function; DNA-protein interactions. *Mailing Add:* Dept Molecular Biophys & Biochem Yale Univ 266 Whitney Ave PO Box 208114 New Haven CT 06520-8114

GRINDLEY, T BRUCE, CARBOHYDRATE CHEMISTRY, MOLECULAR MODELLING. *Current Pos:* From asst prof to assoc prof, 74-95, ASSOC PROF CHEM, DALHOUSIE UNIV, 95- *Personal Data:* b Cornwall, Ont, Nov 22, 43; div; c Jean, Katherine & Mary. *Educ:* Queen's Univ, BSc, Hons, 65, MSc, 67, PhD(chem), 70. *Concurrent Pos:* Regional ed, J Carbohydrate Chem, 90- *Mem:* Fel Chem Inst Can; Am Chem Soc. *Res:* Synthetic carbohydrate chemistry, synthesis of biologically active oligosaccharides, molecular modelling, conformational analysis, nuclear magnetic resonance spectroscopy and stereochemistry. *Mailing Add:* Dept Chem Dalhousie Univ Halifax NS B3H 4J3 Can. *Fax:* 902-494-1310; *E-Mail:* grindley@chem1.chem.dal.ca

GRINDROD, PAUL (EDWARD), FOOD TECHNOLOGY, CHEMICAL ENGINEERING. *Current Pos:* CHIEF PACKAGING RES, OSCAR MAYER & CO, 58- *Personal Data:* b Oconomowoc, Wis, Apr 5, 25; m 45; c 3. *Educ:* Univ Wis, BS, 50, MS, 51, PhD(food tech), 54. *Prof Exp:* Asst food tech, Univ Wis, 51-54; res dir, C J Berst & Co, Wis, 54-58. *Mem:* Am Chem Soc; Am Dairy Sci Asn; Am Inst Chem Engrs; Sigma Xi. *Res:* Food packaging; design and packaging equipment design. *Mailing Add:* 4221 Esch Lane Madison WI 53704

GRINDSTAFF, TEDDY HODGE, PHYSICAL CHEMISTRY, ORGANIC CHEMISTRY. *Current Pos:* res chemist fiber surface, 64-69, res assoc, Dacron Res Lab, 69-86, STAFF CHEMIST, BELLE DEVELOP LAB, E I DU PONT DE NOMOURS & CO, 86- *Personal Data:* b Blount Co, Tenn, Aug 15, 32; m 62; c 1. *Educ:* Univ Tenn, BS, 58, MS, 61, PhD(phys chem), 63. *Prof Exp:* Proj engr prod eval, Celanese Corp Am, NC, 63-64. *Mem:* Fiber Soc; Am Chem Soc. *Res:* Adsorption of fatty acids on copper and nickel single crystals; determination of the kinetics of radioactive fatty soil detergency from polymer materials; surface chemistry; adhesion; computer modeling. *Mailing Add:* 1964 Parkwood Rd Charleston WV 25314

GRINDSTAFF, WYMAN KEITH, INORGANIC CHEMISTRY. *Current Pos:* From asst prof to assoc prof, 65-73, PROF CHEM, SOUTHWEST MO STATE UNIV, 73-, HEAD DEPT, 72- *Personal Data:* b Ada, Okla, May 13, 39; m 62; c 2. *Educ:* E Cent State Col, BS, 59; Univ Okla, MS, 65, PhD(inorg chem), 66. *Mem:* Am Chem Soc; Sigma Xi. *Res:* Synthesis, physical properties, structure and bonding of inorganic coordination compounds; use of computers in chemical education. *Mailing Add:* Dept Chem Southwest Mo State Univ 901 S National Springfield MO 65804-0087

GRINE, DONALD REAVILLE, GEOPHYSICS. *Current Pos:* CONSULT, 89- *Personal Data:* b Dunkirk, NY, Aug 21, 30; m 53; c 2. *Educ:* Mass Inst Technol, BS, 52, MS, 54, PhD(geophys), 59. *Prof Exp:* Physicist, Stanford Res Inst, 59-61; Schlumberger Well Surv Corp, 62-64, sect head, 64-65; dept head, Stanford Res Inst, 65-71; sr res scientist, 71-72, dept head, 72-75, vpres, 75-76, sr vpres & mgr, La Jolla Div, Sci & Software, 76-81; pres, S-Cubed, 82-83; vpres & div mgr, Maxwell Labs, 83-89. *Mem:* AAAS. *Res:* Explosions, shock waves, seismology, ultrasonics, exploration geophysics, instrumentation. *Mailing Add:* 15009 Paso Del Sol Del Mar CA 92014

GRINER, PAUL F, HOSPITAL ADMINISTRATION. *Current Pos:* VPRES & DIR, CTR ASSESSMENT & MGT CHANGE ACAD MED, ASN AM MED COLS, 95- *Personal Data:* b Philadelphia, Pa, 33. *Educ:* Rochester Univ, MD, 59. *Prof Exp:* Med chief resident & fel hemat, Strong Mem Hosp, prof & Samuel E Durand chair med, Rochester Univ, 73-95, gen dir & chief exec officer, 84-95. *Concurrent Pos:* Mem, Mayoral Comn Health & Hosp Corp, New York. *Mem:* Inst Med-Nat Acad Sci; hon mem Venezuela Soc Internal Med; Acad Med Malaysia; Am Col Physicians (pres, 95). *Res:* Author of numerous publications. *Mailing Add:* Asn Am Med Col 2450 N St NW Washington DC 20037-1127

GRINGAUZ, ALEX, MEDICINAL CHEMISTRY, PHARMACY. *Current Pos:* CONSULT. *Personal Data:* b Memel, Lithuania, May 18, 34; US citizen; m 59; c 3. *Educ:* Long Island Univ, BS, 56; Purdue Univ, MS, 58, PhD(pharmaceut chem), 60. *Prof Exp:* Asst org chem, Purdue Univ, 56-58; NIH fel, 60-61; from asst prof to prof org & pharmaceut chem, Brooklyn Col Pharm, Long Island 61-77, actg chmn dept, 70-72, chmn dept, 72-77, chmn, Div Pharmacotherapeut, Arnold & Marie Schwartz Col Pharm, 77-79. *Mem:* Am Chem Soc; Am Pharmaceut Asn. *Res:* Synthesis and stability of organic medicinal agents; synthesis and evaluation of nonsteroidal antiinflammatory drugs. *Mailing Add:* 1055 E Broadway Woodmere NY 11598

GRINKER, JOEL A, PSYCHOLOGY, NUTRITION. *Current Pos:* DIR, PROG HUMAN NUTRIT & PROF NUTRIT, SCH PUB HEALTH, UNIV MICH, 82- *Educ:* New York Univ, PhD(psychol), 67. *Prof Exp:* From asst prof to assoc prof, Rockefeller Univ, NY. *Mem:* Fel AAAS; NY Acad Sci; Am Pharmaceut Asn; Fedn Am Soc Exp Biol; Am Phys Soc. *Res:* Dietary-induced obesity in rodents; changing body composition in older persons. *Mailing Add:* Lab Sci Activite Physics Univ Laval Ste-Foy PQ G1K 7P4 Can

GRINNELL, ALAN DALE, SYNAPTIC NEUROPHYSIOLOGY, ECHOLOCATION. *Current Pos:* from asst prof to prof biol & physiol, 64-78, PROF PHYSIOL, UNIV CALIF, LOS ANGELES, 78-; DIR, JERRY LEWIS NEUROMUSCULAR RES CTR, 78- *Personal Data:* b Minneapolis, Minn, Nov 11, 36; m 62. *Educ:* Harvard Univ, BA, 58, PhD(biol), 62. *Honors & Awards:* Sr Scientist Award, Alexander von Humboldt Inst, WGer, 75, 79; Javits Neurosci Investr Award, 86. *Prof Exp:* NSF fel biophys, Univ Col, Univ London, 62-64. *Concurrent Pos:* Guggenheim fel, 86; Res assoc, Fowler Mus Cult Hist, Univ Calif, Los Angeles. *Mem:* AAAS; Soc Neurosci; NY Acad Sci; Am Physiol Soc. *Res:* Neurophysiology of audition, especially in echolocating bats; synaptic physiology; mechanisms of neurosecretion, development specificity and plasticity in the nervous system. *Mailing Add:* Dept Physiol Univ Calif Los Angeles CA 90095

GRINNELL, FREDERICK, CELL BIOLOGY, BIOCHEMISTRY. *Current Pos:* asst prof, 72-77, assoc prof, 77-81, PROF CELL BIOL & ANAT, SOUTHWESTERN MED SCH, UNIV TEX SOUTHWESTERN CTR, 81- *Personal Data:* b Philadelphia, Pa, Feb 5, 45; m 69; c 3. *Educ:* Clark Univ, AB, 66; Tufts Univ, PhD(biochem), 70. *Prof Exp:* NIH trainee, Biochem Sect, Vet Admin Hosp, Dallas, 70-72 & Tex Cancer Soc fel, 71-72. *Concurrent Pos:* Vis fel, Dept Biol, Yale Univ, 81; Meyerhoff vis prof, Weizmann Inst, Rehovoth, Israel, 84; Furcheimer vis prof, Hebrew Univ, Hadassah Med Sch, 88. *Mem:* Am Soc Cell Biol; Am Soc Biol Chem; Sigma Xi; AAAS. *Res:* Wound healing; biomaterials; cell adhesion; conduct of science; author of one publication. *Mailing Add:* Dept Cell Biol Univ Tex Southwestern Med Sch Dallas TX 75235. *Fax:* 214-648-8694; *E-Mail:* grinne01@utsw.swmed.edc

GRINNELL, ROBIN ROY, INSTRUMENTATION, BIOENGINEERING. *Current Pos:* from asst prof to assoc prof, 67-81, PROF AGR ENG, CALIF POLYTECH STATE UNIV, 81- *Personal Data:* b Palo Alto, Calif, July 21, 32; m 59; c Richard W, Jon E, Scott A & Christopher K. *Educ:* Univ Minn, MS, 61; Purdue Univ, BS, 55, PhD(agr eng), 76. *Prof Exp:* Asst prof, Univ Guelph, 61-67. *Concurrent Pos:* Mem sect comt, Am Standards Inst to Int Orgn Standardization, 66- *Mem:* Am Soc Agr Engrs; Instrument Soc Am; Inst Elec & Electronics Engrs. *Res:* Mechanical properties of biological materials and the development of instrumentation techniques to obtain the measurements and information desired. *Mailing Add:* BioResource & Agr Eng Dept Calif Polytech State Univ San Luis Obispo CA 93407. *Fax:* 805-756-2626; *E-Mail:* rgrinnel@calpoly.edu

GRINSPOON, LESTER, PSYCHIATRY. *Current Pos:* ASSOC PROF PSYCHIAT, HARVARD MED SCH, 68- *Personal Data:* b Newton, Mass, June 24, 28; m 54; c 3. *Educ:* Tufts Col, BS, 51; Harvard Univ, MD, 55. *Prof Exp:* Sr staff, Mass Ment Health Ctr, 61-68. *Mem:* Am Psychiat Asn; AAAS; Group Advan Psychiat. *Res:* Drug abuse. *Mailing Add:* 74 Fernwood Rd Boston MA 02115

GRINSTEIN, REUBEN H, SURFACTANT CHEMISTRY, PROCESS CHEMISTRY. *Current Pos:* TECH MGR, DIAMOND SHAMROCK CORP, 75- *Personal Data:* b Dallas, Tex, Aug 7, 35; m 64; c 2. *Educ:* Southern Methodist Univ, BS, 57; Rice Univ, PhD(phys org chem), 61. *Prof Exp:* Fel chem, Univ Leicester, Eng, 61-62; res chemist, Shell Chem Co, Inc, 62-72; tech mgr, PVO Int, Inc, 72-75. *Mem:* Am Chem Soc; Am Oil Chemists Soc. *Res:* Development and production of surfactants; dispersants; flocculants; lubricants; functional polymers; food chemicals; solvents and catalysts. *Mailing Add:* 5615 N Pontatoc Rd Tucson AZ 85718

GRINSTEIN, SERGIO, ION TRANSPORT, MEMBRANE BIOLOGY. *Current Pos:* asst prof, 79-84, ASSOC PROF PHYSIOL, HOSP SICK CHILDREN, 84-; PROF BIOCHEM, UNIV TORONTO, 85- *Personal Data:* b Mexico City, Mex, May 14, 50; Can citizen; m 76. *Educ:* Polytech Inst, Mexico City, BSc, 72, PhD(physiol), 75. *Honors & Awards:* Scientist Award, Med Res Coun, 85; Averst Award, Can Biochem Soc, 87. *Prof Exp:* Fel, Hosp Sick Children, Toronto, 76-78; res asst, Eidgenossische Technische Hochschule, Zurich, Switz, 78-79. *Concurrent Pos:* Scholar, Med Res Coun Can, 79-84; vis prof, Univ Montreal, 83 & Univ Coimbra, Portugal, 87; assoc prof med biophys, Univ Toronto, 85- & head, Div Cell Biol, 87-; assoc ed, Am J Physiol. *Mem:* Soc Gen Physiologists; Biophys Soc; Can Biophys Soc; Am Physiol Soc. *Res:* Cytoplasmic pH regulation and control of cellular volume; Mechanisms of signal trans in cells of immune system. *Mailing Add:* Div Cell Biol Hosp Sick Children 555 Univ Ave Toronto ON M5G 1X8 Can. *Fax:* 416-813-5028

GRINTER, LINTON E(LIAS), structural engineering; deceased, see previous edition for last biography

GRISAFE, DAVID ANTHONY, CERAMIC SCIENCE, MATERIALS SCIENCE. *Current Pos:* RES ASSOC MAT SCI, KANS GEOL SURV, UNIV KANS, 70- *Personal Data:* b Cincinnati, Ohio, Jan 30, 38; m 66; c 3. *Educ:* Univ Mo, Kansas City, BS, 61; Pa State Univ, MS, 63, PhD(ceramic sci), 68. *Prof Exp:* Res engr luminescent & ceramic mat, Sylvania Elec Prod, 67-70. *Concurrent Pos:* Consult mat & mineral resources, Kans Geol Surv, 71-; reviewer, J Am Ceramic Soc, 76-; contrib ed, Phase Diagrams Ceramists. *Mem:* Am Ceramic Soc; Keramos. *Res:* Physical and chemical properties of building stone; crystal chemistry and color of selected crystal structures; physical properties of construction related materials using clays, cements and ashes; restoration of stone structures and rock art. *Mailing Add:* 2327 Bryce Dr Lawrence KS 66047. *Fax:* 785-864-5317; *E-Mail:* dgrisafe@kgs.ukans.edu

GRISAFFE, SALVATORE J, HIGH TEMPERATURE MATERIALS, PROTECTIVE COATINGS. *Current Pos:* PROJ MGR, OHIO AEROSPACE INST, 95- *Educ:* Univ Ill, BS, 57; Case Inst Technol, MS, 65; Harvard Grad Sch Bus, cert, 76. *Honors & Awards:* Coatings Award, Am Soc Metals, 73. *Prof Exp:* Researcher high temp mat, Nat Adv Comt Aeronaut, NASA, 57-68, head, Coating Sect, 68-72, chief, Surface Protection Br, 72-80, chief, Mat Appl & Composites Br, 80-81, chief, Metallic Mat, 81-83, Chief Mat Div, 83-91, dir, aerospace technol, Lewis Res Ctr, 91-95. *Concurrent Pos:* Mem, Comt Coatings, Nat Mat Adv Bd, 63-65, Comt Erosion, 75-77; consult elec utilities, 70-73; mem adv panel, Lab Surface Sci, State Univ NY, 75-77; head energy conversion, Comn Mat, Nat Res Coun, 77-78; proj officer res & develop high temp mat for automotive engine, Int Energy Agency, 80-81; prog mgr, Mat Adv Turbine Engines, 80-88; mem, Comt Complex Composites, NSF. *Mem:* Fel Am Soc Metals; Am Vacuum Soc; Am Soc Testing & Mat; Am Inst Aeronaut & Astronaut; Am Ceramic Soc. *Res:* Plasma sprayed coatings; ceramics, refractory carbides and oxides; ceramic bearings; oxidation, hot corrosion; gas turbine materials; program management; composites; power generation; aircraft propulsion; space propulsion and power. *Mailing Add:* 2771 Gibson Dr Rocky River OH 44116

GRISAR, JOHANN MARTIN, ORGANIC CHEMISTRY, MEDICINAL CHEMISTRY. *Current Pos:* RETIRED. *Personal Data:* b Gorlitz, Ger, July 10, 29; US citizen; m 60, 83, Gabriele Von Oettingen; c Caia, Margot & Paul. *Educ:* Swiss Fed Inst Technol, BS, 54; Mass Inst Technol, PhD(org chem), 59. *Prof Exp:* Res chemist, Charles Pfizer & Co, Inc, 59-63; proj leader med chem, Marion Merrell Dow Res Inst, Strasbourg Ctr, 63-67, sect head med chem, 67-81, sr scientist, 81-93. *Mem:* Am Chem Soc. *Res:* Medium-sized ring transannular reactions; synthetic neuroleptic, hypolipidemic, anti-thrombotic, and cardiovascular anti-diabetic agents. *Mailing Add:* 7 rue de Mulhouse Wissembourg 67160 France

GRISARU, MARCUS THEODORE, PHYSICS. *Current Pos:* from asst prof to assoc prof, 68-74, PROF PHYSICS, BRANDEIS UNIV, 74- *Personal Data:* b Stefanesti, Romania, May 15, 29; m 64; c 3. *Educ:* Univ Toronto, BASc, 55; Princeton Univ, MA, 57, PhD(physics), 59. *Prof Exp:* Res assoc physics, Univ Ill, 58-60; asst prof, McGill Univ, 60-62. *Res:* Elementary particles physics and quantum field theory; supersymmetry and supergravity. *Mailing Add:* Dept Physics Brandeis Univ PO Box 9110 Waltham MA 02254-2700

GRISCHKOWSKY, DANIEL RICHARD, PHYSICS, OPTOELECTRONICS. *Current Pos:* BELLMAN PROF OPTOELECTRONICS, SCH ELEC & COMPUT ENG, OKLA STATE UNIV, 93- *Personal Data:* b St Helens, Ore, Apr 17, 40; m, Frieda R Bachmann; c Timothy, Stephanie & Daniela. *Educ:* Ore State Univ, BS, 62; Columbia Univ, AM, 65, PhD(physics), 68. *Honors & Awards:* Boris Pregel Award, NY Acad Sci, 85; R W Wood Prize, Optical Soc Am, 89. *Prof Exp:* Res assoc, Columbia Radiation Lab, Columbia Univ, 68-69; res staff mem laser physics, IBM Watson Res Ctr, 69-77, sci adv, dir IBM Res Div, 78, mgr, Atomic Physics Lasers Group, 79-83, mgr, Ultrafast Sci Lasers Group, 83-93. *Mem:* Fel Am Phys Soc; fel Optical Soc Am; fel Inst Elec & Electronics Engrs. *Res:* Interactions of microwaves with paramagnetic spins; interactions of laser light with atomic vapors; nonlinear effects in optical fibers; ultrafast optoelectronics; THz radiation sources; THz time-domain spectroscopy. *Mailing Add:* Sch Elec & Comput Eng Okla State Univ Stillwater OK 74078

GRISCOM, ANDREW, GEOPHYSICS. *Current Pos:* GEOPHYSICIST, BR GEOPHYS, US GEOL SURV, 57- *Personal Data:* b Boston, Mass, Oct 12, 28; c 2. *Educ:* Harvard Univ, AB, 49, MA, 56, PhD, 76. *Mem:* Geol Soc Am; Mineral Soc Am; Am Geophys Union. *Res:* Interpretation of magnetic and gravity data; relationship of petrology to the magnetic properties of rocks. *Mailing Add:* US Geol Surv 345 Middlefield Rd MS 989 Menlo Park CA 94025

GRISCOM, DAVID LAWRENCE, ELECTRON SPIN RESONANCE, STRUCTURE OF GLASSES. *Current Pos:* Nat Res Coun fel, 67-69, head, Radiation Effects Sect, 73-79, RES PHYSICIST, NAVAL RES LAB, 69- *Personal Data:* b Pittsburgh, Pa, Nov 1, 38; m 70, Catherine Godeux; c Laurent & Celine. *Educ:* Carnegie-Mellon Univ, BS, 60; Brown Univ, PhD(physics), 66. *Honors & Awards:* NF Mott Award, J Non-Crystalline Solids, 94; Otto Schott Res Award, Carl-Zeiss-Stiftung, Ger, 95. *Prof Exp:* Res assoc, Brown Univ, 66-67. *Concurrent Pos:* Prin investr, Lunar Sample Prog, NASA, 71-73; mem, Ed Comt, Glass Div, J Am Ceramic Soc, 72-; vis scientist, Univ Lyon/I, France, 75-76; prog mgr, Defense Advan Res Projs Agency, Arlington, Va, 81-83; co-chmn, Mat Res Soc Symp, 85; mem, NASA Microgravity Sci & Appln Discipline Working Group, 88-92; chmn, Glass & Optical Mat Div, Am Ceramic Soc, 91-92; Fulbright scholar, 97. *Mem:* Fel Am Ceramic Soc; fel Am Phys Soc; AAAS; Sigma Xi. *Res:* Physics of optical materials with specialization in radiation effects; electron spin resonance studies of amorphous insulators; author of over 160 articles in books and journals. *Mailing Add:* Code 5612 Naval Res Lab Washington DC 20375. *Fax:* 202-404-8114; *E-Mail:* griscom@nrl.navy.mil

GRISCOM, RICHARD WILLIAM, SYNTHETIC ORGANIC CHEMISTRY. *Current Pos:* RETIRED. *Personal Data:* b Chattanooga, Tenn, Apr 15, 26; wid, Mary Elizabeth Line; c 3. *Educ:* Univ Chattanooga, BS, 45; Univ Tenn, MS, 48. *Prof Exp:* Chemist, Reilly Tar & Chem Corp, Tenn, 45-46, Reilly Labs, Ind, 46 & Phosphate Div, Monsanto Chem Co, Ala, 48-49; res chemist, Res Div, Tenn Prod & Chem Corp, Tenn, 49-63 & Tensyn Div, Velsicol Chem Corp, 63; from res chemist to sr res chemist, Rock Hill Lab, Chemetron Corp, 64-68, res assoc, Rock Hill Lab, Arapahoe Chem Inc, 68-70, sr scientist, 70-74, sr res chemist, 74-80, group leader, 80-85; tech German translator, 85-96. *Mem:* Am Chem Soc; Am Translators Asn. *Res:* Synthetic organic research on pharmaceuticals, pharmaceutical intermediates and fine organic chemicals which includes process development in the field of hydrogenation, esterification, oxidation and halogenation. *Mailing Add:* 2111 Collins St Morristown TN 37814-3232

GRISHAM, CHARLES MILTON, BIOLOGICAL CHEMISTRY. *Current Pos:* from asst prof to assoc prof, 80-87, PROF CHEM, UNIV VA, 87- *Personal Data:* b Minneapolis, Minn, June 29, 47; m 72, Rosemary Jurbala; c David, Emily & Andrew. *Educ:* Ill Inst Technol, BS, 69; Univ Minn, PhD(chem), 72. *Prof Exp:* Res assoc biophys chem, Inst Cancer Res, 72-74. *Concurrent Pos:* NIH/Nat Cancer Inst fel, Inst Cancer Res, 74. *Mem:* Am Chem Soc; Biophys Soc; Am Soc Biochem & Molecular Biol. *Res:* Molecular basis of membrane structure and function; mechanisms of enzyme catalysis; biological application of magnetic resonance spectroscopy, nuclear magnetic resonance imaging and in vivo spectroscopy. *Mailing Add:* Dept Chem Univ Va McCormick Rd Charlottesville VA 22901-1000. *E-Mail:* grisham@virginia.edu

GRISHAM, GENEVIEVE DWYER, nuclear chemistry, for more information see previous edition

GRISHAM, JOE WHEELER, MEDICINE, PATHOLOGY. *Current Pos:* prof path & chmn dept, 73-97, KENAN PROF PATHOL & LAB MED, SCH MED, UNIV NC, CHAPEL HILL, 93- *Personal Data:* b Brush Creek, Tenn, Dec 5, 31; m 55, Evelyn Malone. *Educ:* Vanderbilt Univ, AB, 53, MD, 57. *Prof Exp:* Resident path, Sch Med, Wash Univ, 57-60, from instr to prof path & anat, 60-73. *Concurrent Pos:* Nat Cancer Inst fel, 58-59; Life Ins Med Res Fund fel, 59-61; Markle scholar, 64-69; mem bd sci counsellors, Nat Inst Environ Health Sci, 74-78. *Mem:* Am Asn Cancer Res; Am Asn Study Liver

Dis; Int Acad Path; Am Soc Cell Biol; Am Asn Path (pres, 84-85); Tissue Cult Asn; AMA; Fedn Am Socs Exp Biol (pres, 84-85); Cell Kinetics Soc. *Res:* Liver diseases; chemical carcinogenesis; regulation of cellular proliferation. *Mailing Add:* Dept Path CB 7525 Univ NC Sch Med Chapel Hill NC 27599. *Fax:* 919-966-6718; *E-Mail:* jwg@med.unc.edu

GRISHAM, LARRY RICHARD, PLASMA PHYSICS. *Current Pos:* Res assoc, Princeton Univ, 74-75, res staff physics, 75-82, res physicist, Plasma Physics Lab, 82-89, PRIN RES PHYSICIST, PRINCETON UNIV, 89- *Personal Data:* b Henderson, Tex, Feb 2, 49; m 72, Jacqueline L Criswell; c Austin, Rachel & Hilary. *Educ:* Univ Tex, Austin, BS, 71; Oxford Univ, PhD(physics), 74. *Concurrent Pos:* Indust consult ion-beams & neutral beams, 82-85; Rhodes scholar, 71-74; consult & mem, SDI Rev Panels, US Army Strategic Defense Command, 85-92; head, Neutral Beam Physics Princeton, Plasma Physics Lab, 88-; invited res fel, Japan Atomic Res Inst, 96. *Mem:* Am Phys Soc; AAAS. *Res:* Heating of magnetically confined plasmas by injection of beams of energetic neutral particles; free expansion and energy confinement properties of Tokamak plasmas; physics and technology of neutral beams. *Mailing Add:* Plasma Physics Lab Forrestal Campus Princeton Univ Princeton NJ 08543. *Fax:* 609-243-3248; *E-Mail:* lgrisham@pppl.gov

GRISKEY, R(ICHARD) G(EORGE), CHEMICAL ENGINEERING. *Current Pos:* exec vpres & provost, 85-88, INST PROF, STEVENS INST TECHNOL, 88- *Personal Data:* b Pittsburgh, Pa, Jan 9, 31; m 55, Pauline Becker; c Paula & David. *Educ:* Carnegie Inst Technol, BS, 51, MS, 55, PhD(chem eng), 58. *Honors & Awards:* Except Achievement Award, Am Chem Soc, 91. *Prof Exp:* Sr engr textile fibers, E I du Pont de Nemours & Co Inc, Del, 58-60; asst prof chem eng, Univ Cincinnati, 60-62; prof, Va Polytech Inst & State Univ, 62-66; prof & chmn dept, Univ Denver, 66-68; dir res & prof, Newark Col Eng, 68-71; dean, Col Appl Sci & Eng, Univ Wis-Milwaukee, 71-82, prof eng, 73-82; dean, Sch Eng, Univ Alabama, Huntsville, 82-85. *Concurrent Pos:* Vis prof, Polish Acad Sci, 71, Universidade Estadual Sao Paulo, 73, Monash Univ, 74, Algerian Inst Petrol, 76-77; lectr, Royal Soc Chem (Gt Brit), 85-88; prin investr, grants NSF, NASA, US Dept Com & Environ Protection Agency; consult, Celanese Fibers Co, Res Co, Phillips Petrol, Monsanto, Hewlett-Packard, Litton, US Veterans Admin, Thermo-Tech Inc, Allis-Chalmers, Globe-Union, Rexnord, A O Smith, Donaldson Co, 3M, Hoechst-Celanese, Am Bowling Cong. *Mem:* Fel Am Inst Chem Engrs; fel Am Soc Mech Engrs; fel Am Inst Chemists; Soc Rheology; Am Chem Soc; Am Soc Eng Educ. *Res:* Polymer engineering; physics and chemistry (rheology, heat and mass transfer, chemical kinetics, structure and properties); chemical engineering (thermodynamics, transport processes, chemical kinetics); energy resources; applied chemistry; materials engineering; technology and society. *Mailing Add:* 88 Pine Grove Ave Summit NJ 07901

GRISMORE, ROGER, ENVIRONMENTAL EARTH & MARINE SCIENCES. *Current Pos:* lectr "D" physics, 84-92, RES PROF, CALIF POLYSTATE UNIV, SAN LUIS OBISPO, 92- *Personal Data:* b Ann Arbor, Mich, July 12, 24; m 50, Marilynn A McNinch; c Carol A (Brooks). *Educ:* Univ Mich, BS, 47, MS, 48, PhD(physics), 57; Coleman Col, DS, 79. *Prof Exp:* Asst physicist, Argonne Nat Lab, 56-61, assoc physicist, 61-62; assoc prof physics, Lehigh Univ, 62-67; specialist physics, Scripps Inst Oceanog, Univ Calif, San Diego, 67-71; prof physics, Ind State Univ, Terre Haute, 71-74; specialist physics, Scripps Inst Oceanog, Univ Calif, San Diego, 75-78; sr consult, Potomac Res Inc, 78-79; staff scientist, Jaycor, 79-82, sr scientist, 82-84. *Mem:* Am Phys Soc; Am Geophys Union; Sigma Xi; NY Acad Sci; AAAS. *Res:* Environmental physics; marine radioactivity; lunar sample measurements. *Mailing Add:* 535 Cameo Way Arroyo Grande CA 93420. *Fax:* 805-473-2749; *E-Mail:* rgrismor@cymbal.calpoly.edu

GRISOLI, JOHN JOSEPH, MECHANICAL ENGINEERING. *Current Pos:* RETIRED. *Personal Data:* b New York, NY, Mar 12, 25; m 48, Jeanette Ward; c James, William & Janice (Patel). *Educ:* City Col New York, BME, 54. *Prof Exp:* Assoc mech engr, Brookhaven Nat Lab, 54-64, mech engr, design & electromagnet design, 65-71, sr mech engr & head accelerator oper, 72-75, asst dept chmn admin, 75-77, assoc dept chmn admin, AGS Dept, 77-82, dep div head, Accelerator Div, 83-90. *Res:* High energy particle accelerator design and development. *Mailing Add:* 173 Edgewater Ave Bayport NY 11705

GRISOLIA, SANTIAGO, BIOCHEMISTRY. *Current Pos:* from assoc prof to prof biochem & med, 54-72, chmn dept, 62-72, DISTINGUISHED PROF BIOCHEM, UNIV KANS MED CTR, KANSAS CITY, 73- *Personal Data:* b Jan 6, 23; US citizen; m 49, Frances Thompson; c James & William. *Educ:* Univ Valencia, MD, 44; Univ Madrid, MD, 49. *Hon Degrees:* MD, Univ Salamanca, 67 & Univ Valencia, 72; PhD, Univ Barcelona, 71, Univ Madrid, 73, Univ Siena, 80, Univ Leon, 82, Univ Florence, 88, Basque Country, 88 & Politecnic Univ, Valencia, 91. *Honors & Awards:* Govt of Valencia Prize, Spain, 44; Colosus Award, Valencia, 72; Principe de Asturias Prize in Sci, 90. *Prof Exp:* Asst prof phys chem, Univ Valencia, 44-45; vis asst prof biochem, Univ Chicago, 46-47 & phys chem, Univ Wis, 50-54. *Concurrent Pos:* High Res Coun fels, NY Univ, Univ Chicago & Univ Wis, 45-49; Juan de la Cierva fel, Univ Valencia, 49; fel, Univ Wis, 49, Wis Alumni fel, 50; Am Heart Asn estab investr, Univs Wis & Kans, 54-59; bd, Jimenez-Diaz Found, 67, vpres, Mediter Found, 73-; sec, Valencia Found Adv studies, 79; founding mem, Spanish Soc Emer Univ Prof, 66; dir, Inst Invest Citol Valencia, Spain, 76-92, distinguished prof, 92-; pres organizing comt, workshops human genome proj, 88 & 90; pres exec comt, Jaime I Prizes Sci Econ, Med, 89-; mem exec bd, Club Rome, Spain, 89-; mem sci comt, 1992 Seville Expos, 89-; pres, UNESCO Comn human genome proj, 90-; mem, World Energy Coun, 90-; bd mem, Found Banco de Bilbao Vizcaya, 90-; pres, Spanish Multiple Sclerosis Found, 90- *Mem:* Am Soc Biol Chem; hon mem Span Soc Biochem & Span Soc Physiol; Sigma Xi; foreign hon mem Royal Acad Med Belgium; Neurochem Soc. *Res:* Enzyme regulation; intermediary metabolism; protein turnover. *Mailing Add:* Inst Invest Citol Amadeo de Saboya 4 Valencia 46010 Spain. *Fax:* 34-6-360-1453

GRISSELL, EDWARD ERIC FOWLER, SYSTEMATICS. *Current Pos:* RES ENTOMOLOGIST, SYST ENTOM LAB, AGR RES SERV, USDA, 78- *Personal Data:* b Washington, DC, Aug 10, 44. *Educ:* Univ Calif, Davis, BS, 67, MS, 69, PhD(entom), 73. *Prof Exp:* Taxon entomologist, Fla Dept Agr & Consumer Serv, 73-78. *Mem:* Royal Entom Soc, London; Entom Soc Am; Sigma Xi. *Res:* Systematics of parasitic and aculeate Hymenoptera. *Mailing Add:* c/o US Nat Mus NHB 168 Syst Entom Lab Washington DC 20560

GRISSINGER, EARL H, SOIL SCIENCE, PHYSICS. *Current Pos:* SOIL SCIENTIST, AGR RES SERV, USDA, 60- *Personal Data:* b Lancaster, Pa, Nov 28, 31; m 59; c 4. *Educ:* Pa State Univ, BS, 53, MS, 55, PhD(agron), 57. *Mem:* Am Soc Agron; Soil Conserv Soc Am; Sigma Xi. *Res:* Nature of cohesion of natural soil materials; defining soil properties which determine cohesion. *Mailing Add:* PO Box 1157 Oxford MS 38655

GRISSO, ROBERT DWIGHT, SOFTWARE DEVELOPMENT FOR EXPERT SYSTEMS. *Current Pos:* Asst prof, 85-90, assoc prof & exten engr, 90-96, PROF & EXTEN ENGR, BIOL SYSTS, ENG DEPT, UNIV NEBR, 96- *Personal Data:* b Radford, Va, Feb 24, 56; m 78, Teresa F Gill; c Steven & Lauren. *Educ:* Va Polytech, Inst & State Univ, BS, 78, MS, 80; Auburn Univ, PhD(agr eng), 85. *Concurrent Pos:* Consult engr, Tenn Valley Irrig, Oneonta, Ala, 88-94; mem, Gov Assigned Secondary Containment Legis, State of Nebr, 91-93; chair, Soil Dynamics Res Comt, Am Soc Agr Engrs, 92-94; Agr Pest Control & Fertil Appln Comt, 92-, secy, Exten Comt, 93-94; chair, Tractor Test Bd, Univ Nebr-EMI-Nebr Dept Agr, 94- *Mem:* Am Soc Agr Engrs; Soc Automotive Engrs; Sigma Xi. *Res:* Develop methods to apply pesticides uniformly, accurately and safely to agricultural crops and live stock; to dispose, handle and transport pesticides environmentally safe and to assure little risk of groundwater contamination; develop methods to improve tractive and tillage devices used in agricultural production. *Mailing Add:* Univ Nebr 204 L W Chase Hall Lincoln NE 68583-0726. *Fax:* 402-472-6338; *E-Mail:* bseno35@unlvm.unl.edu

GRISSOM, DAVID, SOLID STATE PHYSICS. *Current Pos:* CONSULT, 89- *Personal Data:* b Dallas, Tex, Aug 22, 35; m 60, 79; c Pinkney O. *Educ:* Univ Tex, BS, 58 & 61, MS, 62, PhD, 65. *Prof Exp:* Assoc engr, Apparatus Div, Tex Instruments Inc, 58-59; res asst, Electronic Mat Res Lab, Univ Tex, 61-65; admin asst res, Nat Geophys Co, 65-67; sr proj engr, Geotech Div, Teledyne Industs, 67-69; chief engr, Rogers Explor, Inc, 69-73; sr engr, Electronics Systs Div, Geosource, 73-76; consult, 76-77, sr engr, N L McCullough, 77-82; sr scientist, Gulf Appl Res, 82-84; sr proj engr, 84-86, consult, Western Res, 86-88; chief engr, Globe Universal Sci, 88-89. *Concurrent Pos:* Consult, Chatlon Inc, Tex, 63-64. *Mem:* Am Soc Mech Engrs; Inst Elec & Electronics Engrs; Sigma Xi. *Res:* Geophysical instruments and oil exploration techniques; digital processing of seismic data; low temperature dielectric loss. *Mailing Add:* 6524 San Felipe St No 253 Houston TX 77057-2611. *E-Mail:* 73021.3276@compuserve.com

GRISSOM, ROBERT LESLIE, INTERNAL MEDICINE. *Current Pos:* from assoc prof to prof, Univ Nebr Med Ctr, Omaha, 53-87, chmn dept, 53-70, head, Div Cardiol, 70-72, EMER PROF MED, UNIV NEBR MED CTR, OMAHA, 87- *Personal Data:* b Macon Co, Ill, Mar 5, 17; m 44, Virginia; c Nancy, Carol, Leslie & Timothy. *Educ:* Univ Ill, BS, 39, MS & MD, 41. *Prof Exp:* From asst to asst prof internal med, Univ Ill, 47-53. *Concurrent Pos:* Markle scholar, 50-55; fel, Coun Clin Cardiol, Am Heart Asn. *Mem:* Fedn Clin Res; master Am Col Physicians; fel Am Col Cardiol; Cent Soc Clin Res; Sigma Xi. *Res:* Cardiovascular diseases. *Mailing Add:* Div Cardiol Univ Nebr Med Ctr 600 S 42nd St Omaha NE 68198-2285

GRISWOLD, BERNARD LEE, fish biology, research administration, for more information see previous edition

GRISWOLD, EDWARD MANSFIELD, mechanical engineering, for more information see previous edition

GRISWOLD, ERNEST, inorganic chemistry; deceased, see previous edition for last biography

GRISWOLD, GEORGE B, GEOLOGICAL & MINING ENGINEERING. *Current Pos:* RETIRED. *Personal Data:* b Ponca City, Okla, Dec 9, 28; m 52; c 4. *Educ:* NMex Inst Mining & Technol, BS, 55; Univ Ariz, MS, 57, PhD, 67. *Honors & Awards:* Spec Achievement Award, US Bur Mines, 92. *Prof Exp:* Jr engr, San Manuel Copper Corp, 55; chief engr, Blackrock Div, Wah Chang Mining Corp, Calif, 55-56; fel & mining engr, US Bur Mines, Ariz, 56-57; mining engr & fac assoc, NMex Inst Mining & Technol, 57-64; NSF trainee mining & geol eng, Univ Ariz, 64-65; assoc prof mining eng, NMex Inst Mining & Technol, 65-70, chmn, Dept Petrol & Mining Eng, 68-70; mgr explor, Western Can & Alaska, Getty Oil Co, 70-73; mem tech staff, Sandia Labs, 74-77; pres, Tecolote Corp, 78-83; chmn, Dept Mining & Geol Eng, NMex Inst Mining & Technol, 84-88. *Concurrent Pos:* Consult, Proj Mohole, Brown & Root Co, 64-67, Westinghouse Corp, 89- & NMex Eval Group, 89-, mining consult, 88- *Mem:* Am Inst Mining, Metall & Petrol Engrs; Soc Econ Geologists; Soc Mining Engrs. *Res:* Rock mechanics; engineering geology; ore deposits; site evaluation for radioactive waste isolation. *Mailing Add:* 6600 Lockhaven Lane NE Albuquerque NM 87111

GRISWOLD, JOSEPH GARLAND, BEHAVIORAL BIOLOGY. *Current Pos:* From asst prof to assoc prof, 71-89, PROF BIOL, CITY COL NEW YORK, 90- *Personal Data:* b Grand Rapids, Mich, June 15, 43; m 66; c 2. *Educ:* Denison Univ, BS, 65; Pa State Univ, MS, 68, PhD(zool), 71. *Concurrent Pos:* Consult. *Mem:* Am Inst Biol Sci; Sigma Xi; Animal Behav Soc; Nat Sci Teachers' Asn; Nat Asn Biol Teachers. *Res:* Behavioral development in dogs and the implications for the human-companion animal bond; innovations in college science teaching. *Mailing Add:* Dept Biol CUNY City Col New York 160 Convent Ave New York NY 10031-9101

GRISWOLD, KENNETH EDWIN, JR, CLINICAL BIOCHEMISTRY, POPULATION GENETICS. *Current Pos:* PROF & HEAD, DEPT CLIN LAB SCI & BACT, LA TECH UNIV, 83-, ASSOC DEAN, COL LIFE SCI, 93- *Personal Data:* b Ruston, La, Oct 22, 43; m 67, Paula R; c Wade & Natalie. *Educ:* La Tech Univ, BS, 65, MS, 67; Univ SC, PhD(biol), 71. *Prof Exp:* Instr chem & physiol, Univ SC, 69-71; instr biochem, Med Ctr, La State Univ, Shreveport, 71-73, mem grad fac path & biochem, 73-83. *Concurrent Pos:* Dir clin chem, Vet Admin Hosp, 71-83, co-dir, Sch Med Technol, 72-83; mem grad fac & prof, La Tech Univ, Ruston; clin assoc prof, Northeastern State Univ, Monroe, La, Centenary Col, Shreveport, La; consult forensic toxicol; clin scientist, Am Soc Clin Pathologists. *Mem:* Am Asn Clin Chem; fel Nat Acad Clin Biochemists; Sigma Xi; Am Soc Clin Pathologists. *Res:* Relationships of protein polymorphisms to population structure; methods development in clinical chemistry; relationship of nucleic acids to disease; toxicology; pathology. *Mailing Add:* PO Box 3053 Ruston LA 71272. *Fax:* 318-257-4288

GRISWOLD, MICHAEL DAVID, BIOCHEMISTRY, DEVELOPMENTAL BIOLOGY. *Current Pos:* ASST PROF CHEM, WASH STATE UNIV, 76- *Personal Data:* b Norman, Okla, Feb 17, 44; m 65; c 2. *Educ:* Univ Wyo, BS, 66, PhD(biochem), 69. *Prof Exp:* Asst prof pharmacol, Baylor Col Med, 73-74; res assoc med res, C Best Inst Med Res, 74-76. *Concurrent Pos:* Nat Cancer Inst fel, Univ Wis-Madison, 69-72; Europ Molecular Biol Orgn fel, Lab Cell Biol, Rome, Italy, 72-73. *Mem:* Soc Develop Biol; NY Acad Sci. *Res:* Biochemistry of metamorphosis and spermatogenesis, primarily RNA polymerase and control of hormone induced processes. *Mailing Add:* Dept Biochem & Biophys Wash State Univ 676 Fulmer Hall Pullman WA 99164-4660. *Fax:* 509-335-9688

GRISWOLD, NORMAN ERNEST, COLLEGE TEACHING. *Current Pos:* From instr to assoc prof, Nebr Wesleyan Univ, 63-79, actg head dept, 67-68, head dept, 79-89, chair, Natural Sci Div, 91-94, PROF CHEM, NEBR WESLEYAN UNIV, 79- *Personal Data:* b Yankton, SDak, July 17, 35; m 59, Ruth E Lill; c Diane E (McCallum) & Debra L (Dooley). *Educ:* Univ Kans, BA, 57; Univ Nebr, MS, 61, PhD(chem), 66. *Concurrent Pos:* Lectr, NSF Summer Inst Introd Phys Sci, 66-69 & 72-75, assoc dir, 70 & 71; vis assoc prof, Univ Ill, Urbana, 70-71 & Purdue Univ, 78-79; instr, NSF Summer Young Scholars Prog, 89-92. *Mem:* Am Chem Soc; Sigma Xi. *Res:* Writer general chemistry. *Mailing Add:* Dept Chem Nebr Wesleyan Univ Lincoln NE 68504-2796. *Fax:* 402-465-2179; *E-Mail:* neg@nebrwesleyan.edu

GRISWOLD, PHILLIP DWIGHT, POLYMER SCIENCE, TECHNOLOGY BUSINESS & PROJECT MANAGEMENT. *Current Pos:* res chemist polymer sci, Tenn Eastman Co, 77-79, sr res chemist, 79-87, develop assoc, 87-88, dept supt, 88-91, div dir, Polymers Res, 91-95, vpres development, 95-97, GEN MGR & VPRES, FLEXIBLE PLASTICS BUS ORGN, EASTMAN CHEM CO, 97- *Personal Data:* b Rutherfordton, NC, Feb 2, 48; m 71, Jeanne Lilly; c Mollie, John & Phillip. *Educ:* NC State Univ, BS, 70, MS, 73, PhD(fiber & polymer sci), 76. *Prof Exp:* Res fel polymer sci & eng, Univ Mass, 76-77. *Mem:* Am Chem Soc; Soc Rheol; Am Soc Qual Control. *Res:* Polymer rheology; fiber formation; morphological characterization of polymers; high modulus fibers; x-ray diffraction of polymers; plastics processing; technology and business management. *Mailing Add:* 4511 Preston Pl Kingsport TN 37764

GRITTINGER, THOMAS FOSTER, ECOLOGY, BOTANY. *Current Pos:* from instr to assoc prof, 68-84, PROF BOT & ZOOL, UNIV WIS, SHEBOYGAN COUNTY CTR, 84- *Personal Data:* b Milwaukee, Wis, Oct 23, 33; m 67; c 3. *Educ:* Univ Wis-Milwaukee, BS, 58, PhD(bot), 69; Univ Wis-Madison, MS, 62. *Prof Exp:* Instr zool, Univ Wis-Milwaukee, 62-65. *Mem:* Ecol Soc Am; Sigma Xi. *Res:* Bog ecology and string bog development; forest ecology, hemlock relicts along Lake Michigan in Wisconsin; scent marking behavior among captive cheetahs; zoology; under water behavior; polar bears. *Mailing Add:* Sheboygan County Ctr Univ Wis One Univ Dr Sheboygan WI 53081

GRITTON, EARL THOMAS, PLANT BREEDING, HORTICULTURE. *Current Pos:* From asst prof to prof, 64-96, EMER PROF AGRON, UNIV WIS-MADISON, 96- *Personal Data:* b Tipton, Iowa, Sept 26, 33; m 52; c 3. *Educ:* Iowa State Univ, BS, 60, MS, 61; NC State Univ, PhD(crop sci), 64. *Concurrent Pos:* Cropping systs agronomist tech adv, Nat Dept Agr Res, The Gambia, WAfrica, 88-90. *Mem:* Am Soc Agron; Crop Sci Soc Am; Pisum Genetics Asn; Soybean Genetics Asn. *Res:* Breeding, genetics and cultural practices for soybeans and processing peas, Pisum sativum; genetic resistance to plant diseases. *Mailing Add:* Dept Agron Univ Wis Madison WI 53706. *Fax:* 608-262-5217

GRITTON, EUGENE CHARLES, NUCLEAR ENGINEERING. *Current Pos:* Res engr, Nuclear Eng & Environ Simulation Modelling & Power Systs Eng, Rand Corp, 66-73, proj leader, Advan Undersea Technol Dev, 73-76, proj leader, Marine Technol, 74-76, head, Phys Sci Dept & Res Admin, 75-77, head, Eng & Appl Sci Dept, 77-86, dep vpres, Res Opers group, 86-90, prog dir appl sci & technol, 76-94, dep vpres, Nat Security Res Div, 86-93 resident scholar technol, 90-93, dir Aquisition & Technol Policy Ctr, 94-97, ACTG DIR, NAT SECURITY RES DIV, RAND CORP, 94- *Personal Data:* b Santa Monica, Calif, Jan 13, 41; m 80; c 2. *Educ:* Univ Calif, Los Angeles, BS, 63, MS, 65, PhD(nuclear eng), 66. *Concurrent Pos:* Vis lectr, Dept Mech Eng, Univ Southern Calif, 67-72 & Dept Energy Kinetics, Univ Calif, Los Angeles, 71-73. *Mem:* Am Nuclear Soc; Am Inst Astronaut & Aeronaut; AAAS. *Res:* Develop and analyze innovative weapon systems concepts; strategic and tactical force management issues; energy systems analyses; advanced science and technology policy analysis. *Mailing Add:* 3616 The Strand C Manhattan Beach CA 90266-3243

GRITZMANN, PETER, CONVEXITY MATHEMATICAL PROGRAMMING, COMPLEXITY THEORY. *Current Pos:* prof, 88-90, Univ Augsburg, WGer, 90-91, PROF MATH, UNIV TRIER, WGER, 91- *Personal Data:* b Dortmund, WGer, Dec 17, 54; m 83, Gitta Hartmann; c Simon C. *Educ:* Univ Dortmund, dipl, 78; Univ Siegen, PhD(math), 80, Habilitation, 84. *Prof Exp:* Prof math, Univ Siegen, WGer, 85-88 & Univ Augsburg, WGer, 90-91. *Concurrent Pos:* vis assoc prof math, Univ Wash, Seattle, 86-87, vis prof, 89-90 & 93; sr res fel, Inst Math & Applns, Minneapolis, 87. *Mem:* Am Math Soc; Soc Indust & Appl Math; Math Prog Soc; Can Math Soc. *Res:* Mathematical programming; operations research; computational convexity; complexity theory; discrete mathematics. *Mailing Add:* Dept Math Univ Trier FB IV 54286 Trier Germany

GRIVETTI, LOUIS EVAN, NUTRITION, GEOGRAPHY. *Current Pos:* from asst prof to assoc prof, 76-87, chmn, 83-87, PROF, DEPT GEOG & DEPT NUTRIT, UNIV CALIF, DAVIS, 87- *Personal Data:* b Billings, Mont, Sept 13, 38; m 67; c 1. *Educ:* Univ Calif, Berkeley, AB, 60, MA, 62; Univ Calif, Davis, PhD(geog), 76. *Honors & Awards:* Bk Award, Nutrit Founds Europe & NAm, 77; Harding lectr, State Univ, Brookings, 85; Inst Food Technologists Sci lectr, 87- *Prof Exp:* Res asst, Dept Biochem, Vanderbilt Univ, 64-70; admin officer, Maternal & Child Health/Family Planning Prog, Meharry Med Col, 73-75. *Concurrent Pos:* Ethel Austin Martin vis prof human nutrit, SDak State Univ, Brookings, 85; Richard Nixon vis prof, Whitter Col, 85; trustee, Freedom from Hunger Found, Davis, Calif; sci lectr, Inst Food Technologists, 87-90. *Mem:* Asn Am Geogrs; Soc Nutrit Educ; Am Inst Nutrit; Am Anthop Asn; Botswana Soc; Int Comn Anthrop Food; Soc Int Nutrit Res. *Res:* Food habits and nutritional implications; history and evolution of human dietary traditions; mechanisms of dietary change; cultural ecology of malnutrition; world food crisis; minority food habits. *Mailing Add:* Dept Nutrit Univ Calif Davis CA 95616. *Fax:* 530-752-4630

GRIVSKY, EUGENE MICHAEL, ORGANIC CHEMISTRY. *Current Pos:* RETIRED. *Personal Data:* b Pskov, Russia, Dec 20, 11; US citizen; m 35; c 2. *Educ:* Free Univ Brussels, BS, 36, MS, 38, DSc, 40. *Prof Exp:* Res assoc phys & org chem with Profs J Timmermans & G Chavanne, Free Univ Brussels & Int Bur Phys Chem Standards, Belgium, 39-40; res chemist & group leader, Pharmaceut Div, Union Chim, Belgium, 41-57; sr org res chemist, Wellcome Res Labs, Burroughs Wellcome Co, 57-78; chem consult, 78-83; res assoc, Dept Chem, Georgetown Univ, 79-83. *Concurrent Pos:* Abstractor, Chem Abstr, 58-70. *Mem:* AAAS; fel Am Inst Chem; NY Acad Sci; Am Chem Soc; Royal Chem Soc; Soc Chem France; Soc German Chemists; Royal Belg Chem Soc. *Res:* Stereochemistry; glycols oxidation by microorganisms; synthetic organic and medicinal chemistry; chemotherapy; sulfonamides; antihistamines; tranquilizers; publications in antidepressant, central muscle relaxant, hypotensive, sympatholytic, anti-inflammatory, antipyretic and anticonvulsant agents; catalysis; mechanism of reactions; patentee in field. *Mailing Add:* 4407 Eastwood Ct Fairfax VA 22032-1838

GRIZZARD, MICHAEL B, pediatrics, infectious disease, for more information see previous edition

GRIZZELL, ROY AMES, JR, FISHERIES MANAGEMENT, FORESTRY. *Current Pos:* CONSULT BIOLOGIST, 78- *Personal Data:* b Sweetwater, Tenn, Mar 14, 18; m 49, Virginia; c Linda & Diane. *Educ:* Univ Ga, BS, 39; Univ Mich, MS, 47, PhD(wildlife mgt), 51. *Prof Exp:* Res biologist, US Fish & Wildlife Serv, 47-49, refuge mgr, 52-55; biologist, Soil Conserv, USDA, 55-78; prof, Sch Forest Resources, Univ Ark, Monticello, 81-90. *Concurrent Pos:* Distinguished fisheries biologist, Catfish Farmers Am, 78. *Mem:* Wildlife Soc; fel Soil & Water Conserv Soc Am; Am Fisheries Soc. *Res:* Fish farming; agriculture; management of soil and water resources for fish and wildlife. *Mailing Add:* 138 Grizzell Lane Monticello AR 71655-9142

GRIZZLE, JAMES ENNIS, BIOSTATISTICS. *Current Pos:* ASSOC HEAD, CANCER PREV RES PROG, PUB HEALTH SCI DIV, FRED HUTCHINSON CANCER RES CTR, 89- *Personal Data:* b Herald, Va, Apr 20, 30; m 51; c 2. *Educ:* Berea Col, BS, 51; Va Polytech Inst, MS, 53; NC State Col, PhD(exp statist), 60. *Prof Exp:* Asst animal husb, Va Polytech Inst, 52-54; anal statistician, White Sands Proving Ground, 54; asst statist, NC State Col, 56; res assoc, Sch Pub Health, Univ NC, Chapel Hill, 57-60, from asst prof to prof biostatist, 60-89, chmn dept, 73-89. *Concurrent Pos:* Statistician, Med Lab, Army Chem Ctr, 55-56 & USPHS. *Mem:* Biomet Soc; Am Statist Asn; Am Pub Health Asn. *Res:* Analysis of categorical data; applications to clinical medicine and other medical research. *Mailing Add:* 10317 Lake Shore Blvd NE Seattle WA 98125

GRIZZLE, JOHN MANUEL, FISH BIOLOGY, FISH PATHOLOGY. *Current Pos:* PROF FISH PATH, DEPT FISHERIES & ALLIED AQUACULT, AUBURN UNIV, 76- *Personal Data:* b Mangum, Okla, June 11, 49; m 69, 87, Cindy Brunner; c Jeffrey. *Educ:* Okla State Univ, BS, 71, MS, 72; Auburn Univ, PhD(fisheries), 76. *Concurrent Pos:* Ed, J Aquatic Animal Health. *Mem:* Am Fisheries Soc; Am Asn Cancer Res. *Res:* Fish histology and histopathology of fish diseases. *Mailing Add:* 323 Lee Rd 48 Opelika AL 36801. *Fax:* 334-844-9208; *E-Mail:* jgrizzle@aghill.ag.auburn.edu

GRMELA, MIROSLAV, PHYSICAL MATHEMATICS. *Current Pos:* VIS MEM MATH FAC, MATH RES CTR, UNIV MONTREAL, 73- *Personal Data:* b Trnava, Czech, May 30, 39; Can citizen; m 62; c 2. *Educ:* Czech Tech Univ, MSc, 61; Czech Acad Sci, PhD(math physics), 66. *Prof Exp:* Res assoc physics, Nuclear Res Inst, Czech Acad Sci, 61-69; res assoc dept physics, Univ BC, 69-71; res assoc math, Carleton Univ, 71-73. *Mem:* Am Math Soc; Can Math Soc. *Res:* Non equilibrium statistical physics; dynamical systems. *Mailing Add:* ECOLE Polytech de Montreal CP 6079 Succ A Montreal PQ H3C 3A7 Can

GROAT, CHARLES GEORGE, ECONOMIC GEOLOGY. *Current Pos:* DIR, COASTAL ENERGY & ENVIRON RES LAB, LA STATE UNIV, 92- *Personal Data:* b Westfield, NY, Mar 25, 40; m 63; c 2. *Educ:* Univ Rochester, AB, 62; Univ Mass, MS, 67; Univ Tex, Austin, PhD(geol), 70. *Prof Exp:* Res geologist, Bur Econ Geol, Univ Tex, Austin 68-71; assoc dir, 71-75, assoc prof, dept geol sci, 71-77, actg dir Bur Econ Geol, 75-77; assoc prof geol sci & chmn, Univ Tex, El Paso, 77-80; dir, LA Geol Survey, 78-90; exec dir, Am Geol Inst, 90-92. *Mem:* Geol Soc Am; Am Asn Petrol Geologists; Soc Environ Geochem. *Res:* Geology of energy resources, especially coal; environmental aspects of resource extraction; geomorphology of coastal and arid areas. *Mailing Add:* 7774 Copperfield Ct Baton Rouge LA 70808

GROAT, RICHARD ARNOLD, surgical pathology, psychology; deceased, see previous edition for last biography

GROB, DAVID, INTERNAL MEDICINE, RESEARCH & ADMINISTRATION. *Current Pos:* dir med serv, 58-89, dir res & educ, 60-89, MED DIR, RES & DEVELOP FOUND, MAIMONIDES MED CTR, 82- *Personal Data:* b New York, NY, Feb 23, 19; m 48, Elizabeth Nussbaum; c Charles, Susan, Emily & Phillip. *Educ:* City Col New York, BS, 37; Johns Hopkins Univ, MD, 42. *Honors & Awards:* Kermit E Osserman Achievement Award, Myasthenia Gravis Found, 82, Kermit E Osserman Res Award, 92; Laureate Award, Am Col Physicians, 93. *Prof Exp:* From intern to asst resident, Johns Hopkins Hosp, 42-48, from instr to assoc prof, Sch Med, 48-58. *Concurrent Pos:* Fel, Johns Hopkins Hosp, 45-48; consult, Nat Cancer Inst, 51-54, Myasthenia Gravis Found, 53-, chmn, 61-63; consult, US Army Hosp, Ft Meade, 53-58 & Surgeon Gen, US Army, 58; fel, Johns Hopkins Hosp, 45-48, physician, 51-58; consult, Bur Med, Food & Drug Admin, 66-78; prof med, State Univ NY Health Sci Ctr, Brooklyn, 58-, assoc dean, 62-89. *Mem:* Am Physiol Soc; Am Soc Clin Invest; Am Soc Pharmacol & Exp Ther; Am Neurol Asn; Asn Am Phys; master Am Col Physicians. *Res:* Neuromuscular disease, physiology and pharmacology; clinical pharmacology, clinical immunology, clinical medicine myasthenia gravis, autoimmune diseases; polymyositis, multiple sclerosis, oncologic diseases, tissue culture. *Mailing Add:* 20 Fern Dr 4802 Tenth Ave Roslyn NY 11576-2202. *Fax:* 718-283-6500

GROB, GERALD N, HISTORY OF MEDICINE. *Current Pos:* SIGERIST PROF HIST MED, RUTGERS UNIV, 69- *Personal Data:* b New York, NY, Apr 25, 31; m 54, Lila E Kronick; c Brad, Evan & Seth. *Educ:* City Col NY, BSS, 51; Columbia Univ, MA, 52; Northwestern Univ, PhD(hist), 58. *Honors & Awards:* William H Welch Medal, Am Asn Hist Med, 86, Garrison Lectr, 86. *Prof Exp:* Prof hist, Clark Univ, 57-69. *Concurrent Pos:* Prin investr, NIMH grant, 60-92; NEH fel, 72-73 & 89-90; mem, Exec Comt, Am Asn Hist Med, 78-81, Prog Comt, 86, 91 & Welch Medal Comt, 85, 89, pres, 96-98; Guggenheim fel, 81; chair, Prog Comt, Orgn Am Historians, 85. *Mem:* Inst Med-Nat Acad Sci; Am Asn Hist Med; Orgn Am Historians. *Res:* History of medicine; history of psychiatry; history of the care and treatment of the mentally ill in America, psychiatry, and public policy; disease and environment. *Mailing Add:* Inst Health Care Policy & Aging Res Rutgers Univ New Brunswick NJ 08903. *Fax:* 732-932-6872; *E-Mail:* ggrob@rci.rutgers.edu

GROB, ROBERT LEE, ANALYTICAL CHEMISTRY, ENVIRONMENTAL SCIENCES. *Current Pos:* from assoc prof to prof, 63-92, EMER PROF ANAL CHEM, VILLANOVA UNIV, 92- *Personal Data:* b Wheeling, WVa, Feb 13, 27; m 52, Marjorie D Sage; c R Kent, G Duane, M Michele, J Allyson & Mattia. *Educ:* Col Steubenville, BS, 51; Univ Va, MS, 54, PhD(chem), 55. *Honors & Awards:* Stephen Dal Nogare Award in Chromatog, 90. *Prof Exp:* Res analytical chemist, Esso Res & Eng Co, 55-57; from assoc prof to assoc prof analytical chem, Wheeling Col, 57-63. *Concurrent Pos:* Consult, analytical & environ chem. *Mem:* Am Chem Soc; fel Am Inst Chemists; Asn Off Analytical Chemists; Sigma Xi. *Res:* Organic reagents for complexing of trace metals; gas chromatography; air and water pollution and control; liquid chromatography; mass spectrometry; gas and high performance liquid chromatography; environmental chemistry. *Mailing Add:* 12 Birch Rd Villanova Univ Malvern PA 19355-1644. *Fax:* 610-650-0132

GROBE, RAINER, COMPUTATIONAL PHYSICS, HIGH INTENSITY LASER-ATOM INTERACTION. *Current Pos:* asst prof, 95-96, ASSOC PROF, ILL STATE UNIV, 97- *Personal Data:* b Essen, Ger, Apr 5, 62; m 89, Monika Fox; c Sebastian & Christian. *Educ:* Univ Essen, Ger, Vordiplom, 83, PhD(physics), 89, Univ Colo, MS, 85. *Honors & Awards:* PHY-9631245 Award, NSF, 96; Cottrel Sci Award, Res Corp, 96. *Prof Exp:* Feodor Lynen res fel, Alexander von Humbolt Found, 89-92; fel, Univ Rochester, 89-90, sr res assoc, 90, asst prof, 93-95; res assoc comput sci & eng, NSF, 91-93. *Mem:* Am Phys Soc. *Res:* Large scale computational studies of strong-laser field matter interactions; propagation of laser pulses in resonant media. *Mailing Add:* Dept Physics Ill State Univ Normal IL 61790-4560

GROBECKER, ALAN J, SPACE PHYSICS, GEOPHYSICS. *Current Pos:* RETIRED. *Personal Data:* b San Diego, Calif, Aug 6, 15; m 40; c 2. *Educ:* Calif Inst Technol, BS, 37, MS, 41; Univ Southern Calif, MS, 49; Univ Calif, Los Angeles, PhD(planetary & space sci), 68. *Prof Exp:* Proj engr, Autonetics Div, NAm Aviation, Inc, 50-59; mem tech staff, Inst Defense Anal, 49-60; mem staff develop planning, Gen Off, NAm Aviation, Inc, 60-61, mgr, 61-62, corp res dir, 62-63, mem tech staff, Sci Ctr, 63-64, scientist, Space Info Systs Div, 64-68; mem tech staff, Inst Defense Anal, 68-71; mem staff, Off of Asst Secy Systs Eng & Technol, Dept Transp, 71-76; dir, Div Atmospheric Sci, NSF, 76-79; vis scholar, Univ Calif, Los Angeles, 79-88. *Concurrent Pos:* Res asst, E O Huburt Ctr Space Res, Naval Res Lab, DC, 65-68; consult, Univ Calif, Los Angeles, 79-86, NASA-Ames, 80- & NASA/GSEC, 84-86. *Mem:* AAAS; Am Meteorol Soc; Am Phys Soc; Am Geophys Union. *Res:* Planetary physics; investigation by rocket borne instrumentation of latitudinal and temporal variation of the homospheric boundary of the upper atmosphere; earth gas magnetism and instrumentation. *Mailing Add:* 25642 Orchard Rim Lane Lake Forest CA 92630

GROBLEWSKI, GERALD EUGENE, PHARMACOLOGY, TOXICOLOGY. *Current Pos:* ADJ PROF BIOL, PARK COL, 86-; ADJ FAC CHEM & BIOL, NMEX STATE UNIV, ALAMOGORDO, 87-; VIS INSTR BIOL, CHAPMAN COL, 87- *Personal Data:* b Nanticoke, Pa, Nov 5, 26; m 53; c 2. *Educ:* Univ Md, BA, 49; Univ Rochester, PhD(pharmacol), 64. *Prof Exp:* Pharmacol technician, Army Chem Ctr, Md, 50-56, physiologist, 56-57; admin asst chem, Distillation Prod Industs, Eastman Kodak Co, 57-59; assoc res biologist, Sterling-Winthrop Res Inst, 63-69; pharmacologist, Spec Proj Div, Woodard Res Corp, 69-73; res assoc toxicol, Inst Comp & Human Toxicol, Albany Med Col, 73-75, res asst prof, 75-76, asst prof, 76-80; mem staff, Int Ctr Environ Safety, 76-80. *Concurrent Pos:* Mem, Coun Thrombosis, Am Heart Asn. *Mem:* AAAS; Am Soc Pharmacol & Exp Therapeut; Int Soc Biochem Pharmacol; Sigma Xi. *Res:* Cardiac automaticity; cardiotonic agents; anticholinesterase agents; thrombosis; psychopharmacology. *Mailing Add:* 1704 Crescent Dr Alamogordo NM 88310-3935

GROBMAN, ARNOLD B(RAMS), HERPETOLOGY, BIOLOGICAL EDUCATION. *Current Pos:* chancellor & prof biol, 75-85, EMER CHANCELLOR & RES PROF BIOL, UNIV MO, ST LOUIS, 85- *Personal Data:* b Newark, NJ, Apr 28, 18; m 44, Hulda Gross; c Marc R & Beth A (Burruss). *Educ:* Univ Mich, BS, 39; Univ Rochester, MS, 41, PhD(zool), 43. *Honors & Awards:* Stoye Prize, 41; Morrison Prize, 44; McAllister Award, 65; Distinguished Serv Award, Am Inst Biol Sci, 84; Commanders Cross, Award of Merit, Fed Repub Ger, 85. *Prof Exp:* Instr zool, Univ Rochester, 43-44; res assoc, Manhattan Dist, Sch Med & Dent, 44-46; from asst prof to assoc prof biol, Univ Fla, 46-58; dir biol sci curric study, Univ Colo, 59-65; dean col arts & sci, Rutgers Univ, 65-67, dean, Rutgers Col, 67-72; vchancellor acad affairs, Univ Ill Chicago Circle, 73-75. *Concurrent Pos:* Res partic, Oak Ridge Inst, 50; dir, Fla State Mus, 52-58; dir, Fla State Mus, 54-59; res partic, Div Biol & Agr, Nat Res Coun, 54-70; chmn, Nat Coun Accreditation Teacher Educ, 70-71; chmn, Div Urban Affairs, Nat Asn State Univ & Land Grant Col, 78-80; adj cur, Fla Mus Natural Hist, 88- *Mem:* Fel AAAS; Herpetologists League; Nat Sci Teachers Asn; Soc Study Amphibians & Reptiles; Nat Asn Biol Teachers (pres, 66); Am Soc Ichthyol & Herpet (pres, 64). *Res:* Herpetology; academic administration; biological education. *Mailing Add:* 855 Live Oak Lane Vero Beach FL 32963. *Fax:* 561-234-8268

GROBMAN, WARREN DAVID, SOLID STATE PHYSICS. *Current Pos:* MGR, ULSI CIRCUIT & DESIGN TECH, MOTOROLA, 93- *Personal Data:* b Philadelphia, Pa, Sept 22, 42; m 65; c 2. *Educ:* Univ Pa, AB, 64; Princeton Univ, MA, 66, PhD(physics), 67. *Prof Exp:* Mem tech staff, Bellcomm Inc, Washington, DC, 67-69; mem tech staff, Appl Res Dept, T J Watson Res Ctr, IBM Corp, 69-80, mgr x-ray lithography, Semiconductor Sci & Technol Dept, 80-93. *Mem:* Inst Elec & Electronics Engrs; Am Phys Soc. *Res:* Geophysical science; experimental and theoretical studies of electronic states in solids; band theory; transport measurements; ultra-high-vacuum electron spectroscopy of surfaces; electron beam and x-ray lithography; applications to fabrication of exploratory devices. *Mailing Add:* ULSI Circuit & Design Technol 3205 Barker Hollow Pass Austin TX 78739

GROBNER, PAUL JOSEF, MATERIALS SCIENCE, CORROSION. *Current Pos:* RETIRED. *Personal Data:* b Prague, Czech, July 16, 19; US citizen; m 59; c 2. *Educ:* Tech Univ, Prague, Czech, MS, 41, PhD(chem eng). *Prof Exp:* Res engr metall, Chem & Metall Corp, Czech, 45-50; scientist corrosion, Res Inst Mat Protection, Czech, 50-59; develop engr mat res, Modransk Eng Works, Czech, 59-66; sr scientist, Res Inst Ferrous Metall, 66-69; sr staff metallurgist mat res, Amax Mat Res Ctr, 69-87. *Mem:* Metall Soc; Am Soc Metals; Nat Asn Corrosion Engrs. *Res:* Elevated temperature corrosion, stress corrosion, heat resistant steels, stainless steels. *Mailing Add:* 5821 S Cliff Rd Evergreen CO 80439

GROBSTEIN, CLIFFORD, BIOLOGY, PUBLIC POLICY. *Current Pos:* prof, Univ Calif, San Diego, 65-87, vchancellor sci & dean, Sch Med, 67-73, vchancellor univ rels, 73-77, prof biol sci & pub policy, 77-87, EMER PROF BIOL SCI & PUB POLICY, UNIV CALIF, SAN DIEGO, 87- *Personal Data:* b New York, NY, July 20, 16; m 38; c 2. *Educ:* City Col New York, BS, 36; Univ Calif, Los Angeles, MA, 38, PhD(zool), 40. *Honors & Awards:* Brachet Award, Belgian Royal Soc. *Prof Exp:* Instr zool, Ore State Col, 40-43; sr res fel, Nat Cancer Inst, 46-47; biologist, USPHS, 47-57; prof biol, Stanford Univ, 58-65. *Mem:* Nat Acad Sci; Am Soc Zoologists (pres, 66); Soc Develop Biol (past pres); Am Acad Arts & Sci; Am Soc Cell Biol; Inst Med. *Res:* Biomedical policy issues, particularly in heredity and development; biomedical policy issues. *Mailing Add:* 6515 LaValle Plateada Rd Rancho Santa Fe CA 92067

GROBSTEIN, PAUL, INTEGRATIVE NEUROBIOLOGY & DEVELOPMENTAL NEUROBIOLOGY. *Current Pos:* PROF, DEPT BIOL, BRYN MAWR COL, 86- *Personal Data:* b Long Beach, Calif, Mar 21, 46; c 2. *Educ:* Harvard Univ, BA, 69; Stanford Univ, MA, 70, PhD(biol), 73. *Prof Exp:* Fel neurobiol, Johns Hopkins Univ, 72-73 & Stanford Univ, 73-74; from asst prof to assoc prof, Dept Pharmacol & Physiol Sci, Univ Chicago, 74-85. *Concurrent Pos:* NIH fel, 72-74; A P Sloan Found fel, 76-80; mem, Comt Space Biol & Med Space Sci Bd, Nat Res Coun, 86-89. *Mem:* Soc Neurosci; Soc Develop Biol; AAAS; Fedn Am Scientists; Int Soc Neurobiol; Sigma Xi. *Res:* Nervous system organization and behavior; nervous system development. *Mailing Add:* Dept Biol Bryn Mawr Col Bryn Mawr PA 19010

GROCE, DAVID EIBEN, MEDICAL PHYSICS, NUCLEAR PHYSICS. *Current Pos:* RETIRED. *Personal Data:* b Wilmar, Calif, July 15, 36; m 61; c 1. *Educ:* Calif Inst Technol, BS, 58, PhD(nuclear physics), 63. *Prof Exp:* Res fel exp nuclear physics, Australian Nat Univ, 63-65; staff assoc res, Gen Atomic Div, Gen Dynamics Corp, 65-67; staff mem, Gulf Gen Atomic, Inc, 67-69; vpres & med consult, Res & Develop, JRB Assocs, Inc, 69-76; div mgr, Sci Appln Int Corp, 69-80, sr scientist appl med res & artificial intel, 80-87; physicist radiation physics, Avalon Inc, 87-90. *Concurrent Pos:* Consult, Nat Comt Radiation Protection, 69-; independent Consult weapons effects, 87-; mem bd trustees, San Diego Natural Hist Mus, 85-90 & 91-97, treas, 89-90; consult, 90- *Mem:* AAAS; Am Phys Soc; Sigma Xi. *Res:* Experimental research in low energy positrons, radioactive pharmaceuticals, fission and neutron yields; Monte Carlo radiation transport, simulation and systems analysis; consulting in cancer therapy and research, accelerators and facility design; neutron physics; radiation shielding; personnel response to external physical forces; diagnostic radiology and nuclear medicine; artificial intelligence and expert systems; decision aids; radiation effects. *Mailing Add:* 8243 Prestwick Dr La Jolla CA 92037-2019. *Fax:* 619-454-8821; *E-Mail:* davefroce@aol.com

GROCE, JOHN WESLEY, BIOCHEMISTRY. *Current Pos:* RETIRED. *Personal Data:* b Stanley, NC, Nov 9, 30; m 59, Joan A Col; c Alisa Marie & Daniel W. *Educ:* Asbury Col, AB, 53; Purdue Univ, MS, 56, PhD, 64. *Prof Exp:* From instr to prof chem, Heidelberg Col, 57-93, chmn dept, 65-93. *Concurrent Pos:* Fel, NC State Univ, 70-71. *Mem:* Am Chem Soc. *Res:* Carbohydrate, polysaccharide chemistry; analytical organic chemistry. *Mailing Add:* 29 Northwood Dr Tiffin OH 44883-1987

GROCE, WILLIAM HENRY (BILL), HAZARDOUS WASTE PROCESSING. *Current Pos:* PRIN CHEMIST, GROCE LABS, INC, 72-, DIR RES, 87- *Personal Data:* b Greer, SC, Sept 21, 40; m 64; c W H IV. *Educ:* Newberry Col, BS, 64. *Prof Exp:* Polymer chemist, Allied Chem Co, 64-66; analytical chemist, US Food & Drug Admin, 66-67; polymer lab mgr, Celanese Corp, 67-72. *Concurrent Pos:* Consult, 72-; lectr, Am Inst Chem Engrs, 83- & SC State Chamber Com, 85-, Univ SC, 87, 88. *Mem:* Am Chem Soc; Am Inst Chem Engrs; fel Am Inst Chemists; Inst Hazardous Mat Mgt; Am Soc Prof Engr. *Res:* Chemical reclamation procedures; chemical detoxification; explosive chemical decomposition by wet chemical oxidation; chemical hazard classification. *Mailing Add:* 203 Melbourne Lane Greenville SC 29615

GROCHOSKI, GREGORY T, RESEARCH ADMINISTRATION. *Current Pos:* Technician res & develop, 64-68, chemist, 68-70, res chemist, 71-72, sr res chemist, 72-73, mgr tech serv, 73-77, mgr personal care, 77-78, admin asst policy admin, 78-79, dir corp develop, 79-82, VPRES, RES & DEVELOP, AMWAY CORP, 82- *Personal Data:* b Grand Rapids, Mich, July 6, 46; c 2. *Educ:* Grand Valley State Col, BS(chem) & BS(econ), 68. *Honors & Awards:* Biomed Res Award, Soap & Detergent Asn, 70. *Concurrent Pos:* US Army Med Corp, Med Field Specialties, 70-75. *Mem:* Soap & Detergent Asn; Chem Specialties Mfg Asn; Cosmetic Toiletry & Fragrances Asn; Soc Cosmetic Chemists; Indust Res Inst; Am Asn Poison Control Ctrs. *Res:* Corporate technical operations including quality assurance, chemical, electrical and package engineering; research and development; analytical, microbiology, technical-regulatory and toxicology departments. *Mailing Add:* Amway Corp 7575 E Fulton Rd Ada MI 49355

GRODBERG, MARCUS GORDON, DRUGS FOR DENTAL & BONE DISEASES. *Current Pos:* dir res & develop, Colgate-Hoyt Labs, Div Colgate-Palmolive Co, Canton, Mass, 58-89, CONSULT, COLGATE ORAL PHARMACEUT, 89- *Personal Data:* b Worcester, Mass, Jan 27, 23; m 51, Shirley F Merkle; c Joel, Kim & Jeremy. *Educ:* Clark Univ, AB, 44; Univ Ill, MS, 48. *Honors & Awards:* Ellis Fund Award, Clare Univ. *Prof Exp:* Jr res chemist, Schenley Labs, Inc, Lawrenceburg, Ind, 44-47; chemist, Marine Prod Co, Boston, 48-50 & Brewer & Co, Inc, Worcester, Mass, 50-55; tech dir, Gray Pharmaceut Co, Newton, Mass, 55-58. *Concurrent Pos:* Consult, Grad Sch Bus Admin, Harvard Univ, 57-58. *Mem:* Int Asn Dent Res; Am Dent Asn; Fedn Dentaire Int; Nat Osteoporosis Found. *Res:* Industrial research and development of pharmaceuticals; fluoride products for dental caries and osteoporosis; patentee, fluoride compositions for treating osteoporosis. *Mailing Add:* 4091 Hearthstone Dr Sarasota FL 34238. *Fax:* 941-925-2946

GRODNER, MARY LASLIE, EMBRYOLOGY, DEVELOPMENTAL BIOLOGY. *Current Pos:* instr, 71-74, ASST PROF, DEPT ZOOL & PHYSIOL, AGR & MECH COL & LA STATE UNIV, BATON ROUGE, 74- *Personal Data:* b Attapulgus, Ga, Jan 5, 35; m 59; c 2. *Educ:* Wesleyan Col, Ga, AB, 55; La State Univ, Baton Rouge, MS, 57, PhD(entom), 73. *Prof Exp:* Instr embryol cell physiol, Otterbein Col, 58-59, 61; agr res technician cotton insects develop, Cotton Insect Physiol Invest, Agr Res Serv, USDA, Baton Rouge, 69, 70. *Mem:* Soc Develop Biol; Electron Micros Soc Am; Am Soc Zoologists; Entom Soc Am; Sigma Xi. *Res:* Developmental biology and reproductive physiology of insects, primarily the cotton boll weevil. *Mailing Add:* Coop Exten Serv La State Univ Baton Rouge LA 70803

GRODNER, ROBERT MAYNARD, FOOD SCIENCE, ZOOLOGY. *Current Pos:* assoc prof, 63-69, PROF FOOD SCI & TECHNOL, LA STATE UNIV, BATON ROUGE, 69- *Personal Data:* b Brooklyn, NY, June 22, 25; m 59; c 2. *Educ:* Brown Univ, AB, 49; Univ Tenn, MSc, 50; La State Univ, PhD(zool, physiol), 59. *Prof Exp:* Instr biol, Berea Col, 51; from asst prof to assoc prof, Otterbein Col, 59-63. *Concurrent Pos:* AEC fels, 64-66. *Mem:* AAAS; Inst Food Technol; Am Inst Biol Sci. *Res:* Autoxidation of unsaturated fatty acids; radiation pasteurization of Gulf Coast shellfish; food toxicology and enzymes; rapid microbiological methodology for assay of Gulf Coast seafood; rapid methodology for determining shrimp decomposition; bacterial survey of fresh commercial seafood. *Mailing Add:* Dept Food Sci La State Univ Baton Rouge LA 70803

GRODSKI, JULIUSZ JAN, TELEROBOTICS, HUMAN FACTORS. *Current Pos:* head diving eng & res, 75-85, HEAD TELEROBOTICS, DEFENSE & CIVIL INST ENVIRON MED, 85- *Personal Data:* b Krosno, Poland, July 9, 39; Can citizen; m 68, Renata Senczuk; c Mark & Tom. *Educ:* Univ Toronto, BSc, 63; Univ Waterloo, MSc, 66, PhD(solid state physics), 71. *Prof Exp:* Assoc res scientist, Ont Res Found, 62-67; Nat Res Coun fel solid state physics, Univ Paris-Sud, 71-73; asst prof physics, Laurentian Univ, 74-75. *Concurrent Pos:* Sci authority, STEAR Prog, Can Space Agency, 90-; adj assoc prof, Indust Eng Dept, Univ Toronto, 93- *Res:* Robotics for unstructured environments involving interfaces with a human operator: sensing and display to facilitate telepresence and actuation with human-like capabilities; development of new technologies (patents); assessment of human factors in various operational environments. *Mailing Add:* 29 Rivercrest Rd Toronto ON M6S 4H4 Can. *Fax:* 416-635-2104; *E-Mail:* jul@dciem.dnd.ca

GRODSKY, GEROLD MORTON, BIOLOGICAL CHEMISTRY, ENDOCRINOLOGY. *Current Pos:* Asst res biochemist, Univ Calif, San Francisco, 56-60, from asst prof to prof, 60-93, EMER PROF BIOCHEM, MED CTR, UNIV CALIF, SAN FRANCISCO, 93- *Personal Data:* b St Louis, Mo, Jan 18, 27; m 51; c 2. *Educ:* Univ Ill, BS, 47, MS, 48; Univ Calif, Berkeley, PhD(biochem), 55. *Honors & Awards:* Somogyi lect, 72; Helen Martin lectr, 76; David Rumbough Int Diabetes Res Award, 84; Mosenthal Hon lectr, 86; Williams-Levine Award, 89. *Concurrent Pos:* Nat Cancer Inst fel biochem, Cambridge Univ, 54-55; consult, various pharmaceut companies & hospitals; vis prof Univ Geneva, 68-69; Univ Paris, 89; mem, Med Adv Bd, Juv Diabetes Found, 75-77 & 80-85; chmn res comt, Am Diabetes Asn, 77-79; chmn acad senate, Univ Calif San Francisco, 77-79; mem adv bd diabetes, US Secy Health, 81-85; mem comt, Am Diabetes Asn, 93-96. *Mem:* Am Soc Biol Chemists; Soc Exp Biol & Med; Am Fedn Clin Res; Am Diabetes Asn. *Res:* Metabolism and immunological aspects of insulin action and secretion; intermediary metabolish of diabetes. *Mailing Add:* Box 0540 Med Metab Unit Univ Calif San Francisco San Francisco CA 94143-0001

GRODY, WAYNE WILLIAM, DIAGNOSTIC MOLECULAR PATHOLOGY, MEDICAL GENETICS. *Current Pos:* Resident lab med, Univ Calif, Los Angeles, 82-85, fel med genetics, 85-86, asst prof, 87-93, ASSOC PROF MED GENETICS & MOLECULAR PATH, SCH MED, UNIV CALIF, LOS ANGELES, 93- *Personal Data:* b Syracuse, NY, Feb 25, 52; m 90, Gaylen Ducker; c Shelby Ross. *Educ:* Johns Hopkins Univ, BA, 74; Baylor Col Med, MD, 77, PhD(cell biol), 81. *Honors & Awards:* Kleiner Mem Award, Am Soc Med Technol, 90. *Concurrent Pos:* Contrib ed, MD Mag, 81-91; consult DNA testing, US Food & Drug Admin, 89-; prin investr, March Dimes Birth Defects Found, 89-92, Nat Inst Child Health & Human Develop, NIH, 89-91; Nat Ctr Human Genome Res, 91-95; mem, Molecular Path Resource Comt, Col Am Path, 89-; chmn, DNA Qual Assurance Comt, Pac Southwest Regional Genetics Network, 89-; mem, DNA Testing Comt, Am Col Med Genetics, 93-; mem, Task Force on Genetic Testing, NIH-Dept Energy, 95. *Mem:* AAAS; AMA; Am Soc Clin Path; Am Soc Human Genetics; Col Am Path; Soc Inherited Metab Dis. *Res:* Molecular genetics of inborn errors of metabolism; application of recombinant DNA technology to clinical diagnosis; cystic fibrosis. *Mailing Add:* Div Med Genetics & Molecular Path Univ Calif Sch Med Los Angeles CA 90095-1732

GRODZICKER, TERRI IRENE, MOLECULAR GENETICS, VIROLOGY. *Current Pos:* staff investr, 73-75, sr staff investr tumor virol, 75-79, SR SCIENTIST, COLD SPRING HARBOR LAB, 79-, ASST DIR, ACAD AFFAIRS, 86- *Personal Data:* b Brooklyn, NY, Nov 18, 42. *Educ:* Wellesley Col, AB, 63; Columbia Univ, MA, 65, PhD(zool), 69. *Prof Exp:* Fel molecular genetics, Harvard Med Sch, 69-72. *Concurrent Pos:* NIH fel, 69-71; adj assoc prof microbiol, Med Sch, State Univ NY, Stony Brook, 81-; NCI Frederick Adv Bd, 82-88; sci adv bd, Damon Runyon, Walter Winchell Cancer Res, 87-91; ed, Genes & Develop, 89- *Mem:* Am Soc Microbiol;

Sigma Xi; AAAS; Am Soc Cell Biol. *Res:* Control of gene expression of viruses and their host cells; tumor viruses-SV40 and adenoviruses. *Mailing Add:* Cold Spring Harbor Lab Bungtown Rd PO Box 100 Cold Spring Harbor NY 11724

GRODZINS, LEE, NUCLEAR PHYSICS. *Current Pos:* from asst prof to assoc prof, 59-66, PROF PHYSICS, MASS INST TECHNOL, 66- *Personal Data:* b Lowell, Mass, July 10, 26; m 56; c 2. *Educ:* Univ NH, BS, 46; Union Col, MS, 48; Purdue Univ, PhD(physics), 54. *Prof Exp:* Res asst physics, Gen Elec Res Lab, 46-48; instr, Purdue Univ, 54-55; from res assoc to assoc physicist, Brookhaven Nat Lab, 55-59. *Concurrent Pos:* Consult, High Voltage Eng Co, 62-70, Avco-Everett Res Lab, 67-72, Los Alamos Nat Labs, 76-, Harvard Univ, 76-77, Brookhaven Nat Labs, 77- & Exxon Nuclear Co, 78-; Guggenheim fel, 64-65 & 71-72. *Mem:* Fel Am Phys Soc; fel Am Acad Arts & Sci. *Res:* Interaction between heavy nuclei; studies of scientific manpower; nuclear spectroscopy, beta decay and Mossbauer scattering. *Mailing Add:* 14 Stratham Rd Lexington MA 02173

GRODZINSKI, BERNARD, PLANT SCIENCE. *Current Pos:* PROF, DEPT HORT SCI, UNIV GUELPH, 80- *Personal Data:* b Stettin, Poland, Jan 28, 46; Can citizen; m 67; c 3. *Educ:* Univ Toronto, BS, 68; York Univ, MS, 71, PhD(biol), 74; Univ Cambridge, MA, 78. *Prof Exp:* Fel, Sch Bot, Oxford Univ, 74-75; demonstr, Sch Bot, Cambridge Univ, 75-79. *Mem:* Can Soc Plant Physiologist; Am Soc Plant Physiologists; Am Asn Hort Sci. *Res:* Biochemical and biophysical nature of photorespiration and glycolate metabolism; the relationship between photosynthesis and plant productivity in horticultural crops. *Mailing Add:* Hort Sci Dept Edmund C Bobey Lab Univ Guelph 50 Stone Rd E Guelph ON N1G 2W1 Can

GRODZINSKY, ALAN J, BIOMEDICAL ENGINEERING. *Current Pos:* Asst prof, Mass Inst Technol, 74-75, Esther & Harold E Edgerton asst prof, Elec & Bioeng, 75-77, assoc prof, Elec & Bioeng, Dept Elec Eng & Computer Sci, 77-84, assoc prof elec & bioeng, 79-84, PROF ELEC & BIOENG, DEPT ELEC ENG & COMPUTER SCI, MASS INST TECHNOL & HARVARD-MASS INST TECHNOL DIV HEALTH SCI & TECHNOL, 84- *Educ:* Mass Inst Technol, SM & SB, 71, ScD, 74. *Honors & Awards:* Giovani Borelli Award, Am Soc Biomech, 87. *Concurrent Pos:* Vis lectr & res assoc, Dept Orthop Surg, Harvard Med Sch & Children's Hosp, Boston, 76-77, vis assoc prof, Biomech Lab, Dept Mech Eng, Rensselaer Polytechnic Inst, 77; Am deleg, Peoples Repub China, Orthop Sci & Bioeng Group, 79; mem sci adv panel, NY Dept Health, 80-87, sci prog comt, Bioelec Res & Growth Soc, 81-86, mem sci coun, 84-86; assoc ed, J Orthop Res, 82-; spec reviewer, Orthop Study Sect, NIH, 85; biomed engr, Dept Biomed Eng, Mass Gen Hosp, 87-; vis prof biochem & orthop, Rush Presby St Lukes Med Ctr, Rush Univ, 89; mem sci adv bds, Nat Inst Arthritis & Musculoskeletal & Skin Dis, NIH, Sci Ctr of Res, grants Osteoarthritis & Osteop; chmn, Gordon Res Conf Bioeng & Orthop Sci, 89-90. *Mem:* Inst Elec & Electronics Engrs, Eng Med & Biol Soc; Bioelec Repair & Growth Soc (pres, 86-87); Bioelectromagnetics Soc; Biomed Eng Soc; Orthop Res Soc; Am Soc Biomech; NY Acad Sci; Biophys Soc; AAAS; Sigma Xi. *Res:* Influence of mechanical and electrical stresses on connective tissue growth; remodeling, repair and pathology; electromechanical and physiochemical properties of connective tissues and polymeric biomaterials; electrically controlled membrane permeability for drug delivery and separation processes; synthesis of physiologically compatible transducers for diagnosis and treatment; fundamental study and modelling of electrical, mechanical and chemical energy conversion in natural and synthetic membranes and in biological tissues; numerous technical publications; patents. *Mailing Add:* Dept Elec Eng & Comput Sci Rm 38-377 Mass Inst Technol 50 Vassar St 38-377 Cambridge MA 02139. *Fax:* 617-258-5239

GROEGER, THEODORE OSKAR, pharmacological chemistry, mechanical engineering, for more information see previous edition

GROEL, JOHN TRUEMAN, MEDICINE. *Current Pos:* RETIRED. *Personal Data:* b Maplewood, NJ, Oct 5, 24; m 88. *Educ:* Yale Univ, MD, 51. *Prof Exp:* Med ed, White Labs, 51-52; from asst med dir to assoc med dir, E R Squibb Corp, 52-60, assoc clin res dir, 60-71, worldwide med dir, 71-72, clin res dir, 72-79, dir, med ed serv, 79-86. *Mem:* AMA. *Res:* Infectious diseases; cardiovascular. *Mailing Add:* 199 Edgemere Way S Naples FL 33999

GROEMER, HELMUT (JOHANN), MATHEMATICS. *Current Pos:* PROF MATH, UNIV ARIZ, 64- *Personal Data:* b Salzburg, Austria, Nov 6, 30; m 57, Helga; c Gerald & Beatrice. *Educ:* Innsbruck Univ, PhD(math & physics), 54. *Prof Exp:* From instr to assoc prof math, Ore State Univ, 57-64. *Concurrent Pos:* NSF res grants, 60- 96. *Mem:* Am Math Soc; Math Asn Am; Austrian Math Soc. *Res:* Convex sets; integral geometry; geometric probability theory; geometric inequalities; spherical harmonics. *Mailing Add:* 6820 E Rosewood Circle Tucson AZ 85710. *E-Mail:* groemer@math.arizona.edu

GROENWEGHE, LEO CARL DENIS, INORGANIC CHEMISTRY, COMPUTER SCIENCES. *Current Pos:* res specialist, Cent Res Dept, 56-66, sr res specialist, 66-73, MGR, COMPUT SERV, CORP RES DEPT, MONSANTO CO, 73- *Personal Data:* b Antwerp, Belg, Aug 31, 25; nat US; m 83; c 5. *Educ:* Univ Ghent, Lic, 48, DSc(inorg & phys chem), 51. *Prof Exp:* Res chemist, Belg Inst Sci Res, 48-53; mem sr staff, Spencer Chem Co, Kans, 53-56. *Mem:* Am Chem Soc; Sigma Xi; Nat Comput Graphics Asn. *Res:* Scientific computation; laboratory automation; inorganic synthetic chemistry, especially uranium, fluorine, nitrogen, and phosphorus compounds; solubility systems; nuclear magnetic resonance; organophosphorus compounds; random reorganization theory; catalysis; statistics; computer applications; computer graphics; technical forecasting; office automation. *Mailing Add:* 229 Greenbriar Estates Dr St Louis MO 63122

GROER, MAUREEN, PHYSIOLOGY. *Current Pos:* PROF NURSING, UNIV TENN, KNOXVILLE, 83- *Personal Data:* b Cambridge, Mass, Nov 27, 44; m; c 3. *Educ:* Univ Ill, PhD(physiol), 75; Univ Tenn, MSN, 81. *Concurrent Pos:* Curriculum Consult. *Mem:* Sigma Xi; Am Nursing Asn; Am Physiol Soc. *Res:* Psychoneuroimmunology; stress. *Mailing Add:* 1501 Rhododendron Ct Knoxville TN 37932

GROER, PETER GEROLD, RADIATION RISK ANALYSIS, BAYESIAN STATISTICS. *Current Pos:* mem staff radiation biol & biostatist, Inst Energy Anal, 78-83, sr scientist, 83-90 , ASSOC PROF, DEPT NUCLEAR ENG, OAK RIDGE ASSOC UNIVS, 90- *Personal Data:* b Vienna, Austria, Jan 27, 41; m 68; c 3. *Educ:* Univ Vienna, PhD(theoret physics), 67. *Prof Exp:* Mem res staff appl nuclear physics & radiation biol, Mass Inst Technol, 67-70; mem staff theoret radiation biol, Argonne Nat Lab, 70-78. *Concurrent Pos:* Consult, UN Sci Comt on Effects of Atomic Radiation, 79, Beir IV Comt, 85-88, Nat Coun Radiation Protection & Measurements Comt, 80-85 Nat Acad Sci, Comt on Interagency Radiation Res & Policy Coord, 85-87; vis scientist, Radiation Effects Res Found, Hiroshima, Japan, 80 & 81. *Mem:* Radiation Res Soc; Soc Risk Anal; Am Statist Asn; Health Physics Soc; Am Math Soc; Am Math Asn. *Res:* Estimation of risk from ionizing radiations; probabilistic models for radiation carcinogenesis; survival (reliability) analysis; competing risk theory; Bayesian statistics. *Mailing Add:* Nuclear Engr Univ Tenn 1345 Circle Park Knoxville TN 37996-0001. *E-Mail:* pgroek@utkvx

GROETSCH, CHARLES WILLIAM, NUMERICAL ANALYSIS, APPROXIMATION THEORY. *Current Pos:* from asst prof to assoc prof, 71-81, PROF MATH, UNIV CINCINNATI, 81-, HEAD DEPT, 85- *Personal Data:* b New Orleans, La, Feb 15, 45; m 66, Sandra Carver; c Kurt & Heidi. *Educ:* Univ New Orleans, BS, 66, MS, 68; La State Univ, PhD(math), 71. *Honors & Awards:* George Polya Award, Math Asn Am, 94. *Prof Exp:* Assoc engr, Boeing Aerospace Corp, 66-67. *Concurrent Pos:* Vis asst prof, Univ RI, 74-75; res assoc, Air Force flight Dynamics Lab, 78; vis scientist, EGer Acad Sci, 79; sr vis fel, Univ Manchester, Eng, 80-81; vis prof, Univ Kaiserslautern, WGer, 83; vis fel, Australian Nat Univ, 86; assoc ed, Numerical Functional Anal & Optimization; Raybould res fel, Univ Queensland, Australia, 96. *Mem:* Am Math Soc; Math Asn Am; Soc Indust & Appl Math. *Res:* Theory of approximate methods for inverse and ill-posed problems, methods for numerical solution of Fredholm integral equations of the first kind; theory of generalized inverses of linear operators. *Mailing Add:* 5320 Engleswatch Ct Cincinnati OH 45230. *Fax:* 513-556-3417; *E-Mail:* groetsch@uc.edu

GROFF, DONALD WILLIAM, GEOENVIRONMENTAL SCIENCE, WATER RESOURCES. *Current Pos:* PROF SOIL SCIENTIST, AM REGISTRY CERT PROF CROP, AGRONOMISTS & SOIL SCIENTISTS, UNIV WIS, MADISON, 78-, CERT PROF GEOLOGIST, 86- *Personal Data:* b Lancaster, Pa, Apr 11, 28; m 57, Mary E Graves; c Dana D. *Educ:* Univ Redlands, BS, 52; Univ Pittsburgh, PhD(geol, geochem), 66. *Prof Exp:* Geophysicist, Western Geophys Co, 52; asst, Pa State Univ, 52-55; instr, Allegheny Col, 55-57; geophysicist, Pickands Mather Co, 57; asst seismologist & instr geol, Univ Pittsburgh, 57-61; assoc prof, Ind Univ, Pa, 61-65; chmn dept, Space & Environ Sci Dept, Western Conn State Col, 65-87, prof geol, 66-87. *Concurrent Pos:* Geol consult, Huntley & Huntley, Inc, 59-61; consult, Earth Sci Serv, Brookfield Ctr, 69-73; mem, Coun Educ Geol Sci, 69-73; dir, Allegheny River Mining Co & Pittsburgh & Shawmut RR Co, 70-75; coun educ geol sci, Am Geol Inst, 70-73; mem, Health Systs Agency, Conn Region V, 75-84; geohydrol consult, Off Planning, Putnam Co, NY, 81-85; chief hydrogeologist, Lawler, Matusky & Skelly Engrs, 87-88, dir geol, 87-91; dep dir environ serv, Storch Assocs, 91-94; environ consult, 95- *Mem:* Comput Oriented Geol Soc; Agron Soc Am; Geol Soc Am; Am Inst Prof Geologists; Asn Groundwater Scientists & Engrs; Nat Water Well Asn. *Res:* Radiometry; spectrochemistry as applied to sediments; soil sciences; water resources; geohydrology field mapper; methods of radioactive measurements; allegheny coal stratigraphy; age dating of bone and GC methodology; quantitative mineral prospecting. *Mailing Add:* 31 Merwin Brook Rd Brookfield CT 06804

GROFF, RONALD PARKE, PHYSICS, APPLICATION DEVELOPMENT. *Current Pos:* SYST DEVELOP CONSULT, DUPONT MERCK PHARMACEUT CO, 93- *Personal Data:* b Lancaster, Pa, Oct 25, 40; m 63; c 2. *Educ:* Lehigh Univ, BS, 62; Univ Rochester, PhD(physics), 67. *Prof Exp:* Res physicist, E I DuPont de Nemours & Co, Inc, 67-93. *Mem:* Am Phys Soc; Sigma Xi; AAAS. *Res:* Infrared; surface physics and chemistry, catalysis; luminescence; molecular crystals; organic conductors. *Mailing Add:* Du Pont Merck Pharmaceut Co Exp Sta Wilmington DE 19880

GROFF, SIDNEY LAVERN, GEOLOGY, GEOPOLITICS. *Current Pos:* RETIRED. *Personal Data:* b Victor, Mont, Apr 7, 19; m 79, Shirley Hand. *Educ:* Mont State Univ, BA, 41, MA, 54; Univ Utah, PhD, 59. *Prof Exp:* USMC Naval Aviator, 41-51; Asst, Mont State Univ, 52-54; chief, Ground Water & Fuels Div, Mont Bur Mines & Geol, 57-71, dir & state geologist, 71-83. *Mem:* Geol Soc Am; Am Asn Petrol Geol; Am Prof Geol Scientists. *Res:* Hydrogeology; coal geology and economics; mineral deposits; reconnaissance geological mapping. *Mailing Add:* 3106 Floral Blvd Butte MT 59701-4623

GROGAN, DONALD E, CELL BIOLOGY. *Personal Data:* b Grogan, Mo, Feb 6, 38; m 62; c 2. *Educ:* Univ Mo, BA, 60, MS, 62, PhD(biochem), 65. *Prof Exp:* Fel protein biochem, Col Med, Baylor Univ, 65-66, res assoc drug metab, 66-68; asst prof, Univ Mo-St Louis, 68-74, assoc prof biol, 74-97. *Res:* Biochemistry of wasps and bees. *Mailing Add:* 7895 Hwy 32 Ste Genevieve MO 63670

GROGAN, JAMES BIGBEE, MICROBIOLOGY. *Current Pos:* supvr surg res bact lab, 57-63, from instr to asst prof surg & microbiol, 63-74, PROF SURG & ASSOC PROF MICROBIOL, SCH MED, UNIV MISS, 74- *Personal Data:* b Edwards, Miss, May 15, 32; m 56; c 2. *Educ:* Miss Col, BS, 55; Univ Wis, MS, 57; Univ Miss, PhD(microbiol), 63. *Prof Exp:* Asst bact, Univ Wis, 55-57. *Mem:* Am Asn Immunologists; Am Soc Microbiol. *Res:* Infections; hosts defense mechanisms; transplantation immunology. *Mailing Add:* Sch Med Univ Miss 2500 N State St Jackson MS 39216-4505

GROGAN, MICHAEL JOHN, PHYSICAL CHEMISTRY. *Current Pos:* chemist, Shell Chem Co, NJ, 67-70, sr chemist, 70-71, sr chemist, Calif, 71-75, sr engr, 75-76, staff engr, 76-77, mgr qual assurance, Ohio, 77-81, supvr sr staff, 81-87, RES MGR, ELASTOMERS RES & DEVELOP, SHELL DEVELOP CO, HOUSTON, 87- *Personal Data:* b Hammond, Ind, Feb 6, 38; m 61, Jean Ablaza; c Lesley. *Educ:* John Carroll Univ, BS, 59; Ill Inst Technol, PhD(chem), 67. *Prof Exp:* Res technician, Dept Med, Univ Chicago, 59-62; chemist, Magnaflux Corp, Ill, 62-63; chemist, Culligan Inc, 63-64; teaching asst phys chem, Ill Inst Technol, 64-67. *Mem:* Am Chem Soc. *Res:* Spectroscopic investigations of metal-olefin complexes, structure and chemistry of titanium III complexes; removal of catalyst residues from polyolefins; determination of the structure and content of ethylene-propylene copolymers by pyrolysis gas chromatography; investigations of the chemistry of propylene polymerization and styrene-butadiene polymerization; elastomer product development; management of futures oriented research on styrenic block copolymers; chemical modification of polymers; product development of styrenic block polymers for automotive uses (SMC, functional parts); polymer modification; thermoset modification; coordinate technical recruiting for polymers. *Mailing Add:* 442 Southchester Lane Houston TX 77079-7007

GROGAN, PAUL J(OSEPH), MECHANICAL ENGINEERING. *Current Pos:* RETIRED. *Personal Data:* b Adrian, Minn, Nov 20, 18; m 45; c 6. *Educ:* Purdue Univ, BS, 43; Univ Wis, MS, 49. *Prof Exp:* From instr to asst prof mech eng, Univ Wis, 47-50; asst prof mech eng, Univ Notre Dame, 50-51; prof & chmn eng exten dept, Univ Wis, 51-66; dir, Off State Tech Serv, US Dept Com, Washington, DC, 66-68; prof eng, Univ Exten, Univ Wis-Madison, 68-85; pvt pract mech eng, 85. *Mem:* Am Soc Eng Educ; Nat Asn Power Engrs. *Res:* Power production and related problems of energy conversion; heat transfer; electrical transmission and distribution; water supply and water conditioning. *Mailing Add:* 18 Southwick Circle Madison WI 53717-1415

GROGAN, RAYMOND GERALD, PLANT PATHOLOGY. *Current Pos:* From instr & jr pathologist to prof & plant pathologist, 48-85, chmn dept, 69-74, EMER PROF PLANT PATH, UNIV CALIF, DAVIS, 85- *Personal Data:* b Emma, Ga, July 22, 20; m 44; c 2. *Educ:* Univ Ga, BSA, 41, MSA, 42; Univ Wis, PhD(plant path), 48. *Mem:* AAAS; Am Phytopath Soc. *Res:* Causes and control of diseases of vegetable crops; plant virology. *Mailing Add:* 2-1921 E Cliff Dr Santa Cruz CA 95062

GROGAN, WILLIAM MCLEAN, LIPID METABOLISM & MEMBRANE STRUCTURAL DYNAMICS, GRADUATE & POSTDOCTORAL TRAINING. *Current Pos:* from asst prof to assoc prof, 75-90, PROF BIOCHEM, DEPT BIOCHEM & MOLECULAR BIOPHYS, VA COMMONWEALTH UNIV, 90- *Personal Data:* b Knoxville, Tenn, Feb 4, 44; m 65; c 2. *Educ:* Belmont Col, BS, 67; Purdue Univ, PhD(biochem), 72. *Prof Exp:* Res assoc biochem, Vanderbilt Univ Sch Med, 72-75. *Concurrent Pos:* Co-dir, Flow Cytometry Lab, Massey Cancer Ctr, 77-; prin investr, NIH res grants, 79-; dir, Laser Cytometry Lab, Sch Basic Health Sci, 91-; assoc ed, Lipids, 91-; mem spec study sect, NIH, 91- *Mem:* Am Soc Biochem & Molecular Biol; Am Oil Chemists Soc; Am Chem Soc; AAAS. *Res:* Investigation of the role of intracellular cholesterol pools in regulation of bile acid metabolism and cholesterol homeostasis; mechanisms for regulation of those pools and effects of cholesterol and other membrane components on membrane structural dynamics and membrane-associated activities; author of 50 publications and one book. *Mailing Add:* Dept Biochem Med Col Va PO Box 614 Richmond VA 23298-0614

GROGAN, WILLIAM R, ELECTRICAL ENGINEERING. *Current Pos:* FAC MEM, WORCESTER POLYTECH INST. *Mem:* Inst Elec & Electronics Engrs. *Mailing Add:* Worcester Polytech Inst 100 Institute Rd Worcester MA 01609

GROGINSKY, HERBERT LEONARD, ELECTRONICS. *Current Pos:* dept mgr appl math, 59-70, TECH DIR, ADVAN DEVELOP LAB, RAYTHEON CO, 70- *Personal Data:* b Newark, NJ, July 10, 30; m 52; c 3. *Educ:* Polytech Inst Brooklyn, BEE, 52; Columbia Univ, MS, 54, EngScD(elec eng), 59. *Prof Exp:* Instr physics, Polytech Inst Brooklyn, 51-52; staff engr, Electronics Res Lab, Columbia Univ, 52-59. *Concurrent Pos:* Instr elec eng, Northeastern Univ, 59-65, adj prof, 65-72, instr, Sch Continuing Educ, 75-; deleg, NASA Active Microwave Workshop, 75-76, mem tech comt atmospherics, 77- *Mem:* AAAS; sr mem Inst Elec & Electronics Engrs; Am Inst Aeronaut & Astronaut; Sigma Xi. *Res:* Radar signal processing; radar meteorology; space based radars. *Mailing Add:* 25 Hillside Rd Wellesley MA 02181

GROH, HAROLD JOHN, PHYSICAL CHEMISTRY. *Current Pos:* RETIRED. *Personal Data:* b New Orleans, La, Jan 28, 28; m 51; c 5. *Educ:* St Louis Univ, BS, 49; Univ Rochester, PhD(phys chem), 52. *Prof Exp:* Res chemist, E I du Pont de Nemours & Co Inc, 52-59, res supvr, 59-67, res mgr, 68, sect dir, 69-78, gen supt, 78-82, prin consult, 82-89. *Concurrent Pos:* Consult, 90- *Mem:* Am Chem Soc; Am Nuclear Soc. *Res:* Radiochemical process development; radiation chemistry; radioisotope production; actinide chemistry. *Mailing Add:* Seven Longwood Dr Aiken SC 29803

GROHSE, EDWARD WILLIAM, MASS AND HEAT TRANSFER. *Current Pos:* PRES, HYDROCARB CORP, 87- *Personal Data:* b New York, NY, Dec 5, 15; m 40; c 2. *Educ:* Cooper Union, BChE, 40; Univ Del, PhD(chem eng), 48. *Hon Degrees:* ChE, Cooper Union, 45. *Prof Exp:* Analytical chemist, 37-40; chem engr, FMC Corp, WVa, 40-44 & NY, 44-45; asst res prof chem eng, Univ Del, 48-49; asst prof, Carnegie Inst Technol, 49-51; sr technologist, Monsanto Chem Co, 51-52; res assoc, Gen Elec Co Res Lab, 52-58, consult engr, Knolls Atomic Power Lab, 58-60; prof chem eng, Univ Ala, Tuscaloosa, 60-65; prof chem eng & head, Energy & Mass Transfer Lab, Univ Ala, Huntsville, 65-80; sr res engr, Brookhaven Nat Lab, 80-82; consult, E W Grohse Assocs, 83- *Concurrent Pos:* Consult, FMC Corp, 60-65, Army Missile Command, 61-63, Brookhaven Nat Lab, 62-63 & 83-, NASA Marshall Space Flight Ctr, 70-80; mem & chmn, Huntsville Air Pollution Control Bd, 69-80. *Mem:* Am Chem Soc; fel Am Inst Chem Engrs; Asn Consult Chemists & Chem Engrs; Sigma Xi. *Res:* Mass and heat transfer; chemical process research and development; distillation, fluidization, heat transfer in nuclear power systems; fuel cell research; metal hydride slurry systems. *Mailing Add:* 75 Clifton Place Port Jefferson Station NY 11776-1139

GROLLMAN, ARTHUR PATRICK, PHARMACOLOGY, MEDICINE. *Current Pos:* PROF PHARMACOL & MED & CHMN DEPT PHARMACOL SCI, STATE UNIV NY, STONY BROOK, 74- *Personal Data:* b Baltimore, Md, May 21, 34; m 59; c 3. *Educ:* Univ Calif, Berkeley, 55; Johns Hopkins Univ, MD, 59. *Prof Exp:* Resident med, Johns Hopkins Hosp, 59-61; res assoc biochem, NIH, 61-63; assoc med & molecular biol, Albert Einstein Col Med, 63-66, asst prof, 66-68, assoc prof pharmacol, molecular biol & med, 68-71, prof pharmacol, 71-74, assoc dean sci & admin affairs, 72-73. *Concurrent Pos:* Career scientist, Health Res Coun, New York, 63-71; consult comt on biol data handling, NIH, 66-70, mem pharmacol study sect, 70-74; attend physician, Bronx Munic Hosp Ctr, 63-74, Northport Vet Admin Hosp, 74- & St Barnabas Hosp, 74-; mem comt on drug safety, Drug Res Bd, 71- *Mem:* Am Soc Pharmacol & Exp Therapeut; Am Soc Biol Chem; Infectious Dis Soc Am; Am Soc Microbiol; Am Physiol Soc. *Res:* Molecular pharmacology; mechanism of drug action; design of chemotherapeutic agents; interaction of drugs with macromolecules. *Mailing Add:* Dept Pharmacol Sci State Univ NY Stony Brook Health Sci Ctr Stony Brook NY 11794-8651. *Fax:* 516-444-7641

GROLLMAN, SIGMUND, PHYSIOLOGY. *Current Pos:* From instr to assoc prof zool & physiol, 49-66, chmn div physiol, 66-73, prof, 66-84, dir grad studies, Zool Dept, 73-84, EMER PROF ZOOL, UNIV MD, COLLEGE PARK, 84- *Personal Data:* b Stevensville, Md, Feb 12, 23. *Educ:* Univ Md, BS, 47, MS, 49, PhD(physiol), 52. *Concurrent Pos:* Consult, Sci Writing & Text Bk Publ. *Mem:* AAAS; Am Soc Exp Biol & Med; NY Acad Sci; fel Am Col Sports Med. *Res:* Tissue and cellular metabolism; exercise and fatigue; aging and lipid metabolism. *Mailing Add:* 4001 N Charles St Baltimore MD 21218

GROMAN, NEAL BENJAMIN, MICROBIOLOGY. *Current Pos:* From instr to prof microbiol, Univ Wash, 50-89, dir, Off Biol Educ, 71-75, actg chmn microbiol, 80-81, EMER PROF MICROBIOL, UNIV WASH, 90- *Personal Data:* b Chisholm, Minn, May 21, 21; m 43, Elaine R Spigle; c JoAnn (Tamarin), Nancy J (Scheffer), Richard P & Ellen J (Fair). *Educ:* Univ Chicago, SB, 47, PhD(bact, parasitol), 50. *Concurrent Pos:* Markle scholar, 55-60; Guggenheim fel, 58-59. *Mem:* Am Soc Microbiol; Am Acad Microbiol. *Res:* Bacteriophage; microbial genetics and physiology; medical microbiology. *Mailing Add:* Dept Microbiol Univ Wash Seattle WA 98195

GROMELSKI, STANLEY JOHN, JR, POLYMER CHEMISTRY, ORGANIC CHEMISTRY. *Current Pos:* VPRES RES & DEVELOP, ANSELL PERRY, OHIO, 90- *Personal Data:* b Haydenville, Mass, Feb 26, 42; m 72; c 1. *Educ:* Univ Mass, Amherst, BS, 65; Ohio State Univ, PhD(org chem), 71. *Prof Exp:* Chemist res training prog, Gen Elec Res & Develop Ctr, 65-67; res chemist, GAF Corp, 73-74, group leader, 74-76, mgr res & develop admin & tech info serv, 76-79, asst to vpres, 76-79, mgr latex res & develop, 79-80, mgr plastics res & develop, 81-84; dir polymer res, Reichhold Chem, Del, 84-86, vpres tech, 86-89. *Concurrent Pos:* Fel dept chem, Univ Ariz, 72-73. *Mem:* AAAS; Am Chem Soc; Tech Asn Pulp & Paper Indust; Soc Plastic Eng. *Res:* Development of medical gloves. *Mailing Add:* 6953 Harbor Dr NW Canton OH 44718-3747

GROMKO, MARK HEDGES, POPULATION GENETICS. *Current Pos:* asst prof genetics, 78-91, PROF POP GENETICS, BOWLING GREEN STATE UNIV, 91- *Personal Data:* b New Haven, Conn, Apr 1, 50. *Educ:* Swarthmore Col, BA, 72; Ind Univ, AM, 75, PhD(pop genetics), 78. *Mem:* Genetics Soc Am; Soc Study Evolution; Am Soc Naturalists; Sigma Xi. *Res:* Genetics of isolated populations of Drosophila in the Bowling Green area; mating patterns in natural populations; behavior genetics; the genetics of repeated mating. *Mailing Add:* 507 Knollwood Dr Bowling Green OH 43402

GROMME, CHARLES SHERMAN, GEOLOGY. *Current Pos:* GEOLOGIST, US GEOL SURV, 65- *Personal Data:* b San Francisco, Calif, Nov 15, 33. *Educ:* Univ Calif, Berkeley, AB, 59, PhD(geol), 63. *Prof Exp:* Asst res geologist, Univ Calif, Berkeley, 63-65. *Mem:* AAAS; Am Geophys Union; Geol Soc Am; Sigma Xi. *Res:* Rock magnetism and paleomagnetism. *Mailing Add:* US Geol Surv MS 937 345 Middlefield Rd Menlo Park CA 94025

GROMOV, MIKHAEL, MATHEMATICS. *Current Pos:* PERM FEL & CHMN MATH DEPT, INST ADV SCIENTIFIC STUDIES, BURES-SUR-YVETTE, FRANCE, 82- *Personal Data:* b Boksitogorsk, USSR, Dec 23, 43. *Educ:* Univ Leningrad, MS, 65, PhD, 69, DSc, 73. *Honors & Awards:* Oswald Veblen Prize Geom, Am Math Soc, 81. *Prof Exp:* Asst prof, Univ Leningrad, 67-74; prof, State Univ NY, Stony Brook, 74-81; prof, Univ Paris, 81-82. *Concurrent Pos:* Lectr, Int Cong Mathematicians, Nice, France, 70, Helsinki, Finland, 78, Warsaw, Poland, 82 & Berkeley, Calif, 86. *Mem:* Foreign assoc Nat Acad Sci; Am Math Soc. *Mailing Add:* Inst Hautes Etudes Sci 35 St Chartres Bvres-sur-Yvette 91440 France

GRONEMEYER, SUZANNE ALSOP, MEDICAL PHYSICS, MAGNETIC RESONANCE IMAGING. *Current Pos:* ASSOC MEM, DIAG IMAGING DEPT, ST JUDE CHILDREN'S RES HOSP, 88-, DIR, PROF ONCOL EDUC PROG. *Personal Data:* b Tulsa, Okla. *Educ:* Washington Univ, St Louis, BA, 64, MA, 67, MA, 75, PhD(nuclear physics), 79. *Prof Exp:* Instr physics, Univ Mo, St Louis, 68-74; prof asst, Physics Div, NSF, 75-76; sr res aide, Argonne Nat Lab, 77-79; res fel radiol physics, Mass Gen Hosp, 79-80; eng physicist, Fermi Nat Accelerator Lab, 80-83; applns scientist, Siemens Med Systs, 83-88; assoc prof radiol, Col Med, Univ Tenn, Memphis, 88- *Mem:* Am Phys Soc; Am Asn Physicists Med; Soc Magnetic Resonance Med; Soc Magnetic Resonance Imaging; Radiol Soc NAm. *Res:* Clinical research and applications of magnetic resonance imaging. *Mailing Add:* Dept Diag Imaging St Jude Childrens Res Hosp 332 N Lauderdale Memphis TN 38105-2794. *Fax:* 901-527-0054; *E-Mail:* suzanne.gronemeyer@stjude.org, gronemey@memphisonline.com

GRONENBORN, ANGELA MARIA, NUCLEAR MAGNETIC RESONANCE, STRUCTURAL BIOLOGY. *Current Pos:* CHIEF STRUCT BIOL, NAT INST DIABETES & DIGESTIVE & KIDNEY DIS, NIH, 88- *Personal Data:* b Cologne, Ger, May 11, 50; Brit citizen; m, G M Clore; c Katharina Rachel Rebecca & Sebastian Aaron Leon. *Educ:* Univ Cologne, Ger, dipl, 75, PhD(org chem), 78. *Prof Exp:* Scientific staff, Nat Inst Med Res, Eng, 78-84; head, Biol Natural Magnetic Remanence Group, Max-Planck Inst, Ger, 84-88. *Concurrent Pos:* Distinguished lectr struct biol, Dartmouth Col, 93. *Mem:* Ger Chem Soc; fel Royal Soc Chem; NY Acad Sci; Am Chem Soc. *Res:* Biological natural magnetic remanence spectroscopy; structure and dynamics of proteins; protein-nucleic acid complexes; natural magnetic remanence methodology. *Mailing Add:* NIDDK-NIH 5503 Lambets Rd Bldg 5 Rm 130 Bethesda MD 20814

GRONER, CARL FRED, ELECTROPHOTOGRAPHY. *Current Pos:* SR RES PHYSICIST ELECTROPHOTOG, EASTMAN KODAK RES LABS, 70- *Personal Data:* b Wilkes-Barre, Pa, July 29, 42; m 65; c 2. *Educ:* Pa State Univ, BS, 63, MS, 66, PhD(solid state sci), 70. *Mem:* Soc Photog Scientists & Engrs. *Res:* Electrophotographic imaging systems. *Mailing Add:* 427 Mt Airy Dr Rochester NY 14617

GRONER, GABRIEL F(REDERICK), ELECTRICAL ENGINEERING, SOFTWARE SYSTEMS. *Current Pos:* PRES, INSIGHT SOLUTIONS, 89- *Personal Data:* b Los Angeles, Calif, May 17, 38; m 64; c 2. *Educ:* Univ Calif, Los Angeles, BS, 60; Stanford Univ, MS, 61, PhD(elec eng), 64. *Prof Exp:* Res asst elec eng, Stanford Univ, 62-64; comput scientist, Rand Corp, 64-78; sr prog mgr, Telesensory Systs Inc, 78-80; vpres & gen mgr, 80-82; vpres eng, Speech Plus Inc, 83-89. *Concurrent Pos:* Lectr, Ext Div, Univ Calif, Los Angeles, 69-72; consult, M D Anderson Hosp, 75-78; prin investr, NIH, 72-79. *Mem:* Inst Elec & Electronics Engrs; Comput Soc; Sigma Xi. *Res:* Pattern recognition; user-oriented interactive computer systems; medical applications of computers; electronic aids for handicapped; electronic speech synthesis. *Mailing Add:* 230 Parkside Dr Palo Alto CA 94306-4530

GRONER, PAUL STEPHEN, ELECTRONICS ENGINEERING. *Current Pos:* GEN MGR & VPRES ENG, SILICON CONTROLS, 89- *Personal Data:* b Binghamton, NY, May 23, 37; m 67; c 2. *Educ:* Polytech Inst Brooklyn, BSEE, 62. *Prof Exp:* Group head, Hughes Aircraft, 69-73; mgr, Sperry Univac, 73-82; dir, Computer Consoles, 82-87; consult engr, McDonnell Douglas, 87-88; dir, AST Res, 88-89. *Concurrent Pos:* Vis lectr, Univ Calif Irvine, 79-84. *Mem:* Inst Elec & Electronics Engrs. *Res:* Developed key silicon including personal computer chip set and risc processor; granted several patents; author of various publications. *Mailing Add:* 2139 N Ross St Santa Ana CA 92706. *Fax:* 714-768-6601; *E-Mail:* pauly@triconex.com

GRONNER, A(LFRED) D(OUGLAS), electrical engineering, for more information see previous edition

GRONOSTAJSKI, RICHARD M, DNA-PROTEIN INTERACTIONS. *Current Pos:* ASSOC STAFF, CLEVELAND CLIN FOUND, 92-; ASSOC PROF BIOCHEM, CASE WESTERN RES UNIV, 92- *Personal Data:* b Trenton, NJ, Mar 3, 54; Can & US citizen; m 83, Christine E Campbell. *Educ:* Va Polytechnic Inst & State Univ, BS, 75, MS, 77; Harvard Univ, PhD(physiol & physics), 82. *Prof Exp:* Asst prof med biophysiol, Univ Toronto, 85-92. *Concurrent Pos:* Staff, Ont Cancer Inst, 85-92; scholar, Nat Res Coun Can, 86-91. *Mem:* Am Asn Cancer Res; Am Soc Biochem & Molecular Biol; AAAS. *Res:* Areas of protein-DNA interactions that regulate DNA replication and transcription. *Mailing Add:* Dept Cancer Biol NN1 Cleveland Clin Found 9500 Euclid Ave Cleveland OH 44195-5178. *Fax:* 216-445-6269; *E-Mail:* gronosr@ccsmtp.ccf.org

GRONSKY, RONALD, MATERIALS SCIENCE, ELECTRON MICROSCOPY. *Current Pos:* Lectr, Dept Mat Sci & Mineral Eng, Univ Calif, 77-79, dep assoc lab dir, Energy Sci, 88-89, chmn, Dept Mat Sci & Mineral Eng, 90-96, SCIENTIST, MAT & MOLECULAR RES DIV, LAWRENCE BERKELEY LAB, UNIV CALIF, BERKELEY, 77-, PROF, DEPT MAT SCI & MINERAL ENG, 81-, OPPENHEIMER CHAIR ADVAN MAT ANALYSIS, 95- *Personal Data:* b Pittsburgh, Pa, July 9, 50; m 70, Andrea; c 4. *Educ:* Univ Pittsburgh, BS, 72; Univ Calif, Berkeley, MS, 74, PhD(mat sci & eng), 77. *Honors & Awards:* First Place Phys Sci, Elec Micros Soc Sci Exhibit, 76; Exhibit Awards, Int Metallographic Soc, 76-78, 82-85; Robert Lansing Hardy Gold Medal, Metall Soc/Am Inst Mech Eng, 79; Burton Medal, Elec Micros Soc Am, 83; Bradley Stoughton Award, Am Soc Metals, 85. *Concurrent Pos:* Mgr Atomic Resolution Micros Proj, Nat Ctr Electron Micros, Berkeley, 79-86; ed, Methods in Mat Res, 96- *Mem:* Am Inst Mining, Metall & Petrol Engrs; Electron Micros Soc Am (secy, 88-90); fel Am Soc Metals Int; AAAS; Mat Res Soc; Microbeam Anal Soc; Am Soc Eng Educ; Sigma Xi. *Res:* Atomic scale microstructural analysis and engineering; electron optics; physical metallurgy; nanostructures, biomaterials. *Mailing Add:* Dept Mat Sci & Mineral Eng Univ Calif Berkeley CA 94720. *Fax:* 510-643-5792; *E-Mail:* rgronsky@garnet.berkeley.edu

GROOD, EDWARD S, BIOMEDICAL ENGINEERING, ORTHOPAEDIC BIOMECHANICS. *Current Pos:* from asst prof to assoc prof, 77-85, PROF ORTHOP RES, MED CTR, UNIV CINCINNATI, 85- *Personal Data:* b Buffalo, NY, Mar 28, 44; m 67; c 2. *Educ:* Rensselaer Polytech Inst, BS, 65; State Univ NY, Buffalo, MS, 68, PhD(mech eng& bioeng), 73. *Prof Exp:* Develop engr, Bell Aerospace Co, 66-72; res assoc mech eng, State Univ NY, Buffalo, 72; sr res engr, Res Inst, Univ Dayton, 72-75. *Concurrent Pos:* Adj asst prof, Univ Dayton, 73-75; res assoc, Miami Valley Chap, Am Heart Asn, 73-75; adj prof biomech, Univ Cincinnati, 76-; dir, Giannestras Biomech Lab. *Mem:* Fel Am Soc Mech Engrs; Orthop Res Soc; Am Soc Biomech; Am Soc Testing & Mat; AAAS; Am Orthop Soc Sports Med; Am Col Sports Med; Biomed Eng Soc. *Res:* Mechanics and kinematics of biological joints; mechanical properties of collagen. *Mailing Add:* 414 Flembrook Ct Cincinnati OH 45231

GROOM, ALAN CLIFFORD, BIOPHYSICS, PHYSIOLOGY. *Current Pos:* assoc prof, Univ Western Ont, 66-72, prof biophys, 72-91, chmn dept, 78-87, hon lectr anesthesia, 70-91, hon lectr physiol, 80-91, EMER PROF BIOPHYS, UNIV WESTERN ONT, 91- *Personal Data:* b London, UK, June 23, 26; m 52, Elizabeth; c 4. *Educ:* Univ London, BSc, 49, PhD(biophys), 57. *Honors & Awards:* Landis Res Award, Microcirculatory Soc, 86. *Prof Exp:* Sr physicist, St Mary's Hosp, London, 49-57, lectr med physics, Med Sch, 58-66; vis res assoc physiol, State Univ NY, Buffalo, 62-63. *Concurrent Pos:* Leverhulme res fel biophys, Univ London, 57-58; hon assoc ed, Can J Physiol & Pharmacol, 69-73. *Mem:* Europ Soc Microcirculation; Int Soc Oxygen Transport Tissue; Microcirculatory Soc. *Res:* Microcirculation and oxygen transport to tissue in skeletal and cardiac muscle; microcirculation of spleen; role of spleen with respect to blood cells; cancer cells and the microcirculation. *Mailing Add:* Dept Med Biophys Univ Western Ont London ON N6A 5C1 Can. *Fax:* 519-661-2123

GROOM, DONALD EUGENE, OBSERVATIONAL COSMOLOGY, HIGH ENERGY PHYSICS INSTRUMENTATION. *Current Pos:* STAFF PHYSICIST, LAWRENCE BERKELEY LAB, 89- *Personal Data:* b Pittsburgh, Pa, Dec 30, 34; m 62, Melinda Flory; c Susanna, Jeremy & Charles. *Educ:* Princeton Univ, AB, 56; Calif Inst Technol, PhD(physics), 65. *Prof Exp:* Res assoc physics, Cornell Univ, 65-66, instr, 66-67, actg asst prof, 67-69; from asst prof to prof, Univ Utah, 69-87; SSC Cent Design Group, 85-89. *Concurrent Pos:* Vis res physicist, Princeton Univ, 75-76. *Mem:* Am Phys Soc; Am Astron Soc. *Res:* Observe at large telescopes and analyzes SNe Ia lightcurves to determine cosmological parameters; radiation environment in hadron collider detectors. *Mailing Add:* Lawrence Berkeley Lab MS 50-308 Berkeley CA 94720. *E-Mail:* deg@lbl.gov

GROOMS, THOMAS ALBIN, ENZYMOLOGY, FERMENTATION. *Current Pos:* PROF, XENIA NAZARENE SCH. *Personal Data:* b Dayton, Ohio, Apr 6, 43; m 69; c 4. *Educ:* Baldwin-Wallace Col, BS; Univ Cincinnati, PhD(biochem), 73. *Prof Exp:* Sr investr, Wilson Pharmaceut & Chem Corp, 73-75; scientist, Leeds & Northrup, 75-76; proj chemist, Yellow Springs Instrument Co, 76-89; sr scientist, Sharon Dr Corp, 89- *Concurrent Pos:* Lectr, Wittenberg Univ, 78-82; nutrit consult, 81-; adj assoc prof, Antioch Univ, 83- *Mem:* Am Asn Clin Chem; NY Acad Sci; Sigma Xi. *Res:* Biochemical sensors; nutritional consulting and evaluation of individuals in order to study the origins of disease and what maintains an individual's health. *Mailing Add:* 1052 N Detroit St Xenia OH 45385

GROOPMAN, JOHN DAVIS, TOXICOLOGY. *Current Pos:* from asst prof to assoc prof toxicol, Johns Hopkins Univ, 81-89, assoc prof, 87-89, assoc prof environ chem, 89-92, PROF, SCH PUB HEALTH, JOHNS HOPKINS UNIV, 92- ANNA M BAETJER PROF & CHMN, 93- *Personal Data:* b New York, NY, Nov 19, 52; m 81; c 3. *Educ:* Elmira Col, BA, 74; Mass Inst Technol, PhD(toxicol), 79. *Prof Exp:* Fel toxicol, Mass Inst Technol, 79-80; staff fel carcinogenesis, Nat Cancer Inst, 80-81. *Concurrent Pos:* Res assoc, Mass Inst Technol, 80-; consult, Sci Adv Bd, Dept Pub Health, State Mass, 81-; lectr epidemiol, Sch Med, Boston Univ, 82- *Mem:* NY Acad Sci; Am Pub Health Asn; Am Asn Cancer Res; Soc Toxicol. *Res:* Non-invasive screening techniques for measuring the exposure of people to chemical carcinogens including immunoassays, and high pressure liquid chromatography. *Mailing Add:* Sch Hyg & Pub Health Dept Environ Health Scis Johns Hopkins Univ 615 N Wolfe St Baltimore MD 21205-2103. *Fax:* 410-955-0617

GROOTES, PIETER MEIERT, physics, geochronology, for more information see previous edition

GROOTES-REUVECAMP, GRADA ALIJDA, medical microbiology, bacterial genetics, for more information see previous edition

GROOVER, MARSHALL EUGENE, JR, medicine, for more information see previous edition

GROOVER, MIKELL, INDUSTRIAL ENGINEERING. *Current Pos:* res asst, Inst Res, 64-66, from instr to assoc prof, 69-78, PROF INDUST ENG, LEHIGH UNIV, 78- *Personal Data:* b Kingsport, Tenn, Sept 8, 39; m 62, Marcia; c Scott, Terri & Kelli. *Educ:* Lehigh Univ, AB, 61, BSME, 62, MSIE, 66, PhD(indust eng), 69. *Prof Exp:* Mfg engr, Eastman Kodak Co, NY, 62-64. *Concurrent Pos:* Pres, Col Indust Coun Mat Handling Educ. *Mem:* Soc Mfg Engrs; Am Inst Indust Engrs; Am Soc Mech Engrs. *Res:* Manufacturing engineering and systems; automation and robotics; manufacturing process technology. *Mailing Add:* Dept Indust Eng Lehigh Univ 200 W Packer Ave Bethlehem PA 18015. *Fax:* 610-758-4886; *E-Mail:* mpgo@lehigh.edu

GROPEN, ARTHUR LOUIS, TOPOLOGY. *Current Pos:* RETIRED. *Personal Data:* b Huntington, NY, May 14, 32; m 86, Patricia Lewis; c Julie, Tim & Miles. *Educ:* Univ Chicago, AB, 52, SB, 53; Duke Univ, PhD(math), 58. *Prof Exp:* Jr engr math, Sperry Gyroscope Corp, 54-55; Fulbright teaching fel, Univ Caen, 58-59; from instr to asst prof, Wellesley Col, 59-62; UNESCO specialist, Univ Satander, 62-63; from asst prof to assoc prof, Carleton Col, 63-74, prof math, 74-84. *Concurrent Pos:* Furniture maker. *Mem:* Am Math Soc; Math Asn Am. *Res:* Point set topology; dimension theory. *Mailing Add:* 809 St Olaf Ave Northfield MN 55057

GROSCH, CHESTER ENRIGHT, PHYSICS. *Current Pos:* SLOVER PROF OCEANOG, DEPT OCEANOG, OLD DOMINION UNIV, 73- *Personal Data:* b Hoboken, NJ, Jan 13, 34; m 56; c 4. *Educ:* Stevens Inst Technol, ME, 56, MS, 59, PhD(physics), 67. *Prof Exp:* Res assoc, Hudson Labs, Columbia Univ, 66-68; scientist, Teledyne-Isotopes, Inc, 68-69; assoc prof comput sci & physics, Pratt Inst, 69-73, chmn dept comput sci, 71-73. *Concurrent Pos:* Consult, Vitro Labs, 63-68, Nuclear Res Assocs, 69-, Advan Res Projs Agency, 70-, TRW Systs, 71-, Inst Defense Anal, 71-, Stanford Res Inst, 73-, Mantech Corp, 75- & Rand Corp, 76-; adj asst prof, Columbia Univ, 68-; pvt consult ocean & atmospheric sci, 70- *Mem:* AAAS; Soc Indust & Appl Math. *Res:* Physics of fluids; kinetic theory; rarefied gas dynamics; viscous flows; boundary layers; hydrodynamic stability; geophysical fluid dynamics; numerical methods in fluid dynamics; algorithms for parallel computing. *Mailing Add:* 1130 Manchester Ave Norfolk VA 23508-1245

GROSCH, DANIEL SWARTWOOD, GENETICS, ZOOLOGY. *Current Pos:* asst prof zool, 46-51, assoc prof genetics, 51-57, PROF GENETICS, NC STATE UNIV, 57- *Personal Data:* b Bethlehem, Pa, Oct 25, 18; m 44; c 5. *Educ:* Moravian Col & Sem, BS, 39; Lehigh Univ, MS, 40; Univ Pa, PhD(zool), 44. *Honors & Awards:* Comenius Award, Moravian Col. *Prof Exp:* Lab instr chem, Moravian Col & Sem, 36-37, asst biol, 37-38; instr zool, Univ Pa, 41-44, prof math, 41-43. *Concurrent Pos:* With Marine Biol Lab, Woods Hole. *Mem:* AAAS; Am Soc Naturalists; Entom Soc Am; Genetics Soc Am; Radiation Res Soc; Sigma Xi. *Res:* Cytology, genetics and radio-biology of habrobracon and brine shrimp; biosatellite research; altered fecundity and fertility from radioisotopes, antimetabolites and mutagenic agents. *Mailing Add:* 1222 Duplin Rd Raleigh NC 27607

GROSCHEL, DIETER HANS MAX, CLINICAL MICROBIOLOGY, INFECTIOUS DISEASES. *Current Pos:* PROF PATH & INTERNAL MED, UNIV VA, CHARLOTTESVILLE, 79- *Personal Data:* b Wurzburg, Ger, May 13, 31; US citizen; m 58; c 2. *Educ:* Univ Cologne, Med, 57; Dr med, 58; Am Bd Microbiol, dipl, 65. *Honors & Awards:* Prof Recognition Award, Am Bd Med Microbiol, 91. *Prof Exp:* Intern med, Univ Cologne, US Army Hosp, Landstuhl & Lutheran Hosp, Cologne, 57-59; asst neurosurg, Univ Cologne, 59-60, res assoc hyg & microbiol, 60-63; assoc microbiol, Wistar Inst, Philadelphia, Pa, 63-65; from asst prof to assoc prof, Sch Med, Temple Univ, 65-68; dir microbiol & infectious dis, Springfield Hosp Med Ctr, 68-71; assoc prof path, Univ Tex M D Anderson Hosp & Tumor Inst, 71-78, prof, 78-79. *Concurrent Pos:* Clin consult lab med, Sch Med, Univ Conn, 70-71; from assoc prof to prof path, Univ Tex Grad Sch Biomed Sci, 72-79; assoc prof med & path, Univ Tex Sch Med, Houston, 73-79; from assoc prof to prof, Univ Tex Sch Allied Health Sci, 77-79. *Mem:* Fel Am Acad Microbiol; Am Soc Microbiol; Ger Soc Hyg & Microbiol; Austrian Soc Hyg Microbiol & Prev Med; fel Infectious Dis Soc Am; Soc Hosp Epidemiol Am; Fedn Am Scientists; Ger Soc Hosp Hyg. *Res:* Clinical microbiology; hospital epidemiology; infectious diseases; medical history. *Mailing Add:* Dept Path Univ Va Sch Med O Hosp Dr Charlottesville VA 22908-0001

GROSE, HERSCHEL GENE, ORGANIC CHEMISTRY. *Current Pos:* from asst prof to prof, 53-77, ERWIN PROF CHEM, MARIETTA COL, 77-, HEAD DEPT, 57- *Personal Data:* b Clinton Co, Ind, Feb 1, 21; m 44; c 6. *Educ:* Ind Cent Col, BS, 42; Ind Univ, PhD(chem), 51. *Prof Exp:* Tech supvr, US Rubber Co, 41-43; res chemist, E I du Pont de Nemours & Co, 52-53. *Mem:* AAAS; Am Chem Soc. *Res:* Chemistry of thiophenes; industrial research in high polymers. *Mailing Add:* 8250 Pheasant Ave NW Canton OH 44720

GROSE, THOMAS LUCIUS TROWBRIDGE, GEOLOGY. *Current Pos:* assoc prof, 64-67, PROF GEOL, COLO SCH MINES, 67- *Personal Data:* b Evanston, Ill, Dec 5, 24; m 47, Barbara Clark; c Clark T & Kathryn (Beymer). *Educ:* Univ Wash, BS, 48, MS, 49; Stanford Univ, PhD(geol), 55. *Prof Exp:* Petrol geologist, Tex Co, 49-52; assoc prof geol, Colo Col, 55-64. *Concurrent Pos:* Consult geologist for indust & govt on energy & mineral explor, 54- *Mem:* Geol Soc Am; Am Asn Petrol Geol; Am Geophys Union; Soc Econ Geologists; Asn Eng Geologists; AAAS. *Res:* Structural and field geology; economic geology; oil, geothermal energy, coal, metals and nuclear facility seismic risk analysis; regional geologic mapping northeast California. *Mailing Add:* 2001 Washington Circle Golden CO 80401

GROSE, WILLIAM LYMAN, ATMOSPHERIC SCIENCE, FLUID MECHANICS. *Current Pos:* Res scientist reentry physics, 61-69, RES SCIENTIST ATMOSPHERIC SCI, NASA, 69- *Personal Data:* b Beckley, WVa, Sept 12, 39; m 61; c 3. *Educ:* Va Polytech Inst, BS, 61, PhD(aerospace eng), 69; Col William & Mary, MS, 66. *Honors & Awards:* Except Sci Achievement Medal, NASA, 86. *Concurrent Pos:* Asst prof lectr, George Washington Univ, 75; vis scientist, Reading Univ, Eng, 76. *Mem:* Am Geophys Union. *Res:* Dynamic meteorology; atmospheric chemistry and transport. *Mailing Add:* 106 Holloway Dr Williamsburg VA 23185

GROSECLOSE, BYRON CLARK, NUCLEAR PHYSICS, RESEARCH ADMINISTRATION. *Current Pos:* physicist, 63-75, assoc div leader, 75-79, dep div leader, 79-80, head, Nuclear Design Dept, 80-84, HEAD, DEFENSE SCI DEPT, LAWRENCE LIVERMORE NAT LAB, UNIV CALIF, 84- *Personal Data:* b Marion, Va, June 11, 34; m 52, Wanda Westman; c Kim, Byron, Eric & Glenn. *Educ:* Emory & Henry Col, BS, 55; Univ Va, MA, 57, PhD(physics), 59. *Prof Exp:* Asst prof physics, Okla State Univ, 59-63 & Kans State Univ, 63. *Concurrent Pos:* Prin investr, US Army Res Off grant, 61-63. *Mem:* Am Phys Soc. *Res:* Elastic and inelastic neutron scattering; positron life-times and intensities; physics design of nuclear explosives for peaceful applications; physics design of nuclear explosives for tactical and strategic weapons applications. *Mailing Add:* Lawrence Livermore Nat Lab L-21 UCL PO Box 808 Livermore CA 94550. *Fax:* 510-422-8672; *E-Mail:* groseclose1@llnl.gov

GROSEWALD, PETER, THIN FILM CRYSTAL GROWTH & SURFACE PREPARATION, ELECTRONIC PACKAGING OPTIMIZATION. *Current Pos:* DIR ENG MGMT PROG, 95- *Personal Data:* b Bronx, NY, May 26, 37; m 59, Carole Weintraub; c Gillian & Carey. *Educ:* City Col New York, BS, 59; Univ Fla, MS, 61; Pa State Univ, PhD(solid state technol), 66. *Honors & Awards:* Productivity Award, US Senate, 84. *Prof Exp:* Mgr physics-engr, Airco, 66-68; IBM Res, IBM Components, 68-76, mgr thin film process engr, Components Div, IBM Corp, 76-79, functional mgr packaging & thermal technol assurance, Systs Div, 79-81, functional mgr, Prod Mfg Ctr, 81-83, chair assignment, New Prof Educ Prog, CHQ Tech Educ Ctr, 83-85, tech ed, Strategic Planning Staff, 85-87, mgr univ progs, 87-94. *Concurrent Pos:* Mem, Indust Exec Adv Bd, Nat Technol Univ, 88-91; home video tutorial chair, Educ Activ Bd, Inst Elec & Electronics Engrs, 89-91; financial chair, 91-94; invited lectr, Frontiers Educ, Austria, Inst Elec & Electronics Engrs, 90-, treas, Educ Soc, 94- *Mem:* Sr mem Inst Elec & Electronics Engrs; Sigma Xi; Am Physics Soc; Am Vacuum Soc. *Res:* Design and development of thin film processes for semiconductor and magnetic film technology; thermal and packaging technologies associated with semiconductors. *Mailing Add:* 87 Mill St Putnam Valley NY 10579. *E-Mail:* p.grosewald@ileee.org

GROSH, DORIS LLOYD, STATISTICS, OPERATIONS RESEARCH. *Current Pos:* asst prof indust eng, 68-75, PROF INDUST ENG, KANS STATE UNIV, 75- *Personal Data:* b Kansas City, Mo, Nov 29, 24; m 50; c 3. *Educ:* Univ Chicago, BS, 46; Kans State Univ, MS, 49, PhD(statist), 69. *Prof Exp:* Instr math, Kans State Univ, 46-49; res asst statist, Purdue Univ, 49-52; instr math, Univ Tulsa, 52-65. *Concurrent Pos:* Actg dept head indust eng, Kans State Univ, 87-88. *Mem:* Am Statist Asn; Am Soc Qual Control; assoc Inst Elec & Electronics Engrs; Am Radio Relay League; Soc Women Engrs. *Res:* Reliability, such as life testing; Bayesian decision theory, hypergeometric distribution and its conjugate beta-binomial distribution. *Mailing Add:* 325 N 14th St Manhattan KS 66502

GROSH, RICHARD J(OSEPH), MECHANICAL ENGINEERING. *Current Pos:* CONSULT, 87- *Personal Data:* b Ft Wayne, Ind, Oct 29, 27; m 50; c 6. *Educ:* Purdue Univ, BSME, 50, MSME, 52, PhD, 53. *Hon Degrees:* DSc, Union Col, 72; DEng, Purdue Univ, 85. *Honors & Awards:* Richards Mem Award, Am Soc Mech Engrs. *Prof Exp:* Jr res engr, Capehart-Farnsworth Corp, 50-51; from asst prof to prof mech eng, Sch Eng Purdue Univ, 53-71, head, Dept Mech Eng, 61-65, assoc dean, 65-67, dean, 67-71; pres, Rensselaer Polytech Inst, 71-76; pres & chmn bd, Ranco Inc, 76-78, chmn & chief exec officer, 79-86. *Concurrent Pos:* Dir indust develop, Purdue Res Park & vpres, McClure Park, 54-71; consult, Allison Div, Gen Motors Corp & Bell Labs, Sterling Drug Inc, AMF Inc, Transway Corp; Westinghouse & Graver res fels, Purdue Univ. *Mem:* Nat Acad Eng; Am Soc Eng Educ; Am Inst Aeronaut & Astronaut; fel Am Soc Mech Engrs. *Res:* Heat transfer; thermodynamics; fluid mechanics. *Mailing Add:* PO Box 2 Brooklin ME 04616

GROSHONG, RICHARD HUGHES, JR, PETROLEUM GEOLOGY. *Current Pos:* assoc prof, 83-86, PROF GEOL, UNIV ALA, 86- *Personal Data:* b Lakewood, Ohio, Aug 10, 43; m 65; c 2. *Educ:* Bucknell Univ, BS, 65; Univ Tex, Austin, MA, 67; Brown Univ, PhD(geol), 71. *Prof Exp:* Asst prof geol, Syracuse Univ, 70-73; res geologist, Cities Serv Co, 73-78, mgr struct geol res, 78-81, sr res assoc, explor & prod res, 81-83. *Concurrent Pos:* NSF grant, 72-73 & 84-86; adj prof geol, Tulsa Univ, 81-82; Oil & Gas Consult Int, 85-; ed, Tectonophys, 81-, geol, 81-90; vis hon chair, Univ Lausanne, 88; distinguished lectr, Am Asn Petrol Geol, 89-90. *Mem:* Fel Geol Soc Am; Am Geophys Union; Am Asn Petrol Geol. *Res:* Geometrical and Kinematic analysis of geological structures; rock deformation mechanisms; comparative structural geology of hydrocarbon accumulations. *Mailing Add:* 10641 Dee Hamner Rd Northport AL 35475

GROSKLAGS, JAMES HENRY, MYCOLOGY. *Current Pos:* Asst prof, 58-68, ASSOC PROF BIOL, NORTHERN ILL UNIV, 68- *Personal Data:* b Milwaukee, Wis, June 20, 29; m 57; c 2. *Educ:* Univ Wis, BS, 51, MS, 55, PhD(bot), 60. *Mem:* AAAS; Mycol Soc Am. *Res:* Ecology of soil fungi. *Mailing Add:* 410 Fairmont Dr De Kalb IL 60115-2336

GROSKY, WILLIAM IRVIN, DATABASE MANAGEMENT, MULTIMEDIA INTERNET. *Current Pos:* assoc prof comput sci, 76-87, actg chmn, 88, PROF COMPUT SCI, WAYNE STATE UNIV, 87-, CHAIR COMPUT SCI, 95- *Personal Data:* b Gulfport, Miss, Aug 4, 44; m 65, Roslyn Balgley; c Sara & Seth. *Educ:* Mass Inst Technol, BS, 65; Brown Univ, MS, 68; Yale Univ, PhD(eng & appl sci), 71. *Prof Exp:* Asst prof comput sci, Ga Inst Technol, 71-76. *Concurrent Pos:* Prin investr grant, IBM Corp, 87 & Ford Motor Co, 90-; consult, US Army, 83-85, 87-90 & 93-94, USAF, 87-88 & UN Indust Develop Org, 89-; ed, Macmillan Encycl Comput, 89-92; vis prof, Ford Motor Co Europe, 90 & 92; assoc ed, Multimedia, Inst Elec & Electronics Engrs, 94- *Mem:* Asn Comput Mach; Am Asn Artificial Intel; Inst Elec & Electronics Engrs. *Res:* Database management systems; object-oriented systems; multimedia information systems. *Mailing Add:* Comput Sci Dept Wayne State Univ Detroit MI 48202. *Fax:* 313-577-3395; *E-Mail:* grosky@cs.wayne.edu

GROSMAN, LOUIS HIRSCH, COMPUTER SCIENCE, INFORMATION SYSTEMS & COMPUTER SECURITY. *Current Pos:* sr systs analyst, US Nuclear Regulatory Comn, 73-81, chief, Info Systs Support Sect, 81-82, sr automated systs security specialist, 82-89, chief, codes & stand, 89-94, SR ADP SECURITY SPEC, US NUCLEAR REGULATORY COMN, 94- *Personal Data:* b Washington, DC, Nov 11, 39; m 65; c Jeffrey & Robin. *Educ:* DC Teachers Col, BS, 65; Am Univ, cert mgt info systs, 72, cert sci & tech info systs, 73, MS, 73. *Prof Exp:* Mathematician, Goddard Space Flight Ctr, NASA, 61-67, NIH fel, 67-70; supvr digital comput programmer, Nat Libr Med, 70-73. *Concurrent Pos:* Instr comput sci, Montgomery Col, Rockville, 74-77; first officer, Safeguards Div, Int Atomic Energy Agency, Vienna, Austria, 77-78. *Mem:* Asn Fed Comput Users. *Mailing Add:* 14809 Flintstone Lane Silver Spring MD 20905. *E-Mail:* lhg@nrc.gov

GROSOF, MIRIAM SCHAPIRO, APPLIED STATISTICS, EDUCATION. *Current Pos:* Res assoc, Yeshiva Univ, 66-68, from asst prof to assoc prof math educ, 68-83, PROF EDUC & STATIST, YESHIVA UNIV, 83-, FAC CHAIR, DIV SOCIAL & BEHAV SCI, 85- *Personal Data:* b New York, NY, Dec 02, 32; div; c Benjamin N & David H. *Educ:* Barnard Col, BA, 52; Columbia Univ, MA, 53; Yeshiva Univ, PhD(math), 66. *Concurrent Pos:* Lectr, Columbia Univ, 53-58; chair, Dept Math Educ, Yeshiva Univ, 72-75; adj assoc prof, Pace Univ, 73-80, adj prof, 80-92; adj prof, Staten Island Col, CUNY, 92- *Mem:* Math Asn Am; Am Statist Asn; Asn Women Math; Nat Coun Teachers Math. *Res:* Small college instruction in statistics; measures of asymmetry in ratings. *Mailing Add:* 875 West End Ave Apt 6B New York NY 10025-4952

GROSS, ALAN JOHN, MATHEMATICAL STATISTICS, BIOLOGICAL STATISTICS. *Current Pos:* PROF BIOMED, MED UNIV SC, 76- *Personal Data:* b Bronx, NY, June 19, 34; m 62, Nancy Norman; c Michael & Andrew. *Educ:* Univ Calif, Los Angeles, BA, 56, MA, 57, PhD(statist), 62. *Prof Exp:* Lectr math, Univ Md, 61-62; lectr, Eindhoven Univ, 63-64; sr scientist, Booz-Allen Appl Res, Inc, 64-66; mathematician, Rand Corp, 66-69; res statistician, Sch Pub Health, Univ Calif, Los Angeles, 69-71; assoc prof pub health, Univ Mass, Amherst, 71-76. *Concurrent Pos:* Lectr, Exten, Univ Calif, Los Angeles, 64-; consult statistician, Opportunity Systs Inc, Washington, DC, 75-76; USPHS training grant biostatist, 75-76; consult statistician, Uniworld Group, Bethesda, Md, 76-78 & Upjohn, Kalamazoo, Mich, 77-84; consult, Covington & Burling, Wash, DC, 89-; res grantee, Am Statist Asn. *Mem:* Fel Am Statist Asn; Inst Math Statist. *Res:* Applications of statistical theory to reliability, biology and information theory problems. *Mailing Add:* Dept Biomet & Epidemiol Med Univ SC 171 Ashley Ave Charleston SC 29425

GROSS, ARTHUR GERALD, APPLIED MATHEMATICS, COMPUTER SCIENCE. *Current Pos:* RETIRED. *Personal Data:* b Amsterdam, NY, Aug 20, 35; m 78; c 4. *Educ:* Rensselaer Polytech Inst, BEE, 56, MS, 59, PhD(appl math), 64. *Prof Exp:* Comput-aided eng design, Comput Networking & Data Commun, Bell Labs, 64-75, supvr, Systs Prog, 75-79, supvr, comput network planning & develop, 79-96. *Mem:* Asn Comput Mach; AAAS; Sigma Xi. *Res:* Numerical analysis; application of digital computers to engineering problems; computer systems design and analysis. *Mailing Add:* 11 Darby Ct New Providence NJ 07974

GROSS, BENJAMIN HARRISON, ORGANIC CHEMISTRY. *Current Pos:* head dept chem, 64-67, from assoc prof to prof, 67-77, GUERRY PROF CHEM & HEAD DEPT, UNIV TENN, CHATTANOOGA, 77- *Personal Data:* b Chattanooga, Tenn, July 23, 30; m 64. *Educ:* Univ Chattanooga, BS, 52; Univ Tenn, MS, 54, PhD(chem), 56. *Prof Exp:* Res chemist, Chattanooga Med Co, 56-64. *Mem:* AAAS; Am Chem Soc; NY Acad Sci; Sigma Xi. *Res:* Synthetic organic chemistry; medicinal chemistry; aluminum alcoholates. *Mailing Add:* Dept of Chem Univ of Tenn Chattanooga TN 37401

GROSS, CHARLES GORDON, NEUROPHYSIOLOGY, NEUROPSYCHOLOGY. *Current Pos:* PROF PSYCHOL, PRINCETON UNIV, 70- *Personal Data:* b New York, NY, Feb 29, 36; m, Greta Berman; c Melanie, Monica (deceased), Derek & Rowena. *Educ:* Harvard Univ, AB, 57; Cambridge Univ, PhD(psychol), 61. *Honors & Awards:* Detor Prize. *Prof Exp:* Fel, Dept Psychol, Mass Inst Technol, 61-62, from lectr to asst prof, 62-65; asst prof, Harvard Univ, 65-68, lectr, 68-70. *Concurrent Pos:* Vis lectr, Dept Psychol, Harvard Univ, 63-65; NIH psychol sci fel rev comt, 69-70 & exp psychol study sect, 70-74; vis scholar, Dept Physiol-Anat, Univ Calif, Berkeley, 70-72; vis prof, Dept Psychol, Mass Inst Technol, 75-76, Depts Biol & Psychol, Beijing Univ, 86; NAS exchange scientist, Shanghai Inst Physiol, 87,; Fulbright researcher/lectr, Rio de Janeiro, 87; vis scientist, US Nat Prog, Shanghai Inst Physiol, 87, Tokyo Metrop Inst Neurosci, 88-89; vis fel, Magdalen Col, Oxford Univ, 90; vis scholar, Wolfson Col, Oxford, 95; McDonnell-Pew fel cognitive neurosci, Oxford Univ, 95. *Mem:* Fel Am Psychol Asn; Soc Neurosci; fel AAAS; fel Soc Exp Psychologists; foreign mem Brazilian Acad Sci. *Res:* Neurophysiology and neuropsychology of primate vision; psychology and physiology of perception; history of neuroscience. *Mailing Add:* 45 Woodside Lane Princeton NJ 08540. *Fax:* 609-258-1113; *E-Mail:* cggross@phoenix.princeton.edu

GROSS, DAVID (JONATHAN), THEORETICAL HIGH ENERGY PHYSICS. *Current Pos:* DIR, INST THEORET PHYSICS, UNIV CALIF, BERKELEY, 96- *Personal Data:* b Washington, DC, Feb 19, 41; m 62; c 2. *Educ:* Hebrew Univ Jerusalem, BSc, 62; Univ Calif, Berkeley, PhD(physics), 66. *Honors & Awards:* J Sakurai Prize, IAPS, 86; MacArthur Found Prize Fel, 87; Dirac Medal, Int Ctr Theoret Physics. *Prof Exp:* Jr fel, Soc Fels, Harvard Univ, 66-69; vis scientist, Europ Orgn Nuclear Res, Switz, 69; from asst prof to assoc prof, Princeton Univ, 69-86, Eugene Higgins prof physics, 86-96. *Concurrent Pos:* Sloan Found fel, 70-75. *Mem:* Nat Acad Sci; Am Acad Arts & Sci; fel Am Phys Soc; fel AAAS. *Res:* High energy particle physics. *Mailing Add:* Inst Theoret Physics Univ Calif Santa Barbara CA 93106-4030

GROSS, DAVID JOHN, CELL MEMBRANES, BIOELECTRICITY. *Current Pos:* asst prof, 86-92, ASSOC PROF, DEPT BIOCHEM, UNIV MASS, AMHERST, 92- *Personal Data:* b Chester, Ill, June 14, 53; m 79. *Educ:* Univ Ill, Urbana-Champaign, BS, 75, MS, 77, PhD(physics), 82. *Prof Exp:* Fel biophys, Cornell Univ Sch Appl & Eng Physics, 82-85, res assoc biophys, 85-86. *Concurrent Pos:* Vis assoc prof, Dept Molecular & Cellular Physiol, Stanford Univ Med Sch, Calif, 93-94. *Mem:* Am Phys Soc; Am Soc Cell Biol; Biophys Soc; AAAS. *Res:* Cell surface receptor dynamics and cell signals are studied at the level of the individual cell by the quantitative optical microscopy; bioelectric effects in non-excitable cells are examined experimentally and theoretically. *Mailing Add:* Dept Biochem Univ Mass Amherst MA 01003. *Fax:* 413-545-3291; *E-Mail:* dave@dgim2.biochem.umass.edu

GROSS, DAVID LEE, GEOLOGY, SCIENCE ADMINISTRATION. *Current Pos:* from asst geologist to assoc geologist, Ill State Geol Surv, 69-80, coordr environ geol, 79-84, geologist, Stratig & Areal Geol Sect, 80-84, geologist & head, Environ Studies & Assessment Sect, 84-89, SR GEOLOGIST & ASST CHIEF, ILL STATE GEOL SURV, 91- *Personal Data:* b Springfield, Ill, Nov 20, 43; m 66, Claudia Cole; c Oliver D & Alexander L. *Educ:* Knox Col, Ill, AB, 65; Univ Ill, MS, 67, PhD(geol), 69. *Prof Exp:* Exec dir, Gov Sci Adv Comt, State Ill, 89-91. *Mem:* Fel Geol Soc Am; Am Inst Prof Geologists; Am Quaternary Asn; fel AAAS. *Res:* Environmental geology; limnogeology; glacial geology of the mid-continent; science policy of State of Illinois and federal government. *Mailing Add:* Ill State Geol Surv 615 E Peabody Dr Champaign IL 61820. *Fax:* 217-244-7004; *E-Mail:* gross@geoserv.isgs.uiuc.edu

GROSS, DAVID ROSS, CARDIOVASCULAR PHYSIOLOGY, PHYSIOLOGICAL FLUID MECHANICS. *Current Pos:* DIR, DEPT VET BIOSCI, UNIV ILL. *Personal Data:* b Cleveland, Ohio, Sept 4, 36; m 60, Rosalie Bockserman; c Theodore S & Jeffrey M. *Educ:* Colo State Univ, BS, 58, DVM, 60; Ohio State Univ, MSc, 72, PhD(physiol), 74. *Prof Exp:* Pvt vet practr, 60-71; from asst prof to prof, Dept Vet Physiol & Pharmacol, Tex A&M Univ, 74-90, dir, Physiol & Appl Physics Lab, 83-90; prof & dir, Cardiovasc & Thoracic Surg Res Labs, Col Med, Univ Ky, 90- *Concurrent Pos:* Consult, Food & Agr Orgn UN, Proj Vet Col, Nat Auton Univ Mex, 67-68; assoc prof, Inst Comp Med, Baylor Col Med, 77-79; adj assoc prof, Dept Civil Eng, Univ Houston, Tex, 77-89; vis prof, Lab Voor Fysiologie, Vrije Univ, Amsterdam, Neth, 87; adj prof physiol, Col Med, Univ Ky, 90-, adj prof biomed eng, 91- *Mem:* Fel Am Inst Ultrasound Med; Am Physiol Soc; Shock Soc; Am Heart Asn. *Res:* Studies on prosthetic aortic valve function, heart and lung preservation for transplantation, neuronal injury associated with open heart surgery, neuropeptide control of vascular function and ventricular-vascular coupling dynamics. *Mailing Add:* Dept Vet Biosci Col Vet Med Univ Ill 2001 Lincoln Ave No 3516 Umms Bldg Urbana IL 61802

GROSS, DELMER FERD, PLANT BREEDING. *Current Pos:* sr sorghum breeder, Trojan Brand, 74-77, WESTERN AREA RES DIR, PFIZER GENETICS, INC, 77- *Personal Data:* b Huron, SDak, Aug 17, 46; m 69; c 1. *Educ:* SDak State Univ, BS, 68, PhD(agron), 74. *Prof Exp:* Instr voc agr, Redfield High Sch, SDak, 68-69. *Mem:* Sigma Xi; Am Soc Agron; Crop Sci Soc Am. *Res:* Development of new inbred lines and hybrids of corn through selection, breeding, testing and statistical interpretation of data. *Mailing Add:* De Kalb Plant Genetics Corn Res Ctr 3100 Sycamore Rd De Kalb IL 60115

GROSS, DENNIS CHARLES, PLANT PATHOLOGY, BACTERIOLOGY. *Current Pos:* asst prof, 79-84, assoc prof, 84-90, PROF PLANT PATH, WASH STATE UNIV, 90- *Personal Data:* b Whittemore, Iowa, Apr 2, 47; m 90, Janet Collins; c Alexander N & Elliot C. *Educ:* Iowa State Univ, BS, 70; Univ Calif, Davis, PhD(plant path), 76. *Honors & Awards:* Stark Award. *Prof Exp:* Res assoc plant path, Univ Nebr, 76-79. *Mem:* Am Phytopath Soc; Am Soc Microbiol; Int Soc Molecular Plant-Microbe Interaction. *Res:* General biology of phytopathogenic bacteria; bacterial ice nucleation;

phytotoxins and bacteriocins produced by bacteria of agronomic importance; biological control of plant pathogens. *Mailing Add:* Dept Plant Path Wash State Univ Pullman WA 99164-6430. *Fax:* 509-335-9581; *E-Mail:* gross@wsunix.wsu.edu

GROSS, DENNIS MICHAEL, CELL BIOLOGY, BIOCHEMISTRY. *Current Pos:* sr res pharmacologist, Merck, Sharp & Dohme Res Labs, 77-81, res fel, 81-82, mgr, 82-87, dir intern strategic & sci planning, 88-90, DIR PROG RESOURCES & LOGISTICS, MERCK RES LABS, 90- *Personal Data:* b Los Angeles, Calif, Sept 12, 47; m 73, Rosemarie Ganly; c Kevin & Alexis. *Educ:* Calif State Univ, Northridge, BA, 69, MSc, 70; Univ Calif, Los Angeles, PhD(cell biol), 74. *Prof Exp:* Teaching asst cell biol, Univ Calif, Los Angeles, 71-72, teaching fel, 72-74; instr pharmacol, Med Sch, Tulane Univ, 76-77. *Concurrent Pos:* Nat Heart, Lung & Blood Inst grant, Med Sch, Tulane Univ, 74-76; from adj asst prof pharmacol to adj assoc prof, Jefferson Med Col, Thomas Jefferson Univ, 77- *Mem:* Am Cell Biol Soc; NY Acad Sci; Soc Exp Biol & Med; Am Heart Asn; Soc Competitor Intel Prof; Sigma Xi. *Res:* B-blockers and hypertension, renin-angiotensin system; computer applications, computer simulation, QSAR. *Mailing Add:* Merck Res Labs West Point PA 19486. *Fax:* 215-652-6913; *E-Mail:* gross@merck.com

GROSS, DONALD, OPERATIONS RESEARCH. *Current Pos:* from asst prof to assoc prof eng & appl sci, George Washington Univ, 65-67, assoc prof opers res, 67-74, chmn dept, 77-88, actg Dean, Sch Eng & Appl Sci, 90-91, assoc vpres res & grad studies, 91-93, PROF OPERS RES, GEORGE WASHINGTON UNIV, 74- *Personal Data:* b Pittsburgh, Pa, Oct 20, 34; m 59, Alice Gold; c 2. *Educ:* Carnegie Inst Technol, BS, 56; Cornell Univ, MS, 59, PhD(opers res), 62. *Prof Exp:* Opers res analyst, Atlantic Refining Co, 61-65. *Concurrent Pos:* Prog dir, NSF, 88-90. *Mem:* Opers Res Soc Am (pres, 89-90); Inst Mgt Sci; Am Inst Indust Engrs; Am Soc Eng Educ; Sigma Xi. *Res:* Queuing theory; inventory control theory; multi-echelon inventory design; queuing analysis of inventory models. *Mailing Add:* 3530 N Rockingham St Arlington VA 22213. *Fax:* 202-994-0245; *E-Mail:* gross@scas.gwu.edu

GROSS, EDWARD EMANUEL, NUCLEAR PHYSICS, NUCLEAR REACTIONS. *Current Pos:* VIS SCIENTIST, TRIANGLE UNIV NUCLEAR LAB, DUKE UNIV, 90- *Personal Data:* b New York, NY, July 11, 26; m 51, Mary A Taylor; c Carolyn, Thomas & Ann. *Educ:* Queens Col, NY, BS, 48; Univ Calif, PhD(physics), 56. *Prof Exp:* Physicist, Radiation Lab, Univ Calif, 50-56; physicist, Oak Ridge Nat Lab, 56-70, dir Cyclotron Lab, 70-76, mgr nuclear res, 76-85, asst dir, Physics Div, 87-90; mgr, Heavy-Ion Physics, Dept Energy, 85-87. *Concurrent Pos:* Prog mgr Div Nuclear Physics, Dept Energy, 85-87. *Mem:* Am Phys Soc. *Res:* Investigation of the nuclear optical potential as revealed by the elastic scattering of pions, nucleons and heavy ions form complex nuclei; nuclear structure by inelastic scattering; experimental nuclear physics. *Mailing Add:* 115 Pitch Pine Lane Chapel Hill NC 27514

GROSS, ELIZABETH LOUISE, PHOTOSYNTHESIS, MEMBRANE BIOCHEMISTRY. *Current Pos:* asst prof, 68-73, assoc prof, 73-79, PROF BIOCHEM, OHIO STATE UNIV, 79- *Personal Data:* b 1940. *Educ:* Univ Calif, Los Angeles, BA, 61, Berkeley, PhD(biophysics), 67. *Prof Exp:* Res assoc biochem, C F Kettening Res Lab, 67-68. *Mem:* Biophys Soc; Am Soc Biol Chemists; Am Soc Plant Physiologists; Am Chem Soc; Int Solar Energy Soc; Sigma Xi. *Res:* Biophysical and biochemical studies of chloroplast membrane proteins including plastocyanin and the pigment-protein complexes; biological solar energy; chloroplast solar battery. *Mailing Add:* Dept Biochem Ohio State Univ 484 W 12th Ave Columbus OH 43210-1328. *Fax:* 614-292-6773

GROSS, FLETCHER, MATHEMATICS. *Current Pos:* assoc prof, 67-77, PROF MATH, UNIV UTAH, 77- *Personal Data:* b Colorado Springs, Colo, Nov 29, 39; m 64; c 3. *Educ:* Calif Inst Technol, BS, 60, PhD(math), 64. *Prof Exp:* Asst prof math, Occidental Col, 63-66; asst prof, Univ Alta, 66-67. *Mem:* Am Math Soc; Math Asn Am. *Res:* Algebra, especially group theory. *Mailing Add:* Dept Math Univ Utah 322 John Widtoe Salt Lake City UT 84112-1193

GROSS, FRANZ LUCRETIUS, THEORETICAL PHYSICS. *Current Pos:* assoc prof, 74-76, PROF PHYSICS, COL WILLIAM & MARY, 76-, DEAN RES & GRAD STUDIES, 96- *Personal Data:* b Minneapolis, Minn, Aug 9, 37. *Educ:* Swarthmore Col, BA, 58; Princeton Univ, PhD(physics), 63. *Honors & Awards:* Sporn Award, 64. *Prof Exp:* Instr & res assoc physics, Cornell Univ, 63-65, actg asst prof, 65-66, asst prof, 66-69; vis assoc prof, Univ Calif, Santa Barbara, 69-70; assoc prof, Col William & Mary, 70-72; phys sci officer, US Arms Control & Disarmament Agency, 72-74. *Concurrent Pos:* Vis prof, Carnegie-Mellon Univ, 81-82, Univ Hannova, Ger, 83; actg assoc dir res, CEBAF, 84-86, sr staff theorist, 86-; vis scientist, INFN, Rome, 89-90, Univ Utrecht, 90, Univ Wash, 91. *Mem:* Fel Am Phys Soc; Sigma Xi. *Res:* Electromagnetic structure; theoretical nuclear and partical physics; relativistic wave equations; deuteron and the nuclear force. *Mailing Add:* Dept Physics Col William & Mary Williamsburg VA 23185. *Fax:* 757-249-7002; *E-Mail:* gross@cebaf.gov

GROSS, FRED, MATHEMATICS. *Current Pos:* PROF MATH, UNIV MD, BALTIMORE CO, 68- *Personal Data:* b Tokay, Hungary, Nov 11, 33; m 58; c 3. *Educ:* Brooklyn Col, BS, 55; Columbia Univ, MA, 57; Univ Calif, Los Angeles, PhD(math), 62. *Prof Exp:* Lectr math, Brooklyn Col, 55-58; mathematician, NAm Aviation, Inc, Calif, 58-59; appl sci rep, IBM, 59-60, univ rep, IBM-Univ Calif, Los Angeles, 62-63; NSF assoc math, Nat Bur Stand, 63-64; res mathematician & consult, Naval Res Lab, 64-66; res mathematician, Bellcomm Inc, 66-68. *Concurrent Pos:* Consult, Naval Res Lab. *Mem:* Math Asn Am. *Res:* Theory of functions; entire and meromorphic functions; functional equations and number theory. *Mailing Add:* 1212 Noyes Dr Silver Spring MD 20910-2717

GROSS, GARRETT JOHN, PHARMACOLOGY. *Current Pos:* from instr to assoc prof, 73-80, PROF PHARMACOL, MED COL WIS, 80-, ACTG CHMN PHARMACOL, 87- *Personal Data:* b Britton, SDak, July 4, 42; m 67. *Educ:* SDak State Univ, BS, 65, MS, 67; Univ Utah, PhD(pharmacol), 72. *Prof Exp:* Fel, Univ Wash, 72-73. *Concurrent Pos:* Fac develop award, Pharmaceut Mfrs Asn, 76-78. *Mem:* AAAS; Am Heart Asn; Am Fedn Clin Res; Am Col Clin Pharmacol; Am Asn Animal Lab Sci. *Res:* Cardiovascular and autonomic pharmacology with general emphasis on drug actions on the coronary circulation. *Mailing Add:* Dept Pharmacol Med Col Wis 8701 W Watertown Plank Rd Milwaukee WI 53226-3548. *Fax:* 414-266-8460

GROSS, GEORGE ALVIN, OSTEOPATHY. *Current Pos:* RETIRED. *Personal Data:* b Detroit, Mich, Feb 5, 33; m 55; c 2. *Educ:* Chicago Col Osteop Med, DO, 61; Univ Mich, MPH, 73. *Prof Exp:* Gen pract, Detroit, Mich, 62-72; med dir, Dexter Clin, Detroit, 68-72; med dir, Barry, Eaton, Ionia Assoc Health Dept, 75; dir, Mich State Univ Col Clin, 75; assoc prof osteop, 73-77, prof community health sci, Mich State Univ, 77-94, emer prof, 94-; dir, Alcoholism Unit, St Lawrence Hosp, 73-94. *Mem:* Asn Teachers Prev Med; Am Pub Health Asn; Am Osteop Asn; Am Med Soc Alcoholism. *Mailing Add:* PO Box 1955 Avon CO 81620

GROSS, GEORGE C(ONRAD), CHEMICAL ENGINEERING. *Current Pos:* CHEM ENGR, E I DU PONT DE NEMOURS & CO, INC, 48- *Personal Data:* b Ginter Park, Va, Aug 14, 14; m 46; c 3. *Educ:* Va Polytech Inst, BS, 36; Purdue Univ, MS, 38, PhD(chem eng), 41. *Prof Exp:* Lab instr chem Purdue Univ, 36-41; chem engr, J T Baker Chem Co, 46-48. *Mem:* AAAS; Am Chem Soc; Am Inst Chem Engrs. *Res:* Chemical engineering plant design and pilot plant work with respect to organic chemicals; preparation of sulfamide; manufacture of synthetic fibers. *Mailing Add:* 1231 Keesling Ave Waynesboro VA 22980-5217

GROSS, GERARDO WOLFGANG, GEOPHYSICS. *Current Pos:* from asst prof to assoc prof geophys, 60-74, PROF GEOPHYS, NMEX INST MINING & TECHNOL, 74-, GEOPHYSICIST, 60- *Personal Data:* b Greifswald, Ger, Sept 1, 23; m 59; c 3. *Educ:* Cordoba Univ, DSc, 48; Pa State Univ, PhD(geophys), 59. *Prof Exp:* Geologist, Nat Fuels Admin, 48-51; geologist, Soc Miniere Penarroya, 51-54; res fel geophys, Pa State Univ, 56-59; geophysicist, Newmont Explor Co, 59; instr sci, Dutchess Community Col, 60. *Mem:* AAAS; Soc Cryobiol; Am Geophys Union; Sigma Xi. *Res:* Geoelectricity; electrochemical properties of ice; groundwater hydrology. *Mailing Add:* Dept Geosci NMex Inst Mining & Technol Campus Sta Socorro NM 87801

GROSS, GUILFORD C, pharmacology; deceased, see previous edition for last biography

GROSS, HARRY DOUGLASS, AGRONOMY. *Current Pos:* RETIRED. *Personal Data:* b Halifax, Pa, Mar 4, 24; m 54, Jeannette Knutsen; c 4. *Educ:* Rutgers Univ, BS, 48, MS, 52; Iowa State Univ, PhD(agron), 56. *Prof Exp:* Teacher, Newport Union Sch Dist, Pa, 48-49; instr farm crops, Rutgers Univ, 49-52; instr agron, Iowa State Univ, 52-56; res asst prof crop sci, NC State Univ, 56-58, proj leader agr mission to Peru, 58-61, res assoc prof, 61-68, res prof crop sci, 68-86; asst dir, Int Prog, Cals, 86-96. *Concurrent Pos:* Prog coordr, Mission to Peru, 67-70. *Mem:* Am Soc Agron. *Res:* Forage crop management, particularly fertilization and cutting practices; forage crop evaluation in vitro and in vivo; sown-pasture and range grazing management; soybean and peanut physiology, particularly as related to light X temperature interactions, root growth, and symbiotic nitrogen fixation. *Mailing Add:* 3417 Horton St Raleigh NC 27607. *Fax:* 919-515-6835; *E-Mail:* doug_gross@msn.com

GROSS, HERBERT MICHAEL, PHARMACEUTICAL CHEMISTRY. *Current Pos:* RETIRED. *Personal Data:* b Milwaukee, Wis, Mar 31, 25; m 51. *Educ:* Univ Wis, BS, 49; Univ Fla, MS, 51, PhD(pharm), 53. *Prof Exp:* Instr pharm, Univ Fla, 49-53; prod supvr, Lincoln Labs, 53; head, Dept Pharmaceut Prod Develop, Com Solvents Corp, 53-56; res pharmacist, Abbott Labs, 56-57, head, Dept Pharmaceut Res, 57-61, dir, New Prod Planning & Develop, 61-68, vpres, Hosp Prod Div, 68-71, pres, 69-71, vpres, Int Sci Affairs, 71-81; consult, 81-88. *Mem:* Am Pharmaceut Asn; Pharmaceut Mfrs Asn. *Res:* Tablets; suppositories; lyophilization; antibiotics; vitamins; flavoring; tablet coatings; research management. *Mailing Add:* 10200 W Bluemound Rd Apt 400 Milwaukee WI 53226-4373

GROSS, IAN, DEVELOPMENTAL BIOLOGY, LUNG DEVELOPMENT. *Current Pos:* fel perinatal med, 73-74, from asst prof to assoc prof, 78-85, PROF PEDIAT, OBSTET & GYNEC, SCH MED, YALE UNIV, 85- *Personal Data:* b Pretoria, SAfrica, Oct 15, 43; US citizen; m 67, Melanie Belman; c David A & Adam C. *Educ:* Univ Witwatersrand, BSc, 63, MB, 67. *Hon Degrees:* MA, Yale Univ, 85. *Prof Exp:* Resident, Univ Witwatersrand Hosps, 68-71; resident pediat, Children's Hosp Med Ctr, Boston, 71-72; fel, Harvard Med Sch, 72-73. *Concurrent Pos:* J H Brown Mem fel, Yale Univ, 73-74; mem, Human Embory & Develop Study Sect, NIH, 81-85; assoc ed, Pediat Res, 93-; ed, Sem Perinatology, 97- *Mem:* Soc Pediat Res; Am Physiol Soc; Am Thoracic Soc; Am Acad Pediat. *Res:* Regulation of gene expression in the developing lung; neonatology; therapies for neonatal lung disease. *Mailing Add:* Dept Pediat 333 Cedar St New Haven CT 06510

GROSS, JAMES RICHARD, ORGANIC CHEMISTRY. *Current Pos:* RES FEL, KIMBERLY-CLARK, 85- *Personal Data:* b Rapid City, SDak, Feb 19, 46; m 67; c 2. *Educ:* SDak Sch Mines & Technol, BS, 68; Univ Ariz, MS, 70. *Prof Exp:* Sr res chemist, Dow Chem Co, 70-80, proj leader, New Prod Res, 80-82, res leader, 82-85. *Mem:* Am Chem Soc. *Res:* Synthesis and applications of polyelectrolytes, particularly cross-linked synthetic polyelectrolytes useful in fluid absorption and retention; synthesis and characterization of new engineering thermoplastics; process design for aromatic polycarbonate. *Mailing Add:* 167 Woodfield Rd SW Calgary AB T2Y 5K5 Can

GROSS, JEROME, DEVELOPMENTAL BIOLOGY, CELL-MATRIX RELATIONSHIP. *Current Pos:* res assoc med, Harvard Med Sch, 50-54, assoc, 54-57, from asst prof to prof, 57-87, EMER PROF MED, HARVARD MED SCH, 87-; BIOLOGIST, MED SERV, MASS GEN HOSP, 66-, DERMAT SERV, 92- *Personal Data:* b New York, NY, Feb 25, 17; m 47; c 3. *Educ:* Mass Inst Technol, BS, 39; NY Univ, MD, 43. *Honors & Awards:* Ludwig Kast Lectr, NY Acad Med, 52, First Paul Klemperer Award, 88; Ciba Found Award for Res Relevant to the Problems of Aging, 59; Spec Award, Soc Cosmetic Chemists, 63; Kappa Delta Award, Am Acad Orthop Surg, 65; Herman Beerman Lectr, Soc Invest Dermat, 66; Harvey Soc Lectr, 73; Lifetime Achievement Award, Wound Healing Soc, 95. *Prof Exp:* Med intern, Long Island Col Hosp, NY, 43-44; capt, Med Corps, US Army, 44-46; res assoc, Dept Biol, Mass Inst Technol, 46-55. *Concurrent Pos:* Fel, Life Ins Med Res Fund, 46-48; clin & res fel med, Mass Gen Hosp, Boston, 48-51, assoc biologist, 51-66, biologist, Med Serv, 66-, chmn comt res, 64-67 & 79-82; mem, Comt Skeletal Syst, Nat Res Coun, 53-62; estab investr, Am Heart Asn, 56-61; mem sci adv comt, Helen Hay Whitney Found, 56-91, bd trustees, 85-; mem, Adv Panel Molecular Biol, NSF, 59-62; mem, Bd Sci Counrs, Nat Inst Dent Res, 62-66, chmn, 63-66; lectr, NIH, 65, mem, Molecular Biol Study Sect, 66-70, Breast Cancer Task Force, 75-78; mem bd dirs, Med Foun Boston, 74-80; Fogarty sr int fel, NIH, 76; mem, Boston Biomed Res Inst, 79-82; Wellcome vis prof, Basic Med Sci, Fed Am Soc Exp Biol, Robert Wood Johnson Med Sch, 82; mem, Sci Affairs Comt, W Alton Jones Cell Sci Ctr, 83-95, mem bd dirs, 86-95, chmn, 89-95; bd trustees, Helen Hay Whitney Found, 84; actg assoc dir res, Cutaneous Res Ctr, Dept Dermat, Mass Gen Hosp, 89-92. *Mem:* Nat Acad Sci; Inst Med-Nat Acad Sci; Am Soc Cell Biol; Am Soc Biol Chem; Int Soc Develop Biol; Am Acad Arts & Sci; Soc Develop Biol; Am Soc Physiologists; Am Soc Cell Biol; Biochem Soc London. *Res:* Developmental and cellular biology; biomedical science; connective tissues and their diseases; aging processes. *Mailing Add:* Mass Gen Hosp Cutaneous Biol Res Ctr E Bldg 149 at 13th St Third Floor Charlestown MA 02129

GROSS, JOHN BURGESS, MEDICINE. *Current Pos:* From assoc prof to prof, Mayo Grad Sch Med, 63-74, PROF MED, MAYO MED SCH, UNIV MINN, 74-, CONSULT, MAYO CLIN & HOSPS, 50- *Personal Data:* b St Louis, Mo, Dec 26, 20; m 45; c 4. *Educ:* DePauw Univ, AB, 42; Western Res Univ, MD, 45; Univ Minn, MS, 49. *Mem:* Am Col Physicians; Am Gastroenterol Asn; Am Soc Human Genetics; Cent Soc Clin Res; affil mem Royal Soc Med; Sigma Xi. *Res:* Diseases of the pancreas, bowel and liver, especially the hereditary form of pancreatitis. *Mailing Add:* Mayo Clin E 19 200 First St SW Rochester MN 55905

GROSS, JONATHAN LIGHT, GRAPH THEORY & ALGORITHMS, MATHEMATICAL MODELING. *Current Pos:* from asst prof to assoc prof, 69-78, PROF MATH STATIST, COLUMBIA UNIV, 78-, PROF COMPUT SCI & MATH, 79- *Personal Data:* b Philadelphia, Pa, June 11, 41; m 76, Susan Kodner; c Aaron, Jessica, Joshua, Rena Lea & Alisa Sharon. *Educ:* Mass Inst Technol, BS, 64; Dartmouth Col, AM, 66, PhD(math), 68. *Prof Exp:* Instr math, Princeton Univ, 68-69. *Concurrent Pos:* Sloan Found res fel, 72-75, IBM fel, 72-73; consult, IBM, Bell Labs, Russell Sage Found, Alfred P Sloan Found, Oak Ridge Nat Lab & Inst Defense Analysis; prin investr, Off Naval Res, NSF, Exxon Found, ARCO Found, Mellon Found. *Mem:* Am Math Soc; Soc Indust & Appl Math; Asn Comput Mach. *Res:* Combinatorics; computer science; social sciences; topology. *Mailing Add:* Dept Math Columbia Univ 450 Comput Sci Bldg New York NY 10027

GROSS, JOSEPH F, BIOMEDICAL ENGINEERING, CHEMICAL ENGINEERING. *Current Pos:* prof chem eng, 72-92, head dept, 75-81, EMER PROF CHEM ENG, UNIV ARIZ, 92- *Personal Data:* b Plauen, Ger, Aug 22, 32; US citizen. *Educ:* Pratt Inst, BChE, 53; Purdue Univ, PhD(chem eng), 56. *Honors & Awards:* Humboldt Prize. *Prof Exp:* Consult, Rand Corp, 56-57, engr, 57-70, res engr, 70-72. *Concurrent Pos:* Fulbright scholar, Thermodyn Inst, Munich Tech & Inst Fluid Dynamics, Brunswick Tech Univ, 56-57; consult, Sch Pharmaceut Sci, 72- & Rand Corp, 72- *Mem:* Am Inst Aeronaut & Astronaut; Am Inst Chem Engrs; Am Soc Mech Engrs; Microcirculatory Soc (pres, 76); fel AAAS; Int Inst Microcirculation (secy treas, 83-). *Res:* Fluid mechanics and mass transfer in the microcirculation; pharmacokinetics of anticancer drugs; boundary layer theory; cell kinetics modelling; tumor microcirculation. *Mailing Add:* Dept Physiol Univ Ariz PO Box 41445 Tucson AZ 85717-1445. *Fax:* 520-299-6713; *E-Mail:* jfgross@ccit.arizona.edu

GROSS, KATHERINE LYNN, PLANT POPULATION & COMMUNITY ECOLOGY. *Current Pos:* ASSOC PROF, KELLOGG BIOL STA, MICH STATE UNIV, 87- *Personal Data:* b Madison, Wis, Oct 28, 53; m 75; c 2. *Educ:* Iowa State Univ, BS, 75; Mich State Univ, PhD(zool & ecol), 80. *Prof Exp:* Res asst ecol, Kellogg Biol Sta, Mich State Univ, 77-80; from asst prof to assoc prof bot & ecol, Ohio State Univ, 80-87. *Concurrent Pos:* Vis scientist, Kellog Biol Sta, 81- *Mem:* Ecol Soc Am; AAAS; Bot Soc Am; Int Soc Plant Pop Biologists; Sigma Xi; Brit Ecol Soc. *Res:* Influence of life history traits on distribution and abundance of co-occuring plant species; root morphology; population biology and community ecology; resource acquisition; competitive ability. *Mailing Add:* Adv Res Dept Hills Petrol Nutriline PO Box 1658 Topeka KS 66601-1658. *Fax:* 913-268-8014

GROSS, KENNETH CHARLES, CELL WALL METABOLISM, POSTHARVEST PHYSIOLOGY. *Current Pos:* PLANT PHYSIOLOGIST, HORT CROPS QUAL LAB, AGR RES SERV, USDA, 81-, RES LEADER, 95- *Personal Data:* b South Kingston, RI, July 20, 54; m 78. *Educ:* Pa State Univ, BS, 76, MS, 78; NC State Univ, PhD(hort), 81. *Honors & Awards:* Krezdon Award, Am Soc Hort Sci, 82. *Concurrent Pos:* Res assoc plant physiol, dept crop sci, NC State Univ, 81. *Mem:* Am Soc Plant Physiologists; Am Soc Hort Sci. *Res:* Cell wall and carbohydrate metabolism in relation to development, ripening and senescence of fruits and vegetables. *Mailing Add:* Hort Crops Qual Lab Bldg 002 Rm 117 USDA Agr Res Serv 10300 Baltimore Ave Beltsville MD 20705

GROSS, KENNETH IRWIN, MATHEMATICAL ANALYSIS. *Current Pos:* dept chair, 89-92, PROF, DEPT MATH & STATIST, UNIV VT, 89- *Personal Data:* b Malden, Mass, Oct 14, 38; m 64; c 1. *Educ:* Brandeis Univ, BA, 60, MA, 62; Wash Univ, PhD(math), 66. *Honors & Awards:* Lester R Ford Prize, Math Asn Am, 79; Chauvenet Prize, Math Asn Am, 80. *Prof Exp:* Asst prof math, Tulane Univ, 66-68 & Dartmouth Col, 68-73; from assoc prof to prof math, Univ NC, Chapel Hill, 73-81; head, Dept Math, Univ Wyo, 81-85; prog dir, NSF, 85-87. *Concurrent Pos:* Vis lectr, Univ Calif, Irvine, 72-73; vis assoc prof, Univ Utah, 77; vis prof, Academia Sinica, Taiwan, 79, Drexel Univ, 88; vis res fel, Macquaire Univ, Australia, 94; univ scholar, Univ Vt, 96. *Mem:* Math Asn Am; Am Math Soc; Asn Women Math. *Res:* Harmonic analysis; infinite-dimensional representation theory; applications to statistics and physics. *Mailing Add:* Dept Math & Statist Univ Vt Burlington VT 05405-1455

GROSS, LEO, BIOPHYSICS. *Current Pos:* CONSULT, 89- *Personal Data:* b Brooklyn, NY, Feb 13, 15; m 40; c Alan, Terry & Jody. *Educ:* Brooklyn Col, BS, 34; Columbia Univ, MA, 36; NY Univ, PhD(biophys), 63. *Prof Exp:* Mem tech staff, Bell Tel Labs, 46-49; chief systs engr, Polarad Electronics Corp, 49-54; pres, Hub Electronics Corp, 54-58; biophysicist, Waldemar Med Res Found, 58-89. *Concurrent Pos:* Physicist, Bur Ord, US Dept Navy, 42-43 & Los Alamos Sci Lab, Univ Calif, 43-46; Nat Acad Sci foreign exchange fel, 73. *Mem:* Am Phys Soc; Inst Elec & Electronics Engrs; Optical Soc Am. *Res:* Biophysics of cell function and change in function in neoplasia. *Mailing Add:* 220 E 67th St New York NY 10021. *Fax:* 212-535-9130; *E-Mail:* 72700.3410@compuserve.com

GROSS, LEONARD, ORGANIC CHEMISTRY, POLYMER SCIENCE. *Current Pos:* chemist, 68-70, sr chemist polymer synthesis, 70-73, group leader polyvinyl chloride resins, 74-77, lab mgr flexible polymers, 78-79, mgr bus develop, 79-80, PROD MGR, POLYVINYL CHLORIDE HOMOPOLYMER, TENNECO CHEM INC, 80- *Personal Data:* b Brooklyn, NY, Oct 13, 41; m 63; c 4. *Educ:* Pratt Inst, BS, 63; Brandeis Univ, MA, 65; Yeshiva Univ, PhD(org chem), 70. *Prof Exp:* Chemist org synthesis, Polaroid Corp, 64-65. *Mem:* Am Chem Soc; Am Soc Testing & Mat; Soc Plastics Engrs. *Res:* Applications research, polyvinyl chloride resins and compounds. *Mailing Add:* 41 Eagle Rd Marlboro NJ 07746-1810

GROSS, LEONARD, MATHEMATICS. *Current Pos:* from asst prof to assoc prof, 60-67, PROF MATH, CORNELL UNIV, 67- *Personal Data:* b Brooklyn, NY, Feb 24, 31; m 56; c 2. *Educ:* Univ Chicago, MS, 54, PhD(math), 58. *Prof Exp:* Instr math, Yale Univ, 57-59, NSF fel, 59-60. *Concurrent Pos:* Guggenheim Found fel, 74. *Mem:* Am Math Soc. *Res:* Classical analysis on Hilbert space; mathematical problems of quantum theories. *Mailing Add:* White Hall Cornell Univ Ithaca NY 14853-7901

GROSS, LUDWIK, CANCER. *Current Pos:* res prof, 71-73, EMER RES PROF MED, MT SINAI SCH MED, 73-; CHIEF CANCER RES, VET ADMIN MED CTR, BRONX, 46- *Personal Data:* b Krakow, Poland, Sept 11, 04; nat US; m 43, Dorothy Nelson; c 1. *Educ:* Iagellon Univ, Poland, MD, 29; Am Bd Internal Med, dipl. *Hon Degrees:* DSc, Mt Sinai Sch Med, City Univ NY, 83. *Honors & Awards:* R R de Villers Found Award, Leukemia Soc, 53; Walker Prize, Royal Col Surgeons Eng, 61; James Award, James Ewing Soc, 62; UN Prize, WHO, 62; Albert Einstein Centennial Medal, 65; Spec Virus Cancer Prog Award, Nat Cancer Inst, 72; William S Middleton Award, Vet Admin, 74; Albert Lasker Basic Med Res Award, 74; Prin Paul Ehrlich-Ludwig Darmstaedter Prize, Frankfurt, 78; Prix Griffuel, Paris, 78; Alfred Jurzykowski Found Award, NY, 85. *Prof Exp:* Cancer res, Pasteur Inst, 32-39; res assoc, Inst Med Res, Christ Hosp, Cincinnati, 41-43. *Concurrent Pos:* Consult, Sloan-Kettering Inst Cancer Res, 53-56, assoc scientist, 57-60; mem, Bd Dir, Am Asn Cancer Res, 73-76; distinguished physician, Vet Admin Med Ctr, Bronx, 77-81. *Mem:* Nat Acad Sci; AAAS; Am Soc Hemat; Soc Exp Biol & Med; Am Asn Cancer Res. *Res:* Experimental cancer and leukemia; discovery of the mouse leukemia virus and the polyoma virus; demonstration that radiation-induced leukemia in mice is caused by activation of a latent virus; experimental immunization against leukemia and cancer sarcoma in guinea pigs and mice. *Mailing Add:* Vet Admin Med Ctr 130 W Kingsbridge Rd Bronx NY 10468

GROSS, M GRANT, JR, OCEANOGRAPHY. *Current Pos:* EXEC DIR, CHESAPEAKE RES CONSORTIUM, 94- *Personal Data:* b Childress, Tex, Jan 5, 33; m 91, Elizabeth Bulleid; c Alison, Jeffrey & Anne. *Educ:* Princeton Univ, AB, 54; Calif Inst Technol, MS, 58, PhD(geochem), 61. *Prof Exp:* From asst prof to assoc prof oceanog, Univ Wash, 61-68; from assoc prof to prof, State Univ NY, Stony Brook, 68-72; dir, Oceanog Serv Off, Nat Oceanic & Atmospheric Admin, 72-73; head, Oceanog Sect, NSF, 73-74; dir, Chesapeake Bay Inst, Johns Hopkins Univ, 74-78; head, Int Decade Ocean Explor, NSF, 78-80, dir, Div Ocean Sci, 80-94. *Concurrent Pos:* Assoc cur sedimentol, Smithsonian Inst, 66-68. *Mem:* Am Soc Limnol & Oceanog; fel Geol Soc Am; Geochem Soc Am; Am Geophys Union; fel AAAS. *Res:*

Marine geochemistry and sedimentary processes in estuarine and coastal ocean waters, especially waste deposits from urban regions. *Mailing Add:* chesapeake Res Consortium 645 Contees Wharf Rd Edgewater MD 21037. *E-Mail:* gross@serc.si.edu

GROSS, MALCOLM EDMUND, CHEMISTRY. *Current Pos:* RETIRED. *Personal Data:* b Brownington, Vt, June 23, 15; m 37; c 2. *Educ:* Middlebury Col, BS, 36; Western Reserve Univ, MS, 46, PhD, 50. *Prof Exp:* Res chemist, B F Goodrich Co, 48, sr res chemist, Res Ctr, 48-66, sect leader, 66-73, sect mgr, 73-76, mgr, Res & Develop Ctr, 76-80. *Concurrent Pos:* Staff scientist, Lockheed Missiles & Space Co, Calif, 63. *Mem:* Am Chem Soc; Soc Advan Mat & Process Eng. *Res:* Structural adhesives for aerospace applications. *Mailing Add:* 5651 RS Hammock Rd C 105 Naples FL 34113

GROSS, MARK WARREN, THEORETICAL PHYSICS, APPLIED MATHEMATICS. *Current Pos:* asst prof, 88-92, interim chair, 94-95, ASSOC PROF, DEPT PHYSICS & ASTRON, CALIF STATE UNIV, 92- *Personal Data:* b Euclid, Ohio, Oct 3, 56; m; Weimin Sun; c Rachel & Daniel. *Educ:* Wash Univ, BS, 77; Univ Chicago, MS, 79, PhD(physics), 83. *Prof Exp:* Postdoctoral fel, Oxford Univ, 83-86 & Cornell Univ, 86-88. *Mem:* Am Phys Soc. *Res:* Structure formation in magnetorhelogical fluids. *Mailing Add:* Dept Physics & Astron Calif State Univ Long Beach CA 90840. *E-Mail:* mgross@csulb.edu

GROSS, MARTIN, MEDICINE. *Current Pos:* resident, 72-75, from asst prof to assoc prof, 75-86, PROF PATH UNIV CHICAGO, 86- *Personal Data:* b New York, NY, Oct 18, 42; m 96, Suzanne Hessefort. *Educ:* Univ Chicago, BS, 64, MD, 69, PhD(biochem), 69. *Prof Exp:* Intern path, Univ Chicago, 69-70; res assoc, NIH, Nat Cancer Inst, 70-72. *Mem:* AAAS; Sigma Xi; Am Soc Biochem & Molecular Biol; Am Soc Invest Path. *Res:* Regulation of protein synthesis in rabbit reticulocyto cell-free preparations. *Mailing Add:* 5841 S Maryland Chicago IL 60637

GROSS, MICHAEL FRED, WETLANDS PLANT ECOLOGY. *Current Pos:* asst prof, 92-96, ASSOC PROF BIOL, GEORGIAN CT COL, 96- *Personal Data:* b Carlisle, Pa, June 6, 60. *Educ:* Lebanon Valley Col, Pa, BS, 82; Univ Del, PhD(marine studies), 87. *Prof Exp:* Postdoctoral fel, Univ Del, 87-88; asst prof biol, Erie-Behrend Col, Pa State Univ, 88-89, Gettysburg Col, 89-90, Elmhurst Col, 90-91, Marshall Univ, 91-92. *Mem:* Ecol Soc Am; Bot Soc Am; Estuarine Res Fedn; Am Inst Biol Sci; AAAS; Torrey Bot Soc. *Res:* Salt marsh plant ecology; biology of the parasitic plant dodder; pinelands plant ecology. *Mailing Add:* Biol Dept Georgian Ct Col Lakewood NJ 08701-2697. *Fax:* 732-905-8571; *E-Mail:* gross@georgian.edu

GROSS, MICHAEL LAWRENCE, ANALYTICAL CHEMISTRY, ORGANIC CHEMISTRY. *Current Pos:* PROF CHEM, WASH UNIV, 93- *Personal Data:* b St Cloud, Minn, Nov 6, 40; div; c Matthew R & Michele R. *Educ:* St John's Univ, Minn, BA, 62; Univ Minn, PhD(org chem), 66. *Prof Exp:* Fel org chem, Univ Pa, 66-67 & Purdue Univ, 67-68; from asst prof to prof, Univ Nebr, Lincoln, 68-88, C Petrus Peterson prof chem, 88-93. *Concurrent Pos:* Dir, Midwest Ctr Mass Spectrometry, 78-94; ed, Mass Spectrometry Revs, 82-90 & J Am Soc Mass Spectrometry, 90-; 3-M alumni prof chem; mem, NIH Study Sect Metallobiochem, 85-88, Nat Res Coun Bd Chem Sci & Technol, 86-91; vis prof, Warwick Univ, 88 & Univ Amsterdam, 90. *Mem:* Am Chem Soc; Am Soc Mass Spectrometry; Sigma Xi. *Res:* Mass spectrometry; structures and properties of gas-phase ions; ion-molecule reactions; fourier transform mass spectrometry; trace analysis of dioxins and related compounds; methods for structural determination of biomolecules. *Mailing Add:* Wash Univ 1 Brookings Dr Campus Box 1134 St Louis MO 63130. *Fax:* 402-472-3109; *E-Mail:* mlg@unl.edu

GROSS, MICHAEL R, computer sciences, for more information see previous edition

GROSS, MICHAEL ROBERT, STRUCTURAL GEOLOGY, TECTONICS. *Current Pos:* ASST PROF STRUCT GEOL, EARTH RESOURCES, ENVIRON GEOL, ROCK FRACTURE MECH & EARTH SCI, FLA INT UNIV, 93- *Personal Data:* b Durham, NC, June 21, 62; m 94, Geula Pancirer. *Educ:* Columbia Univ, AB, 85; Pa State Univ, MS, 89, PhD(geosci), 93. *Prof Exp:* Geol intern, Stand Oil Prod Co, 88, Oryx Energy Co, 90; postdoctoral fel, Ben Gurion Univ, Israel, 93. *Concurrent Pos:* Consult, Occidental Oil Co, 88-89, Mining Explor Co, 96; prin investr, Petrol Res Fund, 94-, US-Israel Binational Sci Found, 95- *Mem:* Geol Soc Am; Am Geophys Union; Am Asn Prof Geologists. *Res:* Field-based quantitative structural geology; brittle deformation; fractural, faults, fold mechanics and geometry; structural development compressional regions and their tectonic implications. *Mailing Add:* Dept Geol Fla Int Univ Miami FL 33199. *Fax:* 305-348-3877; *E-Mail:* grossm@servax.fiu.edu

GROSS, MILDRED LUCILE, MATHEMATICS. *Current Pos:* From assoc prof to prof, 61-86, EMER PROF MATH, DOANE COL, 86- *Personal Data:* b Lancaster Co, Nebr, Nov 16, 20; m 42; c 3. *Educ:* Nebr State Teachers Col, Kearney, BS, 42; Univ Nebr, MS, 59, PhD(math), 63. *Res:* Number theory; use of sieve methods in investigation of prime numbers. *Mailing Add:* 945 Longwood Dr Crete NE 68333-1847

GROSS, PAUL, PATHOLOGY. *Current Pos:* distinguished res prof, 71-75, ADJ PROF PATH, MED UNIV SC, 75- *Personal Data:* b Berlin, Ger, June 8, 02; nat US; m 30; c 4. *Educ:* Western Reserve Univ, AB, 24, MD, 27, MA, 29. *Honors & Awards:* Adolf G Kammer Merit Authorship Award, Indust Med Asn, 67. *Prof Exp:* Pathologist, St Vincent Charity Hosp, 31-35; pathologist, Western Pa Hosp, Pittsburgh, 35-44, Indust Hyg Found, Mellon Inst, 48-54, Indust Health Found, 54-85; from adj prof to res prof, Grad Sch Pub Health, Univ Pittsburgh, 60-71. *Concurrent Pos:* Sr fel, Indust Hyg Found, Mellon Inst, 53-68; pathologist, St Vincent's Charity Hosp, Ohio, 32-35; vol asst, Univ Vienna, 32-33; pathologist, Western Pa Hosp, 35-44, St Joseph's Hosp, 44-54; dir res lab, Indust Health Found, Pittsburgh, 54-85; consult threshold limit comt, Am Conf Govt Hygienists, 68-81. *Mem:* AAAS; Am Col Physicians; Am Soc Clin Path; Am Col Path; Am Asn Path & Bact; AMA; Int Acad Path. *Res:* Pneumoconioses. *Mailing Add:* 28 Maui Circle Naples FL 33962-3722

GROSS, PAUL HANS, ORGANIC CHEMISTRY, PHYSICAL CHEMISTRY. *Current Pos:* assoc prof chem, 66-70, PROF CHEM, UNIV PAC, 70- *Personal Data:* b Berlin, Ger, Apr 17, 31; m 57, Uta Freudiger; c Thomas, Klaus, Michael & Eva. *Educ:* Freie Univ Berlin, dipl, chem, 58, Dr Sci(chem), 61. *Prof Exp:* Res chemist, Schering AG, Ger, 61-62; fel amino-sugar chem, Univ Pac, 62-64; res fel carbohydrate chem, Mass Gen Hosp & Harvard Med Sch, 65-66. *Concurrent Pos:* Grants, NSF, 68 & 69-71, Res Corp, 72-74 & NIH, 87; vis prof, Tech Hschl, Munic, Ger, 73, Frei Univ Berlin, Ger, 78, Univ Autonoma Baja Calif, 80 & Univ Sevilla, Spain, 88; res chemist, Hanover Med Sch, Ger, 83 & 85; consult, Dupont Merck, Cell Pathways & United Pharmaceut. *Mem:* Am Chem Soc; Ger Chem Soc; Sigma Xi. *Res:* C-glycosides, anti cancer compounds; rheology properties of liquids; chemistry of aminosugars; chemistry of peptides. *Mailing Add:* Dept Chem Univ Pac Stockton CA 95211. *Fax:* 209-946-2607

GROSS, PAUL MAGNUS, JR, PHYSICAL CHEMISTRY. *Current Pos:* RETIRED. *Personal Data:* b Durham, NC, Jan 15, 20. *Educ:* Duke Univ, BS, 41; Brown Univ, PhD(chem), 48. *Prof Exp:* Asst dept phys chem, Harvard Med Sch, 42-46; instr chem, Univ Va, 48-51; asst prof gen & phys chem, 51-59; from assoc prof to prof phys chem & coordr honors prog, Wake Forest Univ, 59-87. *Concurrent Pos:* NSF fac fel, Cambridge Univ, 57-58. *Mem:* Am Chem Soc. *Res:* Physical chemistry of hydrogen peroxide-water solutions; dielectric constant measurements of hydrogen peroxide and protein solutions; fractionation and properties of proteins; solubility of strong electrolytes in hydrogen peroxide; vapor pressures of hydrogen peroxide water solutions; formation and stability of hydroperoxidates. *Mailing Add:* PO Box 21 Atlantic Beach NC 28512-0021. *Fax:* 613-545-6191

GROSS, PAUL RANDOLPH, DEVELOPMENTAL BIOLOGY, MOLECULAR BIOLOGY. *Current Pos:* prof biol, 86-89, UNIV PROF LIFE SCI, UNIV VA, 89-, DIR UNIV CTR ADVAN STUDIES, 89-, MOLECULAR BIOL INST, 90-, MARKEY CTR, 90- *Personal Data:* b Philadelphia, Pa, Nov 27, 28; m 64; c 1. *Educ:* Univ Pa, AB, 50, PhD(zool), 54; Brown Univ, MA, 63. *Hon Degrees:* MA, Brown Univ; DSC, Med Col Ohio. *Prof Exp:* From asst prof to assoc prof biol, NY Univ, 54-61; assoc prof, Brown Univ, 62-65; prof biol, Mass Inst Technol, 65-71; chmn dept, Univ Rochester, 72-76, prof biol, 72-78, dean grad studies, 74-78; pres & dir, Marine Biol Lab, Woods Hole, Mass, 78-86. *Concurrent Pos:* Lalor fel, 54-55, NSF sr fel, Univ Edinburgh, 61-62; mem bd trustees, Assoc Univs, Inc, 74-83; chmn cell biol study sect, Div Res Grants, NIH; mem doctoral coun, NY State Dept Educ, 74-; mem corp, Marine Biol Lab, Woods Hole, sci adv comt, Sch Vet Med, Tufts Univ, bd trustees, Univ Rochester, adv comt, Ctr Advan Studies, Univ Virginia, sci adv comn, Doreen Grace Bezeier Ctr, Mashpee, Mass, bd trustees, Sea Educ Asn. *Mem:* Am Physiol Soc; Am Soc Zoologists; Am Soc Cell Biol; Int Soc Cell Biol; AAAS. *Res:* Chemical embryology; molecular biology; cellular physiology; control of gene expression in animal development. *Mailing Add:* Dept Biol Univ Va 229 Gilmer Hall Charlottesville VA 22903

GROSS, PETER A, INFECTIOUS DISEASES, VIROLOGY. *Current Pos:* PROF & VCHMN DEPT MED, J N MED SCH, 80-; CHMN DEPT MED, HACKENSACK MED CTR, 80- *Personal Data:* b Newark, NJ, Nov 18, 38; m 64; c 3. *Educ:* Amherst Col, BA, 60; Yale Univ, MD, 64. *Honors & Awards:* Abbott Award, Infectious Dis Soc Am. *Mem:* Fel Am Col Physicians; fel Infectious Dis Soc Am; fel Am Acad Microbiol; Am Soc Microbiol; Am Fedn Clin Res; Soc Hosp Epidemiol Am (pres). *Res:* Clinical studies on the immune response to influenza vaccine; epidemiologic studies on hospital-acquired infections; health services research on severity of illness indices. *Mailing Add:* 242 Mckinley Pl Ridgewood NJ 07450-4807

GROSS, PETER GEORGE, ASTROPHYSICS, OPHTHALMOLOGY. *Current Pos:* EYE SURGEON & OPHTHALMOLOGIST, 86- *Personal Data:* b Oradea, Rumania, Feb 6, 47; US citizen; m 68, Susan G Roth; c Nicole, Edward, Elissa & Amy. *Educ:* Columbia Univ, BA, 68; Yale Univ, MPhil, 70, PhD(astrophys), 72; Ohio State Univ, MD, 82. *Prof Exp:* Res fel astron, Yale Univ, 72; res fel astrophys, Thomas J Watson Res Ctr, IBM Corp, 72-74; from asst to assoc prof astron, Case Western Res Univ, 74-79; flexible intern, Bryn Mawr Hosp, 82-83; ophthal resident, Sch Med, Univ Pa, 83-86. *Concurrent Pos:* Founder, P G Gross Res Found, 81- *Mem:* Am Astron Soc; Int Astron Union; NY Acad Sci; AMA; AAAS; fel Am Acad Ophthal; Am Col Surgeons. *Res:* Stellar structure; stellar evolution; magnetic fields and mixing in stellar plasmas; atmospheric escape rates; cosmic abundance of helium; glaucoma; rotational mechanics of eye movements and internal ocular forces; clinical measurements of the neuroretinal rim size; physics of the eye. *Mailing Add:* 714 Oxford Rd Bala Cynwyd PA 19004-2112

GROSS, ROBERT ALFRED, PLASMA PHYSICS. *Current Pos:* chmn, Dept Mech Eng, Columbia Univ, 70-76, Dept Appl Physics & Nuclear Eng, 78-81, prof eng sci, 60-80, dean, Sch Eng & Appl Sci, 82-90, HUDSON PROF APPL PHYSICS, COLUMBIA UNIV, 80- *Personal Data:* b Philadelphia, Pa, Oct 31, 27; m 52; c 2. *Educ:* Univ Pa, BS, 49; Harvard Univ, MS, 50, PhD(appl physics), 52. *Honors & Awards:* Waverly Gold Medal Res, 60. *Prof Exp:* Fel & res assoc, Harvard Univ, 53; chief res engr, Fairchild Engine Div, Fairchild Engine & Airplane Corp, 54-59; NSF fel, 59-60. *Concurrent Pos:* Guggenheim & Fulbright fels, 66-67; vis prof, Leiden Univ, 66-67; Australian Acad Sci vis fel, 67; vpres publ, Am Inst Aeronaut & Astronaut, 67-68; ed-in-chief selected reprint series, 68- *Mem:* Fel Am Phys Soc; fel Am Inst Aeronaut & Astronaut (vpres, 65-67). *Res:* High temperature gas dynamics; plasma physics. *Mailing Add:* 173 Deer Run Rd Willow Grove PA 19090-2699

GROSS, ROBERT HENRY, RNA PROCESSING, HEAT SHOCK & THERMOTOLERANCE. *Current Pos:* asst prof biol, 77-83, asst prof, 78-83, ASSOC BIOL, DARTMOUTH COL, 83-, DIR, COMPUTATIONAL CTR, 96- *Personal Data:* b Brooklyn, NY, Mar 6, 45; m 68; c 3. *Educ:* Rensselaer Polytech Inst, Troy, NY, BES, 67, MS, 68; Johns Hopkins Univ, Baltimore, PhD(biophys), 74. *Prof Exp:* Fel molecular biol, Dept Biol, Johns Hopkins Univ, 74-77. *Concurrent Pos:* Mem staff, Norris Cotton Cancer Ctr, Hanover, NH, 79- & Arthritis Ctr, Mary Hitchcock Hosp, 80-; Molecular Genetics Ctr, Darthmouth, 85- *Mem:* AAAS; NY Acad Sci; Am Soc Cell Biol; Am Soc Microbiol. *Res:* Control of gene expression in eukaryotes; control of alternative splicing during development, utilizing liposome mediated introduction; use of computers in research training. *Mailing Add:* Dept Biol Sci Dartmouth Col Hanover NH 03755-2061

GROSS, RUTH T, MEDICINE, PEDIATRICS. *Current Pos:* assoc dean student affairs, Stanford Univ, 73-75, dir gen ambulatory pediat, Sch Med, 75-85, prof pediat, 75-92, dir, Gen Pediat Develop Prog, 79-83, dir, Stanford Children's Ambulatory Care Ctr, 80-85, nat study dir, Infant Health & Develop Prog, 83-92, EMER PROF PEDIAT, STANFORD UNIV, 92- *Personal Data:* b Bryan, Tex, June 24, 20; div; c 1. *Educ:* Columbia Univ, BA, 41, MD, 44. *Prof Exp:* From instr to assoc prof pediat, Sch Med, Stanford Univ, 50-60; from assoc prof to prof, Albert Einstein Col Med, 60-66; dir, Dept Pediat, Mt Zion Hosp & Med Ctr, 66-73. *Concurrent Pos:* Commonwealth fel, 59-60; prin investr, Gen Pediat Acad Develop Prog, Stanford Univ & mem study youth develop, Boys Town Ctr, 78-84; Henry J Kaiser sr fel, Ctr Advan Behav Sci, Stanford, Calif, 80-81. *Mem:* Inst Med-Nat Acad Sci; Soc Res Child Develop; Soc Pediat Res; Am Pediat Soc; Ambulatory Pediat Asn. *Res:* Medical education; interventions for infants at risks for developmental delay. *Mailing Add:* 350 Gulf Mexico Dr No 218 Longboat Key FL 34228

GROSS, SAMSON RICHARD, GENETICS. *Current Pos:* assoc prof microbiol, 60-65, dir prog genetics, 67-77, PROF GENETICS, DEPT BIOCHEM, DUKE UNIV, 65- *Personal Data:* b Brooklyn, NY, July 27, 26; m 52; c 3. *Educ:* NY Univ, BA, 49; Columbia Univ, AM, 51, PhD(genetics, zool), 53. *Prof Exp:* Res assoc biochem genetics, Stanford Univ, 53-56, asst prof genetics, 56-57; asst prof, Rockefeller Inst, 57-60. *Concurrent Pos:* spec spec fel, Weizmann Inst, 69-70; dir undergrad training prog, Cold Spring Harbor Lab, 63 & 64, dir grad studies, Dept Microbiol & Immunol, 64-65; consult, NIH, 75-79; John Simon Guggenheim fel, 85-86. *Mem:* AAAS; Genetics Soc Am; Am Soc Biol Chem. *Res:* Molecular genetics; molecular regulatory mechanisms. *Mailing Add:* Genetics Div Dept Biochem Duke Univ Box 3711 Med Ctr Durham NC 27710-0001

GROSS, STANLEY BURTON, TOXICOLOGY, ENVIRONMENTAL SCIENCES. *Current Pos:* SR TOXICOLOGIST & INDUST HYGIENIST, ENVIRON PROTECTION AGENCY, WASHINGTON, DC, 77- *Personal Data:* b Pittsburgh, Pa, May 24, 31; m 53, 93; c Cheryl, Caren & Gregory. *Educ:* WVa Univ, AB, 54, MS, 57, PhD(biochem), 63; WVa Univ Med Sch, dipl 65; Nat Inst Environ Health Sci, dipl, 69; Am Bd Toxicol, dipl, 82; Am Bd Indust Hyg, dipl 86; Am Col Forensic Examr, dipl, 96. *Prof Exp:* Res assoc agr biochem, WVa Univ, 56-58, res assoc anesthesiol, Med Ctr, 63; res biochemist, Columbus Labs, Battelle Mem Inst, 65-67; asst prof environ health info syst, Univ Cincinnati, 67-69, fel environ toxicol, 69-71, asst prof toxicol, 71-75; sr res inhalation scientist, Hazleton Labs Am, Inc, 75-76; consult toxicol, 76-77. *Concurrent Pos:* Mem, Am Conf Govt Indust Hygienists; Life Sci Adv Comt. *Mem:* Soc Toxicol; Am Chem Soc; Asn Gov Toxicol; Am Indust Hyg Asn; Int Affairs Comt. *Res:* Environmental and occupational toxicology; trace metals; human body burden analyses; automated biomedical information systems; lipid absorption and analysis; pesticides; industrial hygienics; chemical health risks and hazard analysis. *Mailing Add:* 9008 Ft Craig Dr Burke VA 22015-2115. *Fax:* 703-503-4991; *E-Mail:* gross.stanley@epamail.epa.gov

GROSS, THOMAS LESTER, MATERNAL-FETAL MEDICINE. *Current Pos:* ASSOC PROF & CHMN, DEPT OBSTET & GYNEC, UNIV ILL COL MED, PEORIA, 87- *Personal Data:* b Decatur, Ill, Aug 17, 45; m 67, Judy B Osborn; c Elizabeth, Matthew & Joshua. *Educ:* Bluffton Col, BA, 67; Univ Ill Col Med, MD, 71. *Honors & Awards:* Community Hosp Award for Res, Cent Asn Obstetricians & Gynecologists, 81, Ann Prize Award for Res, 82; First Prize for Res, Am Col Obstetricians, & Gynecologist, 84. *Prof Exp:* Intern, St Francis Hosp, Ill, 71-72; residency obstet-gynec, Akron Gen Med Ctr, 74-77; fel maternal-fetal med, Cleveland Metrop Gen Hosp, Case Western Res Univ, 77-79, from asst prof to assoc prof obstet & gynec, 77-86. *Concurrent Pos:* Asst dir, Perinatal Clin Res Ctr, 82-85, actg prog dir, 85-86. *Mem:* Am Col Obstetricians & Gynecologists; Physicians Social Responsibility; Soc Gynec Invest; Soc Perinatal Obstetricians; Perinatal Res Soc; Am Bd Obstetricians & Gynecologists. *Res:* Biochemistry of amniotic fluid; effect of maternal nutrition and metabolism and how they relate to fetal growth; effect of maternal obesity on pregnancy outcome. *Mailing Add:* Univ Ill Col Med 1 Illini Dr PO Box 1649 Peoria IL 61656

GROSS, WALTER BURNHAM, AVIAN PATHOLOGY. *Current Pos:* RETIRED. *Personal Data:* b Sandusky, Ohio, Jan 17, 25; m 53; c 2. *Educ:* Ohio State Univ, DVM, 46; Univ Minn, MS, 52, PhD(animal path), 56. *Prof Exp:* Vet, Bur Animal Indust, USDA, 47-48; assoc animal pathologist, Agr Exp Sta, Va Polytech Inst & State Univ, 49-92, prof vet sci, 56-92. *Mem:* Am Vet Med Asn; Sigma Xi. *Res:* Diseases of poultry. *Mailing Add:* 1509 Lark Lane Blacksburg VA 24060

GROSS, WILLIAM A, TRIBOLOGY, APPLIED MECHANICS. *Current Pos:* prof, 74-93, dean eng, 74-80, EMER PROF ENG, UNIV NMEX, 93- *Personal Data:* b Los Angeles, Calif, Nov 17, 24; m 48, 70, Sharon Philbrick; c Constance (Jackson), Ellen (Door), Mark & David. *Educ:* USCG Acad, BS, 45; Univ Calif, Berkeley, MS, 49, PhD(appl mech), 51. *Honors & Awards:* Centennial Award, Am Soc Mech Engrs. *Prof Exp:* From lectr to instr, Univ Calif, Berkeley, 49-52; asst prof, Iowa State Univ, 52-55; mem tech staff, Bell Tel Labs, 55-56; mgr appl mech, IBM Res Lab, San Jose, Calif, 56-61; vpres advan technol, Ampex Coorp, 61-72. *Concurrent Pos:* Mgr explor, TPC Corp, 94-97. *Mem:* Nat Acad Eng; fel Inst Elec & Electronics Engrs; fel Am Soc Mech Engrs; Am Solar Energy Asn; AAAS; Int Solar Energy Asn. *Mailing Add:* 1401 Las Lomas Rd Albuquerque NM 87106. *Fax:* 505-277-1571

GROSSBECK, MARTIN LESTER, RADIATION EFFECTS, FRACTURE OF METALS & REFRACTORY METALS. *Current Pos:* task leader radiation effects fusion mat, 79-84, RES STAFF MEM, OAK RIDGE NAT LAB, 75- *Personal Data:* b Paterson, NJ, July 5, 44; m 81, Jane Powell. *Educ:* Rensselaer Polytech Inst, BS, 66; Cornell Univ, MS, 68; Univ Ill, PhD(metall eng), 75. *Prof Exp:* Instr reactor physics, US Naval Power Sch, 67-71. *Concurrent Pos:* US coordr, Int Prog Fusion Reactor Mats Irradiation, 81-85; task leader, Radiation Effects Space Reaction Mat, Oak Ridge Nat Lab, 84-86, prin investr, Radiation Effects Tritium Prod Reactor Mat, 89-93; chmn, Mat Sci & Technol Div, Am Nuclear Soc, 88-89. *Mem:* Fel Am Nuclear Soc; Am Soc Metals; Am Vacuum Soc; Sigma Xi. *Res:* Radiation effects in metals; mechanical properties; development of fusion reactor and space nuclear reactor materials; hydrogen embrittlement and gases in metals; refractory metals, gas-cooled reactor fuels; helium embrittlement in metals. *Mailing Add:* Oak Ridge Nat Lab PO Box 2008 Bldg 5500 Oak Ridge TN 37831 6376. *Fax:* 423-574-0641; *E-Mail:* gro@ornl.gov

GROSSBERG, ARNOLD LEWIS, chemical engineering, for more information see previous edition

GROSSBERG, SIDNEY EDWARD, VIROLOGY, ONCOLOGY. *Current Pos:* dep dir, Cancer Ctr, 84-96, PROF MICROBIOL & MED & CHMN DEPT, MED COL WIS, 66- *Personal Data:* b Miami, Fla, Nov 13, 29; m 59, Josette Brugerolle; c Daniel E & Leslie D. *Educ:* Emory Univ, BS, 51, MD, 54. *Prof Exp:* From intern to asst resident med, Duke Univ Hosp, 54-58; from instr to asst prof microbiol, Sch Med, Univ Minn, 59-62; asst prof, Med Col, Cornell Univ, 62-66. *Concurrent Pos:* Virologist, US Army, 55-57; fel, Sch Med, Johns Hopkins Univ, 58-59; Nat Inst Allergy & Infectious Dis fel, 59-61; NIH Res Career Develop Award, 61-66; vis investr, Pasteur Inst, Paris, 64-65 & 74-75; attend physician, NY Hosp, 64-66; Markle scholar acad med, 65-70; assoc mem, Influenza Virus Comn, US Army, 67-70; sr fel, Europ Molecular Biol Orgn, 74-75; Walter Schroeder chair, Microbiol, 83; vis prof, Dept Human Oncol, Univ Wis, Madison, 88-89; Am Cancer Soc Scholar in cancer res, 89; consult, WHO, NIH, Am Cancer Soc, Nat Bd Med Examr Univ Tex, Univ Pittsburgh Sch Pub Health Med Col Pa Grad Schs serono, Berlex Biosci, Biogen, Geiosidus, Schering Plough, Genentech, Rentschler & Athera Diagnostics; ed, Res in Virol. *Mem:* Am Asn Immunol; Am Soc Virol (secy-treas, 84-); Am Soc Microbiol; fel Infectious Dis Soc Am; fel Am Acad Microbiol; French Soc Microbiol; Int Soc Interferon and Cytokine Res; Am Med Sch Microbiol & Immunol chairs (pres, 93-94). *Res:* Host cell-virus relationships; cell biology; interferons; RNA viruses; cytokines. *Mailing Add:* Dept Microbiol Med Col Wis 8701 Watertown Plank Rd Milwaukee WI 53226-4801. *Fax:* 414-266-8522; *E-Mail:* segrossb@post.its.mcw.edu

GROSSBERG, STEPHEN, MATHEMATICAL BIOLOGY. *Current Pos:* PROF MATH, PSYCHOL, BIOMED ENG, BOSTON UNIV, 75-, DIR, CTR ADAPTIVE SYSTS, 83- *Personal Data:* b New York, NY, Dec 31, 39; m 80; c 1. *Educ:* Dartmouth Col, BA, 61; Stanford Univ, MS, 64; Rockefeller Univ, PhD(math), 67. *Prof Exp:* Asst prof appl math, Mass Inst Technol, 67-69, assoc prof, 69-75. *Concurrent Pos:* Ed Math Biosci, 80-, J Theoret Neurobiol, 80-, Behav Processes, 84- & J Math Psychol, 85- *Mem:* Cognitive Sci Soc; Am Math Soc; Soc Math Psychol; Soc Math Biol; Soc Neurosci. *Res:* Models of learning and perception; development, cognition, motor control; psychophysiology; global analysis of dynamical systems. *Mailing Add:* Ctr Adaptive Systs Boston Univ 677 Beacon St Boston MA 02215-2411

GROSSENBACHER, KARL A(LBERT), plant physiology, for more information see previous edition

GROSSER, ARTHUR EDWARD, PHYSICAL CHEMISTRY, FOOD CHEMISTRY. *Current Pos:* asst prof, 65-69, ASSOC PROF CHEM, McGILL UNIV, 69- *Personal Data:* b New York, NY, Nov 30, 34. *Educ:* Cornell Univ, AB, 56; Univ Wis, PhD(phys chem), 63. *Prof Exp:* Alumni Res Found fel, Univ Wis, 63-64, fel phys chem, 64-65. *Mem:* Am Chem Soc; Am Phys Soc; AAAS. *Res:* Molecular beam studies of elastic and reactive collisions. *Mailing Add:* Dept Chem McGill Univ 801 Sherbrooke St W Montreal PQ H3A 2K6 Can

GROSSER, BERNARD IRVING, PSYCHIATRY, NEUROENDOCRINOLOGY. *Current Pos:* Intern med, Affil Hosps, 59-60, resident psychiat, 60-65, from asst prof to assoc prof, Col Med, 67-75, PROF PSYCHIAT, COL MED, UNIV UTAH, 75-, CHMN DEPT PSYCHIAT, 79- *Personal Data:* b Boston, Mass, Apr 19, 29; m 90, Karen; c Steven, Mark & Minda. *Educ:* Univ Mass, BA, 50; Univ Mich, MS, 53; Western Res Univ, MD, 59. *Concurrent Pos:* USPHS training grant, Col Med, Univ Utah, 60-62; USPHS res grants, 62-65 & 67-74; NIMH res career develop awards, 62-65 & 67-73; mem preclin psychopharmacol res rev comt, NIMH, 74-78, mem clin res rev comt, 80-85; mem sci adv bd, Scottish Rite, 78-; sr sci adv, Alcohol & Drug Abuse, Ment Health Admin, 87-88. *Mem:* Int Soc Psychoneuroendocrinol (treas, 74-); Am Psychiat Asn; AMA; Soc Neurosci; NY Acad Sci; Am Col Neuropsychiat. *Res:* Interrelationships between cortico-steroids and brain proteins, especially the role of these hormones in human behavior. *Mailing Add:* Dept Psychiat Univ Utah Sch Med 50 N Medical Dr Salt Lake City UT 84132-1001

GROSSERT, JAMES STUART, ORGANIC CHEMISTRY. *Current Pos:* from asst prof to assoc prof, 67-90, PROF CHEM, DALHOUSIE UNIV, 90- *Personal Data:* b Durban, SAfrica, Jan 28, 40; m 68. *Educ:* Univ Natal, BSc, 60, MSc, 61; PhD(chem), 64. *Prof Exp:* Lab asst, Dyson Perrins Lab, Oxford Univ, 64-65; fel, Brandeis Univ, 65-67. *Concurrent Pos:* Vis fel, Org Chem Lab, Rijks Univ, Groningen, 73-74. *Mem:* Chem Inst Can; Royal Soc Chem; Am Chem Soc. *Res:* Mass spectrometry; organosulfur chemistry; heteroatom chemistry reactions in solution under high pressures; marine and other natural products chemistry. *Mailing Add:* Dept Chem Dalhousie Univ Halifax NS B3H 4J3 Can

GROSSI, CARLO E, surgery; deceased, see previous edition for last biography

GROSSI, MARIO DARIO, RADIO PHYSICS, ENGINEERING. *Current Pos:* staff engr, Equip & Systs Div, Raytheon Co, 58-60, consult scientist, Space & Info Systs Div, 60-65, consult scientist, Equip Div, 65-80, CONSULT SCIENTIST, SUB SIGNAL DIV, RAYTHEON CO, 80-; RADIOPHYSICIST & ENGR, HARVARD-SMITHSONIAN CTR ASTROPHYS, 59-; RES ASSOC, HARVARD COL OBSERV, 65- *Personal Data:* b Giuncarico, Italy, Jan 10, 25; US citizen; m 56; c 2. *Educ:* Univ Pisa, Dr(radio eng), 48; Nat Res Coun, Italy, dipl microwave physics, 49. *Prof Exp:* Res engr, Magneti Marelli Cent Radio Lab, Italy, 49-50; design engr, Ital Marconi, 50-55, design supvr, 55-58. *Concurrent Pos:* Asst prof, Commun Inst, Univ Genoa, 51-58. *Mem:* Sr mem Inst Elec & Electronics Engrs; assoc fel Am Inst Aeronaut & Astronaut; Am Astron Soc. *Res:* Propagation of electromagnetic waves in lithosphere, atmosphere, ionosphere, magnetosphere; remote probing by electromagnetic waves of planetary atmospheres, ionospheres and surfaces. *Mailing Add:* 9 Chauncy Lane Cambridge MA 02138

GROSSIE, JAMES ALLEN, PHYSIOLOGY, NEUROENDOCRINOLOGY. *Current Pos:* ASSOC PROF PHYSIOL, OHIO STATE UNIV, 65- *Personal Data:* b Beaumont, Tex, May 19, 36; m 64. *Educ:* Sam Houston State Col, BS, 58, MA, 59; Univ Mo, PhD(endocrinol), 63. *Prof Exp:* NIH fel, Col Med, Univ Ill, 63-65. *Mem:* Am Physiol Soc. *Res:* Effects of endocrines on the nervous system. *Mailing Add:* Dept Physiol Ohio State Univ Col Med 370 W Ninth Ave Columbus OH 43210-1238

GROSSKREUTZ, JOSEPH CHARLES, ENERGY CONVERSION, SOLAR ENERGY. *Current Pos:* RES PROF PHYSICS, UNIV MO, KANSAS CITY, 89- *Personal Data:* b Springfield, Mo, Jan 5, 22; m 49; c 2. *Educ:* Drury Col, BS, 43; Washington Univ, MS, 48, PhD(physics), 50. *Prof Exp:* Asst physics, Univ Calif, 46-47; asst, Washington Univ, 47-48 & 49-50; res physicist, Calif Res Corp, 50-52; asst prof, Univ Tex, 52-56; sr physicist, 56-59, prin physicist, 59-63, sr adv physics, 63-67, prin adv, Midwest Res Inst, 67-71; chief mech properties sect, Nat Bur Standards, 71-72; mgr, Solar Energy Progs, Black & Veatch Consult Engrs, 72-77; dir, Res & Develop, Solar Energy Res Inst, 77-79; mgr, Advan Technol Proj, Black & Veatch, Engrs-Architects, 79-88. *Mem:* Fel Am Phys Soc; fel Am Soc Testing & Mat. *Res:* Metal physics; plastic deformation; electron microscopy; small angle x-ray scattering; metal fatigue; solar energy conversion to electricity; scanning tanneling and atomic force microscopy. *Mailing Add:* 4306 W 111th Terr Leawood KS 66211

GROSSLING, BERNARDO FREUDENBURG, GEOPHYSICS, OPERATIONS RESEARCH. *Current Pos:* RES GEOPHYSICIST, 85-, SCI ADV APPL GEOPHYS, US GEOL SURV, WASHINGTON, DC. *Personal Data:* b Santiago, Chile, Dec 21, 18; nat US; m 41, 53, Hildegard Romer; c Bernardo, Maria E, Fernando, Jorge & Peter. *Educ:* Univ Chile, CE, 41, EE, 44; Calif Inst Technol, MSc, 45; Univ London, dipl & PhD(geophys), 51. *Honors & Awards:* Marcos Orrego Puelma Prize, Inst Engrs Chile, 41. *Prof Exp:* Asst math, Univ Chile, 38, asst elec eng, 40-42; asst comput, Astron Observ, Chile, 38-40; design engr, Chilian Develop Corp, 40-42, explor geophysicist, 43-44; asst soil mech, Calif Inst Technol, 45-46, Nat Oil Co, Chile, 46-49, consult oil explor, 51-53; from res geophysicist to sr res geophysicist, Calif Res Corp Div, Stand Oil Co Calif, 54-59, res assoc, 59-60; actg chief engr div, Inter-Am Develop Bank, 60-61, engr consult, 61-62, tech adv 62-64; res geophysicist, US Geol Surv, Washington, DC, 64-73, off dir, 73-79; natural resources adv, Int-Am Develop Bank, Washington, DC, 79-85. *Concurrent Pos:* Lectr, Sch Arts & Trades, Univ Chile, 42-43. *Mem:* Soc Explor Geophys; fel Royal Astron Soc; Am Econ Asn; Sigma Xi; NY Acad Sci. *Res:* Mathematical physics; theory of automata; tectonophysics; plasticity; geothermal studies; oil exploration; economics of natural resource exploration and development; unorthodox uses of man's visual system; evaluation of petroleum and coal resources. *Mailing Add:* c/o Cosmos Club 2121 Massachusetts Ave Washington DC 20008

GROSSMAN, ALLEN S, ASTROPHYSICS. *Current Pos:* GROUP LEADER, ATMOSPHERIC PHYSICS, LAWRENCE LIVERMORE NAT LAB, CALIF, 95- *Personal Data:* b New York, NY, Apr 12, 38; m 61; c 2. *Educ:* Hofstra Univ, BS, 61; Adelphi Univ, MS, 64, Ind Univ, PhD(astrophys), 69. *Prof Exp:* Instr electronics, Acad Aeronaut, 58-59; design engr, Brookhaven Nat Lab, 61-64; asst prof, Iowa State Univ, 68-76, assoc prof physics, 76- *Mem:* Am Astron Soc; Royal Astron Soc. *Res:* Stellar evolution; structure of stars of mass less than one half solar mass; astronomical instrumentation. *Mailing Add:* L-103 PO Box 808 Livermore CA 94551

GROSSMAN, BARBARA MULLEN, NUTRITION. *Current Pos:* res asst, Univ Ga, 81-82, teaching asst, 82-83, res technician, 83-85, asst, 85-86, USDA fel, 86-88, post doctoral assoc, 88-93, RES SCIENTIST, DEPT FOODS & NUTRIT, UNIV GA, 93- *Prof Exp:* Staff res assoc, Univ Calif, Davis, 79-81. *Concurrent Pos:* NIH res grant, 92-95. *Mem:* Am Inst Nutrit; Am Diabetes Asn; Soc Ingestive Behav; Soc Neurosci; NAm Asn Study Obesity. *Res:* Author of more than 20 publications. *Mailing Add:* Dept Foods & Nutrit Univ Ga Dawson Hall Athens GA 30602

GROSSMAN, CHARLES JEROME, IMMUNOENDOCRINOLOGY. *Current Pos:* RES PHYSIOLOGIST RES SERV, CINCINNATI VET ADMIN MED STR, 77-; ASSOC PROF BIOL, XAVIER UNIV, CINCINNATI, 77-; ASSOC PROF PHYSIOL & BIOPHYS, COL MED, UNIV CINCINNATI, 85- *Personal Data:* b New York, NY, May 12, 45. *Educ:* Adelphi Univ, Long Island, NY, BA, 68; Univ Cincinnati, MS, 71, PhD(physiol), 77; Xavier Univ, Cincinnati, MBA, 84. *Concurrent Pos:* Prin investr, Res Serv, Med Ctr, Vet Admin, 78- *Mem:* Soc Study Reproduction; Am Physiol Soc; AAAS; Am Asn Univ Professors. *Res:* Regulation of the cell mediated immune response by sex steroids and pituitary and thymic factors. *Mailing Add:* 6700 Fair Acres Dr Cincinnati OH 45213. *Fax:* 513-559-6614

GROSSMAN, DAVID G, CERAMICS & GLASS-CERAMICS. *Current Pos:* sr chemist, 70-85, SR RES ASSOC, CORNING INC, 85- *Personal Data:* b New York, NY, Aug 20, 41; m 71, Ann Streeting; c Jeffrey & Sarah. *Educ:* Rutgers Univ, BS, 63, MS, 64; Univ Sheffield, PhD(glass technol), 67. *Prof Exp:* Asst lectr mat sci, Rugby Col Eng Technol, Eng, 67-69. *Concurrent Pos:* Adj prof mats sci, Med Univ SC, 84- *Mem:* Fel Brit Soc Glass Technol; fel Am Ceramic Soc; fel Int Soc Dental Ceramics; Int Asn Dental Res; assoc mem Am Dental Asn. *Res:* Structure and properties of glass ceramics; 21 US patents. *Mailing Add:* 200 Wall St Corning NY 14830. *Fax:* 607-974-2103

GROSSMAN, GEORGE, MATHEMATICS. *Current Pos:* RETIRED. *Personal Data:* b New York, NY, July 1, 14; wid; c Marsleub D. *Educ:* City Col New York, BS, 34; Columbia Univ, MA, 35. *Prof Exp:* Teacher math, Bd Educ, NY, 35-46, chmn, dept high schs, 46-64, actg dir, 64-68, dir math, 68-78. *Concurrent Pos:* Suppl teacher, Brooklyn Polytech Inst, 44-61, Sci Honors Prog, Columbia Univ, 59-69, Teachers Col, Columbia Univ, 61-69 & City Col New York, 61-62; adj prof, Hunter Col, 73-76 & Webster Col, 74-; consult, IBM Corp & Olivetti Underwood Corp; mem, Nat Coun Teachers Math. *Res:* Computer mathematics; impact of automatic digital computer in mathematical education; multiplicative teacher training. *Mailing Add:* 27000 Grand Central Pkwy Apt 15H Floral Park NY 11005-1104

GROSSMAN, HERBERT JULES, PEDIATRIC NEUROLOGY. *Personal Data:* b Chicago, Ill, June 15, 23; m 54; c 3. *Educ:* Univ Ill, Chicago, BS, 44, MD, 46. *Prof Exp:* Consult, Epilepsy Clin, Univ Ill Neuropsychiat Inst, Chicago, 53-57, pediat neurol, Ctr Handicapped Children, Univ Ill Hosp 56-57, Child Study Ctr, Mt Sinai Hosp, Los Angeles, 57-62, Pac State Hosp, Pomona, 58-62, pediat & neurol, Presby-St Luke's Hosp 65-71 & Neurol, Munic Contagious Dis Hosp, Chicago, 73-; dir pediat neurol, Presby-St Luke's Hosp, 71-76; dir, Ill State Pediat Inst, 62-76. *Mem:* Fel neurol, Univ Calif, Los Angeles, 58-61; distinguished fel Am Psychiat Asn; fel Am Asn Ment Deficiency; Am Acad Ment Retardation (pres, 72-74); Am Acad Pediat. *Mailing Add:* 3738 Middleton Dr Ann Arbor MI 48105-2860

GROSSMAN, HERMAN, RADIOLOGY, PEDIATRICS. *Current Pos:* PROF DIAG RADIOL & PEDIAT, MED COL, DUKE UNIV & ATTEND RADIOLOGIST & PEDIATRICIAN, MED CTR, 71- *Personal Data:* b Waterbury, Conn, Apr 25, 25; m 49; c 3. *Educ:* Univ NC, BA, 47; Wesleyan Univ, MA, 49; Columbia Univ, MD, 53; Am Bd Pediat, dipl, 58; Am Bd Radiol, dipl, 65. *Prof Exp:* Intern pediat, Bellevue Hosp, 53-54; resident, Babies Hosp, NY, 54-56; asst pediatrician, Columbia Univ, 56-61, instr pediat, 61; from asst prof to assoc prof radiol & pediat, Med Col, Cornell Univ, 65-71. *Concurrent Pos:* Fel radiol, Columbia-Presby Med Ctr, 62-65; pvt pract, 56-62; attend physician, Hackensack Hosp, 56-62; asst pediatrician, Presby Hosp & Babies Hosp, NY, 56-62; from assoc attend radiologist to attend radiologist, NY Hosp, 65-71, assoc attend pediatrician, 65-71; from asst attend to attend radiologist & pediatrician, Mem Hosp, 67-71. *Mem:* Asn Univ Radiol; Soc Pediat Radiol. *Res:* Pediatric radiology. *Mailing Add:* Duke Univ Med Ctr Box 3834 Durham NC 27710-0001

GROSSMAN, I G, HYDROGEOLOGY & ECONOMIC GEOLOGY. *Current Pos:* RES SCIENTIST, NJ GEOL SURV, TRENTON, 85- *Personal Data:* b New York City, NY, Mar 4, 17; m 56, Ann Safran; c Barbara, Joshua & Gilbert. *Educ:* Brooklyn Col, BA, 44; Columbia Univ, MA, 47. *Honors & Awards:* Geo Striders Award, US Geol Surv, 82. *Prof Exp:* Hydrogeologist,

US Geol Surv, 49-85. *Concurrent Pos:* Vis prof environ geol, Bejing Univ, China, 87; lectr geol, Rutgers Univ, 88. *Mem:* Fel Geol Soc Am; Soc Econ Geologists; Sigma Xi; Am Geophys Union; ASN Earth Sci Ed; fel AAAS; Asn Geoscientists for Int Develop. *Res:* Review and edit scientific and technical papers and reports on geology, geohydrology and hydrology. *Mailing Add:* 224 S Flint Ct Yardley PA 19067-5716

GROSSMAN, JACOB, NEPHROLOGY, MEDICINE. *Current Pos:* VIS PROF MED, ALBERT EINSTEIN COL MED, 81- *Personal Data:* b NY, Aug 6, 16; m 48, Frances Gaezer; c Arthur, Victor, Daniel & Walter. *Educ:* City Col New York, BS, 35; Columbia Univ, MA, 36; Univ Louisville, MD, 40. *Prof Exp:* Res assoc med, Montefiore Hosp, 52-66; dir med, Hosp Joint Dis & Med Ctr, 66-80; prof clin med, Mt Sinai Sch Med, 68-80. *Concurrent Pos:* Vis prof med, Albert Einstein Col Med, 81- *Mem:* AAAS; fel Am Col Physicians; Am Physiol Soc; Am Soc Nephrol; Soc Exp Biol & Med. *Res:* Cardiovascular and renal physiology; metabolism; clinical investigation. *Mailing Add:* 64 Fayette Rd Scarsdale NY 10583

GROSSMAN, JEFFREY N, COSMOCHEMISTRY, METEORITICS. *Current Pos:* RES CHEMIST, US GEOL SURV, 84- *Personal Data:* b Brooklyn, NY, Nov 6, 55; m 83; c 1. *Educ:* Brown Univ, BS, 77; Univ Calif, Los Angeles, PhD(geochem), 83. *Prof Exp:* Res assoc, Jet Propulsion Lab, 84. *Mem:* Fel Meteoritical Soc. *Res:* Meteorites and the early history of the solar system; trace element geochemistry of igneous and metamorphic rocks; development of methods in neutron activation analysis. *Mailing Add:* 11802 Briar Mill Lane Reston VA 22094-1520

GROSSMAN, JEROME H, MEDICAL ADMINISTRATION. *Current Pos:* CHMN & CHIEF EXEC OFFICER, HEALTH QUAL INC, 96- *Prof Exp:* Fac, Dept Med, Sch Med, Tufts Univ, 88-90; pres & chief exec officer, New Eng Med Ctr, 90-96. *Mem:* Inst Med-Nat Acad Sci. *Mailing Add:* Health Qual Inc 500 Boylston St Suite 550 Boston MA 02116

GROSSMAN, JOHN MARK, PLASMA PHYSICS, COMPUTATIONAL PHYSICS. *Current Pos:* RES SCIENTIST, PLASMA PHYSICS DIV, NAVAL RES LAB, 84- *Personal Data:* b Santiago, Chile, Oct 13, 54; US citizen. *Educ:* Manhattan Col, BA, 74; Univ Md, MA, 80, PhD(appl math), 82. *Prof Exp:* Fel, Nat Res Coun, Los Alamos Nat Acad Sci, 82-84. *Mem:* Am Phys Soc. *Res:* Plasma physics; pulsed power engineering; computer simulation of experiments. *Mailing Add:* 2032 Belmont Rd NW 422 Washington DC 20009

GROSSMAN, LAURENCE ABRAHAM, INTERNAL MEDICINE, CARDIOVASCULAR DISEASES. *Current Pos:* From instr to assoc prof, 47-57, PROF CLIN MED, SCH MED, VANDERBILT UNIV, 57-; ASSOC PROF, MEHARRY MED COL, 48- *Personal Data:* b Nashville, Tenn, Sept 21, 16; m 42; c 4. *Educ:* Vanderbilt Univ, BA, 38, MD, 41. *Concurrent Pos:* Mem bd, exec comt, Vanderbilt Univ Med Ctr, 81-87; vpres, St Thomas Hosp Develop Found, 81-83; pres, Tenn Heart Inst, 84. *Mem:* Fel Am Col Physicians; fel Am Col Cardiol; fel Am Col Chest Physicians. *Res:* Cardiology. *Mailing Add:* 4300 Lilywood Rd Nashville TN 37205

GROSSMAN, LAWRENCE, COSMOCHEMISTRY, GEOCHEMISTRY. *Current Pos:* Asst prof geochem, Dept Geophys Sci, 72-76, asst prof, Enrico Fermi Inst, 74-76, assoc prof, 76-81, PROF GEOPHYS & CHEM, DEPT GEOPHYS SCI & ENRICO FERMI INST, UNIV CHICAGO, 76- *Personal Data:* b Toronto, Ont, Feb 2, 46; m 68; c 2. *Educ:* McMaster Univ, BSc, 68; Yale Univ, MPhil, 70, PhD(geochem), 72. *Honors & Awards:* F W Clarke Medal, Geochem Soc, 74; James B Macelwane Award, Am Geophys Union, 80. *Concurrent Pos:* Consult, Lunar Adv Comt, NASA, 73-76, Lunar Data Synthesis Rev Panel, 73-74 & Mariner Jupiter Orbiter Sci Working Group, Jet Propulsion Lab, 75; consult lunar & planetary rev panel, Lunar & Planetary Inst, 77-79; Alfred P Sloan res fel, 76-78; Lady Davis vis prof, Hebrew Univ, Jerusalem, 81-82. *Mem:* Fel Meteoritical Soc; Geochem Soc; fel Am Geophys Union; fel Mineral Soc Am; Mineral Asn Can. *Res:* Chemical and isotopic compositions of the different petrographic components of chondritic meteorites as clues to the behavior of the elements during the condensation of the solar system; composition and origin of the planets; interstellar grains. *Mailing Add:* Dept Geophys Sci Univ Chicago 5734 Ellis Ave Chicago IL 60637-1433

GROSSMAN, LAWRENCE, BIOCHEMISTRY. *Current Pos:* E V McCollum prof & chmn, 75-89, DISTINGUISHED SERV PROF, DEPT BIOCHEM, SCH HYG & PUB HEALTH, JOHNS HOPKINS UNIV, 89- *Personal Data:* b New York, NY, Jan 23, 24; m 49; c 3. *Educ:* Hofstra Col, BA, 49; Univ Southern Calif, PhD(biochem), 54. *Prof Exp:* NIH fel, McCollum-Pratt Inst, Johns Hopkins Univ, 54-56; res biochemist, NIH, 56-57; from asst prof to prof, Brandies Univ, 67-75. *Concurrent Pos:* Grants, NIH, NSF, AEC & Am Cancer Soc; Commonwealth fel, 63-64, career develop award, NIH, 64-; mem, Sci Adv Comt, Am Cancer Soc, 65-68; chmn adv comt biochem, NIH; Guggenheim fel, 73; ed, Methods Nucleic Acids & Cancer Res, Crit Rev Biochem, J Biol Chem. *Mem:* Am Soc Biol Chem; Biophys Soc. *Res:* Enzymatic mechanisms for the repair of DNA; molecular basis of mutagenesis. *Mailing Add:* Dept Biochem Johns Hopkins Univ Sch Hyg & Pub Health 615 N Wolfe St Baltimore MD 21205-2179. *Fax:* 410-955-2926

GROSSMAN, LAWRENCE I, MOLECULAR BIOLOGY, BIOCHEMISTRY. *Current Pos:* from assoc prof to prof molecular biol & genetics, 86-94, actg chmn, 92, ASSOC CHMN, WAYNE STATE UNIV, 92-, PROF & ASSOC DIR, CTR MOLECULAR MED & GENETICS, 94-, PROF INTERNAL MED, 94- *Personal Data:* b New York, NY, Nov 15, 39; m 70, Esta Shaftel; c Daniel. *Educ:* City Col New York, BS, 61; Albert Einstein Col Med, PhD(genetics & biochem), 70. *Prof Exp:* Res fel biol, Calif Inst Technol, 70-74; asst prof biochem, Sch Med, Wayne State Univ, 74-78; asst prof biol, Univ Mich, 78-85; sr ed, Sci Mag, 85-86. *Concurrent Pos:* Fel, Jane Coffin Childs Mem Fund Med Res fel, 71-73; assoc ed, Theoret & Appl Electrophoresis, 89-93, consult ed, McGraw-Hill Encycl Sci & Technol, 88-, contrib ed, Sci, 87-95; mem, sci adv comt molecular biol & genetics, Am Cancer Soc, 91. *Mem:* Am Soc Biochem & Molecular Biol; Am Soc Microbiol; Am Electrophoresis Soc (treas, 89-); Sigma Xi; AAAS. *Res:* Nucleic acids; structure and function and evolution of mitochondrial DNA; cytochrome c oxidase genes. *Mailing Add:* Wayne State Univ Sch Med Ctr Molecular Med & Genetics Dept 540 East Canfield Detroit MI 48201. *Fax:* 313-577-5218; *E-Mail:* lg@cmb.biosci.wayne.edu

GROSSMAN, LAWRENCE M(ORTON), NUCLEAR ENGINEERING. *Current Pos:* instr mech eng, Univ Calif, Berkeley, 44-46, from lectr to assoc prof, 46-53, chmn dept, 69-74, FAC NUCLEAR ENG, UNIV CALIF, BERKELEY, 59-, CHMN DEPT, 69- *Personal Data:* b New York, NY, Aug 2, 22; m 52; c 1. *Educ:* City Col NY, BChE, 42; Univ Calif, MS, 44, PhD(eng sci), 48. *Prof Exp:* Chem engr, E I du Pont de Nemours & Co, Inc, NY, 42-43. *Concurrent Pos:* Fulbright lectr, Delft, 52-53; NSF sr res fel, 61-62, NATO fel, Saclay Nuclear Res Ctr, France, 74. *Mem:* AAAS; Soc Indust & Appl Math; Am Nuclear Soc. *Res:* Nuclear reactor theory; neutron transport; reactor dynamics and control. *Mailing Add:* 140 Avenida Dr Berkeley CA 94708

GROSSMAN, LEONARD N(ATHAN), lighting science, nuclear fuel science, for more information see previous edition

GROSSMAN, MICHAEL, POPULATION GENETICS, QUANTITATIVE GENETICS. *Current Pos:* From asst prof to assoc prof, 69-85, assoc dean, Grad Col, 89-92, PROF, UNIV ILL, 85- *Personal Data:* b New York, NY, Dec 21, 40; m 70, Margaret Rosso; c Aaron W & Daniel B. *Educ:* City Col NY, BS, 62; Va Polytech Inst & State Univ, MS, 65; Purdue Univ, PhD(genetics), 69. *Concurrent Pos:* Vis prof, Plant Breeding Inst, Nat Inst Agr Technol, Castelar, Arg, 70, Fac Animal Husb, Gadjah Mada Univ, Yogyakarta, Indonesia, 74 & Dept Animal Breeding, Agr Univ Wageningen, Neth, 86-87 & 93-94; Danforth Assoc. *Mem:* Am Dairy Sci Asn; Am Soc Animal Sci; Am Genetic Asn; Biomet Soc; Genetics Soc Am; AAAS. *Res:* Theoretical population and quantitative genetics; mathmatical modeling in the life sciences. *Mailing Add:* Dept Animal Sci Univ Ill Urbana Campus 1207 W Gregory Dr Urbana IL 61801-3838. *Fax:* 217-333-8286; *E-Mail:* mikeg@uiuc.edu

GROSSMAN, NATHANIEL, MATHEMATICS. *Current Pos:* asst prof, 66-70, assoc prof, 70-76, PROF MATH, UNIV CALIF, LOS ANGELES, 76- *Personal Data:* b Chicago, Ill, Apr 17, 37; m 60; c 2. *Educ:* Calif Inst Technol, BS, 58; Univ Minn, PhD(math), 64. *Prof Exp:* Asst, Inst Advan Study, 64-66. *Mem:* AAAS; Am Math Soc; Math Asn Am; Am Geophys Union. *Res:* Differential geometry of manifolds; Riemannian geometry in the large; geodesy. *Mailing Add:* Dept Math Univ Calif Los Angeles CA 90095-1555

GROSSMAN, NORMAN, AERONAUTICAL ENGINEERING. *Current Pos:* MGT CONSULT, 81- *Personal Data:* b New York, NY, Nov 3, 22. *Educ:* NY Univ, BAeroE, 43, MS, 48, PhD(math), 58. *Prof Exp:* Prin res engr, Repub Aviation, Fairchild Industs, Inc, 46-51, asst proj engr, 51-55, staff engr, Fairchild Repub Co, 55-58, chief electronics eng, 58-62, mgr res div, 62-64, chief engr, 64-68, asst gen mgr, 68-69, vpres, 69-76, pres, 76-78, chmn & chief exec officer, 78-80. *Concurrent Pos:* Lectr grad math, Adelphi Col, 51-53; adj prof, Grad Ctr, Polytech Inst Brooklyn, Farmingdale Campus, 67-75. *Mem:* Am Inst Aeronaut & Astronaut; Math Asn Am. *Res:* Design, production and test of high performance military aircraft and aircraft systems. *Mailing Add:* 70 E Tenth St Apt PHL New York NY 10003

GROSSMAN, PERRY L, MECHANICAL ENGINEERING, APPLIED MECHANICS. *Current Pos:* from asst prof to assoc prof, 67-, PROF MECH ENG, COOPER UNION ALBERT NERKEN SCH ENG *Personal Data:* b Brooklyn, NY, Jan 27, 38; m 59; c 2. *Educ:* Polytech Inst Brooklyn, BME, 59, MSME, 63, PhD(mech eng), 68. *Prof Exp:* Instr mech eng, Polytech Inst Brooklyn, 62 66. *Concurrent Pos:* Nat Sci Res initiation grant, 70-71. *Mem:* AAAS. *Res:* Nonlinear vibrations of spherical shells; flexural vibration and pulse-excited response of plates elastically supported at the surface. *Mailing Add:* Dept Mech Eng Cooper Union Albert Nerken Sch Eng 51 Aster Pl New York NY 10003

GROSSMAN, ROBERT G, NEUROSURGERY, NEUROPHYSIOLOGY. *Current Pos:* PROF & CHMN, DEPT NEUROSURG, BAYLOR COL MED, HOUSTON, 80- *Personal Data:* b New York, NY, Jan 24, 33; m 55; c 3. *Educ:* Swarthmore Col, BA, 53; Columbia Univ, MD, 57. *Prof Exp:* From instr to assoc prof, Univ Tex Southwestern Med Sch, 63-69; from assoc prof to prof neurol surg, Albert Einstein Col Med, 69-73; prof neurosurg & chmn div, Univ Tex Med Br Galveston, 73-80. *Concurrent Pos:* Attend neurosurgeon, Univ Tex Med Br Hosp, 73- *Mem:* Am Asn Neurol Surg; Soc Univ Surg; Am Col Surg; Am Electroencephalog Soc; Cong Neurol Surg; Sigma Xi. *Res:* Neurophysiology of cortical neurons and neuroglial cells. *Mailing Add:* Baylor Col Med 6560 Fannin Suite 944 Houston TX 77030-2706

GROSSMAN, SEBASTIAN PETER, PSYCHOBIOLOGY. *Current Pos:* assoc prof biopsychol, 64-67; PROF BIOPSYCHOL & CHMN, UNIV CHICAGO, 67- *Personal Data:* b Coburg, Bavaria, Jan 21, 34; m 55, Lore Bensel. *Educ:* Univ Md, BA, 58; Yale Univ, MS, 59, PhD(psychol), 61. *Prof Exp:* Asst prof physiol psychol, Univ Iowa, 61-64. *Concurrent Pos:* Ed, Physiol & Behav, 66-, Commun Behav Biol, 67-79, Psychopharmacologia, 69-79, J Life Sci, 70-, Biochem Psychol, 70-, Pharmacol Biochem Behav, 73-94 & Neurosci Biobehav Rev, 77-94. *Mem:* Fel AAAS; fel Am Psychol Asn; Am Physiol Soc; Royal Soc Med. *Res:* Physiology and pharmacology of brain mechanisms which mediate psychological processes related to motivation. *Mailing Add:* Dept Psychol Univ Chicago 5848 S University Ave Chicago IL 60637. *Fax:* 773-702-0886; *E-Mail:* lore@midway.uchicago.edu

GROSSMAN, STANLEY I, APPLIED MATHEMATICS. *Current Pos:* ASSOC PROF MATH, UNIV MONT, 75- *Personal Data:* b New York, NY, Sept 25, 42; m 65; c 2. *Educ:* Cornell Univ, BA, 64; Univ Calif, Los Angeles, MA, 65; Brown Univ, PhD(appl math), 69. *Prof Exp:* Asst lectr math, Gothenburg Univ, 65-66; asst prof, McGill Univ, 69-75. *Concurrent Pos:* NSF-Romanian Acad Sci res grant, Iasi, Romania, 71. *Mem:* Am Math Soc; Math Soc Can; Soc Indust & Appl Math. *Res:* Volterra integral and integrodifferential equations; existence, uniqueness, stability and properties of solutions. *Mailing Add:* Dept Math Univ Mont Missoula MT 59812-1032

GROSSMAN, STEVEN HARRIS, PROTEIN FOLDING, FLUORESCENCE. *Current Pos:* ASSOC PROF CHEM, UNIV SFLA, 81- *Personal Data:* b New York, NY, May 18, 45; m 70; c 2. *Educ:* NY Univ, BA, 67; Purdue Univ, PhD(biochem), 72. *Prof Exp:* Fel biochem, Univ Wis, 72-74; res scientist clin chem, Union Carbide Corp, 74-76; asst prof, Univ Southwest La, 78-81. *Mem:* NY Acad Sci; Am Chem Soc; Am Soc Biol Chemists. *Res:* Mechanisms of protein folding, particularly multimeric proteins. *Mailing Add:* Chem Sci 228 Univ SFla 4202 E Fowler Ave Tampa FL 33620-9951

GROSSMAN, WILLIAM, ANIMAL PHYSIOLOGY. *Current Pos:* CHIEF CARDIOL & PROF MED, SCH MED, UNIV CALIF, SAN FRANCISCO, 97- *Personal Data:* b New York, NY, May 24, 40; m 64, Melanie Durand; c Jennifer, Edward & Jessica. *Educ:* Columbia Univ, BA, 61; Yale Univ Sch Med, MD, 65; Am Bd Internal Med, dipl & Subspeciality Cardiovasc Dis, dipl. *Prof Exp:* From asst prof to assoc prof med, Univ NC, Sch Med, Chapel Hill, 71-75; dir, Cardiac Catheterization Lab, Peter Bent Brigham Hosp, 75-81, from assoc prof to prof med Harvard Med Sch, 75-94; chief cardiol, Beth Israel Hosp, 81-94; exec dir to vpres, Clin Res, Merck & Co, 94-96. *Concurrent Pos:* Intern Med, Peter Bent Brigham Hosp, Boston, Mass, 65-66, asst resident med, Harvard Med Sch, 68-69, res fel med, 69-71; peace corps physician, New Delhi, India, 66-68; dir, C V Richardson Cardiac Catheterization Lab, NC Mem Hosp, 71-75; estab investr, Am Heart Asn. *Mem:* Am Soc Clin Invest; Asn Am Physicians; Am Physiol Soc; Am Heart Asn; fel Am Col Cardiol; Am Fed Clin Res; Int Soc Heart Res. *Res:* Congestive heart failure; the role of defective heart muscle relaxation; cardiac hypertrophy; conducted large-scale clinical trials assessing the effects of potent platelet inhibitors in acute coronary ischemic syndromes. *Mailing Add:* Chief Cardiol Med Ctr Univ Calif 505 Parnassus Ave San Francisco CA 94143-0124

GROSSMAN, WILLIAM ELDERKIN LEFFINGWELL, ANALYTICAL CHEMISTRY. *Current Pos:* asst prof chem, 66-74, ASSOC PROF CHEM, HUNTER COL, 74- *Personal Data:* b New York, NY, May 4, 38; m 69; c 3. *Educ:* Princeton Univ, AB, 59; Cornell Univ, PhD(analytical chem), 64. *Prof Exp:* Assoc spectrochem, Inst Atomic Res, Ames Lab, AEC, 63-65; assoc, Univ York, Eng, 65-66. *Mem:* Soc Appl Spectros; Optical Soc Am; Am Chem Soc. *Res:* Raman spectroscopy. *Mailing Add:* Hunter Col 695 Park Ave New York NY 10021-0367

GROSSMANN, ELIHU D(AVID), SAFETY, TOXIC WASTE DISPOSAL. *Current Pos:* Asst, 51-52, from instr to assoc prof, 52-81, PROF CHEM ENG, DREXEL UNIV, 81- *Personal Data:* b Philadelphia, Pa, Nov 29, 27; m 54, Doris Martin; c 3. *Educ:* Drexel Inst Technol, BS, 51, MS, 56; Univ Pa, PhD, 65. *Concurrent Pos:* Consult, US Army, 61-83, var chem, drug & environ co, 52- *Mem:* Am Chem Soc; Am Soc Eng Educ; Am Inst Chem Engrs; Nat Fire Protection Asn; Am Soc Univ Professors; Sigma Xi. *Res:* Abatement of toxic chemical releases the processing conditions required for some hazardous chemical reactions; thermodynamics of solutions; removal of deposited carcinogens from work clothes; process analysis. *Mailing Add:* Dept Chem Eng Drexel Univ 32nd & Chestnut St Philadelphia PA 19104. *E-Mail:* grossman@obis.drexel.edu

GROSSMANN, IGNACIO E, PROCESS OPTIMIZATION, PROCESS SYNTHESIS. *Current Pos:* prof chem eng, 79-90, DEAN & PROF, CHEM ENG, CARNEGIE-MELLON UNIV, 90-, DEPT HEAD, CHEM ENG, 94- *Personal Data:* b Mexico City, Mex, Nov 12, 49; m 77, Blanca Espinal; c Claudia, Andrew & Thomas. *Educ:* Univ Ibero Am, Mexico City, BS, 74; Imp Col, London, MS, 75, PhD(chem eng), 77. *Honors & Awards:* Robert W Vaughn lectr, 84; Presidential Young Investr Award, NSF, 84; Comput Chem Eng Award, Am Inst chem Engrs, 94. *Prof Exp:* Res & develop engr, Mex Inst Petrol, 78-79. *Concurrent Pos:* Acad trustee, CACHE Corp, 84-; Mary Upson vis prof eng, Cornell Univ, 86-87; vis prof, Ctr Poveis Systs Eng, Imperial Col, London, 93-94. *Mem:* Am Inst Chem Engrs; Opers Res Soc Am; Sigma Xi; Am Chem Soc. *Res:* Optimization of chemical processes with particular emphasis on systematic synthesis of chemical process, flowsheets,and multiperiod planning and scheduling of process operations using mixed-integer programming techniques. *Mailing Add:* Dept Chem Eng Carnegie-Mellon Univ Pittsburgh PA 15213. *Fax:* 412-268-7139; *E-Mail:* grossmann@cmu.edu

GROSSMANN, WILLIAM, AERONAUTICAL & ASTRONAUTICAL ENGINEERING. *Current Pos:* sr res scientist, 74-80, from asst dir to assoc dir, Magnetic Fluid Dynamics Div, 74-87, RES PROF, COURANT INST MATH SCI, 80-; DIV MGR & CHIEF SCIENTIST, APPL PHYSICS OPER, SCI APPLN INT CORP, 87- *Personal Data:* b Richmond, Va, Aug 25, 37; m 74; c 2. *Educ:* Va Polytech Inst, BS, 58, MS, 61, PhD(aerospace eng), 64. *Prof Exp:* Aerospace technologist, Langley Res Ctr, NASA, 58-65; assoc res scientist, Courant Inst Math Sci, NY Univ, 64-67; asst prof appl math, Richmond Col, NY, 67-69; sr scientist, Max Planck Inst Plasma Physics, 69-74. *Concurrent Pos:* Lectr, Inst Electronics, Univ Padua, Italy, 71-73; vis sr fel, Ctr for Theoret Physics, Univ Md, 74-75; vis staff mem, Los Alamos Nat Lab, 73-; consult, Bell Aerosysts, 67-69, Sci Appln Inc, 78- & Princeton Plasma Physics Lab, 80-; adj prof, Dept Appl Sci, NY Univ, 78-; univ assoc & mem evaluation panel on alt fusion concepts, Dept Energy, 81; dir plasma physics, Int Ctr Theoret Physics, Trieste, Italy, 83- *Mem:* Am Phys Soc. *Res:* Problems in physics and engineering of controlled fusion research; magnetohydrodynamics; politics and history of science and tec; plasma physics and fluid dynamics. *Mailing Add:* 2853 Ontario Rd NW #322 Washington DC 20009

GROSSO, ANTHONY J, electronics, computer science, for more information see previous edition

GROSSO, JOHN A, PROCESS DEVELOPMENT, PLANT START-UPS. *Current Pos:* RES GROUP LEADER, BRISTOL-MYERS SQUIBB, 90- *Personal Data:* b Hollis, NY, Nov 2, 55; m 83; c 2. *Educ:* New York Univ, BA, 76; Purdue Univ, PhD(med chem), 80. *Prof Exp:* Sr res chemist, Ash-Stevens Inc, 80; res investr, E R Squibb & Sons, 80-86, sr res investr, 86-90. *Concurrent Pos:* Consult. *Mem:* Am Chem Soc; AAAS. *Res:* Preparation and development of organic compounds to be administered as pharmaceuticals, cardiovascular, antimalarial sweetening; anti inflammatory and CNS agents. *Mailing Add:* Bristol-Myers Squibb Co One Squibb Dr PO Box 191 New Brunswick NJ 08903-0191

GROSSWEINER, LEONARD IRWIN, PHOTOBIOLOGY, PHOTOMEDICINE. *Current Pos:* assoc prof, 57-62, chmn dept, 70-81, PROF PHYSICS, ILL INST TECHNOL, 62- *Personal Data:* b Atlantic City, NJ, Aug 16, 24; m 51, Bess Tornheim; c Karen A, Jane (deceased), James B & Eric W. *Educ:* City Col New York, BChE, 47; Ill Inst Technol, MS, 51, PhD(physics), 54. *Prof Exp:* Asst, Argonne Nat Lab, 47-51, from asst physicist to assoc physicist, 51-57. *Concurrent Pos:* Consult, Ravenswood Hosp, 83-; mem, US Nat Comt Photobiol, 78-80, chmn, 80-81; vis prof radiol, Col Med, Stanford Univ, 83-89, physics, Col Med, Univ Ill, 83-, biomed eng, Northwestern Univ Tech Inst, 87-; secy-treas, Div Biol Physics, Am Phys Soc, 72-76, vchmn, 76-77, chmn, 77-78. *Mem:* Fel Am Phys Soc; fel NY Acad Sci; Am Soc Photobiol (secy-treas, 81-86, pres, 87-88, past pres, 88-89); fel Am Soc Lasers Surg & Med. *Res:* Radiation biophysics; photobiology flash photolysis; pulse radiolysis; biological photosensitization; photodynamic tumor therapy; tissue optics and laser interactions with tissues. *Mailing Add:* 231 Wentworth Ave Glencoe IL 60022

GROSTIC, MARVIN FORD, ORGANIC CHEMISTRY. *Current Pos:* VPRES QUAL ASSURANCE, AVTECH LABS, INC, 90- *Personal Data:* b Webberville, Mich, June 16, 26; m 51; c 3. *Educ:* Albion Col, AB, 50; Univ Idaho, PhD(org chem), 65; Univ Ill, 64-65. *Prof Exp:* Infrared spectroscopist, Upjohn Co, 53-61, mass spectroscopist, 64-70, mgr chem prod control, 70-85, dir prod control, 85-86; pharmaceut consult, 86-90. *Concurrent Pos:* Mem rev comt, US Pharmacopeia, 75, 80 & 85. *Mem:* Am Chem Soc; Am Soc Mass Spectrometry. *Res:* Addition to bicyclo hexene-2; mass spectroscopy. *Mailing Add:* 3882 Greenleaf Circle Kalamazoo MI 49008-2509

GROSVENOR, CLARK EDWARD, ZOOLOGY, ENDOCRINOLOGY. *Current Pos:* from asst prof to assoc prof, 59-67, NIH SR RES FEL, UNIV TENN, MEMPHIS, 59-, PROF PHYSIOL, 67-, INSTR BIOCHEM/MOLECULAR BIOL, 95- *Personal Data:* b Piqua, Ohio, May 9, 28; m 50; c 6. *Educ:* Otterbein Col, BS, 50; Univ Cincinnati, MS, 52, PhD(zool), 55. *Prof Exp:* Instr biol, Col Pharm, Univ Cincinnati, 53-54, instr endocrinol, 54-55; asst prof biol, Univ Tenn, 55-56; NIH fel, Univ Mo, 56-59. *Mem:* AAAS; Soc Exp Biol & Med; Am Physiol Soc; Endocrine Soc. *Res:* Neuroendocrinology; lactational physiology. *Mailing Add:* Dept Molecular & Cell Biol Pa State Univ Rm 3-Althouse Labs University Park PA 16802-0001

GROSVENOR, GILBERT MELVILLE, GEOGRAPHY, JOURNALISM. *Current Pos:* Vpres, Nat Geog Soc, 66-80, assoc ed, 67-70, ed, 70-80, pres, 80-96, CHMN BD, NAT GEOG SOC, 87- *Personal Data:* b Washington, DC, May 5, 31; m 79, Wiley Jarman; c Gilbert Hovey II, Alexandra Rowland & Graham Dabney. *Educ:* Yale Univ, BA, 54. *Hon Degrees:* D Pub Serv, George Washington Univ, 83; LLD, Col Wooster, Ohio, 83; LHD, Univ Colo, 83, Curry Col, 84, William & Mary Col, 87, Miami Univ, Oxford Ohio, 88, Syracuse Univ, 89, Rhode Island Col, 91, Old Dominion Univ, 93 & Clark Univ, 95. *Honors & Awards:* Pres Medal, George Washington Univ, 93; Golden Plate Award, Am Acad Achievement, 96. *Concurrent Pos:* Trustee, Nat Wildflower Res Ctr, Fed City Coun, B F Saul Real Estate Trust Saul Ctrs Inc, NY Zool Soc; emer chmn & found bd, Alexander Graham Bell Asn Deaf; bd dirs, Am Farmland Trust, White House Hist Asn, Conserv Fund, Marriot Int Inc, Saul Ctrs Inc & Ethyl Corp. *Mem:* Asn Am Geographers. *Mailing Add:* Nat Geog Soc 1145 17th St NW Washington DC 20036

GROSVENOR, NILES E(ARL), MINING ENGINEERING. *Current Pos:* PRES, GROSVENOR ENG CO, 85- *Personal Data:* b Carbondale, Pa, Feb 14, 22; m 42; c 4. *Educ:* Colo Sch Mines, EM, 50, MS, 52. *Prof Exp:* From instr mining to prof, Colo Sch Mines, 52-70; sr vpres, Gates Eng Co, 70-85. *Mem:* Am Soc Eng Educ; Am Inst Mining, Metall & Petrol Engrs. *Res:* Rock mechanics; mining. *Mailing Add:* 5200 Aspen Dr Littleton CO 80123

GROSZ, BARBARA JEAN, COMPUTER SCIENCE. *Current Pos:* GORDON MCKAY PROF COMPUT SCI, DIV APPL SCI, HARVARD UNIV, 86- *Personal Data:* b Philadelphia, Pa, July 21, 48. *Educ:* Cornell Univ, AB, 69; Univ Calif, Berkeley, MA, 71, PhD(comput sci), 77. *Prof Exp:* Res mathematician, Artificial Intel Ctr, SRI Int, 73-77, comput scientist, 81-82, sr comput scientist, 81-82, prog dir nat lang & representation, 82-83, sr staff scientist, 83-86. *Concurrent Pos:* Organizer & chair panel on discourse, Workshop on Theoretical Issue Nat Lang Processing, Univ Ill, Champaign, 78; rev prog proposals, NSF; vis fac, Dept Comput Sci, Stanford Univ, 82, consult assoc prof comput sci & ling, 84-85, comput sci, 85-87; vis scholar, Dept Comput & Info Sci, Univ Pa, 82; co-founder, mem exec comt & prin researcher, Ctr Study Lang & Info, Stanford Univ & SRI Int, 83-86; conf chair, Int Joint Conf Artificial Intel, chair bd trustees, IJCAI Inc, 89-91. *Mem:* Fel AAAS; fel Am Asn Artificial Intel (pres, 93-); Asn Comput Ling. *Mailing Add:* Div Eng & Appl Sci Harvard Univ Cambridge MA 02138

GROSZ, HANUS JIRI, PSYCHIATRY. *Current Pos:* RETIRED. *Personal Data:* b Brno, Czech, Feb 16, 24; US citizen; m 54, Kirsten Halling; c Anita, Martin & Peter. *Educ:* Univ Wales, BSc, 50, MB BCh, 53; Royal Col Physicians & Surgeons, DPM, 61; Am Bd Psychiat & Neurol, dipl & cert psychiat, 67; Am Col Physicians, FACP, 67; Royal Col Psychiatrists, MRCP, 74. *Honors & Awards:* Achievement Award, John Shaw Billings Hist Med Soc, 69. *Prof Exp:* Intern surg, E Glamorgan Hosp, 53; intern int med, Swansea Gen Hosp, 53-54; resident, Morriston Hosp, Gt Brit, 54-55; resident psychiat, Warren State Hosp, 55-56; sr res fel, Inst Psychiat Res, Med Ctr, Ind Univ, 56-58; USPHS fel & resident neurol, Albert Einstein Col Med, 58-60; resident psychiat, Maudsley & Bethlehem Royal Hosp, London, Eng, 60-62; from asst prof to assoc prof psychiat, Sch Med, Ind Univ, Indianapolis, 62-68, prof & chief psychiat, 68-93, chief psychobiol sect, 72-93. *Concurrent Pos:* Consult, Vet Admin Hosp, 63, Ind Girls' Sch, 64, Div Alcoholism, Ind Dept Ment Health, 66 & Am Asn Foreign Med Grads, 68; mem bd dirs, Community Addiction Serv Agency, Inc, 70; dir alcoholism-drug addiction res, Inst Psychiat Res, 70; pres, Psychiat Clins of Ind, 85-; emer prof clin psychiat. *Mem:* AAAS; Am Psychiat Asn; fel Am Col Physicians; Royal Col Psychiat. *Res:* Alcohol and drug addiction; psychosomatic disorders; delinquency; group process and group interaction. *Mailing Add:* 7233 Lakeside Dr Indianapolis IN 46278-1616

GROSZ, OLIVER, chemistry; deceased, see previous edition for last biography

GROSZMANN, ROBERTO JOSE, GASTROENTEROLOGY. *Current Pos:* asst prof, 75-, PROF MED, YALE UNIV. *Personal Data:* b Buenos Aires, Arg, Aug 17, 39; m 65; c 2. *Educ:* Buenos Aires Univ, BS, 58, MD, 64. *Honors & Awards:* Career Develop Award, Vet Admin, 76. *Prof Exp:* Instr med, Boston Univ, 68-69 & Georgetown Univ, 69-71; asst prof, Buenos Aires Univ, 71-75. *Concurrent Pos:* NIH fel, Arg, 64-65; fel hemodynamics, Georgetown Univ, 69-71 & Med Inst Nat Health, France, 73; investr, Nat Res Coun, Arg, 71-75. *Mem:* Am Asn Study Liver. *Res:* Liver circulation in relation to portal hypertension and cirrhosis of the liver. *Mailing Add:* 33 Pine Ridge Rd Woodbridge CT 06525

GROSZOS, STEPHEN JOSEPH, EDUCATIONAL & RESEARCH ADMINISTRATION. *Current Pos:* dean sci, Col DuPage, 67-70, dir instnl res, 70-80, dir res & planning, 80-82, EMER PROF, COL DUPAGE, 82-; CONSULT CHEMIST, 67- *Personal Data:* b Trenton, NJ, July 1, 20; m 46, Elizabeth F Shanks; c Mark S & Emily J (Ooms). *Educ:* NY Univ, AB, 46; Johns Hopkins Univ, AM, 48, PhD(chem), 51. *Prof Exp:* Instr & consult, Johns Hopkins Univ, 46-50; sr res scientist, Stamford Labs, Am Cyanamid Co, 50-57, mgr resin develop, Formica Corp Div, 57-59; tech dir, Richardson Co, 59-63, dir res & develop, 63-65; vpres, Packer Eng Assocs, Inc, 65-67. *Concurrent Pos:* Res chemist, Polaroid Corp, 49; vis prof, St Procopius Col, 67-68; mem, Ill Nursing Home Adminr Licensure Bd, 69-76; mem bd trustees, Col DuPage Found, 70-82, treas, 73-82; mem & secy bd dirs, Care-Tech, Inc, 73-76; mem, Bd Trustees, Piedmont Environ Ctr, 84-90, treas, 85-87, pres, 87-88; adj fac chem, Guilford Tech Community Col, 89- *Mem:* Am Chem Soc; Soc Plastics Engrs; Sigma Xi. *Res:* Chemistry of rosin, fatty acid derivatives, diazocompounds, aldoketene dimers, organometallics, mold metabolites; condensation and addition polymers; synthesis and study of properties as function of structure; polymers and plastics; molding compounds, laminates, adhesives, coatings, fibers and films. *Mailing Add:* 3843-D Johnson St High Point NC 27265-1372

GROT, WALTHER GUSTAV FREDRICH, ORGANIC POLYMER CHEMISTRY, ELECTROCHEMISTRY. *Current Pos:* TECH DIR, C G PROCESSING INC, 95- *Personal Data:* b Berlin, Ger, June 26, 29; m 57; c 3. *Educ:* Univ Gottingen, BC, 51; Marburg Univ, PhD(chem), 55. *Honors & Awards:* Castner Medal, Soc Chem Indust London, 85. *Prof Exp:* Sr res chemist, Res & Develop Lab, Belle Works, E I DuPont de Nemours & Co Inc, 56-60 & Plastics Dept, Exp Sta, 60-72, res assoc, Plastics Dept, Exp Sta Lab, 72-95. *Concurrent Pos:* Case Western fel, 80. *Mem:* Am Chem Soc; Ger Chem Soc. *Res:* Aliphatic organic chemistry; plastic intermediates; fluorocarbons; polymers; ion exchange membranes; applied electrochemistry. *Mailing Add:* PO Box 133 Rockland DE 19732. *Fax:* 610-388-6974; *E-Mail:* grot@a1.esvax.umc.dupont.com

GROTA, LEE J, PSYCHONEUROIMMUNOLOGY. *Current Pos:* asst prof, 65-71, ASSOC PROF PSYCHIAT & PSYCHOL, SCH MED & DENT, UNIV ROCHESTER, 71- *Personal Data:* b Sturgeon Bay, Wis, May 12, 37; m 59, Mary A Peterson; c Catherine, Steven, Michael & Carl. *Educ:* Marquette Univ, BS, 59; Purdue Univ, MS, 61, PhD(exp psychol), 63. *Prof Exp:* Trainee steroid biochem, Sch Med, Univ Utah, 63-65. *Concurrent Pos:* Vis assoc prof neurosci & psychiat, McMaster Univ, Hamilton, Ont, 77-87. *Mem:* Endocrine Soc; Int Soc Develop Psychobiol; Soc Neurosci; Psychoneuroimmunol Res Soc. *Res:* Neuroendocrinology; psychoneuroimmunology. *Mailing Add:* Dept Psychiat Univ Rochester Med Ctr Rochester NY 14642. *E-Mail:* ljgt@dbl.cc.rochester.edu

GROTCH, HOWARD, THEORETICAL PHYSICS. *Current Pos:* Mem physics fac, 67-76, PROF PHYSICS, PA STATE UNIV, 76- *Personal Data:* b Brooklyn, NY, May 29, 40; m 64; c 3. *Educ:* City Col New York, BS, 62; Cornell Univ, PhD(theoret physics), 67. *Concurrent Pos:* Vis prof, Univ Sussex, Universite d'Aix Marseille & Ben Gurion Univ, Univ Calif-Los Angeles, ITP Santa Barbara. *Mem:* Fel Am Phys Soc; Am Asn Physics Teachers. *Res:* Theoretical work in quantum electrodynamics and its application to atomic systems and to radiative level shifts; research on heavy quark-antiquark spectra and decays. *Mailing Add:* Dept Physics 104 Davey Lab Pa State Univ University Park PA 16802

GROTEFEND, ALAN CHARLES, PRINTING INKS, ADHESIVES. *Current Pos:* Chemist, Richardson Co, 66-69, Meyercord Co, 70-84, TECH DIR, MEYERCORD, 85- *Personal Data:* b Elmhurst, Ill, July 16, 42; m 75, Nancy J Haller; c Brian. *Educ:* Ariz State Univ, BS, 64. *Res:* Formulate inks, coatings and adhesives for gravure and screen printing heat transfer decals to decorate substrates such as glass, metal, wood, and plastics. *Mailing Add:* Meyercord Co 365 E North Ave Carol Stream IL 60188

GROTEN, BARNEY, POLYMER CHEMISTRY, ANALYTICAL CHEMISTRY. *Current Pos:* VPRES, ENERGY INT, INC, 91- *Personal Data:* b Brooklyn, NY, Oct 25, 33; m 55; c 3. *Educ:* Brooklyn Col, BS, 54; Purdue Univ, PhD(org chem), 61. *Prof Exp:* Chemist, Nickel Processing Corp, 55-56, Reaction Motors, Inc, 56-57; instr org chem, Purdue Univ, 57-59, fel, 60-61; sr chemist & group leader, Esso Res & Eng Co, Standard Oil Co, NJ, 61-66, sect head, Esso Res SA, Belg, 66-68, res planning adv, Esso Chem SA, 68-71, planning adv chem specialties, Esso Chem Europe, Inc, 71-73; sr staff adv, Exxon Chem Co, USA, La, 74-75, prod planner, Exxon Chem Co, USA, Houston, Tex, 75-77; sr staff adv, Exxon Chem Co, USA, La, 74-75, prod planner, Houston, Tex, 75-77; dir res & bus develop, Tex Eastern Corp, 77-87; exec vpres, Tex Eastern Develop Corp, 80-87; exec dir, Energy Ctr, Univ Okla, 87-91. *Concurrent Pos:* Secy & treas, Gulf Univ Res Consortium, 81-88. *Mailing Add:* Energy Int Inc 127 Bellevue Way SE Bellevue WA 98004. *Fax:* 425-455-0981; *E-Mail:* bgroten@energyint.com

GROTENHUIS, MARSHALL, PHYSICS, ENVIRONMENTAL SCIENCE & NUCLEAR ENGINEERING. *Current Pos:* RETIRED. *Personal Data:* b Oostburg, Wis, Oct 17, 18; m 46, Marilyn Johnson; c Susan, Alan, Judith & Brian. *Educ:* Milwaukee State Teachers Col, BS, 41; Marquette Univ, MS, 48. *Honors & Awards:* High Qual Award, Nuclear Regulatory Comn, 75; Meritorious Serv Award, Nuclear Regulatory Comn, 80. *Prof Exp:* Instr pub sch, Mich, 41-42; asst physics, Marquette Univ, 46-48, instr, 48-49; assoc physicist, reactor eng, Argonne Nat Lab, 49-56, asst dir, Int Sch, assoc dir, Int Inst, 59-64, dir, Off Indust Coop, 65-67, supt cent shop, 67-70, supt tech serv, 70-71; proj analyst, Div Radiol & Environ Protection, Nuclear Regulatory Comn, 71-75, sr proj mgr, Div Oper Reactors, 76-88. *Mem:* Am Nuclear Soc; Sigma Xi. *Res:* Industrial cooperation; reactor shielding and engineering; nuclear engineering education; nuclear reactor regulation; environmental statement review. *Mailing Add:* 415 Russell Ave Apt 505 Gaithersburg MD 20877-2849

GROTH, EDWARD JOHN, III, ASTROPHYSICS. *Current Pos:* From instr to assoc prof, 71-86, PROF PHYSICS, PRINCETON UNIV, 86- *Personal Data:* b St Louis, Mo, May 13, 46; m 75; c 2. *Educ:* Calif Inst Technol, BS, 68; Princeton Univ, PhD(physics), 71. *Concurrent Pos:* Alfred P Sloan res fel, 73. *Mem:* AAAS; Am Astron Soc; Am Phys Soc; Int Astron Union. *Res:* Pulsars; x-ray sources; space astronomy; evolution of galaxies and clusters of galaxies; systems operations; software. *Mailing Add:* Dept Physics Jadwin Hall Princeton Univ Princeton NJ 08544

GROTH, JAMES VERNON, PLANT PATHOLOGY. *Current Pos:* From asst prof to assoc prof, 72-85, PROF PLANT PATH, UNIV MINN, 85- *Personal Data:* b Minneapolis, Minn, July 13, 45; m 67; c 2. *Educ:* Univ Minn, BS, 67, MS, 69; Univ BC, PhD(bot), 74. *Mem:* Am Phytopath Soc; Sigma Xi. *Res:* Population genetics and quantitative descriptions of host-parasite relationships between higher plants and fungi; genetic diversity of plant pathogenic fungi; fungal pathogens of vegetables. *Mailing Add:* Dept Plant Path Univ Minn 495 Borlaugh Hall 1991 Upper Buford Cir St Paul MN 55108-6024. *Fax:* 612-625-9728; *E-Mail:* jamesg@puccini.crl.umn.edu

GROTH, JOYCE LORRAINE, ANALYTICAL CHEMISTRY. *Current Pos:* INSTR CHEM, NEW BRIT HIGH SCH, 69- *Personal Data:* b Meriden, Conn, Feb 3, 35; m 59, Richard H; c Eileen & Kathleen. *Educ:* Cent Conn State Col, BS, 57; Univ Conn, MS, 59, PhD(analytical chem), 64. *Prof Exp:* Res fel, Wesleyan Univ, 64; asst prof chem, Univ Conn, 64-69. *Concurrent Pos:* Eve lectr, Cent Conn State Col, 68-71. *Res:* Nonaqueous reference systems and polarography; coulometry. *Mailing Add:* 75 Coe Ave Meriden CT 06451-3854

GROTH, RICHARD HENRY, ENVIRONMENTAL CHEMISTRY. *Current Pos:* from assoc prof to prof, 70-92, chmn dept, 75-84, EMER PROF CHEM & LECTR, CENT CONN STATE COL, 92- *Personal Data:* b New Britain, Conn, Oct 14, 29; m 59, Joyce L Weaver; c Eileen & Kathleen. *Educ:* Conn State Col, BS, 51; Ohio State Univ, PhD(org chem), 56. *Prof Exp:* Res assoc, Off Naval Res, Duke Univ, 56-57; from asst prof to assoc prof chem, Univ Hartford, 57-70. *Concurrent Pos:* Consult, United Technol Corp, 61-91. *Mem:* AAAS; Am Chem Soc. *Res:* Gas analysis and chromatography; air pollution measurement technology; carbon dioxide-oxygen control in isolated atmospheres. *Mailing Add:* 75 Coe Ave Meriden CT 06451-3854

GROTHAUS, PAUL GERARD, BIOCONJUGATE CHEMISTRY, ANTIBODY MEDIATED PRODRUG TARGETING CANCER THERAPY. *Current Pos:* GROUP LEADER CHEM, HAWAII BIOTECHNOL GROUP, 88- *Personal Data:* b St Louis, Mo, July 28, 55; m 77, Coraleen T Valdez; c Nina. *Educ:* Creighton Univ Nebr, BS, 77; Purdue Univ Indiana, PhD(org chem), 83. *Prof Exp:* Fel, Univ Wash, 83-84; sr res chemist, Monsanto Agr Co, 84-88. *Concurrent Pos:* Adj asst prof, Cancer Res Ctr Hawaii, 92- *Mem:* Am Chem Soc; AAAS. *Res:* Targeted delivery of cytotoxic natural products or derivatives to tumors and the development of specific monoclonal antibodies to natural products undergoing evaluation as anti-cancer agents. *Mailing Add:* 99-193 Aiea Heights Dr Aiea HI 96701. *E-Mail:* pgrothaus@hibotech.com

GROTHAUS, ROGER HARRY, MEDICAL ENTOMOLOGY. *Current Pos:* MEM STAFF & MGR ENTOM RES, S C JOHNSON & SON, INC, 82- *Personal Data:* b Hamilton, Ohio, Oct 13, 36; m 58; c 2. *Educ:* Earlham Col, BA, 55; Purdue Univ, MS, 62; Okla State Univ, PhD(med entom), 67; Am Registry Prof Entomologists, cert. *Prof Exp:* Chief training div entom, Navy Dis Vector Ecol Control Ctr, Alameda, Calif, 61-64; res entomologist, USN, 64-67, chief opers div, Navy Dis Vector Ecol Control Ctr, Jacksonville, Fla, 67-69, sr med entomologist, Naval Support Activ, Vietnam, 69-70, chief entom div, Naval Med Field Res Lab, Camp Lejeune, NC, 70-75; res liaison officer, Dept Defense, USDA, 75-79, asst exec secy, Armed Forces Pest Mgt Bd, 79-82. *Mem:* Asn Mil Surgeons US; Entom Soc Am; Am Mosquito Control Asn. *Res:* General arthropod ecology and urban entomology. *Mailing Add:* S C Johnson & Son Inc Mail Sta 402 Racine WI 53403

GROTHEER, MORRIS PAUL, ELECTROCHEMISTRY, INDUSTRIAL ELECTROCHEMISTRY. *Current Pos:* RETIRED. *Personal Data:* b Pittsburg, Kans, Dec 15, 28; m 54, Louise Nelson; c Dynnell G (Hein), Timothy, Carla G (Peterman), Sharon G (Strum) & Kathryn. *Educ:* Pittsburg State Univ, BS, 50, MS, 51; Kans State Univ, PhD(analytical chem), 57. *Prof Exp:* Res chemist, Columbia Southern Chem Co, 57-59; sr chemist, Chem Div, Pittsburgh Plate Glass Co, 59-62; supvr electrom develop, Hooker Chem & Plastics Corp, 62-70, mgr sales & mkt, Chlor-Alkali Systs, 70-73, tech mgr, 73-79, mgr com develop, 79-81, prin process engr, Electrochem Div, 81-82, mgr Electrochem Sect, 82-84, tech prog mgr, 84-88, Process Technol, 88-90; mgr, Electrochem Sect, Kerr McGee Corp, 82-84, tech prog mgr, 84-88, dir, Process Technol, 88-90, mgr, Chem Res & Develop, 90-93. *Concurrent Pos:* Consult, 93- *Mem:* Electrochem Soc; Am Chem Soc; Sigma Xi; Am Inst Chem Engrs. *Res:* Fundamental and applied electrochemical research, primarily in brine electrolysis for the production of chlorine, caustic, chlorates and perchlorates; electrolytic manganese dioxide and manganese metal; wide variety of inorganic processes. *Mailing Add:* 3808 Melanie Circle Urbandale IA 50322-2142

GROTJAN, HARVEY EDWARD, JR, ENDOCRINOLOGY, REPRODUCTIVE BIOLOGY. *Current Pos:* ASSOC PROF ANIMAL SCI, UNIV NEBR, 88- *Personal Data:* b Moberly, Mo, July 31, 47; m 69, E Gayle Kothe; c 2. *Educ:* Univ Mo, Columbia, BS, 69, MS, 71; Univ Kans Med Ctr, PhD(physiol), 75. *Prof Exp:* Fel reproductive med, Med Sch, Univ Tex, Houston, 75-77, asst prof, 77-83; assoc prof physiol & pharmacol, Univ SDak, 83-88. *Mem:* Endocrine Soc; AAAS; Soc Study Reproduction; Am Soc Androl; Sigma Xi. *Res:* Biochemistry of the anterior pituitary gonadotropins luteinizing hormone and follicle-stimulating hormone; regulation of gonadal function. *Mailing Add:* Animal Sci Dept Univ Nebr Lincoln NE 68583-0908

GROTTA, HENRY MONROE, ORGANIC CHEMISTRY. *Current Pos:* INDEPENDENT CONSULT, 85- *Personal Data:* b New York, NY, Apr 4, 23; m 48, Mary Littlefield; c Barbara, Virginia, John, Julia & Sarah. *Educ:* NY Univ, BA, 43; Ohio State Univ, PhD(chem), 50. *Prof Exp:* Res chemist org high polymers, Rohm and Haas Co, 50-54; from res chemist to sr chemist, Battelle Mem Inst, 54-68, proj leader, 68-85. *Mem:* Am Chem Soc. *Res:* Synthetic organic chemistry; vinyl polymerization; heterocyclic compounds; coal conversion reactions; agricultural chemicals; hazardous waste treatment. *Mailing Add:* 13238 Miller Rd Mt Vernon OH 43050-9417. *Fax:* 740-392-4907

GROTTE, JEFFREY HARLOW, APPLIED MATHEMATICS, OPERATIONS RESEARCH. *Current Pos:* Mem res staff, 74-83, dep dir, Prog Anal Div, 83-84, DEP DIR, STRATEGY FORCES & RESOURCES DIV, INST DEFENSE ANALYSIS, 84- *Personal Data:* b Youngstown, Ohio, Jan 16, 47; m 73; c 2. *Educ:* Mass Inst Technol, BS, 69; Cornell Univ, MS, 70, PhD(appl math), 74. *Concurrent Pos:* Asst prof lectr, George Wash Univ, 76. *Mem:* AAAS; Soc Indust & Appl Math; Opers Res Soc Am. *Res:* Military applications of operations research; nonlinear optimization; game theory; mathematical aspects of arms control; decision support. *Mailing Add:* Inst Defense Anal 1801 N Beauregard St Alexandria VA 22311-1772. *Fax:* 703-845-2255; *E-Mail:* jgrotte@ida.org

GROTZ, LEONARD CHARLES, PHYSICAL CHEMISTRY. *Current Pos:* assoc prof, 69-74, PROF CHEM, UNIV WIS-WAUKESHA, 74- *Personal Data:* b Chicago, Ill, Nov 8, 27; m 54; c 3. *Educ:* Northwestern Univ, BS, 49; Univ Calif, PhD(phys chem), 52. *Prof Exp:* Res chemist, Glidden Co, 52-54; res fel, Univ Minn, 54-55; res chemist, Union Carbide Chem Co Div, Union Carbide Corp, 55-59; from asst prof to assoc prof chem, Univ Wis-Milwaukee, 59-66; prof, Parsons Col, 66-69. *Concurrent Pos:* Instr, WVa State Col, 57-59. *Mem:* AAAS; Am Chem Soc; Soc Col Sci Teachers; Nat Sci Teachers Asn. *Res:* Surface and polymer chemistry; chemical education. *Mailing Add:* 2701 Lander Lane Waukesha WI 53188

GROTZINGER, PAUL JOHN, SURGERY. *Current Pos:* med dir & chief surgeon, 60-86, EMER MED DIT & CHIEF SURGEON, AM ONCOL HOSP, 86-; PROF CLIN SURG, UNIV PA, 68- *Personal Data:* b Philadelphia, Pa, Oct 23, 18; m 52; c 3. *Educ:* Muhlenberg Col, BS, 39; Hahnemann Med Col, MD, 43. *Prof Exp:* From asst prof to assoc prof surg, Hahnemann Med Col, 50-61, clin prof, 61-68. *Concurrent Pos:* Attend surgeon, Jeanes Hosp, 63- *Mem:* AMA; fel Am Col Surg. *Res:* Cancer and its clinical treatment. *Mailing Add:* 2121 Valley Rd Huntingdon Valley PA 19006-6003

GROUPE, VINCENT, VIROLOGY. *Current Pos:* vpres to pres, 80-89, EMER SCI DIR, NEW LIFE FOUND, 89- *Personal Data:* b Philadelphia, Pa, Sept 13, 18; m 42, Gerry Nash; c David V & Lawrence N. *Educ:* Wesleyan Univ, BA, 39; Univ Pa, PhD(bact), 42. *Prof Exp:* Asst influenza lab, Children's Hosp, Pa, 39-42; from asst bacteriologist to sr bacteriologist, E R Squibb & Sons, NJ, 42-44; res assoc, Squibb Inst Med Res, 44-47; assoc prof virol in animal diseases & in-chg virus lab, Exp Sta, Univ Conn, 47-49; from assoc prof to prof microbiol, Inst Microbiol, Rutgers Univ, 49-68; vpres & sci dir, Life Sci, Inc, 68-76; expert, Nat Cancer Prog, Nat Cancer Inst, 77-80. *Concurrent Pos:* Vis prof, Rutgers Univ, 68-70; pres, Life Sci Res Labs, 73-76. *Mem:* Soc Exp Biol & Med; NY Acad Med; Am Asn Cancer Res; Res Soc Alcohol; Am Acad Microbiol. *Res:* Cancer viruses; alcohol studies; antibiotics; chemotherapy; immunology. *Mailing Add:* 11945 N 143rd St 7202 Lakeview Largo S Largo FL 34644

GROVE, ALVIN RUSSELL, JR, anatomy, morphology; deceased, see previous edition for last biography

GROVE, ANDREW S, ENGINEERING PHYSICS. *Current Pos:* vpres & dir oper, Intel Corp, 68-75, exec vpres, 75-79, chief oper officer, 76-87, PRES & CHIEF EXEC OFFICER, INTEL CORP, 87- *Personal Data:* b Budapest, Hungary, Sept 2, 36; US citizen; m 58; c 2. *Educ:* City Col New York, BS, 60; Univ Calif, Berkeley, PhD, 63. *Hon Degrees:* DSc, City Univ NY, 85; Dr Eng, Worcester Polytech Inst, 89. *Honors & Awards:* Medal Award, Am Inst Chemists, 60; J J Ebers Award, Inst Elec & Electronics Engrs, 74; George Washington Award, Am Hungarian Found, 90. *Prof Exp:* Mem tech staff, Fairchild Semiconductor Res Lab, 63-66, sect head surface & device physics, 66-67, asst dir res & develop, 67-68. *Concurrent Pos:* Lectr, Dept Elec Eng & Comput Sci, Univ Calif, Berkeley, 66-72. *Mem:* Nat Acad Eng; fel Inst Elec & Electronics Engrs; fel Acad Arts & Sci. *Res:* Metal-oxide-semiconductor devices and integrated circuits; large-scale integration technology; transport phenomena, especially fluid dynamics; author of over 40 technical publications. *Mailing Add:* Intel Corp PO Box 58119 2200 Mission College Blvd Santa Clara CA 95052-8119

GROVE, DONALD JONES, NUCLEAR ENGINEERING. *Current Pos:* dep proj mgr, Princeton Univ, 54-80, head, Tokomak Fusion Test Reactor Prog, Plasma Physics Lab, 80-87, prin res physicist & mgr, 82-86, dep dir tech opers, 86-87, CONSULT PHYSICIST, PRINCETON UNIV, 54-; SR CONSULT, EBASCO SERV INC, 87- *Personal Data:* b Pittsburgh, Pa, Oct 8, 19; wid; c Ellen (Petrone), D James & Robert E. *Educ:* Col Wooster, AB, 41; Carnegie Inst Technol, PhD(physics), 53. *Honors & Awards:* Arthur H Compton Prize Physics, 41; Distinguished Assoc Award, Electronic Resources Develop Agency, 76 & US Dept Energy, 86; Outstanding Achievement Award, Am Nuclear Soc, 86. *Prof Exp:* Physicist, Res Labs, Westinghouse Elec Corp, 41-82. *Concurrent Pos:* Mgr, spec projs, 87-89. *Mem:* Fel Am Phys Soc; Am Nuclear Soc; Sigma Xi; fel AAAS. *Res:* Mass spectroscopy, specifically ionization and dissociation of atoms and molecules by electron impact; electronic instrumentation for above; ultra high vacuum techniques; controlled thermonuclear reactor techniques and machine design for controlled fusion reactors. *Mailing Add:* 191 Riverside Dr Princeton NJ 08540

GROVE, EWART LESTER, ANALYTICAL CHEMISTRY, PHYSICAL CHEMISTRY. *Current Pos:* RETIRED. *Personal Data:* b Greensburg, Kans, May 31, 13; m 44; c 2. *Educ:* Ohio State Univ, MA, 45; Western Res Univ, PhD(chem), 51. *Honors & Awards:* Awards for Spec Instrumentation Develop, Nat Adv Comt Aeronaut. *Prof Exp:* Teacher, Pub Sch, Minn, 38-40 & Ohio, 40-47; instr chem, Minn State Teachers Col, St Cloud, 47-48; from asst prof to assoc prof anal chem, Univ Ala, 51-60; res chemist, Ill Inst Tech Res Inst, 60-63, sr chemist, 63-66, mgr anal chem res, 66-71; mem staff, Freeman Labs, Inc, 71-76; sr scientist, IIT Res Inst, 76-90. *Concurrent Pos:* Instr math, Fenn Col, 42-44; res partic, Oak Ridge Nat Lab, 53-54, consult, 54-58. *Mem:* Am Soc Testing & Mat; Am Chem Soc; Am Inst Chemists; Soc Appl Spectros; Sigma Xi. *Res:* Spectrography; spectrophotometry; atomic absorption flame and colorimetric methods as applied to analytical methods. *Mailing Add:* ITT Res Inst 10 W 35th St Chicago IL 60616

GROVE, JOHN AMOS, NUTRITIONAL BIOCHEMISTRY. *Current Pos:* from asst prof to assoc prof, 68-80, PROF CHEM, SDAK STATE UNIV, 80- *Personal Data:* b Youngstown, Ohio, Mar 26, 38; m 62; c 2. *Educ:* Ohio State Univ, BS, 61, MS, 64, PhD(nutrit, biochem), 66. *Prof Exp:* Res fel biochem, Univ Minn, St Paul, 66-68. *Res:* Mechanism of vitamin E action; intermediary metabolism of amino acids. *Mailing Add:* Dept Chem SDak State Univ Box 2202 Brookings SD 57007-0001

GROVE, JOHN SINCLAIR, CHRONIC DISEASE EPIDEMIOLOGY, GENETIC EPIDEMIOLOGY. *Current Pos:* vis investr, Univ Hawaii, 72-74, statistician, 75, assoc prof biostatist, 87-96, PROF BIOSTATIST, SCH PUB HEALTH, UNIV HAWAII, 96- *Personal Data:* b Brownwood, Tex, Nov 27, 43; m 83, Chulee Chawalsilp. *Educ:* Univ Ariz, BA, 64, MS, 66; Univ Hawaii, PhD(genetics), 69. *Prof Exp:* Fel, Univ Wis, 68-70, Ind Sch Med, 70-72; statist consult, Pac Health Res Inst, 76-85; biostatistician, Japan-Hawaii Cancer Ctr, 86-87. *Concurrent Pos:* Instr quant methods, Univ Hawaii Sch Bus, 79-82; vis fac biomet, Mahidol Univ, Bangkok, 80. *Mem:* Am Statist Asn; Biomet Soc; Am Soc Human Genetics; Int Soc Genetic Epidemiol; Am Pub Health Asn. *Res:* Statistical analysis in chronic disease epidemiology and genetic epidemiology. *Mailing Add:* Sch Pub Health Univ Hawaii 1960 East-West Rd Honolulu HI 96822

GROVE, KAREN, SEDIMENTATION & TECTONICS IN AREAS OF ACTIVE FAULTING, COASTAL PROCESSES. *Current Pos:* Lectr, 89-91, asst prof, 92-95, ASSOC PROF GEOL, SAN FRANCISCO STATE UNIV, 95- *Personal Data:* b Hagerstown, Md, June 24, 53; div. *Educ:* Univ Md, BS, 83; Stanford Univ, PhD(geol), 89. *Concurrent Pos:* Stanford fel, US Geol Surv, 87-88; vis scientist, Moss Landing Marine Labs, 91-92; prin investr, Petrol Res Fund grant, 92-94, NSF grant, 95-97. *Mem:* Fel Geol Soc Am; Am Geophys Union; Asn Women Geoscientists; Nat Asn Geol Educ. *Res:* Quaternary sediments and landforms in tectonically active regions to interpret paleo-environments and to evaluate the active faults; coastal sedimentary processes. *Mailing Add:* Dept Geosci San Francisco State Univ San Francisco CA 94132. *Fax:* 415-338-7705; *E-Mail:* kgrove@sfsu.edu

GROVE, LARRY CHARLES, MATHEMATICS. *Current Pos:* assoc prof, 71-76, PROF MATH, UNIV ARIZ, 76- *Personal Data:* b Madison, Minn, Jan 19, 38; m 59; c Sandra & Nathan. *Educ:* Univ Minn, BA, 60, MA, 61, PhD(math), 64. *Prof Exp:* J W Young res instr math, Dartmouth Col, 64-66; asst prof, Univ Ore, 66-69; assoc prof, Syracuse Univ, 69-71. *Mem:* Am Math Soc; Math Asn Am. *Res:* Algebra. *Mailing Add:* Univ Ariz Tucson AZ 85721-0001

GROVE, PATRICIA A, ETHOLOGY. *Current Pos:* assoc prof, 79-89, assoc prof, 90-95, PROF BIOL, COL MT ST VINCENT, 96- *Personal Data:* b Bronx, NY, Oct 3, 52; m 87, Leo M Alves. *Educ:* Col Mt St Vincent, BS, 74; City Col New York, MA, 77; City Univ New York, MPh, 79, PhD(biol), 81. *Prof Exp:* Lectr biol, City Col New York, 74-79 & Mercy Col, 79-80; med writer, Hoffman-La Roche, Inc, 89-90. *Concurrent Pos:* Proj dir, Re-licensing Prog Sch, New York Bd Educ Grant, Manhattan Col, 83-89, adj assoc prof biol, 85-89; consult, Educ Testing Serv & Col Bd, 86- *Mem:* Sigma Xi; Asn Women Sci; Animal Behav Soc; Am Asn Univ Prof; Audubon Soc. *Res:* Use of technology in biology education. *Mailing Add:* Dept Biol Col Mt St Vincent Bronx NY 10471-1093. *Fax:* 718-549-0915; *E-Mail:* pgrove@cmsu.edu

GROVE, STANLEY NEAL, BOTANY, CELL BIOLOGY. *Current Pos:* mem fac, 74-77, ASSOC PROF BIOL, GOSHEN COL, 77- *Personal Data:* b Augusta, Va, Sept 13, 40; m 62; c 2. *Educ:* Goshen Col, BA, 65; Purdue Univ, PhD(bot), 71. *Prof Exp:* Res assoc biochem, Agr Res Serv, USDA, 70-71; fel microbiol, Univ Tex, Austin, 71-74. *Mem:* Bot Soc Am; Mycol Soc Am. *Res:* Structure and function of protoplasmatic and surface components of germinating fungal spores and growing hyphal tips; cytochemical localization of macromolecules, especially enzymes, polysaccharides in fungi and in peanut seeds. *Mailing Add:* Dept Biol Goshen Col Goshen IN 46526

GROVE, THURMAN LEE, SOILS AND SOIL SCIENCE. *Current Pos:* SR ASSOC PROG OFFICER AGROECOL & ENVIRON, WINROCK INT, 91- *Personal Data:* b Lewisburg, Pa, July 22, 43. *Educ:* Wilkes Col, BA, 66; Cornell Univ, PhD(agron), 82. *Prof Exp:* Asst ecol, Cornell Univ, 66-71; proj mgr environ consult, Tex Instruments Inc, 73-75; mgr, Beak Consult Inc, 75-77; res assoc soil sci, Cornell Univ, 70-90. *Concurrent Pos:* Fel ecol, Fed Water Pollution Control Admin, Cornell Univ, 68-70, agroecologist, US Agency Int Develop, 88- *Mem:* AAAS; NY Acad Sci; Am Soc Agron; Soil Sci Soc Am; Soc Conserv Biol; Ecol Soc Am. *Res:* Biogeochemistry, especially transport mechanisms for phosphorus and nitrogen from the landscape to surface waters; biomass energy production; international agricultural development; agroecology. *Mailing Add:* 3320 White Oak Rd Raleigh NC 27609

GROVE, TIMOTHY LYNN, EXPERIMENTAL PETROLOGY & GEOCHEMISTRY. *Current Pos:* from asst prof to assoc prof, 79-91, PROF GEOL, MASS INST TECHNOL, 91- *Personal Data:* b York, Pa, July 15, 49; m, Ann M Reilly; c Matthew B & Michael T. *Educ:* Univ Colo, BA, 71; Harvard Univ, AM, 75, PhD(geol), 76. *Honors & Awards:* Bowen Award, Am Geophys Union, 94. *Prof Exp:* Res assoc earth sci, State Univ NY, Stony Brook 75-79. *Concurrent Pos:* Vis asst prof, Calif Inst Technol, 79; exec ed, Contrib Mineral & Petrol, 90-; vis scientist, Univ Cape Town, 93-94. *Mem:* Geol Soc Am; fel Mineral Soc Am; Am Geophys Union; Geochem Soc. *Res:* Experimental studies of processes lending to chemical differentiation of planetary interiors; phase equilibria, effects of volatiles on magma generation, diffusion and crystal nucleation and growth kinetics. *Mailing Add:* Dept Earth Atmospheric & Planetary Sci Mass Inst Technol Cambridge MA 02139. *Fax:* 617-253-7102; *E-Mail:* tlgrove@mit.edu

GROVENSTEIN, ERLING, JR, ORGANIC CHEMISTRY. *Current Pos:* RETIRED. *Personal Data:* b Miami, Fla, Nov 12, 24; m 54, 62, Lillian A Enloe; c John N & Alfred E. *Educ:* Ga Inst Technol, BS, 44; Mass Inst Technol, PhD(org chem), 48. *Prof Exp:* From asst to res assoc chem, Mass Inst Technol, 45-48; from asst prof to prof, Ga Inst Technol, 48-65, Julius Brown prof chem, 65-88. *Mem:* Am Chem Soc; The Chem Soc; Sigma Xi. *Res:* Organoalkali metal chemistry; organic reaction mechanisms; photochemistry. *Mailing Add:* 2424 Briarmoor Rd Atlanta GA 30345-2112

GROVER, CAROLE LEE, TRANSLATOR OF RESEARCH JOURNALS IN MATH, MANAGEMENT OF COMPUTER INFORMATION SYSTEMS IN HIGHER EDUCATION. *Current Pos:* dean instr, 94-96, DEAN MATH & SCI COMMUNITY COL ALLEGHENY CO, 96- *Personal Data:* b Seattle, Wash, Nov 25, 48; m 77; c 2. *Educ:* Univ Wash, BS, 70, MA, 71; Carnegie Mellon, PhD(math), 78, MPM, 90. *Prof Exp:* Vis asst prof math, Univ Pittsburgh, 76-78; vis instr math, Carnegie Mellon, 80-81; from asst prof to assoc prof math & computer sci, Carlow Col, 81-87, chair, Div Math & Computer Sci, 87-94. *Concurrent Pos:* Translator, Allerton Press, NY, 77-; proj dir, 96- *Mem:* Am Math Soc; Sigma Xi; Math Asn Am; Asn Comput Mach; Nat Woun Instrnl Admin; Math Asn Am. *Res:* Educational reform in undergraduate education in mathematics and computer science, particularly involving women, minority, and continuing education students. *Mailing Add:* 2067 Beechwood Blvd Pittsburgh PA 15217. *Fax:* 412-325-6799; *E-Mail:* cgrover@ccac.edu

GROVER, GARY JAMES, PHYSIOLOGY OF SHOCK. *Current Pos:* SR RES INVESTR PHARMACOL, ER SQUIBB & SONS, 85- *Personal Data:* b Camp Le Jeune, NC, Oct 16, 54; m 79. *Educ:* Rutgers Univ, BS, 76 & MS, 79; Albany Med Col, PhD(physiol), 82. *Prof Exp:* Fel physiol, Rutgers Med Sch, 82-85. *Concurrent Pos:* Adj asst prof, Rutgers Med Sch, 85- *Mem:* Am Heart Asn; Am Physiol Soc; Int Soc Heart Res. *Res:* Efficacy and mechanism of action of novel, pharmacological agents for the treatment of myocardiol ischemia; effect of thromboxane A2 receptor antagonists and calcium antagonists in myocardiol ischemia. *Mailing Add:* Pharmacol Sect Bristol-Myers Squibb Co Rte 206 Princeline Rd Princeton NJ 08543-4000

GROVER, GEORGE MAURICE, engineering physics; deceased, see previous edition for last biography

GROVER, HERBERT DAVID, ECOSYSTEMS. *Current Pos:* PROF BIOL, HARDIN SIMMONS UNIV ,94- *Personal Data:* b Mt Holly, NJ, Feb 20, 51; m 72; c 2. *Educ:* Rider Col, BA, 74; Rutgers Univ, MS, 77; Univ NMex, PhD(ecosysts ecol), 82. *Prof Exp:* Teaching asst biol & ecol, Rutgers Univ, 74-76; field ecologist, Environ Resources Comn, 76; lectr plant ecol, Rider Col, 77; res asst & teaching asst bot & biostatist, Univ NMex, 77-79; res asst, Sandia Labs, 78; res assoc, Ecosyts Res Ctr, Cornell Univ, 81-83; res scientist, Univ NMex, 83-94. *Mem:* AAAS; Ecol Soc Am; Sigma Xi. *Res:* Identification of ecosystem properties that are correlated with the ability of ecosystems to resist or recover from disturbance; clarification of mechanisms that affect ecosystem response to perturbation. *Mailing Add:* PO Box 375 Buffalo Gap TX 79508

GROVER, JAMES ROBB, CHEMICAL PHYSICS, NUCLEAR SCIENCE. *Current Pos:* RES COLLABR, 93- *Personal Data:* b Klamath Falls, Ore, Sept 16, 28; m 57, Barbara J Ton; c Jonathan R & Patricia J. *Educ:* Univ Wash, BS, 52; Univ Calif, Berkeley, PhD, 58. *Prof Exp:* Asst chem, Univ Calif, Berkeley, 52-53, asst nuclear chem, Radiation Lab, 53-57; res assoc, Brookhaven Nat Lab, 57-59, from assoc chemist to sr chemist, 59-93. *Concurrent Pos:* Vis scientist, Lawrence Livermore Lab, 62; Assoc ed, Ann Rev, Inc, Calif, 68-77; vis prof, Inst Molecular Sci, Okazaki, Japan, 86-87; chmn, Div Nuclear Chem & Technol, Am Chem Soc, 89. *Mem:* Am Chem Soc; Am Phys Soc; Sigma Xi. *Res:* Photoionization studies of gaseous molecular complexes; chemical uses of synchrotron light; reactive collisions between molecules; nuclear interactions of synchrotron light. *Mailing Add:* 1536 Pinecrest Terr Ashland OR 97520. *E-Mail:* grover@dynamics.chm.bnl.gov

GROVER, JOHN HARRIS, FISH BIOLOGY. *Current Pos:* from asst prof to assoc prof, 71-84, PROF FISHERIES, AUBURN UNIV, 84- *Personal Data:* b Rockville Centre, NY, Dec 21, 40; m 67; c 4. *Educ:* Univ Utah, BS, 64; Iowa State Univ, MS, 66, PhD(zool), 69. *Prof Exp:* Lectr biol, Univ Libya, 69-71. *Mem:* Am Fisheries Soc; Am Inst Fishery Res Biologists; Am Inst Biol Sci; Sigma Xi. *Res:* Aquaculture and aquatic ecology, especially as practiced in warm fresh waters and the developing world. *Mailing Add:* Dept of Fisheries & Allied Aquacultures Auburn Univ Auburn AL 36849-5419

GROVER, M ROBERTS, JR, MEDICINE. *Current Pos:* RETIRED. *Personal Data:* b Boston, Mass, Dec 5, 27; m 56; c 3. *Educ:* Bowdoin Col, BA, 50; Cornell Univ, MD, 54; Univ Ore, MS, 56. *Prof Exp:* From instr to prof med, Sch Med, Univ Ore, 58-68, dir continuing med educ, 65-76, actg dean, 78-79, assoc dean, 68-83, prof med & psychiat, 83-93. *Concurrent Pos:* Asst med dir hosps & clins, Sch Med, Univ Ore, 58-67, prog coordr, Ore Regional Med Prog, 67-68; mem, Mountain States Regional Med Prog, 67-72. *Mem:* AMA; Asn Am Med Cols. *Res:* Medical education; stress. *Mailing Add:* 7720 SW 91st Ave Portland OR 97223

GROVER, PAUL L, JR, MEDICAL EDUCATION, COMMUNICATION SCIENCE. *Current Pos:* PROF MED EDUC, STATE UNIV NY HEALTH SCI CTR, 75-, ASSOC DEAN, 85- *Personal Data:* b Nunday, NY, Oct 2, 43; m 67; c 3. *Educ:* Univ Rochester, AB, 65, MA, 67; Syracuse Univ,

PhD(instrnl technol), 71. *Prof Exp:* Asst prof med educ & commun, Sch Med & Dent, Univ Rochester, 70-75, asst prof, Sch Nursing, 74-75. *Mem:* Am Educ Res Asn; Asn Educ Commun & Technol. *Res:* Program evaluation; self-instructional techniques; instructional design; problem solving; academic counseling. *Mailing Add:* State Univ NY Health Sci Ctr 750 E Adams St Syracuse NY 13210

GROVER, RAJBANS, ENVIRONMENTAL SCIENCES. *Current Pos:* CONSULT, GROVER CONSULT, INC, 97- *Personal Data:* b Varnasi, India, Oct 18, 27; m 61, Maureen; c Shawn, Susan & Lisa. *Educ:* Panjab Univ, India, BSc, 49; Univ Delhi, MSc, 52; Univ Wash, PhD(phys biochem), 60. *Honors & Awards:* Excellence Weed Sci Award, Dow-Elanco Can. *Prof Exp:* Demonstr, Univ Delhi, 49-50, res asst plant physiol, 52-54; ed asst bot, Publ Div, Sci & Indust Res Coun, India, 54-55; res officer, Forest Nursery Sta, Res Br, Indian Head, Can Dept Agr, 60-63, Exp Farm, Regina, 63-65, res scientist, Res Sta, 65-75, sr res scientist, Environ Chem Res Sta, 75-89, dir, Res Sta, 89-93, guest scientist, 93-97. *Concurrent Pos:* Mem, Sask Weed Adv Coun, Can, 61-76 & Res Appraisal Comt, Western Sect, Can Weed Comt, 62-; vis scientist, Agr Res Coun, Oxford, Eng, 67-68 & USDA, Univ Calif, Riverside, 77-78; prog leader environ chem of herbicides, Can Dept Agr, 71-89; chairperson, Expert Comt Weeds, US, 90-91; adj prof, Univ Regina, SK, 91- *Res:* Environmental chemistry of herbicides; transport persistence and fate of herbicides; air monitoring and drift of herbicides; exposure of applicators to herbicides; non-target deposition of herbicides. *Mailing Add:* Grover Consult Inc 1727 Parker Ave Regina SK S4S 4R9 Can. *Fax:* 306-584-0402

GROVER, ROBERT FREDERIC, MEDICINE, HIGH ALTITUDE. *Current Pos:* instr med & asst dir cardiovasc lab, Med Ctr, Univ Colo, 58-61, from asst prof to prof med, 61-82, dir high altitude res lab, 64-82, dir Cardiovasc Pulmonary Res Lab, 65-82, EMER PROF MED, SCH MED, UNIV COLO, DENVER, 82- *Personal Data:* b Rochester, NY, Feb 25, 24; wid. *Educ:* Univ Rochester, BA, 47; Univ Colo, PhD(physiol), 51, MD, 55. *Honors & Awards:* D W Richards Award, Am Heart Asn, 84; Honor Award, Environ & Exercise Sect, Am Physiol Soc, 92; Trudeau Medalist, Am Thoracic Soc, 95. *Prof Exp:* Intern, St Anthony Hosp, Denver, 55-56. *Concurrent Pos:* NIH study sect, 71-75, Prin Investr res grants, 61-82; vis prof, Univ Calif, Santa Barbara, 78; Biennial Grover Conf Pulmonary Circulation, Pulmonary Circulation Found, 84-; consult, Environ Protection Agency, 89-91. *Mem:* Fel Am Col Cardiol; Am Physiol Soc; fel Am Col Physicians; Am Lung Asn; Am Thoracic Soc. *Res:* Cardiovascular and pulmonary physiology; high altitude; pulmonary circulation; author or coauthor of 170 research reports and 57 books and reviews. *Mailing Add:* 191 Century Ln Arroyo Grande CA 93420. *Fax:* 805-489-6230; *E-Mail:* rgrover@trumpet.aix.calpoly.edu

GROVER, SCOTT DAVID, ENZYME REGULATION. *Current Pos:* from asst prof to assoc prof, 83-93, PROF & CHAIR, BIOCHEM DEPT, CALIF STATE UNIV, LOS ANGELES, 93- *Personal Data:* b Glendale, Calif, Dec 24, 49. *Educ:* Univ Calif, Santa Barbara, BA, 72; Univ Calif, Los Angeles, PhD(biol), 80. *Prof Exp:* Postdoctoral fel, Univ Calif, Riverside, 79-83. *Concurrent Pos:* Vis assoc chem, Calif Inst Technol, 93-94. *Mem:* Sigma Xi; Am Chem Soc; Am Soc Plant Physiologists; Protein Soc; Am Soc Biochem & Molecular Biol. *Res:* Structure-function relationships in regulatory enzymes; regulation of phosphoenolpyruvate carboxylase. *Mailing Add:* Dept Chem & Biochem Calif State Univ Los Angeles CA 90032-8202. *Fax:* 213-343-6490; *E-Mail:* sgrover@calstatela.edu

GROVES, DONALD GEORGE, MATERIALS SCIENCE, SCIENCE ADMINISTRATION. *Current Pos:* TECH CONSULT & PROF FREE LANCE WRITER, 92- *Personal Data:* b Syracuse, NY; m 49, Barbara L Matticks. *Educ:* Syracuse Univ, BSc, 39, MSc, 49. *Hon Degrees:* DSc, Sussex Col, 78. *Honors & Awards:* Freedom Found Nat Award, 70, 73, 74, 87 & 89; Adm Dyer Award, 85. *Prof Exp:* Designer, Hudson Motor Car Co, 41-43; US Naval Officer, 43-47; res grant, Santo Domingo, 49-50; designer & systs engr, Gen Elec Co, 54-61; sr staff scientist mat sci & eng, Nat Acad Sci, 62-88; sr res fel, Inst Technol & Strategic Res, 88-89; sr res consult, Inst Defense Analysis, 88-91, res consult, Naval Res Lab, 91-92. *Concurrent Pos:* Sr staff scientist, Nat Acad Sci comts advan design criteria, 61-62, ceramic mat, 61-62, design with brittle material, 63-64, protective mat aerospace vehicles, 64-65, atomic characterization mat, 64-67, ceramic processing studies, 65-68 & fundamentals amorphous mat, ballistic missile defense hardening, 70-71, infrared, laser-glass & var mat sci & eng studies, Nat Res Coun-Nat Acad Sci, 62-88; US Govt res award, Dominican Rep. *Mem:* Mat Res Soc. *Res:* Natural resource utilization; research and development in materials, ocean science and engineering; scientific administration; author 3 books, published 300 articles and monographs. *Mailing Add:* PO Box 5837 Sun City West AZ 85376

GROVES, ERIC STEDMAN, EXPERIMENTAL HIGH ENERGY PHYSICS, MEDICINE. *Current Pos:* MEM STAFF CELLULAR IMMUNOL, CANCER INST, BETHESDA, MD, 81- *Personal Data:* b Seattle, Wash, Nov 14, 42. *Educ:* Mass Inst Technol, BSc, 65; Univ Pa, PhD(physics), 70; Univ Miami, MD, 78, Am Bd Internal Med, dipl, 81. *Prof Exp:* Res assoc physics, Rutherford Lab, Sci Res Coun, Eng, 70-75; res physicist, Lawrence Berkeley Lab, 75-76; mem staff, Jackson Mem Hosp, Miami, 78-81. *Mem:* Am Phys Soc; Am Med Asn; Am Col Physicians. *Res:* Fundamental structure of hadrons using electronic techniques; high transverse momentum hadron physics at the European Organization for Nuclear Research intersecting storage rings; murine cellular immunology. *Mailing Add:* 22 Rabbit Run Rd Malvern PA 19355

GROVES, IVOR DURHAM, JR, UNDERWATER ACOUSTICS. *Current Pos:* RETIRED. *Personal Data:* b Bowling Green, Ky, Dec 30, 19; m 44, Marjorie Lee; c Ivor III, Carol (Noland) & Gail (Wolven). *Educ:* Rollins Col, BS, 48, MBA, 64. *Prof Exp:* Electronic develop engr, Oak Ridge Nat Lab, 48-51; head transducer div & physicist, Naval Res Lab, 51-69, head transducer br, 69-74, assoc supt underwater sound ref div, 74-79, head transducer br, 77-79. *Concurrent Pos:* Consult, Oak Harbor Marine Assoc, 80-83. *Mem:* Fel Acoust Soc Am. *Res:* Underwater standard transducers for calibration of underwater acoustic devices; underwater electroacoustic transducers. *Mailing Add:* 888 Timber Pond Dr Brandon FL 33510-2945

GROVES, JOHN TAYLOR, III, ORGANIC CHEMISTRY & INORGANIC CHEMISTRY, BIO-ORGANIC & BIO-INORGANIC CHEMISTRY. *Current Pos:* chmn, Dept Chem, 88-93, PROF ORG & INORG CHEM, PRINCETON UNIV, 85-, HUGH STOTT TAYLOR CHAIR CHEM, 91- *Personal Data:* b New Rochelle, NY, Mar 27, 43; m 67, Karen Morrison G; c 2. *Educ:* Mass Inst Technol, SB, 65; Columbia Univ, PhD(org chem), 69. *Honors & Awards:* Spec Creativity Exten Award, NSF, 91. *Prof Exp:* From asst prof to prof org chem, Univ Mich, Ann Arbor, 69-85, dir, Ctr Catalytic Surface Sci, 80-85. *Concurrent Pos:* A C Cope Scholar award, Am Chem Soc, 91; Morris S Kharasch vis prof, Univ Chicago, 93. *Mem:* Fel AAAS; Am Chem Soc; NY Acad Sci; fel Japan Soc Promotion of Sci; fel Am Acad Arts & Sci. *Res:* Physical organic chemistry; bio-organic and bioinorganic chemistry; reaction mechanisms; metals in biology; catalysis; oxidation-reduction; free radical chemistry. *Mailing Add:* Dept Chem Princeton Univ Princeton NJ 08544

GROVES, MICHAEL JOHN, PHYSICS OF DRUG DELIVERY, QUALITY ASSURANCE OF INJECTABLES. *Current Pos:* PROF PHARMACEUT, UNIV ILL, CHICAGO, 83-, DIR INST TUBERCULOSIS RES, 86- *Personal Data:* b Near Birmingham, Warwickshire, UK, Apr 8, 33; US citizen; m 75, Frances Chang; c Clare & David. *Educ:* Nottingham Univ, UK, BPharm, 56, MPharm, 59; Loughborough Univ, UK, PhD(chem eng),67. *Prof Exp:* Scientist, Smith & Nephew Res Ltd, 59-61; group leader, Boots Co, 61-68; lectr pharmaceut, Chelsea Col, Univ London, 68-78; assoc dir, Baxter Health Care, 78-81; sr scientist, G D Searle & Co, 81-83. *Concurrent Pos:* Chair, Particle Size Anal Group, Royal Inst Chem, 74-75; vis prof pharmaceut, RI Univ, 78-79 & Purdue Univ, 82-83. *Mem:* Am Asn Pharmaceut Scientists; Royal Inst Chem; Royal Pharmaceut Soc Gt Brit; Controlled Release Soc. *Res:* Use of bacillus Calmette-Guerin in tuberculosis and cancer; effects of pressure on biologically active proteins; delivery of anti-neoplastics to colon/rectal cancers; physical characterization of phospholipid-stabilized emulsion. *Mailing Add:* 6028 Golfview Dr Gurnee IL 60031. *Fax:* 312-996-4689

GROVES, MONTGOMERY BRALLEY, PROCESS SEQUENCE INTEGRATION, ACOUSTIC FREQUENCY EVALUATION. *Current Pos:* DEVELOP ENGR, ASM AM, 92- *Personal Data:* b Cavite, Phillipines, Oct 3, 53; US citizen; m 96, Darcy M McGuire; c Megan R, Alison R, Brooke N Mahoney & Conrad T Mahoney. *Educ:* Calif State Univ, San Jose, BS, 73, MS, 75. *Prof Exp:* Develop engr, Siltec Corp, 76-86, Cincinnati Milacron, 86-90, Wacker Siltronic, 90-92. *Mem:* Am Vacuum Soc; Am Asn Crystal Growers; Exp Aircraft Asn; Inst Advan Mfg Sci. *Res:* Materials production and improvement of semiconductor wafer productivity; yield enhancement of critical processes; improvement of management process understanding capabilities. *Mailing Add:* 8316 N Lombard Portland OR 97203

GROVES, STEVEN H, SEMICONDUCTOR PHYSICS, CRYSTAL GROWTH. *Current Pos:* STAFF MEM, LINCOLN LABS, MASS INST TECHNOL, 64- *Personal Data:* b Madison, Wis, May 2, 34. *Educ:* Antioch Col, BS, 57; Harvard Univ, MS, 58 & PhD(appl physics), 63. *Mem:* Am Phys Soc. *Res:* Epitaxial growth of 3-4 materials. *Mailing Add:* 18 Winthrop Rd Lexington MA 02173

GROVES, THOMAS HOOPES, PHYSICS. *Current Pos:* RETIRED. *Personal Data:* b Madison, Wis, May 9, 32; m 54; c 4. *Educ:* Antioch Col, BS, 55; Univ Wis, MS, 59, PhD(physics), 62. *Prof Exp:* Asst prof physics, Purdue Univ, 62-66 & Univ Notre Dame, 66-68; assoc physicist, Argonne Nat Lab, Ill, 68-74; asst dir, Fermi Nat Accelerator Lab, 74-80, physicist, 80-96. *Mem:* Am Phys Soc. *Res:* Elementary particle physics. *Mailing Add:* 530 White Oak Rd Naperville IL 60540

GROVES, WILLIAM ERNEST, BIOCHEMISTRY, COMPUTER SCIENCE & CONSULTANT. *Current Pos:* dir, Acad Comput, 86-95, DIR EMERGING TECHNOL RES, 95- *Personal Data:* b Flint, Mich, Sept 8, 35; m 62, Ina Withers; c 3. *Educ:* Southern Methodist Univ, BS, 57; Univ Ill, MS, 59, PhD(biochem), 62; Univ SC, MS, 86. *Prof Exp:* Asst biochem, Univ Ill, 57-62; res biochemist, Lab Biochem Genet, Nat Heart Inst, 62-64; asst prof biochem, Col Med, Univ Tenn, 64-71; asst prof clin path, Med Univ SC, 71-74, assoc prof lab med & biomet, 74-86. *Concurrent Pos:* Res trainee, St Jude Children's Res Hosp, 64-67, asst mem, 67-71; mem grad fac, Memphis State Univ, 69-71. *Mem:* Asn Comput Mach; Inst Elec & Electronics Engrs; Sigma Xi. *Res:* Computer applications in higher education and medicine. *Mailing Add:* Info Technol Serv Univ NC Chapel Hill 103 Abernathy Hall Chapel Hill NC 27599-3420. *E-Mail:* bill_groves@juno.com

GROW, GEORGE COPERNICUS, JR, GEOLOGY, OIL & GAS EXPLORATION. *Current Pos:* PRES, GEORGE C GROW, INC, 81- *Personal Data:* b Stafford, NY, June 10, 16; m 42, Ruth Eber; c Christina R (Shrewsbury) & George C III. *Educ:* Lehigh Univ, AB, 38. *Prof Exp:* From jr geologist to chief geologist, Peoples Natural Gas Co, 38-50; chief geologist,

Eastern Area, Transcontinental Gas Pipe Line Corp, 50-73. *Concurrent Pos:* Mem nat gas surv, Fed Power Comn, 72-; consult geologist, 73- *Mem:* Geol Soc Am; hon mem Am Asn Petrol Geologists; Am Inst Prof Geologists; Soc Petrol Engrs. *Res:* Surface, subsurface, oil and gas geology of the Appalachian area; underground gas storage; geology of eastern United States and offshore. *Mailing Add:* 626 Shadowlawn Dr Westfield NJ 07090

GROW, RICHARD W, MICROWAVE PHYSICS, ELECTRONICS. *Current Pos:* assoc res prof & asst dir, High Velocity Lab, 58-59, assoc res prof & dir, 59-62, from assoc res prof to res prof, 62-66, dir, 60-80, chmn dept, 65-80, PROF ELEC ENG, MICROWAVE DEVICE & PHYS ELECTRONICS LAB, 66- *Personal Data:* b Lynndyl, Utah, Oct 31, 25; m 47; c 4. *Educ:* Univ Utah, BS, 48, MS, 49; Stanford Univ, PhD(elec eng), 55. *Prof Exp:* Electronic scientist, Radio Countermeasures Br, Naval Res Lab, 49-50 & Nucleonics Div, 50-51; res assoc, Stanford Electronics Lab, 53-58. *Concurrent Pos:* Part-time consult, Gen Elec Microwave Lab, 54-59, Litton Industs, 59, 68-, Eitel-McCullough, Inc, 59, Microwave Electronics Corp, 59-, Northrop Corp, 69- & Bur Radiol Health, 70- *Mem:* Sr mem Inst Elec & Electronics Engrs. *Res:* Radar countermeasures; nuclear radiation detectors; traveling-wave tubes; backward-wave oscillators; attenuation in rocket exhausts; masers; lasers; microwave dosimeters; pollution measurements; solid-state plasmas. *Mailing Add:* 1400 E Second St Merrill Eng Bldg 2280 Salt Lake City UT 84124

GROWCOCK, FREDERICK BRUCE, CORROSION SCIENCE, FLUID MECHANICS. *Current Pos:* staff res scientist, 88-93, RES ASSOC, AMOCO CORP, EPTG DRILLING, 93- *Personal Data:* b Monterrey, Mex, May 1, 48; US citizen; m 71, Lou A Wright; c Erick. *Educ:* Univ Tex, Austin, BA & BS, 69; NMex State Univ, MS, 72, PhD(phys chem), 75. *Prof Exp:* Res assoc coal res, Brookhaven Nat Lab, 74-76, from asst scientist to scientist, 76-82; sr res chemist, Dowell Div, Dow Chemical, 82-83; proj leader, Dowell Schlumberger, 83-84, res scientist, 84-88. *Concurrent Pos:* Vis scientist, Oak Ridge Nat Lab, 77; adj prof, Univ Okla, 88- *Mem:* Nat Asn Corrosion Engrs; Soc Petrol Engrs; Am Chem Soc; fel Am Inst Chemists; Electrochem Soc. *Res:* Characterization of coal; kinetics of coal hydrogenation; reaction kinetics of aromatic hydrocarbons; gas-phase kinetics of radical/molecule reactions; characterization and oxidation kinetics of graphite; high temperature nuclear chemistry; corrosion science; corrosion inhibition; surfactant chemistry; properties of foams; oilfield stimulation; electrochemistry; AC impedance spectroscopy; surface analysis; clay chemistry; environmental chemistry; drilling fluids chemistry. *Mailing Add:* 8308 S Fifth St Broken Arrow OK 74011. *Fax:* 418-660-3310; *E-Mail:* fgrowcock@amoco.com

GROZIAK, MICHAEL PETER, NUCLEIC ACID CHEMISTRY, BIOORGANIC CHEMISTRY. *Current Pos:* ASST PROF, SOUTHERN ILL UNIV, 89- *Personal Data:* b Chicago, Ill, Sept 14, 56. *Educ:* Univ Ill, Urbana-Champaign, BS, 77; Northwestern Univ, MS, 78, PhD(chem), 83. *Prof Exp:* Researcher med chem, Univ Mich, 82-85; res assoc, Dept Chem, Univ Ill, Urbana-Champaign, 85-89. *Mem:* Am Chem Soc; Int Soc Heterocyclic Chem; Sigma Xi; AAAS. *Res:* Synthesis of heterocycle and nucleoside analogs of biochemical and medicinal interest, development of new synthetic methodologies and development of enzyme inhibitors. *Mailing Add:* SRI Int 333 Ravenswood Ave Menlo Park CA 94025-3493. *Fax:* 618-453-6408; *E-Mail:* michael_groziak@qm.c_chem.siu.edu

GRUBB, ALAN S, PUBLIC HEALTH, COMMUNITY MEDICINE. *Current Pos:* CHIEF, PROG DEVELOP, OKLA STATE DEPT HEALTH, 84- *Personal Data:* b Poteau, Okla, Apr 3, 39; c 3. *Educ:* Univ Okla, BA, 62, MSPH, 67, PhD(human ecol), 70. *Prof Exp:* Environmentalist, Comanche Co Health Dept, Okla, 62-66; admin consult, Field Training Ctr, Sch Health, Univ Okla, 68-70, instr community health, Cols Health & Med, 70-71, from asst prof to assoc prof family pract & community med, Col Med, 71-84, from asst prof to assoc prof community dent, Col Dent, 70-84. *Mem:* Am Pub Health Asn; Asn Am Med Cols. *Res:* Patterns of health care utilization; levels of health knowledge and health attitudes; evaluation of quality of care. *Mailing Add:* 2513 Meadowbrook Dr Norman OK 73072

GRUBB, H(OMER) V(ERNON), CHEMICAL ENGINEERING. *Current Pos:* From instr to assoc prof, 39-58, from actg dir to dir sch, 58-76, PROF CHEM ENG, GA INST TECHNOL, 58- *Personal Data:* b Rockville, Ind, July 12, 16; m 43; c 1. *Educ:* Purdue Univ, BS, 38, MS, 41; Ga Inst Technol, PhD(chem eng), 51. *Mem:* Am Inst Chem Engrs. *Res:* Heat and mass transfer. *Mailing Add:* 2440 Northside Pkwy NW Atlanta GA 30305

GRUBB, ROBERT LEE, JR, NEUROLOGICAL SURGERY. *Current Pos:* fel neurol surg, Sch Med, Wash Univ, 71-72, Nat Inst Neurol Dis & Stroke fel, 72-73, instr, 73-74, from asst prof to assoc prof, 74-81, PROF NEUROL SURG & RADIOL, SCH MED, WASH UNIV, 81-, HERBERT LAURIE PROF NEUROL SURG, 93. *Personal Data:* b Charlotte, NC, May 9, 40; m 64; c Robert L & Mary Connel. *Educ:* Univ NC, AB, 61, MD, 65. *Honors & Awards:* Grass Award for Res, Soc Neurol Surg, 90. *Prof Exp:* Surg intern, Barnes Hosp, St Louis, 65-66, asst resident gen surg, 66-67, neurol surg, 69-71, sr res, 73. *Concurrent Pos:* Consult, St Louis City Hosp & County Hosp, 73-85, John Cochran Vet Admin Hosp, 73-, St Louis Regional Hosp, 85-; neurosurgeon, Barnes Jewish Hosp & St Louis Children's Hosp, 73-; mem, NIH Study Sect Neurol Dis Prog-Proj Rev A Comt, 79-84, chmn, 82-84; mem sci adv comt, Res Found Am Asn Neurol Surgeons, 82-; ed, Neurosurg, 85-86, J Neurosurg, 86-95. *Mem:* Am Asn Neurol Surgeons; Soc Neurol Surg; Am Acad Neurol Surg; fel Am Col Surgeons; Soc Neurosci; Am Physiol Soc. *Res:* Cerebral blood flow; author of numerous scientific publications. *Mailing Add:* 218 Elm Ave St Louis MO 63122. *Fax:* 314-362-2107

GRUBB, WILLARD THOMAS, PHYSICAL CHEMISTRY. *Current Pos:* RES ASSOC CHEM, RES LAB, GEN ELEC CO, 49- *Personal Data:* b Springfield, Ill, Mar 14, 23; m 50, Emmeline Allen; c Robert. *Educ:* Harvard Univ, SB, 46, PhD(phys chem), 49. *Concurrent Pos:* Coolidge fel, Gen Elec Co, 73. *Mem:* Am Chem Soc. *Res:* Fuel cells; electroless metal plating; electrochemical sensors; ion-selective electrodes; trace element analysis. *Mailing Add:* 2271 Sweetbrier Rd Schenectady NY 12309

GRUBBS, CHARLES LESLIE, PAINTING SYSTEMS, INDUSTRIAL COATING. *Current Pos:* TECH DIR, LILLY CO, 90- *Personal Data:* b Hodgenville, KY, Nov 29, 43; c 1. *Educ:* Univ Louisville, BS, 70. *Prof Exp:* Group leader, Cook Paint, 70-79; asst tech dir, Rockford Coatings, 79-84; tech dir, US Paint-Grow Group, 84-90. *Res:* Environmentally safe coasts; baking enamels. *Mailing Add:* 2957 Charpparl St Ontario CA 91761

GRUBBS, CLINTON JULIAN, MEDICAL PHYSIOLOGY, CANCER. *Current Pos:* DIR, RES NUTRIT & CARCINOGENESIS, UNIV ALA, BIRMINGHAM, 85- *Personal Data:* b Shreveport, La, Mar 7, 45. *Educ:* Univ Miss, BA, 66, MS, 68; Univ Tenn Med Units, PhD(physiol), 73. *Prof Exp:* Res assoc biochem, Ctr Health Sci, Univ Tenn, 73-75, instr physiol, 74-75; sr physiologist, Ill Inst Technol Res Inst, 75-79; sr physiologist, Southern Res Inst, 79-82, head, Cancer Prev Sect, 82-85. *Mem:* Am Asn Cancer Res; Soc Exp Biol & Med. *Res:* Reproductive patho-endocrinology; estrogen receptors; binding of chemical carcinogens; anticarcinogenic effect of retinoids; photo-oxidation of polycyclic hydrocarbons; nutrition and cancer. *Mailing Add:* Compar Med Univ Ala Sch Med 1717 Seventh Ave S Birmingham AL 35294-0001

GRUBBS, DAVID EDWARD, PHYSIOLOGICAL ECOLOGY. *Current Pos:* asst prof biol, 73-76, ASSOC PROF BIOL, CALIF STATE UNIV, FRESNO, 76- *Personal Data:* b Steubenville, Ohio, July 18, 43. *Educ:* Univ Calif, Santa Barbara, BA, 65; Univ Calif, Irvine, PhD(biol), 74. *Prof Exp:* Biol engr, Life Sci Opers, Autonetics Div, NAm Rockwell Corp, 66-69. *Res:* Physiological ecology of vertebrates with particular emphasis on xeric and alpine species; animal behavior and conservation. *Mailing Add:* Dept Biol Calif State Univ Fresno Fresno CA 93740-0073. *Fax:* 209-278-3963; *E-Mail:* david_grubbs@csufresno.edu

GRUBBS, DONALD KEEBLE, GEOLOGY, GEOCHEMISTRY. *Current Pos:* Geologist, Aluminum Co Am, 69-70, sr geologist, Australasian Minerals, Inc, Alcoa, 70-71, sr geologist, Alcoa Minerals Indonesia, 71-72, scientist geochem, 72-74, group leader, 74-81, TECH SPECIALIST, RAW MAT, ALCOA LABS, 81- *Personal Data:* b Pittsburgh, Pa, May 11, 38. *Educ:* Univ Va, BS, 61, MS, 63; Univ Pittsburgh, PhD(geochem), 69. *Mem:* Soc Explor Geochemists. *Res:* Raw materials evaluation; computer usage related to raw material exploration, evaluation, and mining; geochemical research; sulfur reduction in coal. *Mailing Add:* Weaver Mill Rd Rector PA 15677

GRUBBS, EDWARD, PHYSICAL ORGANIC CHEMISTRY. *Current Pos:* from asst prof to assoc prof, 61-68, PROF CHEM, SAN DIEGO STATE UNIV, 68- *Personal Data:* b Los Angeles, Calif, July 22, 34; m 63; c 4. *Educ:* Occidental Col, AB, 56; Mass Inst Technol, PhD(org chem), 59. *Prof Exp:* Fel, Univ Ill, 60-61. *Concurrent Pos:* Vis prof, Ain Shams Univ, Cairo, Egypt, 86. *Mem:* Am Chem Soc. *Res:* Kinetics of molecular rearrangements; stereochemistry; electrostatic interactions of substituents and reaction sites; electrostatic effects on the course of elimination reactions. *Mailing Add:* Dept Chem San Diego State Univ San Diego CA 92182-0001

GRUBBS, FRANK EPHRAIM, MATHEMATICAL STATISTICS, OPERATIONS RESEARCH. *Current Pos:* RETIRED. *Personal Data:* b Montgomery, Ala, Sept 2, 13; m 37; c 1. *Educ:* Auburn Univ, BS, 34, MS, 35; Univ Mich, MA, 40, PhD(math statist), 49. *Honors & Awards:* Samuel S Wilks Mem Medal, 64; Frank Wilcoxon & Jack Youden Technometrics Prizes, 69; Shewart Medal, Am Soc Qual Control, 72; Mil Applns Prize, Opers Res Soc Am, 73 & 77; Merit Award, Am Soc Testing & Mat, 86. *Prof Exp:* From instr to asst prof eng math, Auburn Univ, 34-40; chief, Surveillance Lab, Ballistic Res Labs, US Army Aberdeen Res & Develop Ctr, 41-53, Weapons Systs Lab, 53-62, dep tech dir, Ballistic Res Labs, 62-67, chief opers res anal, 68-75. *Concurrent Pos:* Supvr, Auburn Printing Co, 34-36; prof, Exten Div, Univ Del, 60-61, 62-63 & 67-70; actg chmn, Panel Tracking Data Anal, Nat Acad Sci, 74; chmn, US Army Design Exp Confs. *Mem:* Fel Am Soc Qual Control; Am Soc Testing & Mat; fel Am Statist Asn; fel Inst Math Statist; fel Royal Statist Soc; Int Statist Inst. *Res:* Applied statistics; weapon systems evaluations; reliability; administration of research and development. *Mailing Add:* 4109 Webster Rd Havre de Grace MD 21078

GRUBBS, ROBERT HOWARD, ORGANIC CHEMISTRY, INORGANIC CHEMISTRY. *Current Pos:* PROF ORG CHEM, CALIF INST TECHNOL, 78- *Personal Data:* b Calvert City, Ky, Feb 27, 42; m 67; c 3. *Educ:* Univ Fla, BS, 63, MS, 65; Columbia Univ, PhD(chem), 68. *Honors & Awards:* Organometallic Chem Award, Am Chem Soc, 88; Arthur C Cope Scholar Award, 89. *Prof Exp:* NIH fel, Stanford Univ, 68-69; from asst prof to assoc prof organometallic chem, Mich State Univ, 69-78. *Concurrent Pos:* Sloan Found fel, 74; Alexander von Humboldt fel, 75-; Dreyfus Found teacher-scholar grant, 75. *Mem:* Nat Acad Sci; Am Chem Soc. *Res:* Chemistry and reactions of small ring carbocycles and their metal complexes; polymer synthesis; mechanism and synthetic utility of the olefin dismutation reaction and the development of new synthetic reactions; polymer chemistry. *Mailing Add:* Calif Inst Technol Dept Chem 164-30 Pasadena CA 91125

GRUBE, GEORGE EDWARD, ECOLOGY. *Current Pos:* prof, 65-88, EMER PROF BIOL, DANA COL, 88- *Personal Data:* b Bareville, Pa, Apr 12, 23; m 45; c 2. *Educ:* Muhlenberg Col, BS, 46; Cornell Univ, MS, 49. *Prof Exp:* Instr biol, Franklin & Marshall Col, 46-48 & Gettysburg Col, 49-54; dist rep, Quaker Oats Co, 54-56; assoc prof biol sci, Lock Haven State Col, 57-65. *Concurrent Pos:* NSF partic, Inst Desert Sci, Ariz State Univ, 59, Animal Ecol Inst, Univ Colo, 60 & Inst Trop Ecol & Marine Biol, Univ PR, 66; chmn, East Nebr Nature Conserv, 78- *Mem:* Fel AAAS; Ecol Soc Am; Wilson Ornith Soc; Am Ornith Union. *Res:* Ornithology; ecology of symbiotes. *Mailing Add:* 2106 Grant St Blair NE 68008

GRUBE, GERALDINE JOYCE TERENZONI, THEORETICAL NUCLEAR PHYSICS. *Current Pos:* ASST PROF MATH, NORTHERN VA COMMUNITY COL, 88- *Personal Data:* b Boston, Mass, Sept 2, 42; m 72, Arthur Heinrich. *Educ:* Mass Inst Technol, BS, 66; Fla State Univ, MS, 68; NC State Univ, PhD(physics), 80. *Prof Exp:* Asst physics, Fla State Univ, 66-67; teaching asst physics, NC State Univ, 68-79; asst prof, Northern Ky Univ, 79-80; vis asst prof, Univ Ill, 80; asst prof physics, Ill State Univ, 81-84; at Univ High Sch, 84-85; asst prof physics, Western Ill Univ, 85-86; systems analyst, Fu Assoc, 88-90, prog mgr, 90-91; res assoc, Nat Res Coun, Nat Acad Scis, Bd Radioactive Waste Mgt. *Concurrent Pos:* At Nat Acad Sci, 90-92; prog mgr, res assoc, EIPP, Carlsbad. *Mem:* Sigma Xi; Am Phys Soc. *Res:* Phenomenological investigations into nucleon-nucleon interactions in the region of A-100; investigation into the effect of the spin-orbit interaction in heavy ion physics with a strong emphasis on developing new formalism to simplify calculations and reveal more easily measured symmetries; research in development of ageological site to store radioactive waste (Waste Isolation Pilot Plant). *Mailing Add:* 911 Lira Dr Fort Washington MD 20744-5318

GRUBE, WALTER E, JR, PHYSICALLY & CHEMICALLY DISTURBED LAND & SOIL, SOIL MORPHOLOGY. *Current Pos:* STOCKER PROF CIVIL ENG, OHIO UNIV, 93- *Personal Data:* b Shoemakersville, Pa, Aug 29, 39; c Walter P, Thomas J, John C, Mary F, Norma K, & Paul G. *Educ:* Pa State Univ, BS, 61, MS, 65; WVa Univ, PhD(soil chem), 74. *Prof Exp:* Res aide, Pa State Univ, 61-65; chemist, US Army Cold Regions Res Eng Lab, 65-67; res asst, WVa Univ, 67-74; chemist, Mining Pollution Control Div, US Environ Protection Agency, 74-76, chemist & dir prog opers, Off Res & Develop, Health Effects Res Lab, 76-81, soil scientist & nat expert, 81-91; dir res & develop, Clem Environ Corp, 91-93. *Mem:* Soil Sci Soc Am; Clay Minerals Soc; Am Soc Testing & Mat; Am Soc Civil Engrs; Hazardous Mat Control Res Inst. *Res:* Evaluation of soil engineering technologies applied to waste management facilities, and development of new methods for these evaluations. *Mailing Add:* 3 Andover Ct Athens OH 45701. *E-Mail:* wgrube1@ohiou.edu

GRUBER, ARNOLD, SATELLITE METEOROLOGY. *Current Pos:* res meteorologist, Nat Oceanic & Atmospheric Admin, 70-77, hq staff, 77, chief, Model Appln Br, 77-80, actg dir, 80, CHIEF, ATMOSPHERIC SCI BR, SATELLITE RES LAB, NAT ENVIRON SATELLITE, DATA & INFO SERV, NAT OCEANIC & ATMOSPHERIC ADMIN, 80- *Personal Data:* b New York, NY, Feb 28, 40; m 62; c 2. *Educ:* Brooklyn Col, BS, 62; Fla State Univ, MS, 64, PhD(meteorol), 68. *Prof Exp:* Instr, Meteorol Dept, Fla State Univ, 68-69; res scientist, Boeing Co, Seattle, 69-70. *Concurrent Pos:* Adj assoc prof, Meteorol Dept, Univ Md, 79-; mem, Solar & Earth Radiation Working Group, Nat Climate Prog, 81-; mem, Earth Radiation Budget Environ Sci Team; vis prof, chair remote sensing, US Naval Acad, 90-91. *Mem:* Sigma Xi; fel Am Meteorol Soc; Am Geophys Union; fel Am Meteorol Soc. *Res:* Satellite meteorology; vertical temperature structure refrievals; atmospheric radiation budget and application of quantitative satellite data to problems in weather analysis; forecasting and climate problems. *Mailing Add:* 1225 Port Echo Lane Bowie MD 20716-1843

GRUBER, B(ERNARD) A, ELECTROCHEMICAL ENGINEERING. *Current Pos:* RETIRED. *Personal Data:* b New York, NY, Mar 2, 25; m 68; c 2. *Educ:* Columbia Univ, BS, 45, MS, 47. *Prof Exp:* Res chemist, Harshaw Chem Co, 47-48; res engr, Battelle Mem Inst, 48-51; chief engr rare metals & hydrides, Metal Hydrides, Inc, 51-54; proj leader, Ethyl Corp, 54-56; res mgr, Monsanto Co, Mass, 55-69, res mgr, Mo, 69-70, mgr com develop, 70-79, mgr external res, 79-82. *Concurrent Pos:* Consult, 82- *Mem:* Am Chem Soc; Am Inst Aeronaut & Astronaut; AAAS. *Res:* Electrochemical energy conversion; high temperature materials; extractive metallurgy. *Mailing Add:* 514 Coeur de Royale Creve Coeur MO 63141

GRUBER, CARL L(AWRENCE), SOLID STATE SENSORS. *Current Pos:* RES ASSOC, MICROELECTRONICS LAB, IOWA STATE UNIV, 93- *Personal Data:* b Chicago, Ill, Nov 30, 38; m 59; c Scott & William. *Educ:* Univ Ill, Urbana, BSEE, 60, MS, 61, PhD(shock waves), 67. *Prof Exp:* From asst prof to prof elec eng, SDak Sch Mines & Technol, 64-81; sr prin eng, Honeywell Inc, 81-82, mgr, Adv Sensor Technol, 82-83; prof elec eng & electronic eng technol, Mankato State Univ, 83-93, prog coordr, 83-87, chmn dept, 87-93. *Concurrent Pos:* Am Soc Eng Educ fac fel, NASA-Goddard Space Flight Ctr, 67-68; exchange prof, Bergen, Norway, 72-73; consult, Minn Laser Systs, Honeywell Inc, 81-91, Pheonix Biocomposites, Mitor Inc, 93- *Mem:* Inst Elec & Electronics Engrs; Nat Soc Prof Engrs; Electrochem Soc; Am Soc Eng Educ. *Res:* Laser applications development; solid state sensors; gaseous electronics research; gaseous laser development; solid state materials processing & analysis. *Mailing Add:* Dept Elec Eng & Electronic Eng Technol Mankato State Univ Box 215 Mankato MN 56002. *E-Mail:* gruber@iastate.edu

GRUBER, CHARLES W, AIR POLLUTION. *Current Pos:* assoc prof, 69-77, EMER ASSOC PROF ENVIRON ENG, UNIV CINCINNATI, 77- *Personal Data:* b Cincinnati, Ohio, Mar 5, 10; m 38; c 3. *Educ:* Univ Cincinnati, ME, 32; Environ Eng Intersoc, dipl, 68. *Honors & Awards:* Frank A Chambers Award, Air Pollution Control Asn, 64. *Prof Exp:* Mgr appl eng, Consolidation Coal Co, 34-36 & Bimel Co, 36-38; air pollution control & heating engr, City of Cincinnati, 38-45 & 47-69. *Concurrent Pos:* Mgr eng dept, Floyd & Co, 46-47; spec mem consult, Nat Adv Comn Community Air Pollution Control, USPHS, 52-57, prin investr, res grant, 58-60 & 64-67, dir, USPHS-Nat Ctr Air Pollution Control prog, 67-69; consult, 69- *Mem:* Air Pollution Control Asn (pres, 50-51); Am Soc Mech Engrs; Nat Soc Prof Engrs; Sigma Xi. *Res:* Air pollution control in field of enforcement practices, source measurement, control and administration. *Mailing Add:* 5538 E Galbrath Rd Cincinnati OH 45236

GRUBER, ELBERT EGIDIUS, POLYMER CHEMISTRY. *Current Pos:* RETIRED. *Personal Data:* b Cincinnati, Ohio, Sept 11, 10; m 34; c 4. *Educ:* Xavier Univ, BS, 32; Univ Ill, MS, 34, PhD(org chem), 37. *Hon Degrees:* LLD, Xavier Univ, 75. *Prof Exp:* Res chemist, B F Goodrich Co, 37-43, group leader, 43-46, res supvr, Res Ctr, 46-50; head plastics res, Gen Tire & Rubber Co, 50-55, asst dir res, 55-62, dir res & develop, 62-71, vpres & dir, Res & Develop Div, 71-75; chem consult, 75-87. *Concurrent Pos:* Chmn elastomers, Gordon Res Conf, 57; mem bd dirs, Indust Res Inst, Inc, 73-76 & Textile Res Inst, 73-76; mem, Int Rubber Sci Hall of Fame, Univ Akron & Am Chem Soc, Div Rubber Chem, 76-86, vchmn, 81-86. *Mem:* Sigma Xi; Dirs Indust Res; Am Chem Soc; Soc Plastics Engrs. *Res:* Rubber antioxidants; polymerization; plastics; vinyls; polyurethane foams and elastomers; stereoregulated polymers; solid propellants; rubber and plastics compounding and processing, energy, utilization and supply. *Mailing Add:* 1148 W Market St Apt 422 Akron OH 44313

GRUBER, EUGENE E, JR, PHYSICAL METALLURGY. *Current Pos:* From assoc metallurgist to metallurgist, 63-88, SR SCIENTIST, ARGONNE NAT LAB, 88- *Personal Data:* b Pittsburgh, Pa, Apr 13, 33; m 56, Dorothy Young; c 4. *Educ:* Univ Pa, BS, 59; Carnegie Inst Technol, MS, 62, PhD(metall eng), 64. *Res:* Pores in solids; radiation damage; surface diffusion; capillarity phenomena; computer modeling of transient behavior of nuclear fuel for the fast breeder reactor, including fission-gas effects; fracture toughness testing. *Mailing Add:* Argonne Nat Lab ET/212 9700 S Cass Ave Argonne IL 60439-4838

GRUBER, GEORGE J, BIOENGINEERING, EPIDEMIOLOGY. *Current Pos:* sr res scientist, 71-80, staff scientist, 80-96, CONSULT, SOUTHWEST RES INST, 96- *Personal Data:* b Diosjano, Hungary, Mar 20, 36; US citizen; m 63. *Educ:* Cath Univ, BEE, 59, MS, 60, PhD(physics), 62. *Prof Exp:* Res asst phys acoust, Ultrasonic Lab, Cath Univ, 58-62; dir ultrasonic lab, Chesapeake Instrument Corp, Md, 62-63; asst res prof underwater acoust, Cath Univ, 63-65; asst prof mech eng, Univ Tex, Austin, 65-71. *Concurrent Pos:* Fel, Am Mach & Foundry Co, 62-63; Off Naval Res fel, 63-65; adj assoc prof, Univ Tex Health Sci Ctr, San Antonio, 74-80. *Mem:* Am Indust Hyg Asn; Am Inst Ultrasound Med; Asn Advan Med Instrumentation. *Res:* Human factors engineering; occupational safety and health; medical ultrasonics. *Mailing Add:* PO Drawer 28510 San Antonio TX 78228

GRUBER, GERALD WILLIAM, COATINGS. *Current Pos:* mgr indust coatings, PPG Industs Inc, 83-88, dir automotive coatings, 88-93, chemist, 71-83, dir res & develop chem, 93-95, VPRES RES & DEVELOP, PPG INDUSTS INC, 95- *Personal Data:* b LaCrosse, Wis, Sept 12, 44; m 69, Linette M Walden; c Kelly, Jeff & Scott. *Educ:* Loras Col, BS, 66; Case Western Reserve Univ, PhD(org chem), 70. *Prof Exp:* Nat Cancer Inst fel, Cornell Univ, 70-71. *Mem:* Am Chem Soc. *Res:* Organic synthesis; photochemistry mechanisms; reactive intermediates; radiation polymerization; automotive & industrial coatings; fine and specialty chemical. *Mailing Add:* 405 Heights Dr Gibsonia PA 15044. *Fax:* 412-325-5254

GRUBER, HELEN ELIZABETH, QUANTITATIVE BONE HISTOMORPHOMETRY, ELECTRON MICROSCOPY. *Current Pos:* SR SCIENTIST & DIR RES HISTOL, CAROLINAS MED CTR, CHARLOTTE, NC, 93- *Personal Data:* b Wallace, Idaho, Nov 6, 46. *Educ:* Univ Idaho, BS, 69; Ore State Univ, MS, 74, PhD(cell biol), 76. *Prof Exp:* Teaching asst biol, Ore State Univ, 70-72, res asst radiation biol, 74-76; fel radiation, NW Col & Univ Asn Sci, Richland, Wash, 72-73; res asst, Univ Iowa, 76-78; res asst med, Inst Med, Univ Wash, 78-81; res fel med, Univ Southern Calif, 81-84; res asst prof, Med, 84-86; asst prof, Dept Pediat, Univ Calif, Los Angeles, 86-89, assoc prof, Dept Oral Biol & Pediat, 92-93; res scientist III, Cedars Sinai Med Ctr, Los Angeles, 91-93. *Concurrent Pos:* Adj prof, Dept Biol, Univ NC, Charlotte. *Mem:* AAAS; Am Soc Cell Biol; Am Soc Bone & Mineral Res; Soc Exp Biol & Med; NY Acad Sci; Am Fedn Clin Res. *Res:* Bone and mineral metabolism; metabolic bone disease; primary human bone tumors; fracture healing; bone changes during pregnancy and lactation; biology of bone; electron microscopy; tissue culture of bone and cartilage; histopathology; intervertebral disc. *Mailing Add:* Orthop Res Lab Carolinas Med Ctr PO Box 3286 Charlotte NC 28232-2861. *Fax:* 704-355-2845

GRUBER, JACK, MEDICAL MICROBIOLOGY, VIROLOGY. *Current Pos:* chief off prog resources logistics, viral oncol, Nat Cancer Inst, NIH, 72-78, asst & dep chief, 78-84, chief, Biol Carcinogenesis Br, Div Cancer Etiology, 84-96, CHIEF, DIV CANCER BIOL, NAT CANCER INST, NIH, 96- *Personal Data:* b Brooklyn, NY, Apr 18, 31; m 64, Patricia Mason; c Harry M. *Educ:* Brooklyn Col, City Univ NY, BS, 54; Univ Ky, PhD(microbiol), 63. *Honors & Awards:* Award Merit, NIH, 89, Special Achievement Award, 91 & 92. *Prof Exp:* Asst microbiol, Univ Ky, 55-61; res bacteriologist, US Army Biol Labs, 62-63, microbiologist, Immunol Br, Med Invest Div, Med Sci Lab, Ft Detrick, 63-70; microbiologist, prog admin, Viral Biol Br, Nat Cancer Inst, NIH, 70-72. *Mem:* AAAS; Am Soc Microbiol; Tissue Cult Asn; Sigma Xi; NY Acad Sci; Am Soc Virol. *Res:* Biological carcinogenesis; Viral etiology of cancer; human cancer vaccines; scientific administration; anthropod-borne viruses; experimental viral and bacterial vaccines; AIDS; large-scale production of tumor viruses in tissue culture systems; radioisotope serology; streptococci and rheumatic fever. *Mailing Add:* Biol Carcinogenesis Br Nat Cancer Inst Exec Plaza N Bethesda MD 20892. *Fax:* 301-496-2025; *E-Mail:* gruberj@dcbdcep1.nci.nih.gov

GRUBER, JOHN B, SOLID STATE & OPTICAL PHYSICS, LASER SPECTROSCOPY. *Current Pos:* vpres acad affairs, 84-86, PROF PHYSICS, SAN JOSE STATE UNIV, 84-, DIR, INST MODERN OPTICS, 92- *Personal Data:* b Hershey, Pa, Feb 10, 35; m 61, Judith A Higer; c David P, Karen L & Mark B. *Educ:* Haverford Col, BS, 57; Univ Calif, Berkeley, PhD(chem physics), 61. *Honors & Awards:* Willig Award, 86. *Prof Exp:* Guest prof, Inst Tech Physics, Tech Univ Darmstadt, Repub Ger, 61-62; asst prof physics, Univ Calif, Los Angeles, 62-66; from assoc prof to prof chem physics, Wash State Univ, 66-75, from asst dean to assoc dean, Grad Sch, 68-72; prof physics & dean, Col Sci & Math, NDak State Univ, 75-80; prof physics & chem & vpres acad affairs, Portland State Univ, 80-84. *Concurrent Pos:* NATO fel, 61-62; consult, Aerospace Corp, Calif, 62-65, Missile & Space Systs Div, Douglas Aircraft Co, 63-69, Space & Info Systs Div, NAm Aviation, Inc, 64-66, Pac Northwest Labs, Battelle Mem Inst, 66-69, Douglas Lab, McDonnell Douglas Astronaut Corp, 68-74 & Los Alamos Sci Lab, Univ Calif, 69-71 & 73-74; mem, Lunar Explor Sci Apollo-NASA Task Force, 64-66; consult, Ames Lab, Iowa State Univ, 76-80, US Army Harry Diamond Lab, 80-, Union Carbide Corp, 80-, Naval Weapons Ctr, USN, China Lake, Calif, 84-, US Dept Defense, Washington, DC, 86-, Battelle Res Ctr, Triangle Park, NC, 87- & Gen Tel & Electronics, 87-; gen conf chmn, Fourteenth Rare Earth Res Conf, 79; chmn, Off Naval Technol & Panel Eval Postdoctoral Fel Appln, Am Soc Eng Educ, 87-, session meetings, Nat Meetings Am Phys Soc; pres, Optical Soc Am, Northern Calif Sect, 93-; vis prof, Stanford Univ, 93- *Mem:* Fel Am Phys Soc; AAAS; NY Acad Sci; Sigma Xi; Am Asn Physics Teachers; fel Polish Acad Sci; USSR Acad Sci; fel Am Soc Eng Educ; Optical Soc Am; Int Soc Optical Engrs; fel Uranian Acad Sci; Nat Aerospace Stds. *Res:* Optical and magnetic properties of rare earth and actinide ions in solids; optical spectroscopy; high temperature superconductors, tunable vibonic lasers; science education; engineering physics. *Mailing Add:* Dept Physics San Jose State Univ San Jose CA 95192-0106. *Fax:* 408-924-4815

GRUBER, KENNETH ALLEN, PATHOPHYSIOLOGY, BIOCHEMISTRY. *Current Pos:* PROG ADMINR, DIV COMMUN SCI & DIS, NAT INST DEAFNESS & OTHER COMMUN DIS, NIH, 92- *Personal Data:* b Brooklyn, NY, June 21, 48; m 82, Gail F Miller; c Vanessa & Sarah. *Educ:* NY Univ, BA, 71, PhD(med sci), 74. *Prof Exp:* Fel, Dept Anat, NY Univ, 71-74, Dept Physiol Chem, Roche Inst Molecular Biol, 74-76; asst prof physiol, Bowman Gray Sch Med, 76-80, from asst prof to assoc prof med, 80-89; prof physiol, Med Sci Campus, Univ PR, 89-92. *Concurrent Pos:* Adj assoc prof, Dept Biol, Long Island Univ, 74-75; adj prof, Dept Biol, Middlesex Co Col, 76; foreign travel award, Nat Res Coun, 80 & Am Soc Nephrology, 81; res career develop award, Nat Heart, Lung & Blood Inst, 80; vis prof, Centro Med Docente Trinidad, Venezeula, 83; vis scholar, Univ Iowa, 83-84; vis scientist, Inserm U-7, Necker Hosp, Paris, France, 91. *Mem:* Am Phys Soc. *Res:* Pathophysiology of hypertension as it pertains to neuro-humeral influences, especially the role of natriuretic hormone; endogenous regulators of ion transport; molecular biology of the aditory system; pathology of HIV/AIDS. *Mailing Add:* Nat Inst Deafness & Commun Dis EPS 400C 6120 Executive Blvd Rockville MD 20892. *Fax:* 301-402-6251

GRUBER, PETER JOHANNES, NUCLEAR MATRIX, STRUCTURE & FUNCTION. *Current Pos:* from asst prof to assoc prof, 73-86, PROF BIOL SCI, MOUNT HOLYOKE COL, 86- *Personal Data:* b Stamford, Conn, Aug 23, 41; m 71, Sue E Frederick; c 2. *Educ:* Carleton Col, BA, 62; Univ Wis, PhD(bot), 71. *Prof Exp:* Fel biochem, Mich State Univ, 71-73. *Mem:* Am Soc Plant Physiol; Sigma Xi. *Res:* Organization of plant nuclei; nuclear matrix/lamina proteins--their identification, localization and possible relationship with intermediate filament proteins. *Mailing Add:* Dept Biol Sci Mount Holyoke Col South Hadley MA 01075

GRUBER, SAMUEL HARVEY, BEHAVIORAL & PHYSIOLOGY ECOLOGY, SENSORY PHYSIOLOGY. *Current Pos:* from asst prof to assoc prof behav physiol, 73-84, PROF MARINE SCI, ROSENTIEL SCH MARINE & ATMOSPHERIC SCI, UNIV MIAMI, 84- *Personal Data:* b Brooklyn, NY, May 13, 38; m 69; c 2. *Educ:* Univ Miami, BA, 60, MS, 66, PhD(marine sci), 69. *Prof Exp:* Res scientist visual physiol, Inst Marine Sci, Univ Miami, 69-73. *Concurrent Pos:* Prin investr, Off Naval Res Contract, 69-78, 80-81 & 82-85; NSF grant biol oceanog, 79-89, US-Japan coop res, 83-88, US-Israel Binational Sci Found, 82-85; dir, Bimini Biol Field Sta, 90; pres, Elasmobranch Consult. *Mem:* Am Inst Fishery Res Scientist; Am Fisheries Soc; Am Soc Ichthyologists & Herpetologists; Soc Neurosci; Sigma Xi; distinguished fel Am Elasinobranch Soc, 88; Am Soc Zool. *Res:* Psychophysics and electrophysiology of vision in marine vertebrates and how senses, especially vision, effect the natural behavior of these creatures; bioenergetics; population dynamics and behavioral ecology of sharks; role of apex predators in the marine ecosystem; shark-human interaction especially shark repellent research. *Mailing Add:* 9300 SW 99th St Miami FL 33176

GRUBER, SHELDON, ELECTRICAL ENGINEERING. *Current Pos:* PROF ELEC ENG, CASE WESTERN RES UNIV, 67-, DEPT HEAD. *Personal Data:* b New York, NY, Sept 9, 30; m 55; c 2. *Educ:* Purdue Univ, BSEE, 52; Mass Inst Technol, ScD(elec), 58. *Prof Exp:* Asst prof elec eng, Mass Inst Technol, 59-62; res scientist fusion, Ctr Nuclear Studies, Saclay, France, 62-63; mem res staff plasma physics, Sperry Rand Res Ctr, 63-67. *Concurrent Pos:* Vis scientist, Inst Res, Hydro Que, 74, Ctr Nuclear Studies, Grenoble, France, 74-76 & Inst Prod Automation, Fraun hofer Soc, Stuttgart, WGer, 86. *Mem:* Am Phys Soc; Inst Elec & Electronics Engrs. *Res:* Robot control; industrial inspection; machine vision. *Mailing Add:* Dept Elec Eng Case Western Res Univ University Circle Cleveland OH 44106

GRUBER, WILHELM F, ORGANIC CHEMISTRY. *Current Pos:* RES CHEMIST, ELASTOMERS DEPT, E I DU PONT DE NEMOURS & CO, INC, 56- *Personal Data:* b Bischofshofen, Austria, Aug 2, 13; nat US; m 46. *Educ:* Univ Vienna, PhD(org chem), 39. *Prof Exp:* Instr chem, Univ Vienna, 40-48, asst prof, 48-51; res chemist, Smith, Kline & French Labs, 51-52; res chemist, Res Coun BC, Can, 52-54; res chemist, Univ Ill, 54-56. *Mem:* Am Chem Soc; Sigma Xi. *Res:* Accelerators, antioxidants and antiozonants for rubber; furocoumarins; furochromones and related aromatic derr; pyridine chemistry; sulfur compounds. *Mailing Add:* 2218 Old Orchard Rd Wilmington DE 19810

GRUBIN, HAROLD LEWIS, PHYSICS. *Current Pos:* VPRES SOLID STATE RES, SCI RES ASSOCS, 81- *Personal Data:* b Brooklyn, NY, Mar 1, 39; m 61; c 2. *Educ:* Brooklyn Col, BS, 60; Polytech Inst Brooklyn, MS, 62, PhD(physics), 67. *Prof Exp:* Theoret physicist, United Aircraft Res Labs, 66-68; sr theoret physicist, United Technologies Res Ctr, E Hartford, 68-81. *Mem:* AAAS; Am Phys Soc; Inst Elec & Electronics Engrs. *Res:* Solid state theory, especially on conduction phenomena and device-related physics. *Mailing Add:* 50 Porter Dr West Hartford CT 06117. *Fax:* 860-233-0676; *E-Mail:* hal@srassoc.com

GRUBMAN, MARVIN J, VIROLOGY. *Current Pos:* RES CHEMIST, PLUM ISLAND ANIMAL DIS CTR, 76- *Personal Data:* b Bronx, NY, Nov 4, 45; m 70, Annett Finkelstein; c David & Susan. *Educ:* City Col New York, BS, 67; Univ Pittsburgh, PhD(biochem), 72. *Honors & Awards:* Cleveland Prize, AAAS, 82. *Prof Exp:* Res assoc, Albert Einstein Col Med, 72-76. *Concurrent Pos:* Res fel, NIH, 72-73; US Dept Agr, Agr Res Serv, Plum Island Animal Ctr; mem, Int Comt Taxonomy Virus Picornavirus study group, 83-87; rev panel mem, Molecular Biol & Genetic Mechanisms Biotechnol Prog, USDA competitive Grants Prog, 85 & 93. *Mem:* Am Soc Microbiol; AAAS; Am Soc Virol. *Res:* Replication of foot-and-mouth disease virus; recombinant DNA techniques to produce live-attenuated and recombinant adenovirus and DNA vector based FMDV vaccines; study of the host immune response to FMDV infection. *Mailing Add:* Po BOx 1483 Southold NY 11971. *Fax:* 516-323-2507

GRUBMAN, WALLACE KARL, CORPORATE GENERAL MANAGEMENT. *Current Pos:* DIR, COURTAULDS PLC, 91- *Personal Data:* b New York, NY, Sept 12, 28; m 50, Ruth Winer; c James W (deceased), Steven L & Eric P. *Educ:* Columbia Univ, BS, 50; NY Univ, MS, 54. *Prof Exp:* Chem engr, Nat Starch & Chem Co, 50, mgt, 54-68, vpres, 68-74, group vpres, 75-77, pres & chief oper officer, 78-82, pres & chief exec officer, 81-83, chmn & chief exec officer, 83-85; exec dir, Unilever PLC & NV, 86-91. *Concurrent Pos:* Mem eng adv coun, Columbia Univ, 78- *Mem:* Am Inst Chem Engrs; Soc Chem Industs; Chem Mfrs Asn; Chem Indust Asn UK; fel Inst Chem Engrs London. *Res:* Engineering, manufacturing, marketing and research of a wide spectrum of specialty chemicals. *Mailing Add:* 13 Pitney Dr Mendham NJ 07945

GRUDZIEN, THADDEUS ARTHUR, JR, SYSTEMATICS. *Current Pos:* asst prof, 86-93, ASSOC PROF EVOLUTION, DEPT BIOL SCI, OAKLAND UNIV, 93- *Personal Data:* b Muskegon, Mich, May 3, 51. *Educ:* Cent Mich Univ, BS, 73, MS, 76; Va Polytech Inst & State Univ, PhD(biol), 83. *Honors & Awards:* Stoye Award, Am Soc Ichthyologists & Herpetologists, 82. *Prof Exp:* Adj prof biol, Roanoke Col, 83; res assoc, Wayne State Univ, 84-86. *Mem:* Am Soc Ichthyologists & Herpetologists; Soc Study Evolution; Sigma Xi. *Res:* Evolutionary biology, genetic population structure, dispersal, hybrid zones, phylogenetics, biochemical systematics. *Mailing Add:* Dept Biol Sci Oakland Univ Rochester MI 48309-4401. *E-Mail:* grudzien@oakland.edu

GRUEBELE, MARTIN, LASER INDUCED REACTION DYNAMICS, TIME-RESOLVED PROTEIN FOLDING. *Current Pos:* ASST PROF CHEM, UNIV ILL, 92- *Personal Data:* b Stuttgart, Ger, Jan 10, 64; m 92, Nancy Makri; c Alexander. *Educ:* Univ Calif, Berkeley, BS, 84, PhD(chem), 88. *Honors & Awards:* Cottrell Award. *Prof Exp:* Fel, Calif Inst Technol, 89-92. *Mem:* Sigma Xi; Am Phys Soc; Am Chem Soc. *Res:* Dynamics of molecular vibrational relaxation and its control-theory; folding dynamics of proteins on submillisecond time scales; laser spectroscopy. *Mailing Add:* 505 S Matthews Ave 60-1 Urbana IL 61801. *Fax:* 217-244-3186; *E-Mail:* gruebele@aries.scs.uiuc.edu

GRUEMER, HANNS-DIETER, BIOCHEMISTRY, CLINICAL CHEMISTRY. *Current Pos:* PROF CLIN PATH & DIR SECT CLIN CHEM, MED COL VA, 77- *Personal Data:* b Bochum, Ger, May 25, 24; US citizen. *Educ:* Univ Frankfurt, MD, 49; Am Bd Clin Chem, cert. *Prof Exp:* Res biochemist, Univ Frankfurt, 49-50; sr physician Charite, Univ Berlin, 50-54; res biochemist, Univ Frankfurt, 54-56; biochemist, Pineland Hosp, Pownal, Maine, 56-57, dir, 58-63; asst prof path 63-67, asst prof physiol chem,

64-67, from assoc prof to prof path & physiol chem, Ohio State Univ, 67-77, chief div clin chem, 63-77. *Concurrent Pos:* Instr & res asst, Boston Dispensary, Tufts Univ, 57-63; mem comt clin chem, Nat Acad Sci, 73-75; dir, Am Bd Clin Chem, 74-; mem bd ed, Clin Chem, 74-; dir, Nat Registry Clin Chem, 75- *Mem:* Am Chem Soc; Am Soc Biol Chemists; Am Asn Clin Chemists. *Res:* Membrane disease in muscular dystrophies; clinical enzymology. *Mailing Add:* Med Col Va PO Box 597 MCV Sta Richmond VA 23298-1900. *Fax:* 804-786-7722

GRUEN, DIETER MARTIN, CHEMICAL PHYSICS, SURFACE CHEMISTRY. *Current Pos:* assoc chemist, 47-59, SR CHEMIST, ARGONNE NAT LAB, 60-, ASSOC DIR MAT SCI DIV, 83- *Personal Data:* b Ger, Nov 21, 22; nat US; m 48, Dolores Colen; c Erica, Karen & Jeffery. *Educ:* Northwestern Univ, BS, 44, MS, 47; Univ Chicago, PhD(chem), 51. *Honors & Awards:* Mat Sci Award, Dept Energy, 88. *Prof Exp:* Chemist, Manhattan Proj, Oak Ridge, 44-46. *Concurrent Pos:* Vis scientist, Lawrence Radiation Lab, Univ Calif, 54-55; US deleg, Int Conf Peaceful Uses Atomic Energy, Switz, 58; chmn, Gordon Res Conf Fused Salts, 61; vis prof, Hebrew Univ Jerusalem, 69 & Norweg Tech Univ, 73; chmn, Int Conf Inelastic Ion Surface Collisions, 86; rev comt, Mat Sci Div, Lawrence Livermore Lab, 89. *Mem:* Am Chem Soc; Sigma Xi; Mat Res Soc. *Res:* Physical and surface chemistry; application of lasers to surface science; multiphoton resonance ionization of sputtered atoms; velocity and excited state distributions; ultrasensitive surface analysis; electronic structure of matrix isolated metal clusters; high technetium-superconductors; FTMS of laser desorbed organic molecules; conversion of fullerenes to diamond; plasma enhanced chemical vapor deposition; tin film synthesis. *Mailing Add:* 1324 59th St Downers Grove IL 60515. *Fax:* 630-252-9555

GRUEN, FRED MARTIN, CHEMISTRY. *Current Pos:* assoc prof, 51-61, PROF CHEM & HEAD DEPT, OLIVET COL, 61- *Personal Data:* b Nuernberg, Ger, Feb 4, 15; m 49; c 2. *Educ:* City Col New York, BS, 48; Ill Inst Technol, MS, 50; Mich State Univ, PhD, 64. *Prof Exp:* Res chemist, Schering Corp, NJ, 50-51. *Mem:* Am Chem Soc; Sigma Xi. *Res:* Applicability of Hammett equation to thiophenecarboxylic acids; synthesis and study of decomposition rates of some bis-thenoyl peroxides. *Mailing Add:* Olivet Col Olivet MI 49076

GRUEN, H(AROLD), ELECTRONICS ENGINEERING, COMMUNICATIONS. *Current Pos:* PRES, FAIRCHILD COMM & ELEC CO, 82- *Personal Data:* b Brooklyn, NY, June 4, 31; m 53; c 3. *Educ:* City Col New York, BEE, 52; Univ Pa, MS, 57. *Prof Exp:* Sect head commun eng, Philco Corp, 59-61, mgr, Marine Systs Group, 61-63, dir, Advan Commun Lab, Pa, 63-68, Philco-Ford Corp, 68-69, gen mgr, Sierra Electronic Oper, 69-76; pres, Aydin Vector, 76-82. *Concurrent Pos:* Mem, Franklin Inst, 60- *Mem:* Sr mem Inst Elec & Electronics Engrs. *Res:* Theoretical communications; statistical detection methods; maximal information transfer; coding theory; sensory data processing, for minimum bandwidth. *Mailing Add:* Gruen Investment Co PO Box 3026 Ponte Vedra Beach FL 32004

GRUEN, HANS EDMUND, MYCOLOGY. *Current Pos:* from asst prof to prof, 64-93, EMER PROF BIOL, UNIV SASK, 93- *Personal Data:* b Berlin, Ger, Oct 20, 25; nat US. *Educ:* Brooklyn Col, BS, 51; Harvard Univ, MA, 53, PhD(biol), 57. *Prof Exp:* Asst biol, Harvard Univ, 51, asst mycol, Farlow Herbarium, 52, asst plant physiol, 53-54, Am Cancer Soc res fel, 56-58, res fel, Farlow Herbarium, 59-64. *Concurrent Pos:* Lalor Found fel, Univ Tokyo, 63; assoc ed, Can J Bot, 80-83; actg co-ed, Can J Bot, 82-83. *Mem:* Mycol Soc Am. *Res:* Physiology of fungi, especially growth and development in reproductive structures of fungi. *Mailing Add:* Dept Biol Univ Sask Saskatoon SK S7N 0W0 Can

GRUENBAUM, WILLIAM TOD, SYNTHETIC ORGANIC CHEMISTRY, POLYMER SYNTHESIS. *Current Pos:* Res chemist, 75-80, SR RES CHEMIST, EASTMAN KODAK CO, 80- *Personal Data:* b Columbus, Ohio, Sept 28, 48. *Educ:* Ohio State Univ, BSc, 70; Univ Wis, PhD(org chem), 75. *Mem:* Am Chem Soc. *Res:* Synthesis of chemicals for electrophotographic applications. *Mailing Add:* One Tulley Lane Rochester NY 14626-1630

GRUENBERG, HARRY, ELECTROMAGNETISM. *Current Pos:* RETIRED. *Personal Data:* b Vienna, Austria, Feb 5, 21; US citizen; m 46, Eden J Wayles; c David, Neville & Lisa. *Educ:* Univ BC, BASc, 44; Calif Inst Technol, PhD, 49. *Prof Exp:* Instr elec eng, Calif Inst Technol, 46-49; assoc res officer, Microwave Sect, Nat Res Coun Can, 49-56; from assoc prof to prog elec eng, Syracuse Univ, 56-87. *Concurrent Pos:* Lectr, McGill Univ, 52-56; Fulbright res scholar, Tech Univ, Copenhagen, Denmark, 66-67; vis res scientist, Nat Res Coun Can, 77-78; vis prof, Univ BC, 84-85. *Mem:* Sr mem Inst Elec & Electronics Engrs. *Res:* Electromagnetic theory; antennas and microwave components; aircraft navigational aids. *Mailing Add:* 68 Midlake Circle East Syracuse NY 13057

GRUENBERGER, FRED J(OSEPH), COMPUTER SCIENCE, MATHEMATICS. *Current Pos:* PROF COMPUT SCI, CALIF STATE UNIV, NORTHRIDGE, 77- *Personal Data:* b Milwaukee, Wis, Sept 24, 18; m 42; c 1. *Educ:* Univ Wis, BS, 40, MS, 48. *Prof Exp:* Instr comput, Univ Wis, 48-54; comput programmer, Gen Elec Co, 54-57; assoc mathematician, Rand Corp, 57-67; prof comput sci, San Fernando Valley State Col, 67-77. *Concurrent Pos:* Ed, Popular Comput, 73-81. *Res:* Empirical number theory; computing education. *Mailing Add:* 5000 Beckley Ave Woodland Hills CA 91364

GRUENDLER, JOSEPH R, ANALYSIS & FUNCTIONAL ANALYSIS, APPLIED MATHEMATICS. *Current Pos:* ASSOC PROF CALCULUS, DEPT MATH, NC AGR & TECH STATE UNIV, 68- *Personal Data:* b Madison, Wis, Feb 2, 41. *Educ:* Univ Wis, BS, 63, MS, 64, PhD(eng mech), 68; Univ NC, PhD(math), 82. *Concurrent Pos:* Fulbright grantee math, Comenius Univ, Bratislava, Slovak Repub, 95. *Mem:* Am Math Soc; Soc Indust & Appl Math. *Res:* Homoclinic solutions in ordinary differential equations. *Mailing Add:* Dept Math NC Agr & Tech State Univ Greensboro NC 27411. *E-Mail:* gruendlerj@member.ams.org

GRUENDLER, JOSEPH R, MATHEMATICS ENGINEERING. *Current Pos:* Fac mem, 68-75, PROF MATH, UNIV NC A&T STATE UNIV, 75- *Educ:* Univ Wis, BS, 64, MS, 65, PhD(eng mech), 68; Univ NC, PhD(math), 82. *Concurrent Pos:* Fac res fel, Math Anal Div, Nat Bur Stands, 84-85; Fulbright res fel, Inst Appl Math, Comenius Univ, 95. *Mem:* Analysis; differential equations; variational methods; computational fluid mechanics. *Mailing Add:* Dept Math NC A&T State Univ 102 Markena Hall Greensboro NC 27411. *Fax:* 919-334-7283; *E-Mail:* gruendlj@garfield.ncat.edu

GRUENER, RAPHAEL P, PHYSIOLOGY. *Current Pos:* asst prof, 68-76, assoc prof, 76-80, PROF PHYSIOL, COL MED, UNIV ARIZ, 80- *Personal Data:* b Jerusalem, Israel, Mar 7, 39; m 63; c 2. *Educ:* Univ Calif, Berkeley, BA, 61; Univ Ill, Urbana, MSc, 63, PhD(physiol), 66. *Prof Exp:* NATO fel, 66-67; asst res physiologist, Scripps Inst, Univ Calif, 67-68. *Res:* Muscle physiology and biochemistry; excitation-contraction-coupling; basic mechanisms of myopathies; membrane excitability. *Mailing Add:* Dept Physiol Univ Ariz Col Med Tucson AZ 85724. *Fax:* 520-626-2383

GRUENER, WILLIAM B, COMPUTER SCIENCE PUBLISHING. *Current Pos:* MKT MGR, XYVISION, 88-; PUBL, COMPUT SCI PRESS, W H FREEMAN & CO, 89- *Personal Data:* b Springfield, Mass, 44. *Educ:* Boston Univ, BS, 67. *Prof Exp:* Comput sci ed, Addison Wesley Publ Co Inc, 74-82, exec ed, Comput Sci Div, 82-84, publ, Electronic Educ Prod, 84-86. *Concurrent Pos:* Dir sales & mkt, Avanti Educ Systs, 86; consult, 87-; chair, Publ Bd, Asn Comput Mach, 89- *Mem:* Asn Comput Mach; Inst Elec & Electronics Engrs. *Mailing Add:* 30 Bancroft Rd Andover MA 01810

GRUENHAGEN, RICHARD DALE, WEED SCIENCE, PLANT REGULATORS. *Current Pos:* SR PLANT PHYSIOLOGIST, FMC CORP, 79- *Personal Data:* b Davenport, Iowa, June 9, 41; m 79; c 1. *Educ:* Iowa State Univ, BS, 63; NDak State Univ, MS, 67; NC State Univ, PhD(crop sci & plant physiol), 70. *Prof Exp:* Biologist chem & plastics, Union Carbide Corp, 71-72; sr plant physiologist, Agrichem Proj, 3M Co, 72-77; sr biologist, Agr Prod Div, Union Carbide Corp, 77-79. *Concurrent Pos:* Mem, Plant Growth Regulator Working Group, Nat Acad Sci-Nat Res Coun. *Mem:* AAAS; Weed Sci Soc Am; Am Soc Plant Physiologists; Plant Growth Regulator Soc Am; Sigma Xi. *Res:* Parameters affecting herbicide activity/performance; discovery and evaluation of herbicides and plant regulators; investigation of mechanisms of action and reactors effecting efficacy. *Mailing Add:* 27 Hollybrooke Dr Langhorne PA 19047

GRUENSTEIN, ERIC IAN, CELL BIOLOGY. *Current Pos:* from asst prof to assoc prof, Dept Biol Chem, 74-88, PROF, DEPT MOLECULAR GEN, BIOCHEM & MICRO, MED SCH, UNIV CINCINNATI, 89- *Personal Data:* b New York, NY, Feb 23, 42; m 65, Patricia Jaffe; c 3. *Educ:* Princeton Univ, AB, 64; Duke Univ, PhD(biochem), 70. *Prof Exp:* Fel endocrinol, NIH, 70-72; fel biochem, Mass Inst Technol, 72-74. *Concurrent Pos:* Fogarty Sr Int Fel, 92. *Mem:* Am Soc Cell Biol; Soc Neurosci. *Res:* Signal transduction, especially pathways involving intracellular free calcium and its role in regulation of the cell cycle and neuronal network function. *Mailing Add:* Dept Molecular Gen Biochem & Microbiol Univ Cincinnati Col Med Cincinnati OH 45267-0524. *Fax:* 513-558-8474

GRUENWALD, GEZA, PLASTICS ENGINEERING. *Current Pos:* ENG CONSULT, 80- *Personal Data:* b Budapest, Hungary, Sept 13, 19; US citizen; m 49, Marianne Pabst; c Claudia. *Educ:* Tech Univ Berlin, MS & PhD(org chem), 43. *Prof Exp:* Consult plastic & resins, Ger, 46-51; chemist, Farbwerke Hoechst AG, 51-57; develop chemist, Gen Elec Co, Mass, 57-60, chemist insulation res & develop, 60-68, mgr, Insulation Non-Metals Lab, 68-80. *Mem:* Am Chem Soc; German Chem Soc; Soc Plastics Eng. *Res:* Effect of plasticizers polymer properties; mechanism of crystallization of high polymers; reactivity of epoxy curing agents; fracture mechanism on polymer products; cold forming of polymers with aromatic chain links; solar energy engineering; thermorforming of plastics; author of two books. *Mailing Add:* 36 W 34th St Erie PA 16508. *Fax:* 814-725-8590

GRUENWEDEL, DIETER WOLFGANG, MOLECULAR BIOLOGY, TOXICOLOGY. *Current Pos:* PROF FOOD BIOCHEM & FOOD TOXICOL, UNIV CALIF, DAVIS, 66- *Educ:* Eberhard Karl Univ Tübingen, Germany, PhD(biochem), 53. *Mailing Add:* Dept Food Sci & Tech Univ Calif Davis Davis CA 95616

GRUETT, MONTE DEANE, SYNTHETIC ORGANIC CHEMISTRY. *Current Pos:* From asst res chemist to assoc res chemist, Sterling-Winthrop Res Inst, 58-68, res chemist, 68-75, sr res chemist, 75-90, RES INVESTR, STERLING RES GROUP, 90- *Personal Data:* b Mobridge, SDak, June 2, 33; m 57; c 3. *Educ:* Morningside Col, BS, 55; Univ Minn, MS, 58; Rensselaer Polytech Inst, PhD(org chem), 62. *Mem:* Am Chem Soc. *Res:* Synthesis of new antibacterial and anti viral agents; nitrogen heterocyclics; antiasthmatic agents; cardiotonic anti-hypertensive analgesic agents and antitumor agents. *Mailing Add:* 494 Elliot Rd East Greenbush NY 12061-0304

GRUGEL, RICHARD NELSON, SOLIDIFICATION PROCESSING. *Current Pos:* STAFF SCIENTIST, UNIVS SPACE RES ASN, MSFC, 94- *Personal Data:* b Milwaukee, Wis, Dec 22, 51; m 91, Cynthia Conwill. *Educ:* Univ Wis-Milwaukee, BAG, 76, MS, 80; Mich Technol Univ, PhD(metall eng), 83. *Prof Exp:* Res assoc, Swiss Fed Inst Technol, 83-85 & 87; vis researcher, Northwestern Polytech Univ, Xian, China, 85-87; res asst prof, Vanderbilt Univ, 87-92, res assoc prof, 92-94. *Mem:* Metall Soc; Am Inst Aeronaut & Astronaut. *Res:* Solidification phenomena in dendritic, eutectic and monotectic alloy systems; granted one patent. *Mailing Add:* Univ Space Res Asn c/o MSFC MS-ES75 Huntsville AL 35812. *Fax:* 205-544-8762

GRUGER, EDWARD H, JR, BIO-ORGANIC CHEMISTRY. *Current Pos:* RETIRED. *Personal Data:* b Murfreesboro, Tenn, Jan 21, 28; m 52, Audrey Lindgren; c Sherri J, Lawrence H & Linda G. *Educ:* Univ Wash, BS, 53, MS, 56; Univ Calif, Davis, PhD(agr chem), 68. *Prof Exp:* Chemist fishery technol, US Fish & Wildlife Serv, 53-54; asst gen & org chem, Univ Wash, 54-55; chemist org chem, Technol Lab, US Bur Com Fisheries, 55-59, proj leader marine oil chem, 56-65, supvry chemist, 59-62, res chemist, 62-71; res chemist, Nat Oceanic & Atmospheric Admin, 71-77, supvry res chemist, NW & Alaska Fisheries Ctr, Nat Marine Fisheries Serv, 77-83. *Concurrent Pos:* Res assoc, Agr Exp Sta, Univ Calif, Davis, 65-68; res prof chem, Seattle Univ, 77-82. *Mem:* AAAS; Am Chem Soc; Am Oil Chemists' Soc; Sigma Xi. *Res:* Bio-organic chemistry of marine organisms and studies on effects of organic contaminants in marine life. *Mailing Add:* 3727 NE 193rd St Lake Forest Park WA 98155-2750

GRUHN, JOHN GEORGE, PATHOLOGY, DERMATOPATHOLOGY. *Current Pos:* ASSOC PROF PATH & ASSOC PROF DERMAT, RUSH MED COL, 80- *Personal Data:* b Brooklyn, NY, Sept 8, 18; m 43, Helen Mindelsberg; c George, William, Susan & Paul. *Educ:* Manhattan Col, BS, 41; Long Island Col Med, MD, 44. *Prof Exp:* Res fel med, Long Island Col Med, 47-48; resident, King's Co Hosp, 48-49; asst pathologist & dir blood bank, Montefiore Hosp, 51-55; instr path, Sch Med, Univ Pittsburgh, 56-58, from asst prof to assoc prof, Chicago Med Sch, 58-66, clin prof, 66-81; dir lab, Skokie Valley Community Hosp, 64-81. *Concurrent Pos:* Dir path lab, St Joseph's Hosp, Pittsburgh, Pa, 55-60; pathologist, Mt Sinai Hosp, Chicago, Ill, 60-64. *Mem:* Col Am Path; Am Soc Clin Path; Int Acad Path. *Res:* History of pathology especially lung and breast cancer. *Mailing Add:* Dept Dermat Rush Med Col 1753 W Congress Pkwy Chicago IL 60612. *Fax:* 312-942-7778; *E-Mail:* jgruhn77@aol.com

GRUHN, THOMAS ALBIN, PHYSICAL CHEMISTRY. *Current Pos:* From asst prof to assoc prof, 67-84, PROF CHEM, UNIV SAN FRANCISCO, 84-, CHMN DEPT, 76- *Personal Data:* b Eureka, Calif, Aug 18, 42; m 65; c 2. *Educ:* Univ San Francisco, BS, 64; Univ Calif, Berkeley, PhD(chem), 68. *Mem:* Am Chem Soc. *Res:* Etching mechanisms of solid state particle detectors; radiation chemistry of polymers. *Mailing Add:* Dept Chem Univ San Francisco San Francisco CA 94117

GRULA, MARY MUEDEKING, MICROBIAL ECOLOGY. *Current Pos:* RETIRED. *Personal Data:* b Minneapolis, Minn, Sept 26, 20; m 52; c 4. *Educ:* Univ Minn, BA, 41, PhD(bact, chem), 46. *Prof Exp:* Instr bact, Univ Ky, 46-47, asst prof, 47-52; res assoc, Okla State Univ, 59-80, prof microbiol, 80-90. *Concurrent Pos:* NSF res grant, 63-66 & 69-71; Okla State Univ Res Found grant, 69-71; investr, US Bur Mines-Energy Res & Develop Admin contract, 74-75. *Mem:* AAAS; Am Soc Microbiol; Brit Soc Gen Microbiol. *Res:* Microbial nutrition; cell division and its control in a species of Erwinia; microbiology of deep disposal wells. *Mailing Add:* Dept Microbiol 306 Life Sci East Okla State Univ Stillwater OK 74078. *E-Mail:* 12651.3373@compuserve.com

GRUM, ALLEN FREDERICK, OPERATIONS RESEARCH, DECISION ANALYSIS. *Current Pos:* assoc prof systs & decision analysis, 74-80, PROF & HEAD, DEPT ENG, US MIL ACAD, 81- *Personal Data:* b Washington, DC, Oct 6, 31; m 57; c 5. *Educ:* US Mil Acad, BS, 53; Mass Inst Technol, MS, 58; Stanford Univ, PhD(decision analysis), 76. *Prof Exp:* Res & develop staff officer eng equip, Hq, Dept Army, 68-70. *Concurrent Pos:* Mem Educ Coun, Mass Inst Technol, 77- *Mem:* Mil Opers Res Soc; Inst Mgt Sci; Opers Res Soc Am; Am Soc Eng Educr. *Res:* Application of quantitive methods to defense decision making. *Mailing Add:* 1924 Waverland Dr Macon GA 31211

GRUMBACH, KEVIN LAWRENCE, FAMILY & COMMUNITY MEDICINE. *Current Pos:* fel, 89-91, asst prof, Dept Family Med, 91-96, RES DIR, CTR HEALTH PROFESSIONS, UNIV CALIF, SAN FRANCISCO, 94-, ASSOC PROF, DEPT FAMILY MED, 96- *Personal Data:* b New York, NY, Mar 16, 56. *Educ:* Harvard Univ, AB, 79; Univ Calif, San Francisco, MD, 85; Am Bd Family Pract, cert. *Honors & Awards:* Robert Wood Johnson Found Award, 94. *Prof Exp:* Resident, San Francisco Gen Hosp, 85-89. *Concurrent Pos:* Res dir, PEW Health Professions Comn. *Mem:* Inst Med-Nat Acad Sci; Asn Health Serv Res; Am Pub Health Asn; Physicians Nat Health Prog; Physicians Social Responsibility. *Res:* Contributed articles to professional journals. *Mailing Add:* Univ Calif Box 1364 San Francisco CA 94143-1364

GRUMBACH, LEONARD, PHYSIOLOGY. *Current Pos:* assoc prof, 61-80, PROF PHYSIOL, ALBANY MED COL, 80- *Personal Data:* b Brooklyn, NY, July 24, 14; m 41; c 4. *Educ:* Cornell Univ, AB, 34, AM, 35, PhD(physiol), 39. *Prof Exp:* Col Dent, NY Univ, intr pharmacol, 46-47; prof physiol, Des Moines Still Col Osteop, 47-52; assoc mem, Sterling-Winthrop Res Inst, 52-58, mem, 58-61. *Mem:* AAAS; Am Physiol Soc. *Res:* Pharmacology of analgesics; physiology of pain. *Mailing Add:* Dept Physiol Albany Med Col 47 New Scotland Ave Albany NY 12208-3412

GRUMBACH, MELVIN MALCOLM, PEDIATRICS, MEDICINE. *Current Pos:* chmn dept & dir, Pediat Serv, 66-86, PROF, SCH MED, UNIV CALIF, SAN FRANCISCO, 65-, EDWARD B SHAW PROF PEDIAT, 83- *Personal Data:* b New York, NY, Dec 21, 25; m 51, Madeleine F Butt; c Ethan M, Kevin L & Anthony H. *Educ:* Columbia Univ, MD, 48. *Hon Degrees:* Dr, Geneva, 91. *Honors & Awards:* Joseph Mather Smith Prize, Col Physicians & Surgeons, 62, Bicentennial Silver Medal, 67; Borden Award, Am Acad Pediat, 71; Frederick C Moll lectr, Univ Wash, 79; Canon Eley lectr, Childrens Hosp Med Ctr, Harvard Med Sch, 79; Mali Dittman lectr, Univ Chicago, 80; Robt Williams Distinguished Leadership Award, Endocrine Soc, 80; Frederick M Kenny Mem lectr, Childrens Hosp Pittsburgh, 81; Winthrop Award lectr, Am Fertility Soc, 81; Grover Powers lectr, Yale Univ Sch Med, 81; John Lind lectr, Kawlinska Inst, Stockholm, 84; Bilberbuck lectr, Ore Health Sci Univ, 86; Matthew Steiner lectr, Northwestern Univ, 89; Lifetime Achievement Award, Am Acad Pediats, 96, John Howland Award, 97. *Prof Exp:* Pediat residency, Babies Hosp, Columbia Presby Med Ctr, 49-51; fel & asst pediat, Sch Med, Johns Hopkins Univ, 53-55; instr, Col Physicians & Surgeons, Columbia Univ, 55-56, assoc, 56-57, from asst prof to assoc prof, 57-65. *Concurrent Pos:* Mem, Human Embryol & Develop Study Sect, 62-66, Endocrine Study Sect, 67-71, bd sci counrs, Nat Inst Child Health & Human Develop, NIH, 71-75, Adv Coun NICHD, 92-96; mem basic sci adv comt, 61-, chmn & mem, Clin Res Adv Comt, Nat Found March Dimes, 74-; consult, Letterman Gen Hosp, San Francisco, Childrens Hosp & US Naval Hosp, Oakland; vis prof, Univ Wash, 79, Sch Med, Yale Univ, 81, Univ Calif, 81, Univ NC, 82 & Royal Soc Med, London, 85; mem, Int Sci Coun, Found Princess Marie-Christine, Brussels, 80-; Felton bequests prof, Royal Childrens Hosp, Melbourne, Australia, 83; vis prof, Univ Hong Kong, Peking Union Med Col, 86; Robert N Ganz vis prof, Mass Gen Hosp, 96. *Mem:* Nat Acad Sci; Inst Med-Nat Acad Sci; Am Soc Clin Invest; Soc Pediat Res; Lawson Wilkins Pediat Endocrine Soc (pres, 75-76); Endocrine Soc (pres, 81-82); Am Pediat Soc (pres, 89-90); Am Acad Pediat; Sigma Xi; hon mem Royal Soc Med; fel AAAS; corresp mem Europ Soc Pediat Endocrin. *Res:* Metabolic and endocrine disorders of childhood and adolescence; abnormalities of sex differentiation; effects of hormones on growth and maturation; developmental neuroendocrinology, genetic and chromosome aberrations; human puberty. *Mailing Add:* Dept Pediat Sch Med Univ Calif San Francisco CA 94143-0434. *Fax:* 415-476-4009

GRUMBACH, ROBERT S(TEPHEN), ELECTRICAL ENGINEERING. *Current Pos:* assoc prof, 61-88, EMER PROF ELEC ENG, UNIV AKRON, 88- *Personal Data:* b Morgantown, WVa, Dec 3, 25; m 51; c Robert S Jr & Laura L. *Educ:* Case Inst Technol, BSEE, 47; Univ WVa, MS, 51. *Honors & Awards:* Centennial Medal, Inst Elec & Electronics Engrs, 84. *Prof Exp:* Distribution engr, Monongahela Power Co, 47; instr elec eng, Univ WVa, 47-53; elec engr, Elec Utility Eng Sect, Westinghouse Elec Corp, 53-57; prof elec eng, Tech Inst Bandung, Indonesia, 57-61, head dept, 60-61. *Mem:* Inst Elec & Electronics Engrs. *Res:* Electric utility engineering; generation; transmission and distribution of electrical energy, especially lighting protection and relaying. *Mailing Add:* 1620 26th St Cuyahoga Falls OH 44223

GRUMBINE, ROBERT WALTER, POLAR OCEANOGRAPHY, GLACIOLOGY. *Current Pos:* PHYS SCIENTIST, DATA OPERS CTR/ NAT OCEANIC & ATMOSPHERIC ADMIN/NAT WEATHER SERV/ NCEP, 92. *Personal Data:* b Boulder, Colo, Nov 12, 62. *Educ:* Northwestern Univ, BS, 85; Univ Chicago, MS, 87, PhD(geophys sci), 89. *Prof Exp:* Nat Ctr Atmospheric Res ocean modelling postdoctoral fel, 90-91. *Mem:* Am Meteorol Soc; Am Geophys Union. *Res:* Roles of polar regions in weather, climate and climate change. *Mailing Add:* World Weather Bldg 5200 Auth Rd Rm 209 Camp Springs MD 20746. *E-Mail:* seaice@polar.wwb.noaa.gov

GRUMBLES, JIM BOB, RANGE MANAGEMENT, ECOLOGY. *Current Pos:* RETIRED. *Personal Data:* b San Saba, Tex, Aug 26, 28; m 52; c 3. *Educ:* Southwest Tex State Col, BS, 58; Tex A&M Univ, MS, 61, PhD(range mgt), 64. *Prof Exp:* Jr high sch instr, Tex, 58; asst range mgt, Tex A&M Univ, 58-59; from asst prof to assoc prof, Utah State Univ, 62-68; regional tech specialist, Field Res & Develop Herbicides, Dow Chem Co, Tex, 68-74; mgr res & develop, Agrovet Dept, Dow Quimica Mexicana SAm, 75-76; field res herbicides, Tex div res & develop, Dow Chem Co, 77-93. *Mem:* Int Soc Range Mgt; Sigma Xi. *Res:* Wildlife management; grazing relationship of steers and white-tailed deer in south Texas; grazing management of seeded introduced grasses; studies involving both grazing by livestock and clipping to stimulate grazing. *Mailing Add:* Rte 1 Box 7E Montalba TX 75853-9754. *Fax:* 903-549-2624

GRUMER, EUGENE LAWRENCE, ECONOMICS, PLANNING. *Current Pos:* PLANNING ANALYST, N ATLANTIC REFINING, LTD, 97- *Personal Data:* b New York, NY, May 25, 40; m 64, 84, Diana Ramirez; c Sondra, Elliott & Warren. *Educ:* Pa State Univ, BS, 61, BS, 62; Mass Inst Technol, MS, 64, ChemE, 65. *Prof Exp:* Engr, Celanese Corp, 65-69, sr engr, 69-70; econ engr, Hess Oil Virgin Islands Corp, 71-74; mgr oper planning/econ, 74-83; admin asst to vpres refining, Amerada Hess Corp, 83-85; refinery mgr planning/econ, 85-90, coordr planning & refinery econ, 90-95. *Mem:* Am Chem Soc; Am Inst Chem Engrs; Am Asn Cost Engrs. *Res:* Planning, economic evaluation, fuels blending, budgeting and ranking of research, development and major ventures, particularly for the petrochemical process industry; combustion; explosions; fuels; safety; operations and shipment coordination and planning. *Mailing Add:* Gen Delivery Arnold's Cove NF A0B 1N0 Can. *Fax:* 709-463-8076

GRUMET, ALEX, ELECTRONICS, PHYSICS. *Current Pos:* prof, 83-88, EMER PROF ENG, HOFSTRA UNIV, 88- *Personal Data:* b New York, NY, Sept 1, 19; m 46; c 2. *Educ:* City Col New York, BEE, 42; Polytech Inst Brooklyn, MEE, 58. *Prof Exp:* Jr engr, Signal Corps, Gen Develop Lab, Ft Monmouth, NJ, 42-43; develop engr, Telicon Corp, NY, 46-47; TV instr, NY Tech Inst, NJ, 47-48; design engr, Pilot Radio Corp, NY, 48-49; sr proj engr, Edo Corp, 50-56; prog scientist, Res Div, Repub Aviation Corp, 56-65; staff scientist, Electronics Syst Res, Grumman Aerospace Corp, 65-83. *Mem:* Optical Soc Am; Inst Elect & Electronics Engrs. *Res:* Investigation of nuclear magnetic resonance phenomena in liquids for application as a gyroscopic inertial sensing element; statistical communication theory for improving long-range communication and signal detection; statistical communication theory; optical matched filter processing. *Mailing Add:* 160-20 21st Ave Whitestone NY 11357

GRUMET, MARTIN, DEVELOPMENTAL NEUROBIOLOGY, NEURON GLIAL CELL-CELL INTERACTION. *Current Pos:* ASSOC PROF, NY UNIV MED CTR, 91- *Personal Data:* b Brooklyn, NY, June 30, 54; m 86; c 1. *Educ:* Cooper Union, BS, 76; Johns Hopkins Univ, PhD(biophys), 80. *Prof Exp:* Res assoc, Rockefeller Univ, 80-81, NIH fel, 81-84, asst prof neurobiol, 84-91. *Concurrent Pos:* Prin investr, NIH grant, 84- & Irma T Hirschl Career Scientist Award, 86- *Mem:* AAAS; Am Soc Cell Biol; Soc Neurosci. *Res:* Molecular level transmission of information within and between cells, focusing on defining, isolating and analyzing molecules that mediate interactions at the surfaces of cells from the nervous system. *Mailing Add:* 1349 Lexington Ave New York NY 10128

GRUMMER, ROBERT HENRY, ANIMAL HUSBANDRY. *Current Pos:* From instr to prof, 43-80, chmn dept, 54-63, EMER PROF MEAT & ANIMAL SCI, UNIV WIS-MADISON, 80- *Personal Data:* b Luzerne, Iowa, June 27, 16; m 40; c 2. *Educ:* Iowa State Univ, BS, 39; Univ Wis, MS, 43, PhD(biochem, animal husb), 46. *Mem:* Am Soc Animal Sci. *Res:* Nutrition; genetics; physiology of reproduction and parasitology of swine. *Mailing Add:* 256 Animal Sci Univ Wis 1675 Observatory Dr Madison WI 53706-1205

GRUN, PAUL, CYTOLOGY, CYTOGENETICS. *Current Pos:* from asst prof to assoc prof genetics, 54-63, prof, 64-89, EMER PROF CYTON & CYTOGENETICS, PA STATE UNIV, UNIVERSITY PARK, 89-; CHIEF EXEC OFFICER, VEGENICS, INC, 96- *Personal Data:* b New York, NY, May 14, 23; m, Carmen Moy; c 2. *Educ:* Univ NC, BA, 44; Cornell Univ, PhD(plant breeding), 49. *Prof Exp:* Plant biologist, Carnegie Inst Washington, 49-54. *Concurrent Pos:* Res fel, Inst Cell Res & Genetics, Karolinska Inst, Sweden, 53-54; NIH spec fel, Univ Calif, Los Angeles, 61-62; sabbatical, Univ Calif, Berkeley, 71-72, Louis Pasteur Univ, 83-84. *Mem:* Genetics Soc Am; Soc Study Evolution; Bot Soc Am; Potato Asn Am; Hort Soc Am. *Res:* Cytogenetics of Solanum; cytoplasmic factors in plant evolution; protoplast manipulations of cytoplasmic factors of Solanum; genetics of Capsicum and breeding of Savory Pepper. *Mailing Add:* Dept Hort 102 Tyson Bldg Pa State Univ University Park PA 16802

GRUNBAUM, BENJAMIN WOLF, APPLICATION OF ANALYTICAL BIOCHEMICAL TECHNOLOGY TO THE INDIVIDUALIZATION OF BIOLOGICAL EVIDENCE IN CRIMINAL CASES. *Current Pos:* CONSULT ANALYTICAL BIOCHEM & FORENSIC BIOL, 82- *Personal Data:* b Warsaw, Poland, June 18, 17; US citizen; m, Jean Montgomery; c Daniel, Jon B & Lauren. *Educ:* Univ Calif, Berkeley, BA, 50, MA, 52, PhD(biochem), 54, MCriminol, 64. *Prof Exp:* Res consult, Univ Uppsala, Sweden, 54; res assoc, Dept Physiol Chem, Univ Minn, 55-57; NSF fel, 57-58. *Concurrent Pos:* Consult biochem, Dept Army, LeHerman Hosp, San Francisco, 62-69; vis prof forensic med, Hadassah Med Sch, Israel, 71-72; consult forensic serology, WHO, 72; exchange scholar, Nat Acad Sci & Polish Acad Sci, 77; consult, Alameda Co Sheriffs Dept Crime Lab, Calif, 77-81, Parentage Comt, Am Asn Blood Banks, 80. *Mem:* Sigma Xi; fel Am Inst Chemists; AAAS; Int Soc Forensic Haemogenetics. *Res:* Equipment and methods for clinical use; methods for genetic marker typing in biological evidence materials; over 100 publications in professional journals and granted 2 patents. *Mailing Add:* 112 Turk Dr Moraga CA 94556

GRUNBAUM, BRANKO, POLYHEDRA, TESSELLATIONS. *Current Pos:* PROF MATH, UNIV WASH, 70- *Personal Data:* b Osijek, Yugoslavia, Oct 2, 29; US citizen; m 54; c 2. *Educ:* Hebrew Univ, Jerusalem, MSc, 54, PhD(math), 58. *Honors & Awards:* L R Ford Award, Math Asn Am, 75, C B Allendoerfer Award, 78. *Prof Exp:* Mem, Inst Advan Study, 58-60; vis asst prof math, Univ Wash, 60-61; from asst prof to assoc prof, Hebrew Univ, Jerusalem, 61-65; vis prof, Mich State Univ, 65-66; prof, Univ Wash, 66-69; vis prof, Mich State Univ, 69-70. *Concurrent Pos:* J S Guggenheim Mem Found fel, 81-82. *Mem:* Am Math Soc; Am Math Asn. *Res:* Convexity; combinatorial geometry; graph theory. *Mailing Add:* Univ Wash GN-50 Univ Wash Seattle WA 98195. *E-Mail:* grunbaum@math.washington.edu

GRUNBERG, EMANUEL, chemotherapy; deceased, see previous edition for last biography

GRUNBERG, NEIL EVERETT, MEDICAL PSYCHOLOGY, PSYCHOENDOCRINOLOGY. *Current Pos:* Asst prof, 79-84, ASSOC PROF MED PSYCHOL, UNIFORMED SERVS, UNIV HEALTH SCI, 84- *Personal Data:* b Newark, NJ, Aug 9, 53; m 74; c 1. *Educ:* Stanford Univ, BS, 75; Columbia Univ, MA, 77, MPhil, 79, PhD(psychol), 80. *Concurrent Pos:* Res assoc, Nat Cancer Inst, 82-87. *Mem:* Acad Behav Med Res; Soc Behav Med; Am Psychol Asn; Soc Psychologists in Addictive Behav. *Res:* Behavioral and biological studies of appetitive behaviors, including cigarette smoking and eating behavior; commonalities among substances of abuse and stress. *Mailing Add:* Psychol Dept Uniformed Serv Univ Sch Med 4301 Jones Bridge Rd Bethesda MD 20814-4712

GRUNBERGER, DEZIDER, CHEMICAL CARCINOGENESIS, GENE EXPRESSION. *Current Pos:* PROF BIOCHEM & MOLECULAR BIOPHYS, COL PHYSICIANS & SURGEONS, COLUMBIA UNIV, 68- *Personal Data:* b May 29, 22; m 48, Marta Herman; c George & Ivan. *Educ:* Czechoslovak Acad Sci, PhD(biochem), 56. *Hon Degrees:* DSc, Czech Acad Sci, 68. *Prof Exp:* Dept head, Inst Org Chem & Biochem, Czech Acad Sci, Prague, 50-68. *Concurrent Pos:* Asst prof pharmacol, George Washington Univ, 64-65; prin investr res grants, NIH, Environ Protection Agency & Am Cancer Soc; consult, NIH Study Sect; scholar, Leukemia Soc, 72-77, Rockefeller Found, 82; vis prof, Weizmann Inst, Israel, 83. *Mem:* NY Acad Sci; AAAS; Am Cancer Soc; Harvey Soc; Am Soc Biochem & Molecular Biol; Am Asn Cancer Res. *Res:* The mechanism of action of chemical carcinogens; the correlation between the structure of DNA modified by carcinogens and types of mutations induced in eukoryotic cells on the level of endogenous genes; development of antitumor drugs from propolis. *Mailing Add:* Inst Cancer Res Columbia Univ Col Physicians & Surgeons 701 W 168th St New York NY 10032. *E-Mail:* dg21@columbia.edu

GRUND, VERNON ROGER, PHARMACOLOGY. *Current Pos:* ASSOC PROF PHARMACOL, COL PHARM, UNIV CINCINNATI MED CTR, 78-, CHMN, DIV PHARMACOL & MED CHEM, 85- *Personal Data:* b Baudette, Minn, Oct 27, 46. *Educ:* Univ Minn, BS, 69, PhD(pharmacol), 74. *Prof Exp:* Postdoctorate clin pharmacol, Dept Internal Med, Univ Minn, 74-75; asst prof biochem pharmacol, Sch Pharm, State Univ NY, Buffalo, 75-78. *Concurrent Pos:* Vis assoc prof pharmacol, Univ BC, Can, 89; mem, New Investr Grant Rev Panel, Am Asn Col Pharm & Biol Sci Prog Comt, 90-91, Res & Grad Affairs Comt, 91-92. *Mem:* AAAS; Am Asn Col Pharm; Am Cancer Soc; Am Chem Soc; Am Diabetes Asn; Am Heart Asn; Am Lung Asn; Am Pharmaceut Asn; Am Soc Pharmacol & Exp Therapeut. *Res:* Immunochemical modulation of metabolic homeostasis; causes, complications and treatment of diabetes; influence of stress mediators on free fatty acid mobilization and insulin secretion; cyclic nucleotide changes in hypertension; author of numerous scientific publications. *Mailing Add:* Dept Pharmacol Sci Univ Mont Sch Pharm & Allied Health Sci Missoula MT 59812-1075

GRUNDBACHER, FREDERICK JOHN, HUMAN GENETICS. *Current Pos:* assoc prof, 74-75, actg chmn, 75-84, PROF GENETICS, DEPT BASIC SCI, UNIV ILL COL MED, PEORIA, 74- *Personal Data:* b Switz, Aug 3, 26; US citizen; m 66; c 2. *Educ:* Swiss Fed Inst Technol, dipl, 53; Univ Calif, PhD(genet), 60. *Prof Exp:* Res geneticist & asst specialist, Univ Calif, 60-61; asst prof biol & genetics, Med Col Va, 65-69, assoc prof genetics, 69-74. *Concurrent Pos:* NIH fels human genet, Med Sch, Univ Mich, Ann Arbor, 61-65; NIH grants. *Mem:* AAAS; Am Soc Human Genetics; Soc Exp Biol & Med; Am Asn Blood Banks. *Res:* Immunogenetics of man; quantitative genetics of immunoglobulin and isoantibody levels; variation in erythrocyte and soluble antigens; etiology of ABO hemolytic disease of the newborn; study of a predisposition to allergies; preciptin reactions, mitogenic activity, serologic specificity and biochemistry of lectins, determinant groups of human ABH and related antigens; characterization and inheritance of human mucin antigens; genetics of the tumor-associated antigens Lewis-Y and SSEA-1. *Mailing Add:* Dept Biomed & Therapeut Sci Univ Ill Col Med Box 1649 Peoria IL 61656. *Fax:* 309-671-8403

GRUNDER, ALLAN ANGUS, PHYSIOLOGICAL GENETICS, POULTRY BREEDING. *Current Pos:* leader, Molecular Genetics Team, 92-97, RES SCIENTIST GENETICS, FOOD & ANIMAL RES CTR, CENT EXP FARM, AGR CAN, 66- *Personal Data:* b Kincardine, Ont, Mar 13, 35; m 72, Linda R Marshall; c Laura V. *Educ:* Ont Agr Col, BSA, 58; Univ Alta, MSc, 61; Univ Calif, PhD(genetics), 66. *Honors & Awards:* Award for Excellence in Genetics & Physiol, Can Soc Animal Sci, 91. *Prof Exp:* Drainage surveyor, Ont Dept Agr, 58; salesman, Ogilvy Five Roses Co, 58-59. *Concurrent Pos:* Coordr, Can Animal Biotechnol Network, 92-93. *Mem:* Poultry Sci Asn; Sigma Xi; Genetics Soc Am; Genetics Soc Can; Can Soc Animal Sci; World's Poultry Sci Asn; Am Genetic Asn. *Res:* DNA fingerprinting in geese molecular genetics of avian mitochondria & endogenous viral genes; goose production; chicken meat quality; molecular genetics. *Mailing Add:* Ctr Food & Animal Res Agr Can Ottawa ON K1A 0C6 Can. *E-Mail:* grundera@em.agr.ca

GRUNDER, FRED IRWIN, ENVIRONMENTAL CHEMISTRY, BIOLOGICAL MONITORING. *Current Pos:* DIR LAB ACCREDITATION, PROG AM INDUST HYG ASN, 92- *Personal Data:* b Detroit, Mich, Aug 17, 40; m 66, Barbara Ward; c John & Robert. *Educ:* Univ Mich, BSE, 63, MS, 67. *Prof Exp:* Res assoc indust health, Univ Mich, 60-69; asst lab dir environ chem, George D Clayton & Assocs, 69-72; dir environ chem & toxicol, Bethlehem Steel Corp, 72-85; dir indust hyg, Am Med Labs, 85-92. *Concurrent Pos:* Mem, Subcomt Analytical Procedures, Indust Hyg Comt, Am Iron & Steel Inst, 74 & Subcomt Analytical Methods, Environ Qual Control Comt, 75 & chmn, 79-81; mem, Biol Monitoring Comt, Am Indust Hyg Asn, 84-92; mem toxics planning & oversight panel, Chesapeake Res Consortium, 90. *Mem:* Am Chem Soc; Am Indust Hyg Asn; Am Soc Testing Mat; Coun fel Eng & Sci Soc Exec; Industrial hygiene. *Res:* Environmental chemistry; development of analytical methods; measurement of environmental contaminants absorbed by the body. *Mailing Add:* 4706 Carterwood Dr Fairfax VA 22032. *E-Mail:* fgrunder@arha.org

GRUNDER, HERMANN AUGUST, NUCLEAR STRUCTURE. *Current Pos:* Bevatron mech engr, 59-62, group leader, 88-Inch Cyclotron, 62-64, Bevatron develop group leader, 68-73, group leader, Bevalac Opers, 73-79, LAB ASSOC DIR & HEAD, ACCELERATOR & FUSION RES DIV, LAWRENCE BERKELEY LAB, 79- *Personal Data:* b Basel, Switz, Dec 4, 31; US citizen; m 52; c 3. *Educ:* Tech Hochschule, Ger, MS, 58; Univ Basel,

Switz, PhD(physics), 67. *Concurrent Pos:* Consult, M D Anderson Med Ctr; Sr Scientist Award, Alexander von Humboldt Found, 79. *Mem:* Am Phys Soc; Europ Phys Soc; Swiss Phys Soc. *Res:* Design, construction and operation of accelerators for nuclear science and biomedical research and of neutral beam injectors for fusion energy experiments. *Mailing Add:* 12000 Jefferson Ave Newport News VA 23606

GRUNDLEGER, MELVIN LEWIS, DIABETES. *Current Pos:* RES ANALYST, DEPT LIFE CYCLE INFO MGT, PIONEER HI BRED INT INC, 90- *Personal Data:* b Brooklyn, NY, Nov 21, 47; c 2. *Educ:* Columbia Univ, PhD(nutrit & biochem), 79. *Prof Exp:* Asst prof nutrit, Colo State Univ, 82-90. *Mem:* Am Inst Nutrit; Sigma Xi. *Res:* Fiber; obesity. *Mailing Add:* 2935 NW 133rd Way Des Moines IA 50325-8701

GRUNDMANN, CHRISTOPH JOHANN, CHEMISTRY. *Current Pos:* RETIRED. *Personal Data:* b Berlin, Ger, Dec 29, 08; nat US; m 33; c 1. *Educ:* Univ Berlin, dipl, 31, Dr Phil, 33; Univ Heidelberg, Dr Phil Habil(org chem), 37. *Prof Exp:* Res assoc, Kaiser Wilhelm Inst, Ger, 33-39; res chemist, Deutsche Hydrierwerke, 39-45; assoc prof chem, Univ Halle, 47; prof & head dept, Univ Berlin, 50-52; assoc dir res, Olin Mathieson Chem Corp, NY, 52-58; dir res & develop, Gen Cigar Co, 58-60; prof chem, Carnegie-Mellon Univ, 67-76, sr fel, Mellon Inst, 60-85. *Concurrent Pos:* Privat-docent, Univ Heidelberg, 38; res assoc, Res Found, Ohio State Univ, 52-58; mem patent adv comt, US Secy Com, 60-62. *Mem:* Soc Ger Chem. *Res:* Organic chemistry. *Mailing Add:* 1518 Williamsburg Pl Pittsburgh PA 15235

GRUNDMEIER, ERNEST WINSTON, PHYSICAL CHEMISTRY. *Current Pos:* RETIRED. *Personal Data:* b North Mankato, Minn, Nov 15, 29; m 63. *Educ:* Mankato State Col, BA, 52; Iowa State Univ, MS, 54; Kans State Univ, PhD(chem), 64. *Prof Exp:* Asst chem, Iowa State Univ, 52-54; instr math, Univ NMex, 57; from instr to assoc prof, Mankato State Univ, 58-69, prof chem, 69-90. *Concurrent Pos:* Consult, Mankato Stone Co, 60; fel, Univ Edinburgh, 71. *Mem:* Am Chem Soc; Sigma Xi. *Res:* Kinetics of the benzidine rearrangement and hydrogen isotope effects; kinetics of metal-catalyzed decarboxylations of amino acids; chemistry of combustion. *Mailing Add:* 1331 N Fourth St Mankato MN 56001

GRUNDNER, THOMAS MICHAEL, TELECOMPUTING EDUCATION. *Current Pos:* asst prof, Sch Med, 80-89, dir, Com Telecomput Lab, 89-90, PRES, NAT PUB TELECOMPUT NETWORK, CASE WESTERN RES UNIV, 90- *Personal Data:* b Detroit, Mich, Oct 27, 45; m 81, Mary Lou Monahan. *Educ:* EMich Univ, BS, 67; Inst Behav Res, Silver Spring, Md, MA, 74; Univ Southern Calif, MS, 76, EdD, 78. *Honors & Awards:* Norbert Wiener Award Soc & Prof Responsibility, 95. *Prof Exp:* Asst prof, Marymount Palos Verdes Col, 77-80; adj asst prof, Univ Southern Calif, 79-80. *Res:* Author of two books; contributed to professional journals. *Mailing Add:* 1076 Oxford Rd Cleveland OH 44121-1826. *E-Mail:* tmg@en.com

GRUNDY, SCOTT MONTGOMERY, PHYSIOLOGY, BIOCHEMISTRY. *Current Pos:* prof biochem, 81-95, PROF INTERNAL MED & DIR, CTR HUMAN NUTRIT, UNIV TEX HEALTH SCI CTR, DALLAS, 81-, CHMN, DEPT CLIN NUTRIT, 81- *Personal Data:* b Memphis, Tex, July 10, 33; m 56; c 2. *Educ:* Tex Tech Col, BS, 55; Baylor Univ, MD & MS, 60; Rockefeller Univ, PhD, 66. *Prof Exp:* Instr biochem, Col Med, Baylor Univ, 60-61; asst prof, Rockefeller Univ, 68-70; chief, Phoenix Clin Res Sect, Phoenix Indian Med Ctr, Nat Inst Arthritis, Metab & Digestive Dis, 71-73; prof med in residence, Univ Calif, San Diego, 74-81. *Concurrent Pos:* Chief med serv, Metab Sect, Vet Admin Hosp, San Diego, 74-81. *Mem:* Inst Med-Nat Acad Sci; Asn Am Physicians; Am Soc Clin Invest. *Res:* Plasma lipoprotein structure and interconversions; cholesterol balance in man; cholesterol gallstone; atherosclerosis formation; diabetes mellitus. *Mailing Add:* Ctr Human Nutrit Y3-206 Univ Tex Southwestern Med Ctr 5323 Harry Hines Blvd Dallas TX 75235-8570. *Fax:* 214-648-4837; *E-Mail:* sgrund@mednet.swmed.edu

GRUNER, SOL MICHAEL, BIOLOGICAL PHYSICS, CONDENSED MATTER. *Current Pos:* Res assoc, 77, asst prof, 78-85, ASSOC PROF PHYSICS, PRINCETON UNIV, 85- *Personal Data:* b Vineland, NJ, Oct 4, 50; m; c 2. *Educ:* Mass Inst Technol, BS, 72; Princeton Univ, PhD(physics), 77. *Concurrent Pos:* Danforth Found fel, 72-76; chmn, Nat Synchrotron Light Source Users Subgroup Time-Resolved Diffraction, 82; sci adv, Liposome Co, 84- & Enzymatics Co, 88-; co-chmn, 2nd & 3rd Biann Princeton-Liposome Res Conf, Lipid Membranes, 85 & 87; vis fel, Exxon Res & Eng, 86; vis appointment, Inst Theoret Physics, Univ Calif-Santa Barbara, 89; mem-at-large, Div Biol Physics, Am Phys Soc, 90-; organizer & mem, Princeton Mat Inst, 90- *Mem:* Biophys Soc; fel Am Phys Soc; AAAS. *Res:* Application of physics to problems in biology and condensed matter; one US patent. *Mailing Add:* Dept Physics Princeton Univ PO Box 708 Princeton NJ 08544-0708. *Fax:* 609-258-1115

GRUNES, DAVID LEON, SOIL CHEMISTRY, PLANT NUTRITION. *Current Pos:* soil scientist, Northern Great Plains Res Ctr, USDA, NDak, 50-59, soil phosphorus lab, Colo State Univ, 59-60, soil scientist, Northern Great Plains Res Ctr, USDA, NDak, 60-64, SOIL SCIENTIST, PLANT, SOIL & NUTRIT LAB, USDA, NY, 64-; PROF AGRON, CORNELL UNIV, 67- *Personal Data:* b Paterson, NJ, June 29, 21; m 49, Willa D Freeman; c Lee A, Mitchell R & Rima L. *Educ:* Rutgers Univ, BSc, 44; Univ Calif, PhD(soil chem), 51. *Honors & Awards:* Cert Merit Outstanding Res, US Dept Agr, 59, 82, 89 & 91; Agron Res Award, Am Soc Agron Northeastern Br, 88. *Prof Exp:* Asst soil sci, Univ Calif, 48-50. *Concurrent Pos:* Tech asst expert, Int Atomic Energy Agency, Israel & vis prof, Israel Inst Technol, 63-64; consult ed, McGraw Hill Co, 65-88. *Mem:* Fel AAAS; fel Am Soc Agron; Int Soc Soil Sci; Sigma Xi; Coun Agr Sci & Technol; fel Soil Sci Soc Am. *Res:* Soil chemistry and fertility; plant, animal, and human nutrition; effects of soils, fertilizers and plant species and varieties on crop quality in relation to human and animal nutrition. *Mailing Add:* Soil & Crop/Atmospheric Sci Cornell Univ 236 Emerson Hall Ithaca NY 14853-0001. *Fax:* 607-255-2459

GRUNES, ROBERT LEWIS, METALLURGY, MATERIALS SCIENCE. *Current Pos:* PRES, R L GRUNES & ASSOCS, INC, 70- *Personal Data:* b New York, NY, Aug 15, 41; m 72, Eleonora Grasselli; c Natalie, Daniel & Ian. *Educ:* Polytech Inst Brooklyn, BS, 63, MS, 65, PhD(phys metall), 70. *Prof Exp:* Engr, Mat Develop Lab, Pratt & Whitney Corp, 63; res fel metall, Polytech Inst Brooklyn, 63-64; res engr, Lewis Res Ctr, NASA, 65-66; res assoc metall, Polytech Inst Brooklyn, 66-70. *Mem:* Metall Soc; Am Soc Testing & Mat; Sigma Xi; Am Soc Mech Engrs; Am Soc Civil Engrs. *Res:* Effects of interfaces upon bulk material properties; phase transformations; resource recovery. *Mailing Add:* 18 Oak Ave Tenafly NJ 07670-2646

GRUNEWALD, GARY LAWRENCE, MEDICINAL CHEMISTRY, BIO-ORGANIC CHEMISTRY. *Current Pos:* From asst prof to assoc prof, 66-76, PROF MED CHEM, UNIV KANS, 76- *Personal Data:* b Spokane, Wash, Nov 11, 37. *Educ:* Wash State Univ, BS & BPharm, 60; Univ Wis-Madison, PhD(org chem), 66. *Honors & Awards:* Roland T Lakey lectr, Wayne State Univ, 91. *Concurrent Pos:* Ed, Med Res Ser, Marcel Dekker; chmn, Med Chem & Pharmacog Sect, Acad Pharmaceut Sci, 83-84; vis prof, Victorian Col Pharm, Melbourne, Australia, 84 & 86. *Mem:* AAAS; Am Chem Soc; Soc Neurosci; The Royal Soc Chem; Am Pharmaceut Asn; Am Asn Pharm Scientists. *Res:* Synthesis and mechanism of action of biologically-active compounds; molecular orbital and molecular mechanics calculations and drug action; chemistry of the autonomic nervous system; computer assisted drug design. *Mailing Add:* 1937 Emerald Dr Lawrence KS 66046

GRUNEWALD, KATHARINE KLEVESAHL, EXERCISE, WELLNESS. *Current Pos:* from asst prof to assoc prof, 79-92, PROF NUTRIT, KANS STATE UNIV, 92- *Personal Data:* b Bonduel, Wis, Oct 4, 52; m 75. *Educ:* Univ Wis, BS, 74; Univ Ky, MS, 76, PhD, 79. *Mem:* Am Dietetic Asn; Am Col Sports Med; Am Inst Nutrit. *Res:* Nutrition and exercise; sports nutrition. *Mailing Add:* Dept Foods & Nutrit Kans State Univ Justin Hall Manhattan KS 66506. *Fax:* 785-532-3132; *E-Mail:* humec@ksu.edu

GRUNEWALD, RALPH, BIONUCLEONICS, RADIATION SAFETY. *Current Pos:* asst prof, 66-71, ASSOC PROF BOT, UNIV WIS-MILWAUKEE, 71- *Personal Data:* b Sheboygan, Wis, Nov 17, 36; m 62; c 2. *Educ:* Lakeland Col, BS, 58; Purdue Univ, MS, 64, PhD(health physics), 65. *Honors & Awards:* Kiekhofer Award, 71. *Prof Exp:* Lab technician, A C Electronics Div, Gen Motors Corp, 58-61; chemist IV, Wis State Bd Health, 65-66. *Mem:* AAAS; Health Physics Soc. *Res:* Radiotracer methodology and radioecology studies. *Mailing Add:* Radiation Safety Box 186 Milwaukee Co Med Complex 8700 W Wisconsin Ave Milwaukee WI 53226

GRUNSTEIN, MICHAEL, MOLECULAR BIOLOGY, GENETICS. *Current Pos:* from asst prof to assoc prof, 75-83, PROF, DEPT BIOL, UNIV CALIF, LOS ANGELES, 83- *Personal Data:* b Beclean, Romania, Aug 30, 46; Can citizen; m 67; c 2. *Educ:* McGill Univ, BS, 67; Univ Edinburgh, PhD(molecular biol), 71. *Prof Exp:* Fel molecular biol, Sch Med, Stanford Univ, 72-74, fel, Dept Biochem, 74-75. *Concurrent Pos:* Fac mem, Molecular Biol Inst, Univ Calif, Los Angeles, 75-; NIH grant, 76-79; Nat Found, March of Dimes, 78-79; comt res award, Univ Calif, Los Angeles, 78-79. *Res:* Gene organization and expression during animal cell differentiation; chromosome structure. *Mailing Add:* Dept Biol Univ Calif Los Angeles 405 Hilgard Ave Los Angeles CA 90024-1570. *Fax:* 310-206-9073

GRUNSTEIN, MICHAEL M, PULMONARY PHYSIOLOGY, PEDIATRIC MEDICINE. *Current Pos:* CHIEF, DIV PULMONARY MED & ALLERGY, CHILDREN'S HOSP PHILADELPHIA, 87- *Personal Data:* b Beclan, Romania, Jan 16, 47. *Educ:* Sir George Williams Univ, BS, 70; McGill Univ, MD, 77, PhD(med), 74. *Prof Exp:* sr staff physician, Nat Jewish Ctr Immunol & Respiratory Med, 80-87, dir, Clin Serv, 85-87. *Mem:* Am Physiol Soc; Am Thoracic Soc; Soc Pediat Res. *Mailing Add:* Div Pulmonary Med Childrens Hosp Philadelphia Univ Pa Sch Med 34th & Civic Center Blvd Philadelphia PA 19104. *Fax:* 215-590-3500

GRUNT, JEROME ALVIN, PEDIATRICS, ENDOCRINOLOGY. *Current Pos:* PROF PEDIAT, SCH MED, UNIV MO-KANSAS CITY, 71- *Personal Data:* b Newark, NJ, Apr 6, 23; m 50; c 4. *Educ:* Rutgers Univ, BS, 47, MS, 48; Univ Kans, PhD, 52; Duke Univ, MD, 57. *Prof Exp:* Instr anat, Univ Kans, 48-52 & Duke Univ, 53-59; instr pediat, Harvard Univ, 61-63, from assoc to assoc prof, Yale Univ, 63-71. *Concurrent Pos:* USPHS spec res fel, Duke Univ, 59-60; Med Found fel, Harvard Univ, 60-62, fel pediat endocrinol, 60-63. *Mem:* Lawson Wilkins Pediat Endocrinol Soc; Endocrine Soc; Am Diabetes Asn; Am Pediat Soc; Soc Pediat Res. *Res:* Pediatric endocrinology and growth. *Mailing Add:* Dept Pediat Children's Mercy Hosp Univ Mo Sch Med Kansas City MO 64108

GRUNTFEST, IRVING JAMES, PHYSICAL CHEMISTRY. *Current Pos:* RETIRED. *Personal Data:* b Philadelphia, Pa, Jan 12, 17; m 48; c 2. *Educ:* Brown Univ, ScB, 37, ScM, 38; Cornell Univ, PhD(phys chem), 41. *Prof Exp:* Asst phys chemist, US Bur Mines, Md, 41 & Tenn Valley Authority, Ala, 41-43; mem staff, Bell Tel Labs, NJ, 43; res chemist, Rohm & Haas Co, 43-56; consult chemist, Gen Elec Co, 56-70; mat systs engr, Mat Res Ctr, Allied Chem Corp, Morristown, NJ, 70-74; chemist, Off Toxic Substances, US Environ Protection Agency, 74-84. *Concurrent Pos:* Chmn, Comt High Temp Mat, Mat Adv Bd, 61. *Mem:* Am Chem Soc; Soc Rheology; Am Inst Physics; Am Inst Chem Engrs. *Res:* Catalysis; surface activity; relationship between molecular structure and properties; high strength materials; materials for high temperature service; biomedical materials. *Mailing Add:* 118 Lake Frances Dr West Palm Beach FL 33411-2132

GRUNTHANER, FRANK JOHN, PHYSICAL INORGANIC CHEMISTRY, SOLID STATE CHEMISTRY. *Current Pos:* MEM TECH STAFF SOLID STATE CHEM, JET PROPULSION LAB, 73- *Personal Data:* b St Marys, Pa, Nov 4, 44; m 66; c 2. *Educ:* King's Col, Pa, BS, 66; Calif Inst Technol, PhD(chem), 74. *Prof Exp:* Teaching asst inorg chem, King's Col, Pa, 64-66; from res asst inorg chem to teaching asst introductory chem, Calif Inst Technol, 69-73. *Mem:* Am Chem Soc; Am Vacuum Soc; Am Phys Soc. *Res:* Use of x-ray photoelectron spectroscopy to characterize surface chemistry of microelectronic processing technology; study of active sites of metallo-enzymes (bioinorganic chemistry) and heterogeneous catalysts. *Mailing Add:* 3180 Dragonfly St Glendale CA 91206

GRUNWALD, ERNEST MAX, THERMODYNAMICS & SOLUTION CHEMISTRY. *Current Pos:* prof chem, 64-83, Henry F Fischbach prof, 83-89, EMER PROF CHEM, BRANDEIS UNIV, 89- *Personal Data:* b Wuppertal, Ger, Nov 2, 23; nat US; m 52, Esther Richter; c Judith. *Educ:* Univ Calif, Los Angeles, BS & BA, 44, PhD(chem), 47. *Honors & Awards:* Pure Chem Award, Am Chem Soc, 59. *Prof Exp:* Instr chem, Univ Calif, Los Angeles, 47; res chemist, Portland Cement Asn, 48; Jewett fel, Columbia Univ, 49; from assoc prof to prof, Fla State Univ, 49-61; res chemist, Bell Tel Labs, Inc, 61-64. *Concurrent Pos:* Weizman fel, 55; Sloan fel, 58-61; Guggenheim fel, 75-76. *Mem:* Nat Acad Sci; Am Acad Arts & Sci; Am Chem Soc. *Res:* Structure of liquid solutions; thermodynamics of molecular species; interionic structure of ion pairs. *Mailing Add:* 244 Florence Rd Waltham MA 02154. *Fax:* 781-736-2516; *E-Mail:* eegrun@aol.com

GRUNWALD, GERALD B, CELL INTERACTION IN DEVELOPMENT OF NERVOUS SYSTEM. *Current Pos:* from asst prof to assoc prof, 85-93, PROF ANAT, JEFFERSON MED COL, 93- *Personal Data:* b Brooklyn, NY, Apr 6, 54; m 79, Barbara Lepak; c 2. *Educ:* Cornell Univ, BA, 76; Univ Wis-Madison, MS,; Univ Wis- Madison, PhD(zool), 81. *Prof Exp:* Sr staff fel, Lab Biochem Genetics, NIH, 81-85. *Concurrent Pos:* Mem, Rev Panel Develop Neurosci, NSF, 90-93; Basil O'Connor scholar award, March Dimes; NIH grant awards. *Mem:* Am Soc Cell Biol; Soc Neurosci; Soc Develop Biol; Sigma Xi; Asn Res Vision & Opthal; AAAS. *Res:* Is directed towards understanding the cellular and molecular mechanisms which guide the assembly of the nervous system during embryonic development; major focus on cellular and molecular biology of cadherin cell adhesion molecule structure and function. *Mailing Add:* Dept Anat & Develop Biol Jefferson Med Col 1020 Locust St Philadelphia PA 19107-6731

GRUNWALD, HUBERT PETER, AMORPHOUS SEMICONDUCTORS. *Current Pos:* from asst prof to assoc prof, 70-93, EMER PROF PHYSICS, STATE UNIV NY COL BROCKPORT, 93- *Personal Data:* b Lakota, NDak, Apr 7, 37; m 60; c 2. *Educ:* Wash Univ, BS, 59; Univ Rochester, PhD(solid state physics), 65. *Prof Exp:* Asst prof physics, Union Col, NY, 65-70. *Concurrent Pos:* Consult, Xerox Corp, 83-84. *Mem:* Am Phys Soc; Am Asn Physics Teachers; Sigma Xi. *Res:* High resistivity semiconductors, particularly the study of transport mechanisms of electrical charge through these materials. *Mailing Add:* 144 Ocean Hollow Lane St Augustine FL 32095

GRUNWALD, JOHN J, CHEMICAL MECHANISMS. *Current Pos:* Res chemist, 58-66, dir res & develop, 66-81, VPRES RES, MAC DERMID INC, 81- *Personal Data:* b Berehove, Czech, Aug 24, 31; US citizen; m 60; c 4. *Educ:* Polytech Lausanne, Switz, BSCHE, 56; Columbia Univ, MSCHE, 58; Wayne State Univ, PhD(inorg chem), 64. *Mem:* Am Chem Soc; Am Electrochem Soc; Sigma Xi. *Res:* Electrochemistry of aqueous systems; microphotolithography; catalysis of aqueous systems; electroless deposition on conductors and nonconductors. *Mailing Add:* MacDermid Israel Ltd PO Box 58155 Tel Aviv 61581 Israel

GRUPEN, RODERIC A, COMPUTER SCIENCE. *Current Pos:* ASSOC PROF & CO-DIR, COMPUT SCI LAB PERCEPTUAL ROBOTICS, UNIV MASS, 88- *Educ:* Franklin & Marshall Col, BA; Washington Univ, BS, 80; Pa State Univ, MS, 84; Univ Utah, PhD(comput sci), 88. *Res:* Sensor based modeling and control; dexterous robots; adaptive activation of a control basis; resource allocation; architechtures for real time autonomous systems. *Mailing Add:* Comput Sci Dept Lederle Grad Res Ctr Univ Mass Box 34610 Amherst MA 01003-4610. *E-Mail:* grupen@cs.umass.edu

GRUPEN, WILLIAM BRIGHTMAN, METALLURGY, SOLID STATE PHYSICS. *Current Pos:* mem tech staff, Bell Labs, 64-67, group supvr metallic films, 67-69, dept head,MMat & Process Develop, 69-81, HEAD, DEPT BATTERY RES & DEVELOP, BELL LABS, 81- *Personal Data:* b Pittsburgh, Pa, Mar 30, 30; m 54; c 4. *Educ:* Univ Calif, Los Angeles, BS, 57, MS, 59, PhD(metall), 64. *Prof Exp:* Res engr, Univ Calif, Los Angeles, 58-64. *Mem:* Inst Elec & Electronics Engrs; Am Inst Mining, Metall & Petrol Engrs; Sigma Xi. *Res:* Preprecipitation reactions in aluminum-copper alloys; magnetic properties of 3d transition metals and their alloys; magnetic and electrical properties of thin metal films. *Mailing Add:* 25 Wolf Hill Dr Warren NJ 07059-5327

GRUPP, GUNTER, EXPERIMENTAL MEDICINE, PHYSIOLOGY. *Current Pos:* assoc prof, Univ Cincinnati, 58-65, dir AV activities, 67-69, chmn dept biomed commun, 69-77, PROF EXP MED, PHYSIOL & PHARMACOL, COL MED, UNIV CINCINNATI, 65- *Personal Data:* b Esslingen, Ger, Feb 6, 20; nat US; m 58; c 6. *Educ:* Univ Freiburg, MD, 48, PhD 53. *Prof Exp:* Instr pharmacol, Univ Freiburg, 48-51, asst prof, 51-53, docent, 53-58. *Mem:* Am Soc Physiol; Am Soc Pharmacol & Exp Therapeut; Ger Pharmacol Soc; Cardiac Muscle Soc; Cent Soc Clin Res. *Res:* Pharmacology of calcium antagonists; physiology of cardiac contraction; heat-production of kidney; cardiovascular dynamics; ion-transport of heart and red blood cells; instructional methodology. *Mailing Add:* Physiol & Pharmacol & Cell Biophys Univ Cincinnati Col Med ML 576 231 Bethesda Ave PO Box 670576 Cincinnati OH 45267-0576. *Fax:* 513-558-5738

GRUPP, INGRID L, PHARMACOLOGY, PHYSIOLOGY. *Current Pos:* RESIDENT PEDIAT, COL MED, UNIV CINCINNATI, 59-, ASSOC PROF PHARMACOL & CELL BIOPHYSICS, 84- *Personal Data:* b Hoechenschwand, Ger, Sept 20, 28; US citizen; c 5. *Educ:* Univ Freiburg, Ger, MD, 55. *Prof Exp:* Res fel physiol, Univ Freiburg, Germany, 55-56; resident, Ueberlingen Hosp, Germany, 56-57; resident pediat, Stoneheinring Hosp, Germany, 57-58. *Concurrent Pos:* Mem, Basic Sci & Hypertension Coun, Am Heart Asn. *Mem:* Soc Exp Biol & Med; Am Heart Asn; Am Soc Pharmacol & Exp Therapeut; Cardiac Muscle Soc; Int Soc Heart Res. *Res:* Regulation of cardiac contraction; mechanism of action of cardiac glycosides and non-glycoside cardiotonic agents; comparative pharmacology of Ca; effects on vascular resistance, myocardial contraction and cardiac conduction; cardiovascular adaptation to anemia. *Mailing Add:* Univ Cincinnati Med Ctr Eden & Bethesda Ave Cincinnati OH 45267-0575. *Fax:* 513-558-1169

GRUSHKIN, BERNARD, PHYSICAL CHEMISTRY, ORGANIC CHEMISTRY. *Current Pos:* SR SCIENTIST, XEROX CORP, 67- *Personal Data:* b Brooklyn, NY, Apr 2, 32; m 61; c 3. *Educ:* NY Univ, BA, 53; Univ Tex, MA, 56, PhD(chem), 58. *Prof Exp:* Res chemist, Callery Chem Co, 59-60; sr res chemist, Res Div, W R Grace & Co, 60-67. *Mem:* Am Chem Soc; Soc Photog Scientists & Engrs. *Res:* Solution kinetics; inorganic polymers; phosphorus nitrogen compounds; chemistry of ammonia and its derivatives; organic sulfur-nitrogen and arsenic-selenium compounds and polymers; organic pigments; photoelectric pigments and polymers. *Mailing Add:* Five Old Brick Circle Pittsford NY 14534-4110

GRUSS, PETER H, MOLECULAR GENETICS. *Current Pos:* DIR, DEPT MOLECULAR CELL BIOL, MAX PLANCK INST BIOPHYS CHEM, WGER, 86- *Personal Data:* b Alsfeld, Ger, June 28, 49; m 72, Karin; c 2. *Educ:* Heidelberg Univ, PhD, 77. *Honors & Awards:* Feldberg Prize, 92; Jean Brachet Lectr, Int Soc Differentiation, 92; Butenandt Lectr, Soc Biol Chem, 92; Leibnitz Prize, Deutsche Forschungsgemeinschaft, 94. *Prof Exp:* Fel, Inst Virus Res, Heidelberg Univ, 77-78; fel, Nat Cancer Inst, 78-80, expert, Lab Molecular Virol, 80-81; vis scientist, Lab Molecular Virol, NIH, 81-82; prof microbiol, Heidelberg Univ, 82-86, mem Directorate Ctr Molecular Biol, 83-86. *Concurrent Pos:* Heisenberg grant, 81; hon prof, Univ Gottingen, 90; ed, Mechanism Develop; assoc ed, Cell. *Mem:* Europ Acad Sci; NY Acad Sci; Am Soc Microbiol; Int Soc Differentiation; Europ Molecular Biol Orgn; Int Soc Develop Biol; Ger Soc Develop Biol. *Res:* Elucidation of the molecular mechanisms controlling mammalian development and differentiation processes; transcription factors such as homeobox encoding genes and finger structure encoding genes; molecular control mechanisms of mouse development. *Mailing Add:* Dept Molecular Cell Biol Max Planck Inst Biophys Chem Am Fassberg 37077 Goettingen Germany

GRUSZCZYK, JEROME HENRY, ANIMAL PHYSIOLOGY. *Current Pos:* RETIRED. *Personal Data:* b Jersey City, NJ, Sept 11, 15. *Educ:* Georgetown Univ, AB, 40; Woodstock Col, MD, PhL, 41, STL, 48; Fordham Univ, MS, 51. *Prof Exp:* Instr comp anat, Univ Scranton, 41-42; asst prof human anat & physiol, Le Moyne Col, 51-53; asst prof, Peter's Col, NJ, 53-66, assoc prof, 66-79, emer prof biol, 79- *Mem:* AAAS; Bot Soc Am; Soc Protozool. *Res:* Enzyme activity in muscle tissue. *Mailing Add:* Gothic Towers 50 Glenwood Jersey City NJ 07306

GRUTT, EUGENE WADSWORTH, JR, EXPLORATION GEOLOGY, NATURAL RESOURCES. *Current Pos:* CONSULT URANIUM RAW MAT & PRECIOUS METALS, 78- *Personal Data:* b Hawthorne, Nev, Sept 29, 16; m 50, Rose Symonik; c Eugene & Diane. *Educ:* Univ Nev, BS, 38. *Prof Exp:* Geologist, Nev Victory Mining Co, 38-42; staff geologist, Isbell Construct Co, 48-53; chief, Casper Br, AEC, 53-58, Grants Br, 58-62 & Resources Appraisal Br, 62-67, dir resource div, 67-73, asst mgr, 73-75, mgr, Grand Junction Off, US Dept Energy, 75-78. *Mem:* AAAS; Am Inst Mining, Metall & Petrol Engrs; Geol Soc Am. *Res:* Appraisal of uranium resources and supply; research and development and investigations in geology, geochemistry, exploration technology, and mining methods. *Mailing Add:* 1325 Grand Ave Grand Junction CO 81501-4511

GRUTZNER, JOHN BRANDON, ORGANIC CHEMISTRY. *Current Pos:* from asst prof to assoc prof, 69-88, PROF CHEM, PURDUE UNIV, WEST LAFAYETTE, 88- *Personal Data:* b Melbourne, Australia, Aug 28, 41; m 65; c 2. *Educ:* Univ Melbourne, BS, 63, PhD(chem), 67. *Prof Exp:* Fel chem, Univ Calif, Los Angeles, 67-68 & Calif Inst Technol, 68-69. *Concurrent Pos:* Prog officer, Nat Sci Found, 81-82. *Mem:* Am Chem Soc; AAAS; Sigma Xi; The Chem Soc; Royal Australian Chem Inst; Int Soc Magnetic Resonance. *Res:* Nuclear magnetic resonance spectroscopy; carbanions; organic reaction mechanisms; fluid dynamics; electrophoretic separations/polymers. *Mailing Add:* Dept Chem Purdue Univ 1393 Brown Bldg West Lafayette IN 47907-1393. *E-Mail:* grutzner@chem.purdue.edu

GRUVER, ROBERT MARTIN, CERAMICS ENGINEERING. *Current Pos:* TECH DIR MAT, CERAMIC FINISHING CO, 68- *Personal Data:* b York, Pa, Mar 6, 21; m 46; c 1. *Educ:* Pa State Univ, BS, 43, MS, 48; Univ Mo, PhD(ceramics eng), 56. *Prof Exp:* Res asst ceramics, Pa State Univ, 43-53; proj dir, Linden Labs, Inc, 54-63, tech dir mat, 63-68. *Mem:* AAAS; Am Ceramics Soc; Am Chem Soc. *Res:* Thermal analysis of ceramic materials; investigations of ceramics and glass including strengthening methods, fractography and local impact damage. *Mailing Add:* 1160 Oneida St State College PA 16801-4899

GRUVER, WILLIAM A, ROBOTICS, MANUFACTURING AUTOMATION. *Current Pos:* PROF ENG SCI, SIMON FRASER UNIV, 92- *Personal Data:* b Harrisburg, Pa, July 13, 41; m 70; c 2. *Educ:* Univ Pa, BSEE, 63, MSEE, 66, PhD(elec eng), 70; Univ London, DIC, 65. *Prof Exp:* Instr elec eng, US Naval Acad, Annapolis, 65-67; teaching fel, Moore Sch Elec Eng, Univ Pa, Philadelphia, 67-71; res engr, DFVLR Inst Dynamics Flight Systs, Munich, Ger, 71-73; asst prof elec eng & opers res, NC State Univ, Raleigh, 74-79; vpres res & develop & co-founder, Robotics Systs Div, Logistics Technol Int, Ltd, Torrance, Calif, 79-83; mgr, Indust Electronics Develop Lab, Gen Elec Co, Charlottesville, Va, 83-84 & Gen Elec Indust Automation Ctr, Frankfurt, Ger, 84-86; div pres, IRT Corp, San Diego, 86-88; dir, Ctr Robotics & Mfg Systs & res prof elec eng, Univ Ky, Lexington, 88-92. *Concurrent Pos:* Aerospace engr, Marshall Space Flight Ctr, NASA, 68-71; Alexander von Humboldt Found US sr scientist award, 73; Ger Acad Exchange Serv res award, 78; assoc ed, Inst Elec & Electronics Engrs Trans Systs, Man & Cybernet, 82- & Inst Elec & Electronic Engrs Trans Robotics & Automation, 86; chmn, Robotics Comt, Inst Elec & Electronics Engrs, Systs, Man & Cybernet Soc, 82-88 & Tech Prog, Int Conf Computer Eng, Am Soc Mech Engrs, 84; mem, var tech comts, Inst Elec & Electronics Engrs, 89- *Mem:* Inst Elec & Electronics Engrs Robotics & Automation Soc (secy, 83-95); Inst Elec & Electronics Engrs Systs Man & Cybernet Soc; Am Soc Mech Engrs; Soc Mfg Engrs. *Res:* Manufacturing automation, robotics, control and optimization; sensor-based control of robotic and automated systems; robotics for hazardous environments; programming environments for automation and computer integrated manufacturing, robot hands, walking machines, robot control and path planning; author of 80 technical publications and two books. *Mailing Add:* Sch Eng Sci Simon Fraser Univ Burnaby BC V5A 1S6 Can

GRUY, HENRY JONES, PETROLEUM TECHNOLOGY. *Current Pos:* owner, H J Gruy & Assocs, Petrol Consults, 50-60, chmn & chief exec officer, Gruy Petrol Mgt, Inc, 60-86, Gruy Petrol Technol Inc, 77-86, H J Gruy & Assocs, Inc, 60-86, chmn, Gruy Eng Corp, 86-88, emer chmn, 88-89, co-chmn, 89-92, chmn, H J Gruy & Co, 92-93, PRES, CHIEF EXEC OFFICER & CHMN, H J GRUY & ASSOCS, 93- *Personal Data:* b Victoria, Tex, June 10, 15; m 41; c 3. *Educ:* Tex A&M Univ, BS, 37, PhD(petrol eng), 56. *Honors & Awards:* De Golyer Medal, Soc Petrol Engrs, 83. *Prof Exp:* Field engr, Stand Oil Co Tex, 37-38; exploit engr, Shell Oil Co, 38-42, dist engr, 42-45; geologist & engr, DeGolyer & MacNaughton, 45-50. *Concurrent Pos:* Task force mem, Fed Power Comn, Nat Gas Res, 71-73, Nat Gas Surv, Supply Tech Adv, 75-76, Prospective Exploit & Develop & Supply Additions to Res No4 Comt, Nat Gas Surv Adv Comt, 76-78; mem, Coordinating Sub Comt Nat Petrol, Council Comt Enhanced Oil Recovery, 82-83. *Mem:* Nat Acad Eng; Am Inst Mining, Metall & Petrol Engrs (vpres, 69); Am Asn Petrol Geologists; Soc Petrol Eval Engrs (pres, 64); fel Australasian Inst Mining & Metall; fel Inst Petrol; hon mem Soc Petrol Engrs (treas, 65-67, pres, 68); Soc Independent Prof Earth Scientists; Am Petrol Inst. *Res:* Oil and gas resource analysis; appraisal, producing and non-producing oil and gas interests; author of numerous publications. *Mailing Add:* H J Gruy & Assocs 1200 Smith Suite 3040 Houston TX 77002. *Fax:* 713-739-6112

GRUZALSKI, GREG ROBERT, MATERIALS SCIENCE & THIN FILMS, SOLID STATE PHYSICS. *Current Pos:* STAFF MEM, OAK RIDGE NAT LAB, 80- *Personal Data:* b Chicago, Ill, April 19, 48; m 72; c 3. *Educ:* Western Ill Univ, BS, 70, MS, 71; Univ Nebr, PhD(physics), 77. *Prof Exp:* Res fel physics & mat sci, Harvard Univ, 77-80. *Mem:* Am Physics Soc; Mat Res Soc; Sigma Xi; Am Vacuum Soc. *Res:* Experimental and computational solid state physics and materials science; bulk materials (electronic and magnetic structure), surface science, and synthesis and properties of thin films. *Mailing Add:* Box 2008 Oak Ridge Nat Lab Oak Ridge TN 37831. *Fax:* 423-574-0323; *E-Mail:* grg@ornl.gov.

GRYC, GEORGE, GEOLOGY. *Current Pos:* Field geologist, US Geol Surv, 43-60, staff geologist, 60-63, chief, Br Alaskan Geol, 63-76, regional geologist, 76-77, chief, Off Nat Petrol Res Alaska, 77-81, dirs rep, Western Reg, 77-95, GEN CHMN, CIRCUM-PACIFIC MAP PROJ, US GEOL SURV, 86-, EMER SCIENTIST, 95- *Personal Data:* b St Paul, Minn, July 27, 19; m 42, Jean L Funk; c James A, Stephen M, Christina L, Paula J & Georgina. *Educ:* Univ Minn, BS, 40, MS, 41. *Mem:* Geol Soc Am; Paleont Soc; Am Asn Petrol Geologists; Arctic Inst NAm; Cosmos Club. *Res:* Potential petroleum resources and regional geology of Circum-Pacific Region; paleontology; stratigraphy. *Mailing Add:* US Geol Surv MS-901 Menlo Park CA 94025

GRYDER, JOHN WILLIAM, PHYSICAL CHEMISTRY, INORGANIC CHEMISTRY. *Current Pos:* from instr to assoc prof, 49-66, assoc dean, Fac Arts & Sci, 82-84, PROF CHEM, JOHNS HOPKINS UNIV, 66- *Personal Data:* b Los Angeles, Calif, Nov 6, 26; m 49; c 3. *Educ:* Calif Inst Technol, BS, 46; Columbia Univ, PhD(chem), 50. *Prof Exp:* Jr scientist chem, Brookhaven Nat Lab, 48-49. *Mem:* Am Chem Soc. *Res:* Radiochemistry; kinetics; nature of ionic species in solution; phosphorus chemistry; surface chemistry and catalysis. *Mailing Add:* Dept Chem Johns Hopkins Univ Baltimore MD 21218-2680

GRYDER, ROSA MEYERSBURG, BIOCHEMISTRY, TOXICOLOGY. *Current Pos:* toxicologist, Ctr Food Safety & Nutrit, 82-89, ASSOC DIR RES, NAT CTR TOXICOL RES, FOOD & DRUG ADMIN, 80-; CONSULT TOXICOL, 89- *Personal Data:* b Brooklyn, NY, Aug 23, 26; m 49; c 3. *Educ:* Bucknell Univ, BS, 47; Yale Univ, MS, 49; Johns Hopkins Univ, PhD(biochem), 56. *Prof Exp:* Asst microbiol, Brookhaven Nat Labs, 47-48; res assoc physiol chem, Sch Med, Johns Hopkins Univ, 60-63; from instr to asst prof biochem, Sch Med, Univ Md, Baltimore, 66-74; staff sci adv, Off Assoc Comnr Sci, Food & Drug Admin, 74-80. *Concurrent Pos:* Nat Inst Neurol Dis & Blindness fel, Wilmer Ophthal Inst, 56-59. *Mem:* NY Acad Sci; AAAS; Soc Risk Analysis; Sigma Xi; Soc Toxicol. *Res:* Enzymology; neurochemistry; genetic toxicology. *Mailing Add:* 2006 W Rogers Ave Baltimore MD 21209-4551

GRYNBAUM, BRUCE B, MEDICINE. *Current Pos:* asst prof, 50-58, assoc prof clin phys med & rehab, 58-68, PROF, MED CTR, NY UNIV, 68- *Personal Data:* b Anapa, Russia, May 25, 20; nat US; m 43; c 2. *Educ:* Columbia Univ, MD, 43; Am Bd Phys Med & Rehab, dipl, 52. *Prof Exp:* Intern, Metropolitan Hosp, New York, 44; resident, Mt Sinai Hosp, 47-48. *Concurrent Pos:* Fel, Goldwater Hosp, 49-50; dir phys med & rehab, City Dept Hosps, New York, 50-70; consult, Nat Inst Rehab & Health Serv, 64; mem adv comt auto ins & compensation study, Dept Transp, Washington, DC, 72; consult, Long Island Jewish Hosp, St Vincent's Hosp, Wycoff Heights Hosp & St Claire's Hosp, 78; vis physician, Beekman-Downtown Hosp; mem adv bd, NY State Chap, Arthritis Found; mem exec comt, Cent Labor Rehab Coun, NY, Inc; dir rehab med, Bellevue Hosp; consult dept hosp facilities, US Pub Health Serv; chmn med adv bd, Sidney Hillman Inst, mem med adv bd, St Mary's Children's Hosp, Bayside, NY; dir, Rehab Med Serv, Bellevue Hosp; mem prof adv bd, Inst Crippled & Disabled, sr med consult; mem, Health Task Force, Community Coun; dir, Rehab Med, Beekman Downtown Hosp, mem, Health & Hosp Corp Adv Comt, Amputee, Orthotic, Neuromuscular & Pediat Orthop Prog. *Mem:* AMA; Am Acad Phys Med; Am Cong Rehab Med; Int Asn Rehab Facil; Am Pub Health Asn. *Res:* Physical medicine and rehabilitation; compensation medicine. *Mailing Add:* 400 E 34th St Med Sch New York Univ 550 First Ave New York NY 10016

GRYTING, HAROLD JULIAN, CHEMISTRY. *Current Pos:* CONSULT EXPLOSIVES, PROPELLANTS, & PYROTECHNICS, SOUTHWEST RES INST, 80-; PRES GRYTING ENERGETICS SCI CO, 88-; VPRES ENVIRON ENTERPRISES, INC, 90- *Personal Data:* b Belview, Minn, Dec 31, 19; m 54, Barbara J Ruggles; c Corri & Paul. *Educ:* St Olaf Col, BA, 41; Purdue Univ, PhD(org chem), 47. *Prof Exp:* Grad asst chem, NDak State Col, 41-42; chemist, E I du Pont de Nemours & Co, Ill, 42-43; res chemist, Naval Weapons Ctr, 47-49, head, Properties Sect, 49-51, Properties Br, 52-54, Plastics Br, 54-56, Explosives Res Br, 56-65, tech asst to head, Explosives & Pyrotech Div, 65-72, assoc head, Appl Res & Processing Div, 72-76, res chemist, safety & techn ol coordr & proj mgr, 76-80. *Concurrent Pos:* Mem, Tech Steering Comt, Joint Army, Navy, NASA, Air Force Safety & Environ Protection Working Group; chmn, Triserv Comt Qualification & Performance Test Methods for Explosives; mem Jannaf Propulsion Hazards Subcomt; environ comt, Am Inst Chemists. *Mem:* Fel AAAS; fel Am Inst Chemists; Am Chem Soc; NY Acad Sci; Am Defense Preparedness Asn; Am Inst Astronaut & Aeronaut. *Res:* Alkylation, chloromethylation chlorination and fluorination; synthesis of wetting agents; germicides; high explosives compositions; explosive effects; pollution abatement; polymer chemistry, qualification, recovery and identification of explosives, propellants and pyrotechnics; synthesis of polymers that do not shrink on cure for low vulnerability ammunition propellants; analyzing and selecting explosives and other materials for numerous applications; investigation of accidental detonations/explosions; temperature insensitive explosives; granted 3 US patents. *Mailing Add:* Gryting Energetics Sci Co 7126 Shadow Run San Antonio TX 78250-3483. *Fax:* 210-680-5301

GRZYMALA-BUSSE, JERZY WITOLD, EXPERT SYSTEMS, KNOWLEDGE DISCOVERY. *Current Pos:* prof comput sci, 81-93, PROF ELEC ENG & COMPUT SCI, UNIV KANS, 93- *Personal Data:* b Warsaw, Poland, April 3, 42; m 67, Dobioslawa Thomas; c Anna, Witold & Jan. *Educ:* Tech Univ Poznan, Poland, MS, 64, PhD, 69; Univ Wroclaw, MS, 67; Tech Univ Warsaw, Dr habil, 72. *Honors & Awards:* Award, Minister Sci, Higher Educ & Technol, Poland, 70, 73 & 76; Award, Polish Acad Sci, 81. *Prof Exp:* Instr elec eng, Tech Univ Poznan, 64-70, from asst prof to assoc prof comput sci, 70-80. *Concurrent Pos:* Vis prof comput sci, Univ Kans, 77 & 80-81 & Banach Int Math Ctr, Poland, 74; assoc ed, Found Control Eng, 75-84, ed, Fundamenta Informaticae, 75-90; ed, Found Comput & Decision Sci, 91-, J Comput & Info, 95- *Mem:* Am Asn Artificial Intel; Asn Comput Mach; Europ Asn Theoret Comput Sci. *Res:* Rough set theory; machine learning; expert systems dealing with uncertainty; knowledge acquisition. *Mailing Add:* Dept Elec Eng & Comput Sci Univ Kans Lawrence KS 66045-2192. *E-Mail:* jerzy@eecs.ukans.edu

GSCHNEIDNER, KARL A(LBERT), JR, PHYSICAL METALLURGY, SOLID STATE PHYSICS OF RARE EARTH MATERIALS. *Current Pos:* from assoc prof to prof phys metall, Iowa State Univ, 63-79, dir, Rare-Earth Info Ctr, 66-96, prof, 67-79, prog dir metall & ceramics, 74-79, ANSON MARSTON DISTINGUISHED PROF, AMES LAB & DEPT MAT SCI & ENG, IOWA STATE UNIV, 79- *Personal Data:* b Detroit, Mich, Nov 16, 30; m 57, Melba E Pickenpaugh; c Thomas, David, Edward & Kathryn. *Educ:* Univ Detroit, BS, 52; Iowa State Univ, PhD(phys chem), 57. *Honors & Awards:* William Hume-Rothery Award, Minerals, Metals & Mat Soc, 78; Co-recipient Outstanding Sci Accomplishment in Metall & Ceramics Award, US Dept Energy, 82; Frank H Spedding Prize, Rare Earth Res Conf, 91. *Prof Exp:* Staff mem phys metall, Los Alamos Sci Lab, 57-63, sect leader, 61-63; asst prof solid state physics, Dept Physics & Mat Res Lab, Univ Ill, 62-63. *Concurrent Pos:* Bd dirs, Acta Metallurgica, 92-, chmn bd dir, 96- *Mem:* AAAS; Am Chem Soc; Am Crystallog Asn; fel Minerals, Metals & Mat Soc; Am Phys Soc; Iowa Acad Sci; Sigma Xi; Mat Res Soc; Inst Elect & Electronics Engrs; Magnetics Soc; fel Am Soc Mat Int; hon mem Mat Res Soc India. *Res:* Physical metallurgy of rare-earth metals and alloys; alloy theory; magnetic refrigeration; low temperature heat capacity and magnetic properties of solids; hydrogen in metals and metal hydrides; thermodynamic properties of metals. *Mailing Add:* Ames Lab Iowa State Univ Ames IA 50011-3020. *Fax:* 515-294-9579; *E-Mail:* cagey@ameslab.gov

GSCHWEND, HEINZ W, ORGANIC CHEMISTRY, MEDICINAL CHEMISTRY. *Current Pos:* VPRES RES & DEVELOP INFLAMMATION, ARRIS PHARMACEUT CORP, 92- *Personal Data:* b Unterseen, Switz, Apr 12, 36; m 65; c 2. *Educ:* Swiss Fed Inst Technol, Dipl Ing Chem, 61, Dr Sc Tech(org chem), 64. *Prof Exp:* Res assoc org chem, Swiss Fed Inst Technol, 64-65; res assoc, Harvard Univ, 65-67; sr staff scientist med chem, Ciba-Geigy Corp, 67-70, mgr org chem, 70-72, dir org chem, 73-79, exec dir chem res, 80-86, vpres drug discovery pharmaceut div, 86-88, head, Cent REs Lab, Ciba-Geigy Ltd, 89-91. *Concurrent Pos:* Gen & pharmaceut res mgt. *Mem:* Am Chem Soc; Swiss Chem Soc. *Res:* Synthesis of novel compounds with potential biological activity; general synthetic organic chemistry, in particular intramolecular cycloaddtions, heteroatom directed lithiations, new synthetic methodology; heterocyclic chemistry; drug design. *Mailing Add:* Arris Pharmaceut Corp 385 Oyster Point Blvd Suite 3 South San Francisco CA 94080. *Fax:* 650-737-3560

GSCHWENDTNER, ALFRED BENEDICT, OPTICS. *Current Pos:* staff mem plasma physics, Mass Inst Technol, 64-69, asst group leader infrared systs, 69-71, group leader optical systs, 71-95, SR STAFF, LINCOLN LAB, MASS INST TECHNOL, 95- *Personal Data:* b Altoona, Pa, Dec 16, 36; m 61, Joann McRae. *Educ:* Pa State Univ, BS, 61, MS, 62. *Prof Exp:* Res assoc space physics, Univ Ill, 62-64. *Mem:* Sigma Xi; Am Inst Aeronaut & Astronaut; Am Inst Physics. *Res:* Application of laser and infrared optical systems to tactical problems; theory and application of artificial neural networks. *Mailing Add:* One Harrington Rd Lexington MA 02173. *Fax:* 781-981-4223; *E-Mail:* gsch@ll.mit.edu

GU, BINHE, STABLE ISOTOPE APPLICATIONS TO AQUATIC SCIENCE, NUTRIENT CYCLING IN AQUATIC ECOSYSTEMS. *Current Pos:* RES ASSOC, UNIV FLA, 93- *Personal Data:* b Qingyuam, Guangdong, China, Mar 28, 57; m 85, Le Xu; c Bosi & Diana S. *Educ:* Zhanjiang Fisheries Col China, BS, 81; Nat Network Aquacult Ctr Asia, Dipl, 85; Univ Alaska, Fairbanks, MS, 92, PhD(oceanog), 93. *Prof Exp:* Asst lectr limnol, Zhanjiang Fisheries Col, 81-86, lectr limnol marine planktology, 87-88; res asst, Univ Alaska, Fairbanks, 88-93. *Mem:* Am Soc Linmol & Oceanog; Am Geophys Union. *Res:* Stable isotope analysis of aquatic food webs, biogeochemical response of great lakes to nutrient enrichments; nutrient cycling in lakes, rivers and marine ecosystems. *Mailing Add:* 307 SW 16th Ave Gainesville FL 32601. *Fax:* 904-392-3462; *E-Mail:* binhe@nervm.nerdc.ufl.edu

GU, YAN, ENDOCRINOLOGY & PHYSIOLOGY UTERUS, REPRODUCTIVE TOXICOLOGY. *Current Pos:* RES ASSOC, UNIV ILL, CHICAGO, 90- *Personal Data:* b Peking, Apr 8, 53; m 89, Jwei Y Cheng; c William C. *Educ:* Ohio State Univ, PhD(reprod endocrinol & toxicol), 90. *Concurrent Pos:* Vis scientist, Nat Ctr Toxicol Res/Food & Drug Admin. *Mem:* Soc Study Reprod; AAAS; Endocrine Soc. *Res:* Regulation decidual hormones in uterus during pregnancy; mechanism and toxicity of estrogen on female reproductive track. *Mailing Add:* Nat Ctr Toxicol Res HFT-130 3900 Nat Ctr Toxicol Res Rd Jefferson AR 72079-9502

GUALTIERI, DEVLIN MICHAEL, CRYSTAL GROWTH, MAGNETISM. *Current Pos:* staff physicist, Allied-Signal Inc, 77-81, sr res physicist, 81-83, res assoc, 83-91, SR RES SCIENTIST, ALLIED-SIGNAL INC, MORRISTOWN, NJ, 91- *Personal Data:* b Utica, NY, Dec 11, 47; m 71, Anne V Perretta; c Michael & Marianne. *Educ:* Syracuse Univ, BS, 70, PhD(solid state sci), 74. *Prof Exp:* Res assoc chem, Univ Pittsburgh, 74-76, res asst prof, 76-77. *Concurrent Pos:* Weizmann fel, Dept Chem, Univ Pittsburgh, 76-77. *Mem:* Am Phys Soc; Inst Elec & Electronics Engrs; AAAS; Am Asn Crystal Growth. *Res:* Synthesis of magnetic and optical thin films, especially epitaxy of crystal oxides for optical sensors; device structures based on thin film materials, including magneto-optical sensors. *Mailing Add:* 12 Moore St Ledgewood NJ 07852. *Fax:* 973-455-3008

GUARINO, ANTHONY MICHAEL, RESEARCH ADMINISTRATION, TOXICOLOGY. *Current Pos:* rev scientist, Bur Drugs, 80-84, CHIEF, FISHERY RES BR, FOOD & DRUG ADMIN, DAUPHIN ISLAND, ALA, 84- *Personal Data:* b Framingham, Mass, Dec 11, 34; m 57; c 10. *Educ:* Boston Col, BS, 56; Univ RI, MS, 63, PhD(pharmacol), 66. *Honors & Awards:* Pub Health Serv Commendation Medal, 90. *Prof Exp:* Clin chemist, Chem Lab, Mass Gen Hosp, Boston, 54-57; teaching/res asst, Univ RI, 60-66; res assoc, Pharmacol & Toxicol Prog, Lab Chem Pharmacol, Nat Heart Inst, Md, 66-68; res pharmacologist, Lab Chem Pharmacol, Nat Cancer Inst, 68-73, chief, Lab Toxicol, 73-80. *Concurrent Pos:* Mem fac toxicol, NIH Grad Prog, 68-84, fac chmn, Dept Pharmacol & Toxicol, 80-84; adj prof, Dept Pharmacol, Col Med, Univ Southern Ala, Mobile, 85- *Mem:* Am Soc Pharmacol & Exp Therapeut; Soc Toxicol; Am Chem Soc; NY Acad Sci. *Res:* Drug transport; biliary transport; drug metabolism; marine pharmacology and toxicology; fate and distribution of xenobiotics in aquatic species; regulatory pharmacology and toxicology. *Mailing Add:* Univ SAla Col Med MSB 3130 Mobile AL 36688. *Fax:* 334-460-6798

GUARINO, ARMAND JOHN, BIOCHEMISTRY. *Current Pos:* RETIRED. *Personal Data:* b Beverly, Mass, Jan 24, 26; m 49; c 5. *Educ:* Harvard Univ, BS, 49; Tufts Col, PhD(biochem), 53. *Prof Exp:* Instr biochem & nutrit, Med Sch, Tufts Col, 53-54; res assoc biochem, Mass Inst Technol, 54-55; from asst prof to assoc prof, Sch Med, Univ Mich, 55-63; prof & chmn dept, Woman's Med Col Pa, 63-68; prof biochem & chmn dept, Univ Tex Health Sci Ctr, San Antonio, 68-75, dean Grad Sch Biomed Sci & Sch Allied Health Sci, 73-89. *Mem:* Am Soc Biol Chem. *Res:* Nucleoside and nucleotide metabolism. *Mailing Add:* PO Box 240 Lake Leelanau MI 49653-0261

GUBBINS, KEITH E(DMUND), chemical engineering, physical chemistry; deceased, see previous edition for last biography

GUBER, ALBERT LEE, GEOLOGY. *Current Pos:* NSF fel, Pa State Univ, 62-63, from asst prof to prof geol, 63-83, chmn, Geol Grad Prog, PROF GEOL, PA STATE UNIV, 83-; CONSULT. *Personal Data:* b Heidelberg, Pa, June 17, 35; m 61; c 2. *Educ:* Univ Pittsburgh, BS, 57; Univ Ill, PhD(geol), 62. *Honors & Awards:* Lindback Award. *Concurrent Pos:* Various offices, Marine Sci Consortium, 75- *Mem:* Am Asn Petrol Geol; Paleont Soc; Soc Econ Paleont & Mineral; AAAS; Sigma Xi. *Res:* Coastal geochemistry; Silurian facies of the central and southern Appalachians; compaction and the migration of barrier islands; sedimentology of back-barrier fine-grained sediments. *Mailing Add:* Dept Geosci Pa State Univ University Park PA 16802-1009

GUBERNATIS, JAMES EDWARD, CONDENSED MATTER PHYSICS, COMPUTATIONAL PHYSICS. *Current Pos:* staff mem physics, 75-81, dep group leader, Statist Physics & Mat Theory Group, 81-83, STAFF MEM, LOS ALAMOS NAT LAB, 83- *Personal Data:* b Baltimore, Md, July 22, 45; m 70, Michele A Dulick; c Catherine E & David C. *Educ:* Loyola Col, Md, BS, 67; Case Western Reserve Univ, MS, 69, PhD(physics), 72. *Prof Exp:* Asst prof physics, Ohio Northern Univ, 72-73; res assoc, Lab Atomic & Solid State Physics, Cornell Univ, 73-75. *Concurrent Pos:* Coun Panel Math Sci Appl Mat Sci, Nat Res, 91-93. *Mem:* AAAS; fel Am Phys Soc; Soc Indust & Appl Math. *Res:* Quantum Monte Carlo simulations of strongly correlated electron systems and lower dimensional systems with electron phonon coupling; parallel algorithms for condensed matter physics. *Mailing Add:* Los Alamos Sci Lab T-11 MS B262 PO Box 1663 Los Alamos NM 87545

GUBERSKY, VICTOR R, DERMATOLOGY. *Current Pos:* PVT PRACT, 75- *Personal Data:* b Lamont, Alta, May 17, 35; m 57; c 3. *Educ:* Univ Alta, MD, 59. *Prof Exp:* From intern to resident internal med, Edmonton Gen Hosp, Alta, 59-61; resident dermat, Cleveland Clin Found, Ohio, 61-64; assoc med dir, Inst Clin Med, Syntex Ltd, 64-68, head, Div Inflammatory Dis & Med Dir, 66-68, vpres & gen mgr, 68-75. *Concurrent Pos:* Fel dermat, 59-64. *Mem:* Am Acad Dermat; AMA. *Res:* Basic and clinical dermatological research, especially the effect of corticosteroids on various dermatoses; antimetabolites, antiviral and antiandrogenic agents. *Mailing Add:* 3712 Mission Ave Carmichael CA 95608

GUBLER, CLARK JOHNSON, BIOCHEMISTRY, ENZYMOLOGY. *Current Pos:* from assoc prof to prof, 58-78, EMER PROF CHEM, BRIGHAM YOUNG UNIV, 78- *Personal Data:* b La Verkin, Utah, July 14, 13; m 38, Maurina Kiar; c David C, Kathleen, Ann & Ronald K. *Educ:* Brigham Young Univ, AB, 39; Utah State Univ, MA, 41; Univ Calif, PhD(biochem), 45. *Prof Exp:* Asst chem, Brigham Young Univ, 38-39; asst, Utah State Univ, 39-41; asst biochem, Univ Calif, 41-45; res chemist, El Dorado Oil Works, Calif, 44-46; res assoc med, Sch Med, Univ Utah, 46-52, asst prof, 52-56; USPHS spec res fel, Univ Wis, 56-58. *Concurrent Pos:* Assoc prof, William Col, 44-45; instr, Univ Utah, 51-60; Am Heart Asn advan res fel, 58-60, estab investr, 60-65; vis prof, Univ Freiburg, 64-65; USPHS spec res fel, Univ San Diego, 71-72; vis prof, Univ Kuwait, 82-86, vis prof & Fulbright fel, Sultan Qaboos Univ, Oman, 89-90. *Mem:* AAAS; Am Soc Biol Chemists; Am Inst Nutrit; NY Acad Sci; Am Soc Clin Nutrit; Deutsche Biochemische Gesellschaft. *Res:* Iron, copper metabolism; biological functions and mechanisms of action of thiamin; alpha-keto-acid metabolism; biochemistry of learning and development; nutritional biochemistry; enzymology. *Mailing Add:* Grad Sect Biochem Brigham Young Univ C-421 BNSN Provo UT 84602

GUBLER, DUANE J, VIROLOGY, MOSQUITO-BOURNE DISEASE ECOLOGY PREVENTION & CONTROL. *Current Pos:* DIR, DIV VECTOR-BOURNE INFECTIOUS DIS, CTRS DIS CONTROL & PREV, FT COLLINS, 89- *Personal Data:* b Santa Clara, Utah, June 4, 39; m 58, Bobbie J Carroll; c Justin C & Stuart J. *Educ:* Utah State Univ, BS, 63; Univ Hawaii, MS, 65; Johns Hopkins Univ, ScD, 69. *Hon Degrees:* DSc, SUtah State Univ, 88. *Honors & Awards:* Cert Appreciation, Pres Gerald R Ford, 75; Third Lloyd E Rozeboom lectr, Johns Hopkins Univ, 79, Dean's Lectr,

90; Charles Franklin Craig lectr, Am Soc Trop Med & Hyg, 88. *Prof Exp:* Instr parasitol, Johns Hopkins Univ, 68-69, lectr med entom, 69-70, asst prof, 70-71; from asst prof to assoc prof med entom & parasitol, Univ Hawaii, Honolulu, 71-78; assoc prof med entom, Univ Ill, Urbana, 78-80; res microbiologist virol, Ft Collins, 80-81, dir, San Juan Labs & Chief, Dengue Br, Ctrs Dis Control, USPHS, San Juan, 81-89. *Concurrent Pos:* Head, med entom prog, JHU ICMRT, Calcutta, India, 69-71, guest worker virol, Pac Res Sect, Nat Inst Allergy & Infectious Dis, NIH, 71-75; consult herbicides in Vietnam, Nat Res Coun, Nat Acad Sci, 72; adv, Pan Am Health Orgn, Washington, DC, 73 & 82-96; consult, WHO, New Delhi, 74-80, 82, 86, & 91-96, USAID, Jakarta, 77-, Int Develop Res Ctr, Ottawa, 79-82 & 92-93; head virol dept, US Naval Med Res Unit 2, Jakarta, 75-78; highlights med entom lectr, Enton Soc Am, 80 & 95; adv, Pan Am Health Orgn, Washington, DC, 81-; consult, US Agency Int Develop, Dominican Repub, 83-, Rockefeller Found, 87-96, govts Nepal, Indonesia, Taiwan, Mex, Palau, Vietnam, Philippines, Australia, Thailand, PR, China, Sri Lanka & Venezuela, 88-96; Deans lectr, Johns Hopkins Univ Sch Hygiene & Pub Health, 90, adj prof, Depts Int Health; adj prof, Dept Microbiol, Colo State Univ. *Mem:* AAAS; Am Soc Tropical Med & Hyg; Am Soc Parasitolog; Am Mosquito Control Asn; Entom Soc Am; Sigma Xi; Infectious Dis Soc Am; Soc Ecol Vector. *Res:* Ecology of mosquito-borne diseases; dengue-dengue hemorrhagic fever with primary emphasis on virology, epidemiology, entomology, surveillance, prevention and control. *Mailing Add:* Ctr Dis Control & Prev Div Vector-Bourne Infectious Dis USPHS PO Box 2087 Ft Collins CO 80522. *Fax:* 970-221-6476; *E-Mail:* djg2@cdc.gov

GUBNER, RICHARD S, INTERNAL MEDICINE, CARDIOLOGY. *Current Pos:* CLIN PROF, STATE UNIV NY, DOWNSTATE, MED CTR, 56- *Personal Data:* b New York, NY, July 20, 13; m 49; c 3. *Educ:* Columbia Univ, AB, 33; NY Univ, MD, 36; Am Bd Internal Med, dipl, 44; Am Bd Cardiovasc Dis, dipl, 52. *Prof Exp:* Med dir, Diag Serv Div, Equitable Life Ins Soc US, 41-69. *Concurrent Pos:* Consult physician, Pa RR, 57-69; dir med, Kings County Hosp, Brooklyn, 59-67. *Mem:* Sigma Xi; fel Am Col Physicians. *Res:* Cardiovascular disease. *Mailing Add:* 2905 Mill Stream Ct Clearwater FL 34621

GUBSER, DONALD URBAN, SOLID STATE PHYSICS, SUPERCONDUCTIVITY. *Current Pos:* RES SCIENTIST, NAVAL RES LAB, 69-, SCI MGT & ADMINR, 81- *Personal Data:* b Alton, Ill, Dec 21, 40; m 67, Virginia McCarthy; c Andrea D & Michael D. *Educ:* Univ Ill, BS, 63, MS, 64, PhD(physics), 69. *Concurrent Pos:* Advan grad training, Switz Fed Tech Univ, 76-77; teaching, George Washington Univ, 78-; co-ed, J Superconductivity, 88- *Mem:* Fel Am Phys Soc; Metall Soc; Sigma Xi; Mat Res Soc; Cryog Soc. *Res:* New high temperature superconducting oxides; superintendent of materials division with research in superconductivity, magnetism, physical metallurgy, ceramics and composites and material mechanics. *Mailing Add:* Naval Res Lab Code 6300 4555 Overlook Ave SW Washington DC 20375-5343. *Fax:* 202-404-8009; *E-Mail:* gubser@anvil.nw.navy.mil

GUCCIONE, JULIUS MATTEO, BIOMECHANICS, CARDIAC MECHANICS. *Current Pos:* ASST PROF MECH ENG, WASH UNIV, 93- *Personal Data:* b Chicago, Ill, April 24, 63; m 92, Samira Salehi-Had. *Educ:* Tulane Univ, BS, 85; Univ Calif, San Diego, MS, 87, PhD(bioeng), 90. *Prof Exp:* Res fel, Johns Hopkins Univ, Sch Med, 90-93. *Mem:* Am Soc Mech Engrs; Biomed Eng Soc; Am Acad Mech. *Res:* Application of mechanical engineering principles to the treatment of cardiovascular diseases; advancement of knowledge concerning the mechanical behavior of the intact walls of the heart. *Mailing Add:* 511 S Meramec Ave St Louis MO 63105

GUCHHAIT, RAS BIHARI, BIOCHEMISTRY. *Current Pos:* instr physiol chem, Sch Med, 72-73, ASST PROF EPIDEMIOL, BIOCHEM & BIOPHYS SCI, SCH HYG & PUB HEALTH, JOHNS HOPKINS UNIV, 73- *Personal Data:* b Calcutta, India, May 31, 35; m 56; c 4. *Educ:* Univ Calcutta, BS, 56, MS, 58, PhD, 62. *Prof Exp:* Fel & biochemist, Univ Wis & Vet Admin Hosp, Madison, 63-66; scientist, Univ Calcutta, India, 66-69; fel, NY Univ Med Ctr, 69 & Johns Hopkins Univ, 70-72; sr res scientist, Md Psychiat Res Ctr, 80-89. *Mem:* NY Acad Sci; Soc Neurosci. *Res:* Hormonal and metabolic regulation of enzymes; mechanism of enzyme reactions in relation to subunit structure in mammalian and bacterial systems; regulation of biogenic amine metabolism; cell culture and its application. *Mailing Add:* 1020 Circle Dr Baltimore MD 21227

GUCKEL, GUNTER, FLUID DYNAMICS, FINITE ELEMENT ANALYSIS. *Current Pos:* dir, mgt info systs, 83-, VPRES INFO TECHNOL, ESSEX GROUP INC. *Personal Data:* b Hamburg, Ger, Jan 30, 35; US citizen; m; c 1. *Educ:* Univ Ill, BS, 64, BS, 65, MS, 67. *Prof Exp:* Sr mathematician, United Technol Res Lab, 67-73; systs mgr, Arthur D Little Systs, 73-75; vpres systs mgr, AG Becker, 75-78; mgr mgt info systs, Norden Systs, 78-83. *Concurrent Pos:* Adj fac mem, Univ Hartford, 68-73. *Mem:* Am Phys Soc; Asn Comput Mach. *Res:* Information systems and factory automation. *Mailing Add:* 1601 Wall St Ft Wayne IN 46802

GUCKENHEIMER, JOHN, DYNAMICAL SYSTEMS, BIFURCATION THEORY. *Current Pos:* PROF, CORNELL UNIV, 85-, DIR, CTR APPL MATH, 89- *Personal Data:* b Baton Rouge, La, Sept 26, 45; m 74; c 2. *Educ:* Harvard Univ, BA, 66; Univ Calif, Berkeley, PhD(math), 70. *Prof Exp:* Vis lectr, IMPA, Rio de Janeiro, 69; sr res fel, Univ Warwick, 69-70; mem, Inst Advan Study, 70-72; lectr, Mass Inst Technol, 72-73; from asst prof to prof, Univ Calif, Santa Cruz, 73-85. *Concurrent Pos:* Chmn, math dept, Univ Calif, Santa Cruz, 76-78; vis mem, Courant Inst Math Sci, NY Univ, 79; mem, Inst Hautes Etudes Sci, 80; mem, Math Sci Res Inst, 83-84; mem, Mittag-Leffler Inst; Guggenheim fel, 84; chmn, Univ Calif Coord Comt Nonlinear-Sci, 83-85; bd dirs, Math Sci Res Inst, 82-85. *Mem:* Am Math Soc; Soc Indust & Appl Math. *Res:* Bifurcation theory. *Mailing Add:* White Hall Cornell Univ Ithaca NY 14853-7901

GUCKER, GAIL, MATHEMATICS. *Current Pos:* PROF MATH, ROCHESTER INST TECHNOL, 82- *Personal Data:* b Pa, June 22, 42. *Educ:* State Univ Ny, BA, 73, MS, 78. *Mailing Add:* 60 Nicholson St Rochester NY 14620

GUCWA, PAUL RAMON, GEOLOGY. *Current Pos:* area supvr, 88-91, coord mgr, Domestic Explor, 90-92, US EXPLOR MGR, GULF COAST DIV, N AM FRONTIERS, 92- *Personal Data:* b Buffalo, NY, Jan 26, 47; m, Cheryl Heubach; c Jennifer, Christina & Michael. *Educ:* Franklin & Marshall Col, BA, 69; Univ Tex, Austin, MA, 71, PhD(geol), 74. *Prof Exp:* Res geologist, Denver Res Ctr, Marathon Oil Co, 74-78, area geologist, 78-80; coordr, Sohio Petrol, N Alaska, 80-84, gen mgr, Planning & Bus Develop, 84-85, chief geologist, 85-88. *Mem:* Geol Soc Am; Am Asn Petrol Geologists. *Res:* Structural geology; tectonics; mechanics of deformation of aggregate materials; geology of continental margins; oil and gas exploration. *Mailing Add:* 842 Plainwood Dr Houston TX 77079

GUDAS, LORRAINE J, DEVELOPMENTAL BIOLOGY, BIOCHEMISTRY. *Current Pos:* ASSOC PROF, BIOL CHEM & MOLECULAR PHARMACOL DEPT, HARVARD MED SCH, HARVARD UNIV, 86- *Educ:* Princeton Univ, PhD(biochem), 75. *Mailing Add:* Dept Pharmacol Cornell Univ Med Col 1300 York Ave New York NY 10021-4896. *Fax:* 212-746-8858

GUDAUSKAS, ROBERT THOMAS, VIROLOGY. *Current Pos:* from asst prof to assoc prof, 60-69, PROF PLANT PATH, AUBURN UNIV, 69- *Personal Data:* b Georgetown, Ill, July 26, 34; m 56; c 3. *Educ:* Univ Eastern Ill, BS, 56; Univ Ill, MS, 58, PhD(plant path), 60. *Prof Exp:* Res asst plant path, Univ Ill, 56-60. *Mem:* Am Phytopath Soc; Sigma Xi. *Res:* Plant virology. *Mailing Add:* 813 Heard Ct Auburn AL 36830-6243

GUDDER, STANLEY PHILLIP, MATHEMATICS. *Current Pos:* assoc prof, Univ Denver, 69-74, asst chmn dept, 73-75, chmn dept, 79-84, PROF MATH, UNIV DENVER, 74- *Personal Data:* b Centralia, Ill, Jan 6, 37; m 58; c 3. *Educ:* Wash Univ, BS, 58; Univ Ill, MS, 60, PhD(math), 64. *Prof Exp:* Asst res math, Army Math Res Ctr, Univ Wis-Madison, 64-65, asst prof math, Univ, 65-69. *Concurrent Pos:* Sci Res Coun fel, Gt Brit, 75; sabbatical, Univ Nottingham, 75-76, Univ Bern, Univ Milan & Univ Genoa, 85. *Mem:* Sigma Xi. *Res:* Mathematical foundations of quantum mechanics; functional analysis; operator theory. *Mailing Add:* 1710 S Newport Way Denver CO 80224-2212

GUDE, ARTHUR JAMES, 3RD, MINERALOGY. *Current Pos:* RETIRED. *Personal Data:* b Iowa, Sept 25, 17; m 42; c 1. *Educ:* Colo Sch Mines, Geol Eng, 48, MSc, 49. *Prof Exp:* Geologist, US Geol Surv, 49-52, x-ray crystallogr & mineralogist, 52-76, res geologist, 76-85. *Concurrent Pos:* Lectr, Colo Sch Mines; adv, Geol Surv, Pakistan, 59-61; Fulbright fel, Univ Rio Grande de Sul, Porto Alegre, 85. *Mem:* Fel Mineral Soc Am; Am Crystallog Asn; Am Asn Petrol Geologists; Am Geol Inst; Geochem Soc. *Res:* Clay mineralogy and crystallography; carbonate mineralogy; geochemistry; mineralogy and geochemistry of authigenic zeolites; scanning electron microscopy and spectrography of zeolites; industrial use of zeolites in agriculture, animal husbandry and pollution control. *Mailing Add:* 845 Dudley St Lakewood CO 80215-5410

GUDE, RICHARD HUNTER, ZOOLOGY, ANIMAL BEHAVIOR. *Current Pos:* actg chmn dept biol, Univ Tampa, 68-72, assoc prof, 68-73, chmn, Div Sci & Math, 72-78, PROF BIOL, UNIV TAMPA, 73- *Personal Data:* b Eau Claire, Wis, Sept 16, 37; m 60; c 2. *Educ:* Wis State Univ, Eau Claire, BS, 60; Mich State Univ, MS, 62, PhD(zool), 65. *Prof Exp:* From asst prof to assoc prof biol, Hartwick Col, 64-68. *Mem:* Ecol Soc Am. *Res:* Nesting behavior of Siamese fighting fish, Betta splendens; heavy metal uptake in marine invertebrates. *Mailing Add:* Dept Biol Univ Tampa 401 W Kennedy Blvd Tampa FL 33606-1450

GUDEHUS, DONALD HENRY, OBSERVATIONAL COSMOLOGY, INSTRUMENTATION. *Current Pos:* VIS ASST PROF, DEPT PHYSICS & ASTRON, GA STATE UNIV, 93- *Personal Data:* b Jersey City, NJ, Sept 13, 39; m 68. *Educ:* Mass Inst Technol, BS, 61; Columbia Univ, AM, 63; Univ Calif, Los Angeles, PhD(astron), 71. *Prof Exp:* Engr & scientist, McDonnell Douglas Aerophys Lab, 64-67; scholar, Dept Astron, Univ Calif, Los Angeles, 71-75; asst prof physics, Dept Physics, Los Angeles City Col, 74-81; asst res scientist, Dept Physics & Astron, Univ Mich, 81-89; vis asst prof, Dept Physics, Okla State Univ, 89-92. *Concurrent Pos:* Proj Scientist, 3D Image Technol, Inc, 95. *Mem:* Am Astron Soc. *Res:* Design of instrumentation and the taking of observations for study of structure and evolution of universe; use of CCD to observe distant clusters of galaxies. *Mailing Add:* Dept Physics & Astron Ga State Univ Atlanta GA 30303. *E-Mail:* gudehus@chara.gsu.edu

GUDERLEY, HELGA ELIZABETH, ECOLOGICAL PHYSIOLOGY, COMPARATIVE BIOCHEMISTRY & PHYSIOLOGY. *Current Pos:* prof assoc, 78-79, from asst prof to assoc prof, 79-89, PROF PHYSIOL, UNIV LAVAL, 89- *Personal Data:* b Dayton, Ohio, Sept 24, 49; m 73; c 2. *Educ:* Earlham Col, BA, 71; Univ BC, PhD(zool), 76. *Prof Exp:* Res asst, Univ BC,

72-76; fel, Ore State Univ, 77-78. *Mem:* Am Physiol Soc; Can Soc Zool. *Res:* Evolution of pyruvate kinase isozymes; anaerobic metabolism in Mytilus edulis and short and long term thermal adaptation of fish muscle metabolism. *Mailing Add:* Dept Biol Univ Laval Quebec City PQ G1K 7P4 Can. *Fax:* 418-656-2043

GUDERLEY, KARL GOTTFRIED, MATHEMATICS, AERODYNAMICS. *Current Pos:* RETIRED. *Personal Data:* b Braunsdorf, Ger, June 15, 10; nat US; m 40, Irmgard Delius; c Edith & Helga. *Educ:* DrIng, 38, DrIng habil, 43. *Honors & Awards:* Thurman H Bane Award, 55. *Prof Exp:* Aeronaut res engr, Air Res, Ger, 38-46; aeronaut res engr, Wright Air Develop Ctr, 46-55, chief, Appl Math Br, Aeronaut Res Lab, 55-61, sr scientist, Appl Math Res Lab, Aerospace Res Labs, 61-74. *Res:* Transonic flow; theoretical aerodynamics; applied mathematics. *Mailing Add:* 1645 Countryside Dr Dayton OH 45432

GUDMUNDSEN, RICHARD AUSTIN, PHYSICS, RESEARCH ADMINISTRATION. *Current Pos:* PRES, PERCEPTRIX INC, SANTA ANA, CALIF, 83- *Personal Data:* b Salt Lake City, Utah, Dec 27, 22; m 47, Bernice Sayre; c Joyce, Scott Austin, Mark Richard, Annette, Lee Karl & Eileen. *Educ:* Univ Southern Calif, BE, 47, PhD(physics), 55. *Prof Exp:* Mgr semiconductor labs, Hughes Aircraft Co, 52-59; dir quantum electronics div, Quantatron, Inc, 59-60; pres, Quantum Technol Labs, 60-63; mgr lasers & electrooptics, Autonetics Div, Electronic Res Ctr, Rockwell Int Corp, Anaheim, Calif, 63-69, sci adv to vpres res & technol, 69-70, dir advan technol, 71-83. *Mem:* Am Phys Soc; Am Inst Elec & Electronics Engrs; Sigma Xi; Am Inst Physics. *Res:* Quantum and electro-optics; solid state physics; semiconductor physics and devices; invention and development of physical-electronic devices; noise theory; laser physics, devices and systems; computer memories; heat transfer; instrumentation physics; display technology; information sciences. *Mailing Add:* 12052 Larchwood Lane Santa Ana CA 92705

GUDRY, FREDERICK E, JR, AEROSPACE MEDICINE. *Honors & Awards:* Eric Liljencrantz Award, Aerospace Med Asn, 91. *Mailing Add:* 3861 Ochuse Dr Pensacola FL 32503-3150

GUEFT, BORIS, PATHOLOGY, CYTOCHEMISTRY. *Current Pos:* DIR PATH, UNION HOSP, BRONX, 74- *Personal Data:* b Cannes, France, Nov 10, 16; nat US; m 43; c 3. *Educ:* Columbia Univ, AB, 38; NY Univ, MD, 41. *Prof Exp:* Resident & USPHS asst, New Britain Gen Hosp, Conn, 46-47; instr, Sch Med, Yale Univ, 50-55; asst prof, Med Sch, Univ Cincinnati, 55-58; from assoc prof to prof path, Albert Einstein Col Med, 58-70, clin prof path, 70-87. *Concurrent Pos:* Fel path, Mt Sinai Hosp, New York, 47-50; pathologist, Fairfield State Hosp, Conn, 50-55 & Vet Admin Hosp, Ohio, 55-58; adj prof path, NY Med Col, 78; consult path, Bronx-Lebanon Hosp. *Mem:* Am Asn Path & Bact; AAAS; Int Acad Path; Electron Micros Soc Am. *Res:* Penicillin evaluation; experimental syphilis; cytochemistry of collagen and amyloid disease; microspectrophotometry; electron microscopy; x-ray diffraction. *Mailing Add:* Dept Path NY Med Col 25 Vanderbilt Rd Scarsdale NY 10583-7218

GUEHLER, PAUL FREDERICK, ORGANIC CHEMISTRY. *Current Pos:* Sr chemist, Cent Res Labs, Minn Mining & Mfg Co, 65-67, supvr med prod div, 67-68, supvr tech mkt, New Bus Venture Div, 69-71, develop specialist, 71-74, lab mgr plant care systs, 74-77, RES & DEVELOP MGR, OCCUP HEALTH & SAFETY PROD DIV, 3M CO, 74- *Personal Data:* b Sandwich, Ill, Apr 14, 38; m 61; c 3. *Educ:* Augustana Col, Ill, BA, 60; Univ Minn, Minneapolis, PhD(org chem), 65. *Mem:* Am Chem Soc. *Res:* Efficient delivery systems of nutrients to plants. *Mailing Add:* 7735-100th St N White Bear Lake MN 55110-1441

GUELL, DAVID LEE, highway engineering, for more information see previous edition

GUENGERICH, FREDERICK PETER, BIOCHEMISTRY, TOXICOLOGY. *Current Pos:* PROF BIOCHEM, DEPT BIOCHEM, SCH MED, VANDERBILT UNIV, 75- *Personal Data:* b Pekin, Ill, Jan 1, 49; m 73; c 3. *Educ:* Univ Ill, BS, 70; Vanderbilt Univ, PhD(biochem), 73. *Honors & Awards:* J J Abel Award, Am Soc Pharmacol Exp Therapeut, 84. *Prof Exp:* Res assoc biochem, Sch Med, Univ Mich, 73-75. *Concurrent Pos:* Fel, Nat Inst Gen Med Sci, 74-75; res career develop award, Nat Inst Environ Health Sci, 78-, prin investr, 77-; prin investr, Nat Cancer Inst, 78- *Mem:* Am Soc Biol Chemists; Sigma Xi; Am Chem Soc. *Res:* Enzymic activation and detoxification of foreign chemicals of environmental interest. *Mailing Add:* Dept Biochem Vanderbilt Univ Sch Med Nashville TN 37232-0146. *Fax:* 615-322-3141

GUENNEL, GOTTFRIED KURT, PALYNOLOGY. *Current Pos:* RETIRED. *Personal Data:* b Oelsnitz, Ger, Dec 24, 20; nat US; m 47. *Educ:* Butler Univ, BS, 43, MS, 49; Ind Univ, PhD, 60. *Prof Exp:* Asst prof bot, Franklin Col, 49; paleobotanist, Geol Surv, Ind Univ, 49-61; advan res geologist, Marathon Oil Co, 61-80, sr res geologist, 80-82. *Mem:* AAAS; Bot Soc Am; fel Geol Soc Am; Am Asn Stratig Palynologists. *Res:* Thermal alteration of organic matter in rocks; age-dating and ecology of fossil spores and pollen. *Mailing Add:* 835 Front Range Rd Littleton CO 80120

GUENTHER, ARTHUR HENRY, PULSED POWER TECHNOLOGY & MATERIALS LASERS, OPTICS & TECHNICAL EDUCATION & TECHNOLOGY COMMERCIALIZATION. *Current Pos:* RETIRED. *Personal Data:* b Hoboken, NJ, Apr 20, 31; m 54, Joan Roth; c Wendy K (Gallegos) & Tracie K (O'Geary). *Educ:* Rutgers Univ, BS, 53; Pa State Univ, PhD(chem physics), 57. *Hon Degrees:* DSc, Univ Albuquerque, 73. *Honors & Awards:* Harry Diamond Award, Inst Elec & Electronics Engrs, 71 & Peter Haas Award, 89; Arthur Schalow Medal, Laser Inst Am; Eastman Lectr, Optical Soc Am, 90-91; Ben Dasher Award, Inst Elec & Electronics Engrs. *Prof Exp:* Asst quant analyst, Pa State Univ, 53-55, Spectros Lab, 55-56; proj officer, Physics Br, Air Force Weapons Lab, Kirtland AFB, NMex, 57-59, dir, Pulse Power Lab, 59-62, dir, Mat Dynamics Facil, 62-65, sci adv & chmn, Simulation Group, Sandia Nat Lab, 65-66, sci adv, Effects Br & chmn, Sci Support Group, 66-69, chief, Technol Div, 69-70, sci dir, 70-74, chief scientist, Air Force Weapons Lab, 74-88; chief scientist, Advan Defense Technol, Los Alamos Nat Lab, 88-91. *Concurrent Pos:* Adj prof physics, Air Force Inst Technol, 67- & elec eng & physics, Tex Tech Univ, 71-; consult, Tech Educ Res Ctr, 72-; adj prof chem, physics & elec eng, Univ NMex, 77-; consult, Lawrence Livermore Nat Lab, 78- & Los Alamos Nat Lab, 79-; mem, Int Steering Comt, 87-, chmn, 91-93; mem, Int Conf Ionization Phenomena in Gases; chair, Pulsed Power Conf & numerous other major confs; sci adv, Lab Develop, Sandia Nat Lab & Govt NMex, 88-93; vpres, Int Comt Optics, 96-, chair, US Adv Comt, 97-; mem bd dirs, Soc Photo-Optical Instrumentation Engrs. *Mem:* Fel Optical Soc Am; fel Inst Elec & Electronics Engrs; fel Int Soc Optical Eng; Am Chem Soc; fel Laser Inst Am; Sigma Xi. *Res:* High resolution infrared spectroscopy; fast time instrumentation; exploding wire phenomenology; nuclear weapon phenomena; molecular physics; high temperature properties and equation of state; high energy discharge systems; shock hydrodynamics; lasers; ultrasonics, optics and spectroscopy; simulation of nuclear weapon detonations; pulsed power technology; high power/energy lasers; interaction; laser damage to optical materials; science policy; technology education. *Mailing Add:* 989 Lynx Loop NE Albuquerque NM 87122-1313. *Fax:* 505-881-0536

GUENTHER, BOBBY DEAN, OPTICAL PHYSICS. *Current Pos:* physicist, 79-87, DIR PHYSICS, US ARMY RES OFF, NC, 90- *Personal Data:* b St Louis, Mo, Feb 13, 39; m 61, Sharon Stauder; c Valerie & Brett. *Educ:* Baylor Univ, BS, 60; Univ Mo, MS, 63, PhD(physics), 68. *Prof Exp:* Res asst, McDonnell Douglas Corp, 60-61; res physicist, US Army Missle Command, Redstone Arsenal, Ala, 68-79. *Concurrent Pos:* Rep high energy laser prog, Air Force Weapons Lab, 73-75; adj prof physics, Duke Univ. *Mem:* Fel Am Phys Soc; Am Optical Soc; fel Optical Soc Am. *Res:* Femto second technology; atmospheric propagation of submillimeter waves; coherent imaging problems and optical processing techniques related to imaging; manager of atomic and molecular physics, optics, lasers and opening switch technology and Army research programs. *Mailing Add:* US Army Res Off PO Box 12211 Research Triangle Park NC 27709. *Fax:* 919-549-4310; *E-Mail:* guenther@aro.ncren.net

GUENTHER, DONNA MARIE, PEDIATRICS, IMMUNOLOGY. *Current Pos:* ASST CLIN PROF PEDIAT, UNIV CALIF, SAN DIEGO, 76- *Personal Data:* b Meadville, Pa, Oct 20, 38; m 72. *Educ:* Allegheny Col, BS, 60; Temple Univ, MD, 67. *Prof Exp:* Res technician immunol-transplantation, Mary Imogene Bassett Hosp, Cooperstown, NY, 60-62; res asst, Div Exp Biol, Baylor Col Med, 62-63; intern pediat, St Christopher's Hosp Children, Philadelphia, 67-68, resident, 68-69, chief resident, 69-70; staff pediatrician, Children's Heart Hosp, Philadelphia, 70-71; fel pediat allergy & immunol, Thomas Jefferson Univ, Philadelphia, 70-71; med fel immunol, Univ Minn, Minneapolis, 71-72; resident allergy & fel immunol, Kaiser Found Hosp & Univ Calif Med Ctr, San Francisco, 72-73; chief immunol & allergy, Children's Hosp Med Ctr, Oakland 73-84. *Mem:* Fel Am Acad Pediat; fel Am Acad Allergy; fel Am Col Allergists; Int Soc Exp Hemat; Int Col Pediat. *Res:* Clinical investigation of immunologic parameters in children with allergic disease. *Mailing Add:* Kaiser Permamamte Allergy 3400 Delta Fair Blvd Antioch CA 94509-4004

GUENTHER, FREDERICK OLIVER, CHEMISTRY. *Current Pos:* SR PROJ CHEMIST, TEXACO CHEM CO, INC, 64- *Personal Data:* b Sheboygan, Wis, July 20, 19; m 47; c 2. *Educ:* Univ Wis, BS, 42. *Prof Exp:* Res chemist, US Rubber Co, NJ, 42-47; res asst, Res Lab, Gen Elec Co, 48-56, chemist, Major Appliance Div, 56-64. *Mem:* Am Chem Soc. *Res:* Polymerization; fluid bed coatings; cellular plastics; process development in organic chemicals; organic coatings for wire. *Mailing Add:* 6000 Reims No 2405 Houston TX 77036-3052

GUENTHER, JOHN JAMES, MEAT SCIENCE. *Current Pos:* 58-71, PROF ANIMAL SCI, OKLA STATE UNIV, 71- *Personal Data:* b Birmingham, Ala, Nov 8, 29; m 52; c 2. *Educ:* La State Univ, BS, 51, MS, 53; Tex A&M Univ, PhD(meat sci), 59. *Prof Exp:* Asst, La State Univ, 51-53; asst, Tex A&M, 55-58. *Mem:* Am Soc Animal Sci; Inst Food Technol; Am Meat Sci Asn. *Res:* Beef and pork carcass quality; muscle growth; muscle proteins; meat freezing; irradiation; freeze drying; processing and preservation. *Mailing Add:* 1701 N Jardot Rd Stillwater OK 74075

GUENTHER, PETER T, NUCLEAR STRUCTURE. *Current Pos:* RETIRED. *Personal Data:* b Chicago, Ill, June 30, 35; m 63; c 2. *Educ:* Northwestern Univ, BS, 63; Univ Ill, MS, 68, PhD(physics), 77. *Prof Exp:* Sci asst, Argonne Nat Lab, 67-78, asst physicist, 78-81, physicist, 81-92. *Mem:* Am Phys Soc. *Res:* Fast-neutron physics, particularly experimental work in total, elastic, inelastic-scattering and cross sections; theoretical nuclear models. *Mailing Add:* 4633 Saratoga Ave Downers Grove IL 60515

GUENTHER, R(ICHARD), TELECOMMUNICATIONS, COMPUTER SCIENCE. *Current Pos:* RETIRED. *Personal Data:* b Lodz, Poland, Sept 9, 10; nat US; m 34. *Educ:* Danzig Tech Univ, Dipl Ing, 34, Dr Ing, 37. *Prof Exp:* Asst, Danzig Tech Univ, 34-37; from engr, Commun Lab to mgr eng, Dept Radio Commun & Missile Controls, Siemens & Halske, Inc, Ger, 37-45; consult, 45-47; consult commun instrumentation, US Sig Corps Eng Labs, NJ, 47-52; mem tech staff & systs engr, Bell Tel Labs, Inc, 52-56; mgr, Surface Commun Systs Lab, Systs Eng & Adv Develop, Radio Corp Am, 56-63, chief scientist, Commun Systs Div, 63-65, mgr adv commun technol, Commun Systs Div, 65-68, staff tech adv, Commercial Electronics Systs Div, RCA Corp, 68-70, comput systs architect, Comput Systs Develop Div, 70-72; pres, Commun & Info Systs, Inc, Int Consults, 72-. *Mem:* AAAS; fel Inst Elec & Electronics Engrs. *Res:* Engineering physics, particularly application in modern communication through information theory; network analysis; solid state physics; market analysis; electromagnetic theory; statistical analysis; viscosity of quartz crystals; communication systems analysis. *Mailing Add:* 100 Newbury Ct Apt 310 Concord MA 01742

GUENTHER, RAYMOND A, LOW TEMPERATURE PHYSICS, SOLID STATE PHYSICS. *Current Pos:* vis asst prof, 69, ASSOC PROF PHYSICS, UNIV NEBR, OMAHA, 69-. *Personal Data:* b Chicago, Ill, Mar 13, 32; m 56; c 2. *Educ:* Ill Inst Technol, BS, 55, MS, 57, PhD(physics), 69. *Prof Exp:* Res assoc physics, Argonne Nat Lab, 60-61; instr, Ill Inst Technol, 61-62; res assoc, Argonne Nat Lab, 62-65; instr, Chicago City Jr Col, Bogan Br, 65-66; instr, Ill Inst Technol, 66-69. *Res:* Heat capacity of dysprosium metal; thermal conductivity of irradiated potassium chloride crystals at temperatures between 0.4 and 4 degrees Kelvin. *Mailing Add:* 5603 Jackson Omaha NE 68106

GUENTHER, RONALD BERNARD, MATHEMATICAL PHYSICS. *Current Pos:* from asst prof to assoc prof, 66-76, PROF MATH, ORE STATE UNIV, 76-. *Personal Data:* b North Bend, Ore, Nov 24, 37; m 64. *Educ:* Ore State Univ, BA, 59, MA, 62; Univ Colo, PhD(appl math), 64. *Prof Exp:* Adv res mathematician, Res Ctr, Marathon Oil Co, 64-66. *Concurrent Pos:* Gast prof, Univ Hamburg, 70-71 & 73-74; vis, Hahn-Meituer-Inst, Berlin, 78 & 81. *Mem:* Ger Math Asn. *Res:* Partial differential equations and applied mathematics. *Mailing Add:* Dept Math Ore State Univ Corvallis OR 97331-4605

GUENTHER, WILLIAM BENTON, PHYSICAL CHEMISTRY, INORGANIC CHEMISTRY. *Current Pos:* from asst prof to assoc prof, Univ of the South, 56-68, prof chem, 68-79, F B Williams prof chem, 79-86, EMER PROF, UNIV OF THE SOUTH, 87-. *Personal Data:* b Dayton, Ohio, Sept 27, 28. *Educ:* Oberlin Col, BA, 48; Univ Rochester, MS, 50, PhD(chem), 54. *Prof Exp:* Instr chem, Univ Alaska, 50-52; asst prof, Muhlenberg Col, 54-56. *Concurrent Pos:* Cotrell Res Corp grant, 58; Lilly Endowment res grant, 59. *Mem:* Am Chem Soc; Sigma Xi. *Res:* Inorganic complexes; chemical education; analytical chemistry; published three books and 24 articles. *Mailing Add:* 62A Martin Lane Box 1150 Sewanee TN 37383-1000

GUENTHER, WILLIAM CHARLES, STATISTICS. *Current Pos:* assoc prof, 59-63, PROF STATIST, UNIV WYO, 63-. *Personal Data:* b Stewartville, Minn, Dec 17, 21; m 55; c 4. *Educ:* Univ Iowa, BA, 43, MS, 46; Univ Wash, PhD(math), 52. *Prof Exp:* Instr math, Univ Ark, 48-49; math statistician, US Naval Ord Lab, 52-55. *Concurrent Pos:* NSF fac fel, 62; ed, Bulletin, The Inst Math Statist, 81-86. *Mem:* Math Asn Am; Inst Math Statist; fel Am Statist Asn. *Res:* Mathematical statistics, quality control and nonparametrics. *Mailing Add:* 1515 Kearney Univ Wyo Laramie WY 82070

GUENTHERMAN, ROBERT HENRY, PHYSIOLOGY, PERIODONTOLOGY. *Current Pos:* asst prof physiol & periodont, 68-77, ASSOC PROF PERIODONT, BAYLOR COL DENT, 77-. *Personal Data:* b Chicago, Ill, July 9, 33; m 59; c 2. *Educ:* Baylor Univ, DDS, 65, PhD(physiol), 68. *Honors & Awards:* Merritt-Parks Award, 65. *Prof Exp:* NIH training fel physiol & periodont, 65-68. *Mem:* Am Dent Asn; Am Asn Dent Schs; Int Asn Dent Res; Am Acad Periodont; Sigma Xi. *Res:* Effect of oxygen and oxygenating agents on normal and diseased periodontal tissue; cardiovascular and metabolic physiology and its relationship to the periodontal structure of the oral cavity. *Mailing Add:* 10111 Estate Lane Dallas TX 75238

GUENTZEL, M NEAL, MICROBIOLOGY. *Current Pos:* asst prof, 73-77, ASSOC PROF MICROBIOL, DIV ALLIED HEALTH & LIFE SCI, UNIV TEX, SAN ANTONIO, 77-, ASSOC PROF, DEPT MICROBIOL, HEALTH SCI CTR, 78-. *Personal Data:* b Austin, Tex, Aug 21, 44; m 68; c 3. *Educ:* Univ Tex, Austin, BA, 67, MA, 70, PhD(microbiol), 72. *Prof Exp:* Instr microbiol, Dept Microbiol, Univ Tex, Austin, 71-72, fel, 72-73. *Mem:* Am Soc Microbiol; Int Asn Biol Standardization. *Res:* Virulence factors of enteric bacterial pathogens with concentration on factors affecting colonization and pathogenesis of vibrio cholerae; studies of experimental candidosis and antifungal therapy. *Mailing Add:* Dept Life Sci Univ Tex 6900 N Loop 1604 W San Antonio TX 78249-1130

GUENZER, CHARLES S P, electrical engineering, patent law, for more information see previous edition

GUENZI, WAYNE D, SOIL CHEMISTRY. *Current Pos:* Chemist, 59-66, RES SOIL SCIENTIST, USDA, 66-. *Personal Data:* b Sterling, Colo, Oct 6, 31; m 54; c 3. *Educ:* Colo State Univ, BS, 53, MS, 59; Univ Nebr, PhD(soil sci), 64. *Mem:* AAAS; Am Soc Agron; Soil Sci Soc Am; Sigma Xi. *Res:* Isolation of phytotoxic substances in plants and soils; interactions of chlorinated insecticides with soils, including photodegradation, microbial decomposition and volatilization; formation, release and identification of volatile organic sulfur compounds from animal feedlots and wastes applied to soil. *Mailing Add:* 2210 Mathews St Ft Collins CO 80525

GUERBER, HOWARD P(AUL), COMPUTER SYSTEMS DESIGN, ELECTRICAL ENGINEERING. *Current Pos:* ENG CONSULT, PSS, INC. *Personal Data:* b Rifle, Colo, July 29, 26; m 62, Marlon Brethestone; c Jeffrey R & Eric M. *Educ:* Univ Colo, BS, 47, MS, 54. *Prof Exp:* Develop engr, Westinghouse Elec Corp, 48-50; design & develop engr, RCA Corp, 50-51 & 53-59, supvr systs eng, 59-72; mem tech staff, Mitre Corp, 72-91, System Eng Div, 91-93. *Mem:* Asn Comput Mach; Inst Elec & Electronics Engrs. *Res:* Specification, development and implementation of major communications networks and nodal switching for voice and data. *Mailing Add:* 1904 Abbotsford Dr Vienna VA 22182

GUERIGUIAN, JOHN LEO, PHARMACOGENOLOGY, HISTORY & PHILOSOPHY OF SCIENCE. *Current Pos:* MED OFFICER NEW DRUGS, CTR DRUG EVAL & RES, FOOD & DRUG ADMIN, 78-. *Personal Data:* b Alexandria, Egypt, Sept 20, 35; US citizen; m 69; c 2. *Educ:* Univ Paris, BS, 58, MS, 64, MD, 65. *Prof Exp:* Res fel biochem, Med Sch, Harvard Univ, 65-67; lectr biochem, Med Sch Univ Paris, 67-69; asst prof pharmacol, Med Sch, Univ NC, Chapel Hill, 69-73; assoc prof pharmacol, Sch Med, Univ Minn, Duluth, 73-78. *Concurrent Pos:* Attend Staff, Peter Bent Brigham Hosp, Boston, 65-67; res scientist, Nat Inst Sci Educ & Res Med, 67-69; sci dir, Inst Develop Rationnel Agents Med Teux, 88; mem expert adv panel on biol standardization, WHO, Geneva, 88-; exec secy, endocrinol & metab drugs adv comt, Food & Drug Admin, 90. *Mem:* Endocrine Soc; Am Soc Pharmacol & Exp Therapeut. *Res:* Developing new drugs, biotechnological, reproductive, oncological and antidiabetic, in a rational and efficient manner, taking also into account historical experiences. *Mailing Add:* 14513 Woodcrest Dr Rockville MD 20853

GUERIN, MICHAEL RICHARD, ANALYTICAL CHEMISTRY, CANCER. *Current Pos:* res assoc, analytical chem div, 67-70, group leader, analytical chem div, 70-76, SECT HEAD, ORGANIC CHEM SECT, ANALYTICAL CHEM DIV, OAK RIDGE NAT LAB, 76-. *Personal Data:* b Waukegan, Ill, May 10, 41; m 65; c 2. *Educ:* Northern Ill Univ, BS, 63; Iowa State Univ, PhD(anal chem), 67. *Concurrent Pos:* Prin investr, Nat Inst Cigarette Smoke Chem, 68-, Coun Tobacco Res Cigarette Smoke Chem, 74-78 & 85-, Dept Energy Synfuels Chem, 76-83, Environ Protection Agency Synfuels, 76-79, Dept Defense Fuels & Lubricants, 82-, Dept Energy Complex Mixtures Chem, 83-; consult proposal rev group, Nat Cancer Inst, 70-73, 75 & 81, Nat Inst Environ Health Sci, 76 & 80, Dept Energy, 76, 80 & 84, Environ Protection Agency, 78 & 80, Nat Inst Drug Abuse, 81 & 83, Elec Power Res Inst, 81 & 82; del, Int Group Smoking & Health Res, 70; consult, Chem Carcinogenesis Contract Rev Comt, Nat Cancer Inst, 70, mem tobacco working group, 70-75. *Mem:* AAAS; NY Acad Sci; Sigma Xi; Am Chem Soc; Soc Toxicol. *Res:* Development and application of analytical chemical methodologies to the elucidation of the chemical factors responsible for environmental, fossil energy and tobacco smoke chemical carcinogenesis and mutagenesis. *Mailing Add:* 21 Windhaven Lane Oak Ridge TN 37830-8241

GUERNSEY, DUANE L, MOLECULAR CARCINOGENESIS. *Current Pos:* PROF, DEPT PATH FAC MED SIR CHARLES TUPPER MED BLDG DALHOUSIE, UNIV HALIFAX, 88-. *Educ:* Univ Hawaii, PhD(physiol), 78. *Prof Exp:* asst prof physiol, Col Med, Univ Iowa, 81-88. *Res:* Cellular differentiation. *Mailing Add:* Dept Pathol Sir Charles Tupper Med Bldg Dalhousie Univ Halifax NS B3H 4H7 Can. *Fax:* 902-494-6421

GUERNSEY, EDWIN O(WENS), CHEMICAL ENGINEERING, PHYSICAL CHEMISTRY. *Current Pos:* RETIRED. *Personal Data:* b Washington, DC, Sept 14, 20; m 43; c 3. *Educ:* Univ Ill, BS, 41; Yale Univ, DEng, 49. *Prof Exp:* Sr res chem engr, Cent Res Div, Socony Mobil Oil Co, Inc, 48-54, Socony sponsorship, Oak Ridge Sch Reactor Technol, 54-55, sr res chem engr, Cent Res Div, 55-60, res assoc, 60-65, sr planning assoc, Corp Planning & Econ Dept, Mobil Oil Corp, 65-67, supvr, Mobil Res & Develop Corp, 67-69, spec studies group, 69-84. *Mem:* Am Inst Chem Engrs; Am Chem Soc; fel Am Inst Chem; Sigma Xi. *Res:* Research planning; alternate energy sources; energy conversion; synthetic fuels; nuclear electric power generation. *Mailing Add:* 309 Bridgeboro Rd Apt 1452 Moorestown NJ 08057

GUERNSEY, JANET BROWN, PHYSICS. *Current Pos:* RETIRED. *Personal Data:* b Germantown, Pa, May 2, 13; m 36; c 5. *Educ:* Wellesley Col, AB, 35; Harvard Univ, AM, 48; Mass Inst Technol, PhD(physics), 55. *Prof Exp:* From instr to prof physics, Wellesley Col, 43-75, Louise S McDowell Prof, 70, chmn dept, 67-77. *Concurrent Pos:* Mem gov bd, Am Inst Physics, 74-77. *Mem:* AAAS; Am Asn Physics Teachers (pres, 75-76); Am Inst Physics; Am Phys Soc. *Res:* Neutron physics; electrostatic accelerators. *Mailing Add:* Sabrina Farm Wellesley MA 02181

GUERNSEY, RICHARD MONTGOMERY, ACOUSTICS. *Current Pos:* PRIN, R M GUERNSEY & ASSOCS, 88-. *Personal Data:* b Newton, Mass, Apr 10, 37; m 92, Marilyn Slocum. *Educ:* Wesleyan Univ, Conn, BA, 60. *Prof Exp:* Phys sci asst, Acoust Res Br, Army Human Eng Labs, Aberdeen, Md, 60-62; sr engr, Goodfriend-Ostergaard Assocs, 63-67; contract consult, Donley, Miller & Nowikas, 68-72; consult physicist, Brown-Guernsey Co, 73-74; dir, Cedar Knolls Acoust Labs, 74-88. *Mem:* Acoust Soc Am; Am Soc

Testing & Mat. Res: Acoustical testing and measurement including acoustical properties of materials, generation and transmission of sound, and human response to sound. Mailing Add: R M Guernsey & Assocs PO Box 1517 Morristown NJ 07962-1517. Fax: 973-267-7037; E-Mail: 72707.1450@compuserve.com

GUERRA, JOHN MICHAEL, OPTICAL METROLOGY, OPTICAL MEDICAL INSTRUMENTATION. Current Pos: Supvr, Optical Fabrication Labs, 83-90, prin engr & sr staff, 87-97, PROG MGR NEAR-FIELD OPTICS TECHNOL, POLAROID CORP, 97-, SUPVR, OPTICAL THIN FILMS LAB. Personal Data: b Sept 6, 54. Educ: Univ Mass, Amherst, BS, 76. Honors & Awards: George Eartman Lectr, Optical Soc Am, 91, Eng Excellence Award, 94; Photonics Circle of Excellence Award, 93. Mem: Int Soc Optical Eng; Optical Soc Am. Res: Photon tunneling/near-field research, development and application to microscopy, metrology, lithography and optical data storage; granted 14 patents. Mailing Add: Polaroid Optical Eng Dept 38 Henry St 2A Cambridge MA 02139-3544. Fax: 781-386-3077; E-Mail: guerraj@polaroid.com

GUERRANT, GORDON OWEN, ANALYTICAL CHEMISTRY. Current Pos: RETIRED. Personal Data: b Fulton, Mo, July 11, 23; m 44; c Leslie (Fowler), Libby (Reser), Lori (Jones) & Lyn. Educ: Westminster Col, AB, 44; Univ Ill, PhD(analytical chem), 49. Prof Exp: Asst analytical chem, Univ Ill, 46-49; chemist, Explor & Prod Res Div, Shell Develop Co, Tex, 49-63; sr res chemist, Armour Agr Chem Co, 63-67; supvry res chemist, Ctr Dis Control, USPHS, 67-91. Concurrent Pos: Cert prof chemist, Am Inst Chemists. Mem: Am Chem Soc; fel Am Inst Chem. Res: Spectrophotometry; emission spectroscopy; x-ray diffraction; micromolecular weights; gas chromatography; trace gas analyses; thermal stability of ammonium phosphates; analysis and formulation of public health pesticides; chromatographic analysis of bacterial components. Mailing Add: 1652 Kings Down Circle NE Dunwoody GA 30338

GUERRANT, JOHN LIPPINCOTT, internal medicine, for more information see previous edition

GUERRANT, WILLIAM BARNETT, JR, organic chemistry, for more information see previous edition

GUERRERO, ARIEL HERIBERTO, MICROANALYSIS, SPECTROCHEMISTRY. Current Pos: DIR & CONSULT PROF, SCH CHEM, UNIV DEL SALVADOR, 89-; INDUST CONSULT, 89- Personal Data: b Buenos Aires, Arg, Jan 28, 22; wid; c 2. Educ: Univ Buenos Aires, PhD(chem), 46. Prof Exp: Asst analytical chem, Fac Exact & Natural Sci, Univ Buenos Aires, 42-55, lectr, 56-58, from assoc prof to prof, 58-70, dean fac, 68-69, prof, Fac Agron & Vet Med, 70-88, inorg chem, Fac Eng, 57-59; res worker, Nat Coun Res, Arg, 74-89. Concurrent Pos: Analytical chemist, Nat Direction Chem, 44-46; head, Analysis Lab, Lever Bros, 47-49; Brit Coun fel, Univ Liverpool, 47-48; dir, APA, 50-63; indust consult, A Bonfanti Factory, 53-59; consult, Espiga Co, 60-61; tech secy, Arg Inst Oils & Fats, 62-64; consult solvent extraction eng, 65-68; dir training chem teachers, Nat Res Coun, Ministry Educ & Nat Inst, 62-68, Pan Am Union, 69-73; mem, Conf Chem Educ, Pan Am Union, Buenos Aires, 65, Int Union Pure & Appl Chem, Frascati, 69, Sao Paulo, 71, Wroclaw, 73, Madrid, 75, Liubliana, 77, Perth, 78, Lima, 78, Dublin & Davos, 79, Costa Rica, Maryland & Louvain, 81, Montpellier, 83, Sao Paulo, 85; Arg rep, Comn Teaching Chem, Int Union Pure & Appl Chem, 72-; dir, Sem Teaching Chem, UNESCO, Montevideo, 72-74, Mex, 77; mem, Comt Expert Chem Educ, Pan-Am Union, Honduras, 74; Peruvian Sem Chem Educ, 88; Third World Acad Sci, Caracas, 90. Mem: Arg Chem Asn; Arg Sci Soc; Am Chem Soc; Arg Inst Qual; hon mem Peru Chem Soc; NY Acad Sci. Res: Acetate complexes of lead; rhodamine B as reagent; buffering capacity and regulation; direct estimation of ions; spectrophotometric parameters; Liesegang rings; properties of biological membranes, before and after irradiation; methodology of science, education and creativity; radiation effects on biological membranes. Mailing Add: Avenida Santa Fe 2879 Buenos Aires 1425 Argentina

GUERRERO, E T, PETROLEUM & MECHANICAL ENGINEERING. Current Pos: trustee's prof petrol eng & head dept, 56-66, dean, Col Eng & Phys Sci, 66-76, PROF ENG & PHYS SCI, UNIV TULSA, 66- Personal Data: b Richmond, Tex, Nov 2, 24; m 49; c 4. Educ: Tex A&M Univ, BS, 49, MS, 50, PhD(petrol eng), 53. Prof Exp: Instr petrol eng, Tex A&M Univ, 52-53; petrol reservoir engr, Seeligson Eng Comt, 53-56. Mem: Am Soc Eng Educ; Am Inst Mining, Metall & Petrol Engrs. Res: Relation between capillary pressures and relative permeabilities of large limestone cores; effect of surface and interfacial tensions on the recovery of oil by water flooding. Mailing Add: 1741 S Darlington Ave Tulsa OK 74112

GUERRERO, FELIX DAVID, MOLECULAR BIOLOGY OF INSECTICIDE RESISTANCE, GENE REGULATION OF INSECT HORMONES. Current Pos: RES PHYSIOLOGIST INSECT MOLECULAR BIOL, USDA, AGR RES SERV, 90- Personal Data: b Ft Worth, Tex, May 14, 54; c Michael N. Educ: Stephen F Austin State Univ, BS, 76, MS, 78; Tex A & M Univ, PhD(biochem & biophys), 88. Prof Exp: Environ chemist, Weyerhauser Co, 78-83; res asst, Tex A&M Univ, 83-88; fel, Ciba Geigy Biotechnol Ctr, 88-90. Mem: AAAS; Union Concerned Scientists. Res: Molecular biology and regulation of development of insecticide resistance and interactions between insect pests of livestock and their environment. Mailing Add: USDA Agr Res Serv 2700 Fredericksburg Rd Kerrville TX 78028. Fax: 830-792-0314

GUERRERO, JORGE, parasitology, immunology, for more information see previous edition

GUERRERO, RODRIGO V, SCIENCE HYGIENE. Current Pos: dean, Div Health Sci, Univ Valle, 72-75, dir, Gen Hosp, 76-78, pres, 82-84, PROF, DEPT SOCIAL MED, UNIV VALLE, 68-, REGIONAL ADV HEALTH & VIOLENCE, PAN AM HEALTH ORGN, WASHINGTON. Personal Data: b Cali, Colombia, Sept 8, 37. Educ: Univ Valle, MD, 62; Harvard Univ, MS, 66, DPH, 68. Prof Exp: Asst to exec dir, Found Carvajal, Cali, 63-70, exec dir, 84-92; mem & dir comt, Social Security Inst, 70-72; secy Health, City Calif, 78-80, mayor, 92-94. Concurrent Pos: Pres, Columbian Asn Med Sch, 73-75; founder & dir, 80-94, emer dir, J Columbia Medica, 95- Mem: Inst Med-Nat Acad Sci; Colombian Soc Epidemiol; Nat Acad Med Columbia. Res: Type and time of insemination within the menstrual cycle and human sex ratio at birth; spontaneous abortion. Mailing Add: Pan Am Health Orgn 525 23rd St NW Washington DC 20037

GUERRERO-MUNOZ, FREDERICO, neuropharmacology, for more information see previous edition

GUERRIERO, VINCENT, JR, MYOSIN LIGHT CHAIN KINASE, CALMODULIN. Current Pos: ASST PROF, DEPT ANIMAL SCI, UNIV ARIZ, 86- Personal Data: b Buffalo, NY, 52; m 90. Educ: Syracuse Univ, PhD(cell biol), 79. Prof Exp: res instr, Baylor Col Med, 79-86. Mem: Am Soc Cell Biol. Res: Calcium calmodulin regulation of smooth muscle contraction; function of heat shock proteins. Mailing Add: Dept Animal Sci Univ Ariz Tucson AZ 85721-0001. Fax: 520-621-9435

GUERRINI, ANITA, HISTORY OF MEDICINE, BIOMEDICAL ETHICS. Current Pos: lectr hist, 90-95, ASST PROF, HIST & ENVIRON STUDIES, UNIV CALIF, SANTA BARBARA, 95- Personal Data: b Torrington, Conn, May 23, 53; m 83, Michael A Osborne; c 2. Educ: Conn Col, BA, 75; Oxford Univ, MA, 77; Ind Univ, MA, 80, PhD(hist & philos sci), 83. Prof Exp: Mellon fel, Am Philos Soc, 84-85; Clark fel, Univ Calif, Los Angeles, 85; asst prof hist sci & med, Univ Minn, 85-88. Concurrent Pos: Prin investr, NSF, 87-89; Fletcher Jones fel, Huntington Libr, 89-90; ethics in res lectr, Univ Calif, Santa Barbara, 92; res fel, Ctr Humanities, Ore State Univ, 94-95. Mem: Hist Sci Soc; Am Asn Hist Med; Am Hist Asn; Am Soc Eighteenth-cent Studies; NAm Conf Brit Studies. Res: Early modern medicine; general history of animal and human experimentation; early modern animal experimentation. Mailing Add: Hist Dept Univ Calif Santa Barbara CA 93106-9410. Fax: 805-893-8795; E-Mail: guerrini@humanitas.ucsb.edu

GUERTIN, RALPH FRANCIS, elastic wave propagation, seismic modelling & inversion, for more information see previous edition

GUERTIN, ROBERT POWELL, SOLID STATE PHYSICS, MAGNETISM. Current Pos: From asst prof to assoc prof, 68-74, dean grad, 85-96, PROF PHYSICS, TUFTS UNIV, 74- Personal Data: b Trenton, NJ, July 5, 39; m 66, Margaret Eipper; c 2. Educ: Trinity Col, Conn, BS, 61; Wesleyan Univ, MA, 63; Univ Rochester, PhD(physics), 68. Concurrent Pos: Vis scientist, Francis Bitter Nat Magnetic Lab, Mass Inst Technol, Univ Calif, San Diego, Nat High Magnetic Field Lab, 96-97; chair, Bd Gov, Univ Press New Eng. Mem: Am Phys Soc; Coun Grad Sch; Sigma Xi; AAAS. Res: Transport and high field magnetic properties of nearly ferromagnetic alloys; magnetic properties of superconducting and normal metals and alloys at high pressures and high fields; transition metal oxides-transport and magnetism. Mailing Add: Dept Physics Sci & Technol Ctr Tufts Univ Medford MA 02155. E-Mail: rguertin@infonet.tufts.edu

GUESS, HARRY ADELBERT, BIOSTATISTICS, EPIDEMIOLOGY. Current Pos: SR DIR EPIDEMIOL DEPT, MERCK SHARP & DOHME RES LAB, 82- Personal Data: b New York, NY, Dec 24, 40; m 64; c 2. Educ: Ga Inst Technol, BS & MS, 64; Stanford Univ, MS & PhD(math), 72; Univ Miami, MD, 79; Am Bd Prev Med, cert; Am Bd Pediat, cert. Prof Exp: Asst prof math, Univ Rochester, 72-73; mem tech staff telecommun res, Bell Tel Labs, 73-75; res mathematician, Nat Inst Environ Health Sci, NIH, 75-77; res physician, NC Mem Hosp, 79-82. Concurrent Pos: Consult, sci res syst, 80-82, Hoffman-La Roche Inc, 81-87; vis scientist, Mayo Clinic, 83-; auxiliary prof, epidemiol & biostatist, McGill Univ, 87-; adj assoc prof epidemiol & biostatist, Univ NC, 88-91, adj prof, 91- Mem: Soc Epidemiol Res Serv; AMA; Biomet Soc; fel Am Col Epidemiol; fel Am Col Prev Med; fel Am Acad Pediat. Res: Biostatistics; epidemiology; applications of mathematics and statistics to clinical medicine; pharmacoepidemiology; mathematical popoulation genetics; clinical trial design. Mailing Add: 104 Waterford Pl Chapel Hill NC 27514

GUESS, WALLACE LOUIS, TOXICOLOGY. Current Pos: RETIRED. Personal Data: b Durham, NC, July 18, 24; m 47; c Ginnylu (Guess Cheeb) & Gerrysu (Guess Gebhard). Educ: Univ Tex, BS, 49, MS, 51; Univ Wash, PhD(pharm), 59. Prof Exp: From asst prof to prof pharm, Univ Tex, Austin, 53-71, asst dir, Drug Plastic Res Lab, 63-71; dean, Sch Pharm, Univ Miss, 71-89. Concurrent Pos: Chmn, Panel Over-the-Counter Antimicrobial Agents, Fed Food & Drug Admin, 74-80; consult, Biomed Device. Mem: Am Asn Col Pharm; hon mem Mex Pharmaceut Asn; Soc Toxicol. Res: Toxicology, pharmacology and evaluation of plastics used in medical practice. Mailing Add: 408 CR 102 Oxford MS 38655

GUEST, GARETH E, PLASMA INSTABILITIES THEORETICAL, PLASMA THEORY-WAVE PARTICLE INTERACTIONS FOR RF HEATING. Current Pos: VPRES, APPL MICROWAVE PLASMA CONCEPTS, 81- Personal Data: b Mobile, Ala, June 13, 33; m 54; c 3. Educ: Vanderbilt Univ, BA, 54, MA, 56, PhD(physics/math), 60. Prof Exp: From asst prof to assoc prof physics, N Tex State Univ, 60-63; staff scientist, Oak Ridge Nat Lab, 63-65, group leader, fusion plasma theory, 65-75; dept mgr, Fusion Plasma Theory, Gen Atomic Co, 75-81. *Concurrent Pos:* Lectr, Oak Ridge Inst Nuclear Studies, 65-75. *Mem:* Am Phys Soc (secy/treas, 68-74). *Res:* Theoretical investigations of fusion plasma concepts, including magnetic-mirror systems, the ELMO Bumpy Torus, tokamaks, etc; high-frequency collective phenomena; the theory of electron cyclotron heating and the resulting relativistic-electron plasmas. *Mailing Add:* 5433 Caminito Rosa La Jolla CA 92037

GUEST, GERALD BENTLEY, VETERINARY MEDICINE. *Current Pos:* RETIRED. *Personal Data:* b Hart Co, Ga, July 20, 36; m 62, Anne F Monagham; c Gerald & John. *Educ:* Univ Ga, DVM, 60. *Prof Exp:* Res vet, US Dept Agr, Univ Pa, Kennett Square, 63-70; spec asst to dir, Bur Vet Med, Food & Drug Admin, Rockville, Md, 72-77, assoc dir food safety, 78-83, dep dir bur, 82-86, dir, Bur Vet Med, 86-97. *Concurrent Pos:* Pvt pract vet med, 74-97. *Mem:* Am Vet Med Asn; Nat Asn Fed Vet; Vet Med Asn. *Res:* Veterinary medicine. *Mailing Add:* 19108 Plummer Dr Germantown MD 20876

GUEST, MARY FRANCES, PHYSIOLOGY. *Current Pos:* RETIRED. *Personal Data:* b New Smyrna Beach, Fla, Oct 7, 27. *Educ:* Fla State Univ, BS, 48; Tex Tech Univ, MS, 54; Tulane Univ, PhD(physiol), 64. *Prof Exp:* Instr zool, anat & physiol, Tex Tech Univ, 54-60; res asst surg, Sch Med, Tulane, 63-64; asst prof physiol, Fac Med, Univ Malaya, 64-68; from lectr to asst prof, Sch Vet Med, Univ Calif, Davis, 68-71; asst res parasitologist, G W Hooper Found, Med Ctr, Univ Calif, San Francisco, 71-72; assoc prof, Clarke Col, Iowa, 72-77, dir, Biol Health Prog, 72-92, prof biol, 77-92, chmn, Dept Biol, 81-92. *Mem:* Am Soc Trop Med & Hyg; Am Soc Parasitologists; Sigma Xi; NY Acad Sci. *Res:* Pulmonary physiology; pulmonary pathophysiology related to immune etiologies; immune response to filarial infections. *Mailing Add:* 960 Mayfair Ct Dubuque IA 52001

GUEST, RICHARD W(ILLIAM), AGRICULTURAL ENGINEERING. *Current Pos:* Asst prof, 58-64, assoc prof, 64-84, PROF AGR ENG, CORNELL UNIV, 84- *Personal Data:* b Oklahoma City, Okla, July 7, 32; m 59; c 3. *Educ:* NDak State Univ, BS, 54, MS, 58. *Concurrent Pos:* Staff mem, Ford-New Holland, PA; consult, Alfa-Laval Co, Sweden, 74-75. *Mem:* Am Soc Agr Eng. *Res:* Electrical power and processing; materials handling; agricultural waste management; farm power and machinery. *Mailing Add:* 1801 Dryden Rd Freeville NY 13068

GUEST, WILLIAM C, genetics, for more information see previous edition

GUETHS, JAMES E, SOLID STATE PHYSICS. *Current Pos:* from asst prof to assoc prof, Univ Wis, Oshkosh 66-76, chmn dept, 69-74, asst vchancellor, 74-85, PROF PHYSICS, UNIV WIS-OSHKOSH, 76-, VIS PROF, COL BUS ADMIN, 93- *Personal Data:* b Shawano, Wis, Aug 18, 39; m 61; c 3. *Educ:* Ripon Col, BA, 61; Univ Conn, MS, 63, PhD(physics), 66. *Prof Exp:* Res assoc physics, Univ Conn, 66. *Mem:* Am Phys Soc; Am Asn Higher Educ. *Res:* Transport phenomena in metal and alloy single crystals; learning hierarchies in university science; organizational development. *Mailing Add:* Col Bus Admin Univ Wis 800 Algoma Blvd Oshkosh WI 54901

GUETTER, HARRY HENDRIK, ASTRONOMY, ASTROMETRY. *Current Pos:* ASTRONR, NAVAL OBSERV, 64- *Personal Data:* b Andijk, Holland, Feb 1, 35; US citizen; m 63; c 3. *Educ:* Queen's Univ, Ont, BSc, 61; Univ Toronto, MA, 63. *Prof Exp:* Res asst astron, David Dunlap Observ, Richmond Hill, Ont, 63-64. *Mem:* Am Astron Soc; Int Astron Union; Astron Soc Pac; Am Sci Affil. *Res:* Photoelectric photometry and spectroscopy of early-type stars in associations and clusters; investigations of properties of interstellar matter and distance determinations of stars with small masses. *Mailing Add:* 526 Havasupai Rd Flagstaff AZ 86001

GUEVARA, FRANCISCO A(NTONIO), NUCLEAR ENGINEERING, CHEMICAL ENGINEERING. *Current Pos:* staff mem nuclear res & develop, Radiol Protection Eng, 56-90, RADIOL PROTECTION ENG CONSULT, LOS ALAMOS NAT LAB, 90- *Personal Data:* b Denver, Colo, Jan 10, 24; m 51; c 5. *Educ:* Tex A&M Univ, BS, 50; Univ NMex, MS, 59. *Honors & Awards:* Medal Hon fel Eng, Mex Am Eng Soc. *Prof Exp:* Chem engr, Health & Safety Br, AEC, NMex, 50-56. *Concurrent Pos:* Consult nuclear engr reactor licensing, Effluent Treat Systs Br, Nuclear Regulatory Comn, 72-75; reviewer, Dept Educ Fuel Cycle Facil Safety Analysis Reports, 78- *Mem:* Am Nuclear Soc; Health Physics Soc; Mex Am Eng Soc (nat pres). *Res:* Control systems for decontamination of effluents from nuclear facilities and disposal of radioactive waste. *Mailing Add:* 23 Los Arboles Dr Los Alamos NM 87544

GUEVREMONT, ROGER M, ANALYTICAL CHEMISTRY. *Current Pos:* Assoc res off analytical chem, Marine Analytical Chem Stand Prog, 78-90, SR RES OFF ANALYTICAL CHEM, MEASUREMENT SCI, NAT RES COUN CAN, 90- *Personal Data:* b Thunder Bay, Ont, Jan 20, 51; m 76; c 3. *Educ:* McGill Univ, Can, BSc, 74; Univ Alta, Can, PhD(chem), 78. *Honors & Awards:* Maccoll Prize, 91. *Mem:* Chem Inst Can. *Res:* Methods for trace analysis of environmental samples; reference materials for dioxins and polychlorinated biphenyls; instrumentation development for electrospray mass spectrometry; instrumentation for direct powder introduction inductively coupled plasma emission spectrometry. *Mailing Add:* Inst Environ Chem Nat Res Coun Can Montreal Rd Ottawa ON K1A 0R6 Can

GUGELOT, PIET C, PHYSICS. *Current Pos:* PROF PHYSICS, UNIV VA, 67- *Personal Data:* b Bussum, Neth, Feb 24, 18; US citizen; m 44; c 1. *Educ:* Swiss Fed Inst Technol, dipl physics, 40, PhD(nuclear physics), 45. *Honors & Awards:* Sr Scientist Award, Alexander von Humboldt Found, 82. *Prof Exp:* Res assoc nuclear physics, Swiss Fed Inst Technol, 40-47; res assoc, Palmer Physics Lab, Princeton Univ, 47-49, asst prof, 49-56; prof nuclear physics & dir, Inst Nuclear Physics Res, Univ Amsterdam, 56-66; dir nuclear physics, Space Radiation Effects Lab, 66-67. *Concurrent Pos:* Vis prof, Univ Wash, 55, Oak Ridge Nat Lab, 60, Lawrence Radiation Lab, Univ Calif, Livermore, 60-61, Stanford Univ, 63-64 & Univ Chicago, 69; vis scientist, Ctr Nuclear Physics Res, Saclay, France, 76; guest scientist, Max Planck Inst, 80-88, Tokyo Univ, 84; gus, Japanese Soc Prom Sci. *Mem:* Fel Am Phys Soc; Swiss Phys Soc; Europ Phys Soc. *Res:* Medium energy nuclear physics, particularly nuclear reactions. *Mailing Add:* Dept Physics Univ Va Charlottesville VA 22901

GUGENHEIM, VICTOR KURT ALFRED MORRIS, topology, for more information see previous edition

GUGER, CHARLES EDMUND, JR, PROCESS DEVELOPMENT, PROCESS ENGINEERING. *Current Pos:* ENG SPECIALIST, MOBAY CHEM CORP, 79- *Personal Data:* b Pittsburgh, Pa, Dec 1, 42; m 66; c 2. *Educ:* Carnegie-Mellon Univ, BS, 64, MS, 65, PhD(chem eng), 69. *Prof Exp:* Jr res scientist, Koppers Co Inc, 68-70, proj scientist, 70-72, sr res engr, 72-79. *Mem:* Am Chem Soc; Am Inst Chem Engrs. *Res:* Chemical process simulation; chemical reaction kinetics; chemical thermodynamics; diffusion, mass transfer, and heat transfer pertaining to chemical processing; economic evaluations, process and project engineering. *Mailing Add:* 1359 Foxboro Dr Monroeville PA 15146

GUGGENBERGER, LLOYD JOSEPH, organometallic chemistry, polymer chemistry, for more information see previous edition

GUGGENHEIM, STEPHEN, SILICATE MINERALOGY. *Current Pos:* From asst prof to assoc prof, 76-88, PROF GEOL, UNIV ILL, CHICAGO, 88- *Personal Data:* b New York, NY, June 4, 48; m 74, Linda Brand; c Lauren & David. *Educ:* Marietta Col, BS, 70; State Univ NY, Stony Brook, MS, 72; Univ Wis-Madison, PhD(geol), 76. *Honors & Awards:* Hawley Medal, Mineral Asn, Can, 87; Jackson Mid-Career Clay Sci Award, Clay Minerals Soc Am, 94. *Concurrent Pos:* Vis fel, Australian Nat Univ, Canberra, Australia, 83-84 & 90-91. *Mem:* Am Crystallog Asn; Clay Mineral Soc Am (pres, 96-97); fel Mineral Soc Am (secy, 91-93, 93-95); Mineral Asn Can; Mineral Soc Gt Brit. *Res:* Application of x-ray and electron optical techniques to solve geologic problems; understanding the relationship of crystal structure and crystall chemistry to layer silicate stability. *Mailing Add:* Dept Geol Sci M/C 186 845 W Taylor St Chicago IL 60607-7059. *Fax:* 312-413-2279; *E-Mail:* xtal@uic.edu

GUGGENHEIMER, HEINRICH WALTER, GEOMETRY, ARTIFICIAL INTELLIGENCE COMPUTING. *Current Pos:* prof, 67-90, EMER PROF MATH, LONG ISLAND CTR, POLYTECH UNIV, 90- *Personal Data:* b Nurnberg, Ger, July 21, 24; nat US; m 47, Eva Horowitz; c S Michael, Esther (Furman), Tobias I S & Hannah Y. *Educ:* Swiss Fed Inst Technol, Dipl, 47, DSc(math), 50. *Prof Exp:* Lectr math, Hebrew Univ, Israel, 54-56; prof, Bar Ilan Univ, Israel, 56-59; assoc prof, Wash State Univ, 59-60; from assoc prof to prof, Univ Minn, 60-67. *Mem:* Swiss Math Soc; Math Asn Am; Soc Indust & Appl Math. *Res:* Computer graphics; differential and algebraic geometry; foundations of geometry; history of mathematics; all aspects of geometry, including differential equations; Aramaic linguistics; artificial intelligence. *Mailing Add:* PO Box 401 West Hempstead NY 11552-0401

GUGGENHEIMER, JAMES, ORAL MEDICINE. *Current Pos:* asst prof, 66-76, PROF ORAL MED, SCH DENT MED, UNIV PITTSBURGH, 76- *Personal Data:* b Belgrade, Yugoslavia, Mar 4, 36; US citizen; m 69, Constance Fitzgerald; c 3. *Educ:* City Col New York, BS, 58; Columbia Univ, DDS, 62. *Prof Exp:* Intern dent, Vet Admin Hosp, Albany, NY, 62-63; resident oral surg, Strong Mem Hosp, Rochester, 63-64. *Concurrent Pos:* USPHS fel oral med, Sch Dent Med, Univ Pa & Philadelphia Gen Hosp, 64-66; mem staff det med, Presby Univ Hosp, 67-; consult, Vet Admin Hosp, Oakland, 67-, courtesy staff, Eye & Ear Hosp; clin asst, Dept Oral/Maxillofacial Surg, Montefiore Hosp, 68- *Mem:* Am Asn Dent Res; Am Pub Health Asn; Am Acad Oral Med. *Res:* Oral ulcerations; effects of cancer chemotherapeutic agents; tetracycline stain; use and effects of smokeless tobacco; epidemiology of oral cancer; oral manifestations of diabetes. *Mailing Add:* Sch Dent Med Univ Pittsburgh G137 Pittsburgh PA 15261. *Fax:* 412-383-9142; *E-Mail:* guggent@pitt.edu

GUGIG, WILLIAM, ORGANIC CHEMISTRY. *Current Pos:* RETIRED. *Personal Data:* b New York, NY, Aug 15, 14; m 47; c 4. *Educ:* Long Island Univ, BS, 49; Polytech Inst Brooklyn, MS, 56. *Prof Exp:* From instr to prof chem, Long Island Univ, 50-81. *Concurrent Pos:* NSF fac fel, Long Island Univ, 57-58, adj prof chem, 81- *Mem:* Am Chem Soc; Sigma Xi. *Res:* Properties and structure of cyclopentadienones; rearrangements of aromatic hydrocarbons. *Mailing Add:* 1771 E 14 St Brooklyn NY 11229-2001

GUIDA, VINCENT GEORGE, MARINE ECOLOGY, INVERTEBRATE SYMBIOSIS. *Current Pos:* RES SCIENTIST INVERTEBRATE PATHOBIOL, INST PATHOBIOL, LEHIGH UNIV, 78-, DIR MARINE ECOL, WETLANDS INST, 79- *Personal Data:* b Brooklyn, NY, Sept 2, 48; m 77; c 2. *Educ:* Rensselaer Polytech Inst, BS, 70; NC State Univ,

PhD(marine sci), 77. *Concurrent Pos:* Fel, Inst Pathobiol, Lehigh Univ, 78-80. *Mem:* AAAS. *Res:* Estuarine ecology including community structure and function based on predation, competition, symbiosis and toxic interactions. *Mailing Add:* 565 Brighton St Bethlehem PA 18015

GUIDA, WAYNE CHARLES, ORGANIC CHEMISTRY. *Current Pos:* vis asst prof, 76-77, asst prof, 77-82, ASSOC PROF CHEM, ECKERD COL, 82- *Personal Data:* b Tampa, Fla, Mar 20, 46; div; c 1. *Educ:* Univ SFla, BA, 68, PhD(chem), 76. *Prof Exp:* Fel chem, Duke Univ, 76. *Concurrent Pos:* Vis assoc prof, Univ SC, 83-84; sr fel, Columbia Univ, 85-86. *Mem:* Am Chem Soc; Sigma Xi. *Res:* Chemistry of oxonium ions and their utility as synthetic reagents for organic synthesis; borohydride reductions of organic compounds in non-polar solvents; chemistry of crown ethers; molecular modeling and computational chemistry. *Mailing Add:* Novartis Pharm Corp 556 Morris Ave Summit NJ 07901-1330

GUIDERI, GIANCARLO, PHARMACOLOGY. *Current Pos:* From instr to assoc prof, 69-93, PROF PHARMACOL, NY MED COL, 93- *Personal Data:* b Siena, Italy, Oct 18, 31; US citizen; m 73, Ruth Labhart; c Jessica, Lucas & Danielle. *Educ:* Long Island Univ, BS, 61; NY Univ, MS, 65; NY Med Col, PhD(pharmacol), 69. *Concurrent Pos:* Adj asst prof cell biol, Fordham Univ, 69; adj assoc prof, Inst Int Med Educ, 74-; adj prof, St Johns Univ, 85-; vis prof, Cath Univ Lille, France, 86-88. *Mem:* Am Soc Pharmacol & Exp Therapeut; Am Soc Toxicol. *Res:* Role played by certain drug and central nervous system influences on blood pressure and the development of severe cardiac rhythm disorders; drug-drug interactions. *Mailing Add:* Dept Pharmacol NY Med Col Basic Sci Bldg Valhalla NY 10595

GUIDI, JOHN NEIL, database & information retrieval systems, knowledge representation & reasoning, for more information see previous edition

GUIDICE, DONALD ANTHONY, SPACE SYSTEMS TECHNOLOGY, RADIO ASTRONOMY. *Current Pos:* res physicist, Air Force Cambridge Res Labs, 64-71, radio astronr, 71-82, CHIEF ENGR, SPACE SYST TECHNOL, PHILLIPS LAB, 82- *Personal Data:* b Astoria, NY, Oct 12, 34; m 65; c 4. *Educ:* Manhattan Col, BEE, 56; Ohio State Univ, MS, 59, PhD(elec eng), 69. *Prof Exp:* Electronics engr, Air Force Avionics Lab, Ohio, 56-64. *Mem:* Am Astron Soc; Inst Elec & Electronics Engrs; Int Astron Union; Int Union Radio Sci. *Res:* Ring laser techniques for angular rotation sensing; atmospheric microwave radiometry; spectral characteristics of solar radio bursts; solar microwave instrumentation design; space environment effects on space system technologies. *Mailing Add:* 115 Winchester Rd Arlington MA 02174

GUIDOTTI, CHARLES V, MINERALOGY, PETROLOGY & GEOLOGY. *Current Pos:* PROF GEOL, UNIV MAINE, ORONO, 81- *Personal Data:* b Somerville, Mass, Sept 19, 35; m 61; c 3. *Educ:* Yale Univ, BS, 57; Harvard Univ, PhD(geol), 63. *Prof Exp:* Res asst geol, Univ Minn, 58; lectr, Univ Calif, Davis, 62-63, from asst prof to assoc prof, 63-69; assoc prof to prof, Univ Wis-Madison, 69-81. *Mem:* Am Geophys Union; Mineral Asn Can; fel Geol Soc Am; fel Mineral Soc Am; Mineral Soc Italy; Int Mineral Asn. *Res:* Metamorphic petrology of high-grade pelitic and calc-silicate rocks; stratigraphy and structure of metamorphosed strata in northwest Maine and the central coast of Maine; rock-forming mineralogy; layer silicates. *Mailing Add:* Dept Geol Sci Univ Maine Orono ME 04469. *Fax:* 207-581-2202; *E-Mail:* guidotti@maine.edu

GUIDOTTI, GUIDO, BIOCHEMISTRY. *Current Pos:* asst prof biol, 63-68, assoc prof biol, biochem & molecular biol, 68-69, PROF BIOCHEM, HARVARD UNIV, 69- *Personal Data:* b Florence, Italy, Nov 3, 33. *Educ:* Wash Univ, MD, 57; Rockefeller Inst, PhD(biochem), 63. *Prof Exp:* Intern, Barnes Hosp, 57-58, asst res, 58-59. *Mem:* Am Soc Biochem & Molecular Biol; Am Acad Arts & Sci. *Res:* Interactions of macromolecules in solution; structure and function of proteins; structure and function of biological membranes; mechanism of hormone action. *Mailing Add:* Fairchild Biochem Bldg Harvard Univ 7 Divinity Ave Cambridge MA 02138

GUIDRY, CARLTON LEVON, ORGANIC CHEMISTRY. *Current Pos:* RETIRED. *Personal Data:* b Palacios, Tex, June 23, 33; m 55; c 5. *Educ:* Univ Houston, BS, 58, PhD(biochem), 62. *Prof Exp:* Res chemist, Continental Oil Co, 61-63; from asst to prof prof chem, Sam Houston State Univ, 63-88. *Mailing Add:* 5429 Stone Creek La Porte TX 77571

GUIDRY, CLYDE R, BIOCHEMISTRY. *Current Pos:* fel, Dept Biochem, 86-88, res assoc, 88-90, RES INSTR, DEPTS BIOCHEM & OPHTHAL, UNIV ALA BIRMINGHAM, 90- *Personal Data:* b Paris, Tex, Oct 4, 56. *Educ:* Univ Tex, BS, 81, PhD(cell biol), 86. *Prof Exp:* Teaching asst, Med Histol & Cell Biol, Health Sci Ctr, Univ Tex, Dallas, 84-85. *Concurrent Pos:* Arthritis Found fel, 88-91; Helen Keller Eye Res Inst investr, 90-92. *Res:* Cell biology; numerous technical publications. *Mailing Add:* Dept Ophthal Univ Ala Birmingham Birmingham AL 35294-0001. *Fax:* 205-325-8679

GUIDUCCI, MARIANO A, ORGANIC CHEMISTRY. *Current Pos:* RETIRED. *Personal Data:* b Peckville, Pa, Nov 29, 30; m 54, Marilyn; c 2. *Educ:* Albright Col, BS, 52; Lehigh Univ, MS, 54; Columbia Univ, PhD(org chem), 65. *Prof Exp:* Res asst, Olin Mathieson Chem Corp, 54-56, res asst, Squibb Inst Med Res, 56-61, sr res chemist, 65-70; sr res chemist, Schwarz Biores/Mann Res, 70-74; mgr process res, FMC Corp, 74-81, sr process chemist, 81-83; sr process chemist, Givaudan, 83-89, prod supvr, 90-93. *Mem:* Am Chem Soc. *Res:* Synthetic methods, especially as related to steroids and natural products; scale up of synthesis; peptide synthesis. *Mailing Add:* 68 Eden Ave Edison NJ 08817-3850

GUIER, WILLIAM HOWARD, THEORETICAL PHYSICS. *Current Pos:* Sr staff physicist, 51-58, mem prin staff, Appl Physics Labs, 58-93, ASSOC PROF BIOMED ENG, SCH MED, JOHNS HOPKINS UNIV, 69-, MED (CARDIOL), 88- *Personal Data:* b Wichita, Kans, July 13, 26; m 50; c 1. *Educ:* Northwestern Univ, BS, 48, MS, 50, PhD(physics), 51. *Honors & Awards:* Pioneer Award, Inst Elec & Electronics Engrs, 86; Magellan Prize for Navig, Am Philos Soc, 88. *Mem:* Am Heart Asn; Inst Elec & Electronics Engrs. *Res:* Random function theory and statistical mechanics; geophysics connected with artificial satellites; biomedical engineering; cardiovascular physiology; patient monitoring systems; artificial intelligence. *Mailing Add:* 5146 Mountain Rd Pasadena MD 21122

GUIHER, JOHN KENNETH, FOREST PRODUCTS. *Current Pos:* asst prof, 55-70, ASSOC PROF WOOD TECHNOL & FORESTRY UTILIZATION, UNIV ILL, URBANA, 70- *Personal Data:* b Youngstown, Ohio, Mar 25, 17; m 46; c 1. *Educ:* Mich State Univ, BS, 47, PhD(wood technol), 53; Yale Univ, MF, 48. *Prof Exp:* Instr forest prod, Mich State Univ, 48-52; asst wood technologist, Inst Technol, Wash State Univ, 52-54; prof forestry & head dept, Stephen F Austin State Col, 54-55. *Mem:* Soc Am Foresters; Forest Prod Res Soc; Soc Wood Sci & Technol; Sigma Xi. *Res:* Wood anatomy and identification; wood glues and gluing. *Mailing Add:* 3106 Meadow Brook Dr Champaign IL 61821-6149

GUIKEMA, JAMES ALLEN, PHOTOSYNTHESIS. *Current Pos:* from asst prof to assoc prof, 81-94, PROF BIOL, KANS STATE UNIV, 94- *Personal Data:* b Grand Rapids, Mich, Aug 31, 51; m, Susan J Brown. *Educ:* Calvin Col, BA, 73; Univ Mich, PhD(biol sci), 78. *Prof Exp:* Teaching asst, Univ Mich, 74-78; fel, Univ Mo, 78-81. *Concurrent Pos:* Assoc dir, NASA Specialized Ctr Res & Training in Gravitational Biol, 91- *Mem:* Sigma Xi; Am Soc Plant Physiologists; Am Soc Gravitational Space Biol. *Res:* Physiology of photosynthesis in cyanobacteria using a combination of genetic and biochemical techniques. *Mailing Add:* Div Biol Ackert Hall Kans State Univ Manhattan KS 66506-4901. *Fax:* 785-539-6653; *E-Mail:* guikema@ksuvm.ksu.edu

GUILARTE, TOMAS R, RADIATION HEALTH SCIENCES. *Current Pos:* Res assoc, 80-81, asst prof, 81-87, ASSOC PROF RADIATION HEALTH & TOXICOL SCI, JOHNS HOPKINS UNIV, 87-, ASSOC PROF, JOINT APPT DIV HUMAN NUTRIT, 90- *Personal Data:* b Oriente Cuba, Sept 15, 53; US citizen; m 77; c 3. *Educ:* Univ Fla, BS, 74, MS, 76; Johns Hopkins Univ, PhD(radiation health), 80. *Concurrent Pos:* Affil, Ctr Advan Radiation Educ & Res, Johns Hopkins Univ, 86- *Mem:* Am Inst Nutrit; Soc Nuclear Med; AAAS. *Res:* Effects of maternal vitamin B-6 nutrition on the ontogenesis of neurotransmitter systems in the brain of progeny; discovery of putative endogenous convulsant and neurotoxin and investigation of its mechanism of action; the development and application of analytical methods for the analysis of B-vitamins in complex biological samples. *Mailing Add:* Dept Environ Health Sci Rm 2001 Johns Hopkins Univ Sch Hyg & Pub Health 615 N Wolfe St Baltimore MD 21205-2103. *Fax:* 410-955-6222

GUILBAULT, LAWRENCE JAMES, POLYMER CHEMISTRY. *Current Pos:* tech mgr res & develop, Thiokol Corp, 76-82, VPRES RES & DEVELOP, VENTRON DIV, MORTON INT, 82- *Personal Data:* b Buffalo, NY, Jan 26, 40; m 67; c 3. *Educ:* Kans State Univ, BS, 64; Univ Akron, PhD(polymer sci), 70; Am Inst Chemists, PC-A, 69. *Prof Exp:* Chem technician, Gen Elec Co, 59-62, applns chemist, 64-66; fel, Univ Fla, 70-71; res assoc polymers, Calgon Corp, 71-72, group leader, 72-74, sr group leader polymers, 74-76. *Concurrent Pos:* Lectr ion-containing polymers, Am Chem Soc, 75-; chmn Gordon res conf ion-containing polymers, 83. *Mem:* Am Chem Soc; Tech Asn Pulp & Paper Indust; Soc Plastics Engrs; Controlled Release Soc; Electrochem Soc. *Res:* Synthesis and development of polyelectrolytes for use in water and waste treatment and in oilfield applications; synthesis and application of boron hydrides; antimicrobial additives for plastics; structure-property correlations for water soluble polymers. *Mailing Add:* 396 Ipswich Rd Boxford MA 01921-1510

GUILBEAU, ERIC J, BIOMEDICAL ENGINEERING, CHEMICAL ENGINEERING. *Current Pos:* assoc prof, 77-81, PROF & CHMN CHEM & BIOMED ENG, ARIZ STATE UNIV, 81-, DIR BIOENG, 90- *Personal Data:* b Tullos, La, June 5, 44; m 67; c 3. *Educ:* La Tech Univ, BS, 67, MS, 68, PhD(chem eng), 71. *Prof Exp:* Res assoc chem eng, La Tech Univ, 71-72, res assoc biomed eng, 72-73, from asst prof to assoc prof, 73-77. *Concurrent Pos:* Affil med staff, St Joseph's Hosp, Phoenix, 77- *Mem:* Am Inst Chem Engrs; Am Chem Soc; Sigma Xi; Int Soc Study Oxygen Transport to Tissue; Biomed Eng Soc; Soc Biomat. *Res:* Biomedical engineering, development of transducers for measurement of cellular biological parameters; study transport phenomena in physiological systems; investigation of myocardial protection techniques; development of pericardial substitutes. *Mailing Add:* Dept Chem, Bio Eng & Mats Ariz State Univ Tempe AZ 85287-6006

GUILBERT, JOHN M, PLATE TECTONICS, ECONOMIC PETROLOGY. *Current Pos:* from asst prof to prof, 65-93, EMER PROF, DEPT GEOSCI, UNIV ARIZ, 93-; CHMN BD, JABA, INC, 95- *Personal Data:* b Newton, Mass, May 12, 31; m 54; c 3. *Educ:* Univ NC, BS, 53; Univ Wis, MS, 55, PhD(geol), 62. *Prof Exp:* Res geologist, Geol Res Lab, Anaconda Co, 57-65. *Concurrent Pos:* Consult, 65-95. *Mem:* Soc Econ Geologists; fel Geol Soc Am; fel Mineral Soc Am; Soc Geol Appl Mineral Deposits; Int Asn Genesis Ore Deposits. *Res:* Porphry base metal deposits; precambrian massive sulfide ores; ore deposit-plate tectonic interrelationships; alteration-mineralization petrology. *Mailing Add:* Dept Geosci Univ Ariz Tucson AZ 85721. *Fax:* 520-887-3834; *E-Mail:* guilbert@ccit.arizona.edu

GUILD, LLOYD V, CHEMISTRY. *Current Pos:* FOUNDER & RES DIR, SKC INC, 64- *Personal Data:* b Elmira, NY, July 17, 20; m 41; c 3. *Educ:* Univ Pittsburgh, BS, 48, MS, 61. *Prof Exp:* Vpres res & mfg, Burrell Corp, 41-64. *Mem:* Am Chem Soc; Am Soc Testing & Mat; Instrument Soc Am; Am Indust Hyg Asn; Sigma Xi; Am Carbon Soc. *Res:* Analytical instrumentation and low level determination of chemical hazards; temperature programming and detectors in gas chromatography; 50 patents in analytical chemistry and analytical instrumentation. *Mailing Add:* SKC Inc 863 Valley View Rd Eighty Four PA 15330-9613

GUILD, WALTER RUFUS, MOLECULAR BIOLOGY, GENETICS. *Current Pos:* RETIRED. *Personal Data:* b Ann Arbor, Mich, Oct 25, 23; m 46; c 1. *Educ:* Univ Tex, BS, 48, MA, 49; Yale Univ, PhD(biophys), 51. *Prof Exp:* Instr physics, Yale Univ, 51-54, asst prof biophys, 54-60; from assoc prof to prof biophys, Med Ctr, Duke Univ, 60-86, dir univ prog in genetics, 77-79. *Concurrent Pos:* Mem int fel rev comt, NIH, 68-72; USPHS sr fel, Stanford Univ, 70-71; mem, Microbial Genetics Study Sect, NIH, 81-84; emer prof biophys, Med Ctr, Duke Univ, 87- *Mem:* Am Soc Biol Chem; Biophys Soc; Am Soc Microbiol; Genetics Soc Am; Radiation Res Soc. *Res:* Molecular genetics, primarily mechanisms of gene transfer in bacteria and genetic recombination. *Mailing Add:* 2625 McDowell Rd Durham NC 27710

GUILE, DONALD LLOYD, CERAMICS, MATERIALS SCIENCE. *Current Pos:* RES ENGR, CORNING GLASS WORKS, 64- *Personal Data:* b Olean, NY, Nov 12, 32; m 56; c 4. *Educ:* Alfred Univ, BS, 60, PhD(ceramic sci), 65. *Mem:* Am Ceramic Soc; Brit Ceramic Soc. *Res:* Study of high temperature refractory materials for the glass and metal industries, including particle technology and application of sintering theory. *Mailing Add:* 7 Stonybrook Rd E Horseheads NY 14845

GUILFORD, HARRY GARRETT, ZOOLOGY, PARASITOLOGY. *Current Pos:* from asst prof to prof bot & zool, Univ Wis-Green Bay, 50-69, secy fac, 70-77, dept chmn, 80-84, prof human biol, 69-88, EMER PROF, UNIV WIS-GREEN BAY, 88- *Personal Data:* b Madison, Wis, June 20, 23; m 49; c 2. *Educ:* Univ Wis, PhB, 44, PhM, 46, PhD(zool), 49. *Prof Exp:* Assoc prof biol, Mercer Univ, 49 50. *Mem:* Am Soc Parasitologists; Soc Protozoologists; Sigma Xi. *Res:* Histology and life history of trematodes; myxosporida. *Mailing Add:* 2320 Hawthorne Pl Green Bay WI 54301

GUILFOYLE, RICHARD HOWARD, MATHEMATICS. *Current Pos:* From instr to asst prof, 66-72, assoc prof math/comput sci, 72-87, PROF MATH, MONMOUTH COL, 87- *Personal Data:* b Seaford, NY, Nov 4, 39; m 61; c 3. *Educ:* C W Post Col, BS, 61; Stevens Inst Technol, MS, 63, PhD(math), 72. *Concurrent Pos:* NSF fel, 71-72. *Mem:* Math Asn Am; Sigma Xi. *Res:* Numerical methods for finding zeros of complex functions; variational methods applied to optimal design of switching circuits. *Mailing Add:* Dept Math Monmouth Univ West Long Branch NJ 07764-1898

GUILFOYLE, THOMAS J, MOLECULAR BIOLOGY, PLANT BREEDING & GENETICS. *Current Pos:* PROF, DEPT BIOCHEM, UNIV MO, COLUMBIA, 86- *Personal Data:* b Mendota, Ill, Jan 13, 46. *Educ:* Ill State Univ, BS, 68; Univ Ill, Urbana, MS, 69, PhD, 74. *Prof Exp:* NIH fel, Univ Ga, Athens, 74-76; from asst prof to prof, Dept Bot, Univ Minn, 76-86. *Mem:* Am Soc Biochem & Molecular Biol; Am Soc Plant Physiologists; Am Soc Microbiol; AAAS; Int Soc Plant Molecular Biol. *Res:* Molecular Plant; numerous publications. *Mailing Add:* Dept Biochem Univ Mo 117 Schweitzer Hall Columbia MO 65211-0001. *Fax:* 572-882-5635

GUILLARD, ROBERT RUSSELL LOUIS, BIOLOGICAL OCEANOGRAPHY, PHYTOPLANKTON CULTURE. *Current Pos:* dir, 85-89, EMER DIR, PROVASOLI-GUILLARD CTR CULT MARINE PHYTOPLANKTON, 89-; PRIN INVESTR, BIGELOW LAB OCEAN SCI, 81- *Personal Data:* b New York, NY, Feb 5, 21; m 52, 62, Ruth Fredericks; c David, Mark A & John. *Educ:* City Col New York, BS, 41; Yale Univ, MS, 51, PhD, 54. *Honors & Awards:* Darbaker Award, Bot Soc Am, 68. *Prof Exp:* Elec engr, Navy Yard, NY, 41-46; tutor physics, City Col New York, 46-49; res assoc bot, Univ Hawaii, 54-55; aquatic microbiologist, Oyster Inst NAm, Inc, US Fish & Wildlife Lab, 55-58; res assoc marine biol, Woods Hold Oceanog Inst, 58-61, assoc scientist, 63-73, sr scientist, 73-81. *Mem:* Fel AAAS; Am Soc Limnol & Oceanog; Phycol Soc Am; Int Phycol Soc; Sigma Xi. *Res:* Physiology, ecology and systematics of marine phytoplankton; isolation and culture of algae. *Mailing Add:* Bigelow Lab Ocean Sci West Boothbay Harbor MA 04575

GUILLEMETTE, GAETAN, INTRACELLULAR SIGNALS, SECOND MESSENGERS. *Current Pos:* PROF PHARMACOL, UNIV SHERBROOKE, 87- *Personal Data:* b St-Celestin, Que, Dec 2, 51; m 74, Paule D; c Benoit & Audrey. *Educ:* Univ Que, BSc, 74; Univ Sherbrooke, MSc, 79, PhD(pharmacol), 82. *Concurrent Pos:* Scientist, Med Res Coun Can, 93. *Mem:* Endocrine Soc; AAAS; Am Soc Hypertension; Can Asn Advan Sci. *Res:* Mechanism of action of angiotansin II; activation of phospholipase C; production of diacylglycerol and of inositolphosphates; mobilization of cellularcalcium are the main parameters studied upon stimulation of different cell models including adrenal glomerulosa cells, endothelial cells and pheochromocytoma cells. *Mailing Add:* 3001 12th Ave N Sherbrooke PQ J1H 5N4 Can. *Fax:* 819-564-5400

GUILLEMIN, ROGER (CHARLES LOUIS), PHYSIOLOGY, NEUROENDOCRINOLOGY. *Current Pos:* dir, 93-94, DISTINGUISHED SCIENTIST, WHITTIER INST DIABETES & ENDOCRINOL, 89- *Personal Data:* b Dijon, France, Jan 11, 24; nat US; m 51, Lucienne Jeanne Billard; c Chantal, Francois, Claire, Helene, Elisabeth & Cecile. *Educ:* Dijon Univ, France, BA, 41, BSc, 42; Univ Lyons, MD, 49; Univ Montreal, PhD(exp med & surg), 53. *Hon Degrees:* Numerous from US & foreign univs, 76-89. *Honors & Awards:* Nobel Prize in Physiol or Med, 77; Louis Bonneau Award, Fr Acad Sci, 57, L LaCaze Award, 60; Int Cong Pharmacol Gold Medal, 61; Ayerst-Squibb Award, Endocrine Soc, 70; Lasker Found Award, 75; Passano Award, Borden Award, Asn Am Med Cols, 76; Nat Medal Sci, President of the United States, 77; Barren Gold Medal, 78; Dale Medal, Soc Endocrinol, UK, 78; Nobel Laureat Re-Vis Lectr, Nobel Found, 90. *Prof Exp:* Asst prof & asst dir, Inst Exp Med & Surg, Univ Montreal, 51-53; asst prof physiol, Col Med, Baylor Univ, 53-57, assoc prof, 57-63, prof & dir, Labs Neuroendocrinol, 63-70; res fel & chmn, Labs Neuroendocrinol, Salk Inst Biol Studies, 70-89, dean fac, 72 & 76. *Concurrent Pos:* Markle Found scholar, 52-56; consult, Vet Admin Hosp, Houston, 54-70; lectr, Rice Univ, 58-60; mem study sects, NIH, 59-69 & Int Comt Estab New ACTH Stand, 60; sci prog comt, Int Cong Pharmacol, Stockholm, 60; assoc dir, Dept Exp Endocrinol, Col France, 60-63; consult, Univ Tex, M D Anderson Hosp & Tumor Inst Houston, 67-; vis mem grad fac, Tex A&M Univ, 68-70; mem comt endocrinol, Int Union Physiol Sci Glossary, 69; adj prof, Col Med, Baylor Univ & Univ Calif, San Diego, 70, Salk Inst, La Jolla, 89-; mem, Ctr Pop Res, NIH, 71-74, Panel Nat Pituitary Agency, Nat Acad Sci, 73-75, President's Biomed Res Panel, 75-76, Task Force Conception, Reproduction, Partuition, Contraception & Sex Differentiation, NIH, 78-, President's Comt Nat Medal Sci, 81 & Bd Sci Counselors, Nat Inst Child Health & Human Develop, 83; mem neuroendocrine comt, Fedn Am Socs Exp Biol, 71-75; bd dirs, Sanofi, 82-86, Erbamont NV, 86-92, ICN Pharmaceut, Inc, 87-89 & 94, Counseil de Surveillance, Roussel, 89-90, SPI Pharmaceut Inc, 89-, Whittier Inst, 89-94, Prizm Pharmaceut, 92-, Viratek, 92-; adj prof, Salk Inst, 89-94, Univ Calif, 94- *Mem:* Nat Acad Sci; fel AAAS; Endocrine Soc (pres, 86); fel Am Acad Arts & Sci; Acad des Sci, Arts et Belles-Lettres; Am Physiol Soc; Int Brain Res Orgn; Am Physiol Soc; Soc Exp Biol & Med; hon Can Soc Biol; Am Inst Biol Sci; hon Soc Biol Philos Soc; hon mem Asn Physiologists; Soc Neurosci; Int Soc Neuroendocrine; hon Can Soc Endocrinol & Metabol; Asn Am Physicians; Soc Clin Res; Endocrine Soc (pres-elect, 85, pres, 86); Int Soc Immunol Reprod. *Res:* Physiology and biochemistry of hypothalamic mechanisms controlling secretion of pituitary hormones; improvement of population control techniques with antagonists to hypothalamic hormones; neurochemistry of fundamental brain function. *Mailing Add:* Whittier Inst Diabetes & Endocrinol 9894 Genesee Ave La Jolla CA 92037

GUILLEMIN, VICTOR W, GLOBAL ANALYSIS. *Current Pos:* asst prof, 66-73, PROF MATH, MASS INST TECHNOL, 73- *Personal Data:* b Cambridge, Mass, Oct 15, 37. *Educ:* Harvard Univ, BA, 59, PhD(math), 62; Univ Chicago, MA, 60. *Prof Exp:* Instr math, Columbia Univ, 63-66. *Mem:* Nat Acad Sci; Am Acad Arts & Sci; Am Math Soc. *Mailing Add:* Dept Math Mass Inst Technol Cambridge MA 02139

GUILLEN, MICHAEL ARTHUR, MATHEMATICAL PHYSICS. *Current Pos:* sci ed, Good Morning Am, ABC-TV, 80-, SCI CORRESP & SCI ED, ABC NEWS, NY, 90- *Personal Data:* b Los Angeles, Calif; m 91, Laurel Lucas. *Educ:* Univ Calif, Los Angeles, BS; Cornell Univ, MS, PhD(physics, math & astron), 82. *Honors & Awards:* Broadcast Media Award, Am Inst Aeronaut & Astronaut, 87. *Prof Exp:* Sci tech contribr, CBS Morning News. *Concurrent Pos:* Tech adv, Metro-Goldwyn Mayer; partic numerous educ improv progs; sci consult, MGM/UA; mem, Adv Bd, Am Inst Aeronaut; teacher physics & math core curric prog, Harvard Univ, 85-; sci ed, WCVB-TV, Boston, 85. *Mem:* Nat Acad Sci; AAAS; Leonardo da Vinci Soc. *Res:* Theoretical plasma physics; liquid physics; astrophysics; contributor articles to numerous newspapers and magazines and author. *Mailing Add:* ABC-TV 147 Columbus Ave New York NY 10023

GUILLERY, RAINER WALTER, NEUROANATOMY. *Current Pos:* DR LEE'S PROF ANAT, OXFORD, ENG, 84- *Personal Data:* b Greifswald, Ger, Aug 28, 29; m 54, Margot C Pepper; c Peter, Edward, Philip & Jane. *Educ:* Univ London, BSc, 51, PhD(anat), 54. *Prof Exp:* From asst lectr to lectr, Univ Col, London, 53-63, reader, 63-64; from assoc prof to prof anat, Univ Wis-Madison, 64-77; prof pharmacol & physiol sci, Univ Chicago, 77-84. *Concurrent Pos:* Rockefeller traveling fel neurophysiol, Univ Wis, 60-61; vis prof, Dept Anat, Univ Wis-Madison. *Mem:* Fel Royal Soc; Am Soc Neurosci; Europ Neurosci Asn; Anat Soc Gt Brit & Ireland (pres, 93-95). *Res:* Development of visual and thalermocortical pathways. *Mailing Add:* Dept Anat Sch Med Univ Wis 1300 Univ Ave Madison 53706. *Fax:* 608-262-2327; *E-Mail:* rguiller@facstaff.wisc.edu

GUILLET, JAMES EDWIN, PHYSICAL CHEMISTRY, POLYMER CHEMISTRY. *Current Pos:* from assoc prof to prof, 63-91, EMER PROF CHEM, UNIV TORONTO, 91- *Personal Data:* b Toronto, Ont, Jan 14, 27; m 53; c 4. *Educ:* Univ Toronto, BA, 48; Cambridge Univ, PhD(phys chem), 55, ScD, 74. *Honors & Awards:* Dunlop Lectr, 79. *Prof Exp:* Res chemist, Eastman Kodak Co, 48-50, res chemist, Tenn Eastman Co Div, 50-52, sr res chemist, 55-62, res assoc, 63; assoc dean res & planning, Scarborough Col, 83-84. *Concurrent Pos:* Consult, Glidden Co, Ltd, 64-84, Imp Oil Enterprises, Ltd, 65-83, Royal Packaging, Holland, 72-79, Allied Can, Inc, 82-86 & Res Labs, IBM, 84-85; vis prof, Nat Ctr Sci Res, Strasbourg, France, 70-71, Kyoto Univ, 74, Univ Calif, San Diego, 78-79, Res labs, IBM, San Jose, 80, Univ Mainz, WGer, 81, Univ Calif, Berkeley, 82 & Univ St Andrews, Scotland, 83; dir, Ecoplastics Ltd, 71-85, pres, 75-84; dir, Medipro Sci Ltd, 76-93, pres, 85-89, chmn bd & chief exec officer, 91-93; Guggenheim fel, 81-82; dir, Solarchem Corp, 83-88, pres, 84-85; Killam res fel, 87-89; overseas vis fel, St John's Col, Cambridge Univ; dir & vpres res, Pharmapatch PLC, 93-94. *Mem:*

Am Chem Soc; Chem Soc; fel Chem Inst Can; fel Royal Soc Can; Interam Photochem Soc. *Res:* Structure-property relations in polymers; photochemical and photophysical processes in polymers; solar enrgy conversion; energy storage and migration in polymers; inverse gas chromatography; photo and biodegradable plastics; granted 78 patents in the field of polymers and plastics. *Mailing Add:* Dept Chem Univ Toronto Toronto ON M5S 3H6 Can. *Fax:* 416-978-3591; *E-Mail:* jguillet@alchemy. chem.utoronto.ca

GUILLORY, JACK PAUL, PHYSICAL CHEMISTRY. *Current Pos:* Res chem physicist, Phillips Petrol Co, 65-71, group leader, 71-73, sect supvr, 73-80, br mgr, 80-89, sr br mgr, 89-92, DIV MGR, PHILLIPS PETROL CO, 92- *Personal Data:* b Alexandria, La, Feb 28, 38; m 60; c 3. *Educ:* La State Univ, BS, 60; Iowa State Univ, PhD(phys chem), 65. *Mem:* Am Chem Soc; Catalyst Soc. *Res:* Electron diffraction study of gases; electronic spectroscopy; heterogeneous catalysis; petroleum refining processes; process modeling; analytical chemistry; computational chemistry. *Mailing Add:* 1905 Glynnwood Dr Bartlesville OK 74006

GUILLORY, JAMES KEITH, PHARMACY. *Current Pos:* from asst prof to assoc prof, 64-71, PROF PHARM, UNIV IOWA, 71- *Personal Data:* b Bunkie, La, Feb 4, 35. *Educ:* Loyola Univ, La, BS, 56; Univ Wis, MS, 60, PhD(pharm), 61. *Prof Exp:* Asst prof pharm, Wash State Univ, 61-64. *Concurrent Pos:* Vis Scientist, Burroughs Wellcome Co, 89. *Mem:* Am Chem Soc; fel Am Asn Pharmaceut Scientists. *Res:* Kinetics of degradation of pharmaceuticals; polymorphism; absorption kinetics; thermal analysis; microcalorimetry. *Mailing Add:* Univ Iowa Col Pharm Iowa City IA 52242. *Fax:* 319-335-9418

GUILLORY, RICHARD JOHN, BIOCHEMISTRY. *Current Pos:* chmn dept, 73-76, PROF BIOCHEM & BIOPHYS, SCH MED, UNIV HAWAII, 71- *Personal Data:* b San Diego, Calif, Oct 3, 30; m 56; c 3. *Educ:* Reed Col, BA, 53; Univ Calif, Los Angeles, PhD(biochem), 62. *Prof Exp:* Am Heart Asn res fel, 62-64; from asst prof to assoc prof biochem & molecular biol, Cornell Univ, 66-71. *Concurrent Pos:* Estab investr, Am Heart Asn, 68-73. *Mem:* Am Chem Soc; Brit Biochem Soc; Biophys Soc; Am Soc Biol Chemists; Sigma Xi. *Res:* Bioenergetics; mechanism of enzyme action; oxidative phosphorylation; muscular contraction. *Mailing Add:* Dept Biochem & Biophys Univ Hawaii Sch Med Honolulu HI 96822. *Fax:* 808-956-9498

GUILLORY, WILLIAM ARNOLD, PHYSICAL CHEMISTRY. *Current Pos:* PRES, INNOVATIONS CONSULT, INC, 83- *Personal Data:* b New Orleans, La, Dec 4, 38; m 67; c 1. *Educ:* Dillard Univ, BA, 60; Univ Calif, Berkeley, PhD(chem), 64. *Prof Exp:* NSF fel, Univ Paris, 64-65; asst prof chem, Howard Univ, 65-69; assoc prof, Drexel Univ, 69-75; assoc prof, Univ Utah, 75-76, prof chem & chmn dept, 76-83. *Concurrent Pos:* Res grants, Environ Protection Agency, 69-71, NSF & Dept Energy; consult, Naval Ord Lab, Md, 67-74; Sloan fel, 71-73. *Mem:* AAAS; Am Phys Soc; Am Chem Soc. *Res:* Ultraviolet and infrared spectroscopy, kinetics and photochemistry; elementary photophysical and photochemical processes; low temperature matrix-isolation spectroscopy and molecular structure; applications of infrared and visible ultraviolet lasers in chemistry. *Mailing Add:* PO Box 682423 Park City UT 84068-2423

GUILLOT, DAVID G, ELASTOMERIC ROCKET MOTOR INSULATION. *Current Pos:* scientist, 73-85, SR SCIENTIST, SCI & ENG DIV, THIOKOL CORP, 85- *Personal Data:* b Galveston, Tex, Sept 17, 41; m 62, Rosalie Shaw; c 2. *Educ:* Brigham Young Univ, BS, 62, PhD(phys org chem), 66. *Prof Exp:* Res scientist, Uniroyal Inc, 65-72; lab dir, Terralab, 72-73. *Concurrent Pos:* Pres & dir, TayCon Labs Inc, 73-78; mem, Rubber Div, Am Chem Soc. *Mem:* Am Chem Soc. *Res:* Development of new catalysts for polymerization of polar monomers and the addition of hydroperoxides to butadine; study of pyrolysis of elastomeric compositions and development of elastomeric formulations for specific applications in rocket motors. *Mailing Add:* Thiokol Corp PO Box 707 MS 242 Brigham City UT 84302-0707

GUILMETTE, RAYMOND ALFRED, RADIATION BIOLOGY, HEALTH PHYSICS. *Current Pos:* anal radiochemist, 79-82, RADIOBIOLOGIST, INHALATION TOXICOL RES INST, 77-, MGR, RADIATION TOXICOL PROG, 89- *Personal Data:* b Laconia, NH, May 26, 46; m 69, Patricia M Kerry; c Todd M & Jeremy M. *Educ:* Rensselaer Polytech Inst, BS, 68; NY Univ, MS, 71, PhD(radiol health), 75. *Prof Exp:* Nuclear engr radiation dosimetry, Consol Edison Power Co, 68-69; postdoctoral fel, Argonne Nat Lab, 75-77. *Concurrent Pos:* Assoc ed, Health Physics, 85-90; mem, Sci Comt Dosimetry & Metab Radionuclides, Nat Coun Radiation Protection & Measurements, chmn, Sci Comt Risks Space Appllns Plutonium; mem, Comt Internal Dosimetry Radionuclides, Int Comn Radiol Protection; mem, Radon Sci Initiatives Subcomt, Radiation Adv Comt, Sci Adv Bd, Environ Protection Agency, 93-95, adj prof, Tex A&M Univ, 89-; adj prof, Tex A&M Univ, 89-; bd dir, Health Physics Soc, 91-97. *Mem:* Radiation Res Soc; Health Physics Soc (secy, 94-97); Sigma Xi; Europ Soc Radiation Biol; Am Thoracic Soc; Int Soc Aerosols Med. *Res:* Biokinetics, dosimetry and dose-response relationships for plutonium, other actinides and internal emitters, particularly after inhalation exposure; dosimetry and dose-response modeling, mechanisms of lung clearance, decorporation, therapy; risk assessment, actinide radiochemistry and detection instrumentation; radon dosimetry and biological effects; nasal airway morphometry; dosimetry. *Mailing Add:* Inhalation Toxicol Res Inst PO Box 5890 Albuquerque NM 87185. *Fax:* 505-845-1198; *E-Mail:* rguilmette@lucy.tl1.org

GUIMARAES, ROMEU CARDOSO, ORIGIN OF LIFE, GENETIC CODE. *Current Pos:* PROF GENETICS & EVOLUTION, FED UNIV MINAS GERAIS, 93- *Personal Data:* b Minas Gerais, Brazil, July 29, 43; m 69, Alexandrina Magalhaes. *Educ:* Fed Univ Minas Gerais, MD, 65, DPhil(path), 70. *Prof Exp:* Prof path, Fed Univ Minas Gerais, 66-75; prof genetics, State Univ Sao Paulo, 76-93. *Concurrent Pos:* Fel res grants, Brazilian Nat Res Coun, 68-69 & 76-84 USPHS, 71-73 & Sao Paulo Res Found Aid, 76-; res fel assoc molecular biol, Univ Conn, Storrs, 71 & Univ Tex, Austin, 72-73 & 82; Brit Coun, Univ Kent, Canterbury, 80-81; sr res fel, Brazil Nat Res Coun, 84, consult, 84-; mem gov body, Ctr Study Molecular Evolution, Austin, Tex, 84-86; Inst Biochem, Free Univ Berlin, 87-91; polymer res, Weizmann Inst, Israel, 89-92. *Mem:* Brazilian Asn Advan Sci; Brazilian Soc Genetics; Brazilian Soc Hist Sci; Brazilian Soc Biochem; Int Soc Study Orig Life; Human Genome Orgn. *Res:* Trypanosomatids and fungal taxonomy; cell cycle, karyology; purine metabolism; genetics, cancer; ribosomal RNA; molecular evolution, linguistics; self organization; origin of life; systemic concepts; indeterminacy in biological variation; major evolutionary concepts. *Mailing Add:* Dept Biol ICB-UFMG Belo Horizonte MG 31270-901 Brazil. *Fax:* 55-31-441-5481

GUIMOND, RICHARD JOSEPH, ENVIRONMENTAL SCIENCE. *Current Pos:* CORP DIR RISK MGT, MOTOROLA, 97- *Personal Data:* b Massena, NY, Oct 28, 47; m 71, Sherry L Masis; c Nicole A. *Educ:* Univ Notre Dame, BSME, 69; Rensselaer Polytech Inst, ME, 70; Harvard Univ, MS, 73. *Prof Exp:* Comndg officer, USPHS, 70, adv through grades to rear admiral, 89; spec asst, Off Radiation Progs, Environ Protection Agency, 71-74, dir, Radon Div, 86-88, environ proj leader, Criteria & Stand Div, 74-78, dir, 82-86, chief engr, Off Chem Control, 78-79, chief, Spec Reports Br, Off Toxic Substances, 81, Chem Control Br, 81-82, dir, Off Radiation Protect, 88-91, dep asst adminr, 91-93, actg asst adminr, Off Solid Waste & Emergency Response, 93-97. *Mem:* Health Physics Soc. *Mailing Add:* 1009 Oakland Ct Barrington IL 60019

GUIMOND, ROBERT WILFRID, COMPARATIVE PHYSIOLOGY, MEDICAL PHYSIOLOGY. *Current Pos:* PROF, DEPT BIOL, UNIV MASS, BOSTON, 82- *Personal Data:* b Fall River, Mass, Sept 4, 38; m 63, Elaine Brodie; c Jefferson B & Jameson M. *Educ:* Univ RI, BA, 61, PhD(physiol), 70; New Eng Sch Law, JD, 78. *Prof Exp:* Teacher gen sci, E S Brown Jr High, Swansea, Mass, 61-64; asst prof, Dept Zool, Univ RI, 70-71; from assoc prof to prof, Dept Biol, Boston State Col, 71-82. *Concurrent Pos:* Atty med & environ law specialities, 78- *Mem:* Am Physiol Soc; Am Bar Asn; Am Forestry Asn; Am Soc Law & Med; Sigma Xi; Conserv Law Found. *Res:* General area of comparative respiratory physiology, primarily with amphibious vertebrates; medical-legal problems in regards to the increased use of artificial mechanical life sustaining devices; military medical neglect and the Federal Torts claims act; history of biology and medicine. *Mailing Add:* Dept Biol Univ Mass Boston MA 02125. *Fax:* 781-286-6650

GUINAN, EDWARD F, TROPICAL RAINFORESTS & CLIMATE, STELLAR EVOLUTION & ASTROPHYSICS. *Current Pos:* PROF ASTRON & ASTROPHYS, VILLANOVA UNIV, 77- *Personal Data:* b Philadelphia, Pa, Apr 29, 42; m 69; c 1. *Educ:* Villanova Univ, BS, 64; Univ Pa, PhD(astron & astrophys), 70. *Prof Exp:* Asst prof astron, Villanova Univ, 69-75; vis scientist physics, Shiraz Univ/Biruni Obs, 75-77. *Concurrent Pos:* Vis scientist physics, Shiraz Univ, 77-78; res fel, Harvard-Smithsonian Ctr Astrophys, 82-83, vis scientist, 83-91; prin investr, NASA, 80-91; sci organizing comt, Comn 42, Int Astron Union, 91- *Mem:* Am Astron Soc; Int Astron Union; Am Inst Physics; Rainforest Alliance. *Res:* Observational astrophysics; stellar structure and evolution; binary stars as tests of general relativity; magnetic activity in solar-type stars; variable stars; photoelectric photometry with robotic telescopes; ultraviolet spectroscopy. *Mailing Add:* 100 First Ave Broomall PA 19008

GUINAN, MARY ELIZABETH, MEDICINE, EPIDEMIOLOGY. *Current Pos:* clin res investr venereal dis, Ctr Dis Control, 78-86, asst dir sci, 86-90, spec asst eval HIV/AIDS, 90-95, CHIEF URBAN RES, CTR DIS CONTROL & PREV, 96- *Personal Data:* b New York, NY, Sept 23, 39; div; c Aimee, Erica & Brendan. *Educ:* Univ Tex Med Br, Galveston, PhD(physiol), 69; Johns Hopkins Univ, MD, 72; Am Bd Internal Med, dipl, 78. *Honors & Awards:* Meritorious Serv Medal, US Pub Health Serv. *Prof Exp:* Med epidemiologist hosp infections, Ctr Dis Control, 74-76; fel infectious dis, Univ Utah Med Ctr, 76-78. *Concurrent Pos:* Med epidemiologist, WHO, Delhi, India, 74-75. *Mem:* Am Med Women's Asn; Infectious Dis Soc Am; Am Venereal Dis Asn. *Res:* AIDS; infectious disease; epidemiology of human disease; women's health. *Mailing Add:* Ctr Dis Control 1600 Clifton Rd Atlanta GA 30333

GUINANE, JAMES EDWARD, PEDIATRICS. *Current Pos:* RETIRED. *Personal Data:* b Oak Park, Ill, Mar 16, 32; m 63; c 2. *Educ:* Brown Univ, AB, 53; Calif Inst Technol, MS, 54; Johns Hopkins Univ, MD, 63; Am Bd Pediat, dipl, 68. *Prof Exp:* Intern pediat, NY Univ-Bellevue Med Ctr, 63-64, resident, 64-66; fel pediat neurol, Tufts-New Eng Med Ctr, 69-72, from asst prof to prof pediat, 72-90. *Mem:* Fel Am Acad Pediat; Am Acad Neurol; AAAS. *Res:* Cerebrospinal fluid physiology; experimental hydrocephalus. *Mailing Add:* PO Box 908 Keene NH 03431

GUINASSO, NORMAN LOUIS, JR, OCEANOGRAPHY, COASTAL PHYSICAL OCEANOGRAPHY. *Current Pos:* res assoc oceanog, 72-85, assoc res scientist, 85-93, ASSOC DIR, TEX A&M UNIV, 93- *Personal Data:* b San Francisco, Calif, June 2, 43; m 76, Linda E Ladd. *Educ:* San Jose State Col, BA, 66; Tex A&M Univ, MS, 75, PhD, 84. *Prof Exp:* Assoc scientist physics, Teledyne Isotopes, 66-71. *Concurrent Pos:* Proj scientist, US World

Ocean Circulation Exp, 86-87. *Mem:* AAAS; Am Geophys Union; Sigma Xi. *Res:* Chemical oceanography; geochemistry; physical oceanography. *Mailing Add:* Geochem & Environ Res Group Tex A&M Univ College Station TX 77843-3149. *Fax:* 409-862-1347; *E-Mail:* norman@gergo.tamu.edu

GUINN, DENISE EILEEN, SYNTHETIC ORGANIC CHEMISTRY, MEDICINAL CHEMISTRY. *Current Pos:* CLARE BOOTHE LUCE ASST PROF CHEM, REGIS UNIV, 92- *Personal Data:* b Terra Haute, Ind, Jan 1, 59; m 83, Martin; c Charles M & Scott E. *Educ:* Univ Calif, San Diego, BA, 81; Univ Tex, Austin, PhD(org chem), 86. *Prof Exp:* NIH fel, Harvard univ, 87-88; sr res chemist, Abbott Lab Pharmaceut Discovery, 88-92. *Mem:* Am Chem Soc. *Res:* Synthetic organic chemistry; area of taxol semisynthesis; asymmetric synthesis of Phenyl isoserinates. *Mailing Add:* Chem Dept Regis Univ 3333 Regis Blvd Denver CO 80221. *E-Mail:* guinnd@csn.org

GUINN, GENE, PLANT PHYSIOLOGY. *Current Pos:* RETIRED. *Personal Data:* b Prairie Grove, Ark, Mar 19, 28; m 55; c 2. *Educ:* Univ Ark, BS, 52, MS, 57; Tex A&M Univ, PhD(plant physiol), 61. *Prof Exp:* Agronomist, USDA, Ark, 53-57, res agronomist, Cotton & Cordage Fibers Res Br, Agr Res Serv, Exp Sta, Tex A&M Univ, 57-61, res plant physiologist, USDA & Okla Agr Exp Sta, 61-70; ant physiologist, USDA, 70-77, res leader plant physiologist, 90-92. *Mem:* AAAS; Am Soc Plant Physiologists; Am Soc Agron; Sigma Xi; Crop Sci Soc Am. *Res:* Physiology of cotton, especially fruiting and fruit abscission. *Mailing Add:* 1138 E Balboa Dr Tempe AZ 85282

GUINN, THEODORE, MATHEMATICS. *Current Pos:* RETIRED. *Personal Data:* b Fresno, Calif, Apr 29, 24; m 53; c 2. *Educ:* Fresno State Col, BA, 49; Univ Calif, Los Angeles, MA, 59, PhD(math), 64. *Prof Exp:* Sr scientist, Douglas Aircraft Co, 53-65; asst prof math, Mich State Univ, 65-68; assoc prof math, Univ NMex, 68-83. *Concurrent Pos:* Res asst, Univ Calif, Los Angeles, 62-63, instr, Exten, 63-65, asst res mathematician, 64-65. *Mem:* Soc Indust & Appl Math. *Res:* Calculus of variations and optimum control theory. *Mailing Add:* 1508 Roma Ave NE Albuquerque NM 87106

GUINN, VINCENT PERRY, RADIOCHEMISTRY, FORENSIC CHEMISTRY. *Current Pos:* RETIRED. *Personal Data:* b Los Angeles, Calif, Nov 9, 17; m 38, 91, Maria Gavrilas; c Marjorie C & Terry W. *Educ:* Univ Southern Calif, AB, 39, MS, 41; Harvard Univ, PhD(phys chem), 49. *Honors & Awards:* Spec Award Novel Applns Nuclear Energy, Am Nuclear Soc, 64; Hevesy Medal, radionanal chem, 79. *Prof Exp:* Res chemist, Shell Develop Co, 41-46, 49-61, head radiochem group, 56-61; tech dir activation anal prog, Gen Atomic Co, 61-70; prof radiochem, Univ Calif, Irvine, 70-90; vis prof radiochem, Univ Md, College Park, 90-96. *Concurrent Pos:* Consult on activation analysis; consult & expert witness on forensic activation analysis; consult, Int Atomic Energy Agency. *Mem:* Fel AAAS; fel Am Nuclear Soc; Am Chem Soc; fel Am Acad Forensic Sci; Forensic Sci Soc England. *Res:* Activation analysis; forensic chemistry; radio chemistry; radiotracers. *Mailing Add:* 10490 Graeloch Rd Laurel MD 20723. *Fax:* 301-604-4287

GUINZBURG, ADIEL, FLUID MECHANICS, ROTOR DYNAMICS. *Current Pos:* STAFF RESEARCHER, INGERSOLL DRESSERS PUMPS, 93- *Personal Data:* b Johannesburg, SAfrica, Apr 30, 66; US citizen. *Educ:* Univ Witwatersrand, BSc, 85; Calif Inst Technol, MS, 86, PhD(mech eng), 92. *Prof Exp:* Postdoctoral fel, EPFLL, Switz, 92-93. *Mem:* Am Soc Mech Engrs; Am Inst Aeronaut & Astronaut. *Res:* Design and performance prediction; application of fluid dynamics expertise to improvement of performance and reliability of pumping products; diagnosis of sensor data for the prognosis of the pump. *Mailing Add:* Clinton Gardens No 48 Clinton NJ 08809. *E-Mail:* adiel@alumni.caltech.edu

GUION, ROBERT MORGAN, PSYCHOLOGY. *Current Pos:* Univ prof, 83-85, MEM FAC, BOWLING GREEN STATE UNIV, OHIO, 52-, PROF PSYCHOL, 64-, EMER UNIV PROF, 85- *Personal Data:* b Indianapolis, Ind, Sept 14, 24; m 47, Mary E Firestone; c David M, Diana L, Keith D, Pamela S & Judith E. *Educ:* State Univ Iowa, BA, 48; Purdue Univ, MS, 50, PhD, 52. *Honors & Awards:* James McKeen Cattell Award, Am Psychol Asn, 65 & 81; Distinguished Sci Contrib Award, Soc Indust & Orgn Psychol, 87, Distinguished Serv Award, 93. *Concurrent Pos:* Consult, 54-; vis prof, Univ Calif, Berkeley, 63-64, Univ NMex, 65; tech adv, Dept Personnel Servs, State Hawaii, 70; vis res psychologist, Educ Testing Serv, 71-72. *Mem:* Int Asn Appl Psychol; Am Educ Res Asn; Nat Coun Measurements Educ; fel Am Psychol Soc; fel Am Psychol Asn. *Res:* Psychology. *Mailing Add:* 632 Haskins Rd Bowling Green OH 43402-1615. *Fax:* 419-353-4112

GUIRARD, BEVERLY MARIE, BIOCHEMISTRY. *Current Pos:* RES SCIENTIST ASSOC II, UNIV TEX, AUSTIN, 76- *Personal Data:* b St Martinville, La, Dec 10, 15. *Educ:* Southwestern La Inst, BS, 36; La State Univ, MS, 38; Univ Tex, PhD(bioorg chem), 45. *Prof Exp:* Lab asst, Southwestern La Inst, 36, instr chem, 39-41; teacher pub sch, La, 38-39; tech asst biochem, Inst, Univ Tex, 41-42, asst, 42-45, res assoc, 45-48, res assoc, Dept Bact, 48-52, res scientist biochem, Inst, 52-56; asst res biochemist, Univ Calif, Berkeley, 56-76. *Concurrent Pos:* USPHS spec fel, Physiol Genetics Lab, Ctr Nat Res Sci, France, 63-64. *Mem:* AAAS; Am Chem Soc; Am Soc Biol Chemists; Am Soc Microbiol; Sigma Xi. *Res:* Microbial nutrition and enzymology. *Mailing Add:* 8313 Summer Place Dr Austin TX 78759-8220

GUISELEY, KENNETH B, CARBOHYDRATE CHEMISTRY. *Current Pos:* Sr chemist, Marine Colloids, Inc, FMC Corp, 61-75, dir res, 75-78, dir polymer res, Marine Colloids Div, 78-82, sr res assoc, 82-90, RES FEL, MARINE COLLOIDS DIV, FMC BIO PROD, 90- *Personal Data:* b Auburn, NY, July 20, 33; m 56, Elizabeth A Schnackenberg; c Cynthia A (Guernsey), Pamela J (Sabol) & David L. *Educ:* Hartwick Col, BA, 55; Syracuse Univ, PhD(org chem), 60. *Mem:* Am Chem Soc; fel Am Inst Chemists. *Res:* Extraction of polysaccharides and associated by-products from marine algae; chemical modification of polysaccharides; development of gelling agents for biochemical separations. *Mailing Add:* FMC Bio Prod 191 Thomaston St Rockland ME 04841. *Fax:* 207-594-3426; *E-Mail:* kenneth_guiseley@fmc.com

GUISEPPI-ELIE, ANTHONY, BIOSENSORS, DIAGNOSTICS. *Current Pos:* PRES & SCI DIR, ABTECH SCI INC, 88- *Personal Data:* b Trinidad & Tobago, Oct 8, 54; US citizen; m 77, Annette Wilson; c Adilah. *Educ:* Univ West Indies, BSc, 79; Univ Manchester Inst Sci & Technol, MSc, 80, Mass Inst Technol, ScD(polymer mat sci & eng), 83. *Prof Exp:* Res engr, WR Grace & Co, 83-86; appln specialist, Molecular Electronics Corp, 86-87; dir res, Ohmicron Corp, 87-88. *Concurrent Pos:* Adj prof, Pa State Univ, 91-94; vis scientist, Johns Hopkins Univ, 95-96. *Mem:* AAAS; Am Chem Soc; Mat Res Soc; Sigma Xi; fel Am Inst Chemists; Am Inst Chem Engrs. *Res:* Chemically responsive polymeric materials incorporating bioactivity synthesis, characterization and application; biosensor technology in biomedical diagnostics and environmental monitoring; research management of science and technology policy. *Mailing Add:* PO Box 376 Yardley PA 19067-4032. *Fax:* 215-321-7099

GUITJENS, JOHANNES C, IRRIGATION ENGINEERING, HYDROLOGY. *Current Pos:* From asst prof to assoc prof, 67-78, PROF IRRIG & DRAINAGE ENG, ENVIRON & RESOURCE SCIS DEPT, UNIV NEV, RENO, 78- *Personal Data:* b Heeze, Holland, Jan 24, 35; m 67; c 2. *Educ:* Univ BC, BSA, 61; Univ Calif, Davis, MS, 64, PhD(eng), 68. *Mem:* Sigma Xi; Int Comn Irrig & Drainage; Am Geophys Union; Am Soc Civil Engrs; Am Soc Agr Engr. *Res:* Steady and unsteady flow in viscous flow models; mathematical simulation of ground water flow; water use efficiencies; agricultural drainage; water quality management; total water management. *Mailing Add:* Environ & Resource Scis Dept Univ Nev 1000 Valley Rd Reno NV 89512

GULA, WILLIAM PETER, THEORETICAL PLASMA PHYSICS, LARGE SCIENTIFIC COMPUTER CODE DEVELOPMENT. *Current Pos:* Mem staff, inertial fusion & plasma theory group, Dept Energy, Los Alamos Nat Lab, 72-81, mem staff radiation transport group, 81-90, sci adv, 90-92, staff, assoc dir nuclear weapons technol, 92-94, special tech asst, 93, STAFF RADIATION TRANSPORT GROUP, APPL THEORET PHYSICS DIV, DEPT ENERGY, LOS ALAMOS NAT LAB, 94- *Personal Data:* b Cleveland, Ohio, Dec 5, 39; m 83, Dolores Tory. *Educ:* Spring Hill Col, Mobile, BS, 64; Columbia Univ, MA, 68, PhD(physics), 72. *Mem:* AAAS; Am Phys Soc; Inst Elec & Electronics Engrs; Asn Comput Mach. *Res:* Plasma physics and fluid dynamics problems associated with target designs for controlled thermonuclear fusion by means of lasers and ion beams; transport problems in plasmas. *Mailing Add:* Los Alamos Nat Lab XTM MS B226 Los Alamos NM 87545

GULARI, ESIN, POLYMERS. *Current Pos:* from asst prof to assoc prof, 79-83, prof, 87, CHMN, CHEM ENG & MAT SCI, WAYNE STATE UNIV, 93- *Personal Data:* b Turkey, July 12, 46; US citizen; c Bora. *Educ:* Robert Col, Istanbul, BS, 69; Calif Inst Technol, MS, 70, PhD(chem eng),73. *Honors & Awards:* Henry Ford Technol Award, 95. *Prof Exp:* Instr chem, State Univ NY, Stony Brook, 73-74, res assoc, 76-78; lectr chem, Eastern Mich Univ, 78-79. *Concurrent Pos:* Vis assoc prof, Stanford Univ, 85-86. *Mem:* Am Inst Chem Engrs; Am Chem Soc; Am Phys Soc. *Res:* Phase equilibria and transport properties of polymer solutions, optical methods of emulsions and sprays, processing of polymers with supercritical fluids. *Mailing Add:* Dept Chem Eng Wayne State Univ Detroit MI 48202. *Fax:* 313-577-3810; *E-Mail:* egulari@chem1.eng.wayne.edu

GULATI, ADARSH KUMAR, NEUROSCIENCE. *Current Pos:* ASSOC PROF CELLULAR BIOL & ANAT, MED COL GA, 89- *Personal Data:* b Karnal, India, July 1, 56. *Educ:* Delhi Univ, BS, 75; WVa Univ, PhD(anat), 79. *Prof Exp:* Fel neural develop & regeneration, NIH, 79-81. *Mem:* Am Asn Anatomists. *Res:* Regeneration and repair of nerve and muscle tissues in mammal regeneration of lens and limb in amphibians, neurotrophic interaction; role of basement membrane (fibronectin and laminin) during various regenerative processes. *Mailing Add:* Dept Cell Biol & Anat Med Col Ga Augusta GA 30912-2000

GULATI, SNEH, RELIABILITY NONPARAMETRIC ANALYSIS. *Current Pos:* Asst prof, 91-96, ASSOC PROF STATIST, FLA INT UNIV, 96- *Personal Data:* b Jullundur, India, Dec 3, 63. *Educ:* Delhi Univ, India, BA, 84; Univ SC, MA, 87, PhD(statist), 91. *Concurrent Pos:* Consult, Miami Childrens Hosp, 92-93; chair, Joint Prog Comt, Coun Chapters Sect, Am Statist Asn, 95-96. *Mem:* Am Statist Asn; Inst Math Statist. *Res:* Estimation of the survival function and the hazard function from a type of smooth data called record breaking data; estimation from right censored data and on inference from grouped observations from the exponential distribution. *Mailing Add:* Dept Statist Fla Int Univ Miami FL 33199. *Fax:* 305-348-3879; *E-Mail:* gulati@fiu.edu

GULATI, SUBHASH CHANDER, CANCER RESEARCH. *Current Pos:* MEM FAC, DEPT HEMAT & LYMPHOMA, SLOAN KETTERING CANCER INST, 78- *Personal Data:* b New Delhi, India, Dec 2, 50. *Educ:* NDak State Univ, MS, 71; Columbia Univ, PhD(human genetics), 73; Univ Miami, MD, 76. *Prof Exp:* Mem adv comt, Dept Agron & Genetics, WVa State Univ, 74-76; mem fac, Dept Med, State Univ NY, Buffalo, 76-78. *Concurrent Pos:* Am Cancer Soc clin oncol career develop award, 85-87. *Mem:* Am Col Physicians. *Res:* Understanding molecular changes in neoplastic growth using nucleic acid hybridization and immunological assays; bone marrow transplantation. *Mailing Add:* The New York Hosp Cornell Univ 1300 York Ave New York NY 10021. *Fax:* 212-746-2848

GULATI, SURESH T, MECHANICS, APPLIED MATHEMATICS. *Current Pos:* res scientist, Res & Develop Labs, Corning Inc, 67-69, sr res scientist, 69-76, RES SUPVR, TECHNOL DIV, CORNING INC, 76-, SR RES ASSOC, 79-, RES FEL, 82- *Personal Data:* b West Punjab, Pakistan, Nov 13, 36; m 61, Teresa Davids; c Raj, Prem & Sonya. *Educ:* Univ Bombay, BS, 57; Ill Inst Technol, MS, 59; Univ Colo, PhD(mech), 67. *Prof Exp:* Stress analyst, Continental Can Co, 59-62; instr mech eng, Univ Colo, Boulder, 66-67. *Concurrent Pos:* Vis lectr dept theoret & appl mech, Cornell Univ, 69-70. *Mem:* Sigma Xi; Am Soc Mech Engrs; Am Ceramic Soc; Soc Automotive Engrs. *Res:* Analysis of elastic structures with particular emphasis on plates and shells; deformation and stress analysis of anisotropic elastic materials; application of the principles of mechanics to composite materials and materials science; optical waveguide design, fracture mechanics; cellular ceramics. *Mailing Add:* Suilvan Park RB4 Corning Glass Works Corning NY 14831-0001

GULDEN, TERRY DALE, MATERIALS SCIENCE, CERAMIC ENGINEERING. *Current Pos:* staff mem mat res, Gen Atomic Co, 67-71, mgr, Fuel Mat Br, Fuels & Mat Div, 71-80, mgr, ceramics & chem dept, 80-85, MGR, HIGH TEMPERATURE GAS COOLED REACTOR FUEL DEVELOP DEPT, GEN ATOMIC CO, 80-, DIR, DEFENSE MAT, 85- *Personal Data:* b Seattle, Wash, May 4, 38; m 84; c 1. *Educ:* Univ Wash, BS, 60; Stanford Univ, MS, 62, PhD(mat sci), 65. *Prof Exp:* Ceramist, United Technol Ctr, United Aircraft Corp, 60-61; res assoc radiation effects in mat, Berkeley Nuclear Labs, Cent Elec Generating Bd, Eng, 65-66. *Mem:* AAAS; Am Ceramic Soc; Am Nuclear Soc; Mat Res Soc. *Res:* Radiation effects in solids; transmission electron microscopy; internal friction; chemical vapor deposition; creep and deformation of ceramics and metals; nuclear reactor and composite materials; superconducting materials. *Mailing Add:* 1201 Virginia Way La Jolla CA 92037

GULENS, JANIS, ELECTROANALYTICAL CHEMISTRY, CERAMICS. *Current Pos:* from asst res officer to assoc res officer, 73-83, res officer analytical chem, 83-88, BR MGR, GEN CHEM BR, ATOMIC ENERGY CAN LTD, 88- *Personal Data:* b Rottweil, Ger, Dec 28, 44; Can citizen. *Educ:* Univ Toronto, BSc, 67; Queen's Univ, Ont, PhD(anal chem), 71. *Prof Exp:* Nat Res Coun fel, Calif Inst Technol, 71-73. *Mem:* Fel Chem Inst Can. *Res:* Trace analysis, especially by application of electroanalytical techniques, of materials, solutions and effluents; ion-selective electrodes; fundamentals and applications of ion-conducting ceramics. *Mailing Add:* Chem Div AECL Chalk River ON K0J 1J0 Can. *E-Mail:* gulensj@aecl.ca

GULIANTS, VADIM V, STRUCTURAL CHEMISTRY, INFORMATION SCIENCE & SYSTEMS. *Current Pos:* DEVELOP ASSOC, PRAXAIR INC, 95- *Personal Data:* b Baku, Azerbaijan, Dec 26, 65. *Educ:* Moscow State Univ, dipl, 87; Princeton Univ, MA, 93, PhD(chem), 95; State Univ NY, Buffalo, MBA, 97. *Prof Exp:* Res asst, Moscow State Univ, 87-90. *Concurrent Pos:* Mem, Panel Environ Catalysis, Dept Energy, 96. *Mem:* Am Chem Soc; Mat Res Soc; NAm Catalysis Soc. *Res:* Rational design of micro-mesoporous and layerer materials for sorption and catalysis; combination of molecular modeling, three-dimensional quantitative structure activity relationships and experimental studies of sorption and catalysis, as well as combinatorial chemistry. *Mailing Add:* 175 E Park Dr Tonawanda NY 14151. *Fax:* 716-879-7030; *E-Mail:* vadim_guliants@praxair.com

GULICK, SIDNEY L (DENNY), III, MATHEMATICS. *Current Pos:* from asst prof to assoc prof, 65-73, PROF MATH, UNIV MD, COLLEGE PARK, 73- *Personal Data:* b Oakland, Calif, July 29, 36; m 69, Frances; c David, Barbara & Sharon. *Educ:* Oberlin Col, BA, 58; Yale Univ, MA, 60, PhD(math), 63. *Prof Exp:* Instr math, Univ Pa, 63-65. *Mem:* Math Asn Am; Am Math Soc. *Res:* Theoretical mathematics; linear topological spaces and Banach algebras; chaotic dynamics. *Mailing Add:* Dept Math Univ Md Rm 2103 Bldg 084 College Park MD 20742

GULICK, WALTER LAWRENCE, PSYCHOPHYSICS, PSYCHOPHYSIOLOGY. *Current Pos:* RESIDENT SCHOLAR, UNIV DEL, 88- *Personal Data:* b Summit, NJ, July 4, 27; m 52, Winifred Frazee; c Hans, Tod & Kristina. *Educ:* Hamilton Col, AB, 52; Univ Del, MA, 55; Princeton Univ, PhD(physiol psychol), 57. *Hon Degrees:* MA, Dartmouth Col, 68; LHD, St Lawrence Univ, 89. *Prof Exp:* From asst prof to prof psychol, Univ Del, 57-65, chmn dept, 64-65; prof, Dartmouth Col, 65-73, chmn dept, 70-72, 74-75, class of 25 prof, 73-75; prof psychol, Hamilton Col, 75-81, dean fac, 75-79, William Kenan prof, 79-81; pres, St Lawrence Univ, 81-87. *Concurrent Pos:* Mem coun, Nat Humanities Inst, 75-78; pres, Gulick Assocs, Inc, 88- *Mem:* NY Acad Sci; Psychonomic Soc; Sigma Xi. *Res:* Neurophysiology and electrophysiology; vision; hearing. *Mailing Add:* Psychol Univ Del Newark DE 19717-0001

GULICK, WILSON M, JR, ANALYTICAL CHEMISTRY. *Current Pos:* ASSOC PROF CHEM, MICH TECHNOL UNIV, 77- *Personal Data:* b Plainfield, NJ, Mar 10, 39; m 62, 75, Grace L Swartz; c Wilson C. *Educ:* Harvard Univ, AB, 60; Cornell Univ, PhD(chem), 65. *Prof Exp:* Asst prof chem, State Univ NY Col Cortland, 64-65; res assoc, Cornell Univ, 65-66, asst prof, 66-68; asst prof, Fla State Univ, 68-76. *Mem:* Am Chem Soc; Royal Soc Chem; NY Acad Sci. *Res:* Electrochemistry in non-aqueous media; magnetic resonance and optical spectroscopy of free radicals in solution. *Mailing Add:* Dept Chem Mich Technol Univ Houghton MI 49931-1295. *Fax:* 906-487-2061

GULKIS, SAMUEL, PHYSICS, AERONAUTICAL ENGINEERING. *Current Pos:* SR SCIENTIST PLANETARY & SPACE SCI, JET PROPULSION LAB, 68- *Personal Data:* b West Palm Beach, Fla, Feb 3, 37; m 63, Marjorie Cohen; c Susan R. *Educ:* Univ Fla, BAeroE, 60, MS, 62, PhD(physics), 65. *Honors & Awards:* Sci Achievement Award, NASA, 75 & 84. *Prof Exp:* NASA trainee, 63-65; res assoc radio astron, Arecibo Ionospheric Observ, Cornell Univ, 65-67, asst prof astron, 67-68. *Concurrent Pos:* Co-investr, Voyage Mission Planetary Radio Astron Exp, 81-, Cosmic Background Explorer Satellite; proj scientist, Search for Extraterrestrial Intel, 81-93; distinguished vis scientist, Radiophysics Div, NSW, Australia, Meudon Observ. *Mem:* Am Astron Soc; Int Astron Union; Sigma Xi; Int Union Radio Sci. *Res:* Radio astronomy, particularly planetary radio astronomy and planetary atmospheres; cosmic background radiation. *Mailing Add:* Off Space Sci & Instrumentation JPL 4800 Oak Grove Dr MS 180-701 Pasadena CA 91103

GULL, CLOYD DAKE, INFORMATION SCIENCE. *Current Pos:* RETIRED. *Personal Data:* b Lorain, Ohio, June 17, 15; m 43, Dorothy T Phelps; c Marilyn G (Taggart), Evan H, Janet G (Baxter) & Thomas A. *Educ:* Allegheny Col, AB, 36; Univ Mich, AB, 37, AM, 39. *Prof Exp:* Asst, Gen Libr, Univ Mich, 37-39; periodicals librn, NC State Col, 39-42; from spec asst processing dept to dep chief, Union Catalog Div, Libr Cong, DC, 45-52; tech analyst, Document, Inc, 52-54; admin officer, Div Eng & Indust Res, Nat Acad Sci-Nat Res Coun, 54-58; info systs consult, Gen Elec Co, DC, 58-63; prof libr sci, Ind Univ, Bloomington, 64-67; liaison officer, Nat Libr Task Force, Nat Libr Med, 67-68; rep consult, Document Systs, Inc, 68-69; pres, Cloyd Dake Gull & Assocs, Inc, 69-83. *Concurrent Pos:* Pres, Am Documentation Inst, Am Soc Info Sci, 59-60; chmn, US Nat Comt, Int Fedn Doc, 60-63; vol, Dept Space Hist, Nat Air & Space Mus, Smithsonian Inst, Washington, DC, 85- *Mem:* Am Libr Asn; Spec Libr Asn; Am Soc Info Sci. *Res:* Documentation; information systems; electronic systems for the selection, identification, analysis, storage, retrieval, use and dissemination of information. *Mailing Add:* 8 Pimlico Ct Silver Spring MD 20906. *E-Mail:* 73553.2020@compuserve.com

GULL, DWAIN D, VEGETABLE CROPS. *Current Pos:* PROF VEG PHYSIOL, UNIV FLA, 58-, ASST HORTICULTURIST, EXP STA, 59- *Personal Data:* b Meadow, Utah, Aug 21, 23; m 44; c 4. *Educ:* Utah State Univ, BS, 55; Cornell Univ, MS, 57, PhD(veg crops), 60. *Concurrent Pos:* Adminstr, AID-Fla Contract, El Salvador, 73-75. *Mem:* Am Soc Hort Sci. *Res:* Post harvest physiology; flavor chemistry; quality control physiology; flavor and quality of fresh vegetables as affected by harvest and marketing stresses. *Mailing Add:* 2629 NW 11th Ave Gainesville FL 32605

GULL, THEODORE RAYMOND, ASTRONOMY, SPACE INSTRUMENTATION. *Current Pos:* astrophysicist, Goddard Space Flight Ctr, NASA, 77-82, astro mission scientist, 82-91, proj scientist, Hubble Space Telescope Second Generation Inst, 88-90, ASSOC CHIEF, LAB ASTRON & SOLAR PHYSICS, GODDARD SPACE FLIGHT CTR, NASA, 85- *Personal Data:* b Hot Springs, SDak, Aug 17, 44; m 67, Hazel J Constantine; c Michael & Matthew. *Educ:* Mass Inst Technol, BS, 66; Cornell Univ, PhD(astron), 71; Loyola Col, MBA, 85. *Prof Exp:* Res asst radar astron, Lincoln Lab, Mass Inst Technol, 67; res assoc laser physics, Hughes Res Labs, 69; res assoc astron, Yerkes Observ, Univ Chicago, 70-72; asst astronr, Kitt Peak Nat Observ, 72-75; scientist astron, Lyndon B Johnson Space Ctr, Lockheed Electronics Co, Inc, 75-77. *Concurrent Pos:* Spec consult, Nat Geog Soc, 75-; lectr, Am Astron Soc Shapley Ser, 84- *Mem:* Am Astron Soc; AAAS; Astron Soc Pac; Int Astron Union; Sigma Xi; Am Inst Aeronaut & Aerospace. *Res:* Interstellar medium; observations of emission nebulae especially supernova remnants and interstellar bubbles; development of astronomical instrumentation; development and operation of astronomy facilities on space shuttle; use of International Ultraviolet Explorer and x-ray satellites; management techniques applied to physical sciences. *Mailing Add:* Code 680 Goddard Space Flight Ctr Greenbelt MD 20771. *Fax:* 301-286-1753; *E-Mail:* gullgull@stars.gsfc.nasa.gov

GULLANS, STEVEN R, OSMOREGULATON, STRESS GENES. *Current Pos:* asst prof, 85-91, ASSOC PROF MED, HARVARD MED SCH, 91- *Personal Data:* b Troy, NY, Nov 19, 52; m 76, Stenie Plater; c Emilie & Graham. *Educ:* Union Col, BS, 75; Duke Univ, PhD(physiol), 82. *Mem:* Am Soc Nephrology; Biophys Soc; Am Physiol Soc; Soc Gen Physiol. *Res:* Laboratory studies the program of events associated with adaptation to hyperosmotic stress; studies of stress proteins, transcription factors and ion transporters. *Mailing Add:* Dept Med Renal Div Harvard Med Sch 75 Francis St Boston MA 02115. *Fax:* 617-732-6392; *E-Mail:* gullans@bustoff.bwh.harvard.edu

GULLIKSON, CHARLES WILLIAM, PHYSICS. *Current Pos:* RETIRED. *Personal Data:* b El Dorado, Kans, Sept 11, 28; m 78; c 5. *Educ:* Stanford Univ, BS, 51; Univ Okla, MS, 53, PhD(physics), 57. *Prof Exp:* Asst physics, Univ Okla, 52-56; res physicist, Marathon Oil Co, 56-62; dir res & treas,

Cryogenic Res Co, 62-63; res physicist, Kaman Scis Corp, 63-73; lab dir, Western Environ, Inc, 74-89; lectr, Maui Community Col, 89-90; supvr, Physics Lab, Embry-Riddle Aeronaut Univ, 90-94. *Mem:* Am Phys Soc; Soc Appl Spectros. *Res:* Raman, infrared, ultraviolet, absorption and atomic absorption spectroscopy. *Mailing Add:* 325 Honzoni Prescott AZ 86301

GULLINO, PIETRO M, pathology, for more information see previous edition

GULLIVER, JOHN STEPHEN, ENVIRONMENTAL FLUID MECHANICS. *Current Pos:* asst prof, 81-87, assoc prof, 87-96, PROF, DEPT CIVIL & MINERAL ENG, UNIV MINN, 96- *Personal Data:* b Torrance, Calif, Sept 9, 50; m 72, Karen Lyum; c Djuna, Teigan & Hallon. *Educ:* Univ Calif, Santa Barbara, BS, 74; Univ Minn, MS, 77, PhD(civil eng), 80. *Honors & Awards:* Rickey Medal, Am Soc Civil Engrs, 90. *Prof Exp:* Res assoc, Dept Civil & Mineral Eng, St Anthony Falls Hydraul Lab, 80-81. *Concurrent Pos:* Tech ed, Hydro Rev, 87-, HRW: Hydro Rev Worldwide, 93-; Vis res scientist, US Army Engr Waterways Exp Sta, 90. *Mem:* Int Asn Hydraul Res; Am Soc Civil Engrs; Am Water Resources Asn; Am Geophys Union; Int Asn Water Qual; Asn Environ Eng Prof; Am Soc Eng Educ. *Res:* Mass transfer at the air-water interface in rivers and lakes; hydraulic structures; hydraulics of river flow; hydropower engineering; toxic riverine spills; effects of suspended sediment on stream ecosystems. *Mailing Add:* St Anthony Falls Hydraul Lab Mississippi River at Third Ave SE Minneapolis MN 55414. *Fax:* 612-627-4609; *E-Mail:* gulli003@maroon.tc.umn.edu

GULLIVER, ROBERT DAVID, II, GEOMETRY, PARTIAL DIFFERENTIAL EQUATIONS. *Current Pos:* from asst prof to assoc prof, 73-85, PROF MATH, UNIV MINN, MINNEAPOLIS, 85-, ASSOC DIR, INST MATH & APPLN, 94- *Personal Data:* b Torrance, Calif, July 24, 45; m 86, Kathryn Greulich; c Jacob. *Educ:* Stanford Univ, BS, 67, MS, 69, PhD(differential geom), 71. *Prof Exp:* Lectr math, Univ Calif, Berkeley, 71-73. *Concurrent Pos:* Max Planck Inst Organizer Nonlinear PDE, 86-87. *Mem:* Am Math Soc. *Res:* The immersion question for minimal surfaces of general topological type, solving appropriate variational problems; nonlinear parabolic equations; harmonic maps. *Mailing Add:* Univ Minn Sch Math Minneapolis MN 55455. *Fax:* 612-626-2017; *E-Mail:* gulliver@math.umn.edu

GULLO, VINCENT PHILIP, NATURAL PRODUCT DRUG DISCOVERY, PHARMACEUTICAL RESEARCH. *Current Pos:* assoc dir, 83-89, DIR MICROBIOL PROD, SCHERING PLOUGH RES, 89- *Personal Data:* b New York, NY, Mar 30, 50; m 73; c 1. *Educ:* City Col New York, BS, 71; Columbia Univ, PhD(org chem), 75. *Prof Exp:* sr res chemist, Merck Sharp & Dohme Res Labs, 75-80, res fel natural prod chem, 80-83. *Mem:* Am Chem Soc; Am Soc Microbiol; AAAS; Soc Indust Microbiol. *Res:* Natural product chemistry; chromatography; spectroscopy; structure determinations; antibiotics; pharmacological agents. *Mailing Add:* 33 Darren Woods Dr PO Box 332 Liberty Corner NJ 07938-0332. *Fax:* 908-298-7115; *E-Mail:* vincent.gullo@spcorp.com

GULLY, ARNOLD J(ARVIS), CHEMICAL ENGINEERING. *Current Pos:* RETIRED. *Personal Data:* b Preston, Miss, July 8, 21; m 45; c 4. *Educ:* Auburn Univ, BS, 47; La State Univ, MS, 50, PhD(chem eng), 51. *Prof Exp:* Qual control engr, Hercules Powder Co, 47-48; from assoc prof to prof chem eng, Miss State Univ, 51-59; proj engr, Texaco, Inc, 59-61, res supvr, 61-63; head dept chem eng, Tex Tech Univ, 63-68, prof chem eng, 63-82, assoc dean eng, 68-82. *Mem:* Am Chem Soc; Am Inst Chem Engrs; Am Soc Eng Educ. *Res:* Hydrogenation; petroleum processing; reaction kinetics. *Mailing Add:* 3504 Arthur Dr Nacogdoches TX 75961

GULLY, JOHN HOUSTON, BEARINGS & SEALS, HIGH SPEED CURRENT COLLECTION. *Current Pos:* Res engr, Ctr Electromech, Univ Tex, 76-83, assoc tech dir, 83-85, dep dir, 85-92, DIR, CTR ELECTROMECH, UNIV TEX, 93- *Personal Data:* b Oak Ridge, Tenn, July 27, 52; m 75, Rajean Meester; c Benjamin H & Michael J. *Educ:* Univ Tex, Austin, BS, 76. *Honors & Awards:* IR 100 Award, Res & Develop Mag, 83. *Concurrent Pos:* Prin investr numerous res & develop contracts, 84-; chmn, Opening Switch Panel, Tamarron Workshop, 86 & Power Conditioning Panel, Elec Energy Gun Study, Defense Advan Res Projs Agency, 88-; chmm & ed, Int Current Collector Conf, 88; ed, Superconducting Power Appln Rev Comt, 89; asst dir, Land Systs, Defense Advan Res Projs Agency, Dept Defense. *Mem:* Am Soc Mech Engrs. *Res:* Development of high power electrical systems for military; commercial automotive and commercial utility applications. *Mailing Add:* Ctr Electromech Balcones Res Ctr Univ Tex 10100 Burnet Rd Austin TX 78758. *Fax:* 512-471-0781

GULOTTA, STEPHEN JOSEPH, CARDIOLOGY. *Current Pos:* ASSOC PROF MED, MED COL CORNELL UNIV, 72-; DIR CARDIAC CATHETERIZATION LAB, 82- *Personal Data:* b Brooklyn, NY, Mar 5, 33; m 54; c 3. *Educ:* Brooklyn Col, BS, 54; State Univ NY Downstate Med Ctr, MD, 58. *Prof Exp:* Intern med, Montefiore Hosp, Bronx, 58-59, from jr asst resident to asst resident, 59-61; chief div cardiol, North Shore Hosp, 67-79. *Concurrent Pos:* USPHS fel, NY Hosp, 61-62; attend physician, Mt Vernon Hosp, 62 & North Shore Hosp, 67-; ast attend, NY Hosp, 69-; Nassau & Westchester Heart Asns grant-in-aid, North Shore Hosp, 70-71; fel coun clin cardiol, Am Heart Asn, 71-; attend physician, St Francis Hosp, 79- *Mem:* Am Fedn Clin Res; fel Am Col Physicians; fel Am Col Cardiol; fel Am Col Chest Physicians. *Res:* Conduction disturbances and arrhythmias in man; coronary artery disease. *Mailing Add:* 100 Port Washington Blvd Roslyn NY 11576-1353

GULRAJANI, RAMESH MULCHAND, BIOELECTRIC PHENOMENA, CARDIAC ELECTROPHYSIOLOGY. *Current Pos:* Med Res Coun Can fel neurophysiol, Dept Physiol, Univ Montreal, 73-75, res assoc cardiac electrophysiol, Dept Med, 76-79, res assoc biomed eng, Inst Biomed Eng, 79-87, assoc prof, 87-90, PROF BIOMED ENG, INST BIOMED ENG, UNIV MONTREAL, 90- *Personal Data:* b Patna, India, Dec 12, 44; m 76, Lily T Mani; c Nilima R & Rohan R. *Educ:* Univ Bombay, BE, 64; Ill Inst Technol, MS, 65; Syracuse Univ, MS, 72, PhD(elec eng), 73. *Concurrent Pos:* Res scholar, Can Heart Found, 78-81; sr res scholar, Fonds de la recherch en sante du Que, 86-89; mem, Biomed Eng Grants Comt, Med Res Coun Can, 88-91; spec reviewer, Cardiovasc Study Sect, NIH, 90-92; vis prof, Dept Eng Sci, Auckland Univ, NZ, 92-93. *Mem:* Sr mem Inst Elec & Electronics Engrs; sr mem Biomed Eng Soc. *Res:* Computer models of the electrical activity of the heart; forward and inverse problems of electrocardiography; bioelectric and biomagnetic phenomena. *Mailing Add:* Inst Biomed Eng Univ Montreal PO Box 6128 St A Montreal PQ H3C 3J7 Can

GULRICH, LESLIE WILLIAM, JR, PHYSICAL CHEMISTRY. *Current Pos:* Res chemist, E I Du Pont de Nemours & Co, Inc, 67-76, sr res chemist, 76-87, res assoc, 87-93, SR RES ASSOC, E I DU PONT DE NEMOURS & CO, INC, 93- *Personal Data:* b Chicago, Ill, July 31, 33; m 75; c 3. *Educ:* Kent State Univ, BS, 60, PhD(phys chem), 67. *Mem:* Am Chem Soc. *Res:* Fiber spinning processes; fiber spinning equipment design; fiber structure; polymer molecular weight distribution; polymer solution rheology; computer aided design programming; engineered short fibers & asbestos replacement. *Mailing Add:* 10339 Ashburn Rd Richmond VA 23235-2603

GULTEPE, ISMAIL, AIRCRAFT DATA ANALYSIS, TURBULENCE IN THE ATMOSPHERE. *Current Pos:* FEL, CAN ATMOSPHERIC ENVIRON CLOUD PHYSICS RES DIV, TORONTO, 93- *Personal Data:* b Eskisehir, Turkey, July 10, 57; m 85, Emel Ovunc; c Eren M, Ezel F & Ersen M. *Educ:* Istanbul Tech Univ, Turkey, BS, 79, MS, 81; St Louis Univ, MS, 86, PhD(meteorol), 89. *Prof Exp:* Res assoc, Nat Ctr Atmospheric Res, 87-89, Colo State Univ, 89-90; asst prof, Istanbul Tech Univ, 90-91; fel, Goddard Space Flight Ctr, NASA, 91-93. *Concurrent Pos:* Asst prof meteorol, Istanbul Tech Univ, 80-84 & 90-91. *Mem:* Am Meteorol Soc; Turkish Meteorol Soc; Can Meteorol & Ocean Soc. *Res:* Cloud-climate relationships, cloud physics-cloud dynamic radiation; understanding cloud effect on climate change. *Mailing Add:* Can Atmospheric Environ/Cloud Physics Res Div 4905 Dufferin St Downsview ON M3H 5T4 Can. *Fax:* 416-739-4211

GULYAS, BELA JANOS, CELL & DEVELOPMENTAL BIOLOGY, GAMETE PHYSIOLOGY. *Current Pos:* exec secy NCRR, 88-96, OFF REV DIR NCRR, GEN CLIN RES CTRS, 96- *Personal Data:* b Szekesfehervar, Hungary, Apr 14, 38; US citizen; m 62, Mary B; c Anne M, Lisa G & Catherine E. *Educ:* Moravian Col, BS, 62; WVa Univ, MS, 65; Univ Colo, Boulder, PhD(develop biol), 68. *Honors & Awards:* Merit Award, NIH, 93, Directors Award, 96. *Prof Exp:* Instr histol-cell biol, Georgetown Sch Med & Dent, 70-71; reproductive physiologist & sect chief, Nat Inst Child Health & Human Devel, 71-84. *Concurrent Pos:* Fel, NIH; hon res fel, Mammal Develop Unit, Med Res Coun, London; vis prof histol, George Washington Sch Med, 79-85; exec secy, Div Res Grants Reproductive Endocrinol, NIH, 84-88. *Mem:* Soc Develop Biol; Soc Study Reproduction; Am Soc Cell Biol; Am Asn Anatomists; AAAS; Am Soc Reproductive Med. *Res:* Cellular and developmental aspects of preimplantation mammalian embryos; experimental and fine structural approaches in problems concerning polyspermy, parthenogenesis, and cleavage plane and cleavage furrow formation. *Mailing Add:* NIH Westwood 10A-16 Rockledge 6018 Bethesda MD 20892-7965. *Fax:* 301-594-9193

GULYASSY, PAUL FRANCIS, MEDICINE. *Current Pos:* PROF INTERNAL MED & CHIEF, NEPHROLOGY DIV, UNIV CALIF, DAVIS 72- *Personal Data:* b Bridgeport, Conn, Aug 5, 28; m 60; c 2. *Educ:* Yale Univ, BA, 50; Columbia Univ, MD, 54. *Prof Exp:* From asst prof to assoc prof med, Med Ctr, Univ Calif, San Francisco, 64-72; dir, NCalif Artificial Kidney Ctr & chief, Renal & Electrolyte Sect, San Francisco Gen Hosp, 68-72. *Concurrent Pos:* Am Heart Asn adv res fel med, Renal Lab, Sch Med, Tufts Univ, 60-62 & Cardiovasc Res Inst, Univ Calif, San Francisco, 62-64; res career award, NIH, 65-72, mem, Clin Res Fel Rev Bd, 68-71 & Gen Med B Study Sect, 72- *Mem:* Am Soc Clin Invest; Am Fedn Clin Res; Am Physiol Soc; Am Soc Nephrology. *Mailing Add:* Dept Int Med Div Nephrol Univ Calif Davis 4301 X St Sacramento CA 95817-2280. *Fax:* 916-734-7920

GUM, ERNEST KEMP, JR, MICROBIAL BIOCHEMISTRY, FOOD CHEMISTRY. *Current Pos:* mgr technol develop, Nestle Res & Develop, 85-86, mgr beverage technol, 87-91, mgr nutrit prod develop, 91-94, DIR PROD DEVELOP, NESTLE RES & DEVELOP, 95- *Personal Data:* b Weston, WVa, Feb 1, 49; m 68, Mary Bishop; c Ryan & Stephanie. *Educ:* WVa Univ, BS, 70; Va Polytech Inst & State Univ, PhD(biochem), 74. *Prof Exp:* Res assoc biochem, Va Polytech Inst & State Univ, 74-75, asst prof biochem, 75-77; res scientist, Union Carbide Corp, 77-79; proj specialist, Gen Foods Corp, 79-81, group leader, 82-85. *Mem:* AAAS; Am Chem Soc; Sigma Xi; Inst Food Technologists; Am Soc Microbiol. *Res:* Structure, function and regulation of microbial enzymes; flavor development; beverage development; dietetic product development; food product development. *Mailing Add:* Nestle Res & Develop 221 Housatonic Ave New Milford CT 06776

GUM, JAMES RAYMOND, JR, MOLECULAR CLONING OF MUCINS, COLON CANCER CELL & MOLECULAR BIOLOGY. *Current Pos:* RES BIOCHEMIST, VET ADMIN MED CTR, 84- *Personal Data:* b Cleveland, Ohio; m 74, Elizabeth; c James R III. *Educ:* Univ Ky, BS, 72; Univ Tex, MS, 76, PhD(biochem & molecular biol), 80. *Honors & Awards:* Nat Res Serv

Award, Nat Inst Gen Med Sci, 81. *Prof Exp:* Fel biochem & molecular biol, Univ Wis, 80-84. *Concurrent Pos:* Adj asst prof anat, Univ Calif, San Francisco, 93-, sr scientist, Colorectal Cancer Ctr, 93- *Mem:* Am Soc Biochem & Molecular Biol. *Res:* Molecular biology of colon cancer; molecular cloning of tumor antigen and mucins; characterization of tumor suppressor genes in colon cancer cells. *Mailing Add:* GI Res VA/Med Ctr 4150 Clement St San Francisco CA 94121-1598. *Fax:* 415-750-2177

GUM, MARY LOU, physical chemistry, for more information see previous edition

GUM, OREN BERKLEY, medicine; deceased, see previous edition for last biography

GUM, WILSON FRANKLIN, JR, ORGANIC CHEMISTRY, RESEARCH ADMINISTRATION. *Current Pos:* Spec assignments chemist, Dow Chem Co, 65-67, sr res chemist, 67-68, proj leader, Designed Prod Dept, 68-70, res group leader, Org Chem Prod Res Lab, 70-71, sect head, Org Chem & Intermediates Sect, Tech Serv & Develop, 71-73, div mgr org chem, Tech Serv & Develop, Agr-Org Dept, Freeport, Tex, 74-78, lab dir oxides & intermediates, Tech Serv & Develop, Org Chem Dept, 78, RES & DEVELOP DIR, ORG CHEM DEPT, DOW CHEM USA, 78-, RES & DEVELOP DIR, POLYURETHANES, 84- *Personal Data:* b Pen Argyl, Pa, July 14, 39; m 59; c 4. *Educ:* Muhlenberg Col, BS, 61; Univ Pa, PhD(org chem), 65. *Mem:* Am Chem Soc. *Res:* New product research and development for organic chemicals, resin and polymer intermediates, alkylene oxide and derivatives; polyurethane intermediates; polyurethane products and systems; polymer chemistry and technical management. *Mailing Add:* 26 Lake Ridge Club Dr Burr Ridge IL 60521-7937

GUMAN, WILLIAM J(OHN), AERONAUTICAL ENGINEERING, STRATEGIC PLANNING. *Current Pos:* RETIRED. *Personal Data:* b Greenwich, Conn, June 23, 29; m 54, Elsie R Kramer; c William F & Gloria G. *Educ:* Rensselaer Polytech Inst, BAE, 52, MAE, 54, PhD(aeronaut eng), 65. *Honors & Awards:* Cert Recognition, Nat Aeronaut & Space Admin, 76; Tech Excellence Award, Am Inst Aeronaut & Astronaut, 77. *Prof Exp:* Res asst aeronaut eng, Rensselaer Polytech Inst, 52-54, from instr to asst prof, 54-59; sr sci res engr, Fairchild Industs, 59-60, prin sci res engr, 60-61, spec sci res engr, 61-63, staff engr, 63-65, chief propulsion, 65-79, mgr Indust Res & Develop & Res & Develop Contracts, Fairchild Repub Co, 79-82, dir res & develop, 82-84, dir technol & opers, 84-85, dir adv prod develop, 85-87; dir contract res & develop, Tech Develop, Grumman Corp, 87-90, tech adv strategic planning, 90-95. *Concurrent Pos:* Prin investr 20 res & develop contracts; mem Res & Eng Comt Nat Security Indust Asn, 84-87, bd dirs, 85-87; mem Tech Comt Elec Propulsion, Am Inst Aeronaut & Astronaut, 66-68 & 78-80. *Mem:* Assoc fel Am Inst Aeronaut & Astronaut; Sigma Xi. *Res:* Theoretical and experimental gasdynamics, especially electric space propulsion; management of research and development. *Mailing Add:* 26 Gaymor Lane Commack NY 11725

GUMBINER, BARRY M, PHARMACOLOGY, CELL BIOLOGY. *Current Pos:* ASST PROF, DEPT PHARMACOL, UNIV CALIF, SAN FRANCISCO, 85- *Personal Data:* b Cleveland, Ohio, June 11, 54. *Educ:* Univ Cinncinnati, BS, 76; Univ Calif, PhD(neurosci), 82. *Honors & Awards:* Estab Investr Award, Am Heart Asn, 88-92. *Prof Exp:* Fel, Dept Biol, Mass Inst Technol, Cambridge, 82-83, Dept Cell Biol, Europ Molecular Biol Lab, Heidelberg, WGer, 83-85. *Concurrent Pos:* Mem, cell biol & develop biol grad prog & prog molecular med, Univ Calif, San Francisco, joint appointment, Dept Physiol, fac mem, fel training prog digestive dis & nutrit & nephrol; Helen Hay Whitney fel, 82-85; Estab Investr Award, Am Heart Asn, 88-92. *Mem:* Am Soc Cell Biol; AAAS; Soc Develop Biol. *Res:* Pharmacology; numerous publications. *Mailing Add:* Box 564 Mem Sloan-Kettering Cancer Ctr 1275 York Ave New York NY 10021. *Fax:* 212-717-3047

GUMBS, GODFREY ANTHONY, TRANSPORT & OPTICAL PROPERTIES OF NANOSTRUCTURES, INTENSE MAGNETIC FIELD PHENOMENA. *Current Pos:* PROF, HUNTER COL & GRAD CTR, CITY UNIV NEW YORK. *Personal Data:* b Georgetown, Guyana, Sept 17, 48; m 71, Jean M Sickander; c Anthony, Alexander & Andrew. *Educ:* Trinity Col, Cambridge, Eng, BA, 71; Univ Toronto, MSc, 73, PhD(physics), 78. *Prof Exp:* Res assoc chem, Nat Res Coun, Can, 78-82; asst prof, Dalhousie Univ, Can, 82-86; from assoc prof to prof, Univ Lethbridge, 86-92. *Concurrent Pos:* Alexander von Humboldt fel, 87; vis scientist, Mass Inst Technol, 90-91; adj prof, Stevens Inst Technol. *Mem:* Am Phys Soc. *Res:* Critical phenomena in systems with a surface; the effects due to a surface on a Landau quantized plasma; static shielding of impurities near a surface; collective excitations in two and three dimensions; penetration phenomena in solids, superlattices and heterostructures; transport in mesoscopic systems. *Mailing Add:* Jamaica Estates 182-11 Henley Rd Queens NY 11374. *Fax:* 212-772-5390; *E-Mail:* gogc@cunyvm.cuny.edu

GUMMEL, HERMANN K, SOLID STATE ELECTRONICS. *Current Pos:* CONSULT, 86- *Personal Data:* b Hannover, Ger, July 6, 23; US citizen; m 52; c 2. *Educ:* Syracuse Univ, MS, 52, PhD(physics), 57; Univ Marburg, dipl, 52. *Honors & Awards:* Circuits & Systs Award, Inst Elec & Electronics Engrs, 93. *Prof Exp:* Mem tech staff, Bell Labs, 57-67, head, Design Analysis Dept, from asst dir to dir, Advan Comput Aided Design Test & Studies Lab, AT&T Bell Labs, 82-86. *Mem:* Nat Acad Eng; fel Inst Elec & Electronics Engrs; Sigma Xi; Am Phys Soc. *Res:* Semiconductors; semiconductor devices; computer-aided design. *Mailing Add:* Lucent Technologies 600 Mountain Ave Murray Hill NJ 07974-0636

GUMNICK, JAMES LOUIS, PHYSICS. *Current Pos:* EXEC DIR RES, ST FRANCIS REGIONAL MED CTR, WICHITA, PRES, ST FRANCIS RES INST. *Personal Data:* b Baltimore, Md, Oct 5, 30; m 59, Jean K Lawler; c John, Anne, Edward, Mary, Jane & Elizabeth. *Educ:* Loyola Col, Md, 53; Univ Notre Dame, PhD, 58. *Prof Exp:* Prof physics, Martin-Loyola Col, Baltimore, 57-64; exec dir, Nat Coun Energy Co, 73-76; dir res & develop, Univ Houston, 76-80; gen mgr, Gulf Univs Res Co, Houston, 80-82, pres, 82-84; univ rels dir, Oak Ridge Assoc Univs, 84-87. *Concurrent Pos:* Danforth Found fel, 53; chmn govt prog comt, Pa Gov's Energy Coun, 73-74. *Mem:* Am Physics Soc; Nat Coun Univ Adminrs; AAAS; Soc Res Adminrs; Sigma Xi. *Res:* Inventor multiple reflection photocathode; discoverer cyclic migration of CS on refractory metals. *Mailing Add:* St Francis Regional Med Ctr 929 N St Francis Wichita KS 67214

GUMNIT, ROBERT J, EPILEPSY. *Current Pos:* PRES, MINCEP EPILEPSY CARE; CLIN PROF NEUROL NEUROSURG & PHARM, UNIV MINN. *Personal Data:* b Pittsburgh, Pa, July 4, 31; m, Frances H Graham; c Daniel, Ruth & Stepheu. *Educ:* Univ Pa, MD. *Mem:* Nat Asn Epilepsy Ctrs (pres, 87-); Am Neurol Asn; Am EEG Soc (pres, 83-84); Am Epilepsy Soc (pres, 80-81); Am Asn Neurol. *Res:* Epilepsy; new medical and sugical treatments. *Mailing Add:* Mincep Epilepsy Care 5775 Wayzata Blvd Minneapolis MN 55416

GUMP, BARRY HEMPHILL, ANALYTICAL CHEMISTRY, WINE AND FOOD ANALYSIS. *Current Pos:* From asst prof to assoc prof, 67-74, PROF CHEM, CALIF STATE UNIV, FRESNO, 74-, PROF ENOL & FOOD SCI, 81- *Personal Data:* b Columbus, Ohio, Nov 12, 40; m 63; c 2. *Educ:* Ohio State Univ, BSc, 62; Univ Calif, Los Angeles, PhD(analytical chem), 66. *Concurrent Pos:* Res assoc, Bur Sci, Food & Drug Admin, Washington, DC, 66-67; consult, Cent Calif Med Labs, 69-71; vis scientist, Bioorg Standards Sect, Analysis Div, Nat Bur Standards, 74-76, Danforth Assoc, 81; Fulbright lectr, Univ Repub, Montivideo, Uruguay, 83; assoc referee for sulfur dioxide in wine, AOAC, 86. *Mem:* Am Chem Soc; Am Soc Enologists; Sigma Xi; Am Inst Chemists. *Res:* Separation methods in chemistry, especially chromatographic methods; analytical methods development, trace components in foods and wine; trace hydrocarbon analysis in marine sediment, water and tissue samples. *Mailing Add:* 1053 35th St Sacramento CA 95816

GUMP, DIETER W, INTERNAL MEDICINE, INFECTIOUS DISEASES. *Current Pos:* from instr to asst prof microbiol, 66-71, from asst prof to assoc prof med, 68-80, ASSOC PROF MICROBIOL, UNIV VT, 71-, PROF MED MICROBIOL, 80- *Personal Data:* b Saranac Lake, NY, Mar 28, 33; c 3. *Educ:* Swarthmore Col, BA, 55; Johns Hopkins Univ, MD, 60. *Prof Exp:* Intern, Johns Hopkins Hosp, 60-61; asst resident, Med Ctr, Univ Colo, 61-62 & Johns Hopkins Hosp, 62-63. *Concurrent Pos:* Fel infectious dis, Johns Hopkins Hosp, 63-66. *Mem:* Am Fedn Clin Res; Am Soc Microbiol; Sigma Xi; fel Am Col Physicians; fel Infectious Dis Soc Am. *Res:* Bacterial, mycoplasmal and chlamydial disease; antibiotics. *Mailing Add:* Univ Vt Col Med Given Bldg Burlington VT 05405-0068

GUMP, FRANK E, SURGERY. *Current Pos:* asst prof, 66-69, assoc prof, 69-72, PROF SURG & CHIEF BREAST SERV, COLUMBIA-PRESBY MED CTR, 72- *Personal Data:* b St Louis, Mo, Feb 16, 28; m 59; c 3. *Educ:* Harvard Univ, AB, 51; NY Univ, MD, 55; Am Bd Surg, dipl. *Prof Exp:* NIH res fel, 58-59. *Mem:* Am Col Surg; Asn Acad Surg; Soc Univ Surg; Am Surg Asn; Am Asn Surg of Trauma. *Res:* Breast cancer. *Mailing Add:* Columbia P&S 161 Ft Washington Ave New York NY 10032-3713

GUMP, J R, INORGANIC CHEMISTRY, ANALYTICAL CHEMISTRY. *Current Pos:* from asst prof to prof, 63-87, EMER PROF PHYSICS, CNET MICH UNIV, 87- *Personal Data:* b Ann Arbor, Mich, Apr 1, 21; m 43; c 3. *Educ:* Detroit Inst Technol, BSChE, 43; Wayne State Univ, MS, 47; Univ Ky, PhD(inorg & analytical chem), 52. *Prof Exp:* Instr chem, Lawrence Inst Technol, 47-49 & Univ Ky, 49-52; asst prof, Univ Cincinnati, 52-53; chemist, Inorg Res, Mich Chem Corp, 53-54, supvr, 54-55, group leader, 59-62; res chemist, Victor Chem Co, 62-63. *Concurrent Pos:* Pres, Mitten Chem Inc, 55-67; consult, Sylvania Elec Prod, 67-71. *Mem:* AAAS; Am Chem Soc; Nat Educ Asn; Nat Sci Teachers Asn. *Res:* Brine; bromine; magnesia; rare earths; ion exchange; solvent extraction; yttrium metal; salts and oxides; scandium salts and oxides; ferrates chemistry; secondary and elementary physical science education. *Mailing Add:* 930 Falkirk Rd Alma MI 48801

GUMPERTZ, WERNER H(ERBERT), CIVIL ENGINEERING. *Current Pos:* PRIN CONSULT ENGR & SR PRIN ENGR, SIMPSON GUMPERTZ & HEGER, INC, 57- *Personal Data:* b Berlin, Ger, Dec 26, 17; US citizen; m 49; c 2. *Educ:* Swiss Fed Inst Technol, BCE, 39; Mass Inst Technol, SB, 48, SM, 50, BldgE, 54. *Honors & Awards:* Walter C Voss Award, Am Soc Testing & Mat. *Prof Exp:* Vol engr, Amsterdam, Netherlands, 39-40; instrument man, Lockwood, Kessler & Bartlett, 40-41; field engr, M Shapiro & Sons Construct Co, Inc, 41-43; off engr shipyard, Kaiser Co, 43; struct engr, Corps Engrs, US Army, 47-48; engr, United Engrs & Constructors, 48-49; asst prof civil eng & construct mgt, Mass Inst Technol, 49-57. *Concurrent Pos:* Mem comt adhesives & sealants, Bldg Res Inst, 60-63; mem adv comt, Inst Bldg Res, Pa State Univ, 64-84; mem Nat Bur Standards steering group, US Dept of Energy, 78-85; chmn comt D8 Roofing, Am Soc Testing & Mat. *Mem:* Fel Am Soc Civ; Am Concrete Inst; Am Soc Eng Educ; fel Am Soc Testing & Mat. *Res:* Investigations into physical properties of built-up roofing systems and their components; interrelation between structural building movement and the performance of nonstructural roof membranes; curtain walls; masonry; glass/glazing. *Mailing Add:* 297 Broadway Arlington MA 02174

GUMPF, DAVID JOHN, PLANT VIROLOGY. *Current Pos:* From asst prof & asst plant pathologist to assoc prof & assoc plant pathologist, 70-85, PROF PLANT PATH & PLANT PATHOLOGIST, UNIV CALIF, RIVERSIDE, 85- *Personal Data:* b Billings, Mont, Mar 30, 42; m 64; c 1. *Educ:* Mont State Univ, BS, 64, MS, 66; Univ Nebr, PhD(plant path), 70. *Mem:* Am Phytopath Soc; Int Orgn Mycoplasmology; Int Orgn Citrus Virologists; Sigma Xi; Int Soc Citriculture. *Res:* Purification, characterization and diagnosis of citrus viruses and isolation and cultivation of plant mycoplasmas. *Mailing Add:* Dept Plant Path Univ Calif 900 University Ave Riverside CA 92521-0101

GUMPORT, RICHARD I, BIOCHEMISTRY, NUCLEIC ACID. *Current Pos:* from asst prof to assoc prof biochem, Sch Basic Med Sci & Sch Chem Sci, 71-93, assoc head biochem, 89-93 & 94-97, actg head biochem, 93, PROF BIOCHEM, UNIV ILL, URBANA, 93- *Personal Data:* b Pocatello, Idaho, June 23, 37; m 60, Roberta Kugell; c Susan R & William I. *Educ:* Univ Chicago, BS, 60; PhD(biochem), 68. *Prof Exp:* USPHS fel biochem, Sch Med, Stanford Univ, 68-70, fel, 70-71. *Concurrent Pos:* Vis scholar biochem, Dept Biochem & Molecular Biol, Harvard Univ, 79-80; John Simon Guggenheim Mem fel, 79-80; assoc, Ctr Advan Study, Univ Ill, 85-86; vis prof, Sichuan Univ, Cheug-du, China, 86-; vis fel, Roche Molecular Systs, Emeryville, Calif, 91-92; exec ed, Nucleic Acids Res, 93- *Mem:* AAAS; Am Soc Biol Chem & Molecular Biol; Am Chem Soc; Am Soc Microbiologists; Sigma Xi; Protein Soc. *Res:* Nucleic acid enzymology; restriction endonuclease and modification methylase enzymology; molecular genetics; protein-DNA interaction and site-specific recombination. *Mailing Add:* Dept Biochem Univ Ill 600 S Mathews Ave Urbana IL 61801-3792. Fax: 217-333-8868; E-Mail: gumport@uiuc.edu

GUMPORT, STEPHEN LAWRENCE, surgery; deceased, see previous edition for last biography

GUMPRECHT, WILLIAM HENRY, ORGANIC CHEMISTRY. *Current Pos:* RETIRED. *Personal Data:* b Potsdam, NY, Nov 16, 31; m 78, Elizabeth Nace; c Linda, Mark, Diane & Blake. *Educ:* Univ Ill, BS, 53; Univ Minn, PhD(chem), 57. *Prof Exp:* Res chemist, E I Du Pont de Nemours & Co, Inc, 57-66, sr res chemist, 66-85, res assoc, 85-90, sr res assoc, 90-96. *Mem:* Am Chem Soc. *Res:* Dyes; fluorinated compounds; polymers; telomers. *Mailing Add:* 2606 Stephenson Dr Wilmington DE 19808-3826

GUNASEKARAN, MUTHUKUMARAN, CLINICAL MYCOLOGY, PLANT PATHOLOGY. *Current Pos:* assoc prof, 81-86, PROF BIOL, FISK UNIV, 86- *Personal Data:* b Chidambaram, India, June 6, 42; m 70; c 2. *Educ:* Annamalai Univ, BS, 64; Univ Madras, MS, 66; Tex A&M Univ, PhD(plant path), 70. *Prof Exp:* Asst prof biol, Rust Col, 72-74; asst mem, Infectious Dis Dept, St Jude Children's Res Hosp, 74-81. *Concurrent Pos:* Fel, Brigham Young Univ, 71-72; NIH grant, 76-79, NASA grant, 86-; Fulbright scholar. *Mem:* Am Mycol Soc; Am Soc Microbiol; Indian Phytopath Soc; Soc Indust Microbiol. *Res:* Physiology and rapid diagnostic studies on fungal diseases. *Mailing Add:* Dept Biol Fisk Univ Nashville TN 37208-3051. Fax: 615-329-8677

GUNASEKERA, JAY SARATH, MANUFACTURING PROCESSES, COMPUTER-AIDED DESIGN & COMPUTER-AIDED MANUFACTURING. *Current Pos:* from assoc prof to prof, 83-87, MOSS PROF & CHMN MECH ENG, OHIO UNIV, 87- *Personal Data:* b Kalutara, West Sri Lanka, July 26, 46; US citizen; m 73, Mal Hettiarachchi; c Manisha, Upendri & Yosha. *Educ:* Univ Ceylon, BSc, 67; Univ London, MSc, 70, PhD(mech eng), 72, DSc, 91. *Prof Exp:* Res asst, Imp Col, London, 68-70 & 71-72; teaching asst, McMaster Univ, 70-71; lectr mfg, Univ Sri Lanka, 72-77; sr lectr, Monash Univ, Australia, 77-81 & 82-83; sr res assoc, Nat Res Coun, 81-82. *Concurrent Pos:* Engr, Indust Develop Bd, 75-77; dir, Ceylon Steel Corp, 75-77. *Mem:* Am Soc Mech Engrs; Soc Mining Metall & Explor; Fel Inst Mech Engrs UK; fel Inst Elec Engrs UK. *Res:* Computer simulation of manufacturing processes, primarily forging, rolling and extrusion; tool and die design. *Mailing Add:* 5 Hemlock Dr Athens OH 45701. Fax: 740-593-4684; E-Mail: gsekera@bobcat.ent.ohiou.edu

GUNBERG, DAVID LEO, HEAD & NECK ANATOMY, MAMMALIAN EMBRYO CULTURE. *Current Pos:* prof & chmn anat, 75-88, EMER PROF DEPT ANAT, SCH DENT, ORE HEALTH SCI UNIV, 88- *Personal Data:* b Minneapolis, Minn, May 1, 22; m 64, Jorraine Jacobson; c 4. *Educ:* Univ Redlands, AD, 49; Univ Calif, Berkeley, MS, 52, PhD(anat), 54. *Prof Exp:* Teaching asst anat, Univ Calif, Berkeley, 50-54; instr, Med Sch, Univ Southern Calif, 54-55; from asst prof to prof, Ore Health Sci Univ Med Sch, 55-72; prof & chmn, Univ Malaya Med Fac, Malaysia, 72-75. *Concurrent Pos:* Asst dir, grad prog anat, Ore Health Sci Univ, 60-62 & 64-72; prog dir, postdoctoral training prog anat, AID proj med educ, Airlangga Univ, Indonesia & Univ Calif, 61-67; vis prof, Med Fac, Univ Airlangga, Indonesia, 62-64 & Med Fac, Univ WI, Jamaica, 83-84; external examiner, Univ Kebangsaan Med Fac, Malaysia, 80 & Univ WI Med Fac, Jamaica, 82, 83 & 87. *Mem:* Teratology Soc; Am Asn Anatomists; Europ Teratology Soc; Japanese Teratology Soc; Sigma Xi. *Res:* Causes of congenital defects in mammals; effects of exogenous agents on embryonic and fetal development are studied utilizing morphologic, chemical and metabolic measurements; mammalian teratology. *Mailing Add:* 23950 SW Baker Rd Sherwood OR 97140

GUNCKEL, THOMAS L, II, ELECTRICAL ENGINEERING. *Current Pos:* RETIRED. *Personal Data:* b Dayton, Ohio, Jan 16, 36; m 63; c 2. *Educ:* Calif Inst Technol, BS, 58; Stanford Univ, MS, 59, PhD(elec eng), 61. *Prof Exp:* Res specialist, Autonetics Div, NAm Aviation, Inc, 61-62, supvr phys analysis, 62-63, chief space syst analysis, 63-66, mgr syst analysis, 66-71, mgr navig systs, NAm Rockwell Corp, 71-73, mgr comput & microelectronics, 73-77, mgr systs eng, 77-80, chief engr mx eng, 80-83, chief eng, 83-87, vpres Minuteman & Adv Systs, Strategic Systs Div, 87-89, vpres & gen mgr autonetics, Div, Rockwell Int, 89-94, sr vpres res, eng & opers, Rockwell Int, 94-96. *Res:* Control system theory; space guidance and navigation; optimal control; orbit determination; computer design; systems engineering. *Mailing Add:* 11242 La Vereda Dr Santa Ana CA 92705

GUND, PETER HERMAN LOURIE, MEDICINAL & COMPUTATIONAL CHEMISTRY. *Current Pos:* sci res fel, 73-79, sr res fel, 79-83, dir, 83-90, SR DIR CHEM & BIOL SYSTS, MERCK SHARP & DOHME RES LABS, RAHWAY, NJ, 90- *Personal Data:* b New York, NY, Feb 20, 40; m 67; c 1. *Educ:* Columbia Col, AB, 61; Purdue Univ, MS, 63; Univ Mass, PhD(org chem), 67. *Prof Exp:* Res chemist antiparasitics, Am Cyanamid Agr Div, Princeton, NJ, 67-70; vis res fel, dept chem, Princeton Univ, 70-72; dept biochem, 72-75. *Concurrent Pos:* treas, Div Med Chem, Chem Info & Comput Chem, Am Chem Soc, 87-90. *Mem:* Am Chem Soc; AAAS; Drug Info Asn. *Res:* Computer graphics applications in pharmaceutical chemical research; computer aided new drug design; drug conformation and mechanism of action; computer aided organic synthetic planning; quantitative structure-activity relationships; theoretical chemistry; molecular/macromolecular modeling. *Mailing Add:* MDL Info Systs Inc 1 Sylvan Way Suite 120 Parsippany NJ 07054

GUNDERSEN, JAMES NOVOTNY, ECONOMIC GEOLOGY. *Current Pos:* chmn, Dept Geol, 70-76, PROF GEOL, WICHITA STATE UNIV, 70- *Personal Data:* b Oak Park, Ill, Dec 20, 25; m 56; c 3. *Educ:* Univ Wis, BS, 49; Univ Calif, Los Angeles, MA, 55; Univ Minn, PhD(econ geol), 58. *Prof Exp:* Geol consult, Alamos Mining Co, Mex, 51-53; raw mat engr, Columbia Iron Mining Co, US Steel Corp, Utah, 53-55; asst petrol & mineral, Univ Minn, 57-58, res assoc mining geologist, Mines Exp Sta, 58-61; from asst prof to assoc prof geol & chmn dept, Calif State Col, Los Angeles, 61-68, actg dir res & govt rels, 65; prof, Univ Ariz, 68-70. *Mem:* Am Inst Mining, Metall & Petrol Engrs; Am Inst Prof Geologists; Geol Soc Am; Soc Econ Paleontologists & Mineralogists; Soc Archaeol Sci; Soc Am Archaeol. *Res:* Mining geology, especially taconites and iron ores; petrography and geochemistry of metamorphic and metasomatic rocks; mineral beneficiation; mineralography; hydrothermal alteration; differential thermal analysis; x-ray diffraction; spectroscopy; pre-Cambrian stratigraphy; uranium geology; general geoarchaeometry; provenances of Plains pipestones cathuite and other exotic lithics utilized by Paleoindians; provenances of obsidian raw materials. *Mailing Add:* Geog & Geol Wichita State Univ 1845 Fairmount St Wichita KS 67260-0001

GUNDERSEN, MARTIN ADOLPH, LASERS, SOLID STATE PHYSICS. *Current Pos:* assoc prof, 80-83, PROF, DEPT ELEC ENG & PHYSICS, UNIV SOUTHERN CALIF, 83- *Personal Data:* b Glenwood, Minn, May 19, 40; m 63; c 2. *Educ:* Univ Calif, Berkeley, BA, 65; Univ Southern Calif, MA, 67, PhD(physics), 73. *Prof Exp:* Engr bubble chamber, Lawrence Berkeley Lab, 65; res assoc lasers & solid state physics, Univ Southern Calif, 72-73; asst prof lasers & solid state physics, Dept Elec Eng, Tex Tech Univ, 73-77, assoc prof, 77-80. *Mem:* Am Phys Soc; fel Inst Elec & Electronics Engrs; fel Optical Soc Am. *Res:* Applied physics; spectroscopy; solid state physics; lasers and lasers physics; pulsed power physics. *Mailing Add:* SSC 420 Univ Southern Calif Univ Park Los Angeles CA 90089-0484

GUNDERSEN, RALPH WILHELM, ENTOMOLOGY. *Current Pos:* from asst prof to assoc prof, 64-80, PROF BIOL, ST CLOUD STATE UNIV, 80- *Personal Data:* b Chicago, Ill, Aug 22, 38; m 60; c 2. *Educ:* Hamline Univ, BS, 59; Univ Minn, St Paul, MS, 62, PhD(entom), 68. *Prof Exp:* Instr, Univ Minn, Duluth, 63-64. *Concurrent Pos:* Aquatic insect consult; res assoc, Minn Sci Mus, 77- *Mem:* Coleopterists Soc; Nature Conservancy. *Res:* Taxonomy and life history of aquatic insects principally Coleoptera and Hemiptera. *Mailing Add:* 806 Sixth Ave S St Cloud MN 56301

GUNDERSEN, ROY MELVIN, MATHEMATICS. *Personal Data:* b Ecorse, Mich, May 1, 30. *Educ:* Ill Inst Technol, BS, 51; Univ Wis, MS, 52; Brown Univ, PhD(appl math), 56. *Prof Exp:* Asst math, Univ Wis, 51-52; asst appl math, Brown Univ, 53-55; mathematician, Univ Chicago, 55; dir res, Univ Paris, 55-56; res engr, Boeing Aircraft Co, 56-57; from asst prof to assoc prof math, Ill Inst Technol, 57-63; from asst prof, Univ Wis, Milwaukee, 63-85. *Concurrent Pos:* Consult, Armour Res Found, 57 & 59-60 & Bendix Systs Div, Bendix Corp, 60-61; NSF res grant, 58-60 & 68-72; vis assoc prof, Math Res Ctr, US Army, Univ Wis, 61-62. *Mem:* Soc Natural Philos; Soc Indust & Appl Math. *Res:* Applied mathematics; compressible fluid flow; partial and ordinary differential equations; magnetohydrodynamics. *Mailing Add:* 5801 N Sheridan Rd Chicago IL 60660

GUNDERSON, DONALD RAYMOND, FISH BIOLOGY, RESOURCE SURVEYS. *Current Pos:* from asst prof to assoc prof, 78-94, PROF MARINE FISHERIES, UNIV WASH, 94- *Personal Data:* b La Jolla, Calif, Jan 3, 42; m 85; c 2. *Educ:* Mont State Univ, BS, 63, MS, 66; Univ Wash, PhD(fisheries), 76. *Prof Exp:* Fisheries biologist, Wash State Dept Fisheries, 67-75; res biologist, Nat Marine Fisheries Serv, 75-78. *Concurrent Pos:* Consult, Int Groundfish Comn, US & Can, 71-; mem, Int N Pac Fisheries Comn, Northeast Pac Groundfish Tech Subcomt, 71-75, Pac Fishery Mgt Coun, Groundfish Plan Develop Team, 76-79, Army Corps Engrs, 84-85, Environ Protection Agency, 88, Exxon, 90 & Nat Res Coun, 94. *Mem:* Am Fisheries Soc; Am Inst Fisheries Res Biologists; Sigma Xi. *Res:* Population ecology and population dynamics of marine fish; estimation of stock abundance using trawl and hydroacoustic surveys. *Mailing Add:* 123 Raft Island Gig Harbor WA 98335

GUNDERSON, HANS MAGELSSEN, BIOCHEMISTRY. *Current Pos:* from asst prof to assoc prof, 74-93, PROF CHEM, NORTHERN ARIZ UNIV, 93- *Personal Data:* b Walker, Minn, Oct 10, 38; m 69, Margaret Steeble; c Sharon M. *Educ:* St Olaf Col, BA, 60; Univ NH, MST, 69; Univ NDak, PhD(biochem), 74. *Prof Exp:* Teacher high schs, Minn, New Guinea & Wis, 60-68; teacher chem, Bemidji State Univ, 68-71. *Concurrent Pos:* Sigma Xi grad res award, 74. *Mem:* Am Chem Soc; Sigma Xi; Am Col Sports Med. *Res:* Effect of endurance training on pathways of carbohydrate metabolism, gluconeogenesis and glycogen synthesis. *Mailing Add:* Northern Ariz Univ PO Box 5698 Flagstaff AZ 86011. *Fax:* 520-523-2626; *E-Mail:* hmg@nauvax.ucc.nau.edu

GUNDERSON, NORMAN GUSTAV, MATHEMATICS. *Current Pos:* from instr to assoc prof, Univ Rochester, 46-66, assoc prof educ, 61-66, prof, 66-80, EMER PROF MATH & EDUC, UNIV ROCHESTER, 80- *Personal Data:* b Schenectady, NY, May 29, 17; m 45; c 3. *Educ:* NY State Teachers Col, Albany, AB, 37; Cornell Univ, AM, 41, PhD(math), 48. *Prof Exp:* Teacher, NY Pub Sch, 37-40; asst & instr math, Cornell Univ, 40-46. *Concurrent Pos:* Lectr math, Nazareth Col, 80-83. *Mem:* Am Math Soc; Math Asn Am. *Res:* Number theory; geometry; mathematics curriculum; teaching of mathematics. *Mailing Add:* 2085 W Henrietta Rd Rochester NY 14623-1353

GUNDERSON, NORMAN O, engineering, urban studies; deceased, see previous edition for last biography

GUNDLACH, ROBERT WILLIAM, PHYSICS. *Current Pos:* RETIRED. *Personal Data:* b Buffalo, NY, Sept 7, 26; m 50; c 3. *Educ:* Univ Buffalo, BA, 49. *Honors & Awards:* Ives Jour Award, 64; Inventors Award, Rochester Patent Law Asn, 74; Kosar Award, Soc Photog Scientists & Engrs, 76; Vis Lectr Award, Soc Photog Scientists & Engrs, 85; Carlson Award, 86; Gutenberg Prize, Soc Info Display, 93. *Prof Exp:* Asst physics, Univ Buffalo, 49-51; physicist, Durez Plastics Co, NY, 51-52; physicist, Haloid Co, 52-55, proj leader, 55-57, res assoc, 57-59, sr res assoc, Haloid Xerox, Inc, 59-60, sr scientist, Xerox Corp, 60-63, prin scientist & consult, 63-66, res fel, 66-78, sr res fel, 78-95, mgr, Exite Labs, 89-95. *Mem:* Nat Acad Eng; Soc Imaging Sci & Technol; Electrostatics Soc Am (pres, 77-81). *Res:* Exploratory xerographic research; physical imaging methods, electrophotography; holds over 150 US patents. *Mailing Add:* 2434 Turk Hill Rd Victor NY 14564

GUNDY, SAMUEL CHARLES, BIOLOGY. *Current Pos:* asst prof, 67-81, EMER PROF BIOL, KUTZTOWN STATE COL, 81- *Personal Data:* b Reading, Pa, Mar 28, 18; m 43, Mary Dunkleberger; c Gregory S & Barbara L. *Educ:* Pa State Teachers Col, Kutztown, BS, 46; Cornell Univ, MS, 53. *Prof Exp:* Specialist nature, Reading Recreation Dept, 40-41; teacher entom, vert zool & ornith, Reading Pub Mus & Art Gallery, 41; teacher, Pa Pub Sch, 46-52; from asst dir to dir, Reading Pub Mus & Art Gallery, 53-67. *Concurrent Pos:* Emer dir, Reading Pub Mus & Art Gallery. *Mem:* Am Soc Ichthyologists & Herpetologists; Wilson Ornith Soc; Am Asn Mus. *Res:* Herpetology; ornithology; geology; mineralogy; paleontology. *Mailing Add:* 409 Harvard Blvd Lincoln Park Reading PA 19609

GUNER, OSMAN FATIH, COMPUTATIONAL CHEMISTRY, COMPUTER-AIDED DRUG DESIGN. *Current Pos:* SR SCIENTIST, MDL INFO SYSTS INC, 93- *Personal Data:* b Manisa, Turkey, Feb 25, 56; m 82, Nazli Erbay; c Kurt & Sibel. *Educ:* Middle-East Tech Univ, Turkey, BS, 79, MS, 81; Va Commonwealth Univ, PhD(phys org chem), 86. *Prof Exp:* Fel, Univ Ala, Birmingham, 87-89; sr applns scientist, Molecular Design Ltd, 89-93. *Mem:* Am Chem Soc; fel Am Inst Chemists. *Res:* Three dimensional searching: searching of databases of three dimensional structures; developed and published querying techniques in three dimensional database searching; chemical information management, and computer-aided drug design. *Mailing Add:* Molecular Simulations Inc 9685 Scranton Rd San Diego CA 92121-3752

GUNION, JOHN FRANCIS, HIGH ENERGY PHYSICS, THEORETICAL PHYSICS. *Current Pos:* assoc prof, 75-78, PROF HIGH ENERGY PHYSICS, UNIV CALIF, DAVIS, 78- *Personal Data:* b Washington, DC, July 21, 43; m 67, Ann Hutchings; c Chris & Andrew. *Educ:* Cornell Univ, BS, 65; Univ Calif, San Diego, MS, 68, PhD(physics), 70. *Prof Exp:* Res assoc, Stanford Linear Accelerator, 70-72, Mass Inst Technol, 72-73; from asst prof to assoc prof, Univ Pittsburgh, 73-75. *Concurrent Pos:* NSF res grant, 73-75; Dept Energy grant, 75-; Sloan Found fel, 76-80; NSF Int Collab grant, Univ Warsaw, 79-82; vis prof, Univ Calif, San Diego, 79, Inst Theoret Physics, 79, 88, Stanford Linear Accelerator Ctr, 80, Univ Ore, 85; Europ Orgn Nuclear Res ed, 92, numerous conf proc, 96; Marie-Sklodowski-Curie Fund grant II, 96- *Mem:* Am Inst Physics; fel Am Phys Soc. *Res:* Higgaboson physics and electroweak symmetry breaking; high transverse momentum phenomena; quantum chromodynamics; bound state phenomena; unified theories of the weak and electromagnetic interactions; supersymmetry; collider phenomenology, super-collider phemenology; superstring phenomenology; author of more than 170 publications in scientific journals and over 120 publications in conference/workshop proceedings. *Mailing Add:* Dept Physics Univ Calif Davis CA 95616. *E-Mail:* jfgucd@ucdhep.ucdavis.edu

GUNJI, HIROSHI, MATHEMATICS. *Current Pos:* from asst prof to assoc prof, 66-77, PROF MATH, UNIV-WIS MADISON, 77- *Personal Data:* b Bangkok, Thailand, June 14, 28; m 62; c 1. *Educ:* Univ Tokyo, BA, 54, MA, 56; Johns Hopkins Univ, PhD(math), 62. *Prof Exp:* Instr math, Cornell Univ, 62-64; asst prof, Univ Sask, 64-66. *Concurrent Pos:* NSF math res grants, 62-64 & 66-69. *Res:* Diophantine problem of eliptic curves. *Mailing Add:* 621 Van Vleck Hall Univ-Wis Madison 480 Lincoln Dr Madison WI 53706-1388

GUNKEL, ROBERT JAMES, AERODYNAMICS. *Current Pos:* Design specialist, Missile & Space Systs Div, McDonnell-Douglas Astronaut Co, 47-53, asst supvr missile aerodyn, 53-56, chief aerodyn & astrodyn 56-61, chief res engr, 61-62, adv prog mgr space launch vehicles, 62, mgr sprint systs develop, 62-63, dir prog 437, 63-64, medium launch vehicles, 64, adv manned spacecraft systs, 64-66, dir adv spacecraft & launch systs, Missile & Space Systs Div, 66-68, dir systs develop & integration, Manned Orbiting Lab Subdiv, 68-69, adv space & launch systs, 69-70, dir space shuttle booster, Astronaut Co-West, 70-72, dep dir data processing, 72-76, dir prog eng, space sta design & advan space systs, 76-80, PROG MGR, GPS/PAM DII PROG, MCDONNELL-DOUGLAS ASTRONAUT CO, 80- *Personal Data:* b Chicago, Ill, May 13, 25; m 49; c 5. *Educ:* Univ Mich, BS, 46, MS, 47. *Concurrent Pos:* Mem res & tech adv comt space vehicles, NASA, 66-75; mem, AIAA Launch Vehicles Tech Comt, Spacecraft TC, Space Systs TC & Space Opers & Support TC. *Mem:* AAAS; Am Astron Soc; Am Inst Aeronaut & Astronaut; assoc fel Brit Interplanetary Soc; Sigma Xi. *Res:* Calculations of variational approach to flight mechanics; linearized supersonic wing theory; program management. *Mailing Add:* 1227 Devon Lane Newport Beach CA 92660

GUNKEL, WESLEY W, AGRICULTURAL ENGINEERING. *Current Pos:* From asst prof to prof, 48-92, coordr grad instr, 66-69 & 88-92, EMER PROF AGR ENG, NY STATE COL AGR & LIFE SCI, CORNELL UNIV, 92- *Personal Data:* b Hope, NDak, Oct 17, 21; m 45, Lucille H Peterson; c Sharon & Gerald. *Educ:* NDak State Univ, BSc, 47; Iowa State Univ, MS, 48; Mich State Univ, PhD(agr eng), 57. *Concurrent Pos:* Vis prof & adv, Univ Nigeria, 62-63; consult, Ministry of Agr, Ghana, 65 & Dole Pineapple Co, Hawaii, 69-70; vis scientist, Int Rice Res Inst, Philippines, 76-77. *Mem:* AAAS; fel Am Soc Agr Engrs; Am Soc Eng Educ; Am Chem Soc; Coun for Agr Sci Technol; Nat Safety Coun. *Res:* Energy in agriculture; pest control equipment and methods; harvesting machinery; design of specialized farm and industrial equipment; farm power; agricultural machinery safety; robotics and machine vision. *Mailing Add:* Dept Agr Eng-Riley-Robb Hall Cornell Univ Ithaca NY 14853-5701. *E-Mail:* wwg2@cornell.edu

GUNN, ALBERT EDWARD, MEDICAL ETHICS, MEDICAL LEGAL PROBLEMS. *Current Pos:* med dir, Rehab Ctr, M D Anderson Hosp & Tumor Inst, 75-88, ASSOC PROF INTERNAL MED, MED SCH, UNIV TEX, HOUSTON, 80-, ASSOC PROF PUB HEALTH ADMIN, SCH PUB HEALTH, 81- *Personal Data:* b Port Washington, NY, Oct 31, 33; m 68; c Albert E III, Emily W, Andrew R, Catherine A B, Clare M & Philip D. *Educ:* Fordham Col, BS, 55; Fordham Law Sch, LLB, 58; Nat Univ Ireland, MB, BCh, BAO, 67; LRCP(L) & MRCS(E), 67; Am Bd Int Med, cert, 77. *Prof Exp:* Asst dir govt rel, AMA, 72-74; med dir geriat servs, Suffolk Co Health Servs Dept, NY, 74-75. *Concurrent Pos:* Mem, Nat Adv Health Coun, HEW, 74-77 & Adv Comt, Nat Inst Law Enforcement & Criminal Law, US Dept Justice, 74-76; assoc prof geriat, Syst Cancer Ctr, M D Anderson Hosp & Tumor Inst, Univ Tex, Houston, 79-, asst dean admis, Med Sch, 79-84, assoc dean admis, 84-; mem, Bd Regents, Nat Libr Med, NIH, Dept Health Human Servs, 83-87, chmn, 86-87, chmn lit selection tech rev comt, 88-91; consult, Ctrs Dis Control, 85, Legal Servs Corp, 87. *Mem:* Fel Am Col Physicians; Soc Surg Oncol. *Res:* Geriatrics, particularly in the area of medical and legal problems involved in mental impairment in the elderly. *Mailing Add:* Univ Tex M D Anderson Cancer Ctr 1515 Holcombe Blvd Houston TX 77030. *Fax:* 713-794-5554; *E-Mail:* gunn@dean.med.uth.tmc.edu

GUNN, CHARLES ROBERT, taxonomy, botany, for more information see previous edition

GUNN, CHESTERFIELD GARVIN, JR, INTERNAL MEDICINE, NEUROPHYSIOLOGY. *Current Pos:* asst prof med, physiol & prev med, Univ Oklal, 56-61, asst prof psychiat, neurol & behav sci, 57-62, assoc prof med & physiol, 61-67, prof physiol, 67-, prof med, 68-, prof biol psychol, 71, regents prof med, 85-88, EMER REGENTS PROF MED, UNIV OKLA, 88- *Personal Data:* b Bethany, Mo, Sept 2, 20; m 46; c 3. *Educ:* Univ Mo, AB, 42; Yale Univ, MD, 50. *Prof Exp:* Intern & resident med, Med Ctr, Univ Kans, 50-54; asst res anatomist, Sch Med, Univ Calif, Los Angeles, 54-56. *Concurrent Pos:* Res fels, Am Col Physicians, 53 & Am Heart Asn, 54-56; attend physician, Univ Hosps, 56-; consult physician, Okla VA Hosp, 61- *Mem:* Am Psychosom Soc; Am Col Cardiol; Am Acad Neurol; Cent Soc Clin Res; Sigma Xi. *Res:* Central nervous system mechanisms in normal and pathological cardiovascular function. *Mailing Add:* 1908 NW 20th St Oklahoma City OK 73106

GUNN, JAMES EDWARD, ASTROPHYSICS. *Current Pos:* EUGENE HIGGINS PROF ASTRON, PRINCETON UNIV, 80- *Personal Data:* b Livingstone, Tex, Oct 21, 38; m 61. *Educ:* Rice Univ, BS, 61; Calif Inst Technol, PhD(astrophys), 66. *Honors & Awards:* John & Katherine MacArthur Fel, 83 & MacArthur Award, 86; Heinemann Prize, Am Astron Soc, 88; Gold Medal, Royal Soc, 94. *Prof Exp:* Sr scientist lunar & planetary sci, Jet Propulsion Lab, 66-68; asst prof astrophys, Princeton Univ, 68-70; from assoc prof to prof, Calif Inst Technol, 70-77, prof physics, 77-80. *Concurrent Pos:* Staff mem, Hale Observ, 70-, affil, 77-; mem bd dirs, Astron Soc Pac. *Mem:* Nat Acad Sci; Am Astron Soc. *Res:* Theoretical and observational cosmology; astronomical instrumentation; structure and evaluation of galaxies and clusters; star formation. *Mailing Add:* Dept Astrophys Princeton Univ Princeton NJ 08544-1001

GUNN, JOHN BATTISCOMBE, ENGINEERING PHYSICS. *Current Pos:* staff physicist, IBM Corp, 59-71, mem, Corp Tech Comt, 71-72, IBM fel, 71-92, EMER IBM FEL, RES CTR, IBM CORP, 92- *Personal Data:* b Cairo, Egypt, May 13, 28; wid; c 2. *Educ:* Cambridge Univ, BA, 48. *Honors &*

Awards: Liebmann Prize, Inst Elec & Electronics Engrs, 69; John Scott Award, 71; Valdemar Poulsen Gold Medal, Danish Acad Tech Sci, 72. *Prof Exp:* Res engr, Elliott Bros Ltd, 48-53; jr res fel, Radar Res Estab, 53-56; asst prof physics, Univ BC, 56-59. *Mem:* Nat Acad Eng; fel Inst Elec & Electronics Engrs; fel Am Phys Soc; fel Am Acad Arts & Sci. *Res:* Physics of semiconductors; semiconductor devices; programming language; automotive engineering. *Mailing Add:* 235 Guard Hill Rd Mt Kisco NY 10549. *E-Mail:* gunn@watson.ibm.com

GUNN, JOHN MARTYN, BIOCHEMISTRY. *Current Pos:* from asst prof to assoc prof, 76-85, PROF BIOCHEM, TEX A&M UNIV, 85- *Personal Data:* b Lulworth Cove, Eng, June 27, 45. *Educ:* Inst Biol, MI Biol, 69; Univ Sheffield, PhD(biochem), 72. *Prof Exp:* Res technician biochem, Fison's Pharmaceut Ltd, UK, 63-66; Allen & Hanburys Ltd, UK, 66-69. *Concurrent Pos:* Fel, Temple Univ, 72-76; prin investr, USPHS grants, 78-86; consult, Spec Study Sect, NIH, 78- *Mem:* AAAS; Biochem Soc; Am Soc Biol Chemists; Am Soc Cell Biol; Proc Soc Exp Biol & Med. *Res:* Metabolic regulation; protein turnover; function and mechanism of polypeptide hormones. *Mailing Add:* Dept Biochem & Biophys Tex A&M Univ College Station TX 77843-2128. *Fax:* 409-845-9274; *E-Mail:* jmgunn@bioch.tamu.edu

GUNN, JOHN WILLIAM, JR, FORENSIC SCIENCE, SCIENCE ADMINISTRATION. *Current Pos:* chief labs, Bur Narcotics & Dangerous Drugs, 68-73, actg dir Off Sci & Technol, Drug Enforcement Admin, 74-77, dir, 77-90, DEP ASST ADMINR, OFF ADMIN, DRUG ENFORCEMENT ADMIN, 90- *Personal Data:* b Lynn, Mass, Feb 23, 28; m 60, Barbara Potocki; c Ann, James, Mary, Daniel, Eileen & Michael. *Educ:* Boston Col, BS, 51. *Honors & Awards:* Distinguished Serv Award, Am Acad Forensic Sci, 85. *Prof Exp:* Lab shift supvr, Liberty Powder Defense Corp, 51-54; spec agent, Fed Bur Invest, Dept Justice, 54-62; lab supvr, Chas Pfizer & Co, Inc, 62-63; sr staff chemist, Appl Physics Lab, Johns Hopkins Univ, 63-66; chief investigative serv br, Bur Drug Abuse Control, Food & Drug Admin, 66-68. *Concurrent Pos:* Chmn sci & technol subcomt, Cabinet Comt Int Narcotics Control, 74-76; consult, UN Div on Narcotics, 85 & 87. *Mem:* Am Soc Crime Lab Dirs; fel Am Acad Forensic Sci; Int Asn Chiefs Police; Am Chem Soc; Int Asn Forensic Sci. *Res:* Law enforcement technology; forensic sciences; narcotics and dangerous drugs. *Mailing Add:* 4400 Cherry Valley Dr Rockville MD 20853-1104

GUNN, ROBERT BURNS, TRANSPORT KINETICS, BIOPHYSICS. *Current Pos:* PROF & CHMN DEPT PHYSIOL, SCH MED, EMORY UNIV, 81- *Educ:* Harvard Univ, MD, 66. *Mailing Add:* Dept Physiol Sch Med Emory Univ Physiol Bldg Rm 149 Atlanta GA 30322-3110. *Fax:* 404-727-2648

GUNN, ROBERT DEWEY, CHEMICAL ENGINEERING. *Current Pos:* RETIRED. *Personal Data:* b Leninakhan, Armenia, May 29, 28; US citizen; m 54; c 2. *Educ:* Kans State Univ, BS, 50; Univ Calif, Berkeley, MS, 58, PhD(chem eng), 67. *Prof Exp:* Geophys engr, Robert H Ray Co, Saudi Arabia, 51-53; petrol engr, Mobil Int Oil Co, 55-57; asst prof chem eng, Univ Tex, Austin, 67-71; assoc prof to prof chem eng, Univ Wyo, 71-92. *Concurrent Pos:* Distinguished guest prof, Tech Univ Aachen, WGer. *Mem:* AAAS; fel Am Inst Chem; Soc Petrol Engrs; Am Chem Soc; Am Inst Chem Engrs. *Res:* Mass transport in porous material; thermodynamics and high pressure phase equilibria; underground coal gasification; permafrost. *Mailing Add:* Dept Chem Eng Univ Wyo Laramie WY 82070

GUNN, WALTER JOSEPH, engineering, psychoacoustics, for more information see previous edition

GUNNAR, ROLF MCMILLAN, CARDIOLOGY, INTERNAL MEDICINE. *Current Pos:* clin prof, 72-73, chief, Sect Cardiol, 72-82, PROF MED, STRITCH SCH MED, LOYOLA UNIV, 73-, CHMN DEPT MED, 82- *Personal Data:* b Riverside, Ill, Jan 22, 26; m; c 4. *Educ:* Northwestern Univ, BS, 46, MB, 47, MS, 48, MD, 49; Am Bd Internal Med, dipl, 55; Am Bd Cardiovasc Dis, dipl, 61. *Prof Exp:* From intern to resident, Cook County Hosp, Chicago, Ill, 48-53; from clin instr to clin assoc, Univ Ill Col Med, 54-59, from asst prof to prof med, 59-72, dir cardiol sect, 68-70; Edmund F Foley prof med, Univ Ill Med, 71-72. *Concurrent Pos:* Fel cardiol, New Eng Deaconess Hosp & Children's Med Ctr, 58-59; pvt pract, 54-58 & 59-62; from assoc attend physician to attend physician, Cook County Hosp, 54-, from assoc dir Dept Adult Cardiol to dir, 59-70, dir Div Med, 70-71; chief, Univ Ill Med Div, 62-68, dir Dept Adult Cardiol, 63-64; dir Cardiopulmonary Lab, US Vet Admin Hosp, Hines, Ill, 59, prog dir cardiol, 71-74, consult prog dir, 74-; mem bd dirs, MacNeal Mem Hosp, Berwyn, 66-; actg chief Sect Cardiol, Univ Ill Res & Educ Hosps, 67-68; fel coun clin cardiol, Am Heart Asn. *Mem:* AMA; Am Heart Asn; fel Am Col Physicians; fel Am Col Cardiol. *Res:* Research in the mechanisms of and hemodynamic changes in shock due to myocardial infarction and septic shock; research in vectorcardiography including development and testing of criteria for diagnosis of myocardial infarction. *Mailing Add:* 3722 Harlan Ave Riverside IL 60546

GUNNER, HAIM BERNARD, ENVIRONMENTAL BIOLOGY. *Current Pos:* from asst prof to assoc prof soil microbiol, Univ Mass, 63-71, co-dir, Tech Guid Ctr Indust Environ Control, 68-72, assoc dir res, Ctr Int Agr Studies, 69-72, PROF ENVIRON MICROBIOL & ACTG HEAD DEPT ENVIRON SCI, UNIV MASS, AMHERST, 71- *Personal Data:* b Ottawa, Ont, June 18, 24; m 51; c 2. *Educ:* Univ Toronto, BSA, 46; Univ Man, MSc, 48; Cornell Univ, PhD(soil sci), 62. *Prof Exp:* Field crops supvr, Sasa Coop Farm, Israel, 49-51, farm mgr, 51-53, soil conserv supvr, 53-55; asst coordr agr res, Res Coun Israel, Jerusalem, 55-56, coordr, 56-57; res asst soil microbiol, Cornell Univ, 57-61; res officer, Microbiol Res Inst, Can Dept Agr, Ont, 61-63. *Concurrent Pos:* NSF res grant, 64-66; USPHS grant, 66-69; Off Water Resources Res, Dept Interior res grant, 67-70, 72-76 & 76-80; chmn soil biol sect, Northeast Soil Res Comt, 69; secy, Northeast Regional Res Comt Nitrogen Transformation Soil & Water, 69; past chmn, Northeast Regional Res Comt Pesticides; vis prof, Univ Tel Aviv, 71-; consult, Israel Environ Protection Serv, 71-; US Army Corps Engrs grant, 80-89; found, chmn & chief scientist, EcoSci Labs, Inc, 82-; vis prof, Harvard Univ, 87-88. *Mem:* Am Soc Microbiol; Can Soc Microbiol; Am Soc Agron; Soil Sci Soc Am; Int Orgn Biol Control Noxious Animals & Plants. *Res:* Investigations of inorganic transformations of microbial origin; biochemical and physiological aspects of microfloral interrelations with specific reference to the biological control of soil-borne pathogens; microbial degradation of industrial effluents; microbial ecosystem stress in soil and water; microbial control of insect pests; microbial control of aquatic weeds. *Mailing Add:* Marshall Hall Univ Mass Amherst MA 01002

GUNNESS, R(OBERT) C(HARLES), CHEMICAL ENGINEERING. *Current Pos:* RETIRED. *Personal Data:* b Fargo, NDak, July 28, 11; m 36; c 3. *Educ:* Univ Mass, BS, 32; Mass Inst Technol, MS, 34, ScD(chem eng), 36. *Prof Exp:* From instr to asst prof chem eng, Mass Inst Technol, 35-38; group leader, Stand Oil Co, Ind, 38-43, asst dir res, 43-45, assoc dir, 45-47, mgr, 47-52, mem bd dir, 53-75, asst gen mgr mfg, 52-54, gen mgr, Supply & Transp Dept, 54-56, exec vpres, 56-65, pres, 65-75, corp dir, 75. *Concurrent Pos:* Vchmn res & develop bd, Dept Defense, 51. *Mem:* Nat Acad Eng; Am Inst Chem Engrs; Am Chem Soc. *Res:* Distillation; heat transfer; fluid catalytic cracking; petroleum refinery processing techniques; performance characteristics of a commercial stabilizer for absorption naphtha. *Mailing Add:* PO Box 538 Rancho Sante Fe CA 92067

GUNNING, HARRY EMMET, PHYSICAL CHEMISTRY, PHOTOCHEMISTRY. *Current Pos:* prof & chmn dept, Univ Alta, 57-74, Killam mem prof, 68-82, pres univ, 74-79, EMER PROF CHEM, UNIV ALTA, 82- *Personal Data:* b Toronto, Ont, Dec 16, 16; m 43; c 1. *Educ:* Univ Toronto, BA, 39, MA, 40, PhD(phys chem), 42. *Hon Degrees:* DSc, Univ Guelph, 69 & Queen's Univ, 74; LLD, Univ Victoria, 78, Univ Alta, 83, Univ Sask, 84 & Simon Fraser Univ, 84. *Honors & Awards:* Medal, Chem Inst Can, 67; Officer of the Order of Can, 79. *Prof Exp:* Res fel chem, Nat Res Coun Can, 42-43, from asst res chemist to assoc res chemist, 43-46; asst prof chem, Univ Rochester, 46-48; from asst prof to prof, Ill Inst Technol, 48-57. *Concurrent Pos:* Mem, Nat Res Coun Can, 61-; consult, Syncrude Can Ltd, Imp Oil Enterprises Ltd & Dunlop Can; adv indust develop div, City of Edmonton. *Mem:* Fel AAAS; fel Royal Soc Can; fel Chem Inst Can (pres-elect, 72-74, pres, 73-74); fel NY Acad Sci; Am Chem Soc; Faraday Soc; Am Phys Soc; Can Asn Univ Teachers; Sigma Xi; corresp mem Europ Acad Sci, Arts & Lett. *Res:* Chemical kinetics; photochemistry; isotope separation; reactions of atomic sulphur; sulphur chemistry; mercury photo sensitization; flash photolysis and photo-ionization; kinetic mass spectroscopy; hydrocarbon chemistry. *Mailing Add:* 14815 64th Ave Edmonton AB T6H 4Y1 Can

GUNNING, ROBERT CLIFFORD, COMPLEX ANALYSIS, ALGEBRAIC GEOMETRY. *Current Pos:* from asst prof to assoc prof, Princeton Univ, 57-66, chmn dept, 76-79, dean fac, 89-95, PROF MATH, PRINCETON UNIV, 66- *Personal Data:* b Colo, Nov 27, 31; m 66. *Educ:* Univ Colo, BA, 52; Princeton Univ, PhD(math), 55. *Prof Exp:* NSF fel, Univ Chicago, 55-56. *Concurrent Pos:* Sloan fel, 58-61, Cambridge Univ, 59-60; vis prof, Munich, 67 & Oxford Univ, 68 & 80. *Mem:* Am Math Soc; fel AAAS. *Res:* Complex analysis, particularly functions of several complex variables, Riemann surfaces and theta functions; transcendental algebraic geometry. *Mailing Add:* Fine Hall Princeton Univ Washington Rd Princeton NJ 08544-0001

GUNNINK, RAYMOND, PHYSICAL CHEMISTRY. *Current Pos:* CONSULT, 90- *Personal Data:* b Chandler, Minn, June 28, 32; m 54; c 5. *Educ:* Calvin Col, AB, 54; Purdue Univ, PhD(phys chem), 59. *Prof Exp:* Res scientist, Res Ctr, US Rubber Co, 59-63; group leader, Nuclear Chem Div, Lawrence Livermore Lab, Univ Calif, 63-90. *Mem:* Am Phys Soc; Inst Nuclear Mats Mgt. *Res:* Nuclear decay schemes; computer analysis of X- and gamma ray spectra; activation analysis; absolute counting techniques; gamma ray spectroscopy; plutonium safeguards. *Mailing Add:* 4607 Montecarlo Park Ct Freemont CA 99538

GUNNISON, ALBERT FARRINGTON, ENVIRONMENTAL MEDICINE, TOXICOLOGY. *Current Pos:* USPHS fel environ med, NY Univ Med Ctr, 70-71, assoc res scientist, 71-72, asst prof environ med, 72-77, res assoc prof, 77-79, ASSOC PROF, NY UNIV MED CTR, 79- *Personal Data:* b Crown Point, NY, Oct 20, 39; m 73. *Educ:* Cornell Univ, BS, 64, MS, 66; Pa State Univ, PhD(entom, air pollution), 70. *Prof Exp:* Res asst entom, Cornell Univ, 64-66. *Mem:* Sigma Xi; Soc Toxicol. *Res:* Toxicology of environmental contaminants with emphasis on food additives and air pollution. *Mailing Add:* 57 Old Forge Rd Tuxedo NY 10987

GUNSALUS, IRWIN CLYDE, BIOCHEMISTRY. *Current Pos:* SR RES BIOCHEMIST, ECOL DIV, ENVIRON PROTECTION AGENCY, 93- *Personal Data:* b Sully Co, SDak, June 29, 12; m 35, 51, 70; c 7. *Educ:* Cornell Univ, BS, 35, MS, 37, PhD(bact), 40. *Honors & Awards:* Mead Johnson Award, 46; Selman A Waksman, Nat Acad Sci, 82; William C Ruse Award, Am Soc Biol Chem, 86. *Prof Exp:* From asst instr to prof, Cornell Univ, 35-47; prof bact, Ind Univ, 47-50; prof microbiol, Univ Ill, Urbana-Champaign, 50-55, head, Dept Biochem, 55-65, prof biochem, 55-82, head, Ctr Advan Study, 65-66; asst secy gen, UN Indust Develop Orgn & founding dir, Int Ctr

Genetic Eng & Biotechnol, 86-89. *Concurrent Pos:* Guggenheim fel, 49, 59, 68; asst secy general, UN; dir, Int Ctr for Genetic Eng & Biotechnol, UN Indust Develop Orgn, Trieste, Italy & New Delhi, 86- *Mem:* Nat Acad Sci; AAAS; Am Soc Microbiol; Am Chem Soc; Am Soc Biol Chem (pres, 74-75); Fedn Am Socs Exp Biol (pres, 73-74); foreign mem Fr Sci Acad; Am Acad Arts & Sci; Am Acad Microbiol; Harvey Soc; Japanese Biochem Soc. *Res:* Biochemistry; microbiology; oxygenases-oxidases: reactions intermediates and mechanisms, carbon reactions cycles; P450 heme thiolate reaction center structure, function and genetics; keto acid lipoate: isolation, syntheses, SS-Sh2 reaction cycle and mechanism; amino acid-pyridoxal phosphate: synthesis, structure, enzymes, reaction and mechanism; effects of horizontal gene transfer and consortia competition on biosphere productivity. *Mailing Add:* 420 Roger Adams Lab Univ Ill Urbana IL 61801

GUNSALUS, ROBERT PHILIP, GENETIC REGULATION, ANAEROBIC MICROBIOLOGY. *Current Pos:* asst prof microbiol, Univ Calif, Los Angeles, 81-87, assoc mem, Molecular Biol Inst, 81-89, assoc prof, 87-91, MEM, MOLECULAR BIOL INST, UNIV CALIF, LOS ANGELES, 90-, PROF MICROBIOL, 92- *Personal Data:* b Ithaca, NY, Aug 24, 47. *Educ:* SDak State Univ, BS, 70; Univ Ill, MS, 72, PhD(microbiol), 77. *Prof Exp:* Fel molecular biol, Stanford Univ, 78-81. *Concurrent Pos:* Chmn, Gordon Conf Methanogenesis, 90; mem, NIH Microbiol Physiol Study Sect, 92-96; chmn, Div Gen Microbiol, Am Soc Microbiol, 93. *Mem:* Am Chem Soc; Am Soc Microbiol; AAAS; Am Soc Molecular Biol & Biochem. *Res:* Gene organization and regulation in the procaryotic and archaebacterial organisms; molecular aspects of nitrate sensing; control of change analysis cyle genes; control of anaerobic gene expression in E coli. *Mailing Add:* Dept Microbiol & Molecular Genetics Univ Calif Los Angeles CA 90095. *Fax:* 310-206-5231; *E-Mail:* robg@microbio.lifesci.ucla.edu

GUNSHOR, ROBERT LEWIS, ELECTRICAL ENGINEERING, SEMICONDUCTOR PHYSICS. *Current Pos:* prof elec eng, 68-69, DISTINGUISHED PROF ELEC ENG, PURDUE UNIV, 89- *Personal Data:* b New York, NY, Oct 28, 35; m 59; c 3. *Educ:* New York Univ, BEE, 58; Union Col, MSE, 62; Rensselaer Polytech Inst, PhD(elec eng), 65. *Prof Exp:* Engr, Microwave Assocs, 58-60; asst prof, Union Col, 60-63 & Cornell Univ, 65-66; assoc prof, Rensselaer Polytech Inst, 66-68. *Concurrent Pos:* Consult & vpres, Technol Assocs, 76- *Mem:* Fel Inst Elec & Electronics Engrs; fel Am Phys Soc; Sigma Xi. *Res:* Surface acoustic wave devices; solid state microwave devices; semiconductor devices; molecular beam epitaxy of semiconductors. *Mailing Add:* Sch Elec Eng 1285 Elec Eng Bldg Purdue Univ West Lafayette IN 47907

GUNST, SUSAN JANE, MUSCLE & PULMONARY PHYSIOLOGY. *Current Pos:* ASSOC PROF PHYSICS, IND UNIV, 89- *Educ:* Johns Hopkins Univ, PhD(physiol), 79. *Prof Exp:* Asst prof physiol, Mayo Clin & Found, 83-89. *Res:* Physiology of airway smooth muscle. *Mailing Add:* Ind Univ Sch Med 635 Barnhill Dr Indianapolis IN 46202-5120. *Fax:* 317-274-3318

GUNSUL, CRAIG J W, SOLID STATE PHYSICS. *Current Pos:* From asst prof to assoc prof, 69-88, PROF PHYSICS, WHITMAN COL, 88- *Personal Data:* b Seattle, Wash, May 16, 37; c 1. *Educ:* Reed Col, BA, 63; Univ Del, MS, 66, PhD(physics), 69. *Mem:* Sigma Xi. *Res:* Luminescence. *Mailing Add:* Dept Physics Whitman Col 345 Boyer Ave Walla Walla WA 99362

GUNTAKA, RAMAREDDY V, RETROVIRUSES-VIROLOGY, ONCOGENES. *Current Pos:* assoc prof, 83-87, PROF MOLECULAR MICROBIOL & IMMUNOL, UNIV MO, SCH MED, 87- *Personal Data:* b Bollapadu AP, India, Apr 1, 42; m 69, Swaruparani; c Padmaja & Srikar. *Educ:* Andhra Univ, BSc, 63; UP Agr Univ, MSc, 65; Kans State Univ, PhD(microbiol), 70. *Honors & Awards:* Siromani Award, Am Telugu Asn, 92. *Prof Exp:* Res asst prof, Univ Calif, San Francisco, 73-75; asst prof, Columbia Univ, NY, 75-83. *Concurrent Pos:* Totken expert, UN Develop Prog, Coun Sci & Indust Res, 92; sci adv, Cancer Res Ctr, 92-, Shantha Biotechnol, 93- *Mem:* Am Soc Microbiol; Fedn Am So Exp Biol; AAAS; NY Acad Sci. *Res:* Retroviruses and oncogenes; mechanism of carcinogenesis by environmental pollutants; role of src oncogine in the down regulation of collagen gene expression and molecular characterization of higher mobility group protein of malarial parasite. *Mailing Add:* Molecular Microbiol & Immunol Univ Mo Sch Med Columbia MO 65212-0001. *Fax:* 573-884-4536

GUNTER, CLAUDE RAY, BIOCHEMISTRY, MEDICAL DIAGNOSTIC TEST SYSTEMS. *Current Pos:* CONSULT, MED DIAG TESTS, DRY REAGENT STRIP TESTS, CRG CONSULT SERV, 85-; PRES, TOOLKITS REAGENT TEST DEVELOP, PRAGMATICS INC. *Personal Data:* b Benton, Ill, May 9, 39; c Claude R Jr, Tamera, Kathryn & Christopher. *Educ:* Southern Ill Univ, BA, 61; Northwestern Univ, PhD(chem), 66. *Prof Exp:* M L Bender staff fel enzym, Lab of Chem, Nat Inst Arthritis & Metab Dis, NIH, 65-68; staff scientist biochem, US Army Chem Warfare Ctr, Edgewood Arsenal, 66-68; dir, Urine Chem Lab, Ames Div, Miles Lab Inc, 68-85, Div Sci Serv & Spec Proj, 81-85,. *Concurrent Pos:* Assoc fac, Chem Dept, Ind Univ, South Bend, 75-76; prin, CRG Consult Assocs. *Mem:* Am Asn Clin Chem; Am Chem Soc. *Res:* Development of enzyme methods for clinical chemistry; dry reagent strip tests. *Mailing Add:* 29477 County Rd 16 Elkhart IN 46516

GUNTER, EDGAR JACKSON, JR, ROTOR DYNAMICS, LUBRICATION THEORY. *Current Pos:* assoc prof, 65-75, PROF MECH ENG, UNIV VA, 75- *Personal Data:* b Baltimore, Md, July 4, 34; m 55; c 3. *Educ:* Duke Univ, BSME, 56; Univ Pa, MS, 61, PhD(eng mech), 65. *Prof Exp:* Compressor design engr, Dresser-Clark, 56-59; sr res eng, Franklin Inst, 62-65. *Mem:* Sigma Xi; Am Soc Mech Engrs; Vibration Inst; Am Acad Mech. *Res:* Stability balancing and dynamic response of high speed turbomachinery; author or coauthor of over 100 publications; finite element analyses. *Mailing Add:* 1503 Gordon Ave Univ Va Charlottesville VA 22903

GUNTER, GORDON, ZOOLOGY. *Current Pos:* dir, 55-71, EMER DIR & PROF ZOOL, GULF COAST RES LAB, 72- *Personal Data:* b Goldonna, La, Aug 18, 09; m 32, 57; c 5. *Educ:* La State Norm Col, BA, 29; Univ Tex, MA, 31, PhD(zool), 45. *Prof Exp:* Asst shrimp invest, US Bur Fisheries, 31-33, asst oil pollution invest, 34-35, spec oyster investr, 35-36; com oyster bus, Tex, 36-37; jr aquatic biologist, Debris Dam Fisheries Surv, Calif, US Engrs, 38; marine biologist, Game, Fish & Oyster Comn, Tex, 39-44; res assoc marine fisheries, Inst Marine Sci, Univ Tex, 45-49, actg dir, 49, dir, 54-55. *Concurrent Pos:* Zoologist, La State Dept Conserv, 34; consult to fishery coordr, US Bur Fisheries, 41-45; vchmn comn on treatise on marine ecol, Nat Res Coun, 41-57; adv, Atlantic States Fisheries Comn, 46; vis prof zool, Univ Miami, 46-47; sr marine biologist, Scripps Inst, Univ Calif, 49; mem adv panel, La State Comn Wildlife & Fisheries, 53-55; mem, Gulf States Marine Fisheries Comn, 56-; mem bd sci consult, Wash Pollution Control Comn, 58-59; adv, Fla State Bd Conserv, 62-70; prof, Univ Miss & Miss State Univ, 68-; mem consult team, Impact of Corps Engrs Works on Coastal Ecol, 69-; consult comt deepwater ports, US Army Corps Engrs, 71- & Panama Canal Co, 73- *Mem:* Am Soc Limnol & Oceanog; Ecol Soc Am; Wildlife Soc; Am Soc Zool; Am Soc Naturalists. *Res:* Seasonal movements, distribution related to salinity, life histories and relative abundance of gulf animals; catastrophic mass mortalities; natural history of oysters, fishes, shrimp and marine mammals. *Mailing Add:* Gulf Coast Res Lab PO Box 7000 Ocean Springs MS 39564-7000

GUNTER, KARLENE KLAGES, MEMBRANE TRANSPORT, CALCIUM HOMEOSTASIS & CONTROL OF CELLULAR ATP SYNTHESIS. *Current Pos:* ASST PROF BIOPHYS, UNIV ROCHESTER, 73- *Personal Data:* b Pittsburgh, Pa, Aug 14, 39; m 61, Thomas; c Kerstin, Kari & Kelly. *Educ:* Mass Inst Technol, BS, 61; Univ Calif, Berkeley, PhD(nuclear physics), 68. *Mem:* Sigma Xi; Am Fedn Scientists. *Res:* Calcium hemostasis; calcium transport in mitochondria, submitochondrial particles and a reconstituted system; oxidative phosphorylation; how mitochondria are signaled by the cell to increase or decrease ATP synthesis. *Mailing Add:* Dept Biophys & Biochem Univ Rochester Rochester NY 14642

GUNTER, LAURIE M, GERONTOLOGY. *Current Pos:* RETIRED. *Personal Data:* b May 3, 1922; div; c Lara Elaine (Bonow) & Margo Alyce (Toner). *Educ:* Tenn A&I State Univ, BS, 48; Fisk Univ, MA, 52; Univ Chicago, PhD(human develop), 59. *Prof Exp:* Instr, 50-55, asst prof, 55-57, proj dir, Ment Health Training Grant, 57-58, actg dean, 57-58, dean, Meharry Med Col Sch Nursing, Nashville, 58-61; asst prof, nursing, 61-63, assoc prof, Univ Calif, Los Angeles, 63-65; prof, nursing, Ind Univ Med Ctr, Indianapolis, 65-66; assoc prof, 66-69, prof, Univ Wash, Seattle, 69-71; head, Dept Nursing, Pa State Univ, 71-75, prof, 71-87, emer prof, Nursing & Human Develop, 87. *Concurrent Pos:* Staff nurse, George W Hubbard Hosp, Nashville, 43-44, head nurse, 45-46, staff nurse, 46-47, supvr, 47-48. *Mem:* Inst Med-Nat Acad Sci; AAAS; Am Nurses Asn; Gerontol Soc; Am Asn Univ Prof; Am Pub Health Asn. *Res:* Numerous articles published in various journals. *Mailing Add:* 4008 47th Ave S Seattle WA 98118

GUNTER, THOMAS E, JR, SOLID STATE PHYSICS, BIOPHYSICS. *Current Pos:* Asst prof radiation biol & biophys, 70-77, assoc prof radiation biol & biophys, 77-93, PROF BIOPHYS, UNIV ROCHESTER, 93- *Personal Data:* b Montgomery, Ala, Mar 13, 38; m 61, Karlene Klages; c Kerstin, Kari, Kelly. *Educ:* Mass Inst Technol, BS, 60; Univ Calif, Berkeley, PhD(physics), 66. *Prof Exp:* Researcher, Boeing Aircraft Co, 60; res fel biophys, Donner Lab, Lawrence Radiation Lab, 66-68; NSF fel, Phys-Chem Inst, Uppsala Univ, 68-70. *Mem:* Biophys Soc. *Res:* Applications of physical spectroscopic techniques to problems of interest in bioenergetics. *Mailing Add:* Dept Biochem & Biophys Med Ctr Univ Rochester Rochester NY 14642. *Fax:* 716-275-6007

GUNTHER, GARY RICHARD, BIOCHEMISTRY, CELL BIOLOGY. *Current Pos:* ASST MEM BIOCHEM, ST JUDE CHILDREN'S RES HOSP, 78-; ASST PROF, DEPT PHYSICS & BIOPHYSICS, SCH MED, IND UNIV, 87- *Personal Data:* b Indianapolis, Ind, Mar 30, 48; m 69. *Educ:* Wabash Col, BA, 69; Rockefeller Univ, PhD(biochem), 75. *Prof Exp:* Fel cell biol, Sch Med, Yale Univ, 75-78. *Concurrent Pos:* USPHS fel, 75-77; asst prof anat, Ctr Health Sci, Univ Tenn, 80-84. *Mem:* Am Soc Cell Biol; Am Pancreatic Asn. *Res:* Mechanism of hormone-stimulated secretion in pancreatic acinar cells; role of calcium and cyclic nucleotides in mediating peptide hormone action; interaction of phorbol esters with normal and transformed pancreatic acinar cells. *Mailing Add:* 3734 Willowood Dr Indianapolis IN 46236-3501

GUNTHER, JAY KENNETH, RESEARCH ADMINISTRATION, BIOCHEMICAL PHARMACOLOGY. *Current Pos:* sr scientist, 70-73, sr investr, 73-77, ASSOC DIR DRUG REGULATORY AFFAIRS, MEAD JOHNSON & CO, 77- *Personal Data:* b Chicago, Ill, Dec 19, 38; m 66; c 2. *Educ:* Univ Notre Dame, BS, 61; Univ Ill, PhD(biochem), 66. *Prof Exp:* Trainee molecular biol, Univ Pa, 66-69, res assoc, 69-70. *Mem:* AAAS; Am Chem Soc. *Res:* Bacterial transformation; isolation and characterization of nucleases of Hemophilius influenzae; secretion of pancreatic hormones; control of lipid synthesis and degradation; regulatory affairs. *Mailing Add:* 409 Green Hill Rd Madison CT 06443-2305

GUNTHER, LEON, THEORETICAL CONDENSED MATTER PHYSICS. *Current Pos:* from asst prof to assoc prof, 65-78, PROF PHYSICS, TUFTS UNIV, 78- *Personal Data:* b New York, NY, Aug 22, 39; m 62, 79, Johanna E Cotter; c David, Benjamin, Rachel & Avi. *Educ:* City Col New York, BS, 60; Mass Inst Technol, PhD(physics), 64. *Prof Exp:* Res assoc physics, Mass Inst Technol, 64-65. *Concurrent Pos:* NATO fel, 66-67; vis prof, Technion & Tel Aviv Univs. *Mem:* Am Asn Univ Professors; Am Phys Soc. *Res:* Superconductivity; Brownian motion; mossbauer effect; phase transitions; magnetism; vacancy diffusion; solitons; macrscopic quantum tunneling. *Mailing Add:* Dept Physics Tufts Univ 4 Colby St Medford MA 02155. *Fax:* 617-627-3878; *E-Mail:* lgunther@pearl.tufts.edu

GUNTHER, RONALD GEORGE, ELECTROCHEMISTRY. *Current Pos:* STAFF RES SCIENTIST, GEN MOTORS RES LABS, 76- *Personal Data:* b St Paul, Minn, Jan 22, 33; m 66; c 2. *Educ:* Col St Thomas, BS, 55; Univ St Louis, PhL, 61; Iowa State Univ, MS, 64, PhD(phys chem), 68; Univ New Haven, MBA, 76. *Honors & Awards:* Bronze Medal, Am Inst Chemists, 55. *Prof Exp:* Res assoc fuel cells, Pratt & Whitney Aircraft Div, United Aircraft Corp, 68-70; head fuel cell res, Catalytic Technol Div, Pioneer Systs, 70-71; mgr electrochem systs, Electrochem Res & Develop Group, Yardney Elec Corp, 71-76. *Mem:* Electrochem Soc; Int Soc Electrochem. *Res:* Chemical kinetics; electrolytic solutions; electrode processes; electrochemistry; coordination compounds; battery systems; electrocatalysis; Langmuir-Blodgett films; fuel cells. *Mailing Add:* 3343 Troy Hill Dr Troy MI 48382

GUNTHER, WOLFGANG HANS HEINRICH, SELENIUM TELLURIUM CHEMISTRY. *Current Pos:* CONSULT 95- *Personal Data:* b Gifhorn, Ger, Mar 26, 31; nat US; m 58, Helge L Hoffmann; c Rita D & Bernard M. *Educ:* Brunswick Tech Univ, Cand Chem, 53; Univ Leeds, PhD(org chem), 58. *Prof Exp:* Demonstr org chem, Univ Leeds, 55-58; Brown Mem fel, Yale Univ, 58-59, from res asst to res assoc pharmacol, 59-66, asst prof, 66-67; scientist, Chem Res Lab, Xerox Corp, 67-68, mgr org & polymer chem, 68-80; res assoc & sr staff mem res lab, Sterling-Winthrop Inc, Eastman Kodak Co, 80-83, head, Sensitizing Dye Lab, 83-85, sr res investr, 87-90, sr fel, 90-95. *Mem:* Am Chem Soc; Royal Soc Chem; Sigma Xi. *Res:* Sensitizing dyes; synthesis of metabolically active compounds; synthesis and study of oxygen, sulphur and selenium isologs; electrophotographic imaging materials and processes; organotellurium chemistry. *Mailing Add:* 606 John Anthony Dr West Chester PA 19382-7191. *Fax:* 610-430-8623; *E-Mail:* whhg@aol.com, whhg@bellatlantic.net

GUNTHER-MOHR, GERARD ROBERT, PHYSICS. *Current Pos:* mem staff, Watson Sci Comput Lab, IBM Corp, 53-58, mgr semiconductor res dept, 58-61, dir solid state eng, 62-66, mgr tech develop & assurance, Components Div, 66-67, mgr tech & reliability develop, 67-69, asst to pres, Components Div, 69-74, MGR TECH DEVELOP, IBM CORP, 74- *Personal Data:* b Montclair, NJ, June 8, 22; m 50; c 3. *Educ:* Yale Univ, BS, 43; Columbia Univ, MA, 49, PhD(physics), 53. *Prof Exp:* Researcher, Manhattan Dist, Corps Engrs, US Army & Monsanto Chem Co, 44-46; asst physics, Columbia Univ, 47-50, lectr, 50. *Mem:* Fel Am Phys Soc; sr mem Inst Elec & Electronics Engrs; Sigma Xi. *Res:* Semiconductors. *Mailing Add:* 58 Constitution Hill W Princeton NJ 08540-6776

GUNTHEROTH, WARREN G, PEDIATRIC CARDIOLOGY, CARDIOVASCULAR PHYSIOLOGY. *Current Pos:* from instr to assoc prof, 58-69, head, Div Pediat Cardiol, 62-91, PROF PEDIAT, SCH MED, UNIV WASH, 69- *Personal Data:* b Hominy, Okla, July 27, 27; m 54, Ellie Haglund; c Kurt, Karl & Sten. *Educ:* Harvard Univ, MD, 52; Am Bd Pediat, dipl, 60, cert cardiol, 61. *Prof Exp:* Intern med, Peter Bent Brigham Hosp, Boston, Mass, 52-53; resident pediat, Children's Hosp, 55-56. *Concurrent Pos:* Fel pediat cardiol, Children's Hosp, 53-55; spec fel physiol, Sch Med, Univ Wash, 57; consult cardiol, King Co, Children's Orthop & USPHS Hosps, Seattle, 58- *Mem:* Am Physiol Soc; Biomed Eng Soc; Soc Exp Biol & Med; Am Col Cardiol; Soc Pediat Res. *Res:* Venous return; shock; crib death; physiology of cyanotic-congenital heart disease; electrocardiography; doppler echocardiography. *Mailing Add:* Dept Pediat Box 356320 Sch Med Univ Wash Seattle WA 98195. *Fax:* 206-543-3184; *E-Mail:* wgg@u.washington.edu

GUNTON, JAMES D, THEORETICAL PHYSICS, STATISTICAL MECHANICS. *Current Pos:* dean, Col Arts & Sci, 88-94, PROF PHYSICS, LEHIGH UNIV, 95- *Personal Data:* b Medford, Ore, Mar 28, 37; m 62, Margaret R Taylor; c Deborah J, James T & Michael A. *Educ:* Linfield Col, BA, 58; Oxford Univ, BA, 61; Stanford Univ, PhD(physics), 66. *Prof Exp:* Lectr physics, Univ Western Australia, 65-68; from vis asst prof to assoc prof physics, Temple Univ, 70-76, prof, 76-88; provost, Kenyon Col, 94-95. *Concurrent Pos:* Vis scientist, Kyoto Univ, US-Japan Coop Sci Prog, NSF, 74-75, Univ Geneva, 81, Kernforschungsanlage, WGer, 82, Inst Laue Langevin, Grenoble, 82. *Mem:* Fel Am Phys Soc; Sigma Xi. *Res:* Equilibrium and non-equilibrium theory of first and second order phase transitions; pattern formation in nonlinear nonequilibrium systems. *Mailing Add:* Dept Physics Lehigh Univ Bethlehem PA 18015. *Fax:* 610-758-5730; *E-Mail:* jdg4@lehigh.edu

GUNTON, RAMSAY WILLIS, MEDICINE. *Current Pos:* prof, 66-93, active staff, 72-93, EMER PROF MED, UNIV WESTERN ONT, 93- *Personal Data:* b Lexington, Ky, July 30, 22; Can citizen; m 51; c 4. *Educ:* Univ Western Ont, MD, 45; Oxford Univ, DPhil, 49; FRCP(C), 52. *Honors & Awards:* Hon Fel, Royal Australosian Col Physicians, 88. *Prof Exp:* Sr med res fel, Nat Res Coun Can, 52-56; assoc in med, Fac Med, Univ Toronto, 53-63, assoc prof med, prof therapeut & head dept, 63-66. *Concurrent Pos:* Med res assoc, Ont Heart Found, 56-63; physician, Toronto Gen Hosp, 57-66; mem teaching staff, Victoria Hosp, 66-72; mem, Med Coun Can, 78-; mem coun, Royal Col Physicians & Surgeons; mem coun clin cardiol, Am Heart Asn, Can; pres, Royal Col Physicians & Surgeons, Can, 86-88. *Mem:* Am Fedn Clin Res; fel Am Col Physicians; Can Med Asn; Can Soc Clin Invest (vpres, 61); Can Cardiovasc Soc. *Res:* Clinical investigation; heart disease; therapeutics. *Mailing Add:* 1008 Harrison Ave London ON N5Y 2B2 Can

GUNZBURGER, MAX DONALD, numerical analysis, computational mathematics, for more information see previous edition

GUO, HUA, CHEMISTRY. *Current Pos:* ASST PROF CHEM, UNIV TOLEDO, 90- *Personal Data:* b Sichuan, People's Repub China, Aug 20, 62. *Educ:* Chengdu Inst Electronic Eng, BS, 82; Sichuan Univ, MS, 85; Sussex Univ, PhD(chem), 88. *Prof Exp:* Res assoc chem, Northwestern Univ, 88-90. *Mem:* Am Chem Soc; Am Phys Soc. *Res:* Photodissociation and reaction dynamics calculations. *Mailing Add:* Dept Chem Univ Toledo Toledo OH 43606

GUO, JAMES ZHIQIANG, RELIABILITY ENGINEERING, ADHESION SCIENCE. *Current Pos:* MEM TECH STAFF, HEWLETT-PACKARD CO, 95- *Personal Data:* b Jiannin, Fujian, China, Aug 12, 57; m, Mannu Luo; c Yao & Helena. *Educ:* Nanjing Inst Chem Technol, BS, 82; Zhejiang Univ, MS, 85; Ore State Univ, MS, 93, PhD(mech eng), 94. *Prof Exp:* Lectr reliability & fatigue, Fuzhou Univ, 85-89; consult, Precision Measurement & Instrument Co, 94-95. *Mem:* Am Soc Mech Engrs. *Res:* Fatigue and fracture of pressure vessel; characterization on nickle-titanium superconducting materials; mechanical measurement and modeling on aerospace composite; measuring and modeling thin film stress in electronic devices; investigate adhesion and delamination of polymer adhesive. *Mailing Add:* 1214 NE Conroy Pl Corvallis OR 97330

GUO, JIAN ZHONG, molecular & cellular endocrinology, for more information see previous edition

GUO, PEIXUAN X, VIRAL ASSEMBLY, MOLECULAR VIROLOGY. *Current Pos:* asst prof, 90-93, ASSOC PROF MOLECULAR VIROL & PROJ DIR, PURDUE UNIV, 94- *Personal Data:* m 83, Lini Lu; c Yinyin & Sida. *Educ:* SChina Agr Univ, MS, 83; Univ Minn, PhD(microbiol), 87. *Honors & Awards:* First Award, NIH, 93; Pfizer Distinguished Fac Award Res Excellence, 95. *Prof Exp:* Res scientist virol, NY State Dept Health, 87-88; vis scientist, NIH, 88-89. *Concurrent Pos:* Vis prof molecular virol, Inst Genetics, Chinese Acad Sci, 94-, adv & vis prof, Inst Microbiol, 96-; vis prof molecular biol, SChina Agr Univ, 93- *Mem:* Am Soc Virol; Am Soc Biochem & Molecular Virol; Am Soc Microbiol; AAAS; RNA Soc; Chinese Bioscientists Am. *Res:* Mechanism of viral capsid assembly and genomic DNA packaging involving a ribozyme RNA; construction of gene delivery systems; development of particle or molecular vaccines and methods for antiviral therapy. *Mailing Add:* Purdue Univ West Lafayette IN 47906. *Fax:* 765-496-1795; *E-Mail:* guo@vet.purdue.edu

GUO, QUANXIN, ENGINEERING MECHANICS. *Current Pos:* SR ENGR, TERRATEK INC, 92- *Personal Data:* b Henan Province, China, Sept 8, 62; m 89, Ying Wei; c Emily L. *Educ:* Lanzhou Univ, China, BS, 83; Huazhong Univ, China, MS, 85; Northwestern Univ, PhD(mech eng), 91. *Prof Exp:* Lectr eng mech, Huazhong Univ, China, 85-87; res assoc mat sci, Northwestern Univ, 91-92. *Concurrent Pos:* Lectr eng mech, Huazhong Univ, 87-92. *Mem:* Soc Petrol Engrs. *Res:* Applying fracture mechanics and materials science to failure analysis such as fatigue and failure in microelectronics; applying engineering mechanics and physics to petroleum such as wellbore stability, subsidence, sand production, hydraulic fracturing waste disposal. *Mailing Add:* 400 Wakara Way Salt Lake City UT 84108. *Fax:* 801-584-2432

GUO, SHUMEI, CARDIOVASCULAR EPIDEMIOLOGY, HUMAN GROWTH & DEVELOPMENT. *Current Pos:* RES SCIENTIST & ASSOC PROF, DIV HUMAN BIOL, DEPT COMMUNITY HEALTH, SCH MED, WRIGHT STATE UNIV, 84- *Personal Data:* b Taiwan, Sept 8, 54; m 78; c 1. *Educ:* Nat Taiwan Univ, BPH, 76; State Univ NY, Stony Brook, MS, 80; Univ Pittsburgh, PhD(biostatist), 83. *Honors & Awards:* First Independent Res Support & Transition Award, NIH. *Prof Exp:* Consult statistician, cancer res, Info Mgt Servs, 83-84. *Mem:* Am Statist Asn; Soc Clin Trials. *Res:* Growth, body composition and risk factors; biased estimation; curve fitting and mathematical modelling; survival analysis. *Mailing Add:* 2615 Woodbluff Lane Spring Valley OH 45370-9551. *Fax:* 937-767-6922

GUO, YAN-SHI, CANCER BIOLOGY. *Current Pos:* ASST PROF, GASTROINTESTINAL & ENDOCRINOL, DEPT SURG, MED BR, UNIV TEX, GALVESTON, 84- *Personal Data:* b Jie-Yang, Kwangtung, China, Aug 16, 43; m 70, Gui-Fang Jin; c Jun & Yu. *Educ:* Beijing Med Univ, MD, 64, MS(physiol), 68 & MS(endocrinol), 80. *Prof Exp:* Surgeon, Chen-Guang Hosp, Szechuan, 68-78; instr physiol, Beijing Med Univ, 81-84. *Concurrent Pos:* John Sealy mem endowment award, 92 & 93-94. *Mem:* Chinese Physiol Asn; AAAS; Am Phys Soc; Am Gastrointestinal Asn; Am Endocrine Soc. *Res:* Physiological actions of gastrointestinal hormones and their intracellular mechanisms; regulation of gastrointestinal hormones release; relationship between gastrointestinal hormones and gastrointestinal cancers; insulin-like growth factor in cancer growth and metastasis. *Mailing Add:* Univ Tex Med Br E33 Galveston TX 77550. *Fax:* 409-772-6368

GUPTA, AJAYA KUMAR, NUCLEAR POWER PLANTS, STRUCTURAL ENGINEERING. *Current Pos:* assoc prof, 80-83, PROF CIVIL ENG, NC STATE UNIV, 83-, DIR, CTR NUCLEAR POWER PLANT STRUCT, EQUIP & PIPING, 93- *Personal Data:* b Allahabad, India, Sept 27, 44; US citizen; m 92, Kristine Lanning; c Aparna M, Suvarna (Sona), Sasha Lanning, Kirstin Lanning. *Educ:* Univ Roorkee, BE, 66, ME, 68; Univ Ill, PhD(civil eng), 71. *Honors & Awards:* Huber Res Prize, Am Soc Civil Engrs, 82. *Prof Exp:* Supvr, struct eng, Sargent & Lundy, 71-76; sr res engr, IIT Res Inst, 76-79; assoc prof civil eng, Ill Inst Technol, 79-80. *Concurrent Pos:* Adj assoc prof, Ill Inst Technol, 77-79; adv, Comt Dynamic Response Mats Subjected High Strain Rate Loadings, Nat Mats Adv Bd, Nat Acad Sci, 77-78; vis scholar, Univ Ill, 78; consult, Zurn Indust, 79-, Sargent & Lundy, 79-, IIT Res Inst, 79- & Res Triangle Res Inst, 81-; prin investr, NSF grants, 79-81, 79-82, 82-85 & 85-; chmn, Energy Div, Am Soc Civil Engrs, 90-91. *Mem:* Am Soc Civil Engrs; Am Concrete Inst; Earthquake Eng Res Inst; Am Soc Mech Engrs; Int Asn Shell & Spatial Struct; Int Asn Struct Mech Reactor Technol. *Res:* Nuclear power plants; seismic analysis and design: concrete shells, low-rise buildings; structural analysis and design; author one book. *Mailing Add:* Civil Eng & Ctr Nuclear Power Plant Struct Equip & Piping NC State Univ Raleigh NC 27695-7908. *Fax:* 919-515-7908

GUPTA, ALANKAR, AIRCRAFT LIFE SUPPORT SYSTEMS, AIRCRAFT PROTECTIVE SYSTEMS. *Current Pos:* Sr res engr specialist, 67-86, PRIN ENGR, BOEING AIRPLANE CO, 86- *Personal Data:* b India, Aug 26, 40; US citizen; m, Louise C Hollmann; c Ramon R & Maya R. *Educ:* Delhi Univ, India, BSc, 59; London Univ, BSc, 64; McGill Univ, MS, 68. *Mem:* Fel Am Soc Mech Engrs. *Res:* Development of aircraft life support of protective systems. *Mailing Add:* 18612 Fourth Ave SW Seattle WA 98166. *Fax:* 425-294-7434; *E-Mail:* alankar.gupta@boeing.com

GUPTA, AMITAVA, photochemistry, physical organic chemistry, for more information see previous edition

GUPTA, ARJUN KUMAR, MULTIVARIATE STATISTICAL ANALYSIS. *Current Pos:* assoc prof math, 76-78, PROF MATH & STATIST, BOWLING GREEN STATE UNIV, 78- *Personal Data:* b Purkazi, India, July 10, 38; m 67, Meera; c Alka, Mita & Nisha. *Educ:* Banaras Hindu Univ, BSc & dipl, 57; Univ Poona, BSc Hons, 58, MSc, 59; Purdue Univ, PhD(statist), 68. *Honors & Awards:* Iscamp Res Award, 90. *Prof Exp:* Lectr statist, Agra Univ, 62 & Benaras Hindu Univ, 62-63; asst prof math, Univ Ariz, 68-71; asst prof statist, Univ Mich, Ann Arbor, 71-76; vis fac, Ohio State Univ, Univ Mich, Univ Sao Paulo, Al-Mustansariya Univ, Univ Rajasthan. *Concurrent Pos:* Consult, Univ Ariz, 68-71, Semiconductor Prod Div, Motorola Inc, 69; UN statist consult, 81; vis lectr, Soc Indust & Appl Math, 81; consult, Ed Math Rev, 73-76; chmn, Dept Math & Stat, Bowling Green State Univ, 85-87. *Mem:* Inst Math Statist; fel Am Statist Asn; Royal Statist Soc; Indian Statist Asn; Int Statist Inst. *Res:* Multivariate statistical analysis; classification models; central and non-central distribution problems in multivariate analysis; distribution of second elementary symmetric function and of likelihood ration criterion in the real and complex case; contingency tables; correlation tables; applied statistics. *Mailing Add:* Dept Math & Statist Bowling Green State Univ Bowling Green OH 43403-0221. *E-Mail:* gupta@bgnet.bgu.edu

GUPTA, ASHWANI KUMAR, FUEL TECHNOLOGY, ENVIORNMENTAL MECHANICAL ENGINGEERING. *Current Pos:* assoc prof, 83-87, PROF MECH ENG, UNIV MD, 88- *Personal Data:* b India, Oct 23, 48; US citizen. *Educ:* Panjab Univ, BS, 66; Univ Southampton, UK, MS, 70; Univ Sheffield, UK, PhD(combustion) & DSc, 73. *Hon Degrees:* DSc, Univ Sheffield, 86. *Honors & Awards:* Energy Systs Award, Am Inst Aeronaut & Astronaut, 80. *Prof Exp:* Res engr mech eng, Int Combustion, 67-71; res asst chem eng, Univ Sheffield, UK, 71-73, res assoc & independent res worker chem eng, 73-76; res staff chem eng, Mass Inst Technol, 77-82. *Concurrent Pos:* Consult, NFK Japan, 76, various industs & orgn, 80- *Mem:* Fel Am Inst Aeronaut & Astronaut; Am Soc Mech Eng; Combustion Inst; fel Inst Energy UK; Soc Automotive Engrs. *Res:* Combustion and pollution; fuel sprays; laser diagnostics; alternate fuels; coal, gas, liquid fuels; swirl flows; gas turbine combustion; internal combustion engines; furnaces, modeling, fires, boilers; hazardous waste incineration; waste thermal destruction. *Mailing Add:* Dept Mech Eng Univ Md College Park MD 20742

GUPTA, AYODHYA P, ENTOMOLOGY, IMMUNOLOGY. *Current Pos:* res assoc, Rutgers Univ, 64-66, from asst prof to assoc prof, 66-72, dir grad prog, 81-86, PROF ENTOM, RUTGERS UNIV, 73- *Personal Data:* b India, July 1, 28; m 67, Godaveri Rawat; c Rajeew & Anita. *Educ:* St Andrew's Col, India, BSc, 50; Benares Hindu Univ, MSc, 53; Univ BC, MSc, 61; Univ Idaho, PhD(entom), 64. *Honors & Awards:* Pride of India Award, BS Sanstha, 93. *Prof Exp:* Lectr zool, Besant Col, India, 56-57; asst entomologist, Pub Health Dept, Filaria Unit, 58-59. *Concurrent Pos:* Ed-in-chief, Int J Insect Morphol & Embryol, 71- & Recent Advan Comp Arthropod Morphol, Physiol & Develop, 86-; FAO consult, 74 & 82. *Mem:* AAAS; hon mem Arthropodan Embryol Soc Japan; fel Entom Soc India; Entom Soc Am; Royal Entom Soc London; Am Asn Univ Prof; Electron Microscopy Soc Am; NY Acad Sci. *Res:* Insect morphology and physiology with particular interest in hemocytes; hormones and pheromones, insect ultrastructure; arthropod immunity. *Mailing Add:* Dept Entom Rutgers Univ New Brunswick NJ 08903-0231. *Fax:* 732-932-7229

GUPTA, BHUPENDER SINGH, TEXTILE PHYSICS. *Current Pos:* res instr textile physics, Sch Textiles, NC State Univ, 63-66, from asst to assoc prof textile eng, chem & sci, 66-79, asst head & grad adminr textile eng & sci, 84-90, PROF TEXTILE ENG CHEM & SCI, SCH TEXTILES, NC STATE UNIV, 79-, ASSOC HEAD UNDERGRAD PROG, 90- *Personal Data:* b Delhi, India, Mar 29, 37; m 67, Vasudha; c Sumedha, Apurve & Anoopum. *Educ:* Panjab Univ, India, BSc, 58; Univ Manchester, PhD(textile physics), 63. *Honors & Awards:* Fulbright Lectr Award, India, 85. *Prof Exp:* Supvr prod textile yarns, Spinning Dept, Modi Spinning & Weaving Mills, India, 59-60. *Concurrent Pos:* Develop engr, Fiber Industs, 75. *Mem:* Sigma Xi; Fiber Soc; Brit Textile Inst; Am Chem Soc; Am Asn Textile Technol; fel Textile Inst; Tech Asn Pulp & Paper Indust. *Res:* Knot characteristics of surgical sutures; fiber, yarn and fabrics structure and mechanics; high energy irradiation cross-linking and curing; absorbent non-woven structures; arterial grafts; inter-fiber friction in textiles; impact of textiles on indoor air quality. *Mailing Add:* Col Textiles NC State Univ Raleigh NC 27695-8301. *Fax:* 919-515-6532

GUPTA, BRIJ MOHAN, PHARMACY, CHEMISTRY. *Current Pos:* at RIJ PHARMACEUT CORP, NY. *Personal Data:* b Muzaffar Nagar, India, Mar 16, 47; m 69; c 2. *Educ:* Birla Inst Technol & Sci, Pilani, India, BS, 66; Panjab Univ, MS, 68; Columbia Univ, PhD(pharm), 73. *Prof Exp:* Mfg chemist pharmaceut mfg, Allodial Chem, Meerut, India, 68-69; sr scientist, pharmaceut res & develop, Schering Corp, Bloomfield, 73-, mgr lab res serv, Kenilworth, 80- *Concurrent Pos:* Adj asst prof, Arnold & Marie Schwartz Col Pharm, Long Island Univ, NY, 77- *Mem:* Am Pharmaceut Asn; Am Chem Soc. *Res:* Pharmaceutical formulation research, physical pharmacy; rheology, surface chemistry. *Mailing Add:* 4890 Shasta Dr Nashville TN 37211

GUPTA, CHAITAN PRAKASH, MATHEMATICAL ANALYSIS. *Current Pos:* PROF & CHMN, DEPT MATH, UNIV NEV, RENO, 92- *Personal Data:* b India, Apr 21, 39; m 65; c 3. *Educ:* Univ Delhi, BA, 58, MA, 60; Univ Rochester, PhD(math), 67. *Prof Exp:* Lectr math, Ramjas Col, Delhi, 60-62; asst prof, Univ Va, 66-69; from asst prof to prof math, Northern Ill Univ, 69-92. *Concurrent Pos:* Instr, Univ Chicago, 67-69; NSF res grant, 71-72. *Mem:* Am Math Soc; Math Asn Am. *Res:* Nonlinear analysis; numerical methods for partial differential equations. *Mailing Add:* Dept Math Univ Nev 084 Reno NV 89557. *E-Mail:* gupta@math.umn.edu

GUPTA, DEVENDRA, MATERIALS SCIENCE. *Current Pos:* EMER STAFF SCIENTIST, T J WATSON RES CTR, IBM CORP, 68- *Personal Data:* b Nagina, India, Feb 15, 31; nat US; m 63, Sudha; c Chitra, Sudhir & Deuratna. *Educ:* Univ Delhi, BSc, 50; Banaras Hindu Univ, BSc, 54; NY Univ, MS, 57; Univ Ill, Urbana, PhD(metall), 61. *Prof Exp:* Sr sci officer, Nat Metall Lab, Govt India, 61-63; reader phys metall, Banaras Hindu Univ, 63; asst chief indust res develop, Planning Comn, Govt India, 63-65; fel metall & solid state physics, Univ Ill, Urbana, 65-68. *Concurrent Pos:* Adj prof phys & eng metall, Polytech Inst NY, 78-79; adj prof, Dept Mat Sci & Eng, Lehigh Univ, Pa. *Mem:* Sigma Xi; fel Am Phys Soc; Minerals Metals & Mat Soc. *Res:* Internal friction in metals and alloys; diffusion in materials; ductility and fracture; mass transport in thin films for VLSI applications; epitaxy of thin films; ion implantation; materials for electronic packaging; defects in materials. *Mailing Add:* 3 Morningside Ct Ossining NY 10562. *Fax:* 914-945-2141; *E-Mail:* gupta@watson.ibm.com

GUPTA, DHARAM VIR, PROCESS DEVELOPMENT, ANTIBIOTICS. *Current Pos:* Res engr, Am Cyanamid Co, 74-78, group leader & tech mgr, 79-83, prod mgr, 84-89, SR RES SCIENTIST, AM CYANAMID CO, 89- *Personal Data:* b New Delhi, India, Sept 4, 45; US citizen; m 81, Shobha Karwan; c Mona A, Tina K & Neil H. *Educ:* Univ Delhi, India, BSc(hons), 65; Indian Inst Technol, Kharagpur, BTech(hons), 68; Univ Waterloo, Ont, MS, 70; Worcester Polytech Inst, PhD(chem eng), 75. *Mem:* Am Soc Pharmaceut Engrs; Am Inst Chem Engrs; Am Chem Soc. *Res:* Heterogeneous catalysis; polymer engineering; reactor design; pharmaceutical plant design, trouble shooting and start up. *Mailing Add:* 1937 W Main St Stamford CT 06904

GUPTA, GIAN CHAND, WATER POLLUTION, AIR POLLUTION STRESS ON PLANTS. *Current Pos:* lectr environ sci, 77-78, from asst prof to assoc prof, 79-90, PROF ENVIRON SCI, UNIV MD EASTERN SHORE, 90-, ACTG CHMN NATURAL SCI, 93- *Personal Data:* b Delhi, India, Oct 10, 39; m 72, Hirdesh Bindu; c Tarra & Suneal. *Educ:* Panjab Univ, BSc, 59, BT, 60; Vikaram Univ, MS, 62; Univ Roorkee, PhD(chem), 67. *Prof Exp:* Jr sci asst soil chem, Defense Sci Lab, Delhi, India, 62-63; jr res fel chem, Univ Roorkee, India, 63-66; sr res fel, Cent Rd Res Inst, New Delhi, India, 67-68; res assoc civil eng, Univ Miss, 68-69; assoc prof chem, Rust Col, Miss, 69-70; dir environ health, Medgar Evers Comprehensive Health Ctr, Fayette, Miss, 70-72; dir environ health & educ, Jackson Hinds Comprehensive Health Ctr, Utica, Miss, 72-77. *Concurrent Pos:* Consult res soil chemist, Alcorn A&M Univ, 75-77; guide prof colloid, soil & environ sci, World Open Univ, 75-83; vis scientist, NSF, India, 92. *Mem:* Am Chem Soc; Am Soc Agron; Nat Environ Health Asn; fel Pollution Res Soc India. *Res:* Environmental chemistry/soil science; physio-chemical properties of transformed clay minerals, water and wastewater recycling through land application; disposal of energy related pollutants; toxicology of chicken liter; physiological and biochemical changes in crops following exposure to air pollutants. *Mailing Add:* Dept Natural Sci Univ Md Eastern Shore Princess Anne MD 21853. *Fax:* 410-651-7739; *E-Mail:* ggupta@umes-bird.umd.edu

GUPTA, GOUTAM, COATINGS, ORGANIC-POLYMER. *Current Pos:* sr scientist, Central Res Div, Sherman Williams, 81-84, group leader, 83-84, dir, New Prod Div, 85-88, DIR, APPL RES, CHEM COATING DIV, SHERWIN-WILLIAMS, 88- *Personal Data:* b India, Apr 17, 45; US citizen; m 73; c 2. *Educ:* Jadaupur Univ, Calcutta, MSc, 65; Catholic Univ Am, PhD(org chem) 72. *Prof Exp:* Res assoc, Univ Va, 72-74; chemist, Res Triangle Inst, 74-76; sr res chemist, Corp Res-Ferro Corp, 76-81. *Mem:* Am Chem Soc; Fed Soc Coating Tech. *Res:* New cure systems, polymer, oligomer synthesis for application to high solids coatings uncured coatings development. *Mailing Add:* W R Grace Res Ctr 7500 Grace Dr Bldg 2 Columbia MD 21044

GUPTA, JIWAN DAS, TRAFFIC ENGINEERING, TRANSPORTATION PLANNING & DESIGN. *Current Pos:* PROF CIVIL ENG, UNIV TOLEDO, 80- *Personal Data:* m 69, Meena; c Geetika & Ruchika. *Educ:* Univ Waterloo, PhD(transp eng), 78. *Prof Exp:* Transp engr, MVRPC, 79-80. *Concurrent Pos:* Dir, Creativity & Prob Solving Ctr, Univ Toledo. *Mem:* Inst Transp Engrs; Transp Res Bd; Am Soc Eng Educ; Am Soc Civil Engrs. *Res:* Various aspects of transportation engineering; traffic engineering, planning and pavement design. *Mailing Add:* Civil Eng Dept Univ Toledo Toledo OH 43606. *Fax:* 419-537-2805; *E-Mail:* jgupta@uoft02.utoledo.edu

GUPTA, KAILASH CHANDRA, PROTEIN SYNTHESIS IN EUKARYOTES, STRUCTURE FUNCTION RELATIONSHIP OF RNA POLYMERASE PROTEINS OF PARAMYXOVIRUSES. *Current Pos:* from asst prof to assoc prof, 85-95, PROF VIROL, RUSH MED COL, 95- *Personal Data:* b Madhya Pradesh, India, Sept 6, 43; US citizen; m 68, Ahilya; c Rajesh & Ram. *Educ:* Vikram Univ Ujjain, India, BS, 64, MS 66; Indian Inst Sci, Bangalore, India, PhD(cellbiol), 71. *Prof Exp:* Lectr bot, Banavas Hindu Univ, Varanasi, India, 71-73, Vikram Univ, Ujjain, India, 73-74; UNESCO fel, Biol Res Ctr, Szeged, Hungary, 74-75; fel, Ind Univ, Bloomington, 75-78; res fel, Univ Ala, Birmingham, 78-80; sr res asst, St Judes Childrens Res Hosp, Memphis, 80-82, asst mem, 82-85. *Concurrent Pos:* Prin investr, Am Cancer Soc, 87-, Am Heart Asn, 89-, NIH, 91-; Tokten consult, UN Develop Prog, Anna Univ, Madras, 91-; fel, Japanese Soc Prom Sci, Hokkaido Univ, Sapporo, Japan, 92-; mem, Virol Study Sect, NIH, 96- *Mem:* Am Soc Microbiol; Am Soc Virol; Am Soc Biochem & Molecular Biol; Protein Soc; Am Asn Cancer Res; Am Heart Asn. *Res:* Defining the mechanisms by which viruses usurp the cellular protein systhesizing machinery; functions and structures of viral polymerase proteins. *Mailing Add:* 619 S Wenonah Ave Oak Park IL 60304. *Fax:* 312-942-2808

GUPTA, KRISHANA CHANDARA, MICROBIOLOGY TUMOR BIOLOGY, IMMUNOCHEMISTRY & HYBRIDOMA TECHNOLOGY. *Current Pos:* res mem, 75-81, RES SCIENTIST, CONNAUGHT RES INST, CONNAUGHT LABS LTD, 81- *Personal Data:* b Jammu, Kashmir, India, Feb 22, 27; m 59; c 4. *Educ:* Punjab Univ, BSc, 45; Univ Montreal, MSc, 57, PhD(bact), 59. *Prof Exp:* Head, Dept Microbiol, Drug Res Lab, Univ Jammu & Kashmir, 47-53; res officer tuberc, Patel Chest Dis Inst, Univ Delhi, 53-55; asst dir appl microbiol & antibiotics, Regional Res Lab, Univ Jammu & Kashmir, 60-68; Muskoka Hosp Fund Res Asn fel, 68-71; res assoc immunochem of tuberculo-proteins, Connaught Med Res Lab, Univ Toronto, 71-75. *Concurrent Pos:* Chmn, Session New Antibiotics, Intersci Cong Antimicrobial Agents & Chemother, NYC, 64; prof microbiol & biotechnol, Ryerson Polytech Inst, Toronto, 83-92; consult, Dept Path, Women's Col Hosp, Univ Toronto, Ont, 93- *Mem:* Fel NY Acad Sci; Am Soc Microbiol; Can Soc Microbiol. *Res:* Infection promoting factors; genetic studies in Bacillus Calmette-Guerin; immunochemistry of tuberculo-proteins; taxonomic studies of streptomycetes; antibacterial and antifungal antibiotics; electron microscopic studies of effect of antibiotics on the cytology of tubercule bacilli; protective antigens from pathogenic microorganisms; immunology; development of marine and human monoclonal antibodies to bacterial and viral antigens; anti-idiotype antibodies as vaccines; human monoclonal antibodies to breast carcinoma; tumor biology. *Mailing Add:* 21 Lowbank Ct Toronto ON M2M 3A5 Can

GUPTA, KRISHNA CHANDRA, MECHANISM SYNTHESIS, INDUSTRIAL ROBOTS. *Current Pos:* From asst prof to assoc prof, Univ Ill, Chicago, 74-84, dir grad studies, 82-84, actg dept head, 91-92, PROF MECH ENG, UNIV ILL, CHICAGO, 84- *Personal Data:* b Sept 24, 48; US citizen. *Educ:* Indian Inst Technol, Kanpur, India, BTech, 69; Case Inst Technol, MS, 71; Stanford Univ, PhD(mech eng), 74. *Honors & Awards:* Henry Hess Award, Am Soc Mech Engrs, 79. *Concurrent Pos:* Prin investr, Res Bd Grant, Univ Ill, NSF Grant & US Army Res Off Contracts; assoc ed, J Mech Design, Am Soc Mech Engrs, 81-82; gen conf chmn, Am Soc Mech Engrs, Design Tech Conf, Chicago, 90. *Mem:* Fel Am Soc Mech Engrs. *Res:* Mechanical engineering design; mechanisms; industrial robots; design optimization. *Mailing Add:* Univ Ill Chicago Dept Mech Eng M/C 251 2039 ERE 842 W Taylor St Chicago IL 60607-7022. *E-Mail:* k.c.gupta@uic.edu

GUPTA, KRISHNA MURARI, FUEL CELL ELECTRODES, POROSITY MEASUREMENT. *Current Pos:* PRES, POROUS MAT INC, 78- *Personal Data:* b Kanpur, India, Sept 11, 49; m 76; c 2. *Educ:* Indian Inst Technol, Kanpur, BTech, 70; Mass Inst Technol, SM, 72, ScD, 76. *Prof Exp:* Assoc, Columbia Univ, 76 & Cornell Univ, 76-78. *Mem:* Am Ceramic Soc; NY Acad Sci. *Res:* Development of novel fuel cell electrodes and porosity measurement techniques; creep resistant ceramics. *Mailing Add:* Cornell Univ Res Park Bldg 4 83 Brown Rd Ithaca NY 14850

GUPTA, KULDIP CHAND, COMPUTER-AIDED DESIGN OF MICROWAVE CIRCUITS & MICROSTRIP ANTENNAS. *Current Pos:* PROF ELEC ENG, UNIV COLO, BOULDER, 85- *Personal Data:* b India, Oct 6, 40; m 71; c 3. *Educ:* Punjab Univ, BSc, 58; Indian Inst Sci, Bangalore, BE, 61, ME 62; Birla Inst Sci & Technol, PhD(electronics eng), 69. *Prof Exp:* Res fel, Indian Inst Sci, Bangalore, 63-64; asst prof elec eng, Punjab Eng Col, 64-65; sr res fel, Cent Electronics Eng Res Inst, 65-68; asst prof, Birla Inst Technol & Sci, 68-69 & Indian Inst Technol, Kanpur, 69-75, prof, 75-84. *Concurrent Pos:* Coordr, Advan Ctr Electronics Systs, Indian Inst Technol, 71-79; vis assoc prof, Univ Waterloo, Can, 75-76; vis prof, Fed Polytech Univ Lausanne, Switz, 76, Tech Univ Denmark, 76-77, Eidgenossische Tech Univ, Zurich, 79, Univ Kans, 82-83 & Univ Colo, 83-84; res coordr, Ctr Microwave & Millimeter-Ware Cad, NSF, 87-; ed, Int J Microwave-Millimeter-Wave Computer-Aided Eng, 90- *Mem:* Fel Inst Elec & Electronics Engrs; Int Union Radio Sci; Electromagnetics Acad. *Res:* Computer-aided design techniques for microstrip circuits and microstrip antennas; author of five books and 140 publications. *Mailing Add:* Dept Elec Eng Univ Colo Box 425 Boulder CO 80309

GUPTA, MADAN MOHAN, COMPUTER SCIENCE, CONTROL ENGINEERING. *Current Pos:* from lectr to assoc prof, 67-78, PROF CONTROLS, UNIV SASK, 78-, DIR, INTEL SYSTS RES LAB, 80- *Personal Data:* b Lansdowne, India, Apr 10, 36; m 64, Suman; c Anu, Ashu & Amit. *Educ:* Univ Rajasthan, BE, 61, ME, 62; Univ Warwick, Eng, PhD(controls), 67. *Prof Exp:* Lectr, Univ Roorkee, 62-64. *Concurrent Pos:* Vis prof, Whiteshell Nuclear Res Plant, 68, Defense Res Estab, 71-, Univ BC, 75-76 & Europ Ctr Peace & Develop, Univ Peace, UN; res grant, Nat Res Coun Can, 69-, Med Res Coun Can, 75- & Defence Res Bd Can, 70-76; sr mem, Comt Biol Signal Processing, Inst Elec & Electronics Engrs, 73-; sr indust fel, MacMillan Bloedel Res Ltd, 75-76; chmn, Fuzzy Set Symp, 76-77; assoc ed, Fuzzy Set J, 77-, guest ed, 78-; sr indust res fel, Taipei, 81; vis fel, Electro-Tech Lab, Tsukuba Science City, Japan, 89. *Mem:* Fel Inst Elec & Electronics Engrs; Can Biomed Eng Soc; Can Indust Comput Soc; NY Acad Sci; fel Soc Photo-Optical Instrumentation Engrs; Int Soc Optical Engrs. *Res:* Neuro-vision; neuro-control; fuzzy neural-networks; neuronal-morphology of biological systems; intelligent systems; cognitive information; new paradigms in information theory; inverse biomedical engineering. *Mailing Add:* Intel Systs Res Lab Col Eng Univ Sask Saskatoon SK S7N 5A9 Can. *Fax:* 306-966-8710, 966-5427

GUPTA, MADHU SUDAN, ELECTRONICS ENGINEERING, APPLIED PHYSICS. *Current Pos:* PROF ELEC ENG & CHMN DEPT, ELEC ENG, FLA STATE UNIV, TALLAHASSEE, 95- *Personal Data:* b Lucknow, India, June 13, 45; m 70, Vijaya Lakshmi; c Jay & Vineet. *Educ:* Allahabad Univ, MS, 66; Fla State Univ, MS, 67; Univ Mich, Ann Arbor, MA, 68, PhD(elec eng), 72. *Prof Exp:* Asst prof elec eng, Queen's Univ, Can, 72-73; asst prof, Mass Inst Technol, 73-78, assoc prof, 78-79; sr staff engr, Hughes Aircraft Co, 77-89, prog mgr, 89-93, sr proj mgr, 93-95; assoc prof, Univ Ill, Chicago, 79-84, dir grad studies, 80-83, prof, 84-87. *Concurrent Pos:* Lilly fel, Div Study & Res in Educ, Mass Inst Technol, 74-75, consult, Lincoln Lab, 77-79; vis prof, Univ Calif, Santa Barbara, 85-86. *Mem:* Fel Inst Elec & Electronics Engrs; Sigma Xi; AAAS; Asn Prof Engrs; Am Soc Eng Educ. *Res:* Microwave electronics; solid state electronic devices; noise in circuits and devices; fluctuation phenomenon; thermodynamics of electrical devices; engineering education. *Mailing Add:* Dept Elec Eng Col Eng Fla State Univ 2525 Pottsdamer St Tallahassee FL 32310-6046

GUPTA, MANJULA K, ENDOCRINOLOGY, CLINICAL IMMUNOLOGY. *Current Pos:* Res fel immunopath, Cleveland Clin Found, 69-71, res assoc, 72-73, proj scientist, 73-74, assoc staff, 74-75, STAFF & SECT HEAD IMMUNOPATH, CLEVELAND CLIN FOUND, 75- *Personal Data:* b India, Aug, 17, 42; m 68, Satyendra K; c Seema & Neera. *Educ:* Agra Univ, BS, 59, MS, 61, PhD(zool), 66. *Concurrent Pos:* Adj clin prof, Cleveland State Univ, 77-; staff endocrinol, Cleveland Clin Found, 85- *Mem:* Am Soc Clin Path; Am Asn Clin Chem; Endocrine Soc; Am Thyroid Asn; Am Asn Cancer Res; Am Asn Immunologists. *Res:* Immunology of endocrine diseases in general; role of hormones on cancer development and growth; mechanisms by which hormones initiate cancer cell proliferation and alter immune response. *Mailing Add:* Dept Clin Path One Clin Ctr 9500 Euclid Ave Cleveland Clin Found Cleveland OH 44195-5131

GUPTA, NABA K, BIOCHEMISTRY. *Current Pos:* from asst prof to prof chem, 66-76, mem fac chem, 76-80, PROF CHEM, UNIV NEBR, LINCOLN, 80- *Personal Data:* b Calcutta, India, July 2, 34; m 64. *Educ:* Univ Calcutta, BSc, 54, MSc, 57; Univ Mich, PhD(biochem), 62. *Prof Exp:* Res assoc biochem, Univ Chicago, 62-65; proj assoc, Inst Enzyme Res, Univ Wis, Madison, 65-66. *Mem:* Am Soc Biol Chem. *Res:* Chemistry and biology of nucleic acids. *Mailing Add:* Dept Chem Univ Nebr PO Box 88034 Lincoln NE 68588-0001. *Fax:* 402-472-9402

GUPTA, NAND K, ENGINEERING PHYSICS, SOLID STATE PHYSICS. *Current Pos:* PRES, OMEGA INT TECHNOL, INC, 88- *Personal Data:* b Mathura, UP, India, June 10, 42; m 62; c 3. *Educ:* Agra Univ, BS, 61, MS, 64; Univ Mass, MS, 67, PhD(physics), 69. *Prof Exp:* Proj mgr nuclear detectors, Harshaw Chem Co, 69-74; mkt mgr instruments, Reuter-Stokes Inc, 75-76; sr scientist radiation group, EMI Med Inc, 76-81; sr lab dir eng, Bio-Imaging Res, Inc, 81-87. *Mem:* Am Asn Physicists Med; Soc Nuclear Med. *Res:* Program management and development of large computerized radiation based medical and industrial instruments; CAT scanners and digital radiographic machines for medical applications, large CAT scanners and filmless radiographic machines for aerospace and defense applications. *Mailing Add:* 1506 Bull Creek Dr Libertyville IL 60048

GUPTA, NARAIN DATT, MATHEMATICS. *Current Pos:* PROF MATH, UNIV MAN, 67- *Personal Data:* b India, July 27, 36. *Educ:* Univ Kashmir, India, BA, 56; Australian Nat Univ, Canberra, PhD(math), 65. *Mem:* Math Can Soc; Am Math Soc. *Mailing Add:* Dept Math & Astron Univ Man Winnipeg MB R3T 2N2 Can. *Fax:* 204-275-5011

GUPTA, OM PRAKASH, dentistry, periodontics; deceased, see previous edition for last biography

GUPTA, PRABODH KUMAR, PATHOLOGY. *Current Pos:* DIR CYTOPATH & CYTOMETRY, PA MED CTR, PHILADELPHIA, 88-; PROF PATH & LAB MED, UNIV PA SCH MED, 88- *Personal Data:* b Shorkot, India, Mar 1, 37; m 69; c 1. *Educ:* Panjab Univ, Chandigarh, India, MS & BS, 61; All India Inst Med Sci, MD, 65; Am Bd Path, AB, 75; Am Bd Cytopath, 90. *Prof Exp:* Instr, All India Inst Med Sci, New Delhi, 63-67, asst prof & head, Cytopath Lab & consult, Dept Path, 69-72; res fel, Mass Gen Hosp, 67-68; teaching fel, Harvard Med Sch, 67-78; instr, Sch Med, Johns

Hopkins Univ, 68-69, asst pathologist, 72-74, pathologist & cytopathologist, 74-88, assoc prof path, 79-88. *Concurrent Pos:* Rockefeller Found fel, All India Inst Med Sci, 62-64; USPHS res fel, Mass Gen Hosp, 67-68; asst prof, Sch Health Serv, Johns Hopkins Univ, 73-75, cirric comt, 73-75; mem, Res Rev Comn, Nat Found March Dimes, NY, 75-; vis prof, Univ Mich, 80; lectr, Am Cancer Soc, 80, guest speaker, 81; prof dir, McKee Mem Sem, Univ SC; consult, WHO, 83, UN, 89. *Mem:* Fel Col Am Pathologists; fel Int Acad Cytol; Am Soc Cytol; AAAS; NY Acad Sci; AMA; Am Soc Cytopath (pres, 95-96). *Res:* Morphologic studies of precancerous lesions; biomarker studies with special reference to cytology, automation, bacterial, viral and related infections; molecular pathology. *Mailing Add:* Cytopath Sect Univ Pa Founders Pavilion 3400 Spruce St Philadelphia PA 19104-4220

GUPTA, PRADEEP KUMAR, MECHANICAL ENGINEERING, TRIBOLOGY. *Current Pos:* PRES, PKG INC, 83- *Personal Data:* b Bandikui, India, July 9, 44; m 77; c 2. *Educ:* Birla Inst Technol & Sci, India, BE Hons, 66; Mass Inst Technol, SM, 68, ME, 69, ScD, 71. *Honors & Awards:* Birla Inst Gold Medal, 66; Newkirk Award, Am Soc Mech Engrs, 78; Nat Acad Sci Fel, 83. *Prof Exp:* Res asst mech eng, Mass Inst Technol, 66-70; sr eng scientist tribology, 71-77, program advan technol, 77-79, sr consult scientist, Mech Technol Inc, 79-82. *Mem:* Am Soc Mech Engrs; Sigma Xi; Soc Tribologists & Lubrication Engrs. *Res:* Rolling bearing technology; lubrication mechanics, friction and wear; applied mechanics; surface topography and mechanical interaction of rough surfaces. *Mailing Add:* 117 Southbury Rd Clifton Park NY 12065-7714

GUPTA, RADHEY SHYAM, HEAT SHOCK PROTEINS, MOLECULAR EVOLUTION. *Current Pos:* asst prof med, 78-80, from asst prof to assoc prof biochem, 80-86, PROF BIOCHEM, MCMASTER UNIV, 86- *Personal Data:* b India, Mar 21, 47; m 73; c 2. *Educ:* Agra Univ, India, BSc, 65; Indian Inst Technol, MSc, 68; Univ Bombay, PhD(molecular biol), 73. *Prof Exp:* Vis mem, Tata Inst Fundamental Res, Bombay, 68-73; res assoc, Wash Univ Sch Med, 73-75, Univ Toronto, 75-78. *Concurrent Pos:* MRC scholar, 79-84, scientist, 84-89; assoc ed, Mutagenesis; ed, Drug Resistance in Mammalian Cells. *Mem:* Am Asn Can Res; Genetics Soc Can; Am Soc Microbiol; Can Biochem Soc. *Res:* Evolutionary relationships between prokaryotes and eukaryotes assembly/function of microtubules; origin of eukaryotic cell; cellular functions of the mitochondrial chaperone proteins; cellular resistance to anticancer drugs; role of heat shock proteins in autoimmune diseases. *Mailing Add:* Dept Biochem McMaster Univ Health Sci Ctr 1200 Main St W Hamilton ON L8N 3Z5 Can

GUPTA, RAJ K, NUCLEAR MAGNETIC RESONANCE. *Current Pos:* prof biochem, 82-95, PROF PHYSIOL & BIOPHYS, ALBERT EINSTEIN COL MED, 82- *Personal Data:* b India, Oct 30, 43; m 68, Pratima Govil; c Julie & Lori. *Educ:* Agra Univ, India, BS, 62; Univ Allahabad, MS, 64; Indian Inst Technol, Kanpur, PhD, 69. *Prof Exp:* postdoctoral, IBM Watson Lab, Columbia Univ, 69-71, Thomas J Watson Res Ctr, Yorktown Hts, NY, 71-72; vis scientist, Nat Inst Arthritis, Metab & Digestive Dis, NIH, Bethesda, Md, 72-73; sr res assoc, Inst Cancer Res, Philadelphia, 73-75, assoc mem res staff, 75-78, mem, sr res staff, 78-82. *Concurrent Pos:* Res career develop award, USPHS, 76-81; adj assoc prof biochem & biophys, Univ Pa, 78-82; mem, Biophys & Biophys Chem B Grants Study Sect, NIH, 79-83. *Mem:* Am Soc Biol Chemists; Biophys Soc; Int Soc Magnetic Resonance Med; Am Chem Soc; Am Soc Hypertension. *Res:* Intracellular metal ions in intact cells and tissues, nuclear magnetic resonance; author of numerous scientific publications. *Mailing Add:* Dept Physiol & Biophys Albert Einstein Col Med Bronx NY 10461. *Fax:* 718-430-8819

GUPTA, RAJENDRA, ATOMIC, MOLECULAR & OPTICAL PHYSICS. *Current Pos:* from asst prof to assoc prof, 78-85, chair, 89-95, PROF PHYSICS, UNIV ARK, 85- *Personal Data:* b Mau Ranipir, India, Jan 01, 43; m, Usha Chand; c Tripti & Sangeet. *Educ:* Agra Univ, India, BSc, 59, MSc, 61; Boston Univ, PhD, 70. *Prof Exp:* Res assoc, Columbia Univ, 70-73, lectr, 73-74, asst prof, 74-78. *Concurrent Pos:* Vis prof, Air Force Inst Technol, Wright-Patterson AFB & vis scientist, Air Force Aero Propulsion Lab, 77-78. *Mem:* Am Phys Soc. *Res:* Laser spectroscopy; atomic and molecular physics. *Mailing Add:* Dept Physics Univ Ark Fayetteville AR 72701. *Fax:* 501-575-4580; *E-Mail:* rgupta@comp.uark.edu

GUPTA, RAJESH K, VACCINOLOGY, ADJUVANTS. *Current Pos:* CONSULT, CHIRON VACCINES, 96- *Personal Data:* b Delhi, India, Apr 6, 58; m 81, Chander; c Aarti, Aditi & Himani. *Educ:* Panjab Univ, India, BSc, 77; HP Univ, India, BSc, 80, MSc, 82, MPhil, 85, PhD(microbiol), 88. *Prof Exp:* Tech supvr, Cent Res Inst, India, 77-86, asst tech officer, 86-89; staff scientist, Nat Inst Immunol, India, 89-91; sr res scientist, Mass Pub Health Biol Labs, 91-93, chief lab, 93-94, asst dir, 94-96. *Concurrent Pos:* Vis fel, NIH, 89-91. *Mem:* Int Asn Biol Stand; Int Tetanus Soc; Am Soc Microbiol; AAAS; Inst Soc Vaccines. *Res:* Development of vaccines for human use; development of adjuvants and delivery system for human vaccines; formulation of vaccines. *Mailing Add:* Chiron Vaccines 4560 Horton St Emeryville CA 94608. *Fax:* 510-923-6918; *E-Mail:* rajesh_k_gupta@cc.chiron.com

GUPTA, RAKESH KUMAR, POLYMER SCIENCE, TEXTILE TECHNOLOGY. *Current Pos:* res engr fibers, Hercules Inc, 74-78, prog leader Fiber Fundamentals, 78-81, group leader, 81-84, proj leader, 85-88, proj mgr, Non-Woven Fibers Res & Develop, 89-92, DIR FUNCTIONAL FIBERS, HERCULES INC, 92- *Personal Data:* b Delhi, India, Jan 15, 47; US citizen; m 70; c 2. *Educ:* Indian Inst Technol, BTech, 68; NC State Univ, MS, 70, PhD(fiber & polymer sci), 74. *Prof Exp:* Fiber physicist, Am Cyanamid Co, 70-71. *Mem:* Fiber Soc. *Res:* Fiber and polymer science; fiber physics and mechanics; polymer characterization; fiber melt and wet spinning; polypropylene polymer and fibers; carpet yarn development; upholstery yarn development; non-wovens; thermal bonding fibers; medical barrier fabrics; filtration fibers. *Mailing Add:* Hercules Res Ctr Inc 500 Hercules Rd Wilmington DE 19808-1599. *Fax:* 770-784-3249

GUPTA, RAMESH, REACTORS, FLUID DYNAMICS. *Current Pos:* engr, Exxon Res & Eng Co, 77-78, proj engr, 78-79, sr engr, 79-81, staff engr, 81-82, SR STAFF ENGR, EXXON RES & ENG CO, 82- *Personal Data:* b India, Dec 14, 47; US citizen; m 76; c 1. *Educ:* Indian Inst Technol, BTech, 69; Princeton Univ, MA, 70, PhD(chem eng), 73. *Prof Exp:* Res fel, Chem Eng, Calif Inst Technol, 73-75; res engr, Air Products Inc, 75-77. *Mem:* Am Inst Chem Engrs; Sigma Xi. *Res:* Fluid dynamics, with focus on multiphase chemical reactors for petroleum, chemicals, coal and synthesis fuels. *Mailing Add:* Dept Chem & Biochem So Ill Univ Med Sch Carbondale IL 62901-4413. *Fax:* 618-453-6440

GUPTA, RAMESH C, IMMUNOLOGY. *Current Pos:* ASSOC PROF MED, UNIV TENN, MEMPHIS, 82- *Personal Data:* b Vindhyachal, Uttar Pradesh, India, Feb 12, 44; US citizen; m 79; c 4. *Educ:* Agra Univ, India, BSc, 61; All India Inst Med Sci, New Delhi, MB & BS, 66, MD, 71. *Prof Exp:* House officer med & surg, All India Inst Med Sci, New Delhi, 67, resident med, 68-71; resident med, Memorial Hosp, Med Sch, Univ Mass, Worcester, 71-72; fel med, rheumatology, Univ Colo, Denver, 72-74, instr med, 74-75; res fel & assoc immunol, Mayo Clin & Found, Rochester, Minn, 75-77; asst prof med, Univ Colo, Denver, 77-82. *Concurrent Pos:* Inst med, Mayo Med Sch, Rochester, Minn, 75-77; chief rheumatology serv, Denver Gen Hosp, 77-82; attend physician, City of Memphis Hosps, 82-; consult physician, Vet Admin Hosp, Memphis, 82- *Mem:* Am Asn Immunologists; Am Rheumatism Asn; AAAS. *Res:* Diagnosis, etiology and therapy of autoimmune diseases with particular emphasis on applying the knowledge of immunology, molecular and cell biology. *Mailing Add:* 6005 Park Ave Suite 409 Memphis TN 38119

GUPTA, RAMESH C, TOXICOLOGY. *Current Pos:* TOXICOLOGIST, BREATHITT VET CTR, MURRAY STATE UNIV, 87- *Personal Data:* b Etah, UP, India, Aug 20, 49; US citizen; m 87, Denise; c Rekha. *Educ:* GB Point Univ Agr Technol, India, DVM, 73; Punjab Agr Univ, India, PhD(toxicol), 76. *Prof Exp:* Vis scientist res toxicol, Dept Pharmacol, Mich State Univ, 81-82; toxicologist, Med Ctr, Vanderbilt Univ, 83-86. *Mem:* Int Brain Res Orgn; Soc Toxicol; Soc Pharmacol & Exp Therapeut; Soc Neurosci; Am Vet Med Asn; AAAS. *Res:* Biochemical mechanisms involved in the toxicity and tolerance to organophosphorus and carbamate insecticides and nerve agents; development of novel antidotal treatment; mechanisms involved in the weightlessness. *Mailing Add:* Toxicol Dept Breathitt Vet Ctr Murray State Univ PO Box 2000 N Dr Hopkinsville KY 42241-2000. *Fax:* 502-886-4295; *E-Mail:* a47413f@msumusik.mursuky.edu

GUPTA, RAMESH K, SATELLITE COMMUNICATIONS, MICROWAVE CIRCUIT & SUBSYSTEM DESIGN. *Current Pos:* mem tech staff microwaves, Comsat Labs, Clarksburg, Md, 80-85, staff scientist, 85-87, assoc mgr microwave systs, 87-90, MGR MICROWAVE COMPS, COMSAT LABS, CLARKSBURG, MD, 90-; ADJ ASSOC PROF, GRAD SCH MGT & TECHNOL, UNIV MD UNIV COL. *Personal Data:* b India, Nov 13, 53; US citizen; m 82, Nito; c Raman & Nikhil. *Educ:* Punjab Univ, Chandigarh, India, BS, 74; Univ Alta, Edmonton, Can, MS, 76, PhD(elec eng), 80; Univ Pa, MBA, 89. *Prof Exp:* Teaching assoc microwave, Univ Alta, Edmonton, Can, 74-80. *Concurrent Pos:* Consult, Int Telecommun Satellite Orgn, 82-85; vchmn, Washington Chap, Inst Elec & Electronics Engrs Microwave Theory & Techniques Soc, 87-88, chmn, 88-89; panelist, Small Bus Innovative Res Prog, NSF, 89. *Mem:* Sr mem Inst Elec & Electronics Engrs; Am Inst Aeronaut & Astronaut. *Res:* Gallium arsenic microwave monolithic integrated circuits; advanced microwave hybrid circuit and subsystem development; satellite systems; author of over 50 publications; granted 2 patents. *Mailing Add:* Comsat Labs 22300 Comsat Dr Clarksburg MD 20871. *Fax:* 301-540-8208

GUPTA, RISHAB KUMAR, IMMUNOCHEMISTRY, ONCOLOGY. *Current Pos:* DIR IMMUNODIAGNOSIS, VPRES EDUC, JOHN WAYNE CANCER INST, SANTA MONICA, CALIF, 92-; EMER PROF IMMUNOL & MED MICROBIOL, UNIV CALIF, LOS ANGELES, 94- *Personal Data:* b Nagina, India, Apr 18, 43; m 72, Mridula; c Arvind & Anita. *Educ:* Govind Ballabh Pant Univ, BSc Hon, 63, MSc, 65; Rutgers Univ, MS & PhD(microbiol), 68. *Prof Exp:* Lectr microbiol & immunol, Univ Calif, Los Angeles, 68-70; res assoc microbiol, Yale Univ, 70-71; res biochemist med mycol, Univ Calif, Los Angeles, 71-72; asst res oncologist, 72-75, assoc res oncologist, 75-79, asst prof immunol & med microbiol, 79-81, assoc prof, 81-87, prof, 87-94. *Concurrent Pos:* Teaching & res asst, Govind Ballabh Pant Univ, 63-65; res asst, Rutgers Univ, 65-68; consult microbiologist, Ralph Stone & Co Engrs Inc, 68-; microbiologist, Vet Admin Med Ctr, Sepulveda, 76-; prin investr grants, Nat Cancer Inst, 81-84, Calif Inst Cancer Res, 73-75 & Cancer Res Coord Comt, Univ Calif, 73-75 & 81-82; mem, Grant Review Comt, Nat Inst Health, 88-92; Tobacco Related Dis Res Prog State Calif, 91-94. *Mem:* Am Soc Microbiol; Am Acad Microbiol; Am Asn Cancer Res; Sigma Xi; Am Asn Immunologists; Am Soc Clin Oncol. *Res:* Identification, detection, isolation and purification of tumor antigens (human) to develop sensitive immunologic tests (radioimmunoassay, enzyme immunoassay), for diagnosis and prognostification of cancer in humans; develop hybridoma antibody to purified tumor antigens used for treatment of human cancer, and other bioprobes for application in immunodiagnosis; tumor markers; microbiology; biotechnology; immunodiagnosis. *Mailing Add:* Dept Immunol John Wayne Cancer Inst 2200 Santa Monica Blvd Santa Monica CA 91404

GUPTA, SANJEEV, HEPATOLOGY, GASTROENTEROLOGY. *Current Pos:* sr fel gastroenterol, 87-89, asst prof, 89-94, ASSOC PROF MED, ALBERT EINSTEIN COL MED, 94- *Personal Data:* b Jaipur, India, Apr 23, 54; m 84; c 2. *Educ:* Univ Rajasthan, India, MBBS, 76; Postgrad Inst Med Educ & Res, Chandigarh, India, MD, 80; Royal Col Physicians, UK, MRCP, 82. *Honors & Awards:* Clin Investr Award, NIH; Pfizer Gold Medal; Irma Hirschi Award; Henry L Moses Prize. *Prof Exp:* Registr med, Postgrad Inst Med Educ & Res, Chandigarh, India, 80-81; registr med & gastroenterol, Royal Postgrad Med Sch, Hammersmith Hosp, 81-85; instr hepath, Sch Med, Univ Southern Calif, 85-87. *Concurrent Pos:* Lectr, Brit Postgrad Med Found, 83-85, Royal Postgrad Med Sch, 83-85; clin investr award, NIH, 89; attend physician, Montefiore Med Ctr & Bronx Munic Hosp Ctr, 89- *Mem:* Am Gastroenterol Asn; Am Asn Studies Liver Dis; Brit Soc Gastroenterol; Indian Soc Gastroenterol. *Res:* Liver growth control; hepatocyte transplantation for somatic gene therapy and liver repopulation; prognosis and therapy of alcoholic liver disease; natural history of viral hepatitis. *Mailing Add:* Liver Res Ctr 1300 Morris Park Ave Bronx NY 10461

GUPTA, SATISH CHANDER, SOIL PHYSICS, WATER RESOURCES & NON-POINT SOURCE POLLUTION. *Current Pos:* assoc prof, 85-88, PROF SOIL SCI, UNIV MINN, 88- *Personal Data:* b Poonch, India, July 29, 45. *Educ:* Punjab Agr Univ, BSc, 68, MSc, 69; Utah State Univ, PhD(soil physics), 72. *Prof Exp:* Res fel, Dept Soil Sci, Univ Minn, 72-77; soil scientist, Agr Res Serv, USDA, 77-85. *Mem:* Am Soc Agron; Soil Sci Soc Am; Am Geophys Union; Int Soc Soil Sci; Int Soil & Tillage Res Org; Soc Environ. *Res:* Modelling simultaneous flow of salt and water in soils; effect of mechanical properties of soils on plant growth; heat flow in soils; agricultural value of sewage waste and dredged materials; effect of tillage and compaction on soil physical properties and processes; rainfall effect on soil detachment; role of earthworm macropores on water entry into soil; Tillage and manuse interactions on nutrient teaching, sediment and nutrient transport in surface runoff soil quality; network modeling; percolation theory. *Mailing Add:* 360 Bear Ave S St Paul MN 55127. *Fax:* 612-625-2208; *E-Mail:* sgupta@soils.umn.edu

GUPTA, SHANTI SWARUP, MATHEMATICAL STATISTICS. *Current Pos:* PROF MATH & STATIST, PURDUE UNIV, 62-, HEAD DEPT STATIST, 68- *Personal Data:* b Saunasi, India, Jan 25, 25. *Educ:* Univ Delhi, BA, 46, MA, 49; Univ NC, PhD(math statist), 56. *Prof Exp:* Lectr math, Delhi Col, 49-53; asst, Univ NC, 54-56; mem tech staff, Bell Tel Labs, 56-57, 58-62; assoc prof math, Univ Alta, 57-58; adj assoc prof, Courant Inst Math Sci, NY Univ, 59-61; vis assoc prof, Stanford Univ, 61-62. *Concurrent Pos:* Can Math Cong fel, Queen's Univ, Can, 58; vis prof, Dept Statist & Opers Res, Univ Calif, Berkeley, 68-69; consult, Math Dept, Gen Motors Res Labs, 70-80. *Mem:* Am Math Soc; fel Inst Math Statist; fel Am Statist Asn; fel AAAS; fel Royal Statist Soc. *Res:* Multiple decision rules; order statistics; life testing and reliability; multivariate probabilities. *Mailing Add:* Dept Statist Purdue Univ Math Bldg West Lafayette IN 47907-1399

GUPTA, SHYAM KIRTI, ORGANIC CHEMISTRY, MEDICINAL CHEMISTRY. *Current Pos:* VPRES, TECH SERV, AM SOAP CO, 90- *Personal Data:* b Lucknow, India, Aug 21, 42; m 68, Moyca; c Kip & Kelly. *Educ:* Univ Lucknow, BS, 58, MS, 60, PhD(org chem), 64. *Prof Exp:* Ford Found fel, Cent Drug Res Inst, Univ Lucknow, 64; res assoc, Univ Maine, 64-65; res assoc, Ariz State Univ, 65-67; vis asst prof biochem, Ind Univ, 67-68; res assoc, Purdue Univ, 68-71; from res chemist to sr res chemist process res & develop, Chas Pfizer & Co, Inc, 71-77; group leader personal care technol, Dial Corp, 77-85, mgr, New Technol, 86-90. *Concurrent Pos:* Consult, soaps & detergents. *Mem:* Fel Am Chem Soc; Am Oil Chemists' Soc. *Res:* Natural products; development of new reactions and reagents in organic synthesis; organometallic chemistry; OTC Drug technology; biochemistry of cosmetics; development of new technology for the manufacture of soaps and detergents; research, development and marketing of soaps and other personal care products. *Mailing Add:* Soap Group 5221 E Windrose Dr Scottsdale AZ 85254. *Fax:* 602-996-9700

GUPTA, SOMESHWAR C, ELECTRICAL ENGINEERING. *Current Pos:* PROF ELEC ENG, SOUTHERN METHODIST UNIV, 67-, CHMN DEPT, 82- *Personal Data:* b Ludhiana, India, Apr 23, 35; US citizen; m 58; c 3. *Educ:* Punjab Univ, India, BA, 51, MA, 53; Univ Glasgow, BSc, 57; Univ Calif, Berkeley, MS & PhD(elec eng), 62. *Prof Exp:* Trainee elec eng, Theodore Kiepe, Ger, 54, Brit Elec Authority, Eng, 54 & Elec de France, Paris, 55; trainee electronics, Pye Telecommun, Eng, 55; lab asst acoust, Brunswick Tech, 56; engr, Remington Rand Corp, Glasgow, Scotland, 57; asst lectr elec eng, Univ Glasgow, 57-58; jr res officer nuclear eng, Atomic Energy Estab, Bombay, India, 58; asst prof elec eng, Calif State Polytech Col, 58-60 & Carnegie Inst Technol, 62-63; from assoc prof to prof, Ariz State Univ, 63-67. *Concurrent Pos:* NSF res grants, 64-72; NASA res grants, 67-74; consult, Gen Elec Co, 63, Mil Electronics Div, Motorola Inc, 63-, Electronics Proving Ground, Ft Huachuca, US Army, 65, Collins Radio Co, 67, Tex Instruments, 69, Western Union Co, 82- & Pagenet, 84; consult ed, Int Textbook Co; assoc ed, Int J Systs Sci, 74- *Mem:* Inst Elec & Electronics Engrs; Sigma Xi. *Res:* Space communication, mobile radio communication, computers, digital signal processing, control. *Mailing Add:* Elec Eng Dept Southern Methodist Univ Dallas TX 75275-0001

GUPTA, SUDHIR, IMMUNOLOGY, INTERNAL MEDICINE. *Current Pos:* PROF MED, UNIV CALIF, 82-, PROF PATH, MICROBIOL, MOLECULAR GENETICS & NEUROL, COL MED, 84-, DIR, DIV BASIC & IMMUNOL, 82- *Personal Data:* b Bijnor, India, Apr 14, 44; m 80, Abhas Rohatgi; c Ankmalika & Saurabh. *Educ:* Agra Univ, BS, 61; King George's Med Col, MB, BS, MD, 66, MD, PhD, 70; FRCP(C), 75; Am Bd Allergy & Immunol, dipl, 77; Am Bd Diag Lab Immunol, dipl, 90. *Honors & Awards:* Lifetime Achievement Award, J M Found, 90; Aruthur Manzel Award, 75; R R Misra lectr, 93. *Prof Exp:* Intern, King George's Med Col, 66, resident med, 67-70; resident med, Sir Ganga Ram Hosp, 71 & Mem Hosp, Worcester, 71-72; fel allergy & immunol, Roosevelt Hosp, New York, 72-74; fel immunol, Mem Sloan-Kettering Cancer Ctr, 72-76, assoc, Sloan-Kettering Inst, 76-78; instr med, Med Col, Cornell Univ, 76-77, asst prof biol, 76-78, asst prof med, Med Col, 77-78, assoc prof biol, 78-82, assoc prof med, 79-82. *Concurrent Pos:* Nat Cancer Inst clin res trainee fel, 74-76; clin asst physician, Immunol Serv, Mem Hosp, 76-78; asst attend physician, Mem Hosp Cancer & Allied Dis, 78-79, assoc attend physician, 79-82; staff physician, Univ Calif Irvine Med Ctr, 83-; mem, Allergy & Clin Immunol Comt, NIAID, NIH, 85-89; mem, Adv Panel Med Devices, Food & Drug Admin, 89-93; vis prof, Hematol Res Found, NY, 92. *Mem:* Am Asn Immunologists; Am Asn Pathologists; fel Am Col Physicians; fel Royal Soc Med; fel Am Acad Allergy & Immunol; Am Col Rheumatology; fel Royal Col Physicians & Surgeons Can. *Res:* Lymphocyte biology; AIDS; aging; cancer. *Mailing Add:* Basic & Clin Immunol Med Sci I C-240 Univ Calif Irvine CA 92717-4069. *Fax:* 714-824-4362

GUPTA, SURAJ NARAYAN, THEORETICAL PHYSICS. *Current Pos:* prof, 56-61, DISTINGUISHED PROF PHYSICS, WAYNE STATE UNIV, 61- *Personal Data:* b Haryana, India, Dec 1, 24; nat US; m 48; c 2. *Educ:* St Stephen's Col, BS, 45, MS, 46; Cambridge Univ, PhD(theoret physics), 51. *Prof Exp:* Fel, Imp Chem Industs, Univ Manchester, 51-53; vis prof physics, Purdue Univ, 53-56. *Concurrent Pos:* Vis scientist, Argonne Nat Lab, Brookhaven Nat Lab & Nat Res Coun Can. *Mem:* Fel Am Phys Soc; fel Indian Nat Acad Sci. *Res:* Relativity; gravitation; quantum electrodynamics; field theory; nuclear physics; high energy physics. *Mailing Add:* Dept Physics Wayne State Univ Detroit MI 48202

GUPTA, SURENDRA MOHAN, INDUSTRIAL ENGINEERING, PRODUCTION SYSTEMS. *Current Pos:* asst prof, 78-81, ASSOC PROF INDUST ENG, NORTHEASTERN UNIV, 81- *Personal Data:* b Delhi, India, July 10, 47; US citizen; m 73, Sharda Agarwal; c Monica & Neil. *Educ:* Birla Inst Technol & Sci, India, BEEE, 70; Purdue Univ, MSIE, 72, PhD(indust eng), 77; Bryant Col, MBA, 77. *Prof Exp:* Teaching asst indust eng, Purdue Univ, 71-72, instr, 72-76; asst prof systs mgt, Bryant Col, 76-78. *Concurrent Pos:* Investr, NSF, 74-77; prin investr, Nat Bur Stand, 80 & Northeastern Univ, 80-81 & 89; vis prof, Jilin Univ Technol, China, 84. *Mem:* Inst Indust Eng; Am Prod & Inventory Control Soc; Inst Opers Res & Mgt Sci; Decision Sci Inst. *Res:* Computerized manufacturing systems; applications of computers and operations research; production management; system evaluation; simulation; multi-level production systems; MRP systems; JIT systems; queueing systems; system reliability. *Mailing Add:* Northeastern Univ Dept Mech Indust & Mfg Eng 360 Huntington Ave Boston MA 02115. *Fax:* 617-373-2921; *E-Mail:* gupta@nuhub.neu.edu

GUPTA, TAPAN KUMAR, CERAMICS. *Current Pos:* SR FEL, ALCOA LAB, 85- *Personal Data:* b Barisal, Bangladesh, Aug 2, 39; US citizen; m 69; c 2. *Educ:* Univ Calcutta, BSc, 58, MSc, 61; Mass Inst Technol, SM, 64, ScD(ceramics), 66. *Prof Exp:* Lectr chem, Hooghly Mohosin Col, India, 60-61; res asst ceramics, Mass Inst Technol, 61-66; sr scientist ceramics, Westinghouse Res Labs, 67-74, fel scientist, 74-82, adv scientist, 82-85. *Concurrent Pos:* Mgr eng & develop, Bharat Heavy Elec Ltd, India, 79-80. *Mem:* Fel Am Ceramic Soc; Mat Sci Soc; Inst Elec & Electronics Engrs. *Res:* Processing of ceramics; development of high density high strength oxides; investigation on nonlinear lightning arrester and varistor materials; studies on sintering, microstructure, thermal shock and crack healing; studies on electronic materials. *Mailing Add:* Alcoa Tech Ctr-C Alloa Central PA 15069

GUPTA, UDAIPRAKASH I, DATABASE MANAGEMENT SYSTEMS. *Current Pos:* ASST PROF COMPUT SCI, NORTHWESTERN UNIV, EVANSTON, 78- *Personal Data:* b Alahabad, India, Feb 4, 52. *Educ:* Indian Inst Technol, BTech, 74; Princeton Univ, MS, 75, PhD(comput sci), 78. *Concurrent Pos:* Mem tech staff, Bell Lab, 81. *Mem:* Asn Comput Mach; Inst Elec & Electronics Engrs. *Res:* Theoretical aspects of file organizations and database management systems; theory of algorithms and data structures; graph theory. *Mailing Add:* 133 Hawkins Circle Wheaton IL 60187

GUPTA, UMESH C, SOIL FERTILITY, PLANT NUTRITION. *Current Pos:* RETIRED. *Personal Data:* b Kanpur, India, Oct 25, 37; Can citizen; m 57, Sharda Kumari; c Sharad, Kamal & Subhas. *Educ:* Agr Col, Kanpur, India, BSc, 55, MSc, 57; Purdue Univ, PhD(soil biochem), 61. *Prof Exp:* Nat Res Coun Can fel, Soil Res Inst, Can Dept Agr, Ont, 61-63, res officer soil fertil & plant nutrit, PEI, 63-65, Res Scientist Soil Fertil & Plant Nutrit, 65-96. *Concurrent Pos:* Ed-in-chief, Can J Soil Sci; pres, PEI Inst Agrologists, 90-91. *Mem:* Fel Soil Sci Soc Am; fel Can Soc Soil Sci (pres, 95-96); fel Agr Inst Can; fel Am Soc Agron. *Res:* To characterize various forms of micro-nutrients from soils and determine sufficiency, deficiency and toxicity levels and deficiency and toxicity symptoms of these nutrients in various crops grown in Eastern Canada; to recommend rates of trace element fertilization; selenium enrichment of livestock feeds. *Mailing Add:* Agr & Agr-Food Can Res Ctr Box 1210 Charlottetown PE C1A 7M8 Can. *Fax:* 902-566-6821; *E-Mail:* guptau@em.agr.ca

GUPTA, VAIKUNTH N, SPEECH PROCESSING, DIGITAL ENGINEERING. *Personal Data:* b Sohna, India, Sept 25, 51; m 80. *Educ:* Banaras Hindu Univ, BTech, 74; Univ Ky, MSME, 77, PhD(biomed eng), 80. *Prof Exp:* Engr applications signal processing, Univ Ky, 76-80; mem tech staff speech processing, Comsat Labs, Commun Satellite Corp, 80-82. *Concurrent Pos:* Consult signal processing, Nat Inst Drug Abuse, 79-80. *Res:* Utilize modern digital signal processing techniques for speech compression and transmission. *Mailing Add:* 12509 Palatine Ct Potomac MD 20854-1477

GUPTA, VIDYA SAGAR, BIOCHEMICAL PHARMACOLOGY, VIROLOGY. *Current Pos:* From asst prof to assoc prof, 68-75, PROF PHARMACOL, DEPT VET PHYSIOL SCI, UNIV SASK, 75- *Personal Data:* b Jammu, India, Dec 17, 35; Can citizen; m 62, Shukla B Vaid; c Susan, Shalini & Sanjay. *Educ:* Univ Jammu & Kashmir, BSc, 54; Univ Rajasthan, MSc, 57; Indian Inst Sci, Bangalore, PhD(biochem & pharmcol), 62. *Concurrent Pos:* Res assoc, Dept Biochem, Scripps Clin & Res Found, La Jolla, Calif, 62-66; vis prof, Dept Pharmacol, Sch Med, Yale Univ, 73-74; pres, Trans-Med Technol Ltd (T-Med) Res & Develop Co. *Mem:* NY Acad Sci; Int Soc Antiviral Res. *Res:* Virus and cancer chemotherapy; mode of action of antiviral and anti cancer drugs; enzymology. *Mailing Add:* 326 Auld Pl Saskatoon SK S7H 4X1 Can. *Fax:* 306-966-8747

GUPTA, VIJAI PRAKASH, CHEMICAL ENGINEERING. *Current Pos:* process supvr, Oxirane Chem Co, 72-81, ADVISOR, ARCO CHEM CO, 81- *Personal Data:* b Banaras, India, Aug 2, 38; m 67; c 2. *Educ:* Banaras Hindu Univ, BSc, 56, MS, 58; McGill Univ, PhD(chem eng), 64. *Prof Exp:* Sr sci asst petrol, Cent Fuel Res Inst, India, 58-59; res engr, E I du Pont de Nemours & Co, Inc, Del, 64-68; sr res engr, Gen Motors Corp, Mich, 69-70; res engr, Cities Serv Oil Co, 70-72. *Concurrent Pos:* Holder, many US & foreign chem process patents. *Mem:* Am Chem Soc; Am Inst Chem Engrs. *Res:* Diffusion effects in heterogeneous catalysis; petroleum processing; automobile emissions control; synthetic fibers; chemical processes; holds over 20 process patents worldwide. *Mailing Add:* ARCO Chem Co 3801 W Chester Pike Newton Square PA 19073

GUPTA, VIJAY KUMAR, PHYSICAL CHEMISTRY. *Current Pos:* PROF PHYS CHEM, CENT STATE UNIV, 69-, CHMN, CHEM DEPT, 93- *Personal Data:* b Ambala, India, Apr 27, 41; m 68; Surjit; c Sonia, Angela & Ashish. *Educ:* Panjab Univ, India, BSc, 61, MSc, 62, PhD(chem), 69. *Honors & Awards:* Outstanding Serv to Community Award, India Club Greater Daytona, Ohio, 85; Excellence in Res Award, Cent State Univ, 86, Community Serv Award, 91; Oustanding Sect Chmn Award, Dayton Sect, Am Chem Soc; Res Excellance Award, Cent State Univ, 95. *Prof Exp:* Lectr chem, D A V Col, Chandigarh, 62; lectr appl chem, Punjab Eng Col, 62-64; res asst chem, Punjab Univ, 64-67; asst prof appl chem, Punjab Eng Col, 67-68; res assoc, Wright State Univ, 68-69; chemist, Lawrence Livermore Nat Lab, Calif, 80. *Concurrent Pos:* Consult, Wright Patterson AFB, 81-88, EG&G Mound Labs, 89-90. *Mem:* Am Chem Soc; Nat Inst Sci; Soc Tribology Lubrication Engrs. *Res:* Thermodynamics of binary mixtures consisting of non-electrolytes; thermodynamic and physical properties of pure components and mixtures; energy conversion and storage processes; environmental pollution; high energy density battery systems; spectroscopic methods and their application in the analysis of trace elements; development of advanced aerospace lubricants; development of methanol based fuel cells. *Mailing Add:* Dept Chem Cent State Univ Wilberforce OH 45384. *Fax:* 937-376-6530

GUPTA, VIRENDRA K, TAXONOMY, FAUNISTICS. *Current Pos:* PROF ENTOM, UNIV FLA, 82- *Personal Data:* b Delhi, India, Mar 14, 32; m 61; c 2. *Educ:* Univ Delhi, BSc Hons, 52, MSc, 54; Univ Mich, ScD(zool), 60. *Prof Exp:* Postdoctoral res assoc entom, Univ Mich, 60-61; lectr zool, Univ Delhi, 61-65, reader, 65-78, prof zool, 78-82. *Concurrent Pos:* Ed, Oriental Insects & Publ Am Etom Inst, 67-; prin investr, NSF grant, Am Etom Inst, 90-92. *Mem:* Entom Soc Am. *Res:* Taxonomy of the family Ichneumonidae; monographed the Indo-Australian fauna of Icheumonidae and some groups of US; revising several genera of Icheumonidae on a worldwide basis and surveying the ichneumonid of Florida. *Mailing Add:* 2716 NW 37th Terr Gainesville FL 32605. *Fax:* 904-392-0190; *E-Mail:* vgupta@ifasgnv

GUPTA, VISHNU DAS, PHYSICAL PHARMACY, ANALYTICAL CHEMISTRY. *Current Pos:* from asst prof to assoc prof, 67-76, PROF PHARMACEUT, UNIV HOUSTON, 77- *Personal Data:* b Kalyanpur, India, Nov 6, 31; US citizen; m 57; c 2. *Educ:* Panjab Univ, India, BS, 53, MS, 57; Univ Tex, Austin, MS, 61; Univ Ga, PhD(pharm), 67. *Honors & Awards:* Lunsford Richardson Pharm Res Award, Wm S Merrell Co, Ohio, 67. *Prof Exp:* In charge mfg & lab, Pharmaceut Mfg House, Azad Hind Chem, India, 53-55 & Janta Pharmaceut Works, 57-60; supvr qual control lab, Schlicksup Drug Co, 61-64; dir control lab, Kapco, Inc, 65-66; teaching asst pharmaceut, Univ Ga, 66-67. *Concurrent Pos:* Pharm consult, Harris Co Hosp Dist, Houston, 70- & numerous pharm co. *Mem:* Am Asn Pharmaceut Scientists; Indian Pharmaceut Asn; fel Acad Pharmaceut Scientists. *Res:* Pharmaceutical analysis, especially development of analytical methods in multicomponent dosage forms; physical pharmacy, especially stability studies on dosage forms and distribution coefficients. *Mailing Add:* Dept Pharm Univ Houston Houston TX 77204-0001

GUPTA, YOGENDRA M(OHAN), HIGH PRESSURE PHYSICS, MECHANICS. *Current Pos:* assoc prof, 81-84, PROF, DEPT PHYSICS, WASH STATE UNIV, 84-, DIR SHOCK DYNAMICS CTR, 92- *Personal Data:* b New Delhi, India, July 24, 49; US citizen; m 75, Barbara L McKay; c Anjuli M & Sonia M. *Educ:* Birla Inst Technol & Sci, India, BSc, 66, MSc, 68; Wash State Univ, PhD(physics), 73. *Prof Exp:* Res assoc physics, Wash State Univ, 73 & Brown Univ, 74; from physicist to sr physicist, Shock Physics Dept, SRI INT, 75-80, asst dir, 80-81. *Concurrent Pos:* Vis prof, SRI INT, BARC, India, NRL, WDC, 86-87. *Mem:* Fel Am Phys Soc; AAAS; Am Acad Mech; NY Acad Sci. *Res:* Condensed matter response to shock waves; spectroscopic studies under high dynamic pressures; mechanical properties of solids; chemical reactions in energetic materials; shock wave instrumentation; materials science. *Mailing Add:* Physics Dept Wash State Univ Pullman WA 99164-2814

GUPTE, SHARMILA SHAILA, biophysics, biochemistry, for more information see previous edition

GUPTON, CREIGHTON LEE, GENETICS. *Current Pos:* RES GENETICIST, CROPS RES DIV, AGR RES SERV, US DEPT AGR, 67- *Personal Data:* b Castalia, NC, Nov 12, 33; m 60; c 2. *Educ:* NC State Univ, BS, 57, MAgr, 63, PhD(plant breeding, bot), 67. *Prof Exp:* Teacher, NC High Sch, 57-61; res supvr, NC State Univ, 63-64. *Mem:* AAAS; Am Soc Agron; Sigma Xi. *Res:* Derivation from Nicotiana species and tobacco introductions, and the genetic analysis of resistance to tobacco leaf diseases incited by potato virus Y, etch virus and tobacco vein mottle virus. *Mailing Add:* 705 N Columbia St Poplarville MS 39470

GUPTON, GUY WINFRED, JR, BUILDING SYSTEMS OPERATION & MAINTENANCE, INDOOR AIR QUALITY. *Current Pos:* VPRES, MAY, GUPTON, BLANKENBEKER, 97- *Personal Data:* b Atlanta, Ga, Nov 15, 26; m 48; c 4. *Educ:* Ga State Univ, BBA, 67. *Honors & Awards:* Distinguished Serv Award, Am Soc Heating, Refrig & Air Conditioning Engrs, 82. *Prof Exp:* Assoc, Newcomb & Boyd Consult Engrs, 52-73; partner, Peters-Gupton Assocs, 73-76; pres, Gupton Eng Assocs, Inc, 76-96. *Concurrent Pos:* Lectr mech eng building systs, Ga Inst Technol, 77-85; prin investr, Control Systs Surv, US Army Construct Eng Res Lab, 86-87; investr, VE Study Design Large Aircraft Corrosion Control Facil, Vent Systs, US Army Cofe & USAF, 85. *Mem:* Fel Am Soc Heating, Refrig & Air Conditioning Engrs; Nat Soc Archit Engrs. *Res:* Building systems operation and maintenance with emphasis on systems commissioning, maintenance management, investigation of failures, indoor air quality investigations and system problem solving. *Mailing Add:* May Gupton Blankenbeker 1303 Hightower Trail Atlanta GA 30350

GUPTON, JOHN, ORGANIC CHEMISTRY. *Current Pos:* from asst prof to assoc prof org chem, 78-83, PROF CHEM, UNIV CENT FLA, 86- *Personal Data:* b Norfolk, Va, Jan 4, 46; m 70, Mary Rose; c Emily. *Educ:* Va Mil Inst, BS, 67; Ga Inst Technol, MS, 69, PhD(chem), 75. *Honors & Awards:* Award for Excellence in Research & Scroll Award, Univ Cent Fla. *Prof Exp:* Sr chemist agr res, Ciba-Geigy Corp, 75-78. *Concurrent Pos:* Mem, Coun on Undergrad Res. *Mem:* Am Chem Soc; Sigma Xi; AAAS. *Res:* Synthesis of agricultural chemicals; new synthetic applications of vinamidinium salts; new methods for the incorporation of fluorine into organic molecules. *Mailing Add:* Dept Chem Univ NC Asheville NC 28804. *Fax:* 407-823-2252; *E-Mail:* chem@ucfivm.bitnet

GUPTON, OSCAR WILMOT, botany, for more information see previous edition

GUPTON, PAUL STEPHEN, CORROSION, ELEVATED TEMPERATURE METALLURGY. *Current Pos:* METAL CONSULT, PAUL S GUPTON & ASSOCS INC, 85- *Personal Data:* b Houston, Tex, Dec 30, 34; m 60; c 2. *Educ:* Lamar Univ, BS, 58; Tex A&M Univ, MS, 60. *Prof Exp:* Develop engr, Murphy Eng Lab, 55-57; welding engr, Hughes Tool Co, 57-58; res fel, Tex Eng Exp Sta, Tex A&M Res Ctr, 59-60; sr fel, Monsanto Co, 60-85. *Mem:* Fel Am Soc Metals (treas, 81); Am Soc Nondestructive Testing; Am Soc Testing & Mat; Am Welding Soc; Coating Soc. *Res:* Magnetic properties of the iron, nickel, zinc system not of high temperature alloys. *Mailing Add:* 1100 Deats Rd Dickinson TX 77539

GUR, DAVID, RADIATION PHYSICS, HEALTH PHYSICS. *Current Pos:* fel, Univ Pittsburgh, 75-77, asst prof radiation health, 77-80, assoc prof radiation health & radiol, 80-84, prof, 84-97, SR VPRES & PROF RADIOL, UNIV PITTSBURGH, 97- *Personal Data:* b Haifa, Israel, Apr 7, 47; m 71; c 2. *Educ:* Israel Inst Technol, BSc, 73; Univ Pittsburgh, MS, 76, ScD, 77. *Prof Exp:* Atomic physicist, Israel Inst Technol, 71-74. *Mem:* Health Physics Soc; Am Asn Physicists Med. *Res:* Development of techniques for early diagnosis and dose reduction in breast cancer detection; computerized electronic radiography; dynamic studies with contrast material using CT scanners; radiation bio-effects in human populations. *Mailing Add:* Alleghany Health Educ & Res Found 20900 Fifth Ave Pl 10920 Fifth Ave Pittsburgh PA 15222

GUR, TURGUT M, SOLID STATE ELECTROCHEMISTRY, ELECTROCHEMICAL ENERGY CONVERSION & STORAGE. *Current Pos:* sr res assoc, Dept Mat Sci Eng, 87-90, tech dir, 90-96, ASSOC DIR, CTR MAT RES, STANFORD UNIV CALIF, 96- *Personal Data:* b Istanbul, Turkey; m, Gulay; c Yerman & Doga. *Educ:* Middle E Tech Univ, Ankara, BS, 66, MS, 69; Stanford Univ, MS, 71, MS, 73, PhD(mat sci eng), 76. *Prof Exp:* Asst prof teaching & res, Middle E Tech Univ, 76-79; staff scientist res, Energy Systs Lab, Calif, 80-82; sr scientist res, Raychem Corp, Calif, 82-85; gen mgr mfg, Tusa AS, Istanbul, Turkey, 85-87. *Concurrent Pos:* IBM fel, 87-88. *Mem:* Electrochem Soc; Mat Res Soc; Am Chem Soc; Am Ceramic Soc; Solid State Ionics Soc. *Res:* High temperature electrosynthesis and fuel cells; solid electrolytes; chemical and humidity sensors; heterogeneous catalysis; chemical vapor deposition techniques; solid state ionics; diamond thin films; gas separation membranes. *Mailing Add:* 1595 Walnut Dr Palo Alto CA 94303. *Fax:* 650-723-3044; *E-Mail:* tmgur@ee.stanford.edu

GURALNICH, SIDNEY AARON, CIVIL ENGINEERING. *Current Pos:* dir, Struct Eng Lab, Ill Inst Technol, 68-71, dean, Grad Sch, 71-75, exec vpres provost, 75-82, trustee, 76-82, MEM FAC, ILL INST TECHNOL, CHICAGO, 58-, PROF CIVIL ENG, 67-, DISTINGUISHED PROF ENG, 82-, DIR, ADVAN BLDG MAT & SYSTS CTR, 87- *Personal Data:* b Philadelphis, Pa, Apr 25, 29; m, Eleanor Alban; c Sara D & Jeremy. *Educ:* Drexel Inst Technol, BSc, 52; Cornell Univ, MS, 55, PhD, 58. *Honors & Awards:* Collingwood Prize, Am Soc Chem Eng, 61. *Prof Exp:* From instr to asst prof, Cornell Univ, 52-58, mgr, Struct Res Lab, 56-58; develop engr, Portland Cement Asn, Ill, 59-61. *Concurrent Pos:* McGraw fel, 52-53; fac fel, Ill Inst Technol, 60; trustee, Inst Gas Technol, 76-81, Res Inst Ill, Inst Tech, 76-82; comnr-at-large, NCent Asn Schs & Cols, 85-89; consult & evaluator, 89-; consult govt & indust. *Mem:* Fel Am Soc Chem Eng; Am Concrete Inst; Am Soc Eng Educ; Soc Exp Mech; Sigma Xi. *Res:* Civil engineering; chemical engineering. *Mailing Add:* Ill Inst Technol 3300 S Federal St Chicago IL 60616-3793

GURALNICK, ROBERT MICHAEL, GROUP THEORY, COMMUTATIVE ALGEBRA. *Current Pos:* from asst prof to assoc prof, 79-88, PROF MATH, UNIV SOUTHERN CALIF, 88- *Personal Data:* b Los Angeles, Calif, July 10, 50; m 74. *Educ:* Univ Calif, Los Angeles, BA, 72, MA, 74, PhD(math), 77. *Prof Exp:* Bateman res instr math, Calif Inst Technol, 77-79. *Mem:* Am Math Soc. *Res:* Finite group theory; representations of orders; matrix theory. *Mailing Add:* Univ Southern Calif DRB 155 1042 W 36th Pl Los Angeles CA 90089-1113

GURALNICK, WALTER, MEDICINE. *Current Pos:* instr dent med, Harvard Sch Dent Med, 54-55, instr oral surg, 55-58, from asst clin prof to clin prof & chmn, Dept Oral Surg, 58-74, actg chmn, Dept Dent Med, 66-67, chmn, Dept Oral & Maxillofacial Surg, 74-81, prof, 81-87, EMER PROF, DEPT ORAL & MAXILLOFACIAL SURG, HARVARD SCH DENT MED, 87- *Personal Data:* b Boston, Mass. *Educ:* Mass State Col, BS, 37; Harvard Sch Dent Med, DMD, 41; Am Bd Oral & Maxillofacial Surgeons, dipl, 50. *Honors & Awards:* Award for Distinguished Achievement in Oral & Maxillofacial Surg, William J Gies Found, 87; Oshon Award, 88. *Prof Exp:* Intern oral surg, Boston City Hosp, 41-42; mil serv, 42-46. *Concurrent Pos:* Oral surgeon, Beth Israel Hosp, Boston, 47-82, Mt Auburn Hosp, Cambridge, 48-82, New Eng Deaconess Hosp, Boston, 50-82, Newton-Wellesley Hosp, Mass, 50-82, New Eng Baptist Hosp, Boston, 52-82; actg chief, Oral Surg Serv, Mass Gen Hosp, Boston, 67-68, chief, Oral & Maxillofacial Surg Serv, 68-81, vis oral & maxillofacial surgeon, 81-, exec dir, Ambulatory Care Ctr, 82-83, dir operating rooms, 83-91; vis prof, Columbia Presby Hosp, NY, 81-82; hon prof, Shanghai Second Med Univ, People's Repub China, 85, Xian Med Univ, 86, W China Univ Med Sci, 87. *Mem:* Nat Acad Sci; Am Dent Asn; fel Int Asn Oral Surgeons; assoc mem Brit Asn Oral Surgeons; Int Asn Dent Res; Am Asn Oral & Maxillofacial Surgeons; Am Asn Cancer Educ; Am Asn Dent Schs; Sr mem Inst Med Nat Acad Sci. *Res:* Author of over 60 technical journal articles and publications. *Mailing Add:* Bernard Gold Mass Gen Hosp 55 Fruit St Boston MA 02214. *Fax:* 617-726-2814

GURAM, MALKIAT SINGH, ZOOLOGY, BOTANY. *Current Pos:* prof biol & head dept, 67-68, div chmn, Natural Sci Dept & acad dean, 68-80, prof zool, 80-94, DIV CHMN, NATURAL SCI DEPT, VOORHEES COL, EMER PROF, 94- *Personal Data:* b Ludhiana, India, Jan 4, 28; nat US; m 50; c 3. *Educ:* Punjab Univ, BS, 48, MS, 55; Ohio State Univ, PhD(biol), 67. *Prof Exp:* Lectr zool & entom, Punjab Univ, India, 48-49, res asst, 49-53, lectr, Agr Col, 53-56; asst entomologist, Punjab Agr Dept, 53-60; asst prof zool & entom, Punjab Univ, 62-64. *Mem:* AAAS; Am Inst Biol Sci; Entom Soc Am. *Res:* Toxicology; pesticide residue detection by electron capture gas chromatography. *Mailing Add:* 25 Weed Dr Columbia SC 29212

GURARY, ALEXANDER, METALORGANIC CHEMICAL VAPOR DEPOSITION, HIGH TEMPERATURE SYSTEMS. *Current Pos:* proj leader, 89-94, STAFF SCIENTIST, EMCORE CORP, 94- *Personal Data:* b Kiev, USSR, Nov 23, 57; US citizen; m 88, Inna Gruz; c Michael, Daniel, Ellen & Benjamin. *Educ:* Politech Inst, Russia, BS & MS, 80; Russian Acad Sci, PhD(mat sci), 88. *Prof Exp:* Res engr, Mat Sci Inst, Russia, 84-87, staff scientist, 87-89. *Mem:* Mat Res Soc; Am Vacuum Soc; Mat Info Soc. *Res:* Equipment and methodology for metorganic chemical vapor depositoin for II-V, II-VI, GaN, SiC and oxide epitaxial films, thermal modeling, flow visualization, temperature measurement; development of the elemental vapor transport epitaxy technique; high temperature strength of advanced composite materials. *Mailing Add:* 618 Foothill Rd Bridgewater NJ 08807. *Fax:* 732-271-9686; *E-Mail:* alex@emcore.com

GURBAXANI, SHYAM HASSOMAL, SOLID STATE ELECTRONICS. *Current Pos:* assoc prof, 74-76, PROF ELEC ENG & COMPUT SCI & DIR, LOS ALAMOS GRAD CTR, UNIV NMEX, 76- *Personal Data:* b Karachi, Pakistan, Dec 28, 28; US citizen; m 59, Shannon Howard; c Andrew, Brian & Catherine. *Educ:* Royal Inst Sci, BSc, 49; Stanford Univ, MS, 50; Rutgers Univ, MS, 63, PhD(solid state physics), 65. *Prof Exp:* Elec engr, Gen Elec Co, 50-51 & Kuljian Corp, 51-52; elec engr, Lummus Co, 52-58, chief engr, 58, budget control consult, Lummus Int, Venezuela, 58-59, cent mgt engr, Lummus Co, 59-60, process design engr, 60-64; br head, Res Div, US Naval Air Develop Ctr, 65-66; asst prof physics, Sacramento State Col, 66-67; assoc scientist, Radiation Co, 67-68, chief scientist, 68-69, reentry physics consult, 69-74. *Concurrent Pos:* Consult, Shell Co, Venezuela, 58-59; NSF res partic laser physics, Stanford Univ, 67; asst prof elec eng, Univ NMex, 69-74; Assoc Western Univs res partic, Los Alamos Sci Lab, 71; guest scientist, Los Alamos Sci Lab, 72-76; NSF scientist, Bombay Univ, India, 75; invited vis scientist, Tata Inst Fundamental Res, Dept Atomic Energy, India, 75; vis prof physics, Inst Sci, India, 75; conf chmn, first Amerem 96 Int symp. *Mem:* Am Phys Soc; sr mem Inst Elec & Electronics Engrs; Am Asn Physics Teachers; Sigma Xi. *Res:* Electron spin and nuclear magnetic resonance; radiation damage; cryogenics; microwave physics; electromagnetic-acoustic energy interaction, population inversion in ionized gases and laser physics; solar energy; electromagnetic pulse in nuclear detonation. *Mailing Add:* Dept Elec-Comput Eng Univ NMex 35 Tierra Monte NE Albuquerque NM 87122-2107. *E-Mail:* gurbaxni@unm.edu

GURD, FRANK ROSS NEWMAN, BIOCHEMISTRY. *Current Pos:* prof chem & biochem, 65-79, distinguished prof, 79-86, EMER PROF BIOCHEM & CHEM, IND UNIV, BLOOMINGTON, 86- *Personal Data:* b Montreal, Can, Jan 20, 24; nat US; m 56, Ruth Sights; c Fraser Baillie, Kathleen, Martha Helen & Charles Baillie. *Educ:* McGill Univ, BSc, 45, MSc, 46; Harvard Univ, PhD(biochem), 49. *Prof Exp:* Res assoc phys chem, Harvard Univ, 48-50, instr, 50-51, res assoc, 51-52, asst prof, 52-55; asst prof clin biochem, Med Col, Cornell Univ, 55-60; prof biochem med, Ind Univ, Indianapolis, 60-65. *Concurrent Pos:* Guggenheim & Whitney fels, Wash Univ, 54-55; asst dir bur med res, Equitable Life Assurance Soc US, 55-59; mem biophys & biophys chem B study sect, NIH, 66-70, chmn, 68-70. *Mem:* Am Chem Soc; Am Soc Biol Chemists; Biophys Soc; Harvey Soc; NY Acad Sci. *Res:* Lipoproteins; protein purification; interactions of peptides and proteins with metals; relation of structure to function of proteins; protein modification and sequence determination; magnetic resonance spectroscopy of proteins and peptides; electrostatic interaction in proteins; semisynthesis of proteins. *Mailing Add:* 2032 Quail Run Dr NE Albuquerque NM 87122-1100

GURD, FRASER NEWMAN, SURGERY. *Current Pos:* EMER PROF, FAC MED, McGILL UNIV, 80- *Personal Data:* b Montreal, Que, Mar 19, 14; m 38; c 5. *Educ:* McGill Univ, BA, 34, MD & CM, 39; Univ Pa, MSc, 47; FRCPS(C) & FACS, 48. *Honors & Awards:* Duncan Graham Award, Royal Col Physicians & Surgeons Can, 85; Surg Award for Serv To Safety, Nat Safety Coun, 85; F N G Starr Award, Can Med Asn, 90. *Prof Exp:* Assoc prof surg, McGill Univ, 59-63, prof & chmn dept, 63-71; assoc secy, Royal Col Physicians & Surgeons Can, 72-75, consult, 76-81. *Concurrent Pos:* From sr surgeon to surgeon-in-chief, Montreal Gen Hosp, 59-71; mem coun, 64-72; regent, Am Col Surgeons, 66-74; consult staff, Montreal Gen Hosp, 71- *Mem:* Can Asn Clin Surgeons (pres, 68-70); Am Asn Surg Trauma (pres, 68); Am Surg Asn (vpres, 75); James IV Asn Surgeons (pres, 81-84); Int Surg Group (treas, 72-75); Hon Mem, Canadian Asn Gen Surgeons, 87. *Res:* Surgical physiology; physiology of the liver; surgical shock; physiology of body fluids and electrolytes; gastroenterology; surgical training. *Mailing Add:* 168 Carlyle Ave Montreal PQ H3R 1S9 Can

GURD, JAMES W, BIOCHEMISTRY OF SYNOPTIC FUNCTION, PROTEIN PHOSPHORYLATION. *Current Pos:* PROF BIOCHEM, SCARBOROUGH CAMPUS, UNIV TORONTO, 74. *Personal Data:* b Montreal, Que, June 23, 43. *Educ:* Mt Allison Univ, BA, 64; McGill Univ, PhD(biochem), 69. *Prof Exp:* Med Res Coun fel, Nat Inst Med Res, Mill Hill, UK, 69-72; res assoc, Brain Res Group, Ind Univ, 72-74. *Res:* Biochemistry of synoptic development and function; biochemical changes at the synapse which occur following brief periods of hypoxia; protein tyrosine phosphorylation at the synapse. *Mailing Add:* 1265 Military Trail West Hill ON M1C 1A4 Can

GURD, RUTH SIGHTS, PROTEIN CHEMISTRY, ENDOCRINOLOGY. *Current Pos:* sr res assoc neurochem, 67-71, from asst prof to assoc prof, 72-89, EMER PROF BIOCHEM, SCH MED, IND UNIV, 89- *Personal Data:* b Chicago, Ill, Sept 17, 27; m 56, Frank Ross Newman; c Martha Helen & Charles Baillie. *Educ:* Univ Mich, Ann Arbor, BS, 49; Washington Univ, St Louis, MO, 57. *Prof Exp:* Res assoc biochem, Dept Med, Presby Hosp, Chicago, 50-51 & Dept Surg, Sch Med, Washington Univ, 51-52; fel physiol, Col Med, Cornell Univ, 57-58; med consult, Aerospace Res Appln Ctr, Ind Univ, 62-66. *Mem:* Soc Neurosci; Biophys Soc; Am Soc Biol Chemists; Am Diabetes Asn. *Res:* Structure-function relationships of peptides and proteins with particular interest in diabetes and the structure/function/mechanisms of the hormones which control metabolic fluxes; the structure/function/ mechanisms of the hormones which control metabolic fluxes. *Mailing Add:* 2032 Quail Run Dr NE Albuquerque NM 87122-1100

GUREL, DEMET, ORGANIC CHEMISTRY. *Current Pos:* adj prof, 83-93, ASSOC PROF, TOURO COL, 93-, CHAIR CHEM & PHYSICS, 96- *Personal Data:* b Ankara, Turkey, July 14, 39; m 62; c 2. *Educ:* Am Col Girls, BS, 59; Smith Col, MA, 61; NY Univ, PhD(chem), 73. *Honors & Awards:* Fulbright Fel. *Prof Exp:* Adj asst prof chem, NY Univ, 73-89. *Concurrent Pos:* Adj asst prof, Baruch Col, City Univ New York, 79-; consult, 89- *Mem:* Am Chem Soc; NY Acad Sci; Sigma Xi. *Res:* Chemical oscillations; thyroglobulin iodination; topological mechanics of protein folding. *Mailing Add:* 630 First Ave N Apt 9J New York NY 10016

GUREL, OKAN, BIOMATHEMATICS, BIOPHYSICS. *Current Pos:* CONSULT, 92- *Personal Data:* b Kirkagac, Turkey, Aug 1, 31; m 62; c 2. *Educ:* Tech Univ Istanbul, YMuh, 54; Univ BC, MASc, 57; Stanford Univ, PhD(appl mech), 61. *Honors & Awards:* Fel, NY Acad Sci. *Prof Exp:* Staff mem math, Int Bus Mach Corp, 61-62; asst prof, Mid East Tech Univ, Ankara, 64-66; staff mem, NY Sci Ctr, 66-70, Sci Ctr HQ, IBM Corp, 70-79 & Cambridge Sci Ctr, 80-85; discipline specialist, Life & Health Sci, Acad Info Systs, 85-92. *Concurrent Pos:* Secy, Scientist Training Group, Sci & Technol Res Coun, Turkey, 64-65, mem, 65-66; consult, Ford Found Sci Lycee Proj, Ankara, 65-66; adj prof, Baruch Col, 70-; vis prof, Bosphorus Univ, Istanbul, 77; NATO sr scientist fel, 77; consult, UN Develop Prog, 78. *Mem:* Am Math Soc; Int Soc Chronobiol; NY Acad Sci; Biophys Soc; AAAS. *Res:* Qualitative theory of differential equations and its application; stability theory and bifurcation of dynamical systems; biological systems, particularly molecular and cellular; chemical oscillations; biomathematics and biophysics; cytology; topological mechanics of protein folding. *Mailing Add:* 630 First Ave No 9J 2-J New York NY 10016

GURER, EMIR, IMPURITIES & DEFECTS IN SEMICONDUCTORS, SURFACE PHYSICS. *Current Pos:* teaching asst introductory physics, Physics Dept, 84-86, res asst, 86-90, VIS RES ASSOC, ZETTLEMOYER CTR SURFACE STUDIES, LEHIGH UNIV, 90- *Personal Data:* b Kastamonu, Turkey, Apr 6, 60; m 89. *Educ:* Middle East Tech Univ, Ankara, Turkey, BS, 82, MS, 84; Lehigh Univ, MS, 86, PhD(physics), 90. *Prof Exp:* Teaching asst introductory physics, Middle East Tech Univ, 82-84. *Mem:* Am Phys Soc; Mat Res Soc; NAm Catalysis Soc; Sigma Xi. *Res:* Defects in semiconductors; electronic properties of materials; study of surfaces of single crystal metals using vibrational and electronic spectroscopic techniques. *Mailing Add:* Silicon Valley Group 541 E Trimble Rd San Jose CA 95131

GUREVITCH, JESSICA, PLANT ECOLOGY & ECOLOGICAL STATISTICS, EXPERIMENTAL DESIGN. *Current Pos:* asst prof, 85-92, ASSOC PROF ECOL & EVOLUTION, STATE UNIV NY, STONY BROOK, 92- *Personal Data:* b Brooklyn, NY, Oct 31, 52; m 89, Todd A Postol; c Nathaniel E. *Educ:* Cornell Univ, BS, 73; Univ Ariz, PhD(ecol & evolutionary biol), 82. *Prof Exp:* Fel, Univ Chicago, 83-85; prog dir pop biol, NSF, 92-93. *Concurrent Pos:* Lectr evolutionary ecol, Univ Chicago, 84; Katherine Putnam res fel, Arnold Arboretam, Harvard Univ, 89; prin investr, NSF, 89-94 & 96-; assoc ed, J Vegetation Sci, 92-; elected coun mem, Ecol Soc Am, 90-92; chair, Ecol Soc Am, Eminent Ecol Award Subcomt, 97- *Mem:* Sigma Xi; Ecol Soc Am; Asn Women Sci; Int Asn Vegetation Sci. *Res:* Experimental study of competition in natural plant communities; meta-analysis in ecology; statistical experimental design and analysis; plant physiological ecology and morphometrics; author of 30 publications. *Mailing Add:* Dept Ecol & Evolution State Univ NY Stony Brook NY 11794-5245. *E-Mail:* jgurvtch@life.bio.sunysb.edu

GUREVITCH, MARK, PHYSICS. *Current Pos:* RETIRED. *Personal Data:* b Cleveland, Ohio, Sept 11, 16; wid; c 2. *Educ:* Univ Calif, AB, 38, PhD(physics), 47. *Prof Exp:* Instr physics, Univ Calif, 42-43, res physicist, Off Sci Res & Develop Proj, 43-45; from asst prof to prof physics, Univ Idaho, 47-58; prof physics & chmn dept, Portland State Univ, 58-82. *Concurrent Pos:* NIH fel biophys, 66-67. *Mem:* AAAS; Am Phys Soc; Am Asn Physics Teachers. *Res:* Spectroscopy; properties of thin films; environmental science. *Mailing Add:* Physics Dept Box 751 Portland OR 97207

GURFINKEL, GERMAN R, STRUCTURAL ENGINEERING. *Current Pos:* vis asst prof, 62-63, from instr to assoc prof, 63-74, PROF CIVIL ENG, UNIV ILL, URBANA, 74- *Personal Data:* b La Habana, Cuba, Sept 14, 32; US citizen; m 56, Ana Fainstein; c 4. *Educ:* Univ Havana, Civil Eng, 55; Univ Ill, Urbana, MS, 57, PhD(civil eng), 66. *Honors & Awards:* James F Lincoln Welding Award, 73, 77 & 78-84, 88. *Prof Exp:* Asst prof civil eng, Univ Havana, 59-61. *Concurrent Pos:* Consult struct engr, 55-; consult, NSF-AID, India, summers 67, 68 & 69; NSF res grant, 67-68. *Mem:* Am Soc Civil Engrs; Am Concrete Inst; Am Soc Testing & Mat. *Res:* Nuclear containment structures; wood structures; structural mechanics; numerical methods; tall buildings, silos and bunkers; investigation of structural failures. *Mailing Add:* Dept Civil Eng Univ Ill Urbana Campus 208 N Romine St Urbana IL 61801-2374. *Fax:* 217-333-9464; *E-mail:* ggunfink@uiuc.edu

GURGANUS, KENNETH RUFUS, MATHEMATICS. *Current Pos:* Lectr, 75-76, ASST PROF MATH, UNIV NC, 76- *Personal Data:* b Williamston, NC, Sept 9, 48; m 76; c 1. *Educ:* Univ NC, BS, 70, MS, 72, PhD(math), 76. *Mem:* Am Math Soc; Math Asn Am; Nat Coun Teachers Math. *Res:* Geometric function theory; real analysis. *Mailing Add:* Dept Math Sci Univ NC Wilmington NC 28403-3201

GURIEN, HARVEY, ORGANIC CHEMISTRY. *Current Pos:* RETIRED. *Personal Data:* b Brooklyn, NY, Sept 25, 25; m 50; c 5. *Educ:* Brooklyn Col, BS, 49; Univ Pa, MS, 50; Polytech Inst Brooklyn, PhD, 55. *Prof Exp:* Res chemist, Gen Aniline Works, 53-60, S B Penick & Co, 60-62, Hoffman-La Roche Co, 62-84 & Sterling-Winthrop Res Inst, 85-91. *Concurrent Pos:* Pres, Regulatory Affairs Prof, 79-91. *Mem:* Drug Info Asn; Am Chem Soc; Regulatory Affairs Prof Soc. *Res:* Pharmaceutical developmental research; drug regulatory affairs. *Mailing Add:* 909 Mohegan Rd Niskayuna NY 12309

GURIES, RAYMOND PAUL, CONSERVATION BIOLOGY. *Current Pos:* From asst prof to assoc prof, 77-87, PROF FOREST GENETICS, UNIV WIS-MADISON, 87- *Personal Data:* b Worcester, Mass, Dec 7, 43. *Educ:* Univ Mass, BS, 71; Univ Wash, PhD(forest genetics), 75. *Mem:* AAAS; Soc Study Evolution; Soc Conserv Biol. *Res:* Selection and breeding of woody plants; population genetics and genecology of forest tree species. *Mailing Add:* 1630 Linden Dr Forest 120 Russell Labs Univ Wis-Madison Madison WI 53706-1520

GURIN, SAMUEL, biochemistry; deceased, see previous edition for last biography

GURINSKY, DAVID H(ARRIS), METALLURGY. *Current Pos:* scientist, 47-50, sr scientist & head metall div, 50-78, DEP CHMN, DEPT ENERGY & ENVIRON, BROOKHAVEN NAT LAB, 78- *Personal Data:* b Brooklyn, NY, Apr 26, 14; m 37; c 2. *Educ:* NY Univ, AB, 36, PhD(phys chem), 42. *Honors & Awards:* Studies Award, Am Inst Chem. *Prof Exp:* Asst instr chem physics, NY Univ, 36-42; res assoc metall Univ Chicago, 42-44, res assoc, Inst Study Metals, 46-47; res assoc, Los Alamos Sci Lab, NMex, 44-46. *Concurrent Pos:* Head mat res on high temperature graphite reactor & consult, Gen Atomic Div, Gen Dynamics Corp, 59-60. *Mem:* Fel Am Nuclear Soc; Am Soc Metals; Am Inst Mining, Metall & Petrol Engrs. *Res:* Nuclear fuels; graphite radiation effects; effects of radiation on structural materials; liquid metal corrosion; superconductivity; superconductor materials; superconducting power transmission. *Mailing Add:* 40 Inwood Rd Center Moriches NY 11934

GURK, HERBERT MORTON, MATHEMATICS. *Current Pos:* CONSULT, 95- *Personal Data:* b Philadelphia, Pa, Aug 6, 30; m 52; c 3. *Educ:* Univ Pa, BA, 51, MA, 52, PhD(math), 56. *Prof Exp:* Instr eng res, Univ Pa, 53-56; mathematician, Systems Eng, Radio Corp Am, RCA Corp, 56-58, leader, Systs Analysis Group, 58-61, Space Opers Analysis Group, 62-66, mgr imagery systs progs, 66-68, mgr earth observation systs, 68-74, staff syst scientist, Advan Prog Planning, 75-95. *Mem:* Soc Indust & Appl Math (treas, 61-65); Am Math Soc; Am Inst Aeronaut & Astronaut. *Res:* Theory of games; theory of waiting lines and stochastic processes; numerical analysis; mathematical linguistics; space systems planning and analysis; space meteorological systems. *Mailing Add:* 26 Howe Circle Princeton NJ 08540

GURKLIS, JOHN A(NTHONY), ENVIRONMENTAL ENGINEERING, ELECTROCHEMICAL ENGINEERING. *Current Pos:* prin chem engr, Battelle Mem Inst, 50-56, sr chem engr, Electrochem Eng Dev, 56-76, sr chem engr, Energy & Environ Systs Assessment Sect, 76-82, SR CHEM ENGR, ENVIRON TECHNOL & ASSESSMENT SECT, BATTELLE MEM INST, 82- *Personal Data:* b Waterbury, Conn, July 12, 21; m 58; c 2. *Educ:* Univ Md, BS, 43; Ohio State Univ, MS, 47, PhD(chem eng), 50. *Prof Exp:* Asst chem engr, Ohio State Univ, 43-44 & 49-50. *Mem:* Am Inst Chem Engrs; Am Electroplaters Soc; Soc Mfg Engrs; Am Soc Metals. *Res:* Hazardous waste management, water pollution control, wastewater treatment, industrial waste management, solid waste management, waste minimization, resource recovery, energy conservation; chemical milling; electrodeposition of metals and alloys; electrowinning; electrorefining; electropolishing; chemical engineering; metal finishing; electrochemical machining. *Mailing Add:* 2840 N Star Rd Columbus OH 43221-2959

GURLAND, JOHN, STATISTICS, PROBABILITY. *Current Pos:* prof, Math Res Ctr, 60-63, PROF STATIST, UNIV WIS-MADISON, 63- *Personal Data:* b Can, Jan 6, 17; nat US; m 48; c 2. *Educ:* Univ Toronto, MA, 42; Univ Calif, PhD(math statist), 48. *Prof Exp:* Pierce instr math, Harvard Univ, 48-49; asst prof statist, Univ Chicago, 49-52; from assoc prof to prof, Iowa State Univ, 52-60. *Mem:* Fel AAAS; fel Inst Math Statist; Biomet Soc; fel Am Statist Asn; Math Asn Am. *Res:* Mathematical and applied statistics; probability and distribution theory, estimation and test of fit; regression, biological assay, survival analysis and reliability. *Mailing Add:* Dept Statist Univ Wis 1210 W Dayton St Madison WI 53706

GURLAND, JOSEPH, PHYSICAL METALLURGY. *Current Pos:* from asst prof to assoc prof, 55-64, prof, 64-87, EMER PROF ENG, BROWN UNIV, 88- *Personal Data:* b Berlin, Ger, Jan 26, 23; nat US; m 48, Doris Hurwitch; c Lisa & Johanna. *Educ:* NY Univ, BChE, 44, MS, 47; Mass Inst Technol, ScD, 51. *Honors & Awards:* Plansee Medal, Int Plansee Soc Powder Metal, 89. *Prof Exp:* Res engr, Battelle Mem Inst, 47-48; asst metall, Mass Inst Technol, 48-51; res engr & mgr basic res, Firth-Sterling, Inc, 51-55. *Concurrent Pos:* NATO fel sci, 70; NSF fac fel, 62 & foreign travel award, 78; vis distinguished scientist & adj prof, Dept Mfg Eng, Boston Univ, 90-97. *Mem:* Fel Am Soc Metals; Am Inst Mining Metall & Petrol Engrs; Am Soc Testing & Mat. *Res:* Structure of sintered carbides; composite alloys; fracture of metals; quantitative metallography; history of technology. *Mailing Add:* Div Eng Box D Brown Univ Providence RI 02912-9104. *Fax:* 401-863-1157

GURLEY, LAWRENCE RAY, BIOCHEMISTRY, CHEMICAL ENGINEERING. *Current Pos:* staff biochemist, 64-83, LAB FEL, LOS ALAMOS NAT LAB, UNIV CALIF, 83- *Personal Data:* b Goldsboro, NC, Jan 13, 35; m 58; c 2. *Educ:* NC State Univ, BChE, 58, ChE, 59; Univ NC, PhD(biochem), 64. *Honors & Awards:* Coker Award, Elisha Mitchell Soc, 65. *Prof Exp:* Prod engr, Merck & Co, Va, 58-60. *Concurrent Pos:* Fel, Los Alamos Nat Lab, Univ Calif, Div leader, Life Sci, 86-88. *Mem:* Am Soc Biochem & Molecular Biol; Am Soc Cell Biol; Am Chem Soc; Protein Soc; Int Cell Cycle Soc. *Res:* Chromatin structure; histone chemistry and biology; histone metabolism; tissue culture; biochemistry of the cell life cycle; radiation biology; pulmonary biochemistry; high performance liquid chromatography. *Mailing Add:* Life Sci Div Univ Calif Los Alamos Sci Lab MS-880 Los Alamos NM 87545-0001. *Fax:* 505-665-3024

GURLEY, THOMAS WOOD, ANALYTICAL CHEMISTRY. *Current Pos:* Sr res chemist, 76-82, SECT HEAD, GOODYEAR TIRE & RUBBER CO, 82-; AT ABBOTT LABS, ASHLAND, OHIO. *Personal Data:* b Endicott, NY, May 28, 46; m 68; c 3. *Educ:* Houghton Col, BA, 68; Case Western Res Univ, PhD(chem), 76. *Mem:* Am Chem Soc. *Res:* Development of new analytical methodology using gas chromatography, high performance liquid chromatography and wet chemistry for chemicals related to the rubber industry; polymer analysis; environmental analysis. *Mailing Add:* Abbott Labs 268 E Fourth St Ashland OH 44805-2412

GURLL, NELSON, ENDOCRINOLOGICAL SURGERY. *Current Pos:* asst prof, 76-80, assoc prof surg, 80-83, PROF SURG, COL MED, UNIV IOWA, 83- *Personal Data:* b Providence, RI, Jan 8, 42; m 65. *Educ:* Univ Calif, Berkeley, AB, 63; Univ San Francisco, MD, 67. *Honors & Awards:* AOA. *Prof Exp:* Clin fel surg, Harvard Med Sch, 68-73; res assoc bioeng & mech eng, Mass Inst Technol, 70-71; teaching fel surg, Harvard Med Sch, 72-73; res investr surg gastroenterol, Walter Reed Army Inst Res, 73-76, chief dept, 74-76. *Concurrent Pos:* Intern & resident, Beth Israel Hosp, Boston, 67-73; NIH acad surg trainee, Mass Inst Technol & Beth Israel Hosp, 70-73; resident physician, Clin Res Ctr, Mass Inst Technol, 70-71; attending staff physician, Vet Admin Med Ctr, Iowa City, 76-; staff surgeon, Hosp & Clin, Univ Iowa, 76-; actg chief surg, Vet Admin Med Ctr, Iowa City, 78-79; vis prof path, Univ BC, 85-86. *Mem:* Am Surg Asn; Am Gastroenterol Asn; Am Physiol Soc; fel Am Col Surgeons; Soc Univ Surgeons. *Res:* Investigating role of endorphins in the pathophysiology of shock and in gastrointestinal physiology. *Mailing Add:* Dept Surg Hosp & Clin Col Med Univ Iowa Iowa City IA 52240

GURNETT, DONALD ALFRED, SPACE PLASMA PHYSICS. *Current Pos:* from asst prof to assoc prof, 65-72, PROF PHYSICS, UNIV IOWA, 72- *Personal Data:* b Cedar Rapids, Iowa, Apr 11, 40; m 64; Marie B Schmitz; c Suzanne M & Christina A. *Educ:* Univ Iowa, BS, 62, MS, 63, PhD(physics), 65. *Honors & Awards:* Alexander von Humboldt Sr Scientist Award, 75; J H Dellinger Gold Medal, Int Sci Radio Union, 78; Distinguished Sci Achievement Award, NASA, 80; NASA Space Act Award, 86; J A Fleming Medal, Am Geophys Union, 89; Excellence in Plasma Physics, Am Phys Soc, 89. *Prof Exp:* NASA trainee, Univ Iowa, 62-64 & Stanford Univ, 64-65. *Concurrent Pos:* vis scientist, Max Planck Inst Extraterrestrial Physics, Garching, Ger, 75-76; vis prof, Inst Geophys & Planetary Physics, Univ Calif, Los Angeles, 79-80. *Mem:* Am Geophys Union; Int Sci Radio Union; Am Phys Soc; Int Acad Astronaut. *Res:* Experimental and theoretical investigation of plasma waves and radio emissions in planetary magnetospheres, in the solar wind, and in the solar corona. *Mailing Add:* Dept Physics & Astron Univ Iowa Iowa City IA 52242. *Fax:* 319-335-1753; *E-Mail:* gurnett@iowave.physics.uiowa.edu

GURNEY, CLIFFORD W, internal medicine, for more information see previous edition

GURNEY, ELIZABETH TUCKER GUICE, CELL BIOLOGY, GENETICS. *Current Pos:* NIH fel animal virol, Univ Utah, 75-77, res asst prof, 76-83, res assoc prof, 83-92, assoc dir, Undergrad Res Opportunities Prog, 90-91, ASSOC PROF, UNIV UTAH, 92- *Personal Data:* b Berkeley, Calif, Apr 5, 41; m 66, Theodore Jr; c Frederick Norman. *Educ:* Univ Chicago, AB, 62; Univ Calif, Berkeley, MS, 70, PhD(genetics), 75. *Prof Exp:* Tcch asst biol, Mass Inst Technol, 63-67, teaching asst animal cells & viruses, Cold Spring Harbor Lab, 66; res biochemist, Univ Calif, Berkeley, 70-73. *Mem:* Am Soc Cell Biol; Am Soc Microbiol; AAAS. *Res:* Cellular growth control mechanisms and transformation by tumor viruses; monoclonal antibodies for tumor antigens; DNA rearrangements. *Mailing Add:* Dept Biol Univ Utah Salt Lake City UT 84112. *E-Mail:* tuckergurney@bioscience.utah.edu

GURNEY, RAMSDELL, INTERNAL MEDICINE. *Current Pos:* Asst prof physiol, 47-50, from asst prof to assoc prof med, 50-76, EMER ASSOC PROF MED, STATE UNIV NY, BUFFALO, 76- *Personal Data:* b Buffalo, NY, Aug 2, 03; m 32; c 2. *Educ:* Yale Univ, BA, 25; Univ Buffalo, MD, 29; Am Bd Internal Med, dipl, 42. *Concurrent Pos:* Pvt pract, 32-; attend physician, Buffalo Gen Hosp, 57-71, consult physician, 71- *Mem:* Am Col Physicians. *Res:* Obesity and sweating; cardiovascular disease. *Mailing Add:* 11 Saint Andrews Walk Buffalo NY 14222

GURNEY, THEODORE, JR, CELL BIOLOGY. *Current Pos:* ASSOC PROF BIOL, UNIV UTAH, 74- *Personal Data:* b Hartford, Conn, Oct 14, 38; m 66, Elizabeth Guice; c Frederick Norman. *Educ:* Harvard Col, AB, 59; Yale Univ, MS, 61, PhD(biophys), 65. *Prof Exp:* USPHS fels biol, Mass Inst Technol, 64-67; Jane Coffin Childs Mem Fund med res fel molecular biol, Univ Calif, Berkeley, 67-68, asst prof, Univ Calif, Berkeley, 68-74. *Mem:* AAAS; Am Soc Cell Biol. *Res:* Contact inhibition of growth in cell culture; cell fractionation; RNA processing; DNA rearrangements. *Mailing Add:* Dept Biol Univ Utah Salt Lake City UT 84112. *E-Mail:* tedgurney@bioscience.utah.edu

GURNIS, MICHAEL, GEOLOGY, GEOPHYSICS. *Current Pos:* assoc prof, 94-96, PROF GEOPHYS, CALIF INST TECHNOL, 96- *Personal Data:* b Boston, Mass, Oct 22, 59. *Educ:* Univ Ariz, BS, 82; Australian Nat Univ, PhD, 87. *Honors & Awards:* Presidential Young Investr Award, NSF, 89; Donath Medal, Geol Soc Am, 93; Macelwance Medal, Am Geophys Union, 93. *Prof Exp:* Res fel geophys, Calif Inst Technol, Pasadena, 86-88; from asst prof to assoc prof geol sci, Univ Mich, Ann Arbor, 88-93. *Concurrent Pos:* Fel, David & Lucile Packard Found, 91; assoc dir, Seismol Lab, 95- *Mem:* Fel Am Geophys Union; fel Geol Soc Am. *Res:* Linkage of sedimentary rocks deposited in the interiors of continents to geodynamics processes within the earth; global dynamics, mantle convection, plate tectonics, sea level changes, evolution of mantle and crust; computational and visual fluids mechanics. *Mailing Add:* Seismol Lab Calif Inst Technol Pasadena CA 91125. *E-Mail:* gurnis@caltech.edu

GUROL, MIRAT D, WASTEWATER MANAGEMENT. *Current Pos:* ASST PROF ENVIRON ENG, DREXEL UNIV, 80- *Personal Data:* b Ankara, Turkey, Sept 2, 51; m 75. *Educ:* Middle East Tech Univ, BS, 73; Univ NC, MS, 77, PhD(environ eng), 80. *Prof Exp:* Teaching asst environ eng, Middle East Tech Univ, 73-75; res asst environ eng, Univ NC, 77-79. *Concurrent Pos:* Res scholar award, Drexel Univ, 81. *Mem:* Am Inst Chem Eng; Int Ozone Asn; Water Pollution Coun Fedn; Am Water Works Asn; Am Chem Soc. *Res:* Treatment of industrial wastewaters by chemical oxidation; reuse and recycling possibilities of industrial wastes by physical and chemical treatment; kinetics of treatment processes of water and wastewater. *Mailing Add:* Environ Studies Inst Drexel Univ Philadelphia PA 19104

GURPIDE, ERLIO, BIOCHEMISTRY, BIOPHYSICS. *Current Pos:* PROF BIOCHEM, OBSTET, GYNEC & REPROD SCI, MT SINAI SCH MED, 72- *Personal Data:* b Buenos Aires, Arg, Apr 8, 27; US citizen. *Educ:* Univ Buenos Aires, PhD(chem), 55. *Prof Exp:* Res assoc biochem, Columbia Univ, 59-64, asst prof, 64-69; prof biochem, obstet & gynec, Univ Minn, Minneapolis, 69-72. *Concurrent Pos:* Career scientist, Health Res Coun, NY, 63-69 & 73-; mem endocrinol study sect, NIH, 70-73. *Mem:* Am Soc Biol Chem; Endocrine Soc; Soc Gynec Invest. *Res:* Steroid biochemistry; use of isotopically labeled tracers in biology; endocrinology of reproduction. *Mailing Add:* Dept Biochem Ob-Gyn & Reprod Sci Mt Sinai Sch Med City Univ NY One Gustave Levy Pl Box 1175 New York NY 10029. *Fax:* 212-534-3192

GURR, HENRY S, ELEMENTARY PARTICLE PHYSICS. *Current Pos:* asst prof, 76-78, PROF PHYSICS, UNIV SC, AIKEN, 78- *Personal Data:* b Ohio, Mar 9, 37; m 61; c 3. *Educ:* Case Inst Technol, BS, 59, MS, 64 & PhD(nuclear physics), 67. *Prof Exp:* Res physicist, Univ Calif, Irvine, 67-76. *Concurrent Pos:* Vis prof physics & eng, Univ SC, Aiken, 73-76; res physicist, Univ Calif, Irvine, 78- *Mem:* Am Phys Soc; Sigma Xi; AAAS. *Res:* Experimental proof of the neutrino-electron scattering, (at Department of Energy reactor site); neutrino would recoil from an electron; research participation continues with collaboration in neutrino deuteron neutral current experiment; author of 2 publications on proceedings of international conferences in cosmic rays. *Mailing Add:* Box 29 Dept Phys Sci Univ SC Aiken Aiken SC 29801

GURRY, ROBERT WILTON, PHYSICAL CHEMISTRY. *Current Pos:* RETIRED. *Personal Data:* b Schenectady, NY, Sept 27, 13; m 39, Ruth C Moffatt; c Susan G (Whitaker) & Peter R. *Educ:* Union Univ, NY, BS, 34; Yale Univ, PhD(phys chem), 37. *Prof Exp:* Phys chemist, US Steel Corp, 37-55; phys chemist, Quaker Chem Prod Corp, 55-59; tech dir, Union Steel Corp, Piscataway, 59-72; consult mat sci & failure analysis, 72-88. *Concurrent Pos:* Instr, Stevens Inst Technol, 44-46. *Mem:* Am Chem Soc; Am Soc Metals; Nat Asn Corrosion Engrs; Am Soc Testing & Mat; Welding Res Coun, Am Soc Mech Engrs. *Res:* Surface chemistry of metals; corrosion; failure analysis; materials application; metal processing; author of one publication. *Mailing Add:* 52 Tropicana Dr Punta Gorda FL 33950

GURSKI, THOMAS RICHARD, QUANTUM OPTICS, ELECTROOPTICS. *Current Pos:* PRIN ENGR, RAYTHEON CO, 89- *Personal Data:* b Elizabeth, NJ, Dec 3, 40; m 64; c 6. *Educ:* Loyola Univ, Los Angeles, BS, 62; Univ Mich, MS, 63; Univ Ariz, PhD(optics), 74. *Prof Exp:* Assoc physicist electrooptics, Fed Systs Div, IBM Corp, 64-68; sr physicist optics, Perkin-Elmer corp, 68-69; res assoc optics, Optical Sci Ctr, Univ Ariz, 69-75; consult electrooptics, Kitt Peak Nat Observ, 71-74; mem staff optics, Lincoln Lab, Mass Inst Technol, 75-80; mem staff electrooptics, W J Schafer Asn, 80-83; vpres res & develop, Am Surg Laser Inc, 83-84; pres & chmn, Electro-optical Technol Inc, 85-89. *Mem:* Optical Soc Am; Soc Photo-Optical Instrumentation Engrs. *Res:* Coherent detection at l0.6 microns, laser oscillator frequency stability; passive infrared detection; robotics and program management; laser design and development. *Mailing Add:* 25 Fifth Ave Shrewsbury MA 01545

GURSKY, HERBERT, ASTRONOMY. *Current Pos:* SUPT, SPACE SCI DIV, NAVAL RES LAB, 81- *Personal Data:* b Bronx, NY, May 27, 30; m 58; c 2. *Educ:* Univ Fla, BS, 51; Vanderbilt Univ, MS, 53; Princeton Univ, PhD(physics), 59. *Prof Exp:* Instr physics, Princeton Univ, 57-58; instr, Columbia Univ, 58-61; sr scientist, Am Sci & Eng, Inc, 61-66, proj dir, 66-69, vpres, Space Res Div, 69-73; astrophysicist, Smithsonian Astrophys Oberv, 73-76, assoc dir, Optical & Infrared Astron, Harvard/Smithsonian Ctr Astrophys, 76-81. *Concurrent Pos:* Assoc, Harvard Univ, 71- 75, prof astron, 75-81. *Mem:* AAAS; Am Phys Soc; Am Astron Soc. *Res:* Galactic and extragalactic astronomy using x-ray and visible light observations. *Mailing Add:* Naval Res Lab Code 4100 4555 Overlook Ave SW Washington DC 20375-5352

GURSKY, MARTIN LEWIS, THEORETICAL PHYSICS. *Current Pos:* MEM STAFF, LOS ALAMOS SCI LAB, UNIV CALIF, 54- *Personal Data:* b New York, NY, Mar 19, 27; m 52; c 5. *Educ:* Ga Inst Technol, BS, 48, MS, 51; Vanderbilt Univ, PhD(physics), 58. *Prof Exp:* Instr physics, Ga Inst Technol, 48-50; mem staff, Melpar, Inc, 53-54. *Mem:* Am Phys Soc. *Res:* Nuclear theory. *Mailing Add:* 223 El Viento St Los Alamos NM 87544

GURST, JEROME E, ORGANIC CHEMISTRY. *Current Pos:* from asst prof to assoc prof org chem, 67-77, assoc prof, 77-81, PROF CHEM, UNIV WFLA, 81- *Personal Data:* b Atlantic City, NJ, Aug 9, 38. *Educ:* Dartmouth Col, AB, 60; Stanford Univ, PhD(chem), 65. *Prof Exp:* Fel organoboranes, Purdue Univ, 64-65 & stereochem, Princeton Univ, 65-66; vis asst prof org chem, Univ Ore, 66-67. *Concurrent Pos:* Vis assoc prof, Dartmouth Col, 73-80; vis res prof, Univ Nev, Reno, 80-81. *Mem:* AAAS; Am Chem Soc; Sigma Xi. *Res:* Stereochemistry; steroids; mass spectrometry; optical rotatory dispersion; circular dichroism; natural products. *Mailing Add:* Dept Chem Univ WFla Pensacola FL 32514-5751

GURTIN, MORTON EDWARD, APPLIED MATHEMATICS, MECHANICS. *Current Pos:* dir, Ctr Nonlinear Analysis, 91-94, PROF APPL MATH, CARNEGIE-MELLON UNIV, 66- *Personal Data:* b Jersey City, NJ, Mar 7, 34; div; c Amy L (Winokur) & William R. *Educ:* Rensselaer Polytech Inst, BME, 55; Brown Univ, PhD (appl math), 61. *Hon Degrees:* PhD(civil eng), Univ Rome, 94. *Prof Exp:* Engr struct, Douglas Aircraft Co, Inc, 55-56 & Gen Elec Co, 56-59; res assoc appl math, Brown Univ, 61-62, from asst prof to assoc prof, 62-66. *Concurrent Pos:* Consult, Gen Elec Co,

61-63 & Mech Tech Inc, 62-64; lectr, Nat Univ Mex, 64 & Univ Wash, 65; NSF res grant, 65-; lectr, WVa Univ, 67-68; consult, Sandia Corp, 67-; lectr, Southwestern Mech Lect Series, 68, Wash State Univ, 70, Univ Rio de Janeiro, 70 & Int Ctr Mech Sci, Italy, 71, Simon Fraser Univ, 71 & Univ Pisa, 71 & 74; Sr Fulbright-Hays res fel, Univ Pisa, 74, Guggenheim fel, 74; lectr, Univ Poitiers, France, Univ Glasgow, Univ Strathclyde, Scotland, Univ Florence, Istanbul Univ, 74, Univ Bari, Italy & Midwest Mech Lect Series, 76; consult, United Tech Ctr, 76-; Air Force Off Sci Res grant, 76-81; Army Res Off grant, 78-; consult, Los Alamos Nat Lab, 80-90; lectr, Univ Tenn, 79, Univ Paris, 81 & Univ Houston, 82. *Mem:* Am Math Soc; Soc Natural Philos; Sigma Xi. *Res:* Application of continuum mechanics and analysis of problems in materials science; foundations of continuum mechanics and thermodynamics; elasticity and viscoelasticity theory; wave propagation; population dynamics; partial differential equations; phase transitions. *Mailing Add:* Dept Math Carnegie-Mellon Univ Pittsburgh PA 15213

GURTNER, GAIL H, pulmonary physiology; deceased, see previous edition for last biography

GURUDATA, NEVILLE, PHYSICAL ORGANIC CHEMISTRY. *Current Pos:* chmn, Dept Chem & Chem Technol, Dawson Col, 74-76, prof chem, 74-92, dean sci, 92, ACAD DEAN, DAWSON COL, 92- *Personal Data:* b Berbice, Guyana, Apr 23, 37; m 62, Julie Seelochan; c Andrew, Ian & Tara. *Educ:* Univ St Andrews, BSc, 59, Hons, 60; Univ Western Ont, PhD(chem), 68. *Prof Exp:* Sci officer, Dept Govt Analyst, Guyana, 60-64; res fel, Univ Ottawa, 68-69; lectr & res assoc prof, Sir George Williams Univ, 69-73. *Concurrent Pos:* Instr, Univ Guyana, 63-64; adj asst prof, Concordia Univ, 73-75; mem, Laurenval Sch Bd, 79, chmn coun, 83-84; chmn exec, 86-87. *Mem:* Chem Inst Can. *Res:* Use of nuclear magnetic resonance spectroscopy to determine structure, stereochemistry, thermodynamic parameters; interactions between formally non-conjugated chromophores; relationships between chemical structure, spectra and chemical reactivity; approaches to synthesis of selected organic compounds. *Mailing Add:* Dawson Col 3040 Sherbrook St W Montreal PQ H3Z 1A4 Can. *Fax:* 514-931-5181

GURUSIDDAIAH, SARANGAMAT, ANTIBIOTICS, NATURAL PRODUCTS HERBICIDES. *Current Pos:* Res assoc agr chem, Bioanalysis Ctr, 70-71, mgr, 71-76, from asst scientist to assoc scientist, 76-85, DIR, BIOANALYSIS LAB, WASH STATE UNIV, 80-, SCIENTIST, 86- *Personal Data:* b Chitradurga, India, Mar 18, 37; US citizen; m 64; c 2. *Educ:* Bangalore Univ, India, BSc, 60, MSc, 61; Wash State Univ, Pullman, PhD(plant path), 71. *Concurrent Pos:* Co-prin investr antibiotics, NIH grant, 79-82; prin investr antibiotics, Dow Chem Co grant, 82-86, Hoffman-LaRoche, 87-92. *Mem:* AAAS; Am Physiol Soc; Am Soc Internal Med. *Res:* Isolation and characterization of antifungal, antibacterial, antiviral and antitumor compounds from microorganisms, plants and other natural sources; natural products isolation and characterization. *Mailing Add:* 1230 NW Clifford St Pullman WA 99163

GURWITH, MARC JOSEPH, INFECTIOUS DISEASES. *Current Pos:* ASSOC PROF MED & MICROBIOL & CHIEF, INFECTIOUS DIS SECT, DEPT MED, MICH STATE UNIV, 80- *Personal Data:* b Paris, France, July 29, 39; US citizen; m 70; c 2. *Educ:* Yale Univ, BA, 61; Harvard Med Sch, MD, 65. *Prof Exp:* Intern internal med, Stanford Univ Hosp, 65-66; res assoc infectious dis, Sch Med, Univ Southern Calif, 66-67; epidemiologist, US AID Malaria Eradication Prog, 67-68; resident, Stanford Univ Hosp, 68-69, fel infectious dis, 69-70, resident, 70-71; staff physician, Kaiser Permanente, 71-72; asst prof internal med & med microbiol, Univ Man, 72-77; assoc prof med, Sch Med, Univ Kans, 77-79; assoc prof med, Univ Calif, Los Angeles, 79-80. *Concurrent Pos:* Adj prof microbiol, Univ Man, 77-79; asst chief res, Infectious Dis Sect, Wadsworth Vet Admin Hosp, 79-80. *Mem:* Am Soc Microbiol; Am Fedn Clin Res; Can Soc Clin Invest; Royal Col Physicians & Surgeons Can; Am Col Physicians. *Mailing Add:* 101 Orchard Ridge Dr Gaithersburg MD 20878-1952

GUSBERG, SAUL BERNARD, MEDICINE, EDUCATIONAL & RESEARCH ADMINISTRATION. *Current Pos:* prof & chmn dept, Mt Sinai Sch Med, 68-80, obstetrician & gynecologist-in-chief, 62-80, distinguished serv prof, 80-84, EMER PROF, MT SINAI SCH MED, 84- *Personal Data:* b Newark, NJ, Aug 3, 13; m 38, Dorothy Cushner; c Richard. *Educ:* Harvard Univ, MD, 37; Columbia Univ, ScD, 48. *Hon Degrees:* DSc, Univ Barcelona, 87. *Honors & Awards:* Am Cancer Soc Medal. *Prof Exp:* Fel oncol, Huntington Hosp, Harvard Univ, 38; resident obstet & gynec, Sloane Hosp Women, 46; assoc prof clin obstet & gynec, Col Physicians & Surgeons, Columbia Univ, 54-62, clin prof, 62-68. *Concurrent Pos:* Assoc attend obstetrician & gynecologist, Columbia-Presby Med Ctr; consult med affairs & res, Am Cancer Soc, Mt Sinai Hosp; ed-in-chief, Gynec Oncol, 73-90, emer ed, 90- *Mem:* AAAS; fel Am Gynec Soc; Soc Gynec Oncol (pres, 74-75); fel Am Radium Soc (vpres, 67); Am Soc Cytol (vpres, 59-62); Sigma Xi; Am Gynec & Obstet; NY Acad Med (Past pres); Soc Pelvic Surg (pres, 76); Am Cancer Soc (pres, 81); Sigma Xi; fel NY Acad Scis; fel Royal Col Obstet & Gynec. *Res:* Gynecologic cancer; reproductive biology; author of textbooks on gynecological cancer; oncology. *Mailing Add:* 257 Palisade Ave Dobbs Ferry NY 10522. *Fax:* 212-719-0193

GUSDON, JOHN PAUL, OBSTETRICS & GYNECOLOGY, IMMUNOLOGY. *Current Pos:* from asst prof to prof, 67-90, ASSOC MICROBIOL, BOWMAN GRAY SCH MED, 67-, EMER PROF OBSTET & GYNEC, 90- *Personal Data:* b Cleveland, Ohio, Feb 13, 31; m 56, 89, Carolyn Gallager; c Marguerite, John P & Veronique. *Educ:* Univ Va, BA, 52, MD, 59. *Honors & Awards:* Pres Award, Am Col Obstet & Gynec. *Prof Exp:* From intern to resident, Univ Hosps Cleveland, Ohio, 59-64; from instr to asst prof, Case Western Res Univ, 64-67. *Concurrent Pos:* Fel immunol, Sch Med, Case Western Res Univ, 64-67; Josiah Macy Jr Found fac fel, 66-69. *Mem:* AAAS; Am Asn Immunol; Am Soc Immunol Reproduction (pres & founder, 81-); Am Col Obstet & Gynec; Am Gynec & Obstet Soc; Soc Gynec Invest; Am Soc Reproductive Immunol. *Res:* Immunological aspects of fetal-maternal relationships; immunology of malignancy. *Mailing Add:* 3198 Kings Arms Ct NE Atlanta GA 30345-2153

GUSELLA, JAMES F, GENETICS. *Current Pos:* asst genetics, Neurol Serv, 80-83 asst geneticist, 83-84, ASSOC GENETICIST, NEUROL SERV & DIR, NEUROGENETICS UNIT, MASS GEN HOSP, CHARLESTOWN, 84- *Educ:* Univ Ottawa, BSc, 74; Univ Toronto, MSc, 76; Mass Inst Technol, PhD(genetics), 80. *Honors & Awards:* Jordi Folch Mem Award, Am Soc Neurochem, 86; A Cressy Morrison Nat Sci Award, NY Acad Sci, 87; Bennett Lect Award, Am Neurol Asn, 88; Med Res Award, Met Life Found, 87 & Nat Health Coun, 93. *Concurrent Pos:* Instr neurol, Harvard Med Sch, 80-84, asst prof, 84-87, assoc prof, 87-92, prof, 92-; Mallinckrodt assoc prof genetics, Mass Gen Hosp, 88-92. *Res:* Contributed numerous articles to professional journals. *Mailing Add:* Mass Gen Hosp E Huntingtons Dis Ctr Bldg 149 13th St Charlestown MA 02129

GUSEMAN, LAWRENCE FRANK, JR, MATHEMATICS. *Current Pos:* from asst prof to assoc prof, 68-81, PROF MATH, TEX A&M UNIV, 81-, DIR, OFF GRAD STUDIES, 88- *Personal Data:* b New Iberia, La, Feb 16, 38; m 68; c 2. *Educ:* Tex A&M Univ, BA, 60, MS, 62; Univ Tex, Austin, PhD(math), 68. *Prof Exp:* Appl mathematician, M D Anderson Hosp & Tumor Inst, 62; res mathematician, Theory & Analysis Off, Comput & Analysis Div, NASA Manned Spacecraft Ctr, 64-68. *Concurrent Pos:* Teaching asst, Univ Tex, Austin, 64-66. *Mem:* Am Math Soc; Math Asn Am; Soc Indust & Appl Math; Sigma Xi. *Res:* Functional analysis, non-linear fixed point theory and optimization theory; mathematical techniques in pattern recognition & statistical decision theory. *Mailing Add:* 2801 Cherry Creek Circle Bryan TX 77802

GUSENIUS, EDWIN MAURTIZ, INORGANIC CHEMISTRY. *Current Pos:* prof & chmn dept, 69-81, EMER PROF, FRIENDS UNIV, 81- *Personal Data:* b Bristol, SDak, July 5, 16; m 48; c 2. *Educ:* Gustavus Adolphus Col, BA, 38; Univ SDak, MA, 48; Kans State Univ, PhD(inorg chem), 63. *Prof Exp:* Instr, SDak High Sch, 38-40; chemist, E I du Pont de Nemours & Co, Inc, 41-42, suprv, 42-45; asst chem, Univ SDak, 46-47; instr, Luther Jr Col, 47-54; from asst prof to prof, Bethany Col, Kans, 54-68; prof, Kearney State Col, 68-69. *Mem:* Am Chem Soc. *Res:* Metal complexes. *Mailing Add:* 321 N Second St Lindsborg KS 67456-2006

GUSHEE, BEATRICE ELEANOR, INORGANIC CHEMISTRY. *Current Pos:* from asst prof to assoc prof, 57-89, EMER PROF CHEM, HOLLINS COL, 89- *Personal Data:* b Dorchester, Mass, Sept 22, 18. *Educ:* Simmons Col, BS, 42; Vassar Col, MS, 46; Univ Conn, PhD(inorg chem), 56. *Prof Exp:* Anal chemist, Celanese Corp Am, 42-44; instr chem, Hofstra Col, 46-48; asst, Univ Conn, 48-54; instr, Smith Col, 54-57. *Mem:* Am Chem Soc; Nat Sci Teachers Asn; Sigma Xi. *Res:* High temperature and solid state reactions and transformation; structural inorganic chemistry. *Mailing Add:* Hollins Col PO Box 9675 Roanoke VA 24020-1675

GUSKEY, LOUIS ERNEST, VIROLOGY, MICROBIOLOGY. *Current Pos:* CHIEF, DIV VIROL, MICH DEPT PUB HEALTH, 84- *Personal Data:* b Pittsburgh, Pa, Jan 13, 42; m 65; c 2. *Educ:* Capital Univ, BS, 63; Ohio State Univ, MSc, 67, PhD(microbiol), 71. *Prof Exp:* Fel virol & biochem, Ciba Geigy, Basle, Switz, 71-73; res fel virol & lipid chem, Hormel Inst, 73-75; res asst prof virol, Waksman Inst Microbiol, 75-77; asst prof microbiol, Univ Wis, Milwaukee, 77-84. *Concurrent Pos:* Res fel, Prog Projs Br Nat Heart & Lung Inst, 73-75; res asst prof, Nat Inst Allergy & Infectious Dis, 75-77. *Mem:* Am Soc Microbiol; Tissue Cult Asn; Am Soc Virol. *Res:* Virus-host cell interactions; molecular events that cause the development of viral-induced cytopathologies and lead to cell death; methods for rapid viral diagnosis. *Mailing Add:* 3205 Snowglen Lane Lansing MI 48917

GUSOVSKY, FABIAN, MOLECULAR PHARMACOLOGY. *Current Pos:* vis fel, 85-87, staff fel, 87-88, SR STAFF FEL, BIOORG CHEM LAB, NAT INST DIABETES & DIGESTIVE & KIDNEY DIS, NIH, 88- *Personal Data:* b Buenos Aires, Arg, Jan 15, 57; m 84; c 1. *Educ:* Univ Buenos Aires, dipl pharm, 78, dipl biochem, 80; Rush Med Col, PhD(pharmacol), 84. *Prof Exp:* Res assoc, Psychobiol Lab, Rush-Presby Hosp, Chicago, 81-84. *Mem:* Am Soc Neurosci; Am Soc Pharmacol & Exp Therapeut. *Res:* Biochemistry and pharmacology of signal transduction in mammalian systems; study of second messenger generating systems. *Mailing Add:* Eisai Res Inst Boston Inc 4 Corp Dr Andover MA 01810-2441. *Fax:* 978-794-4910

GUSS, CYRUS OMAR, organic chemistry; deceased, see previous edition for last biography

GUSS, MAURICE LOUIS, SCIENCE ADMINISTRATION. *Current Pos:* CONSULT, 90- *Personal Data:* b Revere, Mass, June 21, 22; m 46, Florence E Hasson; c Samuel, Michael & Tuviah. *Educ:* Boston Col, BS, 47; Univ Mass, MS, 49; Cornell Univ, PhD(bact), 52. *Prof Exp:* Microbiologist, US Army Biol Labs, Ft Detrick, 52-71; consult, Naval Ship Systs Command, US Navy, 71-72; microbiologist, Nat Cancer Inst, 72-83; exec officer, ABL-Basic Res Prog, Fred Cancer Res & Develop Ctr, Frederick, 83-91. *Concurrent Pos:* Consult, Instnl Rev Bd, SAIC, Inc, 92- *Mem:* Sigma Xi. *Res:* Microbial physiology and structure; medical microbiology; biological waste disposal; viral oncology; research administration. *Mailing Add:* 405 Culler Ave Frederick MD 21701

GUSS, WILLIAM C, FUSION PLASMA DIAGNOSTICS, NON-NEUTRAL PLASMAS. *Current Pos:* RES PHYSICIST, MASS INST TECHNOL, 85- *Personal Data:* b Madison, Wis, Aug 26, 46; m 91, Nancy B Gunn. *Educ:* Univ Colo, BS, 68; Univ Wis, MS, 70, PhD(physics), 75. *Prof Exp:* Mem tech staff, TRW, 84-85. *Mem:* Am Phys Soc; Inst Elec & Electronics Engrs. *Res:* Plasma heating, high frequency, high power microwave sources. *Mailing Add:* Sci Res Lab 15 Ward St Somerville MA 02143

GUSSIN, ARNOLD E S, PLANT PHYSIOLOGY, EDUCATION ADMINISTRATION. *Current Pos:* DEAN, GRAD & CONTINUING STUDIES, UNION COL, 85- *Personal Data:* b New York, NY, Dec 23, 35; m 62; c 2. *Educ:* Tulane Univ La, BS, 57, MS, 59; Brown Univ, PhD(biol), 63. *Prof Exp:* NIH fel biol, Yale Univ, 62-64; asst prof zool, Butler Univ, 64-66; from asst prof to assoc prof biol sci, Smith Col, 66-73; coordr, 73-78, asst vpres & dir educ, NY Bot Garden, 78-85. *Concurrent Pos:* NSF fac fel, Albert Einstein Col Med, 69-70; Oliver Cromwell Gorton Arnold biol fel, Brown Univ. *Mem:* Asn Continuing Higher Educ; Am Soc Biol Chem & Molecular Biol; Am Asn Adult & Continuing Educ; Nat Univ Continuing Educ Asn; Sigma Xi. *Res:* Educational procedures in cultural institutions; physiology and kinetics of trehalases. *Mailing Add:* Dept Biol St Francis 180 Remsen St Brooklyn Heights NY 11201. *Fax:* 718-522-1274

GUSSIN, GARY NATHANIEL, MOLECULAR BIOLOGY. *Current Pos:* asst prof, 69-74, assoc prof, 74-80, PROF BIOL, UNIV IOWA, 80- *Personal Data:* b Detroit, Mich, Aug 7, 39; m 86; c 2. *Educ:* Univ Mich, BS, 61; Harvard Univ, PhD(biophys), 66. *Prof Exp:* NSF fels, Stanford Univ, 66-67 & Univ Geneva, 67-68; Am Cancer Soc fel, 68-69. *Res:* Lysogeny of Escherichia coli by bacteriophage lambda; regulation of transcription initiation. *Mailing Add:* Dept Biol Sci Univ Iowa 138 Biol Bldg Iowa City IA 52242-1324. *Fax:* 319-335-1069

GUSSIN, ROBERT Z, PHARMACOLOGY, ADMINISTRATION. *Current Pos:* CORP VPRES, SCI & TECHNOL, JOHNSON & JOHNSON, 86- *Personal Data:* b Pittsburgh, Pa, Jan 5, 38; m 86; c 2. *Educ:* Duquesne Univ, BS, 59, MS, 61; Univ Mich, PhD(pharmacol), 65. *Prof Exp:* Res fel, State Univ NY-Upstate Med Ctr, 65-67; res pharmacologist, Lederle Labs, 67-69, group leader, 69-73, dir, 73-74; exec dir, Res Div, McNeil Labs, 74-77, vpres res & develop, 78-81, vpres sci affairs, McNeil Pharmaceut, 81-86. *Concurrent Pos:* Adj prof, Dept Pharmacol, Mich State Univ Med Sch, 88-; adv bd, David Mahoney Inst Neurol Sci, Univ Pa, 87- *Mem:* AAAS; Am Soc Nephrol; Am Fedn Clin Res; Am Soc Pharmacol & Exp Therapeut; Am Soc Clin Pharmacol & Therapeut. *Res:* Cardiovascular disease, especially hypertension. *Mailing Add:* Johnson & Johnson 410 George St Rm GS 1142 New Brunswick NJ 08901-2020

GUSSOW, W(ILLIA)M C(ARRUTHERS), PETROLEUM EXPLORATION, PETROLEUM RECOVERY. *Current Pos:* SELF-EMPLOYED PETROL CONSULT, 75- *Personal Data:* b London, Eng, Apr 25, 08; Can citizen; m 36, Margaret B Robinson; c Christopher H, David W & James F Robinson. *Educ:* Queen's Univ, Kingston, Ont, BSc, 33, MSc, 35; Mass Inst Technol, PhD(econ & struct geol), 38. *Prof Exp:* Res fel geol, Royal Soc Can, 36-37; instr geol & mining, Royal Military Col, Ont, 38-39; construct engr, Foundation Co, Can, 41-43; resident construct engr, Aluminum Co, Can, 44; chief petroleum geologist, Shell Oil Co, 45-48, explor mgr, 48-50, sr geologist, 50-52; self-employed geologist, 53-55; staff petrolum geologist, Union Oil Co, Calif, 56-60, sr res assoc, 60-71; petroleum consult, Japan Nat Oil Corp, 72-74. *Concurrent Pos:* Geol mapping, Fed & Prov Geol Survs, Ont, Que & NT, 30-39; distinguished lectr, Am Asn Petrol Geologists, 55; guest lectr, Nat Acad Lincei, Milan, 57, Moscow State Univ, 60; mem, Nat Adv Comt Res Geol Sci, Ottawa, 57-59, Nat Acad Sci, Subcomt Geol, Comt Space Progs Earth Observ, Adv US Geol Surv, 66-72; United Nations expert, Res & Training Inst, Oil & Natural Gas Comn, India, 67; guest lectr, People's Rep China, 77. *Mem:* Am Asn Petroleum Geologists; emer Am Inst Prof Geologists; fel Geol Asn Can; fel Royal Soc Can; Soc Econ Geologists; fel Geol Soc Am. *Res:* Differential entrapment, explaining accumulation of gas downdip, oil updip and water only beyond limit of oil migration; Gussow method of enhanced oil recovery; patents. *Mailing Add:* 322-20 Cleary Ave Ottawa ON K2A 3Z9 Can

GUST, J DEVENS, JR, ORGANIC CHEMISTRY. *Current Pos:* from asst prof to assoc prof, 75-85, dir, Ctr Study Early Events Photosynthesis, 91-94, PROF CHEM, ARIZ STATE UNIV, 85- *Personal Data:* b Phoenix, Ariz, Nov 28, 44; m 69, Elaine Leachman; c 2. *Educ:* Stanford Univ, BS, 67; Princeton Univ, MA, 72, PhD(chem), 74. *Prof Exp:* Res fel chem, Calif Inst Technol, 74-75. *Concurrent Pos:* Vis prof biophys, Mus Natural Hist, Paris, France, 82, 85; vis scientist, dept phys chem, Centre d'Etudes Nucleaires de, Saclay, France, 82-84; vis scientist, Katholieke Univ Leuven, Belg, 87, vis prof chem, 89. *Mem:* Am Chem Soc; Am Soc Photobiol; Inter-Am Photochem Soc. *Res:* Solar energy conversion; photosynthesis; organic stereochemistry; molecular electronics. *Mailing Add:* Dept Chem Ariz State Univ Tempe AZ 85287-1604. *Fax:* 602-965-2747; *E-Mail:* gust@asuchm.la.asu.edu

GUSTA, LAWRENCE V, PLANT PHYSIOLOGY. *Current Pos:* SR RES SCIENTIST CROP SCI & PLANT ECOLOGY, CROP DEVELOP CTR, UNIV SASK, 71- *Personal Data:* b Selkirk, Man, July 18, 39; m 62. *Educ:* Univ Man, BSA, 63, MS, 65; Univ Minn, PhD(plant physiol), 70. *Concurrent Pos:* Fel, Univ Minn, 70 & Univ BC, 71. *Res:* Physiology of cold acclimation and low temperature injury in winter annuals. *Mailing Add:* 515 Copland Crescent Saskatoon SK S7H 2Z4 Can. *Fax:* 306-966-5015

GUSTAFSON, ALVAR WALTER, REPRODUCTIVE BIOLOGY, ENDOCRINOLOGY. *Current Pos:* asst prof anat, Tufts Univ, 75-81, actg chmn comp med, 89-90, dir Histol & Histochem Lab, Dept Anat, 76-92, ASSOC PROF ANAT & CELLULAR BIOL & COMP MED, SCH DENT MED & VET MED, TUFTS UNIV, 81- *Personal Data:* b Chicago, Ill, May 6, 46; m 67, E Yvonne Kittelson; c Erik K. *Educ:* Gustavus Adolphus Col, BA, 68; Cornell Univ, PhD(zool), 75. *Prof Exp:* Teaching asst, Cornell Univ, 68-75. *Concurrent Pos:* Vis assoc prof, LHRRB, Harvard Med Sch, 86-87; assoc dean acad affairs, Sch Vet Med, Tufts Univ, 89-93; dir, Multimedia Resource Ctr, Health Sci Educ & Res, 93. *Mem:* AAAS; Sigma Xi; Am Asn Anatomists; Am Soc Zoologists; Am Soc Andrologists; Soc Study Reproduction. *Res:* Structure and function of the male reproductive system; endocrine control of puberty and seasonal reproductive rhythms; hibernation and the endocrines; protein binding of steroid hormones in relation to hormone action; digital imaging. *Mailing Add:* Dept Anat & Cell Biol Sch Med & Vet Med Tufts Univ 136 Harrison Ave Boston MA 02111. *Fax:* 617-636-0974; *E-Mail:* awgustafson@opal.tufts.edu

GUSTAFSON, BO AKE STURE, CELESTIAL MECHANICS, SMALL PARTICLE DYNAMICS. *Current Pos:* asst res scientist astron, Space Astron Lab, 81-89, assoc scientist, 89-94, ASSOC PROF, ASTRON DEPT, UNIV FLA, 94- *Personal Data:* b Karlskrona, Sweden, Mar 28, 53; m 86. *Educ:* Lund Univ, Sweden, Fil Kand, 77, PhD(astron), 81. *Prof Exp:* Res asst astron, Lund Observ, Lund Univ, Sweden, 74-77, Space Astron Lab, State Univ NY, Albany, 77-80. *Concurrent Pos:* Alexander von Humboldt fel, 89-90; mem, Comt Space Res, Int Comn Sci Unions. *Mem:* Int Astron Union; Sigma Xi; Am Astron Soc; Swedish Astron Soc. *Res:* Small particles lightscattering properties; dynamical evolution of interplanetary dust and meteoroids; celestial mechanics of small bodies; evolution of and relation between comets, asteroids, meteoroids and cosmic dust; meteor science. *Mailing Add:* Astron Dept Univ Fla PO Box 112055 Gainsville FL 32611. *Fax:* 352-392-5089; *E-Mail:* gustaf@astro.ufl.edu

GUSTAFSON, BRUCE LEROY, HETEROGENEOUS CATALYSIS, SURFACE CHARACTERIZATION. *Current Pos:* Res chemist, 81-84, sr res chemist, 84-89, RES ASSOC, EASTMAN CHEM CO, 89- *Personal Data:* b Jamestown, NY, Oct 25, 54; m 75; c 2. *Educ:* Univ Cent Fla, BS, 76; Tex A&M Univ, PhD(chem), 81. *Mem:* Am Chem Soc; NAm Catalysis Soc; Sigma Xi. *Res:* Characterization and evaluation of heterogeneous catalysts; surface science; zeolite chemistry. *Mailing Add:* 936 Meadow Lane Kingsport TN 37663-2822

GUSTAFSON, CARL GUSTAF, JR, ORGANIC CHEMISTRY. *Current Pos:* RETIRED. *Personal Data:* b Montclair, NJ, Apr 27, 25; m 51, Lillie M Olson; c Carl G, Cheryl G & Carol G. *Educ:* King's Col, BS, 48; Univ Del, PhD(org chem), 57; Inst NY, MS, 83. *Prof Exp:* Instr chem, King's Col, 48-50; org res chemist, Chem Corps, Med Labs, US Army Chem Ctr, Md, 52-53; asst prof chem, Roberts Wesleyan Col, 56-59; assoc prof, King's Col, NY, 59-63, actg dean, 60-62, chmn, Div Natural Sci, 65-87, prof chem, 63-90, dir acad comput, 87-90. *Concurrent Pos:* Spec fac appointment with Fed Water Qual Admin, Southeast Water Lab, Athens, Ga, 69-70. *Mem:* Am Chem Soc. *Res:* Sulfonic esters of hexitols; organic insecticides; fiber composition of paper; small ring heterscyolis; polyacetals. *Mailing Add:* 5205 Fielding Dr Raleigh NC 27606

GUSTAFSON, DAVID HAROLD, ORGANIC CHEMISTRY. *Current Pos:* RETIRED. *Personal Data:* b Ft Wayne, Ind, Dec 7, 35; m 57, 78; c 1. *Educ:* Purdue Univ, BS, 57; Univ Ill, PhD(org chem), 61. *Prof Exp:* Res chemist, Procter & Gamble Co, 61-64; sr assoc scientist, Marion Merrell Dow Inc, 64-93. *Mem:* Am Chem Soc; NY Acad Sci; Sigma Xi. *Res:* Metallocenes and terpenoid syntheses; spectroscopy; physical organic chemistry. *Mailing Add:* 1392 Keyridge Dr Cincinnati OH 45240

GUSTAFSON, DAVID HAROLD, INDUSTRIAL ENGINEERING, PREVENTIVE MEDICINE. *Current Pos:* asst prof mech eng, Univ Wis-Madison 66-69, from asst prof to assoc prof indust eng, 69-74, asscc prof prev med, 71-74, PROF INDUST ENG & PREV MED, UNIV WIS-MADISON, 74-, DIR, CTR HEALTH SYSTS RES & ANALYSIS, 76- *Personal Data:* b Kane, Pa, Sept 11, 40; m 62; c 3. *Educ:* Univ Mich, BS, 62, MS, 63, PhD(indust eng), 66. *Honors & Awards:* Ragner Onstad Award for Serv to Soc, 88; Excellence in Educ & Prev, Am Med Asn, 89. *Prof Exp:* Dir hosp div, Community Systs Found, 63-64. *Concurrent Pos:* Adv, Wis Gov Health Planning & Policy Task Force, 71-73, mem health policy coun, 73- & comn on educ & health admin, 73-74; dir, Health Systs Eng Prog; sr systs analyst, Decisions & Designs Inc, Va, 74; spec asst to dir, Bur Community Health Serv, Dept Health, Educ & Welfare, 75; consult to numerous health & social serv agencies within fed govt, univs & pvt sector. *Mem:* Opers Res Soc Am. *Res:* Applicability of behavioral decision theory and computer based decision support systems to medical and social systems; development, implementation and evaluation of computer based medical decision systems. *Mailing Add:* Indust Eng 390 Mech Eng Univ Wis 1513 University Ave Madison WI 53706-1572

GUSTAFSON, DONALD ARVID, chemistry; deceased, see previous edition for last biography

GUSTAFSON, DONALD PINK, VETERINARY VIROLOGY, PATHOBIOLOGY. *Current Pos:* from instr to assoc prof, 49-61, PROF VET MED, PURDUE UNIV, 61- *Personal Data:* b Columbus, Ohio, May 21, 20; m 49; c 5. *Educ:* Ohio State Univ, BSc, 41, DVM, 45; Purdue Univ, MS, 51, PhD(vet path), 53; Am Col Vet Microbiol, dipl. *Prof Exp:* Pvt practice, 45-46.

Concurrent Pos: Consult, Com Solvents Corp, 57; Univ Fla, 58 & Eli Lilly & Co, 58-74; mem subcomt standardized methods in vet microbiol, Nat Acad Sci-Nat Res Coun, 67-72; mem, Livestock Conserv Inst, 69-; chmn swine dysentery comt, 71-76; mem, Coun Biol & Therapeut Agents, Am Vet Med Asn, 70-80, vchmn, 71, 73 & 74, chmn, 72 & 75-80, coun on res, 81-; mem res resources comt, Nat Inst Allergy & Infectious Dis, 71-75. *Mem:* Am Asn Immunologists; Am Vet Med Asn; Am Soc Microbiologists; Tissue Cult Asn; NY Acad Sci. *Res:* Infectious diseases of animals; scrapie in sheep; chronic equine diarrhea; myoclonia congenita in swine; pseudorabies. *Mailing Add:* Sch Vet Med Purdue Univ West Lafayette IN 47907

GUSTAFSON, GRANT BERNARD, MATHEMATICAL ANALYSIS. *Current Pos:* Vis prof, 68-69, from asst prof to assoc prof, 69-79, PROF MATH, UNIV UTAH, 80- *Personal Data:* b St Paul, Minn, Mar 5, 44; m 69; c 1. *Educ:* Ariz State Univ, BS, 65, MA, 67, PhD(math), 68. *Mem:* Am Math Soc; Math Asn Am; Soc Ind & Appl Math. *Res:* Ordinary, functional and partial differential equations; nonlinear analysis. *Mailing Add:* Dept Math 233 JWB Univ Utah Salt Lake City UT 84112-1193

GUSTAFSON, HEROLD RICHARD, QUARKS & NEUTRINOS EXPERIMENTAL GRAVITY. *Current Pos:* scholar, Univ Mich, 68-71, res assoc, 71-77, asst res scientist, 77-82, assoc res scientist, 82-90, RES SCIENTIST, UNIV MICH, 91- *Personal Data:* b Grand Coulee, Wash, June 16, 37; m 65, 95, Mary Dryburgh; c Danielle. *Educ:* Calif Inst Technol, BS, 59; Univ Wash, MS, 61, PhD(physics), 68. *Prof Exp:* Elec engr missiles, Boeing Co, 59-61, space physics, 61-64. *Concurrent Pos:* Vis assoc, Caif Inst Technol. *Mem:* Am Phys Soc. *Res:* Prompt neutrino production (beam dump); searching for quarks; investigation of hadron jets; magnetic monopoles; gravity wave detection. *Mailing Add:* Randall Lab Univ Mich Ann Arbor MI 48109. *Fax:* 313-936-1817; *E-Mail:* gustatso@hgo.caltech.edu

GUSTAFSON, JOHN C, SOLID STATE PHYSICS. *Current Pos:* MEM TECH STAFF, OSRAM-SYLVANIA, 73- *Personal Data:* b Worthington, Minn, Nov 7, 44. *Educ:* Univ Minn, BA, 65; Northwestern Univ, PhD(physics), 72. *Prof Exp:* Res assoc physics, McMaster Univ, 72-73. *Mem:* Am Phys Soc; AAAS. *Res:* Studies of magnetic phenomena in amorphous metals; high temperature transport properties in homogenous materials and plasma-surface interactions. *Mailing Add:* Osram-Sylvania 71 Cherry Hill Dr Beverly MA 01923

GUSTAFSON, JOHN PERRY, PLANT BREEDING. *Current Pos:* RES GENETICIST, AGR RES SERV, USDA, 82- *Personal Data:* b Greeley, Colo, Aug 1, 44; m 77; c 2. *Educ:* Colo State Univ, BS, 67, MS, 68; Univ Calif, Davis, PhD(genetics), 72. *Prof Exp:* Res prof genetics, Univ Manitoba, Can, 72-77, assoc prof, 77-82. *Concurrent Pos:* Res assoc, Univ Manitoba, Can, 76-77. *Mem:* Genetics Soc Am; Genetics Soc Can; Am Soc Agron; Am Genetic Asn. *Res:* Understanding and manipulation of genetic mechanisms of control of the phenotype of cereals; interspecific and intergeneric hybrids within the various grass genera. *Mailing Add:* 3103 Crawford St Columbia MO 65203

GUSTAFSON, KARL EDWIN, MATHEMATICS. *Current Pos:* assoc prof, 68-74, fac fel, 71-72, PROF MATH, UNIV COLO, BOULDER, 74- *Personal Data:* b Manchester, Iowa, May 7, 35; m 61; c 1. *Educ:* Univ Colo, BS(eng) & BS(bus), 58; Univ Md, PhD(math), 65. *Prof Exp:* Instr appl math, Univ Colo, 58-60; physicist, Naval Res Lab, 60-61, mathematician, 61-63; NSF-NATO fel math, Inst Battelle, Geneva & Univ Rome, 65-66; asst prof, Univ Minn, 66-68. *Concurrent Pos:* Vis scientist, Inst Battelle, Geneva, 67; vis prof, Fed Polytech Sch, Lausanne, Switz, 71-72. *Mem:* Am Math Soc. *Res:* Computer applications for naval intelligence problems; partial differential equations; functional analysis; operator theory; mathematical physics; nonlinear problems. *Mailing Add:* Univ Colo Boulder CO 80309-0426

GUSTAFSON, LEWIS BRIGHAM, ECONOMIC GEOLOGY, MINERAL DEPOSITS. *Current Pos:* GEOL CONSULT, 86- *Personal Data:* b Timmins, Ont, Sept 4, 33; m 61; c 3. *Educ:* Princeton Univ, BSE, 55; Calif Inst Technol, MS, 58; Harvard Univ, PhD(geol), 62. *Honors & Awards:* Lindgren Award, Soc Econ Geol, 62, Distinguished Lectr, 89; T Lindsey lectr, Soc Econ Geol, 73-74. *Prof Exp:* From geologist to chief geologist, El Salvador Mine, Andes Copper Mining Co, 62-69, from proj geologist to chief geologist, res & technol, Primary Metals Div, Anaconda Co, 69-75; independent consult, 75; prof econ geol, Australian Nat Univ, 75-81; head, Min Res Group, Conoco, Inc, 81-82; chief res geologist, Freeport Explor Co, 82-86; partner, Annapurna Explor & vpres, Rex Resources, Reno, 86-91. *Mem:* Soc Econ Geologists; fel Geol Soc Am; Am Inst Mining & Metall. *Res:* Mineral deposits; mineral exploration; tectonic settings of ore deposits. *Mailing Add:* 5320 Cross Creek Lane Reno NV 89511

GUSTAFSON, MARK EDWARD, MICROBIAL TRANSFORMATIONS. *Current Pos:* Scientist I, 80-81, SCIENTIST II, FERMENTATION PROG, FREDERICK CANCER RES FACIL, NAT CANCER INST, 81- *Personal Data:* b Cedar Rapids, Iowa, Feb 17, 52. *Educ:* Col Pharm, Univ Iowa, BS, 76, PhD(pharm & med chem), 80. *Mem:* Am Chem Soc. *Res:* Isolation and characterization of variety of antitumor agents, including chemotherapeutics and interferon. *Mailing Add:* Monsanto Co GG3M 700 Chesterfield Village Pkwy St Louis MO 63198

GUSTAFSON, PHILIP FELIX, ENVIRONMENTAL SCIENCES. *Current Pos:* dir, Div Environ Res, 83-85, COORDR HAZARDOUS MAT RES, ARGONNE NAT LAB, 85-, DIR, ENVIRON RES PROG, 87- *Personal Data:* b Ann Arbor, Mich, Apr 2, 24; m 49; c 2. *Educ:* Univ Mich, BS, 49; Ill Inst Technol, MS, 54, PhD(physics), 58. *Honors & Awards:* Glover Award, Dizlason Col, 72; Univ Geert Award, Belgium, 74. *Prof Exp:* Res technician physics, Argonne Nat Lab, 49-52, asst physicist, 52-59, assoc physicist, 55-66; nuclear fallout specialist, US Atomic Energy Comn, 66-68; assoc dir radiol physics div, 68-72, sr biophysicist, 71-88, mgr, 72-75, dir environ statement proj, Argonne Nat Lab, 75-80; dir, Dept Nuclear Safety, Ill, 80-83. *Concurrent Pos:* Mem, Ill Comn Atomic Energy, 72-, sci adv, 74- *Mem:* AAAS; Sigma Xi. *Res:* Environmental radiation; radioecology; environmental impact assessment for nuclear facilities; environmental effects and their minimization; hazardous waste management policy. *Mailing Add:* 413 Addison Rd Riverside IL 60546

GUSTAFSON, RALPH ALAN, MYCOLOGY, BACTERIOLOGY. *Current Pos:* PROF BIOL, WINTHROP COL, 74- *Personal Data:* b Denver, Colo, Apr 9, 39; m 61; c 2. *Educ:* Colo State Univ, BS, 62, MEd, 68; Univ Tex, Austin, PhD(bot), 73. *Prof Exp:* Instr biol, Univ Tex, Austin, 72-74. *Mem:* Sigma Xi; Am Soc Microbiol; Nat Environ Health Asn. *Res:* Bacteriological quality of drinking water sources. *Mailing Add:* 2740 Bonnybrook Circle Rock Hill SC 29732-9415

GUSTAFSON, STEVEN CARL, OPTICS, STATISTICS. *Current Pos:* res scientist, 76-84, SR RES PHYSICIST, RES INST, UNIV DAYTON, 84- *Personal Data:* b St Paul, Minn, Mar 8, 45; m 70. *Educ:* Univ Minn, BS, 67; Duke Univ, MA, 69, PhD(physics), 74. *Prof Exp:* Consult, Air Force Mat Lab, 75, vis scientist, 75-76. *Mem:* Am Phys Soc; Inst Elec & Electronics Engrs; Optical Soc Am; Soc Photo-Optical Instrumentation Engrs. *Res:* Optics; statistics; optical processing. *Mailing Add:* 5813 Arlmont Circle Dayton OH 45440-2305

GUSTAFSON, TERRY LEE, RAMAN SPECTROSCOPY, ULTRAFAST SPECTROSCOPY. *Current Pos:* ASST PROF, OHIO STATE UNIV, 89- *Personal Data:* b Brainerd, Minn, May 14, 53. *Educ:* Moorhead State Univ, BS, 75; Purdue Univ, PhD(chem), 79. *Honors & Awards:* Am Inst Chem Medal, 75. *Prof Exp:* Sr res chemist, Sohio Res & Develop, 79-82; proj leader, Stand Oil Co, 82-87; sr proj leader, BP Am Res & Develop, 87-89. *Mem:* Am Chem Soc; Am Phys Soc; Soc Appl Spectros. *Res:* Molecular conformation and dynamics; time-resolved optical characterization of thin film materials; instrumental developments in ultrafast pulsed lasers for quasi-continuous and time-resolved spectroscopy. *Mailing Add:* Dept Chem Ohio State Univ 120 W 18th Ave Columbus OH 43210-1173. *Fax:* 614-292-1685; *E-Mail:* gustafson.5@osu.edu

GUSTAFSON, WILLIAM HOWARD, ALGEBRA. *Current Pos:* from asst prof to assoc prof, 76-86, PROF MATH, TEX TECH UNIV, 86- *Personal Data:* b New Haven, Conn, Sept 9, 44. *Educ:* Wesleyan Univ, BA, 66; Univ Ill, MA, 67, PhD(math), 70. *Honors & Awards:* Lester R Ford Award, Math Asn Am, 77. *Prof Exp:* Asst prof math, Ind Univ, Bloomington, 70-72; vis asst prof math, Brandeis Univ, 72-73; asst prof math, Ind Univ, Bloomington, 73-76. *Mem:* Am Math Soc; Math Asn Am. *Res:* Representation theory and related aspects of matrix theory; number theory and algebraic geometry. *Mailing Add:* Dept Math Tex Tech Univ Lubbock TX 79409-1042

GUSTAFSON, WINTHROP A(DOLPH), AERODYNAMICS, SPACECRAFT DESIGN. *Current Pos:* assoc prof aeronaut & eng sci, 60-66, actg head, Sch Aeronaut & Astronaut, 84-85, PROF AERONAUT & ASTRONAUT, PURDUE UNIV, 66-, ASSOC HEAD, 80- *Personal Data:* b Moline, Ill, Oct 14, 28; m 57, Sarah E Garner; c Charles L, S Scott, John W & Richard N. *Educ:* Univ Ill, BS, 50, MS, 54, PhD(aeronaut eng), 56. *Prof Exp:* Assoc res scientist, Missiles & Space Div, Lockheed Aircraft Corp, Calif, 56-60. *Concurrent Pos:* Consult, Goodyear Aerospace Corp, Ohio, 64; vis prof, Univ Calif, San Diego, 68; fac fel, Dryden Flight Res Ctr, NASA, 76; consult, Los Alamos Sci Lab, 77-79; consult, US Army Aviation, Washington, DC, 85-86. *Mem:* Am Inst Aeronaut & Astronaut; Am Soc Eng Educ. *Res:* Aerodynamics; rarefied gas dynamics; spacecraft design. *Mailing Add:* Sch Aeronaut & Astronaut Purdue Univ West Lafayette IN 47907. *Fax:* 765-494-0307; *E-Mail:* gustafso@gn.ecn.purdue.edu

GUSTAFSSON, JAN-AKE, MOLECULAR ENDOCRINOLOGY, MOLECULAR TOXICOLOGY. *Current Pos:* PROF MED NUTRIT, DEPT MED NUTRIT, KAROLINSKA INST, 79-, CTR BIOTECH, 85- & CTR NUTRIT & TOXICOL, 89- *Personal Data:* b Stockholm, Sweden, Aug 4, 43; c 1. *Educ:* Karolinska Inst, PhD(chem), 68, MD, 71. *Honors & Awards:* Svedberg Prize in Chem, 82. *Prof Exp:* Prof chem, Karolinska Inst, 76-78, Univ Gothenburg, 78-79. *Concurrent Pos:* Mem, Nobel Assembly, Karolinska Inst, 86; found, KaroBio, AB, 87; adj prof, Dept Cell Biol, Baylor Col Med, Houston, Tex, 87. *Mem:* Hon mem Am Soc Biochem & Molecular Biol. *Res:* Mechanism of action of steroid hormones and of growth hormone; structure and function of steriod receptors; regulation and function of cytochrome P-450 in the liver, brain and prostate; formation and biological effects of mutagens in fried foods. *Mailing Add:* Dept Med Nutrit Ctr Biotechnol Karolinska Inst Huddinge Univ Hosp F60 Novum Huddinge S-141-86 Sweden. *Fax:* 46-8-7798795

GUSTAFSSON, TORGNY DANIEL, SURFACE PHYSICS. *Current Pos:* PROF, RUTGERS UNIV, 87- *Personal Data:* b Halmstad, Sweden, Oct 18, 46; m 77, Ingrid; c Marcus, Lovisa, Hanna & Andreas. *Educ:* Chalmers Univ Technol, MSc, 70, PhD(physics), 73. *Honors & Awards:* Nottingham Prize,

Phys Electronics Conf, 74. *Prof Exp:* From res assoc to prof, Univ Pa, 74-87. *Concurrent Pos:* Vis scientist, Univ Wis Synchrotron Radiation Ctr, 76-77, Stanford Univ, 78 & FOM Inst, Amsterdam, 85; Sloan Found fel, 78-82. *Mem:* Fel Am Phys Soc. *Res:* Surface physics, in particular the interaction of clean metals with adsorbed species; surface structure studies with ion scattering. *Mailing Add:* Dept Physics & Astron Rutgers Univ PO Box 849 Piscataway NJ 08855-0849. *Fax:* 732-445-4343; *E-Mail:* gustaf@physics.rutgers.edu

GUSTAV, BONNIE LEE, PHYSICAL ANTHROPOLOGY, ANTHROPOMETRICS. *Current Pos:* asst prof, 72-86, ASSOC PROF ANTHROP, BROOKLYN COL, 87- *Personal Data:* b New York, NY, Feb 10, 44; m 78; c 3. *Educ:* Hunter Col, BA, 64; Univ Mass, PhD(phys anthrop), 72. *Prof Exp:* Lectr anthrop, Hunter Col, 67-68. *Mem:* AAAS; fel Am Asn Phys Anthrop; Am Anthrop Asn. *Res:* Skeletal growth and development; human paleoanthropology; osteology. *Mailing Add:* Dept Anthrop Brooklyn Col City Univ NY Bedford & Ave H Brooklyn NY 11210. *Fax:* 516-466-4145

GUSTAVSON, FRED GEHRUNG, APPLIED MATHEMATICS, COMPUTER SCIENCES. *Current Pos:* RES STAFF MEM MATH SCI, T J WATSON RES CTR, IBM CORP, 63- *Personal Data:* b New York, NY, May 29, 35; m 66; c 2. *Educ:* Rensselaer Polytech Inst, BS, 57, MS, 60, PhD(appl math), 63. *Honors & Awards:* Outstanding Contrib Award, IBM Corp, 68, Outstanding Invention Award, 71. *Prof Exp:* Res asst math, Math Res Ctr, Univ Wis, 61-62; res assoc, Rensselaer Polytech Inst, 62-63. *Mem:* Sigma Xi; Math Asn Am. *Res:* Sparse matrix theory, especially design and implementation of computer algorithms to handle sparse matrices; analysis of algorithms; numerical analysis. *Mailing Add:* Box 218 Yorktown Heights NY 10598-0218

GUSTAVSON, THOMAS CARL, GEOLOGY. *Current Pos:* RES SCIENTIST ENVIRON GEOL, BUR ECON GEOL, UNIV TEX, AUSTIN, 73-, COORDR, LAND RESOURCES LAB, 75- *Personal Data:* b Northampton, Mass, Dec 28, 36; m 59; c 4. *Educ:* Univ Mass, Amherst, BS, 61, PhD(geol), 73; Univ NDak, MS, 64. *Prof Exp:* Geologist, Humble Oil & Refining Co, 64-66 & Phillips Petrol Co, 66; instr geol, Southampton Col, Long Island Univ, 66-69. *Mem:* Geol Soc Am; Soc Econ Paleontologists & Mineralogists; Glaciol Soc; Sigma Xi. *Res:* Environmental geology of the Texas Coastal Plain; environmental aspects of geothermal energy development; fluvial and lacustrine sedimentary processes; geomorphology and engineering characteristics of expansive clay soil terrains; geology and geomorphology related to nuclear waste isolation. *Mailing Add:* 3404 Saddelstring Trail Austin TX 78739

GUSTIN, VAUGHN KENNETH, ANALYTICAL CHEMISTRY. *Current Pos:* sr analytical chemist, Corning Glass Works, 63-64, supvr analytic lab, 65-66, mgr, Chem Serv Dept, 66-70, mgr, Control Technol, 70-, DIR MFR ENG CONSUMER & SCI PROD DIV, CORNING GLASS WORKS. *Personal Data:* b Mansfield, Ohio, June 10, 36; m 57; c 2. *Educ:* Ohio State Univ, BSc, 58, MSc, 60, PhD(analytical chem), 63. *Prof Exp:* Teaching asst, Ohio State Univ, 58-63. *Concurrent Pos:* Partic, Prog for Mgt Develop, Harvard Bus Sch, 68. *Mem:* Am Chem Soc; Soc Appl Spectros (secy, 66); fel Am Inst Chem. *Res:* Chemical composition control of glasses, glass ceramics and associated raw materials and refractories; analytical method development in all phases of analytical chemistry; pollution control. *Mailing Add:* 104 Point Place Dr Westminster SC 29693-6440

GUSTINE, DAVID LAWRENCE, PLANT MOLECULAR BIOLOGY. *Current Pos:* RES PLANT PHYSIOLOGIST, US REGIONAL PASTURE RES LAB, AGR RES SERV, USDA, 71- *Personal Data:* b Battle Creek, Mich, Jan 2, 41; m 61, Diane R DeShon; c 2. *Educ:* Malone Col, BA, 64; Mich State Univ, PhD(biochem), 69. *Prof Exp:* Res fel biochem & pharmacol, Children's Hosp Res Found, Cincinnati, Ohio, 69-71. *Concurrent Pos:* Adj assoc prof crop sci, Pa State Univ. *Mem:* Am Soc Plant Physiol; Phytochem Soc NAm; AAAS; Int Soc Plant Molecular Biologists. *Res:* Plant biochemical mechanisms of disease resistance; molecular biology of apomixis. *Mailing Add:* USDA Agr Res Serv, PSWMRL 109 Pasture Lab Curtin Rd University Park PA 16802

GUSTISON, ROBERT ABDON, INORGANIC CHEMISTRY. *Current Pos:* RETIRED. *Personal Data:* b Springfield, Ohio, Aug 29, 20; m 43; c 3. *Educ:* Univ Chicago, BS, 42. *Prof Exp:* Res chemist, metall lab, Univ Chicago, 42-44; res engr, Int Minerals & Chem Co, 44-46; res chemist & engr, Union Carbide Chem Co Div, Union Carbide Corp, 46-54, mgr minerals & chem eng res, Union Carbide Metals Co Div, 54-61, supvr pilot plants, 61-63; mgr chem processing, Kawecki Berylco Industs, Inc, 64-; sr res scientist, Cabot Inc; consult, 85-93. *Concurrent Pos:* Mem mat adv bd, Nat Acad Sci; metall consult, Ferro-Tech Inc, Pittsburgh, Pa, 75- *Mem:* Am Chem Soc; Am Inst Mining, Metall & Petrol Engrs; fel Am Inst Chemists. *Res:* Extractive metallurgy involving pyrometallurgy; electrometallurgy; halogenations; high pressure and vacuum; Mass transfer operations. *Mailing Add:* 720-D4 Old Mill Rd Wyomissing PA 19610

GUSTMAN, ALAN LESLIE, ECONOMICS, EDUCATION. *Current Pos:* LOREN M BERRY PROF ECONS, DARTMOUTH COL, 69- *Personal Data:* b Brooklyn, NY, Apr 2, 44; m 66, Janice Faye Reiter; c Samuel M, Evelyn B & Mara H. *Educ:* City Col NY, BA, 64; Univ Mich, PhD, 69. *Concurrent Pos:* Grantee, Dept Health Human Servs, 71-72, 74-76 & 92-94, Dept Labor, 81-96, NSF, 86-88, Dept Educ, 89-90, Upjohn Found, 91-94 & Nat Inst Aging, 92-96; spec asst econ affairs, US Dept Labor, 76-77, consult, 75-; res assoc, Nat Bur Econ Res, Cambridge, Mass, 79-; consult, US Dept Educ, 80-83 & 87, Dept Health & Human Servs, 78-80, 88-89, Gen Acct Off, 84-89, Fed Res Bd, 92, Surv Res Ctr, Univ Mich, 90-, adj res scientist, 93- *Mem:* Nat Acad Social Ins. *Mailing Add:* 4 Bridgeman Rd Hanover NH 03755-1302

GUTAY, LASZLO J, HIGH ENERGY NUCLEAR PHYSICS. *Current Pos:* Res assoc, Purdue Univ, 65-67, asst prof, 67-70, assoc prof, 70-75, PROF HIGH ENERGY NUCLEAR PHYSICS, PURDUE UNIV, 75- *Personal Data:* b Fadd, Hungary, Aug 9, 35; US citizen; m 61; c 5. *Educ:* Oxford Univ, BA, 59, MA, 61; Fla State Univ, PhD(physics), 64. *Honors & Awards:* H McCoy Award Science, Purdue Univ. *Concurrent Pos:* Prin investr contract res, Dept Energy, 74. *Mem:* Fel Am Phys Soc. *Res:* Pion-Pion interactions; current algebra; vector meson dominance; high energy, highly inelastic collision; hadronic temperature size; size of centrally produced hadronic matter hadronic phase transactions; super dense radronic matter; quark-gluon plasma. *Mailing Add:* Dept Physics Purdue Univ West Lafayette IN 47907

GUTBERLET, LOUIS CHARLES, ORGANIC CHEMISTRY. *Current Pos:* RETIRED. *Personal Data:* b Chicago, Ill, Mar 29, 28; m 52, Patricia Panka; c Eric & Paul. *Educ:* Ill Inst Technol, BS, 50; Purdue Univ, MS, 54. *Prof Exp:* Asst chem, Purdue Univ, 52-54; chemist, Amoco Res Ctr, Amoco Oil Co, 54-88, res supvr, 82-88. *Mem:* Am Chem Soc. *Res:* Catalytic hydrogenation; heterogeneous catalysis; hydrocarbon conversion processes. *Mailing Add:* 1520 E Wakeman Ave Wheaton IL 60187-3736

GUTBEZAHL, BORIS, POLYMER CHEMISTRY. *Current Pos:* chemist, Rohm & Haas Co, __53-59, head process develop lab, 59-60, head plastics color lab, 60-65, supvr tech serv, 65-78, mgr analysis & color serv, 78-85, QUAL COORDR, ROHM & HAAS CO, 85- *Personal Data:* b Tientsin, China, May 1, 27; US citizen; m 52; c 2. *Educ:* City Col New York, BS, 47; Columbia Univ, AM, 49; Fla State Univ, PhD(chem), 52. *Prof Exp:* Asst chem, Columbia Univ, 52-53. *Mem:* Am Chem Soc; Soc Plastics Eng; Inter-Soc Color Coun; Am Soc Testing & Mat; Am Soc Qual Control. *Res:* Organic mechanisms; polymerization kinetics; product and process development in plastics. *Mailing Add:* 5070 D Nestingway Delray Beach FL 33484

GUTCHO, SIDNEY J, IMMUNOASSAYS, IMMUNOCHEMISTRY. *Current Pos:* Res chemist, Schwarz Labs, Inc, 41-59, head chemist, Schwarz Biores, Inc, 59-70, head chemist, 70-72, assoc dir res & develop, Schwarz/Mann, Becton-Dickinson & Co, 72-77, assoc dir res & develop, 77-87, CONSULT BECTON DICKINSON IMMUNODIAG, 87- *Personal Data:* b Brooklyn, NY, Oct 18, 19; m 49, Marcia Halpern; c Lawrence & Andrew. *Educ:* NY Univ, BA, 40, MS, 41. *Mem:* Clin Ligand Assay Soc; Am Chem Soc; Am Asn Clin Chem. *Res:* Immunochemistry; immunoassays; isolation of biochemicals from yeast and other natural sources; enzymatic preparation of biochemicals; biosynthesis of radioactive compounds; chemistry of nucleic acids and their derivatives. *Mailing Add:* 22 Francis Pl Monsey NY 10952

GUTELIUS, JOHN ROBERT, SURGERY. *Current Pos:* head dept, 73-83, PROF SURG, QUEEN'S UNIV, 73- *Personal Data:* b Montreal, Que, Jan 18, 29; m 55; c 8. *Educ:* Univ Montreal, BA, 50; McGill Univ, MD, 55. *Prof Exp:* Rotating intern, Royal Victoria Hosp, 55-56; from asst resident surgeon to chief resident surgeon, Teaching Hosps, McGill Univ, 56-61, demonstr surg, McGill Univ, 61-63, from asst prof to assoc prof, 63-69, assoc dean postgrad studies & res, 68-69; prof surg & head dept & dean, Sch Med, Univ Sask, 70-73; surgeon-in-chief, Kingston Gen Hosp, Hotel Dieu Hosp, Kingston, Ont, 73-83. *Concurrent Pos:* Fel exp surg, McGill Univ, 57-58; fel surg, Johns Hopkins Univ & Hosp, 59-60; R S McLaughlin Found traveling fel, 59-60; Markle Found scholar, 63-68; from asst surgeon to assoc surgeon, Royal Victoria Hosp, 63-69; mem, Grants Comt Clin Invest, Med Res Coun Can, 70-75 & comt gen surg & exam-gen surg, Royal Col Physicians & Surgeons, 70-; hon consult, Royal Victoria Hosp, Montreal, Que; mem, priorities comt, Med Res Coun Can, 75-79. *Mem:* Am Surg Asn; Soc Univ Surgeons; Int Cardiovasc Soc; Can Soc Clin Invest; Am Col Surg. *Res:* Vascular surgery; techniques; patient selection; water and electrolytes; adrenal function; natural history of peripheral arterial disease. *Mailing Add:* Kingston Gen Hosp Surg Kingston ON K7L 2V7 Can

GUTERMAN, MARTIN MAYR, ALGEBRA. *Current Pos:* from instr to assoc prof 66-87, PROF MATH, TUFTS UNIV, 87- *Personal Data:* b New York, NY, Nov 18, 41; m 64; c 2. *Educ:* Brooklyn Col, BS, 61; Cornell Univ, MS, 64, PhD(finite groups), 68. *Prof Exp:* Asst, Cornell Univ, 61-66. *Mem:* Am Math Soc; Math Asn Am. *Res:* Theory of finite groups. *Mailing Add:* Bromfield-Pearson Hall Tufts Univ Medford MA 02155

GUTERMAN, SONIA KOSOW, MOLECULAR BIOLOGY. *Current Pos:* TECH SPECIALIST, LAHIVE & COCKFIELD LLP, 96- *Personal Data:* b Brooklyn, NY, June 27, 44; m 64, Martin Guterman; c Lila & Beth. *Educ:* Cornell Univ, BS, 64, MS, 67; Mass Inst Technol, PhD(microbiol), 71. *Prof Exp:* NIH fel microbiol, Mass Inst Technol, 66-70, res assoc, 70-71; instr biol, Brandeis Univ, 71-72; NIH fel molecular biol, Sch Med, Tufts Univ, 72-74, res assoc, 74-75, instr, 75-76; from asst prof to assoc prof biol, Boston Univ, 76-84; sr scientist, Biotech Int, 83-87; vpres res, Protein Eng Corp, 87-91; vis scientist, Dana-Barber Cancer Inst, 92-93; technol licensing officer biotech, Mass Inst Technol, 93-96. *Mem:* AAAS; Am Soc Microbiol; Genetics Soc Am; NY Acad Sci. *Res:* Studies of bacterial RNA polymerase mutants to determine functions and interactions of enzyme subunits; phage and colicin receptor genetics as a probe of inner and outer membrane structure; rho protein genetics and enzymology to study functional sites of nucleic acid interaction; cloning secretion signal antibiotic biosynthetic genes, streptomyces; remodeling proteins by mutagenesis and selection. *Mailing Add:* 20 Oakley Rd Belmont MA 02178

468 / GUTFINGER

GUTFINGER, DAN ELI, MACHINE VISION, ARTIFICIAL HEARTS & VENTRICULAR ASSIST DEVICES. *Current Pos:* GEN SURG RESIDENT, ALLEGHENY GEN HOSP, PITTSBURGH, 93- *Personal Data:* b New Haven, Conn, June 17, 64. *Educ:* Univ Calif, Irvine, BS, 83, MS, 86, PhD(elec & computer eng), 90, MD, 96. *Prof Exp:* Eng specialist signal processing, Ford Aerospace & Aeronaut, 84-92; sports statistician, Univ Calif, Irvine, 83, teaching asst computer sci, 84-85, res asst image processing, 89-90, engr, biomed eng, Artificial Heart Prog, 91-92. *Concurrent Pos:* Mem, Heart Rx Subcomt, Am Heart Asn, 91-93. *Res:* Development of machine vision and pattern recognition systems with medical industrial and military applications; clinical evaluation of artificial hearts and ventricular assist devices; analysis of multi-sensor data with emphasis on radar signature data; cardiac surgery in a managed care environment; heart transplantation. *Mailing Add:* 711 Duncan Ave No 704 Pittsburgh PA 15237

GUTFREUND, KURT, SURFACE CHEMISTRY. *Current Pos:* sr scientist, surface chem, 57-86, SCI ADV, IIT RES INST, 86- *Personal Data:* b Bielitz, Ger, April 18, 24; US citizen; m 54, Julie Frisch; c 3. *Educ:* Munich Tech Univ, Ger, dipl, 49; Univ Buffalo, NY, BA, 50; Univ Wis, MSc, 52. *Prof Exp:* Asst chemist, polymers, Union Carbide Corp, 53-55; res physicist, mat sci, Am Can Co, 55-57. *Concurrent Pos:* Mem adv bd, Nat Heart, Blood & Lung Inst, 78-79, Environ Conserv Comn, 88-93. *Mem:* Am Chem Soc; Soc Rheology; Soc Biomat; AAAS. *Res:* Interfacial relationships in fiber-reinforced composites; interaction of polymers with solids; magnetic coatings; thermal degradation of polymers in oxidizing environments; investigation of blood coagulation by light scattering methods; compatibility of cardiovascular devices with blood constituents; effects of laser radiation on organic coatings. *Mailing Add:* 218 Lee St Park Forest IL 60416. *E-Mail:* krtgutfreund@iitvax

GUTH, ALAN HARVEY, COSMOLOGY. *Current Pos:* vis assoc prof, Mass Inst Technol, 80-81, assoc prof, 81-86, prof, 86-89, Jerrold Zacharias prof physics, 89-91, VICTOR WEISSKOPF PROF PHYSICS, MASS INST TECHNOL, 92- *Personal Data:* b New Brunswick, NJ, Feb 27, 47; m 71, Susan Tisch; c Lawrence & Jennifer. *Educ:* Mass Inst Technol, SB & SM, 69, PhD(physics), 72. *Honors & Awards:* Alfred P Sloan Found Fel, 81; Rennie Taylor Award, Am Tentative Soc, 89-90; Oskar Klein Lectr, Stockholm Univ, 91; Julius Edgar Lilienfeld Prize, Am Phys Soc, 92. *Prof Exp:* Instr physics, Princeton Univ, 71-74; res assoc, Columbia Univ, 74-77; res assoc II, Cornell Univ, 77-79; res assoc, Stanford Linear Accelerator Ctr, Stanford Univ, 79-80. *Concurrent Pos:* Physicist, Harvard Smithsonian Ctr Astrophys, 84-90; mem, Exec Comt, Astrophys Div, Am Phys Soc, 86-88, vchmn, 88-89, chmn, 89-90; vis scientist, Harvard Smithsonian Ctr Astrophys, 90-91. *Mem:* Nat Acad Sci; fel Am Phys Soc; Am Astron Soc; fel AAAS; fel Am Acad Arts & Sci. *Res:* Theory of elementary particles; application of particle physics to the very early universe; inflationary cosmology. *Mailing Add:* Ctr Theoret Physics Mass Inst Technol Rm 6-209 Cambridge MA 02139. *Fax:* 617-253-9798; *E-Mail:* guth@mitlns.mit.edu

GUTH, LLOYD, NERVE REGENERATION, SPINAL CORD INJURY. *Current Pos:* RES PROF, DEPT BIOL, COL WILLIAM & MARY, 90-; RES PROF, DEPT NEUROSCI, UNIV VA MED SCH, CHARLOTTESVILLE, VA. *Personal Data:* b New York, NY, Oct 8, 29; m 55; c 2. *Educ:* NY Univ, BA, 49, MD, 53. *Prof Exp:* Asst anat, Col Med, NY Univ, 50-51 & Jackson Mem Lab, 51; intern, Kings County Hosp, 53-54; neuroanatomist, Lab Neuroanat Sci, NIH, 54-61, head sect exp neurol, 61-75; prof & chmn, Dept Anat, Sch Med, Univ Md, 75-90. *Concurrent Pos:* Sen Jacob Javits Award, 89-96. *Mem:* AAAS; Am Asn Anat. *Res:* Experimental neurology; nerve regeneration; neuromuscular interrelationships, structure, function and chemistry; response of the mammalian spinal cord to traumatic injury focusing on mechanisms that restrict or enhance axonal regeneration. *Mailing Add:* 111 Gullane Fords Colony Williamsburg VA 23188. *Fax:* 757-221-6483; *E-Mail:* polguth@mem.po.com

GUTH, PAUL HENRY, INTERNAL MEDICINE, GASTROENTEROLOGY. *Current Pos:* from assoc prof to prof in residence, 69-93, EMER PROF, SCH MED, UNIV CALIF, LOS ANGELES, 94- *Personal Data:* b New York, NY, Mar 15, 27; m 53, Rachael Klonymus; c David, Eve, Esther & Naomi. *Educ:* NY Univ, BS, 48; Howard Univ, MD, 49; Am Bd Internal Med, dipl, 61; Am Bd Gastroenterol, dipl, 65. *Honors & Awards:* Distinguished Investr Award, Effluent Guidelines Div, Am Gastroenterol Asn, 94. *Prof Exp:* Resident internal med, Kings County Hosp, 50-51; res fel gastrointestinal physiol, Fels Res Inst, Temple Univ, 51-52, Am Gastroenterol Asn res fel, 54-55, resident internal med, Temple Univ Hosp, 55-56, resident gastroenterol, 56-57; chief gastroenterol, Orange County Gen Hosp, 57-69, dir med serv, Med Ctr, 67-69. *Concurrent Pos:* From asst clin prof to assoc clin prof, Univ Calif-Calif Col Med, 66-69; asst chief gastroenterol, W Los Angeles Vet Affairs Med Ctr, 69-93. *Mem:* AMA; Am Fedn Clin Res; fel Am Col Physicians; Am Gastroenterol Asn; Am Physiol Soc. *Res:* Gastrointestinal physiology and pathophysiology: gastrointestinal blood flow; experimental ulcer. *Mailing Add:* 3422 Castlewoods Pl Sherman Oaks CA 91403. *Fax:* 818-788-5447

GUTII, PAUL SPENCER, PHARMACOLOGY. *Current Pos:* from asst prof to assoc prof, 60-66, PROF PHARMACOL, SCH MED, TULANE UNIV, 66- *Personal Data:* b May 29, 31; US citizen; m 53, Marilena Terrell; c Douglas M, Gregory D, Bradley O & Derek A. *Educ:* Fordham Univ, BSc, 53; Philadelphia Col Pharm, MSc, 55; Hahnemann Med Col, PhD(pharmacol), 58. *Prof Exp:* Vis researcher pharmacol, Inst Animal Physiol, 58-59; assoc, Hahnemann Med Col, 59-60. *Concurrent Pos:* Fel, Nat Paraplegia Found, 58-59; consult, ICI Am; Wellcome res fel, 72; Fogarty sr int fel, 83; vis prof, Dept Neurobiol, Univ Mex, 90, Dept Bio, Univ Turin, 93, Univ Pavig, 94. *Mem:* AAAS; Am Soc Pharmacol & Exp Therapeut; NY Acad Sci. *Res:* Biochemical aspects of neuropharmacology; auditory pharmacology; acetylcholine storage and release; sensory pharmacology, vesitbular physiology and pharmacology. *Mailing Add:* Dept Pharmacol Tulane Univ Sch Med 1430 Tulane Ave New Orleans LA 70112-2699. *Fax:* 504-588-5283; *E-Mail:* pguth@mailhost.tms.tulane.edu

GUTH, S(HERMAN) LEON, VISION. *Current Pos:* Lectr, 62-63, from instr to assoc prof, 63-70, PROF PSYCHOL, IND UNIV, BLOOMINGTON, 70- *Educ:* Purdue Univ, BS, 59; Univ Ill, MA, 61, PhD(psychol), 63. *Concurrent Pos:* Grants, NSF, 63-82 & NIH, 64-71; NIH spec res fel, Univ Calif, Berkeley, 71-72; NSF rotating prog dir sensory physiol & perception, 77-78; chmn, Dept Visual Sci, Ind Univ, 83-88. *Mem:* AAAS; fel Optical Soc Am; Asn Res Vision & Ophthal. *Res:* Visual psychophysics. *Mailing Add:* Dept Psychol Ind Univ Bloomington IN 47405-1300

GUTH, SYLVESTER KARL, physics, illumination; deceased, see previous edition for last biography

GUTHALS, PAUL ROBERT, ATMOSPHERIC CHEMISTRY & GENERAL ATMOSPHERIC SCIENCES, QUALITY PROGRAM & TECHNICAL MANAGEMENT. *Current Pos:* radio-chem air sampler, Los Alamos Nat Lab, US Dept Educ, 57-59, proj leader, res, 72-75, asst group leader atmospheric studies, 80-85, PROJ LEADER, ATMOSPHERIC RES, LOS ALAMOS NAT LAB, US DEPT EDUC, 75-, QA OFFICER RES & DEVELOP. *Personal Data:* b Fowler, Colo, Mar 29, 29; m 58; c 2. *Educ:* Eastern NMex Univ, BS, 57;. *Prof Exp:* Prog mgr 89, Nev Nuclear Waste Site Invest, 85-88. *Mem:* Am Soc Qual Control. *Res:* Active participant in atmospheric research as involves collection of samples (particulates and gaseous); sample analysis and in-situ atmospheric constituent measurements; nuclear event diagnosis; air mass movement tracing experiments. *Mailing Add:* 1919 Spruce St Los Alamos NM 87544

GUTHE, KARL FREDERICK, MUSCULAR PHYSIOLOGY. *Current Pos:* from instr to prof, 50-85, EMER PROF ZOOL, UNIV MICH, ANN ARBOR, 85- *Personal Data:* b Detroit, Mich, Aug 3, 18; m 46; c 3. *Educ:* Harvard Univ AB, 39, AM, 40, PhD(biol), 51. *Prof Exp:* Physicist, Naval Ord Dept, 41-45; tutor biochem sci, Harvard Univ, 49-50. *Mem:* AAAS; Biophys Soc. *Res:* Physiology of muscle. *Mailing Add:* 1407 Ferdon Univ Mich Ann Arbor MI 48109

GUTHEIL, THOMAS GORDON, FORENSIC PSYCHIATRY, FORENSIC TEACHING. *Current Pos:* Actg dir, adult psychiat serv, 76-80, DIR MED STUDENT TRAINING, MASS MENT HEALTH CTR, 80-; PROF PSYCHIAT, HARVARD MED SCH, 93- *Personal Data:* b New York, NY, June 11, 42; m 85, Shannon Woolley; c 4. *Educ:* Harvard Univ, BA, 63, MD, 67. *Honors & Awards:* Guttmacher Award, Am Psychiat Asn, 83. *Concurrent Pos:* Vis lectr, Harvard Law Sch, 77-; co-dir, Prog Psychiat & Law, Mass Ment Health Ctr, 80- & pres, Law & Psychiat Resource Ctr, 81-; consult, Am Bar Asn, 80- & Risk Mgt Found, Harvard Med Inst, 87- *Mem:* Am Psychiat Asn; Am Acad Psychiat & Law; Int Acad Law & Ment Health (treas, 86-); Am Bd Forensic Psychiatry. *Res:* Liability and liability prevention; medicolegal decision making. *Mailing Add:* Ma Mental Health Ctr 74 Fenwood Rd Boston MA 02115-6106. *Fax:* 617-734-7915

GUTHRIE, CATHERINE SHIRLEY NICHOLSON, GENETICS. *Current Pos:* INDEPENDENT RES SCIENTIST, 92- *Personal Data:* b Jackson, Miss; m 61, George D; c George D Jr. *Educ:* Auburn Univ, BS, 57; Fla State Univ, MS, 60; Ind Univ, Bloomington, PhD(genetics), 72. *Honors & Awards:* First Place Res Award, Ala Acad Sci, 56. *Prof Exp:* Instr physical, Fla State Univ, 60; res asst molecular biol, Calif Inst Technol, 60-62; instr biol, Boston State Col, 63-64; NIH trainee, 67-71; vis asst prof biol, Univ Evansville, 72-73; mem adj fac, Sch Med, Ind Univ, Indianapolis, 74-92. *Concurrent Pos:* Consult, Mead Johnson & Co, 76; Sarah Berliner fel, Am Asn Univ Women, 78-79; mass media sci fel, AAAS, 79; prof staff mem comt sci & tech, US House Rep, 81; consult, comt environ & pub works, US Senate, 81. *Mem:* Sigma Xi; AAAS; Genetics Soc Am. *Res:* Inheritance of chlorophyll and lamellae; GABA receptors; relationship between membrane structure and function. *Mailing Add:* 700 Drexel Dr Evansville IN 47712

GUTHRIE, CHRISTINE, MOLECULAR BIOLOGY, BIOCHEMISTRY. *Current Pos:* from asst prof to assoc prof, 73-93, PROF, DEPT BIOCHEM & BIOPHYS, UNIV CALIF, SAN FRANCISCO, 93- *Personal Data:* b Brooklyn, NY, Apr 27, 45. *Educ:* Univ Mich, BS, 66; Univ Wis, PhD(genetics), 70. *Prof Exp:* Vis scientist, Max Planck Inst Molecular Genetics, Berlin, Ger, 70-71; fel molecular biol, Univ Wis, 71-73. *Mem:* Nat Acad Sci. *Res:* Genetic and biochemical analysis of nucleic acid and protein synthesis. *Mailing Add:* Dept Biochem & Biophys Univ Calif S-964 San Francisco CA 94143

GUTHRIE, DANIEL ALBERT, VERTEBRATE ZOOLOGY. *Current Pos:* Asst prof, 64-69, assoc prof, 69-76, PROF BIOL, PITZER COL, SCRIPPS COL & CLAREMONT MCKENNA COL, 77- *Personal Data:* b Ind, Mar 5, 39; div; c 3. *Educ:* Amherst Col, BA, 60; Harvard Univ, MA, 62; Univ Mass, PhD(biol), 64. *Mem:* AAAS; Nat Audubon Soc; Soc Vert Paleont; Am Soc Mammal; Am Ornithologists Union; Sigma Xi. *Res:* Lower Eocene mammals; carotid arteries in mammals; mammalian paleontology; evolutionary rates; environmental studies; bird population studies; pleistocene avifauna; zooarcheology. *Mailing Add:* W M Keck Sci Ctr 925 N Mills Ave Claremont CA 91711-5916

GUTHRIE, DAVID BURRELL, ORGANIC CHEMISTRY. *Current Pos:* RETIRED. *Personal Data:* b Long Beach, Calif, Feb 10, 20; m 51; c 3. *Educ:* Westminster Col, AB, 41; Univ Ill, PhD, 45. *Prof Exp:* Res chemist, Monsanto Chem Co, 46-59; asst chief chemist, Lucidol Div, Wallace & Tiernan, Inc, NY, 59-61, supvr & group leader, 61-63; group leader, new prod res, Petrolite Res & Develop, Petrolite Corp, 63-64, group leader, hydrocarbon additives & corrosion res, 64-66, supvr, Process Develop Eng Dept, Tretolite Div, 66-85, mgr, Pilot Plant Sect, 85-87, res chemist, 88. *Mem:* Am Chem Soc. *Res:* Organic peroxides; chemistry of petroleum products; synthetic organic and surfactant chemistry. *Mailing Add:* 1148 Ridgelynn Dr St Louis MO 63124-1220

GUTHRIE, DONALD, STATISTICS. *Current Pos:* EMER PROF PSYCHIAT & BIOSTATIST, UNIV CALIF, LOS ANGELES, 73- *Personal Data:* b Eureka, Calif, July 8, 33; m 54, Janet Gordon; c Donald & Sarah. *Educ:* Stanford Univ, BS, 54, PhD(statist), 58; Columbia Univ, MA, 55. *Honors & Awards:* Founders Award, Am Statist Asn, 96. *Prof Exp:* Asst, Stanford Univ, 53-57, res assoc, 57-58; asst prof math mech, US Naval Postgrad Sch, 58-60; mathematician, Stanford Res Inst, 60-63; from assoc prof to prof statist, Ore State Univ, 63-73. *Concurrent Pos:* Consult, Stanford Res Inst, 58-59, 63-; vis assoc prof, Dept Statist, Univ NC, Chapel Hill, 69-70. *Mem:* Fel AAAS; Inst Math Statist; fel Am Statist Asn; Biomet Soc; Am Asn Ment Deficiency; Am Acad Ment Retardation; Soc Psychophysiol Res; Int Statist Inst. *Res:* Application of statistical methods to mental health research. *Mailing Add:* Dept Psychiat Univ Calif 760 Westwood Plaza Los Angeles CA 90024-1759. *Fax:* 310-825-1119; *E-Mail:* dguthrie@ucla.edu

GUTHRIE, DONALD ARTHUR, ORGANIC CHEMISTRY, RADIATION CHEMISTRY. *Current Pos:* VPRES & TREAS, DEMETER BIOTECHNOL LTD. *Personal Data:* b Winnipeg, Man, May 26, 26; US citizen; m 51; c 2. *Educ:* Univ Man, BSc, 47; Univ Toronto, MSc, 49; McGill Univ, PhD(org chem), 52. *Prof Exp:* From res chemist to sr chemist, Esso Res & Eng Co, Standard Oil Co NJ, 51-62; mgr cent res div, Lord Corp, 62-70, vpres corp develop, 70-75; dir composite res, Ciba-Geigy Corp, 75-82; staff mem, Gulf South Res Inst, 83-88; vpres & dir, Helix Biomedix, 88. *Concurrent Pos:* Trustee, Edinboro Col; chmn, Gt Lakes Res Inst. *Mem:* Am Chem Soc; Am Inst Aeronaut & Astronaut; Soc Advan Mat & Process Eng; fel Am Inst Chem; Com Develop Asn. *Res:* Lubricant oxidation and detergency; radiation initiated polymerization; synthesis and application of propellant oxidizers and binders; management of basic research in solid state physics, polymer synthesis, surface and polymer physical chemistry; composite materials science; peptide drugs as therapeutic agents. *Mailing Add:* 109 Dunedin Ct Cary NC 27511-6405. *Fax:* 919-319-1079

GUTHRIE, EUGENE HARDING, MEDICINE, PUBLIC HEALTH. *Current Pos:* RETIRED. *Personal Data:* b Washington, DC, Apr, 9, 24; m 48; c 6. *Educ:* George Washington Univ, MD, 51; Univ Mich, MPH, 55. *Honors & Awards:* Smith-Reed-Russel Med Honor Soc, 51. *Prof Exp:* Intern, USPHS Hosp, Baltimore, Md, 51-52, house officer, 52-53; resident pub health, Montgomery Co Health Dept, Md, 54-55; resident, State Dept Health, Calif, 55-56; chief sch health & rural health activ, Bur State Serv, USPHS, 56-59, chief prog officer, 59-62, chief, Neurol & Sensory Dis Serv Br, 62 & Div Chronic Dis, 62-66, from asst surgeon gen opers to assoc surgeon gen, 66-68; exec dir, Md Comprehensive Health Planning Agency, 68-74; consult health systs planning & develop, Am Health Planning Asn, 74-76, assoc exec dir, 76-78; dep state health officer & health officer, Dorchester & Talbot Cos, 78-86, co health officer, Talbot Co, Md, 86-87; assoc pub health admin, Sch Hyg, Johns Hopkins Univ, 70-76. *Concurrent Pos:* Mem, Interdept Comt Health Sch Aged Child & Comt Agr Migrants, Dept HEW, 57-59; mem working group, President's Comt Migratory Labor & alt mem, Interagency Adv Group, President's Coun Youth Fitness, 57-59; consult, Boy Scouts Am, 58-59; mem, Commissioned Officers Awards Bd, USPHS, 63-64; mem med comt, President's Comn Employ Handicapped, 63-68; staff dir, Surgeon Gen Adv Comt Smoking & Health, 63-64; chmn bd, Am Acad Comprehensive Health Planning, 70-71; mem bd dir, Md Hosp Educ & Res Found, 70-72; regional adv group, Regional Med Prog, Md, 70-74. *Mem:* AMA; Am Pub Health Asn. *Res:* School and rural health; chronic diseases, including heart, cancer, diabetes, arthritis, neurological and sensory; mental retardation; gerontology; preventive medicine; medical administration. *Mailing Add:* 24832 Deepwater Point Dr St Michaels MD 21663

GUTHRIE, FRANK ALBERT, ANALYTICAL CHEMISTRY, CHEMISTRY GENERAL. *Current Pos:* from instr to prof, Rose-Hulman Inst Technol, 52-94, chmn dept, 69-72, chief health profs adv, 75-94, EMER PROF CHEM, ROSE HULMAN INST TECHNOL, 94- *Personal Data:* b Madison, Ind, Feb 16, 27; m 55, Marcella G Farrar; c Mark A, Bruce B, Kent A & Lee F. *Educ:* Hanover Col, BA, 50; Purdue Univ, MS, 52; Ind Univ, PhD(analytical chem), 62. *Prof Exp:* Asst chem, Purdue Univ, 50-52. *Concurrent Pos:* Asst, Ind Univ, 55-56; vis asst prof, Purdue Univ, 58 & Univ Ill, 61, Charles F Kettering vis lectr, 61-62; NSF res partic, Univ Colo, 63-64, Rensselaer Polytech Inst, 66; dir ed, Div Analytical Chem, Am Chem Soc, 65-77, secy, 73-77, chmn elect, 78-79, chmn, 79-80; res assoc, La State Univ, 67; vis prof chem, US Mil Acad, West Point, NY, 87-88 & 93-94; mem, Local Sect Activ Comt, Am Chem Soc, 82-86, vis assoc, Comt Prof Training, 84-, nominations & elections, 88-94, secy, 92-94; chmn, Acad Found Trustees, Ind Acad Sci, 86- *Mem:* Am Chem Soc; Sigma Xi; Coblentz Soc; fel Ind Acad Sci. *Res:* Spectroscopy; chemical instrumentation; coordination compounds. *Mailing Add:* Dept Chem Rose-Hulman Inst Technol 5500 Wabash Ave Terre Haute IN 47803-3999. *Fax:* 812-877-3198; *E-Mail:* frank.guthrie@rose-hulman.edu

GUTHRIE, FRANK EDWIN, entomology; deceased, see previous edition for last biography

GUTHRIE, GEORGE D, JR, MINERALOGY-CRYSTALLOGRAPHY, PETROLOGY-HYDROTHERMAL ALTERATION. *Current Pos:* fel, 89-92, STAFF SCIENTIST, LOS ALAMOS NAT LAB, 92- *Personal Data:* b May 4, 62; m, Suzanne M Stamatov; c Nicholas S. *Educ:* Harvard Univ, AB, 84; Johns Hopkins Univ, MA, 86, PhD(geol), 89. *Prof Exp:* Res asst, Johns Hopkins Univ, 84-89. *Concurrent Pos:* cur asst, Harvard Mineral Mus, 83; Asst teacher, 84, 86 & 87. *Mem:* AAAS; Am Geophys Union; Clay Minerals Soc; Mineral Soc Am; Sigma Xi. *Res:* Compositional and structural order in clay minerals; submicrometer fluid inclusions, using TEM and analytical electron microscopy; hydrothermal alteration; health effects of minerals; transmission and scanning electron microscopies/electron microprobe; x-ray diffraction techniques; ionic modeling of crystal structures. *Mailing Add:* Geol & Geochem MS D462 Los Alamos Nat Lab PO Box 1663 Los Alamos NM 87545. *Fax:* 505-665-3285; *E-Mail:* guthrie@esslab.lanl.gov

GUTHRIE, GEORGE DRAKE, BIOCHEMISTRY, MOLECULAR BIOLOGY. *Current Pos:* from asst prof to prof, 65-97, EMER PROF BIOCHEM & MOLECULAR BIOL, IND UNIV, INDIANAPOLIS, 97- *Personal Data:* b Indianapolis, Ind, Jan 20, 32; m 61, Catherine S Nicholson; c George Jr. *Educ:* Wabash Col, AB, 54; Calif Inst Technol, PhD(biophys), 62. *Prof Exp:* Res assoc, Mass Inst Technol, 62-65. *Concurrent Pos:* Assoc dir, Evansville Ctr Med Educ, Sch Med, Ind Univ, Evansville, 72-93. *Mem:* AAAS; Sigma Xi; Res Soc Alcoholism; Am Soc Biochem & Molecular Biol. *Res:* Metabolic regulation, especially regulation of intermediary metabolism in liver; neurotransmitter binding in bacteria. *Mailing Add:* 700 Drexel Dr Evansville IN 47712. *E-Mail:* gguthrie.ucs@smtp.usi.edu

GUTHRIE, HELEN A, HUMAN NUTRITION. *Current Pos:* From asst prof to prof, Pa State Univ, 79-89, endowed prof, 90-92, EMER PROF NUTRIT, PA STATE UNIV, 92- *Personal Data:* b Sarnia, Ont, Sept 25, 25; m 49; c Barbara (Ford), Jane (Singletary) & James. *Educ:* Univ Western Ont, BS, 46; Mich State Univ, MS, 48; Univ Hawaii, PhD(physiol), 68. *Hon Degrees:* DSc, Univ Western Ont, 83, Univ Guelph, 96. *Honors & Awards:* Borden Award, Am Home Asn, 78; Atwater Award, USDA, 89; Elvjehm Award, Am Inst Nutrit, 89. *Concurrent Pos:* Mem, Food & Nutrit Bd, Nat Acad Sci, 73-76, Recommended Dietary Allowance Comm, 80-85; mem, Joint Nutrit Eval & Monitoring Comt, Dept Health & Human Serv/USDA, 83-85. *Mem:* Am Soc Clin Nutrit; Am Dietetic Asn; Am Pub Health Asn; Am Inst Nutrit (pres, 87-88); Soc Nutrit Educ (pres, 77-78, 87-88). *Res:* Infant nutrition; nutritional evaluation; world nutrition; nutrition and brain development. *Mailing Add:* 1316 S Garner St State College PA 16801-1638. *Fax:* 941-433-2969

GUTHRIE, HUGH D, CHEMICAL ENGINEERING, ECONOMICS. *Current Pos:* dir extraction proj mgt, 89-92, GEN ENGR & PROD MGR FUELS, ENERGY TECHNOL CTR, DEPT ENERGY, MORGANTOWN, 92- *Personal Data:* b Murdo, SDak, May 11, 19; m 50; c Katharine, Gretchen, Melissa, Elizabeth & Emily. *Educ:* Univ Iowa, BS, 43. *Honors & Awards:* Founders Award, Am Inst Chem Engrs, 74; F J Van Antwerpen Award, 86; Robert L Jacks Mem Award, US Govt Dept Energy Meritorious Serv Award, 92. *Prof Exp:* Jr engr, Shell Develop Co, Calif, 43-45, engr, 45-52, sr technologist, Shell Oil Co, 52-54, asst mgr gas dept, 54-56, asst mgr catalytic cracking, 56, sr technologist, 56-57, group leader mfg econ, 57-59, mgr alkylation dept, 59-61, asst to mgr prod econ, 61-66, mgr prod econ mkt, 66-67, asst to gen mgr refineries for mfg, 67-70, sr staff assoc, 70-72, mgr indust analysis, 72-74, spec assignment, 74-76, dir oil, gas & shale technol, US Energy Res & Develop Admin, 76-77; actg dir oil, gas, shale & insitu technol, Dept Energy, 77-78; dir, Energy Ctr, SRI Int, 78-80; mgr technol assessment, Occidental Res Corp, 80-82, vpres licensing, Occidental Develop Co, 82-86. *Concurrent Pos:* Mem bd, United Eng Trustees, 65-, pres, 78-79; mem bd, Eng Found, 66-80. *Mem:* AAAS; Am Chem Soc; Am Inst Chem Engrs (vpres, 68, pres, 69); Soc Petrol Engrs; NY Acad Sci; Sigma Xi. *Res:* Separation processes, particularly distillation; distillation trays; economics, production and marketing; fossil energy technologies, particularly oil, gas, shale and insitu gasification. *Mailing Add:* Morgantown Energy Tech Ctr PO Box 880 Morgantown WV 26507-0880. *Fax:* 304-291-4469

GUTHRIE, JAMES LEVERETTE, ADHESIVES, POLYURETHANES. *Current Pos:* RETIRED. *Personal Data:* b Lawrence, Kans, July 3, 31; m 58, Mayola Pohlmeyer. *Educ:* Oberlin Col, AB, 52; Univ Mo, PhD(org chem), 56. *Honors & Awards:* IR-100 Award, Indust Res Corp, 68 & 75. *Prof Exp:* Res chemist, PPG Corp, 56-61; res supvr, Polymer Dept, Res Div, W R Grace & Co, Clarksville, 61-70, res assoc, 71-91. *Mem:* AAAS; Am Chem Soc; Sigma Xi; NY Acad Sci. *Res:* Chemistry and applications of organic materials; polymers; photosensitive systems; composite structures, urethanes, coatings, adhesives, sealants, foams, plastisols. *Mailing Add:* 1318 Patuxent Dr Ashton MD 20861

GUTHRIE, JAMES PETER, BIO-ORGANIC CHEMISTRY. *Current Pos:* from asst prof to assoc prof, 69-78, PROF CHEM, UNIV WESTERN ONT, 78- *Personal Data:* b Port Elgin, Ont, Feb 3, 42; m 65; c 2. *Educ:* Univ Western Ont, BSc, 64; Harvard Univ, PhD(org chem), 68. *Honors & Awards:* Syntex Award, Can Soc Chem, 95. *Prof Exp:* Nat Res Coun Can fel biochem, Princeton Univ, 68-69. *Concurrent Pos:* Alfred P Sloan fel, 75 & E W R Steacie fel, 80. *Mem:* Am Chem Soc; Chem Inst Can. *Res:* Mechanisms of enzyme catalysis; enzyme model systems; thermodynamics of metastable intermediates; rate-equilibrium correlations. *Mailing Add:* Dept Chem Univ Western Ont London ON N6A 5B7 Can. *Fax:* 519-661-3022; *E-Mail:* peter.guthrie@uwo.ca

GUTHRIE, JAMES WARREN, PHYTOPATHOLOGY. *Current Pos:* RETIRED. *Personal Data:* b Kansas City, Kans, Sept 7, 23; m 47; c 3. *Educ:* Utah State Univ, BS, 49, MS, 50; Univ Wis, PhD(plant path), 52. *Prof Exp:* From asst prof to prof plant path, Univ Idaho, 52-77, prof plant sci, 77-82. *Mem:* Am Phytopath Soc; assoc Asn Off Seed Analysts; Int Seed Testing Asn. *Res:* Seed pathology, particularly Fusarium disease of corn, diseases of Poa prantensis and Pisum arvense; bacterial diseases of Phaseolus vulgaris. *Mailing Add:* 2433 East F St Moscow ID 83843

GUTHRIE, JOHN ERSKINE, ECOLOGY, RADIATION ECOLOGY. *Current Pos:* RETIRED. *Personal Data:* b Montreal, Que, Sept 25, 26; m 52; c 2. *Educ:* McGill Univ, BSc, 50, MSc, 55; Univ Man, PhD(entom), 69. *Prof Exp:* Officer artillery, Can Army Regular, 44-59; res officer monitoring, Chalk River Nuclear Labs, 59-63; br head, environ br, Whiteshell Nuclear Res Estab, Atomic Energy Can Ltd, 63-83. *Concurrent Pos:* Adj prof, Dept Entom, Univ Man, 72- *Mem:* Ecol Soc Am; Entom Soc Can; Health Physics Soc. *Res:* Effects of chronic exposure to low dose rates of ionizing radiation on ecological systems; environmental radiation monitoring; fate of radionuclides in the environment. *Mailing Add:* PO Box 41 Pinawa MB R0E 1L0 Can

GUTHRIE, JOSEPH D, ANALYTICAL CHEMISTRY. *Current Pos:* Res scientist, Alcoa Labs, 66-68, group leader, 68-76, staff scientist analytical chem, 76-80, tech supvr, 80-85, SR TECH SUPVR, ALCOA LABS, 85- *Personal Data:* b Indianapolis, Ind, Apr 13, 42; m 65; c 4. *Educ:* Wabash Col, AB, 64; Ohio Univ, MS, 66. *Mem:* Am Chem Soc. *Res:* Analysis of thin films on aluminum, determination of hydrogen in aluminum and lubrication in aluminum fabrication processes; cleaning, pretreating and organic coating of aluminum. *Mailing Add:* 100 Technical Dr Alcoa Center PA 15069-0001

GUTHRIE, RICHARD LAFAYETTE, INTERNATIONAL AGRICULTURE, SOIL CONSERVATION. *Current Pos:* exten soil specialist, Ala Coop Exten Serv, 74-75, prof & head Dept Agron & Soils, 83-85, actg dean, Col Agr, 85-88, ASSOC DEAN, INT AGR, COL AGR, AUBURN UNIV, 88- *Personal Data:* b Union Springs, Ala, May 29, 41; m 62; c 3. *Educ:* Auburn Univ, BS, 62, MS, 65; Cornell Univ, PhD(soil sci), 68. *Prof Exp:* Asst soil scientist, Soil Conserv Serv, USDA, 71-72, soil correlator, 72-74. *Concurrent Pos:* res asst, Dept Agron & Soils, Auburn Univ, 63-65, Cornell Univ, 65-68; ed, J Soil Surv Horizons, 73-78. *Mem:* Am Soc Agron; Soil Sci Soc Am; Soil & Water Conserv Soc Am; Int Soil Sci Soc. *Res:* Morphology, genesis and classification of soils with particular emphasis on properties that relate to land use; investigation of soil chemistry, soil mineralogy and soil wetness to better predict soil behavior. *Mailing Add:* Col Agr Auburn Univ 103 Comer Hall Auburn AL 36849-5401. *Fax:* 334-844-4814; *E-Mail:* rguthrie@ag.auburn.edu

GUTHRIE, ROBERT, medical genetics, microbiology; deceased, see previous edition for last biography

GUTHRIE, ROBERT D, PHYSICAL ORGANIC CHEMISTRY. *Current Pos:* from asst prof to assoc prof, 65-77, PROF CHEM, UNIV KY, 77- *Personal Data:* b Bronxville, NY, June 27, 36; m 63; c 3. *Educ:* Oberlin Col, BA, 58; Univ Rochester, PhD(org chem), 63. *Prof Exp:* NSF fel, Univ Calif, Los Angeles, 63-64, univ fel, 64, lectr chem, 64-65. *Mem:* Am Chem Soc. *Res:* Carbanion chemistry; electron transfer reactions. *Mailing Add:* Dept Chem Univ Ky Lexington KY 40506-0002

GUTHRIE, ROGER THACKSTON, ORGANIC CHEMISTRY. *Current Pos:* res mgr, M&T Chem Inc, 71-77, mgr special proj mkt, 77-79, tech mgr, mfg, Chem Div, 80-85, coordr, mfg processes, 85-86, TECH ASSOC, INDUST CHEM DIV, M&T CHEM INC, 86- *Personal Data:* b Spartanburg, SC, Dec 5, 24; m 50; c 3. *Educ:* Wofford Col, BS, 49; Univ NC, MA, 52, PhD(chem), 53. *Prof Exp:* Asst, Univ NC, 50-53; res chemist, Am Enka Corp, 53-59, head dielec mat sect, 59-62, head textile yarn develop sect, 63-66; tech mgr, New Prod Explor, Celanese Plastics Co, 66-69, New Prod Develop, 69-70, mgr, New Venture Anal, 70. *Mem:* AAAS; Am Chem Soc; NY Acad Sci; Asn Res Dirs; Soc Plastics Eng; Sigma Xi. *Res:* Polymer chemistry and physics; electrical insulating materials. *Mailing Add:* PO Box 5443 Spartanburg SC 29304

GUTHRIE, ROLAND L, PLANT ANATOMY, DENDROLOGY. *Current Pos:* arboretum asst, 59-61, from instr to asst prof, 61-73, ASSOC PROF BIOL, WVA UNIV, 73-, CUR ARBORETUM, 61- *Personal Data:* b Charleston, WVa, Apr 5, 28; m 54; c 3. *Educ:* WVa Univ, BSF & MS, 53, PhD(bot), 68. *Prof Exp:* Forester & naturalist, Isaac W Bernheim Found, 53-56. *Mem:* Bot Soc Am; Sigma Xi; Int Asn Wood Anatomists. *Res:* Ecological anatomy of woody plants. *Mailing Add:* 424 Linden St Morgantown WV 26505

GUTHRIE, RUFUS KENT, microbial ecology, for more information see previous edition

GUTHRIE, RUSSELL DALE, ZOOLOGY. *Current Pos:* Assoc prof, 63-74, PROF ZOOL, UNIV ALASKA, 74- *Personal Data:* b Nebo, Ill, Oct 27, 36; m 61, 78; c 3. *Educ:* Univ Ill, BS, 58, MS, 59; Univ Chicago, PhD(zool), 63. *Concurrent Pos:* NSF instnl grant, 63-64, res grant, 65-68, grant, 70-72, 72-74, 80-81 & 85-86. *Mem:* AAAS; Soc Study Evolution; Soc Vert Paleont; Am Soc Mammal. *Res:* Evolutionary mechanics; Pleistocene vertebrate paleontology; vertebrate evolution. *Mailing Add:* Inst Arctic Biol Univ Alaska PO Box 757000 Fairbanks AK 99775

GUTHRIE, WILBUR DEAN, ENTOMOLOGY. *Current Pos:* RETIRED. *Personal Data:* b Woodward, Okla, Mar 3, 24; m 46; c 5. *Educ:* Okla State Univ, BS, 50, MS, 51; Ohio State Univ, PhD, 58. *Prof Exp:* Entomologist, Agr Res Serv, USDA, 51-89. *Mem:* Entom Soc Am; Crop Soc Agron. *Res:* Insect resistance in crop plants; relative degree of resistance of inbred lines and hybrid corn to the European corn borer; sources of germ plasm. *Mailing Add:* 58442 260th St Rte 2 PO Box 191 Nevada IA 50201

GUTIERREZ, GUILLERMO, MAGNETIC RESONANCE SPECTROSCOPY, CRITICAL CARE MEDICINE. *Current Pos:* DIR, PULMONARY & CRITICAL CARE DIV, HERMANN HOSP, 90- *Personal Data:* b Palma Soriano, Cuba, Mar 10, 46; US citizen; m 83; c 4. *Educ:* City Col New York, BS, 68; Univ Dayton, MS, 70; Case Western Univ, MD, 77, PhD(biomed eng), 78. *Honors & Awards:* Career Investr Award, Am Lung Assoc, 90. *Prof Exp:* Develop engr, Gen Motors Res Labs, 68-71, sr scientist, 77-78; resident intern med, Univ Mich, 78-71, fel pulmonary med, 81-83; ASSOC PROF PULMONARY MED, UNIV TEX HEALTH CTR, 83- *Concurrent Pos:* Adj prof, Dept Biomed Eng, Rice Univ, Houston. *Mem:* Am Col Physicians; Am Thoracic Soc; Am Col Chest Physicians; Am Physiol Soc; Soc Critical Care Med; Am Soc Clin Invest. *Res:* Determination of parameters governing the transport of oxygen to the tissues and their effect on cellular bioenergetics during hypoxia; sepsis and multiple systems. *Mailing Add:* Dept Internal Med Univ Tex Health Sci Ctr PO Box 20036 Houston TX 77225

GUTIERREZ, LEONARD VILLAPANDO, JR, ENVIRONMENTAL ENGINEERING. *Current Pos:* RETIRED. *Personal Data:* b Tanawan, Batangas, Philippines, Apr 2, 32; US citizen; m 57; c 3. *Educ:* De La Salle Col, Manila, BS, 53; Univ Philippines, BS, 54; Purdue Univ, MS, 56. *Honors & Awards:* Presidential Sci Award, Repub Philippines, 77. *Prof Exp:* Civil engr, Ayres Lewis Norris & May, 56-58; sanit engr, Gannett Fleming Corddry & Carpenter, 58-60, County San Diego, 60-63, Eng Sci Inc, 63-64, County San Diego, 64-66 & Ralph M Parsons, 66-68; sr engr, Camp Dresser & McKee, 68-72, vpres eng, 72-85; pub works engr, City Chandler, Ariz, 85-94. *Mem:* Am Soc Civil Engrs; Am Acad Environ Engrs. *Mailing Add:* City Chandler 200 E Commonwealth Ave Chandler AZ 85225

GUTIERREZ, PETER LUIS, BIOPHYSICS, PHYSICAL PHARMACOLOGY & ONCOPHARMACOLOGY. *Current Pos:* ASSOC PROF BIOCHEM & ONCOL, UNIV MD CANCER CTR, 79- *Personal Data:* b Colombia, SAm, June 9, 39; US citizen; m 66, Sarah A Hanchett; c Fanny E & Ann C. *Educ:* Wheaton Col, BS, 62; Calif State Univ, Los Angeles, MS, 70; Southern Ill Univ, PhD(radiation biophys), 73. *Prof Exp:* Engr asst electronics, Automatic Elec Co, 62-64; engr, Hycon Mfg Co, 66-67; instr phys biochem, Sch Med, Tulane Univ, 72-74; staff biophysicist biol electron spin resonance, Med Col Wis, 74-79. *Mem:* Biophys Soc; Am Asn Cancer Res; Int Soc Free Radical Res; Am Chem Soc; Oxygen Soc; Int Electron Paramagnetic Resonance Soc. *Res:* Free radical metabolites of antitumor agents and other xenobiotics; electron spin resonance in carcinogenesis-free radical and other paramagnetic changes monitored during the development of experimental tumors; spin labeled drugs; membrane fluidity changes in cancer; sonolysis, DNA damage due to oxidative stress. *Mailing Add:* Div Develop Ther Univ Md Cancer Ctr 655 W Baltimore St Baltimore MD 21201. *Fax:* 410-328-6559; *E-Mail:* pgutierr@umcc01.umcc.ab.umd.edu

GUTIERREZ-MIRAVETE, ERNESTO, MATHEMATICAL MODELING, METALS PROCESSING. *Current Pos:* ASST PROF METALL, HARTFORD GRAD CTR, 87- *Personal Data:* b Mexico City, Mex, June 29, 54; m 87. *Educ:* Nat Univ Mex, Chem Metall Eng, 78; Mass Inst Technol, PhD(metall), 85. *Prof Exp:* Lectr mat sci, Nat Univ Mexico, 77-79; postdoctoral assoc metall, Mass Inst Technol, 85-87. *Concurrent Pos:* Consult, Sicartsa, Hylsa, Mex, 79, Cent Bank Mus, Ecuador, 88, United Technol Corp, 89, consult, Olin Corp, 90. *Mem:* AAAS; Sigma Xi; Univ Mat Coun; Mat Res Soc; Minerals, Metals & Mat Soc; Am Soc Mat. *Res:* Apply and develop theoretical and computational tools to the analysis of materials and manufacturing processing operations; forming processes which start from molten and/or particulate matter. *Mailing Add:* Sch Eng & Sci Hartford Grad Ctr 275 Windsor St Hartford CT 06120-2991

GUTJAHR, ALLAN L, STOCHASTIC HYDROLOGY, APPLIED STOCHASTIC PROCESSES. *Current Pos:* from asst prof to assoc prof, NMex Inst Mining & Technol, 71-81, chmn dept, 85-88, assoc vpres acad affairs, 90-92, PROF MATH, NMEX INST MINING & TECHNOL, 81-, RES MATHEMATICIAN, 78-, VPRES RES & ECON DEVELOP, 92- *Personal Data:* b Hosmer, SDak, Mar 20, 38; m 59, 81, Margaret Sjostedt; c Kurt, Eric, Kristin, Meghan (Kofod) & Ted. *Educ:* Univ Wash, BS, 61; Johns Hopkins Univ, MS, 63; Rutgers Univ, PhD(math statist), 70. *Prof Exp:* Mem tech staff, Bell Tel Labs, 62-68; asst statist, Rutgers Univ, 68-69; mem tech staff, Bell Tel Labs, 69-71. *Concurrent Pos:* Vis scientist, Sch Mines, Paris, 79, US Geol Surv, 79 & Stanford Univ, 89. *Mem:* Sigma Xi; Am Geophys Union; Math Asn Am; NAm Coun Geostatist; Am Statist Asn; Am Soc Eng Educ. *Res:* Stochastic models in hydrology; geostatistics; applied statistics; statistical inference in semi-Markov processes and other stochastic processes; queueing theory. *Mailing Add:* 445 Aquina Ct Belen NM 87002. *Fax:* 505-835-5649; *E-Mail:* Red@Prism.nmt.edu

GUTKNECHT, JOHN WILLIAM, PHYSIOLOGY, MARINE BIOLOGY. *Current Pos:* res assoc, 67-69, from asst prof to assoc prof, 69-80, PROF PHYSIOL, MED CTR, DUKE UNIV, 80- *Personal Data:* b Youngstown, Ohio, Apr 13, 37; m 62; c 1. *Educ:* Ohio Wesleyan Univ, BA, 59; Univ NC, PhD(zool), 64. *Prof Exp:* Res biologist, Radiobiol Lab, US Bur Com Fisheries, NC, 63-66; USPHS res fel biophys, Univ EAnglia, 66-67. *Mem:* AAAS; Am

Inst Biol Sci; Am Physiol Soc; Biophys Soc; Soc Gen Physiol. *Res:* Transport of solutes and water across cell membranes; membrane permeability; bioelectricity. *Mailing Add:* Dept Physiol Duke Univ Sch Med Duke Med Ctr Durham NC 27710-7599

GUTMAN, DAVID, PHYSICAL CHEMISTRY. *Current Pos:* From asst prof to prof chem, Ill Inst Technol, 64-88, PROF CHEM & CHMN, CATH UNIV AM, 88- *Personal Data:* b Isle of Malta, Nov 2, 34; US citizen; m 65; c 3. *Educ:* Univ Calif, Berkeley, BS, 60; Univ Ill, PhD(phys chem), 65. *Concurrent Pos:* Prog Dir Chem Dynamics, NSF, Washington, DC, 76-77. *Mem:* Am Chem Soc; Am Phys Soc. *Res:* Chemical kinetics; laser induced reactions; theoretical and experimental studies of gas phase reactions. *Mailing Add:* 1220 North Carolina Ave NE Washington DC 20002

GUTMAN, GEORGE ANDRE, MOLECULAR IMMUNOLOGY, MOLECULAR EVOLUTION. *Current Pos:* from asst prof to assoc prof, 76-89, PROF, DEPT MICROBIOL & MOLECULAR GENETICS, UNIV CALIF, IRVINE, 89- *Personal Data:* b Domme, France, Sept 15, 45; US citizen; m 77, Janis L Schonauer; c Pierre D & Marie E. *Educ:* Columbia Col, AB, 66; Stanford Univ, PhD(biol sci), 73. *Prof Exp:* Res fel, dept path, Stanford Med Sch, 73-74 & Walter & Eliza Hall Inst Med Res, Australia, 74-76. *Concurrent Pos:* Researcher, Jackson Lab, 62, Roswell Park Mem Inst, 63 & Yale Univ, 64; Fulbright scholar, Inst Pasteur, Paris, 66-67; res fel, USPHS, 72-74 & Arthritis Found, 74-77; prin investr, USPHS-Nat Inst Allergy & Infectious Dis res grants, 78-89, Am Cancer Soc res grants, 78-79 Kroc Found grant, 80-82 & Res Car Develop Award, USPHS, 78-83. *Mem:* Am Asn Immunologists; fel AAAS. *Res:* Organization and expression of immunoglobulin genes; evolution of closely related gene families in rodents and primates; ion channel structure and gene organization. *Mailing Add:* Dept Microbiol & Molecular Genetics Univ Calif Irvine Med Sci I Rm B-240 Irvine CA 92717-0001. *Fax:* 714-824-8598; *E-Mail:* gagutman@uci.edu

GUTMAN, GEORGE GARIK, CLIMATOLOGY OF LAND, REMOTE SENSING FROM SATELLITES. *Current Pos:* res assoc, Coop Inst Climate Studies, 87-90, PHYS SCIENTIST, SATELLITE RES LAB, LAND SCI BR, NAT OCEANIC & ATMOSPHERIC ADMIN, NAT ENVIRON SATELLITE DATA & INFO SERV, 90- *Personal Data:* b Leningrad, USSR, Apr 22, 53; US citizen; m 81; c 2. *Educ:* Leningrad Hydrometeorol Inst, MA, 76; Tel Aviv Univ, PhD(climate), 84. *Prof Exp:* Postdoctoral resident res assoc, Nat Res Coun, Nat Acad Sci, 85-87. *Mem:* Am Meteorol Soc. *Res:* Remote sensing techniques for studying land surface-climate interactions; cloud detection from space; rain estimate from space; monitoring earth ecosystems using remote sensing. *Mailing Add:* Nat Oceanic & Atmospheric Admin Nat Environ Satellite Data & Info Serv E/RA1 Rm 712 NsC(WWB) 4700 Silver Hill Rd Washington DC 20233-9910

GUTMANN, HELMUT RUDOLPH, BIOCHEMISTRY. *Current Pos:* from asst prof to prof physiol chem, 52-82, EMER PROF BIOCHEM, UNIV MINN, MINNEAPOLIS, 82- *Personal Data:* b Strasbourg, France, July 31, 11; nat US; m 46, Elizabeth Manuel; c Ruth, David, Michael & Rebecca. *Educ:* Univ Goettingen, MD, 36. *Prof Exp:* Res assoc, Univ Tenn, 48-50; asst prof cancer res, Univ Fla, 50-52. *Concurrent Pos:* Coxe mem fel biochem, Yale Univ, 46-48; USPHS fel biochem, Max-Planck Inst, Munich, 60-61; biochemist, Radioisotope Serv, Vet Admin Hosp, 56-61, Cancer Res Lab, 61-91; prof, Univ Minn, 65-82. *Mem:* AAAS; Am Chem Soc; Am Soc Biol Chem; Am Asn Cancer Res; Royal Soc Chem. *Res:* Metabolism and mechanism of action of carcinogenic and toxic compounds. *Mailing Add:* 3757 Towndale Dr Bloomington MN 55431

GUTMANN, LUDWIG, NEUROLOGY. *Current Pos:* from asst prof to assoc prof neurol, 66-70, asst prof physiol & biophys, 68-70, PROF NEUROL & CHMN DEPT, SCH MED, WVA UNIV, 70-, DIR ELECTROMYOGRAPH LAB, 66-, ASSOC PROF PHYSIOL & BIOPHYS, 70- *Personal Data:* b Frankfurt, Ger, Apr 7, 33; US citizen; m 54; c 3. *Educ:* Princeton Univ, BA, 55; Columbia Univ, MD, 59. *Prof Exp:* From intern med to resident neurol, Med Ctr, Univ Wis-Madison, 59-63; chief neurol, US Air Force Hosp, Scott AFB, Ill, 63-65; Nat Inst Neurol Dis & Blindness fel neurophysiol, Mayo Clin, 65-66. *Concurrent Pos:* Neurol consult, Alton State Hosp, Ill, 63-65; mem, Myasthenia Gravis Found. *Mem:* Am Acad Neurol; Am Asn Electromyog & Electrodiag; Asn Res Nerv & Ment Dis; Asn Univ Prof Neurol; Am Neurol Asn (pres, 84-86). *Res:* Electromyography and neuromuscular diseases. *Mailing Add:* WVa Univ Med Ctr Morgantown WV 26505-9180

GUTMANN, RONALD JAY, SOLID STATE DEVICES & INTEGRATED CIRCUIT TECHNOLOGY. *Current Pos:* res asst, Rensselaer Polytech Inst, 67-69, engr, 69-70, from asst prof to prof, Dept Elec & Systs Engr, 70-81, dir int electronics, 89-94, STAFF MEM ELEC COMP & SYST ENG, CTR INTEGRATED ELECTRONICS, RENSSELAER POLYTECH INST, 83- *Personal Data:* b Brooklyn, NY, Nov 16, 40; m 67, Suzanne Frech; c David & Jennifer. *Educ:* Rensselaer Polytech Inst, BEE, 62, PhD(electrophys), 70; NY Univ, MEE, 64. *Prof Exp:* Mem tech staff, Bell Tel Labs, 62-66; sr engr, Lockheed Electronics Co, 66-67; prog dir, Solid State & Microstruct Eng, NSF, 81-83. *Concurrent Pos:* Consult, govt & various industs, 72-81 & 84-; ed, Continuing Educ Electronics, McGraw Hill Bk Co, 74-78. *Mem:* Inst Elec & Electronics Engrs; Sigma Xi; Am Asn Univ Professors; Mats Res Soc. *Res:* Semiconductor devices; integrated electronics technology; microwave techniques. *Mailing Add:* Elec Comput & Syst Eng Rensselaer Polytech Inst 110 Eighth St Troy NY 12180-3522. *E-Mail:* rgutmann@unix.cie.rpi.edu

GUTOFF, EDGAR B(ENJAMIN), COATING & DRYING TECHNOLOGY, STATISTICAL PROCESS CONTROL. *Current Pos:* CONSULT CHEM ENGR, 88- *Personal Data:* b New York, NY, June 2, 30; m 56, Hinda Oler; c Joshua J & Jonathan M. *Educ:* City Col New York, BChE, 51; Mass Inst Technol, SM, 52, ScD(chem eng), 54. *Honors & Awards:* John A Tallmadge Award for Contrib to Coating Technol, Am Inst Chem Engrs, 94. *Prof Exp:* Chem engr, Fertilizers & Chem, Ltd, Israel, 52; sr process engr, Brown Co, 54-58; sr chem engr, Ionics, Inc, 58-60; sr scientist & sr prin engr, Polaroid Corp, 60-88. *Concurrent Pos:* Instr chem, Ctr Prof Advan, 79-81; part-time lectr, adj prof & vis res prof, Grad Sch Eng, Northeastern Univ, 81-; adj prof, Tufts Univ, 94- *Mem:* Am Chem Soc; fel Am Inst Chem Engrs; fel Soc Imaging Sci & Technol. *Res:* Coating operations; coating defects; coating die design; drying; air entrainment; dynamic contact modeling angles; surface elasticity; colloidal stability; coagulation; coacervation; syneresis; crystallization of silver halides; scale-up. *Mailing Add:* 194 Clark Rd Brookline MA 02146-5824

GUTOWSKI, GERALD EDWARD, RESEARCH & DEVELOPMENT ADMINISTRATION. *Current Pos:* PRES & CHIEF EXEC OFFICER, CORP COMPUT CONNECTION, 90- *Personal Data:* b Jackson, Mich, June 8, 41; m 64, Magda Cysteni; c Annette, David, Mary & Andy. *Educ:* Mich State Univ, BS, 63; Wayne State Univ, PhD(org chem), 67. *Prof Exp:* Res assoc chem, Wayne State Univ, 67-68; sr res chemist, Lilly Res Labs, Eli Lilly & Co, 68-73, res scientist, Chem Res Div, 73-75, mgr prod intro coord, 75-81, res scientist, 81-86, microcomput consult & local area network mgr, Proj Mgt Div, 86-93. *Mem:* Am Chem Soc; Pharmaceut Soc Japan; Sigma Xi. *Res:* Antibiotics; carbohydrates; medicinal chemistry; structure determination; organic synthesis; mechanisms of organic reactions; anti-tumor agents; anti-viral agents; alkaloids; nucleosides; computer analysis of structure activity relationships; hardware and software systs; information science. *Mailing Add:* 7472 Galloway Ct Indianapolis IN 46250. *Fax:* 317-849-9809

GUTOWSKI, PAUL RAMSDEN, SEISMOLOGY. *Current Pos:* Petrol geophysicist petrol explor, Amoco Can Petrol Co Ltd, 74-75, RES SCIENTIST THEORET SEISMOL, AMOCO PROD CO, 75- *Personal Data:* b Rhyll, UK, Apr 22, 47; Can citizen; m 72; c 1. *Educ:* Univ Alta, BSc, 69, MSc, 70, PhD(seismol), 74. *Concurrent Pos:* Adj asst prof, Univ Tulsa, 78- *Mem:* Soc Explor Geophysicists; Seismol Soc Am. *Res:* Wave propagation in the earth; numerical analysis and communication theory as applied to seismology; inverse theory. *Mailing Add:* Amoco Prod Co Res Ctr 4502 E 41st St Tulsa OK 74135

GUTOWSKY, H(ERBERT) S(ANDER), MICROWAVE ROTATIONAL SPECTROSCOPY. *Current Pos:* From instr to prof, Univ Ill, Urbana, 48-56, head div phys chem, 56-62, prof chem, 56-83, head dept chem & chem eng, 67-70, dir, Sch Chem Sci & head, dept chem, 70-83, RES PROF CHEM, UNIV ILL, URBANA, 83-, PROF CHEM, CTR ADVAN STUDY, 83- *Personal Data:* b Bridgman, Mich, Nov 8, 19; m 82, Virginia Warner; c Danial (deceased), Robb E & Christopher C. *Educ:* Ind Univ, AB, 40; Univ Calif Berkeley, MS, 46; Harvard Univ, PhD(phys chem), 49. *Hon Degrees:* DSc, Ind Univ, 83. *Honors & Awards:* Langmuir Prize, Am Chem Soc, 66, Midwest Award, St Louis Sect, 73, Peter Debye Award, 75; Int Soc Magnetic Resonance Award, 74; Nat Medal Sci, 77; G B Kistiakowsky lectr chem, Harvard Univ, 80; Wolf Found Prize, 83; Krug lectr, Univ Ill, 84; Chem Pioneer Award, Am Inst Chemists, 91. *Concurrent Pos:* Guggenheim fel, 54-55; vis prof, Univ Calif, Berkeley, 56; Walker Ames vis prof, Univ Wash, 57. *Mem:* Nat Acad Sci; fel AAAS; Am Chem Soc; fel Am Phys Soc; Am Acad Arts & Sci; Am Philos Soc. *Res:* Developing nuclear magnetic resonance methods for studying chemical phenomena; use of rotational fourier transform spectroscopy to explore the dynamics structure of small, weakly bonded clusters. *Mailing Add:* Dept Chem Univ Ill 600 S Matthews Ave Urbana IL 61801. *Fax:* 217-244-3186

GUTSCHE, CARL DAVID, ORGANIC CHEMISTRY, BIO-ORGANIC CHEMISTRY. *Current Pos:* ROBERT A WELCH PROF, TEX CHRISTIAN UNIV, 89- *Personal Data:* b Oak Park, Ill, Mar 21, 21; m 44, Alice E Carr; c Clara J, Betha L & Christopher G. *Educ:* Oberlin Col, BA, 43; Univ Wis, PhD(org chem), 47. *Honors & Awards:* St Louis Award, Am Chem Soc, 72, Midwest Award, 88. *Prof Exp:* Res assoc biochem, USDA Off Sci Res & Develop, Univ Wis, 43-44; from instr to assoc prof chem, Wash Univ, 47-59, prof, 59-89, chmn dept, 70-76, emer prof chem, Wash Univ, 89- *Concurrent Pos:* Consult, Petrolite Corp, Mo, 51-89 & Monsanto Co, 59-79; mem adv bd, Petrol Res Fund, 72-74; mem, Med Chem Study Sect, NIH, 77-81, chmn, 78-81; Guggenheim fel, 81; mem, Comt Prof Training, Am Chem Soc, 81-90, consult, 90- *Mem:* Fel AAAS; Am Chem Soc; Royal Soc Chem. *Res:* Carbocyclic synthesis with emphasis on ring expansion processes; photochemistry of cyclic carbonyl compounds; chemistry of diazoalkanes and carbenes; polyfunctional catalysts and enzyme models; micellar catalysis; calixarenes. *Mailing Add:* Dept Chem Tex Christian Univ Ft Worth TX 76129. *Fax:* 817-921-7330

GUTSCHE, GRAHAM DENTON, PHYSICS. *Current Pos:* from asst prof to assoc prof, 52-63, prof physics, 63-, EMER PROF PHYSICS, US NAVAL ACAD. *Personal Data:* b Oak Park, Ill, June 29, 25; m 48; c 3. *Educ:* Univ Colo, BS, 50; Univ Minn, MS, 52; Catholic Univ, PhD, 60. *Prof Exp:* Instr, Northwestern Schs, Minn, 50-52. *Concurrent Pos:* Asst, Univ Minn, 51-52; lectr, Univ Md, 59-; NSF fel, Cambridge Univ, 67-68. *Mem:* Am Asn Physics Teachers; Am Astron Soc; Am Sci Affil; Sigma Xi. *Res:* Nuclear reactions; Raman spectroscopy; stellar photometry; determination and analysis of the light curves of fast eclipsing binary star systems. *Mailing Add:* Physics Dept US Naval Acad Annapolis MD 21402

GUTSCHE, STEVEN LYLE, PHYSICS. *Current Pos:* staff scientist, 71-76, group leader, 77-79, DIV LEADER, MISSION RES CORP, SANTA BARBARA, 79-, VPRES, 87-; PRES, 89- *Personal Data:* b St Paul, Minn, Nov 10, 46; m 80, Marilyn D Maloney; c Kristina, Angela, Taylor S & Daniel M. *Educ:* Univ Colo, BS, 68; Univ Calif, Santa Barbara, MS, 70. *Prof Exp:* Physicist, USN Pac Missile Range, Point Mugu, Calif, 68-71. *Concurrent Pos:* Mem bd dirs, Mission Res Corp. *Res:* Physics; contributed articles to technical publications. *Mailing Add:* Mission Res Corp 735 State St Santa Barbara CA 93101-0719

GUTSCHICK, RAYMOND CHARLES, GEOLOGY EDUCATION, MICROPALEONTOLOGY. *Current Pos:* asst prof, Dept Geol, Univ Notre Dame, 47-50, assoc prof, 50-54, prof, 54-79, dept chmn, 56-70, EMER PROF & CONSULT, UNIV NOTRE DAME, 79- *Personal Data:* b Chicago, Ill, Oct 3, 13; m 39, Alice Edna Augusta Lude; c Alice Antonette & Raal Emily. *Educ:* Univ Ill, BS, 38, MS, 39 PhD(geol), 42. *Honors & Awards:* Neil A Miner Award, Nat Asn Geol Teachers, 77; Raymond C Moore Paleont Medal, Soc Sedimentary Geol, 93. *Prof Exp:* Geologist, Mobil-Magnolia Petrol Co, 43-45, Alcoa Aluminum Ore Co, 42 & 46-47 & Gulf Oil Co, 47. *Concurrent Pos:* NSF grantee, 54 & 60; geologist, US Geol Surv, Denver, 75-; consult geol, Rogers Group Inc, 78-, Environ Serv EIS, 83- *Mem:* Fel Geol Soc Am; Nat Asn Geol Teachers (pres, 52 & 58); Am Asn Petrol Geologists; Paleont Soc; Sigma Xi. *Res:* Co-author of one book; contributor and co-contributor of papers and articles to professional journals. *Mailing Add:* Dept Earth Sci Univ Notre Dame Notre Dame IN 46556

GUTSCHICK, VINCENT PETER, PHYSIOLOGICAL ECOLOGY, PHYSIOLOGICAL MODELLING. *Current Pos:* PROF BIOL, NMEX STATE UNIV, 85- *Personal Data:* b Berwyn, Ill, July 24, 45; m 78, Lou E Kay; c David. *Educ:* Univ Notre Dame, BS, 66; Calif Inst Technol, PhD(chem), 71. *Prof Exp:* NSF fel chem, Univ Calif, Berkeley, 71-72; J W Gibbs instr chem, Yale Univ, 72-74, fel chem, 74-75; dir fel, Los Alamos Nat Lab, 75-77, consult environ sci, 77-78, staff mem, 78-85. *Concurrent Pos:* Ger acad exchange fel, Univ Gottingen, 89; vis scientist plant biol, Commonwealth Sci & Indust Res Orgn, Canberra, 91, Carnegie Inst, 92; prog officer, NSF, 92-93. *Mem:* AAAS; Am Inst Biol Sci; Am Phys Soc; Am Soc Plant Physiologists; Ecol Soc Am. *Res:* Plant adaptations in photosynthesis, water use and mineral nutrition, with extensive use of physiological and biophysical models for hypothesis development; responses to global change. *Mailing Add:* Dept Biol NMex State Univ PO Box 30001 Las Cruces NM 88003-8001. *Fax:* 505-646-5665; *E-Mail:* vince@nmsu.edu

GUTSTADT, ALLAN MORTON, GEOLOGY, STRATIGRAPHY. *Current Pos:* from asst prof to assoc prof, 62-71, prof, 71-88, EMER PROF GEOL, CALIF STATE UNIV, NORTHRIDGE, 88- *Personal Data:* b Chicago, Ill, Jan 9, 26; m 56; c 1. *Educ:* Univ Ill, BA, 49; Northwestern Univ, PhD(geol), 54. *Prof Exp:* Geologist stratig, Ind Geol Surv, 53-57 & Creole Petrol Corp, Stand Oil Co, NJ, 57-61. *Mem:* Geol Soc Am. *Res:* Lower Paleozoic stratigraphy, central interior United States; Precambrian sedimentary rocks, southwestern United States; legal aspects of geology. *Mailing Add:* PO Box 8091 Bloomington IN 47407-8091

GUTSTEIN, WILLIAM H, PATHOLOGY, BIOPHYSICS. *Current Pos:* assoc prof, 63-76, PROF PATH, NY MED COL, 76- *Personal Data:* b New York, NY, July 12, 22; m 45; c 2. *Educ:* Univ Wis, AB, 43; NY Univ, MD, 46. *Prof Exp:* Instr path, State Univ NY Downstate Med Ctr, 52-55; pract pathologist, 55-57; asst prof path, NY Univ, 57-63. *Concurrent Pos:* Partic, Nat Conf Cardiovasc Dis, DC, 64. *Mem:* Am Heart Asn; Am Soc Exp Path. *Res:* Biophysical aspects and pathogenesis of atherosclerosis. *Mailing Add:* Dept Path NY Med Col Basic Sci Bldg Valhalla NY 10595-1690

GUTTAY, ANDREW JOHN ROBERT, soil ecology, mycorrhizae, for more information see previous edition

GUTTENDORF, ROBERT JOHN, PHARMACOKINETICS, DRUG METABOLISM. *Current Pos:* scientist, Parke-Davis Pharmaceut Res, 87-90, sr scientist, 90-92, res assoc, 92-93, SR RES ASSOC, PARKE-DAVIS PHARMACEUT RES, 93- *Personal Data:* b Pittsburgh, Pa, Feb 4, 57; m 81, Nancy McClure; c Elisabeth & Nathaniel. *Educ:* WVa Univ, BS, 79; Univ Ky, PhD(pharmaceut scis), 88. *Prof Exp:* Staff pharmacist, Thrift Drug Co, 78-80; chief pharmacist, Super-X Drug Co, 80-82. *Mem:* Am Asn Pharmaceut Scientists. *Res:* Multiple areas within pharmacokinetics and drug metabolism including antiinfectives, antiinflammatories, oral contraceptives and analgesics; bioanalytical chemistry, stereoselective pharmacokinetics/metabolism, polymorphisms in drug metabolism (pharmacogenetics) and drug absorption. *Mailing Add:* 2260 Prairie St Ann Arbor MI 48105. *Fax:* 313-996-5115; *E-Mail:* guttenr@aa.wl.com

GUTTENPLAN, JACK DAVID, CORROSION, ELECTROCHEMISTRY. *Current Pos:* res specialist electrochem & corrosion, Autonetics Div, NAm Rockwell Corp, 62-74, MEM TECH STAFF, AUTONETICS DIV, ROCKWELL INT, 74-, M-X MISSILE GUID & CONTROL, CORROSION PREVENTION & CONTROL REP, 80- *Personal Data:* b Baton Rouge, La, Oct 10, 25; m 49; c 3. *Educ:* Case Inst Technol, BS, 45, MS, 48. *Prof Exp:* Res asst gasoline additives, Case Inst Technol, 47-48; res assoc protective coatings, C F Prutton & Assocs, Ohio, 48-49; group leader electrochem, Chrysler Corp, Mich, 49-61; mgr develop biol electrochem ocean batteries, Magna Corp, Calif, 61-62. *Concurrent Pos:* Lectr, Chrysler Inst Eng, 52-59. *Mem:* Nat Asn Corrosion Eng; fel Am Inst Chem; Sigma Xi; fel Am Soc Metals. *Res:* Electroplating; thin film circuitry; physics of failure of microelectronic components; fuel cell development; bio-electrochemistry; surface potential difference. *Mailing Add:* 2210 W Avalon Santa Ana CA 92706-1307

GUTTENPLAN, JOSEPH B, MUTAGENESIS, CARCINOGENESIS. *Current Pos:* from asst prof to assoc prof, 74-86, PROF BIOCHEM, DENT CTR, NY UNIV, 86-, COORDR, BIOCHEM-MICROBIOL, 91-, DIR, OFF RES, 93- *Personal Data:* b Staten Island, NY; m, Hilde Krohn; c Nils & Alys. *Educ:* Brooklyn Col, BS, 65; Brandeis Univ, MS, 70, PhD(chem), 70; Columbia Univ, MPH, 91. *Prof Exp:* Res asst prof biochem, Mt Sinai Med Ctr, 73-74. *Concurrent Pos:* Res assoc prof environ med, Med Sch, NY Univ, 83-; consult toxicol. *Mem:* Am Asn Cancer Res; Am Soc Biol Chem & Molecular Biol; Environ Mutagen Soc. *Res:* Carcinogenesis; mutagenesis; DNA damage and repair; metabolism of carcinogens; mutational spectra; host-mediated mediated mutagenesis; site-specific mutagenesis by DNA adducts. *Mailing Add:* Dept Biochem Dent Sch NY Univ New York NY 10010

GUTTERMAN, JORDAN U, CLINICAL IMMUNOLOGY. *Current Pos:* Fac assoc, Dept Develop Therapeut, Univ Tex M D Anderson Cancer Ctr, 71-72, from asst prof to assoc prof, 72-81, prof med & dep head, Dept Clin Immunol & Biol Therap, 81-90, VIRGINIA H COCKRELL PROF IMMUNOL, UNIV TEX M D ANDERSON CANCER CTR, 87-, PROF & CHMN, 87- *Personal Data:* b Flandreau, SDak, Oct 15, 38. *Educ:* Univ Va, BA, 60; Med Col Va, MD, 64; Am Bd Internal Med, dipl, 72, dipl hemat, 73. *Concurrent Pos:* NIH Health Res Ctr Develop Award, 74-79; NCI comt French-Am Agreement Therapeut Cancer Res, 77-80; co-chmn, Am Cancer Soc Interferon Comt, 78-84; mem, Lasker Award Jury, Lasker Found, 78-89, Combined Modality Comt, Div Cancer Treatment, Nat Cancer Inst, 78-81, Citizens Comt, Rosalind Russell Med Res Ctr Arthritis, 80-83; Sci Adv Coun Cancer Res Inst, 79-; sr res investr, Clayton Found Res, 81- *Mem:* Am Asn Cancer Res; Am Chem Soc; Am Col Physicians; AAAS; Am Asn Immunologists; Am Fedn Clin Res; AMA; Am Soc Clin Oncol; Am Soc Hemat; Int Soc Exp Hemat; NY Acad Sci. *Res:* Clinical immunology. *Mailing Add:* Dept Clin Immunol & Biol Therap Univ Tex M D Anderson 6723 Bertner St Houston TX 77030-2603

GUTTMAN, BURTON SAMUEL, BIOLOGY. *Current Pos:* MEM FAC, EVERGREEN STATE COL, 72- *Personal Data:* b Minneapolis, Minn, Apr 12, 36; m 63; c 2. *Educ:* Univ Minn, BA, 58; Univ Ore, PhD(biol), 63. *Prof Exp:* NSF res fel biol, Calif Inst Technol, 63-65; asst prof cell biol, Med Ctr, Univ Ky, 65-72. *Mem:* Am Soc Microbiol. *Res:* Regulation of metabolism; bacteriophage development; general biological organization; philosophy of biology; biology teaching strategies. *Mailing Add:* 1709 Carrison St NE Olympia WA 98506

GUTTMAN, CHARLES M, POLYMER SCIENCE. *Current Pos:* RES CHEMIST, NAT INST STAND & TECHNOL, 67- *Personal Data:* b Cincinnati, Ohio, Apr 11, 39; m 60, 76, Evelyne L Barry; c Hannah, Damiana & Harry. *Educ:* Earlham Col, BA, 61; Brandeis Univ, PhD(chem), 67. *Prof Exp:* Mem tech staff, Bell Tel Labs, 66-67. *Concurrent Pos:* Adj prof, Univ Md & John Hopkins Univ. *Mem:* Fel Am Phys Soc; Am Chem Soc; Am Soc Testing & Mat. *Res:* Statistical mechanics of polymeric systems and ionic solutions; properties of polymeric glasses; kinetics of polymer crystallization; polymers on surfaces; thermal analysis; diffusion of small molecules in polymers; effect of pollutant gases on archival molecular weight determination of polymers maldi-tof-ms. *Mailing Add:* Polymer Div Nat Inst Stand & Technol Gaithersburg MD 20899. *Fax:* 301-869-3239; *E-Mail:* charles.guttman@nist.gov

GUTTMAN, FRANK MYRON, surgery, for more information see previous edition

GUTTMAN, HELENE AUGUSTA NATHAN, MICROBIOLOGY, BIOCHEMISTRY. *Current Pos:* prog coordr, Sci Educ Coord Off, Sci & Educ Directorate, USDA, 80-83, assoc dir, Beltsville Human Nutrit Res Ctr, 83-89, ANIMAL CARE COORDR, NAT PROG STAFF, AGR RES SERV, USDA, 89- *Personal Data:* b New York, NY, July 21, 30. *Educ:* Brooklyn Col, BA, 51; Harvard Univ, AM, 56; Columbia Univ, MA, 58; Rutgers Univ, PhD(bact), 60. *Honors & Awards:* Thomas Jefferson Murray Award, Theobalt Smith Soc, 59. *Prof Exp:* Res technician immunol, Pub Health Res Inst New York, 51-52; control bacteriologist, Burroughs-Wellcome Inc, 52-53; asst microbiologist, Haskins Labs, 52-56, res assoc, 56-59, staff mem, 59-64; res assoc, Goucher Col, 60-62; asst prof biochem & cell physiol, Univ Col & Grad Sch Arts & Sci, NY Univ, 62-65, assoc prof, 65-67; from assoc prof to prof biol sci, Univ Ill, Chicago Circle, 67-75, prof microbiol, Col Med, 69-75, fac assoc urban systems lab, Col Eng, 74-75, assoc dir res, 75; expert, Off Dir, Heart, Lung & Blood Inst, Bethesda, Md, 75-77, res resources coordr, Off Prog Planning & Eval, 77-79; dep dir, sci adv bd, US Environ Protection Agency, Washington, DC, 79-80. *Concurrent Pos:* Dazian Found fel, 56; Soc Am Bacteriologists' pres fel, 57; lectr, Queens Col, NY, 56-57; res collabr, Brookhaven Nat Labs, 58; res asst prof, Med Col Va, 60-62; res grants, NIH, 56-69, NSF, 59-60 & 61-63, Tidewater Fund, 61-62, AEC, 65, Hartford Found, 70-73, Fed Water Pollution Control Agency, 70-74, NASA, 72-74, NIH contract, 74-75 & Ill Dept Ment Health, 74-75, chairperson task force, 74-75; mem educ comt, Ill Comn Status Women, 74-75 & bd dirs, DuPage County Comprehensive Health Care Planning Agency, 74-75; consult sci adv bd, US Environ Protection Agency, 75-79, Int Joint Comn, US & Can, 87-; mem ed bd, J Prtotozool, 72-75, J Am Med Women's Asn, 78-81, Nutrit Running & Fit News, 84-; chmn, Educ Policy Comt, Am Soc Cell Biol, 66-69; chmn, Prof Opportunities Women Comn, Am Inst Chemists, 74-78; mem nomination comt, Tissue Culture Asn, 75-76, mem comt, 90-, educ comt, 90-; ed adv bd, Creative Woman, 77-; mem, Civil Serv Affairs Comn, Am Acad Microbiol, 79-85, mem, Status of Women Microbiol Comn, 80-85, mem, Publ Serv Adult Educ Comn, 81-90, prof, Affairs Comn, 87-, Comn on Use Microbiol in Res, 88-89; Tellers/Auditing Comn, Am Soc Clin Nutrit, 79-82; bd dirs, Montgomery Area Sci Fair Asn, 80-85; bd dirs, Am Running &

Fitness Asn, 88-; pres, HNG Assocs, 82-; ed, Scientists Ctr Animal Welfare, 88-, rep to AAAS, 90- *Mem:* Fel Am Inst Chemists; Royal Soc Chem; Am Soc Neurochem; fel Am Acad Microbiol; fel NY Acad Sci; Am Soc Microbiol; Am Soc Biol Chem; Am Soc Cell Biol; fel AAAS; Am Soc Clin Nutrit. *Res:* Behavioral biochemistry; control of inducible synteses, especially small peptides, enzymes and antibody; isolation and purification of bioactive natural products; nutritional biochemistry; drug mode of action at cellular level. *Mailing Add:* 5607 McLean Dr Bethesda MD 20814. *Fax:* 301-656-8980

GUTTMAN, LESTER, SOLID STATE PHYSICS. *Current Pos:* GUEST SCIENTIST, 86- *Personal Data:* b Minneapolis, Minn, Apr 18, 19; m 55. *Educ:* Univ Minn, BChem, 40; Univ Calif, PhD(chem), 43. *Prof Exp:* Asst chem, Univ Calif, 40-42; assoc scientist, Manhattan Eng Dist, US War Dept, NMex, 43-46; res assoc, Inst Study Metals, Univ Chicago, 46-47, from instr to asst prof, 47-55; Guggenheim fel, UK Atomic Energy Authority, Eng, 55-56; phys chemist, Res Lab, Gen Elec Co, 56-60; sr chemist, Argonne Nat Lab, 60-86. *Concurrent Pos:* Assoc ed, J Appl Physics & Appl Physics Lett, 65-73, ed, J Appl Physics, 74-89, consult ed, 90- *Mem:* Fel Am Phys Soc. *Res:* Statistical thermodynamics of alloys; x-ray diffraction from alloys; structure of covalent glasses. *Mailing Add:* 1234 E Madison Park 5W Chicago IL 60615. *E-Mail:* guttman@hexi.msd.anl.gov

GUTTMAN, NEWMAN, PSYCHOACOUSTICS. *Current Pos:* RETIRED. *Personal Data:* b Minneapolis, Minn, Apr 4, 27; m 85, Dorothy T Hantman. *Educ:* Univ Minn, BA, 49; Univ Ill, AM, 51, PhD(speech), 54. *Prof Exp:* Res assoc speech, Univ Ill, 54-55; asst speech, Mass Inst Technol, 55-56; mem tech staff, Bell Tel Labs, Murray Hill & Naperville, 56-89. *Concurrent Pos:* Mem, Sensory Study Sect, Social & Rehab Serv, HEW, 65-69; mem, Subcomt Sensory Aids, Comt Prosthetics Res & Develop, Nat Res Coun, 69-77, adv, Comt Hearing & Bioacoust, 70-89. *Mem:* Fel Acoust Soc Am; fel Am Speech & Hearing Asn. *Res:* Phonetics; speech and hearing science. *Mailing Add:* 2033 Sherman Ave No 501 Evanston IL 60201. *E-Mail:* newdot@worldnet.att.net

GUTTMAN, SHELDON, ZOOLOGY. *Current Pos:* From prof to assoc prof, 67-76, PROF ZOOL, MIAMI UNIV, 76- *Personal Data:* b New York, NY, Mar 9, 41; m 63. *Educ:* City Univ New York, BS, 62; Univ Tex, MA, 65, PhD(evolution), 67. *Mem:* Soc Study Evolution; Soc Study Amphibians & Reptiles. *Res:* Ecology and evolution of the amphibians and reptiles; biochemical genetics and biochemical taxonomy. *Mailing Add:* 112 Country Club Dr Oxford OH 45056

GUTTMANN, MARK, NUCLEAR PHYSICS. *Current Pos:* asst prof, 62-70, ASSOC PROF PHYSICS, LA SALLE COL, 70- *Personal Data:* b Baltimore, Md, Aug 10, 24. *Educ:* Cath Univ, BS, 47, MS, 56; Univ Notre Dame, PhD(physics), 62. *Prof Exp:* Teacher high sch, Pa, 47-53; instr physics, La Salle Col, 53-55 & De La Salle Col, 55-56. *Mem:* Am Phys Soc; Am Asn Physics Teachers; Sigma Xi. *Res:* Beta and gamma ray spectroscopy; optics. *Mailing Add:* Dept Physics & Geol La Salle Univ 1900 W Olney Ave Philadelphia PA 19141

GUTTMANN, RONALD DAVID, IMMUNOGENETICS, MEDICAL DIAGNOSTICS. *Current Pos:* assoc prof, 70-74, PROF MED, MCGILL UNIV, 75-, ASSOC DIR, UNIV CLIN, 80-, DIR, CLIN IMMUNBIOL & TRANSPLANTATION, MCGILL UNIV CTR, 88- *Personal Data:* b Minneapolis, Minn, Aug 16, 36; m 64, Dagmar Bruninghold; c Astrid, Gregory & Carla. *Educ:* Univ Minn, BA, 58, BS & MD, 61. *Honors & Awards:* Med Award, Kidney Found Can, 87; Mary Jane Kugel Award, Juv Diabetes Found Int, 86; Distinguished Achievement Award, Am Soc Transplant Physicians, 96- *Prof Exp:* Instr med, Harvard Med Sch, 69-70; dir transplantation serv, Royal Victoria Hosp, 70-75, dir, Histocompatibility & Immunogenetics Lab, 75-83, vpres res, 83-86. *Concurrent Pos:* Consult, WHO-UN Develop Prog, 82, Pasteur-Merieux S&V, 89-; Bethune exchange prof, China, 82; vchmn bd mgt, Royal Victoria Hosp Res Inst, 83-86; founder, Int Forum Transplant Ethics, 95. *Mem:* Transplantation Soc (vpres, 81-83); Am Soc Transplant Physicians (pres, 82-83); Can Transplantation Soc (pres, 85-86); emer mem Am Soc Clin Invest; Asn Am Physicians; Can Inst Acad Med. *Res:* Immunogenetics and pathophysiology of transplantation and autoimmune diseases; use of monoclonal antibodies and genetic probes in disease models; expert systems and computer applications in medicine; bioprocessing bioreactor research; transplant medicine; host-defense mechanisms, neurobiological probes. *Mailing Add:* McGill Ctr Clin Immunobiol & Transplantation 687 Pine Ave W Montreal PQ H3A 1A1 Can

GUTZKE, WILLIAM H N, ENVIRONMENTAL PHYSIOLOGY, PHYSIOLOGICAL ECOLOGY. *Current Pos:* LECTR BIOL, UNIV TEX, AUSTIN, 84- *Personal Data:* b Richmond, Va, Feb 8, 50; m 79; c 4. *Educ:* Va Commonwealth Univ, BS, 75, MS, 77; Colo State Univ, PhD(zool), 84. *Prof Exp:* Instr biol, Colo State Univ, 83-84. *Mem:* AAAS; Ecol Soc Am; Soc Study Evolution; Am Soc Ichthyologists & Herpetologists; Herpetologists League; Am Soc Zoologists. *Res:* Influence of the environment on embryos and hatchlings of reptiles; sex determining mechanisms. *Mailing Add:* Dept Biol Memphis Univ 3706 Alumni St Memphis TN 38152-0001

GUTZMAN, PHILIP CHARLES, MAINTAINABILITY, LOGISTICS. *Current Pos:* chief advan develop logistics eng, Gen Dynamics Land Systs, 82-85, mgr opers, Global Positioning Syst, 85-88, dir tech, Saudia Arabian Tank Conversion, 88-89, mgr logistics eng, 89-93, FRANKLIN QUEST, GEN DYNAMICS SERV CO, 93- *Personal Data:* b Salmon, Idaho, June 23, 38; m 60; c 2. *Educ:* Univ Ariz, BS(prod mgt) & BS(personnel mgt), 62; Univ Okla, MPA, 77. *Prof Exp:* Res specialist, US Army, 72-76. *Concurrent Pos:* Guest lectr, Polit Sci Hist & Anthrop Dept, Univ San Francisco, 68-69; mgr, Logistics Res, Gen Dynamics Land Systs Div, 84-85. *Mem:* Soc Logistics Engrs; Am Defense Preparedness Asn. *Res:* Effects of extreme climates, tropic, on complex mechanical and electronic systems; long term functional degradation based on environmental influences. *Mailing Add:* 25201 Che Randa Lane Middleton ID 83644

GUTZWILLER, MARTIN CHARLES, THEORETICAL PHYSICS. *Current Pos:* dir, Gen Sci Dept, Watson Lab, 63-70 & 74-77, physicist, 70-93, EMER RES SCIENTIST, IBM CORP, NY, 93- *Personal Data:* b Basel, Switz, Oct 12, 25; m 52; c 2. *Educ:* Swiss Fed Inst Technol, BS, 47, MS, 50; Univ Kans, PhD(physics), 53. *Hon Degrees:* DSc, Univ Lausane, Switz, 95. *Prof Exp:* Physicist, Brown, Boveri & Co, Baden, Switz, 50-51, Explor & Prod Res Div, Shell Develop Co, Tex, 53-60 & Res Div, Int Bus Mach, Zurich, 60-63. *Concurrent Pos:* Adj prof, Columbia Univ. *Mem:* Nat Acad Sci; Am Phys Soc. *Res:* Propagation of waves, solid state physics; quantum and classical mechanics especially the chaotic phenomenum; ergodic theory; applied mathematics. *Mailing Add:* T J Watson Res Ctr IBM Corp PO Box 218 Yorktown Heights NY 10598

GUVEN, NECIP, GEOLOGY, MINERALOGY. *Current Pos:* assoc prof, 72-76, PROF GEOL, TEX TECH UNIV, 76- *Personal Data:* b Boyalik, Turkey, Apr 14, 36; US citizen; m 70; c 5. *Educ:* Univ Gottengen, Dr Sci, 62. *Prof Exp:* Fel mineral, Columbia Univ, 63-65; fel crystallog, Carnegie Inst Geophys Lab, 65-67; asst prof geol, Univ Ill, Urbana, 67-72. *Concurrent Pos:* Assoc ed, Clay Minerals Soc, 75-87, Appl Clay Sci, 86- *Mem:* Mineral Soc Am; Am Crystallog Asn; Clay Minerals Soc (vpres, 87, pres, 88); Electron Micros Soc Am; Am Asn Petrol Geologists. *Res:* Mineralogy and colloid chemistry of clays; x-ray and electron diffraction of clays in reservoir rocks, shales, and in drilling fluids; rheology of clay dispersions. *Mailing Add:* Dept Geosci Tex Tech Univ Lubbock TX 79409-0001

GUY, ALBERT G(LASGOW), THERMODYNAMICS OF SIMPLE GASES, RADIANT ENERGY. *Current Pos:* RES PROF, CHEM DEPT, FLA ATLANTIC UNIV, 96- *Personal Data:* b Chicago, Ill, May 27, 17; m 66, 76; c 2. *Educ:* Univ Chicago, SB, 38; Ohio State Univ, MS, 41; Carnegie Inst Technol, DSc(metall), 46. *Prof Exp:* Res engr, Res Lab, Gen Elec Co, 44-47; assoc prof mech eng, NC State Col, 47-51; chief metall br, Off Ord Res, 51-52; from assoc prof to prof metall, Purdue Univ, 52-60; prof mat sci, Univ Fla, 60-79; vis prof physics, Fla Inst Technol, 79-87; vis prof mech eng, Univ Cent Fla, 89-90; vis prof chem, 91-93. *Concurrent Pos:* Exchange scientist, Baikov Metall Inst, USSR, 58-59 & Inst Metall, Tbilisi, USSR, 74-75; vis prof, Fla Inst Tech, 79-87 & Univ Cent Fla, 87-; Fulbright researcher, Cent Inst Chem, Budapest, Hungary, 82-83 & Tech Univ, Helsinki, Finland, 87. *Mem:* Am Soc Metals; Am Soc Eng Educ; Am Inst Mining, Metall & Petrol Engrs; Brit Inst Metals. *Res:* Basic theory of materials science; interstital metallic systems and thermodynamics. *Mailing Add:* 3939 NE Fifth Ave Boca Raton FL 33431

GUY, GEORGE ANDERSON, METEOROLOGY. *Current Pos:* CONSULT, 81- *Personal Data:* b Love, Miss, Nov 10, 14; m 39, Alice; c Patricia (Hecht). *Educ:* Memphis State Col, BS, 36; Univ Calif, Los Angeles, M; George Wash Univ, MBA, 62. *Prof Exp:* Meteorologist, USAF, 43-49, chief equip develop, Hqs, Air Weather Serv, 49-52, chief meteorol equip develop, Hqs, Air Res & Develop Command, 52-57, chief, Weather Syst Proj Off, 57-62, chief tactical syst prog off, Syst Command, 63-67; sr engr, Hughes Aircraft Co, 67-81. *Mem:* Am Meteorol Soc; Am Geophys Union; NY Acad Sci. *Res:* Meteorological instrumentation; electronic systems program management. *Mailing Add:* 707 Solana Circle E Solana Beach CA 92075

GUY, H ROBERT, MEMBRANE PROTEIN MODELING. *Current Pos:* staff fel, Lab Molecular Biophys, Nat Inst Neurol Communicative Dis Strokes, 80-82, res assoc, Lab Math & Biol, 82-92, RES BIOLOGIST, LAB EXP COMPUTATIONAL BIOL, NAT CANCER INST, NIH, 92- *Personal Data:* m 68, Suzanne Whitten; c Eric W. *Educ:* Okla City Univ, BA, 68; Univ Ill, Urbana-Champaign, PhD(biophys), 74. *Prof Exp:* NIH postdoctoral fel, State Univ NY, Albany, 73-77; staff, Armed Forces Radiobiol Res Inst, US Navy Med Serv Corp, 77-80. *Concurrent Pos:* NAm ed, Receptors & Channels, 96- *Mem:* Biophys Soc. *Res:* Theoretical modeling of membrane protein with emphasis on low channels. *Mailing Add:* NIH LECB Bldg 12B Rm B106 Bethesda MD 20892-5677. *Fax:* 301-402-4724; *E-Mail:* guy@guy.nci.nih.gov

GUY, LEONA RUTH, IMMUNOLOGY. *Current Pos:* clin asst prof microbiol, Univ Tex Health Sci Ctr, 53-62, from asst prof to prof med technol, Sch Allied Health Sci, 62-82, chmn dept, 62-78, from asst prof to prof path, 77-82, EMER PROF PATH, UNIV TEX HEALTH SCI CTR, 82- *Personal Data:* b Kemp, Tex, Mar 17, 13. *Educ:* Baylor Univ, AB, 34, MS, 49; Stanford Univ, PhD, 53. *Honors & Awards:* John Elliott Award, Am Asn Blood Banks, 83; Distinguished Serv Award, Am Soc Clin Path, 89. *Prof Exp:* Instr bact, Sch Dent, Baylor Univ, 48-49. *Concurrent Pos:* Assoc dir blood bank, Parkland Mem Hosp, 53-78; consult, Vet Admin Hosps, Dallas, 62-82 & Temple Vet Admin Hosp, 64-82. *Mem:* Am Soc Microbiol; hon fel Am Soc Clin Path. *Res:* Immunohematology; bacteriology. *Mailing Add:* 5455 La Sierra Dr No 501 Dallas TX 75231-4146

GUY, REED AUGUSTUS, NUCLEAR PHYSICS. *Current Pos:* asst prof, 75-77, ASSOC PROF PHYSICS, SEATTLE UNIV, 77-, CHAIRPERSON DEPT, 78- *Personal Data:* b Andalusia, Ala, Sept 4, 44; m 66; c 2. *Educ:* Univ Ala, BS, 66; Univ Va, PhD(physics), 70. *Prof Exp:* Asst prof physics, Univ Wis-Oshkosh, 70-74. *Mem:* Sigma Xi; Am Phys Soc; Am Asn Physics Teachers. *Res:* Nuclear structure; pion interactions in nuclei; history of physics. *Mailing Add:* Dept Physics Seattle Univ Seattle WA 98122

GUY, WILLIAM THOMAS, JR, MATHEMATICS. *Current Pos:* from instr to asst prof appl math, Univ Tex, Austin, 46-53, from asst prof to assoc prof math & astron, 53-77, actg chmn dept, Univ, 58-59, prof math & astron & chmn dept, 59-77, PROF MATH, UNIV TEX, AUSTIN, 77-, RES SCIENTIST, DEFENSE RES LAB, 53- *Personal Data:* b Abilene, Tex, Dec 11, 19; m 41; c 3. *Educ:* Agr & Mech Col, Tex, BS, 40; Univ Tex, MA, 48; Calif Inst Technol, PhD(math), 51. *Prof Exp:* Design engr, Westinghouse Elec Corp, 40-42; asst, Calif Inst Technol, 48-51. *Mem:* AAAS; Am Math Soc; Math Asn Am. *Res:* Tensor, extensor and functional analysis; integral transforms; applied mathematics. *Mailing Add:* Dept Math Univ Tex Austin TX 78712-1082

GUYDA, HARVEY JOHN, PEDIATRIC ENDOCRINOLOGY. *Current Pos:* teaching fel endocrinol, McGill Univ-Royal Victoria Hosp, 69-71, from asst prof to assoc prof pediat, 71-79, co-dir, Protein Hormone Lab, 73-91, PROF PEDIAT & MED, MCGILL UNIV, 79-,CHMN, DEPT PEDIAT, 96-; DIR ENDOCRINOL, CLIN ENDOCRINOL LAB, MONTREAL CHILDREN'S HOSP, 80-, PHYSICIAN IN CHIEF, 96- *Personal Data:* b Winnipeg, Man, July 5, 38; m 64, Patricia Senecki; c Evan & Marley. *Educ:* Univ Man, BSc & MD, 62. *Honors & Awards:* Distinguished Serv Award, Can Soc Endocrinol & Metab, 95; John P Maclean Lectr, Univ Manitoba, 96. *Prof Exp:* Teaching fel pediat endocrinol, Johns Hopkins Univ, 66-69. *Concurrent Pos:* Asst physician pediat, Montreal Children's Hosp, 71-73, assoc physician, 73-96; travel awards, Schering Ltd-Can Soc Clin Invest, Merck, Sharp & Dohme-Royal Col Physicians & Surgeons & France-Que Exchange Prog, 75; mem panel C, Grants Rev Comt, Nat Cancer Inst Can, 80-84; vis prof, Nat Inst Endocrinol, Havana, Cuba, 83 & Hadassah, Hebrew Univ Jerusalem, 85; dir endocrinol & metab, Montreal Children's Hosp, 86-96; mem, Sci Rev Comt, JDFI, 86-89; mem, Scholar Renewal Co, Alberta Heritage, 91-94; vis prof, Univ Hong Kong, 95- *Mem:* Can Soc Endocrinol & Metab (pres, 82-84); Soc Pediat Res; Can Soc Clin Invest; Endocrine Soc; Can Pediat Soc. *Res:* Use of growth hormone in non-endocrine short stature children. *Mailing Add:* Dept Pediat Montreal Children's Hosp 2300 Tupper St Rm C-414 Montreal PQ H3H 1P3 Can. *Fax:* 514-934-4364; *E-Mail:* hguyend@mchmeds.mchis.mcgill.ca

GUYER, BERNARD, MEDICINE. *Current Pos:* PROF & CHAIR, DEPT MATERNAL & CHILD HEALTH, SCH HYG & PUB HEALTH, JOHNS HOPKINS UNIV, 89- *Prof Exp:* Assoc prof maternal & child health, Harvard Sch Pub Health, dir, MPH Prog & head, Injury Prev Ctr, 86-89; officer & med epidemiologist, Ctr Dis Control. *Concurrent Pos:* Dir, Maternal & Child Health Agency, Mass Dept Pub Health, 79-86. *Mem:* Inst Med-Nat Acad Sci. *Res:* Maternal and child health planning and administration; low birthweight and infant mortality; assessment of primary health care systems; delivery of immunization services; childhood injury and injury prevention; author of more than 100 papers. *Mailing Add:* Dept Matenal & Child Health Johns Hopkins Univ Sch Hyg & Pub Health 624 N Broadway Baltimore MD 21205-1999

GUYER, CHERYL ANN, BIOCHEMISTRY, MOLECULAR BIOLOGY. *Current Pos:* Res assoc, Dept Biochem, Sch Med, Vanderbilt Univ, 85-88, Am Heart Asn fel, Dept Pharmacol, 86-89, res instr, 89-91, RES ASST PROF, DEPT BIOCHEM, SCH MED, VANDERBILT UNIV, 91- *Personal Data:* b Greensboro, NC, Nov 23, 57; m; c 1. *Educ:* Univ NC Greensboro, BS, 79; Vanderbilt Univ, PhD(biochem), 85. *Mem:* Am Soc Biochem & Molecular Biol. *Res:* Epidermal growth factor receptor; structure and mechanism; biochemistry; numerous technical publications. *Mailing Add:* Dept Biochem Vanderbilt Univ Sch Med PO Box 1820 Sta B Nashville TN 37235. *Fax:* 615-343-6767

GUYER, CRAIG, POPULATION ECOLOGY, BIOGEOGRAPHY. *Current Pos:* ASSOC PROF HERPET, AUBURN UNIV, 87- *Personal Data:* b Los Angeles, Calif, Aug 6, 52. *Educ:* Humboldt State Univ, BA, 75; Idaho State Univ, MS, 78; Univ Miami, PhD(biol), 86. *Concurrent Pos:* Adj asst prof, Univ Costa Rica, 88; co-chair, Gopher Tortoise Coun, 93-94. *Mem:* Am Soc Ichthyologists & Herpetologists; Herpetologist's League; Soc Study Amphibians & Reptiles. *Res:* Regulation of population density; ecology and evolution of anoline lizards; neotropical biogeography; effects of land use history on southeastern amphibians and reptiles. *Mailing Add:* Dept Zool Auburn Univ Auburn AL 36849-3501. *Fax:* 334-844-9234; *E-Mail:* craig.guyer@ag.auburn.edu

GUYER, GORDON EARL, ENTOMOLOGY. *Personal Data:* b Kalamazoo, Mich, May 30, 26; m 50; c 1. *Educ:* Mich State Univ, BS, 50, MS, 52, PhD(entom), 54. *Prof Exp:* From asst prof to assoc prof, Mich State Univ, 54-63, chmn, Dept Entom, 63-73, prof entom, asst dean, Col Agr & Natural Resources & dir coop exten serv, 73-93. *Mem:* Am Entom Soc; Entom Soc Can; Sigma Xi. *Res:* Biology and taxonomy of aquatic insects; economic entomology; vegetable and forest insect research. *Mailing Add:* 862 Whitman Rd East Lansing MI 48823

GUYER, KENNETH EUGENE, JR, BIOCHEMISTRY. *Current Pos:* ASSOC PROF BIOCHEM, MARSHALL UNIV, 75- *Personal Data:* b Pampa, Tex, June 11, 34; m 57, Barbara Priddy; c Greta V & Jennifer P. *Educ:* Univ Tex, BA, 55; Ohio State Univ, MSc, 60, PhD(physiol chem), 62. *Prof Exp:* Chemist, Celanese Corp, 56-58; res assoc physiol chem, Ohio State Univ, 63; asst prof biochem, Med Col Va, 64-75. *Concurrent Pos:* Nat Heart Inst fel physiol chem, Sch Med, Johns Hopkins Univ, 63-64. *Mem:* Sigma Xi; Am Chem Soc; Am Oil Chemists' Soc; Soc Exp Biol & Med; AAAS. *Res:* Chemistry and metabolism of minor lipids and fat-soluble vitamins; hypocholesterolemic agents; biochemistry of autism; learning disabilities; attention deficit disorder. *Mailing Add:* Dept Biochem Marshall Univ Sch Med 1542 Spring Valley Dr Huntington WV 25755. *Fax:* 304-696-7253

GUYER, PAUL QUENTIN, ANIMAL SCIENCE AND NUTRITION. *Current Pos:* from asst to assoc exten animal husbandman, 54-62, PROF ANIMAL SCI, UNIV NEBR, LINCOLN, 62- *Personal Data:* b Linn Co, Mo, Mar 31, 23; m 48; c 3. *Educ:* Univ Mo, BS, 48, MA, 49, PhD, 54. *Honors & Awards:* Exten Livestock Specialist Award, Am Soc Animal Sci, 73. *Prof Exp:* Instr animal husb, Univ Mo, 48-54. *Mem:* Fel Am Soc Animal Sci; Sigma Xi. *Res:* Animal nutrition; beef, sheep and swine production. *Mailing Add:* 230 Park Vale St Lincoln NE 68510

GUYKER, WILLIAM C, JR, POWER & TRANSMISSION ENGINEERING, ENERGY RESEARCH. *Current Pos:* VAR POSITIONS, ALLEGHENY POWER SERV CORP, 59-, PRIN ENGR, 83- *Personal Data:* b Donora, Pa, Aug 21, 33; US citizen; m 71; c 1. *Educ:* Mass Inst Technol, BS, 59. *Honors & Awards:* Centennial Medal, Inst Elec & Electronics Engrs, 84. *Concurrent Pos:* Consult, 68-; adj prof elec eng, Univ Pittsburgh & WVa Univ, 68- *Mem:* Fel Inst Elec & Electronics Engrs; AAAS. *Res:* Research and development that supports power, transmission, distribution, and generation engineering; customer utilization service and power quality; nuclear engineering. *Mailing Add:* 56 Forest Ave Greensburg PA 15601

GUYMON, GARY L, GEOHYDROLOGY, MATHEMATICAL MODELING. *Current Pos:* PROF CIVIL ENG, UNIV CALIF, IRVINE, 74- *Personal Data:* m 88, Lucinda A Kemmis; c Gary Jr, Richard, Marisa & Michael. *Educ:* Univ Calif, Davis, BS, 66, MS, 67, PhD(civil eng), 70. *Prof Exp:* NSF trainee, Univ Calif, Davis, 66-69, asst res engr, 69-71; assoc prof civil eng, Univ Alaska, 71-74. *Concurrent Pos:* mem, US Comt Large Dams. *Mem:* Sigma Xi; fel Am Soc Civil Engrs; Am Geophys Union. *Res:* Developing mathematical model of subsurface flow in both the saturated and unsaturated zones; coupled heat and moisture flow and contaminant movement. *Mailing Add:* Dept Civil & Environ Eng Univ Calif Irvine CA 92697

GUYNN, ROBERT WILLIAM, BIOCHEMISTRY. *Current Pos:* from asst prof to assoc prof, 73-83, prof psychiat & vchmn dept, 83-87, PROF PSYCHIAT & INTERIM CHMN DEPT, MED SCH, UNIV TEX, HOUSTON, 87- *Personal Data:* b Streator, Ill, Oct 27, 42. *Educ:* Mich State Univ, BA, 63; Johns Hopkins Univ, MD, 67. *Prof Exp:* Intern internal med, Univ Hosp Cleveland, Ohio, 67-68; resident psychiat, Johns Hopkins Hosp, Phipps Clin, 68-70; clin assoc, NIMH, Washington, DC, 70-73. *Concurrent Pos:* Surgeon, USPHS, 73; prin investr, var fed & private res grants. *Mem:* Am Soc Biol Chemists; Biochem Soc; Am Chem Soc; Res Soc Alcoholism; Am Psychiat Asn. *Res:* Basic biochemistry into the short-term regulation of metabolism with special emphasis on intermediary metabolism and the pathways of serine synthesis and degradation, using as models of focus: alcoholism. *Mailing Add:* PO Box 20708 Houston TX 77225-0708

GUYON, JOHN CARL, ANALYTICAL CHEMISTRY. *Current Pos:* dean Col Sci, 74-76, assoc vpres res & dean grad sch, 76-80, VPRES ACAD AFFAIRS & RES, SOUTHERN ILL UNIV, CARBONDALE, 81- *Personal Data:* b Washington, Pa, Oct 16, 31; m 55; c 2. *Educ:* Washington & Jefferson Col, BA, 55; Univ Toledo, MS, 58; Purdue Univ, PhD(anal chem), 61. *Prof Exp:* Re chemist, Thatcher Glass Mfg Co, NY, 57-58; from asst prof to assoc prof anal chem, Univ Mo, 61-71; prof & chmn dept, Memphis State Univ, 71-74. *Res:* Absorption spectroscopy; organic analytical reagents; fluorescence analysis; chromatography; heteropoly compounds. *Mailing Add:* Off of the Pres Southern Ill Univ Carbondale Carbondale IL 62901-4399

GUYSELMAN, J(OHN) BRUCE, ZOOLOGY. *Current Pos:* RETIRED. *Personal Data:* b Albion, Mich, Mar 17, 24; m 78, Helen S Rodger. *Educ:* Albion Col, AB, 47; Northwestern Univ, PhD(zool), 52. *Prof Exp:* From instr to assoc prof zool, Carleton Col, 52-64; mem fac staff biol, Albion Col, 64-69, prof biol, 69-81. *Concurrent Pos:* Chief reader biol, Advan Placement Prog, Educ Testing Serv, 71-75, trustee NCent Col, Naperville, Ill, 77- *Mem:* Am Soc Zoologists; Am Soc Limnol & Oceanog; Am Physiol Soc; Soc Gen Physiol; Sigma Xi. *Res:* Comparative animal physiology; environmental physiology; biological rhythms. *Mailing Add:* 2701 Pickett Rd Apt 2026 Durham NC 27705. *E-Mail:* guyselman@aol.com

GUYTON, ARTHUR CLIFTON, PHYSIOLOGY. *Current Pos:* assoc prof pharmacol, 47-48, prof & chmn, Dept Physiol & Biophys, 48-90, EMER PROF PHYSIOL, MED CTR, UNIV MISS, 90- *Personal Data:* b Oxford, Miss, Sept 8, 19; m 43, Ruth Weigle; c 10. *Educ:* Univ Miss, BA, 39; Harvard Univ, MD, 43. *Hon Degrees:* DSc, Med Col Wis, 77, Univ Pretoria, SAfrica, 82, Univ Murcia, Spain, 89, EVa Med Sch, 90. *Honors & Awards:* President's Citation, 56; Gould Award, AAAS, 60; ALZA Award, Biomed Eng Soc, 71; Ross McIntyre Award, Univ Nebr, 72; Circulation Group Wiggers' Award, Am Physiol Soc, 72; Annual Distinguished Res Achievement Award, Am Heart Asn, 75; Ciba Award, 80; Merck Int Award, 84. *Prof Exp:* Intern & resident surg, Mass Gen Hosp, 43-44 & 46; actg assoc prof physiol, Univ Tenn, 47. *Concurrent Pos:* Mem coun, Nat Heart & Lung Inst, 71-75. *Mem:* Am Physiol Soc (pres, 74-75); Fedn Am Soc Exp Biol (pres, 75-76); Am Heart Asn; Biomed Eng Soc; hon fel Am Col Cardiol; Russian Acad Sci. *Res:* Medical electronic development; circulatory physiology; high blood pressure research. *Mailing Add:* Dept Physiol & Biophys Univ Miss Med Ctr Jackson MS 39216. *Fax:* 601-984-1917

GUYTON, JAMES W, GEOLOGY. *Current Pos:* asst prof geol, 64-69, assoc prof geol & phys sci, 69-77, PROF GEOL, CALIF STATE UNIV, 77- *Personal Data:* b New Albany, Miss, Nov 3, 32; m 54. *Educ:* Univ Calif, Berkeley, AB, 57; Univ Wyo, MA, 60, PhD(geol), 65. *Prof Exp:* Jr geologist,

Pan Am Petrol Corp, 57-58; seismologist, Geotech Corp, 61-64. *Mem:* Geol Soc Am; Seismol Soc Am. *Res:* Areal geology; microseisms of short period; recent and ancient landslides. *Mailing Add:* Geol Sci Calif State Univ 101 Orange St Chico CA 95929-0001

GUYTON, WILLIAM F, GROUND WATER HYDROLOGY. *Current Pos:* CONSULT GROUND WATER HYDROLOGIST, 50- *Personal Data:* b Oxford, Miss, Oct 15, 17; m 35, 87; c 5. *Educ:* Univ Miss, BA & BS, 38. *Prof Exp:* Hydraul engr, Ground Water Br, US Geol Surv, 39-45; sci consult ground water, US Army, 45; hydraul engr, US Geol Surv, 46-50. *Mem:* Am Geophys Union; Am Soc Civil Engrs; Am Water Works Asn; Nat Soc Prof Engrs; Nat Water Well Asn; Soc Petrol Engrs; Geol Soc Am. *Res:* Ground water hydrology. *Mailing Add:* 1101 S Capital Texas Hwy Suite B220 Austin TX 78746-6437

GUZE, CAROL (KONRAD LYDON), HUMAN GENETICS, CELL BIOLOGY. *Current Pos:* from asst prof to assoc prof biol, Calif State Univ, 67-78, coordr, Biol Grad Prog, 76-78, chmn dept, 78-81, univ grad adv, 81-83, assoc vpres acad affairs, 83-91, PROF BIOL, CALIF STATE UNIV, DOMINGUEZ HILLS, 78- *Personal Data:* b St Louis, Mo, Nov 12, 35; div; c 3. *Educ:* Wash Univ, AB, 57; Univ Calif, Berkeley, PhD(zool), 63, Am Bd Med Genetics, cert, 93. *Prof Exp:* Res biologist, Naval Biol Labs, Univ Calif, Berkeley, 63-64; instr biol, Brandeis Univ, 64-65 & Univ Mass, Boston, 65-66; fel bact, Univ Calif, Los Angeles, 66-67. *Concurrent Pos:* Res assoc med genetics, Harbor Gen Hosp, Med Sch Campus, Univ Calif, Los Angeles, 74-76, fel, Med Genetics Training Prog, 91-93; extramural assoc, NIH, 82 & Inst Educ Mgt, Harvard Univ, 85. *Mem:* Nat Soc Genetic Counrs; Sigma Xi; Am Soc Human Genetics. *Res:* Medical genetics. *Mailing Add:* 31 Ave 28 Venice CA 90291. *Fax:* 310-516-4268; *E-Mail:* cguze@dhvx2o.csudh.edu

GUZE, SAMUEL BARRY, INTERNAL MEDICINE, PSYCHIATRY. *Current Pos:* from instr to asst prof med, Wash Univ, 51-64, from asst prof to prof psychiat, 55-75, asst to dean, Sch Med, 65-71, dir psychiat clin, 55-75, vchancellor med affairs & pres, Med Ctr, 71-89, head, Dept Psychiat, 75-89, ASSOC PROF MED, WASH UNIV, 64-, SPENCER T OLIN PROF PSYCHIAT, 75-, HEAD, DEPT PSYCHIAT, 93- *Personal Data:* b New York, NY, Oct 18, 23; m 46, Joy Campbell; c Jonathan & Jeremy A. *Educ:* Wash Univ, MD, 45; Am Bd Internal Med, dipl, 54; Am Bd Psychiat & Neurol, dipl, 57. *Prof Exp:* Intern med, Barnes Hosp, 45-46, fel med, 46 & 48-49; resident, Vet Admin Hosp, Conn, 49-50. *Concurrent Pos:* Fel psychiat & resident, Barnes Hosp & Wash Univ Sch Med, 50-53, asst physician, 51-, from asst psychiatrist to assoc psychiatrist, 55-75, psychiatrist-in-chief, 75-89 & 93-, psychiatrist, 89-; from asst psychiatrist to assoc psychiatrist, Renard Hosp, 55-75, psychiatrist-in-chief, 75-89 & 93-, psychiatrist 89-; vis physician & consult, St Louis City Hosp, 51-85; consult, H G Phillips Hosp, 54-85. *Mem:* Inst Med-Nat Acad Sci; fel Am Psychiat Asn; fel Am Col Physicians; Am Psychopath Asn; Asn Res Nerv & Ment Dis; fel Royal Col Psychiatrists; Psychiat Res Soc. *Res:* Natural history psychiatric disease; effects of drugs on behavior. *Mailing Add:* Dept Psychiat 4940 Children's Pl Wash Univ Sch Med St Louis MO 63110

GUZELIAN, PHILIP SAMUEL, INTERNAL MEDICINE, DRUG METABOLISM. *Current Pos:* PROF & CHIEF MED TOXICOL & CO-DIR HEPAT BILIARY CTR, UNIV COLO, 92- *Personal Data:* b Milwaukee, Wis, May 21, 41; m 75; c 3. *Educ:* Univ Wis-Madison, BA, 63, MD, 67; Am Bd Internal Med, dipl, 72. *Honors & Awards:* Clin Investr Award, NIH, 75. *Prof Exp:* Resident internal med, Univ Wis, 70-71; USPHS clin fel liver dis, Yale Univ, 71-72; USPHS res fel gastrointestinal, Univ Calif, San Francisco, 72-74; from asst prof to assoc prof med, Med Col Va, 74-92. *Concurrent Pos:* Investr, NIH Liver Metab Prog Proj, 75-; prin investr, Nat Inst Environ Health Sci, 75-, Allied Chem Corp, 76- & Va Environ Endowment, 78- *Mem:* Am Fedn Clin Res; Am Asn Study Liver Dis; Am Asn Biol Chemists. *Res:* Hepatic drug metabolism and toxicity; collagen metabolism in the liver. *Mailing Add:* Dept Med Univ Colo Health Sci Ctr 4200 E Ninth Ave No B146 Denver CO 80262. *Fax:* 303-270-7180

GUZIEC, FRANK STANLEY, JR, ORGANIC & MEDICINAL CHEMISTRY, SYNTHETIC. *Current Pos:* from asst prof to assoc prof, 81-90, PROF CHEM, NMEX STATE UNIV, 90- *Personal Data:* b Chicago, Ill, Sept 16, 46; m 91, Lynn James; c Daniel. *Educ:* Loyola Univ, BSc, 68; Mass Inst Technol, PhD(org chem), 72. *Prof Exp:* Res fel chem, Imp Col, London, 72-74; res assoc, Mass Inst Technol, 75-76 & Wesleyan Univ, 76-77; asst prof chem, Tufts Univ, 77-81. *Concurrent Pos:* Nat Acad Sci-Polish Acad Sci exchange scholar, 93. *Mem:* Am Chem Soc; Chem UK; Polish Chem Soc; Sigma Xi. *Res:* Organic synthesis; peptides, lipids, natural products; chemistry of sterically crowded molecules; synthetic methods; organo selenium chemistry; organo tellurium chemistry; conducting organic materials; medicinal chemistry. *Mailing Add:* Dept Chem Southwestern Univ Georgetown TX 78627. *Fax:* 505-646-2646; *E-Mail:* fguziec@nmsu.edu

GUZIEC, LYNN ERIN, SYNTHESIS OF HIGHLY HINDERED COMPOUNDS, MUSTARDS & QUINONES. *Current Pos:* ASST PROF ORG CHEM, NMEX STATE UNIV, LAS CRUCES, 88- *Personal Data:* b Long Beach, Calif, Aug 18, 51; m 91, Frank Jr. *Educ:* Russell Sage Col, BA, 79; NMex State Univ, PhD(org chem), 88. *Concurrent Pos:* Proj leader, Nat Cancer Inst, 87-88, prin asst, 88-91, co-prin investr, 91-; secy-treas, Rio Grande Valley Sect, Am Chem Soc, 90, chmn, 91. *Mem:* Am Chem Soc. *Res:* Synthesis and reactions of organo-sulfur and organo-selenium compounds, semi-conductors, hindered halogen compounds, strained organic molecules, heterocycles, mustards & quinones; synthetic design and preparation of anti-cancer and anti-aquired immune deficiency syndrome agents. *Mailing Add:* 100 River Rd Georgetown TX 78628-3023

GUZMAN FORESTI, MIGUEL ANGEL, EXPERIMENTAL STATISTICS, PUBLIC HEALTH NUTRITION. *Current Pos:* prof path & biomet, 82-95, PROF BIOMET & PATH, SCH MED, LA STATE UNIV MED CTR & ACTG HEAD BIOMET & GENETICS. *Personal Data:* b San Salvador, El Salvador, Dec 20, 25; m 51; c 4. *Educ:* Univ Tenn, BA, 49; NC State Col, MS, 56, PhD(exp statist), 61. *Honors & Awards:* Inst Nutrit Cent Am & Panama Award, 64, 89 & 95. *Prof Exp:* Chief labs Nutrit Cent Am & Panama, 53-54, chief div statist, 57-82, assoc dir, 75-82. *Concurrent Pos:* Consult, WHO, 59, 66 & 68, E I du Pont de Nemours & Co, Inc, 60 & USDA, 61; vis assoc prof, Dept Nutrit & Food Sci, Mass Inst Technol, 64-65, vis lectr, 66-88; vis res prof, Dept Path, Med Ctr, La State Univ, 71; vis prof, Int Pub Health, Univ Ala, Birmingham, 84-89; sr lectr, Int Pub Health, J J Sporkman Ctr Int Pub Health Educ, Sch Pub Health, Univ Ala, Birmingham. *Mem:* Am Statist Asn; Biomet Soc; Am Inst Nutrit; Latin Am Nutrit Asn; Am Pub Health Asn. *Res:* Atherosclerosis--etiology and epidemiology; human growth and development; mathematical methods in biology--applications to estimation procedures; experimental design--variance components and their application. *Mailing Add:* Dept Biomet & Genetics La State Univ Med Ctr 1901 Perdido St New Orleans LA 70112-1393

GWADZ, ROBERT WALTER, MEDICAL ENTOMOLOGY. *Current Pos:* staff fel, Primate Malaria Unit, NIH, Ga, 72-74, res biologist, 74-80, sr scientist, 80-85, capt, USPHS & head, Med Entom Unit, Lab Parasitic Dis, 85-92, ASST CHIEF & HEAD, SECT INT RES, LAB PARASITIC DIS, NAT INST ALLERGY & INFECTIOUS DIS, 92- *Personal Data:* b Chicago, Ill, Nov 24, 40; m 63, 79, Joyce Trimble; c Marya, Marc & Joel. *Educ:* Univ Notre Dame, BS, 62, PhD(biol), 70. *Prof Exp:* NIH fel, Sch Pub Health, Harvard Univ, 70-72. *Concurrent Pos:* Proj officer, Epidemiol & Control Arthropod-Borne Dis, Egypt, 79-92, Malaria Res & Training Ctr, Bamako, Mali, 90- *Mem:* Am Entom Soc; Am Mosquito Control Asn; Am Soc Trop Med & Hyg; Royal Soc Trop Med Hyg; Am Soc Parasitol; hon mem Egyptian Soc Parasitologists. *Res:* Genetics of vector capacity; malaria; malaria vaccine development; reproductive physiology; biological control; host-parasite relationship. *Mailing Add:* Lab Parasitic Dis Bldg 4 Nat Inst Allergy & Infect Dis Bethesda MD 20892-0425. *Fax:* 301-402-8536; *E-Mail:* rgwadz@at/as.niaid.nih.gov

GWALTNEY, JACK MERRIT, JR, MEDICINE, INFECTIOUS DISEASE. *Current Pos:* chief resident, Univ Va Hosp, 59-60, prof asst respiratory virus res, 62-63, from instr to asst prof, 64-70, assoc prof internal med & head epidemiol & virol, 70-75, PROF MED & WADE HAMPTON FROST PROF EPIDEMIOL, SCH MED, UNIV VA, 75-, DIR, CTR PREV DIS & INJURY, 84- *Personal Data:* b Norfolk, Va, Dec 24, 30; m 54, Sarah Parrott; c 2. *Educ:* Univ Va, BA, 52, MD, 56. *Honors & Awards:* Joseph E Smadel Award, Infectious Dis Soc Am, 87. *Prof Exp:* From intern to resident internal med, Univ Hosps, Cleveland, Ohio, 56-59. *Concurrent Pos:* Res fel med & prev med, Univ Va, 63-64; Trudeau fel, Am Thoracic Soc, 64-67; assoc mem, Comn Acute Respiratory Dis, Armed Forces Epidemiol Bd, 68; mem, Adv Panel Infectious Dis Ther, US Pharmacopeia, 70 & 75-80. *Mem:* Am Fedn Clin Res; Am Pub Health Asn; Am Soc Microbiol; Am Thoracic Soc; fel Am Col Physicians; Sigma Xi. *Res:* Etiology, epidemiology and pathogenesis of the acute respiratory diseases; virology; rhinoviruses; antiviral compounds. *Mailing Add:* Dept Internal Med Health Sci Ctr Univ Va Charlottesville VA 22908

GWATKIN, RALPH BUCHANAN LLOYD, REPRODUCTIVE DEVELOPMENTAL & CELL BIOLOGY. *Current Pos:* DIR REPRODUCTIVE & DEVELOP & DIR CLIN IN VITRO FERTIL LAB CLEVELAND CLIN FOUND, OHIO, 83- *Personal Data:* b Newport, UK, May 23, 29; nat US; m 54; c 3. *Educ:* Univ Toronto, BA, 50; MA, 51; Rutgers Univ, PhD(microbiol), 54. *Honors & Awards:* Rubin Award, Am Fertil Soc; Pac Coast Wyeth Award, Soc Study Reprod. *Prof Exp:* Fel plant path, Univ Ill, 54-55; res assoc, Connaught Med Res Labs, Univ Toronto, 56-58; assoc, Wistar Inst, Univ Pa, 59-62, asst prof reprod physiol, Sch Vet Med, 63-66; dir, Tissue Cult Lab & asst dir microbiol, Merck Sharp & Dohme Res Lab, Rahway, NJ, 67-70, dir physiol, 71-75, sr res fel & dir, Reproductive & Cell Biol, Merck Inst Therapeut Res, 76-81; prof, dept obstet & gyn, Med Fac, McMaster Univ, 82-83. *Concurrent Pos:* NIH career develop award, 64; vis prof biol, dept biol sci, Dartmouth Col, Hanover, NH, 81-82; ed-in-chief, Gamete Res, 78- *Mem:* Soc Study Reprod; Am Soc Cell Biol; Am Fertil Soc; NY Acad Sci; Soc Develop Biol; Molecular Reproduction Develop. *Res:* Sperm-egg interaction and embryonic developments in mammals; tissue and organ culture, both basic and applied. *Mailing Add:* 25460 Bryden Rd Beachwood OH 44122-4164. *Fax:* 216-765-0956

GWAZDAUSKAS, FRANCIS CHARLES, DAIRY SCIENCE, REPRODUCTIVE ENDOCRINOLOGY & BIOTECHNOLOGY. *Current Pos:* From asst prof to assoc prof, 74-86, PROF REPRODUCTIVE PHYSIOL, VA POLYTECH INST & STATE UNIV, 86- *Personal Data:* b Waterbury, Conn, July 25, 43; m 71, Judy Keller; c Jennifer, James (deceased), John & Peter. *Educ:* Univ Conn, BS, 66; Univ Fla, MS, 72, PhD(animal sci), 74. *Honors & Awards:* Pharmacia UpJohn Physiol Res Award, Am Dairy Sci Asn, 96. *Concurrent Pos:* Fulbright fel, 89-90; consult transpharm, 92-; David R & Margaret Lincicome Endowed Prof, 96. *Mem:* Am Dairy Sci Asn; Am Soc Animal Sci; Soc Study Reproduction; Sigma Xi; Soc Exp Biol Med. *Res:* Factors which determine the optimal time for insemination; proteins in normal and abnormal uterine secretions; adrenal responsiveness to ACTH; early bovine embryo development; embryo manipulation and gene insertion; transgenics. *Mailing Add:* Dept Dairy Sci Va Polytech Inst & State Univ Blacksburg VA 24061

GWIAZDA, S(TANLEY) J(OHN), MECHANICAL ENGINEERING, SCIENCE EDUCATION. *Current Pos:* Head counr, 51-61, ASSOC PROF MECH ENG, DREXEL UNIV, 46-, DEAN EVE COL, 63- *Personal Data:* b Philadelphia, Pa, Feb 14, 22; m 44; c 1. *Educ:* Drexel Inst, BS, 44, MS, 52. *Mem:* Am Soc Eng Educ; Asn Cont Higher Educ (pres, 85-86). *Res:* Ordnance mechanisms; stress analysis and machine design problems. *Mailing Add:* 4325 Lauriston St Philadelphia PA 19128

GWILLIAM, GILBERT FRANKLIN, NEUROBIOLOGY, INVERTEBRATE ZOOLOGY. *Current Pos:* from instr to prof, 57-95, EMER PROF BIOL, REED COL, 95- *Personal Data:* b Park City, Utah, Aug 28, 25; m 50, Marjorie Gardner; c Gilbert Franklin III & Tassie Katherine. *Educ:* Univ Calif, AB, 50, PhD(zool), 56. *Prof Exp:* Fel marine biol, Scripps Inst Oceanog, Univ Calif, San Diego, 56-57. *Concurrent Pos:* NSF sr fel, 64-65; spec postdoctoral fel, Nat Inst Neurol Dis & Stroke, NIH, 70-71; vpres & provost, Comt Dis & Stroke, Nat Inst Neurol, 79-82 & 84-85. *Mem:* AAAS; Soc Integrative & Comp Biol; Soc Neurosci. *Res:* Functional morphology of invertebrates; neuromuscular mechanisms in invertebrates; invertebrate sensory physiology; general invertebrate zoology. *Mailing Add:* Dept Biol 3203 E Woodstock Portland OR 97202-8199. *Fax:* 503-777-7773; *E-Mail:* gwill@reed.edu

GWILT, JOHN RUFF, SCIENCE ADMINISTRATION, APPLIED CHEMISTRY. *Current Pos:* PRIN, WELLSTONE CONSULTS, 90- *Personal Data:* b Worcester, Eng, Aug 18, 20; m 45, Joan M Hill; c David, Peter & Stephen. *Educ:* Univ London, BSc, 47, PhD(chem), 53. *Prof Exp:* Chemist, Chas H Phillips Div, Sterling Drug Inc, 47-56, dir, Winthrop Labs Div, 56-67, vpres, Winthrop Prod Div, 67-74, corp dir qual, 74-78, vpres & dir, 78-81, vpres com develop, 81-88. *Concurrent Pos:* Lectr, Acton Tech Col Eng, 49-55. *Mem:* Fel Royal Soc Chem; Brit Inst Mgt; Royal Soc Health; Am Inst Chemists. *Res:* Analytical and synthetic chemistry; biopharmaceutics; quality control philosophies; management of people, particularly scientists. *Mailing Add:* Wellstone House Hartwell Rd Northampton NN7-2NT England

GWIN, REGINALD, PHYSICS. *Current Pos:* PHYSICIST, OAK RIDGE NAT LAB, 55- *Personal Data:* b Chattanooga, Tenn, Jan 14, 24; m 48; c 5. *Educ:* Univ Chattanooga, BS, 48; Emory Univ, MS, 49; Univ Tenn, PhD(physics), 62. *Prof Exp:* Assoc prof physics, Mercer Univ, 49-50; physicist, Gaseous Diffusion Plant, Union Carbide Corp, 50-52 & Y-12 Plant, 52-55. *Mem:* Am Phys Soc; Am Nuclear Soc; Sigma Xi. *Res:* Measurement of capture and fission cross sections of fissile isotopes as a function of energy. *Mailing Add:* 218 Wakefield Rd Knoxville TN 37922-2036

GWINN, JAMES E, GEOLOGY. *Current Pos:* RETIRED. *Personal Data:* b Harvey, WVa, Mar 30, 23; m 43; c 2. *Educ:* WVa Univ, BS, 48, MS, 50. *Prof Exp:* Prod mgr, CNG Transmission Corp, 63-90. *Mem:* Soc Petrol Engrs; Geol Soc Am. *Mailing Add:* 712 Bright Ridge Rd Bridgeport WV 26330

GWINN, JOEL ALDERSON, PHYSICS. *Current Pos:* RETIRED. *Personal Data:* b Quinnimont, WVa, Feb 24, 29; m 54; c 4. *Educ:* WVa Univ, BSEd, 51, MA, 56, MS, 57, PhD(physics), 62. *Prof Exp:* From instr to assoc prof, Univ Louisville, 61-70, prof physics, 70-94. *Mem:* Am Asn Physics Teachers. *Mailing Add:* Dept Physics Univ Louisville Louisville KY 40292

GWINN, JOHN FREDERICK, SCIENCE EDUCATION. *Current Pos:* From instr to asst prof, 72-81, ASSOC PROF BIOL, UNIV AKRON, 81- *Personal Data:* b Dayton, Ohio, June 18, 42; m 93, Jane Bennett. *Educ:* Manchester Col, BA, 64; Purdue Univ, MS, 67; Kent State Univ, PhD(physiol), 72. *Mem:* Nat Asn Res Sci Teaching; Sigma Xi. *Res:* Computer based testing; development of individualized instruction; science education. *Mailing Add:* Dept Biol Univ Akron Akron OH 44325-3908. *Fax:* 330-972-8445; *E-Mail:* gwinn@uakron.edu

GWINN, WILLIAM DULANEY, PHYSICAL CHEMISTRY. *Current Pos:* From instr to assoc prof, Univ Calif, 42-55, res prof, Miller Res Inst, 61-62, prof 55-79, EMER PROF CHEM, UNIV CALIF, BERKELEY, 79-; PRES, ECTEC CORP, EL CERRITO, CALIF. *Personal Data:* b Bloomington, Ill, Sept 28, 16; m 42, 53, Margaret Boothby; c Robert B, Ellen (Hart) & Kathleen (Walsh). *Educ:* Univ Mo, AB, 37, MA, 39; Univ Calif, PhD(chem), 42. *Concurrent Pos:* Res assoc, div 10, Nat Defense Res Comt, 42-44 & Manhattan Dist Proj, 44-45; Guggenheim fel, 54; Sloan res fel, 55-59; vis prof, Univ Minn, Minneapolis, 69-70. *Mem:* Fel Am Phys Soc; Am Chem Soc. *Res:* Microwave spectroscopy and molecular structure; quantum mechanics; astrophysics. *Mailing Add:* ECTEC Corp 8506 Terrace Dr El Cerrito CA 94530-2721

GWINUP, GRANT, INTERNAL MEDICINE. *Current Pos:* ASSOC PROF ENDOCRINOL & CHMN DIV METAB, UNIV CALIF, IRVINE-CALIF COL MED, 65- *Personal Data:* b Denver, Colo, June 28, 29; m 55; c 2. *Educ:* Univ Colo, BA, 53, MD, 56; Am Bd Internal Med, dipl. *Prof Exp:* Instr internal med, Sch Med, Univ Tex, 60-61; asst prof internal med & endocrinol, Health Ctr, Ohio State Univ, 62-65. *Concurrent Pos:* USPHS fel, 59-60; ed, Metabolism, 66- *Mem:* Am Fedn Clin Res; Am Diabetes Asn; Endocrine Soc. *Res:* Endocrinology and metabolism. *Mailing Add:* Univ Calif Irvine Med Orange CA 92668

GWINUP, PAUL D, PHYSICAL CHEMISTRY, INORGANIC CHEMISTRY. *Current Pos:* Asst prof, 65-80, PROF CHEM, ARK STATE UNIV, 80- *Personal Data:* b Shawnee, Okla, Oct 13, 31; m 57; c 3. *Educ:* Okla State Univ, BS, 57, PhD(chem), 67. *Mem:* Am Chem Soc; Sigma Xi. *Res:* Thermoanalytical chemistry; single-crystal x-ray diffraction. *Mailing Add:* 652 Greene Rd Pollard AR 72456

GWIRTZ, PATRICIA ANN, CORONARY CIRCULATION, CARDIAC DYNAMICS. *Current Pos:* ASSOC PROF CORONARY CIRCULATION & GASTROINTESTINAL PHYSIOL, TEX COL OSTEOP MED, 82- *Educ:* Thomas Jefferson Univ, PhD(physiol), 78. *Mem:* Am Physiol Soc; Am Heart Soc; Sigma Xi. *Res:* Neuro-regulation of cardiovascular system. *Mailing Add:* Dept Physiol Tex Col Osteop Med 3500 Camp Bowie Blvd Ft Worth TX 76107-2690. *Fax:* 817-735-1703

GWYN, CHARLES WILLIAM, electrical engineering, computer science, for more information see previous edition

GWYN, J(OHN) E(DWARD), CHEMICAL ENGINEERING, PROCESS RESEARCH & DEVELOP. *Current Pos:* RETIRED. *Personal Data:* b La Junta, Colo, Dec 5, 27; m 47, Helen Tuttle; c Douglas A & David E. *Educ:* Univ Colo, BS, 50; Univ Wis, MS, 52, PhD, 55. *Prof Exp:* Asst chem eng, Univ Wis, 50-52, res assoc eng exp sta, 52-55; res engr, Shell Oil Co, 52-62, sr res engr, 62-67, staff res engr, 67-70, sr staff res engr, 70-77, res consult, 77-90. *Concurrent Pos:* Consult. *Mem:* Am Chem Soc; Nat Soc Prof Engrs; Am Inst Chem Engrs. *Res:* Chemical and petroleum processes; chemical reaction engineering; gas/particulates. *Mailing Add:* 26602 Willow Lane Katy TX 77494-5418

GWYNN, DONALD EUGENE, SYNTHETIC ORGANIC CHEMISTRY. *Current Pos:* CHEMIST, TEX EASTMAN CO, 69- *Personal Data:* b Columbus, Ohio, Aug 28, 35; m 58; c 2. *Educ:* Ohio State Univ, BSc; Univ Ill, PhD(org chem), 62. *Prof Exp:* Res fel, Calif Inst Technol, 62-63; asst prof org chem, Univ Ark, 63-69. *Mem:* Am Chem Soc. *Res:* Organic synthesis. *Mailing Add:* 205 N Pope Dr Overton TX 75684-1529

GWYNN, EDGAR PERCIVAL, CYTOGENETICS. *Current Pos:* from lectr to assoc prof, 53-64, PROF BIOL, WASHINGTON COL, 64-, CHMN DEPT, 69- *Personal Data:* b Baltimore, Md, Jan 23, 23; m 50; c 1. *Educ:* Univ Md, BS, 50; Univ Ky, MS, 51; Johns Hopkins Univ, PhD(biol), 58. *Prof Exp:* Jr instr biol, Johns Hopkins Univ, 51-53. *Mem:* AAAS; Bot Soc Am; Soc Study Evolution; Am Genetic Asn; Sigma Xi. *Res:* Cytology; evolution. *Mailing Add:* PO Box 8C62 Box 184A Mt Desert ME 04660

GWYNN, ROBERT H, physiology, for more information see previous edition

GYAN, NANIK D, DRUGS & MEDICAL DEVICES, BIOPHARMACEUTICAL STUDIES. *Current Pos:* PRES, EURO-AM PHARMA INC, 89- *Personal Data:* Can citizen. *Educ:* Univ Gujarat, India, BS, 57; Univ Freiburg, WGer, PhD(pharmaceut chem), 64. *Prof Exp:* Tech dir, res & develop, Beecham Labs, 71-78; tech dir, res & develop, Cooper Labs, 78-79; dir, new prod develop, Kalipharma Inc, 79-82; sr vpres, Res & Develop, Thermascam Inc, 83-89. *Concurrent Pos:* Fel, health, protection res, Drug Res Labs, Ottawa, 67-69; sr vpres, Baors-Krey Assocs Inc, 83- *Res:* Dosage form design and development; analytical development and clinical investigation. *Mailing Add:* 64 Montrose Ave Fanwood NJ 07023

GYBERG, ARLIN ENOCH, PHYSICAL CHEMISTRY. *Current Pos:* from asst prof to assoc prof, 67-85, PROF CHEM, AUGSBURG COL, 85- *Personal Data:* b Luverne, Minn, Dec 9, 38; m 77, Barbara; c Greg, Jeff & Torsten. *Educ:* Mankato State Col, BS, 61; Univ Minn, PhD(anal chem), 69. *Honors & Awards:* Kohltoff Award. *Prof Exp:* Teacher high sch, Minn, 61-63. *Concurrent Pos:* Consult, chem. *Mem:* AAAS; Sigma Xi; Am Chem Soc. *Res:* Light scattering; optical methods; polymer solutions. *Mailing Add:* Augsburg Col Minneapolis MN 55454-1396

GYFTOPOULOS, ELIAS P(ANAYIOTIS), MECHANICAL & NUCLEAR ENGINEERING. *Current Pos:* Instr elec eng, 54-58, from asst prof to prof elec & nuclear eng, 58-70, Ford Prof Eng, 70-96, EMER PROF ENG, MASS INST TECHNOL, 96- *Personal Data:* b Athens, Greece, July 4, 27; US citizen; m 62, Artemis S Scalleri; c Vasso, Maro & Rena. *Educ:* Tech Univ Athens, dipl, 53; Mass Inst Technol, ScD(elec eng), 58. *Hon Degrees:* Hon Dr, Tech Univ Athens, 92. *Honors & Awards:* James Harry Potter Gold Medal, AM Soc Mech Engrs, 95; Comdr of Order of Honor, Repub Greece, 96. *Concurrent Pos:* Dir, Thermo Electron Corp, Thermo Remediation Corp, Thermo Cardiosystems Corp, Thermo Spectra Corp, Thermo Voltek Corp, Thermo Bio-Anal Corp, Trex Med Corp, ThermoLyte Corp & ThermoLase Corp; chmn, Nat Energy Coun Greece, 75-78; vchmn, Trustees Anatolia Col, 87- *Mem:* Nat Acad Eng; Fel AAAS; Fel Am Nuclear Soc; Fel Acad Athens; fel Am Acad Arts & Sci; fel Am Soc Mech Engrs. *Res:* Nuclear reactor dynamics; physics of ionized gases; surface physics; direct energy conversion; quantum thermodynamics; energy conservation. *Mailing Add:* Dept Nuclear Eng Mass Inst Technol Cambridge MA 02139

GYLES, C L, VETERINARY MICROBIOLOGY. *Current Pos:* from asst prof to assoc prof, Univ Guelph, 69-75, chair, Dept Vet Microbiol & Immunol, 92-96, actg chair pathobiol, 96-97, PROF VET BACT, ONT VET COL, UNIV GUELPH, 75- *Personal Data:* b Jamaica, WI, May 15, 40; m 91,

Jennifer Ogeer; c Carla & Curtis. *Educ:* Univ Toronto, DVM, 64; Univ Guelph, MSc, 66, PhD, 68. *Prof Exp:* Lectr diag bact, Ont Vet Col, Univ Guelph, 64-66; Med Res Coun Can fel, Eng & Denmark, 68-69. *Concurrent Pos:* Deleg cholera panel, US-Japan Coop Med Sci Prog, Japan, 70; dean grad studies, Univ Guelph, 81-86; Ont Coun Univ Affairs, 81-87. *Mem:* Can Vet Med Asn; Am Soc Microbiol. *Res:* Escherichia coli enterotoxins; R factors and other plasmids; pathogenesis of Escherichia coli infections in pigs, calves and chickens; exotoxin of corynebacterium pseudotuberculosis; pathogenesis of salmonellosis in calves; virulence of salmonella; edema disease principle; Shiga-like toxins; cloning and DNA sequencing; Escherichi acoli Shiga-like toxins; E coli vaccines; microbiol food safety. *Mailing Add:* Dept Pathobiol Univ Guelph Guelph ON N1G 2W1 Can. *Fax:* 519-767-0809; *E-Mail:* cgyles@ovcnet.uoguelph.ca

GYLES, NICHOLAS ROY, GENETICS, ANIMAL BREEDING. *Current Pos:* From asst prof to prof poultry genetics, 52-76, PROF ANIMAL SCI, UNIV ARK, FAYETTEVILLE, 76- *Personal Data:* b Jamaica, WI, Jan 30, 22; US citizen; m 55; c 2. *Educ:* Univ BC, BSA, 46, MSA, 49; Univ Mo, PhD(animal breeding), 52. *Concurrent Pos:* Consult geneticist, Peterson Poultry Breeding Farm, Ark, 56- *Mem:* Genetics Soc Am; Poultry Sci Asn; Sigma Xi. *Res:* Effectiveness of selection for economic traits in poultry; genetic mechanisms of resistance to Rous and leukosis viruses in chickens. *Mailing Add:* 1336 Northview Fayetteville AR 72701-2330

GYLYS, JONAS ANTANAS, NEUROPHARMACOLOGY, AUTONOMIC. *Current Pos:* RETIRED. *Personal Data:* b Kaunas, Lithuania, June 27, 28; US citizen. *Educ:* Roosevelt Univ, BS, 51; Loyola Univ, Ill, MS, 54, PhD(pharmacol), 57. *Prof Exp:* Pharmacologist, Bio-Test Labs, North Brook, Ill, 56-58; sr scientist, Warner-Lambert Res Inst, Morris Plains, NJ, 58-66; sr res scientist, Bristol-Myers, Syracuse, NY, 66-68, asst dir, 68-83, assoc dir pharmacol res, 83-87, assoc dir neuropharmacology, Wallingford, Conn, 87-93. *Mem:* AAAS; Am Soc Pharmacol & Exp Therapeut; Sigma Xi. *Res:* Operant behavior; anoretic agents; hypnotics; tranquilizers; antidepressants; stimulants; performance and memory enhancers; antiemetics, migraine drugs; investigational new and new drug application work-up; good laboratory practice implementation. *Mailing Add:* 153 Ciccio Rd Southington CT 06489-2104

GYOREY, GEZA L, NUCLEAR ENGINEERING, TECHNICAL MANAGEMENT. *Current Pos:* RETIRED. *Personal Data:* b Budapest, Hungary, July 31, 33; US citizen; m 57, Elizabeth Fralick; c 2. *Educ:* Univ Mich, BSE, 55, MSE, 57, PhD(nuclear eng), 60. *Prof Exp:* Assoc prof nuclear eng, Univ Mich, 60-66; mgr nuclear methods, Gen Elec Nuclear Energy Group, 66-68, mgr nuclear design, 68-70, mgr nuclear fuel strategic planning, 70-73, mgr uranium enrichment projs, 73-74, mgr reactor licensing, 74-76, mgr design reviews, 76-80, mgr advan fuel progs, 80-90, mgr safety & anal eng, 90-94. *Mem:* Am Nuclear Soc; AAAS. *Res:* Nuclear power reactor and fuel technology, reliability and safety. *Mailing Add:* 19941 Winter Lane Saratoga CA 95070-4402. *E-Mail:* gyorey_g@compuserve.com

GYORGY, ERNST MICHAEL, experimental solid state physics; deceased, see previous edition for last biography

GYORKEY, FERENC, immunopathology, electro-microscopy; deceased, see previous edition for last biography

GYSLING, HENRY J, INORGANIC CHEMISTRY, ORGANOMETALLIC CHEMISTRY. *Current Pos:* sr res chemist, 70-75, RES ASSOC, EASTMAN KODAK CO, 75- *Personal Data:* b Philadelphia, Pa, Dec 29, 41; m 73; c 2. *Educ:* St Joseph's Col, Pa, 63; Univ Del, PhD(inorg chem), 67. *Prof Exp:* Res fel chem, NY Univ, 67-68; res fel inorg chem, Univ Newcastle upon Tyne, 68-70. *Concurrent Pos:* Adj sr res assoc, Pa State Univ, 81; assoc lectr, Univ Rochester, 80-; adj prof, Rochester Inst Technol. *Mem:* Soc Photog Scientists & Engrs; Am Chem Soc; NY Acad Sci; Mat Res Soc. *Res:* Synthetic and physical inorganic chemistry; coordination chemistry; ambidentate ligand chemistry; tellurium chemistry; organometallic chemistry. *Mailing Add:* PO Box 15430 Rochester NY 14615-0430

GYULASSY, MIKLOS, THEORETICAL PHYSICS. *Current Pos:* PROF PHYSICS, COLUMBIA UNIV, 93- *Personal Data:* b Szolnok, Hungary, Mar 9, 49; m 78; c 3. *Educ:* Univ Calif, Berkeley, AB, 70, PhD(physics), 74. *Honors & Awards:* Alexander von Humboldt US Sr Scientist Award, 86; E O Lawrence Mem Award, 87. *Prof Exp:* Fel physics, Gesselschaft Schwerionenforschung, 74-76; fel, Lawrence Berkeley Lab, 76-81, div fel physics & nuclear sci & sr staff scientist, 81-92. *Mem:* Am Phys Soc. *Res:* Physics of dense, highly excited nuclear matter formed in high energy nuclear collisions; nuclear phase transitions, Quark-gluon plasmas. *Mailing Add:* Physics Dept Columbia Univ 538 W 120th St New York NY 10027. *E-Mail:* gyulassy@nt1.phys.columbia.edu

H

HA, TAI-YOU, CELLULAR IMMUNOLOGY, IMMUNOPHARMACOLOGY & ALLERGY. *Current Pos:* assoc prof & chmn microbiol & immunol, 74-79, PROF & CHMN IMMUNOL, MED SCH, CHONBUK NAT UNIV, 79- *Personal Data:* b Youngam, Chonnam, Mar 5, 33; m 64; c 3. *Educ:* Chonnam Nat Univ, MD, 60, Master Med Sci, 62, PhD(bacteriophage), 68. *Prof Exp:* Instr bact, Dept Microbiol, Med Sch, Chonnam Nat Univ, 66-68, from asst prof to assoc prof immunol, 68-74; res assoc immunol, Med Sch Yale Univ, 71-73. *Concurrent Pos:* Vdean, Med Sch, Chonbuk Nat Univ, 74-79, dir, Inst Med Sci, 77-83, dean, 79-80; pres, Asn Korean Med Educ, 80, Korean Soc Microbiol, 84-85 & Korean Soc Immunol, 87-89; adj prof, Immunol Div, Mont State Univ, 81-82; counr, Bact Div, Int Union Microbiol Socs, 82-86, rep, Int Comt Syst Bact, 86- *Mem:* Am Soc Microbiol; Am Asn Immunol; NY Acad Sci; Soc Leukocyte Biol; Int Soc Immunopharmacol; Int Soc Endotoxin. *Res:* Immunoregulation by T and B cells and cytokines; mechanisms of immediate hypersensitivity effects of platelet activation factor and platelet activation factor antagoinists on anaphylaxis; host-parasite relationships; alcohol immunology dealing with infection and tumor. *Mailing Add:* Dept Microbiol & Immunol Chonbuk Nat Univ Med Sch 220 Kum-Ahm Dong Sun Chonju Chonbuk South Korea 560-182. *Fax:* 82-0652-74-9866

HAACKE, GOTTFRIED, III-V COMPOUND SEMICONDUCTORS, DYE ABSORBER TECHNOLOGY. *Current Pos:* res physicist semiconductors, Am Cyanamid Co, 62-68, group leader electrochromism, 68-77, mgr mat res, 77-84, res fel mat res, Cytec Indust, 84-94, SR RES FEL, COATINGS RES, CYTEC INDUST, 94- *Personal Data:* b Bad Lausick, Ger, Nov 27, 30; US citizen; m 63; c 2. *Educ:* Univ Cologne, Ger, dipl physics, 54, PhD(physics), 57. *Prof Exp:* Res physicist semiconductors, AEG, Frankfurt Ger, 58-61. *Mem:* Am Phys Soc; Fed Soc Coatings Technol. *Res:* Semiconductor epitaxy; wide-band gap semiconductors; thermoelectric compounds and devices; electrochromism devices; heterogeneous catalysis, laser hardening; physics of polymer coatings; author of various publications and patents. *Mailing Add:* 1937 W Main St Stamford CT 06904

HAAG, FRED GEORGE, ENGINEERING. *Current Pos:* dir, Bur Tech Serv, Div Air Resources, 72-79, POWER GENERATION PLANNER, PUB SERV COMN, STATE NY, 79- *Personal Data:* b Weehawken, NJ, May 11, 31; m 7, Dorothy Dodson; c Ellen & Catherine. *Educ:* Stevens Inst Technol, ME, 53; Rensselaer Polytech Inst, MS, 58, DrEngSci(mech eng), 64. *Prof Exp:* Reactor studies, Oak Ridge Nat Lab, 53-54; supv engr, Knolls Atomic Power Lab, 54-67; assoc prof mech eng, Union Col, NY, 67-72. *Concurrent Pos:* Adj prof, Union Col, 77- *Mem:* Sigma XI. *Res:* electric power generation; systems analysis; cost engineeing; electric system planning. *Mailing Add:* 10 Parkwood Dr Burnt Hill NY 12027

HAAG, ROBERT EDWIN, GRINDING, PRODUCTION OF METAL COMPONENTS. *Current Pos:* asst prof mfg, 86-93, ASSOC PROF MFG, WATERBURY STATE TECH COL, 93- *Personal Data:* b New Haven, Conn, Mar 23, 54; m 76; c 2. *Educ:* Univ Conn, BS, 75, MS, 77. *Prof Exp:* Metallurgist, Robin Steel Co, 77-80; chief metallurgist, Super Ball Div, Lydall, Inc, 80-83, mgr eng, 83-84; mgr eng, Hoover Universal, B&R Gray, 84-85. *Concurrent Pos:* Consult, 85-; prin investr, NSF/ILI grant, Waterbury State Tech Col, 90-91 & 92-93. *Res:* Metallurgy; precision grinding; bearing production; computers in manufacturing. *Mailing Add:* 15 Pinehurst Rd Unionville CT 06085

HAAG, ROBERT MARLAY, PHYSICAL CHEMISTRY. *Current Pos:* RETIRED. *Personal Data:* b Dayton, Ohio, Mar 2, 22; m 49, Margaret Alme; c 3. *Educ:* Ohio State Univ, BS, 43; Northwestern Univ, MS, 49; Ind Univ, PhD(chem), 52. *Prof Exp:* Asst, Res Found, Ohio State Univ, 43-44; lab asst, Northwestern Univ, 46-47, asst, 47-48; chemist, US Naval Ord Lab, 48; asst, Ind Univ, 48-50; res assoc, Knolls Atomic Power Lab, Gen Elec Co, 50-57, phys chemist, Res Lab, 57-60, prin engr, Aircraft Nuclear Propulsion Dept, 60-61; sr consult scientist res & develop, Avco Systs Div, Avco Corp, 61-71; mem res staff, Ampex Corp, 71-85. *Mem:* Am Ceramic Soc; Combustion Soc. *Res:* Thermodynamics of gases; thermodynamics of solutions; ultrasonic interferometry; gas-metal reactions; magnetic oxides. *Mailing Add:* 1300 Montclaire Way Los Altos CA 94024

HAAG, WERNER O, CATALYSIS, ZEOLITE CATALYSIS. *Current Pos:* CONSULT, 94- *Personal Data:* b Heilbronn, Ger, Jan 28, 26; US citizen; m, Johanna Strunk; c Peter G, Kristine, Werner R & Dirk M. *Educ:* Univ Tuebingen, Ger, dipl org chem, 54; Northwestern Univ, PhD(org chem), 58. *Honors & Awards:* Petrol Chem Award, Am Chem Soc, 88; Ipatieff Lectr, Northwestern Univ, 92; Robert Burwell lectr in Catalysis, 93; A V Humboldt Prize, 93. *Prof Exp:* Res chemist, Swift & Co, 55; res chemist, Mobil Res & Develop Corp, 59-81, sr scientist & lab adv, 81-93. *Mem:* Am Chem Soc; Catalysis Soc; Int Zeolite Asn; Sigma Xi. *Res:* Zeolite catalysis directed towards basic understanding of sorption, diffusion, mechanisms of hydrocarbon conversions and the nature of active sites; exploratory zeolite catalysis towards shape-selective and other novel processes in the petroleum and petrochemical industry. *Mailing Add:* 38 Pine Knoll Dr Lawrenceville NJ 08648. *E-Mail:* whaag@nerc.com

HAAK, RICHARD ARLEN, MEMBRANE BIOPHYSICS. *Current Pos:* vis asst prof biophys, Sch Med, Ind Univ, Indianapolis, 72-73, asst prof med biophysics, 73-78, assoc prof microbiol & immunol, 78-83, PROF MICROBIOL & IMMUNOL, SCH MED, IND UNIV, INDIANAPOLIS, 83- *Personal Data:* b Fairmont, Minn, Sept 14, 44; m 79, Becky Kerlin; c Tim, Kathy, Kristin, Jennifer, Megan, David & Daniel. *Educ:* MacMurray Col, BA, 66; Southern Ill Univ, MA, 68, PhD(molecular sci), 72. *Prof Exp:* Instr physics, Southern Ill Univ, 68-72. *Mem:* Biophys Soc; Am Soc Microbiol. *Res:* Spectroscopy and chlorimetry. *Mailing Add:* Dept Microbiol & Immunol 635 Barnhill Dr Indianapolis IN 46202-5120. *Fax:* 317-274-4090; *E-Mail:* rhaak@indyvax.inpul.edu

HAAKE, EUGENE VINCENT, NUCLEAR & CONTROL ENGINEERING. *Current Pos:* RETIRED. *Personal Data:* b Cleveland, Ohio, Sept 25, 21; m 51; c 3. *Educ:* Western Reserve Univ, BS, 43; Univ Calif, Los Angeles, MA, 48. *Prof Exp:* Assoc physicist, Nepa Div, Fairchild Engine & Airplane Corp, Tenn, 48-50, exp physicist, 50-51; assoc physicist, Oak Ridge Nat Lab, 51-52; sr nuclear engr, Gen Dynamics/Convair, 52-55, nuclear group engr, 55-62; staff mem nuclear power syst design, Gen Atomic Div, Gen Dynamics Corp, 62-65, sect leader, High Temperature Gas Reactor Dept, 65-68; br mgr, Eng Div, Gen Atomic Co, 68-85. *Mem:* Am Phys Soc; Am Nuclear Soc. *Res:* Nuclear instrumentation and measurement; control and instrumentation of nuclear reactors and power plants; nuclear safety; dynamic and performance analysis of nuclear power plants. *Mailing Add:* 3703 Brandywine St San Diego CA 92117

HAAKE, PAUL, HISTORY & PHILOSOPHY OF SCIENCE, PHOSPHORUS CHEMISTRY. *Current Pos:* prof chem, 68-84, PROF MOLECULAR BIOL & BIOCHEM, WESLEYAN UNIV, 84- *Personal Data:* b Winona, Minn, June 28, 32; div; c David A & Philip C. *Educ:* Harvard Univ, AB, 54, PhD(chem), 61. *Prof Exp:* Noyes fel chem, Calif Inst Technol, 60-61; from instr to assoc prof, Univ Calif, Los Angeles, 61-68. *Concurrent Pos:* A P Sloan fel, 64-66; NATO sr fel, 69, NSF fac fel, 74, Wesleyan Ctr Humanities, 76. *Mem:* Hist Sci Soc; Brit Hist Sci Soc; Philos Sci Asn. *Res:* Reaction mechanisms; models for enzymatically catalyzed reactions; organophosphorus chemistry; ascorbic acid; history and philosophy of science. *Mailing Add:* Dept Molecular Biol & Biochem Wesleyan Univ Middletown CT 06457. *Fax:* 860-685-2141; *E-Mail:* phaake@wesleyan.edu

HAAKONSEN, HARRY OLAV, SCIENCE EDUCATION, RESEARCH ADMINISTRATION. *Current Pos:* PROF SCI EDUC, SOUTHERN CONN STATE COL, 69-; PROF CHEM SOUTHERN CONN STATE UNIV, 75- & DIR, CTR ENVIRON. *Personal Data:* b Brooklyn, NY, Mar 12, 41; m 68; c 3. *Educ:* Taylor Univ, BA, 62, BS, 63; Syracuse Univ, MS, 66, PhD(sci educ), 69. *Prof Exp:* Teacher, Warsaw Community Schs, 63-65, chmn, Sci Dept, 64-65; dir, Audio-Tutorial Genetics Prog, Syracuse Univ, 67-69. *Concurrent Pos:* Grants, Conn State Audio-Tutorial Proj, Southern Conn State Col, Audio-Tutorial Drug Educ Proj, & US Off Educ grant environ educ & Proj Disperse; sci consult, Branford, Granby, New Haven, Wallingford & Wilton, Conn Sch Systs; lectr, Univ Conn; dir, Audio-Tutorial Workshop, NSF; coordr environ studies, Southern Conn State Univ, 71-, dir, Conn Marine Studies Consortium, 86-; dir, Land Use Decision Making Proj & Master Plan Metric Educ, US Off Educ; Student Sci Training Prog Marine Studies, NSF; Inst Study & Instr in Sci; co-ed, Conn J Sci Teaching; vis scientist, Marine Biol Lab, Woods Hole, 81 & Fisheries Directorate, Bergen, Norway, 81; dir, NSF Sponsored Inst Sci Instr & Study. *Mem:* Am Sci Affil; Nat Asn Res Sci Teaching; Nat Sci Teachers Asn; Am Chem Soc; Acad Underwater Res; Acad Arts & Scis; NY Acad Sci. *Res:* The effect of individualized approaches to instruction upon student attitude and achievement; ultrasonic strategies for monitoring migratory behavior of Atlantic salmon; enhancement of adult salmon migration in the Farmington River. *Mailing Add:* 41 Morningside Terr Wallingford CT 06492-3505

HAALAND, CARSTEN MEYER, PHYSICS, SYSTEMS ANALYSIS. *Current Pos:* RETIRED. *Personal Data:* b Winnepeg, Man, Apr 9, 27; m 80; c 3. *Educ:* St Olaf Col, Minn, BS, 50; Univ Minn, MS, 55. *Prof Exp:* Engr klystron tubes, Sperry Gyroscope Co, 54-58; physicist physics, ITT Res Inst, 58-66; physicist civil defense, Oak Ridge Nat Lab, 66-88, physicist, 88-96. *Mem:* Am Phys Soc; Health Physics Soc. *Res:* Civil defense; nuclear weapons effects; atmospheric physics and chemistry. *Mailing Add:* 76 Fox Run Dr Dadeville AL 36853

HAALAND, DAVID MICHAEL, CHEMOMETRICS, ANALYTICAL CHEMISTRY. *Current Pos:* MEM TECH STAFF PHYS CHEM, SANDIA LABS, ALBUQUERQUE, NMEX, 72- *Personal Data:* b Chicago, Ill, Mar 16, 46; m 68, Kathleen York; c Ryan Y. *Educ:* Univ NMex, BS, 68; Univ Rochester, PhD(phys chem), 72. *Mem:* Am Chem Soc; AAAS; Soc Appl Spectros; Coblentz Soc. *Res:* Noninvasive near-infrared diagnostics; process monitoring; molecular structure and spectroscopy; surface studies by infrared spectroscopy; catalysis; infrared of microelectronic devices; quantitative infrared spectroscopy, chemometrics. *Mailing Add:* Sandia Labs MS 0342 Albuquerque NM 87185-0342. *Fax:* 505-844-7910

HAALAND, JOHN EDWARD, SCIENCE ADMINISTRATION, BIOPHYSICS. *Current Pos:* PRES, TOTAL FITNESS SYST, INC, 86-; PRES, BIOSYSTEMS, INC, 93-; PRES, PEAR INC, 95- *Personal Data:* b Preeceville, Sask, Sept 12, 35; US citizen; m 58; c Kendra, Bret & Lance. *Educ:* Univ Minn, BA, 57, PhD(zool, phys chem), 68. *Prof Exp:* Res asst biophys, Univ Minn, 61-62; design engr, Apollo Proj Aeronaut Div, Honeywell, Inc, 62-65, res scientist biotech, Res Systs & Res Group, 65-67, sr res scientist, 68-69; res assoc cell biol, Univ Minn, Minneapolis, 69; vpres systs & res, Health Serv Systs Div, Food & Drug Res Labs, Inc, NY, 69-71, dir ecol sci, 70-71; vpres environ systs, Mgt & Environ Systs, Pillsbury Co, 73-76, vpres info, mgt & environ systs, 76-83. *Concurrent Pos:* Res asst, Univ Minn, Minneapolis, 67-68; Stanford Exec Prog, 75; trustee, Midwest Res Inst, 75-, N StarRes Found; Minn Acad Sci, 78-82; mem, Nat Res Coun Eval Panel Energy Conserv Progs, Nat Bur Stand, 77-79, Off Technol Assessment Rev Comt Five Year Plan, Environ Protection Agency, 77, Nat Renewable Energy Lab Adv Bd & Oversight Comt, 82-; vchmn, Archaeus Proj, 86-89; pres, Univ Taekwondo Ctr, 89-; pres & chief exec officer, Agrimax, Inc, 91-93; adj prof, Univ Minn, Minneapolis, 96- *Mem:* NY Acad Sci. *Res:* Energy and food systems; environmental systems; health delivery systems; corporate and technical information systems; long range strategic planning; organizational design and theory; integrative fitness systems for the mind and body; relationships between brain, mind and consciousness. *Mailing Add:* 339 1/2 Irvine Ave St Paul MN 55102. *Fax:* 612-487-3206; *E-Mail:* bpth26a@prodigy.com

HAALAND, RONALD L, PLANT BREEDING, NATURAL RESOURCES & LAND MANAGEMENT. *Current Pos:* PRES, HAALAND CO, 88-; VPRES SPECIALTY EXPORT PROMOTIONS, 94-; PRES, HCO INT, 94- *Personal Data:* b Havre, Mont, Nov 14, 46; m 67; c 2. *Educ:* Mont State Univ, BS, 68, MS, 70; NMex State Univ, PhD(plant breeding), 73. *Prof Exp:* Plant breeder, NAm Plant Breeders, 73-74; asst prof forage breeding, Auburn Univ, 74-79, assoc prof, 79-80; pres, Sun Rise Inc, 80-88 & Sunbelt Export Productions, Inc, 90-94. *Mem:* Am Soc Agron; Crop Sci Soc Am; NY Acad Sci. *Res:* Natural resources management; developing international marketing for pollution control device. *Mailing Add:* Sun Rise Inc PO Box 2085 Auburn AL 36830. *Fax:* 334-821-6209; *E-Mail:* haaland@mindspring.com

HAAN, CHARLES THOMAS, ENGINEERING, HYDROLOGY. *Current Pos:* prof & head dept, 78-84, prof, 85-87, REGENTS PROF & SARKEYS DISTINGUISHED PROF AGR ENG, OKLA STATE UNIV, 87- *Personal Data:* b Randolph Co, Ind, July 10, 41; m 67, Janice K Johnson; c Patricia, Christopher & Pamela. *Educ:* Purdue Univ, BS, 63, MS, 65; Iowa State Univ, PhD(agr eng), 67. *Honors & Awards:* Young Researcher Award, Am Soc Agr Engrs, 75, Hancor Soil & Water Award, 90, John Deere Medal, 97. *Prof Exp:* Res asst agr eng, Purdue Univ, 63-64 & Iowa State Univ, 64-67; from asst prof to prof agr eng, Univ Ky, 67-78. *Concurrent Pos:* Vis prof civil eng, Colo State Univ, 73-74; hydrol eng specialist, Steffen, Robertson & Kirsten Consult Engrs, Johannesburg, SAfrica, 85; consult, 87- *Mem:* Nat Acad Eng; fel Am Soc Agr Engrs; Am Inst Hydrol (pres, 95-98). *Res:* Mathematical, statistical and empirical models of various phases of the hydrologic cycle; hydrology of agricultural, urban, surface mined and forest lands; statistical applications and mathematical modelling in hydrology; erosion and sedimentation; published over 100 articles. *Mailing Add:* 720 W Lakeshore Dr Stillwater OK 74075-1335. *E-Mail:* haan@olesun.agen.okstate.edu

HAAN, STEVEN W, PLASMA PHYSICS. *Current Pos:* staff physicist, X-Div, 81-85, ASSOC DIV LEADER, X-DIV, LAWRENCE LIVERMORE NAT LAB, 85- *Educ:* Calvin Col, BS(math) & BS(physics), 73; Univ Md, PhD(physics), 77. *Prof Exp:* Res assoc, Nat Bureau Stand, Washington, DC, 77-79, lectr & res assoc, Dept Chem, Univ Calif, Berkeley, 79-81. *Res:* Plasma physics. *Mailing Add:* Lawrence Livermore Nat Lab PO Box 808 Livermore CA 94550

HAAR, JACK LUTHER, ANATOMY, ELECTRON MICROSCOPY. *Current Pos:* asst prof, 71-77, ASSOC PROF ANAT, MED COL VA, VA COMMONWEALTH UNIV, 77- *Personal Data:* b Elmore, Ohio, July 9, 42; m 71; c 1. *Educ:* Capital Univ, BSc, 64; Univ Ariz, MSc, 66; Ohio State Univ, PhD(anat), 70. *Honors & Awards:* William & Wilkins Award, Am Asn Anat, 70. *Prof Exp:* Teaching asst anat, Univ Ariz, 65-66; instr biol, Buena Vista Col, 66-67; instr, Capital Univ, 67-71. *Concurrent Pos:* NSF res grant, Col Sci Improv Prog, Ohio State Univ, 70-71; NIH grant. *Mem:* AAAS; Am Inst Biol Sci; Am Asn Anat. *Res:* Isolation of hemopoietic stem cells from yolk sac, fetal liver and adult bone marrow; histochemistry; chemotastic migration, colony-forming assay; tissue culture, immunofluorescence and electron microscopy. *Mailing Add:* Dept Anat Med Col Va PO Box 980 709 MCV Sta Richmond VA 23298-0709. *Fax:* 804-828-3832

HAARD, NORMAN F, POSTMORTEM PHYSIOLOGY FISH. *Current Pos:* PROF FOOD BIOCHEM, UNIV CALIF, DAVIS, 86- *Personal Data:* b Queens, NY, Dec 4, 41; m 63; c 2. *Educ:* Rutgers Univ, BS, 63; Univ Mass, Amherst, PhD(food biochem), 66. *Honors & Awards:* S C Prescott Award, Inst Food Technologists, 73; Fraser Award, Air Pollution Info & Comput Syst, 78. *Prof Exp:* Res fel, Inst Enzyme Res, Univ Wis-Madison, 66-68; assoc prof food biochem, Rutgers Univ, New Brunswick, 68-77; prof biochem & food, Mem Univ Nfld, 77-86. *Mem:* Inst Food Technologists. *Res:* Structure of biological membranes; noncatalytic proteins of mitochondria; mechanism of plant senescence; biochemistry of fruit ripening; mitochondrial-linked reactions in senescing plant tissue; role of peroxidase in plant senescence; hormonal control of plant senescence; stress metabolites in sweet potato; fishery waste utilization. *Mailing Add:* 1819 Amador Ave Davis CA 95616

HAAS, ALBERT B, MEDICINE. *Current Pos:* RETIRED. *Personal Data:* b Hungary, Oct 27, 11; US citizen; m 40; c 1. *Educ:* Royal Hungarian Med Sch, MD, 37. *Honors & Awards:* Legion of Honor, France, 71. *Prof Exp:* Asst prof rehab med, Inst Phys Med & Rehab, Med Ctr, NY Univ, 58-65, assoc prof to prof exp rehab med, 66-89, dir cardiopulmonary serv, 66-89. *Mem:* NY Acad Sci; Am Thoracic Soc; Fr Nat Soc Phys Med. *Res:* Work physiology; pulmonary physiology. *Mailing Add:* Dept Rehab Med NY Univ Med Ctr 400 E 34th St New York NY 10016-4901

HAAS, CAROL KRESSLER, ORGANOMETALLIC CHEMISTRY, CATALYSIS. *Current Pos:* Res chemist organometallic chem, Res Div, E I du Pont de Nemours & Co, 74-77, mem res staff coal chem, Feedstocks Div, 77-78, group leader coal chem, Feedstocks Div, 78-80, RES SUPVR, FEEDSTOCKS DIV, DU PONT CO CENT RES & DEVELOP, 80- *Personal Data:* b Reading, Pa, Mar 8, 48. *Educ:* Ursinus Col, BS, 70; Mass Inst Technol, PhD(org chem), 74. *Mem:* AAAS; Am Chem Soc; Sigma Xi. *Res:* Routes to alternative sources to chemical feedstocks; heterogeneous and homogeneous catalysis. *Mailing Add:* Birkdale 9011 Highgate Hill Dr Chesterfield VA 23832-2460

HAAS, CHARLES GUSTAVUS, JR, INORGANIC CHEMISTRY. *Current Pos:* RETIRED. *Personal Data:* b Portsmouth, Va, May 26, 23; c 2. *Educ:* Va Polytech Inst, BS, 44; Univ Chicago, SM, 49, PhD(chem), 51. *Prof Exp:* Asst chem, Univ Chicago, 47-48; res assoc, Pa State Univ, 50-51, from asst prof to prof, 51-88. *Mem:* Am Chem Soc; Sigma Xi. *Res:* Extraction of metal chlorides by organic solvents; coordination compounds. *Mailing Add:* 325 S Buckhout St State College PA 16801

HAAS, CHARLES JOHN, ROCK MECHANICS. *Current Pos:* Asst res prof rock mech, 64-68, assoc prof eng mech & sr investr rock mech & explosives, 68-76, PROF MINING ENG, UNIV MO, ROLLA, 76- *Personal Data:* b Platteville, Wis, Oct 9, 35; m 62, Jeanette Dorscheid; c Michael, Douglas & Barbara. *Educ:* Wis State Col & Inst Technol, BS, 60; Colo Sch Mines, MS, 62, DSc(rock mech), 64. *Concurrent Pos:* Student coop mem, Geophys Serv Inc, 60; res engr, Colo Sch Mines Res Found, 62, res assoc, 64; chmn sect, Am Soc Testing & Mat, 74- *Mem:* Am Soc Testing & Mat; Int Soc Rock Mech; Soc Mining Metall & Explor. *Res:* Rock mechanics research, specifically the behavior of rock materials subjected to static, dynamic and impulse loading; design and stability of underground structures. *Mailing Add:* 380 Christy Dr Rolla MO 65401. *Fax:* 573-341-6934

HAAS, CHARLES NATHAN, WATER, WASTEWATER & HAZARDOUS WASTE TREATMENT, RISK ASSESSMENT. *Current Pos:* BETZ PROF ENVIRON ENG, DREXEL UNIV, 91- *Personal Data:* b Bronx, NY, Dec 27, 51; m 89, Victoria S Benham. *Educ:* Ill Inst Technol, BS, 73, MS, 74; Univ Ill, Urbana, PhD(environ eng), 78. *Honors & Awards:* Octave Charnute Aware, Western Soc Engrs, 84, Charles Ellett Award, 85. *Prof Exp:* Asst prof environ eng, Rensselaer Polytech Inst, 78-81; from asst prof to prof, Ill Inst Technol, 81-90. *Concurrent Pos:* Mem, US Nat Comn, Int Asn Water Qual, 88-; ed, Water Environ Res, 91-95. *Mem:* Asn Environ Eng Profs; Am Soc Civil Engrs; Am Inst Chem Engrs; Am Water Works Asn; Int Asn Water Qual; Water Environ Fedn. *Res:* Disinfection of water and wastewater; removal and recovery of metals from wastes; risk assessment; environmental statistics. *Mailing Add:* 220 Locust St Philadelphia PA 19106

HAAS, DAVID JEAN, ELECTRONIC SECURITY, SECURITY IDENTIFICATION & CREDENTIALS. *Current Pos:* PRES, TEMTEC, INC, 83- *Personal Data:* b Buffalo, NY, Apr 10, 39; m 62; c Stuart, Joel & Alan. *Educ:* State Univ NY, BS, 62, PhD(biophys), 65. *Prof Exp:* Res physicist, US Naval Res Lab, DC, 65-66; asst prof biol, Purdue Univ, 67-70; prin scientist, x-rays & security systs, Philips Electronics, 70-83. *Concurrent Pos:* NIH fel, Davey Faraday Lab, Royal Inst London, 65-66; consult, Radiation Safety, 71- *Mem:* AAAS; Am Soc Indust Security; Am Inst Physics; Am Crystallog Asn. *Res:* Electronic security screening; access control; x-ray imaging for contraband; security identification and credentials. *Mailing Add:* 175 North St Buffalo NY 14201 *Fax:* 914-368-4099

HAAS, FELIX, MATHEMATICS. *Current Pos:* prof & head, Div Math Sci, Purdue Univ, 62, dean, Sch Sci, 62-74, provost, 74-75, exec vpres & provost, 75-86, ARTHUR G HANSEN DISTINGUISHED PROF MATH, PURDUE UNIV, 86- *Personal Data:* b Vienna, Austria, Apr 20, 21; US citizen; m 48, 87; c 3. *Educ:* Mass Inst Technol, BS, 48, MS, 49, PhD(math), 52. *Prof Exp:* Instr math, Lehigh Univ, 52-53; Fine instr, Princeton Univ, 53-55; asst prof math, Univ Conn, 55-56; from asst prof to prof math, Wayne State Univ, 56-62, head dept, 60-62. *Concurrent Pos:* Consult to indust, 52- *Mem:* Am Math Soc. *Res:* Nonlinear differential equations; transformation groups. *Mailing Add:* 3364 Morgan St West Lafayette IN 47906

HAAS, FRANCIS XAVIER, JR, NUCLEAR PHYSICS. *Current Pos:* res specialist, 77-80, sr res specialist, 85-88, ASSOC SCIENTIST, EG&G ROCKY FLATS, 80- *Personal Data:* b Covington, Ky, June 16, 38; m 62, 86; c 5. *Educ:* Xavier Univ, Ohio, BS, 60; St Louis Univ, MS, 62; Univ Cincinnati, PhD(physics), 69. *Prof Exp:* Res physicist, Mound Lab, Monsanto Res Corp, 62-69, sr res physicist, 69-77. *Mem:* Am Phys Soc; Inst Nuclear Mat Mgt; Am Soc Testing & Mat. *Res:* Nuclear materials safeguards research and development; radiometric nondestructive assay. *Mailing Add:* 3333 E Florida Ave #102 Denver CO 80210

HAAS, FRANK C, inorganic chemistry, metallurgy, for more information see previous edition

HAAS, FREDERICK CARL, CHEMICAL & PULP & PAPER ENGINEERING. *Current Pos:* from tech asst to vpres, Fine Papers Div, Westvaco Corp, New York, 68-72, plant mgr, Pa, 72-74, gen mfg mgr, Kraft Div, 74-76, assoc corp res dir, 77-81, vpres, 79-81, SR VPRES, WESTVACO CORP, 82- *Personal Data:* b Buffalo, NY, Feb 16, 36; m 57; c 3. *Educ:* Purdue Univ, BS, 57; Rensselaer Polytech Inst, MS, 59, PhD(chem eng), 60. *Prof Exp:* Assoc chem engr, Cornell Aeronaut Lab, Inc, 60-62, res engr, 62-63; tech asst to corp res dir, WVa Pulp & Paper, 63-64, tech serv supt, 64-66, tech dir, 66-67; asst prof, Potomac State Col, WVa Univ, 67-68. *Concurrent Pos:* Fel, Tech Asn Pulp & Paper Indust, 94. *Mem:* Am Inst Chem Engrs; Am Chem Soc; Can Pulp & Paper Asn; Nat Soc Prof Engrs. *Res:* Heat transfer; fluid mechanics; heat transfer instrumentation; pulp and paper processes; water and air pollution abatement; coatings; research management. *Mailing Add:* 11 Cutler Rd Greenwich CT 06831-2508

HAAS, GERHARD JULIUS, MICROBIOLOGY, BIOCHEMISTRY. *Current Pos:* sr res assoc, 87-92, HON CUR, NY BOT GARDENS, 92-; RES PROF, FAIRLEIGH DICKINSON UNIV, 92- *Personal Data:* b Munich, Ger, Apr 1, 17; nat US; m 59; c 2. *Educ:* Cambridge Univ, BA, 39, MA, 43; Univ Pa, PhD(microbiol), 52. *Honors & Awards:* Indust Scientist Award, Inst Evol Technol, 95. *Prof Exp:* Org chemist, Hoffmann-La Roche, Inc, 43-50; dir res, Liebmann Breweries, 52-60; chief chemist, Desitin Chem Co, 60-61; prin scientist, Gen Foods Corp, 61-87. *Concurrent Pos:* Adj prof, Lehman Col, 87- *Mem:* Am Soc Microbiol; Am Chem Soc; Soc Indust Microbiol; AAAS; Inst Food Technologists. *Res:* Enzymes; food biochemistry; brewery microbiology; yeast; lactobacilli; food preservation; natural preservatives; microbial plant interface; antibiotics. *Mailing Add:* 28 Arcadia Rd Woodcliff Lake NJ 07675-8299

HAAS, GUSTAV FREDERICK, AUDIOLOGY, BIOMEDICAL ENGINEERING. *Current Pos:* DIR, AUDITORY REHAB ENG, 79- *Personal Data:* b Vienna, Austria, June 15, 27; US citizen; div. *Educ:* Yale Univ, BE, 63, ME, 64; Univ Calif, Los Angeles, PhD(sensory systs), 70; Univ Iowa, MA, 80. *Prof Exp:* Prod planner, Westinghouse Elec Corp, 52-54; field engr commun equip, RCA Serv Co, 54-56; field engr optical character recognition, Intelligent Mach Res Corp, 57-59; proj mgr electronic design & mfg, Epsco, Inc, 59-67; scholar, Univ Calif, 70-72; sr staff officer, Comt Prosthetics Res & Develop, Nat Acad Sci, 72-76; res fel, Univ Iowa, 76-78; specialist res audiol, Univ Calif, San Francisco, 78-79. *Concurrent Pos:* Mem res adv comt, Helen Keller Nat Ctr Deaf-Blind Youths & Adults, 74-84, chmn, 78-84; mem adv comt, Gallaudet Col Rehab Eng Ctr, 82-85. *Mem:* Acoust Soc Am; Am Speech & Hearing Asn; Inst Elec & Electronics Engrs; Am Acad Audiology; Am Nat Standards Inst. *Res:* Speech processing schemes for the hearing-impaired; time-varying-parameter electric networks; sensory aids for the deaf and the blind; audiology and hearing aids; special devices for rehabilitation of the hearing-impaired. *Mailing Add:* Auditory Rehab Eng 1230 Hopkins Ave Redwood City CA 94062. *E-Mail:* ghaasaudio@aol.com

HAAS, HERBERT, geochronology, geochemistry, for more information see previous edition

HAAS, HERBERT FRANK, MICROBIOLOGY. *Current Pos:* RETIRED. *Personal Data:* b Kansas City, Kans, Apr 4, 14; m 36, Oma Smith; c Charles D, Susan & Paula. *Educ:* Kans State Col, BS, 38, MS, 40, PhD(bact), 42. *Prof Exp:* Asst chemist, Sinclair Ref Co, 34-35; lab asst, Univ Wis, 38-39 & Kans State Col, 39-42; res assoc, Am Petrol Inst, Calif, 42-43; asst dir biol prod, Richardson-Merrell, Inc, 43-58, dir, Tissue Cult Prod Develop Lab, 58-63, head biol process develop, Jensen-Salsbery Labs, 63-79. *Mem:* Am Soc Microbiol; Soc Cryobiol; Tissue Cult Asn. *Res:* Bacterial utilization of petroleum products; veterinary biological product and process development; mass culture technique; tissue culture; freeze-drying. *Mailing Add:* 1100 Shawnee Rd Kansas City KS 66103

HAAS, HOWARD CLYDE, POLYMER CHEMISTRY. *Current Pos:* RETIRED. *Personal Data:* b New York, NY, Oct 31, 20; m 48, 71; c 4. *Educ:* City Col New York, BS, 41; Polytech Inst Brooklyn, PhD(chem), 49. *Prof Exp:* Res chemist, Gen Foods, Inc, 41-42, 45-46; res assoc, Polytech Inst Brooklyn, 46-48; supvr polymer res, Polaroid Corp, 49-55, mgr dept, 55-67, res fel, 67-82. *Concurrent Pos:* Adv asst, USAF, Off Naval Res & Nat Res Coun; consult, 82- *Mem:* Am Chem Soc. *Res:* Copolymerization; free radicals; kinetics; graft copolymers; ionic polymerization; tacticity; peroxide decomposition kinetics; novel monomers; microencapsulation; rheology; diffusion transfer photography; reversible gelation; gelatin substitutes; light sensitive systems; photoresists; duplication processes; fluoropolymers; polymer membranes; dyeing. *Mailing Add:* 140 Pleasant St Arlington MA 02174-8152

HAAS, JERE DOUGLAS, HUMAN ADAPTABILITY, HUMAN GROWTH & DEVELOPMENT. *Current Pos:* from asst prof to assoc prof, 75-87, DIR, HUMAN BIOL PROG, CORNELL UNIV, 83-, PROF NUTRIT, 87-, CO-DIR, PROG INT NUTRIT, 93-, NANCY SCHLEGEL MEINIG PROF MATERNAL & CHILD NUTRIT, 95- *Personal Data:* b Lancaster, Pa, Sept 15, 45; m 68, Sharon F Pitt; c Jeremy & Andrew. *Educ:* Franklin & Marshall Col, BA, 67; Pa State Univ, MA, 70 & PhD(anthropol), 73. *Prof Exp:* Instr anthropol, Pa State Univ, 72-73; asst prof, Univ Mass, Amherst, 73-75. *Concurrent Pos:* Hon res fel, Dept Anat, Univ Aberdeen, Scotland, 82; vis prof, Food Res Inst, Stanford Univ, 88-89; consult govt, Bolivia, Indonesia, & Philippines; mem, Comt Nutrit During Pregnancy & Lactation, Nat Acad Sci, 88-90 & Expert Com, Nutrit, WHO, 92-97. *Mem:* Fel AAAS; Am Asn Phys Anthropol; Am Inst Nutrit; Am Soc Clin Nutrit; Soc Int Nutrit Res; fel Human Biol Coun; Am Asn Phys Anthropologists (vpres, 92-94, pres 95-97). *Res:* Effects of under-nutrition on fetal, infant and adolescent growth and development of the capacity for reproduction and physical work as adults in populations living in less developed countries. *Mailing Add:* Div Nutrit Sci Savage Hall Cornell Univ Ithaca NY 14853. *E-Mail:* jdh12@cornell.edu

HAAS, JOHN ARTHUR, KIDNEY PHYSIOLOGY, PATHOPHYSIOLOGY. *Current Pos:* res assoc renal physiol, 71-96, TECHNICIAN, MAYO CLIN, 96- *Educ:* Mo Valley Col, BS, 68. *Res:* Renal hormones. *Mailing Add:* Dept Physiol Mayo Clin 901 Guggenheim Bldg Rochester MN 55905-0001

HAAS, JOHN WILLIAM, JR, PHYSICAL CHEMISTRY, HISTORY OF SCIENCE. *Current Pos:* PROF CHEM, GORDON COL, 61-, CHMN, DEPT CHEM, 80- *Personal Data:* b Philadelphia, Pa, Feb 19, 30; m 53, Ann Sutliff; c John III, Ruth & Mary. *Educ:* King's Col, NY, BS, 53; Univ Del, MS, 55, PhD(chem), 58. *Prof Exp:* Assoc prof chem, Grove City Col, 57-61. *Mem:* Am Chem Soc; Am Sci Affiliation; Hist Sci Soc. *Res:* Carbohydrate structure and reactions; chemiluminescence; sugar complexes in seawater; science and religion. *Mailing Add:* Dept Chem Gordon Col 255 Grapevine Rd Wenham MA 01984. *E-Mail:* haas@gordonc.edu

HAAS, KENNETH BROOKS, JR, VETERINARY MEDICINE. *Current Pos:* RETIRED. *Personal Data:* b Pittsburgh, Pa, Jan 14, 28; m 53; c 4. *Educ:* Ohio State Univ, DVM, 49; Western Mich Univ, MA, 61. *Prof Exp:* Vet in charge, small animal hosp, Christensen Animal Hosp, Ill, 49-53; asst vet, Vet Div, Dept Vet Med, Upjohn Co, 53-63 & Int Vet Opers, 63-67, asst vet, Med Serv, 67-91. *Concurrent Pos:* Asst ed, Vet Med, 53. *Mem:* Am Vet Med Asn. *Mailing Add:* 2722 Carlyle Kalamazoo MI 49008

HAAS, LARRY ALFRED, PHYSICAL CHEMISTRY, CHEMICAL METALLURGY. *Current Pos:* RETIRED. *Personal Data:* b Zeeland, NDak, Nov 28, 35; m 59; c 2. *Educ:* Univ SDak, BS, 57; Univ Minn, MS, 64. *Prof Exp:* Res chemist, Honeywell Corp, 57-62; res chemist, US Bur Mines, 62-70, proj leader chem, 70-95. *Mem:* Am Inst Metall Engrs. *Res:* Thermodynamics, kinetics, catalysis, pyrometallurgy, hydrometallurgy, base metal sulfides and sulfur gases. *Mailing Add:* 9518 W Country Club Dr Sun City AZ 85373-1726

HAAS, MARK, MEMBRANE TRANSPORT. *Current Pos:* ASSOC PROF PATH, UNIV CHICAGO, 93- *Personal Data:* b New York, NY, Jan 30, 55. *Educ:* Duke Univ, AB, 77, PhD(physiol) & MD, 82. *Prof Exp:* Res assoc physiol, Duke Univ Med Ctr, 83; resident physician physiol, Yale-New Haven Hosp, 83-85; fel physiol, Sch Med, Yale Univ, 85-86, asst prof path & physiol, 86-89. *Mem:* Biophys Soc; Soc Gen Physiologists; Sigma Xi; Am Asn Pathologists. *Res:* The physiology and biochemistry of ion transport processes, particularly the co-transport system of red blood cell and renal epithelial cell membranes. *Mailing Add:* Dept Path Univ Chicago 5841 S Maryland Ave MC 3083 Chicago IL 60637-1470. *Fax:* 773-702-9903

HAAS, MERRILL WILBER, PETROLEUM GEOLOGY, GEOLOGY APPLIED ECONOMIC & ENGINEERING. *Current Pos:* PETROL CONSULT, 75- *Personal Data:* b Albert, Kans, July 9, 10; m 44, Maria Lura; c Mariella (Allard), Merrill Jr, Murial C (Barnes) & Frederick H. *Educ:* Univ Mich, BA, 32. *Honors & Awards:* Sidney Powers Mem Award, Am Asn Petrol Geologists, 86. *Prof Exp:* Paleontologist, Humble Oil & Refining Co, Tex, 33-34, Lago Petrol Corp, Venezuela, 34-38 & Stand Oil Co Venezuela, 38-41, div geologist, 41-42; div geologist, Creole Petrol Co, 42-49; area geologist, Stand Oil Co NJ & NY, 49-50; chief geologist, Carter Oil Co, Okla, 50-53, explor mgr, 53-56, dir & explor mgr, 56-57, vpres & dir, 57-58; asst coordr, Stand Oil Co NJ & NY, 58-59; vpres & dir, Carter Oil Co, Okla, 59-60; vpres, Humble Oil & Refining Co, 60-73 & Exxon USA, 73-75. *Concurrent Pos:* Chmn, Manpower Comt, Am Geol Inst, 60-67; chmn comt reserves & prod capacity, Am Petrol Inst, 71-74; Merrill W Haaz distinguished vis prof geol, Univ Kans, 73; trustee, Am Asn Petrol Geologists Found, 76-, chmn, 89-91. *Mem:* Am Geol Inst; Hon mem Am Asn Petrol Geologists (pres, 74-75); Geol Soc Am; Paleont Res Inst (pres, 73-75). *Res:* Geology of petroleum deposits; micropaleontology; stratigraphy; structural geology. *Mailing Add:* 10910 Wickwild Houston TX 77024

HAAS, MICHAEL JOHN, BIOCHEMISTRY, MOLECULAR BIOLOGY. *Current Pos:* FEL, MCARDLE LAB CANCER RES, UNIV WIS-MADISON, 92- *Personal Data:* b Denver, Colo, Mar 2, 64; m 86; c 2. *Educ:* Univ Mo, Rolla, BS, 86; Univ Nebr, PhD(biochem), 91. *Prof Exp:* Adj fac chem, Bellevue Col, 91; grad student biochem, Univ Nebr Med Ctr, 86-92. *Mem:* AAAS. *Res:* Examination of the roles of growth factors and tumor suppressor genes on initiation, promotion, and progression of carcinogenesis in the rat liver in both chemically and transgene-induced neoplasia. *Mailing Add:* 6433 Pheasant Lane Middleton WI 53562

HAAS, PAUL ARNOLD, NUCLEAR FUEL CYCLE CONVERSION PROCESSES, NUCLEAR FUEL MATERIALS PREPARATION. *Current Pos:* CONSULT CHEM ENGR, 51- *Personal Data:* b Rolla, Mo, Aug 11, 29; m 58, Betty Turner; c Barry, Janet, Robert & Alan. *Educ:* Univ Mo, Rolla, BS, 50; Mont State Univ, MS, 51; Univ Tenn, PhD(chem eng), 65. *Prof Exp:* Res engr, Oak Ridge Nat Lab, 52-56, group leader, 57-80, sr res engr, 80-94. *Mem:* Fel Am Inst Chem Engrs; Am Chem Soc; Am Nuclear Soc. *Res:* Development of process flowsheets and equipment for nuclear fuel fabrication, uranium conversion processes, waste treatment processes, nuclear fuel cycles, uranium and thorium chemistry, fused salt chemistry and electrolysis. *Mailing Add:* 1205 Chickering Way Knoxville TN 37923-6629. *E-Mail:* phaas88888@aol.com

HAAS, RICHARD, ETHOLOGY, ZOOLOGY. *Current Pos:* RETIRED. *Personal Data:* b New York, NY, July 6, 29; m 52; c 2. *Educ:* Univ Calif, Los Angeles, AB, 50, MA, 58, PhD(zool), 69. *Prof Exp:* Teacher, pub sch, Calif, 55-64; consult, WHO, 64, 78-79, 81 & 84; from asst prof to prof biol, Calif State Univ, Fresno, 69-73. *Concurrent Pos:* Consult, Dept Path, Sch Med, Univ Calif, Los Angeles, 63-64 & USAID, Sri Lanka, 83, WHO, 64-88. *Mem:* AAAS. *Res:* Immune responses to skin heterografts in fishes and amphibia; reproductive ethology of freshwater fishes; biology of cyprinodontid fishes; behavioral isolating mechanisms in sympatric fishes. *Mailing Add:* 5491 N Fruit Fresno CA 93711

HAAS, TERRY EVANS, INORGANIC CHEMISTRY. *Current Pos:* From asst prof to assoc prof, 63-89, chmn dept, 73-79, PROF INORG CHEM, TUFTS UNIV, 89- *Personal Data:* b East Grand Rapids, Mich, Sept 25, 37; m 62; c 2. *Educ:* Mich State Univ, BS, 58; Mass Inst Technol, PhD(inorg chem), 63. *Concurrent Pos:* Vis prof, Univ Alta, 69-70. *Mem:* Electrochem Soc; Am Chem Soc; Mats Res Soc. *Res:* Solid state ionics; thin film materials and processing; structure of coordination compounds. *Mailing Add:* Dept Chem Tufts Univ 62 Talbot Ave Medford MA 02155-5813. *E-Mail:* thaas@pearl.tufts.edu

HAAS, THOMAS J, HAZARDOUS MATERIALS, HIGHER EDUCATION ADMINISTRATION. *Current Pos:* VPRES, ACAD & STUDENT AFFAIRS, DEAN FAC, WILLIAM PENN COL, 96- *Personal Data:* b Staten Island, NY, Mar 5, 51; m 74, Marcia Knapp; c Eric, Gregory & Sarah. *Educ:* USCG Acad, BS, 73; Univ Mich, MS, 76, MS, 77; Rensselaer Polytech Inst, MS, 83; Univ Conn, PhD(chem), 87. *Prof Exp:* Br chief hazardous mat, Coast Guard Hq, Washington, DC, 77-81; from instr to assoc prof chem, USCG Acad, 81-96. *Concurrent Pos:* Asst dean, USCG Acad, 87-91, sect chief, 91-, assoc dean, 93-; vis prof, Univ Conn, 87-, assoc prof chem, 88-96; Yale fel, 91-92; fel, Am Coun Educ, 92-93. *Mem:* Sigma Xi; NY Acad Sci; Am Conf Indust Hygienists; Am Chem Soc. *Res:* Synthesis, properties and reactions of 1.1 metallocenophanes which have shown to have application to solar energy production. *Mailing Add:* 2411 McMullin Dr Oskaloosa IA 52577-1772. *Fax:* 860-444-8627; *E-Mail:* cdr_t_haas@unixlink.uscga.edu

HAAS, TRICE WALTER, PHYSICAL CHEMISTRY. *Current Pos:* res scientist, 64-71, res group leader, Aerospace Res Labs, 71-75, RES GROUP LEADER & RES FEL, WRIGHT LAB, WRIGHT-PATTERSON AFB, DAYTON, 75- *Personal Data:* b Dallas, Tex, July 24, 32; m 55; c 5. *Educ:* St Mary's Univ, Tex, BS, 54; Iowa State Univ, PhD(phys chem), 60. *Prof Exp:* Sr res chemist, Field Res Lab, Socony Mobil Oil Co, Tex, 60-62; sr res chemist, Nat Cash Register Co, Ohio, 62-64. *Mem:* Am Phys Soc; Sigma Xi. *Res:* Physics and chemistry of solid surfaces; low energy electron diffraction; electron spectroscopy; electronic devices and materials; secondary ion mass spectroscopy; thermionic emission; molecular beam epitaxy. *Mailing Add:* 1431 Ticonderoga Ct Dayton OH 45434

HAAS, WARD JOHN, BIOCHEMISTRY. *Current Pos:* PRIN, INNOVATION MGT, 86- *Personal Data:* b New York, NY, Aug 26, 21; m 43, Jane Corya; c Margaret, Jeffrey & Elizabeth. *Educ:* Mass Inst Technol, BS, 43, PhD, 49. *Prof Exp:* Asst biol, Mass Inst Technol, 46-49; biochemist, Grasselli Tech Dept, E I du Pont de Nemours & Co, 49-51; attache, London Embassy, US Foreign Serv, 51-54; asst to dir agr res & develop, Chas Pfizer & Co, 54-56, opers res group, 56-57, asst to pres, 57-60, dir opers, Pfizer Labs Div, 60-64; assoc prof mgt & dir, Space Sci Res Ctr, Univ Mo, Columbia, 64-68; dir, Warner-Lambert Res Inst, 68-70, vpres res & develop, 69-72; vpres corp res & develop, S C Johnson & Son, Inc, 72-75; vpres res & develop, Chesebrough-Ponds Inc, 75-86. *Concurrent Pos:* AAAS/Sloan fel, Off Sci & Technol Pol, Exec Off Pres, 91-92. *Mem:* Am Chem Soc; Am Inst Chem; Sigma Xi; fel AAAS; fel Am Inst Chem. *Res:* Enzymology; spectroscopy biological materials; antibiotics in nutrition; research management; administration; management of innovation. *Mailing Add:* 8313 West Blvd Dr Alexandria VA 22308

HAAS, WERNER E L, LIQUID CRYSTALS, ELECTROOPTICS. *Current Pos:* RETIRED. *Personal Data:* b Magdeburg, Ger, Sept 14, 28; m 61, Maria De Lourdes Campos Andrada; c Rene, George & John. *Educ:* Univ Lisbon, Portugal, Licenciado, 56. *Prof Exp:* From jr eng to proj scientist, Res Div Philco-Ford Co, 58-66; assoc scientist, Xerox Corp, 66-68, scientist, 68-69, sr scientist, 69-73, prin scientist, 73-78, res fel, 78-81, mgr & sr res fel corp res, 81-94. *Mem:* Fel Soc Photog Scientists & Engrs; Electrochem Soc; fel Soc Info Display. *Res:* Optical and electrooptical properties of liquid crystals; non-impact printing technologies; displays and storage devices; electrooptic effects in ferroelectrics and their applications; anodic oxidation and mechanisms of electrolytic rectification. *Mailing Add:* 768 High Tower Way Webster NY 14580

HAAS, ZYGMUNT, PERFORMANCE EVALUATION OF COMMUNICATION NETWORKS, OPTICAL NETWORKS. *Current Pos:* ASSOC PROF ELEC ENG, CORNELL UNIV. *Personal Data:* b Poland, Oct 19, 56; Israeli citizen. *Educ:* Israel Inst Technol, BSc, 79; Tel-Aviv Univ, MSc, 85; Stanford Univ, PhD(elec eng), 88. *Prof Exp:* Engr digital design, Govt Israel, 79-85; res asst comput commun, Stanford Univ, 85-88; mem tech staff commun networks, AT&T Bell Labs, 88- *Concurrent Pos:* Lectr digital design & comput commun, Tel-Aviv Univ, Israel, 82-85. *Mem:* Sr mem Inst Elec & Electronics Engrs. *Res:* Performance evaluation of computer and communication networks, especially optical networks; interconnection networks and switches; multi-media application of traffic characterization and traffic integration; very high-speed networks; high-speed and high-performance protocols, especially transport protocols. *Mailing Add:* PO Box 4556 Ithaca NY 14852

HAASCH, MARY LYNN, AQUATIC TOXICOLOGY, ECOTOXICOLOGY. *Current Pos:* PROF, UNIV MD, CHESAPEAKE BIOL LAB, SOLOMONS ISLAND, 94- *Personal Data:* b Manitowoc, Wis, Apr 30, 54; m 77, James R; c Andrea L. *Educ:* Univ Wis-Oshkosh, BS, 76; Univ Wis-Milwaukee, PhD(biol sci), 89. *Prof Exp:* Res asst prof pharmacol & toxicol, Med Col Wis, 90-94. *Concurrent Pos:* Student travel award, Soc Toxicol, 89; prin investr, Biomed Res Support Grant, 91-93; co-investr, Nat Inst Environ Health Sci, 91-94. *Mem:* Am Soc Microbiol; Am Acad Microbiol; AAAS; Soc Toxicol; Soc Environ Toxicol & Chem. *Res:* Regulation of gene expression; development of biomarkers of environmental chemical contamination; mechanisms of cytochrome P450 induction, ecotoxicology, molecular toxicology, environmental and aquatic toxicology. *Mailing Add:* 44481 Joy Chapel Rd Hollywood MD 20636. *Fax:* 414-778-4289; *E-Mail:* mhaasch@post.its.mcw.edu

HAASE, ASHLEY THOMSON, VIROLOGY. *Current Pos:* PROF MICROBIOL & HEAD DEPT, MED SCH, UNIV MINN, 84- *Personal Data:* b Evanston, Ill, Dec 8, 39; m 62, Ann DeLong; c Elizabeth, Stephanie & Harris. *Educ:* Lawrence Col, BA, 61; Columbia Col Physicians & Surgeons, MD, 65. *Prof Exp:* Intern, Osler Serv, Johns Hopkins Hosp, 65-66, resident, 66-67; clin assoc & sr clin assoc, NIH, 67-70; vis scientist, Nat Inst Med Res, London, 70-71; from asst prof to prof, Dept Med, Univ Calif, San Francisco, 71-84, Dept Microbiol, 74-84. *Concurrent Pos:* Chief, infectious dis, Vet Admin Med Ctr, San Francisco, 71-84, clin investr, 71-78, med investr, 78-84; prof, Dept Med, Univ Minn, 84-; Anna Fuller Found fel; mem adv coun, Nat Inst Allergy & Infectious Dis, NIH, 86-90; chmn AIDS panel, US-Japan Coop Med Sci Progr, 86-93; ed-in-chief, Virol, Microbiol Pathogenesis, 88-94; gov coun biotechnol, Minn, 85-87; investr, Javits Neurosci, 88-96; merit investr, Nat Inst Allergy & Infectious Dis, 89-99; mem, AIDS Res Adv Comt, 93-96, chair, Vaccine Subcomt, 93- *Mem:* Am Soc Microbiol; Am Soc Virol; Infectious Dis Soc Am; Am Soc Clin Investrs; Sigma Xi; Asn Am Physicians. *Res:* The molecular mechanisms of viral pathogenicity as they relate to diseases of the central nervous system (for example, Alzheimer's disease, multiple sclerosis and acquired immune deficiency syndrome). *Mailing Add:* Dept Microbiol Med Sch Univ Minn Box 196 UMHC 420 Del S E Minneapolis MN 55455. *Fax:* 612-626-0623; *E-Mail:* ashley@lenti.med.umn.edu

HAASE, BRUCE LEE, AQUATIC ECOLOGY, FISHERIES. *Current Pos:* assoc prof, 69-74, PROF BIOL, EAST STROUDSBURG UNIV, 74- *Personal Data:* b Napoleon, Ohio, Dec 18, 38; m 73. *Educ:* Concordia Teachers Col, BS, 61; Bowling Green State Univ, MA, 62; Univ Wis, PhD(zool), 69. *Prof Exp:* Teacher, St Peters Lutheran Sch, 59-60; instr biol, Milwaukee Lutheran High Sch, 62-64. *Concurrent Pos:* Consult, Monroe County Planning Comn, 70-; pres, Marine Sci Consortium. *Mem:* Am Fisheries Soc; Am Soc Limnol & Oceanog. *Res:* Flocking behavior of the common crow; life history of the longnose gar; ecology of selected fishes; general ecology of small, shallow lakes; ecology of aquatic insects; marine and freshwater plankton. *Mailing Add:* Dept Biol East Stroudsburg Univ 200 Prospect St East Stroudsburg PA 18301-2999

HAASE, DAVID GLEN, LOW TEMPERATURE PHYSICS. *Current Pos:* from asst prof to assoc prof, 76-87, PROF PHYSICS, NC STATE UNIV, 87- *Personal Data:* b Baton Rouge, La, Dec 6, 48; m 73; c 1. *Educ:* Rice Univ, BA, 70; Duke Univ, MA, 72, PhD(physics), 75. *Prof Exp:* Res asst physics, Duke Univ, 70-75. *Concurrent Pos:* Staff, Triangle Univs Nuclear Lab, 88-; vis prof physics, LA State Univ, 88; vis asst prof, NC State Univ, 75-76. *Mem:* Am Phys Soc; Sigma Xi; Am Asn Physics Teachers. *Res:* Properties of quantum solids; cryogenic polarized targets. *Mailing Add:* Dept Physics NC State Univ Univ Box 8202 Raleigh NC 27695-8202. *E-Mail:* david_haase@ncsu.edu

HAASE, DONALD J(AMES), CHEMICAL ENGINEERING. *Current Pos:* CHIEF EXEC OFFICER, HERR HAASE INC, 86- *Personal Data:* b Gillett, Tex, Apr 18, 38. *Educ:* Univ Tex, Austin, BS, 60, MS, 62, PhD(chem eng), 65. *Prof Exp:* Res scientist, Continental Oil Co, Okla, 64-67; sr chem engr, Tenneco Chem Inc, 67-70, group leader, 70-77, mgr cosorb technol, 77-78, dir separations technol, 80-83; pres, Conejo Chem Co, 83-86. *Mem:* Am Chem Soc; Am Inst Chem Engrs. *Res:* Reaction kinetics of high temperature partial oxidation systems; gas-solid purification processes and the regeneration of the substrates; applications of digital computers to control high temperature oxidation reactions; general separations technology; chemical separations technologies; research and technology management. *Mailing Add:* HCR 2 Box 48 Nixon TX 78140-9207

HAASE, EDWARD FRANCIS, BOTANY, PLANT ECOLOGY. *Current Pos:* head, Dept Smoke Invest, 76-79, land use & reclamation coordr, 79-85, SR ENVIRON ANALYST, PHELPS DODGE CORP, 85- *Personal Data:* b Milwaukee, Wis, Apr 29, 37; m 65, Joann Meister; c Timothy & Julie. *Educ:* Marquette Univ, BS, 59; Univ Wis-Milwaukee, MS, 65; Univ Ariz, PhD(bot), 69. *Prof Exp:* Res ecologist, Southwest Watershed Res Ctr, Agr Res Serv, 69-70; res assoc & asst prof arid land resources, Off Arid Lands Studies, Univ Ariz, 70-76. *Mem:* AAAS; Air & Waste Mgt Asn. *Res:* Arid lands plant ecology; ecology; utilization of native desert plants; air pollution effects on vegetation; reclamation of surface mined areas; environmental regulation effects on copper mining, milling, smelting and refining. *Mailing Add:* 13420 N 82nd St Scottsdale AZ 85260

HAASE, GUNTER R, neurology, for more information see previous edition

HAASE, JAN RAYMOND, PHOTOGRAPHIC CHEMISTRY. *Current Pos:* LAB HEAD ORG CHEM, EASTMAN KODAK CO RES LABS, 67- *Personal Data:* b Buffalo, NY, June 24, 41; m 63; c 2. *Educ:* State Univ NY Buffalo, BA, 63; NY Univ, PhD(org chem), 68. *Prof Exp:* Chemist, Tech Serv Lab, Union Carbide Corp, 63-64. *Mem:* Am Chem Soc. *Res:* Design and synthesis of organic image forming materials for color photographic applications with emphasis on image dyes. *Mailing Add:* Nine White Birch Circle Rochester NY 14624-3921

HAASE, OSWALD, SOLID STATE PHYSICS. *Current Pos:* prof, 64-90, EMER PROF PHYSICS, FAIRLEIGH DICKINSON UNIV, 90- *Personal Data:* b Berlin, Ger, Oct 4, 25. *Educ:* Univ Hamburg, BSc, 52, MSc, 55, PhD(physics), 60. *Prof Exp:* Mem tech staff res physics, Bell Tel Labs, Inc, 60-62. *Res:* Electron diffraction; thin films and surfaces; epitaxy; oxidation; electron microscopy of lattice defects; x-ray; structure of liquids; diffraction contrast of dislocations in crystals; corrosion; applied optics, light scattering in glass. *Mailing Add:* Dept Physics Fairleigh Dickinson Univ 1000 River Rd Teaneck NJ 07666

HAASE, RICHARD HENRY, APPLIED STATISTICS. *Current Pos:* RETIRED. *Personal Data:* b Cleveland, Ohio, Feb 27, 24; m 51; c 3. *Educ:* Purdue Univ, BS, 45; Tulane Univ, MBA, 49; Univ Calif, Los Angeles, PhD(eng), 61. *Prof Exp:* Design engr, Convair Corp, Calif, 46-47; from appln engr to dist engr, Lamp Div, Gen Elec Co, 47-51; lectr & asst head eng exten, Univ Calif, Los Angeles, 51-61; mem tech staff, Rand Corp, 61-65; systs engr, Missile & Space Div, Gen Elec Co, 65-67; prof statist & chmn dept, Drexel Univ, 67-87. *Concurrent Pos:* Consult, Missile & Space Div, Gen Elec Co, Pa, Ford Motor Co, Campbell Soup Co, Mrs Smith's Frozen Foods, 67- *Mem:* Am Inst Decision Sci; Sigma Xi. *Res:* Applied statistics and decision theory as applied to management decision making in business; innovative education; statistical process control. *Mailing Add:* 3422 SW Bobalink Way Palm City FL 34990

HAASER, NORMAN BRAY, applied mathematics, for more information see previous edition

HAAVELMO, TRYGVE, ECONOMICS. *Current Pos:* prof, 48-79, EMER PROF ECON, UNIV OSLO, 79- *Personal Data:* b Skedsmo, Norway, Dec 13, 11. *Educ:* Univ Oslo, PhD, 46. *Honors & Awards:* Nobel Prize in Econs, 89. *Prof Exp:* Res asst, Cowles Comn, Univ Chicago, 45-46; staff, Norweg Trade Comn, Oslo. *Mem:* Am Econ Asn; Am Acad Arts & Lett. *Mailing Add:* Univ Oslo PO Box 1072 Blindern Oslo 0316 Norway

HAAVIK, CORYCE OZANNE, PHARMACOLOGY. *Current Pos:* asst prof, 71-77, ASSOC PROF PHARMACOL, MED COL WIS, 78-, ASSOC DEAN RES & GRAD STUDIES, 78- *Personal Data:* b St Paul, Minn, Sept 20, 33. *Educ:* Bryn Mawr Col, BA, 54; Univ Wis, PhD(pharmacol), 65. *Prof Exp:* Res assoc, Sch Med, Yale Univ, 54-57; res asst, Univ Tex Southwestern Med Sch, Dallas, 57-59; instr pharmacol, Sch Pharm, Univ Wis, 64-65, asst prof, 65-71. *Mem:* AAAS; Am Soc Pharmacol & Exp Therapeut. *Res:* Cardiovascular and hypothermic effects of tetrahydracannabinol and analogs. *Mailing Add:* Dept Pharmacol Med Col Wis PO Box 26509 Milwaukee WI 53226-0509. *Fax:* 414-266-8460

HABAL, MUTAZ, SURGICAL ONCOLOGY, TRANSATOLOGY. *Current Pos:* prof surg, 78-80, RES PROF MAT SCI, UNIV SFLA, 80- *Personal Data:* b Damascus, Syria, Apr 27, 38; US citizen; m 64, Randa; c Rula & M Bassam. *Educ:* Am Univ Beirut, Lebanon, BS, 59; Am Univ Med, Beirut, MD, 64; Suny Buffalo, MD, 69; Harvard Univ, MD, 72. *Hon Degrees:* Royal Col Surgeons, Can, FRCSC, 74. *Prof Exp:* Asst Prof Surg, Clin Ctr Ind, 72-74; assoc prof surg, Cin develop Fla, 74-78. *Concurrent Pos:* Dir, Tampa Bay Craniofacial Ctr. *Mem:* Am Col Surgeons; Am Acad Pediat; Am Cleft Palate Assoc; Soc Univ Surgeons; Am Soc Plastic Surgeons; Sigma Xi. *Res:* Bone graft induction, utilizing the basic principles for major reconstruction; clinical investigation, the long term follow up research. *Mailing Add:* 6358 MacLaurin Dr Tampa FL 33647-1164. *Fax:* 813-238-1119

HABASHI, FATHI, METALLURGY. *Current Pos:* PROF METALL, LAVAL UNIV, 70- *Personal Data:* b Minia, Egypt, Oct 9, 28; m 58, 82, Nadia Boulos; c Hani & Hatem. *Educ:* Univ Cairo, BSc, 49; Vienna Tech Univ, Dr Technol(inorg chem), 59. *Hon Degrees:* Dsc, St Petersburg Mining Inst, Russia. *Prof Exp:* Supvr, Fertilizer Factory, Suez, UAR, 49-52 & Misr Cotton Mills, Mahalla Kobra, 52-53; asst dir, Munic Chem Lab, Alexandria, 53-56; res fel chem, Vienna, 59-60; fel, Dept Mines & Tech Surv, Ottawa, 60-62; asst ed, Chem Abstr, 63-64; assoc prof metall, Mont Sch Mines, 64-67; sr res engr, Extractive Metall Res Div, Anaconda Co, Ariz, 67-70. *Concurrent Pos:* consult, UN Develop Prog, Cuban Laterite Proj, 89, Fac Metall, Kosice, Czech, 91, Sch Chem, Fed Univ Rio de Janeiro, 92, Nat Univ San Luis, Argentina, 92, Cath Univ N, Antofagasta, Chile, 92, Univ Sonora, Hermosillo, Mex, Inst Technol, Bandung, Indonesia & Univ Port Elizabeth, SAfrica, 93, Univ Rome, Italy, 96; guest lectr, Mining Res Ctr, Havana, 87; academicia, Russian Acad Sci, 94. *Mem:* Am Chem Soc; Can Inst Mining, Metall & Petroleum; Am Inst Mining, Metall & Petrol Engrs; Soc Mining Engrs; Minerals, Metals & Mats Soc; Am Inst Mining Engrs; Chem Inst Can. *Res:* Extractive metallurgy; extraction of uranium and lanthanides from phosphate rock; kinetics of metallurgical processes; chalcopyrite chemistry and metallurgy; mineral resources of Arab countries; chemical reactions of asbestos; history of metallurgy; pollution problems. *Mailing Add:* Dept Mining & Metall Univ Laval Cite Univ Quebec PQ G1K 7P4 Can. *Fax:* 418-656-5343

HABASHI, WAGDI GEORGE, COMPUTATIONAL FLUID DYNAMICS, TRANSONIC AERODYNAMICS & TURBOMACHINERY. *Current Pos:* from asst prof to assoc prof, 75-84, PROF MECH ENG, CONCORDIA UNIV, 84- *Personal Data:* b Egypt, June 29, 46; Can citizen; m 67; c Jenny, Stephanie & Andrew. *Educ:* McGill Univ, BE, 67, ME, 69; Cornell Univ, PhD(aerospace), 75. *Honors & Awards:* Cray Gigaflop Award, 90; Synergy Award, Am Inst Aeronaut & Astronaut. *Prof Exp:* Asst prof mech eng, Stevens Inst Technol, 74-75. *Concurrent Pos:* Aerodyn consult, Pratt & Whitney, Can, 77-; dir, Indust Ctr Res Comput & Applns; prof, Dept Mech Eng, Can Univ; E W R Steacie Mem fel sci achievement, Nat Sci & Eng Res Coun, Can, 88-89. *Mem:* Assoc fel Am Inst Aeronaut & Astronaut; Am Soc Mech Engrs; Sigma Xi; NY Acad Sci. *Res:* Numerical methods for the analysis and design of aerodynamic components in transonic flow; design of transonic turbomachinery. *Mailing Add:* Mech Eng Dept Concordia Univ 1455 de Maisonneuve Blvd W Montreal PQ H3G 1M8 Can. *Fax:* 514-369-3880; *E-Mail:* cfdlab@cfdmac.concordia.ca

HABAYEB, ABDUL RAZZAQ, SYSTEM INTEGRATION, SYSTEM PARTITIONING. *Current Pos:* tactical avionics mgr, 68-81, GUIDANCE & CONTROL TECHNOL MGR, SYSTS ENG, NAVAL AIR SYST COMMAND, 68- *Personal Data:* b Tulkarm, Palestine, Oct 10, 32; US citizen; m 72, Randa Abughazaleh; c Tarik, Juman, Samah & Donya. *Educ:* Kans State Univ, BSc, 56; Univ Kans, MSc, 59, PhD(elec eng), 63. *Prof Exp:* Network design engr, Collins Radio, 56-57; sr sci adv, ITT Indust Lab, 63-66; sr scientist, ARINC Res, 66-68. *Concurrent Pos:* Sr design engr, Honeywell, 60; sr analyst, Allis Chalmer, 62; adj prof, Purdue Univ, 64-66, George Washington Univ, 81 & 89-, Univ Md, 93 & 94. *Mem:* Inst Elec & Electronics

Engrs; Sigma Xi. *Res:* Systems effectiveness; principles of system engineering; system design, architecture, integration, synthesis, partitioning and effectiveness analysis; application of systems science to organizational design; application of system engineering to the design of computer-integrated manufacturing; granted 8 patents. *Mailing Add:* 8201 Falstaff Rd McLean VA 22102

HABBAL, SHADIA RIFAI, SPACE PLASMA PHYSICS. *Current Pos:* PHYSICIST, SMITHSONIAN ASTROPHYS OBSERV, 82- *Personal Data:* b Damascus, Syria, Sept 30, 48; m 70; c 2. *Educ:* Damascus Univ, BS(math) & BS(physics), 70; Am Univ Beirut, MS, 73; Univ Cincinnati, PhD(physics), 77. *Prof Exp:* Fel solar physics, Nat Ctr Atmospheric Res, 77-78; res fel physics, Harvard Col Observ, 78-79, res assoc, 79-82. *Mem:* Am Phys Soc; Am Geophys Union; Asn Women Sci; Am Astron Soc; Int Astron Union. *Res:* Solar physics; space plasma physics. *Mailing Add:* Harvard-Smithsonian Ctr Astrophys 60 Garden St Cambridge MA 02138

HABECK, DALE HERBERT, ENTOMOLOGY. *Current Pos:* RETIRED. *Personal Data:* b Bonduel, Wis, Oct 21, 31; m 59, Phyllis Pake; c Michael. *Educ:* Univ Wis, BS, 53, MS, 54; NC State Univ, PhD(entom), 59. *Prof Exp:* Asst entomologist, Exp Sta, Univ Hawaii, 59-63; from asst entomologist to assoc entomologist, Univ Fla, 63-73, prof entom, 73-96. *Concurrent Pos:* Pres, Bd Dirs Am Entom Inst. *Mem:* Entom Soc Am. *Res:* Biology and immature stages of Lepidoptera; biological control of weeds. *Mailing Add:* Dept Entom Univ Fla Gainesville FL 32611. *Fax:* 904-392-0190

HABECK, JAMES ROBERT, ECOLOGY. *Current Pos:* from asst prof to assoc prof, 60-69, PROF BOT, UNIV MONT, 69- *Personal Data:* b Ashland, Wis, June 3, 32; m 57; c 2. *Educ:* Univ Wis, BS, 54, MA, 56, PhD(bot), 59. *Prof Exp:* Instr biol, Ore Col Educ, 59-60. *Mem:* Ecol Soc Am. *Res:* Phytosociology and dendrochronology; fire ecology; planning uses for fire in forest and wildlife range systems; designing and fulfilling a research natural area system; ecological baseline monitoring. *Mailing Add:* 200 Agnes Ave Missoula MT 59801

HABEEB, AHMED FATHI SAYED AHMED, PROTEIN CHEMISTRY, IMMUNOLOGY. *Current Pos:* PROF BIOCHEM, MED SCI CAMPUS, UNIV PR, 77- *Personal Data:* b Gerga, Egypt, Apr 10, 28; US citizen; m 74, Magda. *Educ:* Univ Cairo, BPharm, 48; Univ London, PhD(pharmaceut), 54, DSc(protein struct & immunol), 76. *Prof Exp:* Fel chem, Yale Univ, 56-58; fel biol, Div Appl Biol, Nat Res Coun Can, 58-60; sr res asst microbiol, Connaught Med Res Labs, Univ Toronto, 60-62; sr cancer res scientist clin biochem, Roswell Park Mem Inst, 62-65; asst prof microbiol, Univ Tenn, 65-68; asst prof, Lab Immunol, St Jude Children's Hosp, 65-68; assoc prof microbiol, Med Ctr, Univ Ala, Birmingham, 68-77. *Mem:* NY Acad Sci; Am Asn Immunol; Am Soc Biol Chemists; Am Soc Trop Med & Hyg. *Res:* Protein structure, isolation and characterization; chemical modification of proteins, antibodies and toxins; Clostridium perfringens antigens; immunochemical studies on S mansoni. *Mailing Add:* Dept Biochem & Nutrit Med Sci Campus Univ PR GPO Box 5067 San Juan PR 00936-5067

HABEL, ROBERT EARL, VETERINARY ANATOMY, ANATOMY OF RUMINANTS. *Current Pos:* from asst prof to prof, 47-78, head dept, 60-75, EMER PROF VET ANAT, NY STATE COL VET MED, CORNELL UNIV, 78- *Personal Data:* b Toledo, Ohio, Aug 8, 18; m 42, Wilma J Fulks; c Stephanie A (Shaw) (deceased) & Gareth R. *Educ:* Ohio State Univ, DVM, 41, MSc, 47; Univ Utrecht, MVD(vet anat), 56. *Honors & Awards:* Outstanding Achievement Award, Am Asn Vet Anatomists, 88. *Prof Exp:* Vet, Bur Animal Indust, USDA, Pa, 41-42; co vet, Fulton Co Bd Health, Ohio, 42; first Lt-Capt, US Army Vet Corps, 43-46; instr vet embryol, histol & anat, Ohio State Univ, 46-47. *Concurrent Pos:* NIH res grant, Univ Utrecht, 53-54; vchmn, Int Comt Vet Anat Nomenclature, 63-80 & chmn, 80-86; fel, Nat Libr Med, NIH, Anat Inst, Vet Col, Vienna, 67-68 & 75-76; vis prof vet anat, Univ Utrecht, 79 & Univ Sydney, 81. *Mem:* Am Vet Med Asn; Am Asn Anatomists; Am Asn Vet Anatomists (pres, 64-65); World Asn Vet Anatomists (pres, 71-75); Europ Asn Vet Anatomists. *Res:* Applied veterinary anatomy; ruminant anatomy; anatomy of the digestive system; microscopic anatomy of domestic animals; comparative medical anatomy; anatomical nomenclature. *Mailing Add:* Dept Anat NY State Col Vet Med Ithaca NY 14853. *Fax:* 607-253-3541

HABENER, JOEL FRANCIS, ENDOCRINOLOGY. *Current Pos:* res fel, 69-71, from instr to assoc prof, 71-89, PROF MED, HARVARD MED SCH, 89- *Personal Data:* b Indianapolis, Ind, June 29, 37; m 62. *Educ:* Univ Redlands, BS, 60; Univ Calif, Los Angeles, MD, 65; Am Bd Internal Med, dipl. *Prof Exp:* From intern to asst resident med & fel, Johns Hopkins Hosp, 65-67; res assoc endocrinol & surgeon, NIH, 67-69. *Concurrent Pos:* Assoc physician, Mass Gen Hosp, 76-, chief, Lab Molecular Endocrinol; USPHS res career develop award, 72-75; investr, Howard Hughes Med Inst, 76- *Mem:* Am Fedn Clin Res; Endocrine Soc; Am Soc Clin Invest; Am Soc Biol Chemists; Am Soc Bone & Bone Mineral Res; Asn Am Physicians. *Res:* Investigations of the molecular biochemistry of peptide hormone synthesis and secretion. *Mailing Add:* Lab Molecular Endocrinol Mass Gen Hosp Boston MA 02114-2698. *Fax:* 617-726-6954

HABENSCHUSS, ANTON, POLYMER PHYSICS. *Current Pos:* res assoc chem eng, 78-80, RES SCIENTIST, OAK RIDGE NAT LAB, OAK RIDGE ASSOC UNIV, 80- *Personal Data:* b Ruma, Yugoslavia, June 1, 44; US citizen. *Educ:* Kent State Univ, BS, 66; Iowa State Univ, PhD(phys chem), 73. *Prof Exp:* Res assoc chem, Iowa State Univ, Ames, 73-78 & Univ Del, 78-80. *Mem:* Am Chem Soc; Sigma Xi; AAAS; Am Phys Soc. *Res:* Polymer chemistry; transport properties; x-ray diffraction; aqueous electrolyte solutions; rare earth solution chemistry; structure of simple fluids; synchrotron radiation; Thermodynamics. *Mailing Add:* Oak Ridge Nat Lab PO Box 2008 Oak Ridge TN 37831-6197

HABER, ALAN HOWARD, RADIATION BOTANY, PLANT PHYSIOLOGY. *Current Pos:* chmn dept, 73-83, PROF BIOL SCI, STATE UNIV NY, BINGHAMTON, 73-; MASTER HINMAN COL, 85- *Personal Data:* b Chicago, Ill, Apr 1, 30; m 56; c 4. *Educ:* Calif Inst Technol, BS, 53; Univ Wis, PhD(bot), 56. *Prof Exp:* Asst, Univ Wis, 53-56; biologist, Oak Ridge Nat Lab, Tenn, 56-73. *Concurrent Pos:* Proj mgr, Elec Power Res Inst, 79-80. *Mem:* AAAS; Radiation Res Soc. *Res:* Radiation biology. *Mailing Add:* Dept Biol Sci State Univ NY-Binghamton PO Box 6000 Binghamton NY 13902-6000

HABER, BERNARD, BIOCHEMISTRY. *Current Pos:* asst biochem & neurol, 70-72, ASSOC PROF HUMAN BIOL CHEM, GENETICS & NEUROL, UNIV TEX MED BR GALVESTON, 72-, CHIEF NEUROCHEM SECT, DIV COMP NEUROBIOL, MARINE BIOMED INST, 70- *Personal Data:* b Lodz, Poland, July 20, 34; US citizen; m 59. *Educ:* McGill Univ, BSc, 56, MSc, 57, PhD(biochem), 62. *Prof Exp:* Res assoc neuropharmacol, Res Lab, Galesburg State Res Hosp, Ill, 62-64; assoc res scientist neurochem, Div Neurosci, City of Hope Med Ctr, Calif, 65-70. *Concurrent Pos:* Ed-in-chief, J Neurosci Res, 79- *Mem:* AAAS; Am Soc Neurochem; Int Soc Neurochem; Am Soc Biol Chem; Int Brain Res Orgn; Sigma Xi. *Res:* Transport of amino acids and sugars; biogenic amines, purification of brain enzymes related to neurotransmitters and their localization in situ; tissue culture of neurons and glia; cellular communication; muscular distrophy, tumor neovascularization; biochemistry of human head injury; mechanisms of central excitation and inhibition. *Mailing Add:* Marine Biomed Inst Univ Tex Med Br 301 University Blvd Galveston TX 77555-1069. *Fax:* 409-772-2920

HABER, EDGAR, IMMUNOLOGY, CARDIOVASCULAR DISEASES. *Current Pos:* from instr to prof, 63-68, CLIN PROF MED, HARVARD MED SCH, 90-; PHYSICIAN, MASS GEN HOSP, 69-; ELKAN R BLOUT PROF BIOL SCI, HARVARD SCH PUB HEALTH, 91- *Personal Data:* b Berlin, Ger, Feb 1, 32; US citizen; m 58, Carol Avery; c Justin A, Graham S & Eben M. *Educ:* Columbia Univ, AB, 52, MD, 56; Univ Oxford, MA, 91; Am Bd Internal Med, dipl. *Hon Degrees:* AM, Harvard Univ, 68. *Honors & Awards:* Franz Volhard Award, Int Soc Hypertension, 80; Otsulca Award Outstanding Res, Int Soc Heart Res, 85; Res Achievement Award, Am Heart Asn, 86; CIBA Award Hypertension Res, Coun High Blood Pressure Res, Am Heart Asn, 89; Distinguished Scientist Award, Am Col Cardiol, 91; Various named lectr from various univs & asns, 73-90. *Concurrent Pos:* Lab res with C Anfinsen, NIH, 58-61; hon clin asst, Cardiac Dept, St George's Hosp & Nat Heart Hosp, London, Eng, 62-63; asst, Mass Gen Hosp, Boston, 63-64 chief cardiac Unit , 64-88 & asst physician, 65-68; mem study sect allergy & immunol, NIH, 65-68; fel coun clin cardiol, Am Heart Asn, 66, mem prog , 66-68, mem exec comn, 68-76, mem res study comn physiol & pharm, 69-72, mem res comt, 70-76 & chmn adult & pediat cardiol res study comn, 70-72, vpres res & chmn res comt, 73-74; vchmn panel on heart & blood vessel dis, Nat Heart Act of 72, NIH, 72-73; mem task force on immunol & dis, Nat Inst Allergy & Infectious Dis, 72-73; mem tissue & organ biol interdisciplinary cluster, President's Biomed Res Panel, 75; mem US deleg, US-USSR Health Exchange; mem ed bd, Clin Immunol & Immunopath, 71-89, Herz, 80-, Hybridoma, 80-, J Hypertense, 82-88; vis prof, Univ Tex, Dallas, 82; Univ Queensland, Brisbane, 85; Stanford Univ, 85; Univ Calif Los Angles, 87 & State Univ NY, Syracuse, 87; mem, Working Group Arteriosclerosis, Nat Heart, Lung & Blood Inst, 78-81 & Comt Frontiers in Basic Sci, 86-; trustee, Life Sci Res Found, 88-; pres, Bristol Myers Squibb Pharm Res Inst, 88-91. *Mem:* Inst Med-Nat Acad Sci; Am Soc Clin Invest; Asn Am Physicians; Asn Univ Cardiol (vpres, 79-80, pres, 80-81); Am Asn Immunol; London Royal Soc Med; fel AAAS; Am Soc Biol Chem; fel Am Acad Arts & Sci. *Res:* Protein chemistry; immunochemistry; cardiology. *Mailing Add:* Dept Biol Sci Harvard Sch Pub Health 677 Huntington Ave Boston MA 02115

HABER, FRED, ELECTRICAL ENGINEERING. *Current Pos:* from instr to prof, 51-87, EMER PROF ELEC ENG, MOORE SCH ELEC ENG, UNIV PA, 87- *Personal Data:* b New York, NY, July 1, 21; m 48, Esther Gershman; c Jill & Carl. *Educ:* Pa State Univ, BS, 48; Univ Pa, MS, 53, PhD(elec eng), 60. *Prof Exp:* Elec engr, Arma Corp, 48 & Radio Corp Am, 48-51. *Concurrent Pos:* Elec engr, Gen Precision, Inc, 62-63; vis prof, Pahlavi Univ, Shiraz, Iran, 68, Eindhoven Univ Technol, Neth, 83-84, Delft Univ Technol, Neth, 87-88. *Mem:* Fel Inst Elec & Electronics Engrs; Sigma Xi. *Res:* Electrical communications theory; modulation systems; statistical methods; interference; effects of electrical noise; sensor array processing. *Mailing Add:* 11060 180th Ct S Boca Raton FL 33498. *E-Mail:* haber@pender.ee.upenn.edu

HABER, HOWARD ELI, THEORETICAL ELEMENTARY PARTICLE PHYSICS. *Current Pos:* asst res physicist, Dept Physics, Univ Calif, Santa Cruz, 82-84, adj asst prof, 84-88, from asst prof to assoc prof, 88-90, PROF, DEPT PHYSICS, UNIV CALIF, SANTA CRUZ, 90- *Personal Data:* b Brooklyn, NY, Feb 3, 52; m, Marjorie Gorker. *Educ:* Mass Inst Technol, SB & SM, 73; Univ Mich, PhD(physics), 78. *Prof Exp:* Comput programmer, Math Lab, Educ Res Ctr, Mass Inst Technol, 72-73; teaching & res physics, Univ Mich, 73-78; fel theoret physics, Lawrence Berkeley Lab, 78-80 & Univ Pa, 80-82. *Concurrent Pos:* Vis physicist, Theoret Physics Group, Stanford Linear Accelerator Ctr, 82-; Outstanding Jr Investr, Dept Energy, 85-88. *Mem:* fel Am Phys Soc; Am Asn Physics Teachers; Sigma Xi. *Res:* High energy physics, theory and phenomenology, especially models of electroweak interactions and grand unification, phenomenology of Higgs particles; low-energy supersymmetry, searches for physics beyond the Standard Model at present and future colliders; field theory at finite temperature and density. *Mailing Add:* Dept Physics Univ Calif Santa Cruz CA 95064. *Fax:* 408-459-3043; *E-Mail:* haber@scipp.ucsc.edu

HABER, IRVING, PLASMA PHYSICS-ACCELERATORS. *Current Pos:* RES PHYSICIST, NAVAL RES LAB, 69- *Personal Data:* b Brooklyn, NY, 1940. *Educ:* Cooper Union BSEE, 61; Polytech Univ, MS, 67, PhD(electro-physics), 69. *Mem:* Am Phys Soc; Inst Elec & Electronics Engrs. *Mailing Add:* 1209 N Belgrade Rd Silver Spring MD 20902

HABER, JAMES EDWARD, MOLECULAR GENETICS. *Current Pos:* From asst prof to assoc prof,72-80, PROF BIOL, DEPT BIOL & ROSENTIEL BASIC MED SCI RES CTR, BRANDEIS UNIV, 80- *Personal Data:* b Pittsburgh, Pa, Feb 23, 43; m 65; c 2. *Educ:* Harvard Col, AB, 65; Univ Calif, Berkeley, PhD(biochem), 69. *Concurrent Pos:* NSF fel, 70. *Mem:* Am Soc Microbiol; Genetics Soc Am; Am Soc Biol Chemists; Am Soc Cell Biol. *Res:* Genetic and biochemical controls of meiosis and cell differentiation, in the yeast Saccharomyces cerevisiae; control of mating type interconversion; regulation of nucleic acid and protein synthesis. *Mailing Add:* Rosenstiel Ctr Brandeis Univ Waltham MA 02254-9110. *Fax:* 781-736-2405

HABER, LYNNE TRACEY, GENETIC TOXICOLOGY, BACTERIAL DNA REPAIR. *Current Pos:* SR ASSOC, CLEMENT INT, 91- *Personal Data:* b Anaheim, Calif, Dec 14, 61. *Educ:* Univ Calif, Los Angeles, BS, 83; Mass Inst Technol, PhD(biol), 90. *Prof Exp:* Staff scientist, Ill Legis Res Unit, 90-91. *Mem:* AAAS; Sigma Xi. *Res:* Genetic toxicology; critical evaluation of human and animal toxicity data to determine the human health effects, and to derive regulatory values for government agencies. *Mailing Add:* 6903 Hutchison St Falls Church VA 22043-1638

HABER, MERYL H, PATHOLOGY. *Current Pos:* prof clin path, 81-85, UNIV LECTR, NORTHWESTERN UNIV MED SCH, 85-; PROF PATH, RUSH UNIV, 82- *Personal Data:* b Cleveland, Ohio, Dec 28, 34; wid; c 3. *Educ:* Northwestern Univ, BS, 56, MS, 58, MD, 59; Am Bd Path, dipl anat, path, 64 & clin path, 65. *Prof Exp:* Instr path, Med Sch, Northwestern Univ, 63-66; from assoc prof to prof, Sch Med, Univ Hawaii, Manoa, 66-73; dir continuing med educ, Sch Med, Univ Nev, Reno, 74-76, prof lab med & chmn dept, 73-80, med dir, Med Technol Prog, 73-80; consult labs, Vet Admin Hosp, 73-80. *Concurrent Pos:* USPHS fel path, Northwestern Univ, 60-64; USPHS fel, Univ Col, Univ London & Wellcome Assoc, Royal Soc Med, 61-62; head, Dept Anat Path, Passavant Mem Hosp, Chicago, 64-66; dir labs, St Francis Hosp, Honolulu, 66-73; vchmn adv coun, Am Soc Clin Pathologists, 72-77, chmn, 77-, dep comnr for regional progs, 73-; dir, CME, Rush Univ, 87- *Mem:* AAAS; Col Am Path. *Res:* Renal disease; urinalysis. *Mailing Add:* Rush Univ Med Col 600 S Paulina St Chicago IL 60612-3832

HABER, MICHAEL J, BIOSTATISTICS. *Current Pos:* assoc prof, Dept Statist & Biometry, Emory Univ, Atlanta, 83-88, Div Biostatist, Dept Epidemiol & Biostatist, 88-90, Sch Pub Health, 90-92, PROF, DEPT BIOSTATIST, ROLLINS SCH PUB HEALTH, EMORY UNIV, ATLANTA, 92- *Personal Data:* b Ramat-Gan, Israel, Oct 3, 43; m 70, Penina Israel; c Edith & Sharon. *Educ:* Hebrew Univ, Jerusalem, BSc, 65, MSc, 68, PhD(statist), 76. *Prof Exp:* Chief statistician, Div Epidemiol, Ministry Health, Jerusalem, 68-69; lectr, Dept Statist, Univ Haifa, Israel, 76-79; from asst prof to assoc prof, Dept Math Sci, Memphis State Univ, 80-83. *Concurrent Pos:* Vis asst prof, Dept Statist, Univ Waterloo, Ont, Can, 79-80; actg/interim chair & dir grad studies, Dept Biostatist, Emory Univ, 94; Fulbright scholar, London Sch Hyg & Trop Med, 95. *Mem:* Am Statist Asn; Biometric Soc. *Res:* Biostatistics; categorical data analysis; statistical models and methods for infectious diseases and vaccine effects; author of numerous publications. *Mailing Add:* Dept Biostatist Sch Pub Health Emory Univ 1518 Clifton Rd NE Atlanta GA 30322. *Fax:* 404-727-1370; *E-Mail:* mhaber@sp.emory.edu

HABER, ROBERT MORTON, MATHEMATICS. *Current Pos:* RETIRED. *Personal Data:* b Cleveland, Ohio, June 8, 32. *Educ:* Ohio State Univ, BSc, 53, MA, 55, PhD(math), 58. *Prof Exp:* From instr to asst prof math, Univ Ill, 58-61; asst prof, Case Inst Technol, 61-65; assoc prof math, Wright State Univ, 65-86. *Res:* Combinatorial analysis. *Mailing Add:* 36065 Pepper Dr Cleveland OH 44139-2444

HABER, SEYMOUR, NUMERICAL ANALYSIS. *Current Pos:* prof, 87-96, EMER PROF, TEMPLE UNIV, PHILADELPHIA, PA, 97- *Personal Data:* b Brooklyn, NY, Oct 7, 29; m 54, Blossom Delman; c 4. *Educ:* Yeshiva Univ, BA, 50; Syracuse Univ, MA, 51; Mass Inst Technol, PhD(math), 54. *Prof Exp:* Asst, Syracuse Univ, 50-51 & Mass Inst Technol, 51-54; res assoc math, Courant Inst Math Sci, NY Univ, 54-55; asst prof, Bar-Ilan Univ, Israel, 55-56; mathematician, Weizmann Inst, 56-57; from instr to assoc prof math, Polytech Inst Brooklyn, 57-60; mathematician, Nat Bur Stand, 60-87. *Concurrent Pos:* Vis Prof, Univ Md, Baltimore Co, 70-71 & Temple Univ, Philadelphia, 83-84; Fulbright-Hayes sr fel, Hebrew Univ Jerusalem, 73-74. *Mem:* Am Math Soc; Soc Indust & Appl Math; Math Asn Am. *Res:* Numerical quadrature; numerical analysis; function theory. *Mailing Add:* Temple Univ Philadelphia PA 19122. *E-Mail:* shaber@vm.temple.edu

HABER, SONJA B, HUMAN FACTORS, EXPERIMENTAL PSYCHOLOGY. *Current Pos:* Res assoc pop genetics, Brookhaven Nat Lab, 76-78, asst scientist, 78-80, assoc scientist, 80-84, SCIENTIST, BROOKHAVEN NAT LAB, 84- *Personal Data:* b New York, NY, Nov 7, 51. *Educ:* State Univ NY, Binghamton, BA, 72; Miami Univ, MA, 75, PhD(psychol), 76. *Concurrent Pos:* Adj asst prof, State Univ NY, Stony Brook, 78-81; adj assoc prof, Miami Univ, 81-; health scientist adminr, Nat Heart, Lung & Blood Inst, NIH, 81-82. *Mem:* Behav Genetics Asn; Soc Study Social Biol (secy, 77-81, treas, 78-81); Sigma Xi; AAAS. *Res:* Behavioral science; behavioral factors in nuclear safety; organizational behavior; methodology and quantitative analysis in experimental psychology. *Mailing Add:* Dept Adv Technol Brookhaven Nat Lab Bldg 475B Upton NY 11973-5000

HABER, STEPHEN B, IMMUNOPHARMACEUTICALS, MEDICINAL CHEMISTRY. *Current Pos:* res chemist, E I DuPont de Nemours & Co, Inc, 78-82, group leader, 82-84, res supvr, 84-86, res mgr, 86-89, mgr clin res, 89-91, assoc med dir, 91-94, med dir, 94-96, DIR, LICENSING & EXTRAMUREL RES, DUPONT MERCK PHARMACEUT CO, 96- *Personal Data:* b Washington, DC, June 18, 50; m 76, Raquel Ruiz; c Micah & Gabrielle. *Educ:* Stanford Univ, BS, 72; Mass Inst Technol, PhD(org chem), 76. *Prof Exp:* Res fel, Syntex Res, 76-78. *Mem:* Am Chem Soc; NY Acad Sci; Sigma Xi; Soc Nuclear Med; AAAS. *Res:* Radiolabeled monoclonal antibodies for diagnosis and therapy; organic synthesis; anti-inflammatories; beta-lactam antibiotics; medicinal chemistry; in-vivo diagnostics; clinical research. *Mailing Add:* DuPont Merck Pharmaceut Co 331 Treble Cove Rd 500-2 North Billerica MA 01862. *E-Mail:* habersb@alumni.stanford.org

HABERFELD, JOSEPH LENNARD, MICROSCOPY, POLYMER CHARACTERIZATION. *Current Pos:* RES CHEMIST, L J BROUTMAN & ASSOC, 90- *Personal Data:* b Cleveland, Ohio, Jan 17, 45; div; c 2. *Educ:* Ohio Univ, BS, 66; Univ Calif, MS, 68; Univ Conn, PhD(polymer chem), 74. *Prof Exp:* Fel, Inst Mat Sci, Univ Conn, 74-75; res chemist, Uniroyal Inc, 75-85, Akzo Coatings, 86-90. *Mem:* Am Chem Soc; Sigma Xi; NY Micros Soc. *Res:* Development of analytical techniques to characterize and improve rubber and polymeric materials. *Mailing Add:* 1143 S Plymouth Ct No 301 Chicago IL 60605-2041

HABERFIELD, PAUL, ORGANIC CHEMISTRY. *Current Pos:* from instr to assoc prof, 61-72, PROF CHEM, BROOKLYN COL, 73- *Personal Data:* b Carnuntum, Czech, May 29, 33; US citizen; m 66, Mamie Birnbaum; c Shulamith, Rebecca, Felicia & Saul. *Educ:* Mass Inst Technol, BS, 55; Univ Calif, Los Angeles, PhD(chem), 60. *Prof Exp:* Fel, Purdue Univ, 60-61. *Mem:* AAAS; Am Chem Soc. *Res:* Solute-solvent interactions in ground and excited states; proximate charge effects on mechanism and equilibria, calorimetry, phototropic molecules. *Mailing Add:* Dept Chem Brooklyn Col Brooklyn NY 11210-2889. *E-Mail:* paulh@brooklyn.cuny.edu

HABERLAND, MARGARET ELIZABETH, MACROPHAGES ATHEROGENESIS, LIPOPROTEIN METABOLISM. *Current Pos:* ASST PROF MED & BIOCHEM, UNIV CALIF, LOS ANGELES, 80- *Educ:* Case Western Reserve Univ, PhD(biochem), 71. *Mailing Add:* Dept Med Div Cardiol Univ Calif Ctr Health Sci CHS 47-123 Los Angeles CA 90095-1679. *Fax:* 310-794-7345

HABERMAN, CHARLES MORRIS, MECHANICAL & AERONAUTICAL ENGINEERING. *Current Pos:* RETIRED. *Personal Data:* b Bakersfield, Calif, Dec 10, 27. *Educ:* Univ Calif, Los Angeles, BS, 51; Univ Southern Calif, MS, 54, MechE, 57, MS, 61. *Prof Exp:* Group engr in charge comput applns, Northrop Aircraft Corp, 51-59; from asst prof to prof eng, Calif State Univ, Los Angeles, 59-69, prof mech eng, 69-91. *Concurrent Pos:* Consult, Northrop Aircraft Corp, 59-61, Rockwell, 62-63, Lockheed, 66 & Aerospace Corp, 78. *Mem:* Am Soc Eng Educ; Am Inst Aeronaut & Astronaut. *Res:* Thermoheat transfer; applied mechanics; aeronautics; computer applications. *Mailing Add:* 1925 Sunnycrest Dr Apt 102 Fullerton CA 92835

HABERMAN, HERBERT FREDERICK, DERMATOLOGY. *Current Pos:* res assoc dermat, 65-66, asst prof, 67-72, ASSOC PROF MED, UNIV TORONTO, 72-; ACTIVE ATTEND STAFF DERMAT, TORONTO WESTERN HOSP, 65-, DIR DIV DER MAT, 75- *Personal Data:* b Toronto, Ont, Apr 29, 34; m 67; c 3. *Educ:* Univ Toronto, MD, 59; FRCPCan, 64; Am Acad Dermat, dipl, 64. *Prof Exp:* Intern & resident med, Univ Toronto, 59-61; resident and res fel dermat, McGill Univ, NY Univ & Montreal Gen Hosp, 61-65. *Concurrent Pos:* Grants, Med Res Coun, 66, Ont Cancer Treatment & Res Found, 65, Nat Cancer Inst Can, 70 & Can Geriat Res Found, 70; Ont Cancer Treat & Res Found; dir, Sexually Transmitted Dis Clin & Dermat, Toronto Western Hosp; consult, Addiction Res Found, 74- & Metrop Toronto Homes for Aged, 74-; assoc, Ont Cancer Treatment & Res Found, 77-, dir Photother & Vitiligo Units, 74- *Mem:* Can Dermat Asn; Soc Investigative Dermat; Am Asn Cancer Res; Am Acad Dermat. *Res:* Pigmentation, especially melanin research and vitiligo phototherapy, photobiology and cutaneous carcinogenesis. *Mailing Add:* Toronto Hosp Western Div EW-542 399 Bathhurst Toronto ON M5T 2S8 Can

HABERMAN, JOHN PHILLIP, DRILLING & CEMENTING. *Current Pos:* RES ASSOC, EXP TECH DEPT, TEXACO INC, 80- *Personal Data:* b Techumseh, Nebr, June 2, 38; m 62, Kathryn L Wollangk; c Jill & Gwen. *Educ:* Univ Nebr, BSc, 60; Univ Wis, PhD(anal chem), 66. *Prof Exp:* Tech staff anal chem & dent res, Procter & Gamble Co, 66-79; chief chem, Ohio River Valley Water Monitoring Comn, 79-80. *Mem:* Am Chem Soc; Soc Petrol Engrs; AAAS. *Res:* Evaluating and developing systems and processes relating to drilling and cementing oil and gas wells and instrumental methods to model them in the laboratory. *Mailing Add:* Texaco EPTD PO Box 770070 Houston TX 77215

HABERMAN, RICHARD, NONLINEAR WAVE PHENOMENA, SINGULAR PERTURBATION METHODS. *Current Pos:* assoc prof, 78-85, PROF MATH, SOUTHERN METHODIST UNIV, 85- *Personal Data:* b Brooklyn, NY, June 27, 45; m 69, Elizabeth Hart; c Ken & Vicki. *Educ:* Mass Inst Technol, BS, 67, PhD(appl math) 71. *Prof Exp:* Asstt, Univ Calif, San Diego, 71-72; asst prof math, Rutgers Univ, 72-77 & Ohio State Univ, 77-78. *Mem:* Soc Indust & Appl Math. *Res:* Nonlinear wave phenomena; hydrodynamic stability; solitons for dispersive waves; slowly varying transitions for ordinary and partial differential equations. *Mailing Add:* Dept Math Southern Methodist Univ Dallas TX 75275-0156. *E-Mail:* rhaberma@post.smu.edu

HABERMAN, WARREN OTTO, ENTOMOLOGY. *Current Pos:* RETIRED. *Personal Data:* b Milwaukee, Wis, Aug 19, 18; m 46, Grace Boettcher; c Thomas & Carol. *Educ:* Univ Wis, BA, 40, MA, 42, PhD(vet entom), 49. *Prof Exp:* Asst, Univ Wis, 46-48, instr vet sci, 48-49; mgr, Biol-Sanit Res Lab, Ralston Purina Co, St Louis, 49-80. *Mem:* AAAS; Am Soc Parasitol; Entom Soc Am; Sigma Xi. *Res:* Biology of Hypoderma bovis and Hypoderma lineatum. *Mailing Add:* 416 Algonquin Dr Ballwin MO 63011

HABERMAN, WILLIAM L(AWRENCE), THERMODYNAMICS, FLUID DYNAMICS. *Current Pos:* CONSULT, 73- *Personal Data:* b Vienna, Austria, May 4, 22; US citizen; m 57. *Educ:* Cooper Union, BS, 49; Univ Md, MS, 52, PhD(viscous flow), 56. *Prof Exp:* Physicist, Bur Ships, US Dept Navy, 49-50, David Taylor Model Basin, 50-57, dep dir gas dynamics div, 57-59, chief res br, 59-61, res physicist, 61-62, dir advan planning div, Off Naval Res, 62-63; sr staff scientist, NASA, 63-71; chmn, Dept Mech Eng, Newark Col Eng, 71-73. *Concurrent Pos:* Lectr, Univ Md, 58-67, vis prof, 67-68, prof, 68-71; prof, Montgomery Col, 73-78. *Mem:* AAAS; Am Phys Soc; Am Inst Aeronaut & Astronaut; Am Geophys Union; Soc Indust & Appl Math. *Res:* Potential theory; viscous and two-phase flows; cavitation; theoretical mechanics; thermal radiation; research administration; planetary sciences. *Mailing Add:* ERC Co PO Box 1723 Rockville MD 20850

HABERMANN, HELEN M, PLANT PHYSIOLOGY. *Current Pos:* from asst prof to prof, Goucher Col, 58-92, chmn dept, 63-66, 68 & 78-79, Lillian Welsh prof, 83-92, EMER PROF BIOL SCI, GOUCHER COL, 92- *Personal Data:* b Brooklyn, NY, Sept 13, 27. *Educ:* State Univ NY, AB, 49; Univ Conn, MS, 51; Univ Minn, PhD, 56. *Prof Exp:* Asst bot, Univ Conn, 49-51; asst, Univ Minn, 51-53, asst plant physiol, 53-55, head residence counr, Comstock Hall, 55-56; res assoc, Res Inst, Univ Chicago, 56-57; res fel, Hopkins Marine Sta, Stanford Univ, 57-58. *Concurrent Pos:* NIH spec res fel, Res Inst Advan Study, Baltimore, 66-67. *Mem:* Fel AAAS; Am Soc Plant Physiol; Scand Soc Plant Physiol; Japanese Soc Plant Physiol; Phytochem Soc NAm (secy, 87-93). *Res:* Photosynthesis; albino physiology; photomorphogenesis; light control of stomatal opening. *Mailing Add:* Dept Biol Sci Goucher Col Towson MD 21204. *Fax:* 410-337-6123

HABER-SCHAIM, URI, PHYSICS, SCIENCE EDUCATION. *Current Pos:* CONSULT & AUTH, 86- *Personal Data:* b Berlin, Ger, Feb 8, 26; m 47; c 3. *Educ:* Hebrew Univ, Jerusalem, MS, 49; Univ Chicago, PhD, 51. *Honors & Awards:* Oersted Medal, Am Asn Physics Teachers, 70. *Prof Exp:* Res physicist, Weizmann Inst Sci, Israel, 51-53 & Univ Bern, 53-55; res assoc, Univ Ill, 55-56; asst prof physics, Mass Inst Technol, 56-61; proj dir, Phys Sci Study Comt, 63-71; dir div sponsored res & phys sci group, Newton Col Sacred Heart, 71-73; prof sci educ & dir phys sci group, Sch Educ, Boston Univ, 74-76, dir, Inst Curric Develop Sci & Math & prof phys & sci educ, 76-84, adj prof phys, 84-86. *Mem:* Am Phys Soc; Am Asn Physics Teachers; fel AAAS. *Res:* Theoretical and high energy physics; teacher training in physics; curriculum development in science and mathematics. *Mailing Add:* 24 Stone Rd Belmont MA 02178

HABERSTICH, ALBERT, MAGNETIC FUSION RESEARCH. *Current Pos:* RETIRED. *Personal Data:* b Basel, Switz, Dec 11, 27; US citizen; m 58; c 2. *Educ:* Univ Md, MS, 58, PhD(physics), 64. *Prof Exp:* Engr electronics, Autophon A G, Solothurn, Switz, 49-56; res asst electronics & physics, Univ Md, 56-64; res assoc, Plasma Physics Lab, Princeton Univ, 64-67; staff mem, Los Alamos Nat Lab, 67-77, assoc group leader, 77-86, dept group leader, 86-89, staff mem, 90, lab assoc, 91-94. *Res:* Experimental research in magnetic fusion. *Mailing Add:* 159 Laguna St Los Alamos NM 87544

HABERSTROH, ROBERT D, MECHANICAL ENGINEERING. *Current Pos:* assoc prof, 64-70, PROF MECH ENG, COLO STATE UNIV, 70- *Personal Data:* b Altoona, Pa, Feb 11, 28; div; c 1. *Educ:* Carnegie Inst Technol, BS, 50; Mass Inst Technol, SM, 51, MechE, 52, ScD(mech eng), 64. *Prof Exp:* Engr, Struct, Inc, Pa, 53-56; indust liaison off admin, Mass Inst Technol, 56-59; asst prof mech eng, Colo State Univ, 59-62; instr, Mass Inst Technol, 62-64. *Mem:* Am Soc Mech Engrs; Am Inst Chem Engrs. *Res:* Heat transfer and fluid mechanics; single-phase heat convection; thermodynamics; drying of solids. *Mailing Add:* Dept Mech Eng Colo State Univ Ft Collins CO 80523-1374

HABETLER, GEORGE JOSEPH, MATHEMATICAL PHYSICS. *Current Pos:* PROF MATH, RENSSELAER POLYTECH INST, 52- *Personal Data:* b McKees Rocks, Pa, Oct 31, 28; m 53; c 3. *Educ:* Duquesne Univ, BA, 49; Carnegie Inst Technol, DSc(math), 52. *Prof Exp:* Asst math, Carnegie Inst Technol, 49-51; res assoc, Knolls Atomic Power Lab, Gen Elec Co, 52. *Mem:* Am Math Soc; Soc Indust & Appl Math. *Res:* Reactor theory; numerical and functional analysis; linear algebra. *Mailing Add:* Dept Math Rensselaer Polytech Inst Troy NY 12181

HABIB, DANIEL, PALYNOLOGY, MICROPALEONTOLOGY. *Current Pos:* Lectr geol, Queens Col, NY, 65-66, asst prof, 66-69, assoc prof geol & grad adv, Dept Geol & Geog, 69-72, PROF & CHMN, DEPT EARTH & ENVIRON SCI, QUEENS COL, NY, 72- *Personal Data:* b New York, NY, Sept 16, 36; m 71. *Educ:* City Col New York, BS, 58; Univ Kans, MA, 60; Pa State Univ, PhD(geol), 65. *Mem:* AAAS; Paleont Soc; Soc Econ Paleont & Mineral; Brit Paleont Asn; Am Asn Stratig Palynologists. *Res:* Sedimentology of organic detritus; palynological age dating and source of sediments in deep sea cores; Carboniferous palynological paleoecology and distribution of palyniterous sediments; palynological age dating of Phanerozoic rocks; Mesozoic dinoflagellate stratigraphy; deep sea drilling. *Mailing Add:* Dept Geol CUNY Queens Col 6530 Kissena Blvd Flushing NY 11367-1575

HABIB, EDMUND J, ELECTRICAL ENGINEERING, PHYSICS. *Current Pos:* PRIN, SYSTS RES & APPL CORP, 87- *Personal Data:* b Dover, NH, May 24, 27; m 54; c 5. *Educ:* Cath Univ Am, BEE, 49. *Honors & Awards:* Vanguard Proj Outstanding Award, US Navy, 58; Aerospace Commun Award, Am Inst Aeronaut & Astronaut, 70. *Prof Exp:* Group leader rocket instrumentation, Naval Res Lab, 50-56, sect head minitrack calibration sect, 56-58; br head, Systs Eval Br, Goddard Space Flight Ctr, NASA, 58-61, asst div chief, Space Data Acquisition Div, 61-63, asst chief, Data Systs Div, 63-65, assoc chief, Info Processing Div, 65-68, assoc chief, Advan Develop Div, 68-76; mgr com prog develop, Comsat Corp, Intelsat Mgt, 76-80; asst vpres eng, Am Stat Corp, 77-82; vpres, Satellite Systs Eng, 82-85; vpres, Fairchild Communs Systs Div, 86-87. *Concurrent Pos:* Mem, Int Telemetry Conf. *Mem:* AAAS; Inst Elec & Electronics Engrs; Sigma Xi. *Res:* Rocket instrumentation; radio tracking and guidance systems; satellite tracking systems; time standards; tracking calibration systems; satellite instrumentation; radio star and sun position determination; computers; electronic data processing systems. *Mailing Add:* 7201 Dear Lake Lane Derwood MD 20855

HABIB, EDWIN EMILE, PHYSICS. *Current Pos:* RETIRED. *Personal Data:* b Trinidad, WI, Dec 23, 27; Can citizen; m 58; c 2. *Educ:* Univ Birmingham, BSc, 55; McMaster Univ, PhD(physics), 61. *Prof Exp:* From lectr to assoc prof physics, Univ Windsor, 59-94. *Concurrent Pos:* Nat Res Coun Can hon res grant, 56-58 & 60- *Mem:* Am Phys Soc. *Res:* Beta and gamma ray spectroscopy; nuclear reactions using the tandem van de Graaf accelerator. *Mailing Add:* 4019 Roseland E Univ Windsor Windsor ON N9S 1Y7 Can

HABIB, IZZEDDIN SALIM, HEAT TRANSFER, APPLIED MATHEMATICS. *Current Pos:* PROF MECH ENG, UNIV MICH, DEARBORN, 69- *Personal Data:* b Tripoli, Lebanon, Nov 16, 34; US citizen; m 62, Nuha S; c Dina & Tania. *Educ:* Am Univ Beirut, BME, 56; Va Polytech Inst, MSME, 61; Univ Calif, Berkeley, PhD(mech eng), 68. *Prof Exp:* Engr, Dept Hydraul, Lebanon, 57-60; instr eng, Univ Mich-Dearborn, 62-64; group leader, Chrysler Corp, 64-66. *Mem:* Fel Am Soc Mech Engrs. *Res:* Heat and mass transfer in turbulent flow; heat transfer with change of phase; heat transfer in radiating gases; flow of high temperature gases. *Mailing Add:* Dept Mech Eng Univ Mich Dearborn MI 48128

HABIBI, KAMRAN, PROJECT ENGINEERING, ENVIRONMENTAL RESEARCH. *Current Pos:* RETIRED. *Personal Data:* b Tehran, Iran, Dec 14, 37; m 65; c 2. *Educ:* Univ Birmingham, BSc, 61, MSc, 62, PhD(chem eng), 63. *Prof Exp:* Tech officer process develop, Midland Silicones, 63-66; supvr automotive technol, E I DuPont de Nemours & Co, Inc, 66-74, mgr proj eng, 74-76, mem staff energy & hydrocarbon planning & develop, 76-78, govt liaison, 78-80, mem staff corp purchasing, 80-91. *Concurrent Pos:* Mem, Coord Res Coun, 70-74. *Mem:* Brit Inst Chem Engrs. *Res:* Preflame reactions, development of instrumentation and analytical techniques in high-speed diesel engines; characterization of particulate emmisions from cars; development of vehicle emmision control systems; environmental impact research and analysis; quality assessment and audits. *Mailing Add:* 719 Taunton Rd Wilmington DE 19803

HABICHT, ERNST ROLLEMANN, JR, ENVIRONMENTAL SCIENCES, ENERGY CONVERSION. *Current Pos:* INDEPENDENT ENERGY ANALYST & CONSULT, 80- *Personal Data:* b Charleston, WVa, Dec 22, 38; m 66. *Educ:* Harvard Univ, AB, 60; Stanford Univ, PhD(chem), 67. *Prof Exp:* Fel, asst prof biol & lectr chem, Univ Calif, San Diego, 67-71; staff scientist & dir, Energy Prog, Environ Defense Fund, 71-80. *Concurrent Pos:* Consult res & develop Presidential report, US Atomic Energy Comn, 75; mem adv coun to chmn NY Pub Serv Comn, 75-; mem, Nat Gas Surv Task Force on Rate Design, Fed Power Comn, 75-77, Nat Coal Pol Proj, 76-80, Mass Inst Tehcnol Energy Lab, 78-80 & Polit Econ Res Ctr, 84- *Mem:* AAAS; Am Chem Soc; Am Econ Asn; NY Acad Sci. *Res:* Economics of energy utilization; energy technology assessment; marginal cost-based pricing and investing policies for regulated utilities. *Mailing Add:* PO Box 65 Port Jefferson NY 11777-0065

HABICHT, GAIL SOREM, IMMUNOLOGY, PHYSIOLOGY. *Current Pos:* from asst prof to assoc prof, 71-88, PROF PATH, SCH MED, STATE UNIV NY, STONY BROOK, 88-, ASSOC PROVOST, 94- *Personal Data:* b Oakland, Calif, Oct 1, 40; m 66, Ernst R Jr; c Peter H R & Michael E R. *Educ:* Stanford Univ, BS, 62, PhD(physiol), 65. *Prof Exp:* USPHS fel immunol, Rockefeller Univ, 65-66, fel immunophysiol, Stanford Univ, 66-67; asst prof biol, Univ San Diego, 67-68; res assoc, Scripps Clin & Res Found, 68-71. *Concurrent Pos:* Lectr, San Diego State Univ, 68-71; guest investr, Brookhaven Nat Lab, 71-83. *Mem:* Am Asn Immunologists; NY Acad Sci; Am Soc Microbiologists; Soc Leukocyte Biol; Comp Immunol Soc. *Res:* Acquired immunological tolerance; autoimmunity; aging; babesiosis; lyme disease; interleukin 1; inflammation; evolution of cytokines. *Mailing Add:* Dept Path Sch Med State Univ NY Stony Brook NY 11794-8691. *Fax:* 516-444-3424; *E-Mail:* ghabicht@path.som.sunysb.edu

HABICHT, JEAN-PIERRE, NUTRITIONAL EPIDEMIOLOGY. *Current Pos:* PROF NUTRIT EPIDEMIOL, DIV NUTRIT SCI, CORNELL UNIV, 77- *Personal Data:* b Geneva, Switz, Dec 15, 34; US citizen; div; c 3. *Educ:* Univs Geneva & Zurich, Switz, MD, 62; Harvard Sch Pub Health, MPH, 68; Mass Inst Technol, PhD(nutrit, biochem & metab), 69. *Prof Exp:* Med officer, Div Human Develop, WHO, Inst de Nutricion de Centro Am y Panama, Guatemala, 69-74; spec asst to dir, Div Health Exam Statist, Nat Ctr Health Statist, 74-77. *Concurrent Pos:* Prof maternal & child health, Univ San Carlos, Guatemala, 73-74; adv, WHO, 75-, Nat Acad Sci, 75-, USDA, 82-, UN, 83-;

prin investr, var grants & contracts. *Mem:* Soc Epidemiol Res; Am Inst Nutrit; fel Am Col Epidemiol; Int Soc Res Human Milk & Lactation; Am Pub Health Asn; Int Epidemiol Asn. *Res:* Maternal and child health in developing countries; primary medical care in poor rural areas; nutritional influences on health in developed and developing countries; ethics of population research; organization of health and nutritional surveillance systems. *Mailing Add:* Div Nutrit Sci Savage Hall Cornell Univ Ithaca NY 14850-6301. *Fax:* 607-255-7906

HABIG, ROBERT L, clinical chemistry, for more information see previous edition

HABIG, WILLIAM HENRY, BACTERIAL VACCINES. *Current Pos:* CHIEF LAB BAC TOXINS & DEP DIR, FOOD & DRUG ADMIN, 75- *Personal Data:* b 1942; m; c 3. *Educ:* Rutgers Univ, BS, 64; Univ Vt, PhD(biochem), 68. *Prof Exp:* Fel, NY State Dept Health, 71-72; staff fel, NIH, 72-75. *Mem:* Am Soc Biochem & Molecular Biol. *Res:* Biochemistry; pharmacology. *Mailing Add:* Centicor Inc 200 Great Valley Pkwy Malvern PA 19355-1307

HABOWSKY, JOSEPH EDMUND JOHANNES, SCIENCE EDUCATION. *Current Pos:* from asst prof to assoc prof, 64-74, PROF BIOL, UNIV WINDSOR, 74- *Personal Data:* b Coburg, Ger, Sept 27, 28; Can citizen; m 68. *Educ:* Univ Munich, BS, 55; Univ Toronto, MS, 58, PhD(zool), 62. *Honors & Awards:* Armour Pharmaceut Award, 73; William J Stickel Award, 74; Achievement Award, Asn Media & Technol Educ Can, 90; Iseta Award, 91. *Prof Exp:* Nat Res Coun Can fel, 62-63; lectr zool, Univ Toronto, 64. *Concurrent Pos:* Teaching fel, 3M, 91. *Mem:* Hon mem Int Soc Exploring Teaching Alternatives; hon mem Soc Teaching & Learning Higher Educ; Int Soc Individual Instr. *Res:* Science education. *Mailing Add:* Dept Biol Sci Univ Windsor Windsor ON N9B 3P4 Can. *Fax:* 519-738-5200

HABTEMARIAM, TSEGAYE, BIOMEDICAL DECISION SUPPORT SYSTEM, SIMULATION MODELING. *Current Pos:* assoc prof, 79-84, PROF EPIDEMIOL, SCH VET MED, TUSKEGEE INST, 84-, DIR, INFO MGT, 82- *Personal Data:* b Addis Ababa, Ethiopia, Apr 25, 42; m 74; c 3. *Educ:* Agr & Mech Col, Ethiopia, BSc, 64; Colo State Univ, DVM, 70; Univ Calif, Davis, MPVM, 77, PhD(epidemiol), 80. *Prof Exp:* Asst prof animal sci, Agr & Mech Col, Ethiopia, 70-74; res assoc epidemiol, Univ Calif, Davis, 77-79. *Concurrent Pos:* Prin investr, Tuskegee Inst, 82- *Mem:* Soc Med Decision Making; Am Vet Comput Soc; Am Vet Med Asn; Sigma Xi. *Res:* Computer modeling of diseases; biomedical decision-making support systems; analytic and quantitative epidemiology; biomedical information management. *Mailing Add:* 611 Roberts Circle Tuskegee Institute AL 36088

HABTE-MARIAM, YITBAREK, BIOPHYSICAL CHEMISTRY, MAGNETIC RESONANCE. *Current Pos:* res assoc, 79-80, ASST PROF CHEM, ATLANTA UNIV, 80- *Personal Data:* b Asella, Ethiopia, Jan 28, 49. *Educ:* Rutgers Univ, BA, 74, PhD(chem), 77. *Prof Exp:* Fel chem, Univ Va, 77-78 & Ga State Univ, 78-79. *Concurrent Pos:* Teaching asst, Rutgers Univ, 74-76; instr chem, NJ Med Sch, 76-77; prin investr, Atlanta Univ, 80- *Mem:* Am Chem Soc. *Res:* Biophysical chemistry and biophysics; multinuclear magnetic resonance spectroscopy; ligand macromolecule interactions; metol ion ligand interactions and solution equilibria; experimental approaches to solution conformation and determination of inter-nuclear distances; motional properties of polymers and biopolymers as probed by nuclear relaxation. *Mailing Add:* Dept Chem Clark Atlanta Univ 223 James Brawley SW Atlanta GA 30314-4358

HAC, LUCILE R, BIOCHEMISTRY, ORGANIC CHEMISTRY. *Current Pos:* assoc prof, 61-77, EMER PROF BIOCHEM, MED SCH, NORTHWESTERN UNIV, CHICAGO, 77- *Personal Data:* b Lincoln, Nebr, May 18, 09. *Educ:* Univ Nebr, BA, 30, MSc, 31; Univ Minn, PhD(org chem), 35. *Prof Exp:* Chem asst, Univ Nebr, 29-31 & Univ Minn, 31-35; assoc bacteriologist, State Dept Health, Md, 35-36; from asst to res assoc gynec, Kuppenheimer Fund, Chicago, 36-43; res chemist, Int Minerals & Chem Corp, Tex, 43-44, prin chemist & supvr sugar beet res, Calif, 44-56, supvr air pollution res, Fla, 56-58, supvr microbiol res, Ill, 58-61. *Concurrent Pos:* Job counr for sr placement, NShore Ind Ctr, Northfield, Ill. *Mem:* AAAS; Am Chem Soc; Am Soc Microbiol; Soc Exp Biol & Med; NY Acad Sci; Sigma Xi. *Res:* Orthoquinones: Eberthella typhi aglutinins; gonococci; chemotherapy; microbiological assay of amino acids; amino acids of sugar beet and sugar beet juices; sugar beet genetics; air pollution; microbial physiology; fermentation; minerals, vitamins and hormonal effects on bone metabolism and fluorosis in bone. *Mailing Add:* 812 Oakwood Ave Wilmette IL 60091-3318

HACH, EDWIN E, JR, PHYSICAL CHEMISTRY. *Current Pos:* asst prof phys chem, 67-70, ASSOC PROF CHEM, ST BONAVENTURE UNIV, 70- *Personal Data:* b Shippenville, Pa, Jan 5, 34; m 55, Betty Orcutt; c Edwin E III & Sara A. *Educ:* Clarion State Col, BS, 59; Univ NH, MS & PhD(phys chem), 67. *Prof Exp:* Instr acad chem, Bradford Area High Sch, 59-62. *Mem:* Am Chem Soc; Sigma Xi. *Res:* Electrochemistry; potentiometric stability constant determinations; non-aqueous polarography; solute species in non-aqueous solutions; titrations in non-aqueous solutions. *Mailing Add:* Dept Chem St Bonaventure Univ St Bonaventure NY 14778

HACH, VLADIMIR, ORGANIC CHEMISTRY, MEDICINAL & PHARMACEUTICAL CHEMISTRY. *Current Pos:* RETIRED. *Personal Data:* b Prague, Czech, Nov 17, 24. *Educ:* Prague Tech Univ, Dipl Ing, 49, DrSc(org chem), 53. *Prof Exp:* Res scientist, Spofa Res Inst Pharm & Biochem, Czech, 53-66 & Org Div, Austrian Nitrogen Works, 66; sr res chemist & group leader, MacMillan Bloedel Res Ltd, 66-70; sr res assoc, Dept Chem, Univ BC, 70-73; group leader process develop, Delmar Chem Ltd, 73-76; tech dir, Whitehall Labs, 77-89. *Mem:* Am Chem Soc; Chem Inst Can. *Res:* Synthetic organic chemistry; synthesis of new compounds; development of synthetic reactions; natural compounds; analytical control methods research and development; stability of pharmaceutical products; cosmetics development; regulatory affairs. *Mailing Add:* 260 Scarlett Rd Apt 1901 Toronto ON M6N 4X6 Can

HACHINSKI, VLADIMIR, NEUROLOGY, STROKE. *Current Pos:* assoc prof, 80-83, PROF NEUROL, UNIV WESTERN ONT, 83-, PROF EIPIDEMIOL & PHYSIOL, 88-; DIR, STROKE & AGING GROUP, ROBARTS RES INST, 84-; RICHARD & BERYL IVEY PROF & CHMN, DEPT CLIN NEUROL SCI, LONDON, ONT, CAN, 90- *Personal Data:* b Zhitomir, Ukraine, Aug 13, 41; m 67; c 3. *Educ:* Univ Toronto, MD, 66; FRCP(C), 72. *Hon Degrees:* MSc, McMasters Univ, MSc, 87; DSc, Univ London, 88. *Honors & Awards:* Trillium Clin Scientist Award; Milton Sky lectr. *Prof Exp:* Lectr neurol, Univ Toronto, 74-76, from asst prof to assoc prof, 76-83. *Concurrent Pos:* Assoc ed, J Archives Neurol, 79- & J Stroke, 84-86; chmn, Steering Comt, AAAS; counr, Am Acad Neurol. *Mem:* Can Stroke Soc (pres, 81); World Fedn Neurol; AAAS; Int Soc Cerebral Blood Flow & Metab; Am Neurol Asn; Am Acad Neurol; Int Stroke Soc. *Res:* Cerebral blood flow and metabolism; multi-infarct dementia; migraine; cerebrovascular diseases; cardiac complications of stroke; Alzheimer's disease. *Mailing Add:* Univ Hosp 339 Windermere Rd London ON N6A 5A5 Can

HACKAM, REUBEN, HIGH VOLTAGE INSULATION, ELECTRIC POWER ENGINEERING. *Current Pos:* chmn, 80-81 & 84-86, PROF ELEC ENG, UNIV WINDSOR, 78- *Personal Data:* b Baghdad, Iraq, Feb 18, 36; Can & Brit citizen; m 64, Estelle; c Judy, David, Abby & Dan. *Educ:* Technion, Israel Inst Technol, BSc, 60; Univ Liverpool, Eng, PhD(elec eng), 64, DEng, 88. *Prof Exp:* Sr engr, Eng Elec-Gen Elec Co, 64-69; lectr, Univ Sheffield, 69-73, sr lectr, 73-74, reader, Dept Elec Eng, 74-78. *Concurrent Pos:* Vis staff math, Staffordshire Polytech, 64-69 & Sheffield City Polytech, 70-78; consult elec, Brit Rail, 75-78, Eng Elec Co, 75-77, Windsor Star, 81-83, Hiram Walker & Sons, 83-86, Corp City Windsor, 83-88, Can Salt Co, 87-, Greenshield Prepaid Serv Inc, 82- *Mem:* Fel Inst Elec & Electronics Engrs. *Res:* Research in gas insulated systems and devices; electromagnetics, polymer insulators, power system planning; weed eradication using electric energy and control of reactive power in power systems; author of various articles. *Mailing Add:* Dept Elec Eng Univ Windsor Windsor ON N9B 3P4 Can. *Fax:* 519-973-7062

HACKEL, DONALD BENJAMIN, pathology; deceased, see previous edition for last biography

HACKEL, EMANUEL, HUMAN GENETICS, TRANSPLANTATION IMMUNOLOGY. *Current Pos:* instr biol sci, Mich State Univ, 49-52, instr natural sci, 52-53, from asst prof to prof natural sci, 53-74, chmn dept, 63-74, PROF, DEPTS MED & ZOOL, MICH STATE UNIV, 74. *Personal Data:* b Brooklyn, NY, June 17, 25; wid, Rachel A Fisher; c Lisa, Meredith, Janet, Daniel, Tabitha & Jessica (Harrison). *Educ:* Univ Mich, BS, 48, MS, 49; Mich State Univ, PhD(zool), 53. *Honors & Awards:* Cooley Mem Award, Am Asn Blood Banks, 69, Elliot Mem Award, 87. *Prof Exp:* Asst zool, Univ Mich, 48-49. *Concurrent Pos:* Vis investr, Blood Group Res Unit, Lister Inst, Eng, 56-57; asst dean, Univ Col, Mich State Univ, 58-63; res fel, Galton Lab, Univ Col, Univ London, 70-71 & 77-78; mem, bd dirs, Am Asn Blood Banks, 83-84; consult, Mem Blood Ctr, Minneapolis, 83- & Blood Bank, Ingham Med Ctr, Lansing, 83- *Mem:* Am Asn Blood Banks; Sigma Xi; Am Soc Human Genetics; Genetics Soc Am; NY Acad Sci; Am Soc Histocompatibility & Immunogenetics. *Res:* Blood groups; immunohematology; immunogenetics; tissue typing; transplantation; genetic counseling. *Mailing Add:* Dept Med Mich State Univ B220 Col Human Med 110 E Fee Hall East Lansing MI 48824-1316. *E-Mail:* 14001exh@msu.edu

HACKEL, LLOYD ANTHONY, HIGH RESOLUTION LASER SPECTROSCOPY, SOLID STATE LASER DEVELOPMENT. *Current Pos:* PHYSICIST, UNIV CALIF, LAWRENCE LIVERMORE NAT LAB, 76- *Personal Data:* b Litte Chute, Wis, Oct 14, 49; m 71; c Catherine, Laura & Amanda. *Educ:* Univ Wis-Madison, BS, 71; Mass Inst Technol, MS, 73, ScD, 74. *Honors & Awards:* R&D 100 Award. *Prof Exp:* Mem staff, Lab Electronics, Mass Inst Technol, 74-76; staff mem, Lockheed Missiles & Space Co, 87-89. *Mem:* Am Phys Soc. *Res:* Atomic vapor laser isotope separation with emphasis on separator pilot plant operation; atomic physics, spectroscopy, pulse propagation and e-beam generation of atomic vapor; hyperfine and automization structure, precision photon absorption cross sections; resonant and non-resonant pulse propagation; solid state laser development with emphasis on industrial applications. *Mailing Add:* 1072 Sherry Way Livermore CA 94550. *E-Mail:* hackel1@llnl.gov

HACKENBERG, ROBERT ALLAN, MEDICAL ANTHROPOLOGY, APPLIED ANTHROPOLOGY. *Current Pos:* PROF ANTHROP, UNIV COLO, BOULDER & PROG DIR, INST BEHAV SCI, 66- *Personal Data:* b Fargo, NDak, Mar 12, 28; m 63. *Educ:* Univ Minn, BA, 50, MA, 51; Cornell Univ, PhD(anthrop), 61. *Prof Exp:* Asst dir, Bur Ethnic Res, Dept Anthrop, Univ Ariz, 58-62; res anthropologist, Demog Sect, Biomet Br, Nat Cancer Inst, 62-66. *Concurrent Pos:* Dir res training prog cult change, Dept Anthrop, Univ Colo, Boulder, 66-, NIMH grant res training cult change, 68-79; Nat Inst Child Health res grants, demog transition without urbanization, Davao City, Philippines, 69-72, social mobility & fertil control, 72-74 & longitudinal fertil in develop city, 77-79; NIMH res grant, ment health epidemiol, Papago Indian Reservation, Ariz, 69-72; mem div behav sci, Nat Res Coun, 72-; mem, pop study sect, Div Res Grants, NIH, 72-, chmn, 73-76; sr fel, East West Pop Inst, East West Ctr, Honolulu, 75-79 & 80. *Mem:* AAAS; fel Am Anthrop Asn; fel Soc Appl Anthrop; Pop Asn Am; Asn Asian Studies. *Res:* Adaptations to ecological stress brought about by population growth and requiring changes in community organization; modernization and urbanization variables related to this problem in the Philippines and American Southwest. *Mailing Add:* Dept Anthrop Univ Colo Boulder Box 233 Boulder CO 80309-0233

HACKENBROCK, CHARLES ROBERT, CELL BIOLOGY, ELECTRON MICROSCOPY. *Current Pos:* PROF & CHMN, DEPT ANAT, UNIV NC SCH MED, 77- *Personal Data:* b Brooklyn, NY, Dec 23, 29; m 56; c 3. *Educ:* Wagner Col, BS, 61; Columbia Univ, PhD(anat), 65. *Prof Exp:* Asst prof anat, Sch Med, Johns Hopkins Univ, 65-68, assoc prof, 68-71; prof cell biol, Univ Tex Southwestern Med Sch, Dallas, 71-77. *Mem:* Am Asn Anat; Am Soc Cell Biol; Am Inst Biol Sci; Am Soc Biol Chemists; NY Acad Sci. *Res:* Ultrastructure and metabolism in mitochondria; membrane structure; bioenergetics. *Mailing Add:* Dept Anat Univ NC Sch Med 108 Taylor Hall Chapel Hill NC 27599-7090. *Fax:* 919-966-1856

HACKER, CARL SIDNEY, population biology, for more information see previous edition

HACKER, DAVID S(OLOMON), CHEMICAL ENGINEERING, PHYSICAL CHEMISTRY. *Current Pos:* RETIRED. *Personal Data:* b Brooklyn, NY, June 9, 25; m 49, Elaine Samson; c Karen Anne & Julie Ruth. *Educ:* Univ Ill, BS, 49; Mass Inst Technol, MS, 50; Northwestern Univ, PhD(chem eng), 54. *Prof Exp:* Res engr, Gen Elec Co, 54-56; sr scientist, Chicago Midway Labs, 56-57; sr scientist & group leader aerochem, Ill Inst Technol Res Inst, 57-61; supvr combustion res, Inst Gas Tech, 61-65; assoc prof energy eng, Univ Ill, Chicago Circle, 65-81; sr staff res engr, Amoco Chem Corp, 81-95. *Concurrent Pos:* Mem, US Army Missile & Rocket Adv Coun, 59-63, consult, Ill Inst Technol Res Inst, 65; mem indust staff, Amoco Oil Co, Chicago, 72; mem res staff, Argonne Nat Lab, 76-78 & 80-81. *Mem:* Am Phys Soc; fel Am Inst Chem Engrs; Combustion Inst; Sigma Xi; fel Am Inst Chem Engrs. *Res:* Aerothermochemistry; high temperature kinetics; heat transfer and fluid mechanics; multiphase flow; chemical process design and economics; chemical hazards; safety evaluation. *Mailing Add:* 343 Beech St Highland Park IL 60035. *E-Mail:* d1hack2@aol.com

HACKER, HERBERT, JR, ELECTRICAL ENGINEERING. *Current Pos:* RETIRED. *Personal Data:* b Cleves, Ohio, June 4, 30; m 55; c 3. *Educ:* Univ Ohio, BS, 57; Princeton Univ, MS, 59; Univ Mich, PhD, 64. *Prof Exp:* Asst elec eng, Princeton Univ, 57-59; asst prof, Univ Ohio, 59-60; res asst, Univ Mich, 60-62, from instr to asst prof, 62-65; asst prof, Duke Univ, 65-68, assoc prof, 68- *Res:* Electromagnetic theory; magnetism; solid state theory; electron paramagnetic resonance studies of amorphous materials. *Mailing Add:* 2836 Chapel Hill Rd No 20F Durham NC 22707

HACKER, MILES PAUL, PHARMACOLOGY. *Current Pos:* ASST PROF PHARMACOL & TOXICITY, UNIV VT, 80- *Educ:* Univ Tenn, PhD(pharmacol), 75. *Res:* Pharmacology of anti-cancer drugs; mechanism of action; mechanisms of toxicity. *Mailing Add:* Dept Pharmacol Univ Vt 85 S Prospect St Burlington VT 05405-0001. *Fax:* 802-656-4523

HACKER, PETER WOLFGANG, PHYSICAL OCEANOGRAPHY. *Current Pos:* RESEARCHER, HAWAII INST GEOPHYS & PLANETOLOGY, UNIV HAWAII, 92- *Personal Data:* b San Francisco, Calif, May 31, 42; m 82; c 4. *Educ:* Univ Calif, Berkeley, BS, 64; Univ Calif, San Diego, MS, 66, PhD(phys oceanog), 73. *Prof Exp:* Asst prof earth & planetary sci, Johns Hopkins Univ, 73-77; phys oceanog prog dir, NSF, DC, 77-80; consult, 80-81; phys oceanog prog dir, NSF, Washington, DC, 81-84; res scientist, Tex A&M Univ, 84-92. *Concurrent Pos:* Prin investr, Chesapeake Bay Inst, Johns Hopkins Univ, 73-77; staff oceanogr, 77-79; sci officer, US TOGA Proj Off, 84-87; vis scientist, Univ Hawaii, 91-92. *Mem:* Am Geophys Union; AAAS; Am Meteorol Soc; Oceanog Soc. *Res:* Dynamics of ocean currents on continental shelf regions; circulation and transport processes in estuaries; oceanic microstructure and mixing processes; equatorial circulation and dynamics. *Mailing Add:* 142A Pauahilani Pl Kailua HI 96734. *Fax:* 808-956-4104; *E-Mail:* hacker@soest.hawaii.edu

HACKERMAN, NORMAN, PHYSICAL CHEMISTRY, INTERFACE CHEMISTRY. *Current Pos:* Emer prof chem & pres, 70-85, EMER PRES & DISTINGUISHED EMER PROF CHEM, RICE UNIV, 85-; EMER PROF CHEM, UNIV TEX, AUSTIN, 85- *Personal Data:* b Baltimore, Md, Mar 2, 12; m 40, Gene A Coulbourn; c Patricia G, Stephen M, Sally G & Katherine E. *Educ:* Johns Hopkins Univ, BA, 32, PhD(chem), 35. *Hon Degrees:* DSc, Austin Col, 75, Tex Christian Univ, 78; LLD, Abilene Christian Univ, 78, St Edward's Univ, 72; Dr, Univ NTex, 93. *Honors & Awards:* Whitney Award, Nat Asn Corrosion Engrs, 56; Palladium Medal, Electrochem Soc, 65, Edward Goodrich Acheson Award, 84; Matiello Mem lectr, 64; Gold Medal, Am Inst Chemists, 78; Edward Goodrich Acheson Award, Electrochem Soc, 84; Charles Lathrop Parsons Award, Am Chem Soc, 87; Philip Hauge Ableson Prize, AAAS, 87; Vannevar Bush Award, Nat Sci Bd, 93; Nat Medal Sci, 93. *Prof Exp:* Asst prof phys chem, Loyola Col, Md, 35-39; asst chemist, USCG, 40-41; asst prof chem, Va Polytech Inst, 41-43; res chemist, Kellex Corp, NY, 44; from asst prof to prof chem, Univ Tex, Austin, 45-70, chmn dept, 52-62, dir corrosion res lab & dean res & sponsored progs, 61-62, vpres & provost, 62-63, vchancellor acad affairs, 63-67, pres, 67-70. *Concurrent Pos:* Res chemist, Colloid Corp, 36-40; res consult, Univ Tex; mem environ pollution panel, President's Sci Adv Comt; chmn, Gordon Res Conf Corrosion, 52 & Conf Chem Interfaces, 59; mem, Int Comt Electrochem Thermodyn & Kinetics; mem, Nat Sci Bd, NSF, 68-80, chmn, 74-80, mem, Defense Sci Bd, 78-85; ed, J Electrochem, 69-; mem, Gordon Conf Res Bd, 70-76; chmn, Sci Adv Bd, Welch Found, 82- & Comn Phys Scis, Math & Appl, Nat Res Coun, 86-92. *Mem:* Nat Acad Sci; AAAS; Am Chem Soc; Electrochem Soc (vpres, 54-57, pres, 57-58); Am Philos Soc; fel Am Acad Arts & Sci. *Res:* Physical chemistry; corrosion of metals; surface chemistry of metals and oxides; passivity; electrical double layer at solid metal-solution interfaces. *Mailing Add:* Dept Chem Rice Univ PO Box 1892 Houston TX 77001. *Fax:* 713-961-5168

HACKERT, MARVIN LEROY, PROTEIN CRYSTALLOGRAPHY. *Current Pos:* from asst prof to assoc prof, 74-86, PROF BIOCHEM, UNIV TEX, AUSTIN, 86- *Personal Data:* b Pella, Iowa, Sept 23, 44; div; c 2. *Educ:* Cent Col, BA, 66; Iowa State Univ, PhD(phys chem), 70. *Prof Exp:* NIH fel biol sci, Purdue Univ, 70-74. *Concurrent Pos:* Sci dir, UIL, 84- *Mem:* Am Chem Soc; Am Crystallog Asn. *Res:* X-ray crystallography and the molecular structure of proteins; relation of enzyme structure and mechanisms; biophysical methods. *Mailing Add:* Dept Chem & Biochem Univ Tex Austin 24th & Speedway Austin TX 78712

HACKERT, RAYMOND L, ANALYTICAL CHEMISTRY. *Current Pos:* From chemist to sr chemist, 51-66, SR RES CHEMIST, E I DU PONT DE NEMOURS & CO, 66- *Personal Data:* b Anamoose, NDak, Mar 27, 27; m 53; c 6. *Educ:* St John's Univ, Minn, BA, 49; Univ Detroit, MS, 51. *Mem:* AAAS; Am Chem Soc; Soc Appl Spectros. *Res:* Spectroscopy; polymer chemistry. *Mailing Add:* 221 North Blvd Salisbury MD 21801-6217

HACKETT, ADELINE J, virology, genetics, for more information see previous edition

HACKETT, COLIN EDWIN, FLUID & THERMAL SCIENCES. *Current Pos:* mem tech staff fluid physics, Exp Fluid Physics Div, Albuquerque, 73-79, SR MEM TECH STAFF, EXP THERMAL & FLUID SCI, SANDIA NAT LABS, CALIF, 80- *Personal Data:* b Birmingham, Eng, Apr 9, 43; m 68; c 3. *Educ:* Cambridge Univ, BA, 65, MA, 68; Brown Univ, PhD(eng mech & appl math), 71. *Prof Exp:* Proj supvr aeronaut, Aircraft Res Asn, Eng, 65-66; engr-scientist, Lockheed Ga Res Lab, 66-67; res assoc fluid mech, Mass Inst Technol, 71-73. *Concurrent Pos:* Fel, Mass Inst Technol, 71-73; tech consult, AVCO Corp, 72-73; adj prof mech eng, Univ NMex, 75-79. *Mem:* Sigma Xi; AAAS; Am Inst Aeronaut & Astronaut. *Res:* Experimental fluid physics; laser diagnostics; airborne tunable laser spectroscopy, diode, molecular and dye lasers; laser fluid velocimetry in turbulent compressible chemically reacting flows, application to high energy chemical laser devices; chemical physics; energy storage; supersonic laser assisted combustion and fuel synthesis; advanced energy conversion and storage systems. *Mailing Add:* 4318 Pomona Way Livermore CA 94550-3449. *Fax:* 510-294-1459; *E-Mail:* cehacke@ca.sandia.gov

HACKETT, EARL R, NEUROLOGY. *Current Pos:* From instr to assoc prof neurol, 62-72, PROF NEUROL & PHYSIOL, SCH MED, LA STATE UNIV MED CTR, 72-, HEAD, DEPT NEUROL, 77- *Personal Data:* b Moulmein, Burma, Feb 16, 32; US citizen; m 53; c 7. *Educ:* Drury Col, BS, 53; Case Western Res Univ, MD, 57. *Concurrent Pos:* Consult, USPHS Hosp, Carville. *Mem:* Fel Am Acad Neurol; Am Asn Electromyography & Electrodiag. *Res:* Factors involved in nerve injury and repair; methods of evaluating nerve injury. *Mailing Add:* Springfield Clin Neurol Assoc Ozarks 1965 S Fremont No 2800 Springfield MO 65804

HACKETT, JAMES E, FLUID MECHANICS, AERODYNAMICS. *Current Pos:* STAFF SPECIALIST, AERODYN RES, LOCKHEED-GA CO, 67- *Personal Data:* b Nottingham, Eng, Feb 10, 36; m 57; c 2. *Educ:* Hatfield Tech Col, BSc, 59; Univ London, DIC & PhD(aeronaut eng), 64. *Prof Exp:* Student apprentice, De-Havilland Aircraft Co, Eng, 54-59; lectr, Hatfield Tech Col, 59-61; from sci officer to sr sci officer aerodyn res, Nat Phys Lab, Teddington, 62-67. *Concurrent Pos:* Secy, Powered Lift Comt, Aeronaut Res Coun, Eng, 63-66. *Mem:* Am Inst Aeronaut & Astronaut. *Res:* Fluid mechanics of flight at low speeds; formation, structure and consequences of trailing vortices behind wings, bodies, and lifting jets; now predominately methods for testing and interpretation of wind tunnel experiments. *Mailing Add:* 1939 Winding Creek Lane Marietta GA 30064

HACKETT, JOHN TAYLOR, NEUROPHYSIOLOGY, NEUROPHARMACOLOGY. *Current Pos:* from asst prof to assoc prof, 73-84, PROF PHYSIOL, SCH MED, UNIV VA, 84- *Personal Data:* b Chicago, Ill, July 24, 41; m 70; c 3. *Educ:* Univ Ill, Urbana, BS, 64; Univ Ill Med Ctr, PhD(pharmacol), 70. *Prof Exp:* Muscular Dystrophy Asn Can fel, Univ BC, 69-72; NIH fel, Univ Iowa, 72-73. *Concurrent Pos:* Res scientist develop award, Nat Inst Drug Abuse, 75-80. *Mem:* Soc Neurosci; Am Physiol Soc. *Res:* Physiology and pharmacology of identifiable central and peripheral synapses. *Mailing Add:* Dept Physiol Univ Va Health Sci Ctr Hosp Dr Charlottesville VA 22908

HACKETT, JOSEPH LEO, MYCOLOGY, HEMATOLOGY & IMMUNOLOGY. *Current Pos:* supvry microbiologist, Stand Div, Food & Drug Admin, 74-77, IDE coordr res, 77-80, chief microbiol & immunol, Stand Br, 80-83, chief microbiol hemat, Path Clin Labs Div, 83-91, ASSOC DIV DIR, IMMUNOL, MICROBIOL & HEMAT, FOOD & DRUG ADMIN,

91- *Personal Data:* b Springfield, Ohio, Jan 11, 37; m 63, Phyllis Boice; c Amy, Ron, Beth & Susan. *Educ:* Ohio State Univ, BSc, 59, MSc, 63, PhD(clin path), 68. *Prof Exp:* Med lab technologist, Bact Lab, Ohio State Univ Hosp, 61-63, res technologist, Infectious Dis Lab, 63-68; dir qual control, Courtland Div, Abbott Labs 68-69, sect head med microbiol, Ref Lab, 69-72; supvry qual control microbiologist, Pfizer Diag, 72-74. *Concurrent Pos:* Clin lab dir, Am Bd Bioanal, 76-86; adv, biol indicators panel, US Pharmacopeia, 81-82; mem, area comt immunol, Nat Comt Clin Lab Devices, 82-85, mem, antimicrobial susceptibility subcomt, 82- *Mem:* Am Soc Microbiol. *Res:* Effectiveness of clinical microbiological and hematological diagnostic devices. *Mailing Add:* 8487 Devon Lane Walkersville MD 21793. *E-Mail:* jlh@fdadr.cdrh.fda.gov

HACKETT, LE ROY HUNTINGTON, JR, MICROELECTRONIC PROCESS ENGINEERING, ELECTRONIC & METALLURGICAL FAILURE ANALYSIS. *Current Pos:* MEM TECH STAFF, HUGHES RES LABS, 86- *Personal Data:* b Long Beach, Calif, Dec 1, 44. *Educ:* Calif State Univ, BS, 74. *Prof Exp:* Technician, MacDonald Douglas Aircraft, 64-65; res assoc, Sci Ctr, Rockwell Int, 65-73; mem tech staff, Hughes Aircraft Co, 73-83; engr, Gigabit Logic, 83-84 & Plesscor Optronics, 84-86. *Mem:* Am Ceramic Soc. *Res:* Integrating micro electro mechanical devices with microwave integrated circuits on III-V materials; process development for microwave monolithic integrated circuits; electron beam lithography on indium phosphide and gallium arsenide; micro electro-mechanical systems; gyroscopes and accelerometers as micromachines. *Mailing Add:* 4238 Torreon Dr Woodland Hills CA 91364

HACKETT, NORA REED, CELL PHYSIOLOGY, CELL KINETICS. *Current Pos:* TECH LIAISON OFFICER, OFF RES, UNIV CALIF, DAVIS, 91- *Personal Data:* b Abington, Pa, June 17, 43; m 68; c 3. *Educ:* Pa State Univ, BS, 64; Brown Univ, ScM, 67, PhD(biol), 69. *Prof Exp:* Res fel biol chem, Harvard Med Sch, 68-69; res fel med, Miriam Hosp, Brown Univ, 69-71; assoc biologist, Inhalation Toxicol Res Inst, Lovelace Found, 75-79; consult, 80-82; patent adv, Off Pres, Univ Calif, 84-87; Lawrence Livermore Nat Lab, 87-91. *Concurrent Pos:* Patent agent, Patent & Trademark Off, 89- *Mem:* Am Physiol Soc; Am Thoracic Soc; Sigma Xi. *Res:* Biotechnology patents; cell physiology; cell kinetics; biochemical regulation and ion transport; toxicology of non-nuclear fuel effluents; lung; kidney; adipose tissue. *Mailing Add:* 4318 Pomona Way Livermore CA 94550

HACKETT, ORWOLL MILTON, GEOLOGY, HYDROLOGY. *Current Pos:* RETIRED. *Personal Data:* b Vayland, SDak, Jan 30, 20; m 46, Marguerite P King; c Cathy (Jelimek), Wendy (Jalbert), Jeffrey M & Laurie (Hollander). *Educ:* Univ Minn, BA, 48. *Prof Exp:* Geologist, US Geol Surv, 49-56, dist geologist, Boston, Mass, 56-61, chief, Ground Water Br, 61-65, chief, Off Water Data Coord, 65-68, assoc chief hydrologist, 68-79, staff hydrologist, 80-90. *Concurrent Pos:* UNESCO tech adv, Jordan, 65; US mem comn hydrol, World Meteorol Orgn, 72-80; alt chmn, US Nat Comt Sci Hydrol, 74-79. *Mem:* Fel Geol Soc Am; Am Inst Prof Geologists; Am Geophys Union. *Res:* Groundwater geology and hydrology. *Mailing Add:* 2908 N Stafford St Arlington VA 22207

HACKETT, PETER ANDREW, LASER CHEMISTRY. *Current Pos:* Res officer chem, 73-80, HEAD, LASER CHEM GROUP, NAT RES COUN CAN, 81- *Personal Data:* b Havering, Eng, July 16, 48; m 70; c 3. *Educ:* Univ Southampton, BSc, 69, PhD(photochem), 72. *Mem:* Chem Inst Can. *Res:* Multiphoton chemistry; laser isotope separation; photofragment spectroscopy; resonant scattering; industrial laser induced processes. *Mailing Add:* 303 Blair Rd Gloucester ON K1J 7M1 Can

HACKETT, RAYMOND LEWIS, PATHOLOGY. *Current Pos:* From instr to assoc prof, 62-72, PROF PATH, COL MED, UNIV FLA, 72-, ASSOC CHMN DEPT, 78- *Personal Data:* b Hartford, Vt, Oct 30, 29; m 55; c 3. *Educ:* Univ Maine, BA, 51; Univ Vt, MD, 55. *Mem:* Am Asn Path & Bact; Asn Exp Path; Int Acad Path. *Res:* Ultrastructure of renal lithiasis. *Mailing Add:* Dept Path Box J-275 JHMHC Univ Fla Gainesville FL 32610

HACKETT, ROBERT M(OORE), COMPUTATIONAL MECHANICS, MECHANICS OF COMPOSITE MATERIALS. *Current Pos:* PROF & CHAIR, DEPT CIVIL ENG, UNIV MISS, 86-, ACTG CHAIR, DEPT GEOL & GEOL ENG, 95- *Personal Data:* b Carthage, Tenn, Feb 10, 36; m 78, Patricia A Keen; c Kimberly E, William D, Leigh-Ann, Jennifer M & Joseph G. *Educ:* Tenn Technol Univ, BS, 60; Carnegie-Mellon Univ, MS, 66, PhD(civil eng), 68. *Prof Exp:* Engr bridge div, Tenn Hwy Dept, 60; civil engr, Steam-Concrete Div, Tenn Valley Auth, 60-62; engr, Facilities & Criteria Br, Brown Eng Co, Inc, 62-64; from asst prof to prof civil eng & eng sci, Vanderbilt Univ, 67-79; res aerospace engr, US Army Missle Lab, 79-82; prof civil eng, Univ Ala, Huntsville, 82-85; Russ prof & chmn, Dept Civil Eng, Ohio Univ, 85-86; staff engr, Univ Tenn Space Inst, 86. *Concurrent Pos:* Consult, Avco Aerostruct Div, 69-70, Battelle Columbus Labs, 75-78, Los Alamos Nat Lab, 82- & Stone Eng Co, 85- *Mem:* Fel Am Soc Civil Engrs; Am Acad Mech; assoc fel Am Inst Aeronaut & Astronaut; Am Soc Eng Educ; Am Soc Testing & Mat; Asn Chmn Dept Mechs. *Res:* Development of computational models to simulate the response of advanced polymer-based composite material systems subjected to thermomechanical loading conditions in order to characterize the interactive micro-mechanistic accumulation of internal damage. *Mailing Add:* 2235 Lee Loop Oxford MS 38655-4919. *Fax:* 601-232-7191; *E-Mail:* cvrmh@olemiss.edu

HACKETT, WESLEY P, HORTICULTURE. *Current Pos:* CONSULT, 78- *Personal Data:* b Modesto, Calif, Apr 28, 30; m 53; c 4. *Educ:* Univ Calif, Davis, BS, 53, MS, 59, PhD(plant physiol), 62. *Honors & Awards:* Alex Laurie Award, Am Soc Hort Sci, 69 & 71. *Prof Exp:* Asst prof ornamental hort, Univ Calif, Los Angeles & asst plant physiologist, Agr Exp Sta, 62-68; assoc prof ornamental hort, Agr Exp Sta, Univ Calif, Davis 68-73, prof ornamental hort & plant physiologist, 73-82, chmn dept, 73-78. *Mem:* Am Soc Hort Sci. *Res:* Environmental physiology; growth and development of ornamental plants. *Mailing Add:* Hort Sci Univ Minn St Paul 305 Alderman Hall St Paul MN 55108-6007

HACKLEMAN, DAVID E, INTEGRATED CIRCUIT PROCESS TECHNOLOGY, MICRO FLUID MECHANICS. *Current Pos:* mem tech staff, Hewlett Packard Integrated Circuits, 78-81, prog mgr res & develop, 81-84, mem tech staff res & develop, 84-85, prog mgr res & develop, Hewlett Packard Ink-Jet Components Div, 85-89, fac loan, 89-90, prog mgr res & develop, Ink-Jet Components Div, 90-94, PROG MGR MFG, INK-JET SUPPLIES BUS UNIT, HEWLETT PACKARD CO, 94- *Personal Data:* b Coos Bay, Ore. *Educ:* Ore State Univ, BS, 73; Univ NC, Chapel Hill, PhD(chem), 78. *Prof Exp:* Mem tech staff, Am Microsysts, Inc. *Concurrent Pos:* Vis lectr, Nat Youth Sci Camp, 78-, phys sci coordr, 90, vis scientist, 91; vis prof elec eng-solid state, City Col New York, 89-90. *Mem:* Electrochem Soc. *Res:* Solid state processes; ink-jet technology; microwave circuits; radio propagation; leadership; engineering empowerment; management; technical research; world education. *Mailing Add:* Hewlett-Packard Co 1000 NE Circle Blvd Corvallis OR 97330

HACKLER, LONNIE ROSS, BIOCHEMISTRY, NUTRITION. *Current Pos:* chmn dept home econ, 84-93, DIR ARTICULATION AGREEMENTS, STATE UNIV COL NY, ONEONTA, 93- *Personal Data:* b Cloud Chief, Okla, Sept 20, 33; m 54; c 3. *Educ:* Okla Agr & Mech Col, BS, 55; Univ Ill, MS, 57, PhD(animal nutrit), 58. *Prof Exp:* Asst, Univ Ill, 55-58; from asst prof to assoc prof biochem & nutrit, NY State Agr Exp Sta, Cornell Univ, 60-79; prof nutrit & head, Dept Foods & Nutrit, Univ Ill, 79-83. *Concurrent Pos:* Vis scientist, Human Nutrit Div, USDA, Md, 68-69; actg chief, Energy Metab Br & asst biol sci, Fitzsimons Gen Hosp, Denver, 59-60. *Mem:* Am Home Econ Asn; Am Inst Nutrit. *Res:* Bioassay procedures for the determination of protein quality; effect of processing procedures on utilization of proteins; metabolism and utilization of amino acids; amino acid methodology; role of dietary fiber in nutrition. *Mailing Add:* Dept Home Econ State Univ Col RD 3 Box 35 Oneonta NY 13820. *Fax:* 607-436-2107

HACKLEY, BRENNIE ELIAS, JR, MEDICAL SCIENCE, PHARMACOLOGY. *Current Pos:* SCIENTIFIC ADVISOR, US ARMY MED RES INST CHEM DEFENSE, 80- *Personal Data:* b Roanoke, Va, July 29, 24; m 48, Ethal Battle; c Michele (Johnson), Michael B & Brennie E III. *Educ:* Wilberforce Univ, BS, 46; Univ Delaware, MS, 54, PhD(chem), 57. *Prof Exp:* Res chemist, Johns Hopkins Univ, 50-52, chief chemother br, Chem Res Develop Lab, 52-62, Med Res Lab, 62-71; asst prof chem, Univ Md, 60-65; sr res scientist, USABML, 71-80. *Concurrent Pos:* assoc prof chem, Univ Md, 60-65. *Mem:* Fel Am Inst Chemists; Am Chem Soc; Soc Neurosci; Am Soc Neurochem; Sigma Xi. *Res:* Research in new biotechnologies in biochemistry, medicinal chemistry, neurochemistry, immunochemistry, molecular biology, and neuroscience applied to drug discovery and medical chemical defense. *Mailing Add:* USA Med Res Inst Chem Defense 300 Fort Hoyle Rd Joppa MD 21085. *Fax:* 410-671-1960; *E-Mail:* hackleybe@mricd. apgea.army.mil

HACKMAN, ELMER ELLSWORTH, III, POLLUTION CONTROL, ENVIRONMENTAL TECHNOLOGY. *Current Pos:* PRES, NST/ ENGRS, INC, 73- *Personal Data:* b Philadelphia, Pa, Mar 22, 28; m 53, Edna L Oaks; c Matthew E & Christian L. *Educ:* Juniata Col, BS, 49; Univ Pa, MS, 57; Univ Del, PhD(chem), 67. *Prof Exp:* Proj engr, Chem Corps, US Army, 50-52; proj chemist, Am Viscose Corp, 53-54; asst mgr spec prod, ARCO Chem, 54-55; mgr res proj, Elkton Div, Thiokol Chem Corp, 58-73. *Concurrent Pos:* Indust consult, Univ Del, 67-73; mem, Gov Sci Advy Bd, Md, 72-74; lectr, Chem Eng Mag & McGraw-Hill, 79-82. *Mem:* Am Chem Soc; Am Inst Chem Engrs. *Res:* Chemical process and equipment design; surfactants; energy conversion; radiation; combustion catalysis; air, water and solid waste treatment and process design; power plant emissions control; control of hazardous materials dissemination; air separation technology. *Mailing Add:* 505 Runnymede Rd Hockessin DE 19707-9123

HACKMAN, JOHN CLEMENT, NEUROPHARMACOLOGY, NEUROPHYSIOLOGY. *Current Pos:* assoc prof pharmacol, 91-96, RES PHYSIOLOGIST NEUROL, VET ADMIN MED CTR, MIAMI, 79-, PROF PHARMACOL, SCH MED, UNIV MIAMI, 96-; *Personal Data:* b Dayton, Ohio, May 16, 47; m 68, Susie Pollard; c Dawn, Jeffrey & Mark. *Educ:* Univ Miami, BS, 69, MS, 76, PhD(biol), 79. *Prof Exp:* Adj asst prof neurol, Sch Med, Univ Miami, 79-81, res asst prof, 81-82, from asst prof to assoc prof neurol & pharmacol, 82-95. *Mem:* Soc Neurosci; AAAS; Am Physiol Asn; Am Soc Pharmacol & Exp Therapeut; NY Acad Sci. *Res:* Basic mechanism of actions of drugs and neurotransmitters in spinal cord function; emphasis has been on inhibiting and excitaton, amino acid transmitters. *Mailing Add:* Dept Neurol D4-5 Sch Med Univ Miami PO Box 16960 Miami FL 33101. *Fax:* 305-545-7166; *E-Mail:* rdavidof@mednet.med. miami.edu

HACKMAN, MARTIN ROBERT, LABORATORY INFORMATION MANAGEMENT SYSTEMS. *Current Pos:* DATA MGT SPECIALIST, ANAQUEST INC, 86-; SR RES SCIENTIST, OHMEDA-PPD INC, 88- *Personal Data:* b New York, NY, Mar 20, 42; m 71; c 1. *Educ:* Brooklyn Col,

BS, 65; City Univ NY, MA, 74. *Prof Exp:* Chemist electrochem, Princeton Appl Res Corp, 68-69; assoc scientist, Hoffmann-La Roche Inc, 69-80, scientist anal chem, 80-85; tech adminr, Whitehall Labs, 85-86. *Concurrent Pos:* Lectr, Ctr Prof Advan, 77-78; mem, Subcomt LIMS, Am Soc Testing & Mat. *Mem:* Am Chem Soc; Am Asn Pharmaceut Scientists. *Res:* Method development of drugs in biological fluids incorporating analytical instrumentation such as gas and liquid chromatography, fluorescence, techniques specializing in electroanalytical chemistry and computerized data reduction; laboratory information management, system management, system analysis and robotics based on implementation of information and method development. *Mailing Add:* 9 Watchung Rd East Brunswick NJ 08816-4137

HACKMAN, ROBERT MARK, NUTRITION RESEARCH, NUTRITION EDUCATION. *Current Pos:* Partic prof geront & phys educ, 82-90, ASSOC PROF NUTRIT, UNIV ORE, 81- *Personal Data:* b Pittsburgh, Pa, May 29, 53. *Educ:* Johns Hopkins Univ, BA, 75; Pa State Univ, MS, 77; Univ Calif, Davis, PhD(nutrit), 81. *Concurrent Pos:* Nutrit consult, US & Russ Olympic Track & Field Teams; sports nutrit adv, Nat Basketball Asn & Other Prof Sports Teams. *Mem:* Soc Nutrit Educ; Am Inst Nutrit; fel Am Col Nutrit; Am Pub Health Asn. *Res:* Nutritional aspects of athletic performance; motivational strategies to help people make better dietary choices. *Mailing Add:* Dept Anthrop Univ Ore 210 Condon Hall Eugene OR 97403-1273. *Fax:* 541-485-2572

HACKNEY, ANTHONY C, EXERCISE PHYSIOLOGY, ENERGY METABOLISM. *Current Pos:* ASSOC PROF EXERCISE PHYSIOL & NUTRIT, UNIV NC, 88- *Personal Data:* m 78, Grace Griffith; c Sarah E & Zachary C. *Educ:* Berea Col, BA, 79; Kent State Univ, MA, 81, PhD(exercise physiol), 86. *Prof Exp:* Fel, Naval Health Res Ctr, 88, Johnson Space Ctr, NASA, 89. *Mem:* Fel Am Col Sports Med; Sigma Xi; Am Physiol Soc; Fed Am Socs Exp Biol. *Res:* Impact of physical activity upon the reproductive hormonal status of men and women. *Mailing Add:* Univ NC CB8700 Chapel Hill NC 27599-8700. *Fax:* 919-962-0489

HACKNEY, CAMERON RAY, FOOD MICROBIOLOGY, FOOD SAFETY. *Current Pos:* ASSOC PROF, VA POLYTECH INST & STATE UNIV, 85-, SUPT SEAFOOD EXP STA, VA POLYTECH INST, 85-, PROF & HEAD, FOOD SCI & TECHNOL. *Personal Data:* b Charleston, WVa, Oct 24, 51; m 74; c 1. *Educ:* WVa Univ, BS, 73, MS, 75; NC State Univ, PhD(food sci), 80. *Prof Exp:* Res asst, NC State Univ, 76-80; from asst prof to assoc prof food microbiol, La State Univ, 80-85. *Concurrent Pos:* Asst instr, WVa Univ, 73-75. *Mem:* Int Asn Milk Food & Environ Sanitation; Am Soc Microbiol; Inst Food Technologists; Sigma Xi. *Res:* Microbial cell injury; survival, recovery and physiology of pathogenic microorganisms; food safety; food quality. *Mailing Add:* Dept Food Sci & Tech Va Polytech State Univ PO Box 0418 Blacksburg VA 24063-0001

HACKNEY, COURTNEY THOMAS, COMMUNITY ECOLOGY. *Current Pos:* from asst prof to assoc prof, 80-88, PROF BIOL, UNIV NC, WILMINGTON, 88- *Personal Data:* b Mt Holly, NJ, Aug 11, 48; c 2. *Educ:* Univ SAla, BS, 70; Emory Univ, MS, 72; Miss State Univ, PhD(zool), 77. *Prof Exp:* Res assoc ecol, Miss State Univ, 77; asst prof biol, Univ Southwestern La, 78-80. *Concurrent Pos:* Mem NC Coastal Resources Comn, 89- *Mem:* Estuarine Res Fedn; Ecol Soc Am; Am Fisheries Soc; Soc Wetland Scientists (vpres, 84-85, pres, 86-87). *Res:* Coastal studies of shallow estuarine communities; productivity and decomposition of marsh plants; energetics of estuarine communities and the effect of human activity on estuarine systems and sea level rise. *Mailing Add:* Dept Biol Univ NC-Wilmington 601 S College Rd Wilmington NC 28403-3201

HACKNEY, DAVID DANIEL, ENZYMOLOGY, BIOENERGETICS. *Current Pos:* asst prof, 78-83, ASSOC PROF BIOCHEM, DEPT BIOL SCI, CARNEGIE-MELLON UNIV, 83- *Personal Data:* b New Orleans, La, Sept 6, 48. *Educ:* La State Univ, New Orleans, BS, 70; Univ Calif, Berkeley, PhD(biochem), 75. *Prof Exp:* Fel, Dept /cem, Molecular Biol Inst, Univ Calif, Los Angeles, 75-78. *Mem:* Am Chem Soc; Biophys Soc; Am Soc Biol Chemists. *Res:* Mechanism, regulation, and structure of enzymes, involving investigation into the molecular basis of cooperativity and allosteric regulation, the mechanism of biological energy coupling, and the organzation of membrane proteins. *Mailing Add:* Dept Biol Sci Carnegie-Mellon Univ 4400 Fifth Ave Pittsburgh PA 15213-2683. *Fax:* 412-268-7129

HACKNEY, JACK DEAN, INTERNAL MEDICINE, PHYSIOLOGY. *Current Pos:* assoc prof, 69-78, PROF MED, UNIV SOUTHERN CALIF, 78-, CHIEF ENVIRON HEALTH SECT, RANCHOS LOS AMIGOS HOSP, 70- *Personal Data:* b Marion, Ill, Oct 11, 24; m 46; c 2. *Educ:* St Louis Univ, MD, 48; Am Bd Internal Med, dipl, 56; Am Toxicol Sci, dipl. *Prof Exp:* Resident internal med, Vet Admin Hosp, Mo, 49-51; resident, White Mem Hosp, 53-54; instr, Loma Linda Univ, 54-56, asst clin prof, 56-57, asst prof, 57-64, from asst prof to assoc prof physiol, 65-69. *Concurrent Pos:* From actg dir to dir pulmonary lab, Los Angeles County Hosp, 54-63; clin physiologist, Rancho Los Amigos Hosp, 62-69, chief pulmonary function lab, 69- *Mem:* Fel Am Col Chest Physicians; fel Am Col Physicians; Am Col Toxicol; Am Physiol Soc; Sigma Xi. *Res:* Environmental health, especially air pollution health effects; experimental pathology of the lung, especially ozone, nitrogen dioxide and oxygen poisoning; pulmonary physiology, clinical application, especially non-invasive measures of important cardiopulmonary parameters. *Mailing Add:* Univ Southern Calif 5181 Duenas Laguna Hills CA 92653

HACKNEY, JOHN FRANKLIN, endocrine pharmacology, teratology, for more information see previous edition

HACKNEY, ROBERT WARD, NEMATOLOGY & HELMINTHOLOGY, TAXONOMY & IDENTIFICATION. *Current Pos:* assoc plant nematologist, 75-85, sr plant nematologist, supvr, 85-89, SR PLANT NEMATOLOGIST, SPECIALIST, CALIF DEPT FOOD & AGR, 89- *Personal Data:* b Louisville, Ky, Dec 11, 42; m 69, 95, Jacqueline M Eisenreich; c Candice C. *Educ:* Northwestern Univ, BA, 65; Murray State Univ, MS, 69; Kans State Univ, PhD(parasitol), 73. *Prof Exp:* Instr histol, Murray State Univ, 67-68, instr zool, 68-69; instr bot, Kans State Univ, 72-73; scholar, Nema Seminars, Univ Calif, Riverside, 73-75. *Concurrent Pos:* Chmn, Calif Nematode Diag Adv Comn, 80-; com arbitrator, Am Arbitration Asn, 80-; prin investr & proj leader, Exotic Pest Res Grant, 86-87; chmn, Soc Nematologists Regulatory Comt, 89-91. *Mem:* Soc Nematologists; Int Coun Study Viruses & Virus Dis Grape; Sigma Xi. *Res:* Plant disease diagnosis and new pest detection; nematode taxonomy and identification using morphology, cytology, cytogenetics, molecular biology and molecular genetics. *Mailing Add:* Calif Dept Food & Agr Plant Pest Diag Ctr 3294 Meadowview Rd Bldg E Sacramento CA 95832-1448

HACKWELL, GLENN ALFRED, ENTOMOLOGY, ECOLOGY. *Current Pos:* Assoc prof biol, 61-71, PROF BIOL, CALIF STATE UNIV, STANISLAUS, 71- *Personal Data:* b Manti, Utah, Jan 20, 31; m 55; c 2. *Educ:* Brigham Young Univ, BS, 57, MS, 58; Ore State Univ, PhD(entom), 67. *Concurrent Pos:* NSF res partic, Ore State Univ, 67; res partic, Univ Calif, Berkeley, 68-70; consult, Fennimore Chem Co, Campbell Soup Co & Food & Agr Orgn, UN. *Mem:* AAAS; Entom Soc Am. *Res:* Biology of Hymenoptera; insect ecology and behavior; eclosion and duration of larval development in the alkali bee, Nomia melanderi Cockerell; revision of bee genus Panurqinus; hydrobiology. *Mailing Add:* Dept Biol Calif State Univ Stanislaus Turlock CA 95380

HACKWELL, JOHN ARTHUR, ASTROPHYSICS, INFRARED INSTRUMENTATION. *Current Pos:* mem tech staff, 85-87, res scientist, 87-92, MGR, BACKGROUND & TARGETS, 92- *Personal Data:* b Ashton-upon Lyne, Lancashire, Eng, May 31, 47; m 76; c 2. *Educ:* Univ London, BSc, 68, PhD(physics), 71. *Prof Exp:* Asst prof physics & astron, Wyo Infrared Observ, 71-77, dir, 77-85, assoc prof physics, 82, prof physics, 82-85. *Mem:* Am Astron Soc; Int Astron Union. *Res:* Observational infrared astronomy and the development of new infrared instrumentation; remote sensing. *Mailing Add:* Aerospace Corp MS M2-266 PO Box 92957 Los Angeles CA 90009

HACKWOOD, SUSAN, ROBOT SENSORS, ROBOT SYSTEM DESIGN. *Current Pos:* DEAN ENG, UNIV CALIF, RIVERSIDE, 85- *Personal Data:* b Liverpool, Eng, May 23, 55. *Educ:* Leicester Polytech, UK, BSc, 76, PhD(solid state ionics), 79. *Prof Exp:* Fel solid state physics, AT&T Bell Labs, 79-81, mem tech staff, 81-82, supvr device robotics, 83, head, Dept Robotic Technol, 84; prof elec eng, Univ Calif, Santa Barbara, 84, dir, Ctr Robotic Systs Microelectronics, 85. *Concurrent Pos:* Ed, J Robotic Systs, 84-; mem adv comt, Div Information, Robotics & Intelligent Systs, NSF, 85-; prin investr, NSF grants, 85-, Delco Electronics GM Robot & Effector for Vacuum Environ, 85- & SRC A Color Syst, 86-87; mem org comt, Int Workshop on Intelligent Systs, Inst Elec & Electronics Engrs, 87- *Mem:* Inst Elec & Electronics Engrs; Electrochem Soc. *Res:* Robot system design; sensory integration preception and organization. *Mailing Add:* Calif Coun Sci & Technol Univ Calif Riverside CA 92521-0001

HACQUEBARD, PETER ALBERTUS, COAL-GEOLOGY. *Current Pos:* ADJ PROF, DEPT GEOL, DALHOUSIE UNIV, 83-; EMER RES SCIENTIST, GEOL SERV CAN, 88- *Personal Data:* b Rotterdam, Holland, Apr 9, 18; nat Can; m 45, Widdershoven; c Alexander, Simone, Bruno & Marcel. *Educ:* State Univ Leiden, BSc, 37, MSc, 40; State Univ Groningen, PhD(coal petrol), 43. *Hon Degrees:* LLD, Dalhousie Univ, 80. *Honors & Awards:* G H Cady Medal, Geol Soc Am, 79; Reinhardt Thiessen Medal, Int Comt Coal Petrol, 79; Distinguished Lectr Award, Can Inst Mining & Metall, 83; Coal Award, 93. *Prof Exp:* Geologist coal petrol, Geol Bur, Heerlen, Holland, 40-44; geologist field proj, Shell Oil Co Can, 46-48; sr geologist chg, Coal Res Sect, Coal Petrol & Palynology, Geol Surv Can, 48-83. *Concurrent Pos:* Mem, Int Comt Coal Petrol, 53- *Mem:* Fel Geol Soc Am; Geol Asn Can; Can Inst Mining & Metall; Royal Soc Can; hon mem Soc Org Petrol. *Res:* Coal geology; coal petrology for stratigraphic, coal utilization and hydrocarbon exploration purposes. *Mailing Add:* Atlantic Geosci Ctr Bedford Inst Oceanog Dartmouth NS B2Y 4A2 Can

HADD, HARRY EARLE, BIOCHEMISTRY, ENDOCRINOLOGY. *Current Pos:* res assoc, Div Endocrinol, Sch Med, Ind Univ-Purdue Univ, 60-65, asst prof urol, 65-66, asst prof obstet & gynec, 66-72, asst prof urol, 73-77, asst prof, 77-81, assoc prof, 81-89, EMER PROF BIOCHEM, NORTHWEST CTR MED EDUC, SCH MED, IND UNIV, 89- *Personal Data:* b Baltimore, Md, Dec 24, 18; m 53, Mildred D'Agostino; c Marc H. *Educ:* Purdue Univ, BS, 46; Temple Univ, MA, 49; Ind Univ, PhD(biochem), 64. *Prof Exp:* Res asst metab, Lankenau Hosp Res Inst, 49-51; metab chemist, Philadelphia Gen Hosp, 51-53; instr, Div Endocrinol, Sch Med, Temple Univ, 53-57; scientist, Worcester Found Exp Biol, 57-60; res assoc, Emory Univ, 89-91. *Concurrent Pos:* USPHS grant, 64-70 & 73-75; staff mem, Worcester Found Exp Biol, 72; consult to dir, Nat Ctr Toxicol Res, Food & Drug Admin, Jefferson, Ark, 77- *Mem:* AAAS; Am Chem Soc; Endocrine Soc; fel Am Inst Chemists. *Res:* Synthesis; biosynthesis and isolation of steroid hormone conjugates, including their role in the biological economy; synthesis prostate imaging agents for early detection prostate cancer in man; synthesis of steroid carboranes for BNCT. *Mailing Add:* 1051B N James Town Rd Decatur GA 30033

HADDAD, ABRAHAM H(ERZL), CONTROL SYSTEMS, ESTIMATION & DETECTION OF SIGNALS. *Current Pos:* Henry & Isabelle Dever prof & chmn elec eng & comput sci, 88-96, HENRY & ISABELLE DEVER PROF & CHMN ELEC & COMPUT ENG, NORTHWESTERN UNIV, ILL, 96- *Personal Data:* b Baghdad, Iraq, Jan 16, 38; US citizen; m 66, Carolyn A Kushner; c Benjamin J, Judith J & Jonathan D. *Educ:* Israel Inst Technol, BSc, 60, MSc, 63; Princeton Univ, MA, 64, PhD(elec eng), 66. *Honors & Awards:* Centennial Medal, Inst Elec & Electronics Engrs, 84. *Prof Exp:* From asst prof to prof elec eng, Univ Ill, Urbana, 66-79; prog dir systs theory, NSF, 79-83; prof elec eng, Ga Inst Technol, 83-88, dir, Comput Integrated Mfg Prog, 87-88. *Concurrent Pos:* Adv, US Army Missile Res & Develop Command, Redstone Arsenal, 69-79; vis assoc prof, Tel Aviv Univ, 72-73; mem sci adv group, US Army Missile Command, 75-76; chmn estimations comt & assoc ed jour, Inst Elec & Electronics Engrs, 77-78; consult, Dynamics Res Corp, 79, Lockheed Ga Co, 84-88. *Mem:* Fel AAAS; fel Inst Elec & Electronics Engrs; fel Inst Elec & Electronics Engrs Control Systs Soc (pres, 92); Am Automatic Control Coun (secy, 90-). *Res:* Analysis, identification and control of systems and processes subject to disturbances and structural changes with application to maneuvering target tracking and industrial processes, as well as other communication and control systems. *Mailing Add:* Dept Elec & Comput Eng Northwestern Univ 2694 Tech Inst Evanston IL 60208-3118. *Fax:* 847-491-4455; *E-Mail:* ahaddad@ece.nwu.edu

HADDAD, GEORGE I, ELECTRICAL ENGINEERING. *Current Pos:* From instr to prof elec eng, Univ Mich, 60-69, dir, Electron Physics Lab, 68-75, chmn dept, 75-87, PROF ELEC ENG, UNIV MICH, ANN ARBOR, 69-, DIR, CTR HIGH FREQUENCY MICROELECTRONICS, 87-, DEPT CHMN, 91- *Personal Data:* b Aindara, Lebanon, Apr 7, 35; US citizen; m 58; c 2. *Educ:* Univ Mich, BS, 56, MS, 58, PhD(elec eng), 63. *Honors & Awards:* Curtis W McGraw Res Award, 70. *Concurrent Pos:* Mem tech prog comt, Int Solid-State Circuits Conf, 68-74; ed, J Transactions Microwave Theory & Techniques, 68-71; Robert J Hiller prof eng, 91- *Mem:* Nat Acad Eng; Am Phys Soc; fel Inst Elec & Electronics Engrs; Am Soc Eng Educ. *Res:* Masers; parametric amplifiers; detectors; microwave electron beam devices; avalanche diodes; microwave solid-state devices; three-five semiconductor devices and integrated circuits; optoelectronic devices and integrated circuits. *Mailing Add:* Dept Elec Engr & Comput Sci Univ Mich 3303 EECS Ann Arbor MI 48109-2122

HADDAD, HESKEL MARSHALL, OPHTHALMOLOGY. *Current Pos:* PROF OPHTHAL, NY MED COL, 71- *Personal Data:* b Baghdad, Iraq, Sept 26, 30; nat US; m 63, Doris I Fatzer; c Ava M, Andreas M & Michael A. *Educ:* Hebrew Univ, Jerusalem, MD, 53; Am Bd Pediat, dipl, Am Bd Ophthal, dipl. *Honors & Awards:* Boswell Prize of Biol. *Prof Exp:* Intern, Donolo Hosp, Jaffo-Tel Aviv, 50-51; rotating intern, Hadassah Univ Hosp, Jerusalem, 51-53; pediat resident, Children's Med Ctr, Boston, 53-56; fel pediat endocrinol, Johns Hopkins Hosp, 56-58; fel clin endocrinol, Br Nat Inst Arthritis & Metab Dis, NIH, 58-59; pediatrician sect clin endocrinol, NIH, 59-60; resident & asst ophthal, Sch Med, Washington Univ, St Louis, 60-64; ophthalmologist, Hosp Beni Messous, Algiers, 64; asst attend ophthal surgeon & asst prof ophthal, Mt Sinai Hosp & Sch Med, NY, 64-67; dir, Dept Ophthal, Beth Israel Med Ctr, NY; assoc prof ophthal, Mt Sinai Sch Med, 67-71. *Concurrent Pos:* asst prof pediat, Sch Med, Howard Univ, Washington, 59-60; fel pediat ophthal, Inst Visual Sci, 62; res fel, Hosp Des Hautes Etudes, Paris, 62-63; ed-in-chief, Metab Ophthal, 76-79, Metab & Pediat Ophthal, 79-82, Metab, Pediat & Systemic Ophthal, 82- *Mem:* Fel Am Chem Soc; fel Am Inst Chemists; Am Fedn Clin Res; Am Endocrine Soc; AMA; Am Res Ophthal & Vision; NY Acad Sci; Soc Eye Surgeons; Int Soc Metab Eye Dis (secy-treas, 73-). *Mailing Add:* 1125 Park Ave New York NY 10128-1243. *Fax:* 212-360-7009

HADDAD, JERRIER ABDO, COMPUTERS, EDUCATION. *Current Pos:* RETIRED. *Personal Data:* b New York, NY, July 17, 22; m 74, Carol McCowen; c 5. *Educ:* Cornell Univ, BEE, 45. *Hon Degrees:* DSc, Union Col, 71, Clarkson Univ, 78. *Honors & Awards:* Order of Cedars Medal, Off Rank, Lebanese Repub, 70. *Prof Exp:* Var positions, Endicott Lab, IBM Corp, 45-50, develop engr, Poughkeepsie, 50-52, mgr component develop, 52-53, engr, 53-54, dir adv mach develop, 54-56, gen mgr, Spec Eng Prod, 56-59 & Adv Systs Develop, 59-61, vpres data systs, 61-62 & data processing, 62-63, dir eng, Prog & Technol, 63-67, vpres eng prog & technol, 67-70, vpres & dir, Poughkeepsie Lab, 70-72, vpres develop systs prod div, 72-75, vpres tech personnel develop, 75-81. *Concurrent Pos:* Mem comput sci & eng bd, Nat Acad Sci, 67-72, vchmn, 71-72; mem adv coun col eng, Cornell Univ, 68-87; trustee, Clarkson Col Technol, 68, Webb Inst Naval Archit, 88-; dir, Am Dist Tel Co, 68-88; chmn, Nat Res Coun Comt Educ & Utilization Engr, 81-85, mem, Bd Army Sci & Technol, 78-82. *Mem:* Nat Acad Eng; fel Inst Elec & Electronics Engrs; Sigma Xi. *Res:* Management in engineering, programming and technology area. *Mailing Add:* 162 Macy Rd Briarcliff Manor NY 10510. *Fax:* 914-941-4868; *E-Mail:* jahaddad@aol.com

HADDAD, JOHN GEORGE, VITAMIN D METABOLISM, METABOLIC BONE DISEASES. *Current Pos:* PROF MED & CHIEF, DEPT ENDOCRINOL, SCH MED, UNIV PA, 80- *Educ:* Tulane Univ, MD, 62. *Mailing Add:* Dept Med 611 CRB Univ Pa Sch Med G2 422 Curie Blvd Philadelphia PA 19104-6149. *Fax:* 215-898-5408

HADDAD, LOUIS CHARLES, ANALYTICAL BIOCHEMISTRY. *Current Pos:* sr res specialist analytical biochem, 78-93, SR PROD DEVELOP SPECIALIST, 3M CO, ST PAUL, MINN, 93- *Personal Data:* b Waterbury, Conn, Dec 15, 48; m 88, Sheri Olsen. *Educ:* Fairfield Univ, BS, 70; Ind Univ, Bloomington, PhD(biol chem), 75. *Prof Exp:* NIH res assoc biophys chem, Univ Minneapolis, 75-77; sr res biochemist, Gen Mills Inc, Minneapolis, 77-78. *Mem:* Am Chem Soc; AAAS. *Res:* Analytical biochemistry, chromatography, enzymology and biotechnology. *Mailing Add:* 687 Wesley Ct Mendota Heights MN 55118. *Fax:* 612-737-4538

HADDAD, RICHARD A, ELECTRICAL ENGINEERING. *Current Pos:* CHAIR, ELEC ENG DEPT, NJ INST TECHNOL, 96- *Personal Data:* b Brooklyn, NY, Nov 26, 34; m 61; c 3. *Educ:* Polytech Inst Brooklyn, BEE, 56, MEE, 58, PhD(elec eng), 62. *Prof Exp:* Res fel, Polytech Inst NY, 56-57, from instr to assoc prof elec eng, 57-78, assoc dean, 80-82, dir, Westchester Grad Ctr, 82-96. *Concurrent Pos:* Lectr indust, Gen Elec Co, Ford Instrument Co, Grumman Aircraft Corp & Am Bosch Arma Corp; consult, Sperry Gyroscope Co, NY, 63-64, Bell Tel Labs, NJ, 62 & 65-69 & Concord Res Corp, Mass, 71-73, Fairchild Camera, Syosset, NY, 75-76 & US Army Armaments Res & Develop Command, Dover, NJ, 74-78 & 81-; head, Div Eng, Inst Nat d'Electricite et d'Electronique, Boumerdes, Algeria, 78-80; US Nat Acad Sci export to Ministry of Educ, Lanzhou Univ, People's Repub China, 85. *Mem:* Inst Elec & Electronics Engrs. *Res:* Feedback control theory; digital and discrete-time system analysis and synthesis; simulation. *Mailing Add:* Dept Elec Eng NJ Inst Technol 323 Martin Luther King Blvd Newark NJ 07102

HADDAD, ZACK H, ALLERGY, IMMUNOLOGY. *Current Pos:* from asst prof to assoc prof pediat, 67-79, PROF PEDIAT, SCH MED, UNIV SOUTHERN CALIF, 79-, DIR RES & TRAINING, 67-, CHIEF, PEDIAT ALLERGY & IMMUNOL CLIN DIV, 67- *Personal Data:* b Jan 27, 38; m 64; c 2. *Educ:* Univ Cairo, BSc, 56; Univ Paris, MD, 61; Am Bd Allergy & Immunol, dipl, 67 & 72; Am Bd Pediat, dipl, 66. *Honors & Awards:* Bela Shick Mem Lectr Award, 81. *Prof Exp:* Resident pediat, Cook County Hosp, Univ Ill, 62-63 & Bellevue Hosp, Med Sch, NY Univ, 64-65; res fel immunol, Children's Hosp Pittsburgh, Med Sch, Univ Pittsburgh, 65-66; USPHS immunol allergy fel, Med Ctr, Univ Calif, San Francisco, 66-67. *Concurrent Pos:* Res assoc path, Children's Hosp of Los Angeles, Med Sch, Univ Pittsburgh, 63-64; attending physician, Pediat Allergy Clin, Children's Hosp Pittsburgh, 65-66; Calif Lung Asn Res & Educ Fund grant, Syntex, Inc clin res grant & Calif Lung Asn gen res fund grant, 72-73; consult various nat & int med facil, 73-; Union Bank pvt grant, 74-75; Astra Labs, Inc clin res grant, 75-76; Pvt Pharm Indust clin res grant, 77-78 & 78; Astra Labs res grant, 78; Pharmacia Int res grant, 78, Sandoz, 80. *Mem:* Fel Am Acad Allergy; fel Am Acad Pediat; fel Am Col Allergists; Soc Pediat Res; fel Am Asn Cert Allergists. *Res:* Mechanisms of immediate hypersensitivity mediated by IgE; immunoglobulin E-IgE sensitization of heterologous mast cells; drug hypersensitivity; immunochemical studies of food allergens and pollen allergens; mechanisms of immunotherapy; cyclic nucleotides in bronchial asthma. *Mailing Add:* 9400 Brighton Way Beverly Hills CA 90210

HADDAWY, PETER F, ARTIFICIAL INTELLIGENCE, DECISION THEORY. *Current Pos:* ASST ADJ PROF RADIOL, UNIV WIS, 94-, ASSOC PROF ELEC ENG & COMPUT SCI & DIR, DECISION SYSTS & ARTIFICIAL INTEL LAB, 95- *Personal Data:* b Madison, Wis, July 26, 59. *Educ:* Pomona Col, BA, 81; Univ Ill, MS, 86, PhD(comput sci), 91. *Prof Exp:* Sci programmer, Desert Res Inst, 81, software eng, 81-82; systs engr, Nixdorf Comput AG, Munich, WGer, 82-83; res assoc, Tech Univ Munich, 83-84 & 85; res asst, Artificial Intel Lab, Dept Comput Sci, Univ Ill, 84-86. *Concurrent Pos:* Grantee, Gen Elec, 89, Univ Wis-Miwaukee Grad Sch, 92-93, 95-96 & 96-97, NSF, 92-95 & 95-98, Sun Microsysts; mem prog comt, Time 94, 95, 96 & 97, Int Workshops Temporal Rep & Reasoning, 94-96, Conf Uncertainty Artificial Intel, 95 & 97, FLAIRS Spec Track Uncertain Reasoning, 96, Nat Conf Artificial Intel, 96 & 97; Fulbright scholar, Nat Inst Develop Admin, Bangkok, 96-97. *Mem:* Asn Comput Mach; Am Asn Artificial Intel. *Mailing Add:* Dept Elec Eng & Comput Sci Univ Wis-Milwaukee Milwaukee WI 53211. *E-Mail:* haddawy@cs.uwm.edu

HADDEN, CHARLES THOMAS, BACTERIAL METABOLISM, BACTERIAL GENETICS. *Current Pos:* STAFF MICROBIOLOGIST, OAK RIDGE RES INST, TENN, 84- *Personal Data:* b Newport News, Va, May 28, 44; m 66; c 4. *Educ:* Univ Chicago, BS, 66; Univ Wash, PhD(microbiol), 70. *Prof Exp:* Res assoc radiation biol, Univ Fla, 71-73; res asst prof radiation biol, Oak Ridge Grad Sch Biomed Sci, Univ Tenn, 74-83, res assoc prof radiation biol, 83-84. *Mem:* AAAS; Am Soc Microbiol. *Res:* Genetics and mechanisms of DNA repair in bacillus subtilis; physiological responses of Bacillus subtilis to chemical mutagens; DNA-mediated transformation and other genetics systems in anaerobes; microbial treatment of wastewater and soil contaminated with heavy metals. *Mailing Add:* 165 Waddell Circle Oak Ridge TN 37830

HADDEN, JOHN WINTHROP, INTERNAL MEDICINE, IMMUNOPHARMACOLOGY. *Current Pos:* PROF MED PHARMACOL & DIR PROG IMMUNOPHARMACOL, MED COL, MED COL, UNIV SFLA, TAMPA, 83- *Personal Data:* b Berkeley, Calif, Oct 23, 39; m 64, Elba Mas; c John W II & Paul J. *Educ:* Yale Univ, BA, 61; Columbia Univ, MD, 65. *Honors & Awards:* Angier Res Prize; Kellog Res Prize. *Prof Exp:* Intern med, Roosevelt Hosp, NY, 65-66, resident, 66-68; USPHS-NIH spec fel, Dept Pediat & Path, Univ Minn, Minneapolis, 69-72, asst prof path, 72-73; assoc prof, Grad Sch Med Sci, Cornell Univ, 73-83; assoc mem & dir lab immunopharmacol, Sloan Kettering Mem Inst, 73-83. *Concurrent Pos:* Am Heart Asn estab investr, 72-77; assoc attend, Mem Hosp, 73-83; assoc ed, Int J Immunopharmacol, 78- *Mem:* Am Asn Pathologists; Am Asn Immunologists; NY Acad Sci; Int Soc Immunopharmacol (pres, 85-88, past pres, 88-91). *Res:* Immunopharmacology; mechanisms of regulation of cellular function by cyclic nucleotides and related cell surface events; biochemistry of lymphocyte activation; mechanisms of thymic hormone action; lymphokines and macrophage proliferation and activation; immunotherapeutic drug development and analysis. *Mailing Add:* Prog Immunopharmacol Univ SFla Med Col 12901 N 30th St Tampa FL 33612. *Fax:* 813-974-2960

HADDOCK, AUBURA GLEN, TOPOLOGY. *Current Pos:* assoc prof, 67-69, chmn dept, 68-81, PROF MATH, UNIV MO, ROLLA, 69- *Personal Data:* b Jasper, Ark, May 29, 35; m 54; c 4. *Educ:* Ark State Teachers Col, BS, 54; Okla State Univ, MS, 58, PhD, 61. *Prof Exp:* Partic, Ark Exp Teacher Educ, 54-55; teacher, pub sch, Ark, 55-57; asst prof math, Ark Col, 58-59; asst, Okla State Univ, 59-61; prof, Ark Col, 61-63, acad dean, 63-65, dean, 65-67. *Concurrent Pos:* NSF prog, Okla State Univ, 57-58; mathematician, Oak Ridge Nat Labs, 78-79. *Mem:* Math Asn Am; Am Math Soc. *Res:* Point set topology; fixed point theorems. *Mailing Add:* 10251 County Rd 3010 Rolla MO 65401

HADDOCK, FREDERICK THEODORE, JR, RADIO ASTRONOMY. *Current Pos:* assoc prof astron & elec eng, Univ Mich, 56-59, prof elec eng, 59-67, prof astron, 59-88, dir, Radio Astron Observ, 61-80, EMER PROF, UNIV MICH, 88- *Personal Data:* b Independence, Mo, May 31, 19; div; c 2. *Educ:* Mass Inst Technol, BS, 41; Univ Md, MS, 50. *Hon Degrees:* DSc, Southwestern at Memphis, 65 & Ripon Col, 66. *Prof Exp:* Physicist & electronic scientist, US Naval Res Lab, 41-56. *Concurrent Pos:* Trustee, Assoc Univs, Inc, 64-68; mem, Space Sci Bd ad hoc comt astron, Nat Acad Sci, 58-62, radio frequency requirement sci res, 61-68, Whitford panel astron facil, 63-64; mem ad hoc panel on US Navy 600 foot radio telescope, President's Sci Adv Comt, 62, Air Force Off Sci Res Arecibo eval panel, Arecibo Observ, 62-69, adv comt planetary & interplanetary sci, Off Space Sci, NASA, 61-62, ad hoc working group on Apollo sci exp & training, 62-63, NASA hq astron subcomt, 67-69; consult, Off Space Sci & Applns, 70-, NASA astron missions bd, Radio Astron Panel, 68-71, ad hoc comt on Nat Astron Space Observ, 70, NASA outer planets grand tour mission, Radio Astron Team, 71-; vis res assoc, Calif Inst Technol, 66; mem, US Navy Eclipse Expeds, Aleutian Islands, 50, Khartoum, 52; mem, Comn Radio Astron, Int Astron Union, 55-, Comn Space Astron, 64-; chmn comn five, Int Sci Radio Union, 54-57, del to assemblies, 58-61, mem nat comt, 58-61. *Mem:* Am Astron Soc (vpres, 61-63); fel Inst Elec & Electronics Eng; Am Inst Aeronaut & Astronaut; fel Royal Astron Soc; Sigma Xi. *Res:* Radio astronomy; extragalactic sources, solar and planets; antennas and radiometers; space research. *Mailing Add:* PO Box 1245 Ann Arbor MI 48106-1245

HADDOCK, GERALD HUGH, GEOLOGY. *Current Pos:* From instr to prof, 71-91, EMER PROF GEOL, WHEATON COL, ILL, 91- *Personal Data:* b Neosho, Mo, Mar 7, 29; m 60, Faith E Winsor; c Mary, Ralph & Frances. *Educ:* Wheaton Col, Ill, BS, 56; State Col Wash, MS, 59; Univ Ore, PhD(geol), 67. *Mem:* Geol Soc Am. *Res:* Petrology of welded tuffs. *Mailing Add:* Dept Physics/Geol Wheaton Col Wheaton IL 60187-5539

HADDOCK, JOHN R, MATHEMATICS. *Current Pos:* Fac mem, Dept Math Sci & interim dean, Col Arts & Sci, 94, DIR GRAD STUDIES & RES, MEMPHIS STATE UNIV, 97- *Mailing Add:* Col Arts & Sci Univ Memphis 213 Mitchell Hall Memphis TN 38152

HADDOCK, JORGE, SIMULATION, PROJECT MANAGEMENT & PRODUCTION PLANNING. *Current Pos:* from asst prof to assoc prof, 86-96, PROF INDUST ENG & OPER RES, RENSSELAER POLYTECH INST, 96- *Personal Data:* b Caguas, PR, Aug 15, 55; m 80; c 2. *Educ:* Univ PR, BS, 78; Rensselaer Polytech Inst, MS, 79; Purdue Univ, PhD(indust eng), 81. *Honors & Awards:* Outstanding Young Indust Eng Award, Inst Indust Engrs, 90. *Prof Exp:* From instr to asst prof, Indust Eng, Univ PR, 78-83; asst prof indust eng, Clemson Univ, 84-86. *Concurrent Pos:* Consult var corp, 78-90; res chmn, Oper Res Div, Inst Indust Engrs, 85-86, newslett ed, 87-88, publ cluster leader, 88-91. *Mem:* Corresp mem Nat Acad Eng Mex; Oper Res Soc Am; Soc Comput Simulation; assoc mem Inst Mgt Sci; sr mem Inst Indust Engrs. *Res:* Modeling of manufacturing/production and inventory control systems, as well as the design and implementation of simulation modeling and analysis tools; author or co-author of over 60 technical publications. *Mailing Add:* 102 Old Coach Rd Clifton Park NY 12065

HADDOCK, LILLIAN, INTERNAL MEDICINE, ENDOCRINOLOGY. *Current Pos:* from assoc to assoc prof med, Sch Med, Univ PR, 59-70, chief sect endocrinol & diabetes, 60, dir endocrinol & diabetes, 60-76, dir med educ, Univ Hosp, 68-72, assoc dean acad affairs, Med Sci Campus, 76-78, dean, 78-85, actg dean med, 77-78, PROF MED, SCH MED, UNIV PR, 70- *Personal Data:* b Naguabo, PR, Feb 25, 29. *Educ:* Univ PR, BS, 50; Temple Univ, MD, 54; Am Bd Internal Med, dipl, 64; Am Bd Endocrinol & Metab, dipl, 72. *Honors & Awards:* PR Acad Arts & Sci Prize Acomplishments Endocrinol, 89. *Prof Exp:* Internship, Bayamon Dist Hosp, PR, 54-55; resident internal med, San Juan City Hosp, 55-57; NIH trainee endocrinol, Johns Hopkins Hosp, 57-59. *Concurrent Pos:* Vis prof, Harvard Med Sch, 73-74 & 86; Nat Comn Diabetes, 75; mem, NLM Biomed Libr Rev Comt, 83-87; mem, Nat Diabetes Adv Bd, 90-93; gov, PR Chap, Am Col Physicians, 92-96. *Mem:* Am Diabetes Asn; Endocrine Soc; Am Fedn Clin Res; fel Am Col Physicians; Pan-Am Med Asn; Am Soc Bone & Mineral Res. *Res:* Metabolism; vitamin D; calcium and phosphorus metabolism; diabetes mellitus; clinical research in all types of endocrine and metabolic diseases. *Mailing Add:* Univ PR Med Sci Campus San Juan PR 00936-5067

HADDOCK, PHILIP GEORGE, FORESTRY. *Current Pos:* from assoc prof to prof, 53-78, EMER PROF FORESTRY, UNIV BC, 78- *Personal Data:* b San Diego, Calif, Mar 19, 13; m 42; c 5. *Educ:* Univ Calif, BS, 34, PhD(plant physiol), 42. *Prof Exp:* Jr forester, Calif Forest & Range Exp Sta, US Forest Serv, 34-36; asst, dept forestry, Univ Calif, 36-39; asst prof forest bot, State Univ NY Col Forestry, Syracuse, 46-47; asst prof forestry, Univ Wash, 47-53. *Mem:* Fel AAAS; Soc Am Foresters; fel Can Inst Forestry; cor mem Ital Acad Forestry Sci. *Mailing Add:* 4620 W Second Ave Vancouver BC V6R 1L1 Can

HADDOCK, ROY P, NUCLEAR PHYSICS. *Current Pos:* Asst res physicist, Univ Calif, Berkeley, 57-59, from asst prof to assoc prof, 59-71, prof nuclear physics, 71-77, PROF PHYSICS, UNIV CALIF, LOS ANGELES, 77- *Personal Data:* b Nogales, Ariz, Mar 30, 28; m 52; c 5. *Educ:* Univ Calif, Berkeley, AB, 52, PhD(physics), 57. *Concurrent Pos:* Consult, Lawrence Berkeley Lab, 59- *Mem:* Fel Am Phys Soc. *Res:* High energy nuclear physics research and instrumentation. *Mailing Add:* Dept Physics Univ Calif Los Angeles CA 90024

HADDON, ROBERT CORT, ORGANIC & THEORETICAL CHEMISTRY, ORGANIC CONDUCTORS & SUPERCONDUCTORS. *Current Pos:* vis scientist org chem, 76-78, mem tech staff chem physics, 78-92, DISTINGUISHED MEM TECH STAFF, AT&T BELL LABS, 92- *Personal Data:* b Sheffield, Eng, Mar 12, 43; Australian citizen; m 83; c 1. *Educ:* Univ Melbourne, BSc Hons, 66; Pa State Univ, PhD(org chem), 71. *Prof Exp:* Res fel theoret org chem, Univ Tex, Austin, 72-73; hon fel, Res Sch Chem, Australian Nat Univ, 73-76. *Concurrent Pos:* Queen Elizabeth II fel, 73-75. *Mem:* Am Chem Soc; Royal Soc Chem; fel Royal Australian Inst; Am Phys Soc; Mat Res Soc; fel AAAS. *Res:* Theoretical chemistry; organic chemistry; organic metals; molecular engineering: theory, design and synthesis of new materials. *Mailing Add:* RM1A-359 AT&T Bell Labs 600 Mountain Ave Murray Hill NJ 07974-0636

HADDON, WILLIAM F, (JR), MASS SPECTROMETRY. *Current Pos:* RES CHEMIST, WESTERN REGIONAL CTR, AGR RES SERV, USDA, 69-, RES LEADER, FOOD SAFETY & HEALTH, 93- *Personal Data:* b Denver, Colo, Jan 5, 42; m 93, Barbara Rapchick; c Jennifer, Adam & Kimberly. *Educ:* Harvey Mudd Col, BS, 64; Purdue Univ, PhD(chem), 68. *Prof Exp:* Res chemist, Celanese Res Co, NJ, 68-69. *Mem:* Am Soc Mass Spectrometry; AAAS. *Res:* Organic mass spectrometry applied to structure elucidation and trace analysis; computer interfacing of chemical instrumentation. *Mailing Add:* 35 Willow Ave Larkspur CA 94939-1321. *Fax:* 510-559-5777; *E-Mail:* haddon@garnet.berkeley.edu

HADDOX, CHARLES HUGH, JR, clinical chemistry; deceased, see previous edition for last biography

HADDOX, MARK, ELECTRONICS. *Current Pos:* Electronics engr, 78-80, chief engr, 80, VPRES ENG, JODON, INC, ANN ARBOR, 80- *Educ:* Ohio State Univ, BS, 75; Univ Mich, BSEE, 77. *Mem:* Inst Elec & Electronics Engrs. *Res:* Diesel engine emissions; measurement of engine cylinder minimum volume and compression ratio; train safety instrumentation. *Mailing Add:* 1243 King George Blvd Ann Arbor MI 48108

HADDY, FRANCIS JOHN, PHYSIOLOGY, INTERNAL MEDICINE. *Current Pos:* chmn dept, 76-87, PROF PHYSIOL, UNIFORMED SERV UNIV, 87- *Personal Data:* b Walters, Minn, Sept 6, 22; m 46, Theresa Brey; c 3. *Educ:* Univ Minn, BS, 43; BM, 46, MD, 47; MS, 49, PhD(physiol), 53. *Honors & Awards:* Wiggers Award, 66; Medal Sci Achievement Award, Am Heart Asn; Annual Award, Am Col Nutrit. *Prof Exp:* Asst prof physiol, Northwestern Univ, 53-55, asst prof med & physiol, 57-61; prof physiol & chmn dept & assoc prof med, Sch Med, Univ Okla, 61-66; prof physiol & chmn dept, Mich State Univ, 66-76. *Concurrent Pos:* Sr grade physician, Vet Admin Res Hosp, Chicago, 53-55, clin investr, 57-59, chief res, 59-61; chief circulation sect, US Army Med Res Lab, Ft Knox, Ky, 55-57. *Mem:* Am Physiol Soc (pres, 81); Am Soc Clin Invest. *Res:* Cardiovascular physiology; regulation of blood flow fluid flux across capillary membrane; ionic action on blood vesssals low ranin hypertension. *Mailing Add:* Dept Physiol Uniformed Serv Univ Health Sci 4301 Jones Bridge Rd Bethesda MD 20814-4799

HADEEN, KENNETH DOYLE, METEOROLOGY, COMPUTER SCIENCE. *Current Pos:* DIR, NAT CLIMATIC DATA CTR, 84- *Personal Data:* b Haxtun, Colo, Mar 8, 31; m 53; c 2. *Educ:* Colo State Univ, BS, 53; Tex A&M Univ, MS, 61, PhD(meteorol), 66. *Honors & Awards:* Merewether Award, Air Weather Serv, Dept Air Force, 70. *Prof Exp:* Chief tech serv div, HQ Air Weather Serv, 72-73; Air Force Global Weather Ctr Opers officer, Air Weather Serv, USAF, 73-75, wing vcomdr, 75-76; assoc dir, First Global Atmospheric Res Prog Global Exp, Dept Defense, HQ USAF, 76-77; dep dir, Ctr Environ Assessment, 77-84. *Mem:* AAAS; Am Meteorol Soc. *Res:* Numerical analysis and forecasting; physical scientist administration. *Mailing Add:* 226 Wildflower Rd Asheville NC 28804

HADEMENOS, JAMES GEORGE, BIOPHYSICS, SCIENCE EDUCATION. *Current Pos:* assoc prof sci educ, 70-74, PROF EDUC & HEAD DEPT, ANGELO STATE UNIV, 74- *Personal Data:* b Houston, Tex, June 13, 31; m 62; c 3. *Educ:* Univ Houston, BS, 58; Univ SDak, MA, 66; Syracuse Univ, PhD(biophys), 70. *Prof Exp:* Teacher, Spring Br Independent Sch Dist, Tex, 58-65; instr physics, Stephen F Austin State Univ, 66-67; teaching asst, Syracuse Univ, 67-69; assoc prof, Lock Haven State Col, 69-70. *Concurrent Pos:* NSF consult, Phys Sci Study Comt Physics, Univ Andhra, India, 67. *Mem:* AAAS. *Res:* Ozone and air ions accompanying biological applications of electric fields; Piaget-type conservation tasks. *Mailing Add:* Dept Educ Angelo State Univ San Angelo TX 76901-0001

HADEN, CLOVIS ROLAND, ELECTRICAL ENGINEERING. *Current Pos:* VICE CHANCELLOR & DEAN ENG, TEX A&M UNIV, COLLEGE STATION, 93- *Personal Data:* b Houston, Tex, Apr 10, 40; m 56, Joyce Weathers; c Cathy (Fuchs), Kim (Jensen) & Clay. *Educ:* Univ Tex, Arlington, BS, 61; Calif Inst Technol, MS, 62; Univ Tex, PhD, 65. *Honors & Awards:* George Washington Medal, Freedom Found, 89. *Prof Exp:* Design engr, Tex

Instruments Inc, 62; res engr scientist, Electronic Mat Res Lab, Univ Tex, 63-64; asst prof elec eng, Univ Okla, 65-68; assoc prof, Tex A&M Univ, 68-71, dir, Inst Solid-State Electronics, 69-72, prof, 71-72; dir, Sch Elec Engr & Comput Sci, Univ Okla, 72-78; dean, Col Eng & Appl Sci, Ariz State Univ, 78-91, vpres acad affairs & provost, 87-89; vice chancellor & provost, La State Univ, 91-93. *Concurrent Pos:* Exec ed, Elec Power Systs Res, 78- *Mem:* Am Soc Eng Educ; Nat Soc Prof Engrs; fel Inst Elec & Electronics Engrs. *Res:* Application of superconductivity; semiconductor devices and physics; electric power systems; engineering education. *Mailing Add:* Col Eng Tex A&M Univ College Station TX 77843-3126. *Fax:* 409-845-4925; *E-Mail:* crh7483@zeus.tamu.edu

HADER, ROBERT JOHN, MATHEMATICAL STATISTICS. *Current Pos:* from assoc prof to prof, 51-82, EMER PROF EXP STATIST, NC STATE UNIV, 83- *Personal Data:* b Hartford, Wis, Apr 13, 19; m 42; c 2. *Educ:* Univ Chicago, BS, 43; NC State Univ, PhD(statist), 49. *Prof Exp:* Instr exp statist, NC State Univ, 49; statistician, Los Alamos Sci Lab, 49-51. *Mem:* Fel Am Statist Asn. *Res:* Sampling acceptance inspection; experimental designs for industrial research. *Mailing Add:* 5009 New Hope Rd No A4 Raleigh NC 27604

HADER, RODNEY N(EAL), SCIENTIFIC & EDUCATIONAL SOCIETY ADMINISTRATION. *Current Pos:* RETIRED. *Personal Data:* b Paris, Mo, Sept 13, 22; m 52, Lottie Gulbranson; c Catherine, Daniel & Stephen. *Educ:* Univ Ill, BS, 44. *Prof Exp:* Partic, Manhattan proj, US Army Corps Engrs, 44-46; develop engr, Firestone Plastics Co, Firestone Tire & Rubber, 44 & 46-50; assoc ed, Appl Publ, Am Chem Soc, 50-56, ed, 56-64, asst to ed dir, 60-62, exec asst to dir publ, 62-70, actg secy, 70-76, exec asst to exec dir, 73-77, dep to exec dir, 79-80, chief operating officer, 80-82, secy, 77-88, dep exec dir, 83-88. *Concurrent Pos:* Actg ed chem, Am Chem Soc, 62-63, J Chem Eng & Data, 64, I&EC Prod Res & Develop, 65-68; mem bd dirs, Centcom, Ltd, 82-88. *Mem:* Am Chem Soc; AAAS; Am Inst Chem Engrs. *Mailing Add:* 907 Kenbrook Dr Silver Spring MD 20902-3228

HADERLIE, EUGENE CLINTON, BIOLOGICAL OCEANOGRAPHY. *Current Pos:* RETIRED. *Personal Data:* b Thayne, Wyo, Mar 23, 21; m 45; c 2. *Educ:* Univ Calif, AB, 43, MA, 48, PhD, 50. *Prof Exp:* From asst to lectr zool, Univ Calif, 47-50; instr biol sci, Monterey Peninsula Col, 50-54, chmn dept, 54-65; assoc prof, 65-68, prof oceanog, Naval Postgrad Sch, 68-86. *Concurrent Pos:* NSF fac fel, Univ Bristol, Eng & Stazione Zoologia, Naples, Italy, 58-59; liaison scientist, Off Naval Res, London, 62-63; actg assoc prof, Hopkins Marine Sta, Stanford Univ, 62, 64 & vis prof, 75; consult, US Dept Energy, Ocean Thermal Progs, 74-78. *Res:* Helminth parasites of the fishes of California; California intertidal invertebrates; marine boring and fouling organisms; marine pollution. *Mailing Add:* Dept Oceanog Naval Postgrad Sch Monterey CA 93940

HADERLIE, LLOYD CONN, WEED SCIENCE. *Current Pos:* RES & CONSULT, AGRA SERV INC, 88- *Personal Data:* b Afton, Wyo, Feb 23, 46; m 71, Sharyl Jensen; c Kristin, Melanie, Paul L, Rachel, David C, Jacob C, Laura & Rebecca. *Educ:* Utah State Univ, BS, 71; Univ Ill, PhD(agron), 75. *Prof Exp:* Asst prof agron, Univ Nebr, Lincoln, 75-81; assoc prof weed sci, Univ Idaho, 81-88. *Mem:* Weed Sci Soc Am; Am Soc Plant Physiologists; AAAS. *Res:* Weed biochemistry and physiology; perennial weed, rhizome; bud dormancy; translocation physiology; herbicide mode of action; weed control in potatoes, sugar beets and cereals; water quality research; fertilizers; pesticide registration. *Mailing Add:* 3243 W Joanna Ct American Falls ID 83211. *Fax:* 208-226-2739

HADERMANN, ALBERT FELIX, PHYSICAL CHEMISTRY, POLYMER CHEMISTRY. *Current Pos:* PRES, HADERMANN CONSULTS, INC, 91- *Personal Data:* b New York, NY, Mar 20, 38; m 62; c 4. *Educ:* City Col New York, BS, 59; Am Univ, MS, 69, PhD(chem), 70. *Prof Exp:* Sr chemist, Melpar, Inc, Va, 63-67; sr scientist, Ctr Environ Anal, Va, 70; asst prof phys chem, American Univ, 71-74; consult, Enviro-Control, Inc, 74-76; consult, JRB Assocs, Inc, 76-82; vpres res & develop, Gen Technol Appln, Inc, 82-91. *Concurrent Pos:* Consult, EAS Sci Inc, Md, 70-, Appl Phys Chem Inc, 70- & Mineral Pigments Co, 71; fel, Am Univ, 71. *Mem:* AAAS; Am Chem Soc; NY Acad Sci; Am Defense Preparedness Asn. *Res:* Magnetically stabilized electrophoresis; photochemistry; electrokinetic behavior at high field strengths; fractionation of biological materials; applications of membrane theory; model biological membranes; properties of macroradicals; oil-spill removal products; composite development. *Mailing Add:* 11609 Browningsville Rd Ijamsville MD 21754

HADFIELD, MICHAEL GALE, INVERTEBRATE ZOOLOGY, MARINE BIOLOGY. *Current Pos:* from asst prof to assoc prof, 68-79, PROF, DEPT ZOOL & PAC BIOMED RES CTR, UNIV HAWAII, 79-, DIR, KEWALO MARINE LAB, 96- *Personal Data:* b Seattle, Wash, Feb 8, 37; m, Carolyn A deJung. *Educ:* Univ Wash, AB, 59, MS, 61; Stanford Univ, PhD(biol sci), 67. *Prof Exp:* Asst prof zool, Pomona Col, 66-68. *Concurrent Pos:* Vis prof, Friday Harbor Labs, 68, 78, 81, 84, 86, 88 & Hopkins Marine Sta, 89; assoc ed, Pac J Sci, Invert Biol. *Mem:* Fel AAAS; Sigma Xi; Western Soc Naturalists; Int Soc Invertebrate Reproduction; Soc Conserv Biol; Soc Integrative & Comp Biol (pres, 95 & 96); Am Soc Molecular Marine Biol & Biotechnol. *Res:* Invertebrate development; embryology larval development and metamorphosis of marine gastropods; evolutionary and conservation biology of Hawaiian tree snails. *Mailing Add:* Kewalo Marine Lab 41 Ahui St Pac Biomed Res Ctr Univ Hawaii Honolulu HI 96813. *Fax:* 808-599-4817; *E-Mail:* hadfield@hawaii.edu

HADIDI, AHMED FAHMY, MOLECULAR BIOLOGY, MICROBIOLOGY. *Current Pos:* MICROBIOLOGIST, USDA, 75- *Personal Data:* b Damanhur, Egypt, Mar 1, 37; US citizen; m 64; c 3. *Educ:* Cairo Univ, BSc Hons, 58; Univ Minn, MS, 62; Kans State Univ, PhD(plant path), 67. *Prof Exp:* Res fel, Univ Ky, 67-68 & Purdue Univ, 68-69; res assoc, Baylor Col Med, 70 & Univ Calif, Berkeley, 70-73; virologist, Litton Bionetics, Inc, 73-75. *Mem:* Am Soc Virol; Am Phytopath Soc; AAAS; NY Acad Sci; Sigma Xi. *Res:* Replication and structure of plant viruses and viroids. *Mailing Add:* 11203 Harborside Dr Largo FL 33773

HADIDIAN, ZAREH, PHARMACOLOGY. *Current Pos:* RETIRED. *Personal Data:* b Aintab, Turkey, Feb 9, 11; US citizen; m 39, Margaret Humeslon; c Ellen, John & Patricia. *Educ:* Rensselaer Polytech Inst, BS, 34, MS, 35; Clark Univ, PhD(gen physiol), 39. *Prof Exp:* Res assoc physiol, Clark Univ, 39-40, instr, 40-41; asst pharmacologist, Lederle Labs, NY, 41-43; instr pharmacol, Albany Med Col, 43-44; physiologist, Mem Found Neuro Endocrine Res, 44-46; biochemist, Worcester Found Exp Biol, 46-48; asst prof pharmacol, Med Sch, Tufts Univ, 48-50, assoc prof, 50-58; liaison officer, Off Naval Res, London, 58-60; dir pharmacol, Mason Res Inst, Pennwalt Corp, 60-66, dir off sci info, Pharmaceut Div, 66-76; consult, Astra Pharmaceut Prod Inc, 76-90. *Mem:* AAAS; Soc Toxicol; Am Physiol Soc; Am Soc Pharmacol & Exp Therapeut; Royal Soc Med. *Res:* Hyaluronic acid; hyaluronidase; snake venoms; toxicology. *Mailing Add:* 126 Country Rd Ipswich MA 01938

HADIMIOGLU, HALDUN, SUPERCOMPUTER SYSTEMS, VERY-LARGE SCALE INTEGRATION NOVEL COMPUTING & HIGH SPEED COMMUNICATION. *Current Pos:* Teaching fel comput sci, 83-85, vis asst prof, 91-93, indust asst prof 91-97, INDUST ASSOC PROF COMPUT SCI, 97- *Personal Data:* b Erzurum, Turkey, Aug 8, 57. *Educ:* Middle East Tech Univ, Turkey, BS, 79, MS, 81; Polytech Univ, PhD(comput sci), 91. *Prof Exp:* Res engr, Prof Electronics Inc, Turkey, 80-82. *Concurrent Pos:* Fel, Sci & Tech Res Coun Turkey, 78-81. *Mem:* Sigma Xi; Asn Comput Mach; Inst Elec and Electronics Engrs; Soc Indust & Appl Math; NY Acad Sci. *Res:* Exploration of input/output structures for such supercomputers as parallel computers, including distributed file system organizations; novel very-large scale integration techniques for high speed computation and communication. *Mailing Add:* 452 Atlantic Ave Apt 4F Brooklyn NY 11217-1773. *E-Mail:* haldun@photon.poly.edu

HADJIAN, RICHARD ALBERT, protein biochemistry, for more information see previous edition

HADJIMICHAEL, EVANGELOS, THEORETICAL NUCLEAR PHYSICS. *Current Pos:* from asst prof to assoc prof, 67-74, PROF PHYSICS, FAIRFIELD UNIV, 74- *Personal Data:* b Thessaloniki, Greece, Aug 16, 37; m 60; c 2. *Educ:* City Col New York, BS, 60; Univ Calif, Berkeley, PhD(physics), 65. *Prof Exp:* Asst prof physics, Calif Polytech Col, 65-66; res assoc, Yale Univ, 66-68. *Concurrent Pos:* NSF grants intermediate energy nuclear physics, nuclear defense & nuclear arms limitations. *Mem:* Am Phys Soc. *Res:* Heavy ion scattering; deuteron photodisintegration; scattering reactions. *Mailing Add:* Dept Physics Fairfield Univ Fairfield CT 06430. *E-Mail:* hadjm@fair1.fairfield.edu

HADLER, HERBERT ISAAC, BIOCHEMISTRY. *Current Pos:* RETIRED. *Personal Data:* b Toronto, Ont, Aug 22, 20; US citizen; m 47; c 3. *Educ:* Univ Toronto, BASc, 42; Univ Wis, PhD, 52. *Honors & Awards:* Parker Award, Chicago Med Sch, 58. *Prof Exp:* Demonstr chem eng, Univ Toronto, 42-43 & 44-45; supvr dryer house, Seagram's Can, 43-44; asst chem, Univ Wis, 47-51; fel, McArdle Mem Lab, 51-53; assoc surg, Chicago Med Sch, 53-54, from asst prof to assoc prof, 54-59; asst prof biochem, Inst Enzyme Res, Univ Wis, 63-66; assoc prof chem, Southern Ill Univ, 66-74, prof chem & biochem, 74-80. *Concurrent Pos:* Fogarty sr int fel, NIH, 79-80. *Mem:* Am Asn Cancer Res; Am Soc Biol Chem; Sigma Xi; Am Col Toxicol; Am Chem Soc. *Res:* Carcinogenesis mitochondrial genes and oxidative phosphorylation. *Mailing Add:* 2177 Upper Saint Dennis Rd St Paul MN 55116

HADLER, NORTIN M, RHEUMATIC DISEASE. *Current Pos:* PROF MED, MICROBIOL & IMMUNOL, UNIV NC, 73- *Personal Data:* b New York, NY, Nov 13, 42; m 65, Carol Spiegel; c Jeffrey Alan & Elana Beth. *Educ:* Yale, AB, 64; Harvard Univ, MD, 68. *Mem:* Am Soc Clin Invest; Am Asn Immunol. *Res:* Industrial rheumatology; clinical investigations on back pain, disability and compensation. *Mailing Add:* Sch Med Univ NC 3330 Thurston Bldg No 7280 Chapel Hill NC 27599-7280. *Fax:* 919-966-1739; *E-Mail:* nmh@med.unc.edu

HADLEY, BRUCE ALAN, PLANT PATHOLOGY, PLANT BREEDING. *Current Pos:* RES PATHOLOGIST PLANT PATH, E I DU PONT DE NEMOURS & CO, INC, 78- *Personal Data:* b Pittsburgh, Pa, Aug 1, 50; m 71; c 1. *Educ:* Pa State Univ, BS, 72, MS, 73; NC State Univ, PhD(plant path), 78. *Prof Exp:* Res technician plant path, NC State Univ, 73-78. *Mem:* Am Phytopath Soc. *Res:* Chemical control of plant diseases. *Mailing Add:* 104 Great Circle Rd Newark DE 19711

HADLEY, DONALD G, SEDIMENTOLOGY, STRATIGRAPHY. *Current Pos:* GEOLOGIST, US GEOL SURV, 67- *Personal Data:* b Artesia, NMex, July 24, 36; m 63; c 3. *Educ:* Eastern NMex Univ, BS, 59; Univ Wis, MS, 63; Johns Hopkins Univ, PhD(geol), 68. *Prof Exp:* Technician biochem, Univ Wis Inst Enzyme Res, 61-63. *Mem:* AAAS; Am Asn Petrol Geologists; fel Geol Soc Am; Soc Econ Paleont & Mineral. *Res:* Paleocurrents, basin analysis, stratigraphy and sedimentary petrography of Precambrian quartzites, Ontario and Quebec, Canada; anthracite, Pennsylvania, and bituminous, West Virginia and Pennsylvania, coal basins; regional geology and structure of the Arabian Shield. *Mailing Add:* 12211 Westwood Hills Dr Herndon VA 20171

HADLEY, ELBERT HAMILTON, CHEMISTRY. *Current Pos:* RETIRED. *Personal Data:* b Springville, NY, July 10, 13; m 41; c 2. *Educ:* Univ Mich, BS, 36, MS, 37; Duke Univ, PhD(chem), 40. *Prof Exp:* Asst, Duke Univ, 38-40; res chemist, Electrochem Dept, E I du Pont de Nemours & Co, Inc, NY, 40-47; assoc prof chem, Col Sci, Southern Ill Univ, Carbondale, 47-55, asst chmn dept, 60-65, asst dean, 65-71, prof chem, 55-71, dean, 71-88. *Concurrent Pos:* Vis prof, Kabul Univ, Afghanistan, 60. *Mem:* AAAS; Am Chem Soc; Electrochem Soc. *Res:* Pharmaceutical synthetic organic chemistry; vapor phase catalytic fluorination; fluid catalytic reactions; electroplating; cyanides. *Mailing Add:* 1002 Briarwood Dr Carbondale IL 62901-2426

HADLEY, EVAN C, GERIATRICS RESEARCH. *Current Pos:* Staff fel, Geront Res Ctr, Nat Inst Aging, NIH, 78-80, health sci adminr, Geriat Res Sect, Biomed Res & Clin Med Prog, 80-82, actg chief, Geriat Br, 82-84, chief, 84-90, ASSOC DIR GERIAT, NAT INST AGING, NIH, 90- *Personal Data:* b Washington, DC, Jan 19, 47; m; c 2. *Educ:* Yale Univ, BA, 71; Univ Pa, MD, 78. *Honors & Awards:* J Marion Sims Lectr, Am Uro-Gynec Soc, 88. *Concurrent Pos:* Mem, Nutrit Coord Comt, Diabetes Mellitus Interagency Coord Comt & Digestive Dis Interagency Coord Comt, 84-87, Arthritis & Musculoskeletal Dis Interagency Coord Comt, 84-; mem, Comt Nat Res Agenda Aging, Nat Acad Sci, 89, res comt, Am Geriat Soc, 89-; chair, Res Task Force, Clin Med Sect, Geront Soc Am, 89- *Mem:* Am Geriat Soc; Geront Soc Am. *Res:* Protein catabolism in human fibroblasts in vitro and effects of proteases on fibroblast proliferation; glycosylated hemoglobins in man in relation to age and other indices of glucose metabolism; formation and removal of carcinogen-DNA abducts in human cells in tissue culture; therapies for urinary incontinence; interventions to reduce physical frailty and fall injuries among older persons. *Mailing Add:* 11825 Trailridge Dr Potomac MD 20854

HADLEY, FRED JUDSON, PHYSICAL CHEMISTRY. *Current Pos:* ASSOC PROF CHEM, ROCKFORD COL, 84- *Personal Data:* b Kansas City, Mo, July 18, 46; m; c 2. *Educ:* Univ Kans, BA, 68; Rice Univ, PhD(chem), 77. *Prof Exp:* Asst instr chem, Tex A&I Univ, 70-73; vis asst prof chem, Univ Ill, Champaign, 76-78; vis asst prof, Wabash Col, 78-80, asst prof chem, 80-84. *Mem:* Am Chem Soc; Sigma Xi. *Res:* Mass spectrometry and gas-phase kinetics; stopped flow solution kinetics; kinetics in non-aqueous media. *Mailing Add:* 424 N Gardiner Rockford IL 61107-4339

HADLEY, GEORGE RONALD, LASER PHYSICS, OPTICS. *Current Pos:* STAFF MEM PHYSICS, SANDIA CORP, 72- *Personal Data:* b Memphis, Tenn, Nov 25, 46; m 67; c 3. *Educ:* Wichita State Univ, BA, 68; Iowa State Univ, PhD(physics), 72. *Mem:* Optical Soc of Am. *Res:* Modelling of semiconductor lasers; nonlinear optics. *Mailing Add:* 6012 Annapolis Rd NE Albuquerque NM 87111

HADLEY, HENRY HULTMAN, genetics, plant breeding, for more information see previous edition

HADLEY, JAMES WARREN, PHYSICS. *Current Pos:* RETIRED. *Personal Data:* b Pasadena, Calif, Nov 15, 24; m 54, Roberta Evans; c Susan, David, Carl, Karen & Richard. *Educ:* Calif Inst Technol, BS, 45; Univ Calif, PhD, 52. *Prof Exp:* Physicist, Lawrence Livermore Lab, 46-65, div leader, 65-68, assoc leader, 68-83, dep leader, 83-87, asst leader, SP Proj Prog, 87-91. *Concurrent Pos:* Sci mgr seismol, Nev Opers, AEC, 69-72. *Res:* Experimental nuclear physics, especially high energy particle scattering; nuclear reactions; reactor design; nuclear and aerospace propulsion; geophysics; seismology. *Mailing Add:* 4355 Emory Way Livermore CA 94550

HADLEY, KATE HILL, geology, for more information see previous edition

HADLEY, LAWRENCE NATHAN, PHYSICAL OPTICS. *Current Pos:* from assoc prof to prof physics, Colo State Univ, 55-87, actg head, 59-61, chmn dept, 65-68, EMER PROF PHYSICS, COLO STATE UNIV, 87- *Personal Data:* b Valley Center, Kans, Oct 14, 16; m 39, 70; c 2. *Educ:* Friends Univ, AB, 37; Univ Okla, MS 39; Univ Mich, PhD(physics), 47. *Prof Exp:* Lab instr physics, Friends Univ, 35-37; lab instr physics, Univ Okla, 37-39; instr physics & math, Northern Okla Jr Col, 39-41; lab instr physics, Univ Mich, 41, res assoc, 42-45; asst prof, Colo Agr & Mech Col, 47; instr, Dartmouth Col, 47-48, asst prof, 48-55. *Concurrent Pos:* Fund adv ed fel, Univ Calif, 54-55; vis staff mem, Los Alamos Sci Labs, 64-65. *Mem:* Am Phys Soc; Sigma Xi; Am Asn Physics Teachers; fel Optical Soc Am. *Res:* Optical properties of metal semiconductor and dielectric films; reflection and transmission interference filters; solar energy utilization. *Mailing Add:* 3417 Canadian Pkwy Ft Collins CO 80524

HADLEY, MAC EUGENE, COMPARATIVE ENDOCRINOLOGY. *Current Pos:* assoc prof cell & develop biol, 68-80, prof gen biol, 80-83, PROF ANAT, UNIV ARIZ, 83- *Personal Data:* b San Jose, Calif, June 16, 30; m 66; c 1. *Educ:* San Jose State Col, BA, 54; Brown Univ, MS, 64, PhD(biol), 66. *Prof Exp:* Teacher high sch, Calif, 59-62; USPHS res fel, 66-68. *Mem:* AAAS; Am Inst Biol Sci. *Res:* Pineal and pituitary roles in vertebrate pigmentation; mechanisms of hormone action; regulation of pars intermedia function; regulation of vertebrate chromatophores. *Mailing Add:* Dept Cell & Molecular Biol Univ Ariz 1600 E University Blvd Tucson AZ 85721-0001

HADLEY, NEIL F, ENVIRONMENTAL PHYSIOLOGY. *Current Pos:* From asst prof to assoc prof, 66-71, assoc dean, Grad Col, 89-92, PROF ZOOL, ARIZ STATE UNIV, 76- *Personal Data:* b Dearborn, Mich, Oct 13, 41; m 75, Mary McCormick; c Cindy & David. *Educ:* Eastern Mich Univ, BA, 63; Univ Colo, PhD(zool), 66. *Honors & Awards:* Cert Merit for Distinguished Contrib Arid Zone Res, AAAS, 86. *Concurrent Pos:* Asst vpres res, 88-89. *Mem:* Am Arachnology Soc; Am Soc Zool; Sigma Xi. *Res:* Structure and function of arthropod cuticle; physiological adaptations of terrestrial arthropods to desert and montane environments; adaptive role of lipids in biological systems; ventilatory patterns and respiratory transpiration. *Mailing Add:* Grad Col Univ NC James Hall Wilmington NC 28403-3927. *Fax:* 602-965-2519

HADLEY, RICHARD FREDERICK, GEOMORPHOLOGY. *Current Pos:* ADJ PROF, DEPT GEOG, UNIV DENVER, 84- *Personal Data:* b Minneapolis, Minn, Jan 4, 24; m 52, Agnes Gervais; c John T & Mary P. *Educ:* Univ Minn, BA, 48, MS, 50. *Honors & Awards:* Meritorious Serv Award, US Dept Interior, 82. *Prof Exp:* Geologist, US Geol Surv, 48-67, chief, Soil & Moisture Conserv Prog, 67-74, chief, Pub Lands Hydrol Prog, 74-80, hydrologist, Water Resources Div, 67-84. *Concurrent Pos:* Vpres, Int Comn Continental Erosion, Int Asn Hydrol Sci, 75-79 & 80-83, secy, 83- 87. *Mem:* Int Asn Hydrol Sci; fel Geol Soc Am; Am Geophys Union; Sigma Xi. *Res:* Hydrology and geomorphology of arid regions; relations of drainage basin characteristics to erosion and sedimentation; aggradation and erosion in stream channels; rehabilitation potential of surface-mined lands. *Mailing Add:* 3784 S Depew St Denver CO 80235

HADLEY, SUSAN JANE, PULMONARY DISEASES, MICROBIOLOGY. *Current Pos:* from instr to prof, 50-86, asst to chmn, 65-85, EMER PROF MED, CORNELL UNIV, 86- *Personal Data:* b Madison, Wis; m 51; c 2. *Educ:* Univ Wis, BA, 41; Cornell Univ, MD, 44. *Prof Exp:* Instr microbiol, Sch Med, NY Univ, 50-51. *Concurrent Pos:* Asst dir labs, New York Hosp-Cornell Med Ctr, 51-64, physician OPIS, 51-55, asst attend physician, 55-63, assoc attend physician & dir lab microbiol, 63-72, attend physician, 72-86; chief pulmonary clin, New York Hosp, 64-86. *Mem:* NY Acad Med (exec secy, 85-86); Am Thoracic Soc. *Res:* Immunology. *Mailing Add:* 1035 Fifth Ave New York NY 10028

HADLEY, WILLIAM KEITH, CLINICAL PATHOLOGY & LABORATORY MEDICINE MICROBIOLOGY. *Current Pos:* resident, Univ Calif, San Francisco, 64-67, lectr clin path, 67, from asst prof to assoc prof clin path & lab med, 67-76, clin prof lab med & microbiol, 76-90, PROF CLIN LAB MED, UNIV CALIF, SAN FRANCISCO, 90-; CHIEF, MICROBIOL DIV, SAN FRANCISCO GEN HOSP, 67- *Personal Data:* b Eugene, Ore, Nov 12, 28; m 53, Marilyn J Norville; c Joan E & Ruth S. *Educ:* Univ Calif, Berkeley, AB, 50, PhD(bact), 67; Yale Univ, MD, 59. *Prof Exp:* Intern med, Yale New Haven Med Ctr, 59-60, from intern to asst resident path, 60-62; jr res bacteriologist, Univ Calif, Berkeley, 62-64. *Concurrent Pos:* Trainee path, Sch Med, Yale Univ, 61-62; trainee bact, Univ Calif, Berkeley, 62-64. *Mem:* Acad Clin Lab Physicians & Scientists; Am Fedn Clin Res; Am Soc Microbiol; fel Infectious Dis Soc Am; Soc Hosp Epidemiologists Am. *Res:* Clinical microbiology; infectious disease; rapid and automated systems for microbiologic identification; antimicrobiol action of therapy; diagnosis of respiratory infections; opportunistic infections of acquired immune deficiency syndrome; pneumocystis and mycobacterial infections. *Mailing Add:* 18 Reed Ranch Rd Tiburon CA 94920-2071. *Fax:* 415-206-3045; *E-Mail:* hadley@pangloss.ucsf.edu

HADLEY, WILLIAM MELVIN, BIOTRANSFORMATION, NASAL MEMBRANES. *Current Pos:* From asst prof to assoc prof pharmacol & toxicol, 72-82, asst dean, 84-86, DEAN, COL PHARM, UNIV NMEX, 86-, PROF PHARMACOL & TOXICOL, 82- *Personal Data:* b San Antonio, Tex, June 4, 42; m 90, Jane Walsh; c 3. *Educ:* Purdue Univ, BS, 67, MS, 71, PhD(toxicol), 72. *Concurrent Pos:* Investr, NIH Minority Schs Biomed Advan, 74-87, NIH ROI, 84-87; vis scientist toxicol, Inhalation Toxicol Res Inst, 81-82; actg dean, Col Pharm, Univ NMex, 85; mem, US Pharmacopeial Conv, 86- & bd dirs, Nat Ctr Toxicol Res Assoc Univ, 90-; adv bd mem, US Dept Energy Waste Educ & Res Consortium, 90-; pres, Rocky Mountain Chap Soc Toxicol, 90-91. *Mem:* Soc Toxicol; Southwestern Asn Toxicologists; Western Pharmacol Soc; AAAS; Am Asn Cols Pharm. *Res:* Biotransformation of xenobiotics in nasal membranes; effects of heavy metals on biotransformation; cadmium; effects of xenobiotics on the immune system. *Mailing Add:* Col Pharm Univ NMex Albuquerque NM 87131. *Fax:* 505-272-8376; *E-Mail:* wmhadley@unmb.edu

HADLEY, WILLIAM OWEN, CIVIL ENGINEERING, ENGINEERING MATERIALS. *Current Pos:* assoc prof, 71-75, PROF CIVIL ENG, LA TECH UNIV, 77-, DIR, MAT RES LAB, 81- *Personal Data:* b Covington, Tenn, Mar 14, 39; m 64; c 3. *Educ:* Univ Tenn, BS, 61; Univ Tex, MS, 68, PhD(civil eng), 72. *Prof Exp:* Asst design engr, Clark Daily & Dietz, 61; design engr, Clark Dietz Painter & Assoc, 63-64; field engr, Leavell-Kiewit, 64-65; res engr, Tippett & Gee, 65-66; res assoc civil engr, Ctr Hwy Res, Univ Tex, 67-71. *Concurrent Pos:* Prin investr fed & state proj, Fundamental Eng Properties Construct Mat, 74- & Gap Graded Concretes, 75-77. *Mem:* Transp Res Bd; Asn Asphalt Paving Technologists; Am Soc Civil Engrs; Am Soc Testing & Mat. *Res:* Material characterization of construction materials; pavement design and analysis; geotechnical engineering. *Mailing Add:* 1220 Rocky Creek Dr Pflugerville TX 78660

HADLOCK, CHARLES ROBERT, RISK ANALYSIS, ENVIRONMENTAL MODELING. *Current Pos:* PROF & CHMN, MATH SCI DEPT, BENTLEY COL, 90-, DIR, ENVIRON MGT PROG, 92- *Personal Data:* b Brooklyn, NY, Apr 19, 47; m 67, Joanne Miscione; c Charles J & Theresa A (Tessa). *Educ:* Providence Col, BS, 67; Univ Ill, Urbana, MA, 68, PhD(math), 70. *Honors & Awards:* Book Prize, Math Asn Am, 85. *Prof Exp:* Asst prof math, Amherst Col, 70-76 & Bowdoin Col, 76-77; sr mem staff, A D Little Inc, 77-80, mgr safety & environ risk, 80-90. *Concurrent Pos:* Sr Fulbright lectr, Colombia, 76; independent environ consult, 90-; vis prof earth atmospheric & planetary sci, Mass Inst Technol, 96-97. *Mem:* Am Soc Mech Eng; Soc Indust & Appl Math; Math Asn Am. *Res:* Risk analysis with emphasis on environmental applications; applied mathematics. *Mailing Add:* Dept Math Sci Bentley Col Waltham MA 02154-4705. *Fax:* 781-891-3410; *E-Mail:* chadlock@bentley.edu

HADLOCK, RONALD K, METEOROLOGY. *Current Pos:* sr res scientist, Batelle Pac Northwest Labs, 73-77, mgr appl meteorol, 77-83, PNL Admin PRECP Prog, 84-85, dir Erica Prog, 85-91, PROG MGR ATMOSPHERIC SCI, BATELLE PAC NORTHWEST LABS, 91- *Personal Data:* b Oneonta, NY, Sept 26, 34; m 61; c 1. *Educ:* State Univ NY Albany, BS, 56, MS, 57; Fla State Univ, PhD(meteorol), 66. *Prof Exp:* Instr physics, State Univ NY Binghamton, 57-60; res assoc meteorol, Fla State Univ, 64-67, asst prof oceanog & meteorol, 67-73. *Mem:* AAAS; Am Meteorol Soc. *Res:* Dynamics of rotating fluids as laboratory models of geophysical prototypes, especially chemical analogs to latent heat release; meteorology of a small heated tropical island; boundary layer structure; power generation meteorology; intensification of oceanic storms; meteorological field programs; meteorological emergency preparedness. *Mailing Add:* 429 Snyder St Richland WA 99352

HADLOW, WILLIAM JOHN, VETERINARY PATHOLOGY. *Current Pos:* RETIRED. *Personal Data:* b West Park, Ohio, Apr 8, 21; m 52; c 2. *Educ:* Ohio State Univ, DVM, 48. *Prof Exp:* Instr vet med, Univ Minn, 48-50; vet pathologist, Rocky Mt Lab, NIH, 52-58; vet pathologist, Animal Dis & Parasite Res Div, USDA, 58-61; res vet, Rocky Mt Lab, NIH, 61-87. *Mem:* Inst Med-Nat Acad Sci; Am Asn Path; Am Col Vet Path; Int Acad Path; Wildlife Dis Asn; Am Vet Med Asn. *Res:* Relation of viruses to chronic progressive disease in man and animals; comparative pathology. *Mailing Add:* 908 S Third St Hamilton MT 59840. *Fax:* 406-363-6406, 363-1677

HADOW, HARLO HERBERT, BEHAVIORAL ECOLOGY, EVOLUTION. *Current Pos:* asst prof, 77-83, ASSOC PROF BIOL, COE COL, 83- *Personal Data:* b Beaver Dam, Wis, Feb 10, 45; m 82. *Educ:* Milton Col, BA, 67; Univ Colo, MA, 72, PhD(biol), 77. *Prof Exp:* Teacher sci, Crowley County High Sch, 68-70; lab asst psychol, Vet Admin Hosp, 70-72; instr biol, Ft Lewis Col, 72-76. *Concurrent Pos:* Instr anat, Arapaho Jr Col, 71-72; consult, Aspen Colo Trout Unlimited, 72 & Iowa Conserv Comn, 78- *Mem:* Cooper Ornith Soc; Wilson Ornith Soc; Am Ornith Union; Ecol Soc Am; Wildlife Soc. *Res:* Growth and development of nesting woodpeckers; woodpecker ecology; audible communication by woodpeckers; mammalian and avian distribution. *Mailing Add:* Dept Biol Coe Col 1220 First Ave NE Cedar Rapids IA 52402-5092

HADWIGER, LEE A, PLANT PATHOLOGY, BIOCHEMISTRY. *Current Pos:* from asst prof to assoc prof, 65-73, PROF PLANT PATH, WASH STATE UNIV, 73- *Personal Data:* b Alva, Okla, Nov 2, 33; m 57; c 4. *Educ:* Okla State Univ, BS, 55, MS, 59; Kans State Univ, PhD(hort), 62. *Honors & Awards:* Asgrow Award, Am Soc Hort Sci, 64. *Prof Exp:* Fel biochem, Okla State Univ, 62-63; fel biochem & biophys, Univ Calif, Davis, 63-65. *Mem:* Am Soc Plant Physiol; Am Phytopath Soc; Am Soc Hort Sci. *Res:* In vitro and in vivo biosynthesis of pyridine compounds, aromatic amino acids, asparagine, B-cyano alanine and orcylalanine in plants; biochemistry of resistant gene action and host-parasite interactions. *Mailing Add:* Dept Plant Path Wash State Univ One SE Stadium Way Pullman WA 99164-0001

HADZERIGA, PABLO, INORGANIC CHEMISTRY. *Current Pos:* INDEPENDENT CONSULT, 78- *Personal Data:* b Buenos Aires, Argentina, Dec 25, 29; US citizen; m 57; c 3. *Educ:* La Plata Univ, BSc, 51; Univ Buenos Aires, MS, 55, PhD(chem), 56. *Prof Exp:* Chemist, Bonneville, Ltd, Utah, 57-59, chief chemist, 59-61, dir res, 61-64; sr process engr, Hazen Res, 64-78. *Mem:* AAAS; Am Inst Mining, Metall & Petrol Eng; Am Chem Soc; NY Acad Sci. *Res:* Phase chemistry of aqueous solutions; fertilizer industry; potash recovery from brines and ores. *Mailing Add:* 6058 Owens St Arvada CO 80004-4645

HADZIJA, BOZENA WESLEY, PHYSICAL PHARMACY, DRUG METABOLISM. *Current Pos:* asst prof, 71-77, ASSOC PROF PHARM, UNIV NC, CHAPEL HILL, 77- *Personal Data:* b Zagreb, Yugoslavia, Jan 5, 28; nat US; m 60; c 2. *Educ:* Univ Zagreb, BS, 49, MS, 51, PhD(biochem), 60. *Prof Exp:* Lectr pharm, Univ Zagreb, 49-56; chief analyst, Pharmaceut Indust, Zagreb, 56-61; fel, Univ Conn, Storrs, 61-63, res asst, 63-64; sr lectr pharm, UST, WAfrica, 64-71. *Mem:* Am Pharmaceut Asn; Am Asn Col Pharm; Asn Prof Sleep Soc; Sigma Xi. *Res:* Pharmacokinetics and bioavailability studies of drugs in vivo; design and application of new analytical methods for quantitation of drugs in biological fluids; metabolic pathways of drugs in animals and humans; stability of drug products. *Mailing Add:* 408 Highview Dr Chapel Hill NC 27514-7915

HADZIYEV, DIMITRI, food science, agriculture; deceased, see previous edition for last biography

HAEBERLE, FREDERICK ROLAND, EXPLORATION GEOLOGY. *Current Pos:* CONSULT GEOLOGIST, 83- *Personal Data:* b Philadelphia, Pa, Oct 6, 19; m 46, Cynthia Davis; c Cynthia F (Roberts) & Frederick E. *Educ:* Yale Univ, BS, 47, MS, 48; Columbia Univ, MBA, 62. *Prof Exp:* Geologist, Stand Oil Co, Tex, 48-52; chief geologist, J J Lynn Oil Div, 52-53; dist mgr petrol exp prod, Mayfair Minerals, Inc, 53-54; prof geol, McMurry Col, 54-57; chief subsurface geologist, Venezuelan Atlantic Refining Co, 57-60; elec data process coordr, Mobil Oil Co, 62-74, coordr spec studies, Libya, 74-77, mem staff explor statist, Explor & Prod Res Div, 77-83. *Concurrent Pos:* Asst prof, Univ Houston, 48-50. *Mem:* Fel Geol Soc Am; Am Asn Petrol Geologists; Soc Prof Well Log Analysts; Am Inst Prof Geologists. *Res:* Carbonates; hydrocarbon gravity; information systems; application of computers to exploration; giant oil fields-discovery and development; reservoirs description. *Mailing Add:* 4036 Northview Lane Dallas TX 75229

HAEBERLI, WILLY, NUCLEAR PHYSICS. *Current Pos:* PROF PHYSICS, UNIV WIS-MADISON, 61- *Personal Data:* b Zurich, Switzerland, June 17, 25; div; c 3. *Educ:* Univ Basel, PhD(physics), 52. *Honors & Awards:* Tom H Bonner Prize, Am Physics Soc, 79. *Prof Exp:* Res assoc physics, Univ Wis, 52-54; vis prof physics, Duke Univ, 54-56. *Mem:* Fel Am Phys Soc; Europ Phys Soc; fel AAAS. *Res:* Elastic scattering and polarization in nuclear reactions; design of polarized-ion sources; nuclear reactions with beams of polarized ions; development of sources of polarized ions; parity violation in nuclear interactions. *Mailing Add:* Dept Physics Univ Wis Madison WI 53706

HAEDER, PAUL ALBERT, APPLIED MATHEMATICS. *Current Pos:* RETIRED. *Personal Data:* b Yale, SDak, July 31, 15; m 39; c 4. *Educ:* Huron Col, BA, 39; Univ SDak, MA, 50; Iowa State Univ, PhD, 68. *Prof Exp:* Supt pub schs, SDak, 41-44; from instr to asst prof math, Univ SDak, 52-59; asst, Iowa State Univ, 56-57, instr, 59-60; assoc prof, Univ SDak, 60-65; instr, Iowa State Univ, 65-68; chmn, Dept Math, Univ Nebr, Omaha, 68-74, prof math, 68-80, emer prof, 80- *Concurrent Pos:* Asst sci aide, Northern Regional Res Lab, US Govt, 42; assoc ed, Am Math Monthly, 78- *Mem:* Math Asn Am. *Res:* Partial differential equations of mathematical physics. *Mailing Add:* 3060 Stephanos Dr Lincoln NE 68516-1642

HAEDRICH, RICHARD L, ICHTHYOLOGY, BIOLOGICAL OCEANOGRAPHY. *Current Pos:* dir, Nfld Inst Cold Ocean Sci, 82-88 & Ocean Sci Ctr, 88-92, PROF FISHERIES BIOL, MEM UNIV NFLD, 79- *Personal Data:* b Wilmington, Del, Dec 12, 38; m 62, Susan Owers; c Tyson, Daniel & Alexandra. *Educ:* Harvard Univ, AB, 61, AM, 63, PhD(biol), 66. *Prof Exp:* Asst scientist, Woods Hole Oceanog Inst, 66-70, assoc scientist, 70-79. *Concurrent Pos:* Assoc, Harvard Univ, 65-; ed-in-chief, Biol Oceanog, 79-89; mem & chmn, pop biol grant selection comt, NSERC, 81-85. *Res:* General biology and evolutionary relationships of fishes; distribution of oceanic animals, especially the establishment of high-seas faunal regions; ecology of mid-water and bottom fishes; patterns in the structure, seasonality, and long-term variation in animal communities; biology of eels; biology of northern aquatic ecosystems; fisheries oceanography. *Mailing Add:* Dept Biol Mem Univ St John's NF A1C 5S7 Can. *Fax:* 709-737-3121; *E-Mail:* haedrich@kean.ucs.mun.ca

HAEFELE, DOUGLAS MONROE, MICROBIAL ECOLOGY, RESEARCH MANAGEMENT. *Current Pos:* Res group leader, Pioneer Hi-Bred Int, Inc, 86-90, res mgr, 90-93, DIR RES & DEVELOP, MICROBIAL ENVIRON SERVS INC, SUBSID PIONEER HI-BRED INT, INC, 93- *Personal Data:* b Chicago, Ill, June 18, 52; m 81, Eileen M Robb; c Douglas R. *Educ:* Univ RI, BS, 76; Yale Univ, MFS, 78; Univ Calif, Berkeley, PhD(phytopath), 85. *Concurrent Pos:* Mem, Seed Path Comt, Am Phytopath Soc, 86-88. *Mem:* AAAS; Am Soc Microbiol; Hazardous Mat Control Resources Inst; Sigma Xi. *Res:* Discovery and application of biological systems able to chemically transform or degrade xenobiotic compounds; anaerobic microbiological systems for the biotransformation of nitroaromatics. *Mailing Add:* Res Develop 7300 NW 67nd Ave PO Box 1004 Johnston IA 50131-1004. *E-Mail:* haefeled@phibred.com

HAEFELI, ROBERT J(AMES), SANITARY ENGINEERING. *Current Pos:* REGIONAL SERV MGR, POST, BUCKLEY, SCHULT & JERNIGAN, INC, 88- *Personal Data:* b Paterson, NJ, Sept 7, 26; m 50; c 2. *Educ:* Univ Mich, BS, 48; Rutgers Univ, MS, 81; Environ Eng Intersoc Bd, dipl. *Prof Exp:* Civil engr, Bur Reclamation, US Dept Interior, Colo, 48-52; engr water resources, 52-54, actg off engr, Bur Reclamation Team, Beirut, Lebanon, 54-57; sr engr, Ebasco Serv, Inc, NY, 57-60; prin engr & proj mgr, Hydrotech Corp, 60-61; vpres & managing engr, 61-66; assoc & water resources engr, Hazen & Sawyer, 66-69; sanit consult engr, 69-72; pres, Frank & Haefeli Assoc, 72-76; pres, Haefeli Eng, 77-79; planning coordr, Havens & Emerson, Inc, 79-85; chief hydraulic engr, N H Bettigole, Pa, 85-88. *Concurrent Pos:* Mem, Int Comn Irrig, Drainage & Flood Control & NJ Dept Environ Protection, 78-; chmn NJ Clean Air Coun, 78-79, NJ Clean Water Coun, 87-; nat dir, Nat Soc Prof Engrs, 83-84 & 86-87; consult. *Mem:* Water Pollution Control Fedn; Am Geophys Union; Am Water Works Asn; Am Soc Civil Engrs; Nat Soc Prof Engrs. *Res:* Hydraulic model studies; photoelastic laboratory studies; hydrodynamic effect of earthquakes on dams; surge suppression analyses; computer applications. *Mailing Add:* 4 Galdwell Terr Marlboro NJ 07746

HAEFNER, A(LBERT) J(OHN), POLYMER CHEMISTRY, PLASTICS. *Current Pos:* RETIRED. *Personal Data:* b Cincinnati, Ohio, Oct 25, 23; m 45, 60; c 5. *Educ:* Univ Cincinnati, ChE, 49, MS, 51, PhD(org chem), 53. *Prof Exp:* Lab asst, Firestone Tire & Rubber Co, 42-43; control chemist,

Hilton-Davis Chem Co, 46-49; res chemist, Ethyl Corp, 53-58, res supvr, 58-63, asst dir chem res, 63-65, assoc dir polymer res, 65-67, dir plastics res & appln, 69-88. Mem: Am Chem Soc. Res: Polymerization of elastomers and resins; chlorination. Mailing Add: 11646 Glenhaven Dr Baton Rouge LA 70815

HAEFNER, PAUL ALOYSIUS, JR, ZOOLOGY, MARINE BIOLOGY. Current Pos: head, 77-83, PROF, DEPT BIOL, ROCHESTER INST TECHNOL, 77- Personal Data: b Lancaster, Pa, Dec 5, 35; m 62; c 3. Educ: Franklin & Marshall Col, BS, 57; Univ Del, MS, 59, PhD(biol), 62. Prof Exp: Asst prof biol, La State Univ, New Orleans, 62-63; fishery biologist, Maine Coop Fishery Unit, US Fish & Wildlife Serv, 63-69; assoc marine scientist, Va Inst Marine Sci, 69-77. Concurrent Pos: Asst prof, Univ Maine, Orono, 63-68; assoc prof zool, Univ Maine, Orono, 68-69; assoc prof, Univ Va & Col William & Mary, 69-77. Mem: Marine Biol Asn UK; Crustacean Soc (secy, 80-87, pres-elect, 88, pres, 89-91). Res: Reproductive biology and physiological ecology of marine and estuarine decapod Crustacea. Mailing Add: Dept Biol Rochester Inst Technol Rochester NY 14623. Fax: 716-475-5766; E-Mail: pahsbi@rit.edu

HAEGEL, NANCY M, SEMICONDUCTOR CHARACTERIZATION. Current Pos: asst prof, 87-89, ASSOC PROF MAT SCI & ENG, UNIV CALIF, LOS ANGELES, 89- Personal Data: b New Haven, Conn, Sept 7, 59; m 91. Educ: Univ Notre Dame, BS, 81; Univ Calif, Berkeley, MS, 83, PhD(mat sci), 85. Honors & Awards: Ross Tucker Award, Am Inst Mining Metall & Petrol Engrs, 85, Hardy Gold Medal, 89. Prof Exp: Res asst, Lawrence Berkeley Lab, 81-85; postdoctoral scientist, Siemens Res Labs, Erlangen, Fed Repub Ger, 86-87. Concurrent Pos: Trustee, Univ Notre Dame, 87-90; mem, fel panel, Nat Res Coun, 88-91; Kellogg fel, Kellogg Found, 90-93. Mem: Mat Res Soc; Am Phys Soc; Am Inst Mining Metall & Petrol Engrs Metall Soc. Res: Optical and electrical characterization of semiconductors and other electronic materials; photoconductivity and photoluminescence; high resistivity transport; infrared detectors. Mailing Add: 7 Caranton St Fairfield CT 06430

HAEGELE, KLAUS D, DRUG METABOLISM, PHENOTYPE & DRUG METABOLISM. Current Pos: DIR STRUCT & ANAL SCI, HOECHST MARION ROUSSEL INC, 93- Personal Data: b Stuttgart, Ger, Oct 7, 41; m 64, Heidi Baeder; c 2. Educ: Univ Tuebingen, Ger, BS, 64, MS, 67, PhD(org chem), 70. Prof Exp: Res asst prof chem, Univ Tubingen, Ger, 70-71; vis asst prof biochem, Baylor Col Med, Houston, 71-75; asst prof pharmacol, Health Sci Ctr, Univ Tex, San Antonio, 75-77, assoc prof, 78-79; dept head drug metab, Marion Merrell Dow Res Inst, Strasbourg, France, 79-90, dir develop resources, 90-93. Mem: Am Soc Pharmacol & Exp Therapeut; Am Soc Clin Chem; NY Acad Sci; Int Soc Study Xenobiotics. Res: Pharmacokinetics and drug metabolism; pharmacodynamics; development of novel analytical techniques. Mailing Add: Hoechst Marion Roussel 2110 E Galbraith Rd Cincinnati OH 45241

HAEGER, BEVERLY JEAN, INORGANIC CHEMISTRY, ENVIRONMENTAL HEALTH & SAFETY. Current Pos: MGR ENG, MARTIN MARIETTA SPECIALTY COMPONENTS, 92- Personal Data: b Gainesville, Ga. Educ: Bethany Nazarene Col, BS, 61; Univ Tenn, Chattanooga, MAT, 63; Univ Ga, PhD(inorg chem), 74. Honors & Awards: Hoover Award, 85. Prof Exp: Asst prof chem, Trevecca Nazarene Col, 67-71; chemist, Neutron Devices Dept, Gen Elec Co, 74-79, prog mgr, Develop Planning & Control, 79-85, mgr, Power Sources Develop, 85-90, mgr, eng oper surety, 90-92. Mem: Am Chem Soc. Res: Synthesis and characterization of thermal battery related materials; scale-up of synthesis processes from laboratory to pilot plant operation; thermal battery electrochemical systems; pulsed neutron generator tube; total quality management. Mailing Add: 10333 125th St Largo FL 34649. Fax: 813-545-6757

HAELTERMAN, EDWARD OMER, VETERINARY VIROLOGY. Current Pos: RETIRED. Personal Data: b Norway, Mich, Oct 14, 18; m 46. Educ: Mich State Univ, DVM, 52; Purdue Univ, MS, 55, PhD(path), 59. Hon Degrees: Hon Dr, Univ Ghent, Belgium, 73. Prof Exp: Instr vet sci, Purdue Univ, 52-59, assoc prof vet microbiol, 59-64, asst dean, Sch Vet Sci & Med, 59-62, prof vet microbiol, 64-84. Concurrent Pos: Vis investr, Rockefeller Inst, 58; USDA res vet, East African Vet Res Orgn, Kenya, 67-68. Mem: AAAS; Am Vet Med Asn; Am Soc Microbiol; Conf Res Workers Animal Dis; Am Asn Swine Practitioners. Res: Enteric disease of swine; investigations on pathogenesis, immunology and epidemiology of transmissible gastroenteritis of swine. Mailing Add: 3007 Soldiers Home Rd West Lafayette IN 47906

HAEN, PETER JOHN, IMMUNOLOGY, ENDOCRINOLOGY. Current Pos: from asst prof to assoc prof, 72-83, chmn dept, 76-84, PROF BIOL, LOYOLA MARYMOUNT UNIV, 83- Personal Data: b Udenhout, Neth, Aug 29, 38; m 74, Annette M Devitt; c Scott & David. Educ: Nat Univ Ireland, BSc(zool), & BSc(psychol), 64, PhD(biol), 67. Prof Exp: Chmn, Dept Biol, Cardinal Otunga Col, Kenya, 67-71; chmn, Dept Sci, Pius X High Sch, Downey, Calif, 71-72. Concurrent Pos: Dir, Rosecrans Chair Conserv Natural Resources, Loyola Marymount Univ, 77-83; bd dirs, Sigma, 89-92, SW regional dir, 89-92. Mem: AAAS; Sigma Xi. Res: Biochemical and immunological taxonomy of animals; relationships between science and theology. Mailing Add: 6346 W 85th St Los Angeles CA 90045. Fax: 310-338-7239

HAENDEL, RICHARD STONE, TECHNICAL MANAGEMENT. Current Pos: Mgr develop eng, Collins Govt Avionics, 82-87, tech staff, 87-90, mgr res & develop, 90-93, sr tech staff, COLLINS AVIONICS DIV, ROCKWELL-INT, 93- Personal Data: b Brooklyn, NY, Nov 10, 39; m 65, Goldene Braverman; c Melissa A & Erica S. Educ: Rensselaer Polytech Inst, BEE, 60; NY Univ, MEE, 63. Concurrent Pos: Lectr internal, Collins Avionics, Rockwell-Int, 82- Mem: Armed Forces Commun & Electronics Asn; Inst Elec & Electronics Engrs; Am Defense Preparedness Asn; Soc Automotive Engrs. Res: Microwave device development; electronic sensing as applied to weather detection for aircraft; radio propagation; avionics systems; receiver and transmitter design for anti-jam communications systems; microwave communications systems. Mailing Add: 400 Collins Rd MS 124-300 Cedar Rapids IA 52498. Fax: 319-295-8823

HAENDLER, BLANCA LOUISE, SURFACE CHEMISTRY. Current Pos: AT CLOROX TECH CTR. Personal Data: b Boston, Mass, Nov 22, 48. Educ: Goucher Col, BA, 69; Johns Hopkins Univ, PhD(phys chem), 74. Prof Exp: Lectr chem, Johns Hopkins Univ, 74-75; asst prof chem, Lafayette Col, 75- Mem: Am Chem Soc; AAAS; Catalysis Soc NAm; Sigma Xi. Res: Study of adsorbed species and reaction mechanisms on solid surfaces and other aspects of heterogeneous catalysis. Mailing Add: 748 Carla St Livermore CA 94550-0618

HAENDLER, HELMUT MAX, INORGANIC CHEMISTRY. Current Pos: from asst prof to prof, 45-78, EMER PROF CHEM, UNIV NH, 78- Personal Data: b Boston, Mass, June 19, 13; m 36, Mildred Bragdon; c Blanca L & Steven A. Educ: Northeastern Univ, BS, 35; Univ Wash, Seattle, PhD(inorg chem), 40. Prof Exp: Assoc chem, Univ Wash, Seattle, 39-40, instr, 40-42; res chemist & supvr div war res, Carbide & Carbon Chem Co & Substitute Alloy Mat Labs, Columbia Univ, 42-45. Concurrent Pos: Fulbright Res Scholar, Max Planck Inst Solid State Res, 72-73. Mem: Fel AAAS; Am Chem Soc; Am Crystallog Asn; Sigma Xi. Res: X-ray applications. Mailing Add: 309 Lee Hook Rd Lee NH 03824-6417

HAENER, JUAN, THEORETICAL PHYSICS, MECHANICAL ENGINEERING. Current Pos: STAFF SCIENTIST & CONSULT, RES & DEVELOP DIV, NARMCO DIV, WHITTAKER CORP, 60- Personal Data: b Hamba, Rumania, Aug 11, 17; US citizen; m 51; c 4. Educ: Tech Univ, Berlin, MS, 43; Tech Univ, Vienna, PhD, 46. Prof Exp: Dynamics engr, Heinkel Aircraft, Ger, 43-45; asst, Inst Theoret Physics, Vienna, 45-48; head dynamics, Inst Aerotech, Cordoba, Arg, 49-56; res scientist in chg dynamics com, mil & helicopter div, Cessna Aircraft Co, 56-58; staff specialist & consult, Dynamics & Stress, Solar Aircraft Co, 58-60. Res: Dynamics of structures; flutter-vibration; development of composite materials. Mailing Add: 8215 Harton Pl San Diego CA 92123

HAENISCH, SIEGFRIED, MATHEMATICS. Current Pos: assoc prof, 68-73, chmn dept, 73-77, PROF MATH, TRENTON STATE COL, 73- Personal Data: b Dresden, Ger, Sept 20, 36; US citizen; m 61; c 2. Educ: Trenton State Col, BS, 58, MA, 61; Rutgers Univ, New Brunswick, EdD, 67. Prof Exp: Teacher high sch, NJ, 58-62; instr math, Trenton State Col, 62-66; asst math educ, Rutgers Univ, New Brunswick, 66-67; guest prof math educ, Goethe Univ, 67-68. Concurrent Pos: Guest instr, Rutgers Univ, 70-; Nat Endowment Humanities fel, Yale, 80. Mem: Math Asn Am; Nat Coun Teachers Math. Res: Foundations of mathematics and its application to the teaching and learning of mathematics. Mailing Add: Dept Math & Statist Trenton Col Holman Hall 206 Trenton NJ 08650

HAENLEIN, GEORGE FRIEDRICH WILHELM, ANIMAL NUTRITION, ANIMAL BREEDING. Current Pos: from asst prof to assoc prof animal sci, Col Agr Sci, 64-74, RES ASSOC & SUPVR DAIRY HERDS, UNIV DEL, 57-, PROF ANIMAL SCI & AGR BIOCHEM, 74- Personal Data: b Mannheim, Ger, Oct 27, 27; nat US; m 54; c 5. Educ: Hohenheim Agr Univ, Dipl, 50, Dr Agr(animal nutrit & breeding), 53; Univ Del, MS, 60; Univ Wis-Madison, PhD(dairy sci, biochem), 72. Prof Exp: Asst animal nutrit res, Exp Sta, Hohenheim Agr Univ, 50-53; asst mgr & herdsman, Zeitler Farms, Inc, Del, 53-57. Concurrent Pos: US State Dept exchange student scholar, 51-52; NSF teaching fel, 65-66; res asst dairy sci, Univ Wis-Madison, 66-67; abstractor, Biol Abstr; chmn comt animal nutrit of goats, Nat Res Coun, 75-; mem, Northeastern Regional Dairy Res Steering Comt, 75-; ed in chief, J Small Ruminant Res; chmn, dairy goat handbook, US Dept Agr SE Exten, 81- Mem: Hon fel, Am Asn Advan Sci; Am Soc Animal Sci; Am Dairy Sci Asn; NY Acad Sci; Nat Mastitis Coun; Sigma Xi. Res: Milk composition; forage evaluation; dairy cattle genetics; animal behavior; dairy goat management. Mailing Add: 32395 Galena Sassafras Rd Galena MD 21635

HAENNI, DAVID RICHARD, X-RAY SPECTROSCOPY, HIGH-SPIN STATES. Current Pos: fel, 76-77, RES SCIENTIST, CYCLOTRON INST, TEX A&M UNIV, 80- Personal Data: b Peoria, Ill, June 6, 47; m 69; c 1. Educ: Washington Univ, AB, 69; Tex A&M Univ, PhD(chem), 75. Prof Exp: Vis scientist, Nuclear Res Estab, Julich, WGer, 77-79; res scientist, Oak Ridge Nat Lab, 79-80. Mem: Am Chem Soc; Am Physical Soc; Inst Elec & Electronics Engrs. Res: In beam ray spectroscopy following massive transfer reactions; decay and reaction ray spectroscopy with both light and heavy ion accelerators; particle accelerator computer control systems. Mailing Add: 2178 FM Apt 1387 Midlothian TX 76065

HAENNI, EDWARD OTTO, ANALYTICAL CHEMISTRY, FOOD CHEMISTRY. Current Pos: RETIRED. Personal Data: b St Louis, Mo, May 25, 07; m 38; c 1. Educ: Wash Univ, St Louis, AB, 29, MS, 31; Univ Md, PhD(org chem), 40. Prof Exp: Asst instr chem, Wash Univ, St Louis, 29-31;

res chemist, Food & Drug Admin, USDA, 31-43; chief solvents sect, Chem Bur, War Prod Bd, Washington, DC, 43-45; chief drugs sect, Civilian Prod Admin, 46; res chemist, Food & Drug Admin, Fed Security Agency, 47-51; res chemist, Entom Res Br, Agr Res Ctr, USDA, 52-56; res chemist, Bur Foods, US Food & Drug Admin, 57-64; chief, Additives & instrumentation Br, 64-71, Dir Chem & Physics Div, 71-73, consult, 74-79. *Mem:* Am Chem Soc; fel Asn Off Analytical Chem; fel Washington Acad Sci. *Res:* Food additives and contaminants; polynuclear hydrocarbons; analytical research and instrumentation; foods and drugs; organic aerosol dispenser development. *Mailing Add:* 7907 Glenbrook Rd Bethesda MD 20814-2403

HAENSEL, VLADIMIR, CATALYSIS. *Current Pos:* Chem engr, Universal Oil Prod Co, 37-45, div coordr, Universal Oil Prod Inc, 45-55, dir refining res, 55-59, dir process res, 60-63, vpres & dir res, 64-72, vpres sci & technol, 72-79, CONSULT, UOP, INC, 79-; PROF CHEM ENG, UNIV MASS, 80- *Personal Data:* b Freiburg, Ger, Sept 1, 14; nat US; m 39; c 2. *Educ:* Northwestern Univ, BS, 35, PhD(chem), 42; Mass Inst Tech, MS, 37. *Hon Degrees:* DSc, Northwestern Univ, 57, Univ Wis-Milwaukee, 79. *Honors & Awards:* Prof Progress Award, Am Inst Chem Engrs, 57; Modern Pioneers in Creative, Nat Asn Mfrs, 65; Perkin Medal Appl Chem, 67; Chem Pioneer Award, Am Inst Chemists, 67; Nat Medal Sci, 73, Indust Award; Eugene J Houdry Award, Appl Catalysis, 77; Nat Acad Sci Award for Chem Serv to Soc, 91; Charles Stark Draper Prize, Nat Acad Eng, 97. *Concurrent Pos:* Tech observer, Petrol Admin for War, 45; mem, Panel Catalysts Automotive Emmission Devices & Petrol Refining, Nat Mat Adv Bd, 73-74; chmn, US-USSR Technol Exchange Chem Catalysis, 76-79; consult, Exxon Res & Eng Co, 80-81, Environ Res & Technol, Inc, 81, Olin Chem, 82-84, Dow Chem Co, 84, Haicon Res, 83-85, Heico, Inc, 85-89, Kiser Res Inc, 86, Mobil, 88-89 & Catalytica, 89-; lectr, R A Welch Conf Chem Res, 81; chmn, Adv Comt Chem Indust Sci & Technol Innovation, NSF, 82-85; bd dirs, Heico Corp, Hollywood, Fla, 84-89. *Mem:* Nat Acad Sci; Nat Acad Eng; Am Chem Soc; Catalysis Soc NAm (pres, 76-80). *Res:* Process and catalysis in petroleum refining and petrochemical field; author of more than 120 scientific and technical papers, over 145 United States patents and over 450 foreign patents. *Mailing Add:* Dept Chem Eng Univ Mass 159 Goessmann Lab Amherst MA 01003

HAENSLY, WILLIAM EDWARD, veterinary medicine, gerontology, for more information see previous edition

HAENSZEL, WILLIAM MANNING, BIOSTATISTICS, EPIDEMIOLOGY. *Current Pos:* PROF EPIDEMIOL, SCH PUB HEALTH, UNIV ILL, 76-; SR EPIDEMIOLOGIST, ILL CANCER COUN, 76- *Personal Data:* b Rochester, NY, June 19, 10; m 46; c 3. *Educ:* Univ Buffalo, BA, 31, MA, 32. *Hon Degrees:* Hon Dr, Univ Valle, Colombia, 70. *Prof Exp:* From jr statistician to statistician, NY State Dept Health, 34-47; dir, Conn Bur Vital Statist, 47-52; head, Biomet Sect, Nat Cancer Inst, NIH, 52-57, assoc chief, 56-60, chief, Biomet Br, 60-76. *Concurrent Pos:* Mem US Nat Comt Vital Health Statistics, 64-67; adj prof, Grad Sch Pub Health, Univ Pittsburgh, 66-82. *Mem:* Biomet Soc; Am Pub Health Asn; Am Statist Asn; Popul Asn Am; Am Epidemiol Soc. *Res:* Vital statistics; epidemiology of cancer; methodology of field investigations in chronic diseases. *Mailing Add:* 341 E Hawthorne Blvd Wheaton IL 60187

HAERER, ARMIN FRIEDRICH, NEUROLOGY. *Current Pos:* from asst prof to assoc prof, 65-76, PROF NEUROL, UNIV MISS, 76- *Personal Data:* b Stuttgart, Ger, Mar 28, 34; US citizen; m 58, Darlene Volkmar; c Alice & Martha. *Educ:* Univ Mich, BS, 57, MD, 59; Am Bd Psychiat & Neurol, dipl neurol, 66. *Prof Exp:* Intern, Univ Mich, 59-60, resident neurol, 60-63; clin instr, Univ Louisville, 63-65. *Concurrent Pos:* Consult neurol, Wayne County Gen Hosp, Mich, 62-63, US Vet Hosp, Jackson, Miss, 67-89 & Gulfport, 69-89; chief neurol, US Vet Hosp, Jackson, Miss, 89. *Mem:* AMA; fel Am Col Physicians; Am Neurol Asn; fel Am Acad Neurol. *Res:* Clinical and basic neurology, especially cerebrospinal fluid and cerbrovascular disorders. *Mailing Add:* US Vet Admin Hosp 1500 E Woodrow Wilson Jackson MS 39216-5199

HAERING, EDWIN RAYMOND, CHEMICAL PROCESS INDUSTRIES, HAZARDOUS MATERIALS MANAGEMENT. *Current Pos:* From instr to prof chem eng, Ohio State Univ, 59-91, vchmn/chmn dept, 73-77, actg chmn, 77-78, EMER PROF CHEM ENG, OHIO STATE UNIV, 91- *Personal Data:* b Columbus, Ohio, Dec 8, 32; m 56, Suzanne Rowe; c Cynthia, David A & Elizabeth. *Educ:* Ohio State Univ, BChE & MS, 56, PhD(chem eng), 66. *Concurrent Pos:* Tech Consult 66- *Mem:* Am Chem Soc; Am Inst Chem Engrs. *Res:* Adsorption; catalysis; kinetics; process development and design; process safety; hazardous material management. *Mailing Add:* Dept Chem Eng Ohio State Univ 701 Stoutenburg Dr Marblehead OH 43440

HAERING, GEORGE, AIR WARFARE, TECHNICAL MANAGEMENT. *Current Pos:* rep to Comdr, Seventh Fleet Opers Eval Group, 61-62, rep to Comdr in Chief Pac Fleet, 65-66, chief Naval Opers, Systs Analytical Div, 67-84, DIR OPERS RES, NAVAL AIR SYSTS COMMAND, DEPT Navy, 85- *Personal Data:* b Rangoon, Burma, Oct 7, 30; US citizen; m 85; c 3. *Educ:* Princeton Univ, AB, 52. *Prof Exp:* Analyst, US Bur Budget, 55-58 & Opers Eval Group, 59-60; asst to dir, Naval Warfare Anal Group, 60-61. *Concurrent Pos:* Consult, Joint Tech Coord Group Munitions Effect, 63-65 & 68-; chmn, Joint Aircraft Attrition Prog, 71-75. *Mem:* AAAS. *Res:* Analysis of combat data from tactical air warfare; development of optimal force structures within constrained budgets; experimentation in dogfights. *Mailing Add:* 209 E Nelson Ave Alexandria VA 22301

HAERING, RUDOLPH ROLAND, experimental & theoretical solid state physics, for more information see previous edition

HAERTEL, JOHN DAVID, AVIAN BIOLOGY. *Current Pos:* PROF ZOOL, SDAK STATE UNIV, 69- *Personal Data:* b Elgin, Ill, Aug 4, 37; m 62, Lois Steben; c Michael & Patrick. *Educ:* Univ Ill, Urbana, BS, 62; Ore State Univ, Corvallis, MS, 67, PhD(zool), 69. *Mem:* Am Inst Biol Sci; Inland Bird Banding Asn; Am Asn Zool Parks & Aquariums. *Res:* Biology of Charadriiformes in South Dakota; food analysis during spring migration. *Mailing Add:* Biol Dept SDak State Univ Brookings SD 57007-0595. *E-Mail:* haertelj@ur.sdstate.edu

HAERTEL, LOIS STEBEN, AQUATIC ECOLOGY. *Current Pos:* from asst prof to assoc prof, 69-88, PROF BIOL, SDAK STATE UNIV, 88- *Personal Data:* b Hinsdale, Ill, Dec 16, 39; m 62; c Michael & Patrick. *Educ:* Univ Ill, Urbana-Champaign, BS, 61, MS, 63; Ore State Univ, PhD(oceanog), 69. *Prof Exp:* Asst oceanog, Ore State Univ, 63-65. *Concurrent Pos:* Res grants, Off Water Resources, SDak State Univ, 70-72, 74-79, 87-89 & 92-93. *Mem:* Am Soc Limnol & Oceanog; Soc Wetland Scientists. *Res:* Aquatic ecology; algae; eutrophication; biological control of algal blooms. *Mailing Add:* Dept Biol SDak State Univ PO Box 22078 Brookings SD 57007. *Fax:* 605-688-6677; *E-Mail:* haertell@ur.sdstate.edu

HAERTLING, GENE HENRY, CERAMICS. *Current Pos:* EMER PROF CERAMICS ENG, CLEMSON UNIV, 87- *Personal Data:* b Old Appleton, Mo, Mar 15, 32; m 58; c 3. *Educ:* Univ Mo-Rolla, BS, 54; Univ Ill, MS, 60, PhD(ceramics), 61. *Honors & Awards:* Pace Award, Nat Inst Ceramic Engrs, 72; Pub Serv Medal, NASA, 93. *Prof Exp:* Res ceramic engr, Ipsen Ceramics Inc, 54-55, plant engr ceramics develop, 57-58; staff mem ceramics res, Sandia Corp, 61-65, div supvr elec ceramics res & develop, 65-73; pres, Optoceram, Inc, Albuquerque, 73-74; mgr, Opto-Ceramics Dept, Motorola Inc, 74-80, officer tech staff, 80-87. *Mem:* Nat Acad Eng; Nat Inst Ceramic Engrs; fel Inst Elec & Electronics Engrs; fel Am Ceramic Soc. *Res:* Electrooptic ceramics; oxide ceramics; ferroelectric and piezoelectric phenomena; sintering studies; hot-pressing of ferroelectrics. *Mailing Add:* Dept Ceramic Eng Clemson Univ Clemson SC 29634. *Fax:* 864-656-1453; *E-Mail:* hgene@ces.clemson.edu

HAESELER, CARL W, POMOLOGY, HORTICULTURE. *Current Pos:* Asst prof pomol & exten pomologist, 61-66, ASSOC PROF POMOL, COL AGR, PA STATE UNIV, 66-, SUPT ERIE COUNTY FIELD RES LAB, 74- *Personal Data:* b Northampton, Mass, Feb 25, 29; m 54; c 3. *Educ:* Univ Mass, BSc, 54; Cornell Univ, MSc, 58; Pa State Univ, PhD(hort), 62. *Mem:* Am Soc Hort Sci; Am Pomol Soc; Am Soc Enol; Sigma Xi. *Res:* Plant physiology; viticulture, primarily cultural techniques, especially nutrition, root-stocks, growth regulators, training and pruning. *Mailing Add:* 156 Lake Cliff Dr Erie PA 16511-1242

HAEUSSERMANN, WALTER, ELECTRICAL & MECHANICAL ENGINEERING, APPLIED PHYSICS. *Current Pos:* CONSULT. *Personal Data:* b Kuenzelsau, Ger, Mar 2, 14; US citizen; m 40, Ruth Knos. *Educ:* Stuttgart Tech Univ, BSE, 35; Darmstadt Inst Technol, ME, 38, Dr Ing(physics, math), 44. *Honors & Awards:* Super Achievement Award, Inst Navig, 70; Medal Merit, Baden-Wuerttemberg, 85; Wernher von Braun Distinction, Ger Aerospace Soc, 88; Medaris Award, US Army, 90. *Prof Exp:* Asst prof elec eng, Darmstadt Tech Univ, 37-39, asst prof appl physics, 42-46, develop engr elec eng, 46-47; chief engr guid control, Peenemuende, Ger, 39-42; supvr aeronaut develop engr, Ord Dept, US Army, Ft Bliss, 47-50 & Ord Mission Lab, Redstone Arsenal, Ala, 50-56, dir guid & control, Army Ballistic Missile Agency, 56-60; dir astronics lab, Marshall Space Flight Ctr, 60-69, dir cent syst eng, 69-72, dir science & eng, 72-75, asst syst engr, Sci & Eng Directorate, 75-78; consult, Bendix Guid Systs, 78-83, Teledyne Brown Eng, 83-86, Appl Res Inc, 86-92. *Concurrent Pos:* Prof elec eng, Auburn Univ, 66-; mem, Int Fedn Automatic Control Space Comt. *Mem:* Fel Am Astronaut Soc; Am Inst Navig; fel Am Inst Aeronaut & Astronaut; Sigma Xi; hon mem Ger Aerospace Soc. *Res:* Development of space control and guidance systems; space system developments. *Mailing Add:* 1607 Sandlin Ave SE Huntsville AL 35801-2067

HAFELE, JOSEPH CARL, RELATIVITY PHYSICS. *Current Pos:* AT DEPT PHYSICS & COMPUT SCI, CHRISTOPHER NEWPORT UNIV, 91- *Personal Data:* b Peoria, Ill, July 25, 33; US citizen; m 58; c 4. *Educ:* Univ Ill, BS, 59, MS, 60, PhD(physics), 64. *Prof Exp:* Res assoc physics, Univ Ill, 64; mem staff, Los Alamos Sci Lab, 64-66; asst prof, Wash Univ, 66-72; mem staff, Res Dept, 72-77, mem, Eng Gen Off, Caterpillar Tractor Co, 77-85; asst prof, Eureka Col, 85-90; consult, 90-91. *Concurrent Pos:* NASA Summer Res Fel, 87-90. *Mem:* AAAS; Am Phys Soc; Sigma Xi; Am Asn Univ Prof. *Res:* Relativity; mathematics. *Mailing Add:* 121 Tide Mill Lane Apt 21B Hampton VA 23666

HAFEMAN, DEAN GARY, BIOCHEMISTRY. *Current Pos:* RES SCIENTIST, MOLECULAR DEVICES CORP, 84- *Personal Data:* b Green Bay, Wis, Aug 19, 49; m 76; c 1. *Educ:* Univ Wis, PhD(biochem), 75. *Concurrent Pos:* Asst prof, Case Western Reserve Univ, 82-84. *Mem:* Biophys Soc; Mats Res Soc; AM Chem Soc; Am Asn Immunologists; Am Soc Cell Biol. *Res:* Analytical and electrochemical reseach. *Mailing Add:* Molecular Devices Corp 1311 Orleans Dr Sunnyvale CA 94089-1136

HAFEMEISTER, DAVID WALTER, SOLID STATE & NUCLEAR PHYSICS. *Current Pos:* PROF PHYSICS, CALIF STATE POLYTECH UNIV, SAN LUIS OBISPO, 69- *Personal Data:* b Chicago, Ill, July 1, 34; m 61, Gina Rohlander; c Andrew, Jason & Heidi. *Educ:* Northwestern Univ, BSME, 57; Univ Ill, MS, 60, PhD(physics), 64. *Honors & Awards:* Szilard Award, Am Phys Soc. *Prof Exp:* Mech engr, Argonne Nat Lab, 57-58; physics asst, Univ Ill, 58-64; physicist & fel, Los Alamos Sci Lab, NMex, 64-66; asst prof physics, Carnegie-Mellon Univ, 66-69. *Concurrent Pos:* Sci Cong fel with Sen John Glenn, 75-76 & sci adv, 76-77; spec asst to Under Secy of State, 77-78; expert consult, State Dept, 78-80, Off Strategic Nuclear Policy, State Dept, 87, Stanford, 88 & Princeton, 89; vis scientist, Mass Inst Technol, 83-84, Lawrence Berkeley, 85; prof staff mem, Senate Foreign Rels Comn, 90-92, Senate Gov Affairs Comn, 92-93, Off Strategic Negotiations, US Arms Control & Disarmament Agency, 97-98; adj prof, Sch Pub Policy, Univ Md, 96-97. *Mem:* AAAS; fel Am Phys Soc; Fedn Am Scientists. *Res:* Mossbauer effect; energy policy; electronic structure of the alkali halides; arms control technology and policy. *Mailing Add:* 553 Serrano San Luis Obispo CA 93405. *Fax:* 805-756-1670; *E-Mail:* dhafemei@calpoly.edu

HAFEN, ELIZABETH SUSAN SCOTT, PARTICLE ASTROPHYSICS. *Current Pos:* From instr to assoc prof physics, 73-83, PRIN RES SCIENTIST, LAB NUCLEAR SCI, MASS INST TECHNOL, 83- *Personal Data:* b Springfield, Mo, July 25, 46; m 70, Clifford H Jr. *Educ:* Iowa State Univ, BS, 68, PhD(physics), 73. *Mem:* Am Phys Soc; AAAS. *Res:* Short-lived resonances produced in hadron collisions as a probe of quark-quark interactions; large underground detectors. *Mailing Add:* Dept Physics Rm 24-522 Mass Inst Technol, 77 Mass Ave Cambridge MA 02139

HAFEN, MARGUERITE, MATHEMATICS. *Current Pos:* asst prof & lectr, 79-84, ASST PROF, COMPUT SCI & ENG DEPT, PA STATE UNIV, 88- *Educ:* Univ NMex, BA, 68; Western State Col, Colo, MS, 71; Tex A&M Univ, PhD(math), 78; Pa State Univ, MFA(English), 94. *Prof Exp:* Instr math, Western State Col, 72-73 & Univ Okla, 76-78; teaching asst, Tex A&M Univ, 73-76; asst prof, Math Sci Dept, Univ Alaska, 84-87. *Concurrent Pos:* Vis asst prof comput sci, Univ Okla, 78; lectr, Tex A&M Univ, 78, Am Math Soc, 79, State Univ NY, Stony Brook, 80, Pa State Univ, 81 & Spec Interest Group Comput & Soc, Asn Comput Mach, 94; grantee, NSF, 80-81; Fulbright scholar, Nicaragua, 94-95; ed, Next. *Res:* Relational data bases; automata and language theory; semigroup—theory; ring theory; object oriented analysis and design; author of several publications. *Mailing Add:* 439 E Foster Ave State College PA 16801

HAFER, LOUIS JAMES, COMPUTER AIDED DESIGN. *Current Pos:* ASST PROF COMPUT SCI, SIMON FRASER UNIV, 81- *Personal Data:* b Youngstown, Ohio, Jan 21, 55; m 80. *Educ:* Carnegie-Mellon Univ, BS, 76, MS, 78, PhD(comput aided design), 81. *Mem:* Inst Elec & Electronics Engrs. *Res:* Automated synthesis of digital system hardware from behavioural descriptions; computer-aided design; hardware descriptive languages. *Mailing Add:* Sch Comput Sci Simon Fraser Univ Burnaby BC V5A 1S6 CAN

HAFF, RICHARD FRANCIS, MICROBIOLOGY. *Current Pos:* VPRES, SCI DEVELOP, WARNER LAMBERT CO, 81- *Personal Data:* b New York, NY, Oct 1, 29; m 53; c 2. *Educ:* Univ NC, BA, 51; Western Res Univ, PhD(microbiol), 57. *Prof Exp:* Microbiologist, Stine Lab, E I du Pont de Nemours & Co, 57-63; virologist, Smith Kline & French Labs, 63-67, assoc dir microbiol, 67-72, sci dir, 72-78, dir new prod eval, Com Develop, 78-81. *Mem:* Am Soc Microbiol. *Res:* Viral chemotherapy; animal virology; tissue culture. *Mailing Add:* 2433 Blueberry Lane Ann Arbor MI 48103

HAFFLEY, PHILIP GENE, ORGANIC CHEMISTRY. *Current Pos:* Assoc prof chem, 67-81, chmn, Div Biol & Phys Sci, 71-81, PROF CHEM & ASST DEAN ACAD AFFAIRS, IND UNIV, 81- *Personal Data:* b Richmond, Ind, Oct 9, 41; m 63; c 3. *Educ:* Ind Univ, BS, 63; Iowa State Univ, PhD(org chem), 67. *Mem:* Am Chem Soc; Nat Sci Teachers Asn. *Res:* Free radical chemistry. *Mailing Add:* Ind Univ 2300 S Washington St PO Box 9003 Kokomo IN 46904-9003

HAFFNER, ALDEN NORMAN, OPTOMETRY. *Current Pos:* vchancellor health sci, 78-88, PRES, COL OPTOM, STATE UNIV NY, ALBANY, 88- *Personal Data:* b Brooklyn, NY. *Educ:* Brooklyn Col, AB, 48; Pa Col Optom, OD, 52; NY Univ, MPA, 60, PhD, 64. *Hon Degrees:* Dr Ocular Sci, Mass Col Optom, 60; LHD, Southern Col Optom, 80. *Honors & Awards:* Carel Koch Award. *Prof Exp:* Dean, Col Optom, 71-76; exec dir, Optom Ctr, State Univ NY Col Optom, 57-80, pres, Col Optom, 76-80. *Mem:* Fel Am Acad Optom; Am Pub Health Asn; Am Sch Health Asn; Am Pub Welfare Asn; Am Soc Pub Admin. *Res:* Public administration of health and social services. *Mailing Add:* 201 E 36th St No 6F New York NY 10016

HAFFNER, RICHARD WILLIAM, SURFACE CHEMISTRY, COMPOSITE MATERIALS. *Current Pos:* sr indust specialist, 80-90, SR SYSTS ENGR, NAT SYSTS MGT CORP, 90- *Personal Data:* b Bucyrus, Ohio, Feb 15, 31; wid; c Katherine S (Bernard), Barbara E (Foltz) & Suzanne J. *Educ:* Ohio Univ, BS, 53; Purdue Univ, MS, 55; George Washington Univ, MBA, 65. *Prof Exp:* Proj officer, Air Force Aero Propulsion Lab, 55-58; proj officer, Air Force Space & Missile Orgn, 58-64; asst prof chem, Air Force Acad, 65-68; prog mgr, Air Force Off Sci Res, 68-72; inspector, Hq Air Force Systs Command, 72-74; prog mgr, Air Force Off Sci Res, 74-80. *Concurrent Pos:* Consult, tech problems related to Dept Defense use of electro-optic night vision devices. *Mem:* Am Chem Soc; Sigma Xi; AAAS. *Res:* Air Force basic research program in surface chemistry including research in areas such as lubrication, corrosion and catalysis. *Mailing Add:* 13020 Chalfont Ave Ft Washington MD 20744. *Fax:* 703-256-1811

HAFFNER, RUDOLPH ERIC, BIOLOGICAL OCEANOGRAPHY. *Current Pos:* dir sci & prof biol, 67-87, EMER PROF BIOL, HARTFORD COL WOMEN, 87- *Personal Data:* b Thorun, Poland, Feb 27, 20; nat US; m 45, Jeanne Lowell; c Anne H (Wahl), Eric W & Peter L. *Educ:* Univ Maine, BA, 42; Yale Univ, PhD(zool), 52. *Prof Exp:* Instr biol, Colby Col, 46-47; instr biol, Wesleyan Univ, 52-53, asst prof, 53-58; assoc prof biol, Bucknell Univ, 58-60; ed dir sci pub, Am Ed Pub, Inc, 60-67. *Mem:* Fel AAAS; NY Acad Sci; Sigma Xi. *Res:* Oceanography. *Mailing Add:* 60 Hickory Hill Rd Simsbury CT 06070-2833

HAFFORD, BRADFORD C, analytical chemistry, inorganic chemistry; deceased, see previous edition for last biography

HAFIZI, BAHMAN, FREE-ELECTRON SOURCES OF RADIATION, ACCELERATORS. *Current Pos:* SCIENTIST & PRES, ICARUS RES, 90- *Personal Data:* b Tehran, Iran, Jan 23, 53; US citizen; m 79, Carmen Marianovich; c Natalia. *Educ:* Imp Col, London, BSc, 74, PhD(physics), 78. *Prof Exp:* Sr scientist, Sci Applns Int Corp, 81-90. *Concurrent Pos:* Consult, Los Alamos Nat Lab, 79-83, Naval Res Lab, 86- *Mem:* Am Phys Soc; Europ Phys Soc. *Res:* Design and anlysis of free-electron sources of radiation; design and analysis of advanced accelerators; application of advanced radiation sources and accelerators to problems in scientific research and technology. *Mailing Add:* Naval Res Lab Code 6790 4555 Overlook Ave SW Washington DC 20375. *Fax:* 202-767-0631; *E-Mail:* hafizi@ppdu.nrl.navy.mil

HAFLEY, WILLIAM LEROY, GROWTH YIELD, MANAGEMENT SCIENCE APPLICATIONS. *Current Pos:* RETIRED. *Personal Data:* b Phila, Pa, Jan 26, 30; m 54; c 3. *Educ:* Pa State Univ, BS, 53; NC State Univ, MF, 57, PhD(exp statist), 60. *Prof Exp:* Staff consult statistician, Aluminum Co, Am, 60-63; sr consult statistician, Westinghouse Elec Corp, Pa, 63-66; prof forestry & statist, NC State Univ, 66-91. *Mem:* Am Statist Asn; Soc Am Foresters. *Res:* Statistical techniques for biological applications. *Mailing Add:* 1312 W Staggs Creek Rd Warrensville NC 28693

HAFNER, EDMUND W, FERMENTATION OF MICROORGANISMS TO PRODUCE ANTIBOTICS, SCREEN MIOCROORGANISMS FROM NATURE TO FIND NEW ANTIBIOTICS. *Current Pos:* sr res scientist, 84-87, sr res investr, 88-94, PRIN RES INVESTR, PRIZER CENT RES, 95- *Personal Data:* b New York, NY, Feb 13, 43; m 66; c 2. *Educ:* Univ Rochester, BA, 64; Harvard Univ, MA, 65; Cornell Univ, PhD(biochem), 74. *Prof Exp:* Teacher chem, Schreiber High Sch, Port Washington, NY, 65-68; staff fel, NIH, 74-79; sr res scientist, Allied Signal Res Ctr, 79-84. *Concurrent Pos:* Vchair, E Lyme Conserv Comn, 95- *Mem:* Am Soc Microbiol; AAAS; Am Soc Biochem & Molecular Biol; Soc Indust Microbiol. *Res:* Genetics of microorganisms that produce antibiotics and search by mutation and genetic engineering to make novel antibiotics; screen natural sources for novel strains making new antibiotics. *Mailing Add:* Pfizer Cent Res Eastern Point Rd Groton CT 06340. *Fax:* 860-441-4119; *E-Mail:* edmund_w_hafner@groton.pfizer.com

HAFNER, ERICH, SOLID STATE PHYSICS. *Current Pos:* PRES, XOTEC CORP. *Personal Data:* b Graz, Austria, July 26, 28; US citizen; wid; c 3. *Educ:* Graz Univ, PhD(physics), 52. *Honors & Awards:* C B Sawyer Mem Award, 83. *Prof Exp:* Res asst theoret physics, Graz Univ, 50-52; res physicist, US Army Command, 53-60, leader frequency control devices, Solid State & Frequency Control Div, 60-81. *Mem:* Am Phys Soc; fel Inst Elec & Electronics Engrs. *Res:* Frequency control and timekeeping; physical and electrical properties of quartz crystals; stable oscillators; noise; physical acoustics; internal friction in dielectrics; lattice theory; microwave theory. *Mailing Add:* 881 Sycamore Ave Tinton Falls NJ 07724. *Fax:* 732-741-0283

HAFNER, GARY STUART, NEUROANATOMY, NEUROCYTOLOGY. *Current Pos:* res assoc neurocytol, 74-76, asst prof, 76-80, ASSOC PROF, SCH OPTOM, IND UNIV, BLOOMINGTON, 81- *Personal Data:* b Greensboro, NC, Aug 25, 43; m 78. *Educ:* Hanover Col, BA, 65; Drake Univ, MA, 67; Ind Univ, Bloomington, PhD(neuroanat), 72. *Prof Exp:* Asst prof biol, Hanover Col, 72. *Concurrent Pos:* Fel neurocytol, Ind Univ, Bloomington, 73; trainee neuroanat, Univ Calif, Los Angeles, 73-74. *Mem:* Am Asn Anatomists; Am Soc Zoologists; Asn Res Vision & Ophthalmol; Soc Neurosci. *Res:* Combined cytological, biochemical and autoradiographic studies of photo- and chemoreceptors in vertebrates and invertebrates, and the distribution of neurofilaments and microtubules in receptors and other central nervous system neurons. *Mailing Add:* Dept Visual Sci Ind Univ Sch Optom Bloomington IN 47401

HAFNER, STEVEN C, SCIENCE ADMINISTRATION. *Current Pos:* USAF, 72-, dep missile combat crew comndr, crew comndr & instr, 90th Strategic Missile Wing, FE Warren AFB, airborne launch control systs comndr, instr & evaluator, 28th Bombardment Wing, Ellsworth AFB, 76-79, exec officer, comndr 4th Air Div, FE Warren AFB, 79-81, missile maintenance officer, Reentry Syst Br, 81-83, command briefer & action officer, Hq, Strategic Air Command, Offutt AFB, 83-86, action officer, Air Staff's Int Affairs Div, Pentagon, 86-88, comndr, Field Missile Maintenance Squadron, Grand Forks AFB, 88-90, dep dir, Strategic Employ Div, dir, Future Concepts Div, Hqs, 90-91, chief, Nuclear Forces Div, dir forces, Off Dep Chief Sttaff Plans & Opers, team chief, Nuclear Deterrence Resource Allocation Team, Pentagon, 92-93, comndr, 90th Logistics Group, FE Warren AFB, 93-95, COMNDR, FIELD COMMAND, DEFENSE SPEC WEAPONS AGENCY, USAF, 95- *Personal Data:* b Hannibel, Mo, July 12, 50; m, Cydney L Lightfoot; c Eric & Lesley. *Educ:* Univ Mo, BS, 72; Univ Wyo, MBA, 75. *Mailing Add:* Field Command Defense Spec Weapons Agency 1680 Texas St SE Kirtland AFB NM 87117-5669

HAFS, HAROLD DAVID, REPRODUCTIVE PHYSIOLOGY, ENDOCRINOLOGY. *Current Pos:* vpres, Animal Sci Res & Develop, 80-90, VPRES, ANIMAL HEALTH SCI AFFAIRS, MERCK & CO INC, 90- *Personal Data:* b Genoa City, Wis, July 2, 31; m 52; c 3. *Educ:* Univ Wis, BS, 53; Cornell Univ, MS, 57, PhD(animal physiol), 59. *Honors & Awards:* Animal Physiol Award, Am Soc Animal Sci, 73; Animal Breeders Award, Am Dairy Sci Asn, 71; Jr Scientist Award, Sigma Xi, Mich State Univ, 71; Sr Scientist Award, 78. *Prof Exp:* From asst prof to prof reprod physiol, Mich State Univ, 59-80, chmn, dept dairy sci, 76-80. *Concurrent Pos:* NIH spec fel, Harvard Univ, 65-66; vis prof, Univ Nottingham, 73-74. *Mem:* Soc Study Reprod (secy, 70-73); Endocrine Soc; Am Soc Animal Sci; Brit Soc Study Fertil; Am Physiol Soc. *Res:* Sperm production; sperm capacitation; seminal plasma and uterine fluid; gonadotropins and reproductive growth at puberty and during estrous cycle; utero-ovarian relationships, pituitary control of testicular function. *Mailing Add:* Dept Animal Sci Rutgers Univ PO Box 231 New Brunswick NJ 08903-0231. *Fax:* 732-932-6996

HAFT, JACOB I, INTERNAL MEDICINE, INVASIVE & NON CARDIOLOGY. *Current Pos:* CHIEF CARDIOL, ST MICHAELS HOSP, 74-; CLIN PROF MED, NJ COL MED. *Personal Data:* b E Orange, NJ, Jan 15, 37; m 64, Gail S Klein; c Ian & Bethanne. *Educ:* Harvard Univ, BA, 58; Col Phys Columbia Univ, MD, 62. *Prof Exp:* Chief cardiol, Bronx Vet Admin Hosp, 69-74; from asst prof to assoc prof med, Mt Sinai Med Sch, 69-74. *Concurrent Pos:* Consult cardiol, Holy Name Hosp, 75-, Hackensack Hosp, 75-, Clara Mass Hosp, 75-; mem, NJ Gov Adv Comt Cardiol, 76-87; mem, Blue Shield Multispecialty Comt Cardiol, 82-; mem, NJ Comnr Health Cardiac Serv Comt, 87-93. *Mem:* Am Col Cardiol fel; Am Col Chest Physicians; Am Col Physicians; Clin Coun Am Heart Assoc fel. *Res:* Clinical research on cardiology, electrophysiology, arrhythmias, platelet function, thrombosis, coronary atheroscilero and its progression, angioplasty and aortic valvuloplasty, echocardiology. *Mailing Add:* 306 King Blvd Newark NJ 07102

HAFTEL, MICHAEL IVAN, ATOMIC & MOLECULAR COLLISION THEORY. *Current Pos:* asst prof physics, 81-91, ASSOC PROF PHYSICS, GEORGE WASHINGTON UNIV, 91-, PHYSICIST, NAVAL RES LAB, 71- *Personal Data:* b Philadelphia, Pa, Mar 22, 43; m 67; c Joy, Joshua, Jonathan & Johanna. *Educ:* Pa State Univ, BS, 65; Univ Pittsburgh, PhD(physics), 69. *Prof Exp:* Nat Res Coun resident physicist, Nat Acad Sci & res assoc nuclear physics, Naval Res Lab, 69-71. *Concurrent Pos:* Fulbright lectr physics, Univ Graz, Austria, 78-79. *Mem:* Am Phys Soc; Mat Res Soc. *Res:* Nuclear few body problems and nuclear forces, especially pertaining to three nucleon bound and scattering states; few body problems in atomic and molecular collisions; molecular dynamics at surfaces. *Mailing Add:* Code 6651 Naval Res Lab Washington DC 20375-5345. *Fax:* 202-767-6980; *E-Mail:* haftel@ccfympel.nrl.navy.mil

HAFTER, ERVIN R, PSYCHOLOGY, EDUCATION. *Current Pos:* PROF, DEPT PSYCHOL, UNIV CALIF, BERKELEY. *Mailing Add:* Dept Psychol Univ Calif Berkeley CA 94720

HAGAN, JAMES JOYCE, CONTRAST AGENTS FOR MAGNETIC RESONANCE IMAGING, RADIOPHARMACEUTICALS. *Current Pos:* RETIRED. *Personal Data:* b Baltimore, Md, Sept 13, 26; m 61, Ida Costigan; c Alice, Caroline & Anne. *Educ:* Upsala Col, AB, 49; Rutgers Univ, MSc, 51; Univ Louisville, PhD(biochem), 66. *Prof Exp:* Chemist, Gen Foods Corp, 50-51 & Lederle Labs-Am Cyanamid, 51-61; Biochemist, Bristol-Myers Squibb Co, 66-93. *Mem:* Am Chem Soc; Soc Magnetic Resonance Med. *Res:* Evaluation and preparation of executive summaries on new diagnostic (in vivo) products or products in various stages of development; assist in merging significant new therapeutic diagnostic technologies with the research/business activities of major pharmaceutical companies. *Mailing Add:* 12 Ardmore Pl Holmdel NJ 07733

HAGAN, JOHN CHARLES, III, CATARACT & INTRA-OCULAR LENS SURGERY, COMPLICATIONS & MANAGEMENT OF SEMI-FLEXIBLE INTRA-OCULAR LENS. *Current Pos:* FOUNDER & DIR, MIDWEST EYE INST KANSAS CITY, INC, 75- *Personal Data:* b Mexico, Mo, Oct 7, 43; m 67, Rebecca J Chapman; c Carol A & Catherine E. *Educ:* Univ Mo, BS, 65; Loyala Univ, MD, 69; Am Bd Ophthal, Cert, 76. *Prof Exp:* Intern, Milwaukee Co Gen Hosp, 69-70; asst clin instr med, Univ NDak Med Sch, 70-72; resident, Dept Ophthal, Grady Mem Hosp, 72-75. *Concurrent Pos:* Med adv & consult, Am Running & Fitness Asn, 70-91; instr, Lions Eye Bank, Atlanta, 72-75; alt coun mem, Am Acad Ophthal, 89-90. *Mem:* Fel Am Acad Ophthal; fel Am Col Surgeons; AMA; Am Occup Med Asn; Am Soc Cataract & Refractive Surg. *Res:* Development of techniques and instruments for cataract and intra-ocular lens surgery for management of complication correct caused by these medical devices. *Mailing Add:* Midwest Eye Inst 2700 Clay Edwards Dr North Kansas City MO 64116-3251. *Fax:* 816-421-6131

HAGAN, MELVIN ROY, MATHEMATICS. *Current Pos:* asst prof, 65-71, ASSOC PROF MATH, NTEX STATE UNIV, 71- *Personal Data:* b Beaver Co, Okla, Jan 20, 34; m 64; c 2. *Educ:* Northwestern State Col, Okla, BS, 59; Okla State Univ, MS, 61, PhD(math), 64. *Prof Exp:* Asst prof math, Stephen F Austin State Col, 64-65. *Mem:* Am Math Soc; Math Asn Am. *Res:* Topology; peripherally continuous functions and connectivity maps. *Mailing Add:* Dept Math Univ NTex Denton TX 76203

HAGAN, ROBERT M(OWER), WATER RESOURCE MANAGEMENT. *Current Pos:* Assoc bot, Exp Sta, Col Agr, Univ Calif, Davis, 37-39, asst soils, 39-40, assoc irrig, 46-48, instr & jr irrigationist, 48-49, instr & asst irrig technologist, 49-50, asst prof & asst irrig technologist, 50-53, assoc prof & assoc irriagtionist, 53-57, chmn dept water sci & eng, 54-63, prof water sci & eng, 57-87, assoc dir, Int Agr Inst, 68-70, EMER PROF WATER SCI & EXTEN WATER SPECIALIST, COL AGR, UNIV CALIF, DAVIS, 87- *Personal Data:* b Oakland, Calif, Dec 5, 16; m 39; c 2. *Educ:* Univ Calif, BS, 37, MS, 42, PhD(soil sci), 48. *Concurrent Pos:* Mem Int Comn Irrig, Drainage & Flood Control, 60-64; pres, Water Educ Found, 90-; bd dirs, Flood Control & Water Conserv Dist, Yolo Co & Water Resources Assoc. *Mem:* Fel AAAS; Soil Sci Soc Am; Am Soc Hort Sci; Soc Int Develop; fel Am Soc Agron; Sigma Xi. *Res:* Water-soil-plant relations; irrigation planning and management; optimizing use of limited water supplies; antitranspirants; irrigation in relation to international agricultural development; water policy. *Mailing Add:* 548 Oak Ave Davis CA 95616

HAGAN, WALLACE WOODROW, GEOLOGY. *Current Pos:* dir & state geologist, 58-78, MEM ADV BD, KY GEOL SURV, UNIV KY, 52-, EMER GEOLOGIST, 78- *Personal Data:* b Griggsville, Ill, Feb 3, 13; m 40, Mary E Levan; c Karen R & Elizabeth A. *Educ:* Univ Ill, BS, 35, MS, 36, PhD(geol), 42. *Honors & Awards:* John Wesley Powell Award, Geol Surv, US Dept Interior, 72; Pub Serv Award, Am Asn Petrol Geologists, 82. *Prof Exp:* Asst geologist, J V Wicklund Develop Co, Mich, 37-39; consult geologist, Ky & Ill, 39-40; geologist in-chg groundwater sect, Div Geol, Ind State Dept Conserv, 42-44; geologist, Sohio Petrol Co, 45-48; Ky chief geologist, Felmont Oil Corp, 48-52. *Concurrent Pos:* Dist geologist, Owensboro, Ky, 45-48; consult geologist, Ky, 52-58 & 78- & Ind, 78-; gov rep res comt, Interstate Oil Compact Comn, 59-; bd dirs, Natural Resources Comt, Ky Conserv Cong, 61-67; statistician, Asn Am State Geologists, 63-66; chmn res comt, 65-66; mem res & policy comt, Ky Water Resources Inst, 65-78; mem, Ky Water Resources Coun, 65-78; Asn Am State Geologists rep, Adv comt Water Data Pub Use, US Dept Interior, 68-78; mem, Mineral Resources subcomt, Lower Miss Region Comprehensive Study, 70-78; mem, Subcomt Radioactive Waste Disposal, Ky Sci & Technol Coun, 71-78; mem adv coun, Inst Mining & Minerals Res, Univ Ky, 71-78; mem, Ky State-Fed Water Resources Adv Coun, 73-78, Maxey Flats Nuclear Waste Disposal Site Decommissioning Plan Adv Bd, Ky, 83-84 & Ky Oil & Gas Asn State Regulatory Comt, 82-86; ex officio mem, Ky Develop Cabinet, 73-78; distinguished scientist award, Ky Acad Sci, 77; pres, Ky Sect, Am Inst Prof Geologists, 82-83; deleg, Ky-Tenn Sect Geol Soc Ky, Am Asn Petrol Geologists, 83-86; hon life mem, Ky Oil & Gas Asn, 86- *Mem:* Hon mem Asn Am State Geologists (vpres, 66-67, pres-elect, 67-68, pres, 68-69); fel Geol Soc Am; Am Asn Petrol Geologists; Am Inst Prof Geologists (pres, Ky Sect, 82-83); Sigma Xi. *Res:* Stratigraphy; petroleum geography; petroleum geology, exploration and development. *Mailing Add:* 317 Jesselin Dr Lexington KY 40503-2016

HAGAN, WILLIAM JOHN, JR, SURFACE CHEMISTRY, CHEMICAL EVOLUTION. *Current Pos:* asst prof, 92-94, ASSOC PROF CHEM, COL ST ROSE, 94- *Personal Data:* b Port Washington, NY, May 17, 56. *Educ:* Bowdoin Col, BA, 78; Rensselaer Polytech Inst, PhD(org chem), 85, MS, 86. *Prof Exp:* Fel biochem, Univ Rochester, 85-87; asst prof chem, St Anselm Col, 87-92. *Concurrent Pos:* Vis assoc prof, Rensselaer Polytech Inst, 88. *Mem:* Am Chem Soc; AAAS; Int Soc Study of Origins of Life; Hist Sci Soc. *Res:* Surface-catalyzed chemical reactions; thermal and photochemical probes of mineral surfaces; history of chemistry. *Mailing Add:* Dept Chem Col St Rose 432 Western Ave Albany NY 12205-1419. *Fax:* 518-458-5446

HAGAN, WILLIAM LEONARD, PLANT BREEDING, PHYTOPATHOLOGY. *Current Pos:* RES ASSOC, UCCE UNIV CALIF, DAVIS. *Personal Data:* b Atkinson, Ill, Mar 21, 36; m 57, Janet McKenzie; c Kent & Kimberly. *Educ:* Univ Ill, BS, 59, MS, 60, PhD(plant genetics & path), 63; John F Kennedy Univ, MBA, 85. *Prof Exp:* Plant breeder, Del Monte Corp, 63-67, mgr agr res & serv, 67-75, mgr agr res, 75-79, mgr plant breeding, 79-83, dir agr res & seed oper, 83-89, dir agr sci & biotechnol, 89-90. *Mem:* Am Phytopath Soc; Am Soc Agron; Am Soc Hort Sci. *Res:* Genetics, diseases and breeding of vegetable and agronic crops; bio-control and biotechnology management; turfgrass variety evaluation and cultural practices research. *Mailing Add:* 17493 Oak Canyon Pl Castro Valley CA 94546. *E-Mail:* wlhagan@aol.com

HAGANS, JAMES ALBERT, BIOSTATISTICS, THERAPEUTICS. *Current Pos:* RETIRED. *Personal Data:* b Cincinnati, Ohio, Nov 9, 22. *Educ:* Marietta Col, AB, 44; Univ Cincinnati, MD, 46; Univ Okla, MS, 58, PhD, 60. *Prof Exp:* Instr med, Col Med, Univ Cincinnati, 51-52; instr, Sch Med, Emory Univ, 54-55; asst prof med & dir exp therapeut unit, Sch Med, Univ Okla, 55-57, instr med, prev med & pub health, 57-60, assoc prof med biostatist, prev med, pub health & med, 60-62; mgr med biostatist, clin pharmacol & med res, Upjohn Co, 63-71; dir epidemiol biostatist & res data systs med affairs, Merck Sharp & Dohme Res Labs, Pa, 71-73; chief coop studies prog, Dept Med & Surg, Vet Admin, 72-85. *Concurrent Pos:* Jr attend, Cincinnati Gen Hosp, 51-52; attend med, Grady Hosp, Atlanta, Ga, 54-55, Vet Admin Hosp, Okla City, 55-62, Cent State Hosp, 55-62 & Sch Med, Univ Okla, 55-62; prof biostat, Dept Epidemiol & Pub Health, Sch Med, Univ Miami, 73-; mem, US Comt, WHO. *Mem:* Fel Am Col Physicians; Am Statist Asn; Am Soc Pharmacol & Exp Therapeut; Am Soc Clin Pharmacol & Therapeut; Soc Clin Trials. *Res:* Clinical and epidemiological biostatistics; clinical pharmacology; experimental therapeutics; internal medicine; biomedical computer sciences. *Mailing Add:* 9201 W Broward Blvd Apt C-115 Ft Lauderdale FL 33324

HAGAR, CHARLES FREDERICK, ASTRONOMY, SCIENCE COMMUNICATIONS. *Current Pos:* PROF ASTRON, SAN FRANCISCO STATE UNIV, 59-, DIR OBSERV & PLANETARIUM, 75- *Personal Data:* b Los Angeles, Calif, Aug 7, 30. *Educ:* Univ Calif, Los Angeles, BA, 54; Univ Calif, Berkeley, MA, 60. *Prof Exp:* Astronr lectr, Griffith Observ, Los Angeles, 52-57; asst dir astron, AF Morrison Planetarium, San Francisco, 57-59. *Concurrent Pos:* Planetarium consult, Carl Zeiss, WGer, 54-, Hong Kong Space Mus, 75-79; sci fac fel, NSF, 67-68; careers ed, Int Planetarium Soc, 75-77. *Mem:* Astron Soc Pacific; Int Planetarium Soc; Pac Planetarium Assoc. *Res:* Planetarium design and operations; planetarium survey. *Mailing Add:* Dept Physics & Astron San Francisco State Univ 1600 Holloway Ave San Francisco CA 94132. *Fax:* 415-338-2178; *E-Mail:* hagar@stars.sfsu.edu

HAGAR, LOWELL PAUL, ENZYMOLOGY, BIOSYNTHESIS. *Current Pos:* assoc prof, 60-65, head dept, 67-88, PROF BIOCHEM, UNIV ILL, 65-, DIR BIOTECHNOL CTR, 88- *Personal Data:* b Girard, Kans, Aug 30, 26; m 49; c 3. *Educ:* Valparaiso Univ, AB, 47; Univ Kans, MA, 50; Univ Ill, PhD(microbiol), 53. *Prof Exp:* Asst prof biochem, Harvard Univ, 55-60. *Concurrent Pos:* Fel Guggenheim Found, 60. *Mem:* Am Chem Soc; Am Soc Biochem & Molecular Biol. *Res:* Enzymology and enzyme mechanisms; biosynthesis of halo metabolites. *Mailing Add:* 801 W Delaware Urbana IL 61801

HAGBERG, ELROY CARL, FOOD SCIENCE. *Current Pos:* RETIRED. *Personal Data:* b Bayfield, Wis, July 15, 19; m 46, Irene Pippel; c Robert C & William C. *Educ:* Univ Wis, BS, 41, MS, 47, PhD(dairy indust), 49. *Prof Exp:* Chemist, dairy & poultry prods control, Wilson & Co, Ill, 41-44; asst, Univ Wis, 46-49; assoc scientist, milk proteins, Nat Dairy Res Labs, Inc, 49-56; res chemist, Campbell Inst Food Res, Campbell Soup Co, Camden, 56-59, div head dairy prods res, 59-77, dir food sci, 77-80, sr res scientist, 80-82. *Mem:* Am Chem Soc; Am Dairy Sci Asn; Inst Food Technol. *Res:* Dairy, cereal and protein products in heat processed and frozen convenience foods. *Mailing Add:* 336 Olde Chapel Trail Pittsburgh PA 15238-1228

HAGBERG, ERIK GORDON, NUCLEI FAR FROM STABILITY, DELAYED PARTICLE DECAYS. *Current Pos:* assoc res officer, 83-84, RES OFFICER ATOMIC ENERGY CAN, LTD, 85- *Personal Data:* b Gothenburg, Sweden, Nov 12, 49; m 86, Lois A Fitzpatrick; c Audrey & Ingrid. *Educ:* Univ Gothenburg, BSc, 72, PhD(nuclear physics), 78, Docent(nuclear physics), 81. *Prof Exp:* Teaching asst, Chalmers Univ Technol, Gothenburg, Sweden, 72-76, res asst, 78; res fel, Europ Coun Nuclear Res, Geneva, Switz, 76-78, Atomic Energy Can Ltd, 78-80; res assoc, Queens Univ, Kingston, Can, 80-82. *Concurrent Pos:* Adj prof, Univ Man, 90-. *Mem:* Am Phys Soc; Can Asn Physicists. *Res:* Structure of nuclei far from stability; experimental studies of the properties of ground states, and highly excited states of far-unstable nuclei and theoretical model calculations of these properties; nuclear weak interaction and the weak vector coupling constant. *Mailing Add:* Atomic Energy Can Ltd Res Chalk River Labs Chalk River ON K0J 1J0 Can. *Fax:* 613-584-1800

HAGE, KEITH DONALD, METEOROLOGY. *Current Pos:* prof, 67-85, EMER PROF GEOG, UNIV ALTA, 85- *Personal Data:* b Kandahar, Sask, Mar 15, 26; m 52; c 3. *Educ:* Univ BC, BA, 49; Univ Toronto, MA, 50; Univ Chicago, PhD(meteor), 57. *Honors & Awards:* Patterson Medal, Atmospheric Environ Serv, Can, 89. *Prof Exp:* Meteorologist, Meteorol Off, Alta, 50-54; asst meteorol, Univ Chicago, 55-57; meteorologist, Suffield Exp Sta, 57-60; sr res scientist, Travelers Res Ctr, Inc, Conn, 60-67. *Mem:* Can Meteorol Soc; fel Am Meteorol Soc; Royal Meteorol Soc; fel Can Soc Agrometeorol. *Res:* Synoptic-dynamic meteorology and micrometeorology; atmospheric diffusion; mesometeorology. *Mailing Add:* 23-51404 Range Rd 264 Spruce Grove AB T7Y 1E4 Can

HAGEAGE, GEORGE JOHN, JR, MEDICAL MICROBIOLOGY. *Current Pos:* CLIN MICROBIOLOGIST, ST VINCENT HOSP & MED CTR, 75- *Personal Data:* b Allentown, Pa, Nov 4, 35; m 60; c 2. *Educ:* Muhlenberg Col, BS, 57; Univ Md, MS, 60, PhD(microbiol), 63; Am Bd Med Microbiol, dipl, 81. *Prof Exp:* Asst prof microbiol, Univ NH, 63-66; staff fel, Lab Histol & Path, Nat Inst Dent Res, 66-68, res microbiologist, Lab Biol Struct, 68-75. *Concurrent Pos:* Prof microbiol, Med Col Ohio, 75-; adj prof biol sci, Bowling Green State Univ, 76- *Mem:* Am Soc Clin Pathologists; Am Soc Microbiol; NY Acad Sci. *Res:* Ultrastructure of microorganisms; oral microbiology; development of techniques for the rapid identification of pathogenic microorganisms. *Mailing Add:* St Vincent Mercy Hosp & Med Ctr 2213 Cherry St Toledo OH 43608

HAGEDORN, ALBERT BERNER, MEDICINE. *Current Pos:* From asst prof to prof, 50-85, EMER PROF MED, MAYO GRAD SCH MED, UNIV MINN, 85- *Personal Data:* b Salt Lake City, Utah, Jan 15, 15; m 44; c 4. *Educ:* Univ Calif, AB, 38; Stanford Univ, MD, 43; Univ Minn, MS, 46. *Concurrent Pos:* Consult, Mayo Clin, 46- & USAR 54-55. *Mem:* Am Soc Hemat; Am Nuclear Soc; AMA; fel Am Col Physicians; Int Soc Hemat; Sigma Xi. *Res:* Hematology; iron therapy and metabolism. *Mailing Add:* 1217 19th Ave NE Rochester MN 55906

HAGEDORN, CHARLES, SOIL MICROBIOLOGY, FOREST ECOLOGY. *Current Pos:* ASSOC PROF, DEPT AGRON, MISS STATE UNIV, 79- *Personal Data:* b Washington, DC, Aug 13, 47; m 69. *Educ:* Kans State Univ, BS, 70; Iowa State Univ, MS, 72, PhD(microbiol), 74. *Prof Exp:* Teaching asst microbiol, Iowa State Univ, 70-73, res asst, 73-74; asst prof, Dept Microbiol, Ore State Univ, 74-79. *Mem:* Am Soc Microbiol; Soc Indust Microbiol; Soil Sci Soc Am; Am Inst Biol Sci; Am Soc Agron. *Res:* Nitrogen fixation and enzymatic activities in agricultural soils; plant decomposition and microbial antagonisms in forest soils and use of sewage sludge as a source of fertilizer for crops. *Mailing Add:* Dept Crop Soil Sci Va Polytech Inst State Univ PO Box 0404 Blacksburg VA 24063-0001

HAGEDORN, DONALD JAMES, PLANT BREEDING, MICROBIOLOGY. *Current Pos:* From asst prof to prof agron & plant path, 48-64, PROF PLANT PATH, UNIV WIS-MADISON, 64- *Personal Data:* b Moscow, Idaho, May 18, 19; m 43, Eloise; c James. *Educ:* Univ Idaho, BS, 41; Univ Wis, MS, 43, PhD(plant path), 48. *Hon Degrees:* DSc, Univ Idaho, 79. *Honors & Awards:* Campbell Award, AAAS, 61; CIBA-Geigy Award, Am Phytopathol Soc, 75; Meritorious Serv Award, Nat Pea Improv Asn, 79, Bean Improv Coop, 79. *Concurrent Pos:* Courtesy prof plant path, Ore State Univ, 72-73; vis scientist plant path, Dept Sci & Indust Res, Lincoln Res Ctr, NZ, 80-81; consult, Hyderabad, India, 79; mem, Plant Variety Protection Bd, USDA, Washington, DC, 77-78. *Mem:* Sigma Xi; fel Am Phytopath Soc. *Res:* Diseases of peas and beans; control of these diseases through breeding for disease resistance. *Mailing Add:* Univ Wis 1630 Linden Dr Madison WI 53706

HAGEDORN, FRED BASSETT, MAGNETISM & OPTICS. *Current Pos:* INDEPENDENT CONSULT PHYSICS, 87- *Personal Data:* b Boone, Iowa, June 8, 28; m 54, Grace Alexander Helms; c Martha Gray (Hagedorn-Krass) & Katherine Johanna. *Educ:* Iowa State Univ, BS, 52; Calif Inst Technol, PhD(physics), 57. *Prof Exp:* Mem tech staff, Bell Tel Labs, Inc, 57-85; dir tech staff, Parks-Jaggers Aerospace, 85-87. *Mem:* Am Phys Soc; Inst Elec & Electronics Engrs; Sigma Xi. *Res:* Low energy nuclear physics; magnetic flux reversal processes; superconducting and ferromagnetic thin films; magnetic materials research; magnetic bubble device research and development; infrared windows; radar absorbing material. *Mailing Add:* 1000 Cordova Dr Orlando FL 32804

HAGEDORN, GEORGE ALLAN, MATHEMATICAL PHYSICS, QUANTUM CHEMISTRY. *Current Pos:* from asst prof to assoc prof, 80-88, PROF, VA POLYTECH INST & STATE UNIV, 88- *Personal Data:* b Santa Monica, Calif, Oct 18, 53; m 77, 93, Mary E Jones; c Charles A. *Educ:* Cornell Univ, BA, 74; Princeton Univ, MA, 75, PhD(math), 78. *Prof Exp:* Res assoc math physics, Rockefeller Univ, 78-80. *Concurrent Pos:* Mem, Am Math Soc prog comt nat meetings, 88-91; chmn, Joint Prog Comt Nat Meeting, Am Math Soc & Math Asn Am, 91. *Mem:* Am Math Soc; Int Asn Math Physics. *Res:* Rigorous results on N particle Schrodinger operators. *Mailing Add:* Va Polytech Inst & State Univ Blacksburg VA 24061-0123. *E-Mail:* hagedorn@math.vt.edu

HAGEDORN, HENRY HOWARD, INSECT REPRODUCTION, INSECT ENDOCRINOLOGY. *Current Pos:* dir, Ctr Insect Sci, 89-93, actg head, 93-95, PROF INSECT PHYSIOL, ENTOM DEPT, UNIV ARIZ, TUCSON, 88- *Personal Data:* b Milwaukee, Wis, Apr 4, 40; m 64, Magdalene Offen; c Katrina L & Michael A. *Educ:* Univ Wis-Madison, BS, 65, MS, 66; Univ Calif, Davis, PhD(entom), 70. *Prof Exp:* Asst prof insect physiol, Entom Dept, Univ Mass, Amherst, 73-77; from assoc prof to prof insect physiol, Entom Dept, Cornell Univ, 77-88. *Concurrent Pos:* Von Humbolt sr scientist, von Humbolt Stiftung, 81. *Mem:* Fel AAAS; Royal Entom Soc; Entom Soc Am; Sigma Xi. *Res:* Endocrinology of mosquito reproduction; peptide hormones and the hormonal control of gene expression. *Mailing Add:* Dept Entom Univ Ariz 410 Forbes Bldg 36 Tucson AZ 85721. *Fax:* 520-621-1150; *E-Mail:* hagedorn@ag.arizona.edu

HAGEE, GEORGE RICHARD, NUCLEAR & RADIOLOGICAL PHYSICS, ENVIRONMENTAL RADIATION. *Current Pos:* CONSULT, ENVIRON RADIATION & MED PHYSICS, 87- *Personal Data:* b Cincinnati, Ohio, July 10, 25; m 50, Dorothy T Selzer; c Richard, Robert, Mark, Jeannine & Maureen. *Educ:* Xavier Univ, Ohio, BS, 49, MS, 54; Univ Cincinnati, PhD(physics), 65; Am Bd Radiol, dipl, 76. *Prof Exp:* Physicist nuclear measurements, USPHS, 50-52; res physicist appl nuclear & health physics, Mound Lab, Monsanto Res Corp, 52-54; electronic physicist, Wright Air Develop Ctr, USAF, 54; res physicist, Div Radiol Health, USPHS, 54-56, chief phys & instrumental methods, 56-59; sr nuclear res physicist, Mound Lab, Monsanto Res Corp, 59-68; assoc prof physics, USAF Inst Technol, Wright-Patterson AFB, 68-80; res sci, Monsanto Mound Lab, 80-85; vis prof, Nuclear Eng, Univ Cincinnati, 86-87. *Concurrent Pos:* USPHS rep, Am Standards Asn Comt Nuclear Instrumentation, 58-59. *Mem:* AAAS; Am Phys Soc; Am Nuclear Soc; Health Physics Soc. *Res:* Low energy nuclear physics and instrumentation; environmental radioactivity; techniques and methodology; tracer applications; nuclear gauging; low level counting; nuclear spectroscopy; nuclear medicine. *Mailing Add:* 5481 E Kemper Rd Cincinnati OH 45241

HAGEL, ROBERT B, REGULATORY COMPLIANCE, ANALYTICAL CHEMISTRY. *Current Pos:* DIR COMPLIANCE, ORTHO BIOTECH, INC, 95- *Personal Data:* b Newark, NJ, Apr 15, 43; m 69, Giuliana Vidris; c Alexandra. *Educ:* Rutgers Univ, Newark, BA, 65, MS, 68, PhD(inorg chem), 69. *Prof Exp:* Instr chem, Rutgers Univ, 68-70; sr chemist, Hoffmann-La Roche Inc, 70-73, group leader, 73-75, tech fel, 75-79, mgr, 79-83, asst dir qual assurance, 83-88, dir, 88-95. *Mem:* Am Chem Soc; Parenteral Drug Asn; Sigma Xi. *Res:* Characterization and analysis of new drug substances and antibiotics. *Mailing Add:* 12 Orchard Lane Lebanon NJ 08833. *E-Mail:* rhagel@ompus.jnj.com

HAGEL, WILLIAM C(ARL), PHYSICAL METALLURGY. *Current Pos:* PRES, ARBORMET LTD, 84- *Personal Data:* b Pittsburgh, Pa, Apr 5, 27; m 54; c 3. *Educ:* Cornell Univ, BMetE, 51; Carnegie-Mellon Univ, PhD(metall), 54. *Prof Exp:* Metallurgist, Metall Div, Oak Ridge Nat Lab, AEC, Tenn, 51; res metallurgist, Metals Res Lab, Carnegie Inst Technol, 52-54 & turbine div lab, Gen Elec Co, NY, 54-58, mgr metall measurements lab, Mass, 58-59, metallurgist, Metall & Ceramics Res Dept, 59-66; prof metall, chmn dept & head metall div, Denver Res Inst, Univ Denver, 66-70; mgr mat develop, Mat & Process Technol Labs, Aircraft Engine Group, Gen Elec Co, 70-72; mgr res, Climax Molybdenum Co, 73-84. *Mem:* Fel Am Soc Metals; Electron Micros Soc; Electrochem Soc; Am Ceramic Soc; Am Inst Mining, Metall & Petrol Engrs. *Res:* Structure of metals; phase transformations in metals; high-temperature alloys; thermoelectric, magnetic and semiconductor materials; surface reactions; diffusion in solids. *Mailing Add:* Arbormet Ltd 685 Skynob Dr Ann Arbor MI 48105

HAGELBARGER, DAVID WILLIAM, COMMUNICATIONS SCIENCE. *Current Pos:* CONSULT, NAT OPTICAL ASTRON OBSERVS, KITT PARK, 88- *Personal Data:* b Kipton, Ohio, May 3, 20; m 44, Ethel Vanliew; c 2. *Educ:* Hiram Col, AB, 42; Calif Inst Technol, PhD(physics), 47. *Prof Exp:* Asst physics, Calif Inst Technol, 42-43, res physicist, Nat Defense Res Comt Proj, 44-45; instr aeronaut eng, Univ Mich, 46-49, res physicist, 48-49; mem tech staff, Bell Labs, 49-86. *Concurrent Pos:* Consult, Study Group 3, 60-64, eng concepts, Curriculum Proj, 65-70. *Mem:* AAAS; Inst Elec & Electronics Engrs; Sigma Xi. *Res:* Computers; electron dynamics; pressure temperature and composition of upper atmosphere; astronomical instrument and telescope design; communication systems; man machine interface. *Mailing Add:* 2180 S Double O Pl Tucson AZ 85713

HAGELBERG, M(YRON) PAUL, EXPERIMENTAL PHYSICS. *Current Pos:* From instr to asst prof, 58-71, chmn dept, 69-86, PROF PHYSICS, WITTENBERG UNIV, 71- *Personal Data:* b Manistee, Mich, Jan 9, 33; m 55, 84; c 2. *Educ:* Mich State Univ, BS, 54, MS, 56, PhD, 61. *Mem:* Acoust Soc Am; Am Phys Soc; Am Asn Physics Teachers; Sigma Xi; AAAS; Optical Soc Am. *Res:* Diffraction of light by ultrasonic waves; sound propagation in liquids and solids; nonlinear acoustic. *Mailing Add:* Dept Physics Wittenberg Univ Springfield OH 45501

HAGELIN, JOHN SAMUEL, TECHNOLOGIES FOR THE DEVELOPMENT OF HUMAN CONSCIOUSNESS. *Current Pos:* assoc prof, 83-84, PROF & DEPT CHMN PHYSICS, MAHARISHI UNIV MGT, 84-, DIR INST SCI, TECHNOL & PUB POLICY, 92- *Personal Data:* b Pittsburgh, Pa, June 9, 54. *Educ:* Dartmouth Univ, AB, 75; Harvard Univ, MA, 76, PhD(physics), 81. *Honors & Awards:* Kilby Young Innovator Award, 92. *Prof Exp:* Sci assoc, Europ Lab Particle Physics, 81-82; res assoc, Stanford Linear Accelerator Ctr, 82-83. *Concurrent Pos:* Dir doctoral prog physics, Maharishi Univ Mgt, 84-; prin investr, NSF Grant, 89-94; pres & dir res, Enlightened Audio Designs Corp, 89-; pres, Maharishi Int Asn Unified Field Scientists, 90- *Mem:* AAAS; Am Inst Physics; Am Phys Soc. *Res:* Supersymmetric unified quantum field theories based on the superstring and on the practical applications of the unified field to the individual and society; author of approximately 60 publications. *Mailing Add:* Inst Sci Technol & Pub Pol Maharishi Univ Mgt 1000 N Fourth St FB 1137 Fairfield IA 52557-1069. *Fax:* 515-472-1165; *E-Mail:* jhagelin@mum.edu

HAGEMAN, DONALD HENRY, PHYSICS, ELECTRICAL ENGINEERING. *Current Pos:* RETIRED. *Personal Data:* b Quincy, Ill, Nov 2, 18; m 42. *Educ:* Northwestern Univ, Ill, BS, 48; Mass Inst Technol, MS, 51; Univ Southern Calif, PhD(physics), 67. *Prof Exp:* Res asst digital circuit design, servomechanisms Lab, Mass Inst Technol, 49-51; res engr, Hughes Aircraft Co, 51-55; asst proj engr, Litton Industs, Inc, 55-59; mem tech staff, Hughes Aircraft Co, 59-63; physicist, Naval Ocean Systs Ctr, 67-88. *Mem:* Am Phys Soc; Sigma Xi. *Res:* Acoustic signal processing, radiation and scattering; ocean acoustics; laser velocimetry; theory and simulation of vehicle motion in fluids. *Mailing Add:* 6673 Aranda Ave La Jolla CA 92037

HAGEMAN, GILBERT ROBERT, CARDIOLOGY. *Current Pos:* Cardiovascular Res Training Ctr, Univ Ala, 74-84, instr physiol, 75-77, asst prof, 77-82, coursemaster, 80-83, instr cardiol, 82-85, assoc prof physiol, Dept Physiol & Biophys, Med Ctr, 82-91, ASSOC PROF MED, UNIV ALA, 85-, SCIENTIST, CARDIOVASC RES TRAINING CTR, 85-, VCHMN ACAD AFFAIRS, 88-, PROF, 91-, ASST DEAN, BASIC SCI EDUC, 94- *Personal Data:* b Covington, Ky, May 21, 47; m 68, Eileen Stewart; c 5. *Educ:* Thomas More Col, AB, 68; Loyola Univ, Chicago, PhD(physiol), 75. *Prof Exp:* Estab investr, Am Heart Asn, 80-85. *Concurrent Pos:* Fel circulation coun, Am Heart Asn, 81- & cardiovasc sect, Am Physiol Soc; mem basic sci coun, Am Heart Asn; fel, Harvard Macy Inst, 96. *Mem:* AAAS; Am Physiol Soc; Sigma Xi; Am Heart Asn; Am Women Sci. *Res:* Neural regulation of the heart during health and disease; neurogenic cardiac arrhythmias and sudden death. *Mailing Add:* Dept Physiol & Biophys BHS 844 UAB Birmingham AL 35294-0005. *Fax:* 205-975-7679; *E-Mail:* hageman@phybio.bhs.uab.edu

HAGEMAN, GREGORY SCOTT, OCULAR RESEARCH. *Current Pos:* ASST PROF MICROBIOL RES, SCH MED, UNIV SOUTHERN CALIF, 83- *Educ:* Univ Southern Calif, PhD(biol), 83. *Mailing Add:* Dept Ophthal Anheuser-Busch Eye Inst 1755 S Grand St St Louis MO 63104. *Fax:* 573-771-0596

HAGEMAN, JAMES HOWARD, BIOCHEMISTRY, BACTERIAL PHYSIOLOGY. *Current Pos:* from asst prof to assoc prof, 71-81, PROF CHEM, NMEX STATE UNIV, 82-, DIR GRAD PROG, MOLECULAR BIOL, 88- *Personal Data:* b Washington, Iowa, Nov 8, 42; m 68; c 8. *Educ:* Univ Bristol, Int, BSc, 61; Univ Ill, BS, 64; Univ Calif, Los Angeles, PhD(biochem), 68. *Prof Exp:* Fel, Am Cancer Soc, Yale Univ, 69-71. *Concurrent Pos:* Mem exam comt biochem, Am Chem Soc, 74-; Intergovt Personnel Act fel, NIH, 78-79. *Mem:* Am Soc Biol Chemists; AAAS; Am Chem Soc; Am Soc Microbiol. *Res:* Metabolic regulation; mechanisms of enzyme regulation; bacterial proteases; protein turnover; control of bacterial sporulation; bacterial calmodulin; nutritive value of forages; applications of boronic acids. *Mailing Add:* Dept Chem & Biochem NMex State Univ Box 30001 Las Cruces NM 88003-8001. *Fax:* 505-646-2649

HAGEMAN, LOUIS ALFRED, MATHEMATICS. *Current Pos:* ADV MATHEMATICIAN, WESTINGHOUSE ELEC CORP, 72- *Personal Data:* b Danville, Ill, Oct 8, 32; m 71, Marilyn Cupps; c Heidi (Smith) & Melissa (McLean). *Educ:* Rose Hulman Inst Technol, BS, 55; Univ Pittsburgh, PhD(math), 62. *Concurrent Pos:* Sr lectr, Carnegie-Mellon Univ, 64-76. *Mem:* Soc Indust & Appl Math. *Res:* Numerical analysis; iterative solution methods. *Mailing Add:* 1628 Citation Dr Library PA 15129-8831

HAGEMAN, RICHARD HARRY, BIOCHEMISTRY. *Current Pos:* from asst prof to prof, 54-84, EMER PROF AGRON, UNIV ILL, URBANA, 84- *Personal Data:* b Powell, Wyo, Apr 14, 17; m 41, Elizabeth Catlett; c James H, Janet A & Peggy D. *Educ:* Kans State Col, BS, 38; Okla Agr & Mech Col, MS, 40; Univ Calif, Berkeley, PhD(biol), 54. *Honors & Awards:* Crop Sci Award, Am Soc Agron, Agron Res Award, 84; Funke Award, Funke Seed Corn Co; Spencer Award, Am Chem Soc, 85; Hoagland Award, Am Soc Plant Physiologists, 85. *Prof Exp:* Asst, Okla Agr & Mech Col, 38-40; asst chemist, Exp Sta, Univ Ky, 40-41 & 46-47; chemist & plant physiologist, Fed Exp Sta, PR, 47-50. *Concurrent Pos:* Rockefeller fel, Long Ashton Res Sta, Bristol; vis prof, Mich State Univ, 67-68; sr res fel, Australian-Am Scholarly Exchange (Fullbright), Melbourne, Australia; Dugger Lectr, Auburn Univ; Am Soc Bot del, Peoples Repub China. *Mem:* Fel Am Soc Agron; Am Chem Soc; Am Soc Plant Physiologists, Fedn Am Socs Exp Biol; fel Crop Sci Soc Am. *Res:* Plant biochemistry; enzymes; minor elements; nitrogen metabolism; enzyme induction, mode of inheritance and genetic control of nitrate reductase. *Mailing Add:* 1302 E McHenry Urbana IL 61801. *E-Mail:* hageman@uiuc.edu

HAGEMAN, STEVEN JAMES, SYSTEMATICS-ECOLOGY & EVOLUTION OF THE PHYLUM BRYOZOA, MICROEVOLUTIONARY PATTERNS & PROCESSES. *Current Pos:* RES ASSOC GEOL, UNIV ADELAIDE, 93- *Personal Data:* b Lawrence, Kans, Oct 31, 62. *Educ:* Univ Kans, BS, 85; Univ Ill, MS, 88, PhD(geol), 92. *Prof Exp:* Lectr geol, Appalachian State Univ, 92-93. *Concurrent Pos:* Counr, Int Bryozool Asn, 92- *Mem:* Geol Soc Am; Paleont Soc; Int Paleont Asn; Int Bryozool Asn; Sigma Xi. *Res:* Morphometric and traditional multivariate statistical methods are applied to systematic and microevolutionary studies of fossil groups that have proven perplexing with other methods. *Mailing Add:* 723 W Second St Maryville SA 5005 Australia

HAGEMAN, WILLIAM E, PHARMACOLOGY, PHYSIOLOGY. *Current Pos:* PRIN SCIENTIST, RWJ PHARMACEUT RES INST, 90- *Personal Data:* b Glendale, Ohio, Sept 2, 39; m 64, Rita Berssenbruegge; c Leticia L, Holly L, Daniel W & Christa J. *Educ:* Univ Cincinnati, BSPh, 63; Univ Pittsburgh, MS, 66, PhD(pharmacol), 68. *Prof Exp:* Sr scientist, McNeil Labs, Inc, 68-73, group leader, 73-77, sect head cardiovasc pharmacol, res fel, 77-82, prin scientist, McNeil Pharmaceut, 82-88; prin scientist, Janssen Res Found, 88-90. *Concurrent Pos:* Mem, Pulmonary Discussion Group, Inflammation Res Asn. *Mem:* Am Soc Pharmacol & Exp Therapeut; Am Soc Bone & Mineral Res; Am Diabetes Asn; Am Asn Lab Animal Sci; Int Soc Immunopharmacol; Endocrinol Soc. *Res:* Cardiovascular pulmonary & inflammation; endocrine pharmacology and physiology pharmacology and physiology. *Mailing Add:* Dept Exp Therapeut R W Johnson Pharmaceut Res Inst Rm B-14 Raritan NJ 08869-0602. *Fax:* 908-704-6469

HAGEN, ARNULF PEDER, INORGANIC CHEMISTRY, SILICON & ASPHALT CHEMISTRY. *Current Pos:* From asst prof to assoc prof, 67-82, PROF CHEM, UNIV OKLA, 82- *Personal Data:* b Tacoma, Wash, June 6, 42; c 3. *Educ:* Univ Wash, Seattle, BSc, 64; Univ Pa, PhD(chem), 68. *Mem:* Am Chem Soc; Sigma Xi; Asn Asphalt Paving Technologists. *Res:* Synthesis of inorganic and organometallic compounds containing silicon, phosphorus, sulfur, boron and fluorine; high pressure syntheses; chemistry of asphalt and coal. *Mailing Add:* PO Box 271 Woodward OK 73802-0271. *Fax:* 405-325-6111

HAGEN, ARTHUR AINSWORTH, PHARMACOLOGY. *Current Pos:* PROF & CHAIRPERSON, DEPT PHYSIOL & PHARMACOL, UNIV SDAK, VERMILLION, 83- *Personal Data:* b Hot Springs, SDak, Oct 9, 33; m 57, Laurin J Kirley; c Kristen K, Karol L, Sandra L & Sharon A. *Educ:* Univ SDak, BA, 55, MA, 57; Univ Tenn, PhD(pharmacol), 61. *Prof Exp:* USPHS trainee steroid biochem, Salt Lake City, Utah, 61-63; Swed Med Res Coun fel, Stockholm, 63-64; from asst prof to prof pharmacol, Col Med, Univ Tenn, Memphis, 65-83. *Mem:* Endocrine Soc; Soc Study Reproduction; Am Soc Pharmacol & Exp Therapeut. *Res:* Endocrinology; prostaglandins; gonadal physiology and biochemistry; cerebral vasospasm. *Mailing Add:* Dept Physiol & Pharmacol Univ SDak Vermillion SD 57069. *Fax:* 605-677-5124

HAGEN, CARL RICHARD, PHYSICS. *Current Pos:* From res assoc to res asst, 63-64, from asst prof to assoc prof, 64-74, PROF PHYSICS, UNIV ROCHESTER, 74- *Personal Data:* b Chicago, Ill, Feb 2, 37; m 65; c 3. *Educ:* Mass Inst Technol, SB & SM, 58, PhD(physics), 62. *Concurrent Pos:* Res fel, Imp Col, Univ London, 64; vis scientist, Int Ctr Theoret Physics, Italy, 67. *Mem:* Am Phys Soc. *Res:* Field theory; particle physics; group theory. *Mailing Add:* Dept Physics Univ Rochester Wilson Blvd Rochester NY 14627-0001

HAGEN, CHARLES ALFRED, MICROBIOLOGY. *Current Pos:* RETIRED. *Personal Data:* b East Rutherford, NJ, Feb 1, 25; m 51, A Diana Wiltse; c Erich C, Kristine A & Susan L. *Educ:* Univ Chicago, AB, 52, MS, 56. *Prof Exp:* Bacteriologist, Bobs Robert Hosp, Univ Chicago Clin, 54-55; sr med technician, Inst Tuberc Res, 55-56; res bacteriologist, Nat Dairy Prod Corp, 56-62; assoc bacteriologist Life Sci Div, IIT Res Inst, 62-65, res bacteriologist, 65-69; lab mgr space biol, Space Systs Div, Avco Corp, 69-71; lab mgr, planetary quarantine, Jet Propulsion Lab, Bionetics Corp, 71-76; chief bacteriologist, Becton Dickinson Labware, 76-79, regulatory affairs officer, 79-86; qual assurance engr, Spectramed Inc, Oxnard, Ca, 86-87, regulatory affairs mgr, 87-90; consult, 90-95. *Mem:* Am Soc Microbiol; Soc Indust Microbiol; Am Soc Qual Control; Asn Adv Med Instrumentation; Regulatory Affairs Prof Soc. *Res:* Anaerobic culture techniques; space biology; industrial microbiological processes; normal microflora of animals; animal disease; pathogenic microorganisms in foods; tuberculosis vaccination; clean room techniques and contamination control; diagnostic medical bacteriology; medical device quality control; radiation and ethylene oxide sterilization processes; medical device manufacturing compliance to State and Federal requirements. *Mailing Add:* 508 Bandera Dr Camarillo CA 93010-6262

HAGEN, CHARLES WILLIAM, JR, academic administration, plant science; deceased, see previous edition for last biography

HAGEN, DANIEL RUSSELL, REPRODUCTIVE PHYSIOLOGY, ENDOCRINOLOGY. *Current Pos:* from asst prof to assoc prof, 78-93, PROF REPRODUCTIVE PHYSIOL, PA STATE UNIV, 93- *Personal Data:* b Springfield, Ill, Sept 29, 52; m 78, Rosemary Simonetta; c Matthew, Mark, Lane & Elise. *Educ:* Univ Ill, Urbana, BS, 74, PhD(animal sci), 78. *Prof Exp:* Res asst, Univ Ill, Urbana, 74-75, fel, 75-77. *Concurrent Pos:* Res assoc, Cornell Univ, 78; vis assoc prof, Univ Wis-Madison, 88-89. *Mem:* Soc Study Reprod; Soc Study Fertil; Am Soc Animal Sci; Sigma Xi. *Res:* Endocrine relationships between dam and fetus affecting prenatal and postnatal growth and survival, including ovarian and placental function; role of somatotropin in reproduction. *Mailing Add:* 324 Henning Bldg University Park PA 16802. *E-Mail:* dhagen@das9.cas.psu.edu

HAGEN, DONALD E, WATER MICROPHYSICS, CLOUD CHAMBER EXPERIMENT. *Current Pos:* fel, 71-74, res assoc, 74-76, RES ASST PROF CLOUD PHYSICS, UNIV MO, ROLLA, 76- *Personal Data:* b Dayton, Ohio, Oct 29, 43; m 69; c 3. *Educ:* Univ Dayton, BS, 65; Purdue Univ, MS, 67, PhD(physics), 70. *Prof Exp:* Fel physics, Battelle Mem Inst, 70-71. *Concurrent Pos:* Consult, NASA, 76-78, prin investr contracts, 78-81 & 82-84. *Mem:* Am Phys Soc. *Res:* Cloud microphysics; the nature of and evolution of small water drops or clusters; computer hardware and software. *Mailing Add:* Dept Physics Univ Mo Rolla MO 65401

HAGEN, DONALD FREDERICK, ANALYTICAL CHEMISTRY, GENERAL CHEMISTRY. *Current Pos:* ANALYTICAL CORP CHEMIST, 3M CO, 63- *Personal Data:* b Boscobel, Wis, Sept 7, 32; m 53; c 4. *Educ:* Univ Wis-Madison, BS, 57; Okla State Univ, MS, 61. *Prof Exp:* Anal res chemist, Continental Oil Co, 57-63. *Concurrent Pos:* Co-founder & dir, Minn Chromatog Forum, 78- *Mem:* Am Chem Soc. *Res:* Analytical chemistry; fluorine chemistry; plasma chromatography; atomic emission detecters; derivatization; elemental tagging for chromatography; membranes for separations, purifications and reactions. *Mailing Add:* 7149 Windgate Rd Woodbury MN 55125-1529

HAGEN, GRETCHEN, DEVELOPMENTAL BIOLOGY, MOLECULAR BOTANY. *Current Pos:* res specialist cell & molecular biol, 78-80, NIH FEL, BOT DEPT, UNIV MINN, 80- *Personal Data:* b Lake Placid, NY, July 23, 48. *Educ:* State Univ NY, Potsdam, BA, 70, State Univ NY Col Environ Sci & Forestry, Syracuse, MS, 73; Univ Ga, PhD(bot), 78. *Prof Exp:* Res asst bot, Univ Ill, 72-74; lab coord eng biol, Univ Ga, 74-75, grad res asst bot, 75-76, grad teaching asst, 76-77, grad res asst, 77-78. *Res:* Molecular mechanisms involved in plant growth and development, specifically at the nucleic acid and protein level; somatic cell senescence. *Mailing Add:* Dept Biochem Univ Mo 117 Schweitzer Hall Columbia MO 65211-0001. *Fax:* 573-882-5635

HAGEN, HAROLD KOLSTOE, FISH BIOLOGY. *Current Pos:* asst prof, 55-60, ASSOC PROF FISHERIES, COLO STATE UNIV, 60- *Personal Data:* b Plummer, Minn, Nov 18, 24; m 48; c 1. *Educ:* Univ Wyo, BS, 49; Univ Wash, Seattle, PhD(fisheries sci), 56. *Prof Exp:* Biologist fisheries, Wyo Game & Fish Comn, 49; trout water biologist, SDak Dept Game, Fish & Parks, 54-55. *Concurrent Pos:* Edmund Niles Huyck fel, 63; Off Water Resources, Dept Interior grant, thermal pollution, Yellowstone Nat Park, 65; pres, Western Fisheries Consults; tech adv US Peace Corps, Peru & Venezuela, dir fishery resources of Guatemala, 75; bd dir, US Trout Farmers Asn, 73-76; fisheries eval Chile, Booz, Allen, Hamilton & World Bank, 75-76; leader tech adv team fisheries, AID/Peru, 76-80; sr consult fisheries, United Nations, Ecuador, 78; consult pvt trout cult, Mex, 78. *Mem:* Am Fisheries Soc; Am Inst Fishery Res Biol. *Res:* Fresh water fisheries; farm and ranch fish ponds in northern latitudes; aquatic weed control; in situ stream nutrient cycling. *Mailing Add:* Dept Fishery & Wildlife Biol Colo State Univ Ft Collins CO 80523

HAGEN, JACK INGVALD, NUCLEAR PHYSICS. *Current Pos:* assoc res prof, 65-80, EMER RES PROF PHYSICS & ELECTROCHEM, DEPT ELEC ENG, UNIV IDAHO, 80- *Personal Data:* b Coeur d'Alene, Idaho, Sept 21, 14. *Educ:* Ore State Univ, BS, 48, MS, 49. *Prof Exp:* Asst res eng extractive metall, Anaconda Copper Co, 49-51; res staff physics, Johns Hopkins Univ, 51-53; sr engr nuclear eng, Atomic Power Div, Westinghouse Elec Corp, 53-57; assoc physicist, Argonne Nat Lab, 57-65. *Concurrent Pos:* Prin investr, NSF, 74-78. *Mem:* Am Phys Soc; Am Nuclear Soc; Sigma Xi. *Res:* Electro catalysis and surface reaction studies in electrochemical energy conversion, concerning metallic and semiconductor electrodes. *Mailing Add:* 1408 Hall Rd Viola ID 83872-9712

HAGEN, JOHN WILLIAM, RESEARCH ADMINISTRATION, SCIENCE ADMINISTRATION. *Current Pos:* Dir, Ctr Human Growth & Develop, 82-93, dir, Reading & Learning Skills Ctr, 87-94, FROM ASST PROF TO PROF PSYCHOL, UNIV MICH, 65- *Personal Data:* b Minneapolis, Minn, May 11, 40; c Darus, Lonny & Fred. *Educ:* Univ Minn, BA, 62; Stanford Univ, PhD(psychol), 65. *Concurrent Pos:* Exec officer, Soc Res Child Develop, 89-; mem, Study Sect Ment Retardation, NIH & chmn, Study Sect Behav & Neurosci, 91. *Mem:* Soc Res Child Develop; fel Am Psychol Asn; Am Psychol Soc; Int Soc Study Behav Develop; fel Int Asn Res Learning Disabilities; Am Educ Res Asn. *Res:* Cognitive development and its relationship to academic and social behavior in children with learning problems or chronic health conditions. *Mailing Add:* 3421 Burbank Dr Ann Arbor MI 48105. *Fax:* 313-998-6569

HAGEN, JON BOYD, RADIOPHYSICS. *Current Pos:* res assoc, 72-93, DIR LAB OPERS, ARECIBO OBSERV, CORNELL UNIV, 94- *Personal Data:* b Moscow, Idaho, Apr 18, 40; m 74. *Educ:* Stanford Univ, BS, 62; Univ Idaho, MS, 64; Cornell Univ, PhD(elec eng), 74. *Prof Exp:* Instr physics, Hampton Inst, 67-69. *Mem:* Am Geophys Union; Sigma Xi; Inst Elec & Electronics Engrs. *Res:* Aeronomy research using incoherent scatter radar. *Mailing Add:* NAIC Dept Cornell Univ 124 Maple Ave Ithaca NY 14850

HAGEN, KENNETH SVERRE, ENTOMOLOGY. *Current Pos:* Lab technician biol control, Exp Sta, Univ Calif, 47-52, jr entomologist, 52-53, asst entomologist, 53-59, assoc entomologist, 59-69, lectr, 64-69, PROF ENTOM & ENTOMOLOGIST, BIOL CONTROL, UNIV CALIF, 69- *Personal Data:* b Oakland, Calif, Nov 26, 19; m 43; c 1. *Educ:* Univ Calif, BS, 43, MS, 48, PhD, 52. *Concurrent Pos:* Collabr, Entom Res Br, Agr Res Serv, USDA, 54; expert, Int Atomic Energy Comn, 61-63. *Mem:* AAAS; Entom Soc Am; Soc Syst Zool; Ecol Soc Am; Entom Soc Can. *Res:* Insect nutrition; biological control of insect pests; ecology of Coccinellidae; systematics of Anthicidae, Coccinellidae and Encyrtidae. *Mailing Add:* 14 Cambridge Way Piedmont CA 94611-4321

HAGEN, LAWRENCE J, WIND EROSION. *Current Pos:* Agr engr, 67-88, res leader, Agr Res Serv Wind Erosion Res Unit, 88-94, AGR ENGR, USDA, 95- *Personal Data:* b Rugby, NDak, Mar 6, 40. *Educ:* NDak State Univ, BS, 63, MS, 67; Kans State Univ, PhD(mech eng), 80. *Concurrent Pos:* Adj prof, Kans State Univ, 70-91. *Mem:* Am Soc Agr Engrs; Soil & Water Conserv Soc; Int Soils & Tillage Res Orgn. *Res:* Modeling and experimental research on wind erosion. *Mailing Add:* Kans State Univ Throckmorton Hall USDA Wind Erosion Res Unit Manhattan KS 66506. *Fax:* 785-532-6528; *E-Mail:* hagen@weru.ksu.edu

HAGEN, OSKAR, SOLID & FLUID MECHANICS. *Current Pos:* RETIRED. *Personal Data:* b Heddal, Norway, Apr 5, 26; US citizen; m 58; c 2. *Educ:* Vienna Tech Univ, Dipl Ing, 54; Univ Pittsburgh, PhD(mech eng), 64. *Prof Exp:* Draftsman, Hq Air Arms Inspection, Norweg Air Force, 46-47; asst engr, Esco Armature Factory, Oslo, 47-49; engr, Norweg Hydrogen Plant, 54 & Elliott Co, Jeannette, Pa, 54-56; engr atomic equip div, Westinghouse Elec Corp, Cheswick, Pa, 56-60, sr engr, 60-64, fel engr, 64-66, lead eng & eng-anal mgr, electro-mech div, 66-90. *Mem:* Am Soc Mech Engrs; Sigma Xi. *Res:* Stress; dynamics; fluid flow; heat transfer. *Mailing Add:* 204 Craig Dr Greensburg PA 15601

HAGEN, PAUL BEO, BIOCHEMISTRY, PHARMACOLOGY. *Current Pos:* dean grad studies, 68-82, prof, 68-86, EMER PROF PHARMACOL, UNIV OTTAWA, 86- *Personal Data:* b Sydney, Australia, Feb 15, 20; m 56, Jean Himms; c Anna & Nina. *Educ:* Univ Sydney, MB, BS, 45. *Honors & Awards:* Centennial Medal, Govt Can, 67; Jubilee Medal, 77; Fulbright Award, 54. *Prof Exp:* Lectr physiol, Univ Sydney, 48-50; sr lectr, 50-51; sr lectr, Univ Queensland, 51-52; Martin fel pharmacol, Oxford Univ, 52-54; Brown fel, Yale Univ, 54-55, asst prof, 55-56; asst prof, Harvard Med Sch, 56-59; prof biochem & head dept, Univ Man, 59-64; prof & head dept, Queen's Univ, Ont, 64-68. *Mem:* Am Soc Pharmacol & Exp Therapeut; fel Chem Inst Can; Brit Pharmacol Soc; Physiol Soc Gt Brit. *Res:* Biochemistry and pharmacology of naturally occuring amines, endocrinology; whole animal metabolism; metabolic regulation. *Mailing Add:* 233 Tudor Pl Ottawa ON K1L 7Y1 Can

HAGEN, RICHARD EUGENE, BIOCHEMISTRY & FOOD SCIENCE, ENVIRONMENTAL SCIENCE. *Current Pos:* VPRES SCI & QUAL ASSURANCE, KOESTER ENVIRON SERV, EVANSVILLE, IND, 94- *Personal Data:* b Hillsboro, Kans, Apr 4, 37; m 62; c 3. *Educ:* Southwestern Col, Kans, BA, 59; Univ Okla, PhD(biochem), 65. *Prof Exp:* Sr develop scientist, Pillsbury Co, Minn, 65-68; dir res, Roman Meal Co, Wash, 68-71; dir res & develop, Universal Foods Corp, 72-77; vpres & mgr, Wash Lab, Nat Food Processors Asn, 77-82; dir qual assurance, US Pharmaceut & Nutrit Group, Bristol Myers, 82-87; mgr & dir environ affairs, 87-94. Concurrent

Pos: Chmn, Environ Comt, Bristol-Myers Squibb Corp, 89-93. *Mem:* Am Chem Soc; Air & Waste Mgt Asn; Sigma Xi; Am Soc Qual Control. *Res:* Nutrient research, ie raw and processed foods, food safety research including spoilage microorganisms, microbial toxins and indirect additives; industrial research and development of new foods and improvement of existing foods and ingredients particularly yeast, cereals, baked goods, engineered foods and citrus flavonoids; quality assurance of infant formulas, enteral foods, pharmaceuticals; environmental sciences especially pollution prevention management practices for industrial applications; remediation technology environmental field sampling, environmental quality control. *Mailing Add:* 7408 E Walnut St Evansville IN 47715

HAGEN, SUSAN JAMES, GASTROENTEROLOGY. *Current Pos:* instr, 84-90, ASST PROF ANAT & CELL BIOL, DEPT MED, HARVARD MED SCH, 91- *Personal Data:* b Detroit, Mich, March 30, 53. *Educ:* Mich State Univ, BS, 75, MS, 79, PhD, 82. *Prof Exp:* Fel, Dept Cell Biol & Anat, Sch Med, Johns Hopkins Univ, 82-84. *Concurrent Pos:* Grad res award, Col Human Med, Mich State Univ, 80; assoc cell biologist, Brigham & Women's Hosp, 84- *Mem:* Am Soc Cell Biol. *Res:* Cell biology of the brush border after damage with lectins; biochemistry of cytoskeletal proteins in developing microvilli; light and EM immunocytochemical localization of proteins within cells; author of numerous scientific publications. *Mailing Add:* Dept Med Gastroenterol Beth Israel Hosp 330 Brookline Ave Dana 815 Boston MA 02115-6195. *Fax:* 617-735-2978

HAGENAUER, FEDOR, CHILD PSYCHIATRY, PSYCHOANALYSIS. *Current Pos:* resident, Univ Cincinnati, 59-60, fel child psychiat, 60-62, from instr to asst prof, 62-69, ASSOC PROF CHILD PSYCHIAT, UNIV CINCINNATI, 69- *Personal Data:* b Zagreb, Yugoslavia, Mar 12, 20; US citizen; m 58; c 3. *Educ:* Univ Zagreb, MD, 49. *Prof Exp:* Resident psychiat, State Res Hosp, Galesburg, Ill, 56-58. *Concurrent Pos:* Staff child psychiatrist, Children's Psychiat Ctr, Cincinnati, 62-73, dir inpatient serv, 73-; consult, Rollman Receiving Hosp, 68-; staff, Cincinnati Inst Psychoanal, 75-, supv & training anal, 81- *Mem:* Fel Am Psychiat Asn; Am Psychoanal Asn; Am Acad Child Psychiat. *Mailing Add:* 3001 Highland Ave Cincinnati OH 45229

HAGENBACH, W(ILLIAM) P(AUL), CHEMICAL ENGINEERING. *Current Pos:* RETIRED. *Personal Data:* b Rochester, NY, Sept 14, 22; m 46, Ruth Landon; c Paul, Patricia & Mark. *Educ:* Univ Rochester, BS, 44, MS, 47; Univ Ill, PhD(chem eng), 51. *Prof Exp:* Res engr, E I du Pont de Nemours & Co, 51-56, process develop engr, 56-60; dir eng res, A E Staley Mfg Co, 60-69, dir eng res & serv, 69-71, environ sci, 72-73, environ sci & energy conserv, 74-83, environ sci & safety, 83-86. *Mem:* Am Chem Soc; Inst Chem Engrs. *Res:* Process development in field of polyester polymers and films; engineering research studies on corn products; plant environmental compliance; energy conservation programs; safety programs. *Mailing Add:* 4560 Williamsburg Ct Decatur IL 62521-2561

HAGENIERS, OMER LEON, MECHANICAL ENGINEERING. *Current Pos:* Vpres, 69-90, PRES, DIFFRACTO LTD, WINDSOR, 90- *Personal Data:* b Stekene, Belg, Nov 12, 44; m 67, Marilyn L Miner; c Michelle L & Amy L. *Educ:* Univ Windsor, Ont, MA, 69, PhD(mech eng), 72. *Mem:* Am Soc Mech Engrs; Soc Mfg Engrs; Soc Photog & Instrumentation Engrs. *Res:* Mechanical engineering; contributed articles to professional journals; granted numerous patents in field. *Mailing Add:* Diffracto Ltd 2835 Kew Windsor ON N8T 3B7 Can

HAGENLOCHER, ARNO KURT, SOLID STATE PHYSICS. *Current Pos:* MGR RES & DEVELOP, ACTON RES CORP, 80- *Personal Data:* b Herrenberg, Ger, May 20, 28; m 67; c 3. *Educ:* Stuttgart Tech Univ, BS, 50, MS, 53, PhD(physics), 58. *Prof Exp:* Res assoc semiconductors, Stuttgart Tech Univ, 54-57; physicist, Telefunken Ulm, Ger, 58-60; mem tech staff, Gen Tel Electronics Corp, 60-74; mgr elec devices, Coulter Systs Corp, 74-80. *Concurrent Pos:* Lectr, Polytech Inst Brooklyn, 62-66. *Mem:* Am Phys Soc; Electrochem Soc; Sigma Xi; Ger Phys Soc; Inst Elec & Electronics Engrs. *Res:* Semiconductors; ferroelectrics; crystal growth; thin films study by epitaxial growth, evaporation and r f sputtering; electrical properties of above materials; plasmas in solids; electron beam semiconductor devices; charge coupled devices, electrophotography; photovoltaics. *Mailing Add:* 4747 Woodview Dr Santa Rosa CA 95405

HAGENLOCKER, EDWARD EMERSON, PHYSICS. *Current Pos:* Sr res scientist, Ford Motor Co, 64-73, chief engr physics, 73-78, chief engr light trucks, 78-79, mgr light truck prof develop, 80-82, VCHMN, FORD MOTOR CO, 96- *Personal Data:* b Marysville, Ohio, Nov, 18, 39; m 58; c 3. *Educ:* Ohio State Univ, BS & MS, 62, PhD(physics), 64. *Mem:* Nat Acad Eng; Soc Automotive Engrs; Sigma Xi; Am Phys Soc. *Res:* Nonlinear optics; semiconductor devices; plasma physics; holography; automotive design and development. *Mailing Add:* 290 Lone Pine Rd Bloomfield Hills MI 48304. *Fax:* 313-248-4940

HAGENMAIER, ROBERT DOLLER, QUALITY CONTROL, BIOCHEMISTRY. *Current Pos:* RES CHEMIST, USDA CITRUS SUBTROP LAB, 88- *Personal Data:* b Mt Gilead, Ohio, May 26, 39; m 62; c 2. *Educ:* Univ Detroit, BS, 65; Purdue Univ, PhD(phys chem), 70. *Prof Exp:* Assoc res chemist, Food Protein Res & Develop Ctr, Tex A&M Univ, 70-75; mgr, Coconut Foods Pilot Plant, Univ San Carlos, Philippines, 75-80; plant mgr, Red V Coconut Prod, Ltd, 80-85; consult, Niro Atomizer S PTE, Singapore, 85-86; qual control mgr, Holly Hill Fruit Prod, 86-88. *Concurrent Pos:* Lectr, Univ San Carlos, 78-79. *Mem:* Am Chem Soc; Inst Food Technologists; Am Asn Milk Food & Environ Sanitarians. *Res:* Processing technology for coconut protein and dried coconut milk, edible coatings. *Mailing Add:* 1891 18th St NW Winter Haven FL 33881-1213

HAGER, ANTHONY WOOD, LATTICE-ORDERED GROUPS, CATEGORICAL TOPOLOGY. *Current Pos:* from asst prof to assoc prof, 68-75, chmn, 76-77, 88-90 & 93, PROF MATH, WESLEYAN UNIV, 75- *Personal Data:* b Marshfield, Wis, Dec 16, 39; c Amanda D. *Educ:* Pa State Univ, BS, 60, PhD(math), 65. *Prof Exp:* Asst scientist, Leeds & Northrup Co, Pa, 60-61; instr math, Univ Rochester, 65-67, asst prof, 67-68. *Concurrent Pos:* Vis prof, Czech Acad Sci, 73 & 75 & Univ Padua, 78. *Mem:* Math Asn Am; Am Math Soc. *Res:* Lattice-ordered algebra, uniform spaces, categorical algebra and topology. *Mailing Add:* Dept Math Wesleyan Univ Middletown CT 06459-0128. *E-Mail:* ahager@eagle.wesleyan.edu

HAGER, BRADFORD HOADLEY, TECTONOPHYSICS, SOLID EARTH GEOPHYSICS. *Current Pos:* CECIL & IDA GREEN PROF EARTH SCI, MASS INST TECHNOL, 89- *Personal Data:* b Johnstown, Pa, June 21, 50; m 72; c 2. *Educ:* Amherst Col, BA, 72, Harvard Univ, AM 76, PhD(geophys), 78. *Honors & Awards:* James B Macelwane Award, Am Geophys Union, 86. *Prof Exp:* Instr physics, Cushing Acad, 72-74; Weizmann fel geophys, Harvard Univ, 78-79; asst prof, State Univ NY, Stony Brook, 79-80; from asst prof to prof geophys, Calif Inst Technol, 80-89. *Concurrent Pos:* Alfred P Sloan res fel, 82-86. *Mem:* Fel Am Geophys Union; AAAS; Sigma Xi. *Res:* Geodynamics; the driving mechanisms for plate motions; mantle convection; rheology of mantle materials; interpretation of the geoid; GPS satellite geodesy; large-scale parallel computations. *Mailing Add:* Dept Earth Atmosphere & Planetary Sci Mass Inst Technol Bldg 54-622 Cambridge MA 02139. *Fax:* 617-253-1699; *E-Mail:* brad@chandler.mit.edu

HAGER, CHESTER BRADLEY, CLINICAL MEDICINE. *Current Pos:* PRES, CTR PHARMACEUT STUDIES. *Personal Data:* b Madison, WVa, Oct 15, 38; m 62, N Jeanine Beane; c Jennifer & Valerie. *Educ:* WVa Univ, AB, 62, MS, 64, PhD(biochem), 66. *Prof Exp:* Radioisotope technician, Miami Valley Hosp, Dayton, Ohio, 60-61, blood bank technician, 62; asst biochem, WVa Univ, 63-64; Nat Inst Child Health & Human Develop res fel biochem regulation, Biol Div, Oak Ridge Nat Lab, 66 & Am Cancer Soc Res Fel, 66-68; res scientist, Miles Labs Inc, 68, asst dir, 68-72, dir, Tech Serv, Ames Co Div, 72-78, dir res, develop & planning, Res Prod Div, 78-81; dir res & develop, Micromedic Systs, Inc, 81-86; dir, Hazleton Biochem Corp, Div Hazleton Labs Am, 86. *Concurrent Pos:* Mem, Med Devices Technol Adv Bd, Am Nat Stand Inst, 74-78; bd dirs, Va Biotechnol Asn; exec vpres/sci dir, Sci China, Inc. *Mem:* Am Asn Clin Chemists; Am Chem Soc; Am Asn Clin Scientists; Sigma Xi; Drug Information Asn. *Res:* Clinical biochemistry, mechanism of protein synthesis; endocrinology; diagnostic medicine, endocrinology. *Mailing Add:* 17400 Tranquility Rd Purcellville VA 20132-9041. *Fax:* 540-338-3119; *E-Mail:* hager_b_mediasoft.net

HAGER, DOUGLAS FRANCIS, DRUG DELIVERY, PROJECT MANAGEMENT. *Current Pos:* INT PROJ MGR, NOVARTIS PHARMACEUT CORP, 94- *Personal Data:* b Plum City, Wis, July 13, 49; m 82, Mary M Hastings; c Marghet & Bettina. *Educ:* Univ Wis, BS, 71; Harvard Univ, AM, 72, PhD(phys chem), 76. *Prof Exp:* Staff chemist, Procter & Gamble Co, 76-81, sect head corp technol, 81-85, sect head paper technol, 85-86; dir drug delivery, Nestle-Alcon Labs, Inc, 87-89; head, Sandoz Res Inst, 89-93, dir, Drug Delivery Systs, 93-94. *Concurrent Pos:* Adj asst prof, dept chem & nuclear eng, Univ Cincinnati, 78-84. *Mem:* Am Chem Soc; Am Phys Soc; Am Inst Chem Engrs; Am Asn Pharm Scientists; Controlled Release Soc. *Res:* The transport of pharmaceuticals to their sites of action; sustaining the duration of effect of peptide drugs; oncology drug development. *Mailing Add:* 9 Jay Dr Randolph NJ 07869-4102. *Fax:* 973-503-6066; *E-Mail:* douglas.hager@gwa.sandoz.com

HAGER, E JANT, AVIAN MYOGENESIS. *Current Pos:* ASSOC RES, YALE UNIV, 96- *Personal Data:* b 1951; m 87. *Educ:* Univ Va, MS, 81, PhD, 87. *Prof Exp:* Res asst biol, Univ Va, 81-87; fel, Div Oncol, Med Ctr, Stanford Univ, 87-94; at Jerry Lewis Muscular Res Ctr, Sch Med, Univ Calif, Los Angeles. *Concurrent Pos:* Comprehensive sci teacher, Glasgow, 74-78. *Mem:* Am Soc Cell Biol. *Res:* Ulrastructural analysis of gene expression in drosophila melanogastes polyterie chromation. *Mailing Add:* Keck Biotech Resource Lab Yale Univ 295 Congress Ave New Haven CT 06520

HAGER, GEORGE PHILIP, JR, MEDICINAL CHEMISTRY. *Current Pos:* dean, 66-74, prof med chem, 66-81, EMER DEAN & PROF, SCH PHARM, UNIV NC, CHAPEL HILL, 81- *Personal Data:* b Baltimore, Md, Mar 16, 16; m 38; c 3. *Educ:* Univ Md, BS, 38, MS, 40, PhD(pharmaceut chem), 42. *Honors & Awards:* Achievement Award Advan of Pharm, Am Pharmaceut Asn, 68. *Prof Exp:* Res org chemist, Eli Lilly & Co, 42-44; prof pharmaceut chem, Univ Md, 44-55; sr scientist, Smith Kline & French Labs, 55-57; dean col pharm, Univ Minn, Minneapolis, 57-65. *Concurrent Pos:* Mem adv bd-cardiovasc lit proj, Nat Res Coun, 56-60; adv comt antiradiation drug prog, Walter Reed Army Inst Res, 59-65; med chem study sect, NIH, 60-64; chmn comt mod methods handling chem info, Nat Acad Sci-Nat Res Coun, 61-66; mem ad hoc panel narcotic addiction & drug abuse, Off Sci & Technol, Exec Off President, 62-63; panel scientist-to-scientist commun, Surgeon Gen Conf Health Commun, USPHS, 62; panel undergrad sci educ prog, NSF, 63; consult chem info & data syst, Army Res Off, 63-65; mem, Nat Adv Comt Selection Physicians, Dentists & Allied Specialists, Selective Serv Syst, 64-68 & Nat Health Resources Adv Comt, 68-70; mem panel handling toxicol info, Off Sci & Technol, Exec Off President, 64-65; gen res support adv comt, Div Res Facil & Resources, NIH, 64-67, pharm rev comt, Bur Health Manpower Educ, 71-73; consult, Off Sci Info Serv, NSF, 65-72; nat civilian consult pharm, Off Surgeon Gen, USAF, 67-76. *Mem:* Fel Acad Pharmaceut Sci (pres, 68-69); Am Pharmaceut Asn; Am Asn Cols Pharm (vpres, 64-65, pres, 65-66); Am Col Apothecaries. *Res:* Chemistry-synthesis and analysis of drugs and medicines; hormones; antibiotics; fluorine substituted aromatic acids; molecular structure-biological activity relationships, especially in agents with effects on the peripheral nervous system; documentation of information and use of modern equipment in handling chemical and biological data in medicinal chemistry research. *Mailing Add:* 106 Duchess Lane Chapel Hill NC 27514

HAGER, GORDON L, ONCOLOGY. *Current Pos:* chief, Viral Immunogenetics Sect, Lab Tumor Virus Genetics, 80-83, CHIEF, HORMONE ACTION & ONCOGENESIS SECT, LAB MOLECULAR VIROL, NAT CANCER INST, NIH, 83- *Personal Data:* b Girard, Kans, Dec 5, 42; m; c 1. *Educ:* Univ Kans, BS, 64; Institut de Biologie Moleculaire, Geneva, Switz, PhD(genetics), 70. *Honors & Awards:* Karlson Lectr, 90. *Prof Exp:* Assoc res biochemist, Dept Biochem & Biophys, Univ Calif, 76. *Concurrent Pos:* Adv panels, Genetics & Biol, NSF, 83-87, NSF Site Visit Panel, Columbia Univ, 88, fel Study Sect, NIH, 90-93, Molecular Biol Study Sect, NIH, 91-94; NATO Int Coop fel, 87. *Mem:* Am Soc Biol Chemists; AAAS; Am Soc Microbiol; Int Asn Breast Cancer Res. *Res:* Regulation of gene expression in eucaroytic cells; chromatin structure and its relationship to gene expression; mechanism of oncogenic transformation; gene therapy; numerous publications. *Mailing Add:* Hormone Action & Oncogenetic Sect Nat Cancer Inst NIH Bldg 44 Rm B500 Bethesda MD 20892-5055. *Fax:* 301-496-4951

HAGER, JOHN P(ATRICK), METALLURGY. *Current Pos:* From asst prof to assoc prof metall, Colo Sch Mines, 66-71, prof & head dept, 71-74, St Joe Minerals Corp prof extractive metall, 74-88, HAZEN RES PROF EXTRACTIVE METALL, COLO SCH MINES, 88- *Personal Data:* b Miles City, Mont, Oct 2, 36; m 61; c 7. *Educ:* Mont Sch Mines, BS, 58; Mo Sch Mines, MS, 60; Mass Inst Technol, ScD(metall), 69. *Mem:* Minerals, Metals, Mat Soc. *Res:* Physical chemistry of extractive metallurgy; extractive metallurgy process analysis and development. *Mailing Add:* 2054 Crestvue Golden CO 80401

HAGER, JUTTA LORE, GEOTECHNICAL INVESTIGATIONS, BEDROCK & SURFICIAL GEOLOGY. *Current Pos:* prin, Hager-Richter Geosci, Inc, 84-93, PRIN, HAGER GEO SCI INC, 93- *Personal Data:* b Frankfurt, Main Ger, Feb 9, 42; c 1. *Educ:* Radcliffe Col, BA, 63; Harvard Univ, MA, 73, PhD(geol sci), 78. *Prof Exp:* Postdoctoral fel geol, Harvard Univ, Cambridge, Mass, 78-79; asst prof geol, Bentley Col, Waltham, Mass, 79-80 & Wellesley Col, Mass, 83-84; prin scientist, Energy Resources Co, Inc, 80-82; assoc, S A Alsup & Assocs, Inc, 82-83. *Concurrent Pos:* Publ comm, 1984 Ann Meeting, Asn Eng Geologists, 82-84, treas, 85-87, chmn, New Eng Sect, 87-89. *Mem:* AAAS; Geol Soc Am; Soc Econ Paleontologists & Mineralogists; Am Inst Prof Geologists; Asn Eng Geologists; Nat Water Well Asn. *Res:* Applications of geophysics to problems in engineering geology and the environmental field; surficial and bedrock geology of the Boston Basin. *Mailing Add:* 63 Gregory St Waltham MA 02154

HAGER, LOWELL PAUL, BIOCHEMISTRY. *Current Pos:* assoc prof, 60-65, dept head, 67-86, PROF CHEM, UNIV ILL, URBANA, 65-, DIR, BIOTECHNOL CTR, 87- *Personal Data:* b Girard, Kans, Aug, 30, 26; m 49; c 3. *Educ:* Valparaiso Univ, AB, 47; Univ Kans, MA, 50; Univ Ill, PhD, 53. *Prof Exp:* Fel, NIH, 53-54; asst biochemist, Mass Gen Hosp, 54-55; asst prof chem, Harvard Univ, 55-60. *Concurrent Pos:* Guggenheim Mem fel, 59; mem, Physiol Chem Study Sect, NIH; vis scientist, Imp Cancer Res Fund Inst, London, 77-83. *Mem:* Nat Acad Sci; Am Chem Soc; Am Soc Biol Chem; Am Soc Microbiol. *Res:* Chemistry of heme proteins; enzymatic activation mechanisms; enzymatic halogenation and epoxidation reactions. *Mailing Add:* 413 Roger Adams Lab Univ Ill 1209 W California Urbana IL 61801. *Fax:* 217-244-5858; *E-Mail:* l-hager@uiuc.edu

HAGER, MARY HASTINGS, DIETETICS. *Current Pos:* assoc prof foods & nutrit, 89-96, PROF FOODS & NUTRIT & ASSOC DEAN, COL ST ELIZABETH, 96- *Personal Data:* b Upland, Calif, Mar 27, 48; m 82, Douglas F; c Marghet & Bettina. *Educ:* Univ Del, BS, 71; Univ Calif, Davis, MS, 73, PhD(nutrit), 78. *Prof Exp:* Staff scientist, Procter & Gamble Co, 78-83, clin biochem, 86-87; asst prof nutrit, Col Mt St Joseph, 83-86; asst prof nutrit & dietetics, Tex Christian Univ, 87-89. *Concurrent Pos:* Adj prof chem, Col Mt St Joseph, 83-86; tech consult, Food & Pharmaceut Industs. *Mem:* AAAS; Am Physiol Soc; Am Inst Nutrit; Am Dietetic Asn. *Res:* Nutrient endocrine interrelationships; physiological and behavioral response to ingestion of nonabsorbable lipids. *Mailing Add:* Nine Jay Dr Randolph NJ 07869. *Fax:* 973-605-7676; *E-Mail:* hager.liza.st-elizabeth.edu

HAGER, RICHARD ARNOLD, PLANT PATHOLOGY, MICROBIOLOGY. *Current Pos:* PESTICIDE CONTROL SPECIALIST, NY DEPT ENVIRON CONSERV, 81- *Personal Data:* b Morgantown, WVa, Oct 10, 32; m 60; c 1. *Educ:* Univ Pittsburgh, BS, 59; WVa Univ, MS, 61; Pa State Univ, PhD(plant path), 66. *Prof Exp:* Dir res plant pathol & microbiol, Frangella Bros Inc, 66-81. *Concurrent Pos:* Consult, Cambridge Valley Mushroom Farm, 84. *Mem:* Am Phytopath Soc; Mycol Soc Am; US Fedn Culture Collections; Sigma Xi. *Res:* Forest pathology; commercial mushroom spawn production; development of mushroom strains, mushroom disease development and control; commercial mushroom production; exotic mushroom production. *Mailing Add:* 52 Biechman Rd Ravena NY 12143

HAGER, STANLEY LEE, THERMAL ANALYSIS, POLYMER CHARACTERIZATION. *Current Pos:* CHEMIST, UNION CARBIDE CORP, 74- *Personal Data:* b Pittsfield, Ill, Apr 25, 46; m 75. *Educ:* Univ Ill, BS, 68; Univ Wis, PhD(chem), 74. *Prof Exp:* Chemist, Hercules, Inc, 68-70. *Mem:* Am Chem Soc; Soc Plastics Engrs; NAm Thermal Analysis Soc. *Res:* Chemical reactions of polymers; thermal analysis of polymers; rheology and dynamic mechanical testing polymers. *Mailing Add:* 5310 Edgebrook Rd Cross Lanes WV 25313-1099

HAGER, WAYNE R, ENGINEERING, CHEMICAL ENGINEERING & ENGINEERING TECHNOLOGY. *Current Pos:* DEPT HEAD, COL ENG, PA STATE UNIV, 88- *Personal Data:* b Baltimore, Md, Sept 6, 41; m 89, Mary A Rees; c Suzanne, Sharon, Brooke, Matthew, Jeffrey & Sara. *Educ:* Univ Utah, BS, 63, Univ Idaho, MS, 70, PhD(chem eng), 72. *Prof Exp:* Res engr, Jackson Lab, E I Du Pont, 66-68, plant supvr, Chambers Works, 68-69; prof chem engr, Col Eng, Univ Idaho, 72-88, prog dir spec summer progs, 81-88, asst dean, 86-88. *Concurrent Pos:* Nat Defense Educ Act fel, 69-72; chmn, Eng Sci Dept, Univ Idaho, 76-85, dir, Inst Resource Mgt, 81-84; consult, Nat Energy Found, Salt Lake City, 76-85, Western Power Admin, Sacramento, 84- & Save The Children, Mauritius & Rodrigues; vis fac, Dept Earth Resources, Pac Lutheran Univ, 80-81; Fulbright sr & exchange scholar, Univ Mauritius, Reduit, 85-86, vis scholar, Sch Indust Technol; Fulbright sr & exchange scholar, Univ Mauritius, Reduit, 85-86, vis scholar, Sch Indust Technol. *Mem:* AAAS; Am Soc Eng Educ. *Res:* Alternative energy technologies, resource assessment and utilization and modelling for developing countries; utilization of bagasse for the production of energy. *Mailing Add:* Col Eng Pa State Univ 245 Hammond Bldg University Park PA 16802

HAGER, WILLIAM WARD, NUMERICAL ANALYSIS, OPTIMAL CONTROL. *Current Pos:* PROF MATH, UNIV FLA, 88- *Personal Data:* b Altadena, Calif, Apr 29, 48; m 80, Georgine Clark; c William & Ann. *Educ:* Harvey Mudd Col, BS, 70; Mass Inst Technol, MS, 71, PhD(math), 74. *Prof Exp:* Asst prof math, Univ SFla, 74-76; asst prof math, Carnegie Mellon Univ, 76-80; from assoc prof to prof math, Pa State Univ, 80-88. *Concurrent Pos:* Ed-in-chief, Comput Optimization & Applications. *Mem:* Soc Indust & Appl Math; Asn Comput Mach; Math Prog Soc. *Res:* Numerical analysis; control theory; optimization. *Mailing Add:* Dept Math Univ Fla Gainesville FL 32611. *Fax:* 352-392-6254; *E-Mail:* hager@math.ufl.edu

HAGERMAN, ANN ELIZABETH, PLANT PHENOLICS, PHYTOCHEMISTRY. *Current Pos:* asst prof 82-87, ASSOC PROF CHEM, MIAMI UNIV, OHIO, 87- *Personal Data:* US citizen. *Educ:* Occidental Col, AB, 76; Purdue Univ, PhD(biochem), 80. *Prof Exp:* Teaching fel bot, Purdue Univ, 80-82. *Mem:* Am Chem Soc; Am Soc Biol Chemists; Sigma Xi. *Res:* Function of secondary products in higher plants; protective role of phenolic compounds; biochemical characterization of the activity of phenolics, lignin and tannin; development of methods for analyzing phenolics in plant tissues. *Mailing Add:* Dept Chem Miami Univ Oxford OH 45056. *Fax:* 513-529-4221; *E-Mail:* aehagerm@miamiu.acs.muohio.edu

HAGERMAN, DONALD CHARLES, PHYSICS. *Current Pos:* Asst div leader, 68-72, MEM STAFF, LOS ALAMOS NAT LAB, 55-, GROUP LEADER, 65-, ASSOC DIV LEADER, 72- *Personal Data:* b Boulder, Colo, May 2, 29; m 51. *Educ:* Univ Colo, BA, 51; Stanford Univ, PhD(physics), 55. *Mem:* Fel Am Phys Soc; Sigma Xi. *Res:* Nuclear physics; plasma physics; controlled thermonuclear reactors; accelerators. *Mailing Add:* PO Box 6037 Battlement Mesa CO 81636

HAGERMAN, DWAIN DOUGLAS, biochemistry, obstetrics & gynecology; deceased, see previous edition for last biography

HAGERMAN, LARRY M, PHARMACOLOGY, NUTRITIONAL BIOCHEMISTRY. *Current Pos:* INFO SPECIALIST CONSULT, 97- *Personal Data:* b Owensboro, Ky, Oct 12, 40; m 79; c 2. *Educ:* Vanderbilt Univ, BA, 61. *Prof Exp:* Assoc prof chem, Mead Johnson, 64-66, scientist, 66-72, sr scientist nutrit, 72-75; res scientist pharmacol, Warren-Teed, 75-77 & Adria/Warren-Teed, 77-96. *Mem:* AAAS; Am Chem Soc; Am Fedn Sci. *Res:* Cholesterol and bile salt metabolism; blood lipids, lipoproteins, cardiovascular disease. *Mailing Add:* 1351 Castleton Rd N Columbus OH 43220

HAGERUP, HENRIK J(OHAN), AERONAUTICS. *Current Pos:* Asst prof, 62-65, ASSOC PROF AERONAUT ENG, RENSSELAER POLYTECH INST, 65- *Personal Data:* b Horten, Norway, Nov 22, 32; US citizen; m 58; c 2. *Educ:* Mass Inst Technol, BSc & SM, 56; Princeton Univ, PhD(aeronaut eng), 63. *Mem:* AAAS; Am Inst Aeronaut & Astronaut. *Res:* Fluid mechanics. *Mailing Add:* Dept Mech Eng & Aeronaut Eng Rensselaer Polytech Inst 110 Eighth St Troy NY 12180-3590

HAGESETH, GAYLORD TERRENCE, PHYSICS. *Current Pos:* From asst prof to assoc prof, 65-75, PROF PHYSICS, UNIV NC, GREENSBORO, 75- *Personal Data:* b Minot, NDak, Aug 13, 35; m 58; c 3. *Educ:* Univ NC, BS, 58; Cath Univ, MS, 62, PhD(physics), 67. *Mem:* AAAS; Am Phys Soc; Am Asn Physics Teachers. *Res:* Low energy nuclear physics, acoustics and chemical physics; solid state physics thermoluminescense in crystals; kinetics and thermodynamics of isothermal seed germination; x-ray damage in crystals. *Mailing Add:* Dept Physics Univ NC 1000 Spring Garden St Greensboro NC 27412

HAGFORS, TOR, ionospheric physics, planetary astronomy, for more information see previous edition

HAGGARD, BRUCE WAYNE, GENETICS. *Current Pos:* From asst prof to assoc prof, 72-88, PROF BIOL, HENDRIX COL, 88- *Personal Data:* b Muncie, Ind, Dec 26, 43; m 63; c 2. *Educ:* Ind Univ, Bloomington, BA, 66, MA, 70, PhD(genetics), 72. *Concurrent Pos:* USPHS genetics training grant, 66-72. *Mem:* Sigma Xi; AAAS; Genetics Soc Am. *Res:* Determination, differentiation and development in the protozoan Paramecium aurelia. *Mailing Add:* Dept Biol Hendrix Col Conway AR 72032-3099

HAGGARD, J D, mathematics, for more information see previous edition

HAGGARD, JAMES HERBERT, biochemistry, for more information see previous edition

HAGGARD, MARY ELLEN, MEDICINE. *Current Pos:* resident, Hosps, 52-54, from instr to assoc prof, 54-69, PROF PEDIAT, UNIV TEX MED BR GALVESTON, 69- & DIR, DIV PEDIAT HEMATOL-ONCOL, 69- *Personal Data:* b Topeka, Kans, Apr 23, 24. *Educ:* Tex Woman's Univ, BA & BS, 45; Univ Tex, MD, 51; Am Bd Pediat, dipl, 56. *Prof Exp:* Intern, Univ Hosp, Ohio State Univ, 51-52. *Concurrent Pos:* Fel hemat, Boston Children's Hosp, 61. *Mem:* AMA; fel Am Acad Pediat; Am Soc Hemat; Sigma Xi. *Res:* Pediatrics; hematology; medical education; chemotherapeutic agents in leukemia and in solid tumors of childhood; folic acid metabolism in hemolytic disease. *Mailing Add:* Dept Pediat Primary Care Pavillion Univ Tex Med Br 400 Harborside Dr Suite 2705 Galveston TX 77550-1119

HAGGARD, PAUL WINTZEL, MATHEMATICS. *Current Pos:* assoc prof, 63-89, PROF MATH, ECAROLINA UNIV, 89- *Personal Data:* b Bennington, Okla, Aug 31, 33; m 60; c John P & Robert F. *Educ:* Southeastern State Col, BS, 53; NTex State Univ, MS, 60. *Prof Exp:* Instr math, Lamar State Col, 58-61; teaching asst math, Univ Tex, 61-63. *Mem:* Math Asn Am; Nat Coun Teachers Math. *Res:* Algebra and topology; metric spaces; number theory; special functions. *Mailing Add:* Dept Math ECarolina Univ Greenville NC 27858

HAGGARD, RICHARD ALLAN, ORGANIC CHEMISTRY, PHYSICAL ORGANIC CHEMISTRY. *Current Pos:* RETIRED. *Personal Data:* b Pittsburgh, Pa, 36; m 58; c 3. *Educ:* Cornell Univ, AB, 58, PhD(org chem), 65. *Prof Exp:* Res chemist & group leader, Rohm & Haas Co, 65-74, res sect mgr, 75-88, res patent liaison, 89-96, US patent agent, 92-96. *Mem:* Sigma Xi. *Res:* Anionic polymerization; solution polymers; general physical organic chemistry; process development; polymer chemistry; plastics. *Mailing Add:* 1207 Nash Dr Ft Washington PA 19034

HAGGARD, WILLIAM HENRY, CLIMATOLOGY. *Current Pos:* PRES, CLIMAT CONSULT CORP, 76- *Personal Data:* b Woodbridge, Conn, Nov 20, 20; m 44; c 2. *Educ:* Yale Univ, BS, 42; Univ Chicago, SM, 46. *Prof Exp:* Instr physics, NC State Col, 46-47; meteorologist, US Weather Bur, 47-51 & 54-61, from dep dir to dir, Nat Weather Records Ctr, 61-70, dir nat climatic ctr, Nat Oceanic & Atmospheric Agency, 70-75. *Mem:* AAAS; Am Meteorol Soc; Am Geophys Union. *Res:* Climatology; extended forecasting; tropical and marine meteorology. *Mailing Add:* 150 Shope Creek Rd Asheville NC 28805

HAGGERTY, HELEN GRAY, IMMUNOTOXICOLOGY, PHARMACEUTICAL DEVELOPMENT. *Current Pos:* res investr II, 93-95, SR RES INVESTR, BRISTOL MYERS SQUIBB, 95- *Personal Data:* b Fairmont, WVa, June 8, 61; m 85, James V Jr; c 1. *Educ:* Univ Richmond, BS, 83; Med Col Va, PhD(pharmacol/toxicol), 89. *Prof Exp:* Res fel, Univ Pa, 90-93. *Mem:* Am Asn Immunologists; Soc Toxicol; Asn Women Sci. *Res:* Assessing toxicity of biologic or immunologic compounds; develop and implement immunologic, biochemical and molecular based assay systems that address the immunomodulatory potential of these compounds; design and conduct experiments to understand mechanisms of toxicity, especially those that may involve the immune system. *Mailing Add:* Bristol-Myers Squibb PO Box 4755 Syracuse NY 13221. *Fax:* 315-432-2172; *E-Mail:* helen_haggerty@ccmail.bms.com

HAGGERTY, JAMES FRANCIS, biochemistry; deceased, see previous edition for last biography

HAGGERTY, JOHN S, PHYSICAL METALLURGY & CERAMICS. *Current Pos:* sr res scientist & proj mgr advan technol, Energy Lab, 77-90, SR RES SCIENTIST, MASS INST TECHNOL, 90- *Personal Data:* b Washington, DC, Oct 23, 38; m 61; c 3. *Educ:* Mass Inst Technol, SB, 61, SM, 63, PhD, 65. *Prof Exp:* Res asst chem, Harvard Univ, 59-60; res asst, Mass Inst Technol, 61-62 & 62-65; sr specialist ceramist, Arthur D Little, Inc, 65-77. *Mem:* Fel Am Ceramic Soc; Am Asn Crystal Growth; Am Solar Energy Soc. *Res:* Crystal growth processes, materials characterization, optical, thermal and mechanical properties, laser processing of materials, solar energy systems and components. *Mailing Add:* Mass Inst Technol Bldg 12-011 Cambridge MA 02139

HAGGERTY, JOHN S, EXPERIMENTAL HIGH ENERGY PHYSICS. *Current Pos:* ASSOC, BROOKHAVEN NAT LAB, 86- *Personal Data:* b Brooklyn, NY. *Educ:* Manhattan Col, BS, 75; Harvard Univ, AM, 77, PhD(physics), 81. *Prof Exp:* Res assoc, Fermi Nat Accelerator Lab, 81-83, Lawrence Berkeley Lab, 83-86. *Mem:* Am Phys Soc. *Res:* Production of bound states of charmed and bottom quarks; data analysis; electronic data acquisition; new partical detectors; rare decays. *Mailing Add:* Bldg 510C Brookhaven Nat Lab Upton NY 11973

HAGGERTY, ROBERT JOHNS, BEHAVIORAL PEDIATRICS. *Current Pos:* EMER PROF PEDIAT, EXEC DIR, INT PEDIAT ASN, 93-, UNIV ROCHESTER, 92- *Personal Data:* b Saranac Lake, NY, Oct 20, 25; m 49; c 4. *Educ:* Cornell Univ, AB, 46, MD, 49; Am Bd Pediat, dipl. *Hon Degrees:* MA, Harvard, DSc, Ind Univ. *Honors & Awards:* Lienhard Award, Inst Med-Nat Acad Sci; M M Eliot Award, Am Pub Health Asn. *Prof Exp:* Intern med, Strong Mem Hosp, Rochester, NY, 49-51; from jr asst res to chief med res, Children's Hosp Med Ctr, Boston, 53-55; asst prof pediat, Harvard Med Sch, 55-64; prof pediat & chmn dept, Sch Med & Dent, Univ Rochester, 64-75; Roger I Lee prof pub health & pediat & head, Dept Health Serv, Harvard Sch Pub Health & Harvard Med Sch, 75-80; William T Grant Found clin prof pediat, Cornell Univ, 80-92. *Concurrent Pos:* Med dir, Boston Poison Info Ctr, 55-64; chief, Child Health Div, Children's Hosp Med Ctr, 58-64; Markle scholar acad med, 61-66; mem, Health Serv Res Study Sect, USPHS, 64-70, chmn 68-70; pediatrician-in-chief, Strong Mem Hosp, Rochester, 64-75; fel, Ctr Advan Study Behav Sci, Stanford, Calif, 74-75; vis prof pediat, Hard Med Sch & dir, Robert Wood Johnson Gen Pediat Acad Develop Prog, 78-; ed, Pediat in Rev, Am Acad Pediat; chmn, Health Serv Sci Res Study Sect, Nat Ctr Health Serv Res. *Mem:* Inst Med-Nat Acad Sci; fel Am Acad Pediat; Am Asn Poison Control Ctrs (pres, 62-64); Am Pub Health Asn; AAAS. *Res:* Preventive pediatrics; health services research; growth and development; accident prevention; infectious and social disease. *Mailing Add:* Dept Pediat Rm 4-8104 Sch Med Univ Rochester 601 Elmwood Ave Rochester NY 14642-8777. *Fax:* 716-273-1038; *E-Mail:* rhaggerty@cc.urmc.rochester.edu

HAGGERTY, STEPHEN E, GEOPHYSICS. *Current Pos:* from asst prof to assoc prof, 71-79, PROF, DEPT GEOSCI, UNIV MASS, AMHERST, 80- *Personal Data:* b Germiston, SAfrica, 1938; US citizen. *Educ:* Univ London, ARSM, 64, PhD & DIC, 68. *Hon Degrees:* DSc, Univ London, 88. *Prof Exp:* Asst, Dept Geophys, Imp Col, 61-63. *Concurrent Pos:* Leith Gold Mining Co, Can, 60; assoc investr, UK Natural Environ Res Coun, 64-67; staff mem, Nat Aeronaut & Space Admin, 69-86; NASA & fac res grantee, Univ Mass, 72-75; mem, Ocean Sci Bd, Nat Acad Sci, 72; prin investr, NSF, 73-; consult, 78-82 & 87; Ministry Petrol & Mineral Resources, Syrian Arab Repub, 87-88; assoc ed, Can Mineralogist, 87-92. *Mem:* Fel Mineral Soc Am; fel Am Geophys Union; Can Mineral Asn; Geochem Soc; Meteoritical Soc; Microbeam Anal Soc; AAAS; NY Acad Sci; Sigma Xi. *Res:* Mineralogy, petrology and geochemistry of the upper mantle; mineral magnetism; author of over 100 publications. *Mailing Add:* Dept Geosci Univ Mass Amherst MA 01003-5820. *Fax:* 413-545-1200

HAGGERTY, WILLIAM JOSEPH, JR, ANALYTICAL CHEMISTRY. *Current Pos:* sr chemist, Midwest Res Inst, 66-73, prin chemist, 73-74, head Bio & Pharmaceut Analysis Sect, 74-78, tech dir, consumer protection prog, Saudi Arabia, 80-86, TECH MGR, LIFE SCIS DEPT, MIDWEST RES INST, 86- *Personal Data:* b Kansas City, Mo, Nov 3, 32; m 67. *Educ:* Rockhurst Col, BS, 54; Univ Mo, Kansas City, MA, 59, PhD(pharmaceut chem), 68; Baxter Univ, MLA, 94. *Honors & Awards:* MRI Prof Award, Midwest Res Inst, 92. *Prof Exp:* Assoc chemist, Midwest Res Inst, 58-65; res assoc anal methods develop, Univ Mo, Kansas City, 65-66. *Mem:* AAAS; Am Chem Soc; Am Pharmaceut Asn; Am Pharmacognesy Soc; Am Inst Food Technol. *Res:* Organic synthesis and structure determination; synthesis and analysis of drugs used for anti-tumor investigation; analytical methods for drug dosage forms; teratogens present in environment; isolation and identification of natural products; development of bioanalytical techniques. *Mailing Add:* 425 Volker Blvd Kansas City MO 64110

HAGGITT, RODGER C, GASTROINTESTINAL PATHOLOGY, SURGICAL PATHOLOGY. *Current Pos:* PROF PATH, ADJ PROF MED & DIR, HOSP PATH, UNIV WASH, 84- *Personal Data:* b Detroit, Mich, Aug 28, 42; m 65, Mary J Dugan; c Kathryn & Scott. *Educ:* Univ Tenn, MD, 67. *Honors & Awards:* Distinguished Serv Award, Am Soc Clin Pathologists, 89. *Prof Exp:* Instr path, Harvard Med Sch, 74-77; clin assoc prof, Univ Tenn, 77-84. *Concurrent Pos:* Dir surg path, Baptist Mem Hosp, Memphis, 77-84; workshop dir, Am Soc Clin Pathologists, 77-, educ course dir, 79-, chmn, Coun Anat Path, 82-85; mem, Anat Path Test Comt, Am Bd Path, 87-94; vis prof, Univ Calif, Los Angeles, San Diego & San Francisco, Harvard Med Sch, Univ Conn, Univ Ill, Univ Tex, Duke Univ, Vanderbilt Univ, Yale Univ & Univ SFla, 87- *Mem:* AAAS; Am Soc Clin Pathologists; Gastrointestinal Path Soc (pres, 81); Am Gastroenterol Asn; Col Am Pathologists. *Res:* Biology of pre-malignant lesions of the gastrointestinal tract using histologic, flow cytometric and molecular genetic techniques. *Mailing Add:* Univ Wash Med Ctr RC-72 1959 NE Pacific St Box 356100 Seattle WA 98195-0001. *Fax:* 206-548-4928

HAGHIGHAT, ALIREZA, NEUTRON TRANSPORT THEORY METHODS, NEUTRONICS & THERMAL-HYDRAULIC MODELING OF POWER REACTORS. *Current Pos:* Res asst, Pa State Univ, 86-88, res assoc, 88-89, asst prof, 89-93, ASSOC PROF NUCLEAR ENG, PA STATE UNIV, 93- *Personal Data:* b Shiraz, Iran, Aug 2, 56; m 78, Mastaneh Javadi; c Aarash H. *Educ:* Shiraz Univ, Iran, BS 78; Univ Wash, Seattle, MS, 81, PhD(nuclear eng), 86. *Mem:* Am Nuclear Soc; Am Soc Eng Educ; Sigma Xi. *Res:* Development of parallel algorithms for the Sn transport theory method; development of a standard methodology for the estimation of the neutron fluence at the reactor pressure vessel; sensitivity analysis and perturbation studies for the neutron fluence studies; developing methods for the estimation of uncertainties in the transport theory calculated results. *Mailing Add:* 430 Canterbury Dr Pa State Univ State College PA 16803

HAGHIRI, FAZ, AGRONOMY. *Current Pos:* RETIRED. *Personal Data:* b Tehran, Iran, Jan 18, 30; m 53; c 3. *Educ:* Univ Nebr, BS, 55, MS, 56, PhD(agron), 59. *Prof Exp:* Asst soil chem, Univ Nebr, 57-59; asst prof agron, Ohio Agr Exp Sta, 59-64; from assoc prof to prof agron, Ohio Agr Res & Develop Ctr & Ohio State Univ, 64-89, assoc chmn dept, 78-89. *Mem:* Soil Sci Soc Am; Am Soc Agron; Int Soil Sci Soc. *Res:* Soil and water pollution; heavy metals in soils and plants. *Mailing Add:* 1665 W Highland Ave Wooster OH 44691-9088

HAGIN, FRANK G, APPLIED MATH. *Current Pos:* prof, 83-94, EMER PROF MATH & COMPUT SCI, COLO SCH MINES, 94- *Personal Data:* b Callaway, Nebr, Mar 30, 33. *Educ:* Bethesda Univ, BA, 54; Southern Methodist Unv, MA, 63; Univ Colo, PhD(appl math), 66. *Prof Exp:* Prof math, Univ Denver, 66-83. *Mem:* Math Asn Am. *Res:* Applied math. *Mailing Add:* 4881 Kings Ridge Blvd Boulder CO 80301

HAGINO, NOBUYOSHI, NEUROENDOCRINOLOGY. *Current Pos:* PROF CELL BIOL, HEALTH SCI CTR, UNIV TEX, 76- *Personal Data:* b Hokkido, Japan, Feb 8, 32. *Educ:* Toyko-Gekei Univ, MD, 57, PhD(neuro endocrinol), 67. *Mem:* Int Soc Neuroendocrinol; Int Brain Res Orgn; Am Asn Anatomists; Am Physiol Soc. *Mailing Add:* Dept Anat Health Sci Ctr Univ Tex 7703 Floyd Curl Dr San Antonio TX 78284-7762. *Fax:* 210-567-3803

HAGINS, WILLIAM, BIOPHYSICS. *Current Pos:* CHEM PHYSICS LAB, NAT INST ARTHRITIS, DIABETES, DIGESTIVE & KIDNEY DIS, NIH. *Mem:* Nat Acad Sci. *Mailing Add:* Nat Inst Arthritis Diabetes Digestive & Kidney Dis NIH Bethesda MD 20892

HAGIS, PETER, JR, MATHEMATICS. *Current Pos:* From instr to prof math, 52-92, EMER PROF, TEMPLE UNIV, 93- *Personal Data:* b Philadelphia, Pa, Jan 16, 26; m 53, Jeanie McGregor; c Joann & Peter S. *Educ:* Temple Univ, BSEd, 50, MA, 52; Univ Pa, PhD(math), 59. *Mem:* Math Asn Am; Am Math Soc; Fibonacci Asn. *Res:* Theory of numbers. *Mailing Add:* 880 Edison Philadelphia PA 19116

HAGLER, ARNOLD T, BIOTECHNOLOGY. *Current Pos:* CHIEF SCI OFFICER, BIOSYM TECHNOLOGIES INC, 84- *Personal Data:* b New York, NY, Dec 6, 41. *Educ:* Cornell Univ, BChE, 65, PhD(biophys chem), 70. *Prof Exp:* Fel, Weizmann Inst Sci, Israel, 70-72, res assoc, 72-75, sr scientist, 75-79, assoc prof, 75-81; chmn biophys, Agouron Inst, 81-89. *Concurrent Pos:* Europ Molecular Biol Orgn vis fel, Univ Manchester, Eng, 75; vis assoc prof, Univ Calif, San Diego, 78 & 79-81, vis scholar, 81-; Europ Molecular Biol Orgn sr vis fel, Univ Libre Bruxelles, Belg, 79; vis scientist, Salk Inst, 84-; consult, Smith Kline & French, Merck Sharp & Dohme, Beckman Instruments & Abbott Labs. *Mem:* Am Chem Soc; Biophys Soc; NY Acad Sci; Am Crystallog Asn. *Mailing Add:* 9685 Scranton Rd San Diego CA 92121-3752. *Fax:* 619-450-5041

HAGLER, JAMES NEIL, MATHEMATICAL ANALYSIS. *Current Pos:* ASST PROF MATH & COMPUT SCI, UNIV DENVER, 88- *Personal Data:* b Denver, Colo, July 18, 45. *Educ:* Cornell Univ, BA, 67; Univ Calif, Berkeley, MA, 69, PhD(math), 72. *Prof Exp:* Vis asst prof math, State Univ NY, Binghamton, 72-73; asst prof math, Cath Univ Am, 73-88. *Mem:* Am Math Soc. *Res:* Isomorphic problems for separable and nonseparable Banach spaces, especially how the structure of an arbitrary Banach space relates to those of the classical spaces. *Mailing Add:* Math & Comput Sci Dept Univ Denver Denver CO 80208-0189

HAGLER, MARION O(THO), PULSED POWER, ENGINEERING EDUCATION. *Current Pos:* from asst prof to prof, Tex Tech Univ, 67-81, dir, Ctr Energy Res, 77-85, chmn, Dept Elec Eng & Comput Sci, 83-86, HORN PROF ELEC ENG, TEX TECH UNIV, 81-, CHMN, DEPT ELEC ENG, 87- *Personal Data:* b Temple, Tex, Sept 7, 39; m 62; c 3. *Educ:* Rice Univ, BA, 62, BS, 63; Univ Tex, Austin, MS, 64, PhD(elec eng), 67. *Prof Exp:* Res engr, Univ Tex, Austin, 66-67. *Mem:* Am Phys Soc; fel Optical Soc Am; fel Inst Elec & Electronics Engrs; Am Soc Eng Educ. *Res:* Pulsed Power; energy; coherent optical systems; engineering education; fusion. *Mailing Add:* 5106 First Place Lubbock TX 79416

HAGLER, THOMAS BENJAMIN, PLANT SCIENCE. *Current Pos:* RETIRED. *Personal Data:* b Louisville, Ala, May 16, 13; m 39; c 3. *Educ:* Auburn Univ, BS, 39, MS, 47; Univ Md, PhD(hort), 54. *Prof Exp:* Pub sch teacher, 39-45; assoc prof hort & assoc horticulturist, Auburn Univ, 45-58; prof hort & head dept, Clemson Univ, 58-60; chmn, Plant Sci Div, Coop Exten Serv, Auburn Univ, 60-76, head exten hort, 76-81. *Mem:* Am Soc Hort Sci; Sigma Xi. *Res:* Coordination of program phases of educational program in horticulture. *Mailing Add:* 489 Cary Dr Auburn AL 36830-3044

HAGLUND, JOHN RICHARD, MICROBIOLOGY. *Current Pos:* RETIRED. *Personal Data:* b Bessemer, Mich, Aug 31, 31; m 54; c 3. *Educ:* Univ Wis, BS, 53, MS, 57; Iowa State Univ, PhD(food microbiol), 65. *Prof Exp:* Asst bact, Univ Wis, 55-57; dir qual control, Country Gardens, Inc, Wis, 57-59; microbiologist, Cent Qual Control Lab, Gen Mills, Inc, 59-62; res assoc food technol, Iowa State Univ, 62-65; res chemist, James Ford Bell Res Ctr, Gen Mills, Inc, Minn, 65-72; microbiologist, Hunt Wesson Foods, Inc, 72-75; consult, 75-78; sr microbiologist, Dole Foods, Inc, 78-96, mgr, Food & Process Safety Develop, 80-96. *Mem:* Am Soc Microbiol; Inst Food Technologists. *Res:* Bacterial food infections; fluorescent antibody; food processing and preservation; food plant sanitation; food spoilage; food chemistry and product development. *Mailing Add:* 700 Skyline Ct Placerville CA 95667

HAGLUND, RICHARD FORSBERG, JR, LASER PHYSICS, NON-LINEAR OPTICS & OPTICAL MATERIALS. *Current Pos:* assoc prof, 84-93, PROF PHYSICS, DEPT PHYSICS & ASTRON, VANDERBILT UNIV, 93- *Personal Data:* b Washington, DC, Sept 17, 42; m 68, Carol A Bagnell; c Kristine, Richard, Evan, James & Erika. *Educ:* Wesleyan Univ, BA, 67; State Univ NY, Stony Brook, MA, 69; Univ NC, PhD(physics), 75. *Prof Exp:* Fel, Los Alamos Nat Lab, 75-77, mem staff, 77-84. *Concurrent Pos:* Alexander von Humbolt Found fel, 82-83; vis prof, Heraeus Found, 91. *Mem:* Am Phys Soc; Optical Soc Am; Mat Res Soc. *Res:* Laser-surface interactions; nonlinear optical materials; photon-stimulated desorption. *Mailing Add:* Dept Physics & Astron Vanderbilt Univ Nashville TN 37235. *Fax:* 615-343-7263; *E-Mail:* haglunrf@ctrvax.vanderbilt.edu

HAGLUND, WILLIAM ARTHUR, PLANT PATHOLOGY. *Current Pos:* From asst plant pathologist to assoc plant pathologist, 60-72, plant pathologist, 72-92, EMER PLANT PATHOLOGIST, NORTHWESTERN EXP STA, WASH STATE UNIV, 92- *Personal Data:* b Minneapolis, Minn, May 3, 30; m 52, Jean C Rallis; c Michael M & Lynne A. *Educ:* Univ Minn, BS, 53, MS, 58, PhD, 60. *Concurrent Pos:* Pvt consult plant path. *Mem:* Am Phytopath Soc; Soc Nematol; Can Pytopath Soc; Am Arbit. *Res:* Root rot complex of vegetable crops and nematodes in relation to development of root rot; nematodes associated with turf grasses. *Mailing Add:* 1229 11th TEE Burlington WA 98233. *Fax:* 360-428-1331

HAGMANN, SIEGBERT JOHANN, CHARGE TRANSFER. *Current Pos:* res assoc, 78-79, asst prof, 79-84, ASSOC PROF, DEPT PHYSICS, KANS STATE UNIV, 84- *Personal Data:* b Neuenhaus, WGer, Apr 9, 48. *Educ:* Westfaelische Wilhelms Univ Muenster, dipl physics, 73; Univ Koln, Dr rer nat, 77. *Prof Exp:* Res scientist, GSI, Darmstadt, 77-78. *Mem:* Am Phys Soc. *Res:* atomic physics; collision dynamics of very heavy and light quasimolecular systems; spectroscopy of very highly excited atomic states. *Mailing Add:* Dept Physics Kans State Univ J R MacDonald Lab Manhattan KS 66506. *E-Mail:* Bitnet: shagmann@ksoum

HAGMANN, WILLIAM KIRK, MEDICINAL CHEMISTRY. *Current Pos:* sr res chemist, 80-86, res fel, 86-89, ASST DIR MED CHEM RES, MERCK & CO, INC, 90- *Personal Data:* b Jamaica, NY, Apr 19, 51. *Educ:* Hobart Col, BS, 73; Cornell Univ, MS, 76, PhD(org chem), 78. *Prof Exp:* NIH fel, Dept Chem, Mass Inst Technol, 78-80. *Mem:* Am Chem Soc. *Res:* Enzyme inhibition, particularly those involved in inflammatory or endocrine processes; serine, thiol and metalloproteinases. *Mailing Add:* 871 Shackmaxo N Dr Westfield NJ 07090-3462. *Fax:* 732-594-5966

HAGNAUER, GARY LEE, POLYMER COMPOSITE MATERIALS RESEARCH & POLYMER MATERIALS TESTING, POLYMER DURABILITY-LIFE PREDICTION. *Current Pos:* Res chemist, Army Mat & Mech Res Ctr, 69-85, supvr res chemist, 85-90, SR RES SCIENTIST, ARMY MAT TECHNOL LAB, 90- *Personal Data:* b Highland, Ill, Oct 13, 43; m 67; c 2. *Educ:* Southern Ill Univ, BA, 65; Univ Iowa, MS, 68, PhD(phys chem), 70. *Mem:* Am Soc Testing & Mat; Soc Plastic Engrs; Am Chem Soc; Sigma Xi. *Res:* Polymer characterization; polymerization behavior; durability, life prediction and structure-property relationships of polymers and composite materials; automation/artificial intelligence technology for processing, testing and evaluation of polymers and composite materials; advanced testing methodology for polymers. *Mailing Add:* 127 Concord St Wayland MA 01778

HAGNI, RICHARD D, ECONOMIC GEOLOGY, PROCESS MINERALOGY. *Current Pos:* instr geol, Univ Mo, Rolla, 56-60, from asst prof to prof, 60-84, Gulf Oil Found prof geol, 84-92, CHMN DEPT GEOL & GEOPHYS, UNIV MO, ROLLA, 85-, CURATOR PROF, 93- *Personal Data:* b Howell, Mich, Apr 29, 31; m 53, Rachael Stutzman; c John, Sandra, Ann & David. *Educ:* Mich State Univ, BS, 53, MS, 54; Univ Mo, PhD(geol), 62. *Concurrent Pos:* Consult explor geologist, Tex Gulf Sulphur Corp, 67-70; consult, Super Mining, 72-73 & Kerr-McGee, 74-75; US Bur Mines grants, 74-93; US Geol Surv grant, 78-79; dir & lectr, Appl Ore Micros, 72-85; vpres, Int Coun Appl Mineral Indust; chmn comn paragenesis, Int Asn Genesis Deposits, 84-; chmn comn appl mineral, Int Mining Asn, 90- *Mem:* Int Geol Cong; Int Asn Genesis Ore Deposits; Geol Soc Am; Soc Econ Geol; Am Inst Mining, Metall & Petrol Eng; Int Mining Asn. *Res:* Mississippi Valley zinc-lead mineral deposits; ore microscopy; paragenesis and genesis of ore deposits; ore microscopic applications to beneficiation and pyrometallurgical problems; fluid inclusion geothermometry. *Mailing Add:* Dept Geol & Geophys Univ Mo Rolla MO 65401. *Fax:* 573-341-6935; *E-Mail:* geology2@umrvmb.umr.edu

HAGOPIAN, CHARLES LEMUEL, TOPOLOGY. *Current Pos:* asst prof, 72-80, PROF MATH, CALIF STATE UNIV, SACRAMENTO, 80- *Personal Data:* b Sacramento, Calif, Nov 25, 40; m 70; c Jon, Robert & Emily. *Educ:* Sacramento State Col, BA, 62; Ariz State Univ, MA, 65, PhD(math), 68. *Prof Exp:* Res fel, Calif Inst Technol, 68-69; asst prof math, Calif State Univ, Sacramento, 69-71; vis prof, Ariz State Univ, 71-72. *Mem:* Am Math Soc; Math Asn Am. *Res:* Geometric topology, in particular, continua theory involving fixed-point properties, homogeneity and various forms of connectivity. *Mailing Add:* Dept Math Calif State Univ Sacramento CA 95819-6000

HAGOPIAN, MIASNIG, ORGANIC CHEMISTRY, BIOLOGICAL CHEMISTRY. *Current Pos:* BIOCHEMIST, MASON RES INST, EG&G, INC, 67- *Personal Data:* b Providence, RI, June 29, 27; m 58; c 4. *Educ:* Univ RI, BS, 50; Clark Univ, MA, 55, PhD(bio-org chem), 65. *Prof Exp:* Res asst biochem, Worcester Found Exp Biol, 51-56, staff scientist, 56-61; res chemist, Mem Hosp, 61-67. *Mem:* AAAS; Am Chem Soc; fel Am Inst Chemists. *Res:* Steroid metabolism; structure determination of natural products; synthesis of radio labelled steroids and catecholamines; biogenesis of catecholamine hormones; drug disposition and metabolism; chemical carcinogenesis; tobacco and marihuana smoke analysis; applied enzymology; lipid biochemistry. *Mailing Add:* 88 Sachem Ave Worcester MA 01606-1854

HAGOPIAN, VASKEN, HIGH ENERGY PHYSICS. *Current Pos:* assoc prof, 70-75, PROF PHYSICS, FLA STATE UNIV, 75- *Personal Data:* b Lebanon, Apr 21, 37; US citizen; m 65; c 1. *Educ:* Am Univ, Beirut, BS, 57; Univ Pa, MS, 60, PhD(physics), 63. *Prof Exp:* Res investr physics, Univ Pa, 63-65; actg asst prof, Univ Calif, Berkeley, 65-66; asst prof, Univ Pa, 66-69. *Mem:* Am Phys Soc. *Res:* Experimental high energy physics using high energy accelerators. *Mailing Add:* Dept Physics B-159 Fla State Univ Keen Bldg Tallahassee FL 32306-3016

HAGSTROM, GEROW RICHARD, AGRONOMY. *Current Pos:* DIR AGRON SERV, WESTERN AG MINERALS CO. *Personal Data:* b New York, NY, Oct 16, 31; m 60; c 2. *Educ:* Univ Conn, BS, 57, MS, 59; Univ Wis, Madison, PhD(soils), 64. *Prof Exp:* Agron serv rep, Int Minerals & Chem Corp, Ill, 64-68; mgr agron serv, Duval Sales Corp, 68-85. *Mem:* Am Soc Agron; Soil Sci Soc Am; Sigma Xi. *Res:* Secondary and micronutrient element requirements of agronomic crops. *Mailing Add:* 14911 Walters Rd Houston TX 77068

HAGSTROM, JACK WALTER CARL, PATHOLOGY. *Current Pos:* RETIRED. *Personal Data:* b Rockford, Ill, Dec 2, 33. *Educ:* Amherst Col, AB, 55; Cornell Univ, MD, 59. *Prof Exp:* Intern path, New York Hosp, Cornell Med Ctr, 59-60, resident, 60-63; from instr to asst prof, Med Col, Cornell Univ, 62-68; assoc prof, Case Western Res Univ & attend pathologist, Univ Hosps, Cleveland, 68-70; assoc prof, Col Physicians & Surgeons, Columbia Univ, 70-75, prof path, 75-91, assoc dir dept; dir, Dept Path Harlem Hosp Ctr, 81-91. *Concurrent Pos:* Attend pathologist, Presby Hosp, 70-91. *Mem:* Am Asn Path & Bact; Am Fedn Clin Res; Harvey Soc; fel Am Col Cardiol; fel Royal Soc Trop Med & Hyg. *Res:* Cardiovascular and pulmonary pathology. *Mailing Add:* PO Box 105 Water Mill NY 11976

HAGSTROM, RAY THEODORE, FRACTIONAL CHARGE SEARCH, INSTRUMENT DEVELOPMENT. *Current Pos:* asst physicist, 80-85, PHYSICIST, ARGONNE NAT LAB, 85- *Personal Data:* b Minneapolis, Minn, Nov 25, 47; m 68. *Educ:* Mass Inst Technol, BS, 69; Univ Wash, MS, 70; Univ Calif, Berkeley, PhD(physics), 79. *Prof Exp:* Fel, Lawrence Berkeley Lab, 79-80. *Mem:* Am Phys Soc; AAAS. *Res:* Fundamental experimental physics investigations without the use of high energy particle accelerators. *Mailing Add:* 823 S Racine St No D Chicago IL 60607

HAGSTROM, STANLEY ALAN, PHYSICAL CHEMISTRY. *Current Pos:* from asst prof to assoc prof, 62-71, actg chmn dept comput sci, 75-77, PROF CHEM & COMPUT SCI, IND UNIV BLOOMINGTON, 71- *Personal Data:* b Lincoln, Nebr, Nov 30, 30; m 56; c 2. *Educ:* Univ Omaha, BA, 52; Iowa State Univ, PhD(chem), 57. *Prof Exp:* Instr chem, Ind Univ, 58-59, asst dir, Res Comput Ctr, 59-60; res scientist, Lockheed Missiles & Space Co, 60-62. *Concurrent Pos:* Sloan fel, 57; indust consult, molecular quantum mech, theoret spectros, radiation transport. *Mem:* Am Phys Soc; Asn Comput Mach. *Res:* Molecular spectroscopy; molecular quantum mechanics; digital computers; numerical analysis. *Mailing Add:* 708 S Woodlawn Ave Bloomington IN 47401

HAGSTROM, STIG BERNT, INDUSTRIAL RESEARCH MANAGEMENT. *Current Pos:* PROF MAT SCI & ENG & CHMN DEPT, STANFORD UNIV, 87- *Personal Data:* b Barkeryd, Sweden, Sept 21, 32; m 57; c 4. *Educ:* Univ Uppsala, Sweden, BSc, 57, MSc, 59, PhD, 61, DSc, 64. *Hon Degrees:* ScD, Univ Linkoping, Sweden, 87. *Prof Exp:* Res assoc physics, Univ Uppsala, 61-64; res assoc chem, Lawrence Berkeley Lab, 65-66; assoc prof physics, Chalmers Univ Technol, 66-69; prof, Linkoping Univ, 69-76; prin scientist, Xerox Palo Alto Res Ctr, 76-77, mgr, 77-87. *Concurrent Pos:* Vchancellor, Linkoping Univ, 70-76; vis prof, Stanford Univ, 73-74; dir, Stanford Ctr Mat Res, 89- *Mem:* Fel Am Phys Soc; AAAS; Europ Phys Soc; Swed Phys Soc; Royal Swed Acad Eng Sci; Royal Norweg Soc Sci & Let. *Res:* Surface studies of electron structure of semiconductors and metals using electron spectroscopic techniques; instrumentation in surface science; synthesis of diamond films; surface magnetism. *Mailing Add:* 1365 Bay Laurel Dr Menlo Park CA 94025

HAGSTRUM, HOMER DUPRE, surface physics; deceased, see previous edition for last biography

HAGY, GEORGE WASHINGTON, GENETICS. *Current Pos:* from asst prof to assoc prof, 57-73, PROF BIOL, BROWN UNIV, 73- *Personal Data:* b San Antonio, Tex, Aug 21, 23; m 54; c 3. *Educ:* Univ Tex, BA, 44, MA, 48, PhD(genetics), 53. *Prof Exp:* Instr microanat, Southwestern Med Sch, Univ Tex, 53-55, asst prof, 55-57. *Mem:* AAAS; Am Soc Human Genetics; Soc Social Biol; Am Genetic Asn. *Res:* Growth and development; allergy; tissue culture. *Mailing Add:* 18 Fireside Dr Barrington RI 02806

HAHIN, RICHARD, ELECTROPHYSIOLOGY, BIOPHYSICS. *Current Pos:* asst prof, 85-91, ASSOC PROF, DEPT BIOL SCI, NORTHERN ILL UNIV, 91- *Personal Data:* b Buffalo, NY, Nov 23, 46. *Educ:* Mich State Univ, BS, 68; Univ Md, PhD(physiol), 77. *Prof Exp:* Elec engr, US Naval Ship Res & Develop Lab, 68-71; assoc, Dept Physiol & Biophys, Univ Iowa, 80-82, vis asst prof, 82-85. *Mem:* AAAS; Soc Gen Physiologists; Soc Neurosci; Biophys Soc; Int Soc Toxinology. *Res:* Kinetic and structural properties of ion channels; neuromuscular disease and altered ion channel function; structure and properties of natural toxins; prediction of toxicity based on chemical structure. *Mailing Add:* Biol Sci Dept Northern Ill Univ De Kalb IL 60115. *Fax:* 815-753-0461

HAHM, TAIK SOO, TRANSPORT IN TOKAMAK PLASMA, PLASMA TURBULENCE. *Current Pos:* from staff res physicist I to res physicist, 86-96, PRIN RES PHYSICIST, PLASMA PHYSICS LAB, PRINCETON UNIV, 96- *Personal Data:* b Seoul, Korea, July 5, 57. *Educ:* Seoul Nat Univ, BS, 80; Princeton Univ, MA, 82, PhD(astrophys), 84. *Prof Exp:* Res fel, Inst Fusion Studies, Univ Tex, Austin, 84-86. *Concurrent Pos:* Vis prof, Dept Nuclear Eng, Seoul Nat Univ, 93. *Mem:* Fel Am Phys Soc. *Res:* Theory of plasma instabilities and turbulence; transport in tokamak; self-organized-criticality in plasma. *Mailing Add:* 509 Raven's Crest Dr Plainsboro NJ 08536. *Fax:* 609-243-2662; *E-Mail:* tshahm@pppl.gov

HAHN, ALEXANDER J, ALGEBRA, MATHEMATICS. *Current Pos:* PROF MATH, UNIV NOTRE DAME, 72- *Personal Data:* b Bielitz, Poland, Sept 9, 43; US citizen; m 72; c 1. *Educ:* Loyola Univ, BS, 65; Univ Notre Dame, PhD(math), 70. *Concurrent Pos:* NSF fel, WGer, 70-71; vis prof, Univ Calif, Santa Barbara, 82-83, Univ Innsbruck, Austria, 88. *Mem:* Am Math Soc. *Res:* The classical groups and K-theory; co-author one book. *Mailing Add:* Univ Notre Dame Notre Dame IN 46556-0398

HAHN, ALLEN W, VETERINARY MEDICINE, BIOMEDICAL ENGINEERING. *Current Pos:* assoc dir, 80-81, PROF VET MED, SURG & BIOENG & INVESTR, DALTON RES CTR, UNIV MO, COLUMBIA, 69-, ADJ PROF COMPUT SCI, 90-, CO-DIR, MED INFORMATICS TRAINING GRANT, 92- *Personal Data:* b St Louis, Mo, Dec 28, 33; m 57, Joan Miller; c Kenneth M, Rebecca D & C Mark. *Educ:* Univ Mo, BS & DVM, 58; Drexel Univ, MS, 64, PhD(chem eng), 68; Am Col Vet Int Med, dipl, 74. *Prof Exp:* Res asst vet med, Auburn Univ, 58-61; res instr med cardiol, Univ Pa, 61-62; instr biol sci, Drexel Univ, 66-68, assoc prof, 68-69. *Concurrent Pos:* Prin co investr grants & contracts, NIH, NSF, US Army, NASA & var com co; sr ed, Eng Med & Biol, Inst Elec & Electronics Engrs. *Mem:* AAAS; Am Vet Med Asn; Am Col Vet Int Med; Inst Elec & Electronics Engrs; Am Physiol Soc; Am Med Informatics Asn. *Res:* Comparative cardiology; computers in veterinary medicine; implantable polymeric materials. *Mailing Add:* 333 Clydesdale Hall Univ Mo Columbia MO 65211-0001. *Fax:* 573-884-5444; *E-Mail:* hahn@vth.vetmed.missouri.edu

HAHN, AMY BETH, HISTOCOMPATIBILITY, IMMUNOGENETICS. *Current Pos:* ASST PROF PATH & LAB MED & DIR, TISSUE TYPING LAB, MED UNIV SC, 93- *Personal Data:* b Pittsburgh, Pa, Sept 4, 63; m 85, Mark A; c Jennifer A. *Educ:* Carnegie-Mellon Univ, BS, 85; Johns Hopkins Sch Med, PhD(immunol), 90. *Prof Exp:* Fel, Johns Hopkins Sch Med, 91-93. *Mem:* Am Soc Histocompatibility & Immunogenetics. *Res:* Determination of HLA antigen allele and haplotype frequencies for various minority populations in the Carolinas; collaborations with clinicians on HLA associations with transplant outcomes and diseases. *Mailing Add:* Dept Path Med Univ SC 171 Ashley Ave Charleston SC 29425-0001. *Fax:* 803-792-0540

HAHN, BENJAMIN DANIEL, ACCOUNTING. *Current Pos:* PRES, NEUROPSYCHIAT INST, FARGO, NDAK, 74- *Personal Data:* b Emden, NDak, Oct 24, 32; m 57, Eleanor B Anseth; c Lezlie, Deann, Bobette, Lara & Amy. *Educ:* Concordia Col, BBA, 60; Univ NDak, MA, 61. *Prof Exp:* Staff accountant, Broeker Hendrickson, Fargo, NDak, 61-63; asst admin & contribr, NDak State Hosp, Jamestown, 63-74. *Concurrent Pos:* fac, Jamestown Col, 63-74; bd dir, Bethany Home, 75-81, S E Ment Health Ctr, 75-81. *Mem:* Fel Am Col Hosp Adminr; Am Inst Cert Pub Accountants; Med Group Mgt Asn. *Mailing Add:* Neuropsychiat Res Inst PO Box 1415 Fargo ND 58107-1415

HAHN, BEVRA H, RHEUMATOLOGY. *Current Pos:* instr prev med, 69-71, asst prof, 71-78, ASSOC PROF MED, SCH MED, WASH UNIV, 78-; PROF MED, UNIV CALIF, LOS ANGELES, 83- *Personal Data:* b Wheeling, WVa, Dec 9, 39; m 64, Theodore J; c 2. *Educ:* Ohio State Univ, BSc, 60; Johns Hopkins Univ, MD, 64. *Honors & Awards:* Carole Nachman Prize Rheumatology Res; Bunim Medal, ACR; Carolyn Duncan Distinguished Women Med Award. *Prof Exp:* Intern med, Barnes Hosp, Wash Univ, 64-65, asst resident med, 65-66; fel med connective tissue div, Johns Hopkins Univ, 66-69. *Concurrent Pos:* Res assoc, Vet Admin Hosp, St Louis, 69-70; consult rheumatology, Montebello State Hosp, 67-69; clin investr, Vet Admin Hosp, St Louis, 70-73. *Mem:* Am Rheumatism Asn; Am Fedn Clin Res; Am Asn Immunol; Am Soc Clin Invest. *Res:* DNA antibodies in human and murine lupas; cellular immunity in SLE; steroid-induced osteopenia; genetics of SLE. *Mailing Add:* Div Rheumatology Univ Calif Los Angeles Sch Med Ctr Health Sci 1000 Veteran Ave Los Angeles CA 90095. *Fax:* 310-825-9707

HAHN, C(HARLES) ARCHIE, JR, MECHANICAL ENGINEERING. *Current Pos:* RETIRED. *Personal Data:* b Walla Walla, Wash, Apr 10, 14; m 40; c 3. *Educ:* Univ Va, BS, 35, BSME, 36. *Prof Exp:* Jr indust engr, Grasselli Chem Dept, E I du Pont de Nemours & Co, 36-40, asst div engr, War Construct Div, 40-42, div engr, 42; indust engr, Remington Arms Co, NY, 42-51; develop engr, E I Du Pont de Nemours & Co, Inc, 51-54, develop proj engr photoprods equip develop, 54, res supvr, Textile Res Lab, 54-56, develop supvr, Eng Develop Lab, 56-66, specialist engr, Design Div, 66-70, sr mech engr, 70-74. *Mem:* Am Soc Mech Engrs. *Res:* Development of specialized equipment. *Mailing Add:* 173 SW 51st St Cape Coral FL 33914

HAHN, DONALD RICHARD, FERMENTATION & PROCESS DEVELOPMENT, BIOLOGICALS & VACCINE DEVELOPMENT. *Current Pos:* RES SCIENTIST, MALLINKRODT, INC, 90- *Personal Data:* b Plainview, Tex, May 14, 60; m 82, Tammy D Brayton; c Michael B & Rachel

E. *Educ:* Bethany Col, BA, 82; Univ Ill, Urbana-Champaign, MS, 85, PhD(microbiol), 88. *Prof Exp:* Res technician, A E Staley Mfg Co, 82; teaching asst, Dept Microbiol, Univ Ill, 82-87, res asst, 83-88; res scientist, Eli Lilly & Co, 88-90. *Concurrent Pos:* Adj asst prof microbiol, Ind Univ Med Sch, 91-93. *Mem:* Am Soc Microbiol; Soc Indust Microbiol; Sigma Xi. *Res:* Molecular genetics of streptomycetes, antibiotic biosynthesis, bacteriophage genetics, antibiotic strain improvement and process development. *Mailing Add:* 3 S Seymour Ave Mundelein IL 60060

HAHN, DOWON, ENDOCRINOLOGY, REPRODUCTIVE PHYSIOLOGY. *Current Pos:* from assoc scientist to sr scientist reproductive physiol, RW Johnson Pharmaceut Res Inst, 68-73, group leader, 73-75, sect head, 75-82, asst dir, 82-87, dir, Reproductive/Endocrine Res, 87-92, DISTINGUISHED RES FEL, RW JOHNSON PHARMACEUT RES INST, 93- *Personal Data:* b Pyung Buck, Korea, Nov 20, 31; m 63, Myung Y Kim; c Charles, Helen & Anna. *Educ:* Mich State Univ, BS, 60, MS, 63; Univ Mo, PhD(endocrinol), 67. *Honors & Awards:* Philip B Hofmann Res Scientist Award, Johnson & Johnson, 73, 85; Johnson medal, 90. *Prof Exp:* Ford Found fel endocrinol, Worcester Found Exp Biol, 67-68. *Concurrent Pos:* Adj prof, Grad Sch, Rutgers Univ & Eastern Va Med Sch. *Mem:* Soc Study Reproduction; Am Fertil Soc; Am Physiol Soc; Endocrine Soc; Soc Gynec Invest. *Res:* Fertility control; investigation and development of new therapeutic agents for gynecologic disorders; pharmacology of contraceptives. *Mailing Add:* RW Johnson Pharmaceut Res Inst Raritan NJ 08869-0602. *Fax:* 908-526-6469

HAHN, ELLIOT F, OPIATE AGONISTS & ANTAGONISTS, STEROID HORMONES. *Current Pos:* PRES, ANDRX CORP, 93- *Personal Data:* b New York, NY, June 28, 44; m 68, Lillian Helfman; c 3. *Educ:* City Col New York, BS, 66; Cornell Univ, PhD(org chem), 70. *Prof Exp:* Vis scientist, Technion-Israel Inst Technol, Haifa, 70-72; res fel, Inst Steroid Res, Montefiore Hosp, Bronx, NY, 72-74, investr, 74-77; asst prof, Albert Einstein Col Med, 76-78; asst prof, Rockefeller Univ, 77-83, assoc prof biochem, 83-88; assoc dir res & develop, Ivax Corp, 88-89, vpres res, Baker Cummins Pharm, Div Ivax Corp, 89-93, vpres sci affairs, Ivax Corp, 90-93. *Concurrent Pos:* Estab fel, NY Heart Asn; res assoc prof, Univ Miami, 88- *Mem:* Am Chem Soc; AAAS; Sigma Xi; NY Acad Sci. *Res:* Chemistry, biochemistry and pharmacology of narcotic agonists and antagonists; biotransformation of androgens in the brain; central nervous system mechanisms regulating hypertension; anti-HIV agents. *Mailing Add:* Andrx Corp 4001 SW 47th Ave Ft Lauderdale FL 33314. *Fax:* 954-792-1034

HAHN, ERIC WALTER, RADIATION BIOLOGY. *Current Pos:* SCIENTIST, GER CANCER RES CTR, 85- *Personal Data:* b New York, NY, June 1, 32; m 56, Janet Krobak; c Eric, Korina & Charles. *Educ:* Univ Ga, BS, 54, MS, 57; Univ Ill, Urbana, PhD(physiol), 60. *Prof Exp:* Asst physiol, Univ Ga, 56-57; asst, Univ Ill, Urbana, 57-60; instr, Univ Rochester, 60-64, asst prof radiation biol & biophys & head, Sect Exp Endocrinol, 64-68; asst prof radiol & dir res, Health Sci Ctr, Univ Minn, Minneapolis, 68-69; head, Sect Radiation Ther, Sloan-Kettering Inst Cancer Res, 69-77, assoc mem, 79-81; prof, Dept Radiother, Mt Sinai Med Ctr, 81-85. *Concurrent Pos:* Fel steroid training prog, Worcester Found Exp Biol, 63-64; adj assoc prof, Cornell Univ, 69-; attend radiobiologist, Mem Hosp, 75-81, adj attend radiobiologist, 81-; chmn, Biol Res Dept, King Faisal Specialist Hosp, Riyadh, Saudi Arabia; adj prof, Dept Radiol, Southwestern Med Sch, Univ Tex; head, Radiation Biol Lab, Ger Cancer Res Ctr. *Mem:* AAAS; Europ Soc Therapeut Radiol Oncol; Radiation Res Soc; Am Physiol Soc; Soc Study Reproduction; NY Acad Sci. *Res:* Basic and applied radiation biology in the treatment of cancer; mechanisms of action of hyperthermia, application in the treatment of cancer and neutrons and the application of stereo tactic radiation. *Mailing Add:* Ger Cancer Res Ctr Neuenheimer Feld 280 69120 Heidelberg Germany. *Fax:* 49-6221-422572, 904-344-0359

HAHN, ERWIN LOUIS, PHYSICS, NUCLEAR MAGNETIC RESONANCE. *Current Pos:* from asst prof to prof, 55-91, EMER PROF PHYSICS, UNIV CALIF, BERKELEY, 91- *Personal Data:* b Sharon, Pa, June 9, 21; m 80, Natalie Woolfolk; c David, Deborah & Katherine. *Educ:* Juniata Col, BS, 43; Univ Ill, MS, 47, PhD(physics), 49. *Hon Degrees:* DSc, Juniata Col, 66; DSc, Purdue Univ, 74. *Honors & Awards:* Buckley Prize, Am Phys Soc; 1971 prize, Int Soc Magnetic Resonance; Wolf Prize in Physics, 84; Hon Fel Brasenose Col, Oxford Univ, 84; Comstock Prize, US Nat Acad Sci, 93. *Prof Exp:* Asst physics, Purdue Univ, 43-44; res assoc, Univ Ill, 50; Nat Res Coun fel, Stanford Univ, 50-51, instr, 51-52; res physicist, Watson Sci Comput Lab, IBM Corp, 52-55. *Concurrent Pos:* Consult, Off Naval Res, Stanford Univ, 50-52; assoc, Columbia Univ, 52-55; consult, Atomic Energy Comn, 55-; assoc prof, Miller Inst Basic Res, 58-59, Prof, 66-67; spec consult, US Navy, 59; Guggenheim & NSF fels, 61-62; mem adv panel, Radio Stand Div, Nat Bur Stand, 61-64; mem comt basic res, Nat Acad Sci-Nat Res Coun; adv, US Army Res Off, Durham; Guggenheim fel, Brasenose Col, Oxford, 69-70; vis lectr, Josef-Stefan Inst, Slovenia, 69; Alexander von Humboldt Award, 76 & 77; traveling lect ser, Can Res Coun, 64 & Japanese Phys Soc, 77; vis Eastman Prof, Balliol Col, Oxford Univ, 88-89. *Mem:* Nat Acad Sci; fel AAAS; fel Am Phys Soc; foreign mem Acad Sci Slovenia; foreign mem Fr Acad Sci. *Res:* Nuclear and electron spin magnetic resonance; electronic instruments; electron and nuclear spin resonance coupling in molecules and solids; laser-physics; non-linear laser optics; discoverer of spin echoes; spin-spin cross-polarization in solids; electromagnetism; co-discoverer of self-induced transparency. *Mailing Add:* Dept Physics Univ Calif Berkeley CA 94720. *Fax:* 510-643-8497; *E-Mail:* hahn@physics.berkeley.edu

HAHN, FLETCHER FREDERICK, INHALATION TOXICOLOGY, RADIOBIOLOGY. *Current Pos:* EXP PATHOLOGIST, INHALATION RES INST, 71-, PATH GROUP SUPVR, 84- *Personal Data:* b Spokane, Wash, May 8, 39; m 61, Laura M Cheatham; c 2. *Educ:* Wash State Univ, BS & DVM, 64; Univ Calif, Davis, PhD(comp path), 71. *Prof Exp:* Vet lab officer, Walter Reed Army Inst Res, 64-66; NIH fel, Univ Calif, Davis, 66-70. *Concurrent Pos:* Clin assoc, Sch Med, Univ NMex, 72-; chmn, Task Group 9, Nat Coun Radiation Protect Comt, 57, 77-; mem, animal models for aging, Nat Acad Sci-Inst Lab Animal Res, 79; fac assoc, Sch Vet Med, Colo State Univ, 84-90 & Purdue Univ, 86-; clin prof, Sch Pharm, Univ NMex, 87-; assoc ed, Radiation Res, 89-93; assoc scientist, Univ Mex Cancer Ctr, 91-; consult, Ctr Environ Toxicol Path, Am Reg Path, 92-; AWU-DOE Lab Distinguished lectr, 93-94. *Mem:* AAAS; Am Col Vet Pathologists; Am Vet Med Asn; Am Asn Zoos & Aquariums; Radiation Res Soc; Soc Tox Path. *Res:* Pathogenesis of early and late biologic effects and dose response relationships of inhaled environmental pollutants, especially radionuclides and metals; induced and spontaneous diseases of laboratory animals. *Mailing Add:* Inhalation Toxicol Res Inst PO Box 5890 Albuquerque NM 87185. *E-Mail:* fhahn@tlc.lucy.org

HAHN, GEORGE, BIOLOGY. *Current Pos:* res assoc, 69, from asst prof to prof, 69-93, EMER PROF RADIOL, SCH MED, STANFORD UNIV, 93- *Personal Data:* b Vienna, Austria, Jan 31, 26; nat US; m 49, Joyce Webb; c Peter, Nina & John. *Educ:* Univ Calif, BA, 52, MA, 54; Stanford Univ, PhD, 65. *Honors & Awards:* Albert Soiland Mem Award; 1st J Eugene Robinson Award. *Prof Exp:* Mathematician, Radiation Lab, Univ Calif, Berkeley, 51-54; physicist, Dalmo Victor Co, Calif, 54-57, head systs group, 58-60; asst head, Electronic Dept, Firestone Tire & Rubber Co, 57-58; assoc prof electronics, US Naval Postgrad Sch, 60-66. *Concurrent Pos:* Consult, Wright Air Develop Ctr, Ohio, USAF, 58, Dalmo Victor Co, 60-69, Ampex Co, 60-65, Hewlett-Packard Co, 77-80, Nat Cancer Inst & NIH, 80-83; ed, Cancer Res, 80-85, Bioelectromagnetics, 84-86 & Int J Hyperthermia, 85-92. *Mem:* Radiation Res Soc; NAm Hyperthermia Soc; Am Soc Thearapeut Radiol & Oncol; AAAS. *Res:* Cell kinetics; radiobiology of mammalian cell cultures; computer simulations of therapy of malignant disease; hyperthermia as modality of cancer treatment. *Mailing Add:* Dept Radiation Oncol Stanford Univ Sch Med CBRL Rm GK103 Stanford CA 94305-5468. *Fax:* 650-723-7382

HAHN, GEORGE LEROY, BIOMETEOROLOGY. *Current Pos:* res engr, 57-61, res leader, 74-77 & 90-96, RES PROJ LEADER, AGR RES SERV, US DEPT AGR, 61- *Personal Data:* b Muncie, Kans, Nov 12, 34; m 55, Clovice Christensen; c Valerie, Cecile, Steven & Melanie. *Educ:* Univ Mo, Columbia, BS, 57, PhD(atmospheric sci), 71; Univ Calif, Davis, MS, 61. *Honors & Awards:* Bioclimatol Award, Am Meteorol Soc, 76; Farm Bldg Award, Am Soc Agr Engrs, 76. *Concurrent Pos:* Prof, Univ Mo, Columbia, 71-78 & Univ Nebr, Lincoln, 78-; res leader, 74-77, tech adv, Agr Res Serv, US Dept Agr, 72-81; dir, Am Soc Agr Engrs, 79-81 & 91-93; vis prof, Agr Univ Norway, 82-83; bd dir, Am Soc Agr Engrs, 79-81 & 91-93. *Mem:* Fel Am Soc Agr Engrs; Am Meteorol Soc; Int Soc Biometeorol; Am Soc Animal Sci; Coun Agr Sci & Technol. *Res:* Development and validation of models for assessing impact of environmental factors (primarily climatic) on farm animal stress, performance and well-being; application of such models in rational decisions concerning environmental modification for farm animals. *Mailing Add:* US Dept Agr PO Box 166 Clay Center NE 68933. *E-Mail:* hahn@marcvm.marc.usda.gov

HAHN, GERALD JOHN, STATISTICS. *Current Pos:* MGR, APPL STATIST PROG, CORP RES & DEVELOP, GEN ELEC CO, 55- *Personal Data:* b Karlsruhe, Ger, Sept 11, 30; m 56; c 3. *Educ:* City Col New York, BBA, 52; Columbia Univ, MS, 53; Union Col, MS, 65; Rensselaer Polytech Inst, PhD(statist & opers res), 71. *Honors & Awards:* Brumbaugh Award, Am Soc Qual Control, 74, 80 & 82, Wilcoxon Prize, 79 & 88, Shewell Prize, 75 & 89, Youden Address, 87. *Concurrent Pos:* Adj prof statist, Union Col, Schenectady, NY, 65-87. *Mem:* Fel Am Statist Asn; fel Am Soc Qual Control; Inst Math Statist; Am Soc Testing & Mat. *Mailing Add:* 1404 Orlyn Dr Niskayuna NY 12309. *E-Mail:* hahn@crd.ge.com

HAHN, HARALD, ACCELERATOR PHYSICS. *Current Pos:* SR PHYSICIST, BROOKHAVEN NAT LAB, 60-, RHIC ASST PROJ HEAD, 91- *Personal Data:* b Constanta, Romania, 1932; Ger citizen; m 66, Sue Schroeder; c Sigrid & Hansjorg. *Educ:* Paris, DSc, 60. *Mem:* Am Phys Soc. *Mailing Add:* Bldg 1005S Brookhaven Nat Lab Upton NY 11973. *Fax:* 516-282-2588; *E-Mail:* hahnh@bnl.gov

HAHN, HAROLD THOMAS, PHYSICAL INORGANIC CHEMISTRY, ELECTROMAGNETIC MATERIALS. *Current Pos:* CONSULT, 92- *Personal Data:* b New York, NY, May 31, 24; m 48, Bennie Turney; c Anita, Beverly, Carol & Harold Jr. *Educ:* Columbia Univ, BS, 44; Univ Tex, PhD(phys inorg chem), 53. *Prof Exp:* Oper foreman, Los Alamos Sci Lab, Calif, 46-47, mem staff, 47-50; sr scientist, Hanford Lab Oper, Gen Elec Co, 53-58; sect chief chem res, Phillips Petrol Co, 58-64; staff engr, Lockheed Missiles & Space Co, 64-73; sr scientist, Lockheed Palo Alto Res Lab, 73-84, sr staff scientist, 84-92. *Concurrent Pos:* Prin investr ferritic mat; judge, Regional & Intl Sci Fair, 60-80. *Mem:* Sigma Xi; fel Am Inst Chemist; sr mem Inst Elec & Electronics Engrs. *Res:* Reactor fuel processing; heavy element chemistry; diffusion; isotope separation; pyrochemistry; plasma chemistry; ammonolysis of carbon halides; surface coatings; space materials; propulsion; ocean mineral processing; ferrites. *Mailing Add:* 661 Teresi Lane Los Altos CA 94024

HAHN, HENRY, materials science, metallurgy, for more information see previous edition

HAHN, HONG THOMAS, COMPOSITE MATERIALS, STRUCTURES. Current Pos: PROF MECH ENGR, UNIV CALIF LOS ANGELES, 92- Personal Data: b Seoul, Korea, Feb 5, 42; US citizen; m 67, Hoon Paek; c Heryun, Hejin & Jeanie. Educ: Seoul Nat Univ, BS, 64; Pa State Univ, MS, 68, PhD(eng mech), 71. Prof Exp: Fel, McMaster Univ, 71-72; res assoc, Air Force Mat Lab, 72-74; res engr, Univ Dayton Res Inst, 74-77 & Air Force Mat Lab, 77-78; mech engr, Lawrence Livermore Nat Lab, 78-79; assoc prof, Washington Univ, St Louis, 79-81, prof mech eng, 81-86; prof eng mech, Pa State Univ, 86-92. Concurrent Pos: Consult, Lawrence Livermore Nat Lab, 79-, Garrett, 89- & Dow, 89-; ed, J Composite Mat, 81-; Harry & Arlene Schell prof, 91. Mem: Am Soc Mech Engrs; Am Inst Aeronaut & Astronaut; Soc Mfg Engrs; Mat Res Soc; Am Soc Eng Educ; Soc Advan Mat & Process Eng. Res: Mechanical behavior of composite materials; fracture and fatigue; reliability; processing; nondestructive testing; manufacturing; design. Mailing Add: Univ Calif Los Angeles, MANE Dept Eng IV Los Angeles CA 90024-1597. Fax: 310-206-2302; E-Mail: hahn@seas.ucla.edu

HAHN, HWA SUK, MATHEMATICS. Current Pos: RETIRED. Personal Data: b Pusan, Korea, Nov 1, 24; m 49. Educ: Seoul Nat Univ, BS, 49; Univ Ore, MS, 57; Univ Ill, PhD(math), 61. Prof Exp: Instr math, Pusan Nat Univ, Korea, 49-51, asst prof, 51-55; asst prof, Pa State Univ, 61-67; from assoc prof to prof math, WGa Col, 67-92. Mem: Am Math Soc; Math Asn Am. Res: Theory of numbers in mathematics. Mailing Add: 108 W Dunwoody Dr Carrollton GA 30117

HAHN, JAMES H, DIGITAL SYSTEMS, SIGNAL PROCESSING & ANALOG CIRCUITS. Current Pos: ASSOC PROF ELEC ENG, UNIV MO, ROLLA, 85-, INTERIM DIR, ENG EDUC CTR, 90- Personal Data: b East Prairie, Mo, June 28, 36; m 59, Mary J Becker; c 5. Educ: Mo Sch Mines & Metall, BS, 59; Univ Pittsburg, MS, 65, Univ Mo, Rolla, PhD(elec eng), 77. Prof Exp: Engr, Westinghouse Elec Corp, 59-65; eng specialist, Monsanto Co, 65-71; vpres, Interface Technol Inc, 72-85. Mem: Inst Elec & Electronics Engrs. Res: Speech processing; acoustic coupling of speech and dual tone modulated frequency signals. Mailing Add: 2 Hawthorne Estates St Louis MO 63131. Fax: 314-553-5734; E-Mail: jhahn@umrvmb.umr.edu

HAHN, KYONG TAIK, MATHEMATICAL ANALYSIS, SEVERAL COMPLEX ANALYSIS. Current Pos: from asst prof to assoc prof, 64-76, PROF MATH, PA STATE UNIV, 76- Personal Data: b Kyong Gi-Do, Korea, Apr 4, 29; m 62; c 2. Educ: Seoul Nat Univ, BS, 56; Yonsei Univ, MS, 58; Stanford Univ, PhD(math), 64. Honors & Awards: Sr Prof Fulbright Res Award, Ger. Prof Exp: Lectr math, Yonsei Univ, Korea, 57-59; res assoc, Stanford Univ, 64. Concurrent Pos: NSF grants, 68-69 & 80-81; vis assoc prof, Univ Calif, Berkeley, 72; AID vis prof, Seoul Nat Univ, Korea, 78-79. Mem: Am Math Soc. Res: Equivalence of the Bergman metric and the invariant pseudometrics of Caratheodory and Kobayashi on various pseudoconvex domains; tangential boundary behavior of holomorphic functions and invariant harmonic functions on bounded domains. Mailing Add: Dept Math Pa Univ University Park PA 16802-6401. Fax: 814-865-3735; E-Mail: kth@psuvm.psu.edu

HAHN, KYOUNG-DONG, PLASMA PHYSICS. Current Pos: STAFF SCIENTIST, LAWRENCE BERKELEY LAB, 88- Personal Data: b Kyungbuk, Korea, Sept 8, 54. Educ: Seoul Nat Univ, BS, 77; Univ Wash; MS, 80, PhD(physics), 88. Mem: Am Phys Soc. Res: Heavy ion fusion driver and beam dynamics of the intense particle beams using analytic and numerical model; transport of particles in a magnetically confined plasma. Mailing Add: MS 47-112 Lawrence Berkeley Lab One Cyclotron Rd Berkeley CA 94720

HAHN, LIANG-SHIN, MATHEMATICS. Current Pos: asst prof, 68-72, ASSOC PROF MATH, UNIV NMEX, 72- Personal Data: b Tainan, Taiwan; m 58, Hwei-Shien; c Samuel Shin-Y, James Shin-J, & Paul Shin-H. Educ: Nat Taiwan Univ, BS, 56; Stanford Univ, PhD(math), 66. Prof Exp: Instr math, Johns Hopkins Univ, 66-68. Concurrent Pos: Vis scholar, Univ Wash, Seattle, 74-76, Nat Taiwan Univ, 79-80, Univ Tokyo, 81-82 & 85-87, Int Christian Univ, Tokyo, 86-87, Sophia Univ, 87. Mem: Am Math Soc; Math Asn Am; Math Soc Japan. Res: Multiplier problem in harmonic analysis; complex analysis; function algebras. Mailing Add: Univ NMex 6801 Leander Ave NE Albuquerque NM 87109-3722

HAHN, MARJORIE G, PROBABILITY. Current Pos: from asst prof to assoc prof, 77-87, PROF MATH, TUFTS UNIV, 87- Personal Data: b Salt Lake City, Utah, Dec 30, 48; m 73, Peter; c Robert. Educ: Stanford Univ, BS, 71; Mass Inst Technol, PhD(math), 75. Prof Exp: Lectr statist, Univ Calif, Berkeley, 75-77. Concurrent Pos: Sr researcher, NSF grants, 78-; vis assoc prof, Univ Calif, Berkeley, 81-82; mem, Comt Appl & Theoret Statist, Bd Math Sci, Nat Res Coun. Mem: Fel Inst Math Statist; Am Math Soc; Mat Asn Am; Sigma Xi. Res: Probability, stochastic processes in particular, central limit theorems in function spaces, random sets, extreme values and large deviations; statistics (osymptotics and maximum likelihood theory). Mailing Add: Dept Math Tufts Univ Medford MA 02155. E-Mail: mhahn@jade.tufts.edu

HAHN, MARTIN EARL, PSYCHOBIOLOGY, BEHAVIORAL GENETICS. Current Pos: asst prof, 73-77, assoc prof, 78-80, PROF BIOL, WILLIAM PATERSON COL, 80- Personal Data: b Cincinnati, Ohio, Apr 8, 43; m 67; c 2. Educ: Ohio State Univ, BA, 66; Miami Univ, MA, 68, PhD(exp psychol), 70. Prof Exp: Grad asst, Miami Univ, 68-69, res asst psychol, 69-70; res assoc behav genetics, State Univ NY Binghamton, 70-72. Concurrent Pos: NIMH trainee, State Univ NY Binghamton, 72-73; prin investr, NIMH grant, 71-72, & NSF Col Fac Prog, 74-75; NSF grant, 76-78. Mem: Sigma Xi; Behav Genetics Asn; Int Soc Develop Psychobiol. Res: Behavior genetics of social behavior; evolution of behavior and brain size. Mailing Add: Dept Biol Sci William Paterson Col 300 Pompton Rd Wayne NJ 07470-2103

HAHN, OTTFRIED J, MECHANICAL & NUCLEAR ENGINEERING. Current Pos: asst prof, 67-77, ASSOC PROF MECH ENG, UNIV KY, 77- Personal Data: b Berlin, Ger, June 21, 35; Can citizen; m 60; c 3. Educ: Univ Alta, BS, 58; Univ WVa, MS, 60; Princeton Univ, MA & PhD(mech eng), 64. Prof Exp: Physicist, Can Gen Elec Co, 64-67. Mem: Am Nuclear Soc; Am Soc Mech Engrs; Am Phys Soc; Am Soc Eng Educ. Res: Properties of nuclear reactors, including lattice measurements and two-phase flow; coal conversion, gasification and coal properties. Mailing Add: Mech Eng Dept Univ Ky Lexington KY 40506-0002

HAHN, PETER, PHYSIOLOGY. Current Pos: assoc prof, 68-72, EMER PROF PEDIAT & OBSTET, UNIV BC, 72- Personal Data: b Berlin, Ger, Nov 8, 23; m 48; c 2. Educ: Charles Univ, Prague, MD, 50; Czech Acad Sci, PhD(physiol), 54, DSc(physiol), 62. Honors & Awards: Award on Aging, Ciba Found, London, 60; Czech Acad Sci Develop Awards, Prague, 62 & 66; Porkyne Medal, Czech, Acad Sci, 96. Prof Exp: Lectr physiol, Charles Univ, Prague, 50-51; researcher, Czech Acad Sci, 51-62, head dept develop nutrit, 62-68. Mem: Perinatal Res Soc; Am Inst Nutrit; Europ Soc Pediat Res; Can Soc Clin Invest; Royal Col Physicians. Res: Human and mammalian development of lipid and carbohydrate metabolism and its regulations. Mailing Add: Dept Obstet Res Ctr 4467 Marine Dr West Vancouver BC V7W 2N8 Can

HAHN, PETER MATHIAS, COMMUNICATION SYSTEMS, QUADRATIC ASSIGNMENT PROBLEM. Current Pos: CONSULT, SCI-TECH SERV, 91- Personal Data: b Vienna, Austria, May 15, 37; m 80, Bonnie H Silver; c 3. Educ: City Col New York, BEE, 58; Univ Pa, MSEE, 62, PhD(elec eng), 68. Prof Exp: Jr engr, Res Div, Philco Corp, Philadelphia, Pa, 58-61; instr elec eng, Moore Sch Elec Eng, Univ Pa, 62-65; radar systs engr, Missile & Surface Radar Div, Radio Corp Am, 65-67; eng specialist, Philco-Ford Corp, 67-68, eng mgr, Commun & Electronics Div, 68-76; unit supvr, Govt Commun Systs, RCA Corp, 76-77; chief engr, Sonic Sci Corp, 77-79; staff tech adv, Govt Systs Div, RCA Corp, 79-84; sr commun engr, Space Systs Div, Gen Elec Co, 84-86; mgr commun anal & simulation, G E Fed Systs, 87-88, mgr technol develop, G E Strategic Systs, 88-89, sr staff engr, 89-90. Concurrent Pos: Adj prof, Drexel Univ, 80-; adj assoc prof, Univ Pa, 84-; vpres, ARI Corp. Mem: Sr mem Inst Elec & Electronics Engrs; Am Soc Eng Educ; Soc Indust & Appl Math. Res: Electronics; information theory; pattern recognition; communication theory; mathematical programming; operations research; probability; statistics; systems science and engineering; signal and data processing; communication networks; satellite communications; postal systems; quadratic assignment problem. Mailing Add: 1416 Park Rd Elverson PA 19520-9533. Fax: 610-286-7705; E-Mail: peter_hahn@compuserve.com

HAHN, RICHARD ALLEN, SYSTEMIC HEMODYNAMICS, MYOCARDIAL FUNCTION. Current Pos: res scientist, 80-85, RES ASSOC, DEPT CARDIOVASC PHARMACOL, LILLY RES LABS, INDIANAPOLIS, 86- Personal Data: b Columbus, Ohio, Aug 30, 38; m 63; c 2. Educ: Ohio State Univ, BS, 62, MS, 64, PhD(pharmacol), 72. Prof Exp: Assoc sr investr, biol res, Smith Kline & French Labs, 73-79, sr investr, 79. Mem: AAAS; Am Heart Asn; NY Acad Sci. Res: Cardiovascular pharmacology; autonomic pharmacology; hypertension. Mailing Add: 5049 Deer Ridge Dr S Carmel IN 46033

HAHN, RICHARD BALSER, CHEMISTRY. Current Pos: from asst prof to prof, 47-79, EMER PROF CHEM & CONSULT, WAYNE STATE UNIV, 79- Personal Data: b Detroit, Mich, July 6, 13; m 38, Constance Lake; c Paul & Thomas. Educ: Wayne State Univ, BS, 35, MS, 36; Univ Mich, PhD(chem), 48. Honors & Awards: Anachem Award, 78. Prof Exp: Teacher pub sch, Mich, 36-42; instr chem, Wayne State Univ, 42-46; instr, Univ Mich, 46-47. Concurrent Pos: Mem res group, Oak Ridge Nat Lab, 50-51; vis scientist, Atomic Energy Res Estab, Eng, 69. Mem: Am Chem Soc; Sigma Xi. Res: Analytical chemistry of zirconium and hafnium; organic analytical reagents; radiochemistry. Mailing Add: 894 W Outer Dr Oak Ridge TN 37830-4898

HAHN, RICHARD DAVID, INTERNAL MEDICINE. Current Pos: Asst prof, Sch Med, Johns Hopkins Univ, 48-70, asst prof, Sch Hyg & Pub Health, 51-58, assoc prof pub health admin, 58-68, ASSOC PROF INTERNAL MED, SCH MED, JOHNS HOPKINS UNIV, 70- Personal Data: b Baltimore, Md, Sept 5, 12; c 2. Educ: Johns Hopkins Univ, AB, 32, MD, 36; Am Bd Internal Med, dipl. Concurrent Pos: Physician, Johns Hopkins Hosp, 47-; med consult, Social Security Admin, 61-; med dir, Baltimore Life Ins Co, 71-80. Mailing Add: 10533 Stevenson Rd Stevenson MD 21153

HAHN, RICHARD LEONARD, NUCLEAR CHEMISTRY, SOLAR NEUTRINO PHYSICS. Current Pos: res assoc nuclear chem, 60-62, chemist, group leader, 87-94, SR CHEMIST/GROUP LEADER, BROOKHAVEN NAT LAB, 94- Personal Data: b New York, NY, May 25, 34; m 56, Sheila Thomas; c Sharyn Kaly, Jill (McAfee) & Pamela (Feigin). Educ: Brooklyn Col, BS, 55; Columbia Univ, MA, 56, PhD(chem), 60. Honors & Awards: Radiation Indust Award, Am Nuclear Soc, 77. Prof Exp: Chemist, Oak Ridge Nat Lab, 62-74, dir transuranium res lab & sect head nuclear chem, chem div, 74-84, sr chemist, 84-87. Concurrent Pos: Vis scientist, Inst Nuclear Physics, Orsay, France, 72-73; Lawrence Berkeley Lab, 74-79 & 84-87, GSI Soc Heavy Ion Res, Darmstadt, Ger, 79 & Lawrence Livermore Nat Lab, 84-87;

mem, Transplutonium Prog Comt, US Dept Energy, 75-80; secy, Am Chem Soc, Div Nuclear Chem & Technol, 78-80, vchmn, 81, chmn, 82; vis scholar, Southwestern Univ, Georgetown, Tex, 83; mem vis comt Isotopes & Nuclear Chem Div, Los Alamos Nat Lab, 84-86, mem int Gallex exp & vis scientist, Gran Sasso Nat Lab, Italy, 86-, vchmn Nuclear Radiochem comt, Nat Res Coun, 87-90; chmn, 90-93; mem, SNO exp & vis scientist, Sudbury Newtrine Observ, Can, 96-. *Mem:* Am Phys Soc; Am Chem Soc; Sigma Xi. *Res:* Solar neutrino research; structures and interactions of ions in solutions; search for and characterization of new elements and radioactive isotopes; co-discoverer of 22 isotopes; nuclear reactions; nuclear fission; scattering with neutrons and synchrotron radiation; chemistry and physics of transuranium elements. *Mailing Add:* Chem Dept Brookhaven Nat Lab Upton NY 11973-5000. *Fax:* 516-344-5815; *E-Mail:* hahn1@bnl.gov

HAHN, RICHARD RAY, AGRICULTURAL ENGINEERING, ADMINISTRATION. *Current Pos:* HEAD, DEPT GRAIN SCI, KANS STATE UNIV, 92- *Personal Data:* b Rapid City, SDak, July 12, 30; m 53, Joan Fager; c David H, Carol L, Donald R & Kathleen J. *Educ:* Bethany Col, BS, 52; Kans State Univ, MS, 54, PhD, 57. *Prof Exp:* Staff, Harvest Queen Mills, 56-67; vpres res & develop, A E Staley Mfg Co, 67-87; asst to dean agr, Univ Ill, Urbana, 87-89; dir, Kans Agr Value Added Processing Ctr, 89-92. *Concurrent Pos:* Consult, Agr Processing & Technol Mgt. *Mem:* Inst Food Technol; Am Asn Cereal Chemists (pres, 88-89). *Mailing Add:* Kans State Univ 202 Shellenberger Hall Manhattan KS 66506-2200

HAHN, ROBERT S(IMPSON), COMPUTER SCIENCE, MECHANICAL ENGINEERING. *Current Pos:* PRES, HAHN ENG INC, 79- *Personal Data:* b New York, NY, Nov 1, 16; m 41; c 3. *Educ:* Univ Cincinnati, ME, 40, MSc, 42, DSc(appl physics), 44. *Honors & Awards:* Am Soc Mech Engrs Medal, 81; Lifetime Achievement Award, Am Soc Prof Engrs, 96. *Prof Exp:* Res Engr, Hearld Div, Cincinnati-Milacron, Worcester, 44-79. *Concurrent Pos:* Consult, 71-79. *Mem:* Nat Acad Eng; Am Soc Mech Engrs; Soc Mfg Engrs; Int Inst Prod Eng Res. *Res:* Lubrication; metal cutting; vibration; dampers to prevent tool vibration during metal cutting; thin lubricating films; high production grinding technology; computer control of machine tools. *Mailing Add:* 160 Southbridge St Auburn MA 01501. *Fax:* 508-752-8803

HAHN, ROGER C, ORGANIC CHEMISTRY. *Current Pos:* asst prof, 65-71, ASSOC PROF CHEM, SYRACUSE UNIV, 71- *Personal Data:* b Cleveland, Ohio, Feb 20, 32; m 62, 85; c 3. *Educ:* Oberlin Col, AB, 53; Ohio State Univ, PhD(org chem), 60. *Prof Exp:* From asst prof to assoc prof chem, Univ SDak, 60-63; NIH fel, Univ Wis, 63-65. *Mem:* Am Chem Soc. *Res:* Homogeneous nucleophile exchange; asymmetric synthesis; synthesis methods. *Mailing Add:* Chem Dept 1-014 CST Syracuse Univ Syracuse NY 13244-4100

HAHN, RUSSELL H, STANDARDS DEVELOPMENT, TECHNICAL SOCIETY ADMINISTRATION. *Current Pos:* DIR STAND & TECH SERVS, AM SOC AGR ENGRS, 67- *Personal Data:* b Youngstown, Ohio, July 15, 35; m 57, Anne Porter; c Russell H, R Michael & Gary D. *Educ:* Ohio State Univ, BAE & MS, 59. *Prof Exp:* Instr, US Army Engrs Sch, 59; proj engr, O M Scott & Sons Co, 60-67. *Concurrent Pos:* Opers officer, US Army Res Ord Battalion, 60-67; secy, comt Stand policy, Am Soc Agr Engrs, 67-; chmn, Stand & Tech Opers Comt, Coun Eng & Sci Soc Execs, 78-80 & 88-90; mem, Stand & Data Servs Comt, Am Nat Stand Inst, 93-; dir, Stand Eng Soc, 94. *Mem:* Am Soc Agr Engrs; Stand Eng Soc; Nat Soc Prog Engrs; Sigma Xi; Coun Eng & Sci Soc Execs. *Res:* Engineering practices and data for agricultural machinery and systems. *Mailing Add:* 815 Oakridge Dr St Joseph MI 49085-3318. *Fax:* 616-429-3852; *E-Mail:* hahn@asae.org

HAHN, SAMUEL WILFRED, MATHEMATICS. *Current Pos:* chmn dept math, Wittenberg Univ, 61-67 & 76-77, assoc dean, 63-65, prof, 60-83, EMER PROF MATH, WITTENBERG UNIV, 83- *Personal Data:* b Columbia, SC, Mar 21, 21; m 47, Martha Strowd; c Stephen S, Dale B & Carol H (Cooper). *Educ:* Lenoir Rhyne Col, AB, 41; Duke Univ, MA, 42, PhD(math), 48. *Honors & Awards:* Cert Meritorious Serv, Math Asn Am. *Prof Exp:* Instr math, Univ Mich, 47-49; asst prof, Wittenberg Univ, 49-51; prof & head dept math, Winthrop Col, 51-59; prof math, Hampden-Sydney Col, 59-60. *Concurrent Pos:* Bd gov, Math Asn Am, 79-82; vis prof, Wake Forest Univ, 83-84, Washington & Lee Univ, 84-85 & SDak Sch Mines & Technol, 85-86, Calif Lutheran Univ, 86-87. *Mem:* Am Math So; Math Asn Am. *Res:* Statistical methods; computer use in teaching undergraduate mathematics. *Mailing Add:* 1019 Redbud Lane Springfield OH 45504-1547

HAHN, THEODORE JOHN, OSTEOPOROSIS. *Current Pos:* ASST CHIEF ENDOCRINOL, VET ADMIN MED CTR & SCH MED, UNIV CALIF, LOS ANGELES, 83- *Educ:* Johns Hopkins Univ, MD, 64. *Mailing Add:* Dept Geriat Wadsworth Va Med Ctr Grecc (W-11G) Wilshire & Sawtelle Blvds Los Angeles CA 90073. *Fax:* 310-268-4842

HAHN, W(ALTER) C(HARLES), JR, metallurgy; deceased, see previous edition for last biography

HAHN, WALTER I, NEUTRON ACTIVATION ANALYSIS. *Current Pos:* RETIRED. *Personal Data:* b Korea, Nov 10, 23; US citizen; m 54; c 2. *Educ:* Seoul Nat Univ, BS, 54; Fla State Univ, MS, 60, PhD(physics), 62. *Prof Exp:* Instr physics, Seoul Nat Univ, 55-58; fel nuclear eng, Univ Fla, 63-64; asst prof physics, State Univ NY, Fredonia, 64-69; prof physics eng, Benedict Col, 70-, dir, 76- *Concurrent Pos:* Prin investr, Minority Biomed Support Prog, NIH, 78- *Mem:* Am Phys Soc. *Res:* Neutron activation analysis of trace elements; analysis of air particulates. *Mailing Add:* PO Box 8342 Columbia SC 29202

HAHN, WALTER LEOPOLD, POLYMER CHEMISTRY. *Current Pos:* sr res chemist, 56-60, RES ASSOC, BENGER LAB, E I DU PONT DE NEMOURS & CO, INC, 60- *Personal Data:* b Duermentigen, Ger, May 1, 26; US citizen; m 50; c 5. *Educ:* Univ Freiburg, dipl, 50, Dr rer nat, 52. *Prof Exp:* Asst lectr chem, State Res Inst Macromolecular Chem, Freiburg, 50-52, asst prof, 52-56. *Concurrent Pos:* Assoc prof, Univ Notre Dame, 70. *Mem:* Am Chem Soc. *Res:* Vinyl polymerization; synthesis of monomers and polymers; kinetics of polymerization; initiators; textile fibers; graft and block copolymers; inorganic and semiorganic polymers; stereo-specific polymers; high temperature polymers; polyurethanes, elastomer products and fibers, safety and regulatory compliance. *Mailing Add:* 1223 Hollins Rd Waynesboro VA 22980

HAHN, WILLIAM EUGENE, MOLECULAR BIOLOGY, CELL BIOLOGY. *Current Pos:* from asst prof to assoc prof, 68-78, PROF ANAT, MED SCH, UNIV COLO, DENVER, 78- *Personal Data:* b Greeley, Colo, June 11, 37; m 57; c 2. *Educ:* Univ Idaho, BS, 60; Tex Tech Univ, MS, 62; Tulane Univ, PhD(cell biol), 65. *Prof Exp:* Res asst prof molecular endocrinol, Univ Wash, 65-68. *Concurrent Pos:* NIH career development award, Med Sch, Univ Colo, Denver. *Mem:* AAAS; Am Soc Cell Biol; Soc Neurosci; Am Asn Anat; Sigma Xi. *Res:* Genetic expression in development of embryos; genomic structure and complexity; RNA synthesis and hormone action; genetic expression in brain and other organs; biogenesis of messenger RNA. *Mailing Add:* Dept Cellular & Struct Biol Univ Colo Sch Med 4200 E Ninth Ave Denver CO 80262-0001. *Fax:* 303-270-4729

HAHN, YU HAK, QUANTUM OPTICS. *Current Pos:* PRES & CHIEF RES EXEC, CVI LASER CORP, 73- *Personal Data:* b Seoul, Korea, Mar 13, 34; US citizen; m 67; c 2. *Educ:* Ky Wesleyan Col, BS, 58; WVa Univ, MS, 61; Pa State Univ, PhD(physics), 67. *Prof Exp:* Asst prof physics, Slippery Rock State Col, 62-64; sr physicist, Bausch & Lomb Co, 67-69; pres, Laser Energy Inc, 70-73. *Mem:* Am Phys Soc; Sigma Xi. *Res:* Quantum optics, especially thin film optics for high power lasers. *Mailing Add:* 200 Dorado Pl SE Albuquerque NM 87123

HAHN, YUKAP, THEORETICAL PHYSICS. *Current Pos:* from asst prof to assoc prof, 65-73, PROF PHYSICS, UNIV CONN, 73- *Personal Data:* b Seoul, Korea, July 28, 32; m 56; c 3. *Educ:* Univ Southern Calif, BA, 56; Yale Univ, MS, 58, PhD(physics), 62. *Prof Exp:* Assoc res scientist physics, NY Univ, 61-65. *Mem:* Am Phys Soc. *Res:* Theory of hyperfine structure and corrections in one and two electron atoms; bounds on the inverse reactance matrix in reaction theory; scattering theory and rearrangement processes; asymptotic behavior in quantum field theory; plasma physics. *Mailing Add:* Dept Physics Univ Conn Storrs CT 06268

HAHNE, ROLF MATHIEU AUGUST, ENVIRONMENTAL HEALTH MANAGEMENT, INDUSTRIAL HYGIENE. *Current Pos:* FAC MEM, DEPT ENVIRON HEALTH, UNIV WASH, 96- *Personal Data:* b Seattle, Wash, Oct 8, 36; m 64; c 2. *Educ:* Stanford Univ, BS, 58; Columbia Univ, AM, 59; Univ Wis, PhD(phys chem), 64. *Prof Exp:* Sci assoc nuclear chem, Nuclear Res Ctr, Julich, Ger, 64-65; asst prof chem, Wittenberg Univ, 65-69 & Kalamazoo Col, 69-72; chief chemist, Kennedy Space Ctr, Pan Am World Airways, 72-74; asst dir Univ Hygienic Lab, Univ Iowa, 74-83; res leader & res assoc health & environ sci, Dow Chem Co, 83-96. *Concurrent Pos:* Am Chem Soc Petrol Res Fund grant, 67-69; vis fel, Radiation Res Lab, AEC, 70; sci assoc, Nuclear Res Ctr, Julich, Ger, 71-72; US Dept Energy grant, 77-80, US Environ Protection Agency grant, 83. *Mem:* AAAS; Am Indust Hyg Asn; Am Chem Soc; Am Acad Indust Hyg. *Res:* Industrial hygiene chemistry. *Mailing Add:* Dept Environ Health Univ Wash Box 357234 Seattle WA 98195-7234

HAHNEL, ALWIN, electronics engineering, for more information see previous edition

HAHNERT, WILLIAM FRANKLIN, INVERTEBRATE ZOOLOGY. *Current Pos:* from asst prof to prof, 34-68, chmn dept, 41-67, EMER PROF ZOOL, OHIO WESLEYAN UNIV, 68- *Personal Data:* b Logansport, Ind, Oct 6, 01; m 28; c 1. *Educ:* DePaul Univ, AB, 27, Johns Hopkins Univ, PhD(zool), 31. *Prof Exp:* Nat Res Coun fel biol, Johns Hopkins Univ, Univ Pa & Marine Biol Lab, Woods Hole, 31-33. *Concurrent Pos:* Vis prof, Stone Lab, Ohio State Univ, 39-48 & 56-58; adminr, Ohio Biol Surv, 68-72. *Mem:* AAAS; Am Soc Zoologists; Soc Syst Zool; Am Soc Limnol & Oceanog; Sigma Xi. *Res:* Invertebrate faunistic studies. *Mailing Add:* 95 Elizabeth St No 212 Delaware OH 43015

HAHS, SHARON K, COORDINATION CHEMISTRY, SCIENCE EDUCATION. *Current Pos:* DEAN HUMANITIES & SCI, UNIV SC, 84- *Personal Data:* b Washington, Ind, Sept 12, 47; m 69; c 2. *Educ:* Ill Wesleyan Univ, BA, 70; Univ NMex, MS, 72, PhD(inorg chem), 74. *Prof Exp:* Prof chem, Metrop State Col, 74-84. *Mem:* Am Chem Soc; Nat Sci Teacher's Asn. *Res:* Transition metal coordination chemistry; educational research in teaching strategies with special emphasis on Piaget's theories of cognitive development. *Mailing Add:* Southern Ill Univ Box 1608 Edwardsville IL 62026

HAI, CHI-MING, CARDIOVASCULAR PHYSIOLOGY, MATHEMATICAL MODELING IN PHYSIOLOGY. *Current Pos:* ASST PROF PHYSIOL, BROWN UNIV, PROVIDENCE, 88- *Personal Data:* b Hong Kong, June 30, 55; c 1. *Educ:* Univ Toronto, BSc, 78; Univ Ottawa, MSc, 80; Johns Hopkins Univ, PhD(physiol), 84. *Prof Exp:* Fel physiol, Univ

Va, Charlottesville, 84-87, instr, 87-88. *Mem:* Am Physiol Soc; Biophys Soc; AAAS. *Res:* Understanding the regulation of smooth muscle contraction at the levels of cytosolic calcium, crossbridge phosphorylation, crossbridge mechanics and force generation. *Mailing Add:* Sect Physiol & Biophys Div Biol & Med Brown Univ PO Box G-B316 Providence RI 02912. *Fax:* 401-863-1222

HAI, FRANCIS, HIGH VOLTAGE TECHNOLOGY. *Current Pos:* mem tech staff, 69-81, RES SCIENTIST & SECT MGR, AEROSPACE CORP, 81- *Personal Data:* b Los Angeles, Calif, July 30, 37; m 71; c 2. *Educ:* Univ Calif, Los Angeles, BA, 60, MA, 61, PhD(physics), 69. *Prof Exp:* Physicist, Rocketdyne, NAm Rockwell Inc, 61-63. *Mem:* Inst Elec & Electronics Engrs. *Res:* Partial discharge phenomena; high voltage effects in materials. *Mailing Add:* Aerospace Corp 2350 E El Segundo Blvd M2 248 El Segundo CA 90245

HAIBEL, GEORGE K, PHARMACOLOGY. *Current Pos:* LEADER, ANTIMICROBIOL DRUGS TEAM, 92- *Personal Data:* b Buffalo, NY, Sept 5, 46. *Educ:* Cornell Univ, DVM, 79. *Mailing Add:* HFV-133 New Animal Drug Eval Off Metro Park N2 7500 Standish Pl Rockville MD 20855

HAID, D(AVID) A(UGUSTUS), PROCESS DEVELOPMENT, GAS APPLICATIONS. *Current Pos:* Develop engr, Union Carbide, 57-58, engr, 58-61, superconductivity, 61-64, group leader, 64-68, supvr, 68-74, mgr prod eng, 74-76, mgr, New Bus Dept, 76-79, asst mgr, Gas Prod Develop, 79-84, ASSOC DIR, INDUST GASES DEVELOP, PRAXAIR INC, 84- *Personal Data:* b New York, NY, Apr 9, 36; m 63; c 7. *Educ:* Stevens Inst Technol, BS, 57; State Univ NY, Buffalo, MS, 65. *Mem:* AAAS; Am Soc Mech Engrs; Sigma Xi; Am Soc Metals. *Res:* Arc welding, superconductivity, arc heating processes; applications of industrial gases to chemicals and materials processing. *Mailing Add:* Praxair Inc 777 Old Sawmill River Rd Tarrytown NY 10591-6714

HAIDAK, GERALD LEWIS, ANATOMY. *Current Pos:* assoc dean & assoc prof thoracic surg, 76-90, ASSOC DEAN & PROF SURG, PROF CELL BIOL & DISTINGUISHED PROF MED EDUC, UNIV MASS MED SCH, WORCESTER, MASS, 91- *Personal Data:* b Paterson, NJ, Mar 6, 17; m 37, Zelda Shapin; c 4. *Educ:* Chicago Med Sch, BS, 40, MD, 42; Univ Pa, MSc, 55. *Prof Exp:* From asst to prof anat, Albany Med Col, 56-76; dir med educ, St Luke's Hosp, 59-76. *Concurrent Pos:* Sr surgeon, Pittsfield Gen Hosp & St Luke's Hosp, 56-59; sr surgeon, Berkshire Med Ctr, 59-90, dir med educ, 76- *Mem:* AAAS; Hist Sci Soc; Am Asn Anat; Am Asn Am Med Cols; fel Am Col Surgeons; Am Asn Surg Anat. *Res:* Gross anatomy; early diagnosis of pulmonary neoplasm utilizing special techniques in bronchography; experimental emphysema. *Mailing Add:* Dept Surg Med Sch Univ Mass 55 Lake Ave N Worcester MA 01655

HAIDLER, WILLIAM B(ERNARD), NUCLEAR ENGINEERING, METALLURGY. *Current Pos:* FAC & CONSULT, INST PROF & CAREER DEVELOP, CENT MICH UNIV, 86- *Personal Data:* b Ann Arbor, Mich, July 11, 26; m 52, Frances H Hirt; c 4. *Educ:* US Naval Acad, BS, 50; NC State Col, MS, 57; Univ Ariz, PhD(nuclear eng), 64. *Prof Exp:* USAF, 57-, nuclear res officer, Propulsion Lab, Wright Air Develop Ctr, 57-59, asst div chief, 59-60, instr mech & gen physics, Air Force Acad, 60-61, asst prof physics & course dir, 61-62, gen physics, 64-65, assoc prof gen physics & dir prescribed physics courses, 65-66, assoc prof physics & dep head dept, 66-69, prof & head dept, 69-71; asst dir res & develop, Div Mil Appln, USAEC, 71-74; dean, Sch Systs & Logistics, USAF Inst Technol, 74-76; asst to pres tech progs, 76-78, dean, Sch Bus, 78-79, asst to pres eng progs, Southwestern Mich Col, 79-87; adj fac, Cent Mich Univ, ICPD, 82-93. *Mem:* Am Asn Physics Teachers; Am Nuclear Soc; Am Soc Eng Educ; Am Asn Univ Professors; Sigma Xi. *Res:* Achievement testing in general physics; high temperature space energy conversion systems for auxiliary power; influence of nuclear reactor radiations on ceramic material; national-international energy requirements and implications; systems analysis. *Mailing Add:* 1055 Joliet Dr Niles MI 49120

HAIG, FRANK RAWLE, THEORETICAL PHYSICS. *Current Pos:* PROF PHYSICS, LOYOLA COL, 87- *Personal Data:* b Philadelphia, Pa, Sept 11, 28. *Educ:* Woodstock Col, AB, 52, STB, 59, STL, 61; Bellarmine Col, PhL, 53; Cath Univ Am, PhD(physics), 59. *Hon Degrees:* LHD, State Univ NY Onondaga Commun Col. *Prof Exp:* Asst prof physics, Wheeling Col, 63-66, pres, 66-72; from asst prof to assoc prof, Loyola Col, 72-81; pres, Lemoyne Col, 81-87. *Concurrent Pos:* NSF fel, Univ Rochester, 62-63; vis fel, Johns Hopkins Univ, 72. *Mem:* Am Phys Soc; Am Asn Physics Teachers. *Res:* Theoretical physics; relativistic astrophysics. *Mailing Add:* Dept Physics Loyola Col 4501 N Charles St Baltimore MD 21210-2699. *Fax:* 410-617-2646; *E-Mail:* haig@loyola.edu

HAIG, JANET, biosystematics; deceased, see previous edition for last biography

HAIG, PIERRE VAHE, RADIATION ONCOLOGY, NUCLEAR MEDICINE. *Current Pos:* RETIRED. *Personal Data:* b Lebanon, Sept 24, 17; US citizen; m 48, Alice Jernazian; c Helen, Mari & Theodore. *Educ:* Occidental Col, AB, 38; Univ Southern Calif, MD, 43; Am Bd Radiol, dipl, 50; Am Bd Nuclear Med, dipl, 57. *Honors & Awards:* Medallion in Nuclear Med, Am Bd Radiol, 57; Service Award, Am Cancer Soc, 76. *Prof Exp:* From instr to clin prof therapeut radiol, Sch Med, Univ Southern Calif, 49-92; from instr to assoc clin prof, Sch Med, Loma Linda Univ, 52-68; dir, Radiother Dept, St Jude Hosp, 70-90; clin prof therapeut radiol, Sch Med, Univ Southern Calif, 84-92. *Concurrent Pos:* Chief therapeut radiologist, Los Angeles Co Gen Hosp, 50-67; radiologist, Good Hope Med Found, 50-67; consult, Long Beach Vet Admin Hosp, 53-80; mem staff, White Mem Med Ctr, 57-71; radiation therapist, Southern Calif Permanente Med Group, 67-70; physician specialist, Orange Co Med Ctr, 67-74; mem, Med Qual Rev Comt, State Calif, 84-93. *Mem:* Soc Nuclear Med; AMA; fel Am Col Radiol; Radiol Soc NAm. *Mailing Add:* 220 Monarch Bay Dana Point CA 92629. *Fax:* 714-499-2045

HAIG, THOMAS O, METEOROLOGY, SPACE SCIENCE. *Current Pos:* SR SCIENTIST, SONICRAFT CORP, CHICAGO, ILL, 79- *Personal Data:* b Ypsilanti, Mich, June 12, 21; m 46; c 5. *Educ:* Univ Ill, Urbana-Champaign, BS, 55; George Washington Univ, MS, 66. *Prof Exp:* Mgr simulation, Gen Elec Co, Valley Forge, 68-69, mgr advan manned space systs, 69-70; exec dir, Space Sci & Eng Ctr, Univ Wis-Madison, 70-79. *Concurrent Pos:* Res mgt consult, 79- *Mem:* Am Meteorol Soc; Sigma Xi. *Res:* Management and direction of space related scientific and operational research programs. *Mailing Add:* 4558 Hwy 78 Black Earth WI 53515

HAIGH, WILLIAM E, MATHEMATICS. *Current Pos:* Assoc prof, 63-73, chmn, Dept Mat, Nat Sci & Health Prof, 78-82, PROF MATH, NORTHERN STATE UNIV, SDAK, 83- *Personal Data:* b Huron, SDak, Nov 6, 37; m 56, 76, Patricia Honecker; c Pamela, Mark & Lisa. *Educ:* Huron Col, SDak, BS, 59; Univ NDak, MS, 63; Ind Univ, EdD, 70. *Mem:* Math Asn Am; Nat Coun Teachers Math; Sch Sci & Math Asn. *Res:* Mathematics education; differential equations; analysis; computer education. *Mailing Add:* Dept Math Northern State Univ Aberdeen SD 57401. *E-Mail:* haighw@wolf.northern.edu

HAIGHT, FRANK AVERY, APPLIED MATHEMATICS. *Current Pos:* ADJ PROF, UNIV CALIF IRVINE, 88- *Personal Data:* b Des Moines, Iowa, Sept 28, 19; m 69; c 2. *Educ:* Univ Iowa, BA, 40, MSc, 41; Univ NZ, PhD(math), 57. *Prof Exp:* Res analyst gen hqs, US Army, Tokyo, Japan, 46-48; sr lectr math, Univ Auckland, 48-57; assoc res mathematician, Univ Calif, Los Angeles, 57-63, res mathematician, 63-69; prof statist & transp, Pa State Univ, 69-88. *Concurrent Pos:* Hon res assoc, Univ London, 56; consult, Rand Corp, 56; Fulbright prof, Royal Inst Tech, Sweden, 62-63. *Res:* Distribution theory; probability models for road traffic, queueing, transportation, accidents; stochastic processes. *Mailing Add:* Inst Transp Studies Univ Calif Irvine CA 92697. *E-Mail:* fhaight@translab.its.uci.edu

HAIGHT, GILBERT PIERCE, JR, INORGANIC CHEMISTRY, SCIENCE EDUCATION. *Current Pos:* prof, 66-87, EMER PROF CHEM, UNIV ILL, URBANA, 87- *Personal Data:* b Seattle, Wash, June 8, 22; m 46, Shirley Grapek; c Jennifer L, Loisanne F, Charlene E (deceased), Charles P, Stephanie L (Kuntze) & Christopher (deceased). *Educ:* Stanford Univ, AB, 43; Princeton Univ, PhD(chem), 47. *Honors & Awards:* Dodge lectr, Franklin Inst, 59; Award in CHem Educ, MCA, 76 & Am Chem Soc, 79. *Prof Exp:* Res assoc chem, Manhattan Proj, Princeton Univ, 43-46; Rhodes scholar, Oxford Univ, 47-48; asst prof chem, Univ Hawaii, 48-49; George Washington Univ, 49-52; Univ Kans, 52-54; assoc prof chem, Swarthmore Col, 54-65; prof chem, Tex A&M Univ, 65-66. *Concurrent Pos:* Consult, US Bur Entom, Honolulu, 48, Naval Res Lab, 51-52 & Stand Oil Co Ind, 53; prof phys & inorg chem, Wagner Free Inst Sci, 55-59; vis prof, Tech Univ Denmark, 60-61; Petrol Res Found fac fel, 65; vis prof, Colo Col, 72; vis scientist, Univ Calif, San Diego, 74-75; vis fel, Australian Nat Univ, 81-82; mem, Int Active Coop Prog-Malaysia, ITM-Midwest Univs Consortium, 86; affil prof chem, Univ Wash, 89- *Mem:* AAAS; Am Chem Soc; Am Asn Univ Profs; Sigma Xi. *Res:* Chemistry of solutions; mechanisms of substitution and oxidation-reduction of oxy-ions; model enzyme systems. *Mailing Add:* 10798 Manitou Park Blvd Bainbridge Island WA 98110. *E-Mail:* haight@macmail.chem.washington.edu

HAIGHT, JOHN RICHARD, NEUROBIOLOGY. *Current Pos:* RETIRED. *Personal Data:* b Chicago, Ill, Sept 8, 38; m 67; c 3. *Educ:* NCent Col, BA, 64; Mich State Univ, MS, 68, PhD(zool), 71. *Prof Exp:* Lectr, Univ Tazmania, 71-74, sr lectr anat, 74-80, reader in anat, 81-, head, Dept Anat, 84- *Concurrent Pos:* Sr res fel, Res Sch Biol Sci, Australian Nat Univ, 80-83. *Mem:* Am Asn Anat; Am Soc Zoologists; Anat Soc Australia & NZ (secy, 75-80); Australian Mammal Soc; Australian Neurosci Soc. *Res:* Evolutionary and comparative functional morphology of mammalian nervous systems. *Mailing Add:* 187 Channels Hwy Tiroona Tas 7001 Australia

HAIGHT, ROBERT CAMERON, NUCLEAR PHYSICS, NUCLEAR ENGINEERING. *Current Pos:* PHYSICIST NUCLEAR PHYSICS, LOS ALAMOS NAT LAB, 85- *Personal Data:* b Ann Arbor, Mich, May 27, 41; m 70; c 2. *Educ:* Yale Univ, BA, 63; Princeton Univ, MS, 65, PhD(physics), 69. *Prof Exp:* Fel & instr nuclear physics, Univ Pittsburgh, 68-70; fel, Los Alamos Sci Lab, 70-72; physicist nuclear physics, Lawrence Livermore Lab, 72-85. *Concurrent Pos:* Mem, subcomt controlled thermonuclear res, US Nuclear Data Comt, 74-76; mem, Nuclear Data Comt, US Dept Energy, 79-85; adv, Int Nuclear Data Comt, 81- *Mem:* Fel Am Phys Soc; AAAS. *Res:* Nuclear physics; neutron interactions; reaction mechanisms; few-body problems; coulomb excitation. *Mailing Add:* MS-H803 LANL Group P-23 Los Alamos NM 87545

HAIGHT, ROBERT E, AGRICULTURAL ENGINEERING. *Current Pos:* RETIRED. *Personal Data:* b David City, Nebr, Jan 24, 31; m, Jean; c Ronald, James & Laurie. *Educ:* Univ Nebr, BSc, 53. *Honors & Awards:* Cyrus Hall McCormick Jerome Increase Case Gold Medal Award, Am Soc Agr Engrs, 95. *Prof Exp:* Staff, Lincoln Steel Works, 50-53; staff, John Deere Prod Eng, 53, eng trainee, 53-55, gen developer, 55-60, proj leader, 70-77, proj mgr, 77-86, sr proj engr, 86-93. *Mem:* Am Soc Agr Engrs; Soc Automotive Engrs. *Mailing Add:* 2760 Edgemont Ave Waterloo IA 50702

HAIGHT, ROGER DEAN, MICROBIOLOGY, BIOCHEMISTRY. *Current Pos:* from asst to assoc prof, 66-74, PROF MICROBIOL, SAN JOSE STATE UNIV, 74- *Personal Data:* b David City, Nebr, Mar 12, 36; m 64; c 1. *Educ:* Univ Nebr, BS, 59, MS, 61; Ore State Univ, PhD(marine microbiol), 65. *Prof Exp:* Fel, NIH, Torry Res Sta, Aberdeen, Scotland, 65-66. *Concurrent Pos:* Grant, Brown-Hazen Fund, 67- & NASA educ consortium, 70- *Mem:* AAAS; Am Soc Microbiol. *Res:* Microbial physiology; thermal injury phenomena in microorganisms. *Mailing Add:* Dept Microbiol San Jose State Univ One Washington Sq San Jose CA 95192-0001

HAIGHT, THOMAS H, BOTANY, BIOMETRICS-BIOSTATISTICS. *Current Pos:* From asst prof to assoc prof, 69-80, PROF BIOL, FRAMINGHAM STATE COL, 80- *Personal Data:* b Poynette, Wis, Nov 3, 36; m 66. *Educ:* Carroll Col, BS, 58; Syracuse Univ, MS, 65, PhD(bot), 69. *Mem:* Can Soc Plant Physiol; Am Soc Mort Sci; AAAS. *Res:* Morphogenesis in cultured fern fronds. *Mailing Add:* 483 Edgell Rd Framingham MA 01701

HAIGLER, HENRY JAMES, SR, NEUROPHARMACOLOGY. *Current Pos:* VIS ASSOC PROF, DEPT PHARMACODYNAMICS, UNIV ILL, CHICAGO, 90- *Personal Data:* b Columbia, SC, July 23, 41; m 64; c 2. *Educ:* Wake Forest Univ, BS, 63; Bowman Gray Sch Med, Wake Forest Univ, PhD(physiol), 69. *Honors & Awards:* Magistral lectr, Headache 80 Neurol Cong, WHO, Florence, Italy, 80. *Prof Exp:* Trainee neurophysiol, Ment Health Res Inst, Univ Mich, 69-71; res assoc neuropharmacol, Sch Med, Yale Univ, 71-74; from asst prof to assoc prof pharmacol, Emory Univ, 74-80, dir grad studies, Dept Pharmacol, 80-82; sect head, Searle Res & Develop, CNS Pharmacol, G D Searle & Co, 82-87; mgr res & develop neurodiag, Abbott Labs, 87-90. *Concurrent Pos:* Ad hoc mem, Neurol Sci Study Sect, 80 & Aging Rev Comt, 80. *Mem:* Soc Neurosci (pres, 81-82); Am Soc Pharmacol & Exp Therapeut; AAAS. *Res:* Site and mechanism of action of narcotic analgesic drugs; effect of morphine and met-enkephalin administered directly, using the technique of microiontophoresis, on neuronal activity evoked by a nociceptive stimulus; development and evaluation of a post-mortem diagnostic assay for Alzheimer's disease; behavioral effects of neurotropic drugs; site and mechanism of action of lysergic acid diethylamide; analgesic effects of dimethyl sulfoxide. *Mailing Add:* NIMH, NIH 5600 Fishers Lane Rm 17-C26 Rockville MD 20857-0001. *Fax:* 301-443-3225

HAIK, GEORGE MICHEL, ophthalmology; deceased, see previous edition for last biography

HAIL, J MICHAEL, OCEANOGRAPHY. *Current Pos:* DIR GLOBAL PROGS, NAT OCEANOG & ATMOSPHERIC ADMIN, 86- *Personal Data:* b Lusk, Wyo, May 28, 43. *Educ:* Rice Univ, BS, 65; Univ Wash, MS, 68, PhD(phys oceanog), 71. *Mailing Add:* Nat Oceanog Atmospheric Admin 110 Wayne Ave Rm 1210 Silver Spring MD 20910-5603

HAILE, CLARENCE LEE, ENVIRONMENTAL CHEMISTRY, ANALYTICAL CHEMISTRY. *Current Pos:* from assoc chemist to sr chemist, Midwest Res Inst, 57-80, prin chemist, 80-85, sect head, 85-88, DEPT MGR, MIDWEST RES INST, 88- *Personal Data:* b Odess, Mo, Aug 9, 48; m 70. *Educ:* Cent Mo State Univ, BS, 70; Univ Wis, MS, 72, PhD(water chem), 77. *Prof Exp:* Res asst, Univ Wis, 73-75. *Concurrent Pos:* Treas, 85-87, chmn elect, 88-, Div Environ Chem, Am Chem Soc. *Mem:* Am Chem Soc; Sigma Xi. *Res:* Emissions and environmental transformations of hazardous organic compounds; methods for sampling and analysis of trace organic contaminants in the environment. *Mailing Add:* Pace Analytical Serv Inc 9800 Kincey Ave Suite 100 Huntersville NC 28078-8415

HAILE, JAMES MITCHELL, MOLECULAR-SCALE COMPUTER SIMULATION, STATISTICAL MECHANICS. *Current Pos:* from asst prof to assoc prof, 76-84, PROF CHEM ENG, CLEMSON UNIV, 84- *Personal Data:* b Atlanta, Ga, Dec 7, 46; m 71; c 1. *Educ:* Vanderbilt Univ, BS, 68; Univ Fla, ME, 74, PhD(chem eng), 76. *Prof Exp:* Dept head chem eng, Univ Tulsa, 88-89. *Concurrent Pos:* Vis res assoc, Physics Dept, Univ Guelph, Ont, 75; vis scientist, Physics Dept, Chalk River Nat Lab, Ont, 82 & Inst Thermo & Fluid Dynamics, Rhur Univ, Bochum, WGer, 86; presidential young investr, NSF, 84; ed, Molecular Simulation, 86-90. *Mem:* Am Inst Chem Engrs; Am Phys Soc; Am Chem Soc; Hist Sci Soc; Sigma Xi. *Res:* Molecular-scale computer simulation of dense fluids; statistical mechanics; thermodynamics of fluid mixtures; classical nonlinear dynamics applied to many-body problems. *Mailing Add:* Chem Eng Dept Colo Sch Mines Golden CO 80401

HAILMAN, JACK PARKER, ETHOLOGY, ANIMAL COMMUNICATION. *Current Pos:* assoc prof, 69-73, PROF ZOOL, UNIV WIS-MADISON, 73- *Personal Data:* b St Louis, Mo, May 6, 36; m 58, Elizabeth B Davis; c Karl A & P Eric. *Educ:* Harvard Univ, AB, 59; Duke Univ, PhD(zool psychol), 64. *Prof Exp:* Fel, Nat Inst Ment Health, 64; instr animal behavior, Rutgers Univ, 64-66; hon res assoc, Vert Dept, Smithsonian Inst, 66-69; asst prof zool, Univ Md, 66-69. *Mem:* Fel AAAS; fel Animal Behavior Soc (pres, 81-82); Am Soc Naturalists; fel Am Ornith Union; fel Norweg Nat Acad. *Res:* Animal behavior; communication, sensory processes, ontogeny, sociality. *Mailing Add:* Dept Zool 145 Noland Hall Univ Wis-Madison 250 N Mills St Madison WI 53706-1794. *E-Mail:* jhailman@macc.wisc.edu

HAILPERN, RAOUL, MATHEMATICS. *Current Pos:* MATH DEPT, PARK SCH, NY, 58- *Personal Data:* b Alexandria, Egypt, July 19, 16; US citizen; m 38, Fanny Spectoroff; c Jocelyn & Doris. *Educ:* Univ London, BA, 54; Univ Buffalo, MA, 59, PhD(math), 62. *Prof Exp:* Bank exec, Barclays Bank, Egypt, 32-57, Eng, 57; from asst prof to prof lectr, Millard Fillmore Col, 63-89. *Concurrent Pos:* Ed dir, Math Asn Am, 67-87. *Mem:* Math Asn Am; Am Math Soc. *Res:* Calculus of finite differences; combinatorial analysis. *Mailing Add:* 63 Garden Ct Amherst NY 14226-3220

HAIM, ALBERT, INORGANIC MECHANISMS, REACTION KINETICS. *Current Pos:* assoc prof, 64-68, PROF CHEM, STATE UNIV NY, STONY BROOK, 68-, ASSOC ED, INORG CHEM, 89- *Personal Data:* b Paris, France, Mar 19, 31; US citizen; m 55; c 2. *Educ:* Univ Southern Calif, PhD(inorg chem), 60. *Prof Exp:* Res asst chem, Univ Southern Calif, 55-59, res assoc, 59-61; res assoc, Stanford Univ, 61-62; from asst prof to assoc prof, Pa State Univ, 62-64. *Concurrent Pos:* Sloan res fel, 65-67; vis chemist, Brookhaven Nat Lab, 65 & 66; Fulbright lectr, Fac Chem, Montevideo Univ, Uruguay, 67, 69, 70 & 78; lectr, Nova Univ, Lisbon, Portugal, 78 & Univ Neuch05tel, Switz, 80 & Univ Tucuman, Arg, 89. *Mem:* Am Chem Soc; Royal Soc Chem. *Res:* Kinetic and mechanistic studies with complex ions in solution; redox, substitution and photochemical reactions; inorganic free radicals in solution. *Mailing Add:* Dept Chem State Univ NY Stony Brook NY 11794h

HAIMES, FLORENCE CATHERINE, CHEMISTRY, HISTORY OF CHEMISTRY. *Current Pos:* RETIRED. *Personal Data:* b San Jose, Calif, June 10, 17. *Educ:* San Jose State Col, AB, 38; Stanford Univ, MA, 40, EdD, 52. *Prof Exp:* Asst, Stanford Univ, 39-40; teacher pub schs, Calif, 40-47; from asst prof to prof chem, San Francisco State Univ, 47-89. *Concurrent Pos:* Mem bd dirs, CACT, 69-81, pres, 68-69. *Mem:* Fel AAAS. *Res:* History of chemistry. *Mailing Add:* 785 Burnett Apt 10 San Francisco CA 94131

HAIMES, HOWARD B, electron microscopy, biochemical cytology, for more information see previous edition

HAIMES, YACOV Y, WATER RESOURCES, RISK MANAGEMENT. *Current Pos:* LAWRENCE R QUARLES PROF, SYSTS ENG & DIR, RISK MGT, UNIV VA, 87- *Personal Data:* b Baghdad, Iraq, June 18, 36; m 68; c 2. *Educ:* Hebrew Univ, Jerusalem, Israel, BS, 64; Univ Calif, Los Angeles, MS, 67, PhD(large scale systs), 70. *Honors & Awards:* Sigma Xi Distinguished Res Award, 76. *Prof Exp:* From asst prof to prof, systs & civil eng, Case Western Reserve Univ, 83-86, dir Water Resources Systs Eng Prog, 72-87, dir, Ctr large scale systs, 80- 84, chmn, Systs Eng, Case Western Reserve Univ, 83-86. *Concurrent Pos:* Jr petrol engr, Ministry Develop, Israel, 62-65, Res asst & res engr, Univ Calif, Los Angeles, 66-70; pres, Environ Systs Mgt, Inc, 74-, chmn, UNESCO/Int Hydrographic Prog, 80-87, mem, Bd Water Sci & Technol, Nat Res Coun, 82-84; chmn, Tech Adv Comt, Int Ground Water Modeling Ctr, Holcomb Res Inst, 85-88, Consult, Congr Off Technol Assessment, 77-89, Sci Adv Bd, Environ Protection Agency, 82- *Mem:* Fel Am Soc Civil Engrs; fel Inst Elec & Electronic Engrs; fel AAAS; fel Int Water Resources Asn; fel Am Water Resources Asn; Am Geophys Union; Oper Res Soc Am; Sigma Xi; Soc Risk Anal; Am Soc Eng Educ. *Res:* Study of large scale systems theory and methodology, with special emphasis on two areas, modeling and optimization involving multilevel hierarchies and multiple objectives, risk assessment and management; author or co-author of five books. *Mailing Add:* Dept Systs Eng Univ Va Thornton Charlottesville VA 22903

HAIMO, DEBORAH TEPPER, MATHEMATICAL ANALYSIS. *Current Pos:* chmn dept, 69-72 & 73-76, PROF MATH, UNIV MO-ST LOUIS, 68- *Personal Data:* b Odessa, Ukraine, July 1, 21; US citizen; m 44; c 5. *Educ:* Radcliffe Col, AB & AM, 43; Harvard Univ, PhD(math), 64. *Hon Degrees:* DSc, Franklin & Marshall Col, 91. *Prof Exp:* Actg head dept math, Lake Erie Col, 43-44; instr, Northeastern Univ, 44-45; lectr math, Wash Univ, 52-61; from lectr to assoc prof math, Southern Ill Univ, Edwardsville, 61-68. *Concurrent Pos:* Sci fac fel, 64-65; grant, NASA, 66-69, NSF, 69-71 & Air Force Off Sci Res, 71-74; mem sci team, US Support Grad Progs, Naval Nat Univ, 74; mem Inst Advan Study, Princeton, NJ, 72-73; NSF Teacher Enhancement grant, 88-91; mem, Harvard Bd Overseers, 90-95. *Mem:* Am Math Soc; Math Asn Am (pres, 91-93); Soc Indust & Appl Math; Asn Women Math; Sigma Xi. *Res:* Harmonic analysis; integral transforms. *Mailing Add:* PO Box 1483 Univ Calif San Diego La Jolla CA 92038-1483. *Fax:* 314-553-6336

HAIMO, LEAH T, CELL MOTILITY, CELL DIVISION. *Current Pos:* ASST PROF CELL BIOL, UNIV CALIF, RIVERSIDE, 80- *Educ:* Yale Univ, PhD(cell biol), 80. *Mailing Add:* Dept Biol Univ Calif Riverside 900 University Ave Riverside CA 92521-0001

HAIMOVICH, BEATRICE, BIOCHEMISTRY. *Current Pos:* Fel, Dept Biochem, 86-88, Dept Microbiol, 88-90, FEL, LAB JOAN BRUGGE, HOWARD HUGHES MED INST, UNIV PA, 90- *Personal Data:* b Romania, May 13, 58. *Educ:* Tel-Aviv Univ, Israel, BSc, 80; Univ Pa, PhD(biochem), 86. *Concurrent Pos:* NIH fel award, 86-87; Muscular Dystrophy Asn fel, 87-89. *Mem:* Am Soc Biol. *Res:* Signalling pathways activated as a result of interactions between extracellular matrix ligands and their specific cell surface receptors in two model systems; PC12 cells and platelets; involvement of integrins in transformation phenotypes induced by Rous sarcoma virus; analysis of the effects of treatment with cytochalasin D and or polyHEMA substrates on the stability of adhesion plaques and generation of transformation-like phenotypes; expression of avian beta-1 integrin and truncation mutants in mouse 3T3 cells; analysis of their function and distribution; generation of antibodies specific for the voltage-dependent sodium channels from rat skeletal muscle; identification of sodium channel sub-types in adult and in vivo and in vitro developing skeletal muscle using immunocytochemistry and pharmacological probes; numerous publications. *Mailing Add:* Dept Gen Surg UMDNJ-RW Johnson Med Sch 1 Robert Wood Johnson CN19 New Brunswick NJ 08903. *Fax:* 732-235-7079

HAIN, FRED PAUL, FOREST ENTOMOLOGY. *Current Pos:* res assoc, NC State Univ, 74-76, from asst prof to assoc prof, 76-85, chmn, Ecol Prog, 89-94, PROF ENTOM, NC STATE UNIV, 85- *Personal Data:* b Milwaukee, Wis, Nov 21, 44; m 73, Dianne Young; c Erika D & Ernst F. *Educ:* Stetson Univ, BS, 69; Duke Univ, MF, 69; Mich State Univ, PhD(entom), 72. *Prof Exp:* Entomologist II, Tex Forest Serv, 72; fel forest entom, Tex A&M Univ, 73-74. *Mem:* Entom Soc Am; Entom Soc Can; Sigma Xi; Soc Am Foresters. *Res:* Population studies on the southern pine beetle; population studies and control measures for insects and mites infesting Fraser fir; natural enemies of gypsy moth. *Mailing Add:* Dept Entom NC State Univ Box 7626 Raleigh NC 27695-7626

HAINDL, MARTIN WILHELM, HISTORY OF PHYSICS, TELECOMMUNICATIONS. *Current Pos:* from asst prof to assoc prof, 68-95, CHMN DEPT, 77-, PROF PHYSICS, JERSEY CITY STATE COL, 95-,. *Personal Data:* b Landshut, Ger, May 17, 40; US citizen; m 72, Priscilla Jean Putman; c Jennifer. *Educ:* Montclair State Univ, BS, 63, MA, 66; NY Univ, PhD(physics, sci educ), 72. *Prof Exp:* Teacher & coordr chem, Glen Rock High Sch, 63-68. *Concurrent Pos:* Consult, physics/phys sci edu. *Mem:* AAAS; Am Asn Physics Teachers; Am Phys Soc; Am Inst Physics. *Res:* History of physics; thermodynamics-structure of materials; physics education and instructional strategies, computer aided instruction; educational applications of telecommunications; physical principles of telecommunications. *Mailing Add:* Dept Physics Jersey City State Col 2039 Kennedy Memorial Blvd Jersey City NJ 07305-1527

HAINES, BERNARD A, PHARMACEUTICAL CHEMISTRY. *Current Pos:* RETIRED. *Personal Data:* b Phila, Pa, Apr 8, 26; m 57; c 2. *Educ:* Phila Col Pharm, BS, 53; Purdue Univ, MS, 58, PhD(phys pharm), 60. *Prof Exp:* Res assoc parenteral pharmaceut, Merck Sharp & Dohme Div, 54-55; sr res scientist, E R Squibb & Sons Div, Olin Mathieson Chem Corp, 60-65, sci coordr, Olin Int, 65-67, dir prod develop, 67-71, dir int regulatory affairs group, E R Squibb & Sons, Inc, 71-89. *Mem:* Am Pharmaceut Asn; Am Chem Soc. *Res:* Surface and colloidal chemistry. *Mailing Add:* 2001 Pheasant Lane Charlottesville VA 22901

HAINES, CHARLES WILLS, APPLIED MATHEMATICS, CONTROLS & VIBRATIONS. *Current Pos:* assoc prof math & mech eng, Rochester Inst Technol, 71-86, Asst Provost, 73-81, assoc dean eng, 82-90, PROF MATH & MECH ENG, ROCHESTER INST TECHNOL, 86-, MECH ENG DEPT HEAD, 90- *Personal Data:* b Philadelphia, Apr 14, 39; m 61, Carolyn H Anderson; c Marie J & Karen L. *Educ:* Earlham Col, AB, 61; Rensselaer Polytech Inst, MS, 63, PhD(appl math), 65. *Honors & Awards:* Centennial Medallion, Am Soc Eng Educ. *Prof Exp:* Instr math, Rensselaer Polytech Inst, 65-66; asst prof, Clarkson Col Technol, 66-71. *Concurrent Pos:* Consult, Xerox Corp, 76 & 77; rev panelist, NSF Sci Fac Prof Develop Prog, 78 & 80; panelist, Navy grad fel, 87-; projs bd, Am Soc Eng Educ. *Mem:* Soc Indust & Appl Math; Math Asn Am; Am Soc Eng Educ; Sigma Xi; Am Soc Mech Eng. *Res:* Stochastic eigenvalue problems; boundary value and eigenvalue problems in general; ordinary and partial differential equations; stochastic aircraft control problems. *Mailing Add:* Dept Mech Eng Rochester Inst Technol Rochester NY 14623. *Fax:* 716-475-7710; *E-Mail:* cwheme@rit.edu

HAINES, DANIEL WEBSTER, FORENSIC ENGINEERING, WOOD QUALITY. *Current Pos:* assoc dean eng, 87-89, PROF MECH ENG, MANHATTAN COL, 83-, CHAIR MECH ENG DEPT, 95- *Personal Data:* b Nashville, Tenn, Nov 8, 37; m 62, Brynne Levinson; c Gordon & Laurel. *Educ:* Rutgers Univ, BS, 59; Lehigh Univ, MS, 61; Columbia Univ, Eng ScD, 68. *Prof Exp:* Res asst civil eng, Lehigh Univ, 59-61; Peace Corps volunteer-teacher math & sci, Govt Col, Ibadan, Nigeria, 61-63; res asst eng mech, Columbia Univ, 64-68; Alfred P Sloan Found vis fel, Princeton Univ, 68-69; from asst prof to prof mech eng, Univ SC, 69-77; res engr, Ciba-Geigy Corp, 77-80, prod eng mgr, 80-81; prin, Midlantic Testing & Consult, 82-87. *Concurrent Pos:* Vis assoc prof, Stevens Inst Technol, 75-76; vis lectr, Yale Univ, 75-76; exec comt chmn, Tech Coun on Forensic Eng, Am Soc Civil Engr, 87-88; ed-in-chief, Cas J, 89-95. *Mem:* Am Soc Civil Eng; Am Soc Mech Eng; Catgut Acoust Soc. *Res:* Elastic wave propagation; vibrations of elastic solids; properties of musical instrument woods, varnishes and wood substitutes; violin and guitar acoustics; mechanics of composite materials; honeycomb sandwich panels; forensic engineering; wood quality. *Mailing Add:* 142 Greenridge Ave White Plains NY 10605

HAINES, DAVID CLARK, MATHEMATICS. *Current Pos:* asst prof, 69-78, ASSOC PROF MATH, BATES COL, 78-, CHMN DEPT, 79- *Personal Data:* b Youngstown, Ohio, Jan 30, 42; m 79. *Educ:* Col Wooster, BA, 64; Ohio State Univ, MSc, 67, PhD(math), 69. *Prof Exp:* Teaching asst math, Ohio State Univ, 64-67; instr, Iowa State Univ, 67-69. *Concurrent Pos:* Andrew W Mellon Found fel, 75; vis scholar, Mass Inst Technol, 77-78. *Mem:* Am Math Soc; Math Asn Am; Asn Comput Mach. *Res:* Theory of commutative rings, boolean rings and p-rings. *Mailing Add:* Dept Math Bates Col Lewiston ME 04240-6042

HAINES, DONALD ARTHUR, WILDFIRE METEOROLOGY. *Current Pos:* CONSULT METEOROLOGIST, HAINES WEATHER SERV, 90- *Personal Data:* b La Crosse, Wis; m, Sandra Krakower; c Mary Jo & Douglas. *Educ:* Univ Wis, BS, 58, MS, 61. *Honors & Awards:* Qual Res Medal, USDA Forest Serv, 84. *Prof Exp:* Res meteorologist satellite meteorol, Nat Environ Satellite Serv, US Dept Com, 61-65, Minn state climatologist, Nat Weather Serv, 65-68; prin res meterologist wildfire res, USDA Forest Serv, 68-89. *Concurrent Pos:* Instr, Dept Independent Study, Univ Fla, 92- *Mem:* Nat Weather Asn; Am Meteorol Soc (secy-treas, 69-70, vpres, 70-71 & treas, 82-84). *Res:* Assessment of the contributions of weather and climatic factors that lead to large or unusual wildfire occurrence and behavior; author of 70 publications. *Mailing Add:* PO Box 6046 Stuart FL 34997

HAINES, DUANE EDWIN, NEUROSCIENCE & NEUROANATOMY. *Current Pos:* PROF ANAT & CHMN, UNIV MISS MED CTR, 85- *Personal Data:* b Springfield, Ohio, May 4, 43; m 83, Gretchen; c Aaron & Kristian. *Educ:* Greenville Col, BA, 65; Mich State Univ, MS, 67, PhD(anat), 69. *Honors & Awards:* MacLachlan Award, WVa Univ, 83. *Prof Exp:* Instr, Mich State Univ, East Lansing, 68-69; asst prof, Med Col Va, 69-73; from assoc prof to prof anat, Sch Med, WVa Univ, 73-85. *Concurrent Pos:* Assoc, ed, J Med Primatol, 77-, Anat Rec, 85-; prin investr, Metab Brain Dis, NIH, 74-85; off historian, Cajal Club, 86-; auth. *Mem:* Am Asn Anatomists; Neurosci Soc; Int Bran Res Org; Fel Royal Anthrop Inst Gt Brit & Ireland; Cajal Club. *Res:* Comparative neuroanatomy of prosimian primates with an emphasis on cerebellar connections; relay nuclei and spinal pathways; research on the neurological bases for the evolution of upright locomotion in primates. *Mailing Add:* Dept Anat Univ Miss Med Ctr 2500 N State St Jackson MS 39216-4505. *Fax:* 601-984-1655

HAINES, HOWARD BODLEY, ZOOLOGY, PHYSIOLOGY. *Current Pos:* from asst to assoc prof, 64-73, PROF ZOOL, UNIV OKLA, 73- *Personal Data:* b Kansas City, Kans, Jan 15, 35; m 56. *Educ:* Univ Tex, BA, 58, MA, 59, PhD(zool), 61. *Prof Exp:* NIH fel, 61-63; instr zool, Duke Univ, 63-64. *Concurrent Pos:* Res grants, NSF, NIH, 65-78, NASA, 68-70, NIH, 80-83. *Mem:* Am Physiol Soc; Am Soc Zool; Sigma Xi. *Res:* Physiology of vertebrates which dwell in arid environments; water balance; metabolism. *Mailing Add:* Dept Zool Univ Okla 730 Van Vleet Oval Rm 222 Norman OK 73019-0001

HAINES, JOHN HALDOR, MYCOLOGY. *Current Pos:* SR SCIENTIST MYCOL, NY STATE MUS & SCI SERV, 69-; MYCOLOGIST, NY STATE BIOL SURV. *Personal Data:* b Aberdeen, Wash, Sept 17, 38; m 64; c 2. *Educ:* Univ Wash, BSc, 64, MSc, 67; Ore State Univ, PhD(mycol), 72. *Mem:* Mycol Soc Am. *Res:* Taxonomy of the Hyaloscyphaceae; identification of airborne fungus spores. *Mailing Add:* 5 Burhans Pl Delmar NY 12054

HAINES, KENNETH A, ENTOMOLOGY. *Current Pos:* RETIRED. *Personal Data:* b Pendleton, Ind, Mar 27, 07; m 36, Helen Evans; c Kenneth H & Thomas R. *Educ:* Purdue Univ, BS, 29; Ohio State Univ, MS, 31. *Prof Exp:* Field asst oriental fruit moth, Ohio Agr Exp Sta, 29-30; field asst codling moth, NJ Agr Exp Sta, 33; agent dutch elm dis eradication, Bur Entom & Plant Quarantine, NJ, Agr Res Serv, USDA, 34-38 & 39-40, entomologist pear psylla control, Wash, 41-47, entomologist, Div Gypsy Moth Control, Pa, 48 & Mass, 49-50, asst div leader, Div Cereal & Forage Insects, Washington, DC, 51-53, asst dir prog appraisal & internal audit, Agr Res Serv, 54-58,; from assoc dir to dir int prog div, Hyattsville, Md, 59-76. *Mem:* AAAS; Entom Soc Am. *Res:* Biology and control of cereal and forage insects; technical direction of control projects on insect vectors of plant diseases and injurious insects; appraising agricultural research; foreign research operations. *Mailing Add:* 900 N Taylor St No 1231 Arlington VA 22203-1858

HAINES, PATRICK A, MESOSCALE DYNAMICS, CUMULUS PARAMETERIZATION. *Current Pos:* SCIENTIST, ARMY RES LAB, 96- *Personal Data:* b Worcester, Mass, Feb 17, 49; m 78, Suzette Viljoen; c Pieter N. *Educ:* Tufts Univ, BS, 71; Fla State Univ, MS, 76; Purdue Univ, PhD, 92. *Prof Exp:* Sr meteorologist, SAfrican Weather Bur, 74-77; res meteorologist, Res Inst, Univ Dayton, 78-84, consult, 84-91; res scientist, Dept Earth Atmospheric Sci, Purdue Univ, 92-94; fac mem, Dept Meteorol, Stockholm Univ, Sweden, 94-96. *Concurrent Pos:* Res asst, Dept Geosci, Purdue Univ, 84-87; NASA grad student, Res Prog, 87-90. *Mem:* Am Meteorol Soc; Am Inst Aeronaut & Astronaut. *Res:* Numerical simulation of mesoscale convective systems; cumulus and stable cloud parameterization for mesoscale systems; boundary layer flow in complex terrain; meteorological conditions associated with aircraft icing; heavy rain and clear air turbulence and their effect on aircraft. *Mailing Add:* 2227 Sunrise Point Rd Las Cruces NM 88011-5210. *Fax:* 765-496-1210; *E-Mail:* djs@muce.cc.purdue.edu

HAINES, RICHARD FOSTER, HUMAN FACTORS RESEARCH & DEVELOPMENT, PSYCHOPHYSICS RESEARCH. *Current Pos:* res fel biotechnol, NASA-Ames Res Ctr, Nat Res Ctr, 64-67, res scientist aerospace human factors, 67-88, chief-Space Human Factors Off, 86-88, COMPUT SCIENTIST, NASA-AMES RES CTR, RECOM TECHNOL INC, 93- *Personal Data:* b Seattle, Wash, May 19, 37; m 61, Carol T; c Cynthia L & Laura A (Martin). *Educ:* Pac Lutheran Col, BA, 60; Mich State Univ, MA, 62, PhD(exp psychol), 64. *Prof Exp:* Predoctoral fel visual psychophys, NIMH, Mich State Univ, 62-63, res fel visual psychophys, Dept Psychol, 63-64; assoc prof psychol, San Jose State Univ, 88-89; scientist telesci technol, Res Inst Advan Computer Sci, 88-90; res scientist, Calspan Corp, 91-92. *Concurrent Pos:* Consult, Dept Prev Med, Stanford Univ, 66-67; mem, Tech Group on Vision, Optical Soc Am, 67-83, Subcomt Electronic Displays, SAE, 83-91 & Man/Systs Integration Adv Panel, NASA, 85-88; consult mem, Comt Vision, Nat Acad Sci-Nat Res Coun, 70-82; chmn, Advan Technol Applications Comt, NASA-CCAIA, 74-79 & Space Sta Human Factors Subcomt, Aerospace Med Asn, 87-89; consult scientist Telesci Technol, Foothill/Deanza Col, 90-92. *Mem:* Sigma Xi; Soc Automotive Engrs; Soc Info Display. *Res:* Visual psychophysics; NASA-Aerospace project research and management; anomalous aerial phenomena research and advanced telescience technology research and development; granted four US patents; author of over 65 articles. *Mailing Add:* PO Box 880 Los Altos CA 94023-0880

HAINES, RICHARD FRANCIS, MICROBIOLOGY. *Current Pos:* RETIRED. *Personal Data:* b Ann Arbor, Mich, Jan 15, 23; m 51; c 3. *Educ:* Univ Mich, BS, 48, MS, 49 & 54, PhD(bact), 59. *Prof Exp:* Asst bact, Univ Mich, 53-57, instr, 57-60, from instr to asst prof surg & microbiol, 60-74, assoc prof microbiol & surg, 74-91, dir, Tissue Typing Lab, 72-91. *Mem:* AAAS; Am Soc Microbiol; Transplantation Soc; Sigma Xi. *Res:* Transplantation immunology; natural antitumor agents; pathogenic fungi. *Mailing Add:* 807 Bruce St Ann Arbor MI 48103

HAINES, ROBERT GORDON, ENTOMOLOGY. *Current Pos:* PRES, AURUM, 96- *Personal Data:* b NJ, Apr 21, 29; m 52; c 6. *Educ:* Rutgers Univ, BSc, 51, MSc, 54, PhD(entom), 55. *Prof Exp:* Asst prof entom, Mich State Univ, 55-60; field res specialist, Calif Chem Co, 60-62; new prod mgr, Union Carbide Corp, 62-81; consult Pesticide Litigation & Turf Mgt, 81-87; pres, Environ Consult Serv, 87-96. *Concurrent Pos:* pres, Pesticide Consult Serv, 87-96. *Mem:* Entom Soc Am; Soc Am Florists. *Mailing Add:* 2317 Locustwood Ct Orange Park FL 32065

HAINES, ROBERT IVOR, NUCLEAR WASTE MANAGEMENT, MINERAL SURFACE CHEMISTRY. *Current Pos:* PROF CHEM, SIR WILFRED GRENFELL COL, MEM UNIV, NFLD. *Personal Data:* b Wales, Feb 13, 53; Brit & Can citizen; m 73; c 2. *Educ:* Leicester Univ, BSc Hons, 74, PhD(chem), 77. *Prof Exp:* Fel inorg chem, Victoria, 77-79; asst prof inorg chem, Univ RI, 79-80, Univ Toronto, 80-81; res officer geochem, Atomic Energy Can, Ltd, 81- *Mem:* Am Chem Soc; Sigma Xi. *Res:* Nuclear waste mineral water interactions utilizing surface analytical techniques to study mineral alteration and radionuclide sorption onto mineral systems; inorganic reaction mechanisms in ion coordination compounds; chemistry of nickel complexes. *Mailing Add:* Chem Sir Wilfred Grenfell Col Mem Univ Nfld University Dr Corner Brook NF A2H 6P9 Can

HAINES, ROLAND ARTHUR, INORGANIC CHEMISTRY. *Current Pos:* asst prof, Univ Western Ont, 65-71, assoc dean sci, 84-89, actg dean sci, 90-91, ASSOC PROF INORG CHEM, UNIV WESTERN ONT, 71-, ASSOC DEAN SCI, 91- *Personal Data:* b Ottawa, Ont, July 4, 39; m 64, Kathleen Carmody; c David, Heather, Lauren & Deborah. *Educ:* Dalhousie Univ, BSc, 60, MSc, 61; Univ Pittsburgh, PhD(inorg chem), 64. *Prof Exp:* Res assoc inorg chem, Univ Southern Calif, 64-65. *Mem:* Am Chem Soc; Chem Inst Can. *Res:* Stability of metal complexes; studies of optically active coordination compounds. *Mailing Add:* Dept Chem Univ Western Ont London ON N6A 5B7 Can. *Fax:* 519-661-3703; *E-Mail:* scirah@uwoadmin.uwo.ca

HAINES, STEPHEN JOHN, PEDIATRIC NEUROSURGERY, SKULL BASE SURGERY. *Current Pos:* From asst prof to assoc prof neurosurg, 82-93, assoc prof otolaryngol, 87-93, HEAD, DIV PEDIAT NEUROSURG, UNIV MINN, 85-, PROF NEUROSURG, OTOLARYNGOL & PEDIAT, 93- *Personal Data:* b Burlington, Vt, Sept 4, 49. *Educ:* Dartmouth Col, AB, 71; Univ Vt, MD, 75. *Concurrent Pos:* Van Wagenen fel, Am Asn Neurol Surgeons, 81. *Mem:* Cong Neurol Surgeons (vpres, 93-94); Am Asn Neurol Surgeons; fel Am Col Surgeons; Neurosurg Soc Am; Soc Neurol Surgeons; Soc Clin Trials. *Res:* Clinical epidemiologic methodology as applied to neurosurgery. *Mailing Add:* Univ Minn Box 96 420 Delaware St SE Minneapolis MN 55455-0374. *E-Mail:* shaines@maroon.tc.umn.edu

HAINES, TERRY ALAN, AQUATIC ECOLOGY. *Current Pos:* assoc prof, 78-82, PROF ZOOL, UNIV MAINE, ORONO, 82-; LEADER FIELD RES UNIT, ORONO, US FISH & WILDLIFE SERV, 78- *Personal Data:* b Lansdale, Pa, Feb 18, 43; m 67; c 2. *Educ:* Pa State Univ, BS, 65, MS, 67; Mich State Univ, PhD(fisheries, wildlife), 71. *Prof Exp:* From asst prof to assoc prof biol sci, State Univ NY Col Brockport, 72-78. *Mem:* Am Fisheries Soc; Soc Environ Toxicol Chem. *Res:* Impact of Contaminants on fish resources; mechanisms of toxicity of metals to fish; Hg biogeochemical cycling. *Mailing Add:* 5751 Murray Hall Univ Maine Orono ME 04469-5751

HAINES, THOMAS HENRY, MEMBRANES & LIPIDS, ION TRANSPORT. *Current Pos:* lectr, City Col New York, 63-64, from asst prof to assoc prof chem, 64-71, actg dir Ctr Biomed Educ, 72-74, PROF CHEM, CITY COL NEW YORK, 71-, PRES & DIR BIOCHEM, CUNY MED SCH, 74- *Personal Data:* b New York, NY, Aug 9, 33; c 1. *Educ:* City Col New York, BS, 57, MA, 59; Rutgers Univ, PhD(biochem), 64. *Prof Exp:* Res biochemist, Boyce Thompson Inst Plant Res, 59-63; asst biochem, Rutgers Univ, 63. *Concurrent Pos:* Grants, USPHS, 64-66, US Dept Interior, 68-70, US Off Educ, 70-71, Petrol Res Fund, 70-72, NSF, 76- & NIH, 77-; vis assoc prof, Univ Calif, Berkeley, 70; NATO sr fel, Inst Natural Prod Chem, France, 70; vis prof, Univ Minn, 79-80,; vis scholar, Mitsubishi Inst Life Sci, Tokyo, 86-87. *Mem:* AAAS; Am Chem Soc; Am Oil Chemists Soc; NY Acad Sci; Am Soc Biochem & Molecular Biol; Biophys Soc Am. *Res:* Structure and function of natural membranes, especially flagellar membranes; chemistry, biochemistry and function of sulfolipids, glycolipids, fatty acids, sterols and natural halogen lipids; mechanism and role of ion transport in living membranes, proton pathway in bioenergenics; origin of membranes on prebiotic earth. *Mailing Add:* Dept Chem City Col New York 139th St & Convent Ave New York NY 10031-9100. *Fax:* 212-650-7798

HAINES, THOMAS WALTON, medical entomology, for more information see previous edition

HAINES, WILLIAM C, FOOD SCIENCE, MICROBIOLOGY. *Current Pos:* DIR, FOOD INDUST INST, 87- *Personal Data:* b Albion, Mich, Aug 29, 42; m 64; c 3. *Educ:* Mich State Univ, BS, 64, MA, 68, PhD(food sci), 72. *Prof Exp:* Teacher chem, Montrose Twp Schs, Mich, 64-67; food technologist food sci, Post Div, Gen Foods Corp, 67-69; dir prod develop, L D Schreiber Cheese Co, Inc, 72-77; res sect leader food sci, Borden Res Ctr, 77-81; lab mgr, Stauffer Chem Co, 81-83; vpres res, Ridgewood Inc, 83-87. *Mem:* Inst Food Technologists; Am Dairy Sci Asn; Sigma Xi; Coun Agr & Sci Tech; AAAS. *Res:* Food technology; cultured foods. *Mailing Add:* Rm 1 Agr Hall Mich State Univ East Lansing MI 48824

HAINES, WILLIAM EMERSON, PETROLEUM CHEMISTRY. *Current Pos:* RETIRED. *Personal Data:* b Evanston, Wyo, Aug 23, 17; m 41, Dorothy Costin; c 4. *Educ:* Univ Wyo, BS, 39. *Prof Exp:* Pub sch teacher, Wyo, 39-42; asst chem, Univ Wyo, 42-43; petrol chemist, Petrol & Oilshale Exp Sta, US Bur Mines, 43-51, chemist, 51-58, proj leader, 58-63, res supvr, Laramie Energy Res Ctr, 63-75, res supvr, Laramie Energy Res Ctr, US Energy Res & Develop Admin, 75-77; mgr, Div Phys Sci, Laramie Energy Technol Ctr, US Dept Energy, 77-80. *Concurrent Pos:* Managing ed, Petrol Div, Am Chem Soc Preprints, 81- *Mem:* Am Chem Soc; Sigma Xi. *Res:* Petroleum separation and analysis; sulfur and nitrogen compounds; asphalt. *Mailing Add:* 520 S 13th St Laramie WY 82070-4103

HAINES, WILLIAM JOSEPH, PHARMACEUTICAL MANAGEMENT, SCIENCE & TECHNOLOGY MANAGEMENT. *Current Pos:* RETIRED. *Personal Data:* b Crawfordsville, Ind, Sept 26, 19; m 43; c 2. *Educ:* Wabash Col, AB, 40; Univ Ill, PhD(biochem), 43. *Hon Degrees:* DSc, Wabash Col, 70. *Honors & Awards:* Upjohn Prize, 52. *Prof Exp:* Rockefeller asst biochem, Univ Ill, 40-43; res biochemist, Upjohn Co, 43-46, group leader endocrinol res, 46-50, head dept, 50-54; tech dir labs div, Armour & Co, Ill, 54-58; vpres & dir res, Ortho Pharmaceut Corp & Ortho Res Found, 58-65, exec vpres, Corp, 65-67; vchmn, Johnson & Johnson Int, 67-79; dir & exec comt mem, 69-79, corp vpres sci & technol, 79-82, vpres Johnson & Johnson, 81-82. *Concurrent Pos:* Laurentian Hormone Conf lectr, 51; mem, Indust Res Inst; mem, Joslin Diabetes Found, 74-79. *Mem:* Fel AAAS; Am Chem Soc; Am Soc Biol Chemists; Endocrine Soc; Soc Exp Biol & Med; Sigma Xi; NY Acad Sci; Soc Chem Indust. *Res:* Biochemistry of natural and synthetic penicillins and steroid hormones; tissue enzymatic and microbiological synthesis of adrenal cortex hormones; chromatographic analysis; automatic chromatographic fraction cutter; fluoroscopic paper-gram scanner camera; metabolism of proteins and amino acids; determination of human requirement for essential amino acids. *Mailing Add:* 5 Bedford Dr Doylestown PA 18901-9463

HAINING, JOSEPH LEO, BIOCHEMISTRY. *Current Pos:* CHIEF BASIC SCI RES LAB, VET ADMIN CTR, 63- *Personal Data:* b Yazoo City, Miss, Feb 18, 32; m 54; c 3. *Educ:* Miss Southern Col, BS, 54; Purdue Univ, MS, 57, PhD(biochem), 59. *Prof Exp:* Asst prof biochem, Sch Med, Univ Miss, 59-63. *Concurrent Pos:* Asst prof, Univ Miss, 63- *Mem:* AAAS; Am Chem Soc; fel Geront Soc; Am Asn Lab Animal Sci; Sigma Xi. *Res:* Enzymology; protein metabolism; gerontology. *Mailing Add:* 1663 Lelia Dr Jackson MS 39216-4818

HAINLINE, ADRIAN, JR, BIOCHEMISTRY & CLINICAL CHEMISTRY. *Current Pos:* CONSULT, 87- *Personal Data:* b Blandinsville, Ill, Mar 16, 21; m 42; c 5. *Educ:* Western Ill State Univ, BEd, 42; Univ Denver, MS, 48; Univ Mich, PhD, 52; Am Bd Clin Chem, dipl. *Prof Exp:* Control chemist, E I du Pont de Nemours & Co, 42-45; clin chemist, Cleveland Clin Found, 51-64; clin chemist, St Luke's Hosp, Kansas City, 65-67; chief, Coronary Drug Proj Lab, Ctr Dis Control, 67-71, chief, Clin Chem Diag Prod Eval, 73-77, chief, Clin Chem Stand Sect, 77-87. *Concurrent Pos:* Dir, Am Bd Clin Chem, 72-78; sci dir, WHO Collaborating Ctr Ref & Res in Blood Lipids, 77-; nat cholesterol educ, Prog Lab Comt, 86. *Mem:* Fel AAAS; Am Chem Soc; Am Asn Clin Chem; Nat Acad Clin Biochem; Sigma Xi. *Res:* Laboratory management; lipid laboratory standardization; quality control. *Mailing Add:* 6 Westgate Circle Jacksonville IL 62650

HAINLINE, LOUISE, PEDIATRIC VISION. *Current Pos:* from asst prof to prof, 72-84, prof, 85-90, BROEKLUNDIAN PROF PSYCHOL, BROOKLYN COL, 91-, ACTG DEAN GRAD STUDIES & RES, 95- *Personal Data:* b New London, Conn, Apr 22, 47. *Educ:* Brown Univ, BA, 69; Harvard Univ, MA, 71, PhD(develop psychol), 73. *Concurrent Pos:* Prin investr, res grants, NIH, 74-; lectr pediat, Downstate Med Ctr, State Univ NY, 79-85. *Mem:* Am Psychol Asn; Soc Res Child Develop; NY Acad Sci; Asn Res Vision & Ophthal; Sigma Xi; Int Soc Study Behav Develop. *Res:* Development of the normal human visual system in young infants and problems that can arise in vision; development of vision and impact of different environmental factors on that development; devising new methods for testing infants. *Mailing Add:* Dept Psychol Brooklyn Col Brooklyn NY 11210

HAINSKI, MARTHA BARRIONUEVO, BIOLOGICAL CHEMISTRY. *Current Pos:* vpres res & develop, Alpha Therapeut Corp, 77-84, PRES, I B B PLASMA, 85- *Personal Data:* b Buenos Aires, Arg, Feb 18, 32; US citizen; m 62, Steven Hainski; c Alexandra. *Educ:* Univ Buenos Aires, PhD(biochem), 57; Pepperdine Univ, MBA, 81. *Honors & Awards:* Presidential Awards, Abbott Labs, 75, 76 & 77. *Prof Exp:* Res assoc physiol chem, Sch Med, Wayne State Univ, 57-58; res assoc biochem, Philadelphia Gen Hosp, 58-63, NIH fel, 63-65; assoc, Clin Lab Med Group, 65-66; dir protein chem res, Hyland Div, Travenol Labs, 66-70; mgr protein chem, Res & Develop, Abbott Sci Prod Div, 70-76. *Concurrent Pos:* Int consult biol bus, 85- *Mem:* Am Chem Soc; fel Am Inst Chemists. *Res:* Plasma protein fractionation; automation and new methods for large scale production of plasma proteins; immune globulins; intravenous gamma globulin; antihemophilic factor; prothrombin complex; hepatitis antibody; plasma expanders; platelets; blood preservation; interferon research; artificial blood research and clinical trials. *Mailing Add:* 1628 Campbell St Glendale CA 91207

HAINSWORTH, FENWICK REED, ZOOLOGY, PHYSIOLOGY. *Current Pos:* from asst prof to assoc prof, 69-78, PROF BIOL, SYRACUSE UNIV, 78- *Personal Data:* b Norfolk, Va, June 25, 41; m 70; c 2. *Educ:* Clark Univ, AB, 63; Univ Pa, PhD(zool), 68. *Prof Exp:* USPHS fel, 67-69. *Mem:* Am Soc Naturalists; Ecol Soc Am; Soc Study Evolution; Sigma Xi. *Res:* Animal behavior; comparative physiology. *Mailing Add:* Dept Biol Syracuse Univ 100 University Pl Syracuse NY 13244-0001

HAIR, JAKIE ALEXANDER, ENTOMOLOGY. *Current Pos:* assoc prof, Okla State Univ, 67-75, prof ecol, biol & insect control, 75-77, prof entom, 77-, EMER PROF, OKLA STATE UNIV. *Personal Data:* b Williston, SC, Aug 31, 40. *Educ:* Clemson Univ, BS, 62, MS, 64; Va Polytech Inst, PhD(entom), 66. *Prof Exp:* Med entomologist, Commun Dis Ctr, USPHS, Atlanta, Ga, 66-67. *Mem:* Entom Soc Am; Am Mosquito Control Asn; Wildlife Soc. *Res:* Control, ecology, biology and bionomics of insects of medical and veterinary importance; bionomics of wildlife parasites; tick investigations. *Mailing Add:* Rte 5 Box 196 Stillwater OK 74074

HAIR, JAY DEE, zoology, forestry, for more information see previous edition

HAIR, MICHAEL L, PHYSICAL CHEMISTRY, INORGANIC CHEMISTRY. *Current Pos:* CONSULT, CONSURE INT, 96- *Personal Data:* b North Shields, Eng, Mar 23, 34; m 58, Judith Bilton; c Geoffrey, Mandy-Jane & Susan. *Educ:* Univ Durham, BSc, 55, PhD(chem), 58. *Honors & Awards:* Charles E Ives Award, Soc Photographic Scientists & Engrs, 82; Ralph K Iler Award in Colloid Sci, Am Chem Soc, 94. *Prof Exp:* Fel, Nat Res Coun Can, 58-60; tech officer, Imp Chem Industs Ltd, Eng, 60-61; res chemist, Corning Glass Works, 61-64, group leader surface chem, 64-69; mgr, Phys Chem Br, Corp Res Ctr, Xerox Corp, NY, 69-74, mgr colloid & interface sci, 74-81, mgr synthesis & explor res, 83-87, res fel, Xerox Res Ctr Can Ltd, 81-96. *Concurrent Pos:* Adj prof, Univ Toronto, 86- *Mem:* Am Chem Soc. *Res:* Surface forces; polymer adsorbtion; chemistry of surfaces; infrared spectroscopy of adsorbed molecules; colloid stability. *Mailing Add:* 167 Caulder Dr Oakville ON L6J 4T2 Can

HAIRSTON, NELSON GEORGE, ECOLOGY, ZOOLOGY. *Current Pos:* CONSULT, 88- *Personal Data:* b Davie Co, NC, Oct 16, 17; m 42, Martha Patton; c Martha P, Nelson G Jr & Margaret E. *Educ:* Univ NC, BA, 37, MA, 39; Northwestern Univ, PhD(zool), 48. *Honors & Awards:* Eminent Ecologist Award, Ecol Soc Am, 91. *Prof Exp:* Lectr sci, Northwestern Univ, 48; from instr to prof zool, Univ Mich, Ann Arbor, 48-67, dir, Mus Zool, 67-75; W R Kenan, Jr, prof zool, Univ NC, Chapel Hill, 75-88. *Concurrent Pos:* Adv & consult, WHO, Philippines, 54-56 & 59, Iraq, 56, Geneva, 56 & 60-, Egypt, Sudan, Tanzania, Zimbabwe, SAfrica, Ghana & Western Samoa; mem expert adv panel parasitic dis, 64-81; consult, NIH, 64-; vchmn adv comt biol & med sci, NSF, 71-72, chmn, 72. *Mem:* Sigma Xi; Brit Ecol Soc; Am Soc Naturalists; Ecol Soc Am; Soc Study Evolution. *Res:* Population and community ecology of salamanders, soil arthropods, paramecium and freshwater snails; epidemiology of schistosomes and other helminths; sampling methods for invertebrates. *Mailing Add:* Dept Biol Univ NC Chapel Hill NC 27599-3280

HAIRSTON, NELSON GEORGE, JR, FRESHWATER ECOLOGY. *Current Pos:* assoc prof, 85-87, PROF ECOL & SYST DEPT, CORNELL UNIV, 88- *Personal Data:* b Asheville, NC, Sept 26, 49; m 74, D Whitaker; c Peter W. *Educ:* Univ Mich, BS, 71; Univ Wash, PhD(zool), 77. *Prof Exp:* From asst prof to assoc prof zool, Univ RI, 77-85. *Concurrent Pos:* NSF grant, 80-82, 83-85, 86-89, 88-90, 89-90, 92-95 & 95-96; US Environ Protection Agency grant, 96- *Mem:* Am Soc Limnol & Oceanog; Freshwater Biol Asn; Soc Int Limnologiae; Ecol Soc Am; Sigma Xi; Soc Study Evolution. *Res:* Zooplankton population dynamics and community structure; evolutionary dynamics of zooplankton populations; freshwater community-ecosystem interactions; fish vision and diet selection. *Mailing Add:* Ecol & Syst Dept Cornell Univ Corson Hall Ithaca NY 14853-2701. *Fax:* 607-255-8088; *E-Mail:* ngh1@cornell.edu

HAIRSTONE, MARCUS A, RESEARCH ADMINISTRATOR, ENVIRONMENTAL TOXICOLOGY. *Current Pos:* DIR, WORLD TECH CONSULTS, 95- *Personal Data:* b Reidsville, NC, Oct 16, 26. *Educ:* Livingstone Col, BS, 49; Duquesne Univ, MS, 50; Univ Pittsburgh, PhD (cell biol), 56. *Prof Exp:* Dir Dental Res Labs, Univ Nebr, 58-60; asst prof chem, Long Island Univ, 60-62; res assoc cytophotometry, Rockefeller Inst, 62-64, Physicians & Surgeons, Columbia Univ, 64-66; prof & dean academics, City Univ NY, 70-71; prof zool, Am Univ, Cairo, Egypt, 72-74; proj mgr, int progs, NSF, 75-76; health sci adminr, Int Progs, NIH, 77-95. *Concurrent Pos:* Lectr & consult math, NSF, 60-62; Fulbright prof conserv med res Inst, Alexandria Univ, Egypt, 66-67; consult biol, India Univ Sci Imiprovement Prog, Nat Sci Found, 69; chair, Comt Develop Regions, Am Soc Pub Adminr, 76; bd mem, Sudan Studies Asn, 82-83; dean, Arts & Sci, Cheyney Univ, 86-87; chief party, USAID, Univ Hisnkages Prog, Cairo, Egypt, 95-96. *Mem:* Am Soc Pub Adminr; AAAS; NY Acad Sci; Sudan Studies Assoc (bd mem, 82-83). *Res:* Characterization of tumor viruses; administration of program planning and management, international coordination for basic research, epidemiological studies, field trials, leading to vaccine development in hepatitis, diarrheal disease, accute respiratory infections, rabies, and polio. *Mailing Add:* PO Box 30163 Bethesda MD 20824. *Fax:* 202-882-4869; *E-Mail:* mhairstone@worldnet.att.net

HAISCH, BERNHARD MICHAEL, STELLAR ATMOSPHERES, SPACE ASTRONOMY. *Current Pos:* res scientist, 79-83, STAFF SCIENTIST, LOCKHEED MARTIN PALO ALTO RES LAB, 83- *Personal Data:* b Stuttgart-Bad Canstatt, Fed Repub Ger, Aug 23, 49; US citizen; m 77, 86, Marsha Sims; c Katherine S & C Taylor. *Educ:* Ind Univ, BS, 71; Univ Wis-Madison, MS, 73, PhD(astrophys), 75. *Prof Exp:* Res assoc, Joint Inst Lab Astrophys, Univ Colo, Boulder, 75-79; vis scientist, Astron Inst, Univ Utrecht, Neth, 77-78. *Concurrent Pos:* Guest investr, NASA IUE, Einstein, Exosat, Rosat progs; chmn, IAU Colloquium no 104 & no 152; prin investr, multilayer res prog; mem rev comts, NASA; ed, J Sci Explor; vis fel, Max Planck Inst Extra Physik, Garching, Ger, 91-94; assoc ed, Astrophys J; dep dir, Ctr EUV Astrophys, Univ Calif, Berkeley, 92-94. *Mem:* Am Astron Soc; fel Royal Astron Soc; Europ Astron Soc; Int Astron Union; Soc Sci Explor; assoc fel Am Inst Aeronaut & Astronaut. *Res:* High energy astrophysics; investigation of solar and stellar atmospheres; space observations of ultraviolet and x-ray emission of chromospheres, coronae and flares; development of concepts for space instrumentation; zero-point field (quantum vacuum) theory. *Mailing Add:* 519 Cringle Dr Redwood City CA 94065. *Fax:* 650-595-4466; *E-Mail:* haisch@sag.space.lockheed.com

HAISLER, WALTER ERVIN, AEROSPACE ENGINEERING. *Current Pos:* From asst prof to assoc prof, 70-80, PROF AEROSPACE ENG, TEX A&M UNIV, 80- *Personal Data:* b Temple, Tex, June 3, 44; m 64; c 2. *Educ:* Tex A&M Univ, BS, 67, MS, 68, PhD(aerospace eng), 70. *Concurrent Pos:* Consult, David Ehrenpreis Engrs, 70-71. *Mem:* Am Inst Aeronaut & Astronaut. *Res:* Finite element analysis of structural and fluid mechanics problems; nonlinear mechanics; numerical analysis. *Mailing Add:* 3647 Citation Ctr Tex A&M Univ College Station TX 77845-8223

HAISSIG, MANFRED, LADLE METALLURGY. *Current Pos:* PRES, FUCHS SYSTS, INC, 90- *Personal Data:* b Vienna, Austria, Jan 2, 42; m 66; c 2. *Educ:* Montan Univ, Loeben, Austria, Dipl, 68. *Honors & Awards:* Charles W Briggs Award, Iron & Steel Soc, 86. *Prof Exp:* Supt meltshop, Boehler Ag, Ger, 73-77, malt testing, 78-86; vpres res & develop & mkt, Steel Casting Eng, Ltd, 82-86, exec vpres, 86-90. *Mem:* Asn Iron & Steel Engrs; Iron & Steel Soc. *Res:* Horizontal casting of steel and secondary metallurgy to improve product quality; development of near net shape casting of wire and sheet. *Mailing Add:* Fuchs Systs Inc PO Box 379 Salisbury NC 28145

HAIT, WILLIAM NEIL, MEDICAL ONCOLOGY. *Current Pos:* chief med oncol, 94-95, PROF MED & PHARMACOL, ROBERT WOOD JOHNSON MED SCH, PISCATAWAY, NJ, 93-, ASSOC DEAN ONCOL PROGS, 94-; DIR, CANCER INST NJ, 93- *Personal Data:* b Newark, NJ, Mar 23, 49; m, Sung-Yon Yoo; c Jane. *Educ:* Univ Pa, BA, 71; Med Col Pa, MD & PhD, 78; Am Bd Internal Med, cert, 82, cert med oncol, 87. *Honors & Awards:* Award Distinguished Serv, Am Fedn Clin Res. *Prof Exp:* Intern, Sch Med, Yale Univ, 78-79, resident internal med, 79-81, chief resident, 81-82, instr, 83-84, asst prof, 84-87, asst prof pharmacol, 86-87, actg chief med oncol, 86-88, assoc dir, Comp Cancer Ctr, 86-92, assoc prof med, 87-92, dir, Breast Cancer Unit, 87-92, co-dir, Lung Cancer Unit, 87-92, chief, Sect Med Oncol, 88-92, assoc prof pharmacol, 88-92. *Concurrent Pos:* Fel med oncol, Sch Med, Yale Univ, 82-83; actg chief, West Haven Vet Admin Hosp, Conn, 91-92; adj prof pharm, Rutgers Univ, 93-; co-dir, NJ Comp Breast Care Ctr, 94-; found assoc ed, J Exp Theraput & Oncol. *Mem:* Am Fedn Clin Res; Am Soc Clin Oncol; Am Asn Cancer Res; AAAS; Am Soc Clin Invest. *Res:* Mechanisms of signal transduction and drug resistance in cancer. *Mailing Add:* Cancer Inst NJ 195 Little Albany St New Brunswick NJ 08901

HAITKO, DEBORAH ANN, INORGANIC & ORGANOMETALLIC CHEMISTRY. *Current Pos:* CONSULT, 80- *Personal Data:* b New Haven, Conn, Sept 22, 51. *Educ:* Albertus Magnus Col, BA, 73; Yale Univ, MS, 74, MPhil, 75, PhD(inorg chem), 78. *Prof Exp:* Teaching asst introductory chem, Yale Univ, 73-74, teaching asst org lab, 74-75, teaching asst inorg grader, 75-77; fel, Princeton Univ, 78; fel chem, Ind Univ, 78-80. *Mem:* Am Chem Soc; Sigma Xi. *Res:* Transition metal chemistry, specifically the activation of organic molecules by coordination to transition metals; synthesis and mechanism; asymmetric synthesis; rearrangement processes of stereochemically nonrigid organometallic species. *Mailing Add:* Gen Elec Corp R&D Ctr One Res Circle Niskayuna NY 12309

HAITZ, ROLAND HERMANN, SOLID STATE PHYSICS. *Current Pos:* res & develop mgr, Optoelectronics Div, 69-84, RES & DEVELOP MGR, COMPONENTS GROUP, HEWLETT PACKARD, 84- *Personal Data:* b Durmersheim, Ger, Oct 6, 35; m 67; c 2. *Educ:* Karlsruhe Tech Univ, BS, 58; Munich Tech Univ, MS, 61, PhD(physics), 63. *Prof Exp:* Sr scientist, Shockley Res Lab, Clevite Corp, 61-64; mem tech staff, Physics Res Lab, Tex Instruments Inc, 64-69. *Concurrent Pos:* Assoc ed, Trans Electon Devices, 70-73, ed, 73-77. *Mem:* Inst Elec & Electronics Engrs. *Res:* Avalanche breakdown in p-n junctions; microplasmas; avalanche noise generators; noise in particle detectors; radiation damage; microwave generation; solid state image sensors; optically coupled isolators; light emitters and numeric displays; integrated photodetectors, fiber optics, optoelectronic devices and systems. *Mailing Add:* Hewlett Packard Co 370 W Trimble Rd San Jose CA 95131

HAJ-AHMAD, YOUSEF, IMMUNOLOGY, MICROBIOLOGY. *Current Pos:* asst prof, 89-92, ASSOC PROF MOLECULAR GENETICS, BROCK UNIV, 93- *Personal Data:* b Mare, Syria, Mar, 1952; Can citizen; m 74; c 2. *Educ:* Brock Univ, BSc, 79, MSc, 81; McMaster Univ, PhD(molecular virol), 86. *Prof Exp:* Fel, McMaster Univ, 86, Lablatt's Res, 86-89. *Concurrent Pos:* Vpres, Vetrogen Corp, 89- *Mem:* Am Soc Microbiol; Am Soc Virol; Can Soc Microbiol; NY Acad Sci. *Res:* Viral victors; gene therapy; recombinant vaccines. *Mailing Add:* Dept Biol Brock Univ 500 Glenridge Ave St Catharines ON L2S 3A1 Can. *Fax:* 905-688-1855

HAJDU, JOSEPH, BIOORGANIC CHEMISTRY, LIPID BIOCHEMISTRY. *Current Pos:* from asst prof to assoc prof, 84-90, PROF CHEM, CALIF STATE UNIV, NORTHRIDGE, 90- *Personal Data:* b Budapest, Hungary, May 5, 41; US citizen; m 88, Carol Fukuda; c Michael. *Educ:* Hebrew Univ, Jerusalem, BSc, 65, MSc, 67; State Univ NY, Stonybrook, PhD(chem), 72. *Prof Exp:* Fel bioorganic chem, Sch Med, Univ Calif, Los Angeles, 73-76; asst prof chem, Boston Col, 76-; group leader, Ayerst Lab, Rouses Point, NY, 83-84. *Concurrent Pos:* Prin investr, NIH, 79-; consult, Smith Kline Beecham Pharmaceut, Hertforshire, Eng, 91-92. *Mem:* Am Chem Soc; Sigma Xi; AAAS. *Res:* Mechanism of organic and biochemical reactions; modification of enzymic active sites; design and synthesis of enzyme inhibitors, phospholipases, role of metal ions in biochemistry. *Mailing Add:* Chem Dept Calif State Univ-Northridge Northridge CA 91330-8262. *Fax:* 818-677-2912; *E-Mail:* joseph.hajdu@csun.edu

HAJDU, STEPHEN, PHYSIOLOGY. *Current Pos:* RETIRED. *Personal Data:* b Hungary, Jan 9, 16; nat US; m 49; c 2. *Educ:* Univ Budapest, MD, 41. *Prof Exp:* Asst prof physiol, Univ Budapest, 39-41, assoc prof, 41-45; res prof, Hungarian Biol Inst, 45-57; lectr, King's Col, Univ London, 48-49; res assoc, Inst Muscle Res, Woods Hole, Mass, 49-54; from surgeon to sr surgeon, Nat Heart Inst, 54-64, med dir, 64-70, head sect exp cardiovasc dis, 65-76. *Concurrent Pos:* Mem, Marine Biol Lab Asn, Woods Hole, Mass; Eszterhazy Found fel, 42 & 43; Brit Coun fel, King's Col, Univ London, 47-48. *Mem:* Am Physiol Soc; Soc Gen Physiol. *Res:* Nutrition; endocrinology; nerve and muscle physiology; heart physiology. *Mailing Add:* 5513 Oak Pl Bethesda MD 20817

HAJDUK, STEPHEN LOUIS, CELL BIOLOGY, PARASITOLOGY. *Current Pos:* asst prof, 83-88, ASSOC PROF, DEPT BIOCHEM, UNIV ALA, BIRMINGHAM, 88- *Personal Data:* b Marietta, Ga, Apr 23, 52; m 75; c 2. *Educ:* Univ Ga, BS, 77; Univ Glasgow, PhD(zool), 80. *Honors & Awards:* S L Hutner Prize, Am Soc Protozoologists, 85. *Prof Exp:* Res asst, Univ Ga, 72-77, Univ Glasgow, 77-80; fel, Sch Med, Johns Hopkins Univ, 81-83. *Concurrent Pos:* Vis scientist, Univ Amsterdam, 77 & 79. *Mem:* Am Soc Cell Biol; Am Soc Protozoologists; Royal Soc Trop Med & Hyg. *Res:* Molecular and cellular biology of protozoan parasites; mitochondrial DNA structure and function in Africa trypanosomes. *Mailing Add:* Dept Biochem Univ Ala Sch Med 1717 Seventh Ave S Birmingham AL 35294-0001

HAJEK, ANN ELIZABETH, INSECT PATHOLOGY, BIOLOGICAL CONTROL. *Current Pos:* res assoc, 90-92, SR RES ASSOC, BOYCE THOMPSON INST, 92- *Personal Data:* b San Francisco, Calif, Apr 27, 52; m 84, James K Liebherr; c Lisa D Liebherr. *Educ:* Univ Calif, Berkeley, 74, MS, 80, PhD(entom), 84. *Prof Exp:* Res affil, Agr Res Serv, USDA, 85-89, res entomologist, 89-90. *Concurrent Pos:* Vis fel, Dept Entom, Cornell Univ, 85 & 93; prin investr, USDA, NRI. *Mem:* Soc Invert Path; Entom Soc AM; Sigma Xi; AAAS. *Res:* Molecular, cellular and organismal level studies of fungal pathogens of insects; epizootiology of a fungal disease of gypsy moth and its use for biological control. *Mailing Add:* Dept Entomol Cornell Univ Comstock Hall Ithaca NY 14853-0901. *Fax:* 607-254-1242

HAJEK, BENJAMIN F, SOIL CLASSIFICATION, SOIL GENESIS. *Current Pos:* from asst prof to assoc prof, 68-78, PROF AGRON & SOILS, AUBURN UNIV, 78- *Personal Data:* b Shiner, Tex, Sept 17, 31; m 55; c 4. *Educ:* Tex A&M Univ, BS, 58; Auburn Univ, MS, 62, PhD(soil sci), 64. *Prof Exp:* Soil scientist, Soil Conserv Serv, USDA, Tex, 58-60, soil scientist, Soil Serv Lab, Md, 64; chemist, Hanford Labs, Gen Elec Co, Wash, 64; res scientist, Pac Northwest Labs, Battelle Mem Inst, 65-68. *Mem:* Soil Sci Soc Am; Clay Minerals Soc; Am Soc Agron; Sigma Xi. *Res:* Adsorption, migration and dispersion of ions in porous media; quantitative clay mineralogy; surface and colloidal chemistry. *Mailing Add:* Dept Agron Auburn Univ Auburn AL 36849-3501

HAJEK, OTOMAR, MATHEMATICS, CONTROL THEORY. *Current Pos:* from assoc prof to prof, 66-95, PROF SYSTS ENG, CASE WESTERN RES UNIV, 88-, EMER PROF MATH, 96- *Personal Data:* b Belgrade, Yugoslavia, Dec 22, 30; m 55, Olga B Nemcova; c Michael F A. *Educ:* Charles Univ, Prague, Dr rer nat(math analysis), 53, Cand Sci, 63. *Honors & Awards:* Sr US Scientist Award, Alexander von Humboldt Stiftung, 75; Fulbright Award, 90. *Prof Exp:* Asst math, Fac Electrotech Eng, Prague Tech Univ, 53-56, sr asst, 56-58; sci officer comput sci, Res Inst Math Mach, 58-65; sr sci officer math, Inst Math, Charles Univ, Prague, 65-66. *Mem:* Am Math Soc. *Res:* Dynamical system theory; qualitative theory of differential equations; control theory; game theory. *Mailing Add:* 11330 Savannah Dr Fredericksburg VA 22407

HAJEK, THOMAS J, AEROSPACE ENGINEERING. *Current Pos:* mgr turbine tech com engine bus unit, 85-89, AREA DIR INT MKT & PROG MGR VAR NASA SPONSORED PROJS, PRATT & WHITNEY, HARTFORD, CONN, 89- *Educ:* Ill Inst Technol, BS, 74, MS, 80. *Honors & Awards:* Gas Turbine Award, Am Soc Mech Engrs, 91. *Prof Exp:* Researcher compressor aerodyn, Borg Warner Res Ctr, 77-81; from turbine aerodyn engr to dept head turbines, CAE, 81-85. *Res:* Effects of rotation on heat transfer in rotating coolant passages, structural analysis, thermal mechanical fatigue, stress analysis, ceramic coatings, experimental heat transfer studies, advanced cooling concepts and cooling systems design. *Mailing Add:* 112 Old Farms Rd South Glastonbury CT 06073

HAJELA, DAN, MATHEMATICAL ECONOMICS & FINANCIAL STRATEGIES, DATA COMMUNICATIONS & NETWORKS. *Current Pos:* PRES, MICROQUANT CAPITAL MGT, 94-; PRES, SARCO HOLDINGS, 96- *Personal Data:* b Shillong, India, Apr 23, 60; US citizen. *Educ:* Ohio State Univ, BS, 75, MS, 78, MS, 81, PhD(math), 83. *Prof Exp:* Lectr math, Ohio State Univ, 76-83, vis prof, 83-84; mgr & sr scientist, Bellcore, 84-90; sr analyst, Bear, Stearns & Co, Inc, 91; sr partner, First Boston/Tech Partners, 91-93; vpres, Bankers Trust, 93-94. *Concurrent Pos:* Consult, Bell Labs, 83; vis prof, Calif Inst Technol, 84. *Mem:* NY Acad Sci; Inst Elec & Electronics Engrs; AAAS. *Res:* Mathematical analysis and computer modeling of financial instruments and arbitrage strategies; data communications; optical communications; local area networks; distributed databases; software development; information theory; neural networks; applied mathematics. *Mailing Add:* 93 Richards Ave Norwalk CT 06854. *Fax:* 212-250-0023

HAJELA, PRABHAT, OPTIMAL STRUCTURAL DESIGN, INTELLIGENT DESIGN SYSTEMS. *Current Pos:* assoc prof, 90-93, PROF AERONAUT ENG, RENSSELAER POLYTECH INST, 93- *Personal Data:* b Kanpur, India, Dec 25, 56; US citizen; m 91, Aparna Melnotra; c Animesh. *Educ:* Indian Inst Technol, Kanpur, BTech, 77; Iowa State Univ, MS, 78; Stanford Univ, MS, 81, PhD(aeronaut & astronaut), 82. *Honors & Awards:* Ralph Teetor Award, Soc Automotive Eng, 87. *Prof Exp:* Res asst aeronaut, Stanford Univ, 79-82; res assoc, Optimal Struct Design, Univ Calif, Los Angeles, 82-83; from asst prof to assoc prof aerospace eng, Univ Fla, Gainesville, 83-90. *Concurrent Pos:* Consult, Univ Calif, Los Angeles & RCA Astro Electronics, 83-84, Occidental Petrol, Columbia, 87; prin investr numerous res grants, 83-; res fel struct design, Eglin Air Force Armament Lab, 86, Lewis Res Ctr, NASA, 89; mem, Am Inst Aeronaut & Astronaut Tech Comt, multidisciplinary design optimization; assoc ed, Am Inst Aeronaut & Astronaut J, 90-94; fac fel, Boeing Welliver, 95. *Mem:* Assoc fel Am Inst Aeronaut & Astronaut; Am Soc Eng Educ; Am Helicopter Soc; Am Soc Mech Engrs; Int Soc Struct & Multidisciplinary Optimization. *Res:* Development of efficient methods for optimal design; adapting genetic algorithms and neural network based optimization strategies; use of smart materials to detect structural damage; machine learning and computational intelligence. *Mailing Add:* 5020 JEC Rensselaer Polytech Univ Troy NY 12180-3590. *Fax:* 518-276-2623; *E-Mail:* hajela@rpi.edu

HAJIAN, ARSHAG B, MATHEMATICS. *Current Pos:* assoc prof, 63-66, PROF MATH, NORTHEASTERN UNIV, 66- *Personal Data:* b Cairo, Egypt, Oct 21, 30; nat US. *Educ:* Univ Chicago, MS, 54; Yale Univ, PhD(math), 57. *Prof Exp:* Instr math, Univ Rochester, 57-59; NSF res fel, Yale Univ, 59-61; asst prof math, Cornell Univ, 61-63. *Mem:* Am Math Soc. *Res:* Analysis; measure, ergodic and information theories; topological dynamics. *Mailing Add:* Dept Math Northeastern Univ 360 Huntington Ave Rm 537, Lake Hall Boston MA 02115-5096

HAJI-SHEIKH, ABDOLHOSSEIN, MECHANICAL ENGINEERING. *Current Pos:* from asst prof to assoc prof, 66-70, PROF MECH ENG, UNIV TEX, ARLINGTON, 70- *Personal Data:* b Dezful, Iran, Nov 27, 33; m 59; c 2. *Educ:* Univ Tehran, Dipl Eng, 56; Univ Mich, MS, 59, MA, 61; Univ Minn, Minneapolis, PhD(mech eng), 65. *Honors & Awards:* Halliburton Award. *Prof Exp:* Instr & res fel mech eng, Univ Minn, 65-66. *Concurrent Pos:* NSF initiation res grant, 67-68 & NSF res grant, 84-86. *Mem:* Am Soc Mech Engrs; Sigma Xi; Am Inst Aeronaut & Astronaut. *Res:* Various numerical methods of solution concerning diffusion equation; film cooling studies in supersonic and subsonic flow; design of space radiator for lunar missions; thermal property measurement; energy conservation; thermal storage systems. *Mailing Add:* Dept Mech Eng Univ Tex PO Box 19023-UTA Sta Arlington TX 76019-0023

HAJIYANI, MEHDI HUSSAIN, PHARMACEUTICAL CHEMISTRY, BIOCHEMISTRY. *Current Pos:* RETIRED. *Personal Data:* b Chital, India, Oct 8, 39; m 61. *Educ:* Osmania Univ, India, BSc, 60; Univ Southern Calif, PhD(pharmaceut & biomed chem), 70. *Prof Exp:* Sr chemist, Calatomic, Calbiochem, Calif, 67-69; NIH sr res assoc natural prod, Howard Univ, 70-71; from asst prof to assoc prof chem, Univ DC, 71-97. *Mem:* AAAS; Am Chem Soc. *Res:* Chemical structure-biological activity correlations; drug design via molecular modifications; syntheses of radioisotopically labeled compounds of biomedicinal and pharmaceutical interest; isoquinoline alkaloids, isolation, identification, structure determination and biogenesis. *Mailing Add:* 1420 Gerard St Rockville MD 20850

HAJJ, IBRAHIM NASRI, COMPUTER-AIDED DESIGN, RELIABILITY. *Current Pos:* from asst prof to assoc prof, 79-85, PROF, UNIV ILL, URBANA-CHAMPAIGN, 85- *Personal Data:* b Lebanon, June 21, 42; US citizen; m 73; c 2. *Educ:* Am Univ Beirut, BE, 64; Univ NMex, Albuquerque, MS, 66; Univ Calif, Berkeley, PhD(elec eng), 70. *Prof Exp:* Asst prof, Univ Waterloo, Can, 73 & 75-78, assoc prof, 79-82; asst prof, Lebanese Univ, Beirut, 73-75. *Concurrent Pos:* Vis prof, Tech Univ Denmark, 87. *Mem:* Fel Inst Elec & Electronics Engrs; Sigma Xi; Asn Comput Mach. *Res:* Computer-aided design and simulation of very large scale integrated (VLSI) circuits; fault simulation and testing; parallel-processing algorithms; statistical analysis; optimization; design automation; reliability analysis; design for reliability. *Mailing Add:* Coord Sci Lab Univ Ill 1308 W Main St Urbana IL 61801. *E-Mail:* i-hajj@uiuc.edu

HAJJAR, DAVID PHILLIP, BIOCHEMISTRY, MOLECULAR BIOLOGY. *Current Pos:* fel, 78-80, from asst prof to assoc prof, 81-89, PROF BIOCHEM, CORNELL UNIV MED COL, 89- *Personal Data:* b Lawrence, Mass, Sept 13, 52; m 84, Katherine Amberson; c E Katherine & Amanda E.

Educ: Am Int Col, BA, 74; Univ NH, MS, 77, PhD(biochem), 78. *Honors & Awards:* Res Investr Award, Am Heart Asn, 81; Warner Lambert/Parke Davis Award, Fedn Am Socs Exp Biol, 91. *Prof Exp:* Fel, Rockefeller Univ, 80-81. *Concurrent Pos:* Vis prof, Univ NH, 85, Harvard Med Sch, 87, Univ Wash, 91 & Vanderbilt Univ, 93; mem, Coun Arteriosclerosis, Am Heart Asn, 85-, Coun Thrombosis, 86-; mem, Study Sect Path A, NIH, 91-; mem, Pub Affairs Comt, Am Asn Invest Pathol, 91- *Mem:* Am Inst Chemists; fel Am Heart Asn; AAAS; Am Chem Soc; Am Soc Biochem & Molecular Biol; Fedn Am Socs Exp Biol. *Res:* Study of arteriosclerosis, primarily on the regulation of cholesterol trafficking in the vessel wall by investigating the structural-functional properties of cholesteryl ester hydrolases in the cell. *Mailing Add:* Dept Biochem Cornell Med Col New York NY 10021-4896. *Fax:* 212-746-8789

HAJJAR, NICOLAS PHILIPPE, PESTICIDE TOXICOLOGY, BIOCHEMICAL TOXICOLOGY. *Current Pos:* DEPT MGR, ROY F WESTON INC, 91- *Personal Data:* b Cairo, Egypt, Nov 17, 46; US citizen; m 72; c 2. *Educ:* Cairo Univ, BSc, 67, MSc, 71; Univ Calif, Berkeley, PhD(entom), 78. *Prof Exp:* Res asst anthrop biochem, US Naval Res Univ No 3, Cairo, Egypt, 67-72; res asst entom, Univ Calif, Berkeley, 72-78; fel biochem toxicol, NC State Univ, Raleigh, 78-80; sr scientist & dept mgr, Health & Environ Res Div, Dynamac Corp, 80-91. *Mem:* AAAS; Am Chem Soc; Soc Toxicol. *Res:* Conduct quantitative risk assessments on the effects of industrial pollutants on human health, prepare scientific support documents; evaluate pesticide metabolism and toxicology data; determine environmental fate and transport of pollutants; pesticide toxicology and insect growth regulators, mode of action, structure-activity relationships and metabolism. *Mailing Add:* 304 Spindle Lane West Chester PA 19380

HAJOS, ZOLTAN GEORGE, ORGANIC CHEMISTRY, PHARMACEUTICAL CHEMISTRY. *Current Pos:* RETIRED. *Personal Data:* b Budapest, Hungary, Mar 3, 26; US citizen; wid. *Educ:* Budapest Tech Univ, dipl, 47, DSc, 49. *Prof Exp:* Asst prof, Budapest Tech Univ, 48-57; res assoc chem, Princeton Univ, 57-60; sr chemist, Res Div, Hoffmann-La Roche, Inc, 60-67; res fel, 67-70; res assoc chem, Univ Vt, 72-73; res assoc pharm, Univ Toronto, 73-74; prin scientist chem res, Ortho Pharmaceut Corp, Raritan, NJ, 75-90. *Mem:* Am Chem Soc; Sigma Xi. *Res:* Synthesis and stereochemical investigation of compounds with physiological interest: glycosides, hydrophenanthrenes, steroidal hormones, heterocyclic compounds, especially alkaloids, furan and dioxane derivatives; asymmetric synthesis of intermediates of natural product chemistry. *Mailing Add:* Pauler U 2 Apt 21 Budapest I 1013 Hungary

HAJRA, AMIYA KUMAR, BIOCHEMISTRY, NEUROSCIENCES. *Current Pos:* Asst res biochemist, Ment Health Res Inst, Univ Mich, 64-68, asst prof, 69-73, assoc res biochemist, 68-77, assoc prof, 73, PROF & RES BIOCHEMIST, NEUROSCI LAB, MENT HEALTH RES INST, UNIV MICH, ANN ARBOR. *Personal Data:* b W Bengal, India, Apr 8, 35; m 65, Marideepa Sinha; c Amitav & Neelav. *Educ:* Univ Calcutta, BSc, 53, MSc, 56; Northwestern Univ, PhD(biochem), 63. *Honors & Awards:* Jacob Javits Award in Neurosci. *Mem:* AAAS; Am Soc Biol Chem. *Res:* Phospholipid metabolism; brain biochemistry; biomembrane structure. *Mailing Add:* Ment Health Res Inst Univ Mich 1103 E Huron Ann Arbor MI 48104-1687. *Fax:* 313-763-2690

HAJRATWALA, BHUPENDRA R, PHYSICAL-INDUSTRIAL PHARMACY. *Current Pos:* PVT TUTOR & FINANCIAL PLANNER, AM EDUC & FINANCIAL SERV, 90- *Personal Data:* b Navsari, India, April 8, 42; US citizen; m 67; c 2. *Educ:* Gujarat Univ, India, BPharm, 62; Univ Colo, MS, 65; Univ Iowa, PhD(phys pharm), 70. *Prof Exp:* Anal chemist, aerosols, George Barr & Co, 65-67; asst instr pharmaceut, Univ Iowa, 67-70; dir res parenterals, Invenex Pharmaceut, 70-72; sr lectr pharmaceut, Univ Otago, NZ, 72-79; assoc prof pharmaceut, Wayne State Univ, 79-90. *Concurrent Pos:* Vis prof, Univ Iowa, 78-79. *Mem:* Am Inst Hist Pharm; Int Asn Financial Planners; Asn Pharm Teachers India; Indian Pharmaceut Asn. *Res:* Kinetics and mechanism of degradation of drugs; color stability; dissolution of drugs and factors affecting unit operations in industrial pharmacy and drug-ethanol and drug-drug interactions; formulation and development of dosage forms; pharmacokinetics; biostatistics. *Mailing Add:* 46133 Amesbury Dr Plymouth MI 48170

HAK, LAWRENCE J, NEPHROLOGY, CLINICAL DRUG RESEARCH. *Current Pos:* AT UNIV TENN. *Personal Data:* b Roanoke, Va, Oct 15, 44; m 74; c 3. *Educ:* Philadelphia Col Pharm & Sci, BS, 67, PharmD(pharm), 71. *Prof Exp:* Resident, Univ Pa Hosp, 69-70; instr clin pharm, Philadelphia Col Pharm & Sci, 71-73; from instr to asst prof, Univ NC, 73-79, clin assoc prof med & assoc prof pharm, 79- *Mem:* Am Soc Hosp Pharmacists; Am Soc Parenteral & Enteral Nutrit; Am Soc Nephrology; Am Col Clin Pharm; Am Asn Pharmaceut Scientists. *Res:* Total parenteral nutrition in rats; drug and nutritional therapy of human patients with chronic renal failure; nephrotoxic and ischemic acute renal failure in rats; drug development research in humans. *Mailing Add:* 26 S Dunlap St Col Pharm Univ Tenn Memphis TN 38163

HAKALA, MAIRE TELLERVO, BIOCHEMICAL PHARMACOLOGY. *Current Pos:* RETIRED. *Personal Data:* b Helsinki, Finland, Feb 15, 17; US citizen; m 56; c 1. *Educ:* Univ Helsinki, MSc, 47; Duke Univ, PhD(biochem), 55. *Prof Exp:* Res asst pharmacol, Yale Univ, 53-56; sr scientist, 56-62, Roswell Park Mem Inst, 59-62, assoc scientist, 62-69, prin scientist, 69-80, assoc chief cancer res sci, 80-83, res prof pharmacol & exp ther, 80-83. *Concurrent Pos:* Jane Coffin Childs Mem Fund fel, Yale Univ, 53-55; USPHS grant, Roswell Park Mem Inst, 58-; assoc res prof, Dept Biochem, State Univ NY Buffalo, 68-80. *Mem:* Am Soc Biol Chemists; Am Chem Soc; Am Asn Cancer Res. *Res:* Cell culture studies on drugs and antimetabolites; cellular uptake, metabolism and site of action of anticancer agents; drug resistance. *Mailing Add:* 260 Lakewood Pkwy Amherst NY 14226-4073

HAKALA, REINO WILLIAM, CHEMICAL PHYSICS, APPLIED MATHEMATICS. *Current Pos:* dean art & sci, 80-81, PROF MATH & COMPUT SCI, SCI DIV, GOVS STATE UNIV, 81- *Personal Data:* b Albany, NY, Aug 25, 23; m 50, Eunice Kazanowski; c Jonathan, Lisa & Christina. *Educ:* Columbia Univ, AB, 46, MA, 47; Syracuse Univ, PhD(phys chem), 65. *Prof Exp:* Instr org chem, Assoc Cols Upper NY, 47-48; teaching asst org chem, Syracuse Univ, 48-49, phys chem, 49-51; instr chem, Pa State Univ, 53-54; instr phys chem & inorg chem, Fairfield Univ, 54-57; asst prof, Earlham Col, 57-59; lectr, Howard Univ, 59-63; from asst prof to assoc prof phys chem, Mich Tech Univ, 64-67, assoc prof math, 65-67; prof math, Oklahoma City Univ, 67-72, chmn dept math & dir lab, 67-70, chmn dept physics, 68-70; prof math, Washington Tech Inst, 72-73; dean sci & technol, 73-77, prof chem & physics, 73-78, prof math & physics, Lake Superior State Col, 78. *Concurrent Pos:* Res Corp grant, 59; Am Chem Soc Petrol Fund grant, 59-63; consult, Am Dent Asn Res Lab, Nat Bur Stand, 63; Mich Tech Univ grant, 67; consult, Universal Kleen-Rite Chem Corp, 70-72. *Res:* Theoretical research on equations of state and variation of physical properties of chemical substances with temperature; oscillatory and chaotic iterations; numerical algorithms; nutritional biochemistry; environmental issues. *Mailing Add:* Governors State Univ Sci Div CAS Rte 54 University Pkwy University Park IL 60466. *Fax:* 708-534-1641

HAKALA, WILLIAM WALTER, CIVIL ENGINEERING, SOIL MECHANICS. *Current Pos:* prog mgr, 72-81, HEAD, EARTHQUAKE HAZARD MITIGATION PROG, NSF, 82- *Personal Data:* b Blackberry, Minn, Aug 5, 35; m 60; c 3. *Educ:* Univ Minn, BS, 58, MSCE, 59; Va Polytech Inst, PhD(civil eng), 65. *Prof Exp:* Assoc res engr, Boeing Co, 60-61; asst prof civil eng, Va Polytech Inst, 61-63 & Univ NMex, 64-68; dep dir eng, Environ Res Corp, 68-70; dir opers, John A Blume & Assocs, 70-72. *Concurrent Pos:* Consult, Sandia Corp, 66-68. *Mem:* Am Soc Civil Engrs; Am Soc Eng Educ. *Res:* Soil and rock dynamics; nuclear effects. *Mailing Add:* 4201 Wilson Blvd Arlington VA 22230

HAKE, CARL (LOUIS), CONSULTING. *Current Pos:* RETIRED. *Personal Data:* b Hoyleton, Ill, Nov 23, 27; m 52, 80; c 4. *Educ:* DePauw Univ, BA, 48; Univ Ill, PhD(chem), 56; Am Bd Toxicol, dipl, 80, 85. *Prof Exp:* Biochemist, Dow Chem Co, 56-61, head, Chem Res Dept, Pitman-Moore Div, 61-65, asst to dir, Human Health Res & Develop Labs, 65-69, admin mgr, 69-72; asst prof, Med Col Wis, 72-74, assoc prof environ med & vchmn dept, 74-78, assoc prof pharmacol & toxicol, 78-81; consult, 80-88. *Concurrent Pos:* sabbatical, Univ Neuchatel, Switz, 78; adj prof pharmacol & toxicol, 81-91. *Mem:* Am Chem Soc; Soc Toxicol; Am Indust Hyg Asn; Am Pub Health Asn. *Res:* Effect of environmental and industrial contaminants upon health. *Mailing Add:* 4969 Cave Point Dr Sturgeon Bay WI 54235-8233

HAKE, RICHARD ROBB, PHYSICS, PHYSICS EDUCATION. *Current Pos:* prof, 70-95, EMER PROF PHYSICS, IND UNIV, BLOOMINGTON, 96- *Personal Data:* b Denver, Colo, July 15, 27; m 55, Audrey Dannhauer; c Clifford, Douglas & Cynthia. *Educ:* Univ Colo, BS, 50; Univ Ill, MS, 51, PhD(physics), 55. *Prof Exp:* Asst, Univ Ill, 51-55, res assoc, 55-56; sr physicist, Atomics Int Div, NAm Aviation, Inc, 56-64, res physicist, Sci Ctr, 64-70. *Concurrent Pos:* Consult, Los Alamos Sci Lab, Univ Calif, 70-75; vis prof, Univ Calif, San Diego, 87-88; vis scholar, Ariz State Univ, 92. *Mem:* Fel Am Phys Soc; Am Asn Physics Teachers. *Res:* Solid state and low temperature physics; electronic properties; superconductivity; magnetism; cryogenics; science education. *Mailing Add:* 24245 Hatteras St Woodland Hills CA 91367. *E-Mail:* hake@ix.netcom.com

HAKEN, WOLFGANG, MATHEMATICS. *Current Pos:* PROF MATH, UNIV ILL, URBANA, 65- *Personal Data:* b Berlin, Ger, June 21, 28; m 53; c 4. *Educ:* Univ Kiel, PhD(math), 53. *Prof Exp:* Microwave engr, Siemens & Halske AG, 54-62; vis prof math, Univ Ill, 62-63; temp mem, Inst Advan Study, 63-65. *Mem:* Am Math Soc; Ger Math Asn. *Res:* Topology of 3-dimensional manifolds. *Mailing Add:* Dept Math Univ Ill Urbana IL 61801-2975

HAKES, SAMUEL D(UNCAN), ELECTRICAL ENGINEERING. *Current Pos:* RETIRED. *Personal Data:* b Colorado Springs, Colo, Aug 17, 30; m 51; c 2. *Educ:* Univ Wyo, BS, 57, MS, 58; Univ Iowa, PhD(elec eng), 69. *Prof Exp:* From asst prof to prof elec eng, Univ Wyo, 59-96, dean, 75-96. *Concurrent Pos:* Consult engr, Digital Comput Ctr, Univ Wyo, 59-64, Ideal Aerosmith, 61-, Wyo Hwy Patrol, 67-68, US Navy Stand Lab, 69-70 & Gates Rubber Co, 70-; NSF sci fac fel, 64, dir grant, 70- *Mem:* Inst Elec & Electronics Engrs; Instrument Soc Am. *Res:* Active network synthesis; precision instrumentation; computer design. *Mailing Add:* PO Box 3295 Univ Wy Laramie WY 82071-3295

HAKEWILL, HENRY, JR, ORGANIC CHEMISTRY, INORGANIC CHEMISTRY. *Current Pos:* RETIRED. *Personal Data:* b Chicago, Ill, Dec 14, 18; m 46, Gertrude M Glave; c Henry IV, Julia M, John W & Timothy R. *Educ:* Elmhurst Col, BS, 41; DePaul Univ, MS, 47. *Prof Exp:* Res chemist, Nubian Paint & Varnish Co, 41-43; Pure Oil Co, 43-44 & Inst Gas Technol, 44-51; chief chemist, Cent Com Co, 51-62; mgr active prod, Multigraphics Div, Addressograph-Multigraph Corp, 62-77. *Concurrent Pos:* Tech Consult, Duraclean Int, Inc, 85- *Mem:* Am Chem Soc; Tech Asn Pulp & Paper Indust; Am Soc Testing & Mat; Sigma Xi. *Res:* Electrophotography; pigmented coatings; resins; gas analysis. *Mailing Add:* 1355 Wilmot Rd Deerfield IL 60015

HAKIM, EDWARD BERNARD, SOLID STATE PHYSICS, ELECTRONICS. *Current Pos:* BR CHIEF, COMPONENT RELIABILITY BR, DEPT ARMY, FT MONMOUTH, 62- *Personal Data:* b Jersey City, NJ, July 11, 36; m 64; c 4. *Educ:* Fairleigh Dickenson Univ, BS, 59; Univ Conn, MS, 62. *Prof Exp:* Res physicist, IBM Corp, 61-62. *Mem:* Inst Elec & Electronics Engrs. *Res:* Microcircuit reliability and physics of failure. *Mailing Add:* Ctr Com Component Insersion 2412 Emerson Ave Spring Lake Heights NJ 07762

HAKIM, MARGARET HEATH, CLINICAL CHEMISTRY. *Current Pos:* SUPVR, LIGAND ASSAY, ST JOHN CLIN LABS, DETROIT, MICH, 85- *Personal Data:* b Lansing, Mich, Nov 29, 38; m 63; c 2. *Educ:* Oberlin Col, AB, 60; Wayne State Univ, MS, 62, PhD(biochem), 66. *Prof Exp:* Res assoc, Wayne County Gen Hosp, 77-84; res coordr, Henry Ford Hosp, Detroit, 84-85. *Mem:* Clin Ligand Assay Soc; Midwest Radio Assay Soc. *Mailing Add:* 21245 Prestwick Ave Harper Woods MI 48225

HAKIM, RAZIEL SAMUEL, DEVELOPMENTAL BIOLOGY, HISTOLOGY. *Current Pos:* asst prof, 77-84, ASSOC PROF ANAT, HOWARD UNIV, 84- *Personal Data:* b New York, NY, Mar 4, 47; m 69, Frances T; c 2. *Educ:* Queens Col, BA, 67; Harvard Univ, MA, 68, PhD(biol), 72. *Prof Exp:* Teaching asst biol, Harvard Univ, 68-71; asst prof, Univ Ky, 71-77. *Concurrent Pos:* Prin investr, Nat Inst Child Health & Human Develop, 73-80; NIH grant, 80-84, NSF grant, 85-88. *Mem:* AAAS; Soc Develop Biol; Am Soc Zool; Sigma Xi; Am Asn Anatomists; Tissue Culture Soc. *Res:* Problems relating to cellular differentiation and cellular determination using 2 insect model systems: salivary glands/midgut; tem cell control and pattern formation. *Mailing Add:* Dept Anat Rm 1105 Col Med Howard Univ 550 W St NW Washington DC 20059. *E-Mail:* raziel@cldc.howard.edu

HAKIMI, JOHN, IMMUNOPHARMACOLOGY. *Current Pos:* sr scientist, 82-88, RES INVESTR, DEPT IMMUNOPHARMACOL, HOFFMANN-LA ROCHE, 88- *Personal Data:* b New York, NY, Dec 4, 50. *Educ:* Univ NY, BA, 72; Univ Rochester, PhD(pharmacol), 77. *Prof Exp:* Fel, Dept Pharmacol, Sch Med, Univ Rochester, 77; fel develop biol & cancer, Albert Einstein Col Med, 79-82. *Concurrent Pos:* Lectr pharmacol nursing students, Sch Med, Univ Rochester, 72 & 77, lab instr pharmacol med students, 74; res fel, Leukemia Soc Am, 79-81. *Mem:* AAAS; Am Chem Soc; Am Soc Cell Biol; NY Acad Sci; Sigma Xi. *Res:* Immunopharmacology; numerous publications. *Mailing Add:* Dept Immunopharmacol Hoffman-La Roche Inc Bldg 86 Rm 616 340 Kingsland St Nutley NJ 07110-1199. *Fax:* 973-235-3429

HAKIMI, S(EIFOLLAH) L(OUIS), ELECTRICAL ENGINEERING, COMPUTER SCIENCE. *Current Pos:* prof & chair, elec eng & comput sci, 86-91, chair, elec & comput eng, 91-96, PROF ELEC & COMPUT ENG, UNIV CALIF, DAVIS, 91- *Personal Data:* b Meshed, Iran, Dec 16, 32; nat US; m 65, Mary Yomtob; c Alan G, Carol L & Diane R. *Educ:* Univ Ill, BS, 55, MS, 57, PhD, 59. *Prof Exp:* Asst, Univ Ill, 55-58, asst prof elec eng, 59-61; from assoc prof to prof elec eng, Northwestern Univ, 61-86, chair, 72-77, prof comput sci, appl math & oper res, 77-86. *Concurrent Pos:* Assoc ed, Trans Circuits & Systs, Inst Elec & Electronics Engrs, 75-77; ed, Japanese Trans Fundamentals Electronics, Commun & Comput Sci, 91-96. *Mem:* Fel Inst Elec & Electronics Engrs; Sigma Xi; Soc Indust & Appl Math. *Res:* Graph theory and combinatonics and their applications to circuits, networks, coding theory, jault-tolerant computing, operations research, location theory and computer science; networks; coding theory; discrete optimization. *Mailing Add:* 27017 E El Macero Dr El Macero CA 95618

HAKKILA, EERO ARNOLD, ANALYTICAL CHEMISTRY, NUCLEAR SAFEGUARDS. *Current Pos:* RETIRED. *Personal Data:* b Canterbury, Conn, Aug 4, 31; m 88, Margaret Woesner; c Jon E, Mark D & Gregg A. *Educ:* Cent Conn State Col, BS, 53; Ohio State Univ, PhD(anal chem), 57. *Honors & Awards:* US Dept Energy Award Excellence, Nuclear Weapons Prog, 92. *Prof Exp:* Staff mem anal chem, Los Alamos Nat Lab, 57-95. *Concurrent Pos:* Dep group leader, Safeguards Syst, 80-82, group leader, 82-83, prog coord, Int Safeguards, 87-95. *Mem:* Am Chem Soc; Am Nuclear Soc; Inst Nuclear Mat Mgt; fel Am Inst Chem; Sigma Xi. *Res:* X-ray absorption and emission; electron microprobe; analytical chemistry of U and Pu; chemistry of irradiated nuclear fuels; analytical chemistry in nuclear safeguards; ion microprobe analysis; international safeguards. *Mailing Add:* PO Box 125 Los Alamos NM 87544-0125. *Fax:* 505-667-7626

HAKKILA, JON ERIC, INTERMEDIATE-MASS PECULIAR ABUNDANCE STARS, SPATIAL DISTRIBUTIONS GAMMA RAY BURSTS. *Current Pos:* from asst prof to assoc prof, 86-94, PROF ASTRON, MANKATO STATE UNIV, 94- *Personal Data:* b Columbus, Ohio, June 27, 57; m 86, Fahn; c Oriane & Leotie. *Educ:* Univ Calif, San Diego, BA(physics) & BA(eng/am lit), 80, NMex State Univ, MS, 85, PhD(astron), 86. *Honors & Awards:* Pres Res Lectr, Mankato State Univ, 94. *Prof Exp:* Electromech technician I & II, Los Alamos Nat Lab, 78-79; teaching asst & eng aid physics, Univ Calif, San Diego, 79-80; res & teaching asst astron, Astron Dept, NMex State Univ, 80-81 & 83-86; math & sci programmer analyst, Comsysts Div, Sci Applications Int Corp, 81-83. *Concurrent Pos:* Lectr physics & astron, Univ San Diego, 82-83; NASA/ASEE summer fac fel, NASA, Space Sci Lab, Huntsville, Ala, 89 & 90; prin investr, Jt Venture Prog, NASA & Mankato State Univ, 90-93; guest investr, Compton Observ Phase 3, 93-94, Compton Observ Cycle 4, 94-95 & Cycle 6, 96-97; Nat Res Coun fel, 94-95. *Mem:* Am Astron Soc; Int Astron Union. *Res:* Stellar kinematics and spatial distributions; infrared and visible photometry; peculiar-abundance stars; mass transfer in evolving binary star systems; spatial distributions of gamma ray bursts. *Mailing Add:* Dept Phys & Astron Mankato State Univ Mankato MN 56002-8400. *Fax:* 507-389-1840; *E-Mail:* jhakk@msus1.msus.edu

HAKKINEN, RAIMO JAAKKO, AERODYNAMICS, FLUID DYNAMICS. *Current Pos:* mem res staff, Mass Inst Technol, 53-56, res engr, Missile & Space Systs Div, Douglas Aircraft Co, Inc, Calif, 56-64, chief scientist, Phys Sci Dept, 64-70, chief scientist flight sci, 70-82, DIR RES, MCDONNELL DOUGLAS RES LABS, 82- *Personal Data:* b Helsinki, Finland, Feb 26, 26; nat US; m 49; c 2. *Educ:* Helsinki Univ Technol, Dipl, 48; Calif Inst Technol, MS, 50, PhD(aeronaut), 54. *Prof Exp:* Engr, Finnish Aeronaut Asn, 48; instr aeronaut & mech eng, Tampere Tech Col, Finland, 49; engr, Aeronaut Div, Valmet Corp, Finland, 49; asst gas dynamics, Calif Inst Technol, 50-53. *Concurrent Pos:* Lectr, Univ Calif, Los Angeles, 57-59; vis assoc prof, Mass Inst Technol, 63-64. *Mem:* Fel Am Inst Aeronaut & Astronaut; Am Phys Soc; Sigma Xi. *Res:* Fluid physics; boundary layers; experimental gas-dynamics. *Mailing Add:* Dept Mech Eng Washington Univ One Brookings Dr CB1185 St Louis MO 63130

HAKKINEN, SIRPA MARJA ANNELI, NUMERICAL MODELING OF COUPLED ICE-OCEAN SYSTEMS, CONVECTION & WATER MASS FORMATION. *Current Pos:* resident res assoc, 85-87, OCEANOGR, NASA GODDARD SPACE FLIGHT CTR, 90- *Personal Data:* b Joutsa, Finland, Oct 13, 51; m 89, G Leonard Johnson. *Educ:* Univ Helsinki, BS, 74, MS, 76, (licentiate ph, 78; Fla State Univ, PhD(geophys fluid dynamics), 84. *Prof Exp:* Scientist, Inst Marine Res, Helsinki, 77-80; scientist, Univ Space Res Asn, NASA, 87-88; res staff, Princeton Univ, 88-90. *Concurrent Pos:* Prin investr, NASA Nat Oceanic & Atmospheric Admin, Off Naval Res, 90-; mem, Comt Polar Ocean & Meteorol, Am Metrol Soc, 93- *Mem:* Am Geophys Union; Oceanog Soc; Finnish Math & Phys Soc; Finnish Geophys Soc. *Res:* Dynamics/thermodynamics of high latitude oceans, convection, water mass formation, coupled global modeling, thermohaline circulation, ecosystem and tracer modeling. *Mailing Add:* Code 971 NASA Goddard Space Flight Ctr Greenbelt MD 20771

HAKOMORI, SEN-ITIROH, BIOCHEMISTRY, IMMUNOCHEMISTRY. *Current Pos:* assoc prof prev med, Sch Med, 68-71, PROF PATHOBIOL & MICROBIOL, MED SCH & SCH PUB HEALTH, UNIV WASH, 71-, PROF IMMUNOL, 77- *Personal Data:* b Sendai City, Japan, Feb 13, 29; m 56; c 3. *Educ:* Tohoku Univ, Japan, MD, 52, DMedSc(biochem), 56. *Honors & Awards:* Philip Levine Immunohemat Award, Amer Soc Clin Path, 84; Asahi Prize Arts & Sci, Japan, 91; Morton Lectr Award, Brit Biochem Soc, 92; Complex Carbohydrate Soc. *Prof Exp:* Asst, Biochem Inst, Tohoku Univ, Japan, 55-56, asst prof, Med Sch, 57-59; prof & chief dept, Inst Cancer Res, Tohoku Col Pharmaceut Sci, 59-63; res assoc, Harvard Med Sch, 63-66; res assoc, Mass Gen Hosp, 63-66; Am Cancer Soc scholar, Brandeis Univ, 66-68. *Concurrent Pos:* Res fel biochem, Harvard Med Sch, 56-57; mem, Fred Hutchinson Cancer Res Ctr, 75-87; dir, Biomembrane Inst, 87- *Mem:* Am Asn Biol Chemists; Am Asn Immunologists; Am Asn Cancer Res. *Res:* Biochemistry and immunochemistry of glycoproteins and glycolipids. *Mailing Add:* Biomembrane Div Pac Northwest Res Found 720 Broadway Seattle WA 98122. *Fax:* 206-281-9893

HALABAN, RUTH, GENETICS, DEVELOPMENTAL BIOLOGY. *Current Pos:* res assoc, 73-81, SR RES ASSOC GENETICS, SCH MED, YALE UNIV, 81- *Personal Data:* b Tel Aviv, Israel, Nov 30, 38; US citizen; m 63; c 2. *Educ:* Hebrew Univ, Israel, BSc, 62, MSc, 64; Princeton Univ, PhD(molecular & develop biol), 68. *Prof Exp:* Instr biol, Princeton Univ, 68-69; res assoc develop biol, Brookhaven Nat Lab, 69-71; res assoc genetics, State Univ NY Albany, 71-73. *Res:* Hormonal regulation of growth and differentiation in cultured somatic cells; analysis of mutants and their hybrid cells; factors involved in transformation to malignancy of normal pigment cells. *Mailing Add:* Dept Dermat Yale Univ Sch Med 500 LCI New Haven CT 06520-8059. *Fax:* 203-785-7234

HALABISKY, LORNE STANLEY, APPLIED MATHEMATICS. *Current Pos:* systs analyst, 76-81, SR SYSTS ANALYST, INS CO BC, 81- *Personal Data:* b Ottawa, Ont, Jan 4, 45. *Educ:* Univ Alta, BSc, 66; Brown Univ, PhD(appl math), 70. *Prof Exp:* Asst prof math, Univ BC, 70-76. *Mem:* Soc Indust & Appl Math; Fedn Am Sci. *Res:* Evolution of finite disturbances in dissipative gas dynamics; boundary valve problems in dissipative gas dynamics. *Mailing Add:* 11791 Pintail Dr Richmond BC V7E 4N7 Can

HALABY, GEORGE ANTON, FOOD TECHNOLOGY, NUTRITION. *Current Pos:* VPRES RES & DEVELOP, SARA LEE, 90- *Personal Data:* b Jaffa, Palestine, Mar 12, 38; US citizen. *Educ:* Alexandria Univ, BS, 62; Columbia Univ, MS, 66; Univ Mass, Amherst, PhD(food technol), 71. *Prof Exp:* Chief chemist chem & pharm, Govt Cent Labs, Ministry of Health, Amman, Jordan, 62-65; res scientist food sci, John Morrell & Co, Chicago, 71-72; mgr, Stokely-Van Camp, Inc, Indianapolis, 72-79, dir, Res Develop & Lab Serv Food Sci, 79-85; vpres res & develop, Quaker Oaks Co, Barrington, 85-90. *Concurrent Pos:* WHO fel, Univ Alexandria, 59-61; Fulbright fel award, Columbia Univ, 65-66; NIH fel, Univ Mass, 67-71. *Mem:* Am Chem Soc; Inst Food Technologists; Am Oil Chemists Soc; fel Col Sports Med. *Res:* Nutrient analysis of foods; nutritional biochemistry; lipid chemistry; thermal processing canning and bacteriology; research and development of special dietary foods; exercise physiology; sports nutrition. *Mailing Add:* 740 Oxbow Lane Barrington IL 60010

HALABY, NAJEEB E, FINANCE, LAW. *Current Pos:* PRES, HALABY INT CORP, 73- *Personal Data:* b Dallas, Tex, Nov 19, 15; wid; c Lisa (Queen Noor of Jordan), Christian & Alexa. *Educ:* Stanford Univ, AB, 37; Yale Univ, LLB, 40. *Hon Degrees:* LLD, Allegheny Col, 67, Loyola Univ, 68, Dowling Col, 85, Embry Riddle Aeronaut Univ, 93. *Honors & Awards:* Legion of Honor, France; Order of Ceders, Lebanon; Medal of Independence, Jordan; Arthur Fleming Award; Godfrey L Cabot Award; Monsanto Air Safety

Award; Glen Gilbert Air Traffic Award; Nat Air & Space Mus Trophy, Smithsonian Inst, 95. *Prof Exp:* Staff, O'Melveny & Myers, 40-42; test pilot, Lockheed Aircraft Corp, 42-43; foreign affairs adv to secy defense, Dept Defense, 48-53; staff, L S Rockefeller & Bros, 53-56; pres, Am Tech Corp; secy treas & coun, Aerospace Corp; pvt pract law, 59-61; fac lectr, Univ Calif Los Angeles, dir & chmn, Defense Studies Prog, Disarmament Conf, 60; adminr, Fed Aviation Admin, 61-65; pres, Pan Am World Airways, 68-72, chmn chief exec officer, 69-72. *Concurrent Pos:* Dept asst to secy of defense, Dept Defense, 52-54; chmn, Dulles Access Rapid Transit Inc, 85-; staff, Nat Ctr Atmospheric Res Found, 85-; trustee, Jones Inst Reproductive Biol & Flight Safety Found; mem adv coun, Brookings Inst, Libr Cong, Smithsonian Inst; asst chief, Fighter Sect, Naval Air Test Ctr, Patuxent River, Md. *Mem:* Am Inst Aeronaut & Astronaut; Soc Exp Test Pilots; Coun Foreign Rels. *Mailing Add:* 175 Chain Bridge Rd McLean VA 22101-1907

HALABY, SAMI ASSAD, PHYSICAL CHEMISTRY, COMPUTER SCIENCE. *Current Pos:* PRES, APPL TECHNOL CONCEPTS INC, 92- *Personal Data:* b Jerusalem, Palestine, Feb 14, 33; US citizen; m 57; c 2. *Educ:* Mich State Univ, BSc, 53; Univ Cincinnati, PhD(phys chem), 59; Harvard Bus Sch, PMD, 69. *Prof Exp:* Asst chem, Univ Cincinnati, 54-57; sr chemist, Corning Glass Works, 59-64, mgr, Electronic Mat Res Dept, 64-70, mgr tech planning, 70-71, res assooc, Tech Staff's Div, 71-75; res physicist, Am Optical Corp, 76-77; mgr systs technol, Warner Lambert Co, 78-84, mgr, Microprocessor Applin, 85-87, dir, Microprocessor Applin & Eng Develop, 87-91. *Concurrent Pos:* Consult, Nat Inst Environ Health, 75-79; Twitchell fel, Univ Cincinnati, 57-58. *Mem:* Am Chem Soc; Sigma Xi; Inst Elec & Electronics Engrs. *Res:* Aqueous electrolyte solutions; thin film research; active electronic film devices; film structure; biomedical instrumentation; computer applications in manufacturing; QC instrumentation. *Mailing Add:* 292 Brook Valley Rd Kinajelon NJ 07405-3322

HALARIS, ANGELOS, BIOLOGICAL PSYCHIATRY, PSYCHOPHARMACOLOGY. *Current Pos:* DEPT PSYCHIAT, CASE-WESTERN RESERVE UNIV & CLEVELAND METRO GEN HOSP. *Personal Data:* b Athens, Greece, Nov 30, 42; US citizen. *Educ:* Univ Munich, MD & PhD(med), 67. *Honors & Awards:* Physician's Recognition Award, AMA, 77. *Prof Exp:* Res asst neurochem, Max Planck Inst Psychiat, Munich, 67-69; fel psychiat, Univ Chicago, 71-74, asst prof, 74-78, assoc prof, 78- *Concurrent Pos:* Found Fund Res Psychiat fel, 71-73; psychiat consult, Michael Reese Hosp & Med Ctr, 77- *Mem:* Am Col Neuropsychopharmacol; Collegium Int Psychopharmacologicum; Am Psychiat Asn; Am Soc Pharmacol & Exp Therapeut; Soc Neurosci. *Res:* Biochemistry of affective disorders and mode of action of psychotropic drugs. *Mailing Add:* Dept Psychiat Human Behavior Univ Miss Med Ctr 2500 N State St Jackson MS 39216-4505. *Fax:* 601-984-5842

HALARNKAR, PREMJIT P, BIOCHEMISTRY. *Current Pos:* FEL, DEPT BIOCHEM, UNIV NEV, 89- *Personal Data:* b Bombay, India, Aug 31, 59; m. *Educ:* Univ Bombay, BSc, 79, MSc, 81, Univ Nev, PhD(biochem), 87. *Prof Exp:* Chemist, Paper Prod Ltd, Bombay, India, 81-82; res asst, Dept Biochem, Univ Nev, Reno, 83-87; fel, Dept Entom, Univ Calif, 87-89. *Mem:* Am Soc Biochem & Molecular Biol; Am Chem Soc; Entom Soc Am. *Res:* Biochemistry; numerous publications. *Mailing Add:* Bayer Corp 17745 S Medcalf Stilwell KS 66085

HALAS, NAOMI J, NANOSCALE SCIENCE & ENGINEERING. *Current Pos:* asst prof, 90-94, ASSOC PROF, ELEC & COMPUT ENG DEPT, RICE UNIV, 94- *Personal Data:* b New Eagle, Pa, Aug 1, 57; m 86. *Educ:* LaSalle Univ, BA, 80; Bryn Mawr Univ, MA, 84, PhD(physics), 86. *Prof Exp:* Res fel, IBM TJ Watson Res Lab, 83-86, AT&T Bell Lab, 87-89. *Mem:* Am Phys Soc; Am Chem Soc. *Res:* Nanoscale engineering, properties and applications of colloids and nanoparticles; molecular electronics. *Mailing Add:* Elec & Comput Eng Dept MS366 Rice Univ 61005 Main Houston TX 77005

HALASA, ADEL F, POLYMER BLENDS. *Current Pos:* RES & DEVELOP FEL, ELASTOMER RES, GOODYEAR TIRE & RUBBER CO, 83- *Personal Data:* b Madaba, Jordan, Dec 24, 33; US citizen; m 54; c 2. *Educ:* Univ Okla, BS, 55; Butler Univ, MS, 59; Purdue Univ, PhD(chem), 64. *Prof Exp:* Group leader elastomer res, Firestone Tire & Rubber Co, 65-68, res assoc, 68-74, sr res assoc, 74-79, dir petrol & petro-chem, Kuwait Inst Sci Res, 80-82. *Concurrent Pos:* Lectr, Purdue Univ, 62-64; chmn, Akron Polymer Lect Group, 74-75; prog dir cent regional meeting, Am Chem Soc, 76-77. *Mem:* Am Chem Soc; Am Inst Chemists; NY Acad Sci; AAAS; Sigma Xi. *Res:* Anionic polymerization for the preparation of novel elastomer with controlled micro and macro structure; studies in the area of miscible and immiscible blends of various elastomers and their effect on physical properties; studies in hydrogenetics of block copolymers; 150 US patents. *Mailing Add:* 5040 Everrett Rd PO Box 825 Bath OH 44210

HALASI-KUN, GEORGE JOSEPH, HYDROLOGY, CARTOGRAPHY. *Current Pos:* CHMN HYDROL, SEM POLLUTION & WATER RES, COLUMBIA UNIV, 68- *Personal Data:* b Zagreb, Austria-Hungary, July 28, 16; US citizen, Elisabeth Szorad; c Beatrice & Georgine. *Educ:* Inst Technol, Budapest, MS, 38; Univ Foreigner, Italy, cert, 38; Slovak Tech Univ, Bratislava, CE, 49; Brunswick Tech Univ, DrEngSc(geohydrol), 68. *Hon Degrees:* DSc, J Pannonius Univ, Pecs, 93, Agr, Univ Godollo, 95. *Prof Exp:* Hwy engr, Bd of Works, Lipt Mikulas, Czech, 46-48; dir water res & prof, Tech Univ Kosice & Col Water Eng, 48-53; mgr chief engr, Pozemne Stavby Construct Co, Kosice, 54-57; proj mgr eng, Columbia Univ, 58-67. *Concurrent Pos:* Mem, Regional Planning Comt, Dept Interior, Prague, Czech, 52-53; res assoc, Dept Civil Eng, Brunswick Tech Univ, 66-69; organizer & speaker, Int Conf on Pollution & Water Resources, 70-; adj prof, Dept Life Sci, NY Inst Technol, 71-76; state topog engr mapping & hydrol, NJ State, 71-91; vis prof, Dept Environ Resources, Rutgers Univ & Fairleigh Dickinson Univ, 76-; Nat Acad Sci fel, researcher geohydrol, WGer, Yugoslavia & Hungary, 77, 82 & 84; Fulbright scholar, Hungary, Czech, 90-91, 91-92, 92-93 & 93-94; hon fac mem, Agr Sci Univ, Hungary, 93. *Mem:* Fel Am Soc Civil Engrs; fel Geol Soc Am; Int Water Resources Asn; Am Cong Surv & Mapping; Am Water Resources Asn; Am Inst Hydrol; Hungarian Acad Sci; Ukrainian Acad Sci. *Res:* Interdisciplinary program studies on pollution and water resources as an environmental problem; extreme surface flow of smaller watersheds including water storage capacity based on permeability of subsurface geology; author of 31 books and over 80 articles. *Mailing Add:* 31 Knowles Ave Pennington NJ 08534

HALASZ, NICHOLAS ALEXIS, SURGERY, ANATOMY. *Current Pos:* assoc prof, 67-70, PROF SURG & DIR, KIDNEY TRANSPLANT UNIT & HEAD, DIV ANAT, UNIV CALIF, SAN DIEGO, 70- *Personal Data:* b Budapest, Hungary, Mar 13, 31; US citizen; m 64; c 2. *Educ:* Trinity Col, BS, 48; Yale Univ, MD, 54. *Prof Exp:* From instr to asst prof surg, Univ Calif, Los Angeles, 62-67. *Concurrent Pos:* Dir, Am Bd Surg, 84; Markle Scholar in Acad Med, 64-69. *Mem:* Am Col Surg; Soc Exp Biol & Med; Soc Univ Surg; Tissue Cult Asn; Transplantation Soc; Am Surg Asn. *Res:* General, pediatric and thoracic surgery; transplantation immunology; antigen pretreatment; transplacental passage of antigen; organ preservation using perfusion, cooling and freezing. *Mailing Add:* 1361 Virginia Way La Jolla CA 92037

HALBACH, KLAUS, PHYSICS. *Current Pos:* mem staff, 60-80, SR STAFF MEM, LAWRENCE BERKELEY LAB, 80- *Personal Data:* b Wuppertal, Ger, Feb 3, 25; US citizen; m 45; c 1. *Educ:* Univ Basel, PhD(physics), 54. *Prof Exp:* Lectr physics, Univ Fribourg, 54-56, Privatdozent, 56-57 & 59-60; res assoc, Stanford Univ, 57-59. *Concurrent Pos:* Consult, LANL, TRW & Varian. *Mem:* Am Phys Soc. *Res:* Accelerator technology; nuclear magnetic resonance; plasma physics. *Mailing Add:* 1492 Grizzly Peak Blvd Berkeley CA 94708

HALBERG, CHARLES JOHN AUGUST, JR, MATHEMATICS. *Current Pos:* from instr to assoc prof, 55-68, PROF MATH, UNIV CALIF, RIVERSIDE, 68- *Personal Data:* b Pasadena, Calif, Sept 24, 21; m 41, 70, 85, Betty Reese; c Ariel A (Walters), Charle T & Niels F, Ulferik H. *Educ:* Pomona Col, BA, 49; Univ Calif, Los Angeles, MA, 53, PhD(math), 55. *Prof Exp:* Instr math, Pomona Col, 49-50; assoc, Univ Calif, Los Angeles, 54-55. *Concurrent Pos:* Lectr, Univ Calif, Los Angeles, 56-; NSF fel, Copenhagen Univ, 61-62; docent, Gothenburg Univ, 69-70. *Mem:* Am Math Soc; Sigma Xi. *Res:* Linear operator theory; spectral theory of bounded linear operators. *Mailing Add:* PO Box 2724 Carlsbad CA 92018-2724

HALBERSTADT, MARCEL LEON, AUTOMOTIVE EMISSIONS, AIR POLLUTION. *Current Pos:* sr staff scientist, 78-80, mgr, Res & Analysis Dept, 81-87, dir, environ dept, 87-93, MGR, RES & ANALYSIS DEPT, MOTOR VEHICLE MFRS ASN, 94- *Personal Data:* b St Raphael, France, June 4, 37; US citizen. *Educ:* City Col New York, BS, 58; Yale Univ, MS, 60, PhD(phys chem), 64. *Prof Exp:* Nat Acad Sci-Nat Res Coun res assoc, Nat Bur Stand, 63-65; asst prof chem, Univ Mo St Louis, 65-72; proj phys chemist, Bendix Res Labs, 72-78. *Mem:* AAAS; Am Chem Soc; Air & Waste Mgt Asn; Soc Automotive Engrs. *Res:* Emissions from internal combustion engines; motor vehicle emissions and air quality. *Mailing Add:* Motor Vehicle Mfrs Asn 7430 Second Ave Suite 300 Detroit MI 48202-2705. *Fax:* 313-872-5400; *E-Mail:* halberml@ix.netcom.com

HALBERSTAM, HEINI, DEVELOPMENT & APPLICATION OF SIEVE METHODS. *Current Pos:* prof & head, Dept Math, 80-88, prof math, 88-96, EMER PROF MATH, UNIV ILL, URBANA-CHAMPAIGN, 96- *Personal Data:* b Most, Czech, Sept 11, 26; Brit citizen; m 50, 72, Doreen Bramley; c 4. *Educ:* London Univ, Univ Col, BSc, 46, MSc, 48, PhD(math), 52. *Honors & Awards:* Fel, Univ Col London, 87. *Prof Exp:* Lectr math, Univ Exeter, Eng, 49-57; reader, Royal Holloway Col, Univ London, 57-62; Erasmus Smith prof math, Trinity Col, Dublin, 62-64; prof, Univ Nottingham, Eng, 64-80. *Concurrent Pos:* Vis instr, Brown Univ, RI, 55-56; vis prof, Univ Mich, Ann Arbor, 66 & Univ Tel Aviv, Israel, 73; co-prin investr, NSF res grants in number theory, 81-89. *Mem:* Am Math Soc. *Res:* Analytic and combinational number theory, especially in sieve theory. *Mailing Add:* Math Dept 1409 W Green St Urbana IL 61801

HALBERT, EDITH CONRAD, THEORETICAL NUCLEAR PHYSICS. *Current Pos:* PHYSICIST, OAK RIDGE NAT LAB, 56- *Personal Data:* b New York, NY, Apr 23, 31; m 51; c 3. *Educ:* Cornell Univ, AB, 51; Univ Rochester, PhD, 57. *Mem:* Fel Am Phys Soc. *Res:* Heavy ion collisions, nuclear structure, effective interactions. *Mailing Add:* Oak Ridge Nat Lab Box 2008 MS6374 Oak Ridge TN 37831

HALBERT, MELVYN LEONARD, NUCLEAR PHYSICS. *Current Pos:* PHYSICIST, OAK RIDGE NAT LAB, 55- *Personal Data:* b Philadelphia, Pa, Aug 12, 29; m 51; Edith Conrad; c Daniel C, Joel M & Alan L. *Educ:* Cornell Univ, AB, 50; Univ Rochester, PhD(physics), 55. *Concurrent Pos:* Exchange scientist, Brookhaven Nat Lab, 71-72 & Niels Bohr Inst, Copenhagen, 74-75. *Mem:* Fel Am Phys Soc; Sigma Xi. *Res:* Heavy-ion nuclear physics; mesonic x-rays; cross-section fluctuations; nuclear spectroscopy; nucleon-nucleon forces; few-nucleon problems. *Mailing Add:* Oak Ridge Nat Lab PO Box 2008 MS-6368 Oak Ridge TN 37831-6368

HALBERT, SEYMOUR PUTTERMAN, MEDICAL MICROBIOLOGY, IMMUNOLOGY. *Current Pos:* RETIRED. *Personal Data:* b Philadelphia, Pa, Mar 20, 17; m 52. *Educ:* Univ NC, BA, 37; Johns Hopkins Univ, MD, 41. *Prof Exp:* Intern, Long Island Col Hosp, 41-42; assoc bact, Sch Med, Univ Pa, 42-45; asst surgeon, NIH, 45-46; asst prof exp med, Sch Pub Health, Univ NC, 46-49; assoc prof microbiol, Col Physicians & Surgeons, Columbia Univ, 49-60, prof ophthal res, 60-65; prof pediat, Sch Med, Univ Miami, 65-78; vpres res & develop, Cordis Labs, 68-89. *Concurrent Pos:* Guggenheim fel, 56; Helen Hay Whitney fel, 56. *Mem:* AAAS; Am Soc Microbiol; Am Chem Soc; Asn Res Vision & Ophthal; Harvey Soc. *Res:* Pneumococcal hemolysin; Shigella vaccines; oil-emulsion vaccine adjuvants; antibiotic-producing intestinal bacteria and ocular flora; streptolysin O; analysis of streptococcal infections; immunology of ocular tissues; biochemical evolution of proteins; pharmacology of bacterial toxins; cystic fibrosis; cardiac auto-immune system; plasma proteins of pregnancy; enzyme labeled immunoassays. *Mailing Add:* 12450 Rock Garden Lane Miami FL 33156

HALBERT, SHERIDAN A, REPRODUCTIVE BIOLOGY, INFERTILITY. *Current Pos:* Fel, Ctr Bioeng, Univ Wash, 73, res assoc, Dept Biol Structure, 74, actg asst prof, 74-76, asst prof, 76-81, ASSOC PROF BIOENG & BIOL STRUCTURE, UNIV WASH, 81-; CONSULT 91-; DIR SCI RES, AVATAR DESIGN & DEVELOP, SEATTLE, 92- *Personal Data:* b Shelton, Wa, July 3, 43. *Educ:* Univ Wash, BS, 65, PhD(physiol & biophys), 72. *Concurrent Pos:* Res affiliate, Regional Primate Res Ctr, Univ Wash, 77-. *Mem:* Am Asn Anatomists; Soc Study Reproduction. *Res:* Structure and function of the mammalian fallopian tube in normal animals and in animal models representing disease states associated with infertility. *Mailing Add:* 2314 184th Pl SE Bothell WA 98012

HALBERT, SUSAN E, APHIDS, PLANT VIRUS EPIDEMIOLOGY. *Current Pos:* AT BIOL SCI & DIV PLANT INDUST, FDACS. *Educ:* De Pauw Univ, BA, 73; Univ Ill, MS, 75. *Prof Exp:* Vis scholar, Nanjing, China, Nat Acad Sci, 81; fel, Wash State Univ, 82-85; res assoc, Aphid Prog, Univ Idaho, 85-92, Aphid surv coordr, 92- *Concurrent Pos:* Biol control expert, USSR, 89 & 91; pres, Russ Wheat Coord Aphid Res Comt, 90 & 91. *Mem:* Entom Soc Am; Asn Appl Biologists; Am Phytopath Soc; Am Registry Prof Entomologists; Am Sci Affil. *Res:* Biology, taxonomy and pest management of aphids; epidemiology of arthropod-transmitted plant pathogens. *Mailing Add:* Div Plant Indust-FDAC 1911 SW 34th St PO Box 147100 Gainesville FL 32614-7100. *Fax:* 208-397-4311

HALBERT, THOMAS RISHER, SOLID STATE CHEMISTRY. *Current Pos:* Res chemist, 77-79, sr chemist, 79-81, STAFF CHEMIST, SOLID STATE CHEM, CORP RES LABS, EXXON RES & ENG CO, 81-, PROJ LEADER, ADVAN CATALYST & HEAVY FEED UPGRADING, EXXON RES & DEVELOP LABS, 88- *Personal Data:* b Schenectady, NY, July 20, 50; m 73; c 3. *Educ:* Rutgers Univ, BA, 72; Stanford Univ, PhD(org chem), 77. *Mem:* Am Chem Soc. *Res:* Transition metal-sulfur cluster chemistry; hydrotreating catalysis; solid state inorganic chemistry; intercalation chemistry; new materials with applications in energy related fields; organometallic chemistry and bioinorganic chemistry. *Mailing Add:* Exxon Res & Develop Labs PO Box 2226 Baton Rouge LA 70822-2226. *Fax:* 504-359-4404

HALBFINGER, GEORGE PHILIP, ELECTROCHEMICAL CORROSION RESEARCH, THERMODYNAMICS OF OXIDE SYSTEMS. *Current Pos:* SR & PRIN ENGR, KAPL INC, LOCKHEED MARTIN CO, 73- *Personal Data:* b Brooklyn, NY, June 4, 46; m 76, Mary Keyser; c Roger H & Adam H. *Educ:* City Col NY, BE, 67, ME, 69; City Univ NY, PhD(chem eng), 72. *Prof Exp:* Res assoc, Dept Geochem, Pa State Univ, 72-73. *Mem:* Nat Asn Corrosion Engrs; Electrochem Soc. *Res:* Corrosion research, by conventional and elctrochemical means; nuclear propulsion systems for the nuclear navy; developing techniques to measure, monitor predict general corrosion, pitting, stress corrosion and cracking at elevated temperatures. *Mailing Add:* 4323 Buckingham Dr Schenectady NY 12304

HALBIG, JOSEPH BENJAMIN, GEOCHEMISTRY, ENVIRONMENTAL GEOLOGY. *Current Pos:* assoc prof, 80-85, PROF GEOL, UNIV HAWAII, HILO, 85- *Personal Data:* b Sparta, Ill, July 19, 38; m 60, 80; c 2. *Educ:* Southern Ill Univ, Carbondale, BS, 62; Pa State Univ, MS, 65, PhD(geochem), 69. *Prof Exp:* Asst prof, State Univ NY Col Geneseo, 69-75. *Mem:* Sigma Xi; Int Asn Geochem & Cosmochem; Soc Environ Geochem & Health; Soc Archeol Sci. *Res:* Geochemistry of natural materials; environmental geology; geoarchaeology. *Mailing Add:* Dept Natural Sci Univ Hawaii Hilo 200 W Kawili St Hilo HI 96720-4075

HALBLEIB, JOHN A, RADIATION TRANSPORT. *Current Pos:* MEM TECH STAFF, SANDIA NAT LABS, 66- *Personal Data:* b Louisville, Ky, Aug 29, 36. *Educ:* Univ Louisville, BS, 58; Carnegie-Mellon Univ, MS, 64, PhD(physics), 66. *Mem:* Am Phys Soc. *Res:* Methods in Monte Carlo radiation transport. *Mailing Add:* 12428 Chelwood Pl NE Albuquerque NM 87112

HALBOUTY, MICHEL THOMAS, PETROLEUM GEOLOGY. *Current Pos:* consult geologist & petrol engr, Halbouty Ctr, 37-81, CHMN & CHIEF EXEC OFFICER, MICHEL T HALBOUTY ENERGY CO, 81- *Personal Data:* b Beaumont, Tex, June 21, 09; m 81, Billye Harper; c 1. *Educ:* Tex A&M Univ, BS, 30, MS, 31. *Hon Degrees:* DEng, Mont Col Mineral Sci & Technol, 66; PhD, USSR Acad Sci, 90. *Honors & Awards:* Anthony F Lucas Gold Medal, Am Inst Mining, Metall & Petrol Engrs, 75; Human Needs Award, Am Asn Petrol Geologists, 75; Sidney Powers Mem Award, Am Asn Petrol Geologists, 77; William T Pecora Award, NASA, 77; Horatio Alger Award, Am Schs & Cols Asn, 78; Hoover Medal, Am Asn Eng Soc, 82. *Prof Exp:* Geologist & petrol engr, Yount-Lee Oil Co, 31-35; chief geologist & petrol engr, Glenn H McCarthy, 35-37. *Concurrent Pos:* Distinguished lectr, Soc Petrol Engrs, Am Inst Mining & Petrol Engrs, 64, rep, Div Earth Sci, Nat Res Coun, Nat Acad Sci, 65-74; distinguished lectr, Am Asn Petrol Geologists, 65-66, sr ed, Geol Giant Petrol Fields, 68-69, spec educ for publ, 68-; chmn, Comt Technol & Water, Nat Acad Sci, 70-71; mem, Nat Energy Study Comt, 70-71 & Gov Energy Adv Coun, State of Tex, 74-; adj prof, Dept Geosci, Tex Tech Univ, 72-; chmn & pres, Circum-Pac Coun Energy & Mineral Resources, 72- *Mem:* Nat Acad Eng; Am Inst Mining, Metall & Petrol Engrs (vpres, 66-67); Geol Soc Am; Soc Independent Prof Earth Scientists; Am Asn Petrol Geologists (pres, 66-67). *Res:* Salt dome geology of Gulf Coast region; remote sensing. *Mailing Add:* Halbouty Ctr 5100 Westheimer Rd Houston TX 77056. *Fax:* 713-622-5360

HALBRENDT, JOHN MARTHON, NEMATOLOGY, MYCOLOGY. *Current Pos:* ASST PROF, PA STATE UNIV, 88- *Personal Data:* b Chicago, Ill, Feb 3, 49; div; c 2. *Educ:* Southern Ill Univ, BS, 72, MS, 74; Univ Mo, PhD(plant path), 85. *Prof Exp:* Teacher biol & advan chem, Stavanger Am Sch, Norway, 74-76; teacher biol & advan biol, Frankfurt Int Sch, WGer, 76-78 & Cairo Am Col, Egypt, 78-80; res asst, Dept Plant Path, Univ Mo, 80-84, res assoc, 85; res scientist, Dept Plant Path, Clemson Univ, 85-88. *Mem:* Am Inst Biol Sci; Soc Nematologists; Sigma Xi; Am Phytopath Soc. *Res:* Fruit crop pathology-diseases caused by nematodes; nematode/virus interaction; graft-transmissible agents; biology of plant parasitic nematodes. *Mailing Add:* Pa State Fruit Res Lab PO Box 309 Biglerville PA 17307-0309

HALDANE, FREDERICK DUNCAN MICHAEL, QUANTUM HALL EFFECT. *Current Pos:* PROF PHYSICS, PRINCETON UNIV, 90- *Personal Data:* b London, Eng, Sept 14, 51. *Educ:* Cambridge Univ, Eng, BA, 73, PhD(physics), 78. *Honors & Awards:* Oliver E Buckley Prize, Am Physics Soc, 93. *Prof Exp:* Physicist, Inst Laue-Langevin, Grenoble, France, 77-81; asst prof physics, Univ Southern Calif, 81-85; mem tech staff, AT&T Bell Labs, Murray Hill, 85-87; prof physics, Univ Calif, San Diego, 87-90. *Concurrent Pos:* Alfred P Sloan Found fel, 84; trustee, Aspen Ctr Physics, 85-90, mem adv bd, 90- *Mem:* Fel Am Physics Soc; Am Acad Arts & Sci. *Res:* Research in theoretical condensed matter physics; contributions to the understanding of quantum magnetism and the fractional quantum Hall effect; contributed articles to professional journals. *Mailing Add:* Dept Physics Jadwin Hall Princeton Univ Princeton NJ 08544. *Fax:* 609-258-6360; *E-Mail:* duncan@puhep1.princeton.edu

HALDAR, DIPAK, CELL BIOLOGY. *Current Pos:* from asst prof to assoc prof, 75-83, PROF BIOL SCI, ST JOHN'S UNIV, NY, 83- *Personal Data:* b Bankura, India, Dec 8, 37; US citizen; m 63, Jaya Sarkar; c Joydeep & Deeya. *Educ:* Univ Calcutta, BSc, 56, MSc, 58, DPhil(biochem), 63; Univ London, PhD(biochem), 66. *Prof Exp:* Res fel biochem, Indian Inst Biochem & Exp Med, Univ Calcutta, 59-63; mem sci staff, Nat Insts Med Res, London, 63-66; fel, McMaster Univ, 66-69; asst mem biochem, St Jude Children's Res Hosp, 69-71; lectr, Calcutta Univ, 71-73; vis res investr, Pub Health Res Inst City of New York, 74-75. *Concurrent Pos:* Vis asst prof, Memphis State Univ, 70-71; vis prof cell biol, Med Ctr, NY Univ, 85. *Mem:* NY Acad Sci; AAAS; Am Chem Soc; Sigma Xi; Am Soc Biochem & Molecular Biol; Am Soc Cell Biol. *Res:* Mitochondria; structure and function of mitochondrid outer membrane; phospholipid metabolism. *Mailing Add:* Dept Biol Sci St John's Univ Jamaica NY 11439-0001. *Fax:* 718-380-8543

HALDAR, JAYA, NEUROHYPOPHYSICAL HORMONES. *Current Pos:* assoc prof, 83-89, PROF BIOL & NEUROPHYSIOL, ST JOHNS UNIV, 89- *Personal Data:* b Calcutta, India, Apr 23, 39; US citizen; m 63; c 2. *Educ:* Nat Inst Med Res, London, Eng, PhD(physiol), 66. *Prof Exp:* Asst prof pharmacol, Columbia Univ, 77-83. *Mem:* NY Acad Sci; Am Physiol Soc; Soc Neurosci; Endocrine Soc; Sigma Xi; Brit Brain Res Asn; Europ Brain & Behav Soc. *Res:* Neuro-endocrinology. *Mailing Add:* Dept Biol Sci St Johns Univ 8000 Utopia Pkwy Jamaica NY 11439-0001. *Fax:* 718-990-5958

HALDE, CARLYN JEAN, MEDICAL MYCOLOGY. *Current Pos:* RETIRED. *Personal Data:* b Calif, June 16, 24. *Educ:* Univ Calif, Los Angeles, BA, 45, MA, 47; Duke Univ, PhD(microbiol), 53. *Prof Exp:* Lectr bact, Univ Hawaii, 48; bacteriologist, Hawaiian Med Lab, US Dept Army, 48-50, Fulbright scholar, Philippines, 50-51; res asst, Sch Med, Stanford Univ, 53-55; jr res microbiologist, Div Dermat, Sch Med, Univ Calif, Los Angeles, 55-57, asst res microbiologist, 57-58, vis asst prof med educ, Univ Proj at Univ Indonesia, 58-60; from asst prof to prof microbiol, Sch Med, Univ Calif, San Francisco, 60-97. *Concurrent Pos:* Giannini Found fel, 54; La State Univ-Inter-Am fel, 58. *Mem:* Med Mycol Soc Am; Am Soc Microbiol; Mycol Soc Am; Int Soc Human & Animal Mycol; Soc Women Geogr. *Res:* Epidemiology of fungal disease. *Mailing Add:* Dept Microbiol Univ Calif San Francisco CA 94143-0414. *Fax:* 415-476-8201

HALDEN, FRANK, CERAMICS, PHYSICS. *Current Pos:* vpres res & develop, 72-80, DIR, CRYSTAL TECHNOL, INC, 67-, EXEC VPRES, 80- *Personal Data:* b Marshalltown, Iowa, Mar 29, 29; m 54; c 4. *Educ:* Iowa State Col, BS, 51; Mass Inst Technol, ScD(ceramics), 54. *Prof Exp:* Asst metal-ceramic interactions, Mass Inst Technol, 51-54; sr ceramist, Stanford Res Inst, 56-65, dir, Ceramics & Metall Div, 65-69, assoc dir mat lab, 69-72. *Mem:* Am Ceramic Soc; Am Asn Crystal Growers. *Res:* High temperature materials, synthesis, fabrication and evaluation; refractory coatings; ultra-high-purity materials; growth and evaluation of refractory single crystals; ceramic materials for the electronic industry; growth, manufacturing and applications of optical acoustic, electro-optic single crystals. *Mailing Add:* 822 Cascade Dr Sunnyvale CA 94087

HALDER, NARAYAN CHANDRA, SOLID STATE PHYSICS. *Current Pos:* assoc prof, 72-75, PROF PHYSICS, UNIV SFLA, TAMPA, 75- *Personal Data:* b Ranchi, India, Aug 9, 39; m 64; c 2. *Educ:* Univ Bihar, BS, 58, MS, 60; Indian Inst Technol, Kharagpur, PhD(physics), 63. *Prof Exp:* Assoc lectr physics, Indian Inst Technol, Kharagpur, 63-64; res assoc mat sci, Yale Univ, 65-67; asst prof physics, State Univ NY Albany, 67-72. *Concurrent Pos:* NY State Res Found grant, 68-71; NSF grants, 72 & 75, USAF grants; Res Award, Sigma Xi, 78. *Mem:* Am Vacuum Soc; fel Am Phys Soc; AAAS; Sigma Xi. *Res:* Line broadening effects in x-ray patterns from solids; electronic properties and tunneling in metal-oxide-ceramics; study of defects in semiconductors and devices. *Mailing Add:* Dept Physics Univ SFla 4202 E Fowler Ave Tampa FL 33620

HALE, BARBARA NELSON, PHYSICS. *Current Pos:* vis asst prof math, Univ Mo-Rolla, 69-71, res assoc physics, 71-73, assoc prof, 73-82, PROF PHYSICS, UNIV MO-ROLLA, 83- *Personal Data:* b Buffalo, NY, Apr 6, 38; m 64. *Educ:* Syracuse Univ, BS, 60; Purdue Univ, MS, 64, PhD(physics), 67. *Prof Exp:* Asst prof physics, Rochester Inst Technol, 68-69. *Concurrent Pos:* NSF res grant, 72-79; NASA res grant, 76-79; NSF res grant, 80-83, 84-87 & 88-91. *Mem:* Am Phys Soc; Am Asn Physics Teachers; Am Meteorol Soc; Sigma Xi. *Res:* Atmospheric physics; theory of nucleation phenomena; molecular modeling of pre-nucleation water clusters; growth and nucleation of ice; computer simulations of water on substrates. *Mailing Add:* 205 Physics Univ MO PO Box 249 Rolla MO 65401. *E-Mail:* hale@hale1physicsomr.edu

HALE, CECIL HARRISON, CHEMISTRY. *Current Pos:* RETIRED. *Personal Data:* b Kilgore, Tex, June 12, 19; m 45, Margie NornHaussen; c Bryan M, Chris A & Connie H (Wise). *Educ:* Trinity Univ, Tex, BS, 38; La State Univ, MS, 40; Purdue Univ, PhD(phys chem), 48. *Prof Exp:* Asst chem, La State Univ, 38-40 & Purdue Univ, 46-48; analytical chemist, Esso Labs, Standard Oil Develop Co, 40-45, res chemist, 48-50; owner, Southwestern Analytical Chem Inc, 50-84. *Concurrent Pos:* Dir, Sachem Inc. *Mem:* Am Chem Soc; fel Am Inst Chem. *Res:* Polarography; spectrophotometry; analytical chemical methods; electrochemistry. *Mailing Add:* Sachem, Inc 821 E Woodward Austin TX 78704. *Fax:* 512-477-4647

HALE, CHRISTIANE BRADFORD HOFFMANN, COMMUNITY HEALTH ASSESSMENT, PROGRAM EVALUATION. *Current Pos:* PRES, HALE & ASSOCS, INC, 94- *Personal Data:* m 89, Irvin Emanuel; c Jennifer. *Educ:* Auburn Univ, BA, 71; Univ Ala, MPH, 74; Univ Cincinnati, PhD(demog & social psychol), 78. *Prof Exp:* From asst prof to prof epidemiol, Univ Ala, Birmingham, 80-91; dir assessment, Tacoma-Pierce Co Health Dept, 91-94. *Concurrent Pos:* From asst prof to assoc prof psychol, Univ Ala, Birmingham, 81-91; affil prof demog, Univ Wash, 91- *Mem:* Am Pub Health Asn; Pop Asn Am. *Res:* Assessment of county and sub-county health indicators; retraining public health workforce to use results to drive community change. *Mailing Add:* 9100 30th Ave NW Seattle WA 98117-2959

HALE, CREIGHTON J, EXERCISE PHYSIOLOGY. *Current Pos:* dir res & vpres, 55-72, pres & chief exec officer, 73-96, SR ADV, LITTLE LEAGUE BASEBALL, INC, 96- *Personal Data:* b Hardy, Nebr, Feb 18, 24. *Educ:* Colgate Univ, BA, 48; Springfield Col, MS, 49; NY Univ, PhD(educ), 51. *Honors & Awards:* Merit Award, Am Soc Testing & Mat. *Prof Exp:* Instr physiol, Springfield Col, 49-51, from asst prof to assoc prof, 51-55. *Concurrent Pos:* Mem, Comt Helmets, Nat Res Coun-Nat Acad Sci. *Mem:* Am Asn Health, Phys Educ & Recreation; Am Soc Testing & Mat; fel Am Col Sports Med; affil Am Orthop Soc Sports Med. *Res:* Child growth and development and various phases of athletics; development of safety equipment. *Mailing Add:* c/o Little League Hq PO Box 3485 Williamsport PA 17701

HALE, EDWARD BOYD, SOLID STATE PHYSICS & MATERIAL SCIENCE. *Current Pos:* from asst prof to assoc prof, Univ Mo, Rolla, 69-82, res assoc, 72-82, assoc dir, Mat Res Ctr, 88-92, PROF PHYSICS, UNIV MO, ROLLA, 82-, CHMN, PHYSICS DEPT, 92- *Personal Data:* b Washington, DC, July 16, 38; m 64, Barbara Nelson. *Educ:* Univ Md, BSEE, 60; Purdue Univ, PhD(physics), 68. *Prof Exp:* Res assoc spin resonance, Dept Physics & Astron, Univ Rochester, 68-69. *Mem:* AAAS; Am Phys Soc; Am Asn Physics Teachers. *Res:* Auger and ESCA surface studies in solids; ion implantation studies in solids; electron-nuclear double resonance studies; defects in semiconductors; spin resonance studies. *Mailing Add:* Dept Physics Univ Mo Rolla MO 65401. *Fax:* 573-341-4715; *E-Mail:* ehale@physics.umr.edu

HALE, FRANCIS JOSEPH, MECHANICAL & AEROSPACE ENGINEERING. *Current Pos:* from assoc prof to prof, 65-89, EMER PROF MECH & AEROSPACE ENG, NC STATE UNIV, 89- *Personal Data:* b Manila, Philippines, Oct 24, 22; US citizen; m 49, 80, Mary Longcrier; c Francis J III, Olin T & Margaret A. *Educ:* US Mil Acad, BS, 44; Mass Inst Technol, SM, 52, ScD(aeronaut, astronaut), 63. *Honors & Awards:* Ralph R Teetor Educ Award, Soc Automotive Engrs, 85. *Prof Exp:* Dep dir, Ballistics Missile Div, US Air Force, 56-59, prof astronaut & head dept, Air Force Acad, 62-63, chief anal group, Directorate Develop Plans, Washington, DC, 63-65. *Concurrent Pos:* Prof lectr, George Washington Univ, 63-65; vis prof mech eng, Middle East Tech Univ, Ankara, Turkey, 73-74; vis prof mech, US Mil Acad, West Point, 77-78; consult, Int Civil Aviation Orgn, Brazil; consult to indust & govt; tech dir, Wrightsville Beach Test Facil, 81-82; secy of naval fel aerospace eng, US Naval Acad, Annapolis, 90-91. *Mem:* Assoc fel Am Inst Aeronaut & Astronaut; Am Soc Eng Educ; Am Soc Mech Engrs; Soc Automotive Engrs. *Res:* Dynamic analysis and control with emphasis on applications to flight vehicles and processes. *Mailing Add:* 2853 Rue Sans Famille Raleigh NC 27607-3048. *Fax:* 919-781-6672; *E-Mail:* fhalez@juno.com

HALE, HARRY W(ILLIAM), ELECTRICAL ENGINEERING. *Current Pos:* prof, 60-91, EMER PROF ELEC ENG, IOWA STATE UNIV, 91- *Personal Data:* b Winslow, Ind, Sept 15, 20; m 85, Margery Bornmueller; c Charles. *Educ:* Purdue Univ, BS, 42, MS, 49, PhD(elec eng), 53. *Prof Exp:* From instr to assoc prof elec eng, Purdue Univ, 48-58; prof & head dept, Wayne State Univ, 58-60. *Mem:* Inst Elec & Electronics Engrs. *Res:* Network theory; systems. *Mailing Add:* Dept Elec Eng Iowa State Univ Ames IA 50011

HALE, HARRY W, JR, SURGERY. *Current Pos:* RETIRED. *Personal Data:* b New York, NY, Feb 3, 17; m 46; c 5. *Educ:* Rensselaer Polytech Inst, BS, 38; Univ Rochester, MD, 43. *Prof Exp:* From instr to prof surg, Sch Med, State Univ NY Buffalo, 52-69; chmn, Dept Surg, Maricopa Co Hosp, 69-86, chief gen surg, 87-93. *Concurrent Pos:* From asst attend surgeon to attend surgeon, E J Meyer Mem Hosp, 52-, assoc dir surg, 59-; Buswell res fel, State Univ NY Buffalo, 56-59; clin prof surg, Univ Ariz, 78- *Mem:* AMA; Am Asn Surg of Trauma; Am Col Surg; Soc Surg Alimentary Tract; Am Burn Asn; Sigma Xi. *Res:* Surgery of trauma; elderly surgery; surgical bacteriology. *Mailing Add:* 3220 E Stanford Dr Paradise Valley AZ 85253

HALE, JACK KENNETH, MATHEMATICS. *Current Pos:* PROF APPL MATH, GA TECH, 88- *Personal Data:* b Dudley, Ky, Oct 3, 28; m 49, Hazel Reynolds. *Educ:* Berea Col, AB, 49; Purdue Univ, MS, 51, PhD(math), 53. *Hon Degrees:* DSc, Univ Ghent, Belgium, 79, Stuttgart, 88, Inst Tecneco Sup Lisboa, 91. *Honors & Awards:* Chauvenet Prize, Am Math Asn, 65. *Prof Exp:* Instr math, Purdue Univ, 53-54; mem staff, Sandia Corp, 54-57; mem staff, Univac, Remington Rand Div, Sperry Rand Corp, Minn, 57-58, Res Inst Advan Study, Martin Co, 58-64; prof appl math, Brown Univ, 64-89. *Concurrent Pos:* Guggenheim fel, 79-80. *Mem:* Am Math Soc; fel Nat Acad Mechs; Sigma Xi; corresp mem Brazilian Acad Sci; foreign mem Polish Acad Sci; corresp mem Brazilian Acad Sci. *Res:* Ordinary, functional and partial differential equations. *Mailing Add:* Sch Math Ga Tech Atlanta GA 30332. *Fax:* 404-894-1726; *E-Mail:* hale@math.gatech.edu

HALE, JOHN, RADIOLOGICAL PHYSICS. *Current Pos:* RETIRED. *Personal Data:* b Chicago, Ill, Nov 13, 21; m 48, 79, Adele; c 2. *Educ:* Duke Univ, AB, 43; Univ Pa, MS, 49, PhD(elec eng), 57; Am Bd Radiol, dipl, 51; Am Bd Health Physics, dipl, 60. *Prof Exp:* Asst physics, Duke Univ, 43; res asst eng, Motorola, Inc, 46-47; asst elec eng, Univ Pa, 48-49, radiation safety physicist, 49-50, from asst prof to prof radiol physics, Med Sch, 57-67, prof elec eng, Moore Sch Elec Eng, 67-74, prof bioeng, Sch Eng & Appl Sci, 74-87, prof, 67-87, emer prof radiol physics, Med Sch, 87-90. *Concurrent Pos:* Am ed, Physics in Med & Biol, 69-76. *Mem:* Am Asn Physicists Med (pres, 61-62); Radiol Soc NAm; Radiation Res Soc; Am Radium Soc; Am Col Radiol. *Res:* Radiation dosimetry and health physics; radiologic physics. *Mailing Add:* 4901 Homestead Littleton CO 80123-1529

HALE, JOHN DEWEY, inorganic & physical chemistry, for more information see previous edition

HALE, KIRK KERMIT, JR, POULTRY SCIENCE, FOOD SCIENCE. *Current Pos:* ASSOC PROF POULTRY SCI, CLEMSON UNIV, 76- *Personal Data:* b Bentonville, Ark, Nov 20, 40; m 61; c 2. *Educ:* Univ Ark, Fayetteville, BSA, 63, MS, 67; Purdue Univ, PhD(food sci), 70. *Prof Exp:* Asst prof poultry prod technol, Univ Ga, 70-76. *Mem:* Poultry Sci Asn; Inst Food Technologists; Am Meat Sci Asn. *Res:* Development and improvement of poultry products; harvesting and processing of poultry and eggs. *Mailing Add:* 6160 Harbor Rd Daytona Beach FL 32127

HALE, LEONARD ALLEN, mechanical engineering, for more information see previous edition

HALE, MARTHA L, VIROLOGY, HEMATOLOGY. *Current Pos:* PRIN INVESTR, ARMED FORCES RADIOBIOL RES INST, 82- *Personal Data:* b San Antonio, Tex, Sept 6, 46. *Educ:* Va Commonwealth Univ, PhD(microbiol), 74. *Prof Exp:* Staff fel, LMG, Nat Inst Child Health & Human Develop, NIH, 74-77; sr assoc, Nat Res Coun, 80-82. *Mem:* Am Asn Microbiol; Am Asn Immunologists. *Res:* Isolation and characterization of the multipotent hematopoietic stem cell; investigation into the differentiation of the hematopoietic stem cell. *Mailing Add:* 902 College Pkwy Rockville MD 20850

HALE, MAYNARD GEORGE, PLANT PHYSIOLOGY. *Current Pos:* assoc prof, 51-85, EMER PROF PLANT PHYSIOL, VA POLYTECH INST & STATE UNIV, 85- *Personal Data:* b Mentor, Ohio, Apr 5, 20; wid; c Patricia & Arthur. *Educ:* Ohio State Univ, BS, 47, MS, 49, PhD(bot), 51. *Prof Exp:* Asst bot, Ohio State Univ, 47-51. *Mem:* Am Soc Plant Physiologists; Sigma Xi. *Res:* Procedures for culturing groups of plants under aseptic conditions; effects of chemicals on root exudations from aseptic plants; alleopathic potential of plants which interact through root exudations; plant growth. *Mailing Add:* 1213 Woodside Terr Blacksburg VA 24060-6234

HALE, PAUL NOLEN, JR, REHABILITATION ENGINEERING, HUMAN FACTORS ENGINEERING. *Current Pos:* asst prof indust eng, La Tech Univ, 66-67 & 71-74, assoc prof, 74-79, prof, 79-84, dept head indust eng & comput sci, 82-83, dept head indust eng, 83-84, dir, Rehab Ctr, 84-85, actg head, Dept Biomed Eng, 84-85, PROF BIOMED ENG, LA TECH UNIV, 84-, DIR CTR REHAB SCI & BIOMED ENG, 85-, DEPT HEAD BIOMED ENG, 87- *Personal Data:* b Galveston, Tex, Dec 5, 41; m 68,

Frances Andrews; c Tammy L & Eric T. *Educ:* Lamar Tech, BS, 65; Univ Ark, MS, 66; Tex A&M Univ, PhD(indust eng), 70. *Honors & Awards:* Centennial Cert, Am Soc Eng Educ, 93. *Prof Exp:* From res assoc to asst prof indust eng, Tex A&M Univ, 67-71. *Concurrent Pos:* Methods & stand engr, Ethyl Corp, 65; spec tech asst, Western Elec, 66; safety & indust hyg consult, Continental Can Co, 72; pres, Mgt Support Corp, 73-; chmn, Biomed Eng Div, Am Soc Eng Educ, 93-94. *Mem:* Alliance Eng Med & Biol; Rehab Eng Soc NAm; Am Soc Eng Educ; Inst Elec & Electronics Engrs; Biomed Eng Soc. *Res:* Development and application of rehabilitation and assistive technology for persons with disabilities. *Mailing Add:* La Tech Univ PO Box 10348 Ruston LA 71272-0046. *E-Mail:* phale@engr.latech.edu

HALE, RAYMOND JOSEPH, chemical engineering, for more information see previous edition

HALE, ROBERT CLARK, AQUATIC ENVIRONMENTAL CHEMISTRY. *Current Pos:* asst prof, 87-93, ASSOC PROF, DEPT ENVIRON SCI, VA INST MARINE SCI, COL WILLIAM & MARY, 93- *Educ:* Wayne State Univ, BS, 79, BA, 79; Col William & Mary, PhD(marine sci), 83. *Prof Exp:* Res chemist, Environ Health & Scis Lab, Mobil Oil Corp, 84-87. *Mem:* Am Chem Soc; Soc Chem & Toxicol. *Res:* Fate and effects of pollutants in the marine and estuarine environment; development and application of analytical techniques for the defection of contaminants. *Mailing Add:* PO Box 1346 Gloucester Point VA 23062. *Fax:* 804-684-7186; *E-Mail:* hale@.vims.edu

HALE, ROBERT E, PHYSICS. *Current Pos:* RETIRED. *Personal Data:* b North Vernon, Ind, Jan 4, 29; m 53; c 4. *Educ:* Ball State Univ, BS, 51, EdD(educ admin), 73; Western Mich Univ, MA, 60. *Prof Exp:* Teacher, White Pigeon Community Schs, 56-60; teacher, Tucson High Sch, 60-61; from asst prof to prof phys sci, Huntington Col, 61-, chmn, Div Sci, 67- *Mem:* Am Asn Physics Teachers; Nat Sci Teachers Asn. *Res:* Aviation weather. *Mailing Add:* 926 Poplar St Huntington IN 46750

HALE, WARREN FREDERICK, POLYMER CHEMISTRY. *Current Pos:* RETIRED. *Personal Data:* b Cambridge, Mass, Aug 1, 29; m 84, Joyce Cittner; c 2. *Educ:* Northeastern Univ, BS, 52; Polytech Inst Brooklyn, MS, 54; Univ Md, PhD(org chem), 58. *Prof Exp:* Chemist plastics res, Union Carbide Corp, 58-66, proj scientist chem & plastics, 66-71, develop scientist, Plastics Div, 71-75, group leader, 75-80, asst to dir, 80-82, mgr FDA liaison, 82-91. *Concurrent Pos:* Regulatory consult, 91- *Mem:* Am Chem Soc; Sigma Xi; Royal Soc Chem. *Res:* Monomer synthesis; polyethers; water miscible polymers, adhesives and sealants. *Mailing Add:* 94 Dreahook Rd Whitehouse Station NJ 08889

HALE, WILLIAM HARRIS, ANIMAL NUTRITION. *Current Pos:* PROF ANIMAL SCI, UNIV ARIZ, 60- *Personal Data:* b Richmond, Ky, Feb 11, 20; m 45; c 5. *Educ:* Univ Ky, BS, 46, MS, 47; Univ Wis, PhD(biochem, animal husb), 50. *Prof Exp:* Asst animal husb, Univ Wis, 47-50; asst prof, Univ Ill, 50-52 & Iowa State Univ, 52-57; nutritionist, Chas Pfizer & Co, Inc, 57-60. *Mem:* AAAS; Am Soc Animal Sci; Am Inst Nutrit; Soc Exp Biol & Med; Am Chem Soc; Sigma Xi. *Res:* Ruminant nutrition; cobalt and sulphur in sheep nutrition; forage utilization by ruminants; synthetic estrogens in growth of ruminants; nutrition of rumen microorganisms; purified rations for ruminants; vitamin A; grain processing for ruminants; fat utilization and metabolism by ruminants. *Mailing Add:* 7412 N Ellison Dr Tucson AZ 85704-3105

HALEMANE, KESHAVA PRASAD, MATHEMATICAL MODELLING & ANALYSIS, OPTIMUM DESIGN OF ENGINEERING SYSTEMS. *Current Pos:* PROF SYST ANALYSIS & COMPUT APPL, KARNATAKA REGIONAL ENG COL, 91- *Personal Data:* b Ednad Village, India, Jan 2, 52; m 77, Vijayalakshmi P S; c Sriwidya Bharati, Sriwidya Ramana & Sriwidya Prawina. *Educ:* Karnataka Regional Eng Col, India, BS, 72; Carnegie-Mellon Univ, MS, 79, PhD(chem eng), 82. *Prof Exp:* Process engr, Mangalore Chem & Fertilizers Ltd, 73-77; sr engr, Westinghouse Res & Develop Ctr, 82-84; mem tech staff, AT&T Bell Labs, 84-86; prof, Chem Eng & Systs Res Ctr, Univ Md, College Park, 86-89; sr scientist, Ctr Artificial Intel & Robotics, DRDO, India, 89-90. *Mem:* Fel Inst Engrs; Indian Soc Tech Educ; Soc Indust & Appl Math; Am Inst Chem Engrs; Inst Elec & Electronics Engrs. *Res:* Application of mathematical and computer modelling, analysis and optimization techniques in the design of engineering systems; optimum design under uncertainty; computational science; information process in decision-making. *Mailing Add:* 3-17-1506 Nanthoor Cross Mangalore 575002 India. *Fax:* 91-824-476090; *E-Mail:* kph@krec.ernet.in

HALEMANE, THIRUMALA RAYA, TELECOMMUNICATIONS, SOFTWARE SYSTEMS. *Personal Data:* b Ednad, India, May 27, 53; m, Usha; c Kavi & Shilpi. *Educ:* Bangalore Univ, BSc, 72; Indian Inst Technol, Madras, MSc, 74; Univ Rochester, MA, 76, MA, 80, PhD(physics), 80. *Prof Exp:* Asst prof, physics, State Univ NY, Fredonia, 81-85; mem tech staff, AT&T Bell Labs, 85-92. *Mem:* Am Phys Soc. *Res:* Theoretical physics; ferroelectrics; lightwave communication system. *Mailing Add:* 62 Yellowstone Lane E Howell NJ 07731

HALES, ALFRED WASHINGTON, MATHEMATICS, ALGEBRA. *Current Pos:* from asst prof to prof, 66-92, EMER PROF MATH, UNIV CALIF, LOS ANGELES, 93-, DIR, CTR COMMUN RES, IDA, 93- *Personal Data:* b Pasadena, Calif, Nov 30, 38; m 62, Virginia D Greene; c Andrew S, Lisa R & Katherine. *Educ:* Calif Inst Technol, BS, 60, PhD(math), 62. *Honors & Awards:* Polya Prize in Combinatorics, Soc Indust & Appl Math, 72. *Prof Exp:* NSF fel, Cambridge Univ, 62-63; Benjamin Peirce instr math, Harvard Univ, 63-66. *Concurrent Pos:* Consult, Jet Propulsion Lab, 66-70 & Inst Defense Analysis, 64-65, 76-90; vis lectr, Univ Wash, 70-71; vis fel, Univ Warwick, 77-78; mem, Math Sci Res Inst, Berkeley, 86-87; bd trustees, 95- *Mem:* Am Math Soc; Math Asn Am; Soc Indust & Appl Math; Sigma Xi. *Res:* Algebra, especially structure of groups, modules and lattices; combinatorial analysis. *Mailing Add:* Ctr Commun Res 4320 Westerra Ct San Diego CA 92121

HALES, CHARLES A, PULMONARY HYPERTENSION, PULMONARY EDEMA. *Current Pos:* clin res fel, Harvard Univ & Mass Gen Hosp, 71-73, from instr to assoc prof med, 73-96, assoc physician, 84-90, PHYSICIAN, HARVARD UNIV & MASS GEN HOSP, 90, PROF MED, 96- *Personal Data:* b Greeley, Colo, Apr 27, 41; m 65, Mary Ann; c Sam, Chris & John. *Educ:* Emory Univ, BA, 62, MD, 66. *Hon Degrees:* MA, Harvard Univ. *Honors & Awards:* Dickenson W Richards Lectr, Am Heart Asn, 94. *Prof Exp:* Intern & resident, Boston City Hosp, 66-68; Lt comdr, USNR, 68-70; med res II, Univ Calif, San Francisco, 70-71. *Concurrent Pos:* Chmn, Cardiopulmonary Coun, Am Heart Asn, 90-93; chmn, Long Range Planning Coun, Pulmonary Circulation Assembly, Am Thoracic Soc. *Mem:* Am Thoracic Soc; Am Physiol Soc; Am Soc Clin Invest; Am Heart Asn. *Res:* Investigation of the mechanism of pulmonary vasoconstriction in response to hypoxia transforming the vessel on chronic basis producing pulmonary hypertension and COR pulmonale; investigation of smoke to determine the toxins producing pulmonary edema. *Mailing Add:* Pulmonary Unit Mass Gen Hosp Boston MA 02114. *Fax:* 617-726-6878; *E-Mail:* hales@helix.mgh.harvard.edu

HALES, DONALD CALEB, FISH BIOLOGY, AQUATIC ECOLOGY. *Current Pos:* CONSULT, 90- *Personal Data:* b American Fork, Utah, May 10, 29; m 48; c 4. *Educ:* Univ Utah, BS, 53, PhD(limnol), 67; Utah State Univ, MS, 55. *Prof Exp:* Fish biologist, Idaho Dept Fish & Game, 55-56; fish biologist, Utah Fish & Game Dept, 56-58, regional fishery mgr, 58-62, asst chief fishery mgt, 62-64; asst unit leader fisheries, Pa Coop Fishery Unit, Pa State Univ, 67-69; unit leader, SDak Coop Fishery Res Unit, Dept Wildlife & Fisheries, SDak State Univ, 70-77; fishery resources coordr, US Fish & Wildlife Serv, Anchorage, 77-80; asst dir, Nat Fishery Res Lab, Wis, 80-83, staff fishery biologist, Washington, DC, 83-86, fishery res biologist, Dexter Nat Fish Hatchery, NMex, 86-90. *Concurrent Pos:* Teaching aquatic invert, Pa State Univ, 67-69; freshwater ecol, Fishery Mgt, SDak State Univ, 70-77. *Mem:* Am Fisheries Soc; NAm Benthological; Sigma Xi; Desert Fishes Coun. *Res:* Aquatic invertebrates; paddlefish; endangered species. *Mailing Add:* 265 S 200 E No 110-1 Ephraim UT 84627-1408

HALES, HUGH B(RADLEY), CHEMICAL ENGINEERING. *Current Pos:* PROF, BRIGHAM YOUNG UNIV, 97- *Personal Data:* b Salt Lake City, Utah, Mar 17, 40; m 63; c 3. *Educ:* Univ Utah, BS, 62, MS, 63; Mass Inst Technol, ScD, 67. *Prof Exp:* Sr res engr, Esso Prod Res Co, 67-68; asst prof chem eng, Mass Inst Technol, 68-70; scientist, Mobil Oil Corp, 70-97. *Concurrent Pos:* Head, Int Reservoir Simulation Res Inst. *Mem:* Am Inst Chem Engrs; Soc Petrol Engrs. *Res:* Fluid mechanics; petroleum resevoir simulation. *Mailing Add:* 3220 S 4800 W West Valley City UT 84120

HALES, J VERN, ATMOSPHERIC PHYSICS. *Current Pos:* RETIRED. *Personal Data:* b Provo, Utah, July 21, 17; m 40, Lucille Farnsworth; c 7. *Educ:* Brigham Young Univ, AB, 38; Calif Inst Technol, MS, 41; Univ Calif, Los Angeles, PhD(meteorol), 52. *Prof Exp:* Observer meteorol, US Weather Bur, 38-41; meteorologist, Pan-Am Grace Airways, Inc, 41-42; weather officer, US Army Air Corps, 42-46; prof, Univ Utah, 46-65, head, Dept Meteorol, 46-63; consult, Gen Elec Co, 65-71; pres, Hales & Co, 54-91. *Concurrent Pos:* Mem, Comt Sci & Arts, Franklin Inst, 73-91, chmn, 85-86; mem, Nat Coun Indust Meteorologists. *Mem:* Am Meteorol Soc. *Res:* Solution of problems in atmospheric physics and chemistry; air quality, diffusion phenomena, cloud physics; meteorological statistics, measurement and analysis methods and equipment development. *Mailing Add:* 8709 Bolzano Ct Las Vegas NV 89117

HALES, JEREMY M(ORGAN), CHEMICAL ENGINEERING. *Current Pos:* ASSOC PROF, DEPT CIVIL ENG, UNIV WASH, 74-, MGR, ATMOSPHERIC SCI DEPT, 84-, DIR, DEPT ENERGY ATMOSPHERIC CHEM PROG, 89- *Personal Data:* b Seattle, Wash, Oct 15, 37; m 62, Kathryn; c Burke & Sarah. *Educ:* Univ Wash, BS, 60, MS, 62; Univ Mich, Ann Arbor, PhD(chem eng), 68. *Prof Exp:* Sanit engr, Div Air Pollution, HEW, 62-64; sr res engr, Battelle-Northwest, 68-74, mgr, Atmos Dynamics & Chem Sect, 74-77, dir, MAP3S/Raine Prog, 79-81, assoc mgr, Earth Sci Dept, 81-84, mgr, Atmospheric Sci Dept. *Concurrent Pos:* Ed, J Appl Meteorol, 76-81; dir, Dept Energy Precp Prog, Univ Wash, 85-89. *Mem:* Am Inst Chem Engrs; Am Meteorol Soc; AAAS. *Res:* Chemical engineering applications in the environmental sciences, particularly with respect to atmospheric sciences, with special emphasis on transport and reaction-rate phenomena. *Mailing Add:* 4811 W 18th Ave Kennewick WA 99337. *Fax:* 509-783-7352; *E-Mail:* jm_hales@pnlg.pnl.gov

HALES, LYNN B, METALLURGY. *Honors & Awards:* Antoine M Gaudin Award, Soc Mining Metall & Explor, 95. *Mailing Add:* 669 W 200 S Salt Lake City UT 84101

HALES, MILTON REYNOLDS, MEDICINE, PATHOLOGY. *Current Pos:* chmn dept, 69-74, prof, 68-84, EMER PROF PATH, SCH MED, WVA UNIV, 84- *Personal Data:* b Springville, Utah, Aug 15, 18; m 42, Harriet Bacon; c Susan, Peter & Martha. *Educ:* Univ Calif, Los Angeles, AB, 40; Univ Southern Calif, MD, 44; Am Bd Path, dipl, 55. *Prof Exp:* Intern, Los Angeles

County Hosp, 43-44; intern path, New Haven Community Hosp, 47-48; James Hudson Brown Mem res fel, Sch Med, Yale Univ, 48-49, instr, 49-50; asst prof, Univ Southern Calif, 50-55; from asst prof to assoc prof, Sch Med, Yale Univ, 55-68. *Concurrent Pos:* From asst resident to resident, New Haven Community Hosp, 48-50. *Mem:* Am Asn Path & Bact; Int Acad Path; Sigma Xi. *Res:* Liver and pulmonary diseases, particularly associated vascular changes. *Mailing Add:* 66 Sherman Ave Morgantown WV 26505

HALES, RALEIGH STANTON, JR, MATHEMATICS, MATHEMATICAL ECONOMICS. *Current Pos:* VPRES ACAD AFFAIRS & PROF MATH, COL WOOSTER, 90- *Personal Data:* b Pasadena, Calif, Mar 16, 42; m 67, Diane C Moore; c Karen G & Christopher. *Educ:* Pomona Col, BA, 64; Harvard Univ, MA, 65, PhD(math), 70. *Prof Exp:* From instr to assoc prof, Pomona Col, 67-85, prof math, 85-90, assoc dean, 73-90. *Concurrent Pos:* Consult, Div Savings & Loan, Calif, 68-69, Irvine Co & Univ Calif, Irvine, 71 & Develop Econ, Inc, 71-73; Wig distinguished prof, 71. *Mem:* Am Math Soc; Math Asn Am. *Res:* Graph theory, including numerical invariants of graphs, especially related to products of graphs; estimation, linear models and multi-dimensional scaling of mathematical economics. *Mailing Add:* Col Wooster Galpin Hall Wooster OH 44691-2363. *E-Mail:* shales@acs.wooster.edu

HALEVY, SIMON, cardiovascular pharmacology, umbilical vasculature pharmacology; deceased, see previous edition for last biography

HALEY, BOYD EUGENE, BIOCHEMISTRY. *Current Pos:* PROF BIOCHEM, UNIV KY, 85- *Personal Data:* b Greensburg, Ind, Sept 22, 40; m 65; c 2. *Educ:* Franklin Col, BA, 63; Univ Idaho, MS, 67; Wash State Univ, PhD(chem), 71. *Prof Exp:* NIH fel physiol, Med Sch, Yale Univ, 71-74; from asst prof to prof biochem, Univ Wyo, 74-85. *Concurrent Pos:* Dreyfus Found vis researcher & lectr, Univ Wis, 75. *Mem:* Am Soc Biol Chemists; AAAS. *Res:* Use of photoaffinity analogs of nucleotides to photolabel nucleotide binding sites of membranes and complex regulatory enzymes. *Mailing Add:* Col Pharm Univ Ky 800 Rose St Lexington KY 40536-0082. *Fax:* 606-257-3040

HALEY, HAROLD BERNARD, SURGERY. *Current Pos:* CONSULT, 93- *Personal Data:* b Madison, Wis, Sept 11, 23; m 45; c 5. *Educ:* St Louis Univ, MD, 46. *Honors & Awards:* Margaret Hays Edwards Achievement Medal, Am Asn Cancer Educ. *Prof Exp:* Intern, Milwaukee Co Hosp, 46-47; resident surg, Methodist Hosp, Madison, 47-48; res fel & Damon Runyon Clin fel, Harvard Med Sch, 50-51; resident, Peter Bent Brigham Hosp, Boston, 51-55; from asst prof to prof, Loyola Univ, Stritch Sch Med, Chicago, 55-69; prof surg & assoc dean student affairs, Med Col Ohio, 69-72, prof social med, 70-72; prof surg & assoc dean clin serv, Univ Va, Sch Med, Roanoke, 72-80; assoc chief staff educ & clin prof surg, 80-90, emer prof, Houston Vet Admin Med Ctr, Baylor Col Med, 90-93. *Mem:* Asn Am Med Cols; Am Col Surg; Am Asn Cancer Educ (pres, 72-73); Am Anthrop Asn; Soc Am Archaeol. *Res:* Physicians attitudes towards cancer; behavioral aspects of medical education; medical anthropology; medical ethics, especially in areas of cancer, death and dying, resource allocation; Precolumbian medicine and death beliefs, with emphasis on Mexican codices; education of resident physicians. *Mailing Add:* 2311 Broadway Ave SW Unit D Roanoke VA 24014

HALEY, KENNETH WILLIAM, CHEMICAL ENGINEERING. *Current Pos:* Res engr, Standard Oil Co Calif, 65-70, sr res engr, Chevron Res Co, 70-86, MGR, ENERGY FORCASTING, CHEVRON, 86- *Personal Data:* b San Francisco, Calif, Sept 6, 39; m 65; c 1. *Educ:* Stanford Univ, BS, 61; Univ Ill, MS, 63, PhD(chem eng), 65. *Concurrent Pos:* Vis lectr, Univ Ariz, 72. *Mem:* Am Inst Chem Engrs. *Res:* Boiling heat transfer. *Mailing Add:* Chevron Corp-Corp Planning 575 Market St 36th Fl San Francisco CA 94105-2856

HALEY, LESLIE ERNEST, GENETICS. *Current Pos:* DEP MINISTER, DEPT AGR & MKT, 96- *Personal Data:* b Windsor, NS, May 2, 38; m 63, S Lorraine Young; c 2. *Educ:* NS Agr Col, dipl, 58; Ont Agr Col, BSA, 60, MSA, 63; Univ Calif, Davis, PhD(genetics), 67. *Prof Exp:* Asst prof biol, Univ Sask, Regina, 67-70; from asst prof to prof biol, Dalhousie Univ 70-96, chmn, Dept Educ, 81-89; prin, Agr Col, 89-96. *Mem:* Genetics Soc Can. *Res:* Agricultural genetics. *Mailing Add:* Dept Agr & Mkt PO Box 190 Halifax NS B3J 2M4 Can. *Fax:* 902-897-9399; *E-Mail:* lhaley@cadmin.nsac.ns.ca

HALEY, NANCY JEAN, BIOCHEMISTRY. *Current Pos:* DIR, MET LIFE LAB, 90-, ASST VPRES, MET LIFE, 94- *Personal Data:* b Huntington, NY, July 3, 48; m 73; c 1. *Educ:* St Joseph's Col, BA, 70; St John's Univ, MS, 72, PhD(biochem), 75. *Prof Exp:* Fel cell biol, Rockefeller Univ, 75-77, res assoc atherosclerosis, 77-80; assoc, Am Health Found, 80-84, assoc chief, Div Nutrit & Endocrinol, 85-90. *Concurrent Pos:* Consult, Int Asn Res Cancer, Lyon, France, Cine-Med, Woodbury, Conn; ed, Am Health Found, NY. *Mem:* Am Asn Cancer Res; Am Soc Prevent Oncol; Am Heart Asn; Am Asn Clin Chem. *Res:* Risk factor analysis including hypercholesterolemia, hypertension and cigarette smoking; nicotine metabolism and passive smoking; assay development for biomarkers of disease risk. *Mailing Add:* Metlife Lab 4 Westchester Plaza Elmsford NY 10523. *Fax:* 914-347-6338

HALEY, SAMUEL RANDOLPH, DEVELOPMENTAL ANATOMY. *Current Pos:* PROF ZOOL, UNIV HAWAII, MANOA, 67- *Personal Data:* b Ft Worth, Tex, July 12, 40; m 66; c 3. *Educ:* Univ Tex, BA, 62, MA, 64, PhD(zool), 67. *Mem:* AAAS; Soc Develop Biol; Am Soc Zool; Sigma Xi; Crustacean Soc. *Res:* Developmental and reproductive biology. *Mailing Add:* Dept Zool-2538 The Mall Univ Hawaii at Manoa Honolulu HI 96822

HALEY, THOMAS JOHN. PHARMACOLOGY. *Current Pos:* RETIRED. *Personal Data:* b Crosby, Minn, Nov 4, 13; m 64; c 2. *Educ:* Univ Southern Calif, BS, 38, MS, 42; Univ Fla, PhD(pharmacol), 45. *Honors & Awards:* Clinton H Thienes Award, Am Acad Clin Toxicol, 82. *Prof Exp:* Instr org chem lab, Col Pharm, Univ Southern Calif, 40-42; asst pharmacol, Sch Pharm, Univ Fla, 42-45; med dir, E S Miller Labs, Los Angeles, 45-47; chief, Div Pharmacol & Toxicol, Atomic Energy Proj, Med Sch, Univ Calif, Los Angeles, 47-59, assoc clin prof indust med, 52-66, chief, Div Pharmacol & Toxicol, Dept & Labs Nuclear Med & Radiation Biol, 59-66; prof pharmacol, Univ Hawaii Sch Med, 66-69; group leader pharmacol & toxicol, Res Triangle Inst, 69-70; pharmacologist, Nat Ctr Toxicol Res, 70-82; prof pharmacol, Med Ctr, Univ Ark, 73-85. *Concurrent Pos:* Fel, Med Sch, Univ Southern Calif, 46-48; Del Amo fel, 55; vis scientist, Sandoz Labs, Switz, 56; adj prof, Univ NC Sch Med; consult, Food & Drug Admin; co-chmn symp response of nervous syst to ionizing radiation, AEC-NIH, 60 & 63; asst to dir, Nat Ctr Toxicol Res. *Mem:* Am Chem Soc; Am Soc Pharmacol & Exp Therapeut; Am Pharmaceut Asn; fel Am Inst Chemists; fel Am Col Clin Pharmacol & Therapeut. *Res:* Radiobiology; toxicology; neurophysiology. *Mailing Add:* 774 Rivertree Dr Oceanside CA 92054-7456

HALFACRE, ROBERT GORDON, HORTICULTURE, LANDSCAPE ARCHITECTURE. *Current Pos:* from assoc prof to prof, 74-90, ALUMNI DISTINGUISHED PROF, CLEMSON UNIV, 90- *Personal Data:* b Newberry, SC, June 22, 41; div; c Angela & Robert. *Educ:* Clemson Univ, BS, 63, MS, 65; Va Polytech Inst, PhD(hort), 68; NC State Univ, MLA, 73. *Honors & Awards:* Sigma Xi Res Award, 68; Julian C Miller Res Award, Am Soc Hort Sci, 68. *Prof Exp:* From asst prof to assoc prof hort, NC State Univ, 68-74. *Concurrent Pos:* Pres, Facul Sen, Clemson Univ, 89-90. *Mem:* Am Soc Hort Sci; Am Soc Landscape Architects. *Res:* Taxonomy and landscape architectural use of plants. *Mailing Add:* Dept Hort Clemson Univ Clemson SC 29634-0375. *Fax:* 864-656-4960; *E-Mail:* rhlfcr@clemson.edu

HALFAR, EDWIN, TOPOLOGY. *Current Pos:* from instr to assoc prof, 47-63, chmn dept, 64-70, PROF MATH, UNIV NEBR-LINCOLN, 63- *Personal Data:* b Alexandria, La, Dec 10, 17; m 39; c 2. *Educ:* Southern Ill Univ, BEd, 39; Univ Iowa, MA, 41, PhD(math), 47. *Prof Exp:* Instr math, Univ Iowa, 43-44; asst mathematician, Naval Ord Lab, DC, 44-45; instr math, Univ Iowa, 45-47. *Mem:* Am Math Soc; Math Asn Am; Am Soc Clin Pharmacol Therapeut. *Res:* General topology. *Mailing Add:* Dept Math Univ Neb 913 Oldfather Lincoln NE 68508

HALFERDAHL, LAURENCE BOWES, EXPLORATION GEOLOGY. *Current Pos:* CONSULT GEOL ENGR, HALFERDAHL & ASSOC LTD, 69- *Personal Data:* b Ottawa, Ont, Sept 14, 30; m 54; c 4. *Educ:* Queen's Univ, Ont, BSc, 52, MSc, 54; Johns Hopkins Univ, PhD, 59. *Prof Exp:* Mineralogist & indust mineralogist, Res Coun Alta, 57-69. *Mem:* Mineral Asn Can; Can Inst Mining & Metall. *Res:* Physical and economic mineralogy; exploration for metallic and industrial minerals; mining geology; coal. *Mailing Add:* 11539 73 Ave Edmonton AB T6G 0E2 Can

HALFF, ALBERT HENRY, SANITARY & CIVIL ENGINEERING. *Current Pos:* owner, Albert H Halff Assoc Engrs, 60-70, pres, 70-83, chmn, 83-91, EMER CHMN & DIR ADVAN PROJS, ALBERT H HALFF ASSOCS, INC, 91- *Personal Data:* b Midland, Tex, Aug 20, 15; m 40, Lee Benson; c Henry M & Bro. *Educ:* Southern Methodist Univ, BSCE, 37; Ill Inst Technol, MSCE, 42; Johns Hopkins Univ, DEng, 50. *Honors & Awards:* Samuel A Greeley Nat Environ Award, Am Soc Civil Engrs, 86; Twichell Hydrol lectr, Am Water Resources Asn, 92. *Prof Exp:* Off asst, Tex Hwy Dept, 36-37; asst off engr, Koch & Fowler Engrs, 37-39; instr Tex Col Arts & Indust, 39-41; instr civil eng, Ill Inst Technol, 40-42; design engr, Charles DeLeuw & Co, 42; engr, Brown & Bellows, 42-43; asst prof, Southern Methodist Univ, 43-46; sanit engr, Brown & Bellows, 50-53; partner, Hundley & Halff, 53-60. *Concurrent Pos:* Indust consult on waste prevention & treatment; vol, Pub Awareness Prog, Water Resources Div, US Geol Surv, 92- *Mem:* AAAS; Am Water Works Asn; hon mem Am Soc Civil Engrs; Water Pollution Control Fedn; NY Acad Sci; Am Acad Environ Engrs; Am Water Works Asn. *Res:* Water desalinization; industrial wastes; ion exchange desalting; hydraulic mechanisms; water recycle; thermal energy conversion. *Mailing Add:* 3514 Rock Creek Dr Dallas TX 75204. *Fax:* 214-739-0095

HALFHILL, JOHN ERIC, ENTOMOLOGY. *Current Pos:* RETIRED. *Personal Data:* b Cedar Rapids, Iowa, Aug 25, 32; m 58; c 1. *Educ:* San Jose State Col, BA, 54; Univ Idaho, PhD(entom), 70. *Prof Exp:* Lab technician, Agr Lab, Stauffer Chem Co, Calif, 54-56; lab technician, Citrus Exp Sta, Univ Calif, Riverside, 56-58; res entomologist, Agr Res Serv, USDA, 63-88. *Mem:* Entom Soc Am; Int Orgn Biol Control. *Res:* Biology and control of vegetable insect pests. *Mailing Add:* 1208 S 28th Ave Yakima WA 98902

HALFMAN, CLARKE JOSEPH, CLINICAL CHEMISTRY, ANALYTICAL BIOCHEMISTRY. *Current Pos:* ASSOC PROF PATH, CHICAGO MED SCH, UNIV HEALTH SCI, 77- *Personal Data:* b Chicago, Ill, Dec 19, 41; m 67; c 1. *Educ:* Univ Ill, Champaign-Urbana, BS, 63, PhD(food chem), 70. *Prof Exp:* Res fel biochem, Georgetown Univ, 70-71, trainee clin chem, Med Sch, 71-72; asst prof path, Emory Univ, 72-75; clin chemist, BioSci Labs, 75-77. *Concurrent Pos:* Consult clin chemist, North Chicago Vet Admin Med Ctr, 77-, res assoc, 78-, co-prin res investr, 79-82; assoc dir clin lab, Chicago Med Sch, Univ Health Sci, 78- *Mem:* Am Asn Clin Chemists; Am Chem Soc; Nat Acad Clin Biochemists; Acad Clin Lab Physicians & Scientists; AAAS; Am Soc Clin Pathologists. *Res:* Binding of small molecules to proteins; physical chemical properties of immunoglobulins; application of fluorescent labels in immunoassays. *Mailing Add:* Dept Path Finch Univ Chicago Med Sch 3333 Green Bay Rd North Chicago IL 60064-3037

HALFON, EFRAIM, ECOLOGICAL MODELLING, FATE OF TOXIC CONTAMINANTS. *Current Pos:* Fel, 75, from res scientist 1 to res scientist 2, 76-92, RES SCIENTIST 3, SYSTS ECOL, CAN CTR INLAND WATERS, 92-; PROF, DEPT BIOL, MCMASTER UNIV, HAMILTON, ONT, 90- *Personal Data:* b Tripoli, Libya, Mar 31, 48; Can citizen; m 71, Silvia Consorelli; c 2. *Educ:* Univ Milan, Laurea, limnol, 71; Univ Ga, PhD(systs ecol), 75. *Concurrent Pos:* Fulbright fel, 71-72; consult, Ecol Environ Adv Comt, Halton Region, Ont, Can, 76-77; guest scholar, Int Inst Appl Systs Analyst, Laxenburg, Austria, 78-; adj assoc prof, State Univ NY Binghamton, 79-82; vis prof, GSF-PUC, Munich, WGer, 87, 90. *Mem:* Int Soc Ecol Modelling (vpres, 82-89); Int Asn Ecol; Sigma Xi. *Res:* Computer generated animations; fate models of toxic substance in lakes and rivers; ranking hazard of toxic contaminants; scientific visualization. *Mailing Add:* Nat Water Res Inst 867 Lakeshore Rd W PO Box 5050 Burlington ON L7R 4A6 Can

HALFON, MARC, CHEMISTRY. *Current Pos:* RES CHEMIST PROC RES & DEVELOP INSECTICIDES, FMC CORP, 76- *Personal Data:* b Brooklyn, NY, Aug 22, 45. *Educ:* Brooklyn Col, BS, 67; Brown Univ, PhD(org chem), 74. *Prof Exp:* Res chemist, Photo Prod Div, E I du Pont de Nemours & Co, Inc, 73-75. *Mem:* Am Chem Soc. *Res:* Research and development of agricultural process chemistry. *Mailing Add:* FMC Corp PO Box 8 Princeton NJ 08540-0008

HALFORD, GARY ROSS, MATERIALS SCIENCE, ENGINEERING MECHANICS. *Current Pos:* SR RES SCIENTIST, LEWIS RES CTR, NASA, 66- *Personal Data:* b Fayette Co, Ill, Dec 7, 37; m 59; c 3. *Educ:* Univ Ill, BS, 60, MS, 61, PhD(eng mech), 66. *Honors & Awards:* Except Eng Achievement Medal, NASA, 82. *Concurrent Pos:* Caterpillar Tractor, 55-57; Deere & Co, 60-61; vis res scientist, Aeronaut Res Lab, Melbourne, Australia, 89-90. *Mem:* Am Soc Testing & Mat; Am Soc Metals; Am Soc Mech Engrs; Am Inst Aeronaut & Astronaut; Soc Automotive Engrs; Metal Properties Coun; Am Acad Mech. *Res:* Analytical and experimental research of cyclic flow, fatigue and fracture of materials under high-temperature; thermal-fatigue exposure as found in gas turbine and rocket engines; developer of life prediction methods for fatigue; author 110 publications; aeronautical & astronautical. *Mailing Add:* 8439 Celianna Dr Strongsville OH 44136

HALFORD, JAKE HALLIE, electrical engineering, solid state physics, for more information see previous edition

HALGREN, LEE A, ENTOMOLOGY, INVERTEBRATE ECOLOGY. *Current Pos:* VCHANCELLOR, UNIV WIS, PLATTEVILLE, 84- *Personal Data:* b Minneapolis, Minn, Nov 5, 42; m 66; c 2. *Educ:* Gustavus Adolphus Col, BS, 64; Kans State Univ, MS, 66, PhD(entom), 68. *Prof Exp:* Res asst entom, Kans State Univ, 64-68; prof biol & chmn dept, Southwest State Univ, 68-79, assoc vpres acad affairs, 79-84. *Mem:* AAAS; Entom Soc Am; Sigma Xi. *Res:* Flight behavior and ecology of aphids; curriculum development in the biological sciences, environmental education. *Mailing Add:* 1580 Lincoln Suite 750 State Col Colo Denver CO 80203

HALGREN, THOMAS ARTHUR, QUANTUM CHEMISTRY, ORGANIC CHEMISTRY. *Current Pos:* asst prof chem, 75-80, ASSOC PROF CHEM, CITY COL, CITY UNIV NEW YORK, 81- *Personal Data:* b Berwyn, Ill, Nov 1, 41; m 78. *Educ:* Wabash Col, AB, 63; Calif Inst Technol, PhD(chem), 68. *Prof Exp:* Res fel chem, Harvard Univ, 68-71; asst prof, Rollins Col, 71-74; res fel, Harvard Univ, 74-75. *Mem:* Am Chem Soc. *Res:* Computational studies of chemical reactions; calculation of reaction pathways; development of computational methods; localized orbital studies of chemical bonding. *Mailing Add:* 566 Highland Ave Upper Montclair NJ 07043-1206

HALIJAK, CHARLES A(UGUST), electrical engineering; deceased, see previous edition for last biography

HALIK, RAYMOND R(ICHARD), CHEMICAL ENGINEERING, SYNTHETIC FUELS. *Current Pos:* CONSULT, 81- *Personal Data:* b Kilkenny, Minn, Feb 10, 17; m 52, Elaine Tkacz; c Raymond Jr, David & Susan. *Educ:* Univ Minn, BChE, 40; Univ Rochester, MS, 41; Carnegie Inst Technol, PhD(chem eng), 48. *Prof Exp:* Asst chem eng, Univ Rochester, 40-41; develop engr, Rohm and Haas Co, Pa, 41-46; instr chem eng, Carnegie Inst Technol, 47; from technologist to sr technologist, Socony Mobil Oil Co, 48-53, res assoc, 53-59, supvr process develop, 59-66, eng consult, Mobil Oil Corp, 66-81. *Mem:* Am Chem Soc; Nat Soc Prof Engrs; Am Inst Chem Engrs. *Res:* Petroleum, petrochemicals and related energy sources, especially planning and economics of processes or entire ventures in oil, synthetic fuels or in uranium. *Mailing Add:* 9 Newcomb Dr New Providence NJ 07974

HALISKY, PHILIP MICHAEL, phytopathology, for more information see previous edition

HALITSKY, JAMES, AIR POLLUTION METEOROLOGY. *Current Pos:* CONSULT AIR POLLUTION CONTROL, 75- *Personal Data:* b New York, NY, Oct 18, 19; wid; c David J & Julie (Woodward). *Educ:* City Col New York, BME, 40; NY Univ, MAE, 42, PhD(meteorol, oceanog), 70. *Prof Exp:* Aeronaut engr, Edo Aircraft Corp, 40-48; sr res scientist, NY Univ, 48-71; assoc prof civil eng, Univ Mass, Amherst, 71-75. *Concurrent Pos:* USPHS grants, 58-60 & 62-65; meteorol consult air pollution problems of industry & pharmaceut res labs; adj prof appl sci, NY Univ & civil eng, City Univ NY, 79- *Mem:* AAAS; Am Meteorol Soc; Air Pollution Control Asn; Sigma Xi. *Res:* Diffusion of airborne pollutants in the atmosphere and the wind tunnel; chimney jets; modeling of atmospheric turbulence. *Mailing Add:* 122 Upper N Highland Pl Croton-on-Hudson NY 10520

HALKET, THOMAS D, COMPUTERS. *Current Pos:* PVT PRACTR LAW, 86- *Personal Data:* b New York, NY, July 20, 48; m 77; c 4. *Educ:* Mass Inst Technol, SB & SM, 71; Columbia Univ, JD, 74. *Prof Exp:* Assoc, Sullivan & Worcester, Boston, 74-78 & Dewey, Ballantine, Bushby, Palmer & Wood, 78-82; atty, Engelhard Corp, 82-83, asst gen counr, 83-86. *Concurrent Pos:* Ed, Antitrust Law J, 79-81; chmn, Sect Sci & Technol, Am Bar Asn, 88-89; mem, NY Sci Pol Asn, NY Acad Sci, 87- *Mem:* Am Bar Asn (secy, 85-86); Comput Law Asn; Am Phys Soc; AAAS; NY Acad Sci; sr mem Am Inst Aeronaut & Astronaut; Sigma Xi; Am Arbit Asn. *Res:* Computer and other technology transactions; author and/or editor of articles on law, science & technology. *Mailing Add:* 72 Shore Dr PO Box 942 Larchmont NY 10538-0942. *Fax:* 914-833-2681

HALKIAS, CHRISTOS, ELECTRONICS. *Current Pos:* PROF ELEC ENG & CHMN DEPT, NAT TECH UNIV ATHENS, 73-, CHAIR ELECTRONICS, 80- *Personal Data:* b Monasterakion Doridos, Greece, Aug 23, 33; US citizen. *Educ:* City Col New York, BEE, 57; Columbia Univ, MS, 58, PhD(elec eng), 62. *Prof Exp:* Prof & dir, Grad & Undergrad Electronics Labs, Columbia Univ, 62-73. *Concurrent Pos:* Nat Sci Found grant, Columbia Univ, 64-70; proj engr, Underwriters Labs, NY, 57; Fulbright vis prof, Greece, 69. *Mem:* Inst Elec & Electronics Engrs. *Res:* Multiport network theory; electronics and instrumentation; digital signal processing. *Mailing Add:* Paleo Psyhico 4 Kosti Palama St Athens 15452 Greece

HALKIAS, DEMETRIOS, MEDICAL MICROBIOLOGY. *Current Pos:* assoc prof, 72-78, PROF MICROBIOL & PATH, UNIV SFLA, 78- *Personal Data:* b Kosma, Greece, Aug 6, 32; US citizen; m 62; c 4. *Educ:* Univ Ill, BS, 57; Loyola Univ, Ill, MS, 59, PhD(microbiol), 64; Am Bd Med Microbiol, dipl. *Prof Exp:* Bacteriologist, Chicago Park Dist, Ill, 60-61; La State Univ-Inter-Am Prog Trop Med & Parasitol fel, 61; instr microbiol & virol, Creighton Univ, 63-67, from asst prof to assoc prof med microbiol, 67-70, path, 70-72. *Concurrent Pos:* Chief microbiol sect, Vet Admin Hosp, Tampa, Fla, 72- *Mem:* Am Soc Microbiol; NY Acad Sci. *Res:* Diagnostic microbiology; tissue culture and radiomimetic drugs. *Mailing Add:* 10413 Butia Pl Tampa FL 33618

HALKIN, HUBERT, MATHEMATICS. *Current Pos:* assoc prof math & assoc res mathematician, Inst Radiation Physics & Aerodyn, 65-69, PROF MATH, UNIV CALIF, SAN DIEGO, 69-, CHAIR DEPT, 81- *Personal Data:* b Liege, Belg, June 5, 36; div; c 2. *Educ:* Univ Liege, Dipl, 60; Stanford Univ, MS, 61, PhD(math), 63. *Prof Exp:* Res assoc, Res Inst Advan Studies, Md, 61-62; mem tech staff, Bell Tel Labs, 63-65. *Concurrent Pos:* Assoc ed, J Optimization Theory & Applns, 68-; Guggenheim Mem Found fel, Univ Calif, San Diego, 71-72; vis prof, Ctr Opers Res & Economet, Cath Univ Louvain, 71-72. *Mem:* Am Math Soc; Soc Indust & Appl Math; Economet Soc. *Res:* Functional analysis; calculus of variations; optimization theory; convexity; control theory; mathematical programming; applications of mathematics to economics. *Mailing Add:* Dept Math Univ Calif San Diego 9500 Gilman Dr La Jolla CA 92093-0001

HALKO, BARBARA TOMLONOVIC, COORDINATION CHEMISTRY. *Current Pos:* SR LECTR CHEM, ST MARTIN'S COL, 81- *Personal Data:* b Des Moines, Iowa, Nov 9, 40; m 76; c 2. *Educ:* Marycrest Col, BA, 65; Wayne State Univ, MS, 70, PhD(chem), 75. *Prof Exp:* Teacher chem & physics, Unihan High Sch, 65-66, St Albert High Sch, 66-67, Walsh High Sch, 67-69 & Bourgade High Sch, 70-72; res assoc, Ore State Univ, 75-76; teaching fel, Univ BC, 76-78; vis asst prof, Univ Idaho, 78-79. *Concurrent Pos:* Res award, Sigma Xi, 75. *Mem:* Am Chem Soc. *Res:* Synthesis, characterization and reactivities of polynuclear transition metal complexes of catalytic and biological interest. *Mailing Add:* 2903 NW Angelica Dr Corvallis OR 97330-3620

HALKO, DAVID JOSEPH, INORGANIC CHEMISTRY, BIOINORGANIC CHEMISTRY. *Current Pos:* RES & DEVELOP CHEMIST, HEWLETT PACKARD, 88- *Personal Data:* b Great Falls, Mont, Feb 17, 45. *Educ:* Col Great Falls, BS, 67; Univ Calif, Davis, PhD(chem), 73. *Prof Exp:* Res assoc chem, Wayne State Univ, 73-75; res assoc chem, Ore Grad Ctr, 75-76; res fel chem, Univ BC, 76-78; asst prof, Univ Idaho, 78-79; res chemist, ITT Rayonier Inc, 79-; mem staff, Rockwell Hanford Opers, Richland. *Mem:* Am Chem Soc. *Res:* Bioinorganic systems and analytical. *Mailing Add:* 2903 NW Angelica Dr Corvallis OR 97330-3620

HALL, A(LLEN) S(TRICKLAND), JR, MECHANICAL ENGINEERING. *Current Pos:* From instr to prof, 39-87, EMER PROF MECH ENG, PURDUE UNIV, 87- *Personal Data:* b Greensboro, Vt, Dec 12, 17; m 40; c 1. *Educ:* Univ Vt, BS, 38; Columbia Univ, MS, 39; Purdue Univ, PhD(eng), 46. *Honors & Awards:* Mach Design Award, Am Soc Mech Engrs, 74. *Concurrent Pos:* Mem, Sci Adv Coun, Picatinny Arsenal, 55-64; vis prof, Univ Calif, Berkeley, 64-65; mem, Munitions Command Adv Group, US Army, 64-68. *Mem:* Am Soc Mech Engrs; Am Soc Eng Educ. *Res:* Kinematics of machines; design of machines. *Mailing Add:* 2941 N Salisbury St West Lafayette IN 47906

HALL, ALAN H, medical toxicology, aerospace medicine, for more information see previous edition

HALL, ALBERT M(ANGOLD), NICKEL & ITS ALLOYS, STAINLESS & HIGH-ALLOY STEELS. *Current Pos:* CONSULT, 86- *Personal Data:* b Brooklyn, NY, Oct 8, 14; m 78; c Charles, David, Peter, Jay & Joan. *Educ:* Columbia Univ, AB, 35, BS, 36, MS, 37. *Honors & Awards:* Fel Am Soc Metals. *Prof Exp:* Asst metall, Columbia Univ, 35 & 36; res metallurgist, Int Nickel Co, WVa, 37-45; res engr, Battelle Mem Inst, 45-46, metallographer in chg, 46-50, asst supvr, 50-53, div chief, 53-67, sr tech adv, 67-69, asst mgr, Metall Dept, Columbus Labs, 69-79; exec dir, Mat Technol Inst Chem Process Indust, 79-86. *Concurrent Pos:* Mem staff, AEC. *Mem:* Am Soc Metals; Am Inst Mining, Metall & Petrol Engrs; Am Soc Testing Mat; Sigma Xi. *Res:* Use of color photography in study of non-metallic inclusions in metals; stainless and high-alloy steels; high-temperature alloys; cast iron-chromium-nickel alloys; new United States coinage; structural materials for coal conversion systems; alloys with special physical properties; physical metallurgy of iron and steel; graphite formation in steel. *Mailing Add:* 6000 Riverside Dr Dublin OH 43017

HALL, ANTHONY ELMITT, CROP PHYSIOLOGY, CROP ECOLOGY. *Current Pos:* from asst prof to assoc prof, 71-81, assoc plant physiologist, Agr Exp Sta, 76-81, PROF PLANT PHYSIOL, UNIV CALIF, RIVERSIDE, 81-, CROP ECOLOGIST, AGR EXP STA, 81- *Personal Data:* b Tickhill, Eng, May 6, 40; m 65, Bretta Reed; c Kerry & Gina. *Educ:* Univ Calif, Davis, BS, 66, PhD(plant physiol), 70. *Prof Exp:* Carnegie Inst Wash fel plant biol, Stanford Univ, 70-71; lectr water sci & eng, Univ Calif, Davis, 71. *Concurrent Pos:* Consult int agr develop, 74- *Mem:* Scand Soc Plant Physiol; Am Soc Plant Physiol; fel Am Soc Agron; fel Crop Sci Soc Am. *Res:* Environmental plant physiology and crop ecology with emphasis on crop adaptation to semi arid environments and the development of improved cultivars and management methods for these. *Mailing Add:* Dept Bot & Plant Sci Univ Calif Riverside CA 92521. *Fax:* 909-787-4437; *E-Mail:* anthony.hall@ucr.edu

HALL, ARTHUR DAVID, III, TELECOMMUNICATIONS, SYSTEMS ENGINEERING. *Current Pos:* PRES, ADVAN DECISION HANDLING INC, 76- *Personal Data:* b Lynchburg, Va, Apr 13, 24; m 47; c 3. *Educ:* Princeton Univ, BSE, 49. *Honors & Awards:* Outstanding Achievement in Systs Sci & Systs Eng Award, Inst Elec & Electronics Engrs, 74. *Prof Exp:* Head, TV Eng Dept, Bell Tel Labs, Inc, 50-66; vpres eng, Jerrold Corp, 66-67; vpres res, Systs Eng & Develop, Smith-Corona Div, SCM Corp, 68-70, pres, Melabs, Inc, Div, 69-70; pres, Arthur D Hall, Inc, 71- *Concurrent Pos:* Vis prof, Univ Pa, 67-69; adj prof, 70-85. *Mem:* Opers Res Soc Am; Inst Mgt Sci; Inst Elec & Electronic Engrs, Systs Man & Cybernet Soc. *Res:* Communication systems; operations research; telecommunication and agricultural systems engineering; education and writings in systems methodology; behavior sciences; public policy issues in telecommunications; real-time computer control of any type of farm. *Mailing Add:* 594 Liberty Grove Rd Port Deposit MD 21904

HALL, BARRY GORDON, MOLECULAR BIOLOGY, EVOLUTION. *Current Pos:* PROF BIOL, UNIV ROCHESTER, 89- *Personal Data:* b New York, NY, July 17, 42; m 64; c 3. *Educ:* Univ Wis-Madison, BS, 68; Univ Wash, PhD(genetics), 71. *Prof Exp:* Res assoc, Inst of Molecular Biol, Univ Ore, 71-72; NIH fel, 72-73; fel genetics, Univ Minn, 73-74; asst prof molecular biol, Fac Med, Mem Univ Nfld, 74-77; from asst prof to assoc prof biol, Univ Conn, 77-85, prof molecular cell biol, 85-89. *Concurrent Pos:* Res Career Develop Awards, NIH, 80-85; Fulbright sr scholar, 84-85; vis prof fel, Univ Wales, 84-85. *Mem:* Genetics Soc Am; Am Soc Microbiol; Am Soc Biol Chemists; Am Soc Naturalists. *Res:* Experimental evolution of new enzymatic functions in bacteria; molecular evolution; microbial evolution. *Mailing Add:* Biol Dept Univ Rochester 500 Joseph C Wilson Rochester NY 14627-9000

HALL, BENJAMIN DOWNS, MOLECULAR GENETICS. *Current Pos:* from assoc prof to prof genetics, 63-90, chmn, Genetics Dept, 80-84, PROF GENETICS & BOT, UNIV WASH, 90- *Personal Data:* b Berkeley, Calif, Dec 9, 32; m 54, Margaret Black; c Anne & Charles. *Educ:* Univ Kans, AB, 54; Harvard Univ, AM, 56, PhD(chem), 59. *Prof Exp:* From instr to assoc prof chem, Univ Ill, 58-63. *Concurrent Pos:* Guggenheim fel, 62; mem, Microbial Chem Study Sect, NIH, 71-75. *Mem:* Genetics Soc; Am Soc Biol Chem; AAAS. *Res:* Molecular genetics of higher plants and of yeast; eukaryotic gene transcription; molecular evolution. *Mailing Add:* Dept Genetics Univ Wash Seattle WA 98195-5325. *Fax:* 206-543-0754; *E-Mail:* bouhall@u.washington.edu

HALL, BEVERLY FENTON, INTERNAL MEDICINE. *Current Pos:* med staff fel, Lab Clin Invest, Nat Inst Allergy & Infectious Dis, NIH, 86-87, med staff fel, Unit Microbiol Pathogenesis, Lab Parasitic Dis, 87-90, VACCINE DEVELOP PROG OFFICER, PARASITOL & TROP DIS BR, DIV MICROBIOL & INFECTIOUS DIS, NIH, 91-; HOST IMMUNITY PROG OFFICER/MED OFFICER, 91- *Personal Data:* b White Plains, NY, Jan 20, 55. *Educ:* Harvard Col, AB, 77; NY Univ, MD, 84, PhD, 85, Am Bd Internal Med, dipl, 90. *Honors & Awards:* Bertram M Gesner Mem Award, Sch Med NY Univ, 84. *Prof Exp:* Jr asst resident, Dept Med. *Concurrent Pos:* Fel, Infectious Dis Sect, Dept Internal Med, Sch Med, Yale Univ, 89-91. *Mem:* AAAS; Am Soc Cell Biol. *Res:* Development and evaluation of vaccines for parasitic diseases; mechanisms of evasion of host immune responses by parasites; cell biology and biochemistry of intracellular parasitism; gene regulation and developmental biology of parasites; numerous publications. *Mailing Add:* Div Microbiol & Infectious Dis Parasitol Int Prog Br NIAID NIH 6003 Executive Blvd Solar Bldg 3A09-Ms 7630 Bethesda MD 20892. *Fax:* 301-402-0804, 203-785-3864

HALL, BRIAN KEITH, DEVELOPMENTAL BIOLOGY. *Current Pos:* from asst prof to assoc prof biol, Dalhousie Univ, 68-75, chmn dept, 78-85, Killiam res prof, 90-95, PROF BIOL, DALHOUSIE UNIV, 75-, PROF PHYSIOTHER, 88-, KILLIAM PROF, 96- *Personal Data:* b Port Kembla, Australia, Oct 28, 41; m 66, June D Priestley; c Derek A & Imogen E. *Educ:* Univ New Eng, Australia, BSc, 63, Hons, 65, PhD(zool), 68, DSc(biol), 78. *Honors & Awards:* Turner Newall Lectr, Univ Manchester, 85; Moyers Lectr, Univ Mich, 87; Nils von Hofsten Lectr, Univ Uppsala; Fry Medal, Can Soc Zool, 94; Sarnat Lectr, Univ Calif Los Angeles, 95. *Prof Exp:* Res asst zool, Univ New Eng, Australia, 63-64. *Concurrent Pos:* Vis prof, Guelph, 75, Toronto, 80, Brisbane, 81 & Southampton, 82; Nuffield Overseas fel, 82; assoc ed, Can J Zool, 82-85; vis lectr, Alta Heritage Found Med Res, 85, 90 & 92; ed, Anat & Embryol, 88-; Warwick James fel, Univ London, 88; frontiers biol lectr, Tex A&M Univ, 92; fel, Inst Human Biol, Univ WAustralia, 93-, Raine vis prof, 93; Miller vis res prof, Univ Calif, Berkeley, 97. *Mem:* Int Asn Dent Res; Int Soc Develop Biol; Can Soc Cell Biol; Am Soc Zool; fel Royal Soc Can; Brit Soc Develop Biol; Int Soc Differentiation. *Res:* Differentiation of bone and cartilage from common germinal cells; morphogenesis of skeletal system neural crest skeleton; avian embryology; evolution and development. *Mailing Add:* Dept Biol Dalhousie Univ Halifax NS B3H 4J1 Can. *Fax:* 902-494-3736; *E-Mail:* bkh@is.dal.ca

HALL, CARL ELDRIDGE, MATHEMATICS. *Current Pos:* ASSOC PROF MATH, UNIV TEX, EL PASO, 69-, CHMN DEPT, 71- *Personal Data:* b Danville, Ark, Mar 7, 37; m 59; c 2. *Educ:* WTex State Univ, BS, 61; NMex State Univ, MS, 63, PhD(math), 65. *Prof Exp:* Asst prof math, Va Polytech Inst, 65-69. *Mem:* Am Math Soc; Math Asn Am. *Res:* Topological algebra, especially topological groups. *Mailing Add:* Dept Math & Scis MC 00514 Univ Tex Bell Hall Rm 200 500 W University Ave El Paso TX 79968

HALL, CARL W(ILLIAM), AGRICULTURAL & MECHANICAL ENGINEERING. *Current Pos:* CONSULT, WORLD BANK, 90- *Personal Data:* b Tiffin, Ohio, Nov 16, 24; m 49, Mildred Wagner; c Claudia. *Educ:* Ohio State Univ, BS & BAE, 48; Univ Del, MME, 50; Mich State Univ, PhD(agr eng), 52, Harvard Univ, SMG, 83. *Honors & Awards:* Massey-Ferguson Gold Medal, Am Soc Agr Engrs, 76, Cyrus Hall McCormick Medal, 84; Max Eyth Medal, Ger, 79; Distinguished Serv Award & Medal, NSF, 88; Food Eng Gold Medal, Int Orthokevatol Soc, 93. *Prof Exp:* Instr agr eng, Univ Del, 48-50, asst prof, 50-51; from asst prof to prof, Mich State Univ, 51-70, chmn dept, 64-70; prof, dean & mech eng, Wash State Univ, 70-82, emer dean, Col Eng, 87-; dep asst dir eng, NSF, 82-90. *Concurrent Pos:* Res adv, Mich State Univ, 56-64; res consult, Univ PR, 57 & 63 & Nat Univ Colombia, 60; collabr, USDA & Dept State Sci Exchange deleg to USSR, 58; dairy eng consult, Ohio State Univ-Govt India, 61; consult, Latin Am, 64-70, vpres, Int Comn Agr Eng, 64-74, pres sect IV, 68-74, UN Spec Fund Proj, 80; mem bd dirs & secy, Eng Coun Prof Develop; mem, Mich State Univ Mission Ecuador, 66; Nat Acad Sci deleg, Brazil, 72, NSF, Brazil, 86 & 87, Indonesia, 78 & Peoples Repub China, 78; dir, Nat Soc Prof Eng, 75-79; founding ed, Drying Tech-Am Int J, 82-89; dep asst dir, NSF, 82-90, actg asst dir, 84 & 88. *Mem:* Nat Acad Eng; fel Am Soc Agr Engrs (pres, 74-75); fel Am Soc Mech Engrs (vpres, 93-95); Nat Soc Prof Engrs; Inst Food Technol; fel AAAS; Am Soc Eng Educ; fel Accreditation Bd Eng & Technol. *Res:* Application of heat and mass transfer principles to engineering of food processing and drying; administration; published 28 books. *Mailing Add:* Eng Info Serv 2454 N Rockingham St Arlington VA 22207-1033

HALL, CAROL KLEIN, CHEMICAL ENGINEERING & CHEMICAL PHYSICS, STATISTICAL THERMODYNAMICS & COMPUTER SIMULATION. *Current Pos:* assoc prof, 85-87, PROF CHEM ENG, NC STATE UNIV, 87- *Personal Data:* b New York, NY, Apr 23, 46; m 67, Thomas; c Katie, Adam & Norah. *Educ:* Cornell Univ, BA, 67; State Univ NY Stony Brook, MA, 69, PhD(physics), 72. *Prof Exp:* Res assoc chem physics, Cornell Univ, 73-76; mem tech staff econ analyst, Bell Tel Labs, 76-77; asst prof chem eng, Princeton Univ, 77-85. *Mem:* Am Phys Soc; Am Inst Chem Engrs; Sigma Xi; Am Chem Soc; AAAS. *Res:* Application of statistical mechanics to fluid and fluid mixtures containing chainlike molecules; polymers and colloids, metal hydrides, gases in zeolites, semiconductor interfaces, and bioseparations. *Mailing Add:* Chem Eng Dept NC State Univ Raleigh NC 27695-7905. *Fax:* 919-515-3465; *E-Mail:* hall@turbo.che.ncsu.edu

HALL, CAROLE L, ENZYMES, FLAVOPROTEINS. *Current Pos:* SR RES SCIENTIST, GA INST TECHNOL, 83- *Educ:* Purdue Univ, PhD(molecular biol), 66. *Res:* Beta-oxidation. *Mailing Add:* 1179 Milmar Dr NW Atlanta GA 30327-1619

HALL, CHARLES A, MEDICINE. *Current Pos:* DIR NUTRIT LAB CLIN ASSESSMENT & RES, VET ADMIN MED CTR. *Personal Data:* b Castine, Maine, Mar 7, 20; m 44, 74; c 5. *Educ:* Univ Maine, BA, 41; Yale Univ, MD, 44. *Prof Exp:* Fel pharmacol, Sch Med, Yale Univ, 47-48; from instr to assoc prof med, 51-66, prof med, Albany Med Col, 66- *Concurrent Pos:* Chief, Hemat Sect, Vet Admin Hosp, Albany, 53-78, chief radioisotope serv, 57-69, assoc chief staff, 62-71, med investr, 71; Fulbright lectr, Turku Univ, 60-61. *Mem:* Am Fedn Clin Res; Am Soc Hemat; Am Soc Clin Nutrit; Soc Exp Biol & Med. *Res:* Clinical and research hematology; vitamin B-12 metabolism; nutrition. *Mailing Add:* Hematology Res Lab Vet Admin Hosp Holland Ave Albany NY 12208

HALL, CHARLES A(INSLEY), CERAMIC ENGINEERING. *Current Pos:* Staff mem ceramic capacitor components, 62-95, CONSULT, SANDIA LAB, 95- *Personal Data:* b Bloomington, Ill, Feb 27, 37; m 66; c 2. *Educ:* Univ Ill, BS, 59, MS, 60, PhD(ceramic eng), 62. *Mem:* Am Ceramic Soc. *Res:* Ceramic and materials technology; ceramic capacitors; ferroelectric materials; electrooptic ceramics and other electrical ceramics. *Mailing Add:* 8407 Aztec Rd NE Albuquerque NM 87111

HALL, CHARLES ADDISON SMITH, SYSTEMS ECOLOGY, GENERAL COMPUTER SCIENCES. *Current Pos:* assoc prof, 87-92, PROF, STATE UNIV NY, SYRACUSE, 92- *Personal Data:* b Hingham, Mass, May 3, 43; m, Myrna Havnaer. *Educ:* Colgate Univ, BA, 65; Pa State Univ, MS, 66; Univ NC, Chapel Hill, PhD(zool), 71. *Prof Exp:* Res assoc ecol, Brookhaven Nat Lab, 70-72, asst ecologist, 73-74; asst scientist, Ecosyst Ctr, Marine Biol Lab, 72-77; vis asst prof, Cornell Univ, 72-76, asst prof, 77-85; res assoc prof, Univ Mont, 85-87. *Concurrent Pos:* Mem panel environ impacts natural resource mgt, Nat Acad Sci, 75-76; rep, Ecolog Soc Am to AAAS; Fulbright fel, 86; Guest of Honor, Nat Univ Argentina. *Mem:* Ecol Soc Am; fel AAAS; Sigma Xi. *Res:* Application of integrative tools of science, including especially empirical simulation modeling, to the understanding and management of complex systems of nature and of people and nature; examination of how organisms and societies invest energy in resource exploitation, and how such investments change as the quality of resources changes; integrative geographical modeling of environments and economies, especially in the tropics. *Mailing Add:* Environ & Forest Biol 320 Bray Hall State Univ NY Environ Sci & Forestry Syracuse NY 13210-2778. *Fax:* 315-490-6934

HALL, CHARLES ALLAN, NUMERICAL ANALYSIS. *Current Pos:* assoc prof, 70-77, interim chair, 96-97, PROF MATH, UNIV PITTSBURGH, 78- *Personal Data:* b Pittsburgh, Pa, Mar 19, 41; m 62, Mary Harris; c Charles Jr, Eric & Katherine. *Educ:* Univ Pittsburgh, BS, 61, MS, 62, PhD(math), 64. *Prof Exp:* Instr math, Univ Pittsburgh, 63-64; mathematician, US Army, 64-66; sr mathematician, Bettis Atomic Power Lab, Westinghouse Elec Corp, 66-70. *Concurrent Pos:* Instr math, NMex State Univ, 65-66; lectr, Univ Pittsburgh, 67-70; consult, Gen Motors Res, 71-, Westinghouse Elec, 74-81 & Pittsburgh Corning, 80-86, Contraves Goerz, 87-88; exec dir, Inst Comput Math & Applns, 78-88. *Res:* Matrix analysis; interpolation and approximation by piecewise polynomial functions; error bounds for interpolating polynomials; finite element methods; computational fluid dynamics; computational mechanics. *Mailing Add:* Dept Math Univ Pittsburgh Thackeray Hall Rm 603 Pittsburgh PA 15260. *Fax:* 412-624-8397; *E-Mail:* hall@vms.cis.pitt.edu

HALL, CHARLES E, VETERINARY MEDICINE, BOVINE REPRODUCTION. *Current Pos:* RETIRED. *Personal Data:* b Flushing, NY, June 9, 26; m 48, Shirley Auringer; c Ruth, David, Steven, Susan, Roger, Nancy, Eric & Margaret. *Educ:* Alfred Univ, AB, 50; Cornell Univ, DVM, 53. *Prof Exp:* Intern med & obstet, Cornell Univ, 53-54; pvt pract, NY State, 54-69; assoc prof reproductive studies, NY State Vet Col, Cornell Univ, 69-88. *Mem:* Am Vet Med Asn; Asn Bovine Practrs; Am Asn Vet Clinicians. *Res:* Reproductive diseases of cattle; immunology. *Mailing Add:* PO Box 0 Ovid NY 14521

HALL, CHARLES ERIC, PHYSIOLOGY, ANATOMY. *Current Pos:* from asst prof to assoc prof, 47-54, PROF PHYSIOL & BIOPHYS, UNIV TEX MED BR GALVESTON, 54- *Personal Data:* b Montreal, Que, Aug 27, 16; m 44. *Educ:* McGill Univ, BSc, 41, MSc, 42, PhD(anat), 46. *Honors & Awards:* Fantham Mem prize, Can, 41. *Prof Exp:* Asst anat, McGill Univ, 45-46; instr psychobiol, Johns Hopkins Hosp, 46-47. *Concurrent Pos:* Sabbatical, Karolinska Inst, Stockholm, Sweeden, 54. *Mem:* Fel AAAS; Am Physiol Soc; Endocrine Soc; Soc Exp Biol & Med; Am Heart Asn. *Res:* Endocrinology; andrenal cortex; pituitary; cardiovascular lesions; hypertension; parabiosis disease; renal enzymes. *Mailing Add:* Dept Physiol Univ Tex Med Sch Galveston 301 University Blvd Galveston TX 77550-2708

HALL, CHARLES MACK, ORGANIC CHEMISTRY. *Current Pos:* res assoc, Upjohn Co, 69-77, res head, 78-84, Dir, Hypersensitivity Dis Res, 84-94, exec dir proj mat, 94-96, PRES, INFECTIOUS DIS DEVELOP, UPJOHN CO, 96- *Personal Data:* b El Dorado, Ark, Sept 18, 41; m 67; c 3. *Educ:* Univ of the South, BA, 63; Univ Minn, PhD(org chem), 67. *Prof Exp:* NIH fel, Univ Munich, 67-68; asst prof, Univ Minn, 68-69. *Mem:* Am Chem Soc; Royal Soc Chem. *Res:* Synthesis of heterocyclic compounds and nucleosides; medicinal chemistry; anti-allergy agents. *Mailing Add:* 3835 Ruthin Rd Kalamazoo MI 49008

HALL, CHARLES THOMAS, microbiology, immunology, for more information see previous edition

HALL, CHARLES VIRDUS, VEGETABLE CROPS, HORTICULTURE. *Current Pos:* prof & head dept, 74-90, EMER PROF HORT, IOWA STATE UNIV, 90- *Personal Data:* b Ash Flat, Ark, June 18, 23; m 49; c 3. *Educ:* Univ Ark, BS, 50, MS, 53; Kans State Univ, PhD(entom, bot), 60. *Honors & Awards:* Asgrow Award, 64; Marion W Meadows Award, 72. *Prof Exp:* Asst, Fruit & Truck Br, Exp Sta, Univ Ark, 51-53; from asst prof to prof hort, Kans State Univ, 53-74. *Mem:* Fel Am Soc Hort Sci; AAAS. *Res:* Vegetable breeding and genetics. *Mailing Add:* 3416 Clinton Ct Ames IA 50010

HALL, CHESLEY BARKER, PLANT PHYSIOLOGY. *Current Pos:* from asst horticulturist to assoc horticulturist, 50-64, actg chmn, Veg Crops Dept, 78-79, HORTICULTURIST, UNIV FLA, 64- *Personal Data:* b Concord, NH, Sept 5, 20; m 43; c 4. *Educ:* Univ NH, BS, 42; Purdue Univ, MS, 48; Cornell Univ, PhD(veg crops), 50. *Prof Exp:* Asst veg crops, Cornell Univ, 48-50. *Mem:* fel Am Soc Hort Sci; Am Soc Plant Physiologists; Int Soc Hort Sci. *Res:* Physiological and biochemical aspects of vegetable quality as affected by environmental factors with emphasis on tomato. *Mailing Add:* 10710 NW 32nd Ave Gainesville FL 32606

HALL, CLARENCE ALBERT, JR, STRATIGRAPHY, TECTONICS. *Current Pos:* from asst prof to assoc prof, 56-68, chmn dept, 74-78, PROF GEOL, UNIV CALIF, LOS ANGELES, 68-, DIR, UNIV CALIF WHITE MOUNTAIN RES STA, 80-, DEAN DIV PHYS SCI, 83- *Personal Data:* b Los Angeles, Calif, Jan 5, 30; div; c 2. *Educ:* Stanford Univ, BS, 52, MS, 53, PhD, 56. *Prof Exp:* Instr geol, Univ Ore, 54-55; instr, Stanford Univ, 56. *Concurrent Pos:* Fulbright res scholar, 63-64 & 70-71. *Mem:* Fel Geol Soc Am; Paleont Soc. *Res:* Structural and stratigraphic geology of western California; large faults along coastal central California and in southern France; geology of the White Mountains and eastern California. *Mailing Add:* Dept Earth & Space Sci Univ Calif Los Angeles 405 Hilgard Ave Los Angeles CA 90024-1301

HALL, CLARENCE CONEY, JR, acarology, for more information see previous edition

HALL, COLBY D(IXON), JR, PHYSICAL CHEMISTRY, PETROLEUM ENGINEERING. *Current Pos:* RETIRED. *Personal Data:* b Ft Worth, Tex, Apr 17, 19; m 53; c 2. *Educ:* Tex Christian Univ, BS, 39, MS, 41; Univ Tex, PhD(chem), 52. *Prof Exp:* Sr chemist res, Dowell Div, Dow Chem Co, 52-55, lab group leader, 55-64, supvr basic res, 64-69; staff res engr, Amoco Prod Co, 69-86. *Mem:* Am Chem Soc; Soc Petrol Engrs. *Res:* Oil well stimulations; rheology of slurries and polymer solutions; enhanced oil recovery. *Mailing Add:* 5005 E 38th Pl Tulsa OK 74135

HALL, COLIN DAVID, AIDS RESEARCH, NEUROMUSCULAR DISEASE. *Current Pos:* from asst prof to assoc prof neurol & med, 72-86, vchair neurol, 86-95, PROF NEUROL & MED, UNIV NC, 86- *Personal Data:* b Chester, Eng, May 11, 41; US citizen. *Educ:* Univ Aberdeen, Scotland, MBChB, 66. *Prof Exp:* House offices, Univ Aberdeen, 66-69. *Concurrent Pos:* Chair, Neurol Comt, NIH Aids Clin Trials Group, 95-97. *Mem:* Fel Am Acad Neurol; AMA; Am Asn Electromyog & Electrodiag. *Res:* Effect of HIV infection on the nervous system and its treatment. *Mailing Add:* Dept Neurol Chapel Hill Sch Med Univ NC Chapel Hill NC 27599-0001. *Fax:* 919-966-2922; *E-Mail:* hallc.neurolog@mhs.unc.edu

HALL, DALE, PHYSICAL CHEMISTRY. *Current Pos:* ACTG DEP DIR, MAT SCI & ENG LAB, NAT INST STAND & TECHNOL, 96- *Personal Data:* b July 1, 47. *Educ:* Rennsealear Polytech Inst, PhD (phys chem), 73. *Mailing Add:* Nat Inst Stand & Technol Bldg 223 Rm B309 Gaithersburg MD 20899-0001

HALL, DAVID ALFRED, ELECTROCHEMISTRY. *Personal Data:* b Warsaw, NY, Aug 12, 40; m 65; c 2. *Educ:* Rochester Inst Technol, BS, 63; Univ Mich, Ann Arbor, MS, 65, PhD(chem), 69. *Prof Exp:* Res scientist electrochem, Eli Lilly Co, 67-80, res assoc, 80-88. *Mem:* Am Chem Soc; Sigma Xi; Electrochem Soc. *Res:* Investigation of the electrochemical redox behavior of pharmaceutically interesting organic compounds; application of the knowledge gained from these mechanistic studies to the electroorganic synthesis of the compounds. *Mailing Add:* 2506 Bluffwood Dr W Indianapolis IN 46228

HALL, DAVID GOODSELL, SR, MEDICAL ENTOMOLOGY, PARASITOLOGY. *Current Pos:* RETIRED. *Personal Data:* b Port Jefferson, Ohio, Aug 7, 03; m 25; c 2. *Educ:* Ohio State Univ, BSc, 26; Kans State Univ, MSc, 29. *Honors & Awards:* Superior Serv Award, USDA, 54; Silver Anvil, Am Pub Rels Asn, 55. *Prof Exp:* Asst entomologist, Univ Ark, 26-28; asst entomologist, USDA, 29-35, assoc, 35-42, med entomologist, CEngrs, USAAF, 42-46; entomologist, USDA, 46-48, asst chief, Insect Pest Surv Info, Bur Entom Plant Quarantine, 48-50, chief, 50-54, chief, Publ Br, Agr Res Serv, 54-66, English ed, Agr Exp Sta, Univ PR, 66-76, coop scientist, Insect Identification & Beneficial Insect Introd Inst, Agr Res Serv, USDA, 76-80. *Mem:* Entom Soc Am; Sigma Xi; Agr Communicators Educ; AAAS. *Res:* Biology and taxonomy of diptera involved in the health of man and animals; bites and stings of insects and related arthropods. *Mailing Add:* RR 1 Rocheport MO 65279

HALL, DAVID GOODSELL, IV, INTEGRATED PEST MANAGEMENT. *Current Pos:* CHIEF ENTOMOLOGIST, RES DEPT, US SUGAR CORP, 81-, MGR, DEPT ENTOM. *Personal Data:* b Charlottesville, Va, Nov 7, 52; m 77; c 2. *Educ:* Univ Mo, BA, 76, MS, 78; Tex A&M Univ, PhD(entom), 81. *Mem:* Sigma Xi; Am Soc Sugar Cane Technologists; Entom Soc Am; Am Registry Prof Entomologists. *Res:* Economic injury levels, biological control, chemical control; management strategies for insect pests of sugar cane and citrus. *Mailing Add:* US Sugar Corp PO Drawer 1207 Clewiston FL 33440

HALL, DAVID JOSEPH, GEOPHYSICS, THREE DIMENSIONAL SEISMIC & POTENTIAL FIELD INTERPRETATION. *Current Pos:* SR TECH ASSOC, TGS CALIBRE GEOPHYS CO, HOUSTON, TX, 91- *Personal Data:* b Morristown, NJ, June 21, 43; m 62, Nancy Lang; c Cynthia, Thomas & Robert. *Educ:* Beloit Col, BS, 65; Univ Mass, MS, 70, PhD(geol & geophys), 74. *Prof Exp:* Lectr geol, Bucknell Univ, 70-71; asst prof earth sci, Adrian Col, 71-73; chmn dept, 73-74; proj geophysicist, Houston Tech Serv Ctr, 74-78, dir, US Explor Interpretation Sect, Gulf Res & Develop Co, 78-79; dir, Seismic Eval Sect, 79-80, dir, Regional Geophys Sect, 80-81, sr staff geophysicist, 81-82; mgr geophys, Zenith Petrol, 82-83; mgr geophys, Int Oil & Gas Corp, 83-86; from sr to chief geophysicist, Total Minatome Corp, Houston, Tex, 86-91. *Mem:* Am Geophys Union; Soc Explor Geophysicists; Am Asn Petrol Geologists; Sigma Xi. *Res:* Integrated analysis of regional geophysical and geological data; development of geotectonic models consistent with multidisciplinary data sets; use of geophysical data in international and domestic exploration for accumulations of hydrocarbons. *Mailing Add:* 15 Twelve Pines Ct Spring TX 77381-2687

HALL, DAVID MICHAEL, TEXTILE CHEMISTRY & ENGINEERING. *Current Pos:* CONSULT, TEXTILE & RELATED INDUSTS, 69- *Personal Data:* b Birmingham, Ala, Mar 26, 36; m 64, Florence Barrett; c David Jr, Mary E, Alma J & Florence C. *Educ:* Auburn Univ, BSTC, 58; Clemson Univ, MSTC, 62; Univ Manchester, PhD(polymer chem), 64. *Prof Exp:* Assoc prof textile eng, Auburn Univ, 65-76, prof, 76-94. *Concurrent Pos:* Fel, Swiss Fed Inst, Zurich, 65; NSF grant, 65-67, Water Resources Res Inst grant, 69-71, ITT Rayonier grant, 79, Off Water Res & Technol grant, 80, Dow Chem grants, 86-88, US Army & USN grants, 90, 91 & 93; fel & chartered technologist, Textile Inst Gt Brit, 74 & fel & chartered colorist, Soc Dyers & Colourists, Gt Brit, 74. *Mem:* Fiber Soc; sr mem Am Asn Textile Chem & Colorists; fel Soc Dyers & Colourists Gt Brit; Nat Soc Prof Engrs; fel Textile Inst; Sigma Xi. *Res:* Fiber and polymer chemistry; carbohydrate chemistry as it relates to fibers and starch; chemistry of dyes and coloring matters; chemistry of natural and man made fibers. *Mailing Add:* Dept Textile Tech Auburn Univ Auburn AL 36849-3501. *Fax:* 334-844-4068

HALL, DENNIS GENE, GUIDED-WAVE OPTICS, SEMICONDUCTORS. *Current Pos:* from asst prof to assoc prof, 82-87, assoc dir, 92-93, PROF OPTICS, INST OPTICS, UNIV ROCHESTER, 87-, DIR, 93- *Personal Data:* b Belleville, Ill, Mar 7, 48; m 70, Rita Winkelmann; c Katherine, Christine & Gregory. *Educ:* Univ Ill, BS, 70; Southern Ill Univ, MS, 72; Univ Tenn, PhD(physics), 76. *Prof Exp:* Asst prof physics, Southern Ill Univ, 76-78; sr engr, McDonnell Douglas Astronautics Co, McDonnell Douglas Corp, 78-80. *Mem:* Am Phys Soc; fel Optical Soc Am; fel Soc Photo-Optical Instrumentation Engrs. *Res:* Integrated optics; optical properties of solids; thin-film phenomena; quantum electronics; surface phenomena; study of optical guided-waves. *Mailing Add:* Inst Optics Univ Rochester 500 Joseph C Wilson Rochester NY 14627-9000. *Fax:* 716-273-1072; *E-Mail:* hall@moe.optics.rochester.edu

HALL, DONALD D, GEOLOGY, INVERTEBRATE PALEONTOLOGY. *Current Pos:* assoc prof geol, 66-80, DIR AREA & INTERDISCIPLINARY STUDIES, CALIF STATE UNIV, CHICO, 66-, PROF GEOL & PHYS SCI, 80- *Personal Data:* b Cincinnati, Ohio, Mar 9, 33; m 56; c 3. *Educ:* Univ Cincinnati, BS, 55, MS, 60; Univ Mich, PhD(geol), 65. *Prof Exp:* Res geologist, Res Ctr, Union Oil Co, Calif, 64-66. *Mem:* AAAS. *Res:* Micropaleontology; Tertiary ostracoda. *Mailing Add:* 381 W Lindo Ave Chico CA 95926

HALL, DONALD EUGENE, PHYSICS, ASTROPHYSICS. *Current Pos:* from asst prof to assoc prof 74-83, PROF PHYSICS, CALIF STATE UNIV, SACRAMENTO, 83- *Personal Data:* b Takoma Park, Md, Oct 27, 40; m 61; c 2. *Educ:* Southern Missionary Col, BA, 61; Univ Iowa, MA, 73; Stanford Univ, MS, 64, PhD(physics), 67. *Prof Exp:* From asst prof to assoc prof physics, Walla Walla Col, 67-73. *Mem:* Acoust Soc Am; Am Guild Organists; Am Asn Physics Teachers; Am Astron Soc. *Res:* Mathematical physics; musical acoustics; astrophysics; plasma theory; nonlinear problems. *Mailing Add:* Dept Physics Calif State Univ 6000 J St Sacramento CA 95819

HALL, DONALD HERBERT, GEOPHYSICS, SCIENTOMETRICS. *Current Pos:* from asst prof to assoc prof, 62-69, head, Dept Earth Sci, 78-87, PROF GEOPHYS, UNIV MAN, 69-, SR SCHOLAR, 96- *Personal Data:* b Maple Creek, Sask, Nov 23, 25; m 55, Esther Crabbe; c Bernard J, Norman G & Judith (Dvora). *Educ:* Univ Alta, BSc, 48; Univ Toronto, MA, 50; Univ BC, PhD(geophys), 59. *Prof Exp:* Lectr, Univ BC, 57-59; asst prof, Univ Sask, 59-62. *Concurrent Pos:* Regional ed, Geoexplor, 63-83; vis prof geophys, Univ Liverpool, UK, 68-69 & Macquarie Univ & North Ryde, Australia, 75-76; res fel, Sci Policy Res Unit, Univ Sussex, UK, 83-84. *Mem:* Am Geophys Union; Can Geophys Union. *Res:* The Earth's lithosphere using surface and spacecraft data; history of geosciences; science policy and its application to the geosciences; scientometric studies of sciences. *Mailing Add:* Dept Geol Sci Univ Man Winnipeg MB R3T 2N2 Can

HALL, DONALD NORMAN BLAKE, ASTRONOMY, SPECTROSCOPY. *Current Pos:* DIR, INST ASTRON, UNIV HAWAII, 84- *Personal Data:* b Sydney, Australia, June 26, 44; m 67; c 2. *Educ:* Univ Sydney, BSc, 66; Harvard Univ, PhD(astron), 70. *Honors & Awards:* Newton Lacey Pierce Prize, Am Astron Soc, 78. *Prof Exp:* Exp officer physics, Div Physics, Commonwealth Sci & Indust Res Orgn, Sydney, 66-67, div studentship astron, 67-70; res assoc, Kitt Peak Nat Observ, 70-72, assoc astronr, 72-76, astronr, 76-81; dep dir, Space Telescope Sci Inst, 82-84. *Concurrent Pos:* Consult, Smithsonian Inst Astrophys Observ, 67-69; teaching fel, Dept Astron, Harvard Univ, 68; mem Space Sci Bd, Nat Acad Sci, 84-; mem Astron Adv Comt, NSF, 84-87; mem Astrophys Coun, NASA, 84-; mem, Space Sci Working Group, 84-; mem, Hubble Space Telescope Sci Working Group, 86- *Mem:* Am Astron Soc; Int Astron Union. *Res:* High resolution infrared spectroscopy (including observations and development of instrumentation) of astronomical sources applied to the detection of interstellar molecules and investigation of both extremely young and highly evolved stars; author of numerous technical publications. *Mailing Add:* Inst Astron Univ Hawaii 2680 Woodlawn Dr Honolulu HI 96822

HALL, DONALD WILLIAM, MEDICAL ENTOMOLOGY. *Current Pos:* from asst prof to assoc prof, 75-80, PROF ENTOM, UNIV FLA, 80- *Personal Data:* b Muncie, Ind, Dec 11, 42; m 65; c 2. *Educ:* Purdue Univ, BS, 64, MS, 67; Univ Fla, PhD(entom), 70. *Prof Exp:* Asst prof entom, Univ Mass, 70-74. *Mem:* Entom Soc Am; Soc Invert Path; Am Mosquito Control Asn. *Res:* Mosquito pathology. *Mailing Add:* Dept Entom Univ Fla PO Box 110620 Gainesville FL 32611-0620

HALL, DOUGLAS LEE, COMPUTER ASSISTED INSTRUCTION, COMPUTER SCIENCE INSTRUCTION. *Current Pos:* CHAIR, COMPUT SCI DEPT, ST MARY'S UNIV, 90. *Personal Data:* b San Antonio, Tex, Feb 5, 47. *Educ:* Univ Tex, Austin, BA, 69; Pan Am Univ, MEd, 77; NTex State Univ, PhD(comput sci), 87. *Prof Exp:* Syst analyst, TMS, 82-83; instr comput sci, NTex State Univ, 83-86. *Mem:* Inst Elec & Electronics Engrs; Am Asn Artificial Intel; Asn Comput Mach. *Res:* Application of intelligent tutoring systems in the instruction of science, especially with minority students. *Mailing Add:* 515 Marquis San Antonio TX 78216-5217. *Fax:* 210-436-3500; *E-Mail:* cshall@vax.stmarytx.edu

HALL, DOUGLAS SCOTT, ASTRONOMY. *Current Pos:* from asst prof to assoc prof, 68-80, PROF PHYSICS & ASTRON, 80-, DIR, ARTHUR J DYER OBSERV, VANDERBILT UNIV, 86- *Personal Data:* b Lexington, Ky, May 30, 40; m 64, 81, Mimi Kemp; c Bruce D & Brandon S. *Educ:* Swarthmore Col, BA, 62; Ind Univ, MA, 64, PhD(astron), 67. *Honors & Awards:* US Sr Scientist Award, Alexander Von Humboldt Found, 73. *Prof Exp:* Res assoc astron, Arthur J Dyer Observ, 67. *Concurrent Pos:* NSF grant, Vanderbilt Univ, 68, 70, 76 & 84; NASA grants, 77, 78, 79, 80 & 81; Res Corp grant, 78; ed, Int Amateur-Prof Photoelec Photom Commun, 80-; adj prof, Tenn State Univ, 91- *Mem:* Am Astron Soc; Astron Soc Pac; Am Asn Variable Star Observers; Int Astron Union; Int Amateur-Prof Photoelec Photom; Sigma Xi. *Res:* Eclipsing binary stars; astronomical photometry; stellar evolution; star clusters; variable stars. *Mailing Add:* Dyer Observ Vanderbilt Univ Nashville TN 37235

HALL, DWIGHT HUBERT, MOLECULAR GENETICS, MICROBIAL GENETICS. *Current Pos:* ASSOC PROF BIOL, GA INST TECHNOL, 77- *Personal Data:* b Rumford, Maine, July 27, 40; m 63. *Educ:* Bowdoin Col, BA, 62; Purdue Univ, MS, 65, PhD(biophys), 67. *Prof Exp:* NSF fel biol, Mass Inst Technol, 66-68; asst prof biochem, Med Ctr, Duke Univ, 68-77. *Concurrent Pos:* NIH res grant genetics, Med Ctr, Duke Univ, 68-77, Ga Inst Technol, 77-, res career develop award, 70-75. *Mem:* AAAS; Am Soc Biol Chemists; Genetics Soc Am; Am Soc Microbiol; Environ Mutagen Soc. *Res:* Biochemical genetics of bacterial viruses; production, isolation and characterization of mutants; organization and expression of the genome of bacteriophage T4; regulation; recombination; biosynthesis and interconversions of pyrimidine nucleotides; mechanisms of resistance to antimetabolites; genetic engineering. *Mailing Add:* Sch Biol Ga Inst Technol Atlanta GA 30332-0230. *Fax:* 404-853-0048; *E-Mail:* dhall@gtrlol.gatech.edu

HALL, EDWARD DALLAS, NEUROPHARMACOLOGY. *Current Pos:* res scientist II, Upjohn Co, 82-84, sr res scientist III, 85-90, sr scientist IV, 90-92, sr scientist v, 92-96, DISTINGUISHED SCIENTIST VI, CENT NERV SYST DIS RES, UPJOHN CO, 96- *Personal Data:* b Bedford, Ohio, June 16, 50; m 70, Marilynn F Gay; c Edward W & Christian D. *Educ:* Mt Union Col, BS, 72; Cornell Univ, PhD(pharmacol), 76. *Honors & Awards:* Kagan Award for Drug Discovery, 88. *Prof Exp:* Fel pharmacol, Med Col, Cornell Univ, 76-77; asst prof biol sci, Kent State Univ, 78-82; from asst prof to assoc prof pharmacol, Col Med, Northeastern Ohio Univ, 78-82. *Concurrent Pos:* Prin investr, NIMH grant, 78-82, Amyotrophic Lateral Sclerosis Soc Am grant, 78-82; adj assoc prof, Physicians Asst Prog, Western Mich Univ, 83-89, adj prof, Biol Scis Dept, 93-; mem, sci adv coun, Am Paralysis Asn, 85-88; adj assoc prof, 85-90, adj prof, Northeastern Ohio Univ Col Med, 90-; assoc ed, J Neurotrauma, 88-96, sect ed 96- *Mem:* Am Soc Pharmacol & Exp Therapeut; Soc Neurosci; NY Acad Sci; Soc Neurotrauma (vpres, 89-90, secy/treas, 93-94); Sigma Xi; Int Soc Cerebral Blood Flow & Metab. *Res:* Acute treatment of central nervous system trauma and stroke; treatment of degenerative neurological diseases; role of oxygen radicals and lipid peroxidation in acute and chronic neuronal degeneration. *Mailing Add:* Cent Nerv Syst Dis Res Unit Pharmacia & Upjohn Inc Kalamazoo MI 49001. *Fax:* 616-833-2525; *E-Mail:* edward.d.hall@am.pnu.com

HALL, ELIZABETH ROSE, bacteriology, for more information see previous edition

HALL, ERIC JOHN, RADIOBIOLOGY. *Current Pos:* PROF RADIOL, COLUMBIA UNIV, 68- *Personal Data:* b Abertillery, Gt Brit, July 5, 33; m 57; c 1. *Educ:* Univ London, BSc, 53; Oxford Univ, DPhil(radiobiol), 62. *Hon Degrees:* MA, Oxford Univ, 66. *Prof Exp:* Prin physicist, Churchill Hosp, Oxford Univ, 55-68. *Mem:* Radiation Res Soc; Brit Hosp Physicist's Asn; Brit Inst Radiol. *Res:* Effects of ionizing radiation on cells in culture; carcinogenesis; applications of radiobiology to cancer therapy. *Mailing Add:* Dept Radiol Oncol Columbia Univ Col Physicians & Surgeons 622 W 168th St New York NY 10032-3784

HALL, ERNEST LENARD, BIOENGINEERING, IMAGE PROCESSING. *Current Pos:* CTR ROBOTICS, UNIV CINCINNATI, 88- *Personal Data:* b Naylor, Mo, Dec 8, 40; m 69, Bettie C Glass; c Donald, Charles, Jeannine & Michael. *Educ:* Univ Mo-Columbia, BS, 65, MS, 66, PhD(bioeng), 71. *Honors & Awards:* Centennial Medal, Inst Elec & Electronics Engrs, 84. *Prof Exp:* Asst prof elec eng, bioeng & radiol, Univ Mo-Columbia, 71-72; asst prof radiol, Yale Univ, 72-73; asst prof elec eng & radiol, Univ Southern Calif, 73-76; from assoc prof to prof elec eng, Univ Tenn, Knoxville, 80-88. *Concurrent Pos:* NSF grant, Yale Univ, 71-72; Nat Inst Occup Safety & Health grant, Univ Southern Calif, 73-; consult, Oak Ridge Nat Lab, Jet Propulsion Lab, Calif Inst Technol, 73- & Lab Radiation Biol, Univ Calif, Los Angeles, 73-, Procter & Gamble, 82-, Gen Elec, 84, Int Comput Robotics Corp, 85- *Mem:* fel Inst Elec & Electronics Engrs; fel Soc Photo-Optical Instrumentation Engrs; Am Asn Physicists Med; sr mem Soc Mech Engrs. *Res:* Automated measurements; pattern recognition and picture processing in medicine; intelligent robotics, industrial robotics and manufacturing systems. *Mailing Add:* 9256 Village Green Dr Cincinnati OH 45242-7539. *Fax:* 513-556-4116; *E-Mail:* elhall@uceng.uc.edu

HALL, ERNEST LEROY, MATERIALS CHARACTERIZATION, ANALYTICAL ELECTRON MICROSCOPY. *Current Pos:* staff scientist, 79-91, MGR, MICROS & MICROANALYSIS PROG, GEN ELEC CORP RES & DEVELOP CTR, 91- *Personal Data:* b Allegany, NY, Jan, 1952; m 77, Carol J Neff; c Brendan R Neff-Hall & Darcy L Neff-Hall. *Educ:* Mass Inst Technol, BS, 73, PhD(mat sci & eng), 77. *Honors & Awards:* Alfred H Geisler Award, Am Soc Metals, 84. *Prof Exp:* Res assoc, Mass Inst Technol, 77, Int Bus Mach fel, 78. *Concurrent Pos:* Adj prof, Rensselaer Polytech Inst, 82-90; Coolidge fel, Gen Elec Corp Res & Develop, 89; vis scientist, Mass Inst Technol, 94; dir, Micros Soc Am, 94-96. *Mem:* Micros Soc Am (secy, 97-); Metall Soc; Mat Res Soc; Microbeam Analysis Soc. *Res:* Application of advanced methods of materials characterization to study structure-property-processing relationships; interface chemistry and structure in metals, ceramics, semiconductors, superconductors; nickel and titanium-based aerospace alloys, stainless steels, high-temperature superconductors. *Mailing Add:* Gen Elec Res & Develop Ctr PO Box 8 K1-2C12 Schenectady NY 12301. *Fax:* 518-387-6972; *E-Mail:* hallel@crd.ge.com

HALL, FORREST G, PHYSICS, REMOTE SENSING. *Current Pos:* PROG MGR, BOREAL ECO-SYST ATMOSPHERIC STUDIES PROG (BOREA), NASA-GODDARD SPACE CTR, 92- *Personal Data:* b La Feria, Tex, June 7, 40; c 2. *Educ:* Univ Tex, BS, 63; Univ Houston, MS, 68, PhD(physics), 70. *Prof Exp:* Aerospace technologist, NASA-Johnson Space Ctr, 63-64, physicist, 64-74, proj scientist, 74-78, chief scientist, Earth Observ Div, 78-80, chief, Scene Analysis Br, Earth Resources Res Div, 80-85. *Mem:* AAAS; Inst Elec & Electronics Engrs. *Res:* Application problems of multispectral remote sensing to large area survey estimates of crop area, yield and production. *Mailing Add:* Goddard Space Ctr Greenbelt MD 20771

HALL, FRANCIS RAMEY, HYDROLOGY. *Current Pos:* assoc prof soil & water sci, Univ NH, 64-71, prof hydrol, Inst Natural & Environ Resources, 71-83, prof hydrogeol, Earth Sci Dept, 83-90, EMER PROF, UNIV NH, 90- *Personal Data:* b Salmon, Idaho, Feb 25, 25; m 60, Carman Frye. *Educ:* Stanford Univ, BS, 49, PhD(geol), 61; Univ Calif, Los Angeles, MA, 53. *Prof Exp:* Ground-water geologist, US Geol Surv, 51-56; tech asst, Stanford Univ, 56-58; ground-water geologist, Stanford Res Inst, 58-59, res geologist in charge geohydrol, 59-61; assoc hydrologist, NMex Inst Mining & Technol, 61-64. *Mem:* AAAS; Geol Soc Am; Am Geophys Union; Am Water Resource Asn; Nat Water Well Asn. *Res:* Ground-water hydrology, applications of digital computers to fluid flow and chemical transport problems; effect of drainage basin parameters on pattern of ground-water outflow; impact of waste disposal on ground water; radon gas in ground water. *Mailing Add:* PO Box Ten Durham NH 03824-0010

HALL, FRANK FOY, BIOCHEMISTRY. *Current Pos:* sci dir & vpres Lab Opers, Dallas, 81-86, VPRES OPERS, INT CLINS LABS, INC, W REGION, IRVING, 86- *Personal Data:* b Seymour, Tex, Apr 2, 40; m 63; c 4. *Educ:* Tex A&M Univ, BS, 62, PhD(biochem), 66; Am Bd Clin Chem, dipl, 73; Am Bd Bioanal, cert lab dir, 75. *Prof Exp:* Res assoc biochem, Tex A&M Univ, 66; chief chem br, Clin Biochem, Med Lab, Ft Sam Houston, Tex, 66-68; fel, Scott & White Mem Hosp, 68-70, clin biochemist, 70-74; tech dir, Damon Med Lab, Inc, 74-75; dir, Bio-Sci Labs, St Louis, 75-76; pres, Int Clin Labs Mo, Inc, St Louis, 76-81. *Concurrent Pos:* Adj asst prof chem, Baylor Univ; NIH grant; assoc prof biochem, Tex Tech Univ Sch Med, 86- *Mem:* AAAS; Am Chem Soc; fel Am Asn Clin Chemists; Sigma Xi; Am Inst Chem. *Res:* Clinical laboratory methodology, clinical laboratory management, medical research, clinical chemistry, clinical biochemistry. *Mailing Add:* 5705 Grand Oak Ct Colleyville TX 76034

HALL, FRANKLIN ROBERT, ENTOMOLOGY. *Current Pos:* ADJ PROF ENTOM, OHIO STATE UNIV, 78- *Personal Data:* b Boston, Mass, Oct 30, 34; m 57; c 2. *Educ:* Univ Mass, Amherst, BS, 56; State Univ NY Col Forestry, Syracuse Univ, MS, 61; Purdue Univ, PhD(entom), 67. *Prof Exp:* Field rep entom, Niagara Chem Co, 60-63; fruit crop specialist, Chevron Chem Co, Stand Oil Co Calif, 67-70; prof develop rep agr, Chemagro Corp, 70; asst prof to prof entom, Ohio Agr Res & Develop Ctr, Ohio State Univ, 70-78. *Concurrent Pos:* Head, Lab Pest Control Appln Technol, 81- *Mem:* Entom Soc Am. *Res:* Biology, ecology and management of insect and mite pests of fruit; crop loss assessments; pesticide application technology; computerized decision support systems. *Mailing Add:* Dept Entom Ohio State Univ 1680 Madison Ave Wooster OH 44691

HALL, FREDERICK COLUMBUS, PLANT ECOLOGY, SUCCESSION & MANAGEMENT. *Current Pos:* Range conservationist, US Forest Serv, 56-58, vis asst prof range mgt, Idaho, 58-60, plant ecologist, 60-72, REGIONAL ECOLOGIST, US FOREST SERV, 72- *Personal Data:* b Milwaukee, Wis, Apr 19, 27; m 84, Virginia M Potter; c 2. *Educ:* Purdue Univ, BS, 51; Ore State Univ, MS, 56, PhD(plant ecol), 65. *Honors & Awards:* Super Serv, USDA, 76, Cert Merit, 78 & 92. *Prof Exp:* Forestry officer, USMC, 51-54. *Concurrent Pos:* Cert sr ecologist, Ecol Soc Am. *Mem:* Soc Range Mgt; Soc Am Foresters; Ecol Soc Am; Wildlife Soc; Soc Ecol Restoration. *Res:* Ecology of forest and range areas; forest community ecology; evaluation of grazing and logging effects; prediction of vegetation reactions; evaluation of total dry matter production; interpretation of data for land management application; long term monitoring. *Mailing Add:* USDA Forest Serv PO Box 3623 Portland OR 97208. *Fax:* 503-326-2469; *E-Mail:* fswais=f.halllou1-r06@mhs.attmail.com

HALL, FREDERICK KEITH, CELLULOSE CHEMISTRY. *Current Pos:* dir tech serv, Int Pulp Sales Corp, Int Paper Co, 66-70, asst dir, Corp Res Ctr, 70-72, dir primary process, 72-75, corp dir res, 75-77, dir, 77-79, dir res, 79-82, CHIEF SCIENTIST, S & T LABS, INT PAPER CO, 79-, DIR SCI & EXPLOR DEVELOP, 82. *Personal Data:* b Leeds, Eng, Jan 3, 30; m 56, Patricia Ellison; c Simon, Stephanie & Andrew. *Educ:* Univ Manchester, BS, 51; Univ Leeds, PhD(textile chem), 55; Harvard Bus Sch, AMP, 79. *Prof Exp:* Res chemist, Courtaulds (Can), Ltd, 56-58, asst tech mgr, 58-60, tech mgr, 60-63, dep plant mgr, 63-66. *Concurrent Pos:* Mem res adv comt, Textile Res Inst, 71-, mem bd trustees, 90-; officer & treas, Empire State Paper Res Asn, 78-; dir, Tech Asn Pulp & Paper Indust, 83-86, from vpres to pres, 89-93. *Mem:* Fel Royal Soc Chem; fel Textile Inst Eng; Chem Inst Can; fel Tech Asn Pulp & Paper Indust; fel Am Inst Chemists. *Res:* Pulp and paper chemistry; textile chemistry; wood chemistry; plastics; fibers; films; biological science, particularly as applied to trees; engineering development as applied to forest products and pulp industries; biomedical engineering. *Mailing Add:* 97 West Lake Rd Tuxedo Park NY 10987. *Fax:* 914-577-7307

HALL, FREEMAN FRANKLIN, JR, ATMOSPHERIC SCIENCES, REMOTE SENSING. *Current Pos:* RETIRED. *Personal Data:* b Kansas City, Mo, Sept 29, 28; m 52; c 4. *Educ:* Occidental Col, BA, 50; Univ Calif, Los Angeles, MS, 57, PhD(meteorol), 67. *Prof Exp:* Physicist, US Naval Ord Test Sta, Calif, 51 & Lockheed Missile Systs Div, 54-57; sr staff mem, ITT Fed Labs Div, Int Tel & Tel Corp, 57-63, assoc lab dir, 63-66; res scientist, Douglas Advan Res Labs, 66-70; res meteorologist, Nat Oceanic & Atmospheric Admin, 70-87; chief scientist, Harrier Consults, 88- *Concurrent Pos:* Expert witness, visibility & audibility. *Mem:* Optical Soc Am; Am Meteorol Soc. *Res:* Optical radiometry; atmospheric scattering, propagation and emission; infrared astronomy; optical instrument design; laser applications; atmospheric acoustics; planetary boundary layer observation and instrumentation; development, application and interpretation of infrared Doppler lidar for atmospheric dynamics studies. *Mailing Add:* 202 Ocean St Solana Beach CA 92075

HALL, GARY R, CORROSION. *Current Pos:* SR CHEMIST CERAMICS & COATINGS, SAUEREISEN CEMENTS, 68- *Personal Data:* b Milledgeville, Ga, Jan 14, 44; m 68; c Colleen. *Educ:* Univ Pittsburgh, BS, 66. *Prof Exp:* Lab technician glass & ceramic, Kopp Glass, 63-64 & alloy & coatings, Alcoa Appl Res & Develop Labs, 64-68. *Mem:* Nat Asn Corrosion Engrs; Am Inst Chem Engrs; Am Soc Testing & Mat; Am Ceramic Soc; Am Concrete Inst. *Res:* Corrosion of metals, concrete, ceramics, polymers and plastics; methods of controlling corrosion, including high temperature corrosion; concrete and ceramic technologies. *Mailing Add:* 233 Ridgewood Ave Apt 12 Pittsburgh PA 15229

HALL, GENE STEPHEN, RADIOANALYTICAL CHEMISTRY, BIO-ENVIRONMENTAL ANALYSIS. *Current Pos:* ASSOC PROF CHEM, RUTGERS UNIV, NJ, 79- *Personal Data:* b Plainfield, NJ, Feb 6, 51. *Educ:* Tusculum Col, BS, 73; Va Tech & State Univ, PhD(chem), 78. *Prof Exp:* Teaching asst, Va Polytech & State Univ, 73-78. *Concurrent Pos:* Prin investr, Rutgers Univ, NJ, 81- *Mem:* Am Chem Soc; Am Optical Soc; Nat Orgn Prof Advan Black Chemists & Chem Engrs. *Res:* Analysis of biological and environmental samples for trace and toxic metals using proton-induced X-ray emission; positronium reactions of chlorophyll and other compounds. *Mailing Add:* 6 Lawton Pl Bridgewater NJ 08807-2146

HALL, GEORGE ARTHUR, JR, PHYSICAL CHEMISTRY, ORNITHOLOGY. *Current Pos:* from asst prof to prof, 50-86, EMER PROF CHEM, WVA UNIV, 86- *Personal Data:* b Parkersburg, WVa, June 16, 20; m 63; c 1. *Educ:* Univ WVa, BS, 41; Ohio State Univ, PhD(phys chem), 45. *Prof Exp:* Instr chem, Ohio State Univ, 44-46 & Univ Wis, 46-50. *Concurrent Pos:* Ed, Wilson Bul, Wilson Ornith Soc, 63-73. *Mem:* AAAS; Am Chem Soc; Wilson Ornith Soc (2nd vpres, 75-77, 1st vpres, 77-79, pres, 79-81); Am Ornith Union. *Res:* Kinetics of solution reactions; distribution and ecology of West Virginian birds. *Mailing Add:* Dept Chem WVa Univ Morgantown WV 26506-6045

HALL, GEORGE E, ORGANIC CHEMISTRY. *Current Pos:* from instr to prof, 46-79, chmn dept, 66-72, EMER PROF CHEM, MT HOLYOKE COL, 79- *Personal Data:* b New Haven, Conn, July 14, 17; m 42, Sage Adams; c Elisabeth, John, Stephen, Hetty, Sarah & Mary. *Educ:* Yale Univ, BS, 38, PhD(org chem), 42. *Prof Exp:* Res chemist, Calco Chem Div, Am Cyanamid Co, NJ, 41. *Concurrent Pos:* Advan Educ fel & vis prof, Calif Inst Technol, 53-54, vis assoc, 69-70; NSF fel & vis lectr, Bristol Univ, 61-62; hon res fel, Univ Col London, 76-77. *Mem:* AAAS; Am Chem Soc; Royal Soc Chem; Sigma Xi. *Res:* Halogenation of ethers; electrical effects of substituents; biphenylene and derivatives; nuclear magnetic resonance. *Mailing Add:* 15 Silverwood Terr South Hadley MA 01075

HALL, GEORGE FREDERICK, SOILS, SOIL SCIENCE. *Current Pos:* from asst prof to assoc prof, 65-79, PROF AGRON, OHIO STATE UNIV, 79- *Personal Data:* b Spickard, Mo, Mar 5, 31; m 58; c 2. *Educ:* Univ Ill, BS, 59, MS, 61; Iowa State Univ, PhD(soil genesis, classification), 65. *Prof Exp:* Res asst agron, Univ Ill, 60-61; soil scientist, Soil Conserv Serv, 64-65. *Concurrent Pos:* Consult, US AID, India, 72-73; res leave, Commonwealth Sci & Indust Res Orgn, Australia, 86-87. *Mem:* AAAS; Am Asn Quaternary Res; Am Soc Agron; Sigma Xi. *Res:* Earth science; soil genesis and classification; strip mine reclamation; soil geomorphology; landscape evolution; Pleistocene geology; Paleosols; landslips; arctic soils; land use. *Mailing Add:* Dept Agron Ohio State Univ 2021 Coffey Rd Columbus OH 43210-1086

HALL, GEORGE LINCOLN, THEORETICAL PHYSICS, SOLID STATE PHYSICS. *Current Pos:* prof, 66-91, EMER PROF PHYSICS, NC STATE UNIV, 91- *Personal Data:* b Brandywine, Va, Feb 18, 26; div; c Gail, Karen & Rose. *Educ:* Col William & Mary, BS, 49; Syracuse Univ, MS, 51; Univ Va, PhD(math physics), 56. *Prof Exp:* Sr engr traveling waves & electron devices, Fed Telecommun Labs, 51-53; theoret physicist info theory, Res Labs, Westinghouse Elec Corp, 56-57; solid state physicist, Res Inst Advan Study, Baltimore, 57-60; instr math statist, Loyola Col, Md, 59-60; from assoc prof to prof physics, Kans State Univ, 60-66. *Mem:* Am Phys Soc. *Res:* Order-disorder phenomena; lattice distortion around vacancies; lattice summation methods; Wigner solids; mathematical physics; casimir effects. *Mailing Add:* Dept Physics NC State Univ Box 8202 Raleigh NC 27695

HALL, GLENN EUGENE, GRAIN QUALITY & DRYING, BIOMASS PRODUCT DEVELOPMENT. *Current Pos:* RES ENG, THE ANDERSONS, 73- *Personal Data:* b Tiffin, Ohio, Apr 21, 31; m 84, Sylvia Avila; c 3. *Educ:* Mich State Univ, BS, 59, MS, 60, PhD(agr eng), 67. *Prof Exp:* Asst prof res, Ohio Agr Res & Develop Ctr, 60-68; asst prof, eng topics, Univ Ill, 68-73. *Mem:* Am Asn Cereal Chemists; Am Soc Mech Engrs; Am Soc Agr Engrs. *Res:* Grain drying, handling, quality, dust control and grain storage areas; biomass product development. *Mailing Add:* 420 W William Maumee OH 43537. *Fax:* 419-891-2910

HALL, GRETCHEN RANDOLPH, ANALYTICAL CHEMISTRY, INORGANIC CHEMISTRY. *Current Pos:* RES ASSOC ANALYTICAL CHEM, MOBIL RES & DEVELOP CORP, 75- *Personal Data:* b Laurel, Md, Jan 16, 49. *Educ:* McGill Univ, BSc, 70; Univ Ill, PhD(chem), 75. *Mem:* Am Chem Soc; Sigma Xi. *Res:* Structure and composition research pertaining to petroleum and lubricants. *Mailing Add:* Mobil Res/Develop Corp Paulsboro NJ 08066

HALL, GUSTAV WESLEY, BOTANY. *Current Pos:* RETIRED. *Personal Data:* b Chillicothe, Ohio, Jan 14, 34; m 56; c 2. *Educ:* Ohio Univ, AB, 55, MS, 57; Ind Univ, PhD(bot), 67. *Prof Exp:* From asst prof to prof biol, Col William & Mary, 63-92. *Mailing Add:* 175 W Valencia Rd Apt 551 Tucson AZ 85706

HALL, HARLAN GLENN, INSECT GENETICS. *Current Pos:* ASST PROF & HONEYBEE GENETICIST, DEPT ANAT & HEMAT, UNIV FLA, GAINESVILLE, 88- *Educ:* Univ Calif, Berkeley, PhD(genetics), 78. *Prof Exp:* Staff scientist, Lawrence Berkeley Labs, Univ Calif, 80-88. *Res:* Analysis of African honeybee DNA. *Mailing Add:* Dept Entom Univ Fla PO Box 110620 Gainesville FL 32611-0620

HALL, HAROLD HERSHEY, THEORETICAL PHYSICS. *Current Pos:* RETIRED. *Personal Data:* b Kinsman, Ohio, July 18, 24; m 48; c 5. *Educ:* SDak State Col, BS, 48; Univ Ore, MS, 49; Univ Wis, PhD(physics), 53. *Prof Exp:* Sr scientist, Theoret Group, Radiation Lab, Univ Calif, 52-54; sr scientist, Missiles & Space Div, Lockheed Aircraft Corp, 54-56; asst dir reentry & space systs, Aeronutronic Div, Philco Corp, Ford Motor Co, 56-64; chief scientist remote area conflict, Advan Res Proj Agency, Dept Defense, 64-65; dir appl res lab, Aeronutronic Div, Philco Ford, 65-68; pres, HRB-Singer, Inc, 68-70, vpres & chief tech off, Aerospace Group, Singer Co, 70-72, mgr, Syst Sci Lab, actg mgr, Xerox Palo Alto Res Ctr, 73-75; vpres, Corp Res Staff, Xerox Corp, 75-88. *Res:* Nuclear physics. *Mailing Add:* 25155 Ave 417 Fulton SD 57340

HALL, HARVEY, RESEARCH ADMINISTRATION, EDUCATION ADMINISTRATION. *Current Pos:* RETIRED. *Personal Data:* b Butte, Mont, Aug 18, 04; m 34; c 3. *Educ:* Occidental Col, BA, 27; Univ Calif Berkeley, MA, 30 & PhD(physics), 31. *Prof Exp:* Instr physics, Columbia Univ, 31-34; lectr math physics, NY Univ, 34-36; asst prof physics, Col City NY, 36-42; prin physicist, Navy Dept, Bur Aeronaut, 42-48; dir, Physics Dept, Fla State Univ, 58-61; chief scientist, Off Manned Space Flight, NASA, 61-73. *Concurrent Pos:* Chmn, Navy Comt Study Feasibility Space Rocketry & pioneer, Early Earth Satellite Prog, Bur Aeronaut, 46-48; mem, Comt Upper Atmosphere, NASA, 46-51; dir, Naval Analyst Div, Off Naval Res, 51-58. *Mem:* AAAS; fel Am Phys Soc. *Res:* Theoretical physics theory of relativistic photo effect; photo disintegration of nucleus; stopping of fast charged particles by matter; coherent scattering of gamma rays. *Mailing Add:* 9000 Belvoir Wood Pkwy Apt 211 Ft Belvoir VA 22060-2702

HALL, HENRY KINGSTON, JR, POLYMER CHEMISTRY. *Current Pos:* head dept, 70-73, PROF CHEM, UNIV ARIZ, 69- *Personal Data:* b New York, NY, Dec 7, 24; m 51, Alene (Wini); c Doug, Joan & Lillian. *Educ:* Brooklyn Polytech Inst, BS, 44; Pa State Col, MS, 46; Univ Ill, PhD(chem), 49. *Honors & Awards:* Award for Polymer Chemistry, Am Chem Soc, 96; Distinguished Serv Advan Polymer Sci, Am Chem Soc, Japan, 96. *Prof Exp:* Res assoc phys chem, Cornell Univ, 49-50; res assoc phys org chem, Univ Calif, Los Angeles, 50-52; res chemist, Textile Fibers Div, E I Du Pont de Nemours & Co, Inc, 52-58, sr chemist, 58-65, group leader, Cent Res Dept, 65-69. *Concurrent Pos:* Sr vis fel, Japan Soc Prom Sci, 81; consult, Hoechst-Celanese Co, 78-, Eastman Kodak Co, 80-, Ethicon Co, 79-, Exxon Co, 81-, Amoco Chems Co, 77- & Chevron Co, 76-; vis prof, Imperial Col, London, 76, Nagoya Univ, Japan, 81 & Mainz, Ger, 88. *Mem:* Am Chem Soc. *Res:* Mechanisms of polymerizations; synthesis and polymerization of novel monomers and high polymers. *Mailing Add:* Dept Chem Univ Ariz Tucson AZ 85721. *Fax:* 520-621-8407; *E-Mail:* jmeredith@arizona.edu

HALL, HERBERT JOSEPH, ELECTROSTATIC PRECIPITATION, HIGH VOLTAGE POWER SUPPLIES. *Current Pos:* PRES, H J HALL ASSOCS, INC, 73- *Personal Data:* b Springfield, Mass, Sept 30, 16; m 49; c 3. *Educ:* Trinity Col, Conn, BS, 39; Univ Mich, Ann Arbor, MS, 40. *Prof Exp:* Mem staff, Radiation Lab, Mass Inst Technol, 41-45; sr physicist, Research-Cottrell, Inc, 45-54, asst dir res, 55-58, dir res & develop, 62-68, consult scientist aerosol physics, electrostatic precipitation & air pollution control systs & equip, 68-69; vpres, Recon Systs, Inc, 69-72. *Concurrent Pos:* H E Russell fel, Trinity Col, 39; physicist, Bikini Tests, AEC, Los Alamos Lab, 46; sci consult, 59-62. *Mem:* Am Phys Soc; AAAS; NY Acad Sci; Air Pollution Control Asn; int fel Inst Electrostatics Japan. *Res:* Electrostatic precipitation; aerosol physics; physical electronics; high voltage electromagnetic components. *Mailing Add:* 258 Opossum Rd Skillman NJ 08558

HALL, HOMER JAMES, INFORMATION SCIENCE. *Current Pos:* NSF proj dir, Grad Sch Libr & Info Studies, 78-82, VIS RES PROF, RUTGERS UNIV, 81- *Personal Data:* b Uniontown, Pa, Dec 12, 11; m 41; c 5. *Educ:* Marietta Col, AB, 31; Ohio State Univ, MSc, 32, PhD(org chem), 35. *Prof Exp:* Lab asst biol & chem, Marietta Col, 27-31; asst, dept chem, Ohio State Univ, 31-35; res chemist, Res Div, Esso Labs, Standard Oil Develop Co, 35-48, group head, 43-48, tech adv & expert witness, Patent Div, Esso Res, 48-59, gen secy, Patent Comt, 53-59, head indust technol, Tech Info Div, Exxon Res & Eng Co, 59-63, head chem info, 63-65, spec ed, 65-67, info analyst, 67-68, proj mgr, Govt Res Labs, Linden, 68-77. *Concurrent Pos:* Dir, Wainwright House Develop Human Resources, 70-80, trustee, 80-; mem toxic substances subcomt, Sci Adv Bd, Environ Protection Agency, 80-82; chmn, Union County Cultural & Heritage Bd, 85-90. *Mem:* Fel AAAS; Am Chem Soc; Am Inst Chemists (chmn, secy, 75-80); Am Soc Info Sci; Air Pollution Control Asn; NY Acad Sci. *Res:* Pure hydrocarbons, distillation and analysis; petroleum processing; fluidized solids; technical analysis of patents and inventions; air pollution technology United States and foreign; trace elements in coal; problems in the evaluation of information as distinct from technology producing it; training of information analysts; information strategy; multi-dimensional interactions of value systems; professional ethics and codes. *Mailing Add:* 260 Prospect St Westfield NJ 07090-4016

HALL, HOWARD TRACY, HIGH PRESSURE PHYSICS. *Current Pos:* dir res, 55-67, fac lectr, 64, DISTINGUISHED PROF CHEM, BRIGHAM YOUNG UNIV, 67- *Personal Data:* b Ogden, Utah, Oct 20, 19; m 41, Ida-Rose Langford; c 7. *Educ:* Univ Utah, BS, 42, MS, 43, PhD(phys chem), 48. *Hon Degrees:* DSc, Brigham Young Univ, 71; DHumanities, Weber State Univ, 87. *Honors & Awards:* Res Medal, Am Soc Tool & Mfg Eng, 62; Olin Mathiesen lectr, Yale Univ, 64; James E Talmage Sci Achievement Award, Brigham Young Univ, 65; Pioneer Chem Award, Am Inst Chem, 70. *Prof Exp:* Asst, US Bur Mines, Utah, 42-44, res assoc, 46; res assoc, Gen Elec Co, 48-55. *Concurrent Pos:* Alfred P Sloan res fel, 59-63; govt & indust consult. *Mem:* Fel AAAS; Am Chem Soc; fel Am Inst Chemists. *Res:* Ultra high pressure; high temperature technique and phenomena; synthesis of diamonds. *Mailing Add:* 1711 N Lambert Lane Provo UT 84604

HALL, HUGH DAVID, ORAL & MAXILLOFACIAL SURGERY, PHYSIOLOGY. *Current Pos:* PROF ORAL SURG & CHMN DEPT, SCH MED, VANDERBILT UNIV, 68- *Personal Data:* b Henryetta, Okla, May 15, 31; m 60, Katherine Suydam; c Steven D, Andrew D & Brian S. *Educ:* Univ Okla, BS, 53; Harvard Univ, DMD, 57; Am Bd Oral & Maxillofacial Surg, dipl, 65; Univ Ala, MD, 77. *Prof Exp:* From instr to asst prof oral surg, Sch Dent, Univ Ala, Birmingham, 61-65, assoc prof & chmn dept, 65-68. *Concurrent Pos:* Fel oral surg, Med Ctr, Univ Ala, Birmingham, 59-62; USPHS grants, 60-67, res career develop award, 62-64, dir training grants, 64-68; vis assoc prof physiol & biophysics, Univ Ala, 70-93; consult oral surg, US Army, Ft Campbell, Ky, 71-75; examr, Am Bd Oral & Maxillofacial Surg, 80-85. *Mem:* Int Asn Dent Res; Am Physiol Soc; Am Asn Oral & Maxillofacial Surgeons; Sigma Xi; Int Asn Oral & Maxillofacial Surgeons; Soc Educ Oral & Maxillofacial Surg (founding mem); Am Soc Temporomandibular Joint Surgeons (founding mem). *Res:* Clin oral and maxillofacial surgery, neural regulation of salivary gland growth and function. *Mailing Add:* Dept Oral Surg Vanderbilt Univ Sch Med Nashville TN 37232. *Fax:* 615-343-9397

HALL, IAN WAVELL, ELECTRON MICROSCOPY, METAL MATRIX COMPOSITES. *Current Pos:* CHMN MAT SCI, MAT SCI PROG, UNIV DEL, 88-, ASSOC PROF MECH ENG, 97- *Personal Data:* b Leeds, UK. *Educ:* Univ Leeds, BSc, 70, PhD(metall), 74. *Prof Exp:* Fel metall, Leeds Univ, 74-75; lectr metall, Tech Univ Denmark, 75-78; res fel mat sci, Technion-Israel Inst Technol, 78-80; asst prof mat sci, Univ Del, 80-86. *Concurrent Pos:* Res scientist, Univ Bordeaux, 89. *Mem:* Mat Res Soc; Am Soc Metals Int; Electron Micros Soc Am; Metall Soc Am Inst Mech Engrs; Nat Asn Corrosion Engrs; Am Soc Eng Educ. *Res:* Studies of the relationship between structure and properties in metal matrix composites with emphasis on fiber/matrix interfaces. *Mailing Add:* Spencer Lab Univ Del Newark DE 19716. *Fax:* 302-831-4545

HALL, IRIS BERYL HADDON, CELL PHYSIOLOGY, BIOCHEMISTRY. *Current Pos:* from instr to asst prof, 70-77, assoc prof med chem, 77-83, PROF MED CHEM & NATURAL PROD, SCH PHARM, UNIV NC, CHAPEL HILL, 83- *Personal Data:* b Richmond, Va, Nov 19, 37; m 64; c 4. *Educ:* James Madison Univ, Va, BS, 59; Univ Tenn, Knoxville, MS, 61; Univ NC, Chapel Hill, PhD(physiol), 65. *Prof Exp:* Asst zool & physiol, Univ Tenn, Knoxville, 60-61; asst physiol, Sch Med, Univ NC, 61-65; USPHS fel radiobiol, Med Ctr, Duke Univ, 65-66, assoc radiol, 66-67; biochemist & physiologist, Chem & Life Sci Lab, Res Triangle Inst, 67-70. *Mem:* AAAS; Am Asn Cols Pharm; Am Chem Soc; Am Inst Chemists; Sigma Xi; Am Oil Chemist. *Res:* Anoxic, hyperbaric, drug, hormonal radiation toxicological effects on cellular metabolism and enzymes; pharmacokinetics & distribution of radioactive drugs; identification of active contraceptive agents, antitumor, anti-inflammatory and hypocholesteremic agents; athersclerosis LDL & HDL receptor activity; serum lipiproteins; mechanism of action of these agents. *Mailing Add:* Med Chem Parm Sch CB 7360 Univ NC Chapel Hill NC 27599-7360

HALL, IVAN VICTOR, BOTANY. *Current Pos:* RETIRED. *Personal Data:* b Parrsboro, NS, Aug 24, 27; m 53, Carol Haff; c Dorothy, Helen, Peter & John. *Educ:* Acadia Univ, BSc, 48, MSc, 49; Cornell Univ, PhD(bot), 53. *Prof Exp:* Botanist, Kentvile Res Sta Can Dept Agr, 49-88. *Concurrent Pos:* Asst, Cornell Univ, 51-52. *Mem:* Am Soc Hort Sci; Agr Inst Can. *Res:* Ecology of native lowbush blueberries; factors influencing cranberry production in Eastern Canada. *Mailing Add:* 59 Elm Ave Kentville NS B4N 1Z2 Can

HALL, J(AMES) A(LEXANDER), physics, electrical engineering, for more information see previous edition

HALL, J(OHN) GORDON, FLUID MECHANICS, HEAT TRANSFER. *Current Pos:* RETIRED. *Personal Data:* b Westview, BC, Oct 14, 25; nat US; m 50; c 2. *Educ:* Univ BC, BASc, 50; Univ Toronto, MASc, 51, PhD(aeronaut eng, aerophys), 54. *Prof Exp:* Asst aerophys, Univ Toronto, 50-54, res assoc & asst prof aeronaut eng, 54-58; res aerodynamicist, Cornell Aeronaut Lab Inc, 58-59, prin aerodynamicist, 59-61, asst head, Aerodyn Res Dept, 61-66, head dept, 66-69; prof eng & appl sci & dir, Fluid & Thermal Sci Lab, State Univ NY, Buffalo, 69-76, prof mech eng, 76-95. *Mem:* Am Inst Aeronaut & Astronaut; Am Soc Mech Engrs; Am Phys Soc. *Res:* Environmental transport phenomena. *Mailing Add:* Dept Mech & Aerospace Eng State Univ NY Buffalo NY 14260-0001

HALL, J HERBERT, organic chemistry; deceased, see previous edition for last biography

HALL, JAMES CONRAD, CELL METABOLISM, CARCINOGENESIS. *Current Pos:* from instr to prof biol, Rutgers Univ, 47-62, prof physiol, 72-86, assoc dean, Grad Sch, 80-82, EMER PROF PHYSIOL, RUTGERS UNIV, 86- *Personal Data:* b Ont, Apr 26, 19; m 45, 86; c 2. *Educ:* Univ Toronto, BA, 40, PhD(physiol zool), 46; Univ Western Ont, MA, 42. *Prof Exp:* Asst prof biol, Univ New Brunswick, 45-47. *Concurrent Pos:* Vis prof, Univ Nebr Col Med, 70 & Baylor Med Sch, 71; chmn, Dept Zool & Physiol, Rutgers Univ, Newark, 62-69; consult, NIH, USPHS, 66-80; prin investr, NIH grant, 60-82; dir, Grad Prog Zool, Rutgers Univ, Newark, 75-78 & 79-81. *Mem:* Am Physiol Soc; Am Soc Cell Biol; Soc Exp Biol & Med; Am Zool Soc; Can Zool Soc; Sigma Xi. *Res:* Effects of hormones, especially insulin, on cellular respiration and metabolism; liver regeneration; effects of carcinogenic agents, pollutants, drugs on cell structure and function; oncogenesis; atherosclerosis; membrane structure. *Mailing Add:* Rutgers State Univ Newark NJ 07102

HALL, JAMES DANE, FISH BIOLOGY. *Current Pos:* from asst to assoc prof, 63-82, PROF FISHERIES, ORE STATE UNIV 82- *Personal Data:* b Columbus, Ohio, Aug 31, 33; m 55; c 2. *Educ:* Univ Calif, Berkeley, AB, 55; Univ Mich, MS, 60, PhD(fisheries), 63. *Prof Exp:* Res fel fisheries, Inst Fisheries Res, Mich Dept Conserv, 58-62; res instr, Fisheries Res Inst, Univ Wash, 62-63. *Concurrent Pos:* Teaching fel zool, Univ Mich, 59-60. *Mem:* Am Fisheries Soc; Ecol Soc Am. *Res:* Population dynamics of freshwater fish; effects of watershed practices on streams; stream ecology. *Mailing Add:* Dept Fisheries & Wildlife Ore State Univ Corvallis OR 97331

HALL, JAMES E, COMPUTER SOFTWARE. *Current Pos:* CHMN, ASIA PAC PARTNERS LTD, MALVERN, PA, 89- *Personal Data:* b Philadelphia, Pa, Aug 27, 33; m 55, Evelyn James; c Elizabeth A Shelton & James E Jr. *Educ:* Albright Col, BS, 55. *Honors & Awards:* Soichiro Honda Medal, Am Soc Mech Engrs, 94. *Prof Exp:* Staff, IBM, Philadelphia, 55-65, adv, Japan Div, Tokyo, 62-63; mkt mgr, Syracuse, 63-65; pres, Datamedia Corp, Endicott, NY, 65-70 & Educators Processing Serv, Swathmore, Pa, 70-74; sr vpres, Shared Med Systs Corp, Malvern, 74-84; pres, Info Tech Corp, Malvern, 84-87; pres & chief exec officer, Rabbit Software Corp, 87-89. *Concurrent Pos:* Exec vpres, Multimedia Med Systs Inc. *Mailing Add:* RR 1 Box 144 Malvern PA 19355-9801

HALL, JAMES EDISON, NUCLEAR PHYSICS. *Current Pos:* GEN MGR, DANIEL FLOW PRODUCTS INC, HOUSTON, 90- *Personal Data:* b Ft Worth, Tex, June 19, 42; m 64; c 2. *Educ:* Tex Christian Univ, BA, 64; Iowa State Univ, MS, 66, PhD(nuclear physics), 70. *Prof Exp:* Res asst nuclear physics, Ames Lab, AEC, 64-70; assoc, Swiss Fed Inst Technol, 70-72; develop proj mgr, Schlumberger Technol Corp, 72-76, sect mgr nuclear physics, 76-79, head, Eng Physics Dept, 79-82, eng dept, 83-86, dir eng, Statham Transducer Div, 86-90. *Mem:* Am Phys Soc; Soc Prof Well Log Analysts; Soc Petrol Engrs; Inst ELec & Electronic Engrs; Instrument Soc Am. *Res:* Design and development of pressure transducers & transmitters for use in aerospace instrumentation, process control systems and nuclear reactor environments. *Mailing Add:* Daniel Indust 9753 Pine Lake Dr PO Box 55435 Houston TX 77055

HALL, JAMES EMERSON, MATHEMATICS. *Current Pos:* PROF MATH, WESMINISTER UNIV. *Personal Data:* b Berwyn, Ill, Oct 3, 36; m 59; c 3. *Educ:* Northern Ill Univ, BS, 58; Harvard Univ, AM, 59; Univ Wis, PhD(math), 65. *Prof Exp:* Instr math, Northern Ill Univ, 59-61; from asst prof to assoc prof, Univ Wis-Madison, 65-77, prof math, 77- *Mem:* Am Math Soc; Math Asn Am; Sigma Xi. *Res:* Stability of ordinary differential equations. *Mailing Add:* Dept Math Westminister Col Box 23 New Wilmington PA 16172-0001

HALL, JAMES EWBANK, BIOPHYSICS. *Current Pos:* assoc prof, 78-84, PROF PHYSIOL, UNIV CALIF, IRVINE, 84- *Personal Data:* b Sewannee, Tenn, June 2, 41. *Educ:* Pomona Col, BA, 63; Univ Calif, Riverside, MA, 65, PhD(physics), 68. *Prof Exp:* Research physics, US Army, 68-70; res fel biophysics, Calif Inst Technol, 70-74; asst prof biophys, Duke Univ, 74-77. *Concurrent Pos:* Physiol Study Sect, NIH, 86-90. *Mem:* Biophys Soc; Soc Gen Physiologists; AAAS. *Res:* Investigation of the molecular mechanisms of voltage-dependent conductances in membranes; gap junctions. *Mailing Add:* Dept Physiol & Biophysics Univ Calif Irvine Irvine CA 92717. *Fax:* 714-856-8540

HALL, JAMES LAWRENCE, anatomy, for more information see previous edition

HALL, JAMES LOUIS, inorganic chemistry; deceased, see previous edition for last biography

HALL, JAMES TIMOTHY, THIN FILM OPTICS, IR DETECTOR MATERIALS. *Current Pos:* STAFF PHYSICIST, TRW ELEC. *Personal Data:* b Los Angeles, Calif, June 12, 50; m 78, Joanie Brown; c Jocelyn, Jonathan & Jason. *Educ:* Stanford Univ, BS, 72; Univ Calif, Santa Barbara, MA, 77, PhD(physics), 78. *Prof Exp:* Res asst physics, Univ Calif, Santa Barbara, 75-78; physicist, Nat Bur Stand, 78-80; physicist, Hughes Aircraft Co, 80-87, prog mgr, 81-87; staff physicist, prin investr & sr tech specialist, Northrop Electronics Systs Div, 87- *Concurrent Pos:* Res assoc, Nat Res Coun, 78-80; mem res tech staff & group leader, Northrop Res & Technol Ctr, 87-90. *Mem:* Am Phys Soc. *Res:* Thin film deposition technology; characterization spectroscopies; superconductors; semiconductors; chemical vapor; thin films for device applications; research and development scientist; materials scientist; holographer; diffractive optics; multilayer optical coatings. *Mailing Add:* 4010 Merrill St Torrance CA 90503. *Fax:* 213-600-4099; *E-Mail:* jhall@world.nad.northrop.com

HALL, JAMES WESLEY, EDUCATIONAL ADMINISTRATION. *Current Pos:* prof math, 75-97, CHAIR MATH & COMPUT SCI DEPT, PARKLAND COL, 97- *Personal Data:* b Effingham, Ill, Nov 4, 46; m 68, Peggy Probst; c Manette, Mason & Jesse. *Educ:* Eastern Ill Univ, BSEd, 68, MA, 69; Okla State Univ, EdD(math), 73. *Prof Exp:* Instr math, Northern Ariz Univ, 69-70; asst prof, Clayton State Univ, 73-75. *Mem:* Math Asn Am; Nat Coun Teachers Math; Am Math Asn Two Year Col (pres, 96). *Mailing Add:* 1202 Oak Creek Rd Mahomet IL 61853. *Fax:* 217-373-3898; *E-Mail:* jhall@parkland.cc.il.us

HALL, JEFFREY CONNOR, BEHAVIORAL GENETICS, NEUROBIOLOGY. *Current Pos:* from asst prof to assoc prof, 74-79, PROF BIOL, BRANDEIS UNIV, 79- *Personal Data:* b Brooklyn, NY, May 3, 45. *Educ:* Amherst Col, AB, 67; Univ Wash, MS, 69, PhD(genetics), 71. *Prof Exp:* Fel behav genetics, Calif Inst Technol, 71-73. *Mem:* Genetics Soc Am; Soc Neurosci. *Res:* Behavioral genetics of Drosophila; studies of reproductive behavior in mutant and mosaic insects; developmental, physiological, and behavioral abnormalities induced by neurochemical mutants in Drosophila. *Mailing Add:* Dept Biol Brandeis Univ 415 South St Waltham MA 02154-2700

HALL, JENNIFER DEAN, MOLECULAR BIOLOGY. *Current Pos:* asst prof cell develop biol, 76-82, ASSOC PROF MOLECULAR CELL BIOL, UNIV ARIZ, 82- *Personal Data:* b Bethesda, Md, Dec 15, 44; c 3. *Educ:* Harvard Univ, BA, 67; Yale Univ, PhD(molecular biophys & biochem), 74. *Prof Exp:* Fel biochem sci, Princeton Univ, 74-76. *Concurrent Pos:* Fel, Am Cancer Soc, 74-76; NIH grant, 77-; scholars grant, Am Cancer Soc, 84. *Mem:* AAAS. *Res:* DNA replication in mammalian cells; animal viruses. *Mailing Add:* Dept Molecular Cellular Biol Univ Ariz 1600 E University Blvd Tucson AZ 85721-0001

HALL, JEROME WILLIAM, PHYSICS, CIVIL ENGINEERING. *Current Pos:* asst dean eng, 85-88, PROF CIVIL ENG, UNIV NMEX, 80-, CHMN, CIVIL ENG DEPT, 90- *Personal Data:* b Brunswick, Ga, Dec 1, 43; m 65, Loretta E Hood; c Jennifer, Bridget & Bernadette. *Educ:* Harvey Mudd Col, BS, 65; Univ Wash, MS, 68, PhD(civil eng), 69. *Prof Exp:* Instr, Univ Wash, 69-70; from asst prof to assoc prof civil eng, Univ Md, College Park, 70-77. *Concurrent Pos:* Vpres, Transp Planning & Eng, Seattle, 67-70; hwy safety specialist, Fed Hwy Admin, 71; mem, Transp Res Bd, Nat Acad Sci-Nat Res Coun, 71-; consult hwy eng, 81-; int dir, Inst Transp Engrs, 93-95. *Mem:* Fel Inst Transp Engrs; Am Soc Eng Educ; Am Rd & Transp Builders Asn. *Res:* Transportation systems safety and operation. *Mailing Add:* Dept Civil Eng Univ NMex Albuquerque NM 87131-1351. *E-Mail:* jerome@.unm.edu

HALL, JERRY LEE, MECHANICAL & AEROSPACE ENGINEERING. *Current Pos:* From instr to assoc prof, 60-77, PROF MECH ENG, IOWA STATE UNIV, 77- *Personal Data:* b Boulder, Colo, Feb 2, 38; m 57; c 3. *Educ:* Iowa State Univ, BS, 59, MS, 63, PhD(mech & aerospace eng, math), 67. *Honors & Awards:* Ralph Teetor Award, Soc Automotive Engrs, 77. *Mem:* Am Soc Mech Engrs; Am Soc Eng Educ; Soc Automotive Engrs; Am Inst Aeronaut & Astronaut; Nat Fire Protection Asn. *Res:* Gas dynamics; instrumentation and measurements; shock tube flows; design of experiments; environmental emissions; combustion; fires. *Mailing Add:* RR 4 Ames IA 50014-9804

HALL, JOHN B, ORGANIC CHEMISTRY. *Current Pos:* RETIRED. *Personal Data:* b New York, Oct 12, 18; m 57; c 2. *Educ:* Cornell Univ, PhD(chem), 50. *Prof Exp:* Org chemist, Air Reduction Co, 53-57; proj leader, Int Flavors & Fragrances Inc, 58-65, res assoc, 65-68, assoc dir, 68-73, dir, 73-75, vpres res & develop, 75-85. *Mem:* Am Chem Soc. *Res:* Fragrance chemistry; terpenes; relationship between structure and odor. *Mailing Add:* PO Box 404 Rumson NJ 07760-0404

HALL, JOHN BRADLEY, MICROBIAL PHYSIOLOGY. *Current Pos:* from asst prof to assoc prof, 62-73, PROF MICROBIOL, UNIV HAWAII, MANOA, 73- *Personal Data:* b Denver, Colo, Nov 2, 33; m 63. *Educ:* Univ Kans, BA, 56; Univ Calif, Berkeley, PhD(biochem), 60. *Prof Exp:* NIH fel biochem, Calif Inst Technol, 60-62. *Concurrent Pos:* NIH res grant, 63-65; Damon Runyon res grant, 64-65. *Mem:* Am Soc Microbiol; Sigma Xi. *Res:* Energy metabolism in anaerobic bacteria. *Mailing Add:* 5326 Keikilani Circle Honolulu HI 96821

HALL, JOHN EDGAR, ZOOLOGY, PARASITOLOGY. *Current Pos:* from instr to prof, 58-96, EMER PROF MICROBIOL, SCH MED, WVA UNIV, 97- *Personal Data:* b Meadville, Pa, Dec 28, 29; m 57, Judith Chatfield; c Martha (Gach), Kathryn (de Giraaf) & John M. *Educ:* Univ NH, BS, 51, MS, 53; Purdue Univ, PhD(parasitol), 58. *Prof Exp:* Asst zool, Univ NH, 51-52; asst, Purdue Univ, 55-56. *Concurrent Pos:* Inter-Am fel trop med & parasitol, La State Univ, 60; NIH res career develop award, 62-67. *Mem:* AAAS; Am Micros Soc; Am Soc Parasitol; Am Soc Trop Med & Hyg; Entom Soc Am. *Res:* Medical parasitology; morphology, life history and host-parasite relationships of helminths; reactions of insects to helminth parasites; endosymbionts of pathogenic freshwater amebae; medical entomology; lyme disease surveillance. *Mailing Add:* 648 Vista Pl Morgantown WV 26505. *Fax:* 303-293-7823; *E-Mail:* jhall2@wvu.edu

HALL, JOHN EDWARD, HYPERTENSION, BLOOD PRESSURE REGULATION. *Current Pos:* From instr to assoc prof, 75-82, dir grad prog, 80-93, PROF, DEPT PHYSIOL & BIOPHYSICS, UNIV MISS MED CTR, 82-, CHMN, DEPT PHYSIOL & BIOPHYS, 89- *Personal Data:* b Aug 8, 46; c 3. *Educ:* Kent State Univ, BS, 68; Mich State Univ, PhD(physiol), 74. *Honors & Awards:* Goldblatt Award, Am Heart Asn, Louis Dahl Award; Marion Award, Am Soc Hypertension. *Concurrent Pos:* Fel, NIH nat Res Serv Award, Dept Physiol & Biophysics, Univ Miss Med Ctr, 74-75; coun high blood pressure res, Am Heart Asn; mem grad fac, Dept Physiol & Biophysics, Univ Miss Med Ctr, 77-; vchmn, Dept Physiol & Biophysics, Univ Miss Med Ctr, 88-89 & 96-, chmn, 89-; assoc ed, Am J Physiol, 90-96, ed, 96-; mem, Cardiovasc & Renal Study Sect, NIH, 90-94; counr, Am Physiol Soc, 91, chmn, Water & Elec Homeostasis Sect, 91-94. *Mem:* Am Physiol Soc; Am Soc Nephrology; Int Soc Nephrology; Am Soc Hypertension; Int Soc Hypertension; Int Am Soc Hypertension (treas, 93-). *Res:* Renal and cardiovascular physiology; hypertension; obesity, insulin resistance. *Mailing Add:* Dept Physiol & Biophys Univ Miss Med Ctr 2500 N State St Jackson MS 39216. *Fax:* 601-984-1817; *E-Mail:* jeh@fiona.umsmed.edu

HALL, JOHN EMMETT, ORTHOPEDIC SURGERY. *Current Pos:* CHIEF CLIN SERV, DEPT ORTHOP SURG, CHILDREN'S HOSP MED CTR, BOSTON, 71-, CLIN PROF ORTHOP SURG, CHIEF ORTHOP SURGEON, 86- *Personal Data:* b Wadena, Sask, Apr 23, 25; m 52; c 6. *Educ:* Univ Sask, BA, 48; McGill Univ, MD, CM, 52; FRCS(C), 57. *Prof Exp:* Assoc surg, Univ Toronto, 58-68, asst prof, 68-71; prof orthop surg, Harvard Med Sch, 71- *Concurrent Pos:* Orthop consult, Ont Crippled Children's Ctr, 58-68; asst surgeon, Hosp for Sick Children, 58-68, chief div orthop surg, 68-71. *Mem:* Can Med Asn; Can Orthop Asn; fel Am Col Surg. *Res:* Prosthetics; development of myoelectric arm; spinal curvatures. *Mailing Add:* Dept Orthop Surg Childrens Hosp 300 Longwood Ave Boston MA 02115-5737

HALL, JOHN JAY, SOLID STATE PHYSICS. *Current Pos:* RETIRED. *Personal Data:* b Cambridge, Mass, Oct 20, 31; m 53; c 2. *Educ:* Columbia Univ, BS, 56, MA, 58, PhD(physics), 62. *Prof Exp:* Res assoc physics, Watson Res Labs, IBM Corp, Columbia, 62-63, res staff mem, Res Ctr, 63-80; managing partner, Shearwater Co, 80-94. *Mem:* Inst Elec & Electronics Engrs. *Res:* Display technologies; transport properties of semiconductors and semi-metals; ultrasonic properties of insulating and semiconducting crystals; piezoelectric and ferroelectric materials; electrical discharges in gases. *Mailing Add:* 3030 Emmons Ave 2B Shearwater Co Brooklyn NY 11235-2233

HALL, JOHN L, LASERS, OPTICS. *Current Pos:* Nat Res Coun fel, Nat Bur Stand, 61-62, physicist, 62-71; SR SCIENTIST, NAT INST STAND & TECHNOL, 71-; LECTR, PHYSICS DEPT, UNIV COLO, 67-, SR SCIENTIST, JOINT INST LAB ASTROPHYS. *Personal Data:* b Denver, Colo, Aug 21, 34; m 58; c 3. *Educ:* Carnegie Inst Technol, BS, 56, MS, 58, PhD(physics), 61. *Hon Degrees:* Dr, Univ Paris Nord, 89. *Honors & Awards:* Gold Medal, US Dept Com, 69 & 74; Samuel Wesley Stratton Award, Nat Bur Stand, 71, E U Condon Award, 79; Charles H Townes Award, Optical Soc Am, 84, Frederic Eyes Medal, 91; Davisson-Germer Award, Am Phys Soc, 88, Arthur L Schawlow Award, 93. *Concurrent Pos:* Fel, Joint Inst Lab Astrophys, 64-; mem, Comn VII, Int Union Radio Sci; deleg, Consultative Comt Definition Meter, Sevres, France, 70-; mem, Comt Recommendations, NAC-Army Res Off, 76-79; mem, Nat Res Comt Fundamental Constants, Nat Res Coun-Nat Acad Sci, 76-79; mem, Prog Comt, Tenth Int Conf Quantum Electronics, 78. *Mem:* Nat Acad Sci; fel Am Phys Soc; fel Optical Soc Am; Sigma Xi. *Res:* Laser and solid state physics; negative ion photodetachment; nonlinear optics; laser stabilization; application of precision measurement techniques to fundamental physical measurements; granted 5 patents. *Mailing Add:* Univ Colo Campus Box 440 Boulder CO 80309-0440

HALL, JOHN SYLVESTER, ZOOLOGY. *Current Pos:* From asst prof to assoc prof, 60-71, prof biol, 71-, EMER PROF BIOL, ALBRIGHT COL. *Personal Data:* b Westfield, Mass, July 15, 30; m 54; c 5. *Educ:* Univ Mass, BS, 51, MA, 56; Univ Ill, PhD(zool), 60. *Mem:* AAAS; Am Soc Mammalogists; Nat Spleleol Soc; Animal Behav Soc. *Res:* Mammalian ecology and evolution, especially population ecology of bats; osteometric variation of mammals; Pleistocene distribution of mammals; behavior of bats and rodents. *Mailing Add:* Dept Biol Albright Col PO Box 15234 Reading PA 19612-5234

HALL, JOHN WILFRED, STATISTICS. *Current Pos:* statistician, 77-84, STATIST SCIENTIST, RES BR, AGR CAN, 84- *Personal Data:* b Midland, Ont, May 30, 41. *Educ:* Univ Toronto, BSc, 65, MSc, 69; Va Polytech Inst & State Univ, PhD(statist), 73. *Honors & Awards:* C H Bishop Award, 91. *Prof Exp:* Res asst statist, Connaught Biosci, 66-69; consult, Health Protection Br, Health & Welfare Can, 72-74; sect head, 74-77. *Mem:* Am Statist Asn; Biomet Soc; Can Statist Soc. *Res:* Statistical methods for agricultural and medical research. *Mailing Add:* Pacific Agri-Food Res Ctr Agr & Agri-Food Canada Summerland BC V0H 1Z0 Can. *E-Mail:* Hall@pargua.agrica

HALL, JON K, SOIL CHEMISTRY, ENVIRONMENTAL QUALITY. *Current Pos:* Instr agron, 65-66, asst prof soil chem, 66-73, ASSOC PROF SOIL CHEM, PA STATE UNIV, UNIVERSITY PARK, 73- *Personal Data:* b Derby, Conn, June 23, 37; m 60, Elsie Pearson; c David K, Kenneth C, Eric S & Karen A. *Educ:* Univ Conn, BS, 58; Pa State Univ, MS, 63, PhD(agron), 66. *Mem:* Am Soc Agron; Soil Sci Soc Am; Sigma Xi. *Res:* Chemistry, mobility and persistence of herbicides in soils and tillage systems. *Mailing Add:* Dept Agron Pa State Univ 116 Agr Sci Ind Bldg University Park PA 16802. *Fax:* 814-863-7043

HALL, JOSEPH GLENN, VERTEBRATE ZOOLOGY. *Current Pos:* RETIRED. *Personal Data:* b Cincinnati, Ohio, July 22, 23; m 50; c 4. *Educ:* Princeton Univ, AB, 48; Univ Colo, MA, 50; Univ Calif, PhD(zool), 56. *Prof Exp:* Asst prof zool, Colo State Univ, 56-57; from instr to prof biol, San Francisco State Univ, 57-82. *Mem:* Am Soc Mammal; Wildlife Soc; Ecol Soc Am; Cooper Ornith Soc. *Res:* Wildlife ecology. *Mailing Add:* 1907 Monument Canyon Dr Grand Junction CO 81503

HALL, JOSEPH L, HEARING. *Current Pos:* MEM TECH STAFF, LUCENT TECHNOL, 66- *Personal Data:* b Boston, Mass, Jan 22, 36; m 61; c 4. *Educ:* Williams Col, BA, 59; Mass Inst Tech, SB, 59, SM, 59, PhD(elec eng), 63. *Prof Exp:* Asst prof commun theory, Mass Inst Tech, 63-64 & Johns Hopkins Univ, 64-66. *Concurrent Pos:* Chmn, Tech Comt Physiol & Psychol Acoust, Acoust Soc Am, 78-79; assoc ed, J Acoust Soc Am, 81-83; mem, Exec Coun, Acoust Soc Am, 88-91. *Mem:* Fel Acoust Soc Am. *Res:* Application of communication theory to auditory information processing; models for information processing at the auditory periphery. *Mailing Add:* 20 Kinnan Way Basking Ridge NJ 07920

HALL, JUDD LEWIS, POLYMER CHEMISTRY. *Current Pos:* Res chemist, Surety Rubber Co, 56-62, res dir, 62-64, exec vpres, 64-73, PRES, SURETY RUBBER CO, 73- *Personal Data:* b Canton, Ohio, Sept 2, 34. *Educ:* Capital Univ, BS, 56; Akron Univ, MS, 57, PhD(polymer chem), 62. *Mem:* Am Chem Soc. *Res:* Anionic polymerization of styrene, kinetic and synthesis studies; mechanical and physical studies of thin films of natural and synthetic rubbers; chemical resistance studies of thin polymer films. *Mailing Add:* 944 Thomas Ave NW Carrollton OH 44615-9441

HALL, JUDY DALE (MRS RICHARD MODAFFERI), CELL BIOLOGY, ELECTRON MICROSCOPY. *Current Pos:* ELECTRON MICROSCOPIST, DEPT PATH, ROBERT PACKER HOSP, SAYRE PA, 81- *Personal Data:* b Chicago, Ill, July 15, 43; m 77; c 1. *Educ:* Ill Wesleyan Univ, BA, 64; Smith Col, MA, 66; Purdue Univ, PhD(biol), 71. *Prof Exp:* Electron microscopist, Dept Path & Toxicol, Human Health Res & Develop Labs, Dow Chem Co, 71-72; res fel, Boston Biomed Res Inst, 72-74; asst prof biol, State Univ NY Binghamton, 74-81. *Mem:* AAAS; Am Soc Cell Biol; Sigma Xi; Electron Micros Soc Am. *Res:* biological and diagnostic electron microscopy. *Mailing Add:* Dept Path Robert Packer Hosp Sayre PA 18840-1698 ●

HALL, KENNETH DALAND, ANESTHESIOLOGY. *Current Pos:* from asst prof to assoc prof, 58-68, PROF ANESTHESIOL, DUKE UNIV, 68- *Personal Data:* b Durham, NC, Oct 26, 26; m 54; c 4. *Educ:* Duke Univ, AB, 49, MD, 53. *Prof Exp:* Head neuroanesthesiol, Nat Inst Neurol Dis & Blindness, 56-58. *Concurrent Pos:* Consult, Vet Admin Hosp, Durham &

Womack Army Hosp, Ft Bragg, NC. *Mem:* AAAS; Am Soc Anesthesiol; Aerospace Med Asn. *Res:* Physiology of respiration; clinical hypothermia; physiology of halogenated anesthetics. *Mailing Add:* Duke Univ Med Ctr Box 3094 Durham NC 27715-3094

HALL, KENNETH LYNN, PHYSICAL INORGANIC CHEMISTRY. *Current Pos:* RETIRED. *Personal Data:* b Great Falls, Mont, Aug 23, 27; m 52; c Randall Wayne, Mark Steven & Kristin (Andersen). *Educ:* Reed Col, BA, 49; Univ Calif, MS, 51; Univ Mich, PhD(chem), 55. *Prof Exp:* Asst nuclear chem, Radiation Lab, Univ Calif, 49-51; asst, Univ Mich, 51-55; res chemist, Calif Res Corp, 55-64; sr res chemist, Chevron Res Co, 64-68, sr res assoc, 68-86. *Mem:* Am Chem Soc; Sigma Xi. *Res:* Corrosion and wear; petroleum products; internal combustion engines. *Mailing Add:* 16 Sussex Ct San Rafael CA 94903

HALL, KENNETH NOBLE, FOOD SCIENCE, NUTRITION. *Current Pos:* From asst prof to assoc prof, 66-72, PROF NUTRIT SCI, UNIV CONN, 83- *Personal Data:* b Lawrence, Mass, Sept 18, 35; m 58, Juanita M Conover; c 4. *Educ:* Univ Maine, BS, 57; Univ Md, MS, 60; Wash State Univ, PhD(food sci), 64. *Concurrent Pos:* Coord res & develop, Food Sci Lab, US Army Natick Develop Ctr, 68-79; staff officer, Office Dep Chief of Staff for Res & Develop Acquisition, Pentagon, 80-85; regional communicator, Off Sci & Pub Affairs, Inst Food Technologists, 81-; mem adv bd, Nutrit Res News Letter, Lyda Assoc, 82-, corresp, Food Safety Notebk, Lyda Asn, 90; Coun Agr Sci & Technol; interim nat prog leader, Exten Serv, USDA, 90-91 & 94. *Mem:* Inst Food Technologists; Poultry Sci Asn; Sigma Xi. *Res:* Poultry products technology; egg and poultry meat quality; microwave cooking; cooked meat quality. *Mailing Add:* Dept Nutrit Sci Univ Conn U-17 3624 Horsebarn Storrs CT 06269-4017. *Fax:* 860-486-3674; *E-Mail:* khall@canr1.cag.uconn.edu

HALL, KENNETH RICHARD, THERMODYNAMICS. *Current Pos:* PROF CHEM ENG, TEX A&M UNIV, 78-; DIR, THERMODYN RES CTR, 97- *Personal Data:* b Tulsa, Okla, Nov 5, 39; m 76; c Tara, Deirdre, Kent, Keith & Krysta. *Educ:* Univ Tulsa, BSChE, 62; Univ Calif, Berkeley, MS, 64; Univ Okla, PhD(chem eng), 67. *Honors & Awards:* Katz Award, Gas Processors Asn. *Prof Exp:* Asst prof chem eng, Univ Va, Charlottesville, 67-70 & 72-74; asst to pres, ChemShare, 70; sr res engr, Amoco Prod Co, 70-71; assoc prof, Thermodyn Res Ctr, 74-78, dir, 79-85; from asst dir to assoc dir, 85-88, dep dir, Tex Eng Exp Sta, 89-, assoc dep chancellor, 90-94. *Concurrent Pos:* NATO fel, Cath Univ Louvain, 71-72; interim head chem eng, 94, dir, Chem & Trans Syst Div, NSF, 94-96. *Mem:* Fel Am Inst Chem Engrs; Am Chem Soc; Am Soc Eng Educ; Am Soc Testing & Mat. *Res:* Chemical engineering thermodynamics covering: precise data on PVT, enthalpy and VLE; equations of state; critical region modeling. *Mailing Add:* Dept Chem Eng Tex A&M Univ College Station TX 77843-3122. *Fax:* 409-845-6446

HALL, KENT D, REPRODUCTIVE PHYSIOLOGY, ENVIRONMENTAL BIOLOGY. *Current Pos:* asst prof reproductive & ecol physiol, 68-74, ASSOC PROF BIOL, UNIV WIS-STEVENS POINT, 74- *Personal Data:* b Versailles, Mo, Aug 3, 37; m 61; c 2. *Educ:* Cent Mo Univ, BS, 60; Emporia Kans State Col, MS, 64; Univ Kans, PhD(zool), 69. *Prof Exp:* Teacher biol & gen sci, Jr High Sch, Kans, 60-62 & Sr High Sch, 62-63; instr biol, Univ Kans, 64-67. *Mem:* Am Inst Biol Sci. *Res:* Hibernation in 13-lined ground squirrel; premarital pregnancy and abortion problems. *Mailing Add:* 200 Pine Bluff Rd Stevens Point WI 54481

HALL, KIMBALL PARKER, MARINE ENGINEERING. *Current Pos:* SR TECHNOL ADV, OUTBOARD MARINE CORP. *Personal Data:* b Richmond, Va, Nov 7, 14; m 42, Elise La Fevre; c Katherine, Daniel & Christine. *Educ:* Dartmouth Col, AB, 37; Cornell Univ, PhD(org chem), 42. *Prof Exp:* Asst chem, Cornell Univ, 37-40 & 41-42, Nat Defense Res Comt Proj, 40-41; res chemist, Eastman Kodak Co, NY, 42-43; res lab analyst, Lockheed Aircraft Corp, Calif, 43-44, process engr, 44-45; dir aircraft specialty develop, Coast Paint & Chem Co, 45-47; sr res engr, Jet Propulsion Lab, Calif Inst Technol, 47-55; res assoc, Guggenheim Lab Aerospace Propulsion Sci, Princeton Univ, 57-61, consult, 62-63; tech consult, Rocket Power Inc, Ariz, 62-63; consult, Precision Devices & Eng Co, Inc, NJ, 64-67; sr scientist, Princeton Combustion Labs, NJ, 75-76, bus mgr, 76-77; gen engr, Naval Ord Sta, 77-93; pres, Hall Marine Corp, 67-96. *Concurrent Pos:* Consult, Greyrad Corp, 67-71. *Mem:* Assoc fel Am Inst Aeronaut & Astronaut; Am Chem Soc; AAAS; Sigma Xi. *Res:* Sealing compounds and coatings; solid rocket propellant development; combustion processes; underwater propulsion; developed and received multiple patents on a safe propulsion device for small water craft; device in use by Marine Corps. *Mailing Add:* 6 Osprey Lane Setauket NY 11733-4061. *Fax:* 516-689-7816

HALL, LARRY CULLY, ANALYTICAL CHEMISTRY, ELECTROCHEMISTRY. *Current Pos:* ASSOC PROF CHEM, VANDERBILT UNIV, 56-, COORDR GEN CHEM, 77- *Personal Data:* b Akron, Ohio, Apr 6, 30; m 53; c 4. *Educ:* Bowling Green State Univ, BA, 52; Univ Ill, PhD(chem, metall), 56. *Prof Exp:* Asst chem & elec eng, Univ Ill, 52-53, chem, 53-56. *Mem:* Am Chem Soc; Am Soc Metals; Nat Asn Corrosion Engrs. *Res:* Electrochemistry in molten salts and organic solvents; methods of analyzing pharmaceutical compounds; trace analysis studies in semiconductor materials. *Mailing Add:* Box 1530 B Vanderbilt Univ Nashville TN 37202-1530

HALL, LAURANCE DAVID, CARBOHYDRATE CHEMISTRY, NUCLEAR MAGNETIC RESONANCE IMAGING & SPECTROSCOPY. *Current Pos:* HERCHEL SMITH PROF MED CHEM, UNIV CAMBRIDGE, 84- *Personal Data:* b London, Eng, Mar 18, 38; Brit & Can citizen; m 62, Winifred Golding; c Gwendolen, Juliet, Dominic & D'Arcy. *Educ:* Bristol Univ, Eng, BSc, 59, PhD(chem), 62. *Hon Degrees:* MA, Cambridge Univ, 90. *Honors & Awards:* Tate & Lyle Award, Chem Soc, 74; Merck, Sharpe & Dohme lectr, Chem Inst Can, 75; Corday Morgan Medal & Prize, Chem Soc, 76; Barringer Award, Spectros Soc Can, 81; Award for Chem Analysis & Instrumentation, Royal Soc Chem, 90. *Prof Exp:* Fel, Ottawa Univ, 62-63; prof, Univ BC, 63-84. *Concurrent Pos:* Vis prof, Univ Cape Town, 74, Northwestern Univ, 82; I W Killam res fel, Univ BC, 79-80; Can Coun Killam res fel, 82-84. *Mem:* Fel Royal Soc Can; fel Royal Soc Chem. *Res:* Development and applications of magnetic resonance imaging and spectroscopy to problems in medicine and industries such as polymers, oil, food and pharmaceutical. *Mailing Add:* Herchel Smith Lab Med Chem Univ Forvie Site Robinson Way Cambridge CB2 2PZ England. *Fax:* 44-1223-336748; *E-Mail:* ldhll@hslmc.cam.ac.uk

HALL, LAURENCE STANFORD, PLASMA PHYSICS, MAGNETOHYDRODYNAMICS & NON-LINEAR THEORY. *Current Pos:* RETIRED. *Personal Data:* b Winona, Minn, July 24, 29; m 51, 68; c David, Dana, Ole & Quincy. *Educ:* Univ Minn, BA & BPhysics, 53; Univ Calif, Berkeley, MA, 58, PhD(plasma physics), 61. *Prof Exp:* Physicist, Lawrence Livermore Lab, Univ Calif, Livermore, 54-88. *Concurrent Pos:* Lectr, Dept Appl Sci; Univ Calif, Davis. *Mem:* Am Phys Soc. *Res:* Theoretical plasma physics; microinstabilities; equilibria; arc discharges; statistical mechanics; statistical transport theory; non-linear theory. *Mailing Add:* 7695 Crest Ave Oakland CA 94605-3030. *Fax:* 510-635-2270

HALL, LAWRENCE JOHN, PARTICLE PHYSICS, COSMOLOGY. *Current Pos:* Miller fel, 81-83, from asst prof to assoc prof, 86-90, PROF PHYSICS, UNIV CALIF, BERKELEY, 90- *Personal Data:* b London, Eng, Sept 9, 55; m 82; c 2. *Educ:* Oxford Univ, UK, BA, 77; Harvard Univ, PhD(physics), 81. *Prof Exp:* From asst prof to assoc prof physics, Harvard Univ, 83-86. *Concurrent Pos:* Sloan fel, Sloan Found, 84-89; NSF presidential young investr, 86-91. *Mem:* Fel Am Phys Soc. *Res:* Extending the standard model of elementary particles to understand fermion masses, the scale of weak interactions, CP violations and neutrino masses; tests of these theories at high energy collider experiments and via precission measurements. *Mailing Add:* Physics Dept Univ Calif Berkeley CA 94720

HALL, LAWRENCE O'HIGGINS, FUZZY LOGIC & LEARNING, MEDICAL IMAGING. *Current Pos:* from asst prof to assoc prof comput sci, 86-96, PROF COMPUT SCI & ENG, UNIV SFLA, 96- *Personal Data:* b Washington, DC, June 19, 58. *Educ:* Fla Inst Technol, BS, 80; Fla State Univ, PhD(comput & info sci), 86. *Prof Exp:* Software engr, ECI Div, E-Stysts, 82-84. *Concurrent Pos:* NASA-Am Soc Eng Educ fac fel, NASA-Ames Res Ctr, 87 & 88; fac res prog, Naval Res Lab, 89 & Wright-Patterson AFB, 90. *Mem:* NAm Fuzzy Info Processing Soc (pres 94-); Int Fuzzy Systs Asn; Am Asn Artificial Intel; Inst Elec & Electronics Engrs; Asn Comput Mach. *Res:* Integration of approximate knowledge in medical imaging; the use of fuzzy logic in pattern recognition and machine learning; symbolic neural networks. *Mailing Add:* Dept Comput Sci & Eng 118 Univ USFla 4202 Fowler Ave Tampa FL 33620-9900. *Fax:* 813-974-5456; *E-Mail:* hall@csee.usf.edu

HALL, LEO MCALOON, BIOCHEMISTRY, MOLECULAR BIOLOGY OF ALGAE. *Current Pos:* assoc prof, 58-70, PROF BIOCHEM, UNIV ALA, BIRMINGHAM, 77-, ASSOC PROF PATH, 94- *Personal Data:* b Denver, Colo, Jan 28, 29; m 53; c Mikhael, Jeanne, Timothy, Kira, Christopher & Jeffrey. *Educ:* Creighton Univ, BS, 51; Okla State Univ, MS, 53; Univ Wis, PhD(physiol chem), 57. *Prof Exp:* Biochemist, Res Div, Am Cyanamid Co, NY, 57-58. *Concurrent Pos:* Biochemist, Univ Va Sch Med, Charlottesville. *Mem:* Am Chem Soc; AAAS. *Res:* Molecular biology of prokaryote and lukaryote algae. *Mailing Add:* Dept Biochem & Molecular Genetics Univ Ala 520 Community Health Sci Bldg 933 S 19th St Birmingham AL 35294-2041. *E-Mail:* hall@orion.cmc.uab.edu

HALL, LEO TERRY, MICROBIOLOGY. *Current Pos:* from asst prof to assoc prof, 68-80, PROF BIOL, PHILLIPS UNIV, ENID, OKLA, 80- *Personal Data:* b Gettysburg, SDak, Apr 5, 41; m 67; c 3. *Educ:* Northern State Col SDak, BS, 63; Okla State Univ, PhD(microbiol), 73. *Prof Exp:* Sci math teacher, Clarkfield High Sch, Minn, 63; NDEA fel microbiol, Okla State Univ, 63-66, NIH fel, 66-68. *Concurrent Pos:* Vis res assoc, Okla Med Res Found, 75; res assoc, Biochem Dept, Okla State Univ, 77, 79, 80 & 89; chmn, Div Sci & Math, Phillips Univ, Enid, Okla, 80-83, Samuel Roberts Endowed chair, Biol Dept, 86-97; consult, Hillcrest Infertility Ctr, Hillcrest Hosp, Tulsa, Okla, 83-86; vis prof, Biol Dept, Univ Md, Baltimore Co, 84-85; prin investr, NIH Acad Res Enhancement Award, 85-87. *Mem:* Am Soc Microbiol. *Res:* Regulation of fusidic acid and streptomycin resistance in Staphylococcus aureus. *Mailing Add:* Dept Math & Sci Phillips Univ 100 S University Ave Enid OK 73701-6439

HALL, LEON MORRIS, JR, DIFFERENTIAL EQUATIONS. *Current Pos:* FROM ASSOC PROF TO PROF MATH, UNIV MO, ROLLA, 85- *Personal Data:* b Springfield, Mo, July 31, 46; m 67, Pennye Nichols; c Eric & Laura. *Educ:* Univ Mo, Columbia, BS(educ), 69, Univ Mo, Rolla, BS(appl math), 69, MS, 71, PhD(math), 74. *Prof Exp:* Teacher high sch, St Louis, Mo, 69-70; from asst prof to assoc prof math, Univ Mo, Rolla, Univ Nebr, Lincoln, 74-85. *Concurrent Pos:* NSF grant, 75-; assoc ed, Mo J Math Scis. *Mem:* Math Asn Am; Sigma Xi; Nat Coun Teachers Maths. *Res:* Solvability of ordinary and functional differential equations in the neighborhood of a singular point; functional analysis techniques applied to differential equations; difference equations; analytic geometry of curves. *Mailing Add:* Dept Math Univ Mo Rolla Rolla MO 65401. *E-Mail:* co635@umrvmb.umr.edu

HALL, LOWELL HEADLEY, II, PHYSICAL & PHARMACEUTICAL CHEMISTRY, STRUCTURE-ACTIVITY RELATIONS. *Current Pos:* assoc prof, 67-71, PROF CHEM, EASTERN NAZARENE COL, 71-, HEAD DEPT CHEM, 67-, CHMN DIV SCI & MATH, 78- *Personal Data:* b Akron, Ohio, Sept 29, 37; m 60, Dorla D Drumm; c 2. *Educ:* Eastern Nazarene Col, BS, 59; Johns Hopkins Univ, MA, 61, PhD(phys chem), 63. *Prof Exp:* Res assoc x-ray crystallog, Nat Bur Stand, 63-64; asst prof chem, Fla Atlantic Univ, 64-67. *Concurrent Pos:* NSF Col Coop Sci consult, City of Quincy & Minnemast Sci Progs, 70-73; adj prof, Mass Col Pharm, 74-; mem, Acad Adv Coun, GTE Labs, 81-83; Environ Protection Agency grant, 81-84; consult, GTE Labs, Allied Signal Corp, Eastman Pharmaceut; fel, NRC. *Mem:* AAAS; Am Chem Soc; Am Crystallog Asn; NY Acad Sci. *Res:* X-ray crystallogrphy; mass spectrometry; boron hydrides; structural inorganic chemistry; molecular structure by x-ray diffraction techniques; quantitative relation of molecular structure to properties and drug activity (SAR); development of molecular connectivity; semiempirical MO calculations; development of Molconn software; author of three books. *Mailing Add:* Dean & Dir Summer Sch Eastern Nazarene Col 23 E Elm Ave Wollaston MA 02170-2905. *Fax:* 617-773-6324

HALL, LUTHER AXTELL RICHARD, SCIENCE WRITING, ORGANIC CHEMISTRY. *Current Pos:* res assoc, Geigy Chem Corp, 64-66, dir polymer res, 66-69, asst to res dir, Plastics & Additives Div, 69-74, SR PATENT AGENT, CIBA-GEIGY CORP, 74- *Personal Data:* b Pittsburgh, Pa, Oct 19, 24; m 51; c 2. *Educ:* Wesleyan Univ, BA, 44; Calif Inst Technol, MS, 46; Univ Kans, PhD(org chem), 50. *Prof Exp:* Res chemist, Gen Chem Co, 46-47; fel, Sch Pharm, Univ Kans, 50-51; res chemist, E I du Pont de Nemours & Co, 51-64. *Mem:* Am Chem Soc. *Res:* Synthesis, fabrication and analysis of vinyls, polyamides, polyolefins, polyurethanes, polyesters and polyhydrocarbons; organic phosphorus chemistry; physical chemistry of polymers; process development on polymer systems; organic chemical products and processes. *Mailing Add:* 36 Old Farms Rd Woodcliff Lake NJ 07675

HALL, LYLE CLARENCE, PHYSICAL CHEMISTRY. *Current Pos:* from asst prof to assoc prof, 65-81, PROF CHEM, UNIV WIS-RIVER FALLS, 81- *Personal Data:* b Mason City, Iowa, Feb 12, 35. *Educ:* Luther Col, Iowa, BA, 56; Univ Iowa, MS, 60, PhD(phys chem), 61. *Prof Exp:* Res fel phys chem, Univ Minn, 61-64; admin asst to exec secy, Minn State Jr Col Bd, State Minn, 64-65. *Concurrent Pos:* Vis prof, Univ Cape Town, 69, Univ Witwatersrand, 70, Monash Univ, 70, Univ New South Wales, 71 & Univ PR, Mayaguez, 84, Univ Costa Rica, 87-88. *Res:* Infrared spectroscopy; science education. *Mailing Add:* Dept Chem Univ Wis River Falls WI 54022

HALL, MADELINE MOLNAR, PHARMACOLOGY. *Current Pos:* asst prof ,73-78, ASSOC PROF, DEPT BIOL, CLEVELAND STATE UNIV 78- *Personal Data:* b Cleveland, Ohio, June 16, 36; m 77; c 2. *Educ:* Ohio State Univ, BS, 64, PhD(pharmacol), 70. *Honors & Awards:* Lower Prize, 73. *Prof Exp:* Fel pharmacol, Univ Chicago, 70-72; res fel cardiovasc, Cleveland Clin Found, 72-73, staff mem, 73-77. *Mem:* AAAS; Am Soc Pharmacol & Exp Therapeut; NY Acad Sci. *Res:* The interrelationships between angiotensin and prostaglandins in the various tissues, brain, uterus, stomach and aorta; naltrexone-treated animals; effect of adrenalectomy in obese rats. *Mailing Add:* 3793 Bushnell Rd University Heights OH 44118-3109. *Fax:* 216-687-5443

HALL, MARGARET (MARGOT) JEAN, TEACHING & RESEARCH IN BIOCHEMISTRY & ONCOLOGY. *Current Pos:* asst prof clin chem, 85-91, ASSOC PROF CLIN BIOCHEM, UNIV SOUTHERN MISS, 91- *Personal Data:* b Boston, Mass, Mar 25, 42. *Educ:* Univ NC, Chapel Hill, AB, 64, PhD(biochem), 84; Univ Denver, MS, 71. *Prof Exp:* Med technologist, Univ NC, Chapel Hill, 63-65, res asst, 65-68 & 71-84, fel, 84-85; res asst, Univ Colo Med Ctr, 70-71. *Concurrent Pos:* Lectr biochem, William Carey Col, 87-; consult, Miss State Univ, 91; prin investr, US Dept Com, Nat Oceanic & Atmospheric Admin & Nat Marine Fisheries Serv, 93-94. *Mem:* Am Inst Chemists; Sigma Xi; Am Asn Clin Chem; Am Soc Clin Pathologists; Am Chem Soc; Royal Soc Chem. *Res:* Expression of oncofetal proteins, serologic tumor markers and the development of clinical biochemical test systems; isolation and characterization of clinically important enzymes; development of a rapid test for histamine for use by the seafood industry. *Mailing Add:* Univ Southern Miss 104 Kensington Dr Hattiesburg MS 39402. *Fax:* 601-266-5829

HALL, MARION TRUFANT, TAXONOMY, CYTOGENETICS. *Current Pos:* RETIRED. *Personal Data:* b Gorman, Tex, Sept 6, 20; m 44; c 3. *Educ:* Univ Okla, BS, 43, MS, 48; Washington Univ, PhD(bot), 51. *Prof Exp:* Ranger, Nat Park Serv, USDA, 42; instr bot, Univ Okla, 46-47, asst zool, Washington Univ, 48-50; prof bot & head dept, Butler Univ, 56-62; dir, Stovall Mus, Univ Okla, 62-66; dir, Morton Arboretom, 66-90. *Concurrent Pos:* Collabr, Dept Bot, Univ Mich, 50-56; adj prof biol sci, Univ Ill, Chicago Circle, prof hort, Univ Ill, Urbana; adj prof biol, Northern Ill Univ. *Mem:* Am Soc Plant Taxon; Ecol Soc Am; Soc Study Evolution; Int Soc Plant Taxon. *Res:* Taxonomy and cytogenetics of flowering plants; variation and evolution in cupressaeeae and angiosperms; plant ecology; land use management. *Mailing Add:* 1885 Southcliff Dr Maryville TN 37803-7529

HALL, MICHAEL BISHOP, MOLECULAR ORBITAL CALCULATIONS ON ORGANOMETALIC REACTIONS, ELECTRON CORRELATION IN INORGANIC STRUCTURAL & MECHANISTIC CHEMISTRY. *Current Pos:* PROF CHEM & DEPT HEAD, TEX A&M UNIV, 75- *Personal Data:* b Philadelphia, Pa, Oct 21, 44; m 67, Carolyn V Dale; c Whitney D. *Educ:* Juniata Col, BS, 66; Univ Wis-Madison, PhD(chem), 71. *Prof Exp:* AEI fel, Univ Manchester, UK, 71-73; assoc, Univ Wis-Madison, 73-74; asst prof chem, Adelphia Univ, 74-75. *Concurrent Pos:* Vis assoc, Clare Hall, Cambridge, UK, 82-83. *Mem:* Am Chem Soc; Sigma Xi. *Res:* Theoretical studies of the electronic structure of inorganic complexes, organometallic compounds and cluster systems; relationship between electronic structure and chemical behavior especially catalysis. *Mailing Add:* Dept Chem Tex A&M Univ College Station TX 77843-3255

HALL, MICHAEL OAKLEY, BIOCHEMISTRY, OPHTHALMOLOGY. *Current Pos:* asst res biol chemist, Jules Stein Eye Inst, Univ Calif, Los Angeles, 63-67, asst prof surg, 67-69, assoc prof ophthal, 69-80, RES PROF OPHTHAL & ASSOC DIR, JULES STEIN EYE INST, UNIV CALIF, LOS ANGELES, 80- *Personal Data:* b Pretoria, SAfrica, Dec 14, 36; US citizen; m 63; c 2. *Educ:* Univ Natal, BSc, 57; Univ Calif, Los Angeles, PhD(biochem), 61. *Prof Exp:* Lectr biochem, Univ Natal, 61-62. *Concurrent Pos:* NSF Univ Res Coun grant, 63-64; Nat Coun Combat Blindness grants, 64-66; Nat Inst Neurol Dis & Blindness grant, 64-67; partic investr, USPHS Prog Proj grant, Jules Stein Eye Inst, Univ Calif, Los Angeles, 66-73; Nat Eye Inst grants, 69-82. *Mem:* AAAS; Asn Res Vision & Ophthal. *Res:* Biochemistry of the retina; visual pigments; retinal degeneration; electron microscopy of the retina. *Mailing Add:* Dept Ophthal Univ Calif Los Angeles Sch Med 10833 Le Conte Ave Los Angeles CA 90024-1300. *Fax:* 310-206-3652

HALL, NANCY K, PATHOLOGY. *Current Pos:* ASSOC PROF IMMUNOL, HEALTH SCI CTR, OKLA UNIV, 81- *Personal Data:* b Washington, DC, July 7, 47. *Educ:* Kans State Univ, PhD(immunol), 76. *Mem:* Med Mycol Soc Am; Am Soc Microbiol; Int Asn Pathologists; Sigma Xi. *Mailing Add:* Univ Okla Col Med PO Box 26901 BMSB 357 Oklahoma City OK 73190-0001

HALL, NATHAN ALBERT, PHARMACOLOGY. *Current Pos:* RETIRED. *Personal Data:* b Bozeman, Mont, July 3, 18; c 2. *Educ:* Univ Wash, BSc, 39, PhD(pharmaceut chem), 48. *Prof Exp:* Instr pharmaceut chem, Univ Wash, 49; asst prof pharm, Philadelphia Col Pharm, 49-50; pharmaceut chemist, Eli Lilly & Co, 50-51; res chemist, Univ Wash, 51-52, asst prof pharmaceut chem, 52-54, asst prof pharm, 54-56, assoc prof, 56-62, prof pharm, 62-85. *Concurrent Pos:* Fulbright lectr, Univ Malaya, 59-60; vis prof, Univ Sydney, 68. *Mem:* Fel AAAS; Am Pharmaceut Asn; Am Asn Cols Pharm; Acad Pharmaceut Sci. *Res:* Self-medication; folk medicine. *Mailing Add:* 10553 41st Pl NE Seattle WA 98125

HALL, NEWMAN A(RNOLD), MECHANICAL ENGINEERING. *Current Pos:* RETIRED. *Personal Data:* b Uniontown, Pa, June 14, 13; m 38; c 2. *Educ:* Marietta Col, AB, 34; Calif Inst Technol, PhD(math), 38. *Hon Degrees:* ScD, Marietta Col, 59; MA, Yale Univ, 56. *Prof Exp:* Instr, Queens Col NY, 38-41; res mathematician, Chance Vought Div, United Aircraft Corp, Conn, 41-42, supvr, Eng Personnel, 42-43, power plant analyst engr, 43-44, head, Thermodyn Group, Res Dept, 44-46, analyst sect, 46-47; prof mech eng & in charge, Heat Power Div, Univ Minn, 47-55; prof mech eng & asst dean in charge, Grad Div, Sch Eng, NY Univ, 55-56; prof mech eng, Yale Univ, 56-58, Strathcona prof, 58-64, chmn dept, 56-64; exec dir, Comn Eng Educ, 62-68 & Nat Acad Eng, 68-71; Secy M Eng, Am Asn Arts & Sci, 64-74; sci adv, USAID Mission, Korea, 72-74; consult, Ministry Sci & Technol, Repub Korea, 74-75; consult eng & educ, 76-77. *Concurrent Pos:* Dir, Div Eng Sci, Off Ord Res, US Army, 52-53; hon dir, Int Combustion Inst, 65- *Mem:* Am Soc Mech Engrs; Soc Automotive Engrs; Am Soc Eng Educ (vpres, 60-62); assoc fel Am Inst Aeronaut & Astronaut; Int Combustion Inst. *Res:* Thermodynamics; fluid mechanics; gas dynamics; heat transfer; combustion; administration of engineering education. *Mailing Add:* 511 Town Hill Rd New Hartford CT 06057-2516

HALL, OTIS F, FOREST MANAGEMENT, FOREST ECONOMICS. *Current Pos:* RETIRED. *Personal Data:* b Cleveland, Ohio, Oct 5, 21; m 58, Helen Pilcher; c Geoffrey, Elizabeth & Barbara. *Educ:* Oberlin Col, AB, 43; Yale Univ, MF, 48; Univ Minn, PhD(forest econ), 54. *Prof Exp:* Instr & asst prof forestry, Univ Minn, 48-57; prof forest mgt, Purdue Univ, 57-68; prof forestry & head dept, Univ NH, 68-74; prof & head dept, Va Polytech Inst, 74-84, endowed prof forestry, 84-91. *Mem:* Fel Am Foresters; Union Concerned Scientists. *Res:* Forest management, economic analysis and impact, computer applications; expert systems. *Mailing Add:* 816 McBryde Dr Blacksburg VA 24060

HALL, PETER, PHYSIOLOGY, PHARMACOLOGY, ANESTHESIA. *Current Pos:* PROF PHYSIOL, ST GEORGE SCH MED, GRENADA, WEST INDIES, 79- *Personal Data:* b Whangarei, NZ, Oct 17, 26; m 84; c 1. *Educ:* Univ Otago, NZ, MB, ChB, 50; Royal Col Surgeons, fel fac anesthetists, 55. *Prof Exp:* Jr house surgeon med, Auckland Hosp, Bd, NZ, 50, sr house surgeon, 51, jr registr anesthesia, 52-53; jr house officer, Univ Col Hosp, Univ London, 54-55 & Hosp for Sick Children, Eng, 55-56; locum sr registr, Royal Free Hosp, 56; intern, Bispebjerg Hosp, Copenhagen, Denmark, 57, first resident, 58; instr, Univ Pa Hosp, 59-60, instr pharmacol, Sch Med, 60-64, assoc, 64-68; assoc prof physiol & biophys, Colo State Univ, 68-78. *Concurrent Pos:* USPHS grants, 60-62 & fel, 62-63, assoc pharmacol training grant, 63-64, training grant, 64-65; Pa Plan scholar, 65-68; consult, Coun Drugs, AMA, 61, 63 & 64; physician to Univ Pa Underwater Archaeol Exped, 62; vis prof, Dept Anesthesia, Univ Hosp Wales, Cardiff, UK, 82; vis scholar, Dept Res Med Educ, Univ Southern Calif, 76, anesthesiolgist, Gen Hosp Grenada, 87-90. *Mem:* Fel Royal Soc Health; NY Acad Sci. *Res:* Chemical control of respiration and cerebral blood flow in man; hyperbaric oxygen in research and therapy; chemoreceptor responses; altitude physiology; diving physiology. *Mailing Add:* PO Box 7 St Georges St Georges Univ Med Sch St Georges Grenada

HALL, PETER FRANCIS, PHYSIOLOGY, ENDOCRINOLOGY. *Current Pos:* PROF MED & CHMN ENDOCRINOL, UNIV NSW, 86- *Personal Data:* b Sydney, Australia, Dec 13, 24; m 69, Helen Ruth Godfrey; c David & Warwick. *Educ:* Univ Sydney, MB, BS, 47, MD, 56; Univ Utah, PhD(biochem), 61. *Prof Exp:* Jr resident med officer, Royal Prince Alfred Hosp, Sydney, Australia, 47-48, sr resident med officer, 48-50; pvt pract internal med, Australia, 50-52 & Postgrad Sch Med, London, 52; registr, Maudsley Hosp, London, 53; registr, asst lectr & asst dir student health, Guy's Hosp & Guy's Hosp Med Sch, London, 53-55; asst lectr physiol, Univ Sydney, 55-59; USPHS trainee steroid biochem, Sch Med, Univ Utah, 59-61 & res fel biochem, 61-62; asst prof physiol, Sch Med, Univ Pittsburgh, 62-66; prof biochem, Univ Melbourne, 66-71; prof physiol, Univ Calif, Irvine, 71-79, chmn dept, 71-78; prin scientist, Worcester Found Exp Biol, 79-86. *Concurrent Pos:* Asst physician, Sydney Hosp, Australia, 55-59; consult endocrinologist, Prince of Wales Hosp, 55-59; pvt pract, 55-59. *Mem:* Am Physiol Soc; Australian Biochem Soc; Am Soc Biol Chemists; Am Soc Cell Biol. *Res:* Mechanisms by which trophic hormones stimulate steroidogenesis; metabolism of testis; action of follicle-stimulating hormone; biochemistry; role of cytoskeleton in steroid synthesis. *Mailing Add:* Dept Endocrinol Prince of Wales Hosp Avoca St Randwick Sydney NSW 2031 Australia. *Fax:* 320-398-9887

HALL, PETER M, PHYSICS, PROPERTIES OF SOLIDS. *Current Pos:* DISTINGUISHED PROF PHYSICS, JOHNSON C SMITH UNIV, CHARLOTTE, NC, 90-, DIR, DUAL-DEGREE ENG PROG. *Personal Data:* b Belmont, NY, July 31, 34; m 56; c 4. *Educ:* Hobart Col, BA, 54; Iowa State Univ, MS, 56, PhD(physics), 59. *Prof Exp:* Res physics, Iowa State Univ, 54-59; distinguished mem tech staff, Bell Tel Labs, Allentown, 59-90. *Concurrent Pos:* Fel, Bell Labs. *Mem:* Am Phys Soc; fel Inst Elec & Electronics Engrs; Int Soc Hybrid Microelectronics; Soc Exp Mech; Am Soc Mech Eng; Sigma Xi. *Res:* Solid state physics, especially magnetic and electrical properties of matter; thin films; packaging of electronic circuits. *Mailing Add:* Dept Phys Chem JC Smith Univ 100 Beatties Ford Dr Charlotte NC 28216. *Fax:* 704-378-1281; *E-Mail:* phall@mosaic.uncc.edu

HALL, PHILIP LAYTON, BIOORGANIC CHEMISTRY. *Current Pos:* vpres acad affairs & dean, 85-93, PROVOST, MARY WASHINGTON COL, 93- *Personal Data:* b Orange, NJ, Dec 12, 40; m 64; c 2. *Educ:* Col Wooster, AB, 63; Univ Chicago, SM, 65, PhD(chem), 67. *Prof Exp:* NIH fel, Columbia Univ, 67-68; from asst prof to assoc prof chem, Va Polytech Inst & State Univ, 68-79, asst univ provost, 79-84, assoc univ provost, 84-85. *Mem:* Am Chem Soc; Sigma Xi; AAAS. *Res:* Organic reaction mechanisms of biological interest; mechanisms of enzyme action; the chemistry and biochemistry of lignin biodegradation; enzyme model system. *Mailing Add:* Off Provost Mary Washington Col Fredericksburg VA 22401-5358

HALL, PHILIP WELLS, III, MEDICINE, PHYSIOLOGY. *Current Pos:* from instr to assoc prof, 59-81, prof med, 81-, EMER PROF MED, SCH MED, CASE WESTERN RES UNIV, ASSOC DEAN CURRIC. *Personal Data:* b Cranford, NJ, June 11, 25; m 49; c 5. *Educ:* Bethany Col, WVa, BS, 48; Western Reserve Univ, MS, 52, MD, 55. *Prof Exp:* Demonstr physiol, Western Reserve Univ, 54-55; Arthritis & Rheumatism Found fel & asst med, Sch Med, Boston Univ, 56-58. *Concurrent Pos:* Estab investr, Am Heart Asn, 62-67; dir nephrology, Cleveland Metrop Gen Hosp; Porter fel, Am Physiol Soc, 51-52. *Mem:* Soc Exp Biol & Med; Am Fedn Clin Res; Am Soc Nephrol; Int Soc Nephrol. *Res:* Kidney physiology; acid-base physiology and electrolytes; clinical nephrology; environmental toxicology and epidemiology. *Mailing Add:* 1965 Mornington Lane No 10 Cleveland Heights OH 44106-2800

HALL, R(OYAL) GLENN, JR, ASTRONOMY. *Current Pos:* RETIRED. *Personal Data:* b Koloa, Hawaii, June 23, 21; m 43, Mary M Mowry; c Carol Anne, Robert Glenn & Thomas Martin. *Educ:* Park Col, BA, 41; Univ Chicago, PhD(astron), 49. *Prof Exp:* Instr, Univ Chicago, 49-52, res assoc, 53; astronomer, US Naval Observ 53-81. *Mem:* Int Astron Union; Am Astron Soc; AAAS. *Res:* Mass ratios of binary stars; orbits of binary stars; time. *Mailing Add:* 3612 Spring St Chevy Chase MD 20815

HALL, RAYMOND G, JR, CELL PHYSIOLOGY. *Current Pos:* Instr physiol & biophys, 68-70, ASSOC PROF PHYSIOL & PHARMACOL, LOMA LINDA UNIV, 70- *Personal Data:* b Sherman, Tex, Mar 11, 37; m 59; c 2. *Educ:* Union Col, Nebr, BA, 59; Walla Walla Col, MA, 62; Loma Linda Univ, PhD(physiol, biophys), 68. *Concurrent Pos:* Am Cancer Soc fel, Dept Molecular, Cellular & Develop Biol, Boulder, Colo, 69-70. *Mem:* Am Soc Cell Biol; Sigma Xi. *Res:* Regulatory mechanisms in bone. *Mailing Add:* Dept Physiol Loma Linda Univ Loma Linda CA 92350-0001. *Fax:* 909-478-4119

HALL, RICHARD BRIAN, FOREST GENETICS, SILVICULTURE. *Current Pos:* From asst prof to assoc prof, 74-82, PROF FORESTRY, IOWA STATE UNIV, 82- *Personal Data:* b Mendota, Ill, Mar 24, 47; m 67; c 2. *Educ:* Iowa State Univ, BS, 69; Univ Wis-Madison, PhD(plant breeding & genetics), 74. *Mem:* AAAS; Sigma Xi; Soc Am Foresters. *Res:* The development of improved selection and breeding techniques for Populus species and Alnus glutinosa; genetic and cultural improvement of nitrogen fixation in Alnus; variation in DNA content and redundancy in tree genomes. *Mailing Add:* Dept Forestry Iowa State Univ 251 Bessey Hall Ames IA 50011

HALL, RICHARD CHANDLER, ASTRONOMY. *Current Pos:* Asst prof, 65-71, ASSOC PROF PHYSICS & ASTRON, NORTHERN ARIZ UNIV, 65- *Personal Data:* b Northampton, Mass, Apr 12, 39; m 67; c 2. *Educ:* Amherst Col, AB, 60; Ind Univ, PhD(astron), 65. *Mem:* Fel AAAS; Am Astron Soc. *Res:* Image tubes; photometry; polarization; cinematography; Orion Nebula polarization. *Mailing Add:* 1089 Coy Dr Flagstaff AZ 86001

HALL, RICHARD EUGENE, INORGANIC CHEMISTRY. *Current Pos:* From res chemist to sr res chemist, 69-79, res assoc, 79-88, SR RES ASSOC, FMC CORP, 88- *Personal Data:* b Sioux City, Iowa, Jan 19, 43; m 68; c 2. *Educ:* Univ SDak, BA, 64; Ohio State Univ, MS, 67, PhD(inorg chem), 69. *Res:* Synthesis and characterization of molecular hydride complexes containing boron and aluminum; investigation and development of reaction catalysts and process and product development in peroxide, phosphorus and sodium chemicals. *Mailing Add:* FMC Corp PO Box 8 Princeton NJ 08543

HALL, RICHARD EUGENE, neurophysiology; deceased, see previous edition for last biography

HALL, RICHARD HAROLD, ORGANIC CHEMISTRY, CHEMICAL ENGINEERING. *Current Pos:* res chemist, Dow Chem Co, 53-67, group leader, Polymer Res Lab, 67-69, sr res engr, Phys Res Lab, 69-73, proj mgr imbiber systs eng & metal prod, 73-76, proj mgr functional prod & systs, 76-79, RES LEADER, NEW MONOMERS & POLYMERS, DOW CHEM CO, 79- *Personal Data:* b Akron, Ohio, Jan 12, 27; m 54; c 2. *Educ:* Case Inst Technol, BSChE, 50; Univ Del, MS, 51, PhD(chem), 53. *Prof Exp:* Chemist, B F Goodrich Co, 52; lab instr org chem, Univ Del, 52-53. *Mem:* Am Chem Soc; Am Inst Chem Engrs; Sigma Xi; Royal Soc Chem. *Res:* Petrochemical processes; industrial organic chemistry; synthesis; oxidation of hydrocarbons; monomers and polymerization; reinforced plastics and laminating resins; plastic foams; t-butylstyrene, chlorostyrene, vinylbenzyl chloride; imbibing or absorbing polymers; pollution control; systems to protect the environment; economic evaluation. *Mailing Add:* Rte 2 1187 Steward Rd Midland MI 48640-9503

HALL, RICHARD L, mathematics, physics, for more information see previous edition

HALL, RICHARD LELAND, FLAVOR CHEMISTRY & TECHNOLOGY, NATURAL TOXICANTS. *Current Pos:* CONSULT 88- *Personal Data:* b Roseland, Nebr, June 14, 23; m 48, Barbara A Goodspeed; c Ann H (Dorr) & Nancy. *Educ:* Harvard Univ, SB, 43, AM, 48, PhD(chem), 51. *Honors & Awards:* Nicolas Appert Award, Inst Food Technologists, 77, Int Award, 86 & Carl Fellers Award, 90. *Prof Exp:* Res chemist & dir res, McCormick & Co, Inc, 50-57, dir res & develop, 57-68, vpres res & develop, 68-75, vpres sci & technol, 75-88. *Concurrent Pos:* Mem panel chem & health, Pres Sci Adv Comt, 70-73; mem exec comt, Int Union Food Sci & Technol, 75-78, vpres, 78-83, pres, 83-87; pres, Int Food Biotechnol Coun, 88-91. *Mem:* Hon mem Soc Flavor Chemists; fel Inst Food Technologists (pres, 71-72); Soc Toxicol; Am Chem Soc; fel AAAS. *Res:* Flavor and odor constituents of spices and other natural products; food toxicology and safety evaluation; food science; naturally-occurring toxicants. *Mailing Add:* 7004 Wellington Ct Baltimore MD 21212-1929

HALL, RICHARD S, NUMBER THEORY. *Current Pos:* PROF, DEPT MATH, WILLAMETTE UNIV, 74- *Personal Data:* b Eaton Rapids, Mich, Apr 13, 40. *Educ:* Albion Col, BS, 62; Univ Ill, MS, 63, PhD(math), 67. *Mem:* Math Asn Am; Int Asn Cryptologyc Res; Consort Peace Res Educ & Develop. *Res:* Number theory. *Mailing Add:* Math Dept Willamette Univ Salem OR 97301

HALL, RICHARD TRAVIS, automotive research, automotive development, for more information see previous edition

HALL, ROBERT, FIELD CROP DISEASES. *Current Pos:* from asst prof to assoc prof, 62-80, PROF PLANT PATH, UNIV GUELPH, 80- *Personal Data:* b Melbourne, Australia, Mar 26, 39; m 63; c 2. *Educ:* Univ Melbourne, BAgrSc, 61, PhD(bot), 64. *Prof Exp:* Univ Adelaide fel bot, Waite Agr Res Inst, 64-66; res plant pathologist, Univ Calif, Riverside, 66-67. *Concurrent Pos:* Ed, Can J Plant Path, 90- *Mem:* Am Phytopath Soc; fel Can Phytopath Soc (pres, 87-88). *Res:* Pathology, physiology, taxonomy of plant pathogenic fungi; chemical taxonomy of fungi; pathology of field crops; environmental plant pathology. *Mailing Add:* Dept Environ Biol Univ Guelph Guelph ON N1G 2W1 Can

HALL, ROBERT B, PHOTOVOLTAICS. *Current Pos:* dir solar cell develop, 83-89, VPRES RES & DEVELOP, ASTROPOWER INC, 89- *Personal Data:* b Philadelphia, Pa, Mar 24, 41; m 64, Janet Dreves; c Kevin R, Kely E & Brian C. *Educ:* Gettysburg Col, BA, 63; Univ Del, MS, 66, PhD(physics), 72. *Prof Exp:* Res asst, Gen Elec Res & Develop Ctr, 66-68; asst prof, Juniata Col, 71-75; sr scientist, Inst Energy Conserv, Univ Del, 75-78, mgr solar cell develop, 78-83. *Concurrent Pos:* Prin investr, PVMat/AstroPower Proj, 91- *Mem:* Am Phys Soc; Am Vacuum Soc; AAAS; Sigma Xi. *Res:* Research and product development of materials and advanced device structure for the achievement of high performance, low-cost solar cells for terrestrial applications. *Mailing Add:* 807 Rock Lane Newark DE 19713. *Fax:* 302-368-6474

HALL, ROBERT DICKINSON, MEDICAL & VETERINARY ENTOMOLOGY, MEDICOCRIMINAL ENTOMOLOGY. *Current Pos:* From asst prof to assoc prof, 77-89, PROF ENTOM, UNIV MO, COLUMBIA, 89- *Personal Data:* b Washington, DC, Mar 6, 47; m 68, 90, Melba Richterkessing; c Emily D & Pamela O. *Educ:* Univ Md, College Park, BA, 73; Va Polytech Inst & State Univ, MS, 75, PhD(entom), 77; Univ Mo, JD, 97. *Concurrent Pos:* Med entomologist, US Army Reserve, 77- *Mem:* Entom Soc Am; Sigma Xi; Am Acad Forensic Sci; Am Bd Forensic Entom.

Res: Taxonomy, biology and control of arthropods affecting man and animals, with particular interest in Diptera (Calliphoridae, Muscidae, Sarcophagidae) and their use in forensic science and judicial proceedings. *Mailing Add:* Dept Entom 1-87 Agr Bldg Univ Mo Columbia MO 65211. *Fax:* 573-882-1469; *E-Mail:* agrhall@muccmail.missouri.edu

HALL, ROBERT DILWYN, PHYSIOLOGICAL PSYCHOLOGY, NEUROBIOLOGY. *Current Pos:* AUDITORY PROTHESIS RES LAB, DEPT OTOLARYNGOL, MASS EYE & EAR INFIRMARY. *Personal Data:* b Philadelphia, Pa, Jan 19, 29; m 62; c 3. *Educ:* Dartmouth Col, AB, 56; Brown Univ, MA, 58, PhD(psychol), 60. *Prof Exp:* Instr psychol, Brown Univ, 59-60; res fel commun biophys, Res Lab Electronics, Mass Inst Technol, 60-63, res assoc, 63-68, staff scientist, 68-74, staff scientist, Neurosci Res Prog, 74-76; staff scientist neurobiol, Worcester Found Exp Biol, 76-83; vis prof psychol, Bourdoin Col, 83-84. *Mem:* Aero Sci Soc; Soc Neurosci; AAAS; Sigma Xi. *Res:* Cochlear implants; animal auditory psychophysics; auditory psychophysics. *Mailing Add:* Mass Eye & Ear Infirmary 243 Charles St Boston MA 02114-3002

HALL, ROBERT EARL, PHYSICAL OCEANOGRAPHY, GEOPHYSICAL FLUID DYNAMICS. *Current Pos:* SR SCIENTIST, SCI APPLNS INC. *Personal Data:* b Philadelphia, Pa, Aug 1, 49. *Educ:* Calif Inst Technol, BS, 71; Univ Calif, San Diego, PhD(eng physics), 76. *Prof Exp:* Asst prof geophys, Yale Univ, 76-81, res assoc, Dept Geol & Geophys, 81- *Mem:* Am Geophys Union; Am Meteorol Soc. *Res:* Theoretical and observational studies in physical oceanography. *Mailing Add:* Sci Appln Inc 10260 Campus Point Dr Mail Stop C4 San Diego CA 92121

HALL, ROBERT EVERETT, VETERINARY MEDICINE. *Current Pos:* RETIRED. *Personal Data:* b Sioux City, Iowa, Apr 27, 24; m 49; c 3. *Educ:* Iowa State Univ, DVM, 50; Univ Wis, MS, 64. *Prof Exp:* Vet Mo, 50-51; field supvr regulatory progs, Wis State Dept Agr, 51-52, diagnostician, Animal Health Lab, 52-59, chief diagnostician, 59-61; exten vet, Univ Wis-Madison, 61-80. *Mem:* Am Vet Med Asn; Am Asn Swine Practitioners; Am Asn Exten Vet. *Res:* Prevention, treatment, control and eradication of livestock diseases. *Mailing Add:* 5718 Dogwood Pl Madison WI 53705

HALL, ROBERT JOSEPH, CARDIOLOGY. *Current Pos:* RETIRED. *Personal Data:* b Buffalo, NY, June 4, 26; m 48, Dorothy Nowak; c Thomas, Kathleen, Mary, Michael & Steven. *Educ:* Univ Buffalo, MD, 48; Am Bd Internal Med & Am Bd Cardiovasc Dis, dipl. *Prof Exp:* Intern, Mercy Hosp, Buffalo, NY, 48; chief med serv, Hosps, Korea & Japan, US Army, 52-55, internist, Valley Forge Hosp, 55-56, mem cardiol serv, Walter Reed Army Hosp & Inst Res, 56-61, chief, Brooke Gen Hosp, 61-66, chief, Walter Reed Gen Hosp, 66-69; med dir, Tex Heart Inst, 69-95; chief cardiol serv, St Luke's Hosp, Houston, 69-95. *Concurrent Pos:* Clin prof med, Baylor Col Med & Univ Tex Med Sch, Houston; dir educ cardiol, St Luke's Episcopal Hosp & Tex Heart Inst; consult cardiol, Vet Admin Hosp, Houston & US Army; fel, Coun Clin Cardiol, Am Heart Asn. *Mem:* Fel Am Col Physicians; fel Am Col Cardiol; AMA; Am Heart Asn. *Res:* Coronary heart disease; electrocardiography; exercise testing; antianhythemic agents; phonocardiography; prosthetic heart valves; coronary bypass surgery; coronary circulation. *Mailing Add:* St Luke's Med Tower 6624 Fannin Suite 2480 Houston TX 77030. *Fax:* 713-791-1786

HALL, ROBERT LESTER, MATHEMATICAL ANALYSIS. *Current Pos:* asst prof, 67-71, ASSOC PROF MATH, UNIV WIS-MILWAUKEE, 71-, CHAIRPERSON DEPT, 80-, ASSOC DEAN, 82- *Personal Data:* b Little Rock, Ark, Dec 17, 39; m 62. *Educ:* Univ Ark, BS, 61; Rice Univ, MA, 63, PhD(math), 65. *Prof Exp:* Ritt instr math, Columbia Univ, 65-67. *Mem:* Math Asn Am. *Res:* Boundary behavior of functions analysis in the unit disc. *Mailing Add:* 430 E Hampton Rd Whitefish Bay WI 53217-5927

HALL, ROBERT NOEL, SEMICONDUCTORS. *Current Pos:* RETIRED. *Personal Data:* b New Haven, Conn, Dec 25, 19; m 41, Dora Siechert; c Richard & Elaine. *Educ:* Calif Inst Technol, BS, 42, PhD(physics), 48. *Honors & Awards:* David Sarnoff Award, Inst Elec & Electronics Engrs, 63; Jack A Morton Award, Inst Elec & Electronics Engrs, 76; Solid State Sci & Tech Award, Electrochem Soc, 77; Nat Inventors Hall Fame, 94. *Prof Exp:* Lab asst, Corp Res & Develop Ctr, Gen Elec Co, 42-46, res assoc, 48-52, physicist, res lab, 52-87. *Concurrent Pos:* Marconi int fel, 89. *Mem:* Nat Acad Sci; Nat Acad Eng; fel Inst Elec & Electronics Engrs; fel Am Phys Soc; Electrochem Soc. *Res:* Semiconductor physics; device technology; recombination; solar cells; junction lasers; gamma detectors. *Mailing Add:* 2315 Gurenson Lane Niskayuna NY 12309-5908. *E-Mail:* 74242.2573@compuserve.com

HALL, RONALD HENRY, spectrochemistry, analytical chemistry, for more information see previous edition

HALL, ROSS HUME, BIOCHEMISTRY, ENVIRONMENTAL MANAGEMENT. *Current Pos:* RETIRED. *Personal Data:* b Winnipeg, Man, Nov 22, 26; nat US; m 50; c 3. *Educ:* Univ BC, BA, 48; Toronto Univ, MA, 50; Cambridge Univ, PhD(chem), 53. *Prof Exp:* Fel, Univ BC, 53-54; res chemist, Lederle Labs Div, Am Cyanamid Co, 54-58; prin scientist cancer res, Roswell Park Mem Inst, 58-67; assoc prof biochem, State Univ NY Buffalo, 65-67; prof biochem & chmn dept, McMaster Univ, 67-88. *Concurrent Pos:* Mem grants rev comt, Med Res Coun Can; mem, Can Environ Adv Coun, 75-81; co-founder & dir, En-Trophy Inst Advan Study Food, Nutrit & Food Policy, 77; chmn & mem, bd dirs, Pollution Probe Found, Toronto, Ont, 83-87; chmn, ministers panel selectional priority substances, Dept Environ, Govt Can; co-chmn, health comt, Int Joint Comn, 90- *Mem:* Am Soc Plant Physiologists; Can Biochem Soc (pres, 72-73); Am Chem Soc; Am Soc Biol Chem; Am Asn Cancer Res; Inst Food Technol. *Res:* Assessment of effects of biological technologies; food processing, agriculture, drug, medical technologies; study of cellular mechanisms for processing information. *Mailing Add:* PO Box 239 Danby VT 05739

HALL, RUSSELL P, DERMATOLOGY. *Current Pos:* asst prof, 84-90, ASSOC PROF, DEPT MED, DUKE UNIV, 90- *Educ:* Univ Mo, MD, 75. *Mem:* Am Asn Immunologists; Am Acad Dermatology; Soc Invest Dermat. *Res:* Pathogenesis of auto-immune diseases. *Mailing Add:* Dept Med Duke Univ Box 3135 Durham NC 27710-0001. *Fax:* 919-684-3002

HALL, SEYMOUR GERALD, TEXTILE CHEMISTRY. *Current Pos:* PRES, PROCHEM, 79- *Personal Data:* b Brooklyn, NY, June 30, 40; m 63; c 2. *Educ:* Elon Col, BS, 64; Appalachian State Univ, MA, 66; Univ NC, Greensboro, PhD(textiles), 75. *Prof Exp:* Process chemist, E I du Pont de Nemours & Co, Inc, 66-68; mgr res & develop, Cone Mills Corp, 68-76; vpres oper, Chemonic Indust, 76-79. *Mem:* Am Chem Soc; Am Asn Textile Chemists & Colorists; Air Pollution Control Asn; Synthetic Org Chem Mfrs Asn. *Res:* Developing textile finishing and dyeing chemicals; flame retardant research; water and air pollution development projects; surfactants; esterification reactions. *Mailing Add:* 510 W Grimes Ave High Point NC 27260-6545

HALL, STAN STANLEY, ORGANIC CHEMISTRY, BIO-ORGANIC CHEMISTRY. *Current Pos:* from asst prof org chem to assoc prof chem, 68-78, PROF CHEM, RUTGERS UNIV, 78- *Personal Data:* b Platteville, Wis, July 4, 38; div; c 2. *Educ:* Univ Wis, Madison, BS, 63; Mass Inst Technol, PhD(org chem), 67. *Honors & Awards:* Geigy Award, Chem Indust, Summit, NJ, 80. *Prof Exp:* NIH fel & res assoc chem, Stanford Univ, 67-68. *Concurrent Pos:* NIH spec fel, Scripps Inst Oceanog, 72-73. *Mem:* Am Chem Soc; Sigma Xi. *Res:* Synthetic methods; chemistry of natural products; metal-ammonia reductions; model enzyme studies; molecular rearrangements. *Mailing Add:* Dept Chem Rutgers Univ NWK Campus 175 University Ave Newark NJ 07102-1814

HALL, STANTON HARRIS, BIOCHEMISTRY OF EXTRACELLULAR MATRIX. *Current Pos:* asst prof, 79-85, CUN ASSOC PROF ORTHOD, UNIV WASH, 85- *Personal Data:* b Boise, Idaho, 1940; m 62; c 3. *Educ:* Northwestern Univ, MS & DDS, 67; Univ Wash, PhD(exp path), 74, cert orthod, 79; Am Bd Orthod, dipl, 91. *Prof Exp:* Capt, Wilford Hall USAF Hosp, Lackland AFB, Tex, 67-69; trainee exp path, Univ Wash, 69-74; res assoc, Lab Molecular Genetics, Nat Inst Child Health & Human Develop, NIH, 74-77. *Concurrent Pos:* USPHS trainee, Univ Wash, 70, res grant & co-prin investr, Dept Orthod, 81-86. *Mem:* AAAS; Am Soc Bone & Mineral Res; Am Asn Dent Res; Am Asn Orthodontists. *Res:* Morphogenesis of craniofacial sutures and the modulation of phenotypic expression accompanying osteodifferentiation. *Mailing Add:* 12817 120th Ave NE Kirkland WA 98034

HALL, STEPHEN AUSTIN, QUATERNARY GEOLOGY, PALYNOLOGY. *Current Pos:* assoc prof, 85-97, PROF EARTH SCI, UNIV TEX, AUSTIN, 97- *Personal Data:* b Ponca City, Okla, Aug 11, 42; m 68, Ann Alley; c John D & James A. *Educ:* Univ Okla, BS, 67; Univ Iowa, MS, 71, Univ Mich, PhD(geol), 75. *Prof Exp:* Asst prof earth sci, NTex State Univ, 77-85. *Concurrent Pos:* Chmn, Comm Aerobiol, Int Union Biol Sci, 86-90; chmn, Gordon Res Conf Aerobiol, 87; co-leader, Friends of the Pleistocene, South-Cent, 87, 89 & 94; dir-at-large, Am Asn Stratig Palynologists, 88-89. *Mem:* Int Asn Aerobiol (secy & vice pres, 82-90); Am Asn Stratig Palynologists; Int Union Biol Sci; fel Geol Soc Am; AAAS; Soc Am Archaeol. *Res:* Quaternary vegetational, geomorphic and climatic history of the southern Great Plains and Southwest, including applications of geology and paleoecology to the archologic record. *Mailing Add:* Dept Geog Univ Tex Austin TX 78712-1098

HALL, STEPHEN KENNETH, industrial hygiene, environmental chemistry, for more information see previous edition

HALL, THEODORE (ALVIN), biophysics, for more information see previous edition

HALL, THOMAS KENNETH, ORGANIC CHEMISTRY. *Current Pos:* PRES & FINANCIAL MGR, T K HALL ENTERPRISES, INC, 78- *Personal Data:* b Minneapolis, Minn, Sept 28, 36; m 59; c 5. *Educ:* Univ Santa Clara, BS, 61; Iowa State Univ, PhD(org chem), 65. *Prof Exp:* Asst prof, Chico State Col, 65-66; from assoc to asst prof, Univ Ga, 66-68; sr res chemist, Eastman Kodak Co, 68-70; asst prof chem, Rochester Inst Technol, 70-71; prof chem, West Valley Col, 71-78. *Mem:* Am Chem Soc; Royal Soc Chem. *Res:* Organic photochemistry; oxidation mechanisms; ozonide decomposition. *Mailing Add:* 1620 Knollwood Ave San Jose CA 95125

HALL, THOMAS LIVINGSTON, PUBLIC HEALTH, MEDICINE. *Current Pos:* HEALTH CARE CONSULT, CTR AIDS PREV STUDIES, UNIV CALIF, SAN FRANCISCO, 87- *Personal Data:* b Great Barrington, Mass, Aug 14, 31; m 90, Elizabeth McLoughlin; c Eric L, Tefel A & Rachel F. *Educ:* Harvard Univ, AB, 53, MD, 57, MPH, 61; Johns Hopkins Univ, DrPh, 67; Am Bd Prev Med & Pub Health, Cert. *Prof Exp:* Med dir, Castaner Gen Hosp, PR, 58-60; dir training & res, Community Teaching Health Ctr, Guaynabo,

PR, 61-62; res assoc pub health, Sch Hyg, Johns Hopkins Univ, 63-67, from asst prof to assoc prof, 67-71; dep dir, Carolina Pop Ctr & assoc prof health admin, Univ, 71-74, actg dir, 74-75, dir, Carolina Pop Ctr, Univ NC, 75-77, prof, Dept Health Admin, Sch Pub Health, 74-79; prof health admin, Univ NC, Chapel Hill, 74-79; vis prof, Sch Pub Health & Community Med, Univ Wash, 79-80; exec dir, Puget Sound Health Systs Agency, Seattle, 80-82; health care consult, 82-84, prin med officer res, Dept Health, Wellington, NZ, 85-86 & 86-88. *Concurrent Pos:* Consult, Md State Comt Med Care, 65, Pan Am Health Orgn, 65 & 66 & WHO, 70-; AID consult, Chile, 66 & Chilean Nat Health Serv, 67-70, World Bank, 88-; comt, Int Health, Inst Med, 77-80; lectr, Dept Epidemiol & Biostatist, Sch Med, Univ Calif, San Francisco; gov coun, Am Pub Health Asn, 87-89; dir postdoctoral training, Ctr AIDS Prev Studies, Univ Calif, San Francisco, 89-95. *Mem:* Fel Am Pub Health Asn. *Res:* Public health administration; medical care; health manpower and general health planning; population dynamics and family planning program administration; AIDS program planning; Research about and development of instruments to facilitate the development of human resources for health; author of numerous publications and major reports. *Mailing Add:* 1515 16th Ave San Francisco CA 94122. *Fax:* 415-476-6014

HALL, TIMOTHY COUZENS, PLANT VIROLOGY, PLANT BIOCHEMISTRY. *Current Pos:* distinguished prof & head, Dept Biol, 84-92, DISTINGUISHED PROF & DIR, INST DEVELOP & MOLECULAR BIOL, TEX A&M UNIV, 92- *Personal Data:* b Darlington, Eng, Aug 29, 37; m 60; c 3. *Educ:* Univ Nottingham, BSc, 62, PhD(bot), 65. *Prof Exp:* Res fel, Dept Hort Sci, Univ Minn, St Paul, 65-66; from asst prof to prof hort, Univ Wis-Madison, 66-82. *Concurrent Pos:* Prin investr, NSF, NIH, USDA, Sci Educ Admin & Herman Frasch Found grants; sabbatical leave, vpres & dir advan res, Agrigenetics Corp, 81-84. *Mem:* AAAS; Am Soc Microbiol; Am Soc Plant Physiologists; Brit Biochem Soc; Am Soc Virol; Agr Soc Biochem & Molecular Biol; Sigma Xi. *Res:* Gene cloning, isolation and expression; biosynthesis, structure and function of legume seed proteins; transformation and regeneration of rice; replication of viral RNAs. *Mailing Add:* Inst Develop & Molecular Biol Tex A&M Univ College Station TX 77843-3155. *Fax:* 409-862-4098; *E-Mail:* tim@bio.tamu.edu

HALL, W(ILLIAM) J(OEL), EARTHQUAKE ENGINEERING, STRUCTURAL ENGINEERING. *Current Pos:* res asst, Univ Ill, Urbana, 49-52, res assoc, 52-54, from asst prof to assoc prof civil eng, 54-59, assoc mem, Inst Advan Study, 63-64, prof, 59-93, head dept, 84-91, EMER PROF CIVIL ENG, UNIV ILL, URBANA, 93- *Personal Data:* b Berkeley, Calif, Apr 13, 26; m 48, Elaine Thalman; c Martha J (Sigler), James F & Carolyn M (Vandendriessche). *Educ:* Univ Kans, BS, 48; Univ Ill, MS, 51, PhD(struct eng), 54. *Honors & Awards:* A Epstein Mem Award, 58; Walter L Huber Res Award, Am Soc Civil Engrs, 63, Newmark Medal & E E Howard Award, 84, Martin Duke Award, 91. *Prof Exp:* Asst civil eng, Univ Kans, 47-48; engr, Sohio Pipe Line Co, Mo, 48-49. *Concurrent Pos:* Consult, numerous indust orgn & govt agencies, 70-; mem & chmn, numerous sci & adv comts, Nat Acad Sci, Nat Acad Eng, Nat Res Coun, NSF, US Geol Surv & Am Soc Civil Engrs. *Mem:* Nat Acad Eng; hon mem Am Soc Civil Engrs; Am Concrete Inst; Earthquake Eng Res Inst; fel AAAS; Am Soc Mech Engrs; Am Soc Testing & Mat. *Res:* Structural analysis and design; structural dynamics; plasticity; brittle fracture; earthquake and nuclear effects; author or co-author of more than 200 technical publications. *Mailing Add:* 2106 Newmark Civil Eng Lab Univ Ill 205 N Mathew Ave Urbana IL 61801. *Fax:* 217-333-9464

HALL, W KEITH, PHYSICAL CHEMISTRY, CATALYSIS. *Current Pos:* DISTINGUISHED RES PROF, UNIV PITTSBURGH, 85- *Personal Data:* b McComb, Ohio, June 30, 18; m 45; c 1. *Educ:* Emory Univ, BS, 40; Carnegie Inst Technol, MS, 48; Univ Pittsburgh, PhD(chem), 56. *Hon Degrees:* DSc, Emory Univ, 74; Dr, Katholieke Univ Leuven, Belg, 77; PHU, Univ Santa Fe, Arg, 80. *Honors & Awards:* Kendall Award, Am Chem Soc, 74, Petrol Award, 87; Von Humboldt Award, 84; Exxon Award Excellence Catalysis, 90. *Prof Exp:* Res assoc chem, Nat Defense Res Coun, Div VIII, 41-45; phys chemist, US Bur Mines, 45-51; fel, Mellon Inst, 51-56, sr fel, 56-70; sr scientist, Gulf Res & Develop Co, 70-85, distinguished prof chem, Univ Wis-Milwaukee, 73-85. *Concurrent Pos:* Mem, Petrol Res Adv Bd, Am Chem Soc, 72-75; coordr, US-USSR Exchange Prog chem catalysis, 72-78; mem, Advan Res Prop Agency Conf, res needs Dept Defense, 73; co-organizer, NSF Workshop Catalysis Related to Energy Prod, Houston, 74; exec comn, Colloid & Surface Chem Div, Am Chem Soc, 74-81, chmn div, 79; mem, Comt Direction, Nat Ctr Sci Res, Res Ctr, Crystalline Solids, France, 75-79; ed, J Catalysis, 76-89; bd Trustee, Gordon Res Conf, 81-87. *Mem:* Am Chem Soc; Catalysis Soc NAm (pres, 81-85). *Res:* Chemistry; surface chemistry; energy; solar energy; petroleum chemistry; automotive emissions control. *Mailing Add:* PO Box 97 Mill Run PA 15464-0097

HALL, W(ILLIAM) M(OTT), electrical engineering; deceased, see previous edition for last biography

HALL, WARREN G, PSYCHOBIOLOGY, NEUROBIOLOGY. *Current Pos:* AT DEPT PSYCHOL, DUKE UNIV. *Personal Data:* b Urbana, Ohio, July 14, 48. *Educ:* Univ Ariz, BA, 71; Johns Hopkins Univ, MA, 73, PhD(physiol psychiat), 75. *Prof Exp:* Fel develop psychobiol, Inst Animal Behav, Rutgers, 75-77; res scientist, NC Div Ment Health, Dorothea Dix Hosp, 77- *Mem:* Int Soc Develop Psychobiol; Animal Behav Soc; Am Psychol Asn; Soc Neurosci. *Res:* Developmental psychobiology and neurobiology of motivation and learning. *Mailing Add:* Dept Psychol Duke Univ Durham NC 27706-8001

HALL, WAYNE CLARK, plant physiology, for more information see previous edition

HALL, WAYNE HAWKINS, MATHEMATICS EDUCATION. *Current Pos:* asst prof math educ, Eastern Wash Univ, 70-73, assoc prof math & educ, 73-80, co-dir, Ctr Safety Educ, 74, PROF MATH & EDUC, EASTERN WASH UNIV, 80- *Personal Data:* b Fairland, Okla, Apr 4, 36; m 55; c 3. *Educ:* Kans State Col Pittsburg, BS, 58, MS, 64; George Peabody Col, PhD(math, educ-psychol), 70. *Prof Exp:* Teacher math, High Schs, Kans, 59-66; instr, Kans State Col Pittsburgh, 66-67. *Mem:* Sigma Xi. *Res:* Mathematics education, especially the effect on performance of number of exercises; feedback and detail; investigation of two instructional variables in learning non-metric geometry. *Mailing Add:* Dept Math 526 Fifth St Eastern Wash Univ Cheney WA 99004

HALL, WENDELL HOWARD, INTERNAL MEDICINE, INFECTIOUS DISEASES. *Current Pos:* RETIRED. *Personal Data:* b Redfield, SDak, May 18, 16; m 48, Muriel H Griffith; c David H, Donald B, Joan (Hyrkas) & John W. *Educ:* Univ Minn, BS, 38, MB, 40, MD, 41, PhD(med), 50; Am Bd Internal Med, dipl. *Prof Exp:* Intern, Detroit Receiving Hosp, 40-41; intern internal med, Univ Minn Hosp, 41-42, asst, 43-45, instr, 45-47, from asst prof to assoc prof internal med & microbiol, 47-61, prof internal med & microbiol, 61-86. *Concurrent Pos:* Chief bact lab, Vet Admin Hosp, 49-52, chief clin labs, 52-60, chief med serv, 60-71, chief infectious dis serv, 71-80. *Mem:* Am Soc Clin Invest; Am Col Physicians; Infectious Dis Soc Am. *Res:* Infectious diseases; brucellosis; tuberculosis; antibiotics; immunology. *Mailing Add:* 6609 Galway Dr Minneapolis MN 55439

HALL, WILLIAM BARTLETT, GEOLOGY, PHOTOGEOLOGY. *Current Pos:* from assoc prof to prof, 65-91, EMER PROF GEOL, UNIV IDAHO, 91- *Personal Data:* b Cincinnati, Ohio, July 12, 25; m 51; c 3. *Educ:* Princeton Univ, AB, 50; Univ Cincinnati, MS, 51; Univ Wyo, PhD, 61. *Prof Exp:* Geologist, Pure Oil Co, 51-54; asst geol, Univ Wyo, 54-57, instr, 58; asst prof, Mont Sch Mines, 58-65. *Concurrent Pos:* Mem, Fourth Int Field Inst, Italy, 64; dir, Geophotography & Remote Sensing Ctr, Univ Idaho, 67-91, co-dir, Remote Sensing Res Unit, 72-91. *Mem:* Geol Soc Am; Am Soc Photogram; Am Asn Petrol Geologists; Am Inst Prof Geologists. *Res:* Montana geology; geomorphology; photogeology; photogrammetry; engineering geology; aerial photography. *Mailing Add:* 2343 Wallen Rd Moscow ID 83843

HALL, WILLIAM CHARLES, NEUROPSYCHOLOGY, NEUROANATOMY. *Current Pos:* ASSOC PROF ANAT, DUKE UNIV, 70- *Personal Data:* b Peoria, Ill, Aug 2, 40; m 62; c 1. *Educ:* Duke Univ, BA, 62, PhD(physiol psychol), 67. *Honors & Awards:* C J Herrick Award, Am Asn Anat, 72. *Prof Exp:* NIMH fel, Duke Univ, 67-68; Nat Inst Neurol Dis & Stroke fel, Brown Univ, 68-70. *Concurrent Pos:* NIMH res scientist career develop award, 71-; Nat Inst Neurol Dis & Stroke res grant award, 71-; NSF res grant award, 75- *Mem:* AAAS; Am Asn Anat; Neurosci Soc. *Res:* Structure and function of neocortex, especially the use of comparative technique; identification and comparison of particular structure in a variety of species to determine how structures vary in response to the particular ecological niches of species and as a function of the evolutionary history of species. *Mailing Add:* Dept Psych Duke Univ Durham NC 27706-8001

HALL, WILLIAM EARL, PHARMACY, PHYSICAL CHEMISTRY. *Current Pos:* group leader, Burroughs Wellcome Co, 73-74, sect head, 74-77, dept head, 77-84, DEPT HEAD, PHARMACEUT RES DEVELOP LAB, QUAL ASSURANCE DIV, BURROUGHS WELLCOME CO, 84- *Personal Data:* b Fayetteville, Ark, Mar 2, 38; m 79, Sandra Crandel; c William E Jr, Sherri L & Kristin A. *Educ:* Univ Ark, BS, 61; Univ Wis, MS, 64, PhD(pharm), 67. *Prof Exp:* Instr pharm, Univ Wis, 65-66; asst prof, Sch Pharm, Univ NC, Chapel Hill, 66-73. *Mem:* Am Asn Pharmaceut Scientists; Am Soc Qual Control; Parenteral Drug Asn. *Res:* Computer optimization of pharmaceutical formulations, microscopy of particulate matter, sustained release of drug dosage forms, image analysis, regulatory compliance in the pharmaceutical industry; validation of pharmaceutical processes; cleaning in pharmaceutical operations. *Mailing Add:* Burroughs Wellcome PO Box 1887 Greenville NC 27834

HALL, WILLIAM FRANCIS, speech pathology; deceased, see previous edition for last biography

HALL, WILLIAM HEINLEN, CHEMISTRY. *Current Pos:* from instr to prof chem, 36-76, chmn, Dept Chem, 54-72, EMER PROF CHEM, BOWLING GREEN STATE UNIV, 76- *Personal Data:* b Cairo, WVa, June 19, 10; m 38; c 2. *Educ:* Muskingum Col, AB, 32; Ohio State Univ, PhD(phys chem), 39. *Prof Exp:* Asst chem, Ohio State Univ, 32-36. *Concurrent Pos:* Consult, Chem Info. *Mem:* Fel AAAS; Am Chem Soc. *Mailing Add:* 324 Pennsylvania Ave Kutztown PA 19530

HALL, WILLIAM JACKSON, STATISTICS, BIOSTATISTICS. *Current Pos:* chmn, Dept Statist, 69-81 & 95-97, actg dir, Div Biostatist, 87-90, PROF STATIST & BIOSTATIST, UNIV ROCHESTER, 69- *Personal Data:* b Beltsville, Md, Nov 13, 29; m 54; c 4. *Educ:* Johns Hopkins Univ, AB, 50; Univ Mich, MA, 51; Univ NC, PhD(statist), 55. *Prof Exp:* Mem tech staff probability & statist, Bell Tel Labs, 54-55; asst chief polio surveillance unit, Commun Dis Ctr, USPHS, 55-57; from asst prof to prof, Univ NC, Chapel Hill, 57-69. *Concurrent Pos:* Vis prof, Stanford Univ, Univ Calif, Berkeley, 67-69 & Univ Wash, 82. *Mem:* Fel AAAS; fel Am Statist Asn; fel Inst Math Statist; Royal Statist Soc. *Res:* Statistical inference. *Mailing Add:* 75 Chelmsford Rd Rochester NY 14618

HALL, WILLIAM SPENCER, APPLIED MATHEMATICS. *Current Pos:* Asst prof, 68-74, ASSOC PROF MATH, UNIV PITTSBURGH, 75- *Personal Data:* b Ancon, Panama, Oct 9, 35; m 63. *Educ:* Univ Va, BEE, 58; Cambridge Univ, BA, 65, MA, 70; Brown Univ, PhD(appl math), 68. *Concurrent Pos:* Lectr, Dept Math, Univ Col, Galway, Ireland, 73-74; Joint Int Res & Exchange Bd & Nat Acad Sci Scholar, Czech Acad Sci, 75-76 & 78-79. *Mem:* Am Math Soc; Sigma Xi. *Res:* Periodic solutions of partial differential equations. *Mailing Add:* 5621 Maple Heights Ct Pittsburgh PA 15232

HALL, ZACH WINTER, PHYSIOLOGY GENERAL. *Current Pos:* DIR, NAT INST NEUROL DIS & STROKE & CHIEF, SECT SYNAPTIC MECHANISMS, LAB CELL BIOL, NIH, 94- *Personal Data:* b Atlanta, Ga, Sept 15, 37; m; Julie Giacobassi; c Charles & Rebecca. *Educ:* Yale Univ, BA, 58; Harvard Univ, PhD(biochem), 66. *Honors & Awards:* Grass Lectr, Univ NC, 78; Louis B Flexner Lectr, Inst Neurol Sci, Univ Pa, 84, Lowell O Randall Lectr, Dept Pharmacol, 91; Dunaway-Burnham Lectr, Dartmouth Med Sch, 91; Steven Schuetze Lectr, Columbia Univ, 93; Alexander Forbes Lectr, Grass Found, Marine Biol Lab, Woods Hole, Mass, 94. *Prof Exp:* Fel biochem, Sch Med, Stanford Univ, 66-68; from asst prof to assoc prof, Dept Neurobiol, Harvard Med Sch, 68-76; prof physiol, Univ Calif, San Francisco, 76-94. *Concurrent Pos:* Res Career Develop Award, Nat Inst Neurol Dis & Stroke, 72-76; head, Div Neurobiol & Neurosci Grad Prog, Univ Calif, San Francisco, 76-88, chmn, Dept Physiol, 87-94, Jack & DeLoris Lange prof physiol, 92-94, head, Biomed Sci Grad Prog, 92-94. *Mem:* Inst Med-Nat Acad Sci; Soc Neurosci; Am Soc Biol Chemists; Am Soc Cell Biol; hon mem Am Neurol Asn; fel Am Acad Arts & Sci; AAAS. *Res:* Structure and function of the acetylcholine receptor; development of the neuromuscular junction. *Mailing Add:* Nat Inst Neurol Dis & Stroke NIH Bldg 31 Rm 8A52 31 Center Dr Bethesda MD 20892-2540. *Fax:* 301-496-0296; *E-Mail:* zach_hall@nih.gov

HALLADA, CALVIN JAMES, INDUSTRIAL CHEMISTRY, METALLURGY. *Current Pos:* sr res chemist, Climax Molybdenum Co, 65-66, group leader chem & extractive metall, 66-70, supvr, 70-74, mgr, Chem & Process Res, 74-84, dir chem develop, 87-89, DIR CHEM SALES & DEVELOP, CLIMAX MOLYBDENUM CO, 89- *Personal Data:* b Grand Forks, NDak, Oct 16, 33; m 57; c Mark, Katharine & Patricia. *Educ:* Univ NDak, BA, 56; Univ Mich, Ann Arbor, MS, 58, PhD(chem), 61. *Prof Exp:* Res chemist, Union Carbide Corp, 61-62 & Lawrence Radiation Lab, 62-63; group leader chem, Conductron, Inc, 63-65. *Concurrent Pos:* Lectr, Univ Calif, Berkeley, 62-63. *Mem:* Am Chem Soc; NAm Catalyst Soc. *Res:* Chemistry of transition metals as it applies to extraction of the metals and their use in catalysis, lubrication, pigments, flame retardants and aqueous corrosion inhibitors; energy storage materials. *Mailing Add:* Climax Molybdenum Co PO Box 407 Ypsilanti MI 48197

HALLAHAN, WILLIAM LASKEY, BIOLOGY, ETHOLOGY. *Current Pos:* ASST PROF BIOL, NAZARETH COL, ROCHESTER, 76- *Personal Data:* b Philadelphia, Pa, Dec 19, 46. *Educ:* Colo Col, BA, 69; Duke Univ, PhD(zool), 76. *Mem:* AAAS; Am Inst Biol Sci; Animal Behav Soc; Nat Sci Teachers Asn. *Res:* Ecology; endocrinology. *Mailing Add:* Dept Biol Nazareth Col Rochester 4245 East Ave Rochester NY 14618-3703

HALLAM, THOMAS GUY, MATHEMATICS. *Current Pos:* PROF MATH & ECOL, UNIV TENN, KNOXVILLE, 77- *Personal Data:* b Chicago, Ill, Sept 3, 37; m 64; c 2. *Educ:* Univ Southern Ill, BA, 59, MA, 61; Univ Mo, PhD(math), 65. *Prof Exp:* From asst prof to prof math, Fla State Univ, 65-76; vis prof math & zool, Univ Ga, 76-77. *Concurrent Pos:* Vis assoc prof, Univ RI, 70-71; vis prof, Inst Math Sci, Univ Sao Paulo, Brazil, 74. *Mem:* Ecol Soc Am; AAAS; Soc Indust & Appl Math. *Res:* Ordinary and functional differential equations; asymptotic behavior; stability theory; mathematical modelling; magnetohydrodynamics, rotating fluid flows, ecological systems; ecotoxicology; mathematical ecology. *Mailing Add:* Dept Math Univ Tenn Knoxville 1345 Circle Park Knoxville TN 37996-0001

HALLANGER, LAWRENCE WILLIAM, OCEAN ENGINEERING, RESEARCH ADMINISTRATION. *Current Pos:* PROG MGR, SAIC, 84- *Personal Data:* b Oakland, Calif, Aug 9, 39; m 91, Mary Ann Martin; c 1. *Educ:* Harvey Mudd Col, BS, 61; Calif Inst Technol, MS, 62, PhD(appl mech), 67. *Prof Exp:* Proj engr, US Naval Civil Eng Lab, 65-79; proj mgr, Seacoast Test Fac, Seaco, Hawaii, 79-81, actg exec dir, Natural Energy Lab, 80-82, sr prog engr, 82-84. *Mem:* Am Soc Mech Engrs; Marine Technol Soc. *Res:* Diver work systems and techniques; alternate energy applications; undersea surveillance systems. *Mailing Add:* SAIC 2111 Eisenhower Suite 200 Alexandria VA 22314

HALLANGER, NORMAN LAWRENCE, METEOROLOGY. *Current Pos:* RETIRED. *Personal Data:* b Salt Lake City, Utah, June 13, 12; m 35; c 2. *Educ:* Calif Inst Technol, BS, 34, MS, 36. *Prof Exp:* Meteorologist, United Airlines, 36-39; meteorologist, Pan Am Airways, 39-52, asst supt meteorol, 44-50; chief meteorologist, R M Parsons Co, 52-54, prin scientist, Booz, Allen Appl Res, Inc, 57-71; sr scientist & mgr indust meteorol, Meteorol Res, Inc, 71-77; consult, 77-83. *Mem:* Fel Am Meteorol Soc; Nat Coun Indust Meteorol. *Res:* Micrometeorology; atmospheric diffusion; industrial meteorology; tropical meteorology; forecast system development. *Mailing Add:* 2200 W Acacia Ave Apt W202 Hemet CA 92545-3748

HALLAS, LAURENCE EDWARD, ENVIRONMENTAL MICROBIOLOGY, MICROBIAL ECOLOGY. *Current Pos:* MONSANTO AGR CO, 82- *Personal Data:* b Montgomery, Ala, Feb 10, 54; m 78; c 2. *Educ:* Miami Univ, Ohio, BA, 75; Univ Cincinnati, MS, 77; Univ Md, PhD(microbiol), 81. *Prof Exp:* Fel toxicol, Cornell Univ, 81-82. *Mem:* Am Soc Microbiol; Soc Indust Microbiol; Sigma Xi. *Res:* Environmental microbiology and toxicology; heavy metal biotransformations; biodegradation of industrial and agricultural chemical. *Mailing Add:* Monsanto Agr Co T4G 800 N Lindbergh Blvd St Louis MO 63141-7843

HALLAUER, ARNEL ROY, PLANT BREEDING. *Current Pos:* prof, 77-90, DISTINGUISHED PROF AGRON, IOWA STATE UNIV, 91- *Personal Data:* b Netawaka, Kans, May 4, 32; m 64; c Elizabeth & Paul. *Educ:* Kans State Univ, BS, 54; Iowa State Univ, MS, 58, PhD(crop breeding), 60. *Honors & Awards:* Crop Sci Award, Crop Sci Soc Am, 81, DeKalb-Pfizer Crop Sci Distinguished Career Award, 90; Appl Res & Exten Award, Iowa Agr Exp Sta, 81; Res Recognition Award, Northop-King, 84; Nat Coun Com Plant Breeders Award, 84; Scientist of Year Award, Agr Res Serv, USDA, 85; Agron Achievement Award, Am Soc Agron, 89; Gov Sci Award, 89; Henry A Wallace Award, 92; Agron Res Award, Am Soc Agron, 92. *Prof Exp:* Res agronomist, USDA, 58-61, res geneticist, 61-89. *Mem:* Nat Acad Sci; fel Crop Sci Soc Am; Am Genetics Asn; Biometric Soc; fel Am Soc Agron. *Res:* Experimental quantitative genetic studies and their relation to corn breeding methodology. *Mailing Add:* 516 Luther Dr Ames IA 50010-4735. *Fax:* 515-294-3163; *E-Mail:* hallaner@iastate.edu

HALLBERG, CARL WILLIAM, PARASITOLOGY, EMBRYOLOGY. *Current Pos:* RETIRED. *Personal Data:* b Detroit, Mich, July 13, 18; m 42; c 3. *Educ:* Univ Mich, BS, 47, MS, 48, PhD(zool), 52. *Prof Exp:* From asst prof to prof biol, Bowling Green State Univ, 51-83, actg chmn biol sci, 74-75. *Concurrent Pos:* Adj prof, Col Health & Community Serv, Bowling Green State Univ, 84-87. *Mem:* Am Soc Parasitologists; Am Asn Adv Health; Am Micros Soc; Am Inst Biol Scientists; AAAS; Sigma Xi; Audubon Soc; Nat Geog Soc; Am Mus Natural Hist. *Res:* Studies of migration routes to kidneys of mammals and resultant pathology caused by Dioctophyma renale; giant kidney worm of man; germ cell cyclein digenetic trematodes. *Mailing Add:* 1109 Clark Bowling Green OH 43402-3518

HALLBERG, GEORGE ROBERT, ENVIRONMENTAL GEOLOGY, SUSTAINABLE AGRICULTURE. *Current Pos:* CHIEF, ENVIRON RES, OAKDALE HALL, UNIV HYG LAB, IOWA CITY, 93-, ASSOC DIR, 95- *Personal Data:* b Chicago, Ill, Nov 11, 47; m 70, Lillian Gruenwald; c Abbey & Aaron. *Educ:* Augustana Col, BA, 70; Univ Iowa, PhD(geol), 75. *Prof Exp:* Res geologist, Quaternary Geol & Earth Resources Observ Satellite & coordr remote sensing, Iowa Geol Surv, 71-73, sr res geologist quaternary geol, 73-75, chief, Res Div, 75-79, chief geol studies, 79-86, chief, environ geol, 86-93. *Concurrent Pos:* Adj prof geol, Univ Iowa, 75-, civil & environ eng, 94-, prev med & environ health, 96-; assoc prof geol collabr, Iowa State Univ, 78-; liason rep, Geol Soc Am, 78-81; mgt adv group, Off Water, US Environ Protection Agency, 90-92, mem, Nat Adv Coun, environ policy & technol, 96-; assoc ed, Water Resources Bull, Am Water Res Asn, 92-96; mem bd agr, Nat Acad Sci & Nat Res Coun, 96- *Mem:* Fel Geol Soc Am; Soil Sci Soc Am; Am Quaternary Asn; Asn Ground Water Scientists & Engrs; Prof Soil Classifiers. *Res:* Environmental exposure assessment; gound water quality; agriculture and nonpoint source pollution; stratigraphy, engineering geology and hydrology of quaternary deposits. *Mailing Add:* Univ Hyg Lab Oakdale Hall Iowa City IA 52242. *Fax:* 573-335-4600

HALLE, MORRIS, LINGUISTICS. *Current Pos:* From asst prof to prof mod lang, Mass Inst Technol, 51-76, Ferrari P Ward prof mod lang & ling, 76-81, actg head, Dept Foreign Lang & Ling, 76, inst prof, 81-96, EMER PROF, MASS INST TECHNOL, 96- *Personal Data:* b Liepaja, Latvia, July 23, 23; nat US; m 55, Rosamond T Strong; c David, John & Timothy. *Educ:* Univ Chicago, MA, 48; Harvard Univ, PhD(ling), 55. *Hon Degrees:* DSc, Brandeis Univ, 89; DHL, Chicago Univ, 92. *Honors & Awards:* James R Killian Jr lectr, 78. *Concurrent Pos:* J S Guggenheim Found fel, 60-61; fel, Ctr Advan Study Behav Sci, 60-61; vis prof, Col France, 87. *Mem:* Nat Acad Sci; Am Acad Arts & Sci; Ling Soc Am (vpres, 73, pres, 74). *Res:* What do the sounds of language tell us about the nature of the human mind and body. *Mailing Add:* Dept Ling 20D219 Mass Inst Technol 77 Massachusetts Ave Cambridge MA 02139

HALLECK, FRANK EUGENE, BIOMEDICAL ENGINEERING. *Current Pos:* CONSULT, 90- *Personal Data:* b Waterbury, Conn, Dec 9, 27; m 56; c 2. *Educ:* Wesleyan Univ, BA, 48, MA, 49; Rutgers Univ, PhD(microbiol, biochem), 52. *Prof Exp:* Res assoc, Univ Md, 52-53; assoc prof microbiol & bact, Loyola Univ, Ill, 53-60; res assoc, Pillsbury Co, 60-64; res dir, Proprietaries & Hosp Prod, Chesebrough Ponds Inc, 64-72; vpres, Cytomed Labs, Inc, 73; corp dir, Sci Affair, Am Sterilizer Co, Inc, Pa, 73-84; pres, Tech Consult Ltd, 84-87; sr dir qual assurance, Faberge & Elizabeth Arden, Inc, 87-90. *Concurrent Pos:* Res consult, Wahl-Henius Inst, 53-55; prof, Worsham Col Mortuary Sci, 57-58; consult, Oppenheimer Casing Co, 57-59, Res Armour Co, 55-57 & numerous med & pharmacol co. *Mem:* Parenteral Drug Asn; Soc Indust Microbiol; AAAS; Am Soc Microbiol; NY Acad Sci; Am Chem Soc. *Res:* Microbial fermentaitons and metabolism; chemical composition of polysaccharides of microbial origin; factors influencing microbial growth; food spoilage problems; product development of hospital and proprietary ethical and over-the-counter products; business development through acquisition evaluations; regulatory liaison; microbiological deterioration of cosmetic products; health care products, hardware and disposable products; antibacteerial products; enzyme drugs. *Mailing Add:* 5026 Upland Game Rd Roanoke VA 24014

HALLECK, MARGARET S, CELL BIOLOGY. *Current Pos:* RES INSTR, DEPT PHARMACOL, SCH MED, UNIV TEX, HOUSTON, 86- *Personal Data:* b 1937. *Educ:* Univ NMex, PhD(biol), 80. *Res:* Red cell-mediated injection; chromatin structure. *Mailing Add:* Dept Molecular & Cell Biol Penn State Univ 101 S Frear Bldg University Park PA 16802

HALLECK, SEYMOUR LEON, PSYCHIATRY. *Current Pos:* PROF PSYCHIAT & DIR RESIDENT TRAINING, SCH MED, UNIV NC, CHAPEL HILL, 72- *Personal Data:* b Chicago, Ill, Apr 16, 29; c 3. *Educ:* Univ Chicago, PhB, 48, BS, 50, MD, 52. *Hon Degrees:* ScD, Rockford Univ, 69. *Prof Exp:* Clin asst path, Sch Med, Univ Chicago, 49-51; intern, USPHS Hosp, San Francisco, 52-53; staff psychiatrist, Dept Justice, Med Ctr Fed Prisoners, Springfield, Mo, 53-55; resident psychiat, Menninger Found, Topeka, Kans, 55-58; asst prof psychiat, Univ Wis, 58-60, clin asst prof, 60-63, lectr sociol, 63-64, from assoc prof to prof psychiat, 63-72, actg chmn dept, 71-72. *Concurrent Pos:* Psychiat consult, Wis Diag Ctr, 58-60 & Wis Sch Girls, 58-60; coordr inst serv, Psychiat Serv, Div Corrections, 60-61, chief psychiat serv, 61-63; chief psychiat consult, Wis Div Corrections, 62-72; mem adv comt, Cent State Hosp, 60-72; columnist, Madison Capital Times & Chapel Hill Newspaper, 71-73. *Res:* Student mental health and adolescent adjustment. *Mailing Add:* Dept Psychiat Univ NC Sch Med Chapel Hill NC 27514

HALLEEN, ROBERT M(ARVIN), mechanical engineering, for more information see previous edition

HALLENBECK, PATRICK CLARK, NITROGEN FIXATION, ANAEROBIC METABOLISM. *Current Pos:* invited prof, 87-89, ASSOC PROF MICROBIOL, UNIV MONTREAL, 89- *Personal Data:* b Hornell, NY, Apr 17, 51; m, Carole Gellman; c Jessica & Gaelen. *Educ:* Syracuse Univ, BSc, 72; Univ Calif, Berkeley, PhD(biophys), 78. *Prof Exp:* Fel microbiol, Dept Sanit Eng, Univ Calif, Berkeley, 79; nuclear engr biochem, Ctr Nuclear Studies, Grenoble, 79-81; fel, Univ Calif, Davis, 81-87. *Concurrent Pos:* Prin investr, Med Res Coun Can & Natural Sci & Eng Res Coun, 88- *Mem:* Am Soc Microbiol; Can Soc Microbiologists; Am Soc Biochem & Molecular Biol. *Res:* Physiology and genetics of bacterial anaerobic metabolism; biochemical and physiological basis of bacterial nitrogen fixation; purification and characterization of iron-sulfur proteins. *Mailing Add:* Dept Microbiol & Immunol Univ Montreal CP 6128 Succursale A Montreal PQ H3C 3J7 Can. *Fax:* 514-343-5701; *E-Mail:* hallenbe@ere.umontreal.ca

HALLENBECK, WILLIAM H, ENVIRONMENTAL SCIENCE, CHEMISTRY. *Current Pos:* instr, Univ Ill, Chicago, 73-77, asst prof environ sci, 77-80, assoc prof, 80-90, PROF ENVIRON SCI, UNIV ILL CHICAGO, 90- *Personal Data:* b Albany, NY, Sept 14, 45; m, Carolyn S Hesse. *Educ:* State Univ NY Albany, BS, 67, MS, 69; Univ NC, MSPH, 73; Univ Ill Med Ctr, DrPH, 77. *Prof Exp:* Chemist food chem, NY State Dept Agr & Mkt, 70-72. *Mem:* Am Nuclear Soc; Health Physics Soc. *Res:* Asbestos, food, drinking water and air pollution; solid waste; hazardous waste; risk assessment; radiation protection. *Mailing Add:* Sch Pub Health Univ Ill M/C 922 Chicago IL 60612-7260. *Fax:* 312-413-9898

HALLER, CHARLES REGIS, PETROLEUM GEOLOGY. *Current Pos:* RETIRED. *Personal Data:* b Kansas City, Kans, Nov 21, 31; m 64, Evelyn Munchow; c Sabrina (Wagner). *Educ:* Univ Mo, Columbia, AB, 53, MA, 57; Univ Calif, Berkeley, PhD(paleont), 64. *Prof Exp:* Paleontologist, Amerada Petrol Corp, 59-60 & Oasis Oil Co of Libya, Inc, 60-62; sr paleontologist, Amoco Int Oil Co, 65-74; sr geologist petrol explor, Marathon Petrol Norte Brazil, 74-80, chief geologist, 80-81, explor mgr, 81-85; explor mgr, Clam Petrol Co, 85-88; sr proj coordr, Marathon Oil Co, 88-92. *Mailing Add:* Postfach 1353 55383 Bingen Germany

HALLER, EDWIN WOLFGANG, PHYSIOLOGY, NEUROENDOCRINOLOGY. *Current Pos:* asst prof physiol, 71-72, ASSOC PROF PHYSIOL & BIOL, SCH MED, UNIV MINN, DULUTH, 72- *Personal Data:* b Stuttgart, Ger, May 19, 36; US citizen; c 2. *Educ:* Park Col, BA, 59; Western Reserve Univ, PhD(physiol), 67. *Prof Exp:* Res & develop chemist, Lucidol Div, Wallace & Tiernan, Inc, 59-61; res assoc physiol, Sch Med, Univ Md, Baltimore, 67-69, asst prof, 69-71. *Concurrent Pos:* Vis scientist, Inst Animal Physiol, Agr Res Coun, Cambridge, Eng, 77-78; consult, Am Asn Accreditation Lab Animal Care, 78-88, Coun Accreditation, 88-; vis prof, Health Sci Ctr, State Univ NY, Syracuse, 90. *Mem:* Sigma Xi; AAAS; Endocrine Soc; Soc Neurosci. *Res:* Central nervous system regulation of gonadotropin secretion; neurophysiological aspects of neurosecretion; regulation of secretion of vasopressin and oxytocin from the posterior pituitary. *Mailing Add:* 5021 Peabody St Duluth MN 55804

HALLER, ELDEN D, CHEMICAL ENGINEERING. *Current Pos:* RETIRED. *Personal Data:* b Chillicothe, Ohio, Oct 20, 09; c 1. *Educ:* Ohio State Univ, BChE, 33, MSc, 35, PhD(chem eng), 40. *Prof Exp:* Pvt jobber, 27-34; asst chem eng, Ohio State Univ, 35, asst, Mach Lab, 37-39; chief chemist & chem engr, Nat Lime & Stone Co, 40; tech ed, Ord Dept, Washington, DC, 41; chem engr, Nat Tech Labs, 41-52; eastern sales mgr, Beckman Instruments, Inc, 52-54; from consult to asst to pres, Arthur H Thomas Co, 54-59, vpres & sales mgr, 59-74. *Concurrent Pos:* Consult, 74- *Mem:* Am Chem Soc; Instrument Soc Am; Soc Appl Spectros; Am Inst Chem Engrs. *Res:* Instrumentation; spectrophotometric pH control and radiation; corrosion of galvanized iron. *Mailing Add:* 8505 Hazelwood Dr Bethesda MD 20814-1407

HALLER, EUGENE ERNEST, SEMICONDUCTOR PHYSICS, ELECTRONIC MATERIALS & DEVICES. *Current Pos:* fel solid state res, Lawrence Berkeley Lab, 71-73, staff scientist, 75-80, sen staff scientist, 75-80, assoc prof, 80-82, PROF, DEPT MAT SCI & MINERAL ENG, UNIV CALIF, BERKELEY, 82-, FAC SR SCIENTIST, LAWRENCE BERKELEY LAB, 80- *Personal Data:* b Basel, Switz, Jan 5, 43; US citizen; m 73, Marianne E Schlittler; c Nicole & Isabelle. *Educ:* Univ Basel, Switz, dipl, 67, PhD(physics), 70. *Honors & Awards:* US Sr Scientist Award, Alexander von Humboldt Found, 86; Max-Planck Res Prize, 94. *Prof Exp:* Res & teaching asst physics, Inst Appl Physics, Univ Basel, 67-71. *Concurrent Pos:* Prog leader, Ctr Advan Mat, Lawrence Berkeley Lab, 84-; prin investr, Space Infrared Telescope Facil, NASA, 85-; res prof, Miller Found Basic Res Sci, 90; vis prof, Imp Col, London, 91. *Mem:* Fel Am Phys Soc; Mat Res Soc; Swiss Phys Soc; Sigma X. *Res:* Spectroscopic and electronic characterization of one and two dimensional defects in semi-conductors; growth of ultra-pure and doped thin film and bulk single crystals of germanium, Gan and GaAs; advanced far infrared, x-ray and gamma ray semiconductor detectors; author of numerous publications; granted 2 patents. *Mailing Add:* 1054 Mariposa Ave Berkeley CA 94707

HALLER, GARY LEE, PHYSICAL CHEMISTRY. *Current Pos:* from asst prof to assoc prof eng & appl sci, Yale Univ, 67-80, Becton prof eng & appl sci, 84-87, dep provost phys sci & eng, 87-89, PROF CHEM ENG & CHEM, YALE UNIV, 80-, HENRY PRENTISS BECTON PROF ENG APPL SCI, 84-, MASTER, JONATHAN EDWARDS COL, 97- *Personal Data:* b Loup City, Nebr, July 10, 41; m 62, Sandra S Krueger; c Jared, Sarah & Joshua. *Educ:* Kearney State Col, BA, 62; Northwestern Univ, PhD(chem), 66. *Honors & Awards:* Donald Fox Lectr, Univ Nebr, Kearney, 82; Robert Burwell Lectr, Catalysis Soc N Am, 95; Harny Fair Lectr, Univ Okla, 95; Lacy Lectr, Cal Inst Technol, 96; Ipatieff Lectr, Northwestern Univ, 96. *Prof Exp:* NATO fel phys chem, Oxford Univ, 66-67. *Mem:* Am Chem Soc; Am Inst Chem Eng; Catalysis Soc NAm; AAAS. *Res:* Heterogeneous catalysis; kinetics and mechanisms of catalyzed reactions; surface chemistry and structure of solid catalysts; environmental problems; air pollution. *Mailing Add:* Dept Chem Eng Yale Univ 8286 Yale Sta New Haven CT 06520-8286. *Fax:* 203-432-4387; *E-Mail:* gary.haller@yale.edu

HALLER, IVAN, PHYSICAL & GASEOUS ION CHEMISTRY, MASS SPECTROMETRY. *Current Pos:* DIR, CORE LAB, GEN CLIN RES CTR, MED COL, CORNELL UNIV, 96- *Personal Data:* b Budapest, Hungary, June 8, 34; US citizen; m 65, Laura Woolf; c Paul & Drew. *Educ:* Budapest Technol Univ, BS, 56; Univ Calif, Berkeley, PhD(chem), 61. *Prof Exp:* Asst, Univ Calif, Berkeley, 57-59; assoc mem staff, T J Watson Res Ctr, IBM Corp, 60-61, mem staff, 61-93; chemist, Clin Res Assocs, NY, 94-95. *Concurrent Pos:* Vis scientist, Biol Mass Spectrometry Fac, Rockefeller Univ, 93- *Mem:* Am Chem Soc; Am Inst Chemists; Am Soc Mass Spectrometry. *Res:* Materials science of electronic materials; photon, charged particle; beam and plasma induced chemical processes; spectroscopy and molecular structure; mass spectrometry of biopolymers. *Mailing Add:* 901 Hardscrabble Rd Chappaqua NY 10514. *E-Mail:* ihaller@mail.med.cornell.edu

HALLER, KURT, THEORETICAL HIGH ENERGY PHYSICS. *Current Pos:* assoc prof, Univ Conn, 64-70, actg dept head, 81-82 & 92-93, interim dept head, 86, PROF PHYSICS, UNIV CONN, 70- *Personal Data:* b Vienna, Austria, May 6, 28; nat US; m 52, Lottie Schlegel; c Paul B & Geoffrey S. *Educ:* Columbia Univ, AB, 49, PhD(physics), 58. *Honors & Awards:* Sr Fulbright lectr, Univ Graz, Austria, 73. *Prof Exp:* Instr physics, Newark Col Arts & Sci, Rutgers Univ, 53-54; instr, Newark Col Eng, 54-56; res asst, Columbia Univ, 56-57; res assoc, Wash Univ, 57-59; from asst prof to assoc prof, NY Univ, 59-64. *Concurrent Pos:* Vis prof, Inst Theoret Physics, 73. *Mem:* Fel Am Phys Soc. *Res:* Elementary particle theory; quantum field theory. *Mailing Add:* Dept Physics U-46 Univ Conn 2152 Hillside Rd Storrs CT 06269-3046. *Fax:* 860-486-3346; *E-Mail:* khaller@uconnvm.uconn.edu

HALLER, WILLIAM T, AQUATIC BOTANY, PLANT PHYSIOLOGY. *Current Pos:* Res assoc aquatic ecol, Agr Res Ctr, Univ Fla, 71-72, from asst prof to assoc prof aquatic bot, 74-84, dir, Ctr Aquatic Weeds, 83-85, PROF AGRON, UNIV FLA, 84- *Personal Data:* b Watertown, NY, June 28, 47; m 68; c 3. *Educ:* Cornell Univ, BS, 69; Univ Fla, MS, 71, PhD(agron), 74. *Concurrent Pos:* Prin investr, Fla Dept Natural Resources grants, 73-, US Army Corps Engrs grants, 77-, US Environ Protection Agency grant, 78-81 & US Agency Int Develop grant, 81-85; ed, Aquatic Plant Mgt Soc. *Mem:* Weed Sci Soc Am; Int Asn Aquatic Plant Biologists; Aquatic Plant Mgt Soc. *Res:* Aquatic weed control and effects of chemical, mechanical and biological aquatic weed control on the ecology of lakes and rivers; physiology of aquatic plants and interrelationships of aquatic plants and fish. *Mailing Add:* 3454 NW Tenth Ave Gainesville FL 32605

HALLER, WOLFGANG KARL, PHYSICAL CHEMISTRY, GLASS TECHNOLOGY. *Current Pos:* RES ASSOC & CONSULT, MAT SCI & ENG LAB, NAT INST STANDARDS & TECHNOL, WASHINGTON, DC, 84- *Personal Data:* b Vienna, Austria, Dec 9, 22; nat US. *Educ:* Univ Vienna, PhD(chem), 50. *Honors & Awards:* Gold Medal, US Dept Com, 73; Alexander von Humboldt Award, Ministry for Res & Technol, Fed Repub Ger, 75; Presidential Sci Medal, Rep Austria, 96. *Prof Exp:* Res assoc, Univ Vienna. 49-51; res chemist & Fulbright fel, Univ Wash, 51-52; res assoc, Univ Calif, Berkeley, 52-53; prof phys chem, Inst Silicate Res, Univ Toledo, 53-57; physicist, Inst Mat Sci & Technol, Nat Bur Standards, Washington, DC, 58-66, chief, Inorg Glass & Optical Mat Sect, 66-84. *Concurrent Pos:* vis prof, Max Planck Inst Protein Res, Munich, Ger, 68-69 & Inst Appl Phys & Chem, Univ Heidelburg, Ger, 75. *Mem:* Am Ceramic Soc; Brit Soc Glass Technol; Am Soc Microbiol. *Res:* Structure of glass; physics of surfaces; separation science; chromatography; microbiology. *Mailing Add:* 4620 N Park Ave Chevy Chase MD 20815-4557

HALLESY, DUANE WESLEY, ENVIRONMENTAL HEALTH. *Current Pos:* RETIRED. *Personal Data:* b Denton, Mont, Feb 2, 28; m 56, Mary E Althoen; c Duane M, Peter M & John D. *Educ:* Mont State Col, BS, 53; Univ Chicago, PhD(pharmacol), 56. *Prof Exp:* Res assoc pharmacol, Univ Chicago,

56-57; res pharmacologist, Lederle Labs Div, Am Cyanamid Co, 57-63, sr res pharmacologist & group leader, 63-65; sr indust toxicologist, Stand Oil Co Calif, 65-69; toxicologist, 69-71, mgr toxicol sect, 71-73, head, Toxicol Dept, 73-83, dir toxicol, Syntex Res Div, Syntex Corp, 83-88. *Mem:* AAAS; Soc Toxicol. *Res:* Preclinical safety evaluation of proposed new therapeutic agents. *Mailing Add:* 1555 S Mission Rd Tucson AZ 85746

HALLET, BERNARD, GEOLOGY, GLACIOLOGY. *Current Pos:* PROF, DEPT GEOL & QUATERNARY RES CTR, UNIV WASH, SEATTLE, 80- *Personal Data:* b Ciney, Belg, Sept 28, 48; m 74, Amy Heyneman; c Amber, Emily & Johnathon. *Educ:* Univ Calif, Los Angeles, BS, 70, PhD(geol), 75. *Prof Exp:* Asst prof geol & appl earth sci, Stanford Univ, 75-80. *Mem:* Int Glaciol Soc; Am Geophys Union; Geol Soc Am. *Res:* Glacial and periglacial geomorphology and permafrost studies; processes that shape landscape in arctic and alpine areas; glaciology. *Mailing Add:* Quaternary Res Ctr Box 351360 Univ Wash Seattle WA 98195-1360. *Fax:* 206-543-3836; *E-Mail:* hallet@u.washington.edu

HALLET, RAYMON WILLIAM, JR, THERMODYNAMICS, NUCLEAR ENGINEERING. *Current Pos:* CONSULT, 86- *Personal Data:* b Chicago, Ill, Nov 21, 20; m 44, Mary E Zried; c Julianna, Raymon W III & Christine. *Educ:* Purdue Univ, BS, 42; Univ Calif, Los Angeles, MS, 58. *Prof Exp:* Chief nuclear eng, Douglas Aircraft Co, McDonnell Douglas Corp, 62-64, dir res & develop, 64-66, vpres & dep gen mgr, Douglas United Nuclear, 66-70, dir energy systs, 72-74, prog mgr design integration, Univ I Pilot Plant, 78-84, dir solar progs, 84-86. *Concurrent Pos:* Consult, NSF, 73-74; mem solar energy rev bd, NSF, 73-75. *Mem:* Am Inst Aeronaut & Astronaut. *Res:* Application of solar energy to thermal electric power generation involving development of heliostats, solar boilers and thermal storage subsystems; nuclear propulsion systems. *Mailing Add:* 1906 Holiday Rd Newport Beach CA 92660

HALLETT, FREDERICK ROSS, BIOPHYSICS. *Current Pos:* From asst prof to assoc prof, 69-82, PROF PHYSICS, UNIV GUELPH, 82- *Personal Data:* b High River, Alta, July 14, 42; m 67, Barbara P Polisse; c Andrew & Amy. *Educ:* Univ Calgary, BSc, 63, MSc, 66; Pa State Univ, PhD(biophys), 69. *Concurrent Pos:* Dir, Guelph-Waterloo Prog Grad Work Physics, 90-93. *Mem:* Biophys Soc; Can Asn Physicists; Biophys Soc Can (pres, 93-94). *Res:* Photon correlation spectroscopic and small angle neutron scattering of vesicles and biopolymers in solution. *Mailing Add:* Dept Physics Univ Guelph Guelph ON N1G 2W1 Can. *Fax:* 519-836-9967; *E-Mail:* frh@physics.uoguelph.ca

HALLETT, JOHN, CLOUD PHYSICS. *Current Pos:* RES PROF ATMOSPHERIC PHYSICS, UNIV NEV, RENO, 66-, MARSTON CHAIR ATMOSPHERIC PHYSICS, 79-, DENT RES INST. *Personal Data:* b Bristol, UK, Dec 2, 29; m 60; c 4. *Educ:* Bristol Univ, BSc, 53; Imp Col, dipl, 54, Univ London, PhD(meteorol), 58. *Honors & Awards:* Dandini Medal Sci, 95. *Prof Exp:* Asst lectr meteorol, Imp Col, London, 58-60; asst prof, Univ Calif, Los Angeles, 60-62; lectr physics, Imp Col, London, 62-66. *Concurrent Pos:* Vis prof physics, Univ Manchester, Eng, 78; vis fel, Japan Soc Promotion Sci, 85. *Mem:* Fel Am Meteorol Soc; Glaciol Soc; fel Royal Meteorol Soc. *Res:* Laboratory studies of the mechanism of ice crystal growth from vapor and liquid; ice phase evolution in convective clouds in the atmosphere and its influence on cloud electrification; combustion aerosol physics and chemistry; role of aircraft exhaust on cirrus and climate. *Mailing Add:* Dept Physics Univ Nev Reno NV 89557

HALLETT, MARK, HUMAN MOTOR CONTROL, CLINICAL NEUROPHYSIOLOGY. *Current Pos:* CLIN PROF NEUROL, UNIFORMED SERVS UNIV HEALTH SCI, 87- *Personal Data:* b Philadelphia, Pa, Oct 22, 43; m 66, Judith Peller; c Nicholas & Victoria. *Educ:* Harvard Univ, BA, 65, MD, 69. *Prof Exp:* Intern med, Peter Bent Brigham Hosp, Boston, 69-70; staff assoc, Lab Neurobiol, NIMH, 70-72; resident neurol, Mass Gen Hosp, 72-74, chief resident, 74-75; dir, Neurophysiol Labs, Sect Neurol, Peter Bent Brigham Hosp, 76-84. *Concurrent Pos:* Clin fel med, Harvard Med Sch, 69-70, clin fel neurol, 72-75; from instr to assoc prof neurol, 76-84; guest lectr physiol, Howard Med Sch, 70-72; staff physician, Mass Rehab Hosp, Boston, 73-74, New Eng Baptist Hosp, 78-84, Parker Hill Hosp, 79-84, Brigham & Women's Hosp, 82-84; Moseley traveling fel-Harvard Med Sch, Dept Neurol, Inst Psychiat, London, Eng, 75-76; jr assoc med/neurol, Peter Bent Brigham Hosp, 76-77, assoc, 77-82; consult neurol, Robert Breck Brigham Hosp, 76-80 & Naval Hosp, Bethesda, Md, 84-; dir, Children's Hosp Med Ctr-Affil Hosps Ctr Inc Muscular Dystrophy Clin, 80-84, Neurol Div, Acute Rehab Unit, Brigham & Women's Hosp, 82-84; clin assoc prof neurol, Uniformed Servs Univ Health Sci, 84-86; clin dir, Nat Inst Neurol & Commun Dis & Stroke, NIH, 84-, chief, Human Motor Control Sect, dir, Clin Neurosci Prog, Div Intramural Res, 87-; assoc dir intramural res prog, Nat Inst Neurol & Commun Disorders & Stroke, NIH, 86-87; Carmichael fel, Inst Neurol, London, 96; Silversides vis prof, Univ Toronto. *Mem:* Fel Am Acad Neurol; Am Neurol Asn; Soc Neurosci; Am EEG Soc; Am Asn Electromyography & Electrodiag (secy-treas, 87-); Int Med Soc Motor Disturbances (pres, 88-). *Res:* Physiology of how the brain controls movement in humans; studies of normal physiology of and pathophysiology of both disordered voluntary movements and involuntary movements; myoclonus, bradykinesia and ataxia. *Mailing Add:* 5147 Westbard Ave Bethesda MD 20816. *Fax:* 301-402-1007; *E-Mail:* hallett@codon.nih.gov

HALLETT, PETER EDWARD, VISUAL PSYCHOPHYSICS, EYE MOVEMENTS & VISION THEORY. *Current Pos:* PROF PHYSIOL, UNIV TORONTO, 75-, PROF ZOOL, 79- *Personal Data:* b Sliemma, Malta, Apr 30, 37; Brit & Can citizen; m 60; c 3. *Educ:* Univ Oxford, BA, 58, BSc, 60, BM, 62, MA, 62. *Prof Exp:* Asst lectr physiol, Univ Col London, 63-65; asst prof, Univ Alta, 65-69. *Concurrent Pos:* Prof Biomed Eng, Univ Toronto, 85. *Mem:* Physiol Soc; Can Physiol Soc; Asn Res Vision & Ophthal; Optical Soc Am. *Res:* Behavioral and non-invasive approaches to human peripheral vision and its clinical assessment; human night vision and eye movements; optics, visual neuroanatomy and computational models. *Mailing Add:* Dept Physiol Univ Toronto Toronto ON M5S 1A8 Can

HALLEY, JAMES WOODS, (JR), THEORETICAL PHYSICS. *Current Pos:* assoc prof, 68-77, PROF PHYSICS, UNIV MINN, MINNEAPOLIS, 77- *Personal Data:* b Chicago, Ill, Nov 16, 38; m 70; c 2. *Educ:* Mass Inst Technol, BS, 61; Univ Calif, Berkeley, PhD(physics), 65. *Prof Exp:* NSF fel, Fac Sci, Orsay Ctr, Univ Paris, 65-66; asst prof physics, Univ Calif, Berkeley, 66-68. *Concurrent Pos:* Prin investr, NSF, Corrosion Res Ctr, 79-, Dept Energy, 91- & 93-, NASA, 93-96; vis scientist, Harvard, 79, Mich State Univ, 80 & 81, Argonne Nat Lab, 81-96, Univ Calif, Santa Barbara, 83-84, Australian Nat Univ, 88 & Univ Calif, Berkeley, 93; Bush fel, 83-84, Paul Flory IBM Sabbatical, 87, Nat Renewable Energy Lab, 94-97. *Mem:* Am Phys Soc; AAAS. *Res:* Theory of optical and other properties of normal and superfluid liquids; percolation theory; magnetic phase transitions and optical properties of magnetic materials; physics of human motion and human powered technology; polymers; physics of electrochemistry; electronic structure of oxides; high temperature superconductivity. *Mailing Add:* Dept Physics Univ Minn Minneapolis MN 55455. *E-Mail:* woods%jwh@vx.cis.umn.edu

HALLEY, ROBERT, UNDERWATER ACOUSTICS. *Current Pos:* RETIRED. *Personal Data:* b San Diego, Calif, Jan 5, 20; m 43, 63, Harriet Garfield; c 3. *Educ:* San Diego State Col, AB, 41; Univ Calif, Los Angeles, MA, 49. *Prof Exp:* Jr physicist, Div War Res, Univ Calif, 45-46; instr math & physics, San Diego State Col, 46 & 49-50; physicist, US Naval Ocean Systs Ctr, 49 & 50-77; physicist, Comput Sci Corp, 78-90. *Mem:* Acoust Soc Am. *Res:* Underwater sound, especially ambient sea noise and ship noise measurement; passive sonar target classification; information processing for classification. *Mailing Add:* 1714 Malden St San Diego CA 92109

HALLEY, ROBERT BRUCE, SEDIMENTOLOGY. *Current Pos:* GEOLOGIST, US GEOL SURV, 74- *Personal Data:* b Englewood, NJ, June 2, 47; m 68; c 1. *Educ:* Oberlin Col, AB, 69; Brown Univ, MS, 71; State Univ NY Stony Brook, PhD(geol), 74. *Prof Exp:* Res assoc geol, State Univ NY, Binghamton, 73-74. *Mem:* Sigma Xi; Soc Econ Paleontologists & Mineralogists; Am Asn Petrol Geologists. *Res:* Deposition and diagenesis of carbonate sediments. *Mailing Add:* 1153 Williams Dr S St Petersburg FL 33705

HALLFORD, DENNIS MURRAY, REPRODUCTIVE PHYSIOLOGY, ENDOCRINOLOGY. *Current Pos:* from asst prof to assoc prof, 75-83, PROF ANIMAL SCI, NMEX STATE UNIV, 83- *Personal Data:* b Abilene, Tex, Feb 11, 48; m 71, Marilyn Williams; c Amy. *Educ:* Tarleton State Univ, BS, 70; Okla State Univ, MS, 73, PhD(animal breeding), 75. *Prof Exp:* Instr animal sci, Tarleton State Univ, 70-71. *Mem:* Am Soc Animal Sci; Sigma Xi; Soc Study Reproduction. *Res:* Improving reproductive performance in domestic animals. *Mailing Add:* Dept Animal & Range Sci NMex State Univ Box 3I Las Cruces NM 88003

HALLFRISCH, JUDITH, NUTRITION, PUBLIC HEALTH & EPIDEMIOLOGY. *Current Pos:* sr staff fel, Nat Inst Aging, Beltsville Nutrit Ctr, NIH, 84-90, mem nutrit coordr comt, 87-91, res leader, Carbohydrate Lab, 91-93, Metab Lab, 93-97, RES LEADER, DIET & HUMAN PERFORMANCE, NAT INST AGING, BELTSVILLE NUTRIT CTR, NIH, 97- *Personal Data:* b Gary, Ind. *Educ:* Ind Univ, AB; Univ Md, PhD(nutrit sci). *Prof Exp:* Res nutritionist, Nutrit Inst, USDA, 74-84. *Concurrent Pos:* Prin investr, Geront Nutrit Study, Baltimore Longitudinal Study, 84-91; asst prof nutrit biochem, Univ Md, 84-; vis prof nutrit biochem, Med Sch, Johns Hopkins Univ, 86-, continuing educ prog, 86-87, asst prof med, 88. *Mem:* Am Asn Cereal Chemists; Am Col Nutrit; Am Inst Nutrit; Am Soc Clin Nutrit; Am Chem Soc; AAAS; Geront Soc Am. *Res:* Effects of various dietary carbohydrates on cardiac risk factors and diabetes indicators; effects of fiber on cardiac risk factors, mortality from heart disease and copper and zinc status in chronically ill patients; diet and performance in master's athletes over 50; bioavailability of ingested lead. *Mailing Add:* Carbohydrate Lab USDA ARS Human Nutrit Res Ctr Bldg 307 Rm 323 Beltsville MD 20705

HALLGREN, ALVIN ROLAND, FORESTRY, FOREST MANAGEMENT. *Current Pos:* RETIRED. *Personal Data:* b Aug 24, 19; US citizen; m 48, Dorothy Primmer; c Stephen W & Katherine J (Liverman). *Educ:* Univ Minn, BS, 49, PhD(forestry), 67; Yale Univ, MF, 50. *Prof Exp:* Asst dist forester, Crossett Co, 50-52, conserv forester, 53-55, asst wood mgt, 56-59, assoc prof, Cloquet Forestry Ctr, Univ Minn, 59-75, coordr & prof forestry, 75-87. *Concurrent Pos:* Chmn, Minn Timber Law Comt, 56-; forestry consult, St Paul Bd Water Comnrs, Minn, 57-75. *Res:* Timber laws; effects of mechanized harvesting. *Mailing Add:* 909 Jasper St Cloquet MN 55720

HALLGREN, HELEN M, HUMAN AGING. *Current Pos:* Asst prof, 76-84, ASSOC PROF IMMUNOL, UNIV MINN, 84- *Personal Data:* b Lancaster, Minn, Jan 6, 40; m 59; c 2. *Educ:* Univ Minn, MS, 75. *Honors & Awards:* Sci Creativity Award, Am Soc Med Technol, 87. *Mem:* Am Asn Immunologists; NY Acad Sci; AAAS; Acad Clin Lab Physicians & Scientists; Am Soc Med Technol. *Res:* Determination of the mechanisms underlying the decline in immune functions in aging humans. *Mailing Add:* Dept Lab Med & Path Univ Minn Box 609 UMHC 420 Delaware St SE Minneapolis MN 55455-0392. *Fax:* 612-625-5901; *E-Mail:* hallg001@maroon.tc.umn.edu

HALLGREN, RICHARD E, METEOROLOGY, PHYSICS. *Current Pos:* EXEC DIR, AM METEOROL SOC, 88- *Personal Data:* b Kersey, Pa, Mar 15, 32; m 54, Maxine H Anderson; c Scott, Douglas & Lynette. *Educ:* Pa State Univ, BS, 53, PhD(meteorol), 60. *Hon Degrees:* DSc, State Univ NY. *Honors & Awards:* Arthur S Fleming Award, 68; Gold Medal, US Dept Com, 69; Charles F Brooks Award, Am Meteorol Soc, 86; Int Meteorol Prize, World Meteorol Orgn, 90. *Prof Exp:* Res asst cloud physics, Pa State Univ, 56-60; opers res analyst, IBM Corp, 60-63, mgr meteorol systs, 63-64; sci adv to asst secy com, US Govt, 64-66; dir world weather systs, Environ Sci Serv Admin, 66-69; asst adminr environ systs, 69-71; assoc adminr environ monitoring & prediction, Nat Oceanic & Atmospheric Admin, 71-73; dep dir, Nat Weather Serv, 73-77; dep asst adminr, Oceanic & Atmospheric Servs, Nat Oceanic & Atmospheric Admin, 77-79; dir, 79-83, asst Adminr Weather Serv, Nat Weather Serv, 83-88. *Concurrent Pos:* US Rep, World Meteorol Orgn, 81-88. *Mem:* Fel Am Meteorol Soc (pres, 82); fel AAAS; Am Geophys Union; Oceanog Soc. *Res:* Cloud physics; atmospheric electricity; meteorological systems. *Mailing Add:* 11428 Cedar Ridge Dr Potomac MD 20854. *Fax:* 202-682-9298; *E-Mail:* hallgren@de.ametsoc.org

HALLIBURTON, LARRY EUGENE, SOLID STATE PHYSICS. *Current Pos:* from asst prof to assoc prof, 71-81, PROF PHYSICS, OKLA STATE UNIV, 81- *Personal Data:* b Cairo, Mo, Oct 13, 43; m 65; c 2. *Educ:* Univ Mo-Columbia, BS, 65, MS, 67, PhD(physics), 71. *Prof Exp:* Engr scientist microwave stand, Douglas Aircraft Co, 65-66. *Mem:* Am Phys Soc; Sigma Xi. *Res:* Investigations of impurities and other point defects in electro-optic, electro-acoustic, and laser materials using electron spin resonance, electron-nuclear double resonance, optical absorption, and luminescence techniques. *Mailing Add:* Dept Phys WVa Univ PO Box 6315 Morgantown WV 26506

HALLIDAY, IAN, METEORITICS, ASTROPHYSICS. *Current Pos:* res officer, 70-90, GUEST WORKER, NAT RES COUN CAN, 90- *Personal Data:* b Lloydminster, Sask, Nov 10, 28; m 51, Norma L Mobley; c John D & Janet E. *Educ:* Univ Toronto, BA, 49, MA, 50, PhD(astron), 54. *Honors & Awards:* Gold Medal, Royal Astron Soc Can, 49; Minor planet named in honor, 3944 Halliday, 86. *Prof Exp:* Astrophysicist, Dom Observ, Can Dept Mines & Tech Surv, 52-70. *Concurrent Pos:* Lectr, St Patrick's Col, 58-60; ed, Royal Astron Soc Can J, 70-75; mem steering group, Int Halley Watch, 81-90, chmn, 85-90. *Mem:* Int Astron Union; Am Astron Soc; Royal Astron Soc Can (pres, 80-82, hon pres, 89-93); Meteoritical Soc; Can Astron Soc; Planetary Soc; fel Royal Astron Soc Can. *Res:* Stellar and meteor spectra; positional astronomy; meteors; meteorite craters; diameter of Pluto; meteor spectroscopy; meteorite astronomy and recovery; comets. *Mailing Add:* Herzberg Inst Astrophys Nat Res Coun Can Ottawa ON K1A 0R6 Can

HALLIDAY, ROBERT WILLIAM, INORGANIC CHEMISTRY. *Current Pos:* RETIRED. *Personal Data:* b New York, NY, July 17, 42; m 64; c 3. *Educ:* Bates Col, BS, 64; Wesleyan Univ, MA, 66; Wayne State Univ, PhD(inorg chem), 69. *Prof Exp:* Asst prof, Adelphi Univ, 69-77, assoc prof inorg chem, 77-91. *Concurrent Pos:* Cottrell Corp res grant, Adelphi Univ, 70- *Res:* Preparation and characterization of inorganic coordination compounds; optical and magnetic properties of inorganic complexes; conformation and configuration of optically active coordination compounds. *Mailing Add:* 38 Park Way Sea Cliff NY 11579

HALLINAN, EDWARD JOSEPH, BIOLOGY. *Current Pos:* PROF, MORAVIAN COL, 94- *Personal Data:* b Bryn Mawr, Pa, Mar 27, 37. *Educ:* Niagara Univ, BS, 61; Cath Univ, MS, 65; Univ Notre Dame, PhD(biol), 76. *Prof Exp:* Instr biol, Allentown Col, 66-69; sci consult genetic control, WHO, Indian Coun Med Res Unit Genetic Control Culicine Mosquitoes, 73-74; asst prof biol, Allentown Col,74-76 assoc prof & chmn dept, 76-; at dept biol, Va Commonwealth Univ, 83-94. *Concurrent Pos:* Res grant, Div Parasitol & Entom, Univ Calif, Berkeley, 76-; vis lectr, XV Int Cong Entom, 76-; fel, Nat Endowment Humanities Sem Technol, Univ Calif, Los Angeles, 78-79. *Mem:* Entom Soc Am; Nat Sci Teacher Asn; Genetics Soc Am. *Res:* Cytogenetics of Aedes aegyptii; genetic control of insect pest species; radiation induced sterility in Culicine mosquitoes. *Mailing Add:* 2 Manor Dr East Stroudsburg PA 18301

HALLINAN, JOHN CORNELIUS, MECHANICAL ENGINEERING. *Current Pos:* ENG CONSULT, WASHINGTON, ILL, 85- *Personal Data:* b Philadelphia, Pa, Feb 12, 19; m 45, Eleanor R Denny; c Ann, Mary, Kathleen, Claire, Joan, John, Patricia, Mark, Michael, Joseph, William & Theresa. *Educ:* Villanova Univ, BSME, 40. *Honors & Awards:* Internal Combustion Engine Award, Am Soc Mech Engrs, 95. *Prof Exp:* Design & lab engr, Am Bosch, Springfield, Mass, 46-47; lab mgr, Baldwin Lima Hamilton, Eddystone, Pa, 47-54; res engr, Caterpillar Inc, Peoria, 54-62, lab mgr, 62-72, eng mgr, 72-85. *Mem:* Am Soc Mech Engrs; Soc Automotive Engrs. *Res:* Direction and management of the design and development of large engines; turbocharging of engines; conversion of diesel to spark ignited engines. *Mailing Add:* 700 Crestview Dr Washington IL 61571-1605

HALLINAN, THOMAS JAMES, AURORAL PHYSICS. *Current Pos:* engr TV, 65-76, asst prof, 76-81, ASSOC PROF GEOPHYSICS, UNIV ALASKA, 81- *Personal Data:* b Albany, NY, Sept 30, 41; m 64; c 2. *Educ:* Cornell Univ, BS, 64; Univ Alaska, MS, 69, PhD(geophysics), 76. *Prof Exp:* Engr TV, Cornell Univ, 64; engr TV, Aero-Geo-Astro, 64-65. *Mem:* Am Geophys Union; AAAS; Archaeol Inst Am; Nat Speleol Soc. *Res:* Detailed morphology of the Aurora Polaris using a stereo pair of low-light-level television cameras; experiments in space, including explosive chemical releases and accelerated electron beams. *Mailing Add:* 1617 Wolverine Lane Fairbanks AK 99709

HALLIWELL, ROBERT STANLEY, PLANT VIROLOGY. *Current Pos:* from asst prof to assoc prof, 62-71, PROF PLANT VIROL, TEX A&M UNIV, 71- *Personal Data:* b Lovell, Wyo, Sept 8, 31; m 54; c 3. *Educ:* Univ Wyo, BS, 56, MS, 59; Ore State Univ, PhD(plant path, biochem), 62. *Prof Exp:* Instr plant path, Ore State Univ, 60-62. *Concurrent Pos:* Consult, Food & Agr Orgn, UN, Korea, 74-75. *Mem:* Am Phytopath Soc. *Res:* Physiology of virus diseased plants; plant virus disease effects on individual cells. *Mailing Add:* 6069 Halliwell Lyda Rd Bryan TX 77808

HALLOCK, GILBERT VINTON, PSYCHIATRY. *Current Pos:* RETIRED. *Personal Data:* b Worcester, Mass, Oct 23, 25; c Candyce (Cummings) & Jason P. *Educ:* Harvard Univ, BA, 50; Tufts Univ, MD, 54. *Prof Exp:* Med Dir, Dir Prof Serv & Prof Info, Astra Pharmaceut Prod Inc, 56-73; dir Med Serv, Dome Labs Div, Miles Labs, 74; assoc med dir & assoc dir, Prof Serv, Lederle Labs Div, Am Cyanamid Co, 74-78; staff physician, Worcester State Hosp, 80-83. *Concurrent Pos:* Assoc med staff, Worcester City Hosp, 69-83, consult pharmacol, 77-83; consult pharmacol, Worcester Mem Hosp, 65-83; charter mem & dir, Drug Info Asn, 72-74. *Mem:* Drug Info Asn; Aerospace Med Asn; AMA; Am Med Writers Asn; Am Pub Health Asn; Am Col Gen Practice. *Res:* Research and development in the field of anesthetics, hematinics, dermatologicals and antibiotics. *Mailing Add:* 16 Duncannon Ave Apt 2 Worcester MA 01604-5128

HALLOCK, JAMES A, PEDIATRICS. *Current Pos:* DEAN, SCH MED, ECAROLINA UNIV, 88-, VCHANCELLOR HEALTH SCI, 90- *Personal Data:* b Paterson, NJ, Oct 28, 42; m 65, Jeanne La Rossa; c 3. *Educ:* Seton Hall Univ, AB, 63; Georgetown Univ, MD, 67. *Prof Exp:* Dir, Pediat Ambulatory Serv, Univ SFla, 75-77, asst med dir, Ambulatory Care Ctr, 76-77, assoc dean, Sch Med, 77-83 & 87-88, dep dean, 83-85, exec dean, 85-87. *Concurrent Pos:* Rep, Accreditation Coun Continuing Med Educ, 91-; vchmn, NC Joint Conf Med Care, 92. *Mem:* Southern Med Asn; AMA; Asn Am Med Cols; fel Am Acad Pediat; Nat Bd Med Examrs. *Res:* Medical education and health care delivery. *Mailing Add:* Sch Med ECarolina Univ Brody Bldg AD-48 Greenville NC 27858-4354

HALLOCK, ROBERT B, LOW TEMPERATURE PHYSICS, CONDENSED MATTER PHYSICS. *Current Pos:* from asst prof to assoc prof physics, 70-79, head, Dept Physics & Astron, 85-93, PROF PHYSICS, UNIV MASS, AMHERST, 79- *Personal Data:* b Washington, DC, Dec 9, 43; m 65, Norma; c Robert W & Kevin F. *Educ:* Univ Mass, BS, 65; Stanford Univ, MS, 67, PhD(physics), 69. *Prof Exp:* Air Force Off Sci Res-Nat Res Coun fel, Stanford Univ, 69-70. *Concurrent Pos:* A P Sloan res fel, Univ Mass, Amherst, 72-76; prin investr, NSF Grants, 72-; vis prof, Brown Univ, 74, Cornell Univ, 77-78; Fulbright fel, 77-78; adj prof polymer sci & eng, Univ Mass, 85-; J S Guggenheim fel, 92-93; mem, NASA low temperature steering group, 92-96; NASA fundamental physics steering group, 96- *Mem:* Fel Am Phys Soc; Am Asn Physics Teachers. *Res:* Macroscopic quantization effects in He II; nuclear magnetic resonance in 3He-4He mixtures; properties of persistent currents and third sound in helium films; super fluid onset; conducting polymers; classical localization of helium waves; polarized quantum systems; viscosity and boundary kinetics of polymer solutions; antibody-antigen kinetics at surfaces; transport measurements in novel conducting systems; porous media; capillary condensation; wetting phenomena. *Mailing Add:* Dept Physics & Astron Univ Mass Amherst MA 01003. *Fax:* 413-545-1691; *E-Mail:* hallock@phast.umass.edu

HALLOCK, ZACHARIAH R, PHYSICS. *Current Pos:* PHYS OCEANOGR, NAVAL OCEANOG & ATMOSPHERIC RES LAB, 81- *Personal Data:* b Southampton, NY, June 27, 42; m 66; c 2. *Educ:* Polytech Inst Brooklyn, BS, 70; Univ Miami, MS, 73, PhD(phys oceanog), 77. *Prof Exp:* Phys oceanogr, US Naval Oceanog Off, 77-81. *Mem:* Am Geophys Union. *Res:* Design and implementation of oceanographic measurement programs; analysis and interpretation of data from oceanographic observations and evaluation of theoretical predictions. *Mailing Add:* 5546 Pecan Haven Lane Long Beach MS 39560. *Fax:* 228-688-5997; *E-Mail:* hallock@zrh.nrlssc.navy.mil

HALLOCK-MULLER, PAMELA, CARBONATE SEDIMENTOLOGY, CORAL REEF ECOLOGY. *Current Pos:* assoc prof, 83-88, PROF MARINE SCI, UNIV SFLA, 88- *Personal Data:* b Pierre, SDak, June 2, 48; m 69, Robert G. *Educ:* Univ Mont, BA, 69; Univ Hawaii, Manoa, MS, 72, PhD(oceanog), 77. *Honors & Awards:* W Storrs Cole Mem Award, Geol Soc Am, 94. *Prof Exp:* Asst prof, earth sci, Univ Tex, Permian Basin, 78-83. *Concurrent Pos:* Environ consult, Hawaiian Elec Co Inc, 75-77; res fel, Univ Copenhagen, 78 & Kiel Univ, 79 & Gollard Space Flight Ctr, 87; consult, Cities Serv Co, 81; prin investr, NSF grants, 81-94; assoc ed, J Foraminiferal Res; consult, Continental Shelf Asn, 88-89; bd dirs, Cushman Found Foraminiferal Res, 90- *Mem:* Fel Geol Soc Am; Soc Sedimentary Geologists; Asn Women Geoscientists; Paleont Soc; fel Cushman Found Foraminiferal Res(vpres, 92 & 94, pres, 95-96). *Res:* Role of nutrients in coral reefs, carbonate sedimentology and paleoceanography; role of algal symbiosis in carbonate production, community structure and evolution; larger foraminiferal ecology/paleoecology and response to ultraviolet B. *Mailing Add:* Dept Marine Sci Univ SFla St Petersburg FL 33701. *Fax:* 813-893-9189; *E-Mail:* pmuller@.marine.usf.edu

HALLOIN, JOHN MCDONELL, PLANT PHYSIOLOGY, PLANT PATHOLOGY. *Current Pos:* res plant physiologist, Nat Cotton Path Res Lab, Col Sta, Tex, 72-87, RES PLANT PHYSIOLOGIST, USDA, AGR RES SERV, E LANSING, MICH, 87- *Personal Data:* b Green Bay, Wis, Aug 14, 38; m 67; c 2. *Educ:* Univ Wis-Madison, BS, 60; Univ Minn, St Paul, MS, 64; Mich State Univ, PhD(bot), 68. *Prof Exp:* Asst plant physiol, Univ Minn, St Paul, 60-64; res fel plant path, Univ Wis, 68-71; asst prof bot, Mich State Univ,

71; res assoc biochem, Iowa State Univ, 71-72. *Concurrent Pos:* Mem grad fac, Tex A&M Univ, 73-87; mem fac, Mich State Univ, 88- *Mem:* Am Phytopath Soc; Am Soc Sugar-Beet Technologists; Am Soc Agron; Crop Sci Soc Am; Sigma Xi. *Res:* Studies the nature and heritability of resistance to sugarbeet diseases; nuclear magnetic resonance imaging of plants and independent research and consulting on seed quality and the nature and heritability of resistance to seed deterioration and seedling disease. *Mailing Add:* 4805 Arapaho Trail Okemos MI 48864

HALLORAN, HOBART, POULTRY NUTRITION, ANIMAL NUTRITION. *Current Pos:* RETIRED. *Personal Data:* b San Francisco, Calif, Jan 8, 16; m 38; c 1. *Educ:* Univ Calif, Berkeley, BS, 37. *Honors & Awards:* Poultry Scientist of Year, Pac Egg & Poultry Asn. *Prof Exp:* Chemist & salesman, Adhesive Prod, Inc, 38-39; chemist & plant mgr, Farallone Div, Borden Co, 39-43; vpres & mgr, Feed Prod Div, Collett-Week-Nibecker, Inc, 43-48; res dir, Poultry Producers Cent Calif, 48-56; pres, Halloran Consult, 56-90. *Concurrent Pos:* Mem, Agr Adv Comt, Univ Calif, 64-67; assoc ed, Poultry Sci; life mem, Nutrit Coun, Am Feed Indust Asn; nutrit consult. *Mem:* Fel Poultry Sci Asn; Am Chem Soc; Animal Nutrit Res Coun; Am Inst Nutrit; Worlds Poultry Sci Asn. *Res:* Poultry feed ingredients; new ingredient development; ingredient improvement; computer evaluation; research planning and reviewing; technical service functions. *Mailing Add:* 8801 Bainbridge Pl Stockton CA 95209

HALLORAN, PHILIP FRANCIS, MEDICINE, SURGERY. *Current Pos:* DIR, DIV NEPHROL/IMMUNOL, UNIV ALTA, 91- *Personal Data:* b Ont, Can, June 44; c 3. *Educ:* Univ Toronto, MD, 68, FKCP(C), 73; Univ London, PhD(immunol), 76. *Prof Exp:* Assoc prof med, 80-87, assoc prof surg, Univ Toronto, 81-, prof med, 87- *Concurrent Pos:* Staff physician, Mt Sinai & Toronto Gen Hosp, 75-; dir renal transplantation, Tri-Hosp Nephrol Serv, 75- *Mem:* Can Soc Immunologists; Can Soc Nephrology; Am Soc Nephrol; Am Fedn Clin Res; Am Asn Immunologists; Am Soc Clin Invest. *Mailing Add:* Div Nephrol & Immunol Univ Alberta Rm 205 8249 114th St Edmonton AB T6G 2R8 Can. *Fax:* 403-431-0461

HALLS, LOWELL KEITH, RANGE CONSERVATION. *Current Pos:* RETIRED. *Personal Data:* b Monticello, Utah, May 7, 18; m 46; c 5. *Educ:* Colo State Univ, BS, 47; Tex A&M Univ, MS, 48. *Honors & Awards:* Outstanding Forest Res, Tex Forestry Asn, 73. *Prof Exp:* Instr range mgt, Colo State Univ, 48-49; range conservationist, Southeastern Forest Exp Sta, Ga, 49-57, res forester, Southern Forest & Range Exp Sta, La, 57-61, range conservationist, Forest Serv, USDA, 61-81. *Concurrent Pos:* Part-time instr, Sch Forestry, Stephen F Austin State Univ, 69-79. *Mem:* Soc Range Mgt; Wildlife Soc; Soc Am Foresters. *Res:* Forest wildlife habitat; grazing on forest lands; coordination of wildlife, cattle and timber production. *Mailing Add:* 2720 Dogwood Dr Nacogdoches TX 75961

HALLUM, CECIL RALPH, APPLIED STATISTICS, MEDICAL STATISTICS. *Current Pos:* AT DEPT MATH, UNIV HOUSTON, CLEAR LAKE. *Personal Data:* b Stamford, Tex, Jan 6, 44; m 64; c 2. *Educ:* Tex Tech Univ, BS, 66, MS, 69, PhD(math statist), 72. *Prof Exp:* Teaching asst math, Tex Tech Univ, 66-68, consult statistician, 68-72; assoc prof math, Loyola Univ, La, 72-78; aerospace technician, Earth Observ Div, Johnson Space Flight Ctr, NASA, 78- *Concurrent Pos:* NASA traineeship, 67-69; consult statist, La State Univ Med Ctr. *Mem:* Am Statist Asn; Int Inst Statist. *Res:* Remote sensing in the area of medical statistics, experimental designs and music therapy. *Mailing Add:* Dept Math Sam Houston State Univ Huntsville TX 77341-1001

HALLUM, JULES VERNE, virology, for more information see previous edition

HALM, DAN ROBERT, EPITHELIAL ION TRANSPORT. *Current Pos:* Res fel, 81-85, RES ASST PROF PHYSIOL, DEPT PHYSIOL, UNIV ALA BIRMINGHAM, 85- *Personal Data:* b Fort Dodge, Iowa, Apr, 25, 55; m 86; c 1. *Educ:* Univ Iowa, BA, 77 & PhD(physiol), 81. *Concurrent Pos:* Prin investr, Nat Inst Healt grants. *Mem:* Am Physiol Soc; Biophys Soc. *Res:* Regulation of electrolyte transport across epithelial tissues; measurement of ion flow across the epithelium and the membranes of epithelial cells during activiation of these processes. *Mailing Add:* Dept Physiol Ohio State Univ 1645 Neil Ave Columbus OH 43210-1239

HALMI, NICHOLAS STEPHEN, ENDOCRINOLOGY. *Current Pos:* DEPT ANAT, MT SINAI SCH MED, NY. *Personal Data:* b Budapest, Hungary, June 6, 22; nat US; m 63; c 2. *Educ:* Univ Budapest, MD, 47. *Honors & Awards:* Ciba Award, Endocrine Soc, 57. *Prof Exp:* Asst path, St Johns Hosp, Budapest, 45-47; asst anat, Univ Pecs, 47-49; instr, Univ Chicago, 49-50; from instr to assoc prof, 50-58, prof anta, 58-, prof physiol, 66-, prof endocrinol, 69- *Concurrent Pos:* NSF sr fel, 61-62; mem endocrinol study sect, NIH, 62-66. *Mem:* AAAS; Soc Exp Biol & Med; Am Asn Anat; Am Thyroid Soc; Am Physiol Soc. *Res:* Pituitary histophysiology; hypothalamic regulation of adenohypophysis; thyroid regulation; staining techniques; morphogenesis of pituitary tumors; metabolism of iodide. *Mailing Add:* 200 Winston Dr No 707 Cliffside Park NJ 07010-3214

HALMOS, PAUL RICHARD, PURE MATHEMATICS. *Current Pos:* prof, 84-96, EMER PROF MATH, SANTA CLARA UNIV, 96- *Personal Data:* b Budapest, Hungary, Mar 3, 16; nat US; m 45. *Educ:* Univ Ill, BS, 34, MS, 35, PhD(math), 38. *Hon Degrees:* DSc, Univ St Andrews, 80, DePauw Univ, 80, LHD, Kalamazoo Col, 86. *Prof Exp:* Asst math, Univ Ill, 35-36, instr, 38-39, assoc, 42-43; fel, Inst Advan Study, 39-40, asst, 40-42; asst prof math, Syracuse Univ, 43-46; from asst prof to prof, Univ Chicago, 46-61; prof, Univ Mich, 61-68; prof & chmn dept, Univ Hawaii, 68-69; prof, Ind Univ, Bloomington, 69-70, distinguished prof math, 70-84. *Concurrent Pos:* Mem staff, Radiation Lab, Mass Inst Technol, 45; Guggenheim fel, Inst Advan Study, 47-48; prof, Univ Montevideo, 51-52, Univ Calif, Santa Barbara, 76-78. *Mem:* Am Math Soc; Math Asn Am; fel Royal Soc Edinburgh; Hungarian Acad Sci. *Res:* Measure theory; Hilbert space; algebraic logic. *Mailing Add:* 2155 Emory St San Jose CA 95128. *Fax:* 408-554-2370; *E-Mail:* phalmos@scuacc.scu.edu

HALONEN, MARILYN JEAN, IMMUNOLOGY. *Current Pos:* technician biochem, Univ Ariz, 68-69, from res asst to res assoc immunol, 69-77, adj asst prof med, 77-83, res assoc prof internal med, 83-92, assoc prof, 87-92, PROF PHARMACOL, UNIV ARIZ, 92- *Personal Data:* b Duluth, Minn, July 8, 41; m 80; c 1. *Educ:* Univ Minn, BS, 63; Iowa State Univ, MS, 68; Univ Ariz, PhD(molecular biol), 74. *Honors & Awards:* Res Career Develop Award, NIH, 78. *Prof Exp:* Instr hemat, State Univ NY, Buffalo, 63-64; technician org chem, Univ Chicago, 64-65; med technologist clin path, Mercy Hosp, Des Moines, Iowa, 65-66. *Concurrent Pos:* Prin investr NIH grant, 77- *Mem:* Am Asn Immunologists; Int Soc Immunopharmacol; Am Thoracic Soc; Am Acad Allergy & Immunol; Am Soc Pharmacol & Exp Therapeut. *Res:* Mechanism of IgE-induced acute allergic reactions; the capacity of IgE to alter neuronal regulation of airways; relationship of IgE to asthma. *Mailing Add:* Respiratory Sci Ctr Univ Ariz 1501 N Campbell Tucson AZ 85724-0001. *Fax:* 520-626-6970

HALOULAKOS, VASSILIOS E, ENGINEERING, APPLIED MATHEMATICS. *Current Pos:* PRES, CONSULT SERV 21ST CENTURY TECHNOL & EDUC PROGS, VEH ASSOC/CONSULT, 96- *Personal Data:* b Gytheion, Greece, Jan 13, 31; US citizen; m 53; c 1. *Educ:* Univ Southern Calif, BSME, 59, MSAE, 62, EngrD(aeronaut eng), 65. *Hon Degrees:* LHD, WCoast Univ, 95. *Prof Exp:* Sr engr, Rocketdyne Div, NAm Rockwell Corp, 59- 66, spec lectr, 65-66; sr staff mem, Mech Res, Inc, 66; supvr res & develop propulsion, McDonnell Douglas Space Systs, 66-77, propulsion specialist, exotic propulsion, 77-96. *Concurrent Pos:* Sr lectr, WCoast Univ, 66-, mem bd trustees, 81-85; spec consult math, Los Angeles Sch Dist; vpres bd dir, Calif Acad Decathalon. *Mem:* Assoc fel Am Inst Aeronaut & Astronaut; fel Inst Advan Eng; Nat Space Soc. *Res:* Propulsion, flight mechanics, space nuclear power and propulsion, spacecraft control dynamics and systems analysis; uses of new mathematical techniques in solution of novel-type problems; missile propulsion; energy management systems; organized and lectured national courses on nuclear propulsion; physics; science education; airplane accident investigations and resolutions rockets and space vehicle malfunction expert. *Mailing Add:* 1031 Fairmount Rd Burbank CA 91501. *Fax:* 818-563-1541

HALPER, JAROSLAVA, CELL BIOLOGY. *Current Pos:* asst prof path, 86-91, ASSOC PROF PATH, COL VET MED, UNIV GA, 91- *Personal Data:* b Prague, Czech, Aug 1, 53; Can citizen; m 79, Edward C; c 3. *Educ:* Univ Toronto, MD, 80; Univ Minn, PhD(path), 86. *Prof Exp:* Resident path, Albert Einstein Col Med, 80-81; fel exp path, Mayo Clin/Found, 81-82, resident path, 82-86. *Concurrent Pos:* Clinician-investr, Mayo Clin/Found, 84-86; res assoc cell biol, Vanderbilt Univ, 85-86. *Mem:* AAAS; Wound Healing Soc; Am Soc Cell Biol; US Acad Path; Am Soc Invest Path; Can Acad Path. *Res:* Characterization of a novel (transforming) growth factor; cell and molecular biology; protein purification; biochemistry; growth factors in growth, development and wound healing. *Mailing Add:* Dept Path Col Vet Med Univ Ga Athens GA 30602-7388. *Fax:* 706-542-5828; *E-Mail:* halper.j@calc.vet.uga.edu

HALPERIN, BERTRAND ISRAEL, SOLID STATE PHYSICS, STATISTICAL MECHANICS. *Current Pos:* chmn, Physics Dept, 88-91, PROF PHYSICS, HARVARD UNIV, 76-, HOLLIS PROF MATH & NATURAL PHILOS. *Personal Data:* b Brooklyn, NY, Dec 6, 41; m 62, Helena S French; c Jeffery A & Julia S. *Educ:* Harvard Univ, AB, 61; Univ Calif, Berkeley, MA, 63, PhD(physics), 65. *Honors & Awards:* Oliver Buckley Prize, Am Phys Soc, 82. *Prof Exp:* NSF fel physics, Univ Paris, 65-66; mem tech staff, Bell Tel Labs, 66-76. *Concurrent Pos:* Lectr, Harvard Univ, 69-70; assoc ed, Rev Modern Physics, 73-80. *Mem:* Nat Acad Sci; Am Phys Soc; Am Acad Arts & Sci; Am Philos Soc. *Res:* Theory of disordered systems, critical phenomena, magnetism, metal-insulator transitions, two-dimensional systems and electrons in strong magnetic fields. *Mailing Add:* Dept Physics Harvard Univ Cambridge MA 02138. *Fax:* 617-495-0416

HALPERIN, JANET R P, NEURAL MODELLING OF ADAPTIVE BEHAVIOR, AUTONOMOUS BIO-MIMIC ROBOTICS DESIGN. *Current Pos:* res assoc, Dept Zool, 90-92, Ethology, 93-94, ADJ PROF, DEPT ZOOL, UNIV TORONTO, 94- *Personal Data:* b Winnipeg, Man, Mar 17, 50; c 2. *Educ:* Univ Toronto, BSc, MSc, 80, PhD(zool), 90. *Prof Exp:* Leverhulme fel, Dept Artificial Intel, Univ Edinburgh, 92-93. *Concurrent Pos:* Assoc ed, Adaptive Behav, 91-; dir res, Neurobotics Inc, 93- *Res:* Principles of adaptive behavior, and neural mechanisms to achieve adapted, autonomous behavior. *Mailing Add:* Dept Zool Univ Toronto 25 Harbord St Toronto ON M5S 1A1 Can. *Fax:* 416-978-8532; *E-Mail:* janh@zoo.toronto.edu

HALPERIN, JOSEPH, INORGANIC CHEMISTRY, NUCLEAR CHEMISTRY. *Current Pos:* RETIRED. *Personal Data:* b Gomel, Russia, Apr 1, 23; nat US; m 51; c 4. *Educ:* Univ Chicago, BS, 43, MS, 50, PhD(chem), 51. *Prof Exp:* Asst chem, Metall Lab, Univ Chicago, 43; assoc chemist, Clinton Lab, Tenn, 44-46; chemist, Oak Ridge Nat Lab, 51-87. *Mem:* AAAS; Am Chem Soc; Sigma Xi; Am Phys Soc; Am Nuclear Soc. *Res:* Heavy element chemistry and physics. *Mailing Add:* 8904 SW 42d Pl Gainesville FL 32608-4417

HALPERIN, STEPHEN, RATIONAL HOMOTOPY THEORY. *Current Pos:* From asst prof to assoc prof, 70-79, PROF MATH, UNIV TORONTO, 79- *Personal Data:* b Kingston, Ont, Feb 1, 42; m 79, Janet; c Nicole & Adam. *Educ:* Univ Toronto, BSc, 65, MSC, 66; Cornell Univ, PhD(math), 70. *Honors & Awards:* Jeffery-Williams Lectr, Can Math Soc. *Concurrent Pos:* Vis scientist, Univ Bonn, 81; vis prof, Univ de Nice, 86, Univ de Lille, 95; bol dir, Fields Inst, Res Math Sci, 95-96; mem, Reallocations Comt, Natural Sci & Eng Res Coun, 97- *Mem:* Fel Royal Soc Can; Can Math Soc; Am Math Soc. *Res:* Rational homotopy theory, with a particular interest in the loop spaces of finite complexes. *Mailing Add:* Dept Math Univ Toronto Toronto ON M5S 1A1 Can. *E-Mail:* nalper@math.toronto.edu

HALPERIN, WALTER, BOTANY. *Current Pos:* from asst prof to assoc prof, 68-88, PROF BOT, UNIV WASH, 88- *Personal Data:* b San Jose, Calif, Oct 20, 32; m 56; c 2. *Educ:* Brown Univ, AB, 54; Univ Conn, PhD(bot), 65. *Prof Exp:* Asst prof bot, Univ Mass, 66-68. *Mem:* AAAS; Bot Soc Am; Am Soc Plant Physiol. *Res:* Physiology of growth and development in plants. *Mailing Add:* Dept Bot KB-15 Univ Wash 3900 Seventh Ave NE Seattle WA 98195-0001

HALPERIN, WILLIAM PAUL, LOW TEMPERATURE PHYSICS, NUCLEAR MAGNETIC RESONANCE. *Current Pos:* from asst prof to assoc prof, 75-86, chmn, Dept Physics & Astron, 90-95, PROF PHYSICS, NORTHWESTERN UNIV, EVANSTON, 86- *Personal Data:* b Ottawa, Ont, July 16, 45; m 68, Eileen A Yamamoto; c Milo, Chrisitina & Lise. *Educ:* Queen's Univ, Ont, BSc, 67; Univ Toronto, MSc, 68; Cornell Univ, PhD(physics), 75. *Prof Exp:* Fel physics, Cornell Univ, 74-75. *Concurrent Pos:* Fac res partic, Argonne Nat Lab, 75-; Alfred P Sloan fel, 77; Yamada Found fel, 84. *Mem:* Fel Am Phys Soc. *Res:* Thermal and magnetic properties of liquid helium 3, solid helium 3, solutions of helium 3 in helium 4; superfluidity; superconductivity; cryogenic devices; absolute thermometry; nuclear magnetic resonance; platinum metal particles; molecular diffusion; organic; metals and magnets; porous materials; cementitious materials; vortex dynamics in superconductors; molecular magnets and conductors. *Mailing Add:* Dept Physics Northwestern Univ Evanston IL 60208. *E-Mail:* w-halperin@nwu.edu

HALPERIN-MAYA, MIRIAM PATRICIA, PURE MATHEMATICS. *Current Pos:* SYST DESIGNER, INTERLEAF, 92- *Personal Data:* b Brooklyn, NY, July 1, 45; c 2. *Educ:* Radcliffe Col, AB, 66; Brandeis Univ, MA, 68, PhD(math), 73. *Prof Exp:* Asst prof math, Univ Md, College Park, 72-74 & Tufts Univ, 74-80; syst designer, Camex Co, 80-88, consult, 88-92. *Mem:* Asn Comput Mach; Math Asn Am; Asn Women in Math. *Res:* Singularities of algebraic and complex analytic varieties; equisingularities; equivalence of zerocycles on algebraic varieties; computer graphics including scan conversion, splines, image representations and manipulations. *Mailing Add:* 25 Marshall St Brookline MA 02146

HALPERIN, ALVIN M, ATOMIC PHYSICS. *Current Pos:* from instr to assoc prof, 65-74, chmn dept, 80-90, PROF PHYSICS, BROOKLYN COL, 75-, EXEC DIR, APPL SCI INST, 90- *Personal Data:* b New York, NY, July 17, 38; m 66; c 2. *Educ:* Columbia Col, AB, 59; Columbia Univ, MA, 61, PhD(physics), 65. *Prof Exp:* Instr physics, Pratt Inst, 64-65. *Concurrent Pos:* Recipient & dir, NSF educ grants, 70-71 & 72-74, co-prin investr, NSF res grant, 78-80 & 80-82; vis guest scientist, Internat Ctr Theoret Physics, Trieste, Italy & Theoret Chem Dept, Oxford Univ, 73. *Mem:* Am Phys Soc; Am Asn Physics Teachers; AAAS; NY Acad Sci. *Res:* Theoretical studies of atomic scattering processes, especially charge transfer, charge exchange, excitation, and ionization of atoms and ions. *Mailing Add:* Dept Physics Brooklyn Col Brooklyn NY 11210

HALPERIN, ARTHUR MERRILL, PHYSICAL CHEMISTRY, SPECTROSCOPY. *Current Pos:* PROF & CHMN, IND STATE UNIV, 90- *Personal Data:* b Bayonne, NJ, Aug 4, 43; m 66; c 4. *Educ:* Rutgers Univ, New Brunswick, BA, 64; Northeastern Univ, PhD(phys chem), 68. *Prof Exp:* Fel, Univ Minn, Minneapolis, 68-70; vis mem staff, Bell Tel Labs, 70; asst prof chem, NY Univ, Bronx, 70-73; from asst prof to prof chem, Northeastern Univ, 73-90. *Concurrent Pos:* Indust consult; Alfred P Sloan res fel, 74-76; sr sci fel, NATO, 80. *Mem:* Am Chem Soc; AAAS; Am Phys Soc; Europ Photochem Asn; Inter-Am Photochem Soc. *Res:* Photophysics of organic molecules especially saturated amines; measurement of fast luminescence phenomena; photokinetics/photoassociation; laser spectroscopy; chemical education. *Mailing Add:* Dept Chem Ind State Univ Terre Haute IN 47809-0001

HALPERIN, BENJAMIN DAVID, CHEMISTRY, CHEMICAL ENGINEERING. *Current Pos:* PRES, POLYSCI INC, 63- *Personal Data:* b Malden, Mass, May 19, 21; m 51; c 5. *Educ:* Mass Inst Technol, BS, 43; Univ Notre Dame, PhD(chem), 49. *Prof Exp:* Chem engr & proj leader polymerization, Rohm & Haas Co, 43-49; res dir med specialties, Dajac Labs, 49-55; res dir, Borden Chem Co, 55-63. *Concurrent Pos:* Mem staff, Monomer-Polymer, Inc, 49-51, treas, 51-53, secy & pres, 53-55; vis prof, Hahnemann Med Col; pres, Polaron Instruments, Inc. *Mem:* Am Chem Soc; NY Acad Sci; Electron Micros Soc; Asn Consult Chemists & Chem Engrs (past pres); Histochem Soc. *Res:* Polymers; monomers; organic intermediates; monomer synthesis; polymerization; medical specialties; medical application of polymers; materials and chemicals for life sciences. *Mailing Add:* Materia Medica Inc PO Box 4040 Rydal PA 19046

HALPERN, BERNARD, BACTERIOLOGY. *Current Pos:* RETIRED. *Personal Data:* b Chicago, Ill, Feb 13, 18; m 41; c 3. *Educ:* Univ Ill, BS, 39, MS, 42; Northwestern Univ, PhD(bact), 57. *Prof Exp:* Jr bacteriologist, Michael Reese Hosp, 39-43; res bacteriologist, St Luke's Hosp, 46-51; from asst prof to assoc prof microbiol, Obstet & Gynec, Med Sch, Northwestern Univ, Chicago, 62-88. *Mem:* Am Soc Microbiol. *Res:* Immunology research, especially carbohydrate metabolism, choriocarcinoma (trophoblastic disease) and amebiasis; growth of mycobacteria tuberculosis. *Mailing Add:* 17725 Stonebridge Dr Hazel Crest IL 60429

HALPERN, BRUCE PETER, NEUROSCIENCES, TASTE. *Current Pos:* assoc prof psychol & biol, Cornell Univ, 66-73, field rep psychol, Grad Sch, 70-73, chmn, Dept Psychol, 74-80 & 90-95, SUSAN LINN SAGE PROF PSYCHOL, NEUROBIOL & BEHAV, CORNELL UNIV, 95- *Personal Data:* b Newark, NJ, Aug 18, 33; m 56, Pauline T; c Michael T & Stacey R. *Educ:* Rutgers Univ, AB, 55; Brown Univ, ScM, 57, PhD(physiol psychol), 59. *Prof Exp:* NIH vis fel physiol, Cornell Univ, 59-61, res assoc, 59-60, lectr, 60-61; asst prof, Health Sci Ctr, State Univ NY, 61-66. *Concurrent Pos:* Consult, Behav Sci Div, Food Sci Lab, US Army Natick Develop Ctr, 73, vis scientist, 73-74; consult, NSF Sensory Physiol & Perception Prog, 77-79; mem commun bi panel, Nat Inst Neurol & Commun Dis & Stroke, NIH, 77-79; Fogarty Sr Int fel, Osaka Univ, 82; mem, Sensory Prog Adv Comt, NIH, 84-87; exec ed, Chem Senses, 84-88; chmn, Gordon Conf Chem Senses, 87-90; mem, Int Comn Olfaction & Taste, 85-94; vis scientist, Monell Chem Senses Ctr, 96-97. *Mem:* Asn Chemoreception Sci; Am Physiol Soc. *Res:* Sensory physiology; sensory function, especially in gustation; relation between environmental energy, neural responses and chemosensory behavior. *Mailing Add:* Dept Psychol Uris Hall Cornell Univ Ithaca NY 14853-7601. *Fax:* 607-255-8433; *E-Mail:* bph1@cornell.edu

HALPERN, DANIEL, MEDICINE. *Current Pos:* RETIRED. *Personal Data:* b New York, NY, May 28, 17; m 43; c 3. *Educ:* NY Univ, BA, 36; Chicago Med Sch, MD, 43. *Prof Exp:* Pvt pract, 48-58; instr phys med & rehab, Bird S Coler Hosp, New York Med Col, 61-62; from asst prof to assoc prof, Children's Rehab Ctr, Univ Hosps, Univ Minn, 62-74, prof phys med & rehab, 74-80. *Concurrent Pos:* Mem, Interdisciplinary Adv Comt Active Nursing Home Care, Minneapolis Dept Health, 63; consult, Minneapolis Area Study Educ Serv, Multiply Handicapped Sch Children, 68; med consult, St Paul Sch Syst, 71-; mem, Comt Nursing Home Rehab & Stand, Minn Dept Welfare, 72; consult, Educ Prog Handicapped Children, St Paul Sch Syst, 72-74; mem spec consult comt, Dakota's Children's Nursing Home, Hill Found, 73-74; adj prof rehab med, Univ Wis-Madison Med Sch, 80- *Mem:* Am Acad Pediat; Am Acad Phys Med & Rehab; Am Acad Cerebral Palsy; Am Cong Phys Med & Rehab. *Res:* Learning of motor skills in handicapped and normal individuals; mechanisms of abnormal muscle tone and evaluation of treatment; special learning disabilities in handicapped children. *Mailing Add:* 200 Tanglewood Dr South Chatham MA 02659-1426

HALPERN, DAVID, PHYSICAL OCEANOGRAPHY, OCEAN-ATMOSPHERE INTERATIONS. *Current Pos:* SR RES SCIENTIST, JET PROPULSION LAB, CALIF INST TECHNOL, PASADENA, 88-; ADJ PROF, ATMOSPHERIC SCI, UNIV CALIF, LOS ANGELES, 89-, MGR, JPL CLIMATE VARIABILITY PROG, 96- *Personal Data:* b Montreal, Que, June 24, 42; m 66, Tema Kovack; c Michael & Lisa. *Educ:* McGill Univ, BSc, 64; Mass Inst Technol, PhD(phys oceanog), 69. *Honors & Awards:* Graham Medal, 62-63; Silver Medal, Dept Com, 81. *Prof Exp:* Res assoc phys oceanog, Mass Inst Technol, 69; oceanogr, Pac Oceanog Labs, Nat Oceanic & Atmospheric Admin, 69-74; proj supvr, Ocean-Atmospheric Response Studies, Pac Marine Environ Lab, Nat Oceanic & Atmospheric Admin, 74-81, sr scientist, 81-85; prin res assoc, Atmospheric Sci Dept & Sch Oceanog, Univ Wash, 85-86. *Concurrent Pos:* Affil prof oceanog & atmospheric sci, Univ Wash, 81-85; ed, Trop Ocean-Atmospheric Newsletter, 79-84, assoc ed, Tropicale Oceanologie; mem, Adv Panel Trop Oceans & Global Atmosphere, Nat Res Coun, Nat Acad Sci. *Mem:* AAAS; fel Am Geophys Union; fel Am Meteorol Soc; Sigma Xi. *Res:* Near-surface circulation; coastal and equatorial upwelling; ocean-atmosphere response studies; wind and current measurements; oceanography of tropical and equatorial waters, satellite observations of wind, ocean color and sea surface temperature; author or coauthor of over 100 publications. *Mailing Add:* Jet Propulsion Lab M/S 300-323 Calif Inst Tech 4800 Oak Grove Dr Pasadena CA 91109. *Fax:* 818-393-6720; *E-Mail:* david.halpern@jpl.nasa.gov

HALPERN, DONALD, ORGANOMETALLIC CHEMISTRY, ORGANOFLUORINE CHEMISTRY. *Current Pos:* CONSULT, 93- *Personal Data:* b New York, NY, May 9, 36; c Peter. *Educ:* Queen's Col, BS, 59, MA, 64; City Univ New York, PhD(chem), 71. *Prof Exp:* Chemist, Sun Chem Corp, 60-64; instr chem, Queen's Col, 64-73; sr scientist, Bio-Med Sci, 73; tech serv mgr, Tuck Indust, 74; res scientist, Anaquest Div, BOC Healthcare Inc, 75-81, group leader, 82-84, sr scientist, 84-88, consult scientist, 88-93. *Mem:* Am Chem Soc; Asn Consult Chemists & Chem Engrs. *Res:* Product oriented organic synthesis, pharmaceutical research and development; use of computers in research; chlorofluorocarbon replacements; fluorine chemistry; enantromeric separations. *Mailing Add:* 44 Murray Hill Sq Murray Hill NJ 07974

HALPERN, FRANCIS ROBERT, THEORETICAL PHYSICS. *Current Pos:* RETIRED. *Personal Data:* b New York, NY, Mar 5, 29; m 51; c 2. *Educ:* Cornell Univ, AB, 49; Univ Chicago, MS, 49; Univ Calif, PhD(physics), 57. *Prof Exp:* Dynamics engr, Bell Aircraft Corp, 49-50; instr res engr, Armour Res Found, Ill Inst Technol, 50-52; instr physics, Princeton Univ, 57-61; from asst prof to assoc prof physics, Univ Calif, San Diego, 61-80, prof, 80-84; lectr, Univ MD, 85-87. *Concurrent Pos:* Fulbright fel, Italy, 59-60. *Mem:* Am Phys Soc. *Res:* Field theory; electrodynamics and pi meson physics. *Mailing Add:* 4024 Quartz Dr Santa Rosa CA 95405

HALPERN, HOWARD S, PHYSICS, SYSTEMS ENGINEERING. *Current Pos:* CONSULT, 90- *Personal Data:* b Newark, NJ, July 7, 25; m 49; c 3. *Educ:* Union Col NY, BS, 46; Univ Md, MS, 53. *Prof Exp:* Physicist commun & radar, Naval Res Lab, 47-50; electronic scientist, Naval Gun Factory, 50-53; res engr radar, pinspotter, Am Mach & Foundry Co, 53-55; chief physics & chem sect, Avco Res & Advan Develop, 55-56; mem staff res & planning mil syst radar, Norden Syst Inc, Subsid United Technol Corp, 56-90. *Mem:* Assoc fel Am Inst Aeronaut & Astronaut; Inst Elec & Electronics Engrs; Am Phys Soc. *Res:* Military electronics systems and equipments; radar; cosmology; seven patents. *Mailing Add:* 182 Clay Hill Rd Stamford CT 06905

HALPERN, ISAAC, PHYSICS. *Current Pos:* from asst prof to prof, 53-93, EMER PROF PHYSICS, UNIV WASH, 93- *Personal Data:* b New York, NY, May 15, 23; m 51; c 3. *Educ:* City Col New York, BS, 43; Mass Inst Technol, PhD(physics), 48. *Prof Exp:* Instr physics, Princeton Univ, 43-44; res assoc, Nuclear Lab, Mass Inst Technol, 46-53. *Mem:* Am Phys Soc. *Res:* Nuclear physics; nuclear reactions; fission; interactions of mesons and photons with nuclei. *Mailing Add:* Dept Physics 351560 Univ Wash Seattle WA 98195

HALPERN, JACK, INORGANIC CHEMISTRY, ORGANOMETALLIC CHEMISTRY. *Current Pos:* prof, 62-71, LOUIS BLOCK DISTINGUISHED SERV PROF CHEM, UNIV CHICAGO, 71- *Personal Data:* b Poland, Jan 19, 25; nat US; m 49, Helen Peritz; c Janice & Nina. *Educ:* McGill Univ, BSc, 46, PhD(chem), 49. *Hon Degrees:* DSc, Univ BC, 86, McGill Univ, 97. *Honors & Awards:* Inorg Chem Award, Am Chem Soc, 68 & 85, Award Organometallic Chem, 95; Catalysis Award, Chem Soc London, 76; Humboldt Award, 77; Willard Gibbs Medal, 86; Von Hoffmann Medal, Ger Chem Soc, 88; Chem Pioneer Award, Am Inst Chemists, 91; Paracelsus Prize, Swiss Chem Soc, 92. *Prof Exp:* Nat Res Coun Can fel, Univ Manchester, 49-50; from instr to prof chem, Univ BC, 50-62. *Concurrent Pos:* Nuffield Found traveling fel, Cambridge Univ, 59-60; Sloan fel, 59-63; vis prof, Univ Minn, 62, Harvard Univ, 66-67, Calif Inst Technol, 69, Princeton Univ, 70-71, Univ Copenhagen, 78 & Univ Sheffield, 81-82; mem adv panel chem, NSF, 67-70; bd trustees, Gordon Res Conf, 68-70; Chem Rev Comt, Argonne Nat Lab, 70-72; mem adv bd, Am Chem Soc Petrol Res Fund, 72-74; mem, NIH Med Chem B Study Sect, 75-78; assoc ed, J Am Chem Soc & Inorganica Chimica Acta; guest scholar, Kyoto Univ, 81; consult, Monsanto Co, Argonne Nat Lab, IBM, Air Prods & Chem & Eni Chem, Enimont & Rohm & Haas; R B Woodward vis prof, Harvard Univ, 91. *Mem:* Nat Acad Sci (vpres, 93-); fel Am Acad Arts & Sci; fel NY Acad Sci; fel Royal Soc London; fel AAAS; Max Planck Soc; hon fel Royal Soc Chem. *Res:* Kinetics and mechanisms of inorganic reactions; organometallic chemistry; electron transfer processes; catalytic phenomena; fast reactions; bioinorganic chemistry. *Mailing Add:* Dept Chem Univ Chicago 5735 S Ellis Ave Chicago IL 60637. *Fax:* 773-702-8809; *E-Mail:* jhjh@midway.uchicago.edu

HALPERN, JAMES DANIEL, MATHEMATICAL LOGIC. *Current Pos:* VIS SCHOLAR COMPUT SCI, UNIV CALIF, BERKELEY, 93- *Personal Data:* b Detroit, Mich, Aug 4, 34; m 59; c 2. *Educ:* Univ Mich, AB, 55, MS, 56; Univ Calif, Berkeley, PhD(math), 62. *Prof Exp:* Bateman res fel math, Calif Inst Technol, 62-64, instr, 64-65; mem, Inst Advan Study, 65-66; asst prof math, Univ Mich, Ann Arbor, 66-70; assoc prof, Univ Toledo, 69-74; prof math, Univ Ala, Birmingham, 74-82; mem tech staff, Mitre Corp, Boston, 82-84 & Sytek Corp, Mountainview, Calif, 85-87; staff engr, Sun Micro Systs, 88-92; consult, Software Eng, 92-93. *Concurrent Pos:* Consult, Math Rev, 71-74. *Mem:* Am Math Soc. *Res:* Foundations of set theory; independence problems involving axiom of choice; combinatorial set theory. *Mailing Add:* 1060 Continentals Way No 416 Belmont CA 94002

HALPERN, JOSHUA BARUCH, PHOTOCHEMISTRY, SPECTROSCOPY. *Current Pos:* res asst prof chem, 76-79, asst prof, 79-84, ASSOC PROF CHEM, HOWARD UNIV, 84- *Personal Data:* b Brooklyn, NY, Jan 21, 46; m 74. *Educ:* Johns Hopkins Univ, BA, 66; Brown Univ, PhD(physics), 72. *Prof Exp:* Teaching assoc, Notre Dame Radiation Lab, 71-73; sci assoc physics, Univ Bielefeld, 73-76. *Mem:* Am Chem Soc; Optical Soc Am. *Res:* Photochemistry and spectroscopy of small molecules and free radicals using laser generation and detection techniques. *Mailing Add:* Chem Dept Howard Univ Washington DC 20059-9998

HALPERN, LAWRENCE MAYER, PHARMACOLOGY, NEUROPHARMACOLOGY. *Current Pos:* asst prof, 65-68, ASSOC PROF PHARMACOL, SCH MED, UNIV WASH, 69- *Personal Data:* b New York, NY, July 3, 31; m 52; c 3. *Educ:* Brooklyn Col, BSc, 53; Albert Einstein Col Med, PhD(pharmacol), 61. *Prof Exp:* Unit head neuropharmacol, Merck Inst Therapeut Res, 63-65. *Concurrent Pos:* Vis scientist, NIH & consult, Dir Nat Inst Neurol Dis & Blindness, 67-75; clin consult, Univ Wash Hosp, 70-; dir, Drug Abuse Info Serv, Univ Wash, 68-75. *Mem:* NY Acad Sci; Am Soc Pharmacol & Exp Therapeut; Soc Neurosci; Am Pain Soc. *Res:* Epileptogenesis in cerebral cortex and anticonvulsant drugs; antidepressants, analgesics and psychosedative agents; electrophysiology in pharmacology and behavior; addiction behavior; chronic pain medicines. *Mailing Add:* Univ Wash SJ-30 HSB F-436 Seattle WA 98195-7280. *Fax:* 206-685-3822

HALPERN, LEOPOLD (ERNST), GRAVITATIONAL THEORY, THEORETICAL PHYSICS. *Current Pos:* SR RES ASSOC THEORET PHYSICS, FLA STATE UNIV, 74- *Personal Data:* b Vienna, Austria, Feb 17, 25. *Educ:* Brit Inst Eng Technol, AM, 47; Univ Vienna, PhD(physics), 52. *Prof Exp:* Asst theoret physics, Univ Vienna, 56-59; res assoc, Europ Orgn Nuclear Res, Geneva, 59-60 & Inst Field Physics, Univ NC, 60-61; fel, Niels Bohr Inst, Copenhagen, 62-63; vis prof, Univ Stockholm, 63-66; vis researcher, Inst H Poincare, Paris, 66-67; assoc prof, Univ Windsor, Can, 67-79; researcher, Univ Libre, Bruxelles, Belg, 70-73 & Univ Amsterdam, 73-74. *Concurrent Pos:* Sr res assoc, Jet Propulsion Lab, Calif Inst Technol, Nat Res Coun Grantee, 86-88. *Mem:* Am Phys Soc. *Res:* Gravitational theory and its relation to elementary particle physics and the quantum theory; foundation of generalizations of the general theory of relativity based on local covariance with respect to semisimple lie groups. *Mailing Add:* Dept Physics Fla State Univ Keen Bldg Tallahassee FL 32306-3016

HALPERN, MARTIN, petroleum exploration, geochronology, for more information see previous edition

HALPERN, MARTIN B, THEORETICAL HIGH ENERGY PHYSICS. *Current Pos:* from asst prof to assoc prof, 67-73, PROF PHYSICS, UNIV CALIF, BERKELEY, 73- *Personal Data:* b Newark, NJ, Aug 26, 39; m 87, Penelope Dutton; c Tamar. *Educ:* Univ Ariz, BS, 60; Harvard Univ, AM, 61, PhD(physics), 64. *Honors & Awards:* Sci Talent Search Winner, Westinghouse, 56. *Prof Exp:* Fel physics, Europ Orgn Nuclear Res, Switz, 64-65; Univ Calif, Berkeley, 65-66 & Inst Advan Study, Princeton Univ, 66-67. *Mem:* Am Phys Soc. *Res:* Theory of elementary particles; high energy theoretical physics. *Mailing Add:* Dept Physics Univ Calif Berkeley CA 94720

HALPERN, MIMI, NEUROSCIENCE, PSYCHOBIOLOGY. *Current Pos:* From instr to asst prof anat, State Univ NY, Downstate Med Ctr, 69-74, assoc prof, 74-79, asst dean, Sch Grad Studies, 75-83, dir, Grad Prog Biol Psychol, 76-85, assoc dean, Sch Grad Studies, 83-90, co-dir, Grad Prog Neurol Behav Sci, 85-90, PROF ANAT & CELL BIOL, STATE UNIV NY, DOWNSTATE MED CTR, 79- *Personal Data:* b Antwerp, Belg, June 19, 38; US citizen; m 61; c 2. *Educ:* Oberlin Col, AB, 60; Adelphi Univ, PhD(psychol), 64. *Mem:* Fel Am Psychol Asn; Am Asn Anatomists; Soc Neurosci; Am Asn Zoologists; Sigma Xi; fel AAAS. *Res:* Biological basis of behavior; comparative neuropsychology; visual and limbic systems of vertebrates; chemical communication; reptilian neuroanatomy and behavior. *Mailing Add:* 262 Central Park W Apt 8-A New York NY 10024

HALPERN, MYRON HERBERT, ANATOMY, HISTOLOGY. *Current Pos:* RETIRED. *Personal Data:* b New York, NY, May 12, 24; m 60; c 2. *Educ:* Ind Univ, AB, 44; WVa Univ, ScM, 47; Univ Mich, PhD(anat), 52. *Prof Exp:* Dir biol labs, Univ Rochester, 47-49; asst anat, Med Sch, Univ Mich, 49-52; asst prof, Hahnemann Med Col, 52-57; dir, Info Res Sect & admin dir, Common Cold & Virus Res Prog, Nat Drug Co, 57-61; dir life sci & space med, RCA, 61-63; pres, Bio-Med Res Corp, 63-67; chmn, Div Allied Health Sci, Camden Co Col, 68-72, dean instr, 69-71, prof biol, 67-92. *Mem:* Am Soc Ichthyol & Herpet; Sigma Xi. *Mailing Add:* 109 Leeds Rd Mt Laurel NJ 08054

HALPERN, PAUL H, MATHEMATICS. *Current Pos:* ASSOC PROF PHYSICS, DEPT MATH & PHYSICS, PHILADELPHIA COL PHARM & SCI, 88- *Personal Data:* b Philadelphia, Pa, Jan 15, 61; m 94, Felicia Hurewitz; c Eli. *Educ:* Temple Univ, BA, 82; State Univ NY, Stony Brook, MA, 84, PhD(theoret, phys), 87. *Prof Exp:* Vis asst prof physics, Hamilton Col, 87-88. *Concurrent Pos:* Fulbright scholar, Humboldt Univ, Berlin, Ger, 96. *Mem:* Am Phys Soc; Sigma Xi. *Res:* Published in the fields of chaos in general relativity and complex systems. *Mailing Add:* Dept Math & Physics Philadelphia Col Pharm & Sci 600 S 43rd St Philadelphia PA 19104. *Fax:* 215-895-1100; *E-Mail:* halpern@shrsys.hslc.org

HALPERN, TEODORO, SOLID STATE PHYSICS, INSTRUMENTATION. *Current Pos:* from asst prof to assoc prof, Sch Theoret & Appl Sci, Ramapo Col, NJ, 74-78, dir, 78-79, dean of schs & actg vpres acad affairs, 79-82, PROF PHYSICS, SCH THEORET & APPL SCI, RAMAPO COL, NJ, 78- *Personal Data:* b Buenos Aires, Arg, Sept 5, 31; m 56; c 2. *Educ:* Nat Univ La Plata, BSc, 54; Nat Univ Cuyo, MSc, 58; Univ Stuttgart, MSc & Dr rer nat(physics), 61. *Prof Exp:* Researcher, Arg AEC, 58-64; from asst prof to assoc prof solid state physics, Nat Univ Cuyo, 58-63; prof phys metall, Nat Univ La Plata, 63-64; res assoc physics, Univ Chicago, 64-67; vis scientist, Argonne Nat Lab, 68-70; vis assoc prof solid state physics, Yeshiva Univ, 70-74. *Concurrent Pos:* Sci consult, lasers in med, Yeshiva Univ, 81-, semiconductors, Stauffer Chem, 82-; Fred & Florence Thomases fac award, 82; fel, Princeton Univ, 83 & Am Cyanamid, 84-90; educ consult, 90-; exec secy, Inter-Am Coun Physics Educ, 90- *Mem:* AAAS; Sigma Xi; Ger Soc Metall; Arg Soc Metals; NY Acad Sci; Am Asn Physics Teachers. *Res:* Optical properties of solids; electroreflectance; high pressure optical spectroscopy; semiconductor to metal transition; high voltage, high speed pulse-induced semiconductor to metal transition; quantum states in sputtered metal dispersions in semiconductor phases; lasers in medicine; international energy; bio-engineering; semiconductor crystal growth plasma enhanced chemical vapor deposition; epitaxial growth; diffusion. *Mailing Add:* 760 Cottage Pl Teaneck NJ 07666-2215

HALPERN, WILLIAM, HYPERTENSION, CORONARY & BRAIN ISCHEMIA. *Current Pos:* EMER PROF MED INSTRUMENTATION, DEPT PHYSIOL & BIOPHYS, COL MED, UNIV VT, 69- *Personal Data:* b Oct 27, 23; c 2. *Educ:* Univ Vt, PhD(physiol & biophys), 69. *Mailing Add:* Dept Physiol & Biophys Univ Vt 156 Battery St Burlington VT 05401-5276. *Fax:* 802-863-8057

HALPERT, JAMES ROBERT, DRUG-METABOLIZING ENZYMES, ENZYME INHIBITORS. *Current Pos:* asst prof, 83-87, ASSOC PROF PHARMACOL & TOXICOL, DEPT PHARM & TOXICOL, UNIV ARIZ, 87- *Personal Data:* b Los Angeles, Calif, Dec 5, 49. *Educ:* Univ Calif, BA, 71; Uppsala Univ, PhD, 77, MSc, 78. *Prof Exp:* Res assoc, Dept Pharmacol, Karolinska Inst, 77-78, Vanderbilt Univ, 78-80. *Mem:* Int Soc Toxicol; Am Soc Pharmacol & Exp Therapeut; Am Soc Biochem & Molecular Biol. *Res:* Structure and function of mammalian hepatic cytochromes P-450 with special emphasis on the use of specific irreversible inhibitors as probes and modulators of P-450 function. *Mailing Add:* Dept Pharmacol & Toxicol Univ Ariz Col Pharm Tucson AZ 85721-0001. *Fax:* 520-626-2466

HALPIN, DANIEL WILLIAM, ENGINEERING MANAGEMENT, CIVIL ENGINEERING. *Current Pos:* DIV HEAD, SCH ENG, PURDUE UNIV, 87- *Personal Data:* b Covington, Ky, Sept 29, 38; m 63, Maria Kirchner; c Rainer. *Educ:* US Mil Acad, BS, 61; Univ Ill, Urbana, MS, 69, PhD(civil eng), 73. *Honors & Awards:* Huber Res Prize, Am Soc Civil Engrs, 79, Peurifoy Construct Res Prize, 92. *Prof Exp:* Opers res analyst, Construct Eng Res Lab, Champaign, Ill, 70-72; mem fac civil eng, Univ Ill, 72-73; prof civil eng, Ga Inst Technol, 81-85, mem fac civil eng, 73-85; Clark chair prof, Univ Md, 85-87. *Concurrent Pos:* Proj dir res proj, Dept Energy, 76-78; vis scholar, Tech Univ Munich, Ger, 79; vis assoc prof civil eng, Univ Sydney, Australia, 81; chmn const res coun, Am Soc Civil Engrs, 84-86; vis prof, Swiss Tech Inst (ETH), Zurich, 85; consult, Off Tech Assessment, 86 & Tenn Valley Authority. *Mem:* Am Soc Civil Engrs; Am Soc Eng Educ; Sigma Xi. *Res:* Simulation of construction operations; data base management for complex construction projects, impact of international competition on construction technology; author or co-author of 5 engineering textbooks. *Mailing Add:* Head Div Construct Eng Mgt Purdue Univ Civil Eng Bldg West Lafayette IN 47907

HALPIN, JOSEPH JOHN, PHYSICS, ELECTRONICS. *Current Pos:* tech specialist, 71-75, BR CHIEF NUCLEAR WEAPONS EFFECTS, ARMY RES LAB, US ARMY, 75- *Personal Data:* b Philadelphia, Pa, Nov 10, 39; m 61; c 4. *Educ:* St Joseph's Col, Philadelphia, BS, 61; Georgetown Univ, MS, 71. *Prof Exp:* Res asst, Georgetown Univ, 64-66; res physicist, US Naval Res Lab, 66-71. *Mem:* Sr mem Inst Elec & Electronics Engrs; Sigma Xi. *Res:* Nuclear weapons effects to include blast, thermal radiation, electromagnetic pulse and transient radiation-induced effects on materials, components and systems; technical and managerial aspects of nuclear effects phenomena. *Mailing Add:* 15208 Red Gate Dr Silver Spring MD 20905

HALPRIN, ARTHUR, PHYSICS. *Current Pos:* Asst prof, 64-69, assoc prof, 69-80, PROF PHYSICS, UNIV DEL, 80- *Personal Data:* b Portsmouth, NH, Aug 11, 35; m 58. *Educ:* Univ NH, BS, 57; Worcester Polytech Inst, MS, 59; Univ Pa, PhD(physics), 65. *Mem:* Am Phys Soc. *Res:* Particle physics. *Mailing Add:* Dept Physics & Astron Univ Del Newark DE 19716. *Fax:* 302-831-1637; *E-Mail:* Bitnet: hesly@physcolumbia.edu

HALPRIN, KENNETH M, DERMATOLOGY, BIOCHEMISTRY. *Current Pos:* assoc prof, 68-71, PROF DERMAT, SCH MED, UNIV MIAMI, 71-; CHIEF DERMAT, MIAMI VET ADMIN HOSP, 68- *Personal Data:* b Brooklyn, NY, Mar 19, 31. *Educ:* Univ Chicago, BA, 50, MD, 55. *Prof Exp:* Intern, Univ Chicago Clins, 55-56, resident dermat, 56-59; NSF fel, St John's Hosp, London, 61-62; asst prof dermat, Univ Chicago, 63; from asst prof to assoc prof, Med Sch, Univ Ore, 64-68. *Mem:* Am Acad Dermat; Soc Invest Dermat; Am Fedn Clin Res; NY Acad Sci. *Res:* Enzymology; carbohydrate metabolism; carcinogenesis. *Mailing Add:* 1550 NW Tenth Ave Miami FL 33136-1031

HALPRYN, BRUCE, CARDIOLOGY. *Current Pos:* SECT HEAD/PROJ LEADER, DIV PROCTER & GAMBLE, NORWICH PHARMACEUT INC, 86- *Personal Data:* b New York, Mar 5, 57. *Educ:* State Univ NY, BS, 79, PhD(biol & pharmacol), 83. *Prof Exp:* Nat Res Coun fel, Cardiac Res Labs, NASA/Ames, 83-86. *Concurrent Pos:* Mem bd dir, Nonprofit Community Health Clin, Our Health Ctr, 82-84. *Mem:* Am Physiol Soc. *Res:* Development of novel inotropic agents for congestive heart failure. *Mailing Add:* Dept Cardia C Prod Develop Procter & Gamble Pharmaceut 11450 Grooms Rd Cincinnati OH 45242. *Fax:* 513-626-3434

HALS, FINN, MECHANICAL ENGINEERING. *Current Pos:* prin res engr, 60-87, CONSULT, AVCO-EVERETT RES LAB, 87- *Personal Data:* b Trondheim, Norway, July 1, 24; m 60; c 3. *Educ:* Tech Univ Norway, MSc, 51. *Prof Exp:* Consult engr, Asn Norweg Steam Power Generators, 51-55; mgr, G Hartman Inc, Norway, 55-57; asst power supt, WVa Pulp & Paper Co, Pa, 57-58; mech engr, Stone & Webster Eng Corp, Mass, 58-60. *Mem:* Am Soc Mech Engrs; AAAS. *Res:* Magnetohydrodynamic electrical power generation; coal combustion and utilization; pollution control. *Mailing Add:* 140 Vine St Lexington MA 02173

HALSALL, H(ALLEN) BRIAN, PROTEIN SCIENCE. *Current Pos:* asst prof, 74-81, assoc prof, 81-87, PROF CHEM, UNIV CINCINNATI, 87- *Personal Data:* b Eng, Apr 13, 43; m 70; c 2. *Educ:* Univ Birmingham, Eng, BSc, 64, PhD(phys biochem), 67. *Prof Exp:* Post doctoral scholar, Univ Calif, Los Angeles, 67-69, actg asst prof biochem, 69-70; staff mem & consult phys biochem, Oak Ridge Nat Lab, 70-74. *Mem:* Biophys Soc; Brit Biophys Soc; Am Chem Soc; Sigma Xi; Protein Soc; Am Asn Clin Chemists. *Res:* Biophysical studies of protein-ligand interactions, particularly therapeutic drugs with orosomucoid; application of electrochemical techniques to immunoassay methodology; glycoprotein structure and function. *Mailing Add:* Dept Chem Univ Cincinnati Cincinnati OH 45221-0172. *Fax:* 513-556-9239; *E-Mail:* halsalhb@ucbeh.san.uc.edu

HALSEY, BRENTON S, CHEMICAL ENGINEERING. *Current Pos:* mem staff, 70-77, CHMN BD, JAMES RIVER PAPER CORP, 77- *Personal Data:* b Newport News, Va, Apr 8, 27; m 54; c 4. *Educ:* Univ Va, BChE, 51; Inst Paper Chem, Lawrence Col, cert. *Prof Exp:* Res engr, Va-Carolina Chem Corp, 53-55; process develop engr, Albemarle Paper Mfg Co, 55-57, asst tech dir, 57-60, dir res & develop, 60-63, vpres planning, 63-70. *Mem:* Am Chem Soc; Tech Asn Pulp & Paper Indust; Am Inst Chem Engrs. *Res:* Pulp and paper; wood chemistry; plastics; heat transfer; fluid flow. *Mailing Add:* 213 Ampthill Rd Richmond VA 23226

HALSEY, GEORGE DAWSON, JR, PHYSICAL CHEMISTRY. *Current Pos:* from asst prof to assoc prof chem, 51-58, PROF CHEM, UNIV WASH, 58- *Personal Data:* b Washington, DC, May 28, 25. *Educ:* Univ SC, BS, 43; Princeton Univ, PhD(chem), 48. *Honors & Awards:* Kendall Award, Am Chem Soc, 65. *Prof Exp:* Jr fel, Soc Fels, Harvard Univ, 48-51. *Mem:* Am Chem Soc. *Res:* Adsorption; catalysis; viscous elasticity; statistical mechanics; solutions. *Mailing Add:* 5819 17th Ave NE Seattle WA 98105-2511

HALSEY, JAMES H, JR, NEUROLOGY. *Current Pos:* assoc prof & dir div, 69-72, chmn dept, 73-85, PROF NEUROL, UNIV ALA MED CTR, BIRMINGHAM, 72- *Personal Data:* b Paris, France, Sept 3, 33; US citizen; c 2. *Educ:* Univ Bridgeport, BA, 55; Yale Univ, MD, 59. *Prof Exp:* From instr to assoc prof neurol, 65-69. *Concurrent Pos:* Mem, Res Comt, Am Heart Asn, 71-75; mem, Prog Proj Comt, Nat Inst Neurol Dis & Stroke, 73-77. *Mem:* Am Neurol Asn; Int Soc Oxygen Transp Tissue; Am Acad Neurol; AMA; Am Heart Asn; Int Soc Cerebral Blood Flow & Metab. *Res:* Cerebrovascular disease and clinical neurophysiology. *Mailing Add:* Univ Hosp Hillman Clin Birmingham AL 35203

HALSEY, JOHN FREDERICK, CLINICAL IMMUNOLOGY. *Current Pos:* PRES, PROGENE CORP, 83- *Personal Data:* b St Petersburg, Fla, Feb 8, 42; m 67; c 2. *Educ:* Univ Fla, BS, 65, MS, 67; Johns Hopkins Univ, PhD(biochem), 73. *Prof Exp:* Res assoc phys biochem, Univ Va, 73-75; instr molecular pharmacol, Med Univ SC, 75-76; asst prof microbiol, Univ Okla, 76-78; asst prof biochem, Med Ctr, Univ Kans, 78-83. *Concurrent Pos:* Consult, Int Diag Inc; prin investr, NIH grant. *Mem:* Am Chem Soc; Am Asn Immunologists; Am Soc Microbiol. *Res:* Immunochemistry, immunology and biochemistry. *Mailing Add:* Progene Corp 10453 W 84th Terr Lenexa KS 66214

HALSEY, JOHN JOSEPH, CHEMISTRY, OPERATIONS RESEARCH. *Current Pos:* RETIRED. *Personal Data:* b Jersey City, NJ, Dec 26, 18; m 44, Harriet Lutton; c Martina, Valerie, Adrienne & Gregory. *Educ:* St Peters Col, BS, 40; NY Univ, MS, 48, MBA, 59. *Prof Exp:* Prod chemist, Calco Chem Div, Am Cyanamid Corp, 40; anal chemist, Brooklyn Army Base, 41-42; chief, Chem Prods Br, Qm Depot, NJ, 42-44; chief, Chem Sect, Merck & Co, Inc, 46-47, mgr, Qual Standards Dept, 48-54 & Testing & Inspection Dept, 54-57; mgr, Qual Servs Dept, 57-63, spec proj, 63-64 & opers analyst, 64-68; dir, mgt sci dept, Gen Foods Corp, 69-82. *Concurrent Pos:* Mem bd dir, Extrudo Film Corp, NY, 59-62; dir, Neuwirth Fund, Inc, 68-91, Winthrop Focus Funds, 91- *Mem:* Am Chem Soc; Am Soc Qual Control. *Res:* Analytical chemistry; testing methods; statistics in chemistry; management of technical operations; management sciences; operations research; financial and portfolio management. *Mailing Add:* 9600 S Ocean Dr Suite 1405 Jensen Beach FL 34957

HALSTEAD, BRUCE W, CHEMISTRY, NUTRITION. *Current Pos:* DIR, WORLD LIFE INST, 58- *Personal Data:* b San Francisco, Calif, Mar 28, 20; m 41, Terri Holcomb; c Linda, Sandy, David, Larry, Claudia & Shari. *Educ:* Univ Calif, BA, 43; Loma Linda Univ, MD, 48. *Prof Exp:* Asst surgeon, USPHS, 47-48; instr path & med zoologist, Sch Trop & Prev Med, Loma Linda Univ, 48-58, asst prof prev med & pub health, Sch Med & head, Dept Biotoxicol, Sch Trop & Prev Med, 54-58. *Concurrent Pos:* Mem, Great Barrier Reef Comt, Australia, 68; mem, Adv Coun, Life Bound, 71; consult, NIH, Bur Med & Surg, USN, Marine Colloids, Inc, NAm Aviation, Inc, W J Voit Rubber Co, Dow Chem Co, Tempo, Gen Elec Co, 70; mem, Joint Group Experts Sci Aspects Marine Pollution, WHO, UN, Paris, 70; partic, Fishery Develop Proj, Food & Agr Orgn, UN, Mauritius, 70; mem, Sci Adv Bd, Environ Defense Fund, 71 & Expert Adv Panel Food Additives, WHO, 71; med dir, Rancho Mediterranean Med Clin. *Mem:* AAAS; Marine Technol Soc; Am Inst Chem; Royal Soc Health; fel NY Acad Sci. *Res:* Poisonous and venomous marine animals; natural product chemistry; author or coauthor of numerous publications; preventive medicine; traditional medicine and nutrition. *Mailing Add:* World Life Res Inst 23000 Grand Terr Rd Colton CA 92324. *Fax:* 909-783-3477

HALSTEAD, CHARLES LEMUEL, ORAL PATHOLOGY, ORAL MEDICINE. *Current Pos:* assoc prof oral med & chmn dept, 66-71, PROF ORAL PATH & CHMN DEPT, EMORY UNIV, 71-; CLIN PROF ORAL PATH, UNIV VA, 89- *Personal Data:* b Norfolk, Va, Aug 24, 28; m 52, Jean Roberts; c 3. *Educ:* Univ Va, BA, 49; Med Col Va, DDS, 54; Emory Univ, MS, 66; Am Bd Oral Path, dipl, 69. *Prof Exp:* USN Dent Corps, 54-57; pvt pract gen dent, Norfolk, Va, 57-64. *Concurrent Pos:* Consult, Ga Dept Human Resources, 70-; NIH grant, 73-; consult, Conn Int Exchange Scholars, 78- & Univ Lampinas, Brazil, 94- *Mem:* Am Acad Oral Path; Int Asn Dent Res; Soc Teachers Oral Path; Am Asn Dent Schs (secy, 74-75). *Res:* Oral cancer, particular fluorescent antibody studies and chemical carcinogenesis; inorganic bone and dental pulps; ceramic implants; differential diagnosis of soft tissue diseases utilizing computer assistance; Diagnostic Aid and Resource Tool - computer aid for head and neck pathology; Oral Pathologic Electronic Resource Atlas - cd-rom atlas of head and neck pathology. *Mailing Add:* 825 Emerson Dr Charlottesville VA 22901

HALSTEAD, RONALD LAWRENCE, SOIL FERTILITY, SOIL CHEMISTRY. *Current Pos:* RETIRED. *Personal Data:* b Alta, Can, Sept 18, 23. *Educ:* Univ Man, BSA, 50; Univ Wis-Madison, PhD(soil sci & microbiol), 54. *Prof Exp:* Res scientist, Chem Div, Can Dept Agr, 54-59, Soil Res Inst, 59-75, res coordr, Planning & Eval Directorate, Res Br & Cent Exp Farm, 75-82, dir gen, Prog Coordr Directorate, 82-85, dir gen insts, 85-87. *Mem:* Int Soc Soil Sci; fel Can Soc Soil Sci; Agr Inst Can. *Res:* Soil organic and inorganic phosphorous; sewage sludge disposal in soils. *Mailing Add:* 1094 Bedbrook St Ottawa ON K2C 2R7 Can

HALSTEAD, SCOTT BARKER, MEDICAL MICROBIOLOGY, TROPICAL MEDICINE. *Current Pos:* DEP DIR, HEALTH SCI DIV, ROCKEFELLER FOUND. *Personal Data:* b Lucknow, India, Jan 23, 30; m 55, Edna Fishburn; c Rodd, Layne & Geoffrey. *Educ:* Yale Univ, BA, 51; Columbia Univ, MD, 55; Am Bd Med Microbiol, dipl, 64; Am Bd Prev Med, dipl, 73. *Hon Degrees:* DrMedS, Mahidol Univ, Bangkok. *Honors & Awards:* Langmuir Lectr, Ctr Dis Control, 81. *Prof Exp:* Intern, Bellevue Hosp, New York, 55-56, resident internal med, 56-57; chief virol, Dept Virus & Rickettsial Dis, 406th Med Gen Lab, Japan, 57-59; mem, Dept Virus Dis, Walter Reed Army Inst Res, 59-61; chief, Virol Dept, SEATO Med Res Lab, Thailand, 61-65; res assoc virol, Yale Univ, 65-68; prof trop med, med microbiol & chmn dept, John A Burns Sch Med, Univ Hawaii, 68-83. *Concurrent Pos:* Prof pub health, Sch Pub Health, Univ Hawaii; assoc mem, Armed Forces Epidemiol Bd, Comn Virus Dis, 68-73; consult epidemiol & control dengue hemorrhagic fever, WHO, 67-; expert consult, Southeast Asia Regional Off, WHO, 74-83; Fogarty Int Fel, 75-76; mem, Armed Forces Epidemiol Bd, 87-93; mem HIV Vaccine Selection Comt, NIH, 89-; mem infectious dis adv bd, Ctr Dis Control, 89-; mem, WHO Sci Adv Group of Experts, Prog for Vaccine Develop, 88- *Mem:* Am Asn Immunologists; Am Epidemiol Soc; Am Soc Trop Med & Hyg (pres, 92); AAAS; Inf Dis Soc Am; Soc Epidemiol Res; Int Fedn Trop Med (pres, 92-). *Res:* Japanese encephalitis ecology; clinical, epidemiological and virological studies of dengue hemorrhagic fever; epidemiology of primary bladder stone disease; development and evaluation of live virus vaccines; vaccine technology transfer; science-based development. *Mailing Add:* Nat Naval Med Ctr Rockefeller Found 1133 Ave Americas Bethesda MD 20889-5606. Fax: 212 764 3468

HALSTEAD, THORA WATERS, gravitational & space biology, cell biology, for more information see previous edition

HALSTED, A(BEL) STEVENS, ELECTRICAL ENGINEERING, APPLIED PHYSICS. *Current Pos:* PROG MGR, SANTA BARBARA RES CTR, 87- *Personal Data:* b Pasadena, Calif, Jan 18, 38; m 59; c 2. *Educ:* Stanford Univ, BS, 59, MS, 60, PhD(elec eng), 65. *Prof Exp:* Res asst plasma physics, Electronics Lab, Stanford Univ, 62-65; sr mem tech staff gas lasers & head ion laser sect, Hughes Res Labs, 65-70, mgr, Laser Dept & Laser Prod Line, Electron Dynamics Div, Hughes Aircraft Co, 70-75; prog mgr, Electra-Optical & Data Systs Group, Huges Aircraft Co, 75-87. *Concurrent Pos:* Mem comt, Int Electron Devices Conf, 67-71; mem tech prog comts, Int Electron Devices Conf, 67-70; mem, Electron Device Res Conf, 70 & Conf Laser Eng & Appln, 71. *Mem:* Inst Elec & Electronics Engrs; Sigma Xi. *Res:* Electron devices; microwave tubes and devices; plasma physics; quantum electronics; lasers, infrared systems. *Mailing Add:* 1599 E Valley Rd Santa Barbara CA 93108

HALSTED, CHARLES H, CLINICAL NUTRITION. *Current Pos:* PROF INTERNAL MED, UNIV CALIF, DAVIS. *Personal Data:* b Cambridge, Mass, Oct 2, 36. *Educ:* Univ Rochester, MD, 62. *Mem:* Am Soc Clin Invest; Am Soc Clin Nutrit; Am Gastroesterol Asn. *Mailing Add:* Div Clin Nutrit Univ Calif Davis Sch Med TB156 Davis CA 95616. Fax: 530-752-3470

HALTER, JEFFREY BRIAN, ENDOCRINOLOGY, METABOLISM. *Current Pos:* CHIEF, INST GERIAT, UNIV MICH MED CTR, 84- *Personal Data:* b Minneapolis, Minn, Aug 25, 45; c 2. *Educ:* Univ Minn, BA, 66, BS & MD, 69. *Prof Exp:* Res asst metab, Univ Minn Sch Med, 64-68; physician & surgeon internal med, USPHS Outpatient Clin, Washington, 71-73; staff physician, Seattle Vet Admin Med Ctr, 74-75, advan spec resident endocrinol & metab, 75-77; acting instr, Univ Wash, 74-77, from asst prof to assoc prof med, 77-84; assoc dir geriat res, Educ & Clin Ctr, Seattle Vet Admin Med Ctr, 78-84. *Concurrent Pos:* Res & educ assoc, Seattle Vet Admin Med Ctr, 77-78; NIH grants, 77- *Mem:* Am Diabetes Asn; Am Fedn Clin Res. *Res:* Autonomic nervous system function and insulin secretion in diabetes mellitus; neuroendocrine responses in aging. *Mailing Add:* Dept Med Geriat Univ Mich Med Ctr 300 N Ingalls N13A03 Ann Arbor MI 48109-0405. Fax: 313-763-2064

HALTERLEIN, ANTHONY J, HORTICULTURE. *Current Pos:* ASST PROF, MIDDLE TENN STATE UNIV, 81- *Personal Data:* US citizen. *Educ:* Univ Mo, BS, 72, MS, 74; Kans State Univ, PhD(hort), 78. *Prof Exp:* Asst res horticulturist, Delta Br, Miss Agr & Forestry Exp Sta, 78-81. *Mem:* Am Soc Hort Sci. *Res:* Cultural practices. *Mailing Add:* Dept Agr Middle Tenn State Univ Murfreesboro TN 37132-0001

HALTERMAN, JERRY J, AGRICULTURAL ENGINEERING. *Current Pos:* prof agr educ, 68-76, PROF ENG EDUC, OHIO STATE UNIV, 76-; AT DEPT AGR, RICKS COL. *Personal Data:* b Parowan, Utah, May 7, 22; m 44; c 4. *Educ:* Univ Calif, Davis, BS, 50, MEd, 55; Ohio State Univ, PhD(agr educ & eng), 64. *Prof Exp:* Instr agr, Red Bluff Union High Sch, 51-55 & Modesto Jr Col, 55-65; res asst agr educ, Ohio State Univ, 63-65; coordr agr, Chico State Col, 65-68; prof agr educ, Ohio State Univ, 68-76, prof eng educ, 76- *Concurrent Pos:* Consult, Ctr Voc & Tech Educ, Columbus, Ohio, 65 & 67 & Off Educ, Washington, DC, 66; mem, Conf Undergrad Educ Biol Sci Students in Agr & Natural Sci, 66; dir, Agr Tech Inst, 68- *Res:* Educational needs of vocational, technical and professional workers in the agricultural manpower force. *Mailing Add:* 14 N Millhollow Rd Rexburg ID 83440

HALTINER, GEORGE JOSEPH, METEOROLOGY. *Current Pos:* RETIRED. *Personal Data:* b St Paul, Minn, Nov 26, 18; m 47, Mary Wahl; c Mary L, Jeffrey, Kathleen, Jean & Michele M. *Educ:* Col St Thomas, BS, 40; Univ Wis, PhM, 42, PhD(math), 48. *Honors & Awards:* Cleveland Abbe Award, Am Meteorol Soc; Distinguished Civilian Award, USN. *Prof Exp:* Asst math, Univ Wis, 40-42; from asst prof to prof aerological eng, US Naval Postgrad Sch, 46-69, chmn, Dept Meteorol & Oceanog, 64-68, actg dean sci & eng, 77-78, distinguished prof meteorol, 69-81, chmn, Dept Meteorol, 68-81. *Concurrent Pos:* Mem tech adv comt, Air Pollution Control Dist, Monterey & Santa Cruz counties. *Mem:* Fel Am Meteorol Soc; Royal Meteorol Soc. *Res:* Dynamical meteorology and numerical weather prediction. *Mailing Add:* 1134 Alta Mesa Rd Monterey CA 93940

HALTIWANGER, JOHN D(AVID), STRUCTURAL ENGINEERING. *Current Pos:* from asst to assoc prof, 48-59, PROF CIVIL ENG, UNIV ILL, URBANA, 59-, ASSOC HEAD DEPT, 67-84. *Personal Data:* b Irmo, SC, June 10, 25; m 54; c 2. *Educ:* Univ SC, BS, 45; Univ Ill, MS, 49, PhD(civil eng), 57. *Honors & Awards:* Bliss Medal, Soc Am Military Engrs, 80. *Prof Exp:* Instr civil eng, Ala Polytech Inst, 46-48, asst prof, 49-51. *Concurrent Pos:* Consult, Strategic Structures Div, Targets Div, Defense Nuclear Agency, US Dept Defense, 81-92 & Defense Nuclear Facil Safety Bd; mem adv comt, US Off Civil Defense, 66-70; mem, Ill State Tech Serv Adv Coun, 67-70 & USCG Acad Adv Comt, 80-83. *Mem:* Am Soc Civil Engrs; Am Soc Eng Educ; Am Concrete Inst; Sigma Xi. *Res:* Structural analysis and design; design of structures for blast-induced loads. *Mailing Add:* 2207 Vawter St Urbana IL 61801

HALTNER, ARTHUR JOHN, PHYSICAL CHEMISTRY. *Current Pos:* CONSULT, ASTRO SPACE DIV, LOCKHEED-MARTIN, 92- *Personal Data:* b Milwaukee, Wis, Aug 28, 27. *Educ:* Univ Wis, BS, 51; Univ Calif, PhD(phys chem), 55. *Prof Exp:* Asst phys chem, Univ Wis, 51; assoc chem, Univ Calif, 51-53; phys chemist, Res Lab, Gen Elec Co, 55-64, surface physicist, Space Sci Lab, 64-69, consult surface physicist, Astro Space Div, 69-92. *Mem:* Am Chem Soc; sr mem Am Vacuum Soc; fel Soc Tribologists & Lubrication Engrs. *Res:* Friction, wear and adhesion of solid surfaces in space environment; ultrahigh vacuum. *Mailing Add:* 194 Chandler Dr West Chester PA 19380

HALTON, JOHN HENRY, MATHEMATICS, COMPUTER SCIENCE. *Current Pos:* PROF COMPUT SCI, UNIV NC, CHAPEL HILL, 84- *Personal Data:* b Brussels, Belg, Aug 25, 31; m 77; c 2. *Educ:* Cambridge Univ, BA, 53, MA, 57; Oxford Univ, BA, 56, MA, 57, DPhil(math), 60. *Prof Exp:* Physicist, Mech Eng Lab, Eng Elec Co, 54-56; res officer, Clarendon Lab, Oxford Univ, 60-62; vis lectr math & comput sci, Univ Colo, 62-64; mathematician, Brookhaven Nat Lab, 64-66; from assoc prof to prof comput sci, Univ Wis-Madison, 66-83; prin engr, Advan Technol Dept, Harris Corp, Melbourne, 83-84. *Concurrent Pos:* Consult, Rand Corp, 63, C-E-I-R Corp, 66, Lawrence Livermore Nat Lab, 83 & Los Alamos Nat Lab, 85; fel math & physics, Cambridge Philos Soc, 54; pres, Tedco, 80- *Mem:* Am Math Soc; Asn Comput Mach; Math Asn Am; Soc Indust & Appl Math; Sigma Xi; sr mem Inst Elec & Electronics Engrs; fel Inst Math & Applns; fel Brit Comput Soc. *Res:* Monte Carlo method; mathematical analysis; probability theory; combinatorial theory; theory of algorithms, computer networks and very large scale integration. *Mailing Add:* 108 Carolina Forest Chapel Hill NC 27516

HALUSHKA, PERRY VICTOR, PHARMACOLOGY, MEDICINE. *Current Pos:* from asst prof to assoc prof, 74-81, PROF PHARM & MED, MED UNIV SC, 81-, DIR, DIV CLIN PHARMACOL. *Personal Data:* b Chicago, Ill, June 4, 41; m 64, Joan R Boris; c Francine, Marc & Suzanne. *Educ:* Univ Ill, Chicago, BS, 63, PhD(pharmacol), 67; Univ Chicago, MD, 70. *Honors & Awards:* Found Fac Develop Award, Pharmaceut Mfg Asn, 75. *Prof Exp:* Teaching asst pharmacol, Univ Chicago, 67-69; from intern to jr asst resident, Grady Med Hosp, Atlanta, Ga, 70-72; res assoc pharmacol & toxicol, Nat Heart & Lung Inst, NIH, 72-74. *Mem:* Am Soc Pharmacol & Exp Therapeut; Am Soc Clin Pharmacol & Therapeut; Am Fedn Clin Res; Am Soc Clin Invest. *Res:* Regulation and structure-function of Thromboxane A2 receptors. *Mailing Add:* Dept Pharmacol Med Univ SC Charleston SC 29425-0001. Fax: 803-792-0816

HALVER, JOHN EMIL, NUTRITION. *Current Pos:* instr, Sch Fisheries, Univ Wash, 49-50, dir, Western Fish Nutrit Lab, Bur Sport Fisheries & Wildlife, 50-75, US Fish & Wildlife prof, 75-78, sr fisheries, 78-92, EMER PROF, UNIV WASH, 92- *Personal Data:* b Woodinville, Wash, Apr 21, 22; m 44, Jane Loren; c 5. *Educ:* Wash State Univ, BSc, 44, MSc, 49; Univ Wash, PhD(biochem), 53. *Prof Exp:* Plant chemist, Asn Frozen Foods, Inc, Wash, 46; asst chem, Wash State Univ, 46-47; asst chemist, State Chemists Off, Purdue, 48-49. *Concurrent Pos:* Pres, Halver Corp, 78-, Fisheries Develop Technol, Seattle, Wash, 80-90. *Mem:* Nat Acad Sci; fel Am Inst Fisheries Res Biologists; fel Am Inst Nutrit; Am Fisheries Soc; Am Chem Soc. *Res:* Fundamental nutrition, metabolism and comparative biochemistry of fish and other experimental animals; basic nutritional requirements and specific functions of each in metabolism. *Mailing Add:* 16502 41st Ave NE Seattle WA 98155

HALVERSON, ANDREW WAYNE, agricultural chemistry, for more information see previous edition

HALVERSON, FREDERICK, CHEMISTRY. *Current Pos:* RETIRED. *Personal Data:* b West Prairie, Wis, Sept 8, 17; m 46, Edith L. *Educ:* Luther Col, BA, 39; Johns Hopkins Univ, PhD(phys chem), 43. *Prof Exp:* Asst chem, Johns Hopkins Univ, 40-43, instr, 43-46, res chemist, USN Proj, 44; res chemist, Nat Defense Res Comt & US Army Proj, 45; res physicist, Am Cynamid Co, 46-51, theoret chemist, 51-53, group leader phys chem, 53-54, mgr, Basic Res Sect, 54-62, res fel, 62-68, sr res fel, 68-82. *Concurrent Pos:* Am Cyanamid Co sr res award, 57-58; vis scientist, Cambridge Univ, 57-58. *Mem:* Am Phys Soc; Faraday Soc; Am Chem Soc; Am Optical Soc; Sigma Xi. *Res:* Electronic energy transfer; structural inorganic chemistry; raman, ultraviolet and infrared spectroscopy; use of deuterium in analysis of molecular spectra, flocculation, water treating, enhanced oil recovery. *Mailing Add:* 206 Janes Lane Stamford CT 06903-4821

HALVORSON, ARDELL DAVID, SOIL SCIENCE, CHEMISTRY. *Current Pos:* SOIL SCIENTIST, AGR RES SERV, USDA, 71-, RES LEADER, 88-, LAB DIR, 94- *Personal Data:* b Rugby, NDak, May 31, 45; m 66; c 2. *Educ:* NDak State Univ, BS, 67; Colo State Univ, MS, 69, PhD(soil sci), 71. *Honors & Awards:* Cert of Merit, USDA, 90; Commendation Award, Soil Water Conserv Soc, 93. *Mem:* Sigma Xi; fel Am Soc Agron; fel Soil Sci Soc Am; fel Soil Water Conserv Soc; Crop Sci Soc Am. *Res:* Soil chemistry, reclamation of saline land under semiarid conditions; soil fertility and plant nutrition; nitrogen, phosphorous, potassium and trace elements for sugarbeets, corn, beans and small grains; dryland cropping systems. *Mailing Add:* Agr Res Serv USDA PO Box 459 Mandan ND 58554-0459

HALVORSON, GARY ALFRED, SOIL SCIENCE, MINE LAND RECLAMATION. *Current Pos:* assoc soil scientist, 79-83, SOIL SCIENTIST, NDAK STATE UNIV, MANDAN, 89- *Personal Data:* b Klamath Falls, Ore, July 18, 49; m 76, Bonita R Hill; c Janet, Daniel, Anne & Clifford. *Educ:* St Olaf Col, Minn, 71; Ore State Univ, MS, 75, PhD, 79. *Honors & Awards:* Reclamation Researcher of Year, Am Soc Surface Mining & Reclamation. *Concurrent Pos:* Timeryazov Agr Acad res fel, Moscow, 78; interim supt, Land Reclamation Res Ctr, 91-, dir, 94; dir, Land Reclamation Res Ctr, 93- *Mem:* Am Soc Agron; Soil Sci Soc Am; Am Soc Surface Mining & Reclamation. *Res:* Soil science; agronomy; mine land reclamation. *Mailing Add:* NDak State Univ PO Box 459 Mandan ND 58554-0459. *E-Mail:* halvorson@mandan.ars.usda.gov

HALVORSON, HARLYN ODELL, MICROBIOLOGY. *Current Pos:* PROF BIOL & DIR ROSENSTIEL BASIC MED SCI RES CTR, BRANDEIS UNIV, 71- *Personal Data:* b Minneapolis, Minn, May 17, 25; m 54; c 2. *Educ:* Univ Minn, BS, 48, MS, 50; Univ Ill, PhD(bact), 52. *Prof Exp:* Instr bact, Univ Mich, 52-54, asst prof, 54-56; Merck sr fel, Pasteur Inst, Paris, 55-56; from assoc prof to prof bact, 56-71, Univ Wis-Madison, prof molecular biol, 64-71, actg dir, Molecular Biol Lab, 64-66, chmn, 66-71. *Concurrent Pos:* Mem NSF adv panel, Qm Corps, 58-64; fel panel biochem & nutrit, NIH, 61-64, mycol & microbiol, 64-; instr, Marine Biol Lab, Woods Hole Biol Inst, 62-65 & 67, investr, 68-70, trustee & mem exec comt; instr, Hebrew Univ, 65, Univ Naples, 66 & Univ Bergen, 68; mem Nat Acad Sci Res Adv Comt to USDA; consult, NASA Comt Mariner Sterilization. *Mem:* Am Soc Microbiol (vpres, 75-76, pres, 76-77); Am Chem Soc; Am Soc Biol Chemists; Am Acad Microbiol; Am Acad Arts & Sci. *Res:* Induced enzyme synthesis; sporulation, physiology and germination of aerobic spores; cell cycle in yeast, nucleic acid synthesis, genetics and physiology of bacterial spores; regulation of gene expression at the molecular level. *Mailing Add:* Policy Ctr Marine Biosci & Technol Univ Mass Dartmouth North Dartmouth MA 02747-2300. *Fax:* 508-540-1030

HALVORSON, HERBERT RUSSELL, BIOPHYSICAL CHEMISTRY. *Current Pos:* STAFF INVESTR BIOCHEM, EDSEL B FORD INST MED RES, 75- *Personal Data:* b Fergus Falls, Minn, Aug 18, 40; m 68; c 1. *Educ:* Univ Minn, BS, 63; Univ Va, PhD(biophys), 71. *Prof Exp:* Mgr tech commun, Medtronics, Inc, 66-68; NIH fel chem, Univ Mass, 71-73; res assoc biochem, Univ Va, 73-74. *Concurrent Pos:* NIH study sect biophys & biophys chem, 77-; adj fac biol, Wayne State Univ, 78- *Mem:* Sigma Xi; NY Acad Sci; Fedn Am Scientists; Biophys Soc; AAAS; Am Chem Soc. *Res:* Macromolecular interactions as typified by oligomeric proteins, particularly ligand-mediated subunit association; application of physical techniques to the study of biochemical systems. *Mailing Add:* 4661 Devonshire Rd Detroit MI 48224-3639

HALVORSON, LLOYD CHESTER, AGRICULTURAL ECONOMICS. *Current Pos:* PRIN AGR ECONOMIST, COOP STATE RES SERV, USDA, 57- *Personal Data:* b Swift County, Minn, Feb 7, 18; m 42; c 4. *Educ:* Univ Minn, BS, 39, PhD(agr econ), 43. *Prof Exp:* Economist credit, Farm Credit Admin, 42-45; economist agr policy, Nat Grange, 45-57. *Mem:* Am Agr Econ Asn. *Res:* Marketing and production economics. *Mailing Add:* 931 Douglass Dr McLean VA 22101

HALZEN, FRANCIS, THEORETICAL PHYSICS. *Current Pos:* MEM FAC PHYSICS, UNIV WIS-MADISON, 72- *Personal Data:* b Tienen, Belg, Mar 23, 44; m 68; c 1. *Educ:* Cath Univ Louvain, MS, 66, PhD(physics), 69. *Prof Exp:* Fel physics, Europ Ctr Nuclear Res, 69-71. *Concurrent Pos:* Consult, Argonne Nat Lab, 73; Brookhaven Nat Lab, 75, Rutherford Lab, 77 & Europ Orgn for Nuclear Res, 77. *Res:* High energy physics (theory). *Mailing Add:* Dept Physics Univ Wis-Madison 1150 University Ave Madison WI 53706. *E-Mail:* Bitnet: halzen@wiscphen

HAM, FRANK SLAGLE, POINT DEFECTS IN SEMICONDUCTORS, JAHN-TELLER EFFECT. *Current Pos:* VIS PROF PHYSICS, LEHIGH UNIV, 83- *Personal Data:* b Bronxville, NY, Aug 15, 28; m 60, Joan Kellogg; c William K & Peter S. *Educ:* Harvard Univ, AB, 50, AM, 51, PhD(physics), 55. *Prof Exp:* Nat Res Coun fel physics, Univ Ill, 54-55; res assoc, Corp Res & Develop Ctr, Gen Elec Co, 55-83. *Concurrent Pos:* Guggenheim fel theoret studies solid state physics, Oxford Univ, 71-72; alumni vis prof physics, Clemson Univ, 76-77. *Mem:* Am Phys Soc; Fedn Am Scientists; Sigma Xi. *Res:* Solid state physics; theory; spectroscopy of point defects; ribronic interactions; Jahn-Teller effect. *Mailing Add:* 1445 Valencia Rd Schenectady NY 12309-4317

HAM, GEORGE EDWARD, ORGANIC CHEMISTRY. *Current Pos:* Res chemist, Tex Org Res Dept, Dow Chem Co, 55-58, sr res chemist, 58-62, res specialist, 62-67, res specialist, Tex Amines Res Dept, 67-71, ASSOC SCIENTIST, TEX AMINES RES DEPT, DOW CHEM CO, 71- *Personal Data:* b Jacksboro, Tex, May 19, 31; m 59; c 3. *Educ:* Baylor Univ, BS, 51; Purdue Univ, MS, 53, PhD(org chem), 56. *Mem:* Am Chem Soc. *Res:* Organic synthesis; physical organic chemistry. *Mailing Add:* 112 Begonia St Lake Jackson TX 77566-0373

HAM, GEORGE ELDON, SOIL MICROBIOLOGY, AGRONOMY. *Current Pos:* prof agron & head dept, 80-89, ASSOC DEAN & ASSOC DIR, AGR EXP STA, KANS STATE UNIV, MANHATTAN, 89- *Personal Data:* b Ft Dodge, Iowa, May 22, 39; m 64; c 3. *Educ:* Iowa State Univ, BS, 61, MS, 63, PhD(soil microbiol), 67. *Prof Exp:* Res assoc soil microbiol, Iowa State Univ, 65-67; from asst prof to prof soil microbiol, Univ Minn, St Paul, 67-80. *Mem:* Fel AAAS; fel Soil Sci Soc Am; fel Am Soc Agron. *Res:* Ecology and significance of Rhizobium japonicum and its impact on the nitrogen nutrition of the soybean plant. *Mailing Add:* 2957 Nevada St Manhattan KS 66502

HAM, INYONG, MECHANICAL & INDUSTRIAL ENGINEERING. *Current Pos:* asst prof indust eng, Pa State Univ, 58-59, from asst prof to assoc prof, 63-69, distinguished prof, 91-95, DISTINGUISHED PROF EMER, 95-, PA STATE UNIV, PROF INDUST ENG, 69-, FANUC PROF, 89-, DIR MFG RES CTR, 90- *Personal Data:* b Korea, Dec 22, 25; US citizen; m 49, Hyancak; c 2. *Educ:* Seoul Nat Univ, BEng, 48; Univ Nebr, MSc, 56; Univ Wis, PhD(mech eng), 58. *Honors & Awards:* CAM-I Award, Comput Aided Mfg-Int, 78; Sargent Progress Award, 90. *Prof Exp:* Instr mech eng, Seoul Nat Univ, 48-50; asst, Univ Nebr, 54-56; res asst & instr, Univ Wis, 56-58; dir indust & asst minister, Repub SKorea Ministry Com & Indust, 60-62. *Concurrent Pos:* Adv, Korea Inst Sci & Technol, 73-83; consult prof, Xian Jiaotong Univ, China, 81 & Beijing Inst Technol, 84; Fulbright prof, Ga Polytech Inst, USSR, 81; chair vis prof, Univ Tokyo, 89, Korea Advan Sci & Technol I Seoul Nat Univ. *Mem:* Fel Am Soc Mech Engrs; fel Soc Mfg Engrs; Int Inst Prod Eng Res (vpres, 94-95); fel Inst Indust Engrs; Korean Sci & Eng Asn Am (pres, 74-75); NAm Mfg Res Inst (pres, 85-86). *Res:* Analysis of manufacturing problems; metal cutting theory and experiments; machinability evaluation; optimization of manufacturing conditions; design of cutting tools, jigs, and fixtures; group technology application; computer integrated manufacturing; manufacturing systems engineering. *Mailing Add:* Dept Indust & Mfg Eng 207 Hammond Bldg Pa State Univ University Park PA 16802

HAM, JAMES M(ILTON), ELECTRICAL ENGINEERING. *Current Pos:* from assoc prof to prof elec eng, Univ Toronto, 52-88, dean fac eng, 66-73, chmn res bd, 77-76, dean, Grad Sch, 76-78, pres, 78-88, HEAD DEPT, UNIV TORONTO, 64-, EMER PROF, 88-, EMER PRES, 88- *Personal Data:* b Coboconk, Ont, Sept 21, 20; m 55; c 3. *Educ:* Univ Toronto, BASc, 43; Mass Inst Technol, SM, 47, ScD(elec eng), 52. *Honors & Awards:* Centennial Medal of Can. *Prof Exp:* Asst prof, Mass Inst Technol, 51-52. *Concurrent Pos:* Vis scientist, Cambridge Univ, 60-61; mem, Nat Res Coun Can; bd gov, Ont Res Found; chmn comt educ, World Fedn Eng Orgn. *Mem:* Fel Inst Elec & Electronics Engrs; fel Eng Inst Can; Sigma Xi. *Res:* Feedback control systems; computer applications in industrial process control. *Mailing Add:* 135 Glencairn Ave Toronto ON M4R 1N1 Can

HAM, JOE STROTHER, PHYSICS, CHEMISTRY. *Current Pos:* from asst prof to prof physics, 56-63, prof chem, 67-78, PROF PHYSICS, TEX A&M UNIV, 63- *Personal Data:* b Okmulgee, Okla, Mar 12, 28; m 52, Florence Seeger; c Alice (Clark) & Susan (Janek). *Educ:* Univ Chicago, PhB, 48, MS, 51, PhD(physics), 54. *Prof Exp:* Res chemist, Jackson Lab, E I Du Pont de Nemours & Co, 53-56. *Concurrent Pos:* Res physicist, Ford Motor Co, 61-62; vis scientist, TNO, Delft, Neth, 71; consult, Shell Develop Co, 78-80; vis scientist, Air Force Mats Labs, 80-81. *Mem:* Am Phys Soc; Am Asn Physics Teachers; Sigma Xi. *Res:* Molecular spectra; thermosetting resins; polymer solutions; composite materials. *Mailing Add:* Dept Physics Tex A&M Univ College Station TX 77843-4242. *Fax:* 409-845-2590; *E-Mail:* ham@phys.tamw.edu

HAM, LEE EDWARD, URBAN PLANNING, NEW TOWN DESIGN. *Current Pos:* PRES, WILSEY & HAM CONSULT ENG, 45-, CHMN BD. *Personal Data:* b San Francisco, Calif, Dec 19, 19; m 86; c 4. *Educ:* Univ Calif, Berkeley, BS, 42. *Concurrent Pos:* Prin in charge, Design Foster City, Calif, 60-, Design of North Star, Tahoe, Calif, 74-80 & Design of Las Positas New Town, 80-84; distinguished engr, Am Pub Works Asn, 74. *Mem:* Fel Am Soc Civil Engrs; Am Pub Works Asn; fel Am Consult Engrs Coun; Urban Land Inst. *Res:* Development of new towns; determining optimum location and how to finance the infrastructure. *Mailing Add:* PO Box H San Mateo CA 94402

HAM, RICHARD GEORGE, CELL BIOLOGY, CELL GROWTH REQUIREMENTS. *Current Pos:* res assoc, Inst Develop Biol, 65-66, from asst prof to assoc prof, 66-76, PROF MOLECULAR, CELLULAR & DEVELOP BIOL, UNIV COLO, BOULDER, 76- *Personal Data:* b Tacoma, Wash, Feb 10, 32; m 53; c 4. *Educ:* Calif Inst Technol, BS, 53; Univ Tex, PhD(biochem), 57. *Prof Exp:* Res scientist biochem, Biochem Inst, Univ Tex, 57-58; instr biophys, Med Ctr, Univ Colo, Denver, 58-60, asst prof, 60-65. *Mem:* Am Soc Cell Biol; Soc Develop Biol; Tissue Cult Asn. *Res:* Growth requirements of cultured mammalian and avian cells; mechanisms of cellular differentiation; aging at the cellular level; effects of malignancy on cellular growth requirements. *Mailing Add:* Dept Molecular Cell & Develop Biol Univ Colo Campus Box 347 Boulder CO 80309-0347. *Fax:* 303-492-7744

HAM, RICHARD JOHN, GERIATRICS, FAMILY PRACTICE. *Current Pos:* DISTINGUISHED CHAIR, GERIAT MED, HEALTH SCI CTR, STATE UNIV NY, 87- *Personal Data:* b Chester, Eng, June 14, 46; m 67, Joanna Price; c Jason, Zoe & Gabriel. *Educ:* Univ London, BS & MB, 69; Ray Col Obstetricians & Gynecologists, DObs RCOG, 72; Royal Col Gen Practitioners, MRCGP, 74; Med Col Can, LMCC, 85. *Prof Exp:* Asst prof geriat & family med & chief, Div Geriat, Dept Family Practice, Sch Med, Southern Ill Univ, 77-82; assoc prof geriat, Dept Family Med & Suncoast Geront Ctr, Univ SFla, 82-84; Mt Pleasant Legion prof community geriat & dir, Div Community Geriat, Dept Family Pract, Univ BC, 84-86. *Concurrent Pos:* Ed, Geriat Med Ann, 83-87; dir, Short Term Assessment & Treatment Ctr, Vancouver Gen Hosp, 84-86; co-dir, Statewide Resource Ctr Geriat Educ, 87-94; dir, Alzheimers Dis Assistance Ctr, Cent NY, 88-94. *Mem:* Fel Am Geriat Soc (pres, 88-89); Am Acad Family Physicians; Soc Teachers Family Med; fel Geront Soc Am. *Res:* Interrelationship of dementia and depression; impact of dementia on caregivers; effect of environment and familiarity on behaviors in dementia; neuroleptics in dementia management. *Mailing Add:* Dept Med State Univ NY Health Sci Col Med 750 E Adams St Syracuse NY 13210-2306. *Fax:* 315-464-1771

HAM, RUSSELL ALLEN, GEOPRESSURED GEOTHERMAL ENERGY. *Current Pos:* PROF CHEM, MCNEESE STATE UNIV, 70- *Personal Data:* b Belvidere, Ill, March 18, 40; m 65. *Educ:* Northern Ill Univ, BS, 66; Univ Iowa, MS, 68, PhD(chem), 70. *Mem:* Am Chem Soc; Soc Col Sci Teachers. *Res:* Composition of gas and fluids obtained from geopressure geothermal resevoirs in Louisiana and Texas to determine potential for energy production. *Mailing Add:* Box 90455 Chem Dept McNeese State Univ Lake Charles LA 70609-9998

HAM, WILLIAM TAYLOR, JR, PHYSICS, PHOTOBIOLOGY. *Current Pos:* from assoc prof to prof, 48-76, head dept, 53-76, EMER PROF BIOPHYS, VA COMMONWEALTH UNIV, 76- *Personal Data:* b Norfolk, Va, Sept 20, 08; m 40; c 2. *Educ:* Univ Va, BSE, 31, MS, 33, PhD(physics), 35. *Prof Exp:* Instr physics, Columbia Univ, 36-37; res physicist, Kendall Mills, NC, 37-38; pres, W T Ham & Co, Inc, Va, 38-40; res assoc, Univ Va, 40-43; head, Div Physics, Inst Textile Technol, 46-48. *Concurrent Pos:* Mem, Radiation Cataract Comt, Nat Acad Sci-Nat Res Coun, 54-57, Atomic Bomb Casualty Comt, 56-58; NSF panel on fels, 55-58; mem, Electromagnetic Radiation Mgt Adv Coun, exec off pres, 68-75; Nat Coun Radiation Protection & Measurements; chmn, AEC spec fel bd, 66-67, chmn, Gordon Conf Lasers Med & Biol, 70. *Mem:* Fel Am Phys Soc; Biophys Soc; Health Phys Soc (pres, 63-64); Asn Res Vision Ophthal; fel AAAS; Am Soc Photobiol; Bioelectromagnetic Soc; Optical Soc Am. *Res:* Nuclear physics; separation uranium isotopes; radiation dosimetry; radiation cataract; radiobiology; health physics; thermal injury; biological effects of lasers; ultraviolet, visible and infrared radiation effects on the eye. *Mailing Add:* 8653 Cherokee Rd Richmond VA 23235-1515

HAMA, FRANCIS R(YOSUKE), AERODYNAMICS. *Personal Data:* b Tokyo, Japan, Dec 6, 17; nat US; m 76, Liselotte Hama-Nonweiler; c Mary & Michiko. *Educ:* Tokyo Imp Univ, ME, 40, ScD(aerodyn), 52. *Honors & Awards:* A V Humboldt Stiftung Sr Am Scientist Prize; Soc of Scholars, Johns Hopkins Univ. *Prof Exp:* Asst prof, Tokyo Imp Univ, 43-50; asst, Johns Hopkins Univ, 50-52; res engr, Inst Hydraul Res, Univ Iowa, 52-54; from asst res prof to res prof, Inst Fluid Dynamics & Appl Math, Univ Md, 54-63; staff scientist, Jet Propulsion Lab, Calif Inst Technol, 63-68; sr res scientist, lectr & prof, Mech & Aerospace Eng Dept, Princeton Univ, 68-81. *Concurrent Pos:* Vis prof, Stuttgart Univ, 81- *Mem:* Am Phys Soc; Am Inst Aeronaut & Astronaut; Ger Asn Appl Math & Mech; Ger Soc Air & Space Travel; Japan Soc Fluid Mechs. *Res:* Supersonic aerodynamics; boundary layer. *Mailing Add:* Wilramstr 17 81669 Munich Germany

HAMACHER, HORST W, combinatorial optimization, for more information see previous edition

HAMACHER, V(INCENT) CARL, ELECTRICAL ENGINEERING, COMPUTER SCIENCE. *Current Pos:* DEAN, FAC APPL SCI, QUEEN'S UNIV, 91- *Personal Data:* b London, Ont, Sept 28, 39; m 65; c 2. *Educ:* Univ Waterloo, BASc, 63; Queen's Univ, Ont, MSc, 65; Syracuse Univ, PhD(elec eng), 68. *Prof Exp:* Asst prof elec eng, Univ Toronto, 68-72; from assoc prof to prof elec eng & comput sci, 72-82. *Concurrent Pos:* Nat Res Coun Can res grant, 68- *Mem:* Inst Elec & Electronics Engrs; Asn Comput Mach. *Res:* Computer organization; computer communication networks; real time systems. *Mailing Add:* 2 Beverley St Kingston ON K7L 3Y4 Can

HAMADA, HAROLD SEICHI, CIVIL ENGINEERING, APPLIED MECHANICS. *Current Pos:* assoc prof, 67-76, chmn dept, 90-94, PROF CIVIL ENG, UNIV HAWAII, 94- *Personal Data:* b Honolulu, Hawaii, Nov 1, 35; m 58, Lucy Igawa; c LeeAnn (Kakuda) & Kyle. *Educ:* Univ Hawaii, BS, 57; Univ Ill, PhD, 62. *Prof Exp:* Proj off, Air Force Weapons Lab, Kirtland AFB, NMex, 62-65; engr, Theoret Physics Div, Lawrence Radiation Lab, Calif, 65-67. *Mem:* Am Soc Civil Engrs; Am Concrete Inst; Sigma Xi. *Res:* Numerical techniques for the solution of fluid or solid mechanics problems, creep and shrinkage of concrete. *Mailing Add:* Dept Civil Eng Univ Hawaii at Manoa Honolulu HI 96822. *Fax:* 808-956-5014; *E-Mail:* hamada@wiliki.eng

HAMADA, SPENCER HIROSHI, DEVELOPMENTAL BIOLOGY, CELL BIOLOGY. *Current Pos:* asst prof, 78-81, ASSOC PROF BIOL, WGA COL, 81- *Personal Data:* b Honolulu, Hawaii, Mar 31, 43. *Educ:* Univ Hawaii, BA, 68; Ore State Univ, MS, 72, PhD(zool), 75. *Prof Exp:* Instr zool, Ore State Univ, 73; lectr biol, Calif Polytech State Univ, 74; asst prof, Fordham Univ, 76. *Concurrent Pos:* Grant, Fordham Univ, 76; Ga fac grant, 78-79; Dept Energy grant; res scientist, Med Univ SC, 82. *Mem:* AAAS; Am Inst Biol Sci; Soc Develop Biol; Tissue Cult Asn; Electron Micros Soc. *Res:* Development of neurons and glial cells in culture; self-reassembly of embryos in culture. *Mailing Add:* Dept Biol WGa Col 1601 Maple St Carrollton GA 30118-0001

HAMAI, JAMES Y, MANUFACTURING REPRESENTATIVE. *Current Pos:* exec vpres, corp secy & mem bd dirs, Concrete Cutting Industs, 69-72, pres, 73-79, BD CHMN, CONCRETE CUTTING INDUSTS, INC, 80- *Personal Data:* b Los Angeles, Calif, Oct 14, 26; m 54; c 1. *Educ:* Univ Southern Calif, BS, 52, MS, 55. *Prof Exp:* From process engr to sr process engr, Fluor Corp Ltd, 54-64; sr proj mgr, Cent Res Dept, Monsanto Co, 64-67, mgr res, develop & eng, Graphic Systs Dept, 67-68, mgr commercial develop & mgr, Brisbane Tech Ctr, 68-69. *Concurrent Pos:* Lectr chem eng, Univ Southern Calif, 63-64; consult, Fluor Corp, 70-75, Japan bus, 76- *Mem:* Am Inst Chem Engrs. *Res:* Research management and planning; technical and commercial liaison; process design of petroleum, petrochemical and chemical plant complexes; general management. *Mailing Add:* 6600 Via La Paloma Rancho Palos Verdes CA 90274

HAMAKER, JOHN C, JR, AEROSPACE APPLICATIONS. *Current Pos:* OWNER, JCH INC & PLH INC, AUTO PARTS MFRS, 81- *Personal Data:* b Canton, Ohio, Apr 21, 24; m 47; c 2. *Educ:* Univ Mich, BS, 45, MS, 47, PhD(metall eng), 52. *Prof Exp:* Plant engr, Stearns-Roger Mfg Co, Denver, 51-53; dir res & eng, Basco Metals Corp, Latrobe, Pa, 53-61, vpres & dir, 61-68; pres, Teledyne Rodney Metals, New Bedford, Mass, 68-70; group pres, Whittaker Corp, Los Angeles, 70-71; group exec & chmn, Teledyne Can, 71; group vpres, Automation Industs Inc, Los Angeles, 71-75; sr vpres, SSP Industs, Burbank, 75-77. *Concurrent Pos:* Mem mat adv bd, Nat Acad Sci; lectr, Pa State Univ, Univ Hawaii, Univ Wis; trustee, Am Soc Metals Int. *Mem:* Am Soc Metals Int; Am Soc Testing & Mat; Am Inst Mining Metall & Petrol Engrs; Am Iron & Steel Inst; Am Chem Soc. *Res:* Development and properties of tool steels; heat treatment of special steels and alloys; superstrength steels. *Mailing Add:* 795 Kumukahi Pl Honolulu HI 96825-1114

HAMAKER, JOHN WARREN, AGRICULTURAL CHEMISTRY. *Current Pos:* RETIRED. *Personal Data:* b Montreal, Que, Oct 25, 17; m 44; c 4. *Educ:* Univ Calif, Los Angeles, BA, 40; Univ Calif, PhD(chem), 44. *Prof Exp:* Res assoc chem, Univ Calif, 44-45; instr, Napa Jr Col, 45-47; from asst prof to assoc prof, Whittier Col, 47-55; chemist, Dow Chem Co, 55-86. *Concurrent Pos:* With AEC; with Off Sci Res & Develop, 44; vis assoc prof, Univ Chicago, 53. *Mem:* Am Chem Soc; Sigma Xi. *Res:* Microchemical technique of qualitative analysis; analytical microchemistry; radioactive or tracer chemistry; environmental fate of pesticides. *Mailing Add:* 125 Conifer Lane Walnut Creek CA 94598

HAMANN, BERND, COMPUTER SCIENCE. *Current Pos:* actg assoc prof comput sci, 95-97, CO-DIR, CTR IMAGE PROCESSING & INTEGRATED COMPUT, UNIV CALIF, DAVIS, 97-, ASSOC PROF, 97- *Personal Data:* b Ger, Dec 24, 63. *Educ:* Tech Univ, Ger, BS, 85, 86, MS, 88; Ariz State Univ, PhD(comput sci), 91. *Prof Exp:* Appl programmer, Stahlwerke Peine-Salzgitter AG, Ger, 85-86. *Concurrent Pos:* From asst prof to assoc prof comput sci, Miss State Univ, 91-95, res fac mem sci visualization thrust, NSF Res Ctr Comput Field, Simulation, 91-95, adj prof comput sci, 95- *Mem:* Asn Comput Mach; Inst Elec & Electronics Engrs Comput Soc; Soc Indust & Appl Math. *Res:* Computer-aided geometric design; scientific visualization and computer graphics; grid/mesh generation (triangulation methods); computer vision (edge/feature detection); robotics. *Mailing Add:* Dept Comput Sci Univ Calif Davis CA 95616-8562

HAMANN, DONALD DALE, engineering mechanics, food technology; deceased, see previous edition for last biography

HAMANN, DONALD ROBERT, PHYSICS. *Current Pos:* mem tech staff, 65-78, head, Dept Theoret Physics, 78-81, HEAD, SURFACE PHYSICS RES DEPT, AT&T BELL LABS, 81- *Personal Data:* b Valley Stream, NY, May 16, 39; m 66, Ruth Halpert; c Hillary B. *Educ:* Mass Inst Technol, BS, 61, PhD(elec eng), 65. *Honors & Awards:* Davisson-Germer Prize, Am Phys Soc. *Prof Exp:* Staff scientist theoret physics, Ford Motor Co Sci Lab, 64-65. *Mem:* Fel Am Phys Soc; Sigma Xi. *Res:* Theoretical solid state physics; surface physics; computational physics. *Mailing Add:* AT&T Bell Labs 600 Mountain Ave PO Box 261 Rm 1C-327 Murray Hill NJ 07974. *E-Mail:* drh@physics.att.com

HAMAR, DWAYNE WALTER, BIOCHEMISTRY. *Current Pos:* From instr to asst prof, 63-70, ASSOC PROF PATH, COLO STATE UNIV, 70-, QUAL ASSURANCE CONSULT. *Personal Data:* b Lexington, Nebr, Mar 28, 37; m 90, Cindi Hoffman; c Mitch. *Educ:* Nebr State Teachers Col, Kearney, BA, 58; Univ Nebr, MS, 61, PhD(biochem), 64. *Mem:* Fel Am Inst Chem; Soc Qual Assurance. *Res:* Chemical pathology; metabolism. *Mailing Add:* Dept Path Colo State Univ Ft Collins CO 80523. *Fax:* 970-491-0603

HAMARNEH, SAMI KHALAF, HISTORY OF MEDICAL SCIENCES. *Current Pos:* Assoc cur, Div Med Sci, Smithsonian Inst, 59-61, cur-in-chg, 61-72, res historian, Dept Sci & Technol, 73-78 & pharm, 72-78, field expert, 79, EMER CUR, SMITHSONIAN INST, 78- *Personal Data:* b Madaba, Jordan, Feb 2, 25; nat US; m 48; c 1. *Educ:* Syrian Univ, Damascus, Syria, BS, 48; NDak State Univ, MS, 56; Univ Wis, PhD(hist pharm & sci), 59. *Honors & Awards:* Star of Jordan Medal, 65; Ed Kremers Award, 66. *Concurrent Pos:* Vis assoc prof, George Washington Univ, 63-64; vis prof, Univ Pa, 69 & Univ Aleppo, Syria, 79; sci adv, Arab Soc Hist Pharm, 77-; prof hist med sci, King Abdulaziz Univ, Jeddah, Saudi Arabia, 82-83; prof hist med sci, Sch Pub Health, Yarmouk Univ, Irbid, Jordan, 84-90. *Mem:* Int Acad Pharm; Am Inst Hist Pharm; Arab Soc Hist Pharm; Arab Acad. *Res:* Health field in Islam; history of Arabic medicine, pharmacy and public health and the Arab physicians who contributed to it. *Mailing Add:* 4631 Massachusetts Ave NW Washington DC 20016

HAMASAKI, DUCO I, OPHTHALMOLOGY. *Current Pos:* from instr to assoc prof, 62-79, PROF OPHTHAL, UNIV MIAMI, 79- *Personal Data:* b Maui, Hawaii, July 1, 29; m 67; c 2. *Educ:* Washington Univ, AB, 50; Univ Calif, Berkeley, MOptom, 54, PhD(physiol optics), 59. *Prof Exp:* Asst physiol optics, Univ Calif, Berkeley, 53-59, physiol opticist, 59-61. *Concurrent Pos:* NIH fel physiol, Cambridge Univ, 61-62; NIH grant, 63-64; vis scientist physiol, Tohoku Univ, Sendai, Japan, 77-78. *Mem:* Asn Res Vision & Ophthal. *Res:* Visual physiology. *Mailing Add:* 9841 SW 60th Ct Miami FL 33156

HAMAWY, MAJED MAHMOOD, IMMUNOLOGY, ALLERGY & SIGNAL TRANSDUCTION. *Current Pos:* IRTA fel, NIH, 89-91, staff fel, 92-93, sr staff fel, 94-96, BIOLOGIST, NIH, 97- *Personal Data:* b Kuwait City, Kuwait, Jan 25, 58; US citizen; m 87, Sonia Wailand; c Faysal & Nawal. *Educ:* Univ Jordan, BS, 80; Univ London, MS, 84; Univ Ariz, PhD(immunol & pharmacol), 88. *Honors & Awards:* Allergy Res Found Award, Pharmacia Inc, 96. *Concurrent Pos:* Intramural res training award, NIH, 89, fels award res excellence, 97. *Mem:* Am Asn Immunologists; AAAS. *Res:* Identifying molecules important for cell signaling. *Mailing Add:* 20226 Grazing Way Gaithersburg MD 20879. *E-Mail:* mh101v@nih.gov

HAMB, FREDRICK LYNN, ORGANIC POLYMER CHEMISTRY, TECHNICAL MANAGEMENT. *Current Pos:* Sr res chemist, Eastman Kodak Co, 63-69, res assoc, 69-71, lab head, Res Labs, 71-75, asst dir, Photog Res Div, 75-78, asst dir, 78-80, dir, Black & White Photog Div, 80-89, mgr, Regional Bus Unit, 90-95, SR VPRES & CHIEF TECH OFFICER, INT IMAGING MATS, JAPANESE REGION, EASTMAN KODAK CO, 95- *Personal Data:* b Mt Gay, WVa, May 28, 37; m 60, Joan Vannoy; c Christopher & Kelly. *Educ:* WVa Univ, BS, 60, MS, 62, PhD(org chem), 64. *Mem:* Am Chem Soc; NY Acad Sci; Sigma Xi. *Res:* Condensation and addition polymers; chemistry of cyclopentadienes; Diels-Alder reaction; polymers for photography; non-silver photography; silver halide photography; non-impact electronic imaging. *Mailing Add:* Eastman Kodak 343 State St NJ160 Rochester NY 14650. *Fax:* 716-691-2424

HAMBIDGE, K MICHAEL, PEDIATRICS. *Current Pos:* Res fel pediat, Health Sci Ctr, Univ Colo, 66-67, asst dir, Children's Clin Res Ctr, 67-68, from instr to assoc prof, 67-77, PROF PEDIAT, HEALTH SCI CTR, UNIV COLO, 78-, DIR, CHILDREN'S CLIN RES CTR, 85- & CTR HUMAN NUTRIT, 88- *Personal Data:* b Oct 28, 32. *Educ:* Cambridge Univ, Eng, BA, 56; Westminster Med Sch, MB & BChir, 60. *Hon Degrees:* ScD, Univ Cambridge, 88. *Honors & Awards:* Borden Award, Am Inst Nutrit, 79; Nutrit Award, Am Acad Pediat, 87. *Concurrent Pos:* Co-dir, Children's Clin Res Ctr, Univ Colo, 75-84. *Res:* Childhood nutrition; author of numerous scientific publications. *Mailing Add:* Dept Pediat Health Sci Ctr Univ Colo 4200 E Ninth Ave PO Box C-225 Denver CO 80262-0001. *Fax:* 303-270-3273

HAMBLEN, DAVID GORDON, EXPERIMENTAL PHYSICS. *Current Pos:* VPRES, ADVAN FUEL RES, INC, 80- *Personal Data:* b Norwalk, Conn, Apr 20, 40; m 64; c 2. *Educ:* Williams Col, BA, 62; Univ Ill, Urbana, MS, 63, PhD(physics), 69. *Prof Exp:* Exp physicist, United Technol Res Ctr, 69-80. *Mem:* Am Phys Soc; Inst Elec & Electronics Engrs; Sigma Xi. *Mailing Add:* Advan Fuel Res 87 Church St East Hartford CT 06108-3742

HAMBLEN, DAVID PHILIP, CLINICAL ANALYZERS, ION ETCHING. *Current Pos:* RES ASSOC SR STAFF, EASTMAN KODAK RES LABS, 67- *Personal Data:* b Chicago, Ill, Sept 12, 28; m 59, Frances Winfree; c Mary A & Susan E. *Educ:* NMex Mil Inst, BS, 51; Tulane Univ La, BS, 55; Univ Tenn, MS, 60; Univ Rochester, MS, 65. *Prof Exp:* Assoc physicist, Union Carbide Nuclear Co, 56-58 & Oak Ridge Nat Lab, 58-61; sr scientist, Bausch & Lomb, Inc, 61-67. *Concurrent Pos:* Consult, Redstone Arsenal, asst, Tulane Univ La, 55-56; consult, Atomic Energy Proj, US AEC-Univ Rochester, 66-67. *Mem:* Am Optical Soc. *Res:* Development of radiation scanner for tumor localization; atomic reactor experimentation; thermonuclear fusion research; abiotic synthesis of biological molecules; gas laser development; production of gradient-index optical materials; electrochemical and liquid-crystal display systems; liquid photographic devices; clinical diagnostic instrumentation; emulsion research; microelectronics development. *Mailing Add:* 42 Gateway Rd Rochester NY 14624. *Fax:* 716-477-0757

HAMBLEN, JOHN WESLEY, COMPUTER SCIENCE, GENEALOGY. *Current Pos:* chmn comput sci, 72-81, prof, 72-87, EMER PROF, UNIV MO, ROLLA, 87- *Personal Data:* b Story, Ind, Sept 25, 24; m 87, Marianne Muhlbauer; c James O. *Educ:* Ind Univ, AB, 47; Purdue Univ, MS, 52, PhD(math), 55. *Honors & Awards:* Asn Educ Data Systs Award, 71; Outstanding Contrib Comput Sci Educ, Am Comput Mech, 90. *Prof Exp:* From asst prof to assoc prof math, Okla State Univ, 55-58, dir, Comput Ctr, 57-58; assoc prof statist & dir, Comput Ctr, Univ Ky, 58-61; prof math & technol & dir, Data Processing & Comput Ctr, Southern Ill Univ, 61-65; proj dir comput sci, Southern Regional Educ Bd, 65-72. *Concurrent Pos:* Consult, D-X Sunray Oil Co, 57-58; lectr, IBM Corp, 57, Asn Comput Mach-NSF vis scientist, 60; consult, Systs Develop Corp & prof, Ga Inst Technol, 65-66; ed, J Asn Ed Data Systs, 67-68; mem, Data Base Panel, Comput Sci & Eng Bd, Nat Acad Sci, 69-71 & 79-80; chmn, Educ Comt, Am Fedn Info Processing Socs, 71-72 & 79-84; consult, NSF, 75-76; vis scientist, Ctr Appl Math, Nat Bur Stand, 81-83; assoc prog dir, SEE/DMDRI/AAT, NSF, 85-86. *Mem:* Fel AAAS; Asn Comput Mach (secy, 72-76); Nat Geneal Soc; Asn Educ Data Systs (pres, 68-69). *Res:* Distributions of combinations of random variables; application of digital computers; information systems design; genealogy. *Mailing Add:* 4432 Carya Sq Columbus IN 47201-4944. *E-Mail:* hamblen@uno.com

HAMBLETON, WILLIAM WELDON, GEOLOGY, GEOPHYSICS. *Current Pos:* instr, 49, from asst prof to assoc prof, 51-62, PROF GEOL, UNIV KANS, 62-, STATE GEOLOGIST & DIR, KANS GEOL SURV, 70- *Personal Data:* b Lancaster, Pa, Sept 10, 21; m 46; c 2. *Educ:* Franklin & Marshall Col, BS, 43; Northwestern Univ, MS, 47; Univ Kans, PhD(geol), 51. *Prof Exp:* Geologist, Pa Geol Surv, 46 & 51. *Concurrent Pos:* Chem petrographer, US Bur Mines, 49; asst dir, Kans Geol Surv, 54-56, assoc dir, 56-70, assoc dean, Grad Sch, Univ Kans, 67-68, fac, 68-70; geophysicist, Chevron Oil Co, 55; vis scientist, Lamont Geol Observ, Columbia Univ, 59-60; mem, Bd Dirs, Mid-Continent Res & Develop Coun; Bd Dirs, Kans Sch Relig, Energy Comt, Interstate Oil Compact Comn, Mineral Resources Comt, Nat Asn State Univ & Land Grant Cols, Energy Adv Coun, Kans Energy Off, Exec Adv Comt, Nat Gas Surv, Gov Task Force Water Resources; chmn, Kans Comt Midwest Gov Conf Task Energy & Natural Resources, Gov Rev Group nuclear waste disposal, Dept Energy; vchmn adv bd, Kans Univ Sch Fine Arts. *Mem:* Geol Soc Am; Am Soc Explor Geol; Am Asn Petrol Geol; Am Asn Geol Teachers; Sigma Xi. *Res:* Geophysics, gravity and magnetism; igneous petrography; economic geology. *Mailing Add:* 1312 Raintree Pl Lawrence KS 66044-4536

HAMBLIN, WILLIAM KENNETH, GEOLOGY. *Current Pos:* PROF GEOL, BRIGHAM YOUNG UNIV, 63- *Personal Data:* b Lyman, Wyo, May 22, 28; m 52; c 4. *Educ:* Brigham Young Univ, BA, 53, MS, 54; Univ Mich, PhD(geol), 58. *Prof Exp:* Asst prof geol, Univ Kans, 57-62; assoc prof, Univ Ga, 62-63. *Mem:* Geol Soc Am; Soc Econ Paleont & Mineral; Am Asn Petrol Geol. *Res:* Stratigraphy and sedimentation. *Mailing Add:* Dept Geol Brigham Young Univ 209 Page Provo UT 84602

HAMBOURGER, PAUL DAVID, EXPERIMENTAL SOLID STATE PHYSICS. *Current Pos:* asst prof, 71-75, ASSOC PROF PHYSICS, CLEVELAND STATE UNIV, 75- *Personal Data:* b Cleveland, Ohio, Dec 26, 39; m 76. *Educ:* Harvard Univ, BA, 62; Northwestern Univ, PhD(physics), 69. *Prof Exp:* Res assoc physics, Univ Pa, 69-71. *Mem:* Am Phys Soc. *Res:* Low temperature solid state physics and applied physics; high-pressure physics; electronic and magnetic properties of solids; reduced-dimensionality materials; solid-state phase transitions; superconductivity; conductor-insulator composite materials. *Mailing Add:* Dept Physics Cleveland State Univ Euclid Ave at E 24th St Cleveland OH 44115

HAMBRECHT, FREDERICK TERRY, BIOMEDICAL ENGINEERING. *Current Pos:* RES ASSOC NEURAL CONTROL, 69- & PROG DIR NEURAL PROSTHESIS, NIH, 72- *Personal Data:* b Galesburg, Ill, Aug 18, 39; m 65; c 2. *Educ:* Purdue Univ, BS, 61; Mass Inst Technol, MS, 63; Johns Hopkins Univ, MD, 68. *Honors & Awards:* Commendation Medal, USPHS, 75; Meritorious Serv Medal, 80, Distinguished Serv Medal, 86. *Prof Exp:* Res assoc biomed eng, Mass Inst Technol, 61-63; intern surg, Med Ctr, Duke Univ, 68-69. *Mem:* Soc Neurosci; Biomed Eng Soc. *Res:* Application of engineering to clinical medicine, neural prostheses, neural control and neurophysiology. *Mailing Add:* 14015 Manorvale Rd Rockville MD 20853

HAMBRICK, GEORGE WALTER, JR, MEDICINE, DERMATOLOGY. *Current Pos:* prof, 81-95, EMER PROF, MED COL, CORNELL UNIV, 95- *Personal Data:* b Charlottesville, Va, Dec 4, 22. *Educ:* Concord Col, BS, 44; Univ Va, MD, 46; Am Bd Dermat, dipl, 53, dipl dermatopath, 75. *Prof Exp:* Intern, Univ Iowa Hosp, 47; resident dermat, Univ Va Hosp, 48; resident, Columbia-Presby Med Ctr, 51; instr, Duke Univ Hosp, 51-52, assoc, 52-53; instr, Col Physicians & Surgeons, Columbia Univ, 53-55; from assoc to assoc prof, Sch Med, Univ Pa, 55-66, chief dermat, Clin Hosp, 56-65; from assoc prof to prof, Sch Med, Johns Hopkins Univ, 66-76, dir dermat, 67-76; prof dermat & dir dept, Univ Cincinnati, 76-81. *Concurrent Pos:* Fel, Duke Univ Hosp, 51-52; mem, Attend Staff, Philadelphia Gen Hosp, 55-66; consult, US Naval Hosp, Philadelphia, 59-66 & NIH, 67-75; chief, NY Hosp, 81-95; consult, 88- *Mem:* Hon mem Soc Invest Dermat (secy-treas, 65-69, pres, 71-); Am Dermat Asn; AMA; Am Acad Dermat; Am Col Physicians; Am Skin Asn (pres, 88-93). *Res:* Clinical dermatology and anatomy of the skin. *Mailing Add:* 916 E High Sparesh Office Charlottesville VA 22902. *Fax:* 804-970-2205

HAMBURG, BEATRIX A M, CHILD PSYCHIATRY, PEDIATRICS. *Current Pos:* dir, Div Child & Adolescent Psychiat, 88-92, PROF PSYCHIAT & PEDIAT, MT SINAI HOSP, 83-; PRES, WILLIAM T GRANT FOUND, 92- *Personal Data:* b Jacksonville, Fla, Oct 19, 23; m 51; c 2. *Educ:* Vassar Col, AB, 44; Yale Univ, MD, 48. *Hon Degrees:* DHL, Northwestern Univ, 94. *Honors & Awards:* T Roswell Gallagher Award, Adolescent Med. *Prof Exp:* Intern, Grace-New Haven Hosp, 48-49; resident, Yale Psychiat Inst, 49-50, Children's Hosp, 50-51 & Inst Juv Res, 51-53; res assoc, Med Sch, Stanford Univ, 61-71, assoc prof psychiat, 76-80; assoc prof, Sch Med, Harvard Univ, 80-83, exec dir, Health Policy Res Div, 81-83. *Concurrent Pos:* Mem, Comn Behav & Social Sci, Nat Acad Sci; mem, NY State Pub Health Coun; dir, Bush Found; trustee, William T Grant Found; mem, Adolescent Comt, Am Pub Health Asn, 77-81; bd dirs, AAAS, 87-91. *Mem:* Inst Med-Nat Acad Sci; Soc Adolescent Med; Am Pub Health Asn; fel Am Acad Child Psychiat; Soc Prof Child Psychiat; AAAS; Acad Res Behav Med; Soc Study Soc Biol; NIMH. *Res:* Biomedical-behavioral factors in diabetes; normal development and developmental psychopathology of adolescents; health policy research. *Mailing Add:* William T Grant Found 515 Madison Ave 6th Floor New York NY 10022-5403. *Fax:* 212-752-1398

HAMBURG, DAVID ALAN, BEHAVIORAL SCIENCE. *Current Pos:* pres, 83-97, EMER PRES, CARNEGIE CORP NY, 97- *Personal Data:* b Evansville, Ind, Oct 1, 25; m 51; c 2. *Educ:* Ind Univ, AB, 44, MD, 47; Am Bd Psychiat & Neurol, cert, 53. *Hon Degrees:* DSc, Ind Univ, 76, Rush Univ, 77, City Univ NY, 80, Univ Rochester, 81, Univ Ill, 84, Albert Einstein Sch Med, 85, Univ Southern Calif, Hahnemann Univ, 86 & Univ Pittsburgh, 86. *Honors & Awards:* Menninger Award, Am Col Physicians, 76; Vestermark Award, Am Psychiat Asn, 77; Rosenhaus Award, Am Pub Health Asn, 78; John P McGovern Award, Sigma Xi, 86; Health for All Medal, WHO, 88. *Prof Exp:* Asst psychiat, Sch Med, Yale Univ, 48-49; resident psychiatrist, Michael Reese Hosp, Chicago, 49-50; staff psychiatrist, Brooke Army Hosp, Tex, 50-52; resident psychiatrist, Walter Reed Army Inst Res, DC, 52-53; assoc dir inst psychosom & psychiat res & training, Michael Reese Hosp, 53-56; chief, Adult Psychiat Br, NIMH, 58-61; exec head dept, Sch Med, Stanford Univ, 61-69, prof psychiat, 61-76, chmn dept, 69-76; pres, Inst Med, Nat Acad Sci, 75-80; J D MacArthur prof health policy & dir, Div Health Policy Res & Educ, Harvard Univ, 80-82. *Concurrent Pos:* Consult, Walter Reed Army Inst Res, 54-57, Nat Adv Comt Res Psychiat, Neurol & Psychol, Vet Admin, 64-68, UNESCO, 69-70; fel, Ctr Advan Study Behav Sci, 57; mem bd dirs, Found Fund Res Psychiat, 57-60, Comt Res Probs Sex, Nat Acad Sci, Nat Res Coun, 58-61, Res Career Award Comt, NIMH, 61-65, Behav & Social Sci Surv Comt & Comt Life Sci & Social Policy, Nat Acad Sci, 66-73, gov bd, Nat Res Coun, 75-80, Bd Ment Health & Behav Med, Inst Med-Nat Acad Sci & Comt Int Security & Arms Control, 81-; assoc ed, J Psychiat Res, 60-; chmn var sci comts, NIMH, HEW, WHO & Nat Acad Sci, 61-; clin prof psychiat & behav sci, George Washington Univ, 76-80; adj prof pub policy & clin prof psychiat, Duke Univ, 78-80; sr adv, Ctr Social Policy Studies Israel, 83- *Mem:* Inst Med-Nat Acad Sci (pres, 75-80); AAAS (pres, 84-85); Am Psychosom Soc; Am Psychiat Asn; Am Soc Human Genetics; Soc Neurosci; Am Philos Soc. *Res:* Psychological stress and endocrine function; adaptive behavior under stress; psychotherapy in crisis; genetics, hormones and behavior; author of numerous technical publications. *Mailing Add:* Carnegie Corp NY 437 Madison Ave New York NY 10022. *Fax:* 212-753-0395

HAMBURG, JOSEPH, HEALTH ADMINISTRATION. *Current Pos:* from asst prof to dean, 63-66, prof med, Community Med & Allied Health Educ, 71-91, DEAN & EMER PROF, COL ALLIED HEALTH PROFESSIONS, UNIV KY, 92- *Personal Data:* b Philadelphia, Pa, Sept 9, 22. *Educ:* Hahnemann Med Col, MD, 51. *Hon Degrees:* DSc, Hahnemann Med Col, 79; LHD, Thomas Jefferson Univ, 93. *Concurrent Pos:* Chmn, Nat Coun Educ Health Profs, Health Prom, 86- *Mem:* Inst Med-Nat Acad Sci; Am Soc Allied Health Professions (pres, 72); AMA; Am Acad Family Pract. *Mailing Add:* 3212 S Ocean Blvd 608A Highland Beach FL 33487

HAMBURG, MARGARET ANN, INTERNAL MEDICINE. *Current Pos:* dep comnr, Family Health Servs, 90-91, HEALTH COMNR, NY CITY DEPT HEALTH, 91- *Personal Data:* b Chicago, Ill, July 12, 55. *Educ:* Harvard Univ, BA, 78, MD, 83; Am Bd Internal Med, dipl, 86. *Honors & Awards:* John P McGovern MD Award, Am Asn Cols Nursing, 94. *Prof Exp:* Intern/resident, Internal Med, NY Hosp, Cornell Univ Med Col, 83-86; spec asst to dir, Off Dis Prev & Health Promotion, Off of Asst Secy Health, US Dept Health & Human Servs, 86-88; spec asst to dir, Nat Inst Allergy & Infectious Dis, NIH, 88-89, asst dir, 89-90. *Concurrent Pos:* Guest investr, Rockefeller Univ, 85-86; mem, Prev Coordr Comt, NIH, 86-88; clin instr, Dept Med, Georgetown Univ Sch Med, 86-90; vol attending physician, Washington Free Clin, 88-90; mem, Med Sci Sect Comt, AAAS, 89-; mem, Steering Comt on Women & AIDS, NIH, 91; adj asst prof med, Cornell Univ Med Col, 91-; asst prof, Clin Pub Health, Columbia Univ Sch Pub Health, 91-; scholar, Pub Health Leadership Inst, Ctr Dis Control, Univ Calif, 92; mem, Comt Substance Abuse & Ment Health Issues in AIDS Res, Inst Med, 93-, Comt Prev & Control Sexually Transmitted Dis, 95- *Mem:* Inst Med-Nat Acad Sci; Soc Social Biol; NY Acad Med; AAAS; Am Col Physicians; Am Med Women's Asn; Am Pub Health Asn. *Res:* Published numerous articles in professional journals. *Mailing Add:* New York City Dept Health 125 Worth St New York NY 10013

HAMBURGER, ANNE W, cell biology, experimental hematology, for more information see previous edition

HAMBURGER, MICHAEL WILE, SEISMOLOGY, TECTONOPHYSICS. *Current Pos:* ASSOC PROF GEOPHYS, IND UNIV, 86- *Personal Data:* b Rochester, NY, Dec 17, 53; m 83; c 1. *Educ:* Wesleyan Univ, BA, 75; Cornell Univ, MS, 82 & PhD(geol), 86. *Prof Exp:* Sr res asst seismol, Lamont-Doherty Geol Observ, 76-80; grad res asst seismol, Cornell Univ, 80-86. *Concurrent Pos:* Mem, US-USSR work group on exchange in earthquake prediction, 86-88, earthquake adv panel, Ind Dept Civil Defense. *Mem:* Am Geophysical Union; Geol Soc Am; Seismol Soc Am. *Res:* Spatial and temporal distribution of earthquakes in a collisional plate boundary, Soviet Central Asia; seismicity of the Fiji Islands; tectonics of the southwest pacific. *Mailing Add:* Dept Geol Sci Ind Univ Bloomington Bloomington IN 47405. *E-Mail:* hamburg@indiana.edu

HAMBURGER, RICHARD, GEOLOGY. *Current Pos:* CONSULT, 74- *Personal Data:* b Baltimore, Md, Dec 30, 15; m 43; c 1. *Educ:* Univ Mich, AB, 38. *Prof Exp:* Geologist & engr, Inspiration Consol Copper Co, 46-55; geol engr, Div Raw Mat, AEC, 55-58, mining engr, Div Mil Appln, 58-60, asst chief, Div Peaceful Nuclear Explosives, 60-61, asst dir tech opers, 61-74. *Mem:* Am Inst Mining, Metall & Petrol Engrs; Health Physics Soc; Geol Soc Am; Soc Econ Geologists. *Res:* Occurrence of mineral deposits; evaluation of ore deposits and of exploration techniques with emphasis on statistical analysis; site investigations. *Mailing Add:* 14900 Springfield Rd Germantown MD 20874

HAMBURGER, ROBERT NEWFIELD, PEDIATRICS, ALLERGY & IMMUNOLOGY. *Current Pos:* vis assoc prof, Univ Calif, San Diego, 63-64, assoc prof pediat & asst dean, Sch Med, 64-67, head, Div Pediat Immunol & Allergy, 70-90, prof, 67-90, EMER PROF PEDIAT, SCH MED, UNIV CALIF, SAN DIEGO, 90-, LAB DIR, ALLERGY IMMUNOL LAB, 90- *Personal Data:* b New York, NY, Jan 26, 23; m 43; Sonia Gross; c Hilary, Lisa & Toya. *Educ:* Univ NC, BA, 47; Yale Univ, MD, 51; Am Bd Pediat, dipl, 58; Am Bd Allergy & Immunol, dipl, 74. *Prof Exp:* Intern & asst resident pediat, Strong Mem Hosp, 51-53; asst resident, New Haven Hosp, Conn, 53-54; clin instr, Sch Med, Yale Univ, 54-58, asst clin prof, 58-60. *Concurrent Pos:* Spec fel, NIH, Yale Univ & Univ Calif, San Diego, 60-63; instr pediat, Univ Rochester, 51-53; practicing pediatrician, 54-60; chief pediat serv, Milford Hosp, 59-60; Fulbright fel, 78; pres, RNA Co, Inc; bd dirs, La Jolla Diag, Inc. *Mem:* Sigma Xi; Am Acad Allergy & Immunol; Soc Pediat Res; Am Asn Immunologists; Am Col Allergy Asthma & Immunol. *Res:* Lupus erythematosus; immunology; genetics; pediatric growth and development; laboratory allergy immunology; cancer diagnostics. *Mailing Add:* Univ Calif San Diego 9485 La Jolla Shores Dr La Jolla CA 92037-1149. *E-Mail:* rhamburger@ucsd.edu

HAMBURGER, VIKTOR, ZOOLOGY. *Current Pos:* from asst prof to prof, Washington Univ, 35-69, actg head dept, 42-44, chmn dept, 44-66, EMER PROF BIOL, WASHINGTON UNIV, 69- *Personal Data:* b Landeshut, Ger, July 9, 00; nat US; m 28; c 2. *Educ:* Univ Freiburg, PhD(zool), 25. *Hon Degrees:* PhD, Wash Univ, 76 & Univ Uppsala, Sweden, 84. *Honors & Awards:* Wakeman Award, 78; Harrison Prize, 81; Louise Gross Horwitz Prize, Cell Biol & Develop Neurobiol, Columbia Univ, 83; Nat Medal Sci, 89; Karl Lashley Award, 90. *Prof Exp:* Asst, Kaiser Wilhelm Inst, Berlin, 26-27; instr zool & privatdocent, Dept Zool, Univ Freiburg, 27-32; Rockefeller res fel, Univ Chicago, 32-33, instr zool, 33-35. *Concurrent Pos:* Fel, NIH, 47. *Mem:* Nat Acad Sci; AAAS; Am Soc Naturalists; Am Soc Zool (pres, 55); Soc Develop Biol (pres, 50-51); Neurosci Soc. *Res:* Experimental neuro-embryology; mode of gene action in development; embryology of behavior. *Mailing Add:* Dept Biol Washington Univ 740 Trinity Ave St Louis MO 63130

HAMBY, DAME SCOTT, TEXTILE ENGINEERING. *Current Pos:* prof textile technol, NC State Univ, 48-65, head dept, 65-72, assoc dean, Textile Exten & Continuing Educ, 75-81, dean, Sch Textiles, 81-87, EMER DEAN, NC STATE UNIV, 87- *Personal Data:* b Macon, Ga, July 8, 20; m 43; c 2. *Educ:* Auburn Univ, BS, 46. *Hon Degrees:* Dr Textiles, Philadelphia Col Textile & Sci, 84. *Prof Exp:* Prod trainee textile testing & qual control, Goodyear Tire & Rubber Co, 37-42; textile engr res & develop, Celanese Corp, 43-45, B F Goodrich Co, 47-48. *Concurrent Pos:* Chmn, Hamby Textile Res Labs. *Mem:* Fel AAAS; fel Brit Textile Inst; fel Am Soc Qual Control; Sigma Xi; fel Am Soc Testing & Mat. *Res:* Performance of textile materials; process evaluation and control. *Mailing Add:* 2904 Allenby Dr Raleigh NC 27604

HAMBY, DRANNAN CARSON, ELECTROCHEMISTRY. *Current Pos:* Asst prof physics, Linfield Col, 62-69, dir, Res Inst, 62-78, assoc prof physics & chem, 69-74, chmn, Div Math & Natural Sci, 79-83, CHEMIST, LINFIELD RES INST, LINFIELD COL, 56-, PROF PHYSICS & CHEM, 74- *Personal Data:* b Duncan, Okla, Nov 16, 33; m 52, Beverly Reinhart; c Mark & Marcy. *Educ:* Linfield Col, BA, 55; Ore State Univ, MA, 61, PhD, 68. *Concurrent Pos:* Chemist, Field Emission Corp, 61-62; vis assoc res engr, Univ Calif, Los Angeles, 74-75, Brigham Young Univ, 81 & 91-92. *Mem:* Am Chem Soc; Electrochem Soc; Sigma Xi. *Res:* High temperature batteries; thermodynamics of fused salts; electrochemical machining of refractory metals; alkaline zinc secondary electrode; charging of sealed lead-acid batteries; nickel secondary electrode. *Mailing Add:* 232 Oregan Way McMinnville OR 97128

HAMBY, ROBERT KEITH, PRODUCT DEVELOPMENT. *Current Pos:* SR RES SCIENTIST, BIO-RAD LABS, 94- *Personal Data:* b Mobile, Ala, Nov 25, 56. *Educ:* Auburn Univ, BS, 78; Va Inst Technol, MS, 84; La State Univ, PhD(biochem), 90. *Prof Exp:* Chem engr, Dow Chem USA, 78-82; instr comput, Va Inst Technol, 84. *Mem:* AAAS. *Res:* New product development and product support. *Mailing Add:* 2248 Mira Vista Dr El Cerrito CA 94530. *Fax:* 510-741-1058; *E-Mail:* khamby@bio_rad.com

HAMDAN, MOHAMMAD HAFIZ, COMPUTATIONAL FLUID DYNAMICS, FLOW THROUGH POROUS MEDIA & ENVIRONMENTAL FLOWS. *Current Pos:* asst prof, 91-93, chmn, Dept Math, Statist & Compt Sci, 94-97, ASSOC PROF MATH, UNIV NEW BRUNSWICK, 93- *Personal Data:* b Howara, Nablus, West Bank, Apr 21, 59; Can citizen; m 85, Carol Dale; c Nadia, Fadia & Hafiz. *Educ:* Univ Windsor, Can, BSc, 83, MSc, 86, PhD(appl math), 89. *Prof Exp:* Asst prof, Mt Allison Univ, 89-91. *Concurrent Pos:* Coordr environ studies, Univ New Brunswick, 92-94. *Mem:* Am Acad Mech; Can Math Soc. *Res:* Analysis and modelling of single and multiphase flow through porous media; numerical analysis of the von Mises transformation and its extension to multiphase flow; oil spill simulation and modelling sediment contamination by hydrocarbons. *Mailing Add:* PO Box 5050 St John NB E2L 4L5 Can. *Fax:* 506-648-5799; *E-Mail:* hamdan@unbsj.ca

HAMDEN, MOHAMMAD HAFIZ, COMPUTATIONAL FLUID DYNAMICS, ENVIRONMENTAL FLOWS. *Current Pos:* asst prof, 91-93, ASSOC PROF MATH, UNIV NB, 93- *Personal Data:* b Howara, West Bank, Apr 21, 59; Can citizen; m 85, Carol Dale; c Nadia, Fadia & Hafiz. *Educ:* Col Swindon, Eng, dipl, 79; Univ Windsor, BSc, 83, MSc, 86, PhD(appl math), 89. *Prof Exp:* Asst prof, Mt Allison Univ, 89-91. *Concurrent Pos:* Coordr environ studies, Univ NB, 92-94, chmn, Dept Math, Statist & Comput Sci, 94-97; mem, Int Affairs Comt, Can Math Soc, 97- *Mem:* Am Acad Mech; Can Math Soc. *Res:* Analysis and modelling of single and multiphase flow through porous media; numerical analysis of the von Mises transformation and its extension to multiphase flow; oil spill simulation and modelling sediment contamination by hydrocarbons. *Mailing Add:* PO Box 5050 St John NB E2L 4L5 Can. *Fax:* 506-648-5799; *E-Mail:* hamdan@unbsj.ca

HAMDY, MOHAMED YOUSRY, POWER & MACHINERY, ENERGY. *Current Pos:* from res assoc to prof, 63-89, EMER PROF AGR ENG, OHIO STATE UNIV, 89- *Personal Data:* b Cairo, Egypt, Apr 17, 38; m 93, Safaa Hegazy; c Tarek. *Educ:* Cairo Univ, BSc, 59; Mich State Univ, MS, 62; Ohio State Univ, PhD(agr eng), 65. *Prof Exp:* Instr mech eng, Cairo Univ, 59-61. *Concurrent Pos:* Consult, USAID & Pioneer Hi-Bred Int, 79- *Mem:* Am Soc Agr Engrs. *Res:* Mathematical modeling of engineering systems in agriculture: power and machinery, energy, grain drying, falling water tables. *Mailing Add:* 2488 Lytham Rd Columbus OH 43220

HAMDY, MOSTAFA KAMAL, BACTERIOLOGY. *Current Pos:* from asst prof bact & biochem to prof food sci, 58-91, EMER PROF FOOD SCI, UNIV GA, 91- *Personal Data:* b Cairo, Egypt, May 27, 21; nat US; m 54, Kathryn R; c 2. *Educ:* Cairo Univ, BSc, 44, MSc, 49; Ohio State Univ, PhD, 53. *Honors & Awards:* PR for Excellence in Microbiol, Am Soc Microbiol & Soc Exp Biol & Med, 85; Spec Citation, Food & Drug Admin, 91. *Prof Exp:* Instr bot, Univ Alexandria, 44-47; instr bact, Cairo Univ, 47-49; asst waste treatment lab, Eng Exp Sta, Ohio State Univ, 51-52, res assoc bact, 52-53, Muellhaupt fel, 53-54, res assoc biochem, 54-58. *Concurrent Pos:* Dir res, Col Agr, 88; sci adv, Food & Drug Admin, 93. *Mem:* Fel Am Soc Microbiol; Soc Exp Biol & Med; fel Inst Food Technol; fel Am Acad Microbiol. *Res:* Pathogenesis of salmonella; effect of radiation and radioprotectors on the lysosomal enzymes in rats; effect of staphylococcus infection on the biochemistry of bruised and infected tissues; effect of anthocyanin on bacteria; mercury biotransformation polychlorinated biphenyl pollution control, alcohol fermentation, biotechnology, PCR for detections of pathogens; polychlorinated biphenyl. *Mailing Add:* Dept Food Sci Univ Ga Athens GA 30602. *Fax:* 706-542-1050

HAMED, AWATEF A, TURBOMACHINERY, TWO-PHASE FLOWS. *Current Pos:* grad teaching & res asst, 68-72, from asst prof to assoc prof, 73-80, PROF AEROSPACE ENG, UNIV CINCINNATI, 80- *Personal Data:* b El-Mansoura, Egypt, June 17, 44; US citizen. *Educ:* Cairo Univ, BSc, 65; Univ Cincinnati, MSc, 69, PhD(eng), 72. *Honors & Awards:* Tech Innovation Award, NASA, 83; Amelia Gerhart fel, 67, 69 & 70. *Prof Exp:* Design engr, Helwan Aircraft Estab, Egyptian Gen Aero Orgn, 65-67. *Concurrent Pos:* Prin investr, NASA, Air Force Off Sci Res, Dept Energy, Dept Navy, Army Res Off & NSF; consult to indust & govt agencies; assoc ed, J Fluids Eng, 82-85; collateral prof, Ohio Aerospace Inst, 90-; ed, Int J Computational Fluid Mech, 94- *Mem:* Fel Am Inst Aeronaut & Astronaut; fel Am Soc Mech Engrs; Sigma Xi. *Res:* Gas turbine engine aerothermodynamics; laser doppler velocimetry measurements in three dimensional and two phase flows; prediction of turbomachinery single and two phase flows, erosion, performance deterioration and engine life; probablistic modeling of propulsion systems; noise associated with jet engines. *Mailing Add:* Dept Aerospace Eng Univ Cincinnati Cincinnati OH 45221-0002. *Fax:* 513-556-5038; *E-Mail:* ahamed@uceng.uc.edu

HAMED, GARY RAY, POLYMER CHEMISTRY. *Current Pos:* asst prof, 80-88, PROF, UNIV AKRON, 88- *Personal Data:* b Jonesboro, Ark, July 3, 50; m 74, Jean Coberly; c Greg & Chris. *Educ:* Cornell Univ, BS, 72, MS, 73; Univ Akron, PhD(polymers), 78. *Honors & Awards:* Sparks-Thomas Award, Am Chem Soc, 87. *Prof Exp:* Res scientist, Firestone, 76-78, sr res scientist, 78-80. *Mem:* Am Chem Soc; Adhesion Soc; Tire Soc. *Res:* Mechanical properties of polymers, especially tack fracture and adhesion of elastomers. *Mailing Add:* 3301 N Dover Rd Stow OH 44224-2423. *Fax:* 330-972-5290

HAMEED, SULTAN, ATMOSPHERIC SCIENCE. *Current Pos:* assoc prof, 76-86, PROF ATMOSPHERIC SCI, STATE UNIV NY, STONY BROOK, 86- *Personal Data:* b Ambala, India, Sept 8, 41; m 63; c 3. *Educ:* Univ Karachi, Pakistan, BSc & MS, 61; Univ Manchester, Eng, PhD(physics), 68. *Prof Exp:* Res assoc atomic physics, Belfer Grad Sch, Yeshiva Univ, NY, 68-70; res assoc, Physics Dept, Columbia Univ, 70-72; sr res assoc atmospheric sci, Inst Space Studies, NASA, NY, 72-76. *Concurrent Pos:* Consult, Pub Div, Am Inst Physics, New York, 70-91, Lawrence Livermore Nat Lab, 90- *Mem:* Am Geophys Union; Am Meteorol Soc. *Res:* Many-electron effects in atomic and molecular structure; changes in atmospheric composition, cycles of trace gases in the atmosphere, climate change and boundary layer phenomena. *Mailing Add:* Inst Terrestrial & Planetary Atmosphere State Univ NY Stony Brook NY 11794-5000

HAMEKA, HENDRIK FREDERIK, THEORETICAL CHEMISTRY. *Current Pos:* assoc prof, 62-67, PROF CHEM, UNIV PA, 67- *Personal Data:* b Rotterdam, Neth, May 25, 31; US citizen; m 72; c 2. *Educ:* Univ Leiden, Drs, 53, DSc(chem), 56. *Hon Degrees:* MA, Univ Pa, 71. *Honors & Awards:* Alexander von Humboldt Prize, 82. *Prof Exp:* Asst chem, Univ Leiden, 55-56 & Univ Rome, 56-57; fel, Carnegie Inst, 57-58; res physicist, Philips Lamps Labs, 58-60; asst prof chem, Johns Hopkins Univ, 60-62. *Concurrent Pos:* Consult, Bombrini-Parodi Delfino, Italy, 57; Sloan Found res fel, 62-66; distinguished vis res prof, USAF Acad, 86-87. *Res:* Quantum theory of molecules and radiation fields; interactions between molecules and electromagnetic fields. *Mailing Add:* 1503 Argyle Rd Berwyn PA 19312-1905

HAMEL, COLEMAN RODNEY, HETEROCYCLIC CHEMISTRY. *Current Pos:* assoc prof, 70-73, chmn, Dept Phys Sci, 77-82, PROF CHEM, KUTZTOWN UNIV, PA, 73- *Personal Data:* b Massena, NY, June 9, 37; m 60; c 3. *Educ:* Clarkson Col Technol, BChE, 57; Bucknell Univ, MS, 63; Lehigh Univ, PhD(chem), 69. *Prof Exp:* Chemist, Merck & Co, 58-65; teaching asst, Lehigh Univ, 66-67; asst prof chem, Lafayette Col, 69-70. *Concurrent Pos:* Consult, J T Baker Chem Co, 79-84, Connaught Labs, 84-, Air Prod & Chem, Inc, 84- & Lemmon Chem Co, 85; mem, health & safety comt, Am Chem Soc, 80-86, Wright Lab, 88- *Mem:* Am Chem Soc; fel Am Inst Chem; AAAS; NY Acad Sci. *Res:* Heterocyclic chemistry; hazardous chemical safety. *Mailing Add:* Dept Phys Sci Kutztown Univ Pa 1407 W Union Blvd Bethlehem PA 18018

HAMEL, EARL GREGORY, JR, ANATOMY. *Current Pos:* instr, 59-64, assoc prof, 64-70, PROF ANAT & CHMN DEPT, MED CTR, UNIV ALA, BIRMINGHAM, 70- *Personal Data:* b Pensacola, Fla, Nov 30, 28; m 55; c 4. *Educ:* Spring Hill Col, BS, 51; St Louis Univ, MS, 53; Univ Iowa, PhD(anat), 59. *Prof Exp:* Instr anat, Univ Tex, 51-53; instr, Univ Iowa, 58-59. *Res:* Neuroanatomy; comparative neurology; motor disturbances and behavior. *Mailing Add:* Dept Anat Sch Med Univ Ala University Sta Birmingham AL 35294. *Fax:* 205-934-7029

HAMEL, EDWARD E, ORGANIC CHEMISTRY. *Current Pos:* RETIRED. *Personal Data:* b Alta, Can, Feb 18, 26; US citizen; m 54; c 8. *Educ:* Univ Notre Dame, BS, 47; Univ Calif, Berkeley, PhD(org chem), 52. *Prof Exp:* Res chemist, E I du Pont de Nemours & Co, 51-57; res supvr chem, Aerojet Solid Propulsion Co, 57-74, mgr res & develop, Cordova Chem Co, 74-81; dir chem opers, Aerojet Strategic Propulsion, Co, 81; vpres & gen mgr, chem opers, Aerojet Propulsion Co, 81-88. *Mem:* Am Chem Soc; Sigma Xi; NY Acad Sci. *Res:* Aliphatic polynitro compounds; process research; continuous processing; catalytic hydrogenation; monomer synthesis; antimalarial synthesis; medicinal chemistry; aziridings; anticancer synthesis. *Mailing Add:* 7592 Lakeshore Dr Granite Bay CA 95746

HAMEL, JAMES V(ICTOR), GEOTECHNICAL ENGINEERING, ENGINEERING GEOLOGY. *Current Pos:* CONSULT ENGR, HAMEL GEOTECH CONSULTS, 73- *Personal Data:* b Rochester, NY, Apr 21, 44; m 67, Betsy (Mecke); c Omar. *Educ:* Univ Pittsburgh, BS, 65, PhD(geotech eng), 70; Mass Inst Technol, SM, 66. *Prof Exp:* Res engr, Univ Pittsburgh, 67-69; asst prof civil eng, SDak Sch Mines & Technol, 69-72; proj engr, Gen Anal, Inc, Monroeville, Pa, 72-73. *Concurrent Pos:* Consult, Mo River Div, US Army CEngrs, Nebr, 70-73; adj assoc prof civil engr, Univ Pittsburgh, 74-85, adj prof, 94- *Mem:* Am Soc Civil Engrs; Asn Eng Geologists; Int Soc Rock Mech; US Comt Large Dams; Am Inst Mining, Metall & Petrol Engrs; Int Soc Soil Mech & Found Engr; Int Asn Eng Geol. *Res:* Stability and long-term behavior of natural and excavated slopes in soil and rock; stability and behavior of rock foundations and abutments of dams; disposal of solid wastes from mining, industrial, and energy generation processes; river bank instability. *Mailing Add:* 1992 Butler Dr Monroeville PA 15146-3918

HAMEL, RAY O, COMPUTER SCIENCE. *Current Pos:* PROF & CHAIR, COMPUT SCI DEPT, EASTERN WASH UNIV, 70- *Personal Data:* B Madison, Wis, Oct 29, 39. *Educ:* Univ Wis, BS, 63, MS, 64; Univ Ore, PhD(math), 68. *Mem:* Math Asn Am; Inst Elec & Electronics Engrs; Sigma Xi. *Res:* Computer Science. *Mailing Add:* Math & Comp Sci Dept MS 86 Eastern Wash Univ Cheney WA 99004

HAMELIN, CLAUDE, VIROLOGY, MOLECULAR GENETICS. *Current Pos:* asst prof, 78-85, dir res & develop biotics, 85-86, PROF VIROL, ARMAND-FRAPPIER INST, UNIV QUE, 87- *Personal Data:* b Montreal, Que, Aug 25, 43; m 70; c 2. *Educ:* Univ Montreal, BPed, 65, BSc, 70, MSc, 72, PhD(genetics), 75. *Prof Exp:* Fels, Stanford Univ, 75-76, Armand-Frappier Inst, Univ Quebec, 76-77 & Pasteur Inst, 77-78. *Mem:* Am Soc Microbiol; Can Col Microbiologists; Genetics Soc Am; Genetics Soc Can; NY Acad Sci; Can Soc Microbiologists; French-Can Asn Advan Sci. *Res:* Biochemical analysis of the human cytomegalovirus genome; researches on the persistence, latency, late reactivation and oncogenic potential of this virus in humans; development of biosensors, bioprobes and biochips. *Mailing Add:* Dept Virol Inst Armand-Frappier 531 Blvd Des Prairies PO Box 100 Laval PQ H7N 4Z7 Can. *Fax:* 514-686-5501

HAMER, DEAN H, BIOCHEMISTRY, MOLECULAR GENETICS. *Current Pos:* sr staff fel, 80-89, CHIEF, SECT GENE STRUCT & REGULATION, NAT CANCER INST, 90- *Personal Data:* b Montclair, NJ, May 29, 51; c 1. *Educ:* Trinity Col, BA, 72; Harvard Univ, PhD(biochem), 77. *Prof Exp:* Staff fel molecular genetics, Nat Inst Child Health & Human Develop, 77-78; staff fel, Nat Inst Allergy & Infectious Dis, 78-80. *Res:* Molecular basis of gene expression; recombinant DNA technology. *Mailing Add:* Gene Struct & Regulation Sect Biochem Lab NIH Nat Cancer Inst Bldg 37 Rm 4A-13 Bethesda MD 20897-0001

HAMER, JAN, CHEMISTRY. *Current Pos:* RETIRED. *Personal Data:* b Gombong, Indonesia, May 2, 27; m 56; c 2. *Educ:* Univ Leyden, BS, 49, Drs, 55, Dr(chem), 56. *Prof Exp:* Res assoc chem, Tulane Univ, 53-55 & 56-57; assoc prof, Dillard Univ, 58-60; from asst prof to assoc prof chem, Tulane Univ, 60-86. *Concurrent Pos:* Consult, USDA, 62- *Mem:* AAAS; Am Chem Soc. *Res:* Cycloaddition reactions; stereochemistry and kinetics of four-center reactions; synthesis of azahexahelicene. *Mailing Add:* 299 Walnut St New Orleans LA 70118

HAMER, JUSTIN CHARLES, ORGANIC CHEMISTRY & QUALITATIVE ANALYSIS, ORGANO-METALLIC COMPLEXES PHTHALOCYANINES. *Current Pos:* RES CONSULT & SCI TEACHER, CENT AM VOL COL, COSTA RICA, 93- *Personal Data:* b Oct 2, 14; US citizen; wid, Evelyn Lorntz (dec); c Judith, James, Jon, Joyce & William. *Educ:* Pac Union Col, BA, 49, MA, 49; Univ NMex, PhD(chem), 61. *Prof Exp:* Sci teacher chem & math, Sandia View Acad, NMex, 53-56; head, Sci Dept, Col of the Antillas, Cuba, 56-58; chmn, Chem Dept, Columbia Union Col, 60-68; chmn, Div Sci & Chem, MidE Col, Beirut, Lebanon, 68-74; prof chem, Oakwood Col, 75-93. *Concurrent Pos:* Sci teacher, Voc Col, Alajuela, Costa Rica; res asst, Univ Md, 65-68; sr res fel, Col Med, Howard Univ, 74-75. *Mem:* Sigma Xi; Am Chem Soc. *Res:* Biochemistry of lipids; lipids in body fluids; amino acid derivatives of salicylic acid; synthesis of metal phthallocyanines. *Mailing Add:* 4113 Nelson Dr NW Huntsville AL 35810

HAMER, MARTIN, ORGANIC CHEMISTRY. *Current Pos:* RETIRED. *Personal Data:* b Indianapolis, Ind, Sept 17, 28; m 54, Joanne Kushner; c 2. *Educ:* Ind Univ, BS, 49; Purdue Univ, MS, 51, PhD(org chem), 53. *Prof Exp:* Res chemist, Stand Oil Co Ind, 53-60; res chemist, Int Minerals & Chem Corp, 60-74, mgr process & prod res, 74-77, corp toxicity coordr, 77-81, mgr, tech mkt serv, 81-82 RES DIR BISCO INC, 83-91; res dir, Bisco Inc, 83-91. *Mem:* Am Chem Soc. *Res:* Heterocyclics; fuels; pesticides; medicinals; organic phosphorus compounds; improved processes for phosphate flotation; dental materials. *Mailing Add:* 8423 N Karlov Skokie IL 60076-2102

HAMER, WALTER JAY, ELECTROCHEMISTRY, ELECTRICAL ENGINEERING. *Current Pos:* CHEM CONSULT & SCI WRITER, 72- *Personal Data:* b Altoona, Pa, Nov 5, 07; m 41, Alma Robison; c Margaret J. *Educ:* Juniata Col, BS, 29; Yale Univ, PhD(phys chem), 32. *Hon Degrees:* DSc, Juniata Col. 66. *Honors & Awards:* Manhattan Proj Award, 45; Superior Awards, 54, 62 & 65, Gold Medal Award, 65, US Dept Com; Robert T Foley Award, Electrochem Soc, 91. *Prof Exp:* Asst instr, Juniata Col, 27-29; asst, Yale Univ, 29-32; USN res fel, 32-34; res assoc chem, Mass Inst Technol, 34-35; chemist, Nat Bur Stand, 35-50, chief electrochem sect, 50-70, consult electrochem & dir electrolyte ctr, 70-72. *Concurrent Pos:* Lectr grad sch, USDA, 40-49, Nat Bur Stand, 44-45, 52-53, Cath Univ, 44-45 & Georgetown Univ, 47-50; res chemist, Nat Defense Res Comn, Off Sci Res & Develop & Manhattan Proj, Nat Bur Standards, 43-44; consult res & develop bd, US Dept Defense, 51-53; mem comn electrochem, Int Union Pure & Appl Chem, 57-71; tech adv, Int Electrotech Comn, 50-67; chmn, dry cell comt, Am Standards Asn, 50-68; pres, Yale Chem Assoc, 58-61; adv, coun electrochem, Univ Pa, 62-63. *Mem:* Fel AAAS; fel Am Inst Chem; Am Phys Soc; hon mem Electrochem Soc (vpres, 60-63, pres, 63-64); fel Inst Elec & Electronics Eng; fel NY Acad Sci; Sigma Xi. *Res:* Standard cells; primary and secondary batteries; electrolytic solutions; standardization of pH scale; fused salts and thermal batteries; electromotive series for molten electrolytes; critical evaluation of electrochemical data; Faraday determination. *Mailing Add:* 407 Russell Ave No 305 Gaithersburg MD 20877

HAMERLY, ROBERT GLENN, PHYSICS. *Current Pos:* RETIRED. *Personal Data:* b Apr 4, 31; US citizen; m 55; c 2. *Educ:* Western Ill Univ, BS, 55; Univ Ill, Urbana, MS, 57; Colo State Univ, PhD(physics), 69. *Prof Exp:* Mem tech staff systs analyst, Hughes Aircraft Corp, Calif, 59-60; from assoc prof to prof physics, Univ Northern Colo, 60-90. *Mem:* Am Asn Physics Teachers; Sigma Xi. *Res:* Solid state physics; transport properties of semiconductors. *Mailing Add:* 260 Bell Dr Crescent Apt N Green Valley AZ 85614

HAMERMAN, DAVID JAY, INTERNAL MEDICINE. *Current Pos:* From asst prof to assoc prof, 56-68, chmn dept, 68-81, DISTINGUISHED UNIV PROF MED, MONTEFIORE HOSP & MED CTR, ALBERT EINSTEIN COL MED, 90- *Personal Data:* b New York, NY, Apr 20, 25; m 89, Laura Friedman; c Alan, Jean & Frederick. *Educ:* NY Univ, MD, 48. *Honors & Awards:* Whitmore Mem Lectr, Baylor Col Med, 94. *Concurrent Pos:* Dazian fel chem, Col Med, NY Univ, 52-53; Markle scholar med sci, 58; Sinsheimer scholar med sci, 63; Fogarty Int fel, 81. *Mem:* Am Soc Clin Invest; Am Rheumatism Asn; Asn Am Physicians; fel Am Col Physicians; fel Am Geriat Soc. *Res:* Joint structure and function in the normal state, in aging and in osteoarthritis. *Mailing Add:* Dept Med Albert Einstein Col Med 1300 Morris Park Ave Bronx NY 10461

HAMERMESH, BERNARD, PHYSICS. *Current Pos:* RETIRED. *Personal Data:* b Brooklyn, NY, Dec 25, 19; m 41, Sylvia Molberger; c Judith G, Richard G & Kenneth S. *Educ:* City Col New York, BS, 40, NY Univ, MS, 42, PhD(physics), 44. *Prof Exp:* Tutor, City Col New York, 41-42; instr, NY Univ, 43-46; Nat Res Coun fel, Calif Inst Technol, 46-48; assoc physicist, Argonne Nat Lab, 48-58, sr physicist, 58-59; sr tech adv, Res Lab, TRW Inc, 59-60 & Space Tech Labs, 60-65, sr staff physicist, TRW Systs, 65-68; prof physics & chmn dept, Cleveland State Univ, 68- *Concurrent Pos:* Fel, Nat Res Coun, 46-48; vis prof physics, Univ Calif, Los Angeles, 87- *Mem:* Am Phys Soc. *Res:* Electron scattering; hygrometry; cosmic ray neutrons; cosmic ray meson energy spectrum; photo-neutron reactions; gamma rays from neutron capture; micrometeoroids; micrometeoroid accelerators. *Mailing Add:* 10433 Wilshire Blvd Apt 906 Los Angeles CA 90024

HAMERMESH, MORTON, PHYSICS. *Current Pos:* RETIRED. *Personal Data:* b New York, NY, Dec 27, 15; m 41, Madeline Goldberg; c Daniel, Deborah & Lawrence. *Educ:* City Col New York, BS, 36; NY Univ, PhD(physics), 40. *Honors & Awards:* Townsend Harris Medal. *Prof Exp:* Tutor physics, City Col New York, 36-37; instr, 41; from asst to assoc prof, NY Univ, 37-47; instr, Stanford Univ, 41-43, res assoc, 42-43; res assoc, Radio Res Lab, Harvard Univ, 43-45; assoc prof, NY Univ, 47-48; sr physicist, Argonne Nat Lab, 48-50, assoc dir, Physics Div, 50-59, dir, 59-63, assoc dir, Lab, 63-65; head, Sch Physics & Astron, Univ Minn, Minneapolis, 65-69; head, Physics Dept, State Univ NY, Stony Brook, 69-70; head, Sch Physics & Astron, 70-75, prof physics & astron, Univ Minn, Minneapolis, 75-86. *Concurrent Pos:* Off Sci Res & Develop, 44; consult, Brookhaven Nat Lab, 47-; ed, J Math Physics, 70-79; mem bd trustees, Argonne Univs Asn, 72-76. *Mem:* AAAS; fel Am Phys Soc; Am Asn Univ Professors. *Res:* Theoretical nuclear physics; electromagnetic theory; longwave search antenna array; passage of neutrons through crystals and polycrystals; group theory; elementary particle physics; nonlinear phenomena; theory of solitons; symmetry principles. *Mailing Add:* Physics Dept Univ Minn Minneapolis MN 55455

HAMERS, ROBERT J, CHEMISTRY. *Current Pos:* PROF CHEM, UNIV WIS-MADISON. *Honors & Awards:* Peter Mark Mem Award, Am Vacuum Soc, 94. *Concurrent Pos:* NSF fel, 92-97. *Mailing Add:* Dept Chem 1307 Univ Wis 1101 University Ave Madison WI 53706-1322

HAMERSKI, JULIAN JOSEPH, INORGANIC CHEMISTRY. *Current Pos:* ASSOC PROF CHEM, EASTERN ILL UNIV, 63- *Personal Data:* b Winona, Minn, May 21, 30; m 55; c 6. *Educ:* St Mary's Col, BS, 52, MA, 57; Univ of Pac, PhD(chem), 63. *Prof Exp:* Res chemist, Am Can Co, 52-53; teacher high schs, Minn, 53-56; chem instr, Worthington Jr Col, Minn, 56-61; teacher high sch, Calif, 62-63. *Mem:* Am Chem Soc. *Res:* Iron transition metal carbonyl phosphine complexes. *Mailing Add:* RR 4 Charleston IL 61920

HAMERSTROM, FRANCES, BIOLOGY, BOOK WRITING. *Current Pos:* ADJ PROF, UNIV WIS-STEVENS POINT, 82- *Personal Data:* b Needham, Mass, Dec 17, 07; m 31, Frederick N; c Alan & Elva (Paulson). *Educ:* Iowa State Col, BS, 35; Univ Wis-Madison, MS, 40. *Hon Degrees:* DSc, Carroll Col, 61. *Honors & Awards:* Awards, Wildlife Soc, 40 & 57; Josselyn Van Tyne Award, Am Ornithologist's Union, 60; Chapman Award, Am Mus Natural Hist, 64; United Peregrine Soc Conserv Award, 80; Edwards Prize, Wilson Ornith Soc, 85. *Prof Exp:* Biologist game, Wis Dept Natural Resources, 49-72. *Concurrent Pos:* Dir, Raptor Res Found, 74-76; mem sci bd, Wis Peregrine Soc, 90- *Mem:* Corresp mem Ger Ornith Soc; Wilson Ornith Soc; Wildlife Soc; hon mem, Ger Falconry Asn; fel Am Ornithologist's Union. *Res:* Ecology and behavior of raptors; hunting ethics and habits of primative peoples of the tropical rain forests. *Mailing Add:* N 6789 Third Ave Plainfield WI 54966

HAMERTON, JOHN LAURENCE, HUMAN GENETICS, CELL BIOLOGY. *Current Pos:* from assoc prof to prof pediat & anat, Fac Med, Univ Man, 69-84, assoc dean, 77-81, prof & head, Dept Human Genetics, 85-87, DISTINGUISHED PROF, UNIV MAN, 87- *Personal Data:* b Brighton, Eng, Sept 23, 29. *Educ:* Univ London, BSc, 51, DSc(human genetics), 68. *Honors & Awards:* Robert Roessler DeVilliers Award, Leukemia Soc Am, 56; Huxley Mem Medal, Imp Col, London Univ, 58; Teddy Award, Childrens Hosp Winnipeg Res Found, 88. *Prof Exp:* Sci staff mem mammal cytogenetics group, Radiobiol Res Unit, Med Res Coun, 51-56; sr sci officer, Zool Dept, Brit Mus Natural Hist, HM Sci Civil Serv, 59-60; sr lectr, Cytogenetics Sect, Pediat Res Unit, Guy's Hosp Med Sch, 60-69, head sect, 62-69. *Concurrent Pos:* Consult, Psychiat Genetics Res Unit, Med Res Coun, 62-69; adv human cytogenetics, WHO, 67; chmn, Working Group Prenatal Diag Genetic Dis & mem, Grants Panel Genetics, Med Res Coun Can, 71, res prof, 81-82; chmn, Int Standing Comt Human Cytogenetics, 71-76; dir, Dept Genetics, Children's Ctr Winnipeg, 69-80. *Mem:* Royal Soc Med; Soc Pediat Res; Genetics Soc Can (pres, 77-78); Am Soc Human Genetics (pres, 75). *Res:* Human & mammalian cytogenetics; somatic cell genetics; gene mapping; molecular genetics. *Mailing Add:* Dept Human Genetics 770 Bannatyne Ave Rm T250 Winnipeg MB R3C 0W3 Can

HAMES, F(REDERICK) A(RTHUR), METALLURGICAL ENGINEERING. *Current Pos:* RETIRED. *Personal Data:* b Assiniboia, Sask, July 22, 19; m 44; c 2. *Educ:* Mont Sch Mines, BS, 40; Queen's Univ, Ont, MSc, 46; Univ Mo, PhD(metall eng), 48. *Prof Exp:* Asst prof metall, Univ BC, 48-50; prof & head dept, Mont Sch Mines, 50-57; prof metall eng, Queen's Univ, Ont, 57-84. *Mem:* Am Soc Metals; Am Inst Mining, Metall & Petrol Engrs. *Res:* Magnetic materials; constitution and structure of alloys; x-ray diffraction. *Mailing Add:* 2132 Colinwood Rd Sidney BC V8L 4H5 Can

HAMET, PAVEL, ENDROCRINOLOGY. *Current Pos:* DIR, RES CTR, HOTEL DIEU DE MONTREAL, 90-, CHIEF, MOLECULAR MED SERV, 93- *Personal Data:* b Klatovy, Czech, June 13, 43; m, Johanne Tremblay; c 4. *Educ:* Charles Univ, MD,67; McGill Univ, PhD, 72. *Hon Degrees:* Montreal Univ, CSPd; Royal Col, FRCP(C). *Honors & Awards:* Res Award, Can Cardiovasc Soc; Astra Award, Can Hypertension Soc; Harry Goldblatt Award, Am Heart Asn, 90. *Prof Exp:* Dir, Clin Res Lab, 75-90. *Concurrent Pos:* Mem, Endocrinol, Hotel Dieu Montreal; prof, Montreal Univ; assoc mem, McGill Univ; Centennial Fel, Med Res Coun Can; hon prof, Shanghai Second Med Univ, China, 94. *Mem:* Asn Med Lang Francaise Can; AAAS; Can Med Asn; Can Soc Endocrinol & Metab; Am Fedn Clin Res; Endocrine Soc; Can Soc Clin Invest; Am Heart Asn; Can Diabetes Asn; Can Health Res; Int Soc Hypertension (secy, 93-); Can Hypertension Soc (pres). *Res:* Mechanism of action of atrial natriuretic factor; studies on nutritional calcium in hypertension; studies on heat stress proteins in hypertension; growth control of vascular smooth muscle in diabetes mellitus and hypertension; platelet functions and cyclic nucleotide metabolism in hypertension and diabetes mellitus. *Mailing Add:* Res Ctr Hotel Dieu de Montreal Pavillon Marie de la Ferre 3850 St-Urbain Montreal PQ H2W 1R8 Can. *Fax:* 514-843-2753

HAMID, MICHAEL, ELECTRICAL ENGINEERING. *Current Pos:* from asst prof to assoc prof, 65-70, PROF ELEC ENG, UNIV MAN, 70-, HEAD ANTENNA LAB, 67- *Personal Data:* b June 7, 34; Can citizen. *Educ:* McGill Univ, BEng, 60, MEng, 62; Univ Toronto, PhD(elec eng), 66. *Prof Exp:* Res asst elec eng, McGill Univ, 60-61; sr consult engr, Sinclair Radio Labs, 62-66. *Concurrent Pos:* Treas, assoc ed & mem bd gov, Int Microwave Power Inst, 69-, pres, 71-; gen chmn, Microwave Power Symposium, Monterey, 71; pres, Indust Microwave Res Assoc, Winnipeg, 71-75; mem, Nat Res Coun Can assoc comn on bird hazards to aircraft, 72-77; mem, Man Res Coun; consult, Defense Res Bd Can, 72-; vis prof, Naval Postgrad Sch, Monterey, Calif, 79-81; mem, Can deleg to Int Union Radio Sci, 65-; chmn grad studies, Univ Man, 83-88. *Mem:* Sr mem & fel Inst Elec & Electronics Engrs; Int Union Radio Sci; Can Med & Biol Eng Soc; fel Inst Electronic Eng; Int Microwave Power Inst; Med Prod Inst. *Res:* Antennas; diffraction; scattering; inverse scattering; microwave techniques; microwave power; acoustics; electromagnetic theory; transmission lines; biological effect of electromagnetic energy. *Mailing Add:* Dept Elec Eng Univ S Ala EE375 Mobile AL 36688

HAMIELEC, ALVIN EDWARD, CHEMICAL ENGINEERING, POLYMER SCIENCE. *Current Pos:* from asst prof to prof, 63-91, EMER PROF CHEM ENG, MCMASTER UNIV, 91- *Personal Data:* b Cracow, Poland, Jan 10, 35; Can citizen; m 55; c 3. *Educ:* Univ Toronto, BASc, 57, MASc, 58, PhD(mass transfer), 61. *Honors & Awards:* ERCO Award, Can Soc Chem Eng, 74; Protective Coatings Award, Chem Inst Can, 78; Dunlop Award, Macro Sci/Eng, 87. *Prof Exp:* Res engr chem, Cent Res Labs, Can Industs Ltd, Que, 61-63. *Concurrent Pos:* Dir, McMaster Inst Polymer Prod Technol, McMaster Univ. *Mem:* Am Inst Chem Engrs; Chem Inst Can; Am Chem Soc; Can Soc Chem Engrs; Fel Royal Soc Can. *Res:* Polymer production technology; polymer synthesis and characterization; polymer reactors and production technology. *Mailing Add:* 99 Rennick Rd Burlington ON L7R 3X5 Can. *Fax:* 905-528-5114

HAMIL, MARTHA M, STRUCTURAL GEOLOGY, MINERALOGY. *Current Pos:* MEM STAFF, ENGELHARD MINERALS & CHEM, 79- *Personal Data:* b New Edinburg, Ark, Jan 14, 39. *Educ:* La State Univ, BS, 59, MS, 65; Univ Mo-Columbia, PhD(geol), 71. *Prof Exp:* Asst prof geol, Rutgers Univ, 72-79. *Concurrent Pos:* Fel, Va Polytech Inst, 70-71, Univ Calif, Berkeley, 72. *Mem:* AAAS; Am Geophys Union; Geol Soc Am; Geol Soc London; Mineral Soc Am. *Res:* Hercynian tectonics of Central Morocco; fabric analysis; planar structures; tectonic-mineralogic interface; fracture mechanisms in rocks; distortions of metal-oxygen polyhedra in crystal structures. *Mailing Add:* PO Box 254 Lyle WA 98635

HAMILL, DENNIS W, SOLID STATE PHYSICS. *Current Pos:* res mgr physics, 71-77, tech dir, Info Mgt Div, 77-80, TECH DIR, ELEC & MECH RES DIV, 3M CO, 80- *Personal Data:* b Cedar Rapids, Iowa, Dec 7, 40; m 60; c 2. *Educ:* Univ Wis-Madison, BS, 62, MS, 63; Boston Univ, PhD(physics), 68. *Prof Exp:* Staff physicist, Forest Prod Lab, USDA, 63; physicist semiconductors, Dow Corning Corp, 63-65, group leader, 68-70; vpres opers, High Performance Technol Inc, 70-71. *Concurrent Pos:* Fac mem, Dept Physics, Saginaw Valley Col, 64-69. *Mem:* Am Phys Soc; Int Soc Hybrid Microelectronics. *Res:* Semiconductor materials and devices; role of impurities in silicon and other bulk semiconductors and films; Mossbauer effect. *Mailing Add:* A130-2N-07, 3M Ctr 6801 River Pl Blvd Austin TX 78726

HAMILL, JAMES JUNIOR, CHEMISTRY, CHEMICAL MICROSCOPY. *Current Pos:* RETIRED. *Personal Data:* b Griswold, Iowa, Dec 7, 21; m 47, Donna Brooks; c James M & Christy S. *Educ:* Univ Colo, BA, 50. *Honors & Awards:* R P Dinsmore Res Award, 59. *Prof Exp:* Microscopist, Res Div, Goodyear Tire & Rubber Co, 50-56, sr microscopist, 56-64, res scientist, 64-65, head, Micros Sect, Res Div, 65-80. *Mem:* Am Chem Soc. *Res:* Chemical and industrial microscopy; development of new or improved processes for synthetic rubber, plastics, rubber chemicals or other products of interest to the rubber and plastics industry; high impact plastics. *Mailing Add:* 105 Audubon Rd SE Winter Haven FL 33884-2503

HAMILL, PATRICK JAMES, CELESTIAL MECHANICS, AEROSOL PHYSICS. *Current Pos:* PROF PHYSICS, SAN JOSE STATE UNIV, CALIF, 81- *Personal Data:* b Salt Lake City, Utah; m, Elsa Li; c Carla A & Candace J. *Educ:* St Edward's Univ, Austin, BS, 59; Univ Ariz, MS, 68, PhD(physics), 71. *Honors & Awards:* Julian Allen Award, NASA. *Prof Exp:* Vis prof physics, Univ Trujillo, Peru, 62-66; fel geophys, Univ Chicago, 71-72; asst prof physics, Clark Col, Atlanta, 72-74; res assoc, Ames Res Ctr, NASA, 74-78; scientist, Systs & Appl Sci Corp, 78-81. *Concurrent Pos:* Pres scholar, San Jose State Univ, 96. *Mem:* Am Phys Soc; Am Geophy Union. *Res:* Celestial mechanics and aerosol physics; author of 70 journal articles on topics ranging from the rings of Saturn to the formation of stratospheric aerosol particles and the ozone hole. *Mailing Add:* 10300 Moretti Dr Cupertino CA 95014

HAMILL, PETER VAN VECHTEN, EPIDEMIOLOGY, PREVENTIVE MEDICINE. *Current Pos:* CONSULT EPIDEMIOLOGIST PREV MED, HAMILL ASSOCS, INC, 78- *Personal Data:* b Baltimore, Md, Apr 16, 26; m 52, Margot J Henry; c Jan, Peter Jr, Hanna E & Bill. *Educ:* Univ Mich, BA, 47, MD, 53; Johns Hopkins Univ, MPH, 62. *Prof Exp:* Med officer in charge, Alaska Native Hosp, Tanana, 55-57; med dir, USPHS, 55-78, chief epidemiol studies air pollution, 58-60, sci dir surgeon gen study smoking & health, 62-64, chief med adv, US Nat Health Exam Surv, 64-78. *Concurrent Pos:* Consult, Nat Ctr Health Statist, USPHS, 78-; sr consult, SRI-Int, 78-84; consult epidemiologist, Olin Corp, 78-; chmn, sci adv comt, Aleutian-Bering Sea Inst, 66-79; vis prof, Epidemiol & Pub Health, Univ Mass, Amherst, 78-79; prof epidemiol & prev med, Med Sch, Univ Md, Baltimore, 79-81, adj prof, 81-; sr med consult, Occidental Chem, 86- *Mem:* Soc Epidemiol Res; Soc Study Human Biol; fel Am Acad Occup Med; fel Am Col Prev Med; Asn Teachers Prev Med; fel Am Col Epidemiol. *Res:* Pulmonary disease, chronic, non-infectious, malignant and nonmalignant; environmental health, especially air pollution, smoking and occupational health; epidemiology of occupational diseases; preventive medicine in occupational diseases; chronic lung diseases. *Mailing Add:* 1001 Whitehall Cove Annapolis MD 21401

HAMILL, ROBERT L, NATURAL PRODUCTS CHEMISTRY, BIOCHEMISTRY. *Current Pos:* sr biochemist, Eli Lilly & Co, 55-64, res scientist, 64-69, res assoc, 69-83, group leader antibiotic isolation, 70-83, RES ADVISOR ANTIBIOTIC ISOLATION, ELI LILLY & CO, 83- *Personal Data:* b Youngstown, Ohio, Mar 13, 27; m 53, 76; c 2. *Educ:* Ohio Univ, BS, 50; Mich State Univ, MS, 53, PhD(biochem), 55. *Prof Exp:* Res asst, Mich State Univ, 50-51 & 52-55. *Concurrent Pos:* Chemist, Mich Dept Health Lab, 54-55; ed, J Antibiotics, 75- & Antimicrobial Agents & Chemother, 80-85, vchmn, Int Conf Antimicrobial Agents & Chemother, 84-87, chmn, 88- *Mem:* Am Chem Soc; Am Soc Microbiol; Sigma Xi; NY Acad Sci; AAAS. *Res:* Antibiotic isolation and purification; blood coagulation; transmethylation and methylation in higher plants and animals; fibrinolysis. *Mailing Add:* 617 Brookview Dr Greenwood IN 46142-1802

HAMILL, ROBERT W, NEUROLOGY, NEUROSCIENCE. *Current Pos:* DIR NEUROL, MONROE COMMUNITY HOSP, 80- *Personal Data:* b Hartford, Conn, July 30, 42; m 66; c 3. *Educ:* Springfield Col, BS, 64; Wake Forest Univ, MD, 68. *Prof Exp:* Med intern & resident, Sch Med & Dent, Univ Rochester, 68-70; med officer-internist, USN, 70-73; resident neurol, Med Col, Cornell Univ, 73-75, instr, 75-76, asst prof, 76-80; asst prof, 80-85, assoc prof neurol, Sch Med & Dent, Univ Rochester, 85- *Concurrent Pos:* Alfred P Sloan Found fel, 76; Nat Res Serv Award, Nat Inst Neurol Commun Dis & Stroke, 76-78, teacher investr develop award, 78-80; Jordan res fel, Nat Paraplegia Found, 77. *Mem:* Soc Neurosci; Am Acad Neurol; AAAS; Asn Res Nervous & Ment Dis; NY Acad Sci. *Res:* Growth and development, function, aging, and hormonal control of the autonomic nervous system; neurodegenerative disorders and autonomic dysfunction. *Mailing Add:* Fletcher Allen Health Care MCHV Campus Brown 313 Burlington VT 05401

HAMILL, WILLIAM HENRY, PHYSICAL CHEMISTRY. *Current Pos:* prof, 38-74, EMER PROF PHYS CHEM, UNIV NOTRE DAME, 74- *Personal Data:* b Oswego, NY, June 13, 08; m 34; c 5. *Educ:* Univ Notre Dame, BS, 30, MS, 31; Columbia Univ, PhD(phys chem), 36. *Prof Exp:* Asst prof phys chem, Fordham Univ, 31-38. *Mem:* Am Chem Soc; The Chem Soc. *Res:* Ionic processes in radiation chemistry; mass spectrometry; slow electron impact phenomena for thin-film dielectric solids; electron transport in disordered solids. *Mailing Add:* 3602 S Ironwood Dr South Bend IN 46614

HAMILTON, ANGUS CAMERON, GEODESY. *Current Pos:* chmn dept, 71-85, prof, 71-86, EMER PROF SURV ENG, UNIV NB, 86- *Personal Data:* b Listowel, Ont, Apr 18, 22; m 49; c 5. *Educ:* Univ Toronto, BASc, 49, MASc, 51. *Honors & Awards:* Earle Fernell Award, Am Cong Surv Mapping, 83; Champlain Award, Can Coun Land Surveyors. *Prof Exp:* Chief shoran sect, Geod Surv Can, 54-57, electronics sect, 57-58; sr sci officer, Can Dept Mines & Tech Surv, 58-67; coordr res & training, Surv & Mapping Br, Can Dept Energy, Mines & Resources, 67-71. *Mem:* Hon mem Can Inst Surv & Mapping. *Res:* Application of electronic distance measuring methods to geodetic surveying; application of gravity measurements to geoidal and isostatic studies; development of land information systems; development of studies in surveying engineering economy. *Mailing Add:* Dept Geod & Geomatic Eng Univ NB Fredericton NB E3B 5A3 Can

HAMILTON, BRUCE KING, BIOCHEMICAL ENGINEERING, CHEMICAL PROCESS DEVELOPMENT. *Current Pos:* PRES, BIODEVELOP ASSOC, INC, 95- *Personal Data:* b Easton, Pa, May 26, 47; m 83, Judith A Johnson; c Michael & Katharine. *Educ:* Mass Inst Technol, BS, 74, PhD(biochem eng), 74. *Prof Exp:* Res assoc biochem eng, Mass Inst Technol, 74-75; group leader, Frederick Cancer Res Ctr, 75-77, sect head fermentation technol, 78-80; dir process develop, Genex Corp, 80-81, vpres process develop, 82-85; dir process develop, W R Grace & Co, 85-92, dir bioprod & bioprocess res & develop, Res Div, 92-95. *Concurrent Pos:* Mem, bd dir, Md Bioprocessing Ctr, Inc; adj fac, Grad Sch Mgt & Technol, Univ Md. *Mem:* AAAS; Am Inst Chem Engrs; Am Chem Soc. *Res:* Biochemical engineering; biotechnology process design, development, and scale-up; biotechnology plant start-up and toubleshooting; design of biotechnology plant operating and maintenance systems. *Mailing Add:* 15229 Watergate Rd Silver Spring MD 20905. *E-Mail:* bhamilto@polaris.umuc.edu

HAMILTON, BRUCE M, METALLURGY. *Current Pos:* RETIRED. *Personal Data:* b Hamilton, Ont, Apr 20, 20. *Educ:* Queens Univ, BSc, 43. *Prof Exp:* Res analyst, Dept Mines & Resources, Ottawa, 43-44; chief metallurgist, supt melting & primary rolling & dir metall, Atlas Steel Corp, Welland, Ont, 44-64; dir metall, Crucible Steel Corp, Pittsburgh, 66-67, works mgr, 67-68; pres, Colt Indust, 68-71; pres & chief exec officer, Slater Steels Corp, Hamilton, Ont, 71-86; pres, Bruce Hamilton Consult Inc, Burlington, Ont, 86-87; vpres & gen mgr, Atlas Specialty Steels, Welland, Ont, 87-88, pres, 88-89; consult to chmn, Sammi Steel Co, Seoul, Korea, 89-90; chmn bd, Sydney Steel Corp, NS, 91-93. *Concurrent Pos:* Bd dirs, numerous corp & orgn, 75-90. *Res:* Alloy specialty steels; automotive steels; fatigue in mining and construction steels; application and selection of specialty steels. *Mailing Add:* 584 North Shore Blvd E Burlington ON L7T 1X2 Can

HAMILTON, BYRON BRUCE, PHARMACOLOGY, MEDICINE & RESEARCH ADMINISTRATION. *Current Pos:* ASSOC CLIN PROF, DEPT MED, DIV GERIAT, DUKE UNIV MED CTR, 94-; DIR REHAB SERV RES & DEVELOP UNIT, DEPT VER AFFAIRS MED CTR, DURHAM, 94- *Personal Data:* b New Brighton, Pa, July 6, 34; m 58; c 2. *Educ:* Syracuse Univ, AB, 56; State Univ NY, MD, 59, PhD(pharmacol), 71. *Honors & Awards:* Licht Award. *Prof Exp:* Intern med, Boston City Hosp, 59-60; asst prof pharmacol & rehab, State Univ NY Upstate Med Ctr, 67-70; from asst prof to assoc prof, clin rehab, Sch Med, Northwestern Univ, 70-84; clin assoc prof, Rehab Med Sch Med & Biomed Sci, Dept Rehab Med, State Univ NY, Buffalo, 84-94 *Concurrent Pos:* USPHS fels, State Univ NY Upstate Med Ctr, 60-61 & 63-67; dir res, Nat Inst Handicapped Res, Rehab Res & Training Ctr, Northwestern Univ-Rehab Inst Chicago, 70-84. *Mem:* Am Eval Asn; Am Rheumatism Asn; Am Cong Rehab Med. *Res:* Physiology of cell cation transport; renal acid and base transport; rehabilitation outcomes management research; rehabilitation research administration. *Mailing Add:* Rehab Serv Res & Develop Unit Vet Affairs Med Ctr 841 508 Fulton St Durham NC 27705. *Fax:* 919-286-6048

HAMILTON, C HOWARD, MECHANICAL METALLURGY, SHAPING & FORMING. *Current Pos:* PROF MAT SCI, WASH STATE UNIV, 84- *Personal Data:* b Pueblo, Colo, Mar 17, 35; m 68; c 3. *Educ:* Colo Sch Mines, BS, 59; Univ Southern Calif, MS, 65; Case Western Res Univ, PhD(metall), 68. *Honors & Awards:* IR 100 Award. *Prof Exp:* Mem tech staff, Mat Lab, La Div, Rockwell Int, 68-76, Metals Processing Sci Ctr, 76-78, group mgr, 78-80, prin scientist mat, 80-81, dir, 81-84. *Concurrent Pos:* Mem, Shaping-Forming Comt, Minerals, Metals & Mat Soc, 78-; ed, J Mat Shaping Technol, 86-88; dep ed, Scripta Metallurgica, 89-95. *Mem:* Minerals Metals & Mat Soc; fel Am Soc Metals Int; Sigma Xi; Mat Res Soc. *Res:* Deformation processing and forming, especially at elevated temperatures, including superplasticity, superplastic forming, diffusion bonding and thermomechanical processing; number of publications and patents. *Mailing Add:* Wash State Univ Pullman WA 99164-2920. *Fax:* 509-335-4662; *E-Mail:* hamilton@mme.wsu.edu

HAMILTON, CAROLE LOIS, ENERGY CONVERSION; SYSTEMS ANALYSIS. *Current Pos:* mem tech staff, 74-78, TECH GROUP SUPVR, JET PROPULSION LAB, 79- *Personal Data:* b Butte, Mont, Jan 25, 37; m 62; c 2. *Educ:* Colo State Univ, BS, 58; Calif Inst Technol, PhD(chem), 63. *Prof Exp:* Res fel chem, Calif Inst Technol, 62-65; res fel, Stanford Univ, 65-68, lectr, 68-71; with Environ Qual Lab, Calif Inst Technol, 71-74. *Mem:* Am Chem Soc; Sigma Xi. *Res:* Rearrangements in organometallic compounds; analysis of specificity alpha-chymotrypsin; spin-labeled biomolecules; energy systems engineering. *Mailing Add:* 2269 Midwock Dr Altadena CA 91001-2844

HAMILTON, CHARLEEN MARIE, GENE CLONING & SEQUENCING, IN VITRO PROTEIN EXPRESSION. *Current Pos:* FEL, DEPT CELL BIOL & NEUROSCI, UNIV TEX SOUTHWESTERN MED CTR, 91- *Personal Data:* b Allentown, Pa, Apr 12, 62; m 90, Roger S Davis. *Educ:* Ohio State Univ, BS, 84; Texas A&M Univ, PhD(med microbiol-genetics), 91. *Mem:* Am Soc Cell Biol. *Res:* Dissection of the cellular processes regulating membrane trafficking, especially microtubule-based motors and anchor proteins; in vivo and in vitro analysis of these proteins. *Mailing Add:* 209 Bacon St Waltham MA 02154. *E-Mail:* hamilton@utsw.swmed.edu

HAMILTON, CHARLES LEROY, GEOLOGY. *Current Pos:* assoc prof, 69-81, PROF GEOL, MONTCLAIR STATE COL, 81- *Personal Data:* b Nyack, NY, Feb 19, 32; m 54; c 3. *Educ:* Lehigh Univ, BA, 53; Dartmouth Col, MA, 54; Va Polytech Inst, PhD(geol), 64. *Prof Exp:* Explor geologist, NJ Zinc Co, Va, 56-58; from instr to asst prof, Rutgers Univ, 60-69. *Mem:* Nat Asn Geol Teachers; Mineral Soc Am; Sigma Xi; Geol Soc Am. *Res:* Igneous and metamorphic petrology. *Mailing Add:* Three Lafayette Ct Wayne NJ 07470-2716

HAMILTON, CHARLES R, HEMISPHERIC SPECIALIZATION, VISUAL PERCEPTION. *Current Pos:* RES SCIENTIST, COL MED, TEX A&M UNIV, 91- *Personal Data:* b Chicago, Ill, Sept 27, 35; m 64, Carole Olson; c Catherine & Christopher. *Educ:* Univ of the South, BS, 57; Calif Inst Technol, PhD(biol), 64. *Prof Exp:* Res fel psychobiol, Calif Inst Technol, 64-65; asst prof psychol, Stanford Univ, 65-71; sr res fel, Calif Inst Technol, 71-74, from res assoc to sr res assoc biol, 74-90. *Mem:* AAAS; Am Psychol Soc; Am Psychol Asn; Soc Neurosci; Sigma Xi; Int Primatological Soc. *Res:* Behavioral testing of split-brain monkeys and humans; study cerebral lateralization, interhemispheric relations and visual perception. *Mailing Add:* Human Anat & Med Neurobiol Col Med Tex A&M Univ College Station TX 77843-1114. *E-Mail:* chamilton@tamu.edu

HAMILTON, CHARLES WILLIAM, CHEMISTRY. *Current Pos:* RETIRED. *Personal Data:* b Chicago, Ill, Sept 6, 19; m 43; c 4. *Educ:* Cent YMCA Col, BS, 41; Northwestern Univ, MS, 43. *Prof Exp:* Res chemist, Armour Res Found, 43-44; assoc res chemist, Columbia-Southern Chem Corp, 46-52; asst div chief rubber & plastics chem, Battelle Mem Inst, 52-60, assoc dir, New Prod Res, Continental Can Co, Inc, 60-69; mgr, Prod Develop & Tech Serv, Foster Grant Co, Inc, 69-80; dir, Develop Lab Plastics Div, Am Hoechst Corp, 80-83. *Mem:* Emer mem Am Chem Soc. *Res:* Polymer chemistry; synthesis and processing of thermoplastics; properties of crystalline polymers; electrical applications of plastics; condensation polymers; plastics packaging. *Mailing Add:* 118 Prospect St Leominster MA 01453-3050

HAMILTON, CLARA EDDY, ZOOLOGY, PHYSIOLOGY. *Current Pos:* RETIRED. *Personal Data:* b New Haven, Conn, Mar 14, 23; m 55. *Educ:* Univ Ga, BS, 42; Univ Ill, MA, 44, PhD(zool), 46. *Prof Exp:* Asst prof zool, Univ Ga, 46-55, assoc prof, 55-56; physiologist, Div res grants, NIH, 56-78. *Mem:* AAAS; Am Soc Zoologists; Am Physiol Soc. *Res:* Physiology of reproduction; endocrinology. *Mailing Add:* 15424 Tierra Dr Silver Spring MD 20906-1266

HAMILTON, D(EWITT) C(LINTON), JR, MECHANICAL ENGINEERING. *Current Pos:* head dept, 65-74, prof, 65-86, EMER PROF MECH ENG, TULANE UNIV, LA, 86- *Personal Data:* b Eufaula, Okla, Dec 4, 18; m 42. *Educ:* Univ Okla, BS(mech eng) & BS(petrol eng), 41; Univ Calif, MS, 46; Purdue Univ, PhD(mech eng), 49. *Prof Exp:* Res & develop engr, Power Plant Lab, Wright Field, 46-47; res asst, Purdue Univ, 47-48, instr heat transfer & thermodyn, 48-49, asst prof heat transfer, 49-51; sr develop engr, Oak Ridge Nat Lab, 51-52, prin develop engr, 52-56; lectr in chg reactor eng, Oak Ridge Sch Reactor Technol, 56-65. *Concurrent Pos:* Spec lectr, Ga Inst Technol, 64. *Mem:* Am Soc Mech Engrs Int. *Res:* Thermodynamics; heat transfer; solar thermal systems. *Mailing Add:* 2311 Prancer St New Orleans LA 70131

HAMILTON, DAVID WHITMAN, DEVELOPMENTAL BIOLOGY. *Current Pos:* PROF CELL BIOL & NEUROANAT & HEAD DEPT, UNIV MINN, MINNEAPOLIS, 77-, DIR GRAD STUDIES, 80- *Personal Data:* b Anaconda, Mont, Nov 29, 35; m 59. *Educ:* Harvard Univ, AB, 57; Univ Kans, MA, 60; Cambridge Univ, PhD(anat), 64. *Prof Exp:* Instr anat, Univ Kans, 59-60; fel, Harvard Med Sch, 63-65, from instr to assoc prof, 65-77, Lawrence J Henderson assoc prof health sci & technol, 74-77. *Mem:* Am Soc Cell Biol; Soc Study Reproduction; Am Asn Anat. *Res:* Cell and reproductive biology. *Mailing Add:* Dept Cell Biol & Neuroanat Univ Minn Jackson Hall 321 Church St SE Minneapolis MN 55455. *E-Mail:* hamilton@umnhnue

HAMILTON, DOUGLAS J(AMES), ELECTRICAL ENGINEERING. *Current Pos:* assoc prof, 59-62, actg dir, Solid State Eng Lab, 65, PROF ELEC ENG, UNIV ARIZ, 62- *Personal Data:* b Canton, Ohio, Dec 6, 30; m 53; c 2. *Educ:* Case Western Reserve Univ, BS, 53; Univ Calif, Los Angeles, MS, 56; Stanford Univ, PhD, 59. *Prof Exp:* Mem tech staff, Hughes Aircraft Co, 53-57; design engr comput lab, Gen Elec Co, 57-58; asst elec eng, Stanford Univ, 58-59. *Concurrent Pos:* Consult, Lockheed Missile Syst Div, 59 & Motorola Semiconductor Prod, Inc, 60- *Res:* Solid-state circuit techniques and devices; integrated circuits. *Mailing Add:* Dept Elec Comp Eng Univ Ariz Tucson AZ 85721

HAMILTON, DOUGLAS STUART, PHYSICS. *Current Pos:* PROF PHYSICS, UNIV CONN, 80- *Personal Data:* b Ft Collins, Colo, June 28, 49. *Educ:* Univ Colo, Boulder, BA, 71; Univ Wis-Madison, PhD(physics), 76. *Prof Exp:* Res assoc physics, Univ Wis, 77; res assoc, Univ Southern Calif, 77-80. *Mem:* Am Phys Soc; Am Asn Physics Teachers; Sigma Xi. *Res:* Dynamical interactions between light and condensed media. *Mailing Add:* Dept Physics 2152 Hillside Rd Univ Conn Storrs CT 06269. *Fax:* 860-486-3346; *E-Mail:* hamilton@mainphysuconn.edu

HAMILTON, EDWIN LEE, MARINE GEOLOGY, ACOUSTIC PROPERTIES OF SEDIMENTS. *Current Pos:* RETIRED. *Personal Data:* b Sherman, Tex, Dec 20, 14; m 38; c 3. *Educ:* Tex Agr & Mech Col, BS, 36; Stanford Univ, MS, 50, PhD(geol), 52. *Honors & Awards:* Curl Mem Award, Naval Undersea Ctr, 71. *Prof Exp:* Lectr geol, Univ Wash, 51; marine geologist, US Navy Electronics Lab, 51-77; marine geologist, Naval Ocean Systs Ctr, 77-84, emer marine geologist, 84-85. *Mem:* Geol Soc Am; Soc Econ Paleont & Mineral; Am Asn Petrol Geologists; Am Geophys Union; Sigma Xi; Acoust Soc Am. *Res:* Marine geology; sediments, geomorphology of the sea floor; acoustic properties of the sea floor. *Mailing Add:* 3594 DuPont St San Diego CA 92106

HAMILTON, FRANKLIN D, PROTEIN & ENZYME CHEMISTRY. *Current Pos:* DIR, DIV SPONSORED RES, FLA A&M UNIV. *Personal Data:* b Aulcila, Fla, Oct 30, 42; c 3. *Educ:* Univ Pittsburgh, PhD(biochem); Fla A&M Univ, BS. *Prof Exp:* Assoc prof chem, Atlanta Univ, 79- *Concurrent Pos:* Asst prof biomed sci, 71-74, assoc prof biomed sci, Grad Sch Bio Med Sci, Univ Tenn-Oak Ridge, 74-79; food found fel, USPHS fel; mem, NIH-MARC rev comt, Nat Acad Sci-NSF; fel rev panel, sci & tech adv comt, Nat Asn Equal Opportunity Higher Ed, vchair; vis lectr, FASEB Minority Inst, Prague. *Mem:* Am Soc Biol Chemists; AAAS; Am Soc Cell Biol. *Mailing Add:* Div Sponsored Res Dept Chem Fla A&M Univ Tallahassee FL 32307. *Fax:* 850-599-3952

HAMILTON, GORDON ANDREW, BIO-ORGANIC CHEMISTRY. *Current Pos:* assoc prof, 66-72, PROF ORG CHEM, PA STATE UNIV, 72- *Personal Data:* b Cobden, Ont, Mar 15, 35; m 68, Falene E Fink; c 1. *Educ:* Queen's Univ, Ont, BA, 56; Harvard Univ, MA, 57, PhD(org chem), 59. *Prof Exp:* Res assoc org chem, Ill Inst Technol, 59-60; from instr to asst prof, Princeton Univ, 60-66. *Concurrent Pos:* Sloan res fel, 67-69; mem, Biochem Study Sect, NIH, 71-74; NIH spec res fel, Kyoto, Japan, 75; ed, Bioorganic Chem, 83-; mem, Comt Prof Training, Am Chem Soc. *Mem:* AAAS; Am Chem Soc; Am Soc Biol Chemists; Sigma Xi. *Res:* Mechanisms of organic and enzymatic reactions, especially oxidation-reduction reactions; peroxisomal oxidases and their role in metabolism; mechanism of insulin and growth factor action; role of oxalyl thidesters in controlling metabolism. *Mailing Add:* Dept Chem Pa State Univ 152 Davey University Park PA 16802-6300. *Fax:* 814-863-8403; *E-Mail:* gah4@psuvm.psu.edu

HAMILTON, GORDON WAYNE, plasma physics, civil engineering, for more information see previous edition

HAMILTON, HARRY LEMUEL, JR, MICROMETEOROLOGY. *Current Pos:* PROVOST, CHAPMAN UNIV, 90- *Personal Data:* b Charleston, SC, May 26, 38; c David & Lisa. *Educ:* Beloit Col, BA, 60; Univ Wis, MS, 62, PhD(meteorol), 65. *Prof Exp:* From asst prof to assoc prof atmospheric sci, State Univ NY, Albany, 65-90, chmn dept, 76-83. *Concurrent Pos:* Environ analyst, Gen Elec Gas Turbine Div, 79, environ consult, 75-79. *Mem:* AAAS; Sigma Xi; Am Meteorol Soc. *Res:* Micrometeorologic instrumentation; determination of diffuse solar radiation. *Mailing Add:* Off Provost Chapman Univ Orange CA 92666

HAMILTON, HOBART GORDON, JR, INORGANIC CHEMISTRY. *Current Pos:* from asst prof to assoc prof, Calif State Univ, Stanislaus, 68-74, chmn dept, 72-73, assoc vpres acad affairs, 73-81, PROF CHEM, CALIF STATE UNIV, STANISLAUS, 75-; INTERIM PROVOST VPRES ACAD AFFAIRS, 94- *Personal Data:* b Washington, DC, Feb 8, 39; m 64, Mary Kline; c Laurissa & Elise. *Educ:* Univ Tex, El Paso, BS, 61; NMex State Univ, MS, 63, PhD(chem), 68. *Prof Exp:* Radiochemist, Gen Elec Co, 63-64; res assoc analytical chem, Univ Ariz, 67-68. *Mem:* Am Chem Soc; Sigma Xi. *Res:* Synthesis and stereochemistry of multidentate ligand transition metal complexes. *Mailing Add:* 2010 Sconyers Ct Turlock CA 95382

HAMILTON, HOWARD BRITTON, ELECTRICAL ENGINEERING, ELECTRIC POWER & MACHINERY. *Current Pos:* prof, 66-86, chmn dept, 66-73 & 83-86, EMER PROF ELEC ENG, UNIV PITTSBURGH, 86- *Personal Data:* b Augusta, Kans, Oct 28, 23; m 43, Geraldine Karr; c John, Stephen, Jana & Christopher. *Educ:* Kans State, BS, 49; Univ Minn, MS, 55; Okla State Univ, PhD(elec eng), 62. *Honors & Awards:* Centennial Award, Inst Elec & Electronics Engrs. *Prof Exp:* Engr, Gen Elec Co, 49-53; instr mech eng, Univ Wichita, 53-54, assoc prof elec eng & head dept, 55-58; unit chief mfg res, Boeing Co, 58-60; prof, Wichita State Univ, 60-65; adj prof & chief at party Univ Pittsburgh at Valparaiso Santa Maria Univ, Chile, 65-66. *Mem:* Fel Inst Elec & Electronics Engrs. *Res:* Power systems; electric machinery and current limiting devices. *Mailing Add:* Elec Eng Dept 348 Benedum Univ Pittsburgh Pittsburgh PA 15261

HAMILTON, HOWARD LAVERNE, DEVELOPMENTAL BIOLOGY. *Current Pos:* prof, 62-82, EMER PROF BIOL, UNIV VA, 82- *Personal Data:* b Lone Tree, Iowa, July 20, 16; m 45, 75, Elizabeth Bentley; c Christina H, Phillips H, Martha J, Elizabeth M & Catherine R. *Educ:* Univ Iowa, BA, 34, MS, 38; Johns Hopkins Univ, PhD(biol), 41. *Prof Exp:* From asst prof to prof zool, Iowa State Univ, 46-62, actg head, Dept Zool & Entom, 60-61, chmn dept, 61-62. *Concurrent Pos:* Mem corp, Marine Biol Lab, Woods Hole, 46-; managing ed, Am Zoologist, Am Soc Zool, 66-70. *Mem:* Soc Develop Biol; Am Soc Naturalists; Am Soc Zool; Int Soc Develop Biol; Am Inst Biol Sci. *Res:* Pigmentation in birds; culture of viruses and rickettsiae; chemotherapy in rickettsial diseases; experimental embryology; developmental effects of rare earths; chemical control of organogenesis. *Mailing Add:* Jumping Branch Farm Rte 16 Box 401 Charlottesville VA 22901

HAMILTON, IAN ROBERT, MICROBIOLOGY, BIOCHEMISTRY. *Current Pos:* Asst prof biochem, Univ Man, 64-67, assoc prof oral biol, 67-71, prof, 71-81, HEAD ORAL BIOL, FAC DENT, UNIV MAN, 81-85 & 90- *Personal Data:* b Ft Frances, Ont, July 1, 32; m 59; c 3. *Educ:* Ont Agr Col, BSc, 58, MSc, 60; Univ Wis, PhD(microbiol, biochem), 63. *Concurrent Pos:* Nat Res Coun Can res fel biochem, Oxford Univ, 63-64. *Mem:* Am Soc Microbiol; Can Soc Microbiol; Int Asn Dent Res; Can Asn Dent Res. *Res:* Carbohydrate formation and utilization by oral microorganisms; bioenergetics of sugar transport by bacteria; microbial gluconeogenesis; mechanism of antibacterial effects of fluoride; growth of oral pathogens in continuous culture. *Mailing Add:* Dept Oral Biol Univ Man Fac Dent Winnipeg MB R3E 0W2 Can

HAMILTON, J(AMES) HUGH, electrical & chemical engineering, for more information see previous edition

HAMILTON, JAMES ARTHUR, NUCLEAR MAGNETIC RESONANCE SPECTROSCOPY. *Current Pos:* from asst prof to assoc prof chem, 78-90, PROF BIOPHYSICS, BOSTON UNIV SCH MED, 91- *Personal Data:* b Oct 21, 47; m 83, Melinda McLendon; c Lianna. *Educ:* Juniata Col, BS, 69; Ind Univ, PhD(chem), 74. *Prof Exp:* Res asst, Eastman Kodak, 69; assoc instr, Ind Univ, 71-75, fel chem, 75-78. *Concurrent Pos:* Vis prof, Juniata Col, 76; nat res serv award, NIH, 76. *Mem:* Biophys Soc; Am Chem Soc; Sigma Xi. *Res:* High resolution and solid state nuclear magnetic spectroscopy of lipids in membranes, plasma lipoproteins and atherosclerotic lesions; interaction of lipids with proteins and the movement of lipids between membranes and proteins; application of NMR methods to lipid enzymatic reactions, such as the phosphdipose A2 and C reactions. *Mailing Add:* Biophys Dept Boston Univ Sch Med 80 E Concord St Boston MA 02118-2394

HAMILTON, JAMES ARTHUR ROY, FISH BIOLOGY. *Current Pos:* RETIRED. *Personal Data:* b Eng, May 1, 19; m 46; c 3. *Educ:* Univ BC, BA, 44, MA, 47; Univ Wash, PhD(fisheries), 55. *Prof Exp:* Sr biologist, Int Pac Salmon Fisheries Comn, Can, 43-56; sr biologist fisheries, Pac Power & Light Co, 56-70, environ coordr, 71-84. *Concurrent Pos:* Consult, US CEngr & Wash Dept Fisheries. *Mem:* Am Fisheries Soc; Am Soc Limnol & Oceanog; Am Inst Fishery Res Biologists. *Res:* Limnology and fresh water ecology, especially reservoir and salmon populations. *Mailing Add:* 10345 SW Homestead Lane Beaverton OR 97008

HAMILTON, JAMES BECLONE, inorganic chemistry; deceased, see previous edition for last biography

HAMILTON, JAMES F(RANCIS), MECHANICAL ENGINEERING. *Current Pos:* assoc prof, 65-70, PROF MECH ENG, PURDUE UNIV, 70- *Personal Data:* b Edinburg, Ind, Apr 8, 27; m 48; c 3. *Educ:* Purdue Univ, BSME, 51, PhD(eng), 63; Cornell Univ, MME, 54. *Prof Exp:* Instr mech eng, Cornell Univ, 51-54; sr res engr, Clevite Res Ctr, 54-55; prof mech eng, WVa Univ, 55-65. *Mem:* Am Soc Mech Engrs. *Res:* Experimental stress analysis; structural vibrations; analysis and design; system analysis; noise control. *Mailing Add:* 1401 Warren Pl Lafayette IN 47905

HAMILTON, JAMES GUTHRIE, BIOCHEMISTRY. *Current Pos:* RETIRED. *Personal Data:* b Eagletown, Okla, Jan 30, 23; m 50; c 4. *Educ:* Okla State Univ, BS, 48, MS, 50; Univ Minn, PhD(biochem), 53. *Prof Exp:* Asst prof exp med, Univ Tex Southwestern Med Ctr, 54-57; asst prof biochem & med, Sch Med, Tulane Univ, 57-61, assoc prof, 61-68; mem staff, Hoffman-LaRoche, Inc, 68-72, group chief, Dept Biochem Nutrit, 72-88. *Mem:* Am Chem Soc; Am Soc Microbiol; Am Inst Nutrit; Am Oil Chem Soc. *Res:* Chemistry and metabolism of lipids and bile acids. *Mailing Add:* 2976 Heather Bow Sarasota FL 34235-7201

HAMILTON, JAMES WILBURN, BIOCHEMISTRY. *Current Pos:* ASSOC PROF BIOCHEM, MED SCH, UNIV KANS, 79- *Personal Data:* b Louisville, Ky, Sept 20, 36; m 55; c 5. *Educ:* Univ Louisville, AB, 61, PhD(biochem), 65. *Prof Exp:* Res asst biochem, Med Sch, Univ Louisville, 58-61; fel pharmacol, Baylor Med Sch, 65-66; asst prof, biochem, Sch Dent, Univ Mo-Kansas City, 66-71, assoc prof, 71-77; co dir Calcium Res Lab, 68-82, res biochemist, Vet Admin Hosp, Kansas City, Mo, 66-, dir calcium res lab, 82- *Mem:* AAAS; Am Chem Soc; Am Soc Biol Chemists; Endocrine Soc. *Res:* Parathyroid hormone biosynthesis; structure-function studies of vitamin D-dependent calcium binding protein. *Mailing Add:* Dept Biochem Res Serv Vet Admin Hosp 4801 Linwood Blvd Kansas City MO 64128-2295. *Fax:* 816-861-1110

HAMILTON, JANET V, PHYSICAL CHEMISTRY. *Current Pos:* PROF CHEM, TARRANT COUNTY JR COL, 66- *Personal Data:* b Decatur, Ill, Nov 11, 36; m 60, Walter; c Karen & Susan. *Educ:* Millikin Univ, AB, 58; Tulane Univ, PhD(phys chem), 63. *Prof Exp:* Sr res engr thermochem, Rocketdyne Div, NAm Aviation, Inc, 63-66. *Mem:* AAAS; Am Chem Soc; Sigma Xi. *Res:* Heat of formation, reaction and ablation; bond energies; heat capacity; surface tension; viscosities. *Mailing Add:* Rte 1 Box 272 Sanger TX 76266

HAMILTON, JEFFERSON MERRITT, JR, FLUORINE CHEMISTRY. *Current Pos:* RETIRED. *Personal Data:* b Minneapolis, Minn, Aug 31, 18; m 42; c 2. *Educ:* Johns Hopkins Univ, AB, 40, PhD(phys chem), 44. *Prof Exp:* Res supvr, Manhattan Dist, Johns Hopkins Univ, 43-46; res chemist, E I du Pont de Nemours & Co, Inc, 46-53, res supvr, 53-60, head, Res & Develop Div, 60-82, consult, 82-88. *Concurrent Pos:* Civilian with Off Sci Res & Develop, 44. *Mem:* AAAS; Am Chem Soc. *Res:* Organic fluorine compounds; acetylene chemistry; catalytic processes. *Mailing Add:* 4031 Kennett Pike Box 56 Wilmington DE 19807

HAMILTON, JOHN FREDERICK, SOLID STATE PHYSICS. *Current Pos:* RETIRED. *Personal Data:* b Knoxville, Tenn, Mar 19, 28; m 50; c 3. *Educ:* Univ Tenn, BS, 50. *Prof Exp:* Sr res physicist, Eastman Kodak Co, 50-60, res assoc, 60-71, sr res assoc, 71-82, res fel, 82-86. *Concurrent Pos:* Instr, Inst Optics, Univ Rochester. *Mem:* Fel AAAS; Electron Micros Soc Am; fel Am Phys Soc; fel & hon mem Soc Photog Sci & Eng; Am Vacuum Soc. *Res:* Formation of photographic latent image; electrical and structural properties of silver halides, using the electron microscope and related equipment; imperfections in crystalline solids; heterogeneous catalysis; nucleation phenomena. *Mailing Add:* 211 Glenn Abbey Johns Island SC 29455

HAMILTON, JOHN MEACHAM, BIOLOGY. *Current Pos:* RETIRED. *Personal Data:* b Gifford, Ill, Feb 20, 12; wid; c 2. *Educ:* Oberlin Col, AB, 35; Wesleyan Univ, MA, 37; Yale Univ, MS, 42; Univ Iowa, PhD(zool), 51. *Prof Exp:* Asst neurophysiol res, Yale Univ, 37-41; sci master, Asheville Sch for Boys, NC, 42-46; from asst prof to prof biol, Park Col, 46-77, head dept, 49-64, actg chmn, Sci Div, 51-53, chmn, Sci Div, 59-64, actg dean col, 55-56 & 64-67, emer prof biol, 77. *Concurrent Pos:* NSF fac fel, Univ Calif, Los Angeles, 58-59; vis lectr, Inter-Am Univ PR, 67-68; scholar, Univ Calif, Davis, 71-72. *Mem:* Nat Asn Biol Teachers; Sigma Xi. *Res:* Fresh water protozoology and ecology; history of evolution. *Mailing Add:* 6500 Wexford Pl Kansas City MO 64151

HAMILTON, JOHN ROBERT, WOOD SCIENCE & TECHNOLOGY. *Current Pos:* prof, 64-87, EMER PROF WOOD SCI & WOOD SCIENTIST, WVA UNIV, 97- *Personal Data:* b Atlanta, Ga, Apr 22, 25; m 46; c 2. *Educ:* Univ Ga, BSF, 48, MSF, 49; NC State Col, PhD, 60. *Prof Exp:* Co forester, Ga Forestry Comn, 49-50; assoc forester, Ga Exp Sta, 50-53, head, Dept Forestry, 53-55; asst, NC State Col, 55-57; assoc prof, Univ Ga, 57-64. *Concurrent Pos:* Ga Forest Res Coun grants, 60-64, Nat Plant Food Inst grant, 61-62; US AEC grant, 61-64 & 65-; Soc Am Wood Preservers grant, 62-63. *Mem:* Soc Am Foresters; Forest Prod Res Soc; Soc Wood Sci & Technol; Sigma Xi. *Res:* Wood anatomy. *Mailing Add:* One Bates Rd Morgantown WV 26505

HAMILTON, JOSEPH H, JR, EXPERIMENTAL NUCLEAR PHYSICS. *Current Pos:* From asst prof to prof physics, Vanderbilt Univ, 58-81, chmn dept, 79-85, Landon C Garland prof, 81-92, LANDON C GARLAND DISTINGUISHED PROF PHYSICS, VANDERBILT UNIV, 92- *Personal Data:* b Ferriday, La, Aug 14, 32; m 60, Jannelle L; c Melissa C & Christopher L. *Educ:* Miss Col, BS, 54; Ind Univ, MS, 56, PhD(physics), 58. *Hon Degrees:* DSc, Miss Col, 82; DPhil Nat, J W Goethe Univ Franfort, 92. *Honors & Awards:* Jesse Beams Gold Medal, 75; Earl Southerland Award, 88; George Pegram Gold Medal, 88; Guy & Rebecca Forman Award, 90; Award for Int Sci Coop, AAAS, 96. *Concurrent Pos:* NSF fel, Univ Uppsala, 58-59; res appointment, Inst Nuclear Physics Res, Amsterdam, Neth, 62-63; chmn, Int Conf Internal Conversion Processes, 65; chmn, Int Conf Radioactivity in Nuclear Spectros, Mod Tech & Appln, 69, mem, Nat Acad Sci Sub-Comt Nuclear Physics, Mgt & Costs, 70; chmn, Univ Isotope Separator Group, Oak Ridge Nat Lab, 71-73, 82-83, 90-92 & nat policy bd, Nat Heavy Accelerator Lab, 75-82; mem planning comt, Int Conf on Reactions between Complex Nuclei, 73-74; chmn, Int Conf Future Directions Studies Nuclei Far From Stability, 79; Alexander von Humboldt sr fel, Frankfurt, 79-80; guest prof, Univ Frankfort, 79-80, 87 & Univ Louis Pasteur Stratsbourg, 91; dir, Joint Inst Heavy Ion Res, 83-92; H Branscomb distinguished prof, 83; chmn, Int Symposium, Directions in Nuclear Struct Res, 84; adj prof, Tsing-Hue Univ, Beijing, 86-; hon adv prof, Fudan Univ, Shanghai, 88-; policy coun, Nuclear Sci Adv Comn & Long Range Planning Comn, 89; chmn, Int Symposium Reflection & Direction in Nuclear Res, 91; dir, Vanderbilt Summer Sci Collab, 91-; conc, Am Physiol Soc, 95; conc, Am Physiol Soc, 95. *Mem:* Fel Am Phys Soc; Sigma Xi; fel AAAS; Am Asn Physics Teachers. *Res:* Nuclear structure studies via beta- and gamma-ray spectroscopy of nuclei far from stability with heavy ions and isotope separator; Coulomb excitation; in-beam spectroscopy following heavy-ion nuclear reactions. *Mailing Add:* PO Box H1807 Sta B Vanderbilt Univ Nashville TN 37235. *Fax:* 615-343-7263

HAMILTON, KENNETH GAVIN ANDREW, ENTOMOLOGY. *Current Pos:* RES SCIENTIST ENTOM, AGR CAN, 72- *Personal Data:* b Nottingham, Eng, Mar 13, 46; Can citizen; m 77. *Educ:* Univ Man, BSA Hons, 68; Univ Ga, MS, 70, Phd(entom), 72. *Mem:* Entom Soc Can; Sigma Xi. *Res:* Taxonomy of Homoptera-Auchenorrhyncha; morphology of Insecta; phylogeny of Insecta; palaeontology of Insecta. *Mailing Add:* ECORC K W Neatby Bldg Carling Ave Ottawa ON K1A 0C6 Can

HAMILTON, KEVIN, DYNAMICAL METEOROLOGY, ATMOSPHERIC MODELLING. *Current Pos:* res scientist, Atmospheric & Oceanic Sci Prog, 87-88, RES SCIENTIST, GEOPHYS FLUID DYNAMICS LAB, PRINCETON UNIV, 88-, ASSOC PROF, ATMOSPHERIC & OCEANIC SCI PROG, 88- *Personal Data:* b Calgary, Alta, Can, Feb 10, 56. *Educ:* Queen's Univ, BSc, 76; McMaster Univ, MSc, 77; Princeton Univ, MA, 79, PhD(geophys fluid dynamics), 81. *Honors & Awards:* Pres Prize, Can Meteorol & Oceanog Soc, 93; Meisinger Award, Am Meteorol Soc, 94. *Prof Exp:* Fel, Nat Ctr Atmospheric Res, 81-82; NSERC Univ res fel, Dept Oceanog, Univ BC, 82-85; asst prof, Dept Meteorol, McGill Univ, Can, 85-87. *Mem:* Am Meteorol Soc; Can Meteorol & Oceanog Soc. *Res:* General circulation of the stratosphere and mesosphere; dynamics of atmospheric waves; interannual variability of the ocean and atmosphere; author several articles and publications. *Mailing Add:* Geophys Fluid Dynamics Lab Princeton Univ PO Box 308 Princeton NJ 08542

HAMILTON, LAWRENCE STANLEY, FORESTRY, WATERSHED MANAGEMENT. *Current Pos:* exten forester, Cornell Univ, 51-54, from asst prof to assoc prof, 54-66, prof, 65-80, EMER PROF FORESTRY, CORNELL UNIV, 80- *Personal Data:* b Toronto, Ont, June 5, 25; nat US; m 47, Linda Schenck; c Blair, Bruce, Anne & Lynne. *Educ:* Univ Toronto, BScF, 48; State Univ NY, MF, 50; Univ Mich, PhD, 62. *Honors & Awards:* Fulbright Awards, 69 & 78. *Prof Exp:* Zone forester, Dept Lands & Forests, Can, 48-51; res assoc, East West Ctr, Honolulu, 80-89, sr fel, 89-93. *Concurrent Pos:* NSF fel, 64-65; mem panel nat res sci, Nat Acad Sci-Nat Res Coun, 65-67, comt soc sci educ, 67-70; Fulbright lectr, Univ New Eng, Australia, 69-70 & Univ Walkato, NZ, 78; vis lectr, Univ Queensland, 72; dir, Venezuelan Trop Rainforest Study, 74-75; consult, UNESCO, Australia, 80, Asn Rural Develop, Costa Rica, 85, Int Union Conserv Nature & Natural Resources, 88; fel, East West Ctr, 79; Comn Ecol, Int Union Conserv Nature, 78-, comn Nat Parks & Protected Areas, 88-; counr, Int Mountain Soc, 90-; vchair mountains, Comn Nat Parks & Protected Areas, Int Union Conserv Nature, 91-; consult, World Bank, Bhutan, 96. *Mem:* Soc Am Foresters; Int Soc Trop Foresters; Int Union Conserv Nature & Natural Resources; Int Mountain Soc. *Res:* Ecological base for land and water planning; watershed land use; international natural resources programs; tropical forests and protected areas; sustainable mountain development; mountain protected area management. *Mailing Add:* Island & Highlands Environ Consult 342 Bittersweet Lane Charlotte VT 05445. *E-Mail:* lsx2_hamilton@together.org

HAMILTON, LEONARD DERWENT, EXPERIMENTAL MEDICINE. *Current Pos:* attend physician, Hosp Med Res Ctr, 64-85, HEAD, BIOMED & ENVIRON ASSESSMENT DIV, BROOKHAVEN NAT LAB, 73- *Personal Data:* b Manchester, Eng, May 7, 21; nat US; m 45; c 3. *Educ:* Oxford Univ, BA, 43, BM & BCh, 45, MA, 46, DM, 51; Cambridge Univ, MA, 48, PhD, 52. *Prof Exp:* Jr asst pathologist, Radcliffe Infirmary, Oxford Univ, 45-46; resident med officer, Radiotherapeut Ctr & house physician, Dept Med, Addenbrooke's Hosp, 46; res student path, Dept Radiotherapeut, Cambridge Univ, 46-49; from asst to assoc, Sloan-Kettering Inst, 50-64, head, Isotope Studies Sect, 57-64, assoc scientist, 65-79. *Concurrent Pos:* Fel med, Salt Lake Gen Hosp, 49-50; spec fel, Mem Hosp, New York, 51-53, spec fel radiation ther, 53; clin asst radiation therapist & clin asst med, Chemother Serv, Mem Hosp, NY, 54-58, asst attend physician, 58-65; consult, Off Under-Secy Spec Polit Affairs, Sci Comt Effects Atomic Radiation, UN, 60-62; mem, NY Mayor's Tech Adv Comt Radiation, 63-77; prof med, Health Sci Ctr, State Univ NY, Stony Brook, 68-; vis fel, St Catherine's Col, Oxford Univ, 72-73; mem panel, Fossil Fuel, UN Environ Prog, 78, Nuclear Energy, 78-79, Renewable Sources, 80, Comp Assessment Different Sources, 80; mem, NY Comnr Health Tech Adv Comt Radiation, 78; mem, Expert Adv Panel Environ Hazards & Focal Pt Health & Environ Effects energy systs, 83- *Mem:* Am Asn Pathologists; Am Soc Clin Invest; Am Asn Cancer Res; Harvey Soc; Soc Risk Anal. *Res:* Structure and functions of nucleic acids; lymphocytes; biomedical and environmental effects of energy systems; hazards evaluation; biological effects of ionizing radiations. *Mailing Add:* Brookhaven Nat Lab Bldg 490D Uptown NY 11973-5000. *Fax:* 516 282-7867

HAMILTON, LEROY LESLIE, BIOMEDICAL ENGINEERING, ELECTRICAL ENGINEERING. *Current Pos:* PRES, HAMILTON PROGS, 84- *Personal Data:* b Fresno, Calif, Aug 31, 34; c 4. *Educ:* Univ Calif, Berkeley, BSEE, 58; Cath Univ Am, MEE, 60; Case Western Res Univ, PhD(Med eng), 67. *Prof Exp:* Electronic engr, US Dept Defense, 58-63; res assoc med eng, Highland View Hosp, Ohio, 63-68; assoc prof elec eng, Cath Univ Am, 68-74; engr, Bur Med Devices, Food & Drug Admin, Rockville, 74-76; dir med eng & electronics, Health Indust Mfrs Asn, Washington, DC, 76-83; pres, Hamilton Med Equip, Inc, 87-89. *Concurrent Pos:* Prof lectr, Med Sch, Georgetown Univ, 69-; consult comput applns, Silver Spring, MD, 84- *Mem:* Inst Elec & Electronics Engrs; Asn Advan Med Instrumentation; Bioelectromagnetics Soc. *Res:* Analysis and modeling of human cardiovascular control system, especially postural reflexes. *Mailing Add:* 13002 Autumn Dr Silver Spring MD 20904

HAMILTON, LEWIS R, ORGANIC CHEMISTRY. *Current Pos:* CHEMIST, EASTMAN KODAK CO, 70- *Personal Data:* b Wilmington, Ohio, Apr 19, 41; m 61; c 2. *Educ:* Ohio State Univ, BS, 63, PhD(chem), 67. *Prof Exp:* Chemist, Miami Valley Labs, Procter & Gamble Co, 67-70. *Mem:* Am Chem Soc; Soc Photog Scientists & Engrs. *Res:* Photochemical and excited state behavior of dyes; color photographic chemistry. *Mailing Add:* 215 Rogers Pkwy Rochester NY 14617-4207

HAMILTON, LYLE HOWARD, PHYSIOLOGY. *Current Pos:* PRES, QUINTRON INSTR CO, 87- *Personal Data:* b Superior, Nebr, June 11, 24; m 85; c 1. *Educ:* Willamette Univ, AB, 50; Univ Iowa, MS, 52, PhD(physiol), 54. *Prof Exp:* Asst prof physiol, Univ Sask, 54-57, admin asst to dean, 56-57; from asst prof to assoc prof physiol, Sch Med, Marquette Univ, 57-66; chief, Physiol Sect, Zablocki Vet Admin Med Ctr, 57-61, prin scientist, 61-86; emer prof physiol, Med Col Wis, 87- *Concurrent Pos:* Prof physiol & dir clin physiol, Med Col Wis, 67-87; external examr physiol, Univ West Indies, 79-81, 83-84 & 86. *Mem:* Am Physiol Soc; Soc Exp Biol & Med; Biomed Eng Soc; Can Physiol Soc; Instrument Soc Am. *Res:* Respiration (mechanics of ventilation); development of instruments for physiological studies; exercise physiology. *Mailing Add:* Dept Physiol Med Col Wis 19245-B McAllister Lane Wauwatosa WI 53045. *Fax:* 414-645-4222

HAMILTON, MARY JANE GILL, PHYSICAL BIOCHEMISTRY. *Current Pos:* PROF CHEM, DIV SCI & MATH, COL LINCOLN CTR, FORDHAM UNIV, 82- *Personal Data:* b Buffalo, NY, Sept 9, 25; m 48, Hubert R. *Educ:* Univ Buffalo, BA, 47; Polytech Inst Brooklyn, MS, 50; Cornell Univ, PhD(biochem), 61. *Prof Exp:* From asst to res assoc biochem, Sloan-Kettering Inst Cancer Res, 49-64; from instr to asst prof biochem, Sloan-Kettering Div, Grad Sch Med Sci, Cornell Univ, 64-71, assoc prof, 71-82, assoc mem, Sloan-Kettering Inst Cancer Res, 64-82. *Concurrent Pos:* Fel biochem, Sloan-Kettering Inst Cancer Res, 56-60; Nat Cancer Inst fel, Nat Inst Med Res, London, 61-63. *Mem:* Am Chem Soc; NY Acad Sci; Am Soc Biol Chemists; AAAS. *Res:* Structure of hemocyanins and other invertebrate proteins; structure and function of ribosomes; physical chemical characterization of proteins, nucleic acids and viruses. *Mailing Add:* Div Sci & Math Fordham Univ 113 W 60th St New York NY 10023-7484. *Fax:* 212-581-1284

HAMILTON, PAT BROOKS, MICROBIOLOGY, MYCOTOXICOLOGY. *Current Pos:* assoc prof, 67-71, prof microbiol & poultry sci, 71-, EMER PROF MICROBIOL & POULTRY SCI, NC STATE UNIV. *Personal Data:* b Haskell, Okla, Sept 25, 30; m 55, Dolores M Wanores; c Jeffrey C, Cynthia A & Matthew L. *Educ:* Northeastern State Col, BS, 51; Univ Wis, MS, 54, PhD(bact), 62. *Hon Degrees:* Dr Hon Causa, Marcilio Ficino Free Univ Sci, Bologna, Italy. *Honors & Awards:* Int Award, Corn Prod Coun, 76. *Prof Exp:* Assoc res biochemist, Sterling-Winthrop Res Inst, 60-62; sr res microbiologist, Continental Oil Co, 62-64; sr microbiologist, Res Triangle Inst, 64-67. *Concurrent Pos:* Exchange Scholar, Hebrew Univ, Jerusalem, Israel, 81. *Mem:* Am Soc Microbiol; Soc Indust Microbiol; Am Chem Soc; fel Poultry Sci Asn; Am Acad Microbiol. *Res:* Mycotoxins; fungicides; carotenoids; microbial transformations; mycotoxicoses; poultry physiology and toxicology; poultry pigmentation. *Mailing Add:* Dept Poultry Sci NC State Univ Box 7608 Raleigh NC 27609-7608. *Fax:* 919-515-2625

HAMILTON, RALPH WEST, PLASTIC SURGERY. *Current Pos:* From asst instr to instr surg, Univ Pa, 60-65, from instr to assoc prof plastic surg, 65-69, from asst prof to assoc prof, 69-74, PROF SURG, UNIV PA, 74- *Personal Data:* b Raleigh, NC, Aug 16, 33; m 58; c 3. *Educ:* Lehigh Univ, BS, 55; Univ Pa, MD, 59. *Mem:* Am Soc Plastic & Reconstruct Surgeons; Am Asn Plastic Surgeons; Plastic Surg Res Coun; Soc Univ Surgeons; Soc Head & Neck Surgeons. *Res:* Biology of wound healing; frozen organ preservation. *Mailing Add:* Univ Pa 3400 Spruce St Philadelphia PA 19104-4219

HAMILTON, ROBERT BRUCE, WILDLIFE ECOLOGY, ORNITHOLOGY. *Current Pos:* Asst prof, 72-77, ASSOC PROF WILDLIFE MGT, LA STATE UNIV, BATON ROUGE, 77- *Personal Data:* b Nashville, Tenn, Aug 8, 36; m 63. *Educ:* Univ Tenn, Knoxville, BS, 60; Univ Calif, Berkeley, PhD(zool), 69. *Prof Exp:* Asst prof biol sci, Northwestern State Univ, 69-72. *Mem:* Wildlife Soc; Ecol Soc Am; Am Ornithologists Union; Wilson Ornith Soc; Cooper Ornith Soc; Sigma Xi. *Res:* Avian community ecology; population ecology of herons, rails, and shorebirds. *Mailing Add:* 1167 Verdun Dr Baton Rouge LA 70810-4684

HAMILTON, ROBERT DUNCAN, aquatic microbiology; deceased, see previous edition for last biography

HAMILTON, ROBERT HILLERY, JR, PLANT PHYSIOLOGY. *Current Pos:* from asst prof to prof, 61-, EMER PROF BOT, PA STATE UNIV. *Personal Data:* b Thompsonville, Ill, Apr 24. 29; m 59; c 2. *Educ:* Univ Ill, BS, 50; Rutgers Univ, MS, 52; Mich State Univ, PhD, 60. *Prof Exp:* Plant physiologist, Agr Res Serv, USDA, Mich State Univ, 55-60 & NC State Col, 60-61. *Mem:* AAAS; Am Soc Plant Physiologists; Weed Sci Soc Am; Japan Soc Plant Physiol. *Res:* Plant growth and development; biosynthetic mechanisms in plants; plant growth substances. *Mailing Add:* 324 Puddintown Rd State College PA 16801

HAMILTON, ROBERT L, JR, PLASMA LIPOPROTEIN METABOLISM. *Current Pos:* from asst prof to assoc prof, 70-84, assoc staff, cardiovasc Res Inst, 71-81, PROF ANAT, MED SCH, UNIV CALIF, SAN FRANCISCO, 84-, SR STAFF, CARDIOVASC RES INST, 81- *Personal Data:* b Muba City, Calif, Dec 25, 34; m 60, Dottie Towle; c Beth L, Susan A & Karen A. *Educ:* Tenn Polytech Univ, BS, 57; Vanderbilt Sch Med, PhD(anat), 64. *Prof Exp:* Instr anat, Vanderbilt Univ Sch Med, 65-67, asst prof anat, 67-70. *Concurrent Pos:* Res Career Develop Award, 71-76; mem, Coun Arteriosclerosis, Am Heart Asn. *Mem:* Am Asn Anatomists; AAAS; Am Soc Biochem & Molecular Biol; Am Heart Asn; Am Soc Cell Biol; Fedn Am Socs Exp Biol. *Res:* Assembly of plasma lipoproteins; receptor-mediated uptake and processing of plasma lipoproteins; pulmonary surfactant assembly by alveolar type II cells; mechanisms of hepatocytic assembly and secretion of plasma lipoproteins that are involved in atherogenisis or its regressions; mechanisms of high-density lipoprotein and low-density lipoproteins delivery of cholesterol into the pathway by which lung type II cells assemble lamellar bodies which becomes pulmonary surfactant. *Mailing Add:* Univ Calif San Francisco Med Ctr Anat Box 0452 & CVRI 10304 M Third & Parnassus San Francisco CA 94143-0001

HAMILTON, ROBERT MILTON GREGORY, POULTRY NUTRITION, POULTRY PRODUCTION. *Current Pos:* from res scientist III to sr res scientist IV, 89-93, sect head poultry, 89-93, PROG LEADER POULTRY, ATLANTIC FOOD & HORT RES CTR, AGRI & AGR-FOOD CAN, KENTVILLE, NS, 93- *Personal Data:* b Ottawa, Ont, Dec 15, 39; c Lorraine C & Louise E. *Educ:* McGill Univ, BSc, 66, MSc, 68; Univ Western Ont, PhD(biochem), 72. *Honors & Awards:* Poultry Sci Asn Award, 81. *Prof Exp:* Fel biochem, Univ Western Ont, 72-73; from res scientist I to res scientist III, Animal Res Ctr, Agr Can, 73-89, chmn, Poultry Nutrit Prog, 79-84. *Concurrent Pos:* Scholar, Nat Res Coun Can, 66; fel, Med Res Coun Can, 68 & Ont Prov Govt, 70; mem, NS Inst Agrologists; mem, Sta Mgt Comt, Agri & Agri-Food Can, 91-93; adj prof, Atlantic Vet Col, UPEI, Charlottown, PEI, 92-, NS Agr Col, Truro, NS, 95- *Mem:* Agr Inst Can; Can Soc Animal Sci; Poultry Sci Asn; World Poultry Sci Asn. *Res:* Elucidation of nutritional and management factors that influence economic returns of poultry production. *Mailing Add:* Dept Animal Sci NS Agr Col Truro NS B2N 5E3 Can

HAMILTON, ROBERT MORRISON, GEOPHYSICS. *Current Pos:* geophysicist, US Geol Surv, 68-72, dep earthquake geophysicist, 72-73, chief off earthquake studies, 73-78, RES GEOPHYSICIST, US GEOL SURV, 78- *Personal Data:* b Houston, Tex, June 20, 36. *Educ:* Colo Sch Mines, BSc, 58; Univ Calif, Berkeley, MA, 63, PhD(geophys), 65. *Prof Exp:* Res seismologist, Geophys Div, Dept Sci & Indust Res, NZ, 65-68. *Mem:* Seismol Soc Am; Am Geophys Union; Earthquake Eng Res Inst; AAAS; Geol Soc Am. *Res:* Electrical properties of minerals; seismicity of geothermal areas; explosion and earthquake seismology; seismicity of eastern United States. *Mailing Add:* US Geol Surv MS-955 12201 Sunrise Valley Rd Reston VA 20192

HAMILTON, ROBERT W, ENTOMOLOGY. *Current Pos:* From asst prof to assoc prof, 69-82, PROF BIOL, LOYOLA UNIV CHICAGO, 82- *Personal Data:* b Davenport, Iowa, Dec 6, 39; m 80; c 4. *Educ:* Parsons Col, BSc, 62; Ohio State Univ, MSc, 64, PhD(entom), 69. *Concurrent Pos:* Mem, Am Mus Natural Hist-Lerner Marine Lab Exped, Bahama Islands, 65 & Loyola Univ Chicago Entom Exped Southwest US, 71; consult pest control, 71-; Type Species Study, London, Eng & Hamburg, W Ger, 89; entom exped Chiapas, Mex, 96; Am Latin Am Studies, Coleoptera proJ, Costa Rica, 97. *Mem:* Coleopterists Soc Am; Entom Soc Am; Am Entom Soc. *Res:* Arthropod biodiversity; entomology, taxonomy and morphology of weevils (Coleoptera: Rhynchophora: Attelabidae and Rhynchitidae). *Mailing Add:* 554 Briarwood Dr Wheeling IL 60090

HAMILTON, ROBERT WILLIAM, ENVIRONMENTAL MEDICINE. *Current Pos:* PRES & SR CONSULT, HAMILTON RES, LTD, 77- *Personal Data:* b Stanton, Tex, June 5, 30; m 72, Kathryn Faulkner; c 3. *Educ:* Univ Tex, BA, 51; Tex A&M Univ, MS, 58; Univ Minn, PhD(physiol), 64. *Honors & Awards:* Stover-Link Award, Undersea Med Soc; Oceaneering Award, Undersea & Hyperbaric Med Soc, 88; N001 Award, Acad Underwater Arts & Sci. *Prof Exp:* Instr physiol, Med Ctr, Univ Kans, 61-63; res physiologist, Linde Div, Union Carbide Corp, 64-67, sr res physiologist, 67-68, res supvr, Ocean Systs Inc, Tarrytown Tech Ctr, 69-74, dir res, Tarrytown Labs, Ltd, 74-76. *Concurrent Pos:* Ed, Pressure. *Mem:* Aerospace Med Asn; Am Physiol Soc; Undersea & Hyperbaric Med Soc (secy, 81-82); NY Acad Sci; AAAS; Europ Underwater & Baromed Soc. *Res:* Development of practical procedures for decompression; commercial and scientific diving, aerospace, and medical therapy aspects; life support and human performance in stress environments: pressure, gases, thermal; hyperbaric medicine; human performance; life support systems; decompression and decompression sickness; effects of various inert gas atmospheres at low, normal and high pressures; diving physiology; G-forces. *Mailing Add:* 80 Grove St Tarrytown NY 10591-4138. *Fax:* 914-631-6134; *E-Mail:* 70521.1613@compuserve. com, rwhamilton@compuserve.com

HAMILTON, STANLEY R, GASTROINTESTINAL PATHOLOGY. *Current Pos:* Intern & resident path & lab med, 73-79, asst prof, 79-83, ASSOC PROF PATH, SCH MED & HOSP, JOHNS HOPKINS UNIV, 83-, ASSOC PROF ONCOL, 86- *Personal Data:* b Ft Wayne, Ind, Dec 2, 48; m 71; c 3. *Educ:* Ind Univ, AB, 70, MD, 73. *Concurrent Pos:* Sr fel, Nat Found Ileitis & Colitis, 79-81; prin investr, Nat Cancer Inst res grant, NIH, Dept Health & Human Servs, 81-; Am Cancer Soc Nat Adv Comt & Task Force Colorectal Cancer, 89- *Mem:* Int Acad Path; Am Gastroenterol Asn; Gastrointestinal Path Soc; Am Asn Cancer Res; Am Asn Pathologists. *Res:* Colorectal carcinogenesis; Barrett esophagus; inflammatory bowel diseases; pathology and pathogenesis of colorectal carcinoma in human beings and experimental models, particularly relating to dietary factors, chemoprevention and molecular and medical genetics; dysplasia and carcinoma in Barrett esophagus. *Mailing Add:* Dept Path Johns Hopkins Univ Sch Med 730 Rutland Ave Baltimore MD 21205-2182

HAMILTON, STEVEN J, AQUATIC TOXICOLOGY. *Current Pos:* Res fishery biologist, Columbia Nat Fisheries Res Lab, 81-84, RES FISHERY BIOLOGIST, NAT FISHERIES CONTAMINANT RES CTR, US FISH & WILDLIFE SERV, COLUMBIA, MO, 84- *Personal Data:* b Sacramento, Calif, Jan 8, 47; m 68, Pamela J Ashmore; c Heather. *Educ:* Humboldt State Univ, BS, 74; Univ Mo, Columbia, MS, 80, PhD(fish & wildlife), 85. *Concurrent Pos:* Adj assoc prof, Univ SDak, Vermillion, 87-, SDak State Univ, Brookings, 90- *Mem:* Am Fisheries Soc; Sigma Xi; Soc Environ Toxicol & Chem. *Res:* Determine the biological effects of aquatic contaminants on warm and coldwater fish and aquatic invertebrates; development of new, complex techniques and original approaches to address resource contamination problems in the United States. *Mailing Add:* Midwest Sci Ctr US Geol Yankton SD 57078-9214. *Fax:* 605-665-9335; *E-Mail:* steve_hamilton@nbs.gov

HAMILTON, THOMAS ALAN, MONONUCLEAR PHAGOCYTE BIOLOGY. *Current Pos:* HEAD SECT IMMUNOL, RES INST, CLEVELAND CLIN FOUND, 89- *Personal Data:* b Philadelphia, Pa, Feb 2, 50; m 73; c 2. *Educ:* Univ Colo, BA, 71; Univ Ore Health Sci, PhD(biochem), 76. *Prof Exp:* Fel path, Stanford Univ Med Ctr, 76-80; res assoc immunol, St Jude Childrens Res Hosp, 80-82; from asst prof to assoc prof path, Duke Univ Med Ctr, 82-87. *Mem:* Am Asn Immunologists; Reticuloendothelial Soc; AAAS. *Res:* The biology and biochemistry of mononuclear phagocytes and their activation for performance of multiple functions including host defense homeostasis and inflammation; particular emphasis is placed upon defining the genes which are expressed selectively during maerophage activation and examining the transmembrane signalling mechanisms which regulate their expression. *Mailing Add:* Cleveland Clin Found NN1-06 9500 Euclid Ave Cleveland OH 44195-7178. *Fax:* 216-444-9329

HAMILTON, THOMAS CHARLES, ANALYTICAL PROBLEM SOLVING, DECISION ANALYSIS. *Current Pos:* CHIEF TECH STRATEGIST, CENT INTEL AGENCY, 97- *Personal Data:* b Chicago, Ill, Apr 24, 47; m 69. *Educ:* Mich State Univ, BS, 68, MS, 71, PhD(biophys), 72. *Prof Exp:* Fel neurophys, Univ Tex, Austin, 72-73; Res analyst life sci, US Govt, 74-79, instr info sci, 79-81, scientist, advan concepts staff, 81-83, chief life sci, 83-85, dept chief sci & technol, 85-87. *Concurrent Pos:* Inst environ sci, Univ Va, Northern Va Exten Campus, 75. *Res:* Problem solving techniques and strategies for intelligence analysts; decision analysis; strategies for management and allocation of government resources; application of technical advances in biophysical and life sciences. *Mailing Add:* 6506 Heather Brook Ct McLean VA 22101

HAMILTON, THOMAS DUDLEY, QUATERNARY GEOLOGY, GLACIAL GEOLOGY. *Current Pos:* GEOLOGIST, US GEOL SURV, 75- *Personal Data:* b White Plains, NY, Jan 17, 36; m 62; c 2. *Educ:* Univ Idaho, BS, 60; Univ Wis, MS, 63; Univ Wash, PhD(geol), 66. *Prof Exp:* From asst prof to assoc prof geol, Univ Alaska, 66-75. *Concurrent Pos:* Consult geologist, Trans-Alaska Pipeline Syst, 69-70 & 74. *Mem:* AAAS; Arctic Inst NAm; Geol Soc Am; Glaciol Soc; Am Quaternary Asn. *Res:* Arctic and alpine geomorphology; environmental geology; late Cenozoic geology, chronology and environments; environmental reconstructions, early man sites. *Mailing Add:* 3918 Wesleyan Dr Anchorage AK 99508

HAMILTON, THOMAS REID, MICROBIOLOGY, PATHOLOGY. *Current Pos:* prof & head, 72-78, prof, 78-81, EMER PROF MED MICROBIOL & IMMUNOL, MED SCH, UNIV MINN, DULUTH, 81- *Personal Data:* b Kansas City, Mo, Apr 30, 11; m 41; c 3. *Educ:* Univ Mo, AB, 32; Univ Kans, MD, 35, MS, 41; Am Bd Path, dipl & cert anat path & clin microbiol; Am Bd Med Microbiol, dipl & cert med lab & pub health. *Prof Exp:* Intern, Univ Hosp, Univ Iowa, 35-36; resident, St Joseph Hosp, Kansas City, 36-37; from asst to assoc prof path, Sch Med, Univ Kans, 37-50, prof microbiol & path & lectr hist med, 50-69; prof path, Sch Med, Washington Univ, 69-72; prof biol, microbiol & path, Med Sch, Univ Mo-Kansas City & actg dir, Div Microbiol, Truman Med Ctr, 81-83. *Concurrent Pos:* Resident, Univ Hosp, Univ Kans, 37-39, clin bacteriologist, 38-42, chmn, Dept Med Microbiol, 51-61; pathologist, Providence Hosp, 39-42, dir, Develop Prog, 56-58; mem, Training Grant Comt, Nat Inst Allergy & Infectious Dis; consult, US Vet Admin Hosp, Mo, 46- & Kans, 47; assoc prof, Univ Minn, 48-51, vis prof, 62-63; chief, Lab Serv, St Louis Vet Admin Hosp, 69-72; consult, Children's Cardiac Ctr & Mercy Hosp, Kansas City, Mo. *Mem:* Am Soc Microbiol; Am Soc Clin Path; Soc Exp Biol & Med; Am Asn Path. *Res:* Pathogenesis and prophylaxis of rheumatic and granulomatous disease; biology of streptococcus and L-forms as slow agents; asbestos and immune response. *Mailing Add:* Dept Path & Microbiol Univ Mo Sch Med 2411 Holmes St Kansas City MO 64108

HAMILTON, WALTER S, PHYSICAL CHEMISTRY. *Current Pos:* asst prof, 66-75, ASSOC PROF PHYS CHEM, TEX WOMAN'S UNIV, 75- *Personal Data:* b Hattiesburg, Miss, Dec 12, 31; m 60, Janet V Walmsley; c Karen A & Susan K. *Educ:* Univ Southern Miss, BS, 54; Tulane Univ, PhD(phys chem), 63. *Prof Exp:* Sr res engr, Rocketdyne Div, NAm Aviation, Inc, 63-66. *Mem:* AAAS; Am Chem Soc. *Res:* Solvent effect in kinetics; growth of ice crystals; electrochemical demineralization of brackish water; thermodynamics and thermochemistry. *Mailing Add:* Dept Chem Tex Woman's Univ PO Box 425859 Denton TX 76204-3859

HAMILTON, WARREN BELL, GEOLOGY, TECTONICS. *Current Pos:* ADJ PROF GEOPHYS, COLO SCH MINES, 96- *Personal Data:* b Los Angeles, Calif, May 13, 25; m 47, Alicita Koenig; c Lawrence, Kathryn & James. *Educ:* Univ Calif, Los Angeles, AB, 45, PhD(geol), 51; Univ Southern Calif, MS, 49. *Honors & Awards:* Distinguished Serv Award, US Dept Interior, 81; Wilbert lectr, La State Univ, 85; Penrose Medal Geol Sc Am, 89; Hookes Distinguished lectr, McMaster Univ, 90 & Nat Acad Sci, 89. *Prof Exp:* Lectr geol, Univ Calif, Los Angeles, 49 & 51; asst prof, Univ Okla, 51-52; geologist, US Geol Surv, 52-61, res geologist, 61-81, sr scientist, 82-95, emer Pecora fel, 95-96. *Concurrent Pos:* Sr exchange scientist, USSR, 67; vis prof, Scripps Inst Oceanog, 68 & 79, Calif Inst Technol, 73, Yale, 80 & Univ Amsterdam, 81 & Plate Tetonics Deleg China, 79; distinguished lectr, Am Asn Petrol Geol, 84-85; vis scholar, Western Mich Univ, 85; regents lectr, Univ Calif Santa Barbara, 86, Univ Calif Los Angeles, 88, Univ Calif San Diego, 90; chmn, Cordilleran Sect, Geol Soc Am, 87-88. *Mem:* Fel Geol Soc Am; Am Geophys Union; Geol Soc Am. *Res:* Structural geology and tectonics Western North America, Antarctica, Indonesia, Melanesia, Southeast Asia, USSR; plate tectonics; marine geophysics; igneous and metamorphic petrology; crustal evolution. *Mailing Add:* Dept Geophys Colo Sch Mines Golden CO 80401. *Fax:* 303-273-3478

HAMILTON, WILLARD CHARLSON, SURFACE CHEMISTRY, PRODUCT DEVELOPMENT. *Current Pos:* PRES, WILLARD C HAMILTON ASSOC, INC, 83- *Personal Data:* b Auburn, NY, Sept 29, 42; m 63; c Tracy, Wendy, Melanie & Bradley. *Educ:* Cornell Univ, BS, 64; Univ Calif, Davis, PhD(chem), 67. *Prof Exp:* NSF res assoc, Ctr Surface & Coatings Res, Lehigh Univ, 67-68; res chemist, Res Inst, Gillette Co, 68-69, proj supvr res & develop, 69-72; mgr, Spec Mat Technol Ctr, Xerox Corp, 72-75; dir res & develop, Johnson & Johnson Co, 75-83. *Mem:* Sigma Xi; Am Chem Soc. *Res:* Biotechnology; medical device development; pharmaceutical development; clinical trials. *Mailing Add:* 4905 Marlborough Way Durham NC 27713

HAMILTON, WILLIAM DONALD, EVOLUTIONARY BIOLOGY. *Current Pos:* ROYAL SOC RES PROF, DEPT ZOOL, UNIV OXFORD, UK, 84- *Personal Data:* b Cairo, Egypt, Aug 1, 36; Brit citizen; m 67; c 3. *Educ:* Cambridge Univ, BA, 60; Univ London, PhD(genetics), 68. *Honors & Awards:* Sci Medal, Zool Soc London, 75; Newcomb Cleveland Prize, AAAS, 81; Darwin Medal, Royal Soc, 88; Scientific Medal, Linnaean Soc, 89; Frink Medal, Zool Soc London, 91; Albert Wander Fdn Prize, 92; Kyoto Prize, 93; Crafoord Prize, Royal Swed Acad Sci, 93. *Prof Exp:* Lectr genetics, Imp Col Sci & Technol, Univ London, 64-77; prof evolutionary biol, Mus Zool, Div Biol Sci, Univ Mich, Ann Arbor, 77-84. *Mem:* Brit Genetical Soc; Am Soc Naturalists; foreign hon mem Am Acad Arts & Sci; mem Royal Soc Sci Uppsala; corres mem Brazilian Acad Sci, 93. *Res:* Evolution of social behavior, population genetics, sex ratio, evolution of sex and sexual selection. *Mailing Add:* Dept Zool Univ Oxford S Parks Rd Oxford OX1 3PS England. *Fax:* 44-1865-310447

HAMILTON, WILLIAM EUGENE, JR, CONTROL THEORY, OPTIMIZATION. *Current Pos:* sr res engr, 83-87, STAFF RES ENGR, GEN MOTORS RES LABS, 87- *Personal Data:* b Washington, DC, Sept 14, 42; m 73; c 2. *Educ:* Iowa State Univ, BS, 64; Purdue Univ, MS, 66, PhD(elec eng), 70. *Prof Exp:* Systs engr, Comptek Res, Inc, 72-75 & Sierra Res Corp, 75-78; sect head, Hydra-Pt Div, Maeg Inc, 78-79, mgr systs engr, 79-81, consult, 81-82, staff engr, Aircraft Controls Div, 82-83. *Mem:* Inst Elec & Electronics Engrs; Am Sci Affil. *Res:* Simulation and control of electromechanical systems; optimization; digital signal processing. *Mailing Add:* General Motors Res Labs 30500 Mound Rd PO Box 9055 Warren MI 48090

HAMILTON, WILLIAM HOWARD, ELECTRICAL & NUCLEAR ENGINEERING. *Current Pos:* CONSULT ENGR, 79- *Personal Data:* b Greenville, Pa, Apr 2, 18; m 44, Ellinor Kistler; c 2. *Educ:* Wash & Jefferson Col, BS, 40; Univ Pittsburgh, MS, 48. *Prof Exp:* Res engr electronics, Res Labs, Westinghouse Elec Corp, 45-50, eng mgr, Nuclear Reactor Plants, 50-65, mgr, Operating Plants, 65-70, gen mgr, Bettis Atomic Power Lab, 70-79. *Mem:* Fel Inst Elec & Electronics Engrs; Am Nuclear Soc. *Res:* Development, design, installation and operation of nuclear reactor propulsion and power plants. *Mailing Add:* 410 E Church St Ligonier PA 15658

HAMILTON, WILLIAM KENNON, CLINICAL MEDICINE, ANESTHESIOLOGY. *Current Pos:* PROF ANESTHESIA & CHMN DEPT, UNIV CALIF, SAN FRANCISCO, 67-, ASSOC DEAN AFFAIRS, 78- *Personal Data:* b Guthrie Center, Iowa, Dec 15, 22; m 46; c 2. *Educ:* Univ Iowa, BA, 43, MD, 46; Am Bd Anesthesiol, dipl, 54. *Prof Exp:* Intern, St Luke's Hosp, Duluth, Minn, 46-47; resident, Div Anesthesiol, Col Med, Univ Iowa, 49-51, clin instr, 51-53, from asst prof to prof surg, 53-67, chmn div, 58-67. *Concurrent Pos:* Chief anesthesiologist, Vet Admin Hosp, Iowa City, 51-53, consult, 58-; consult, Vet Admin Hosp, Des Moines, 58- & US Naval Hosp, Oakland & US Vet Admin Hosp, San Francisco; dir, Am Bd Anesthesiol, 64- *Mem:* Soc Exp Biol & Med; Am Soc Anesthesiol; AMA; Asn Univ Anesthetists. *Res:* Respiratory physiology, especially acute changes during anesthesia and surgery and in the postoperative period; care and management of acute and chronic respiratory insufficiency; venous physiology, especially role of the veins in adjusting blood volume. *Mailing Add:* Dept Anesthesia Univ Calilf San Francisco Med Sch 513 Parnassus Ave San Francisco CA 94122-2722

HAMILTON, WILLIAM LANDER, ORGANIC CHEMISTRY, POLYMER CHEMISTRY. *Current Pos:* Res chemist, Film Dept, E I du Pont de Nemours & Co, Inc, 69-72, res chemist, 72-75, sr chemist, 75-79, supvr, Photo Prod Dept, 79-81, mgr, Com Systs Develop, 81-83, bus mgr, PCM Div, Du Pont Japan Ltd, 83-88, SR RES ASSOC, DU PONT ELECTRONICS, 88- *Personal Data:* b New York, NY, May 3, 43; m 65; c 2. *Educ:* Columbia Univ, AB, 64; Yale Univ, MS, 65, PhD(chem), 69. *Mem:* Am Chem Soc. *Res:* Photoresists for printed circuit industry; physical structure and chemistry of natural and synthetic macromolecules; high temperature polymers; radiation chemistry; photo-initiated polymerization. *Mailing Add:* 52 Leicester Way Chesapeake City MD 21915-1808

HAMILTON, WILLIAM OLIVER, EXPERIMENTAL GENERAL RELATIVITY. *Current Pos:* assoc prof, 70-76, PROF PHYSICS, LA STATE UNIV, BATON ROUGE, 76- *Personal Data:* b Lawrence, Kans, Sept 5, 33; m 56, Mary H Kelson; c Eric W, Christopher D & Ann E. *Educ:* Stanford Univ, BS, 55, PhD(physics), 63. *Prof Exp:* Res assoc physics, Stanford Univ, 63-65, actg asst prof, 65-67, asst prof, 67-70. *Concurrent Pos:* NSF fel, 63-65; vis prof, Univ Rochester, 78. *Mem:* Am Phys Soc; Am Asn Physics Teachers; AAAS. *Res:* Experimental gravitational measurements; electron paramagentic resonance in organic free radicals; magnetism; cryogenics; properties of superconductors; thin film technology; Josephson effect; infrared detection. *Mailing Add:* Dept Physics & Astron La State Univ Baton Rouge LA 70803-4001. *E-Mail:* hamilton@phgrav.phys.lsu.edu

HAMILTON, WILLIAM THORNE, AERONAUTICAL ENGINEERING. *Current Pos:* RETIRED. *Personal Data:* b Marion Center, Pa, July 26, 17; m 41; c 3. *Educ:* Wash Univ, Seattle, BS, 41, MS, 47. *Prof Exp:* Res engr, Ames Lab, Nat Adv Comt Aeronaut, 41-48; mem aeronaut staff & aerodyn & propulsion staff engr, Boeing Co, 48-58, chief flight tech, 58-62, chief tech staff, Airplane Div, 62-65, dir develop proj, 65-71, mgr res eng, Boeing Aerospace Co, 72-74, vpres eng, 74-75, vpres-mgr, YC-14 Prog, 75-76, vpres eng, 77-78, vpres res & eng, Boeing Com Airplane Co, 78-80, vpres & chief scientist, Boeing Mil Airplane Co, 81-82, consult, 82-92. *Concurrent Pos:* Mem, Res Adv Comt Aerodyn, NASA, 56-78; mem, Flight Mech Panel, Adv Group Aerospace Res & Develop, NATO. *Mem:* Nat Acad Eng; Flight Mech Panel; Am Inst Aeronaut & Astronaut; Asn Unmanned Vehicle Systs. *Res:* Aerodynamics; aeroelasticity; dynamic stability. *Mailing Add:* PO Box 88 Copalis Beach WA 98535

HAMILTON-KEMP, THOMAS ROGERS, NATURAL PRODUCTS, ANTIMICROBIAL COMPOUNDS. *Current Pos:* From asst prof to assoc prof, 70-84, PROF, DEPT HORT, UNIV KY, 84- *Personal Data:* b Lebanon, Ky, May 13, 42; m 80, Lois A Groce. *Educ:* Univ Ky, BA, 64, PhD(org chem), 70. *Concurrent Pos:* Asst prof, Dept Food Sci & Nutrit, Univ Ky, 70. *Mem:* Am Chem Soc; AAAS; Am Soc Hort Sci; Sigma Xi. *Res:* Isolation, identification and biological evaluation of natural chemicals, especially volatile compounds which have antimicrobial properties; characterization of compounds such as lipoxygenase-derived volatiles from plants which inhibit the growth of bacteria and fungi which cause disease. *Mailing Add:* 2025 Williamsburg Rd Lexington KY 40504. *Fax:* 606-257-2859

HAMILTON-STEINRAUT, JEAN A, X-RAY CRYSTALLOGRAPHY, BIOCHEMISTRY. *Current Pos:* Instr, 66-68, asst prof, 68-80, PROF BIOCHEM, IND UNIV SCH MED, INDIANAPOLIS, 80- *Personal Data:* b Airdrie, Scotland, Feb 5, 38; m 67; c 2. *Educ:* Univ Glasgow, BSc, 59, PhD(chem), 62. *Concurrent Pos:* Fels, Dept Chem, Univ Ill, Urbana, 62-64 & Dept Biochem, Ind Univ, Indianapolis, 64-66; NIH career develop award, 66. *Mem:* Royal Soc Chem. *Res:* X-ray crystallography of biologically important substances, such as proteins, antibiotics and hormones. *Mailing Add:* Dept Biochem Ind Univ Sch Med 635 Barnhill Dr Indianapolis IN 46202-5122

HAMIT, HAROLD F, SURGERY. *Current Pos:* clin prof, 75-85, EMER PROF CLIN SURG, UNIV NC, CHAPEL HILL, 85- *Personal Data:* b Stockton, Kans, Dec 29, 13; m 35, Cordelia Granger; c Francis G & Elaine M. *Educ:* NY Univ, AB, 42, MD, 45; Univ Colo, MS, 55; Am Bd Surg, dipl, 56 & 80; Am Bd Thoracic Surg, dipl, 63. *Prof Exp:* Chief obstet & gynec, Med Corps, US Army Hosp, Ft Bragg, NC, 48, resident gen surg, Oliver Gen Hosp, Augusta, Ga, 49-50, chief post-oper sect, 1st Mobile Army Surg, Korea, 50-51, comdr, Army Hosp, Camp Leroy Johnson, La, 51-53, resident gen surg, Fitzsimons Gen Hosp, Denver, 53-55, chief gen surg serv, Army Hosp, Ft Hood, Tex, 55-56, chief surg res, Army Med Res & Develop Command, 57-60, resident thoracic surg, Letterman Gen Hosp, San Francisco, 60-62, comdr, 121st Evacuation Hosp, Ascom, Korea, 62-63, res assoc prof surg, Baylor Col Med, 63-65, chief gen surg serv, Brooke Gen Hosp, San Antonio, 65-67, dir, Div Surg, Walter Reed Army Inst Res, DC, 67-68; assoc dir clin res, Baxter Labs, Inc, 68-70; assoc dir surg, Charlotte Mem Hosp, 70-85. *Concurrent Pos:* Mem, Surg Study Sect, USPHS, 58-60; vis oper surgeon, Korean Nat Res Cross Hosp, Seoul, 62-63; consult, Eighth Army Surgeon, 62-63; lectr, Dept Surg, Northwestern Univ, 68-70. *Mem:* AAAS; fel Am Col Surg; fel Am Asn Surg Trauma; Asn Mil Surgeons US; NY Acad Sci; AMA; Pan Am Med Soc. *Res:* General, thoracic and cardiovascular surgery; trauma; burns; shock; bacterial enzymes; esophageal physiology; plasma volume expanders; tissue adhesives; antibiotics; hemodynamics of brain. *Mailing Add:* 1309 Providence Rd Charlotte NC 28207

HAMJIAN, HARRY J, METALLURGY. *Current Pos:* RETIRED. *Personal Data:* b Auburn, NY, July 8, 23; m 49. *Educ:* Univ Mich, BSE, 44, MSE, 47. *Prof Exp:* Chem engr, Pilot Plant, Houdaille Hershey Corp, 44-45, supvr gas opers, 45-46; scientist mat res, NASA, 47-52; mgr powder metall, Utica Drop Forge & Tool Corp, 52-53, mgr opers, 53-56 & Kelsey Hayes Corp, 56-61; vpres metall, Spec Metals, Inc, 61-65; mgr process metall, Carpenter Steel Co, 65-67, asst mgr labs, Carpenter Technol Corp, 67-69, mgr process metall res, 69-77; from vpres metall opers to sr vpres mat tech group, Howmet, 77-86. *Mem:* Am Inst Mining, Metall & Petrol Engrs; Am Soc Metals; Am Vacuum Soc; Newcomen Soc. *Res:* Vacuum metallurgy; high temperature alloys; powder metallurgy; high temperature alloys and tool steels. *Mailing Add:* 170 Blackberry Dr Stanford CT 06903

HAMKALO, BARBARA ANN, GENETICS, CELL BIOLOGY. *Current Pos:* from asst prof to assoc prof, biol sci, Dept Molecular Biol & Biochem, 79-86, assoc dean grad studies & res, 81-84, PROF MOLECULAR BIOL, UNIV CALIF, IRVINE, 86- *Personal Data:* b New York, NY, July 4, 44. *Educ:* Univ Mass, PhD(radiation biophys), 68. *Prof Exp:* Nat Cancer Inst fel biochem, Harvard Med Sch, 68-70; res assoc, Biol Div, Oak Ridge Nat Lab, 70-71, staff mem, 71-73. *Mem:* Am Soc Cell Biol; Am Soc Biochem & Molecular Biol. *Res:* Structure and function of chromosomes in eukaryotes; regulation of gene expression. *Mailing Add:* Dept Molecular Biol & Biochem Univ Calif Irvine Irvine CA 92717-3900. *Fax:* 714-824-8551

HAMLET, RICHARD GRAHAM, COMPUTER SCIENCE, SOFTWARE ENGINEERING. *Current Pos:* PROF, DEPT COMPUT SCI, PORTLAND STATE UNIV, 88-, CHMN, 97- *Personal Data:* b Minneapolis, Minn, Mar 27, 38; m 58, 86, Corinne McWilliams; c 2. *Educ:* Univ Wis-Madison, BS, 59; Cornell Univ, MS, 64; Univ Wash, PhD(comput sci), 71. *Prof Exp:* Intern, Shimer Col, 62-64; systs supvr, Comput Ctr, Univ Wash, 66-68; dir systs prog, Comput Ctr Corp, 68-70; from asst prof to assoc prof comput sci, Univ Md, 71-83; prof, Dept Comput Sci, Ore Grad Ctr, 83-88. *Concurrent Pos:* Consult, Naval Res Lab, 76-78, IBM, 78-83; vis prof, Univ Melbourne, 82, Univ Col, Galway, 95. *Mem:* Asn Comput Mach; Inst Elec & Electronics Engrs. *Res:* Theory of program testing; software engineering; computability theory; theory of programming; Godel numberings; systems programming; programming languages. *Mailing Add:* Comput Sci Dept Portland State Univ PO Box 751 Portland OR 97207. *E-Mail:* hamlet@cs.pdx.edu

HAMLET, ZACHARIAS, ORGANIC CHEMISTRY. *Current Pos:* asst prof, 66-69, ASSOC PROF CHEM, CONCORDIA UNIV, 69- *Personal Data:* b Pulincunnu, India, Nov 19, 30. *Educ:* Loyola Col, Madras, India, BSc, 50; Victoria Col, Agra, MSc, 52; Univ Notre Dame, PhD(org chem), 60. *Prof Exp:* Lectr chem, St Joseph's Col, Darjeeling, India, 52-56; res assoc, Univ Southern Calif, 60-61 & State Univ NY Stony Brook, 61-62; fel, Nat Res Coun Can, 62-64; res asst, Univ Montreal, 64-66. *Concurrent Pos:* Vis assoc, Calif Inst Technol & Stanford Univ, 72-73; vis colleague, Univ Hawaii, Manoa, 80-81. *Mem:* Am Chem Soc; Royal Soc Chem; Chem Inst Can. *Res:* Organic free radical chemistry; organic photochemistry; organophosphorus and organosulfur chemistry; synthesis and reaction mechanisms. *Mailing Add:* Concordia Univ 1455 de Maisonneuve Blvd W Montreal PQ H3G 1M8 Can

HAMLIN, DANIEL ALLEN, ATMOSPHERIC PHYSICS. *Current Pos:* SCIENTIST 4, SCI APPLNS, INC, LA JOLLA, CALIF, 69- *Personal Data:* b Burbank, Calif, June 21, 26; m 52; c 2. *Educ:* Univ Calif, Berkeley, AB, 47, PhD(physics), 54. *Prof Exp:* Sr res engr, Gen Dynamics/Convair, 55-59, design specialist, 59-60, staff scientist, 60-63, sr staff scientist, 63-64, chief theoret physics group, 64-69. *Mem:* AAAS; Am Phys Soc; Am Geophys Union; Am Optical Soc; Sigma Xi. *Res:* Elementary particle and nuclear physics; atomic properties and processes; equation of state of high temperature gases; radiation transport; opacity; penetration of atomic particles through matter; aeronomy; infrared physics; geomagnetism. *Mailing Add:* 3224 Oliphant St San Diego CA 92106-1942

HAMLIN, GRIFFITH ASKEW, JR, COMPUTER SCIENCES. *Current Pos:* CO-FOUND, DES SCI INC, 87- *Personal Data:* b Wilson, NC, Oct 31, 45; m 66; c 1. *Educ:* Westminster Col, BA, 68; Univ NC, MS, 70, PhD(comput sci), 75. *Prof Exp:* Instr math, William Woods Col, 69-72; vis scientist comput sci, Inst Comput Applns Sci & Eng, Univs Space Res Asn, 75-77; mem staff, Los Alamos Sci Lab, 77-83; sr scientist, Unicad Inc, Boulder, Co, 83-87. *Mem:* Asn Comput Mach. *Res:* Distributed computing research related to interactive satellite computer graphics; design of user interface management system software. *Mailing Add:* 6397 Pitcairn St Cypress CA 90630

HAMLIN, JAMES T, III, INTERNAL MEDICINE. *Current Pos:* prof med, 73-88, dean, Sch Med, 75-88, EMER PROF, TULANE UNIV MED CTR, 89-, EMER DEAN, 89- *Personal Data:* b Danville, Va, Feb 6, 29; m 55, Mary Caperton; c Helen (Tharrington), Mary D & James T IV. *Educ:* Va Mil Inst, AB, 51; Univ Va, MD, 55. *Prof Exp:* Intern, Peter Bent Brigham Hosp, 55-56; instr med, NY Med Col, 59-60; guest investr, Rockefeller Inst, 60-62; from asst prof to assoc prof, Med Col Ga, 62-66; assoc prof med, Sch Med, Univ Va, 66-73, from asst dean to actg dean, 70-73. *Concurrent Pos:* Dir, Clin Res Ctr, Univ Va Hosp, 66-71. *Mem:* Am Fedn Clin Res; AMA; Sigma Xi. *Res:* Lipid metabolism and atherosclerotic disease. *Mailing Add:* 199 Fairmont Circle Danville VA 24541. *E-Mail:* jth@ns.qamcwood.net

HAMLIN, JOYCE LIBBY, DNA REPLICATION, GENE AMPLIFICATION. *Current Pos:* ASSOC PROF BIOCHEM, SCH MED, UNIV VA, 84- *Personal Data:* b Apr 15, 39; div. *Educ:* Univ Calif, Los Angeles, PhD(molecular biol), 71. *Concurrent Pos:* fac res award, Am Cancer Soc. *Res:* Mammalian genome organization; DNA replication. *Mailing Add:* Biochem Dept Univ Va Sch Med Jordan Med Educ Bldg Box 440 Charlottesville VA 22908-0001. *Fax:* 804-924-1789

HAMLIN, KENNETH ELDRED, JR, CHEMISTRY, RESEARCH ADMINISTRATION. *Current Pos:* RETIRED. *Personal Data:* b Baltimore, Md, Mar 27, 17; m 41; c 2. *Educ:* Univ Md, BS, 38, PhD(pharmaceut chem), 41. *Prof Exp:* Pharmacist, Univ Md, 38-41; fel & spec asst chem, Univ Ill, 41-42; instr org chem, Univ Md, 42-43; res chemist, Abbott Labs, 43-54, from asst head to head org res, 54-57, from asst dir to dir chem res, 57-61, dir res, 61-66; vpres res, Cutter Labs Inc, 66-73, vpres res & qual assurance, 73-74, sr vpres sci opers, 74-81. *Concurrent Pos:* Mem bd dirs, Cutters Labs, 67-81, vchmn, 79-81. *Mem:* AAAS; Am Pharmaceut Asn; Am Chem Soc. *Res:* Synthesis of amino acids; monocrotaline and related alkaloids; antimalarials; synthetic organic medicinals. *Mailing Add:* 3270 Terra Granada Dr Apt 1A Walnut Creek CA 94595-3526

HAMLIN, ROBERT LOUIS, CARDIOVASCULAR PHYSIOLOGY. *Current Pos:* From asst prof to assoc prof, 62-69, PROF VET PHYSIOL, OHIO STATE UNIV, 69- *Personal Data:* b Cleveland, Ohio, Mar 18, 33; m 60; c 2. *Educ:* Ohio State Univ, BSc, 56, DVM, 58, MSc, 60, PhD(physiol), 62. *Concurrent Pos:* NIH career develop award, 62- *Mem:* AAAS; Am Heart Asn; Am Physiol Soc; Am Vet Med Asn. *Res:* Ventricular activation processes of many species; simultaneous indicator-dilution curves for detection of mitral regurgitation; electrocardiographic and hemodynamic characteristics of sinus arrhythmia in the dog. *Mailing Add:* 1520 Grenoble Rd Columbus OH 43221-3847

HAMLIN, WILLIAM EARL, INDUSTRIAL PHARMACY. *Current Pos:* RETIRED. *Personal Data:* b Wautoma, Wis, July 3, 22; m 51, Charlotte Buckallew; c William & Charlene. *Educ:* Lawrence Col, BA, 44; Univ Ill, MS, 47, PhD(chem), 49. *Prof Exp:* Res chemist, Schenley Labs, Inc, 49-50 & Upjohn Co, 50-84. *Mem:* Am Chem Soc; Sigma Xi. *Res:* Pharmaceutical research; product development. *Mailing Add:* 2601 Hill-n-Brook Dr Kalamazoo MI 49008-3454

HAMLOW, EUGENE EMANUEL, PHARMACY. *Current Pos:* RETIRED. *Personal Data:* b Bloomington, Ill, Feb 22, 27; m 54; c 3. *Educ:* Purdue Univ, BS, 50, MS, 53, PhD, 58. *Prof Exp:* Control chemist, Upjohn Co, 52-55; sect leader, Bristol-Myers Squibb Co, 58-70, dir pharmaceut res & develop, 70-92. *Mem:* Am Chem Soc; Soc Cosmetic Chem; Sigma Xi; Am Pharmaceut Asn; Am Asn Pharmaceut Scientists. *Res:* Pharmaceutical research and development. *Mailing Add:* 2800 Pennsylvania St Evansville IN 47712

HAMM, DONALD IVAN, ORGANIC CHEMISTRY. *Current Pos:* RETIRED. *Personal Data:* b Wellington, Kans, Jan 11, 28; m 50, Jean A Ewing; c Jeffrey L, Cheryl L (Leonard), Dena J (Perkins), David E & James R. *Educ:* Univ Okla, BS, 49, PhD(chem), 56; Purdue Univ, MS, 51. *Prof Exp:* Asst prof chem, Southwestern State Col, Okla, 51-53; asst, Okla Med Res Found, 53-56; from assoc prof to prof chem, Southwestern Okla State Univ, 56-89, chmn dept, 70-79, dean, Sch Arts & Sci, 78-89. *Concurrent Pos:* Vis prof, Mich State Univ, 69-70. *Mem:* Am Chem Soc. *Mailing Add:* 1533 Chisholm Trail Weatherford OK 73096

HAMM, KENNETH LEE, ORGANIC CHEMISTRY. *Current Pos:* RETIRED. *Personal Data:* b Princeton, Ill, Nov 12, 23; m 49, Janice Vanzile; c Diane & Janet. *Educ:* Carthage Col, BA, 47; Univ Ill, MA, 48; Univ Iowa, PhD, 57. *Prof Exp:* From assoc prof to prof chem, Carthage Col, 48-89. *Mem:* Am Chem Soc; Sigma Xi. *Res:* Synthesis and oxidation of unsymmetrical bibenzyl hydrazines. *Mailing Add:* 4210 Farmington Lane Racine WI 53403-4082

HAMM, RANDALL EARL, PHYSICAL CHEMISTRY. *Current Pos:* prof analytical chem, 63-78, EMER PROF ANALYTICAL CHEM, WASH STATE UNIV, 78- *Personal Data:* b Auburn, Wash, May 9, 13; m 37, Vivian M; c Jacqueline, Thomas & Terrance. *Educ:* Univ Wash, BS, 35, MS, 37, PhD(chem), 40. *Prof Exp:* Res assoc oceanog, Univ Wash, 40-41; asst chemist, Puget Sound Navy Yard, US Dept Navy, 40-42; instr phys sci, Western Wash Col Educ, 42; from instr to prof analytical chem, Univ Utah, 42-63. *Mem:* Am Chem Soc. *Res:* Electrochemistry; dissolved gases in solution; amperometric titrations; analytical polarography; structure and reactions of complex ions; kinetics of complex ion reactions. *Mailing Add:* Dept Chem Wash State Univ Pullman WA 99164-4630

HAMM, THOMAS EDWARD, JR, LABORATORY ANIMAL MEDICINE & ANIMAL MODELS OF DISEASE, COMPARATIVE PATHOLOGY. *Current Pos:* DIR, LAB ANIMAL RESOURCES, NC STATE UNIV. *Personal Data:* b Denver, Colo, Dec 26, 42; m 70, Diane L Mauck; c Jonathan. *Educ:* Univ Colo, Boulder, BA, 64; Colo State Univ, DVM, 68, MS, 72; Am Col Lab Animal Med, dipl, 74; Bowman Gray Med Sch, PhD, 80. *Prof Exp:* Fel lab animal med, Colo State Univ, 70-72; NIH fel comp path, Bowman Gray Sch Med, 72 75; asst prof path, Med Ctr, Univ Colo, 75-78; expert consult lab animal med, Nat Cancer Inst, 78-80, chief, Toxicol Br, 79-80; head, Dept Toxicol, Chem Indust Inst Toxicol, 80-84; prof & chmn, Dept Comp Med, Stanford Univ, 84- *Concurrent Pos:* Consult animal care, Wake Forest Univ, 74-75, Colo State Univ, 75-76, Univ Colo, Boulder & Nat Jewish Hosp, 75-78; affil fac path, Colo State Univ, 75-78; consult, Am Asn Accreditations Lab Animal Care, 78-; affil fac, NC State Univ, 81- *Mem:* Am Vet Med Asn; Am Asn Lab Animal Sci; Am Soc Lab Animal Practr; Am Col Lab Animal Med; Soc Toxicol; Soc Investigative Pathologists. *Res:* Development of animal models of human diseases, especially atherosclerosis and carcinogenesis; toxicology. *Mailing Add:* Col Vet Med NC State Univ 4700 Hillsborough St Raleigh NC 27606. *Fax:* 919-829-4283; *E-Mail:* tom_hamm@ncsu.edu

HAMM, WILLIAM JOSEPH, PHYSICS. *Current Pos:* from asst prof to assoc prof, 42-58, PROF PHYSICS, ST MARY'S UNIV, TEX, 58- *Personal Data:* b Belleville, Ill, July 26, 10. *Educ:* Univ Dayton, BSc, 31; Cath Univ Am, MSc, 35; Wash Univ, PhD(physics), 42. *Prof Exp:* Instr physics, St Mary's Univ, Tex, 35-37 & Maryhurst Norm Col, 37-40. *Concurrent Pos:* Extramural assoc, NIH, 78; sr res assoc, USAF Sch Aerospace Med, Brooks AFB, Tex, 79. *Mem:* Fel Inst Elec & Electronics Engrs; Am Phys Soc. *Res:* Collision processes in gases, particularly energy loss retardation of positive ions shot through gases; electronic circuitry. *Mailing Add:* Dept Physics St Mary's Univ San Antonio TX 78284. *Fax:* 210-431-6740; *E-Mail:* whamm@stmarytx.edu

HAMMACK, WILLIAM S, CHEMMICAL ENGINEERING. *Current Pos:* Asst prof, 88-93, ASSOC PROF, DEPT CHEM ENG, CARNEGIE-MELLON UNIV, 93- *Personal Data:* b Greencastle, Ind, Nov 2, 61. *Educ:* Mich Technol Univ, BSChE, 84; Univ Ill, Urbana, MSChE, 86, PhD(chem eng), 88. *Honors & Awards:* Exxon Solid State Chem Fel Award, 93. *Concurrent Pos:* Mem, ChemCARS comt, Adv Photon Source, Argonne; mem adv bd, nat high pressure facil, CHESS; reviewer, Ben Franklin Tech Ctr, Sci Mag, J Physics & Chem Solids. *Mem:* AAAS; Am Inst Chem Eng; Am Chem Soc; Am Phys Soc; Am Crystallograph Asn; Am Geophys Union; Mat Res Soc. *Res:* Pressure-induced amorphization using in situ x-ray diffraction and Raman spectroscopy; schemes in halide glasses; ionic glasses and amorphous molecular solids; solid state amorphizations; production of amorphous metallic alloys at ambient temperatures; the fundamental ordering in quasicrystalline and amorphous alloys. *Mailing Add:* Dept Chem Eng Carnegie-Mellon Univ 5000 Forbes Ave Pittsburgh PA 15213-3890

HAMMAKER, ROBERT MICHAEL, HADAMARD TRANSFORM SPECTROMETRY, VOLATILE ORGANIC COMPOUNDS IN THE ATMOSPHERE. *Current Pos:* from asst prof to prof chem, 61-74, assoc head dept, 68-76, PROF CHEM, KANS STATE UNIV, 74- *Personal Data:* b Evanston, Ill, Feb 9, 34; div; c Lucy & Barry. *Educ:* Trinity Col, Conn, BS, 56; Northwestern Univ, PhD(phys chem), 60. *Prof Exp:* Sr chemist, Res Lab, Texaco, Inc, NY, 60-61. *Concurrent Pos:* Sr vis fel, Univ East Anglia, England, 76-77; sabbatical, Univ Calif, Riverside, 87-88. *Mem:* AAAS; Am Chem Soc; Am Phys Soc; Royal Soc Chem; Soc Appl Spectros. *Res:* Molecular spectroscopy (infrared); development of Hadamard transform spectrometry; detection of volatile organic compounds using Fourier transform infrared spectrometry. *Mailing Add:* Dept Chem Willard Hall Kans State Univ Manhattan KS 66506-3701

HAMMAM, M SHAWKY, ELECTRICAL ENGINEERING. *Current Pos:* RETIRED. *Prof Exp:* Fac mem, Elec Eng Dept, Clarkson Univ, 92. *Mem:* Inst Elec & Electronics Engrs. *Mailing Add:* 53 May Rd Potsdam NY 13676

HAMMANN, JOHN WILLIAM, ELECTRICAL ASPECTS OF SOLAR ENERGY, ALTERNATE ENERGY SOURCES. *Current Pos:* assoc prof, 78-85, EMER PROF ELEC TECHNOL, IND UNIV-PURDUE UNIV, INDIANAPOLIS, 85- *Personal Data:* b St Louis, Mo, Oct 21, 14; div; c Sandra L (Todd). *Educ:* Purdue Univ, BSEE, 36; Mo Sch Mines & Metall, MSEE, 48; Univ Grenoble, dipl higher educ, 52; Wash Univ, PhD(elec eng), 60. *Prof Exp:* Instr elec eng, Mo Sch Mines & Metall, 46-48; lectr, Wash Univ, 48-51 & 52-56; engr, Emerson Elec & Mfg Co, 56-59; assoc elec engr, Argonne Nat Lab, 60-67; from asst prof to assoc prof, Calumet Campus, Purdue Univ, 67-75, assoc prof elec technol, 77-78. *Mem:* Inst Elec & Electronics Engrs; Am Soc Eng Educ; Sigma Xi. *Res:* Electrical aspects of solar energy; alternate energy sources, such as solar, wind, tidal, atomic and geothermal power. *Mailing Add:* 5316 Acorn Lane Indianapolis IN 46254-1351. *E-Mail:* jhammann@champion.iupui.edu

HAMMANN, WILLIAM CURL, ANIMAL GROWTH PROMOTANTS, FOOD & FEED CHEMICALS. *Current Pos:* CONSULT, 86- *Personal Data:* b Little Rock, Ark, Apr 22, 25; m 55, Kupperstein; c Mark G, Joyce & Scott J. *Educ:* Univ Minn, BChem, 47; Univ Ill, PhD(chem), 51. *Prof Exp:* Fulbright fel, Univ Paris, 51-52; Swiss-Am fel, Swiss Fed Inst Technol, 52-53; res chemist, Monsanto Co, 53-60, group leader, 60-67, res mgr, New Enterprises Div, Res Ctr, 67-69, mgr com develop, foods & fine chem bus group, 69-75, mgr res functional prod bus group, 75-77, dir, Res Spec Chem Div, 77-80, dir res & develop, Nutrit Chem Div, 80-85. *Concurrent Pos:* Instr, Univ Dayton, 55-61. *Mem:* AAAS; Sigma Xi; Soc Chem Indust; Am Chem Soc. *Res:* Synthetic functional fluids; thermal stability of organic compounds; polyphenyl ethers; organic syntheses; food additives; fine chemicals; water treatment chemicals; feed additives; growth promotants. *Mailing Add:* 438 Fourwynd Dr St Louis MO 63141

HAMMAR, ALLAN H, MICROBIOLOGY, ZOOLOGY. *Current Pos:* RETIRED. *Personal Data:* b Springfield, Mass, June 5, 23; m 48, Ruth Rayno; c Ellen (Leitch) & Nancy (Brooker). *Educ:* Univ Conn, BS, 50, MS, 51. *Prof Exp:* Instr virus res animal dis, Univ Conn, 51-53; biologist, Lederle Labs, Am Cyanamid Co, 53-57, dept head virus vaccine prod, 57-60, supt tissue cult vaccine prod, 60-63, supt virus prod & vacuum drying, 63-70; microbiol biol res mgr, Bayer USA, 70-76, asst to vpres, 77-86, res & develop qual assurance mgr, 86-88. *Mem:* Am Soc Microbiol. *Res:* Experimental embryology; virus research in animal diseases; rickettsial and human virus vaccines; tissue culture and production activities in virus vaccines; development and study of effectiveness of new hyperimmune globulins. *Mailing Add:* 120 Florence Ave Mill Valley CA 94941

HAMMAR, SHERREL L, PEDIATRICS, ADOLESCENT MEDICINE. *Current Pos:* assoc prof, 71-73, chmn dept, 73-97, PROF PEDIAT, SCH MED, UNIV HAWAII, MANOA, 73-, INTERIM DEAN, 97- *Personal Data:* b Caldwell, Idaho, May 21, 31; m 56, Shirley Gose; c Kathryn M (Pryor) & David J. *Educ:* Col Idaho, BA, 53; Univ Wash, MD, 57. *Prof Exp:* From instr to assoc prof pediat, Univ Wash, 62-71, asst dir, Div Child Health, 65-71. *Concurrent Pos:* Res fel growth & develop, Univ Wash, 60-62; med consult, Luther Burbank Sch, 60-66 & Echo Glenn Children's Ctr, 67-71; dir ambulatory serv, Kauikeolani Children's Hosp, 71-73, chief pediat, 73-; lectr, Am Bd Pediat; chmn, Kopioloni Med Spcialists, 94. *Mem:* Fel Am Acad Pediat; Soc Adolescent Med (pres, 80); Ambulatory Pediat Asn; Am Pediat Soc; AMA. *Res:* Adolescent medicine and obesity; school learning problems; mental retardation and growth disorders. *Mailing Add:* Off Dean Univ Hawaii Sch Med 1960 Eastwest Rd Honolulu HI 96822. *Fax:* 808-956-5506; *E-Mail:* hammars@jabson.biomed.hawaii.edu

HAMMAR, WALTON JAMES, ORGANIC CHEMISTRY. *Current Pos:* res specialist drug res, Riker Labs, 69-76, STAFF SCIENTIST, LIFE SCI LAB, 3M CO, 76- *Personal Data:* b Waverly, Iowa, Apr 25, 41; m 63; c 4. *Educ:* Iowa State Univ, BS, 63; Purdue Univ, PhD(org chem), 67. *Prof Exp:* NIH fel, Cornell Univ, 67-69. *Mem:* Am Chem Soc; Soc Biomat; Sigma Xi. *Res:* Organic cation chemistry; photochemistry; small ring chemistry; chemotherapeutic agents; central nervous system agents; biomaterials; nonthrombogenic surfaces; polymer chemistry. *Mailing Add:* Cent Res 201-2W-17 3M Ctr St Paul MN 55144-1000

HAMMARLUND, EDWIN ROY, PHARMACY. *Current Pos:* assoc prof, 60-62, PROF PHARM, UNIV WASH, 62- *Personal Data:* b Seattle, Wash, Aug 24, 22; m 47; c 3. *Educ:* Univ Wash, BS, 43, MS, 49, PhD(pharm), 51. *Prof Exp:* From asst prof to assoc prof pharm, Wash State Univ, 51-60. *Concurrent Pos:* Pfeiffer Mem res fel, Copenhagen, 58-59; WHO fel drug abuse, London, Stockholm & Copenhagen, 71; US Info Serv lectr drug abuse, WGer, 71. *Mem:* Am Pharmaceut Asn; Am Asn Cols Pharm. *Res:* Surface active agents; antacids; isosmotic solutions; blood hemolysis; drug abuse education. *Mailing Add:* 12512 Eighth Ave NW Seattle WA 98177

HAMME, JOHN VALENTINE, MINERAL & CERAMIC ENGINEERING. *Current Pos:* res asst, NC State Univ, 58-63, assoc prof, 63-83, dir coop eng educ, 69-83, EMER ASSOC PROF CERAMIC ENG, NC STATE UNIV, 83- *Personal Data:* b Oxford, NC, May 14, 19; m 47; c 2. *Educ:* NC State Col, BS, 40; Univ Utah, MS, 42; NC State Univ, PhD(ceramic eng), 63. *Prof Exp:* Metallurgist, Columbia Steel Co Div, US Steel Corp, 42-44; engr, Tungsten Mining Corp, NC, 47-50, asst mill supt, 50-51, mill supt, 51-55, chem plant supt, 55-58. *Mem:* Am Inst Mining, Metall & Petrol Engrs; Sigma Xi. *Res:* Mineral exploration; mineral beneficiation; nuclear fuel materials research. *Mailing Add:* 1312 Onslow Rd Raleigh NC 27606-2745

HAMMEL, EDWARD FREDERIC, PHYSICAL CHEMISTRY. *Current Pos:* CONSULT ENERGY, LOW TEMPERATURE PHYSICS, CRYOENG, 79- *Personal Data:* b New York, NY, Jan 6, 18; m 42; c 3. *Educ:* Dartmouth Col AB, 39; Princeton Univ, PhD(phys chem), 44. *Honors & Awards:* Am Chem Soc Award, 55; Samuel C Collins Award, Cryogenic Eng Conf, 73; Wilbur T Pentzer Award, Int Inst Refrig, 85. *Prof Exp:* Res assoc heterogeneous catalysis, Princeton Univ, 41-42, sr scientist, 42-44; sect leader plutonium remelting, alloying & casting, high vacuum, Los Alamos Nat Lab, Univ Calif, 44-45, group leader metal physics & low temperature physics, 45-70, mem staff low temperature physics, 70-72, prog mgr superconducting transmission line & energy storage, 72-73, assoc div leader, Energy Div, 73-74, asst dir energy, 74-79. *Mem:* Sigma Xi; fel Am Phys Soc. *Res:* Low temperature physics. *Mailing Add:* 99 Rim Rd Los Alamos NM 87544

HAMMEL, EUGENE A, SOCIAL ANTHROPOLOGY, DEMOGRAPHY. *Current Pos:* from asst prof to prof, 61-78, PROF ANTHROP & CHAIR, DEPT DEMOG, UNIV CALIF, BERKELEY, 78- *Personal Data:* b New York, NY, Mar 18, 30; m 51; c 4. *Educ:* Univ Calif, Berkeley, AB, 51, PhD(anthrop), 59. *Prof Exp:* Asst prof anthrop, Univ NMex, 59-61. *Mem:* Nat Acad Sci; Am Ethnol Soc (pres, 83-85); Am Anthrop Asn; Pop Asn Am. *Mailing Add:* Dept Demog Univ Calif 2232 Piedmont Ave Berkeley CA 94720

HAMMEL, HAROLD THEODORE, PHYSIOLOGY & BIOPHYSICS. *Current Pos:* ADJ PROF PHYSIOL & BIOPHYS, IND UNIV, BLOOMINGTON, 88- *Personal Data:* b Huntington, Ind, May 8, 21; m 48, Dorothy King; c Nannette & Heidi. *Educ:* Purdue Univ, BS, 43; Cornell Univ, MS, 50, PhD(zool), 53. *Honors & Awards:* Hon Award, Environ & Exercise Physiol Sect, Am Physiol Soc, 96. *Prof Exp:* Jr physicist, Los Alamos Sci Lab, Univ Calif, Los Angeles, 44-46, staff physicist, 48-49; from instr to asst prof physiol, Sch Med, Univ Pa, 53-61; assoc prof, Yale Univ, 61-67; prof physiol, Univ Calif, San Diego, 67-88. *Concurrent Pos:* Fel, John B Pierce Found Lab, 61-67; panelist regulatory biol, NSF, 68-71; foreign sci mem, Max Planck Inst Physiol & Clin Res; Alexander von Humboldt Found US sr scientist award, 81-82. *Mem:* Am Phys Soc; Am Soc Mammal; Am Physiol Soc; fel AAAS; Norweg Acad Sci & Lett. *Res:* Osmoregulation and regulation of body temperature in vertebrates; water relations in vascular plants; physical chemistry of osmosis. *Mailing Add:* 1605 Ridgeway Dr Ellettsville IN 47429-9474. *Fax:* 812-855-4436; *E-Mail:* hhammel@indiana.edu

HAMMEL, JAY MORRIS, MICROBIOLOGY, BIOCHEMISTRY. *Current Pos:* From instr to asst prof, 65-81, ASSOC PROF MICROBIOL, HAHNEMANN MED COL, 81- *Personal Data:* b New York, NY, Mar 14, 38; m 70, Deborah Meltzer; c Geoffrey. *Educ:* City Col New York, BS, 60; Pa State Univ, MS, 62, PhD(microbiol), 65. *Concurrent Pos:* Vis prof, Dept Micro & Immunol, Ore Health Sci Univ, 81-82. *Mem:* AAAS; Am Soc Microbiol; NY Acad Sci; Sigma Xi. *Res:* Microbial physiology, especially protein synthesis; control mechanisms; extracellular enzyme synthesis; legionella pneumophila; mechanisms of pathogenesis; environmental microbiology. *Mailing Add:* Dept Microbiol Hahnemann Univ Sch Med Broad & Vine Sts Philadelphia PA 19102-1178

HAMMEL, P CHRIS, CORRELATED ELECTRONIC SYSTEMS, NUCLEAR MAGNETIC RESONANCE. *Current Pos:* J R Oppenheimer fel, 86-89, STAFF MEM, LOS ALAMOS NAT LAB, 89- *Personal Data:* b Los Alamos, NMex, Apr 14, 54. *Educ:* Univ Calif, San Diego, BS, 77; Cornell Univ, PhD(physics), 84. *Prof Exp:* Res fel, Mass Inst Technol, 84-86. *Mem:* Am Phys Soc. *Res:* Electronic, magnetic and structural properties of correlated electronic systems, including cuprate superconductors by application of nuclear magnetic resonance techniques. *Mailing Add:* Los Alamos Nat Lab MST 10 K764 PO Box 1663 Los Alamos NM 87545

HAMMEN, CARL SCHLEE, INVERTEBRATE PHYSIOLOGY, COMPARATIVE BIOCHEMISTRY. *Current Pos:* RETIRED. *Personal Data:* b Newark, NJ, Aug 26, 23; m 49, 62, Susan Lum; c Scott, Carol, John & Elizabeth. *Educ:* St John's Col, Md, BA, 47; Columbia Univ, MA, 49; Univ Chicago, SM, 52; Duke Univ, PhD(zool), 58. *Prof Exp:* Instr biol & chem, Mitchell Col, NC, 49-51; prof biol & math, Cedarville Col, 52-53; biologist, Vet Admin Ctr, WVa, 53-54 & Army Chem Ctr, Md, 54-56; assoc prof biol, Newark State Col, 58-60 & Adelphi Col, 60-63; from asst prof to emer prof, Univ RI, 63-97. *Concurrent Pos:* NSF res grants, Newark State Col, 59-60, Adelphi Col, 61-63 & Univ RI, 64-66; Fulbright fel, Morocco, 84. *Mem:* Am Physiol Soc; Am Soc Zoologists; Sigma Xi. *Res:* Metabolism of marine invertebrates, particularly bivalve mollusks and brachiopods. *Mailing Add:* 449 Golden Gate Pt Sarasota FL 34236

HAMMEN-WINN, SUSAN LUM, POPULATION BIOLOGY OF FERNS, NOCTURNAL REEF FISH & SEAGRASSES. *Current Pos:* INSTR BOT, COL CONTINUING EDUC, UNIV RI, 89- *Personal Data:* b Summit, NJ, Mar 15, 36; m 62, 92; c John & Elizabeth. *Educ:* Mt Holyoke Col, BA, 58; NY Univ, MS, 63; Univ RI, PhD(bot), 89. *Prof Exp:* Res asst, Kidney Lab, P B Brigham Hosp, Harvard Med Sch, 58-60 & physiol, Adelphi Univ, Garden City, 60-63. *Concurrent Pos:* Instr, Prog Excellence Teaching Sci, Univ RI, 89-93, adj prof biol. *Mem:* Am Fern Soc; Bot Soc Am; Sigma Xi. *Res:* Population biology of the hay-scented fern, Dennstaedtia Punctilobula, including intraspecific variation, morphology, resource allocation, and defoliation and transport of mineral nutrients. *Mailing Add:* 45 Willer Rd Saunderstown RI 02874. *E-Mail:* swinn@uriacc.uri.edu

HAMMER, CARL, COMPUTER SCIENCES. *Current Pos:* CONSULT, 81- *Personal Data:* b Chicago, Ill, May 10, 14; m 44. *Educ:* Univ Munich, dipl, 36, PhD(math statist), 38. *Honors & Awards:* Comput Sci Man-of-the-Yr Award, Data Processing Mgt Asn, 73. *Prof Exp:* Statistician, Res Labs, Tex Co, NY, 38-43 & foreign div, Pillsbury Mills, Inc, 44-47; chmn div tech educ, Walter Hervey Jr Col, 47-50; res assoc, Columbia Univ, 50-52; sr res engr, Franklin Inst, 52-55; dir, Univac Europ Comput Ctr, Ger, 55-57; staff consult, Electronic Systs Div, Sylvania Elec Prod, Inc, Mass, 57-59; adminr tech proj coord, Surface Commun Eng, Radio Corp Am, 59-61, mgr sci comput appln, 61-63; dir comput sci, Sperry Univac, 63-81. *Concurrent Pos:* Adj prof, Am Univ, 63-81; vis prof, Indust Col Armed Forces, 65-; mem, Nat Defense Exec Reserve, 70- *Mem:* Fel AAAS; Am Math Soc; Soc Indust & Appl Math (treas, 53-55); Am Statist Asn; Am Soc Cybernet (pres, 69-71); fel Inst Elec & Electronics Engrs. *Res:* Engineering and mathematical-statistical analysis; quantal response studies; evaluation of computing systems; design of experiments; cryptology. *Mailing Add:* 3263 O Dr NW Washington DC 20007-2843

HAMMER, CARL HELMAN, biochemistry of complement, for more information see previous edition

HAMMER, CHARLES F, ORGANIC CHEMISTRY, CHEMICAL INSTRUMENTATION. *Current Pos:* from asst prof to prof, 63-95, dir, Inst Advan Analytical Chem, 63-74, EMER PROF CHEM, GEORGETOWN UNIV, 95-; DIR, HOYA/NMEX SCH CHEMOBILE, 95- *Personal Data:* b Fremont, Ohio, July 22, 33; m 57, Lois Reel; c Laurence N. *Educ:* Bowling Green State Univ, BA, 55; Univ Minn, PhD(org chem), 59. *Honors & Awards:* Alan Berman Res Publ Award, NRL, 87. *Prof Exp:* Res chemist, Proctor & Gamble, 59; NIHPD fel, x-ray crystallog & steroids, Brandeis Univ, 61-63. *Concurrent Pos:* Mem, ChemTec Writing Team, Am Chem Soc, 70-72; vis prof, Dept Hydrocarbon Chem, Sch Eng, Kyoto Nat Univ, Japan, 71-72, Dept Chem, Nanjing Univ, 94; vis scholar, Dept Chem, Univ Calif, Berkeley, 78, Nat Inst Diabetes, Digestive & Kidney Dis, NIH, 86, Inst Chem, Ljubljana, Slovenia, 93. *Mem:* AAAS; Am Chem Soc; Am Soc Mass Spectrometry; Soc Appl Spectros; Am Soc Testing & Mat; Sigma Xi. *Res:* Chemistry and mechanisms in nitrogen heterocyclics and steroids; bromination-dehydrobromination reactions; structure elucidation of natural products by instrumental methods; complete structure by 2D-nuclear magnetic resonance; isotope ratio kinetics by mass spectrometry; computer software applications to spectrometric analysis; synthesis of plant growth hormones and antitumor agents. *Mailing Add:* 2017 Calle Lejano Santa Fe NM 87501-8747. *Fax:* 505-989-1176

HAMMER, CHARLES LAWRENCE, ELEMENTARY PARTICLE PHYSICS, MATHEMATICAL PHYSICS. *Current Pos:* RETIRED. *Personal Data:* b Buffalo, NY, June 30, 22; m 48; c 4. *Educ:* Univ Mich, BS, 48, MS, 50, PhD(physics), 54. *Prof Exp:* Instr physics, Univ Mich, 53-54; res assoc, Iowa State Univ, 54-55, from asst prof to assoc prof, 55-61, prof, 61-88. *Concurrent Pos:* Consult, Allis Chalmers Mfg Co, 57-67 & Midwestern Univs Res Asn, 59-70; mem adv coun, NSF, 78-82. *Mem:* Am Phys Soc. *Res:* Nuclear and theoretical physics; quantum field theories and applications to coherent phenomenon. *Mailing Add:* Dept Physics Iowa State Univ Ames IA 50011

HAMMER, CHARLES RANKIN, ORGANIC CHEMISTRY. *Current Pos:* RETIRED. *Personal Data:* b Memphis, Tenn, Aug 7, 27; m 56; c 2. *Educ:* Univ Utah, BA, 49, PhD(org chem), 57. *Prof Exp:* Asst prof chem, Westminster Col, Utah, 56-60 & Idaho State Univ, 60-64; from asst prof to assoc prof, Univ Southern Calif, 64-93. *Mem:* Am Chem Soc. *Res:* Condensation of phenols with formaldehyde and primary amines; Mannich reactions involving primary amines; synthesis of heterocyclic compounds. *Mailing Add:* 1208 Liberty Lane Pueblo CO 81001-4901

HAMMER, CLARENCE FREDERICK, JR, POLYMER SCIENCE. *Current Pos:* CONSULT, 81- *Personal Data:* b Toledo, Ohio, Nov 24, 19; m 42; c 3. *Educ:* Miami Univ, BA, 40; Univ Wis, PhM, 42, PhD(chem physics), 48. *Honors & Awards:* Award for Creative Invention, Am Chem Soc, 90. *Prof Exp:* Jr physicist, Naval Ord Lab, 42-44, assoc physicist, 45, elec engr, 45-46; res asst physics, Univ Wis, 46-48; physicist, 58-51, group leader, Polychem Dept, E I du Pont de Nemours & Co, Inc, 51-55, supvr, 55-61, res assoc, Electrochem Dept, 61-71, res assoc, Plastics Dept, 71-78, res fel, Plastics Prod & Resins Dept, 78-81. *Mem:* Am Phys Soc; Sigma Xi; Am Chem Soc; AAAS. *Res:* Infrared studies of molecular structures; theoretical depolymerization mechanisms of high polymers; crystalline structure and physical properties of high polymers; physical properties of high polymers; polymer compatibility; invented "Elvaloy" non-migrating polymeric plasticizer for PVC, "Elvaloy" weather resistant impact modifier for PVC, polymeric toughener for phenolic and epoxy resins, highly novel and versatile graft copolymers. *Mailing Add:* 5349 Delano Ct Cape Coral FL 33904

HAMMER, DAVID ANDREW, PLASMA PHYSICS, INTENSE PARTICLE BEAMS. *Current Pos:* assoc prof, Cornell Univ, 77-84, prof nuclear sci & eng, 84-95, dir, Lab Plasma Studies, 85-95, J CARLTON WARD PROF NUCLEAR ENERGY ENG, CORNELL UNIV, 91-, PROF ELEC ENG, 95- *Personal Data:* b New York, NY, Apr 5, 43; m 68, Tove Helland; c Cailin (Benedicte) & Thomas Alden. *Educ:* Calif Inst Technol, BS, 64; Cornell Univ, PhD(appl physics), 69. *Prof Exp:* Res physicist, Naval Res Lab, Washington, DC, 69-76; assoc prof elec sci & eng, Univ Calif, Los Angeles, 77. *Concurrent Pos:* Vis assoc prof, Univ Md, 73-76; sr vis fel, Imp Col, London, Eng, 77, 83-84 & 91; consult, Physical Dynamics, 77-79, Lawrence Livermore Nat Lab, 79-, Sci Applns Int Corp, 79-, SRI Int-Jason, 80-82 & Mitre-Jason, 82-; div assoc ed phys rev lett, 88-91, assoc ed, Phys

Plasmas, 92- *Mem:* Fel Am Phys Soc; AAAS; sr mem Inst Elec & Electronics Engrs; Sigma Xi. *Res:* Intense electron and ion beams and their application to plasma physics and controlled fusion; physics of intense pulsed plasma radiation sources and their application to research and industry; controlled fusion. *Mailing Add:* Lab Plasma Studies Upson Hall Cornell Univ Ithaca NY 14853

HAMMER, GARY G, PHYSICAL ORGANIC CHEMISTRY. *Current Pos:* from asst prof to assoc prof, 67-74, chmn dept, 69-76, PROF CHEM, CHRISTOPHER NEWPORT COL, 74- *Personal Data:* b Wichita, Kans, Jan 9, 34; m 53; c 3. *Educ:* Wichita State Univ, BS, 55, MS, 57; Ga Inst Technol, PhD(chem), 62. *Prof Exp:* Res chemist, Dow Badische Co, 61-67. *Mem:* AAAS; Am Chem Soc. *Res:* Polymerization kinetics; mechanisms of addition to nitriles. *Mailing Add:* 684 Winthrop Rd Williamsburg VA 26185-4742

HAMMER, HENRY FELIX, PHARMACEUTICAL CHEMISTRY. *Current Pos:* RETIRED. *Personal Data:* b Brooklyn, NY, Oct 3, 21; m 48, Annette M Kelly; c Mary (Story), Henry F Jr & John J. *Educ:* Polytech Inst Brooklyn, BS, 43; Rensselaer Polytech Inst, PhD(org chem), 51. *Prof Exp:* Res chemist, Sterling-Withrop Res Inst, 43-46; asst & instr, Rensselaer Polytech Inst, 46-51; res chemist, Pfizer Inc, 51-58, pharmaceut res supvr, 58-62, mgr pharmaceut res, 62-64, from asst dir to dir qual control, 64-72, vpres, 72-86. *Mem:* Sigma Xi; Am Chem Soc. *Res:* Antibiotics; synthetic medicinals; vitamins and nutritional products; pharmaceutical dosage forms. *Mailing Add:* 29 Sea Marsh Rd Amelia Island FL 32034

HAMMER, JACOB, MATHEMATICAL SYSTEM THEORY, CONTROL THEORY. *Current Pos:* assoc prof, 87-90, PROF ELEC ENG, UNIV FLA, 91- *Personal Data:* b Bucarest, Rumania, Apr 30, 50; US citizen; m 84, Ivy S Gaines; c Mark M, Rachel T & Talia B. *Educ:* Technion-Israel Inst Technol, BSc, 74, MSc, 77, DSc(elec eng), 80. *Prof Exp:* Lectr eng, Technion-Israel Inst Technol, 79-80; res fel syst theory, Univ Fla, Gainesville, 80-82; asst prof math, Case Western Reserve Univ, 82-87. *Mem:* Am Math Soc; fel Inst Elec & Electronics Engrs. *Res:* Nonlinear control theory; linear control theory; nonlinear filtering. *Mailing Add:* Dept Elec Eng Univ Fla Gainesville FL 32611. *Fax:* 904-392-0044; *E-Mail:* hammer@lea.ee.ufl.edu

HAMMER, JACOB MEYER, SEMICONDUCTOR LASERS, OPTICAL WAVEGUIDES. *Current Pos:* PRES, PHOTONICS CONSULT, 88- *Personal Data:* b New York, NY, Sept 14, 27; m 51, 82, Katrina Schuyler; c Daniel, Jonathan, Miriam & David Reisberg. *Educ:* NY Univ, BS, 50, PhD(physics), 56; Univ Ill, MS, 51. *Prof Exp:* Asst physics, NY Univ, 51-55; mem tech staff, Bell Tel Labs, 56-59 & RCA Labs, 59-87. *Concurrent Pos:* Sr visitor, Cavendish Lab, Cambridge, Eng, 68-69; adj prof elec eng, Polytech Inst NY, 81. *Mem:* Am Phys Soc; fel Inst Elec & Electronics Engrs; Optical Soc Am. *Res:* Photonics; optoelectronics; semiconductor lasers; integration of optical isolators with semiconductor lasers and waveguides. *Mailing Add:* 42 City Gate Lane Annapolis MD 21401. *E-Mail:* jakehammer@aol.com

HAMMER, JOHN A, CELL MOTILITY, GENE REGULATION. *Current Pos:* SR STAFF FEL, CELL BIOL LAB, NIH, 82- *Educ:* Pa State Univ, PhD(physiol), 80. *Mailing Add:* Cell Biol Lab Nat Heart Lung Blood Inst NIH Bldg 3 Rm B1-22 Bethesda MD 20892-0001. *Fax:* 617-636-8934

HAMMER, LOWELL CLARKE, SPEECH PATHOLOGY, AUDIOLOGY. *Current Pos:* RETIRED. *Personal Data:* b Council Bluffs, Iowa, Jan 7, 30; m 49; c 2. *Educ:* Wichita State Univ, BA, 52; Univ Fla, PhD(speech path), 65. *Prof Exp:* Staff speech pathologist, Inst Logopedics, Wichita, Kans, 52-55; dir speech path, Children's Rehab Inst, Reisterstown, Md, 55-60; from instr speech path & audiol to asst prof, Univ Fla, 63-70, assoc prof speech path, 70-75, prof commun dis & speech, 75-94. *Concurrent Pos:* Chief, Dept Commun Dis & Chief speech path, Shands Hosp, 65-94; consult, Fla Crippled Childrens Comn, 66-; assoc dean Col Health Related Professions, 71- *Mem:* AAAS; Am Speech & Hearing Asn. *Res:* Clinical research in neurological diseases affecting speech and language processes; physiological research, especially electromyography of the speech mechanism. *Mailing Add:* 4909 NW 18th Ave Gainesville FL 32605

HAMMER, MARK J(OHN), CIVIL ENGINEERING. *Current Pos:* assoc prof civil eng, 64-69, acting chmn dept, 68-69, PROF CIVIL ENG, UNIV NEBR, 69- *Personal Data:* b Fond du Lac, Wis, Apr 26, 31; m 55; c 4. *Educ:* Northwestern Univ, BS, 55, MS, 56; Univ Mich, PhD(civil eng), 64. *Prof Exp:* Proj engr, Shannon & Wilson, consult engr, Wash, 60-61. *Mem:* Water Pollution Control Fedn; Am Water Works Asn. *Res:* Biological waste treatment, nitrogen and phosphorus removal from waste water, eutrophication of reservoirs; sanitary engineering and technology. *Mailing Add:* 1810 S 77th St Lincoln NE 68506

HAMMER, RICHARD BENJAMIN, NEW PRODUCT MANAGEMENT & DEVELOPMENT. *Current Pos:* DEVELOP ENG & MGR, IBM CORP, 81- *Personal Data:* b Hornell, NY, Sept 18, 43; m 86, L Karen; c Sarah J. *Educ:* Alfred Univ, BA, 66; Syracuse Univ, PhD(org chem), 72. *Honors & Awards:* Alfred Hitchcock Award. *Prof Exp:* Res asst, Syracuse Univ, 71-72, State Univ NY Col Environ Sci & Forestry, 72-73; group leader basic res cellulose chem & technol, ITT Rayonier Inc, 73-81. *Concurrent Pos:* Res assoc supvr, ITT Rayonier Inc, 81. *Mem:* Am Chem Soc; The Chem Soc; Sigma Xi. *Res:* Basic cellulose chemistry derivative, fiber spinning and processing, polymer chemistry, pulping, ceramic engineering, circuit design, photolithography; new product and process development; polymer & colloidal chemistry; computer chip packaging and development. *Mailing Add:* 522 Hilton Rd Apalachin NY 13732-9765. *Fax:* 607-755-2850; *E-Mail:* hammerrb@endvms.vnet.ibm.com

HAMMER, RICHARD HARTMAN, PHARMACEUTICAL CHEMISTRY, ORGANIC CHEMISTRY. *Current Pos:* From asst prof to assoc prof, Univ Fla, 63-76, chmn dept, 75-79, asst dean, 79-84, PROF PHARMACEUT CHEM, UNIV FLA, 76- *Personal Data:* b Latrobe, Pa, May 24, 33; m 62; c 2. *Educ:* Univ Ariz, BS, 59, PhD(pharmaceut chem), 63. *Concurrent Pos:* Am Cancer Soc grant, 64-67. *Mem:* Am Pharmaceut Asn; Am Chem Soc; Am Asn Pharmaceut Scientists. *Res:* Design and synthesis of drugs; drug metabolism. *Mailing Add:* 1704 NW 68th Terr Gainesville FL 32605

HAMMER, ROBERT NELSON, INORGANIC CHEMISTRY. *Current Pos:* from asst prof to assoc prof, 54-77, PROF CHEM, MICH STATE UNIV, 77- *Personal Data:* b Kansas City, Kans, Sept 15, 24. *Educ:* Univ Kans, AB, 47, MA, 49; Univ Ill, PhD(chem), 54. *Prof Exp:* Instr chem, Ark State Col, 49-51. *Concurrent Pos:* Assoc dir hons col, Mich State Univ, 66-70. *Mem:* AAAS; Am Chem Soc; Brit Chem Soc. *Res:* Nonaqueous solvents; voltammetry in liquid ammonia; acid-base equilibria in nonaqueous solvents; metallosiloxane synthesis. *Mailing Add:* 4953 S Okemos Rd East Lansing MI 48823-2922

HAMMER, ROBERT RUSSELL, PHYSICAL INORGANIC CHEMISTRY. *Current Pos:* RETIRED. *Personal Data:* b Red Bluff, Calif, Aug 5, 36. *Educ:* Chico State Col, AB, 58; Univ Wash, PhD(inorg chem), 63. *Prof Exp:* Res chemist, Phillips Petrol Co, 64-66; res chemist, Idaho Nuclear Corp, 66-70; assoc res scientist, Allied Chem Corp, 70-79, Exxon Nuclear Corp, 79-84, Westinghouse Idaho Nuclear Corp, 84-87. *Concurrent Pos:* Consult, 88. *Mem:* Am Chem Soc; Sigma Xi. *Res:* Fluoride complexes of various metal ions, their stability constants, rates of formation and thermodynamic properties; computer simulation of chemical processes. *Mailing Add:* 605 Tendoy Dr Idaho Falls ID 83401-4132

HAMMER, RONALD PAGE, JR, NEUROENDOCRINOLOGY, NEUROPHARMACOLOGY. *Current Pos:* PROF PSYCHIAT, PHARMACOL & ANAT, TUFTS UNIV, BOSTON, 94- *Personal Data:* b Philadelphia, Pa, Feb 21, 53; m 86, Sandra Jacobson. *Educ:* Univ Calif, Berkeley, AB, 80; Univ Calif, Los Angeles, PhD(anat), 84. *Honors & Awards:* Res Career Develop Award, NIH, 87. *Prof Exp:* Teaching fel psychiat, Univ Calif, Los Angeles, 80; staff fel neurosci, NIMH, 80-83, sr res fel, 83-84; assoc prof anat, Univ Hawaii, Manoa, Honolulu, 84-93, prof anat & pharmacol, 93-94. *Concurrent Pos:* Instr, Montgomery Col, Md, 80-83; mem adv comt, Am Asn Anatomists, 84-87. *Mem:* Soc Neurosci; Am Asn Anatomists; AAAS; Int Soc Develop Neurosci; Soc Biol Psychiat; Soc Neuroendocrinol. *Res:* Brain development; modulation by neuropeptide factors; drug effects on brain metabolism; biological substrates for drug function; drugs of abuse; neuroendocrine effects on reproductive behavior; addiction medicine. *Mailing Add:* Dept Psychiat Tufts Univ New Eng Med Ctr NEMC Box 1007 750 Washington St Boston MA 02111

HAMMER, ULRICH THEODORE, LIMNOLOGY. *Current Pos:* instr, Univ Sask, 61-62, lectr, 62-63, from asst prof to assoc prof, 63-71, chmn, Water Studies Inst, 67-69, prof, 71-91, head dept, 73-76, EMER PROF BIOL, UNIV SASK, 91- *Personal Data:* b Maple Creek, Sask, Mar 25, 24; m 54; c Debra & Philip. *Educ:* Univ Sask, BEd, 50, BA, 56, PhD(limnol), 63; Mont State Univ, MS, 59. *Prof Exp:* Teacher elem schs, Sask, 46-47 & 48-49 & Alta, 50-51 & high schs, 51-58. *Concurrent Pos:* Woods Hole Oceanog Inst fel, 63; sabbatical vis lectr, Monash Univ, Australia, 69-70; San Diego State Univ, 90; Sask res coun scholar, 60-61 & 61-62; fel Rawson Acad Aquatic Sci, 79, dir, 86-92. *Mem:* Am Soc Limnol & Oceanog; Int Soc Limnol; Soc Can Limnol; Int Consortium Salt Lake Res. *Res:* Ecology of bloom-forming blue-green algae; eutrophication; primary productivity of inland lakes; chemical, physical and biological limnology of saline lakes; bioaccumulation and cycling of heavy metals. *Mailing Add:* Dept Biol Univ Sask 112 Science Pl Saskatoon SK S7N 5E2 Can. *Fax:* 306-966-4461; *E-Mail:* hammer@usask.sask.ca

HAMMERLI, MARTIN, electrochemistry, for more information see previous edition

HAMMERLING, JAMES SOLOMON, MEDICINE, OTOLARYNGOLOGY. *Current Pos:* RETIRED. *Personal Data:* b Philadelphia, Pa, Aug 17, 07; m 36; c 2. *Educ:* City Col New York, BSc, 29; NY Med Col, MD, 33. *Prof Exp:* Prof otolaryngol, fac med, Dalhousie Univ, 64-76. *Concurrent Pos:* Consult, Izaak Walton Killam Hosp Children, Camp Hill Hosp & Halifax Infirmary, 64-76. *Mem:* Am Col Surgeons; Am Acad Ophthal & Otolaryngol; Can Otolaryngol Soc; Can Med Asn. *Mailing Add:* 6777 Quinpool Rd Halifax NS B3L 1C2 Can

HAMMERLING, ULRICH, IMMUNOCHEMISTRY, IMMUNOGENETICS. *Current Pos:* MEM STAFF, MEM SLOAN-KETTERING INST, 83- *Educ:* Univ Freiburg, Ger, PhD(immunol), 65. *Mailing Add:* Dept Immunol Sloan-Kettering Cancer Ctr 1275 York Ave New York NY 10021-6006. *Fax:* 212-794-4019

HAMMERMAN, DAVID LEWIS, PHYSIOLOGY, PATHOLOGY & ANATOMY. *Current Pos:* from asst prof to assoc prof, 62-71, adj prof health sci, 81-89, PROF BIOL, LONG ISLAND UNIV, 71-, ADJ PROF SPORTS SCI, 83- *Personal Data:* b Brooklyn, NY, Dec 19, 35; m 63, Gail Stern; c Craig, Robin & Evan. *Educ:* City Col New York, BS, 57; NY Univ, MS, 59, PhD(biol), 62. *Prof Exp:* Asst med, NY Univ, 58-59, instr biol, 62. *Concurrent Pos:* Consult Div Natural Sci, Brooklyn Children's Mus, Inst Arts & Sci, 63, Saunders Col Publ, 89. *Mem:* AAAS; Sigma Xi; Am Soc Zool. *Res:* Vertebrate morphogenesis; sensory physiology; physiogenesis of taste. *Mailing Add:* Dept Biol Long Island Univ Brooklyn NY 11201-5372

HAMMERMAN, IRA SAUL, BIOPHYSICS, BIOLOGICAL STRUCTURE. *Current Pos:* FAC MEM, ELTA DEPT, ISRAEL AIRCRAFT INDUST, 77- *Personal Data:* b New York, NY, May 15, 42; m 65; c 4. *Educ:* Brandeis Univ, BA, 64; Princeton Univ, MA, 66, PhD(physics), 69. *Prof Exp:* Res assoc elem particles, Nevis Labs, 69-71; res assoc, Technion-Israel, Inst Technol, 71-72; res assoc, Dept Biol Sci, Columbia Univ, 72-74; lectr, Dept Life Sci, Bar Ilan Univ, Israel, 74-77. *Mem:* Am Phys Soc; Israel Electron Micros Soc. *Res:* Three-dimensional reconstruction of cell ultrastructure; sex determination in fish; ribosome structure; statistical fluctuations in polymerization. *Mailing Add:* 8 Taran Rehovot 76248 Israel

HAMMERMAN, MARC R, CELL PHYSIOLOGY. *Current Pos:* Asst prof, 79-84, ASSOC PROF INTERNAL MED, WASH UNIV SCH MED, 84- *Personal Data:* b St Louis, Mo, Sept 29, 47. *Educ:* Washington Univ, St Louis, MD, 72. *Mem:* Am Fedn Clin Res; Am Physiol Soc; Am Soc Clin Invest; Am Soc Nephrology; Cent Soc Clin Res. *Mailing Add:* Renal Div Wash Univ Sch Med Box 8126 660 S Euclid Ave St Louis MO 63110-1093. *Fax:* 314-362-8237

HAMMERMEISTER, KARL E, CARDIOLOGY. *Current Pos:* asst chief, 71, CHIEF, CARDIOVASC DIS SERV, VET ADMIN HOSP, SEATTLE. *Personal Data:* b Baguio, Philippines, Sept 10, 39; US citizen. *Educ:* Univ Wash, BS, 60, MD, 64. *Prof Exp:* Asst chief med cardiol, USPHS Hosp, Baltimore, Md, 68-70; asst chief cardiol & dir, Cardiovasc Lab, Vet Admin Hosp, Denver & asst prof med, Univ Colo Med Ctr, 70-71. *Concurrent Pos:* Cardiol fel, Sch Med, Univ Wash, 67-68, asst prof med, 71-75 & assoc prof med, 75-; fel, Coun Clin Cardiol, Am Heart Asn, 74- *Mem:* Am Fedn Clin Res; Am Heart Asn; fel Am Col Cardiol. *Res:* Effect of left ventricular function on surgical and late mortality in patients with cardiac disease. *Mailing Add:* Vet Admin Med Ctr Cardiol Denver CO 80220

HAMMERNESS, FRANCIS CARL, PHARMACY. *Current Pos:* assoc prof pharm admin, 57-66, prof pharm admin & dir Ctr Drug Mkt Res, 66-87, EMER PROF, UNIV COLO, BOULDER, 87- *Personal Data:* b Glasgow, Mont, Aug 8, 22; m 46. *Educ:* Mont State Univ, BS, 47, MS, 51; Univ NC, PhD(pharm), 56. *Prof Exp:* Instr pharm, Mont State Univ, 48-51; instr, Univ NC, 51-55, lectr, 55-56, asst prof, 56-57. *Mem:* Am Asn Cols Pharm; Am Pharmaceut Asn. *Res:* Pharmaceutical product development and marketing studies. *Mailing Add:* 3251 E Rd Clifton CO 81520

HAMMERSCHLAG, RICHARD, NEUROCHEMISTRY, CELL BIOLOGY. *Current Pos:* from asst res scientist to assoc res scientist, 70-84, RES SCIENTIST NEUROCHEM, DIV NEUROSCI, BECKMAN RES INST, CITY OF HOPE, 84- *Personal Data:* b New York, NY, June 12, 39; div; c 1. *Educ:* Mass Inst Technol, BS(humanities & sci), 60 & BS(chem), 61; Brandeis Univ, PhD(biochem), 67. *Prof Exp:* Fel neurochem, Dept Biophysics, Univ Col London, 67-69. *Mem:* Am Soc Neurochem; Int Soc Neurochem; Soc Neurosci; Am Soc Cell Biol. *Res:* Mechanisms and functions of axonal transport; neurotrophic phenomena. *Mailing Add:* Div Neurosci Beckman Res Inst City Hope 1450 E Duarte Rd Duarte CA 91010-0269

HAMMERSMITH, JOHN L(EO), SPACE SCIENCE, NUMERICAL ANALYSIS. *Current Pos:* RETIRED. *Personal Data:* b Massillon, Ohio, Apr 4, 29; m 51, Frances M; c Lynn H (Wyvill) & Ann F. *Educ:* Univ Mich, BS, 51. *Prof Exp:* Mathematician, US Naval Res Lab, 51-60; mathematician, Theoret Div, Goddard Space Flight Ctr, NASA, 60-61, space sci & eng assignments, Off Manned Space Flight, 61-63, mission analyst, Gemini Prog Off, NASA Hq, 63-66, sr engr, Manned Space Flight, Advan Missions Prog, 66-70, chief engr payload planning, 70-72, head payload accomodations, Space Shuttle Prog, 72-79, sr systs engr, Space Transp Syst Prog, 79-83, staff engr, Space Shuttle Opers, NASA Hq, 83-87. *Concurrent Pos:* Radio reportage of US Space Prog, Voice of Am. *Mem:* Assoc fel Am Inst Aeronaut & Astronaut. *Res:* Manned space flight mission planning; systems engineering; numerical analysis. *Mailing Add:* PO Box 430 Upper Marlboro MD 20773

HAMMERSTEDT, ROY H, BIOCHEMISTRY, REPRODUCTIVE PHYSIOLOGY. *Current Pos:* from asst prof to assoc prof, 70-83, PROF BIOCHEM, PA STATE UNIV, UNIVERSITY PARK, 83- *Personal Data:* b Duluth, Minn, June 17, 41; m 66; c 2. *Educ:* Univ Minn, BA, 63, PhD(biochem), 68. *Prof Exp:* NIH res fel biochem, Mich State Univ, 68-70. *Concurrent Pos:* Vis prof, Univ Wis, 78 & Cornell Univ, 86. *Mem:* Sigma Xi; Am Chem Soc; Am Soc Biol Chemists; AAAS; Am Soc Andrology; Soc Study Reproduction; Soc Cryobiol. *Res:* Biochemical characterization of spermatozoa; bioenergetics; membrane structure and function; lipid metabolism and cryobiology; effect of microgravity on cell function. *Mailing Add:* 406 Althouse Lab Pa State Univ University Park PA 16802-0001. *Fax:* 814-863-7024

HAMMERSTROM, HAROLD ELMORE, ANALYTICAL CHEMISTRY, INORGANIC CHEMISTRY. *Current Pos:* RETIRED. *Personal Data:* b Davis, SDak, Apr 7, 27; m 49; c 4. *Educ:* SDak State Col, BS, 53; Univ SDak, MA, 55; Univ of the Pac, PhD(chem), 68. *Prof Exp:* Prin, Linn Grove Consol Sch, Iowa, 54-57; prof chem, Northwestern Col, 57- *Mem:* Am Chem Soc. *Res:* Radiometric titrations. *Mailing Add:* 2525 Francis Sites Dr Spirit Lake IA 51360

HAMMES, GORDON G, BIOCHEMISTRY, BIOPHYSICS. *Current Pos:* PROF BIOCHEM & VCHANCELLOR ACAD AFFAIRS, MED CTR, DUKE UNIV, 91- *Personal Data:* b Fond du Lac, Wis, Aug 10, 34; m 59; c 3. *Educ:* Princeton Univ, BA, 56; Univ Wis, PhD(chem), 59. *Honors & Awards:* Award Biol Chem, Am Chem Soc, 67. *Prof Exp:* NSF fel, 59-60; from instr to assoc prof chem, Mass Inst Technol, 60-65; prof, Cornell Univ, 65-75, chmn dept, 70-75, Horace White prof chem & biochem, 75-88, dir, Biotechnol Prog, 83-88; prof chem & vchancellor acad affairs, Univ Calif, Santa Barbara, 88-91. *Concurrent Pos:* Mem adv panel, NIH, 67-80 & 86-88; NSF sr fel, 68-69; NIH Fogarty scholar, 75-76. *Mem:* Nat Acad Sci; Am Acad Arts & Sci; Am Chem Soc; Am Soc Biochem & Molecular Biol (pres, 94-). *Res:* Biophysical chemistry, especially enzyme kinetics and mechanisms; biochemical control mechanisms and membrane structure and function. *Mailing Add:* 11 Staley Pl Durham NC 27705-2421

HAMMETT, MICHAEL E, MATHEMATICS. *Current Pos:* asst prof, 67-70, assoc prof, 70-79, PROF MATH, FURMAN UNIV, 79- *Personal Data:* b Cowpens, SC, Dec 5, 37; m 59; c 2. *Educ:* Furman Univ, BS, 59; Auburn Univ, MS, 61, PhD(math), 67. *Prof Exp:* Asst prof math, Furman Univ, 62-65; asst prof, Auburn Univ, 65-67. *Mem:* Math Asn Am. *Res:* Mathematical analysis; ordinary differential equations. *Mailing Add:* Dept Math Furman Univ Greenville SC 29613-0001

HAMMILL, TERRENCE MICHAEL, MYCOLOGY, CYTOLOGY. *Current Pos:* from asst prof to assoc prof, 71-85, prof biol, 85-90, DISTINGUISHED TEACHING PROF BIOL, COL ARTS & SCI, STATE UNIV NY, OSWEGO, 90-, CHAIR BIOL, 91- *Personal Data:* b Potsdam, NY, Dec 28, 40; m 63; c 2. *Educ:* State Univ NY, Col Potsdam, BS, 63; Univ Ga, MEd, 68; State Univ NY, Col Forestry, Syracuse, PhD(bot), 71; Syracuse Univ, PhD(biol), 71. *Prof Exp:* Teacher biol, Indian River Cent High Sch, 63-67. *Concurrent Pos:* Res grant, Res Corp, 73; NSF grant, 74, 80. *Mem:* AAAS; Am Inst Biol Sci; Bot Soc Am; Electron Micros Soc Am; Mycol Soc Am; NY Acad Sci; Sigma Xi; Am Soc Microbiol. *Res:* Light and electron microscopy of fungi and fungal development; human sexuality. *Mailing Add:* Dept Biol State Univ NY Col Oswego Oswego NY 13126-3599

HAMMING, KENNETH W, ENGINEERING. *Current Pos:* RETIRED. *Personal Data:* b 1918; US citizen. *Educ:* Univ Ill, BS, 40. *Prof Exp:* Mech engr, Sargent & Lundy, 40-56, partner, 56-66, mgr, Mech & Nuclear Dept, 64-65, dir eng, 65-66, sr partner, 66-77. *Mem:* Nat Acad Eng; Am Soc Mech Eng. *Res:* Company planning, organization, direction and administration. *Mailing Add:* 565 Portsmouth Ct Naples FL 33963-8687

HAMMING, MYNARD C, SPECTROCHEMISTRY. *Current Pos:* res chemist, 60-67, SR RES SCIENTIST, CONOCO INC, 67- *Personal Data:* b McBain, Mich, Nov 1, 21; m 53; c 2. *Educ:* Mich State Univ, BS, 50. *Prof Exp:* Chemist, Dow Chem Co, Mich, 51-54, Phillips Petrol Co, 54-55 & Koppers Co, 55-60. *Mem:* Am Chem Soc; Am Soc Testing & Mat. *Res:* Analytical applications of high and low mass spectrometry, microprobe mass spectrometry; complex computer matrices; computer programming; gas chromatography; fossil fuel chemistry. *Mailing Add:* 1410 Reveille Dr Ponca City OK 74604-4438

HAMMING, RICHARD W, COMPUTER SCIENCE. *Current Pos:* RETIRED. *Personal Data:* b Chicago, Ill, Feb 11, 15; m 42. *Educ:* Univ Chicago, BS, 37; Univ Nebr, MA, 39; Univ Ill, PhD(math), 42. *Honors & Awards:* Piore Prize, Inst Elec & Electronics Engrs, 49, Hamming Medal named in honor, 91; Turing Prize lectr, 68; Pender Prize, 81; Rhein Found Prize, 96. *Prof Exp:* Instr math, Univ Ill, 42-44; asst prof, Univ Louisville, 44-45; mem staff, Manhattan Proj, Los Alamos Sci Lab, 45-46; mem tech staff, Bell Labs, Inc, 46-64, head, Numerical Methods Res Dept, 64-67, head, Comput Sci Res Dept, 67-77; adj prof, Dept Comput Sci, Naval Postgrad Sch, 76-97. *Mem:* Nat Acad Eng; Math Asn Am; Asn Comput Mach; fel Inst Elec & Electronics Engrs. *Res:* Numerical methods; error detecting and error correcting codes; automatic coding systems; statistics; digital filters. *Mailing Add:* Dept Comput Sci Naval Postgrad Sch Monterey CA 93940

HAMMOCK, BRUCE DUPREE, TOXICOLOGY, ENDOCRINOLOGY. *Current Pos:* from asst prof to assoc prof entom, 74-80, ASSOC PROF ENTOM & ENVIRON TOXICOL, UNIV CALIF, DAVIS, 80- *Personal Data:* b Little Rock, Ark, Aug 13, 47; m 72; c 3. *Educ:* La State Univ, Baton Rouge, BS, 69; Univ Calif, Berkeley, PhD(entom), 73. *Honors & Awards:* Frash Found Award; Burrough Wellcome Toxicol Scholar. *Prof Exp:* Fel endocrinol, Dept Biol, Northwestern Univ, 73-74. *Concurrent Pos:* Fel, Rockefeller Found, 73-74; res career develop award, 78-83; NSF, USDA, NIH & Environ Protection Agency grants; prin invester, Superfund Nat Inst Environ Health Sci Proj; vis fel, Lady Margaret Hall, Oxford Univ; fel, Fogarty Int. *Mem:* AAAS; Am Chem Soc; Entom Soc Am; Sox Toxicol; Soc Environ Toxicol. *Res:* Biochemistry of endocrine control of insect development; effects of xenobiotics on organisms and xenobiotic metabolism; immunoassay. *Mailing Add:* Dept Entom Univ Calif Davis CA 95616-5224

HAMMOND, ABNER M, JR, ENTOMOLOGY. *Current Pos:* from asst prof to prof, 68-77, PROF INSECT PHYSIOL, LA STATE UNIV, BATON ROUGE, 77- *Personal Data:* b Marks, Miss, Jan 17, 39; m 61; c 2. *Educ:* Miss State Univ, BS, 61, MS, 63; La State Univ, PhD(entom), 67. *Prof Exp:* Res entomologist, Southern Res Inst, 67-68. *Concurrent Pos:* Int consult. *Mem:* Entom Soc Am, Int Insect Chemoreception Workshop; Sigma Xi. *Res:* Physiological ecology of migrant noctuid moths; chemistry and behavior of lepidopterous insect pheromones; plant/insect interactions, including the role of endophytic fungi in regulating insect pest populations. *Mailing Add:* Dept Entom La State Univ Baton Rouge Baton Rouge LA 70803-0001

HAMMOND, ALLEN LEE, ENVIRONMENTAL POLICY RESEARCH. *Current Pos:* ED, WORLD RESOURCES, 90-; DIR, PROG RESOURCE & ENVIRON INFO, 90- *Personal Data:* b W Chicago, Ill, Sept 6, 43; m 69, Alice Rajchman; c Ross & Lily. *Educ:* Stanford Univ, BS, 66; Harvard Univ, MA, 67, PhD(appl math), 70. *Prof Exp:* Res news ed, AAAS, 70-79, ed Sci, 80-86; pres, ALH & Assoc Inc, 86-90. *Concurrent Pos:* Consult, Nat Acad Sci, 83-86; ed, I Sci & Tech, 84-86, Sci Impact Letter, 87-89, Off Sci & Technol Policy, 89-90. *Mem:* Fel AAAS; Sigma Xi. *Res:* Environmental indicators; writing on environmental policy; constraints on global sustainability. *Mailing Add:* 9612 E Bexhill Dr Kensington MD 20895. *E-Mail:* allen@wri.org

HAMMOND, ANDREW CHARLES, RUMINANT NUTRITION. *Current Pos:* RES LEADER, SUBTROP AGR RES STA, US DEPT AGR, BROOKSVILLE, FLA, 85- *Personal Data:* b Glendale, Calif, May 25, 49; m 73, Renee Ruzol; c Andrew & Matthew. *Educ:* Ore State Univ, BS, 71; Wash State Univ, MS, 77, PhD(nutrit), 79. *Prof Exp:* Res assoc, Dept Animal Sci, Wash State Univ, 79-80; res animal scientist, Beltsville Agr Res Ctr, US Dept Agr, Md, 80-85. *Concurrent Pos:* Courtesy prof, Univ Fla, 85- *Mem:* AAAS; Am Inst Nutrit; Am Soc Animal Sci; Coun Agr Sci Technol; Am Registry Cert Animal Scientists; Am Dairy Sci Asn; Soc Exp Biol & Med; Am Forage & Grasslands Coun; Sigma Xi. *Res:* Beef cattle nutrition; growth biology; nutritional toxicology. *Mailing Add:* USDA Agr Res Serv 22271 Chinsegut Hill Rd Brooksville FL 34601-4672. *Fax:* 352-796-2930; *E-Mail:* ach@gnv.ifas.ufl.edu

HAMMOND, BENJAMIN FRANKLIN, MEDICAL MICROBIOLOGY. *Current Pos:* RETIRED. *Personal Data:* b Austin, Tex, Feb 28, 34. *Educ:* Univ Kans, AB, 54; Meharry Med Col, DDS, 58; Univ Pa, PhD(microbiol), 62. *Honors & Awards:* Hatton Award, Int Asn Dent Res, 59; Medaille d'Argent, Paris, 78; Pres lectr, Univ Pa, 81; Turpin Mem lectr, Meharry Med Col, 85. *Prof Exp:* USPHS fel, Sch Dent Med, Univ Pa, 58-62, from asst instr to prof microbiol, 58-91, chmn dept, 72-85, dean acad affairs, 84-91; prof microbiol, Med Col Pa, 91-97. *Concurrent Pos:* USPHS career develop award, 66; consult, Coun Dent Educ & USPHS, NSF & Am Fund Dent Educ, 74-; mem study sect, Nat Inst Dent Res, mem, Nat Adv Dent Res Coun, NIH, 81-; Ralph Metcalf chair-distinguished vis prof, Marquette Univ, 85-86. *Mem:* Am Soc Microbiol; Int Asn Dent Res; Sigma Xi; Am Asn Dent Res (pres, 77-78). *Res:* Oral microbiology with emphasis on the physiology and molecular biology of periodontopathic bacteria; precise physico-chemical definition of how specific bacteria produce human periodontal disease; characterization & mechanisms of action of cytotoxic macromolecules and their effects on the microbial ecology of the gingival crevice; DNA probes. *Mailing Add:* 560 N 23rd St Philadelphia PA 19130

HAMMOND, CHARLES BESSELLIEU, OBSTETRICS, GYNECOLOGY. *Current Pos:* Intern surg, Duke Univ Med Ctr, 61-62, resident obstet & gynec, 62-64 & 66-69, from asst prof to prof, 69-80, E C HAMBLEN PROF OBSTET & GYNEC & CHMN DEPT, MED CTR, DUKE UNIV, 80- *Personal Data:* b Ft Leavenworth, Kans, July 24, 36; m 58, Peggy Adams; c 2. *Educ:* Duke Univ, BS, 60, MD, 61. *Concurrent Pos:* Fel reproductive endocrinol, NIH, Bethesda, Md, 64-66; dir, Am Bd Obstet & Gynec, 78-90. *Mem:* Am Fertil Soc (pres, 84-85); fel Am Col Obstet & Gynec; fel Soc Gynec Invest; Am Gynec & Obstet Soc (pres, 93-94). *Res:* Menopause, including hormonal replacement, osteoporosis and cardiovascular disease; prolactin disorders; reproductive endocrinopathy; malignant trophoblastic disease. *Mailing Add:* Dept Obstet-Gynec Duke Univ Sch Med Duke Med Ctr Durham NC 27710-7599. *Fax:* 919-684-6161

HAMMOND, CHARLES E, DIGITAL SYSTEM DESIGN. *Current Pos:* PRES & CONSULT, TRONEX CORP, 83- *Personal Data:* US citizen. *Educ:* Univ Md, BSEE, 75; Loyola Col, MSES, 81. *Prof Exp:* Staff engr, Univ Md, 75-77; elec engr, Nat Bur Standards, 77-79; sr engr, Gould Inc, 79-82. *Mem:* Inst Elec & Electronics Engrs. *Res:* Advanced computer architecture development. *Mailing Add:* Tronex Corp PO Box 6029 Annapolis MD 21401

HAMMOND, CHARLES EUGENE, DYNAMICS, AEROELASTICITY. *Current Pos:* prin engr, Martin Marietta Orlando Aerospace, 85-91, DIR MECH ENG, LOCKHEED MARTIN, 91- *Personal Data:* b Lithonia, Ga, Dec 21, 40; m 62; c 2. *Educ:* Ga Inst Technol, BAE, 62, MSAE, 68, PhD(aero eng), 70. *Honors & Awards:* Spec Achievement Award, NASA, 75, Group Achievement Award, 78. *Prof Exp:* Aero engr, US Naval Weapons Lab, 65-70; leader rotor aero group, Res & Technol Labs, US Army, 71-80, chief aeromech, Appl Technol Lab, 80-85. *Concurrent Pos:* Lectr math, Thomas Nelson Community Col, 73-; ad hoc fac mem, Univ Kans, 75-77. *Mem:* Am Inst Aeronaut & Astronaut; Howard Hughes Award, Am Helicopter Soc, 83. *Res:* Helicopters, aeroelasticity, structural dynamics, wind tunnel testing; digital data acquisition and analysis. *Mailing Add:* 100 Cove Colony Rd Maitland FL 32751

HAMMOND, CHARLES THOMAS, BIOLOGY, CYTOLOGY, CELL BIOLOGY, BOTANY. *Current Pos:* from asst prof to assoc prof, 77-86, PROF BIOL, ST MEINRAD COL, 86- *Personal Data:* b Moline, Ill, July 11, 44; m 67; c 3. *Educ:* Western Ill Univ, BSEd, 66; Ohio State Univ, MS, 69; Ind Univ, Bloomington, PhD, 77. *Prof Exp:* Teaching assoc bot & biol, Ohio State Univ, 67-69; assoc instr bot, Ind Univ, 69-72; asst prof biol, Wabash Col, 73-77. *Mem:* AAAS; Bot Soc Am. *Res:* Development, function and fine structure of the glandular secretory system in Cannabis stavia; biogenesis of cannabinoid precursors in cannabis; structure and function of glandular systems in plants. *Mailing Add:* Dept Biol St Meinrad Col St Meinrad IN 47577

HAMMOND, DAVID G, CIVIL ENGINEERING. *Current Pos:* vpres, 73-85, CONSULT ENG, DANIEL, MANN, JOHNSON & MENDENHALL, 85- *Personal Data:* b Paterson, NJ, Sept 8, 13; m 47; c 3. *Educ:* Pa State Univ, BS, 34; Cornell Univ, MSCE, 39. *Prof Exp:* Engr, US Army CEngr, 37-64; asst gen mgr oper engrs, San Francisco Rapid Transit, 64-73. *Mem:* Nat Acad Eng; fel Am Soc Civil Engrs; Am Pub Transit Asn. *Mailing Add:* Daniel Mann Johnson & Mendenhall 3250 Wilshire Blvd Los Angeles CA 90010

HAMMOND, DONALD L, PHYSICAL SCIENCE. *Current Pos:* RETIRED. *Personal Data:* b Kansas City, Mo, Aug 7, 27. *Educ:* Colo State Col, BS, 50, MS, 52. *Prof Exp:* Chief, Crystal Res Sect, Frequency Control Br, US Army Signal Eng Labs, 53-57; dir res, Sci Electronic Prod, 57-59; consult, Corp Develop Dept, Hewlett Packard, 88-91. *Concurrent Pos:* Bd dirs, Colo Crystal Corp, 87-96, Mid Penninsla Bank, 88-, Iris Med Corp, 90- & Nellcor Puritan Bennett, 90-; chmn, New Hope & Ivy Land RR, 90-; adv bd, Idaho Nat Eng Labs, 91-92. *Mem:* Nat Acad Eng; fel Inst Elec & Electronics Engrs. *Mailing Add:* 12660 Corte Madera Lane Los Altos Hills CA 94022. *Fax:* 650-941-6102

HAMMOND, DOUGLAS ELLENWOOD, MARINE CHEMISTRY, GEOCHEMISTRY. *Current Pos:* from asst prof to assoc prof, 75-89, chmn, 91-94, PROF GEOL, UNIV SOUTHERN CALIF, 89- *Personal Data:* b New York, NY, Jan 12, 46; m 79, Ayshe Ege; c Timur & Altay. *Educ:* Univ Rochester, BA, 67, MS, 70; Columbia Univ, PhD(geol), 75. *Concurrent Pos:* Sr NATO fel, 88-89; adj vis prof, Univ Bologna, 96. *Mem:* AAAS; Am Geophys Union; Geochem Soc. *Res:* Aqueous geochemistry; estuarine chemistry; application of stable and radioisotopes to the study of accumulation and diagenesis of recent sediments, dissolved gases, nutrient cycles, circulation and mixing; groundwater chemistry. *Mailing Add:* Dept Earth Sci Univ Southern Calif Los Angeles CA 90089-0740. *Fax:* 213-740-8801; *E-Mail:* hammond@usc.edu

HAMMOND, EARL GULLETTE, FOOD CHEMISTRY, BIOCHEMISTRY. *Current Pos:* Assoc prof dairy & food indust, biochem & biophys, 53-70, chmn food technol, 85-90, prof food technol, biochem & biophys, 70-90, PROF FOOD SCI & HUMAN NUTRIT, IOWA STATE UNIV 90- *Personal Data:* b Terrell, Tex, Nov 21, 26; m 51, Johnie Wright; c Bruce G, Linda C, Pamela K & Christopher A. *Educ:* Univ Tex, BS, 48, MA, 50; Univ Minn, PhD(biochem), 53. *Hon Degrees:* Dhc, Univ Agr & Biotechnol, Olsztyn Poland, 90. *Honors & Awards:* Pfizer Award, Am Dairy Sci Asn, 80; Hon Medal, Univ Agr & Technol, Olsztyn, Poland, 86; Chang Award, Am Oil Chem Soc, 92, A E Bailey Award, 93; Res & Develop 100 Award, Rest Develop Mag, 91; Utilization Res Award, Am Soybean Asn, 93. *Mem:* Am Chem Soc; Am Oil Chem Soc; Am Dairy Sci Asn; Inst Food Technol; AAAS; Sigma Xi. *Res:* Chemistry and analysis of lipids; autoxidation of fats; glyceride structure of fats; cheese chemistry; odor pollution; fermentations. *Mailing Add:* 3431 Ross Rd Ames IA 50010. *Fax:* 515-294-8181; *E-Mail:* hammond@iastate.edu

HAMMOND, GEORGE SIMMS, ORGANIC CHEMISTRY, PHYSICAL CHEMISTRY. *Current Pos:* CONSULT, 88-; DIR MAT SCI, BOWLING GREEN STATE UNIV, 91-, DISTINGUISHED VIS RES PROF, 92- *Personal Data:* b Auburn, Maine, May 22, 21; m 45, 77, Eva Menger; c Kenric, Janet (Starks), Steven, Barbara (Bennett), Kirsten & Lenore. *Educ:* Bates Col, BS, 43; Harvard Univ, MS & PhD(chem), 47. *Hon Degrees:* DSc, Wittenberg Univ, 72, Bates Col, 73; Dr State Univ Ghent, 73, Georgetown Univ, 85, Bowling Green State Univ, 90 & Weizmann Inst Sci, 93. *Honors & Awards:* Award Petrol Chem, Am Chem Soc, 61, James Flack Norris Award Phys Org Chem, 68, Award Chem Educ, 74 & Priestley Medal, 76; E Harris Harbison Award Gifted Teaching, Danforth Found, 71; Nat Medal Sci, 94. *Prof Exp:* Asst, Rohm and Haas Co, Pa, 43; res assoc insect repellants, Off Sci Res & Develop, Harvard Univ, 45; Off Naval Res fel, Univ Calif, Los Angeles, 48; from asst prof to prof chem, Iowa State Univ, 48-58; prof org chem, Calif Inst Technol, 58-64, Arthur Amos Noyes prof chem, 64-72, chmn, Div Chem & Chem Eng, 68-72; vchancellor, Div Natural Sci, Univ Calif, Santa Cruz, 72-75, prof chem, 72-78; foreign secy, Nat Acad Sci, 74-78; assoc dir, Allied Corp, 78-79, dir, Integrated Chem Systs, 79-85, exec dir biosci metals & ceramics, 85-88. *Concurrent Pos:* Vis prof, Georgetown Univ. *Mem:* Nat Acad Sci; Am Chem Soc; Chem Soc; Mat Res Soc; Int Asn Photochemical Scientists. *Res:* Mechanisms of free radical reaction; solution photochemistry; theories of reaction rates; materials science. *Mailing Add:* 27 Timber Lane Painted Post NY 14870. *Fax:* 607-937-8311

HAMMOND, GORDON LEON, SPECTRAL LINE BROADENING. *Current Pos:* PROF MATH, UNIV SFLA, 87- *Personal Data:* b Portsmouth, NH, Nov 6, 31; wid; c 3. *Educ:* Univ NH, BS, 58; Univ Md, MS, 62, PhD(astrophys), 74. *Prof Exp:* physicist, US Naval Ord Lab, 58-66, res physicist, 66-74, res physicist, Naval Surface Weapons Ctr, 74-86. *Concurrent Pos:* Consult, Dept Defense, 75-86. *Mem:* Int Astron Union; Am Astron Soc. *Res:* Neutral atom interactions; spectral line broadening; stellar atmospheres; plasma diagnostics; explosives properties and phenomenology; shock wave physics. *Mailing Add:* 5944 Plazaview Dr Zephyrhills FL 33541. *E-Mail:* hammond@math.usf.edu

HAMMOND, H DAVID, BOTANY, PLANT PHYSIOLOGY. *Current Pos:* RETIRED. *Personal Data:* b Philadelphia, Pa, Feb 10, 24; div; c Julia E (Wagner). *Educ:* Rutgers Univ, BS, 45, MS, 47; Univ Pa, PhD(bot), 52. *Prof Exp:* Res assoc biochem, Long Island Jewish Hosp, 55-57; asst prof physiol, Univ Del, 57-58; asst prof bot, Howard Univ, 58-68; from asst prof to assoc prof biol sci, State Univ NY Col Brockport, 68-83; assoc ed, NY Bot Gardens, 84-92. *Concurrent Pos:* Sigma Xi res grant, 64-65; NSF grant, 70-72; State

Univ NY Found grant, 70-72; ed, Bull of the Torrey Bot Club, 76-82, 88-92. *Mem:* Torrey Bot Soc; Bot Soc Am; Am Inst Biol Sci; Sigma Xi. *Res:* Plant morphogenesis; function of boron; herbarium development; evolution; plant growth and development; chemotaxonomy. *Mailing Add:* 4025 Lake Mary Rd Apt 33 Flagstaff AZ 86001-8608

HAMMOND, HAROLD LOGAN, ORAL & MAXILLOFACIAL PATHOLOGY. *Current Pos:* from asst prof to assoc prof oral diag & oral path, 67-83, head, Div Oral Diag, 73-75, PROF ORAL PATH, COL DENT, UNIV IOWA, 83-, DIR, SURG ORAL PATH SERV, 80- *Personal Data:* b Hillsboro, Ill, Mar 18, 34; m 86, Pat J Palmer; c Connie. *Educ:* Loyola Univ Chicago, DDS, 62; Univ Chicago, MS, 67; Am Bd Oral & Maxillofacial Path, dipl, 72. *Prof Exp:* Intern dent, Univ Chicago Hosps, 62-63, Zoller fel oral path, Univ Chicago Hosps & W G Zoller Mem Dent Clin, 63-65; USPHS res fel, 65-67. *Concurrent Pos:* Consult pathologist, Gen Hosp Managua, Nicaragua, 70-89; consult ed, Odontol Fedn Rev, Cent Am & Panama, 71-77, J Am Dent Asn, 79-89; consult oral path, Vet Admin Hosp, Iowa City, 77- *Mem:* Fel AAAS; Int Asn Oral Pathologists; Int Asn Dent Res; fel Am Acad Oral & Maxillofacial Path; NY Acad Sci; Am Asn Dent Res. *Res:* Salivary gland disease; oral manifestations of systemic disease; odontogenic tumors. *Mailing Add:* 1732 Brown Deer Rd Coralville IA 52241-1157. *Fax:* 319-335-7351; *E-Mail:* harold-hammond@uiowa.edu

HAMMOND, JAMES ALEXANDER, JR, ORGANIC CHEMISTRY. *Current Pos:* Res chemist, 63-70, SR RES CHEMIST, NYLON TECH SECT, TEXTILE FIBERS DEPT, E I DU PONT DE NEMOURS & CO, INC, 70- *Personal Data:* b Trion, Ga, Mar 10, 36; m 59; c 2. *Educ:* Ga Inst Technol, BS, 59, PhD(chem), 63. *Mem:* Am Chem Soc. *Res:* Natural product and polymer chemistry. *Mailing Add:* 1010 Pacific St Redlands CA 92373-6623

HAMMOND, JAMES B, INTERNAL MEDICINE, GASTROENTEROLOGY. *Current Pos:* VET ADMIN MED CTR, NORTH CHICAGO; CHIEF GASTROENTEROL SECT, MED SERV, UNIV HEALTH SERVS CHICAGO MED SCH, 93-, PROF CLIN MED, CHIEF, DIV GASTROENTEROL, ASSOC PROF, DEPT PHYSIOL. *Personal Data:* b Salt Lake City, Utah, Sept 27, 21. *Educ:* Univ Utah, BA, 43, MD, 46. *Prof Exp:* From assoc to instr, Sch Med, Ind Univ, 53-61; asst prof med, Chicago Med Sch, 62-63, assoc prof med, 81-93; assoc prof med, Med Sch, Northwestern Univ, Chicago, 63-81. *Concurrent Pos:* Fel biochem, Mass Inst Technol, 61-62 & Chicago Med Sch, 62-63; physician, Div Clin Res, Eli Lilly & Co, 53-61; attend physician, Marion County Gen Hosp, Indianapolis, 53-61; chief gastroenterol serv, Vet Admin Lakeside Hosp, 63-70, clin investr, 71-72, physician, 72-81; chief, Gastroenterol Serv, Vet Admin Med Ctr, North Chicago, 80- *Mem:* Am Gastroenterol Asn; fel Am Col Physicians; Am Asn Study Liver Dis; Am Soc Clin Nutrit; Am Soc Parenteral & Enteral Nutrit; Am Pub Health Asn. *Res:* Gastric and small intestinal disease including electron microscopy of endocrine cells and enzyme deficiency; pancreatitis; drug effects on gastric secretion; colonic motility studied by namometry; carbohydrate deficient serum; nutrition. *Mailing Add:* Vet Admin Med Ctr 111 G North Chicago IL 60064-3095

HAMMOND, JAMES JACOB, AGRONOMY. *Current Pos:* from asst prof to assoc prof, 70-79, PROF AGRON, NDAK STATE UNIV, 79- *Personal Data:* b West Union, Ill, Dec 11, 41; m 69; c 2. *Educ:* Univ Ill, BS, 63, MS, 65; Univ Nebr, PhD(agron), 70. *Mem:* Am Soc Agron; Crop Sci Soc Am. *Res:* Flax breeding and genetics. *Mailing Add:* Crop & Weed Sci NDak State Univ Main Campus Fargo ND 58105

HAMMOND, JAMES W, CHEMISTRY, CHEMICAL ENGINEERING. *Current Pos:* indust hygienist, 47-58, chief indust hygienist, 58-63, DIR INDUST HYG, HUMBLE OIL & REFINING CO, 63- *Personal Data:* b Winona, Miss, Feb 2, 13; m 37; c 2. *Educ:* Miss State Univ, BS, 35, ChE, 50; La State Univ, MS, 37. *Prof Exp:* Asst chemist, Univ Tenn, 36-41 & USPHS, 41-46; asst dir indust hyg, Ga State Dept Health, 47. *Concurrent Pos:* Asst prof, Col Med, Baylor Univ, 48-67; instr, Post-Grad Sch Med, Univ Tex, 50-67; asst prof, Sch Pub Health, Univ Tex, Houston, 67-72, assoc prof, 72- *Mem:* Am Indust Hyg Asn; Am Acad Indust Hyg (pres, 76-77). *Res:* Industrial environment science related to health conditions in work and occupation areas; industrial toxicology; chemical testing; ventilation; personal protective measures and equipment. *Mailing Add:* 1010 Town Place St Houston TX 77057

HAMMOND, JOSEPH LANGHORNE, JR, COMPUTER NETWORKS, COMMUNICATION NETWORKS. *Current Pos:* prof elec & comput eng, 85-95, EMER PROF ELEC & COMPUT ENG, CLEMSON UNIV, 95- *Personal Data:* b Birmingham, Ala, Oct 16, 27; m 49; c 3. *Educ:* Mass Inst Technol, BS & MS, 52; Ga Inst Technol, PhD(elec eng), 61. *Prof Exp:* Asst instrumentation, Air Force Cambridge Res Ctr, 49-52; elec engr, Southern Res Inst, 52-55; from asst prof to prof elec eng, Ga Inst Technol, 55-84. *Concurrent Pos:* Instr, Univ Ala, 54 & Redstone Arsenal, 55; consult, Lockheed Ga Corp, 77 & 80-81 & Sci Atlanta Inc, 78-79; prin investr, NSF grant, 81-83; consult, Lockheed Ga Corp, 84-85. *Mem:* Inst Elec & Electronics Engrs; Sigma Xi. *Res:* Instrumentation; application of random processes; computer applications; systems theory; digital communication systems; design of local computer networks. *Mailing Add:* Elec & Comput Eng Dept Clemson Univ 207 Riggs Hall Clemson SC 29634-0915

HAMMOND, LUTHER CARLISLE, WATER & SOLUTE TRANSPORT, CROP WATER PRODUCTION FUNCTIONS. *Current Pos:* from asst prof & asst soil physicist to prof & soil physicist, 50-92, EMER PROF SOILS, UNIV FLA, 92- *Personal Data:* b Seneca, SC, Jan 17, 21; m 47, Dorothy Swanson; c 4. *Educ:* Clemson Univ, BS, 42; Iowa State Univ, MS, 47, PhD, 49. *Mem:* Fel AAAS; Am Soc Agron; Soil Sci Soc Am; Am Geophys Union. *Res:* Soil-water-plant relationships; irrigation water management; crop-water production functions; water and solute transport in soils; modeling water balance; plant water use efficiency; soil spatial variability. *Mailing Add:* 1018 SW 25th Pl Gainesville FL 32601

HAMMOND, MARTIN L, materials science, for more information see previous edition

HAMMOND, MARVIN H, JR, ELECTRICAL ENGINEERING. *Current Pos:* MGR ELEC ENG, BATTELLE MEM INST, 76- *Personal Data:* b Great Bend, Kans, Sept 28, 39; m 66; c 2. *Educ:* Kans State Univ, BSEE & BS(math), 62, MS, 63; Ohio State Univ, PhD(elec eng), 68. *Prof Exp:* Mem tech staff, NAm Rockwell Corp, Ohio, 65-69 & Inst Defense Anal, 69-76. *Mem:* Inst Elec & Electronics Engrs; Nat Soc Prof Engrs; Sigma Xi. *Res:* Optimal control systems; pattern recognition; guidance and control systems. *Mailing Add:* 11691 Benngtn Woods Rd Reston VA 22090

HAMMOND, MARY ELIZABETH HALE, IMMUNOPATHOLOGY. *Current Pos:* DIR EM LAB, LDS HOSP, 77-, CHMN, PATH DEPT, 92; PROF PATH, COL MED, UNIV UTAH, 90- *Personal Data:* b Salt Lake City, Utah, Jan 5, 42; m 64, John M; c Jonathan H, Thomas H & Kathleen H. *Educ:* Univ Utah, BS, 63, MD, 67. *Prof Exp:* Intern path, Univ Hosp, Univ Utah, 67-68; fel tumor biol, Karolinska Inst, Sweden, 68-69; resident path, Mass Gen Hosp, 70-73, fel immunopath, 73-74, asst path, 74-77. *Concurrent Pos:* Teaching fel, Harvard Med Sch, 70-74, instr, 74-76, asst prof, 76-77; Am Cancer Soc res scholar, 74-77; from asst prof to assoc prof path, Col Med, Univ Utah, 77-90; dir EM LAB, Vet Admin Ctr, 84-87; cardiac pathologist, Utah Cardiac Transplant Prog, 85- *Mem:* Am Asn Immunologists; Am Asn Pathologists; Col Am Path; Am Soc Clin Path; Int Acad Path; Int Soc Heart Lung Transplant; Transplantation Soc. *Res:* Role of macrophage in cell mediated and tumor immunity, especially related to cell membrane surface changes; role of clotting system in cell mediated immunity; ultrastructure of human tumors; immunopathology of tumors, hearts and kidney; ultrastructure of heart and kidney disease; immunopathology of transplantation, especially heart, kidney and liver. *Mailing Add:* EM Lab LDS Hosp Eighth Ave & C St Salt Lake City UT 84143

HAMMOND, PAUL B, toxicology, for more information see previous edition

HAMMOND, PAUL ELLSWORTH, GEOLOGY. *Current Pos:* from asst prof to assoc prof, 63-90, PROF GEOL, PORTLAND STATE UNIV, 90- *Personal Data:* b Oakland, Calif, Jan 28, 29; m 56; c 3. *Educ:* Univ Colo, AB, 52; Univ Calif, Los Angeles, MA, 58; Univ Wash, PhD(geol), 63. *Prof Exp:* Mining geologist, Northern Pac Rwy Co, 56-60. *Mem:* Geol Soc Am; Geol Soc London; Am Geophys Union. *Res:* Volcanic stratigraphy; structure of volcanic rock terrain; geology of the Pacific Northwest and of geothermal resources. *Mailing Add:* Geol Dept Portland State Univ PO Box 751 Portland OR 97207-0751

HAMMOND, R PHILIP, SEAWATER DESALINATION, NUCLEAR SAFETY. *Current Pos:* CONSULT, 86-; HEAD DESIGN TEAM, ADV SEAWATER EVAPORATORS, METROP WATER DIST SCALIF. *Personal Data:* b Creston, Iowa, May 28, 16; m 41; c 4. *Educ:* Univ Southern Calif, BS, 38; Univ Chicago, PhD(inorg chem), 47. *Prof Exp:* Chief chemist, Lindsay Chem Co, Ill, 38-46; mem staff, Los Alamos Sci Lab, 47-58, asst dir, Reactor Div, 58-64; dir nuclear desalination prog, Oak Ridge Nat Lab, 62-74; energy staff, R & D Assocs, 74-86. *Concurrent Pos:* Adv, US Deleg, Geneva Conf Peaceful Uses Atomic Energy, 55, 64 & 71; adj prof eng, Univ Calif, Los Angeles, 85- *Mem:* Am Nuclear Soc. *Res:* Design, engineering and economics of nuclear reactors and sea water evaporators; mobile fuel reactors; nuclear fuel reprocessing; effect of energy on environment; fusion energy process from underground containment of thermonuclear reactions, storage of nuclear waste, and energy storage systems; nuclear power plant safety; ocean thermal energy; liquid nitrogen automobile; chill-vent filter system; marine structures; engineering systems; design of ultra-efficient, compact seawater distillation plant. *Mailing Add:* PO Box 1735 Santa Monica CA 90406. *E-Mail:* hammondp@worldnet.att.net

HAMMOND, RAY KENNETH, BIOCHEMISTRY, MICROBIOLOGY. *Current Pos:* from asst prof to assoc prof, 72-86, vpres & dean students, 88-93, PROF BIOL & BIOCHEM, CENT COL, 86-, DIR ATHLETICS, HEALTH & RECREATION, 93- *Personal Data:* b Lake Charles, La, Oct 3, 43; m 66, Carolyn Gray; c Jason & Drew. *Educ:* Cent Col, BS, 65; Univ Ky, PhD(biochem), 69. *Prof Exp:* Res assoc biochem, Mich State Univ, 70-72. *Concurrent Pos:* Vis prof biol, Silliman Univ, Philippines, 80-81; vis prof biochem, Sch Med, St Georges Univ, WI, 81-83; vis lectr, Chulalongkorn Univ, Bangkok, Thailand, 86. *Mem:* Nat Asn Adv Health Professions; Nat Sci Teachers Asn. *Res:* Microbial degradation of agricultural pesticides and function of lipids in insect development; metabolism of yeast phosphoinositides; exercise biochemistry. *Mailing Add:* 600 W Walnut St Cent Coll Danville KY 40422

HAMMOND, ROBERT BRUCE, SOLID STATE PHYSICS, SUPERCONDUCTORS & SEMICONDUCTORS. *Current Pos:* VPRES, SUPERCONDUCTOR TECHNOLOGIES INC, 87- *Personal Data:* b Bethesda, Md, Mar 27, 48; m 87, Christine A Seeman. *Educ:* Calif Inst Technol, BS, 71, MS, 72, PhD(appl physics), 75. *Prof Exp:* Staff physicist laser physics, USAF Weapons Lab, NMex, 75-76; dep group leader, electronics res, Los Alamos Sci Lab, Univ Calif, 76-87. *Mem:* Am Phys Soc; Inst Elec & Electronics Engrs. *Res:* Study of excitons and electron-hole liquid in semiconductors; photoluminescence studies of impurities and defects in semiconductors; thermo-electric power of semiconductors; picosecond photoconductivity and device applications; microwave superconductivity. *Mailing Add:* Superconductor Technologies Inc 460-F Ward Dr Santa Barbara CA 93111. *Fax:* 805-683-8527

HAMMOND, ROBERT GRENFELL, MATHEMATICS. *Current Pos:* ASSOC PROF MATH, UTAH STATE UNIV, 56- *Personal Data:* b Portland, Ore, Feb 14, 17; m 43; c 3. *Educ:* Utah State Univ, BS, 48, MS, 52. *Concurrent Pos:* NSF fels, Univ Wyo, 59 & Harvard Univ, 60-61. *Mem:* Math Asn Am. *Res:* Development of teaching methods of mathematics in college and secondary school; logics; fundamental concepts of mathematics. *Mailing Add:* 8266 Yarrow Ct Arvada CO 80005-2530

HAMMOND, ROBERT HUGH, PHYSICS. *Current Pos:* CONSULT, 90- *Personal Data:* b Fullerton, Calif, May 11, 30; m 55; c 3. *Educ:* Univ Calif, Berkeley, BS, 53, PhD(physics), 60. *Prof Exp:* Res & develop staff mem, Gen Atomic Div, Gen Dynamics Corp, 60-68; physicist, Lawrence Radiation Lab, Univ Calif, 68-71; sr res physicist, Stanford Univ, 71-90. *Concurrent Pos:* Lectr, Univ Calif, Berkeley, 67-71. *Mem:* Am Phys Soc. *Res:* Solid state and low temperature physics; superconductivity; nuclear magnetic resonance; thin films; synthesis of new superconducting materials. *Mailing Add:* Ginzton Physics Lab Stanford Univ Stanford CA 94305. *Fax:* 650-725-2533; *E-Mail:* hammond@sierrastanford.edu

HAMMOND, SALLY KATHARINE, OCCUPATIONAL HEALTH, INDUSTRIAL HYGIENE. *Current Pos:* asst prof, 85-89, ASSOC PROF, MED SCH, UNIV MASS, 89-, DIR, ENVIRON HEALTH DIV, 93- *Personal Data:* b Philadelphia, Pa, Feb 6, 49; m 72. *Educ:* Oberlin Col, BA, 71; Brandeis Univ, PhD(inorg chem), 76; Harvard Sch Pub Health, MS, 81. *Prof Exp:* Instr chem, physics, meteorol & astron, Boston Univ, 75-76; asst prof chem, Wheaton Col, 76-80; res assoc, Harvard Sch Pub Health, 80-84. *Concurrent Pos:* Vis investr, New Eng Aquarium, 75-; lectr indust hyg, Harvard Sch Pub Health, 85-, mem, Chem Substance Threshold Limit Valve Comt, 92- *Mem:* Am Chem Soc; AAAS; Am Indust Hyg Asn; Am Coun Govt Indust Hygienists; Am Pub Health Asn; Int Soc Exposure Anal. *Res:* Occupational health; effects of various industrial chemicals on workers; solvents; polycyclic aramatic compounds; epidemiological studies; methods of sample collection and analysis; environmental tobacco smoke; diesel exhaust. *Mailing Add:* Dept Family & Community Med Med Sch Univ 55 LakeAve N Worcester MA 01655-0002. *Fax:* 508-856-1212; *E-Mail:* khammond@umassmed.ummed.edu

HAMMOND, WILLIAM EDWARD, biomedical engineering, computer sciences, for more information see previous edition

HAMMOND, WILLIAM MARION, COMMUNICATIONS, COMPUTER SYSTEMS. *Current Pos:* PROF ELEC ENG, BRADLEY UNIV, 66- , DIR TECHNOL CTR, 85- *Personal Data:* b South Bend, Ind, Nov 24, 30; m 59, 88; c 3. *Educ:* Purdue Univ, BSEE, 57, PhD(elec eng), 66; Bradley Univ, MSEE, 60. *Prof Exp:* Asst prof elec eng, Bradley Univ, 57-63; instr, Purdue Univ, 63-66. *Concurrent Pos:* Consult, Surface Radar Br, Apparatus Div, Tex Instruments, Inc, Tex, 66-67; prin investr, NASA contracts, 67-68; dir & res adv, Continental Mgt Co, Ill, 68-71; pres & mem, Bd Dirs, Comput Corp Am, 69-71 & ADS, Inc, 74-; NSF grant, 71-72; consult, Caterpillar Tractor Co, 73-85. *Mem:* Am Soc Eng Educ; Inst Elec & Electronics Engrs. *Res:* Statistical communications; microelectronics; computer application systems. *Mailing Add:* 333 Job St Bradley Univ Peoria IL 61625-0002

HAMMOND, WILLIS BURDETTE, COMPUTATIONAL CHEMISTRY, POLYMER MODELING. *Current Pos:* sr res chemist, 75-81, RES ASSOC, ALLIED CORP, 81- *Personal Data:* b Truman, Minn, Sept 29, 42; m 71; c 2. *Educ:* Northwestern Univ, BA, 64; Columbia Univ, MA, 66, PhD(chem), 67. *Prof Exp:* NIH fel, Calif Inst Technol, 67-68; asst prof chem, Yale Univ, 68-75. *Mem:* AAAS; Am Chem Soc. *Res:* Organic photochemistry; organic spectroscopy; laser chemistry; polymer characterization; organic spectroscopy; polymer characterization; organic photochemistry; currently developing computer modeling of polymers for purpose of predicting polymer structures and properties; spectroscopic characterization of polymers with special emphasis on nuclear magnetic resonance, organic synthesis and organic photochemistry. *Mailing Add:* 128 Center Ave Chatham NJ 07928

HAMMONS, JAMES HUTCHINSON, PHYSICAL ORGANIC CHEMISTRY. *Current Pos:* from instr to assoc prof, 64-76, chmn dept, 76-81, PROF CHEM, SWARTHMORE COL, 76- *Personal Data:* b Chicago, Ill, Aug 8, 34; m 56, Elisabeth Netherwood; c Laura N & James B. *Educ:* Amherst Col, BA, 56; Johns Hopkins Univ, MA, 58, PhD(chem), 62. *Prof Exp:* Fel chem, Univ Southern Calif, 62-63 & Univ Calif, Berkeley, 63-64. *Concurrent Pos:* Fel, Swiss Fed Inst Technol, 68-69; vis res prof, Univ Calif, Berkeley, 72-73 & Univ Geneva, Switz, 77-78; vis fel, Yale Univ, 81-82; NSF Sci Fac Develop Grant, 81-82; vis res prof, Univ Wash, 89. *Res:* Molecular orbital theory; electron spin resonance; Jahn-Teller distortions of organic radicals and radical ions. *Mailing Add:* Dept Chem Swarthmore Col 500 College Ave Swarthmore PA 19081-1390. *Fax:* 610-328-7355; *E-Mail:* jhammonl@cc.swarthmore.edu

HAMMONS, RAY OTTO, GENETICS, AGRONOMY. *Current Pos:* RETIRED. *Personal Data:* b Miss, Oct 2, 19; m 42; c 4. *Educ:* Miss State Univ, BS, 47, MS, 48; NC State Univ, PhD(agron), 53. *Honors & Awards:* Golden Peanut Res Award, Nat Peanut Coun, 75. *Prof Exp:* Res instr peanut radiation genetics, NC State Univ, 49-53, assoc genetics, 52-53; asst prof forage breeding, Purdue Univ, 53-55; geneticist, Agr Res Serv, USDA, 55-63, res geneticist, 63-72, tech adv peanuts, 73-81, res leader crops, 72-84, supvry res geneticist, 75-84; collabr, Agr Res Serv, USDA, 84-87; consult, Univ Ga, 89-. *Concurrent Pos:* Assoc prof, Univ Ga, 55-84, mem grad fac, 59-82; plant explorer, SAm, 68; agr consult, USAID, West Pakistan, 71; ed, Peanut Res, 72-82; consult, Int Progs Div, USDA, Israel, India & Pakistan, 73; assoc ed, Agron J, Am Soc Agron, 75-77; vis scientist award, Am Soc Agron, 81-82; consult, UN Conference Trade & Develop, Geneva & Rome, 80 & Int Crops Res Inst Semi-Arid Tropics, India, 79, 80 & 84; assoc ed, Peanut Sci, Am Peanut Res & Educ Soc, 79-85 & Crop Sci, Crop Sci Soc Am, 81-84; UN Food & Agr Orgn deleg, Int Symp Groundnut, Africa, Gambia, 82. *Mem:* Fel Am Soc Agron; fel Crop Sci Soc Am; Am Genetic Asn; fel Am Peanut Res Educ Soc; Sigma Xi. *Res:* Peanut genetics, breeding, origin, history; evolutionary development in Arachis; production research on tobacco, ornamentals, tomato and peanuts. *Mailing Add:* 1203 Lake Dr Tifton GA 31794

HAMMOSH, MAMOUN AHMED, BOUNDARY ELEMENT ANALYSIS, FINITE ELEMENT METHOD. *Current Pos:* PROF MATH, DAMASCUS UNIV, 86- *Personal Data:* b Damascus, Syria, June 19, 62; m 86, Zoubida B Smsmieh; c Asma, Aeshah, Moaz & Kadejah. *Educ:* Univ Damascus, Syria, BSc(math) & BSc(civil eng), 85; Okla State Univ, MSc, 88, MSc, 89; Univ Ark, PhD(math), 93. *Concurrent Pos:* Specialist engr bridge design, Tech Inst Bridge Eng, 86- *Res:* Dynamical systems and functional integro-differential equations with delay studying the parameter dependence of those systems. *Mailing Add:* Col Civil Eng Univ Damascus Damascus Syria

HAMNER, CHARLES EDWARD, JR, BIOCHEMISTRY, VETERINARY MEDICINE. *Current Pos:* asst prof exp surg & dir vivarium, Univ Va, 64-67, assoc prof obstet & gynec, 67-77, from asst vpres to assoc vpres Health Serv, 77-88, PROF OBSTET & GYNEC, SCH MED, UNIV VA, 77- *Personal Data:* b Schuyler, Va, Mar 26, 35; m 61; c Cliff & Diana. *Educ:* Va Polytech Inst, BS, 56; Univ Ga, DVM, 60, MS, 62, PhD(biochem), 64. *Honors & Awards:* Res Career Develop Award, NIH, 71. *Concurrent Pos:* Morris Animal Found fel, Univ Ga, 60-61, Nat Inst Gen Med Sci fel, 61-64; consult, Pharmaceut Res & Develop Mgt, WHO, NIH, 71-; dir prog coord, A H Robins Co, 74-77; pres, NC Biotechnol Ctr, 88- *Mem:* Soc Study Reproduction; Drug Info Asn; Brit Soc Study Fertil; AAAS. *Res:* Sperm metabolism, composition of female reproductive tract secretions; drug development; industrial management. *Mailing Add:* NC Biotechnol Ctr PO Box 13547 Research Triangle Park NC 27709-3457. *Fax:* 919-549-9544

HAMNER, MARTIN E, PHARMACY. *Current Pos:* prof & chmn dept, Univ Tenn, Memphis, 59-63, assoc dean, Col Pharm, 63-81, actg dean, 75, prof, 83-88, EMER PROF PHARMACEUT, UNIV TENN, MEMPHIS, 88. *Personal Data:* b Castor, La, July 28, 18; m 46; c 3. *Educ:* Univ Colo, BS, 49, MS, 51, PhD(pharm), 55. *Prof Exp:* Instr pharm, Univ Fla, 51-53 & Univ Colo, 53-55; assoc prof, Southwestern State Col, Okla, 55-59. *Concurrent Pos:* Parenteral & Sterilr Prod Lab, 86-88. *Mem:* Am Asn Col Pharm; Am Pharmaceut Asn. *Res:* Bacteriology and antibiotics with emphasis on synergism and drug action; larvae and larvicidal agents; tracer studies on contamination and cleaning of contact lenses; completation retinoic acid with cyclodextrims. *Mailing Add:* 4806 Craigmont Dr Memphis TN 38128

HAMNER, WILLIAM FREDERICK, POLYMER CHEMISTRY, ENVIRONMENTAL REGULATIONS. *Current Pos:* HEAD, PERMITTING BR, HAZARDOUS WASTE SECT, NC DEPT ENVIRON HEALTH & NATURAL RESOURCES, 84- *Personal Data:* b Pharr, Tex, Sept 25, 22; m 49; c William F III, Marie D, Mary C & Martha G. *Educ:* Centenary Col, BS, 43; Univ Tex, MA, 47, PhD(phys chem), 50. *Prof Exp:* Asst prof phys chem, Univ Ala, 49-51; res chemist, Monsanto Co, 51-52; from asst res group leader to res group leader, 52-59, res sect leader, 59-63, group leader, Chemstrand Res Ctr, 63-65, mgr, 65-74, mgr res & develop, 74-80, mgr tech serv & phys sci, Monsanto Triangle Park Develop Ctr, 80- 84. *Mem:* Am Chem Soc; Am Inst Chem; Sigma Xi. *Res:* Spectroscopy; instrumental analysis; textiles and fibers; synthetic turf; research and development of synthetic recreational surfaces, polyurethane chemistry, analytical chemistry. *Mailing Add:* 724 Catawba St Raleigh NC 27609

HAMOLSKY, MILTON WILLIAM, INTERNAL MEDICINE. *Current Pos:* PROF MED, BROWN UNIV, 63-; DIR, DIV MED RES, RI HOSP, 75- *Personal Data:* b Lynn, Mass, May 25, 21; m 45, 79; c 3. *Educ:* Harvard Univ, AB, 43, Harvard Med Sch, MD, 46; Am Bd Internal Med, dipl, 56. *Prof Exp:* Asst med, Beth Israel Hosp, 51-52; from asst to asst prof, Harvard Med Sch, 52-63. *Concurrent Pos:* Assoc med res, Beth Israel Hosp, 52-63, head, Endocrine Clin, 58-63, asst vis physician, 57-59, assoc vis physician, 59-63, consult, 63-; tutor, Harvard Med Sch, 57-62, lectr, 63; vis res asst prof, Brandeis Univ, 58-59; physician-in-chief, Med Serv, RI Hosp, 63-; consult, Miriam Hosp, Roger Williams Hosp, Bradley Hosp & Vet Admin Hosp, 63-; chief, Dept Med, Women & Infants Hosp, 81- *Mem:* AAAS; Am Physiol Soc; fel Am Col Physicians; Am Soc Clin Invest; Am Thyroid Asn; Endocrine Soc. *Res:* Endocrinology; clinical thyroid physiology; biochemistry; pathology. *Mailing Add:* RI Dept Health Providence RI 02908

HAMON, AVAS BURDETTE, COCCOIDEA, ALEYRODIDAE. *Current Pos:* TAXON ENTOMOLOGIST, DEPT AGR & CONSUMER SERV, FLA, 76- *Personal Data:* b Ripley WVa, Mar 8, 40; m 65. *Educ:* Morris Harvey Col, BS, 68; Marshall Univ, MS, 69; Va Polytech Inst & State Univ,

PhD(entom), 76. *Concurrent Pos:* Adj asst prof, Dept Entom & Nematol, Univ Fla, 78- *Mem:* Entom Soc Am; Sigma Xi; Am Registry Prof Entomologists. *Res:* Taxonomy and systematics of Coccoidea and Aleyrodidae. *Mailing Add:* 2030 NW 14th Ave Gainesville FL 32605

HAMON, J HILL, AVIAN ANATOMY, PALEONTOLOGY. *Current Pos:* PROF BIOL, TRANSYLVANIA UNIV, 68-, CHMN BIOL DEPT, 87- *Personal Data:* b Junction City, Ky, July 30, 31; m 51; c 3. *Educ:* East Ky State Col, BS, 52; Univ Ky, MS, 53; Univ Fla, PhD(biol), 61. *Prof Exp:* Asst prof biol, Jacksonville Univ, 60-61; assoc prof, Ind State Univ, 61-68. *Mem:* Sigma Xi. *Res:* Avian anatomy and paleontology; history and philosophy of science. *Mailing Add:* Div Natural Sci & Math Transylvania Univ 300 N Broadway Lexington KY 40508-1797

HAMOR, GLENN HERBERT, MEDICINAL CHEMISTY. *Current Pos:* from asst prof to prof, 52-88, EMER PROF PHARMACEUT CHEM, UNIV SOUTHERN CALIF, 88- *Personal Data:* b Kootenai, Idaho, May 14, 20; m 47, Eileen Deegan; c Patricia, Ellen, Kathleen & Timothy. *Educ:* Univ Mont, BS, 41, MS, 47; Univ Minn, PhD(pharmaceut chem), 52. *Prof Exp:* Instr pharm, Univ Mont, 47-48; asst, Univ Minn, 48-51. *Concurrent Pos:* Cotrell res grant, 53-54; Pfeiffer Mem res fel, Univ Trieste, 66-67; vis prof, Sch Pharm, Trinity Col, Dublin, Ireland, 81-82. *Mem:* Fel AAAS; Am Chem Soc; Am Pharmaceut Asn; Am Asn Col Pharm. *Res:* Synthesis of medicinally active pharmaceutical agents; design of enzyme inhibitors; antiinflammatory, antiepileptic and sweetening agents; heterocyclic chemistry; histidine decarboxylase; inhibition of histamine biosynthesis; literary perceptions of pharmacists. *Mailing Add:* 6519 W 87th St Los Angeles CA 90045

HAMORI, EUGENE, BIOCHEMISTRY, PHYSICAL CHEMISTRY. *Current Pos:* PROF BIOCHEM, SCH MED, TULANE UNIV, 82- *Personal Data:* b Gyor, Hungary, Aug 27, 33; US citizen; m 58; c 2. *Educ:* Sci Univ Budapest, dipl chem, 56; Univ Pa, PhD(phys chem), 64. *Prof Exp:* Asst prof chem, Univ Del, 66-72. *Concurrent Pos:* NIH grant biophys chem, Cornell Univ, 64-66; vis prof, Max-Planck Inst Biophys Chem, Goettingen, WGer, 79-80. *Mem:* Am Chem Soc; NY Acad Sci; Am Soc Biol Chemists; Biophys Soc. *Res:* Nucleic acids; kinetics of conformation changes of biopolymers; computer study of DNA sequences. *Mailing Add:* Dept Biochem Tulane Univ Sch Med 1430 Tulane Ave New Orleans LA 70112. *E-Mail:* eha@bioc.tulane.edu

HAMOSH, MARGIT, PHYSIOLOGY & BIOCHEMISTRY, DEVELOPMENTAL BIOLOGY. *Current Pos:* res assoc, 74-78, assoc prof pediat, 78-84, PROF PEDIAT, MED SCH, GEORGETOWN UNIV, 84-, CHIEF, DIV DEVELOP BIOL NUTRIT, 88- *Personal Data:* b Dresden, Ger, Aug 13, 33; US citizen; m 54, Paul; c Ada, Leora & Tamar. *Educ:* Hebrew Univ, Israel, MSc, 56, PhD(biochem), 59. *Prof Exp:* Fel biochem, Hadassah Med Sch, Hebrew Univ, Israel, 59-61, from instr to asst prof biochem, 61-65; sabbatical, NIMH, Bethesda, Md, 65-67, vis scientist endocrinol, NIH, Nat Inst Arthritis & Metab Dis, 67-74. *Concurrent Pos:* Mem, Pulmonary Dis Adv Comt, NIH, 80-84; Pediat Coun, Am Col Nutrit, 82-84; Coun Perinatal Res Soc; Nat Res Rev Comt, Am Thoracic Soc, 84-90 & Maternal & Child Health Res Comt, Nat Inst Child Health & Human Develop, NIH, 86-90; Proj Hope adv, Poland, 85; Heritage prof, Alta, Can, 86; chair, Subcomt Nutrit during Lactation, Nat Acad Sci, 88-90; mem, Comt Nutrit During Pregnancy & Lactation, Nat Acad Sci, 89-91. *Mem:* Am Physiol Soc; Endocrine Soc; Soc Exp Biol & Med; Am Fedn Clin Res; Am Thoracic Soc; Perinatal Res Soc; Am Inst Nutrit; Am Col Nutrit; Am Soc Clin Nutrit; Int Soc Res Human Milk Lactation (pres, 88-90). *Res:* Developmental physiology; lipid transport; development of digestive functions; lung maturation; endocrine control of organ development; role of lipoprotein lipase in lipid uptake by extrahepatic tissues; lipid digestion and clearing of lipids from the circulation system; biologic and nutritional aspects of milk (human and other species); developmental biology. *Mailing Add:* Pediat 2 PHC Med Ctr Georgetown Univ 3800 Reservoir Rd NW Washington DC 20007. *Fax:* 202-687-7757

HAMOSH, PAUL, NEUROSCIENCES, NUTRITION. *Current Pos:* from asst prof to assoc prof, 72-85, PROF PHYSIOL BIOPHYS & PEDIAT, GEORGETOWN UNIV, 85- *Personal Data:* b Subotica, Yugoslavia, Apr 4, 31; US citizen; m 54, Margit Segenreich; c Ada, Leora & Tamar. *Educ:* Hebrew Univ, Jerusalem, MD, 59. *Prof Exp:* Resident, Hadassa Univ Hosp, Jerusalem, 58-63; fel hematol, Tel Aviv Munic Univ Hosp, 63-65; fel respiration, Georgetown Univ & Vet Admin Hosp, Washington, DC, 65-68; res assoc hemodynamics, Vet Admin Hosp, Washington, DC, 68-70; asst prof med, George Washington Univ, 70-72. *Concurrent Pos:* Dir, Pulmonary Function Lab, Vet Admin Hosp, Washington, DC, 69-72, Dept Pediat, Georgetown Univ Hosp, 80-84. *Mem:* Am Physiol Soc; Biophys Soc; Am Fedn Clin Res; Int Asn Study Lung Cancer; fel AAAS. *Res:* Respiration physiology, control and mechanics; infant digestion: lipases in human milk and upper gastrointestinal tract; lung metabolism and hormonal control of lung maturation; neurotransmitters. *Mailing Add:* Sch Med Georgetown Univ 3900 Reservoir Rd NW Washington DC 20007. *E-Mail:* hamoshp@medlib.georgetown.edu

HAMPAR, BERGE, VIROLOGY, ADMINISTRATION. *Current Pos:* PRES, BIO-MOLECULAR TECH, INC, 86- *Personal Data:* b New York, NY, Aug 20, 32; div. *Educ:* Columbia Univ, BA, 54, DDS, 60; Univ Baltimore, JD, 84. *Prof Exp:* Res microbiologist, NIH, 62-67, asst chief, Lab Molecular Virol & head, Microbiol Sect, 75-81, dent dir, Nat Cancer Inst, 67-86, gen mgr, Frederick Cancer Res Fac, 81-86. *Concurrent Pos:* Res fel microbiol, Columbia Univ, 60-62, USPHS fel, 60-63; head, Solid-Tumor Virus Sect, Nat Cancer Inst, 73-75. *Mem:* Am Asn Immunologists; Am Soc Virol. *Res:* Herpes viruses with emphasis on immunology, biological properties, oncogenesis and genetics; biology of cell transformation; monoclonal antibodies to virion and non-virion antigens. *Mailing Add:* Bio-Molecular Tech Inc 5340 Spectrum Dr Frederick MD 21703. *Fax:* 301-695-0824

HAMPARIAN, VINCENT, VIROLOGY. *Current Pos:* EXEC DIR, CHILDREN'S HOSP RES FOUND, 73- *Personal Data:* b New York, NY, July 30, 27; m 55; c 4. *Educ:* Wayne State Univ, BA, 50, MS, 51; Univ Pa, PhD(med microbiol), 58. *Prof Exp:* Instr pub health & prev med, Univ Pa, 58; res assoc virol, Chas Pfizer & Co, 58; res assoc, Merck Inst Therapeut Res, Pa, 58-64; prod pediat & med microbiol, Col Med, Ohio State Univ, 64-, prof emer. *Concurrent Pos:* Mem res staff, Children's Hosp, Philadelphia, 58; mem, Res Resources Comt, Nat Inst Allergy & Infectious Dis, 67-71, chmn, 70-71. *Mem:* AAAS; Am Asn Immunol; Am Soc Microbiol. *Res:* Respiratory viruses; immunology and serology, particularly laboratory diagnosis of viral infections. *Mailing Add:* Res Serv Children's Hosp 700 Childrens Dr Columbus OH 43205-2696

HAMPEL, ARNOLD E, BIOCHEMISTRY, MOLECULAR BIOLOGY. *Current Pos:* asst prof to assoc prof, 70-78, PROF BIOL & CHEM, NORTHERN ILL UNIV, 78- *Personal Data:* b Burlington, Ill, Sept 10, 39; m 62; c 3. *Educ:* Northern Ill Univ, BS, 63; Univ Wis-Madison, PhD(biochem), 69. *Prof Exp:* Fel, Los Alamos Nat Lab, Univ Calif, 69-70. *Concurrent Pos:* NIH career develop award, 72; vis assoc prof, Salk Inst, 75-76; vis prof, Univ Calif Davis, 85-86. *Mem:* AAAS; Am Chem Soc; Biophys Soc; Am Soc Biochem & Molecular Biol. *Res:* Catalytic RNA, the "Hairpin" Ribozyme. *Mailing Add:* Dept Biol Sci & Chem Northern Ill Univ De Kalb IL 60115-2854. *Fax:* 815-753-0461

HAMPEL, CLIFFORD ALLEN, CHEMISTRY. *Current Pos:* CONSULT CHEM ENGR, 58- *Personal Data:* b Minneapolis, Minn, Mar 15, 12; m 35; c 1. *Educ:* Univ Minn, BChE, 34. *Prof Exp:* Res chemist, Mathieson Alkali Works, Inc, NY, 36-42 & Diamond Alkali Co, Ohio, 42-43; res scientist, Manhattan Dist Proj, SAM Labs, Columbia Univ, 43-44; res chemist, Minn Mining & Mfg Co, 44-45; asst chief chemist, Cardox Corp, Ill, 45-46; chem engr, Armour Res Found, Ill Inst Technol, 46-48, supvr inorg technol, 48-49, extraction metall, 49-52; consult chem engr, Ill, 52-53 & 55; proj engr, Morton Salt Co, 53-54; mgr, Chem Equip Div, Fansteel Metall Corp, Ill, 55-58. *Concurrent Pos:* Consult, USN & USCG, 47-49; lectr, Milan Polytech Univ, 50. *Mem:* Fel AAAS; Am Chem Soc; Electrochem Soc; fel Am Inst Chemists; Am Soc Metals. *Res:* Production and uses of chlorine compounds; equilibria in heterogeneous salt systems; industrial chemicals; electrochemical processes and products; sea water and natural salts; economic and market surveys on inorganic chemicals and metals; fluorine compounds; heavy chemicals; rare metals. *Mailing Add:* 169 Sunnyside Ave Crystal Lake IL 60014-5253

HAMPSON, MICHAEL CHISNALL, MYCOLOGY, HORTICULTURE. *Current Pos:* RETIRED. *Personal Data:* b Lancashire, Eng, July 29, 30; c 2. *Educ:* Univ Col NWales, BSc, 52, dipl educ, 53; McGill Univ, MSc, 60; Cornell Univ, PhD(plant path), 69. *Prof Exp:* Teacher sci, Eng, 56-58; community teacher, Govt Can, 60-61; photo tech, McGill Univ, 61-62; teaching specialist biol, Greater Montreal, 62-65; res scientist plant path, Agr Can Res Br, 69-97. *Concurrent Pos:* Lectr biol, Mem Univ NFld, 71-72; mem, Atlanta Comt Crops, 72-; adj prof biol, Mem Univ NFla. *Mem:* Am Phytopath Soc; Can Phytopath Soc; Sigma Xi; Mycol Soc Am; Brit Soc Plant Path. *Res:* Studies on the biological control and eradication of wart disease of potatoes and studies on the life-history and biology of its causal agent Synchtrium endobioticum. *Mailing Add:* 38 Long Pond Rd St John's NF A1B 1N7 Can. *Fax:* 709-772-6064; *E-Mail:* hampson@nfrssj.agr.va

HAMPSON, ROBERT F, JR, PHYSICAL CHEMISTRY. *Current Pos:* res chemist, Inorg Solids Div, 59-61, RES CHEMIST, PHYS CHEM DIV, NAT BUR STANDARDS, 61- *Personal Data:* b Washington, DC, May 4, 30; m 66; c 1. *Educ:* Cath Univ Am, AB, 51, MS, 57, PhD(chem), 59. *Prof Exp:* Res chemist, US Naval Propellant Plant, Md, 51-52. *Mem:* AAAS; Am Chem Soc; Am Phys Soc. *Res:* Vacuum-ultraviolet photochemistry; chemical kinetics; high-temperature and quantum chemistry. *Mailing Add:* 18913 Whetstone Circle Gaithersburg MD 20879

HAMPTON, CAROLYN HUTCHINS, ZOOLOGY, PARASITOLOGY. *Current Pos:* assoc prof, 70-76, PROF SCI EDUC, ECAROLINA UNIV, 76- *Personal Data:* b Burke Co, NC, Dec 11, 36; m 63; c 1. *Educ:* Appalachian State Teachers Col, BS, 59; Univ Tenn, MS, 61, PhD(zool), 63. *Honors & Awards:* Gustaf-Ohaus Award, Nat Sci Teachers Asn, 74. *Prof Exp:* Asst zool, Univ Tenn, 59-61, instr, Exten Sch, 62-63; asst prof biol, Charlotte Col, 63-65 & Longwood Col, 65-70. *Concurrent Pos:* Consult, NSF In-Serv Coop Prog High Sch Biol, 64-65 & Sch Sci Inst Coop Col, 69-70, dir, NSF Inst, 69-70 & NSF Implementation Proj, 74-75, partic, NSF Leadership Confs, 72 & 74; dir, Title I Community Serv grant, 74-77, Title IV-C ESEA grant, 79-82; NC State Dept Pub Instr, Summer Sci Inst Mid Sch Teachers, 83-85. *Mem:* Sigma Xi; Nat Sci Teachers Asn; Am Inst Biol Sci; Am Asn Univ Professors. *Res:* Environmental education; teaching materials; field equipment; biological education; marine education. *Mailing Add:* Dean Phys Ed ECarolina Univ 1000 W Fifth St Greenville NC 27834-3006

HAMPTON, CHARLES ROBERT, MATHEMATICS. *Current Pos:* asst prof, 72-79, assoc prof, 79-87, PROF MATH, COL WOOSTER, 87- *Personal Data:* b Weeksville, NC, July 22, 45; m 68; c 3. *Educ:* Univ Mich, BS, 67; Univ Wis, MA, 68, PhD(math), 72. *Prof Exp:* Teaching asst math, Univ Wis, 67-72. *Concurrent Pos:* Fulbright-Hays lectr, Liberia, West Africa, 77-78; vis scholar, Cambridge Univ, Eng, 84-85. *Mem:* Am Math Soc; Math Asn Am; Asn Christians in Math Sci. *Res:* Structure theory of group rings; philosophy of mathematics, particularly epistemological questions; mathematics in political science, particularly redistricting and gerrymandering issues. *Mailing Add:* Dept Math Col Wooster Wooster OH 44691. *E-Mail:* Hampton@acs.wooster.edu

HAMPTON, DAVID CLARK, ORGANIC CHEMISTRY, BIOCHEMISTRY. *Current Pos:* from asst prof to assoc prof, 62-72, CHMN DEPT, WARTBURG COL, 66-, OTTO DISTINGUISHED PROF CHEM, 72- *Personal Data:* b Mason City, Iowa, Nov 25, 34; m 57, Carolyn; c 2. *Educ:* St Olaf Col, BA, 56; Univ NDak, MS, 58; Purdue Univ, PhD(org chem), 63. *Prof Exp:* Instr chem, Luther Col, Iowa, 61-62. *Concurrent Pos:* Consult, North Cent Asn; researcher, Ore State Univ, 64, 65, Ind Univ, 66, Ames Res Labs, NASA, 70 & 71; prin investr, NASA, sr res grant, 72-73; chair, Iowa Sect, Am Chem Soc; bd dir, Iowa Acad Sci. *Mem:* AAAS; Am Chem Soc; Sigma Xi; Nat Asn Adv Health Professions; Int Union Pure & Appl Chem. *Res:* Organic reaction mechanisms; organosulfur, organic oxidation, organometallic and hydrocarbon chemistry; computers in chemical education. *Mailing Add:* Dept Chem Wartburg Col Waverly IA 50677. *Fax:* 319-352-8394; *E-Mail:* hampton@wartburg.edu

HAMPTON, DELON, CIVIL ENGINEERING. *Current Pos:* CHMN, DELON HAMPTON & ASSOCS, 73- *Personal Data:* b Jefferson, Tex, Aug 23, 33; m 93, Sonia M Guevara. *Educ:* Univ Ill, BSCE, 54; Purdue Univ, MSCE, 58, PhD(civil eng), 61. *Hon Degrees:* DEng, Purdue Univ, 94, DS, NJ Inst Technol, 96. *Prof Exp:* Instr civil eng, Prairie View Agr & Mech Col, 54-55; asst prof, Univ Kans, 61-64; sr res engr, IIT Res Inst, 64-68; prof, Howard Univ, 68-85. *Concurrent Pos:* Actg head soil mech res, E H Wang Civil Eng Res Facil, Univ NMex, 62-63; pvt consult, 68-70; pres, Gnaedinger Baker Hampton & Assocs, 70-74; mem, Hwy Res Bd, Nat Acad Sci-Nat Res Coun; mem, US Nat Comt Tunneling Technol, 76-78. *Mem:* Nat Acad Eng; hon mem Am Soc Civil Engrs; Am Soc Testing & Mat; Int Soc Soil Mech & Found Engrs; Am Pub Transit Asn; Am Soc Eng Educ. *Res:* Soil dynamics; stress wave propagation; dynamic properties of soils; foundation vibrations; soil properties; tunneling; pavement design. *Mailing Add:* Delon Hampton & Assocs 800 K St NW Suite 720 N Lobby Washington DC 20001. *Fax:* 202-371-2073

HAMPTON, JAMES WILBURN, HEMATOLOGY, MEDICAL ONCOLOGY. *Current Pos:* From clin asst to assoc prof, Univ Okla, 60-71, head hemat oncol, Col Med, 72-77, prof med, Sch Med, 71-77, head, Hemat Sect, 69-72, head, Hemat Lab, Okla Med Res Found, 71-77, dir med oncol, 77-83, CLIN PROF MED, SCII MED, UNIV OKLA, 77-, MED DIR CANCER CTR, SW BAPTIST MED CTR, 85- *Personal Data:* b Durant, Okla, Sept 15, 31; m 58, Carol; c Jaime, Clay, Diana (Locher) & Neal. *Educ:* Univ Okla, BA, 52, MD, 56. *Concurrent Pos:* NIH career develop award, 66-76; Angiol Res Found honors achievement award, 67-68; attend, Vet Admin Hosp, Oklahoma City 63-; consult, Tinker AFB Hosp, 65-; NIH chair, Network Cancer Control in Am Indians & Alaskan Natives, 90- *Mem:* Asn Am Pathologists; Cent Soc Clin Res; Am Soc Hemat; Am Physiol Soc; Am Psychosom Soc; Am Soc Clin Oncol; Sigma Xi; fel Am Col Physicians. *Res:* Physiology and pathophysiology of hemostasis, thrombosis, leukemia, multiple myeloma and paraneoplastic syndromes; epidemiology of cancer in native Americans. *Mailing Add:* Baptist Med Ctr 3366 NW Expressway Suite 200 Oklahoma City OK 73112-4414

HAMPTON, JOHN KYLE, JR, PHYSIOLOGY. *Current Pos:* RETIRED. *Personal Data:* b Okalona, Miss, Nov 9, 23; m 44, 61; c 1. *Educ:* Millsaps Col, BS, 47; Tulane Univ, PhD(physiol), 49. *Prof Exp:* From instr to prof physiol, Tulane Univ, 49-66; prof & mem, Univ Tex Dent Sci Inst & prof, Grad Sch Biomed Sci, Houston, 66-73; prof biol & chmn dept, Adelphi Univ, 73-76; head dept, Calif Polytech State Univ, San Luis Obispo, Calif, 76-83, prof, Biol Sci Dept, 76-89. *Concurrent Pos:* Markle scholar, 51-56. *Mem:* AAAS; Am Physiol Soc; Geront Soc Am; Am Geront Soc. *Res:* Primatology; reproductive biology; gerontology. *Mailing Add:* 20213 Rimrock Rd Monroe WA 98272

HAMPTON, LOYD DONALD, PHYSICS, OCEANOGRAPHY. *Current Pos:* Res physicist, Univ Tex, Austin, 51-65, head, Signal Physics Br, 65-70, asst dir, 70-75, assoc dir, 75-80, DIR, APPL RES LAB, UNIV TEX, AUSTIN, 80- *Personal Data:* b Santa Anna, Tex, Aug 23, 30; m 58; c 2. *Educ:* Univ Tex, BS, 52, MA, 59; Tex A&M Univ, PhD(phys oceanog), 67. *Mem:* Sigma Xi; fel Acoust Soc Am. *Res:* Acoustics; underwater sound; physical oceanography. *Mailing Add:* 6507 River Pl Blvd No 1 Austin TX 78730

HAMPTON, RAYMOND EARL, plant pathology; deceased, see previous edition for last biography

HAMPTON, RICHARD OWEN, PLANT PATHOLOGY. *Current Pos:* RETIRED. *Personal Data:* b Dalhart, Tex, Feb 17, 30; m 54, Willa M Johnson; c Kevin R & Audrey C. *Educ:* Univ Ark, BSAgr, 51; Iowa State Univ, MS, 54, PhD(plant path), 57. *Honors & Awards:* Meritorious Serv Award, Nat Pea Improv Asn, 91. *Prof Exp:* Teaching asst, Iowa State Univ, 52-54, res asst, 54-57; asst plant pathologist, Irrig Agr Res & Exten Ctr, Wash State Univ, 57-61; res plant pathologist, Irrig Agr Res & Exten Ctr, Agr Res Serv, USDA, Wash, 61-65, Dept Bot & Plant Path, Agr Res Serv, 65-95. *Concurrent Pos:* Asst plant path, virol, seed-borne viruses, germplasm-born viruses & genetic resistance to viruses, Third World. *Mem:* Am Phytopath Soc; Int Soc Plant Pathologists. *Res:* Virus-induced diseases of food legumes; virology of legume viruses; genetic resistance to viral diseases; mechanisms of viral transmission through seeds. *Mailing Add:* 2170 Bonnie Dr Payette ID 83661. *Fax:* 541-737-3573; *E-Mail:* hamptonr@bcc.orst.edu

HAMPTON, SUZANNE HARVEY, DEVELOPMENTAL BIOLOGY, GENETICS. *Current Pos:* ASSOC DIR, REGULATORY AFFAIRS, BERLEX LABS, 87- *Personal Data:* b Ogdensburg, NY, Oct 27, 34; m 61. *Educ:* Drew Univ, BA, 56; Tulane Univ, MS, 59; Univ Tex, Houston, PhD(biomed sci), 70. *Prof Exp:* Res assoc physiol, Tulane Univ, 59-66; res asst, Univ Tex Dent Sci Inst Houston, 66-70, asst mem, 70-72; asst prof biol, York Col, 72-75, assoc prof, 75-77; asst prof biol, Barnard Col, 80-84; sr med writer, Ayerst Labs, 84-87. *Concurrent Pos:* Prin investr, Dept Health, Educ & Welfare grant, 71-77. *Mem:* Drug Info Asn; Regulatory Affairs Prof Soc; Soc Study Reproduction. *Res:* Developmental biology of marmosets; sex determination; gametogenesis; husbandry of primates; reproductive biology. *Mailing Add:* 47 Tulip Ave Ringwood NJ 07456

HAMRE, HAROLD THOMAS, BIOLOGY. *Current Pos:* RETIRED. *Personal Data:* b Wautoma, Wis, Jan 1, 10; m 52; c 1. *Educ:* Univ Wis, BS, 33, MS, 34; Ohio State Univ, PhD(physiol), 61. *Prof Exp:* Instr zool, Wittenburg Col, 34-35; instr biol, Shenandoah Col, 35-38; from instr to asst prof biol, Bowling Green State Univ, 46-61, assoc prof, 61-79. *Mem:* AAAS. *Res:* Physiology; circulation. *Mailing Add:* 227 Biddle St Bowling Green OH 43402

HAMRE, MELVIN L, FOOD SCIENCE, POULTRY SCIENCE. *Current Pos:* from asst prof to assoc prof, 65-73, PROF POULTRY, DEPT ANIMAL SCI, UNIV MINN, ST PAUL, 73-, EXTEN SPECIALIST, 65- *Personal Data:* b Tacoma, Wash, Nov 8, 32. *Educ:* Wash State Univ, BS, 54, MEd, 60; Purdue Univ, MS, 63, PhD(food technol), 66. *Prof Exp:* Asst poultry sci, Purdue Univ, 60-65. *Mem:* Poultry Sci Asn; Inst Food Technologists. *Res:* Maintenance of shell egg quality; poultry management and nutrition. *Mailing Add:* 1425 Terrace Dr St Paul MN 55113

HAMRICK, ANNA KATHERINE BARR, MATHEMATICS, MATHEMATICS EDUCATION. *Current Pos:* asst prof, 76-96, PROF MATH, AUGUSTA STATE UNIV, 96- *Personal Data:* b Atlanta, Ga, Aug 29, 47; m 69; c 1. *Educ:* Univ Ga, BSEd, 69, MEd, 74, EdD(math), 76. *Prof Exp:* Res asst math, Res & Develop Ctr, Univ Ga, 69-70; teacher math, US Army Dependent Sch Syst, 71-72, Big Bend Community Col, 72-73 & Continuing Educ, Univ Ga, 75-76, teaching asst math educ, 73-76. *Concurrent Pos:* Curric evaluator, Lincoln Co Sch Syst, 77- *Mem:* Nat Coun Teachers Math. *Res:* How computational skills contribute to the meaningful learning of arithmetic; beginning programming languages. *Mailing Add:* Dept Math & Comput Sci Augusta State Univ 2500 Walton Way Augusta GA 30904-2200

HAMRICK, JAMES LEWIS, POPULATION BIOLOGY. *Current Pos:* PROF BOT & GENETICS, UNIV GA, 85- *Personal Data:* b Hopewell, Va, Feb 26, 42; m 74; c 1. *Educ:* NC State Univ, BS, 64; Univ Calif, Berkeley, MS, 66, PhD(genetics), 70. *Prof Exp:* Fel genetics, Univ Calif, Davis, 70-71; asst prof bot, Univ Kans, 71-75, assoc prof, 75-79, prof bot & syst & ecol, 79-85. *Mem:* Genetics Soc Am; Soc Study Evolution; Ecol Soc Am; Am Genetic Asn; Am Soc Naturalists. *Res:* Population genetics and ecology of natural plant populations. *Mailing Add:* Dept Bot Univ Ga 1180 E Broad St Athens GA 30601-3040

HAMRICK, JOSEPH THOMAS, PUBLIC HEALTH, PREVENTIVE MEDICINE. *Current Pos:* assoc prof pub health admin, 66-67 & health serv admin, 67-70, chmn dept, 68-71 & 73-77, PROF HEALTH SERV ADMIN, SCH PUB HEALTH & TULANE UNIV, 70-, PROF & DIR, PROG COMMUNITY MED, 80- *Personal Data:* b Meridian, Miss, Oct 4, 33; m 54, Nina Smith; c Janet Leslie, Joseph Jr & Mark Daniel. *Educ:* Univ Tenn, MD, 57; Tulane Univ, MPH, 62. *Prof Exp:* Dir, Copiah Simpson County Health Dept, Miss, 59-61; res div county health work, Miss State Bd Health, 62-64, supvr tuberc control unit, 64-65, dir div tuberc control, 65-66. *Concurrent Pos:* Vis prof, Sch Nursing, Univ Southern Miss, 67-79; consult, USPHS Hosp, New Orleans, La, La State Dept Hosps, Health Educ Authority, La, La Regional Med Prog, New Orleans City Health Dept & Sch Nursing, Univ Southern Miss; dep, State Health Off, 79-80; actg dean, Tulane Univ, Sch Pub Health, 87-91, assoc dean, 87; med dir, Willowwood Home Jewish Aged, Jefferson parish Correctional Ctr, Expert Correctional Health Care, 90- *Mem:* Am Asn Univ Prof; Am Pub Health Asn; Am Col Prev Med; Am Pub Health Asn; Asn Teachers Prev Med; Soc Correctional Physicians. *Res:* Community day care cancer clinic; promoting quality care in nursing homes; sexually transmitted disease research screening in jails. *Mailing Add:* Dept Community Med Sch Med Tulane Univ 1430 Tulane Ave New Orleans LA 70112-2699

HAMRICK, JOSEPH THOMAS, POWER GENERATING SYSTEMS, BIOMASS PROCESSING. *Current Pos:* PRES, AEROSPACE RES CORP, 61- *Personal Data:* b Carrollton, Ga, Mar 20, 21; m 48, Doroth Jones; c Thomas M, Jane E (Kneisley) & Nancy A (Owen). *Educ:* Ga Inst Technol, BME, 46, MSME, 48. *Honors & Awards:* Tech Achievement Award, US Dept Energy, 84. *Prof Exp:* Aeronaut res scientist, Nat Adv Comt Aeronaut, 55-84. *Concurrent Pos:* Chief res engr, Thompson Prod, 55-61. *Mem:* Am Soc Mech Engrs. *Res:* Compressor and pump; biomass fueled gas turbine. *Mailing Add:* 4353 Windy Gap Dr Roanoke VA 24014

HAMRIN, CHARLES E(DWARD), JR, CHEMICAL ENGINEERING. *Current Pos:* assoc prof, 68-78, actg chair, 88-89, PROF CHEM ENG, UNIV KY, 78-, CHAIR, 89- *Personal Data:* b Chicago, Ill, Jan 12, 34; m 56; c 3. *Educ:* Northwestern Univ, BS, 56, MS, 57, PhD(chem eng), 64. *Prof Exp:* Develop specialist, Nuclear Div, Y-12 Plant, Union Carbide Corp, 60-66; asst prof chem eng & res engr, Denver Res Inst, Univ Denver, 66-68. *Concurrent Pos:* Consult, Rocky Flats Plant Dow Chem Co, 67-68; vis prof, Chalmers Univ Technol, Sweden, 79-80. *Mem:* Am Inst Chem Engrs. *Res:* Chemical vapor deposition; thermodynamic and transport properties; fluidized beds; biomedical and enzyme engineering; wastewater treatment; catalysis; materials processing. *Mailing Add:* 3311 Coldstream Dr Lexington KY 40517

HAMSA, WILLIAM RUDOLPH, ORTHOPEDIC SURGERY. *Current Pos:* from instr to assoc prof, 37-49, chmn dept, 49-69, prof orthop surg, Univ Nebr Med Ctr, Omaha, 49-65, ORTHOP SURG, CACLARKSON HOSP, 65- *Personal Data:* b Stanton, Nebr, Dec 18, 03; m 31; c 2. *Educ:* Univ Nebr, BSc, 27, MD, 29; Am Bd Orthop Surg, dipl, 37. *Prof Exp:* Asst orthop surg, Univ Iowa, 33-36, assoc, 36-37. *Concurrent Pos:* Attend orthop surgeon, Nebr Orthop Hosp, Lincoln; consult, Vet Admin Hosp, Omaha. *Mem:* Clin Orthop Soc; AMA; Am Col Surg; Am Acad Orthop Surg. *Res:* Reconstructive orthopedic surgery, especially related to crippled children. *Mailing Add:* 6401 Rainwood Rd Omaha NE 68152

HAMSHER, JAMES J, BIO-ORGANIC CHEMISTRY. *Current Pos:* PRES & CHIEF EXEC OFFICER, HAMSHER ASSOCS INT, 93- *Personal Data:* b Nappanee, Ind, Oct 7, 40. *Educ:* Wabash Col, BA, 63; Southern Ill Univ, Carbondale, MA, 65; Purdue Univ, PhD(org chem), 69. *Prof Exp:* Res chemist, Pfizer, Inc, 69-72, proj leader, 72-75, mgr, 75-77, asst dir, 77-93. *Mem:* Am Chem Soc. *Res:* Enzymology; use of enzyme transformations in organic synthesis. *Mailing Add:* 54 Trumbull Rd Waterford CT 06385

HAMSHER, KERRY DE SANDOZ, NEUROPSYCHOLOGY. *Current Pos:* asst prof, 79-84, ASSOC PROF NEUROL, UNIV WIS MED SCH, 84- *Personal Data:* b Long Br, NJ, Dec 10, 46; div. *Educ:* Trinity Col, BS, 70; Univ Iowa, MA, 74 & PhD(psychol), 77. *Prof Exp:* Asst res scientist neurol, Univ Iowa, 77-79. *Concurrent Pos:* Mem, US Dept Educ Nat Invitational Conf Traumatic Brain Injury Res, 87, Vet Admin Merit Rev Bd Neurobiol, 87-89, res group dementias, World Fed Neurol, 85-; chmn, Dict Comt, Int Neuropsychol Soc, 87- *Mem:* Fel Am Psychol Asn; Sigma Xi; Am Acad Neurol; Am Psychol Asn; Int Neuropsychol Soc; Royal Soc Med; World Fed Neurol. *Res:* Aging and brain disease; attention, audition, memory sequencing, spatial and facial perception and stereopsis; development of neuropsychological assessment instruments; language disorders; neuroaromatic basis of confusion; objective research criteria for neurobehavioral syndromes. *Mailing Add:* 1218 W Kilbourn Ave Suite 415 Milwaukee WI 53203

HAMSON, ALVIN RUSSELL, VEGETABLE CROPS. *Current Pos:* RETIRED. *Personal Data:* b Lava Hot Springs, Idaho, Sept 11, 24; m 46; c 4. *Educ:* Utah State Univ, BS, 48; Cornell Univ, PhD(veg crops), 52. *Prof Exp:* Asst veg crops, Cornell Univ, 48-52; from asst prof to assoc prof, Utah State Univ, 52-55, horticulturist, 55-58, prof hort, 59-90. *Concurrent Pos:* Actg head, Dept Hort, Utah State Univ, 58-60 & 65. *Mem:* Am Soc Hort Sci; Weed Sci Soc Am. *Res:* Cultural research on vegetable crops; plant breeding of vegetable crops; varietal testing of vegetable crops. *Mailing Add:* 1780 N 1200 E Logan UT 84341

HAMSTROM, MARY-ELIZABETH, PURE MATHEMATICS. *Current Pos:* assoc prof, 57-66, PROF MATH, UNIV ILL, URBANA, 66- *Personal Data:* b Pittsburgh, Pa, May 24, 27. *Educ:* Univ Pa, AB, 48; Univ Tex, PhD(pure math), 52. *Prof Exp:* Instr pure math, Univ Tex, 49-52; from asst prof to assoc prof math, Goucher Col, 52-57. *Concurrent Pos:* Mem, Inst Advan Study, 56-57. *Mem:* Am Math Soc. *Res:* Set theoretic topology; regular mappings; space homeomorphisms on manifolds. *Mailing Add:* Univ Ill 1409 W Green St Urbana IL 61801-2917. *Fax:* 217-344-5656

HAMTIL, CHARLES NORBERT, physics, for more information see previous edition

HAMZA, MOHAMED HAMED, AUTOMATIC CONTROL SYSTEMS, OPERATIONS RESEARCH. *Current Pos:* assoc prof, 68-75, PROF ELEC ENG, UNIV CALGARY, 75- *Personal Data:* b Heliopolis, Egypt, Oct 17, 36. *Educ:* Mass Inst Technol, BSc, 58; Swiss Fed Inst Technol, Dr tech sci, 63; Univ Zurich, PhD(math), 66. *Prof Exp:* Res asst, Inst Opers Res & Electronic Data Processing, Univ Zurich, 64-68. *Concurrent Pos:* Consult, Univ Fribourg, 66-68; ed jour, Automatic Control Theory & Appln; pres, Icord Ltd; pres, Int Asn Sci & Technol Develop. *Mem:* Inst Elec & Electronics Engrs; Int Soc Min & Micro Computers. *Res:* Expert systems; adaptive, optimum, and stochastic control systems; mathematical programming; simulation. *Mailing Add:* 4500 16th Ave NW Calgary AB T3B 0M6 Can

HAN, BYUNG JOON, catalysis, polymer rheology, for more information see previous edition

HAN, CHANG DAE, CHEMICAL & ELECTRICAL ENGINEERING. *Current Pos:* PROF CHEM ENG, POLYTECH INST NY, 72-, HEAD DEPT, 74- *Personal Data:* b Seoul, Korea, Sept 28, 35; US citizen; m 62; c 3. *Educ:* Seoul Nat Univ, BS, 58; Mass Inst Technol, MS, 62, ScD(chem eng), 64; Newark Col Eng, MS, 68; NY Univ, MS, 71. *Prof Exp:* Process analyst, Am Cyanamid Co, 64-66; systs engr, Esso Res & Eng Co, 66-67; assoc prof chem eng, Polytech Inst Brooklyn, 67-72. *Mem:* Am Inst Chem Engrs; Am Chem Soc; Soc Rheology; Soc Plastics Engrs. *Res:* Rheology; mathematical modelling; applied mathematics; polymer processing. *Mailing Add:* Inst Polymer Eng Univ Akron Akron OH 44325-0301

HAN, CHARLES CHIH-CHAO, POLYMER CHEMISTRY. *Current Pos:* RES CHEMIST, NAT BUR STAND, 74- *Personal Data:* b Szuchuan, China, Jan 18, 44; m 70; c 3. *Educ:* Univ Houston, MS, 69; Univ Wis, PhD(polymer chem), 74. *Mem:* Am Chem Soc; Am Phys Soc. *Res:* Neutron scattering and quasielastic light scattering of polymer solutions; polymer characterization; block copolymers. *Mailing Add:* Polymer Div B210/224 Nat Inst Stand & Technol Gaithersburg MD 20899

HAN, CHIEN-PAI, STATISTICS. *Current Pos:* PROF MATH, UNIV TEX, ARLINGTON, 82- *Personal Data:* b Hunan, China, Dec 17, 36; m 66, Maria L; c Richard & Julie. *Educ:* Nat Taiwan Univ, BA, 58; Univ Minn, MA, 62; Harvard Univ, PhD(statist), 67. *Prof Exp:* From asst prof to prof statist, Iowa State Univ, 67-82. *Concurrent Pos:* Vis asst prof statist, Harvard Univ, 70; assoc ed, Commun Statist, 93- *Mem:* Am Statist Asn; Inst Math Statist; Int Statist Inst; Int Chinese Statist Asn; Sigma Xi. *Res:* Multivariate analysis; sample survey. *Mailing Add:* Dept Math Univ Tex Arlington TX 76019

HAN, JANG HYUN, HEPATITIS C VIRUS RESEARCH, VIROLOGY. *Current Pos:* ASSOC DIR BIOCHEM & MOLECULAR BIOL, CHIRON, 89- *Personal Data:* b Seoul, Korea, July 22, 45; m 74, Kyung Hee; c John & Christine. *Educ:* Seoul Nat Univ, BS, 70, MS, 72; Univ Tenn, PhD(biol), 79. *Prof Exp:* Fel, Columbia Univ, 80-83; res asst biochemist, Univ Calif, San Francisco, 83-86; sr biochemist, Merck Sharp & Dohme, 86-88. *Mem:* AAAS; Am Soc Microbiol; NY Acad Sci. *Res:* Hepatitis C virus research including cloning and characterization of viral genome, study on control mechanism for viral translation and replication and development of diagnostics, vaccine and therapeutics. *Mailing Add:* 4560 Horton St Chiron Corp Emeryville CA 94608. *Fax:* 510-601-3347; *E-Mail:* hanj@chiron.com

HAN, JAOK, CARDIOLOGY, PHYSIOLOGY. *Current Pos:* from asst prof to assoc prof, 68-73, PROF MED & DIR ELECTROCARDIOGRAPHY, ALBANY MED COL, 73- *Personal Data:* b Chinnampo, Korea, July 16, 30; US citizen; m 61, Yangsook Chun; c Sylvia, Julia & Andrew. *Educ:* Kyung-Pook Nat Univ, Korea, MD, 51; State Univ NY, PhD(physiol), 61. *Prof Exp:* Intern med, Jersey City Med Ctr, NJ, 55-56; med resident, Mercy Hosp, Pittsburgh, 56-57; res assoc cardiol, Masonic Med Res Lab, NY, 60-66. *Concurrent Pos:* Res fel physiol, State Univ NY Upstate Med Ctr, 57-60; Int Soc Cardiol Found fel, 60-61; Masonic Found Med Res & Human Welfare fel, 61-63; Am Heart Asn & NIH grants, 63-90; cardiol fel, Univ Rochester Med Ctr, 66-67; attend physician & cardiologist, Albany Med Ctr Hosp, 68-; mem res comt, Am Heart Asn, NY State Affil, 69-72 & 76-79, pres, NE NY Chap, 80-84; mem comt, Sudden Cardiac Death, Nat Heart, Lung & Blood Inst, 71, Ischemic Heart Dis, 74, Beta Blocker Heart Attack Trial, 78, Cardiol Adv Comt, 81-85 & Cardiac Rhythm Studies, 85. *Mem:* Am Fedn Clin Res; Am Physiol Soc; fel Am Col Cardiol; fel Am Heart Asn. *Res:* Clinical and research cardiology, especially electrophysiology of cardiac arrhythmias. *Mailing Add:* Dept Med Albany Med Col Albany NY 12208. *Fax:* 518-262-4944

HAN, KENNETH N, HYDROMETALLURGY, MINERAL BENEFICIATION. *Current Pos:* assoc prof, 81-84, DISTINGUISHED PROF METALL, SDAK SCH MINES & TECHNOL, 84-, HEAD, DEPT METALL ENG & DIR, INST MINING & METALL, 87-, DEAN, COL CHEM, PHYS & MAT SCI & ENG, 94- *Personal Data:* b Seoul, Korea, July 3, 38; US citizen; m 67, Helen Rho; c Iris, Vincent & Alison. *Educ:* Seoul Nat Univ, BS, 61, MS, 63; Univ Ill, Urbana, MS, 67; Univ Calif, Berkeley, PhD(metall), 71. *Honors & Awards:* Ernest L Buckley Award, 94; Milton Wadsworth Award, Soc Mining, Metall & Explor, 95. *Prof Exp:* Res asst beneficiation, Res Inst Mining & Metall, Seoul, 61-63; res assoc mining, Seoul Nat Univ, 63-65; lectr chem eng, Monash Univ, Melbourne, Australia, 71-74, sr lectr, 74-80; SDak dir, Exper Prog Simulate Compet Res, NSF, 89-92. *Concurrent Pos:* Vis lectr, Univ Calif, Berkeley, 74, vis assoc prof, 79; res investr, Korean Inst Sci & Technol, 79-80; ed-in-chief, Mineral Processing & Extractive Metall Rev, 86-; dir, Epscor State SDak, 89-; consult, Inst Mineral & Energy Res, Taiwan, 89- *Mem:* Nat Acad Eng; Soc Mining Metall & Explor; Minerals Metals & Mat Soc. *Res:* Geochemistry and extraction of marine manganese nodules; fine particle recovery; leaching and cementation mechanisms; metal recovery from solutions; transport phenomena on metal ions in solutions; treatment of gold refractory ores; solubility of gases in solutions; corrosion. *Mailing Add:* Dept Metall Eng SDak Sch Mines & Technol Rapid City SD 57701. *Fax:* 605-394-3369; *E-Mail:* khan@silver.sdsmt.edu

HAN, L(IT) S(IEN), MECHANICAL ENGINEERING, GAS TURBINE TECHNOLOGY. *Current Pos:* RETIRED. *Personal Data:* b Shanghai, China, May 5, 23; m 53, Bonnie Shen; c Barbara (Lia) & Derek. *Educ:* Chiao Tung Univ, BSc, 45; Ohio State Univ, MS, 48, PhD, 54. *Honors & Awards:* McQuigg Award, Am Soc Mech Engrs. *Prof Exp:* Jr engr, Shanghai Rwy Admin, 45-47; asst res found, Ohio State Univ, 47-50, res assoc, 50-54, from instr to prof eng mech, 54-90. *Concurrent Pos:* NSF sr fel & vis prof, Max Planck Inst Fluid Mech Res, Gottingen, 62-63; consult, Battelle Mem Inst, 63- & Flight Dynamics Lab, USAF, 69-; sen scientist, Lockheed Missiles & Space Co, Palo Alto, CA, 86-91; res prof, Santa Clara Univ, CA, 87- *Mem:* Am Soc Mech Engrs. *Res:* Applied mechanics; thermodynamics; heat transfer; gas turbine technology; composite materials. *Mailing Add:* 520 Shelby Lane Los Altos CA 94024-4160

HAN, MOO-YOUNG, PARTICLE PHYSICS, THEORETICAL PHYSICS. *Current Pos:* from asst prof to assoc prof, 67-77, PROF PHYSICS, DUKE UNIV, 77- *Personal Data:* b Seoul, Korea, Nov 30, 34; US citizen; m 59, Chang K Hong; c Grace, Chris & Anthony. *Educ:* Carroll Col, Wis, BS, 57; Univ Rochester, PhD(physics), 63. *Prof Exp:* Res assoc physics, Boston Univ, 63-64; res assoc, Syracuse Univ, 64-65; asst prof, Univ Pittsburgh, 65-67. *Concurrent Pos:* Distinguished foreign scholar, Kyoto Univ, 74; vis prof, Korea Advan Inst Sci, 82. *Mem:* Am Phys Soc. *Res:* Quantum electrodynamics; symmetries of strong interactions; quark models; quantum chromodynamics; author of two books. *Mailing Add:* 615 Duluth St Durham NC 27705. *E-Mail:* myhan@phy.duke.edu

HAN, SEONG S, CELL BIOLOGY, SCIENCE EDUCATION. *Current Pos:* Res assoc anat, Univ Mich, 60-61, from asst prof to assoc prof dent, 61-68, prof dent, Sch Dent, 68-87, prof anat, Med Sch, 70-87, EMER PROF, DEPT ANAT & CELL BIOL, SCH MED, UNIV MICH, ANN ARBOR, 87-, EMER PROF, SCH DENT, 87-; CHMN BD, YURIN SOC WORLD-WIDE, INC, ANN ARBOR, 88- *Personal Data:* b Seoul, Korea, May 12, 33; m 60; c 3. *Educ:* Seoul Nat Univ, DDS, 56; Univ Mich, PhD(anat), 61. *Concurrent Pos:* Consult res, Vet Admin Hosp, 68-87; mem, Spec Study Sect, NIH, 71-87; consult, Khmer Repub, 71 & Ministry Sci & Technol, Repub Korea, 73; mem fac, Interdept Prog Cell & Molecular Biol, Univ Mich, Ann Arbor, 71-87, chmn, Grad Prog Anat, 72-74 & Reproductive Endocrinol Prog, 74-87, dir, Interdisciplinary Prog Biol Aging, 75-87; res scientist dir, Prog Biol Aging, 80-87; vpres & chancellor, Med Ctr, Dong-A Univ, Korea, 87-89, prof anat, 87-; dean, Med Sch, Life Sci Res Inst, Dong-A Univ, 87-89, dir, 87- *Mem:* Fel Am Asn Anatomists; Am Soc Cell Biol; Geront Soc; Soc Exp Biol & Med; Int Asn Dent Res. *Res:* Cellular mechanism of exocrine and endocrine secretion; membrane receptors to protein hormones; molecular biology of membrane aging; development of educational technology. *Mailing Add:* 1225 Lincolnshire Lane Ann Arbor MI 48103. *Fax:* 613-769-1441

HAN, SHU-TANG, chemical engineering; deceased, see previous edition for last biography

HAN, TAO, THEORETICAL PHYSICS. *Current Pos:* asst prof, 93-97, ASSOC PROF PHYSICS, UNIV CALIF, DAVIS, 97- *Personal Data:* b Jiamusi, China, May 3, 56; m 84, Dandan Sun; c Crystal. *Educ:* Nankai Univ, China, BS, 80, MS, 83; Univ Wis-Madison, PhD(physics), 90. *Prof Exp:* Postdoctoral fel, Fermi Nat Accelerator Lab, 90-93, SSC fel, 91-92. *Concurrent Pos:* Prin investr, High Energy Physics Grant, Dept Energy, 94- *Res:* Theoretical high energy physics; high energy collider phenomenology; fundamental interactions for elementary particles. *Mailing Add:* Dept Physics Univ Calif Davis CA 95616

HAN, TIN, IMMUNOLOGY, HEMATOLOGY. *Current Pos:* DIR MED ONCOL, E AMHERST MED CTR, 90- *Personal Data:* b Mergui, Burma, May 23, 33; US citizen. *Educ:* Rangoon Univ, ISc, 53, MD, 58. *Prof Exp:* Intern, Worcester City Hosp, Mass, 60-61; first yr resident internal med, Union Mem Hosp, Baltimore, Md, 61-62; second yr resident, Roswell Park Mem Inst, Buffalo, NY, 62-63; third yr resident, French Hosp, New York, 63-64; sr cancer res clinician, Roswell Park Mem Inst, 64-72, cancer res clinician II, 72-74; res instr, State Univ NY Buffalo, 68-70, asst res prof, 70-75, assoc res prof med, 70-75; assoc chief cancer res clinician, Roswell Park Mem Inst, 74-90. *Concurrent Pos:* Nat Cancer Inst grants, 72-78 & 73-76. *Mem:* AAAS; Am Asn Cancer Res; Am Soc Clin Oncol; Am Soc Hemat; Am Asn Immunologists. *Res:* Basic research in T lymphocytes, B lymphocytes and macrophages participation in cell-mediated immunity; immunological studies in patients with cancer; immunotherapy of cancer. *Mailing Add:* E Amherst Med Ctr 1150 Youngs Rd Suite 206 Williamsville NY 14221-8024. *Fax:* 716-636-0012

HAN, YURI WHA-YUL, ORGANIC CHEMISTRY, POLYMER CHEMISTRY. *Current Pos:* PROF CHEM, EAST LOS ANGELES COL, 69-, CHMN DEPT, 74- *Personal Data:* b Seoul, Korea, Oct 15, 32; US citizen; m 55; c 1. *Educ:* Austin Col, BA, 55; Univ Tex, Austin, PhD(chem), 60. *Prof Exp:* xes fel chem, Univ Tex, 60-61; res assoc, Univ Southern Calif, 61-62; asst prof, Mt St Mary's Col, Calif, 61-64; sr res engr, Rye Canyon Res Lab, Lockheed-Calif Co, 64-68. *Mem:* Sigma Xi; Am Chem Soc. *Res:* Rearrangements of alkylaryl hydrocarbons; aromatic-heterocyclic polymer chemistry. *Mailing Add:* Dept Chem East Los Angeles Col 1301 Avenida Cesar Chavez Monterey Park CA 91754

HANAFEE, JAMES EUGENE, METALLURGY, MATERIALS SCIENCE & ENGINEERING. *Current Pos:* PROJ MGR, LAWRENCE LIVERMORE LAB, 71- *Personal Data:* b Chicago, Ill, Jan 8, 37; m 62; c 2. *Educ:* Univ Ill, Urbana-Champaign, BS, 58, MS, 60; Case Western Res Univ, PhD(metall), 66. *Prof Exp:* Res metallurgist, Int Nickel Co, 60-63; sr res metallurgist, Franklin Inst, Pa, 66-71. *Concurrent Pos:* Contrib ed, PCM-PCE, 71-73; US chmn, Joint Working Group 22B, 80-; high sch sci teacher, 96- *Mem:* Am Soc Metals. *Res:* Science education; mechanical properties; fabrication; beryllium; aluminum; failure analysis; prototype development, laser machining/welding; technical management. *Mailing Add:* Lawrence Livermore Lab Univ Calif Livermore CA 94550. *E-Mail:* hanafee1@llnl.gov

HANAFEE, WILLIAM NORMAN, radiology, for more information see previous edition

HANAFUSA, HIDESABURO, VIRAL ONCOLOGY. *Current Pos:* PROF, ROCKEFELLER UNIV, 73- *Personal Data:* b Nishinomiya, Japan, Dec 1, 29; m 58; c 1. *Educ:* Osaka Univ, BS, 53, PhD(biochem), 60. *Honors & Awards:* Howard Taylor Ricketts Award, Univ Chicago, 81; Albert Lasker Basic Med Res Award, Lasker Found, 82; Asahi Prize, Asahi Press, 84; Clowes Mem Award, Am Asn Cancer Res, 86; Sloan Prize, Gen Motors Cancer Res Found, 93; Order of Culture, Japan, 95. *Prof Exp:* Res assoc, Res Inst Microbial Dis, Osaka Univ, 58-61; fel, Univ Calif, Berkeley, 61-64; vis scientist, Col France, Paris, 64-66; assoc mem & chief, Dept Viral Oncol, Pub Health Res Inst City of New York, Inc, 66-68, mem, 68-73. *Mem:* Nat Acad Sci; Am Soc Microbiol; Am Soc Biol Chemists; Am Asn Cancer Res; NY Acad Sci; Am Soc Virol; Am Soc Cell Biol. *Res:* RNA tumor viruses; mechanism of cell transformation; function of viral and cellular oncogenes. *Mailing Add:* Rockefeller Univ 1230 York Ave New York NY 10021

HANAHAN, DONALD JAMES, BIOCHEMISTRY. *Current Pos:* chmn dept biochem, 76-83, PROF BIOCHEM, UNIV TEX HEALTH SCI CTR, SAN ANTONIO, 76- *Personal Data:* b Springfield, Ill, May 13, 19; m 47; c 5. *Educ:* Univ Ill, BS, 41, PhD, 44. *Prof Exp:* Res assoc, Manhattan Proj, Univ Chicago, 44; res assoc, E I du Pont de Nemours & Co, 45; res assoc physiol, Univ Calif, 45-48; instr chem, Univ Wash, 48-49, asst prof, 49-50, from asst prof to prof biochem, 50-60; prof & chmn, Dept Biochem, Col Med, Univ Ariz, 67-75. *Concurrent Pos:* Guggenheim fel, 55; NIH spec fel, 65-66; Macy fac scholar, 74. *Mem:* Am Soc Biol Chemists; Am Chem Soc. *Res:* Simple and complex lipids; lipolytic action, lipid chemical mediators. *Mailing Add:* Dept Biochem Univ Tex Health Sci Ctr 7703 Floyd Curl Dr San Antonio TX 78284-7760. *Fax:* 210-567-6595

HANAK, JOSEPH J, SOLID STATE SCIENCE. *Current Pos:* RETIRED. *Personal Data:* b Tarrytown, NY, Mar 21, 30; m 55; c 6. *Educ:* Manhattan Col, BS, 53; Univ Detroit, MS, 56; Iowa State Univ, PhD(phys chem), 59. *Honors & Awards:* David Sarnoff Award & John A Roebling Award, Am Soc Metals, 65; Best Sem Award, Soc Info Display, 75. *Prof Exp:* Asst chem, Univ Detroit, 53-55; chemist, Ethyl Corp, Mich, 55; asst rare earth res, Inst Atomic Res, Iowa State Univ, 55-59; mem tech staff mat res, Radio Corp Am, RCA Labs, 59-71, fel tech staff, 71-94. *Mem:* Am Vacuum Soc; Soc Info Display; Sigma Xi. *Res:* Chemistry and metallurgy of rare earth elements; superconducting materials research; chemical vapor deposition of niobium-tin used in construction of high field superconducting solenoids; radio frequency co-sputtering of multicomponent systems; microwave; acoustic delay lines; electroluminescence; magnetic recording heads; video disc development; photovoltaic amorphous silicon solar cells. *Mailing Add:* 240 Raphael Ave Apt 9 Ames IA 50014-7777

HANAN, BARRY BENTON, HEAVY ISOTOPE GEOCHEMISTRY. *Current Pos:* GRAD SCH OCEANOG, UNIV RI. *Personal Data:* b Morgantown, WVa, Mar 10, 49; m 78; c 2. *Educ:* Univ Kans, BS, 73; Va Polytech Inst & State Univ, MS, 77, PhD(geol), 80. *Prof Exp:* Fel geol & geochem, Univ Calif, Santa Barbara, 80- *Mem:* Am Geophys Union; Geol Soc Am; Mineral Soc Am; AAAS; Geochem Soc; Sigma Xi. *Res:* Investigation of the early history of the solar system by experimentation with the uranium, thorium, lead and rubidium strontium isotopic systems in meteorites and lunar rocks. *Mailing Add:* 9121 Sinsonte Lane Lakeside CA 92040-4625

HANAN, JOE JOHN, GREENHOUSE PRODUCTION, PLANT ENVIRONMENTAL CONTROL. *Current Pos:* asst horticulturist, Colo State Univ, 63-64, from asst prof to prof hort, 65-89, leader floricult invests, 74-82, leader & bulletin ed, 82-89, EMER PROF HORT, COLO STATE UNIV, 89- *Personal Data:* b Buffalo, NY, Jan 22, 31; m 56, Julia Watkins; c John W, Ernest L & S Lois. *Educ:* Univ Mo, BS, 52; Colo State Univ, MS, 59; Cornell Univ, PhD(hort), 63. *Honors & Awards:* Alex Laurie Award, Am Soc Hort Sci, 63, 82, Kenneth Post Award, 65 and 76. *Prof Exp:* Res asst hort, Colo State Univ, 57-59; res asst floricult, Cornell Univ, 59-62, res assoc, 62-63. *Mem:* Fel Am Soc Hort Sci; Int Hort Soc; Sigma Xi. *Res:* Effects of temperature on plant growth and development; oxygen diffusion in soils; storage of horticultural products; air pollution; environmental control and measurement; carbon dioxide utilization by plants; water relationships of plants; greenhouse management and nutrition; computer control of plant environments. *Mailing Add:* 1508 Briarwood Ft Collins CO 80521. *E-Mail:* jjhanan@lamar.colostate.edu

HANAU, RICHARD, OPTICS. *Current Pos:* RETIRED. *Personal Data:* b New York, NY, Aug 1, 17; m 41, Laia Pearlmutter; c Loren M. *Educ:* Mass Inst Technol, SB, 39; Univ Mich, MS, 40, PhD(physics), 47. *Prof Exp:* From assoc prof to prof physics, Univ Ky, 47-83. *Concurrent Pos:* Vis prof, Univ PR, 53-54; prof, Univ Indonesia, 56-58; asst, Univ Rochester, 58-59; vis scholar, Opt Sci Ctr, Univ Ariz, 73-74. *Mem:* Optical Soc Am; Am Phys Soc. *Res:* Visible and ultraviolet spectrochemical analysis; geometrical optics and lens design. *Mailing Add:* RR 4-46 Stage Coach Rd Patterson NY 12563-9504

HANAUER, RICHARD, ANALYTICAL CHEMISTRY, BIOCHEMISTRY. *Current Pos:* Sr chemist fibers, Pate Rohn & Hass Co, 68-70, sr chemist petrol additives, 70-80, sr chemist process res, Agr Chemicals & Biocides, 80-87, SR CHEMIST AGR RES RESIDUE/METAB/ENVIRON, PATE ROHM & HAAS, CO, 87- *Personal Data:* b Brooklyn, NY, Feb 10, 43; m 68; c 2. *Educ:* Columbia Univ, BS, 63; Univ Wis, PhD(org chem), 68. *Mem:* Am Chem Soc. *Res:* Process research of agricultural chemicals and biocides. *Mailing Add:* 3094 Cloverly Dr Furlong PA 18925-1231

HANAUER, STEPHEN B, MEDICINE. *Current Pos:* Resident, internal med, 77-80, gastroenterol, 80-82, asst prof, 82-88, ASSOC PROF MED, UNIV CHICAGO, 88- *Personal Data:* b Chicago, Ill, Jan 1, 52; m 72; c 3. *Educ:* Univ Mich, BS, 73; Univ Ill, 77. *Concurrent Pos:* Am Col Physicians fel, 86; mem, Food & Drug Admin Gastrointestinal Adv Panel, 87-; Am Col Gastroenterol fel, 87. *Mem:* Am Col Physicians; Am Gastroenterol Asn; Am Col Gastroenterol; AMA. *Res:* Clinical research in gastroenterology with specific interest in management and new medical therapies of inflammatory bowel diseases. *Mailing Add:* Univ Chicago Pritzker Sch Med 5841 Maryland Ave Chicago IL 60637-1463

HANAUER, STEPHEN H(ENRY), nuclear engineering, for more information see previous edition

HANAWALT, PHILIP COURTLAND, PHOTOBIOLOGY, DNA REPAIR. *Current Pos:* res assoc & lectr, Biophys Lab, Stanford Univ, 61-65, assoc prof biol, 65-70, dir, Biophys Grad Prog, 68-85, chmn, Dept Biol Sci, 82-89, PROF BIOL, STANFORD UNIV, 70-, DIR, GRAD STUDIES BIOL, 90- *Personal Data:* b Akron, Ohio, Aug 25, 31; m 57, 78, Graciela Spivale; c David, Steven, Alex & Lisa. *Educ:* Oberlin Col, BA, 54; Yale Univ, MS, 55, PhD(biophys), 59. *Hon Degrees:* ScD, Oberlin Col, 97. *Honors & Awards:* Hans Falk Lectr, Nat Inst Environ Health Sci, 90; Ann Res Award, Environ Mutagen Soc, 92; Res Award, Am Soc Photobiol, 96. *Prof Exp:* USPHS fel, Microbiol Inst, Univ Copenhagen, 58-60; Am Cancer Soc fel biophys, Calif Inst Technol, 60-61. *Concurrent Pos:* Fel, NIH & Am Cancer Soc, 58-61; mem, Physiol Chem Study Sect, NIH, 66-70, Chem Path Study Sect, 81-84, bd sci counselors, Nat Inst Environ Health Sci, 87-90, Outstanding Investr Res Award, Nat Cancer Inst, 87-; mem adv comt, Nucleic Acids & Protein Synthesis, Am Cancer Soc, 72-76; prog dir, Cell-Molecular Biol, Training Prog, Stanford Univ, 73-84, chmn, Admin Panel Radiol Hazards, 78-80; vis prof, Dept Molecular Biol, Univ Calif, Berkeley, 76; fel rev panel, NSF, 85; outstanding investr res award, Nat Cancer Inst, 87-; counr, Environ Mutagen Soc, 88-91; mem, Carcinogen Identification Comn, Environ Protection Agency, Calif, 95- *Mem:* Nat Acad Sci; fel AAAS; Am Acad Microbiol; Genetics Soc; Biophys Soc; Am Soc Biochem & Molecular Biol; Environ Mutagen Soc (pres, 93-94); Radiation Res Soc. *Res:* Molecular mechanism and control of repair and tolerance of damaged DNA (including: ultraviolet, psoralens and chemical carcinogens), in bacteria and mammalian cells; selective repair in defined genes; co-discovery of DNA excision-repair and transcription-coupled DNA. *Mailing Add:* Dept Biol Sci Stanford Univ Stanford CA 94305-5020

HANBAUER, INGEBORG, PHARMACOLOGY, NEUROSCIENCE. *Current Pos:* vis fel, Lab Clin Sci, NIMH, NIH, 71-74, sr staff fel, Sect Biochem Pharmacol, Hypertension-Endocrine Br, Nat Heart Lung & Blood Inst, 74-79, pharmacologist, 79-89, PHARMACOLOGIST, LAB CHEM PHARMACOL, NAT HEART LUNG & BLOOD INST, NIH, 89- *Personal Data:* b Austria, July 30, 43; nat US. *Educ:* Univ Vienna, PhD, 69. *Prof Exp:* Sr res fel, NY State Res Inst, Ward's Island, 69-71. *Concurrent Pos:* Vis assoc, Lab Clin Sci, NIMH, NIH, 74. *Mem:* Am Soc Neurochem; Soc Neurosci; Am Soc Pharmacol & Exp Therapeut. *Res:* Pharmacology; numerous publications. *Mailing Add:* Lab Chem Pharmacol NHLB1 NIH Bldg 10 Rm 8N102 Bethesda MD 20892-0001. *Fax:* 301-402-0171

HANBY, JOHN ESTES, JR, PAPER SCIENCE & ENGINEERING. *Current Pos:* dir, Fiber Res & Develop, 94-96, VPRES TECHNOL, POTLATCH CORP, CLOQUET, MINN, 96- *Personal Data:* b Washington, DC, May 3, 41; m 68, Elaine; c John & Christina. *Educ:* Ga Inst Technol, BChE, 63; Lawrence Univ, MS, 65, PhD(phys inorg chem), 68. *Prof Exp:* Res eng, James River Corp, 70-75, suprvr prod develop, Cent Res Div, Camas, Wash, 75-76, tech mgr, 77-78, plant mgr, 78-80, mgr div mfg, 80-81, asst resident mgr, 81-89, vpres tech, Commun Papers, 89-94. *Mem:* Tech Asn Pulp & Paper Indust; Am Inst Chem Engrs; Paper Indust Mgt Asn. *Res:* Management of research and technology; technology strategy development. *Mailing Add:* Potlatch Corp PO Box 503 Cloquet MN 55720-0503

HANCE, ANTHONY JAMES, NEUROPHARMACOLOGY. *Current Pos:* assoc prof, 68-94, EMER PROF PHARMACOL, SCH MED, UNIV CALIF, DAVIS, 94- *Personal Data:* b Bournemouth, Eng, Aug 19, 32; m 54, Ruth A Martin; c David, Peter & John. *Educ:* Univ Birmingham, BSc, 53, PhD(neuropharmacol), 56. *Prof Exp:* Jr res pharmacologist, Univ Calif, Los Angeles, 59, asst res pharmacologist, 59-62; res assoc pharmacol, Stanford Univ, 62-65, asst prof, 65-68. *Concurrent Pos:* Res fel electrophysiol, Univ Birmingham, 57-58; consult pharmacologist, Riker Labs, Inc, Calif, 59-60; consult, Stanford Res Inst, 63-65 & Ampex Corp, 64-65; mem, Comt Psycho-pharmacol, NIMH, 65-69. *Mem:* Am Soc Pharmacol & Exp Therapeut; Asn Comput Mach; Biomed Eng Soc. *Res:* Electrical activity of central nervous system of mammals and its modification by drugs and during learning. *Mailing Add:* Dept Med Pharmacol & Toxicol Univ Calif Sch Med Davis CA 95616-8654. *Fax:* 530-752-7710

HANCE, ROBERT LEE, SURFACE CHEMISTRY, ELECTRON SPECTROSCOPY. *Current Pos:* TECH STAFF, MOTOROLA, INC, 84- *Personal Data:* b El Paso, Tex, Mar 1, 43; m 63; c 5. *Educ:* Abilene Christian Univ, BS, 66; Mass Inst Technol, PhD(phys chem), 70. *Prof Exp:* From asst prof to prof chem, Abiline Christian Univ, 70-83. *Concurrent Pos:* Vis assoc prof chem, Univ Tex, 78-79, res assoc, 81; res grants, Robert A Welch Found, Res Corp & NSF. *Mem:* Am Chem Soc; Am Phys Soc; Am Vacuum Soc. *Res:* Interaction of atoms and molecules at catalytic surfaces investigated by electron spectroscopy; programmed thermal desorption techniques; semiconductor materials analysis and characterization. *Mailing Add:* 8805 El Rey Blvd Austin TX 78737-1330

HANCK, KENNETH WILLIAM, ANALYTICAL CHEMISTRY. *Current Pos:* From asst prof to assoc prof, 69-78, PROF CHEM, NC STATE UNIV, 78-, HEAD DEPT, 84- *Personal Data:* b Danvers, Ill, Dec 6, 42; m 87. *Educ:* Ill State Univ, BS, 64; Univ Ill, MS, 66, PhD(chem), 69. *Concurrent Pos:* Sr Fulbright scholar, Australia, 80. *Mem:* Am Chem Soc. *Res:* Electrochemistry of transition metal complexes; development of analytical chemical techniques for the solution of specific chemical problems. *Mailing Add:* Dept Chem NC State Univ PO Box 8204 Raleigh NC 27695-8204

HANCOCK, ANTHONY JOHN, BIOCHEMISTRY, ORGANIC CHEMISTRY. *Current Pos:* DIR SCI PARTNERSHIPS, HOECHST MARION ROUSSEL, 90- *Personal Data:* b Smethwick, Eng, May 7, 36; m 75, Judith A; c Rebecca A. *Educ:* Univ Nottingham, BSc, 57, Dipl Ed, 58; Univ Ottawa, Can, PhD(biochem), 72. *Prof Exp:* Lectr chem, Univ Ottawa, 69-71; res assoc biochem, Case Western Res Univ, Sch Med, 72-75; from asst prof to assoc prof chem & med, Univ Mo, Kansas City, 75-83; res & develop proj mgr, Marion Labs, Inc, 83-88, dir sponsored external res, 88-90. *Concurrent Pos:* Bd chmn, Univ Kans Med Ctr Res Inst, 95- *Mem:* AAAS; Am Chem Soc; NY Acad Sci. *Res:* Chemical synthesis of lipid analogs; isolation and structure elucidation of natural lipids; physical and biochemical properties of lipids; membrane lipid-protein interaction. *Mailing Add:* Hoechst Marion Roussel PO Box 9627 Kansas City MO 64134-0627. *Fax:* 816-966-4400; *E-Mail:* thancock@hmri.com

HANCOCK, DEANA LORI, RUMINANT NUTRITION, GROWTH & DEVELOPMENT. *Current Pos:* STAFF MEM, ALANCO, 95- *Personal Data:* b Sedalia, Mo, Jan 23, 61; m 81, Michael. *Educ:* Univ Mo, Columbia, BS, 83, MS, 86; Tex Tech Univ, Lubbock, PhD(animal sci), 89. *Prof Exp:* Res scientist animal nutrit & physiol, Lilly Res Labs, 89-90; asst prof ruminant nutrit growth & develop, Purdue Univ, 90-95. *Mem:* Am Soc Animal Sci; Am Dairy Sci Asn; AAAS. *Res:* Ruminant nutrition with an emphasis on cellular and molecular regulation of nutrient utilization, growth, protein accretion, lactation and their interactions; author of numerous publications. *Mailing Add:* Alanco Ani Health Div Eli-Lilly & Co 2001 W Main St Greenfield IN 46140. *Fax:* 317-277-4532; *E-Mail:* dhancock@hub.ansc.purdue.edu

HANCOCK, GEORGE WHITMORE, PHYSICS TEACHING. *Current Pos:* From instr to assoc prof, 68-90, PROF PHYSICS DEPT, MARIETTA COL, 90- *Personal Data:* b Richmond, Va, Apr 25, 42; m 80, Carole Wylie. *Educ:* Univ Va, BA, 63, PhD(physics), 73. *Mem:* Am Asn Physics Teachers; assoc Sigma Xi. *Mailing Add:* 105 Keyser St Marietta OH 45750

HANCOCK, HAROLD E(DWIN), ELECTRICAL ENGINEERING. *Current Pos:* OWNER, H E HANCOCK ASSOCS, 65-; PRES, HAST INDUST INC, 74- *Personal Data:* b Norwood, Ohio, Apr 8, 21; m 46; c 2. *Educ:* Univ Cincinnati, EE, 43, MS, 45, DSc, 48. *Prof Exp:* Consult, Askania Regulator Co, 44-49; partner, Eng Specialties, Madeira, 49-65. *Concurrent Pos:* Instr, Univ Cincinnati, 43-45 & 48-49, eve col, 43-49, res engr, 43-45; consult, Wright Field, 46-47; gen mgr, Environ Instruments Div,Ohmart Corp, 71-73. *Mem:* AAAS; sr mem Inst Elec & Electronics Engrs. *Res:* Design of electronic control equipment and magnetic amplifiers for control; development of underwater logistics; electrical, electronic and mechanical research, development and manufacturing; design of nuclear instrumentation for reactor control pruposes; design and manufacture of robot monitors for water quality analysis; development of arc-less contactors. *Mailing Add:* 5209 Kenridge Dr Cincinnati OH 45242

HANCOCK, JAMES FINDLEY, JR, PLANT EVOLUTION, PLANT BREEDING. *Current Pos:* from asst prof to assoc prof, 80-89, PROF HORT, MICH STATE UNIV, 89- *Personal Data:* b Cleveland, Ohio, Jan 20, 50; m 75, Ann Randall. *Educ:* Baldwin-Wallace Col, BS, 72; Miami Univ, MS, 74; Univ Calif, Davis, PhD(genetics), 77. *Prof Exp:* Lab asst biol, Baldwin-Wallace Col, 70-72; teaching asst bot, Miami Univ, 72-74; res asst genetics, Univ Calif, Davis, 74-77; asst prof biol, Univ SC, 77-80. *Concurrent Pos:* Fulbright fel, Univ Talca, Chile, 94. *Mem:* Bot Soc Am; Am Soc Hort Sci. *Res:* Artificial and natural selection in blueberries and strawberries; polyploidy; ecological genetics; gene flow; breeding for disease resistance and physiological traits. *Mailing Add:* Dept Hort Mich State Univ 347 Plant & Soil Sci East Lansing MI 48824-1325. *Fax:* 517-353-0890; *E-Mail:* hancock@pilot.msu.edu

HANCOCK, JOHN C(OULTER), ELECTRICAL ENGINEERING. *Current Pos:* PVT CONSULT, 88- *Personal Data:* b Martinsville, Ind, Oct 21, 29; m 49; c 4. *Educ:* Purdue Univ, BS, 51, MS, 55, PhD, 57. *Honors & Awards:* Lamme Award, Inst Elec & Electronics Engrs, 80. *Prof Exp:* Res engr, US Naval Avionics Facil, Ind, 51-57; from asst prof to prof elec eng, Purdue Univ, 57-80, dir, Electronics Systs Res Lab, 64-65, head sch, 65-80, dir, Appl Electronics Res Lab, 66-80, dean, Sch Eng, 72-80; exec vpres, United Telecommun, 80-88. *Concurrent Pos:* Mem, Nat Sci Bd, Inst Elec & Electronics Engrs. *Mem:* Nat Acad Eng; fel Am Soc Eng Educ; Inst Elec & Electronics Engrs; fel Nat Asn State Univ & Land Grant Col. *Res:* Communication theory. *Mailing Add:* 7056 Spotted Fawn Ct Ft Myers FL 33908. *E-Mail:* jhan33908@aol.com

HANCOCK, JOHN CHARLES, NEURO-CARDIOVASCULAR PHARMACOLOGY, ELECTRO PHYSIOLOGY. *Current Pos:* PROF, INTERIM CHMN & ASSOC CHMN PHARMACOL, ETENN STATE COL MED, 78- *Personal Data:* b Lockwood, Mo, Aug 20, 38. *Educ:* Univ Mo, Kansas City, BS, 62; Univ Tex, MS, 65, PhD(pharmacol), 67. *Prof Exp:* From res assoc to asst prof pharmacol, Health Ctr, Univ Conn, 67-71; assoc prof, Med Ctr, La State Univ, 72-78. *Mem:* AAAS; Sigma Xi; Am Soc Pharmacol & Exp Therapeut; Soc Neurosci; Am Heart Asn. *Res:* Regulation of cardiovascular function by endogenous vasoactive peptides and the changes in blood vessel responsiveness and transmitter release in the hypertensive rat. *Mailing Add:* 3010 Newbern Dr Johnson City TN 37604

HANCOCK, JOSEPH GRISCOM, JR, PLANT PATHOLOGY, SOIL MICROBIOLOGY. *Current Pos:* From asst prof to assoc prof, Univ Calif, Berkeley, 64-76, from asst plant pathologist to assoc plant pathologist, 64-76, chmn, Dept Conserv & Resource Studies, 74-76 & 83-84, actg chmn, Dept Plant Path, 84-85, chmn dept, 85-89, PROF PLANT PATH & PLANT PATHOLOGIST, UNIV CALIF, BERKELEY, 76- *Personal Data:* b Bridgeton, NJ, Apr 8, 38; m 60, 87; c Leita & Mara. *Educ:* Rutgers Univ, BS, 60; Cornell Univ, MS, 63, PhD(plant path), 64. *Concurrent Pos:* Vis prof, Imp

Col, Univ London, 70. *Mem:* Am Phytopath Soc; Mycol Soc Am. *Res:* Physiological aspects of plant disease; ecology of soil-borne plant pathogenic fungi; rhizosphere biology; biological control; integrated pest management. *Mailing Add:* Div Insect Biol Univ Calif 201 Wellman Hall Berkeley CA 94720-3112. *Fax:* 510-642-3845

HANCOCK, KENNETH FARRELL, BIOLOGY. *Current Pos:* From asst prof to assoc prof, 60-67, chmn dept, 62-85, CHARLES A DANA PROF BIOL, BERRY COL, 67- *Personal Data:* b Alexander City, Ala, Apr 17, 30; m 59; c 2. *Educ:* Jacksonville State Col, BS, 50; George Peabody Col, MA, 51; Univ Ala, PhD(biol), 60. *Res:* Plant morphology; phycology. *Mailing Add:* Dept Biol Berry Col One Mount Berry Sta Mt Berry GA 30149-0001

HANCOCK, MICHAEL B, NEUROPHYSIOLOGY. *Current Pos:* ASST PROF ANAT, UNIV TEX MED BR GALVESTON, 69- *Personal Data:* b Dallas, Tex, Mar 11, 39; m 69. *Educ:* Arlington State Col, BS, 62; Univ Tex Southwestern Med Sch Dallas, PhD(neurophysiol), 69. *Prof Exp:* Fel anat, Univ Tex Southwestern Med Sch Dallas, 68-69. *Res:* Spinal cord physiology; interactions of visceral and somatic pathways at the spinal level. *Mailing Add:* Dept Anat Univ Tx Med Sch 301 University Blvd Galveston TX 77550-2708

HANCOCK, PETER ADRIAN, HUMAN FACTORS, STRESS. *Current Pos:* ASSOC PROF, UNIV MINN, 89- *Personal Data:* b Berkley, Eng, March 9, 53; m 79, Frances Martinez; c Susan A & Gabriella M. *Educ:* Loughborough Univ, Eng, BEd, 76, MSc, 78; Univ Ill, PhD(human performance), 83. *Prof Exp:* Res assoc, Univ Ill, 82-83; asst prof safety sci, Univ Southern Calif, 83-89. *Concurrent Pos:* Res grantee, NASA, 86-93; consult, Calif Comn Police Training, 87-, Los Angeles Cty Sheriffs Dept, 87-, Shell Oil Co, 86- & Thermacor Inc, 86-; lectr, Southern Calif Safety Inst, 87- *Mem:* Human Factors Soc; Psychonomic Soc; Am Soc Safety Engrs; Inst Elec & Electronics Engrs; AAAS. *Res:* Human performance under extremes of stress; time dilation and contraction in life-threat conditions and how to engineer human-machine interfaces to cope with such demands. *Mailing Add:* HFRL 141 Mariucci Arena Univ Minn 1901 Fourth St SE Minneapolis MN 55455

HANCOCK, ROBERT ERNEST WILLIAM, MICROBIOLOGY, BIOCHEMISTRY. *Current Pos:* From asst prof to assoc prof, 78-86, sci dir, Can Bact Dis Network, 90-96, PROF MICROBIOL, UNIV BC, 86- *Personal Data:* b Merton, Eng, Mar 23, 49; Can & Brit citizen; m 73, Elizabeth J Hunter; c David G & Lynn M. *Educ:* Univ Adelaide, BSc Hons, 71, PhD(microbiol), 75. *Honors & Awards:* Can Soc Microbiologists Award, 87; Can 125 Silver Medal, 93. *Concurrent Pos:* Consult, Bristol-Myers Squibb & Co, Ltd, 84-91, Genta Inc, 93-94; vis scholar, Monash Univ, 86-87; chmn exec, Med Sci Adv Comt, Can Cystic Fibrosis Found, 90-93; bd dirs, Micrologix Biotechnol Inc, 93-94. *Mem:* Am Soc Microbiol; Infectious Dis Soc Am; Can Soc Microbiologists. *Res:* Role of the outer membranes of gram negative bacteria in bacterial antibiotic resistance, barrier function, pathogenesis and interaction with macrophages; cationic antimicrobial peptides, design and mechanism of action. *Mailing Add:* Dept Microbiol Univ BC Vancouver BC V6T 1Z3 Can. *Fax:* 604-822-6041; *E-Mail:* bob@chdn.ca

HANCOCK, RONALD LEE, BIOCHEMISTRY. *Current Pos:* ASSOC PROF MED BIOCHEM, FAC MED, UNIV CALGARY, 70- *Personal Data:* b St Joseph, Mo, Nov 24, 31; m 55; c 1. *Educ:* Univ Kansas City, BA, 52; Univ Kans, MD, 59. *Prof Exp:* Assoc staff scientist, Jackson Lab, Maine, 64-66, staff scientist, 66-70. *Concurrent Pos:* Fel biochem, Ben May Lab Cancer Res, Univ Chicago, 59-63, USPHS fel, 60-63; Am Cancer Soc Janice M Blood Mem grant cancer res, Jackson Lab, Maine, 64-66, Nat Cancer Inst grant, 66-70; Med Res Coun Can grant, Fac Med, Univ Calgary, 70- *Mem:* Am Chem Soc; Biochem Soc; Can Biochem Soc; fel Royal Soc Health; NY Acad Sci. *Res:* Biochemistry of carcinogenesis; alkylation of transfer RNA. *Mailing Add:* Cancer Res Ctr Hotel-Dieu Hosp 1 Rue de L'Arsenal Quebec City PQ G1R 2J6 Can. *Fax:* 418-691-5439

HANCOCK, V(ERNON) RAY, ALGEBRA. *Current Pos:* chmn dept, 63-74, prof, 63-91, EMER PROF MATH, EMORY & HENRY COL, 91- *Personal Data:* b Baltimore, Md, July 10, 26; m 50, Ruth A Farnham; c Dale K & Clark T. *Educ:* Va Polytech Inst, BS, 49; Johns Hopkins Univ, MA, 51; Tulane Univ, PhD(math), 60. *Prof Exp:* Jr instr, Johns Hopkins Univ, 50-51; from instr to asst prof math, Va Polytech Inst, 52-56; instr, Tulane Univ, 56-60; from asst prof to assoc prof, Va Polytech Inst, 60-63. *Concurrent Pos:* Consult, US Naval Res Lab, 54-59; visitor, Tulane Univ, 70-71; adj prof math, Va Highlands Community Col, 96- *Mem:* Am Math Soc; Math Asn Am. *Res:* Algebraic semigroups. *Mailing Add:* PO Box Y Emory VA 24327-0965

HANCOX, WILLIAM THOMAS, THERMAL-HYDRAULICS, NUMERICAL FLUID MECHANICS. *Current Pos:* sect head, Appl Math & Comput Reactor Analyst Br, 73-76, br head thermalhydraul res, 76-78, dir, Appl Sci Div, 78-84, dir, Local Energy Systs Bus Unit, 84-86, VPRES, ATOMIC ENERGY CAN LTD, 86- *Personal Data:* b New Westminister, BC, Mar 19, 40; m 63; c 2. *Educ:* Carleton Univ, Ont, BEng, 66, MEng, 67; Univ Waterloo, Ont, PhD(mech eng), 71. *Prof Exp:* Res eng, Atomic Power Div, Westinghouse Can, 67-73. *Concurrent Pos:* Adj prof, Univ Waterloo, 71-73. *Mem:* Can Nuclear Soc; Am Nuclear Soc. *Res:* Aspects of candu reactor safety; reprocessing of uranium and thorium fuels; disposal of radioactive waste; radioactive waste management. *Mailing Add:* 128 Dunbarton Ct Ottawa ON K1K 4L6 Can

HAND, ARTHUR RALPH, CELL BIOLOGY, CYTOCHEMISTRY. *Current Pos:* res investr, 68-78, CHIEF, LAB BIOL STRUCT, NAT INST DENT RES, NIH, USPHS, 78- *Personal Data:* b Los Angeles, Calif, May 15, 43; m 61; c 2. *Educ:* Univ Calif, Los Angeles, DDS, 68. *Honors & Awards:* Commendation Medal, USPHS, 75; Basic Res Oral Sci Award, Int Asn Dent Res, 78. *Concurrent Pos:* Vis prof, Dept Anat, McGill Univ, 76-77. *Mem:* Am Soc Cell Biol; Int Asn Dent Res; Sigma Xi; Histochem Soc; AAAS. *Res:* Ultrastructure, cytochemistry and function of cellular organelles; mechanisms of exocrine secretion. *Mailing Add:* Dept Pediat Dent & Orthod Univ Conn Health Ctr Farmington CT 06030. *Fax:* 860-679-4078

HAND, BRYCE MOYER, SEDIMENTOLOGY. *Current Pos:* PROF GEOL, SYRACUSE UNIV, 69- *Personal Data:* b Jersey City, NJ, Mar 22, 36; m 63; c 2. *Educ:* Antioch Col, BA, 58; Univ Southern Calif, MS, 61; Pa State Univ, PhD(geol), 64. *Prof Exp:* Asst prof geol, Amherst Col, 64-69. *Mem:* AAAS; fel Geol Soc Am; Am Asn Petrol Geol; Soc Econ Paleont & Mineral. *Res:* Sediment transport; bedform dynamics. *Mailing Add:* Dept Geol Syracuse Univ Heroy Geol Lab Syracuse NY 13244

HAND, CADET HAMMOND, JR, INVERTEBRATE ZOOLOGY. *Current Pos:* from asst prof to prof, 53-85, dir, Bodega Marine Lab, 61-85, EMER PROF ZOOL, UNIV CALIF, BERKELEY, 85- *Personal Data:* b Patchogue, NY, Apr 23, 20; m 42, Winifred Werdelin; c Cadet H III & Gary A. *Educ:* Univ Conn, BS, 46; Univ Calif, MA, 48, PhD(zool), 51. *Prof Exp:* From instr to asst prof zool, Mills Col, 48-51; asst res zoologist, Scripps Inst, Univ Calif, 51-53. *Concurrent Pos:* Mem, Pac Sci Bd Res Exped to Kapingamarangi Atoll, Caroline Islands, 54; NSF sr fel, NZ & Australia, 59-60; consult, NIH, 63-66 & NSF, 63-67; John Simon Guggenheim Mem Found fel, 67-68; mem, Nuclear Regulatory Comn, Atomic Safety & Licensing Bd Panel, 71-93; admin judge, US Nuclear Regulatory Comn, 80-93. *Mem:* Soc Syst Zool; Am Soc Limnol & Oceanog; Ecol Soc Am; Soc Integrative & Comp Biol. *Res:* Systematic and natural history studies of invertebrates, particularly hydroids and sea anemones; symbiosis, particularly in hydroids. *Mailing Add:* Bodega Marine Lab PO Box 247 Bodega Bay CA 94923

HAND, CLIFFORD WARREN, PHYSICAL CHEMISTRY. *Current Pos:* ASSOC PROF CHEM, UNIV ALA, 69 *Personal Data:* b Philadelphia, Pa, Jan 3, 36; m 60. *Educ:* Cornell Univ, AB, 57; Harvard Univ, PhD(phys chem), 61. *Prof Exp:* Res assoc chem, Princeton Univ, 61-62; fel, Carnegie-Mellon Univ, 63-67, asst prof, 67-69. *Mem:* Am Chem Soc; Am Phys Soc; Sigma Xi. *Res:* Gas phase kinetics; fast reactions; flash photolysis; mass spectroscopy. *Mailing Add:* 9 Fairway Dr Tuscaloosa AL 35405

HAND, GEORGE SAMUEL, JR, EXPERIMENTAL EMBRYOLOGY. *Current Pos:* asst prof, 69, assoc dir med admis, 85-94, ASSOC PROF ANAT, UNIV ALA, BIRMINGHAM, 75-, ASST DEAN ADMIS, 95- *Personal Data:* b Perryville, Mo, Aug 22, 36; m 61, Judith Hayes; c Emily K & Gregory S. *Educ:* Southeast Mo State Col, BS, 58; Washington Univ, MA, 61; Univ NC, PhD(zool), 67. *Prof Exp:* NIH res fel embryol, Calif Inst Technol, 67-69. *Concurrent Pos:* Lectr, Univ Calif, Los Angeles, 69. *Mem:* AAAS; Am Soc Zoologists; Soc Development Biol; Sigma Xi. *Res:* Macromolecular synthesis during early development; comparative histophysiology of endometrium; fertilization physiology; RNA and protein synthesis during early development; embryonic induction. *Mailing Add:* Med Student Serv Univ Ala Sch Med P100 Volker Hall Birmingham AL 35294-0019. *Fax:* 205-934-8724; *E-Mail:* ghand@uasom.meis.uab.edu

HAND, JAMES HENRY, CHEMICAL ENGINEERING. *Current Pos:* assoc proc consult, 81-94, PROCESS ENG SCIENTIST, DOW CORNING CORP, 94. *Personal Data:* b Jersey City, NJ, Jan 2, 43. *Educ:* Newark Col Eng, BS, 66; Univ Calif, Berkeley, PhD(chem eng), 71. *Prof Exp:* From asst prof to assoc prof, Univ Mich, Ann Arbor, 77-81. *Mem:* Am Inst Chem Engrs. *Res:* Mathematical modeling of polymerization reactors; applied statistical mechanics and thermodynamics. *Mailing Add:* 715 Shorefront Circle Midland MI 48640-7245

HAND, LOUIS NEFF, HIGH ENERGY PHYSICS, ACCELERATOR PHYSICS. *Current Pos:* assoc prof, 65-71, PROF PHYSICS, CORNELL UNIV, 71- *Personal Data:* b Hollywood, Calif, Oct 16, 33; m 56, Elizabeth Kasanin; c Jonathan, Brooke, Pattie & Sonya. *Educ:* Swarthmore Col, BA, 55; Stanford Univ, PhD(physics), 61. *Prof Exp:* Res fel physics, Harvard Univ, 61-62, instr, 62-64, asst prof, 64-65. *Concurrent Pos:* Alfred P Sloan fel, 64-66; John Simon Guggenheim Mem fel, 80-81; Sci Res Coun vis fel, Oxford, 80-81; vis foreign scientist, Deutsches Elektronec-Synchrotron, 86-88. *Mem:* Am Phys Soc; AAAS. *Res:* Experimental high energy nuclear physics; accelerator physics. *Mailing Add:* Dept Physics Cornell Univ Clark Hall Ithaca NY 14853. *E-Mail:* lnh1@cornell.edu

HAND, PETER JAMES, NEUROBIOLOGY. *Current Pos:* head, Dept Anat, 80-87 & 91-97, MEM FAC, UNIV PA, 64-, PROF ANAT, 79- *Personal Data:* b Oak Park, Ill, Jan 5, 37; m 58, 76, 86, Christine L Arnold; c Katherine Patricia, Carol Jane, Margaret Anne, Robin Lynn, Stephen Douglas & Peter James. *Educ:* Univ Pa, VMD, 61, PhD(neuroanat), 64. *Concurrent Pos:* Grantee, NIH, 70-82, 86-92 & 95-98; mem rev comt, Regional Primate Ctrs, NIH, 85-89. *Mem:* Am Asn Anatomists; Am Asn Vet Anatomists; Soc Neurosci; Int Brain Res Orgn; World Asn Vet Anatomists; Int Asn Study Pain; Am Soc Acupuncture (pres-elect, 95-96); Sigma Xi. *Res:* Published articles on neurobiology, specifically neuroplasticity and acupuncture-produced analgesia mechanisms. *Mailing Add:* PO Box 144 Wycombe PA 18980. *Fax:* 215-898-9923

HAND, ROGER, INTERNAL MEDICINE, HEALTH CARE SERVICES RESEARCH. *Current Pos:* PROF MED, UNIV ILL, CHICAGO, 84-, PROF HEALTH POLICY & ADMIN, 95- *Personal Data:* b Brooklyn, NY, Sept 25, 38; c Christopher & Jessica. *Educ:* NY Univ, BS, 59, MD, 62. *Prof Exp:* Clin asst prof med, Med Sch, Cornell Univ, 70-73; asst attend physician, Mem Hosp Cancer & Allied Dis, McGill Univ, 72-73, from asst prof to assoc prof, Dept Med & Microbiol, 73-78, from asst physician to assoc physician, Royal Victoria Hosp, 73-78, prof med, Dept Med, Cancer Ctr, 78-84, dir, Cancer Ctr, 80-84; chmn, Dept Med, Ill Masonic Med Ctr, 84-88; chief, Sect Gen Internal Med, Univ Ill Chicago Col Med, 88-95. *Concurrent Pos:* Sr investr, NY Heart Asn, Rockefeller Univ, 72-73; transfer receipt & vis prof, Univ Bern, 77; assoc ed, Clin & Investigative Med, 81-84; vis scientist, Int Cancer Res Technol, NIH, 83; mem bd dirs, Am Cancer Soc, Ill Div, 87-93; prin clin coordr, Ill Health Care Qual Improvement Prog. *Mem:* Am Soc Clin Invest; Am Soc Biol Chemists; Am Soc Clin Oncol; Am Soc Cell Biol; Am Asn Cancer Res; Asn Health Serv Res. *Res:* Health care outcomes, access to health care, clinical guidelines and standards of health care; basic research in biochemistry of DNA. *Mailing Add:* Sect Gen Internal Med Rm 720S CSIS Col Med Univ Ill Chicago 787 840 S Wood St Chicago IL 60612. *E-Mail:* rphand@uic.edu

HAND, STEVEN CRAIG, METABOLIC REGULATION, COMPARATIVE BIOCHEMISTRY. *Current Pos:* asst prof biol, 86-89, ASSOC PROF BIOL, UNIV COLO, 89- *Educ:* Ore State Univ, PhD(physiol), 80. *Prof Exp:* Asst prof biol, Univ Southwestern La, 82-86. *Mailing Add:* Dept Environ Pop & Org Biol Univ Colo Campus PO Box B-334 Boulder CO 80309-0334. *Fax:* 303-492-8699

HAND, THOMAS, FORTH ENVIRONMENTS, EXTENSIBLE SOFTWARE. *Current Pos:* CHMN, GRAD COMPUT SCI, FLA INST TECHNOL, 81- *Personal Data:* b Olean, NY, Feb 28, 43; m 66; c 1. *Educ:* Fla Southern Col, BS, 64; Okla Univ, PhD(math), 72. *Prof Exp:* Prof comput sci, Ind State Univ, 72-78; consult, Software Environ, 78-81. *Mem:* Asn Comput Mach; Inst Elec & Electronics Engrs. *Res:* expert systems, relational data base systems, operating systems, compilers and other extensions to FORTH. *Mailing Add:* 617 Manor Pl Melbourne FL 32904

HANDA, PAUL, THERMODYNAMICS & MATERIAL PROPERTIES, PHYSICAL CHEMISTRY. *Current Pos:* RES OFFICER CHEM, NAT RES COUN, CAN, 82- *Personal Data:* b Lucknow, India, Dec 9, 50; Can citizen; m 78, Tina Passi; c Amy & Anita. *Educ:* Punjab Univ, BSc, 70, MSc, 72; Univ Otago, NZ, PhD(chem), 75. *Prof Exp:* Fel chem, Univ Calif, Los Angeles, 75-76; fel, Wright State Univ, Dayton, 76-77; res assoc, Nat Res Coun, Can, 77-81; res chemist, Allied Chem Co, Buffalo, 81-82. *Res:* Thermodynamic properties of solids and fluids; stability, structure and thermophysical properties of inclusion compounds especially gas hydrates; pressure and thermally induced phase transitions; materials; climate change; gas separation membranes. *Mailing Add:* Inst Environ Chem Nat Res Coun Ottawa ON K1A 0R6 Can. *Fax:* 613-952-1275; *E-Mail:* paul@iec.lan.nrc.ca

HANDA, V(IRENDER) K(UMAR), CONSTRUCTION, CIVIL ENGINEERING. *Current Pos:* lectr civil eng, 60-64, from asst prof to assoc prof, 64-69, PROF CIVIL ENG, UNIV WATERLOO, 69- *Personal Data:* b India, Dec 28, 31; m 62; c 2. *Educ:* Univ Calcutta, BSc, 49; Univ London, BSc, 54; Queen's Univ, Ont, MASc, 58; Univ Waterloo, MSc, 62, PhD(civil eng), 64. *Honors & Awards:* Peurifoy Construct Res Award, Am Soc Civil Engrs, 94. *Prof Exp:* Staff photographer, The Spotlight, India, 49-50; eng trainee, K Hajnal Konyi, 53-54; civil engr, William H Laithwaite, 54-56; teaching asst, Queen's Univ, Ont, 56-58; asst construct engr, Eldorado Mining & Refining Ltd, 58; proj engr soils, Racey McCallum & Assocs, Ltd, 59-60. *Concurrent Pos:* Nat Res Coun Can grants, 62-; consult, Nat House-Builders Asn Can, 64-; vis prof & chmn, Dept Civil Eng, Univ Petrol & Minerals, Dhahran, Saudi Arabia, 69-70 & Polytech Sch, Fed Univ Paraiba, Brazil, 71; vis prof Inter Am Comt Agr Develop, Univ West Indies, 74-75, 77; mem comn W.65, Int Coun Building Res & Documentation, 74-, coordr, 89-; mem, steering comt indust building construct, Can Standards Asn, 74-, vchmn, 90-; head econ group, construct indust study proj group, Ministry Planning & Develop, Govt Trinidad & Tobago, 75-77; guest prof, Swiss Fed Inst Technol, Zurich, 79; adv, Cree Housing Corp, 80-87; adv, Secondary Sch Bldg Prog, Gov Trinidad, Tobago, 77-79; external examnr, Fac eng, Univ WI, 85; UN Tokten expert, Govt India, 85-; mem, Fire Code Comn, Govt Ont, 90-95. *Mem:* Can Stand Asn; fel Inst Engrs India; Am Soc Civil Engrs; Prof Engrs Ont; Asn Researchers Construct UK; Construct Mgt Asn Am. *Res:* Construction: organization, productivity, project management, planning and control process; economics; resource allocation; operations research; econometrics; cold regions northern engineering; industrialized buildings; housing; educational planning; training in developing countries; energy, small scale low-head hydro power. *Mailing Add:* Dept Civil Eng Univ Waterloo Waterloo ON N2L 3G1 Can. *Fax:* 519-749-0127

HANDEL, DAVID, TOPOLOGY. *Current Pos:* assoc prof, 72-78, PROF MATH, WAYNE STATE UNIV, 78- *Personal Data:* b Brooklyn, NY, June 20, 38; m 63, 70; c 2. *Educ:* Calif Inst Technol, BS, 59; Univ Chicago, MS, 60, PhD(math), 65. *Prof Exp:* NSF fel, Univ Calif, Berkeley, 65-66, actg asst prof math, 66-67, lectr, 67-68; asst prof, Univ Wash, 68-72. *Mem:* Am Math Soc. *Res:* Algebraic topology; embeddings and immersions of manifolds in Euclidean space; nonsingular bilinear maps; K theory; topological methods in approximation theory; thom modules. *Mailing Add:* Dept Math Wayne State Univ Detroit MI 48202-9861

HANDEL, MARK DAVID, TROPICAL CYCLONE DYNAMICS, CLIMATE CHANGE. *Current Pos:* SR STAFF OFFICER, NAT RES COUN, 93- *Personal Data:* b Queens, NY, June 20, 57. *Educ:* Univ Chicago, AB, 79; Mass Inst Technol, SM, 84, ScD(atmospheric physics), 91. *Prof Exp:* Res meteorologist, Hurricane Res Div, Nat Oceanic & Atmospheric Admin, 87; geophys scholar, Phillips Lab, USAF, 91-92. *Concurrent Pos:* Sr consult, Tigger Co, 76-93; mem, Hurricane Andrew Disaster Surv Team, Nat Oceanic & Atmospheric Admin, 92-93, Hurricane Iniki Disaster Surv Team, 92-93. *Mem:* Am Meteorol Soc; Am Geophys Union; Natural Hazards Soc; AAAS; Am Phys Soc. *Res:* Policy issues across the atmospheric sciences; tropical cyclone dynamics, in particular cyclone formation and intensification; integrated assessments of climate change and the history of the science of the greenhouse effect. *Mailing Add:* Nat Acad Sci 2101 Constitution Ave NW Washington DC 20418. *Fax:* 202-334-3825; *E-Mail:* mhandel@nas.edu

HANDEL, MARY ANN, CELL BIOLOGY. *Current Pos:* from asst prof to assoc prof, 73-88, PROF ZOOL, UNIV TENN, 88- *Personal Data:* b New Haven, Conn, Feb 27, 43; m 67; c 1. *Educ:* Goucher Col, BA, 65; Johns Hopkins Univ, MS, 67; Kans State Univ, PhD(biol), 70. *Prof Exp:* Fel biol, Oak Ridge Nat Lab, 70-73. *Concurrent Pos:* Am Cancer Soc fel, 70. *Mem:* AAAS; Soc Study Reproduction; Am Soc Cell Biol; Soc Develop Biol; Genetics Soc Am. *Res:* Cytological and genetic aspects of cell differentiation during spermatogenesis. *Mailing Add:* Dept Zool Univ Tenn Knoxville TN 37996-0840. *Fax:* 423-974-6306

HANDELMAN, DAVID E, MATHEMATICS, OPERATOR ALGEBRAS. *Current Pos:* PROF, DEPT MATH, UNIV OTTAWA, 77- *Personal Data:* b Toronto, Ont, Nov, 22, 50; m 75, Rochelle Gold; c Michael & Daniel. *Educ:* Univ Toronto, BS, 72; McGill Univ, MS, 73, PhD(math), 75. *Concurrent Pos:* Steacie mem fel, Natural Sci & Eng Res Coun Can, 85; Killam res fel, Can Coun, 91. *Mem:* Royal Soc Can. *Res:* Mathematics; connections between classification of W-algebra ergodic tronst, zandum walks and choquet theory. *Mailing Add:* Dept Math Univ Ottawa Ottawa ON K1N 6N5 Can. *E-Mail:* dehsg@uottawa.ca

HANDELMAN, EILEEN T, MICROWAVE SPECTROSCOPY. *Current Pos:* RETIRED. *Personal Data:* b Holyoke, Mass, Dec 11, 28; m 59, Robert B; c Audrey (Kalman). *Educ:* Mt Holyoke Col, BA, 50, MA, 52; Univ Calif, Berkeley, PhD(phys chem), 55. *Prof Exp:* NSF fel, Univ Copenhagen, Denmark, 55-56; mem tech staff, Bell Tel Labs, Murray Hill, 56-66; prof physics & dean sci, Simon's Rock Col, 68- *Mem:* Am Asn Physics Teachers. *Res:* Microwave spectroscopy; molecular structure; solid state and semiconductor physics; author of numerous publications; awarded several patents. *Mailing Add:* Dept Natural Sci Simon's Rock Col Great Barrington MA 01230. *Fax:* 413-528-7365

HANDELMAN, GEORGE HERMAN, APPLIED MATHEMATICS. *Current Pos:* chmn dept, Rensselaer Polytech Inst, 60-72, prof appl math, 55-78, dean, Sch Sci, 72-78, Amos Eaton prof, 78-90, EMER AMOS EATON PROF APPL MATH, RENSSELAER POLYTECH INST, 90- *Personal Data:* b Pittsburgh, Pa, Mar 24, 21; m 49, Marcia M; c Nancy M & Louise S (Sanito). *Educ:* Harvard Univ, AB, 41, AM, 42; Brown Univ, PhD(appl math), 46. *Prof Exp:* Res assoc appl math, Brown Univ, 43-47, asst prof eng, 47-48; from asst prof to assoc prof math, Carnegie Inst Technol, 48-55. *Concurrent Pos:* Mem, US Nat Comt Theoret & Appl Mech, 71-77; book rev ed, Soc Indust & Appl Math, Rev & Soc Indust Appl Math, News. *Mem:* Am Math Soc; Soc Indust & Appl Math; fel Am Soc Mech Eng. *Res:* Elasticity; vibrations; stability; wave motion; math problems in biology. *Mailing Add:* 6 Clinton Pl Troy NY 12180-6805

HANDELSMAN, JACOB C, SURGERY. *Current Pos:* Asst prof, 54-63, surg dir, Same Day Surg, Hopkins Hosp, 90-96, SURGEON & IN CHG OUTPATIENT CLIN, SCH MED, JOHNS HOPKINS UNIV, 50-, ASSOC PROF SURG, 63- *Personal Data:* b Elizabeth, NJ, Jan 20, 19; m 43, Shirley Silverberg; c Stephen, Bruce, Walter & Jane. *Educ:* Johns Hopkins Univ, AB, 40, MD, 43. *Honors & Awards:* Arnold Seligman Lectr, Sinai, 94. *Concurrent Pos:* Attend surgeon, Sinai Hosp, 51-, chief surg, 77-78. *Mem:* Soc Univ Surgeons; Am Col Surg. *Res:* Surgical teaching; pediatric and general surgery; writings on various surgical subject; cardiac pediatric, general surgery inflammatory bowel disease, patient evaluation for surgery. *Mailing Add:* 220 W Cold Spring Lane Baltimore MD 21210

HANDELSMAN, JO, MOLECULAR BIOLOGY. *Current Pos:* from asst prof to assoc prof, 85-95, PROF PLANT PATH, UNIV WIS, 95- *Personal Data:* b New York, NY, Mar 19, 59. *Educ:* Cornell Univ, BS, 79; Univ Wis, PhD(molecular biol), 83. *Prof Exp:* Res fel, Am Cancer Soc, 84 & NIH, 84-85. *Mem:* Am Soc Microbiol; Am Phytopath Soc. *Res:* Molecular basis of competitiveness of Rhizobium phaseoli in nodulation of beans; elucidating the mechanism of attachment of Agrobacterium tumefaciens to its host plant; mechanisms of biocontrol of root rot pathogens of crop plants. *Mailing Add:* Dept Plant Path Univ Wis 284 Russell Labs 1630 Linden Dr Madison WI 53706

HANDIN, ROBERT I, HEMATOLOGY, HEMOSTASIS. *Current Pos:* fel, Harvard Med Sch, 71-73, instr, 73-74, from asst prof to assoc prof, 74-93, PROF MED, HARVARD MED SCH, 93- *Personal Data:* b New York, NY, June 20, 41; m 67; c Marcia Rew; c David & Mark. *Educ:* Univ Calif, Berkeley, AB, 63; Univ Calif Med Ctr, San Francisco, MD, 67. *Hon Degrees:* AM, Harvard Univ, 93. *Honors & Awards:* Merit Award & Res Career Develop Award, NIH. *Prof Exp:* Resident, Peter Bent Brigham Hosp, 67-69; lt comdr res, Naval Blood Res Lab, USNR, 69-71. *Concurrent Pos:* Sr physician & dir,

Hemat & Oncol Div, Brigham & Womens Hosp. *Mem:* Am Soc Clin Invest; Am Soc Hemat; Am Soc Biol Chemists; Am Fedn Clin Res; Am Asn Physicians. *Res:* Role of platelets in hemostasis and thrombosis. *Mailing Add:* Hemat-Oncol Div Brigham & Women's Hosp Boston MA 02115. *Fax:* 617-732-5706; *E-Mail:* handin@calvin.harvard.edu

HANDLER, BARBARA HERSHEY, COMPUTER BASED INSTRUCTION, ADOPT A SCHOOL PROGRAM. *Current Pos:* CONSULT, 96- *Personal Data:* b Detroit, Mich, Sept 10, 39; m 61, Leonard; c Charles A & Amy E. *Educ:* Mich State Univ, BS, 61, MA, 64; Univ Tenn, EdD, 82. *Prof Exp:* Instr, Univ Tenn, 70-85; develop assoc, Lockheed Martin Energy Systs Inc, 85-96. *Mem:* Nat Mgt Asn (secy, 95-96); Math Asn Am; Am Asn Univ Prof; Women Math Educ; Am Mgt Asn; Nat Coun Teachers & Mathematics. *Res:* Science, mathematics, computer science education in schools for both students and instructors; development of computer based instruction and use of computer systems in education. *Mailing Add:* 1800 Kinglet Lane Knoxville TN 37919. *E-Mail:* bhhandler@aol.com

HANDLER, EVELYN ERIKA, cell biology, for more information see previous edition

HANDLER, JOSEPH S, INTERNAL MEDICINE. *Current Pos:* sr investr renal physiol, Nat Heart Inst, 60-67, head membrane metab unit, 67-76, SECT HEAD, LAB KIDNEY & ELECTROLYTE METAB, NAT HEART LUNG & BLOOD INST, 76- *Personal Data:* b New York, NY, Apr 19, 29; m 55. *Educ:* Univ Pa, AB, 50, MD, 54. *Prof Exp:* Instr med, Univ Pa, 57-60. *Mem:* Am Fedn Clin Res; Am Physiol Soc; Soc Gen Physiol; Am Soc Clin Invest. *Res:* Renal physiology. *Mailing Add:* Dept Med Div Nephrol Johns Hopkins Univ Sch Med 720 Rutland Ave Ross Bldg 958 Baltimore MD 21205-2196. *Fax:* 410-955-0485

HANDLER, PAUL, CLIMATE. *Current Pos:* Res assoc, 54-56, from asst prof to prof, 56-92, EMER PROF PHYSICS, UNIV ILL, URBANA, 92- *Personal Data:* b Newark, NJ, Apr 24, 29; m 52; c 3. *Educ:* Univ Chicago, PhD, 54. *Concurrent Pos:* Guggenheim fel, 60-61. *Mem:* Am Meteorol Soc; Am Phys Soc. *Res:* Climate and long range weather and crop forecasting; computer-assisted instruction. *Mailing Add:* Dept Physics Univ Ill 1110 W Green St Urbana IL 61801

HANDLER, SHIRLEY WOLZ, BIOLOGY, GENETICS. *Current Pos:* RETIRED. *Personal Data:* b Marshall, Tex, Jan 2, 25. *Educ:* Univ Tex, BA, 45, MA, 47; Univ Okla, PhD(biol educ), 58. *Prof Exp:* Asst genetics, Univ Tex, 44-47; assoc prof chem, E Tex Baptist Col, 47-49 & biol, 49-51 & 53-58, chmn, Div Sci & Math, 71-79, prof biol & head dept, 58-90, adj prof & chief health adv, 90-96. *Mem:* AAAS; Am Chem Soc; Am Soc Human Genetics; Am Genetic Asn; Nat Asn Biol Teachers. *Res:* Master's chromosomal aberration in Drosophila melanogaster as produced by x-ray; teaching methods in college biology. *Mailing Add:* 203 E Crockett Marshall TX 75670

HANDLEY, DEAN A, CARDIOVASCULAR PHARMACOLOGY, ATHEROSCLEROSIS INFLAMMATION. *Current Pos:* SR RES SCIENTIST, SANDOZ RES INST, 81- *Personal Data:* b Salisbury, Md, Sept 20, 49. *Educ:* Rutgers Univ, PhD(microbiol), 78. *Concurrent Pos:* Mem, Coun Arteriosclerosis, Am Heart Asn. *Mem:* Am Soc Microbiol; Am Soc Cell Biol; Am Physiol Soc; Am Asn Pathologists; Soc Exp Biol & Med; Am Heart Asn. *Mailing Add:* 17 Garfield Dr Westborough MA 01581

HANDLIN, DALE L, POLYMER MORPHOLOGY, STRUCTURE PROPERTY RELATIONSHIPS. *Current Pos:* sr res chemist, 82-94, STAFF RES CHEMIST, SHELL DEVELOP, 94- *Personal Data:* b Clemson, SC, Sept 4, 56; m 78. *Educ:* Clemson Univ, BS, 78; Univ Mass, MS, 81, PhD(polymer sci & eng), 83. *Mem:* Am Phys Soc; Am Chem Soc. *Res:* Structure property relationships of multi-phase composite matrix materials and block co-polymers. *Mailing Add:* Shell Develop Co PO Box 1380 Houston TX 77251

HANDMAN, STANLEY E, SAFETY IN PROCESSING SYSTEMS & EQUIPMENT DESIGN & OPERATION, INNOVATIVE MECHANICAL DESIGN. *Current Pos:* OWNER, S E HANDMAN CONSULTS, 86- *Personal Data:* b New York, NY, Jan 17, 23; m 49, Emily Bonvicino. *Educ:* Polytech Univ, Brooklyn, BME, 44; MME, 50. *Honors & Awards:* Centennial Award, Am Soc Mech Engrs, 80; Distinguished Serv Award, Welding Res Coun, 87. *Prof Exp:* Develop test eng, Gen Elec Co, 46-47; instr mech eng, Polytech Inst Brooklyn, 47-51; anal engr, M W Kellogg Co, 51-59, supvr, Mech Eng Develop Lab, Res & Develop, 59-61, sect head mech eng develop, 61-64, mgr, Mech Eng Develop Div, Res & Develop Dept, 64-73, chief mech eng, 73-78, chief engr, 78-86. *Concurrent Pos:* Adj instr mech eng, Polytech Inst, Brooklyn, 51-54; mem exec comt, Safety Div, Am Soc Mech Engrs, 67-72, chmn, 71-72; mem, Bd Safety Codes & Stand, Am Soc Mech Engrs, 72-84; mem bd dir, welding res coun 78-86, mem exec comm bd, 82-86. *Mem:* Am Soc Mech Engrs; Nat Soc Prof Engrs; NY Acad Sci; Sigma Xi; AAAS. *Res:* Development of equipment and systems for the chemical, petroleum petrochemical and liquified fuel gas industries with emphasis on safety and economical designs to meet industries needs. *Mailing Add:* 32 Joyce Rd Plainview NY 11803

HANDORF, CHARLES RUSSELL, NEUROPSYCHOPHARMACOLOGY, TRACE METAL RESEARCH. *Current Pos:* sect chief toxicol, 82-91, ASSOC DIR, MED EXPRESS LABS, 85-; CHMN & DIR LABS, METHODIST HOSPS MEMPHIS, 88- *Personal Data:* b Memphis, Tenn, Jan 1, 51; m 76; c 2. *Educ:* Rice Univ, BA, 73; Univ Tenn, MD, 77, PhD(chem), 81; Am Bd Path, cert, 82. *Prof Exp:* Resident path, Univ Tenn & Methodist Hosps Memphis, 78-82. *Concurrent Pos:* Marion res fel, Marion Labs, 73; adj instr, Univ Tenn, 78-80, clin instr, 83-; nat med dir, Personal Blood Storage, 91- *Mem:* Sigma Xi; AMA; Col Am Pathologists; Am Soc Clin Pathologists. *Res:* Neuropsychopharmacology; trace metal research; urine drug screening technology. *Mailing Add:* 1591 Peabody Ave Memphis TN 38104-6654. *Fax:* 901-726-7182

HANDSCHUMACHER, ROBERT EDMUND, PHARMACOLOGY. *Current Pos:* From instr to assoc prof pharmacol, Sch Med, Yale Univ, 56-64, dir grad studies, 63-70, dir, Div Biol Sci, 69-71, chmn dept, 74-77, PROF PHARMACOL, SCH MED, YALE UNIV, 64- *Personal Data:* b Glenside, Pa, Oct 16, 27; m 49, 81; c 2. *Educ:* Drexel Univ, BS, 49; Univ Wis, MS, 51, PhD(biochem), 53. *Concurrent Pos:* Nat Found Infantile Paralysis fel, Lister Inst Prev Med, London, 53-54; Squibb fel, Sch Med, Yale Univ, 55-56, scholar cancer res, 57-62; Eleanor Roosevelt sr fel, Prague & London, 62-63; sci consult, Am Cancer Soc, 63-, career prof, 64-74; consult, Anna Fuller Fund, 65-73, sci adv, 73-88; consult, Nat Cancer Inst, 65- *Mem:* Fel AAAS; Am Chem Soc; Am Asn Cancer Res; Am Soc Biol Chemists; Am Soc Pharmacol & Exp Therapeut. *Res:* Biochemical pharmacology; nucleic acid and amino acid metabolism; development of antimetabolites and enzymes for chemotherapy; pharmacological control of the immune response. *Mailing Add:* Dept Pharmacol Yale Univ Sch Med PO Box 208066 New Haven CT 06520-8066. *Fax:* 203-785-7670

HANDWERGER, BARRY S, RHEUMATOLOGY, IMMUNOLOGY. *Current Pos:* HEAD, DIV RHEUMATOL & CLIN IMMUNOL & PROF MED & MICROBIOL, SCH MED, UNIV MD, BALTIMORE, 85- *Personal Data:* b Baltimore, Md, Apr 25, 43; m 67, Marilyn Greenfield; c Adam & Korie. *Educ:* Johns Hopkins Hosp, BA, 64; Univ Md, MD, 68; Am Bd Internal Med, cert, 79; Am Bd Med Lab Immunol, cert, 80. *Prof Exp:* Clin assoc, Gerontol Res Ctr, NICHD, NIH, 70-72, sr staff fel, Immunol Br, Nat Cancer Inst, 72-74; asst prof med, Sect Rheumatology/Immunol Dept Med, Sch Med, Univ Minn, 74-81, asst prof microbiol, 74-85; assoc prof med & immunol, Mayo Med Sch, Rochester, head, Rheumatol Res Unit, Mayo Clin/ Mayo Found & consult, Dept Med Rheumatol/Immunol, 81-85. *Concurrent Pos:* Mem, Ctr Grants Study Sect, Nat Arthritis Found, 79-84 & 86-87, med sci comt, Arthritis Found, 75-85, res grant rev comt, Am Diabetes Asn, 83-85, legis subcomt Res Coun, Am Col Rheumatol, 89-91. *Mem:* Fel Am Rheumatism Asn; Am Asn Immunologists; Am Fedn Clin Res; fel Am Col Rheumatol; Cent Soc Clin Res. *Res:* Basic rheumatology and immunology; immunology of systemic lupus erthematosus and diabetes mellitus; biochemistry and cell biology of T cell activation; numerous technical publications; immunology of aging. *Mailing Add:* Dept Med Univ Md Sch Med Baltimore MD 21201-1192. *Fax:* 410-706-0231

HANDWERGER, STUART, DEVELOPMENTAL & FETAL ENDOCRINOLOGY. *Current Pos:* PROF PEDIAT & PHYSIOL, DUKE UNIV, 71- *Personal Data:* b Baltimore, Md, Dec 10, 38; m 64, Roberta Blaker; c David & Rachel. *Educ:* Johns Hopkins Univ, AB, 60; Univ Md, MD, 64. *Prof Exp:* Intern pediat, Jacobi Hosp, Bronx, NY, 64-65; resident, Mt Sinai Hosp, NY, 65-66; clin assoc metab, NIH, Bethesda, Md, 66-68; fel endocrinol, Harvard Med Sch, Childrens Hosp Med Ctr, 68-69, Beth Israel Hosp, Boston, 69-71. *Concurrent Pos:* prin investr, NIH grants, 72-, res career develop award, 74-79; mem, Nat Adv Coun, Nat Inst Child Health & Human Develop Award, 74-79; mem, Human Embryol & Develop Study Sect, NIH, 78-84; vis scientist & Guggenheim fel, Weizmann Inst Sci, Israel, 79-80; assoc ed, J Clin Endocrinol & Metab, 84; bd sci adv, Barbara Davis Diabetes Ctr, Univ Colo, Denver, 87- *Mem:* Am Soc Clin Invest; Am Pediat Soc; Soc Pediat Res; Endocrine Soc; Am Acad Pediat; AAAS. *Res:* Physiology of prolactin, placental lactogen and growth factors in the mother and fetus during pregnancy; regulation of the synthesis and secretion of these hormones and factors. *Mailing Add:* Div Pediat Endocrinol Childrens Hosp Med Ctr Elland & Bethesda Aves Cincinnati OH 45229-2883. *Fax:* 513-636-7486; *E-Mail:* stuart.handwerger@chmcc.org

HANDWERKER, CAROL, CERAMICS ENGINEERING. *Current Pos:* CHIEF, METALL DIV, NAT INST STAND & TECHNOL, 96- *Personal Data:* b Feb 28, 51. *Educ:* Mass Inst Technol, PhD(ceramics), 83. *Mailing Add:* Nat Inst Stand & Technol Rte 270 Bldg 223 Rm B261 Gaithersburg MD 20895

HANDWERKER, THOMAS SAMUEL, TREE FRUITS, POMOLOGY. *Current Pos:* PROF HORT & HEAD AGR & AQUACULT PROGS, UNIV MD-EASTERN SHORE, 87- *Personal Data:* b Little Rock, Ark, Dec 9, 51; m 80; c 1. *Educ:* Univ Tenn, BS, 73; Cornell Univ, MS, 76, PhD(pomol), 79. *Prof Exp:* Exten horticulturist pomol, Tex Agr Exten Serv, Tex A&M Univ, 79-87. *Mem:* Am Soc Hort Sci; Am Pomol Soc. *Res:* Fruit crops. *Mailing Add:* Dept Agr Univ Md-Eastern Shore Princess Anne MD 21853-1299

HANDY, CARLETON THOMAS, TEXTILE CHEMISTRY. *Current Pos:* RETIRED. *Personal Data:* b Cataumet, Mass, July 16, 18; m 43, Ruth Lees; c Margaret (Isenberg), Alice & Carol. *Educ:* Yale Univ, BS, 40, PhD(org chem), 43. *Prof Exp:* Res chemist, Exp Sta, E I du Pont de Nemours & Co Inc, 43-57, sr res chemist, Textile Fibers Dept, 57-60, res supvr, 60-70, asst to tech dir, Textile Fibers Dept, 70-78, asst to res & develop dir, 79-81. *Mem:* Fel AAAS; Am Chem Soc; Fiber Soc (pres, 73). *Res:* Synthetic organic chemistry; organic peroxides; polyester and polyamide fibers; fabric construction, finishing and performance characterization. *Mailing Add:* PO Box 727 Cataumet MA 02534

HANDY, LYMAN LEE, RESERVOIR ENGINEERING, SURFACE CHEMISTRY. *Current Pos:* prof & chmn, Petrol Eng Dept, 66-88, EMER PROF CHEM & PETROL ENG, UNIV SOUTHERN CALIF, 88- *Personal Data:* b Payette, Idaho, Aug 4, 19; wid; c Mark R & C Eileen. *Educ:* Univ Wash, BS, 42, PhD(chem), 51. *Prof Exp:* Res assoc, Calif Res Corp, Stand Oil Co, Calif, 51-66. *Mem:* Am Chem Soc; Am Inst Chem Engrs; Soc Petrol Engrs. *Res:* Colloid and surface chemistry; multiphase flow of fluids in porous media; enhanced oil recovery; structural and thermodynamic properties of certain inorganic compounds. *Mailing Add:* 1401 E Dana Pl Fullerton CA 92631-1110

HANDY, RICHARD L(INCOLN), GEOTECHNICAL ENGINEERING. *Current Pos:* From asst prof to assoc prof, Iowa State Univ, 56-63, prof civil eng & head geotech res lab, 63-91, Anson Marston distinguished prof, 87-91, EMER DISTINGUISHED PROF CIVIL ENG, IOWA STATE UNIV, 91- *Personal Data:* b Chariton, Iowa, Feb 12, 29; m 64, 82, Kathryn E Claussen; c Beth. *Educ:* Iowa State Univ, BS, 51, MS, 53, PhD(geol, soil eng), 56. *Honors & Awards:* T A Middlebrooks Award, Am Soc Civil Engrs, 85. *Concurrent Pos:* Res consult. *Mem:* Fel AAAS; Soil Sci Soc Am; Am Soc Civil Engrs; fel Geol Soc Am. *Res:* Geotechnical engineering; soil mechanics; development soil and rock testing devices; Pleistocene geology and geomorphology. *Mailing Add:* 1502 270th St Madrid IA 50156. *Fax:* 515-795-3998

HANDY, ROBERT M(AXWELL), ELECTRICAL ENGINEERING, SOLID STATE PHYSICS. *Current Pos:* dir bus & tech planning, Integrated Circuits Div, Motorola, Inc, 76-80, patent agt & semiconductor technol specialist, 80-84, patent atty, 84-91, GROUP INTELLECTUAL PROPERTY COUN, MOTOROLA, INC, 91- *Personal Data:* b Buffalo, NY, Apr 1, 31; m 55; c 3. *Educ:* Trinity Col, BS, 53; Northwestern Univ, MS, 58, PhD(elec eng), 62. *Prof Exp:* Sr engr, Westinghouse Res Labs, 61-65, mgr oxides & surfaces res, 65-68, mgr solid state devices res, 68-69, mgr prod planning & develop, Semiconductor Div, Westinghouse Elec Corp, 69; prod mgr, Semiconductor Div, Motorola, Inc, Phoenix, Ariz, 69-72, corp dir res, 72-75; exec dir, Ariz Solar Energy Res Commn, 75-76. *Concurrent Pos:* Lectr, Carnegie Inst Technol, 64-65. *Mem:* Inst Elec & Electronics Engrs; Am Phys Soc. *Res:* Solid state electronics; semiconductors; thin films; tunneling; hot electron effects in solids; surface effects on semiconductors; semiconductor devices. *Mailing Add:* Motorola Inc Patent Dept R3108 PO Box 10219 Scottsdale AZ 85271

HANE, CARL EDWARD, SEVERE THUNDERSTORMS. *Current Pos:* METEOROLOGIST ATMOSPHERIC RES, NAT SEVERE STORMS LAB, ENVIRON RES LABS, NAT OCEANIC & ATMOSPHERIC ADMIN, DEPT COM, 76- *Personal Data:* b Leavenworth, Kans, Mar 19, 43; m 66, Nancy Meyn; c Elizabeth & Andrew. *Educ:* Univ Kans, BA & BS, 66; Fla State Univ, MS, 68, PhD(meteorol), 72. *Prof Exp:* Fel, Nat Ctr Atmospheric Res, 72-73; atmospheric res scientist, Battelle Northwest Lab, Battelle Mem Inst, 73-76. *Concurrent Pos:* Adj assoc prof meteorol, Univ Okla. *Mem:* Am Meteorol Soc; fel Cooperative Inst Mesoscale Meteorol Studies. *Res:* Numerical modelling of convective clouds; analysis of observations from severe thunderstorms; planning and execution of severe storms observational programs. *Mailing Add:* Nat Severe Storms Lab 1313 Halley Circle Norman OK 73069. *E-Mail:* hane@nssl.voknor.edu

HANEBRINK, EARL L, ORNITHOLOGY, ANIMAL ECOLOGY. *Current Pos:* RETIRED. *Personal Data:* b Mar 24, 24; US citizen; wid; c Lisa & Kay (Noell). *Educ:* Southeast Mo State Col, BSE, 48; Univ Miss, MS, 55; Okla State Univ, EdD(zool), 65. *Prof Exp:* Sci instr high sch, Mo, 48-57; from instr to prof biol, Ark State Univ, 58-93. *Concurrent Pos:* NSF lectr, Southeast Mo State Univ, 62- *Mem:* Am Ornith Union; Wilson Ornith Soc; Nat Audubon Soc; Sigma Xi; Am Birding Asn. *Res:* Heronry in Mississippi County, Arkansas; bird populations and habitat selections of birds in northeastern Arkansas; pigeon milk and pigeon behavior studies; environmental surveys. *Mailing Add:* Dept Biol Sci Ark State Univ PO Box 67 State University AR 72467

HANEGAN, JAMES L, COMPARATIVE PHYSIOLOGY. *Current Pos:* from asst prof to assoc prof, 70-81, chmn dept, 74-76, PROF BIOL, EASTERN WASH UNIV, 81- *Personal Data:* b Chicago, Ill, Apr 11, 44; m 65; c 2. *Educ:* Northern Ill Univ, BS, 66; Univ Maine, MS, 68; Univ Ill, PhD(physiol), 70. *Concurrent Pos:* Fel, NASA-Ames Res Ctr, 72-73. *Mem:* AAAS; Am Soc Zool; Sigma Xi. *Res:* Neurophysiology of insect flight; insect temperature regulation; central nervous system control of mammalian thermoregulation. *Mailing Add:* PO Box 2170 Medical Lake WA 99022

HANEL, RUDOLF A, ATMOSPHERIC PHYSICS. *Current Pos:* consult, Aeronomy & Meteorol Div, 59-65, chief scientist, Lab Planetary Atmospheres, 65-77, SR SCIENTIST LAB EXTRA TERRESTRIAL PHYSICS, GODDARD SPACE FLIGHT CTR, NASA, 77- *Personal Data:* b Krems, Austria, July 14, 22; US citizen; m 58; c 2. *Educ:* Vienna Tech Univ, BS, 48, MS, 50, PhD(physics), 53. *Honors & Awards:* Spec Serv Award, NASA Group Achievement Award & Sustained Super Performance Award, 63. *Prof Exp:* Asst prof electronics, Vienna Tech Univ, 50-53; res physicist, US Army Res & Develop Lab, Ft Monmouth, NJ, 53-59. *Res:* Ultrasonics; space electronics; physics of planetary atmospheres; infrared; Fourier spectroscopy. *Mailing Add:* 31 Brinkwood Rd Brookeville MD 20833

HANES, DARCY ELIZABETH, BACTERIAL ADHERENCE & INVASION, TISSUE CULTURE. *Current Pos:* MICROBIOLOGIST, FOOD & DRUG ADMIN, 87- *Personal Data:* m 86, Joseph A Martin. *Educ:* St Bonaventure Univ, BS, 82; State Univ NY, Buffalo, MA, 86, PhD(microbiol), 89. *Mem:* Am Soc Microbiol. *Res:* Determining the attachment and invasion factors of food-borne pathogens and the genes that code for them; determine the control mechanism for expression of these genes. *Mailing Add:* 3609 Pocono Pl Beltsville MD 20705. *Fax:* 202-205-4185; *E-Mail:* deh@vax8.cfsan.fda.gov

HANES, DEANNE MEREDITH, BIOLOGY, IMMUNOLOGY. *Current Pos:* NIH fel, 70-73, RES IMMUNOLOGIST, DEPT SURGERY, TRANSPLANT UNIT, HISTOCOMPATIBILITY LAB, MED CTR, UNIV CALIF, SAN FRANCISCO, 73- *Personal Data:* b Weehawken, NJ, Aug 7, 42. *Educ:* Hunter Col, BA, 64; Univ Calif, Davis, PhD(nutrit, biochem), 70. *Concurrent Pos:* Res asst lysosomal biochem, Univ Calif, Davis, 66-70. *Mem:* AAAS; Sigma Xi; Am Soc Human Genetics. *Res:* Transplantation immunology; aspects of immunology at the cellular level. *Mailing Add:* 317 Michelle Lane Daly City CA 94015-2880

HANES, HAROLD, MATHEMATICS. *Current Pos:* From asst prof to assoc prof, 62-71, PROF MATH, EARLHAM COL, 71- *Personal Data:* b Thebes, Ill, Apr 10, 31; m 56, Mary A Woolsey; c Ann E & Harold M. *Educ:* Tex Christian Univ, BA, 57; Univ Kans, MA, 59, PhD(math), 67. *Mem:* Asn Comput Mach; Math Asn Am; Am Math Soc; Soc Indust & Appl Math. *Res:* Theory of finite groups, specifically factorizability. *Mailing Add:* Dept Math Earlham Col Richmond IN 47374. *E-Mail:* haroldh@yang.earlham.edu

HANES, N BRUCE, ENVIRONMENTAL ENGINEERING. *Current Pos:* RETIRED. *Personal Data:* b Minot, NDak, Jan 24, 34; m 54; c 5. *Educ:* NDak State Univ, BS, 54; Univ Wis, MS, 57, PhD(civil eng), 61. *Prof Exp:* Instr sanit eng, Univ Wis, 55-57; instr environ eng, Mont State Col, 57-59; from asst prof to prof environ eng, Tufts Univ, 61-93, chmn, Dept Civil Eng, 69-81. *Concurrent Pos:* Consult, Nat Coun Stream Improv, 63-64; US Public Health Serv, Environ Protection Agency, & NSF. *Mem:* Am Water Works Asn; Water Pollution Control Fedn; Am Acad Environ Engrs; Asn Environ Eng Professors (past pres). *Res:* Water pollution, survival of indicator bacteria in water and oxygen demand of benthal deposits. *Mailing Add:* 40 Kingston Ct Gibsonville NC 27249

HANES, RONNIE MICHAEL, ORGANIC CHEMISTRY, CATALYSIS. *Current Pos:* sr res chemist, 77-87, group leader, US Indust Chem, 87-90, SECT LEADER, QUANTUM CHEM, 90- *Personal Data:* b Birmingham, Ala, Apr 15, 49; m 71; c 2. *Educ:* Univ Ala, BS, 72, PhD(org chem), 76. *Prof Exp:* Res assoc, Dept Chem, Univ Ga, 76-77. *Mem:* Am Chem Soc; Catalysis Soc. *Res:* Organic synthesis via homogeneous catalysis; supported homogeneous catalysts. *Mailing Add:* 11530 N Lake Dr Cincinnati OH 45249. *Fax:* 513-530-4206

HANES, SHEILA DELFELD, PALEOBOTANY, PALYNOLOGY. *Current Pos:* asst prof, 76-, ASSOC PROF BIOL, ECKERD COL. *Personal Data:* b Dallas, Tex, Feb 26, 39; m 73. *Educ:* Baylor Univ, BA, 61; Univ Ill, Chicago Circle, MS, 69; Ohio Univ, PhD(bot), 75. *Prof Exp:* Res asst bot, Univ Tex, Austin, 61-64; res asst anat, Univ Mo Med Sch, 64-65; res asst bot, Univ Iowa, 65-66, res asst zool, 66-67. *Mem:* Sigma Xi (secy-treas, 78-79); Bot Soc Am; Am Asn Stratig Palynologists; Torrey Bot Club; Int Orgn Paleobot. *Res:* Structure and morphology of living and fossil lycopods; ferns and gymnospermous plants; transmission and scanning electron microscopy of fossil and extant pollen and spores. *Mailing Add:* Div Natural Sci Eckerd Col PO Box 12560 St Petersburg FL 33733

HANES, TED L, PLANT ECOLOGY. *Current Pos:* RETIRED. *Personal Data:* b Los Angeles, Calif, Mar 31, 28; m 60; c 4. *Educ:* Univ Calif, Los Angeles, BS, 50, MS & PhD(plant ecol), 63; Claremont Grad Sch, MA, 58. *Prof Exp:* Teacher high sch, Calif, 55-57; biologist, Citrus Jr Col, 57-69; prof, Calif State Univ, Fullerton, 69-93, dir, Arboretum, 80-85. *Concurrent Pos:* Environ consult, NSF res grant, 66-68, Ultrasysts, Inc, 73- & numerous environ firms. *Mem:* AAAS; Ecol Soc Am; Nat Audubon Soc. *Res:* Ecology of chaparral vegetation; chaparral succession after fire in the mountains of southern California; natural areas; environmental assessment and impact studies; vegetation community structure and dynamics. *Mailing Add:* 680 S Walnut St San Dimas CA 91773

HANESIAN, DERAN, CHEMICAL ENGINEERING, REACTOR DESIGN. *Current Pos:* from asst prof to assoc prof, 63-70, chmn dept, 75-88, PROF CHEM ENG, CHEM & ENVIRON SCI, NJ INST TECHNOL, 63- *Personal Data:* b Niagara Falls, NY, Sept 26, 27; m 86, Eva G Pogosian. *Educ:* Cornell Univ, BChE & PhD(chem eng), 61. *Honors & Awards:* Mid-Atlantic AT&T Found Award, Am Soc Eng Educ, 86, John Fluke Award, 94. *Prof Exp:* Engr, E I du Pont de Nemours & Co Inc, 52-57, res engr, 60-63. *Concurrent Pos:* Consult, E I du Pont de Nemours, 64-66, Exxon Affil, 67-70, NJ Inst Technol, 72-74, Celanese Corp, 77 & 80, Ctr Plastics Recycling Res, Rutgers, State Univ, 88-93, Johnson & Johnson, 93-, Napp Technol, 94 & Elan Chem Co, 95; grant, NSF, 67-69 & 72-74, German Acad Exchange Serv, 81-82; mem, Adv Bd J Int Chem Eng, Am Inst Chem Engrs, 73-79, Tech prog comt, 67 & 77, prof develop comt, 70-86, nat prog comt, 74-86, secy, vchmn & chmn, 74-79, educ projs comt, 69-, vchmn, 80-82, chmn, 83-85, past chmn, 86; invited lectr, Algerian Petrol Inst, 78; secy, Div Exp & Lab Oriented Studies, Am Soc Eng Educ, 78-80, prog chmn/chmn-elect, 80-81, chmn, 82-83, past chmn 83-84, nominating comt chmn, 86; vis prof, Univ Edinburgh, Scotland, 81, Ctr Plastics Recycling Res, Rutgers, State Univ NJ,

89-90; Fulbright scholar, USSR, 82; vchmn, Chem Eng Div, Am Soc Eng Educ, 83-84, chmn, 84-85, past chmn, 85-86, mem comt, 85-87, nominating comt, 85-88. *Mem:* Am Inst Chem Eng; Am Chem Soc; Am Soc Eng Educ; Sigma Xi. *Res:* Chemical kinetics and chemical reaction engineering; process dynamics, simulation and control optimization of chemical reactor systems; plastics recycling, in-situ soil remediation. *Mailing Add:* Dept Chem Eng Chem & Environ Sci NJ Inst Technol 323 Dr Martin Luther King Jr Blvd Newark NJ 07102. *Fax:* 973-596-8436; *E-Mail:* hanesian@tesla.njit.edu

HANESSIAN, STEPHEN, ORGANIC CHEMISTRY. *Current Pos:* assoc prof, 68-70, PROF CHEM, UNIV MONTREAL, 70- *Personal Data:* b Alexandria, Egypt, Apr 25, 35; US citizen; m 57; c 3. *Educ:* Univ Alexandria, BSc, 56; Ohio State Univ, PhD(chem), 60. *Honors & Awards:* Merck Sharpe & Dohme Award, Chem Inst Can, 74. *Prof Exp:* Res chemist, Starch Prod Co, 56-57; NIH fel, 57-59; Charles Kettering fel, 59-60; res chemist, Parke, Davis & Co, 61-68. *Mem:* Am Chem Soc. *Res:* Carbohydrates; antibiotics; natural products. *Mailing Add:* Dept Chem Univerite de Montreal CP 6128 Station A Montreal PQ H3C 3J7 Can. *Fax:* 514-343-5728

HANEY, ALAN WILLIAM, PLANT ECOLOGY. *Current Pos:* PROF FORESTRY & DEAN, COL NATURAL RESOURCES, UNIV WIS-STEVENS POINT, 88- *Personal Data:* b Portsmouth, Ohio, Oct 12, 41; div; c Ryan Steven. *Educ:* Ohio State Univ, BS, 63; Yale Univ, MF, 65; State Univ NY, PhD(forest ecol), 68. *Prof Exp:* From asst prof to assoc prof bot, Univ Ill, Urbana, 68-77; prof biol & chmn, Div Natural Sci, Warren Wilson Col, 77-88. *Concurrent Pos:* Grant ecol wild marijuana in Ill, 69-70 & grant effects wildlife & logging on bird pop; mem, Wis Natural Areas Comn; sci adv, Sand Co Found. *Mem:* Ecol Soc Am; Soc Am Foresters; Am Orinthologist's Union. *Res:* Ecology of colonizing species; mechanisms of plant interactions, especially plant succession; chemical interactions between weed and crop plants; population dynamics and community structure in disturbed forest communities. *Mailing Add:* Col Natural Resources Univ Wis Stevens Point WI 54481

HANEY, DAVID N, COMPUTATIONAL CHEMISTRY, DRUG DISCOVERY. *Current Pos:* CONSULT & PRES, HANEY ASSOC, 93- *Personal Data:* b Springfield, Ill, Feb 10, 53; m 74, Nancy Burritt; c Seth & Sean. *Educ:* Boston Univ, BA, 75; Northwestern Univ, MS, 79, PhD(chem), 81. *Prof Exp:* Res scientist, Harvard Med Sch, 75-76; res assoc, Brookhaven Nat Lab, 80-82; mgr pioneering res & innovation, Kimberly-Clark Corp, 82-87; dir sci support, Biosym Technol, Corning Inc, 87-93. *Concurrent Pos:* NIH teaching fel, 79, NATO fel, 89; vis prof comput chem, Va Med Col, 90, 91, 92 & 93. *Mem:* Am Chem Soc; Sigma Xi; NY Acad Sci; AAAS; Am Inst Chemists; Royal Soc Chem; Drug Info Asn. *Res:* Utilize biochemistry, medicinal chemistry and computational chemistry methods to study specific drug discovery problems; studies result in potential new drugs and new methods for drug discovery; published 15 papers and granted 2 patents. *Mailing Add:* Haney Assoc 4212 93rd Ave SE Mercer Island WA 98040. *Fax:* 206-236-5268; *E-Mail:* haney@hbond.com

HANEY, DONALD C, GEOLOGY, SOILS. *Current Pos:* MEM FAC, DIR & STATE GEOLOGIST, GEOL SURV, UNIV KY, 80- *Personal Data:* b Ferguson, Ky, July 2, 34; m 56; c 2. *Educ:* Univ Ky, BS, 60, MS, 62; Univ Tenn, PhD(geol), 66. *Prof Exp:* Instr geol, Campbellsville Col, 60-62; from instr to assoc prof geol, Eastern Ky Univ, 62-76, chmn dept, 68-80, prof, 76-80. *Mem:* Geol Soc Am. *Res:* Structural geology of east Tennessee; research with Pennsylvanian's sediments in eastern Kentucky, including structure, sedimentology and coal resources. *Mailing Add:* 185 Adams Lane Richmond KY 40475

HANEY, JAMES FILMORE, LIMNOLOGY, STREAM ECOLOGY. *Current Pos:* from asst prof to assoc prof, 72-86, PROF ZOOL, UNIV NH, 86- *Personal Data:* b Bergholz, Ohio, May 20, 38; c 3. *Educ:* Miami Univ, BA, 61, MA, 63; Univ Toronto, PhD(limnol), 70. *Prof Exp:* Instr zool, Miami Univ, 65-66; res assoc limnol, Kellog Biol Sta, Mich State Univ, 70-72. *Concurrent Pos:* Consult, Radiol & Environ Res Div, Argonne Nat Lab, 74-; co-dir, NH Lakes Lay Monitoring Prog, 79- *Mem:* Am Soc Limnol & Oceanog; Int Soc Theoret & Appl Limnol. *Res:* Interactions of zooplankton and phytoplankton communities; feeding relationships of zooplankton; factors which regulate and consequences of diel vertical migration. *Mailing Add:* Dept Zool Univ NH Spaulding Hall Durham NH 03824-4724

HANEY, ROBERT LEE, METEOROLOGY, OCEANOGRAPHY. *Current Pos:* From asst prof to assoc prof meteorol, 70-83, PROF METEOROL, NAVAL POSTGRAD SCH, 83- *Personal Data:* b Newport News, Va, Oct 14, 38; m 66; c 1. *Educ:* George Wash Univ, BA, 64; Univ Calif, Los Angeles, PhD(meteorol), 71. *Concurrent Pos:* Vis prof, Univ Hawaii, 83-84; co-ed, J Phys Oceanog, 83-88. *Mem:* Am Meteorol Soc; Sigma Xi; Nat Geog Soc. *Res:* Numerical modelling and analysis of coastal oceanography. *Mailing Add:* 17 Caribou Ct Monterey CA 93940

HANFF, ERNEST SALO, ELECTRICAL ENGINEERING. *Current Pos:* From asst res officer to assoc res officer, 71-81, SR RES OFFICER, NAT RES COUN, 82- *Personal Data:* b Santiago, Chile, July 16, 40; Can citizen; m 64; c 2. *Educ:* Univ Toronto, BASc, 65; Univ Western Ontario, MESc, 67, PhD(elec eng), 71. *Concurrent Pos:* Lectr, Algonquin Col Technol, 74-77; chmn comt instrumentation, Aerospace Simulation Facilities, Inst Elec & Electronics Engrs, 77- *Mem:* Inst Elec & Electronics Engrs; Am Inst Aeronaut & Astronaut. *Res:* Data handling; signal extraction and instrumentation particularly as applied to studies of the dynamic stability and performance of aircraft. *Mailing Add:* NRC 1500 Montreal Rd Bldg M-10 Ottawa ON K1A 0R6 Can

HANFORD, WILLIAM EDWARD, CHEMISTRY. *Current Pos:* RETIRED. *Personal Data:* b Bristol, Pa, Dec 9, 08; m 39, Lorraine Easom; c William Jr. *Educ:* Philadelphia Col Pharm, BS, 30; Univ Ill, MS, 32, PhD(org chem), 35. *Hon Degrees:* DSc, Philadelphia Col Pharm, 56, Alfred Univ, 59. *Honors & Awards:* Gold Medal, Am Inst Chemists, 74. *Prof Exp:* Analyst chemist, Rohm and Haas, Pa, 30-31; asst chem, Univ Ill, 32-35; res chemist, Exp Sta, E I du Pont de Nemours & Co, Del, 35-36, group leader, 36-42; from asst dir res to dir res, Gen Aniline & Film Corp, Pa, 42-46; tech consult, M W Kellogg Co, 46-47, dir petrol & chem res, 48-50, vpres, dir res & mem bd dirs, 50-57; asst to pres, Olin Corp, NY, 57, vpres res & develop, Conn, 57-73; consult, World Water Resources Inc, 73-85. *Mem:* AAAS; Am Chem Soc; Soc Indust Chem; Am Inst Chem Engrs. *Res:* Synthetic organic chemistry; high pressure reactions; polymerization; petroleum chemistry; granted one patent. *Mailing Add:* 4956 Sentinel Dr Apt 306 Bethesda MD 20816

HANFT, RUTH S, HEALTH POLICY, HEALTH ECONOMICS. *Current Pos:* RETIRED. *Personal Data:* b New York, NY, July 12, 29; m 51; c 2. *Educ:* Cornell Univ, BS, 49; Hunter Col, MA, 63; George Washington Univ, PhD, 89. *Hon Degrees:* ScD, Univ Osteop Med & Health Sci. *Prof Exp:* Pub admin intern & consult mgt, NY State Dept Social Welfare, 51-54; res assoc health econ, Health Res Coun, 62-63; social sci analyst, Social Security Admin, 64-66; prog analyst, Health Care Off Econ Opportunity, 66-68, Health Care & Econ, HEW, 68-71, spec asst to asst secy health financing, 71-72; sr res assoc, Health Econ Inst Med, 72-76; consult health policy-self employ, 76-77; dep asst secy, Health Policy, HEW, 77-78, dep asst secy health res statist technol, 79-81; consult, 81-91; res prof, Dept Health Mgt & Policy, George Washington Univ, 88-91, prof, 91-93. *Concurrent Pos:* Consult health econ, DC Dept Health, 64; vis prof, Health Policy, Dartmouth Col, 76- *Mem:* Inst Med-Nat Acad Sci; fel Hastings Inst. *Res:* Health care financing; health manpower. *Mailing Add:* 3609 Cameron Mills Rd Alexandria VA 22305

HANG, DANIEL F, ENGINEERING ECONOMICS. *Current Pos:* prof, 47-84, dir, Nuclear Reactor Lab, 92-94, EMER PROF ELEC & NUCLEAR ENG, UNIV ILL, URBANA, 84-; PRES, HTH ASSOCS, 78- *Personal Data:* b Cleveland, Ohio, July 17, 18; m 41, Ruth Ann McGaughey; c 2. *Educ:* Univ Ill, BS, 41, MS, 49. *Honors & Awards:* Distinguished Serv Award, Nat Coun Examiners Eng & Surv, 90. *Prof Exp:* Proj engr, Gen Elec Co, NY, 41-47. *Concurrent Pos:* Consult, Argonne Nat Lab, 61-80, Commonwealth Edison Co & US Army Corps Eng, 71-76, Nat Coun Examiners Eng & Surv, 84-; mem, Ill State Prof Eng Exam Comt, 71- & Ill Atomic Energy Comn, 78-85. *Mem:* Nat Soc Prof Engrs; Inst Elec & Electronics Engrs; Am Soc Eng Educ; Am Nuclear Soc; Nat Coun Examiners Eng & Surv. *Res:* Engineering economy; nuclear fuel cycle; nuclear fuel management; electrical engineering; power systems. *Mailing Add:* 2012 Boudreau Dr Urbana IL 61801. *Fax:* 217-333-2906; *E-Mail:* d_hang@uiue.edu

HANG, YONG DENG, FOOD SCIENCE, WATER POLLUTION. *Current Pos:* Res assoc plant proteins, NY State Agr Exp Sta, Cornell Univ, 68-70, res assoc water pollution, 70-76, from asst prof to assoc prof, 76-90, PROF FOOD SCI, CORNELL UNIV, 90- *Personal Data:* b Kampot, Cambodia. *Educ:* Nat Taiwan Univ, BS, 62; Univ Alta, MS, 65; McGill Univ, PhD(microbiol), 68. *Mem:* Inst Food Technologists; Am Soc Microbiol; Sigma Xi. *Res:* Microbial degradation of phenolic compounds; development of practical methods of isolation, processing and utilization of plant proteins; effects of processing conditions on fruit and vegetable effluents; biological treatment of processing effluents; utilization of agricultural and industrial wastes; production of fuels, chemicals and biologics from waste materials; solid-state fermentation systems. *Mailing Add:* 26 Maxwell Dr Geneva NY 14456

HANGARTER, ROGER PAUL, PLANT PHOTOSENSORY SYSTEMS, PLANT DEVELOPMENT. *Current Pos:* ASSOC PROF BIOL, IND UNIV, 95- *Personal Data:* b Flushing, NY, Nov 28, 52. *Educ:* State Univ Col Geneseo, BA, 75; Mich State Univ, MS, 77, PhD(plant physiol), 81. *Prof Exp:* Res assoc, Mich State Univ, 81-83, Univ Ill, 83-86; from asst prof to assoc prof plant biol, Ohio State Univ, 86-95. *Mem:* Am Soc Plant Physiologists; Sigma Xi; Int Soc Plant Molecular Biol; AAAS. *Res:* Genetics and physiological approaches are used to investigate the photosensory systems that regulate photomorphogenesis in plants and how plants integrate the information from multiple sensory system to coordinate their development programs. *Mailing Add:* Dept Biol Indiana Univ Jordan Hall Bloomington IN 47405-6801. *E-Mail:* rhangart@bio.indiana.edu

HANGARTNER, THOMAS NIKLAUS, QUANTITATIVE BONE MEASUREMENTS, OSTEOPOROSIS. *Current Pos:* assoc prof biomed eng & med, 86-94, PROF BIOMED, MED & PHYSICS, WRIGHT STATE UNIV, 94- *Personal Data:* b Brunnen, Switz, Aug 9, 49; US, Swiss & Can citizen; m 75, Elisabeth Everts; c Lilian. *Educ:* Stiftsschule, Einsiedeln, Switz, Matriculation, 70; Swiss Fed Inst Technol, dipl phys eth physics, 75, teaching cert second educ, 75, Dr sc nat, 78. *Honors & Awards:* Cert merit, Radiol Soc NAm, 89. *Prof Exp:* Asst prof appl sci med, Univ Alta, 79-82, assoc prof, 82-85. *Concurrent Pos:* Reviewer & cnslt, Am Inst Biol Sci, 83, Inst Arthritis, Muscular, Skeletal & Skin Dis, NIH, 87, small Bus Innovative Res, NIH, 88, Inst Aging, NIH, 91; mem, Am Asn Phys Med, Standing Comt Diag Radiol, 88-91 & Nat Ctr Health Statist, 88 & 97. *Mem:* Am Asn Phys Med; Am Inst Physics; NY Acad Sci. *Res:* Development and application of highly precise bone measurement methods; computed tomography; changes in bone density due to osteoporosis; disuse, spinal-cord injury, stroke; osteogenesis imperfecta; granted one US patent. *Mailing Add:* 504 E Bldg 1 Wyoming St Dayton OH 45409. *Fax:* 937-208-2278; *E-Mail:* thangart@delta.cs.wright.edu

HANGGI, EVELYN BETTY, ACOUSTICS & DATA ANALYSIS, ANIMAL COGNITION. *Current Pos:* RESEARCHER, UNIV CALIF, SANTA CRUZ, 93-, FOUNDER & HEAD, EQUINE COGNITION PROJ, 93- *Personal Data:* b Chicago, Ill, Oct 13, 59. *Educ:* San Jose State Univ, BS, 81; Univ Calif, Santa Cruz, BA, 86, MS, 88, PhD(biol), 92. *Prof Exp:* Res chemist, Timex, 82-83; res asst, Sea Lion Cognition Proj, Univ Calif, Santa Cruz, 85-91, res asst & lab mgr, 91-92; res marine biologist, Biosoc Res Found, 92-93. *Concurrent Pos:* Res biologist, Biosoc Res Found, 93-; prin investr, Harbor Seal Bioacoust Proj, 93- *Mem:* Animal Behav Soc; Soc Marine Mammal; Nat Geog Soc. *Res:* Studying the breeding behavior of harbor seals and how their underwater vocalizations are used during the reproductive season; cognition in harbor seals and sea lions as well as other species; fluctuating asymmetry in pinnipeds and lizards; cognition in horses-specifically how they make association, process information, and encode stimuli in memory. *Mailing Add:* 3861 Trout Gulch Rd Aptos CA 95003. *Fax:* 408-423-4271

HANIG, JOSEPH PETER, NEUROPHARMACOLOGY, TOXICOLOGY. *Current Pos:* Pharmacologist & proj leader, Div Pharmacol, Bur Sci, 68-70, pharmacologist & proj leader, 70-73, group leader, 73-93, br chief, 93-95, DEP DIV DIR, CTR DRUG EVAL & RES, DIV RES & TESTING, US FOOD & DRUG ADMIN, 96- *Personal Data:* b New York, NY, Apr 29, 41; m 69, Jill; c 3. *Educ:* Rutgers Univ, BS, 62; NY Med Col, MS, 65, PhD(pharmacol), 68; Am Bd Toxicol, dipl, 80, recert, 85, 90 & 95; Acad Toxicol Sci, dipl, 84, recert, 89 & 94. *Concurrent Pos:* NIH fel, 68; Nat Acad Sci-Nat Res Coun res assoc, 68-70; adj asst prof pharmacol, New York Med Col, 74-75; vis lectr toxicol, Sch Med, Howard Univ, 75-81, vis assoc prof toxicol, 81-89, vis prof toxicol, 89-; adj assoc prof pharmacol, New York Med Col, 75- *Mem:* AAAS; Am Soc Pharmacol & Exp Therapeut; Soc Exp Biol & Med; Sigma Xi; Acad Toxicol Sci (vpres, 94-95); Soc Toxicol; Asn Govt Toxicologists. *Res:* Blood-brain barrier permeability; drug effects, pharmacologic mechanisms; biogenic amine and ethanol-biogenic amine interactions in brain; neurochemistry, effects on behavior; studies of putative neurotransmitter substances; drug toxicity; drug interactions, adverse effects; effects of drugs on intracranial pressure; adrenergic receptor sensitivity in hypertension; effects of nutrition on drug toxicity. *Mailing Add:* Ctr Drug Eval & Res FDA Div Testing & Appl Analytical Develop HFD 926 8301 Muirkirk Rd MOD 1 Laurel MD 20708. *Fax:* 301-594-3037; *E-Mail:* hanig@cder.fda.gov

HANIN, ISRAEL, PSYCHOPHARMACOLOGY, NEUROPHARMACOLOGY. *Current Pos:* PROF & CHMN, DEPT PHARMACOL & DIR, NEUROSCI & AGING INST, STRITCH SCH MED, LOYOLA UNIV CHICAGO, 86- *Personal Data:* b Shanghai, China, Mar 29, 37; US citizen; m 60, Leda T Wermer; c Adam & Darlia. *Educ:* Univ Calif, Los Angeles, BS, 62, MS, 65, PhD(pharmacol), 68. *Prof Exp:* Vis res scientist, Dept Toxicol, Karolinska Inst, Sweden, 68; NIMH fel & pharmacologist, Lab Preclin Pharmacol, NIMH, St Elizabeth Hosp, Washington, DC, 69-73; prog dir psychopharmacol, Dept Psychiat, Western Psychiat Inst & Clin, Sch Med, Univ Pittsburgh, 73-86, from asst prof to prof psychiat & pharmacol, 73-86. *Mem:* Am Chem Soc; fel Am Col Neuropsychopharmacol; Am Soc Neurochem; Am Soc Pharmacol & Exp Therapeut (pres, 90-92); Soc Neurosci; Collegium Int Psychopharmacol. *Res:* Measurement of the extent of neurotransmitter involvement, particularly of acetylcholine, in various psychiatric disorders; measurement and correlation of the neurochemical findings with effects of drug therapy on clinical course; investigation in research animals of the effect of psychoactive drugs on the neurotransmitter mechanisms under investigation; development of animal models of neuropsychiatric disease states; animal models of Alzheimer's disease; cholinotoxins; nootropic drugs. *Mailing Add:* Dept Pharmacology Loyola Univ Chicago Stritch Sch Med 2160 S First Ave Maywood IL 60153. *Fax:* 708-216-6596

HANING, BLANCHE COURNOYER, PHYTOPATHOLOGY, EDUCATIONAL ADMINISTRATION. *Current Pos:* ACAD COORDR PEST MGT & ASSOC PROF PLANT PATH, NC STATE UNIV, 77-, ASSOC PROF ENTOM, 80- *Personal Data:* b Paxton, Mass, Mar 7, 43; m 70. *Educ:* Univ Mass, BS, 65; Iowa State Univ, MS, 67, PhD(plant path), 70. *Prof Exp:* Fel plant path, De Kalb AgRes, Inc, 70-74; asst prof biol sci, Northern Ill Univ, 75-76. *Concurrent Pos:* Mem comt, Nat Constraints Work Group, Off Technol Assessment, 78-79; mem, Food & Agr Systs Analysis, Col & Univ Fac Develop Workshop, 86; assoc prof biol sci, NC State Univ. *Mem:* Am Phytopath Soc; Entom Soc Am. *Mailing Add:* Plant Path NC State Univ PO Box 7616 Raleigh NC 27695-0001

HANIS, CRAIG L, GENETIC EPIDEMIOLOGY. *Current Pos:* Res instr human genetics, Grad Sch Biomed Sci, 81-83, from asst prof to assoc prof, 83-91, ASSOC PROF EPIDEMIOL, SCH PUB HEALTH, UNIV TEX HEALTH SCI CTR, 87-, PROF, GRAD SCH BIOMED SCI, 91- *Personal Data:* b Seattle, Wash, Apr 11, 52; m 74; c 4. *Educ:* Brigham Young Univ, BS, 74, MS, 77; Univ Mich, MA, 81, PhD(human genetics), 81. *Concurrent Pos:* Res career develop award, NIH, 87; acting dir, Ctr Demographic & Pop Genetics & Med Genetics Ctr, Grad Sch Biomed Sci, Univ Tex Health Sci Ctr, 90- *Mem:* Am Soc Human Genetics; Am Diabetes Asn. *Res:* Genetics and epidemiology of common chronic diseases, including diabetes, cardiovascular disease and gallbladder disease; chronic disease among Mexican Americans. *Mailing Add:* 4745 Spellman Rd Houston TX 77035

HANJAN, SATNAM S, IMMUNO DIAGNOSTICS, HYBRIDOMA TECHNOLOGY & ASSOCIATED FIELDS. *Current Pos:* GROUP LEADER, BECTON DICKINSON ADVAN DIAG, 91- *Personal Data:* m 82, Tina Jatinder; c Grace & Rick P. *Educ:* Panjab Univ, BS, 67; All India Inst Med Sci, MS, 72, PhD(immunol), 76. *Prof Exp:* Chemist, All India Inst Med Sci, New Delhi, 77-79; sr res assoc, Comprehensive Cancer Ctr, Univ Ala, Birmingham, 79-81; head immunobiol, Kallestad, Labs, Austin, Tex, 81-83; sr immunologist, Div Syntex Corp, Syva Co, Palo Alto, Calif, 83-87; res investr, Boehringer Mannheim Diag, 87-88; sr proj immunochemist, CIBA Corning Diag Corp, 88-90. *Concurrent Pos:* Course instr, WHO-ICMR Ctr Immunol, All India Inst Med Sci, 72-78; charge res, Insirm, Nancy, France, 76; WHO consult, Indian Inst Immunol, 87. *Mem:* Am Asn Immunol; Am Asn Clin Chem; Indian Immunol Soc. *Res:* Study of human lymphoctes based on their surface charge, antigen and receptors for drugs, hormones and adjuvants; research and development of assays for therapeutic drug monitoring, drugs of abuse, lymphocyte and surface tumor antigens, infectious diseases, anemia and cardiac markers. *Mailing Add:* 14823 SW 74th Pl Miami FL 33158-2134. *Fax:* 410-316-3690

HANKA, LADISLAV JAMES, MICROBIOLOGY. *Current Pos:* res assoc analyst microbiol, 58-67 & biochem res, 67-71, SR RES SCIENTIST CANCER RES, UPJOHN CO, 71- *Personal Data:* b Mnetice, Czech, July 31, 20; nat US; m 48; c 2. *Educ:* Prague Tech Univ, Ing, 46; Iowa State Col, MS, 56, PhD(bact), 58. *Prof Exp:* Teacher high sch, Czech, 42-45; agr adminr, 47-50; asst bact, Iowa State Col, 56-58. *Mem:* Am Soc Microbiol; Am Asn Cancer. *Res:* Am Chem Soc. *Res:* Analytical microbiology; microbiological assay; antibiotics; reproduction physiology; fermentations; cryobiology; antimetabolites in cancer chemotherapy; methods of finding new antitumor drugs; international cooperation in cancer research. *Mailing Add:* 2917 Grace Rd Kalamazoo MI 49006

HANKEN, JAMES, EVOLUTIONARY MORPHOLOGY, HERPETOLOGY. *Current Pos:* asst prof, 83-90, ASSOC PROF BIOL, UNIV COLO, BOULDER, 90- *Personal Data:* b New York, NY, July 14, 52; m 85, Sally E Susnowitz; c Daniel & Alexandra. *Educ:* Univ Calif, Berkeley, AB, 73, PhD(zool), 80. *Honors & Awards:* Early Career Develop Award, NIH. *Prof Exp:* Killam res fel, Dalhousie Univ, 80-83. *Concurrent Pos:* Mem bd gov, Am Soc Ichthyologists & Herpetologists, 83-88 & publ secy, 85-88; prog officer, Am Soc Zoologists, Div Vert Morphol, 88-89 & chair-elect, 91-92; assoc ed, J Morphol, 88- & Evolution, 91-94; ed, Am Zoologist, 96- *Mem:* Soc Study Evolution; Sigma Xi; Am Soc Ichthyologists & Herpetologists; Soc Integrative & Comp Biol; AAAS. *Res:* Evolutionary morphology of vetebrates; developmental and evolutionary questions about the skull and limb skeleton. *Mailing Add:* Dept Environ Pop & Organismic Biol Campus PO Box 334 Univ Col Boulder CO 80309-0334. *Fax:* 303-492-8699; *E-Mail:* james.hanken@colorado.edu

HANKER, JACOB S, HISTOCHEMISTRY, CELL BIOLOGY. *Current Pos:* prof neurobiol prog, Univ, 69-77, PROF ORAL SURG & ORAL BIOL, DENT RES CTR, SCH DENT, UNIV NC, CHAPEL HILL, 69- *Personal Data:* b Philadelphia, Pa, Feb 23, 25; m 51; c 3. *Educ:* St Joseph's Col, Pa, BS, 48; Univ Md, PhD(med chem), 69. *Prof Exp:* Group leader org chem, US Army Chem Welfare Labs, 52-60; supvr surg res labs, Sinai Hosp, Baltimore, Md, 60-69. *Concurrent Pos:* Consult, Polysci, Inc, Pa, 65-; asst in surg, Sch Med, Johns Hopkins Univ, 67-69; consult, NIMH, 71 & Papanicolaou Cancer Res Inst, UN Navy; adj assoc prof path, Duke Univ Med Ctr, 81- *Mem:* AAAS; Am Chem Soc; Histochem Soc; Sigma Xi; Am Soc Cell Biol. *Res:* Development of cytochemical staining methods for the light and electron miroscopic study of leukocytes in health and disease, especially leukemia, granuloma and malignancy. *Mailing Add:* 733 Tinkerbell Rd Chapel Hill NC 27514

HANKES, GERALD H, VETERINARY SURGERY. *Current Pos:* PROF SMALL ANIMAL SURG & MED, AUBURN UNIV, 69- *Personal Data:* b Aurora, Ill, Aug 27, 36; m 59; c 4. *Educ:* Univ Ill, Urbana, BS, 59, DVM, 61; Colo State Univ, MS, 67, PhD(cardiovasc surg & physiol), 69. *Prof Exp:* Gen pract large & small animals, Ill, 61-62; instr small animal surg & med, Colo State Univ, 64-65; NIH fels, Nat Inst Arthritis & Metab Dis, 65-68 & Nat Heart Inst, 68-69. *Mem:* Am Vet Med Asn. *Res:* Cardiovascular surgery and physiology; intensive patient care; anesthesiology; malignant neoplasia. *Mailing Add:* 1220 Sanders St Auburn AL 36830

HANKES, LAWRENCE VALENTINE, BIOCHEMISTRY, NEUROSCIENCES. *Current Pos:* BIOCHEMIST & HEAD CLIN CHEM DEPT, BROOKHAVEN NAT LAB, 51-, SR CLIN SCIENTIST, 68- *Personal Data:* b Chicago, Ill, Nov 24, 19; m 51, Mary Cay; c Lawrence, Catherine & Matthew. *Educ:* DePauw Univ, AB, 42; Mich State Col, MS, 43; Univ Wis, PhD, 49. *Prof Exp:* Biochemist, Vet Admin Hosp, 50. *Concurrent Pos:* Mem, Nat Registry Clin Chemists; vis clin scientist, SAfrican Coun Sci & Indust Res, 65, sr clin scientist, SAfrican Atomic Energy Bd & SAfrican Med Res Coun, 68, 69, 72, 73, 75, Inst Med, Kernforschungsanlage, WGer, 87 & 88; USA partic, Int Study Group Tryptophan Res, Padova, Italy, 74, Madison, Wis, 77, Kyoto, Japan, 80 & Munich, Ger, 83, Baltimore, Md, 89, Nagoya, Japan, 92, Padova, Italy, 95; qual assurance consult, 84- *Mem:* Am Soc Biol Chemists; Am Chem Soc; Soc Exp Biol & Med; Am Asn Clin Chemists; Nat Acad Clin Biochem; Asn Clin Scientists. *Res:* Animal nutrition; amino acid interrelationships; vitamins; synthetic and analytical radiochemistry; radiation effects on enzymes; neoplastic diseases metabolism; Trichinella spiralis larvae metabolism; quantitative clinical chemistry; tryptophan metabolism in scurvy, pellagra, scleroderma, dementia, Alzheimers, Huntingtons, and cancer; I-inositol meabolism in Pentosuria. *Mailing Add:* PO Box 1056 Setauket NY 11733-0804

HANKEY, WILBUR LEASON, JR, AERONAUTICAL ENGINEERING. *Current Pos:* prof, 85-97, EMER PROF, WRIGHT STATE UNIV, DAYTON, OHIO, 97- *Personal Data:* b New Kensington, Pa, Oct 31, 29; m 54, Eleanor C Annese; c Robert L, Judith A & Mary E. *Educ:* Pa State Univ,

BS, 51; Mass Inst Technol, SM, 53; Ohio State Univ, MS, 58, PhD(aeronaut eng), 62. *Honors & Awards:* Primus AFSC Award. *Prof Exp:* Res asst fluid mech, Mass Inst Technol, 51-53; proj engr, transonic wind tunnel, US Dept Air Force, Wright-Patterson AFB, 53-58, aerothermodyn chief, 58-60, aerodyn chief, Dynasoar Proj, 60-64, group leader hypersonics res, Aerospace Res Labs, 64-75, group leader, Flight Dynamics Lab, 75-84. *Concurrent Pos:* Adj prof, USAF Inst Technol, 64- *Mem:* Fel Am Inst Aeronaut & Astronaut; Sigma Xi; Am Soc Mech Engrs. *Res:* Optimization studies of hypersonic lifting bodies; boundary layer-shock interactions in supersonic flow; trajectory and aerodynamic studies of hypersonic lifting vehicles; computational fluid dynamics; unsteady flows. *Mailing Add:* 5738 Thatchwood Circle Dayton OH 45431

HANKIN, JEAN H, NUTRITION, EPIDEMIOLOGY. *Current Pos:* prof pub health, Manoa, 69-88, prof family pract & community health, Sch Med, 80-88, NUTRIT RESEARCHER & PROF PUB HEALTH, EPIDEMIOL PROG, CANCER RES CTR, UNIV HAWAII, 88- *Personal Data:* b Ewen, Mich, May 7, 23. *Educ:* Milwaukee-Downer Col, BS, 45; Univ Tenn, Knoxville, MS, 54; Univ Calif, Berkeley, MPH, 63, MPH & DrPH(nutrit, epidemiol), 66. *Honors & Awards:* Cottes Gen Foods Lectr, Australia, 80; Plenary lectr, Nutrit Soc Australia, 83; Lenna Frances Cooper lectr, Am Dietetic Asn, 85. *Prof Exp:* Dietetic intern, Cincinnati Gen Hosp, 46; supvry dietitian, Cook County Hosp, Chicago, 46-48; dietician, Milwaukee Children's Hosp, 48-50 & Detroit Children's Hosp, 51-52; nutrit apprentice, Mich Dept Health, 52-53; pub health nutritionist, City Milwaukee Health Dept, 54-59; nutrit consult, Heart Dis Control Prog, USPHS, 59-60 & RI Dept Health, 60-62; instr pub health & res nutritionist, Univ Calif, Berkeley, 67-69. *Concurrent Pos:* Mem, Coun Epidemiol, Am Heart Asn, 69; dir proj grants, Pub Health Nutrit Training Prog, 75-83; prin investr & co-prin investr, diet & cancer epidemiol studies, Cancer Res Ctr, Univ Hawaii. *Mem:* Am Dietetic Asn; Soc Nutrit Educ; fel Am Pub Health Asn; Am Heart Asn; Am Inst Nutrit; Am Soc Clin Nutrit; Soc Epidemiol Res. *Res:* Diet and breast cancer; dietary methods in epidemiological studies; diet, ethnicity & cancer risk; use of scientific methods for planning, conducting and evaluating applied nutrition programs. *Mailing Add:* Epidemiol Prog Cancer Res Ctr Univ Hawaii 1236 Lauhala Honolulu HI 96813. *Fax:* 808-586-2982

HANKIN, LESTER, FOOD SCIENCE & TECHNOLOGY. *Current Pos:* RETIRED. *Personal Data:* b Norwich, Conn, Feb 23, 26; m 49; c 3. *Educ:* Univ Conn, BS, 49, MS, 51; NC State Col, PhD(food sci), 54. *Prof Exp:* Asst dairy bact, NC State Col, 51-54; from asst biochemist to biochemist, Conn Agr Exp Sta, 54-83, head, Dept Anal Chem, 84-92. *Mem:* Am Soc Microbiol; Asn Off Anal Chem; Int Asn Milk, Food & Environ Sanit; Am Chem Soc; Asn Food & Drug Off. *Res:* Interrelationship of nutrients to growth; methods in food analysis; solid waste recycling; environmental pollutants. *Mailing Add:* 88 Charlton Hill Rd Hamden CT 06518

HANKINS, B(OBBY) E(UGENE), ANALYTICAL CHEMISTRY, GEOPRESSURED-GEOTHERMAL ENERGY. *Current Pos:* from asst prof to assoc prof, McNeese State Univ, 59-63, chmn dept, 70-80, dean col sci, 80-87, PROF CHEM, MCNEESE STATE UNIV, 64-, VPRES ACAD AFFAIRS, 87- *Personal Data:* b Wilson, Ark, Feb 22, 29; m 58, Lynn Fuson; c Robert. *Educ:* Univ Cent Ark, BS, 51; Univ Mo, MA, 53, PhD(chem), 57. *Prof Exp:* Asst, Univ Mo, 51-57; chemist, Union Carbide Nuclear Co, 57-59. *Concurrent Pos:* Consult Dept Energy, 80-88. *Mem:* Am Chem Soc; fel Am Inst Chemists; fel Royal Soc Chem; Am Asn State Col & Univ; Int Union Pure & Appl Chem. *Res:* Instrumental analysis; chemical concentration of trace elements; geopressured-geothermal energy; analysis. *Mailing Add:* 1317 Covey Lane Lake Charles LA 70605. *Fax:* 318-475-5012

HANKINS, GEORGE THOMAS, ELECTRICAL ENGINEERING. *Current Pos:* from assoc prof to prof, 80-91, EMER PROF ELEC ENG, UNIV PAC, 91- *Personal Data:* b England, Ark, Nov 10, 25; m 51, Virginia L Lotts; c Jeff R, Thomas C, Rebecca (Guillot), Wren A, Douglas E & Julie Z. *Educ:* USAF Inst Technol, BS, 55; Southern Methodist Univ, MS, 61; Union Grad Sch, PhD(elec eng, educ), 77. *Honors & Awards:* Western Elec fund award, 78. *Prof Exp:* Pilot, USAF, 47-53, engr, Airborne Radar Systs, 51-53, proj engr, Long Range Radar Syst, Air Tech Intel Ctr, 55-59, br chief instrumentation data analysis, Foreign Technol Div, Air Force Systs Command, 61-63, div chief, Space Explor Systs, 63-64, chief engr, Space Systs, 64-68; from asst prof to assoc prof, Wright State Univ, 69-80. *Mem:* AAAS; Am Inst Elec & Electronics Engrs; Am Soc Eng Educ. *Res:* Radar systems; spaceborne electronic systems; digital systems; social dynamics of technology; engineering education methods; quantum mechanic effects. *Mailing Add:* Univ Pac Stockton CA 95211. *Fax:* 209-946-3086

HANKINS, GERALD ROBERT, MOLECULAR BIOLOGY OF TUMOR SUPPRESSOR GENES. *Current Pos:* RES ASSOC, DUKE UNIV MED CTR, 91- *Personal Data:* b Pensacola, Fla, Mar 28, 48. *Educ:* Fla State Univ, BS, 72; George Washington Univ, MA, 78; Univ Va, PhD(biol), 91. *Prof Exp:* Asst statistician, Mortgage Bankers Asn Am, 72-74; statistician, Gillette Med Eval Labs, Gillette Co, 74-78, res statistician, 78-82. *Concurrent Pos:* Instr anat & physiol, Alamance Community Col, 93- *Mem:* Genetics Soc Am; AAAS. *Res:* Study of the function of mammalian and drosophila tumor suppressor genes in normal development and tumorigenesis. *Mailing Add:* Univ VA Dept Neurosurg Charlottsville VA 22903. *Fax:* 919-684-5584

HANKINS, HESTERLY G, III, preventive health care initiatives, telecommunications & systems design & implementation, for more information see previous edition

HANKINS, TIMOTHY HAMILTON, RADIO ASTRONOMY, SIGNAL PROCESSING. *Current Pos:* assoc prof, 88-90, PROF NMEX TECH, 90- *Personal Data:* b Miami, Fla, Mar 13, 41; m 77, Mary E Nutt; c 2. *Educ:* Dartmouth Col, BA, 62, MS, 67; Univ Calif, San Diego, PhD(astron), 71. *Prof Exp:* Res physicist radio astron, Univ Calif, San Diego, 71-74; res assoc radio astron, Arecibo Observ, 74-81; assoc prof, Dartmouth Col, 81-88. *Concurrent Pos:* Lectr physics, Univ Calif, San Diego, 71-75; Alexander von Humbolt fel, 78-79; vis scientist, Nat Radio Astron Observ. *Mem:* Am Astron Soc; Int Sci Radio Union; Int Astron Union. *Res:* Radio observations of pulsars, including high-time resolution, polarization, microstructure dispersion measurement, hardware and software dispersion removal and signal processing; electronic engineering instrumentation. *Mailing Add:* Physics Dept NMex Tech Socorro NM 87801

HANKINS, WILLIAM ALFRED, virology, for more information see previous edition

HANKINSON, DENZEL J, FOOD SCIENCE. *Current Pos:* prof dairy & animal sci & head dept, 48-64, prof food sci & technol, 64-75, EMER PROF FOOD SCI & TECHNOL, UNIV MASS, AMHERST, 75- *Personal Data:* b Morrice, Mich, June 24, 15; m 38, Clarinda E Winegar; c Judith A, Denzel G, Richard E, James A, Nancy J & Thomas R. *Educ:* Mich State Univ, BS, 37; Univ Conn, MS, 39; Pa State Univ, PhD(dairy mfg), 42. *Prof Exp:* Asst prof dairy indust, Univ Conn, 42-44; fieldman, Sealtest, Inc, NY, 44-46; assoc prof dairy husb, Agr & Mech Col Tex, 46-48. *Concurrent Pos:* Consult dairy products & processing. *Mem:* Am Dairy Sci Asn. *Res:* Detection of neutralized cream; shrinkage of ice cream; comeup time milk pasteurization; automation cleaning. *Mailing Add:* 110 Jacaranda Dr Leesburg FL 34748-8805

HANKINSON, OLIVER, GENE CLONING, SOMATIC CELL GENETICS. *Current Pos:* from asst prof to assoc prof, 79-91, PROF PATH, UNIV CALIF, LOS ANGELES, 91- *Personal Data:* b Reading, Eng, Jan 5, 46; US citizen. *Educ:* Univ Edinburgh, BSc, 67; Univ Cambridge, PhD(genetics), 72. *Prof Exp:* Res fel genetics, Med Sch, Harvard Univ, 72-74, Med Ctr, Univ Colo, Denver, 74-75 & Univ Calif, Berkeley, 75-79. *Concurrent Pos:* Prin investr, Nat Cancer Inst grant, Calif, 79- & Margaret E Early Med Res trust grant, 88- *Mem:* Am Soc Cell Biol; Tissue Cult Asn; Sigma Xi. *Res:* Genetic and molecular biological analysis of the process of induction of cytochrome P-450 and other xenobiotic metabolizing enzymes with emphasis on cloning the genes involved, and their relation to cancer induction by environmental pollutants. *Mailing Add:* Dept Path Univ Calif Los Angeles Sch Med 10833 Le Conte Ave Los Angeles CA 90024-1300

HANKOFF, LEON DUDLEY, PSYCHIATRY, SUICIDOLOGY. *Current Pos:* CLIN PROF PSYCHIAT, MED SCH, UNIV MED & DENT NJ, 89- *Personal Data:* b Baltimore, Md, June 17, 27; m 57, Selma Mervis; c Eve, Sarah, Rachel & Rebecca. *Educ:* Univ Md, BS, 50, MD, 52. *Prof Exp:* From instr to assoc prof psychiat, Col Med, State Univ NY Downstate Med Ctr, 56-71; chmn psychiat, Misericordia Hosp & Misericordia-Fordham Affil, Bronx, 70-78, prof psychiat, NY Med Col, 71-78; prof & dir, Div Clin Psychiat, Sch Med, State Univ NY, Stony Brook, 78-81. *Concurrent Pos:* Psychiatrist, Kings County Hosp, 56, 58-64; dir psychiat, Queens Hosp Ctr, Jamaica, NY, 64-68; actg dir psychiat, Shaar Menashe Hosp, Israel, 68-69; prog planning consult, First Dept Comnr, New York Dept Ment Health & Ment Retardation Serv, 69-70; clin dir psychiat, Elizabeth Gen Med Ctr, NJ. *Mem:* AAAS; Sigma Xi; NY Acad Sci; Am Psychiat Asn; Asn Orthodox Jewish Scientists. *Res:* Community psychiatry; suicide; history of psychiatry; memory mechanisms. *Mailing Add:* Elizabeth Gen Med Ctr-Psych 925 E Jersey St Elizabeth NJ 07201. *Fax:* 908-965-7457

HANKS, ALAN RAY, REGULATORY CHEMISTRY, PESTICIDE RESIDUE & FORMULATION CHEMISTRY. *Current Pos:* PROF AGR CHEM & STATE CHEMIST, PURDUE UNIV, 82- *Personal Data:* b Baltimore, Md, Nov 30, 39; m 61, Beverly J Henson; c James C, Letz E (Cruse) & Sheral D (Kuciemba). *Educ:* W Tex State Univ, BS, 62; NMex Highlands Univ, MS, 64; Pa State Univ, PhD(biophys), 67. *Prof Exp:* Nuclear med sci Officer, Armed Forces Inst Path, 67-69; prof biochem & biophys, Tex A&M Univ, 69-82. *Concurrent Pos:* Asn Off Analyst Chemists liaison, Collab Pesticide Analyst Coun; mem, Expert Panel Pesticide Specif, Food & Agr Orgn & WHO. *Mem:* Fel Asn Off Analyst Chemists (pres-elect, 93-94, pres, 94-95); Asn Am Plant Food Control Officials (pres, 92-93); Asn Am Feed Control Officials; AAAS; Am Chem Soc; Asn Am Pesticide Control Officials. *Res:* Pesticide product analysis; drug in feed analysis; general pesticide residue analysis. *Mailing Add:* Purdue Univ 1154 Biochem Bldg West Lafayette IN 47907-1154

HANKS, CARL THOMAS, ORAL PATHOLOGY. *Current Pos:* Nat Inst Dent Res grant, 71-76, from asst prof to assoc prof, Sch Dent & Dent Res Inst, 70-80, PROF ORAL PATH, SCH DENT, UNIV MICH, ANN ARBOR 79-, ASSOC PROF PATH, SCH MED, 78- *Personal Data:* b Cushing, Okla, Aug 10, 39; m 61; c 2. *Educ:* Phillips Univ, BS, 61; Wash Univ, DDS, 64; State Univ NY Buffalo, PhD(exp path), 70. *Prof Exp:* USPHS training fel, Univ Pittsburgh, 64-66; Nat Inst Dent Res fel, 66-69; asst prof oral path, Sch Dent, State Univ NY Buffalo, 69-70. *Mem:* AAAS; Am Acad Oral Path; Int Asn Dent Res; Tissue Cult Asn. *Res:* Cell differentiation in salivary glands associated with development and neoplasia; wound healing; growth and differentiation of epithelial and connective tissue in vivo and in vitro; electromagnetic stimulation of metabolic processes in mammalian cells; influence of extracellular matrix on cellular differentiation of osteoblasts and odontoblasts; in vitro testing of biocompatibility of dental materials. *Mailing Add:* 1276 Kuehnle Ct Ann Arbor MI 48103-2628

HANKS, JAMES ELDEN, MARINE BIOLOGY. *Current Pos:* RETIRED. *Personal Data:* b Augusta, Maine, Apr 24, 24; m 46; c 1. *Educ:* Univ NH, BA, 52, MS, 53, PhD(marine zool), 60. *Prof Exp:* Asst marine biol, Woods Hole Oceanog Inst, Mass, 52-53, fel, 57-60; asst zool, Univ Hawaii, 53-55; fishery res biologist, US Fish & Wildlife Serv, 55-56; asst dir, Marine Biol Lab, US Bur Com Fisheries, Oxford, Md, 60-62, lab dir, Milford, 62-69; liaison scientist marine biol, Off Naval Res, US Navy, Eng, 69-70; dir biol lab, Nat Marine Fisheries Serv, US Dept Com, 70-84, liaison scientist aquacul, 84-91. *Mem:* Nat Shellfisheries Asn. *Res:* Marine ecology; life histories of benthic marine invertebrates; reproduction and larval development of pelecypod and gastropod mollusks; predator-prey relationships in marine inter-tidal communities. *Mailing Add:* 200 Valley Rd Bethany CT 06524

HANKS, RICHARD DONALD, CHEMISTRY. *Current Pos:* RETIRED. *Personal Data:* b Cincinnati, Ohio, Mar 9, 18; m 44; c 4. *Educ:* Ohio State Univ, BA, 40, MSc, 46. *Prof Exp:* Chemist, McGean Chem Co, Ohio, 41-42; res engr, Battelle Mem Inst, 42-48; asst ed, Chem Abstracts, 48-53, assoc ed, 53-61, head, Abstracting Dept, 61-65, sr assoc ed, 65-69, sr ed, 69-80. *Mem:* Am Chem Soc. *Res:* Organic syntheses; polarography; patent research; economic survey; separation and purification of olefins; synthesis of organo-selenium compounds; chemical literature. *Mailing Add:* 3939 Karl Rd Apt 101 Columbus OH 43224-2400

HANKS, RICHARD W(YLIE), NON-NEWTONIAN FLUID MECHANICS. *Current Pos:* from asst prof to assoc prof chem eng, Brigham Young Univ, 63-72, Ctr Thermochem Studies, 70-71, chmn dept, 78-84, PROF CHEM ENG, BRIGHAM YOUNG UNIV, 72-; PRES, RICHARD W HANKS ASSOCS, INC, 80-; PRIN, PROCESS SIMULATION CORP, 90- *Personal Data:* b St Petersburg, Fla, Oct 16, 35; m 55; c 6. *Educ:* Yale Univ, BE, 57; Univ Utah, PhD(chem eng), 60. *Prof Exp:* Res engr, Oak Ridge Gaseous Diffusion Plant, Union Carbide Nuclear Co, 60-63. *Concurrent Pos:* NSF grants, 65-71; consult, Gen Elec Co, Wash, 65-69, Douglas United Nuclear Co, 66-70, Bechtel, Inc, Calif, 71-78, Marathon Oil Co, 76, Oak Ridge Nat Lab, 78-79, Pipline Systems Inc, Orinda, Calif, 79-80, AMAX Extractive Res & Develop, Golden, Colo, 79-80, Arthur D Little, Cambridge, Mass, 80-86, Marconaflo, Salt Lake City, 80-82, CarbonFuels, Denver, 83-89, United Conveyor, Waukegan, 87-, Eastern Generation/Transmission, NH, 90- *Mem:* Am Inst Chem Engrs; Soc Rheol; Coal & Slurry Technol Asn. *Res:* Fluid mechanics and heat transfer; turbulent and transitional flow; stability, particularly non-Newtonian fluids; non-ideal solution thermodynamics; slurry hydraulics and rheology. *Mailing Add:* 495 E 1010 S Orem UT 84907

HANKS, ROBERT WILLIAM, PLANT CHEMISTRY, PHYTOPATHOLOGY. *Current Pos:* RETIRED. *Personal Data:* b Hurley, NMex, July 6, 15; m 42, Lois Paceley; c Katherine Ann (Eyl) & Sara J. *Educ:* Univ NMex, BS, 37, MS, 38; Univ Chicago, PhD(plant physiol), 46. *Prof Exp:* Chemist, Kennecott Copper Co, NMex, 39-40; asst prof bot, Univ Miami, 46-49 & Fla State Univ, 49-53; biologist, Fla State Plant Bd, 54-55; from asst plant physiologist to assoc plant physiologist, Agr Res & Educ Ctr, Univ Fla, 55-81, assoc prof, 80-81. *Mem:* Am Soc Plant Physiol; Am Phytopath Soc. *Res:* Mineral nutrition of plants; systemic chemicals; physiology of host-pathogen relationships. *Mailing Add:* 650 N Lake Howard Dr Apt 2-I Winter Haven FL 33881-3133

HANKS, ROBERT WILLIAM, FISHERIES MANAGEMENT, RESEARCH ADMINISTRATION. *Current Pos:* fisheries res biologist marine invert zool, Bur Com Fisheries, US Fish & Wildlife Serv, Maine, 55-63, fisheries res biologist & leader shellfish ecol & physiol prog, Biol Lab, 63-68, prog coordr, Nat Oceanic & Atmospheric Admin, 68-71, prog analyst, Nat Marine Fisheries Serv, Washington, DC, 71-74, asst regional dir, Nat Marine Fisheries Serv, Gloucester, Mass, 74-81, NEW ENGLAND LIAISON OFFICER, NAT MARINE FISHERIES SERV, PORTLAND, MAINE, 81- *Personal Data:* b Springfield, Mass, May 17, 28; m 51; c 5. *Educ:* Univ NH, BA, 52, MSc, 60, PhD(zool), 69. *Prof Exp:* Proj leader test mach design, Assoc Engrs Inc, 52-54; asst biol, Univ NH, 54-55. *Res:* Marine invertebrate ecology; bottom fauna; invertebrate taxonomy. *Mailing Add:* Summer Harbor Rd Winter Harbor ME 04693

HANKS, RONALD JOHN, SOIL PHYSICS. *Current Pos:* PROF SOIL & BIOMETEOROL, UTAH STATE UNIV, 68- *Personal Data:* b Salem, Utah, Aug 4, 27; m 48; c 5. *Educ:* Brigham Young Univ, BS, 50; Univ Wis, MS, 52, PhD(soils), 53. *Prof Exp:* Soil scientist, USDA, 53-68. *Concurrent Pos:* Am Soc Agron vis scientist, 68-69; Fulbright sr scholar, Australia, 78. *Mem:* Fel Am Soc Agron; Soil Sci Soc Am; Soil Conserv Soc Am. *Res:* Evaporation of water from soils and plants; water conservation; irrigation water management; evapotranspiration; soil temperature; heat flow; modelling soil-plant-atmosphere systems. *Mailing Add:* 1305 E 2050 N Logan UT 84321

HANKS, THOMAS COLGROVE, GEOPHYSICS. *Current Pos:* GEOPHYSICIST, US GEOL SURV, 74- *Personal Data:* b Washington, DC, Nov 29, 44; m 68; c 2. *Educ:* Princeton Univ, BSE, 66; Calif Inst Technol, PhD(geophys), 72. *Prof Exp:* Res fel, Calif Inst Technol, 72-74. *Concurrent Pos:* Vis assoc appl sci & geophys, Calif Inst Technol, 77; vis sr scientist, Lamont-Doherty Geol Observ, 79-80; G K Gilbert fel, US Geol Surv, 82-84; bd dir, Am Seismol Soc. *Mem:* Fel Am Geophys Union; Seismol Soc Am. *Res:* Cause and effect of earthquakes; strong ground motion; fault-scarp geomorphology. *Mailing Add:* 860 Hamilton Ave Palo Alto CA 94301

HANLE, PAUL ARTHUR, HISTORY OF PHYSICS, SPACE SCIENCES. *Current Pos:* EXEC DIR, MD ACAD SCIS, 87- *Personal Data:* b Newark, NJ, Oct 27, 47; m 79, Joan Burroughs; c John & Juliana. *Educ:* Princeton Univ, AB, 69; Yale Univ, MS, 72, PhD(hist sci), 75. *Prof Exp:* From assoc cur to cur, Sci & Technol, Nat Air & Space Mus, Smithsonian Inst, 74-80, actg chmn, Space Sci & Explor, 80-81, chmn, 81-84, assoc dir res, Space Sci & Explor, 84-87. *Concurrent Pos:* Mem, Inst Advan Study, Princeton, 83-84. *Mem:* Am Phys Soc; Sigma Xi; Hist Sci Soc; Soc Hist Technol; AAAS. *Res:* History of quantum theory; German and American aerodynamics between the wars; space science. *Mailing Add:* Maryland Acad Sci 6 01 Light St Baltimore MD 21230. *Fax:* 410-837-8840

HANLEY, ARNOLD V, analytical chemistry, for more information see previous edition

HANLEY, DANIEL F, JR, NEUROLOGY. *Current Pos:* resident neurol, Johns Hopkins Hosp, 79-81, res fel, Depts Neurol & Anesthesia, Johns Hopkins Med Insts, 81-83, asst prof, Depts Neurol, Neurosurg & Anesthesia-Critical Med, 83, co-dir, Neurol Resident Training Prog, 87 & 90, DIR, NEUROSCI CRITICAL CARE UNIT, JOHNS HOPKINS MED INSTS, 83-, ASSOC PROF, DEPT NEUROL, 90- *Personal Data:* b Portland, Maine, May 17, 49; m 82; c 3. *Educ:* Williams Col, BA, 71; Cornell Univ, MD, 75; Am Bd Internal Med, dipl, 78; Am Bd Neurol & Psychiat, dipl, 90. *Prof Exp:* Med intern, NY Hosp, New York, 75-76, resident, 76-78; Kettering res fel, Sloan-Kettering Inst, 78. *Concurrent Pos:* Prin investr, Am Heart Asn, 83-85, Charles Dana Found, 84-86, NIH, 86-88 & 87-92; prin collabr, Nat Inst Neurol & Communicative Disorders & Stroke, 83-87; collabr, Collab Antiviral Study Group, Nat Inst Allergy & Infectious Dis, 83-89; clinician-scientist award, Johns Hopkins Med Inst, 86-88; vis prof med, Univ Hawaii, 87; vis consult neurocritical care, Univ Va, 87, Univ Rochester Med Col, 88, Mayo Clin, 90; head, Sect Emergency & Critical Care Neurol, Am Acad Neurol, 88, mem exec bd, 91, mem, Therapeut & Technol Assessment Subcom, 91, Neurol Self Assessment Task Force, 91. *Mem:* AMA; Am Acad Neurol; Am Soc Neurol Invest (secy-treas, 87, pres, 88); Soc Neurosci; Am Physiol Soc; Soc Critical Care Med; Am Neurol Asn; Soc Cerebral Blood Flow & Metab. *Res:* Acute care of the neurologically impaired patient; mechanisms of cerebrovascular regulation; author of numerous publications. *Mailing Add:* Dept Neurol Johns Hopkins Hosp Med Inst Meyer 8-140 600 N Wolfe St Baltimore MD 21287-7840. *Fax:* 410-955-4925

HANLEY, HOWARD JAMES MASON, STATISTICAL MECHANICS, NEUTRON SCATTERING. *Current Pos:* phys chemist, Cryogenics Div, 65-78, Thermophysics Div, 78-82, FEL, NAT INST STAND & TECHNOL, 82- *Personal Data:* b Hove, Eng, Aug 19, 37; nat US; m 64, Janet Kettlewell; c Elizabeth. *Educ:* Univ London, BSc, 59, PhD(chem), 63. *Honors & Awards:* Gold Medal, Dept Com, 85; Humboldt Res Prize, 92. *Prof Exp:* Res assoc, Pa State Univ, 63-65. *Concurrent Pos:* Vis fel, Australian Nat Univ, 73-74, 78-79 & 87; adj prof, Dept Chem, Univ Colo, 75-; vis scientist, Inst Laue-Langeuin, 84, 85; NBS fel, 83; fel, Wissenschaftskolleg Zu Berlin, 89-90; adj prof, Res Sch Chem, Australian Nat Univ, 93- *Mem:* Fel Royal Chem Soc. *Res:* Statistical mechanics and thermodynamics; study of fluids via computer simulation; non linear fluid behavior; structure of liquids by neutron scattering. *Mailing Add:* Phys & Chem Properties Div Nat Inst Standards & Technol Boulder CO 80303

HANLEY, JAMES RICHARD, JR, TERPENE CHEMISTRY. *Current Pos:* PROF CHEM, FLA COMMUNITY COL, JACKSONVILLE, 72- *Personal Data:* b Dorchester, Mass, Apr 21, 29; m 51; c 1. *Educ:* Univ RI, BS, 56; Univ Ill, PhD(chem), 59. *Prof Exp:* Propellant chemist, US Naval Propellant Plant, Md, 51-52; org chemist, Univ RI, 55-56, lab instr, 56; asst org & polymer chem, Univ Ill, 56-59; assoc technologist, Gen Foods Res Ctr, NY, 59-60; res chemist, Fla Citrus Canners Coop, 60-61 & Nelio Chem Inc, 61-64; res chemist, Org Chem Div, Glidden Co, 64-72. *Mem:* AAAS; Am Chem Soc; Am Inst Chem; Royal Soc Chem; Chem Soc Japan. *Res:* Terpenes; essential oils; thermally stable polymers; waste recycling and utilization. *Mailing Add:* 1043 Natures Hammock Rd N Jacksonville FL 32259

HANLEY, KEVIN JOSEPH, ORTHODONTICS. *Current Pos:* ORTHODONTIST, KEVIN J HANLEY, DDS, 87- *Personal Data:* b Utica, NY, Oct 25, 52; m 78; c 1. *Educ:* State Univ NY, Buffalo, BA, 74, DDS, 78. *Prof Exp:* Asst prof, Sch Dent Med, Univ Conn, Farmington, 80-83, asst clin prof orthod, 83-; orthodontist, Orthod Assocs, 83-86. *Mem:* Am Dent Asn; Am Asn Orthodontists. *Res:* Effects of pulsating electromagnetic fields on bone cell growth, specifically its effect on the proliferation of DNA. *Mailing Add:* 7 Englewood Ave Buffalo NY 14214

HANLEY, LUKE, MASS SPECTROMETRY, SURFACE SCIENCE. *Current Pos:* asst prof, 90-96, ASSOC PROF CHEM, UNIV ILL, CHICAGO, 96- *Personal Data:* b Mt Kisco, NY, Aug 25, 61; m, Debrah M Rowland. *Educ:* Univ Toronto, BSc, 83; State Univ NY, Stony Brook, PhD(chem), 88. *Honors & Awards:* Young Investr Award Chem, NSF, 94. *Prof Exp:* NSF postdoctoral fel, Univ Pittsburgh, 88-90. *Concurrent Pos:* Guest assoc, Argonne Nat Labs, 96- *Mem:* Am Chem Soc; Am Vacuum Soc; Am Soc Mass Spectrometry; Sigma Xi. *Res:* Collisions of polyatomic ions with surfaces as applied to mass spectrometry and materials science; development of mass spectrometric methods for the analysis of surfaces. *Mailing Add:* Chem Dept Univ Ill 845 W Taylor St Chicago IL 60607-7061. *E-Mail:* lhanley@uic.edu

HANLEY, THOMAS ANDREW, FORAGING ECOLOGY, RIPARIAN FOREST ECOLOGY. *Current Pos:* res wildlife biologist, 80-, PRIN WILDLIFE BIOLOGIST, PAC NW FOREST & RANGE EXP STA, FOREST SERV, USDA. *Personal Data:* b Chicago, Ill, Jan 24, 51; div; c Elizabeth M. *Educ:* Ariz State Univ, BS, 73, MS, 76; Univ Wash, PhD(forest wildlife ecol), 80. *Prof Exp:* Wildlife biologist, Bur Land Mgt, US Dept Interior, 76-77. *Concurrent Pos:* Res asst, Div Agr, Ariz State Univ, 74-76 & Col Forest Resources, Univ Wash, 77-80; wildlife biologist, Forest Serv, USDA, 80; affil assoc prof wildlife biol, Dept Biol, Fisheries & Wildlife, Univ Alaska, Fairbanks, 84-, Col Forest Resources, Univ Wash, Seattle, 90-; adj assoc prof wildlife biol, Dept Natural Resources Sci, Wash State Univ, 85-; assoc ed, J Range Mgt, Soc Range Mgt, 85-89; mem high latitude ecosyst directorate, US Man & Biosphere Prog, Washington, DC, 92- *Mem:* AAAS; Am Soc Naturalists; Ecol Soc Am; Soc Range Mgt; Wildlife Soc. *Res:* Effects of forest management practices on habitat quality for animals, particularly regarding ungulate-vegetation interactions; food and habitat selection by ungulates; ruminant nutrition and bioenergetics; forest community structure and productivity; ecology of riparian forest ecosystems; interactions between terrestrial and aquatic systems. *Mailing Add:* Forest Sci Lab US Forest Serv PO Box 20909 2770 Sherwood Lane Suite 2A Juneau AK 99801. *Fax:* 907-586-7848

HANLEY, THOMAS RICHARD, REACTIVE MIXING, BIOENGINEERING. *Current Pos:* DEAN ENG, SPEED SCI SCH, UNIV LOUISVILLE, 91- *Personal Data:* b Logan, WVa, July 26, 45; m 79, Norma Decker; c Thomas J, Alan M, Andrew R & Cactlin M. *Educ:* Va Polytech Inst, BS, 67, MS, 71, PhD(chem eng), 72; Wright State Univ, MBA, 75. *Honors & Awards:* Ralph R Teetor Educ Award, Soc Automotive Engrs, 89. *Prof Exp:* Develop engr & chem engr, USAF mat lab, 72-75; asst prof, chem eng, Tulane Univ, 75-79; assoc prof, chem eng, Rose-Hulman Inst Technol, 79-83; prof & head chem eng, La Tech Univ, 83-85; prof & chmn chem eng, Fla State Univ/Fla A&M Univ, 85-91. *Concurrent Pos:* Chem eng consult, Edgewood Arsenal, 76-77, Solar Energy Res Inst, 80, El Paso Polyolefins Co, 82-84, Int Minerals & Chem Corp, 82-84, Fla Dept Revenue, 86-87, Olin Corp, 86-91, Fla Attorney Gen, 87, Chevron, 88-89, Kraft Inc, 89-90, Kyy Fried Chicken, 91, Brown & Williamson, 92-93, Little Tykes, Fosroc, Swan Blomas & LG & E, 92-93; div adv, Chem, Biochem & Thermal Div, NSF, 87-89, Biol & Critical Systs Div, 89-92; bd mem, Ky Bd Regents Prof Engrs & Land Surveyors, 91-; bd dirs, Louisville Advan Technol Coun, 92, Louisville Sci Ctr, 93-, Ky Partners Pollution Prev Ctr, 94- & Louisville Area Chamber Com, 96; counr, Univ Louisville, Oak Ridge, Assoc Univ, 96- *Mem:* Fel Am Inst Chem Engrs; Am Soc Eng Educ; Nat Soc Prof Engrs; Sigma Xi. *Res:* Reactive mixing in chemical, biomedical and biochemical systems including simulation using computational fluid dynamics; author of over 45 papers; over 150 technical presentations. *Mailing Add:* Speed Sci Sch Univ Louisville Louisville KY 40292. *Fax:* 502-852-7033; *E-Mail:* trhanl01@ulkyvm.louisville.edu

HANLEY, WAYNE STEWART, BIO-ORGANIC CHEMISTRY. *Current Pos:* CONSULT, CONWOOD CORP, 74-, DIR, RES & DEVELOP; ECKO GLACO. *Personal Data:* b Edinburgh, Scotland, Oct 30, 45; US citizen; m 68; c 2. *Educ:* Tarkio Col, BA, 66; Vanderbilt Univ, PhD(org chem), 71. *Prof Exp:* Fel med chem, Univ Minn, 70-71; fel, Dept Chem, Vanderbilt Univ, 71-72; asst prof chem, Georgetown Col, 72-76. *Concurrent Pos:* Res grant, Am Chem Soc, 74; dir, Res & Develop, Conwood Corp, 76-80; plant mgr, Kilgore Corp, 80- *Mem:* Am Chem Soc; Sigma Xi. *Res:* Study of synthesis, stability and reactions of organic sulfenyl iodides; preparation of penicillamine analogs as potential antiarthritic agents; synthesis of organic sulfur compounds as antihistoplasmosis agents. *Mailing Add:* 407 SW Woodlawn Ave Topeka KS 66606

HANLIN, RICHARD THOMAS, MYCOLOGY. *Current Pos:* assoc prof, 67-71, PROF MYCOL, UNIV GA, 71- *Personal Data:* b Hammond, Ind, May 10, 31; m 55; c 3. *Educ:* Univ Mich, BS, 53, MS, 55, PhD(bot), 60. *Prof Exp:* Asst plant pathologist, Ga Exp Sta, 60-66. *Mem:* AAAS; Bot Soc Am; Mycol Soc Am; Am Phytopath Soc; Brit Mycol Soc. *Res:* Morphological development and taxonomy of the Pyrenomycetes, especially the Hypocreales. *Mailing Add:* Dept Plant Path Univ Ga 4309 Plant Sci Bldg Athens GA 30602. *Fax:* 706-542-1262; *E-Mail:* rhanlin@uga.cc.uga.edu

HANLON, C ROLLINS, SURGERY. *Current Pos:* prof, 69-85, EMER PROF SURG, MED SCH, NORTHWESTERN UNIV, CHICAGO, 85- *Personal Data:* b Baltimore, Md, Feb 8, 15; m 49; c 8. *Educ:* Loyola Col, Md, AB, 34; Johns Hopkins Univ, MD, 38; Am Bd Surg, dipl; Am Bd Thoracic Surg, dipl. *Hon Degrees:* DSc, Georgetown Univ, 76, St Louis Univ & Univ Ill, 86. *Prof Exp:* From instr to assoc prof surg, Johns Hopkins Univ, 46-50; prof & dir dept, Sch Med, St Louis Univ, 50-69. *Concurrent Pos:* W S Halsted fel, Johns Hopkins Univ, 39-40; William H Vogt Lectr, 51; mem surg study sect, NIH, 61-65, chmn, 65-; pres, Coun Med Spec Soc, 74-75; chmn, Coord Coun Med Educ, 76-77; gov, Am Col Surgeons, 57-59, Regent, 67-69, dir, 69-86, pres elect, 86-87, pres, 87-88, exec consult, 86- *Mem:* Soc Univ Surgeons (secy, 53, pres, 58-59); Am Asn Thoracic Surg (treas, 62-68); Int Cardiovasc Soc (pres, 63-64); Am Thoracic Soc; Am Surg Asn (pres, 81-82); hon mem Am Hosp Asn; hon mem Soc Thoracic Surgeons; hon mem Am Urol Asn; hon mem Am Col Radiol. *Res:* Shock; cardiovascular and pulmonary diseases. *Mailing Add:* Am Col Surg 55 E Erie St Chicago IL 60611-2731

HANLON, EDWARD A, SOIL FERTILITY, NUTRIENT MANAGEMENT. *Current Pos:* from asst prof to prof, 84-96, EXTEN SOIL MGT SPECIALIST, UNIV FLA, 84-; DIR, SOUTHWEST FLA RES & EDUC CTR, 97- *Personal Data:* m 71, Elizabeth. *Educ:* Univ Ariz, BS, 69, MS, 77; Okla State Univ, PhD(soil & water sci), 83. *Prof Exp:* Lab supvr, Okla State Univ, 77-84. *Concurrent Pos:* Secy, Soil & Plant Analysis Regional Comt, Soil Sci Soc Am, 91-92, chair, S-877 Soil Testing & Plant Analysis, 93, S899 Soil Methodology; assoc ed, Agron J, Am Soc Agron, 93- *Mem:* Soil Sci Soc Am; Am Soc Agron. *Res:* Define and extend efficient nutrient management strategies for commercial agriculture to increase or maintain high quality production and minimize environmental implications. *Mailing Add:* Univ Fla PO Box 110510 Gainesville FL 32611. *Fax:* 904-392-3399; *E-Mail:* hanlon@gnv.1fas.ufl.edu

HANLON, MARY SUE, BIOCHEMISTRY. *Current Pos:* asst prof biol chem, 66-69, assoc prof biochem, 69-76, PROF BIOCHEM, UNIV ILL COL MED, 76- *Personal Data:* b New Orleans, La, Sept 14, 33; m 66; c 1. *Educ:* La State Univ, BS, 54; Univ Calif, Berkeley, PhD(biochem), 61. *Prof Exp:* Instr biochem, Chicago Med Sch, 63-64, asst prof, 64-66. *Concurrent Pos:* NSF fel, 61-62; NIH fel, 62-63. *Mem:* Am Chem Soc; Am Soc Cell Biol; Am Soc Biol Chemists; Biophys Soc; fel AAAS. *Res:* Physical biochemistry; conformation and chemical interaction properties of biologically important macromolecules. *Mailing Add:* Dept Biochem MC 536 Univ Ill Col Med 1819 W Polk St Chicago IL 60612-4316. *Fax:* 312-413-0364

HANLON, ROGER THOMAS, CEPHALOPOD BEHAVIOR. *Current Pos:* asst prof, 82-85, ASSOC PROF, MARINE BIOMED INST, UNIV TEX MED BR, 85-, CHIEF, DIV BIOL & MARINE RESOURCES, 83- *Personal Data:* b Frankfurt, Germany, May 17, 47; US citizen; m 79; c 2. *Educ:* Fla State Univ, BS, 69; Univ Miami, MS, 75, PhD(marine sci), 78. *Prof Exp:* Res assoc, Marine Biomed Inst, Med Br, Univ Tex, 75-80; NATO res fel, Dept Zool, Univ Cambridge, 81-82. *Mem:* Am Soc Zoologists; Animal Behav Soc; Marine Biol Asn UK; Am Malacol Union; Sigma Xi. *Res:* Ethology of cephalopods, with particular emphasis on the functional morphology of the neurally controlled chromatophore system; mariculture of cephalopods. *Mailing Add:* Marine Biol Lab Marine Resources Ctr Water St Woods Hole MA 02543

HANLON, THOMAS LEE, PHYSICAL CHEMISTRY. *Current Pos:* SR APPLNS CHEMIST, ETHYL CORP, 80- *Personal Data:* b Durbin, WVa, May 10, 37; m 62; c 2. *Educ:* Randolph-Macon Col, BS, 59; Princeton Univ, PhD(phys chem), 63. *Prof Exp:* Sr res chemist synthetic rubber, Goodyear Tire & Rubber Co, 63-75, res scientist, 75-80. *Mem:* Am Chem Soc. *Res:* Stereospecific polymerizations, especially dienes; ionic copolymerization; Ziegler-Natta type catalysis; emulsion polymerization and copolymerization. *Mailing Add:* Albemarle Corp 8000 GSRI Ave Baton Rouge LA 70820-7403

HANLY, W CAREY, BIOCHEMISTRY, IMMUNOLOGY. *Current Pos:* res assoc, 70-73, asst prof, 73-77, ASSOC PROF IMMUNOL, UNIV ILL MED CTR, 77- *Personal Data:* b Wharton, Tex, Aug 6, 36. *Educ:* Rice Univ, BA, 58, PhD(biochem), 64. *Prof Exp:* Res biochemist, Bowman Gray Sch Med, 58-60; Nat Acad Sci-Nat Res Coun res associateship biochem, Aeromed Res Lab, Holloman AFB, NMex, 64-66, res biochemist, 66-70. *Concurrent Pos:* Lectr, Holloman Exten, Univ NMex, 66-67; instr, Alamogordo Community Col, NMex State Univ, 67-68. *Mem:* Am Asn Immunologists; AAAS; Sigma Xi; NY Acad Sci. *Res:* Chemistry, genetic variation and function of immunoglobulin A; comparative biochemistry of primates, hemoglobin, red cell antigens and serum proteins; dihydroxyphenylalanine-decarboxylase and functional properties. *Mailing Add:* Dept Microbiol & Immunol Univ Ill M/C 790 835 S Wolcott Ave Chicago IL 60612-7344. *Fax:* 312-996-6415

HANN, DAVID WILLIAM, FOREST MENSURATION, FOREST BIOMETRY. *Current Pos:* ASSOC PROF FOREST MENSURATION, COL FORESTRY, ORE STATE UNIV, 78- *Personal Data:* b Oakland, Calif. *Educ:* Ore State Univ, BS, 68, MS, 70; Univ Wash, PhD(forest mensuration), 78. *Prof Exp:* Res forester forest mensuration, Intermountain Forest & Range Exp Sta, US Forest Serv, USDA, 71-78. *Mem:* Soc Am Foresters; Am Statist Asn; Biomet Soc. *Res:* Development of mathematical tools useful to forest managers, especially modeling of stand and tree dynamics, and the prediction of stand yield and of the tree product potential. *Mailing Add:* Col Forestry Ore State Univ 140 Peavy Hall Corvallis OR 97331-5710

HANN, G(EORGE) C(HARLES), GENERAL MANAGEMENT. *Current Pos:* dir res & prod develop, 66-68, VPRES, APACHE CORP, 68- *Personal Data:* b United States, June 25, 24; m 47; c 5. *Educ:* Univ Minn, BChemE, 45, MS, 51. *Prof Exp:* Asst chem, Univ Minn, 47-48; from res engr glass tech to proj mgr systs prod, Minn Mining & Mfg Co, 49-66. *Mem:* AAAS; fel Am Inst Chem; Am Chem Soc; Am Inst Chem Engrs; Sigma Xi. *Res:* Fluid mechanics; fluidization; high refractive index glasses; ion exchange. *Mailing Add:* 5615 Woodcrest Dr Minneapolis MN 55424

HANN, HIE-WON L, PEDIATRICS, PEDIATRIC ONCOLOGY. *Current Pos:* PROF MED, JEFFERSON MED COL, PHILADELPHIA, 88- *Personal Data:* b Seoul, Korea, Mar 9, 36; m 66, Richard Suhung; c Christine & Carolyn. *Educ:* Seoul Nat Univ, MD, 61; Am Bd Pediat, dipl, 71. *Prof Exp:* Intern, Worcester City Hosp, Mass, 63-64; resident pediat, Children's Hosp Med Ctr, Harvard Med Sch, Boston, Mass, 64-65, resident pediat path, 65-66, resident pediat, 66-68, fel pediat oncol, 68-71; instr to asst prof, Sch Med, Univ Pa, 72-80, assoc prof pediat, 81-88. *Concurrent Pos:* Res physician, Inst Cancer Res, Philadelphia, 71-88; asst physician oncol, Children's Hosp Philadelphia, 72-75, assoc physician, 75-; assoc staff, Am Oncol Hosp, Philadelphia, 72-88; assoc med staff, Jeanes Hosp, Philadelphia, 72-88; dir, Liver Dis Prev Ctr, Thomas Jefferson Univ Hosp, Philadelphia, 88- *Mem:* Nat Acad Sci; Am Soc Clin Oncol; Am Fedn Clin Res; Am Acad Pediat; Am Asn Study Liver Dis; Am Asn Cancer Res. *Res:* Biology of isoferritins in cancer; immunology and biochemistry of neuroblastoma; hepatitis B virus, hepatitis C virus and hepatoma; effect of iron on cancer and alcoholic liver disease. *Mailing Add:* Jefferson Med Col 1025 Walnut St Philadelphia PA 19107. *Fax:* 215-923-7697

HANN, ROY WILLIAM, JR, CIVIL ENGINEERING. *Current Pos:* head environ eng div, 71-75, dir, Sea Grant Prog, 75-77, PROF CIVIL ENG, ENVIRON ENG DIV, TEX A&M UNIV, 65- *Personal Data:* b Oklahoma City, Okla, Mar 21, 34; m 84; c 6. *Educ:* Univ Okla, BSCE, 56, MCE, 57, PhD(eng sci), 63. *Honors & Awards:* Palladium Medal, Nat Aubudon Soc, 83. *Prof Exp:* Civil engr, US Pub Health Serv, 57-59 & C H Guernsey & Co, 59-60; prof civil eng, Univ SC, 62-65. *Concurrent Pos:* Consult civil eng, 60-; pres, Civil Eng Systs, Inc, Hann Enterprises & Int Spill Technol Corp. *Mem:* Fel Am Soc Civil Engrs; Nat Soc Prof Engrs; Am Soc Eng Educ; Water Pollution Control Fedn; Am Water Works Asn. *Res:* Environmental engineering; prevention and control of oil spills; mathematical simulation of aquatic systems; digital computer applications in civil engineering; design, operation and management of water resources projects. *Mailing Add:* 1300 Walton Dr College Station TX 77840

HANNA, ADEL, geotechnical engineering, foundation engineering, for more information see previous edition

HANNA, BRIAN DALE, ONTOGENY OF THE AUTONOMIC NERVOUS SYSTEM, AUTONOMIC NEURAL CONTROL OF THE HEART. *Current Pos:* PEDIAT CARDIOLOGIST, RUSH UNIV. *Personal Data:* b Lloydminster, Sask, Dec 26, 49; Can citizen; m 85, Rafzelle Zinman. *Educ:* Univ BC, BSc, 75; McGill Univ, MDCM, 83, PhD(physiol), 89. *Prof Exp:* Pediat residency, Montreal Childrens Hosp, 83-86, pediat cardiol fel, 86-87; pediat cardiol fel, Boston Childrens Hosp, 87-89; asst prof pediat physiol & biophys, Dalhousie Univ, 90-; dir, Cardiac Lab, Izaak Walton Killam Hosp Children, 93- *Concurrent Pos:* Staff pediat cardiologist, Izaak Walton Killam Hosp Children, 90-, staff pediat pathologist cardiac, 90-; consult cardiol, Chalmers Hosp, Moncton City Hosp, Med Asn, 90-; vchmn, Pediat Sect, NS Med Soc, 92-; prin investr, Heart & Stroke Found, Can, 92- *Mem:* Can Med Asn; Fel Can Pediat Soc; Can Cardiovasc Soc; NY Acad Sci; fel Am Acad Pediat; Am Physiol Soc. *Res:* The functional development autonomic nervous system and its role in cardiovascular control is investigated in acute studies on anesthetized piglets using direct recordings of nerve activity and in longitudinal studies of well and ill human infants using frequency-domain analysis of cardiovascular, respiratory and neurological variables. *Mailing Add:* Dept Pediat Rush Univ 1653 W Congress Pkwy Chicago IL 60612. *Fax:* 902-425-2481

HANNA, CALVIN, PHARMACOLOGY. *Current Pos:* RETIRED. *Personal Data:* b Danville, Ill, May 1, 23; m 46, Alverta May Anderson; c 2. *Educ:* Univ Ill, BS, 49; Univ Iowa, MS, 50, PhD(pharmacol), 53. *Prof Exp:* Asst pharmacol, Univ Iowa, 49-52; instr, Col Med, Univ Tenn, 53-54, asst prof, 54-55; from asst prof to assoc prof, Col Med, Univ Vt, 55-61; from assoc prof to prof pharmacol, Col Med, Univ Ark, Little Rock, 61-89, emer prof, 89- *Concurrent Pos:* Lederle fac award, 63-66; mem, Visual Sci Study Sect, Div Res Grants, NIH, 62-65; mem, OTC Opthal Panel, Food & Drug Admin, 75-80. *Mem:* Am Chem Soc; Am Soc Pharmacol & Exp Therapeut; Soc Exp Biol & Med. *Res:* Ophthalmology; relation of chemical structure to biological action; synthesis of physiologically active materials; tachyphylaxis; mechanism of action of drugs, radiation biology, drug toxicology. *Mailing Add:* 74 Glemere Rd Little Rock AR 72204

HANNA, EDGAR E(THELBERT), JR, MICROBIOLOGY & IMMUNOLOGY, INFECTIOUS DISEASES. *Current Pos:* sr investr, NIH, 75-83, immunobiologist, Lab Molecular Genetics, 70-83, chief, immunoregulation & cellular control sect, Develop & Molecular Immunity Lab, 83-90, SR MICROBIOL, DIV SCI REV, NAT INST CHILD & HUMAN DEVELOP, NIH, 90- *Personal Data:* b Anniston, Ala, Sept 2, 33; m 59, Norma Rushen; c Natalie, Monica & Charles E. *Educ:* Tuskegee Inst, BSc, 59; Univ Minn, MS, 63, PhD(microbiol, immunol), 67. *Honors & Awards:* Sustained High Qual Res Award, NIH, 77; Becton-Dickinson-Traveling Lectr Award, Am Soc Microbiol, 82. *Prof Exp:* Asst microbiol, Tuskegee Inst, 57-59; asst, Med Sch, Univ Minn, 60-64; asst prof, Health Sci Div, Va Commonwealth Univ, 69-70. *Concurrent Pos:* USPHS res fel, Lab Immunol, Nat Inst Allergy & Infectious Dis, 67-69; fel, NIH, 67-69; lectr, Howard Univ, 68-69; Nat Inst Allergy & Infectious Dis grant, 70-72; sect ed, Microbiology, 80 & 82; chmn, Immunol Div, Am Soc Microbiol, 80-82 & counr, Div Group I, 84-86; lectr, Found Microbiol, 84-85; elect bd gov, Am Acad Microbiol, 85-88; vis prof, Wellcome Found, 86; King, Chavez & Parks vis prof, Wayne State Univ, Sch Med, 89-90. *Mem:* AAAS; Am Asn Immunologists; Am Soc Microbiol; fel Am Acad Microbiol; Int Endotoxin Soc; Sigma Xi. *Res:* Genetic, cellular and subcellular mechanisms of the antibody response; microbiological superantigens and the immune system, pioneer studies and research; regulatory mechanisms of antibody biosynthesis; pathways of antibody biosynthesis in dispersed cell culture; cell fusion and regulatory cell hybridomas; molecular biology; functional precursor T-cell hybridomas; cloned from nude (athymic mice) as models for understanding development of the T-cell phenotype. *Mailing Add:* Nat Inst Child Health & Human Develop NIH 61E Rm SE010 Bethesda MD 20892. *Fax:* 301-402-4104; *E-Mail:* hannae@hd01.nichd.nih.gov

HANNA, GEOFFREY CHALMERS, NUCLEAR PHYSICS. *Current Pos:* RETIRED. *Personal Data:* b Stretford, Eng, Oct 5, 20; Can citizen; m 51, Barbara Scott; c Christopher, David & Jeremy. *Educ:* Cambridge Univ, BA, 41, MA, 43. *Hon Degrees:* DSc, McGill Univ, 1983. *Prof Exp:* Exp officer, Brit Ministry Supply, 41-45; sci officer, Brit Mission to Can, 45-50; asst res officer, Nat Res Coun Can, 50-52; assoc res officer, Chalk River Nuclear Lab, Atomic Energy Can Ltd, 52-57, sr res officer, 57-64, prin res officer, 64-67, res dir, Physics Div, 67-71, res dir, 71-85. *Mem:* Fel Royal Soc Can; Can Asn Physicists. *Mailing Add:* 5 Tweedsmuir Pl PO Box 194 Deep River ON K0J 1P0 Can. *Fax:* 613-584-2852

HANNA, GEORGE P, JR, WATER QUALITY CONTROL. *Current Pos:* PROF CIVIL ENG, CALIF STATE UNIV, FRESNO, 79- *Personal Data:* b Manhattan, Kans, Mar 25, 18; m 44; c 2. *Educ:* Ill Inst Technol, BS, 40; NY Univ, MS, 42; Univ Cincinnati, PhD, 68. *Prof Exp:* Asst sanit engr, dist off, US Army Engrs, Pa, 42-43; design engr, Holmes, O'Brien & Gere, consult engrs, NY, 46-48; sanit engr & dir bur sanit, Dept Health, Syracuse, 48-50; asst prof civil eng, Syracuse Univ, 50-52; chief engr, Mat Handling Prod Corp, 52-53; design engr, Nussbaumer, Clarke & Velzy, consult engrs, 53; civil engr, Creole Petrol Corp, Venezuela, 54-59; from assoc prof to prof civil eng & dir water resources ctr, Ohio State Univ, 59-69; prof civil eng & chmn dept, Univ Nebr, Lincoln, 69-72, interim dean, Col Eng, 71-72, dean, Col Eng & Technol, 72-79. *Concurrent Pos:* NSF sci fac fel, 68-69; mem, Nebr Environ Control Coun, 71-72; vis prof, South China Inst Technol, Guangzhou, People's Repub China, 85. *Mem:* Am Soc Civil Engrs; Am Water Works Asn; Am Acad Environ Engrs (pres, 81-82); Am Soc Eng Educ; Nat Soc Prof Engrs (vpres, 78-79). *Res:* Industrial wastes treatment; water quality studies involving aggressive water neutralization, activated carbon adsorption of contaminants from groundwaters, and agricultural drainwater desalination. *Mailing Add:* 7389 N Bond Ave Fresno CA 93720-3005

HANNA, GEORGE R, NEUROLOGY, NEUROPHYSIOLOGY. *Current Pos:* From asst prof to assoc prof, 63-74, PROF NEUROL, SCH MED, UNIV VA, 74- *Personal Data:* b Boonville, Mo, July 27, 31; m 56; c 3. *Educ:* Cent Methodist Col, AB, 52; Univ Mo, BSc, 54; McGill Univ, MD & CM, 56. *Concurrent Pos:* Fel neuroanat, Col Physicians & Surgeons, Columbia Univ, 60-61; prin investr, Dept Health, Educ & Welfare grants, Voc Rehab Admin, 65-69, Nat Heart & Lung Inst, 72- & Nat Inst Neurol Dis & Stroke, 73- *Mem:* Fel Am Acad Neurol; Am Neurol Asn; Am Epilepsy Soc; Asn Res Nerv & Ment Dis; Soc Neurosci. *Res:* Neuroanatomy; abnormal movements and control of ocular movements; neurophysiology of auditory and vestibular systems; neural control of motor systems; mechanisms of epilepsy; cerebrovascular disease. *Mailing Add:* Dept Neurol Univ Va Hosp Charlottesville VA 22903

HANNA, JEFF, TECHNICAL & ENGINEERING MANAGEMENT, ASTONAUTICAL ENGINEERING. *Current Pos:* Assoc res engr, Boeing Co, Seattle, 60-62, res engr, 62-67, res specialist, Washington, DC, 67-72, prod mgr, Seattle, 72-82, dir prod develop, Boeing Assoc Prod, 82-95, CONSULT BOEING CO, SEATTLE, 95- *Personal Data:* b Atlanta, Ga, Aug 2, 31; m 89, Gayle Roecks; c 5. *Educ:* Va Mil Inst, BS, 52; Rice Univ, MA, 60. *Honors & Awards:* Apollo Achievement Award, NASA, 70. *Prof Exp:* Engr, Westinghouse, 52; navigator, USAF, 52-56, res & develop engr, 56-58, sr navigator & tech intell officer, USAF Res, 58-82. *Mem:* Sr mem Inst Elec & Electronics Engrs; Am Phys Soc; assoc mem Sigma Xi. *Res:* Search for, evaluation, and preparation for marketing of technical by-products. *Mailing Add:* 03013 126th Ave E Puyallup WA 98374-3659

HANNA, JOEL MICHAEL, PHYSICAL ANTHROPOLOGY. *Current Pos:* asst prof, 68-74, ASSOC PROF ANTHROP & PHYSIOL, DEPT PHYSIOL, UNIV HAWAII, MANOA, 74- *Personal Data:* b Lock Haven, Pa, Dec 6, 38; m 62; c 1. *Educ:* Pa State Univ, BS, 61, MA, 65; Univ Ariz, PhD(anthrop), 68. *Prof Exp:* Field dir anthrop, Field Lab, Pa State Univ, Peru, 66-67. *Concurrent Pos:* Assoc prof, Pa State Univ, 71-; coordr, Int Biol Prog, 71- *Mem:* Am Asn Phys Anthrop; Am Anthrop Asn; Brit Soc Study Human Biol. *Res:* Human biology and ecology; environmental physiology. *Mailing Add:* Dept Physiol Univ Hawaii Burns Med Sch 1960 East-West Rd Honolulu HI 96822-2319

HANNA, MARTIN SLAFTER, MATHEMATICS. *Current Pos:* Asst prof, 63-68, ASSOC PROF MATH, UNIV KANS, 68- *Personal Data:* b Detroit, Mich, Aug 8, 32; m 60; c 3. *Educ:* Harvard Univ, AB, 53; NY Univ, MS, 59; Univ Wis, PhD(math), 63. *Mem:* Am Math Soc; Math Asn Am; Soc Indust & Appl Math; Asn Comput Mach. *Res:* Numerical methods; partial differential equations; functional analysis. *Mailing Add:* Dept Math Univ Kans Lawrence KS 66044-3155

HANNA, MELVIN WESLEY, PHYSICAL CHEMISTRY. *Current Pos:* from asst prof to assoc prof, 61-66, PROF CHEM, UNIV COLO, BOULDER, 66- *Personal Data:* b Glendale, Calif, Oct 1, 32; m 56, Sarah Nordstrom; c Gregory J, Steven R & John M. *Educ:* Univ Calif, Los Angeles, BS, 54; Univ Minn, PhD(chem), 59. *Prof Exp:* NSF fel, Calif Inst Technol, 59-60, Noyes teaching fel, 60-61. *Concurrent Pos:* Alfred Sloan fel, 65-67. *Mem:* AAAS; Am Chem Soc. *Res:* Electron and nuclear magnetic resonance spectroscopy; chemical education. *Mailing Add:* 8150 S Humboldt Circle Littleton CO 80122

HANNA, MICHAEL G, JR, IMMUNOBIOLOGY. *Current Pos:* PRES & CHIEF EXEC OFFICER, PERIMMUNE INC, 94- *Personal Data:* b Cleveland, Ohio, July 7, 36; m 58; c 3. *Educ:* Baldwin-Wallace Col, BSc, 58; Univ Notre Dame, MSc, 60; Univ Tenn, PhD(radiation biol), 64. *Honors & Awards:* Delafield Lectr, Columbia Univ, 72; Wadsworth Mem Lectr, Rush Med Col, 83. *Prof Exp:* Res assoc chem co-carcinogenesis, Oak Ridge Nat Lab, 64-65, res biol, 65-68, dir, Immunol Carcinogenesis Group, 68-75; res psychiatrist, Lab Psychol, NIMH, 70-72, Ment Health Study Ctr, 72-74, asst chief, 74, actg chief, 74-75, chief, Ment Health Study Ctr, 75-84, chief, Clin Infant/Child Develop Res Ctr, Health Resources & Servs Admin & NIMH, 84-92; dir, Cancer Biol Prog, Frederick Cancer Res Facility, 75-79, dir, 79-82; dir, Litton Inst Appl Biotechnol, Litton Bionetics Inc, 82-85; sr vpres, Organon Teknika Corp & dir, Biotechnol Res Inst, 85-92, chief operating officer & sr vpres, 92-94. *Concurrent Pos:* Gen ed, Contemp Topics Immunol, 71; co-chmn educ comt, Am Asn Immunologist, 78-80, chmn, 80-82; distinguished oncologist lectr, Dayton Oncol Soc, 82. *Mem:* NY Acad Sci;

Am Asn Pathologists; Am Asn Cancer Res; Am Asn Immunologists; AAAS. *Res:* Immunology; immunopathology; immunotherapy; clinical applications for vaccine-based active specific immunotherapy (ASI) and the development, clinical application and manufacture of human moncional antitbodies (HMAB's). *Mailing Add:* PerImmune Inc 1330 Piccard Dr Rockville MD 20850-4373. Fax: 301-840-2161

HANNA, MILFORD A, FOOD ENGINEERING, PROPERTIES OF BIOLOGICAL MATERIALS. *Current Pos:* from asst prof to assoc prof agr eng, 75-85, PROF BIOL SYST ENG, UNIV NEBR, LINCOLN, 85- *Personal Data:* b West Middlesex, Pa, Feb 26, 47; m 78; c 4. *Educ:* Pa State Univ, BS, 69, MS, 71 & PhD(agr eng), 73. *Prof Exp:* Asst prof agr eng, Calif Polytech State Univ, 73-75. *Concurrent Pos:* Morrison prof food eng, 90. *Mem:* Am Soc Agr Engrs; Inst Food Technologists; Sigma Xi. *Res:* High-temperature short-time extrusion cooking effects on the quality attributes of food constituents; proteins and starches; value added processing. *Mailing Add:* Dept Biol-Eng Univ Nebr E Campus Lincoln NE 68583

HANNA, OWEN TITUS, STATISTICS, COMPUTATIONAL METHODS. *Current Pos:* assoc prof chem eng, Univ Calif, Santa Barbara, 67-74, chmn dept, 71-73, 81-84, prof, 74-93, EMER PROF CHEM ENG, UNIV CALIF, SANTA BARBARA, 93- *Personal Data:* b Chicago, Ill, June 8, 35; m 57, Zetta Hole; c Michael, Christopher, Adrian, Rebecca & Patrick. *Educ:* Purdue Univ, BSChE, 57, PhD(chem eng), 61. *Prof Exp:* Asst prof chem eng, Rensselaer Polytech Inst, 62-65; sr res engr, Boeing Co, 65-67. *Concurrent Pos:* Consult, US Naval Missile Ctr, 67-89, Lawrence Livermore Nat Lab, 82-93 & Los Alamos Nat Lab, 86-89. *Res:* Applied mathematics; heat, mass and momentum transfer; computational methods; engineering statistics. *Mailing Add:* Dept Chem Eng Univ Calif Santa Barbara CA 93106. E-Mail: hanna@engineering.ucsb.edu

HANNA, PATRICK E, MEDICINAL CHEMISTRY, PHARMACOLOGY. *Current Pos:* From asst prof to assoc prof, 69-84, PROF MED CHEM & PHARMACOL, UNIV MINN, MINNEAPOLIS, 84- *Personal Data:* b Little River, Kans, Oct 13, 40; c 1. *Educ:* Creighton Univ, BS, 63; Univ Kans, PhD(med chem), 69. *Concurrent Pos:* Vchmn, Med Chem Div, Am Chem Soc, 85, chmn. 86. *Mem:* AAAS; Am Chem Soc; Soc Toxicol; Am Asn Cols Pharm; Am Soc Pharmacol & Exp Therapeut; Int Soc Study of Xenobiotics. *Res:* Bioactivation processes and drug metabolism; carcinogen metabolism; enzyme inhibitors; drug design. *Mailing Add:* 8-101 Weaver Densford Hall Med Chem Dept Univ Minn Minneapolis MN 55455. Fax: 612-624-2974; E-Mail: hanna002@maroon.tc.umn.edu

HANNA, SAMIR A, PHARMACEUTICAL & ANALYTICAL CHEMISTRY. *Current Pos:* dir, Analytical Res Dept Pharaceut, Res & Develop Div, Bristol- Myers Co, 83-85, vpres qual assurance, Indust Div, 85-90, VPRES QUAL CONTROL, BRISTOL-MYERS SQUIBB CO, 90- *Personal Data:* b Egypt, May 1, 34; US citizen; m 66; c 2. *Educ:* Cairo Univ, BS, 56, MS, 67; Assiut Univ, PhD(pharmaceut sci), 70. *Prof Exp:* Pharmacist, Pharmacy Fikry, 56-63; analytical chemist, Morgan's Chem Co, 60-63; group leader pharmaceut, Drug Res & Control Ctr, 63-70; dir, Control Dept Pharmaceut, Natcon Chem Co, 71-74; dir, Analytical Res & Develop Dept Pharmaceut, Endo Lab, Inc, 74-79; dir, Analytical Res & Develop Dept Pharmaceut, Bristol Lab, 79-83. *Concurrent Pos:* Teaching, Sch Pharm, NDak State Univ, 72; lectr, Ctr Prof Advan, NJ, 78. *Mem:* Am Chem Soc; Am Pharmaceut Asn; Acad Pharmaceut Sci; Parenteral Drug Asn; Asn Anal Chem. *Res:* Drug analysis; automated analysis; biopharmaceutics and pharmacodynamics. *Mailing Add:* Bristol Myers Co Bldg 102 PO Box 1912 New Brunswick NJ 08903-0191

HANNA, STANLEY SWEET, NUCLEAR PHYSICS, SOLID STATE PHYSICS. *Current Pos:* PROF PHYSICS, STANFORD UNIV, 63- *Personal Data:* b Sagaing, Burma, May 17, 20; m 42; c 3. *Educ:* Denison Univ, AB, 41; Johns Hopkins Univ, PhD(physics), 47. *Hon Degrees:* DSc, Denison Univ, 70. *Honors & Awards:* Humboldt Award, 77 & 89. *Prof Exp:* Instr physics, Johns Hopkins Univ, 43-44 & 46-48, asst, 44-45, asst prof, 48-55; assoc physicist, Argonne Nat Lab, 55-60, sr physicist, 60-63. *Concurrent Pos:* Guggenheim fel, 58-59; chmn, Nuclear Physics Panel, Comt Physics, Nat Acad Sci-Nat Res Coun, 64-65; mem, Comt Intermediate Energy Physics, NSF-AEC, 74; chmn, Div Nuclear Physics, Am Physics Soc, 76-77, mem coun, 78-82. *Mem:* Fel Am Phys Soc; Sigma Xi. *Res:* Nuclear physics and structure; giant resonances; polarizations of nuclear radiations; lifetimes of nuclear states; resonance absorption; Mossbauer effect; nuclear moments; analog states; photonuclear reactions; hyperfine interactions; magnetism; electron scattering; intermediate energy physics weak interactions. *Mailing Add:* Dept Physics Stanford Univ Stanford CA 94305

HANNA, STEVEN J(OHN), CIVIL ENGINEERING, TRANSPORTATION. *Current Pos:* assoc prof, Southern Ill Univ, 73-77, chmn, Dept Eng & Technol, 81-83, actg asst dean eng & actg chmn civil eng, 83-84, asst dean eng, 84-87, PROF ENG, SOUTHERN ILL UNIV, EDWARDSVILLE, 77-, ACTG ASST DEAN, 93- *Personal Data:* b Indianapolis, Ind, Dec 24, 37; m 60, Mary L Daringer; c Philip, Christopher, Benjamin, Susan & Michael. *Educ:* Purdue Univ, BS, 60, MS, 62, PhD(civil eng), 68. *Prof Exp:* From asst prof to assoc prof civil eng, Univ Wyo, 67-73. *Concurrent Pos:* Mem, Transp Res Bd, Nat Res Coun. *Mem:* Am Soc Testing & Mat; Am Soc Civil Engrs; Am Soc Eng Educ; Nat Soc Prof Engrs. *Res:* Statistical analysis and quality control for highway construction materials and test methods; investigation of origin and growth of critical cracks in hardened portland cement paste; highway safety; engineering materials; soils. *Mailing Add:* 13517 St Rose Rd Highland IL 62249-4557. Fax: 618-692-3374

HANNA, STEVEN ROGERS, METEOROLOGY. *Current Pos:* RES METEOROLOGIST, SIGMA RES CORP, 85- *Personal Data:* b Rutland, Vt, June 26, 43; m 65; c 5. *Educ:* Pa State Univ, BS, 64, MS, 66, PhD(meteorol), 67. *Prof Exp:* Res meteorologist, Nat Oceanic & Atmospheric Admin, 67-81; res meteorologist, Environ Res & Technol, Inc, 81-85. *Mem:* Am Meteorol Soc. *Res:* Atmospheric boundary layer turbulence and diffusion. *Mailing Add:* 160 Baker Ave Concord MA 01742

HANNA, WAYNE WILLIAM, PLANT GENETICS. *Current Pos:* RES GENETICIST, COASTAL PLAIN EXP STA, USDA, 71- *Personal Data:* b Flatonia, Tex, Apr 20, 43; m 67; c 1. *Educ:* Tex A&M Univ, BS, 66, MS, 68, PhD(genetics), 70. *Prof Exp:* Asst prof plant breeding, Univ Fla, 70-71. *Mem:* AAAS; Am Soc Agron; Crop Sci Soc Am. *Res:* Apomixis, chromosome manipulation and reproductive behavior in plants as related to plant improvement. *Mailing Add:* Agron Dept Coastal Plain Exp Sta PO Box 748 Tifton GA 31793

HANNA, WILLIAM F, GEOPHYSICS. *Current Pos:* dep chief, Off Geochem & Geophys, 74-77, chief, Br Regional Geophysics, 78-82, GEOPHYSICIST, US GEOL SURV, 65- *Personal Data:* b Chicago, Ill, July 27, 38; m 77, Naomi V Purdy; c Kenneth A Spedden & James E Spedden. *Educ:* Ind Univ, BS, 60, AM, 62, PhD(geophys), 65. *Prof Exp:* Vis asst prof geophys, Stanford Univ, 64-65. *Mem:* AAAS; Am Geophys Union; Sigma Xi; Soc Explor Geophys; fel Geol Soc Am. *Res:* Solid-earth geophysics; gravity, aeromagnetic and rock magnetic interpretation. *Mailing Add:* 2081 Cobblestone Lane Reston VA 20191

HANNA, WILLIAM J(OHNSON), ELECTRIC POWER, TRANSMISSION & MACHINES. *Current Pos:* From instr to prof, 46-91, EMER PROF ELEC ENG, UNIV COLO, BOULDER, 91- *Personal Data:* b Longmont, Colo, Feb 7, 22; m 96, Helen Yaeger; c Daniel A & Paul W. *Educ:* Univ Colo, BS, 43, MS, 48, EE, 50. *Honors & Awards:* Archimedes Award, Calif Soc Prof Engrs, 78; Distinguished Serv Award, Nat Coun Eng Examr, 79; Alfred J Ryan Award, 78; Distinguished Serv Award, Spec Commendation, Nat Coun Eng Examr Soc, 90. *Concurrent Pos:* Res engr, eng labs, 44-46; consult bd adv, Electronics Assocs, Colo, 59-63 & Los Alamos Sci Lab, 65-85; mem, State Bd Regist Prof Engrs & Land Survrs, 73-84; pres, Nat Coun Eng Examrs, 77-78. *Mem:* Am Soc Eng Educ; Inst Elec & Electronics Engrs; Nat Soc Prof Engrs. *Res:* Use of foils, especially aluminum, in electromagnetic applications; generation and transmission of electric power. *Mailing Add:* 27 Silver Spruce-NSR Boulder CO 80302-9604

HANNAH, HAROLD WINFORD, VETERINARY MEDICINE LAW. *Current Pos:* dir admin, Div Spec Serv War Vet, 45-47, prof agr law, 47-54, EMER PROF, UNIV ILL; ADJ PROF LAW, SOUTHERN ILL UNIV. *Personal Data:* b White Heath, Ill, Jan 16, 11; m 32; c 5. *Educ:* Univ Ill, BS, 32; Univ Agr & Technol, India, 74. *Hon Degrees:* JD, Univ Ill, 35. *Prof Exp:* Asst to dean, admin, Col Agr, Univ Ill, 35-39, asst prof agr, 39-41; mil officer, 101st Airborne, 41-45. *Concurrent Pos:* Exec secy, Ill Soil Conserv Dist, 39-41, res dir, Mich "Little Hoover Comt", agr, 52, group leader, Univ Ill Contract term, India, 55-57, adv, GP Pant Univ, India, 59, team mem, comn post-sec & higher educ, Nigeria, 60, adv; Ford Found Term, Pakistan, 62, author books on struct of univs in develop countries, 64-65, adv United Nations Develop Prog, Agr Univ, Malaysia, 72. *Mem:* Hon mem, Am Vet Asn; Am Bar Asn; Am Agr Law Asn. *Res:* Laws and internal structures of universities in developing countries; veterinary law; agricultural law; water law; landlord and tenant law. *Mailing Add:* RFD Rte 1 Texico IL 62889

HANNAH, JOHN, ORGANIC CHEMISTRY. *Current Pos:* RETIRED. *Personal Data:* b Kilwinning, Scotland, Aug 1, 31; m 56; c 2. *Educ:* Glasgow Univ, BSc, 53; Imp Col, dipl, 56; Univ London, PhD(org chem), 56. *Prof Exp:* Harwell fel org chem, Imp Col, Univ London, 56-57; Harvard fel, Harvard Univ, 57-58; sr res chemist, Merck & Co, Rahway, 60-66, res fel, 66-71, sr res fel, 71-82, sr investr, 82-93. *Mem:* Am Chem Soc. *Res:* Nitrogen heterocyclic compounds; steroids; antibiotics; natural products. *Mailing Add:* Strathmore AT 155 Idlebrook Lane Matawan NJ 07747-1744

HANNAH, SIDNEY ALLISON, ENVIRONMENTAL CHEMISTRY. *Current Pos:* res chemist, USPHS, 63-67, Fed Water Pollution Control Admin, 67-69 & Fed Water Qual Admin, 69-70, SUPVRY RES CHEMIST, ENVIRON PROTECTION AGENCY, 70- *Personal Data:* b Clifton Forge, Va, Apr 9, 30. *Educ:* Va Mil Inst, BS, 51; Univ Fla, MS, 60, PhD(chem), 62. *Prof Exp:* Chemist, Gen Chem Div, Allied Chem & Dye Corp, 51-52 & Am Viscose Corp, 56-58; res asst, Univ Fla, 58-62. *Mem:* AAAS; Am Chem Soc; Am Water Works Asn; Fed Water Qual Asn. *Res:* Water treatment, particularly removal of dissolved and suspended solids; physical and chemical methods for wastewater purification; water quality monitoring; control of toxic substances in wastewater; pollution control research project management. *Mailing Add:* 1648 Dell Terr Cincinnati OH 45230-2022

HANNAN, HERBERT HERRICK, ZOOLOGY, LIMNOLOGY. *Current Pos:* from instr to asst prof, Southwest Tex State Col, 60-65, chmn dept, 70-76, dir, Aquatic Sta, 76-79, ASSOC PROF BIOL, SOUTHWEST TEX STATE UNIV, 68-, CHEM DEPT, 80- *Personal Data:* b Liberty, Maine, Apr 3, 29; m 52; c 2. *Educ:* Southwest Tex State Col, BS, 57, MA, 63; Brown Univ, MAT, 61; Okla State Univ, PhD, 67. *Prof Exp:* Sci coordr, Dickinson Independent Sch Dist, 57-59. *Mem:* Am Inst Biol Sci; Am Soc Limnol & Oceanog. *Res:* Limnology, primary productivity, plant succession, eutrophication; physiology, endocrinology. *Mailing Add:* Dept Biol Southwest Tex State Univ San Marcos TX 78666-4602

HANNAN, JAMES FRANCIS, MATHEMATICAL STATISTICS. *Current Pos:* asst prof, Mich State Univ, 53-55, statist, 55-57, assoc prof, 57-66, PROF STATIST, MICH STATE UNIV, 66- *Personal Data:* b Holyoke, Mass, Sept 14, 22; m 51. *Educ:* St Michael's Col, PhB, 43; Harvard Univ, AM, 47; Univ NC, PhD(math statist), 53. *Prof Exp:* Instr math, Cath Univ, 50-53. *Mem:* Am Math Soc; Economet Soc; Math Asn Am; Am Statist Asn; fel Inst Math Statist. *Res:* Statistical decision theory; asymptotic distribution theory. *Mailing Add:* Dept Statist Mich State Univ East Lansing MI 48824-0001

HANNAWAY, DAVID BRYON, NITROGEN FIXATION, FORAGE QUALITY. *Current Pos:* FORAGE AGRONOMIST, CROP SCI DEPT, ORE STATE UNIV, 79- *Personal Data:* b Philadelphia, Pa, Sept 14, 51; m 75. *Educ:* Univ Del, BS, 73; Univ Tenn, MS, 75; Univ Ky, PhD(plant physiol), 79. *Mem:* Am Soc Agron; Crop Sci Soc Am; Am Forage & Grassland Coun. *Res:* Nitrogen fixation and mineral nutrition of forage legumes; forage physiology; forage quality; hay quality standards. *Mailing Add:* Crop & Soil Sci Dept Ore State Univ 3017 Ag Life Science Corvallis OR 97331-7306

HANNAY, DAVID G, INFORMATION SYSTEMS, THEORY OF COMPUTING. *Current Pos:* assoc prof, 78-84, CHMN COMPUT SCI, UNION COL, NY, 84- *Personal Data:* b Catskill, NY, July 2, 45; m 65; c 2. *Educ:* Wheaton Col, Ill, BS, 66; State Univ NY Stony Brook, MA, 67, MS, 70; Rensselaer Polytechnic Inst, PhD(comput Sci), 73. *Prof Exp:* Asst dir, Comput Ctr, State Univ NY Albany, 67-70, lectr comput sci, 70-73; dir comput serv, Russell Sage Col, 73-76; sr software specialist, Digital Equip Corp, 76-78. *Concurrent Pos:* Consult, 67-90, vpres info systs, Hannay Reels, 90-; exec dir, Computator Assoc, 90- *Mem:* Asn Comput Mach; Sigma Xi; Inst Elec & Electronics Engrs. *Res:* Making computer theory more accessible via such methods as hypercard animations. *Mailing Add:* Comput Sci Dept Union Col Schenectady NY 12308

HANNAY, NORMAN BRUCE, solid state chemistry & physics, physical chemistry; deceased, see previous edition for last biography

HANNE, JOHN R, DOCUMENTATION AUTOMATION, ENGINEERING AUTOMATION. *Current Pos:* PRES, CHMN & CHIEF EXEC OFFICER, J&B IMAGING SERV INC, 88- *Personal Data:* b St Louis, Mo, Aug 25, 36; m 58, Patricic Kerby; c Paul & Evelyn H (Anastos). *Educ:* Dartmouth Col, AB, 58; Univ Mich, MS, 59 & 61, PhD(commun sci), 64. *Prof Exp:* Engr, Bendix Systs Div, 59-61; res asst automatic speech recognition, Commun Sci Lab, Univ Mich, 61-64, res assoc, 64-65; mem corp tech staff, Tex Instruments Inc, 65-67, mgr, Design Automation Dept, 67-76, mgr prod develop, Comput Systs Div, 76-80, asst vpres & mgr advan technol res & develop, Digital Syst Group, 80-82, vpres, 82-83; vpres eng, Osborne Comput, 83; vpres comput aided design, Microelectronics & Comput Technol Corp, 83-88. *Concurrent Pos:* Chmn design automation comt, Inst Printed Circuits, 67-70; secy & treas, spec interest group design automation, Asn Comput Mach; chmn, comput sci adv comt, Univ Tex, Austin. *Mem:* Inst Elec & Electronics Engrs; Asn Comput Mach; Sigma Xi. *Res:* Computer aided design; automation in document creation ortransformation; automated in data base data entry. *Mailing Add:* 11000 Spicewood Pkwy Austin TX 78750. *Fax:* 512-219-9517

HANNEKEN, CLEMENS, MATHEMATICS. *Current Pos:* From asst prof to assoc prof, 53-67, chmn dept, 64-70, PROF MATH, MARQUETTE UNIV, 67- *Personal Data:* b Ramsey, Ill, Oct 10, 23; m 55; c 6. *Educ:* Eastern Ill Univ, BS, 45; Univ Ill, MS, 48, PhD, 52. *Mem:* Am Math Soc; Math Asn Am. *Res:* Metabelian groups; classification of irreducible congruences. *Mailing Add:* Dept MSCS Marquette Univ PO Box 1881 Milwaukee WI 53201-1881

HANNEMAN, RODNEY E, MATERIALS SCIENCE, METALLURGY. *Current Pos:* vpres res, develop & energy resources, 81-85, VPRES QUAL ASSURANCE & TECHNOL, REYNOLDS METAL CO, 85- *Personal Data:* b Spokane, Wash, Mar 14, 36; m 59, 81; c 2. *Educ:* Wash State Univ, BS, 59; Mass Inst Technol, MS, 61, PhD(phys metall), 64. *Honors & Awards:* Geisler Award, Am Soc Metals, 71; Edison Medallion, 79; Engr Nat Achievement Award, Am Soc Metals, 73. *Prof Exp:* Metallurgist, Hanford Labs, Wash, Gen Elec Co, 59; staff assoc electronic mat res, Lincoln Lab, Mass Inst Technol, 59-63; metallurgist, Gen Elec Co, 63-68, acting mgr, Ceramics Br, 68, mgr, Inorganic Mat & Reactions Br, 68-75, mgr, BWR struct mat, 75-77, mgr, Mat Character Lab, Res & Develop Ctr, 77-80, mgr mat prog, 80-81. *Concurrent Pos:* Dir, Environ Struct Inc, 71-73; mem, Elec Power Res Inst, Corrosion Adv Comt, 75-80; mem adv bd, Mat Process Ctr, Mass Inst Technol, 80-; chmn, Res Coord Coun, Gas Res Inst, 82-; mem bd, Metal Properties Coun, 82- *Mem:* Am Chem Soc; Am Soc Metals; Am Inst Mining, Metall & Petrol Engrs; NY Acad Sci; AAAS. *Res:* Nuclear technology, thermodynamics; kinetics; phase stability; diffusion; x-ray; high pressure; diamonds; material removal technology; surfaces; light sources; environment effects; analytical chemistry; aluminum technology. *Mailing Add:* 3801 Old Gun Rd W Midlothian VA 23113. *Fax:* 804-281-2823

HANNIBAL, JOSEPH TIMOTHY, FOSSIL MYRIAPODS, FOSSIL CRUSTACEA. *Current Pos:* assoc cur, 83-90, CUR INVERT PALEONT, CLEVELAND MUS NATURAL HIST, 90- *Personal Data:* b Cleveland, Ohio, Jan 24, 50; m, Kathleen Farago; c Ivan & Roberta. *Educ:* Kent State Univ, BA, 72, MLS, 73, MS, 80, PhD(appl geol), 90. *Prof Exp:* Librn, Cleveland Pub Libr, 73-77; geologist, Amerada Hess Corp, 81-83. *Concurrent Pos:* Co-ed, Kirtlandia, 90-92, ed, 92- *Mem:* AAAS; Geol Soc Am; Paleont Soc; Asn Study Marble & Other Stones in Antiquity; Nat Asn Geosci Teachers. *Res:* Fossil myriapods and crustacea; numerous articles and reviews. *Mailing Add:* Cleveland Mus Natural Hist 1 Wade Oval Dr Cleveland OH 44106-1767. *Fax:* 216-231-5919

HANNON, BRUCE MICHAEL, ENERGY, ECONOMIC & ECOLOGICAL MODELING. *Current Pos:* instr eng, 66-70, from asst prof to assoc prof Off Vchancellor Res, 70-80, PROF GEOG, UNIV ILL, URBANA, 80- *Personal Data:* b Ivesdale, Ill, Aug 14, 34; m 56; c Claire, Laura, & Brian. *Educ:* Univ Ill, Urbana, BS, 56, MS, 66, PhD(theoret & appl mech), 70. *Honors & Awards:* Mitchell Prize Award, Club of Rome, 75. *Prof Exp:* Proj & res engr, US Indust Chem Corp, 56-66. *Concurrent Pos:* Consult, US Indust Chem Corp, 66-67, Inst Environ Qual, Ill, 70-77, Ford Found, 72-73, Dept Transp, Ill, 74-75, Fed Energy Agency, Wash, DC, 74-76, Off Technol Assessment, US Cong, 75-; prin investr grants, NSF, US Energy Res & Develop Admin, Dept of Energy, Coun on Environ Qual, 71-78; Bioengineering & Hon Fac, Affil Scientist, Ill; Natural Hist Surv, 82-; Jubilee prof lib arts & sci, Univ Ill, Urbana. *Mem:* Int Soc Ecol Econ. *Res:* Modeling the flow of natural resources through society and through ecosystems. *Mailing Add:* Dept Geog Univ Ill 220 Daven Hall Urbana IL 61801. *Fax:* 217-244-1785; *E-Mail:* b-hannon@uiuc.edu

HANNON, JAMES PATRICK, THEORETICAL SOLID STATE PHYSICS. *Current Pos:* from asst prof to assoc prof, 70-77, PROF PHYSICS, RICE UNIV, 77-; ASSOC, WEISS COL, 76- *Personal Data:* b Houston, Tex, Mar 27, 40; m 66; c 2. *Educ:* Rice Univ, BA, 62, MA, 65, PhD(physics), 67. *Prof Exp:* Fel physics, AEK Riso, Denmark, 66-67; fel, Rice Univ, 67-69; fel, Tech Univ Munich, 69-70. *Concurrent Pos:* Exchange scientist to USSR, Nat Acad Sci, 78; vis res scientist, Tech Univ Munich, 78-79 & Univ Hamburg, 78-79 & 81. *Mem:* Am Phys Soc. *Res:* Gamma ray optics; theoretical Mossbauer effect studies; quantum optics; magnetism; cooperative effects. *Mailing Add:* Dept Physics Rice Univ PO Box 1892 Houston TX 77251. *Fax:* 713-285-5245; *E-Mail:* Bitnet: hannon@riceum.1

HANNON, MARTIN J, POLYMER SCIENCE. *Current Pos:* QUALITY, BUS & MKT MGR, HOECHST-CELANESE, ENG PLASTICS DIV, 88- *Personal Data:* b New York, NY, Dec 20, 42; m 69; c 2. *Educ:* Manhattan Col, BChE, 64; Case Western Reserve Univ, MS, 66, PhD(polymer sci, eng), 69. *Prof Exp:* Res chemist, Celanese Res Co, 68-70, sr res chemist, 70-74, group leader, 77-80, mem tech staff planning mgt, Celanese Plastics & Specialities Co, 80-88. *Mem:* Am Chem Soc; Am Inst Physics; Soc Rheology; Soc Plastics Eng. *Res:* Rheological studies of polymer melts; polymer solid state structure and morphology; infrared spectroscopy and theoretical studies of molecular vibrations; mechanical and physical properties of polymers; fiber physics; powder coatings. *Mailing Add:* 103 Pomeroy Rd Madison NJ 07940

HANNON, WILLARD JAMES, JR, GEOPHYSICS. *Current Pos:* leader, Geophys Sect, 80-82, PHYSICIST, LAWRENCE LIVERMORE NAT LAB, 69-, PROG MGR, SEISMIC MONITORING RES, 82- *Personal Data:* b Jacksonville, Ill, July 9, 38; m 60; c 3. *Educ:* St Louis Univ, BSc, 59, PhD(geophys), 64. *Prof Exp:* Inst mech, St Louis Univ, 61-64; asst prof geophys, Wash Univ, 65-69. *Concurrent Pos:* Fel, Calif Inst Technol, 65. *Mem:* Seismol Soc Am; Am Geophys Union. *Res:* Elastic wave propagation; nuclear test ban monitoring. *Mailing Add:* 309 Pearl Dr Livermore CA 94550-3935. *Fax:* 510-423-4077; *E-Mail:* hannon2@llnl.gov

HANNON, WILLIAM HARRY, BIOCHEMISTRY, CHEMISTRY. *Current Pos:* Lab staff, 61-82, CHIEF, CLIN BIOCHEM BR, DIV ENVIRON HEALTH LAB SCI, CTR DIS CONTROL & PREV, GA, 82- *Educ:* Ga State, Univ, BS, 65; Univ Tenn, PhD(biochem), 72. *Concurrent Pos:* Postdoctoral, Oak Ridge Nat Lab; mem, Newborn Screening Comt, Coun Regional Networks Genetic Servs, 89-; Ctr Dis Control Liaison, Newborn Screening Comt, Asn State & Territorial Pub Health Lab Dirs, 91- *Mem:* Int Soc Newborn Screening. *Res:* Over 150 publications in scientific journals. *Mailing Add:* Clin Biochem Br Div Environ Health Lab Sci Nat Ctr Environ Health Ctr Dis Control & Prev 4770 Buford Hwy NE Atlanta GA 30341-3724

HANNSGEN, KENNETH BRUCE, VOLTERRA INTEGRAL EQUATIONS. *Current Pos:* from asst prof to assoc prof, 72-80, PROF MATH, VA POLYTECH INST & STATE UNIV, 80- *Personal Data:* b New York, NY, May 27, 42; m 63; c 1. *Educ:* Dartmouth Col, BA, 64; Univ Wis-Madison, MA, 65, PhD(math), 68. *Prof Exp:* Asst prof math, Univ Calif, Los Angeles, 68-72. *Mem:* Am Math Soc; Soc Indust & Appl Math. *Res:* Asymptotic behavior of solutions of integral equations and applications to stabilization of mechanical systems. *Mailing Add:* Va Polytech Inst & State Univ Blacksburg VA 24061-0123. *Fax:* 540-231-5960; *E-Mail:* hannsgen@math.vt.edu

HANNUM, STEVEN EARL, PHYSICAL CHEMISTRY. *Current Pos:* ASSOC PROF CHEM, GEORGE FOX COL, 85- *Personal Data:* b Long Beach, Calif, July 18, 41; m 66; c 2. *Educ:* Wheaton Col, Ill, BS, 63; Univ Ky, PhD(phys chem), 69. *Prof Exp:* Res assoc, Univ SC, 69-70; from asst prof to assoc prof chem, Aurora Col, 70-78; assoc prof, Asbury Col, 78-85, chmn, Sci Div, 78-84. *Mem:* Am Chem Soc. *Res:* Computers and chemistry; interfacing chemical instrumentation to computers. *Mailing Add:* Dept Chem George Fox Univ Newberg OR 97132. *E-Mail:* shannum@georgefox.edu

HANOVER, JAMES W, forest genetics; deceased, see previous edition for last biography

HANOVER, JOHN ALLAN, GLYCOPROTEIN RESEARCH, CELL BIOLOGY. *Current Pos:* Sr staff, Nat Cancer Inst, 81-85, RES CHEMIST, NAT INST DIABETES, DIGESTIVE & KIDNEY DIS, NIH, 85- *Personal Data:* b Tulsa, Okla, May 19, 53; m 87; c 2. *Educ:* Univ Tulsa, BS, 76; Johns

Hopkins Univ, PhD(biochem), 81. *Concurrent Pos:* Exec ed, Anal Biochem, 88-; lectr, Univ Ky, 90; ed, Arch Biochem & Biophysics, 90-, Glycobiol, 90-. *Mem:* Am Soc Biochem & Molecular Biol; Am Soc Cell Biol. *Res:* Molecular characterization of nuclear pore glycoproteins. *Mailing Add:* Biochem & Metab Lab NIDDK NIH Bldg 10 Rm 9B07 9000 Rockville Pike Bethesda MD 20892-0850. *Fax:* 301-496-9431

HANRAHAN, EDWARD S, PHYSICAL CHEMISTRY. *Current Pos:* from asst prof to prof chem, Marshall Univ, 63-78, chmn dept, 67-78, dean, 77-94, DISTINGUISHED PROF CHEM, COL SCI, MARSHALL UNIV, 94-. *Personal Data:* b Marietta, Ohio, Dec 8, 29; m 52; c 3. *Educ:* Univ Miss, BS, 51; WVa Univ, MS, 56, PhD(chem), 59. *Prof Exp:* Instr chem, WVa Univ, 57-58; chemist, E I Du Pont de Nemours & Co, 58-63. *Concurrent Pos:* Consult, Polan Indust, Inc, 63-65; mem, Comt Chem Educ, Am Chem Soc, 72-78. *Mem:* AAAS; Am Chem Soc; NY Acad Sci; Sigma Xi. *Res:* Decarboxylation of organic di-acids; hydrogen bonding; phase transitions in solids; surface chemistry. *Mailing Add:* Dept Chem Marshall Univ Huntington WV 25755-2520

HANRAHAN, JOHN J, UNDERWATER ACOUSTICS. *Current Pos:* BBN SYSTS & TECHNOL, 87- *Personal Data:* b New London, Conn, Mar 19, 32; m 57; c 4. *Educ:* Univ Conn, BA, 54, MS, 62. *Prof Exp:* Actuarial trainee, Travelers Ins Co, 54-55; jr engr, US Navy Underwater Sound Lab, 57-60; math analyst, Elec Boat Div, Gen Dynamics Corp, 60-62; opers res analyst, US Naval Underwater Systs Ctr, 62-71, head, oper systs anal & assessment, 71-83, head, Oper Systs & Spec Projs Off, 83-87. *Concurrent Pos:* Exchange scientist, Admiralty Underwater Weapons Estab, Eng, 64-65; adj prof, Naval Postgrad Sch, Monterey, Calif, 83. *Mem:* Fel Acoust Soc Am. *Res:* Propagation and scattering aspects of underwater sound; performance prediction studies and new system concepts. *Mailing Add:* 4 Seabreeze Dr Waterford CT 06385

HANRAHAN, ROBERT JOSEPH, PHYSICAL CHEMISTRY, RADIATION CHEMISTRY. *Current Pos:* from asst prof to assoc prof, 58-71, PROF CHEM, UNIV FLA, 71- *Personal Data:* b Chicago, Ill, Jan 7, 32; m 57, Mary E Hogan; c Ann M, Sheila F, Robert J Jr & Margaret E. *Educ:* Loyola Univ, Ill, BS, 53; Univ Wis, PhD, 58. *Prof Exp:* Asst, Univ Wis, 53-56; res fel, NSF, Univ Leeds, 57-58. *Concurrent Pos:* Vis scientist, Hahn-Meitner Inst Nuclear Res, Berlin, 76. *Mem:* AAAS; Am Chem Soc; Radiation Res Soc; Am Soc Mass Spectrometry; Am Phys Soc; Int Am Photochem Soc. *Res:* Kinetics and mechanisms of reactions; radiochemistry; radiation chemistry, especially the effects of ionizing radiation on pure organic compounds; mass spectrometry; application of small computers in chemistry; photochemistry; chemical aspeids of solar energy. *Mailing Add:* Dept Chem Univ Fla Gainesville FL 32611. *E-Mail:* hanrahan@chem.ufl.edu

HANRATTY, THOMAS J(OSEPH), CHEMICAL ENGINEERING, FLUID DYNAMICS. *Current Pos:* from asst prof to assoc prof, 53-63, PROF CHEM ENG, UNIV ILL, URBANA, 63-, JAMES W WESTWATER PROF, 88- *Personal Data:* b Philadelphia, Pa, Nov 9, 26; m 56, Joan Hertel; c John, Vincent, Maria, Michael & Peter. *Educ:* Villanova Col, BChE, 47; Ohio State Univ, MS, 50; Princeton Univ, PhD(chem eng), 53. *Hon Degrees:* Dr, Villanova Univ, 79. *Honors & Awards:* Colburn Award, 57, William H Walker Award, 64 & Prof Prog award, 67, Am Inst Chem Engrs; Curtis W McGraw res award, Am Soc Eng Educ, 63; Sr Res Award, Am Soc Eng Educ, 79; Ernest Thiele Award, Am Inst Chem Eng, 86. *Prof Exp:* Engr, Fischer & Procter Co, 47-48; res engr, Battelle Mem Inst, 48-50. *Concurrent Pos:* NSF fel, 62-63; Shell distinguished prof, 81-86. *Mem:* Nat Acad Eng; Am Inst Chem Engrs; fel Am Phys Soc; Am Chem Soc; fel Am Acad Mech. *Res:* Physics of turbulence and multiphase flows. *Mailing Add:* Dept Chem Eng Univ Ill 205 RAL 600 S Mathews Ave Urbana IL 61801-3792. *Fax:* 217-294-8068

HANSARD, SAMUEL L, II, ANIMAL SCIENCES, NEW DRUG EVALUATION. *Current Pos:* ANIMAL SCIENTIST NUTRIT, CTR VET MED, FOOD & DRUG ADMIN, 76- *Personal Data:* b Ft Sill, Okla, Feb 20, 44; m 80, Sharon C Ashley; c Tammy, Timothy, Tracy & Sarah E. *Educ:* Univ Tenn, BS, 66; Univ Fla, MS, 68, PhD(animal sci), 75. *Concurrent Pos:* Consult, Nat Heart, Lung & Blood Inst & NIH, 85. *Mem:* NY Acad Sci; Am Soc Animal Sci; Sigma Xi. *Mailing Add:* Rte 2 PO Box 166 Charles Town WV 25414-9643. *Fax:* 304-728-3749; *E-Mail:* shansard@bangate.fda.gov

HANSARD, SAMUEL LEROY, NUTRITION. *Current Pos:* RETIRED. *Personal Data:* b Knoxville, Tenn, June 5, 14; m 41; c 3. *Educ:* Univ Tenn, BSA, 37; Ohio State Univ, MS, 38; Univ Fla, PhD, 52. *Honors & Awards:* Nutrit Award, Am Soc Animal Sci, 66; Trace Mineral Award, 70; Morrison Award, 76; Distinguished Serv Award, 77. *Prof Exp:* From instr to assoc prof animal husb, 46-50, prof & sr scientist nutrit, 51-57; prof animal sci & dir, Nutrit Radioisotope Labs, La State Univ, 57-68; prof animal sci, Univ Tenn, Knoxville, 68-80, head dept, 78-80, emer prof, 80- *Concurrent Pos:* Travel award, Am Inst Nutrit, 63, 66, 69, 75 & 78; Gamma Sigma Delta res award, 63; travel fel award, Calcium Carbonate Co, 65. *Mem:* Fel AAAS; Soc Exp Biol & Med; Am Inst Nutrit; NY Acad Sci; Am Soc Animal Sci (pres, 74). *Res:* Mineral metabolism; placental transfer and body composition studies in farm and laboratory animals; radioisotope procedures for biological availability; fission product partition; response measurements and nutritional interrelationships; nature of farm animal anemias. *Mailing Add:* 320 Seven Oaks Trail Knoxville TN 37922

HANSCH, CORWIN HERMAN, CHEMISTRY. *Current Pos:* from asst prof to assoc prof, 46-56, PROF ORG CHEM, POMONA COL, 56-, EMER PROF, 90- *Personal Data:* b Kenmare, NDak, Oct 6, 18; m 44, Gloria Tomasulo; c Clifford & Carol. *Educ:* Univ Ill, BS, 40; NY Univ, PhD(chem), 44. *Honors & Awards:* Edward E Smissman-Bristol Labs Award, Am Chem Soc, 75; Res Achievement Award Pharmaceut & Med Chem, Am Pharmaceut Asn Found, 69; Medal Ital Soc Pharmaceut Sci, Ital Pharmaceut Soc, 67; Tolman Award, Am Chem Soc, 76, Undergrad Res Award, 85. *Prof Exp:* Asst chem, NY Univ, 40-44; mem staff, Manhattan Proj, Univ Chicago, 44, group leader, Richland, Wash, 44-45; res chemist, E I du Pont de Nemours & Co, Del, 45-46. *Concurrent Pos:* Guggenheim fel, Fed Inst Technol, Zurich, 52-53; fel, Petrol Res Fund, Am Chem Soc, Munich, 59-60; Guggenheim fel, 66-67; hon prof, Beijing Med Univ, China, 88. *Mem:* Am Chem Soc; hon fel Royal Soc Chem. *Res:* Nitrogen and sulfur heterocycles; vapor phase catalysis; correlation of chemical structure and biological activity. *Mailing Add:* Dept Chem Pomona Col Claremont CA 91711

HANSCH, THEODOR WOLFGANG, PHYSICS. *Current Pos:* PROF PHYSICS, UNIV MUNICH, 86-; DIR, MAX PLANCK INST QUANTUM OPTICS, GARCHING, GER, 86- *Personal Data:* b Heidelberg, Ger, Oct 30, 41. *Educ:* Univ Heidelberg, MS, 66, PhD(physics), 69. *Honors & Awards:* Otto Klung Award, 80; Cyrus B Comstock Prize, Nat Acad Sci, 83; Herbert Broida Prize, AM Phys Soc, 83; Am Phys Soc, 83, A I Schawlow Price, 96; Michelson Medal, Franklin Inst, 86; Italgas Prize Res & Innovation, 87; Gottfried Wilhelm Leibniz Prize, Ger Sci Found, 88; King Faisal Int Prize for Sci, 89; Einstein Medal Laser Sci, 95. *Prof Exp:* Asst prof physics, Univ Heidelberg, 69-70; NATO fel, Stanford Univ, 70-72; assoc prof, Stanford Univ, 72-75, prof 75-78. *Concurrent Pos:* Alfred P Sloan fel, 73-75; sr US scientist award, Alexander von Humboldt, 78-79; prog co-chmn, 14th Int Quantum Electronics Conf, San Francisco, CA, 86; consult & prof, Stanford Univ, 88- *Mem:* Fel Am Phys Soc; fel Optical Soc Am; Am Acad Arts & Sci; Sigma Xi; Bavarian Acad Sci; Ger Phys Soc. *Res:* Spectroscopy and quantum electronics; developed powerful monochromatic pulsed dye lasers; techniques for high resolution nonlinear spectroscopy of atoms and molecules; co-inventor of the method of lasercooling; published over 250 articles to professional journals; granted 10 patents. *Mailing Add:* Max Planck Inst Hans Kopfermann Str 1 85748 Garching Germany. *Fax:* 49-89-32905-712

HANSEBOUT, ROBERT ROGER, SURGICAL NEUROLOGY, HOSPITAL & UNIVERSITY ADMINISTRATION. *Current Pos:* assoc prof, 79-82, PROF SURG, MCMASTER UNIV, 82- *Personal Data:* b Ont, Can, Jan 11, 35; m 81, Agnes; c Diane-Marie & Christopher. *Educ:* Univ Western Ont, MD, 60; McGill Univ, MSc, 64, dipl, 66; FRCS. *Prof Exp:* Res assoc, Univ Ottawa, 67-68; asst prof neurosurg, Hahnemann Med Col, 68-69; from asst prof to assoc prof, McGill Univ, 69-79. *Concurrent Pos:* Consult neurosurg, Nat Defense Med Ctr, 67-68; neurosurgeon, Montreal Neurol Inst, 69-79; asst dir prof serv, Montreal Neurol Hosp, 78-79, vpres, Coun Physicians, 79-; head neurosurg co-dir, St Joseph's Hosp, Hamilton, Ont, 79-; co-dir Spinal Injury Unit, Montreal Neurol Hosp, 76-79; affiliate surgeon, Hamilton Civic & Chedoke-McMaster Hosp, 79-; prof & chair, Dept surg, McMaster Univ, 89-; chief surg, Chedoke McMaster Hosp, 89-93. *Mem:* Am Asn Neurol Surgeons; Congress Neurol Surgeons; Can Neurosurg Soc; Sigma Xi; Soc Surg Chairs. *Res:* Pathogenesis and treatment of severe spinal cord injuries; investigation of methods to improve quality of life of patients with spinal cord injury. *Mailing Add:* St Joseph's Hosp 50 Charlton Ave E Hamilton ON L8N 4A6 Can. *Fax:* 905-521-6138; *E-Mail:* hansebou@fhs.mcmaster.ca

HANSEL, PAUL G(EORGE), ENGINEERING PHYSICS. *Current Pos:* CONSULT ADV TECHNOL, 79- *Personal Data:* b Grand Island, Nebr, June 22, 17; m 46; c 3. *Educ:* Univ Kans, BS, 46. *Honors & Awards:* US War Dept civilian serv commendation, 46; Apollo Achievement Award, NASA, 69; Pioneer Award, Inst Elec & Electronics Engrs, 70. *Prof Exp:* Radio engr, US Army Signal Corps Labs, NJ, 41-47; chief radio engr, Servo Corp Am, 47-61; vpres eng, Electronic Commun, 61-70, asst gen mgr, 64-70, vpres & gen mgr aerospace electronics, 70, vpres res & eng, 71-79. *Mem:* Fel Inst Elec & Electronics Engrs; NY Acad Sci; AAAS. *Res:* Radio direction finding and navigation; frequency control; receivers; transmitters; electronic instrumentation; light modulators; communication systems; radiation health effects. *Mailing Add:* 1374 Monterey Blvd NE St Petersburg FL 33704

HANSEL, WILLIAM, ANIMAL BIOTECHNOLOGY, REPRODUCTIVE BIOLOGY. *Current Pos:* GORDON D CAIN PROF ANIMAL PHYSIOL, LA STATE UNIV, 90- *Personal Data:* b Vale Summit, Md, Sept 16, 18; m 42; c 2. *Educ:* Univ Md, BS, 40; Cornell Univ, MS, 47, PhD(animal physiol), 49. *Honors & Awards:* Soc Animal Sci Award Physiol & Endocrinol, Am Soc Animal Sci, 62 & NY Farmers Award, 64 & 65; Borden Award, 72; Nat Asn Animal Breeders Award, 73; Morrison Award, Am Soc Animal Sci, 79; Carl Hartman Award, Soc Study Reproduction, 80; W Henry Hatch Award, 86. *Prof Exp:* Asst animal husb, Cornell Univ, 46-49, from assoc prof to prof animal physiol, 49-90, chmn physiol, 78-84. *Concurrent Pos:* Guggenheim fel, Univ Chicago, 58; NSF sr fel, Commonwealth Sci Res Orgn, Australia, 66-67; Liberty Hyde Bailey Professorship, 78; consult, Merck Sharpe & Dohme, 81-83, Smith Kline Buchman, 86; vis prof, Univ Guelph, Can, 84. *Mem:* AAAS; Am Soc Animal Sci; Am Dairy Sci Asn; Am Physiol Soc; Brit Soc Study Fertil; Soc Study Reproduction (pres, 75-76); Endocrinol Soc. *Res:* Dairy cattle sterility; mechanism of the control of ovulation in farm animals; pituitary hypothalamic interrelationships; corpus luteum function; early pregnancy recognition. *Mailing Add:* Dept Vet Sci 251 Dalrymple Hall La State Univ Baton Rouge LA 70808-4124. *Fax:* 504-763-2525

HANSELL, MARGARET MARY, ANATOMY. *Current Pos:* lectr anat, 69-71, asst prof, 71-76, ASSOC PROF ANAT, DALHOUSIE UNIV, 76- *Personal Data:* b Weston, Ont, Feb 1, 41. *Educ:* Univ Toronto, BSc, 63; Univ Calif, Riverside, PhD(biol), 68. *Prof Exp:* Nat Res Coun Can fel bot, Univ Toronto, 68-69. *Mem:* Can Asn Anat; Can Soc Cell Biol. *Res:* Electron microscopy of mammalian respiratory system, liver and kidney; pollution effects. *Mailing Add:* Dept Anat & Neurobiol Dalhousie Univ Halifax NS B3H 4H7 Can

HANSELMAN, RAYMOND BUSH, ANALYTICAL CHEMISTRY, PHOTOGRAPHIC CHEMISTRY. *Current Pos:* dir chem res, 85-90, DIR CUSTOMER SATISFACTION & QUAL ASSURANCE, CHEM PROD, WATERS CHROMATOGRAPHY DIV, MILLIPORE CORP, 90- *Personal Data:* b New York, NY, Dec 29, 32; m 58; c 3. *Educ:* Amherst Col, BA, 54; Mass Inst Technol, PhD(analytical chem), 59. *Prof Exp:* Group leader analytical chem, Plastics Div, Union Carbide Corp, 59-64; mgr environ technol, Space Systs Div, Avco Corp, 64-67; mgr res lab, Polaroid Corp, 67-85. *Mem:* AAAS; Am Chem Soc. *Res:* Photographic sciences; polymer physical chemistry; chemical instrumentation and space sciences; oceanography; chromatography. *Mailing Add:* 132 Deacon Haynes Rd Concord MA 01742-4712

HANSEN, AFTON M, BIOLOGY, GENETICS. *Current Pos:* RETIRED. *Personal Data:* b Mayfield, Utah, Sept 25, 25. *Educ:* Brigham Young Univ, BS, 52, MS, 53; Utah State Univ, PhD(zool), 62. *Hon Degrees:* DSc, Show Col, 85. *Prof Exp:* From instr to prof & chmn, Div Agr & Life Sci, Snow Col, 53- 72, prof & chmn, Div Natural Sci, 72-75, prof biol sci, 75-89. *Concurrent Pos:* Forestry aid, US Forest Serv, 54-57; range conservationist, Great Basin Res Ctr, 64-54; range scientist, 65-66. *Res:* Drasophila genetics eye abnormatities. *Mailing Add:* PO Box 96 Mayfield UT 84643

HANSEN, ANTHONY DAVID ANDERS, ATMOSPHERIC PHYSICS, INSTRUMENTATION. *Current Pos:* res assoc physics, 74-77, STAFF SCIENTIST ATMOSPHERIC PHYSICS, LAWRENCE BERKELEY LAB, UNIV CALIF, BERKELEY, 77- *Personal Data:* b London, Eng, May 12, 51; c 1. *Educ:* Oxford Univ, Eng, BA, 72; Univ Calif, Berkeley, PhD(physics), 77. *Hon Degrees:* MA, Oxford Univ, Eng, 78. *Prof Exp:* Technician instrumentation, Nuclear Physics Lab, Univ Oxford, 70-72 & Europ Orgn Nuclear Res, Geneva, 72. *Mem:* Am Phys Soc; Optical Soc Am. *Res:* Particulate air pollution; physical and chemical transformation of particles; development and validation of instrumentation, experimental techniques and data analysis. *Mailing Add:* 1829 Francisco St Berkeley CA 94703

HANSEN, ANTON JUERGEN, HORTICULTURE, ENVIRONMENTAL SCIENCE. *Current Pos:* CONSULT, ENVIRON & AGR, 91- *Personal Data:* b Hamburg, Ger, Dec 23, 28; m 61; c Ingrid & Tanya C. *Educ:* Univ Gottingen, dipl, 54; Univ Wis, PhD(plant path), 58. *Prof Exp:* Asst, Max Planck Inst Res Plant Breeding, Ger, 54-55; asst plant path, Univ Wis, 55-58, res fel, 63-65; plant pathologist, Int-Am Inst Agr Sci, 58-63; plant pathologist, Res Br, Can Dept Agr, 65-91. *Concurrent Pos:* Adj prof, Simon Fraser Univ; pres, Green Group. *Mem:* Am Phytopath Soc; Am Hort Soc. *Res:* Virus diseases of stone fruits, pome fruits and grapes; diseases of grapes and tropical crops; agricultural business and management. *Mailing Add:* RR No 4 Site 106 C16 Summerland BC V0H 1Z0 Can

HANSEN, ARTHUR G(ENE), MECHANICAL ENGINEERING, APPLIED MATHEMATICS. *Current Pos:* RETIRED. *Personal Data:* b Sturgeon Bay, Wis, Feb 28, 25; m 72, Nancy Tucker; c James, Geoffrey, Ruth, Christine & Paul. *Educ:* Purdue Univ, BS, 46, MS, 48; Case Western Res Univ, PhD(math), 58. *Hon Degrees:* DEng, Purdue Univ, 70; DSc, Ind Univ, 82; Dr, Int Univ Kyrgyatan, 96. *Honors & Awards:* Medal Pub Serv, Dept Defense, 86. *Prof Exp:* Instr math, Purdue Univ, 46-48; res engr fluid mech, Lewis Lab, Nat Adv Comt Aeronaut, 48-49, aeronaut res scientist, 50-58; head nucleonics sect, Cornell Aeronaut Lab, Inc, 58-59; prof mech eng & chmn dept, Univ Mich, 59-66; dean eng, Ga Inst Technol, 66-69, pres, 69-71; pres, Purdue Univ, 71-82; chancellor, Tex A&M Syst, 82-86; dir res, Hudson Inst, 87-88. *Concurrent Pos:* Instr math, Univ Md, 49-50; lectr, John Carroll Univ, 56-57 & Baldwin-Wallace Col, 57-58; consult engr, Deming Pump Co, 61-65; lectr, Ford Motor Co, 64; vis prof, Tuskegee Inst, 65; mem bd dirs, Eng Joint Coun, 70-72; subcomt Prof Sci & Technol Manpower, US Dept Labor, 71-73; consult, 86-; chmn, Corp Educ Technol, 93-96; vchmn, Ind Comn Higher Educ. *Mem:* Nat Acad Eng; Am Soc Eng Educ; AAAS. *Res:* Viscous fluid flow, particularly three-dimensional boundary-layer theory; theoretical fluid mechanics; partial differential equations; pump design. *Mailing Add:* 815 Suagrbush Ridge Zionsville IN 46077. *Fax:* 317-873-1937; *E-Mail:* hansen@pop.iquest.net

HANSEN, AXEL C, OPHTHALMOLOGY. *Current Pos:* From instr to prof surg ophthal, Meharry Med Col, 49-74, head, Div Ophthal, 60-74, prof ophthal & chmn dept, 74-85, DISTINGUISHED EMER PROF OPHTHAL, MEHARRY MED COL, 85- *Personal Data:* b VI, Mar 4, 19; m 46. *Educ:* Fisk Univ, BA, 41; Meharry Med Col, MD, 44; Am Bd Opthal, dipl, 53. *Hon Degrees:* DHL, Fisk Univ, 90. *Concurrent Pos:* Insular ophthalmologist & consult to children's serv, Dept Health, VI, 56-59, consult ophthalmologist, 69-74; consult, Tenn Dept Health & Environ, Georges W Hubbard Hosp, Mecharry Med Col & Alvin York Med, Ctr Vet Admin, Murfreesboro, TN. *Mem:* Fel AAAS; Nat Med Asn; Nat Soc Prev Blindness; Am Med Asn; fel Am Acad Opthamol; fel Am Col Surgeons. *Mailing Add:* 1716 Windover Dr Nashville TN 37218

HANSEN, BARBARA CALEEN, ENDOCRINOLOGY, OBESITY. *Current Pos:* prof physiol, psychol & vpres, 86-90, PROF PHYSIOL, SCH MED & DIR OBESITY & DIABETES RES CTR, UNIV MD, 90- *Personal Data:* b Boston, Mass, Nov 24, 41; m 76; c 1. *Educ:* Univ Calif, Los Angeles, BS, 64, MS, 65; Univ Wash, Seattle, PhD(physiol & psychol), 71. *Honors & Awards:* Rod Rose Award. *Prof Exp:* From asst prof to assoc prof physiol & nursing, Sch Med & Sch Nursing, Univ Wash, 71-76; from assoc prof to prof, Sch Med & Sch Nursing, Univ Mich, 76-82; prof physiol & psychol, assoc vpres res & dean, Grad Sch, Southern Ill Univ, 82-85. *Concurrent Pos:* Prin investr, NIH res grants, 73-; mem, Dir Adv Comt & Nutrit Study Sect, NIH, 79-83; mem, Inst Med-Nat Acad Sci, 81- *Mem:* Inst Med-Nat Acad Sci; Am Physiol Soc; Am Soc Nutrit Sci; NAm Asn Study Obesity (pres); Nat Asn Univ Res Admin; Am Inst Nutrit; Am Soc Clin Nutrit; Int Asn Study Obesity (pres). *Res:* Non-human primates in the study of aging, obesity and the regulation of appetite, diabetes, endocrinology and behavior. *Mailing Add:* Obesity & Diabetes Res Ctr Sch Med Univ Md 10 Pine St No 600 Baltimore MD 21201

HANSEN, BERNARD LYLE, PHYSICS. *Current Pos:* RES ASSOC, UNIV NEBR-LINCOLN, 74- *Personal Data:* b Providence, Utah, July 27, 16; m 38; c 1. *Educ:* Brigham Young Univ, BS, 40. *Hon Degrees:* PhD honoris causa, Univ Bern, 77. *Honors & Awards:* Seligman Crystal Award, Int Glaciol Soc, 72. *Prof Exp:* Instrument engr, US Weather Bur, Washington, DC, 42-45, physicist, Instrument Div, 45-47; physicist & dir, Snow Lab, Calif, 47-49; res assoc, Univ Minn, 49-51; physicist, Snow, Ice & Permafrost Res Estab, Wilmette, 52-60; chief tech serv div, US Army Cold Regions Res & Eng Lab, Hanover, 61-73. *Mem:* Am Meteorol Soc; Am Geophys Union; Int Glaciol Soc. *Res:* Design of new instruments and equipment to determine physical properties of snow, ice and frozen ground; geophysical applications of infra-red radiation; deep core drilling in ice. *Mailing Add:* 530 Hazelwood Dr Lincoln NE 68510

HANSEN, CARL JOHN, ASTROPHYSICS, PHYSICS. *Current Pos:* res assoc, 66-68, from asst prof to assoc prof, 68-74, PROF ASTROPHYS, JOINT INST LAB ASTROPHYS, UNIV COLO, BOULDER, 74-, FEL, 69- *Personal Data:* b Brooklyn, NY, Dec 21, 33; m 60; c 1. *Educ:* Queens Col, NY, BS, 56; Yale Univ, MS, 61, PhD(physics), 66. *Prof Exp:* Reactor analyst, Combustion Eng Inc, Conn, 56-60. *Res:* Evolution and stability of highly evolved stars; nuclear astrophysics. *Mailing Add:* Dept Astrophys & Geophys Univ Colo Jila Campus Box 440 Boulder CO 80309

HANSEN, CARL TAMS, GENETICS. *Current Pos:* GENETICIST, NAT CTR RES RESOURCES, NIH, 64- *Personal Data:* b Greeley, Colo, July 22, 29; m 62; c 2. *Educ:* Colo State Univ, BS, 51; SDak State Univ, MS, 59; Univ Wis-Madison, PhD(genetics), 66. *Mem:* AAAS; Am Genetic Asn; Genetics Soc Am. *Res:* Developing rodent models for the study of cardiovascular disorders, metabolic diseases, parasitic and infectious diseases, immunology, cancer, endocrine disorders and behavior. *Mailing Add:* Vet Res Prog Nat Ctr Res Resources NIH Bldg 14 G Rm 101 Bethesda MD 20892-5590

HANSEN, DALE J, SCIENCE ADMINISTRATION. *Current Pos:* DIR RES & DEVELOP, THATCHER CO, 93- *Personal Data:* b Idaho Falls, Idaho, Sept 3, 39; m 65, Ruth L Wheeler; c Evan, Eric, Ryan & Kristi. *Educ:* Univ Idaho, BS, 63, MS, 66; Ohio State Univ, PhD(plant physiol), 69. *Prof Exp:* Fel, Univ Ill, Urbana, 69-72; scientist, Monsanto Corp, St Louis, 72-81; res dir, Agrigenetics Res Corp, 81-87, pres, 82-86; dir res & develop, Agridyne Techs Inc, Salt Lake City, 87-93. *Mem:* AAAS; Am Soc Agron; Plant Growth Regulator Soc (pres), 84); Sigma Xi. *Mailing Add:* Thatcher Co 1900 W Fortune Rd Salt Lake City UT 84104

HANSEN, DAVID ELLIOTT, ENZYMOLOGY, ANTIBODY CATALYSIS. *Current Pos:* From asst prof to assoc prof, 86-96, PROF CHEM, AMHERST COL, 96-; ADJ PROF, PROG MOLECULAR & CELLULAR BIOL, UNIV MASS, 90- *Personal Data:* b Brooklyn, NY, July 18, 58; m 88; c 1. *Educ:* Brown Univ, ScB, 79; Harvard Univ, PhD (chem), 86. *Hon Degrees:* MA, Amherst Col, 96. *Concurrent Pos:* NSF presidential young investr award, 89; Camille & Henry Dreyfus teacher-scholar, 91, scholar, 96. *Mem:* Am Chem Soc; AAAS. *Res:* Strategies for the isolation of antibodies with sequence- specific protease activity. *Mailing Add:* Dept Chem Amherst Col Amherst MA 01002. *Fax:* 413-542-2731; *E-Mail:* dehansen@amherst.edu

HANSEN, DAVID HENRY, PHYSIOLOGICAL ECOLOGY, COMMUNITY ECOLOGY. *Current Pos:* From asst prof to assoc prof, 74-81, PROF BIOL, PAC LUTHERAN UNIV, 89- *Personal Data:* b Corvallis, Ore, May 8, 45; m 68; c 2. *Educ:* Ore State Univ, BS, 68; Univ Utah, MS, 69; Univ Calif, Irvine, PhD(pop, environ biol), 74. *Concurrent Pos:* Vis assoc prof, Univ Hawaii, Monoa, 81. *Mem:* AAAS; Bot Soc Am; Ecol Soc Am. *Res:* Physiological plant ecology with specific interests in comparative leaf physiology related to invasion and persistance strategics. *Mailing Add:* Dept Biol Pac Luthern Univ 12180 Park Ave S Tacoma WA 98447-0001. *Fax:* 253-536-5055; *E-Mail:* hansen.d@plu.bitnet

HANSEN, DEBORAH KAY, TOXICOLOGY, GENETICS. *Current Pos:* RES BIOLOGIST, DIV REPRODUCTIVE & DEVELOP, 85- *Personal Data:* b Springfield, Ill, June 17, 52. *Educ:* Eastern Ill Univ, BS, 74; Iowa State Univ, MS, 76; Ind Univ, PhD(med genetics), 81. *Concurrent Pos:* Fel, Dept Epidemiol & Pub Health, Yale Univ, 81-82; fel, Dept Pharmacol, Univ Tex, 82-85; adj asst prof, Dept Pharmacol & Interdisciplinary, Ark Med Sci, 86- *Mem:* Soc Toxicol; Sigma Xi; AAAS; Teratol Soc; Soc Exp Biol & Med; Asn Women Sci. *Res:* Research interest focus on mechanisms whereby drugs and or chemicals induce developmental toxicity. *Mailing Add:* 9817 Johnson Rd Mabelvale AR 72013

HANSEN, DONALD JOSEPH, MATHEMATICS. *Current Pos:* RETIRED. *Personal Data:* b Kansas City, Mo, June 14, 32. *Educ:* Southern Methodist Univ, BS, 54, MS, 55; Univ Tex, PhD(math), 62. *Prof Exp:* Lectr math, Southern Methodist Univ, 55-56; spec instr, Univ Tex, 58-62; asst prof math, NC State Univ, 62-96. *Mem:* Am Math Soc; Math Asn Am. *Res:* Ordered algebraic systems; lattice theory; functional equations. *Mailing Add:* Dept Math NC State Univ Raleigh NC 27695-8205

HANSEN, DONALD VERNON, OCEAN CIRCULATION, AIR-SEA INTERACTION. *Current Pos:* SR RES ASSOC, UNIV MIAMI, 93- *Personal Data:* b Seattle, Wash, Jan 18, 31; m 58, Eva Busemann; c 3. *Educ:* Univ Wash, BS, 54, MS, 61, PhD(oceanog), 64. *Prof Exp:* Engr, Boeing Airplane Co, Seattle, 56-57; teacher sci pub schs, Seattle, 57-58; asst oceanog, Univ Wash, Seattle, 59-61, res asst, 61-64, res asst prof, 64-65; res oceanogr, Environ Sci Serv Admin, Nat Oceanic & Atmospheric Admin, US Dept Commerce, 66-69, dir, Phy Oceanog Div, 69-93, supvry oceanogr, 70-93, actg dir, Atlantic Oceanog & Meteorol Labs, Miami, 78-80. *Concurrent Pos:* Adj prof, Univ Miami, 69- *Mem:* Am Geophys Union; Am Soc Limnol & Oceanog; fel AAAS; Sigma Xi. *Res:* Currents and general circulation in coastal and oceanic waters; dynamics and theory of estuarine and inshore waters; ocean processes in climate. *Mailing Add:* 5900 SW 104th St Miami FL 33156. *Fax:* 305-361-4392; *E-Mail:* hansen@aoml.noaa.gov

HANSEN, DONALD WILLIS, JR, MEDICINAL CHEMISTRY, ORGANIC CHEMISTRY. *Current Pos:* SR RES SCIENTIST & GROUP LEADER PHARMACEUT CHEM, G D SEARLE & CO, 74- *Personal Data:* b Springfield, Ill, June 12, 43; m 73, Sue-Ann; c Kevin. *Educ:* Univ Wis, BS, 65; Pa State Univ, PhD(org chem), 71. *Honors & Awards:* G D Searle Spec Recognition Award. *Prof Exp:* Scholar, Dept Chem, Univ Mich, 71-73, scholar, Dept Med Chem, 72-73, lectr org chem, 73-74. *Concurrent Pos:* Adj asst prof med chem, Univ Ill, Chicago. *Mem:* Am Chem Soc; AAAS; Soc Neurosci. *Res:* Design and synthesis of new pharmacologically active substances and the development of new synthetic methods and transformations in organic chemistry. *Mailing Add:* 5250 W Brown St Skokie IL 60077-3616

HANSEN, DOUGLAS BRAYSHAW, CHILD PSYCHIATRY, PSYCHOANALYSIS. *Current Pos:* asst prof, Baylor Col Med, 64-72, dir, Child Psychiat Training Prog, 64-80, assoc prof psychiat, Child Psychiat & Pediat, 76-86, PROF CLIN PSYCHIAT, BAYLOR COL MED, 85-, TRAINING PSYCHOANALYST, HOUSTON-GALVESTON PSYCHOANAL INST, 80- *Personal Data:* b Neenah, Wis, Apr 30, 29; m 57; c 3. *Educ:* Antioch Col, AB, 51; Univ Rochester, MD, 55; Am Bd Psychiat & Neurol, dipl & cert psychiat, 65 & cert child psychiat, 66. *Prof Exp:* Intern med, Barnes Hosp, Wash Univ, 55-56; res assoc cerebral metab, NIMH, 56-58; resident psychiat & child psychiat, Columbia Univ & NY State Psychiat Inst, 58-62; instr child psychiat, Columbia Univ, 62-64. *Concurrent Pos:* Chief psychiatrist, Rice Univ, 64-65; chief child psychiatrist, Tex Res Inst Ment Sci, 65-74; fel psychoanal, New Orleans Psychoanal Inst, La, 71, mem fac psychoanal, 72-73, teaching analyst, 73-80; mem, Regional Coun, Am Acad Child Psychiat, 71-; Am Soc Adolescent Psychiat liaison, Am Asn Psychiat Serv Children, 72-; mem Comt Adolescent Psychiat, Am Acad Child Psychiat, 72-; training & supv psychoanalyst, Houston-Galveston Psychoanal Inst, 77-; psychiatrist-in-chief, Tex Childrens Hosp, 75-86; St Lukes Episcopal Hosp, 78-79; pres med staff, Psychiat Inst, Houston, 81-83, med dir, 85-87; pres, Houston Psychoanal Soc, 73-75, 82-84; vpres, Houston-Galveston Psychoanal Inst, 92- *Mem:* Fel Am Psychiat Asn; Am Orthopsychiat Asn; Am Psychoanal Asn; Am Group Psychother Asn; Am Soc Adolescent Psychiat; fel Am Col Psychiat; fel Am Acad Child Psychiat. *Res:* Child development and thesies of the mind. *Mailing Add:* 2240 Looscan Lane Houston TX 77019-1414

HANSEN, EDER LINDSAY, PHARMACOLOGY. *Current Pos:* RETIRED. *Personal Data:* b Melbourne, Australia, Jan 7, 14; m 44, James W; c Stuart & Mary-Louise. *Educ:* Univ Melbourne, BAgrSc, 35, MAgrSc, 38; Univ Calif, MS, 40, PhD, 49. *Prof Exp:* Asst bot, Univ Melbourne, 36-39; mem res staff indust hyg, Dept Labor & Nat Serv, Australia, 42-44; asst & assoc pharmacol, Univ Calif, 44-50; asst, Kaiser Found Res Inst, 56-60, assoc, 60-66; mem res staff, Clin Pharmacol Res Inst, 66-80. *Mem:* Am Soc Pharmacol & Exp Therapeut; Am Soc Trop Med & Hyg; Soc Exp Biol & Med; Am Soc Parasitologists. *Res:* Experimental biology; tropical medicine. *Mailing Add:* 561 Santa Barbara Rd Berkeley CA 94707

HANSEN, EVERETT MATHEW, FOREST PATHOLOGY. *Current Pos:* Res assoc, 72-75, from asst prof to assoc prof, 75-88, PROF FOREST PATH, ORE STATE UNIV, 81- *Personal Data:* b Portland, Ore, Sept 8, 46; m 77; c 3. *Educ:* Ore State Univ, BS, 68; Univ Wis-Madison, MS, 70, PhD(plant path), 72. *Concurrent Pos:* Assoc ed, Phytopath, Am Phytopath Soc, 85-88, chair, Forest Path Comt, 88. *Mem:* Am Phytopath Soc; Sigma Xi; Brit Myological Soc. *Res:* Biology, ecology and management of fungi causing diseases of forest trees, particularly root disease; cytology and sexuality and subsequent influences on population patterns and development of host specialization. *Mailing Add:* Dept Bot & Path Ore State Univ Corvallis OR 97331. *Fax:* 541-737-3573; *E-Mail:* hansene@cgrb.orst.edu

HANSEN, GERALD DELBERT, JR, PHYSICAL CHEMISTRY. *Current Pos:* SR CONSULT, CHEMLINK CO, 87- *Personal Data:* b Oil City, Pa, May 27, 21; m 49; c 3. *Educ:* Thiel Col, BS, 46. *Prof Exp:* Res chemist rubber, Lord Mfg Co, Pa, 46-47; asst chem, Duquesne Univ, 47-49; res chemist rheol, Hagan Chem & Controls, Inc, 50-56, proj leader, 56-57, group leader surface chem, 57-64, Calgon Corp, 64-65; boiler res group, Betz Labs, 65-66, group leader surface chem, 66-69, res assoc surface chem, 69-73; pres, G D Hansen Assocs, 73-77; sr chemist, Arco Chem, 77-78, prod mgr, Arco Performance Chem Co, 78-79, dir cent res, 80-87. *Mem:* AAAS; Soc Rheol; Royal Soc Chem; fel Am Inst Chem. *Res:* Thermodynamics and electrokinetics of interfaces and the relationship between these properties and the rheology of dispersed systems. *Mailing Add:* PO Box 127 Holicong PA 18928-0127

HANSEN, GRANT LEWIS, ELECTRICAL ENGINEERING, TECHNICAL MANAGEMENT. *Current Pos:* RETIRED. *Personal Data:* b Bancroft, Idaho, Nov 5, 21; m 45, Iris R Heyden; c Alan, Brian, Carol, David & Ellen. *Educ:* Ill Inst Technol, BSEE, 48. *Hon Degrees:* DSc, Nat Univ, 78. *Prof Exp:* Mem staff, Douglas Aircraft Co, 48-60, vpres & prog dir for Centaur, Convair Div, 60-65; vpres launch vehicle progs, Convair Div, gen Dynamics Corp, 65-69, gen mgr, 73-74, corp vpres, 74-78; asst secy Airforce for res & develop, 69-73; vpres, Gen Dynamics Corp, San Diego, 74-78, vpres & gen mgr, Convair Div, 73-78; pres, Systs Develop Corp, 78-86. *Concurrent Pos:* US deleg, NATO Adv Group Aerospace Res & Develop, 69-73; US mem sci comt nat reps, SHAPE Tech Ctr, The Hague, Netherlands, 69-73; mem res & tech adv coun, NASA, 71-73; mem sci adv bd, Dept Air Force, 76-83. *Mem:* Nat Acad Eng; fel Am Inst Aeronaut & Astronaut (pres, 75); AAAS; fel Int Acad Astronaut; sr mem Inst Elec & Electronics Engrs. *Res:* Liquid hydrogen propulsion; space launch vehicles; missiles; knowledge based computer systems. *Mailing Add:* 10737 Fuerte Dr La Mesa CA 91941-5740

HANSEN, HANS JOHN, ANTIBODY THERAPY. *Current Pos:* Dir cell biol, 85-87, VPRES, EXPLOR RES, IMMUNOMEDICS, INC, 87- *Educ:* Tulane Univ, PhD(biochem), 60. *Res:* In vitro and in vivo diagnosis; cancer research. *Mailing Add:* Immunomedics Inc 300 American Rd Morris Plains NJ 07950. *Fax:* 973-605-1103

HANSEN, HARRY LOUIS, entomology, biology, for more information see previous edition

HANSEN, HOWARD EDWARD, CHILD PSYCHIATRY, PSYCHOANALYSIS. *Current Pos:* assoc prof, 67-88, EMER ASSOC PROF PEDIAT PSYCHIAT & BEHAV SCI, SCH MED, UNIV SOUTHERN CALIF, 88-; MED DIR, CHILD STUDY CTR, ST JOHN'S HOSP & HEALTH CTR, 90- *Personal Data:* b Lincoln, Nebr, Jan 28, 23; m 62; c 2. *Educ:* Univ Nebr, BS & MD, 47. *Prof Exp:* Asst pediat, Childrens Hosp, Los Angeles & Univ Southern Calif, 54-55; chief, Pediat Serv 7520 USAF Hosp, London, Eng, 56-59; pvt practr psychiat, Calif, 60-68; asst attending pediat & psychiat, Childrens Hosp, Los Angeles, 61-67; asst clin prof, Univ Southern Calif, 62-65, asst prof, 65-67; head psychiat & dir child psychiat, Children's Hosp, Los Angeles, 68-88. *Concurrent Pos:* Dir child psychiat, Cedars Lebanon Hosp, Los Angeles, 61-64, assoc attend psychiat & adj pediat, Med Ctr, 61-70; med dir psychiat, Julia Ann Singer Presch Ctr, 61-64, mem, Prof Adv Comt, Psychiat Clin, 65-; sr staff psychiatrist, Mt Sinai Hosp, 61-64, adj pediat, Med Ctr, 61-70; mem attend staff, Los Angeles Co Gen Hosp, 61-70; mem, Prof Adv Coun, Dubnoff Sch Educ Ther, 62-; psychiat consult, Ment Retardation Community Serv Clin, Childrens Hosp, Los Angeles, 63-; clin assoc psychoanal, Southern Calif Psychoanal Inst, 64-; coordr, Child Psychiat Training, Los Angeles Co-Univ Southern Calif Med Ctr, 65-68; mem, Adv Comt, Dept Child Psychiat, Cedars Sinai Med Ctr, 65-; mem adv bd, Park Cent Sch, 68-; mem, Med Adv Comt, Calif State Dept Ment Hyg, 70-71, mem, Task Force 5 Yr Plan, Subcomt Child & Adolescent Psychiat, 71-; mem, Citizens Comt Bd & Care, Los Angeles City Coun, 71-72; mem, Ment Health Adv Bd, Welfare Planning Coun, 71-; co-investr, NIMH grant & contract, 71-, prin investr, Grants Found, Inc grant, 71-; mem bd dirs, Ment Health Asn, Los Angeles, 74-, Edgemont Hosp, 78-; med dir, Child Study Ctr, St John's Hosp & Health Ctr, 90- *Mem:* Am Psychoanal Asn; AMA; fel Am Acad Pediat; fel Am Psychiat Asn; fel Am Acad Child Psychiat. *Res:* Emotional reactions to natural disasters; psychological preparation and care of amputees; renal dialysis and transplant patients; cancer patients; fatally ill child and his family; extreme cases of psycho-social isolation; suicide and self endangering behaviors of children; Gilles de la Tourette Syndrome. *Mailing Add:* 1268 Oceanfront Santa Monica CA 90401

HANSEN, HUGH J, ENERGY MANAGEMENT, AGRICULTURAL ENGINEERING. *Current Pos:* PROF ENG, AGR ENG DEPT, ORE STATE UNIV, 78- *Personal Data:* b Thief River Falls, Minn, March 30, 23; m 49; c 3. *Educ:* NDak State Univ, BSAE, 51; Cornell Univ, MSAE, 52. *Prof Exp:* Asst prof eng, Agr Eng Dept, Purdue Univ, 52-55; ed tech eng, Reuben H Donnelley Corp, NY, 55-62; publ, Dun-Donnelley Publ Corp, 62-74; mgr, Western Regional Agr Eng Serv, 74-78. *Concurrent Pos:* Exec mgr, Nat Food & Energy Coun, 72-74. *Mem:* Fel Am Soc Agr Engrs (pres, 71-72); Irrigation Asn. *Mailing Add:* 886 Laiqua Lane Santa Barbara CA 93110

HANSEN, J RICHARD, ELECTROOPTICS. *Current Pos:* RETIRED. *Personal Data:* b Sioux City, Iowa, Sept 21, 22; m 48; c 2. *Educ:* Univ Mo, BS, 44. *Prof Exp:* Sr res engr, Res Labs, Westinghouse Elec Corp, 47-66, sr res scientist, 66-87. *Mem:* Sr mem Inst Elec & Electronics Engrs; Am Astron Soc. *Res:* Electronic circuitry; imaging devices, especially electronic; infrared detection; liquid crystals; x-ray and neutron activation nondestructive testing; fiber optics. *Mailing Add:* 1462 Jefferson Heights Rd Pittsburgh PA 15235

HANSEN, JAMES E, PULMONARY DISEASES, ENVIRONMENTAL PHYSIOLOGY. *Current Pos:* from assoc prof to prof 76-86, EMER PROF MED, UNIV CALIF, LOS ANGELES, 86- *Personal Data:* b Green Bay, Wis, Sept 4, 26; m 48; c 4. *Educ:* Johns Hopkins Univ, MD, 49. *Prof Exp:* From intern to resident internal med, US Army, Letterman Gen Hosp, San Francisco, 49-53, asst chief med serv, US Army Hosp, Ft Riley, Kans, 53-56, surgeon, 32 AAA Brigade, England, 56-57, chief med serv, 34th Gen Hosp,

Orleans, France, 57-59, resident pulmonary dis, Fitzsimons Gen Hosp, Denver, 60-61, chief tuberc serv, 61-62, chief med training team, Jordan Arab Army, 62, chief physiol div, US Army Med Res & Nutrit Lab, 62-65, commanding officer & sci dir, US Army Res Inst Environ Med, Mass, 65-71, chief clin invest serv, Tripler Army Med Ctr, 71-75; fel pulmonary dis, Harbor-Univ Calif, Los Angeles Med Ctr, Torrance, 75-76, head clin respiratory physiol lab, 76-86. *Concurrent Pos:* Instr, Univ Colo, 62-65; lectr, Johns Hopkins Univ, 66-71; clin prof physiol, Univ Hawaii, 72-75; assoc prof med, Univ Calif, Los Angeles, 76-78, prof, 78- *Mem:* Fel Am Col Physicians; Am Thoracic Soc; Am Physiol Soc; Am Fedn Clin Res; fel Am Col Chest Physicians. *Res:* Clinical medicine; pulmonary and infectious diseases; exercise physiology; altitude physiology. *Mailing Add:* Respiratory Physiol & Med Div Univ Calif Los Angeles Med Ctr Box 24 1692 Morse Dr Torrance CA 90509. *Fax:* 310-832-8452

HANSEN, JAMES E, PHYSICS, METEOROLOGY. *Current Pos:* Nat Acad Sci-Nat Res Coun resident res assoc, 67-69, mem staff, space scientist & mgr, Planetary & Climate Progs, 72-81, HEAD, GODDARD INST SPACE STUDIES, 81- *Personal Data:* b Mar 29, 41. *Educ:* Univ Iowa, BA, 63, MS, 65, PhD(physics), 67. *Honors & Awards:* Goddard Spec Achievement Award, 77; Group Achievement Award, NASA, 82, 93, Except Serv Medal, 84, Pres Rank Award, 90; William Nordberg Achievement Award, 96. *Prof Exp:* NSF fel, Leiden Observ, Neth, 69; res assoc, Columbia Univ, 69-72. *Concurrent Pos:* Co-prin investr, AER-OPOL Proj, 71-74; co-investr, Voyager Photopolarimeter Exp, 72-85; prin investr, Pioneer Venus Cloud-Photopolarimeter Exp, 74-78, co-investr, 78-; prin investr, Galileo Photopolarimeter Radiometer Exp, 77-, Earth Observ Interdisciplinary Invest, 89-; adj assoc prof geol sci, Columbia Univ, 78-85, adj prof, 85-; Am Geophys Union fel, 92. *Mem:* Nat Acad Sci. *Res:* Radiative transfer in planetary atmospheres; interpretation of remote sounding of planetary atmospheres; development of simplified climate models and 3-D global climate models; current climate trends from observational data and projections of man's impact on climate. *Mailing Add:* NASA Goddard Inst Space Studies 2880 Broadway New York NY 10025

HANSEN, JOHN C, COMPUTER SCIENCE. *Current Pos:* ENGR, YORK INT CORP, 88- *Personal Data:* b Miami, Fla, Mar 3, 47. *Educ:* Univ Miami, BA, 68; Mich State Univ, PhD(comput sci), 74. *Prof Exp:* Assoc prof comput sci, Xavier Univ, 81-83; prof comput sci, Cent Mich Univ, 83-88. *Mem:* Math Asn Am; Inst Elec & Electronics Engrs; Asn Comput Mach. *Mailing Add:* 7503 Oak Lane Ft Wayne IN 46804

HANSEN, JOHN FREDERICK, ORGANIC CHEMISTRY. *Current Pos:* ASSOC PROF CHEM, ILL STATE UNIV, 72- *Personal Data:* b Turtle Lake, Wis, Mar 21, 42. *Educ:* Wis State Univ, River Falls, BA, 64; Duke Univ, AM, 67, PhD(org chem), 69. *Prof Exp:* Fel chem, Ohio State Univ, 68-69, Univ Notre Dame, 69-71 & Wayne State Univ, 71-72. *Mem:* Am Chem Soc; Sigma Xi. *Res:* Chemistry of organic heterocyclic compounds. *Mailing Add:* Dept Chem 4160 Ill State Univ Normal IL 61761-4160

HANSEN, JOHN NORMAN, BIOCHEMISTRY, MOLECULAR BIOLOGY. *Current Pos:* from asst prof to assoc prof, 71-78, PROF BIOCHEM, UNIV MD, COLLEGE PARK, 78- *Personal Data:* b Kearney, Nebr, July 15, 42; m 66; c 2. *Educ:* Drake Univ, BA, 64; Univ Calif, Los Angeles, PhD(biochem), 68. *Prof Exp:* USPHS fel, Univ Wis, Madison, 68-71. *Mem:* Am Chem Soc; Sigma Xi; AAAS; Am Soc Microbiol. *Res:* Spore outgrowth; control of development; chromosome structure and organization; molecular genetics and mechanism of action of ribosomally-synthesized peptide antibiotics. *Mailing Add:* Dept Chem & Biochem Univ Md College Park MD 20740-2021

HANSEN, JOHN PAUL, MATERIALS SCIENCE ENGINEERING, CHEMICAL ENGINEERING. *Current Pos:* head, Dept Chem & Metall Eng, 70-73, prof, 70-87, EMER PROF METALL ENG, UNIV ALA, TUSCALOOSA, 87- *Personal Data:* b Bain, Minn, Feb 11, 28; m 50, Doris A Dropps; c Steven, Bradley & Kurt. *Educ:* Univ Minn, BS, 54, MS, 55, PhD(metall eng), 58. *Prof Exp:* Res fel, Univ Minn, 55-58; res metallurgist, US Bur Mines, 58-63; prof metall eng, Univ Ala, Tuscaloosa, 63-67; chief, Tuscaloosa Metall Res Lab, US Bur Mines, 67-70. *Concurrent Pos:* Consult, US Army Res Off, NC, Bur Mines, Ala & Ores Res Lab, Mich. *Mem:* Am Inst Mining, Metall & Petrol Engrs; Am Inst Chem Engrs. *Res:* Reaction kinetics of heterogeneous systems; thermodynamics. *Mailing Add:* 1245 Highpoint E Springfield MO 65804

HANSEN, JOHN THEODORE, ANATOMY, CELL BIOLOGY. *Current Pos:* instr, 75-76, asst prof anat, 76-80, ASSOC PROF, MED SCH, UNIV TEX, SAN ANTONIO, 80- *Personal Data:* b Sheboygan Falls, Wis, Oct 10, 47; m 70; c 2. *Educ:* Beloit Col, BA, 70; Creighton Univ, MS, 72; Tulane Univ, PhD(anat), 74. *Prof Exp:* Adj instr anat, Tulane Univ Med Sch, 74-75. *Mem:* AAAS; Am Asn Anat; Am Soc Cell Biol; Am Heart Asn; Soc Neurosci. *Res:* Ultrastructure of paraneurons, chromaffin tissues and cardiovascular system; cardiovascular neurobiology. *Mailing Add:* Dept Neurol Anat Univ Rochester 601 Elmwood Ave Rochester NY 14642

HANSEN, KEITH LEYTON, BIOLOGY. *Current Pos:* RETIRED. *Personal Data:* b Gainesville, Fla, Nov 14, 25; m 47, 83, Genevieve M Horan; c Cynthia L (Cara) & Kimberly J (Finn). *Educ:* Stetson Univ, BS, 49, MS, 50; Univ Fla, PhD, 55. *Prof Exp:* Instr, Stetson Univ, 50-55, from assoc prof to prof, 55-88, res prof biol, 88- *Concurrent Pos:* Consult ecol, Ecosyst Anal. *Mem:* Am Soc Icthyol & Herpet; Ecol Soc Am. *Res:* Freshwater ecology; ecology of anurans and reptiles; radiological research of trophic relations in aquatic communities; heavy metal detection in marine coastal fauna; reproductive and endocrine physiology of anura; systems ecology; ecology of Florida. *Mailing Add:* 4075 Hwy 11 N De Land FL 32724-9720

HANSEN, KENT F(ORREST), NUCLEAR ENGINEERING. *Current Pos:* Res assoc, comput ctr, 59-60, Ford fel, 60-61, from asst prof to assoc prof nuclear eng, 60-69, assoc dean eng, 79-82, PROF NUCLEAR ENG, MASS INST TECHNOL, 69- *Personal Data:* b Chicago, Ill, Aug 10, 31; m 59; c 2. *Educ:* Mass Inst Technol, SB, 53, ScD(nuclear eng), 59. *Honors & Awards:* A H Compton Award, Am Nuclear Soc, 78. *Concurrent Pos:* Consult, US Nuclear Regulatory Comn, 75-89; sci adv comn, EG&G, Idaho, 77-92. *Mem:* Nat Acad Eng; Am Nuclear Soc; Asn Comput Mach; Am Soc Eng Educ. *Res:* Numerical methods of reactor analysis; reactor theory; numerical mathematics; radiation shielding. *Mailing Add:* Dept Nuclear Eng Mass Inst Technol Cambridge MA 02139

HANSEN, KENT W(ENDRICH), CERAMIC ENGINEERING, METALLURGY. *Current Pos:* eng specialist glass & ceramic res, Semiconductor Prod Div, Motorola, Inc, 67-70, mgr glass & ceramics, 70-76, mem tech staff, 76-77, sect mgr, Semiconductor Res & Develop Labs, 77-79, mgr, Mat Tech Lab, 79-85, MGR, PHYS ELECTRONICS & PACKAGING LAB, SEMICONDUCTOR RES & DEVELOP LABS, MOTOROLA, INC, 85- *Personal Data:* b Salt Lake City, Utah, Apr 28, 36; m 56; c 3. *Educ:* Univ Utah, BS, 58, PhD(ceramic eng, metall), 62. *Prof Exp:* Sr engr, Corning Glass Works, 62-65, res engr, 65-67, res assoc ceramics, 67. *Concurrent Pos:* Assoc mem sci adv bd, Motorola, 72. *Mem:* Am Phys Soc; Am Ceramic Soc; Soc Glass Technol; Sigma Xi; Inst Elec & Electronics Engrs. *Res:* Electrical properties of materials, particularly ceramics and glasses; sintering mechanisms in oxides; surface area and pore structure of porous materials; glass technology; semiconductor materials and packaging; glass-metal reactions and sealing; electronic packaging. *Mailing Add:* Motorola Semiconductor Prod Sector 5005 E McDowell Rd Phoenix AZ 85008

HANSEN, LARRY GEORGE, ENVIRONMENTAL TOXICOLOGY. *Current Pos:* res assoc zool, Univ Ill, Urbana, 70-71, asst prof physiol & pharmacol, Col Vet Med, 71-76, assoc prof vet pharmacol, 76-80, PROF VET TOXICOL, UNIV ILL, URBANA, 80- *Personal Data:* b Omaha, Nebr, July 16, 41. *Educ:* Creighton Univ, BS, 63; Univ Nebr, Omaha, MS, 66; NC State Univ, PhD(entom, toxicol), 70. *Prof Exp:* Teacher high sch, Iowa, 63-65. *Concurrent Pos:* Res fel toxicol, Wageningen, The Neth, 80. *Mem:* Soc Toxicol. *Res:* Environmental toxicology; residue transmission; chlorinated hydrocarbons; cadmium; pollution in developing countries; endocrine disruption. *Mailing Add:* Dept Vet Biosci Univ Ill 2001 S Lincoln Urbana IL 61801. *Fax:* 217-333-4628

HANSEN, LEE DUANE, GENERAL CHEMISTRY, PLANT RESPIRATION. *Current Pos:* assoc prof dept chem & Ctr Thermochem Studies, 72-78, PROF CHEM, BRIGHAM YOUNG UNIV, 78- *Personal Data:* b Brigham City, Utah, Apr 13, 40; m 60, Judith Woolstenhulme; c Velinda D, Thea J, Clifford W, Judith A, Jared R, Karina A, Jeremiah J & Benjamin L. *Educ:* Brigham Young Univ, BS, 62, PhD(inorg chem), 65. *Honors & Awards:* J J Christensen Award Innovation Calorimetry, US Calorimetry Conf, 93; Lavoisier Medal, Int Soc Biol Calorimetry, 94. *Prof Exp:* From asst prof to assoc prof chem, Univ NMex, 65-72. *Concurrent Pos:* USPHS career develop award, 69-72; James Prof Chem, St Francis Xavier Univ, 85-86; vis prof, UC Davis, 79-80 & 88; W F James chair pure & appl sci, St Francis Xavier Univ, Antigonish, NS, Can, 86-87. *Mem:* AAAS; Sigma Xi; Chem Soc; Am Asn Pharmaceut Sci; Am Soc Plant Physiol. *Res:* Thermodynamics; proton ionization; metal ion complexation; chemical speciation in air pollutants; multiple equilibria of proteins; metabolism in plants; shelf-life prediction for organic materials; calorimetry. *Mailing Add:* Dept Chem Brigham Young Univ Provo UT 84602-1022. *Fax:* 801-378-5474

HANSEN, LEON A, PLANT BREEDING. *Current Pos:* VPRES RES, ROGERS NK SEED CO, 91- *Personal Data:* b Idaho Falls, Idaho, Sept 15, 43; div; c Rita. *Educ:* Univ Idaho, BS, 65, MS, 67; Ore State Univ, PhD(hort plant breeding), 76. *Honors & Awards:* Nat Food Processors Asn Award, 78. *Prof Exp:* Fieldman, Rogers Bros Seed Co, 67-69, field dept mgr, 69-72, res asst, 72-75, plant breeder, 75-79, dir sweet corn res, 79-85, dir corp res, 85-87, vpres res, 87-94. *Mem:* Am Soc Hort Sci; Am Soc Crop Sci; Nat Sweet Corn Breeders Asn. *Res:* Management of all company research. *Mailing Add:* Rogers NK Seed Co Res Ctr 6338 Hwy 20-26 Nampa ID 83687

HANSEN, LESLIE BENNETT, ANIMAL BREEDING, BIOMETRICS. *Current Pos:* From asst prof to assoc prof, 81-90, PROF DAIRY CATTLE BREEDING, UNIV MINN, 90- *Personal Data:* b Blooming Prairie, Minn, Aug 30, 51. *Educ:* Univ Minn, BS, 73, MS, 78; Iowa State Univ, PhD(animal breeding), 81. *Concurrent Pos:* Mem, Coun Agr Sci & Technol; assoc ed, J Dairy Sci. *Mem:* Am Dairy Sci Asn; Am Soc Animal Sci. *Res:* Population genetics of dairy cattle with special emphasis on management traits, health traits, type traits and other non-production traits; linear statistical models, especially mixed models having random and fixed effects. *Mailing Add:* Dept Animal Sci 122 Peters Hall Univ Minn St Paul 1404 Gortner Ave St Paul MN 55108-6160

HANSEN, LOWELL JOHN, MATHEMATICAL ANALYSIS. *Current Pos:* Asst prof, 69-73, ASSOC PROF MATH, WAYNE STATE UNIV, 73- *Personal Data:* b Bemidji, Minn, Oct 3, 41; m 64; c 4. *Educ:* Bemidji State Col, BA, 65; Univ Ill, Urbana, MA, 66, PhD(math), 69. *Res:* Complex analysis; Hardy Classes; cluster sets; univalent functions; potential theory. *Mailing Add:* Dept Math Wayne State Univ 6050 Cass Ave Detroit MI 48202

HANSEN, LUISA FERNANDEZ, NUCLEAR PHYSICS, HIGH ENERGY PHYSICS. *Current Pos:* SR PHYSICIST, LAWRENCE LIVERMORE NAT LAB, UNIV CALIF, 59- *Personal Data:* b Santiago, Chile; US citizen; m 54, William L; c George A. *Educ:* Univ Chile, BS, 49; Univ Calif, Berkeley, MS, 57, PhD(nuclear physics), 59. *Prof Exp:* Teaching asst physics, Univ Chile, 47-52, asst prof math & physics & statistical cosmic rays, 50-55; res asst physics, Univ Calif, Berkeley, 55-59. *Concurrent Pos:* Consult res & eng, Bechtel Corp, 76-78 & Dept Fusion Power Systs, Westinghouse Elec Corp, 76-77; mem, Bay Area Women Sci Network, 75- *Mem:* Am Phys Soc; fel Am Nuclear Soc; Sigma Xi. *Res:* Neutron and charged particle interactions; measurements and calculations of neutron and gamma ray transport for shielding applications weapon systems and fusion reactors; author of over 150 publications. *Mailing Add:* Lawrence Livermore Nat Lab PO Box 808 L-56 Livermore CA 94550. *Fax:* 510-423-8086; *E-Mail:* hansen13@llnl.gov

HANSEN, MARC F, PEDIATRICS. *Current Pos:* PRES & CHMN BD, U-CARE HMO INC, 90-; EMER PROF, FAMILY PRACT DEPT, UNIV WIS. *Personal Data:* b Marshfield, Wis, Sept 19, 30; c 2. *Educ:* Harvard Univ, AB, 52, MD, 56; Am Bd Pediat, dipl, 61. *Prof Exp:* Intern, Boston City Hosps, 56-57; resident, Univ Hosps, Univ Wis-Madison, 57-59, from asst prof to assoc prof pediat, Med Ctr, 63-74, asst prof, Dept Rehab Med, 67-69, asst dean clin affairs, 70, prof family med, 74-90. *Concurrent Pos:* Fel, Univ & Inst Enzyme Res, Univ Wis-Madison, 61-62; Lederle award, 66; staff physician, Univ Hosps, Med Ctr, Univ Wis-Madison, 63-90, dir pediat outpatient serv & univ child health serv, 66-68, dir univ family health serv, 68-69, dir progm primary care, 69; prin policy adv & mem mgt group, Gov Health Planning & Policy Task Force, 71-72; prog dir, Family Med Prog, Univ Wis, 85-89, actg chair, Dept Family Med, Wilwaukee Clin Campus, 90- *Mem:* Am Acad Pediat; AMA. *Res:* Health system study; health policy and planning; organization and curriculum of primary care; health service resources. *Mailing Add:* Family Pract Dept Univ Wis 777 S Mills St Madison WI 53715

HANSEN, MERLE FREDRICK, PARASITOLOGY. *Current Pos:* prof & parasitologist, 50-82, assoc dir, Div Biol, 74-82, EMER PROF PARASITOL, AGR EXP STA, KANS STATE UNIV, 82- *Personal Data:* b Minneapolis, Minn, Jan 9, 17; m 46; c 3. *Educ:* Univ Minn, BA, 39, MA, 41; Univ Nebr, PhD(zool), 48. *Prof Exp:* Asst zool, Univ Nebr, 46, instr, 46-47; assoc parasitologist, Dept Animal Path, Univ Ky, 48-50. *Concurrent Pos:* Sr scientist, USPHS, 57-79. *Mem:* Am Soc Parasitol; Am Inst Biol Sci. *Res:* Animal parasitology. *Mailing Add:* 2025 Thackery Manhattan KS 66502

HANSEN, MICHAEL ROY, BONDING AT POLYMER-POLYMER INTERFACES, MECHANISMS OF HYDROPHILLIC POLYMER HYDRATION. *Current Pos:* Proj technician, 88-92, RES SCIENTIST, WEYERHAUSER, 92- *Personal Data:* b Bremerton, Wash, July 27, 53; m 84, Valerie J Paulson; c Ryan E. *Educ:* Univ Wash, BS(chem) & BS(molecular biol), 78. *Concurrent Pos:* Chem instr, Highline Community Col, 91- *Mem:* Am Chem Soc; AAAS; NY Acad Sci. *Res:* Mechanisms of bonding and adhesion of polymer/polymer interfaces and how they might be used to design and manufacture new products; granted 16 US patents. *Mailing Add:* 32901 Weyerhaeuser Way S Federal Way WA 98003. *E-Mail:* hansenm1@wdni.com

HANSEN, MIKE, VETERINARY MEDICINE. *Current Pos:* pres, 81-96, SECY, POULTRY & TELEMETRICS, 96- *Personal Data:* b Rockville, Minn, Nov 31, 31; m 58; c 3. *Educ:* Univ Minn, DVM, 57. *Prof Exp:* Field vet, Minn Livestock Sanit Bd, 57-58; gen practr, 58-60; res veterinarian, Land O'Lakes Creameries, Inc, 60-71 & Land O'Lakes, Inc, 71-73; turkey prod mgr, Koronis Mill & Supply Co, 73-81. *Mem:* Am Vet Med Asn; Am Dairy Sci Asn; Am Poultry Sci Asn; Am Soc Animal Sci. *Res:* Feed management and health programs and program development for turkeys, laying hens, pullets and chicks. *Mailing Add:* 53190 532nd Ave Painesville MN 56362

HANSEN, NIELS, METALLURGY. *Current Pos:* Researcher, 57-61, sect leader, 61-64, HEAD, DEPT METALL, RISO NAT LAB, DENMARK, 64- *Personal Data:* b Elsinore, Denmark, Dec 2, 33; m 64, Annette F Bierfreund. *Educ:* Danish Tech Univ, MS, 57, DTech, 71; Inst Nat Sci & Technol, France, DEA, 58. *Mem:* Foreign assoc Nat Acad Eng; fel Am Soc Metals; Danish Acad Tech Sci; Acad Europaea; hon mem Metall Soc France. *Mailing Add:* Frederiksborgvej 131C Roskilde DK-4000 Denmark

HANSEN, OLE, HIGH ENERGY HEAVY ION PHYSICS. *Current Pos:* Teaching asst physics, Niel Bohrs Inst Denmark, 60-62; lectr, 62-68 & 72-74, prof exp physics, 74-82, DIR, NIELS BOHR INST ASTRON, PHYSICS & GEOPHYS, 93- *Personal Data:* b Frederiksberg, Denmark, May 14, 34; m 58; c 4. *Educ:* Univ Copenhagen, Mag Scient, 58, DrPhil(physics), 67. *Honors & Awards:* Prize, Ole Rohmer Found, Denmark, 68; von Humboldt Sr Sci Award, 88. *Prof Exp:* Prof physics, Univ Pa, 69-70; mem staff, Los Alamos Sci Lab, 70-72; sr scientist, Brookhaven Nat Lab, 81-92, group leader heavy ion res, 84-88. *Concurrent Pos:* Res assoc, Mass Inst Technol, 64-65 & Rutgers Univ, NJ, 65-66; mem staff, Los Alamos Sci Lab, 69-70 & 74-75, adv, P-Div, 82-88; mem, Natural Sci Coun, Denmark, 79-81; prog adv, Oak Ridge Nat Lab, 83-85; mem, Nuclear Sci Adv Comt, NSF-Dept Energy, 83-88; chmn, Danish Physics Surv, Ministry Educ, Denmark, 90-92; mem bd dirs, Danish Res Found, 91; Danish Space Res Inst, 94-; Nordic Inst Theoret Physics, 96- *Res:* Collisions between nuclei at high energies to search for new forms of matter. *Mailing Add:* Niel Bohr Inst Blegdamsvej 17 DK-2100 Copenhagen Denmark. *E-Mail:* oleh@nbi.dk

HANSEN, PAUL B(ERNARD), CHEMICAL ENGINEERING. *Current Pos:* RETIRED. *Personal Data:* b Mont, Nov 23, 13; m 44, Jane Fletcher; c Ann, Catherine, Timothy & James. *Educ:* State Col Wash, BS, 37; Lawrence Col, MS, 41, PhD(chem eng), 43. *Prof Exp:* Mem res staff, Schweitzer Paper Co, 43-44; tech dir, Bergstrom Paper Co, 44-53; prod process develop, Kimberly-Clark Corp, 53-64, mgr tech info systs, 64-68, res chemist pioneering res, 68-70, mgr res & eng tech infor serv, 70-73. *Concurrent Pos:* Spec proj Kimberly-Clark, 74-88; instr pulp & paper, Local Tech Col, 85-88. *Mem:* Tech Asn Pulp & Paper Indust. *Res:* Paper and high polymer technology; electrical papers; product development and applied science. *Mailing Add:* 740 Chestnut Neenah WI 54956

HANSEN, PAUL VINCENT, JR, PHYSICAL CHEMISTRY. *Current Pos:* from asst prof to prof, 62-94, PROF CHEM, CARTHAGE COL, 94- *Personal Data:* b Salt Lake City, Utah, May 18, 31; m 55; c 3. *Educ:* Dana Col, BS, 52; Northwestern Univ, MS, 54; Univ Nebr, PhD, 65. *Prof Exp:* Res chemist, Swift & Co, Ill, 54-56; from instr to asst prof chem, Dana Col, 56-60. *Mem:* Am Chem Soc; Sigma Xi. *Res:* Hydrogen bonding and association; application of phase rule and phase diagrams; ultraviolet and infrared spectroscopy. *Mailing Add:* 7840 42nd Ave Kenosha WI 53142

HANSEN, PETER GARDNER, ENGINEERING MECHANICS, THEORETICAL MECHANICS. *Current Pos:* from assoc prof to prof eng mech, 60-90, chmn dept, 71-88, EMER PROF ENG MECH, UNIV MO, ROLLA, 90- *Personal Data:* b Curryville, Mo, Nov 2, 27; m 54; c 3. *Educ:* Mo Sch Mines, BS, 53, MS, 57; Wash Univ, ScD, 63. *Prof Exp:* From instr to asst prof mech, Mo Sch Mines, 53-60. *Concurrent Pos:* Grant, Univ Mo, 69 & Bur Mines, US Dept Interior, 70-71. *Mem:* Soc Exp Mech; Am Acad Mech; Am Soc Eng Educ; Am Soc Metals. *Res:* Experimental stress analysis; structural analysis; materials. *Mailing Add:* Dept Eng & Mech Univ Mo G3D Basic Eng Bldg Rolla MO 65401

HANSEN, PETER J, REPRODUCTIVE PHYSIOLOGY, ENVIRONMENTAL PHYSIOLOGY. *Current Pos:* Res assoc, Dept Biochem, Univ Fla, 83-84, asst prof, Dept Reprod, 84-86, from asst prof to assoc prof, 86-93, PROF, DAIRY SCI DEPT, UNIV FLA, 93- *Personal Data:* b Oak Park, Ill, Nov 23, 56; m 80, Nancy Donovan; c Meghan. *Educ:* Univ Ill, BS, 78; Univ Wis, MS, 80, PhD(endocrinol-reprod physiol), 83. *Honors & Awards:* Agway, Inc Young Scientist Award, Am Dairy Sci Asn, 91; Young Scientist Award, Am Soc Animal Sci, 94. *Concurrent Pos:* Assoc grad fac, Ont Vet Col, 88-92; panel mem, USDA Competitve Grants Prog, 90 & 93. *Mem:* Am Soc Animal Sci; Am Dairy Sci Asn; Soc Study Reprod; Am Soc Reprod Immunol; Am Soc Cell Biol; AAAS. *Res:* Methods of improving reproductive function of domestic animals; uterine immunologic function and effects of heat stress on embryonic survival. *Mailing Add:* Univ Fla IFAS PO Box 920 Gainesville FL 32611-0920. *Fax:* 904-392-5592; *E-Mail:* hansen@animal.ufl.edu

HANSEN, PETER JACOB, COMPUTATIONAL CHEMISTRY, CHEMICAL EDUCATION & KINETICS. *Current Pos:* assoc prof chem, 69-93, PROF CHEM, NORTHWESTERN COL, 94- *Personal Data:* b Willmar, Minn, Feb 27, 39; m 64, Kathryn Wirth. *Educ:* St Olaf Col, BA, 61; Iowa State Univ, PhD(phys chem), 66. *Prof Exp:* Lectr phys chem, Univ Ife, Nigeria, 67-68. *Concurrent Pos:* Lectr chem, Makerere Univ, Uganda, 76-77; adj prof, Ariz State Univ, Tempe, 79-80; vis assoc prof, Penn State Univ, 86-87. *Mem:* AAAS; Am Chem Soc; Am Asn Univ Professors; NAm Int Chemometrics Soc. *Res:* Kinetics of organometallic catalysis. *Mailing Add:* Box 256 Orange City IA 51041-0256. *E-Mail:* pjhansen@nwciowa.edu

HANSEN, POUL M T, FOOD SCIENCE, DAIRY TECHNOLOGY. *Current Pos:* res assoc, 64-65, from asst prof to assoc prof, 65-75, PROF DAIRY TECHNOL, OHIO STATE UNIV, 75- *Personal Data:* b Vejle, Denmark, Sept 24, 29; m 57; c 3. *Educ:* Royal Vet & Agr Col, Copenhagen, BSc, 56; Univ Ill, MSc, 58, PhD(food technol), 60. *Prof Exp:* Res off dairy res, Commonwealth Sci & Indust Res Orgn, Australia, 60-63. *Mem:* AAAS; Am Chem Soc; Inst Food Technol; Am Dairy Sci Asn; Am Asn Cereal Chem. *Res:* Milk technology; heat effects on milk proteins; hydrophilic colloids and their interactions. *Mailing Add:* 1330 Lakeshore Dr Apt A Columbus OH 43204

HANSEN, R(OBERT) J(OSEPH), CIVIL ENGINEERING. *Current Pos:* res assoc, 47-48, from asst prof to prof struct eng, 48-75, EMER PROF CIVIL ENG, MASS INST TECHNOL, 75- *Personal Data:* b Tacoma, Wash, May 27, 18; m 48, Eleanor S Welch; c Eric & Karen. *Educ:* Univ Wash, Seattle, BS, 40; Mass Inst Technol, ScD(civil eng), 48. *Honors & Awards:* Moisseiff Award, Reese Prize, Innovation Civil Eng, Am Soc Civil Engrs. *Prof Exp:* Res engr, Nat Res Coun, Washington, DC, 40-43; Princeton Univ, 43-44 & Arthur D Little Co, 45. *Concurrent Pos:* Partner, Hansen, Holley & Biggs, 55-88, prin, 75-88; mem security resources panel, Exec Off President, 57; proj harbor, Nat Acad Sci, 64. *Mem:* Am Soc Civil Engrs. *Res:* Structural dynamics; experimental techniques for stuctural design; design of tall buildings; earthquake design of nuclear power reactors; effects of wind on constructed facilities; properties and behavior of glass. *Mailing Add:* 25 Cambridge St Winchester MA 13201

HANSEN, RALPH HOLM, PLASTICS CHEMISTRY & PROCESSING. *Current Pos:* RETIRED. *Personal Data:* b Brooklyn, NY, Jan 23, 23; m 45, Vera Herzog; c Ralph E, Bradley H, Wesley C & Randall S. *Educ:* Cornell Univ, AB, 44; NY Univ, MS, 49, PhD(org chem), 52. *Honors & Awards:* Mobay Award, Soc Plastics Indust, 65; Union Carbide Chem Award, Am Chem Soc, 66; Polyolefins Award, Soc Plastics Engrs, 76. *Prof Exp:* Res

HANSEN, chemist, Heyden Chem Corp, 44-47; asst chem, NY Univ, 48-52; supvr appl org res, Bell Labs, 52-68; dir chem finishing & explor technol, J P Stevens & Co, 68-69; dir develop, Raychem Corp, 69-70; supvr plastics deterioration & stabilization, Bell Labs, 70-81; sr res assoc, Chomerics, Inc, 81-83; sr res assoc, Canusa Coating Systs, 83-86; plastics consult, Rave Consult Assoc, 86-96. *Concurrent Pos:* Chmn, Conf Chem & Physics Cellular Mat, Gordon Res Conf, 66; mem vis comt, Chem Dept, NY Univ; dir, Polymer Durability Ctr, Polytech Univ, 87-91, res prof, 87- *Mem:* Am Chem Soc; fel Soc Plastics Engrs; fel NY Acad Sci; Asn Res Dir; fel Am Inst Chemists. *Res:* Studies of the modification and optimization of polymer properties by physical and chemical techniques, by use of composite structures, and by development of new and improved additives for polymers; flame retardants, antioxidants, and blowing agents. *Mailing Add:* 114 Castleton Rd Princeton NJ 08540

HANSEN, RALPH W(ALDO), agricultural engineering, for more information see previous edition

HANSEN, RICHARD LEE, physical chemistry, for more information see previous edition

HANSEN, RICHARD M, ZOOLOGY. *Current Pos:* RETIRED. *Personal Data:* b Goshen, Utah, Jan 11, 24; m 45; c 3. *Educ:* Univ Utah, BS, 50, MS, 51, PhD(vert zool), 54. *Prof Exp:* Lab asst, Univ Utah, 50-51, lab instr, 51-52; asst prof zool, Exp Sta, Col State Univ, 54-55, asst biologist, Exp Sta, 55-61, assoc biologist, 61-68, prof biol, 68-74, prof range sci, 74-85; res scientist, Kiboko Range Res Sta, Kenya, 83-86. *Mem:* Am Soc Mammal; Ecol Soc Am; Wildlife Soc; Soc Range Mgt. *Res:* Ecology and distribution of mammals and vertebrates; vertebrate management; evolution and physiology; food-habits quantification techniques; conflicts and complementary effects of herbivores and the partitioning of range plants to animals and microorganisms. *Mailing Add:* 720 E Stuart St Ft Collins CO 80525

HANSEN, RICHARD OLAF, POTENTIAL FIELDS. *Current Pos:* CHIEF GEOPHYSICIST, PEARSON DE RIDDLER & JOHNSON, INC, 95- *Personal Data:* b Ottawa, Ont, Oct 4, 46; US citizen; m 68, Kathleen J Thoms. *Educ:* Carleton Univ, BSc, 68; Univ Chicago, MS, 69, PhD(physics), 73. *Prof Exp:* Res assoc physics, Univ Pittsburgh, 73-75; res asst math, Univ Oxford, 75-76; lectr math, Univ Calif, Berkeley, 76-78; numerical analyst, EG&G Geometrics, 79-81; staff scientist, 81-85; res assoc prof, Colo Sch Mines, 85-88, res prof geophys, 88-95. *Concurrent Pos:* Assoc ed, Geophysics, 87-91. *Mem:* Soc Explor Geophysicists; Am Geophys Union; Europ Asn Explor Geophysicists; Am Phys Soc; Am Math Soc; Soc Indust & Appl Math. *Res:* Numerical methods for processing and interpretation of gravity and magnetic data applied to resource exploration. *Mailing Add:* Pearson, deRidder & Johnson, Inc 12640 W Cedar Dr Suite 100 Lakewood CO 80228. *Fax:* 303-273-3478; *E-Mail:* rhansen@mines.colorado.edu

HANSEN, ROBERT C(LINTON), ANTENNAS & ELECTROMAGNETICS. *Current Pos:* PRES & CONSULT, R C HANSEN INC, 71- *Personal Data:* b St Louis, Mo, Aug 3, 26; m 52, Dorothy Hays; c Mary K & Margaret E. *Educ:* Univ Mo, BS, 49; Univ Ill, MS, 50, PhD(elec eng), 55. *Hon Degrees:* DEng, Univ Mo, Rolla, 75. *Honors & Awards:* Barry Carlton Prize, Inst Elec & Electronics Engrs, 91. *Prof Exp:* Res assoc, Antenna Lab, Univ Ill, 50-55; sr staff engr, Microwave Lab, Hughes Aircraft Co, 55-59 & telecommun lab, Space Technol Labs, 59-60; dir test mission anal off, Aerospace Corp, Calif, 60-67; head electronics div, KMS Technol Ctr, 67-71. *Concurrent Pos:* Mem Comn B, Int Sci Radio Union, chmn, Inst Elec & Electronics Engrs Antennas & Propagation Soc, 64 & 80; ed, Microwave Scanning Antennas, 64-66. *Mem:* Nat Acad Eng; Am Phys Soc; Sigma Xi; fel Inst Elec Eng, London; fel Inst Elec & Electronics Engrs. *Res:* Electromagnetic theory applied to surface waves; slot arrays; antennas and near field studies; electronic scanning antennas and systems; ferrite loop antennas; data processing antenna systems; adaptive antenna systems; satellite telemetry and command systems; software systems for satellite command and data handling; computer solutions to electromagnetic problems. *Mailing Add:* 18651 Wells Dr Tarzana CA 91356

HANSEN, ROBERT CONRAD, ANALYTICAL CHEMISTRY, INORGANIC CHEMISTRY. *Current Pos:* Assoc prof, 59-67, PROF CHEM, UNIV WIS-PLATTEVILLE, 67- *Personal Data:* b Rice Lake, Wis, Nov 3, 31; m 60; c 2. *Educ:* Wis State Col, Eau Claire, BS, 53; Univ Wis, MS, 56, PhD(chem), 63. *Mem:* Am Chem Soc; AAAS; Sigma Xi. *Res:* Physical chemistry of electrolytic solutions; complexes and analytical methods for transition metals; design and development of instruments for teaching instrumental analysis; trace metals in water. *Mailing Add:* 607 Mitchell Hollow Rd Platteville WI 53818

HANSEN, ROBERT DOUGLAS, PHYSICAL CHEMISTRY. *Current Pos:* RETIRED. *Personal Data:* b Quincy, Ill, Feb 25, 29; m 50; c 3. *Educ:* Valparaiso Univ, BS, 50; Iowa State Univ, PhD(chem), 53. *Honors & Awards:* Vaaler Award, 80. *Prof Exp:* Proj leader, Dow Chem Co, 53-71, sr res specialist, Phys Res Lab, 71-79, res assoc, Specialty Prod Res Lab, 79-82, res assoc, Mining Prods Res & Develop Lab, 83-88, res assoc, Mineral Reagents Int, 88-95. *Mem:* Am Chem Soc; Sci Res Soc Am; Am Inst Mining, Metall & Petrol Engrs. *Res:* Ion exchange; surface chemistry; hydrometallurgy; solvent extraction; powder metallurgy; emulsion polymerization; emulsion polymers for use in dielectric papers, and as binders in nonwoven fabrics; mineral and coal flotation; frothers and collectors for mineral flotation. *Mailing Add:* 2350 North Trail Rd Midland MI 48642

HANSEN, ROBERT JACK, HYDRODYNAMICS. *Current Pos:* STAFF MEM, AMES RES CTR, NASA, 92- *Personal Data:* b Houston, Tex, July 14, 40; m 66; c 1. *Educ:* Stanford Univ, BS, 62; Mass Inst Technol, MS, 64, ScD, 69. *Prof Exp:* Nat Res Coun fel, Off Naval Res, 68-70, res mech engr, 70-78, head boundary layer hydrodyn, 78-86, dep dir, Lab Comput Physics & Fluid Dynamics & Naval Res Lab & prog mgr, 86-87, head, Defense Sci Div, 87-92. *Concurrent Pos:* Adj asst prof, Dept Physics, Univ Md, 71-72. *Mem:* Am Soc Mech Engrs; Sigma Xi. *Res:* Transitional and turbulent boundary layer flows and associated flow-induced vibration and acoustic phenomena. *Mailing Add:* Ames Res Ctr NASA MS200-3 Mountain View CA 94035

HANSEN, ROBERT JOHN, PHYSIOLOGICAL CHEMISTRY, ENDOCRINOLOGY. *Current Pos:* ASSOC DEAN STUDENT SERV, SCH VET MED, 82- *Personal Data:* b Harvey, Ill, July 2, 37; m 59; c 2. *Educ:* George Williams Col, BS, 60, MS, 62; Univ Chicago, PhD(physiol), 69. *Prof Exp:* Instr biol & phys educ, George Williams Col, 62-63; from asst prof to assoc prof, Univ Calif, Davis, 68-84, prof physiol chem, 84- *Concurrent Pos:* Von Humboldt Found fel & guest prof, Biochem Inst, Freiburg, Ger, 75. *Mem:* AAAS; Am Physiol Soc; Am Diabetes Soc. *Res:* Action of insulin on protein turnover in animal tissues. *Mailing Add:* Dept Vet Med Molecular Biosci Univ Calif Davis CA 95616

HANSEN, ROBERT JOSEPH, BIOMECHANICS, STRUCTURAL DESIGN. *Current Pos:* res assoc, 47-48, dept dir proj transp, 64-67, MEM FAC, MASS INST TECHNOL, 48, PROF CIVIL ENG, 57- *Personal Data:* b Tacoma, Wash, May 27, 18; m 48, Eleanor Swaim Welch; c Eric Charles & Karen Welch. *Educ:* Univ Wash, BS, 40; Mass Inst Technol, ScD, 48. *Honors & Awards:* Moisseiff Award, Am Soc Civil Engrs, 74; Raymond C Reese Res Prize, 75, Innovation Civil Eng Award, 89. *Prof Exp:* Res engr, Nat Res Coun, 40-43; Princeton Univ, 43-45; Arthur D Little Co, 45. *Concurrent Pos:* Partner, Hansen, Holley & Biggs Inc, 55-88, prin, 75-88; consult biochem, Mass Gen Hosp, 56-60; mem secy resources panel, Exec Off of Pres, 57; partner, Newmark, Hansen & Assoc, 58-68; mem sr adv panel, Air Force Ballistic Div, USAF, 58-60. *Mem:* Sigma Xi; fel Am Soc Civil Engrs. *Mailing Add:* 25 Cambridge St Winchester MA 01890-3703

HANSEN, ROBERT M(ARIUS), CHEMICAL ENGINEERING. *Current Pos:* RETIRED. *Personal Data:* b Gulfport, Miss, Jan 19, 24; m 46; c 2. *Educ:* La State Univ, BS, 50, PhD(chem eng), 55; Newark Col Eng, MS, 52. *Prof Exp:* Chem engr, Victor Div, Radio Corp Am, 50-52; asst, La State Univ, 52-55; sr chem engr, Res Dept, Baton Rouge, Kaiser Aluminum & Chem Corp, 55-56, group leader, Prod Control Dept, 56-57, prod control supt, 57-58, proj supvr, Develop Dept, 58-59, from asst mgr to mgr process develop, 59-61, tech supt, Gramercy, 61-68, prod supt, 63, prod mgr, 69-72, tech mgr, 73-74, environ mgr, alumina, coke & chem plants, 75-81, mgr, field develop & bauxite coord, 81-83, mgr, Lab Res & Develop, 83-84. *Concurrent Pos:* On site, tech asst, Hindalco Alumina Plant, India, 70; plpnt stsrt-up Euralumina, 74. *Res:* Chemical processing; production control; technical service and development; supervision of scientific personnel; production and plant management. *Mailing Add:* 9621 N Parkview Dr Baton Rouge LA 70815

HANSEN, ROBERT SUTTLE, PHYSICAL CHEMISTRY. *Current Pos:* From asst prof to prof, Iowa State Univ, 48-67, distinguished prof chem, Col Sci & Humanities, 67-88, dir, Ames Lab, 68-88, EMER DISTINGUISHED PROF, COL LIB ARTS & SCI, IOWA STATE UNIV, 88-, ASSOC, AMES LAB, 88- *Personal Data:* b Salt Lake City, Utah, June 17, 18; m 39, Gilda Cappannari; c Edward C. *Educ:* Univ Mich, BA, 40, MS, 41, PhD(phys chem), 48. *Hon Degrees:* DSc, Lehigh Univ, 78. *Honors & Awards:* Award Colloid & Surface Chem, Am Chem Soc, 66; Midwest Award, Am Chem Soc, 80; Iowa Award, Am Chem Soc, 87. *Concurrent Pos:* Assoc chemist, Ames Lab, 48-55, sr chemist, 55-65, chief chem div, 65-68, chmn dep chem, Iowa State Univ, 65-68; consult, Union Carbide & Carbon Corp, 52-86, Interchem Corp, 56-68; NSF sr fel, Univ Utrecht & Univ Southern Calif, 59-60; consult, Procter & Gamble Co, 62-86; mem NSF Adv Panels chem, 70-75 & mat sci, 76-80. *Mem:* AAAS; Am Chem Soc; Am Phys Soc. *Res:* Adsorption, boundary tensions; surface thermodynamics; thermodynamics of nonelectrolytic solutions; surface chemistry and electrochemistry; catalysis. *Mailing Add:* Ames Lab US Dept Energy & Inst Phys Res & Technol Iowa State Univ Ames IA 50011

HANSEN, RODNEY THOR, MATHEMATICS, STATISTICS. *Current Pos:* assoc prof, 81-85, ASSOC DEAN UNDERGRAD AFFAIRS, WHITWORTH COL, 84-, PROF MATH, 85- *Personal Data:* b Spokane, Wash, Mar 27, 40; m 64; c 3. *Educ:* Whitworth Col, BS, 62; Univ Wash, MA, 64; Wash State Univ, PhD(math), 67. *Prof Exp:* From asst prof to assoc prof math, Mont State Univ, 67-82. *Concurrent Pos:* Vis assoc prof math, Univ Ore, 76. *Res:* Combinatorial number theory; combinatorics. *Mailing Add:* Dept Math & Comput Sci Whitworth Col Spokane WA 99251-3702

HANSEN, ROGER GAURTH, NUTRITIONAL BIOCHEMISTRY. *Current Pos:* RETIRED. *Personal Data:* b Smithfield, Utah, Aug 18, 20; m 43; c 3. *Educ:* Univ Wis, BS, 44, MS, 46, PhD(biochem), 48. *Honors & Awards:* Borden Award, Am Inst Nutrit. *Prof Exp:* Asst prof biochem, Univ Utah, 48-50; from assoc prof to prof, Univ Ill, 50-57; prof & head dept, Mich State Univ, 57-68; provost, Utah State Univ, 68-85, prof biochem, nutrit & food sci, 68-91. *Concurrent Pos:* Mem, Nutrit Study Sect, NIH, Coun Foods & Nutrit, AMA & Food & Nutrit Bd, Nat Res Coun. *Mem:* Am Soc Biol Chem; Am Chem Soc; Soc Exp Biol & Med; Am Inst Nutrit. *Res:* General biochemistry and nutrition of animals; formation and utilization of galactose and hereditary disorders of metabolism; human requirements for nutrients. *Mailing Add:* 1676 E 1030 North Logan UT 84321

HANSEN, SHARON LEE, MICROBIOLOGY, EPIDEMIOLOGY. *Current Pos:* sr sci reviewer, 90-91, MICROBIOL BR CHIEF, DIV CLIN LAB DEVICES, OFF DEVICE EVAL, CTR DEVICES & RADIOL HEALTH, FOOD & DRUG ADMIN, 91- *Personal Data:* b Corry, Pa. *Educ:* Beaver Col, BS, 60; Univ Md, MA, 70, PhD(path), 80. *Prof Exp:* Microbiol res technologist, Univ Pa Hosp, 60-61; supvr, Microbiol Lab, Franklin Sq Hosp, Md, 61-62 & Clin Res Ctr, Univ Md Hosp, 62-63; asst & head qual control, Baltimore Biol Lab, 63-68 & 70-71; supvr, Microbiol, Urinal & Serol Sect, Vet Admin Med Ctr, Baltimore, 71-90, actg chief clin path, 87-89. *Concurrent Pos:* Res assoc, Dept Med, Sch Med, Univ Md, 73-81, from asst prof to assoc prof, Dept Path, 81-93, from asst prof to assoc prof, Dept Med, 81-93; mem, Nat Comt Clin Lab Stand, 80-, Pub & Sci Affairs Bd, Am Acad Microbiol, 84-90, Comt Lab Pract, Am Soc Microbiol, 91-; ed, Am J Infection Control, 81-96. *Mem:* Am Acad Microbiol; Am Soc Microbiol; Am Soc Clin Pathologists; Acad Clin Lab Physicians & Scientists. *Res:* Detection and control of Nosoconual infections; automation in clinical microbiology; anaerobic infections and methodology; in vitro susceptibility testing; blood cultures and resin devices; epidemiology and detection of heteroresistant staphylococcus aureus; rapid methods diagnosis of infectious disease. *Mailing Add:* 2749 Deerfield Dr Ellicott City MD 21043

HANSEN, STEVEN M, FIBER SCIENCE & ENGINEERING, POLYESTER FIBERS. *Current Pos:* res asst, DuPont Dacron, 81-85, SR RES ASST, DACRON TECH, E I DUPONT DE NEMOURS & CO, INC, 87- *Personal Data:* b St Paul, Minn, June 15, 53; m 77, Sharon Walker; c Kathryn D. *Educ:* Univ Ala, BS, 75, PhD(chem eng), 81. *Prof Exp:* Assoc chem engr, Texaco Prod Res Lab, 77-78; instr, Univ Ala, 78-81; asst prof textile eng, Ga Inst Technol, 85-87. *Concurrent Pos:* Indust lectr, Fiber Soc, 96-97. *Mem:* Fiber Soc. *Res:* Polyester copolymerization kinetics and material properties; synthetic fiber formation processes; nonwoven fabric mechanic and manufacturing processes; yarn structure and mechanics; composite materials and manufacturing processes. *Mailing Add:* 7008 Eschol Ct Wilmington NC 28409. *E-Mail:* hansensm@cfoc01.dnet.dupont.com

HANSEN, TED HOWARD, IMMUNOLOGY, GENETICS. *Current Pos:* AT DEPT GENETICS, UNIV WASHINGTON. *Personal Data:* b Madison, Wis, June 6, 47. *Educ:* Univ Mich, PhD(human genetics), 75. *Prof Exp:* Sr staff fel, Transplantation Sect, Immunol Br, Nat Cancer Inst, NIH, 78-80; res fel, Merck Inst Therapeut Res, 80- *Mem:* Sigma Xi; Am Asn Immunol; Fedn Am Socs Exp Biol. *Res:* Immunogenetics; transplantation; immunochemistry. *Mailing Add:* Dept Genetics Wash Univ Sch Med PO Box 8232 660 S Euclid Ave St Louis MO 63110-1093. *Fax:* 314-362-4137

HANSEN, TIMOTHY RAY, MEDICAL PHYSIOLOGY. *Current Pos:* ASST PROF PHYSIOL, UNIV HEALTH SCI-CHICAGO MED SCH, 75- *Personal Data:* b Detroit, Mich, Aug 25, 45; m 67; c 1. *Educ:* Univ Mich, Ann Arbor, BS, 67, PhD(physiol), 73. *Prof Exp:* Teaching fel physiol, Med Sch, Univ Mich, Ann Arbor, 70-73; res fel, Harvard Med Sch, 73-75. *Mem:* Assoc Am Physiol Soc. *Res:* Physiology of vascular smooth muscle in cardiovascular disease. *Mailing Add:* 74 S Seventh Ave La Grange IL 60525-2503

HANSEN, TORBEN CHRISTEN, concrete, cement, for more information see previous edition

HANSEN, UWE JENS, MUSICAL ACOUSTICS. *Current Pos:* assoc prof, Ind State Univ, 68-77, interim chmn dept, 80-83, chairperson, 94-97, PROF PHYSICS, IND STATE UNIV, 77- *Personal Data:* b Kiel, Ger, June 7, 33; US citizen; m 59, Louise Brimhail; c Ruth & Mark. *Educ:* Brigham Young Univ, BS, 54, MA, 61, PhD(physics), 66. *Prof Exp:* Nat Acad Sci-Nat Res Coun res assoc, US Naval Res Lab, 66-68, res physicist, 68. *Concurrent Pos:* Vis prof physics, Northern Ill Univ, 91; vis scientist, PTB, Ger, 92. *Mem:* Am Phys Soc; Am Soc Metals; Am Asn Physics Teachers; fel Acoust Soc Am; Ger Acoust Soc; Sigma Xi. *Res:* Vibrational studies of musical instruments using holographic interferometry and modal analysis. *Mailing Add:* 715 S 34th St Terre Haute IN 47803. *Fax:* 812-237-4396; *E-Mail:* phhanse@scifac.indstate.edu

HANSEN, VAUGHN ERNEST, WATER RESOURCES, IRRIGATION ENGINEERING. *Current Pos:* RETIRED. *Personal Data:* b Syracuse, Utah, July 26, 21; m 41; c 10. *Educ:* Utah State Univ, BS, 43, MS, 47; State Univ Iowa, PhD(mech eng & hydrol) 49. *Honors & Awards:* Collingwood Prize, Am Soc Civil Engrs, 54. *Prof Exp:* Prof eng, Utah State Univ, 55-66, dir res eng exp sta, 58-64; coordr resource develop, Inter-Am Ctr Land & Water, 64-66; dir water res lab, Utah State Univ, 64-66; gen consult, Vaughn Hansen Assoc, 66-74, consult engr water resources, 74-88. *Concurrent Pos:* Consult, numerous foreign countries, 54-, NSF, 64-68; pres, Agr Develop & Eng Serv, 54-61; vpres, Western Admixture Co, 58-66; consult, numerous foreign countries, 54-93. *Mem:* Sigma Xi; Consult Engrs Coun; Am Water Resources Asn. *Res:* Water resource development; irrigation; ground water development. *Mailing Add:* 5297 Cottonwood Club Circle Salt Lake City UT 84117

HANSEN, VICKI L, STRUCTURAL GEOLOGY. *Current Pos:* from asst prof to assoc prof, 87-97, PROF, SOUTHERN METHODIST UNIV, 97- *Educ:* Carleton Col, BA, 80; Univ Mont, MS, 83; Univ Calif, Los Angeles, PhD(geol), 87. *Prof Exp:* Geol field asst, US Geol Surv, 80-83. *Mem:* Geol Soc Am; Am Asn Univ Women; Am Geophys Union; Geol Asn Can; Int Asn Struct/Tectonic Geologists; Nat Asn Geol Teachers; Sigma Xi. *Res:* Application of the concepts and techniques of structural geology, metamorphic petrology and isotope geochemistry to tectonic problems on Earth and Venus. *Mailing Add:* Dept Geol Sci Southern Methodist Univ Dallas TX 75275-0395. *Fax:* 214-768-2701; *E-Mail:* vhansen@mail.smu.edu

HANSEN, WAYNE RICHARD, RADIOECOLOGY, HEALTH PHYSICS. *Current Pos:* staff mem, environ surveillance, Los Alamos Nat Lab, 77-78, group leader, 78-84, dep leader, Div Health Safety & Environ, 84-87, prog mgr, 87-90, GROUP LEADER, ENVIRON SCI, LOS ALAMOS NAT LAB, 90- *Personal Data:* b Rice Lake, Wis, Aug 6, 39; m 60, Nancy Rohde; c Richard & William. *Educ:* Univ Wis-Eau Claire, BS, 61; Univ Kans, MS, 63; Colo State Univ, PhD(radiation biol), 70; Am Bd Health Physics, dipl, 72. *Prof Exp:* Health physicist, Univ Colo, 63-67, Health Educ & Welfare, Food & Drug Admin & Bur Radiation Health, 70-71 & Environ Protection Agency & Off Radiation Prog, 71-75; sr radiobiologist, Nuclear Regulatory Comn, 75-77. *Concurrent Pos:* Consult, Fed Res Biol & Health Effects of Ionizing Radiations, Nat Acad Sci, 80, EG&G, Idaho, 81-88; mem, NMex Radiation Technol Adv Coun, 83-93; lectr, US Air Force Interservice Nuclear Weapons Sch, Dept Defense, 84-92; mem, NCRP Scientific Comt-64, 87-; consult, Dept Energy Nuclear Facil Safety Comt, 88-92. *Mem:* Fel AAAS; Int Radiation Protection Asn; Health Physics Soc; Sigma Xi. *Res:* Environmental behavior of radionuclides and hazardous chemicals; transuranic elements and polonium in ecosystems or waste sites. *Mailing Add:* Los Alamos Nat Lab M5 J495 Environ Sci Los Alamos NM 87545. *Fax:* 505-665-3866

HANSEN, WILFORD NELS, SURFACE PHYSICS, SPECTROSCOPY. *Current Pos:* prof physics, 68-73, PROF PHYSICS, CHEM & BIOCHEM, UTAH STATE UNIV, 73- *Personal Data:* b Cardston, Alta, May 30, 28; US citizen; m 51; c 6. *Educ:* Brigham Young Univ, BS, 50; Iowa State Univ, PhD(chem), 56. *Prof Exp:* Sr chemist, Atomics Int, NAm Aviation, Inc, 56-57; res assoc chem, Iowa State Univ, 57-58; asst prof, Brigham Young Univ, 58-60; res specialist, Atomics Int Div, NAm Rockwell Corp, 60-62, mem tech staff, Sci Ctr, Calif, 62-68. *Concurrent Pos:* Consult, Atomics Int Div, 59-62, NAm Aviation, Inc, 62-69 & Southern Res Inst, 70-72, Los Alamos Nat Lab, 82- *Mem:* Am Chem Soc; Electrochem Soc; Am Phys Soc. *Res:* Surface physics and chemistry; optics and spectroscopy of surface regions; electrochemistry. *Mailing Add:* Dept Physics Utah State Univ 5305 Logan UT 84322-4415

HANSEN, WILLIAM ANTHONY, COMPUTER SCIENCES. *Current Pos:* PRES, HANSEN TRAINING SYSTS, INC, 80-; VPRES, MANTA TECHNOL INC, 93- *Personal Data:* b Chicago, Ill, July 14, 48; m 69, Sandra Stuebner; c 4. *Educ:* Ill Inst Technol, BS, 70; Northwestern Univ, MS, 71, PhD(math), 74. *Prof Exp:* Training coordr, Comput Serv Div, Abbott Labs, 72-74; asst prof comput sci & math, Wilkes Col, 74-76; prod mgr, Deltak, Inc, 76-78, mgr qual assurance, 78-80. *Res:* Computer calculation of the homology of the lambda algebra; computer science education, particulary learner paced modules utilizing text, computer-based instruction and video tapes. *Mailing Add:* 1981 Abbotsford Dr Barrington IL 60010-5560. *Fax:* 847-382-7199; *E-Mail:* whmanta@aol.com

HANSEN-SMITH, FEONA MAY, MUSCLE DEVELOPMENT, EXTRA-CELLULAR MATRIX. *Current Pos:* Asst prof human anat & gen histol, Oakland Univ, 85-86. *Educ:* Med Col Wis, PhD(physiol), 74. *Res:* Neuromuscular biology. *Mailing Add:* Dept Biol Sci Oakland Univ Rochester MI 48309-4401. *Fax:* 248-370-4225

HANSFORD, RICHARD GEOFFREY, ION TRANSPORT, ENZYMOLOGY. *Current Pos:* vis assoc & scientist, 73-79, res chemist, 79-86, SECT CHIEF ENERGY METAB & BIOENERGETICS SECT, LAB CARDIOVASC SCI, NAT INST AGING, NIH, 86- *Personal Data:* b Market Bosworth, UK, Apr 29, 44; US citizen; div; c 3. *Educ:* Univ Bristol, UK, BSc, 65, PhD(biochem), 69. *Prof Exp:* Fel, dept physiol chem, Johns Hopkins Univ, 69-70; lectr biochem, Univ Col, Cardiff, Wales, 70-73. *Concurrent Pos:* Assoc prof med, Johns Hopkins Univ, 90- *Mem:* Am Soc Biol Chemists; Biophys Soc. *Res:* Control of energy metabolism, especially by calcium ions; isolated mitochondria and cells; impact of senescence on metabolism. *Mailing Add:* Energy Metab & Bioenerget Sec Francis Scott Key Med Ctr Baltimore MD 21224-2700. *Fax:* 410-558-8150

HANSFORD, ROWLAND CURTIS, PHYSICAL CHEMISTRY. *Current Pos:* RETIRED. *Personal Data:* b Belington, WVa, Jan 26, 12; m 53. *Educ:* Davis & Elkins Col, BS, 33; George Washington Univ, MA, 37. *Hon Degrees:* DSc, Davis & Elkins Col, 71. *Honors & Awards:* Tolman Medal, Am Chem Soc, 71; Philadelphia Catalysis Club Award, 74; Chem Pioneer Award, Am Inst Chemists, 76. *Prof Exp:* Works chemist, E I du Pont de Nemours & Co, WVa, 33-35; res chemist, Socony-Vacuum Oil Co, NJ, 37-44, res assoc, 44-52; res assoc, Union Oil Co Calif, 52-57, sr res assoc, 57-65, staff consult, 65-77. *Mem:* Fel AAAS; Am Chem Soc; Catalysis Soc; fel Am Inst Chemists. *Res:* Catalysis in petroleum conversion; fundamentals of catalysis. *Mailing Add:* 5470A Paseo Del Lago E Laguna Hills CA 92653

HANSHAW, BRUCE BUSSER, GEOCHEMISTRY. *Current Pos:* sr staff scientist, 91-95, CONSULT, NAT ACAD SCI-NAT RES COUN, 95- *Personal Data:* b Harrisburg, Pa, May 7, 30; m 54; c 2. *Educ:* Mass Inst Technol, ScB, 53; Univ Colo, MS, 58; Harvard Univ, PhD(geochem), 62. *Honors & Awards:* O E Meinzer Award, Geol Soc Am, 73. *Prof Exp:* Geologist, US AEC, 53-54 & 56 & Petrol Res Corp, 58-61; geologist, Water Resources Div, US Geol Surv, 61-70, staff scientist, Off Dir, Washington, DC, 70-73, geochemist, 73-81, asst dir, 81-85. *Concurrent Pos:* Mem comt pollution, Nat Acad Sci-Nat Res Coun, 65-67, mem US nat comt, Int Hydrol Decade, 67. *Mem:* Fel AAAS; Geol Soc Am; Geochem Soc; Am Geophys Union; Am Chem Soc; Sigma Xi; hon fel Geol Soc Africa. *Res:* Isotope chemistry; membrane phenomena applied to clay minerals; mineral-solution equilibria; factors affecting natural water chemistry; paleoclimate. *Mailing Add:* 1868 Massachusetts Ave McLean VA 22101

HANSHAW, JAMES BARRY, PEDIATRICS, VIROLOGY. *Current Pos:* chair, Dept Pediat, Univ Mass, 75-85, interim vchancellor & acad dean, 85-86, dean & provost, 86-89, PROF PEDIAT, UNIV MASS, 75-, CHAIR DEPT PEDIAT, MEM HEALTH CARE, 93- *Personal Data:* b Scarsdale, NY, Dec 23, 28; m 54, Marian C Kernan; c Thomas, Lee, Elizabeth, John & Margaret. *Educ:* Syracuse Univ, AB, 50; State Univ NY Upstate Med Ctr, MD, 53; Am Bd Pediat, dipl, 61. *Hon Degrees:* DSc, Syracuse Health Sci Ctr, State Univ NY, 91. *Prof Exp:* Nat Found fel, Sch Pub Health, Harvard Univ, 58-60; USPHS career res develop award, 62-72, prof pediat & microbiol, Sch Med & Dent, Univ Rochester, 72-75. *Concurrent Pos:* Pediatrician-in-chief, Genesee Hosp, 72-75, dir med educ, 73-75, chmn med bd, 74-75; vis prof pediat, Inst Child Health, Univ London; lectr pediat, Harvard Med Sch, 75- *Mem:* AAAS; Am Acad Pediat; AMA; Infectious Dis Soc Am; Am Pediat Soc; Soc Pediat Res; Am Orothop Asn. *Res:* Seroepidemiological studies of cytomegaloviruses and other herpes viruses; congenital infections in man and their effect on the development of the central nervous system. *Mailing Add:* Mem Health Care 119 Belmont St Worcester MA 01605. *Fax:* 508-793-5573

HANSMA, PAUL KENNETH, SOLID STATE PHYSICS, INSTRUMENTATION BIOPHYSICS. *Current Pos:* From asst prof to assoc prof, 72-80, PROF PHYSICS, UNIV CALIF, SANTA BARBARA, 80- *Personal Data:* b Salt Lake City, Utah, Apr 28, 46; m 68, Helen Greenwood; c Scott & Joy. *Educ:* New Col, Fla, BA, 67; Univ Calif, Berkeley, PhD(physics), 72. *Honors & Awards:* Max Planck Award. *Concurrent Pos:* Res fel, Alfred P Sloan Found, 75. *Mem:* Fel Am Phys Soc; fel AAAS. *Res:* Scanning ion conductance microscopy; atomic force microscopy; watching individual protein molecules in action; biomineralization in shells and diatoms. *Mailing Add:* Dept Physics Univ Calif Santa Barbara CA 93106. *Fax:* 805-893-8315; *E-Mail:* prasant@physics.ucsh.edu

HANSMAN, ROBERT JOHN, JR, AERONAUTICS, ASTRONAUTICS. *Current Pos:* res asst, Dept Physics, 76-82, lectr, Dept Astronaut & Aeronaut, 82-83, PROF, DEPT ASTRONAUT & AERONAUT, MASS INST TECHNOL, 83-, DIR AERO SYSTS LAB, 88-, HEAD, DIV HUMANS & AUTOMATION, 93- *Personal Data:* b Brockton, Mass, Oct 13, 54; m 83, Laura Ann Wernick; c Heather Ann & Christopher John. *Educ:* Cornell Univ, AB, 76; Mass Inst Technol, MS, 80, PhD, 82. *Honors & Awards:* Gold C with 2 Diamonds, Fedn Aeronaut Int, 80; Presidential Young Investr Award, NSF, 80; Losey Atmospheric Sci Award, Am Inst Aeronaut & Astronaut, 94; Excellence in Aviation Award, Fed Aviation Admin, 97. *Prof Exp:* Pilot, Schweizer Aircraft Co, 76. *Concurrent Pos:* Consult, Cambridge, Mass, 82-; mem, US Cong Aero Adv Comt, 87-89; dir, Int Ctr Air Transp, 95- *Mem:* Sigma Xi; fel Am Inst Aeronaut & Astronaut; Am Meteorol Soc; Soc Automotive Engrs; Am Phys Soc; Human Factors Soc. *Res:* Flight safety; human-automation systems; air traffic control; aviation weather; Ice prevention; ice measurement; liquid monitoring in tanks; published numerous articles and granted several patents. *Mailing Add:* Dept Aeronaut & Astronaut 33-115 Mass Inst Technol Cambridge MA 02139. *Fax:* 617-253-4196

HANSMANN, EUGENE WILLIAM, AQUATIC ECOLOGY, ALGOLOGY. *Current Pos:* wetland coordr, 77-79, PROG MGR, ENVIRON CONTAMINANTS, FISH & WILDLIFE SERV REGION SIX, 79- *Personal Data:* b Whiting, Ind, Dec 20, 33; m 62; c 2. *Educ:* Mich State Univ, BS, 56, MS, 63; Ore State Univ, PhD(bot), 69. *Prof Exp:* Biologist, Plankton Lab, USPHS, Cincinnati, 62-63; botanist, NASA, 63-65; asst prof biol, Univ Conn, 68-71; NSF fel biol, Univ NMex, 71-77. *Concurrent Pos:* Grants, Inst Water Resources, Univ Conn, 69 & 70 & US Dept Interior, 71. *Mem:* AAAS. *Res:* Algal ecology of streams and reservoirs including productivity; community change; biomass accumulation as affected by watershed practices and eutrophication; algal taxonomy. *Mailing Add:* 971 S Arbutus St Lakewood CO 80228

HANSON, ALBERT L, NUCLEAR ANALYTICAL METHODS, X-RAY PHYSICS. *Current Pos:* Fel, Brookhaven Nat Lab, 79-81, asst scientist physics dept, 81-83, assoc physicist dept appl sci, 83-85, physicist dept appl sci, 85-89, PHYSICIST, DEPT ADVAN TECHNOL, BROOKHAVEN NAT LAB, 89- *Personal Data:* b Gainesville, Fla, July 9, 52; m 81, Anita Lopiccolo; c Christopher & Gregory. *Educ:* NC State Univ, BS, 74; Univ Mich, MSE, 76, PhD(nuclear sci), 79. *Honors & Awards:* R & D 100 Award, 88. *Mem:* Am Phys Soc; Am Nuclear Soc; AAAS; Int Soc Radiation Physics. *Res:* Development of analytical techniques, mostly synchrotron radiation and ion beam based, utilizing nuclear and atomic physics for materials characterization, energy sciences and biological sciences; x-ray physics. *Mailing Add:* Bldg 130 Dept Nuclear Energy Brookhaven Nat Lab PO Box 5000 Upton NY 11973-5000. *Fax:* 516-344-5730; *E-Mail:* alh@bnl.gov

HANSON, ALFRED OLAF, EXPERIMENTAL NUCLEAR PHYSICS. *Current Pos:* from asst prof to assoc prof, 46-51, PROF PHYSICS, UNIV ILL, URBANA, 51- *Personal Data:* b Braddock, NDak, Sept 26, 14; m 42, Elisabeth Miller; c Andrew Jorgen, Donald Farnessd, Ardith (Field) & Craig Demorest. *Educ:* Univ NDak, BS, 36, MA, 38; Univ Wis, PhD(physics), 42. *Prof Exp:* Teacher pub sch, 36-37; asst, Off Sci Res & Develop, Univ Wis, 42-43; scientist, Los Alamos Sci Lab, Univ Calif, NMex, 43-46. *Concurrent Pos:* Fulbright scholar, Torino, Italy, 55-56; Fulbright lectr, Sao Paolo, 60 & Brookhaven Nat Lab, NY, 61-62. *Mem:* Fel Am Phys Soc; Sigma Xi. *Res:* Nuclear physics with electrostatic generator and betatron; rotating target for neutron sources; neutron detector with uniform response; electron scattering; photonuclear reactions; accelerator development. *Mailing Add:* Dept Physics Univ Ill Urbana IL 61801

HANSON, ALLEN LOUIS, PHYSICAL CHEMISTRY. *Current Pos:* from assoc prof to prof, 52-80, EMER PROF CHEM, ST OLAF COL, 80- *Personal Data:* b Crookston, Minn, Aug 7, 15; m 44; c 2. *Educ:* Concordia Col, BA, 35; Univ Iowa, MS, 40, PhD(phys chem), 42. *Prof Exp:* Instr pub schs, NDak, 35-37 & Minn, 37-39; res chemist, Photoprod Dept, E I du Pont de Nemours & Co, 42-43; prof chem, Concordia Col, 46-52. *Concurrent Pos:* Chmn deptr chem, St Olaf Col, 64-70 & div natural sci & math, 73-77; vis prof, Univ Lancaster, 70-71. *Mem:* Am Chem Soc. *Res:* Properties of gelatin; activity of solutes from vapor pressure lowering; electrochemistry, especially electrodeposition from nonaqueous solvents; gamma radiolysis; photolysis and x-radiolysis of alkyl halides; enzyme kinetics. *Mailing Add:* Dept Chem St Olaf Col Northfield MN 55057

HANSON, ANDREW JORGEN, SCIENTIFIC VISUALIZATION, ARTIFICIAL INTELLIGENCE. *Current Pos:* assoc prof, 89-95, PROF COMPUT SCI, IND UNIV, BLOOMINGTON, 95- *Personal Data:* b Los Alamos, NMex, Feb 22, 44; m 68; c 2. *Educ:* Harvard Col, BA, 66; Mass Inst Technol, PhD(physics), 71. *Prof Exp:* Res assoc, Inst Advan Study, 71-73, Cornell Univ, 73-74; Stanford Linear Accelerator Ctr, 74-76 & Lawrence Berkeley Lab, 76-78; proj scientist, Inst Advan Comput, 79-80; comput scientist, Artificial Intel Ctr, SRI Int, 80-89. *Concurrent Pos:* NSF fel, 71-72; proj coordr & consult, Explor Sci Mus, 76-78. *Mem:* Am Phys Soc; Sigma Xi; Asn Comput Mach; Inst Elec & Electronics Engrs; Am Asn Artificial Intel; Am Math Soc. *Res:* Theoretical elementary particle physics; gauge theories and gravitation; mathematical physics; applications of artificial intelligence to machine vision; interactive computer-based tools for scientific visualization and intuition development. *Mailing Add:* Comput Sci Dept Ind Univ Bloomington IN 47405

HANSON, ANGUS ALEXANDER, AGRONOMY, PLANT BREEDING. *Current Pos:* dir res & vpres, W-L Res, Inc, 80-86, vpres, 87-88, bd dir, 89-92, CONSULT, W-L RES, INC, 92- *Personal Data:* b Chilliwack, BC, Jan 1, 22; US citizen; m 48, Helen Crook; c Bruce A, Brian E & Margot R. *Educ:* Univ BC, BSA, 44; McGill Univ, MSc, 46; Pa State Col, PhD(agron), 51. *Honors & Awards:* Medallian Award, Am Forage & Grassland Coun, 71. *Prof Exp:* Asst, McGill Univ, 44-46, lectr agron, 46-48, asst prof, 48-49; agt, US Regional Pasture Res Lab, Agr Res Serv, USDA, Pa, 49-52, agronomist, 52, sr agronomist, Forage & Range Br, Plant Sci Res Div, 53-54; prin agronomist, 54-57, head grass & turf invests, 57-65, chief br, Plant Indust Sta, 65-72, dir, Beltsville Agr Res Ctr, 72-79. *Concurrent Pos:* Assoc prof, Pa State Col, 51-52; ed, Crop Sci, 62-64, Turfgrass Sci, 69, J Environ Qual, 71-73, Alfalfa & Alfalfa Improv, 88, Practical Handbk Agr Sci, 90. *Mem:* Fel AAAS; fel Am Soc Agron; fel Crop Sci Soc Am (pres, 67); hon mem Asn Off Seed Certifying Agencies. *Res:* Inheritance of economic characters in forage grasses; cytogenetic investigations; development of proprietary alfalfa cultivars; technique studies, including methods of determining combining ability and methods of isolating disease resistant lines, research organization and management. *Mailing Add:* 10411 Sweetbriar Pkwy Silver Spring MD 20903

HANSON, AUSTIN MOE, BIOCHEMISTRY. *Current Pos:* RETIRED. *Personal Data:* b Roland, Iowa, Feb 26, 17; m 44; c 2. *Educ:* Luther Col, Iowa, BA, 39; Univ Wis, MS, 41, PhD(bact), 44. *Prof Exp:* Head bact sect, Res Labs, Western Condensing Co, 44-51; tech dir, Grain Processing Corp, 51-63, mgr res admin, 63-64; dir, Nutrit Res Lab, Kent Feeds, Inc, 64-78, vpres, 78-89; vpres, Grain Processing Corp, 79-89. *Mem:* Am Soc Microbiol; Am Chem Soc. *Res:* Production of microbial products and starch derivatives; enzymatic conversion of starch to syrups and dextrose; dextrose crystallization. *Mailing Add:* 2815 Termini Dr Muscatine IA 52761

HANSON, BARBARA ANN, MICROBIAL BIOCHEMISTRY, MICROBIAL PHYSIOLOGY. *Current Pos:* fel microbiol biochem, Med Ctr, 77-80, ASST PROF, SCH BIOL SCI, UNIV KY, 80- *Personal Data:* b San Francisco, Calif, Nov 2, 48. *Educ:* Stanford Univ, BA, 70; Univ Calif, San Diego, PhD(biol), 75. *Prof Exp:* Fel microbial biochem, Univ Calif, Irvine, 76-77. *Mem:* Am Soc Microbiol; Sigma Xi. *Res:* Regulation of lipid and cell wall biosynthesis in Sacecharomyces, Neurospora, and a pathogenic yeast, Candida albicans. *Mailing Add:* 682 Richmond Ave Apt A Buffalo NY 14222

HANSON, BERNOLD M, PETROLEUM, ENVIRONMENTAL & FORENSIC GEOLOGY. *Current Pos:* CONSULT GEOLOGIST, 60-; PRES, HANSON CORP, 66- *Personal Data:* b Mayville, NDak, May 7, 28; m 51, Marilyn Miller; c Karen (Flowers), Gretchen H (Bakke). *Educ:* Univ NDak, BS 51; Univ Wyo, MA, 54. *Hon Degrees:* LLD, Univ Wyo, 87. *Prof Exp:* Geologist, Magnolia Petrol Mobil, 51-52; First Lt topog mapping, US Army, 52-53; lab instr geol, Univ Wyo, 53-54; geologist, Humble Oil & Refining, Exxon, 55-60. *Concurrent Pos:* Chmn adv bd, Am Asn Petrol Geologists, 87-88; pres, Div Environ Geosci, Am Asn Petrol Geologists. *Mem:* Hon mem Am Asn Petrol Geologists (secy, 73-75, pres, 86-87); Soc Independent Prof Earth Scientists; Am Inst Prof Geologists; fel Sigma Xi; Soc Petrol Engrs. *Res:* Economic geology of the Permian Basin describing in detail the reservoir of the oil and gas producing zones and their economic input, plus environmental studies on problem areas in the US. *Mailing Add:* PO Drawer 1269 Midland TX 79702-1269. *Fax:* 915-684-6136

HANSON, CARL VEITH, MOLECULAR VIROLOGY, DIAGNOSTIC VIROLOGY. *Current Pos:* res specialist virol, 77-82, RES SCIENTIST, VIRAL & RICKETTSIAL DIS LAB, CALIF DEPT HEALTH SERV, 82- *Personal Data:* b Pueblo, Colo, Nov 19, 43; m 73; c 2. *Educ:* Harvard Univ, BA, 65; Stanford Univ, PhD(biophysics), 70. *Prof Exp:* Fel phys chem, Univ Calif, 71-76. *Concurrent Pos:* Instr, UNESCO Cell Biol Training Course, Szeged, Hungary, 74; prin investr, US Army Res Contract, 77-81. *Mem:* Am Soc Microbiol; Pan Am Group Rapid Viral Diag. *Res:* Development of inactivated viral vaccines and immunodiagnostic reagents; photochemical inactivation of viruses; structural probes for use in molecular virology; novel methods for the rapid immunodiagnosis of viral disease; development of immunoassays for the detection of mutagens, carcinogens, pesticides and toxins in humans; AIDS diagnostic methods; HIV neutralizing antibodies. *Mailing Add:* Calif Dept Health Servs VRDL 2151 Berkeley Way Berkeley CA 94704

HANSON, D(ONALD) N(ORMAN), CHEMICAL ENGINEERING. *Current Pos:* from asst prof to prof, 47-97, chmn dept, 63-66, EMER PROF CHEM ENG, UNIV CALIF, BERKELEY, 97- *Personal Data:* b Minooka, Ill, Aug 3, 18; m 43; c 3. *Educ:* Univ Ill, BS, 40; Univ Wis, MS, 41, PhD, 43. *Prof Exp:* Instr chem eng, Univ Wis, 43-44, chem engr, Shell Develop Co, Calif, 44-46 & 47; asst prof, Kans State Col, 46-47. *Mem:* Am Chem Soc; Am Inst Chem Eng. *Res:* Calculation and design of distillation columns; process development for energy conservation. *Mailing Add:* Dept Chem Eng Univ Calif Berkeley CA 94720

HANSON, DANIEL JAMES, PATHOLOGY. *Current Pos:* Assoc pathologist, 61-65, chief of staff, 73-75, DIR, PATH SERV, MERCY HOSP, 65- *Personal Data:* b Faribault, Minn, Oct 7, 28; m 53; c 2. *Educ:* Univ Minn, BA, 50, BS, 51, MD, 53. *Concurrent Pos:* Pathologist, Path Labs, Toledo, Ohio, 61-; consult pathologist, Res Inst, Mercy Hosp, 61-; consult, Pharmaceut Firms, 61-; adj prof, Univ Toledo, 62-; clin assoc prof path, Med Col Ohio, 69- *Mem:* Am Soc Clin Path; Col Am Path; AMA; Pan-Am Med Asn; Int Acad Path; Am Chem Soc. *Res:* Anatomical, chemical, gynecological and clinical pathology; instrumentation techniques; drug toxicity; hemolytic disease; pharmaceutical evaluation; injection complications. *Mailing Add:* 2200 Jefferson Ave Toledo OH 43624-1120

HANSON, DANIEL RALPH, BEHAVIORAL GENETICS, EXPERIMENTAL PSYCHOPATHOLOGY. *Current Pos:* STAFF PSYCHIATRIST, RAMSEY CLIN, 90-, CHIEF, DEPT PSYCHIAT, 91- *Personal Data:* b Fargo, NDak, Jan 26, 47; m 69; c 3. *Educ:* Univ Minn, BA, 69, PhD(psychol), 74, MD, 83. *Prof Exp:* Asst prof psychol & psychiat, McMaster Univ, 74-77; fel human genetics, Univ Minn, 77-79, asst prof, Dept Psychiat, 87-90. *Concurrent Pos:* Sr fel human genetics, Univ Wash, 76-77 *Mem:* Am Soc Human Genetics; Behav Genetics Asn; Soc Study Social Biol; Am Psychiat Asn; fel Am Psychopath Asn. *Res:* Biological and genetic bases of abnormal behavior; antecedents of adult psychopathology. *Mailing Add:* Dept Psychiat Ramsey Clin 640 Jackson St St Paul MN 55101

HANSON, DAVID LEE, PROBABILITY STATISTICS, MATHEMATICS. *Current Pos:* PROF MATH SCI, STATE UNIV NY BINGHAMTON, 73-, CHMN DEPT, 83- *Personal Data:* b Minneapolis, Minn, July 14, 35; m 56, Alison W Robbins; c Linda, Sharon, Scott & Carol. *Educ:* Mass Inst Technol, BS, 56; Ind Univ, MA, 59, PhD(probability statist), 60. *Prof Exp:* Staff mathematician, Int Bus Mach Corp, 60-61 & Sandia Corp, 61-63; assoc prof statist, 63-64, from assoc prof to prof statist & math, Univ Mo, Columbia, 64-73, chmn dept statist, 71-73. *Concurrent Pos:* Assoc ed, Ann Math Statist, 67-72 & Ann Probability & Ann Statist, 72-79; prog dir statists & probability, NSF, Washington, DC, 79-80. *Mem:* Am Math Soc; fel Inst Math Statist. *Res:* Probability theory; convergence rates; non-parametric regression; stochastic approximation; utility theory. *Mailing Add:* Dept Math Sci State Univ NY Binghamton NY 13902-6000. *Fax:* 607-777-2450; *E-Mail:* hanson@math.binghamton.edu

HANSON, DAVID M, PHYSICAL CHEMISTRY. *Current Pos:* From asst prof to assoc prof, 69-78, PROF CHEM, STATE UNIV NY STONY BROOK, 78- *Personal Data:* b Waseca, Minn, June 22, 42; m 64; c 2. *Educ:* Dartmouth Col, AB, 64; Calif Inst Technol, PhD(chem), 68. *Concurrent Pos:* NATO fel, Munich Tech Univ, 68-69; Alfred P Sloan Found res fel, 72; fel, Synchrotron Ultraviolet Radiation Facil, Nat Bur Stand, 80-81; vis scientist, Inst Molecular Sci, Okazaki, Japan, 85. *Mem:* Am Chem Soc; Am Phys Soc. *Res:* Soft x-ray spcetroscopy and molecular fragmentation processes. *Mailing Add:* Dept Chem State Univ NY Stony Brook NY 11794-3400

HANSON, DONALD BURNETT, ANALYTICAL ENGINEERING. *Current Pos:* analytical engr, Hamilton Stand, Div United Technol Corp, 64-72, sr analytical engr, 72-82, prin res engr, 82-88, SR PRIN RES ENGR, HAMILTON STAND, DIV UNITED TECHNOL CORP, 88- *Personal Data:* b Niagara Falls, NY, July 9, 38; m 69, Monique Marie Rose Dewinter; c Natalie & Erika. *Educ:* Univ Del, BS, 62; Univ Pa, MS, 64; Univ Conn, MME, 69, PhD(appl mech), 73. *Honors & Awards:* Gas Turbine Power Award, Am Soc Mech Engrs, 74; Aeroacoust Award, Am Inst Aeronaut & Astronaut, 95. *Mem:* Fel Am Inst Aeronaut & Astronaut. *Res:* Contributed articles to professional journals. *Mailing Add:* 11 Sunset Ave Chester CT 06412-1323

HANSON, DONALD FARNESS, ELECTRICAL ENGINEERING. *Current Pos:* asst prof, 77-83, ASSOC PROF ELEC ENG, UNIV MISS, 84- *Personal Data:* b Urbana, Ill, Mar 5, 46. *Educ:* Univ Ill, Urbana-Champaign, BS, 69, MS, 72, PhD(elec eng), 76. *Prof Exp:* Res asst comput sci, Univ Ill, Urbana-Champaign, 69-71, teaching asst elec eng, 71-73, lectr archit, 73-74, instr elec eng, 74-76; asst prof, Iowa State Univ, 76-77; assoc prof elec eng, Syracuse Univ, 83-84. *Concurrent Pos:* Consult, Electronics Technol & Devices Lab, US Army, Ft Monmouth, NJ, 90-91. *Mem:* Inst Elec & Electronics Engrs; Asn Comput Mach. *Res:* Electromagnetic field theory, especially numerical methods, scattering and applications; applications of digital and analog electronics and microprocessors; applications of computer science; hardware description languages. *Mailing Add:* 201 News Hill Cove Oxford MS 38655. *Fax:* 601-232-7231; *E-Mail:* eehanson@olemiss.edu

HANSON, DONALD WAYNE, SATELLITE COMMUNICATIONS, TIME & FREQUENCY METROLOGY. *Current Pos:* ENGR, NAT INST STAND & TECHNOL, 63- *Personal Data:* b Denver, Colo, Feb 9, 37; m 63; c 2. *Educ:* Univ Colo, BS, 59; Stanford Univ MS(elec eng), 61. *Honors & Awards:* M Barr Carlton Award, Inst Elec & Electronic Engrs, 75. *Prof Exp:* Scientist, Lockheed Missile & Space Co, 59-61; engr, Ford Western Develop Labs, 61-63. *Concurrent Pos:* Consult, BDM Corp, 83- *Mem:* Fel Inst Elec & Electronics Engrs. *Res:* Application of advanced communication techniques for high accuracy transfer of time and frequency information; spread spectrum signals; encryption of data; tracking of satellites; use of satellites for broadcasting and point-to-point distribution; corrections for atmospheric dispersion of radio signals. *Mailing Add:* 735 Jonquil Pl Boulder CO 80304

HANSON, EARLE WILLIAM, PLANT PATHOLOGY, FIELD CROPS. *Current Pos:* RETIRED. *Personal Data:* b Wheaton, Minn, Oct 18, 10; m 41; c 2. *Educ:* Univ Minn, BS, 33, MS, 39, PhD(plant path), 41. *Prof Exp:* Asst plant path, Univ Minn, 34-35; pathologist, Bur Plant Indust, Soils & Agr Eng, USDA, Minn, 37-46 & Agr Res Serv, Wis, 46-51; from asst prof to prof plant path, Univ Wis-Madison, 51-92, plant pathologist, Univ Wis-Exten, 72-76. *Concurrent Pos:* Ed, Phytopath, Am Phytopath Soc, 55-58; mem bd dirs, Am Grassland Coun, 62-65; mem, Univ Wis-US AID Team, Univ Ife, Nigeria, 67-71, chief of party, 68-71. *Mem:* AAAS; Am Phytopath Soc; Am Soc Agron; Crop Sci Soc Am; Am Inst Biol Sci. *Res:* Plant disease diagnosis; legume viruses; crop seed microflora; field crop diseases; breeding for disease resistance. *Mailing Add:* 6209 Mineral Point Rd Madison WI 53705

HANSON, ERIC, COMPUTER & INFORMATION SCIENCE. *Current Pos:* FAC MEM, COMPUT & INFO SCI & ENG DEPT, UNIV FLA. *Res:* Active database management systems; ariel/optimization of active database rule condition testing; phalanx parallel active database project; triggerman asynchronous trigger processing project; interactiion between databases and applications. *Mailing Add:* Comput & Info Sci & Eng Dept Univ Fla PO Box 116120 Gainesville FL 32611. *E-Mail:* hanson@cis.ufl.edu

HANSON, FLOYD BLISS, APPLIED MATHEMATICS, COMPUTER SCIENCE. *Current Pos:* from asst prof to assoc prof, 69-83, PROF MATH, UNIV ILL, CHICAGO, 83- *Personal Data:* b Brooklyn, NY, Mar 9, 39; m 62, Ethel H; c Lisa. *Educ:* Antioch Col, BS, 62; Brown Univ, MS, 64, PhD(eng), 68. *Prof Exp:* Tech asst phys chem, Space Physics Dept, Convair Astronaut, 61; appl mathematician, High Temperature Physics Group, Arthur D Little, Inc, 61; physicist, Plasma Physics Lab, Aeronaut Res Lab, Wright-Patterson AFB, Dayton, Ohio, 62; assoc res scientist, Courant Inst Math Sci, NY Univ, 67-69. *Concurrent Pos:* Proj dir equip grant, NSF, 73, assoc investr res grant, 70-84, prin investr, 88-; fac res partic, Argonne Nat Lab, 85, 86 & 87-88; vis prof, Div Applied Math, Brown Univ, 94; vis fac, Civil & Environ Eng Sch, Cornell Univ, 95. *Mem:* Soc Indust & Appl Math; Inst Elect & Electronics Engrs; Resource Modeling Asn. *Res:* Parallel computer computations; application of stochastic differential equations; mathematical biology; kinetic theory, separated flows, laminar boundary layer analysis; asymptotic analysis; integral equations; computational control; stochastic modeling; resource management; manufacturing processes. *Mailing Add:* Dept Math M/C 249 Univ Ill Chicago 851 Morgan St Rm 3225EO Chicago IL 60607-7045. *Fax:* 312-996-1491; *E-Mail:* hanson@uic.edu

HANSON, FRANK EDWIN, NEUROSCIENCES, BEHAVIORAL PHYSIOLOGY. *Current Pos:* assoc prof, 72-81, PROF BIOL SCI, UNIV MD BALTIMORE COUNTY, 81- *Personal Data:* b Bryan, Tex, Mar 14, 38; m, Barbara Allen; c Valerie & Erik. *Educ:* Univ Iowa, BA, 60; Univ Pa, PhD(zool), 65. *Prof Exp:* Sr asst scientist biol, NIH, 64-66; USPHS fel, Univ Pa, 66-67; asst prof zool, Univ Tex, Austin, 68-72. *Mem:* Am Soc Entom. *Res:* Insect chemoreceptor physiology; insect feeding behavior; behavioral physiology of bioluminescent communication mechanisms. *Mailing Add:* Dept Biol Sci Univ Md Baltimore County Campus 5401 Wilkins Ave Catonsville MD 21228-5329. *E-Mail:* hanson@umbc.edu

HANSON, GAIL G, ELEMENTARY PARTICLE PHYSICS. *Current Pos:* PROF PHYSICS, IND UNIV, 89- *Personal Data:* b Dayton, Ohio, Feb 22, 47; m 68; c Russell & Sonya. *Educ:* Mass Inst Technol, BS, 68, PhD(physics), 73. *Honors & Awards:* W R H Panotsky Prize, Am Phys Soc, 96. *Prof Exp:* Res assoc, Stanford Univ, 73-76, staff physicist high energy physics, Stanford Linear Accelerator Ctr, 76-89. *Concurrent Pos:* Guggenheim fel, 95. *Mem:* Fel Am Phys Soc; fel AAAS. *Res:* Experimental high energy physics; e+ e- colliding beams; jet structures in final state; topologies associated with new particle production; particle detectors; wire chambers; hadron collider physics and detectors. *Mailing Add:* Physics Dept Ind Univ Swain Hall W-117 Bloomington IN 47405. *Fax:* 812-855-0440; *E-Mail:* gail@indiana.edu

HANSON, GEORGE PETER, PLANT BREEDING. *Current Pos:* RETIRED. *Personal Data:* b Conde, SDak, July 20, 33; m 58, 69; c 3. *Educ:* SDak State Univ, BS, 56, MS, 58; Ind Univ, PhD(genetics), 65. *Prof Exp:* Asst prof biol, Thiel Col, 62-65; asst prof bot, Butler Univ, 65-67; asst prof, Eastern Ill Univ, 67-68; biologist, Los Angeles State & Co Arboretum, 68-70, sr biologist, 70-80. *Concurrent Pos:* Consult, Comn Undergrad Educ Biol Sci, 66. *Mem:* AAAS; Am Genetics Soc; Am Inst Biol Sci; Bot Soc Am. *Res:* B-chromosome effects upon crossing over and mutation in maize; ornamental plant breeding; air pollution, especially the effects on plants; guayule breeding and research. *Mailing Add:* 1725 S Nogales Apt 101 Rowland Heights CA 91748

HANSON, GILBERT N, PETROLOGY, GEOCHEMISTRY. *Current Pos:* from asst prof to assoc prof, 66-75, chmn, Earth & Space Sci Dept, 83-93, PROF GEOCHEM, STATE UNIV NY STONY BROOK, 75- *Personal Data:* b Minneapolis, Minn, Apr 30, 36; m 63, Janet R; c Lynn C, Kevin A & Darlene A. *Educ:* Univ Minn, BA, 58, MA, 62, PhD(geol), 64. *Prof Exp:* Res assoc geochem, Minn Geol Surv, 64-65; res assoc, Swiss Fed Inst Technol, 65-66. *Mem:* AAAS; Am Geophys Union; Geol Soc Am; Geol Soc India; Geochem Soc. *Res:* Application of geochemical data to petrogenetic problems in igneous and sedimentary systems; geochemical and geochronological studies of geologic terranes. *Mailing Add:* Dept Earth & Space Sci State Univ NY Stony Brook NY 11794-2100. Fax: 516-632-8240; E-Mail: ghanson@ccmail.sunysb.edu

HANSON, HAROLD PALMER, GOVERNMENT ADMINISTRATION. *Current Pos:* from instr to assoc prof, Univ Fla, 48-54, dean grad sch, 69-71, vpres acad affairs, 71-74, exec vpres, 74-78, ADJ PROF PHYSICS & EMER EXEC VPRES, UNIV FLA, 90- *Personal Data:* b Virginia, Minn, Dec 27, 21; m 44, Mary J Stevenson; c Steven B & Barbara J. *Educ:* Super State Teachers Col, BS, 42; Univ Wis, MS, 44, PhD(physics), 48. *Honors & Awards:* St Olav Medal, 76; Franklin Medal, NSF, 90. *Prof Exp:* Res physicist, Naval Ord Lab, USNR, 44-46; WARF fel, Univ Wis, 46-48, vis lectr, 57; from assoc prof to prof, Univ Tex, 54-69, chmn dept physics, 61-69, dir, Ctr Struct Studies, 67-69; provost, Boston Univ, 78-80, Wayne State Univ, 82-84. *Concurrent Pos:* Res physicist, Lincoln Lab, Mass Inst Technol, 53; Fulbright res fel, Univ Oslo, 60-61, NAVF fel, 68; consult, Gen Atomic, 64; exec dir, US House Rep Comt Sci, Space & Technol, 80-82 & 84-90; chmn, Sr Res Adv Bd, Fla Inst Technol; ed, Delos, 91- *Mem:* Am Phys Soc; Am Asn Physics Teachers; AAAS; Sigma Xi. *Res:* X-ray spectroscopy; electron and x-ray atomic form factors. *Mailing Add:* Univ Fla 215 Williamson Hall Gainesville FL 32605. E-Mail: hanson@ufhepa.phys.ufl.edu

HANSON, HARVEY MYRON, THEORETICAL PHYSICS. *Current Pos:* RETIRED. *Personal Data:* b Akron, Ohio, Mar 24, 31; m 53; c 2. *Educ:* Univ Akron, BS, 52; Ohio State Univ, MSc, 54, PhD(physics), 56. *Prof Exp:* Res fel physics, Ohio State Univ, 56-57; asst prof, Univ Akron, 57-60; assoc prof, Southwestern at Memphis, 60-65; prof physics, Wright State Univ, 65-96. *Concurrent Pos:* Chmn dept physics, 65-77. *Res:* Theoretical and experimental aspects of molecular spectra in the infrared region. *Mailing Add:* 5607 Red Coach Dr Dayton OH 45429

HANSON, HENRY W A, III, SEDIMENTOLOGY. *Current Pos:* Asst prof, 66, ASSOC PROF GEOL, DICKINSON COL, 66- *Personal Data:* b Hagerstown, Md, Aug 2, 32; m 54; c 2. *Educ:* Univ Alaska, BS, 60; Pa State Univ, MS, 65, PhD(geol), 68. *Mem:* Geol Soc Am; Soc Econ Paleontologists & Mineralogists; Sigma Xi. *Res:* Environmental system and processes of barrier islands. *Mailing Add:* 133 N College St Carlisle PA 17013

HANSON, HIRAM STANLEY, GEOLOGY, GEOCHEMISTRY. *Current Pos:* RETIRED. *Personal Data:* b Whitesburg, Ga, July 26, 23; m 47; c 1. *Educ:* Emory Univ, BA, 46, MS, 49, MA, 59; Univ Ariz, PhD, 66. *Prof Exp:* Asst chemist, Bell Aircraft Corp, 44-45; res inorg chemist, Tenn Corp, 47-48; asst prof chem, Middle Ga Col, 48-49; instr sci, Reinhardt Col, 49-54; asst geol, Emory Univ, 54-56, instr chem & geol, 56-58; asst prof, Sul Ross State Col, 58-61; asst geol, Univ Ariz, 61-64; from asst prof to prof geol, Ga Southern Col, 67-88, head dept, 69-88. *Concurrent Pos:* Shell merit fel, 70. *Mem:* Geol Soc Am; Mineral Soc Am; Nat Asn Geol Teachers; Geochem Soc; Sigma Xi. *Res:* Igneous and metamorphic petrology and petrography. *Mailing Add:* 13 E Moore St Statesboro GA 30458

HANSON, HOWARD GRANT, PHYSICS. *Current Pos:* RETIRED. *Personal Data:* b Nelson, Minn, Jan 22, 20; m 45; c 4. *Educ:* St Cloud State Teachers Col, BS, 43; Univ Wis, PhD(physics), 48. *Prof Exp:* From asst prof to prof physics, Univ Minn, Duluth, 47-85, head dept, 50-85. *Concurrent Pos:* NSF fac fel, Univ Stockholm, 63. *Mem:* Am Phys Soc; Am Asn Physics Teachers. *Res:* Quenching and exciting of fluorescence by different gases; spectra of scintillating crystals; tesselations of random sphere aggregations. *Mailing Add:* 5120 Crosley Ave Duluth MN 55811

HANSON, HOWARD P(AUL), ATMOSPHERE-OCEAN INTERACTION, CLIMATE DYNAMICS. *Current Pos:* res assoc, 81-91, FEL, COOP INST RES ENVIRON SCI, UNIV COLO, BOULDER, 85-, SR RES ASSOC UNIV, 91-, EXEC ASSOC DIR INST, 93- *Personal Data:* b Peoria, Ill, Jan 1, 50; m 83, Claire Smith. *Educ:* Univ Ill, BS, 72; Univ Miami, PhD(atmospheric sci), 79. *Prof Exp:* Resident res assoc, Nat Res Coun, 79-81. *Mem:* AAAS; Am Geophys Union; Am Meteorol Soc; Sigma Xi; Oceanog Soc. *Res:* Theoretical and observational work on interaction of atmosphere and ocean with focus on process studies that are relevant to climate change; computer simulation and modeling, field programs and data analyses. *Mailing Add:* Coop Inst Res Environ Sci Univ Colo Boulder CO 80309-0216. Fax: 303-492-1149; E-Mail: hph@cires.coloredo.edu

HANSON, HUGH, animal ecology, community & ecosystem ecology; deceased, see previous edition for last biography

HANSON, JAMES CHARLES, CELL BIOLOGY, DEVELOPMENTAL BIOLOGY. *Current Pos:* Chmn, Div Sci & Math, 60-62, Dept Biol Sci, 60-66 & 71-74, assoc prof biol sci, 68-72, PROF BIOL SCI, STANISLAUS STATE COL, 72- *Personal Data:* b Modesto, Calif, Jan 6, 31; m 56; c 2. *Educ:* Univ of the Pac, BA, 55, MA, 57; Ore State Univ, PhD, 67. *Res:* Early development and cell division in marine invertebrates, especially the fertilization process and the first mitotic period. *Mailing Add:* Dept Biol Sci Calif State Univ Stanislaus 801 W Monte Vista Ave Turlock CA 95382-0256

HANSON, JAMES EDWARD, TECHNICAL STAFF ADMINISTRATION. *Current Pos:* ASSOC PROF, SETON HALL, 91- *Personal Data:* b Wichita, Kans, Mar 25, 62. *Educ:* Tex Christian Univ, BS, 84; Calif Inst Technol, PhD(chem), 90. *Prof Exp:* Mem tech staff, AT&T Bell Labs, 89-91. *Mem:* Sigma Xi; Am Chem Soc. *Res:* Design and synthesis of new materials, including polymers for microelectronics manufacturing and dencritic polymers. *Mailing Add:* Dept Chem Seton Hall South Orange NJ 07079-2694

HANSON, JERRY LEE, ELECTRICAL ENGINEERING. *Current Pos:* assoc prof physics, 77-83, RES ASSOC, AUGUSTANA RES INST, 75-; CHMN COMPUT SCI DEPT, AUGUSTANA COL, 83- *Personal Data:* b Belmond, Iowa, Aug 6, 32; m 54; c 3. *Educ:* St Olaf Col, BA, 54; US Air Force Inst Technol, BS, 61; Univ Ill, MS, 62, PhD(elec eng), 70. *Prof Exp:* From instr to assoc prof, US Air Force Acad, 62-67, from asst prof to assoc prof, USAF Inst Technol, 70-74, chief, Electronics Div, Foreign Technol Div, Air Force Systs Command, 74-75. *Mem:* Inst Elec & Electronics Engrs. *Res:* Linear systems; circuits; digital systems; microprocessor and microcomputer systems. *Mailing Add:* Comput Sci Physics Dept Augustana Col Gilbert Sci Ctr 204 Sioux Falls SD 57105

HANSON, JOE A, resource management, science writing, for more information see previous edition

HANSON, JOHN BERNARD, PLANT PHYSIOLOGY. *Current Pos:* from asst prof to prof, 53-85, head dept bot, 67-77, EMER PROF AGRON & PLANT BIOL, UNIV ILL, URBANA, 85- *Personal Data:* b Denver, Colo, Mar 24, 18; m 43; c 3. *Educ:* Univ Colo, BA, 48; State Col Wash, MS, 50, PhD(bot), 52. *Honors & Awards:* Barnes Award, Am Soc Plant Physiol, 80, Gude Award, 89. *Prof Exp:* Asst, State Col Wash, 48-51; Nat Res Coun fel, Calif Inst Technol, 52-53. *Concurrent Pos:* Fulbright res scholar, Waite Agr Exp Sta, Australia, 59-60; NATO sr fel, Univ East Anglia, 68. *Mem:* Am Soc Plant Physiologists (pres, 73-74). *Res:* Mineral absorption; respiration. *Mailing Add:* 610 Burkwood Ct E Urbana IL 61801

HANSON, JOHN ELBERT, INORGANIC CHEMISTRY. *Current Pos:* From asst prof to assoc prof, 61-70, PROF CHEM, OLIVET NAZARENE COL, 70-, CHMN DEPT, 71- *Personal Data:* b Toledo, Ohio, Mar 5, 35; m 59, Esther Johnson; c Heidi & Heather. *Educ:* Olivet Nazarene Col, AB, 57; Purdue Univ, PhD(chem), 64. *Concurrent Pos:* Res assoc, Univ Chicago, 74; vis prof, Univ Wis, 84-85. *Mem:* Am Chem Soc. *Res:* Organosilicon chemistry; coordination compounds; bioinorganic chemistry. *Mailing Add:* Olivet Nazarene Univ Kankakee IL 60901. Fax: 815-939-5071

HANSON, JOHN M, STRUCTURAL ENGINEERING, FAILURE ANALYSIS. *Current Pos:* DISTINGUISHED PROF CIVIL ENG & CONSTRUCT, UNIV NC, 93- *Personal Data:* b Brookings, SDak, Nov 16, 32; m 60; c 4. *Educ:* SDak State Univ, BS, 53; Iowa State Univ, MS, 57; Lehigh Univ, PhD(civil eng), 64. *Honors & Awards:* State-of-the-Art Civil Eng Award, Am Soc Civil Engrs, 74, Raymond C Reese Award, 76, T Y Lin Award, 79; Distinguished Serv Award, Am Concrete Inst, 76, Henry Crown Award, Ill Sect, 93; Martin P Korn Award, Prestressed Concrete Inst, 78. *Prof Exp:* Jr engr, Boeing Airplane Co, 53; designer-detailer, Sverdrup & Parcel, Inc, 55-56; engr, J T Banner & Assocs, 57-58 & Phillips-Carter-Osborn, Inc, 58-60; res instr civil eng, Lehigh Univ, 60-64, asst res prof, 64-65; sr develop engr & prin res engr, Portland Cement Asn, 65-69, asst mgr struct res sect, 69-72; vpres opers, 79, pres, Wiss, Janney, Elstner & Assocs, 79-92. *Mem:* Fel Am Soc Civil Engrs; fel Am Concrete Inst (pres, 90-91); Prestressed Concrete Inst; Int Asn Bridge & Struct Eng (pres, 93-97). *Res:* Behavior and ultimate strength, particularly shear strength of concrete beams; structural concrete members in general. *Mailing Add:* Dept Civil Eng NC State Univ Box 7908 Raleigh NC 27695

HANSON, JOHN MARK, POPULATION & COMMUNITY ECOLOGY & BIOLOGY, MARINE INVERTEBRATES & FISH. *Current Pos:* vis fel, 89-90, RES SCIENTIST, GULF FISHERIES CTR, DEPT FISHERIES & OCEANS, 90- *Personal Data:* b Ottawa, Ont, Apr 14, 55; m 80, Catherine M Merlin; c Margaret A, Jennifer T & Brian J. *Educ:* Univ Ottawa, BSc, 78, MSc, 80; McGill Univ, PhD(biol), 85. *Prof Exp:* Natural Sci & Eng Res Coun Can fel, Univ Alta, 86-88, sci writer/ed, Alta Environ, 88-89. *Concurrent Pos:* Mem, Groundfish Subcomt, Can Atlantic Fisheries Sci Adv Comt, 90-93; mem, Groundfish Comt & Fisheries Oceanog Comt, Atlantic Stock Assessment Comt, 93-96; mem, Invert Fisheries Comt & Fisheries, Oceanog Comt, 96. *Mem:* Am Fisheries Soc; Ecol Soc Am; Am Soc Naturalists; Can Soc Zool. *Res:* Interactions between Atlantic cod and their competitors and prey; effects of size-selective fishing and environmental changes on fish growth; competitive and predator-prey relations between commercially important marine invertebrates. *Mailing Add:* Gulf Fisheries Ctr PO Box 5030 Moncton NB E1C 9B6 Can. Fax: 506-851-2387; E-Mail: hansonm@gfl.dfo.ca

HANSON, JONATHAN C, COMPUTER AUTOMATION, COMPUTER GRAPHICS. *Current Pos:* res assoc, 77-79, comput analyst, 79-92, CHEMIST, BROOKHAVEN NAT LAB, 92- *Personal Data:* b Chicago, Ill, Sept 11, 41; m 69, Louise Kurle; c Jeffrey & Christina. *Educ:* Northwestern Univ, BS, 63; Univ Mich, Ann Arbor, PhD(chem), 69. *Prof Exp:* Res assoc chem, Univ Wash, 69-70, res assoc biol struct, 70-73, res assoc biophys, Johns Hopkins Univ, 73-77. *Mem:* Am Crystallog Asn. *Res:* Automation of physical chemical experiments, crystallographic computing and molecular graphics; molecular interactions from an experimental and theoretical standpoint. *Mailing Add:* Dept Chem Bldg 555A Brookhaven Nat Lab Upton NY 11973. E-Mail: hanson@X7b.chm.bnl.gov

HANSON, KENNETH MARVIN, PHYSIOLOGY. *Current Pos:* asst prof, 66-71, assoc prof, 71-76, PROF PHYSIOL, OHIO STATE UNIV, 76- *Personal Data:* b Brookings, SDak, Feb 21, 27; c 2. *Educ:* Sioux Falls Col, BS, 51; Ind Univ, MS, 63, PhD(physiol), 65. *Prof Exp:* Teaching asst biol, Augustana Col, 45-49; lab technician, Univ Minn, 54-57; res asst physiol, Ind Univ, 57-63, res assoc, 63-65, instr, 65-66. *Mem:* Am Physiol Soc; Sigma Xi; Soc Exp Biol & Med; Am Heart Asn. *Res:* Regional blood flow; vascular physiology; liver function and blood flow; gastrointestinal physiology. *Mailing Add:* Dept Physiol Ohio State Univ Col Med 1645 Neil Ave Columbus OH 43210

HANSON, KENNETH MERRILL, RADIOGRAPHIC IMAGING, TOMOGRAPHIC RECONSTRUCTION. *Current Pos:* STAFF MEM IMAGE SCI, LOS ALAMOS NAT LAB, 75- *Personal Data:* b Mt Vernon, NY, Apr 17, 40; m 96, Jeannene Masterson; c Jennifer A & Keith M. *Educ:* Cornell Univ, BEng Phys, 63; Harvard Univ, MS, 67, PhD(physics), 70. *Honors & Awards:* Nuclear Weapons Prog Award of Excellence, 87 & 92. *Prof Exp:* Res assoc nuclear physics, Cornell Univ, 70-75. *Concurrent Pos:* Consult, tomographic reconstruction; sabbatical, Thomson GGR, 86-87. *Mem:* Am Phys Soc; sr mem Inst Elec & Electronics Engrs; Soc Photog Instr Eng. *Res:* Industrial and medical imaging; tomographic reconstruction and image analysis; detection of signals in radiographic images; interactive image processing and image display techniques. *Mailing Add:* Los Alamos Nat Lab MS-P940 Los Alamos NM 87545. *E-Mail:* kmh@lanl.gov

HANSON, KENNETH RALPH, BIOCHEMISTRY. *Current Pos:* from asst biochemist to biochemist, 60-74, SR BIOCHEMIST, CONN AGR EXP STA, 74- *Personal Data:* b Birmingham, Eng, Sept 7, 30; m 58; c 2. *Educ:* Univ Liverpool, BSc, 51, PhD(org chem), 54. *Prof Exp:* Fel enzym, Nat Res Coun Can, 56-58; Jane Coffin Childs fel biochem, Sch Med, NY Univ, 58-60. *Concurrent Pos:* Lectr, Japan Soc Promotion Sci, 80. *Mem:* Am Soc Biol Chem; Am Soc Plant Physiol; Am Chem Soc; Phytochem Soc NAm (pres, 72-73). *Res:* Stereochemistry and mechanisms of enzymatic reactions; aromatic amino acids and plant phenols and their biosynthesis and regulation; stereochemical concepts; photosynthetic metabolism; use of stereospecifically tritiated glyceric acid to study loss during photorespiration of CO_2 fixed by photosynthesis in C-3 plants (such as wheat and tobacco); isolation and characterization of a starchless mutant of Nicotiana Sylvestris in which plastid phosphoglucomutase is altered. *Mailing Add:* 595-Saddle Ridge Rd Orange CT 06477-2024. *Fax:* 203-789-7232

HANSON, KENNETH WARREN, HORTICULTURE. *Current Pos:* RETIRED. *Personal Data:* b Graceville, Minn, July 15, 22; m 46; c 4. *Educ:* Univ Minn, BS, 48, MS, 51, PhD(hort), 52. *Prof Exp:* Field agent fruit res, USDA, Univ Minn, 42-43 & 46-51; asst horticulturist, Univ Ga, 52, assoc horticulturist, 52-54; asst prof pomol, Geneva Agr Exp Sta, Cornell Univ, 54-60; assoc prof hort, Am Univ, Beirut, 60-63; dir & horticulturist, Mo State Fruit Exp Sta, 63-84. *Concurrent Pos:* Consult, Int Exec Serv Corps, 85- *Mem:* AAAS; Am Soc Hort Sci; Am Inst Biol Sci; Sigma Xi. *Res:* Pomology; the creation of new varieties of fruits through breeding. *Mailing Add:* 15275 Royal St Gulfport MS 39503-2818

HANSON, LESTER EUGENE, animal science; deceased, see previous edition for last biography

HANSON, LOUISE I KARLE, BIOPHYSICS, QUANTUM CHEMISTRY. *Current Pos:* sr res assoc, 77-78, asst chemist, 78-80, CHEMIST, BROOKHAVEN NAT LAB, 80- *Personal Data:* b Washington, DC, Aug 26, 46; m 69; c 1. *Educ:* Univ Mich, BS, 67, MS, 69; Univ Wash, PhD(chem), 73. *Prof Exp:* Fel & res chemist, NIH, 73-77. *Concurrent Pos:* Prof lectr, Chem Dept, The Am Univ, Washington, 77. *Mem:* Am Chem Soc; Biophys Soc. *Res:* Elucidation of the electronic structure of biological chromophores (chlorophyll, heme derivatives and flavins) both in vivo and model systems, and the role of these compounds in mediating photosynthetic and biochemical processes. *Mailing Add:* Bldg 480 Brookhaven Nat Lab Upton NY 11973-5000

HANSON, LYLE EUGENE, VETERINARY MICROBIOLOGY. *Current Pos:* from instr to prof vet path & hyg, Col Vet Med, Univ Ill, Urbana, 61-85, head dept, 67-79, assoc dean res, 79-85, EMER PROF, UNIV ILL, URBANA, 85- *Personal Data:* b Sarona, Wis, Oct 2, 20; m 45, Ruth Magnider; c Bruce, Karen (Malocha), Craig & Jane (Becker). *Educ:* Northland Col, PhB, 42; Mich State Univ, DVM, 50; Univ Ill, MS, 53, PhD(vet path), 57. *Prof Exp:* Veterinarian, Wis Dept Agr, 50. *Concurrent Pos:* Consult, US Army Med Corps & PAHO. *Mem:* Am Vet Med Asn; Am Asn Avian Path; US Animal Health Asn; Am Col Vet Microbiol. *Res:* Animal virology, microbiology; development of polyvalent leptospires; investigated the epizootiology of leptospiral strains in the US and Jamaica. *Mailing Add:* 1908 Shelly Ct Urbana IL 61802

HANSON, MARVIN WAYNE, ANALYTICAL CHEMISTRY. *Current Pos:* CHEMIST & ENGR, BAYOU STATE OIL CORP, 79- *Personal Data:* b Longstreet, La, May 12, 28; m 65, 81, Loretta Palmer; c Kim, Lisa & Wayne Jr. *Educ:* Centenary Col, BS, 50; Univ Houston, MS, 53, PhD(chem), 64. *Prof Exp:* Asst prof chem, McNeese State Col, 54-55 & 57-59; assoc prof, Centenary Col La, 59-71, chmn dept, 68-78, prof, 71-78; prof chem, Monroe Community Col, 78-79. *Res:* Analytical chemistry; spectroscopy and spectrophotometry; qualitative organic and reaction mechanisms. *Mailing Add:* Bayou State Oil Co PO Box 7886 Shreveport LA 71137-7886

HANSON, MAUREEN REBECCA, ORGANELLE GENETICS, PLANT MOLECULAR BIOLOGY. *Current Pos:* from assoc prof to prof, 85-96, LIBERTY HYDE BAILEY PROF, CORNELL UNIV, 96- *Personal Data:* b Washington, DC, Dec 7, 49. *Educ:* Duke Univ, BS, 71; Harvard Univ, PhD(cell & molecular biol), 76. *Prof Exp:* NIH fel, Harvard Univ, 76-79; asst prof, Univ Va, 79-85. *Concurrent Pos:* Assoc ed, Genetics, 84-; assoc dir, Cornell Biotech Prog, 88-92; dir, Cornell NSF/Dept Educ/USDA Plant Sci Ctr, 88- *Mem:* Fel AAAS; Am Soc Plant Physiol; Genetics Soc Am; Int Soc Plant Molecular Biol. *Res:* Nuclear-organelle interactions; RNA editing in plant organelles; molecular mechanisms of cytoplasmic male sterility and fertility restoration, subcellular protein localization, and mitochondrial gene expression. *Mailing Add:* Genetics/Cornell Univ Biotech Bldg Ithaca NY 14853. *Fax:* 607-255-2428; *E-Mail:* mrhs@cornell.edu

HANSON, MERLE EDWIN, PHYSICS, ENGINEERING. *Current Pos:* CONSULT, 92- *Personal Data:* b Oakes, NDak, July 8, 34; m 58, Marlys C Cudworth; c 2. *Educ:* NDak State Univ, BS, 61, MS, 62; NMex Inst Mining & Technol, PhD(physics), 73. *Prof Exp:* Teaching asst eng, NDak State Univ, 61-62; res engr mech eng, NAm Aviation, 62-65; sr res engr continuum mech, NMex Inst Mining & Technol, 65-73; physicist, Lawrence Livermore Lab, 73-82; dir res & develop, Hunter Geophys, 82-84; vpres, Comdisco Resources, 84-89; vpres, Duncan Energy Co, 89-92. *Mem:* Soc Petrol Engrs. *Res:* Fracture mechanics and continuum mechanics; early time detonation phenomena and interaction of explosives with other material; reservoir stimulation phenomena; secondary oil recovery. *Mailing Add:* 1134 Geneva Livermore CA 94550

HANSON, MERVIN PAUL, PHYSICAL CHEMISTRY. *Current Pos:* PROF CHEM, HUMBOLDT STATE COL, 65- *Personal Data:* b Skellytown, Tex, Sept 14, 37; m 64; c 2. *Educ:* Humboldt State Col, BS, 61; Cornell Univ, PhD(chem), 66. *Mem:* Am Chem Soc. *Res:* Irreversible thermodynamics. *Mailing Add:* Dept Chem Humboldt State Col Arcata CA 95521

HANSON, MILTON PAUL, CHEMISTRY. *Current Pos:* From asst prof to assoc prof, 64-78, PROF CHEM, AUGUSTANA COL, SDAK, 78- *Personal Data:* b Mitchell, SDak, Aug 22, 38; m 61, Marjorie Niedringhaus; c Paul & Peter. *Educ:* Augustana Col, SDak, BA, 60; Rice Univ, PhD(org chem), 64. *Concurrent Pos:* Vis lectr, Univ Ill, Urbana-Champaign, 69-70; vis assoc prof, Univ Ariz, 78; post doctoral assoc, Univ Ga, Athens, Ga, 85-86; hon fel, Univ Wis-Madison, 97. *Mem:* Am Chem Soc; Sigma Xi. *Res:* Organic chemistry; reaction mechanisms; polymers; quantative structure-property relationships. *Mailing Add:* Dept Chem Augustana Col Sioux Falls SD 57197. *E-Mail:* mhanson@inst.augie.edu

HANSON, MORGAN A, OPERATIONS RESEARCH, STATISTICS. *Current Pos:* RETIRED. *Personal Data:* b Wowan, Australia, Jan 28, 30; m 54; c 5. *Educ:* Univ Queensland, BSc, 52; Univ Melbourne, MSc, 55; Univ New South Wales, PhD(statist), 64. *Honors & Awards:* Stevenson Prize for Maths, Queensland Univ, 60. *Prof Exp:* Physicist, Imp Chem Industs, Ltd, 55; mathematician, Lysaght's Works Ltd, Australia, 56; opers res analyst, Australian Gas Light Co, 56-58; from lectr to sr lectr math & statist, Univ New South Wales, 58-64; vis assoc prof statist, Fla State Univ, 65; from assoc prof to prof math, Queen's Univ, Ont, 66-68; prof statist, Fla State Univ, 68-96. *Concurrent Pos:* Can Nat Res Coun res grants math prog, 66-68; consult, Aerospace Res Labs, USAF, 66-; Off Naval Res grant, weather modification, 80; vis fel, La Trobe Univ, Australia, 80 & 92, Melbourne Univ, Australia, 91. *Mem:* Am Math Soc; Math Prog Soc; Int Statist Inst. *Res:* Mathematical programming; approximation theory; economic optimization; control theory; calculus of variations. *Mailing Add:* Dept Statist Fla State Univ Tallahassee FL 32306. *Fax:* 850-644-5271

HANSON, NORMAN WALTER, STRUCTURAL ENGINEERING, APPLIED MECHANICS. *Current Pos:* RETIRED. *Personal Data:* b Manistique, Mich, Jan 18, 25; m 51, Lorraine V Malm; c Ann & Laurie. *Educ:* Univ NMex, BS, 50; Kans State Univ, MS, 53. *Prof Exp:* Test engr aircraft struct, NAm Aviation, 51-52; res asst struct, Kans State Univ, 52-53; asst to sr develop engr, Construct Technol Labs, Portland Cement Asn, 53-68, prin struct engr, 68-86, prin engr, 86-89. *Mem:* Fel Am Concrete Inst; Am Soc Civil Engrs; Instrument Soc Am. *Res:* Structural reinforced concrete; seismic resistance; masonry buildings; testing methods; instrumentation. *Mailing Add:* 3026E Dodgelake Rd Manistique MI 49854

HANSON, PAUL ELIOT, taxonomy, biological control, for more information see previous edition

HANSON, PER ROLAND, ELECTRONICS, ELECTRICAL ENGINEERING. *Current Pos:* RETIRED. *Personal Data:* b Medford, Mass, Aug 30, 12; m 40, Mabel Thorburn; c Joyce E & Richard E. *Educ:* Mass Inst Technol, BS, 35; Northeastern Univ, MS, 59. *Prof Exp:* Receiving tube engr, Champion Radio Works, 35-39; receiving tube engr, Raytheon Mfg Co, Newton, 39-42, mgr eng & mfg groups, Power Tube Div, Waltham, 42-61; mgr eng & mfg groups, Bomac Div, Varian Assoc, Beverly, 61-66; prin engr, Spec Microwave Devices Oper, Raytheon Co, Burlington, 66-77, consult, 78-82; consult, 82-87. *Mem:* Inst Elec & Electronics Engrs. *Res:* Microwave tubes and components engineering and manufacturing. *Mailing Add:* 7 Wadleigh Point Rd Kingston NH 03848

HANSON, PETER, EXERCISE PHYSIOLOGY, CARDIOLOGY. *Current Pos:* PROF, MED SCH, UNIV WIS, 74-, CLIN DIR, PREV CARDIOL PROG, 78- *Personal Data:* b Appleton, Wis, Oct 9, 35; m, Mary Morton; c Karoline, Elizabeth & Helen. *Educ:* Univ Wis-Madison, BS, 58; Univ Ill, Urbana, MS, 62; Univ NMex, MD, 71. *Mem:* Am Physiol Soc; Am Col Sports Med; Am Heart Asn; Am Soc Hypertension. *Res:* Physiological responses to exercise in cardiovascular disease. *Mailing Add:* Cardiology Dept Univ Wis Clin Sci Ctr 600 Highland Ave Madison WI 53792-0001. *E-Mail:* pg.hanson@uwmsg.hosp.wisc.edu

HANSON, RICHARD E, PRECAMBRIAN GEOLOGY, PETROLOGY. *Current Pos:* asst prof, 88-94, ASSOC PROF, DEPT GEOL, TEX CHRISTIAN UNIV, 94- *Educ:* Okla State Univ, BS(zool) & BS(geol), 75, MS, 77; Columbia Univ, PhD(geol), 83. *Prof Exp:* Lectr, Dept Geol, Sch Mines, Univ Zambia, 83-85; adj asst prof, Dept Geol Sci, Ohio State Univ, 85-88. *Concurrent Pos:* Grantee, NSF, 83, 90, 94 & 95, Tex Christian Univ, 89-90 & 94; fulbright scholar award, African Reg Res Prog, 95. *Mem:* Geol Soc Am; Soc Sedimentary Geol; Geol Soc Zimbabwe. *Res:* Authored several papers in technical journals. *Mailing Add:* Dept Geol Tex Christian Univ PO Box 298830 Ft Worth TX 76129

HANSON, RICHARD STEVEN, MICROBIOL PHYSIOLOGY, MOLECULAR BIOLOGY. *Current Pos:* dir, 81-91, PROF MICROBIOL, GRAY FRESHWATER BIOL RES INST, UNIV MINN, 81- *Personal Data:* b Platte, SDak, Nov 14, 35; m 56; c 3. *Educ:* SDak State Univ, BS, 59; Univ Ill, PhD(microbiol), 62. *Honors & Awards:* Res Award, Charles Lindberg Found, 84. *Prof Exp:* Nat Acad Sci fel microbiol chem, Pioneering Labs, Northern Regional Res Labs, Agr Res Serv, USDA, 62-63; USPHS fel biochem, Enzymol Lab, Nat Ctr Sci Res, Gif Sur Yvette, France, 63-64; asst prof biochem, Med Ctr, Univ Ill, Chicago, 64-65; from asst prof to prof bact, Univ Wis-Madison, 65-81, chmn dept bact, 73-76. *Mem:* AAAS; Am Soc Microbiol; Fedn Am Soc Exp Biol. *Res:* Regulation of enzyme synthesis in bacteria and the biochemistry of sporulation and its control in bacteria; chemolithotrophic bacteria; biochemistry, ecology and genetics of methanotrophic bacteria; biological degradation of xenobiotic chemicals. *Mailing Add:* Univ Minn Med Sch Box 196 Mayo Mem Bldg 1420 Delaware St SE Minneapolis MN 55455. *Fax:* 612-626-0623

HANSON, RICHARD W, BIOCHEMISTRY. *Current Pos:* prof, 78-93, CHMN DEPT, CASE WESTERN RES UNIV, 78-, LEONARD & JEAN SHEGGS PROF BIOCHEM, 93- *Personal Data:* b Oxford, NY, Nov 10, 35; m 61, Gloria M Lucchin; c Paul, Benjamin & Daria. *Educ:* Northeastern Univ, BS, 59; Brown Univ, MS, 61, PhD(biol), 63. *Honors & Awards:* Mead Johnson Award, Am Inst Nutrit, 71; Kaiser-Permanente Award, 82; Merit Award, Nat Inst Diabetes, & Digestive & Kidney Dis, 87; Maurice Saltyman Award, 91; Leonard & Jean Skaggs Prof Biochem, 91. *Prof Exp:* From asst prof to prof biochem, Fels Res Inst, Med Sch, Temple Univ, 75-77. *Concurrent Pos:* USPHS fel, 65-66; Nat Inst Arthritis & Metab Dis career develop award, 70-74; mem, Biochem Study Sect, NIH, 74-78; mem, Comn Life Sci, Nat Res Coun; assoc ed, J Biol Chem, 85- *Mem:* AAAS; Am Inst Nutrit; Am Soc Biochem & Molecular Biol; Am Soc Microbiol. *Res:* Hormonal regulation of gene expression; development of metabolic processes; regulation of gluconeogenesis in mammalian liver and kidney. *Mailing Add:* Dept Biochem Case Western Res Univ Sch Med Cleveland OH 44106-4935. *Fax:* 216-368-4544

HANSON, ROBERT BRUCE, ASTROMETRY, STATISTICAL ASTRONOMY. *Current Pos:* from asst res astronr to assoc res astronr, 80-93, RES ASTRONOMER, LICK OBSERV, UNIV CALIF, SANTA CRUZ, 93- *Personal Data:* b Minneapolis, Minn, Jan 26, 47; m 71, Nancy J Perlman; c Robert & Katherine. *Educ:* Carleton Col, BA, 67; Univ Calif, Santa Cruz, PhD(astron), 74. *Honors & Awards:* Trumpler Award, Astron Soc Pac, 76. *Prof Exp:* Lectr astron, Dept Astron, Yale Univ, 75-76, res staff astronr, 76-78; sr res fel, Royal Greenwich Observ, Herstmonceux, Eng, 78-80. *Mem:* Am Astron Soc; Astron Soc Pac; Sigma Xi; Royal Astron Soc; Int Astron Union. *Res:* Astrometry: proper motions and parallaxes; statistical astronomy: stellar luminosities and kinematics; stellar populations; galactic structure; cosmic distance scale. *Mailing Add:* Lick Observ Univ Calif Santa Cruz CA 95064. *E-Mail:* hanson@ucolick.org

HANSON, ROBERT C, AUTONOMIC PHARMACOLOGY. *Current Pos:* sect head autonomic pharmacol, 85-87, MGR LIC & RES PLANNING, NOVA PHARMACEUT CORP, 87- *Personal Data:* b Berwyn, Ill, Aug 13, 44; m; c 2. *Educ:* Cornell Col, BA, 66; De Paul Univ, MS, 70; Univ Mo, PhD(physiol), 73; Univ Evansville, MBA, 83. *Prof Exp:* Sr res assoc, pharmaceut res & develop, cardiovasc pharmacol, Bristol-Myers, 78-85. *Mem:* Am Physiol Soc; Int Soc Nephrology; Am Soc Nephrology; Am Heart Asn; Am Soc Zoologists; Licensing Execs Soc. *Mailing Add:* Dept Bus Develop 3M Pharmaceut 3M Ctr Bldg 275-3W-01 PO Box 33275 St Paul MN 55133-3275. *Fax:* 612-737-4556

HANSON, ROBERT D(UANE), STRUCTURAL ENGINEERING, EARTHQUAKE ENGINEERING. *Current Pos:* consult, 92-94, SR EARTHQUAKE ENGR, FED EMERGENCY MGT AGENCY, 94- *Personal Data:* b Albert Lea, Minn, July 27, 35; m 59, Kaye Nielsen; c Craig R & Eric N. *Educ:* Univ Minn, BS, 57, MSCE, 58; Calif Inst Technol, PhD(civil eng), 65. *Honors & Awards:* Reese Res Award, Am Soc Civil Engrs, 80; Attwood Eng Excellence Award, 86. *Prof Exp:* Asst prof civil eng, Univ NDak, 59-61; asst prof eng, Univ Calif, Davis, 65-66; from asst prof to prof civil eng, Univ Mich, Ann Arbor, 66-94, chmn dept, 76-84. *Concurrent Pos:* UNESCO expert, Int Inst Seismol & Earthquake Eng, Tokyo, 70-71; consult, NSF, 79-88 & 92-94; Bechtel Corp, 76-87; Sensei Engrs, 77-90; Bldg Seismic Safety Coun, 88-94; div dir, NSF, Washington, DC, 89-90; vis prof civil eng & actg dir, Earthquake Eng Res Ctr, Univ Calif, Berkeley, 91. *Mem:* Nat Acad Eng; Earthquake Eng Res Inst (vpres, 77-79, pres elect, 88, pres, 89-91); Am Soc Civil Engrs. *Res:* Structural dynamics; earthquake resistant design; building failure and repair; mechanical damping systems for buildings; active control of buildings subjected to wind storms and earthquakes. *Mailing Add:* 2256 N Middlecoff Dr Mesa AZ 85215. *Fax:* 313-764-4292; *E-Mail:* rdhanson@um.cc.umich.edu

HANSON, ROBERT JACK, microbiology; deceased, see previous edition for last biography

HANSON, ROGER BRIAN, marine microbiology, for more information see previous edition

HANSON, ROGER JAMES, MUSICAL ACOUSTICS, NUCLEAR SPECTROSCOPY. *Current Pos:* head, Dept Physics, 69-80, PROF PHYSICS, UNIV NORTHERN IOWA, 69- *Personal Data:* b Hutchinson, Minn, Oct 27, 27; m 50; c 4. *Educ:* Gustavus Adolphus Col, BS, 50; Univ Nebr, MA, 53, PhD(physics), 56. *Prof Exp:* From asst prof to prof physics, Grinnell Col, 56-69. *Concurrent Pos:* NSF fac fel, Harvard Univ, 61-62; res assoc, Inst Physics, Aarhus Univ, 66-67. *Mem:* Acoust Soc Am; Catgut Acoust Soc; Am Asn Physics Teachers; Sigma Xi. *Res:* Musical acoustics. *Mailing Add:* Dept Physics Univ Northern Iowa Cedar Falls IA 50614-0150

HANSON, ROGER WAYNE, BIOLOGY & CELL BIOLOGY, PHARMACOLOGY & PARASITOLOGY. *Current Pos:* from instr to assoc prof, Med Col, Univ Ala, Birmingham, 54-67, chmn, Div Natural Sci & Math, Univ Col, 67-73, prof pharmacol, Med Col & prof biol, Univ Col, 67-81, dean, Sch Natural Sci & Math, Univ Col, 73-81, dir & coordr curricula, Basic Allied Health Sci, 81-85, EMER PROF PHARMACOL & BIOL, UNIV ALA, 85- *Personal Data:* b Minn, Sept 3, 22; m 48, Bette R Johnson; c Heidi Ann & Eric R. *Educ:* Univ Iowa, BA, 46, MA, 48; Univ Calif, Los Angeles, PhD, 52. *Prof Exp:* Asst zool, Univ Iowa, 47-48; asst, Univ Calif, Los Angeles, 48-52; lectr biol, Univ Calif, Santa Barbara, 52-53. *Concurrent Pos:* NSF fel, Med Col, Univ Ala, Birmingham, 53-54, USPHS fel, 55-57; NIH fel, La State Univ Inter-Am Prog Trop Med, Cent Am, 61; vis assoc prof, Med Col, Univ Calif, San Francisco, 64-65; contract assoc prof, Sch Med, Univ Calif, San Francisco-AID Proj, Indonesia. *Mem:* Fel AAAS; Am Physiol Soc; Nat Sci Teachers Asn; Am Asn Allied Health Prof. *Res:* Intermediary metabolism and metabolic effect of endocrines and organic salivary secretions and mechanisms of salivation. *Mailing Add:* 2765 Hanover Circle Birmingham AL 35205

HANSON, ROLAND CLEMENTS, EXPERIMENTAL SOLID STATE PHYSICS. *Current Pos:* from asst prof to assoc prof, 66-76, PROF PHYSICS, ARIZ STATE UNIV, 77- *Personal Data:* b Moose Lake, Minn, Mar 23, 34; m 62; c 4. *Educ:* Mich Technol Univ, BS, 55; Univ Ill, MS, 56, PhD(physics), 60. *Prof Exp:* Asst prof physics, Reed Col, 60-63; res assoc eng physics, Cornell Univ, 63-66. *Concurrent Pos:* Guest scientist, Max Planck Inst Solid State Res, Stuttgart, WGer, 73-74. *Mem:* Am Phys Soc; Am Asn Physics Teachers. *Res:* Silver and copper halides; elastic constants; Raman scattering; high pressure; condensed gases. *Mailing Add:* Dept Physics Ariz State Univ PO Box 871504 Tempe AZ 85287. *Fax:* 602-965-7954

HANSON, RONALD LEE, BIOCHEMISTRY. *Current Pos:* sr res investr, 87-96, PRIN SCIENTIST, BRISTOL-MYERS SQUIBB, 96- *Personal Data:* b Lincoln, Nebr, Feb 2, 44. *Educ:* Univ Minn, BA, 65; Univ Wis, PhD(biochem), 70. *Prof Exp:* Asst prof biochem, Col Physicians & Surgeons, Columbia Univ, 72-79; mem sr sci staff, Sandoz Res Inst, 79-87. *Concurrent Pos:* NIH fel, Harvard Med Sch, 70-72. *Mem:* Am Soc Biochem & Molecular Biol; Am Chem Soc. *Res:* Biotransformation of organic compounds by enzymes and microbial cells; enzymology. *Mailing Add:* Bristol Myers Squibb One Squibb Dr New Brunswick NJ 08903

HANSON, TREVOR RUSSELL, interactive systems, programming environments, for more information see previous edition

HANSON, VIRGIL, MEDICINE. *Current Pos:* from asst prof to assoc prof, 60-73, PROF PEDIAT, SCH MED, UNIV SOUTHERN CALIF, 73- *Personal Data:* b Lima, Peru, June 30, 20; US citizen; m 43; c 2. *Educ:* Univ Calif, Los Angeles, BA, 42; Johns Hopkins Univ, MD, 45. *Prof Exp:* Resident pediat, Children's Hosp, Los Angeles, 50-52, chief resident, 52-53; pvt pract, Riverside, Calif, 53-56; instr pediat, Children's Hosp, Los Angeles, 56-57, asst clin prof, 57-60. *Concurrent Pos:* Consult, Calif State Dept Health, 54-60; Nat Found Congenital Defect Ctr, 62-63; Arthritis Found grant, 63-65. *Mem:* AAAS; Am Rheumatism Asn; Am Acad Pediat. *Res:* Rheumatology; rheumatic diseases in childhood. *Mailing Add:* Childrens Hosp Los Angeles 4650 Sunset Blvd Los Angeles CA 90027-6016

HANSON, WARREN DURWARD, plant genetics, quantitative genetics, for more information see previous edition

HANSON, WAYNE CARLYLE, WILDLIFE MANAGEMENT, RADIATION ECOLOGY. *Current Pos:* VPRES, HANSON ENVIRON RES SERV, 84- *Personal Data:* b Kennewick, Wash, Sept 5, 23; m 70, Mary Ann Moser; c Christian & Eric. *Educ:* Wash State Univ, BS, 49; Colo State Univ, MS, 71, PhD, 73. *Honors & Awards:* Arthur S Einarsen Award,

Wildlife Soc, 80. *Prof Exp:* Biol scientist, Biol Lab, Gen Elec Co, 49-61, sr scientist, 61-64; sr res scientist, Pac Northwest Lab, Battelle Mem Inst, 65-70; res asst, Colo State Univ, 70-73; alt group leader environ study group, Los Alamos Sci Lab, 73-78; sr scientist, Pac Northwest Lab, Battelle Mem Inst, 78-81; sr ecologist, Ertec Northwest Inc, 81-82; assoc, Dames & Moore Co, 82-84. *Mem:* Wildlife Soc; Ecol Soc Am; Am Soc Mammal; Am Ornith Union; Cooper Ornith Soc; Sigma Xi. *Res:* Radionuclide cycling in Arctic ecosystems; ecological implications and arctic resource development; biological monitoring. *Mailing Add:* 1902 Yew St Rd Bellingham WA 98226-8944

HANSON, WILLIAM A, ELECTRICAL ENGINEERING, SYSTEMS DESIGN. *Current Pos:* SR SYSTS ARCHITECT, IBM CORP. *Personal Data:* b Ft Rucker, Ala, Sept 27, 51. *Educ:* Rensselaer Polytech Inst, BS, 73, MS, 76. *Prof Exp:* Assoc programmer, Software Dept, IBM Corp, Oswego, NY, 76-78, staff engr, Systs Eng Develop Dept, 78, assoc engr, 78-82, staff engr, Adv Systs Eng Dept, 82, mem staff, Palo Alto Sci Ctr, 86-87, chief designer, Image Sci Appl Dept, 87-92; chief scientist high performance comput, Loral Fed Systs, 92- *Concurrent Pos:* Prin investr, NASA Landsat 4 & 5 Earth Observ Satellite Projs, 86-87, Sanford Univ, 87-92, Dartmouth Col, 87-92. *Mem:* Inst Elec & Electronics Engrs. *Res:* Design and implementation of the Computational Network Environment System; medical image processing on IBM mainframes; information theory; analysing earth observation data to study spruce trees stress syndrome supected to be caused by acid rain; author of numerous books articles and reviews on image processing. *Mailing Add:* IBM 6710 Rockledge Dr Bethesda MD 20817. *E-Mail:* hansonwa@lfs.loral.com

HANSON, WILLIAM BERT, planetary atmospheres, space science; deceased, see previous edition for last biography

HANSON, WILLIAM LEWIS, PARASITOLOGY, PROTOZOOLOGY. *Current Pos:* res assoc zool, 65-67, from asst prof to assoc prof vet path & parasitol, Sch Vet Med, 67-76, PROF PARASITOL, UNIV GA, 76-, HEAD DEPT, 74- *Personal Data:* b Rutledge, Ga, Mar 21, 31; m 63. *Educ:* Univ Ga, BS, 57, MS, 60, PhD(zool), 63. *Prof Exp:* Fel parasitol, Rutgers Univ, 63-65. *Mem:* Soc Protozool; Am Soc Parasitol; Am Soc Trop Med & Hyg. *Res:* Biology, morphology, physiology, immunology and taxonomy of Protozoa of the family Trypanosomatidae. *Mailing Add:* Dept Parasitol & Vet Med Univ Ga 1180 E Broad St Athens GA 30601-3040

HANSON, WILLIS DALE, FISH BIOLOGY. *Current Pos:* RETIRED. *Personal Data:* b Omaha, Nebr, July 23, 26; m 50; c 2. *Educ:* Univ Mo, AB, 54, MA, 56. *Prof Exp:* Fishery biologist, Mo Dept Conserv, 63-75, sr fisheries res biologist, 75- *Mem:* Am Fisheries Soc. *Res:* Fish population dynamics, water quality, habitat and environmental changes in small to large reservoirs; fish distribution, movement and production of small streams; creel census; recreational use studies; channel catfish studies. *Mailing Add:* 420 Hwy 124 Box No 436 Hallsville MO 65255

HANSROTE, CHARLES JOHNSON, JR, POLYMER CHEMISTRY, MEDICINAL CHEMISTRY. *Current Pos:* RETIRED. *Personal Data:* b Bowling Green, Md, Nov 22, 30; m 53, Melva Hardinger; c Charles 3rd. *Educ:* Va Mil Inst, BS, 52; Univ Richmond, MS, 55; Univ Va, PhD(chem), 58. *Honors & Awards:* Gene Wise Award, Blue Ridge Sect, Am Chem Soc, 91. *Prof Exp:* Asst instr chem, Va Mil Inst, 52-53; asst chem lab, Univ Va, 55-57; res chemist, E I du Pont de Nemours & Co, 58-62; from assoc prof to prof chem, Frostburg State Col, 62-65; chmn dept, Lynchberg Col, 70, 72-83 & 89, chmn phys sci & math, 82-92, prof chem, 65-96. *Concurrent Pos:* Vis prof, Va Commonwealth Univ, 68; Hopwood Scholars Prog, Lynchburg Col, 79, 82 & 89; curric consult, Lynchburg City Sch Sci Dept, 82. *Mem:* Am Chem Soc. *Res:* Tetrazolium compounds; schiff bases; reactions of diphenyl methylene norcamphor; amino acid uptake and release by larvae of American oyster crassostrea Virginica; detection of amino ethyl phosphoric acid in marine sediments; monomer preparation; polymer preparation; dyeing of yarns; physical testing of yarns; science education. *Mailing Add:* Lynchburg Col Lakeside Dr Lynchburg VA 24501

HANSSEN, GEORGE LYLE, OCEANOGRAPHY. *Current Pos:* SR SCIENTIST OCEANOG & METEOROL, SCI APPLICATIONS INT INC, 80- *Personal Data:* b Monticello, Iowa, Dec 19, 27; m 54; c 3. *Educ:* Okla State Univ, BS, 52. *Honors & Awards:* First Annual Sci & Eng Award, US Naval Oceanog Off, 74. *Prof Exp:* Meteorologist, US Navy Hydrographic Off, 52-55, oceanogr, 55-60; head forecaster, US Naval Oceanog Off, 60-71, proj mgr, Integrated Command Antisubmarine Warfare Prediction Syst & head, Environ Div, 71-78, liaison to Naval Air Systs Command, 78-80. *Mem:* Am Meteorol Asn; Am Geophys Union. *Res:* The development of the Integrated Command Antisubmarine Warfare Prediction System; the first real time numerical support system to use on-scene environmental data. *Mailing Add:* 14900 W Ridge Rd Accokeek MD 20607

HANSSON, CAROLYN M, concrete reinforcement corrosion, surface treatment & properties, for more information see previous edition

HANSSON, GORAN K, CARDIOVASCULAR DISEASES, CELLULAR IMMUNOLOGY. *Current Pos:* PROF CARDIOVASC RES, KAROLINSKA INST, 95- *Personal Data:* b Lysekil, Sweden, Nov 2, 51; m 73, Margareta; c Emil & Axel. *Educ:* Gothenburg Univ, MD, 77, PhD(cell biol), 80. *Honors & Awards:* Fernstrom Prize, 92. *Prof Exp:* Res assoc med, Gothenburg Univ, Sweden, 80-81; fel path, Univ Wash, 81-82; resident med, Sahlgren's Hosp, Gathenburg, 83-85; from asst prof to assoc prof, Lab Med, Gothenburg Univ, 85-95, sr scientist, Med Res Coun, 90-95, prof cell biol, 94-95. *Concurrent Pos:* Mem, Nobel Assembly, 97- *Mem:* Am Asn Pathologists; Int Soc Appl Vascular Biol; Scand Soc Immunol; Am Asn Immunol; Europ Vascular Biol Asn (secy, 95-). *Res:* Interactions between immune system and blood vessels; immunologic responses in cardiovascular diseases; cytokine effects on cell growth and metabolism; pathogenesis of altherosclerosis. *Mailing Add:* Ctr Molecular Med Korolinska Hosp Stockholm S-17176 Sweden. *Fax:* 46-8-313147; *E-Mail:* gkh@instmed.ks.se

HANTHORN, HOWARD E(UGENE), chemical engineering; deceased, see previous edition for last biography

HANTMAN, ROBERT GARY, MATERIALS & PROCESSES APPLICATION DEVELOPMENT, ENGINEERING TOOLS & TECHNIQUE DEVELOPMENT. *Current Pos:* mech engr fluid mech, Res & Develop Ctr, Gen Elec Corp, 78-82, liaison scientist, Res & Develop Ctr, 82-84, mgr advan mfg technol, GE Lighting Bus Group, 84-89, MGR APPLIANCE TECHNOLOGIES, GE APPLIANCES, 91- *Personal Data:* b New York, NY, Feb 9, 41; m 70, Susan Levesque; c Aaron & Daniel. *Educ:* Case Inst Technol, BS, 62, MS, 66; Case Western Res Univ, PhD(eng), 68. *Prof Exp:* Res engr turbomach, Pratt & Whitney Aircraft, United Technologies, 68-74; res engr energy conversion, Argonne Nat Labs, 74-77; eng mgr, STD Res Corp, 77-78; vpres biomech, Nat Ctr Mfg Sci, 89-91. *Mem:* Sigma Xi; Am Soc Mech Engrs; Soc Mfg Eng. *Res:* Material and process applications and test, including appropriate manufacturing technologies developments to support introduction of new technology into rpoduction of new products; development of broad-based computer-aided-engineering tools for use in design and manufacturing systems disciplines. *Mailing Add:* 2209 Whisperwood Dr Prospect KY 40059

HANTO, DOUGLAS W, SURGERY. *Current Pos:* ASSOC PROF SURG, UNIV CINCINNATI, 91- *Mailing Add:* Dept Surg Div Transplant Univ Cincinnati Col Med 231 Bethesda Ave Cincinnati OH 45267-0558. *Fax:* 513-558-3580

HANTON, JOHN PATRICK, ELECTRICAL ENGINEERING. *Current Pos:* From asst prof to assoc prof, 64-77, PROF ELEC ENG, MONT STATE UNIV, 77- *Personal Data:* b St Paul, Minn, Apr 5, 35. *Educ:* Univ Minn, BS, 57, MS, 59, PhD(elec eng), 64. *Concurrent Pos:* NSF res grant, 65-67. *Res:* Field of magnetic materials. *Mailing Add:* 9440 Hodgeman Canyon Dr Bozeman MT 59715

HANUKOGLU, ISRAEL, CYTOCHROME P FOUR HUNDRED FIFTY, MOLECULAR BIOLOGY. *Current Pos:* PROF BIOCHEM & MOLECULAR BIOL & HEAD, SOCIAL & LIFE SCI DIV, RES INST, COL JUDEA & SAMARIA, ISRAEL, 95- *Personal Data:* b Istanbul, Turkey, Mar 14, 52; Israeli citizen; m 96, Sarah Leitman; c Liora. *Educ:* Hebrew Univ Jerusalem, BA, 74; Univ Wis-Madison, MSc, 76, PhD(endocrinol-biochem), 80. *Honors & Awards:* Henri Gutwirth Award, Technion-Israel Inst Technol, 84; Hans Lindner Prize in Biochem Endocrinol, Israel Endocrine Soc, 88; Lubell Prize, Weizman Inst Sci, Sci Coun, 91. *Prof Exp:* Res asst, Univ Wis-Madison, 75-80; res fel & assoc molecular biol, Univ Chicago, 80-83; lectr biochem & molecular biol, Technion-Israel Inst Technol, 84-87, sr lectr, 86-87; sr scientist, Weizmann Inst Sci, 87-91, assoc prof biochem & molecular biol, 92-95. *Concurrent Pos:* Chmn, Int Symp Molecular View of Steroid Biosynthesis & Metab, 91; vchmn, Ninth Int Symp Microsomes & Drug Oxidations, 92; sci adv to Israeli Prime Minister, 96- *Mem:* Am Soc Biochem & Molecular Biol; Endocrine Soc; Israel Biochem Soc; Int Soc Study Xenobiotics. *Res:* Trophic hormone regulation of gene expression in steroidogenic tissues; structure, function analysis of cytochrome P450 system electron transport enzymes; molecular genetics of pseudohypoaldesteronism. *Mailing Add:* Res Inst Col Judea & Samaria Ariel 44837 Israel. *Fax:* 972-3-9640956; *E-Mail:* israel@research.yosh.ac.il

HANUMARA, RAMACHANDRA CHOUDARY, STATISTICS. *Current Pos:* from asst prof to assoc prof, 68-88, PROF STATISTICS, UNIV RI, 88- *Personal Data:* b Peyyeru, India, Aug 28, 37; m 68, Hilary Clancy; c Nevan. *Educ:* Univ Madras, BA, 56; Guzarat Univ India, MA, 58; Mich State Univ, MS, 62; Fla State Univ, PhD(statist), 68. *Prof Exp:* Res asst statist, Govt of India, 59-61; res asst, Mich State Univ, 61-63 & Fla State Univ, 63-68. *Mem:* Inst Math Statist; Am Statist Asn; Sigma Xi. *Res:* Theory and applications of statistics. *Mailing Add:* Dept Comp Sci Univ RI Tyler Hall Kingston RI 02881

HANUSA, TIMOTHY PAUL, MAIN GROUP CHEMISTRY, MATERIALS SYNTHESIS. *Current Pos:* Asst prof, 85-92, ASSOC PROF CHEM, VANDERBILT UNIV, 92- *Personal Data:* b Council Bluffs, Iowa, July 1, 56. *Educ:* Cornell Col, AB, 78; Ind Univ, PhD(chem), 83. *Mem:* AAAS; Am Chem Soc; fel Am Inst Chemists; NY Acad Sci; Sigma Xi. *Res:* Synthesis, structural characterization and reactivity studies of main group compounds of importance for materials and catalytic science; organometallic complexes of the heavy alkali and alkaline-earth metals; single crystal x-ray differaction studies. *Mailing Add:* Vanderbilt Univ Nashville TN 37235. *E-Mail:* hanvsat@ctrvax.vanderbilt.edu

HANWAY, DONALD GRANT, GENETICS, PLANT BREEDING & GENETICS. *Current Pos:* RETIRED. *Personal Data:* b Broadwater, Nebr, Aug 6, 18; m 42, Blanche E Larson; c Donald G Jr, Wayne E & Janice K (Jimenez). *Educ:* Univ Nebr, BSc, 42, MSc, 48; Iowa State Col, PhD, 54.

Honors & Awards: Honor Award, Soil Conserv Soc Am, 73; Agron Serv Award, Am Soc Agron, 82; Exten Educ Award, Am Soy Asn, 85. *Prof Exp:* From instr to prof agron, 48-76, chmn dept, 55-76, prof agron & extension crops specialist, Univ Nebr, 76-84. *Concurrent Pos:* Chief of party, AID-Univ Nebr group, Ataturk Univ, Turkey, 65-67; consult, agronomists & AID-Nebr prog, 68 & 70; coordr, Morocco Dryland Farming Prog, 80-82. *Mem:* Fel Am Acad Sci; fel Am Soc Agron; fel Crop Sci Soc Am; Am Inst Biol Sci; Soil Conserv Soc Am. *Res:* Soybean breeding; genetics; production practices; administration of research in crop breeding, crop production systems, soil and water conservation and soil science. *Mailing Add:* 6025 Madison Ave Lincoln NE 68507-2461

HANWAY, JOHN E(DGAR), JR, CHEMICAL ENGINEERING. *Current Pos:* PRES, JECON ENGRS, INC, 74- *Personal Data:* b Fairmont, WVa, May 14, 22; m 46. *Educ:* WVa Univ, BSChE, 49, MSChE, 51. *Prof Exp:* Asst, Eng Exp Sta, WVa Univ, 49-51; prin chem engr, Battelle Mem Inst, 51-57, asst div chief, 57-61, div chief, 61-65; dir eng, Copeland Process Corp, Ill, 65-67, vpres eng, 67-68; asst dir res, Chicago Bridge & Iron Co, 68-74. *Mem:* Am Inst Chem Engrs; Am Inst Mining, Metall & Petrol Engrs. *Res:* Waste effluent treatment; paper and pulp industry; non-ferrous extractive metallurgy; metallurgical and other applications of fluidized-bed reactor systems; chloride chemistry; design of chemical processing systems. *Mailing Add:* 13179 White River Trail Wautoma WI 54982

HANWAY, JOHN JOSEPH, SOILS. *Current Pos:* RETIRED. *Personal Data:* b Broadwater, Nebr, Dec 22, 20; m 43, Barbara Cary Baldwin; c Laurel (Kimball), John Jr, Rodney, Kevin, Craig, Bruce & Christopher. *Educ:* Univ Nebr, BS, 42, MS, 48; Iowa State Univ, PhD(soil fertility), 54. *Prof Exp:* Chemist & supvr explosives, E I du Pont de Nemours & Co, Okla, 42-45; asst soils, Univ Nebr, 45-50, from asst prof to assoc prof, 50-58; prof soils, Iowa State Univ, 58-85. *Concurrent Pos:* Sr officer, Joint FAO-IAEA Div, Int Atomic Energy Agency, Vienna, Austria, 66-68. *Mem:* Fel Am Soc Agron; Soil Sci Soc Am; Int Soc Soil Sci. *Res:* Soil chemistry and fertility; soil testing; plant analysis; soil-plant relations. *Mailing Add:* 215 Parkridge Circle Ames IA 50014

HANYSZ, EUGENE ARTHUR, electrical engineering, for more information see previous edition

HANZEL, ROBERT STEPHEN, ORGANIC CHEMISTRY, TEXTILE TECHNOLOGY. *Current Pos:* RETIRED. *Personal Data:* b Johnstown, Pa, July 18, 32; m 59; c 2. *Educ:* St Vincent Col, BS, 53; Univ Notre Dame, MS, 55, PhD(org chem), 60. *Prof Exp:* Res chemist, E I du Pont de Nemours & Co, 59-67, tech serv rep, 67-74, tech serv specialist, Textile Fibers Dept, 74-84, sr tech mkt specialist, 84-90. *Mem:* Am Chem Soc. *Res:* Textile fibers developments; textured fibers development in spandex elastomeic fibers and applications to fabric formation. *Mailing Add:* 336 Hampton Rd Wilmington DE 19803-2420

HANZELY, LASZLO, BOTANY, CYTOLOGY. *Current Pos:* PROF BIOL, NORTHERN ILL UNIV, 69- *Personal Data:* b Satoraljaujhely, Hungary, June 29, 39; US citizen; m 68; c 2. *Educ:* Colo State Univ, BS, 62, MS, 64; Southern Ill Univ, PhD(bot), 69. *Mem:* Electron Micros Soc Am; Bot Soc Am; Sigma Xi. *Res:* Ultrastructural plant anatomy and cytology. *Mailing Add:* Dept Biol Sci Northern Ill Univ De Kalb IL 60115

HANZELY, STEPHEN, PHYSICS. *Current Pos:* asst prof, Youngstown State Univ, 68-73, assoc prof, 73-80, chmn dept, 74-79, PROF, PHYSICS & ASTRON, YOUNGSTOWN STATE UNIV, 80-, DIR FAC REL, 93- *Personal Data:* b Satoraljaujhely, Hungary, Dec 30, 40; US citizen; m 62; c 2. *Educ:* Kent State Univ, BS, 62; Univ Toledo, MS, 64; NMex State Univ, MS, 67, PhD(physics), 69. *Prof Exp:* Owens-Ill Glass Co asst, Univ Toledo, 62-64; asst, NMex State Univ, 64-68, NASA asst, 67. *Concurrent Pos:* Fulbright fel, Hungary, 94. *Mem:* Am Inst Physics; Am Asn Physics Teachers; Sigma Xi; Am Phys Soc; Nat Educ Asn. *Res:* Study of x-ray emission spectra of the first series transition elements under threshold level excitation; x-ray spectroscopy. *Mailing Add:* Dept Physics & Astron Youngstown State Univ Youngstown OH 44555. *Fax:* 330-742-1579; *E-Mail:* fr080201@ysub.ysu.edu

HANZLIK, ROBERT PAUL, MEDICINAL CHEMISTRY. *Current Pos:* from asst prof to assoc prof, 71-79, PROF MED CHEM, UNIV KANS, 80- *Personal Data:* b Chicago, Ill, Nov 4, 43; m 65, Lois Anne Lang. *Educ:* Southern Ill Univ, BA, 66; Stanford Univ, PhD(org chem), 70. *Honors & Awards:* Sato Mem Int Award, FAES & Pharmaceut Soc Japan, 90. *Prof Exp:* NATO res fel & US Hon Ramsay Mem fel, Cambridge Univ, 70-71. *Concurrent Pos:* Mem, Bioorg & Natural Prods Study Sect, NIH, 87-91. *Mem:* AAAS; Royal Soc Chem; Am Chem Soc; Soc Toxicol; Int Soc Study Xenobiotics (pres, 96-97). *Res:* Drug metabolism; biochemical toxicology; enzyme mechanisms and inhibition; drug design. *Mailing Add:* Dept Med Chem Univ Kans Lawrence KS 66045-2506. *Fax:* 785-864-5326

HAO, JIANXIU, EFFICIENT ALGORITHMS DEVELOPMENT, GEOGRAPHIC INFORMATION SYSTEMS. *Current Pos:* Sr mem tech staff, 89-92, PRIN MEM TECH STAFF, GTE LABS, 93- *Personal Data:* b Hebei, China, May 20, 57; m 82; c 2. *Educ:* Univ Sci & Technol, Beijing, BS, 82; Columbia Univ, MS, 85, MPhil, 86, PhD(opers res), 89. *Res:* Develop efficient algorithms for routing, scheduling, combinatorial optimization and geographic information systems; algorithms adapted to real software systems. *Mailing Add:* GTE Labs 40 Sylvan Rd Waltham MA 02254. *Fax:* 781-890-9320; *E-Mail:* jhao@gte.com

HAO, OLIVER J, WASTE WATER MANAGEMENT. *Current Pos:* from asst prof to assoc prof, 82-94, PROF ENVIRON ENG, UNIV MD, 94- *Personal Data:* b China, May 11, 46; US citizen; m 79, Cathy C Tang; c Melissa & Christina. *Educ:* Cheng Kung Univ, Taiwan, BS, 68; Colo State Univ, MS, 71; Univ Calif, Berkeley, PhD, 82. *Prof Exp:* Dir res, Sieco Inc, 73-78. *Concurrent Pos:* Assoc ed, JEE, Am Soc Civil Engrs, 90- & Critical Rev Environ Sci & Technol, 97- *Mem:* Water Environ Fedn; Am Water Works Asn; fel Am Soc Civil Engrs; Int Asn Water Qual; Am Acad Environ Engrs. *Res:* Biological wastewater treatment. *Mailing Add:* Dept Civil Eng Univ Md College Park MD 20742. *Fax:* 301-405-2585; *E-Mail:* ojhl@eng.umd.edu

HAPAI, MARLENE NACHBAR, ECOLOGY, BIOLOGICAL CONTROL. *Current Pos:* teacher & curric writer physiol & entom, Manoa, Univ Hawaii, 79-82, researcher ecol, Natural Energy Inst, Manoa, 85-86, instr biol & ecol, Hawaii Community Col, 82-86, asst prof biol sci educ, 86-89, asst dir, Ctr Gifted & Talented Native Hawaiian Children, 89-92, ASSOC PROF BIOL SCI EDUC, UNIV HAWAII, HILO & MANOA, 89-, COORDR, NATURAL SCI MAJOR & NATURAL SCI CERT PROG. *Personal Data:* b Honokaa, Hawaii, July 19, 48; m 72, Archie III; c Archie IV & Alicia M. *Educ:* Gonzaga Univ, BA, 70; Univ Hawaii, Manoa, MS, 77, PhD(entom), 81. *Honors & Awards:* Frances Davis Mem Award, Univ Hawaii, 85. *Prof Exp:* Teacher biol, physiol & earth sci, Kohala High Sch, 70-76; teacher biol & chem, Hilo High Sch, 78-79. *Mem:* Entom Soc Am; Sigma Xi; AAAS; Nat Sci Teachers Asn; Nat Asn Gifted Children. *Res:* Insect cecidogenesis; biological science curriculum; acid precipitation; physiology; science education. *Mailing Add:* Univ Hawaii Natural Sci Div 200 W Kawila St Hilo HI 96720-4053. *Fax:* 808-933-3693

HAPKE, BERN, NUCLEAR MEDICINE. *Current Pos:* SR CHEMIST NUCLEAR MED, 3M CO, 73- *Personal Data:* b Berlin, Ger, June 4, 43; US citizen. *Educ:* Univ Ill, BSc, 65; Univ Mich, MS, 68, PhD(med chem), 70. *Prof Exp:* Fel, Northwestern Univ, 70-73. *Mem:* AAAS; Soc Nuclear Med. *Res:* Diagnostic procedures in medicine; nuclear medical diagnosis and in vitro radioassays. *Mailing Add:* 7590 62nd St N St Paul MN 55115

HAPKE, BRUCE W, PLANETARY SCIENCES, REMOTE SENSING. *Current Pos:* assoc prof, 67-76, PROF GEOL & PLANETARY SCI, UNIV PITTSBURGH, 77- *Personal Data:* b Racine, Wis, Feb 17, 31; m 54, Joyce Zellinger; c Kevin, Jeffrey & Cheryl. *Educ:* Univ Wis, BS, 53; Cornell Univ, PhD(eng physics), 62. *Prof Exp:* Sr res assoc astrophys, Cornell Univ, 60-67. *Concurrent Pos:* Chair, Div Planetary Sci, Am Astron Soc, 88-89; res assoc, Carnegie Mus Natural Hist, Pittsburgh, Pa; consult, NASA. *Mem:* AAAS; Am Astron Soc; Fel Am Geophys Union; Int Astron Union. *Res:* Nature and origin of planets; nature of planetary surfaces; theory of scattering and emission of electromagnetic radiation from planetary surfaces. *Mailing Add:* Dept Geol & Planetary Sci Univ Pittsburgh Pittsburgh PA 15260. *Fax:* 412-624-8876; *E-Mail:* hapke@vms.cis.pitt.edu

HAPNER, KENNETH D, BIOCHEMISTRY. *Current Pos:* from asst prof to assoc prof, 69-84, PROF CHEM, MONT STATE UNIV, 84- *Personal Data:* b Goshen, Ind, May 7, 39; m 66; c 2. *Educ:* Ind Univ, Indianapolis, PhD(biochem), 66. *Prof Exp:* NIH fel, Sch Med, Ind Univ, Indianapolis, 65-66 & Univ Wash, 66-67; actg asst prof biochem, Univ Wash, 67-69. *Concurrent Pos:* Res grants, Agr Exp Sta, 69 & 74, USDA, 76 & NSF, 78, 85. *Mem:* Am Soc Biochem & Molecular Biol; Entom Soc Am; Soc Invert Path. *Res:* Structural and functional roles of amino acids, proteins, and enzymes; isolation and characterization of naturally occurring proteinase inhibitors; protein primary structure; affinity chromatography; phytohemagglutinins; insect agglutinins, immunology; molecular cloning; DNA sequence. *Mailing Add:* Dept Chem Mont State Univ Bozeman MT 59717

HAPP, GEORGE MOVIUS, INSECT PHYSIOLOGY, DEVELOPMENTAL BIOLOGY. *Current Pos:* interim vprovost, 90-91, PROF ZOOL & CHMN DEPT, UNIV VT, 78- *Personal Data:* b St Louis, Mo, May 18, 36. *Educ:* Principia Col, BS, 58; Cornell Univ, PhD(animal physiol), 64. *Prof Exp:* Asst prof biol, Cath Univ Am, 65-67; from asst prof to assoc prof, NY Univ, 67-72; from assoc prof to prof zool & entom, Colo State Univ, 72-78. *Concurrent Pos:* NIH fel, 64-65. *Mem:* AAAS; Entom Soc Am; Am Soc Cell Biol; Am Soc Zool; Int Soc Develop Biol. *Res:* Insect endocrinology and reproductive development; histochemistry, ultrastructure and development of exocrine glands. *Mailing Add:* Dept Zool Marsh Life Sci Univ Vt Burlington VT 05405-0001

HAPP, HARVEY HEINZ, APPLIED MATHEMATICS, OPERATIONS RESEARCH. *Current Pos:* CONSULT, NY STATE DEPT PUB SERV, 88- *Personal Data:* b Berlin, Ger, June 27, 28; US citizen; m 51, Ruth Hollander; c Deborah (Yablon) & Sandra (Klein). *Educ:* Ill Inst Technol, BSEE, 53; Rensselaer Polytech Inst, MEE, 58; Univ Belgrade, DSc(appl sci), 62. *Prof Exp:* Engr, High Voltage Lab, Gen Elec Co, 54-56, anal engr, Elec Utility Eng Oper, 56-68, sr engr, 68-72, mgr, Anal Eng Serv, 72-77, mgr, Advan Syst Technol, 77-82, mgr, Syst Anal, 82-87; consult, 87-88. *Concurrent Pos:* Lectr various cols & univs; co-founder, Power Syst Computations Conf, 62. *Mem:* Fel Inst Elec & Electronics Engrs; Power Syst Computations Conf; Tensor Soc Gt Brit (vpres, 73-); Conf Int Des Grands Reseaux Electriques; Sigma Xi. *Res:* Basic understanding of new and advanced technologies for power system analysis and synthesis and incorporate the use of these technologies to benefit electric utilities and consumers of electric energy; author of numerous books and contributor to numerous articles and book reviews to professional journals, chapters to technical books. *Mailing Add:* 2211 Webster Dr Niskayuna NY 12309

HAPPEL, JOHN, CATALYSIS, PROCESS ECONOMICS. *Current Pos:* PRES, CATALYSIS RES CORP, 73- *Personal Data:* b New York, NY, Apr 1, 08; m 51, Dorothy Merriam; c 3. *Educ:* Mass Inst Technol, BS, 29, MS, 30; Polytech Inst NY, PhD(chem), 48. *Honors & Awards:* Founders Award, Am Inst Chem Engrs, 87. *Prof Exp:* Chem engr, Mobil Oil Corp, 30-48; prof, 48-72, EMER PROF CHEM ENG, NEW YORK UNIV, 72- *Concurrent Pos:* Spec res assoc chem eng, Columbia Univ, 73- *Mem:* Nat Acad Eng; NY Acad Sci; Am Chem Soc; Am Inst Chem Engrs. *Res:* Development of catalysts and catalytic processes, especially as related to petrochemicals and energy; chemical process economics; fluid-solid dynamics. *Mailing Add:* 69 Tompkins Ave Hastings-on-Hudson NY 10706. *Fax:* 914-478-2549

HAPPEL, LEO THEODORE, JR, NEUROPHYSIOLOGY. *Current Pos:* Instr, 72-74, ASST PROF PHYSIOL, NEUROL & NEUROSURG, LA STATE UNIV MED CTR, NEW ORLEANS, 74- *Personal Data:* b New Orleans, La, Aug 5, 43; m 66; c 2. *Educ:* Tulane Univ, BS, 66, MS, 70; La State Univ Med Ctr, New Orleans, PhD(physiol), 72. *Mem:* Soc Neurosci. *Res:* Spinal cord; computer analysis of bioelectric potentials; pain; stroke. *Mailing Add:* La State Univ Sch Med 1542 Tulane Ave New Orleans LA 70112-2825

HAPPER, WILLIAM, JR, ATOMIC PHYSICS. *Current Pos:* prof, 80-93, PROF PHYSICS, PRINCETON UNIV, 93- *Personal Data:* b Vellore, India, July 27, 39; US citizen; m 67, Barbara Baker; c James & Gladys. *Educ:* Univ NC, BSc, 60; Princeton Univ, PhD(physics), 64. *Honors & Awards:* Alexander von Humboldt Award, 75; Broida Prize, 97. *Prof Exp:* Res physicist, Columbia Univ, 64-65, from instr to prof, Radiation Lab, 65-80, dir, 71-78; prof, Princeton Univ, 80-91; dir, Off Energy Res, US Dept Energy, 91-93. *Concurrent Pos:* Sloan fel, 66-; trustee, Mitre Corp, 88- *Mem:* Nat Acad Sci; fel Am Phys Soc; Am Acad Arts & Sci; AAAS. *Res:* Atomic beams; optical double resonance and level crossing spectroscopy; optically pumped microwave masers; laser spectroscopy; spin polarized atoms and nuclei; medical imaging with laser-polarized noblegases. *Mailing Add:* 559 Riverside Dr Princeton NJ 08540. *Fax:* 609-258-2496; *E-Mail:* happer@pupgg.princeton.edu

HAQ, BILAL U, ENVIRONMENTAL SCIENCE, EARTH & MARINE SCIENCE. *Current Pos:* DIR MARINE GEOL & GEOPHYSICS PROG, NSF, 88- *Personal Data:* US citizen. *Educ:* Panjab Univ, Pakistan, BS, 61, MS, 63; Univ Stockholm, Sweden, PhD(marine geol), 67, DSc, 72. *Prof Exp:* Lectr paleont, Panjab Univ, Pakistan, 63-64; UNESCO res assoc micropaleont, Geol Surv Austria, 64-65; res fellow, Swed Int Develop Agency, Univ Stockholm, Sweden, 66-70; asst & assoc scientist, Woods Hole Oceanog Inst, 70-82; sr res specialist, 82-84, res assoc, Exxon Prod Res Co, 84-88. *Concurrent Pos:* Adj docent, Univ Stockholm, 72-; co-chief scientist, Deep Sea Drilling Proj, 73; chief ed, Marine Micropaleont J, 76-90; vis res scientist, Soc Nat Elf, Aquitaine, France, 78-79; vis scholar, Univ Paris, 79; assoc ed, Micropaleont, Am Mus Natural Hist, 80-; mem, Geophys Study Comt, Nat Res Coun, Nat Acad Sci; chmn subcomt oceans non-living resources, Int Union Geol Sci/Comn Marine Geol; coordr, environ issue, Exxon Prod Res Co, 86-88; mem guiding group, experts ocean resources, UNESCO, co-chief scientist, Ocean Drilling Prog, 88; distinguished lectr, Am Asn Petrol Geologists, 88-89; vis prof, Univ Copenhagen, Denmark, 91-92; mem, UK Natural Environ Res Coun vis comn Brit Geol Surv, 91; off mgt & budget, White House, 92-93; World Bank, 93; sr exec, Serv Selectee Prog, 93. *Mem:* Fel Geol Soc Am; Am Geophys Union; AAAS; Am Asn Petrol Geol; Geol Soc Sweden; fel Geol Soc London; Oceanog Soc. *Res:* Marine geology and geophysics; biostratigraphy; paleobiogeography; paleoceanography; petroleum geology; paleontology; global stratigraphy; global change. *Mailing Add:* 6128 Massachusetts Ave Bethesda MD 20816

HAQ, M SAFIUL, MATHEMATICAL STATISTICS. *Current Pos:* asst prof math, 67-70, assoc prof, 70-80, PROF STATIST, UNIV WESTERN ONT, 80- *Personal Data:* b Bangladesh, Feb 1, 35; Can citizen; m 73, Sitara Begum; c Khaledul, Shahnaz & Mahbubal. *Educ:* Univ Dhaka, BSc, 54, MSc, 55; Univ Toronto, MA, 64, PhD(math), 66. *Prof Exp:* Statistician II, Food & Agr Coun Pakistan, Karachi, 56-58, statistician I, Agr Census, 58-59; lectr statist, Univ Dhaka, 59-60; dep dir statist, Small Industs Corp, Bangladesh, 60-62; sr lectr, Rajshahi Univ, 62-67. *Mem:* Inst Math Statist; fel Royal Statist Soc; Statist Soc Can; Int Statist Inst. *Res:* Predicitive inference; multivariate statistical analysis; marginal likelihood inference. *Mailing Add:* Dept Statist & Actuarial Sci Univ Western Ont London ON N6A 5B7 Can

HAQUE, RIZWANUL, ENVIRONMENTAL CHEMISTRY, ENVIRONMENTAL TOXICOLOGY. *Current Pos:* PRES & CHIEF EXEC OFFICER, ASCI CORP, 86- *Personal Data:* b India, Dec 15, 40; m 69; c 1. *Educ:* Aligarh Muslim Univ, India, MS, 59; Univ BC, PhD(chem), 66. *Prof Exp:* From asst prof to assoc prof agr chem, Ore State Univ, 66-74; US Environ Protection Agency, 74-86. *Mem:* Am Chem Soc; fel Am Inst Chem; Sigma Xi; AAAS; Soc Environ Toxicol & Chem. *Res:* Physical chemistry and its application to environmental problems; transport and fate of toxic substances; modeling, regulation, exposure assessment and hazard assessment of toxic chemicals; pesticide chemistry; hazardous waste. *Mailing Add:* ASCI Corp 1365 Beverly Rd McLean VA 22101-3603

HARA, SABURO, PEDIATRICS, HEMATOLOGY. *Current Pos:* from instr to assoc prof pediat, 59-71, asst proj dir, 63-64, co-dir res lab ment retardation demonstration clin, 66-69, PROF PEDIAT, MEHARRY MED COL, 71-, DIR, DIAG & TRAINING LAB, 69- *Personal Data:* b Yamanashi, Japan, Feb 16, 28; US citizen; m 58; c 1. *Educ:* Tokyo Med Col, MD, 53; Am Bd Pediat, dipl. *Prof Exp:* Intern, Bronson Methodist Hosp, Kalamazoo, Mich, 55; resident pediat, Res & Educ Hosp, Univ Ill, 58, asst, Col Med, 58-59. *Concurrent Pos:* Res fel pediat & hemat, Univ Ill Col Med, 59. *Mem:* Fel Am Acad Pediat; Am Soc Human Genetics. *Res:* Medical and clinical science; human genetics. *Mailing Add:* Dept Pediat Meharry Med Col Sch Med 1005 Dr DB Todd Blvd Nashville TN 37208-3501

HARA, TOSHIAKI J, GENERAL BIOLOGY, GENERAL PHYSIOLOGY. *Current Pos:* res scientist, 69-96, EMER RES SCIENTIST, FRESHWATER INST, CAN DEPT FISHERIES & OCEANS, 97- *Personal Data:* b Kumamoto, Japan, Aug 22, 32; m 59, Shizuko Ukai; c Ryo. *Educ:* Yokohama Munic Univ, BS, 56; Univ Tokyo, MS, 58, PhD(zool), 63. *Prof Exp:* NIH fels, Columbia Univ, 63 & Univ Wash, 63-66; instr physiol, Med Sch, Kumamoto Univ, 67-69. *Concurrent Pos:* Adj prof zool, Univ Man, 78- *Mem:* Soc Neurosci; Asn Chemoreception Sci. *Res:* Neurobiological study of chemosensory, olfactory and gustatory, processes in fishes and its application to aquaculture and environmental pollution researches. *Mailing Add:* Dept Fisheries & Oceans Freshwater Inst Winnipeg MB R3T 2N6 Can. *Fax:* 204-984-6587; *E-Mail:* thara@cc.umanitoba.ca

HARACZ, RICHARD DANIEL, EDUCATIONAL SCIENCE & ENGINEERING. *Current Pos:* Head, Dept Physics & Atmospheric Sci, 89-96, PROF, DREXEL UNIV, 67-, ASSOC PROVOST RES & GRAD STUDIES, 96- *Personal Data:* m, Eleanor; c Richard Jr & Robert. *Educ:* Wayne State Univ, BS, 60, MS, 61, PhD(physics), 64. *Mem:* Am Phys Soc. *Res:* Quantum Field Theory and nuclear forces; atomic scattering; scattering of electromagnetic radiation by nonspherical dielectric particles. *Mailing Add:* 216 Morlyn Ave Bryn Mawr PA 19010. *Fax:* 215-895-1056; *E-Mail:* haraczrd@duvm.ocs.drexel.edu

HARAGAN, DONALD ROBERT, ATMOSPHERIC SCIENCE, HYDROLOGY & WATER RESOURCES. *Current Pos:* from asst prof to prof atmospheric sci, Tex Tech Univ, 69-82, chmn dept, 72-82, assoc dean, A&S, 82-85, interim vpres, 85-87, vpres acad affairs & res, 86-89, EXEC VPRES & PROVOST, TEX TECH UNIV, 89- *Personal Data:* b Houston, Tex, Apr 15, 36; m 66; c 2. *Educ:* Univ Tex, Austin, BS, 59, PhD(atmospheric sci), 70; Tex A&M Univ, MS, 60. *Prof Exp:* Res scientist meteorol, Tex A&M Univ, 59-60; res scientist meteorol, Elec Eng Res Lab, Univ Tex, Austin, 60-66, instr, 62-69. *Concurrent Pos:* Res grants, US Dept of Interior, Tex Dept Water Resources & Int Ctr Study Arid & Semi-arid Lands, 70- *Mem:* Am Meteorol Soc; AAAS; Am Water Res Asn; Am Soc Civil Eng. *Res:* Physics and dynamics of severe storms; cloud physics and atmospheric water resources; precipitation processes; clouds and precipitation in arid and semi-arid environments. *Mailing Add:* 6914 Nashville Dr Lubbock TX 79413

HARAKAL, CONCETTA, PHARMACOLOGY. *Current Pos:* From instr to assoc prof, 62-76, PROF PHARMACOL, SCH MED, TEMPLE UNIV, 76- *Personal Data:* b Chieti, Italy, Nov 25, 23; US citizen; m 48. *Educ:* Univ Pa, AB, 45; Temple Univ, MS, 50, PhD(pharmacol), 62. *Honors & Awards:* Sowell Award, Temple Univ Sch Med, 79, 90; Lindbach Award, Temple Univ, 80. *Mem:* AAAS; Am Soc Pharmacol & Exp Therapeut; Am Heart Asn; NY Acad Sci; Sigma Xi. *Res:* Cardiovascular and renal pharmacology; hemodynamic effects of adrenalectomy; medical education; effect of drugs on vascular smooth muscle. *Mailing Add:* Dept Pharmacol Temple Univ Sch Med Philadelphia PA 19140

HARAKAS, N(ICHOLAS) KONSTANTINOS, CHEMICAL ENGINEERING, BIOCHEMICAL ENGINEERING. *Current Pos:* BIOTECHNOL CONSULT, HARAKAS TECHNE, INC, 94- *Personal Data:* b Karyai, Greece, July 15, 34; US citizen; m 63; c Dean & George. *Educ:* Clemson Univ, BS, 58; NC State Univ, MS, 60, PhD(chem eng), 62. *Prof Exp:* Res chem engr, Am Cyanamid Co, 62-63; res chem engr, Chemstrand Res Ctr, Inc, 63-69, group leader, Monsanto Co, 69-73, sr res specialist, 73-77, sr res group leader, 77-88, biotech consult, 88-94. *Concurrent Pos:* Monsanto vis scientist, Med Ctr, Univ Ala, Birmingham, 75-76; affil prof, Chem Eng Dept, Washington Univ, St Louis, Mo, 90- *Mem:* Am Inst Chem Engrs; Am Chem Soc. *Res:* Heat transfer to particulate solids; synthetic fiber spinning and morphology; polymerization, fiber reinforced composites; epoxy resins; thermodynamics of steel refining; inviscid melt spinning of steel; gas carburization of steel sheet; crystallization of steel sheet; steel tire cord adhesion; phosphate conversion coatings; silane coupling agents; mammalian cell culture technology; protein fractionation; construction and operation of recombinant DNA facilities; fibrinolysis and hemostasis; cellular immunology; neovascularization; monoclonal antibodies; industrial scale mammalian cell culture facilities operation; growth factors; diagnostics; bone healing; biospecific affiniity chromatography. *Mailing Add:* Harakas Techne Inc 15611 Sugar Lake Ct Chesterfield MO 63017-5217

HARALICK, ROBERT M, ELECTRICAL ENGINEERING. *Current Pos:* BOEING CLAIRMONT EGTVEDT PROF ELEC ENG & ADJ PROF COMPUT SCI, UNIV WASH, 86-, ADJ PROF CTR BIOENG, 88- *Personal Data:* b Brooklyn, NY, Sept 30, 43; m 93, Ihsin T Phillips; c 1. *Educ:* Univ Kans, BA, 64, BS, 66, MS, 67, PhD(elec eng), 69. *Honors & Awards:* Young Outstanding Fac Award, Dow Chem, Am Eng Educ, 75. *Prof Exp:* From asst prof to assoc prof, Univ Kans, 69-75, prof elec eng & adj prof comput sci, 75-78; prof elec eng & comput sci, Va Polytech Inst & State Univ, 79-84; vpres res, Mach Vision Int, 84-86. *Concurrent Pos:* Assoc ed, Comput Vision, Graphics & Image Processing, 75-93, Pattern Recognition, 77-93, IEEE Trans Systs, Man & Cybernet, 79-88, Commun ACM Image Processing, 82-92; mem, Comput Soc Pattern Anal Mach Intel & Tech Comt, Inst Elec & Electronics Engrs, 75-, Pattern Recognition Tech Subcomt, 75-81, Data Struct & Pattern Recognition Subcomt, 75-81, Biomed Pattern Recognition Comt, 75-81, prog comt, Pattern Recognition & Image Processing Conf, 78; co-dir, Advan Study Inst Imaging Processing, NATO, 78, co-chair, 80, dir, Advan Study Inst Pictorial Data Anal, 82. *Mem:* Fel Inst Elec & Electronics Engrs; Soc Gen Systs Res; Pattern Recognition Soc; Asn Comput Mach; Am Asn Artificial Intel; Inst Elec & Electronics Engrs Comput Soc; Acoustics Signals & Speech Processing Soc; Systems Man & Cybernet Soc. *Res:* Pattern recognition; clustering techniques as well as discrimination techniques, particularly as they apply to image patterns; general systems research and scene analysis; artificial intelligence; computer vision; author of 4 books, 36 book chapters, 132 journal articles and 176 conference papers. *Mailing Add:* Dept Elec Eng Univ Wash Seattle WA 98195. *Fax:* 206-543-3842; *E-Mail:* haralick@ee.washington.edu

HARAMAKI, CHIKO, ORNAMENTAL HORTICULTURE, WEED SCIENCE. *Current Pos:* Asst prof hort, 57-68, from assoc prof to prof ornamental hort, 68-86, EMER PROF ORNAMENTAL HORT, PA STATE UNIV, 86- *Personal Data:* b Hayward, Calif, Oct 3, 25. *Educ:* Ore State Col, BS, 52; Univ Ill, MS, 53; Ohio State Univ, PhD(hort), 57. *Concurrent Pos:* Assoc exp sta, Univ Calif, Riverside, 70-71; vis prof, Univ Peradeniya, Sri Lanka, 85. *Mem:* AAAS; Am Soc Hort Sci; NY Acad Sci; Int Soc Hort Sci; Int Plant Propagators Soc; Sigma Xi. *Res:* Herbicides; asexual propagation of ornamental plants; arboriculture; tissue culture. *Mailing Add:* 7012 Seventh Ave Blvd NW Bradenton FL 34209-1547

HARAMATI, AVIAD, RENAL PHYSIOLOGY, MEDICAL EDUCATION. *Current Pos:* from asst prof to assoc prof physiol, 85-92, assoc prof med, 90-92, PROF PHYSIOL & MED, GEORGETOWN UNIV SCH MED, 92-, DIR EDUC PHYSIOL, 95- *Personal Data:* b Jerusalem, Israel, Jan 25, 54; US citizen. *Educ:* Brooklyn Col, BS, 75; Univ Cincinnati, PhD(physiol), 79. *Honors & Awards:* Day Mem Rgs Award, Nat Kidney Found. *Prof Exp:* Asst prof physiol, Mayo Clin, 82-85. *Mem:* Am Physiol Soc; Am Soc Nephrol; Int Soc Nephrol; Nat Kidney Found; Endocrine Soc; Asn Am Med Coll. *Res:* Understanding the role of the kidneys in regulating water and electrolyte homeostasis during growth and in pathophysiological stages such as heart failure. *Mailing Add:* Dept Physiol & Biophys Georgetown Univ Sch Med 3900 Reservoir Rd NW Washington DC 20007-2187. *E-Mail:* haramata@gunet.georgetown.edu

HARARI, HAIM, PHYSICS. *Current Pos:* Assoc prof, 67-70, ANNENBERG PROF HIGH ENERGY PHYSICS, WEIZMANN INST SCI, 70-, PRES, 88- *Personal Data:* b Jerusalem, Israel; m 61, Aviva Levidov; c Ayelet, Sharon & Guri. *Educ:* Hebrew Univ, MS, 61, PhD, 65. *Hon Degrees:* PhD, Ben Gurion Univ, 87, Univ Bordeaux, 93. *Honors & Awards:* Rothschild Prize Physics, Jerusalem, 76; Israel Prize, Exact Scis. *Concurrent Pos:* Vis prof, Stanford Univ, Harvard Univ, Cornell Univ, Rockefeller Univ, Univ Calif, Berkeley, Hebrew Univ, Fermi Nat Lab & Europ Res Ctr Particle Physics; mem, Coun Higher Educ, Israel, 75-85, Nat Coun Res & Develop, 82-90; hon fel, Open Univ, Tel Aviv, 95. *Mem:* Israel Acad Scis & Humanities. *Mailing Add:* Weizmann Inst Sci P O Box 26 76100 Rehovot Israel

HARARY, FRANK, EDUCATING THE GIFTED, DISCOVERING NEW RESEARCH TOPICS. *Current Pos:* DISTINGUISHED PROF COMPUTER SCI, NMEX STATE UNIV, LAS CRUCES, 86- *Personal Data:* b New York, NY, Mar 11, 21. *Educ:* Brooklyn Col, BA, 41, MA, 45; Univ Calif, Berkeley, PhD(math), 48. *Hon Degrees:* DSc & MSc, Univ Aberdeen, Scotland, 75; Fil Dr, Univ Lund, Sweden, 78; DSc, Univ Exer, Eng, 92. *Honors & Awards:* C E Cullis Mem Lectr, Calcutta Math Soc, 86; R N Prasad Mem Lectr, Allahabad Math Soc, 86. *Prof Exp:* Prof math, Univ Mich, Ann Arbor, 48-86. *Concurrent Pos:* Vis prof & lectr, numerous foreign & US univs & socs, 57-; founding ed, J Combinatorial Theory, 66- & J Graph Theory, 77-; vis fel, Wolfsen Col, Oxford Univ, 73-74; scientist-in-residence, NY Acad Sci, 77; Humboldt sr US scientist award, Munich, 78; overseas fel, Churchill Col, Cambridge Univ, 80-81; Ulam chair math, Univ Colo, 82; res prof, Stevens Inst Technol, 84; distinguished vis prof, Indian Statist Inst, Calcutta, 86. *Mem:* Am Math Soc; Can Math Soc; Math Asn Am; Soc Indust & Appl Math. *Res:* Graph theory applications to computer science, chemistry, mechanical engineering, geography, social networks, mathematical games, pedagogy, knot theory and group theory; author of seven books, almost 700 publications.. *Mailing Add:* Computer Sci Dept NMex State Univ Las Cruces NM 88003-0105

HARARY, ISAAC, BIOCHEMISTRY. *Current Pos:* asst prof biol chem, biophys & nuclear med, 58-60, assoc prof, 60-64, PROF BIOL CHEM, SCH MED, UNIV CALIF, LOS ANGELES, 64- *Personal Data:* b New York, NY, Mar 15, 23; m 48; c 1. *Educ:* Brooklyn Col, BA, 45; NY Univ, PhD(biochem), 52. *Prof Exp:* Asst dir radioisotope unit, Vet Admin Hosp, Calif, 55-58. *Concurrent Pos:* Am Cancer Soc fel, Univ Chicago, 52-54; NIH fel, 54-55. *Mem:* Am Chem Soc; Am Soc Biol Chem. *Res:* Enzymology and intermediary metabolism; carbon dioxide fixation; cholesterol synthesis; metabolism of nicotinic acid and acetoin in bacteria; control of glycolysis; acyl phosphates and thyroxin action; enzymes of cellular differentiation; control of specific function and protein synthesis in developing heart cells in culture. *Mailing Add:* Dept Biol-Chem Univ Calif Los Angeles Sch Med 900 Veteran Ave Los Angeles CA 90024-2703

HARB, JOSEPH MARSHALL, CELL BIOLOGY, DIAGNOSTIC ELECTRON MICROSCOPY. *Current Pos:* ASSOC PROF PEDIAT, MED COL WIS-MILWAUKEE, 81- *Personal Data:* b Oakland, Calif, Dec 20, 38; m 72; c 1. *Educ:* Oglethorpe Univ, BS, 61; Tulane Univ, MS, 66, PhD(biol), 69. *Prof Exp:* Tech res specialist cell biol, Tulane Univ, 63-69, instr med, Cardiovascular Lab, Med Sch, 69-72, asst prof med, Cardiovasc Lab, Med Ctr, Tulane Univ, 72-76; dir, Electron Micros Lab, Vet Admin Hosp, 76-80; dir, Electron Micros Serv, Children's Hosp Wis, 80- *Concurrent Pos:* Consult, Dept Path Electron Micros, Delta Regional Primate Ctr, 65; USPHS fel, Tulane Univ, 73-75; adj instr path, Wayne State Med Sch, 76-80; planning & exec comt, Vet Admin Coop Study No 147, 80-; adj instr, Anat Dept, Univ Detroit Sch Med, 80-; ed, Electron Micros Soc Am Bull. *Mem:* Am Soc Cell Biol; Electron Micros Soc Am. *Res:* Ultrastructure of myxomycete cells; ultrastructure of pseudobranchs and gills; cardiac, hepatic, renal, pancreatic, and aortic diseases of viral cause; diagnostic electron microscopy. *Mailing Add:* 14655 Eastview Ct Brookfield WI 53005

HARBACH, RALPH EDWARD, MEDICAL ENTOMOLOGY, MOSQUITO SYSTEMATICS. *Current Pos:* INT ADV, MOMORIAS DO INST OSWAIDO CRUZ, 95- *Personal Data:* b Streator, Ill, Mar 23, 48; m 70; c 2. *Educ:* Western Ill Univ, BS, 71, MS, 72; Univ Ill, PhD(entom), 76. *Prof Exp:* Res assoc entom, NC State Univ, 76-79; entomologist, Walter Reed Army Inst Res, 80-84; med entomologist & taxonomist, Armed Forces Res Inst Med Sci, Thailand, 85-88; med entomologist, Mosquito systematist & mgr, Biosyst Unit, Walter Reed Army Inst Res, 88-92. *Concurrent Pos:* Res assoc, Smithsonian Inst; co-ed, Mosquito Syst, 88-93, Syst Entom, 95- *Mem:* Am Mosquito Control Asn; Royal Entom Soc; Sigma Xi. *Res:* Biosystematic research on mosquito vectors of disease including taxonomy, morphology, bionomics and medical importance. *Mailing Add:* Natural Hist Mus Cromwell Rd London SW7 5BD England

HARBATER, DAVID, ALGEBRAIC GEOMETRY, ARITHMETIC GEOMETRY. *Current Pos:* from asst prof to assoc prof 78-91, PROF MATH, UNIV PA, 91-, E OTIS KENDALL PROF, 96- *Personal Data:* b New York, NY, Dec 19, 52. *Educ:* Harvard Univ, AB, 74; Brandeis Univ, MA, 75; Mass Inst Technol, PhD(math), 78. *Hon Degrees:* MA, Univ Pa, 84. *Honors & Awards:* Cole Prize, Am Math Soc, 95. *Concurrent Pos:* Fel, Am Math Soc, 78-79, NSF, 82-83; NSF grantee, 79-82 & 83-86; Sloan Found fel, 84-87; vis mem, Math Sci Res Inst, 86-87 & 92-93, Nat Sect grantee, 90-; invited lectr, Int Cong Math, 94. *Mem:* Am Math Soc; Sigma Xi; Math Asn Am. *Res:* Algebric geometry research and its connections to number theory, Galois theory and topology. *Mailing Add:* Dept Math Univ Pa Philadelphia PA 19104-6395. *E-Mail:* harbater@rademacher.math.upenn.edu

HARBAUGH, ALLAN WILSON, OPERATIONS RESEARCH, PHYSICS. *Current Pos:* RETIRED. *Personal Data:* b Houston, Tex, Oct 22, 26; m 60, Joan Loye. *Educ:* Univ Tex, Austin, BS, 47, PhD(eng), 53; Univ Mich, MEng, 49; Univ Calif, Los Angeles, MBA, 61. *Prof Exp:* Geophysicist oil explor, Shell Oil Co, 49-50; res engr electromagnetics, Appl Res Lab, Univ Tex, 50-56; scientist opers res, Rand Corp, 56-59; sr staff mem space res, Space-Gen Corp, 59-62; mgr opers res, Comput Sci Corp, 62-65; mgr mgt systs, Tex Instruments Inc, 65-67; asst to vpres finance, LTV Corp, 67-72; consult opers res, 72-83; prof physics, Richland Col, 83-91. *Res:* Application of mathematical methods to industry and finance, options analysis, and financial management. *Mailing Add:* 7009 Meadowcreek Dr Dallas TX 75240-2712

HARBAUGH, BRENT KALEN, ORNAMENTAL HORTICULTURE, ENTOMOLOGY. *Current Pos:* From asst prof to assoc prof, 75-86, PROF ORNAMENTAL HORT, GULF COAST RES & EDUC CTR, 86- *Personal Data:* b Topeka, Kans, Feb 15, 48; m 69; c 4. *Educ:* Washburn Univ, BS, 70; Kans State Univ, MS, 72, PhD(hort), 75. *Mem:* Am Soc Hort Sci. *Res:* Development of production systems for ornamental crops, encompassing plant nutrition, cultural practices, water management, photoperiod, media, growth regulators, pest management and post harvest techniques. *Mailing Add:* 2204 40th St W Bradenton FL 34205

HARBAUGH, DANIEL DAVID, ANIMAL NUTRITION, PURCHASING. *Current Pos:* field nutritionist, Arbie Mineral Feed Co, 71-76, bd dirs, 76, formulation & nutrit consult, 76-78, formulation & purchasing consult, 78-85, dir formulation & purchasing & mkt consult, 85-94, VPRES NUTRIT & TECH SERV, ARBIE MINERAL FEED CO, 94- *Personal Data:* b Prairie du Rocher, Ill, Jan 2, 42; m 66, Ellen L Stork; c James H & Thomas D. *Educ:* Southern Ill Univ, Carbondale, BS, 65, MS, 66; Kans State Univ, PhD(animal nutrit), 70. *Prof Exp:* Dir nutrit res & develop, Fermbionics, Inc, Mo, 70-71. *Concurrent Pos:* Lectr, Feed Ingredient Inst, 82-83; mem & chmn elect, Comput Usage Comt, Am Feed Industs Asn, 80-84. *Mem:* Poultry Sci Asn; Sigma Xi; Am Soc Animal Sci; Am Feed Industs Asn. *Res:* Recycling of animal waste; nutritional consulting; feed technology. *Mailing Add:* Arbie Mineral Feed Co 409 S Center Marshalltown IA 50158. *Fax:* 515-752-7628

HARBAUGH, JOHN WARVELLE, ECONOMIC GEOLOGY. *Current Pos:* from asst prof to assoc prof, 55-66, chmn dept, 69-72, PROF GEOL SCI, STANFORD UNIV, 66- *Personal Data:* b Madison, Wis, Aug 6, 26; wid; c 3. *Educ:* Univ Kans, BS, 48, MS, 50; Univ Wis, PhD(geol), 55. *Honors & Awards:* Levorsen Award, Am Asn Petrol Geol, Distinguished Serv Award. *Prof Exp:* Prod geologist, Carter Oil Co, Okla, 51-53. *Mem:* Fel Geol Soc Am; Soc Econ Paleont & Mineral; Am Asn Petrol Geol. *Res:* Petroleum geology; application of digital computers in analysis and simulation of geologic processes and exploration for petroleum and coal; decision analysis in oil exploration. *Mailing Add:* Dept Geol Sci Stanford Univ Stanford CA 94305-2115. *Fax:* 650-725-0979; *E-Mail:* harbaugh@pangea.stanford.edu

HARBECK, RONALD JOSEPH, DIAGNOSTIC AND CLINICAL IMMUNOLOGY, IMMUNOPATHOLOGY. *Current Pos:* DIR CLIN LABS, NAT JEWISH CTR IMMUNOL & RESPIRATORY MED, DENVER, COLO, 83- *Personal Data:* b Nov 7, 42; m 65, Delores Manning; c Lisa M (Kihn) & Andrea Lynn. *Educ:* Univ SDak, PhD(microbiol), 71. *Concurrent Pos:* Prof, Dept Microbiol, Immunol, Path & Med Univ of Colo, Health Sci Ctr; chairperson, Diag & Clin Immunol Div, Am Soc Microbiol, 91. *Mem:* Am Asn Immunologists; Am Soc Microbiol; Clin Immunol Soc. *Res:* Gamma-delta T cell receptors; diagnostic immunology. *Mailing Add:* Dept Med J115 423 Nat Jewish Hosp & Respiratory Ctr 1400 Jackson St Denver CO 80206-1900. *E-Mail:* harbeckr@njc.org

HARBER, LEONARD C, DERMATOLOGY. *Current Pos:* PROF DERMAT & CHMN DEPT, COL PHYSICIANS & SURGEONS, COLUMBIA UNIV, 73- *Personal Data:* b New York, NY, June 22, 27; m 62; c 2. *Educ:* Johns Hopkins Univ, AB, 49; NY Univ, MD, 53, MS, 58. *Honors & Awards:* Husik Award, 60. *Prof Exp:* From instr to prof dermat, Sch Med, NY Univ, 58-73. *Concurrent Pos:* Fulbright res scholar dermat & syphil, Univ Copenhagen, 56-57; fel dermat, Post-Grad Med Sch, NY Univ, 57-58; guest investr, Rockefeller Univ, 70; consult, Dermat Adv Comt, Food & Drug Admin, 76-79. *Mem:* Soc Invest Dermat; Am Med Writers' Asn; Am Dermat Asn; Am Soc Clin Invest; Am Acad Dermat. *Res:* Clinical and research problems associated with adverse skin reactions following sun exposure, porphyria, drug photosensitivity; protoporphyria; drug photoallergy. *Mailing Add:* Columbia Presby Med Ctr 630 W 168th St New York NY 10032-3702

HARBERS, CAROLE ANN Z, FOOD SCIENCES, NUTRITION. *Current Pos:* asst prof, 79-84, ASSOC PROF FOODS & NUTRIT, KANS STATE UNIV, 84- *Personal Data:* b Ironton, Ohio, Mar 19, 43; m 78, Leniel H. *Educ:* Ohio Univ, BS, 69; Va Polytech Inst & State Univ, MS, 76; Kans State Univ, PhD(foods & nutrit), 79. *Prof Exp:* Vocational home econ teacher, Ironton City Sch, 69-74. *Mem:* Inst Food Technologists; Am Dietetics Asn; Sigma Xi. *Res:* Physical, chemical, sensory and nutritional aspects of corn-based products including ethnic food, products containing high fructose corn syrup and red meats; food color; food losses and conservation. *Mailing Add:* Dept Foods & Nutrit Justin Hall Kans State Univ Manhattan KS 66506. *Fax:* 785-532-3132; *E-Mail:* harbers@humec.ksu.edu

HARBERS, LENIEL H, ANIMAL NUTRITION, FOOD SCIENCE. *Current Pos:* assoc prof, 64-76, asst dean, 88-89, PROF ANIMAL NUTRIT, SKANS STATE UNIV, 76-, CHAIR, FOOD SCI GRAD PROG, GRAD SCH, 90- *Personal Data:* b La Grange, Tex, Nov 11, 34; m 78, Carole Zimmerman; c Julia, Sarah & Jennifer (deceased). *Educ:* Tex A&M Univ, BS, 57, MS, 58; Okla State Univ, PhD(nutrit), 61. *Prof Exp:* Univ fel pharmacol, Univ Chicago, 61-62, USPHS fel, 62-63; assoc chemist, Am Meat Inst Found, 63-64. *Concurrent Pos:* AID consult to Nigeria, 66-68; consult to Bulgaria, UN Food & Agr Org, 75; vpres, Kans-Paraguay Partners, 87-89, pres, 91-94. *Mem:* Am Inst Nutrit; Am Soc Animal Sci. *Res:* Monogastric and ruminant nutrition; scanning electron microscopy; near infrared spectroscopical analysis of foods and feeds. *Mailing Add:* Dept Animal Sci Kans State Univ Manhattan KS 66506. *Fax:* 785-532-5681; *E-Mail:* lharbers@oz.oznet.ksu.edu

HARBERT, CHARLES A, ORGANIC CHEMISTRY, MEDICINAL CHEMISTRY. *Current Pos:* res chemist, Pfizer Inc, 69-72, proj leader, 72-76, mgr, 76-81, dir cent res, 81-84, exec dir res cent, 84-91, sr exec dir, 91-93, VPRES, PFIZER INC, 93- *Personal Data:* b Indianapolis, Ind, Apr 7, 40; m 61; c 2. *Educ:* Univ Colo, BA, 62; Univ Mo-Columbia, PhD(org chem), 67. *Prof Exp:* NIH fel org chem, Stanford Univ, 67-69. *Concurrent Pos:* Chair, Med Chem Gordon Res Conf, 90; alt counr, Am Chem Soc, 94-96. *Mem:* Am Chem Soc; Sigma Xi. *Res:* Heterocycles; natural products. *Mailing Add:* 7 Westwood Dr Waterford CT 06385-3826

HARBIN, WILLIAM T(HOMAS), CHEMICAL ENGINEERING. *Current Pos:* RETIRED. *Personal Data:* b Wheeler Co, Ga, July 6, 08; m 30, Virginia Frith; c 3. *Educ:* Ga Inst Technol, BS, 38. *Prof Exp:* Chem engr, Hercules Powder Co, Ga, 37-38, Union Bag & Paper Co, 38-39 & Chatham Processes Co, 39-40; head, Dept Eng, E R Squibb & Sons, NJ, 40-46; asst supt, Celanese Corp of Am, 46-49, plant supt, Chem Div, 49-54; plasticizer plant supt, Kolker Chem Corp, 54-58, prod mgr, 58-61; plant mgr, Thompson Chem Co, 61-65, asst plant mgr, Thompson Apex Co Div, Continental Oil Co, 65-67, plant mgr, Teknor Apex Co, 67-73. *Concurrent Pos:* Consult engr, 73- *Mem:* AAAS; Am Chem Soc; fel Am Inst Chem Engrs. *Res:* Terpene compounds and chemistry; sulfa drugs and related chemicals; plasticizers; chlorinated products; resins; peroxides. *Mailing Add:* 3922 Gail Dr Oakwood GA 30566-2217

HARBISON, G RICHARD, MARINE BIOLOGY, BIOLOGICAL OCEANOGRAPHY. *Current Pos:* from asst scientist to assoc scientist, 72-86, SR SCIENTIST, WOODS HOLE OCEANOG INST, 86- *Personal Data:* b Miami, Fla, Mar 4, 41; m 89, Judith Lindsey. *Educ:* Columbia Col, AB, 66; Fla State Univ, PhD(biochem), 71. *Concurrent Pos:* Prin res scientist, Australian Inst Marine Sci, 80-82; dir, Div Marine Sci, Harbor Br Oceanog Inst, 87-89. *Mem:* Am Soc Limnol & Oceanog; Am Soc Zoologists; Crustacean Soc; Oceanog Soc; Soc Syst Zool; Systematics Asn. *Res:* Biology of gelatinous zooplankton; systematics, physiology and ecology; associations between amphipods and gelatinous zooplankton; behavior of mesopelagic organisms. *Mailing Add:* Woods Hole Oceanog Inst Woods Hole MA 02543. *E-Mail:* gharbison@whoi.edu

HARBISON, GERARD STANISLAUS, PHYSICAL CHEMISTRY, BIOLOGICAL CHEMISTRY. *Current Pos:* PROF CHEM, UNIV NEBR, LINCOLN. *Personal Data:* b Manchester, Eng, Jan 1, 58; m 80; c 3. *Educ:* Univ Dublin, BA (MOD), 77; Harvard Univ, PhD (biophys), 84. *Prof Exp:* Asst prof chem, State Univ NY, Stonybrook, 86-92. *Concurrent Pos:* NSF presidential young investr, 90. *Res:* Nuclear magnetic resonance and nuclear quadruple resonance spectroscopy; structure and dynamics of DNA and proteins. *Mailing Add:* Dept Chem Univ Nebr Lincoln NE 68588-0304

HARBISON, JAMES PRESCOTT, CRYSTAL GROWTH, SEMICONDUCTOR PHYSICS. *Current Pos:* MEM TECH STAFF, BELLCORE, 84- *Personal Data:* b Philadelphia, Pa, Apr 5, 51; m 73; c 3. *Educ:* Harvard Col, AB, 73; Harvard Univ, PhD(appl physics), 77. *Prof Exp:* IBM fel, Div Appl Sci, Harvard Univ, 77-78; mem tech staff, Bell Labs, Murray Hill, NJ, 78-83. *Mem:* Am Phys Soc; Am Vacuum Soc; Mat Res Soc; Minerals Metals & Mat Soc. *Res:* Crystal growth of thin films of semiconductors and metals; molecular beam epitaxy. *Mailing Add:* Bell Comm Res 331 Newman Springs Rd Red Bank NJ 07701. *E-Mail:* hariso@ccbellcore.com

HARBISON, RAYMOND D, PHARMACOLOGY & TOXICOLOGY, RISK ANALYSIS & MANAGEMENT. *Current Pos:* PROF ENVIRON & OCCUP HEALTH COL PUB HEALTH & PROF PHARMACOL, COL MED, UNIV SFLA, 95- *Personal Data:* b Peru, Ill, Jan 1, 43; m 62, Holly Hosutt; c John, Matthew, Andrew & Stephen. *Educ:* Drake Univ, BS, 65; Univ Iowa, MS, 67, PhD(pharmacol), 69. *Honors & Awards:* Achievement Award, Soc Toxicol, 78. *Prof Exp:* Instr pharmacol, Sch Med, Tulane Univ, 69-70, asst prof, 71-72; asst prof pharmacol & biochem, Sch Med, Vanderbilt Univ, 72-76, assoc prof, 77-80; prof pharmacol & toxicol, Sch Med Sci, Univ Ark, Little Rock, 80-88; prof toxicol & pharmacol, Univ Fla, 88-95. *Concurrent Pos:* Mem, Narcotic Addiction & Drug Abuse Rev Comt, NIMH, 71-73; mem, Nat Inst Drug Abuse Rev Comt, 73-75, Nat Inst Occup Safety & Health Rev Comt, 80-88, Nat Inst Environ Health Sci Rev Comt, 89-93. *Mem:* Soc Toxicol; Am Soc Pharmacol & Exp Therapeut; AAAS; Teratology Soc; Soc Risk Anal. *Res:* Teratology; developmental pharmacology; hazardous materials; drug metabolism; toxicology; occupational medicine. *Mailing Add:* Ctr Risk Anal & Mgt Col Pub Health Univ SFla 13201 Bruce B Downs Blvd Tampa FL 33612-3805. *Fax:* 813-974-5311; *E-Mail:* rharbiso@com1.med.usf.edu

HARBISON, S P, SOFTWARE SYSTEMS, COMPILERS. *Current Pos:* Res programmer, 74-77, asst, 78-80, RES COMPUT SCIENTIST, DEPT COMPUT SCI, CARNEGIE-MELLON UNIV, 80- *Personal Data:* b Pittsburgh, Pa, Jan 26, 52; m 82. *Educ:* Princeton Univ, AB, 74; Carnegie-Mellon Univ, Pittsburgh, PhD(comput sci), 80. *Mem:* Asn Comput Mach; AAAS; Sigma Xi. *Res:* Operating systems; software engineering; personalized computing environments. *Mailing Add:* 840 Canterbury Ln Pittsburgh PA 15232

HARBO, JOHN RUSSELL, APICULTURE. *Current Pos:* RES ENTOMOLOGIST APICULTURE, BEE BREEDING & STOCK CTR LAB, AGR RES SERV, USDA, 71- *Personal Data:* b Tracy, Minn, Nov 20, 43; m 66; c 2. *Educ:* Gustavus Adolphus Col, BA, 65; Mich Technol Univ, MS, 67; Cornell Univ, PhD(entom), 71. *Concurrent Pos:* Mem, Am Bee Res Conf. *Mem:* Entom Soc Am; Bee Res Asn. *Res:* Reproductive physiology of honey bees. *Mailing Add:* 7240 Palmetto Dr Baton Rouge LA 70808

HARBORDT, C(HARLES) MICHAEL, ENVIRONMENTAL MANAGEMENT & ENGINEERING, PHYSICAL ORGANIC CHEMISTRY. *Current Pos:* dir, environ affairs, Temple-Eastex Inc, 75-89, dir Environ Affairs, 80-88, vpres Temple-Inland FPC, 90-96, VPRES, TEMPLE-INLAND INC, 96- *Personal Data:* b Houston, Tex, Apr 8, 42; m 60; c 3. *Educ:* Stephen F Austin State Univ, BS, 63; Southern Methodist Univ, MS, 65; Tex A&M Univ, PhD(phys chem), 70. *Prof Exp:* Assoc chemist, Texaco, Inc, 65-67, sr chemist, 70-71; dir environ control, Temple Industs, Diboll, 71-75. *Mem:* AAAS; Air Pollution Control Asn; Water Pollution Control Fedn; Tech Asn Pulp & Paper Indust; fel Am Inst Chemists. *Res:* Waste water treatment technology; air pollution; pollution control, industrial hygiene, assessment. *Mailing Add:* Temple-Inland Inc PO Drawer N Diboll TX 75941

HARBOTTLE, GARMAN, NUCLEAR CHEMISTRY. *Current Pos:* SR SCIENTIST, BROOKHAVEN NAT LAB, 68- *Personal Data:* b Dayton, Ohio, Sept 25, 23; m 49, Naomi Perkiss; c Laura. *Educ:* Calif Inst Technol, BS, 44; Columbia Univ, PhD(chem), 49. *Honors & Awards:* George von Hevesy Medal, 84; Roald Fryxell Medal, Soc Am Archaeol, 94; Glenn Seaborg Medal, Am Nucl Soc, 95. *Prof Exp:* From asst chemist to assoc chemist, Brookhaven Nat Lab, 49-54, chemist, 54-65; dir div res & labs, Int Atomic Energy Agency, Vienna, Austria, 65-67. *Concurrent Pos:* Fel, AEC, 51-52; Guggenheim fel, 57-58; res assoc, Metrop Mus Art, 90- *Mem:* Soc Am Archaeol; AAAS; Mex Soc Archaeol; Soc Archaeol Sci (pres, 88-89). *Res:* Chemical consequences of nuclear transformations; application of nuclear techniques to archaeology and radon; forensic science. *Mailing Add:* Brookhaven Nat Lab Upton NY 11973. *Fax:* 516-282-5815; *E-Mail:* garman@bnl.gov

HARBOUR, JERRY, GEOLOGY. *Current Pos:* CONSULT, 91- *Personal Data:* b Coleman, Tex, Nov 24, 27; m 51; c 3. *Educ:* Univ NMex, AB, 51, MS, 57; Univ Ariz, PhD, 66. *Prof Exp:* Instr geol, WTex State Univ, 57-59; geologist, US Geol Surv, Va, 62-69; geologist sci & technol div, Inst Defense Anal, 69-71; eng geologist, Environ Safety Br, US AEC, 71-75; br chief, Site Safety Res Br, US Nuclear Regulatory Comn, 75-81, admin judge, Atomic Safety & Licensing Bd Panel, 81-90. *Concurrent Pos:* Consult, Mus NMex, Santa Fe, 61-62. *Mem:* Soc Vert Paleont. *Mailing Add:* 308 Poplar Dr Falls Church VA 22046

HARBOUR, JOHN RICHARD, COLLOIDS & INTERFACES. *Current Pos:* ADV SCIENTIST, DEFENSE WASTE PROCESSING TECHNOL, WESTINGHOUSE, 88- *Personal Data:* b Portage, Wis, May 5, 44; div; c 1. *Educ:* Univ Wis, Eau Claire, BS, 66; Univ Wyo, PhD(chem), 71. *Prof Exp:* Fel chem, Univ Ariz, 71-73 & Univ Western Ont, 73-74; from scientist to sr scientist, Xerox Res Ctr Can, 74-84, mgr develop physics & characterization, 85-88. *Mem:* Am Chem Soc; Mat Res Soc. *Res:* Radioactive waste management; electron spin resonance spectroscopy; ultrifiliation. *Mailing Add:* Westinghouse Savannah River Co Bldg 773-43A PO Box 616 Aiken SC 29802. *Fax:* 803-725-4704; *E-Mail:* john.harbour@srs.gov

HARBOURT, CYRUS OSCAR, ELECTRICAL ENGINEERING. *Current Pos:* prof elec eng, 67-77, dir eng exten, 82-86 & 87-96, EMER PROF, UNIV MO, COLUMBIA, 96- *Personal Data:* b Baton Rouge, La, June 1, 31; m 52; c 5. *Educ:* La State Univ, BS, 52; Mass Inst Technol, MS, 55; Syracuse Univ, PhD(elec eng), 61. *Prof Exp:* Asst, Mass Inst Technol, 52-54; instr elec eng, La State Univ, 54-55, Univ Del, 56-57 & Syracuse Univ, 57-61; from asst prof to assoc prof, Univ Tex, 61-67. *Concurrent Pos:* NSF grant, Univ Tex, 62-65; elec eng, Bonneville Power Admin, 77-78; interim dean eng, Univ Mo, Columbia, 86-87. *Mem:* Inst Elec & Electronics Engrs; Am Soc Eng Educ; Nat Soc Prof Engrs. *Res:* Active and nonlinear circuit analysis and design; solid state device applications; power systems. *Mailing Add:* 2306 Ridgefield Rd Columbia MO 65203

HARBRON, THOMAS RICHARD, COMPUTER SCIENCES. *Current Pos:* Instr physics, Anderson Univ, 61-65, asst prof, 65-70, assoc prof physics & comput sci, 70-77, chmn, Comput Sci Dept, 80-90, dir, Comput Ctr, 65-93, PROF COMPUT SCI, ANDERSON UNIV, 77- *Personal Data:* b Clinton, Iowa, Dec 16, 37; m 64, Jean L Phillips; c 3. *Educ:* Iowa State Univ, BS, 60, MS, 61. *Concurrent Pos:* Mem bd, Interex (Hewlett-Packard Users Group), 74-78, chmn bd, 78-79; consult. *Mem:* Inst Elec & Electronics Engrs; Inst Elec & Electronics Engrs Comput Soc; Asn Comput Mach. *Res:* File systems; database systems; programming methods; algorithms. *Mailing Add:* Dept Comput Sci Anderson Univ Anderson IN 46012

HARBURY, HENRY ALEXANDER, BIOCHEMISTRY. *Current Pos:* chmn dept biochem, 72-89, prof, 72-96, EMER PROF BIOCHEM, DARTMOUTH MED SCH, 96- *Personal Data:* b The Hague, Neth, Dec 11, 27; nat US; m 47, Dorothy Harley; c Katharine, Jennifer, Olin & Alexander. *Educ:* Cornell Univ, AB, 47; Johns Hopkins Univ, PhD(biochem), 53. *Prof Exp:* From instr to assoc prof biochem, Yale Univ, 53-67; prof biochem & chmn sect biochem & molecular biol, Dept Biol Sci, Univ Calif, Santa Barbara, 67-72, chmn dept, 69-72. *Concurrent Pos:* Markle scholar med sci, 56-61; pres, Dartmouth-Hitchcock Med Ctr, 80-91. *Mem:* AAAS; Am Chem Soc; Am Soc Biochem & Molecular Biol. *Res:* Structure and function of proteins; oxidative enzymes. *Mailing Add:* Dept Biochem Dartmouth Med Sch Hanover NH 03755

HARCLERODE, JACK E, ZOOLOGY. *Current Pos:* from asst prof, 65-72, chmn, Dept Biol, 68-78 & 86-90, PROF BIOL, BUCKNELL UNIV, 72- *Personal Data:* b Everett, Pa, June 29, 35; m 60; c Jake, Jill & Jan. *Educ:* Shippensburg State Col, BS, 57; Pa State Univ, MS, 58, PhD(zool), 62. *Prof Exp:* Asst prof zool, Univ Ohio, 62-65. *Concurrent Pos:* Herbert L Spencer prof, 77. *Mem:* Endocrine Soc. *Res:* Comparative thyroid physiology in birds, reptiles and mammals; pharmacology of marihuana phencyclidine and cocaine. *Mailing Add:* Dept Biol Bucknell Univ Lewisburg PA 17837-2029

HARCOMBE, PAUL ALBIN, PLANT ECOLOGY. *Current Pos:* From asst prof to assoc prof, 72-87, chair, Dept Ecol & Evolutionary Biol, 89-95, PROF BIOL, RICE UNIV, 87- *Personal Data:* b McMinnville, Ore, Oct 13, 45; m 69, Elnora Smith; c Mary K & William. *Educ:* Mich State Univ, BS, 67; Yale Univ, PhD(biol), 73. *Concurrent Pos:* Res assoc & consult, Rice Ctr Community Design & Res, 73-76; assoc ed, Ecol & Ecol Monograph, 78-80, ed, 80-82; mem, Bd Prof Cert, Ecol Soc Am, 83-86; chair, Vegetation Sect, Ecol Soc Am, 93-94. *Mem:* Ecol Soc Am; Brit Ecol Soc; Soc Conserv Biol; Nat Areas Asn. *Res:* Structure and dynamics of coastal plain forest vegetation; woody plant demography; global change. *Mailing Add:* Dept Ecol & Evolutionary Biol Rice Univ 6100 Main Houston TX 77005. *Fax:* 713-285-5232; *E-Mail:* harcomb@rice.edu

HARCOURT, DOUGLAS GEORGE, INSECT ECOLOGY, INTEGRATED PEST MANAGEMENT. *Current Pos:* RETIRED. *Personal Data:* b Toronto, Ont, Mar 23, 26; m 49, Barbara A Ruliff; c Margaret, Scott & Peter. *Educ:* Univ Toronto, BA; Cornell Univ, PhD(econ entom), 54. *Prof Exp:* Tech officer, Entom Div, Can Dept Agr, 49-51, res officer, Entom Res Inst, 54-65, res scientist, 65-70, chief, Entom Sect, 70-77, sect head, 78-89, prin res scientist, Ottawa Res Sta, 82-91, proj leader, Pest Mgt, Plant Res Ctr, 89-91. *Concurrent Pos:* Adj prof, Carleton Univ, 68- & Guelph Univ, 80-; vis prof, Univ Parana, Brazil, 72; consult, UN Food & Agr Orgn, Arg, 74-79, Taiwan Nat Coun Agr, 85, Embrapa, Brazil, 81; vis prof, Univ Tucuman, Arg, 88; consult, CESO, 91- *Mem:* Entom Soc Am; Japanese Soc Pop Ecol; fel Entom Soc Can. *Res:* Population dynamics of insects attacking forage crops; spatial pattern and sequential sampling of crop insects; pest management. *Mailing Add:* 25 Okanagan Dr Nepean ON K2H 7E9 Can. *Fax:* 613-952-9295

HARD, CECIL GUSTAV, HORTICULTURE. *Current Pos:* PROF HORT & EXTEN HORTICULTURIST, UNIV MINN, ST PAUL, 54, PROF LANDSCAPE ARCHIT, 78- *Personal Data:* b Ill, June 2, 23; m 56; c 3. *Educ:* Mich State Univ, BS, 51, MS, 52, PhD(hort), 54. *Res:* Ornamental horticulture; landscape design. *Mailing Add:* 1937 Autumn St St Paul MN 55113

HARD, GORDON CHARLES, KIDNEY TOXICOLOGY & CARCINOGENESIS, CANCER RESEARCH & MECHANISMAS. *Current Pos:* SR TOXICOLOGIST & PATHOLOGIST, DIR ADMIN, AM HEALTH FOUND, NY, 91- *Personal Data:* b Auckland, NZ, July 5, 31; Australian citizen; m 70, Sally A Bowman; c Cassandra, James & Nicolas. *Educ:* Univ Sydney, Australia, BVSc, 59, PhD(vet path, bact & toxicol), 69; Univ Melbourne, DSc(toxicol path), 78; FRCVS, 86; FRCPath, 86. *Prof Exp:* Large animal vet, Taihape Vet Club, NZ, 59-63; staff scientist, Med Res Coun, UK, 68-71; sr res fel, Anti-Cancer Coun Victoria, Australia, 71-78; assoc dir, Fels Res Inst, Philadelphia, 78-85; exec dir, Brit Indust Biol Res Asn, UK, 85-88. *Concurrent Pos:* Prof path, Temple Univ Med Sch, Pa, 78-85; consult, var pharmaceut & chem corp, 82-, US Environ Protection Agency, 89-; joint ed-in-chief, Food & Chem Toxicol, 85-90 & Toxicol In Vitro, 86-90; prof comp path & toxicol, Surrey Univ, UK, 86-90; vis prof, Med Res Coun, UK, 88-91; res fel, Med Col NY. *Mem:* Am Asn Cancer Res; Soc Toxicol; Soc Toxicol Pathologists. *Res:* Biomedical research specializing in carcinogenesis, toxicology and pathology of the kidney, liver and other organs particularly with nitroso compounds, mycotoxins and chemopreventive agents (eg tamoxifer). *Mailing Add:* 9 Brundige Dr Goldens Bridge NY 10526. *Fax:* 914-592-6317

HARD, JEFFREY JOHN, QUANTITATIVE GENETICS, CONSERVATION BIOLOGY. *Current Pos:* fishery res biologist, 82-86, FISHERY RES BIOLOGIST, NAT MARINE FISHERIES SERV, 92- *Personal Data:* b Bangor, Maine, May 11, 56; m 82, Emilie Thompson; c Alyson & Andrew. *Educ:* Ore State Univ, BS, 79; Univ Alaska, Juneau, MS, 84; Univ Ore, PhD(biol), 91. *Honors & Awards:* Bronze Medal, US Dept Com, 96. *Prof Exp:* Teaching fel biol & ecol, Univ Ore, 86-88, res fel, 88-91. *Concurrent Pos:* Res consult, Nat Marine Fisheries Serv, 87-88 & 90-91. *Mem:* Assoc mem Sigma Xi; Am Inst Fishery Res Biologists; Am Fisheries Soc; AAAS. *Res:* Conservation biology of fishes; genetic and ecological consequences of artificial propagation of fishes; evolution of fish life histories; quantitative genetic basis of life-history variation. *Mailing Add:* Northwest Fisheries Sci Ctr CZES Div 2725 Montlake Blvd E Seattle WA 98112. *E-Mail:* jeff.hard@noaa.gov

HARD, MARGARET MCGREGOR, FOOD SCIENCE, NUTRITION. *Current Pos:* Res chemist, 42-45, asst prof & asst home economist, 45-51, assoc home economist, 51-60, actg dean, Col Home Econ, 73-75, CHMN, DEPT HOME ECON, AGR EXP STA, WASH STATE UNIV, 51-, PROF FOODS & NUTRIT, COL HOME ECON, 60- *Personal Data:* b Can, June 26, 19; nat US; m 48; c 2. *Educ:* Univ Sask, BHSc, 40; Univ Wis, MS, 42. *Concurrent Pos:* Mem, Comt of Nine, USDA, 74-77. *Mem:* AAAS; Am Chem Soc; Am Home Econ Asn; Inst Food Technol. *Res:* Food processing; availability of nutrients for humans; nutritional status of population groups in Washington state; consumer food quality. *Mailing Add:* SE 1000 Spring Pullman WA 99163

HARD, RICHARD C, JR, BONE MARROW TRANSPLANTATION, AIDS. *Current Pos:* ASSOC PROF PATH, MED COL VA, 65- *Personal Data:* b May 14, 33; m 97, Maria Bourlos. *Educ:* St Louis Univ, MD, 58. *Concurrent Pos:* Assoc prof Microbiol & Immunol, Med Col Va, Va Commonwealth Univ,. *Mem:* Am Asn Immunologists; AMA. *Res:* Materno-setol transmission of HIV-1; host versus graft reactions in bone marrow transplantation. *Mailing Add:* Dept Path Med Col Va Box 662 Richmond VA 23298-0662. *Fax:* 804-828-9749

HARD, ROBERT PAUL, CELL BIOLOGY. *Current Pos:* ASSOC PROF, ANAT SCI/CELL BIOL, STATE UNIV NY, BUFFALO, 85- *Personal Data:* b Seattle, Wash, Oct 16, 44; m 64; c 2. *Educ:* Univ Wash, BS, 67, MS, 70; State Univ NY, Albany, PhD(biol), 75. *Prof Exp:* Res assoc cell biol, Dartmouth Col, 75 & Univ Ore, 75-78; asst prof zool, Ore State Univ, 78-85. *Concurrent Pos:* Trainee cell biol, NIH, State Univ NY, 71-75. *Mem:* Am Soc Cell Biol. *Res:* Nature of microtubule-dynein interactions in the mechanism of ciliary movement and the role of microtubules in the mechanism of chromosome movement during mitosis. *Mailing Add:* Dept Anat Sci/Cell Biol State Univ NY Sch Med Buffalo NY 14214-3000. *Fax:* 716-829-2915

HARD, THOMAS MICHAEL, PHYSICAL CHEMISTRY, OPTICS. *Current Pos:* RES FEL, PORTLAND STATE UNIV, 77- *Personal Data:* b Florence, Italy, Nov 25, 37; US citizen. *Educ:* Harvard Univ, AB, 60; Univ Wis, Madison, PhD(chem), 65. *Prof Exp:* Res assoc chem, Mass Inst Technol, 65-67; physicist, Electronics Res Ctr, NASA, 67-70; chemist, US Dept Transp, 70-76. *Mem:* AAAS; Optical Soc Am; Am Chem Soc; Sigma Xi. *Res:* Atmospheric chemistry; determination of trace constituents; laser spectroscopic methods; interference suppression in detection of weak light signals; chemistry of tropospheric free radicals. *Mailing Add:* 3258 SE Sherman Portland OR 97214-5748

HARDAGE, BOB ADRIAN, EARTH SCIENCES. *Current Pos:* RES SCIENTIST, BUR ECON GEOL, AUSTIN, 91- *Personal Data:* b Checotah, Okla, Apr 5, 39. *Educ:* Okla State Univ, BS, 61, MS, 67, PhD(physics), 67. *Prof Exp:* Res geophysicist, Phillips Petrol Co, 66-80, chief geophysicist seismic stratig, 80-85, chief geophysicist, Europe-Africa, 85-86, explor mgr, Asia-Latin Am, 86-88; vpres geophys devel & mktg, Atlas Wireline Serv, 88-91. *Concurrent Pos:* Ed, Geophys, 93-95. *Mem:* Soc Explor Geophys; Am Asn Petrol Geol. *Res:* Wave propagation in earth materials; well logging; synthetic seismograms; numerical modeling; seismic data processing; geological interpretation of seismic data; 3D seismic technology; borehole seismic measurements; crosswell profiling. *Mailing Add:* Univ Tex Univ Sta Box X Bldg 130 Austin TX 78713-8924. *Fax:* 512-471-0140

HARDAWAY, ERNEST, II, ORAL & MAXILLOFACIAL SURGERY. *Current Pos:* CHIEF, POLICY COORD BR, BUR MED SERV, DEPT HEALTH & HUMAN SERV, 77-, DEP DIR, BUR MED SERV, PUB HEALTH SERV, 81- *Personal Data:* b Columbus, Ga, Mar 3, 34. *Educ:* Howard Univ, BS, 57, DDS, 66, cert(oral surg), 72; Johns Hopkins Univ, MPH, 73. *Prof Exp:* Prof staff, Comt Ways & Means, US Cong, 72; proj officer, Bur Qual Assurance, 74-75, dent off, 75-77. *Concurrent Pos:* Exec asst to dir, DC Govt, Div Human Resources, 70-71; chief resident oral surg, Howard Univ Med Ctr, 71-72; asst prof, 74-75; spec asst to dir, Off Policy Planning & Eval, Off Asst Secy, Dept HEW, 72-73; comnr pub health, Washington DC, 84-; regional dir, Fed Occup Health, 86- *Mem:* Am Asn Oral & Maxillofacial Surgeons; Am Dent Asn; Nat Dent Asn; Am Col Dentists; Acad Dent Int; Am Pub Health Asn. *Res:* Health care policy and administration. *Mailing Add:* 88 W Schiller No 1204 Chicago IL 60610

HARDAWAY, JOHN E(VANS), HYDROLOGY, GEOLOGICAL ENGINEERING. *Current Pos:* MGR ENVIRON AFFAIRS, INDEPENDENCE MINING CO (PIKES PEAK MINING CO), 93- *Personal Data:* b Philadelphia, Pa, Mar 2, 36; m 63, Ann Tilson; c Robert & James. *Educ:* Princeton Univ, BSE, 59, MSE, 63. *Honors & Awards:* Gold Medal, US Environ Protection Agency. *Prof Exp:* Jr geologist, NJ Geol Surv, 59; geophysicist, Geotech & Resources, Inc, 59; asst geophys, Princeton Univ, 62-63; hydrologist, Desert Res Inst, Univ Nev, 63-64; hydrologist, Isotopes, Teledyne, Inc, 64-67; geol engr-hydrologist, 67-69; hydrologist, Fed Water Pollution Control Admin, 69-71; phys sci adminr, Environ Protection Agency, 71-78, asst regional dir tech anal & res, Off Surface Mining, 78-81; mgr regional environ affairs, Tosco Corp, 81-83; scientist, Kaman Tempo, 83-84; tech mgr environ affairs, Homestake Mining Co, 84-93. *Concurrent Pos:* Consult, Resource Conserv & Control Act, Superfund; cochair, Water Qual Subcomt, Colo Mining Asn. *Mem:* AAAS; Am Geophys Union; Soc Petrol Engrs; Geol Soc Am; Sigma Xi. *Res:* Characteristics and control of liquid effluents; mine drainage; oil shale development; heavy metal pollution; hydrology; environmental data base management; environmental (multidisciplinary) management. *Mailing Add:* PO Box 1628 Wheat Ridge CO 80034-1628

HARDAWAY, ROBERT M, III, SURGERY. *Current Pos:* PROF SURG, SCH MED, TEX TECH UNIV, 76- *Personal Data:* b Camp John Hay, Philippines, Jan 9, 16; US citizen; m 39, Lee Harkey; c Robert M IV, E Joan, Thomas G & Christopher L. *Educ:* Univ Denver, AB, 36; Washington Univ, MD, 39; Am Bd Surg, dipl, 52. *Prof Exp:* Dir, Div Surg, Med Corps, Walter Reed Army Inst Res, Washington, DC, 60-67, commanding officer, 97th Gen Hosp, NY, 67-71, commanding gen, William Beaumont Army Med Ctr, El Paso, 70-75. *Mem:* AMA; Asn Mil Surgeons US; Am Col Surg; Am Asn Surg Trauma; Am Col Angiol; Int Soc Surg; Int Trauma & Surg Intensive Care Soc. *Res:* Surgical research, particularly with regard to shock and disseminated intravascular coagulation; critical care medicine. *Mailing Add:* 6121 Pinehurst Dr El Paso TX 79912. *Fax:* 915-545-6864

HARDBERGER, FLORIAN MAX, ZOOLOGY, BOTANY. *Current Pos:* RETIRED. *Personal Data:* b Atlanta, La, Dec 18, 14; m 44, Dorris M Windham; c Florian M Jr, Karl W & Dorris W. *Educ:* Northwestern State Col, La, BS, 42; La State Univ, MS, 50. *Prof Exp:* From asst prof to assoc prof, Nicholls State Univ, 50-71, head, Dept Biol Sci, 61-73, prof zool, 71-80. *Res:* Affects of heat on mammalian reproduction. *Mailing Add:* 1706 Lynn Ave Thibodaux LA 70301

HARDCASTLE, DONALD LEE, COMPUTER SCIENCE, NUMERICAL METHODS. *Current Pos:* from asst prof to assoc prof, 67-81, PROF PHYSICS & DIR COMPUT & INFO SYSTS, BAYLOR UNIV, 81- *Personal Data:* b Wheeler, Tex, July 20, 38; m 59; c 4. *Educ:* Tex Tech Col, BS, 60, MS, 62; Tex A&M Univ, PhD(physics), 67. *Prof Exp:* Instr physics, South Plains Jr Col, 61-62, Tex Tech Col, 62-63 & Tex A&M Univ, 63-65. *Mem:* Am Phys Soc; Am Asn Physics Teachers; Sigma Xi. *Res:* Theoretical physics. *Mailing Add:* RR1 Waco TX 76798. *E-Mail:* don__hardcastle@baylor.edu

HARDCASTLE, JAMES EDWARD, RADIOCHEMISTRY, BIOCHEMISTRY. *Current Pos:* asst prof, 68-83, assoc prof biochem, 83-, PROF BIOCHEM, TEX WOMAN'S UNIV. *Personal Data:* b San Diego, Calif, Aug 14, 32; m 70; c 6. *Educ:* Col William & Mary, BS, 53; Univ Richmond, MS, 60; Univ Ariz, PhD(agr chem), 67. *Prof Exp:* Res chemist, Philip Morris, Inc, 58-63; res assoc radiochem, Univ Ariz, 63-67; asst prof chem & biol, Rocky Mt Col, 67-68. *Mem:* Am Chem Soc. *Res:* Analytical biochemistry; metal ions in biological systems; the uptake and metabolism of metal ions by algae and fungi; leukotriene production in macrophage cell cultures. *Mailing Add:* Dept Chem Tex Woman's Univ Box 425859 Denton TX 76204-3859

HARDCASTLE, KENNETH IRVIN, INORGANIC CHEMISTRY, STRUCTURAL CHEMISTRY. *Current Pos:* PROF CHEM, CALIF STATE UNIV, NORTHRIDGE, 63- *Personal Data:* b San Jose, Calif, Jan 2, 31; m 60; c 3. *Educ:* San Jose State Col, AB, 52; Univ Miss, MS, 54; Univ Southern Calif, PhD(chem), 61. *Prof Exp:* Chemist, Peninsula Labs, 54-56; res assoc chem, Tufts Univ, 61-63. *Concurrent Pos:* NSF fac fel, Mass Inst Technol, 71-72; vis fac, Univ Sussex, 74, Univ Parma, 80 & 83 & Univ Col London, 85; Fulbright fel, 83. *Mem:* Am Crystallog Asn; Sigma Xi; Am Chem Soc. *Res:* Metal hydrides; non-stoichiometric compounds; rare earths; x-ray and neutron diffraction studies; crystallographic structure determinations. *Mailing Add:* Dept Chem Calif State Univ 18111 Nordhoff St Northridge CA 91330. *Fax:* 818-677-2912; *E-Mail:* ken.hardcastle@csun.edu

HARDCASTLE, WILLIS SANTFORD, WEED SCIENCE. *Current Pos:* asst agronomist, 61-80, ASSOC AGRONOMIST, GA EXP STA, 80- *Personal Data:* b Homer, La, June 16, 21; m 55; c 5. *Educ:* La State Univ, BS, 50, MS, 52, PhD(plant path), 58. *Prof Exp:* Biologist, La Wildlife & Fisheries Comn, 55-61. *Mem:* Weed Sci Soc Am; Am Soc Agron. *Res:* Laboratory, field and greenhouse evaluations of herbicides in agronomic crops, pastures, non-crop and aquatic areas; soil-herbicide interactions; physiological and life cycle studies on crops and weeds receiving herbicide applications. *Mailing Add:* 217 Hillandale Dr Griffin GA 30224

HARDEBECK, ELLEN JEAN, RADIO ASTRONOMY. *Current Pos:* AIR POLLUTION CONTROL OFFICER, GREAT BASIN AIR POLLUTION CONTROL DIST, 85- *Personal Data:* b Chicago, Ill, July 25, 39; m 68; c 1. *Educ:* Univ Chicago, BS, 61; Harvard Univ, MS, 63, PhD(astron), 65. *Prof Exp:* Res assoc radio astron, Cornell Univ, 65-69; res fel, Calif Inst Technol, 69-72. *Mem:* Am Astron Soc; Int Astron Union; Int Union Radio Sci; Air Pollution Control Asn. *Res:* Interstellar medium; interstellar molecules; interplanetary scintillations studies with radio astronomical techniques. *Mailing Add:* 3106 Tumbleweed Rd Bishop CA 93514

HARDEE, DICKY DAN, ENTOMOLOGY, ECOLOGY. *Current Pos:* lab dir, Agr Res Serv, 88-97, RES LEADER, USDA, 97- *Personal Data:* b Snyder, Tex, July 21, 38; m 86, Frieda Houston; c Steven & Stefanie. *Educ:* Tex Tech Col, BS, 60; Cornell Univ, MS, 62, PhD(entom), 64. *Prof Exp:* Res asst entom, Cornell Univ, 60-64; res entomologist, Boll Weevil Res Lab, USDA, 64-74; pres, Pest Mgt Specialists Inc, 74-88. *Mem:* AAAS; Entom Soc Am. *Res:* Development and use of non-insecticidal approaches to management of insect pests of cotton, pecan and soybean. *Mailing Add:* 905 N Deer Creek Dr E Leland MS 38756

HARDEGREE, MARY CAROLYN, PEDIATRICS, IMMUNOLOGY. *Current Pos:* med officer, Div Biologics Stand, 62-68, chief, Bact Toxins Sect, 68-72; DIR, BACT TOXINS BR, BUR BIOLOGICS, NIH, FOOD & DRUG ADMIN, 72-, DIR, OFF VACCINES RES & REVIEW. *Personal Data:* b Wichita Falls, Tex, Oct 2, 33; m 61; c 2. *Educ:* Baylor Univ, BS, 55; Univ Tex, MD, 58; Am Bd Pediat, dipl. *Prof Exp:* Rotating intern, Minneapolis Gen Hosp, Minn, 58-59; resident pediat, Sch Med, Univ Minn, Minneapolis, 59-61, med fel specialist, 61-62. *Mem:* Infectious Dis Soc Am; Am Asn Immunol; Soc Pediat Res; Am Soc Microbiol; fel Am Acad Pediat. *Res:* Bacterial toxins and toxoids; adjuvants; tetanus. *Mailing Add:* Vaccines Res & Review Ctr Biol Eval & Res Food & Drug Admin 1401 Rockville Pike HFN400 Rockville MD 20852-1448

HARDEKOPF, ROBERT ALLEN, NUCLEAR PHYSICS, RESEARCH ADMINISTRATION. *Current Pos:* STAFF MEM PHYSICS, LOS ALAMOS NAT LAB, UNIV CALIF, 72- *Personal Data:* b St Louis, Mo, Oct 14, 40; m 62, Priscilla; c Catherine, David & Kenneth. *Educ:* Auburn Univ, BS, 62; Duke Univ, PhD(physics), 72. *Mem:* Am Phys Soc. *Res:* Polarization phenomena in nuclear reactions, including experimental research and design, development of polarized ion sources; acceleration and beam physics; technical management. *Mailing Add:* DOD-PO MS F-613 Los Alamos Nat Lab Los Alamos NM 87545. *Fax:* 505-655-5739; *E-Mail:* hardekopfr@lanl.gov

HARDELL, WILLIAM JOHN, MATHEMATICS. *Current Pos:* from asst prof to assoc prof, 60-67, PROF MATH, WORCESTER POLYTECH INST, 67- *Personal Data:* b Chicago, Ill, May 28, 28; m 56; c 1. *Educ:* Northwestern Univ, BS, 50; Mich State Univ, MS, 53, PhD(math), 59. *Prof Exp:* Mathematician, Univac Div, Sperry-Rand Corp, Minn, 56-59; systs engr, Defense Electronic Prod Div, Radio Corp Am, NJ, 59-60. *Mem:* Am Math Soc; Math Asn Am; Inst Mgt Sci; Sigma Xi. *Res:* Associative algebras. *Mailing Add:* 7 Neptune Dr Shrewsbury MA 01545

HARDEN, DARREL GROVER, THERMODYNAMICS. *Current Pos:* asst prof, 63-67, ASSOC PROF MECH ENG, UNIV OKLA, 67- *Personal Data:* b Fay, Okla, Dec 29, 30; m 58; c 3. *Educ:* Univ Okla, BS, 57; Southern Methodist Univ, MS, 60; Okla State Univ, PhD(mech eng), 63. *Prof Exp:* Res assoc heat transfer, Argonne Nat Lab, 62-63. *Mem:* Am Soc Mech Engrs; Am Soc Eng Educ. *Res:* Dynamic response of fluid flow systems with heat addition, including nuclear reactors and combustion instability. *Mailing Add:* 2114 Briggs St Norman OK 73072

HARDEN, PHILIP HOWARD, ENTOMOLOGY. *Current Pos:* prof, 61-74, EMER PROF BIOL, ROBERTS WESLEYAN COL, 74- *Personal Data:* b SDak, May 17, 08; m 39, 59; c 1. *Educ:* Greenville Col, AB, 35; Univ Minn, PhD(zool, entom), 49. *Prof Exp:* Asst zool, Univ Minn, 47-49; chmn div sci, Pasadena Col, 49-57; pres, Wessington Springs Col, 57-61. *Res:* Medical entomology; plecoptera. *Mailing Add:* 810 S Elm McPherson KS 67460

HARDEN, VICTORIA ANGELA, HISTORY OF TWENTIETH-CENTURY BIOMEDICAL RESEARCH, HISTORY OF INFECTIOUS DISEASES. *Current Pos:* HISTORIAN, NIH & DIR, STETTEN MUS, 86- *Personal Data:* b Savannah, Ga, Jan 10, 44; m 81, Robert L Berger; c Charles D McDonell III & Emily V McDonell. *Educ:* Emory Univ, BA, 66, PhD(Am hist), 83; Univ Fla, MA, 68. *Honors & Awards:* Henry Adams Prize, Soc Hist Fed Govt, 91. *Prof Exp:* Instr soc sci, Huston-Tillotson Col, 68-72; teacher, Dixie Co Fla High Sch, 74-75 & Marietta High Sch, Ga, 75-79; historian, Nat Inst Allergy & Infectious Dis, 84-86. *Concurrent Pos:* Fel, Nat Mus Am Hist, Smithsonian Inst, 81-82 & Inst Hist Med, Johns Hopkins Med Sch, 83-84; prin investr, NIH, 81-84; adj assoc prof hist med, Univ Md, 84-87; fac mem hist med, FAES, NIH, 87-90. *Mem:* Am Asn Hist Med; Hist Sci Soc; Soc Hist Technol; Soc Hist Fed Govt; Orgn Am Historians; Am Hist Asn. *Res:* Twentieth century biomedical research, instruments and technologies; biomedical research policy; Rocky Mountain spotted fever. *Mailing Add:* 4503 Avamere St Bethesda MD 20814-3930

HARDENBURG, ROBERT EARLE, HORTICULTURE STORAGE, POSTHARVEST PHYSIOLOGY. *Current Pos:* RETIRED. *Personal Data:* b Ithaca, NY, July 27, 19; m 43, Jean Swett; c Kathryn & Mary. *Educ:* Cornell Univ, BS, 41, MS, 47, PhD(veg crops), 49. *Honors & Awards:* Distinguished

Serv Award, Produce Mkt Asn, 63. *Prof Exp:* Assoc horticulturist, Plant Indust Sta, USDA, 49-53, horticulturist, Biol Sci Br, Agr Mkt Serv, 53-55, sr horticulturist, 56-59, prin horticulturist, 59-67, invests leader, 67-72, chief, Hort Crops Mkt Lab, Hort Crops Inst, 72-81. *Concurrent Pos:* Sci adv coun, Refrig Res Found, 75-91. *Mem:* AAAS; fel Am Soc Hort Sci; Produce Mkt Asn; Int Inst Refrig. *Res:* Post-harvest horticulture and physiology of fruits and vegetables; prepackaging; handling and storage. *Mailing Add:* 648 Bird Bay Circle Venice FL 34292-4027

HARDER, DAVID RAE, PHYSIOLOGY, ELECTROPHYSIOLOGY. *Current Pos:* ASSOC PROF NEUROL & PHYSICS, MED COL WIS, MILWAUKEE, 83- , DIR NEUROL RES, 84- *Personal Data:* b Marshfield, Wis, Jan 10, 50; m 71; c 3. *Educ:* Univ Wis, BA, 72; Med Col Wis, MS, 75, PhD(physiol), 76. *Prof Exp:* Lectr physiol, Univ Wis-Milwaukee, 76-77; res assoc, Med Col Wis, 76-77; fel electrophysiol, Med Sch, Univ Va, 77-78; asst prof physiol, Sch Med, E Tenn State Univ, 78-80; res asst prof physics & biophys, Univ Vt, Burlington, 80-83. *Concurrent Pos:* Consult scientist, Cleveland Clin Found, 77; estab investr, Am Heart Asn, mem sci coun; res career scientist, Vet Admin, 85. *Mem:* Sigma Xi; Am Physiol Soc; Fedn Am Soc Exp Biol; Soc Gen Physiologists; Biophys Soc; Int Soc Heart Res. *Res:* Electrophysiology of excitable cells; ionic conductances across cell membranes; control of vascular smooth muscle. *Mailing Add:* Dept Physiol Med Col Wis 8701 Watertown Plank Rd Milwaukee WI 53226-0509. *Fax:* 414-266-8712

HARDER, DONALD EDWALD, PLANT PATHOLOGY, CELL BIOLOGY. *Current Pos:* RES SCIENTIST PLANT PATH, RES BR, AGR CAN, 73- *Personal Data:* b Bassano, Alta, May 17, 39; m 65; c 2. *Educ:* Univ Alta, BSc, 62, MSc, 64; Wash State Univ, PhD(plant path), 68. *Prof Exp:* Fel plant sci, Univ Man, 68-69, asst prof agr, 69-73. *Concurrent Pos:* Adj prof, Dept Bot, Res Admin, Univ Man. *Mem:* Am Phytopath Soc; Can Phytopath Soc. *Res:* Genetics of host parasite relations in the cereal rust diseases; physiology, ultrastructure and cytochemistry of host parasite relations in the cereal rusts. *Mailing Add:* Agr Can Res Sta 195 Dafoe Rd Winnipeg MB R3T 2M9 Can. *Fax:* 204-983-4604; *E-Mail:* dharder@em.agr.ca

HARDER, EDWIN L, ELECTRICAL ENGINEERING. *Current Pos:* SR CONSULT, WESTINGHOUSE ELEC CO, 70- *Personal Data:* b Buffalo, NY, 1905. *Educ:* Cornell Univ, EE, 26; Univ Pittsburgh, MS, 30, PhD, 46. *Honors & Awards:* Lamme Award, Am Inst Elec Engrs; Distinguished Serv Award, Am Fedn Info Processing Socs; Centennial Award, Am Inst Elec Engrs, Nat Acad Engrs, 76, 90. *Concurrent Pos:* Res & writing energy resources, processes & basic fundamentals. *Mem:* Nat Acad Eng; Am Inst Elec Engrs; Am Math Soc. *Res:* Railroad electrification; electric power engineering; computers; advanced system engineering; power system problems. *Mailing Add:* 1204 Milton Ave Pittsburgh PA 15218

HARDER, HAROLD CECIL, PHARMACOLOGY, CANCER. *Current Pos:* PRES, BLESSINGS INT, 85- *Personal Data:* b Lansing, Mich, Feb 27, 43; m 65, Linda J; c David L, Harold D & Leanna M. *Educ:* Alma Col, BS, 64; Mich State Univ, MS, 66, PhD(biophys), 70. *Prof Exp:* Fel pharmacol, Yale Univ, 70-72; asst prof pharmacol, George Washington Univ, 72-78; assoc prof pharmacol, Oral Roberts Univ, 78-85. *Mem:* Am Asn Cancer Res; Sigma Xi; Am Soc Pharmacol & Exp Therapeut. *Res:* Cancer chemotherapy, drug effects on mammalian cell cycle kinetics, drug induced DNA damage and repair, template activity of drug treated DNA and polynucleotides, heavy metal pharmacology and toxicology, drug metabolism, drug interactions, pharmacokinetics; coauthor of two model acts (laws) that relieve liability for treatment of indigent patients in the United States; active in health care reform debate. *Mailing Add:* 5881 S Garnett Tulsa OK 74146-6812. *Fax:* 918-250-1281

HARDER, JAMES ALBERT, ENGINEERING SCIENCE. *Current Pos:* res engr, Univ Calif, Berkeley, 52-57, asst prof hydraul eng, 57-62, assoc prof civil eng, 62-69, PROF HYDRAUL ENG, UNIV CALIF, BERKELEY, 69- *Personal Data:* b Fullerton, Calif, Dec 2, 26; m 95, Cedar Carrier; c 3. *Educ:* Calif Inst Technol, BS, 48; Univ Calif, Berkeley, MS, 52, PhD(fluid mech), 57. *Prof Exp:* Design engr, Soil Conserv Serv, USDA, 48-50. *Concurrent Pos:* Hydrologist, Aquatechnics, San Francisco. *Mem:* Fel AAAS; Am Soc Civil Engrs; Soc Sci Explor. *Res:* Pollution travel in pipe networks; non-linear system analysis; feedback control of canal systems; flood propagation; extraterrestrial science and societies. *Mailing Add:* Dept Civil Eng Univ Calif Berkeley CA 94720

HARDER, JOHN DWIGHT, REPRODUCTIVE PHYSIOLOGY, WILDLIFE BIOLOGY. *Current Pos:* ASSOC PROF ZOOL, OHIO STATE UNIV, 73- *Personal Data:* b O'Neill, Nebr, May 21, 43; m 66; c 2. *Educ:* Hastings Col, BA, 65; Colo State Univ, MS, 67; Ohio State Univ, PhD(zool), 71. *Prof Exp:* Res asst wildlife biol, Colo Coop Wildlife Res Unit, Colo State Univ, 65-67; asst prof, State Univ NY Col Oswego, 70-73. *Mem:* Am Soc Mammal; Wildlife Soc; Soc Study Reproduction. *Res:* Reproductive endocrinology of mammals; population biology; wildlife ecology; ovariectomy, ovarian analysis; radio immunoassay of ovarian steroids; physiology regulations of estrus; ovulation and partarition. *Mailing Add:* Dept Zool Ohio State Univ 1735 Neil Ave 063 B-Z Columbus OH 43210. *Fax:* 614-292-2030; *E-Mail:* harder.2@osu.edu

HARDER, ROGER WEHE, SOIL CONSERVATION, SOIL FERTILITY. *Current Pos:* RETIRED. *Personal Data:* b Fond du Lac, Wis, May 26, 17; m 46; c 3. *Educ:* Univ Wis, BA, 42, MS, 47. *Prof Exp:* From asst prof to assoc prof agron, Univ Idaho, 47-64, assoc prof agr biochem & soils, 64-72, assoc prof & assoc soil scientist, 72-77, prof plant & soil scientist soil fertil, 77-83. *Mem:* Soil Conserv Soc Am; Soil Sci Soc Am; Am Soc Agron. *Res:* Soil erosion control and management; need for phosphorus and sulfur on erouded hill tops; need for sulphur for wheat production in palouse soils; need for lime for maxium alealea growth on acidic forest soils. *Mailing Add:* 314 E Seventh St Moscow ID 83843

HARDESTY, BOYD A, BIOCHEMISTRY. *Current Pos:* from asst prof to assoc prof, 63-74, PROF CHEM, UNIV TEX, AUSTIN, 74- *Personal Data:* b Cheney, Wash, May 15, 32; m 52; c 3. *Educ:* Wash State Univ, BS, 53, MS, 56; Calif Inst Technol, PhD(biochem), 60. *Prof Exp:* NSF fel, Med Sch, Yale Univ, 61; NSF fel, Med Sch, Univ Ky, 60-62, USPHS fel, 62-63. *Mem:* AAAS; Am Chem Soc; Am Soc Biol Chem. *Res:* Hemoglobin biosynthesis and polyribosomes in rabbit reticulocytes; ribosome structure and functions; translational control in normal and transformed erythroid cells. *Mailing Add:* Dept Chem Univ Tex Austin TX 78712. *Fax:* 512-471-8696

HARDESTY, GEORGE K(IRWAN) C(OLLISON), APPLIED OPTICS, ILLUMINATING ENGINEERING. *Current Pos:* CONSULT ENG, 69- *Personal Data:* b Mayo, Md, Nov 15, 09; m 32, Elizabeth Sterba; c Kathleen (Hull). *Prof Exp:* Asst to supt Interior Commun Div, US Naval Res Lab, 41-43, asst supt, 43-47, head, Indicators Sect, 47-49, head, Interior Commun Br, 50-56, electronic scientist, 56-60, electronics engr, 60-61, res electronics engr, US Navy Marine Eng Lab, 61-65; consult & display engr, 65-69. *Concurrent Pos:* Consult Polaris Proj Off, Navy Bur Weapons, 61-65, Miller Co, Conn, 62-65 & Belsinger-Signtific Display Div, Md, 64-65; vpres, Caysea Eng Corp, 81-93; pres, Warwick River Lab, 90- *Mem:* Soc Automotive Engrs; fel Illum Eng Soc; Optical Soc Am; sr mem Instrument Soc Am. *Res:* Information display systems; instrument and display illumination; work space surveys, proposals; colored signal specifications and evaluations; spectroradiometry and colorimetry; human factors interface problems; invention development, tutorial writings; expository technical writing; approximately 40 US & foreign patents awarded; electro-optics, electro-mechanical product design; security-system keyed locks; safety systems. *Mailing Add:* PO Box 355 Secretary MD 21664

HARDESTY, LINDA HOWELL, AGROFORESTRY, LAND MANAGEMENT SYSTEMS. *Current Pos:* ASSOC PROF, WASH STATE UNIV, 85- *Personal Data:* b Argentia, Nfld, June 15, 52; US & Can citizen. *Educ:* Univ Idaho, BS, 74; Utah State Univ, MS, 81, PhD(range mgt), 87. *Prof Exp:* Inventory specialist, Idaho Dept Lands, 75, range mgr, 76-80; res assoc, Utah State Univ, 80-85. *Concurrent Pos:* Proj leader, Idaho Dept Fish & Game, 76; consult, US Feed Grains Coun, 84, World Bank, 88, Region 10 Environ Protection Agency, 89 & Bureau Land Mgt, 90; prin investr, USDA. *Mem:* Soc Range Mgt; Am Asn Women Sci; Soc Am Foresters. *Res:* Study of the impacts of glazing on forest site productivity in the US, Brazil and Tanzania. *Mailing Add:* Dept Natural Resource Wash State Univ One SE Stadium Way Pullman WA 99164-0001

HARDESTY, PATRICK THOMAS, CHEMISTRY. *Current Pos:* Res chemist, Monsanto Co, 75-77, RES CHEMIST, E I DU PONT DE NEMOURS & CO, INC, 80- *Personal Data:* b Owensboro, Ky, Feb 9, 51; m 77. *Educ:* Brescia Col, BA, 73; Purdue Univ, MS, 74; Univ Ill, PhD(anal chem), 80. *Mem:* Am Chem Soc; Sigma Xi. *Res:* Metabolism research to determine the environmental fate of pesticides. *Mailing Add:* 822 Starvegut Rd Kennett Square PA 19348-2528

HARDGROVE, GEORGE LIND, JR, PHYSICAL CHEMISTRY. *Current Pos:* From asst prof to assoc prof, 59-71, PROF CHEM, ST OLAF COL, 71- *Personal Data:* b Barberton, Ohio, Dec 2, 33; m 61, Gretchen M Grosenick; c George W & Anne E. *Educ:* Oberlin Col, AB, 56; Univ Calif, Berkeley, PhD(chem), 59. *Concurrent Pos:* NIH spec fel, Oxford Univ, 65-66; vis prof, Univ Fla, 73-74; vis consult, Oak Ridge Nat Lab, 81-82; res fel, Univ Durham, Eng, 88-89. *Mem:* Am Crystallog Asn; Am Chem Soc. *Res:* Molecular structure determination by NMR and x-ray diffraction. *Mailing Add:* Dept Chem St Olaf Col Northfield MN 55057-1098

HARDHAM, WILLIAM MORGAN, PHOTOGRAPHIC CHEMISTRY, ORGANIC CHEMISTRY. *Current Pos:* res chemist, E I Du Pont de Nemours & Co, Inc, 65-69, res supvr, Photo Prod Dept, 69-87, asst to dir res, Electronics Dept, 87-93, staff consult, Res & Develop, 93-94, LAB MGR/HR CONSULT, DUPONT P & EM, 94- *Personal Data:* b Philadelphia, Pa, Oct 19, 39; m 61, 71, 93, Lorena C Meunier; c William D, John M & Erin E. *Educ:* Pa State Univ, BS, 61; Calif Inst Technol, PhD(chem), 65. *Prof Exp:* NIH fel, 64-65. *Mem:* Am Chem Soc. *Res:* Photochemistry of maleic anhydride; ketone photoreductions; mechanism of the photoreaction of orthoquinone monoimines with arylmethanes; sensitized and direct photodecomposition of bimidazoles; silver halide emulsions. *Mailing Add:* Du Pont P&Em Exp Sta PO Box 80334 Wilmington DE 19880-0334

HARDIE, EDITH L, CARDIOPULMONARY PHYSIOLOGY. *Personal Data:* b Ancon, CZ, Oct 1, 31. *Educ:* Georgetown Univ, BSN, 54; Med Col Va, PhD(physiol), 69. *Prof Exp:* Head nurse, Med-Surg Unit, Med Col Va, Va Commonwealth Univ, 54-56, head nurse-technician, Pulmonary Function Lab, 56-61, instr, 69-71, asst prof physiol, 71-83, nurse, 90-93. *Concurrent Pos:* Richmond Area Heart Asn fel, Med Col Va, 70-71, A D William Fund fels, 71-72 & 73-74; Va Heart Asn fel, 72-73; vis scientist, Stritch Sch Med, Loyola Univ, Ill, 75-76. *Mem:* Sigma Xi; assoc mem Am Physiol Soc; AAAS. *Res:* Cardiac and pulmonary receptors and their reflex effects on circulation and respiration; experimental pulmonary embolism; location of atrial subsidiary pacemakers. *Mailing Add:* 5701 Monument Ave Richmond VA 23226-1825

HARDIE, GERALD, NUCLEAR PHYSICS. *Current Pos:* asst prof, 65-67, assoc prof, 67-72, PROF PHYSICS, WESTERN MICH UNIV, 72- *Personal Data:* b Winnipeg, Man, Feb 7, 31; US citizen. *Educ:* Univ Man, BS, 55, MS, 57; Univ Wis, PhD(physics), 62. *Prof Exp:* Assoc physicist, IIT Res Inst, 62-64, res physicist, 64-65. *Mem:* Am Phys Soc. *Res:* Low energy nuclear physics. *Mailing Add:* Dept Physics Western Mich Univ 1128 EVR Kalamazoo MI 49008. *Fax:* 616-387-4948

HARDIE, WILLIAM GEORGE, low dielectric constant materials, high temperature polymers, for more information see previous edition

HARDIN, BOBBY OTT, CIVIL ENGINEERING. *Current Pos:* from instr to assoc prof, 56-67, PROF CIVIL ENG, UNIV KY, 67- *Personal Data:* b Lexington, Ky, Sept 9, 35; m 60, Anita J Stoten; c Kenneth O & Cynthia J (Gibson). *Educ:* Univ Ky, BS, 56, MS, 58; Univ Fla, PhD, 61. *Honors & Awards:* Alfred Noble Prize, 66; Walter Huber Res Prize, Am Soc Civil Engrs, 68, Norman Medal 73, & Thomas A Middlebrooks Award, 79; C A Hogentogler Award, Am Soc Testing & Mat, 79; J James R Croes Medal, 90. *Prof Exp:* Hwy engr, Ky Dept Hwys, 55-56. *Concurrent Pos:* Struct design engr, Gregg & Assocs, 57-; asst, Univ Fla, 59; Ford Found resident engr, Tenn Valley Authority, Nickajack Proj, 65-66. *Mem:* Fel Am Soc Civil Engrs; Am Soc Testing & Mat. *Res:* Soil dynamics; constitutive equations. *Mailing Add:* Dept Civil Eng Univ Ky Lexington KY 40506

HARDIN, CLIFFORD MORRIS, AGRICULTURAL ECONOMICS. *Current Pos:* RETIRED. *Personal Data:* b Knightstown, Ind, Oct 9, 15; m 39; c 5. *Educ:* Purdue Univ, BS, 37, MS, 39, PhD(agr econ), 41. *Hon Degrees:* DSc, Purdue Univ, 53, NDak State Univ, 69, Mich State Univ, 69; Dr, Nat Univ Colombia, 68; LLD, Creighton Univ, 56, Ill State Univ, 73; DHumL, Univ Nebr, 78, Okla Christian Col, 79. *Prof Exp:* Res assoc prof agr econ, Univ Wis, 41-44; prof dir & dean agr, Mich State Univ Col Agr, 44-55; chancellor, Univ Nebr, 54-69; secy, USDA, 69-71; vchmn & dir corp res, Ralston Purina Co, 71-80; scholar-in-residence, Wash Univ, 80-81 & 83-85, dir, Ctr Study Am Bus, 81-82; consult, Stifel Nicolaus & Co, Inc, 80-90. *Concurrent Pos:* Mem, NSF Bd, 66-69; bd dir, Ralston Purina Co, 71-81 & Ralston Purina Can, 71-80; bd trustees, Rockefeller Found, 61-81, Int Agr Develop Serv, 75-85, Farm Found, 73-84, Am Assembly, 75-, Univ Nebr Found, 75-; mem bd dir, 81-; trustee, Kettering Found, 80-, Winrock Int Inst Agr Develop, 85- *Mailing Add:* 10 Roan Lane St Louis MO 63124

HARDIN, CLYDE D, ELECTRONICS ENGINEERING. *Current Pos:* CONSULT, 81- *Personal Data:* b Ft Worth, Tex, May 26, 25; m 48; c 3. *Educ:* Wake Forest Col, BS, 48. *Honors & Awards:* Secy Defense Meritorious Serv Medal, 73; Republic Korea Pres Cheonsu Medal, 76; Asn Old Crows Nat Medal Electronic Warfare Mgt, 76; Res & Develop Achievement Award, Dept Army, 69, Army Meritorious Serv Medal, 71. *Prof Exp:* Asst staff engr electronics, Inst Coop Res, Johns Hopkins Univ, 48; res physicist & group leader, Nat Bur Stands, 48-53; group leader & sect chief, Harry Diamond Labs, 53-58, chief adv res lab, 58-65, develop lab, 65-69; spec asst on SE Asia, to Asst Secy Army, Res & Develop, 69-72, dir defense res, develop, test & eval counterpart group, Korea, 72-73; dir, US Army Electronics Warfare Lab, 73-80, tech dir, US Army Electronics Res & Develop Command, 80-81; vpres, Int Opers, J S Lee Assocs Inc, 85-86. *Mem:* Fel Inst Elec & Electronics Engrs; AAAS; Am Defense Preparedness Asn; Asn Old Crows; Armed Forces Commun & Electronics Asn. *Res:* Military electronics; radar; guidance; fuzing and communications systems and techniques. *Mailing Add:* One Sorrelwood Cross Savannah GA 31411

HARDIN, GARRETT (JAMES), BIOLOGY, HUMAN ECOLOGY. *Current Pos:* asst prof bact, Univ Calif, Santa Barbara, 46-50, assoc prof biol, 50-57, prof, 57-63, prof human ecol, 63-78, EMER PROF HUMAN ECOL, UNIV CALIF, SANTA BARBARA, 78- *Personal Data:* b Dallas, Tex, Apr 21, 15; m 41; c Hylz, Peter, Sharon & David. *Educ:* Univ Chicago, ScB, 36; Stanford Univ, PhD(biol), 41. *Hon Degrees:* DHH, Puget Sound Univ, 75; LHD, Northland Col, 76. *Honors & Awards:* Margaret Sanger Award, 80. *Prof Exp:* Asst, Chicago City Jr Col, 38; mem staff, Div Plant Biol, Carnegie Inst, 42-46. *Concurrent Pos:* Actg asst prof, Stanford Univ, 45, vis prof, 48; sr res assoc, Calif Inst Technol, 52-53; vis prof, Univ Calif, Los Angeles, 61, Berkeley, 64 & Univ Chicago, 70; pres, Environ Fund, 80-81; emer bd mem, Fedn Am Immigration Reform. *Mem:* AAAS; Ecol Soc Am; Am Philos Soc; Am Acad Arts & Sci; Int Soc Ecol Econ. *Res:* Evolution; human ecology. *Mailing Add:* Dept Biol Sci Univ Calif Santa Barbara CA 93106. *Fax:* 805-967-2715

HARDIN, GEORGE C, JR, GEOLOGY. *Current Pos:* RETIRED. *Personal Data:* b Oakwood, Tex, Oct 6, 20; m 42; c 2. *Educ:* Agr & Mech Col, Univ Tex, BS, 41; Univ Wis, PhM, 42. *Prof Exp:* Geologist & mining engr, Victory Fluorspar Co, Ill, 42; geologist, US Geol Surv, Washington, DC, 42-45 & Carter-Gragg Oil Co, Tex, 45-46; geologist & petrol engr, Michel T Halbouty, 46-51, explor & prod mgr, Michel T Halbouty Oil & Gas Interests, 51-59, gen mgr, 59-61; partner, Hardin & Hardin, Consult Geologists, 61-64; mgr oil & gas explor, Kerr-McGee Oil Industs, Inc, 64-65, vpres, NAm Oil & Gas Explor, Kerr-McGee Corp, 65-67, explor, 67-68; pres, Royal Resources Corp, 68-71; pres, Ashland Explor Co, 71-80, sr vpres, Ashland, Inc, 71-80; vchmn & dir, Integrated Energy, Inc, 81-84; dir, Am Gas & Oil Investors, 81-82. *Concurrent Pos:* Exec vpres, Halbouty Alaska Oil Co, 58-61; vis geoscientist, Am Geol Inst, 63. *Mem:* Am Asn Petrol Geol (secy-treas, 64-66); Geol Soc Am; Nat Soc Prof Eng; Soc Econ Paleont & Mineral; Soc Explor Geophys. *Res:* Petroleum geology; sedimentation; stratigraphy. *Mailing Add:* 204 Arborway St Houston TX 77057

HARDIN, HILLIARD FRANCES, microbiology, mycology; deceased, see previous edition for last biography

HARDIN, IAN RUSSELL, TEXTILE CHEMISTRY, POLYMER SCIENCE. *Current Pos:* asst prof textiles, 71-76, dept head consumer affairs, 77-82, ASSOC PROF TEXTILES, AUBURN UNIV, 76-; CONSULT. *Personal Data:* b Glasgow, Scotland, Aug 3, 44; US citizen; m 67; c 2. *Educ:* Auburn Univ, BS, 65; Inst Textile Technol, MS, 67; Clemson Univ, PhD(chem), 70. *Prof Exp:* Fel polymers, Univ Mich, 70-71. *Concurrent Pos:* Chmn, Gen Fac & Univ Senate, Auburn Univ, 85-86. *Mem:* Am Chem Soc; Am Asn Textile Chemists & Colorists; Am Home Econ Asn; Sigma Xi; Fiber Soc; AAAS. *Res:* Textile flammability; morphology of polymers; photochemical effects in fibers. *Mailing Add:* Univ Ga 303 Dawson Hall Athens GA 30602-3622

HARDIN, JAMES T, INDUSTRIAL CONTROLS, POWER ELECTRONICS. *Current Pos:* MGR OPERS, INNOVATIVE APPLNS CORP, 92- *Personal Data:* b Peoria, Ill, Sept 28, 34; m 57, Jane Christensen; c Kathy L, Kelly J & Joseph E. *Educ:* Bradley Univ, BS, 56, MS, 63. *Prof Exp:* Proj engr, Lockheed Aircraft Corp, 56-57; grad asst circuit anal, Bradley Univ, 61-63; mgr & vpres eng, Prestolite Div, Allied Signal Corp, 64-85; chief engr, Septor Electronics Corp, 85-90; pres, Terawmar Technologies, Inc, 90-92. *Concurrent Pos:* Chmn, Ignition Comt, Soc Automotive Engrs, 80-85; mem, US deleg Int Standards Orgn, 80-85. *Mem:* Inst Elec & Electronics Engrs; Soc Automotive Engrs. *Res:* Developed and patented electronic ignition systems, voltage regulators and alternators for automotive and marine engines; developed unique machine control system hardware based on digital computer techniques and logic. *Mailing Add:* 205 Morning Star Dr Santa Teresa NM 88008. *Fax:* 915-778-1491

HARDIN, JAMES W, MOLECULAR ENDOCRINOLOGY, MOLECULAR PATHOLOGY. *Current Pos:* ASSOC PROF MED & BIOCHEM, UNIV ARK MED SCI, 80-, PROF PATH INTERNAL MED, 96-; ASSOC DIR RES, ARK CANCER RES CTR, 88- *Personal Data:* b Baton Rouge, La, Nov 16, 46; m 72, Gwendolyn Stafford; c James & Margaret. *Educ:* La State Univ, BSc, 68; Purdue Univ, PhD(biochem), 72. *Prof Exp:* Asst prof, Baylor Col Med, 77-79. *Concurrent Pos:* Reviewer, Nat Cancer Inst & Am Chem Soc. *Mem:* AAAS; Am Soc Cell Biol; Sigma Xi; Am Soc Microbiol. *Res:* Molecular biology of hormone and proto oncogene activity; molecular mechanisms radiation injury. *Mailing Add:* Ark Cancer Res Ctr Univ Ark Med Sci Slot 623 4301 W Markham St Little Rock AK 72205-7107. *Fax:* 501-686-7861; *E-Mail:* jwhardin@acro.uams.edu

HARDIN, JAMES WALKER, SYSTEMATIC BOTANY, DENDROLOGY. *Current Pos:* from asst prof to prof, 57-96, cur herbarium, 57-96, EMER PROF BOT, NC STATE UNIV, 96- *Personal Data:* b Charlotte, NC, Mar 31, 29; m 57, Dorthy Struck; c Elizabeth, Patricia & Catherine. *Educ:* Fla Southern Col, BS, 50; Univ Tenn, MS, 51; Univ Mich, PhD(bot), 57. *Honors & Awards:* Cooley Award, Am Soc Plant Taxon, 58. *Prof Exp:* Instr bot, Univ Mich, 56-57. *Concurrent Pos:* Vis prof, Mt Lake Biol Sta, Va, 62, 64 & 83; pres, Highlands Biol Sta, 63-69; consult, Res Triangle Inst, 64-70; vis prof biol sta, Univ Okla, 67 & 70; ed, ASB Bull, 80-86, Systematic Bot, 85-91. *Mem:* Am Soc Plant Taxon (pres, 92-93); Bot Soc Am; Int Asn Plant Taxon; Soc Econ Bot; Asn Southeastern Biol (pres, 79-80). *Res:* Taxonomic botany; taxonomy of woody Angiosperms; flora of the southeastern United States; endangered species; poisonous plants; scanning electron microscopy of foliar surfaces. *Mailing Add:* Dept Bot NC State Univ Raleigh NC 27695-7612. *Fax:* 919-515-3436

HARDIN, JAMES WILLIAM, VERTEBRATE ECOLOGY, ANIMAL BEHAVIOR. *Current Pos:* from asst prof to assoc prof, 78-85, PROF WILDLIFE, COL NATURAL RESOURCES, UNIV WIS, STEVENS POINT, 85- *Personal Data:* b Paintsville, Ky, July 16, 43. *Educ:* Univ Ky, BS, 65, MS, 67; Southern Ill Univ, PhD(zool), 74. *Prof Exp:* Instr biol, Memphis State Univ, 67-69; researcher, Southern Ill Univ, 74, asst dir, Wildlife Res Lab, 74-78, asst prof zool, 74-78. *Mem:* Am Soc Mammalogists; Wildlife Soc; Ecol Soc Am; Wilson Ornith Soc. *Res:* Life history, population dynamics and behavior of vertebrates emphasizing the roles that these parameters play in enabling populations to exist in the wild. *Mailing Add:* Col Natural Resources Univ Wis Stevens Point 2100 Main St Stevens Point WI 54481-3871

HARDIN, JAY CHARLES, ACOUSTICS, FLUID MECHANICS. *Current Pos:* Scientist acoust, 69-90, CHIEF SCIENTIST ACOUST DIV, NASA, 90- *Personal Data:* b Indianapolis, Ind, Oct 22, 42; m 64, Ellen Huey; c Lance, Shane & Brooke. *Educ:* Purdue Univ, BS, 64, MS, 65, PhD(eng sci), 69. *Concurrent Pos:* Fel, Inst of Sound & Vibration Res, Southampton, Eng, 72; prof, George Washington Univ, 70-, Christopher Newport Col, 81- & Old Dom Univ, 83- *Mem:* Sigma Xi. *Res:* Aeroacoustics; stochastic processes; computational fluid mechanics. *Mailing Add:* 116 Mistletoe Dr Newport News VA 23606

HARDIN, JOHN AVERY, RHEUMATOLOGY. *Current Pos:* PROF MED & CHMN, DEPT MED, MED COL GA, 91- *Personal Data:* b Washington, Ga, Aug 12, 43. *Educ:* Med Col Ga, MD, 69. *Prof Exp:* From asst prof to prof med, Sch Med, Yale Univ, 76-91. *Concurrent Pos:* Chief, Rheumatology Sect, Sch Med, Yale Univ, 88-91. *Mem:* Am Soc Clin Invest. *Mailing Add:* Dept Med Med Col Ga 1120 15th St B1W456 Augusta GA 30912-3100

HARDIN, ROBERT TOOMBS, BIOMETRICS, POULTRY BREEDING. *Current Pos:* RETIRED. *Personal Data:* b Dyas, Ga, Sept 14, 31; m 57; c 3. *Educ:* Univ Ga, BSA, 56; Purdue Univ, MS, 60, PhD(genetics), 62. *Prof Exp:* From asst prof to prof poultry & genetics, Univ Alta, 62-97, chmn, Dept Animal Sci, 82-89. *Res:* Data analysis; design and analysis of agricultural experiments. *Mailing Add:* Dept Agr Food & Nutrit Sci Univ Alta Edmonton AB T6G 2P5 Can

HARDING, BOYD W, BIOCHEMISTRY, ENDOCRINOLOGY. *Current Pos:* Am Cancer Soc fel endocrinol, 59-61, from instr med to assoc prof 60-70, PROF MED & BIOCHEM, SCH MED, UNIV SOUTHERN CALIF, 70- *Personal Data:* b Provo, Utah, June 4, 26; m 55; c 4. *Educ:* Brigham Young Univ, BS, 50; Univ Utah, MD, 54, PhD(biochem), 61. *Prof Exp:* USPHS fel biochem, Univ Utah, 57-58 & Cambridge Univ, 58-59. *Concurrent Pos:* USPHS res develop award gen med sci, 65-69; mem, Endocrine Study Sect, NIH, 73-77. *Mem:* AAAS; Am Soc Biol Chem; Am Fedn Clin Res; Endocrine Soc. *Res:* Hydroxylation reactions; control of adrenal cortex. *Mailing Add:* Dept Med & Biochem EM 2916 Commercial Ave Suite 230 Anacortes WA 98221-2998

HARDING, CHARLES ENOCH, PHYSICAL ORGANIC CHEMISTRY. *Current Pos:* asst prof, 71-73, assoc prof, 73-80, PROF CHEM, UNIV TENN, MARTIN, 73-, CHMN DEPT, 80- *Personal Data:* b Paris, Tenn, Nov 30, 42; m 66; c 2. *Educ:* Univ Tenn, Martin, BS, 64; Knoxville, PhD(chem), 69. *Prof Exp:* Alexander von Humboldt fel, Univ Tübingen, 69-70. *Mem:* Am Chem Soc; Am Inst Chemists; Sigma Xi. *Res:* Experimental studies in organic reaction mechanisms. *Mailing Add:* Dept Chem Univ Tenn Martin TN 38238-0001

HARDING, CLIFFORD VINCENT, JR, CELL PHYSIOLOGY. *Current Pos:* RETIRED. *Personal Data:* b Cranston, RI, Apr 27, 25; m 48, Drusilla Van Hoesen; c Clifford III & Richard H. *Educ:* Brown Univ, AB, 46; Yale Univ, MS, 48; Univ Pa, PhD(zool), 50. *Honors & Awards:* Fight-for-Sight Citation, 82. *Prof Exp:* Lab asst zool, Yale Univ, 46-48; asst instr, Univ Pa, 48-49; NIH fel cell physiol, Wenner-Grens Inst, Stockholm & Zool Sta, Naples, 50-52; asst prof zool, Univ Southern Calif, 52-54 & Univ Pa, 54-58; physiologist & asst to chief, Med Br, Div Biol & Med, US AEC, 56-57; from asst prof to assoc prof physiol, Col Physicians & Surgeons, Columbia Univ, 58-64; prof biol & chmn dept, Oakland Univ, 64-73; prof ophthal & dir res, Kresge Eye Inst, Sch Med, Wayne State Univ, 73-88. *Concurrent Pos:* Lalor fel, 58; mem corp, Marine Biol Lab, Woods Hole, Mass; NIH career develop award, 63-64; adj prof, Oakland Univ, 73- *Mem:* Am Soc Cell Biol; Tissue Cult Asn; Soc Develop Biol; Int Soc Cell Biol; Asn Res Vision & Opthal; Int Soc Eye Res. *Res:* Cell nucleus; fertilization proteins in hybrid embryos; radiation on cell division; DNA and mitosis; control of cell division and growth in ocular tissues; lens, cornea, ocular vasculature and human cataracts; energy dispersive X-ray analysis of eye tissue elements. *Mailing Add:* 54 Two Ponds Rd Falmouth MA 02540

HARDING, CLIFFORD VINCENT, III, IMMUNOLOGY, CELL BIOLOGY. *Current Pos:* asst prof, 93-96, ASSOC PROF, PATH DEPT, CASE WESTERN RES UNIV, CLEVELAND, 96- *Personal Data:* b Arlington, Va, Jan 31, 57; m 83, Mina Kay Chung; c Clifford V IV & Andrew R. *Educ:* Harvard Col, BA, 79; Washington Univ, St Louis, PhD(cell biol) & MD, 85. *Honors & Awards:* Exp Pathologist in Training Award, 89; Pfizer Scholar Award, 91; Am Cancer Soc J Fac Res Am Asn Pathologists, 91. *Prof Exp:* Resident path, Washington Univ & Barnes Hosp, 85-89, chief resident, 89-90, asst prof, Path Dept, 90-93. *Mem:* Am Soc Cell Biol; Am Asn Immunologist; Am Soc Invest Path; AAAS. *Res:* Antigen processing, MHC molecule function, receptor-mediated endocytosis; intracellular protein processing and transport; roles of endosomal compartments. *Mailing Add:* Inst Path Case Western Res Univ 2085 Adelbert Rd Cleveland OH 44106-4907. *Fax:* 216-368-0495; *E-Mail:* cvh3@po.cwru.edu

HARDING, DUANE DOUGLASS, FORECASTING, BROADCASTING METEOROLOGY. *Personal Data:* b Damarascotta, Maine, Dec 14, 47. *Educ:* Univ Mich, BS, 69, PhD(atmospheric sci), 77. *Prof Exp:* Asst res meteorol, Univ Mich, 71-78; res meteorologist, Mauna Lao Observ, Nat Oceanic & Atmospheric Admin, 78-79; asst prof, Eastern Ky Univ, 79-; broadcast meteorologist & sci producer, WKYT, Lexington, Ky, 84-86; chief meteorologist, WVEC, Norfolk, Va, 86-90; chief meteorologist, WKYT, Norfolk, Va, 90-96. *Concurrent Pos:* Adj prof, Old Dominion Univ, 88- *Mem:* Am Meteorol Soc; Sigma Xi; Nat Weather Asn. *Res:* Meteorology. *Mailing Add:* 5301 Stewart Dr Virginia Beach VA 23464

HARDING, FANN, ANATOMY. *Current Pos:* ASST TO DIR DIV BLOOD DIS & RESOURCES, NAT HEART, LUNG & BLOOD INST, 74- *Personal Data:* b Henderson, Ky, Jan 29, 30; m 56; c Mary Breckinridge. *Educ:* Coker Col, AB, 51; Med Univ SC, MS, 54, PhD(anat), 58. *Honors & Awards:* Ruth Patrick Award, 51; NIH Award Sustained Performance, 73; Distinguished Serv Award, Am Asn Blood Banks, 90; Award of Merit, NIH, 93. *Prof Exp:* Teaching & res fel anat, Med Col SC, 53-58; pub health res prog analyst, Extramural Prog, Nat Heart Inst, 58-61, health scientist adminr, res & training grants br, 61-64, sr health scientist adminr, sect chief, Res Grant Br Sect, 64-69, sr health scientist adminr Thrombosis & Hemorrhagic Dis Br & Arteriosclerosis Dis Br, Nat Heart & Lung Inst, 69-74. *Concurrent Pos:* Consult, James F Mitchell Found, Washington, DC, 62-67, Wash Vet Admin Hosp, 68-70; mem, Nat Heart Inst Fel Bd, 66-68; mem, Civil Serv Qual Rev Bd, NIH, 71-, Women's Action Prog adv coun, US Dept Health Educ & Welfare, 71-72; founding pres, Fedn Orgn Prof Women, 72-; mem staff, res training & res career develop & transfusion med, Prob Area US-USSR Health Exchange, Blood Dis & Res Adv Comt; prog dir, Extramural Res Training & Career Develop Blood Dis & Transfusion Med, Nat Heart, Lung & Blood Inst, exec secy, Blood Dis & Resources Adv Comt; asn Women US Edn Found, 73-74, mem bd dirs, Lupus Found Am, 85-88; asst coordr, US-USSR Health Exchange Prog, 74-; bd visitors, Coker Col, 74-78. *Mem:* Int Soc Thrombosis & Haemostasis; Microcirc Soc; Reticuloendothelial Soc; Am Heart Asn; Am Asn Blood Banks; Int Soc Blood Transfusion; AAAS. *Res:* Histology and physiology of liver; normal and pathologic microcirculatory physiology. *Mailing Add:* 1870 Wyoming Ave NW Washington DC 20009. *Fax:* 301-496-1817

HARDING, GODFREY KYNARD MATTHEW, INFECTIOUS DISEASES. *Current Pos:* asst microbiologist, Health Sci Ctr, 75-81, asst prof med & med microbiol, 75-80, assoc prof, 80-87, PROF MED & MED MICROBIOL, UNIV MAN, 87-; HEAD INFECTIOUS DIS, ST BONIFACE GEN HOSP, 81- *Personal Data:* b Trinidad, W Indies, Sept 21, 42; Can citizen; m 69; c 2. *Educ:* Univ Man, BSc & MD, 69; FRCPS(C), 74; Am Bd Internal Med, dipl, 74; FACP, 85. *Prof Exp:* Fel infectious dis, Univ Man, 72-73; fel Univ Calif, Los Angeles, 73-74. *Concurrent Pos:* Consult, St Boniface Gen Hosp, 75-81, Health Sci Ctr, 75-; grants, Med Res Coun Can, 76-83, Health & Welfare Can, Nat Health Res Develop Prog, 82- *Mem:* Am Soc Microbiol; fel Royal Col Physicians Can; Can Soc Clin Invest; Can Infectious Dis Soc; fel Infectious Dis Soc Am; fel Am Col Physicians. *Res:* Pathogenesis and management of recurrent urinary tract infections; anaerobic infections; hospital-acquired infections. *Mailing Add:* Dept Infectious Dis St Boniface Gen Hosp 409 Tache Ave Winnipeg MB R2H 2A6 Can

HARDING, HOMER ROBERT, endocrinology, for more information see previous edition

HARDING, JAMES A, GENETICS, HORTICULTURE. *Current Pos:* Lab technician agron, Univ Calif, Davis, 57-65, asst prof landscape hort, 65-71, assoc prof environ hort, 71-76, PROF ENVIRON HORT, UNIV CALIF, DAVIS, 71- *Personal Data:* b Tustin, Calif, Jan 20, 35; m 55, 62, 72, 86; c 3. *Educ:* Univ Calif, Davis, BS, 57, PhD(genetics), 65. *Concurrent Pos:* Assoc ed, Euphytica. *Mem:* Am Soc Hort Sci. *Res:* Quantitative genetics; genetic structure of natural and artificial populations of plants; multi-trait selection in ornamental species. *Mailing Add:* Dept Environ Hort Univ Calif Davis CA 95616-5224

HARDING, JAMES LOMBARD, GEOLOGICAL OCEANOGRAPHY. *Current Pos:* assoc dir, Sea Grant Prog, Univ Ga, 74-77, dir, Marine Exten Serv, 77-85, assoc dir res, 85-87, ASSOC DIR RES, MARINE EXTEN SERV, UNIV GA, 90- *Personal Data:* b Harvey, Ill, Aug 4, 29; m 54. *Educ:* Miss Southern Col, BS, 56; Univ Tenn, MS, 57; Tex A&M Univ, PhD(oceanog), 64. *Prof Exp:* Instr geol, Univ Tenn, 56-59; asst prof, Miss Southern Col, 59-60; res scientist, Tex A&M Univ, 63-64; vpres, Oceanonics, Inc, 64-71; oceanogr, Marine Resources Ctr, Skidway Inst Oceanog, 71-74; sr geologist, UNDP/ESCHP, Bangkok, Thailand, 88-89. *Concurrent Pos:* Prof earth sci, Nicholls State Univ, 65-68; consult, major oil co, US, 61-71, 78-84. *Mem:* Fel Geol Soc Am; Soc Econ Paleont & Mineral; Am Inst Prof Geol; Am Inst Mining & Metall Engrs; Sigma Xi. *Res:* Marine sedimentation; coral reef geology and oceanography; coastal oceanography; carbonate petrology and sedimentation; applied marine geophysics; applied coastal oceanography; exploration and marine mining; applied marine geotechnics and soils mechanics. *Mailing Add:* 21 Ogeechee Dr Richmond Hill GA 31324

HARDING, JOSEPH WARREN, JR, NEUROCHEMISTRY. *Current Pos:* res assoc, Dept Vet Microbiol & Path, 76-77, asst prof path, 77-79, from asst prof to assoc prof, 79-, PROF NEUROSCI & PHYSIOL, DEPT VET & COMP ANAT, PHARMACOL & PHYSIOL, WASH STATE UNIV, 79- *Personal Data:* b Orange, NJ, Feb 9, 48; m 69; c 2. *Educ:* Alegheny Col, BS, 70; Univ Del, PhD(biochem), 75. *Prof Exp:* Fel neurochem, Roche Inst Molecular Biol, 74-76. *Concurrent Pos:* Adj prof, Prog Biochem & Biophys, Wash State Univ, 78- & Dept Psychol, 80- *Mem:* Soc Neurosci. *Res:* Neural control of cardiovascular function: brain-angiotensiun interactions; neural regeneration and plasticity: the primary olfactory system as a model; mechanisms of neurotransmitter release. *Mailing Add:* Dept Vet & Comp Anat Pharmacol & Physiol Wash State Univ Pullman WA 99164-6520

HARDING, KENN E, ORGANIC CHEMISTRY. *Current Pos:* asst prof, 69-76, assoc prof, 76-86, PROF CHEM, TEX A&M UNIV, 86- *Personal Data:* b Ponca City, Okla, Oct 2, 42; m 64, 76; c 1. *Educ:* Okla State Univ, BS, 64; Stanford Univ, PhD(org chem), 68. *Prof Exp:* NIH fel chem, Harvard Univ, 68-69. *Concurrent Pos:* Dir, Synthetic Org Chem Prog, NSF, 85-86. *Mem:* Am Chem Soc. *Res:* Organic synthesis; biogenetic-like olefin cyclizations; alkaloid synthesis; natural products synthesis; stereoselective and enantioselective synthesis. *Mailing Add:* Dept Chem Tex A&M Univ College Station TX 77843

HARDING, MAURICE JAMES CHARLES, PESTICIDES. *Current Pos:* sr res chemist, 75-79, PROCESS DEVELOP MGR, AGR CHEM GROUP, FMC CORP, 79- *Personal Data:* b Surrey, Eng, Dec 29, 38; wid; c Justin & Jason. *Educ:* Univ London, BS, 60, PhD(org chem), 63. *Prof Exp:* Res fel, Johns Hopkins Univ, 63-65; sr chemist, Laporte Chem Ltd, Luton, Eng, 65-68; res scientist, Res & Develop Div, Union Camp Corp, 68-75. *Mem:* Am Chem Soc; The Chem Soc. *Res:* Peroxides; peroxyacids; epoxides; nitrogen heterocycles; pyrroles; porphyrins; imidazoles; chemiluminescence; singlet oxygen; musk compounds; catalytic hydrogenation; sulfur chemistry; clay catalysis; pesticide chemistry; statistical design of experiments; process development in pyrethroids and herbicide chemistry; scale-up and commercialization of specialty chemicals, agrochemicals, etc. *Mailing Add:* 28 Fisher Ave Princeton NJ 08540

HARDING, PAUL GEORGE RICHARD, REPRODUCTIVE PHYSIOLOGY, PERINATOLOGY. *Current Pos:* Med Res Coun Can fel, 66-67, scholar, 67-71, ASSOC PROF PHYSIOL, OBSTET & GYNEC, UNIV WESTERN ONT, 70-, ASSOC DEAN RES MED. *Personal Data:* b Kitchener, Ont. *Educ:* Univ Western Ont, MD, 58, MSc, 61; FRCS(C), 63. *Mem:* Can Physiol Soc; Soc Obstet & Gynec Can. *Res:* Fetal and placental physiology, particularly energy metabolism in the fetus. *Mailing Add:* Res Off Fac Med Rm H103 Health Sci Addition Univ Western Ont London ON N6A 5C1 Can

HARDING, R(ONALD) H(UGH), NEW PRODUCT SYSTEMS DEVELOPMENT. *Current Pos:* PVT CONSULT, 86- *Personal Data:* b Chicago, Ill, June 26, 31; m 60, Mary E Skelly; c Robert J & Ellen M. *Educ:* Purdue Univ, BS, 53, PhD(chem eng), 58. *Prof Exp:* Asst, Purdue Univ, 52-53; asst, Lilly Varnish Co, 54-57; proj chemist, Res Dept, Chem Div, Union Carbide Corp, 57-62, group leader, Res & Develop Dept, 63-72, technol mgr, 69-72, mkt mgr, Mkt Dept, 70-72, prod mkt mgr, Latex Opers Dept, Chem & Plastics Div, 73-75, bus develop mgr, 76-77, sr develop scientist, 78-85. *Concurrent Pos:* Counr, Men's Residence Halls, Purdue Univ, 53-57. *Mem:* Am Chem Soc. *Res:* Applications research, product development and technical service of elastomers, urethane foams, water-soluble polymers, oil production chemicals, leather chemicals, latexes, adhesives, mining and water treatment chemicals. *Mailing Add:* 5 Janson Dr Westport CT 06880

HARDING, ROY WOODROW, JR, BIOCHEMISTRY. *Current Pos:* PROF BIOCHEM, IND UNIV PA, 87- *Personal Data:* b Arthurdale, WVa, Sept 16, 40; m 61; c 3. *Educ:* George Washington Univ, BS, 62; Calif Inst Technol, PhD(biochem), 68. *Prof Exp:* Fel, Univ Tex, Austin, 68-70; res scientist, Smithsonian Inst, 70-87. *Mem:* Am Soc Plant Physiologists; Am Soc Photobiol; Am Soc Biochem & Molecular Biol; Plant Growth Regulator Soc Am. *Res:* Light mediated biological responses; carotenoid biosynthesis; regulation of metabolic pathways. *Mailing Add:* Dept Chem Ind Univ Pa Indiana PA 15705-0001. *Fax:* 412-357-5700

HARDING, SAMUEL WILLIAM, PHYSICS. *Current Pos:* from asst prof to prof, 47-81, asst head, Dept Physics & Astron, 71-81, dir, Sci & Math Teaching Ctr, 74-78, EMER PROF PHYSICS, UNIV WYO, 81- *Personal Data:* b Salt Lake Co, Utah, Feb 18, 15; m 39, 79; c 2. *Educ:* Utah State Agr Col, BS, 39; Pa State Col, MS, 42, PhD(physics), 47. *Prof Exp:* Asst physics, Utah State Agr Col, 39-40; asst, Pa State Col, 40-42, instr, 42-46, res assoc, 46-47. *Concurrent Pos:* Consult, Optical Res Lab, Tex, 48-51. *Mem:* Am Phys Soc; Optical Soc Am; Am Asn Physics Teachers; fel AAAS. *Res:* Geometrical and physical optics with emphasis on resolution of optical instruments and thin films; science education. *Mailing Add:* 2317 Sunset Dr Lewiston ID 83501

HARDING, THOMAS HAGUE, NEUROPHYSIOLOGY, NEUROSCIENCE. *Current Pos:* PRIMARY INVESTR, UNIVERSAL ENERGY CORP, 94-, PROG MGR, 95- *Personal Data:* b Oxford, Miss, Mar 1, 45; m 85. *Educ:* Tex A&M Univ, BS, 67, MS, 71; Purdue Univ, PhD(neurophysiol), 77. *Prof Exp:* Teaching asst psychol & res asst, Tex A&M Univ, College Station, 70-71; David Ross res fel, Purdue Univ, West Lafayette, 71-74; traveling scholar, Biomed Eng Ctr, Technol Inst, Northwestern Univ, 75-77; vis fel, Australian Nat Univ, 77-79; res neurophysiologist, US Army Aeromed Res Lab, Ft Rucker, Ala, 79-82, chief, Sensory Neurosci Br, 82-93. *Mem:* Asn Res in Vision & Ophthal; AAAS. *Res:* Neurophysiology of the visual system; visual psychophysics; computer vision; visual perception; expert systems. *Mailing Add:* c/o USAARL Universal Energy Systs PO Box 577 Ft Rucker AL 36362

HARDING, WINFRED MOOD, BIOLOGICAL CHEMISTRY. *Current Pos:* RETIRED. *Personal Data:* b Huntsville, Tex, May 23, 20; m 44; c 2. *Educ:* Sam Houston State Col, BS, 41; Univ Tex, MA, 46, PhD(chem), 49. *Prof Exp:* Teacher pub sch, Tex, 42-43; asst chemist, Dow Chem Co, 43-44; asst, Univ Tex, 44-47; assoc prof chem, Southwest Tex State Col, 48-59; assoc prof, Sam Houston State Univ, 59-80, prof chem, 80-88. *Concurrent Pos:* Lab tutor, Univ Tex, 44-45. *Mem:* Am Chem Soc; Am Soc Microbiol; Sigma Xi. *Res:* Microbiological metabolism. *Mailing Add:* 2030 Ave Q Huntsville TX 77340

HARDING-BARLOW, INGEBORG, CHEMISTRY, PATHOLOGY. *Personal Data:* b Johannesburg, SAfrica, June 14, 38. *Educ:* Univ Cape Town, BSc, 57, Hons, 58, PhD(chem), 61. *Prof Exp:* Instr chem, Univ Cape Town, 59-61; res assoc physics, Univ Tenn, 61; Am Asn Univ Women int fel & res investr path, Univ Tex M D Anderson Hosp & Tumor Inst, 61-62; res assoc internal med, Washington Univ, 63, res instr, 63-65; res assoc path, Stanford Univ, 65-69; consult, Ames Res Ctr, NASA, 69-72; sr res assoc, Inst Chem Biol, Univ San Francisco, 72-80. *Mem:* Am Chem Soc; Soc Appl Spectros; assoc Royal Inst Chem; Royal Soc Health; Soc Environ Geochem & Health. *Res:* Emission spectroscopy; amounts and functions of trace metals in humans and animals, analytical chemistry; toxicity and carcinogenicity of trace elements; mass spectroscopy; laser microprobe spectroscopy. *Mailing Add:* 3717 Laguna Ave Palo Alto CA 94306-2625

HARDINGE, MERVYN GILBERT, PHARMACOLOGY, HEALTH PROMOTION. *Current Pos:* RETIRED. *Personal Data:* b July 29, 14. *Educ:* Pac Union Col, BS, 39; Loma Linda Univ Sch Med, MD, 42; Harvard Univ, MPH, 49, DrPH(nutrit), 51; Stanford Univ, MA, 52, PhD(pharmacol), 56. *Prof Exp:* Prof health prom, Loma Linda Univ, Calif, 43-80. *Res:* Vegetarian dieteries. *Mailing Add:* 382 B Valley Rd Brewster WA 98812

HARDIS, LEONARD, MECHANICAL ENGINEERING. *Current Pos:* DESIGN CONSULT, 84- *Personal Data:* b New York, NY, Sept 9, 16; m 52; c 2. *Educ:* Carnegie Inst Technol, BS, 38; Univ Md, MS, 53. *Prof Exp:* Asst, Carnegie Inst Technol, 38-39; ord engr, Naval Gun Factory, 39-48; supvr mech eng, US Naval Ord Lab, 48-60, chief gen eng div, 60-61; staff engr, orbiting geophys observ proj, Goddard Space Flight Ctr, NASA, 61-69, resources technol satellite, 69-77; Systs Engr, OAO Corp, 77-84. *Res:* Design of naval ordnance; experimental stress analysis; rocket blast measurement; design and development of spacecraft. *Mailing Add:* 1316 Midwood Pl Silver Spring MD 20910

HARDISON, JOHN ROBERT, PLANT PATHOLOGY. *Current Pos:* PROF PLANT PATH, ORE STATE UNIV, 81-; PRES, AG TECH, INC, 85- *Personal Data:* b Yakima, Wash, Jan 12, 18; m 37, 88, Janet L O'Connor; c J Robert, Catherine A, Mary E & Patrick J. *Educ:* State Col Wash, BS, 39; Univ Mich, MS, 40, PhD(mycol), 42. *Prof Exp:* Asst forage crop invests, Exp Sta, Univ Ky, 42-44; res pathologist, Forage & Range Res Br, Plant Sci Res Div, Agr Res Serv, USDA, 44-72, res leader, legume & grass seed prod, 71-72. *Mem:* Am Phytopath Soc; Mycol Soc Am; Am Soc Agron; Crop Sci Soc Am. *Res:* Biology and control of diseases of forage crops. *Mailing Add:* Bot & Plant Path Dept Ore State Univ Corvallis OR 97331

HARDISON, ROSS CAMERON, BIOCHEMISTRY, MOLECULAR GENETICS. *Current Pos:* from asst prof to assoc prof biochem, Dept Molecular & Cell Biol, 80-91, PROF, DEPT BIOCHEM & MOLECULAR BIOL, PA STATE UNIV, 91-, DIR, CTR GENE REGULATION, 92- *Personal Data:* b Nashville, Tenn, Mar 29, 51; m 91, Deborah Smith; c Alexander. *Educ:* Vanderbilt Univ, BA, 73; Univ Iowa, PhD(biochem), 77. *Prof Exp:* Res fel molecular biol, Div Biol, Calif Inst Technol, 77-80. *Concurrent Pos:* Fel, Jane Coffin Childs Mem Fund Med Res, 77-79; prin investr on NIH funded grants, 80-; res career develop award, NIH, 86-91; vis prof, Biomed Res Centre, Univ BC, Vancouver, Can, 88; assoc ed, Genomics, 92- *Mem:* Am Chem Soc; Am Soc Biochem & Molecular Biol; Am Soc Microbiol; Soc Molecular Biol & Eval; Am Soc Human Genetics. *Res:* Molecular basis for control of gene expression; mammalian globin gene evolution and regulation. *Mailing Add:* Dept Biochem & Molecular Biol Pa State Univ University Park PA 16802

HARDISON, WESLEY AUREL, ANIMAL NUTRITION. *Current Pos:* RETIRED. *Personal Data:* b Barren Co, Ky, May 24, 25; m 46; c 2. *Educ:* Western Ky State Col, BS, 47; Univ Ky, MS, 49; Cornell Univ, PhD, 52. *Honors & Awards:* Am Feed Mfrs Award, 60. *Prof Exp:* Asst dairy husb, Univ Ky, 48-49; asst animal husb, Cornell Univ, 49-52; assoc prof dairy sci, Va Polytech Inst, 53-62; prod officer, Food & Agr Orgn, UN, 62-67; proj specialist fodder & animal prod, Ford Found, 67-74; livestock specialist, Int Agr Develop, World Bank, 74-87. *Concurrent Pos:* Consult livestock prod, 87-92. *Mem:* Am Soc Animal Sci; Am Inst Nutrit; Am Dairy Sci Asn. *Res:* Forage utilization, including pasture herbage, with special emphasis on use of indicator techniques; dairy calif nutrition. *Mailing Add:* 4600 Connecticut Ave NW No 606 Washington DC 20008

HARDISON, WILLIAM GERRY MORGAN, INTERNAL MEDICINE. *Current Pos:* asst prof med, Sect Gastroenterol, Vet Admin Hosp, 68-70, chief, 74-92, clin investr, 78-81, ACTG CHIEF, DIV GASTROENTEROL, VET ADMIN HOSP, 95-; PROF MED, UNIV CALIF, SAN DIEGO, 80- *Personal Data:* b San Diego, Calif, Oct 15, 33. *Educ:* Harvard Univ, AB, 55, MD, 59; Am Bd Internal Med, dipl, 68. *Honors & Awards:* Fulbright Lectr Gastroenterol, Univ Tirana, Albania, 94-95. *Prof Exp:* Intern, Boston City Hosp, 59-60, from asst resident to sr resident, 60-64, res fel, Thorndike Mem Lab, 64-67, chief res, 66-67. *Concurrent Pos:* Gen med officer, US Naval Dispensary, Washington, DC, 61-63; res fel med, Harvard Med Sch, 64-67; vis worker, Dept Biochem, NIH, 83-94; assoc ed liver, Am J Physiol, 86-91; grantee, NIH, 88, 89, 90, 92 & 94; actg assoc chief staff res, Vet Admin Hosp, San Diego, 91-92. *Mem:* Am Fedn Clin Res; Am Phys Soc; Am Gastroenterol Asn; fel Am Col Physicians; Am Asn Study Liver Dis; Am Soc Clin Invest. *Mailing Add:* Dept Med Vet Admin Med Ctr Univ Calif San Diego CA 92161

HARDMAN, BRUCE BERTOLETTE, MATERIALS QUALITY MANAGEMENT, ENVIRONMENTAL REGULATORY COMPLIANCE. *Current Pos:* mgr, qual opers, 90-93, QUAL & COMPLIANCE DIR, PCR, INC, GAINESVILLE, FLA, 93- *Personal Data:* b Mineola, NY, Jan 18, 42; m; c David E & Daniel G. *Educ:* Union Col, NY, BS, 64; Rensselaer Polytech Inst, PhD(phys chem), 67. *Prof Exp:* Res chemist, Gen Elec Co, 67-74, chem develop specialist, 74-77, mgr, Anal Servs, 77-78, mgr RTV Qual Control, 78-79, mgr, Process Qual, 80-81, mgr, Anal Serv & Process Qual, 81-84, mgr environ testing & anal, Silicone Prod Bus Div, 84-89. *Mem:* AAAS; Am Chem Soc; Chem Soc; Royal Inst Chem. *Res:* Quality management systems; chemical process technology; environmental science and technology; organosilane and silicone technology. *Mailing Add:* 3756 NW 53rd Rd Gainesville FL 32653

HARDMAN, CARL CHARLES, ELECTROCHEMISTRY. *Current Pos:* SR ENGR, WESTINGHOUSE RES LAB, 63- *Personal Data:* b Atlantic City, NJ, Aug 30, 19; m 48, Annette Schinasi; c Wendy, Craig & Robin. *Educ:* Pa State Univ, BS, 41; Univ Wis, MS, 47. *Prof Exp:* Engr, INCO, 41-43; res chemist, Union Carbide Co, 50-53; res chemist, Diamond Shamrock, 53-59; div scientist electrochem, Aerovox, 60-63. *Mem:* Am Chem Soc; Electrochem Soc. *Res:* Alkaline and acid batteries; electrolytic capacitors. *Mailing Add:* 6564 Rosemoor Dr Pittsburgh PA 15217

HARDMAN, HAROLD FRANCIS, PHARMACOLOGY. *Current Pos:* from assoc prof to assoc dean, 68-70, prof & chmn dept, 62-88, EMER PROF PHARMACOL, MED COL WIS, 92- *Personal Data:* b East Orange, NJ, Aug, 2, 27; m 50; c 4. *Educ:* Rutgers Univ, BSc, 49; Univ Ill, MSc, 51; Univ Mich, PhD, 54, MD, 58. *Prof Exp:* Instr pharmacol, Med Sch, Univ Mich, 54-58, asst prof, 58-60. *Concurrent Pos:* Vis prof, Cali, Colombia, 65-66; Markle scholar med sci, 58-62. *Mem:* AAAS; Am Soc Clin Pharmacol & Therapeut; Am Soc Pharmacol & Exp Therapeut (pres, 82-83); Fedn Am Soc Exp Biol (pres, 83-84). *Res:* Effect of pH and drug ionization on the pharmacological action of drugs affecting the heart; physiology of oxygen utilization by the heart; pharmacology of theophylline, barbiturates, epinephrine, procaine derivatives and antianginal agents; pharmacology of marijuana and derivatives. *Mailing Add:* Dept Pharmacol Med Col Wis 8701 Watertown Plank Rd Milwaukee WI 53226-4801

HARDMAN, JOEL G, MOLECULAR PHARMACOLOGY. *Current Pos:* instr physiol, Sch Med, Vanderbilt Univ, 64-67, from asst prof to prof, 67-75, prof pharmacol & chmn dept, 75-90, ASSOC VCHANCELLOR HEALTH AFFAIRS, VANDERBILT UNIV MED CTR, 91- *Personal Data:* b Colbert, Ga, Nov 7, 33; m 55, Georgette Johnson; c Pamela, Frances, Mary G & Joel. *Educ:* Univ Ga, BS, 54, MS, 59; Emory Univ, PhD(pharmacol), 64. *Honors & Awards:* H B Van Dyke Award, Columbia Univ, 81; John V Croker Mem Lectr, Am Soc Pharmacol & Exp Therapeut, 93. *Prof Exp:* Instr pharm, Univ Ga, 57-60. *Concurrent Pos:* Mem adv bd, Advan Cyclic Nucleotide Res, 73-; Francqui Foreign vis prof, Free Univ Brussels, 74; mem, pharmacol study sect, NIH, 75-77, chmn, 77-79; ed, Molecular Pharmacol, 83-86; mem, res comt, Am Heart Asn, 79-84, mem, Coun Basic Sci; chmn, Bd Publ Trustees, Am Soc Pharmacol & Exp Therapeut, 90-92; mem exec comt, Int Union Pharmacol, 90- *Mem:* Am Soc Pharmacol & Exp Therapeut (pres, 93-94); Am Soc Biol Chemists; Am Heart Asn; AAAS. *Res:* Regulation of cyclic nucleotide metabolism; mechanisms of drug and hormone action. *Mailing Add:* D-3300 MCN Vanderbilt Univ Med Ctr Nashville TN 37232-2104. *Fax:* 615-343-2447

HARDMAN, JOHN KEMPER, BIOCHEMISTRY, MOLECULAR GENETICS. *Current Pos:* assoc prof, 72-76, PROF BIOL, UNIV ALA, 76- *Personal Data:* b Waynesboro, Pa, Aug 11, 34; m 67; c 3. *Educ:* Mt St Mary's Col, Md, BS, 56; Georgetown Univ, MS, 59; Univ Md, PhD(microbiol, biochem), 62. *Prof Exp:* Chemist, NIH, 58-62; Nat Acad Sci fel, Stanford Univ, 62-63, NIH fel, 63-65; asst prof biol, Dept Biol & McCollum-Pratt Inst, Johns Hopkins Univ, 65-72. *Mem:* AAAS; Am Chem Soc; Sigma Xi; Am Soc Biochem & Molecular Biol. *Res:* Structure-function relationships in proteins. *Mailing Add:* Dept Biol & Biochem Biol Univ Ala Tuscaloosa AL 35487-0344. *Fax:* 205-348-1786

HARDMAN, JOHN M, PATHOLOGY. *Current Pos:* PROF & CHMN, DEPT PATH, JOHN A BURNS SCH MED, UNIV HAWAII, MANOA, 77-, PROG DIR, INTEGRATED PATH RESIDENCY PROG, 78- *Personal Data:* b Matheson, Colo, Jan 15, 33; m 78; c 2. *Educ:* Univ Colo, BS, 54, MD, 58; Baylor Univ, MS, 65; Am Bd Path, cert anat & clin path, 63, cert, neuropath, 67. *Honors & Awards:* Sir Henry Wellcome Medal, Scroll & Prize, Asn Mil Surgeons US, 68. *Prof Exp:* Intern, Walter Reed Army Med Ctr, Washington, DC, 58-59; resident anat & clin path, Brooke Gen Hosp, San Antonio, Tex, 59-63; fel neuropath, Armed Forces Inst Path, 65-67; assoc clin & clin prof, John A Burns Sch Med, Univ Hawaii, 70-75; clin prof, Georgetown Univ, 76-77. *Concurrent Pos:* Neuropath consult, Nat Naval Med Ctr, 66-68; vis prof neuropath, William Beaumont Gen Hosp, El Paso, Tex, 66, 68, 71 & 75, Madigan Gen Hosp, Tacoma, Wash, 70 & 74; dir-at-large, Am Cancer Soc, 71-75 & 82-; liaison mem, Army Med Dept-NIH Study Group Sect Path B, 76-77; neuropath consult, St Francis Hosp, Tripler Army Med Ctr & Med Examr City & County Honolulu, 78-; dir labs, Kapiolani-Children's Med Ctr, 78-85; dir educ & res, Dept Labs, Kapiolani Med Ctr for Women & Children, 85-; bd dirs, Alzheimer's Dis & Related Disorders Asn, Inc, 87- *Mem:* Col Am Pathologists; Am Soc Clin Path; Am Asn Neuropathologists; Am Asn Pathologists & Bacteriologists; Int Acad Path; Am Asn Pathologists; Sigma Xi; Soc Neurosci; AMA. *Res:* Effects of traumatic injury on the nervous system; diagnosis of central nervous system diseases, particularly brain tumors and dementias; acute nervous system decompression sickness in dogs. *Mailing Add:* Dept Path Univ Hawaii Honolulu HI 96822-2319. *Fax:* 808-956-5465

HARDMAN, JOHN MICHAEL, INSECT ECOLOGY. *Current Pos:* RES SCIENTIST, TREE FRUIT ENTOM, KENTVILLE, NS, 82- *Personal Data:* b Exeter, Ont, Oct 31, 47; m 71; c 1. *Educ:* Dalhousie Univ, BSc Hons, 68; Imp Col, Univ London, MSc & DIC, 69; Simon Fraser Univ, PhD(insect ecol), 73. *Prof Exp:* Res scientist insect ecol, Div Entom, Commonwealth Sci & Indust Res Org, Canberra, Australia, 73-77; res assoc, Pestology Ctr, Simon Fraser Univ, 77; res scientist grasshopper ecol, Agr Can Res Sta, Lethbridge, 77-82. *Mem:* Entom Soc Can; Ecol Soc Am; Brit Ecol Soc. *Res:* Use of systems analysis and simulation models in management of insect pests. *Mailing Add:* Res Sta Agr Can 32 Main St Kentville NS B4N 1J5 Can

HARDT, ALFRED BLACK, PHYSIOLOGY. *Current Pos:* RETIRED. *Personal Data:* b Fond du Lac, Wis, Nov 7, 30. *Educ:* Iowa State Univ, BS, 53; San Jose State Col, MA, 60; Univ Colo, PhD(physiol), 69. *Prof Exp:* Asst prof zool, Univ Wyo, 68-72; assoc prof oral biol, Univ Nebr, Lincoln, 72-90. *Mem:* AAAS; Int Asn Dent Res. *Res:* Hard tissue physiology. *Mailing Add:* 11 Trout Pond Lane SW Bandon OR 97411

HARDT, DANIEL, COMPUTING SCIENCES, ARTIFICIAL INTELLIGENCE. *Current Pos:* ASST PROF, DEPT COMPUT SCI, VILLANOVA UNIV. *Educ:* Curtis Inst Music, BM, 80; Swarthmore Col, BA, 81; Univ Pa, PhD(comput & info sci), 93. *Concurrent Pos:* Prin investr, Fac Early Career Develop Prog, NSF, 95- *Res:* Natural language processing such as semantics, discourse processing, syntax, applied natural language processing; programming languages; cognitive science. *Mailing Add:* Dept Comput Sci Villanova Univ 800 Lancaster Ave Villanova PA 19805

HARDT, DAVID EDGAR, CONTROL SYSTEMS, MANUFACTURING. *Current Pos:* Res assoc, Mass Inst Technol, 78-79, from asst prof to assoc prof, 79-92, dir, Lab Mfg, 85-94, PROF MECH ENG, MASS INST TECHNOL, 92- *Personal Data:* b Bryn Mawr, Pa, Sept 11, 50; m 74, Susan Mitchell; c 4. *Educ:* Lafayette Col, BSME, 72; Mass Inst Technol, MS, 74, PhD(mech eng), 78. *Honors & Awards:* Adam Mem Membership Award, Am Welding Soc. *Mem:* Am Soc Mech Engrs; Am Welding Soc; Soc Mfg Engrs. *Res:* Application of system dynamics and control to batch manufacturing processes, design/manufacturing integration; process design for control; control of thermal processes. *Mailing Add:* Dept Mech Eng Mass Inst Technol Rm 35-132 Cambridge MA 02139-4307

HARDT, ROBERT MILLER, MATHEMATICS. *Current Pos:* WILLIAM MOODY PROF MATH, RICE UNIV, 88- *Personal Data:* b Pittsburgh, Pa, June 24, 45; m 68, Louise M Ryder; c Susanna L, Stephen L & Heidi F. *Educ:* Mass Inst Technol, BS, 67; Brown Univ, PhD, 71. *Prof Exp:* Res assoc, Brown Univ, 71; from instr to prof, Univ Minn, Minneapolis, 71-82. *Concurrent Pos:* NSF grant, Minneapolis & Houston, 71-; vis mem, Inst Adv Study, Princeton, 76, Inst des Hautes Etudes Sci, Bures-sur-Yvette, France, 78, 81; vis prof, Univ Melbourne, 79, Univ Wuppertal, Ger, 84, Stanford Univ, 87. *Mem:* Am Math Soc. *Mailing Add:* Math Dept Rice Univ PO Box 1892 Houston TX 77251

HARDTKE, FRED CHARLES, JR, CHEMISTRY. *Current Pos:* ASST PROF CHEM, UNIV MO-ROLLA, 65- *Personal Data:* b Chicago, Ill, Aug 30, 31. *Educ:* Ill Inst Technol, BS, 53; Ore State Univ, PhD(phys chem), 59. *Prof Exp:* Anal chemist, Sci Control Lab, 53-54; instr, Ore State Univ, 57-58; appointee, Inst Nuclear Sci & Eng, Argonne Nat Lab, 58-60, asst chemist, Remote Control Div, 60-65. *Mem:* Am Chem Soc; Am Nuclear Soc. *Res:* Photoconductivity; electrets; compton current; cyclic voltommetry. *Mailing Add:* 14525 State Rt 4 Rolla MO 65401

HARDTMANN, GOETZ E, ORGANIC CHEMISTRY, MEDICINAL CHEMISTRY. *Current Pos:* sr res chemist, 63-68, res group leader med chem, 69-71, res sect head med chem, 71-77, DIR CHEM DEVELOP, SANDOZ PHARMACEUT, 77- *Personal Data:* b Leipzig, Ger, Oct 4, 32; US citizen; m 61; c 3. *Educ:* Brunswick Tech Univ, Dipl, 59, PhD(chem), 61. *Prof Exp:* Res assoc org chem, Brunswick Tech Univ, 61 & Univ Wis, 61-63. *Mem:* Am Chem Soc; Ger Chem Soc. *Res:* Total synthesis of Terramycin; synthesis of medicinal agents; heterocyclics; metallorganics. *Mailing Add:* PO Box 505 Earlysville VA 22936-0505

HARDWICK, DAVID FRANCIS, PATHOLOGY, PEDIATRICS. *Current Pos:* clin instr path, Univ BC, 63-65, from asst prof to assoc prof, 65-74, head, Dept Path, 76-90, assoc dean, Res & Planning, 90-96, PROF PATH, UNIV BC, 74-, HEAD DEPT PATH, CHILDREN'S HOSP, VANCOUVER, 69-, DIR, INTERINSTITUTIONAL PLANNING, 90- *Personal Data:* b Vancouver, BC, Jan 24, 34; m 56, Margaret M; c 3. *Educ:* Univ BC, MD, 57; FRCP(C), 65; Am Bd Path, cert anat & clin path, 65. *Honors & Awards:* Queen Elizabeth II Medal, 78; F K Mostofi Award, US & Can Acad Pathol. *Prof Exp:* Res assoc physiol, Univ Southern Calif, 60-62. *Concurrent Pos:* Asst clin chemist, Vancouver Gen Hosp, 63-64, from asst pathologist to assoc pathologist, 65-72, pediat pathologist, 72-; consult, Ministry Health, Prov of BC, 69-; mem senate, Univ BC, 69-75; Nat Inst Neurol Dis & Blindness trainee, Children's Hosp, Los Angeles, 60-62; chief med staff, Children's Hosp, Vancouver, 70-86. *Mem:* Can Asn Path; Can Med Asn; fel Col Am Path; Int Acad Path (pres, 92-94); NY Acad Sci; Soc Pediat Pathol; US & Can Acad Pathol (pres, 90). *Res:* Pediatric neonatal pathology; metabolic diseases; laboratory direction and administration; tumor tissue fluid flow dynamics. *Mailing Add:* Dean's Off Fac Med 317-2194 Health Sci Mall Univ BC Vancouver BC V6T 1W5 Can. *Fax:* 604-822-6061

HARDWICK, JOHN LAFAYETTE, PHYSICAL CHEMISTRY, SPECTROSCOPY. *Current Pos:* SR RES ASSOC, DEPT PHYSICS, UNIV ORE, 85- *Personal Data:* b Atlanta, Ga, June 28, 44; m 70; c 2. *Educ:* Princeton Univ, AB, 66; Ga Inst Technol, PhD(chem), 72. *Prof Exp:* Fel chem, Univ Western Ont, 72-75; res assoc spectros, Herzberg Inst Astrophys, 75-78; vis asst prof chem, Univ Colo, 78-79; asst prof specialist, Radiation Lab, Univ Notre Dame, 79-85. *Mem:* Am Chem Soc. *Mailing Add:* Dept Physics Univ Ore Eugene OR 97403-1274

HARDWICK, MARTIN, ENERGY DATA BASE SYSTEMS, DATA PROTOCOLS INDUSTRIAL VIRTUAL ENTERPRISES. *Current Pos:* PROF COMPUT SCI, RENSSELAER POLYTECH INST, 93- *Personal Data:* b Enfield, Eng, Jan 13, 57. *Educ:* Bristol Univ, BA, PhD(math & comput sci). *Prof Exp:* Elec engr, Tex Tech, 83-87; pres & founder, Step Tools, Inc, 91. *Mem:* Asn Comput Mach; Inst Elec & Electronics Engrs Comput Sci. *Mailing Add:* Comput Sci Dept Rensselaer Polytech Inst 110 Eighth St Rm 7015 CII Bldg Troy NY 12180

HARDWICKE, JAMES ERNEST, JR, ORGANIC CHEMISTRY. *Current Pos:* HARWICKE CONSULT, 88- *Personal Data:* b Winston-Salem, NC, Oct 21, 24; m 50; c 5. *Educ:* Univ NC, BS, 47; Northwestern Univ, MS, 48; Univ Calif, PhD(org chem), 51. *Prof Exp:* Asst chem, Northwestern Univ, 47-48 & Univ Calif, 48-51; res chemist, Tenn Eastman Co, 51-55; mgr, Org Res Lab, Shulton Inc, 55-58; dir res & develop, Cardinal Mfg Co, 58-63, gen mgr, Cardinal Chem Co & pres, Cardinal Stabilizers, Inc, 64-67, vpres, 67; pres, Hardwicke Chem Co, 67-88. *Concurrent Pos:* Mem bd dirs, McLaughlin Gormley King Co, Minneapolis, Minn, 75; mem, Chem & Specialties Mfrs Coun. *Mem:* AAAS; Am Chem Soc; Sigma Xi. *Res:* Synthetic organic chemistry in general; synthetic insecticidal synergists; perfumery synthetics; high pressure synthesis; organotin chemistry; vinyl stabilizers; fire retardants; pyrethrim substitutes intermediates for synthetic pyrethroids; surface active agents; carbamates; N-alkyl anilines; benzyl chemicals; insect repellents. *Mailing Add:* 805 Kilbourne Rd Columbia SC 29205-2049

HARDWICKE, NORMAN LAWSON, POLYMER CHEMISTRY. *Current Pos:* RETIRED. *Personal Data:* b Winnipeg, MB, May 21, 24; Can & US citizen; m 50; c 3. *Educ:* Tex Col Arts & Indust, BS(chem eng) & BS(chem), 49; Univ Okla, MChE, 51, PhD(chem eng), 67. *Prof Exp:* Res engr, Monsanto Co, 51-58, group leader polymers, 58-63, res specialist, 66-67, group leader, 67-72, res specialist, 72-79, sr technol specialist, 79-82. *Mem:* Am Inst Chem Eng; Am Chem Soc. *Res:* Vinyl monomers; vinyl polymers; polymer stabilization; reaction simulation; analog and digital model development; liquid diffusion. *Mailing Add:* 1867 Taylor St Victoria BC V8R 3G3 Can

HARDWIDGE, EDWARD ALBERT, PHARMACEUTICAL CHEMISTRY. *Current Pos:* DIR, QUAL CONTROL, CATER-WALLACE INC, 89- *Personal Data:* b Chicago, Ill, June 16, 46; m 68; c 2. *Educ:* Ill Inst Technol, BS, 67; Univ Wash, PhD(chem), 72. *Prof Exp:* Res assoc chem, Univ Alta, 72-74; scientist, UpJohn Co, 74-76, lab head quality control, 76-77, res head, 77-84, mgr packaging eng, 84-86, group mgr, exp clin prod, 86-89. *Mem:* Am Soc Qual Control; Am Chem Soc. *Res:* Bioavailability of oral dosage forms of drugs and correlations between bioavailability and in vitro physical tests; physical and particulate properties of parenteral drugs. *Mailing Add:* 1256 W Ravina Park Rd Decatur IL 62526

HARDY, CLYDE THOMAS, STRUCTURAL GEOLOGY. *Current Pos:* From asst prof to assoc prof, 50-66, head dept, 68-82, PROF GEOL, UTAH STATE UNIV, 67- *Personal Data:* b Fremont, Ohio, Apr 23, 21. *Educ:* Ohio State Univ, BA, 43, MS, 48, PhD(geol), 49. *Mem:* Geol Soc Am; Am Asn Petrol Geol; Am Geophys Union. *Mailing Add:* PO Box 3790 Logan UT 84323-3790

HARDY, D ELMO, ENTOMOLOGY. *Current Pos:* from prof to sr prof, 48-80, from assoc entomologist to entomologist, 48-60, sr entomologist, 60-80, chmn dept, 58-68, EMER PROF ENTOM, UNIV HAWAII, 81- *Personal Data:* b Lehi, Utah, Sept 3, 14; m 35; c 4. *Educ:* Brigham Young Univ, AB 37; Utah State Univ, 38; Univ Kans, PhD(entom), 41. *Prof Exp:* Field entomologist, Exp Sta, Utah State Col, 37-38; asst instr entom, Univ Kans, 38-41, fel taxon, 41-42; asst state entomologist, Iowa State Col, 45-48. *Concurrent Pos:* State nursery inspector, Kans, 39-41; dep state entomologist, Kans Entom Comn, 42; med entomologist, US Army, 42-45; hon assoc & mem, BP Bishop Mus entom exped, New Guinea, 57; mem, State of Hawaii Natural Area Reserves Comn, 70-76 & Animal Species Adv Coun, 78-80. *Mem:* AAAS; assoc Soc Syst Zool; assoc Entom Soc Am. *Res:* Diptera taxonomy; taxonomy of the Bibionidae and Dorilaidae of the world; Diptera of Hawaii; Tephritidae of the Orient and Pacific. *Mailing Add:* 500 University Ave PH6 Honolulu HI 96826

HARDY, DAREL W, ALGEBRA. *Current Pos:* PROF, DEPT MATH, COLO STATE UNIV, 67- *Educ:* Mex State Univ, BS, 62, MS, 64, PhD(math), 67. *Mem:* Am Math Soc; Math Asn Am. *Res:* Algebra. *Mailing Add:* 1301 Front Nine Dr Ft Collins CO 80523-0001

HARDY, EDGAR ERWIN, CHEMISTRY. *Current Pos:* ADJ PROF, CHEM & NATURAL SCI DEPTS, SAN DIEGO STATE UNIV, 84- *Personal Data:* b Charlottenburg, Ger, July 6, 13; nat US; m 41; c 4. *Educ:* Univ Zurich, PhD(law), 35; Univ Minn, BS, 38, MS, 40. *Prof Exp:* From res chemist to res group leader, Monsanto Chem Co, 42-45, from org res supvr, Phosphate Div, to asst dir res, 45-53, asst dir, Org Div, 54; res dir, Mobay Chem Co, 54-59; from develop assoc, Plastics Div, to assoc dir res, Monsanto Res Corp, Monsanto Co, 59-63, dir develop, Plastic Prod & Resins Div, 64-65, dir, Dayton Lab, 65-78; prof chem, Wright Univ, 78-80; prof chem, Calif State Polytech Univ, 80-84. *Concurrent Pos:* Instr, Wright State Univ. *Mem:* Am Chem Soc. *Res:* Polyurethanes; plastic foams and coatings composites; synthetic rubber; organic isocyanates; organic phosphorus compounds; detergent synthesis and application; organic fluorine compounds. *Mailing Add:* 3655 Jackdaw St San Diego CA 92103

HARDY, H(ENRY) REGINALD, JR, ENGINEERING MECHANICS. *Current Pos:* assoc prof, 66-70, PROF MINING, PA STATE UNIV, 70- *Personal Data:* b Ottawa, Ont, Aug 19, 31; m 54, Margaret M; c William R & David A. *Educ:* McGill Univ, BSc, 53; Univ Ottawa, MSc, 62; Va Polytech Inst, PhD(eng mech), 65. *Honors & Awards:* Templin Award, Am Soc Testing & Mat, 68 & C A Hogentogler Award, 83; Gold Award, Acoustic Emission Working Group, 88. *Prof Exp:* Sci officer rock mech, Mines Br, Can Dept Mines & Tech Survs, 53-60, rock physics, 60-66. *Concurrent Pos:* Deutsche Forschungsgemeinschaft vis prof, Univ Aachem, WGer, 80; sr vis fel, Japanese Soc Promotion Sci, Tohoku Univ, Sendai, Japan, 86; vis prof, Silesian Univ, Poland, 89 & Nottingham Univ, Eng. *Mem:* Can Asn Physicists; Soc Exp Stress Anal; Am Geophys Union; Am Soc Testing & Mat; Am Soc Nondestructive Testing; Int Soc Rock Mech. *Res:* Stress and strain in earth's crust particularly problems of mining at depth; deformation of geologic materials especially their viscoelastic properties; mechanics of underground gas storage, mechanical behavior of salt, design of structures in salt; acoustic emission/microseismic studies of geologic materials. *Mailing Add:* State Col 1250 S Garner St University Park PA 16801-6326. *Fax:* 814-865-3240

HARDY, JAMES C, SPEECH PATHOLOGY. *Current Pos:* speech therapist, Univ Hosp Sch, Univ Iowa, 56-57, supvr speech & hearing, 57-67, from asst prof to assoc prof, 61-69, PROF, DEPT SPEECH PATH, AUDIOL & DEPT PEDIAT, UNIV IOWA, 69-, DIR SPEECH & HEARING CLIN, 72-, DIR PROF SERV, DIV DEVELOP DISABILITIES, 79-, DIR, IOWA PROG ASSISTIVE TECHNOL, 90- *Personal Data:* b Salina, Kans, Apr 14, 30; m 53; c 3. *Educ:* Northeast Mo State Col, BS, 51; Univ Iowa, MA, 57, PhD(speech path), 61. *Prof Exp:* Speech therapist, Pub Schs, Mo, 51-52, 54-55. *Concurrent Pos:* Prin investr, Nat Inst Neurol Dis & Blindness res grant, 60-73; consult, Nat Inst Dent Res grants, 63- *Mem:* AAAS; Am Speech & Hearing Asn; Am Acad Cerebral Palsy. *Res:* Speech physiology and neurology of speech; speech disorders associated with trauma and pathologies of nervous system. *Mailing Add:* Dept Pediatrics & Speech Path Univ Iowa Iowa City IA 52242

HARDY, JAMES D, SURGERY, BIOCHEMISTRY. *Current Pos:* RETIRED. *Personal Data:* b Birmingham, Ala, May 14, 18; m 49; c 4. *Educ:* Univ Ala, BA, 38; Univ Pa, MD, 42, MS, 51; Am Bd Surg, dipl, 50; Bd Thoracic Surg, dipl, 52. *Honors & Awards:* Smithy Mem Lectr, Med Col SC, 56; Agnew Lectr, Sch Med, Univ Pa, 57; Elkin Lectr, Emory Univ, 60; Banks Mem Lectr, Univ Liverpool, 63; John L Madden Lectr, Hershey Med Sch, 81; Emmett B Frazier Lectr, Univ S Ala, 83; Walter Estelle Lee Lectr, Grad Hosp, Univ Pa, 84. *Prof Exp:* Asst instr med, Univ Pa, 43-44, asst instr surg, 46-49, instr, 49-51; from asst prof to assoc prof, Col Med, Univ Tenn, 51-55, dir surg labs, 51-55; prof surg & chmn dept, Univ Miss, Sch Med, 55-, dir surg res, Med Ctr, 55-, emer prof surg. *Concurrent Pos:* Consult, Oak Ridge Inst Nuclear Sci, 51-54; surgeon-in-chief, Univ Hosp, Univ Miss, 55-; chief surg consult, Jackson Vet Hosp, 55-; vis prof, Univ SC, 56, Emory Univ, 60, Hartford Hosp, Conn, 61, St Louis City & Los Angeles Co Hosps, 62, Univ Calif, San Francisco, 62, Tulane Univ, 64 & Honolulu Hosps, 65; mem, Adv Comt Res Ther, Am Cancer Soc, 63-66; mem adv bd, Am Bd Surg, 64-70; mem, Anesthesiol Training Comt, NIH, 66-69; vchmn, Am Bd Surg, 69-79. *Mem:* AAAS; Soc Univ Surg (secy, 56-58, pres, 61-62); Am Surg Asn (pres, 75-76); Soc Surg Chmn (secy-treas, 72-74, vpres, 74-76, pres, 76-78); Int Cardiovasc Soc; Am Heart Asn; Sigma Xi; Am Asn Surg Trauma; Am Asn Thoracic Surg; Am Col Surg. *Res:* Systemic response to injury; body fluid metabolism and composition; surgical endocrinology; dynamics of the circulation. *Mailing Add:* Dept Surg Univ Miss Sch Med 2500 N State St Jackson MS 39216-4505

HARDY, JAMES EDWARD, THEORETICAL PHYSICS. *Current Pos:* from asst prof to assoc prof, 63-94, PROF PHYSICS, CARLETON UNIV, 94- *Personal Data:* b Salmon Arm, BC, Mar 21, 32; m 73; c 2. *Educ:* Univ BC, BA, 55, MSc, 57; Princeton Univ, PhD(theoret physics), 62. *Prof Exp:* Asst res officer, Nat Res Coun Can, 62-63. *Mem:* Can Asn Physicists. *Res:* Quantum field theory. *Mailing Add:* Dept Physics Carleton Univ Colonel By Dr Ottawa ON K1S 5B6 Can

HARDY, JOHN CHRISTOPHER, NUCLEAR PHYSICS, ELECTROWEAK INTERACTIONS. *Current Pos:* PROF, PHYSICS DEPT, TEX A&M UNIV, 97- *Personal Data:* b Montreal, Que, July 10, 41; m 64, 97, June Dennis; c Ericka, Kirsten, Bruce, Alana, Benjamin & Samantha. *Educ:* McGill Univ, BSc, 61, MSc, 63, PhD(nuclear physics), 65. *Honors & Awards:* Ambridge Prize, 65; Herzberg Medal, 76; Rutherford Medal, 81. *Prof Exp:* Nat Res Coun Can overseas fel nuclear physics, Oxford Univ, 65-67; Miller fel, Lawrence Radiation Lab, Univ Calif, Berkeley, 67-69, physicist, 69-70; assoc res officer, Chalk River Labs, AECL Res, 70-74, sr res officer, 75-83, head, Nuclear Physics Br, 83-85, asst vpres, 86-88, dir, Tandem Accelerator Superconducting Cyclotron Div, 89-97. *Concurrent Pos:* Sci assoc, CERN, 76-; chmn, Bd of Dir, Deep River Sci Acad, 87-97; ed, N Runfrew Times, 72-97. *Mem:* Can Asn Physicists; fel Am Phys Soc; fel Royal Soc Can (vpres, 92). *Res:* Nuclear spectroscopy; beta-decay; delayed proton radioactivity; transfer reactions; nuclear isospin; nuclei far from stability. *Mailing Add:* Cyclotron Inst Tex A&M Univ College Station TX 77843. *Fax:* 409-845-1899; *E-Mail:* hardy@comp.tamu.edu

HARDY, JOHN R, CONDENSED MATTER PHYSICS. *Current Pos:* vis assoc prof physics, 66-67, assoc prof, 67-68, PROF PHYSICS, UNIV NEBR, 68-, COURTESY APPT PROF, COL ENG & TECHNOL, 90- *Personal Data:* b Jan 9, 35. *Educ:* Bristol Univ, Eng, BSc, 56, PhD, 59. *Prof Exp:* Theoret res, Bristol Univ, 56-59; res fel, Assoc Elec Indust, Univ Reading, 59-62, Harwell, 62-65; sr sci off & res fel, Atomic Energy Res Estab, Harwell, Didcot, Berkshire, Eng, 65-66. *Concurrent Pos:* Vis scholar, Mich State Univ & Univ Pa, 64; vis scientist, Lawrence Livermore Lab, 76, 77; George Holmes distinguished prof physics & astron, 93. *Mem:* Sigma Xi; fel Am Phys Soc. *Res:* Lattice dynamics of perfect and imperfect alkali halides, point defect studies in alkali halides and metals; theory of ferroelectricity; shock dynamics of solids; superconductivity. *Mailing Add:* Physics Dept Behlen Lab Univ Nebr Lincoln NE 68588

HARDY, JOHN THOMAS, NUMBER THEORY. *Current Pos:* vis asst prof, 69-70, asst prof, 70-72, ASSOC PROF MATH, UNIV HOUSTON, 72- *Personal Data:* b Booneville, Miss, Oct 30, 38; m 66; c 2. *Educ:* Univ Miss, BS, 60; La State Univ, MS, 62, PhD(math), 65. *Prof Exp:* Asst prof math, Southwestern La Univ, 65-66 & Univ Ga, 66-69. *Mem:* Am Math Soc. *Res:* Algebra; rings of integers in the Cayley algebra; quadratic forms; sums of two squares in quadratic rings; quaternions. *Mailing Add:* Dept Math Univ Houston Houston TX 77004-3476

HARDY, JOHN THOMAS, AQUATIC TOXICOLOGY, RESEARCH MANAGEMENT. *Current Pos:* DIR, CTR ENVIRON SCI, WESTERN WASH UNIV, 93- *Personal Data:* b Detroit, Mich, June 3, 41; m 66; c 1. *Educ:* Univ Calif, Santa Barbara, BA, 64; Ore State Univ, MS, 66; Univ Wash, PhD(marine bot) & PhD(aquatic ecol), 71. *Prof Exp:* Res fel, Univ Wash, 69-71; asst prof marine sci, Am Univ Beirut, 72-75; dir, Environ Consult Serv, 75-79; group leader, Battelle NW, 79-88; from assoc prof to prof, Ore State Univ, 88-93. *Concurrent Pos:* Affil prof, Sch Fisheries, Univ Wash, 84-; dir, Ctr Aquatic Surface Res, 85-88. *Mem:* Fel AAAS; Am Soc Limnol & Oceanog. *Res:* Biological oceanography; dynamics processes at the sediment-water and atmosphere-water interfaces; photochemistry; biological community analysis and primary productivity, effects of UV-B radiation; coral reef ecology. *Mailing Add:* Ctr Environ Sci Western Wash Univ Bellingham WA 98225

HARDY, JOHN W, JR, MATHEMATICS, COMPUTER SCIENCE. *Current Pos:* PROF MATH, CALIF STATE COL, BAKERSFIELD, 71- *Personal Data:* b Tucson, Ariz, Apr 21, 27; m 51; c 2. *Educ:* Stanford Univ, BS, 49, MS, 52, PhD(math), 55. *Prof Exp:* Mathematician, Kaiser Electronics Lab, 55 & Lawrence Radiation Lab, 55-71. *Concurrent Pos:* Consult, 777 Lock & Eng Corp, 63-68 & Madsen Corp, Calif, 64-65; vpres res & develop, Resource Data Corp, 66-69. *Mem:* Am Math Soc; Sigma Xi. *Res:* Numerical analysis; analysis. *Mailing Add:* 4617 Chadborn St Bakersfield CA 93307-5156

HARDY, JOHN WILLIAM, ORNITHOLOGY. *Current Pos:* chmn dept, 73-78, prof zool & curornith, Dept Natural Sci, Fla State Mus, 73-, EMER PROF ZOOL, UNIV FLA. *Personal Data:* b Murphysboro, Ill, Jan 12, 30; c 2. *Educ:* Univ Southern Ill, BS, 52; Mich State Univ, MS, 54; Univ Kans, PhD, 59. *Honors & Awards:* Tucker Award, Am Ornith Union, 58. *Prof Exp:* Asst zool, Mich State Univ, 52-54; asst zool, Univ Kans, 54-57; ed, Bullentin, Kans Ornith Soc, 57-59; asst res zoologist, Univ Calif, Los Angeles, 60-61, from asst prof to assoc prof biol, Occidental Col & dir, Moore Lab, 61-73. *Concurrent Pos:* Chapman Mem Fund res grant, Am Mus Natural Hist, 56; Kans Acad Sci fel, 55; NSF fel, Marine Lab, Duke Univ, 57; ed recent lit, Auk, Am Ornith Union, 62-64, ed, Am Ornith Union Monographs, 72-78; Nat Geog Soc res grant, 73, 78 & 81; NSF res grant, 74-78. *Mem:* Wilson Ornith Soc; Cooper Ornith Soc (treas, 64-); Am Ornith Union; AAAS. *Res:* Ornithology; behavior; phylogeny; behavior and phylogeny of New World jays; behavior of parrots, ecology; life history studies; fossil birds; communal social behavior of neotropic jays; avian bioacoustics. *Mailing Add:* 2803 NW 83rd St Gainesville FL 32606

HARDY, JUDSON, JR, NUCLEAR PHYSICS, REACTOR PHYSICS. *Current Pos:* RETIRED. *Personal Data:* b New Orleans, La, Nov 8, 31; m 54; c 3. *Educ:* Univ NC, BS, 53; Princeton Univ, PhD(physics), 58. *Prof Exp:* Adv scientist, Bettis Atomic Power Lab, Westinghouse Elec Corp, 58-90. *Mem:* Am Phys Soc; Am Nuclear Soc. *Mailing Add:* 3226 Kennebec Rd Pittsburgh PA 15241

HARDY, KENNETH REGINALD, SATELLITE METEOROLOGY. *Current Pos:* CONSULT, AS&T, 96- *Personal Data:* b Saskatoon, Sask, July 30, 29; US citizen; m 57, Helga N Hohme; c Kevin & Sabina. *Educ:* Univ Sask, BA, 50, Hons, 52; Univ Toronto, MA, 53; Univ Mich, PhD(meteorol), 63. *Honors & Awards:* Darton Prize, Royal Meteorol Soc, 63. *Prof Exp:* Meteorologist, Can Meteorol Serv, 52-56 & Weather Eng Corp Can, 57-58; res assoc meteorol, Univ Mich, 58-62; res physicist, Air Force Cambridge Res Labs, 63-66, chief, Weather Radar Br, 66-70 & 71-74; div mgr, Environ Res & Technol, Inc, 74-81; chief Satellite Meteorol Br, Air Force Geophys Lab, 81-90; sr staff scientist, Res & Develop Div, Lockheed, 90-96. *Concurrent Pos:* Vis assoc prof, Univ Wash, 70-71. *Mem:* Fel Am Meteorol Soc; Am Geophys Union. *Res:* Cloud physics; growth of precipitation and raindrop size distributions; clear air turbulence and clear air atmospheric structure as deduced from radar and other meteorological observations; satellite remote sensing of the atmosphere and earth's surface. *Mailing Add:* AS&T 1520-208 Sand Hill Rd Palo Alto CA 94304-2060. *E-Mail:* khardy@batnet.com

HARDY, LAURENCE MCNEIL, SYSTEMATIC HERPETOLOGY, ANATOMY. *Current Pos:* Asst prof, 68-71, assoc prof, 71-78, PROF BIOL, LA STATE UNIV SHREVEPORT, 78- *Personal Data:* b Tulsa, Okla, Feb 24, 39; m 60; c 2. *Educ:* NMex State Univ, BS, 62; Univ Kans, MA, 65; Univ NMex, PhD(biol), 69. *Mem:* Am Soc Ichthyol & Herpet; Soc Study Amphibians & Reptiles; Soc Study Evolution; Am Soc Syst Zool; Herpetologists League (treas); Sigma Xi. *Res:* Systematic studies of colubrid snakes, especially from the New World; karyotypes of snakes; reproductive biology and population dynamics of salamanders; biogeography of amphibians and reptiles; reproductive anatomy of reptiles. *Mailing Add:* Biol Sci Dept La State Univ 1 University Pl Shreveport LA 71115-2399

HARDY, MATTHEW PHILLIP, STEROID BIOCHEMISTRY. *Current Pos:* staff scientist, 91-97, SCIENTIST, POP COUN, 97-; ASST PROF, ROCKEFELLER UNIV, 93- *Personal Data:* b Evanston, Ill, Feb 7, 57; m 84, Dianne Oshiro. *Educ:* Oberlin Col, BA, 79; Univ Va, PhD(biol), 85. *Prof Exp:* Fel, Sch Hyg & Pub Health, Johns Hopkins Univ, 85-89, res assoc, 90-91. *Mem:* Sigma Xi; Am Soc Andrologists; Endocrine Soc; Soc Study Reproduction; AAAS. *Res:* Differentiation of Leydig cells during puberty; stress and leydig cell steroidogenic function. *Mailing Add:* Population Coun 1230 York Ave New York NY 10021. *Fax:* 212-327-7678

HARDY, PAUL WILSON, CHEMISTRY. *Current Pos:* RETIRED. *Personal Data:* b Waukesha, Wis, Apr 18, 27; m 48; c 4. *Educ:* Carroll Col, Wis, BA, 48. *Prof Exp:* From sr res chemist to group leader, Am Can Co, 48-65, res assoc 65-78, sr res assoc, 78-82. *Mem:* Am Chem Soc. *Res:* Exploratory research; color and color measurement; ceramics. *Mailing Add:* PO Box 4096 University Park NM 88003-4096

HARDY, RALPH WILBUR FREDERICK, SCIENCE POLICY, BIOCHEMISTRY. *Current Pos:* PRES, NAT AGR BIOTECHNOL COUN, 96- *Personal Data:* b Lindsay, Ont, July 27, 34; m 54, Jacqueline M Thayer; c Steven J, Christopher F, Barbara J, Ralph W & Jonathan D. *Educ:* Univ Toronto, BSA, 56; Univ Wis, MS, 58, PhD(biochem), 59. *Hon Degrees:* DSc, Univ Guplph, 97. *Honors & Awards:* Gov Gen Silver Medal, Am Chem Soc, 56, Delaware Award, 68 & Hendricks Medal & Award, 86. *Prof Exp:* Asst prof biochem, Univ Guelph, 60-63; res biochemist, Cent Res & Develop Dept, Exp Sta, E I Du Pont De Nemours & Co, Inc, 60 & 63-67, res supvr, 67-74, assoc dir res, 74-79, dir life sci, 79-84; pres, Biotech Int Inc, 84-86, dep chmn, 86-90; pres & chief exec officer, Boyce Thompson Inst, Plant Res Inc, 86-95. *Concurrent Pos:* Int Coun Sci Unions comt genetic experimentation, 81-90; exec comt mem, Bd Agr, Nat Res Coun, 83-88, mem Comn Life Sci, 84-90, Bd Basic Biol, 84-90, Comt Biotechnol, 88-94, Bd Sci Technol Int Develop, 90-93; vis prof life sci, Cornell, 84-86; bd mem & consult, Biotechnic Int Inc, Kansas City, 84-; mem bd, Biotech Int Inc, 85- & Indust Biotechnol Asn, 86-89; mem, Alt Agr Res Commercialization Agency, USDA, 92-96; bd mem, Boyce Thompson Inst Plant Res Inc, Ithaca, NY, 86 & Boyce Thompson Southwestern Arboretum, Superior, Ariz, 86-; mem gov bd, Agr Res Inst, 88-91; mem, Dept Energy Basic Sci Adv Comt, 91-; sr bd mem, Corp Secy Alt Asn Res & Comm Corp, 96- *Mem:* Am Soc Plant Physiologists (treas, 73-76); Am Soc Biol Chemists & Molecular Biologists; Am Soc Agron; Am Chem Soc (secy, Biol Chem Div, 78-81); Am Soc Microbiol; AAAS. *Res:* Plant biology and biochemistry including nitrogen and carbon inputs into major crops, nitrogen fixation, photosynthesis and partitioning of assimilates. *Mailing Add:* 330 The Parkway Ithaca NY 14850. *Fax:* 607-257-3381

HARDY, RICHARD ALLEN, mechanical engineering, for more information see previous edition

HARDY, ROBERT J, PHYSICS. *Current Pos:* from asst prof to assoc prof, 71-76, PROF PHYSICS, UNIV NEBR, LINCOLN, 76-, VCHMN, PHYSICS & ASTRON, 84- *Personal Data:* b Port Angeles, Wash, Jan 26, 35; m 70. *Educ:* Reed Col, BA, 56; Lehigh Univ, MS, 58, PhD(physics), 62. *Prof Exp:* Physicist, US Naval Radiol Defense Lab, Calif, 62; res assoc physics, Lehigh Univ, 62-63; vis prof ctr res & adv studies, Nat Polytech Inst, Mex, 64; res assoc & instr, Univ Ore, 65-67. *Concurrent Pos:* Consult, Lawrence Livermore Lab, 70- *Mem:* Am Phys Soc; Am Asn Physics Teachers; Am Asn Univ Prof. *Res:* Theory of equilibrium and transport properties of crystal lattices; statistical mechanics; theory of conduction electrons in magnetic fields; solid state physics. *Mailing Add:* Dept Physics & Astron Univ Nebr Lincoln NE 68588. *E-Mail:* rharoy@unlinfounl.edu

HARDY, ROBERT W, DIABETES, PATHOLOGY. *Current Pos:* fel, 90-91, RES INSTR & ASSOC CLIN CHEM, PATH DEPT, UNIV ALA, BIRMINGHAM, 91- *Personal Data:* b Brantford, Ont, June 8, 52. *Educ:* Univ Waterloo, BSc, 75; Univ Toronto, MSc, 82, PhD(clin biochem), 88. *Honors & Awards:* Med-Chem Award, Can Soc Clin Chemists, 86. *Prof Exp:* Technologist chem, Can Med Labs, 76-80, Sunnybrook Med Ctr, Toronto, 80-82, Hosp for Sick Children, Toronto, 85-87; fel, Clin Chem Prog, Sch Med, Washington Univ, St Louis, Mo, 87-90. *Concurrent Pos:* Fel, Can Diabetes Asn, 88-; young investr award, Acad Clin Lab Physicians & Scientists, 89. *Res:* Interaction of calmodulin and polylysine; regulation of glucose transport. *Mailing Add:* Dept Path Univ Ala Birmingham LHR Rm 511 701 S 19th St Birmingham AL 35294-0001

HARDY, ROLLAND L(EE), GEODESY, MATHEMATICAL PHYSICS. *Current Pos:* CONSULT, 91- *Personal Data:* b Carthage, Ill, May 2, 20; m 44, 53, 90, Betty J Devore; c Rosalyn, Timothy & Melinda. *Educ:* Univ Ill, BS, 47; Univ Mo, Rolla, BSCE, 50, CE, 56; Karlsruhe Tech Univ, Dr Ing, 63. *Honors & Awards:* Performance Award Cert, US Dept Army, 59 & 60; Earle Fennel Award, Am Cong Surv & Mapping, 86. *Prof Exp:* Field engr, US Geol Surv, 47-51; supvr geod engr, map serv, US Army, 51-52, civil engr, Eng Res & Develop Labs, 52-55; asst prof civil eng, George Washington Univ, 56-58; hwy res engr, Bur Pub Rds, Dept Commerce, 58-59; geod engr, AID, US Opers Mission, Sudan, 59-61; gen engr adv systs off, mapping, charting & geod directorate, Dept Defense, 63-67; geodesist, Geod Res Lab, Inst Earth Sci, Environ Sci Serv Admin, 67; prof civil eng, Iowa State Univ, 67-85, prof-in-chg geod, photogram & surv, 80-88; pres, Int Inst Sci & Technol, Monroe, La, 90-97. *Concurrent Pos:* Lectr, Northern Va Ctr, Univ Va, 56-58; consult, 55-58; dir geod & cartographic sci prog, George Washington Univ, 63-66; lectr, Darmstadt & Univ Stuttgart, Ger, 89. *Mem:* Fel Am Soc Civil Engrs; fel Am Cong Surv & Mapping; Am Geophys Union; Am Soc Photogram & Remote Sensing; Sigma Xi. *Res:* Design of engineering instruments; development of advanced geodetic and photogrammetric systems; data reduction; satellite geodesy and photogrammetry; multiquadric analysis; biharmonic potential theory. *Mailing Add:* 1213 Wanda Ave Seaside CA 93955

HARDY, RONALD W, FISH NUTRITION. *Current Pos:* ASSOC PROF FISHERIES, UNIV WASH, 78-; SUPVRY RES CHEMIST, NAT MARINE FISHERIES SERV, NAT OCEANIC & ATMOSPHERIC ADMIN, 83- *Personal Data:* b Vancouver, BC; US citizen; m 70; c 2. *Educ:* Univ Wash, BS, 69, PhD(fisheries), 78; Wash State Univ, MS, 73. *Concurrent Pos:* Mem subcomt nutrient requirements warmwater fishes, Nat Res Ctr, Nat Acad Sci. *Mem:* Am Fisheries Soc; World Maricult Soc; Am Inst Nutrit. *Res:* Diet and disease resistance, diet development for aquaculture, nutritional requirements, lipid composition of fish. *Mailing Add:* UR Div Nat Marine Fish Serv 2725 Montlake Blvd E Seattle WA 98122-2013. *Fax:* 206-553-4304

HARDY, VERNON E, ELECTRONICS ENGINEERING. *Current Pos:* CONSULT, VEH CONSULT, 93- *Personal Data:* b Oklahoma City, Okla, Apr 5, 37; m 66, Kate Garrison; c Laura M & Staphani L. *Educ:* Univ Okla, BSEE, 60, MSEE, 62. *Prof Exp:* Grad asst electronics, Univ Okla, 60-62; engr & sect mgr, Tex Instruments, 62-69; staff engr & sect mgr, Electronic Memories & Magnetics, 69-71; eng mgr & dir eng, Stand Memories-Trendata, 71-73; dir eng, MSI Data, 83-87; eng mgr, Rockwell Int, 87-89, group mgr, CMC Div, 89-93. *Concurrent Pos:* Consult, ElectroCom Automation, 87. *Mem:* Inst Elec & Electronics Engrs. *Mailing Add:* 18912 Santa Mariana Fountain Valley CA 92708

HARDY, WALTER NEWBOLD, SOLID STATE PHYSICS, SUPERCONDUCTIVITY. *Current Pos:* assoc prof, 71-80, PROF PHYSICS, UNIV BC, 80- *Personal Data:* b Vancouver, BC, Mar 25, 40; m 59, Sheila Lorraine; c Kevin James & Steven Wayne. *Educ:* Univ BC, BSc, 61, PhD(physics), 65. *Honors & Awards:* Steacie Prize, Nat Sci & Eng Res Coun, 78; Herzberg Medal, Can Asn Physicists, 78, Medal of Achievement, 93. *Prof Exp:* Nat Res Coun Can fel, Saclay Nuclear Res Ctr, France, 64-66; mem tech staff, Sci Ctr, NAm Rockwell Corp, Calif, 66-71. *Concurrent Pos:* Alfred P Sloan fel, 72-74; vis prof, Ecole Normale Superieure, Paris, 80-81, 85, 88 & 95, Univ Groningen, Holland, 96; Can Coun Sr Killam fel, 84-86; Killam Res prize, 86-88. *Mem:* Am Phys Soc; Royal Soc Can; Can Asn Physicists. *Res:* Cryogenics; microwave properties of high temperature superconductors; superconductivity. *Mailing Add:* Dept Physics Univ BC Vancouver BC V6T 1Z1 Can. *Fax:* 604-822-5324

HARDY, WILLIAM LYLE, BIOPHYSICS, PHYSIOLOGY. *Current Pos:* RETIRED. *Personal Data:* b BC, June 18, 36; m 60. *Educ:* Univ BC, BASc, 59, MSc, 61; Univ Wash, PhD(physiol, biophys), 69. *Prof Exp:* Asst physicist radiol physics, BC Cancer Inst, 61-63; USPHS fel, Dept Physiol & Biophys, Univ Wash, 69-71; asst prof physiol & cardiol, Sch Med, Boston Univ, 71-85. *Concurrent Pos:* Comput consult, Worchester Found Exp Biol, 72. *Mem:* AAAS. *Res:* Excitable membrane biophysics of nerve and muscle; excitation-contraction coupling; pacemaker activity in cardiac cells; digital computer applications in teaching and in clinical and biological research. *Mailing Add:* 508 Border St Boston MA 02128

HARDY, YVAN J, FORESTRY ENTOMOLGY, SILVICULTURE. *Current Pos:* ASST DEP MINISTER, CAN FORESTRY SERV & NATURAL RESOURCES. *Personal Data:* b Quebec City, Can, Aug 11, 41; m 67; c 2. *Educ:* Laval Univ, BScA, 65, MSc, 68; State Univ NY, Syracuse, PhD(forest entom), 71. *Prof Exp:* From asst prof to prof forest entom, Fac Forestry & Geod, Laval Univ, 70-85, chmn dept forest mgt, 75-78, vice dean, 79-80, dean, 80-85; dir gen, Que Region, Can Forestry Serv, 85- *Concurrent Pos:* Consult forest entom, Dept Lands & Forest, Que, 71-76; dir res, Forest Res & Develop Found, 76-82; working group leader Can-USA Prog, USDA Forest Serv, 77-80; vis prof, Univ Maine, Orono, 78-79; mem adv comt forest res, Que Dept Energy & Resources, 81-86; ad hoc comnr, Que Pub Hearing Bur Environ, 82-83; guest lectr, Universite de Quebec, Laval Univ, 85-; pres, Int Seminar on Private Woodlot Mgt, FAO, 87; rapporteur, Nat Forum Sustainable Forest Develop, Halifax, 89. *Mem:* Entom Soc Can; Sigma Xi; Can Inst Forestry. *Res:* Epidemiology of the spruce budworm in relation to bioregions and dynamics of forest cover; host-insect relationships; vulnerability and susceptibility of host species in various ecological environments; methodology in private woodlot management. *Mailing Add:* 580 Booth St Ottowa ON K1A 0E4 Can

HARE, CURTIS R, INORGANIC CHEMISTRY, PHYSICAL CHEMISTRY. *Current Pos:* ASSOC PROF, UNIV MIAMI, 69- *Personal Data:* b Collingdale, Pa, Dec 13, 33; m 57; c 1. *Educ:* Pa State Univ, BS, 55; Mich State Univ, PhD(inorg chem), 61. *Prof Exp:* Asst chem, Pa State Univ, 55 & Mich State Univ, 57-59, 60-61; NSF fel, Inst Phys Chem, Copenhagen Univ, 61-62, res assoc, 62-63; from asst prof to assoc prof, State Univ NY Buffalo, 63-69. *Mem:* AAAS; Am Inst Chem; Am Chem Soc; Royal Soc Chem; Am Crystallog Asn. *Res:* Spectral and magnetic properties of transition metal complexes; ligand field theory; inorganic stereochemistry. *Mailing Add:* Dept Chem Univ Miami PO Box 248106 Miami FL 33124-8106

HARE, FREDERICK KENNETH, PUBLIC INQUIRIES. *Current Pos:* provost, 79-86, EMER UNIV PROF, TRINITY COL, 84-; CHANCELLOR, TRENT UNIV, 88- *Personal Data:* b Wylye, Eng, Feb 5, 19; Can citizen; m 53; c 3. *Educ:* Univ London, 39; Univ Montreal, PhD(geog), 50. *Hon Degrees:* LLD, Queen's Univ, 64, Univ Western Ont, 68, Trent Univ, 79; DSc, McGill Univ, 69, Adelaide, 74, York Univ, 78; DS Litt, Thorneloe Col, 83; DLitt, Mem Univ, 85; LID, Toronto, 87; DSc, Windsor 88. *Honors & Awards:* Dawson Medal, Royal Soc Can, 87; Companion, Order of Can; Int Meteorol Orgn Prize, 88. *Prof Exp:* Asst lectr geography/meteorol, Univ Manchester, 40-41; asst prof geog & meteorol, McGill Univ, 45-49, assoc prof, 50-52, prof, 52-62, dept chmn, 50-62, dean arts & sci, 62-64; prof, King's Col, Univ London, 64-66, master, Birkbeck Col, 66-68; pres, Univ BC, 68-69; prof geog & physics, Univ Toronto, 69-84, Univ prof, 76-84. *Concurrent Pos:* Chmn, Can Climate Planning Bd, 79-90; comnr, Ontario Nuclear Safety Rev, 86-88; chair, adv bd, Int Prog, Univ Toronto, 90. *Mem:* Can Asn Geographers; Asn Am Geographers; Royal Geog Soc; fel Royal Soc Can; Royal Meteorol Soc (pres, 67-68); Sigma Xi. *Res:* High latitude climatology and biogeography; behavior of the stratosphere; water and energy balance of North America; aspects of climatic change; arid zone climates. *Mailing Add:* 301 Lakeshore Rd W Oakville ON L6K 1G2 Can. *Fax:* 905-849-4954

HARE, JAMES FREDERIC, MEMBRANES, CELL BIOLOGY. *Current Pos:* asst prof, 77-82, ASSOC PROF BIOCHEM, HEALTH SCI CTR, UNIV ORE, 82- *Personal Data:* b Philadelphia, Pa, June 4, 45; m 75; c 2. *Educ:* Lafayette Col, AB, 67; Univ NH, MS, 69; Purdue Univ, PhD(biol sci), 73. *Prof Exp:* Teach asst zool & cell biol, Purdue Univ, 69-73; res assoc biochem, Harvard Med Sch, 73-75; res assoc biochem, Calif Inst Technol, 75-77. *Mem:* Am Chem Soc; Am Soc Biochem & Molecular Biol. *Res:* Biosynthesis and degradation of the proteins of biological membranes; mechanisms of protein degradation. *Mailing Add:* Dept Biochem Ore Health Sci Ctr Univ 3181 SW Sam Jackson Park Dr Portland OR 97201-3098. *Fax:* 503-494-8393

HARE, JOAN CONWAY, PHYCOLOGY, MARINE BOTANY. *Current Pos:* chem tutor, 76-83, INSTR, CONT EDUC, UNIV MASS, 81- *Personal Data:* b Berlin, NH, June 6, 43; m 72. *Educ:* Univ NH, BA, 67; Univ Mass, MS, 72, PhD(bot), 76. *Prof Exp:* NATO fel marine bot, Biologische Anstalt Helgoland, 78-79. *Concurrent Pos:* Consult algae, Mass Inst Technol, 81. *Mem:* Bot Soc Am; Phycol Soc Am; Int Phycol Soc; Brit Phycol Soc. *Res:* Development, morphogenesis and life histories of algae; photobiology and nutrition of algae; environmental control of algal development and morphology. *Mailing Add:* 1 Chadwick Ct Amherst MA 01002

HARE, JOHN DANIEL, III, INSECT ECOLOGY, EVOLUTIONARY ECOLOGY. *Current Pos:* from asst prof to assoc prof, 84-94, PROF, DEPT ENTOM, UNIV CALIF, RIVERSIDE, 94- *Personal Data:* b Fresno, Calif, Jan 30, 48; m 82; c 2. *Educ:* Stanford Univ, BA, 70; State Univ NY Stony Brook, PhD(ecol & evolution), 78. *Prof Exp:* Asst entomologist, Conn Agr Exp Sta, 77-84. *Mem:* Int Soc Chem Ecol; Entom Soc Am; Ecol Soc Am; Soc Study Evolution. *Res:* Plant-insect interactions; chemical ecology; co-evolution; tritrophic interactions. *Mailing Add:* Dept Entom Univ Calif 900 University Ave Riverside CA 92521. *Fax:* 909-787-3086; *E-Mail:* harejd@ucrsc1.ucr.edu

HARE, JOHN DONALD, VIROLOGY. *Current Pos:* from instr med & bact to assoc prof microbiol, 59-71, PROF MICROBIOL, MED CTR, UNIV ROCHESTER, 71- *Personal Data:* b Rochester, NY, Jan 23, 28; m 52; c 3. *Educ:* Harvard Univ, BA, 50; Univ Rochester, MS, 53, MD, 55. *Prof Exp:* Intern med, Harvard Serv, Boston City Hosp, Mass, 55-56, asst resident, 58-59. *Mem:* Infectious Dis Soc Am; Am Soc Microbiol; Am Asn Cancer Res. *Res:* Viral oncogenesis; cellular metabolism; infectious diseases; immunology. *Mailing Add:* Univ Rochester Med Ctr Rochester NY 14642

HARE, LEONARD N, PLANT PHYSIOLOGY. *Current Pos:* assoc prof, 61-70, PROF BIOL, ANDREWS UNIV, 70- *Personal Data:* b Rangoon, Burma, Dec 5, 21; US citizen; m 44; c 2. *Educ:* Pac Union Col, BA, 44; Univ Md, MA, 59, PhD(plant physiol), 61. *Prof Exp:* Prin, Burma Union Training Sch, 46-48, Tenasserim Mission Sch, Burma, 48-50 & Raymond Mem Training Sch, India, 51-56. *Res:* Effects of environment, especially light duration and quality, on differentiation, elongation, metabolism and free amino acid content of plant cells. *Mailing Add:* 2283 Wilderness Trail Berrien Springs MI 49103

HARE, MARY LOUISE ECKLES, cytology, botany, for more information see previous edition

HARE, PETER EDGAR, ORGANIC GEOCHEMISTRY. *Current Pos:* STAFF MEM, CARNEGIE INST GEOPHYS LAB, 63- *Personal Data:* b Maymyo, Burma, Apr 14, 33; US citizen; m 54; c 2. *Educ:* Pac Union Col, BS, 54; Univ Calif, Berkeley, MS, 55; Calif Inst Technol, PhD(geochem), 62. *Prof Exp:* Instr chem, Pac Union Col, 55-58; res fel, Calif Inst Technol, 62-63. *Concurrent Pos:* Regents lectr, Univ Calif, Riverside, 94. *Mem:* Geol Soc Am. *Res:* High sensitivity amino acid analysis including D & L amino acid isomers; application fo geochemical systems; amino acid sequence of fossil peptides; development of chiral separations in liquid chromatography; stable isotopes of nitrogen and carbon in amino acids from fossils; paleodiets and paleoenvironments of fossils. *Mailing Add:* Carnegie Inst Washington Geophys Lab 5251 Broad Branch Rd NW Washington DC 20015-1305. *Fax:* 202-686-2419; *E-Mail:* hare@gl.ciw.edu

HARE, ROBERT RITZINGER, JR, APPLIED MATHEMATICS, OPERATIONS RESEARCH. *Current Pos:* from assoc prof to prof, 69-90, EMER PROF MATH, NDAK STATE UNIV, 90- *Personal Data:* b Indianapolis, Ind, Feb 23, 25; m 47; c 4. *Educ:* DePauw Univ, AB, 48, MA, 49. *Prof Exp:* Mathematician & chief math anal sect, USAF Missile Test Ctr, Patrick AFB, Fla, 51-53; mem staff math, Opers Res Off, Johns Hopkins Univ, 53-57; sr scientist, Opers Res Inc, Md, 57-69. *Concurrent Pos:* Instr, Rollins Col, 52, Univ Fla, 52-53 & Montgomery Jr Col, 56-57; consult, Army Res Off, 70. *Mem:* AAAS; Am Math Soc; Opers Res Soc Am. *Res:* Systems analysis and operations research in military and transportation fields; applied probability theory; computer applications, simulation. *Mailing Add:* 2832 Longfellow Rd Fargo ND 58102-1717

HARE, WILLIAM CURRIE DOUGLAS, EMBRYOS, CYTOGENETICS. *Current Pos:* ED-IN-CHIEF, CAN VET J, 91- *Personal Data:* b Edinburgh, Scotland, Jan 10, 25; m 75, Wendy E Hirst; c Sara, Simon & Alastair. *Educ:* Univ Edinburgh, BSc, 50, PhD(vet anat), 53, DVM & S, 60. *Hon Degrees:* MA, Univ Pa, 71. *Prof Exp:* Asst lectr vet anat, Royal Sch Vet Studies, Univ Edinburgh, 50-53, lectr, 53-55; assoc prof, Ont Vet Col, 55-58; from assoc prof to prof vet anat, Sch Vet Med, Univ Pa, 58-74; res scientist, Food Prod & Inspection Br, Agr Can, 74-92. *Mem:* Can Vet Med Asn; fel Royal Col Vet Surgeons; Coun Biol Ed; Sigma Xi; Am Med Writers Asn. *Res:* Veterinary cytogenetics; embryo transfer; disease control. *Mailing Add:* Can Vet J 339 Booth St Ottawa ON K1R 7K1 Can. *Fax:* 613-236-9681; *E-Mail:* jnlsevma@magi.com

HARE, WILLIAM RAY, JR, MATHEMATICS. *Current Pos:* assoc prof, 64-74, PROF MATH & HEAD DEPT, CLEMSON UNIV, 74- *Personal Data:* b Murfreesboro, Ark, June 29, 36; m 61; c 3. *Educ:* Henderson State Teachers Col, BS, 57; Univ Fla, MS, 59, PhD(math), 61. *Prof Exp:* From instr to asst prof math, Duke Univ, 61-64. *Mem:* Am Math Soc; Math Asn Am. *Res:* Topological and combinatorial convexity; generalizations of convexity. *Mailing Add:* Dept Math Clemson Univ Clemson SC 29634

HAREIN, PHILLIP KEITH, entomology, for more information see previous edition

HARES, GEORGE BIGELOW, INORGANIC CHEMISTRY. *Current Pos:* Sr res chemist, 52-59, res assoc chem, 59-67, SR RES ASSOC CHEM, CORNING GLASS WORKS, 67- *Personal Data:* b Corning, NY, Jan 11, 21; m 45; c 2. *Educ:* Syracuse Univ, BS, 48, MS, 49; Pa State Col, PhD(chem), 52. *Mem:* Am Chem Soc; Am Ceramic Soc; Brit Soc Glass Technol; fel Am Inst Chem. *Res:* Chemistry of glass. *Mailing Add:* 31 E Fourth St Corning NY 14830-3115

HARESIGN, THOMAS, ZOOLOGY. *Current Pos:* from asst prof to assoc prof, 64-74, PROF BIOL, SOUTHAMPTON COL, LONG ISLAND UNIV & DIR NAT SCI DIV, 74- *Personal Data:* b Sandy Creek, NY, Sept 4, 32; m 57, Marlene BuschKampes; c Tim, Lincoln & Athena. *Educ:* State Univ NY Albany, BS, 57, MS, 59; Univ Mass, PhD(zool), 64. *Prof Exp:* Instr biol, Marist Col, 62-64. *Concurrent Pos:* Worcester Found fel exp biol, 70-71. *Mem:* AAAS. *Res:* Endocrinology; steroid biochemistry; computer applications. *Mailing Add:* Dept Biol Southampton Col Long Island Univ Southampton NY 11968

HAREWOOD, KEN RUPERT, MOLECULAR GENETICS, CANCER RESEARCH. *Current Pos:* PRIN RES INVESTR, MOLECULAR GENETICS RES DEPT, PFIZER INC, GROTON, CONN, 71- *Educ:* City Univ New York, PhD(biochem), 70. *Concurrent Pos:* Mem, educ task force, Pfizer Inc. *Mem:* Am Soc Biochem & Molecular Biol; Harvey Soc. *Res:* Biochemistry. *Mailing Add:* Cent Res Div Pfizer Inc Groton CT 06340

HARFENIST, MORTON, ORGANIC CHEMISTRY, MEDICINAL CHEMISTRY. *Current Pos:* RETIRED. *Personal Data:* b New York, NY, Dec 6, 22; div; c 3. *Educ:* City Col New York, BS, 42; Polytech Inst Brooklyn, MS, 46; Univ Ill, PhD(chem), 48. *Prof Exp:* Jr chemist, Wellcome Res Labs, 43-44; res chemist, Chas Pfizer & Co, Inc, 48-52; sr org hemist, Wellcome Res Lab, 52-70, group leader, 70-74, actg head, Org Chem Dept, 74-77, group leader, 77-88, sect head, 88-96. *Concurrent Pos:* Naval med res, US Navy, 45-46. *Mem:* Am Chem Soc. *Res:* Medicinal synthetic organic chemistry. *Mailing Add:* 6406 C Farrington Rd Chapel Hill NC 27514

HARFORD, JAMES J, MECHANICAL ENGINEERING, SPACE HISTORY. *Current Pos:* exec dir, 64-89, EMER EXEC DIR, AM INST AERONAUT & ASTRONAUT, 89- *Personal Data:* b Jersey City, NJ, Aug 19, 24; m 52; c Susan, James Jr, Jennifer & Christopher. *Educ:* Yale Univ, BE, 45. *Honors & Awards:* Pub Serv Award, NASA, 85; Distinguished Serv Award, Am Inst Aeronaut & Astronaut, 87. *Prof Exp:* Appln engr fluid mach, Worthington Corp, 46-49; assoc ed indust prod methods, Mod Indust, 50-52; free lance writer, 52-53; exec secy astronaut, Am Rocket Soc, 53-63. *Concurrent Pos:* Verville fel, Nat Air & Space Mus, 92-93. *Mem:* Fel AAAS; fel Brit Interplanetary Soc; fel Am Inst Aeronaut & Astronaut; assoc fel Royal Aeronaut Soc; Inst Elec & Electronics Engrs. *Res:* Technical society administration, technical publishing and journalism; researching history of Soviet space program. *Mailing Add:* 601 Lake Dr Princeton NJ 08540. *E-Mail:* 71053.1525@compuserve.com

HARFORD, JOE BRYAN, PROTEIN SYNTHESIS, IRON METABOLISM. *Current Pos:* DIR BIOCHEM & CELL BIOL, RIBO GENE INC, 93- *Personal Data:* b Montgomery, WVa, Nov 4, 51; m 74, Esther Chang; c Leah E. *Educ:* Ohio Univ, BS, 73; Univ Md, PhD(biochem), 79. *Prof Exp:* Unit leader, Cell Biol & Metab Br, Nat Inst Child Health & Human Develop, NIH, 84-93. *Mem:* Am Soc Cell Biol. *Res:* Post-transcriptional control of gene expression; translational control and regulated mRNA stability; genes involved in cellular iron metabolism; translation-targeted therapeutics for viral infections, fungal infections and cancer. *Mailing Add:* 31 Center Dr MSC 2590 Bldg 31 Rm 11A48 Bethesda MD 20892-2590. *Fax:* 562-402-0338

HARGENS, CHARLES WILLIAM, III, ELECTRICAL ENGINEERING, BIO-MEDICAL ENGINEERING. *Current Pos:* RETIRED. *Personal Data:* b Philadelphia, Pa, Oct 21, 18; m 41, Mary K Johnson; c William J, Mary V (Vicberman) & Rogers. *Educ:* Mass Inst Technol, SB, 41. *Honors & Awards:* Sect Award, Inst Elec & Electronics Engrs, 72. *Prof Exp:* Design engr, Lockheed Aircraft Corp, 41-42; proj engr, Gilfillan Bros, Inc, Calif, 42-45; group leader adv develop, RCA, NJ, 46-47; sr staff engr, 48-59, head, Bio-Electronics Br, 59-60, tech dir labs in charge elec eng, 60-68, fel, res labs, Franklin Inst, 68-88. *Concurrent Pos:* Vis mem staff, radiation lab, Mass Inst Technol, 42-44; res assoc, Wills Eye Hosp, 70-; adj assoc prof acoust, Temple Univ, 76 & 77 & Drexel Univ, 78-87; lectr acoust, Philadelphia Col Art, 81; expert witness, acousts & bioeng; mem, Franklin Inst Comn Sci & Arts, 81- *Mem:* Sigma Xi; fel Inst Elec & Electronics Engrs. *Res:* Electrical instrumentation; medical and biological applications; electrical communication engineering; acoustics; granted 12 US patents; contributed chapters in books on bioengineering; numerous journal publications in instrumentation field of specialties. *Mailing Add:* 1006 Preston Rd Erdenheim PA 19038

HARGER, ROBERT OWENS, ELECTRICAL ENGINEERING. *Current Pos:* assoc prof, 68-75, chmn dept, 75-80, PROF ELEC ENG, UNIV MD, COLLEGE PARK, 75- *Personal Data:* b Flint, Mich, Sept 15, 32; m 60; c 4. *Educ:* Univ Mich, Ann Arbor, BSE, 55, MS, 59, PhD(elec eng), 61. *Honors & Awards:* Barry Carlton Award, Inst Elec & Electronics Engrs, 77. *Prof Exp:* Res engr, Inst Sci & Technol, Univ Mich, Ann Arbor, 61-68, asst prof elec eng, 63-66. *Concurrent Pos:* Consult var org, including NASA, 69-72, Dept Defense, 73-75 & Environ Res Inst Mich, 77- *Mem:* Fel Inst Elec & Electronics Engrs; Int Radio Sci Union; AAAS. *Res:* Signal and image processing; radar and remote sensing systems. *Mailing Add:* Dept Elec Eng Univ Md 23 Watchwater Way Rockville MD 20850. *Fax:* 301-314-9281; *E-Mail:* harger@eng.und.edu

HARGEST, THOMAS SEWELL, BIOMEDICAL ENGINEERING. *Current Pos:* RETIRED. *Personal Data:* b Phillipsburg, NJ, Jan 3, 25; m 45; c 4. *Educ:* Lafayette Col, BA, 50. *Prof Exp:* Geophysicist, Stand Oil & Gas Co, 51-53; opers mgr, Oil & Gas Div, Brown Container Co, 53-56; vpres, Slade Oil & Gas, Inc, 56-58; pres, Overland, Inc, 58-60; vpres, Western Oil Corp, 60-62; pres, Metcon, Inc, 62-63; dir res, Metcon Div, Chatleff Controls, 63-64; dir eng develop sect, Shriners Burn Inst, 64-65; dir, Div Clin Eng, Dept Surg, Med Univ SC, 65-76, from asst prof to assoc prof surg, 70-80, prof surg & biomet, 80-85. *Concurrent Pos:* Consult, Vet Admin Hosp, Charleston, SC & SC Retarded Children's Rehabilitation Ctr, Ladson, Support Syst Int, SA, Montpellier, France, Am Hosp Supply Corp, Evanston, Ill, Kum Klao Proj, Royal Thai Air Force, Bangkok, Thailand. *Mem:* Asn Advan Med Instrumentation; Am Burn Asn; Am Soc Artificial Internal Organs; Sigma Xi. *Res:* Development of systems and devices to improve the care and well-being of the patient. *Mailing Add:* 14 Lockwood Dr No 10J Charleston SC 29401

HARGIS, I GLEN, PHYSICAL CHEMISTRY, POLYMER CHEMISTRY. *Current Pos:* sr res chemist, Gencorp, 66-71, res scientist, Res & Develop Ctr, 71-72, group leader, Res Div, 72-81, sect head, 81-89, SR RES ASSOC, GENCORP, 89- *Personal Data:* b Hail, Ky, June 5, 39; m 61; c 3. *Educ:* Kent State Univ, BS, 61; Ohio Univ, PhD(chem), 66. *Prof Exp:* Sr res chemist, Monsanto Res Corp, 65-66. *Mem:* Am Chem Soc. *Res:* Materials chemistry; polymer characterization; elastomer synthesis and characterization; identifying structural and morphological parameters which significantly contribute to vulcanizate performance; synthesis and evaluation of organometallic initiator catalyst systems. *Mailing Add:* 679 Atwood Dr Tallmadge OH 44278-1104

HARGIS, J HOWARD, ORGANIC CHEMISTRY. *Current Pos:* asst prof, 70-78, ASSOC PROF CHEM, AUBURN UNIV, 70- *Personal Data:* b Fayetteville, Ark, Nov 2, 42; m 64; c 1. *Educ:* Eastern NMex Univ, BS, 64; Univ Utah, PhD(org chem), 69. *Prof Exp:* Res assoc org chem, Univ Ill, Urbana, 69-70. *Mem:* Am Chem Soc. *Res:* Free radical chemistry; mechanistic organophosphorus chemistry; conformational analysis. *Mailing Add:* Dept Chem Auburn Univ Auburn AL 36849

HARGIS, LARRY G, ANALYTICAL CHEMISTRY. *Current Pos:* asst prof, 65-69, ASSOC PROF CHEM, UNIV NEW ORLEANS, 69- *Personal Data:* b Ferndale, Mich, Nov 22, 39; m 61; c 2. *Educ:* Wayne State Univ, BS, 61, MS, 63, PhD(anal chem), 64. *Prof Exp:* Fel, Purdue Univ, 64-65. *Mem:* Am Chem Soc. *Res:* Ultraviolet and visible absorption spectroscopy; chemistry of heteropoly acids; analytical applications of solution kinetics; chemical applications of on-line computer systems. *Mailing Add:* Acad Affairs Univ New Orleans New Orleans LA 70148

HARGIS, PHILIP JOSEPH, JR, QUANTUM OPTICS. *Current Pos:* MEM TECH STAFF OPTICS, SANDIA LABS, 72- *Personal Data:* b New Orleans, La, Nov 28, 44; m 64; c 3. *Educ:* Univ New Orleans, BS, 66; Univ Pa, MS, 68, PhD(physics), 72. *Mem:* Optical Soc Am. *Res:* Application of tunable lasers to atomic and molecular spectroscopy; laser induced molecular photodissociation; laser radar; laser based diagnostics for chemical vapor deposition and plasma etching studies. *Mailing Add:* Dept 1128 Sandia Nat Labs Albuquerque NM 87185-5800

HARGIS, WILLIAM JENNINGS, JR, BIOLOGICAL OCEANOGRAPHY, PARASITOLOGY. *Current Pos:* mem staff, 79-92, EMER PROF, SCH MARINE SCI, COL WILLIAM & MARY, 92- *Personal Data:* b Lebanon, Va, Nov 24, 23; m 79. *Educ:* Univ Richmond, AB, 50, MA, 51; Fla State Univ, PhD(zool), 54. *Prof Exp:* Asst prof biol & chem, The Citadel, 54-55; assoc marine scientist, Va Inst Marine Sci, 55-59, dir, 59-69; from assoc prof to prof marine sci, Col William & Mary, 55-69; dean sch, Univ Va, 60-79, prof marine sci & chmn dept, 63-79. *Concurrent Pos:* Mem nat tech adv comt on water qual criteria, Fed Water Pollution Control Admin, Dept Interior; co-chmn adv comt, Atlantic States Marine Fisheries Comn, 59-; mem, Ocean Affairs Adv Comt, US State Dept, 71-; mem adv comt, Coastal Plains Regional Comn Marine Resources, 75-; voting mem & chmn, S&S comt, Mid-Atlantic Mgt Coun, 76-; mem, Comt Offshore Technol, Nat Acad Sci, 78- *Mem:* Fel AAAS; Am Soc Limnol & Oceanog; Soc Syst Zool; Am Soc Parasitol; fel Marine Technol Soc (pres, 78-); Sigma Xi. *Res:* Resource and environmental management; information management; science administration; coastal zone management; fisheries. *Mailing Add:* 220 Mastin Ave Seaford VA 23696

HARGITAY, BARTHOLOMEW, PHYSICAL CHEMISTRY, POLYMER CHEMISTRY. *Current Pos:* staff scientist, 81-92, CONSULT, TECHNICON INSTRUMENT CO, 92- *Personal Data:* b Arad, Romania, Aug 25, 24; US citizen; m 67, Elinor. *Educ:* Pazmany Peter Univ, Budapest, BS, 46; Univ Basel, MS & PhD(phys chem), 50. *Prof Exp:* Fel, Fritz Hoffmann La Roche Found, Basel, 50-52; fel chem, Harvard Univ, 52-54; group leader polymers, Europ Res Assocs, Brussels, Belg, 54-65; sr scientist, Corp Res Lab, Union Carbide Corp, 65-81. *Res:* Physico-chemical processes that make up physiology, particularly effects due to the polymeric and colloidal nature of biological systems; contractility; kidney action; semipermeability and separations; topochemical effects in catalysis; materials used in clinical diagnostics; diagnostics. *Mailing Add:* 15 Edna St White Plains NY 10606

HARGRAVE, PAUL ALLAN, BIOCHEMISTRY. *Current Pos:* PROF OPHTHAL & BIOCHEM, SCH MED, UNIV FLA, 85- *Personal Data:* b Clifton Springs, NY, Nov 30, 38; m 67, Doris Dayton; c Elizabeth & David. *Educ:* Colgate Univ, AB, 60; Univ EAfrica, Dipl, 62; Univ Ill, MS, 66; Univ Minn, PhD(biochem), 70. *Prof Exp:* From asst prof to prof biochem, Sch

Med, Southern Ill Univ, 73-84. *Concurrent Pos:* Am Cancer Soc fel, Calif Inst Technol, 70-72, NIH fel, 72-73; mem visual disorders study sect, NIH, 81-85. *Mem:* AAAS; Am Chem Soc; Asn Res Vision & Ophthal; Am Soc Photobiol; Am Soc Biol Chemists. *Res:* Protein biochemistry; structure and function of membrane proteins; rhodopsin biochemistry. *Mailing Add:* Ophthal Dept Univ Fla Box 100 284 JHMHC Bldg Gainesville FL 32610. *Fax:* 352-392-0573; *E-Mail:* hargrave@eye1.eye.ufl.edu

HARGRAVES, PAUL E, BIOLOGICAL OCEANOGRAPHY, MARINE PHYTOPLANKTON. *Current Pos:* cur, Univ RI, 68-69, res assoc, 69-70, asst prof, 71-77, PROF OCEANOG & BOT, NARRAGANSETT MARINE LAB, UNIV RI, 86- *Personal Data:* b Providence, RI, July 27, 41; m 63, 92; c 3. *Educ:* Univ RI, BS, 63, MS, 65; Col William & Mary, PhD(marine sci), 68. *Prof Exp:* Res scientist, Lamont Geol Observ, Columbia Univ, 67-68. *Concurrent Pos:* Vis prof, Nat Univ Costa Rica, 79 & Univ Salzburg, Austria, 95. *Mem:* Int Phycol Soc; Plankton Soc Japan; Am Soc Limnol & Oceanog; Phycol Soc Am; Am Inst Biol Sci. *Res:* Systematics and ecology of marine microalgae and phytoplankton, especially diatoms; ecology of marine algae. *Mailing Add:* Bay Campus Univ RI Narragansett RI 02882-1197

HARGRAVES, ROBERT BERO, GEOLOGY. *Current Pos:* from asst prof to assoc prof, 61-71, PROF GEOL, PRINCETON UNIV, 71- *Personal Data:* b Durban, SAfrica, Aug 11, 28; US citizen; m 55; c 3. *Educ:* Univ Natal, BSc, 48, Hons, 49, MSc, 52; Princeton Univ, PhD(geol), 59. *Prof Exp:* Geologist, Uruwira Minerals Ltd, Tanganyika, 49-50, Union Corp Ltd, SAfrica, 50-52 & Newmont Mining Corp, NY, 53-54; res fel geol, Econ Geol Res Unit, Univ Witwatersrand, 59-61. *Mem:* Mineral Soc Am; Geol Soc Am; Geol Soc SAfrica; Am Geophys Union. *Res:* Igneous petrology, rock and paleomagnetism; economic geology, Precambrian geology. *Mailing Add:* 747 Great Rd Princeton NJ 08540

HARGREAVES, GEORGE H(ENRY), CIVIL ENGINEERING, SOIL SCIENCE. *Current Pos:* res engr, Dept Agr & Irrig Eng, 70-86, EMER RES PROF, UTAH STATE UNIV, 86- *Personal Data:* b Chico, Calif, Apr 2, 16; m 51, Sara Romero; c Margaret (Stolpmann), Mark, Sonia (Hart) & George L. *Educ:* Univ Calif, BS, 39; Univ Wyo, BS, 43. *Prof Exp:* Soil surveyor, Univ Calif, 40; rural rehab supvr, Farm Security Admin, Calif. 40-41; soils technologist, Bur Reclamation, US Dept Interior, 41-42, hydraul engr, 46-48; reclamation engr, NAtlantic Div, US Army CEngrs, Greece, 48-49 & Econ Coop Admin, 49-50; agr irrig engr, Inst Inter-Am Affairs, 50-51 & Haiti, Foreign Opers Admin, 51-56; Int Coop Admin, Philippines, 56-57, water resources adv, 57-60, agr irrig engr, US Agency Int Develop, Brazil, 60-62, water resources adv, 62-65, agr adv, Colombia, 65-68; chief, Civil Eng Br, Nat Resources Div, Inter-Am Geod Surv, US Army, Ft Clayton, CZ, 68-70. *Concurrent Pos:* Asst, Univ Wyo, 42-43; mem, Regional Water Resources Conf, US Del to UN, Manila, 57; US Nat Comt, Int Comn Irrig & Drainage. *Mem:* Fel Am Soc Civil Engrs; Am Soc Agr Engrs. *Res:* Water resources planning and development, especially irrigation; hydrology. *Mailing Add:* Dept Agr & Irrig Eng Utah State Univ Logan UT 84322-4150. *Fax:* 435-797-1248

HARGREAVES, LEON ABRAHAM, JR, FORESTRY. *Current Pos:* PROF FORESTRY, UNIV GA, 62-, DEAN, 80- *Personal Data:* b Pearson, Ga, Jan 11, 21; m 46; c 3. *Educ:* Univ Ga, BSF, 46, MSF, 47; Univ Mich, MPA & PhD(forestry), 53. *Prof Exp:* Forestry specialist, Agr Exten Serv, Univ Ga, 47-49, asst prof, Sch Forestry, 49-54; asst dir, Ga State Forestry Comn, 54-60; asst admin mgt lands & forests, St Regis Paper Co, 60-62. *Mem:* Soc Am Foresters; Sigma Xi. *Res:* Operations analysis; valuation; property taxes. *Mailing Add:* 240 Terrell Dr Athens GA 30606

HARGREAVES, RONALD THOMAS, ORGANIC CHEMISTRY. *Current Pos:* Res chemist spectros, 74-80, sr res chemist, 80-81, MGR TECH REGULATORY AFFAIRS, MED RES DIV, LEDERLE LABS, AM CYANAMID CO, 81- *Personal Data:* b Manchester, Eng, Mar 3, 46; m 72; c 2. *Educ:* Univ EAnglia, BSc, 67, MSc, 68; Univ Rochester, PhD(chem), 74. *Concurrent Pos:* Fel, Univ Ill, Urbana, 72-74. *Res:* Mass spectrometry, structural studies of natural products, chromatography. *Mailing Add:* 1 Yellowstone Dr West Nyack NY 10994

HARGROVE, CLIFFORD KINGSTON, EXPERIMENTAL HIGH ENERGY PHYSICS, MUON PHYSICS. *Current Pos:* EMER RES SCIENTIST, CTR RES PARTICLE PHYSICS, CARLETON UNIV, 90- *Personal Data:* b St John, NB, Nov 22, 28; m 53; c Ian K. *Educ:* Univ NB, BA, 49; McGill Univ, BSc, 55, MSc, 57, PhD(nuclear physics), 61. *Prof Exp:* Asst res officer, Nat Res Coun, Ottawa, Can, 61-65, assoc res officer, 65-73, sr res officer, 73-84, prin res officer, 84-90. *Concurrent Pos:* Adj prof, Carleton Univ, 73- *Mem:* Inst Particle Physics; Can Asn Physicists; fel Am Phys Soc. *Res:* Muon and pion physics with emphasis on elementary particle aspects; lepton conservation laws, and rare decays of muons; instrumentation for particle physics with emphasis on gas counters; Operation Alert detector; solar-neutrino physics. *Mailing Add:* Carleton Univ Ctr Res Particle Physics 1125 Colonel By Dr Herzberg Bldg Rm 222 Ottawa ON K1S 5B6 Can

HARGROVE, GEORGE LYNN, QUANTITATIVE GENETICS, STATISTICS. *Current Pos:* From asst prof to assoc prof, 70-83, PROF DAIRY SCI, PA STATE UNIV, UNIVERSITY PARK, 83- *Personal Data:* b Cantril, Iowa, Sept 20, 35; m 64; c 2. *Educ:* Iowa State Univ, BS, 65; NC State Univ, MS, 68, PhD(animal sci), 70. *Concurrent Pos:* USAID, Uruguay, 68. *Mem:* Am Dairy Sci Asn. *Res:* Dairy cattle production and genetics. *Mailing Add:* Dept Dairy & Animal Sci Pa State Univ 324 Henning Bldg University Park PA 16802-3503

HARGROVE, JAMES LEE, COMPUTER MODELING OF GENE EXPRESSION, EFFECTS OF DIET ON GENE EXPRESSION. *Current Pos:* ASSOC PROF, DEPT FOOD & NUTRIT, UNIV GA, 90- *Personal Data:* b Vallejo, Calif, July 25, 46; m 75, Diane K Hartle; c Katharine I & John J. *Educ:* Univ Wash, BS, 69; Utah Univ, MS, 73, PhD(zool & biol), 75. *Honors & Awards:* Cosmos Achievement Award, NASA, 89. *Prof Exp:* Fel biochem, Univ Minn, 75-76; fel, Univ Iowa, 76-79, res assoc, 79-82; from asst prof to assoc prof, Sch Med, Emory Univ, 82-89. *Mem:* Am Inst Nutrit; Am Soc Biochem & Molecular Biol; Sigma Xi. *Res:* Influence of dietary protein on blood coagulation and enzyme synthesis; computer modeling of gene expression; transaminase enzymology. *Mailing Add:* Dept Foods & Nutrit Dawson Hall Univ Ga Athens GA 30602. *Fax:* 706-542-5059; *E-Mail:* jhargrov@hestia.fcs.uga.edu

HARGROVE, LOGAN EZRAL, ACOUSTICS, OPTICS. *Current Pos:* physicist, Physic Div, 76-94, PHYSICIST, CHEM & PHYSICS DIV, OFF NAVAL RES, 94- *Personal Data:* b Spiro, Okla, Mar 3, 35; div; c Paul H & David H. *Educ:* Okla State Univ, BS, 56, MS, 57; Mich State Univ, PhD(physics), 61. *Honors & Awards:* Biennial Award, Acoust Soc, 70. *Prof Exp:* Res assoc, Ultrasonics Lab, Mich State Univ, 61-62, mem tech staff, Mech Res Dept, Bell Tel Labs, 62-69, mem tech staff, Guided Wave Res Lab, 69-76. *Concurrent Pos:* Fel, Dept Mat Sci & Eng, Johns Hopkins Univ, 89- *Mem:* Fel Acoust Soc Am; Optical Soc Am; fel Am Phys Soc; sr mem Inst Elec & Electronics Engrs; AAAS. *Res:* Physical acoustics and optics. *Mailing Add:* Off Naval Res Chem & Physics Div ONR331 800 N Quincy St Arlington VA 22217-5660. *Fax:* 703-696-2611; *E-Mail:* hargrove@onr-hq.navy.mil

HARGROVE, ROBERT JOHN, ORGANIC CHEMISTRY, ENVIRONMENTAL TOXICOLOGY. *Current Pos:* asst prof, 75-81, chmn dept, 79-81, PROF CHEM, MERCER UNIV, 81-, CHMN, DEPT CHEM, 88- *Personal Data:* b Willard, Ohio, June 12, 42; m 67, Carolyn Ballard; c 2. *Educ:* Ohio Wesleyan Univ, BA, 64; Univ Utah, PhD(org chem), 74; Univ Ala, Birmingham, MPH, 87. *Honors & Awards:* Sr Fulbright-Hays lectr, Cultington Univ, 81-82. *Prof Exp:* Comn officer, USN, 64-68; teaching fel chem, Univ Utah, 69-74; asst prof chem, Dickinson Col, 74-75. *Concurrent Pos:* Title III proj coordr, Mercer Univ, 82-84, dean protem, Col Liberal Arts, 84-86; vis prof, Colo Sch Mines, Golden, Colo, 94-95; William C Foster vis scientist, US Arms Control & Disarmament Agency, Washington, DC, 95-96. *Mem:* AAAS; Am Chem Soc. *Res:* Mechanistic organic chemistry, history of chemical education, vinyl trifluoromethane-sulfonate chemistry; pesticide residues in human adipose tissue. *Mailing Add:* Dept Chem Mercer Univ Macon GA 31207-0003

HARI, V, VIROLOGY, MOLECULAR BIOLOGY. *Current Pos:* res assoc virol, 73-76, asst prof biol, 76-81, ASSOC PROF BIOL, WAYNE STATE UNIV, 81- *Personal Data:* b Trichur, India, June 23, 36; m 67; c 1. *Educ:* Annamalai Univ, Madras, BSc, 58; Madras Univ, MSc, 59, PhD(bot, virol), 64. *Prof Exp:* Fel virol, Waite Agr Res Inst, Australia, 64-65; res assoc, Univ Ariz, 65-70; officer scientist pool, Univ Madras, 70-71; asst virologist, Univ Calif, Berkeley, 71-73. *Mem:* Am Soc Virol; Plant Molecular Biol Asn; Sigma Xi. *Res:* Structure and replication of plant viruses by molecular techniques including gene cloning and sequencing; introduction of genes into plants using vectors; viral immunodiagnostics including HIV. *Mailing Add:* Dept Biol Sci 210 Sci Hall Wayne State Univ Detroit MI 48202-3940

HARING, OLGA M, MEDICINE. *Current Pos:* assoc prof, 70-75, prof, Dept Med & Community Health & Prev Med, Med Sch, 75-87, dir cardio-pulmonary-renal clins, 65-85, EMER PROF, NORTHWESTERN UNIV, CHICAGO, 87- *Personal Data:* b Oradea, Romania, Aug 25, 17; US citizen; m 38; c 1. *Educ:* Univ Vienna, MD, 38; Am Bd Internal Med, dipl, 64. *Prof Exp:* Dir med, Health Ctr 1, Dept Pub Health, Nicaragua, 40-46; foreign asst cardiol, Sorbonne, 47-49; assoc, Div Cardiol, Chicago Med Sch, 50-56; assoc attend, Cook County Hosp, Chicago, 64-65. *Concurrent Pos:* Fel coun clin cardiol, Am Heart Asn; UN Children's Emergency Fund fel, 48; Hektoen Inst pediat cardiol fel, 51-52. *Mem:* AAAS; fel Am Col Cardiol; fel Am Col Physicians. *Res:* Experimental production of cardiac malformations by prenatal hypercapnea in the rat and in the chicken; medical records; application of computers in medicine; clinical trials in cardiology. *Mailing Add:* 1201 Judson Evanston IL 60202

HARINGTON, CHARLES RICHARD, MAMMALOGY. *Current Pos:* chief, Paleobiol Div, 82-91, CUR QUATERNARY ZOOL, CAN MUS NATURE, 65- *Personal Data:* b Calgary, Alta, May 22, 33; m 94, Gail Doreen Wollacott. *Educ:* Univ Alta, BA, 54, BSc, 57, PhD, 77; McGill Univ, MSc, 61. *Honors & Awards:* Can Asn Geographers Prize, 57; Massey Medal, 87. *Prof Exp:* Wildlife biologist, Can Wildlife Serv, 60-65. *Concurrent Pos:* Res assoc, Can Mus Civilization, 92- *Mem:* AAAS; Am Soc Mammal; fel Arctic Inst NAm; fel Royal Geog Soc; fel Royal Can Geog Soc. *Res:* Canadian Pleistocene and Pliocene mammals; life history, distribution, ecology and evolution of the muskoxen and polar bear; climatic change in Canada during the Quaternary. *Mailing Add:* Paleobiol Can Mus Nature Ottawa ON K1P 6P4 Can

HARITATOS, NICHOLAS JOHN, PETROCHEMICAL PROCESS ENGINEERING. *Current Pos:* Res engr, Chevron Res & Technol Co, 56-61, group supvr, 61-65, sr eng assoc, 65-81, sr supv process engr, 81-87, ENG CONSULT, CHEVRON RES & TECHNOL CO, RICHMOND, CALIF, 88- *Personal Data:* b Rome, NY, May 29, 31; m 61, Nancy J Pierce; c Christopher & Edith. *Educ:* Mass Inst Technol, SB, 52, SM, 53, ScD(chem eng), 56. *Mem:* Am Chem Soc; Am Inst Chem Engrs. *Mailing Add:* 1354 Contra Costa Dr El Cerrito CA 94530. *Fax:* 510-242-1502

HARJU, PHILIP HERMAN, PHYSICAL CHEMISTRY. *Current Pos:* sr res scientist phys chem, 69-73, sr proj scientist, 73-75, GROUP MGR CATALYSIS, KOPPERS CO, INC, 75- *Personal Data:* b Bismarck, NDak, Aug 2, 30; m 54; c 5. *Educ:* NDak State Univ, BS, 56, MS, 57; Univ Pittsburgh, PhD(phys chem), 69. *Prof Exp:* Res assoc petrol, Mellon Inst Technol, 57-59, jr fel, 60-64. *Mem:* Am Chem Soc. *Res:* Catalysis; chemical kinetics; interfacial chemistry; photochemistry and photopolymerization; organic geochemistry and organometallics; water pollution. *Mailing Add:* 6 Maple Dr Spring Church PA 15686-9712

HARKAVY, ALLAN ABRAHAM, MAGNETIC RESONANCE, VISUAL PHYSIOLOGY. *Current Pos:* ASSOC PROF-PROF PHYSICS, STATE UNIV NY, NEW PALTZ, 64- *Personal Data:* b New York, NY, Mar 16, 25; m 52; c 2. *Educ:* City Col New York, BS, 49; New Sch Social Res, MA, 55; NY Univ, MS, 58, PhD(physics), 67. *Prof Exp:* Scientist, Westinghouse Atomic Power Div, 57-59; instr physics, Hofstra Col, 59-64. *Mem:* Am Phys Soc. *Res:* Theory of lateral geniculate body and visual cortex; theory of physical basis of human will; magnetic resonance. *Mailing Add:* 14 Prospect St New Paltz NY 12561

HARKE, DOUGLAS J, PHYSICS, SCIENCE EDUCATION. *Current Pos:* dean grad studies & res, 74-88, ASST PROF PHYSICS, STATE UNIV NY COL, GENESEO, 69-, DIR RES, 88- *Personal Data:* b Edmonton, Alta, Apr 18, 42; m 64; c 3. *Educ:* Univ Alta, BSc, 63; Wash Univ, MAEd, 64; Purdue Univ, MS & PhD(sci educ), 69. *Prof Exp:* Teacher high sch, Leduc, Alta, 64-65 & South Bend, Ind, 65-67. *Mem:* Am Asn Physics Teachers; Nat Asn Res Sci Teaching. *Res:* Physics achievement testing and computerized grading of physics tests; evaluation of training programs for secondary physics teachers; student evaluation of college teachers. *Mailing Add:* Dir Res State Univ NY Geneseo NY 14454-1401. *E-Mail:* harke@uno.cc.geneseo.edu

HARKER, J M, ENGINEERING. *Current Pos:* RETIRED. *Personal Data:* b San Francisco, Calif, June 30, 26; m 50; c 3. *Educ:* Swarthmore Col, BSME, 50; Univ Calif, Berkeley, MSE, 51; Stanford Univ, MSEE, 62. *Honors & Awards:* Reynold B Johnson Info Storage Award, Inst Elec & Electronics Engrs, 93. *Prof Exp:* IBM fel, IBM Corp, 52-87. *Mem:* Fel Inst Elec & Electronics Engrs. *Res:* Authored 6 publications; 6 issued US patents. *Mailing Add:* 840 Melville Ave Palo Alto CA 94301

HARKER, KENNETH JAMES, NUMERICAL ELECTROMAGNETICS. *Current Pos:* SR RES PHYSICIST, SRI INT, 81- *Personal Data:* b Long Beach, Calif, July 4, 27; wid; c Elizabeth & Kathryn. *Educ:* Univ Calif, Los Angeles, AB, 48, MA, 50, PhD(physics), 54. *Prof Exp:* Mem tech staff, Bell Tel Labs, 54-59; res physicist, Hansen Phys Lab, Stanford Univ, 59-75, sr res assoc, 75-89, consult prof elec eng, 89-90. *Concurrent Pos:* Consult, Varian Assocs, Sylvania Elec Prod, Sperry Rand, Microwave Assocs, 59-63. *Mem:* Fel Am Phys Soc; sr mem Inst Elec & Electronics Engrs; Int Asn Geomagnetism & Aeronomy; Am Geophys Union. *Res:* Plasma physics; wave phenomena; numerical electromagnetics. *Mailing Add:* 694 Camellia Way Los Altos CA 94024. *Fax:* 650-859-4121; *E-Mail:* harker@sri.com

HARKER, ROBERT IAN, geology; deceased, see previous edition for last biography

HARKER, YALE DEON, REACTOR PHYSICS. *Current Pos:* adv scientist, 94-96, CONSULT SCIENTIST, NUCLEAR & RADIATION PHYSICS DEPT, LOCKHEED-MARTIN, IDAHO TECH, 95- *Personal Data:* b Idaho Falls, Idaho, June 11, 37; m 59, Bonnie B Millward; c Shane D, Michael S, Julie A, David R, & Daniel Y. *Educ:* Idaho State Univ, BS, 59; Case Western Res Univ, MS, 62; Colo State Univ, PhD(physics), 69. *Prof Exp:* Res scientist, Phillips Petrol Co, Idaho, 62-66 & Idaho Nuclear Corp, 66-71; res scientist, Reactor Develop Br, 71-72, res & eng supvr, Nuclear Physics Br, Aerojet Nuclear Co, 72-76; res & eng supvr, Nuclear Physics Br, EG&G Idaho Inc, 76-80, sr scientist, 80-83, sci specialist, Nuclear Sci Unit, 83-94. *Concurrent Pos:* Adj prof physics, Idaho State Univ, Pocatello. *Mem:* Am Nuclear Soc. *Res:* Physics constants for fast reactor technology; high pressure solid state research; Raman scattering from crystalline solids; laser development research; study of the liquid and low temperature solid state; neutron spectrometry; radiation dosimetry; neutron scattering; non-destructive radioassay. *Mailing Add:* Nuclear & Radiation Physics 2114 Idaho Nat Eng Lab Idaho Falls ID 83415. *Fax:* 208-526-5208; *E-Mail:* ydh@inel.gov

HARKEY, JACK W, MECHANICAL ENGINEERING. *Current Pos:* From instr to assoc prof, 46-70, dir coop prof, 53-67, PROF MECH ENG, SOUTHERN METHODIST UNIV, 70- *Personal Data:* b Mar 17, 21; US citizen; m 47; c 2. *Educ:* Southern Methodist Univ, BSME, 44. *Concurrent Pos:* Consult & designer, D C Pfeiffer & Assocs, 50-53. *Mem:* Am Soc Eng Educ. *Res:* Environmental aspects of fallout shelter habitability; photoelastic analysis of sucker rod joints. *Mailing Add:* 2815 Amherst Ave Dallas TX 75225

HARKIN, JAMES C, PATHOLOGY, NEUROPATHOLOGY. *Current Pos:* assoc prof, 62-69, PROF PATH & ANAT, SCH MED, TULANE UNIV, 69- *Personal Data:* b Fayette, Miss, Dec 9, 26; m 52, Gerda Van Leeuwen; c Graham. *Educ:* Univ Nebr, BS & MD, 51. *Prof Exp:* Intern med, Univ Hosp, Univ Cleveland, 51-52; resident path, Inst Path, Western Res Univ, 52-55, demonstr, 54-55; instr, Sch Med, Wash Univ, 55-57, asst prof, 57-59; asst prof, Med Col, Cornell Univ, 61-62. *Concurrent Pos:* Asst pathologist, Barnes & St Louis Children's Hosps, 55-59; fel neuropath, Montefiore Hosp, NY, 56-57; assoc dir labs, Hosp Spec Surg, New York, 59-62; asst attend pathologist, New York Hosp, 61-62; vis pathologist, Charity Hosp, 62-; USPHS res career prog award, 63-72; vis scientist, Oxford Univ, 65; mem ed adv bd, Armed Forces Inst Path; consult, Int Ctr Med Res & Training, Univ Valle, Columbia, 68-78. *Mem:* Am Asn Neuropath; Am Asn Path; fel Col Am Path. *Res:* Pathology and experimental pathology; neuroanatomy; electron microscopy; tumors of the peripheral nervous system. *Mailing Add:* Sch Med Tulane Univ 1430 Tulane Ave New Orleans LA 70112-2699

HARKIN, JOHN MCLAY, ORGANIC CHEMISTRY, BIOCHEMISTRY. *Current Pos:* assoc prof soil sci, 74-77, PROF WATER RESOURCES & SOILS, UNIV WIS-MADISON, 77- *Personal Data:* b Paisley, Scotland, Apr 7, 33; US citizen; m 55; c 3. *Educ:* Glasgow Univ, BSc, 55; Univ Heidelberg, Dr rer nat(chem), 59. *Prof Exp:* Res asst, Res Inst Chem Wood & Polysaccharides, Univ Heidelberg, 55-66; proj leader lignin chem, US Forest Prod Lab, Wis, 66-74. *Mem:* Am Chem Soc; Tech Asn Pulp & Paper Indust. *Res:* Lignin structure and utilization; anatomy, physiology, chemistry and biochemistry of wood; pulping reactions and byproducts; nature and fate of natural and synthetic organic compounds in soil and water. *Mailing Add:* 3991 Plymouth Circle Madison WI 53705-5214

HARKINS, CARL GIRVIN, PHYSICAL CHEMISTRY, MATERIALS SCIENCE. *Current Pos:* mem tech staff, 78-85, PROJ MGR, HEWLETT-PACKARD LABS, 85-; WOLTSON INDUST FEL, UNIV OXFORD, 95- *Personal Data:* b Colorado City, Tex, June 14, 39; m 60; c 3. *Educ:* McMurry Col, BA, 60; Johns Hopkins Univ, MA, 62, PhD(phys chem), 64. *Prof Exp:* Res assoc chem eng, Univ Calif, Berkeley, 64-65; res fel, Rice Univ, 65-66; asst prof chem, Mat Res Div, Southwest Ctr Advan Studies, 66-68, actg head dept, 67-68; sr res scientist, Rice Univ, 68-73, adj prof mat sci, 73-85. *Mem:* Am Chem Soc; Nat Asn Corrosion Eng; Sigma Xi. *Res:* Surface chemistry; catalysis and photocatalysis; corrosion and stress corrosion; tribology; magnetic recording technology; computational materials science. *Mailing Add:* Hewlett-Packard Labs 1501 Page Mill Rd Palo Alto CA 94304

HARKINS, ROBERT W, NUTRITION, PHYSIOLOGICAL CHEMISTRY. *Current Pos:* dir res & develop, 79-87, VPRES, RES & DEVELOP, MCNEIL SPECIALTY PROD CO, DIV JOHNSON & JOHNSON, 87- *Personal Data:* b Chester, Pa, Oct 18, 35; m 58; c 3. *Educ:* Pa State Univ, BS, 57; Wayne State Univ, PhD(chem), 61. *Prof Exp:* Assoc scientist antibiotic develop, Parke Davis & Co, 57-58; sr scientist nutrit res, Mead Johnson & Co, 61-64, group leader, 64-66; dir sect food sci, Dept Foods & Nutrit & secy food indust liaison comt, AMA, 66-68; dir nutrit res, Ross Labs, 68-70; dir sci affairs, Grocery Mfg Am, Inc, 70-79, vpres sci affairs, 74-79. *Mem:* NY Acad Sci; Am Inst Nutrit; fel Am Inst Chem; Am Chem Soc. *Res:* Absorption and utilization of nutrients; rate of growth and body composition-mental development; safety and regulation of food ingredients. *Mailing Add:* 1575 Mirian Dr North Brunswick NJ 08902-3019. *Fax:* 732-247-3519

HARKINS, THOMAS REGIS, CHEMISTRY. *Current Pos:* PRES, HARKINS INT, INC, 95- *Personal Data:* b McKeesport, Pa, Jan 5, 29; m 61; c 3. *Educ:* Univ Pittsburgh, BS, 52, PhD(chem), 56. *Prof Exp:* Analytical res chemist, E I du Pont de Nemours & Co, 56-59; supvr chem & mech testing sect, Res Ctr, 59-62, proj supvr stainless steels, 62-64, res assoc, 64-65, sr develop engr, Sales Develop Dept, 65-69, mgr indust sales process equip & construct, 69-71, mkt dir stainless & specialty steel plate, Allegheny Ludlum Steel Corp, 71-76, dist sales mgr, Houston, 76-77; vpres sales & mkt, Spec Metals Corp, 77-82; gen sales mgr & exec vpres, Affival, 82-89; mgr prod develop, Claremont Trading Corp, 89-95. *Mem:* Am Chem Soc; Am Soc Metals; Am Ord Asn. *Res:* Analytical chemistry and applied spectroscopy; infrared spectroscopy; chelates and chelating agents; organic coatings; electrodeposition; corrosion; stainless steels and specialty metals. *Mailing Add:* Sta One Unit 6A Wrightsville Beach NC 28480

HARKLESS, GENE ELIZABETH, NURSING. *Current Pos:* ASSOC PROF NURSING DEPT NURSING, UNIV NH, 85- *Educ:* Duke Univ, BSN, 76; Vanderbilt Univ, MSN, 80; Boston Univ, DNSc, 91. *Prof Exp:* staff nurse, Indian Health Serv, Owyhee, Nev, 76-77; Victoria Gen Hosp, BC, 77-78; community health nurse, Churchill Health Ctr, Manitoba, 78-79; clin coordr, Maternal-Child & Occup Health Servs, 81-82; hemophilia nurse coordr, Hitchcock Clin Hemat/Oncol, Dartmouth-Hitchcock Med Ctr, 82-84, nurse practr, Pediat Oncol Prog, 83-85. *Concurrent Pos:* Nurse practr, Planned Parenthood, NH, 84-85; corresp mem, Clin Pract Comt, Oncol Nursing Soc, 84-85; vol comp nurse, New Eng Hemophilia Asn, 88 & 89; consult, Health Dimensions PA, 93-; family nurse practr, Lamprey Health Care, 93-; core fac, NH Alliance Maternal & Child Health Leadership Develop Prog, 94-95; adj assoc prof pediat, Dartmouth Med Sch, 94-; Fulbright scholar, Univ Oslo, 97. *Mem:* Am Acad Nurse Practr. *Mailing Add:* Dept Nursing Univ NH Durham NH 03824

HARKLESS, LAWRENCE BERNARD, PODIATRIC MEDICINE & SURGERY, DIABETES & ITS COMPLICATIONS. *Current Pos:* DIR PODIATRY RESIDENCY TRAINING, UNIV TEX HEALTH SCI CTR, SAN ANTONIO, 77- *Personal Data:* b Longview, Tex, Jan, 51; m 80; c 2. *Educ:* Cal Col Podiatric Med, BS & DPM, 75. *Res:* Foot disorders caused by diabetes. *Mailing Add:* Family Med Univ Tex Med Sch San Antonio 7703 Floyd Curl Dr San Antonio TX 78284-6200

HARKNESS, DONALD R, HEMATOLOGY, BIOCHEMISTRY. *Current Pos:* PROF & CHMN DEPT MED, UNIV WIS-MADISON, 80- *Personal Data:* b Mitchell, SDak, Aug 23, 32; m 54; c 4. *Educ:* Univ Calif, Berkeley, BA, 54; Wash Univ, MD, 58. *Prof Exp:* Intern med, Wash Univ, 58-59, resident internal med, 59-60; res assoc, Nat Inst Arthritis & Metab Dis, 60-63; Am Cancer Soc fel, 63, NIH spec res fel, 64; from asst prof to prof med, Univ Miami Sch Med, 64-80, assoc prof biochem, 69-75, mem grad fac, 70-80; chief hemat, Vet Admin Hosp, 68-80. *Concurrent Pos:* John & Mary Markle scholar, 66; dir, Miami Comprehensive Sickle Ctr, 73-78; chmn, Bd-u Care, Univ HMO, 84- *Mem:* Am Soc Hematol; Am Fedn Clin Res; Am Soc Clin Invest; Asn Am Phys; Sigma Xi. *Res:* Biochemistry and enzymology of erythrocytes; control of hemoglobin function, 2, 3-diphosphoglycerate and inositol polyphosphate metabolism; hemoglobinopathy; sickle cell anemia. *Mailing Add:* 110 Standish Ct Madison WI 53705

HARKNESS, SAMUEL DACKE, METALLURGY, NUCLEAR ENGINEERING. *Current Pos:* GEN MGR SYSTS, PROCESS & TECHNOL DIV, WESTINGHOUSE SCI & TECHNOL CTR, 90- *Personal Data:* b Richmond, Va, Oct 28, 40; m 63, Christine Hotchkiss; c Samuel, Laura & Matthew. *Educ:* Cornell Univ, BMetEng, 63; Univ Fla, PhD(metall eng), 67; Univ Pittsburgh, MBA, 83. *Honors & Awards:* Robert Lansing Hardy Gold Medal, Am Inst Mining, Metall & Petrol Engrs, 69. *Prof Exp:* Res engr, Atomics Int Div, NAm Aviation, Inc, 63-64; assoc metalurgist & group leader radiation effects, Argonne Nat Lab, 67-73, mgr mat technol, Nuclear Power Systs Div, combustion eng, 73-76, assoc dir fusion power, 76-79; mgr fuel develop, Bettis Atomic Power Lab, 79-86, mgr, Mat Technol Div, 86-90. *Concurrent Pos:* Mem fusion mat coord comn, Off Fusion Energy, Dept Energy, 77-79, ITER Indust Coun, 91- *Mem:* Fel Am Soc Metals; fel Am Nuclear Soc; Indust Res Inst. *Res:* Energy systems; radiation damage to materials; nuclear fuel performance and corrosion of reactor cladding materials; design of fusion reactor systems; performance of steam generators. *Mailing Add:* Sci & Technol Ctr Westinghouse Elec Corp 1310 Beulah Rd Pittsburgh PA 15235. *Fax:* 412-256-1310; *E-Mail:* harkness.s.d.@wec.com

HARKNESS, WILLIAM LEONARD, STATISTICS, APPLIED STATISTICS. *Current Pos:* from asst prof to assoc prof math, Pa State Univ, University Park, 59-69, actg head dept statist, 69-70, head dept, 70-87, PROF STATIST, PA STATE UNIV, UNIVERSITY PARK, 69- *Personal Data:* b Lansing, Mich, June 25, 34; m 56, 80; c 3. *Educ:* Mich State Univ, BS, 55, MA, 56, PhD(statist), 59. *Prof Exp:* Res mathematician, Inst Air Weapons Res, 57; res asst statist, Mich State Univ, 57-59, instr, 59. *Concurrent Pos:* Vis assoc prof statist, Calif State Univ, Hayward, 67; NIH consult, 77 ; vis prof statist, Stanford Univ, 79-80. *Mem:* Fel Am Statist Asn; fel Inst Math Statist (prog secy, 74-80); Biomet Soc; Royal Statist Soc; Math Asn Am. *Res:* Contingency tables; distribution theory; sociometry; applied probability theory. *Mailing Add:* 1877 Millson Circle State College PA 16801

HARKRIDER, DAVID GARRISON, SEISMOLOGY. *Current Pos:* assoc dir, Seismol Lab, 77-79, assoc prof, 70-78, PROF GEOPHYS, CALIF INST TECHNOL, 79- *Personal Data:* b Houston, Tex, Sept 25, 31; div; c 2. *Educ:* Rice Univ, BA, 53, MA, 57; Calif Inst Technol, PhD(geophys), 63. *Prof Exp:* Res fel geophys, Calif Inst Technol, 63-65; from asst prof to assoc prof, Brown Univ, 65-70. *Concurrent Pos:* Elect pres Seismol Soc Am, 87-88. *Mem:* Fel Am Geophys Union; Seismol Soc Am. *Res:* Elastic wave propagation and infrasonics; coupling and excitation of surface waves, especially Rayleigh, Love, acoustic-gravity waves and tsunamis. *Mailing Add:* Geol & Planetary Sci 170-25 Calif Inst Technol 1201 E California Pasadena CA 91125-0001

HARLAN, HORACE DAVID, physical chemistry, organic chemistry, for more information see previous edition

HARLAN, JACK RODNEY, ARCHEOBOTANY. *Current Pos:* prof, 66-84, EMER PROF AGRON, UNIV ILL, URBANA, 84- *Personal Data:* b Washington, DC, June 7, 17; m 39; c 4. *Educ:* George Washington Univ, BS, 38; Univ Calif, PhD(genetics), 42. *Honors & Awards:* Frank N Meyer Mem Medal, Am Genetic Soc; Crop Sci Award, Am Soc Agron, 71 & Int Ser Agron Award, 76; Meyer Medal, Am Genetic Asn Am. *Prof Exp:* Agronomist, Div Forage Crops & Diseases, USDA, 42-51 & Agr Exp Sta, Okla State Univ, 51-66. *Concurrent Pos:* John Simon Guggenheim Mem fel, 59; vis scientist, Am Soc Agron, 63; vis prof, Univ Calif, Davis, 75, Univ Calif, Riverside, 76 & Univ Nagoya, Japan, 79. *Mem:* Nat Acad Sci; fel AAAS; fel Am Soc Agron; Crop Sci Soc Am (pres, 65-66); Soc Econ Bot; fel Am Acad Arts & Sci. *Res:* Origin and evolution of cultivated plants, biosystematics, germ plasm conservation, genetics and evolution. *Mailing Add:* 3201 St Charles Ave No 219 New Orleans LA 70115

HARLAN, JOHN MARSHALL, HEMATOLOGY, ONCOLOGY. *Current Pos:* From asst prof to prof, 78-88, PROF MED, UNIV WASH, 89-, HEAD DIV HEMAT, 90- *Personal Data:* b Chicago, Ill, July 18, 47; m 73, Joanne; c 2. *Educ:* Loyola Univ, BS, 69; Univ Chicago, MD, 73; Am Bd Internal Med, cert hemat, 78, cert oncol, 80. *Concurrent Pos:* Clin scientist, Am Heart Asn, 80-85, estab investr, 86-91; consult, Biogen Corp, 88-90, Cytel Corp, 90-; assoc ed, J Immunol, 88-, Blood J, 90; adj prof path, Univ Wash, 89-; vis prof, numerous univs & biotechnol co. *Mem:* Am Soc Clin Invest; Asn Am Physicians. *Res:* Cell biology of vessel wall focusing on interaction of leukocytes with endothelial cells. *Mailing Add:* Div Hemat Univ Wash MS 357710 Seattle WA 98195-7710. *Fax:* 206-543-3560; *E-Mail:* jharlan@u.washington.edu

HARLAN, PHILLIP WALKER, SOIL MANAGEMENT. *Current Pos:* INT TRAINING SPECIALIST, OFF INT COOP & DEVELOP, INT TRAINING DIV, USDA, 75- *Personal Data:* b McCook, Nebr, Oct 6, 44; m 70. *Educ:* Univ Nebr, BS, 67; Purdue Univ, MS, 72, PhD(soils), 75. *Mem:* Soil Sci Soc Am; Am Soc Agron; Soil Conserv Soc Am; Sigma Xi. *Res:* Loess soils; defining and evaluating their natural soil characteristics which influence or are influenced by different uses and farming practices. *Mailing Add:* 1200 N Quantico St Arlington VA 22205-1736

HARLAN, RONALD A, NUCLEAR CHEMISTRY, NON-DESTRUCTIVE ASSAY. *Current Pos:* CONSULT. *Personal Data:* b Mansfield, La, Dec 25, 37; m 57, N Sandra Smith; c Allen B, Jay W & Jon C. *Educ:* Northwestern State Col, La, BS, 58; Fla State Univ, PhD(nuclear chem), 63. *Prof Exp:* Asst prof chem, Univ Ark, 63-66; sr nuclear chemist, Idaho Nuclear Corp, 66-67, assoc scientist, 67-69; sr res chemist, Dow Chem Co, Rocky Flats Div, 70-73, res specialist, 73-75; res specialist II, EG&G, Rocky Flats, Inc, 75-81, sr res specialist, Rockwell Int Energy Systs Group, Rocky Flats Plant, 81-89, sr res specialist, 90-93, develop assoc scientist, 93-96. *Concurrent Pos:* Consult, Energy Co, 83; prin investr, various instrumentation develop, 83-; standardized writing groups, Am Soc Testing & Mat, 88-; mem, Inst Nuclear Mat Mgt-9 Nondestructive Assay, Am Nat Stand Inst, 74-88, chmn, 88- *Mem:* Am Chem Soc; Inst Nuclear Mat Mgt; Sigma Xi; Am Nuclear Soc. *Res:* Nuclear safeguards and accountability; nuclear spectroscopy and models; environmental chemistry and detection of low activity radionuclides. *Mailing Add:* 1156 Crestmoor Dr Boulder CO 80303. *Fax:* 303-966-5305

HARLAN, WILLIAM R, JR, MEDICINE. *Current Pos:* dir, Div Epidemiol & Clin Appl, Nat Heart Lung & Blood Inst, 88-91, ASSOC DIR DIS PREV, NIH, 91- *Personal Data:* b Richmond, Va, Nov 1, 30; m 81; c 4. *Educ:* Univ Va, BA, 51; Med Col Va, MD, 55. *Prof Exp:* Resident internal med, Duke Univ, 58-61; asst prof med, Med Col Va, 63-67, dir, Clin Res Ctr, 63-71, assoc prof, 67-70; prof med & assoc dean, Sch Med, Univ Ala, Birmingham, 71-73; prof med & community health sci, Duke Univ, 73-75; prof & chmn, Dept Post Grad Med, Med Sch, Univ Mich, 75-82, prof internal med, 75-88. *Concurrent Pos:* Consult, Nat Ctr Health Statist, 75-, Atherosclerosis & Hypertension Adv Ctr, Nat Heart & Lung Inst, 75-79, NIH Epidemiol & Dis Control Study Sect, 71-74, World Bank, 81-82; dir, Physicians Asst Training Prog & Medex Training Prog, USAF sci adv bd, 79-85, Armed Forces Epidemiol Bd, 81-; NIH res fel, Dept Biochem, Duke Univ, 61-63; Markle scholar, 64. *Mem:* Sigma Xi; AAAS; Am Col Physicians; Am Heart Asn. *Res:* Medical research; lipid metabolism; blood pressure regulation; epidemiology of cardiovascular disease; prevention research. *Mailing Add:* NIH Dis Prev Bethesda MD 20892

HARLAND, BARBARA FERGUSON, NUTRITION. *Current Pos:* PROF NUTRIT, HOWARD UNIV, 84- *Personal Data:* b Chicago, Ill; m 47, James W; c Joseph, Jane (Bates) & Janet (Edmonds). *Educ:* Iowa State Univ, BS, 46; Univ Wash, MS, 49; Univ Md, PhD(nutrit), 71. *Prof Exp:* Head dietitian, Lakeview Mem Hosp, 46-47; food serv asst, Univ Northern Iowa, 47; nutrit instr, Univ Md, College Park, 64-69; res biologist nutrit, Food & Drug Admin, Washington, DC, 68-84. *Concurrent Pos:* Assoc referee phytate, Asn Anal Chemists. *Mem:* Am Inst Nutrit; Am Chem Soc; Am Dietetic Asn; Soc Exp Biol & Med; Soc Nutrit Educ; Am Soc Clin Nutrit; Sigma Xi. *Res:* The effects of phytate and dietary fiber on mineral interactions in human and animal nutrition. *Mailing Add:* Dept Nutrit Sci Howard Univ Col Allied Health Sci Rm 337 Washington DC 20059. *Fax:* 202-806-9233; *E-Mail:* bfh@cldc.howard.edu

HARLAND, GLEN EUGENE, JR, SOLID STATE PHYSICS. *Current Pos:* PROF, PURDUE UNIV, 86- *Personal Data:* b Salina, Kans, Jan 30, 33; m 56; c 2. *Educ:* Kans State Univ, BS, 58, MS, 60, PhD(physics), 64. *Prof Exp:* Instr physics, Kans State Univ, 60-64; sr physicist, Delco Radio Div, Delco Electronics, Gen Motors Corp, 64-72, staff engr, 72-87. *Concurrent Pos:* Mem assoc fac, Ind Univ, 64- *Mem:* Soc Automotive Eng; Inst Elec & Electronics Engrs; Int Soc Hybrid Microelectronics; Sigma Xi. *Res:* Semiconductor physics; materials research; x-ray diffraction phenomena. *Mailing Add:* 2301 Willow Spring Rd Kokomo IN 46902

HARLAND, RONALD SCOTT, CONTROLLD RELEASE, CONSUMER PRODUCTS. *Current Pos:* PRES, HARLAND TECHNOL, Inc, 93-; SR APPLN SPECIALIST, ROQUETTE AM, 95- *Personal Data:* b Rochester, NY, May 25, 62; m, Marcia D Stevens; c Nicole, Alexandra, Rebecca & Ronnie. *Educ:* Purdue Univ, BS, 83, MS, 85, PhD(chem eng), 88. *Prof Exp:* Engr, IBM Inc, 83; res asst & teaching asst chem eng, Purdue Univ, 83-88; res scientist, Kimberly-Clark Corp, 88-89, sr appln specialist, 90; mgr basic res, KV Pharmaceut Co, 90-93. *Concurrent Pos:* Session chair, Am Inst Chem Engrs, 88- *Mem:* Am Inst Chem Engrs; Am Chem Soc; Sigma Xi; Controlled Release Soc. *Res:* Inventor of aqueous-based and thermal-based controlled-release (24 hour) oral devices; inventor of osmotic superabsorbents, proteinaceous (blood) superabsorbents, heterogeneous absorbents and absorbent microfiber absorbents. *Mailing Add:* 904 Grand Ave Keokuk IA 52632. *Fax:* 319-526-2320

HARLE, THOMAS STANLEY, RADIOLOGY. *Current Pos:* AT DEPT RADIOL, UNIV TEX HEALTH & SCI CTR. *Personal Data:* b Detroit, Mich, Aug 17, 32; m 60; c 2. *Educ:* Northwestern Univ, BS, 54, MD, 57. *Prof Exp:* Radiologist, Ft Detrick, Md, 61-62; chief radiol, Irwin Army Hosp, Ft Riley, Kans, 62-64; chief radiol, Brooke Army Hosp, Ft Sam Houston, Tex, 64-65; from instr to assoc prof radiol, Baylor Col Med, 65-69; prof, Med Sch, Duke Univ, 69-71; prof radiol, Univ Tex Med Sch Houston, 71-78; prof radiol, Mich State Univ, 78- *Concurrent Pos:* Radiologist, Kelsey-Seybold Clin, Houston, 65-66; asst radiologist, Univ Tex M D Anderson Hosp & Tumor Inst Houston, 65-66; chief, Radiol Serv, Vet Admin Hosp, Durham, 69-71; consult, Res Triangle Inst, 70- & Brooke Army Hosp, 74-; prof radiol & assoc radiologist, Univ Tex M D Anderson Hosp & Tumor Inst Houston, 71-78. *Mem:* Asn Univ Radiologists; AMA; Radiol Soc NAm; Am Col Radiol. *Res:* Xeroradiography. *Mailing Add:* Univ Tex M D Anderson Cancer Ctr 1515 Holcomb Blvd Houston TX 77030-4009

HARLEMAN, DONALD R(OBERT) F(ERGUSSON), ENVIRONMENTAL ENGINEERING. *Current Pos:* asst fluid mech, Mass Inst Technol, 45-47, res assoc, 47-50, asst prof hydraul, 50-56, assoc prof, 56-63, dir, R M Parsons Lab Water Resources, 73-83, Ford prof eng, 75-91, PROF CIVIL ENG, MASS INST TECHNOL, 63-, EMER FORD PROF ENVIRON ENG, 91- *Personal Data:* b Palmerton, Pa, Dec 5, 22; m 50, Martha Havens; c Robert, Kathleen & Anne. *Educ:* Pa State Univ, BS, 43; Mass Inst Technol, SM, 47, ScD(civil eng), 50. *Honors & Awards:* Res Prize, Am Soc Civil Engrs, 60, Karl Emil Hilgard Prize, 71 & 73, First Hunter Rouse Hydraul Eng Lectr, 80. *Prof Exp:* Design engr, Curtiss-Wright Corp, 44-45. *Concurrent Pos:* Vis prof, Calif Inst Technol, 62-63; sr visitor, Dept Appl Math & Theoret Physics, Cambridge Univ, 68-69; Guggenheim fel, 68-69; consult, Tenn Valley Auth, US Army CEngrs, E I du Pont de Nemours & Co, Inc, Arthur D Little & Consol Edison, NY, Environ Protection Agency. *Mem:* Nat Acad Eng; Am Soc Civil Engrs; Am Geophys Union; Int Asn Hydraul Res; Water Pollution Control Fedn. *Res:* Fluid mechanics; stratified flow; heat disposal from power generation; temperature distributions in lakes and reservoirs; water quality control; tidal motion; mixing processes in lakes, estuaries and coastal waters; innovative waste water treatment using coagulants and flocculants. *Mailing Add:* R M Parsons Lab Rm 48-311 Mass Inst Technol Cambridge MA 02139. *Fax:* 617-258-8850; *E-Mail:* drfh@mit.edu

HARLESS, WILLIAM H, SPACE NUCLEAR POWER. *Current Pos:* res specialist, Astron Div, 90-92, RES SPECIALIST, MISSILES & SPACE DIV, LOCKHEED MISSILES & SPACE CO, SUNNYVALE, CALIF, 92- *Educ:* Univ Calif, Los Angeles, AB; Stanford Univ, MS, PhD(physics). *Prof Exp:* Prin engr advan nuclear technol, Gen Elec Co, 82-90. *Mem:* Am Phys Soc; Am Neurotology Soc; Am Asn Physics Teachers; Am Geol Union. *Res:* Survivability, lethality and hardening; catalytic transfer hydrogenation hydrocode analysis for missile penetrator and heat shield erosion studies; natural and induced space environments and nuclear weapons environments; determining nuclear radiation and space radiation environments. *Mailing Add:* 595 Camellia Way Los Altos CA 94024

HARLETT, JOHN CHARLES, OCEANOGRAPHY. *Current Pos:* ASST DIR PROGS, APPL PHYSICS LAB, UNIV WASH, 82- *Personal Data:* b Tiffin, Ohio, Apr 7, 36; m 63; c 3. *Educ:* Ohio State Univ, BSc, 60; US Navy Postgrad Sch, MS, 67; Ore State Univ, PhD(oceanog), 71. *Prof Exp:* Engr, US Navy, 61-68; instr oceanog, US Naval Acad, 71-74; cmndg officer, Oceanog Unit One, 74-75; oceanogr, Off Naval Res, Boston, 75-77, cmndg officer, 77-79; mem staff, Off Oceanogr Navy, Off Naval Technol, 79-82. *Mem:* Sigma Xi; Am Geophys Union; US Naval Inst. *Res:* Continental shelf and deep ocean sedimentation processes; bottom currents; bottom boundary layer; shore processes and prediction of beach changes. *Mailing Add:* 11601 NE 143rd Pl Kirkland WA 98034

HARLEY, JOHN BARKER, INTERNAL MEDICINE, IMMUNOLOGY. *Current Pos:* clin assoc, 79-82, asst prof, 82-87, ASSOC PROF, DEPT MED, NAT INST ALLERGY & INFECTIOUS DIS, USPHS, 87- *Personal Data:* b Baltimore, Md, Sept 13, 49; m 72. *Educ:* Dickinson Col, BS, 71; Univ Pa, MD, 75, PhD(biochem), 76. *Honors & Awards:* Baldwin-Lucke Award, Univ Pa. *Prof Exp:* Fel, Nat Inst Allergy & Infectious Dis, Univ Pa & Imp Cancer Res Fund Lab, London, 76-77; intern, Yale Univ, 77-78, res internal med, 78-79. *Concurrent Pos:* Adj asst prof, Dept Microbiol & Immunol, Health Sci Ctr, Univ Okla, 82-88, adj assoc prof, 88-; affil asst prof, assoc mem, Okla Med Res Found, Okla City, 82-89; chem investr, Dept Vet Affairs, Okla City, 87- *Mem:* Am Fed Clin Res; Sigma Xi. *Res:* Etiology and puterogenesis of autoimmune rheumatic diseases. *Mailing Add:* Okla Med Res Found 825 NE 13th St Oklahoma City OK 73104-5097. *Fax:* 405-271-4110

HARLEY, NAOMI HALLDEN, RADIATION CARCINOGENESIS, RADIATION MEASUREMENT & RADIATION DOSIMETRY. *Current Pos:* RES PROF RADIATION PHYSICS, MEASUREMENT & DOSIMETRY, MED CTR, NY UNIV, 67- *Personal Data:* b NY, Aug 4, 32; m 64, John H. *Educ:* Cooper Union, BSEE, 59; Grad Sch Eng & Sci, NY Univ, MS, 67, PhD(radiation health), 71. *Prof Exp:* Phys scientist radioactivity measurement, AEC, 51-65. *Concurrent Pos:* Prin investr, Environ Protection Agency, US Dept Energy & other grants, 71-; mem, Nat Coun Radiation Protection & Measurement; adv, Sci Comt Effects Atomic Radiation, UN. *Mem:* AAAS; fel Health Physics Soc; NY Acad Sci; Am Statist Asn; Am Asn Aerosol Res. *Res:* Environmental radon study to determine mechanisms for entry and removal in homes; radiation carcinogenesis; lung cancer risk from environmental radon daughter exposure; environmental radioactivity measurement; radiation risk analysis. *Mailing Add:* Dept Environ Med NY Univ Sch Med 550 First Ave New York NY 10016

HARLEY, PETER W, III, MATHEMATICS. *Current Pos:* from asst prof to assoc prof math, comput sci & statist, 69-84, ASSOC PROF MATH, UNIV SC, 84- *Personal Data:* b St George, SC, Oct 4, 40; m 62; c 3. *Educ:* Wofford Col, AB, 62; Univ Ga, MA, 65, PhD(math), 66. *Prof Exp:* Asst prof math, Univ Ga, 66-67. *Mem:* Am Math Soc. *Res:* Topology and set theory. *Mailing Add:* Dept Math Univ SC Columbia SC 29208-0001

HARLEY, ROBISON DOOLING, OPHTHALMOLOGY. *Current Pos:* RETIRED. *Personal Data:* b Pleasantville, NJ, Feb 27, 11; m 44; c 7. *Educ:* Rutgers Univ, BSc, 32; Univ Pa, MD, 36; Univ Minn, PhD(neurol), 41. *Honors & Awards:* Antonio Navasl Lectr, PR, 72; Al Morgan lectr, Toronto, 74; Frank Costenbaker lectr, Wash, 79; Honor & Sr Honor Awards, Am Acad Ophthal, 87; Honor Award, Am Asn Pediat Ophthal & Strabismus, 90; Vasso Nunez de Balboa-Legion of Honor, Repub Panama. *Prof Exp:* Resident physician, Philadelphia Gen Hosp, 36-38; asst ophthal, Mayo Clin, 41-42; from assoc to assoc prof ophthal, Temple Univ, 47-68, prof & chmn dept, 68-78; attend surgeon & dir pediat ophthal & motility, Willis Eye Hosp, 68-80. *Concurrent Pos:* Asst chief ophthal, Atlantic City Hosp, 47-50, chief, 50-68; attend surgeon, St Christopher's Hosp for Children; consult, Shore Mem Hosp, 48-50, Children's Hosp, Philadelphia, Children's Seashore Home & Betty Bacharach Home for Children; mem med bd, Proj Hope, Proj Orbis; adj prof ophthal, Thomas Jefferson Univ; mem med bd, Nat Found Retinitis Pigmentosa; consult surgeon, Wills Eye Hosp; prof pediat, St Christophers Hosp Children. *Mem:* Am Ophthal Soc; fel Asn Res Vision & Ophthal; fel Am Col Surg; Am Acad Ophthal & Otolaryngol; Am Orthoptic Coun. *Res:* Clinical research in ophthalmology; medicine; author of 152 publications in textbooks, chapters and journal articles. *Mailing Add:* 1910 Academy Pl Wilmington DE 19806

HARLIN, MARILYN MILER, ALGOLOGY, ECOLOGY. *Current Pos:* from asst prof to assoc prof, 71-83, PROF, UNIV RI, 83-; CONSULT, APPL SCI ASN, 87- *Personal Data:* b Oakland, Calif, May 30, 34; wid; c John & Andrea (Cilento). *Educ:* Stanford Univ, AB, 56, MA, 57; Univ Wash, PhD(bot), 71. *Prof Exp:* Teacher biol, Leysin Am Sch, Switz, 62-66. *Concurrent Pos:* Instr, Am Col Switz, 65-66; NSF fel, 71; NSF travel award, 74; res grants, Sea Grant, 75-82, Environ Protection Agency, 83-84; guest scientist, Atlantic Regional Lab, Dalhousie, 78; vis prof bot, La Trobe Univ, Australia, 84; res assoc, Univ Calif, Santa Cruz, 93. *Mem:* AAAS; Phycol Soc Am; Int Phycol Soc; Aust Soc Phycol & Aquatic Bot; Am Soc Limnol & Oceanog; Int Asn Aquatic & Vascular Plant Biologist. *Res:* Physiological ecology of marine macroalgae; epiphytic algae; nitrogen uptake by marine macroalgae; algal development on artificial substrata; attachment mechanisms in red algae; marine botany. *Mailing Add:* Dept Biol Sci Univ RI Kingston RI 02881. *Fax:* 401-874-5974; *E-Mail:* harlin@uriacc.uri.edu

HARLIN, VIVIAN KRAUSE, PUBLIC HEALTH ADMINISTRATION. *Current Pos:* RETIRED. *Personal Data:* b Seattle, Wash, Dec 26, 24; m 48; c 3. *Educ:* Univ Wash, BS, 46, MS, 70; Univ Ore, MD, 50. *Honors & Awards:* Physicians Recognition Award, AMA, 70-73; William A Howe Award, Am Sch Health Asn, 79. *Prof Exp:* Pvt pract, Seattle, Wash, 52-53; exam physician, Seattle Pub Schs, 53-57, dir health serv, 57-79; dir health serv, Off Supt Pub Instr, Tumwater, 79-84; immunization consult, Wash Dept Social & Health Serv, 87-90. *Concurrent Pos:* Clin physician, Snohomish County Health Dept, 53; clin instr, Sch Pub Health & Community Med, Univ Wash, 67-, sr fel dept prev med, 68-69. *Mem:* Am Med Womens Asn (vpres, 78, pres, 81); Am Sch Health Asn (vpres, 73, pres-elect, 74, pres, 75). *Mailing Add:* PO Box 340 Ravensdale WA 98051

HARLING, OTTO KARL, NUCLEAR ENGINEERING, NUCLEAR PHYSICS. *Current Pos:* DIR NUCLEAR REACTOR LAB & PROF NUCLEAR ENG, MASS INST TECHNOL, 76- *Personal Data:* b Staten Island, NY, Oct 1, 31; m 57; c 4. *Educ:* Ill Inst Technol, BS, 53; Univ Heidelberg, dipl, 55; Pa State Univ, PhD(physics), 62. *Prof Exp:* Physicist, Curtiss-Wright Res Div, 56-59; staff physicist, H R B-Singer, Inc, 59-62; sr physicist, Hanford Labs, Gen Elec Co, 62-65; staff scientist, Pac Northwest Lab, Battelle Mem Inst, 65-76. *Concurrent Pos:* Assoc prof, Joint Ctr Grad Studies, Richland, 63-; adj assoc prof, Wash State Univ. *Mem:* Am Phys Soc; Am Nuclear Soc. *Res:* Nuclear materials research reactors; nuclear medicine; expert in the use of research reactors, in nuclear measurements, nuclear materials testing and in neutron capture therapy for cancer treatment; surface science. *Mailing Add:* 46 Gardner St Hingham MA 02043-3744

HARLOW, CHARLES ALTON, ELECTRICAL ENGINEERING. *Current Pos:* PROF ELEC ENG, LA STATE UNIV, 78-, DIR REMOTE SENSING & IMAGE PROCESSING LAB, 79- *Personal Data:* b New Boston, Tex, Mar 14, 40; m 61; c 2. *Educ:* Univ Tex, Austin, BS, 63, PhD(elec eng), 67. *Prof Exp:* From asst prof to prof elec eng, Univ Mo, Columbia, 67-78. *Mem:* Inst Elec & Electronics Engrs; Asn Comput Mach. *Res:* Computer engineering and logical design; image analysis; pattern recognition. *Mailing Add:* Elec Eng Dept La State Univ Boyd Hall Baton Rouge LA 70803

HARLOW, EDWARD E, MOLECULAR GENETICS. *Current Pos:* PROF GENETICS, HARVARD MED SCH, 91-, AM CANCER SOC RES PROF MOLECULAR GENETICS, 92- *Personal Data:* b Manhattan Beach, Calif, Apr 27, 52. *Educ:* Univ Okla, BS, 74, MS, 78; Imp Cancer Res Fund Lab, PhD, 82. *Honors & Awards:* Wallace P Rowe Award, 89; Milken Family Med Found Cancer Res Award, 89; Richard C Parker Mem lectr, Columbia Univ, 93; Alfred P Sloan Jr Prize, Gen Motors Cancer Res Found, 95; William Sokolow Vis lectr, Univ Calif, San Francisco, 95; Eudoxia Dutkevich Mem lectr, Univ Toronto, 96; Howard Hughes lectr, Mass Inst Technol, 96; Lila Graber Cancer Res Award, 97. *Prof Exp:* Res microbiologist, McDonnell Douglas Aerospace, St Louis, 74-75; fel, Lady Tata Mem Trust, Imp Cancer Res Fund Labs, London, 78-81, vis fel, 80-82; staff investr, Cold Spring Harbor Lab, 82-94, sr staff investr, 85-88, sr staff scientist, 88-91. *Concurrent Pos:* Adj asst prof, Dept Microbiol, State Univ NY, 86-91; molecular biologist, Mass Gen Hosp, Charlestown, 90-; Eppley vis prof, Univ Neb Med Ctr, 91; Ralph R Braund vis prof, Forum Cancer Res, 93; Charles L Spurr prof oncol, Wake Forest Univ, 94; Charles B Smith vis res prof, Mem Sloan-Kettering Cancer Ctr, 96; vis prof, Huffington Ctr Aging, Baylor Col Med, 96. *Mem:* Inst Med Nat Acad Sci; Am Acad Microbiol; fel AAAS. *Mailing Add:* Mass Gen Hosp Cancer Ctr Bldg 1497330 13th St Charlestown MA 02129

HARLOW, FRANCIS HARVEY, JR, ANALYTICAL FLUID DYNAMICS, NUMERICAL FLUID DYNAMICS. *Current Pos:* Group leader, 59-73, MEM STAFF, LOS ALAMOS NAT LAB, 53-, FEL, 81- *Personal Data:* b Seattle, Wash, Jan 22, 28; m 52; c 4. *Educ:* Univ Wash, BS, 49, PhD(physics), 53. *Res:* Multiphase flow, turbulence transport theory and numerical approximation methods for partial differential equations. *Mailing Add:* 1407 11th St Los Alamos NM 87544

HARLOW, H(ENRY) GILBERT, CIVIL ENGINEERING. *Current Pos:* From instr to prof, 40-79, chmn dept, 50-79, EMER PROF CIVIL ENG, UNION UNIV, NY, 80- *Personal Data:* b Plymouth, Mass, Apr 27, 14; m 40; c 5. *Educ:* Tufts Univ, BCE, 37; Harvard Univ, MS, 40. *Concurrent Pos:* Consult, 40- *Mem:* Am Soc Civil Engrs. *Res:* Foundations and soil mechanics; plant genetics; nuclear shielding; plant tissue culture. *Mailing Add:* 17 Front St Schenectady NY 12305

HARLOW, RICHARD FESSENDEN, WILDLIFE ECOLOGY, PLANT ECOLOGY. *Current Pos:* RETIRED. *Personal Data:* b Boston, Mass, Dec 16, 19; m 42; c 3. *Educ:* Univ Maine, BS, 47, MS, 48; Va Polytech Inst & State Univ, MS, 71; Clemson Univ, PhD, 92. *Prof Exp:* Game technician, Maine Inland Fisheries & Game, 49-50; soil conservationist, Soil Conserv Serv, USDA, 50-52; asst proj leader wildlife, Fla Game & Fresh Water Fish Comn, 52-62, proj leader wildlife res, 62-64, asst chief game div, 64-65; res wildlife biologist, Forest Serv, USDA, 66-85. *Mem:* Hon mem Wildlife Soc; Sigma Xi. *Res:* Food habits of game species; influence of land use practices and other environmental changes on wildlife habitat, especially white-tailed deer and non game and endangered wildlife species. *Mailing Add:* 100 Ft Rutledge Rd Clemson SC 29631-1819

HARLOW, RICHARD LESLIE, X-RAY CRYSTALLOGRAPHY. *Current Pos:* chemist, 77-79, supvr, 79-85, SR RES ASSOC, E I DU PONT DE NEMOURS & CO, INC, 85- *Personal Data:* b Schenectady, NY, Nov 6, 42; m 77; c 3. *Educ:* Union Col, BS, 64; Univ Ill, MS, 66; Syracuse Univ, PhD(chem), 71. *Prof Exp:* Lectr chem, Univ Zambia, 70-73; res asst, Syracuse Univ, 73; fel chem, Univ Tex, Austin, 73-77. *Concurrent Pos:* Adj prof, Univ Del, 81- *Mem:* Am Crystallog Asn; Am Chem Soc; Sigma Xi. *Res:* Molecular structure determinations (via x-ray diffraction) of inorganic and organometallic complexes; powder diffraction software and analyses; synchrotron studies. *Mailing Add:* Cent Res & Develop Exp Sta E228/316D E I du Pont de Nemours & Co Inc Wilmington DE 19880. *Fax:* 302-695-1351; *E-Mail:* harlow@esvax.dnet.dupont.com

HARMAN, CHARLES M(ORGAN), THERMODYNAMICS, POWER GENERATION. *Current Pos:* from asst to prof mech eng, Duke Univ, 61-86, coordr res, 68-70, assoc dean grad sch, 70-80, PROF & DIR GRAD STUDIES, DUKE UNIV, 81- *Personal Data:* b Canonsburg, Pa, July 25, 29; m 56; c 3. *Educ:* Univ Md, BS, 54; Univ NDak, MS, 57; Univ Wis, PhD(mech eng), 61. *Prof Exp:* Instr mech eng, Univ NDak, 54-57 & Univ Wis, 57-59. *Concurrent Pos:* Sr sci adv, Army Res Off, 64-77; assoc prog dir, NSF, 67-68; co-ed, J Advan Transp, 77-; assoc dir, Inst Prod Safety, 82-87. *Mem:* Am Soc Mech Engrs; Advan Transit Asn. *Res:* Fluid mechanics; transportation; energy systems. *Mailing Add:* Duke Univ Sch Eng Box 90301 Durham NC 27708-0301. *Fax:* 919-660-8963; *E-Mail:* cmh@egr.duke.edu

HARMAN, DENHAM, BIOCHEMISTRY. *Current Pos:* res assoc, Donner Lab, Univ Calif, instr assoc med & assoc prof biochem, 58-62, asst prof med, 62-68, PROF BIOCHEM, MED SCH, UNIV NEBR AT OMAHA, 62-, PROF MED, 68- *Personal Data:* b San Francisco, Calif, Feb 14, 16; m 43; c 4. *Educ:* Univ Calif, BS, 40, PhD(chem), 43; Stanford Univ, MD, 54. *Prof Exp:* Chemist, Shell Develop Co, 43-49. *Mem:* AAAS; Am Chem Soc; AMA; fel Am Col Physicians; Am Aging Asn. *Res:* Use of radioactive tracers in organic reactions; free radical reactions; organic chemistry of phosphorus and sulphur; arteriosclerosis; aging and cancer. *Mailing Add:* Univ Nebr Med Ctr 600 S 42nd St Omaha NE 68198-4635

HARMAN, GARY ELVAN, PLANT PATHOLOGY, MICROBIOLOGY. *Current Pos:* from asst to assoc prof, 70-84, chmn, Dept Hort Sci, 83-84, PROF SEED MICROBIOL, NY STATE AGR EXP STA, CORNELL UNIV, 84- *Personal Data:* b La Junta, Colo, Nov 13, 44; m 65; c 3. *Educ:* Colo State Univ, BS, 66; Ore State Univ, PhD(plant path & biochem), 70. *Honors & Awards:* Award of Merit, Am Phytopath Soc. *Prof Exp:* Res assoc plant path & biochem, NC State Univ, 69-70. *Concurrent Pos:* Dir res, TGT Inc, Geneva, NY. *Mem:* Sigma Xi; Am Phytopath Soc. *Res:* Development of large-scale production and delivery systems for biocontrol fungi; biological control of seed and root-attacking microorganisms; isolation and cloning of genes and gene products for the control of plant pests; genetics of brocontrol fungi. *Mailing Add:* PO Box 462 NY State Exp Sta Geneva NY 14456. *Fax:* 315-787-2246; *E-Mail:* gary_harman@cornell.edu

HARMAN, GEORGE GIBSON, JR, PHYSICS, ENGINEERING. *Current Pos:* Electronic engr microwave measurements, Electron Tube Lab, Nat Inst Stand & Technol, 50-53, physicist, Semiconductor Mat Sect, 53-63, physicist hot carriers semiconductors, Electronic Technol Div, 63-70 & semiconductor packaging & assembly tech, 70-74, sr res scientist acoust emission semiconductor devices, Semiconductor Devices Div, 75-93, FEL MICROELECTRONICS PACKAGING & RELIABILITY, NAT INST STAND & TECHNOL, 93- *Personal Data:* b Norfolk, Va, Dec 7, 24; div; c 3. *Educ:* Va Polytech Inst, BS, 49; Univ Md, MS, 59. *Honors & Awards:* Silver Medal, US Dept Com, 73, Gold Medal, 79; Tech Achievement Award, Int Soc Hybrid Microelectronics, 81, Lewis F Miller Award, 84, Distinguished Serv Award, 86 & 87, Daniel C Hughes Award, 89, Educ Found Distinguished Serv Award, 90; Centennial Medal, Inst Elec & Electronics Engrs, 84, CPMT Outstanding Contrib Award, 93, Harry Diamond Mem Award, 96; Achievement Award, Int Electronic Packaging Soc, 98. *Concurrent Pos:* Res fel, Dept Physics, Univ Reading, 62-63. *Mem:* Am Phys Soc; fel Inst Elec & Electronics Engrs; Am Soc Testing & Mat; fel Int Soc Hybrid Microelectronics (pres, 94); Sigma Xi; Int Electronic Packaging Soc. *Res:* Microelectronics reliability; microelectronics assembly and packaging technology; acoustic emission; ultrasonics; semiconductor materials; hybrids microelectronics. *Mailing Add:* Semiconductor Electronics Div 812 Nat Inst Stand & Technol Gaithersburg MD 20899

HARMAN, T(HEODORE) C(ARTER), MATERIALS SCIENCE, CRYSTAL GROWTH THERMODELECTRICITY. *Current Pos:* asst group leader, 66-78, sr staff, 78-87, STAFF, LINCOLN LAB, MASS INST TECHNOL, 87- *Personal Data:* b Ind, July 22, 29; m 57, Marilyn Axline; c Elizabeth, Janet, Kathryn & Thomas. *Educ:* Manchester Col, AB, 51; Purdue Univ, MS, 53. *Prof Exp:* Proj leader, Battelle Mem Inst, 53-59; asst group leader, Lincoln Lab, Mass Inst Technol, 59-65; prog mgr, Adv Proj Res Agency, US Dept Defense, 65, 66. *Concurrent Pos:* Ed, J Electronic Mat, 72- *Mem:* Fel Am Phys Soc; Inst Elec & Electronics Engrs; sr mem Minerals, Metals, & Mat Soc. *Res:* Preparation of compound semiconductors; physical properties of semimetals and semiconductors; various solid state devices; crystal growth; diffusion and defects in semiconductors; thermoelectric and thermomagnetic materials and devices. *Mailing Add:* Lincoln Lab Mass Inst Technol Lexington MA 02173-9108. *Fax:* 781-981-0122; *E-Mail:* tharman@ll.mit.edu

HARMAN, WALTER JAMES, ZOOLOGY. *Current Pos:* RETIRED. *Personal Data:* b Strong, Ark, Feb 25, 28; m 54; c 2. *Educ:* La Polytech Inst, BS, 48; Univ Ark, MA, 50; Univ Ill, PhD, 59. *Prof Exp:* From instr to assoc prof zool, La Polytech Inst, 52-61; chmn dept, La State Univ, Baton Rouge, 63-78, from asst prof to prof zool, 66-89. *Mem:* Am Micros Soc; Am Soc Zool; Soc Syst Zool. *Res:* Taxonomy and ecology of Oligochaeta. *Mailing Add:* 5988 S Pollard Pkwy Baton Rouge LA 70808

HARMAN, WILLARD NELSON, FRESHWATER ECOLOGY, MALACOLOGY. *Current Pos:* From asst prof to assoc prof, 68-76, chmn, 80-89, PROF BIOL, STATE UNIV NY ONEONTA, 76-, DIR, BIOL FIELD STA. *Personal Data:* b Geneva, NY, Apr 20, 37; m 65, 80, Barbara Stong; c Rebecca M, Willard W, Jessica M & Samuel W. *Educ:* State Univ NY, BS, 65; Cornell Univ, PhD(limnol), 68. *Honors & Awards:* Environ Qual Award, US Environ Protection Agency, 90. *Concurrent Pos:* Ecol Resource Adv, NY State Dept Environ Conserv, NY State, 74- *Mem:* AAAS; Soc Limnol & Oceanog; Am Malacol Union; Soc Exp & Descriptive Malacol. *Res:* Descriptive malacology in freshwater ecosystems. *Mailing Add:* State Univ NY Oneonta Biol Field Sta RD 2 Box 1066 Cooperstown NY 13326. *Fax:* 607-547-8926

HARMEL, MEREL H, ANESTHESIOLOGY. *Current Pos:* CHMN, DEPT ANESTHESIOL, MED CTR, DUKE UNIV, 71- *Personal Data:* b Cleveland, Ohio, May 19, 17; m 44; c 4. *Educ:* Johns Hopkins Univ, BA, 38, MD, 43. *Prof Exp:* Asst instr surg, Johns Hopkins Univ, 44, instr, 45-47; assoc anesthesiol-in-surg, Univ Pa, 47-48; assoc prof anesthesia & assoc pharmacol, Albany Med Col, Union Univ, NY, 48-52; prof anesthesia & chmn dept, Col Med, State Univ NY, Downstate Med Ctr, 52-68; chmn, Dept Anesthesiol, Pritzker Sch Med, Univ Chicago, 68-71. *Concurrent Pos:* Nat Res Coun fel, Johns Hopkins Univ, 46-47; vis prof, Sch Med, Yale Univ, 59; anesthesiologist-in-chief, State Univ Hosp, 66-68. *Mem:* Am Soc Anesthesiologists; AMA; Am Sci Affil; NY Acad Sci. *Res:* Action of drugs on the central nervous system. *Mailing Add:* Anesthesiol Duke Univ Med Ctr Durham NC 27710

HARMER, DAVID EDWARD, RADIATION CHEMISTRY, NUCLEAR DECONTAMINATION. *Current Pos:* INDEPENDENT CONSULT, D H TECH ASSOC, 95- *Personal Data:* b Grand Rapids, Mich, Apr 8, 29; m 57, Janice L Gockel; c David M & Shelley L. *Educ:* Albion Col, AB, 50; Univ Mich, MS, 52, PhD(org chem), 55. *Prof Exp:* Fel chem, Univ Mich, 50-51, res asst, Eng Res Inst, 51-55; chemist org synthesis, Dow Chem Co, 55-56, head radiation chem sect, 56-71, group leader, Phys Res Lab, 71-74, proj mgr, Dow Nuclear Serv, 74-82; gen mgr, Nuclear & Mixed Waste Eng Serv, It Corp, 83-95. *Mem:* AAAS; Am Chem Soc; Am Inst Chem Eng; Sigma Xi; Am Nuclear Soc. *Res:* Radiation chemistry, dosimetry and calculations; engineering management; radiation chemical engineering; polymer chemistry; nuclear reactor decontamination; nuclear waste remediation. *Mailing Add:* 916 Westcourt Dr Knoxville TN 37919-7100

HARMER, DON STUTLER, NUCLEAR CHEMISTRY, NUCLEAR & NEUTRINO PHYSICS. *Current Pos:* spec res scientist, Eng Exp Sta, 59-60, assoc prof physics, 60-67, PROF PHYSICS, SCH PHYSICS, GA INST TECHNOL, 67- *Personal Data:* b Washington, DC, Mar 11, 28; m 52, 65, Lee DeLoache; c Diana, Katherine, Nancy, David, Muffin & Jonathan. *Educ:* George Washington Univ, BS, 52; Univ Calif, Los Angeles, PhD(nuclear chem), 56. *Prof Exp:* Asst, George Washington Univ, 51-52 & Univ Calif, Los Angeles, 52-56; res assoc, Brookhaven Nat Lab, 56-58. *Mem:* Am Phys Soc; Am Nuclear Soc; fel Am Inst Chem. *Res:* On-line applications of small computers in teaching and research; radiation shielding; neutron radiography; biomedical neutron radiography; bioengineering; nuclear and cosmic ray physics, neutrinos. *Mailing Add:* Sch Phys Ga Inst Technol 225 North Ave NW Atlanta GA 30332-0430. *Fax:* 404-894-9958; *E-Mail:* don.harmer@physics.gatech.edu

HARMER, MARTIN PAUL, CERAMIC PROCESSING, ELECTRONIC CERAMICS. *Current Pos:* From asst prof to assoc prof, 80-87, PROF MAT SCI, LEHIGH UNIV, 87-, DIR, CERAMICS RES LAB, MAT RES CTR, 87- *Personal Data:* b Hull, Eng, Aug 7, 54. *Educ:* Leeds Univ, Eng, BSc, 76, PhD(ceramics), 80. *Honors & Awards:* IBM Award, 84; DuPont Award, 88. *Concurrent Pos:* Presidential young investr, White House, 84; assoc ed, J Am Ceramic Soc, 84-; chmn, Kraner Award Symp, 85-; secy, Basic Sci Div, Am Ceramic Soc, 91. *Mem:* Am Ceramic Soc. *Res:* Processing of advanced ceramics; science of sintering; microstructure and properties of advanced structural and electronic (dielectric and ferroelectric) ceramics. *Mailing Add:* 1843 Valley Forge Rd Allentown PA 18104

HARMER, RICHARD SHARPLESS, MATERIALS SCIENCE, CERAMIC ENGINEERING. *Current Pos:* asst prof mat sci, 70-77, ASSOC PROF MAT SCI, UNIV DAYTON, 77-, RES CERAMIST, RES INST, 70- *Personal Data:* b Whittier, Calif, Sept 14, 41; m 66; c 2. *Educ:* Univ Ill, BS, 63, MS, 67, PhD(ceramic eng), 71. *Prof Exp:* Instr electron micros, Univ Ill, 66-68. *Mem:* Am Soc Metals. *Res:* Electron microprobe; scanning electron microscopy; materials characterization; x-ray diffraction; rare earth-cobalt magnetic materials. *Mailing Add:* Dept Mech & Aerospace Eng Univ Dayton 300 College Park Ave Rm KL121 Dayton OH 45469-0210

HARMET, KENNETH HERMAN, ION TRANSPORT, RAPID GROWTH RESPONSES. *Current Pos:* instr, 55-61, asst prof, 61-71, ASSOC PROF BIOL & PLANT PHYSIOL, NORTHERN ILL UNIV, 71- *Personal Data:* b Chicago, Ill, Aug 1, 24; m 73; c 3. *Educ:* Coe Col, BS, 49; Northwestern Univ, MS, 53; Univ Chicago, PhD(biol), 69. *Prof Exp:* Instr biol, Geneva High Sch, Ill, 50-52; Biol & Bot, East High Sch, 52-55. *Concurrent Pos:* Consult, De Kalb Agres Inc, 69-73. *Mem:* Am Soc Plant Physiologists; Sigma Xi; AAAS. *Res:* Effects of mineral nutrients and rare earth ions on the rapid growth responses of AVENA coleoptile segments; membranes and ion transport; seedling physiology with emphasis on amides and cyanogenic glycosides. *Mailing Add:* 8380 Ebenezer Ovil Rd Hopkinsville KY 42240

HARMON, ALAN DALE, PHARMACOGNOSY, ORGANIC CHEMISTRY. *Current Pos:* staff fel, 77-80, ASST PROF MED CHEM & PHARMACOG, NIH, 80- *Personal Data:* b Macon, Ga, Nov 11, 44; m 71; c 1. *Educ:* Idaho State Univ, BS, 68; Univ Conn, MS, 75, PhD(pharmacog), 77. *Prof Exp:* Pharmacist qual control pharmaceut, USPHS, 69-72. *Mem:* Am Soc Pharmacog; Am Chem Soc; Sigma Xi. *Res:* Biosynthesis of secondary natural products; elucidation of structures and synthesis of biologically active organic molecules; stereochemistry of enzyme reactions. *Mailing Add:* McCormormick & Co Inc 200 Wight Ave Hunt Valley MD 21031-1501

HARMON, BRUCE NORMAN, COMPUTATIONAL PHYSICS. *Current Pos:* from instr to prof, 74-95, DISTINGUISHED PROF PHYSICS, IOWA STATE UNIV, 95-, PROG DIR SOLID STATE PHYSICS DIV, 83-; DEP DIR, AMES LAB, 95- *Personal Data:* b Grand Rapids, Mich, 1947; m 69; c Dion & Alyssa. *Educ:* Ill Inst Technol, BS, 68; Northwestern Univ, MS, 69, PhD(physics), 73. *Prof Exp:* Lectr physics, Northwestern Univ, 69-71; fel physics, Ames Lab, 73-74. *Concurrent Pos:* Scientist, Res Estab Riso, Denmark, 76, Kernforschumgszentrum, Karlsruch, Ger, 81; ESRF, Grenoble, France, 90. *Mem:* Fel Am Phys Soc; Am Asn Physics Teachers; Mat Res Soc; Minerals, Metals & Mat Soc. *Res:* Superconductivity, electronic, optical and magnetic properties of metals, hydrogen in metals, high temperature conductors, electron-phonon interaction, metal surfaces and rare earth metals and compounds; martensitic phase transformations. *Mailing Add:* Dept Physics Iowa State Univ Ames IA 50011. *Fax:* 515-294-0689; *E-Mail:* harmon@ameslab.gov

HARMON, BUD GENE, ANIMAL SCIENCE, ANIMAL NUTRITION. *Current Pos:* DEPT HEAD ANIMAL SCI, PURDUE UNIV, 85- *Personal Data:* b Camden, Ind, July 2, 31; m 53; c 3. *Educ:* Purdue Univ, BS, 58; Mich State Univ, PhD(animal nutrit), 62. *Honors & Awards:* Am Soc Animal Sci Teaching Award, 71; Distillers Feed Res Coun Distinguished Nutrit Award, 74. *Prof Exp:* From asst prof to prof animal nutrit, Univ Ill, Urbana, 62-75; dir monogastric res, Ralston Purina, 75-85. *Concurrent Pos:* Mem comt, Nat Acad Sci Comn Educ in Agr & Natural Resources, 67- *Mem:* AAAS; Am Soc Animal Sci; Am Inst Nutrit; Animal Nutrit Coun. *Res:* Mineral nutrition. *Mailing Add:* Dept Animal Sci Purdue Univ West Lafayette IN 47907-1968

HARMON, DALE JOSEPH, POLYMER CHEMISTRY. *Current Pos:* RETIRED. *Personal Data:* b Cuyahoga Falls, Ohio, Mar 1, 27; m 51, Betty Phillips; c Phillip, Paul & Perry. *Educ:* Kent State Univ, BS, 51; Univ Akron, MS, 60. *Prof Exp:* Sr res chemist, B F Goodrich Res Ctr, Breckville, 51-68, res assoc, 68-79, sr res assoc, 79-92. *Mem:* Am Chem Soc; Am Soc Testing & Mat. *Res:* Physical structure of polymers and the relationship of the structure to processing and mechanical properties; gel permeation and liquid chromatography; solution properties of polymers. *Mailing Add:* 993 Cotswold Dr Copley OH 44321

HARMON, DAVID ELMER, JR, PETROLEUM EXPLORATION, NON-METALLIC MINERAL EXPLORATION. *Current Pos:* CONSULT, 84- *Personal Data:* b Kittanning, Pa, Aug 12, 32; m 60, Paula Younker; c David M, Sabrina M, John M Wills, Patrick K, Paul C & Robert J. *Educ:* Marietta Col, Ohio, AB, 54. *Prof Exp:* Geologist, BH Putnam Oil Producer, 54-58; chief geologist, FE Moran Oil Co, 58-67, Guernsey Petrol Corp, 69-73; chief engr, Jefferson Country, Ky, 67-69; chief geologist, Guernsey Petrol Corp, 69-73; vpres, Johnston Petrol Corp, 73-75 & O'Neal Petrol Inc, 75-83; founder & pres, Concord Energy Inc, 83-84. *Concurrent Pos:* Am Asn Petrol Geologist, 77-87. *Mem:* Am Asn Petrol Geologists; Am Inst Prof Geologists; fel Geol Soc Am; Geol Soc Am; Soc Petrol Engr. *Res:* Exploration for and exploitation of oil and gas deposits domestically and internationally. *Mailing Add:* PO Box 1 New Concord OH 43762-0001. *Fax:* 740-452-1655

HARMON, G LAMAR, CONCEPT & DESIGN OF AVIONICS, ELECTRO OPTICAL & AUTOMATION SYSTEMS. *Current Pos:* CONSULT, EO SYSTS, EYE TRACKING & VIRTUAL REALITY SYSTS, 93- *Personal Data:* b Baltimore, Md, Feb 21, 31; m 57, Jean Palmer; c Virgina Palmer & Mark Lamar. *Educ:* Emory Univ, AB, 52, MS, 54; Vanderbilt Univ, PhD(physics), 57. *Honors & Awards:* Inventor of the Year, Martin Marietta Corp, 66. *Prof Exp:* Mgr, New Guidance Systs, Martin Marietta Corp, Orlando, 57-71, proj mgr, Helicopter Fire Control Exp, 71, div staff engr electronics, 72-74, mgr systs eng res & technol & eng mgr, Lantirn Navigation Pad Develop, 74-81, mgr avionics res & technol, 81-92. *Res:* Automation for nighttime pilot situational awareness enhancement; target recognition automation; precision laser target designation systems; correlation guidance systems angle; angle rate ordinance delivery; loop control and display techology; eye and helmet trackers and their interconnection. *Mailing Add:* 1362 Granville Dr Winter Park FL 32789-1423

HARMON, GEORGE ANDREW, BIOCHEMISTRY, MICROBIOLOGY. *Current Pos:* RETIRED. *Personal Data:* b Lewisville, Idaho, Aug 31, 23; m 54; c 2. *Educ:* Univ Calif, Los Angeles, AB, 48; Stanford Univ, MA, 50, PhD, 58. *Prof Exp:* Instr microbiol, Univ Calif, Santa Barbara, 58-59; res biochemist, Med Res Serv, Vet Admin Ctr, 59-61; asst to exec head dept biol sci, Stanford Univ, 62-66; prof biol, Clarion State Col, 66-88. *Mem:* AAAS; Am Chem Soc. *Res:* Microbial intermediary metabolism; nucleic acid structure. *Mailing Add:* 709 S Brandywine St West Chester PA 19382

HARMON, GLYNN, INFORMATION SCIENCE. *Current Pos:* assoc prof, 70-75, PROF INFO, UNIV TEX, AUSTIN, 75- *Personal Data:* b Hollister, Calif, Nov 4, 33; div. *Educ:* Univ Calif, Berkeley, BA, 60, MA, 63; Case Western Res Univ, MS, 65, PhD(info sci), 69; Southwest Tex Univ, MBA, 73. *Prof Exp:* Res info, Case Western Reserve Univ, 64-65; librn & instr govt, Calif State Univ, Chico, 65-66; asst prof info, Univ Denver, 66-70. *Concurrent Pos:* Res assoc, Case Western Res Univ, 65-72. *Mem:* Am Soc Info Sci; Am Asn Artificial Intel; Am Med Informatics Asn. *Res:* Education; public and private investment; systems theory, management information systems, medical information and cognition. *Mailing Add:* 6910 Hart Lane Austin TX 78731

HARMON, H JAMES, BIOENERGETICS, BIOPHYSICS. *Current Pos:* from asst prof to assoc prof biol & physics, Okla State Univ, 77-88, prof zool & physics, 88-90, adj prof physics, 90-93, PROF MICROBIOL, OKLA STATE UNIV, 90-, COORDR INTELLECTUAL PROPERTIES, 92-, PROF PHYSICS, 93- *Personal Data:* b Granite City, Ill, Sept 14, 46; m 69; c 3. *Educ:* Purdue Univ, BS, 68, MS, 71, PhD(biol), 74. *Prof Exp:* Instr biol, dept biol sci, Purdue Univ, 69-72; res bioenergetics, Johnson Res Found, Univ Pa, 74-77. *Concurrent Pos:* Researcher, Johnson Res Found, Univ Pa, NIH, 75-77, Am Heart Asn, 80-82; prin investr, USAF, 84-88 & 89-90. *Mem:* Biophys Soc; AAAS; Am Soc Biochem & Molecular Biol; Sigma Xi. *Res:* Structure-function of inner mitochondrial membrane; instrumentation/ spectrophotometer design; mechanism of mitochondrial transport; membrane topography; effect of drugs on protein structure; aging of heart and brain; effects of environmental contaminants on bioenergetic systems; proton interaction with cytochrome oxidase; rapid enzyme kinetics; spectroscopy and spectrometry. *Mailing Add:* Dept Microbiol & Molecular Genetics Okla State Univ Stillwater OK 74078. *E-Mail:* jharmon@vm1.ucc.okstate.edu

HARMON, J FRANK, PHYSICS, CHEMICAL PHYSICS. *Current Pos:* from asst prof to assoc prof, 69-79, chmn dept, 71-76, PROF PHYSICS, IDAHO STATE UNIV, 80-, CHAIR DEPT, 83- *Personal Data:* b Van Wert, Ohio, Feb 23, 39; m 63; c 3. *Educ:* Portland State Univ, BS, 63; Univ Wyo, MS, 65, PhD(physics), 68. *Prof Exp:* Res assoc physics, Univ Utah, 68-69. *Concurrent Pos:* NSF fel, Univ Wyo, 70; assoc Western Univ fac fel, Los Alamos Sci Labs, 71 & Argonne Nat Lab W, 81; consult, Los Alamos Nat Lab, 79-84, Idaho Nat Eng Lab, 86- *Mem:* Sigma Xi; Int Soc Magnetic Resonance. *Res:* Magnetic resonance; molecular motions in condensed phases; generation and application of charged particle and photon beams to materials analysis. *Mailing Add:* Dept Physics Idaho State Univ Box 8106 Pocatello ID 83209

HARMON, JOAN T, DIABETES. *Current Pos:* RES ASSOC & SCIENTIST II, BIOMED RES & DEVELOP LAB, AM RED CROSS, 84- *Personal Data:* b Staten Island, NY. *Educ:* Univ Rochester, PhD(biochem), 76. *Mem:* Am Soc Biol Chemists; Sigma Xi. *Mailing Add:* Diabetes Res Sect NIH Natcher Bldg Rm 5AN-18G Bethesda MD 20892-6600

HARMON, JOHN W, SURGICAL GASTROENTEROLOGY, ENDOCRINOLOGY. *Current Pos:* CHMN, SECT SURG SCI, JOHNS HOPKINS BAYVIEW MED CTR, VCHMN, DEPT SURG, SCH MED, JOHNS HOPKINS UNIV. *Personal Data:* b White Plains, NY, Apr 22, 43; m 66, Gail McGreevy; c James Milton & Eve Page. *Educ:* Harvard Col, BA, 65; Columbia Univ, MD, 69. *Honors & Awards:* William Beaumont Prize Gastroenterol, US Army, 82. *Prof Exp:* Surg resident, Harvard Surg Serv, Boston City Hosp & New Eng Deaconess Hosp, 69-75; investr surg gastroenterol, Walter Reed Army Inst Res, 75-77, chief dept, 77-81 & dir div surg, 82-85; chief surg serv, Wash Vet Admin Med Ctr, 85- *Concurrent Pos:* staff surgeon, Walter Reed Army Med Ctr, 78-85; chief acad surg, Uniformed Serv Univ Health Sci, 78-85; prof surg, Georgetown Univ, George Washington Univ & Uniformed Serv Univ; clin prof surg, Howard Univ; Harvard res fel surg gastroenterol, Beth Israel Hosp, Mass, 72; fel gastrointestinal & endocrine surg, Lahey Clin, Mass, 73. *Mem:* NY Acad Sci; Am Physiol Soc; Am Col Surgeons; Soc Univ Surgeons; Am Gastroenterol Asn; Am Surg Asn. *Res:* Surgical gastroenterology and endocrinology; mechanisms of tissue and cellular injury and repair; peptic ulcer disease and reflux esophagitis. *Mailing Add:* Johns Hopkins Bayview Med Ctr 4940 Eastern Ave Baltimore MO 21224

HARMON, KENNETH MILLARD, INORGANIC CHEMISTRY. *Current Pos:* PROF CHEM, OAKLAND UNIV, 69- *Personal Data:* b Washington, DC, May 16, 29; m 49; c 2. *Educ:* San Jose State Col, BA, 54; Univ Wash, PhD(org chem), 58. *Prof Exp:* From instr to assoc prof chem, Harvey Mudd Col, 58-69, actg chmn dept, 63-64. *Concurrent Pos:* Petrol Res Fund res fel, 64-65. *Mem:* Am Chem Soc; Sigma Xi. *Res:* Infrared study of strong hydrogen bonds; organoborane chemistry. *Mailing Add:* Dept Chem Oakland Univ Rochester MI 48309

HARMON, LAURENCE GEORGE, FOOD SCIENCE, MICROBIOLOGY. *Current Pos:* from asst prof to assoc prof dairy indust, 54-60, prof food sci, 60-70, assoc chmn dept, 71-79, prof, 70-80, EMER PROF FOOD SCI & HUMAN NUTRIT, MICH STATE UNIV, 80- *Personal Data:* b Mountain Grove, Mo, Mar 18, 13; m 39, Inez Rose; c Patricia N. *Educ:* Kans State Univ, BS, 36; Tex Tech Univ, MS, 40; Iowa State Univ, PhD, 54. *Honors & Awards:* Pfizer Award, Am Dairy Sci Asn, 66, Award of Hon, 79; Distinguished Serv Award, Int Asn Sanitarians, 80. *Prof Exp:* From instr to prof dairy indust, Tex Tech Univ, 36-54. *Concurrent Pos:* Consult, Dairy Res Inc, 71-82. *Mem:* Am Dairy Sci Asn (pres, 75-76); Inst Food Technol; Int Asn Sanitarians. *Res:* Food microbiology and processing. *Mailing Add:* 5204 E Brookfield Dr East Lansing MI 48823

HARMON, ROBERT E, ORGANIC CHEMISTRY, MEDICINAL CHEMISTRY. *Current Pos:* From asst prof to assoc prof, 61-71, PROF ORG CHEM, WESTERN MICH UNIV, 71- *Personal Data:* b Conrad, Mont, Jan 22, 31; m 89, Renee M Bussing; c Greg, Eric, Jeff, Heidi, Andrea & Michael. *Educ:* Wash State Univ, BS, 54; Wayne State Univ, PhD(org chem), 59. *Concurrent Pos:* Consult, chem notations study, Nat Acad Sci-Nat Res Coun, 61-63 & Rohm & Haas, 85- *Mem:* Am Chem Soc; Brit Chem Soc; NY Acad Sci; Ger Chem Soc. *Res:* Cancer chemotherapy; reaction mechanisms in organic chemistry, particularly in the fields of heterocyclics and carbohydrates. *Mailing Add:* Dept Chem Western Mich Univ 1201 Oliver St Kalamazoo MI 49008-3804. *Fax:* 616-387-2943; *E-Mail:* harmon@wmich.edu

HARMON, ROBERT WAYNE, INSULATION APPLICATION, HI-VOLTAGE ENGINEERING & ELECTRIC SHOCK. *Current Pos:* CONSULT, 91- *Personal Data:* b Winchester, Ind, Oct 22, 29; m 51, Mary Cobb; c Wayne C, Keith R, Arthur D & Frederic B. *Educ:* Purdue Univ, BSEE, 51, MSEE, 55. *Prof Exp:* Dir, New Prod Develop, Ohio Brass Co, 55-68; chief engr, AB Chance Co, 68-94. *Concurrent Pos:* Lectr, Univ Belo Horizonte, Brazil, 74-76, Univ Mo, 70-85; expert witness, litigation consult, 80-94. *Mem:* Fel Inst Elec & Electronics Engrs; Am Soc Testing Mat; Electro-Tech Comn; Am Nat Stand Inst. *Res:* Insulation, forensic engineering; electrical shock hazards, protective grounding, insulation design, shock protection of cranes, vehicles, insulators for power lines; over 25 United States patents in insulation, hot line tools, protective devices. *Mailing Add:* 19001 N Jay Jay Centralia MO 65240. *Fax:* 573-682-2840; *E-Mail:* robermon@aol.com

HARMON, WALLACE MORROW, PARASITOLOGY, PROTOZOOLOGY. *Current Pos:* from asst prof to assoc prof, 65-74, PROF ZOOL, CALIF STATE UNIV, FRESNO, 74- *Personal Data:* b Colorado Springs, Colo, June 1, 33; m 58; c 4. *Educ:* Colo Col, BS, 55; Univ Calif, Los Angeles, PhD(parasitol), 63; Syracuse Univ, MS, 65. *Prof Exp:* NIH fel biol, Rice Univ, 63-65. *Mem:* Soc Protozool. *Res:* Parasites of man in Nigeria; avian hematozoa. *Mailing Add:* Dept Biol Calif State Univ Fresno 2555 E San Ramon Fresno CA 93740-8034

HARMON, WILLIAM LEWIS, PHYSICS. *Current Pos:* RETIRED. *Personal Data:* b Grove City, Pa, Aug 22, 28; m 55, Naomi R Donaghy; c William L III, Bruce R, Hawley P & Robyn L. *Educ:* Ohio State Univ, BSc, 49, MSc, 55. *Prof Exp:* Jr physicist physics, Commun & Navigation Lab, 49-56; electronic scientist, Air Force Avionics Lab, 56-61, sr physicist, 61-66; laser field engr, Cloudcroft Electro-optical Site, 66-69; sr physicist lasers, Air Force Avionics Lab, 69-90. *Mem:* Inst Elec & Electronics Engrs. *Res:* Management of carbon dioxide laser radar programs for strategic and tactical aircraft weapon delivery applications. *Mailing Add:* 5907 Rosebury Dr Dayton OH 45424-4355

HARMONY, JUDITH A K, BIOCHEMISTRY. *Current Pos:* ASSOC PROF ANAT & CELL BIOL, COL MED, UNIV CINCINNATI, 80- *Personal Data:* Decatur, Ill, Sept 29, 43. *Educ:* Kans Univ, BA, 65, MA, 67, PhD(chem), 71. *Prof Exp:* Fel biochem, Kans Univ, 71-75, dir, Enzyme Lab, 73-74; fel chem, Ind Univ, 75-76, asst prof biochem, 76-80, adj asst prof med sci, 78-80. *Concurrent Pos:* Estab investr, Am Heart Asn, 80-85, fel, Coun Arteriosclerosis, 81-82. *Mem:* Am Heart Asn; Am Soc Biol Chemists; Am Asn Immunologist; Am Soc Cell Biol; AAAS. *Res:* Mechanism of action of immunoregulatory human plasma lipoproteins as it relates to lipoprotein structure and to cell-cell collaboration; structures and physiological importance of lipid transfer proteins which exist in human plasma. *Mailing Add:* Pharmacol Dept ML 575 Univ Cincinnati Col Med 231 Bethesda Ave Cincinnati OH 45267-0575. *Fax:* 513-558-1169

HARMONY, MARLIN D, MICROWAVE SPECTROSCOPY, MOLECULAR SPECTROSCOPY. *Current Pos:* from asst prof to assoc prof, 62-67, chmn dept, 80-88, PROF CHEM, UNIV KANS, 71- *Personal Data:* b Lincoln, Nebr, Mar 2, 36; m 84, Nancy M Malody. *Educ:* Univ Kans, BS, 58; Univ Calif, Berkeley, PhD(chem), 61. *Prof Exp:* NSF fel, Harvard Univ, 61-62. *Concurrent Pos:* Mem, Comt Gas-Phase Interatomic Distances, Nat Bur Stand, 70-79; vis res assoc, Cambridge Univ, 71. *Mem:* Fel AAAS; Am Chem Soc; Am Phys Soc; Sigma Xi; Am Asn Univ Prof. *Res:* Studies in molecular structure using microwave and laser spectroscopy. *Mailing Add:* Dept Chem Univ Kans Lawrence KS 66044. *Fax:* 785-864-5396; *E-Mail:* harmony@kuhub.cc.ukans.edu

HARMS, ARCHIE A, NUCLEAR ENGINEERING, ENGINEERING PHYSICS. *Current Pos:* assoc prof, 69-80, PROF ENG PHYSICS, MCMASTER UNIV, 80- *Personal Data:* b Apr 18, 34; Can citizen; m 57; c 3. *Educ:* Univ BC, BSc, 63; Univ Wash, MSE, 65, PhD(nuclear eng), 69. *Prof Exp:* Mathematician, Int Power & Eng Consults, 63-65; lectr eng mech, Univ Wash, 65-66. *Concurrent Pos:* Consult, Int Atomic Energy Agency & various industs. *Mem:* Am Nuclear Soc; Am Phys Soc; Can Nuclear Soc. *Res:* Fusion-fission-spallation energy systems; nuclear reactor physics; neutron diagnostics; science & engineering education; engineering mathematics. *Mailing Add:* Dept Eng Physics Fac Eng McMaster Univ Hamilton ON L8S 4M1 Can

HARMS, BENJAMIN C, ELEMENTARY PARTICLE PHYSICS. *Current Pos:* vis prof, 70-71, PROF PHYSICS, UNIV ALA, 85- *Personal Data:* b Gladbrook, Iowa, June 1, 39; m 68; c 2. *Educ:* Iowa State Univ, BS; Univ Vt, MS, 64; Fla State Univ, PhD(physics), 69. *Prof Exp:* Res assoc physics, Fla State Univ, 69-70. *Concurrent Pos:* Cottrell Found Res Corp res grant, 71-72; NSF teaching grant, 75-77, DOE res grant, 84- *Mem:* Am Phys Soc; Sigma Xi. *Res:* Superstring theory. *Mailing Add:* Dept Phys & Astron Univ Ala Box 870324 Tuscaloosa AL 35487-0324. *E-Mail:* Bitnet: bharmsuaiumua.edu

HARMS, CLARENCE EUGENE, PARASITOLOGY. *Current Pos:* assoc prof, Westminster Col, Pa, 69-73, dean col, 85-87, chmn dept, 69-85, PROF BIOL, WESTMINSTER COL, PA, 73-, CHMN DEPT, 89- *Personal Data:* b Ulysses, Kans, Jan 22, 34; m 54; c 5. *Educ:* Tabor Col, BA, 55; Univ Kans, MA, 57; Univ Minn, PhD(zool), 62. *Prof Exp:* From instr to prof biol, Tabor Col, 57-69. *Concurrent Pos:* NSF res grants bact transformation, 64-66 & axenic cultivation, 65-67; NIH res grant, 65-68; Fulbright Scholar, 88-89; Nat Inst Oceanog, Pakistan, 88-89. *Mem:* Sigma Xi; AAAS; Am Soc Parasitologists. *Res:* Morphogenesis and nutrition of acanthocephalans; parasites of marine fishes. *Mailing Add:* Dept Biol Westminster Col 319 S Market St New Wilmington PA 16172-0001

HARMS, JEROME SCOTT, MOLECULAR IMMUNOLOGY OF THE MAJOR HISTOCOMPATIBILITY COMPLEX CLASS I. *Current Pos:* RES SCIENTIST, UNIV WIS-MADISON, 86- *Personal Data:* b Port Washington, Wis, Mar 23, 60. *Educ:* Univ Wis, BBA, 84, MS, 90, PhD(molecular immunol), 94. *Res:* Comprehensive cellular and molecular examination of cattle major histocompatibility complex class I transcription regulation. *Mailing Add:* 2120 University Ave Madison WI 53705. *Fax:* 608-262-7420; *E-Mail:* jsh@zeus.ahabs.wisc.edu

HARMS, JOHN CONRAD, GEOLOGY. *Current Pos:* CONSULT, HARMS & BRADY GEOL CONSULTS INC, 82- *Personal Data:* b Albuquerque, NMex, July 29, 30; m 52; c 3. *Educ:* Columbia Univ, BA, 51; Univ Colo, PhD(geol), 59. *Prof Exp:* Geologist, Continental Oil Co, 52-54; res geologist, Marathon Oil Co, 59-80, assoc res geologist & mgr regional explor dept, 80-82. *Mem:* Geol Soc Am; Am Asn Petrol Geol; Sigma Xi; Soc Explor Paleontologists & Mineralogists; AAAS. *Res:* Detrital sedimentary rocks; structural geology. *Mailing Add:* 855 Front Range Rd Littleton CO 80120. *E-Mail:* hbgeolcons@aol.com

HARMS, PAUL G, REPRODUCTIVE ENDOCRINOLOGY. *Current Pos:* from assoc prof to assoc prof, 74-82, PROF PHYSIOL, DEPT ANIMAL SCI, TEX A&M UNIV, 82- *Personal Data:* b Fairbury, Ill, Nov 21, 41; m 66; c 2. *Educ:* Univ Ill, BS, 63, MS, 65; Purdue Univ, PhD(animal physiol), 69. *Prof Exp:* Res physiologist, Capt USAF, USAF Sch Aerospace Med, Brooks AFB, Tex, 68-72; fel neroendocrinol, dept physiol, Univ Tex SW Med Sch, Dallas, 72-74. *Mem:* Am Soc Animal Sci; Am Physiol Soc; Endocrine Soc; Soc Study Reprod; Int Soc Neuroendocrinol; Soc Study Fertil. *Res:* Hypothalamic pituitary control of reproduction. *Mailing Add:* Dept Lab Animal Sci Texas A&M Univ College Station TX 77843-2471

HARMS, ROBERT HENRY, POULTRY NUTRITION. *Current Pos:* from assoc prof to prof, 57-64, chmn dept poultry sci, 64-82, GRAD RES PROF, UNIV FLA, 83- *Personal Data:* b Dover, Ark, Sept 27, 23; m 44; c 2. *Educ:* Univ Ark, BS, 53, MS, 54; Agr & Mech Col Tex, PhD(poultry nutrit), 56. *Honors & Awards:* Am Feed Mfg Award, Poultry Sci Asn, 65, Broiler Res Award, 84. *Prof Exp:* Pub sch teacher, Ark, 46-51; asst poultry, Univ Ark, 52-53 & Agr & Mech Col Tex, 53-55; asst prof, Univ Tenn, 55-57. *Mem:* Fel Poultry Sci Asn; Soc Exp Biol & Med; Am Inst Nutrit. *Res:* Protein, minerals and energy requirements of broilers and laying hens; vitamin A; vitamin K; unidentified factors. *Mailing Add:* Dept Poultry Sci Univ Fla Gainesville FL 32601

HARMS, VERNON LEE, SYSTEMATIC BOTANY & PHYTOGEOGRAPHY. *Current Pos:* assoc prof, 69-75, PROF BOT & CUR, FRASER HERBARIUM, UNIV SASK, 69- *Personal Data:* b Newton, Kans, May 31, 30; m 55, Ramona Waltner; c Sharon S (Delorme), Daryl D, Janelle J & Loren L. *Educ:* Bethel Col, Kans, BS, 55; Kans State Univ, MS, 59; Univ Kans, PhD(bot), 63. *Prof Exp:* From asst prof to assoc prof, Univ Alaska, 63-69, cur herbarium, 63-69. *Mem:* Bot Soc Am; Am Soc Plant Taxon; Int Asn Plant Taxon; Can Bot Asn. *Res:* Plant biosystematics; arctic, subarctic, and boreal Canadian grasslands phytogeography; biosystematics of Heterotheca, Petasites and Sparganium; flora of Saskatchewan; Saskatchewan rare native plants. *Mailing Add:* Agr Bldg Univ Sask 51 Campus Dr Saskatoon SK S7N 5A8 Can. *Fax:* 306-966-5015

HARMS, WILLIAM OTTO, PHYSICAL METALLURGY. *Current Pos:* RETIRED. *Personal Data:* b Alton, Ill, Sept 27, 23; m 41, Mary Grace Luer; c Benjamin William, Elizabeth Grace & Lawrence David. *Educ:* Wayne State Univ, BS, 48; Univ Minn, MS, 50, PhD(phys metall), 53. *Prof Exp:* Metallurgist, Oak Ridge Nat Lab, 53-55; assoc prof metall eng, Univ Tenn, 55-60; head ceramics lab, Metals & Ceramics Div, Oak Ridge Nat Lab, 60-65, asst sect chief res & develop, 65-66, sect chief, 66-72, mgr fast reactor progs, 69-72, dir, Breeder Reactor Prog, 72-77, dir, nuclear reactor technol progs, 77-85, dir mats & structs technol mgt ctr, 79-84. *Concurrent Pos:* Lectr & in-charge mat course, Oak Ridge Sch Reactor Tech, 55-56; consult, Oak Ridge Nat Lab, 55-60. *Mem:* Fel Am Soc Metals Int; Am Inst Mining, Metall & Petrol Engrs; fel Am Nuclear Soc; Sigma Xi. *Res:* Engineering mechanics; properties of materials; metallurgy and metallurgical engineering; radiation effects; reactor fuels; metallography; nuclear reactor engineering; fuel element design and development; physical chemistry; phase equilibria; thermodynamics. *Mailing Add:* 4029 Hiawatha Dr Knoxville TN 37919

HARMSEN, RUDOLF, COMMUNITY ECOLOGY, BIOLOGICAL CONTROL. *Current Pos:* from asst prof to assoc prof, 66-80, PROF BIOL, QUEEN'S UNIV, 80- *Personal Data:* b Medemblik, Neth, Mar 11, 33; m 60; c 2. *Educ:* Univ Toronto, BA, 59, MA, 60; Cambridge Univ, PhD(insect physiol), 63. *Prof Exp:* Rockefeller sr res fel parasitol, Univ Col, Nairobi, Kenya, 63-66. *Mem:* Entom Soc Am; Entom Soc Can; Entom Soc Ont. *Res:* Control systems in biology; ecological and behavior genetics; integrative population biology; community structure. *Mailing Add:* Dept Biol Queen's Univ Kingston ON K7L 3N6 Can. *Fax:* 613-545-6617; *E-Mail:* harmsenr@biology.queensu.ca

HARMUTH, HENNING FRIEDOLF, ELECTROMAGNETIC SIGNALS. *Current Pos:* PROF ELEC ENG, CATH UNIV AM, 72- *Personal Data:* b Vienna, Austria, July 27, 28; US citizen; m 57, Anne B Stragins; c Ursula. *Educ:* Vienna Tech Univ, dipl, 51, Dr tech Sci(elec eng), 53. *Prof Exp:* Scientist, Signal Corps Eng Labs, 53-55 & Gen Elec, 55-59; sect head commun, Gen Dynamics, 59-60; researcher physics, Nat Univ Mex & Tokyo Univ, 60-61. *Concurrent Pos:* Var positions, Battelle Inst, Frankfurt, 61-65; consult electronics, 65-71; lectr, Univ Karlsruhe, 65-68; assoc prof, Univ Md, 69-71; guest lectr, Stanford Univ, 71; consult UNESCO, Warangal Univ, India, 72; guest prof, Australian Nat Univ, 73, Northwest Telecommun Eng Inst, Xi'an, China, 81, Univ Witwatersrand, SAfrica, 83, Univ Sydney, Australia, 84, 90, Kuwait Univ, 85, 89, Beijing Inst Aeronaut & Astronaut, China, 87 & Tech Univ Dresden, Ger, 88; exchange scientist, USSR Acad Sci, 79. *Mem:* Inst Elec & Electronics Engrs. *Res:* Nonsinusoidal electromagnetic waves; author of 10 scientific books on nonsinusoidal electromagnetic waves and electromagnetic signals; correction of Maxwell's equations for signals; numerous paper awards. *Mailing Add:* 10905 Picasso Lane Potomac MD 20854. *Fax:* 202-319-4499

HARN, STANTON DOUGLAS, ANATOMY. *Current Pos:* ASSOC PROF ORAL BIOL & CUR DENT MUS, COL DENT, UNIV NEBR-LINCOLN, 72- *Personal Data:* b Pomona, Calif, Mar 14, 45; m 87; c 5. *Educ:* La Verne Col, BA, 67; Univ Utah, PhD(anat), 72. *Mem:* Am Asn Anatomists; Int Asn Dent Res; Am Acad Hist Dent; Sigma Xi; Am Asn Clin Anatomists; Am Asn Dent Schs. *Res:* Anesthesia; mandibular nerve; history of dentistry. *Mailing Add:* Dept Oral Biol Univ Nebr Col Dent Lincoln NE 68583-0740

HARNDEN, JOHN D, JR, ELECTRONICS ENGINEERING. *Current Pos:* Develop engr electronics, 50-59, proj engr, 60-78, MGR TECHNOL ADVAN ELECTRONICS PROD, GEN ELEC CO, 79- *Personal Data:* b Schenectady, NY, Sept 20, 28; m 74; c 2. *Educ:* Union Col, BS, 50. *Mem:* Fel Inst Elec & Electronics Engrs; Am Soc Inventors; Radio Club Am. *Res:* Developing the next generation of solid state devices, with impact on new components (senses and power control) as well as new products with emphasis on consumer markets. *Mailing Add:* 1078 Parkwood Blvd Schenectady NY 12305

HARNED, HERBERT SPENCER, JR, MEDICINE. *Current Pos:* RETIRED. *Personal Data:* b Philadelphia, Pa, Feb 1, 21; m 47, Jean Goldfuss; c Richard S, Douglas A & Thomas G. *Educ:* Yale Univ, BS, 42, MD, 45. *Prof Exp:* Intern pediat, Johns Hopkins Hosp, 45-46; resident, Boston Children's Hosp, 48-50; asst clin prof pediat, Sch Med, Yale Univ, 52-54, asst prof, 54-58; from asst prof to prof pediat, Sch Med, Univ NC, Chapel Hill, 58-92. *Mem:* Am Pediat Soc; AMA; Am Fedn Clin Res. *Res:* Pediatric cardiology; newborn circulation; newborn respiratory physiology pediatric; pulmonary heart disease. *Mailing Add:* Spring Dell Lane Chapel Hill NC 27514

HARNEST, GRANT HOPKINS, ORGANIC CHEMISTRY. *Current Pos:* Instr, Middlebury Col, 43-45, asst prof, 45-47, chmn, Dept Chem, 53-70, prof, 56-82, chmn, Natural Sci Div, 66-77, EMER PROF CHEM, MIDDLEBURY COL, 82- *Personal Data:* b Carthage, Ill, Nov 23, 16; m 45, Kathryn I Hampson. *Educ:* Knox Col, AB, 39; Middlebury Col, MS, 41; Univ Va, PhD(org chem), 46. *Honors & Awards:* James Flack Norris Award, Am Chem Soc, 74. *Prof Exp:* Res assoc, Off Sci Res & Develop contract, Univ Va, 45-46. *Concurrent Pos:* Bd of vis res award, Univ, Va, 47; bd dirs, Porter Med Cgtr, 85-87. *Mem:* Am Chem Soc. *Res:* Synthetic antimalarials and analgesics; heterocyclic amino alcohols; synthesis of antimalarials. *Mailing Add:* 125 S Main Middlebury VT 05753-1324

HARNETT, R MICHAEL, LARGE-SCALE SYSTEMS OPTIMIZATION. *Current Pos:* DEPT HEAD INDUST ENG, KANS STATE UNIV, 88- *Personal Data:* b Winnfield, La, June 3, 44; m 68; c 2. *Educ:* La Polytech Inst, BS, 68; Univ Ala, Huntsville, MS, 72, PhD(indust & systs eng), 74. *Prof Exp:* Engr, Northrop Space Labs, 67-70; OR analyst, Safeguard Systs Command, 70-74; from asst prof to assoc prof systs eng, Clemson Univ, 74-83; assoc dean eng, La Tech Univ, 83-88. *Concurrent Pos:* Res fel, Air Force Off Sci Res, 81. *Mem:* Opers Res Soc Am; Inst Indust Engrs; Am Soc Eng Educr; Soc Mfg Engrs. *Res:* Large-scale systems optimization; methods of economic analysis; biological system modelling, especially humans in cold stress situations. *Mailing Add:* 2483 Oregon Lane Manhattan KS 66502

HARNEY, BRIAN MICHAEL, OIL SHALE TECHNOLOGY. *Current Pos:* sr assoc engr, Mobil Res & Develop Corp, 81-84, mgr groundwater progs, 84-88, mgr polit & environ affairs, 89-90, mgr policy fed legis & regulations, 91-95, MGR POLICY & ISSUES MGT, MOBIL OIL CORP, 96- *Personal Data:* b New York, NY, Jan 20, 44; m 67; c 2. *Educ:* Manhattan Col, BS, 65; Univ Pittsburgh, PhD(phys chem), 70. *Prof Exp:* Res chemist, US Bur of Mines, 70-72, staff res coordr, 72-74; br chief, Div Fossil Energy Res, US Energy Res & Develop Admin, 75-77; dir, Div Technol Assessment, Off Shale Resource Applns, US Dept Energy, 78-79, Off Oil Shale, 79-81. *Mem:* Am Chem Soc. *Res:* Synthetic fuels engineering with emphasis on eastern and western oil shale; infrared and Raman spectroscopy to determine molecular structure and to perform vibrational analyses; remote sensing of air pollution; conversion of coal and oil shale to clean liquid fuels; hazardous waste management. *Mailing Add:* 6612 Jill Ct McLean VA 22101-1613

HARNEY, ROBERT CHARLES, LASER PHYSICS, SENSOR SYSTEMS. *Current Pos:* SR PRIN ENGR, CONTRAVES, INC, 94- *Personal Data:* b Pasadena, Calif, Sept 28, 49; m 72, Jane Withers; c Elizabeth, Catherine & Robert J. *Educ:* Harvey Mudd Col, BS(chem) & BS(physics), 71; Univ Calif, Davis, MS, 72, PhD(appl sci), 76. *Honors & Awards:* Outstanding Engr Award, Inst Elec & Electronics Engrs, 90. *Prof Exp:* Physicist, Lawrence Livermore Lab, Univ Calif, 71-76; staff scientist, Lincoln Lab, Mass Inst Technol, 76-82; mem prof staff, Martin Marietta, Orlando, 82-85, sr mem prof staff, 85-93; consult, Los Alamos Nat Lab, 93-94. *Concurrent Pos:* Fel, Fannie & John Hertz Found, 72-76; consult, Lawrence Livermore Lab, Univ Calif, 76-81; lectr, Appl Physics, Univ Lowell, 80-82. *Mem:* Am Asn Physics Teachers; Am Chem Soc; Inst Elec & Electronics Engrs; Soc Photo-Optical Instrumentation Engrs; Optical Soc Am. *Res:* Application of laser techniques to investigation of problems in physics, chemistry and biology; laser radar systems and multisensor integration. *Mailing Add:* Naval Post Grad Sch Code PH/HA Monterey CA 93943. *Fax:* 412-967-7973

HARNSBERGER, HUGH FRANCIS, PHYSICAL CHEMISTRY. *Current Pos:* CATALYST & TECHNOL CONSULT, HARNSBERGER ASSOCS, INC, 83- *Personal Data:* b Taizhou, Jiangsu, China, Jan 3, 24; US citizen; m 43; c 4. *Educ:* Col William & Mary, BS, 44; Univ Calif, Berkeley, MS, 47, PhD(phys chem), 50. *Prof Exp:* From asst prof to assoc prof chem, Duquesne Univ, 49-52; res chemist, Chevron Res Co, 52-57, group supvr, 57-64, sr res assoc, head catalyst res group, 64-79; proj leader, Technol Acquisition, 79-83. *Concurrent Pos:* Chmn, Gordon Conf Catalysis, 72; guest scientist microanal, Mass Inst Technol, Cambridge, 66-67, Univ Louvain, 73 & Mat Panel, Proj Rev Bd, Stanford Synchrotron Radiation Lab, 83-86; founder & pres, ICI Ebonex Technol Inc, Emeryville, Calif, 83-86, dir & consult, 87- *Mem:* AAAS; Am Chem Soc; Catalysis Soc; Microbeam Anal Soc; Am Ceramic Soc; Mat Res Soc. *Res:* Kinetics of inorganic reactions; physical, chemical and surface studies of solid microporous catalysts; electron microprobe-scanning electron microscope catalyst research. *Mailing Add:* 501 Via Casitas Greenbrae CA 94904

HARNSBERGER, PAUL MICHAEL, ASPHALT CHEMISTRY-PHYSICAL PROPERTY RELATIONSHIPS, PETROLEUM, HEAVY OIL-SYNCRUDE CHEMICAL CHARACTERIZATION. *Current Pos:* technician II, Western Res Inst, 84-85, scientist II, 85-87, res scientist, 87-93, SR RES SCIENTIST, WESTERN RES INST, 93- *Personal Data:* b Washington, DC, Oct 16, 52; m 85, Susan J Sullivan; c Eric & Kelly. *Educ:* Univ Wyo, BS, 75. *Prof Exp:* Phys sci technician, US Energy Res & Develop Admin, 75-76; chemist/toxicologist II, State Wyo Pub Health Lab, 77-80; asphalt supvr, STC Construction Inc, 80-83. *Mem:* Am Chem Soc. *Res:* Investigation of the relationship between asphalt chemical composition and physical properties, mainly focusing on rheological properties; asphalt chemical components and compound types involved in associations to form polymer-like molecules. *Mailing Add:* 5947 Bill Nye Laramie WY 82070-5325. *Fax:* 307-721-2300; *E-Mail:* mikeharns@aol.com

HAROIAN, ALAN JAMES, NEUROANATOMY. *Current Pos:* Instr hist & neuroanat, 78-79, sr instr gross anat & neuroanat, 79-82, ASST PROF NEUROANAT, HAHNEMANN UNIV, 82- *Personal Data:* b Hartford, Conn, Sept 28, 50; c 2. *Educ:* Drew Univ, BA, 72; St Louis Univ, PhD(anat), 78. *Mem:* Soc Neurosci; Am Asn Anatomists. *Res:* Neuroanatomical studies of the afferent and efferent connections of the rat cerebellum using autoradiographic and horseradish peroxidase techniques; developmental plasticity of the cerebellothalamic system. *Mailing Add:* Dept Anat Allegheny Univ Hahnemann Med Col 85230 N Broad St Philadelphia PA 19102. *Fax:* 970-491-0494

HAROLD, FRANKLIN MARCEL, CELL BIOLOGY, BIOENERGETICS. *Current Pos:* sr scientist, 89-96, EMER PROF, COLO STATE UNIV, FT COLLINS, 96- *Personal Data:* b Frankfurt-on-Main, Ger, Mar 16, 29; nat US; m 54, Ruth L Catsiff; c Lynn S. *Educ:* City Col, BS, 52; Univ Calif, PhD(comp biochem), 55. *Hon Degrees:* DSc, Univ Osnabruck, WGer, 84. *Prof Exp:* Asst, Univ Calif, 52-55; res biochemist, Nat Jewish Hosp, Denver, Colo, 59-62, chief dept exp chem, 62-68; from asst prof to assoc prof microbiol, Sch Med, Univ Colo, Denver, 63-74, prof biochem, 74-89. *Concurrent Pos:* NSF res fel, Calif Inst Technol, 57-58, USPHS res fel, 58-59; sr biochemist, Nat Jewish Ctr, 68-89. *Mem:* Am Soc Biol Chem; Am Soc Microbiol. *Res:* Bioenergetics and physiology of microorganisms; ion currents in relation to growth and development; morphogenesis. *Mailing Add:* Dept Biochem Colo State Univ Ft Collins CO 80524

HAROLD, RUTH L, BIOLOGY OF FUNGI. *Current Pos:* RETIRED. *Personal Data:* b New York, NY, July 16, 31; m 54, Franklin M; c Stephanie L. *Educ:* Univ Ariz, BA, 52; Univ Calif, Berkeley, MA, 54. *Prof Exp:* Lab technician, Calif Inst Technol & var other univs, 54-61; res assoc, Nat Jewish Ctr Immunol & Respiratory Med, 62-72 & 78-89; res assoc, Colo State Univ, 89-95, facil affil, 95- *Mem:* Am Soc Microbiol; Mycol Soc Am. *Res:* Cellular physiology of zoosporic fungi; apical growth and branching in Achlya and Saprolegnia. *Mailing Add:* Dept Biochem & Molecular Biol Colo State Univ Ft Collins CO 80523. *Fax:* 970-491-0494; *E-Mail:* harold@vines.colostate.edu

HAROWITZ, CHARLES LICHTENBERG, ORGANIC CHEMISTRY. *Current Pos:* RETIRED. *Personal Data:* b Newport News, Va, Sept 24, 26; m 48, Florine Siff; c Charles L Jr, Michael A & Richard E. *Educ:* Va Polytech Inst, BS, 48. *Prof Exp:* From res chemist to sr chemist, Va-Carolina Chem Corp, 48-56, sect leader, 56-58, mgr org prod, 58; mgr indust chem div, Mobil Chem Co, 58-67, mkt mgr phosphorus chem & cleaners, chem div, 67-69, gen sales mgr, Indust Chem Div, 69-74, gen mkt mgr, 74-83, mgr bus develop, 83-84. *Concurrent Pos:* Independent mgt consult, 84- *Mem:* Am Chem Soc; Com Develop Asn; AAAS. *Res:* Organic phosphorus compounds; urethane polymers; agricultural chemicals; metal process chemicals. *Mailing Add:* 8207 Shelley Rd Richmond VA 23229

HARP, GEORGE LEMAUL, ZOOLOGY, LIMNOLOGY. *Current Pos:* from asst prof to assoc prof, 67-79, prof zool, 79-93, PROF ENVIRON BIOL, ARK STATE UNIV, 93- *Personal Data:* b Butler, Mo, Oct 21, 36; m 65, Phoebe A Pigg; c Heather D & Geoffrey R. *Educ:* Univ Kans, AB, 58; Univ Mo, MA, 63, PhD(zool), 69. *Prof Exp:* Instr aquatic entom, Univ Mo, 67. *Concurrent Pos:* Consult, US Army Corps Engrs, 72-74, 78-80, US Soil Conserv Serv, 74-80, Ark Eastman Co, 74, Ark Power & Light Co, 78 & Frit Indust, 83-87, Ark Game & Fish Comm, 91-, USDA Forest Serv, 93- *Mem:* Odonatologica; N Am Benthological Soc; Brit Freshwater Biol Asn. *Res:* Ecology of altered freshwater ecosystems; taxonomy and ecology of aquatic insects. *Mailing Add:* Dept Biol Ark State Univ PO Box 599 State University AR 72467. *Fax:* 870-972-2638; *E-Mail:* glharp@navajo.astate.edu

HARP, JAMES A, MICROBIOLOGY. *Current Pos:* microbiologist, 84-88, lead scientist, Immunol Ruminant Perinatal Dis Proj, 88-93, SUPVRY MICROBIOLOGIST, NAT ANIMAL DIS CTR, AGR RES SERV, USDA, AMES, IOWA, 93- *Educ:* Univ Ill, BS, 67; Southern Ill Univ, MA, 69; Mont State Univ, PhD(microbiol), 83. *Prof Exp:* Microbiologist, Ill Dept Pub Health, Chicago, 69-76, Vet Res Lab, Mont State Univ, Bozeman, 77-80; fel path-immunol, Stanford Univ Med Sch, 83-84. *Concurrent Pos:* Asst prof/collabr, Dept Microbiol, Iowa State Univ, Ames. *Mem:* Am Asn Vet Immunologists; Sigma Xi. *Res:* Mechanisms of regulation and modulation of the immune system in domestic animals; immunologic mechanisms of resistance and recovery from protozoan parasites, particularly cryptosporidium parvum. *Mailing Add:* Nat Animal Dis Ctr PO Box 70 Ames IA 50010. *Fax:* 515-839-8458

HARP, JIMMY FRANK, CIVIL ENGINEERING. *Current Pos:* RETIRED. *Personal Data:* b Mar 2, 33; US citizen; m 58; c 2. *Educ:* Univ Ark, BS, 55, MS, 59; Univ Ariz, PhD(civil eng), 63. *Prof Exp:* Instr eng mech, Univ Ark, 57-60; instr civil eng, Univ Ariz, 60-63; from assoc prof to prof civil eng, Univ Okla, 76-94. *Mem:* Am Soc Civil Engrs; Am Soc Eng Educ. *Res:* Hydraulics; hydrology. *Mailing Add:* 3217 Cotswold Sq Norman OK 73072

HARP, WILLIAM R, JR, SPECTROSCOPY. *Current Pos:* RETIRED. *Personal Data:* b Roanoke, Va, Nov 28, 19; m 41; c 2. *Educ:* Roanoke Col, BS, 41; Tulane Univ, MS, 43. *Prof Exp:* Asst physics, Tulane Univ, 41-43; molecular spectroscopist, Shell Develop Co, 43-57, supvr analytical res, 57-60 & spectros res, 60-61, from asst to head analytical dept, 61-65, mgr serv div, 65-69, mgr analytical dept, 69-72, mgr analytical chem dept, 72-76, mgr health, safety & environ, 76-80. *Mem:* Am Chem Soc. *Res:* Analytical absorption spectroscopy; molecular structure determination using spectroscopic techniques. *Mailing Add:* 2210 Sewell Lane Roanoke VA 24015

HARPAVAT, GANESH LAL, FLUID MECHANICS. *Current Pos:* assoc scientist res div, 68-70, scientist, 70-74, SR SCIENTIST, XEROX WEBSTER RES CTR, 75-; VIS ASSOC PROF, DEPT BUS COMPUT INFO SYST, N TEX STATE UNIV. *Personal Data:* b Udaipur, India, May 13, 44; m 70. *Educ:* Univ Jodhpur, BE, 65; Univ Rochester, MS, 67, PhD(fluid mech), 68; Univ Dallas, MBA, 78. *Prof Exp:* Mech engr, Birla Jute Mfg Co, India, 65; teaching & res assoc mech, Univ Rochester, 65-68. *Mem:* Am Soc Mech Engrs; Am Inst Aeronaut & Astronaut; Inst Elec & Electronics Engrs. *Res:* Ink jet technology; science of xerographic development; transfer, fusing, and cleaning; system simulation and modeling; fluid mechanics and hydrodynamic stability; applied math; computers. *Mailing Add:* 560 W Main St Lewisville TX 75057

HARPELL, GARY ALLAN, POLYMER SCIENCE, PHYSICAL CHEMISTRY. *Current Pos:* RES ASSOC POLYMER SCI, ALLIED CHEM CORP, 77- *Personal Data:* b Kingston, Ont, Sept 20, 37; m 65; c 3. *Educ:* Queen's Univ, BSc, 60, MSc, 61; Univ Leeds, PhD(phys chem), 65. *Prof Exp:* Res chemist rubber, B F Goodrich Co, 65-71; mgr appln peroxide uses, Lucidol Div, Pennwalt Corp, 71-77. *Mem:* Am Chem Soc. *Res:* Free radical polymerizations and thermoset resin systems; structure property relationships of polymeric systems; the evaluation of ballistic phenomena, with particular emphasis on optimization of ballistic resistant composites and fabric structures; polymerization processes; thermoset care systems; structure property relationships of polymeric systems. *Mailing Add:* 19 Elder Dr Morristown NJ 07960-2805

HARPENDING, HENRY COSAD, BIOLOGICAL ANTHROPOLOGY. *Current Pos:* PROF ANTHROP, PA STATE UNIV. *Personal Data:* b Penn Yan, NY, Jan 13, 44; m 66; c 1. *Educ:* Hamilton Col, AB, 64; Harvard Univ, MA, 65, PhD(anthrop), 72. *Prof Exp:* Asst prof anthrop, Yale Univ, 71-72; from asst prof to prof anthrop, Univ NMex, 72- *Mem:* Nat Acad Sci; Am Asn Phys Anthrop; Am Asn Athrop Genetics; Human Behav Evolution Soc. *Res:* Human population genetics; numerical methods in anthropology. *Mailing Add:* Dept Anthrop 318 Carpenter Bldg Pa State Univ Main Campus University Park PA 16802. *E-Mail:* hxh5@psu.edu

HARPER, ALEXANDER MAITLAND, ECONOMIC ENTOMOLOGY, ECOLOGY. *Current Pos:* RETIRED. *Personal Data:* b Lethbridge, Alta, Mar 10, 26; m 56, Georgean Hirst; c Bradley, Shawna, Paula & Liana. *Educ:* Univ Alta, BSc, 48, MSc, 51; Wash State Univ, PhD(entom), 57. *Prof Exp:* Res scientist entom, Sci Serv Lab, 48-59; res scientist, Res Sta Agr Can, 59-86, emer scientist entom, 87-89. *Concurrent Pos:* Mem, Entom Soc Alta. *Mem:* Entom Soc Am; Entom Soc Can; Can Nature Fedn. *Res:* Biology, ecology, and control of forage insects, sugar beet insects, and aphids; insect transmission of plant diseases. *Mailing Add:* 1654 Scenic Heights S Lethbridge AB T1K 1N5 Can

HARPER, ALFRED EDWIN, BIOCHEMISTRY. *Current Pos:* PROF BIOCHEM, UNIV WIS-MADISON, 65-, PROF NUTRIT SCI & CHMN DEPT, 68- *Personal Data:* b Lethbridge, Alta, Aug 14, 22; nat US; m 48; c 2. *Educ:* Univ Alta, BSc, 45, MSc, 47; Univ Wis, PhD(biochem), 53. *Honors & Awards:* Borden Award, Am Inst Nutrit, 65; Storer Lectr, Life Sci, Univ Calif, Davis, 81. *Prof Exp:* Instr biochem, Univ Alta, 48-49, lectr, 49-52, asst prof, 52-54, NSF-Nat Res Coun res fel, Cambridge Univ, 55-56; from asst prof to assoc prof, Univ Wis, 56-61; prof nutrit, Mass Inst Technol, 61-65. *Concurrent Pos:* Mem, comt amino acids, Food & Nutrit Bd, Nat Res Coun, Nat Acad Sci, 56-70, chmn, 63-70, dietary allowances comt, 65-74, chmn, 69-74, dietary guidelines comt, 77-, mem bd, 61-71 & 77-, chmn, 78-81; mem metab study sect, NIH, 63-67; mem nutrit training comt, Nat Inst Gen Med Sci, 67-71, chmn, 68-71; comt dietary guidelines, 77-79; chmn Food & Nutrit Bd, 78- *Mem:* Fel AAAS; Am Soc Biol Chem; Biochem Soc; Am Chem Soc; Am Inst Nutrit (pres, 70). *Res:* Amino acid metabolism and interrelationships; amino acid transport; control of food intake; metabolic adaptations. *Mailing Add:* 3600 86th Ave SE Mercer Island WA 98040

HARPER, C(HARLES) A(RTHUR), MATERIALS SCIENCE, CHEMICAL ENGINEERING. *Current Pos:* RETIRED. *Personal Data:* b Ridgeley, WVa, June 21, 26; m 50; c 3. *Educ:* Johns Hopkins Univ, BChemE, 49. *Prof Exp:* Res engr, Glidden Co, Md, 49-50; mfg engr, Point Breeze Works, Western Elec Co, 52-55; mat engr, Aerospace Div, Westinghouse Elec Corp, 55-57, sr engr, 57-63, fel engr, 63-66, prog mgr, 66-87. *Concurrent Pos:* Tech adv, numerous nat & int tech conferences; lectr & keynote speaker, numerous seminars & conferences. *Mem:* Inst Elec & Electronics Engrs; Soc Plastics Engrs. *Res:* Materials engineering; plastics; electronics. *Mailing Add:* Technol Seminars Inc Box 487 Lutherville MD 21094

HARPER, CHARLES WOODS, JR, INVERTEBRATE PALEONTOLOGY. *Current Pos:* asst prof, 67-70, PROF GEOL, UNIV OKLA, 70- *Personal Data:* b San Antonio, Tex, Jan 10, 38; m 59; c 1. *Educ:* Mass Inst Technol, SB, 59, SM, 61; Calif Inst Technol, PhD(geol), 64. *Prof Exp:* NSF fel geol, Univ Col Swansea, Wales, 64-65; vis res assoc paleont, Smithsonian Inst, 65-66. *Mem:* Paleont Soc; Sigma Xi. *Res:* Evolution, taxonomy and distribution in time and space of lower paleozoic brachiopods; evolutionary paleontology; quantitative methods. *Mailing Add:* Dept Geol Univ Okla Main Campus 900 Asp Ave Norman OK 73019-4050

HARPER, CURTIS, PHARMACOLOGY. *Current Pos:* ASSOC PROF PHARMACOL, UNIV NC, 76- *Personal Data:* b Auburn, Ala, May 13, 37. *Educ:* Tuskegee Inst, BS, 59, MS, 61; Iowa State Univ, MS, 63; Univ Mo, PhD(biochem), 69. *Prof Exp:* Fel biochem, Yale Univ, 69-70, Univ NC, 70-71; instr pharmacol, Univ NC, 71-72; sr staff fel, NIH, 72-76. *Mem:* Am Chem Soc; AAAS; Sigma Xi; Soc Toxicol; Am Soc Pharmacol & Exp Therapeut. *Res:* Metabolism of drugs and other chemicals by pulmonary microsomal enzymes; pulmonary toxicity of halogenated hydrocarbons; biochemical toxicology; oxidative stress and ischemic lung injury. *Mailing Add:* Dept Pharmacol Flob CB No 7365 Univ NC Sch Med Chapel Hill NC 27599-0001

HARPER, DEAN OWEN, CHEMICAL ENGINEERING, POLYMER SCIENCE & ENGINEERING. *Current Pos:* assoc prof, 69-83, PROF CHEM ENG, UNIV LOUISVILLE, 83- *Personal Data:* b Cincinnati, Ohio, Dec 1, 34; m 59; c 3. *Educ:* Purdue Univ, BSChE, 56, MS, 59; Univ Cincinnati, PhD(chem eng), 67. *Prof Exp:* Jr engr, Redstone Arsenal, Thiokol Chem Corp, 56-57; asst prof chem eng, WVa Univ, 63-69. *Concurrent Pos:* Consult, US Bur Mines, 67-69, E I du Pont de Nemours & Co, 69, Gen Elec, Appliance Park, Louisville, 72 & 81 & Brown & Williamson Tobacco Corp, 84 & 85. *Mem:* Am Inst Chem Engrs; Am Soc Eng Educ; Soc Plastics Engrs; Fedn Soc Coatings Technol; Soc Rheology; Nat Soc Prof Engrs. *Res:* Interfacial phenomena; properties of polymers and polymer processing; rheology; fluidization; fluid dynamics; numerical solution of partial differential equations; organic paints and coatings; interstitial composite materials. *Mailing Add:* Dept Chem Eng Univ Louisville Louisville KY 40292

HARPER, DOYAL ALEXANDER, JR, ASTRONOMY. *Current Pos:* AT YERKES OBSERV, WILLIAMS BAY, WI. *Personal Data:* b Atlanta, Ga, Oct 9, 44; m 67; c 3. *Educ:* Rice Univ, BA, 66, PhD(space sci), 71. *Prof Exp:* Asst prof, 71-77, assoc prof astron, Univ Chicago, 71- *Mem:* Am Astron Soc.

Res: Far infrared astronomy; investigations of regions of star formation, active galactic nuclei, interstellar medium, infrared stars and planetary atmospheres. *Mailing Add:* Astron & Astrophys Box 0258 Univ Chicago 5640 Ellis Ave Chicago IL 60637

HARPER, EDWIN T, ORGANIC CHEMISTRY, BIOCHEMISTRY. *Current Pos:* asst prof biochem, 70-74, ASSOC PROF BIOCHEM, MED CTR, IND UNIV-PURDUE UNIV, INDIANAPOLIS, 74- *Personal Data:* b Chicago, Ill, May 4, 35; m 57; c 3. *Educ:* Grinnell Col, BA, 55; Univ Minn, PhD(org chem), 59. *Prof Exp:* Res assoc org chem, Univ Minn, 59-60; NIH fel, 62-64; asst prof chem, Clarkson Col Technol, 64-70. *Mem:* AAAS; Am Chem Soc; Sigma Xi. *Res:* Reaction mechanisms; mechanism of enzyme action. *Mailing Add:* 635 Barnhill Dr Ind Univ Sch Med Indianapolis IN 46202-5122. *Fax:* 317-274-4686

HARPER, ELVIN, BIOCHEMISTRY. *Current Pos:* assoc prof, 73-81, PROF CHEM, UNIV CALIF, SAN DIEGO, 81- *Personal Data:* b New York, NY, Nov 19, 30; m 76; c 2. *Educ:* City Col New York, BS, 52; Brooklyn Col, MA, 61; Albert Einstein Col Med, PhD(biochem), 66. *Honors & Awards:* John E Fogarty Sr Int Scholar Award, 80. *Prof Exp:* From instr to assoc prof biol chem, Harvard Med Sch, 68-73. *Concurrent Pos:* NIH fel, Weizmann Inst Sci, 66-67; res fel biol chem, Harvard Med Sch, 67-68, Arthritis Found fel, 69-71; USPHS res career develop award, 71-76. *Mem:* AAAS; Am Chem Soc; NY Acad Sci; Am Rheumatism Asn; Am Soc Biol Chem; Sigma Xi. *Res:* Mechanism of action of enzymes utilizing structural proteins as substrates, in particular the structural protein collagen and the enzyme collagenase. *Mailing Add:* Dept Chem D-0506 Univ Calif San Diego 9500 Gilman Dr La Jolla CA 92093-0506. *Fax:* 619-534-4864

HARPER, FRANCIS EDWARD, SEMICONDUCTOR ENGINEERING, ENGINEERING SCIENCE. *Current Pos:* PROJ MGR, WESTERN DIGITAL, 80- *Personal Data:* b Boston, Mass, Feb 28, 36; m 58; c 2. *Educ:* Univ Calif, Berkeley, BS, 61, MS, 62, PhD(eng sci), 66. *Prof Exp:* Mem tech staff, Bell Tel Labs, Inc, NJ, 66-69; sr physicist, KEV Electronics Corp, 69-71; staff scientist, Technol Inc, 71-72; eng mgr, Solitron 72-73; supvry engr, Fairchild Semiconductor, 73-74; eng mgr, Eurosil Intermetall Gmbh, 74-76; staff consult, ITT, 76-78; mgr advan projs, Rockwell Int, 78-79; staff scientist, Hughes Aircraft, 79-80. *Mem:* Am Phys Soc; Inst Elec & Electronics Engrs. *Res:* Solid state research; semiconductor processing. *Mailing Add:* 390 Elan Village Lane No 212 San Jose CA 95134

HARPER, HENRY AMOS, JR, nuclear engineering, reactor physics, for more information see previous edition

HARPER, JAMES ARTHUR, POULTRY SCIENCE. *Current Pos:* Instr, 42, prof in chg turkey res, Poultry Sci Dept, 42-82, EMER PROF POULTRY SCI, ORE STATE UNIV, 82- *Personal Data:* b Delemar, Idaho, Nov 18, 16; m 42; c 2. *Educ:* Ore State Univ, BS, 40; Pa State Univ, MS, 42. *Honors & Awards:* Res Award, Nat Turkey Fedn, 51; Hamilton, Lyons, Michell Award. *Mem:* Poultry Sci Asn; Worlds Poultry Sci Asn; Am Genetics Asn. *Res:* Physiology of reproduction in turkeys; nutrition and breeding problems of turkeys. *Mailing Add:* 1545 Dixon Corvallis OR 97330-4650

HARPER, JAMES DOUGLAS, INSECT PATHOLOGY, BIOLOGICAL CONTROL. *Current Pos:* From asst prof to prof insect path, 69-89, HEAD, DEPT ENTOM, AUBURN UNIV, 89-; HEAD, DEPT ENTOM, NC STATE UNIV, 96- *Personal Data:* b Havre-de-Grace, Md, Sept 9, 42; m 60; c Tanya, Jeffrey & Kelly. *Educ:* Univ Ill, BS, 64, MS, 65; Ore State Univ, PhD(insect path), 69. *Mem:* Soc Invert Path (treas, 80-82); Entom Soc Am; Int Orgn Biol Control. *Res:* Theoretical and applied research with insect pathogens, especially viruses, bacteria and fungi. *Mailing Add:* Dept Entom NC State Univ Box 7613 Raleigh NC 27695-7613

HARPER, JAMES EUGENE, PLANT PHYSIOLOGY, AGRONOMY. *Current Pos:* plant physiologist, 68-91, SUPVRY PLANT PHYSIOLOGIST, RES LEADER & LOCATION COORDR, AGR RES SERV, USDA, 91- *Personal Data:* b Syracuse, Kans, Jan 19, 40; m 64; c 2. *Educ:* Kans State Univ, BS, 62, MS, 66, PhD(plant physiol), 68. *Honors & Awards:* Am Soybean Asn Res Tour. *Prof Exp:* From asst prof to prof plant physiol, Univ Ill, Urbana, 68-86. *Concurrent Pos:* Assoc ed, Crop Sci, 81-83, tech ed, 84-86; vis scientist, Commonwealth Sci Indust Res Org, 81-82; assoc ed, Plant Physiol, 84-91. *Mem:* Am Soc Plant Physiologists; fel Am Soc Agron; fel Crop Sci Soc. *Res:* Mineral nutrition of soybean; fertility, nutrient uptake and metabolism; nitrogen nutrition involving nitrate reductase and symbiotic nitrogen fixation. *Mailing Add:* 1173 County Rd 2400E St Joseph IL 61873. *Fax:* 217-333-6089; *E-Mail:* j-harper@staff.uiuc.edu

HARPER, JOHN DAVID, STRATIGRAPHY, SEDIMENTOLOGY. *Current Pos:* MGR GEOL, CONCEPT RESOURCES, INC, 80-; PROF GEOL, MEM UNIV NFLD, 87- *Personal Data:* b Toronto, Ont, Mar 21, 39; m 62; c 2. *Educ:* Univ Toronto, BASc, 61, MASc, 64; Brown Univ, PhD(geol), 69. *Prof Exp:* Teacher, Danforth Tech Inst, 61-62; res geologist, Shell Develop Co, Calif, 68-70, sr geologist, Shell Oil Co, Midland Tex, 70-73, sr geologist, Shell Can, Ltd, 73-76; vpres, Trend Explor Ltd, 76-80. *Concurrent Pos:* Consult, 80- *Mem:* Am Asn Petrol Geologists; Soc Econ Paleontologists & Mineralogists; Int Asn Sedimentologists; fel Geol Soc Am; Can Soc Petrol Geologists. *Res:* Carbonate and clastic sedimentology; related paleoecology; exploration of petroleum; computer applications to geology. *Mailing Add:* Earth Sci Memorial Univ Nfld Box 420 St John's NF A1C 5S7 Can

HARPER, JON JAY, INDUSTRIAL ORGANIC CHEMISTRY. *Current Pos:* Chemist, 68-73, sr res chemist, 73-89, ASSOC SR RES CHEMIST, AMOCO CHEM CORP, 89- *Personal Data:* b Cleveland, Ohio, May 28, 41; m 67; c 2. *Educ:* Col Wooster, BA, 63; Princeton Univ, MA, 65, PhD(chem), 68 Midwest Col of Eng, MChE, 83. *Mem:* Am Chem Soc; Sigma Xi. *Res:* Study processes for the preparation of polyester intermediates, especially terephthalic acid. *Mailing Add:* 1120 Birkdale Ct Naperville IL 60563-2406

HARPER, JUDITH JEAN, biochemistry, for more information see previous edition

HARPER, JUDSON M(ORSE), EXTRUSION, FOOD ENGINEERING. *Current Pos:* prof agr & chem eng & head dept, 70-82, int pres, 89-90, VPRES RES, COLO STATE UNIV, 82- *Personal Data:* b Lincoln, Nebr, Aug 25, 36; m 58, Patricia A Kennedy; c Jayson K, Stuart H & Neal K. *Educ:* Iowa State Univ, BS, 58, MS, 60, PhD(food technol), 63. *Honors & Awards:* Food Eng Award, Dairy & Food Ind Supply Asn & Am Soc Agr Engrs, 83; Cert Merit, Off Int Coop & Develop, USDA, 83; Int Award, Inst Food Technologists, 90. *Prof Exp:* Instr food technol, Iowa State Univ, 58-64; res assoc food, Gen Mills, Inc, Minn, 64-68, dept head eng sci, 68-69, venture mgr nylon polymers, 69-70. *Concurrent Pos:* Sabbatical leave, Technion, Haifa, Israel; Fulbright-Hayes Scholar, 78. *Mem:* AAAS; Am Soc Agr Engrs; Inst Food Technologists; Am Inst Chem Engrs; Am Soc Eng Educ; Am Chem Soc. *Res:* Food processing including drying, thermoprocessing and extrusion; application of operations research techniques to food processes; the effect of processing on the nutritive value of food; new feeding systems including school lunch. *Mailing Add:* 1818 Westview Rd Ft Collins CO 80524-1891. *Fax:* 970-491-5541; *E-Mail:* jharper@vines.colostate.edu

HARPER, KENNARD W(ATSON), mechanical engineering; deceased, see previous edition for last biography

HARPER, KIMBALL T, BOTANY, SOIL SCIENCE. *Current Pos:* chmn dept, 73-76, PROF BOT & RANGE SCI, BRIGHAM YOUNG UNIV, 73- *Personal Data:* b Oakley, Idaho, Feb 15, 31; m 58, Caroline Stepp; c Ruth, James, Gay, Denise, Karla & Steven. *Educ:* Brigham Young Univ, BS, 58, MS, 60; Univ Wis, PhD(bot), 63. *Honors & Awards:* Pres Pub Serv Award, Nature Conservancy, 87. *Prof Exp:* Range technician, US Forest Serv, 57-60; asst prof bot, Univ Utah, 63-68, assoc prof biol, 68-73. *Concurrent Pos:* Adj prof geog, Univ Utah. *Mem:* Fel AAAS; Brit Ecol Soc; Ecol Soc Am; Soc Range Mgt; Bot Soc Am. *Res:* Community ecology; plant reproduction biology; rare plant conservation. *Mailing Add:* Dept Bot & Range Sci Brigham Young Univ Provo UT 84602

HARPER, LAURA JANE, nutrition, human physiology; deceased, see previous edition for last biography

HARPER, LAURENCE RAYMOND, JR, MATHEMATICS. *Current Pos:* Instr, 56-59, asst prof, 59-97, ASSOC PROF MATH, UNIV MINN, MINNEAPOLIS, 97- *Personal Data:* b Atlanta, Ga, Dec 10, 29; m 56; c 4. *Educ:* Talladega Col, AB, 50; Univ Chicago, SM, 53, PhD(math), 59. *Res:* Structure theory of non-associative algebras; number theory. *Mailing Add:* Dept Math Univ Minn 206 Church St SE Rm 105 Vincent Hall Minneapolis MN 55455-0487

HARPER, LAWRENCE HUESTON, MATHEMATICS, THEORY. *Current Pos:* assoc prof, 70-80, PROF MATH, UNIV CALIF, RIVERSIDE, 80- *Personal Data:* b Hemet, Calif, Aug 24, 38; m 90; c 3. *Educ:* Univ Calif, Berkeley, BA, 61; Univ Ore, MA, 63, PhD(math), 65. *Prof Exp:* Res assoc math, Rockefeller Univ, 65-66, asst prof, 66-70. *Concurrent Pos:* Part time employee, Commun Res Div, Jet Propulsion Lab, 70-74. *Mem:* Am Math Soc. *Res:* Combinatorial optimization using combinatorial; algebraic and analytic methods; complexity theory in computer science. *Mailing Add:* Dept Math Univ Calif Riverside 900 University Ave Riverside CA 92521

HARPER, MICHAEL JOHN KENNEDY, REPRODUCTIVE PHYSIOLOGY, ENDOCRINOLOGY. *Current Pos:* assoc prof, 75-81, PROF OBSTET, GYNEC & PHYSIOL, & CHIEF DIV REPRODUCTIVE BIOL, DEPT OBSTET & GYNEC, UNIV TEX HEALTH SCI CTR, SAN ANTONIO, 81- *Personal Data:* b London, Eng, Feb 25, 35; US citizen; m 85; c 4. *Educ:* Cambridge Univ, BA, 57, MA, 61, PhD(reproductive physiol), 62, ScD, 79; Univ Reading, 57-58, dipl, 58; Univ Tex, San Antonio, MBA, 84. *Honors & Awards:* Res Career Develop Award, Nat Inst Child Health & Human Develop, 69-72. *Prof Exp:* Tech officer, Pharmaceut Div, Imp Chem Industs, Ltd, Eng, 61-64; staff scientist, Worcester Found Exp Biol, 64-65; tech officer, Pharmaceut Div, Imp Chem Industs, Ltd, 65-66; staff scientist, Worcester Found Exp Biol, 66-68; sr scientist, 68-70, prog dir prostaglandin res, 70-72; med officer, Human Reprod Unit, WHO, Switz, 72-75; found scientist, Southwest Found Res & Educ, San Antonio, 75-76. *Concurrent Pos:* Lectr, Clark Univ, 71; mem med adv comt int fertil res prog, Carolina Pop Ctr, 71; mem steering comt, 75-81, chmn Spec Prog, Human Reprod Task Force, 83, Task Force, Postovulatory Methods Birth Control, WHO, 84-87; Nat Inst Child Health & Human Develop res career develop award, 69-72; mem Nat Inst Child Health & Human Develop, Contraceptive Develop Contract Review, 77-78; consult, US Agency Int Dev, Contraceptive Dev Br, Nat Inst Child Health & Human Develop; grant reviewer, NIH, USAID, NSF, & USDA; manuscript reviewer, Biol Reprod, J Reprod & Fertil, J Med Chem, Am J Physiol, Fertil & Steril Endocrinology, Prostaglandins, J Lipid Res, J Neurochem & J Cellular Biochem; mem adv comt, Family Health Int, 86- *Mem:* Soc Study Reprod; Am Fertil Soc; Endocrine Soc; Am Asn Anat;

Brit Soc Study Fertil; Am Physiol Soc; Soc Gynec Invest; Soc Study Reprod; Am Pub Health Asn. *Res:* Ovum development and uterine preparation for blastocyst implantation in animals and primates; prostaglandins as regulators of reproductive function; development of contraceptive agents; platelet-activating factor in reproduction; two US and one UK patent. *Mailing Add:* Dept Obstet & Gynec E Va Med Sch Conrad Prog 1611 N Kent St Suite 806 Arlington VA 22209. *Fax:* 703-524-4770

HARPER, PAUL ALVA, MATERNAL & CHILD HEALTH. *Current Pos:* assoc prof pub health admin, 47-51, prof, 51-65, assoc prof pediat, Sch Med, 59-75, EMER PROF MATERNAL & CHILD HEALTH & POP DYNAMICS, SCH HYG & PUB HEALTH, JOHNS HOPKINS UNIV, 75- *Personal Data:* b Watertown, Conn, Sept 18, 04; m 52; c 3. *Educ:* Dartmouth Col, AB, 26; Yale Univ, MD, 31; Johns Hopkins Univ, MPH, 47. *Prof Exp:* Instr pediat, Sch Med, Yale Univ, 34-35, clin instr, 35-42. *Mem:* Am Pediat Soc; Am Pub Health Asn; AMA; Am Acad Pediat. *Res:* Study of prematurely born children; population problems. *Mailing Add:* 13801 York Rd Apt B6 Cockeysville MD 21030

HARPER, PAUL VINCENT, SURGERY. *Current Pos:* From instr to assoc prof, 49-60, prof surg, 60-80, prof radiol, 72-80, PROF SURG & MEM STAFF, FRANKLIN MCLEAN MEM RES INST, UNIV CHICAGO, 80- *Personal Data:* b Chicago, Ill, July 27, 15; m 39; c 4. *Educ:* Harvard Univ, AB, 39, MD, 41. *Concurrent Pos:* Assoc dir, Argonne Cancer Res Hosp, 63-67. *Mem:* AAAS; Soc Exp Biol & Med; Soc Nuclear Med; Am Physiol Soc; Radiation Res Soc. *Res:* Applications of the methods of nuclear medicine of problems in clinical and experimental surgery. *Mailing Add:* FMI Box 433 5841 S Maryland Ave Chicago IL 60637-1463

HARPER, PIERRE (PETER) PAUL, AQUATIC ENTOMOLOGY. *Current Pos:* From asst prof to assoc prof, 70-75, dir, Biol Sta, 75-86, PROF BIOL, UNIV MONTREAL, 81- *Personal Data:* b Masson, Que, Sept 4, 42; m 67, Francoise Delorme; c Catherine. *Educ:* Laval Univ, BA, 63; Univ Montreal, BSc, 66, MSc, 67; Univ Waterloo, PhD(biol), 71. *Concurrent Pos:* Fel, Paul Sabatier Univ, France, 71; consult, Can Agency Int Develop, 75-77; sabbatical leave, Ore State Univ, Corvallis, 80, Max-Planck Inst, Schlitz, Ger, 92-93. *Mem:* Entom Soc Can; NAm Benthological Soc. *Res:* Ecology of stream ecosystems particularly with regard to the benthic fauna; taxonomy and ecology of aquatic insects. *Mailing Add:* Dept Biol Sci Univ Montreal Montreal PQ H3C 3J7 Can. *Fax:* 514-343-2293

HARPER, RICHARD ALLAN, BIOPHYSICS, PHYSICS. *Current Pos:* asst prof, 71-76, ASSOC PROF PHYSICS, RENSSELAER POLYTECH INST, 76- *Personal Data:* b Anderson, Ind; m 64; c 1. *Educ:* Univ Chicago, SB, 63; NY Univ, MS, 65, PhD(physics), 70. *Prof Exp:* Physicist & asst res, NIH, 62-63, scientist & asst hosp spec surg, Res Lab, 63-71. *Mem:* AAAS; Am Crystallog Asn; Int Asn Dent Res; Sigma Xi. *Res:* X-ray scattering; biological structure; biological mineralization. *Mailing Add:* Dept Physics Rensselaer Polytech Inst 110 Eighth St Troy NY 12180-3522

HARPER, RICHARD WALTZ, SYNTHETIC ORGANIC CHEMISTRY. *Current Pos:* Org chemist, 67-69, SR ORG CHEMIST, ELI LILLY & CO, 73- *Personal Data:* b Portland, Ore, July 21, 43; m 92, Maude E Glore; c Jennifer C, Jill M, Jonathan G, Robert H (Hux), William L (Hux) & Benjamin M (Hux). *Educ:* Willamette Univ, BA, 65; Ore State Univ, MS, 68; Mass Inst Technol, PhD(org chem), 73. *Mem:* Am Chem Soc; Royal Soc Chem; Asn Comput Mach. *Res:* Synthesis of novel, biologically-active heterocyclic compounds; computer-assisted drug design. *Mailing Add:* Eli Lilly & Co Lilly Res Labs Lilly Corp Ctr Indianapolis IN 46285-0528. *E-Mail:* rwharper@acm.org

HARPER, ROBERT JOHN, JR, CELLULOSE CHEMISTRY, TEXTILE CHEMISTRY. *Current Pos:* res chemist, 63-73, res leader, cellulose chem, 73-85, LEAD SCIENTIST, SOUTHERN REGIONAL RES CTR, 85- *Personal Data:* b Savannah, Ga, Aug 16, 30; m 56; c 6. *Educ:* Fordham Univ, BS, 52; Ohio State Univ, PhD(org chem), 57. *Prof Exp:* Res chemist organo/metallic chem, Ethyl Corp, Baton Rouge, 58-62; res chemist fluoroaromatic chem, Mat Lab, Wright-Patterson AFB, Ohio, 62-63. *Mem:* Am Chem Soc; Am Asn Textile Chemists & Colorists. *Res:* Cellulose and textile chemistry with emphasis on durable press, flame retardant, smolder resistance, speciality dyeing and weather resistance; organo metallics; organo synthesis; flouroaromatic chemistry. *Mailing Add:* 4701 Page Dr Metairie LA 70001-1129

HARPER, VERNE LESTER, FOREST MANAGEMENT, FOREST RESEARCH ADMINISTRATION. *Current Pos:* prof, 66-73, EMER PROF FORESTRY, UNIV FLA, 73- *Personal Data:* b Monroe, SDak, Aug 13, 02; m 27; c 1. *Educ:* Univ Calif, BS, 26, MS, 27; Duke Univ, PhD(forestry), 43. *Hon Degrees:* DSc, NC State Univ, 67. *Honors & Awards:* Distinguished Serv Award, USDA, 61; Fernow Int Forestry Award, Am Forestry Asn, 65; Forest Farmers Asn Award, 68. *Prof Exp:* Asst, Univ Calif, 26-27; jr forester, Southern Forest Exp Sta, US Forest Serv, 27-29, leader field studies, 29-35, chief, Field Div Forest Mgr Res, 35-37, asst chief, Div Silvicult, Washington, DC, 37-43, chief, Div Forest Econ, 43-45, dir, Forest Serv, Northeast Exp Sta, 45-51, dep chief chg res, Washington, DC, 51-66. *Concurrent Pos:* Mem, Permanent Comt, Int Union Forest Res Orgn, 56-61, vpres, 61-67; chmn, World Forestry Comt, Soc Am Foresters, 56-67; chmn, Latin Am Forest Res Comt, UN Food & Agr Orgn, 58-61; pres, Int Union Soc Foresters, 69-75. *Mem:* Fel Soc Am Foresters; Am Forestry Asn; fel Int Union Soc Foresters; hon mem Int Union Forestry Res Orgn. *Res:* Silviculture; forest economics; naval stores production. *Mailing Add:* 1812 SW Sixth Terr Gainesville FL 32601-8406

HARPER, W(ILLIS) JAMES, DAIRY FOODS. *Current Pos:* PROF & J T PARHER CHAIR DAIRY FOODS, OHIO STATE UNIV, 92- *Personal Data:* b Lafayette, Ind, June 9, 23; m 45, Elaine Bushnell; c Kenneth J, D Scott & Virginia F. *Educ:* Purdue Univ, BS, 46; Univ Wis, MS, 47, PhD(dairy indust), 49. *Honors & Awards:* Borden Award, 46, 58. *Prof Exp:* From asst prof to prof dairy tech, Ohio State Univ, 49-67, assoc prof biochem & molecular biol, 67-71, prof biochem, 71-80; res fel, NZ Dairy Res Inst, 81-86. *Mem:* Am Chem Soc; Am Dairy Sci Asn; Inst Food Technologists. *Res:* Food ingredient characterization and functionality; flavor of dairy foods; cheese ripening. *Mailing Add:* 3563 S Old 3-C Rd Galena OH 43021-9436. *Fax:* 614-292-0218; *E-Mail:* harper.a@osu.edu

HARPOLD, MICHAEL ALAN, BIO-ORGANIC CHEMISTRY. *Current Pos:* PRES & CHIEF EXEC OFFICER, LIPOMED INC, 97- *Personal Data:* b Charleston, WVa, June 24, 40; c 2. *Educ:* WVa State Col, BS, 63; Univ NC, Chapel Hill, PhD(org chem), 67. *Prof Exp:* NIH fel, Lab Chem Biodyn, Univ Calif, Berkeley, 67-68; res chemist, Res & Develop Dept, Union Carbide Tech Ctr, 68-73, mkt mgr biochem intermediates, 73-77, sr group leader, Corp Res Dept, 77-78, mgr systs commercialization, Med Prod Div, Union Carbide Corp, 78-79, dir res & develop, 79-81; plant mgr, Baker Instruments Corp, 81-82; dir process technol, Technicon Instruments Corp, 82-86, dir clin biochem, 86-89; dir qual assurance develop, Miles Inc, 89-92, vpres diabetes prod develop, 92-93; vpres bus develop, Andcare, Inc, 94-96. *Mem:* Am Chem Soc; NY Acad Sci; AAAS; Am Asn Clin Chem. *Res:* Management of clinical chemistry research and development activities, including development and technology transfer. *Mailing Add:* 508 Wellingham Dr Durham NC 27713

HARPP, DAVID NOBLE, CHEMISTRY. *Current Pos:* from asst prof to assoc prof, 66-75, PROF CHEM, MCGILL UNIV, 75- *Personal Data:* b Albany, NY, Jan 20, 37; m 61, 94, Bonnie Folkins; c Karen & Emily. *Educ:* Middlebury Col, AB, 59; Wesleyan Univ, MA, 62; Univ NC, PhD(chem), 65. *Honors & Awards:* Union Carbide Award Chem Educ, 82; Michael Smith Award, Govtt Can, 86; Nat Award Chem Mfrs Asn, 88; McNeil Award, Royal Soc Can, 93; Edward Leete Award, Chem Soc, 95. *Prof Exp:* Fel org chem, Cornell Univ, 65-66. *Mem:* Am Chem Soc; Can Soc Chem; AAAS; The Chem Soc. *Res:* Organic synthesis; sulfur and silicon compounds; new methods; teaching innovations. *Mailing Add:* 40 King St Warrensburg NY 12885-1318

HARPST, JERRY ADAMS, PHYSICAL BIOCHEMISTRY. *Current Pos:* asst prof, 65-71, ASSOC PROF BIOCHEM, SCH MED, CASE WESTERN RESERVE UNIV, 71- *Personal Data:* b Glasgow, Ky, Sept 27, 36; m 61, Bethalee June Brandenberger; c Lisa Lynnelle & Tamara Lee. *Educ:* Wabash Col, AB, 58; Yale Univ, MS, 60, PhD(phys chem), 62. *Prof Exp:* USPHS fel, Univ Calif, San Diego, 62-63, res assoc traineeship, 63-64, NIH fel biophys chem, 62-64. *Concurrent Pos:* USPHS career develop award, 67-77; vis scientist, Nat Inst Med Res, Mill Hill, London, 71-72; vis assoc prof biochem & biophys, Ore State Univ, 80-81. *Mem:* Am Chem Soc; Am Soc Biol Chemists; Biophys Soc. *Res:* Physical biochemistry of DNA, proteins and DNA-protein interactions; DNA-protein interactions; structure-function relationships of biological macromolecules; nucleoprotein structure and DNA replication in adenovirus. *Mailing Add:* Dept Biochem Case Western Res Univ Sch Med Cleveland OH 44106-4935. *E-Mail:* jah8@po.cwra.edu

HARPSTEAD, DALE D, GENETICS, PLANT BREEDING. *Current Pos:* chmn dept crop & soil sci, 69-84, PROF CROP & SOIL SCI, MICH STATE UNIV, 85- *Personal Data:* b Sioux Falls, SDak, Sept 10, 26; m 48; c 5. *Educ:* SDak State Col, BSc, 50, MS, 53; Univ Nebr, PhD(genetics), 61. *Prof Exp:* Plant breeder, SDak State Col, 53-61; assoc geneticist, Rockefeller Found, 61-69. *Concurrent Pos:* Mem bd, Int Food & Agr Develop, Dept State, Washington, DC, 84-86, mem, Coun Agr Sci & Technol. *Mem:* Am Soc Agron; Crop Sci Soc Am. *Res:* Improved yield; quality and adaptation of maize; world food supply, agricultural development. *Mailing Add:* 2646 Raphael Rd East Lansing MI 48823

HARPSTEAD, MILO I, SOILS. *Current Pos:* PROF SOIL SCI, UNIV WIS, STEVENS POINT, 61- *Personal Data:* b Wilmot, SDak, Sept 28, 30; m 63. *Educ:* SDak State Col, BSc, 53, MSc, 57; Univ Minn, PhD(soils), 62. *Prof Exp:* Instr soils, Univ Minn, 57-60. *Concurrent Pos:* Prof, Univ Ife, Nigeria, 68-70. *Res:* Soil genesis, morphology and fertility. *Mailing Add:* 612 Fieldcrest Ave Stevens Point WI 54481

HARPSTER, JOSEPH, FLUIDS APPLIED PHYSICS, ELECTRICAL ENGINEERING. *Current Pos:* PRES, INTEK INC, WESTERVILLE, OHIO, 77- *Personal Data:* b Sewickley, Pa, June 29, 32; m 75, Marilyn Fu; c Jodean A, Bradford C, Brian K & Timothy J. *Educ:* Geneva Col, BS, 59; Case Western Reserve Univ, MS, 64; Ohio State Univ, PhD(nuclear eng), 71. *Honors & Awards:* Apollo Soyuz Medallion Award, NASA, Marshall Space Flight Ctr, 76. *Prof Exp:* Plant engr phys chem, Ashland Oil, Freedom, Pa, 54-59; proj leader solid state physics, Harshaw Chem Co, Cleveland, 60-62; res assoc physics, Horizons Inc, 62-63; mgr solid state physics, Ohio Semiconductors Inc, Columbus, 63-65; lab supvr appl physics, Ohio State Univ, 65-72; vpres res & develop appl sci, Ohio Semitronics Inc, Columbus, 72-77. *Concurrent Pos:* Comt mem, Am Soc Testing & Mat, 63-65, ISA, 77-, Ohio Acad Sci. *Mem:* Am Phys Soc; Am Asn Small Businesses; Sigma Xi; Instrument Soc Am. *Res:* Industrial process controls; applied electronics; space manufacturing; experimentation hardware; semiconductor materials; applied chemistry; military equipment; ocean wave energy conversion; thermoelectric systems; electrooptics; electric power monitoring. *Mailing Add:* 11450 Overbrook Lane Galena OH 43021. *Fax:* 614-895-0319

HARPSTER, ROBERT E, CLAY MINERALOGY, SEISMIC GEOLOGY. *Current Pos:* mgt assessment & qual assurance consult, 93-95, CONSULT, CER, 95- *Personal Data:* b Olney, Ill, Sept 25, 30; m, Carol A. *Educ:* Beloit Col, BS, 52; Univ Tex, MA, 57. *Prof Exp:* Proj geologist, Bechtel Corp, 56-57; sr proj eng geologist, Calif Dept Water Resources, 57-71; from sr res scientist to vpres & dir qual assurance, Woodward-Clyde Consult, 71-87; mgt assessment & qual assurance consult, Mactec, 87-93. *Concurrent Pos:* Instr earthquake anal & soil eng, Antelope Valley Community Col, 70-72; mem, US Comt Large Dams; tech fel, Woodland-Clyde Consult; res grant, US Geol Surv. *Mem:* Fel Geol Soc Am; Am Soc Civil Engrs; Am Asn Petrol Geologists; Am Soc Qual Control; Clay Mineral Soc. *Res:* Study of the earth with respect to seismic events (seismic geology); study of the earth and younger materials to assess relative activity of faulting (neotectonics). *Mailing Add:* 5735 Buena Vista Ave Oakland CA 94618-2120

HARPUR, ROBERT PETER, BIOCHEMISTRY. *Current Pos:* RETIRED. *Personal Data:* b Marton, NZ, Dec 20, 21; m 47, 92, Alida Johanny; c Douglas, Kathleen & Arthur. *Educ:* Univ NZ, BSc, 42; McGill Univ, MSc, 47, PhD(biochem), 49. *Prof Exp:* Asst prof, MacDonald Col, McGill Univ, 50-71, assoc prof, Inst Parasitol, 71-81. *Mem:* Am Chem Soc. *Res:* Biochemistry of parasites. *Mailing Add:* 10 Koromiko Rd Waikanae 6454 New Zealand

HARR, MILTON EDWARD, GEOTECHNICAL ENGINEERING. *Educ:* Northeastern Univ, BS, 49; Rutgers Univ, MS, 55; Purdue Univ, PhD, 58. *Hon Degrees:* Dr, Univ Brussels, 87. *Honors & Awards:* Bechtel Award, 83; Shaw Lectr, NC State Univ, 84. *Prof Exp:* Engr, State Hwy Dept, Mass, 49-53; asst instr, Rutgers Univ, 53-55; instr, Purdue Univ, 55-58, from asst prof to assoc prof civil eng, 58-63, from prof to area head soil mech, 63-72, prof civil eng, 72-91, area head geotech eng, 91-94, PROF GEOTECH ENG, PURDUE UNIV, 94- *Concurrent Pos:* Chmn, Pavement Design Div, 64-70, Track Struct Syst Design Comt, 76-79; bd dirs, Ind Joint Hwy Res Proj, 69-72; lectr, Cross Canada Tour, 81; distinguished eng lectr, Univ Alberta, Edmonton, 83, Carleton Univ, Ottawa, 87. *Mem:* Nat Acad Eng; Am Soc Civil Engrs; Sigma Xi. *Res:* Granted one US patent; author of many publications. *Mailing Add:* 2201 Indian Trail Dr West Lafayette IN 47906

HARR, ROBERT DENNIS, hydrology, for more information see previous edition

HARRACH, ROBERT JAMES, LASER PHYSICS, ATOMIC & MOLECULAR PHYSICS. *Current Pos:* SR PHYSICIST, LAWRENCE LIVERMORE NAT LAB, 66- *Personal Data:* b Holyoke, Colo, Mar 30, 37; m 62, Nadine Ginther; c David & Benjamin. *Educ:* Dartmouth Col, AB, 60; Univ Colo, MS, 62, PhD(physics), 65. *Prof Exp:* Res physicist, Nat Bur Stand, Boulder, 62-66. *Concurrent Pos:* Lectr, Univ Calif Davis, Livermore, 69-74; vis assoc prof physics, Dartmouth Col, 78-79. *Mem:* Am Phys Soc; Am Asn Physics Teachers. *Res:* Lasers, laser-matter interactions; atomic beam spectroscopy; fluid dynamics; radiation transport; environmental science; pollution transport; dose and risk assessment. *Mailing Add:* 255 Kottinger dr Pleasanton CA 94566. *Fax:* 510-422-2748

HARRAR, JACKSON ELWOOD, ELECTROCHEMISTRY, ANALYTICAL CHEMISTRY. *Current Pos:* CHEMIST & GROUP LEADER, LAWRENCE LIVERMORE NAT LAB, UNIV CALIF, 58- *Personal Data:* b Boulder, Colo, June 8, 30; m 61, Knight; c 4. *Educ:* Purdue Univ, BS, 52; Univ Wash, PhD(chem), 58. *Honors & Awards:* Weapons Award, Dept Energy, 85. *Prof Exp:* Asst, Los Alamos Sci Lab, 54. *Concurrent Pos:* US Army Arctic Test Team, 54-56. *Mem:* Electrochem Soc; Am Chem Soc; Sigma Xi; Soc Electroanal Chem. *Res:* Electroanalytical chemistry including polarography, potentiometric titrations, coulometry and mechanisms of electrode processes; automated measurement instrument design; geothermal chemistry; corrosion measurements; electrosynthesis; field analytical chemistry; quality assurance. *Mailing Add:* 4977 Proctor Rd Castro Valley CA 94546. *Fax:* 510-423-9014

HARRAWOOD, PAUL, CIVIL ENGINEERING, HYDRAULICS. *Current Pos:* assoc prof & assoc dean, Vanderbilt Univ, 67-70, dir, Eng Sci Div, 67-71, actg dean, 70-71, assoc dean & dep sch eng, 71-79, prof, 70-97, dean Sch Eng, 79-97, EMER PROF ENG & DEAN, VANDERBILT UNIV, 97- *Personal Data:* b Akin, Ill, Aug 28, 28; m 53; c 1. *Educ:* Univ Mo, Rolla, BS, 51, MS, 56; NC State Univ, PhD(civil eng), 67. *Prof Exp:* Instr civil eng, Univ Mo, Rolla, 54-56; from instr to asst prof, Duke Univ, 56-67. *Concurrent Pos:* Test engr eng stress anal, McDonnell Aircraft Corp, 57; engr construct mgt, US Army Corps Eng, 58. *Mem:* AAAS; Am Soc Civil Engrs; Soc Am Mil Engrs; Am Soc Eng Educ; Am Asn Higher Educ; Sigma Xi. *Res:* Fluid mechanics, steady and unsteady flow; open channel flow; effects of construction on hydrologic environment; environmental propulsion systems. *Mailing Add:* 5314 Camelot Ct Brentwood TN 37027

HARRELL, EVANS MALOTT, II, SCHRODINGER OPERATORS, SPECTRAL GEOMETRY. *Current Pos:* PROF MATH, GA INST TECHNOL, 83- *Personal Data:* b Indianapolis, Ind, July 26, 50; m 77, Charity Scott; c Peter E & Constance S. *Educ:* Stanford Univ, BS, 72; Princeton Univ, PhD(math physics), 76. *Prof Exp:* NSF fel physics, Princeton Univ, 72-75; asst prof, Haverford Col, 76-77; vis prof, Univ Vienna, 7-78; NSF Nat Needs fel math, Mass Inst Technol, 78-79; asst prof math, Johns Hopkins Univ, 79-83. *Concurrent Pos:* Fel, Alfred Sloan Found, 83-85; vis scholar, Univ de Toulon et du Var & Schrodinger Inst, Vienna, 93. *Mem:* Am Math Soc; Int Asn Math Physicists; Am Phys Soc; AAAS. *Res:* Use rigorous mathematics to investigate quantum mechanics and the semiclassical limit; study the connections between geometry and eigen-valves of differential equations. *Mailing Add:* Sch Math Ga Inst Technol Atlanta GA 30332-0160. *Fax:* 404-853-9112; *E-Mail:* harrell@math.gatech.edu

HARRELL, GEORGE T, MEDICINE, EDUCATION FACILITIES. *Current Pos:* RETIRED. *Personal Data:* b Washington, DC, June 16, 08; m 37, Janet Griffin; c George T III & Robert. *Educ:* Duke Univ, AB, 32, MD, 36. *Hon Degrees:* DSc, Univ Fla, 80, Georgetown Univ, 83; LLD, Duke Univ, 83. *Honors & Awards:* Abraham Flexner Medal, Asn Am Med Col, 73. *Prof Exp:* Resident med & path, Duke Hosp, 36-41; instr med, Duke Med Sch, 39-41; from asst prof to res prof med, Bowman Gray Sch Med, Wake Forest Univ, 41-53, dir, Dept Internal Med, 43-52; found dean & prof med, Col Med, Univ Fla, Gainesville, 54-64; found dean, prof med & dir, Milton S Hershey Med Ctr, Pa State Univ, Hershey, 64-72, vpres med sci, 72-73, emer vpres, 73- *Concurrent Pos:* Emer dean, Col Med, Univ Fla, Gainesville, 64-; mem adv coun & panels, Nat Acad Sci, USPHS, Vet Admin & others. *Mem:* Inst Med-Nat Acad Sci; Sigma Xi; Am Soc Clin Invest; AAAS; Master Am Col Physicians. *Res:* Infectious diseases; radioisotopes; chemotherapy; fluid balance; myxedema; facilities for medical education; animal care; over 300 publications. *Mailing Add:* 2701 Pickett Rd Apt 2050 Durham NC 27705

HARRELL, JAMES W, JR, MAGNETIC MATERIALS. *Current Pos:* assoc prof, 80-88, PROF PHYSICS, UNIV ALA, 88-, CHAIRPERSON, 91- *Personal Data:* b Rose Hill, NC, July 14, 42; m 64, Elizabeth Bullard; c 2. *Educ:* Univ NC, Chapel Hill, BS, 64, PhD(physics), 69. *Prof Exp:* Asst prof, Univ NDak, 69-75, assoc prof physics, 75-80. *Mem:* Am Phys Soc; Inst Elec & Electronics Engrs Magnetics Soc; Am Asn Physics Teachers. *Res:* Characterization of particulate magnetic media for information storage. *Mailing Add:* Dept Physics & Astron Univ Ala Tuscaloosa AL 35487-0324. *Fax:* 205-348-5051; *E-Mail:* jharrell@ua1vm.ua.edu

HARRELL, JERALD RICE, POLYMER CHEMISTRY. *Current Pos:* Res chemist, Film Dept, 59-64, res chemist, Elastomer Chems Dept, 64-80, RES ASSOC, POLYMER PRODS DEPT, E I DU PONT DE NEMOURS & CO, 80- *Personal Data:* b Greenup, Ky, Jan 21, 35; m 56; c 2. *Educ:* Univ Louisville, BS, 56, PhD(chem), 59. *Mem:* Am Chem Soc; Res Soc Am; Sigma Xi. *Res:* Radiation chemistry; films; elastomers; polymerization. *Mailing Add:* 1708 Forestdale Dr Wilmington DE 19803

HARRELL, REGINAL M, CONSERVATION BIOLOGY, FISH GENETICS. *Current Pos:* from asst prof to assoc prof, 85-95, STATE FISHERIES & BIOTECHNOL SPECIALIST, COOP EXTEN SERV, UNIV MD, 85-, PROF, CTR ENVIRON & ESTUARINE STUDIES, 95- *Personal Data:* b Hemingway, SC, Aug 18, 53; m 76, Ann Brown; c Kaitlyn E. *Educ:* Clemson Univ, BS, 75, MS, 77; Univ SC, PhD(biol), 84. *Prof Exp:* State biologist, SC Wildlife & Marine Resources Dept, 77-84, actg chief, 84. *Concurrent Pos:* Vis assoc prof, Univ SC, 91-92; affil prof, Univ Md Biotechnol Inst; adj prof, Col Marine Studies, Univ Del. *Mem:* Am Fisheries Soc; Am Inst Fisheries Res Biologists; Soc Conserv Biol; World Aquacult Soc. *Res:* Aquaculture genetics and conservation biology of fish; polyploidy induction; molecular genetics; stock discrimination using molecular techniques, quantitative and qualitative genetics, and aquaculture production. *Mailing Add:* Univ Md Horn Pt Environ Lab PO Box 775 Cambridge MD 21613. *Fax:* 410-221-8456; *E-Mail:* harrell@hpel.cees.edu

HARRELL, RONALD EARL, PURE MATHEMATICS. *Current Pos:* ASST PROF MATH, ALLEGHENY COL, 71- *Personal Data:* b Sanford, Fla, Nov 17, 44; m 66; c 1. *Educ:* Univ Maine, BA, 66; Univ Md, MA, 69, PhD(math), 71. *Mem:* Am Math Soc; Math Asn Am. *Res:* Geometry in Banach spaces and how it is related to the classification of Banach spaces; biomathematics, specifically, ecosystem models and population dynamics. *Mailing Add:* Dept Math Allegheny Col Meadville PA 16335-3902

HARRELL, T GIBSON, ANALYTICAL CHEMISTRY. *Current Pos:* RETIRED. *Personal Data:* b Charleston, SC, June 6, 16; m 49; c 2. *Prof Exp:* Technician chem, R J Reynolds Indusrs, Inc, 41-56, from jr chemist to chemist, 56-66, group leader chem, Res Dept, 66-78. *Mem:* Am Chem Soc. *Res:* General analytical chemistry; nonaqueous titration; spectroscopy; food chemistry; ion-selective electrodes. *Mailing Add:* 2535 Amesbury Rd Winston-Salem NC 27103

HARRELL, WILLIAM BROOMFIELD, MEDICINAL CHEMISTRY. *Current Pos:* Asst prof pharm, 49-53, assoc prof pharmaceut chem, 53-68, PROF MED CHEM, TEX SOUTHERN UNIV, 68- *Personal Data:* b New Orleans, La, Sept 18, 28; m 57; c 2. *Educ:* Univ Wash, BS, 49; Univ Tex, MS, 53; Ore State Univ, PhD(pharmaceut chem), 66. *Mem:* Am Chem Soc; Am Pharmaceut Asn. *Res:* Synthesis and pharmacological screening of indolizines in a search for new medicinal agents with special emphasis on Mannich bases derived from indolizines. *Mailing Add:* Dept Pharm Tex Southern Univ 3100 Cleburne Ave Houston TX 77004-4501

HARREN, RICHARD EDWARD, CHEMISTRY. *Current Pos:* RETIRED. *Personal Data:* b New York, NY, Dec 14, 22; m 49; c 5. *Educ:* Queen's Col, NY, BS, 47. *Prof Exp:* Chemist prod & develop, Nat Starch Prod, Inc, NY, 47-49; with tech sales, Mallinckrodt Chem Co, 49-50; chemist prod develop, Randolph Prod Co, 50-55; lab head, Rohm & Haas Co, 55-64, res supvr polymer res & develop, 64-73, dir coatings res, 73-87. *Mem:* Am Chem Soc. *Res:* Solution, dispersion and solution high polymers for coatings, floor polishes, cement, additives. *Mailing Add:* 68 Hillcrest Dr Doylestown PA 18901-2955

HARRENSTIEN, HOWARD P(AUL), STRUCTURAL ENGINEERING. *Current Pos:* PROF, DEPT ENG, UNIV MIAMI, 77- *Personal Data:* b Kansas City, Mo, Jan 14, 31; m 52; c 4. *Educ:* Kans State Univ, BS, 53, BArch, 54; Iowa State Univ, MS, 56, PhD(theoret & appl mech), 59. *Prof Exp:* Asst appl mech, Kans State Univ, 53-54; asst theoret & appl mech, Iowa State Univ, 54-55, instr, 55-56, from instr to asst prof civil eng, 56-60; from assoc prof to prof, Univ Ariz, 60-67; prof, assoc dean & dir, Ctr Eng Res, Univ Hawaii, 67-77. *Mem:* Int Asn Shell Struct; Am Soc Civil Engrs; Am Concrete Inst; Am Soc Eng Educ; Sigma Xi. *Res:* Expression of structure in architecture; structural research in the areas of plate and shell structures; development of models and model testing laboratories; shelter research in civil defense. *Mailing Add:* 6731 SW 88th Terr Miami FL 33156

HARRIES, HINRICH, ECOLOGY, SOIL SCIENCE. *Current Pos:* asst prof, 63-69, ASSOC PROF BIOL, MT ALLISON UNIV, 69- *Personal Data:* b Berlin, Ger, June 29, 28; m 61; c 2. *Educ:* Rutgers Univ, MSc, 60, PhD(soil sci), 65. *Prof Exp:* Instr biol, Dartmouth Col, 62-63. *Concurrent Pos:* Nat Res Coun Can operating res grant, 67-68; Can Wildlife Serv res contract, 67-68. *Mem:* Can Wildlife Fedn; Ecol Soc Am; Can Bot Asn. *Res:* Ecosystem ecology of forests and wetlands, with emphasis on soil-vegetation interrelationships, humus studies and soil genesis. *Mailing Add:* Dept Biol Mt Allison Univ Sackville NB E0A 3C0 Can

HARRIES, WYNFORD LEWIS, PHYSICS. *Current Pos:* prof, 70-93, EMER PROF PHYSICS, OLD DOM UNIV, 93- *Personal Data:* b Llannon, Wales, June 1, 23; nat US; m 58, Natalie Gratkowski. *Educ:* Univ Wales, BSc, 49; Oxford Univ, DPhil(physics), 53. *Prof Exp:* Res assoc biophys, Mass Inst Technol, 53-54; asst dir res, Transistor Prod, Inc, Clevite Corp, Mass, 54-56; sr proj engr, Phys Sci & Mat Lab, IT&T Corp, 56-60; mem res staff, Plasma Physics Lab, Princeton Univ, 60-70. *Concurrent Pos:* Consult, Sch Ophthal, New York Col Med & IT&T Corp. *Mem:* Fel Am Phys Soc; life sr mem Inst Elec & Electronics Engrs; fel Brit Inst Physics; fel Brit Inst Elec Engrs. *Res:* Electrical discharges in gases; semiconductors; plasma physics; energy conversion; lasers; polymer physics. *Mailing Add:* 258 N Blake Norfolk VA 23505. *Fax:* 757-683-3038

HARRILL, ROBERT W, ENVIRONMENTAL SCIENCE, GLOBAL CHANGE ISSUES. *Current Pos:* EXEC DIR, LIGHTHAWK, SANTA FE, NMEX, 92- *Personal Data:* b Denver, Colo, Sept 30, 41; m 75; c 2. *Educ:* Grinnell Col, BA, 63; Univ Calif, Los Angeles, PhD(biog chem), 67. *Prof Exp:* Asst prof chem, Univ Calif, Los Angeles, 67-68 & New Col, 68-70; assoc prof environ sci, Prescott Col, 70-75, vpres acad affairs, 73-74, actg pres, 74-75; acad dean, Antioch Col W, 77-78; vpres inst advan, Bryant Col, 85-87; sr assoc, Woods Hole Res Ctr, 87-92. *Res:* Biotic aspects of global and regional environmental problems, including global warming, land use in the tropics, biotic impoverishment. *Mailing Add:* 22 Abanico Rd Santa Fe NM 87505

HARRIMAN, BENJAMIN RAMAGE, ORGANIC CHEMISTRY. *Current Pos:* RETIRED. *Personal Data:* b Monroe Bridge, Mass, Aug 9, 13; m 37; c 2. *Educ:* Dartmouth Col, AB, 35; Pa State Univ, MS, 36, PhD(org chem), 39. *Prof Exp:* Asst, Pa State Univ, 36-37; res chemist, Wm S Merrell Co, Ohio, 38-41; res chemist, Ansco Div, Gen Aniline & Film Corp, 41-45, group leader, 45-46, mgr coating develop, 47-55; mgr photo prods res & develop, Haloid Xerox, Inc, 55-60; mgr chem res imaging res, 3M Co, 60-68 & Europ sci & tech liaison, 68-76, with spec assignments in corp res & develop, 76-78. *Concurrent Pos:* Teacher & naturalist, Dodge Nature Ctr, 78-; mem, Minn Water Resources Bd, 79-84; consult, Univ Wis-Stout, 81. *Mem:* Fel AAAS; Am Chem Soc; Royal Soc Chem; Royal Inst London. *Res:* Organic syntheses; photographic science and technology; research and development administration; scientific and technical liaison; technical planning and coordination. *Mailing Add:* 1335 Pinehurst Ave St Paul MN 55116

HARRIMAN, JOHN E, CHEMICAL PHYSICS, QUANTUM CHEMISTRY. *Current Pos:* From asst prof to assoc prof phys chem, 64-76, ASSOC CHMN, DEPT CHEM, UNIV WIS-MADISON, 70-72 & 89-, PROF CHEM, 76- *Personal Data:* b Appleton, Wis, Dec 17, 36; m 68, Mary Sue Weinman; c David. *Educ:* Univ Wis, BS, 59; Harvard Univ, PhD(chem physics), 63. *Concurrent Pos:* NSF fel quantum chem group, Univ Uppsala, 62-64; Sloan Found fel, 68-70. *Mem:* AAAS; Am Phys Soc. *Res:* Molecular quantum mechanics; reduced density matrices; density functional theory; phase space descriptions of quantum mechanics. *Mailing Add:* Dept Chem Bldg Univ Wis Madison 1101 University Ave Madison WI 53706. *E-Mail:* harriman@chem.wisc.edu

HARRIMAN, NEIL ARTHUR, PLANT TAXONOMY. *Current Pos:* from asst prof to assoc prof, 64-74, PROF BIOL, UNIV WIS-OSHKOSH, 74- *Personal Data:* b St Louis, Mo, Aug 1, 38; m 63. *Educ:* Colo Col, BA, 60; Vanderbilt Univ, PhD(bot), 65. *Prof Exp:* Vis lectr bot, Colo Col, 61. *Concurrent Pos:* Vis lectr, Univ Wis, 67. *Mem:* Am Soc Plant Taxon; Int Asn Plant Taxon. *Res:* Taxonomy of Cruciferae and Juncaceae. *Mailing Add:* Dept Biol Univ Wis-Oskosh 800 Algoma Blvd Oshkosh WI 54901-3551

HARRIMAN, PHILIP DARLING, MICROBIAL GENETICS, BIOPHYSICS. *Current Pos:* sr sci assoc to asst res dir biol, Behav & Soc Sci, 81, PROG DIR GENETIC BIOL, NSF, ARLINGTON, VA, 77- *Personal Data:* b San Rafael, Calif, Nov 24, 37; m 59, Jenny Flack; c Marco. *Educ:* Calif Inst Technol, BS, 59; Univ Calif, Berkeley, PhD(biophys), 64. *Prof Exp:* Asst prof biochem, Med Ctr, Duke Univ, 68-75; from assoc prof to assoc prof biol, Univ Mo, Kansas City, 75-79. *Concurrent Pos:* USPHS fel, Genetics Inst, Univ Cologne, 64-65 & Lab Pasteur, Paris, 65-66; Am Cancer Soc fel, Cold Spring Harbor Lab, NY, 66-68; Cong fel, 80-81; vis fac mem, Dept Molecular Biol & Genetics, Med Sch, Johns Hopkins Univ, Baltimore, Md, 87-88. *Mem:* Genetics Soc Am; Am Soc Microbiol; fel AAAS. *Res:* Genetics of bacteria and bacterial viruses. *Mailing Add:* Genetics Prog Dir NSF DMB Rm 655 4201 Wilson Blvd Arlington VA 22230. *Fax:* 703-306-0355; *E-Mail:* pharrima@nsf.gov

HARRINGTON, CHARLENE A, SOCIOLOGY. *Current Pos:* from asst to assoc prof, Dept Social & Behav Sci, Univ Calif, San Francisco, 83-89, dept vchair, 89-92, chair, 93-96, PROF, DEPT SOCIAL & BEHAV SCI, UNIV CALIF, SAN FRANCISCO, 89- *Personal Data:* b Sept 28, 41; m 76, Ben Yerger. *Educ:* Univ Kans, BS, 63; Univ Wash, MA, 68; Univ Calif, Berkeley, PhD(sociol/higher educ), 75. *Prof Exp:* Spec asst to dir, Calif State Dept Health, 75-76, dep dir, Div Licensing & Cert, 76-77; exec dir, Golden Empire Health Systs Agency, 78-80; assoc dir, Inst Health & Aging, Sch Nursing, Univ Calif, San Francisco, 81-93. *Mem:* Inst Med-Nat Acad Sci; Am Acad Nursing. *Res:* Published numerous articles in professional journals. *Mailing Add:* Dept Social & Behav Sci Univ Calif Rm N631 Box 0612 San Francisco CA 94143-0612. *Fax:* 415-476-6552; *E-Mail:* chas@itsa.ucsf.edu

HARRINGTON, DALTON, BOTANY, PHYCOLOGY. *Current Pos:* RETIRED. *Personal Data:* b Rice Lake, Wis, June 12, 34; m 59; c 2. *Educ:* Univ Omaha, BA, 61; Univ Mo, Kansas City, MS, 65; Univ Nebr, Lincoln, PhD(bot), 69. *Prof Exp:* Instr bot, Univ Nebr, Lincoln, 68-69; from asst prof to assoc prof, 69-77, assoc prof biol & chmn dept, 73-77, prof biol, 77- *Concurrent Pos:* Dir, Calif State Univ & Col Desert Res Ctr, Mojave Desert, 75- *Mem:* Am Inst Biol Sci; Bot Soc Am; Phycol Soc Am; Am Soc Limnol & Oceanog; Sigma Xi. *Res:* Ecology of aquatic plants, particularly members of Division Charophyta, studies of their excretion products and effect of these on other members of the aquatic biota. *Mailing Add:* Dept Biol Calif State Univ 5500 State Univ Pkwy San Bernardino CA 92407

HARRINGTON, DANIEL DALE, VETERINARY PATHOLOGY. *Current Pos:* ASSOC PROF VET PATH, PURDUE UNIV, 73- *Personal Data:* b Flint, Mich, Aug 12, 37; m 64; c 3. *Educ:* Mich State Univ, DVM, 62, MSc, 63; Mass Inst Technol, PhD(nutrit path), 69. *Prof Exp:* NIH fel, Mass Inst Technol, 63-69; asst prof nutrit path, Univ Ky, 69-73. *Mem:* Am Vet Med Asn; Asn Am Vet Col; Am Col Vet Path. *Res:* Nutritional diseases with emphasis on vitamin and mineral associated pathology, especially of the cardiovascular system. *Mailing Add:* 51 Edgewood Ct West Lafayette IN 47906

HARRINGTON, DAVID HOLMAN, FARM FINANCIAL MANAGEMENT. *Current Pos:* br chief, 79-86, dep dir, Econ Res Serv, 86-94, BR CHIEF, FARM & RURAL ECONOMY, USDA, 94- *Personal Data:* b Laconia, NH, Feb 13, 37; m 75; c 3. *Educ:* Cornell Univ, BS, 59; Univ NH, MS, 64; Purdue Univ, PhD(agr econ), 73. *Prof Exp:* Agr econ, econ res serv, USDA, 64-73; agr econ, Agr Can, 73-77; exec dir, Canfarm, Agr, Can, 77-79. *Mem:* Am Arg Econ Asn. *Res:* Research on structure of agriculture, farm financial management, financial conditions of American agriculture and farm rural economy linkages. *Mailing Add:* Red USDA Rm 940 C 1301 New York Ave NW Washington DC 20250

HARRINGTON, DAVID ROGERS, PHYSICS. *Current Pos:* from asst prof to assoc prof, 64-84, grad dir, 89-93, PROF PHYSICS, RUTGERS UNIV, 84- *Personal Data:* b North Tonawanda, NY, Sept 23, 35; m 63, 88, Rosemarie Mihlan; c Dominic. *Educ:* Carnegie Inst Technol, BS, 57, MS, 59, PhD(physics), 61. *Prof Exp:* NSF fel, 61-62; instr & res assoc physics, Cornell Univ, 62-63, actg asst prof, 63-64. *Mem:* Am Phys Soc; AAAS. *Res:* Theoretical nuclear physics. *Mailing Add:* Dept Physics & Astron Rutgers Univ PO Box 849 Piscataway NJ 08855-0849. *E-Mail:* drharr@physics.rutgers.edu

HARRINGTON, DEAN BUTLER, ELECTRICAL ENGINEERING, ELECTROMAGNETIC PHENOMENA. *Current Pos:* RETIRED. *Personal Data:* b Schenectady, NY; m 49, Barbara Stibbe; c Kim, Kevin & Jeffrey. *Educ:* Mass Inst Technol, BS, 44. *Honors & Awards:* Charles P Steinmetz Award, Gen Elec Co, 77; Nikola Tesla Award, Inst Elec & Electronics Engrs, 81. *Prof Exp:* Engr, Gen Elec Co, 44-67, mgr generator advan eng, 67-82. *Concurrent Pos:* Consult, elec eng, 82- *Mem:* Nat Acad Eng; fel Inst Elec & Electronics Engrs. *Res:* Electric power engineering; electric machine theory. *Mailing Add:* 22 Via Maria Dr Scotia NY 12302. *Fax:* 518-399-1314

HARRINGTON, EDMUND ALOYSIUS, JR, TELECOMMUNICATIONS SCIENCE, TELECOMMUNICATIONS ENGINEERING. *Current Pos:* DIR, CALIF MICROWAVE LABS. *Personal Data:* b Wareham, Mass, Dec 23, 43; m 70; c 1. *Educ:* Providence Col, BS, 65; Univ Notre Dame, PhD(physics), 70. *Honors & Awards:* Distinguished Serv Award, Armed Forces Commun & Electronics Asn, 77. *Prof Exp:* Mem tech staff switching, Bell Tel Labs, 70-71; eng specialist telecommun, GTE Sylvania Inc, 72- *Concurrent Pos:* Lectr, Northeastern Univ, 74-75, 79- & Boston Univ, 78-; nat sem leader, Telephony Publ Corp & Info Gatekeepers Inc, 78- *Mem:* Inst Elec & Electronics Engrs; Am Inst Physics; Am Phys Soc; Sigma Xi. *Res:* Telecommunication networks; computer communications; fiber optics; satellite communications. *Mailing Add:* GTE Gov Systs 77 A St Needham MA 02194

HARRINGTON, FRED HADDOX, ETHOLOGY, BEHAVIORAL ECOLOGY. *Current Pos:* from asst prof to assoc prof, 77-87, PROF, DEPT PSYCHOL, MT ST VINCENT UNIV, 87- *Personal Data:* b Albany, Calif, Nov 2, 47; m 72, 90, Karen Hollett; c Ian A & Justin P. *Educ:* Univ Del, BA, 69; State Univ NY, Stony Brook, PhD(biol), 75. *Prof Exp:* Fel ethology, Dalhousie Univ, 75-77. *Concurrent Pos:* Consult, Nfld-Labrador Wildlife Dir, 86-93, Labrador Inuit Asn, 88- & Parks Can, 93- *Mem:* Animal Behav Soc; Soc Conserv Biol; Int Soc Behav Ecol; Am Soc Naturalists. *Res:* Canid behavior and communication and their relation to ecology; social and environmental influences on olfactory and acoustic communication in wolves and coyotes; human attitudes toward animals; behavioral ecology of Caribou and Black Bear. *Mailing Add:* Dept Psychol Mt St Vincent Univ Halifax NS B3M 2J6 Can. *Fax:* 902-445-3960; *E-Mail:* fred.harrington@msvu.ca

HARRINGTON, GEORGE WILLIAM, ANALYTICAL CHEMISTRY. *Current Pos:* from instr to assoc prof, Temple Univ, 59-67, assoc dean, Col Lib Arts, 68-71, chmn dept, 78-81, PROF CHEM, TEMPLE UNIV, 67- *Personal Data:* b New York, NY, Nov 13, 29; m 55; c 2. *Educ:* NY Univ, AB, 54, PhD(chem), 59. *Prof Exp:* Asst chem, NY Univ, 57-59; proj engr, Philco Corp, 59. *Mem:* Am Chem Soc; Am Inst Chemists. *Res:* Electroanalytical chemistry; N-nitrosamines; instrumentation. *Mailing Add:* 1326 Meetinghouse Rd Jenkintown PA 19046

HARRINGTON, GLENN WILLIAM, PARASITOLOGY, MICROBIOLOGY. *Current Pos:* PROF MICROBIOL, WEBER STATE UNIV, OGDEN, UTAH, 93- *Personal Data:* b Los Angeles, Calif, Oct 13, 32; m 75, Marilyn Shreve; c 2. *Educ:* Univ Calif, Los Angeles, BA, 54, MA, 61; Rice Univ, PhD(parasitol, biol), 64. *Prof Exp:* Asst prof microbiol, State Univ NY Upstate Med Ctr, 66-70; asst prof, Univ Health Sci, 70-73; assoc prof, Univ Mo, Kansas City, 73-92. *Concurrent Pos:* NIH fel microbiol, State Univ NY Upstate Med Ctr, 64-66. *Mem:* Am Soc Parasitol; Soc Protozool; Am Soc Microbiol; Am Soc Clin Path. *Res:* Lipid chemistry and metabolism of tapeworms and algae; dental microbiology. *Mailing Add:* Dept Microbiol Weber State Univ 3750 Harrison Blvd Ogden UT 84408-0001

HARRINGTON, JAMES FOSTER, OLERICULTURE. *Current Pos:* asst prof truck crops & asst olericulturist, 46-50, assoc prof veg crops & assoc olericulturist, 50-58, prof, 58-80, EMER PROF VEG CROPS & OLERICULTURIST, UNIV CALIF, DAVIS, 80- *Personal Data:* b Newark, NJ, Nov 24, 16; m 39; c 3. *Educ:* Ohio State Univ, BS, 39, MS, 40; Cornell Univ, PhD(veg crops), 44. *Prof Exp:* Asst res prof hort, Iowa State Col, 44-46. *Concurrent Pos:* Fels, Fulbright, 54-55 & USDA, 62-63; consult, Agency Int Develop, Brazil, 65-66, Food Agr Org, Egypt, 69 & Rockefeller Found, India, 69. *Mem:* AAAS; Am Soc Hort Sci; Am Soc Plant Physiol; Am Soc Agron. *Res:* Seed physiology; vegetable crops; aging of seeds. *Mailing Add:* Dept Veg Crops Univ Calif Davis CA 95616

HARRINGTON, JAMES PATRICK, ASTROPHYSICS. *Current Pos:* Asst prof, 67-74, ASSOC PROF ASTRON, UNIV MD, COLLEGE PARK, 74- *Personal Data:* b Salem, Ohio, Dec 21, 39; m 66; c 3. *Educ:* Univ Chicago, SB, 61; Ohio State Univ, MSc, 64, PhD(astron), 67. *Mem:* Am Astron Soc; Int Astron Union; Royal Astron Soc. *Res:* Gaseous nebulae; radiative transfer; stellar atmospheres. *Mailing Add:* Astron Prog Space Sci Bldg 224 Univ Md College Park MD 20742

HARRINGTON, JOHN VINCENT, physics, electrical engineering, for more information see previous edition

HARRINGTON, JOSEPH ANTHONY, COMBUSTION. *Current Pos:* SR RES PHYSICIST, ENG & ENVIRON RES, AMOCO OIL CO, 81- *Personal Data:* b Monroe, Mich, Aug 23, 39; m 65; c 1. *Educ:* Univ Mich, Ann Arbor, BS, 62; Northeastern Univ, MS, 70; York Univ, PhD(physics), 70. *Prof Exp:* Sr scientist, Systs Div, Avco Corp, 62-67; staff scientist, 69-70; prin res scientist assoc, res staff, Ford Motor Co, 70-81. *Mem:* Combustion Inst; Sigma Xi; Am Asn Artificial Intel; Inst Elec & Electronics Engrs. *Res:* Determination of fundamental chemical and radiative properties of gases or their diagnostic applications; hydrocarbon fuel combustion and phase transition kinetics; combustion of solid matter; artificial intelligence-expert systems. *Mailing Add:* HDS Computers Inc 2012 Ogden Ave Lisle IL 60532

HARRINGTON, JOSEPH D, ZOOLOGY, PHYSIOLOGY. *Current Pos:* Asst prof biol, 60-69, acad dean, 65-69, pres, 69-74, PROF BIOL, CARROLL COL, MONT, 74- *Personal Data:* b Butte, Mont, Aug 24, 30. *Educ:* Carroll Col, Mont, AB, 52; Cath Univ Am, MS, 58, PhD(biol), 60. *Mem:* AAAS; Am Inst Biol Sci; Sigma Xi; Am Soc Microbiol. *Mailing Add:* Dept Biol & Chem Carroll Col 1601 N Benton Ave Helena MT 59625-0001

HARRINGTON, JOSEPH DONALD, AGRONOMY. *Current Pos:* RETIRED. *Personal Data:* b Washington, DC, Oct 6, 26; m 51, Jean Frances Duvall; c Daniel M & Nancy J (deceased). *Educ:* Univ Md, BS, 53; Pa State Univ, MS, 55, PhD(agron), 59. *Prof Exp:* From asst prof to prof agron, Pa State Univ, University Park, 53-92. *Mem:* Am Soc Agron; Potato Asn Am. *Res:* Cultural evaluations and ecological factors influencing the quantity and quality of white potatoes for fresh market and processing purposes. *Mailing Add:* 806 S Sparks St State College PA 16801

HARRINGTON, MARSHALL CATHCART, optics, for more information see previous edition

HARRINGTON, ROBERT D(EAN), METROLOGY, STANDARDS. *Current Pos:* RETIRED. *Personal Data:* b Philip, SDak, Apr 23, 28; m 50, Eilene Smathers; c Donald & Diane. *Educ:* Univ Colo, BS, 51, MS, 52. *Prof Exp:* Physicist, Naval Res Lab, 52-53; physicist, Nat Bur Stand, Boulder Labs, 53-67, asst div chief, 67-68, asst chief tech admin & coord, 68-70, prog coordr, 70-88. *Mem:* Am Sci Affil; Sigma Xi. *Res:* Magnetic materials, measurements and phenomena at radio, microwave and optical frequencies; lasers; metrology and standards; administration. *Mailing Add:* 5321 Holmes Pl Boulder CO 80303

HARRINGTON, ROBERT JOSEPH, POWER SYSTEMS ANALYSIS, TRANSIENT PHENOMENA ANALYSIS. *Current Pos:* assoc prof, 80-85, PROF ELEC ENG, GEORGE WASHINGTON UNIV, WASHINGTON, DC, 85-, CHMN, 91- *Personal Data:* b Rochdale, Eng, July 6, 41; US citizen; m 64; c 4. *Educ:* Univ Liverpool, BEng, 62, PhD(elec eng), 67. *Prof Exp:* Res eng elec power, Nelson Res Labs, English Elec Co, 66-67; lectr elec eng, Univ Newcastle Upon Tyne, UK, 68-69. *Concurrent Pos:* Expert witness, elec equip. *Mem:* Sr mem Inst Elec & Electronics Engrs; fel Gt Brit Inst Elec Engrs. *Res:* Transient analysis of electrical power systems and machinery; traveling wave phenomena on power transmissions systems; corona and field effects of extra high voltage systems. *Mailing Add:* Dept Elec Eng & Comput Sci Acad Ctr Rm 609 George Washington Univ Washington DC 20052

HARRINGTON, RODNEY B, ANIMAL SCIENCE, STATISTICS. *Current Pos:* from instr to assoc prof, 62-69, PROF ANIMAL SCI, PURDUE UNIV, 69- *Personal Data:* b Bethel, Maine, Apr 30, 31; m 59; c 2. *Educ:* Univ Maine, BS, 54; Okla State Univ, MS, 57, PhD(animal breeding, statist), 63; Univ New South Wales, MSc, 62. *Prof Exp:* Asst animal sci, Okla State Univ, 56-57, 59-62; tech officer, Univ New South Wales, 57-59. *Concurrent Pos:* Vis sr res fel, Dept Animal Breeding, Agr Univ, Wageningen, Neth. *Mem:* Am Soc Animal Sci; Biomet Soc; AAAS. *Res:* Design of experiments and applications of computers in animal science; population genetics. *Mailing Add:* Dept Animal Sci Purdue Univ West Lafayette IN 47907-1968

HARRINGTON, RODNEY E, BIOCHEMISTRY, PHYSICAL CHEMISTRY. *Current Pos:* prof chem, 72-81, chmn dept, 72-76, PROF BIOCHEM, UNIV NEV, RENO, 81- *Personal Data:* b Mayville, NDak, Jan 9, 32; m 79, Ilga Winicov; c 2. *Educ:* Univ SDak, BA, 53; Univ Wash, PhD(phys chem), 60. *Prof Exp:* Res chemist, Ames Lab, AEC, 53-56; res assoc biophys, Univ Calif, San Diego, 60-62; asst prof chem, Univ Ariz, 62-65; from asst prof to prof, Univ Calif, Davis, 65-72. *Mem:* Am Chem Soc; Am Phys Soc; AAAS; Fed Am Socs Exp Biol. *Res:* DNA sequence-dependent structure and nucleoprotein complexes; transcriptional regulation. *Mailing Add:* Dept Biochem Univ Nev Reno NV 89507-0014

HARRINGTON, ROGER F(ULLER), ELECTRICAL ENGINEERING. *Current Pos:* From instr to prof, 48-68, DISTINGUISHED PROF ELEC ENG, SYRACUSE UNIV, 68- *Personal Data:* b Buffalo, NY, Dec 24, 25; m 54; c 4. *Educ:* Syracuse Univ, BS, 48; Ohio State Univ, PhD(elec eng), 52. *Honors & Awards:* Sigma Xi Res Award, 71; Schlesinger Award, Inst Elec & Electronics Engrs, Distinguished Achievement Award, 89. *Concurrent Pos:* Vis prof, Univ Calif, Berkeley, 64-65, E China Normal Univ, 83; guest prof, Tech Univ Denmark, 69-70; vis scientist, Yugoslavian Academies Sci, 72. *Mem:* Fel Inst Elec & Electronics Engrs; Int Sci Radio Union; Am Asn Univ Professors. *Res:* Electromagnetic field theory; electric network theory; applied mathematics. *Mailing Add:* 5424 N Strada De Rubinot Tucson AZ 85750

HARRINGTON, ROY VICTOR, INORGANIC CHEMISTRY. *Current Pos:* assoc dir res, 68-72, VPRES & CORP DIR RES, FERRO CORP, 72- *Personal Data:* b Brooklyn, NY, Sept 28, 28; m 52; c 3. *Educ:* Polytech Inst Brooklyn, BS, 49; Univ Colo, PhD(chem), 56. *Prof Exp:* Chemist, Gen Foods Corp, 49-52; chemist, Corning Glass Works, 55-58, supvr, 58-63, mgr appl res glass, 63-64, mgr mat res, 64-66, mgr appl chem res, 66-68. *Concurrent Pos:* Panel mem, Nuclear Waste Disposal, Nat Acad Sci. *Mem:* Am Chem Soc; Am Ceramic Soc; Indust Res Inst. *Res:* Research management; chemistry and physics of glassy state; high temperature inorganic chemistry; frit; color; fiber glass; refractories; abrasives; composites. *Mailing Add:* 6821 Rosemont Dr Brecksville OH 44141-2613

HARRINGTON, SANDRA SERENA, GASTROINTESTINAL PHYSIOLOGY-ESOPHAGEAL MOTILITY, RESPIRATORY PHYSIOLOGY-CONTROL OF BREATHING. *Current Pos:* ASST PROF BIOL, CARTHAGE COL, 92- *Personal Data:* b Washington DC, May 30, 60; m 89, Thomas J. *Educ:* Col William & Mary, BS, 81; Univ Va, ME, 85, PhD(biomed eng), 89. *Prof Exp:* Polysomnographic technologist, Stanford Univ, Sleep Dis Clin & Res Ctr, 81-83; res assoc, Dept Internal Med, Univ Va, 89-90; asst prof radiol, Med Col Wis, 90-92. *Concurrent Pos:* Instr biomed eng, Marquette Univ, 91; adj instr biol, Univ Wis-Parkside, 91-92; lectr human anat & physiol, Carthage Col, 92. *Mem:* Biomed Eng Soc; Sigma Xi. *Res:* Role of smooth muscle in esophageal motility and relaxation of the lower esophageal sphincter. *Mailing Add:* 7310 Third Ave Kenosha WI 53143-5537. *Fax:* 414-551-6208; *E-Mail:* sandy@.cns.carthage.edu

HARRINGTON, STEVEN JAY, COMPUTER GRAPHICS, SYSTEMS DESIGN. *Current Pos:* PRIN SCIENTIST, XEROX CORP, 81- *Personal Data:* b Portland, Ore, Nov 28, 47; m 69. *Educ:* Ore State Univ, BS(physics) & BS(math), 68; Univ Wash, MS(physics) & MS(comput sci), 69, PhD(physics), 76. *Prof Exp:* Res assoc prof comput physics, Univ Utah, 76-78; asst prof comput sci, State Univ NY, Brockport, 78-81. *Mem:* Asn Comput Mach; Inst Elec & Electronics Engrs; Soc Info Display. *Res:* Architectures, algorithms, and system design for electronic imaging. *Mailing Add:* Xerox Xerox Square Rochester NY 14644-0001

HARRINGTON, WALTER JOEL, MATHEMATICS. *Current Pos:* RETIRED. *Personal Data:* b Salamanca, NY, Nov 9, 16; m 41; c 2. *Educ:* Cornell Univ, AB, 37, AM, 38, PhD(math), 41. *Prof Exp:* Instr math, Pa State Univ, 41-44; res assoc, Allegheny Ballistics Lab, Md, 44-46; vis asst prof, Cornell Univ, 46-47; from asst prof to assoc prof math, Pa State Univ, 47-57; prof math, NC State Univ, 57-82, actg head dept, 79-80, emer prof, 82- *Concurrent Pos:* Dir, Dept Defense Res Proj, 67-72. *Mem:* Am Math Soc; Soc Indust & Appl Math; Math Asn Am; Sigma Xi. *Res:* Number theory; analysis of exterior ballistics; analysis and operational mathematics. *Mailing Add:* 3010 Ruffin St Raleigh NC 27607-4060

HARRINGTON, WILLIAM J, JR, LEUKEMIA, LYMPHOMA. *Current Pos:* internship & residency, Jackson Mem Med Ctr, Univ Miami, 84-87, clin fel, Dept Med, Div Hemat, 87-89, res fel, 89-91, ASST PROF MED, SCH MED, UNIV MIAMI, 91- *Educ:* Fla Int Univ, Miami, BS, 80; Univ Miami, PhD(med), 84; Am Bd Internal Med, dipl, 87. *Concurrent Pos:* Fulbright grantee, Fed Univ Bahia, Brazil, 94; prog dir viral oncol, Sylvester Cancer Ctr, 96. *Mem:* Am Col Physicians; Leukemia Soc Am; Am Soc Hemat; Am Soc Clin Res. *Mailing Add:* Sch Med Univ Miami Miami FL 33136

HARRIOTT, PETER, CHEMICAL ENGINEERING. *Current Pos:* From asst prof to prof, 53-66, FRED H RHODES PROF CHEM ENG, CORNELL UNIV, 75- *Personal Data:* b Ithaca, NY, July 21, 27; m 53, Mary White; c George, James, John, Paul & Douglas. *Educ:* Cornell Univ, BCE, 49; Mass Inst Technol, ScD, 52. *Mem:* Am Chem Soc; Am Inst Chem Engrs; Sigma Xi. *Res:* Chemical kinetics; reactor design; membrane separation; air pollution control. *Mailing Add:* 139 Ellis Hollow Creek Rd Ithaca NY 14850

HARRIS (NOEL), ANN, ENVIRONMENTAL GEOLOGY. *Current Pos:* PROF GEOL, YOUNGSTOWN STATE UNIV, 61-; CONSULT, 77- *Personal Data:* b Cleveland, Ohio, Sept 6, 34; m 53, 80; c 2. *Educ:* Kent State Univ, BS, 56; Miami Univ, MS, 58. *Prof Exp:* Res engr micros anal, Ferro Corp, 58-59; geol aide field mapping & res, US Geol Surv, 59-60; asst chem, Summer Inst, Wis State Col, Superior, 60-61. *Concurrent Pos:* Adv, Struthers Total Environ Educ Prog, 73-; Environ Rev Comt, 75-; mem, adv comt energy, app by Gov Richard Celeste, Ohio, 84-87. *Mem:* NAm Thermal Anal Soc; Nat Asn Geol Teachers; Geol Soc Am; Am Inst Prof Geologist. *Res:* The location, history and layout of abandoned deep coal and/or clay mines; engineering methods best suited for the stabilization of these mines when subsidence occurs or the sealing of the dangerous drift, slope or shaft openings. *Mailing Add:* Dept Geol Youngstown State Univ 1 Univ Plaza Youngstown OH 44555

HARRIS, ALAN WILLIAM, ASTRONOMY, PLANETARY PHYSICS. *Current Pos:* Supvr, Earth & Planetary Physics Group, 83-92, RES SCIENTIST, JET PROPULSION LAB, 80-, SR MEM TECH STAFF, 92- *Personal Data:* b Portland, Ore, Aug 3, 44; m 70, Rose M Spitt; c W Donald, David S & Catherine R. *Educ:* Calif Inst Technol, BS, 66; Univ Calif, Los Angeles, MS, 67, PhD(planetary & space sci), 75. *Honors & Awards:* Asteroid 2929 Harris Named in Recognition of Planetary Res. *Concurrent Pos:* Mem tech staff, Jet Propulsion Lab, 74-92; prin investr, Lunar & Planetary Prog, NASA, 76-; vis prof physics, Univ Calif, Santa Barbara, 78; vis prof earth & space sci, Univ Calif, Los Angeles, 79; pres, Comn 15 Int Astron Union, 91-94; chmn, Div Dynamics, Am Astron Soc, 91-92, secy/treas, Div Planetary Sci, 95- *Mem:* Am Astron Soc; Am Geophys Union; Int Astron Union. *Res:* Dynamical evolution of the solar system, origin and evolution of satellite and ring systems; physical studies of asteroids; author of one book and over 50 technical papers in books, journals, conference proceedings, etc. *Mailing Add:* Jet Propulsion Lab MS 183-501 4800 Oak Grove Dr Pasadena CA 91109. *Fax:* 818-354-0966; *E-Mail:* awharris@lithos.jpl.nasa.gov

HARRIS, ALBERT KENNETH, JR, EMBRYOLOGY, CELL BIOLOGY. *Current Pos:* from asst prof to assoc prof zool, 72-83, PROF BIOL, UNIV NC, CHAPEL HILL, 83- *Personal Data:* b Colorado Springs, Colo, Nov 5, 43; m 65, Elizabeth Holder; c Hannah, Thomas & Frieda. *Educ:* Swarthmore Col, BA, 65; Yale Univ, MPhil, 70, PhD(biol), 71. *Prof Exp:* Damon Runyon-Walter Winchell Mem Fund res fel cancer res, Strangeways Res Lab, Eng, 71-72. *Concurrent Pos:* Distinguished vis prof zool, Univ Calif, Davis, 91. *Mem:* Am Soc Cell Biol; Soc Develop Biol. *Res:* Mechanism of locomotion of tissue cells in embryonic development, cancer and cell sorting; role of adhesion in cell motility; connective tissue morphogenesis; mechanism of contractile ring formation in cytokinesis. *Mailing Add:* Univ NC Dept Biol Coker Hall CB 3280 Chapel Hill NC 27599-3280. *Fax:* 919-962-1625; *E-Mail:* akharris@med.unc.edu

HARRIS, ALEX L, biochemical pharmacology, enzymology, for more information see previous edition

HARRIS, ALEXANDER L, PHYSICAL CHEMISTRY. *Current Pos:* Mem tech staff, Bell Labs Lucent Technols, 85-93, distinguished mem tech staff, 93-95, res tech mgr, 95-96, DEPT HEAD, MAT RES CHEM, BELL LABS LUCENT TECHNOLS, 96. *Personal Data:* b Madison, Wis, Jan 27, 54; m 87, Annemarie Drummey; c Kendall. *Educ:* Swarthmore Col, BA, 78; Univ Calif, Berkeley, PhD(phys chem), 85. *Mem:* Am Phys Soc; Am Chem Soc; AAAS; Sigma Xi; Optical Soc Am. *Res:* Physical chemistry of interfaces and surfaces; polymer physical chemistry especially for optical applications; holographic data storage. *Mailing Add:* Bell Labs Lucent Technols Rm 1D-346 Murray Hill NJ 07974. *Fax:* 908-582-3958; *E-Mail:* alexh@bell-labs.com

HARRIS, ANDREW LEONARD, NEUROPHYSIOLOGY, MEMBRANE ION CHANNELS. *Current Pos:* asst prof, 85-91, ASSOC PROF, DEPT BIOPHYS, JOHNS HOPKINS UNIV, 91- *Personal Data:* b Saranac Lake, NY, Oct 18, 51. *Educ:* Univ Calif, San Diego, BA, 72; Stanford Univ, PhD(neurosci), 79. *Prof Exp:* Fel, Dept Neurosci, Albert Einstein Col Med, 79-82; res assoc, Dept Biol Sci, Stanford Univ, 82-84; res assoc, Dept Anat, Harvard Med Sch, 84-85. *Concurrent Pos:* Staff fel, Div Comput Res & Technol, Nat Inst Arthritis, Diabetes & Digestive & Kidney Dis, NIH, 85. *Mem:* Biophys Soc; Soc Neurosci; Am Soc Cell Biol; AAAS; Soc Gen Physiologists. *Res:* Cellular neurophysiology; ion channels biophysics; regulation and gating of gap junction channels in native membranes and reconstituted systems. *Mailing Add:* Dept Biophys Johns Hopkins Univ 3400 N Charles St Baltimore MD 21218

HARRIS, ARLO DEAN, INORGANIC CHEMISTRY, SYMMETRY GROUP THEORY. *Current Pos:* from asst prof to assoc prof chem, 67-78, prog inorg chem, 79-88, EMER PROF INORG CHEM, CALIF STATE UNIV, SAN BERNARDINO, 88- *Personal Data:* b Dayton, Ohio, Sept 17, 34. *Educ:* Univ Dayton, BSc, 61; Tulane Univ, PhD(chem), 64. *Prof Exp:* Instr chem, Univ Dayton, 59-61; teaching asst, Tulane Univ, 61-64; fel, Univ Calif, Berkeley, 64-65; asst prof chem, Calif State Col, Fullerton, 65-67. *Concurrent Pos:* Vis lectr, Univ Nottingham, 69-70; res assoc, Univ London, King's Col, 78-79; vis prof, Univ Khartoum, Sudan, 80 & Univ Queensland, Brisbane Australia, 82, 84 & 87. *Mem:* Am Chem Soc; Royal Soc Chem; fel Am Int Chemists; NY Acad Sci; Am Acad Arts & Sci. *Res:* Hydride complexes of platinum metals; cancer chemotherapy of cis-platin derivatives. *Mailing Add:* 1005 Chelsea Ave Dayton OH 45420-2726

HARRIS, ARTHUR BROOKS, SOLID STATE PHYSICS. *Current Pos:* from asst prof to assoc prof, 65-77, PROF PHYSICS, UNIV PA, 77- *Personal Data:* b Boston, Mass, Mar 25, 35; m 58; c 3. *Educ:* Harvard Univ, AB, 56, AM, 59, PhD(solid state physics), 62. *Prof Exp:* Asst physics, Harvard Univ, 57-58, res asst, 58-61; res assoc, Duke Univ, 61-62, instr, 62-64; res assoc, UK Atomic Energy Auth, 64-65. *Mem:* Am Phys Soc. *Res:* Calorimetric determination of energy levels in magnetic compounds; static and dynamic properties of the chemical shift tensor; theory of metals in the narrow band limit. *Mailing Add:* Dept Physics Univ Pa Philadelphia PA 19132

HARRIS, ARTHUR HORNE, VERTEBRATE PALEOBIOLOGY, VERTEBRATE ZOOLOGY. *Current Pos:* from asst prof to assoc prof, 65-71, PROF BIOL, UNIV TEX, EL PASO, 71- *Personal Data:* b Middleborough, Mass, May 18, 31; div; c 3. *Educ:* Univ NMex, BA, 58, MS, 59, PhD(vert zool), 65. *Prof Exp:* Asst prof vert zool, Ft Hays Kans State Col, 63-65. *Concurrent Pos:* Cur vert paleobiol, Lab Environ Biol, 76-, co-dir resource collections, 80-; managing ed, Southwestern Naturalist, 78-82. *Mem:* Am Soc Mammal; Soc Vert Paleont; Am Quaternary Asn; Sigma Xi. *Res:* Distribution and ecology of modern Southwestern vertebrates; past distributions and environments as interpreted from fossil and archaeological faunas, particularly of the late Pleistocene and post-Pleistocene. *Mailing Add:* Dept Biol Sci Univ Tex 500 W University Ave El Paso TX 79968-8900

HARRIS, B(ENJAMIN) L(OUIS), CHEMICAL ENGINEERING. *Current Pos:* RETIRED. *Personal Data:* b Savannah, Ga, Aug 1, 17; m 42, Janet Diekmann; c Benjamin S II, Stefanie (Hunt), Deborah (Kommalan), Penelope (Clifton) & Rebecca (Gutim). *Educ:* Johns Hopkins Univ, BE, 38, PhD(chem eng), 41. *Prof Exp:* Res asst to Dr Frankenburg, Johns Hopkins Univ, 41, asst prof chem eng, 46-53; pres, Eng Res Co, Md, 47-53; chief plants br & dep asst chief, Toxic Chem Warfare Div, Res & Eng Command, 52-55; asst to sci dir, Chem Warfare Labs, 55-60, dep dir develop, 60-62, dir develop support, 62-66, chief systs anal div, Army Chem Res & Develop Labs, 66, dep asst dir, Off of Dir Defense Res & Eng, 66-70, tech dir, Edgewood Arsenal, 70-77; dep dir & tech dir, US Army Chem Systs Lab, 77-81; pres & chief exec officer, Eng Res Co, Glen Arm, Md, 81-87. *Concurrent Pos:* Mem comt hazardous mat, Nat Acad Sci-Nat Res Coun, chmn risk anal panel, 67-76; consult, 87- *Mem:* Fel AAAS; Am Chem Soc; fel Am Inst Chem Engrs; Sigma Xi; Am Defense Preparedness Asn. *Res:* Adsorption of gases by solids; adsorption from solution; permeability of organic films to water and gases; physical constants; stability and corrosion of chemical agents; operations research; engineering evaluation; mass transfer; management of research, development and engineering. *Mailing Add:* 11323 Glen Arm Rd Glen Arm MD 21057

HARRIS, BARNEY, JR, DAIRY SCIENCE. *Current Pos:* RETIRED. *Personal Data:* b Prescott, Ark, Dec 20, 31; m 64; c 3. *Educ:* Okla State Univ, BS, 54, PhD(dairy nutrit), 64; La State Univ, MS, 56. *Prof Exp:* Instr dairy, Southern State Col, 58-60; from asst prof to prof dairy sci, Univ Fla, 63-94, exten dairy nutritionist, Fla Coop Exten Serv, 63-69. *Concurrent Pos:* Chmn, Fla Dairy Indust Tech Coun, 71- & Fla Prod Conf, 71-88. *Mem:* Am Dairy Sci Asn. *Res:* Effect of parakeratosis on ruminant absorption in dairy calves; aueromycin feeding to dairy calves; nutrient requirements for high milk production; feeding and herd arrangements; studies with roughage by-products for dairy cattle; the value of sodium bicarbonate, fat and enzymes in dairy rations; mineral needs of dairy cattle; protein sources for dairy cattle; personnel management on large dairies; feed additives for dairy cattle; feeding and management of dairy goats. *Mailing Add:* 1817 NW 22nd Dr Gainesville FL 32605

HARRIS, BEN GERALD, ENZYMOLOGY. *Current Pos:* asst prof, 68-73, assoc prof, depts basic health sci & biol sci, 73-77, PROF DEPT BIOCHEM, NTEX STATE UNIV, 77- & TEX COL OSTEOP MED, 77- *Personal Data:* b Altus, Okla, Sept 25, 40; m 63; c 2. *Educ:* Southwestern State Col, Okla, BS, 62; Okla State Univ, MS, 65, PhD(physiol), 67. *Prof Exp:* NIH & univ fels physiol, Rice Univ, 67-68. *Mem:* Am Chem Soc; Am Soc Biol Chemists;

Am Soc Parasitologists. *Res:* Structure and function of enzymes; protein associations with cell organelles; metabolism of parasite enzymes; control mechanisms in parasites. *Mailing Add:* Dept Biochem Tex Col Osteo Med NTex State Univ 3500 Camp Bowie Blvd Ft Worth TX 76107-2699. *Fax:* 817-735-2133

HARRIS, BERNARD, MATHEMATICAL STATISTICS, COMBINATORICS. *Current Pos:* PROF MATH & STATIST, DEPT STATIST, UNIV WIS-MADISON, 64- *Personal Data:* b New York, NY, June 20, 26; m 49, 83; c 6. *Educ:* City Col NY, BBA, 46; George Washington Univ, MA, 53; Stanford Univ, PhD(statist), 58. *Honors & Awards:* Wilks Mem Medal, 82. *Prof Exp:* Statistician, Richard Manville Assocs, 47; dir, Res Dept, Statist Serv Bur, NY, 48-50; math statistician, US Census Bur, 50-52; mathematician, Nat Security Agency, 52-58; from asst prof to assoc prof math, Univ Nebr, 58-64. *Concurrent Pos:* Instr, George Washington Univ, 52-57; prof & lectr, Am Univ, 57-58; consult, Agr Res Serv, USDA, 59-63; vis prof, Eindhoven Technol Univ, 70- & Tech Univ Munich, 73-74; vchmn, Comt Nuclear Regulatory Res, Am Statist Asn, chmn, comt on AIDS, statist working group, Mil Handbook Plastics Aerospace Vehicles. *Mem:* Economet Soc; fel Am Statist Asn; fel Inst Math Statist; Am Math Soc; Int Statist Inst; AAAS; Bernoulli Soc. *Res:* Discrete stochastic processes; moment inequalities; combinatorial methods in probability and statistics; reliability theory; statistical decision theory. *Mailing Add:* Dept Statist Univ Wis 1210 W Dayton St Madison WI 53706

HARRIS, BERNARD, ELECTRICAL ENGINEERING. *Current Pos:* PRES, HARRIS SCI SERV, 79- *Personal Data:* b New York, NY, Oct 13, 27; m 52, 72, Maria; c Richard, Lynn, Clifford, Robert, Bernard, Peter, Steven, Barbara & William. *Educ:* Cooper Union, BEE, 49; Columbia Univ, MS, 51, EngScD, 61; Pace Univ, MBA, 78. *Prof Exp:* Design engr, RCA Lab Div, 51-54; res scientist syst, NY Univ, 54-63; tech & mgt staff, Sperry Rand Corp, 63-65; res scientist oceanog, Hudson Lab, Columbia Univ, 65-68; chief engr microwaves, Polarad Electronics Corp, 68; vpres, Ocean & Atmospheric Sci, Inc, 68-79. *Concurrent Pos:* Adj assoc prof, NY Univ, Pratt Inst & Manhattan Col, 60-70 assoc prof, Manhattan Col, 79- *Mem:* Acoust Soc Am; Inst Elec & Electronics Engrs; Oper Res Soc Am; AAAS; Am Soc Eng Educ; Sigma Xi. *Res:* Applications of atmospheric and oceanographic acoustics to such diverse fields as noise pollution and Navy oceanography. *Mailing Add:* 15 Overlook Rd Dobbs Ferry NY 10522-3209

HARRIS, BEVERLY HOWARD, MATHEMATICAL ANALYSIS. *Current Pos:* RETIRED. *Personal Data:* b Lee's Summit, Mo, Aug 22, 27; m 50, Zorene Pruitt; c Susan A (Spurgeon), Steven H & Joy A (Crow). *Educ:* Southwest Mo State Univ, BS, 49; Univ Mo, MA, 53, DEd, 63. *Prof Exp:* High sch teacher, 49-51; instr, Southwest Baptist Univ, 52-64, prof math & chmn dept, 64-89. *Mem:* Math Asn Am. *Res:* Mathematics education; undergraduate mathematics, specifically elementary and intermediate analysis; summation of infinite series in intermediate analysis. *Mailing Add:* 910 E Division Bolivar MO 65613

HARRIS, BRUNO, MATHEMATICS. *Current Pos:* assoc prof, 61-65, PROF MATH, BROWN UNIV, 65- *Personal Data:* b Ploesti, Romania, Mar 1, 32; nat US. *Educ:* Calif Inst Technol, BS, 52; Yale Univ, PhD, 56. *Prof Exp:* NSF fel math, Yale Univ, 56-57; from instr to asst prof, Northwestern Univ, 57-60; Air Force Off Sci Res res assoc, Inst Advan Study, 60-61. *Concurrent Pos:* Mem, Inst Advan Study, 64-65; vis prof math, Princeton Univ, 81. *Mem:* Am Math Soc. *Res:* Algebra; geometry; homogeneous spaces; vector bundles and k-theory. *Mailing Add:* Dept Math Brown Univ Brown Sta Box 1917 Providence RI 02912

HARRIS, C EARL, JR, GEOLOGY, MINERALOGY & PETROLOGY. *Current Pos:* chmn, Dept Geol, 61-77, from assoc prof to prof, 75-92, EMER PROF ADJ PROF GEOL, YOUNGSTOWN STATE UNIV, 92- *Personal Data:* b Mineral Point, Wis, May 1, 30; div; c 2. *Educ:* Kent State Univ, BS, 57; Miami Univ, MS, 58; Sussex Col Technol, PhD, 70. *Hon Degrees:* DSc, Ohio Christian Col, 70. *Prof Exp:* Areal geologist, US Geol Surv, 58-59; instr geol, Wis State Univ, Superior, 59-61. *Concurrent Pos:* Geol consult, Columbiana County Prosecutor's Off, 74-75; mem screening comt prof cert, Am Inst Prof Geologists. *Mem:* AAAS; fel Geol Soc Am; Am Inst Prof Geologists; Am Geol Inst; Sigma Xi. *Res:* Subsurface stratigraphy of Louisiana; structural geology of Grandfather Mountain Region, North Carolina; geology of Catskill Mountains, New York; Ohio Devonian biostratigraphy; origin of salt domes; influence of industrial wastes on surface-subsurface water. *Mailing Add:* 3333 Kiwatha Rd Youngstown OH 44511

HARRIS, C(HARLES) LEON, NEUROBIOLOGY. *Current Pos:* From asst prof to assoc prof, 70-81, PROF BIOL, STATE UNIV NY COL PLATTSBURGH, 81- *Personal Data:* b Christiansburg, Va, Jan 3, 43; m 71, Mary J Zewe. *Educ:* Va Polytech Inst, BS, 66; Pa State Univ, MS, 67, PhD(biophys), 69. *Mem:* AAAS; Soc Integrative & Comp Biol; Sigma Xi; Am Inst Biol Sci. *Res:* Mechanisms of learning and memory; history and philosophy of biology. *Mailing Add:* Dept Biol Sci State Univ NY Plattsburgh NY 12901. *Fax:* 518-561-2685; *E-Mail:* harriscl@splava.cc.plattsburgh.edu

HARRIS, CARL MATTHEW, OPERATIONS RESEARCH, SYSTEMS ENGINEERING. *Current Pos:* BDM PROF OPER RES & ENG & ASSOC DEAN, SCH INFO, TECHNOL & ENG, GEORGE MASON UNIV, 85- *Personal Data:* b Brooklyn, NY, Mar 29, 40; m 69, Alice Follender; c Naomi & Margo. *Educ:* Queens Col, NY, BS, 60; Polytech Inst Brooklyn, MS, 62, PhD(math), 66. *Prof Exp:* Instr math, St John's Univ, NY, 63-65; sr res mathematician, Eng Res Ctr, Western Elec Co, 65-67; mem tech staff, Adv Res Dept, Res Anal Corp, 67-70; assoc prof opers res, George Washington Univ, 70-75; prof indust eng & opers res & chmn dept, Syracuse Univ, 75-78, consult, 78-81; prof systs eng, Univ Va, 81-85. *Concurrent Pos:* Instr, Rutgers Univ, 66; assoc prof lectr, George Washington Univ, 67-70; consult, US Dept Energy, Washington, DC, Dept Corrections, Syracuse Police Dept, US Dept Justice, US Dept Com & US Dept State, Nat Inst Standards & Technol, US Dept Treas, NASA. *Mem:* Sigma Xi; Inst Indust Engrs; Am Statist Asn; Am Soc Eng Educ; Inst Opers Res & Mgt Sci (secy, 87-90, pres, 90-91); Math Asn Am; Inst Opers Res & Mgt Sci. *Res:* Methodological research in applied probability and statistics with emphasis on queuing theory and digital simulation; applied research in analysis of public systems. *Mailing Add:* 12016 Whippoorwill Lane Rockville MD 20852. *Fax:* 703-993-1521; *E-Mail:* charris@.gmu.edu

HARRIS, CECIL CRAIG, NUCLEAR MEDICINE. *Current Pos:* assoc prof, 71-92, EMER PROF RADIOL, DIV NUCLEAR MED, DUKE UNIV, MED CTR, 92- *Personal Data:* b Raymond, Miss, Feb 20, 25; m 47; c 3. *Educ:* Univ Tenn, BS, 49, MS, 51. *Prof Exp:* Instr elec eng, Miss State Univ, 49-50; jr develop engr, Oak Ridge Sch Reactor Tech, 50-52, develop engr, Physics Div, Oak Ridge 3949 Lab, 52-57, res staff mem, Thermonuclear Div, 57-67. *Concurrent Pos:* Mem, Task Group Scanning, Int Comn Radiation Units & Measurements, 63-68. *Mem:* Soc Nuclear Med (secy, 62-65, vpres, 66-67, pres, 68-69); Am Col Nuclear Med; fel Am Col Nuclear Physicians; fel Am Col Radiol; Radiol Soc NAm. *Res:* Development of training materials and methodology in nuclear medicine science; development of instrumentation for evaluation of coronary artery hemodynamics by radionuclide means; development of multi-port clinical data processing systems for nuclear medicine. *Mailing Add:* 2910 Welcome Dr Durham NC 27705-5576

HARRIS, CHARLES, PATHOLOGY. *Current Pos:* RETIRED. *Personal Data:* b New York, NY, Jan 7, 23; m 49; c 3. *Educ:* Cornell Univ, BA, 43; Long Island Col Med, MD, 46. *Prof Exp:* NIH fel, Fels Res Inst, Sch Med, Temple Univ, 50-51, pathologist, Fels Res Inst & assoc path, Sch Med, 54-62; mem staff, Geront Res Inst, Philadelphia Geriat Ctr, 62-69; dir clin labs, 69-88; consult, 88-95. *Concurrent Pos:* Vis asst prof, Woman's Med Col Pa, 64-69. *Mem:* AAAS; Am Soc Exp Path; Am Soc Hemat; Am Asn Path & Bact; AMA. *Res:* Breast cancer; leukemia. *Mailing Add:* 16 Highland Bend PO Box C Island Heights NJ 08732

HARRIS, CHARLES BONNER, PHYSICAL CHEMISTRY. *Current Pos:* PROF CHEM, UNIV CALIF & PRIN INVESTR, LAWRENCE BERKELEY LAB, 67- *Personal Data:* b New York, NY, Apr 24, 40. *Educ:* Univ Mich, BS, 63; Mass Inst Technol, PhD(chem), 66. *Prof Exp:* AEC fel physics, 66-67. *Concurrent Pos:* Alfred P Sloan Found fel, 70-74; Humboldt sr scientist award, 80. *Mem:* Am Chem Soc; Am Phys Soc. *Res:* General studies of coherence and coherent properties of matter and radiation; energy transfer processes in condensed phase and on metal surfaces; laser spectroscopy. *Mailing Add:* Chem D-87 Hildebrand Bldg Univ Calif Berkeley CA 94720

HARRIS, CHARLES LAWRENCE, MICROBIOLOGY. *Current Pos:* from asst prof to assoc prof, 72-82, PROF BIOCHEM, WVA UNIV, 82- *Personal Data:* b Chicago, Ill, Nov 13, 42; m 63; c 3. *Educ:* Univ Ill, Urbana, BS, 66, PhD(biochem), 70. *Prof Exp:* Res assoc biochem, Col Med, Univ Ill, 70; fel neurochem, Ill State Psychiat Inst, 70-72. *Mem:* AAAS; Am Soc Biochem & Molecular Biol. *Res:* Structure, biosynthesis and function of transfer RNA; role and synthesis of modified nucleotides in RNA; synthetase complex, aminoacyl and RNA. *Mailing Add:* Dept Biochem WVa Univ Sch Med Morgantown WV 26506-9142. *Fax:* 304-293-6846

HARRIS, CHARLES RONALD, INTEGRATED PEST MANAGEMENT, ENVIRONMENTAL TOXICOLOGY. *Current Pos:* RETIRED. *Personal Data:* b Kimberley, BC, Oct 3, 32; m 57, Carol R Smith; c Brenda & Shelley. *Educ:* Univ BC, BA, 54, MA, 56; Univ Wis, PhD(entom), 61. *Honors & Awards:* Bussart Award, Entom Soc Am, 68. *Prof Exp:* Res scientist, Can Dept Agr, 56-90, head, Soil Pesticide Sect, 66-90; prof & chair, Univ Guelph, 90-97. *Concurrent Pos:* Hon lectr, Univ Western Ont, 66-90; fac assoc, Univ Guelph, 69-90; mem, Ont Pesticides Adv Comt, 72-92; vis res fel, NSW Dept Agr, 86-87; vis prof, Univ Sydney, 95-96. *Mem:* Fel Entom Soc Can (pres, 74-75); Entom Soc Am. *Res:* Efficacy, behaviour and fate of insecticides in soil; insect resistance to insecticides; control of soil insect pests. *Mailing Add:* Dept Environ Biol Univ Guelph Guelph ON N1G 2W1 Can. *Fax:* 519-837-0442

HARRIS, CLARE I, PLANT SCIENCE. *Current Pos:* AGR CONSULT. *Personal Data:* b Canandaigua, NY, May 20, 33; m 55, Marjorie Herendeen; c Gregory S, Paul R & Amy J (Truly). *Educ:* Cornell Univ, BS, 55; Purdue Univ, MS, 60, PhD(hort), 62. *Prof Exp:* Instr hort, Purdue Univ, 59-62; soil scientist, Agr Res Serv, USDA, 62-67, prin horticulturist, Coop State Res Serv, 67-70; res assoc, Univ Calif, Davis, 70-71; dir plant sci res prog, USDA, 71-74, dep adminr, 74-85, assoc adminr, Coop State Res Serv, 85-94. *Mem:* AAAS; Am Chem Soc; Am Soc Hort Sci. *Res:* Agriculture; agricultural research administration. *Mailing Add:* 14410 Northwyn Dr Silver Spring MD 20904-5934

HARRIS, COLIN C(YRIL), MINERAL ENGINEERING, COAL PREPARATION & PARTICLE TECHNOLOGY. *Current Pos:* from asst prof to prof, 60-70, PROF MINERAL ENG, COLUMBIA UNIV, 70- *Personal Data:* b Leeds, Eng, Jan 9, 28; wid. *Educ:* Univ London, BSc, 52; Univ Leeds, PhD(mineral eng & coal preparation), 59. *Honors & Awards:*

Gaudin Award, Am Inst Mining, Metall & Petrol Engrs, 90. *Prof Exp:* Res asst coal preparation & mineral eng, Univ Leeds, 52-56, lectr, 57-60, 62-63. *Concurrent Pos:* Consult, MacMillan & Co, 63 & Envirotech, 77-83; supvr res proj, Am Iron & Steel Inst, 67-71, Cities Serv Co, 73-, Asarco, Inc, 77- & Dept Energy, 88-; assoc ed, Int J Mineral Processing; adv fac appointments, res & grad prog to US & foreign univs; adv res proposals to govt funding agencies; adv & consult to mining, res & mfg co; mem organizing comts for int conf on mineral processing. *Mem:* Brit Oper Res Soc; Brit Inst Mining & Metall; Am Inst Mining, Metall & Petrol Engrs, Soc Mining, Metall & Explor. *Res:* Powder technology; fine particle statistics and measurement; fracture of brittle materials; comminution kinetics; flotation machine hydrodynamics; flotation kinetics; fluid flow and retention in porous media; sedimentation; design and scale-up of processing machinery; coal preparation and mineral processing; ceramics engineering. *Mailing Add:* 907 Eng Ctr Columbia Univ New York NY 10027

HARRIS, CURTIS C, CARCINOGENESIS, CLINICAL ONCOLOGY. *Current Pos:* CHIEF, LAB HUMAN CARCINOGENESIS, NAT CANCER INST, 80- *Personal Data:* b Anthony, Kans, Jan 9, 43. *Educ:* Univ Kans, MD, 69. *Mem:* Am Asn Cancer Res; Am Soc Cell Biol; Am Asn Path; Am Soc Clin Invest. *Mailing Add:* Lab Human Carcinogenesis Nat Cancer Inst Bldg 37 Rm 2C05 37 Convent Dr Bethesda MD 20892-4255. *Fax:* 301-496-0497

HARRIS, CYRIL MANTON, ACOUSTICS. *Current Pos:* from assoc prof to prof elec eng, 52-76, Charles Batchelor prof, 76-87, CHARLES BATCHELOR EMER PROF ELEC ENG & EMER PROF ARCHIT, COLUMBIA UNIV, 87- *Personal Data:* b Detroit, Mich; m 49; c 2. *Educ:* Univ Calif, Los Angeles, BA, 38, MA, 40; Mass Inst Technol, PhD(physics), 45. *Hon Degrees:* ScD, NJ Inst Technol, 81, Northwestern Univ, 89. *Honors & Awards:* Emile Berliner Maker of Microphone Award, 77; Franklin Medal, 77; Wallace Clement Sabine Medal, 79; Medal, Am Inst Architects, 80; Gold Medal, Audio Eng Soc, 84; Gold Medal, Acoust Soc Am, 87. *Prof Exp:* Asst, Univ Calif, Los Angeles, 39-40; mem staff war res, Carnegie Inst of Wash, 41; mem staff war res, Nat Defense Res Comt & teaching fel, Mass Inst Technol, 41-45; res engr, Bell Tel Labs, Inc, 45-51; sci consult, London Br, Off Naval Res, 51; Fulbright lectr, Delft Univ Technol, 51-52. *Concurrent Pos:* Fulbright vis prof, Univ Tokyo, 60; S Charles Lee vis prof, Univ Calif, Los Angeles, 91-; chmn bd, NY Acad Sci, 92-94. *Mem:* Nat Acad Sci; Nat Acad Eng; fel Inst Elec & Electronics Engrs; hon mem Audio Eng Soc; fel Acoust Soc Am (vpres, 60-61, pres 64-65); Am Soc Testing & Mat; NY Acad Sci (pres, 91-93); Am Philos Soc; Sigma Xi; Am Inst Physics. *Res:* Architectural acoustics; noise control. *Mailing Add:* S W Mudd Bldg Columbia Univ New York NY 10027

HARRIS, D LEE, OCEANOGRAPHY, METEOROLOGY. *Current Pos:* RETIRED. *Personal Data:* b Jenkinjones, WVa, July 11, 16; m 43, Mary B Blowers; c David R. *Educ:* Concord State Col, AB, 37; George Washington Univ, MS, 51; Univ Mich, PhD(meteorol), 65. *Prof Exp:* Res meteorologist, US Weather Bur, 49-65, res meteorologist, ESSA, 65-67, chief oceanog br, 67-78, sr scientist, Coastal Eng Res Ctr, 78-80; mem fac, Coastal & Oceanog Engr Dept, Univ Fla, 80-85. *Mem:* Am Meteorol Soc. *Res:* Coastal oceanography; sea surface waves; storm surges; astronomical tides. *Mailing Add:* 3870 NW 25th Circle Gainesville FL 32606

HARRIS, DANIEL CHARLES, BIOPHYSICAL CHEMISTRY. *Current Pos:* OPTICAL & ELECTRONIC MAT, NAVAL WEAPONS CTR, 83- *Personal Data:* b New York, NY, May 30, 48. *Educ:* Mass Inst Technol, SB, 68; Calif Inst Technol, PhD(chem), 73. *Honors & Awards:* Meller Award Basic Med Res, Albert Einstein Col Med, 75. *Prof Exp:* Instr, Calif Inst Technol, 72-73; res fel, Albert Einstein Col Med, 73-75; asst prof chem, Univ Calif, Davis, 75-80; assoc prof chem, Franklin & Marshall Col, 80-83. *Mem:* Am Chem Soc; Am Ceramic Soc. *Res:* Optical and electronic materials; analytical chemistry textbook writing. *Mailing Add:* Naval Air Warfare Ctr Code 3854 China Lake CA 93535-6001

HARRIS, DANIEL EVERETT, RADIO ASTRONOMY. *Current Pos:* ASTRONOMER, SMITHSONIAN ASTROPHYS OBSERV, MASS, 80- *Personal Data:* b Summit, NJ, Aug 5, 34; m 67; c 3. *Educ:* Haverford Col, BA, 56; Calif Inst Technol, MS, 57, PhD(astron & physics), 61. *Prof Exp:* Res assoc, Inst di Fisica, Bologna, Italy, 61-64 & Arecibo Observ, Cornell Univ, PR, 65-69; sci investr, Inst Argentino di Radioastron, 69-70; res assoc & lectr, Harvard Col Observ, 70-73; prin sci res officer, Radiosterrenwach, Neth Found Radioastron, 74-77; res assoc astron, Dom Radio Astrophys Observ, Nat Res Coun, 77-80. *Mem:* Am Astron Soc. *Res:* Non-thermal astrophysics. *Mailing Add:* 60 Garden St Cambridge MA 02138

HARRIS, DAVID OWEN, CHEMICAL PHYSICS, MOLECULAR SPECTROSCOPY. *Current Pos:* From asst prof to assoc prof, 65-75, chmn dept, 80-82, PROF CHEM, UNIV CALIF, SANTA BARBARA, 75- *Personal Data:* b Price, Utah, July 2, 39; div; c 2. *Educ:* Univ Calif, Berkeley, PhD, 65. *Mem:* Am Phys Soc. *Res:* Laser spectroscopy; molecular structure. *Mailing Add:* Dept Chem Univ Calif Santa Barbara CA 93106

HARRIS, DAVID R, PHYSICAL CHEMISTRY. *Current Pos:* from assoc prof to prof, 69-91, EMER PROF COMPUT SCI, CALIF STATE UNIV, CHICO, 91- *Personal Data:* b Schenectady, NY, Aug 17, 32. *Educ:* Univ Colo, BA, 57, PhD(phys chem), 63. *Prof Exp:* Sr cancer res scientist biophys, Roswell Park Mem Inst, 62-65; asst prof comput sci, Utah State Univ, 65-69. *Mem:* AAAS; Am Crystallog Asn. *Res:* X-ray structure analysis of organic and biological compounds; protein structure; adaptation of scientific problems to digital computers; artificial intelligence. *Mailing Add:* 6159 County Rd 3 Orland CA 95963

HARRIS, DAVID THOMAS, TRANSPLANTATION, GENE THERAPY OF CANCER. *Current Pos:* assoc prof, 89-96, PROF IMMUNOL, UNIV ARIZ, 96- *Personal Data:* b Jonesboro, Ark, May 9, 56; m 89, Francoise Besencon; c Alexandre & Stefanie. *Educ:* Wake Forest Univ, BS, 78; Bowman Gray Med Sch, MS 79, PhD(immunol), 82. *Prof Exp:* Fel, Ludwig Inst Cancer Res, 82-85; res asst prof, Univ NC, 85-89. *Concurrent Pos:* Staff immunologist, EMSI Inc, 85; prin investr, Nat Cancer Inst, 88-94, Ariz Dis Control Res Comn, 92-, Am Cancer Soc, 93-, Ariz Elks Res Award, 93-, Vical Inc, 93-94, Cryo-Cell Int, 93-94, World Med Match Inc, 93-94; clin scientist, Ariz Arthritis Ctr, 90-; consult, Teltech Inc, 90-; mem, Ariz Cancer Ctr, 93-, Steele Mem Children's Res Ctr, 93-; dir, Cord Blood Bank, 92- *Mem:* Am Asn Immunol; Reticuloendothelial Soc; AAAS; Int Soc Develop Comp Immunol; Sigma Xi; Int Soc Hematother & Graft Eng. *Res:* Use of umbilical cord blood instead of bone marrow for transplantation, especially for ethnic minorities; use of gene therapy for the treatment of cancer and the correction of genetic diseases. *Mailing Add:* Univ Ariz Bldg No 90 Tucson AZ 85721. *Fax:* 520-621-6366; *E-Mail:* davidh@aruba.ccit.arizona.edu

HARRIS, DELBERT LINN, VETERINARY MICROBIOLOGY. *Current Pos:* CHMN & PROF, DEPT MICROBIOL, IMMUNOL & PREV MED, IOWA STATE UNIV, 92- *Personal Data:* b Boone, Iowa, Sept 24, 43; m 61; c 4. *Educ:* Iowa State Univ, DVM, 67, PhD(vet microbiol), 70. *Honors & Awards:* H Dunne Mem, Am Asn Swine Practr. *Prof Exp:* Prof vet microbiol, Iowa State Univ, 70-82; vpres, Pig Improv Co, Inc, 85-92. *Concurrent Pos:* Consult, Merck, Sharp & Dohme Co, 75-76, Pig Improv Co, 76- *Mem:* Am Vet Med Asn; Am Soc Microbiol; Int Pig Vet Soc; Conf Res Workers Animal Dis; Am Asn Swine Practr. *Res:* Bacterial diseases of the respiratory and digestive tract; swine dysentery; effect of environment on pig and human health; 3 site production of pigs. *Mailing Add:* Dept Microbiol Iowa State Univ Ames IA 50011-2010

HARRIS, DENNIS GEORGE, ATOMIC & MOLECULAR PHYSICS, OPTICS. *Current Pos:* MEM TECH STAFF, ROCKETDYNE DIV, ROCKWELL INT, 79- *Personal Data:* b Indiana, Pa. *Educ:* Cornell Univ, BS, 70, PhD(appl physics), 80; Univ Ill, MS, 72. *Concurrent Pos:* Res assoc, Coord Sci Lab, Univ Ill, 72-74. *Mem:* Am Phys Soc. *Res:* The molecular energy transfer, as well as the visible, ultraviolet and vacuum ultraviolet spectroscopy of small molecules; visible and ultraviolet lasers. *Mailing Add:* 4193 Minnecota Thousand Oaks CA 91360

HARRIS, DENNY OLAN, PHYCOLOGY, MICROBIOLOGY. *Current Pos:* asst prof, 67-71, ASSOC PROF BIOL SCI, UNIV KY, 71- *Personal Data:* b Louisville, Ky, May 2, 37; m 62, Patricia Ann Appling; c Lisa (Diluna), Bradley & Gregory. *Educ:* Univ Louisville, BA, 61, MS, 63; Ind Univ, Bloomington, PhD(microbiol), 67. *Prof Exp:* Instr biol, Univ Louisville, 61-63; USPHS res fel microbiol, Ind Univ, Bloomington, 63-67. *Concurrent Pos:* US Dept Interior res grant, 68-; vis prof, Cambridge Univ, 73, Oxford Univ, 91. *Mem:* Int Phycol Soc; Am Phycol Soc. *Res:* Fresh water algology, especially the study of inhibitory products produced by the algae to include the chemistry, biochemistry and ecology of algal inhibition and the effects of naturally occurring algicides upon algae, protozoans, bacteria and other forms of aquatic life. *Mailing Add:* Dept Biol Sci Univ Ky Lexington KY 40506. *Fax:* 606-257-1717

HARRIS, DEVERLE PORTER, MINERAL RESOURCES APPRAISAL, MINERAL SUPPLY SYSTEMS. *Current Pos:* PROF & DIR MINERAL ECON, DEPT MINING & GEOL ENG, UNIV ARIZ, 74- *Personal Data:* b Lovell, Wyo, Jan 21, 31; m 67; c 6. *Educ:* Brigham Univ, BS, 56, MS, 58; Pa State Univ, PhD(mineral econ), 65. *Prof Exp:* Struct & photogeologist, Geophoto Serv, Inc, Denver, Colo, 57-59, Calgary, Can, 59-60; res asst opers res, Dept Mineral Econ, Pa State Univ, 62-65; res geologist & geostatistician, res dept, Union Oil Co Calif, 65-66; from asst prof to prof mineral econ, Dept Mineral Econ, Pa State Univ, 66-74. *Concurrent Pos:* Chmn, Adv Task Force, Fed Power Comn Appraisal Resource Base Natural Gas, 76; mem adv comt, Joint US Dept Energy & US Geol Surv Prog Appraisal Uranium Resources, 79-81; mem, Comt Tech Aspects Critical & Strategic Mat, Nat Res Coun Nat Acad Sci, 79-81, Panel Rev Statist Prog US Bur Mines, 81-83; elected mem, US Nat Comt, Int Asn Math Geol, 85- *Mem:* Soc Mining Engrs; Am Econ Asn; Int Asn Energy Economists; Soc Econ Geologists; Int Asn Math Geol. *Res:* Development of concepts and quantitative methods for the estimation of undiscovered mineral and energy resources; design and implementation of computer systems to simulate exploration, development and production of mineral resources and provide a means of describing the potential supply stock and future supply flows. *Mailing Add:* 3330 N Jackson Ave Tucson AZ 85719

HARRIS, DEWEY LYNN, ANIMAL GENETICS, STATISTICS. *Current Pos:* res geneticist, W Lafayette, 76-86, RES GENETICIST, US MEAT ANIMAL RES CTR, CLAY CTR, AGR RES SERV, USDA, NEBR, 86- *Personal Data:* b Red Rock, Tex, June 23, 33; m 55, Jeanne; c Scott, Jeff & Todd. *Educ:* Tex A&M Univ, BS, 54, MS, 58; Iowa State Univ, PhD(animal breeding), 61. *Honors & Awards:* Rockefeller Prentice Mem Award, Am Soc Animal Sci, 92; Distinguished Serv Award, Nat Swine Improv Asn, 95. *Prof Exp:* Asst county agr agent, Tex Agr Exten Serv, 54-55; asst genetics, Tex A&M Univ, 57-58; asst animal breeding, Iowa State Univ, 58-60, from instr to asst prof statist, 60-64; biomet geneticist, De Kalb Agr Asn, Inc, 64-69, asst dir, De Kalb Agr Res, Inc, 69-71, dir poultry res, 71-74; chief, Sect Animal & Poultry Genetics, Agr Can, 74-76. *Mem:* Am Dairy Sci Asn; Poultry Sci Asn; Am Soc Animal Sci; Am Genetic Asn. *Res:* Systems analysis of livestock production with emphasis on simulation modelling as a tool for livestock systems; design of genetic improvement systems for livestock species. *Mailing Add:* USDA Agr Res Serv US Meat Animal Res Ctr Clay Center NE 68933-0166. *Fax:* 402-762-4155; *E-Mail:* harris@marcum.marc.usda.gov

HARRIS, DON NAVARRO, BIOCHEMISTRY, PHYSIOLOGY. *Current Pos:* sr res investr biochem, 65-84, res fel, 84-90, RES FEL, HUM RESOURCES CONSULT, BRISTOL-MYERS SQUIBB, PHARMACEUT RES ISNT, 90- *Personal Data:* b New York, NY, June 17, 29; wid; c Donna M, John C & Scott A. *Educ:* Lincoln Univ, Pa, AB, 51; Rutgers Univ, MS, 59, PhD(biochem), 63. *Prof Exp:* Sr res chemist, Colgate Palmolive Res Ctr, 63-64; asst res specialist biochem, Rutgers Univ, 64-65. *Concurrent Pos:* Coadjutant assoc prof biochem, Univ Col, Rutgers Univ, 75-80; adj assoc prof pharmacol, Temple Univ Sch Med, 90- *Mem:* AAAS; Am Chem Soc; NY Acad Sci; Am Soc Pharmacol & Exp Therapeutics; Am Heart Asn; Sigma Xi. *Res:* Biosynthesis of cholesterol; mechanism of action of platelet aggregation, arachidonic acid metabolites and cyclic adenosinemonophosphate; isolation and purification of nucleic acids; effect of hormones on nucleic acids and protein synthesis. *Mailing Add:* 26 Summerall Rd Somerset NJ 08873-2210

HARRIS, DONALD C, MINERALOGY. *Current Pos:* RES SCIENTIST, ECON GEOL MINERAL DIV, GEOL SURV CAN, 81- *Personal Data:* b NS, Can, Jan 3, 36. *Educ:* Acadia Univ, BSc, 58; Univ Toronto, MA, 61, PhD(geol), 64. *Prof Exp:* Mine geologist, Stanrock Uranium Mine, 58-59; asst cur mineral, Royal Ont Mus, 63-67; res scientist, Mineral Sci Div, Canmet, 67-81. *Mem:* Mineral Soc Am; Mineral Soc Can. *Res:* Mineralogy of ore minerals and deposits, electron microprobe. *Mailing Add:* Econ Geol Mineral Div Geol Surv Can 601 Booth St Ottawa ON K1A 0E8 Can

HARRIS, DONALD R, JR, PHYSICS. *Current Pos:* res engr, 75-77, ASSOC PROF NUCLEAR ENG & DIR RPI REACTOR, RENSSELAER POLYTECH INST, 77- *Personal Data:* b Johnstown, Pa, Nov 29, 25; m 54, Janet Helen Bradley; c Sally, Gwen, Andrew, Daniel, Julia, Katherina & Laura. *Educ:* Carnegie Inst Technol, BS, 48, MS, 49; Princeton Univ, MA, 52; Rensselaer Polytech Inst, PhD, 76. *Honors & Awards:* Meritorious Performance in Reactor Opers Award, Am Nuclear Soc. *Prof Exp:* Asst math, Carnegie Inst Technol, 48-49; asst physics, Princeton Univ, 50-54; sr scientist, Bettis Atomic Power Lab, Westinghouse Elec Corp, 54-61, fel scientist, 61-68; staff mem, Los Alamos Sci Lab, Univ Calif, 68-71, group leader theoret div, 71-75. *Mem:* Am Phys Soc; fel Am Nuclear Soc; Am Anthrop Asn; Soc Am Archaeol. *Res:* Reactor physics; nuclear cross sections; transport methods; shielding; Monte Carlo; systems analysis. *Mailing Add:* Dept Environ & Energy Eng Rensselaer Polytech Inst Troy NY 12181. *Fax:* 518-276-4832; *E-Mail:* harrisdr@rpi.edu

HARRIS, DONALD WAYNE, BIO-ORGANIC CHEMISTRY. *Current Pos:* RES FEL, A E STALEY MFG CO, 84- *Personal Data:* b Ft Scott, Kans, Sept 23, 42; m 64; c 3. *Educ:* Univ Mo, BS, 66, MS, 68, PhD(agr chem), 74. *Prof Exp:* Lab technician, Chemagro Corp, 64-65; phys sci asst, US Army, 68-70; res chemist, Clinton Corn Processing Co, 74-77, mgr carbohydrate polymer res, 77-84. *Mem:* Am Chem Soc. *Res:* Research and development concerning new products derived from polymers associated with corn. *Mailing Add:* 5208 Cameron Lane Lafayette IN 47905

HARRIS, DOROTHY VIRGINIA, exercise physiology, sport psychology; deceased, see previous edition for last biography

HARRIS, DURWARD SMITH, BIO-ORGANIC CHEMISTRY. *Current Pos:* from asst prof to assoc prof, 62-69, chmn dept, 79-85, PROF CHEM, AUSTIN PEAY STATE UNIV, 69- *Personal Data:* b Dickson, Tenn, Mar 30, 31; m 68; c 1. *Educ:* Austin Peay State Col, BS, 54; Univ Tenn, MS, 61, PhD(proteins), 63. *Prof Exp:* Anal chemist, Tenn Valley Auth, 54-57. *Mem:* AAAS; Am Chem Soc; Sigma Xi. *Res:* Separation and identification of protein mixtures by ion-exchange. *Mailing Add:* Dept Chem Austin Peay State Univ 601 College St Clarksville TN 37044-0001

HARRIS, EDWARD DAVID, BIOCHEMISTRY, COPPER. *Current Pos:* asst prof, 73-80, PROF BIOCHEM & NUTRIT, TEX A&M UNIV, 80- *Personal Data:* b Chicago, Ill, Dec 1, 38; m 60, Janet Weith; c Terri, Scot & Dan. *Educ:* Univ Ill, Urbana, AB, 60, MS, 65, PhD(biochem), 68. *Prof Exp:* Res asst biochem, Univ Ill, 63-68; NIH fel, Univ Chicago, 68-70; USPHS res assoc biochem & instr, Univ Mo, Columbia, 70-73. *Concurrent Pos:* Sr Fulbright award, Australia, 84-85. *Mem:* Am Soc Biol Chemists; Am Inst Nutrit; Soc Exp Biol & Med; Int Soc Trace Elem Res Humans. *Res:* Human nutrition; biochemical function of copper. *Mailing Add:* Dept Biochem & Biophys Tex A&M Univ College Station TX 77843-2128. *Fax:* 409-845-9274; *E-Mail:* eharris@bioch.tamu.edu

HARRIS, EDWARD DAY, JR, MEDICINE, RHEUMATOLOGY. *Current Pos:* Arthur L Bloomfield prof & chmn, Dept Med & chief med serv, 88-95, GEORGE DEFOREST BARNETT PROF MED, STANFORD UNIV HOSP, 95- *Personal Data:* b Philadelphia, Pa, July 7, 37; m 58, Joan Z Lonergan; c Ned, Tom & Chandler. *Educ:* Dartmouth Col, AB, 58; Harvard Univ, MD, 62. *Honors & Awards:* Quadrennial CIBA-GEIGY Prize for Excellence in Rheumatology Res, 77. *Prof Exp:* Intern med, Mass Gen Hosp, Boston, 62-64, resident, 66-67; from instr to asst prof, Harvard Med Sch, 69-70; from assoc prof to assoc prof med & chief, Connective Tissue Dis Sect Dartmouth Med Sch, 70-82, dir, Multipurpose Arthritis Ctr, 77-82, Eugene W Leonard prof med, 80; prof & chmn, Dept Med, Univ Med & Dent NJ-Rutgers Med Sch, 83-88. *Concurrent Pos:* Asst physician, Mass Gen Hosp, Boston, 69-70; Nat Inst Arthritis & Metab Dis spec fel, Mass Gen Hosp, Boston, 67-69 & res career develop award, Dartmouth Med Sch, 70-75. *Mem:* Am Rheumatism Asn (pres, 85-86); Asn Am Physicians; Am Soc Clin Invest; Am Col Rheumatol; Am Fed Clin Res; Am Bd Int Med; Arthritis Found. *Res:* Mechanisms of destruction of connective tissue in man. *Mailing Add:* 1000 Welch Rd Suite 203 Palo Alto CA 94304-1808. *Fax:* 650-723-9656; *E-Mail:* madera@leland.stanford.edu

HARRIS, EDWARD FREDERICK, GROWTH & DEVELOPMENT, HUMAN VARIATION. *Current Pos:* PROF ORTHOD & PEDIAT DENT, UNIV TENN, 80- *Personal Data:* b San Jose, Calif, Oct 2, 47; m, Betsy D Barcroft; c Jeremy T & Emily J. *Educ:* San Jose State Col, BA; Ariz State Univ, MA & PhD(anthrop). *Mem:* Am Asn Phys Anthropologists; Int Asn Dent Res; Am Cleft Palate-Craniofacial Asn. *Res:* Quantification of the effects of genetic and environmental factors on growth and development of the craniofacial complexes. *Mailing Add:* 870 Union Ave Memphis TN 38163. *Fax:* 901-448-8745; *E-Mail:* eharris@utmem1.utmem.edu

HARRIS, EDWARD GRANT, THEORETICAL PHYSICS. *Current Pos:* from asst prof to assoc prof, 57-64, PROF PHYSICS, UNIV TENN, KNOXVILLE, 64- *Personal Data:* b Morristown, Tenn, Mar 10, 24; m 62, Sara Waldron; c Heather A. *Educ:* Univ Tenn, BS, 48, MS, 50, PhD(physics), 53. *Prof Exp:* Physicist, Naval Res Lab, 53-57. *Concurrent Pos:* Consult, Oak Ridge Nat Lab, 57-80. *Mem:* Am Phys Soc; Am Asn Physics Teachers; Sigma Xi. *Res:* Plasma physics; quantum physics; relativity. *Mailing Add:* Dept Physics Univ Tenn Knoxville TN 37996-1200

HARRIS, EDWARD LYNDOL, physical chemistry, for more information see previous edition

HARRIS, EDWIN RANDALL, ORGANIC CHEMISTRY. *Current Pos:* from asst prof to assoc prof, 59-70, PROF CHEM, CALIF STATE COL, LONG BEACH, 70- *Personal Data:* b Little Rock, Ark, Aug 15, 32; m 58. *Educ:* Univ Okla, BS, 53, MS, 56; Univ Calif, PhD(chem), 59. *Prof Exp:* Asst chem, Univs Okla & Calif, 53-59, assoc, Univ Calif, 58-59. *Concurrent Pos:* Fulbright grant, Univs Tbingen & Hamburg, 54-55. *Mem:* Am Chem Soc. *Res:* Analysis and structure elucidation of terpenoid natural products from plants; chemistry of marine animals; mechanisms of rearrangements. *Mailing Add:* Dept Chem Calif State Univ Long Beach Long Beach CA 90840-0004

HARRIS, ELIZABETH FORSYTH, ENVIRONMENTAL MICROBIOLOGY, IMMUNOLOGY. *Current Pos:* chmn dept, 70-83, ASSOC PROF MICROBIOL & IMMUNOL, TEX COL OSTEOP MED, 70- *Personal Data:* b Kilgore, Tex, Aug 14, 35; m 56; c 4. *Educ:* Tex Wesleyan Col, BA, 56; Tex Christian Univ, MA, 64; Univ Tex Southwestern Med Sch, PhD(microbiol), 70; Am Bd Med Microbiol, cert. *Prof Exp:* Bacteriologist, Ft Worth Water Dept, 57; teacher math & sci, Hurst-Euless-Bedford Schs, 58-62; lab instr biol, Tex Christian Univ, 62-63; teacher sci, New Orleans Pub Schs, 64-65; instr biol, La State Univ, New Orleans, 65-66. *Concurrent Pos:* Microbiol consult, Nat Bd Examrs Osteop Physicians & Surgeons, 73-86; consult, air conditioning & heat pump mfrs. *Mem:* Am Soc Microbiol. *Res:* Biofilms in air conditioning systems; hormones, stress and immunity; hyperbaric oxygen effects; depression and natural killer cells. *Mailing Add:* Dept Microbiol Tex Col Osteop Med 3500 Camp Bowie Blvd Ft Worth TX 76107-2644

HARRIS, ELIZABETH HOLDER, GENETICS, MOLECULAR BIOLOGY. *Current Pos:* RES ASSOC GENETICS, DEPT BOT, DUKE UNIV, 72-, SR RES SCIENTIST, 83-, ASSOC RES PROF, 91- *Personal Data:* b Winston-Salem, NC, Oct 1, 44; m 65, Albert; c Hannah, Thomas & Frieda. *Educ:* Swarthmore Col, BA, 65; Yale Univ, PhD(microbiol), 71. *Mem:* Int Soc Plant Molecular Biol; Genetics Soc Am; Asn Women Sci; Phycological Soc Am. *Res:* Genetic control of organelle biogenesis; genetics of Chlamydomonas reinhardtii; plant molecular biology. *Mailing Add:* Dept Bot Duke Univ Durham NC 27706-8001

HARRIS, ELLIOTT STANLEY, RESEARCH ADMINISTRATION, OCCUPATIONAL HEALTH. *Current Pos:* ADJ ASSOC PROF ENVIRON & OCCUP HEALTH, EMORY UNIV, 84- *Personal Data:* b New York, NY, June 27, 22; m 45, Almeda Butler; c Jennifer J & Catherine A. *Educ:* Univ Colo, BA, 48; Univ Southern Calif, MS, 50, PhD(biochem), 54; Nat Registry Clin Chem, cert. *Prof Exp:* Instr biochem, Dent Sch, Univ Southern Calif, 48-52, res assoc, Sch Med, 54; Hodgkins res fel, Roswell Park Mem Inst, Buffalo, 54-55, sr cancer res scientist clin biochem, 55-56; sr res scientist biochem, Wyeth Inst Med Res, 56-63; chief toxicol lab, Manned Spacecraft Ctr, NASA, 63-73; dir, Div Biomed & Behav Sci, Nat Inst Occup Safety & Health, 73-81; adj assoc prof toxicol, Sch Med, Univ Cincinnati, 74-81; dep dir, Nat Inst Occup Safety & Health, 81-86. *Concurrent Pos:* Vis prof, Univ Ariz, 80-81; consult, 86- *Mem:* NY Acad Sci; Am Indust Hyg Asn; Soc Toxicol; Sigma Xi; Am Conf Govt Indust Hygienists. *Res:* Enzyme isolation and characterization; neurochemistry; enzymology; inhalation and biochemical toxicology particularly with respect to long term low level continuous exposures. *Mailing Add:* 3215 Bolero Pass Atlanta GA 30341

HARRIS, EMMETT DEWITT, JR, ECONOMIC ENTOMOLOGY. *Current Pos:* exten entomologist & pesticides chems coordr, Coop Exten Serv, 66-87, EMER PROF ENTOM, UNIV GA, 87- *Personal Data:* b Orlando, Fla, July 27, 25; m 48, Marjorie Garland; c Heather & Jeffrey. *Educ:* Univ Fla, BSA, 51; Cornell Univ, PhD(econ entom), 56. *Prof Exp:* Lab technician, Citrus Exp Sta, Univ Fla, 51-52; asst entom, Cornell Univ, 52-55; from asst entomologist to assoc entomologist, Everglades Exp Sta, Univ Fla, 56-66. *Mem:* Entom Soc Am. *Res:* Coordination of pesticide information and policies; vegetable insect control. *Mailing Add:* 178 Spruce Valley Rd Athens GA 30605

HARRIS, ERNEST JAMES, ENTOMOLOGY. *Current Pos:* RES LEADER ENTOM, AGR RES SERV, USDA, HONOLULU, 72-, TECH ADV, NAT RES PROG INSECT CONTROL FRUITS & VEG, 75- *Personal Data:* b North Little Rock, Ark, May 24, 28; m 54; c 3. *Educ:* Univ Ark, Pine Bluff, BS, 51; Univ Minn, St Paul, MS, 59; Univ Hawaii, Manoa, PhD(entom), 75. *Prof Exp:* Teacher biol, Univ Ark, Pine Bluff, 59-62; res entomologist, Agr Res Serv, USDA, Hawaii, 62-69; leader-coordr entom, US AID, Tunis, Tunisia & Rabat, Morocco, 69-72. *Mem:* Sigma Xi; Entom Soc Am. *Res:* Basic and applied research to develop methods for the detection, control and eradication of fruit flies to improve food production. *Mailing Add:* 45-170 Ohaha Pl Kaneohe HI 96744

HARRIS, EVA, MOLECULAR & CELL BIOLOGY. *Current Pos:* Postdoctoral fel, 93-97, DIR, APPL MOLECULAR BIOL/APPROPRIATE TECHNOL TRANSFER PROG, UNIV CALIF, SAN FRANCISCO, 93-, ASST ADJ PROF, PROG MOLECULAR PATHOGENESIS, 97- *Personal Data:* b New York, NY, Aug 6, 65. *Educ:* Harvard Univ, BA, 87; Univ Calif, Berkeley, PhD(molecular & cell biol), 93. *Concurrent Pos:* Invited lectr, Stanford Univ, 93, New Eng Biolabs, 93, Ctr Genetic Eng & Biotechnol, 94, Int Health Network, 95, San Francisco State Univ, 95, Univ Calif, San Francisco, 95 & 96, Col Pa, 95, Ministry Health, San Salvador, El Salvador, 95, Univ Fla, 95, Centro de Investy Estudios de la Salud, 96, Univ Ore, 96, Yale Univ Sch Med, 96, San Francisco State Univ, 96, San Francisco Gen Hosp, 97, Skyline Col, 97 & Univ Calif, Berkeley, 97; prof, Masters Prog, Mayor Univ San Andres, Boliva, 97-, vis prof, 97-; MacArthur fel, John D & Catherine T MacArthur Found, 97. *Mem:* Am Soc Microbiol; AAAS. *Res:* Infectious disease research both at the basic and applied levels; basic science focus using dengue virus as a disease model for studying pathogenesis; development of a simple and low-cost methodology for the application of molecular techniques to infectious disease problems on site in developing countries. *Mailing Add:* Univ Calif 521 Parnassus Ave C740 Box 0422 San Francisco CA 94143-0422. *E-Mail:* eharris@cgl.ucsf.edu

HARRIS, FRANCIS LAURIE, ORGANIC CHEMISTRY. *Current Pos:* from asst prof to assoc prof, 68-77, PROF CHEM, CALIF STATE UNIV, NORTHRIDGE, 77- *Personal Data:* b Nebraska City, Nebr, July 2, 39. *Educ:* Univ Tulsa, BCh, 61; Univ Calif, Los Angeles, PhD(org chem), 66. *Prof Exp:* Fel, Harvard Univ, 67-68 *Mem:* Am Chem Soc. *Res:* Carbonium ion reactions and mechanisms; synthesis of spin labels; synthetic methods. *Mailing Add:* PO Box 9129 Horseshoe Bay TX 78654

HARRIS, FRANK BOWER, JR, PHYSICS. *Current Pos:* RETIRED. *Personal Data:* b New York, NY, May 24, 27; m 49, Lillian Abood; c Susan, Lisa & Frank. *Educ:* Mass Inst Technol, BS, 49, PhD(physics), 55. *Prof Exp:* Mem staff, Div Indust Coop, Mass Inst Technol, 49-50, asst, 50-53; from asst prof to assoc prof physics, Utica Col, 53-58; res engr, Stanford Res Inst, 58-62; sr supvry engr, TRG-West, 62-67; res scientist, Granger Assocs, 67-68; mgr data processing & comput applns & tech adv, TCI Inc, Mountain View, 68-87; comput software consult, 87-91. *Mem:* Inst Elec & Electronics Engrs. *Res:* Electromagnetic theory; computer applications and systems; antennas; structural engineering. *Mailing Add:* 196 Meadowood Dr Portola Valley CA 94028-7651

HARRIS, FRANK EPHRAIM, JR, CHEMICAL PHYSICS. *Current Pos:* dean, Col Sci, 73-75, PROF PHYSICS, UNIV UTAH, 68-, PROF CHEM, 69- *Personal Data:* b Boston, Mass, Aug 26, 29; m 52. *Educ:* Harvard Univ, AB, 51; Univ Calif, PhD(chem), 54. *Prof Exp:* Instr chem, Harvard Univ, 53-56; asst prof, Univ Calif, 56-59; from asst prof to assoc prof, Stanford Univ, 59-68. *Concurrent Pos:* Sloan Found fel, Univ Calif, 57-59; mem planning comt study nat ctr comput in chem, Nat Res Coun, 72-73. *Mem:* Am Chem Soc; Am Phys Soc. *Res:* Statistical mechanics; quantum mechanics; solid state theory. *Mailing Add:* Dept Chem Univ Utah 2020H Eyring Blvd Salt Lake City UT 84112-1107

HARRIS, FRANK WAYNE, POLYMER CHEMISTRY, ORGANIC CHEMISTRY. *Current Pos:* PROF, DEPT POLYMER SCI, UNIV AKRON, 83- *Personal Data:* b St Louis, Mo, Jan 28, 42; m 70; c 2. *Educ:* Univ Mo, BS, 64; Univ Iowa, MS, 66, PhD(org chem), 68. *Honors & Awards:* Space Act Award, NASA. *Prof Exp:* Captain, US Army Environ Hyg Agency, 68-70; instr org chem, Towson State Col, 69-70; prof chem, Wright State Univ, 70-83. *Concurrent Pos:* Consult, Ethyl Corp, Goodyear Tire & Rubber Co & W H Brady Co. *Mem:* Am Chem Soc; Controlled Release Soc. *Res:* Polymer synthesis and characterization with emphasis on polymer structure property relationships; preparation and development of controlled-release formulations. *Mailing Add:* Dept Polymer Sci Univ Akron Akron OH 44325-3909

HARRIS, FRANKLIN STEWART, JR, OPTICS. *Current Pos:* CONSULT, 78- *Personal Data:* b Logan, Utah, May 24, 12; m 36; c 11. *Educ:* Brigham Young Univ, AB, 31, MA, 36; Calif Inst Technol, PhD(physics), 41. *Honors & Awards:* Distinguished Serv Award, Optical Soc Am, 88. *Prof Exp:* Asst, Brigham Young Univ, 35-36 & Calif Inst Technol, 37-41; lectr physics, Univ BC, 41-43; from asst prof to prof, Univ Utah, 43-63 & BYU, 80-81; mem tech staff, Aerospace Corp, 63-70; sr scientist, Dept Chem & Inst Oceanog, Old Dominion Univ, 71-73, res prof physics, Geophys Sci & Oceanog, 73-78. *Concurrent Pos:* Consult, Sperry Utah Co, 59-62, Intermt Weather Inc, 61-63 & Nat Oceanog Atmospheric Admin, 77-79. *Mem:* Fel AAAS; fel Optical Soc Am; Am Meteorol Soc; fel Brit Inst Phys; Am Asn Physics Teachers. *Res:* Mass spectroscopy; oligodynamic effect of silver; diffraction of visible light; polarization by diffraction; cloud physics; infrared radiation; atmospheric optics; visibility; information retrieval; air pollution. *Mailing Add:* 81 W Main St Rockville UT 84763

HARRIS, GALE ION, NUCLEAR PHYSICS, MEDICAL PHYSICS. *Current Pos:* assoc chmn, Dept Radiol, 80-85, assoc dir, Inst Res & Advan Studies, 81-82, ASSOC PROF PHYSICS & RADIOL, MICH STATE UNIV, 75- *Personal Data:* b Arlington, Calif, Aug 7, 35; m 56, Bonnie Jean Hazlett; c 2. *Educ:* Univ Kans, BS, 57, MS, 59, PhD(physics), 62; Mass Inst Technol, SM, 73; Cooley Law Sch, JD, 85. *Prof Exp:* Group leader nuclear physics, Aerospace Res Labs, USAF, 62-69, actg dir, Gen Physics Res Lab, 69-72, dep dir, Solid State Physics Lab, 73-74; dir, Off Mgt Res, Med Sch, Johns Hopkins Univ, 74-75. *Concurrent Pos:* Mem, Nuclear Physics Subpanel, Off Aerospace Res, 64-70; adminr & asst prof, Dept Radiol, Johns Hopkins Univ, 74-75; consult, US Dept Energy, 74-82, NIH, 85-; mem, Energy Res & Develop Admin Task Force Nuclear Med, 75-77; trustee & pres, Mich Res Ctr, Inc, East Lansing, 75-77; dir, Am Technetronic Corp, 82-86. *Mem:* AAAS; fel Am Phys Soc; Soc Nuclear Med; Am Asn Physicists Med; Sigma Xi; Asn Univ Radiologists; Soc Magnetic Resource Med. *Res:* Nuclear structure physics; proton capture reactions; technology transfer from physics to medicine; application of imageing methods to medical research and diagnosis. *Mailing Add:* Dept Radiol Mich State Univ B220 Clin Ctr East Lansing MI 48824

HARRIS, GRANT ANDERSON, RANGE ECOLOGY. *Current Pos:* assoc prof, 56-67, chmn dept & extensionist, 67-80, RES SCIENTIST RANGE MGT, WASH STATE UNIV, 56-, PROF, 67-, EMER EXTENSIONIST COOP PROGS & CONSULT, 80-; CHMN BD, DECAGON DEVICES INC, SCI CONSULT, PULLMAN, WASH, 82- *Personal Data:* b Logan, Utah, July 13, 14; m 39, Jennabee Ballif; c Judith (Campbell), Patricia (Oak), Joseph B & Halli (Stone). *Educ:* Utah State Univ, BS, 39, PhD(range mgt), 65; Univ Idaho, MS, 41. *Prof Exp:* Res scientist, US Forest Serv, 38-40 & 41-52; asst prof & exten forester, Utah State Univ, 52-56. *Concurrent Pos:* Potlach fel, Univ Idaho, 40-41; consult, Wash Dept Natural Resources, 60-80, WPakistan Agr Univ & sr ecologist consult, Am Ecol Soc, 83; mem, Gov Tech Comt NCascades Recreation Study Team, 63-65; arid land ecol sci comt, AEC, 64-75, chmn, 70; mem, Coun Forest Sch Exec, 67-80; chmn, Inland Empire For Adv Coun, 67-80; chmn res adv comt, Intermountain Forest & Range Exp Sta, 67-80; chmn res adv comt, Pac NW Forest & Range Exp Sta, 67-80; local contact, President's Coun Environ Qual; chmn, Coun Agr Sci & Technol, 76; team leader, US AID Eval Econ Feasibility Range Forage Seed Prod, Morocco, 77; mem agr prog, Yemen, Arab Repub, 79 & agr exten prog, Chile, 80; cert range consult, Soc Range Mgt, 80-; sr ecologist, Ecol Soc Am, 83- *Mem:* Fel AAAS; Soc Am Foresters; fel Soc Range Mgt; Sigma Xi, Ecol Soc Am. *Res:* Genecology of and competition between annual and perennial range grasses; range ecosystems; plant genecology; soil-plant-water relations; rangeland fire influences. *Mailing Add:* Dept Natural Res Sci Wash State Univ Pullman WA 99164-6410. *Fax:* 509-335-7867; *E-Mail:* gaharris@turbonct.com

HARRIS, GROVER CLEVELAND, JR, ANIMAL PHYSIOLOGY, ENVIRONMENTAL PHYSIOLOGY. *Current Pos:* from asst prof to assoc prof, 60-70, PROF PHYSIOL, UNIV ARK, FAYETTEVILLE, 70- *Personal Data:* b Belington, WVa, Mar 24, 31; m 51; c 3. *Educ:* WVa Univ, BS, 52, MS, 56; Univ Md, PhD(avian physiol), 60. *Honors & Awards:* Poultry Sci Res Award, 63; Univ Ark Fac Teaching & Res Award, 69. *Prof Exp:* Asst poultry breeding, WVa Univ, 54-56; instr poultry sci, Univ Md, 56-60. *Concurrent Pos:* Vis scientist, UK Poultry Res Ctr, Edinburgh, Scotland, 82; founder, Univ Teaching Acad. *Mem:* Fel AAAS; fel Poultry Sci Asn; World Poultry Sci Asn; Soc Study Reprod. *Res:* Cryobiology; reproductive physiology; environmental physiology. *Mailing Add:* 617 Edna St Fayetteville AR 72703

HARRIS, GUY H, ORGANIC CHEMISTRY. *Current Pos:* ASSOC SCIENTIST, DOW CHEM CO, 64- *Personal Data:* b Calif, Oct 2, 14; m 40; c 4. *Educ:* Univ Calif, BS, 37; Stanford Univ, AM, 39, PhD(chem), 41. *Prof Exp:* Lab asst, Shell Develop Co, 37-38; org chemist, William S Merrell Co, 41-45 & Fiberboard Paper Prod Inc, 45-46; org chemist, Dow Chem Co, 46-59, assoc scientist, 59-62; lectr, Univ Ghana, 62-63, sr lectr, 63-64,. *Concurrent Pos:* Chmn dept chem, John F Kennedy Univ, 65-72. *Mem:* AAAS; Am Inst Mining, Metall & Petrol Eng; The Chem Soc; WAfrican Sci Asn; Am Chem Soc. *Res:* Mining chemicals. *Mailing Add:* Merck & Co Inc PO Box 2000 MS RY804-340 Rahway NJ 07065-0900

HARRIS, HAROLD H, PHYSICAL CHEMISTRY. *Current Pos:* asst prof, 70-75, ASSOC PROF CHEM, UNIV MO, ST LOUIS, 75- *Personal Data:* b Council Bluffs, Iowa, Mar 12, 40; m 66, Mary Cline; c Matthew & Jill. *Educ:* Harvey Mudd Col, BS, 62; Mich State Univ, PhD(phys chem), 67. *Prof Exp:* Fel phys chem, Univ Calif, Irvine, 66-67, instr chem, 67-70. *Concurrent Pos:* Vis prof, Solar Energy Res Inst, 85; vis scientist, Univ Chicago, 78; fac res partic, Wright-Patterson Air Force Lab, 91. *Mem:* AAAS; Am Chem Soc; Am Phys Soc; Fedn Am Scientists; Combustion Inst; Am Asn Physics Teachers. *Res:* Chemical kinetics and dynamics; modeling chemical systems; flame chemistry and dynamics; self-organizing systems. *Mailing Add:* Dept Chem Univ Mo St Louis MO 63121. *Fax:* 314-553-5342; *E-Mail:* hharris@umsl.edu

HARRIS, HAROLD JOSEPH, psychiatry, child psychiatry, for more information see previous edition

HARRIS, HENRY EARL, ORGANIC CHEMISTRY, BIOCHEMISTRY. *Current Pos:* assoc prof, 66-71, PROF CHEM, ARMSTRONG STATE COL, 71-, ASST DEAN, SCH ARTS SCI. *Personal Data:* b Ft Valley, Ga, Jan 28, 36; m 62; c 1. *Educ:* Ga Inst Technol, BS, 59, PhD(org chem), 63. *Prof Exp:* Res chemist, Chemstrand Res Ctr, Inc, 62-66. *Concurrent Pos:* Consult biochemist, St Josephs Hosp, Savannah, Ga, 69- *Mem:* AAAS; Am Chem Soc; Am Asn Clin Chemists. *Res:* Structure reactivity correlations; free-radical reactions; linear free energy relationships; polymer chemistry; clinical chemistry. *Mailing Add:* Dept Chem Armstrong Atlantic State Univ Abercom Ext Rd Savannah GA 31406

HARRIS, HENRY WILLIAM, MEDICINE. *Current Pos:* PROF CLIN MED, SCH MED, NY UNIV, 71- *Personal Data:* b Catawba, NC, Jan 6, 19; m 51; c 3. *Educ:* Univ NC, AB, 40; Harvard Univ, MD, 43; Am Bd Internal Med & Am Bd Pulmonary Dis, dipl, 51. *Prof Exp:* Med intern, Fourth Med Serv, Thorndike Mem Lab, Boston City Hosp, 44-45, asst resident med, 45-46; resident, Chest Serv, Bellevue Hosp, NY, 47; staff mem, Dept Med, Gundersen Clin, Wis, 48-53; asst prof med, Col Med, Univ Utah, 55-59, assoc prof, 59-60; prof & chmn dept, Woman's Med Col Pa, 60-67; chmn dept med, Cath Med Ctr, Brooklyn & Queens, 67-71; dir chest serv, Bellevue Hosp, 83-90, dir, Grad Training Prog, 71-90. *Concurrent Pos:* Chief pulmonary dis serv, Vet Admin Hosp, Salt Lake City, 55-57 & 59-60, chief med serv, 58-59; chief med serv, Hosp Woman's Med Col, 60-67; consult, Philadelphia Gen Hosp, Philadelphia & Wilmington Vet Admin Hosps, Valley-Forge Army Hosp, Phoenixville, Pa & Londis State Hosp; res fel, Thorndike Mem Lab, Boston City Hosp, 44 & 46; consult, Cath Med Ctr Brooklyn-Queens, 71- & NY Vet Admin Hosp, 73-; attending physician, Univ Hosp, NY Univ Med Ctr, 71- *Mem:* Am Thoracic Soc; Am Lung Asn; Am Bur Med Advan, China (pres, 87); fel Am Col Physicians. *Res:* Pulmonary diseases; human genetics; internal medicine. *Mailing Add:* Bellevue Hosp 462 First Ave New York NY 10016

HARRIS, HENSON, MATHEMATICS, ACADEMIC ADMINISTRATION. *Current Pos:* vpres acad affairs & prof math, 66-80, EMER DEAN, CULVER STOCKTON COL, 80- *Personal Data:* b Graves Co, Ky, Dec 12, 12; m 34; c 2. *Educ:* Murray State Col, BS, 34; Vanderbilt Univ, MA, 41; Univ Okla, EdD(math, educ), 53. *Prof Exp:* Instr pub schs, Fla, 35-41; head dept math, Campbell Col, 41-42; instr math & physics, Maxwell AFB, 42; instr math, Univ Tenn, 46 & Univ Ill, 47; prof & chmn dept, Okla Baptist Univ, 47-54; acad dean, Wayland Col, 54-57; admin vpres & dean, Georgetown Col, 57-62; dean instr, Slippery Rock State Col, 62-65; exec vpres & dean, Union Univ, Tenn, 65-66. *Concurrent Pos:* Asst, Vanderbilt Univ, 40-41. *Mem:* Am Math Soc. *Res:* Mathematics and education. *Mailing Add:* Whispering Oaks Circle Rte 1 Box 417 Mayfield KY 42066

HARRIS, HERBERT H, medicine; deceased, see previous edition for last biography

HARRIS, HOLLIS LOYD, AERONAUTICS. *Current Pos:* vchmn, 92-93, PRES & CHIEF EXEC OFFICER, AIR CAN, 92-, CHMN, 93- *Personal Data:* b Carrollton, Ga, Nov 25, 31; m 55, Joyce Entrekin; c Patricia S, David L & Michael J. *Educ:* Ga Inst Technol, BA, 61. *Prof Exp:* Staff, Delta Air Lines, 54-90, asst vpres facil, 68-71, asst vpres eng, 71-72, asst vpres, Inflight Serv Dept, 72-73, sr vpres, Passenger Serv, 73-85, sr vpres opers, 85-87, pres & chief oper officer, 87-90; pres & chief exec officer, Continental Airline Holdings & Continental Airlines, 90-91; chmn & chief exec officer, Air Eagle Holdings Inc, 91-92. *Mem:* Am Inst Aeronaut & Astronaut; Int Transport Asn. *Mailing Add:* Air Canada Air Can Ctr PO Box 14000 St Laurent PQ H4Y 1H4 Can

HARRIS, HOLLY ANN, GROUP THEORY GRAPH MEMORY AS APPLIED TO SOLID STATE STRUCTURES, HISTORY OF WOMEN IN SCIENCE. *Current Pos:* ASST PROF PHYS CHEM, CREIGHTON UNIV, 90- *Personal Data:* b Denver, Colo. *Educ:* Harvey Mudd Col, Calif, BS, 82; Univ Wis-Madison, PhD(chem), 88. *Prof Exp:* Res assoc crystallog, Univ Wis-Madison, 88; asst prof inorg phys chem, Grinnell Col, Iowa, 88-90. *Concurrent Pos:* Clare Booth Luce prof sci, Luce Found, 90. *Mem:* Am Chem Soc; Sigma Xi. *Res:* Electronic structure and bonding relationship in novel main group organo-metalic and inorganic molecules; electronic structure of bio-inorganic molecules; group theory memory as applied to solid state structures. *Mailing Add:* Chem Dept Creighton Univ Omaha NE 68178-0001

HARRIS, HUBERT ANDREW, PHYTOPATHOLOGY, MYCOLOGY. *Current Pos:* RETIRED. *Personal Data:* b Durant, Okla, July 18, 09; m 39, Pauline Mary Clay; c Sue. *Educ:* Southeastern State Col, AB, 30; Univ Ill, MS, 32, PhD(bot), 38. *Prof Exp:* Asst biol, Southeastern State Col, 28-30, assoc prof biol, 38-42; asst botanist, Ill State Natural Hist Surv, 30-33; asst bot, Univ Ill, 35-37; asst prof, SDak State Col, 42-43, assoc plant pathologist, Exp Sta, 43; plant pathologist, Bur Plant Indust, Soils & Agr Eng, USDA, 43-44; prof biol, Univ PR, 44-46; asst prof biol, Univ Colo, 46-49; prof bot, San Jose State Univ, 49-76. *Mem:* AAAS; Bot Soc Am; Am Phytopath Soc; Mycol Soc Am. *Res:* Mycology; antibiotics. *Mailing Add:* 1145 Husted Ave San Jose CA 95125

HARRIS, HUGH COURTNEY, ASTROPHYSICS. *Current Pos:* ASTRONOMER, US NAVAL OBSERV, 85- *Personal Data:* b New Rochelle, NY, Dec 21, 47; m 90, Diane Notarianni. *Educ:* Cornell Univ, BS, 70; Univ Wash, PhD(astron), 80. *Prof Exp:* Vis res fel, Dominion Astrophys Observ, 80-85. *Concurrent Pos:* Res fel, McMaster Univ, 82-84. *Mem:* Am Astron Soc; Astron Soc Pac. *Res:* Motions and chemical abundances in stars; star clusters; variable stars; structure of galaxy and Magellanic clouds; globular clusters. *Mailing Add:* US Naval Observ PO Box 1149 Flagstaff AZ 86002

HARRIS, J DOUGLAS, COMPUTER NETWORKING, DATABASE. *Current Pos:* Chmn dept, 79, PROF MATH, MARQUETTE UNIV, 69- *Personal Data:* b Dallas, Tex, Apr 13, 39; m 65; c 2. *Educ:* Univ Kans, BA, 66, MA, 67, PhD(math), 69. *Mem:* Am Math Soc; Math Asn Am; Asn Comput Mach. *Res:* Topology; mathematical logic; computer language; applying topological ideas to computer networks and distributed databases; data flow architectures and languages. *Mailing Add:* Dept Math Marquette Univ Dept MSCS PO Box 1881 Milwaukee WI 53201-1881

HARRIS, J(OHN) S(TERLING), chemical engineering; deceased, see previous edition for last biography

HARRIS, JACK KENYON, CELL BIOLOGY. *Current Pos:* ASSOC PROF BIOL, RUSSELL SAGE COL, 79- *Personal Data:* b Albuquerque, NMex, May 2, 45; m 67; c 1. *Educ:* Columbia Univ, BA, 67; Harvard Univ, MAT, 70; State Univ NY, Albany, PhD(biol), 80. *Mem:* AAAS; Optical Soc Am. *Res:* Light-optical techniques to localize and quantitate forces produced by biomolecules, cells, and organisms. *Mailing Add:* Biol Dept Russell Sage Col Troy NY 12180

HARRIS, JACK R, ELECTRICAL ENGINEERING, PHYSICS. *Current Pos:* CONSULT, 87- *Personal Data:* b Saginaw, Mich, Oct 17, 30; m 53; c 3. *Educ:* Univ Mich, Ann Arbor, BS, 52; US Naval Postgrad Sch, MS, 60, PhD(elec eng), 65. *Prof Exp:* US Navy pilot, 52-57, sonics engr, Naval Air Develop Squadron, VXI, 62-64, instr physics, US Naval Postgrad Sch, 64-66, spec proj mgr, Naval Air Develop Ctr, 66-68, dep dir syst anal & eng dept, 68-71, sci off, 71-74; vpres, Pinkerton Comput Const, 74-79; sr dir, Tracop Inc, 79-87. *Concurrent Pos:* Chmn, acoust working group, Dept Defense, 67-71. *Mem:* Opers Res Soc Am; Inst Elec & Electronics Engrs; Radio Club Am; Acoust Eng Soc; Sigma Xi. *Res:* Systems engineering emphasizing computers with acoustical processing applications. *Mailing Add:* 20400 Highland Hall Dr Gaithersburg MD 20879-4005

HARRIS, JAMES EDWARD, ORTHODONTICS, GENETICS. *Current Pos:* RETIRED. *Personal Data:* b Ann Arbor, Mich, Aug 25, 28. *Educ:* Univ Mich, AB, 50, DDS, 54, MS, 60 & 63. *Prof Exp:* Res assoc orthod, Univ Mich, Ann Arbor, 63-64, from asst prof to assoc prof orthod & human genetics, 64-70, prof orthod & chmn dept, 69-82. *Concurrent Pos:* Consult, Plymouth State Hosp, Mich, 65-; NIH career develop award, 64-82; dir field projs, Egypt, 82-; lectr & writer. *Mem:* Am Asn Orthodontists; Am Dent Asn; Am Asn Phys Anthrop; Am Soc Human Genetics; Sigma Xi; Int Col Dentists. *Res:* Inheritance of the craniofacial complex; study of malocclusion; facial growth; effect of orthodontic treatment on mandibular growth; the x-ray investigation of the royal mummies of Egypt; study of ancient skeletal record and modern Nubian population; application of genetics to orthodontic diagnosis and treatment. *Mailing Add:* 1918 Scottwood Ann Arbor MI 48104

HARRIS, JAMES JOSEPH, INORGANIC CHEMISTRY. *Current Pos:* lab mgr, 87-88, mgr, surfactant synthesis, 87-88, CHEM SERV, CHUBB NAT FOAM, 88-, MGR, CHEM SYNTHESIS, CHEM SERV, 88- *Personal Data:* b Chicago, Ill, Jan 27, 30; m 61, Marilyn Canon; c 2. *Educ:* Miami Univ Ohio, AB, 52; Univ Fla, PhD(chem), 58. *Prof Exp:* Chemist, Union Carbide Corp, WVa, 53; sr scientist, Koppers Co, Inc, 58-74; sr proj scientist, Arco Chem, 74-75, sr group mgr, 75-86. *Mem:* Am Chem Soc. *Res:* Organometallic compounds; metallic fluorides; polymerization catalysis; polyolefins; organic chemistry; pesticide synthesis. *Mailing Add:* 1523 High Meadow Lane West Chester PA 19380

HARRIS, JAMES RIDOUT, SYSTEMS ENGINEERING, COMPUTER COMMUNICATIONS. *Current Pos:* RETIRED. *Personal Data:* b Lockhart, Tex, Apr 14, 20; m 43, Frances E Wiley; c Richard W, Betty A & Beverly J. *Educ:* Univ Richmond, BS, 41; Polytech Univ, MEE, 48. *Prof Exp:* Eng asst, Chesapeake & Potomac Tel Co, Va, 41-42; mem tech staff res & develop, 42-53, supvr comput res, 53-56, head dept data processing & data commun develop, 56-61, dir data systs eng, 61-62, dir data transmission systs eng, 62-65, dir customer switching eng ctr, 65-69, dir govt & spec systs eng ctr, 69-70, dir govt commun planning ctr, 70-71, dir customer equip studies ctr, 71-81, dir data network spec studies ctr, Bell Tel Labs, 81; dir spec studies ctr, Info Systs Labs, AT&T, 82-83. *Concurrent Pos:* Mem admin comt, Comput Soc, Inst Elec & Electronics Engrs, 62-65. *Mem:* Inst Elec & Electronics Engrs; Am Phys Soc; Sigma Xi. *Res:* Airborne communications; solid state devices and circuits; data processing; data communication; communications networks. *Mailing Add:* 8 Dogwood Lane Rumson NJ 07760-1412

HARRIS, JAMES STEWART, JR, SEMICONDUCTOR PHYSICS, MOLECULAR BEAM EPITAXY. *Current Pos:* PROF ELEC ENG, STANFORD UNIV, 82-, DIR SOLID STATE LAB, 84-, DIR, JOINT SERV ELEC PROG, 84- *Personal Data:* b Portland, Ore, Aug 22, 42; m 65, Joyce Christensen; c Geoffrey S & Gregory A. *Educ:* Stanford Univ, BS, 64, MS, 65, PhD(elec eng), 69. *Prof Exp:* Instr elec eng, Stanford Univ, 68; mem tech staff semiconductor physics, Rockwell Int Sci Ctr, 69-72, group leader infrared devices, 72-80, prin scientist, 80-81, dir, Optoelectronics Dept, 81-82. *Concurrent Pos:* Consult, Varian Asn; mem Inst Elec & Electronics Engrs Electron Device Soc, 83-; vis prof, Ecole Polytechnique, Lausanne, Switz, 92. *Mem:* Fel Inst Elec & Electronics Engrs; fel Am Phys Soc; Electrochem Soc; Am Vacuum Soc; Mat Res Soc; Sigma Xi. *Res:* Semiconductor device physics; molecular beam, epitaxial growth of III-V compounds; electro-optical devices; lasers; resonant tunneling devices; quantum well optical modulators; non-linear optical devices; super lattice structures; single electron transport and Coulomb blockade. *Mailing Add:* Dept Elec Eng McCullough 224 Stanford CA 94305-4055. *Fax:* 650-723-4659; *E-Mail:* harris@sierra.stanford.edu

HARRIS, JANE E, ONCOGENICITY, NEUROTOXICITY. *Current Pos:* SR DIR TOXICOL, AM CYANAMID, 86- *Personal Data:* b New York, NY, Feb 26, 46; m 76, Joseph Longind; c Tristan & Moira. *Educ:* Cornell Univ, BS, 65; Yale Univ, PhD(pharmacol), 71. *Prof Exp:* Toxicologist, Food & Drug Admin, 78-84; surpvry toxicoligist, Environ Protection Agency, 84-86. *Mem:* Am Soc Pharmacol & Exp Therapeut; Soc Neurosci; Int Soc Regulatory Toxicol & Pharmacol; Am Col Toxicol. *Res:* Toxicological research. *Mailing Add:* Am Cyanamid Co PO Box 400 Princeton NJ 08543-0400. *Fax:* 609-275-3578; *E-Mail:* harnsj@pt.cyanamid.com

HARRIS, JAY H, ELECTRICAL ENGINEERING, BIOMEDICAL ENGINEERING. *Current Pos:* DIR, ELEC ENG DEPT, SAN DIEGO STATE UNIV. *Personal Data:* b Newark, NJ, June 3, 36; m 63; c 1. *Educ:* Polytech Inst Brooklyn, BEE, 58; Calif Inst Technol, MS, 59; Univ Calif, Los Angeles, PhD(electromagnetics), 65. *Prof Exp:* Mem tech staff antennas & propagation, Hughes Aircraft Co, 58-65; asst prof elec eng, Univ Wash, 66-70, assoc prof, 70-76; prog dir, Nat Sci Found Eng, 76- *Concurrent Pos:* Fulbright-Hays fel, Paris, 65-66; consult urol, Sch Med Univ Wash, 67-76. *Mem:* Inst Elec & Electronics Engrs. *Res:* Radio wave propagation; antennas; plasmas; electro-optics; biomedical ultrasonics; optical spectroscopy. *Mailing Add:* Elec Eng Dept San Diego State Univ San Diego CA 92182

HARRIS, JEAN LOUISE, INTERNAL MEDICINE, ALLERGY. *Current Pos:* SR ASSOC DIR & DIR MED AFFAIRS, UNIV MINN HOSP & CLIN, 92-; MAYOR, EDEN PRAIRE, MINN, 94- *Personal Data:* b Richmond, Va, Nov 24, 31; m 55; c 3. *Educ:* Va Union Univ, BS, 51; Med Col Va, MD, 55. *Hon Degrees:* DSc, Univ Richmond, 81. *Prof Exp:* Intern, Med Col Va, 55-56, resident internal med, 56-57, fel, 57-58; fel, Strong Mem Hosp-Sch Med, Univ Rochester, 58-60; instr med, Col Med, Howard Univ, 60-68, asst prof community health pract, 69-72; prof, Va Commonwealth Univ, 73-78, clin prof family pract, 78-82; vpres, State Marketing Progs, Control Data Corp, 82-84, vpres, State Govt Affairs, 86-88; pres & chief exec officer, Ramsey Found, 88-92. *Concurrent Pos:* Res assoc, Walter Reed Army Inst Res, Washington, DC, 60-63; pvt pract internal med & allergy, 64-71; chief, Bur Resources Develop, Washington DC Dept Health, 67-69; dir, Ctr Community Health Consults, Div Health Manpower Intel, HEW, 69-77; asst clin prof community med, Charles R Drew Postgrad Med Sch, Los Angeles, 70-72; exec dir, Nat Med Asn Found, Washington, DC, 70-73; consult, Nat Ctr Health Statist, HEW, 71-72, Div Med Care Stand, Health Serv & Ment Health Admin, 73, Vet Admin, 73, Vet Admin Hosp Health Care Study, Nat Acad Sci, 76 & US Aid, 77; lectr, Dept Med Care & Hosps, Johns Hopkins Univ, 71-73; mem, Adv Coun Sickle Cell Prog, Nat Heart Lung & Blood Inst, 75-79, Recombinant DNA Adv Comt, NIH, 79-82 & President's Task Force Pvt Sector Initiatives, 81-82; secy human resources, Commonwealth Va, 78-82; state liaison, US Coun Int Yr Dis Persons, 81. *Mem:* Inst Med-Nat Acad Sci; fel Royal Soc Health; Am Acad Med Adminr; Am Pub Health Asn; Am Acad Family Pract; Sigma Xi. *Mailing Add:* 10860 Forestview Circle Eden Prairie MN 55347

HARRIS, JEFFREY R, PUBLIC HEALTH & EPIDEMIOLOGY. *Current Pos:* epidemic intel serv officer, 81, ACTG ASSOC DIR, POLICY PLANNING & EVAL, CTR DIS CONTROL & PREV. *Educ:* Johns Hopkins Univ, MPH; Am Bd Internal Med, cert; Am Bd Prev Med, cert. *Prof Exp:* Dir, AIDS Prev Prog, Agency Int Develop. *Mailing Add:* Ctrs Dis Control Prev Bldg 16 Rm D-23 1600 Clifton Rd NE Atlanta GA 30333

HARRIS, JEROME SYLVAN, PEDIATRICS. *Current Pos:* RETIRED. *Personal Data:* b New York, NY, Feb 27, 09; m 58, Jacqueline Hijmans. *Educ:* Dartmouth Col, AB, 29; Harvard Univ, MD, 33. *Prof Exp:* From instr to prof pediat & biochem, Sch Med, Duke Univ, 37-79, pediatrician, Univ Hosp, 37-79, chmn dept pediat, 54-68. *Mem:* Fel Soc Pediat Res; fel Am Soc Clin Invest; fel Am Pediat Soc; fel Am Acad Pediat. *Res:* Biochemistry; metabolic disturbances in children. *Mailing Add:* 1701 Pleasant Green Rd Durham NC 27705

HARRIS, JESSE RAY, PHYSICAL CHEMISTRY, CERAMIC ENGINEERING. *Current Pos:* SR CHEMIST, PHILLIPS PETROL CO, 66- *Personal Data:* b Spokane, Wash, Apr 26, 37; m 70; c 2. *Educ:* Univ Wash, BS, 59, MS, 62; Alfred Univ, PhD(ceramic sci), 67. *Mem:* Am Ceramic Soc; Nat Inst Ceramic Eng; Am Chem Soc. *Res:* Catalytic reactions of olefins; thermodynamics of adsorption. *Mailing Add:* 3409 Willowood Dr Bartlesville OK 74006-4433

HARRIS, JOEL MARK, SPECTROSCOPY. *Current Pos:* From asst prof to assoc prof, 76-85, PROF CHEM, UNIV UTAH, 85- *Personal Data:* b Charleston, WVa, Aug 27, 50; m 72, Frances Nicrosi; c Peter. *Educ:* Duke Univ, BS, 72; Purdue Univ, PhD(chem), 76. *Honors & Awards:* Coblentz Award Molecular Spectros, 86; Award in Chem Instrumentation, Anal Chem Div, Am Chem Soc, 91. *Concurrent Pos:* From adj asst prof to adj prof bioeng, Univ Utah, 80-88; Alfred P Sloan fel, 85-87. *Mem:* Am Chem Soc; Optical Soc Am; Soc Appl Spectros; Coblentz Soc. *Res:* Analytical molecular spectroscopy: application of lasers to chemical analysis, time-resolved fluorescence and Raman spectroscopy; spectroscopic studies of liquid-solid interfaces. *Mailing Add:* Dept Chem Univ Utah Salt Lake City UT 84112-1102. *Fax:* 801-581-8433; *E-Mail:* harrisj@chemistry.chem.utah.edu

HARRIS, JOHN FERGUSON, JR, ORGANIC SYNTHESIS, POLYMER SYNTHESIS. *Current Pos:* RES CHEMIST, CENT RES & DEVELOP DEPT, E I DU PONT DE NEMOURS & CO, INC, 52- *Personal Data:* b Stroudsburg, Pa, Apr 15, 25; m 49; c 3. *Educ:* Univ Pa, AB, 48, MS, 50, PhD(org chem), 53. *Concurrent Pos:* Guggenheim fel, 63-64. *Mem:* Am Chem Soc; Sigma Xi; AAAS. *Res:* Organic sulfur and fluorine chemistry; free radical chemistry; photochemistry; polymer chemistry. *Mailing Add:* 333 Hampton Rd Wilmington DE 19803-2425

HARRIS, JOHN KENNETH, TOPOLOGY. *Current Pos:* From asst prof to assoc prof, 62-73, asst dean grad studies, asst dean acad affairs, 71-74, PROF MATH, PORTLAND STATE UNIV, 73-, DIR BUDGET, 75- *Personal Data:* b Reno, Nev, Jan 7, 34; m 55, Charlotte Olsen; c John F, Maryellen & Elizabeth S. *Educ:* Fresno State Col, AB, 58, MS, 59; Univ Ore, PhD(math), 62. *Mem:* Am Math Soc. *Res:* Point set topology; number theory; algebra. *Mailing Add:* Budget Off Portland State Univ PO Box 751 Portland OR 97207-0751. *Fax:* 503-725-5800; *E-Mail:* ken@bud.pdx.edu

HARRIS, JOHN MICHAEL, MAMMALIAN PALEONTOLOGY. *Personal Data:* b London, UK, Dec 6, 42; m 73; c 2. *Educ:* Univ Leicester, BSc, 64; Univ Tex, Austin, MA, 67; Univ Bristol, PhD(geol), 70. *Prof Exp:* Lectr geol, Ahmadu Bello Univ, Nigeria, 70; sr palaeontologist, Ctr Prehistory & Palaeont, Nairobi, 71-72; dir paleont, Nat Mus Kenya, 72-79; head, Earth Sci Div, Los Angeles Co Mus Natural Hist, 80-93. *Concurrent Pos:* Consult paleontologist, Koobi Fora Res Proj, Nat Mus Kenya, 72-; hon lectr, Dept Zool, Univ Nairobi, 76-79. *Mem:* Geol Soc London; Linnean Soc; Soc Vert Paleont; Sigma Xi. *Res:* Systematics, biostratigraphy and functional morphology of Miocene, Pliocene and Pleistocene mammals from Africa particularly fossil ungulates from sub-Saharan Africa. *Mailing Add:* Natural Hist Mus 900 Exposition Blvd Los Angeles CA 90007. *Fax:* 801-581-7065; *E-Mail:* harrisjm@aol.com

HARRIS, JOHN WALLACE, BIOLOGY. *Current Pos:* From asst prof to assoc prof, 68-80, dir honors prog, 78-83, PROF BIOL, TENN TECHNOL UNIV, 80- *Personal Data:* b Peoria, Ill, Aug 28, 41; m 79, Caroline Edwards; c Mary, John & Larry. *Educ:* Western Ill Univ, BSEd, 63; Ind Univ, AM, 65, PhD(genetics), 68. *Concurrent Pos:* Fulbright fel, India, 91-92. *Mem:* Sigma Xi. *Res:* Biochemical genetics and systematics. *Mailing Add:* 1615 Bilbrey Park Dr Cookeville TN 38501

HARRIS, JOHN WAYNE, RADIATION THERAPY, RADIATION BIOLOGY. *Current Pos:* AT DEPT RADIATION ONCOL, ST JOSEPH'S HOSP. *Personal Data:* b Syracuse, NY, Jan 8, 37; m 60; c 4. *Educ:* Syracuse Univ, BA, 58, MS, 62; Univ Rochester, PhD(radiation biol), 65; Univ Calif, San Francisco, MD, 78. *Prof Exp:* Teacher, Baldwinsville Acad, 59-61; Australian Inst Nuclear Sci & Eng fel, 65-67; asst prof radiol, dept radiation oncol, Univ Calif, San Francisco, 67-71, assoc prof, 71- *Mem:* AAAS; Am Soc Cell Biol; Radiation Res Soc; Biophys Soc; Am Asn Cancer Res. *Res:* Cellular sulfhydryl groups; tumor growth; radiation and drug effects; cellular immunology; radiation therapy. *Mailing Add:* Dept Radiation Oncol St Joseph's Hosp 2700 Dolbeer St Eureka CA 95501-4736

HARRIS, JOHN WILLIAM, CLINICAL MEDICINE, HEMATOLOGY. *Current Pos:* from sr instr to assoc prof, 52-62, PROF MED, CASE WESTERN RESERVE UNIV, 62- *Personal Data:* b Boston, Mass, Mar 30, 20; m 51, Stephanie Bunting; c Wendy A, Stephen B & Alison D. *Educ:* Trinity Col, Conn, BS, 41; Harvard Univ, MD, 44; Am Bd Internal Med, dipl, 54. *Honors & Awards:* Martin Luther King Jr Med Award, 72. *Prof Exp:* Res assoc med, Harvard Med Sch, 51-52. *Concurrent Pos:* Res fel med, Med Sch, Harvard Univ, 48-51; Stengel res fel, Am Col Physicians, 51-52; hematologist, Cleveland Metrop Gen Hosp, 52-, assoc dir, med dept, 66-81; attend physician, Crile Vet Admin Hosp, 53-58, sr attend physician, 58-; Markle scholar, 55-60; USPHS res career award, 62. *Mem:* Am Soc Hemat (vpres, 78-79, pres-elect, 79-81, pres, 81-82); Am Soc Clin Invest (vpres, 64-65); fel Am Col Physicians; Am Fedn Clin Res; Asn Am Physicians; fel Int Soc Hemat. *Res:* Internal medicine; hematology; hemolytic anemias; sickle cell anemia; nutritional and pernicious anemia. *Mailing Add:* MetroHealth Med Ctr 2500 MetroHealth Dr Cleveland OH 44109-1998. *Fax:* 216-778-5825; *E-Mail:* jwh2@po.cwru.edu

HARRIS, JOSEPH, BIOPHYSICS, NEUROCHEMISTRY. *Current Pos:* lectr chem, Ariz State Univ, 62-65, res prof, 65-75, prof chem & assoc chmn dept, 75-89, EMER PROF, ARIZ STATE UNIV, 89- *Personal Data:* b Baltimore, Md, Dec 2, 19; m 44, Irene D Brown; c Donald J & Mark L. *Educ:* Univ Md, BS, 47; Johns Hopkins Univ, MA, 49, PhD(physiol chem), 52. *Prof Exp:* Instr biochem, Johns Hopkins Univ, 52; responsible invest, Baxter Labs, Inc, 52-54; instr, Sch Med, Univ Colo, 54-55; asst prof, Albany Med Col, 55-62; chief lab neurochem, Barrow Neurol Inst, 62-75. *Concurrent Pos:* Vis prof, Inst Med Res, Royal NShore Hosp, Sydney, Australia, 69; exchange scientist, US-Hungary Nat Acad Sci, 71; vis prof, Biochem Dept, Oxford Univ, 81. *Mem:* Fel AAAS; fel NY Acad Sci; Am Chem Soc; Am Asn Clin Chemists; Biochem Soc; Biophys Soc. *Res:* Neurochemistry; metal ions effect on and mechanisms of action in cellular processes; biological membrane structure and neurotoxins; mechanism of drug action; biochemistry of exercise. *Mailing Add:* 2131 E Geneva Dr Tempe AZ 85282-4039. *Fax:* 602-965-2747

HARRIS, JOSEPH BELKNAP, cytology, for more information see previous edition

HARRIS, JUDITH ANNE VAN COUVERING, VERTEBRATE PALEONTOLOGY. *Current Pos:* ASSOC PROF GEOL, UNIV COLO, BOULDER, 77-; CUR FOSSIL VERTEBRATES & ASSOC PROF NATURAL HIST, UNIV COLO MUS, 77- *Personal Data:* b Tulsa, Okla, Feb 20, 38; div; c 4. *Educ:* Univ Calif, Berkeley, BA, 60; Univ Cambridge, PhD(geol), 72. *Mem:* Soc Vertebrate Paleont; fel Linnean Soc. *Res:* African tertiary faunas and paleoenvironments; origin of modern terrestrial communities; biogeography; evolutionary problems cichlid fish evolution; science and philosophy; feminist science. *Mailing Add:* Geol Box 250 Univ Colo Boulder Boulder CO 80309-0250

HARRIS, JULES ELI, ONCOLOGY, IMMUNOLOGY. *Current Pos:* RETIRED. *Personal Data:* b Toronto, Ont, Oct 12, 34; m 72; c 6. *Educ:* Univ Toronto, MD, 59; FRCPS(C), 65, FACP, 66. *Prof Exp:* Asst prof med, Univ Tex, Houston, 66-69; from assoc prof to prof med, Univ Ottawa, 72-77, prof med & dir sect med oncol, 78-93; dir, Rush Med Cancer Ctr, 86-92. *Concurrent Pos:* Res fel med, Ont Cancer Inst, 61-62 & Brit Med Res Coun, 62-63; consult, Ont Cancer Treat & Res Found, Nat Defense Med Ctr, Ottawa, 69, 71-77; sci officer, Med Res Coun Can, 70-72. *Mem:* Am Soc Clin

Oncol; fel Am Col Physicians; Am Soc Hemat; Am Asn Cancer Res; NY Acad Sci; Sigma Xi. *Res:* Tumor immunology; effect of chemotherapy on immune response. *Mailing Add:* Rush Med Col 1725 W Harrison St Chicago IL 60612

HARRIS, KENNETH, SUPERALLOY METALLURGY, MELTING REFINING & CASTING METALLURGY. *Current Pos:* VPRES & DIR TECHNOL, CANNON-MUSKEGON CORP, 82- *Personal Data:* b Manchester, UK, Dec 26, 43; m 66; c 2. *Educ:* Royal Sch Mines, BS, 65; Univ London, ARSM, 65. *Prof Exp:* Mgr tech qual, Superalloys Div, Union Carbide UK Ltd, 65-75. *Mem:* Metal Soc; Am Soc Metals. *Res:* Developed technology to electro-slag refine wrought nickel-base precipitation hardened superalloys; developed vacuum induction refining technology for premium quality nickel-base; gamma prime strengthened cast and PM superalloys; inventor and developer of the CMSX series of single crystal superalloys. *Mailing Add:* Cannon-Muskegon Corp PO Box 506 2875 Lincoln St Muskegon MI 49443-0506

HARRIS, KERRY FRANCIS PATRICK, VIROLOGY. *Current Pos:* PROF ENTOM & VIROL, TEX A&M UNIV, 76-, DIR VIRUS-VECTOR RES LAB, 93- *Personal Data:* b New Orleans, La, Aug 6, 43; m 65. *Educ:* New Orleans Univ, BS, 64; Loyola Univ, MS, 68; Mich State Univ, PhD(entom & virol), 71. *Honors & Awards:* Sigma Xi Award, 71. *Prof Exp:* Instr biol sci, New Orleans Sch Bd, 63-65; res assoc, Loyola Univ, 65-67; res fel entom & virol, NSF, 68, NIH, 68-71, virus-vector interactions, Nat Res Coun, Can, 71-72 & NIH, 72-73. *Concurrent Pos:* Fulbright scholar & res fel, 69; prin investr & prog leader, Nat Sci Found, 72-75; res scientist, Int Sorghum-Millet Improv Prog, 77-81 & Coop Regional Res Proj Viral & Mycoplasmal Dis Corn & Sorghum, 76-; assoc ed, J Econ Entom, 77-; res scientist, Int Working Group Legume Viruses, 77-, mem, Nat Medal Sci Comt, 79-82; lectr, Int Maize & Wheat Improv Ctr, Mex, 81-, invited lectr, People's Rep China, 88 & Int lectr, WHO, Indonesia, 88; assoc ed, Plant Dis, 81-; ed, Aphids as Virus Vectors, 77, Leafhopper Vectors & Plant Agents, 79, Vectors of Plant Pathogens, 80, Plant Dis & Vectors: Ecol & Epidemiol, 81, Current Topics Vector Res, 81-88, Pathogens, Vector & Plant Dis: Approaches to Control, 82, Adv in Dis Vector Res, 88- *Mem:* Am Phytopath Soc; Entom Soc Am; Sigma Xi; Am Soc Microbiol; Am Soc Virol; Soc Vector Ecol. *Res:* Pathogen-Vector-Host interactions with special emphasis on virus transmission mechanisms, determinants of virus-vector specificity phenomena and the fates of noncirculative and circulative viruses in their vectors; molecular biology of insect-transmitted plant viruses. *Mailing Add:* Dept Entomol Tex A&M Univ College Station TX 77843-2475

HARRIS, LAWRENCE DEAN, ANIMAL ECOLOGY, RESOURCE MANAGEMENT. *Current Pos:* ASST PROF WILDLIFE ECOL, UNIV FLA, 72- *Personal Data:* b Avoca, Iowa, Sept 20, 42; div; c 4. *Educ:* Iowa State Univ, BSc, 64; Mich State Univ, MSc, 68, PhD(ecol), 70. *Prof Exp:* Wildlife mgt officer, Tanzania Game Div, 64-66, wildlife biologist, 66-67; res assoc systs ecol, Colo State Univ, 70-72. *Concurrent Pos:* Fel US int biol prog, Colo State Univ, 70-72; res grant US forest serv, Southeastern Forest Exp Sta, 73-74, US Nat Park Serv, 74-76, US Dept Transp, 74-75 & Fla Game Fish Comn, NSF, 73-; task force recreation & wildlife res priorities, USDA, 73-74; long range plan comn, Wildlife Soc, 77-78. *Mem:* Am Soc Mammal; AAAS; Ecol Soc Am; Sigma Xi; Wildlife Soc. *Res:* Quantitative and conceptual aspects of renewable resource management with special emphasis on decision making and mathematical modelling. *Mailing Add:* Wildlife Ecol & Conserv Univ Fla 118 Newins-Zieler Hall Gainesville FL 32611

HARRIS, LAWSON P(ARKS), ELECTRICAL ENGINEERING. *Current Pos:* ELEC ENGR, GEN ELEC RES & DEVELOP CTR, 59- *Personal Data:* b Providence, RI, Aug 28, 29; m 57, Priscilla L Bird; c Susan (Bates), Janet L (Harris-Parillo) & Carolyn L. *Educ:* Mass Inst Technol, BS, 50, MS, 56, ScD(elec eng), 59. *Prof Exp:* Develop engr, RCA-Victor, 50-51; res asst, Mass Inst Technol, 54-56, res engr, 56-57, instr elec eng, 57-59. *Concurrent Pos:* Chmn, Gaseous Electronics Conf, 80-82. *Mem:* Am Soc Mech Engrs; Inst Elec & Electronics Engrs; Am Phys Soc. *Res:* Control systems theory; magneto-hydrodynamics; energy conversion; gaseous electronics; electric arcs; industrial applications of electric arcs in vacuum and high-pressure electric switchgear, lighting, arc welding and plasma jets; factory automation; aircraft engine controls; modeling for control design. *Mailing Add:* Gen Elec Res & Develop Ctr KW-D212 PO Box 8 Schenectady NY 12301. *Fax:* 518-387-5164; *E-Mail:* harrislp@crd.ge.com

HARRIS, LEE ERROL, HYDROGRAPHIC SURVEYING, COASTAL & OCEANOGRAPHIC ENGINEERING. *Current Pos:* chmn, Eng Sci Div, 80-87, ASSOC PROF OCEAN ENG & OCEANOG, FLA INST TECHNOL, MELBOURNE, 80- *Personal Data:* b Ft Pierce, Fla, Oct 29, 53; m 75; c 2. *Educ:* Fla Atlantic Univ, BS, 74; Univ Fla, MS, 75. *Prof Exp:* Res asst, Coastal & Oceanog Eng Lab, Univ Fla, 74-75; coastal engr, Jacksonville Dist, US Army Corps Engrs, 75-77. *Concurrent Pos:* Consult engr & survr, 77- *Mem:* Marine Technol Soc; Am Shore & Beach Preserv Asn. *Res:* Coastal engineering including tidal inlet hydrodynamics; beach erosion; hydrographic surveying and coastal structures. *Mailing Add:* 310 Ormond Ave Indialantic FL 32903-3432

HARRIS, LELAND, BIOORGANIC CHEMISTRY, SCIENCE EDUCATION. *Current Pos:* ADJ PROF, DEPT CHEM, UNIV ARIZ. *Personal Data:* b Warren, Ohio, Sept 9, 24; m 55; c 3. *Educ:* Univ Mich, BS, 50; Univ Ariz, MS, 52; Univ Iowa, PhD(org chem), 55. *Prof Exp:* Res chemist, E I du Pont de Nemours & Co, Va, 55-57; from asst prof to prof chem, Knox Col, 57-71, chmn dept, 59-77, Herbert E Griffith prof, 71- *Concurrent Pos:* NSF sci fac fel chem, Calif Inst Technol, 68-69 & Duke Univ, 78; vis prof biochem, Rush Med Col, 72- *Mem:* AAAS; Am Chem Soc; Sigma Xi. *Res:* Pigment variations and morphological changes in various genotypes of soybeans and peanuts using HPLC and electron microscopy; synthesis and nuclear magnetic resonance studies of substituted conjugated unsaturated acids; design and curriculum studies of first year medical programs; variable temperature nuclear magnetic resonance studies of cyclohexene systems; kinetics of transition from protochlorophyll to chlorophyll. *Mailing Add:* Dept Chem Univ Ariz Tucson AZ 85721-0001

HARRIS, LEONARD ANDREW, CIVIL ENGINEERING, APPLIED MECHANICS. *Current Pos:* MGR MAT & STRUCT, OFF AERONAUT & SPACE ADMIN, NASA, 72- *Personal Data:* b San Francisco, Calif, Apr 11, 28; m 55; c 3. *Educ:* Stanford Univ, BS, 50; Univ Ill, MS, 53, PhD(eng), 54. *Prof Exp:* Res assoc civil eng, Univ Ill, 53-54; from engr to sr eng specialist appl mech, Space & Info Systs Div, NAm Aviation Corp, 54-58, supvr, 58-59, prin scientist struct sci, 59-61, dir, 61-67, asst mgr sci & technol, 67-68, mgr struct & design, NAm Rockwell Corp, 68-70, mgr shuttle technol, 70-72. *Concurrent Pos:* Lectr aeronaut eng, Univ Southern Calif, 56-60; guest lectr, Univ Calif, Los Angeles, 59-65; mem indust adv comt mil handbk on sandwich construct, 59-65; mem ad hoc comt design with brittle mat, Mat Adv Bd, Nat Acad Sci, 64; mem res adv comt space vehicle struct, NASA, 65-67. *Mem:* Assoc fel Int Aeronaut & Astronaut; Am Soc Civil Engrs. *Res:* Experimental and theoretical studies of buckling of plates and shells; static and fatigue strength of welds in structural materials; brittle behavior of materials. *Mailing Add:* NASA-Aeronaut & Space Technol 300 E St NW Washington DC 20546

HARRIS, LEONCE EVERETT, PROPULSION, PROPELLANTS & EXPLOSIVES. *Current Pos:* RES CHEMIST, US ARMY ARMAMENT RES & DEVELOP COMMAND, 70- *Personal Data:* b New Orleans, La, July 31, 41; m 69; c 2. *Educ:* La State Univ, BS, 64, PhD(chem), 68. *Prof Exp:* Teaching asst chem, La State Univ, 64-68, vis asst prof, 68-70. *Concurrent Pos:* Prin investr, US Army Ardec, 70-80, group leader, 80-85, exec fel, Off Tech Dir, 86-87, proj mgr, 87-; secy Army fel, Royal Inst Gt Brit, Davy-Faraday Lab, 75-76; chmn, Joint Army, Navy, NASA, AF(JANNAF) Workshop on Combustion Diag, 89; res supvr postdoctoral students, Nat Res Coun, 83. *Mem:* Fel Roy Soc Chem; Am Chem Soc; AAAS. *Res:* Electrothermal and chemical propulsion; evaluation and identification of propellants; glucidation of the mechanism of propellant and plasma interaction using combustion diagnostics and modelling; direction of propulsion aspects of system integration. *Mailing Add:* 92 Tomahawk Trail Sparta NJ 07871

HARRIS, LESTER EARLE, JR, HERPETOLOGY, ISLAND BIOGEOGRAPHY & EVOLUTIONARY BIOLOGY. *Current Pos:* prof, Loma Linda Univ, Riverside, 76-89, prof 90-94, EMER PROF BIOL, LA SIERRA UNIV, 94- *Personal Data:* b Washington, DC, June 4, 22; m 49, Majorie Schultz; c Lester III, Deborah J, Charles C & Julia E. *Educ:* Columbia Union Col, BA, 49, PedD, 70; Univ Md, MS, 51. *Prof Exp:* From instr to prof, Columbia Union Col, 51-73, chmn dept, 53-73. *Mem:* Soc Study Amphibians & Reptiles. *Res:* Ecology; snake anatomy; 22 year study of Galapagos biology and evolution with geologied history; specific research in genus microlophys of fam iqanidai. *Mailing Add:* Dept Biol La Sierra Univ Riverside CA 92515. *Fax:* 714-785-7111; *E-Mail:* lharris@lasierra.edu

HARRIS, LEWIS ELDON, PHARMACEUTICAL CHEMISTRY. *Current Pos:* Dir lab, 33-67, PRES, HARRIS LABS, INC, 67- *Personal Data:* b Cedar, Kans, Dec 3, 10; m 35; c 2. *Educ:* Univ Nebr, BSc, 32, MSc, 33. *Hon Degrees:* ScD, Univ Nebr, 70. *Concurrent Pos:* Pres, Norden Labs, Inc, 39-69; instr, Sch Nursing, Univ Nebr, 41- *Mem:* Am Pharmaceut Asn; fel Am Inst Chem. *Res:* Stabilization of calcium gluconate solutions and calcium glycerophosphate solutions; stability and antioxidant studies in powdered dairy products; stability in stabilizing vitamin A in alfalfa; soluble glucosides of sulfonamides. *Mailing Add:* 7134 South St Lincoln NE 68506-6552

HARRIS, LOUIS SELIG, NEUROPHARMACOLOGY, PSYCHOPHARMACOLOGY. *Current Pos:* HARVEY HAAG PROF & CHMN, DEPT PHARMACOL, VA COMMONWEALTH UNIV, 72-, ASSOC VPRES HEALTH SCI, 96- *Personal Data:* b Boston, Mass, Mar 27, 27; m 52, Ruth I Schaufus; c Charles A. *Educ:* Harvard Univ, BA, 54, MA, 56, PhD(pharmacol), 58. *Honors & Awards:* Res Achievement Award Pharmacol, Am Pharmaceut Asn Found-Acad Pharmaceut Sci, 77; Hartung Mem Award, Univ NC, 81; Nathan B Eddy Mem Award, 85; Abe Wilker Award, 91; Gov's Award Drug Abuse Res, 92. *Prof Exp:* Sr res biologist & sect head, Sterling-Winthrop Res Inst, 58-66; assoc prof pharmacol, Sch Med, Univ NC, Chapel Hill, 66-70, assoc prof, Sch Pharm, 67-70, prof, Sch Med & Sch Pharm, 70-72. *Concurrent Pos:* Vis lectr, Albany Med Col, 60-66; mem, Psychotomimetic Agents Adv Comt, NIMH, 70-72, chmn, 71-72; trustee, Sisa Inst Res, 70-84; mem, Presidential Biomed Res Panel, Nat Acad Sci-Nat Res Coun, 75-76, Comt Clin Eval Narcotic Antagonists, 76-78, Comt Probs Drug Dependence, 76- & chmn, 90-; mem, Comt Revision Analgesics, US Pharmacopeial Conv, 80-85; Comt Public Concern, US Pharmacop Conv, 80-85; Bd Scientific Counrs, Nat Inst Drug Abuse Chmn, 83-86; sr sci adv to dir, Nat Inst Drug Abuse, 87-88, mem, Extramural Sci Adv Bd, 91; hon prof pharmacol, Beijing China, 90. *Mem:* AAAS; Am Soc Pharmacol & Exp Therapeut; Am Col Neuropsychopharm; Am Chem Soc; Soc Neurosci; Col Probs Drug Dependency. *Res:* Central stimulants and depressants; analgesics; psychopharmacology; pharmacology of marijuana and its active constituents; drug development; opioids; drug dependence. *Mailing Add:* Dept Pharmacol Va Commonwealth Univ MCV Sta PO Box 980027 Richmond VA 23298-0027. *Fax:* 804-828-1532; *E-Mail:* harris@gems.vcu.edu

HARRIS, LOWELL DEE, biophysics, bioengineering, for more information see previous edition

HARRIS, LOYD ERVIN, PHARMACEUTICAL CHEMISTRY. *Current Pos:* prof pharm & dean, Col Pharm, 63-70, EMER PROF PHARM & EMER DEAN, COL PHARM, UNIV OKLA, 70- *Personal Data:* b Ryan, Okla, Sept 21, 00; m 23; c 2. *Educ:* Univ Okla, BS, 22, MS, 24; Univ Wis, PhD(pharmaceut chem), 26. *Prof Exp:* Asst pharm, Univ Okla, 19-23, from asst prof to prof chem, 23-46; prof pharm, Ohio State Univ, 46-63. *Mem:* Am Pharmaceut Asn. *Res:* Phytochemical studies. *Mailing Add:* 2514 S Pickard Ave Norman OK 73072

HARRIS, MARTIN H, PETROLEUM ENGINEERING. *Current Pos:* TECH MGR, BRIT PETROL CO, 83- *Personal Data:* b Pittsburgh, Pa, Oct 11, 37; m 2. *Educ:* Pa State Univ, BS, 59, MS, 61. *Honors & Awards:* Rossiter W Raymond Mem Award, Am Inst Mining, Metall & Petrol Engrs, 67. *Prof Exp:* Engr, Gulf Res & Develop Co, Gulf Oil Corp, 61-65, from res engr to sr res engr, 65-70, sect supvr, 70-83. *Mem:* Soc Petrol Engrs. *Res:* Natural gas engineering; well stimulation, completion and logging; petrophysics and fluid flow in porous media; application of digital computers to petroleum exploration and data processing. *Mailing Add:* 5107 Queensloch St Houston TX 77096

HARRIS, MARVIN KIRK, ENTOMOLOGY. *Current Pos:* ASSOC PROF ENTOM, TEX A&M UNIV, 72- *Personal Data:* b Genoa, Nebr, Aug 15, 43; m 64; c 3. *Educ:* Dana Col, BS, 68; Cornell Univ, PhD(entom), 72. *Prof Exp:* Res asst econ entom, Cornell Univ, 68-72. *Mem:* Entom Soc Am; Sigma Xi; AAAS. *Res:* Biology and pest management of pecan insects; pecan domestication as it affects the pecan insect complex; host-plant resistance to insects in agriculture; insect-plant co-evolution. *Mailing Add:* Dept Entom Tex A&M Univ College Station TX 77843

HARRIS, MARY STYLES, GENETICS, PUBLIC HEALTH & EPIDEMIOLOGY. *Current Pos:* PRES, BIOTECH COMMUNS, 87- *Personal Data:* b Nashville, Tenn, June 26, 49; m 71. *Educ:* Lincoln Univ, BA, 71; Cornell Univ, PhD(genetics), 75. *Prof Exp:* Instr genetics, Sch Med, Morehouse Col, 78- & dir admin, Sickle Cell Found Ga, Inc, 77-; asst dir sci & pub policy, Atlanta Univ, 81-82; pres, Harris & Assocs Ltd, 86-87. *Concurrent Pos:* Ford Found fel, 71-75; res assoc tumor virol, Rutgers Med Sch, 75-77; NSF Residency, 79-80; scientist in residence, WGTV, 79, adj pub serv asst, 79-80; instr human genetics, Emory Univ, 82; dir genetic serv, Ga Dept Human Resources, 82-85. *Mem:* Am Pub Health Asn; Am Soc Human Genetics. *Res:* Investigation of the induction of cellular DNA synthesis by Adenovirus type 2; regulation of the synthesis of fetal hemoglobin in adult patients producing hemoglobin F; developing statewide genetic screening programs; dissemination of health care information using cable television technology. *Mailing Add:* 2058 N Mills Ave Suite 214 Claremont CA 91711

HARRIS, MATTHEW N, SURGERY, ONCOLOGY. *Current Pos:* PROF SURG & DIR DIV ONCOL, DEPT SURG, NY UNIV SCH MED, 79- *Personal Data:* b New York, NY, Dec 20, 31; m 54, Frances Wicentowski; c Amy R (Pollack), Julie R (Silverstein) & Daniel C. *Educ:* NY Univ, BA, 52; Chicago Med Sch, MD, 56; Am Bd Surgery, dipl, 64. *Honors & Awards:* Meritorious Achievement Award, Am Col Surgeons, 91. *Prof Exp:* Intern med & surg, 3rd NY Univ Surg Div, Bellevue Hosp Ctr, 56-57, resident gen surg, 57-58, 60-63, Am Cancer Soc fel, 61-63, USPHS sr clin trainee cancer, 63-64; teaching asst surg, Sch Med, NY Univ, 64-65, from instr to assoc prof, 65-75, prof clin surg, 75-79. *Concurrent Pos:* Vis surgeon, Bellevue Hosp Ctr; attend surgeon, Tisch Hosp, Med Ctr, NY Univ, 76; consult, Manhattan Vet Admin Hosp; NY State chmn surgeon liaison prog, Cancer Comn, Am Col Surgeons. *Mem:* Fel Am Col Surgeons; Am Soc Clin Oncol; Asn Acad Surg; Soc Surg Oncol; Sigma Xi; Am Radium Soc. *Res:* Surgical oncology; malignant melanoma; carcinoma of the breast and soft tissue tumors. *Mailing Add:* NY Univ Med Ctr 530 First Ave New York NY 10016. *Fax:* 212-263-7581

HARRIS, MAUREEN ISABELLE, PUBLIC HEALTH, EPIDEMIOLOGY. *Current Pos:* staff res scientist ribosome biochem, Nat Inst Arthritis & Metab Dis, NIH, 68-70, health scientist adminr, Fogarty Int Ctr, 71-76, res prog analyst, Kidney & Urol Dis, 76-77, DIR, NAT DIABETES DATA GROUP, NAT INST DIABETES, DIGESTIVE & KIDNEY DIS, NIH, 77-, DIR, WHO COLLABORATING CTR DIABETES, 85- *Personal Data:* b Anniston, Ala, Mar 21, 43. *Educ:* George Washington Univ, BS, 64; Yale Univ, PhD(biochem), 68; Johns Hopkins Univ, MPH, 75. *Honors & Awards:* Hildebrand Jr Award, Am Chem Soc, 64; Spec Recognition Award, USPHS, 85; Award of Merit, NIH, 87. *Prof Exp:* Phys sci aide, US Army CEngr, 64. *Mem:* Am Diabetes Asn; Soc Epidemiol Res. *Res:* Epidemiology of diabetes. *Mailing Add:* Nat Diabetes Data Group Nat Inst Diabetes Digestive & Kidney Dis NIH Rm SAN24 45 Center Dr Bethesda MD 20892

HARRIS, MILES FITZGERALD, METEOROLOGY, SCIENCE WRITING. *Current Pos:* RETIRED. *Personal Data:* b Brunswick, Ga, Feb 2, 13; m 38; c 3. *Educ:* NY Univ, BS, 44, MS, 57. *Prof Exp:* Asst observer, US Weather Bur, 32-35 & 37-43, analyst, 43-45, hurricane forecaster, 45-47, supv meteorologist, 47-48, spec projs meteorologist, 48-51, res meteorologist, Meteorol Statist Sect, 51-61, meteorologist, Ed Sect & head, Editing & Pub Br, 61-66, phys scientist & chief, Sci Info Anal Br, Environ Sci Serv Admin, 66-68, ed, Monthly Weather Rev, 68-70; tech ed, Bull of the Am Meteorol Soc & Spec Projs Off, 70-74, tech ed, Monthly Weather Rev, 74-75. *Mem:* Am Meteorol Soc. *Res:* Investigating the earth; popularization of meteorology. *Mailing Add:* 40 Lothrop St Beverly MA 01915

HARRIS, MORGAN, CELL BIOLOGY. *Current Pos:* from instr to prof zool, 45-83, from vchmn to chmn dept, 52-63, EMER PROF ZOOL, UNIV CALIF, BERKELEY, 82- *Personal Data:* b St Anthony, Idaho, May 25, 16; m 89, Lola Jeanne; c Roger Mason & Ronald Morgan Harris-Warrick. *Educ:* Univ Calif, AB, 38, PhD(zool), 41. *Prof Exp:* Harrison fel, Univ Pa, 41-42; asst zool, Stanford Univ, 42-44; instr, Univ Wash, 44-45. *Concurrent Pos:* Merck sr fel, Univ Paris, 53-54; mem cell biol study sect, NIH, 58-60, 61-63, nat adv gen med sci coun, 63-65; prof, Miller Inst Basic Res, 63-65; Guggenheim fel, Cambridge Univ, 60-61. *Mem:* Am Soc Zoologists; Soc Gen Physiol; Tissue Cult Asn (pres, 58-60); Am Soc Cell Biol. *Res:* Cell growth and nutrition; somatic cell genetics; tumor biology. *Mailing Add:* MCB-CDB LSA No 5 Univ Calif Berkeley CA 94720

HARRIS, MORTON E, ALGEBRA. *Current Pos:* PROF MATH, UNIV MINN, 73- *Personal Data:* b Apr 27, 34; m 67. *Educ:* Yale Univ, BS, 55; Harvard Univ, MA, 56, PhD(math), 60. *Prof Exp:* Asst prof math, Clark Univ, 60-61 & Tufts Univ, 61-65; from asst prof to assoc prof, Univ Ill, Chicago Circle, 65-73. *Concurrent Pos:* NSF res grants, 71-72. *Mem:* Am Math Soc; Math Asn Am. *Res:* Problems in the classification of finite simple groups. *Mailing Add:* Sch Math Univ Minn 127 Vincent Hall Minneapolis MN 55455-0488

HARRIS, NATHOLYN DALTON, FOOD SCIENCE. *Current Pos:* from asst prof to assoc prof, 71-86, PROF FOOD SCI, FLA STATE UNIV, 86- *Personal Data:* b Calvary, Ga, Feb 26, 39; m 67, Ronald; c Rhonda & Scott. *Educ:* Berry Col, BS, 61; Ohio State Univ, MS, 62; Univ Wis, PhD(food, nutrit), 67. *Prof Exp:* Instr food & nutrit, Berry Col, 62-63; lectr food sci, Univ Wis, 66-71. *Mem:* Inst Food Technologists; Am Asn Family & Consumer Sci; Am Chem Soc; Int Asn Milk, Food & Environ Sanitarians. *Res:* Microbiological aspects of food; food flavor; quality changes in food. *Mailing Add:* 413 Sandels Bldg Fla State Univ Tallahassee FL 32306. *Fax:* 850-644-0700; *E-Mail:* nharris@mailer.fsu.edu

HARRIS, NORMAN OLIVER, PREVENTIVE DENTISTRY. *Current Pos:* RETIRED. *Personal Data:* b Shinglehouse, Pa, May 27, 17; m 55; c 1. *Educ:* Temple Univ, DDS, 39; Ohio State Univ, MSD, 53. *Prof Exp:* Intern, USPHS, 39 40; UN Relief & Rchab Agency adv, Nationalist China, 46-47; chief exp dent, USAF Sch Aviation Med, 55-61, chief res & prev dent, USAF, PR, 61-63; dir res activ, Sch Dent, Univ PR, San Juan, 63-76; prof, Dept Community Dent, Dent Sch, Univ Tex, 76-87. *Concurrent Pos:* Prof honoris causa, Univ Pernambuco, Brazil. *Mem:* Am Dent Asn; Int Asn Dent Res; Am Col Dentists. *Res:* Basic and applied research in preventive dentistry; research administration; interhemispheric integration of research, teaching and public health administration; professional communications; programmed learning. *Mailing Add:* 11020 Huebner Oaks Apt 2021 San Antonio TX 78230-1145

HARRIS, P(HILIP) J(OHN), STRUCTURAL ENGINEERING. *Current Pos:* PROF CIVIL ENG & ENG MECHS, MCMASTER UNIV, 91- *Personal Data:* b Montreal, Que, Mar 22, 26; m 53; c Elizabeth J (Richardson) & Janet C. *Educ:* Univ Man, BSc, 48; McGill Univ, MEng, 49, PhD(struct shells), 64. *Honors & Awards:* Univ Gold Medal, Civil Eng, 48. *Prof Exp:* Struct designer, Dom Bridge Co, Ltd, 49-51; chief civil engr, C D Howe Co Ltd, 51-58; from asst prof to assoc prof civil eng, McGill Univ, 58-73, prof civil eng & appl mech, 73-91, chmn dept, 77-84, emer prof, 93. *Concurrent Pos:* Consult engr, 58-; mem, Univ Senate, 71-91 & Univ Bd Gov, 75-82. *Mem:* Am Soc Civil Engrs; Am Concrete Inst; fel Eng Inst Can; fel Can Soc Civil Eng; Can Stand Asn. *Res:* Structural engineering. *Mailing Add:* 1153 Flynn Rd Hamilton 2001 New Zealand

HARRIS, PAMELA ANN, soil microbiology, biological weed control, for more information see previous edition

HARRIS, PATRICIA J, CELL BIOLOGY, ELECTRON MICROSCOPY. *Current Pos:* adj assoc prof, 73-81, ADJ PROF BIOL, UNIV ORE, 81- *Personal Data:* b Seattle, Wash, Sept 2, 21; m 73. *Educ:* Univ Calif, Berkeley, BA, 54, PhD(zool), 62; Yale Univ, MS, 58. *Prof Exp:* Phys sci aide in chg electron microscope lab, Naval Radiol Defense Lab, Calif, 48-52; technician fish endocrinol, Bingham Oceanog Lab, Yale Univ, 54-58; technician cell biol & electron micros, Univ Calif, Berkeley, 58-62, asst res zoologist, 62-64; from asst prof to assoc prof zool, Ore State Univ, 64-73. *Mem:* Am Soc Cell Biol; Electron Micros Soc Am; Am Soc Develop Biol; Am Soc Zoologists; fel AAAS. *Res:* Fine structure studies of mitosis in both animal and plant cells; experimental modification of mitosis and normal development, particularly in marine invertebrate embryos. *Mailing Add:* Dept Biol Univ Ore Eugene OR 94703-1210. *Fax:* 541-346-2364

HARRIS, PATRICK DONALD, PHYSIOLOGY, ELECTRICAL ENGINEERING. *Current Pos:* PROF & CHMN, PHYSIOL & BIOPHYS, UNIV LOUISVILLE, 81- *Personal Data:* b Nebraska City, Nebr, Mar 30, 40; m 59; c 3. *Educ:* Univ Mo, BSEE, 62, MSEE, 63; Northwestern Univ, PhD(physiol), 67. *Honors & Awards:* Microcirculatory Soc Award, 66. *Prof Exp:* NIH fel physiol, Med Ctr, Ind Univ, 67-68; from asst prof to prof physiol, Univ Mo, Columbia, 68-80; assoc dir, Dalton Res Ctr, 80-81. *Concurrent Pos:* NIH spec fel, 70-72; vis assoc biomed eng, Calif Inst Technol, 77-78. *Mem:* Am Physiol Soc; Inst Elec & Electronics Eng; Microcirc Soc; Am Heart Asn; Biomed Eng Soc; Shock Soc; Sigma Xi; Europ Microcirculatory Soc; US Microcirculatory Soc (pres, 86). *Res:* Hormonal control of small vessel diameters during hypertension, hemorrhagic shock, sepsis and anesthesia. *Mailing Add:* Dept Physiol Univ Louisville Louisville KY 40292-0001. *Fax:* 502-852-6239

HARRIS, PAUL CHAPPELL, POULTRY SCIENCE. *Current Pos:* from asst prof to assoc prof, 59-94, EMER PROF POULTRY SCI, UNIV MAINE, ORONO, 94- *Personal Data:* b Nova Scotia, Can, Oct 30, 30; US citizen; m 55; c 3. *Educ:* McGill Univ, BSc, 52; Univ Md, MS, 56, PhD(poultry husb), 60. *Prof Exp:* Poultry fieldman, NS Dept Agr, Can, 52-54; asst, Univ Md, 54-59. *Mem:* Fel AAAS; Poultry Sci Asn; World Poultry Sci Asn; Sigma Xi. *Res:* Physiology of egg production; egg quality and diet utilization; layer management. *Mailing Add:* 7 Averill St Orono ME 04473

HARRIS, PAUL JONATHAN, COATING TECHNOLOGY, PHOSPHAZENE CHEMISTRY. *Current Pos:* RES ASSOC, BASF COATINGS, DIV, 87- *Personal Data:* b Park Royal, Eng, July 8, 53. *Educ:* Univ Bath, Eng, BSc, 74; Bristol Univ, PhD(chem), 78. *Prof Exp:* Res asst, Pa State Univ, 77-80; asst prof chem, Va Polytech Inst & State Univ, 80-87. *Mem:* Am Chem Soc; Royal Soc Chem. *Res:* Fundamental aspects of automotive coating technology. *Mailing Add:* BASF Coatings Div 26701 Telegraph Rd Southfield MI 48034-2442

HARRIS, PAUL ROBERT, CHEMICAL ENGINEERING. *Current Pos:* VPRES COM DEVELOP, LEE LABS, INC, 84- *Personal Data:* b Charlotte, NC, Nov 8, 42; m 68; c 4. *Educ:* Ga Inst Technol, BChE, 63; Northwestern Univ, MS, 64; Mich State Univ, PhD(chem eng), 67. *Prof Exp:* Res engr, Eastern Res Ctr, Stauffer Chem Co, 67-68, sr res engr, 70-71, plant engr, Energy Prod Dept, 71-76; supt, Plains Co-op Oil Mill, 76-77; prog mgr, Pillsbury Co, 77-79; mgr-engr, Am Maize Prod Co, 79-84. *Mem:* Am Chem Soc; Am Inst Chem Engrs; Sigma Xi; Int Oil Mill Supt Asn. *Res:* Chemical reactor design; photochemical reactor design; reaction kinetics; spray drying; unusual separation techniques. *Mailing Add:* 11114 Sithean Way Richmond VA 23233-2222

HARRIS, PETER, WEED SCIENCE, CLASSICAL BIOLOGICAL CONTROL. *Current Pos:* RETIRED. *Personal Data:* b Cambridge, Eng, Oct 19, 30; Can citizen; m 57; c 3. *Educ:* Univ BC, BSF, 55; Univ London, DIC & PhD(zool), 58. *Honors & Awards:* Commendation Medal 125th Anniv Can Fedn. *Prof Exp:* Res scientist, Agr Can, 59-93. *Mem:* Fel Entom Soc Can. *Res:* Establishing procedures for the biological control of weeds with introduced insects; control of the following weed in Canada: Hypericum perforatum, Carduus nutans, Centaurea diffusa and Centaurea maculosa, Euphorbia esula and Euphorbia cyparissias, Senecio jacobaea. *Mailing Add:* Res Can Agr & Agri Food Can PO Box 3000 Lethbridge AB T1J 4B1 Can

HARRIS, RAE LAWRENCE, JR, GEOLOGY. *Current Pos:* from asst prof to prof, 57-89, EMER PROF GEOL, TEX TECH UNIV, 89- *Personal Data:* b Laurel, Miss, Apr 8, 26; m 47; c 3. *Educ:* Ore State Col, BS, 50; Columbia Univ, PhD(geol), 57. *Prof Exp:* Lectr geol, Columbia Univ, 55-57. *Mem:* AAAS; Geol Soc Am; Am Geophys Union; Sigma Xi. *Res:* Petrology and structure of granite rocks; economic and engineering geology. *Mailing Add:* 6118 Louisville Dr Lubbock TX 79413

HARRIS, RALPH ROGERS, ANIMAL NUTRITION, DAIRY SCIENCE. *Current Pos:* asst animal nutritionist, Auburn Univ, 60-64, assoc prof animal sci, 64-73, prof animal nutrit, 73-91, DEPT HEAD, AUBURN UNIV, 92- *Personal Data:* b Winfield, Ala, Mar 9, 29; m 51; c 3. *Educ:* Auburn Univ, BS, 51, MS, 52; Agr & Mech Col Tex, PhD(dairy sci), 59. *Prof Exp:* Asst animal husb & nutrit, Auburn Univ, 51-52, animal husbandman, 55; asst, Agr & Mech Col Tex, 56, dairy specialist voc agr, 59-60. *Mem:* Am Dairy Sci Asn; Am Soc Animal Sci. *Res:* Forage utilization by beef and dairy cattle; environmental effects upon response of beef and dairy cows. *Mailing Add:* Dept Animal Sci Auburn Univ Auburn AL 36849-3501

HARRIS, REECE THOMAS, MATHEMATICS, THEORY OF LANGUAGE. *Current Pos:* TUTOR, ST JOHN'S COL, NMEX, 68- *Personal Data:* b Shreveport, La, Aug 10, 32; m 60; Julia B; c Lycia & Derwyn. *Educ:* Reed Col, BS, 55; Univ Ill, MA, 56, Phd(math), 59. *Prof Exp:* Res assoc math, Duke Univ, 59-60, asst prof, 60-65; assoc prof, Univ Md, 65-68. *Concurrent Pos:* Vis asst prof, Univ Calif, Berkeley, 62-63; vis assoc prof, NY Univ, 67-68; consult, India Proj, NSF, 67 & IBM Corp Hq, NY; vis prof, UCSC Math Dept, 85-86 & 88. *Mem:* Am Math Soc; AAAS. *Res:* Functional and harmonic analysis; spectral theory; history of science; catastrophe theory; computer science. *Mailing Add:* 4 Mariposa Rd Santa Fe NM 87505. *E-Mail:* rtharris@delphi.com

HARRIS, RICHARD, SOLID STATE PHYSICS. *Current Pos:* asst prof, 70-76, ASSOC PROF PHYSICS, MCGILL UNIV, 76- *Personal Data:* b London, Eng, Jan 19, 44; Brit & Can citizen. *Educ:* Oxford Univ, BA, 65; Univ Sussex, DPhil, 68. *Prof Exp:* Res asst physics, Imp Col, Univ London, 68-70. *Mem:* Am Phys Soc; Brit Inst Physics. *Res:* Magnetic and structural properties of amorphous metals and other glassy solids. *Mailing Add:* Rutherford Physics Bldg McGill Univ 3600 University St Montreal PQ H3A 2T8 Can

HARRIS, RICHARD ELGIN, SOLID STATE PHYSICS, LOW TEMPERATURE PHYSICS. *Current Pos:* PHYSICIST, NAT INST STAND & TECHNOL, 75-, DIV CHIEF, 95- *Personal Data:* b Kansas City, Mo, May 28, 41; m 67; c 1. *Educ:* Univ Rochester, BS, 63; Univ Ill, MS, 65, PhD(physics), 69. *Prof Exp:* Exp physicist, United Technol Res Ctr, 69-75. *Mem:* Am Phys Soc; Sigma Xi; AAAS. *Res:* Superconducting electronics; Josephson effect, experiment and theory. *Mailing Add:* US Dept Com Div 81400 Nat Inst Stand & Technol 325 Broadway Boulder CO 80303

HARRIS, RICHARD WILSON, LANDSCAPE HORTICULTURE. *Current Pos:* instr & jr pomologist, Univ Calif, Davis, 50-52, asst prof & asst pomologist, 52-57, assoc prof landscape hort & assoc horticulturist, 58-64, chmn, Dept Environ Hort, 58-65 & 78-83, prof environ hort & horticulturist, 64-86, EMER PROF ENVIRON HORT, UNIV CALIF, DAVIS, 86- *Personal Data:* b Fresno, Calif, July 26, 20; m 46; c Dan R, Craig W & Martha C (Saylor). *Educ:* Univ Calif, BS, 42, MS, 47; Cornell Univ, PhD, 50. *Honors & Awards:* Norman Jay Colman Award, Am Asn Nurserymen; Sci Award, Am Hort Soc. *Prof Exp:* Asst pomol, Univ Calif, 46-47 & Cornell Univ, 47-50. *Concurrent Pos:* Consult, tree safety, tree appraisal. *Mem:* Int Soc Arboricult (pres, 86-87). *Res:* Culture of landscape plants; arboriculture; management of landscape maintenance. *Mailing Add:* 602 Sunset Ct Davis CA 95616. *Fax:* 530-752-1819; *E-Mail:* rwharris@ucdavis.edu

HARRIS, ROBERT A, THEORETICAL CHEMISTRY, CHEMICAL PHYSICS. *Current Pos:* from asst prof to assoc prof, 63-74, PROF CHEM, UNIV CALIF, BERKELEY, 74- *Personal Data:* b Chicago, Ill, Aug 9, 36; m 58; c 3. *Educ:* Univ Ill, BS, 57; Univ Chicago, MS, 59, PhD(chem), 60. *Prof Exp:* Jr fel, Harvard Soc Fels, Harvard Univ, 60-63. *Concurrent Pos:* Sloan Found fel, 65-67; NSF sr fel, 68-69; Humboldt sr Am scientist award, 77-78; J S Guggenheim found fel, 82-83. *Res:* Electronic properties of molecules and polymers; polymer hydrodynamics, interaction of radiation with matter, general problems of quantum theory. *Mailing Add:* Dept Chem Univ Calif Berkeley 419 Latimer Hall Berkeley CA 94720-1401

HARRIS, ROBERT ALLISON, BIOCHEMISTRY. *Current Pos:* assoc prof, 70-74, prof & assoc chmn, 75-88, PROF BIOCHEM & CHMN, SCH MED, IND UNIV, INDIANAPOLIS, 88- *Personal Data:* b Boone, Iowa, Nov 10, 39; m 59; c 4. *Educ:* Iowa State Univ, BS, 62; Purdue Univ, MS, 64, PhD(biochem), 65. *Prof Exp:* Asst res prof, Inst Enzyme Res, Univ Wis-Madison, 69-70. *Concurrent Pos:* Multiple Sclerosis fel, Inst Enzyme Res, Univ Wis-Madison, 66-70; estab investr, Am Heart Asn, Sch Med, Ind Univ, Indianapolis, 70-74; vis fel, Metab Res Lab, Oxford Univ, 73-74; assoc ed, Lipids, 73-87; res biochemist, Nat Inst Alcohol Abuse & Alcoholism, 80. *Mem:* Am Oil Chem Soc; Brit Biochem Soc; Am Heart Asn; Am Soc Biol Chem; Am Rust Nutrit. *Res:* Regulation of metabolic processes; application of recombinant DNA techniques in the regulation of branched chain amino acid catabolism. *Mailing Add:* Dept Biochem Ind Univ Sch Med 635 Barnhill Rd Indianapolis IN 46202-5122. *Fax:* 317-274-4686

HARRIS, ROBERT HUTCHISON, INORGANIC CHEMISTRY. *Current Pos:* from instr to prof, 51-90, EMER PROF CHEM, UNIV NEBR, LINCOLN, 90- *Personal Data:* b St Louis, Mo, Mar 17, 20; m 46; c 3. *Educ:* Calif Inst Technol, BS, 47; Purdue Univ, PhD(chem), 52. *Prof Exp:* Chem engr, Thompson Aircraft Prods Co, 42-45. *Mem:* Am Chem Soc. *Res:* P-block structures and reactions. *Mailing Add:* Dept Chem Univ Nebr Lincoln NE 68588-0304

HARRIS, ROBERT L, ORGANIC POLYMER CHEMISTRY. *Current Pos:* CONSULT, W&F MFG CO, 83- *Personal Data:* b Pontiac, Ill, Feb 6, 29; m 60; c 1. *Educ:* Univ Ill, BSc, 51; Mass Inst Technol, PhD(org chem), 56. *Prof Exp:* Res chemist, Visking Co Div Union Carbide Corp, 56-61, Minn Mining & Mfg Co, 61-63 & Devoe & Raynolds Co, Div Celanese Corp, 63-66; sr res scientist, Oxford Paper Co, Div Ethyl Corp, 66-68; sr res chemist, Ecusta Paper Co, Div Olin Corp, 68-74; res dir, Imperial Paper Co, 74-78; sr res chemist, Moore Bus Forms Inc, 78-80. *Concurrent Pos:* Lectr, Ind Univ, 65. *Mem:* Am Chem Soc; Tech Asn Pulp & Paper Indust; Soc Plastics Engrs; NY Acad Sci. *Res:* New monomers and polymers for coating applications; coatings for marking and decorative systems; flexographic and gravure inks; plastisol coatings; coatings for printing papers and wallpapers; water-based coatings. *Mailing Add:* 4480 Darcy Lane Williamsville NY 14221-6695

HARRIS, ROBERT L, JR, OCCUPATIONAL HEALTH. *Current Pos:* assoc prof, 73-76, dir, Occup Health Studies Group, 74-84, PROF ENVIRON SCI & ENG, SCH PUB HEALTH, UNIV NC, CHAPEL HILL, 76- *Personal Data:* b Hollister, Mo, July 18, 24; c 3. *Educ:* Univ Ark, BS, 49; Harvard Univ, MS, 54; Univ NC, Chapel Hill, PhD(environ sci & eng), 72. *Honors & Awards:* Henry F Smyth Award, Am Acad Indust Hyg, 85; Meritorious Achievement Award, Am Conf Govt Indust Hygienists, 91; Donald E Cummings Mem Award, Am Indust Hyg Asn, 94. *Prof Exp:* Jr engr, Div Indust Hyg, USPHS, 49-50, asst engr, Environ Health Ctr, 50-52, engr, Div Spec Health Serv, 52-57, engr, Occup Health Field Sta, Div Occup Health, 57-60, chief, Eng Sect, 60-64, chief, Field Invests, Abatement Prog, Nat Air Pollution Control Admin, 64-68, dir, Bur Abatement & Control, 68-70. *Mem:* Am Indust Hyg Asn; Am Conf Govt Indust Hygienists; Sigma Xi; Am Acad Indust Hyg; Brit Occup Hyg Soc. *Res:* Assessment of occupational exposures for exposure control and for occupational epidemiology. *Mailing Add:* Dept Environ Sci & Eng CB No 7400 Rosenau Hall Univ NC Chapel Hill NC 27599-7400

HARRIS, ROBERT LAURENCE, PHYSICAL CHEMISTRY. *Current Pos:* Res chemist, Cent Res Lab, 51-52, proj leader, 53-58, mgr lab res, 59-64, asst dir res & develop, 65-66, sr tech assoc, Cent Res Lab, 66-69, res mgr, Corp Res Div, 69-71, sr scientist, 71-76, SR RES ASSOC, DEPT TOXICOL, CORP RES DIV, ALLIED CORP, 77- *Personal Data:* b Melrose, Mass, May 16, 23; m 46; c 2. *Educ:* Bates Col, BS, 47; Univ Wis, PhD(chem), 51. *Mem:* Am Chem Soc; AAAS. *Res:* Building products from plastics; x-ray diffraction; structure of salts in the liquid state; catalytic hydrogenation; liquid phase oxidation. *Mailing Add:* PO Box 11 Sunset ME 04683-0011

HARRIS, ROBERT MARTIN, PHYSIOLOGICAL GENETICS. *Current Pos:* RETIRED. *Personal Data:* b Atlantic City, NJ, Dec 5, 21; m 44; c 4. *Educ:* Univ Calif, BA, 49, PhD(bot sci), 53. *Prof Exp:* Asst bot, Univ Calif, 50-53; from instr to prof biol sci, Univ Ariz, 53-84, chmn comt genetics, 66-84. *Concurrent Pos:* Ed, J Ariz-Nev Acad Sci, 56-78. *Mem:* Fel AAAS; Am Genetics Soc; Am Genetics Asn. *Res:* Physiological genetics of stature mutants of corn; genetics of blue-green algae. *Mailing Add:* 841 E Alta Vista St Tucson AZ 85719-2914

HARRIS, ROGER MASON, NEUROANATOMY. *Current Pos:* AT DEPT BIOL STRUCT, SCH MED, UNIV WASH. *Personal Data:* b Berkeley, Calif, Mar 22, 46; m 70; c 2. *Educ:* Stanford Univ, BS, 68; Univ Wash, PhD(physics), 75. *Prof Exp:* Res assoc physics, Fermi Nat Accelerator Lab, 74-77; res assoc neurobiol, Wash Univ Sch Med, 77-80; fel, Sch Med, Univ Calif, San Francisco, 80-82. *Mem:* AAAS; Soc Neurosci. *Res:* High energy bubble chamber physics; mouse cortical barrels; computer-assisted neuroanatomy; rat somatosensory thalamus; recovery from spinal cord injury. *Mailing Add:* Dept Biol Struct Unvi Wash Sch Med 3900 Seventh Ave NE Seattle WA 98195-0001

HARRIS, RONALD A, STRUCTURAL GEOLOGY. *Current Pos:* asst prof, 89-95, ASSOC PROF GEOL, WVA UNIV, 95- *Personal Data:* b Springfield, Ore, June 29, 57; c 4. *Educ:* Univ Ore, BSc, 82; Univ Alaska, MSc, 85; Univ London, PhD, 89. *Prof Exp:* Geologist intern, Unocal Oil Co, 82; geologist, Alaska Div Geol & Geophys Surv, 83; geol consult, US Geol Surv & US Bur Mines, Alaska, 86-90, geologist, Br Alaskan Geol, US Geol Surv, 91-95. *Concurrent Pos:* Fulbright res fel, Indonesia, 97. *Mem:* Geol Soc Am; Am Geophys Union; Int Asn Struct Tectonic Geologists; Nat Asn Geol Teachers. *Res:* Neotectonic hazard mitigation; contributed numerous publications to professional journals. *Mailing Add:* Dept Geol WVa Univ PO Box 6300 Morgantown WV 26506

HARRIS, RONALD DAVID, FOOD SCIENCE, CHEMICAL ENGINEERING. *Current Pos:* ADJ PROF & ASSOC DIR EXEC EDUC, OHIO STATE UNIV, 96- *Personal Data:* b Norman, Okla, Apr 9, 38; m 62, Judith Wright; c Todd D (deceased), Scott H & Susanna K. *Educ:* Ohio State Univ, BChE & MSc, 61; Univ Cincinnati, MBA, 70. *Prof Exp:* Res engr foods, Procter & Gamble Co, 61-62 & 64-66, group leader, 66-71; sect mgr, Clorox Co, 71-72, dept mgr, 72-73, dir res & develop, 73-77; vpres res & develop, Anderson Clayton Foods, Anderson, Clayton & Co, 77-87; vpres, Kraft, Inc, 87-96. *Mem:* Inst Food Technologists; Am Chem Soc; Am Oil Chemists Soc. *Res:* Food science; consumer food products; edible fats and oils; dairy products; dairy analogs; shelf stable packaged foods; fresh prepared refrigerated foods; cheese. *Mailing Add:* 1250 Cascade Ct Lake Forest IL 60045-3614

HARRIS, RONALD WILBERT, OPTICS. *Current Pos:* from assoc prof to prof, 70-85, chmn dept, 70-76, ADJ PROF PHYSICS, LOYOLA UNIV CHICAGO, 85-; OWNER, SLADCO INC, EUNICE, LA, 75- *Personal Data:* b Houston, Tex, May 23, 38; m 56; c 2. *Educ:* Southwestern La Univ, BS, 63; Univ Ark, MS & PhD(physics), 67. *Prof Exp:* Physicist, Comput Graphics Res, Shell Develop Co, Tex, 66-67, proj dir optical info processing, 67-68; assoc prof physics & chmn dept, Drury Col, 68-70. *Concurrent Pos:* Lectr, Univ Houston, 67-68; chmn bd, Sladco, Inc, Eunice LA, 75- *Mem:* Am Phys Soc; Inst Elec & Electronics Engrs; Optical Soc Am; Soc Photog Scientists & Engr. *Res:* Image enhancement; optical and acoustical holography; data filtering and displays; determination of liquid structure by means of x-ray diffraction. *Mailing Add:* Sladco Inc PO Box 1289 Eunice LA 70535

HARRIS, RONNEY D, ELECTRICAL ENGINEERING. *Current Pos:* from asst prof to prof elect eng 64-69, DIR CTR ATMOSPHERIC & SPACE SCI, 80- *Personal Data:* b Tremonton, Utah, Sept 8, 32; m 55; c 4. *Educ:* Univ Utah, BS, 54, PhD(elec eng), 64. *Prof Exp:* Proj engr, Microwave Tube Div, Litton Industs, Inc, 60-63. *Mem:* Inst Elec & Electronics Engrs; Am Geophys Union. *Res:* Generation and focusing of large diameter electron beams; numerical solutions of charged particle trajectories; characteristics and formation of sporadic E ionization; wave propagation in ionospheric plasmas. *Mailing Add:* Dept Elec Eng Utah State Univ Logan UT 84322-4120

HARRIS, ROY H, AIRBORNE & GROUND RADAR, UNDERWATER SONAR & TELECOMMUNICATIONS. *Current Pos:* PRES, TRIAD TECHNOL, GREENSBORO, NC, 87- *Personal Data:* b Madison, Ga, Dec 17, 28; m 51, Margaret Pitman; c Kathryn (Humble) & Audrey (Bowen). *Educ:* Ga Inst Technol, 51; Polytech Inst, MEE, 56. *Honors & Awards:* Mgr of Year Award, Inst Elec & Electronics Engrs Mgt Soc, 84. *Prof Exp:* Engr, Hazeltine Elec Corp, 51-56; mem tech staff, Bell Tel Lab, Burlington NC, 56-60, supvr, Nike Hecules design & prod eng, 60-62, supvr, Uncom, 62-64; Eng Mgr, Guid Systs, Western Elec Co, 65-68, mgr mil systs eng, 68-72, mgr mil eng Navy, 72-82; dir, Fed Systs Div, AT&T Technol, Greensboro, NC, 82-86, vpres advan technol systs, 86-87. *Concurrent Pos:* Bd dir, Southcon, 79-82 & 90-91; mem, Undersea Surveillance & Oceanog Sub Comt; mem bd trustees, NC AT&T State Univ; Eng Sch Indust Adv Group, 83- *Mem:* Fel Inst Elec & Electronics Engrs; Nat Security Industr Asn. *Res:* Systems for airborne and ground radar, missile guidance, underwater sonar and telecommunications. *Mailing Add:* 2025 Nottingham Lane Burlington NC 27215. *E-Mail:* r.harris@ieee.org

HARRIS, RUDOLPH, CELL BIOLOGY. *Current Pos:* consumer safety officer, 77-92, CHIEF, NOVEL INGREDIENTS BR, FOOD & DRUG ADMIN, 92- *Personal Data:* b Shreveport, La, Nov 21, 35; m 62, Janette Hoston; c Rylan & Junie. *Educ:* Southern Univ, BS, 56; Cath Univ Am, PhD(cell biol), 73. *Prof Exp:* Asst prof biol, Fed City Col, 71-73; staff fel virol, Nat Cancer Inst, 74-77. *Mem:* Am Soc Cell Biol; Sigma Xi; AAAS. *Res:* Analysis of the transport of ions across the membrane of cells in culture which has been transformed by oncogenic viruses. *Mailing Add:* Food & Drug Admin 200 C St SW Washington DC 20204. *Fax:* 202-418-3131; *E-Mail:* rxh@fdacf.ssw.dhhs.gov

HARRIS, RUTH B S, food intake regulation, for more information see previous edition

HARRIS, RUTH CAMERON, PEDIATRICS. *Current Pos:* RETIRED. *Personal Data:* b Mt Vernon, NY, Apr 23, 16; m 52; c 2. *Educ:* Columbia Univ, AB, 37, MD, 43. *Prof Exp:* Intern, Philadelphia Gen Hosp, 43-44; resident, Willard Parker Hosp, New York, 44-45; asst resident, Babies Hosp, 45-47; from asst to assoc pediat, Columbia Univ, 47-55, asst prof, 55-72, assoc prof clin pediat, Col Physicians & Surgeons, 72-76; prof pediat & chmn dept, Sch Med, Marshall Univ, 76-81, emer prof, 81-90. *Concurrent Pos:* From asst pediatrician to asst attend pediatrician, Babies Hosp, 47-72, from actg dir to dir chem lab, 53-65, attend pediatrician, 72-; from asst pediatrician to asst attend pediatrician, Vanderbilt Clin, 47-72, attend pediatrician, 72-; guest prof, Yonsei Univ, Korea, 68-70. *Mem:* Soc Pediat Res; Am Soc Human Genetics; Am Asn Study Liver Dis; Am Pediat Soc; Am Acad Pediat. *Res:* Liver disease in childhood. *Mailing Add:* 317 Sycamore Glen Dr No 412 Miamisburg OH 45342

HARRIS, SAMUEL M(ELVIN), THEORETICAL NUCLEAR PHYSICS, QUANTUM OPTICS. *Current Pos:* asst prof, 64-67, ASSOC PROF PHYSICS, PURDUE UNIV, 67- *Personal Data:* b Chicago, Ill, Mar 25, 33; m 60, Muriel Goldsmith; c Rebecca & David. *Educ:* Univ Ill, BS, 55, MS, 56, PhD(physics), 61. *Prof Exp:* NSF vis scientist, Univ Bonn, 60-61; from res assoc to sr res assoc physics, Columbia Univ, 62-64. *Mem:* Am Phys Soc. *Res:* Theory of nuclear structure; collective states of deformed nuclei; quantum theory; quantum optics. *Mailing Add:* Dept Physics Purdue Univ Lafayette IN 47907-1396. *E-Mail:* smh@physics.purdue.edu

HARRIS, SAMUEL WILLIAM, TRIBIOLOGY CHEMISTRY. *Current Pos:* RETIRED. *Personal Data:* b Chicago, Ill, Jan 27, 30; m 67; c 2. *Educ:* Miami Univ Ohio, BA, 52, MS, 53; Ohio State Univ, PhD(chem), 56. *Prof Exp:* Res chemist, Whiting Labs, Stand Oil Ind, 56-62, proj chemist, Propellants Div, 62-65, proj chemist, 65-77; sr res chemist, Amoco Res Ctr, Amoco Chem Corp, 77- 92. *Mem:* Am Chem Soc; Sigma Xi. *Res:* Boron hydride and nitrogen oxide chemistry; heterogeneous catalysis; catalytic petroleum and solid propellant technology; lubricant chemistry. *Mailing Add:* 10 S 181 Alago Rd Naperville IL 60564-9623

HARRIS, SIGMUND PAUL, PHYSICS. *Current Pos:* RETIRED. *Personal Data:* b Buffalo, NY, Oct 12, 21; m 48, Florence Katcoff; c Roslyn. *Educ:* Univ Buffalo, BA, 41, MA, 43; Ill Inst Technol, PhD(physics), 54. *Prof Exp:* Asst physics, Univ Buffalo, 41-43 & Yale Univ, 43; jr physicist, Metall Lab, Univ Chicago, 43-44; jr scientist, Los Alamos Sci Lab, 44-46; assoc physicist, Argonne Nat Lab, 46-53; proj engr, Stewart-Warner Corp, 53-54; sr physicist, Tracerlab, Inc, 54-56; sr res engr, Atomics Int Div, NAm Aviation Inc, 56-64; head physics sect, Res Div, Maremont Corp, 64-66; from instr to assoc prof, Pierce Col, 66-79, prof physics, 79-86. *Concurrent Pos:* Indust consult. *Mem:* Am Phys Soc; Am Nuclear Soc; Sigma Xi; Am Asn Physics Teachers. *Res:* Neutron physics; transient radiation effects; space electrical propulsion; air pollution; inventor of 3 US patents and 1 Canadian patent. *Mailing Add:* 5831 Saloma Ave Van Nuys CA 91411

HARRIS, STANLEY EDWARDS, JR, GEOLOGY NATURAL AREAS. *Current Pos:* from assoc prof to prof, 49-82, chmn dept, 55-66, EMER PROF GEOL, SOUTHERN ILL UNIV, 82- *Personal Data:* b Basking Ridge, NJ, Mar 5, 18; m 40; c 4. *Educ:* Princeton Univ, BA, 40; Univ Iowa, MS, 42, PhD(geol), 47. *Prof Exp:* Lab asst, Iowa Geol Surv, 40-41, from jr geologist to geologist, 42-48; asst geol, Univ Iowa, 41-42; vis asst prof, Univ Mo, 48-49. *Concurrent Pos:* Guest docent, Univ Hamburg, 57-58; mem, Ill State Nature Preserves Comn, 76-78. *Mem:* AAAS; Sigma Xi. *Res:* Physiography of central United States; teaching of earth science; environmental geology; Pleistocene geology; Paleozoic stratigraphy; study of natural areas. *Mailing Add:* 98 Edgewood Lane Carbondale IL 62901

HARRIS, STANLEY WARREN, WILDLIFE MANAGEMENT, ORNITHOLOGY. *Current Pos:* from asst prof to prof, 59-92, EMER PROF WILDLIFE MGT, HUMBOLDT STATE UNIV, 92- *Personal Data:* b Dodson, Mont, Sept 18, 28; m 50, Lorene Johnson; c Tonna Jean (Hailer) & Michael H. *Educ:* Wash State Univ, BS, 50, MS, 52; Univ Minn, PhD, 57. *Prof Exp:* Asst, Wash State Univ, 50-52 & Univ Minn, 52-54; res biologist, Game & Fish Div, State Minn, 56-59. *Concurrent Pos:* Res biologist III, Alaska Fish & Game Dept, 73-75 & Calif Condor, 81-85; mem, Adv Comt Shorebirds, Calif Fish & Game Dept, 73-75, Adv Comt Calif Condor, 81-85. *Mem:* Wildlife Soc. *Res:* Waterfowl and seabirds, especially their population dynamics and life history; ornithology; wetland ecology and management. *Mailing Add:* 1595 Charles Ave Arcata CA 95521

HARRIS, STEPHEN ERNEST, ELECTRICAL ENGINEERING. *Current Pos:* from asst prof to prof elec eng, Stanford Univ, 63-79, dir, Edward L Ginzton Lab, 83-88, chair, Dept Appl Physics, 93-96, PROF ELEC ENG & APPL PHYSICS, STANFORD UNIV, CALIF, 79- *Personal Data:* b Brooklyn, NY, Nov 29, 36; m 59; c 2. *Educ:* Rensselaer Polytech Inst, BEE, 59; Stanford Univ, MS, 61, PhD(elec eng), 63. *Honors & Awards:* Nobel Prize, 65; Curtis W McGraw Res Award, 73; David Sarnoff Award, 78; Charles Hard Townes Award, Optical Soc Am, 85; Einstein Prize Laser Sci, 91; Quantum Electronics Award, Inst Elec & Electronics Engrs. *Prof Exp:* Mem tech staff, Bell Tel Labs, 59-60. *Concurrent Pos:* Consult, Optical Device Group, Sylvania Electronic Systs, Calif, 63-68 & Chromatix, Inc, Calif, 68-; Guggenheim fel, 76; dir, Joint Serv Electronics Prog, Edward L Ginzton Lab, 84-91; Barbara & Kenneth Oshman prof eng, 88. *Mem:* Nat Acad Sci; Nat Acad Eng; fel Optical Soc Am; fel Inst Elec & Electronics Engrs; fel Am Phys Soc; Nat Acad Eng; fel AAAS; Am Acad Arts & Sci. *Res:* Quantum electronics; lasers; nonlinear optics; acousto-optics; XUV radiation sources; spectroscopy; publications in more than 170 professional journals and conference proceedings; 14 US patents granted. *Mailing Add:* Edward L Ginzton Lab Stanford Univ Stanford CA 94305

HARRIS, STEPHEN EUBANK, MOLECULAR BIOLOGY, BIOCHEMISTRY. *Current Pos:* ASSOC PROF MED, DEPT MED, UNIV TEX HEALTH SCI CTR, SAN ANTONIO, 90- *Personal Data:* b New Orleans, La, June 30, 42; m 74, Marie A Melton; c Micheleen. *Educ:* Univ Tex, Austin, BA, 65, MA, 66, PhD(zool), 70. *Prof Exp:* Res instr, Baylor Col Med, Houston, Tex, 73-76; sr staff fel, Nat Inst Environ Health Sci, NC, 76-83; sr scientist molecular biol, W Alton Jones Cell Sci Ctr, NY, 83-90. *Concurrent Pos:* Mem, Cancer Ctr, Univ NC, Chapel Hill, 77-; mem, Cancer Inst, San Antonio; adj assoc prof, Dept Cellular & Struct Biol. *Mem:* Fel AAAS; Endocrine Soc; Soc Bone & Mineral Res. *Res:* Molecular biology of steroid hormone gene expression in growth and differentiation; cell biology; cell and molecular biology of osteoblast differentiation and bone morphogenetic protein action. *Mailing Add:* Health Sci Ctr Univ Tex 7730 Floyd Curl Dr San Antonio TX 78284-7877

HARRIS, STEPHEN JOEL, PHYSICAL CHEMISTRY. *Current Pos:* RES CHEMIST PHYS CHEM, GEN MOTORS RES LABS, 77- *Personal Data:* b Los Angeles, Calif, July 9, 49; m 77; c 2. *Educ:* Univ Calif, Los Angeles, BS, 71; Harvard Univ, MA, 72, PhD(chem), 75. *Concurrent Pos:* Fel, Miller Inst Basic Res Sci, Univ Calif, Berkeley, 75-77. *Mem:* Am Phys Soc. *Res:* Laser kinetics and spectroscopy; intracavity techniques; soot formation; diamond films. *Mailing Add:* Dept Phys Chem Gen Motors Res Labs Warren MI 48090

HARRIS, STEVEN H, PETROLEUM GEOLOGY, SEDIMENTOLOGY. *Current Pos:* PRES PETROL, CAMARGO CORP, 65-, OIL PROD, PRADERA DEL NORTE INC, 81-; PRES, TURMOIL, INC, 88- *Personal Data:* b Cincinnati, Ohio, Nov 18, 24; m 55, Mary K Broderick; c Steven B, Bruce, Terry, Wayne & Genevieve D. *Educ:* Univ Cincinnati, BA, 48, MS, 50. *Honors & Awards:* Distinguished Serv Award, Am Asn Petrol Geologists, 92. *Prof Exp:* Geologist, Shell Oil Co, 50-52, consult geol Harris & Brown, 52-60; instr geol, Bismarck Jr Col, 58-64, consult geol, Harris, Brown & Klemer, 60-90; vpres, Condor Resources, 85-92. *Concurrent Pos:* Pres, NDak Geol Soc, 65 & 72, rep, Interstate Oil Compact Comn, 68-72, vpres exec comt, Independent Petrol Assn Am, 81-84; rep, Interstate Oil & Gas Compact Comn, 92- *Mem:* Am Asn Petrol Geologists; fel Geol Soc Am; Soc Paleontologists & Mineralogists; Am Inst Prof Geologists; Sigma Xi. *Res:* Author of numerous technical articles dealing primarily with petroleum exploration of the Williston Basin. *Mailing Add:* PO Box 5 Bismarck ND 58502-0005

HARRIS, STEWART, STATISTICAL MECHANICS. *Current Pos:* from asst prof to assoc prof, 66-78, chmn dept, 79-81, PROF MECH, STATE UNIV NY STONY BROOK, 78-, DEAN, COL ENG & APPL SCI, 81- *Personal Data:* b Cleveland, Ohio, Jan 11, 37; m 63; c 2. *Educ:* Case Inst Technol, BS, 59; Northwestern Univ, MS, 60, PhD(physics of fluids), 64. *Prof Exp:* Assoc res scientist, Courant Inst Math Sci, NY Univ, 64-66. *Concurrent Pos:* Sci res coun sr vis fel, Dept Physics, Univ Surrey, UK, 72-73; SRC fel, 72; vis fel, Univ Surv, 79; vis, Univ Berlin & fel, 79-80. *Mem:* Am Phys Soc; Am Soc Mech Engrs. *Res:* Kinetic theory of monatomic gases; Brownian motion; environmental physics; non-equilibrium statistical mechanics; suspensions. *Mailing Add:* Dept Mech State Univ NY Stony Brook Stony Brook NY 11794-2300

HARRIS, SUSANNA, MICROBIOLOGY, IMMUNOLOGY. *Current Pos:* Instr bact, 48-52, from asst prof to assoc prof, 58-81, EMER ASSOC PROF IMMUNOL PEDIAT, SCH MED, UNIV PA, 81- *Personal Data:* b Brooklyn, NY, May 11, 19; m 40, T N; c Joseph D & Elizabeth H (Tape). *Educ:* Brooklyn Col, BA, 40; Drexel Inst, BS, 42; Univ Pa, PhD(med bact), 48. *Concurrent Pos:* Mem dept res, Children's Hosp, Philadelphia, Pa. *Mem:* Am Soc Microbiol; Am Asn Immunol; Sigma Xi. *Res:* Formation of antibodies. *Mailing Add:* 50 Belmont Ave No 502 Bala Cynwyd PA 19004

HARRIS, SUZANNE STRAIGHT, NUTRITION, MICRONUTRIENTS. *Current Pos:* DIR, HUMAN NUTRIT INST, INT LIFE SCI RES FOUND, 89- *Personal Data:* b Miami, Fla, Nov 18, 44; m 74, William D; c William & Jonathan. *Educ:* Vanderbilt Univ, BA, 66; Univ Ala, Birmingham, PhD(biochem), 76. *Prof Exp:* Assoc biochemist, Southern Res Inst, Birmingham, Ala, 66-73; investr, Inst Dent Res, Univ Ala, Birmingham, 76-85; from instr to asst prof, Dept Nutrit Sci, 80-85, asst prof, Dept Comp Med, 81-85, asst prof, Dept Int Pub Health, 84-85; admnr, Human Nutrit Info Serv, USDA, 85, dep asst secy, Food & Consumer Serv, 85-89; *Concurrent Pos:* Fel, Nat Inst Dent Res, NIH, 74-77; mem, Long Term Care Subcomt, Nat Comt Vital & Health Statist, Dept Health & Human Serv, 83-86; Nat Nutri Monitoring Adv Comt, 92- *Mem:* Sigma Xi; Am Soc Nutrit Scientists. *Res:* Relationship between vitamin A deficiency and calcification of bones and teeth. *Mailing Add:* Int Life Sci Inst 1126 16th St NW Suite 200 Washington DC 20036

HARRIS, THEODORE EDWARD, MATHEMATICS. *Current Pos:* prof, 66-89, EMER PROF MATH & ELEC ENG, UNIV SOUTHERN CALIF, 89- *Personal Data:* b Philadelphia, Pa, Jan 11, 19; m 47; c 2. *Educ:* Univ Tex, BA, 39; Princeton Univ, MA, 46, PhD(math), 47. *Hon Degrees:* DrTechnol, Chalmers Inst Technol, Gothenburg, Sweden. *Prof Exp:* Mathematician, Rand Corp, 47-66, head, Math Dept, 59-66. *Concurrent Pos:* Vis assoc prof, Columbia Univ, 53; ed, Ann Math Statist, Inst Math Statist, 55-58; vis prof, Stanford Univ, 63. *Mem:* Nat Acad Sci; Am Math Soc; fel Inst Math Statist (pres elect, 65-66, pres, 66-67); fel AAAS. *Res:* Probability, stochastic processes. *Mailing Add:* Dept Math DRB 155 Univ Southern Calif 1042 W 36th Pl Los Angeles CA 90089-1113. *E-Mail:* tharris@mtha.usc.edu

HARRIS, THOMAS DAVID, organic chemistry, for more information see previous edition

HARRIS, THOMAS MASON, EMBRYOLOGY, HISTOLOGY. *Current Pos:* RETIRED. *Personal Data:* b Louisville, Ky, Mar 30, 28; m 50; c 2. *Educ:* Emory Univ, BA, 49; Univ NC, PhD(zool), 62. *Prof Exp:* Asst prof biol, Richmond Univ, 61-64; from asst prof to assoc prof anat, Med Col Va, 64-75, prof, 75- *Mem:* Am Soc Zool; Am Asn Anat. *Res:* Mechanisms of embryonic histogenesis analyzed by descriptive and experimental techniques; reinvestigation and documentation of normal developmental events and correlation with embryonic anamolies. *Mailing Add:* 9501 Newhall Rd Ridge VA 23229

HARRIS, THOMAS MUNSON, ORGANIC CHEMISTRY. *Current Pos:* from asst prof to prof, 70-84, CENTENNIAL PROF CHEM & ASSOC DIR, MOLECULAR TOXICOL, VANDERBILT UNIV, 84- *Personal Data:* b Niagara Falls, NY, May 29, 34; m 58, Constance Malmar; c Mary & Jennifer. *Educ:* Univ Rochester, BS, 55; Duke Univ, PhD(chem), 59. *Prof Exp:* Res proj chemist, Union Carbide Chem Co Div, Union Carbide Corp, 58-61; res assoc chem, Duke Univ, 61-63, USPHS spec fel biochem, Med Ctr, 63-64. *Concurrent Pos:* Alfred P Sloan fel, 67-69; USPHS res career develop award, 67-72. *Mem:* Am Chem Soc. *Res:* Polycarbonyl compounds; biogenetic-type syntheses of polyketide compounds; biosynthesis of natural products; glycopeptide antibiotics; mycotoxins; DNA-carcinogen interactions. *Mailing Add:* Vanderbilt Univ 2201 W End Ave Nashville TN 37240-0001

HARRIS, THOMAS R(AYMOND), BIOMEDICAL ENGINEERING, CHEMICAL ENGINEERING. *Current Pos:* from asst prof to assoc prof chem eng, 64-75, asst prof med, 74-80, prof biomed & chem eng & dir, Biomed Eng Prog, 75-87, assoc prof med, 80-86, CHMN, DEPT BIOMED ENG, VANDERBILT UNIV, 88-, PROF MED, 86- *Personal Data:* b San Angelo, Tex, Feb 19, 37; m 63; c 2. *Educ:* Tex A&M Univ, BS, 58, MS, 62; Tulane Univ, PhD(chem eng), 64; Vanderbilt Univ, MD, 74. *Prof Exp:* Design engr, Stand Oil Co Calif, 58-60. *Concurrent Pos:* Res assoc sch med, Vanderbilt Univ, 65. *Mem:* Am Inst Chem Engrs; Biomed Eng Soc (pres, 86); Am Heart Asn; Am Soc Clin Res; Sigma Xi. *Res:* Cardiovascular transport phenomena; physiological systems analysis; pulmonary edema. *Mailing Add:* Dept Med Vanderbilt Univ PO Box 1724 Sta B Nashville TN 37235. *Fax:* 615-343-7919

HARRIS, TZVEE N, IMMUNOLOGY. *Current Pos:* Instr bact, Sch Med, 38-41, from instr to asst res prof pediat, 41-48, from assoc prof to prof, 48-81, EMER PROF IMMUNOL, DEPT PEDIAT, UNIV PA, 81- *Personal Data:* b Russia, Aug 31, 12; US citizen; m 40, Susanna Shapiro; c Joseph D & Elizabeth H (Tape). *Educ:* Univ Pa, BA, 33, MD, 36. *Mem:* AAAS; Am Soc Microbiol; Am Asn Immunol. *Res:* Etiology of rheumatic fever; formation of antibodies; transplantation immunology. *Mailing Add:* 50 Belmont Ave No 502 Bala Cynwyd PA 19004

HARRIS, WALLACE WAYNE, AGRONOMY, SOIL FERTILITY. *Current Pos:* RETIRED. *Personal Data:* b Americus, Kans, Sept 15, 25; m 50; c 3. *Educ:* Kans State Univ, BS, 51, MS, 55; Iowa State Univ, PhD(soil fertil), 70. *Prof Exp:* Asst agronomist, Colby Br Exp Sta, Kans State Univ, 55-70; from asst prof to prof soils, Ft Hays Kans State Univ, 70-88, chmn, Dept Agr, 73-88. *Mem:* Am Soc Agron; Soil Sci Soc Am; Soil Conserv Soc Am. *Res:* Dryland and irrigated soil management and fertility. *Mailing Add:* 653 Rd 230 Americus KS 66835

HARRIS, WALTER EDGAR, ANALYTICAL CHEMISTRY. *Current Pos:* from asst prof to prof, 46-80, chmn dept, 74-79, EMER PROF CHEM, UNIV ALTA, 80- *Personal Data:* b Alta, June 9, 15; wid; c Margaret & William. *Educ:* Univ Alta, BSc, 38, MSc, 39; Univ Minn, PhD(chem), 44. *Hon Degrees:* DSc, Univ Waterloo, 87 & Univ Alberta, 91. *Honors & Awards:* Fisher Award, Chem Educ Award, Chem Inst Can. *Prof Exp:* Res fel synthetic rubber, Univ Minn, 43-46. *Concurrent Pos:* Anal ed, Can J Chem, 74-79; chmn pres adv comt campus reviews, Univ Alta, 80-90. *Mem:* Am Chem Soc; fel Chem Inst Can; Sigma Xi; fel Royal Soc Can; fel AAAS. *Res:* Polarography; modifiers in synthetic rubber; electrochemistry of uranium; amperometric titrations; chromatography; chemical effects of nuclear transformations; programmed temperature gas chromatography; sampling and other uncertainties in the analytical process; hazardous waste; risks. *Mailing Add:* Dept Chem Univ Alta Edmonton AB T6G 2E1 Can

HARRIS, WAYNE G, BIONUCLEONICS, BIOCHEMISTRY. *Current Pos:* MGR ANALYTIC DIV, NEW ENG NUCLEAR CORP, 69- *Personal Data:* b Alexandria, Minn, July 14, 33; m 54; c 2. *Educ:* Purdue Univ, BS, 61, MS, 62, PhD(bionucleonics), 64. *Prof Exp:* Asst prof pharmaceut chem, SDak State Univ, 64-67; assoc prof, NDak State Univ, 67-69. *Mem:* AAAS; Am Chem Soc. *Res:* Development of analytical methods for evaluation of labeled chemicals; theory and applications in liquid scintillation counting. *Mailing Add:* 670 Overlook Dr W Framingham MA 01701-3395

HARRIS, WESLEY LAMAR, AGRICULTURAL ENGINEERING. *Current Pos:* AGR ENGR, USDA, 88- *Personal Data:* b Taylorsville, Ga, Nov 12, 31; m 53; c 4. *Educ:* Univ Ga, BSAE, 53, MS, 58; Mich State Univ, PhD(agr eng), 60. *Prof Exp:* Instr agr eng, Univ Ga, 56-58; asst, Mich State Univ, 58-60; from asst prof to assoc prof agr eng, Univ Md, College Park, 60-69, prof, 69-76 & 87-88, chmn dept, 74-76, dir, Md Agr Exp Sta, 76-87. *Mem:* Am Soc Agr Engrs; Am Soc Eng Educ. *Res:* Development of a strain-stress relationship for soils; basic relationships required for design of pneumatic handling systems for non-free flowing materials; application of thermal energy for control of insects; development of sweet potato harvester. *Mailing Add:* 29 Valerian Ct North Bethesda MD 20852

HARRIS, WESLEY LEROY, AEROSPACE ENGINEERING, COMPUTATIONAL FLUID DYNAMICS. *Current Pos:* PROF AERONAUT & ASTRONAUT, MASS INST TECHNOL, 95- *Personal Data:* b Richmond, Va, Oct 29, 41; m 60, 85, Sandra M Butler; c Wesley Jr, Zelda, Kamau, Kalomo & Tosha. *Educ:* Univ Va, BAeroEng, 64; Princeton Univ, MA, 66, PhD(aerospace eng), 68. *Hon Degrees:* LHD, Lane Col, Jackson Tenn 94; EngrD, Milwaukee Sch Eng, 94; ScD, Old Dominion Univ, 95. *Honors & Awards:* Irwin Sizer Award, 79; Herberts & Jane Gregory Distinguished lectr, Univ Fla Col Eng, 92. *Prof Exp:* NASA trainee aerospace eng, Princeton Univ, 64-66; asst prof aerospace eng, Univ Va, 68-70; assoc prof physics, Southern Univ, 70-71; asst prof aerospace eng, Univ Va, 71-72; assoc prof aeronaut & astronaut & ocean eng, Mass Inst Technol, 72-81, prof aeronaut & astronaut, 81-85; dean, Sch Eng, Univ Conn, 85-90; vpres & prof mech eng, Univ Tenn Space Inst, 90-93; assoc adminr aeronaut, NASA Hq, 93-95. *Concurrent Pos:* Consult, Res Labs Eng Sci, 70-73; staff mem, Nuclear Div, Union Carbide Corp, 71-76; mem, US Army Sci Bd, 79-85, 89-93; eminent scholar, Norfolk State Univ, 81-82, mem, NSF Eng Adv Comt, 89-93. *Mem:* Nat Acad Eng; Am Phys Soc; Soc Indust & Appl Math; Sigma Xi; fel Am Helicopter Soc; Nat Tech Asn; Am Soc Eng Educ; fel Am Inst Aeronaut & Astronaut. *Res:* Shock structure in gas mixtures; quasi-linear techniques applied to aerodynamic noise analysis; uranium separation in gas dynamic flows; hypersonic flow analysis; transonic flow analysis; helicopter rotor acoustics; computational fluid dynamics. *Mailing Add:* Dept Aeronaut & Astronaut Mass Inst Technol Cambridge MA 02139. *Fax:* 617-258-7845; *E-Mail:* weslhar@mit.edu

HARRIS, WILLIAM BIRCH, CHEMICAL ENGINEERING. *Current Pos:* assoc prof & assoc res engr, 53-77, PROF CHEM ENG, TEX A&M UNIV, 77- *Personal Data:* b Loveland, Colo, Sept 26, 19; m 42; c 2. *Educ:* Univ Colo, BS, 41; Agr & Mech Col, Tex, MS, 60; Colo State Univ, PhD, 73. *Prof Exp:* Res chemist, Nat Aniline Div, Allied Chem & Dye Corp, 41-48; asst tech dir, Apache Powder Co, 48-53. *Mem:* Fel Am Inst Chem Eng. *Res:* Cottonseed products; catalysis; alternative fuels; solar energy. *Mailing Add:* 2512 Club Lake Trail McKinney TX 75069

HARRIS, WILLIAM BURLEIGH, PETROLOGY, STRATIGRAPHY. *Current Pos:* PROF GEOL, UNIV NC, WILMINGTON, 84- *Personal Data:* b Norfolk, Va, July 2, 43; m 65, Sharon; c Daniel & Timothy. *Educ:* Campbell Univ, BS, 66; WVa Univ, MS, 68; Univ NC, Chapel Hill, PhD(geol), 75. *Prof Exp:* Explor geologist, Texaco, Inc, 68-70; econ geologist, Va Div Mineral Resources, 70-72; teaching asst geol, Univ NC, Chapel Hill, 72-74; from instr to assoc prof, Univ NC, Wilmington, 74-82; res specialist, Exxon Prod Res Co, 82-83. *Concurrent Pos:* Proj dir & prin investr grant, NC Bd Sci & Technol, 76-78; consult geologist, E I du Pont de Nemours & Co, Inc, & Westinghouse Savannah River Co, Savannah River Lab, 78, 81, 87, 88, 89 & 90; dir & prin investr, US Dept Energy grant, 82; consult geologist, Arco Oil & Gas Co, 85, 86, 87 & 88 & US Army Corps Engrs, 93; US Dept Energy grant, 90. *Mem:* Soc Econ Paleont & Mineral; Sigma Xi; Geol Soc Am. *Res:* Stratigraphic and structural relations of the Atlantic and Gulf Coastal Plain Province, glauconite radiometric dating, carbonate petrology and depositional sedimentary environments; carbonate cement origins, isotopic compositions and dolomitization; application of the seismic sequence concepts to outcrops and core holes. *Mailing Add:* Dept Earth Sci Univ NC 601 S Col Rd Wilmington NC 28403. *Fax:* 910-962-7077; *E-Mail:* harrisw@uncw.edu

HARRIS, WILLIAM CHARLES, PHYSICAL CHEMISTRY, SPECTROSCOPY. *Current Pos:* prog dir struct chem & thermodyn, NSF, 77-87, assoc dir, 87-88, prog dir phys chem, 87-88, dir off sci & technol, 88-89, asst to NSF dir sci & technol, 89-91, ASST DIR MATH & PHYS SCI, NSF, 92- *Personal Data:* b New York, NY, Nov 4, 44; m 67; c 2. *Educ:* William & Mary Col, BS, 66; Univ SC, PhD(chem), 70. *Prof Exp:* Nat Inst Arthritis & Metab Dis fel, 70-71; from asst prof to assoc prof chem, Furman Univ, 71-79. *Concurrent Pos:* Petrol res fund grant, Res Corp, NSF, 71-74; vis prof chem, Univ NC, Chapel Hill, 75; Dreyfus teacher scholar, 75-80; fac fel, NSF, 77; guest res, Lab Chem Physics, NIH, 78- *Mem:* Am Phys Soc; Am Chem Soc; Coblent Soc (pres, 81-83); Soc Appl Spectros. *Res:* Application of mid- and far- infrared, as well as laser Raman spectroscopy, to the study of molecular conformations; matrix isolation studies of reactive molecules; molecular dynamics and force field calculations of large molecules; lipid membranes. *Mailing Add:* Biosphere Ctr Columbia Univ 32540 S Biosphere Rd PO Box 689 Oracle AZ 85623

HARRIS, WILLIAM EDGAR, ASTRONOMY. *Current Pos:* from asst prof to assoc prof, 76-84, PROF PHYSICS, MCMASTER UNIV, 84- *Personal Data:* b Edmonton, Alta, Nov 28, 47. *Educ:* Univ Alta, BSc, 69; Univ Toronto, MSc, 70, PhD(astron), 74. *Prof Exp:* Fel astron, Yale Univ Observ, 74-76. *Concurrent Pos:* Scientific adv coun, Can-France-Hawaii Telescope, 84-86, chmn, 85-86; Grant Selection Comt, Space & Astron, Nat Sci & Eng Res Coun Can, 90-93. *Mem:* Can Astron Soc; Am Astron Soc; Astron Soc Pac. *Res:* Photometry in star clusters and nearby galaxies; observational stellar evolution; galactic structure. *Mailing Add:* McMaster Univ Dept Physics & Astron Hamilton ON L8S 4M1 Can

HARRIS, WILLIAM FRANKLIN, III, ENVIRONMENTAL SCIENCES. *Current Pos:* DIR & PROF, DIV BIOL, UNIV TENN, KNOXVILLE, 93- *Personal Data:* b Jacksonville, Fla, Sept 27, 42; m 66, Marilyn Wohlleber; c James G & Steven F. *Educ:* Wabash Col, BA, 64; Univ Tenn, Knoxville, MS, 66, PhD(bot), 70. *Honors & Awards:* Presidential Rank Award, Meritorious Exec, US Govt, 92. *Prof Exp:* Res ecologist, Oak Ridge Nat Lab, 70-73, res group leader, 73-76, sect head, 76-80; prog dir, NSF, 80-81, dep div dir, 81-87, exec officer, 87-92, dep asst dir biol, 92-93. *Mem:* Ecol Soc Am; fel AAAS; Am Inst Biol Sci. *Res:* University administration biological sciences; emphasizing terrestrial and freshwater ecosystems. *Mailing Add:* 810 Glensprings Dr Knoxville TN 37922. *Fax:* 423-974-0978; *E-Mail:* wfharris@utk.edu

HARRIS, WILLIAM J, TRANSPORTATION, FAILURE ANALYSIS. *Current Pos:* Snead distinguished prof, Dept Civil Eng, 85-95, assoc dir, Tex Transp Inst, 87-95, DISTINGUISHED EMER PROF/SNEAD EMER PROF TRANSP ENG, TEX A&M UNIV, 95-, SR RES ENGR, TEX TRANSP INST, 95- *Personal Data:* b South Bend, Ind, June 17, 18; m 44, 78; c 2. *Educ:* Purdue Univ, BS & MS, 40; Mass Inst Technol, DSc, 48. *Hon Degrees:* DEng, Purdue Univ, 78. *Honors & Awards:* Mathewson Medal, Am Inst Metall, Mining & Petrol Engrs, 50; Carey Award, Transp Res Bd, 78, Crum Award, 89; Distinguished Res Award, Transp Res Forum, 84. *Prof Exp:* Head, Ferrous Alloys Br, Metall Div, Naval Res Lab, 47-51; asst secy, Div Eng, Nat Acad Sci-Nat Res Coun, 60-62; asst dir, Battelle Mem Inst, 54-57, asst to vpres, 62-67; asst dir technol, Columbus Labs, 67-69; vpres res, Res & Test Dept, Asn Am RR, 70-85. *Concurrent Pos:* Pres, W J Harris, Inc, 85-; mem, Pres Comt Critical Infrastruct Protection, 97- *Mem:* Nat Acad Eng; fel Metall Soc (pres, 69-70); fel Am Soc Metals; fel Am Soc Mech Engrs; hon mem Nat Security Indust Asn; Am Inst Mining Metall & Petrol Engrs; Found Eng Technols; Int Heavy Haul Asn. *Res:* Type, thickness and arrangement of aircraft armor; shop failure analysis; brittle fracture; rocket motor failure analysis; re-entry materials; advanced structural materials; railroad wheel failures; track train dynamic interactions; labor management productivity; transportation planning and analysis. *Mailing Add:* 415 Chimney Hill Dr College Station TX 77840-1833

HARRIS, WILLIAM M, PLANT ANATOMY. *Current Pos:* asst prof, 68-73, ASSOC PROF BOT, UNIV ARK, FAYETTEVILLE, 73- *Personal Data:* b Fresno, Calif, Mar 23, 40; m 64; c 2. *Educ:* Fresno State Col, BA, 63; Univ Calif, Davis, PhD(bot), 68. *Mem:* AAAS; Am Inst Biol Sci; Bot Soc Am. *Res:* Morphogenesis of plastids in ripening solanaceous fruits, primarily at the ultrastructure level; plastid mutants; ultrastructure of gymnosperm leaves; root hair structure and function. *Mailing Add:* Biol Sci Univ Ark 632 Sci-Eng Fayetteville AR 72701-1202

HARRISBERGER, EDGAR LEE, MECHANICAL ENGINEERING. *Current Pos:* RETIRED. *Personal Data:* b Denver, Colo, Sept 24, 24; m 69, Ruth H Surgeson; c Russ, Ron, Dianne, Judy & David. *Educ:* Univ Okla, BS, 45; Univ Colo, MS, 50; Purdue Univ, PhD(mech eng), 63. *Honors & Awards:* Fred Merry Field Award Excellence Eng Design, Am Soc Eng Educ, 84; Chester F Carlson Award, Am Soc Eng Educ, 86. *Prof Exp:* Instr eng, Murray State Agr Col, 46-49; asst prof mech eng, Univ Utah, 50-54; assoc prof, NC State Univ, 54-60; NSF fel, 60-61; assoc prof mech eng, Okla State Univ, 63-65, Halliburton prof & dir, Ctr Teaching, 65-71, head, Sch Mech & Aerospace Eng, 66-71; dean col sci & eng, Univ Tex of the Permian Basin, 71-75; Andrew Carnegie vis prof, Cooper Union, 76-77; prof mech eng & dir, Mech Eng Design Clin, Univ Ala, 77-88, head, Mech Eng Dept, 83-88, co-dir, Venture Clin, 83-86; distinguished vis prof eng educ, Univ Cincinnati, 88, head, Mech Indust, Nuclear Eng Dept, 89-91. *Concurrent Pos:* Ed, MEN Mag, 65-71, ERM Mag, 68-71. *Mem:* Fel Am Soc Mech Engrs; hon mem & fel Am Soc Eng Educ (vpres, pres). *Res:* Mechanism and machine design; kinematics; engineering design; author one book. *Mailing Add:* 15511 Walden Rd Tampa FL 33618

HARRISES, ANTONIO EFTHEMIOS, PARASITOLOGY, ZOOLOGY. *Current Pos:* PROF BIOL, SALEM STATE COL, 70-, PROG DIR, NUCLEAR MED TECHNOL PROG. *Personal Data:* b Manchester, NH, Sept 12, 26; m 57; c Anthony, Gregory, Stephan, Sally & Susan. *Educ:* St Anselm's Col, AB, 50; Univ NH, MS, 52; Univ Notre Dame, PhD, 57. *Prof Exp:* From asst prof to prof biol, Univ Southern Miss, 57-70. *Mem:* Sigma Xi; Am Soc Parasitol. *Res:* Taxonomy of freshwater monogenetic trematodes; culture methods. *Mailing Add:* 447 Laydon St Manchester NH 03109

HARRISON, AIX B, EXERCISE PHYSIOLOGY. *Current Pos:* from asst prof to assoc prof, 50-68, PROF PHYS EDUC & PROG DIR HEALTH & FITNESS CTR, OKLA STATE UNIV, 58- *Personal Data:* b Zearing, Iowa, Feb 14, 25; m 50; c 2. *Educ:* Univ Ill, BS, 49, MS, 50; Mich State Univ, PhD(phys educ), 59. *Prof Exp:* Teacher, Galva Ill Community Schs, 49-50. *Mem:* Am Col Sports Med; Sigma Xi. *Res:* Training programs for producing maximal oxygen consumption; training for and measuring maximal oxygen debts; logitudinal study of adult physical fitness; fitness and aging. *Mailing Add:* Okla State Univ 2135 W University Stillwater OK 74074-2547

HARRISON, ALEXANDER GEORGE, PHYSICAL CHEMISTRY, ANALYTICAL CHEMISTRY. *Current Pos:* lectr chem, 59-60, from asst prof to assoc prof, 60-67, assoc chmn dept, 71-74, PROF CHEM, UNIV TORONTO, 67- *Personal Data:* b Peterborough, Ont, Apr 1, 31; m 55; c 2. *Educ:* Univ Western Ont, BSc, 52, MSc, 53; McMaster Univ, PhD(chem), 56. *Honors & Awards:* Noranda Lect Award, Chem Inst Can, 71. *Prof Exp:* Fel, McMaster Univ, 56-57; Nat Res Coun Can fel chem, 57-59. *Concurrent Pos:* Alfred P Sloan res fel, 62-64; Killam res fel, 85-87. *Mem:* Chem Inst Can; Am Chem Soc; Am Soc Mass Spectrometry. *Res:* Mechanistic studies in electron impact and chemical ionization mass spectrometry; collisional spectroscopy of gaseous ions; analytical applications of mass spectrometry. *Mailing Add:* Dept Chem Univ Toronto Toronto ON M5S 1A1 Can

HARRISON, ALINE MARGARET, CHEMISTRY. *Current Pos:* asst instr, 79-81, asst prof, 81-90, ASSOC PROF CHEM, YORK COL PA, 90- *Personal Data:* b Lincoln, Nebr, Aug 30, 40; m 66, Ernest A Harrison Jr; c 1. *Educ:* Univ Mich, BS, 62; Univ Md, MS, 67, PhD(org chem), 81. *Prof Exp:* Res org chemist, Agr Res Serv, USDA, 62-63; instr chem, Northern Mich Univ, 66-68; lab instr & admin coun, Pa State Univ, York Campus, 70-72; teaching asst, Univ Md, 72-76, res asst, 76-78; asst prof, Dickinson Col, 78-79. *Mem:* Am Chem Soc; Sigma Xi; AAAS. *Res:* Synthesis of potential analgesics for replacement of morphine; immunocompetence of the human immune system under stress, in conjunction with psychological state and of cancer patients having various psychological states. *Mailing Add:* Country Club Rd York PA 17405

HARRISON, ANNA JANE, PHYSICAL CHEMISTRY. *Current Pos:* from asst prof to assoc prof, Mt Holyoke Col, 45-50, chmn dept, 60-66, prof chem, 50-76, William R Kenan, Jr, prof, 76-79, EMER PROF CHEM, MT HOLYOKE COL, 79- *Personal Data:* b Benton City, Mo, Dec 23, 12. *Educ:* Univ Mo, AB, 33, MA, 37, PhD(phys chem), 40. *Hon Degrees:* DSc, Tulane Univ Y Smith Col, 75, Vincennes Univ, Am Int Col & Williams Col, 78, Suffolk Univ, Worcester Polytech Inst, Hartford Univ, Hood Col & Leigh Univ, 79, Univ Mo & Eastern Mich Univ, 83, Russell Sage Col & Mt Holyoke Col, 84, Mills Col, 85; LHD, Lindenwood Col, 77, Emmanuel Col, 83, St Joseph Col & Elms Col, 85, Rhodes Col, 90. *Honors & Awards:* Frank Forrest Award, 49; Petrol Res Fund Int Award, Nat Res Coun Can, 59-60; Award, Mfg Chem Asn, 69; James Flack Norris Award, Am Chem Soc, 77 & Award Chem Educ, 82. *Prof Exp:* From instr to asst prof chem, Newcomb Col, Tulane Univ, 40-45. *Concurrent Pos:* Berliner res fel, Am Asn Univ Women, Cambridge Univ, 52-53; mem, Nat Sci Bd, 72-78; distinguished vis prof, US Naval Acad, 80; chmn bd, AAAS, 83; bd dirs, Sigma Xi, 88-91; mem bd, Int Union Pure & Appl Chem, 78-81 & Vol in Tech Assistance, 90-94. *Mem:* AAAS (pres 83-84); Am Chem Soc (pres, 78); Sigma Xi; Int Union Pure & Appl Chem; Nat Sci Teachers Asn. *Res:* Vacuum ultraviolet spectroscopy. *Mailing Add:* 14 Ashfield Lane Mt Holyoke Col South Hadley MA 01075

HARRISON, ARNOLD MYRON, PHYSICAL ORGANIC CHEMISTRY. *Current Pos:* SR RES SCIENTIST, RES & DEVELOP, UNION CARBIDE TECH CTR, 75- *Personal Data:* b Pittsburgh, Pa, Sept 25, 46. *Educ:* Princeton Univ, AB, 68; Univ Chicago, MS, 70, PhD(org chem), 75. *Mem:* Am Chem Soc; AAAS; Sigma Xi. *Res:* Physical organic chemistry; nuclear magnetic resonance and catalysis. *Mailing Add:* PO Box 8361 South Charleston WV 25303

HARRISON, ARTHUR PENNOYER, JR, MICROBIOLOGY HISTORY OF ELECTRONICS-RADIO. *Current Pos:* RETIRED. *Personal Data:* b Takoma Park, Md, Oct 15, 22; m 58. *Educ:* Univ Md, BS, 48, MS, 49, PhD(bact), 52. *Prof Exp:* Res assoc, Univ Md, 52-53; from asst prof to assoc prof biol, Vanderbilt Univ, 53-63; mem staff, Biol Div, Oak Ridge Nat Lab, 63-68; prof bot, Univ Mo, Columbia, 68-90. *Concurrent Pos:* Vis investr, Oxford Univ, 57-58. *Res:* Bacterial physiology and taxonomy. *Mailing Add:* 20 Suttlers Row Port Royal Plantation Hilton Head Island SC 29928

HARRISON, BEN, CHEMISTRY. *Current Pos:* INDEPENDENT CONSULT, 82- *Personal Data:* b Chicago, Ill, Apr 12, 30. *Educ:* Ill Inst Technol, BA, 54, MA, 63; Alta Col, PhD(chem), 68. *Mem:* Am Inst Chemists. *Mailing Add:* Chem Consult Servs 18842 Jamie Ct Homewood IL 60430

HARRISON, BENJAMIN KEITH, CHEMICAL PROCESS SIMULATION, THERMODYNAMICS. *Current Pos:* PROF CHEM ENG, UNIV S ALA, 86- *Personal Data:* b Macon, Ga, July 29, 47; m 71, Nancy Kelly; c 1. *Educ:* Ga Inst Technol, BS, 69, MS, 71, MS, 77; Univ Mo, Rolla, PhD(chem eng), 84. *Honors & Awards:* Halliburton Educ Found Award of Excellence, 89. *Prof Exp:* Eng specialist, Monsanto Co, 77-86. *Concurrent Pos:* Consult, Ciba Geigy Corp, 87-; prin investr, Cray Res, 88-; mem, Sci Adv Comt, Gulf Coast Hazardous Substance Res Ctr, 88-; vchmn comt, Am Soc Testing & Mat, 90- *Mem:* Am Inst Chem Eng; Am Soc Testing & Mat; Am Chem Soc. *Res:* Chemical process simulation, often involving supercomputers; thermodynamic physical property prediction, often in connection with hazard predictions. *Mailing Add:* Dept Chem Eng EGLB 248 Univ SAla Mobile AL 36688

HARRISON, BERTRAND FEREDAY, PLANT PHYSIOLOGY, AGROSTOLOGY. *Current Pos:* RETIRED. *Personal Data:* b Springville, Utah, Feb 20, 08; m 31, Lorna Jensen; c Bertrand K, Linnaea, Leon C & Philip A. *Educ:* Brigham Young Univ, BS, 30, MS, 31; Univ Chicago, PhD(plant physiol), 37. *Prof Exp:* Ranger naturalist, Yellowstone Nat Park, 31; from instr to prof, Brigham Young Univ, 31-74, emer prof bot, 74-88. *Concurrent Pos:* Asst, Univ Chicago, 36-37; res assoc, Agr Res Lab, Am Smelting & Ref Co, 42 & 43; consult intermountain res, Nat Resources Res, Mgt Consult, Provo, 76-88. *Mem:* Am Soc Plant Physiol; Bot Soc Am; Sigma Xi. *Res:* Physiology of range grasses, especially water and mineral requirements. *Mailing Add:* 655 N 1130 E Provo UT 84606

HARRISON, BERTRAND KENT, THEORETICAL PHYSICS. *Current Pos:* from asst prof to assoc prof, 64-71, PROF PHYSICS & ASTRON, BRIGHAM YOUNG UNIV, 71- *Personal Data:* b Provo, Utah, July 21, 34; m 54; c 4. *Educ:* Brigham Young Univ, BS, 55; Princeton Univ, AM, 57, PhD(theoret physics), 59. *Prof Exp:* Asst physics, Princeton Univ, 56-59; staff mem, Los Alamos Sci Lab, Calif, 59-64. *Concurrent Pos:* Nat Sci Found grant, res res grant gravitation & electromagnetism, 65-67; Nat Acad Sci-Nat Res Coun sr resident res assoc, 68-70; res affil, Jet Propulsion Lab Calif Inst Technol, 77-, pres, Fac Adv Coun, Brigham Young Univ, 75-76. *Mem:* Am Phys Soc; Sigma Xi; NY Acad Sci. *Res:* General relativity and gravitation with particular emphasis on exact solutions of field equations, and superdense stars; plasma physics; applied mathematics. *Mailing Add:* Dept Physics & Astron Brigham Young Univ Provo UT 84602

HARRISON, BETTINA HALL, CYTOLOGY, IMMUNOLOGY. *Current Pos:* asst prof, 67-74, ASSOC PROF BIOL, UNIV MASS, BOSTON, 74- *Personal Data:* b Foxboro, Mass; m 41; c 3. *Educ:* Univ Mass, BS; Radcliffe Col, AM; Boston Univ, PhD(cytol), 68. *Prof Exp:* Fac mem med technol, Lasell Jr Col, Mass, 40-41; res microscopist, Maine Mills Labs, 41-43 & 50-51; fac mem med technol, Lasell Jr Col, 59-65. *Concurrent Pos:* Fac res grants, 68-70, 71-72 & 72-74; res fel, Tufts-New Eng Med Ctr Hosp, 76-77; res grant, Nat Leukemia Asn, 77, Healy grant, Univ Mass, Boston, 86-87. *Mem:* AAAS; Am Soc Cell Biol; Soc Develop Biol; NY Acad Sci; Int Soc Immunol. *Res:* Cytological development of lymphocytes; functional aspects of palatine tonsils; ultrastructure of ozonated pollen; regeneration of bone marrow; cytological effects of acid rain on leaf structures; various publications. *Mailing Add:* 19 Priscilla Lane Medford MA 02155-1516

HARRISON, CHARLES WAGNER, JR, APPLIED PHYSICS, ELECTRICAL ENGINEERING. *Current Pos:* CONSULT, 73- *Personal Data:* b Farmville, Va, Sept 15, 13; m 40; c 2. *Educ:* Univ Va, BSE, 39, EE, 40; Harvard Univ, SM, 42, ME, 52, PhD(appl physics), 54. *Honors & Awards:* Electronics Achievement Award, Inst Elec & Electronics Engrs, 66. *Prof Exp:* Instr, Univ Va, 39-40; res engr antenna res, Bur Ships, Dept Navy, 39-41; physicist, US Naval Res Lab, 44-46; electronics officer repair & installation, Philadelphia Naval Ship Yard, 46-48; asst dir electronics res, Electronics Design & Develop Div, Bur Ships, 48-50; prog officer radio div I, US Naval Res Lab, 50-51; electronics officer electronics equip eval, Comdr Oper Develop Force, US Navy, 53-55, electronics officer res & heat studies, Staff, Comndg Gen, Armed Forces Spec Weapons Proj, 55-57; res physicist antenna & electromagnetics compatibility studies, Sandia Labs, 57-73. *Concurrent Pos:* Lectr, Harvard Univ, 42-43; Princeton Univ, 43-44; vis prof, Christian Heritage Col, El Cajon, Calif, 76; auth; mem, Int Union Radio Sci, comn B. *Mem:* Fel Inst Elec & Electronics Engrs; Int Union Radio Sci; Sigma Xi. *Res:* Electromagnetics; acoustics; astronomy; contributed numerous articles to professional journals; author; numerous articles in the field of astrophysics. *Mailing Add:* 2808 Alcazar St NE Albuquerque NM 87110-3516

HARRISON, CHRISTOPHER GEORGE ALICK, GEOPHYSICS. *Current Pos:* from asst prof to assoc prof, Univ Miami, 67-74, chmn div marine geol & geophys, 76-83, interim dean, 86-89, PROF GEOPHYS, ROSENSTIEL SCH MARINE & ATMOSPHERIC SCI, UNIV MIAMI, 74- *Personal Data:* b Oxford, Eng, Dec 29, 36; m 64; c Ewen & Ariel. *Educ:* Cambridge Univ, BA, 60, MA, 64, PhD(geophys), 66, ScD,89. *Honors & Awards:* Group Achievement Award, Magnetic Field Satellite Sci Invest Team, NASA, 83. *Prof Exp:* Res geophysicist, Scripps Inst Oceanog, 61-67. *Concurrent Pos:* Assoc ed, J Geophys Res, 73-75; mem panel, NSF, 75-77; ed, Earth & Planetary Sci Lett, 78-86; mem, sea level change panel, Nat Res Coun, 84-86, panel on solid earth aspects of global change, 90-91; mem, US Nat Comt, Int Union Geod & Geophys, 84-, chair, 91-96, vchair, 96- *Mem:* Fel AAAS; fel Am Geophys Union (gen secy, 91-97); fel Royal Astron Soc; Sigma Xi. *Res:* Paleomagnetism of deep sea sediments and other rocks; magnetic anomalies; plate tectonics; remote sensing; sea level change. *Mailing Add:* 3851 Braganza Ave Miami FL 33133. *Fax:* 305-361-4632; *E-Mail:* charrison@rsmas.miami.edu

HARRISON, DALTON S(IDNEY), AGRICULTURAL ENGINEERING. *Current Pos:* RETIRED. *Personal Data:* b Darlington, Fla, Oct 10, 20; m 49; c 2. *Educ:* Univ Fla, BSA, 50, MSA, 53. *Prof Exp:* Asst agr engr, Inst Food & Agr Sci, Univ Fla, 53-60, from asst prof & assoc agr exten serv to prof agr eng & agr engr, 60-88. *Mem:* Am Soc Agr Engrs; sr mem Nat Soc Prof Engrs. *Res:* Drainage and irrigation. *Mailing Add:* 300 SW 41st St Gainesville FL 32607

HARRISON, DAVID ELLSWORTH, MECHANISMS OF AGING, PRIMITIVE STEM CELLS. *Current Pos:* Fel, Jackson Lab, 69-70, assoc staff scientist, 70-73, staff scientist, 73-81, SR STAFF SCIENTIST PHYSIOL GENETICS, JACKSON LAB, 81- *Personal Data:* b New Haven, Conn, June 26, 42; m 67; c 3. *Educ:* Bates Col, BS, 64; Stanford Univ, PhD(inorg chem), 69. *Concurrent Pos:* Mem mouse subcomt, Animal Models Res, Aging Comn, Nat Res Coun, 78-80; site evaluator, Aging Rev Comn, Nat Inst Aging & Vet Admin; ed biol sci, J Gerontol, 84-87, Growth, 87-; chmn, Biol, Gerontol Soc Am, 89-91; dir training, Jackson Lab, 90-; Prin investr, NIH, RO1 grants, 72- *Mem:* Soc Develop Biol; Int Soc Exp Hemat; Gerontol Soc Am; Am Asn Immunologists; Am Aging Asn; Am Soc Hemat. *Res:* Hemopoietic and immunopoietic early precursor cells; stem cells as gene transfer vehicles; marrow grafts; aging tissue transplantations; physiological age measurements evaluating antiaging treatments; causes of senescence; senetics of longevity. *Mailing Add:* Jackson Lab Bar Harbor ME 04609. *Fax:* 207-288-6079; *E-Mail:* deh@aretha.jax.org

HARRISON, DAVID KENT, mathematics, for more information see previous edition

HARRISON, DEBIA, CHEMISTRY. *Current Pos:* PROF CHEM, UNIV FLA. *Honors & Awards:* Lester W Strock Award, Soc Appl Spectros, 94. *Mailing Add:* Chem Dept Univ Fla Gainesville FL 32611

HARRISON, DON EDMUNDS, physical oceanography, applied mathematics, for more information see previous edition

HARRISON, DON EDWARD, CERAMICS, MATERIALS SCIENCE. *Current Pos:* RETIRED. *Personal Data:* b Dennison, Ohio, Oct 29, 28; m 61, Mary Irene Newby; c David William. *Educ:* Pa State Univ, BS, 52, MS, 53, PhD(ceramics), 55. *Prof Exp:* Asst lectr ceramics, Univ Leeds, 55-56; assoc chem luminescence, Lamp Div, Gen Elec Co, 56-59; fel engr crystal growth, Res & Develop Ctr, Westinghouse Elec Corp, 59-65; coordr adv group tech assessment, Regional Indust Develop Corp Southwestern Pa, 65-66; mgr mat sci, Res & Develop Ctr, Westinghouse Elec Corp, 66-71, lab mgr, Westinghouse Res Lab-Europe, Brussels, Belg, 72-74, res adv, Iran-Westinghouse Prog Ctr, Tehran, 75, mgr, Nuclear Mat Dept, Res & Develop Ctr, 76-84, mgr, mat sci div, Res & Devel Ctr, 84-87, dir res & develop, Energy & Utility Syst Group, 88-89. *Mem:* Am Chem Soc; Sigma Xi. *Res:* High temperature ceramics, crystal growth, solidification, luminescence, phase equilibria; nuclear waste management. *Mailing Add:* 3809 Edinburg Dr Murrysville PA 15668-1013

HARRISON, DONALD C, CARDIOLOGY, CARDIOVASCULAR PHYSIOLOGY. *Current Pos:* SR VPRES PROVOST HEALTH AFFAIRS, UNIV CINCINNATI MED CTR, 86-, CHIEF EXEC OFF, COL MED, 95-, PROF MED & CARDIOL. *Personal Data:* b Blount Co, Ala, Feb 24, 34; m 55, Laura McAnnally; c Douglas, Elizabeth & Donna M. *Educ:* Birmingham Southern Col, BS, 54; Med Col Ala, MD, 58. *Prof Exp:* Intern asst resident, Peter Bent Brigham Hosp, 58-60; fel cardiol, Harvard Univ, 61, NIH, 61-63; mem fac, Med Sch, Stanford Univ, 63-86, chief, Div Cardiol, 67-86, prof med, 71-86. *Concurrent Pos:* Chief cardiol, Stanford Univ Hosp, 67-86; William G Irwin prof cardiol, 72-86. *Mem:* Am Soc Pharmacol & Exp Therapeut; fel Am Col Cardiol; Am Asn Physicians; Asn Univ Cardiol; Am Clin & Clin Assoc; Brit Cardiac Soc; Am Heart Asn. *Res:* Pharmacology. *Mailing Add:* Sr Vpres Health Affairs Univ Cincinnati Med Ctr ML 663 250 Health Prof Bldg Cincinnati OH 45267-0663. Fax: 513-558-2962

HARRISON, DOUGLAS P, CHEMICAL ENGINEERING. *Current Pos:* from asst prof to prof, La State Univ, 69-89, chmn dept, 77-80, alumni prof, 89-96, VOORHIES PROF CHEM ENG, LA STATE UNIV, 96- *Personal Data:* b Frost, Tex, Nov 19, 37; m 65, Kay; c Carol & Steve. *Educ:* Univ Tex, Austin, BSChE, 61, PhD(chem eng), 66. *Prof Exp:* Res engr, Monsanto Co, 66-69. *Mem:* Am Inst Chem Engrs; Am Soc Eng Educ; Air Pollution Control Asn. *Res:* Reactor design; catalysis; pollution control. *Mailing Add:* Dept Chem Eng La State Univ 312 Chem Engr Bldg Baton Rouge LA 70803. Fax: 504-388-1476

HARRISON, EDWARD ROBERT, PHYSICS, ASTROPHYSICS. *Current Pos:* prof astrophys, 66-87, DISTINGUISHED PROF PHYSICS & ASTRON, UNIV MASS, AMHERST, 87- *Personal Data:* b London, Eng, Jan 8, 19; m 45; c 2. *Honors & Awards:* Melcher Award, 85; Melville S Green lectr, 87. *Prof Exp:* Prin scientist, Atomic Energy Res Estab, Eng, 47-65; Nat Acad res assoc, Goddard Space Flight Ctr, Md, 65-66. *Concurrent Pos:* Vis scientist, Europ Orgn Nuclear Res, 59-60, Trieste Inst Theoret Physics, 73, Nat Radio Astron Observ, 76; vis prof, Woods Hole Oceanog Inst, 69, Inst Astron, Cambridge, Eng, 70, 71, 76, 84 & 90, Univ Sussex, Eng, 73, Univ Va, 76, Univ Wellington, NZ, 81 & Univ NC, 87; Chancellor's lect award, 78. *Mem:* Fel AAAS; fel Am Inst Physics; Am Astron Soc; Int Astron Union; fel Royal Astron Soc. *Res:* Cosmology, particle physics, history of science and author of books on cosmology, history of science and the riddle of cosmic darkness; cosmology. *Mailing Add:* Astron Prog Grad Res Tower B Univ Mass Amherst MA 01003

HARRISON, ERNEST AUGUSTUS, JR, ORGANIC CHEMISTRY. *Current Pos:* from asst prof to assoc prof, 68-81, PROF CHEM, PA STATE UNIV, 81- *Personal Data:* b Boston, Mass, May 25, 34; m 66; c 1. *Educ:* Boston Univ, BA, 57; Univ Md, MS, 62, PhD(org chem), 66. *Prof Exp:* Instr chem, Univ Md, 65; asst prof, Northern Mich Univ, 65-68. *Concurrent Pos:* Vis chemist, NIH-Nat Inst Diabetes, Digestive & Kidney Dis, Lab Chem, Med Chem Sect, 75-76 & 82-83, spec expert, med chem sect, 83. *Mem:* Am Chem Soc; NY Acad Sci. *Res:* Synthesis of heterocyclic compounds and molecules of potential medicinal interest; chemistry and photochemistry of bridge-carbonyl systems; development of experiments for use in the undergraduate organic laboratory. *Mailing Add:* 1031 Edgecomb Ave York PA 17403

HARRISON, FLORENCE LOUISE, COMPARATIVE PHYSIOLOGY, MARINE BIOLOGY. *Current Pos:* ENVIRON SCIENTIST, ENVIRON SCI DIV, LAWRENCE LIVERMORE NAT LAB, 64- *Personal Data:* b Oil City, Pa, Sept 6, 26; m 45, Melvin A; c Leslie A & David A. *Educ:* Greenville Col, BS, 47; Univ Wash, MS, 53, PhD(zool), 54. *Prof Exp:* Instr zool & chem, Seattle Pac Col, 54-55; res assoc zool, Univ Wash, 55-56; NIH fel, Stanford Univ, 56-57. *Mem:* Am Soc Zool; Am Physiol Soc; Am Chem Soc. *Res:* Evaluation of the quantities present, the rates of turnover, and the potential toxic effects of energy-related pollutants, particularly radionuclides, heavy metals and hydrocarbons in marine and freshwater molluscs, crustaceans, and fishes. *Mailing Add:* Health Ecol Assessment Div L286 Univ Calif Lawrence Livermore Nat Lab PO Box 5507 Livermore CA 94550. *E-Mail:* floharri@rockisland.com

HARRISON, FRANK, ANATOMY, NEUROPHYSIOLOGY. *Current Pos:* RETIRED. *Personal Data:* b Dallas, Tex, Nov 21, 13; m 46, Elsie Claire Redfearn; c James R, Frank & Susan C. *Educ:* Southern Methodist Univ, BS, 35; Northwestern Univ, MS, 36, PhD(neuroanat), 38; Univ Tex Southwestern Med Sch, Dallas, MD, 56. *Prof Exp:* From instr to prof & chief div anat, Univ Tenn, 38-51; prof, Univ Tex Southwestern Med Sch, Dallas, 52-68, assoc dean, 56-68, assoc dean grad studies, 58-68; actg pres, Univ Tex, Arlington, 68-69, pres, 69-72; pres, Univ Tex Health Sci Ctr, San Antonio, 72-85. *Concurrent Pos:* Assoc dean grad studies, Univ Tex, Arlington, 65-68; adj prof, Southern Methodist Univ, 64-70. *Mem:* AAAS; Am Physiol Soc; Soc Exp Biol & Med; Biophys Soc; Am Asn Anat. *Res:* Neuroanatomy; neurophysiology. *Mailing Add:* 4168 Valley Ridge Dallas TX 75220

HARRISON, FRANK W, JR, GEOLOGY. *Honors & Awards:* Ben H Parker Award, Inst Prof Geologists, 94. *Mailing Add:* PO Box 51943 Lafayette LA 70505

HARRISON, FREDERICK WILLIAMS, BIOLOGY, INVERTEBRATE MICROSCOPIC ANATOMY. *Current Pos:* head biol dept, 77-89, PROF BIOL, WESTERN CAROLINA UNIV, 77- *Personal Data:* b Macon, Ga, Apr 14, 38; m 65, Marion Boyd; c 2. *Educ:* Univ SC, BS, 60, MS, 62, PhD(biol), 69. *Prof Exp:* Assoc prof biol, Presby Col, 66-73; from asst to assoc prof anat, Albany Med Col, 73-77. *Concurrent Pos:* Vis res scholar, Sch Biol Sci, Univ Sydney, 73-74; assoc ed, J Morphology, 78-; vis scientist, Yunnan Univ, Peoples Repub China, 83; proj adv, Sponges in Space, Space Shuttle 5; counr, Coun Undergrad Res, 89-93. *Mem:* Am Soc Zool; Am Micros Soc (secy, 83-88, pres, 90); Sigma Xi; fel AAAS. *Res:* Developmental cytology; systematics, paleolimnology of Porifera; invertebrate microscopic anatomy. *Mailing Add:* Dept Biol Western Carolina Univ Cullowhee NC 28723

HARRISON, GAIL GRIGSBY, HUMAN NUTRITION, PHYSICAL ANTHROPOLOGY. *Current Pos:* PROF, UNIV CALIF MED SCH, LOS ANGELES, 92- *Personal Data:* b Denver, Colo, June 8, 43; m, Osmar M Galaf; c 4. *Educ:* Univ Calif, BA, 65; Cornell Univ, MNS, 67; Univ Ariz, PhD(anthrop), 76. *Honors & Awards:* Future Leaders Award, Nutrit Found, Inc, 78. *Prof Exp:* Exten assoc nutrit, Cornell Univ, 67-70; instr med dietetics, Ohio State Univ, 70-72; from lectr to prof community med, Univ Ariz, 76-92. *Concurrent Pos:* Mem, World Food & Nutrit Study, Nat Acad Sci, 76-77 & comt food consumption patterns, Food & Nutrit Bd, 78-81; comt Int Nutrit Progs NAS/NRS, 87-90. *Mem:* Am Pub Health Asn; Am Dietetic Asn; fel Am Anthrop Asn; Soc Pediat Res; Soc Int Nutrit Res (pres, 92-94); Am Soc Nutrit Sci. *Res:* Growth and development of children; international nutrition; dietary methodology. *Mailing Add:* Sch Pub Health Univ Calif 10833 LeConte Ave Los Angeles CA 90024-1602. Fax: 310-794-1805; *E-Mail:* gailh@ucla.edu

HARRISON, GEORGE H, RADIOBIOLOGY, RADIATION PHYSICS. *Current Pos:* res asst nuclear physics, Cyclotron Lab, Univ Md, 69-72, res assoc radiobiol, 72-73, asst prof radiobiol, 73-78, ASSOC PROF RADIATION THER, SCH MED, UNIV MD, 78- *Personal Data:* b Newark, NJ, Mar 13, 43; m 67; c 1. *Educ:* Tufts Univ, BA, 65; Univ Md, MS, 69, PhD(nuclear physics), 72. *Prof Exp:* Comput systs analyst, Goddard Space Flight Ctr, NASA, 66-69. *Concurrent Pos:* Res assoc nuclear physics, Cyclotron Lab, Univ Md, 72-; tutor technol, Univ Col, 73-; NSF Presidential internship, 73. *Mem:* Radiation Res Soc; Inst Elec & Electronics Engrs. *Res:* Physics and bioeffects of high energy neutrons; neutron production and dosimetry; study of microwaves and ultrasound for use in cancer therapy; ultrasonic transducer design and bio-effect studies. *Mailing Add:* Radiation Res Div/6-015 BRB Univ Md Sch Med 655 W Baltimore St Baltimore MD 21201. Fax: 410-328-5279

HARRISON, GORDON R, PHYSICS, ELECTRICAL ENGINEERING. *Current Pos:* vpres mat & new technol, 83-91; TECH CONSULT, ELECTROMAGNETIC SCI, 91- *Personal Data:* b Wister, Okla, Dec 14, 31; m 57, Barbara Ann Herndon; c William A, Melissa H (McCormick), Lori J (Cora) & Amanda R (Flanter). *Educ:* Ark State Teachers Col, BS, 52, Vanderbilt Univ, MS, 54, PhD(physics), 58. *Prof Exp:* Sr staff engr, Sperry Microwave Electronics Div, 57-62, eng staff consult, 62-64, res sect head, 64-68, eng mgr, 68-71; prin res scientist, Ga Inst Technol, 71-83, dir, Appl Sci Lab, 72-78, sr staff, Dir Off, 78-83. *Concurrent Pos:* Health physicist, Oak Ridge Nat Lab, 53, physicist, 54 & Gen Dynamics/Convair, 55. *Mem:* Inst Elec & Electronics Engrs. *Res:* Ferrimagnetic materials; microwave components; solid state and nuclear physics. *Mailing Add:* 2915 Greenrock Trail Doraville GA 30340

HARRISON, GUNYON M, PEDIATRICS. *Current Pos:* instr pediat, 55-57, asst prof pediat & rehab, 57-64, assoc prof, 64-77, PROF PEDIAT & REHAB, BAYLOR COL MED, 77- *Personal Data:* b Fredericksburg, Va, Mar 6, 21; div; c 2. *Educ:* Va Mil Inst, BS, 43; Univ Va, MD, 46; Am Bd Pediat, dipl, 56. *Prof Exp:* Intern, St Joseph's Hosp, Baltimore, 46-47; pediat intern, Duke Univ Hosp, Durham, NC, 51-52, resident, 52-53, fel, 53; resident, Jefferson Davis Hosp, Houston, 53-54; resident, Baylor Col Med & Tex Children's Hosp, 54-55. *Concurrent Pos:* Asst instr, Baylor Col Med, 53-55; fel, Polio Respiratory Ctr, Nat Found Infantile Paralysis, Houston, 55-56; dir cystic fibrosis clin, Tex Children's Hosp, 55-61, chief respiratory ther, 68-, mem active med staff; mem med staff, Tex Children's Hosp, 58-; dir, Cystic Fibrosis & Related Pulmonary Dis Ctr, Baylor Col Med, Inst Rehab & Res & Tex Children's Hosp, 61-; chief chest clin, Tex Children's Hosp, 69-, pulmonary med, 72-; mem attend staff, Ben Taub Gen Hosp, 77-, courtesy staff, Methodist Hosp, 71- & St Luke's Hosp, 72-; consult physician, Pediat Chest Clin, Ben Taub Gen Hosp, assoc attend staff; assoc consult, Methodist Hosp & Cystic Fibrosis Clin, Baptist Mem Hosp, San Antonio; assoc attend staff, Harris Co Hosp Dist. *Mem:* Am Acad Pediat; Am Thoracic Soc; Am Asn Respiratory Ther; Asn Advan Med Instrumentation. *Res:* Pulmonary pediatric diseases; cystic fibrosis of the pancreas. *Mailing Add:* Baylor Col Med Tex Med Ctr One Baylor Plaza Pediat Pulmonary Sect Houston TX 77030-3411

HARRISON, H KEITH, PLANT ANATOMY. *Current Pos:* assoc prof, 67-74, PROF BOT & DIR MUS NATURAL HIST, WEBER STATE COL, 74- *Personal Data:* b Springville, Utah, Dec 10, 19; c 3. *Educ:* Univ Calif, Berkeley, AB, 53, PhD(bot), 59. *Prof Exp:* Res botanist, Univ Calif, 59-60; asst prof bot, Mont State Univ, 60-67. *Concurrent Pos:* Vis asst prof, Univ Wis, 63. *Mem:* Bot Soc Am; Torrey Bot Club; Am Soc Plant Taxonomists; Sigma Xi; NY Acad Sci. *Mailing Add:* Dept Bot Weber State Col 3850 Harrison Blvd Ogden UT 84408

HARRISON, HALSTEAD, ATMOSPHERIC CHEMISTRY. *Current Pos:* sr res assoc air chem, 71-73, ASSOC PROF ATMOSPHERIC SCI, UNIV WASH, 73- *Personal Data:* b Annapolis, Md, Apr 4, 31; m 60; c 3. *Educ:* Stanford Univ, BS, 55, PhD(chem), 60. *Prof Exp:* Staff scientist, Gen Atomic Div, Gen Dynamics Corp, 60-62; res assoc atomic & molecular beams, Univ Mich, 62; NSF fel, Inst Appl Physics, Univ Bonn, 63; staff scientist, Boeing Sci Res Labs, Wash, 63-71. *Mem:* Am Chem Soc; Am Phys Soc; Am Meteorol Soc; AAAS; Am Geophys Union. *Mailing Add:* Dept Atmospheric Sci A K-40 Univ Wash 3900 Seventh Ave NE Seattle WA 98195-0001

HARRISON, HELEN CONNOLLY, HORTICULTURAL SCIENCE. *Current Pos:* from asst prof to assoc prof, 80-91, PROF HORT, UNIV WIS, 91- *Personal Data:* b Annapolis, Md, Apr 15, 49; m 77, Richard; c Christopher, Peter & Jessi Eileen. *Educ:* NC State Univ, BA, 71; Ohio State Univ, MS, 76; Penn State Univ, PhD (hort), 79. *Mem:* Int Soc Hort Sci; fel Am Soc Hort Sci; Am Soc Agron; fel AAAS. *Res:* Environmental horticulture; major program areas such as mulching alternatives for small-scale food producers, row covers and other non-chemical alternatives for pest protection, heavy metal toxic problems relating to growing vegetables on contaminated soils, specialty vegetables cultivarevaluation, ginseng, snapbeans and melons. *Mailing Add:* Dept Hort Univ Wis Madison WI 53706. *Fax:* 608-262-4743; *E-Mail:* hcharris@facstaff.wisc.edu

HARRISON, HELEN COPLAN, BIOCHEMISTRY. *Current Pos:* res asst, 47-58, res assoc, 58-59, from asst prof to assoc prof, 59-78, EMER ASSOC PROF PEDIAT, MED SCH, JOHNS HOPKINS UNIV, 78- *Personal Data:* b Baltimore, Md, Sept 29, 11; wid; c 2. *Educ:* Goucher Col, AB, 31; Smith Col, MA, 34; Yale Univ, PhD(physiol chem), 39. *Hon Degrees:* DSc, Goucher Col, 96. *Honors & Awards:* Mead-Johnson Award, Am Acad Pediat, 42; Howland Award, Am Pediat Soc, 83. *Prof Exp:* Asst biol, Goucher Col, 31-33; asst physiol chem, Yale Univ, 35-37; res asst pediat, Med Col, Cornell Univ, 38-42; instr physiol chem, Yale Univ, 44-45. *Concurrent Pos:* Coxe fel biochem, Yale Univ, 42; scholar, Woods Hole Marine Biol Lab, Mass. *Mem:* Am Physiol Soc; Soc Exp Biol & Med; Am Pediat Soc. *Res:* Nutrition; endocrinology; renal physiology; physiology of calcium and phosphorus. *Mailing Add:* 111 Hamlet Hill Rd No 606 Baltimore MD 21210

HARRISON, IAN ROLAND, POLYMER SCIENCE. *Current Pos:* from asst prof to assoc prof, 71-81, PROF POLYMER SCI, PA STATE UNIV, UNIV PARK, 81- *Personal Data:* b Manchester, Eng, Apr 3, 43; US citizen; m 66; c 2. *Educ:* Univ Leeds, BSc, 64; Case Western Reserve Univ, MS, 69, PhD(macromolecular sci), 71. *Prof Exp:* Chemist, Dow Chem Co, 64-66; res grant, Case Western Reserve Univ, 71. *Mem:* NAm Thermal Anal Soc; Am Inst Physics; Am Phys Soc; Am Chem Soc; Sigma Xi; Soc Plastics Engrs. *Res:* Fold surface reactions of polymers; polymer characterization; thermal analysis of polymers; influence of polymer morphology on carbon structure; polymer crystallite size; small angle x-ray diffraction of polymers; deformation mechanisms; morphological control of diffusion polymer films. *Mailing Add:* Pa State Univ 325 Steidle Bldg University Park PA 16802-5007

HARRISON, IRENE R, SOFTWARE SYSTEMS. *Current Pos:* asst res engr, United Technologies Res Ctr, 76-80, assoc res engr, 80-84, assoc anal engr, 84-86, PROG ANALYST, UNITED TECHNOLOGIES RES CTR, 86- *Personal Data:* b Bronx, NY, Mar 20, 52. *Educ:* Univ NY, Binghamton, BA, 74; Univ Ariz, MS, 76; Rensselaer Polytech Inst, MS, 86. *Prof Exp:* Res asst optical sci, Univ Ariz, 74-76. *Mem:* Optical Soc Am; Asn Women Sci; Asn Comput Mach. *Res:* Computer programming in the sciences; simulations of processes and controls; graphics and implementation of theoretical equations; recipient of one patent. *Mailing Add:* United Technologies Res Ctr 411 Silver Lane East Hartford CT 06108

HARRISON, J(OHN) D(AVID), METALLURGY. *Current Pos:* CONSULT METALL, 81- *Personal Data:* b Pittsburgh, Pa, Oct 11, 30; m 55, Rose McCormick; c Richard A, Jeffrey S & Tamberly (Petrovich). *Educ:* Pa State Univ, BS, 52, MS, 53; Mass Inst Technol, ScD(metall), 58. *Prof Exp:* Res assoc, Fritz Haber Inst, Max Planck Inst, Berlin, Ger, 58-59; res metallurgist, Westinghouse Elec Corp, 59-66; res staff mem, Raychem Corp, 66-77, tech mgr, Metal Prod Group, 77-81. *Mem:* Am Chem Soc; Am Inst Mining, Metall & Petrol Engrs; Am Soc Metals Int. *Res:* Corrosion of solid alloys by liquid metals; ice interface morphology during freezing; high pressure seeded growth and etch-pit studies of hexagonal selenium single crystals; shape memory in TiNi and other alloys. *Mailing Add:* 13801 Hutchings Ct Watsonville CA 95076-5333

HARRISON, JACK EDWARD, regional geology; deceased, see previous edition for last biography

HARRISON, JACK LAMAR, geology, for more information see previous edition

HARRISON, JAMES BECKMAN, ORGANIC PEROXIDES, CATALYSTS. *Current Pos:* PRES, R&A SPECIALTY CHEM CO INC, 81- *Personal Data:* b Pittsburgh, Pa, May 25, 23; m 46; c 3. *Educ:* Allegheny Col, BS, 43; Carnegie Inst Technol, MS, 46; Univ Pittsburgh, PhD, 52. *Prof Exp:* Chemist, Lucidol Corp, 43-45, res chemist, Lucidol Div, Novadel-Agene Corp, 46-47; asst, Mellon Inst, 48-50 & Univ Pittsburgh, 50-52; from asst chief chemist to chief chemist, Wallace & Tiernan, Inc, 52-58, mgr res & develop, 58-60, dir, 60-62; pres, Aztec Chem Inc, 63-68, Aztec Chem, Div Rexall Drug & Chem Co, 69-70 & Div Dart Industs Inc, 70-74, vpres com develop, Chem Group, Dart Industs Inc, 74-79. *Mem:* AAAS; Com Develop Asn; Am Chem Soc; Soc Plastics Eng. *Res:* Organic peroxides and peroxy compounds; polymerization initiators; fats and oils. *Mailing Add:* 812 E 43rd St Brooklyn NY 11210

HARRISON, JAMES FRANCIS, THEORETICAL CHEMISTRY, QUANTUM CHEMISTRY. *Current Pos:* from asst prof to assoc prof, 68-81, PROF CHEM, MICH STATE UNIV, 81- *Personal Data:* b Philadelphia, Pa, Jan 19, 40; c Christopher & Kenneth. *Educ:* Drexel Univ, BS, 62; Princeton Univ, MA, 64, PhD(chem), 66. *Honors & Awards:* Camille & Henry Dreyfus Award, The Camille & Henry Dreyfus Found, NY, 72. *Prof Exp:* NSF fel, Ind Univ, Bloomington, 66-67, res assoc chem, 66-68. *Concurrent Pos:* Resident scientist, Argonne Nat Lab, 80-81. *Mem:* Am Chem Soc; Am Phys Soc. *Res:* Molecular electronic structure theory. *Mailing Add:* Dept Chem Mich State Univ East Lansing MI 48824-1322. *Fax:* 517-353-1793; *E-Mail:* harrison@cemvax.cem.msu.edu

HARRISON, JAMES OSTELLE, ENTOMOLOGY. *Current Pos:* from asst prof to prof, 62-85, EMER PROF BIOL, MERCER UNIV, 85- *Personal Data:* b Harrison, Ga, June 17, 20; m 42; c 2. *Educ:* Mercer Univ, BA, 49; Univ Ga, MA, 53; Cornell Univ, PhD(ecol), 62. *Prof Exp:* From asst entomologist to assoc entomologist, United Fruit Co, 56-62. *Concurrent Pos:* Chmn, Energy Adv Comt, City Macon, Ga; chmn, Water Qual Adv Comt, Mid Ga Area Planning & Develop Comn. *Mem:* Entom Soc Am; Ecol Soc Am. *Res:* Biology of banana insect pests and natural control of insect populations. *Mailing Add:* 1179 Matthews Pl Macon GA 31210

HARRISON, JOHN CHRISTOPHER, GEOPHYSICS. *Current Pos:* SR STAFF, GEODYNAMICS CORP, 83- *Personal Data:* b Co Durham, Eng, May 20, 29; US citizen; m 60, Elaine C Millar; c Kirsteen, Fiona & Keith. *Educ:* Cambridge Univ, BA, 50, PhD(geophys), 53. *Honors & Awards:* Sr US Scientist Award, Alexander von Humboldt Found, WGer, 75-76. *Prof Exp:* Jr res geophysicist, Inst Geophys & Planetary Physics, Univ Calif, Los Angeles, 53-55, from asst res geophysicist to assoc res geophysicist, 57-61; mem tech staff geophys & oceanog, Hughes Res Labs, 61-65; from assoc prof to prof geol, Univ Colo, Boulder, 65-83, dir, Coop Inst Res Environ Sci, 69-72, assoc dir, 72-83. *Concurrent Pos:* Lectr, Univ Calif, Santa Barbara. *Mem:* Am Geophys Union; Royal Astron Soc; Soc Explor Geophysicists. *Res:* Measurement of gravity, especially at sea and in the air; earth tides and free oscillations of the earth; physical geodesy; earth tilt. *Mailing Add:* 224 Merida Dr Santa Barbara CA 93111. *Fax:* 805-964-1070

HARRISON, JOHN HENRY, IV, information science & systems, for more information see previous edition

HARRISON, JOHN MICHAEL, BEHAVIOR-ETHOLOGY. *Current Pos:* Prof, 62-80, EMER PROF PSYCHOL, BOSTON UNIV, 80-; SR RES FEL, CAMBRIDGE CTR BEHAV STUDIES, 85- *Personal Data:* b London, Feb 2, 15; US citizen; m 46. *Educ:* Univ London, dipl psychol, 47. *Prof Exp:* Prof, 62-80, EMER PROF PSYCHOL, BOSTON UNIV, 80- *Concurrent Pos:* Mem, Int Brain Res Orgn, UNESCO; univ lectr, Boston Univ, 79; mem, Bd Trustees Cambridge Ctr for Behav Studies, 86-90. *Mem:* Am Asn Anat; fel Am Psychol Asn; fel Brit Psychol Soc. *Res:* Physiological psychology; investigation of relation between neural structure and behavior; comparative neuroanatomy of the auditory system and comparative study of hearing in mammals. *Mailing Add:* Dept Psychol Boston Univ 48 Sparks St Cambridge MA 02238

HARRISON, JOHN PATRICK, LOW TEMPERATURE PHYSICS. *Current Pos:* from asst prof to assoc prof, 69-78, PROF PHYSICS, QUEEN'S UNIV, ONT, 78- *Personal Data:* b Watford, Eng, May 5, 40; Can citizen; m 62; c 4. *Educ:* Univ Leeds, BSc, 61, PhD(physics), 64. *Prof Exp:* Res assoc, Cornell Univ, 64-67; fel, Univ Sussex, 67-69. *Mem:* Can Asn Physicists; Am Phys Soc. *Res:* Quantum fluids at very low temperatures; thermal properties of solids at low temperatures; superconductivity. *Mailing Add:* Dept Physics Queen's Univ Kingston ON K7L 3N6 Can. *E-Mail:* harrisjp@qucdn.bitnet

HARRISON, JONAS P, petroleum chemistry, chemical engineering, for more information see previous edition

HARRISON, JULIAN R, III, HERPETOLOGY, MALACOLOGY. *Current Pos:* RETIRED. *Personal Data:* b Charleston, SC, Aug 23, 34; m 60, Margaret Marquardt; c Charles A & Susan G. *Educ:* Col Charleston, BS, 56; Duke Univ, AM, 59; Notre Dame Univ, PhD(zool), 64. *Prof Exp:* Instr biol, Western Carolina Col, 60-61; from asst prof to prof biol, Col Charleston, 63-94. *Concurrent Pos:* Res assoc herpetol, The Charleston Mus, 72- *Mem:* Am Soc Ichthyologists & Herpetologists; Soc Study Amphibians & Reptiles; Herpetologists' League; Am Malacological Union. *Res:* Biology, taxonomy and evolution of reptiles and amphibians in the southeastern United States; systematics and ecology of prosobranch and pulmonate mollusks of the southeastern United States. *Mailing Add:* Dept Biol Col Charleston Charleston SC 29424. *E-Mail:* harrisonj@cofc.edu

HARRISON, LIONEL GEORGE, PHYSICAL CHEMISTRY. *Current Pos:* instr, 57-59, from asst prof to assoc prof, 59-67, PROF CHEM, UNIV BC, 67- *Personal Data:* b Liverpool, Eng, May 29, 29; m 53; c 1. *Educ:* Univ Liverpool, BSc, 49, PhD(chem), 52. *Prof Exp:* Tech officer res, Nobel Div, Imp Chem Industs, Ltd, Scotland, 52-55; Nat Res Coun Can fel pure chem, 55-57. *Mem:* Faraday Soc; Brit Chem Soc. *Res:* Surface structure and bulk imperfections of solids; adsorption; gas-solid exchange reactions; diffusion; conductivity; thermal decomposition. *Mailing Add:* Dept Chem Univ BC 2329 West Mall Vancouver BC V6T 1W5 Can

HARRISON, LURA ANN, PHYSIOLOGY. *Current Pos:* RETIRED. *Personal Data:* b Enid, Okla, June 26, 42; m 69; c 2. *Educ:* Univ Okla, BS, 65, PhD(physiol), 69. *Prof Exp:* NIH fel, Med Ctr, Univ Okla, 69-70; NIH training grant cardiol, 70-72; res assoc, Nat Heart & Lung Inst, NIH, 72-74; res assoc med, Med Ctr, Duke Univ, 74-79; asst prof, Okla Univ Health Sci Ctr, 79- *Mem:* Am Physiol Soc; Am Col Cardiol; NY Acad Sci. *Res:* Effects of endotoxin on the cardiovascular system; cardiac electrophysiology and mechanisms of cardiac arrhythmias; influence of sympathetic neurohormones on electrophysiology of the myocardium; hormonal control of gastric secretions. *Mailing Add:* 48 Colony Rd Gretna LA 70056

HARRISON, MALCOLM CHARLES, COMPUTER SCIENCE. *Current Pos:* from adj asst prof to assoc prof, 65-73, dir grad studies,76-84, PROF COMPUT SCI, NY UNIV, 73- *Personal Data:* b St Helens, Eng, July 17, 37; m 62; c 3. *Educ:* Cambridge Univ, BA, 59; Leeds Univ, PhD(math), 62. *Prof Exp:* Div sponsored res staff mem, Solid State & Molecular Theory Group, Mass Inst Technol, 62-63; staff mem res lab electronics, 63-64. *Mem:* Asn Comput Mach. *Res:* Artificial intelligence; parallel computer systems; programming languages; operating systems. *Mailing Add:* Dept Comp Sci NY Univ 719 Broadway New York NY 10003

HARRISON, MARK, PHYSICS. *Current Pos:* PROF PHYSICS & CHMN DEPT, AM UNIV, 60- *Personal Data:* b Paris, Mo, Nov 21, 19; m 42; c 2. *Educ:* Northeast Mo State Col, BS, 42; Cath Univ Am, PhD(physics), 52. *Prof Exp:* Res assoc, Columbia Univ, 42-45; res physicist, David Taylor Model Basin, 46-60. *Mem:* Am Phys Soc; Acoust Soc Am. *Res:* Theoretical physics; acoustics; quantum and fluid mechanics; scattering; cavitation; underwater sound; turbulence. *Mailing Add:* 1511 Kingsmill Dr Salem VA 24153

HARRISON, MELVIN ARNOLD, PHYSICS. *Current Pos:* RETIRED. *Personal Data:* b Seattle, Wash, Nov 16, 24; m 45; c 2. *Educ:* Greenville Col, BA, 47; Univ Wash, PhD(physics), 53. *Prof Exp:* Asst prof physics, Seattle Pac Col, 53-56; assoc prof physics, Western Wash State Col, 61-62; physicist, Lawrence Livermore Lab, Univ Calif, 56-61 & 62-86. *Concurrent Pos:* Sci officer, AEC, 68-75. *Mem:* Am Phys Soc; Asn Comput Mach. *Res:* Conduction of electricity through gases; nuclear explosive physics; plasma physics. *Mailing Add:* PO Box 2419 Friday Harbor WA 98250-2419

HARRISON, MERLE E(DWARD), BIOCHEMISTRY, CHEMISTRY. *Current Pos:* RETIRED. *Personal Data:* b Durango, Colo, May 4, 33; m 67. *Educ:* Brigham Young Univ, BS, 55; Colo State Univ, MS, 57, PhD(biochem), 60. *Prof Exp:* Instr chem, Colo State Univ, 60-61; asst prof pharm, Am Univ Beirut, 61-64; dir lab biochem, Crops Res Div, Agr Res Serv, USDA, 65-67; head dept biochem, Univ Nangrahar, Afghanistan, 67-68; asst prof, Ft Lewis Col, 68-70, chmn, Dept Chem, 69-73, assoc prof biochem & gen chem, 70-88. *Concurrent Pos:* Fulbright lectr biochem, 67-68. *Res:* Resistance of plants to attacks of fungal diseases; clinical tests for cysts; analysis for trace elements. *Mailing Add:* 1539 W Third Ave Durango CO 81301

HARRISON, MICHAEL A, PROGRAMMING ENVIRONMENTS, MULTIMEDIA SYSTEMS. *Current Pos:* from asst prof to assoc prof elec eng, 63-66, assoc prof comput sci, 66-71, PROF COMPUT SCI, UNIV CALIF, BERKELEY, 71- *Personal Data:* b Philadelphia, Pa, Apr 11, 36; m 71, Susan Graham; c Craig. *Educ:* Case Inst Technol, BS, 58, MS, 59; Univ Mich, PhD(commun sci), 63. *Prof Exp:* Lectr elec eng, Univ Mich, 62-63. *Concurrent Pos:* Consult numerous cos & govt agencies, 63-; vis prof, Mass Inst Technol, 69, Hebrew Univ, Jerusalem, 70 & Stanford Univ; Guggenheim fel, 69-70; mem, Asn Comput Mach coun, 78-82 & 85-; founder & chmn bd, Gain Technol, Inc. *Mem:* Asn Comput Mach (vpres, 80-82); fel Inst Elec & Electronics Eng; fel AAAS. *Res:* Research in programming environments user interfaces, and electronic publishing; multimedia systems; theoretical computer science. *Mailing Add:* Comput Sci Div Univ Calif Berkeley CA 94720. *E-Mail:* harrison@cs.berkeley.edu

HARRISON, MICHAEL JAY, THEORETICAL CONDENSED MATTER PHYSICS, THEORETICAL EPIDEMIOLOGY & IMMUNOLOGY. *Current Pos:* from asst prof to assoc prof, Mich State Univ, 61-68, fac grievance officer, 72-73, dean, Lyman Briggs Col, 73-81, PROF PHYSICS, MICH STATE UNIV, 68-, ADJ PROJ INTERNAL MED, 93- *Personal Data:* b Chicago, Ill, Aug 20, 32; m 70, Ann Tukey. *Educ:* Harvard Univ, AB, 54; Univ Chicago, MSc, 56, PhD(physics), 60. *Prof Exp:* Res fel math physics, Univ Birmingham, Eng, 59-61. *Concurrent Pos:* NSF fel, Univ Chicago, 57-59; consult, UK Atomic Energy Authority, Harwell Lab, 60, Sarnoff Labs, RCA, NJ, 62-64 & United Aircraft Res Labs, Conn, 64-66; Am Coun Educ fel, Univ Calif, Los Angeles, 70-71; vis res physicist, Inst Theoret Physics, Univ Calif, Santa Barbara, 80-81; res affil, Theoret Biol & Biophys, Los Alamos Nat Lab, 87-88. *Mem:* Fel Am Phys Soc; Sigma Xi. *Res:* Quantum theory of condensed matter; transport phenomena in solids; plasma physics and non-equilibrium processes in many-particle systems; quantum optics and retarded Van der Waals interactions in biological tissues, surface physics, theoretical epidemiology and immunology. *Mailing Add:* Dept Physics & Astron Mich State Univ East Lansing MI 48824-1116. *Fax:* 517-353-0690; *E-Mail:* harrison@msupa.pa.msu.edu

HARRISON, MICHAEL R, PEDIATRIC SURGERY, FETAL SURGERY. *Current Pos:* from asst prof to assoc prof, 78-88, PROF, UNIV CALIF, SAN FRANCISCO, 88- *Personal Data:* b Portland, Ore, May 5, 43; m 66; c 4. *Educ:* Yale Univ, BA, 65; Harvard Med Sch, MD, 69. *Prof Exp:* Internship surg, Mass Gen Hosp, 69-70, resident II, 70-71; res assoc, Lab Immunol, Nat Inst Allergy & Infections Dis, NIH, 71-73; resident II-IV, Mass Gen Hosp, 73-75; fel, Pediat Surg, Children's Hosp, Los Angeles, 76-77. *Concurrent Pos:* Attend surgeon, Univ Calif Hosp, San Francisco Gen Hosp, Children's Hosp, Mt Zion Hosp & Kaiser-Permenente Med Ctr, 78- *Mem:* Am Col Surgeons; Am Pediat Surg Asn; AMA; Am Acad Pediat. *Res:* Research on physiology of fetal malformations and their correction before birth; animal models of congenital diaphragmatic hernia, hydronephrosis, hydrocephalus, and intrauterine growth retardation; clinical applications of fetal surgery; transplantation of fetal tissues and organs. *Mailing Add:* 406 Pacheco St San Francisco CA 94116

HARRISON, MONTY DEVERL, PLANT PATHOLOGY. *Current Pos:* From asst plant pathologist to assoc plant pathologist, Colo State Univ, 62-68, assoc prof bot & plant path, 68-73, plant pathologist, Col Natural Sci, 68-84, prof plant path, 73-90, assoc dean, 79-85, actg assoc dean, Col Agr Sci, 85, EMER PROF PLANT PATH, COLO STATE UNIV, 90- *Personal Data:* b Afton, Wyo, June 18, 34; m 53; c 4. *Educ:* Univ Wyo, BS, 57, MS, 58; Univ Minn, PhD(plant path), 62. *Concurrent Pos:* Consult, PRECODEPA, CID; prin investr fungus & bact dis potatoes, 64-90; legal expert-plant dis. *Mem:* Am Phytopath Soc; Potato Asn Am. *Res:* Bacteria and air diseases of potatoes; bacterial diseases; epidemiology, bacterial ecology soil borne fungal pathogens; soil microbiology; disease control. *Mailing Add:* 1818 Manchester Dr Ft Collins CO 80526

HARRISON, NANCY EVELYN KING, ALGEBRA. *Current Pos:* from asst prof to assoc prof, 79-83, chairperson, 86-89, PROF MATH & COMPUT SCI, MERCY COL, 88- *Personal Data:* b Haverhill, Mass, Apr 26, 43; m 70, Daniel; c Scott S. *Educ:* Smith Col, BA, 64; Univ Mich, Ann Arbor, MA, 65, PhD(math), 69. *Prof Exp:* Asst prof math, Univ Mo, Columbia, 69-70; asst prof math, Brooklyn Col, 70-75 & John Jay Col Criminal Justice, City Univ New York, 75-79. *Concurrent Pos:* Prof Res Fund grant, Univ Mo, Columbia, 70; consult, Dowling Col, 92; Tensor Found grant, Career Mentorship Prog, 95- *Mem:* Math Asn Am; Nat Coun Teachers Math. *Res:* Structure theorems for groups with length functions into the real numbers; evaluation of undergraduate mathematics programs using technology in teaching calculus; author of professional papers and book reviews. *Mailing Add:* 2455 Bound Brook Lane Yorktown Heights NY 10598. *E-Mail:* merlin.mercynet.edu

HARRISON, PAUL C, ENVIRONMENTAL HEALTH. *Current Pos:* PROF ANIMAL PHYSIOL, UNIV ILL, URBANA, 73- *Personal Data:* b Houston, Tex, Oct 1, 36; m 60; c 4. *Educ:* Sam Houston State Univ, BS, 61; Univ Mo, MS, 64, PhD(agr), 66. *Honors & Awards:* Nat Poultry Res Award, Poultry Sci Asn, 70. *Prof Exp:* Res asst poultry sci, Univ Mo, 61-63; from asst prof to assoc prof animal physiol, Wash State Univ, 66-73. *Mem:* Fel Poultry Sci Asn; Soc Exp Biol & Med; Am Soc Animal Sci; Am Asn Lab Animal Sci. *Res:* Incorporate the beneficial innate physiological and behavioral responses of various farm animal species into new management equipment and practices. *Mailing Add:* Dept Animal Sci Univ Ill Urbana 1301 W Gregory Dr Urbana IL 61801-3608

HARRISON, R(OLAND) H(ENRY), PHYSICAL CHEMISTRY, CHEMICAL ENGINEERING. *Current Pos:* RETIRED. *Personal Data:* b Austin, Tex, July 30, 27; m 51, Mary Fewell; c Margaret, Cecelia, Roland Jr, Thomas, Elizabeth, Robert & William. *Educ:* Univ Tex, BS, 49, MS, 52, PhD(chem eng), 55. *Prof Exp:* Res engr, Univ Tex, 54-55; chem engr res & develop, Esso Stand Oil Co, 55-58; phys chemist, US Bur Mines, 58-75, Energy Res & Develop Admin, 75-77 & Dept Energy, Bartlesville Energy Technol Ctr, 77-83; sr engr, Nat Inst Petrol & Energy Res, 83-86; consult, 87-93. *Mem:* Am Chem Soc; Am Inst Chem Engrs. *Res:* Compressibility of gases and thermodynamic properties; vapor-liquid equilibrium in coal liquefaction processes. *Mailing Add:* 2312 Parkway St Bartlesville OK 74006

HARRISON, RALPH JOSEPH, solid state theory, computer molecular dynamics, for more information see previous edition

HARRISON, RICHARD GERALD, EVOLUTIONARY BIOLOGY. *Current Pos:* PROF BIOL, DEPT BIOL, CORNELL UNIV, 86- *Personal Data:* b Baltimore, Md, Nov 19, 45; m 71; c 2. *Educ:* Harvard Univ, BA, 67; Cornell Univ, PhD(ecol & evolution), 77. *Prof Exp:* From asst prof to assoc prof biol, Yale Univ, 77-86. *Mem:* Soc Study Evolution; Genetics Soc Am; Am Soc Naturalists. *Res:* Speciation in insects; evolution of barriers to gene exchange between closely related species; evolutionary dynamics of animal m; molecular evolution. *Mailing Add:* Sect Ecol E145 Corson Bldg Cornell Univ Ithaca NY 14853-0001

HARRISON, RICHARD MILLER, REPRODUCTIVE PHYSIOLOGY, PRIMATOLOGY. *Current Pos:* res fel reproductive physiol, 73-75, assoc scientist reproductive physiol, 75, RES SCIENTIST UROL & REPRODUCTIVE PHYSIOL, DELTA REGIONAL PRIMATE RES CTR, TULANE UNIV, 78-, RES SCIENTIST UROL & VET SCI, 92- *Personal Data:* b Pineville, Ky, Apr 8, 39; m 62, Joanna Schafer; c Brian G & Byron G. *Educ:* Univ Ky, BA, 62; Mich State Univ, MS, 71, PhD(physiol), 73. *Honors & Awards:* Sigma Xi Res Award, 73. *Prof Exp:* Assoc scientist biochem, Mead Johnson Res Ctr, 63-67, scientist pharmacol, 67-69. *Concurrent Pos:* Adj asst prof urol, Tulane Univ, 73-78, adj asst prof physiol, 75-80, from asst prof to assoc prof urol, 80-86, adj assoc prof physiol, 80-;

historian, Am Soc Primatol, 85-94. *Mem:* Am Soc Primatol; Soc Exp Biol & Med; Sigma Xi; Am Soc Andrology (pres & vpres, 80-82); Soc Study Reproduction; Am Soc Reproductive Med. *Res:* Male fertility problems; pregnancies from limited mating sessions; in vitro fertilization of non-human primate ova; utilizing laparoscopy for ovulation detection; use of ultrasonography to detect early pregnancies and monitor fetal growth. *Mailing Add:* Tulane Regional Primate Res Ctr 18703 Three Rivers Rd Covington LA 70433. *Fax:* 504-893-1352; *E-Mail:* harrison@tpc.tulane.edu

HARRISON, ROBERT CAMERON, SURGERY. *Current Pos:* PROF SURG & HEAD DEPT, UNIV BC, 66- *Personal Data:* b Lamont, Alta, Aug 2, 20; m 47; c 5. *Educ:* Univ Alta, MD, 43; Univ Toronto, MS, 51; FRCPS(C), 50. *Prof Exp:* From assoc prof to prof surg, Univ Alta, 60-67, dir surg res, 51-67. *Concurrent Pos:* Consult, Dept Vet Affairs, Can. *Mem:* Fel Am Col Surg; Soc Univ Surg; Am Surg Asn. *Res:* Gastrointestinal and related research. *Mailing Add:* Fac Med Univ BC 2211 Wesbrook Mall Vancouver BC V6T 2B5 Can

HARRISON, ROBERT EDWIN, NEMATOLOGY, BIOLOGICAL CONTROL. *Current Pos:* PROF, DEPT AGR SCI, TENN STATE UNIV, 87- *Personal Data:* b Shreveport, La, Mar 11, 47. *Educ:* La Tech Univ, BS, 70, MS, 72; Univ Fla, PhD(nematol), 75. *Prof Exp:* Nematologist, Div Plant Industs, Tenn Dept Agr, 75-87. *Res:* Taxonomy of entomopathogenic nematodes. *Mailing Add:* Dept Agr Sci 3500 John Merritt Blvd Nashville TN 37209-1561

HARRISON, ROBERT J, AUDIOLOGY, SPEECH PATHOLOGY. *Current Pos:* RETIRED. *Personal Data:* b Anthony, Kans, Nov 22, 28; m 52; c 3. *Educ:* Univ Wichita, BA, 51; Northwestern Univ, PhD(audiol), 62. *Prof Exp:* Logopedist, Inst Logopedics, 51-53; dir, Hearing & Speech Ctr, Kans, 55-56; instr audiol, Med Col Ala, 56-58; asst prof audiol, Sch Med, Univ Miami, 61-72, prof otolaryngol, 71-94, chief audiol-speech path, 61-94. *Concurrent Pos:* Nat Inst Neurol Dis & Stroke grant audiol, 63-; Int Audiol Cong grant, HEW, 64 & Voc Rehab Admin Workshop, 64-65. *Mem:* Fel Am Speech & Hearing Asn; Am Acad Otolaryngol; Am Acad Audiol; Am Auditory Soc. *Res:* Meniere's disease; cleft palate; retrocochlear neoplasms; middle ear impedance; licensing of professionals; cochlear otospongiosis. *Mailing Add:* 446 Alhambra Circle Miami FL 33134

HARRISON, ROBERT LOUIS, AGRONOMY. *Current Pos:* RETIRED. *Personal Data:* b Poteau, Okla, July 29, 29; m 50; c 4. *Educ:* Okla State Univ, BSc, 54, MSc, 57; Univ Ill, PhD(agron), 61. *Prof Exp:* Asst secy, Okla Crop Improv Assoc, 55-56; secy mgr, Okla Found Seed Stocks, Inc, 56-58; asst prof agron, NDak State Univ, 61-64; mem staff, Va Polytech Inst & State Univ, 64-89, prof agron, 74-89. *Res:* Seed production. *Mailing Add:* 621 Watson Lane Blacksburg VA 24060

HARRISON, ROBERT VICTOR, AUDITORY PHYSIOLOGY, OTOLARYNGOLOGY. *Current Pos:* assoc prof, 84-89, PROF, DEPT OTOLARYNGOL & PHYSIOL, UNIV TORONTO, 89-; SR SCIENTIST, DEPT OTOLARYNGOL, HOSP SICK CHILDREN, 88- *Personal Data:* b Bristol, Eng, Oct 11, 51; Can & Brit citizen; m, Debra Bertollo. *Educ:* Univ Birmingham, UK, BSc, 73, DSc, 91; Univ Keele, UK, PhD(commun & neurosci), 78. *Prof Exp:* Researcher, Nat Inst Health & Med Res, France, 81-83, sr researcher, 83-84. *Concurrent Pos:* Grants & awards comt, Med Res Coun, Can, 89-92; dir, Auditory Sci Lab, Hosp Sick Children, Toronto, 84-, Pediat Cochlear Implant Prog, 89-; dir, Inst Med Sci, Univ Toronto, 84-, Sch Grad Studies, 85-, Inst Biomed Eng, 91-, mem coun, fac med, 92- *Mem:* Acoust Soc Am; Asn Res Otolaryngol; Sigma Xi; Soc Neurosci; Int Brain Res Org; Can Acoust Soc. *Res:* Physiology and pathophysiology of the auditory system, including studies on hearing loss and developmental plasticity of central auditory pathways; cochlear implant related research. *Mailing Add:* Dept Otolaryngol Hosp Sick Children 555 University Ave Toronto ON M5G 1X8 Can. *Fax:* 416-813-5036; *E-Mail:* rvh@sickkids.on.ca

HARRISON, ROBERT W, METALLURGY. *Current Pos:* CONSULT, OAK RIDGE NAT LABS, 96- *Personal Data:* b Brooklyn, NY, Feb 29, 36. *Educ:* Xavier Univ, BS, 57, MS, 59, MBA, 75. *Prof Exp:* Mgr mat compatibility space power & propulsion, Gen Elec Aircraft Engines, 64-70, mgr technol transfer, 70-91, consult technol transfer mat & processes, 91-96. *Concurrent Pos:* Dir, Technol Transfer Soc, 90- *Mem:* Fel Am Soc Metals; Technol Transfer Soc; Metall Soc. *Mailing Add:* 4502 Longwood Ct Liberty Township OH 45011

HARRISON, ROBERT WALKER, III, ENDOCRINOLOGY, BIOCHEMISTRY. *Current Pos:* Asst prof, 74-81, ASSOC PROF MED, SCH MED, VANDERBILT UNIV, 81- *Personal Data:* b Natchez, Miss, Oct 13, 41; m 63; c 2. *Educ:* Tougaloo Col, BS, 61; Northwestern Univ, MD, 66. *Concurrent Pos:* Investr, Howard Hughes Med Inst, 77- *Mem:* Endocrine Soc; Am Col Physicians; Am Fedn Clin Res. *Res:* Biochemistry of steroid hormone effects on sensitive tissues. *Mailing Add:* Div Endocrinol Univ Rochester 601 Elmwood PO Box 693 Rochester NY 14643. *Fax:* 716-256-2789

HARRISON, ROBERT WILLIAM, ZOOLOGY, PHYSIOLOGY & AVIATION. *Current Pos:* from instr to prof, Univ RI, 49-77, chmn, Fac Senate, 63-64, assoc dean, Div Univ Exten, 68-69, actg dean, 69-70, actg chmn, Dept Zool, 74-75, EMER PROF ZOOL, UNIV RI, 77- *Personal Data:* b Napoleon, Ohio, Nov 3, 15; div; c Suzanne (Marchetti), Elizabeth A (Greene) & Barbara A (DiOrio). *Educ:* Oberlin Col, AB, 38; Wesleyan Univ, MA, 41; Yale Univ, MS, 42, PhD(zool), 49. *Prof Exp:* Asst biol, Springfield Col, 38-39 & Wesleyan Univ, 39-41; asst zool, Yale Univ, 41-42 & 46-48. *Concurrent Pos:* From Private to Corporal, 148th Infantry, Ohio Nat Guard, 32-40; officer aviation physiol, US Naval Res, 42-46; res fel, Nat Cancer Inst, Yale Univ, 49; mem/comndg officer, USNR Res Co, Kingston, RI, 53-70; vis assoc prof, Wesleyan Univ, 57; vis spec instr, Brown Univ, 58; res fel, Am Physiol Soc, Univ Ill, 59; Atomic Energy Comn grantee, 62; hon life mem, RI Asn Health Phys Educ Recreation & Dance, 82; from Lt to Capt, Med Serv Corps. *Mem:* AAAS; Am Soc Zoologists; Am Inst Biol Sci; Am Col Sports Med; Sigma Xi. *Res:* Genetics of Lebistes; survival and rescue in aviation emergencies; physiology of growth and development; chemical mediators; forensic science; physiology of exercise and diet effects on serum cholesterol and atherosclerosis. *Mailing Add:* 40 Dockray Wakefield RI 02879-3915

HARRISON, SAMUEL S, HYDROLOGY & WATER RESOURCES. *Current Pos:* OWNER, HARRISON HYDROSCI, 82- *Personal Data:* b Union City, Pa, Feb 19, 41; m 63; c 3. *Educ:* Allegheny Col, BS, 63; Univ NDak, Grand Forks, MS, 65, PhD(geol), 68. *Prof Exp:* Asst prof geol, Wis State Univ, Oshkosh, 68-70; from asst prof to assoc prof geol, Allegheny Col, 70-81, prof geol & environ sci, 81-82, chairperson, Environ Sci Dept, 75-82. *Concurrent Pos:* Prin investr, Off Water Resources Res grant, Wis State Univ, 68-69; res assoc, Limnol Lab, 68-70; consult soils & ground water, 74- *Mem:* Soc Econ Paleont & Mineral; Soil Conserv Soc Am; Am Geol Inst; Am Inst Prof Geologists; Asn Prof Groundwater Scientists & Engrs. *Res:* Fluvial processes; groundwater monitoring; groundwater contamination; hydrogeology of hazardous waste sites' groundwater; soils; environmental geology; hydrogeologic investigations of contaminated groundwater and hazardous-waste disposal sites. *Mailing Add:* 18450 Black Rd Saegertown PA 16433

HARRISON, SAUL I, PSYCHIATRY, CHILD & ADOLESCENT PSYCHIATRY. *Current Pos:* from asst prof to prof, 56-84, dir child & adolescent psychiat educ, Med Ctr, 56-83, EMER PROF PSYCHIAT, UNIV MICH, ANN ARBOR, 84- *Personal Data:* b New York, NY, Nov 4, 25; c Susan (Hoff), Richard & Rebecca. *Educ:* Univ Mich, MD, 48. *Honors & Awards:* Agnes Purcell McGavin Award, Am Psychiat Asn. *Prof Exp:* Resident psychiat & child psychiat, Hosp & Med Sch, Temple Univ, 50-52 & 54-55, instr psychiat, 54-56. *Concurrent Pos:* Asst attend neuropsychiatrist, St Christopher's Hosp for Children, Philadelphia; Commonwealth Fund fel & Grant Found award, Hampstead Clin, London & Western Europ Child Psychiat Ctrs, 66; prof & dir child & adolescent psychiat, Harbor-Univ Calif Los Angeles Med Ctr, Torrance, 84-91. *Mem:* Am Psychoanal Asn; fel Am Psychiat Asn; fel Am Acad Child Psychiat; fel Am Orthopsychiat Asn; fel Am Col Psychiatrists. *Res:* Psychopathology, psychiatric treatment. *Mailing Add:* 1916 Palisades Dr Pacific Palisades CA 90272-1918. *Fax:* 310-454-7319

HARRISON, SHIRLEY WANDA, CHEMICAL PHYSICS. *Current Pos:* instr, 78-80, from asst prof to assoc prof, 81-89, chair dept, 86-89, EMER PROF PHYS SCI DEPT, NASSAU COMMUNITY COL, 90- *Personal Data:* b Patchogue, NY, Oct 18, 23; m 46; c 3. *Educ:* Barnard Col, AB, 44, Columbia Univ, AM, 46; City Univ New York, PhD(physics), 70. *Prof Exp:* Lectr math, Barnard Col, Columbia Univ, 44-45; res physicist, Gen Tel & Electronics Lab, 46-61; instr physics, Queens Col, NY, 70-71; res asst chem, Hunter Col, 71-72; asst prof sci, Mahattan Community Col, 72-75; res assoc, Hunter Col, 75-77; asst prof physics, US Merchant Marine Acad, 78. *Concurrent Pos:* Guest jr res assoc, Brookhaven Nat Lab, 67-71; City Univ New York Res Found new fac res award, 72; mem, Doctoral Fac Physics, City Univ New York, 75-76; res assoc, Hunter Col, 84-85 & Queens Col, 90- *Mem:* Am Phys Soc; Am Asn Univ Women. *Res:* Theoretical studies of environmental effects on structure, properties and chemical reactions in liquids and solids; quantum mechanical calculations of structure and properties of molecules, particularly hydrazoic acid and lithium fluoride; contributions of women to physics, astronomy and space science. *Mailing Add:* 42-40 208 St Bayside NY 11361-2743

HARRISON, STANLEY L, ANALYTICAL CHEMISTRY, ENVIRONMENTAL SCIENCES. *Current Pos:* RETIRED. *Personal Data:* b Philadelphia, Pa, May 12, 35; m 58; c 1. *Educ:* Drexel Univ, BS, 60. *Prof Exp:* Assoc scientist anal chem, Rohm & Haas Co, 60-67; assoc scientist anal chem, Amchem Prod, 67-73, mgr, Anal Res Lab, Amchem Prod Inc, 73-78; group leader, Union Carbide Agr Prod Co Inc, 78-84, mgr regist anal chem, 84-86; mgr environ chem, Phone-Poulenc Ag Co, 87-89, mgr, Food Safety & Residue Progs, 90-93. *Mem:* Am Chem Soc; AAAS. *Res:* Metabolism and environmental chemistry of and development of residue analytical procedures for insecticides, fungicides, herbicides, plant regulators in plant, animal and environmental matrices. *Mailing Add:* 4717 Pemberton Dr Raleigh NC 27609

HARRISON, STEPHEN COPLAN, BIOPHYSICAL CHEMISTRY. *Current Pos:* from asst prof to assoc prof biochem, 71-77, PROF, DEPT MOLECULAR & CELLULAR BIOL, HARVARD UNIV, 77- *Personal Data:* b New Haven, Conn, June 4, 43. *Educ:* Harvard Univ, AB, 63, PhD(biophys), 68. *Honors & Awards:* Wallace P Rowe Award, Nat Inst Allergy Infectious Dis, 88. *Prof Exp:* Res assoc struct molecular biol, Children's Cancer Res Found, Boston, 68-71. *Concurrent Pos:* Harvard Univ Soc Fels jr fel, 68-71; vis scientist biophys, Max Planck Inst Med Res, 71; investr, Howard Hughes Med Inst, 87- *Mem:* Nat Acad Sci; Am Crystallog Asn; Am Soc Microbiol; AAAS. *Res:* Structure and assembly of viruses and membranes; protein-nucleic acid interactions; applications of x-ray diffraction and electron microscopy to biomolecular structure. *Mailing Add:* Fairchild Biochem Bldg Harvard Univ Cambridge MA 02138

HARRISON, STUART AMOS, CHEMISTRY. *Current Pos:* RETIRED. *Personal Data:* b Carver Co, Minn, Jan 21, 12; m 40; c 6. *Educ:* Univ Minn, BChE, 35, PhD(org chem), 39. *Prof Exp:* Res chemist, B F Goodrich Co, Ohio, 40-47; res chemist, Gen Mills, Inc, 47-53, head process develop sect, Chem Res Dept, 53-61, res assoc, 61-77. *Mem:* Am Chem Soc. *Res:* Fatty nitrogen compounds; organic coatings; polymerization; detergents; polyamides; radiation curing; acrylic resins; azophenols; plasticizers; vinyl stabilizers. *Mailing Add:* 2515 W 40th St Minneapolis MN 55410-1214

HARRISON, THOMAS J, ELECTRICAL ENGINEERING EDUCATION, COMPUTER ENGINEERING. *Current Pos:* PROF ELEC ENG, FLA A&M UNIV/FLA STATE UNIV, COL ENG, 87-, CHMN, 88- *Personal Data:* b Wausau, Wis, May 13, 35; m; c 2. *Educ:* Carnegie-Mellon Univ, BS, 57, MS, 58; Stanford Univ, PhD(elec eng), 70. *Prof Exp:* Consult, acad specialist, IBM Corp, 58-87. *Mem:* Fel Inst Elec & Electronics Engrs; fel Instruments Soc Am (pres, 86); Am Soc Eng Educ; Asn Comput Mach; Indust Comput Soc. *Res:* Small computer architecture; real time computer systems; computer process control; small computers in electrical engineering education. *Mailing Add:* Dept Elec Eng Fla State Univ Col Eng 2525 Tallahassee FL 32310-6046. *Fax:* 850-487-6479; *E-Mail:* harrison@evax.eng.fsu.edu

HARRISON, TIMOTHY STONE, SURGERY. *Current Pos:* PROF SURG & PHYSIOL, COL MED, MILTON S HERSHEY MED CTR, PA STATE UNIV, 75- *Personal Data:* b Kodaikanal, India, July 13, 27; US citizen; m 61; c 2. *Educ:* Hope Col, AB, 49; Johns Hopkins Univ, MD, 53. *Prof Exp:* Instr surg, Sch Med, Yale Univ, 61-62; from asst prof to prof surg, Med Sch, Univ Mich, Ann Arbor, 62-75. *Concurrent Pos:* Consult, Ann Arbor Vet Admin Hosp, Mich, 64-; consult ed med sci, Blaisdell Publ Co, NY, 64-70; prof & chmn dept surg, Am Univ Beirut, 68-71; USPHS fel, Nat Inst Arthritis & Metab Dis, 56-57, spec fel, 59-60. *Mem:* AAAS; Am Fedn Clin Res; fel Am Col Surg; NY Acad Sci; Am Thyroid Asn. *Res:* Magnesium and calcium metabolism; adrenal medullary and catechol amine physiology; central nervous system control of endocrine function; adrenal medullary-thyroid relationships. *Mailing Add:* Milton S Hershey Med Ctr Hershey PA 17033

HARRISON, WALTER ASHLEY, SOLID STATE PHYSICS. *Current Pos:* PROF APPL PHYSICS, STANFORD UNIV, 65- *Personal Data:* b Flushing, NY, Apr 26, 30; m 54, Lucille Carley; c Richard, John, William & Robert. *Educ:* Cornell Univ, BE, 53; Univ Ill, MS, 54, PhD(physics), 56. *Honors & Awards:* Sr US Scientist Award, von Humboldt Found, 82. *Prof Exp:* Physicist, Res Lab, Gen Elec Co, NY, 56-65. *Mem:* Fel Am Phys Soc; Europ Phys Soc; Mat Res Soc. *Res:* Quantum theory of solids; theory of molecular bonding and structures. *Mailing Add:* Dept Appl Physics Stanford Univ Stanford CA 94305. *Fax:* 650-725-2533; *E-Mail:* harrison@ee.stanford.edu

HARRISON, WILKS DOUGLAS, GEOMORPHOLOGY, METEOROLOGY. *Current Pos:* RETIRED. *Personal Data:* b Tyler, Tex, Nov 19, 32; m 56; c 4. *Educ:* NTex State Univ, BA, 57; Stephen F Austin State Univ, MA, 60; Univ NC, Chapel Hill, PhD(geog), 70. *Prof Exp:* Asst prof geog, Pembroke State Univ, 61-65; instr, Univ NC, Chapel Hill, 67-68; assoc prof geog, Moorhead State Univ, 68-83, assoc prof geol, 73-83. *Mem:* Asn Am Geogr; Am Soc Photogram; Am Meteorol Soc; Geol Soc Am. *Res:* Geography of iron ore, iron and steel; storm development; tropical climates; origin of mound topography. *Mailing Add:* 1420 Pettit Dr Tyler TX 75701

HARRISON, WILLARD WAYNE, ANALYTICAL CHEMISTRY. *Current Pos:* From asst prof to prof anal chem, 64-88, chmn dept chem, 78-88, DEAN LIBERAL ARTS & SCI & PROF, UNIV VA, 88- *Personal Data:* b McLeansboro, Ill, July 28, 37; m 59; c 4. *Educ:* Southern Ill Univ, BA, 58, MA, 60; Univ Ill, PhD(atomic absorption), 64. *Mem:* Am Chem Soc. *Res:* Atomic absorption; mass spectrometry; hollow cathode discharge. *Mailing Add:* Chem Dept 200 Leigh Hall Univ Fla Gainesville FL 32611

HARRISON, WILLIAM ASHLEY, ORGANIC CHEMISTRY. *Current Pos:* res chemist, 66-76, SR RES SCIENTIST, RES LABS, UNIROYAL LTD, 76- *Personal Data:* b Kentville, NS, Apr 26, 33. *Educ:* Acadia Univ, BSc, 54, Hons, 55; McMaster Univ, MSc, 57, PhD(org chem), 60. *Prof Exp:* Nat Res Coun Can overseas fel org chem, Oxford Univ, 60-62; res chemist, Res Labs, Dominion Rubber Co, 63-66. *Mem:* Am Chem Soc; Chem Inst Can. *Res:* Lycopodium alkaloids; steroids; organic synthesis; agricultural chemicals. *Mailing Add:* Uniroyal Chem Ltd PO Box 1120 Guelph ON N1H 6N3 Can

HARRISON, WILLIAM EARL, ORGANIC & PETROLEUM GEOCHEMISTRY, ENVIRONMENTAL CHARACTERIZATION & REMEDIATION. *Current Pos:* MGR, GEOSCI, LOCKHEED-MARTIN IDAHO, 89- *Personal Data:* b Galveston, Tex, Apr 7, 42; m 85, Cynthia A Shilling; c Scott, Joy & Julie. *Educ:* Lamar State Col Technol, BS, 66; Univ Okla, MS, 68; La State Univ, PhD, 76. *Prof Exp:* Geologist, Shell Oil Co, 68-71; Okla Geol Surv, 75-84; sr res geochemist, Atlantic Richfield, 74-75; grad fac, Okla Univ, 75-84; res dir, Atlantic Richfield Co, 84-89. *Mem:* Am Asn Petrol Geologists; Geochem Soc; Sigma Xi; Am Inst Prof Geologists; Soc Econ Paleontologists & Mineralogists. *Res:* Paleothermometry of sediments utilizing organic compounds; thermally-controlled diagenesis of organic matter in sediments; lipid geochemistry of ancient and modern sediments; quantitative basin analysis and modeling; environmental/site characterization studies; surface and subsurface remediation. *Mailing Add:* Lockheed-Martin PO Box 1625 MS 2107 Idaho Falls ID 83401. *Fax:* 208-526-9822; *E-Mail:* weh@inel.gov

HARRISON, WILLIAM HENRY, BIOCHEMISTRY. *Current Pos:* assoc prof, 71-73, PROF BIOCHEM & NEUROSCI, MED COL, RUSH UNIV, 73- *Personal Data:* b Aberdeen, SDak, Feb 24, 24; m 60; c 4. *Educ:* Univ Minn, BA, 48, MS, 51, PhD(biochem), 54. *Prof Exp:* Sr biochemist antibiotics, Res Lab, Eli Lilly Co, Ind, 54-58; asst prof biochem & neurol, 63-64; from asst prof to assoc prof biochem & neurol, Univ Ill Col Med, 64-71. *Concurrent Pos:* Neurobiologist, Rush-Presby-St Luke's Med Ctr, 64-68, dir neurochem unit, 68-; spec fel, Columbia Univ, 58-63. *Mem:* AAAS; Am Soc Biol Chemists; Soc Neurosci; Am Chem Soc. *Res:* Vitamin E; enzymatic phosphate transfer mechanism; antibiotic isolation and characterization; biochemistry of nerve action; catecholamine metabolism and function. *Mailing Add:* Presby-St Luke's Med Ctr 1753 W Congress Pkwy Chicago IL 60612

HARRISON, WILLIAM PAUL, SOIL MECHANICS. *Current Pos:* RETIRED. *Personal Data:* b Hebden Bridge, Eng, Feb 1, 20; US citizen; m 46; c 5. *Educ:* Dartmouth Col, AB, 44; Clarkson Col Technol, BCE, 57; Purdue Univ, MSCE, 59. *Prof Exp:* Teacher pub sch, Mass, 46-48; from instr to assoc prof civil eng, Clarkson Col Technol, 48-85, exec officer, Civil & Environ Eng Dept, 74-85. *Concurrent Pos:* NSF fel, 58-59. *Mem:* Am Soc Civil Engrs. *Res:* Thixotrophy and structure of sensitive clay; foundation engineering; groundwater and seepage model study and correlation with theory in earth and masonry dams; frost action; lateral earth pressure. *Mailing Add:* 102 Wheeler Rd Potsdam NY 13676

HARRISON, WYMAN, APPLIED GEOSCIENCE, APPLIED GEOENGINEERING. *Current Pos:* dir, Water Resources Res Prog, 75-76, assoc dir geosci & eng, Energy & Environ Systs Div, 78-87, SPEC PROJS GROUP, ENERGY SYSTS DIV, ARGONNE NAT LAB, 89- *Personal Data:* b Chicago, Ill, Mar 18, 31; m 55; c 2. *Educ:* Univ Chicago, SB, 53, SM, 54, PhD(geol), 56. *Honors & Awards:* Distinguished Authorship Award, US Environ Sci Serv Admin, 69. *Prof Exp:* Geologist, Ind Geol Surv, 56-59; asst prof geol, Dartmouth Col, 59-60; assoc prof & chmn dept, Norfolk Div, Col William & Mary, 60-62; assoc prof, Va Inst Marine Sci, Univ Va, 62-64; oceanogr & dir, Land & Sea Interaction Lab, Inst Oceanog, Environ Sci Serv Admin, Va, 64-69; asst prof marine sci, Univ Va & chmn, Dept Phys Chem & Geol Oceanog, Va Inst Marine Sci, 69-71; prof geog, Univ Toronto, 71-74. *Concurrent Pos:* Assoc prof, Col William & Mary, 69-71; pres, Environ Res Assocs, Inc, 69-, sr prog mgr, 87- *Mem:* Am Asn Petrol Geologists; Am Geophys Union; Am Inst Prof Geologists; Asn Eng Geologists. *Res:* Fate of energy-related environmental contaminants; environmental aspects of coal-conversion processes; man as a geological agent; geotechnology; beach process, responses, and protection; geologic isolation of high level nuclear wastes. *Mailing Add:* 2577 Alta Ct Lisle IL 60532

HARRISON-JOHNSON, YVONNE E, biochemical pharmacology, drug metabolism, for more information see previous edition

HARRISS, DONALD K, PHYSICAL CHEMISTRY. *Current Pos:* From asst prof to assoc prof, Univ Minn, Duluth, 63-68, vchancellor acad admin, 83-86, head, Dept Chem, 88-92, PROF CHEM, UNIV MINN, DULUTH, 75- *Personal Data:* b Zeigler, Ill, Sept 24, 34; m 87, Pat Merrier; c Vicki, Kyle, Joan & Hugh. *Educ:* Southern Ill Univ, BA, 59; Northwestern Univ, PhD(phys chem), 63. *Mem:* Am Chem Soc; Sigma Xi. *Res:* Quantum chemistry; non-integration methods; quantitative structure-activity relationship. *Mailing Add:* 246 Chem Bldg Univ Minn Duluth Duluth MN 55812. *Fax:* 218-726-7394; *E-Mail:* dharriss@madonna.d.umn.edu

HARRIST, RONALD BAXTER, STATISTICS, MATHEMATICS. *Current Pos:* ASSOC PROF BIOMET, SCH PUB HEALTH, UNIV TEX, HOUSTON, 72- *Personal Data:* b Dec 24, 36; US citizen; m 59; c 3. *Educ:* Tex Tech Univ, BS, 59, MS, 63; Southern Methodist Univ, PhD(statist), 71. *Prof Exp:* Instr math, Lubbock Christian Col, 60-66; mem tech staff, TRW Systs, 66-67; instr math, Angelo State Univ, 67-68; instr comput sci, Baylor Col Med, 71-72. *Concurrent Pos:* NSF acad year inst math teachers, La State Univ, 64-65; NSF fel, Angelo State Univ, 68-69; NIH trainee statist, Southern Methodist Univ, 68-71; res asst prof biomet, Prog Neurol & asst prof, Dept Biomed Commun, Med Sch, Univ Tex, Houston, 73- *Mem:* Math Asn Am; Biomet Soc; Am Statist Asn. *Res:* Applications of statistics in public health and medicine. *Mailing Add:* UTHSC-SPH 1200 Herman Pressler Suite E-801 Houston TX 77030

HARRIS-WARRICK, RONALD MORGAN, NEUROCHEMISTRY, NEUROPHYSIOLOGY. *Current Pos:* asst prof, Cornell Univ, 80-86, assoc prof, 86-92, assoc chmn, 87-90, PROF NEUROBIOL, SECT NEUROBIOL & BEHAV, CORNELL UNIV, 92- *Personal Data:* b Berkeley, Calif, July 28, 49; m 75, Rebecca; c Sheridan & Thomas. *Educ:* Stanford Univ, BA, 70, Med Sch, PhD(genetics), 76. *Honors & Awards:* Stephen Fox Award, Stanford Univ, 70. *Prof Exp:* Fel, Dept Neurobiol, Med Sch, Stanford Univ, 76-78 & Harvard Med Sch, 78-80. *Concurrent Pos:* Guggenheim fel, 86-87; vis scientist, Ecole Normale Superieure, Paris, 86-87; vis prof, Stanford Univ Sch Med, 94. *Mem:* Soc Neurosci; AAAS; Int Soc Neuroethology. *Res:* Cellular and molecular mechanisms of behavior; biochemical action of neuromodulators in simple invertebrate nervous systems; control of locomotion; neuropharmacology; cloning of ion channel genes. *Mailing Add:* Sect Neurobiol & Behav Cornell Univ Ithaca NY 14853. *Fax:* 607-254-4308; *E-Mail:* rmh4@cornell.edu

HARROD, JOHN FRANK, INORGANIC SYNTHESIS, PHYSICAL CHEMISTRY. *Current Pos:* from asst prof to assoc prof, 66-73, PROF CHEM, MCGILL UNIV, 73-, TOMLINSON CHAIR MAT CHEM, 94- *Personal Data:* b Coventry, Eng, July 15, 34; m 58. *Educ:* Univ Birmingham, BSc, 55, PhD(chem), 58. *Honors & Awards:* Alan Lectr Award, Can Inst Chem, 97. *Prof Exp:* Fel chem, Univ BC, 58-60; mem staff, Res Lab, Gen Elec Co, NY, 60-66. *Concurrent Pos:* Consult, Dow Chem Co, 67-80; vis prof, Ecole Nat Superieure De Chimie, 82-83 & 89-90; Killam fel, Can Coun, 95-97. *Mem:* AAAS; Can Inst Chem; Am Chem Soc. *Res:* Coordination chemistry; catalytic activation of simple, inert molecules; heterogeneous catalysis; organometalic synthesis. *Mailing Add:* Dept Chem 801 Sherbrooke St W Montreal PQ H3A 2K6 Can. *Fax:* 514-398-3797; *E-Mail:* harrod@omc.lan.mcgill.ca

HARROLD, ROBERT LEE, ANIMAL NUTRITION. *Current Pos:* assoc prof, 68-74, PROF ANIMAL NUTRIT, NDAK STATE UNIV, 80- *Personal Data:* b Newcastle, Ind, Oct 5, 40; m 65; c 3. *Educ:* Purdue Univ, BS, 62, MS, 64, PhD(animal nutrit), 67. *Prof Exp:* Fel nutrit & physiol, Ohio Agr Res & Develop Ctr, Ohio State Univ, 67-68. *Mem:* Am Soc Animal Sci; Sigma Xi; Am Asn Lab Animal Sci; Animal Nutrit Res Coun. *Res:* Physiology of nutrition; nutrition of monogastric animals; nutrient requirements; utilization and nutritive value of atypical feedstuffs; analysis of amino acids in biological specimens. *Mailing Add:* Animal Sci NDak State Univ Main Campus Fargo ND 58105

HARROLD, RONALD THOMAS, ACOUSTIC WAVEGUIDE TECHNOLOGY, VAPOR-MIST DIELECTRICS. *Current Pos:* sr res engr, Westinghouse, 63-75, fel res engr, 75-87, adv scientist high voltage corona, Westinghouse Sci & Technol Ctr, 75-96, CONSULT SCIENTIST, WESTINGHOUSE, 96- *Personal Data:* b Fulham, London, Eng, Apr 4, 33; US citizen; m 55, Whitley; c Lesley A & Linda J. *Educ:* Twickenham Col Technol, Eng, BS, 55; Chelmsford Col Technol, Eng, BS, 62. *Honors & Awards:* Indust Res-100 Award, 81, 83 & 84; Inst Elec & Electronics Engrs fel, 82. *Prof Exp:* Student apprentice high voltage switchgear, Brit Thomson-Houston Co, 50-55; lectr radar technol, Army Sch Electronics, 55-57; develop engr cathode ray tubes, Eng Elec Valve Co, 57-61; res engr color TV, Sylvania Thorn Color TV Lab, 61-63. *Concurrent Pos:* Mem, conf elec insulation & dielectric phenomena, Inst Elec & Electronics Engrs, 74-96; mem comt radio-elec coord, Am Nat Stand Inst, Inc, 75- *Mem:* Brit Inst Elec Engrs; fel Inst Elec & Electronics Engrs; Brit Coun Eng Inst. *Res:* The detection, measurement, location and interpretation of high voltage corona and electrical discharges; acoustic waveguide technology; cure and stress monitoring of composite materials; vapor-mist dielectrics for high voltage insulation; environmental engineering. *Mailing Add:* Westinghouse Sci & Technol Ctr Beulah Rd Pittsburgh PA 15235

HARROP, RONALD, COMPUTER APPLICATIONS IN MEDICAL IMAGING. *Current Pos:* head dept, Simon Fraser Univ, 64-68, prof math, 64-91, prof comput sci, 74-91, EMER PROF MATH & COMPUT SCI, SIMON FRASER UNIV, 91- *Personal Data:* b Manchester, Eng, May 3, 26; Can citizen; m 52, Olive J Cutten; c John C & Timothy P. *Educ:* Cambridge Univ, BA, 46, MA, 50, PhD(math), 53. *Prof Exp:* Jr sci officer, Royal Aircraft Estab, Farnborough, 45-48; lectr math, King's Col, Univ Durham, 51-61, sr lectr, 61-65. *Concurrent Pos:* Vis asst prof, Pa State Univ, 57-58; vis prof, Univ Munich, 69 & Univ Leicester, 70; vis prof radiol, Univ Southern Calif, 78-91; hon prof pharmaceut sci, Univ BC, 83-87, adj prof (hon) pharmaceut sci, 88-91. *Mem:* Am Math Soc; Soc Nuclear Med; Asn Symbolic Logic; Asn Comput Mach; Can Info Processing Soc; Inst Elec & Electronics Engrs. *Res:* Medical applications of computing; positron emission tomography; mathematical logic; automata theory. *Mailing Add:* Dept Math Simon Fraser Univ Burnaby BC V5A 1S6 Can. *Fax:* 604-291-4947; *E-Mail:* harrop@cs.sfu.ca

HARROW, LEE SALEM, PHYSICAL CHEMISTRY, CHEMICAL ENGINEERING. *Current Pos:* FOOD INDUST CONSULT, 88- *Personal Data:* b Washington, DC, Oct 20, 26; m 46, Phyllis Steuer; c Jeffrey J, Bruce I, Arthur S & Sarah A (Harlan). *Educ:* George Washington Univ, BS, 46; Georgetown Univ, MS, 52, PhD(phys chem), 53. *Prof Exp:* Engr plastics lab, US Naval Ord Lab, 46; chemist & engr org dyes spectros, Spec Proj Br, US Food & Drug Admin, 46-55; supvr & mgr instruments mass spectros, Philip Morris Res Lab, 55-60; chief engr & tech dir metals & metal coatings, Am Safety Razor, 60-64; lab mgr instr org chem phys chem eng, Gen Food Corp, 64-67; vpres & tech dir, Coca-Cola Co, 68-73; vpres & corp tech dir, World Hq, H J Heinz Co, 73-88. *Concurrent Pos:* Instr, USDA Grad Sch, 48-55, Georgetown Univ, 53; vis prof & dir, NSF, 58-68. *Mem:* Am Chem Soc; Inst Food Technol; Am Inst Chem Engrs; NY Acad Sci. *Res:* Absorption and mass spectroscopy, structure versus spectra; ion exchange, chemical equilibrium; waste utilization, enzymatic conversions of pectins, carbohydrates; technical management systems, systems analysis; hygienic practice and construction. *Mailing Add:* 412 Cezanne Dr Osprey FL 34229

HARRY, GEORGE YOST, MAMMALOGY, FISHERIES. *Current Pos:* RETIRED. *Personal Data:* b Portland, Ore, Jan 14, 19; m 42; c 2. *Educ:* Ore State Col, BS, 40; Univ Mich, MS, 41; Univ Wash, PhD(fisheries), 56. *Prof Exp:* Marine fisheries biologist, State Fish Comn, Ore, 47-52, dir res, 52-57, asst state fisheries dir, 58; dir, Auke Bay Biol Lab, US Bur Com Fisheries, 58-67 & Great Lakes Fishery Lab, 67-70; dir, Marine Mammal Div, Northwest Fisheries Ctr, Nat Marine Fisheries Serv, 70-80; pres, Aqua Sci Inc, 81-80, consult, Univ Mich, 67-70. *Mem:* Am Fisheries Soc; Soc Marine Mammal; Am Inst Fishery Res Biol. *Res:* Conservation of marine mammals and fish. *Mailing Add:* 4259 133th Ave SE Bellevue WA 98006

HARRY, HAROLD WILLIAM, invertebrate zoology; deceased, see previous edition for last biography

HARSANYI, JOHN C, ECONOMICS EDUCATION. *Current Pos:* prof, 64-90, EMER PROF BUS ADMIN, UNIV CALIF, BERKELEY, 90- *Personal Data:* b Budapest, Hungary, May 29, 20; m 51, Anne Klauber; c Tom Peter. *Educ:* Univ Budapest, Dr Phil, 47; Sydney Univ, MA, 53; Stanford Univ, PhD, 59. *Hon Degrees:* DSc, Northwestern Univ, 89. *Honors & Awards:* Nobel Prize in Econs, 94. *Prof Exp:* Univ asst, Univ Budapest, 47-48; lectr econs, Univ Queensland, Australia, 54-56; vis asst prof, Stanford Univ, 58; sr fel, Australian Nat Univ, 59-61; prof econs, Wayne State Univ, 61-63. *Concurrent Pos:* NSF grantee, 63-85; fel, Ctr Advan Study Behav Sci, 65-66. *Mem:* Nat Acad Sci; Am Acad Arts & Sci; fel Economet Soc; Am Econ Asn. *Mailing Add:* 14 Parnassus Rd Berkeley CA 94708-2041

HARSCH, HAROLD H, PSYCHOPHARMACOLOGY, BEHAVIORAL MEDICINE & GEROPSYCHIATRY. *Current Pos:* PSYCHIATRIST, MILWAUKEE COUNTY MED COMPLEX, 82-, MED DIR, 83- *Personal Data:* b Bachnung, WGer, Oct 15, 50; US citizen. *Educ:* Marquette Univ, BS, 72; Med Col Wis, MD, 76. *Prof Exp:* Psychiat training, Stanford Univ, 76-80, NIMH fel, Med Ctr, 79-80. *Concurrent Pos:* Assoc staff, Milwaukee Psychiat Hosp, 82-88; Human Res & Rev Comt, Milwaukee Co Med Complex, 84-88, Med Audit Comt, Froedert Mem Lutheran, 84-88, Impaired Residents Comt, Med Col Wis, 84-91, chmn, 88-90; asst prof med, Med Col Wis, 82-88, assoc prof, 89- *Mem:* AMA; Am Psychiat Asn; fel Acad Psychosomat Med; Physicians Soc Responsibility; Asn Acad Psychiat. *Res:* Develop of medical-psychiatry units; use of functional brain imaging; clinical use of novel antidepressants; psychiatric teaching in medical school, phase II & III; Food & Drug Admin drug studies; functional MRI. *Mailing Add:* Froedert Mem Lutheran Hosp Psychiat E 6-W 9200 W Wisconsin Ave Milwaukee WI 53226. *Fax:* 414-257-5241

HARSHBARGER, BOYD, MATHEMATICAL STATISTICS. *Current Pos:* RETIRED. *Personal Data:* b Weyers Cave, Va, Feb 15, 06; m 35; c 2. *Educ:* Bridgewater Col, BA, 28; Va Polytech Inst, MS, 31; Univ Ill, MA, 35; George Washington Univ, PhD(math statist), 42. *Hon Degrees:* DSc, Bridgewater Col, 50. *Honors & Awards:* Wilks Award, 89. *Prof Exp:* Teacher, Miller Sch, Va, 28-29; from instr to assoc prof math, Va Polytech Inst & State Univ, 31-39, assoc prof statist, 41-48, in charge statist lab, 48-72, prof statist & head dept, 48-76, emer prof, 76-85. *Concurrent Pos:* Statist consult adv, Va Legis Comt, 47-53; founder & ed, Va J Sci, 50-55; NATO sr sci fel, 69. *Mem:* AAAS; Biomet Soc; fel Am Statist Asn; fel Inst Math Statist. *Res:* Mathematics involved in developing of new statistical designs; mathematical theory of area sampling; application of statistical designs to agriculture and engineering research. *Mailing Add:* 213 Country Club Dr SE Blacksburg VA 24060-5515

HARSHBARGER, JOHN CARL, JR, PATHOBIOLOGY, COMPARATIVE ONCOLOGY. *Current Pos:* PROF PATH & DIR REGISTRY TUMORS IN LOWER ANIMALS, GEORGE WASH UNIV MED CTR, 95- *Personal Data:* b Weyers Cave, Va, May 9, 36; m, Deborah L Hixon; c Alys Amelia. *Educ:* Bridgewater Col, BA, 57; Va Polytech Inst, MS, 59; Rutgers Univ, PhD(entom), 62. *Honors & Awards:* Prince Hitachi Prize, Japanese Found Cancer Res, 96. *Prof Exp:* NSF res assoc, Insect Path Pioneering Res Lab, USDA, Md, 62-64; asst res pathobiologist invert path, Univ Calif, Irvine, 64-67; dir, Registry Tumors in Lower Animals, Mus Natural Hist, Smithsonian Inst, 67-95. *Mem:* Fel AAAS; Sigma Xi; Soc Invert Path (secy, 74-76, vpres, 84-86, pres, 86-88); Am Asn Cancer Res; NY Acad Sci; Am Soc Zoologists; Am Fisheries Soc. *Res:* Etiology, epidemiology and comparative pathology of neoplasms and related diseases of invertebrate and cold blooded vertebrate animals. *Mailing Add:* Dept Path George Wash Univ Med Ctr Ross Hall 520 2300 I St NW Washington DC 20037

HARSHBARGER, KENNETH E, DAIRY SCIENCE. *Current Pos:* from asst prof to prof, 46-80, dept head, 69-79, EMER PROF DAIRY SCI, UNIV ILL, URBANA, 80- *Personal Data:* b Arcola, Ill, Nov 12, 14; m 57, Elsie Brown; c Lee, Keven, Kent & Karen. *Educ:* Univ Ill, BS, 37, MS, 39, PhD, 60. *Prof Exp:* Teacher pub sch, Ill, 37-38; asst dairy prod, Univ Ill, 38-41, asst prof, 46-54. *Concurrent Pos:* Officer, Med Dept, US Army, 41-46; asst prof animal husb, Cornell Univ, 54-55; consult, Inter-Dept Comt Nutrit for Nat Defense, 57-71; dir, Higher Educ Proj Indonesia, Midwest Univ Consortium, 79-82. *Mem:* Am Dairy Sci Asn; Am Inst Nutrit; Sigma Xi. *Res:* Dairy cattle nutrition and feeding; automation of dairy cattle feeding; human nutrition. *Mailing Add:* 502 E Pennsylvania Ave Urbana IL 61801

HARSHMAN, ELBERT NELSON, ECONOMIC GEOLOGY. *Current Pos:* CONSULT MINING GEOL, 75- *Personal Data:* b Los Angeles, Calif, July 10, 10; m 39, Anita E Wichman; c Oro L, Charlene M, Anita J, James N & Keith D. *Educ:* Calif Inst Technol, BS, 32, MS, 33; Univ Ariz, PhD(geol), 40. *Prof Exp:* Chief geologist, Cadiz Mining Co, Calif, 34; teaching fel, Univ Ariz, 34-36; chief geologist, Nielson Co, Inc, Philippines, 36-45; liaison geologist, US Bur Reclamation, 45-52; geologist, US Geol Surv, 52-75. *Concurrent Pos:* Civilian internee, Philippines, 42-45; partic panel uranium explor geol, Int Atomic Energy Agency, Vienna, 70 & Athens, 74; mem comt sedimentary basins & sandstone-type uranium deposits, Int Atomic Energy Agency, 70- *Mem:* Geol Soc Am; Soc Econ Geologists. *Res:* Economic and engineering geology; exploration for ore deposits. *Mailing Add:* 360 Brentwood St Denver CO 80226-1354

HARSHMAN, RICHARD C(ALVERT), CHEMICAL ENGINEERING. *Current Pos:* assoc prof chem eng, 60-71, prof, 71-84, EMER PROF CHEM ENG, CLEMSON UNIV, 84- *Personal Data:* b Columbus, Ohio, July 31, 22; wid; c Anne (Snider), David, Janet (Sprouse), Paul & Philip. *Educ:* Ohio Wesleyan Univ, BA, 47; Ohio State Univ, MS, 49, PhD(chem eng), 51. *Prof Exp:* Tech asst, Inst Paper Chem, 43-46; asst chem eng, Ohio State Univ,

47-50, res assoc, 50-51; sr res engr, Mathieson Chem Corp, 51-56, sect chief process develop eng, Indust Chem Div, Olin Mathieson Chem Corp, 56-60. *Mem:* Am Chem Soc; Am Inst Chem Engrs. *Res:* Process development; reaction kinetics; design. *Mailing Add:* 1000 Keystone Lane Clemson SC 29631

HARSHMAN, SIDNEY, BIOCHEMISTRY, MICROBIOLOGY. *Current Pos:* from instr to assoc prof, 59-78, assoc dean Grad Sch, 75-81, PROF MICROBIOL, SCH MED, VANDERBILT UNIV, 78- *Personal Data:* b Youngstown, Ohio, Nov 14, 30; m 50, Joan Schwartz; c Amy, David & Rachel. *Educ:* Western Reserve Univ, BS, 50; Johns Hopkins Univ, ScD, 59. *Mem:* AAAS; Am Chem Soc; Am Soc Microbiol; Am Soc Biol Chem; Sigma Xi. *Res:* Chemistry of normal and transformed cell membranes; biological and chemical properties of staphylococcal and alpha toxin; immunochemistry. *Mailing Add:* Dept Microbiol Vanderbilt Univ Sch Med Nashville TN 37203. *Fax:* 615-343-7392; *E-Mail:* harshms@ctrvax.vanderbilt.edu

HART, BENJAMIN LESLIE, ANIMAL BEHAVIOR. *Current Pos:* Prof anat, 75-78, asst prof anat & psychol, 64-69, assoc prof anat, 69-75, PROF PHYSIOL BEHAV, UNIV CALIF, DAVIS, 78- *Personal Data:* b Kansas City, Mo, Aug 12, 35; m 81; c 2. *Educ:* Univ Minn, BS, 58, DVM, 60, PhD(physiol psychol), 64. *Concurrent Pos:* Assoc ed, Hormones & Behavior, 71-; consult ed, Appl Animal Ethology, 73- *Mem:* Animal Behav Soc; Am Physiol Soc; Am Vet Med Asn. *Res:* Reproductive behavior; animal behavior and disease management. *Mailing Add:* 38 College Park Davis CA 95616

HART, CHARLES WILLARD, JR, AQUATIC BIOLOGY. *Current Pos:* RETIRED. *Personal Data:* b Farmville, Va, Jan 30, 28; m 62, Dabney Gardner. *Educ:* Hampden-Sydney Col, BA & BS, 49; Univ Va, MA, 51. *Prof Exp:* Asst physiol, Fla State Univ, 51-52; asst instr, Kirksville Col Osteop & Surg, 52-53; asst physiol, Fla State Univ, 53-54; instr biol, Washington Col, Md, 54-55 & Randolph-Macon Woman's Col, 55-56; med ed, Smith Kline & Fr Labs, 56-58; ed sci pubs, Acad Natural Sci, 58-71, invert zoologist, 62-71, adminr, Consult Progs, 69-72; dir consult progs, Acad Natural Sci Philadelphia, 72-74; prog limnologist, Smithsonian Inst, 74, asst to dir, 74-79, res scientist, Dept Invert Zool, Nat Mus Natural Hist, chmn, Dept Invert Zool, 88-91. *Concurrent Pos:* Coun Educ Biol (treas, 69-71); consult, Mediter Marine Sorting Ctr, Tunisia, 70; ed, Proc Biol Soc Wash, 78-79. *Mem:* Fel AAAS; Coun Biol Ed (treas, 69-71); Am Soc Zool; Asn Southeastern Biol (pres, 70-71); Sigma Xi; Crustacean Soc (treas, 81-84). *Res:* Administration; freshwater and marine crustacea; limnology of Jamaica, Puerto Rico and Dominica; pollution ecology of freshwater and estuarine invertebrates; biological bibliography and lexicography. *Mailing Add:* 6449 Walter Woods Dr Falls Church VA 22044. *Fax:* 202-357-3043

HART, CLARENCE ARTHUR, FORESTRY. *Current Pos:* Wood technologist, 54-57, from asst prof to assoc prof, 57-69, prof wood physics, 69-80, PROF WOOD & PAPER SCI, NC STATE UNIV, 80- *Personal Data:* b Norton, Va, Nov 14, 27. *Educ:* Va Polytech Inst, BS, 52; NC State Col, MS, 54, PhD(wood technol), 57. *Mem:* Soc Wood Sci & Technol; Forest Prod Res Soc. *Res:* Wood technology; wood physics, especially wood moisture relations. *Mailing Add:* Dept Wood & Paper Sci NC State Univ Box 8005 Raleigh NC 27695-0001

HART, DABNEY GARDNER, HAZARDOUS WASTE MANAGEMENT, ENVIRONMENTAL POLICY. *Current Pos:* sr writer-ed, Mitre Corp, 75-76, mem tech staff, Dept Environ Assessment & Planning, Metrek Div, 76-80, group leader, 80-96, SR STAFF, ENERGY, RESOURCES & ENVIRON SYSTS, MITRE TEK, 96- *Personal Data:* b Jackson, Miss, Dec 3, 40; m 62. *Educ:* Bryn Mawr Col, AB, 62, MA, 70; Am Univ, MS, 84, PhD, 89. *Prof Exp:* Biologist, Acad Natural Sci Philadelphia, 62-63, res assoc ostracod taxon, 63-67, co investr, 67-73, spec proj ed, 73-75. *Concurrent Pos:* Partic, Bredin-Archbold-Smithsonian Exped to Dominica, 64 & 66, Invests in Marine Shallow Water Ecosyst Prog, Smithsonian Inst, Carrie Bow Cay, Belize, 76; consult, Mediter Marine Sorting Ctr, Khereddine, Tunisia, 70; mem, Sci Adv Bd, US Environ Protection Agency, 78-82. *Mem:* Sigma Xi; AAAS; Asn Women Sci. *Res:* Environmental regulation, legislation, and policy, especially as related to hazardous waste; computer security. *Mailing Add:* Mitre Tek Systs 1820 Dolley Madison Blvd McLean VA 22102-3481

HART, DAVID ARTHUR, IMMUNOLOGY, BIOCHEMISTRY. *Current Pos:* PROF MICROBIOL, INFECTIOUS DIS & MED, UNIV CALGARY HEALTH SCI CTR. *Personal Data:* b Marquette, Mich, Aug 6, 42. *Educ:* Northern Mich Univ, BA, 64; Mich State Univ, PhD(biochem), 69. *Prof Exp:* Res assoc, Univ Ill Med Ctr, 69-72; from asst prof to assoc prof immunol, Univ Tex Health Sci Ctr, Dallas, 72-78. *Concurrent Pos:* Chmn, McCaig Ctr Joint Injury & Arthritis Res. *Mem:* Am Asn Immunologists; Am Soc Microbiol; Am Soc Biochem & Molecular Biol Soc; Can Soc Clin Invest. *Res:* Plasminogen activators and their inhibitors; role of proteinases in inflammation processes; connective tissue biochemistry and cell biology. *Mailing Add:* Dept Microbiol & Infect Dis Univ Calgary 3330 Hosp Dr NW Calgary AB T2N 4N1 Can. *Fax:* 403-283-7742

HART, DAVID CHARLES, DYNAMICAL SYSTEMS, GRID GENERATION. *Current Pos:* ASST PROF MATH, UNIV CINCINNATI, 86- *Personal Data:* b Cincinnati, Ohio, July 8, 47; m 72; c 2. *Educ:* Purdue Univ, BS, 72; Univ Calif, Berkeley, PhD(math), 80. *Prof Exp:* Asst prof math, Univ Fla, 80-86. *Concurrent Pos:* Consult, USAF, 85 & 87, NASA, 86. *Mem:* Am Math Soc; Soc Indust & Appl Math. *Res:* Dynamical systems; grid generation. *Mailing Add:* 1422 E Elliston Dr Bloomington IN 47401-8745

HART, DAVID DICKINSON, AQUATIC ECOLOGY, WATER RESOURCE MANAGEMENT. *Current Pos:* Ruth Patrick scholar, Acad Natural Sci, 83-85, sr scientist ecol, 85-86, assoc curator, 86-90, CURATOR, ACAD NATURAL SCI, PHILADELPHIA, 91-, DIR, PATRICK CTR ENVIRON RES, 96- *Personal Data:* b Santa Rosa, Calif, Sept 17, 52; m 72, Sally Millner; c Allison M. *Educ:* Univ Calif, Santa Cruz, BA, 74; Univ Calif, Davis, PhD(ecol), 79. *Prof Exp:* Fel ecol, W K Kellogg Biol Sta, Mich State Univ, 79-80, asst vis prof, 80-83. *Concurrent Pos:* Adj asst prof, Dept Biol, Univ Pa, 84-90, adj prof, 92-; vis assoc prof, Swarthmore Col, 89-90; mem, Working Group Lake & Reservoir Bioassessment, US Environ Protection Agency, 93- *Mem:* AAAS; NAm Benthological Soc; Ecol Soc Am. *Res:* Processes that control patterns of distribution, abundance and dynamics especially in streams and rivers; how biological monitoring of aquatic ecosystems can yield more powerful insights regarding environmental quality. *Mailing Add:* Patrick Ctr Environ Res Acad Natural Sci 1900 Ben Franklin Pkwy Philadelphia PA 19064. *E-Mail:* hart@acnatsci.org

HART, DAVID JOEL, ORGANIC CHEMISTRY. *Current Pos:* asst prof, 78-83, ASSOC PROF CHEM, OHIO STATE UNIV, 83- *Personal Data:* b Lansing, Mich, May 15, 48. *Educ:* Univ Mich, Ann Arbor, BS, 72; Univ Calif, Berkeley, PhD(chem), 76. *Honors & Awards:* Stuart Pharmaceut Award, 86. *Prof Exp:* NIH fel chem, Calif Inst Technol, 76-78. *Concurrent Pos:* Eli Lilly fel, Eli Lilly Co, 82-84; Alfred P Sloan Found fel, 83-87. *Mem:* Am Chem Soc; AAAS. *Res:* Synthetic organic chemistry including the development of synthetic methods, reaction mechanisms, stereochemistry, asymmetric induction, free radical chemistry and natural products total synthesis. *Mailing Add:* Dept Chem Ohio State Univ Columbus OH 43210

HART, DAVID R, CHEMICAL ENGINEERING, CHEMISTRY. *Current Pos:* RETIRED. *Personal Data:* b Denbo, Pa, July 26, 26; m 50, Carol Jo Dorrough; c John M & Jody C (Gonzalez). *Educ:* Auburn Univ, BS, 51; Univ Ala, Tuscaloosa, MS, 70, PhD(chem eng), 75. *Prof Exp:* Res chemist, Monsanto Chem Co, 51-55; area supvr, Liberty Powder Defense Corp, 55-56; proj engr, Cramet Inc, 56-58; chem engr, Allied Chem Co, 58-59; res chem engr, US Pipe & Foundry Co, 59-68, dir chem res, 70-76; proj mgr & secy, Harmon Eng, 76-77; proj engr, Rust Int Corp, Birmingham, 77-78, gen mgr, Albany, Ore, 78-80, prog mgr, Allentown, PA, 80-81, proj mgr, Birmingham, AL, 81-93. *Concurrent Pos:* Adj assoc prof chem eng, Auburn Univ, 73-77 & 83-, mech eng, Univ Ala, Birmingham, 83-, chem eng, Univ Ala, 93- *Mem:* Fel Am Inst Chem Engrs. *Mailing Add:* 2630 Greenmont Dr Birmingham AL 35226

HART, DONALD JOHN, INDUSTRIAL HYGIENE, TOXICOLOGY. *Current Pos:* Assoc sr res chemist, Gen Motors Corp, 73-80, sr res scientist, res labs, 80-83, staff indust hyg, chemist, 83-87, mgr, Indust Hyg Lab, 87-92, SR ADMINR, GEN MOTORS CORP, 92- *Personal Data:* b Montreal, Que, Mar 23, 48; m 75, 88, Cynthia Morgan; c Lisa (Hopwood), Christopher & Daniel. *Educ:* Oakland Univ, BS, 69; Univ Ill, Urbana, PhD(org chem), 74; Wayne State Univ, MS, 85. *Concurrent Pos:* Chmn, Lab Accreditation Comt, Am Indust Hyg Asn. *Mem:* Am Indust Hyg Asn; Am Bd Indust Hyg. *Res:* Health studies of chemicals in the workplace. *Mailing Add:* 35279 Davison St Sterling Heights MI 48310

HART, EARL W, QUATERNARY GEOLOGY, PALEOSEISMICITY. *Current Pos:* RETIRED. *Personal Data:* b Los Angeles, Calif, Oct 13, 27; m 56, Donna J Olson; c William, John & Amy. *Educ:* Univ Calif, Los Angeles, BA, 50; Univ Calif, Berkeley, MA, 71. *Prof Exp:* Field geologist mud logging & well drilling, Litho Log Inc, 52-53; geologist econ geol, Calif Div Mines & Geol, 54-65, field mapping, 65-73, sr geologist & mgr, fault eval prog, 73-94, emer geologist, 95-97. *Concurrent Pos:* Consult, geol res, 96-97. *Mem:* Fel Geol Soc Am; Asn Eng Geologists; Seismol Soc Am; Am Geophys Union; Earthquake Eng Res Inst. *Res:* Evaluation of active faults; regulatory zoning; earthquake-induced ground deformation. *Mailing Add:* 6 Vista Ct Corte Madera CA 94925. *Fax:* 415-904-7715

HART, EDWARD LEON, HIGH ENERGY PHYSICS. *Current Pos:* assoc prof, 69-77, PROF PHYSICS, UNIV TENN, KNOXVILLE, 77- *Personal Data:* b Brooklyn, NY, Nov 10, 30; m 65, 94, Barbara Flynn; c Philip & Jason. *Educ:* City Col New York, BS, 52; Cornell Univ, PhD(physics), 59. *Prof Exp:* Instr physics, Cornell Univ, 58-59; from asst physicist to assoc physicist, Bubble Chamber Group, Brookhaven Nat Lab, 59-66; lectr physics, Univ Calif, Riverside, 66-69. *Concurrent Pos:* Res fel, Univ Pisa, 64-65; consult, Oak Ridge Nat Lab, 69-76, part-time res staff mem, 76-82. *Mem:* Am Phys Soc. *Res:* High energy, particle physics; bubble chamber research and data processing. *Mailing Add:* Dept Physics Univ Tenn Knoxville TN 37996-1200. *Fax:* 423-974-7843; *E-Mail:* lhart@utk.edu

HART, EDWARD WALTER, THEORETICAL PHYSICS, MATERIALS SCIENCE. *Current Pos:* prof, 76-88, EMER PROF MECH & MAT SCI, CORNELL UNIV, 88- *Personal Data:* b Easton, Pa, Jan 14, 18; m 40, 78; c 2. *Educ:* City Col New York, BS, 38; Univ Calif, PhD(physics), 50. *Honors & Awards:* Sr US Scientist Award, Alexander von Humboldt Found, 82. *Prof Exp:* Physicist degaussing & magnetic compass, US Navy Dept, 40-45; asst physics, Univ Calif, 46-47, physicist theoret physics, Radiation Lab, 47-51; physicist, Gen Elec Res & Develop Ctr, 51-76. *Concurrent Pos:* Vis lectr, Rensselaer Polytech Inst, 52-63, adj prof, 63-64; consult, Adv Comt Perspectives Mat Res, Nat Acad Sci-Nat Res Coun, 59; Battelle vis prof, Ohio State Univ, 73; vis prof mech & mat sci, Cornell Univ, 75-76; vis scientist, Nat Bur Stand, 81, Tech Univ, Braunschweig, 82 & Tech Univ, Darmstadt, 86. *Mem:* Fel Am Phys Soc; Am Soc Mech Engrs; Am Inst Mining & Metall Eng. *Res:* Magnetic compass; nuclear forces; field theory; plastic deformation of metals; metal physics; thermodynamics of inhomogeneous systems; fracture and failure of materials. *Mailing Add:* 228 Bard Hall Cornell Univ Ithaca NY 14853

HART, ELWOOD ROY, FOREST ENTOMOLOGY. *Current Pos:* from asst prof to assoc prof, 74-86, PROF ENTOM, IOWA STATE UNIV, 86-, PROF FORESTRY, 89- *Personal Data:* b Sioux City, Iowa, Mar 6, 38; m 79, Nancy L Fues; c Curtis. *Educ:* Cornell Col, BA, 59; Tex A&M Univ, MEd, 65, PhD(entom), 72. *Prof Exp:* Fel forest entom, Tex A&M Univ, 72-74. *Concurrent Pos:* Vis scientist, Univ Calif, Berkeley, 85. *Mem:* Entom Soc Am; Sigma Xi; Soc Am Forestry. *Res:* Biology and management of pests of forest and shade trees; pest management in short-rotation woody crops systems. *Mailing Add:* Dept Entom 401 Sci II Iowa State Univ Ames IA 50011. *Fax:* 515-294-5957; *E-Mail:* ehart@iastate.edu

HART, FREDERICK LEWIS, ENVIRONMENTAL ENGINEERING. *Current Pos:* asst prof, 74-75 & 78-80, ASSOC PROF ENVIRON ENG, WORCESTER POLYTECH INST, 80- *Personal Data:* b New Britain, Conn, Jan 6, 45; m 71. *Educ:* Univ Conn, BS, 69, MS, 71, PhD(environ), 74. *Prof Exp:* Sanit engr wastewater treat, Conn Health Dept, 69-71; asst prof, McGill Univ, 75-78. *Concurrent Pos:* Consult, Pluritec Consults, 76, SNC Group, 77; prin investr, Nat Res Coun Can, 76- & Am Soc Civil Engrs, 78- *Mem:* Water Pollution Control Fedn; Can Soc Civil Engrs. *Mailing Add:* Dept Civil & Environ Eng Worcester Polytechnic Inst 100 Institute Rd Worcester MA 01609

HART, GARRY DEWAINE, MATHEMATICS. *Current Pos:* Assoc prof math & coordr acad adv, 70-85, PROF MATH & CHMN MATH DEPT, CALIF STATE UNIV, DOMINGUEZ HILLS, 85- *Personal Data:* b Los Angeles, Calif, June 18, 44; m 65. *Educ:* Univ Calif, Riverside, BA, 66; Univ Ore, MA, 68; Kans State Univ, PhD(math), 70. *Mem:* Am Math Soc; Math Asn Am. *Res:* Functional analysis and measure theory. *Mailing Add:* Dept Math Calif Univ Dominquez Hills Carson CA 90747-0001. *Fax:* 310-516-3627; *E-Mail:* ghart@dhvxzo.csudh.edu

HART, GARY ELWOOD, GENETICS. *Current Pos:* asst prof, 66-71, assoc prof, 71-79, PROF GENETICS, TEX A&M UNIV, 79- *Personal Data:* b Langdon, NDak, Jan 12, 34; m 62; c 2. *Educ:* NDak State Univ, BS, 55; Univ Calif, Berkeley, PhD(genetics), 65. *Prof Exp:* Res assoc genetics, Brookhaven Nat Lab, NY, 65-66. *Mem:* AAAS; Genetics Soc Am; Soc Study Evolution; Crop Sci Soc; Am Inst Biol Sci; Sigma Xi. *Res:* Evolutionary biology; developmental genetics; cytogenetics. *Mailing Add:* Soil & Crop Sci Dept Tex A&M Univ College Station TX 77843-0100

HART, GERALD WARREN, BIOLOGICAL CHEMISTRY. *Current Pos:* Postdoctoral, 77-79, from asst prof to assoc prof, 79-88, PROF BIOL CHEM, SCH MED, JOHNS HOPKINS UNIV, 88-, DIR MED SCH BIOCHEM COURSE, 85- *Personal Data:* b Topeka, Kans, July 16, 49; m 73; c 2. *Educ:* Washburn Univ, BS, 71; Kans State Univ, PhD(develop biol), 77. *Honors & Awards:* H H Haymaker Award, 75; Winzler Mem Lectr, Univ Fla, 89. *Concurrent Pos:* Estab investr, Am Heart Asn, 83-88; ed-in-chief, J Glycobiol, 87-89. *Mem:* Soc Develop Biol; Am Soc Biol Chem & Molecular Biol; Sigma Xi; Soc Complex Carbohydrates; Am Soc Cell Biol; AAAS. *Res:* Biological chemistry. *Mailing Add:* Dept Biol Chem & Molecular Genetics Univ Ala Birmingham Sch Med & Dent UAB Sta BHS Bldg 1918 University Ave Birmingham AL 35294-0005. *Fax:* 205-975-6685

HART, HAL, SOFTWARE ENGINEERING. *Current Pos:* comput scientist, 74-79, Ada technol mgr, 79-90, SOFTWARE PROCESSING ENGR, TRW, 90- *Personal Data:* b Salt Lake City, Utah, Apr 7, 45. *Educ:* Carlton Col, BA, 67; Purdue Univ, MS, 69. *Prof Exp:* Instr comput sci, Purdue Univ, 69-74. *Mem:* Asn Comput Mach; Inst Elec & Electronics Engrs. *Mailing Add:* TRW DH5/1638 1 Space Park Redondo Beach CA 90278. *Fax:* 310-764-6255; *E-Mail:* hal.hart@acm.org

HART, HAROLD, ORGANIC CHEMISTRY, PHOTOCHEMISTRY. *Current Pos:* from instr to prof, 46-87, EMER PROF CHEM, MICH STATE UNIV, 87- *Personal Data:* b New York, NY, May 14, 22; m 42, Geraldine M Cohen; c Leslie (Craine), David, Diana (Johnson) & Ariel (Anderson). *Educ:* Univ Ill, BS, 41; Pa State Col, MS, 43, PhD(org chem), 47. *Honors & Awards:* Petrol Chem Award, Am Chem Soc, 62. *Prof Exp:* Asst, Petrol Refining Lab, Pa State Col, 42-46. *Concurrent Pos:* Guggenheim fel, Harvard Univ, 55-56; NSF sr fel, Cambridge Univ, 62-63; ed-in-chief, Chem Rev, 67-76. *Mem:* Am Chem Soc; Royal Soc Chem; fel AAAS. *Res:* Mechanisms of organic reactions; molecular rearrangements; small ring compounds; carbocations ions; organic synthesis; organic photochemistry; host-guest chemistry. *Mailing Add:* Dept Chem Mich State Univ East Lansing MI 48824. *Fax:* 517-353-1793

HART, HAROLD BIRD, THEORETICAL PHYSICS. *Current Pos:* From asst prof to assoc prof, 69-84, PROF PHYSICS, WESTERN ILL UNIV, 84- *Personal Data:* b Washington, DC, July 19, 40; m 64; c 4. *Educ:* Univ Utah, BA, 65; Brigham Young Univ, PhD(theoret physics), 69. *Res:* Conservation laws and symmetry properties of scalar-tensor gravitational theories. *Mailing Add:* Dept Physics Western Ill Univ Macomb IL 61455

HART, HAROLD M(ARTIN), ELECTRONICS. *Current Pos:* CONSULT ELECTRONICS, 77- *Personal Data:* b Cherokee, Okla, Nov 9, 13; m 38; c 2. *Educ:* Univ Buffalo, AB, 34; Univ Okla, MS, 36. *Prof Exp:* Res assoc, Submarine Signal Co, 38-39, chief engr radar, Raytheon Co, 39-49, head radar systs eng, 49-55, mgr radar dept, Wayland Lab, 55-57, dir adv develop & asst mgr, 57-59, gen mgr systs mgt sub-div, 59-60, gen mgr surface radar & navig oper, 60-66, vpres & asst gen mgr, Equip Div, 66-75, vpres eng, 75-77. *Mem:* Fel & sr mem Inst Elec & Electronics Engrs; Am Inst Aeronaut & Astronaut. *Res:* Military radio, radar and direction finding equipment and commercial air traffic control radar and displays. *Mailing Add:* 5 Marvin Rd Wellesley MA 02181

HART, HASKELL VINCENT, SPECTROSCOPY. *Current Pos:* sr res chemist, 81-85, supvr, 85-87, RES MGR, SHELL DEVELOP CO, 87- *Personal Data:* b Chicago, Ill, Apr 17, 43; div; c 2. *Educ:* Univ Ill, BS, 65; Harvard Univ, AM, 66, PhD(chem), 73. *Prof Exp:* Asst actg chief chem, Univ NC, Wilmington, 71-79, assoc prof, 79-81. *Mem:* Am Chem Soc; Soc Appl Spectros. *Res:* Spectroscopic analysis. *Mailing Add:* 13211 Chipman Glen Dr Houston TX 77082-5009

HART, HIRAM, PHYSICS. *Current Pos:* from instr to prof physics, 53-93, EMER PROF, CITY COL NEW YORK, 93-; CHIEF PHYSICIST, MONTEFIORE HOSP, 68-; PROF NUCLEAR MED, ALBERT EINSTEIN COL MED, 72- *Personal Data:* b Brooklyn, NY, May 29, 24. *Educ:* City Col New York, BS, 43; NY Univ, PhD(physics), 52. *Prof Exp:* Physicist optical design, Universal Camera Corp, 43-46; instr, Bd Educ, NY, 46-53; physicist, Montefiore Hosp, 52-61, chief med physics lab, 62-68. *Concurrent Pos:* NSF fel, Yale Univ, 59-60; consult, Walter Reed Inst Res, 60-62; res assoc, Brookhaven Nat Lab, 64-67 & 71-75; assoc ed, Bull Math Biol, 73-90; mem bd dirs, Soc Math Biol, 76-90; assoc ed, Med Physics 79-92. *Mem:* AAAS; fel Am Phys Soc; Biophys Soc; Am Asn Physicists in Med; fel NY Acad Sci; Sigma Xi. *Res:* Meson theory and scattering problems; radioisotopes in tracer and therapeutic applications; theory of perturbation-tracer experiments; x-ray and optical diffraction; circulatory physiology; radiobiology; radioisotope scanning; diffusion-interaction phenomena; scintillation proximity assay. *Mailing Add:* 3394 Wayne Ave Bronx NY 10467

HART, HOWARD ROSCOE, JR, SOLID STATE PHYSICS, NUCLEAR MAGNETIC RESONANCE. *Current Pos:* CONSULT, 95- *Personal Data:* b Fayetteville, NC, Dec 6, 29; m 58, Emily Sawyer; c Evelyn, Alice & Susan. *Educ:* Cornell Univ, BEng, 52; Univ Ill, MS, 55, PhD(physics), 60. *Prof Exp:* Physicist, E I du Pont de Nemours & Co, 52-54; res assoc, Univ Ill, 60; physicist, Gen Elec Res & Develop Ctr, 60-94. *Concurrent Pos:* Consult, 95- *Mem:* Nat Acad Eng; fel Am Phys Soc; Am Geophys Union. *Res:* Low temperature physics; high field superconductivity; cosmic rays; geochronology; mineral exploration; nuclear magnetic resonance; medical imaging. *Mailing Add:* 2159 Rankin Rd Schenectady NY 12309-4220

HART, JAYNE THOMPSON, PHYSIOLOGY, PHARMACOLOGY. *Current Pos:* asst prof, 74-78, asst dean, Col Arts & Scis, 90-93, ASSOC PROF BIOL, GEORGE MASON UNIV, 78- *Personal Data:* b Aurora, Ill, Apr 30, 42; m 71. *Educ:* NCent Col, Ill, BA, 64; Univ Wis-Madison, MS, 66, PhD(physiol), 69. *Prof Exp:* Instr physiol, Univ Wis-Madison, 68-70; res pharmacologist, Med Res Labs, Pfizer, Inc, Conn, 70-71; asst prof physiol & pharmacol, Univ Hawaii, Manoa, 72-73. *Concurrent Pos:* Guest scientist, Naval Med Res Inst, Bethesda, 75-77; vis assoc prof, Uniformed Serv Univ Health Sci, Bethesda, Md, 85- *Mem:* Am Physiol Soc; Am Inst Biol Sci; Sigma Xi; Am Heart Asn. *Res:* Physiology of pregnancy; cardiovascular physiology; vascular reactivity; neurovascular interactions. *Mailing Add:* Dept Biol 3E1 George Mason Univ 4400 University Dr Fairfax VA 22030. *E-Mail:* jmarz@gmu.edu

HART, JOHN BIRDSALL, PHYSICS. *Current Pos:* From instr to assoc prof math & physics, Xavier Univ, 50-68, actg chmn, Dept Physics, 58-61, chmn, 61-71 & 82-83, PROF MATH & PHYSICS, XAVIER UNIV, OHIO, 68- *Personal Data:* b Hamilton, Ohio, Aug 24, 24; m 48, Agnes M Roegner; c Mary A McLain. *Educ:* Xavier Univ, Ohio, BS, 48, MS, 50. *Concurrent Pos:* Mgr Conf Found Quantum Mech, 62; lectr, Univ Cincinnati, 55-56; vis prof, Fla State Univ, 67-68; consult prof, Ohio Univ, 70-71; educ & com TV lectr sci; teacher navig, USNR Officer Can Schs. *Mem:* Am Asn Physics Teachers. *Res:* Pedagogy of physics; classical mechanics. *Mailing Add:* Dept Physics Xavier Univ Cincinnati OH 45207-1096

HART, JOHN HENDERSON, TREE PATHOLOGY, FOREST ECOLOGY. *Current Pos:* From asst prof to assoc prof, 63-75, PROF PLANT PATH & FORESTRY, MICH STATE UNIV, 75- *Personal Data:* b Kansas City, Mo, June 18, 36; m 59; c 3. *Educ:* Dartmouth Col, BA, 58; Iowa State Univ, MS, 60, PhD(plant path), 63; Mich State Univ, MS, 85. *Concurrent Pos:* Vis res fel, Div Appl Chem, Commonwealth Sci & Indust Res Orgn, Melbourne, Australia, 70-71; vis scientist, Pac Forest Res Ctr, Environ Can, Victoria, BC, 77-78; vis prof, Rocky Mt Forest & Range Exp Sta, US Forest Serv, Ft Collins, Colo, 85. *Mem:* Am Phytopath Soc; Wildlife Soc; Soc Am Foresters; Ecol Soc Am; Walnut Coun (pres, 91-92). *Res:* Diseases of woody plants; effect of herbivory on forest ecosystems. *Mailing Add:* Dept Bot 166 Plant Biol Mich State Univ East Lansing MI 48824-1312

HART, KENNETH HOWELL, PHYSICS. *Current Pos:* RETIRED. *Personal Data:* b Edmonton, Alta, Apr 5, 24; m 48; c 4. *Educ:* Univ Alta, BSc, 46, MSc, 48; Univ Toronto, PhD(physics), 53. *Prof Exp:* Lectr physics, Univ Alta, 47-48; asst prof, Acadia Univ, 48-51; assoc res officer, Nat Res Coun, 53-80, sr res officer physics, 80-84. *Res:* Low temperature physics; properties of liquid helium; optical physics; metrology. *Mailing Add:* 46526 McCafferty Blvd Chilliwack BC V2P 1E5 Can

HART, LARRY GLEN, PHARMACOLOGY. *Current Pos:* asst chief, Pharmacol Br, Nat Inst Environ Health Sci, 72-77, actg chief lab pharmacokinetics, 78-80, asst dir, 80-82, asst to sci dir, 77-80, asst to dir, 80-92, TOXICOLOGIST, NAT INST ENVIRON HEALTH SCI, 92- *Personal Data:* b Los Angeles, Calif, Dec 6, 32; m 57, Martha Olson; c David M, Thomas C & Mary K. *Educ:* Univ Iowa, BS, 60, MS, 62, PhD(pharmacol), 64. *Prof Exp:* Res pharmacologist, Lab Chem Pharmacol, Nat Cancer Inst, 66-68; supvr biochem pharmacol, Bio-Med Res Labs, ICI Am Inc, 68-72.

Concurrent Pos: Staff fel pharmacol, Nat Heart Inst, 64-66. *Mem:* Soc Exp Biol & Med; Am Soc Pharmacol & Exp Therapeut; Sigma Xi. *Res:* Biochemical pharmacology and drug metabolism; toxicology; drug transport, primarily foreign compounds, insecticides on hepatic drug metabolizing enzymes; stimulation of drug metabolism in newborn animals. *Mailing Add:* Environ Toxicol Prog Hew-Pub Health Serv PO Box 12233 Research Triangle Park NC 27709. *Fax:* 919-541-0295; *E-Mail:* hart@niehs.nih.gov

HART, LAWRENCE ALAN, PURE MATHEMATICS. *Current Pos:* instr math, 55-58, from asst prof to assoc prof, 58-70, PROF MATH, LORAS COL, 70- *Personal Data:* b Eagle Grove, Iowa, Sept 22, 30. *Educ:* Loras Col, BS, 53. *Prof Exp:* Sec teacher, Iowa, 53-55. *Concurrent Pos:* NSF fel, Univ Wyo, 59; instr & dir, NSF Inst, dir, Allied Health Prog, 77-, study, Univ Iowa, 65-66; NSF fac fel, 66-67. *Mem:* Math Asn Am. *Res:* Undergraduate mathematics; analysis; topology; algebra. *Mailing Add:* 2130 Sunnyview Dr Dubuque IA 52001

HART, LEWIS THOMAS, MICROBIOLOGY, BIOCHEMISTRY. *Current Pos:* assoc prof, 68-80, PROF VET SCI, LA STATE UNIV, BATON ROUGE, 80- *Personal Data:* b Chesbrough, La, Feb 2, 33; m 58; c 2. *Educ:* Southeastern La Col, BS, 59; La State Univ, Baton Rouge, MS, 64, PhD(microbiol), 67. *Prof Exp:* Fel, Univ Iowa, 67-68. *Mem:* Am Soc Microbiol; Sigma Xi. *Res:* Microbial physiology; nitrate reduction; effect of herbicides on microbial organisms; hydrocarbon oxidation by microbes; alteration of lipid biosynthesis in anemic diseases of animals; fatty acid metabolism. *Mailing Add:* 337 Baird Dr Baton Rouge LA 70808

HART, LYNN PATRICK, PLANT PATHOLOGY. *Current Pos:* Assoc prof, 84-88, PROF PLANT PATH, MICH STATE UNIV, 87- *Personal Data:* b Kalamazoo, Mich, Jan 2, 42; m 68, 86; c 4. *Educ:* Calif State Polytech Univ, Pomona, BS, 73; Univ Calif, Riverside, PhD(plant path), 78. *Mem:* Am Phytopath Soc. *Res:* Genetic and physiological bases of host-pathogen interactions. *Mailing Add:* Dept Bot & Plant Path 105 Pest Res Ctr Mich State Univ East Lansing MI 48824

HART, LYNN W, PHYSICS. *Current Pos:* PHYSICIST, APPL PHYSICS LAB, JOHNS HOPKINS UNIV, 72- *Personal Data:* b Logan, Utah, Oct 25, 42; div; c 5. *Educ:* Brigham Young Univ, BS, 67; Iowa State Univ, PhD(physics), 71. *Prof Exp:* Fel physics, Kent State Univ, 71-72. *Mem:* Am Phys Soc. *Res:* Magnetism; electromagnetic propagation; biomedical engineering; acoustics. *Mailing Add:* 6177 Prophecy Pl Columbia MD 21045

HART, MARY KATE, T-CELL IMMUNOLOGY, MUCOSAL IMMUNE RESPONSES. *Current Pos:* MICROBIOLOGIST, US ARMY MED RES INST INFECTIOUS DIS, 91- *Personal Data:* b Wilmington, Del, Dec 10, 59. *Educ:* St Josephs Univ, BS, 81; Univ Pa, PhD(immunol), 88. *Prof Exp:* Fel, Duke Univ Med Ctr, 88-90, res assoc, 90-91. *Mem:* AAAS; Soc Mucosal Immunol; Am Soc Trop Med & Hyg. *Res:* Evaluate systemic and mucosal immune responses to viral vaccines and vaccine candidates; identify T and B cell epitopes critical for the induction of protective immune responses and the major histocompatibility complex molecules that restrict responses. *Mailing Add:* USAMRIID Div Virol Ft Detrick Frederick MD 21702

HART, MAURICE I, JR, PHYSICAL CHEMISTRY. *Current Pos:* from asst prof to assoc prof, 63-71, PROF PHYS CHEM, UNIV SCRANTON, 71- *Personal Data:* b New York, NY, Feb 3, 34; m 59; c 7. *Educ:* Maryknoll Col, AB, 55; Fordham Univ, MS, 59, PhD(phys chem), 62. *Prof Exp:* Sr chemist, Melpar Inc, Va, 62-63. *Mem:* Am Chem Soc; Electrochem Soc; Sigma Xi. *Res:* Thermodynamic properties of clathrate compounds; electrochemistry in non-aqueous solvent systems; irreversible thermodynamics-thermocells. *Mailing Add:* Dept Chem Univ Scranton Scranton PA 18510

HART, MICHAEL H, ASTRONOMY, ATMOSPHERIC SCIENCE. *Current Pos:* asst prof, 87-92, ASSOC PROF ASTRON, SCI DIV, ANNE ARUNDEL CC, 92- *Personal Data:* b New York, NY, Apr 28, 32; m 63; c Robert & Richard. *Educ:* Cornell Univ, AB, 52; Adelphi Univ, MS, 69; Princeton Univ, PhD(astron), 72. *Prof Exp:* Res fel astron, Hale Observ, 72-74; res fel planetary atmospheres, Nat Ctr Atmospheric Res, 74-75 & NASA Goddard Space Flight Ctr, 75-77; sr staff scientist climat, Syst & Appl Sci Corp, 77; asst prof, Dept Meteorol, Univ Md, 78; asst prof physics & astron, Dept Physics, Trinity Univ, 78-82. *Concurrent Pos:* Fel Carnegie Inst Wash, 72-74; Nat Res Coun fel, NASA, 75-77. *Mem:* Int Astron Union. *Res:* Planetary atmospheres and their evolution; early atmosphere of the earth; history of science and its impact on society; possible abundance of life in the galaxy; climate modeling. *Mailing Add:* Sci Div Anne Arvndel Community Col 101 College Pkwy Arnold MD 21012

HART, NATHAN HOULT, EXPERIMENTAL MORPHOLOGY & DEVELOPMENTAL BIOLOGY. *Current Pos:* PROF BIOL SCI, RUTGERS UNIV, 88- *Personal Data:* b Torrington, Conn, Jan 29, 36; m 60; c 2. *Educ:* Clark Univ, AB, 58; Harvard Univ, MA, 59, PhD(biol), 63. *Prof Exp:* Nat Heart Inst fel, 63-64; asst prof biol, Union Col, NY, 64-66; from asst prof to assoc prof zool, Rutgers Univ, New Brunswick, 66-71. *Concurrent Pos:* NIH res grant, 65-68 & 83-86, NSF, 87-88. *Mem:* Soc Develop Biol; Am Soc Zoologists; Sigma Xi; Am Soc Cell Biol. *Res:* Fish embryology; fertilization and the cortical reaction; ultrastructure and freeze fracture; developmental biology; sperm-egg interactions; egg cytoskeleton. *Mailing Add:* Dept Biol Sci Nelson Biol Labs Rutgers Univ PO Box 1059 Piscataway NJ 08855-1059. *Fax:* 732-445-5870

HART, PATRICK E(UGENE), CERAMIC ENGINEERING. *Current Pos:* Sr res scientist, Battelle Mem Inst, 67-78, tech leader nuclear ceramics, 78-80, mgr, Ceramics & Polymers Develop Sect, 80-85, assoc, Mat Sci & Technol Dept, 80-87, oper mgr, Appl Physics Ctr, 87-94, STAND-BASED MGT SYST PROJ MGR, BATTELLE MEM INST, 94- *Personal Data:* b Portland, Ore, Jan 8, 40; m 63, Marian; c 1. *Educ:* Univ Wash, BS, 62; Univ Calif, Berkeley, MS, 64, PhD(ceramic eng), 67. *Mem:* Fel Am Ceramic Soc; Sigma Xi. *Res:* Thermal-mechanical behavior of ceramic systems including oxides and composites; fabrication techniques. *Mailing Add:* 103205 N Harrington West Richland WA 99353

HART, PAUL ROBERT, DEMULSIFICATION, SOLIDS CONTROL. *Current Pos:* scientist energy chem, Betz Dearborn Inc, 83-85, res scientist process chem, 85-93, sr res scientist energy & process chem, 93-96, SR RES SCIENTIST, HYDROCARBON PROCESS GROUP, BETZ DEARBORN INC, 96- *Personal Data:* b Sacramento, Calif, Feb 28, 56; m 86, Rosalie B Shassetz; c James E & Emily B. *Educ:* Univ Wash, BS, 77. *Prof Exp:* Chemist, Rocket Res Div, Olin, 79-80; res chemist, Chem Div, BASF, 80-83. *Concurrent Pos:* Sr consult, S & T Serv, 82-83; pres, Hart Fund, 90- *Mem:* Am Chem Soc. *Res:* Development of chemicals to break water-in-oil and oil-in-water emulsions, settle or disperse solids in petroleum fluids, break aqueous and non-aqueaous foams, including the relevant application and selection technology; granted 14 US patents. *Mailing Add:* 2710 Echo The Woodlands TX 77380. *Fax:* 281-383-7780; *E-Mail:* paulhart@worldnet.att.net

HART, PEMBROKE J, GEOPHYSICS, SEISMOLOGY. *Current Pos:* mem staff geophys, 58-89, CONSULT, NAT ACAD SCI, 90- *Personal Data:* b Chicago, Ill, Jan 20, 29; m 76. *Educ:* Harvard Univ, AB, 50, AM, 52, PhD(geophys), 55. *Prof Exp:* Instr geol, Vanderbilt Univ, 56-58. *Concurrent Pos:* Guest investr, Carnegie Inst Dept Terrestrial Magnetism, 65 & 68; prog officer geophys, NSF, 69-70. *Mem:* Fel AAAS; Am Geophys Union; Seismol Soc Am; fel Geol Soc Am. *Res:* Seismic refraction studies of earth's crust and upper mantle; propagation of seismic waves; structure and composition of the earth's interior. *Mailing Add:* 3252 O St NW Washington DC 20007-2847

HART, PETER E(LLIOT), COMPUTER SCIENCE. *Current Pos:* SR VPRES, RICOH CORP, 91- *Personal Data:* b Brooklyn, NY, Feb 27, 41; m 64. *Educ:* Rensselaer Polytech Inst, BEE, 62; Stanford Univ, MS, 63, PhD(elec eng), 66. *Prof Exp:* Res engr artificial intel, SRI Int, 66-74, dir, Artificial Intel Ctr, 74-80; mgr, Artificial Intel Res Lab, Fairchild Camera & Instrument Corp, 80-83; sr vpres, Syntelligence Inc, 83-90. *Mem:* AAAS; Asn Comput Mach; fel Inst Elec & Electronics Engrs; fel Am Asn Artificial Intel. *Res:* Artificial intelligence; pattern recognition; computer modelling; statistical decision theory. *Mailing Add:* 301 Arbor Rd Menlo Park CA 94025

HART, PHILLIP A, ORGANIC CHEMISTRY. *Current Pos:* from asst prof to assoc prof, 63-79, PROF PHARMACEUT CHEM, UNIV WIS-MADISON, 79- *Personal Data:* b San Jose, Calif, Mar 2, 33; m 55; c 2. *Educ:* San Jose State Col, BA, 55; Univ Wash, MS, 57; Stanford Univ, PhD(org chem), 64. *Prof Exp:* Chemist, US Fish & Wildlife Serv, 57-58 & Stanford Res Inst, 58-61. *Mem:* Am Chem Soc; AAAS. *Res:* Nucleic acid structure and function as studied by instrumental and biological techniques. *Mailing Add:* 505 Gunthrie St Ashland OR 97520

HART, R NEAL, ABELIAN GROUPS. *Current Pos:* from asst prof to PROF MATH, SAM HOUSTON STATE UNIV, 71- *Personal Data:* b Jacksonville, Ill, Feb 19, 38; m 61; c Mikal Neal, Damon Lane & Shannon Jean. *Educ:* Ill Col, AB, 60; Univ Calif, Los Angeles, MA, 63; NMex State Univ, PhD(math), 69. *Prof Exp:* Comput analyst, Douglas Aircraft Corp, 62-63; math instr, MacMurray Col, 63-65; math lectr, Univ Nairobi, 69-71. *Concurrent Pos:* Int student adv, Sam Houston State Univ, 74-77; sr lectr math, Univ Bostwana & Swaziland, 77-78, actg chmn dept math, 78; Fulbright prof math, Univ Liberia, 81-82, Sultan Qaboos Univ, 90-92; educ specialist math, Egyptian Air Force Acad, 86-88; Peace Corps vol, 94- *Mem:* Am Math Soc; Math Asn Am. *Res:* Study of generalization of Ulm's theorem to totally projective groups and quotient categories of abelian groups modulo bounded groups. *Mailing Add:* Math Dept Sam Houston Univ Huntsville TX 77341-2206. *E-Mail:* mth___rnh@shsu.edu

HART, RAYMOND KENNETH, METALLURGICAL FAILURE ANALYSIS, ELECTRON MICROSCOPY. *Current Pos:* DIR FORENSIC METALL, RAYMOND K HART LTD, GA, 91- *Personal Data:* b Newcastle, Australia, Feb 15, 28; US citizen; m 52, Betty J Bingemann; c Timothy K & Rowena J. *Educ:* Sydney Tech Col, Australia, ASTC, 49; Univ, London, DIC, 51; Univ Cambridge, England, PhD(metall), 55; Kennedy Western Univ, JD, 91. *Honors & Awards:* President's Award, Midwest Soc Electron Microscopists, 86; Distinguished Scientist Award, Southeastern Electron Micros Soc, 93; Morton D Maqser Distinguished Serv Award, Micros Soc Am, 95. *Prof Exp:* Sci officer metall, Aeronaut Res Labs, Australia, 55-58; assoc scientist, 59-67, sr scientist metall, Argonne Nat Lab, Ill, 68-69; prin res scientist phys sci, Ga Tech, 70-75; dir forensic metall, Pasat Res Assocs, Inc, Ga, 75-91. *Concurrent Pos:* Dir phys sci, Electron Micros Am, 69-72; prin investr, NASA, NSG-9040, 74-75; consult, Jet Propulsion Lab, Pasadena, 77-82; exec officer, Nat Defense Exec Reserve, 90-95. *Mem:* Fel Am Acad Forensic Sci; Am Phys Soc; Am Soc Metals Int; Micros Soc Am; Sigma Xi. *Res:* Composition, structure and strength of metal alloys, and the relationship of these properties to their performance characteristics in service environments. *Mailing Add:* Raymond K Hart Ltd 145 Grogan's Lake Dr Atlanta GA 30350-3115

HART, RICHARD ALLEN, SCIENCE EDUCATION. *Current Pos:* from instr to prof, 62-90, EMER PROF BIOL, NORTHWEST MO STATE UNIV, 90- *Personal Data:* b Nora Springs, Iowa, Dec 6, 30; m 58, Margaret Lee; c Jeffrey, James & Mary L. *Educ:* Univ Mo, BS, 58, MS, 60, PhD(entom), 65. *Prof Exp:* Asst entom, Univ Mo, 58-62. *Concurrent Pos:* Entomologist, Fruit Fly Lab, Agr Res Serv, USDA, 66-68; biologist, IPA appointee, Environ Protection Agency region VIII, 78-80; consult, Nine-Patch Software, 90- *Mem:* Entom Soc Am; Sigma Xi. *Res:* Computer supplemented science courses; testing for quantity and quality; retraining passive pupils into self-correcting scholars; scoring by knowledge and judgment. *Mailing Add:* 315 S Alco Maryville MO 64468-2033. *Fax:* 660-582-8589; *E-Mail:* 71222.3565@compuserve.com

HART, RICHARD CULLEN, SCIENCE POLICY, ASTRONOMY. *Current Pos:* RETIRED. *Personal Data:* b Brooklyn, NY, Nov 7, 45; m 71; c 2. *Educ:* Wagner Col, BS, 67; Boston Univ, MS, 69, PhD(physics & astron), 73. *Prof Exp:* Lectr astron, Bentley Col, 72-74; lectr astron & physics, Boston Univ, 72-74; staff officer, Space Sci Bd, Nat Acad Sci, 74-95. *Mem:* Am Astron Soc; Am Geophys Union; AAAS. *Res:* Solar and space physics; space astronomy; data management and computation. *Mailing Add:* 2232 William & Mary Dr Alexandria VA 22308

HART, RICHARD HAROLD, RANGE SCIENCE, AGRONOMY. *Current Pos:* res agronomist, 62-86, RANGE SCIENTIST, AGR RES SERV, USDA, 86- *Personal Data:* b Villisca, Iowa, July 23, 33; m 60, Helen Wetter; c James & Kelley. *Educ:* Iowa State Univ, BS, 54, MS, 58; Ore State Univ, PhD, 61. *Honors & Awards:* Am Forage & Grassland Coun Merit Cert, 82; Outstanding Achievement Award, Soc Range Mgt, 89, Chapline Res Award, 92. *Prof Exp:* Asst agronomist, Coastal Plain Exp Sta, Univ Ga, 61-62. *Concurrent Pos:* Mem grad fac, Univ Wyo & Colo State Univ, 74- *Mem:* Fel Am Soc Agron; Soc Range Mgt; Coun Agr Sci & Technol; Am Forage & Grassland Coun. *Res:* Forage and range management systems; stocking rate theory; plant responses to grazing; crop ecology; computer modeling. *Mailing Add:* High Plains Grasslands Res Sta 8408 Hildreth Rd Cheyenne WY 82009. *Fax:* 307-637-6124

HART, RICHARD ROYCE, GEOLOGY, STRATIGRAPHY. *Current Pos:* RETIRED. *Personal Data:* b Chicago, Ill, Nov 30, 33; m 56; c 2. *Educ:* Cornell Col, BA, 56; Univ Iowa, MS, 59, PhD(geol), 63. *Prof Exp:* Asst geol, Univ Iowa, 56-61; from asst prof to assoc prof geol, Ill State Univ, 61-88. *Mem:* AAAS; Geol Soc Am; Paleont Soc; Nat Asn Geol Teachers. *Res:* Lower Paleozoic conodonts and biostratigraphy of mid-continent. *Mailing Add:* 404 E Vernon Apt 4 Normal IL 61761

HART, ROBERT GERALD, REPRODUCTIVE PHYSIOLOGY. *Current Pos:* Assoc prof, 67-77, PROF BIOL & CHMN DEPT, SLIPPERY ROCK STATE COL, 77- *Personal Data:* b Cumberland, Md, Feb 20, 37; m 59; c 4. *Educ:* Duquesne Univ, BS, 63, MS, 65; Univ Ill, PhD(reproductive physiol), 67. *Concurrent Pos:* Nat Sci Found travel grant, 68; Sigma Xi res grant, 68-69; res assoc reproductive physiol, Univ Ill, 69. *Mem:* AAAS; Am Soc Zool; Soc Study Reproduction; Brit Soc Study Fertil. *Res:* Biochemistry of semen coagulation; effect of age on spermatozoa. *Mailing Add:* 1253 Highland Green Dr Venice FL 34292

HART, ROBERT JOHN, PHYSICS. *Current Pos:* from assoc prof to prof, 56-89, EMER PROF PHYSICS, STATE UNIV NY, BINGHAMTON, 89- *Personal Data:* b Utica, NY, Aug 16, 23; m 47; c 3. *Educ:* Syracuse Univ, BA, 44, MA, 51, PhD, 55. *Prof Exp:* From asst prof to assoc prof physics, Col William & Mary, 51-56. *Concurrent Pos:* Consult, IBM, 60. *Res:* Science in general education; energy transfer. *Mailing Add:* 57 Hawthorn Rd Binghamton NY 13903

HART, ROBERT WARREN, THEORETICAL PHYSICS. *Current Pos:* RETIRED. *Personal Data:* b Yankton, SDak, Aug 17, 22; m 44, Maxine H Fisher; c Douglas. *Educ:* Univ Iowa, BS, 44, MS, 46; Univ Pittsburgh, PhD(physics), 49. *Prof Exp:* Instr physics, Cath Univ Am, 49-50; sr physicist, Appl Physics Lab, Johns Hopkins Univ, 50-54, group supvr, 54-75, chmn, Res Ctr, 72-83, asst dir explor develop, 78-83, mem prin staff, Appl Physics Lab, 55-89, asst dir res & explor develop, 83-89. *Concurrent Pos:* Assoc prof ophthal, Sch Med, Johns Hopkins Univ, 71-89. *Mem:* Am Phys Soc. *Res:* Scattering theory; medical physics; statistical mechanics. *Mailing Add:* 4205 SW 20th Ave Ocala FL 34474

HART, RONALD WILSON, NUTRITIONAL TOXICOLOGY. *Current Pos:* dir, 80-91, DISTINGUISHED SCIENTIST RESIDENCE, NAT CTR TOXICOL RES, 91- *Personal Data:* b Syracuse, NY, Mar 23, 42; m 74; c 2. *Educ:* Syracuse Univ, BS, 67; Univ Ill, MS, 69, PhD(physiol), 71. *Honors & Awards:* Karl-August-Forster Award, Germany, 80; FDA Award, 82, 85 & 86; Bose Medal, 94. *Prof Exp:* Prof radiol & dir chem & biomed environ res group, Ohio State Univ, 71-82, joint appointment biophys, pharmacol & pathobiol & dir div radiol res, 72-82. *Concurrent Pos:* Mem, Argonne Univ Assoc-Argonne Nat Labs Biomed Comt, 75, chmn, Argonne Univ Assoc-Biol Comt, 76-78; consult, Brookhaven Nat Lab, 75-78; mem bd toxicol & environ health, Nat Acad Sci, 76-83; chmn, Interagency Staff Group, Off Sci & Technol Policy, 83-85, Comt Coord Environ & Health Related Progs, Dept Health & Human Serv, 85-, Task Force Risk Assessment & Risk Mgt Toxic Substances, 85; chmn bd dirs, Ark Sci & Technol Authority, 83-84, mem, 85-; mem Res Bd Visitors, Memphis State Univ, 84-, Res Ctr Adv Comt, Fla A&M Univ, 85-; chmn, Agt Orange Working Group Sci Panel; vchmn, Exec Working Group Interagency Comt, Fed Lab Tech; distinguished prof, Guangzhou Med Col, 88, Moscow State, 88, Cario Univ, 89. *Mem:* Fel AAAS; fel Geront Soc; fel Am Col Toxicol (pres, 81); Sr Exec Asn (pres, 90); Soc Toxicol. *Res:* Determination of the mechanism by which dietary intake modulates the rate of occurance of endogenously and exogenously induced degenerative disease processes including cancer, heart disease, aging, etc. *Mailing Add:* Dir Nat Ctr Toxicol Res Jefferson AR 72079

HART, STANLEY ROBERT, GEOLOGY, GEOCHEMISTRY. *Current Pos:* SR SCIENTIST, WOODS HOLE OCEANOG INST, 89- *Personal Data:* b Swampscott, Mass, June 20, 35; m 80, Pamela Calouras; c Jolene, Elizabeth & Nathaniel. *Educ:* Mass Inst Technol, SB, 56, PhD(geol), 60; Calif Inst Technol, MS, 57. *Honors & Awards:* Goldschmidt Medal, Geochem Soc; H Hess Medal, Am Geophys Union, 97. *Prof Exp:* Fel geochem, Carnegie Inst Dept Terrestrial Magnetism, 60-61, staff mem geochem & geophys, 61-75; prof geol & geochem, Mass Inst Technol, 75-89. *Concurrent Pos:* Vis assoc prof earth sci, Univ Calif, San Diego, 66-67; assoc ed, Rev of Geophys, 70-72 & Geochimica et Cosmochimica Acta, 71-76; mem earth sci adv panel, NSF, 70-73; chmn 75-76 US Nat Comt Geochem, 73-76; mem, US Nat Comt for Int Geol Correls Prog, 74-76; mem ocean crust panel, Int Phase of Ocean Drilling, 74-76; assoc ed, Physics of Earth & Planetary Interiors, 75-; adv ed, Earth & Planetary Sci Letters, 78-87; Iselin chair, Woods Hole Oceanog Inst. *Mem:* Nat Acad Sci; fel Geol Soc Am; fel Am Geophys Union; fel Geochem Soc (vpres, 83-85, pres, 85-87); fel Europ Asn Geochem. *Res:* Applications of radioactive age determination to geologic problems; Sr, Nd and Pb isotope geochemistry of volcanic rocks; geochemical evolution of earth's mantle, and the oceanic lithosphere. *Mailing Add:* 53 Quonset Rd Falmouth MA 02540-1656. *Fax:* 508-457-2175; *E-Mail:* shart@whoi.edu

HART, TERRY JONATHAN, COMMUNICATIONS. *Current Pos:* PRES, LORAL SKYNET, 97- *Personal Data:* b Pittsburgh, Pa, Oct 27, 46; m 75, Wendy M Eberhardt; c Amy & Lori. *Educ:* Lehigh Univ, BS, 68; Mass Inst Technol, MS, 69; Rutgers Univ, MS, 78. *Hon Degrees:* DEng, Lehigh Univ, 88. *Prof Exp:* Mem tech staff, AT&T Bell Labs, 68-69 & Electronic Power Systs Lab, 73-78, supvr, 84-91, dir, Govt Data Systs Div, Sweden, 91, dir, Satellite Eng & Opers, 91-97; astronaut, Johnson Space Ctr, NASA, 78-84, captured solar maximum satellite, 84, div mgr, Telstar 4 Satellite Prog. *Mem:* Inst Elec & Electronics Engrs; Sigma Xi; Am Inst Aeronaut & Astronaut. *Res:* Patentee in field. *Mailing Add:* Loral Skynet 900 Rte 202/206 N Rm 2A118 Bedminster NJ 07921

HART, WILLIAM FORRIS, organic chemistry, for more information see previous edition

HART, WILLIAM JAMES, JR, FOOD SCIENCE. *Current Pos:* CONSULT, 87- *Personal Data:* b Holyoke, Mass, June 20, 23; m 45, 79; c 7. *Educ:* Univ Mass, BS, 44, MS, 47. *Prof Exp:* Dir res & qual control, Pan Am Foods, Inc, Tex, 47-48; assoc horticulturist, Va Polytech Inst, 48-49; chief food technologist, Dulany Foods, Inc, Md, 49-63, vpres, 63-67; vpres res, Ibec Foods Inc, NY, 67-71; dir res, Am Home Foods Inc, 71-73 vpres res & develop, 73-85, sr vpres technol, 85-87. *Mem:* AAAS; Am Chem Soc; Inst Food Technol; fel Am Inst Chem. *Res:* Fruits, vegetables, meats and seafoods as they apply to processed foods; water for processing foods and industrial waste disposal. *Mailing Add:* 2 Riverfield Dr Westport CT 06880

HARTBERG, WARREN KEITH, ENTOMOLOGY, GENETICS. *Current Pos:* CHMN DEPT BIOL & PROF BIOL, BAYLOR UNIV. *Personal Data:* b Watseka, Ill, Jan 24, 41; m 64, Rebecca Crosby; c Gretchen, Adam & Joanna. *Educ:* Wabash Col, AB, 63; Univ Notre Dame, MSc, 65, PhD(biol), 68. *Prof Exp:* Teaching asst, Univ Notre Dame, 63-66, res asst, 66-68; entomologist-geneticist, EAfrican Aedes Res Unit, WHO, 68-70; coordr inst arthopodology & parasitol, Ga Southern Col, 71-83, from asst prof to prof biol, 70-86. *Concurrent Pos:* Fac res fund grants, Ga Southern Col, 70-71 & 73-80; grant-in-aid, Sigma Xi, 71, NSF grant, 80-83; mem bd dirs, Biol Res Inst Am, Inc, 73-; mem bd dirs, Baylor Res Inst, 87-89, Tex Mosquito Control Asn, 91-; adv comt, Brazos Basin Tech, 91- *Mem:* Am Mosquito Control Asn; Sigma Xi; Soc Vector Ecologists. *Res:* Culicidae; genetics, cytogenetics, reproductive biology, behavior, physiology, evolution, bionomics and systematics; genetic control of insects; vector-borne diseases; vector genetics. *Mailing Add:* Dept Biol Baylor Univ PO Box 97388 Waco TX 76706-9989. *Fax:* 254-755-2969; *E-Mail:* keith_hartberg@baylor.edu

HARTE, JOHN, MATHEMATICS MODELING. *Current Pos:* PROF, ENERGY & RESOURCES GROUP, UNIV CALIF, BERKELEY. *Personal Data:* b July 8, 39; US citizen; m 84, Mary E Lindenfelser; c Julia, Alexis & David. *Educ:* Harvard Col, BA, 61; Univ Wis, PhD(physics), 65. *Prof Exp:* NSF fel physics, Europ Orgn Nuclear Res, Geneva, Switz, 65-66; AEC fel, Univ Calif, Berkeley, 66-68; asst prof, Yale Univ, 68-74. *Concurrent Pos:* Pew Scholar's Prize, conservation & environ; Guggenhein fel; mem, Calif Acad Sci; prin investr, Rocky Mountain Biol Lab; assoc ed, Annual Rev Energy & Environ, 92- *Mem:* Fel Am Phys Soc; Ecol Soc Am; Soc Conserv Biol; AAAS. *Res:* Ecological consequences of climate change; conservation biology and biodiversity; biogeochemistry. *Mailing Add:* Energy & Resources Group 310 Barrows Hall Univ Calif Berkeley CA 94720. *Fax:* 510-642-1085; *E-Mail:* jharte@violet.berkeley.edu

HARTE, KENNETH J, ELECTRON OPTICS, ULTRAVIOLET OPTICS. *Current Pos:* chief scientist, Lithography Prods Div, 84-85, CONSULT ELECTRON ION & PHOTON BEAM TECHNOL, VARIAN ASSOC, 85- *Personal Data:* b New York, NY, June 16, 35; m 56, 63; c 3. *Educ:* Rensselaer Polytech Inst, BS, 58; Harvard Univ, AM, 60, PhD(physics), 65. *Prof Exp:* Staff mem, Lincoln Lab, Mass Inst Technol, 62-69; founder & vpres, Micro-Bit Corp, 69-78, mgr theoret design dept, Micro-Bit Div Control Data

Corp, 78-84. *Mem:* Am Phys Soc; Inst Elec & Electronic Engrs; Int Soc Optical Eng; Am Optical Soc; Am Ornith Union. *Res:* Theoretical electron optics; development of electron beam accessed memory; design of electron-beam lithography systems; design of far-ultraviolet optical systems. *Mailing Add:* 64 Estabrook Rd Carlisle MA 01741

HARTENBERG, RICHARD S(CHEUNEMANN), MECHANICAL ENGINEERING, HISTORY OF TECHNOLOGY. *Current Pos:* from asst prof to prof, 41-75, EMER PROF MECH ENG, NORTHWESTERN UNIV, 75- *Personal Data:* b Chicago, Ill, Feb 27, 07; m 33, Elna Mygdal; c Richard M & Elna A. *Educ:* Univ Wis, BS, 28, MS, 33, PhD(eng mech), 41. *Honors & Awards:* Mechanisms Award, Am Soc Mech Engrs, 74; Centennial lectr, Am Soc Mech Engrs, 80. *Prof Exp:* Instr mech, Univ Wis, 30-41. *Concurrent Pos:* Ground sch instr, civilian pilot training prog, Univ Wis, 40-41; sr consult engr, Forest Prod Lab, US Dept Agr, 42-44; asst dir, Off Nat Defense Res & Develop, 43-45; staff engr & ed, Bur Aeronaut Proj, 45-50; tech rep, USAF, Wright Field, 45; vis prof, La State Univ, 76. *Mem:* Fel Am Soc Mech Engrs; Sigma Xi; Soc Hist Technol; fel Brit Inst Mech Engrs; Asn Ger Engrs. *Res:* Kinematics; machine design; history of technology. *Mailing Add:* 726 Laurel Ave Wilmette IL 60091

HARTER, DONALD HARRY, NEUROLOGY, VIROLOGY. *Current Pos:* SR SCI OFF, HOWARD HUGHES MED INST, 87-, DIR, NAT INST HEALTH RES SCHOLAR PROG, 89-; CLIN PROF NEUROL, SCH MED & HEALTH SCI, GEORGE WASHINGTON UNIV, 87- *Personal Data:* b Breslau, Ger, May 16, 33; US citizen; m 90, Marjorie Brandt; c Kathryne, Jennifer, Amy & David. *Educ:* Univ Pa, AB, 53; Columbia Univ, MD, 57. *Honors & Awards:* Joseph Mather Smith prize, Columbia Univ, 70. *Prof Exp:* Intern med, Grace-New Haven Community Hosp, 57-58; from asst resident to resident neurol, New York Neurol Inst, 58-61; guest investr, Rockefeller Univ, 63-66; from asst prof to prof neurol & microbiol, Col Physicians & Surgeons, Columbia Univ, 66-75; Charles L Mix prof, Med Sch, Northwestern Univ, 75-85, chmn dept, 75-87, Benjamin & Virginia T Boshes prof neurol, 85-87. *Concurrent Pos:* Mem nat comt venereal dis, Dept Health, Educ & Welfare, 70-72; Am Cancer Soc scholar, 73-74; Guggenheim fel, 73; vis fel, Clare Hall, Cambridge Univ, 73-74; vis sci officer, Howard Hughes Med Inst, 86-87; mem, Sci Rev Comt, Amyotrophic Lateral Sclerosis Asn, 87-91, chmn, 89-91, sr sci adv, 92-; mem, Bd Sci Coun, Nat Inst Dental Res, NIH, Dept Health & Human Serv, 90- *Mem:* Am Psychiat Asn; fel Infectious Dis Soc; Am Soc Virol; Am Soc Microbiol; Am Neurol Asn; fel Am Acad Neurol; Am Soc Clin Invest. *Res:* Viral infections of the nervous system; virus-cell interaction; motor neuron disease. *Mailing Add:* Howard Hughes Med Inst 1 Cloister Ct Bethesda MD 20814-1460

HARTER, GEORGE A, DEFENSE & AEROSPACE SYSTEMS. *Current Pos:* RETIRED. *Personal Data:* c 2. *Educ:* Purdue Univ, BS & MS; Ohio State Univ, MS. *Prof Exp:* Var tech, mgt & exec positions, TRW Inc, 57-85, vpres & asst gen mgr, Electronics & Defense Sector, 85. *Mem:* Nat Acad Eng; Sigma Xi; assoc fel Am Inst Aeronaut. *Mailing Add:* 38-654 Wisteria Dr Palm Desert CA 92211

HARTER, H(ARMAN) LEON, ORDER STATISTICS, STATISTICAL TABLES. *Current Pos:* RETIRED. *Personal Data:* b Keokuk, Iowa, Aug 15, 19; m 43, Alice L Madden. *Educ:* Carthage Col, AB, 40; Univ Ill, AM, 41; Purdue Univ, PhD(math statist), 49. *Prof Exp:* Asst math, Univ Ill, 41-43; prof physics, Mo Valley Col, 43-44; instr math, Purdue Univ, 46-48; asst prof, Mich State Col, 49-52; math statistician, Appl Math Res Lab, Aerospace Res Labs, Wright-Patterson AFB, 52-64, sr scientist math statist, 64-75, sr scientist math statist, Appl Math Group Air Force Flight Dynamics Lab, 75-76, mathematician, 76-78; res prof, Wright State Univ, 79-84; consult, 84-88. *Concurrent Pos:* Co-ed, Selected Tables, Inst Math Statist, 68-75; vis prof, Air Force Inst Technol, 82-84; chmn, Sect Phys & Eng Sci, Am Statist Asn, 64; writer, 84- *Mem:* Fel Am Statist Asn; fel Inst Math Statist; Int Statist Inst; Soc Indust & Appl Math. *Res:* Order statistics and their use in testing and estimation; computation and compilation of statistical tables; reliability and life testing; chronological annotated bibliography on order statistics. *Mailing Add:* 203 N McKinley Ave Champaign IL 61821-3251

HARTER, JAMES A(NDREW), ELECTRICAL ENGINEERING. *Current Pos:* RETIRED. *Personal Data:* b Bellefonte, Pa, Sept 13, 22; m 49, Ann Garner; c Barbara & Bob. *Educ:* Pa State Col, BS, 43. *Prof Exp:* Test engr, Gen Elec Co, NY, 43-44; elec engr, Tenn Eastman Corp, 44-47; health physicist, Health Physics Div, Oak Ridge Nat Lab, 47-56, eng leader, 56-72, develop specialist, Instrumentation & Controls Div, 72-85. *Mem:* Health Physics Soc; sr mem Inst Elec & Electronics Engrs. *Res:* Radiation instrument design and development; radiation physics; radiation dosimetry instrumentation; basic measurement science; nuclear medicine instrumentation. *Mailing Add:* 6004 Grove Park Rd Knoxville TN 37918

HARTER, ROBERT DUANE, SOIL CHEMISTRY. *Current Pos:* from asst prof to assoc prof, 69-83, PROF SOIL CHEM, UNIV NH, 83- *Personal Data:* b Muskegon, Mich, July 6, 36; m 69; c 3. *Educ:* Ohio State Univ, BS, 61, MS, 62; Purdue Univ, PhD(soil chem), 66. *Prof Exp:* Asst soil scientist, Conn Agr Exp Sta, 66-68; assoc res scientist clay surface chem, NY Univ, 68-69. *Concurrent Pos:* Vis prof, Pa State Univ, 76, Agr Univ, Netherlands, 83-84; chmn soil chem div, Soil Sci Soc Am, 82; assoc ed, Soil Sci Soc Am J, 88- *Mem:* Fel Soil Sci Soc Am; Am Soc Agron; Int Soc Soil Sci. *Res:* Clay surface chemistry and the kinetics and thermodynamics of heavy metal adsorption by soils and clays; soil inorganic chemistry, especially phosphorous interactions in soil; nutrient cycling in forest soils. *Mailing Add:* Dept Natural Resources James Hall Univ NH Durham NH 03824-4724

HARTER, WILLIAM GEORGE, QUANTUM ELECTRONICS. *Current Pos:* PROF PHYSICS, UNIV ARK, 84- *Personal Data:* b Lancaster, Pa, July 18, 43; m 74, Margot Williams; c Alexander, Thomas & Daniel. *Educ:* Hiram Col, BA, 64; Univ Calif, Irvine, PhD(physics), 67. *Prof Exp:* Asst prof physics, Univ Southern Calif, 69-74; assoc prof physics, Univ Estadual de Campinas, Brazil, 74-76; vis fel physics, Joint Inst Lab Astrophysics, Univ Colo, 76-78; from asst prof to assoc prof physics, Ga Inst Technol, 78-84. *Concurrent Pos:* Vpres, Earth-ings Corp, 80-; consult, Los Alamos Nat Lab, 81- *Mem:* Fel Am Phys Soc. *Res:* Group theory for symmetry analysis of laser spectroscopy; new methods for studying the dynamics of molecular rotations and vibrations; high resolution spectroscopy; computer graphics; spectroscopic properties of fullerenes; optimal control of atoms and molecules; computer simulations for teaching. *Mailing Add:* Dept Physics Univ Ark Fayetteville AR 72701. *E-Mail:* wharte@comp.uark.edu

HARTFIEL, DARALD JOSEPH, MATRIX THEORY. *Current Pos:* From asst prof to assoc prof, 69-81, PROF MATH, TEX A&M UNIV, 81- *Personal Data:* b Ray Point, Tex, Oct 10, 39; m 62, Faye Melton; c Andra & Simone. *Educ:* Southwest Tex State Univ, BS, 62; Univ Houston, MS, 66, PhD(math), 69. *Mem:* Am Math Soc; Soc Indust & Appl Math. *Res:* Mathematical systems with imprecise data. *Mailing Add:* Dept Math Tex A&M Univ College Station TX 77843. *Fax:* 409-845-6028; *E-Mail:* hartfiel@math.tamu.edu

HARTFORD, WINSLOW H, CHEMISTRY & TECHNOLOGY OF CHROMIUM, WOOD PRESERVATION. *Current Pos:* chmn dept, 72-76, assoc prof, 70-78, EMER PROF ENVIRON SCI, BELMONT ABBEY COL, 79- *Personal Data:* b Newton, Mass, June 1, 10; m 39, Mary Haviland; c Douglas B & Janet W (Clifford). *Educ:* Boston Univ, AB, 28; Mass Inst Technol, SB, 30, PhD(inorg chem), 33. *Honors & Awards:* Colley Mem Lectr, Am Wood Preservers Asn, 93. *Prof Exp:* Asst, Mass Inst Technol, 30-33; res assoc, Mutual Chem Co Am, Mass, 33-34, res chemist, Md, 34-45, res supvr, 45-54, res supvr, Mutual Chem Div, Allied Chem & Dye Corp, 55-57, res supvr, Solvay Process Div, Allied Chem Corp, 58-63, sr scientist, 63-66, sr scientist, Indust Chem Div, 66-69. *Concurrent Pos:* Gen consult, 69-; adj prof environ sci, Queens Col, 81-82. *Mem:* AAAS; Am Chem Soc; Am Inst Chemists; Int Res Group Wood Preserv; Sigma Xi; Int Soc Ecotoxicology. *Res:* Chemistry and technology of chromium and its compounds; inorganic wood preservatives; statistical evaluation of wood preservatives and treating methods; relation of thermodynamics to economics and environment; biochemical causes of acid rain; energy conservation; biospecificity of inorganic compounds; structural inorganic chemistry and biological activity. *Mailing Add:* 5800 Old Providence Rd Apt 3310 Charlotte NC 28226

HARTGERINK, RONALD LEE, CATALYSIS, PETROLEUM CHEMISTRY. *Current Pos:* res chemist, Exxon Res & Eng Co, 69-71, sr res chemist, 71-77, res assoc & sect head, 77-82, LAB DIR, EXXON RES & ENG CO, 82-; PRES, WYCKOFF CHEM CO. *Personal Data:* b Zeeland, Mich, Mar 21, 42; m 64; c 3. *Educ:* Hope Col, AB, 64; Univ Calif, Berkeley, PhD(chem), 68. *Prof Exp:* Lectr chem, Univ Calif, Berkeley, 68-69. *Mem:* Am Chem Soc. *Res:* Rates and mechanisms of organic and organometallic reactions; organic synthesis; petroleum chemistry; synthetic fuels. *Mailing Add:* c/o Wyckoff Chem Co 1421 Kalamazoo St South Haven MI 49090

HARTH, ERICH MARTIN, NEUROSCIENCES, MATHEMATICAL BIOPHYSICS. *Current Pos:* from asst prof to prof, 57-90, EMER PROF PHYSICS, SYRACUSE UNIV, 90- *Personal Data:* b Vienna, Austria, Nov 16, 19; nat US; m 51; c 2. *Educ:* Syracuse Univ, AB, 43, MS, 48, PhD(physics), 51. *Prof Exp:* Physicist, Nucleonics Div, Naval Res Lab, 51-54; res assoc, Duke Univ, 54-57. *Mem:* AAAS; Biophys Soc; Am Phys Soc; Biophys Soc; Soc Neurosci. *Res:* Elementary particles; bubble chambers; dynamics and information processing in neural systems; visual perception; neural mechanisms in higher brain functions, optimization processes. *Mailing Add:* 4451 Lafayette Rd Syracuse Univ Jamesville NY 13078

HARTIG, ELMER OTTO, PHYSICS. *Current Pos:* RETIRED. *Personal Data:* b Evansville, Ind, Jan 28, 23; m 49; c 4. *Educ:* Univ NH, BS, 46; Harvard Univ, MS, 47, PhD(appl physics), 50. *Prof Exp:* Group leader microwave & antennas, Goodyear Aerospace Corp, Ohio, 50-53, sect head, Radiation Systs, 54-55, asst mgr, Aerophys Dept, 55-63, mgr, Electronics Eng Div, 63-66, chief engr, Ariz Div, 66-76, vpres res & eng, 76-81, vpres opers, defense & energy, 81-85, vpres eng & res, 85-88. *Concurrent Pos:* Consult, Sci Adv Bd Guid & Control Panel, USAF, 64-78; mem, Ariz AEC, 70-75; mem, US Army Sci Bd, 80-; mem adv comt, Univ Akron, 82- *Mem:* Fel Inst Elec & Electronics Engrs; Am Inst Aeronaut & Astronaut; Sigma Xi; Aerospace Industs Asn Am. *Res:* Microwaves; antennas; radar systems; radomes; guidance systems; data processing. *Mailing Add:* 826 E Meadow Lane Phoenix AZ 85022

HARTIG, PAUL RICHARD, NEUROCHEMISTRY. *Current Pos:* ASST PROF BIOL, JOHNS HOPKINS UNIV, 79-; SR DIR, CENT NERV SYST DISEASES RES, DUPONT MERCK, 9+ *Personal Data:* b St Louis, Mo, Oct 19, 49. *Educ:* St Louis Univ, AB, 71; Univ Calif, Berkeley, PhD(biophys), 76. *Prof Exp:* Fel neurochem, Calif Inst Technol, 76-79. *Mem:* Soc Neurosci; Am Soc Biol Chemists; Am Soc Neurochem. *Res:* Molecular level characterization of serotonin. *Mailing Add:* Dupont Merck Res & Develop Exp Sta E-400-4352 PO Box 80400 Wilmington DE 19880-0400

HARTIGAN, JOHN A, MATHEMATICAL STATISTICS. *Current Pos:* assoc prof, 70-74, chmn dept, 74-80, PROF STATIST, YALE UNIV, 74- *Personal Data:* b Sydney, Austrailia, July 2, 37; m 59; c 3. *Educ:* Sydney Univ, BSc, 59, MSc, 60; Princeton Univ, PhD(math statist), 62. *Prof Exp:* Instr math, Princeton Univ, 62-63; vis lectr statist, Cambridge Univ, 63-64; asst prof, Princeton Univ, 64-66, statistician, 66-67, assoc prof statist & asst chmn dept, 67-70. *Mem:* Inst Math Statist; Royal Statist Soc. *Res:* Statistical inference, similarity principles, error analysis. *Mailing Add:* Dept Statist PO Box 208290 Yale Univ New Haven CT 06520-8290

HARTIGAN, MARTIN JOSEPH, ANALYTICAL CHEMISTRY. *Current Pos:* DIR, THERMO SEPARATION PROD. *Personal Data:* b Providence, RI, Apr 20, 43; m 66; c 2. *Educ:* Univ RI, BS, 66, PhD(chem), 71. *Prof Exp:* Sr res chemist anal chem, Ethyl Corp, 70-72; sr appl chemist gas chromatography, Perkin-Elmer Corp, Norwalk, 72-78; mkt mgr, Spectra-Physics Corp, San Jose 78- *Mem:* Am Chem Soc; Am Soc Testing & Mat. *Res:* High resolution glass capillary columns and specific detectors for gas chromatography; microprocessor based gas chromatographs. *Mailing Add:* Thermo Separation Prod PO Box 49031 San Jose CA 95161-9031

HARTILL, DONALD L, PHYSICS. *Current Pos:* asst prof, 68-74, assoc prof, 74-80, PROF PHYSICS, CORNELL UNIV, 80- *Personal Data:* b Chewelah, Wash, Mar 25, 39; m 66. *Educ:* Mass Inst Technol, BS, 61; Calif Inst Technol, PhD(physics), 67. *Prof Exp:* Res assoc physics, CERN, 67-68. *Concurrent Pos:* Alfred P Sloan Found res fel, 72-76. *Res:* Experimental high energy particle physics. *Mailing Add:* Dept Physics Cornell Univ Newman Lab Ithaca NY 14853

HARTKE, JEROME L, SOLID STATE PHYSICS. *Current Pos:* CONSULT, 83- *Personal Data:* b Wichita, Kans, Oct 26, 32; m 56; c 3. *Educ:* Kans State Univ, BS, 55, MS, 56; Univ Ill, PhD(solid state physics), 61. *Prof Exp:* Scientist photoconductor res, Xerox Corp, 61-67; group leader solid state physics, Ion Physics Corp, 67-68; mgr advan develop, KEV Electronics Corp, 68-71, gen mgr, Semiconductor Div, 71-72; pres, KSW Electronics Inc 72-75, pres, KSW Electronics Corp, 76-81; gen mgr, Semiconductor Div, Frequency Sources Inc, 81-82. *Res:* Semiconductor devices. *Mailing Add:* 119 Fairbank Rd Sudbury MA 01776

HARTKOPF, ARLEIGH VAN, POLYMER ANALYTICAL CHEMISTRY. *Current Pos:* sr res chemist, 76-80, ASSOC, MOBIL CHEM CO, 80- *Personal Data:* b Glendale, Calif, Apr 3, 42; m 68; c 3. *Educ:* Harvey Mudd Col, BS, 64; Northeastern Univ, MS, 68, PhD(anal chem), 70. *Prof Exp:* Asst prof chem, Weber State Col, 70-71 & Wayne State Univ, 71-74; staff scientist, Northeastern Univ, 74-76. *Concurrent Pos:* Petrol Res Fund grant, Weber State Col & Wayne State Univ, 70-73. *Mem:* Am Chem Soc; Sigma Xi. *Res:* Chromatography; spectroscopy; polymer analysis. *Mailing Add:* 21 Tanglewood Lane East Brunswick NJ 08816

HARTL, DANIEL L, POPULATION GENETICS. *Current Pos:* PROF, OFF EVOLUTION & BIOL, HARVARD UNIV, 93- *Personal Data:* b Marshfield, Wis, Jan 1, 43; m 64, 80; c 3. *Educ:* Univ Wis, BS, 65, PhD(genet), 68. *Prof Exp:* Trainee, Univ Calif, Berkeley, 68-69; from asst prof to assoc prof genetics, Univ Minn, St Paul, 69-74; from assoc prof to prof biol, Purdue Univ, Lafayette, Ind, 74-81; prof genetics, Sch Med, Washington Univ, St Louis, Mo, 81-93, dept head, 84-93. *Concurrent Pos:* NIH res career develop award, 75-79; assoc ed, BioSci, Am Inst Biol Sci, 75-78, Theoret Pop Biol, 76-80, Brazilian J Genetics, 77-82, Genetics, 80-88. *Mem:* Genetics Soc Am (pres, 89); Am Soc Study Evolution. *Res:* Genetics and population genetics; evolutionary biology. *Mailing Add:* Organismic & Evolutionary Biol Dept Harvard Univ 16 Divinity Ave Cambridge MA 02138

HARTLAGE, JAMES ALBERT, ORGANIC CHEMISTRY, INDUSTRIAL CHEMISTRY. *Current Pos:* dir res & develop, 77-80, VPRES TECHNOL, STEPAN CHEM CO, 80- *Personal Data:* b New Albany, Ind, Jan 22, 38; m 64; c 3. *Educ:* Bellarmine Col, BS, 59; Xavier Univ, MS, 61; Mich State Univ, PhD(org chem), 65. *Prof Exp:* Res chemist, ADM Chem Co, 65-69; sr res chemist, Ashland Chem Co, 69-71, mgr indust chem, 71-77. *Concurrent Pos:* Steering comt mem, Soap & Detergent Assoc, 78- *Mem:* Am Inst Mining, Metall & Petrol Engrs; Am Chem Soc. *Res:* Synthesis and application of anionic and cationic surfactants; a broad range of industrially useful surface active agents, especially amines and detergent sulfonates; materials having mildness and efficacy in personal case products. *Mailing Add:* 3926 Brittany Dr Northbrook IL 60062-2106

HARTLAGE, LAWRENCE CLIFTON, NEUROPSYCHOLOGY. *Current Pos:* MED ADV & VOC EXPERT, BUR HEARINGS & APPEALS, SSA, 73- *Personal Data:* b Portsmouth, Ohio, May 11, 34; m 67, Hughes; c 2. *Educ:* Ohio State Univ, BSc, 59; Univ Louisville, MA, 62, PhD(psychol), 68. *Honors & Awards:* Outstanding Contrib Award, Nat Acad Neuropsychologists, 81, 85 & Am Psychol Asn, 85; Inaugral Award Distinguished Contrib to Clin Pract in Child Neuropsychol, Am Bd Prof Neuropsychol, 84. *Prof Exp:* Prof neurol, Med Col Ga, 72-85; Marie Wilson Howell prof, Univ Ark, 85-86. *Concurrent Pos:* Consult, HEW, 71-, Vet Admin Hosp, 74-85, Eisenhower Army Med Ctr, 75, US Surgeon Gen, 73-80 & Agency Toxic Substances Dis Registry, US Dept Health & Human Servs, 93- *Mem:* Fel Nat Acad Neuropsychol (pres); Sigma Xi; fel Am Psychol Soc. *Res:* Human clinical neuropsychology; traumatic brain injury; neurotoxic substance effects on behavior. *Mailing Add:* 4227 Evans Lock Rd Evans GA 30809. *Fax:* 706-860-5363

HARTLE, JAMES BURKETT, PHYSICS. *Current Pos:* from asst prof to assoc prof, 66-72, PROF PHYSICS, UNIV CALIF, SANTA BARBARA, 72- *Personal Data:* b Baltimore, Md, Aug 20, 39; m 84. *Educ:* Princeton Univ, AB, 60; Calif Inst Technol, PhD(physics), 64. *Honors & Awards:* F A Matson Endowed Regents Lectr, Univ Tex, 97. *Prof Exp:* Mem, Inst Advan Study, 63-64; instr physics, Princeton Univ, 64-66. *Concurrent Pos:* Alfred P Sloan fel, 70-72; vis prof, Univ Chicago, 79, prof physics, 81-83; mem, Int Comt Gen Relativity & Gravitation, 86-95; Rothchild vis prof, Isaac Newton Inst Math Studies, 94; G C Stenard vis fel math, Gonville & Caius Col, Cambridge, 94; dir, Inst Theoret Physics, Univ Calif, Santa Barbara, 95-97. *Mem:* Nat Acad Sci; Am Astron Soc; fel Am Phys Soc; fel Am Acad Arts & Sci. *Res:* Relativity; astrophysics. *Mailing Add:* Dept Physics Univ Calif Santa Barbara CA 93106

HARTLE, RICHARD EASTHAM, EARTH SCIENCES, ASTROPHYSICS. *Current Pos:* Nat Acad Sci-Nat Res Coun resident res assoc, Ames Res Ctr, NASA, 64-67, head, Planetary Aeronomy Br, Goddard Space Flight Ctr, 76-85, RES SCIENTIST, LAB ATMOSPHERES, GODDARD SPACE FLIGHT CTR, NASA, 67-, ASST CHIEF, 85- *Personal Data:* b Royal Oak, Mich, May 17, 36; m 59; c 2. *Educ:* Univ Mich, Ann Arbor, BSE, 59; Pa State Univ, PhD(physics), 64. *Concurrent Pos:* Proj scientist, Earth Observing Syst, Goddard Space Flight Ctr, NASA, 83-87. *Mem:* Am Phys Soc; Am Geophys Union. *Res:* Electromagnetic theory; high pressure physics; solar wind; interaction of solar wind with planetary atmospheres; planetary ionospheres; atmospheric escape and evolution; plasma physics. *Mailing Add:* 11756 Morning Mist Lane Columbia MD 21044

HARTLEY, ARNOLD MANCHESTER, ANALYTICAL CHEMISTRY. *Current Pos:* RETIRED. *Personal Data:* b Cranston, RI, Oct 14, 26; m 61; c 3. *Educ:* Univ RI, BS, 51; Harvard Univ, AM, 53, PhD(anal chem), 55. *Prof Exp:* From instr to assoc prof anal chem, Univ Ill, Urbana, 55-78, dir environ res lab, 71-78; dir chem, Environ Qual Lab Inc, 78-89. *Mem:* Am Chem Soc. *Res:* Analytical chemistry; atomic spectrometry. *Mailing Add:* 411 Lebeth St Port Charlotte FL 33980-2203

HARTLEY, CHARLES LEROY, FLUID PHYSICS. *Current Pos:* ASST PROF PHYSICS, HARTWICK COL, 75- *Personal Data:* b Oregon City, Ore, Sept 9, 44; m 72. *Educ:* Portland State Col, BS, 66; Univ Colo, PhD(physics), 74. *Prof Exp:* Asst prof physics, Middlebury Col, 74-75. *Mem:* Am Asn Physics Teachers. *Res:* Critical point phenomena; dynamics of the bursting of gas bubbles at a liquid gas interface. *Mailing Add:* Dept Physics Hartwick Col Oneonta NY 13820

HARTLEY, CRAIG JAY, ULTRASONIC INSTRUMENTATION, IMPLANTABLE SENSORS. *Current Pos:* From instr to assoc prof, 73-86, PROF MED, DEPT MED, SECT CARDIOVASC SCI, BAYLOR COL MED, HOUSTON, 86- *Personal Data:* b Spokane, Wash, Apr 2, 44; m 68, Kathleen Tietsort; c Kevin, Eric & Ryan. *Educ:* Univ Wash, Seattle, BS, 66, PhD(elec eng), 70. *Honors & Awards:* Merit Award, NIH, 91; Laufman Prize, Asn Advan Med Instr, 93. *Prof Exp:* Postdoctoral bioeng, Rice Univ, Houston, 70-71, res engr, 71-73. *Concurrent Pos:* Adj asst prof, Elec Eng Dept, Rice Univ, Houston, 72-73; prin investr, NIH, 76-; adj prof elec & mech eng, Univ Houston, 81- *Mem:* Inst Elec & Electronics Engrs; Am Inst Ultrasound Med; Am Physiol Soc; Cardiovasc Syst Dynamics Soc; Am Heart Asn. *Res:* Design, development, and application of ultrasonic instrumentation and sensors for cardiovascular research especially intravascular and implantable devices; methods for measuring blood flow and dimensions in animals and in man. *Mailing Add:* Dept Med Sect Cardiovasc Sci Baylor Col Med Houston TX 77030. *Fax:* 713-796-0015

HARTLEY, CRAIG SHERIDAN, MECHANICAL BEHAVIOR METALS, DEFORMATION PROCESSING METALLIC MATERIALS. *Current Pos:* PROF & DEAN MECH ENG, FLA ATLANTIC UNIV, 90- *Personal Data:* b Quantico, Va, Dec 9, 37; m 58, Cornelia M McMann; c Margaret A, Katherine J & David B. *Educ:* Rensselaer Polytech Inst, BMetE, 58; Ohio State Univ, MS, 60, PhD(metall eng), 65; Univ Fla, MFA, 80. *Prof Exp:* Metallurgist, Nuclear Metals, Inc, Concord, Mass, 58-59; proj engr lieutenant, Mat Lab, USAF Ohio, 59-62, res phys metallurgist, 62-66; from asst prof to prof mat sci & eng, Univ Fla, 66-80; prof & chair mat sci & eng, State Univ NY, Stony Brook, NY, 80-82; assoc dean & prof mech eng, La State Univ & A&M Col, 82-87; prof & chair mat sci & eng, Univ Ala, Birmingham, 87-90; serving as prog dir, Mechs & Mats, NSF, Arlington, Va, 96-98. *Concurrent Pos:* Postdoctoral fel, NSF-Birmingham Univ, Eng, 65-66; acad visitor, UKAEA, AERE, Harwell, 69, 73 & 78 & Imp Col Sci & Technol, 72-73; Oak Ridge Assoc Univ fel, Savannah River Lab, 70; NSF fel, Lockheed Palo Alto Res Ctr, 75 & Westinghouse Res & Develop Ctr, 76; fac fel, Sandia Lab, 80; prog dir, NSF, 86-87; chair, E&PD Comt, Mining, Metall & Mat Soc, 90-92. *Mem:* Fel Am Soc Metals Int; Metall Soc; Soc Exp Mech; Am Soc Eng Educ; fel AAAS; Am Soc Mech Engrs. *Res:* Author or co-author of approximately 75 articles in technical journals in the areas of dislocation theory, materials processing, mechanical behavior of materials and diffusion in metals; co-edited 2 volumes of conference proceedings; experimental and theoretical investigations on defects in crystals, dislocations, mechanical behavior of solids, metal deformation processing; analytical and experimental studies of residual stresses in deformed metals and composites; dislocation theory. *Mailing Add:* 900 N Stafford St No 2131 Arlington VA 22203. *Fax:* 703-306-0291; *E-Mail:* chartley@nsf.gov

HARTLEY, DANNY L, COMBUSTION SCIENCE, ENERGY RESEARCH. *Current Pos:* staff mem res, Sandia Nat Lab, 68-72, supvr aero res, 72-76, mgr combustion res, 76-81, dir appl res, 81-86, VPRES ENERGY & ENVIRON PROG, SANDIA NAT LAB, 86- *Personal Data:* b North

Little Rock, Ark, Sept 10, 41; c 2. *Educ:* Ga Inst Technol, BS, 63, PhD(aeroeng), 67. *Prof Exp:* Assoc engr res, Lockheed Missile & Space Corp, 63-64; res & teaching fel, Von Karman Inst, 67-68. *Concurrent Pos:* Tech rep, US Combustion Group, Int Energy Agency, 77-; mem rev comt, Lawrence Livermore Nat Labs, 79-82, NASA, 81, Lawrence Berkeley Lab, 82, Agena Control Systs, 85 & US Dept Treas, 86; mem bd dirs, Combustion Inst, 82-; mem, Cont High Temperature Sci & Tech Res Coun, 83-85. *Mem:* Am Inst Aeronaut & Astronaut; Combustion Inst. *Res:* Fluid mechanics, gasdynamics, diagnostics, computational methods, combustion and energy systems; materials and applied physics. *Mailing Add:* 11113 Double Eagle NE Albuquerque NM 87111

HARTLEY, HAROLD V, JR, AUDIOLOGY, SPEECH PATHOLOGY. *Current Pos:* RETIRED. *Personal Data:* b Lenoxville, Pa, Feb 5, 31; m 56; c 3. *Educ:* Bloomsburg State Col, BS, 52; Pa State Univ, MEd, 58; Kent State Univ, PhD(audiol), 72. *Prof Exp:* Clinician speech & hearing, Mercer Co Crippled Children's Soc, 54-55 & Sharon Pub Sch, 55-62; audiologist, Pa State Univ, 62-63; chmn, Dept Speech & Hearing, Clarion Univ, 73-78, prof audiol, 63-90. *Concurrent Pos:* Clinician speech & hearing, Sharon Med Ctr, 55-60; consult, Sch Med, Univ PR, San Juan, 69; consult audiol, Polk State Sch & Hosp, 69-87, Lawrence Co Crippled Children's Soc, 69-71 & Easter Seal Soc, 74-75. *Mem:* Acoust Soc Am; Am Speech & Hearing Asn; Am Auditory Soc. *Res:* Physiological response to auditory signals. *Mailing Add:* RD 1 Box 60 Cranberry PA 16319

HARTLEY, JANET WILSON, VIROLOGY. *Current Pos:* from med bacteriologist to res med bacteriologist, Lab Infectious Dis, 53-63, microbiologist, 63-68, RES MICROBIOLOGIST, LAB VIRAL DIS, NAT INST ALLERGY & INFECTIOUS DIS, 68- *Personal Data:* b Washington, DC, Mar 25, 28. *Educ:* Univ Md, BS, 49; George Washington Univ, MS, 51, PhD(virol), 57. *Prof Exp:* Asst bacteriologist, Am Type Cult Collection, 52-53. *Concurrent Pos:* Mem, Virol & Cell Biol Comt, Am Cancer Soc, 72-76. *Mem:* Sigma Xi; AAAS. *Res:* Tumor virology, especially characterization of C-type murine RNA viruses, studies of their natural history, transmission, and role in disease. *Mailing Add:* 3513 Idaho Ave NW Washington DC 20016-3151

HARTLEY, MARSHALL WENDELL, ZOOLOGY, PHYSIOLOGY. *Current Pos:* instr anat & path, 59-62, from asst prof to assoc prof path, 62-72, PROF PATH, MED CTR, UNIV ALA, BIRMINGHAM, 72- *Personal Data:* b Madison, Wis, Sept 16, 25; m 48; c 4. *Educ:* Univ Wis, BS, 50, MS, 54, PhD(zool), 59. *Prof Exp:* Asst zool, Univ Wis, 52-56, sr asst, 56-57, instr med physiol, 57-59. *Mem:* AAAS; Electron Micros Soc Am; Am Soc Cell Biol; AMA; NY Acad Sci; Sigma Xi. *Res:* Functional ultrastructural relationships; pathogenesis of renal diseases; pituitary cytology. *Mailing Add:* Dept Path Univ Ala Birmingham UAB Sta Birmingham AL 35294-0007

HARTLEY, ROBERT WILLIAM, PROTEIN CHEMISTRY. *Current Pos:* physicist, Nat Cancer Inst, 59-69, PHYSICIST, NAT INST ARTHRITIS & METAB DIS, 69- *Personal Data:* b Memphis, Tenn, Apr 9, 27; m 56, Dorothy White; c Ralph, Henry, George & Albert. *Educ:* Yale Univ, BS, 49; Mass Inst Technol, PhD(biophys), 58. *Prof Exp:* Res assoc biol, Mass Inst Technol, 58-59. *Concurrent Pos:* Wellcome fel, Med Res Coun Lab Molecular Biol, Cambridge Univ, 71-72. *Mem:* Am Chem Soc; Sigma Xi; Am Soc Biochem & Molecular Biol; Protein Soc. *Res:* Experimental approaches to the protein folding problem and to protein-protein recognition using the family of microbial ribonucleases and their inhibitors as models. *Mailing Add:* NIDDK NIH Bethesda MD 20892-0001. *Fax:* 301-496-5239; *E-Mail:* hartley@helix.nih.gov

HARTLINE, BEVERLY KARPLUS, TECHNICAL MANAGEMENT, PRECOLLEGE SCIENCE & MATH EDUCATION. *Current Pos:* sci asst to dir, 85-87, asst dir info & anal, 87-89, ASSOC DIR & PROJ MGR, THOMAS JEFFERSON NAT ACCELERATOR FACIL, 89- *Personal Data:* b Princeton, NJ, June 13, 50; m 72, Fred Hartline; c Jason & Jeff. *Educ:* Reed Col, BA, 71; Univ Wash, PhD(geophys), 78. *Prof Exp:* Vis asst prof geophys, Hampshire Col, 77-78; sci writer, Sci Mag, 78-80; phys scientist, Goddard Space Flight Ctr, NASA, 80-82; sr tech writer, Lawrence Berkeley Lab, 83, sci asst planning & develop, 83-85. *Concurrent Pos:* Mem, Comt Status Women Physics, Am Phys Soc, 93-95, Forum on Educ, 95-98, chair, 98; asst dir, Phys Sci & Eng Office Sci & Technol Policy, 96- *Mem:* AAAS; Am Phys Soc; Nat Sci Teachers Asn; Am Asn Physics Teachers; Am Women Sci; Am Geophys Union. *Res:* Project management of major scientific user facility; precollege science and math education; national science policy. *Mailing Add:* Thomas Jefferson Nat Accelerator Facil 12000 Jefferson Ave Newport News VA 23606. *E-Mail:* hartline@jlab.org

HARTLINE, DANIEL KEFFER, NEUROPHYSIOLOGY, BIOPHYSICS. *Current Pos:* ASSOC RESEARCHER, UNIV HAWAII, MANOA, 78- *Personal Data:* b Philadelphia, Pa, Dec 1, 39. *Educ:* Swarthmore Col, BA, 61; Harvard Univ, MA, 66, PhD(biol), 67. *Prof Exp:* NIH fel, Stanford Univ, 68-70; asst prof biol, Univ Calif, San Diego, 70-78. *Concurrent Pos:* NIH-NSF res grants, Univ Calif, San Diego, 71- *Mem:* AAAS; Soc Neurosci. *Res:* Quantitative analysis and modeling of integration in simple nerve nets, especially crustacean cardiac and stomatogastric ganglia; computer techniques in neuroscience. *Mailing Add:* Dept Zool Univ Hawaii Manoa Honolulu HI 96822-2270

HARTLINE, PETER HALDAN, NEUROPHYSIOLOGY, ANIMAL BEHAVIOR. *Current Pos:* CHIEF SCIENTIST, NOVA SCI, BEVERLY, MASS, 91-, PRES, MILLENNIUM INFO TECHNOL INC, 94- *Personal Data:* b Philadelphia, Pa, Jan 26, 42; m; c 2. *Educ:* Swarthmore Col, BA, 64; Harvard Univ, MA, 66; Univ Calif, San Diego, PhD(neurosci), 69. *Prof Exp:* Asst res neuroscientist, Univ Calif, San Diego, 69-74; asst prof physiol, Univ Ill, Urbana, 74-77; assoc scientist, Charles Schepens, Eye Res Inst, Boston, 77-85, sr scientist, 85-91. *Concurrent Pos:* Consult, Commun Res Mach, Inc, 71-72; NIH fel, Univ Calif, San Diego, 71-74; grants, NIH & NSF, 74-89; mem, Sensory Physiol & Perception Adv Panel, NSF, 83-85. *Mem:* Sigma Xi. *Res:* Information processing by neurons in sensory systems of vertebrates and invertebrates; control of animal behavior by the nervous system; cephalopods vision; infrared and visual senses in rattlesnakes; especially auditory visual integration in cats; automated control of experiments; expert systems application to experiment control and clinical testing. *Mailing Add:* 160 Woodland Meade Hamilton MA 01982

HARTLINE, RICHARD, BIOCHEMISTRY, ORGANIC CHEMISTRY. *Current Pos:* ASST PROF BIOCHEM, IND UNIV, PA, 67- *Personal Data:* b Reading, Pa, July 21, 32; m. *Educ:* Kutztown State Col, BS, 58; Univ Ariz, MS, 61; Univ Calif, PhD(biochem), 66. *Prof Exp:* Fel biochem, Univ Ill, 66-67. *Mem:* Am Chem Soc; Am Soc Microbiol; Fedn Am Soc Exp Biol; Am Soc Biol Chem. *Res:* Microbial metabolism and metabolic control; bacterial transport. *Mailing Add:* Dept Chem Ind Univ Pa Indiana PA 15705-0001

HARTMAN, ARTHUR DALTON, PHARMACOLOGY, CLINICAL SCIENCE. *Current Pos:* VPRES, NEW DRUG SERVS, 93- *Personal Data:* b Mar 22, 41; m 64, Pamela Shaffer; c Thomas A. *Educ:* Univ Tenn, PhD(physiol), 68. *Prof Exp:* Prof physiol, La State Univ Med Sch, 85-87; med res dir, Controlled Therapeut Corp, 88-91; dir med affairs, Valley Pharmaceut, 91-92. *Mem:* Am Physiol Soc; Am Med Writers Asn; NY Acad Sci; AAAS. *Res:* Metabolism. *Mailing Add:* New Drug Servs Longwood Corp Ctr S 415 McFarlan Rd Suite 201 Kennett Square PA 19348

HARTMAN, BOYD KENT, PSYCHIATRY, NEUROCHEMISTRY. *Current Pos:* PROF CELL BIOL & NEUROANAT, DONALD W HASTING PROF & DIR NEUROSCI PSYCHOL, UNIV MINN, 87- *Personal Data:* b Oct 21, 39; US citizen; m 60; c 2. *Educ:* Univ Kans, AB, 62, MD, 66. *Honors & Awards:* Shernd-Stanford Award, Am Soc Clin Path, 66; A E Bennett Award, Soc Biol Psychiat, 71. *Prof Exp:* Intern path, Sch Med, Wash Univ, 66-67, res psychologist, 69-72, from asst prof to prof psychol, 72-87, from assoc prof to prof neurobiol, 75-87. *Concurrent Pos:* USPHS res assoc pharmacol & toxicol, Lab Clin Biochem, Nat Heart Inst, 67-69. *Mem:* Am Psychiat Asn; Soc Neurosci; Am Soc Neurochem; Am Soc Biol Chemists; Am Soc Pharmacol & Exp Therapeut; Int Soc Cerebral Blood Flow & Metab. *Res:* Enzymes regulating catecholamine synthesis and degradation using biochemical and immunochemical methods. *Mailing Add:* Dept Psychiat Univ Minn Mayo 420 Delaware St SE PO Box 392 Minneapolis MN 55455-0392. *Fax:* 612-624-8935

HARTMAN, CHARLES WILLIAM, plasma physics, controlled fusion research, for more information see previous edition

HARTMAN, DAVID ROBERT, CHEMICAL EDUCATION, ENZYMOLOGY. *Current Pos:* From asst prof to assoc prof, 66-90, PROF CHEM, WESTERN KY UNIV, 90- *Personal Data:* b Streator, Ill, Sept 17, 40; m 62, Sandra Ann Davis; c Timothy J & Stephen V. *Educ:* NCent Col, Ill, BS, 62; Va Polytech Inst, MS, 64, PhD(biochem), 67. *Concurrent Pos:* Teacher chem, Health Careers Opportunity Prog, Univ Ky, 84-85. *Mem:* Am Chem Soc; Sigma Xi. *Res:* Economical electrophoresis apparatus-design and construction; studies on the esterase activity of the greater wax moth larvae. *Mailing Add:* Dept Chem Western Ky Univ Bowling Green KY 42101

HARTMAN, EMILY LOU, BOTANY. *Current Pos:* RETIRED. *Personal Data:* b Kansas City, Mo, Dec 19, 30. *Educ:* Univ Kans, BA, 53, MA, 55, PhD(bot), 57. *Prof Exp:* Instr biol sci, Calif State Polytech Col, 57-58; asst prof biol, Kans State Teachers Col, 58-61 & Southwest Mo State Col, 61-67; from asst prof to assoc prof, Univ Colo, Denver, 67-71, prof biol, 71- *Mem:* Am Bryol & Lichenolog Soc; Am Soc Plant Taxonomists; Nat Asn Biol Teachers. *Res:* Alpine tundra floristics. *Mailing Add:* 119 Meadow Brook Ct Paonia CO 81428

HARTMAN, FRANCIS THOMAS, MANAGEMENT OF TECHNOLOGY & TECHNOLOGICAL CHANGE, PROJECT MANAGEMENT. *Current Pos:* PROF PROJ MGT, UNIV CALGARY, 91- *Personal Data:* b Moshi, Tanzania, May 1, 50; Can & Brit citizen; m 74, Margaret Marshall; c Tamsin, Richard, Christopher & Kirsten. *Educ:* Brighton Univ, UK, BSc, 72, Loughborough Univ Technol, UK, MSc, 80, PhD(construct mgt), 93. *Prof Exp:* Engr, Sir William Halcrow & Partners, UK, 72-79; prof mgr, Wright Engrs Ltd, 80-81; mgr proj serv, 81-83; vpres proj mgt, Tectonic Controls Inc, San Jose, Calif, 84-85; dir & gen mgr, PM3-Inducon, Toronto, Ont, 85-87; vpres & gen mgr, Vanbots Construct Corp, Toronto, Ont, 88-91. *Concurrent Pos:* Adj prof proj mgt, Univ BC, 82-85, Univ Toronto, 86-92, fac mgt, Univ Calgary, 95- *Mem:* Can Soc Mgt Technol; Inst Mgt UK; fel Can Soc Eng Mgt; fel Eng Inst Can; Inst Civil Engrs UK. *Res:* Improved effectiveness of project management; project risk; faster time to market for new products; virtual teams; alliances, partnering and contract incentives. *Mailing Add:* Proj Mgt Rm R262 Eng Fac 2500 University Dr NW Calgary AB T2N 1N4 Can. *Fax:* 403-282-7026, 239-0207; *E-Mail:* fhartman@acs.ucalgary.ca

HARTMAN, FRED OSCAR, POMOLOGY. *Current Pos:* Asst, Ohio State Univ, 40-42, 46-48, instr, 48-51, secy plant inst, 50-53, from asst prof to assoc prof, 51-62, prof, 62-83, EMER PROF HORT & FORESTRY, 83- *Personal Data:* b Toledo, Ohio, Oct 20, 15; m 43, 59, Joan G Hartman; c Sharon M (Bartkus). *Educ:* Univ Toledo, BS, 37; Ohio State Univ, MSc, 41, PhD(hort), 51. *Concurrent Pos:* Partic fruit prod study, Mex, 68. *Mem:* Am Soc Hort Sci. *Res:* Fruit setting; anatomy and morphology; propagation; rootstocks. *Mailing Add:* Dept Hort Ohio State Univ 2001 Fyffe Ct Columbus OH 43210-1096

HARTMAN, FREDERICK COOPER, BIOCHEMISTRY, PROTEIN CHEMISTRY. *Current Pos:* sect head, Molecular & Cellular Sci, 80-88, SR RES BIOCHEMIST, OAK RIDGE NAT LAB, 66-, DIR, BIOL DIV, 88- *Personal Data:* b Memphis, Tenn, Aug 17, 39; m 61, Patricia Ballard; c Suzanne & Sheila. *Educ:* Memphis State Univ, BS, 60; Univ Tenn, Memphis, PhD(biochem), 64. *Honors & Awards:* Pfizer Award Enzyme Chem, 79. *Prof Exp:* NIH fel, Univ Ill, 64-66. *Mem:* AAAS; Am Soc Biol Chem; Protein Soc; Am Chem Soc; Sigma Xi. *Res:* Chemical modification of proteins as method of correlating structure and function; design and use of active-site specific reagents; site-directed mutagenesis. *Mailing Add:* 103 Dansworth Lane PO Box 2009 Oak Ridge TN 37831. *Fax:* 423-574-9297

HARTMAN, HERMAN BERNARD, COMPARATIVE PHYSIOLOGY. *Current Pos:* CHMN & PROF, DEPT BIOL SCI, DUQUESNE UNIV, 89- *Personal Data:* b Baltimore, Md, Jan 1, 34; m 57, 72, Makiko Suda; c Lica & Naomi. *Educ:* Univ Md, BS, 60; Am Univ, MS, 62; Univ Conn, PhD(physiol), 65. *Prof Exp:* Asst physiol, Am Univ, 60-62 & Univ Conn, 62-64; fel, Inst Cellular Biol, Univ Conn, 64-65; fel entom, US Army Natick Labs, 65-67; asst prof zool, Univ Iowa, 67-72; asst prof biol, Univ Maine, 73-75; assoc prof, Tex Tech Univ, 75-86, prof biol, 87-89. *Concurrent Pos:* Mem, Corp Marine Biol Lab, Woodshole, Mass; vis scientist, Ore Inst Marine Biol, 73-75 & 84- & Friday Harbor Labs, 96. *Mem:* AAAS; Am Soc Zool; Sigma Xi; Soc Neurosci; Crustacean Soc. *Res:* Stridulation by cockroaches; physiology of arthropod movement, position, and tension receptors; neurophysiology of simple behaviors; equilibrium reception insects; regeneration of limbs. *Mailing Add:* Dept Biol Sci Duquesne Univ Pittsburgh PA 15282. *Fax:* 412-396-5907; *E-Mail:* hartman@duq3.cc.duq.edu

HARTMAN, HOWARD L(EVI), MINING ENGINEERING. *Current Pos:* CONSULT MINING ENG, 89- *Personal Data:* b Indianapolis, Ind, Aug 7, 24; m 47; c 2. *Educ:* Pa State Univ, BS, 46, MS, 47; Univ Minn, PhD(mining eng), 53. *Honors & Awards:* 57th Warren Lectr, Univ Minn, 65; Mineral Industs Educ Award, Am Inst Mining, Metall & Petrol Engrs, 65; Pub Bd Award, Soc Mining, Metall & Explor, 82, Jackling Award, 90, Eavanson Award, 93. *Prof Exp:* Instr mining eng, Pa State Col, 47-48; jr mining engr, Phelps Dodge Corp, Ariz, 48-49; state mine dust engr, Ariz State Mine Inspectors Off, 49-50; instr mining eng, Univ Minn, 50-54; from asst prof to assoc prof, Colo Sch Mines, 54-57; prof mining & head dept, Pa State Univ, 57-63, from assoc dean to actg dean eng, 63-67; dean eng, Sacramento State Col, 67-71, Vanderbilt Univ, 71-80; prof, Univ Ala, 80-89. *Concurrent Pos:* Consult, Minn Tax Comn, 51-54, US Dept Justice, 54-57, Colo State Hwy Dept, 55, Am Peoples Encycl, 58, US Steel Corp, 60, Stand Oil Co NJ, 60-65, H E Fletcher Co, 61-65, Ingersoll-Rand Co, 63-66, Martin Co, 66-67 & Aerojet-Gen Corp, 69-70; chmn, Fed Mine & Nonmetallic Mine Safety Bd Rev, 71-75; mem, US Nat Comt Tunneling Technol, 74-77, Bechtel Corp, 82-84, NRiver Energy Co, 86-88. *Mem:* Nat Acad Eng; Am Soc Eng Educ; Am Inst Mining, Metall & Petrol Engrs; Soc Mining Mettal & Explor. *Res:* Mine dust control, ventilation, environmental control; rock drilling, mechanics; rapid excavation; engineering education. *Mailing Add:* 4052 Alex Lane Carmichael CA 95608

HARTMAN, ICLAL SIREL, BIOCHEMISTRY. *Current Pos:* from instr to assoc prof, 59-74, PROF CHEM, SIMMONS COL, 74-, CHAIR CHEM DEPT, 85- *Personal Data:* b Elazig, Turkey, Dec 22, 30; US citizen; m 57; c 2. *Educ:* Mt Holyoke Col, AB, 50, MA, 51; Univ Fla, PhD(biochem), 63. *Prof Exp:* Head qual control chem anal, E R Squibb & Sons, 51-55; instr chem, Regis Col, Mass, 57-58 & Wellesley Col, 58-59. *Mem:* Am Chem Soc. *Res:* Steroids, gas chromatographic analysis; biochemical basis of folk medicine. *Mailing Add:* Dept Chem Simmons Col 300 Fenway Boston MA 02115-5898

HARTMAN, JAMES AUSTIN, GEOLOGY. *Current Pos:* INDEPENDENT GEOLOGIST, 86- *Personal Data:* b Lanark, Ill, Jan 29, 28; m 51, Zoe Wiley; c Victoria & Lester. *Educ:* Beloit Col, BS, 51; Univ Wis, MS, 55, PhD(geol), 57. *Honors & Awards:* Distinguished Serv Award, Am Asn Petrol Geologists, 85. *Prof Exp:* Resident geologist, Reynolds Jamaica Mines, Ltd, 51-53; geologist, Union Carbide Ore Co, 56-57; exploitation engr, Shell Oil Co, 57-64, sr prod geologist, 64-65 & Shell Develop Co, 65-66, staff prod geologist, 66-68, div exploitation engr, 68-70, regional geol engr southern region, 70-76, sr staff geol engr, 71-80, geol engr adv, 80-81, geol engr consult, 81-86, field studies task force leader, 76-86. *Mem:* Sigma Xi; hon mem Am Asn Petrol Geologists (secy, 81-83); Soc Petrol Engrs; fel Geol Soc Am; Am Inst Prof Geologists; Soc Independent Prof Earth Scientists. *Res:* Origin of Jamaican bauxite; titanium mineralogy of bauxites; salt dome research; Gulf Coast oil and gas fields. *Mailing Add:* 4512 Newlands St Metairie LA 70006-4318

HARTMAN, JAMES KEITH, electromagnetism, modeling & simulation; deceased, see previous edition for last biography

HARTMAN, JAMES XAVIER, MICROBIOLOGY, PHYTOPATHOLOGY. *Current Pos:* From asst prof to assoc prof, 71-80, PROF MICROBIOL, FLA ATLANTIC UNIV, 80- *Personal Data:* b Chicago, Ill, Sept 28, 42; m 66; c 2. *Educ:* Aquinas Col, BS, 64; Mich State Univ, MS, 67, PhD(phytopath), 71. *Mem:* Am Phytopath Soc. *Res:* Plant viruses-infection of plant tissue culture cells and protoplasts. *Mailing Add:* 424 NE 28th Rd Boca Raton FL 33431

HARTMAN, JOHN ALAN, ORGANIC CHEMISTRY. *Current Pos:* RETIRED. *Personal Data:* b Toledo, Ohio, Feb 4, 20; m 44. *Educ:* Univ Toledo, BS, 46; Wayne State Univ, MS, 55, PhD(org chem), 63. *Prof Exp:* Sr technician, Henry Ford Hosp, Detroit, Mich, 46-48; res asst org chem, Detroit Inst Cancer Res, 49-56; sr chemist, Grass Lakes Platers, Mich, 56-57; res chemist, Metal & Thermit Corp, Mich, 57-60; asst org chem, Wayne State Univ, 60-61; asst prof, Wheeling Col, 63-67; from assoc prof to prof org chem, Mansfield State Col, 67-84, chmn dept, 72-77. *Concurrent Pos:* NSF res fel, 65-67. *Mem:* Am Chem Soc; Sigma Xi. *Res:* Synthesis of terpenoid natural products; electro organic chemistry. *Mailing Add:* 806 William Penn Ct Pittsburgh PA 15221

HARTMAN, JOHN DAVID, NEUROPATHOLOGY, CARDIOVASCULAR PATHOLOGY. *Current Pos:* Attend pathologist, 67-81, SR ATTEND PATHOLOGIST, ALBERT EINSTEIN MED CTR, 81- *Personal Data:* b Peninsula, Ohio, 1922; m 44, Mary E Tharp; c Augustine, Stephen & Daniel. *Educ:* Case Western Res Univ, MD, 46. *Concurrent Pos:* Qual assurance coordr, Dept Lab & Clin Med, Albert Einstein Med Ctr, 90. *Mem:* Am Asn Path; Am Heart Asn. *Res:* Role of smooth muscle cells in cardiovascular pathology. *Mailing Add:* Dept Path Albert Einstein Med Ctr Northern Div Philadelphia PA 19141

HARTMAN, JOHN H, COMPUTER HARDWARE SYSTEMS. *Current Pos:* ASST PROF COMPUT SCI, UNIV ARIZ, 94- *Educ:* Brown Univ, ScB, 87; Univ Calif, Berkeley, MS, 90, PhD (comput sci), 94. *Concurrent Pos:* Intern, Microsoft Corp, 87 & 88; co-prin investr, Intel Corp, 95-96; fac assoc, Advan Res Proj Agency, 95-, co-prin investr, 96-; contrib investr, NSF, 95-, prin investr, 96-; prin investr, AT&T Found, 95-96. *Mem:* Asn Comput Mach; Inst Elec & Electronics Engrs. *Res:* Distributed systems; file systems; operating systems; computer networks; computer architecture. *Mailing Add:* Dept Comput Sci Univ Ariz Tucson AZ 85721

HARTMAN, JOHN L(OUIS), FLUID MECHANICS, HEAT TRANSFER. *Current Pos:* syst planning engr, Allison Div, Gen Motors Corp, 59, asst nuclear eng, 60-63, chief, Advan Power Systs, 63-67, head, Elec Power Plants Dept, Res Labs, 67-69, head, Electrochem Dept, 69-85, FACIL MGR, RES LABS, GEN MOTORS CORP, 85- *Personal Data:* b Elgin, Ill, Aug 7, 30; m 57; c 4. *Educ:* Purdue Univ, BS, 52, MS, 53, PhD, 56. *Prof Exp:* Sr engr, Aircraft Nuclear Propulsion Dept, Gen Elec Co, 55-57; mem tech staff rocket propulsion, Ramo-Wooldridge Corp, 57-58; staff mem nuclear propulsion, Los Alamos Sci Lab, 58-59. *Mem:* Am Mgt Asn; Am Inst Plant Engrs; Int Facil Mgt Asn. *Res:* Energy conversion research and development of power propulsion systems; specific emphasis directed upon advanced electrochemical energy conversion for future vehicular applications. *Mailing Add:* 688 Balfour Rd Grosse Pointe MI 48230

HARTMAN, JOHN PAUL, ENGINEERING EDUCATION, ENGINEERING HISTORY. *Current Pos:* from asst prof to assoc prof, 68-76, asst dean eng, 78-89, PROF ENG, UNIV CENT FLA, 76- *Personal Data:* b Glasgow, Mont, Aug 15, 36; m 61; c 2. *Educ:* Principia Col, BS, 57; Washington Univ, St Louis, BSCE, 59; Harvard Univ, SM, 60; Univ Fla, PhD(civil eng), 74. *Honors & Awards:* Western Elec Fund Award, Am Soc Eng Educ, 81. *Prof Exp:* Instr heat transfer, US Naval Nuclear Power Sch, 61-65; soils engr civil eng, Ardaman & Assocs, 65; sr engr nuclear effects, Martin-Marietta Co, 65-68. *Concurrent Pos:* NSF res grant, 75-77; bd dir, Am Soc Eng Educ, 81-83, vpres Prof Interest Couns, 82-83; Nat Hist & Heritage Comt, Am Soc Mech Engrs, 76- *Mem:* Fel Am Soc Civil Engrs; fel Am Soc Mech Engrs; Nat Soc Prof Engrs; Soc Hist Technol; Am Soc Eng Educ; Soc Indust Archeol. *Res:* Engineering and industrial history; impact of engineering and technology on society; geotechnical engineering. *Mailing Add:* Col Eng Univ Cent Fla Orlando FL 32816-2456

HARTMAN, JOHN STEPHEN, NUCLEAR MAGNETIC RESONANCE SPECTROSCOPY. *Current Pos:* from asst prof to assoc prof, 68-81, dept chmn, 85-88, PROF INORG CHEM, BROCK UNIV, 81- *Personal Data:* b Toronto, Ont, July 18, 38; m, Sandra E; c 2. *Educ:* Queen's Univ, Ont, BSc, 61; Univ Ottawa, MSc, 63; McMaster Univ, PhD(inorg chem), 67. *Prof Exp:* Nat Res Coun fel, Phys Chem Lab, Oxford Univ, 67-68. *Concurrent Pos:* Adj prof, Dept Chem, McMaster Univ. *Mem:* Am Chem Soc; Chem Inst Can; Mat Res Soc. *Res:* High-resolution solid-state nuclear magnetic resonance spectroscopy with magic angle spinning, applied to inorganic solids and minerals; nuclear magnetic resonance spectroscopy applied to coordination chemistry. *Mailing Add:* Dept Chem Brock Univ St Catharines ON L2S 3A1 Can. *Fax:* 905-682-9020; *E-Mail:* shartman@chemiris.labs.brocku.ca

HARTMAN, KARL AUGUST, PHYSICAL BIOCHEMISTRY. *Current Pos:* from asst prof to assoc prof, 70-76, PROF BIOCHEM, UNIV RI, 76- *Personal Data:* b Wilmington, Del, Nov 30, 35; m 61; c 3. *Educ:* Lehigh Univ, BS, 58; Mass Inst Technol, PhD(phys chem), 62. *Prof Exp:* Res assoc chem, Mass Inst Technol, 62-63; res chemist, E I du Pont de Nemours & Co, Inc, Del, 63-67. *Mem:* Am Chem Soc; Biophys Soc; Am Asn Univ Professors. *Res:* Structure, stability and interaction of nucleic acids, proteins and viruses; infrared and Raman spectroscopy. *Mailing Add:* 131 Cherry Rd Kingston RI 02881

HARTMAN, KENNETH EUGENE, ORGANIC CHEMISTRY, MEDICINAL CHEMISTRY. *Current Pos:* From instr to asst prof, 68-74, assoc prof, 74-79, PROF CHEM, GENEVA COL, 80- *Personal Data:* b Johnstown, Pa, Dec 6, 42; m 67. *Educ:* Geneva Col, BS, 63; Univ Pa, PhD(chem), 69. *Mem:* Am Chem Soc. *Res:* Synthesis of isoquinoline antimalarials; group shift effects in nuclear magnetic resonance spectrometry; aromatic substitution patterns by infrared spectroscopy; reactions of quinuclidine and triethylenediammine. *Mailing Add:* 2401 Clayton Rd Beaver Falls PA 15010

HARTMAN, KENNETH OWEN, PHYSICAL CHEMISTRY. *Current Pos:* sr res chemist, Technol Mkt, 67-73, supvr, 73-78, supt, 78-84, sr scientist, 85-88, mgr, 88-90, TECH DIR, TECHNOL MKT, 91- *Personal Data:* b Philadelphia, Pa, Oct 20, 39; m 65; c 2. *Educ:* Lehigh Univ, BS, 61; Pa State Univ, PhD(chem), 65. *Prof Exp:* Fel chem, Mellon Inst, 65-67. *Mem:* Am Chem Soc. *Res:* Kinetics and mechanisms of solid state and combustion reactions; matrix isolation of transient species; urethane polymerization kinetics; thermal stability of propellants; explosives development; jet plasma characterization; infrared and Raman spectroscopy; transport properties; polymer and slurry rheology; synthesis of energetic materials; insensitive munitions. *Mailing Add:* 609 N Second St Lavale MD 21502-7234

HARTMAN, MARVIS EDGAR, POLYMER CHEMISTRY, ORGANIC CHEMISTRY. *Current Pos:* Scientist, PPG Indust Inc, 63-81. *Personal Data:* b Oshkosh, Wis, Sept 30, 40; m 61; c 4. *Educ:* Univ Wis-Madison, BS, 63; Carnegie-Mellon Univ, PhD(org chem), 72. *Mem:* Am Chem Soc. *Res:* Synthesis of new polymers for coatings; functional group manipulations on polymers, particularly acrylics, polyesters and polyarethanes; synthesis of polymers containing unique functionality. *Mailing Add:* 144 Rawlins Run Rd C/O M L Jordon 1 PPG Pl Pittsburgh PA 15272

HARTMAN, NILE FRANKLIN, INTEGRATED OPTICS, FIBER OPTICS. *Current Pos:* Sr res scientist, Columbus Labs, Battelle Mem Inst, 61-86, SR RES SCIENTIST, GA TECH RES INST, 86- *Personal Data:* b New Marshfield, Ohio, Nov 24, 39; m 65; c 1. *Educ:* Ohio Univ, BS, 61. *Honors & Awards:* IR-100 Award, 82. *Mem:* Optical Soc Am; Soc Photo-Optical Instrumentation Engrs. *Res:* Sensor systems; optical inspect and sensing systems. *Mailing Add:* 5595 Southern Pines Ct Stone Mountain GA 30087-5262

HARTMAN, PATRICK JAMES, STOCHASTIC SIMULATION, SYSTEMS DESIGN & SYSTEMS SCIENCE. *Current Pos:* SR MECH ENGR, US NAVY, WASHINGTON, DC, 80-; ADJ PROF, GEORGE WASHINGTON UNIV, FAIRFAX, VA, 91- *Personal Data:* b Ann Arbor, Mich, Dec 5, 44; m 68; c 2. *Educ:* Marquette Univ, BME, 68; Univ RI, MS, 74, PhD(eng), 76. *Honors & Awards:* Bausch & Lomb Sci Award, 63; Gold Cert, Am Soc Mech Engrs, Ocean Eng Div, 85. *Prof Exp:* Mech engr, USCG, Washington, DC, 68-72; researcher eng, Univ RI, 72-76; res engr, E I du Pont de Nemours, 76-79; sr ocean engr, Gould, Inc, 79-80. *Concurrent Pos:* Officer, USCG Res, 69-72; bd gov cert, Am Soc Mech Engrs, 85. *Mem:* Am Soc Mech Engrs; Nat Soc Prof Engrs; USN Asn Scientists & Engrs; Soc Reliability Engrs. *Res:* Efficient software tailored to increased speed of simulation of very large reliability and maintainability systems; artificial intelligence and expert systems; increased precision in stochastic simulations. *Mailing Add:* 5070 Durham Rd W Columbia MD 21044

HARTMAN, PAUL ARTHUR, food & agricultural microbiology; deceased, see previous edition for last biography

HARTMAN, PAUL LEON, EXPERIMENTAL PHYSICS. *Current Pos:* prof physics, 46-83, assoc dir appl & eng physics, 72-78, EMER PROF PHYSICS, CORNELL UNIV, 83- *Personal Data:* b Reno, Nev, July 13, 13; m 41, Margaret D Lockwood; c Barbara A, Laurel L & Sara W. *Educ:* Univ Nev, BS, 34; Cornell Univ, PhD(physics), 38. *Prof Exp:* Instr physics, Cornell Univ, 38-39; mem tech staff, Bell Tel Lab, 39-46. *Concurrent Pos:* Vis staff mem, Los Alamos Sci Lab, NMex, 60-61, 66-67 & 73-74. *Mem:* Am Phys Soc. *Res:* Magnetrons; vacuum ultraviolet; synchrotron radiation optics; alkali halides; air fluorescence. *Mailing Add:* Dept Physics & Eng Physics Cornell Univ Ithaca NY 14853

HARTMAN, PHILIP EMIL, MICROBIOLOGY. *Current Pos:* from asst prof to assoc prof, 57-65, PROF BIOL, JOHNS HOPKINS UNIV, 65-, WILLIAM D GILL PROF BIOL, 75- *Personal Data:* b Baltimore, Md, Nov 23, 26; m 55; c 3. *Educ:* Univ Ill, BS, 49; Univ Pa, PhD(med microbiol), 53. *Honors & Awards:* Ann Award, Environ Mutagen Soc, 85. *Prof Exp:* Instr med microbiol, Univ Pa, 53-54; NIH fel, Carnegie Inst, 54-55; at dept bact & immunol, Harvard Med Sch, 55-56; Am Cancer Soc fel, Animal Morphol Lab, Univ Brussels, 56-57. *Mem:* Am Soc Photobiol; Environ Mutagen Soc. *Res:* Bacterial genetics; gene action; chemical mutagenesis; antimutagens. *Mailing Add:* Dept Biol Johns Hopkins Univ 3400 N Charles St Baltimore MD 21218-2608

HARTMAN, RICHARD LEON, OPTICAL PHYSICS, SOLID STATE PHYSICS. *Current Pos:* Res physicist, Phys Sci Lab, 65-74, actg dir, Aeroballistics Directorate, 74-75, dir, Phys Sci Directorate, 76-77, DIR, ARMY MISSILE LAB, REDSTONE ARSENAL, 77- *Personal Data:* b Pittsburgh, Pa, July 5, 37; m 64; c 2. *Educ:* Carnegie Inst Technol, BS, 58, MS, 61, PhD(physics), 65; Mass Inst Technol, SM, 73. *Honors & Awards:* Army Res & Develop Achievement Award, 69. *Concurrent Pos:* Sloan Found fel, Mass Inst Technol, 72. *Mem:* AAAS; Am Phys Soc; Optical Soc Am; Soc Photo-Optical Instrumentation Engrs; Sigma Xi. *Res:* Spin lattice relaxation; electron paramagnetic resonance; nuclear quadrupole and magnetic resonance; optical spectroscopy; semiconductors; holography; optical data processing; laser radar; submillimeter physics. *Mailing Add:* Advan Optical Systs Inc 1103 Deborah Dr SE Huntsville AL 35801-1412

HARTMAN, RICHARD THOMAS, PLANT ECOLOGY. *Current Pos:* asst biol sci, Univ Pittsburgh, 47-48, instr bot, 48-52, from asst prof to prof, 52-87, dir, Pymatuning Lab Ecol, 73-87, EMER PROF, UNIV PITTSBURGH, 87- *Personal Data:* b Sligo, Pa, Feb 10, 21; m 44; c 2. *Educ:* Clarion State Col, BS, 42; Pittsburgh Univ, MS, 47, PhD(bot), 52. *Prof Exp:* Teacher pub sch, Pa, 42-43, 45-46. *Concurrent Pos:* Res assoc, Carnegie Mus Natural Hist, 65-; acad dean, semester at sea, 85. *Mem:* AAAS; Ecol Soc Am; Orgn Biol Field Stas; Am Soc Limnol & Oceanog; Am Inst Biol Sci. *Res:* Physiological ecology of algae and vascular aquatic plants; fresh water algal communities; eutrophication processes in lakes. *Mailing Add:* 124 Wetzel Rd Glenshaw PA 15116

HARTMAN, ROBERT CHARLES, HIGH ENERGY ASTROPHYSICS. *Current Pos:* Nat Acad Sci res assoc, 68-69, ASTROPHYSICIST, GODDARD SPACE FLIGHT CTR, NASA, 69- *Personal Data:* b Bartlesville, Okla, Aug 24, 38; m 60; c 3. *Educ:* Rice Inst, BA, 60; Univ Chicago, SM, 62, PhD(physics), 67. *Prof Exp:* Res assoc space sci, Enrico Fermi Inst, Univ Chicago, 67-68. *Mem:* Am Astron Soc; Am Phys Soc. *Res:* Primary cosmic ray electron-positron ratio and fluxes; high energy gamma ray astronomy. *Mailing Add:* Code 662 Goddard Space Flight Ctr NASA Greenbelt MD 20771

HARTMAN, ROGER DUANE, SOLID STATE PHYSICS, MEDICAL PHYSICS. *Current Pos:* PRES, ESTHART RES & DEVELOP CORP, 88-; PROF PHYSICS, SCH MED, ORAL ROBERTS UNIV, 88- *Personal Data:* b Kansas City, Mo, Nov 4, 35; m 55; c 1. *Educ:* William Jewell Col, AB, 58; Univ Ark, MS, 60; Okla State Univ, PhD(physics), 67. *Prof Exp:* Asst physics, Univ Ark, 58-60; instr phys sci, Evangel Col, 60-61; instr physics, Univ Ark, 61 62; from asst prof to assoc prof, Univ Tulsa, 62 72; vpres med & regulatory affairs, Tech Eval & Mgt Systs, Inc, 86-88; chmn, Nat Sci Div, Sch Med, Oral Roberts Univ, 73-77, prof physics, 72-78, dir, Off Res & Grants, 73-78, dir, Res & Develop, 78-81, prof radiol & assoc dean res grants, 81-86. *Concurrent Pos:* Consult, Los Alamos Sci Lab, 62-66; NSF Sci Fac fel, 65-66. *Mem:* Am Phys Soc; Optical Soc Am; Nat Coun Univ Res Adminr; Am Asn Physicists Med; Soc Res Adminr (pres elect, 79-80, pres, 80-81). *Res:* Molecular solids; optical and electrical properties of materials; radiation biology; biomedical engineering; medical ethics; medical physics; radiation therapy; medical and regulatory clinical trials. *Mailing Add:* Dept Eng Sci Oral Roberts Univ 7777 S Lewis Tulsa OK 74171-0001

HARTMAN, STANDISH CHARD, BIOCHEMISTRY. *Current Pos:* assoc prof, 68-73, PROF CHEM, BOSTON UNIV, 73- *Personal Data:* b Philadelphia, Pa, Nov 24, 31; m 57, 78; c 4. *Educ:* Mass Inst Technol, SB & SM, 54, PhD(biochem), 57. *Prof Exp:* Instr biochem, Mass Inst Technol, 57-59; asst prof, Harvard Med Sch, 59-68. *Concurrent Pos:* USPHS develop award, 60-68. *Mem:* Am Soc Biol Chem. *Res:* Enzymic reactions of purine biosynthesis; mechanisms of enzyme action. *Mailing Add:* Dept Chem Boston Univ 590 Commonwealth Ave Boston MA 02215. *Fax:* 617-353-6466

HARTMAN, WARREN EMERY, FOOD TECHNOLOGY, PROTEIN STRUCTURING. *Current Pos:* dir res, 46-60, vpres res & develop, 60-79, EMER BD DIRS, WORTHINGTON FOODS, INC, 79- *Personal Data:* b Hawthorne, Calif, May 12, 14; m 40; c 3. *Educ:* Andrews Univ, BA, 40; Univ Mich, Ann Arbor, MS, 45. *Prof Exp:* Bacteriologist, Mich State Dept Health, 40-42, anal chemist, 42-44; instr lab pract, USPHS, 45-46. *Concurrent Pos:* Consult, USAID, 60-70; mem, Protein Technol Adv Comt, White House Conf Food & Nutrit, 70. *Mem:* AAAS; Inst Food Technol; Am Asn Cereal Chemists; AMA. *Mailing Add:* 1046 Morning St Worthington OH 43085

HARTMAN, WILBUR LEE, FISHERY SCIENCE, LIMNOLOGY. *Current Pos:* RETIRED. *Personal Data:* b Northampton, Mass, June 22, 31; m 68; c 4. *Educ:* Amherst Col, BA, 52, MA, 53; Cornell Univ, PhD(fishery biol), 58. *Prof Exp:* Fishery aide biol, NY Dept Conserv, Cornell Univ, 54-58; fishery scientist, US Bur Com Fisheries, 58-68, supvry fishery scientist, 68-71; supvry fishery scientist biol, US Fish & Wildlife Serv, 71-89. *Concurrent Pos:* Adj assoc prof, Ohio State Univ, 69-74; sci adv, Ohio Gov's Task Force Fishery Mgt, 73-74. *Mem:* Am Fisheries Soc; Am Soc Limnol & Oceanog. *Res:* Dynamics Great Lakes fish resources; biology and behavior of fishes; fishery management; environmental stresses on fish stocks; limnology oligotrophic lakes. *Mailing Add:* 11520 Dunlavy Lane Whitmore Lake MI 48189

HARTMAN, WILLARD DANIEL, INVERTEBRATE ZOOLOGY. *Current Pos:* from asst prof & assoc cur to assoc prof & cur, 53-73, dir biol grad studies, 76-79, PROF BIOL & CUR INVERT ZOOL, YALE UNIV, 73- *Personal Data:* b Cincinnati, Ohio, Sept 26, 21; m 60. *Educ:* Yale Univ, BS, 43, MS, 44, PhD(zool), 50. *Prof Exp:* Lab asst biol, Yale Univ, 43-44 & 46-49; instr zool, Yale Univ, 50-53. *Concurrent Pos:* Mem, Yale Univ Seychelles Exped, 57-58; actg dir, Peabody Museum, 87-89. *Mem:* Am Soc Zool; Soc Syst Zool; Am Soc Limnol & Oceanog; Marine Biol Asn UK; Sigma Xi; Int Soc Reef Studies. *Res:* Systematics, ecology and evolution of sponges. *Mailing Add:* Peabody Mus Natural Hist Yale Univ PO Box 208118 New Haven CT 06520

HARTMANIS, JURIS, MATHEMATICS, COMPUTER SCIENCE. *Current Pos:* chmn dept, 65-71, prof comput sci, 65-70, WALTER R REED PROF ENG, CORNELL UNIV, 81-; ASST DIR, CONSORTIUM INT STUDIES EDUC, 96- *Personal Data:* b Riga, Latvia, July 5, 28; nat US; m 59; c 3. *Educ:* Univ Marburg, Cand Phil, 49; Univ Kansas City, MA, 51; Calif Inst Technol, PhD(math), 55. *Hon Degrees:* Dah, Univ Dortmund, 95. *Honors & Awards:* Turning Award, Asn Comput Mach, 93; B Blozano Gold Medal, Nat Acad Sci, Czech Repub, 95. *Prof Exp:* Asst math, Calif Inst Technol, 51-55; instr, Cornell Univ, 55-57; asst prof, Ohio State Univ, 57-58; res scientist, Res Lab, Gen Elec Co, 58-65. *Concurrent Pos:* Assoc ed, J Comput & Systs Sci, 69 & Soc Indust & Appl Math J Comput, 72- *Mem:* Nat Acad Eng; Math Asn Am; Asn Comput Mach; Am Math Soc; NY Acad Sci. *Res:* Electronic computers; automata theory; theory of computing. *Mailing Add:* Upson Hall Cornell Univ Ithaca NY 14853

HARTMANN, ALOIS J(OSEPH), CIVIL ENGINEERING. *Current Pos:* sr engr, 74-84, FEL ENG, WESTINGHOUSE ELEC CORP, 84- *Personal Data:* b Cincinnati, Ohio, Mar 16, 36; m 62; c 2. *Educ:* Manhattan Col, BCE, 58; Lehigh Univ, MS, 60; Univ Ill, PhD(struct), 64. *Prof Exp:* Ford of Can fel, Univ Western Ont, 64-65; asst prof eng sci, 65-66; from asst prof to assoc prof civil eng, Marquette Univ, 66-74. *Mem:* Am Soc Civil Engrs; Am Concrete Inst; Am Soc Mech Engrs; Sigma Xi; Struct Stability Res Coun. *Res:* Stability of structures; dynamics of structures; structural design; computer code development. *Mailing Add:* 185 Regal Ct Monroeville PA 15146-4735

HARTMANN, BRUCE, POLYMER PHYSICS, MATERIALS SCIENCE ENGINEERING. *Current Pos:* Mem staff physics, 60-75, HEAD POLYMER PHYSICS GROUP, NAVAL SURFACE WARFARE CTR, 75- *Personal Data:* b St Louis, Mo, June 30, 38; m 62, Judith A Bryan; c Eric, Lisa & Kevin. *Educ:* Cath Univ Am, AB, 60; Univ Md, College Park, MS, 66; Am Univ, PhD(physics), 71. *Mem:* Am Phys Soc; Soc Rheology; Acoust Soc Am. *Res:* Experimental and theoretical structure-property relations in polymers. *Mailing Add:* 15006 Hunter Mountain Lane Silver Spring MD 20906. *Fax:* 301-394-2414

HARTMANN, DENNIS LEE, ATMOSPHERIC SCIENCES, CLIMATOLOGY. *Current Pos:* from asst prof to assoc prof, 77-88, PROF ATMOSPHERIC SCI, UNIV WASH, 88- *Personal Data:* b Salem, Ore, Apr 23, 49; m; c 2. *Educ:* Univ Portland, BS, 71; Princeton Univ, MA, 73, PhD(geophys & fluid dynamics), 75. *Prof Exp:* Res assoc meteorol, McGill Univ, 75-76; vis scientist, Nat Ctr Atmospheric Res, 76-77. *Concurrent Pos:* Assoc ed, J Atmospheric Sci & J Geophys Res: Athmospheres. *Mem:* Am Meteorol Soc; AAAS. *Res:* Stratospheric dynamics and chemistry; theoretical climatology. *Mailing Add:* Dept Atmospheric Sci Box 351640 Univ Wash Seattle WA 98195-1640

HARTMANN, ERNEST LOUIS, SLEEP & SLEEP DISORDERS, DREAMING. *Current Pos:* PROF PSYCHIAT, SCH MED, TUFTS UNIV, 75-; SR PSYCHIATRIST & DIR, SLEEP LAB, WEST-ROS-PARK MENT HEALTH CTR, 78-; DIR, SLEEP RES LAB, LEMUEL SHATTUCK HOSP, 80-; DIR, SLEEP DIS CTR, NEWTON WELLESLEY HOSP, 84- *Personal Data:* b Vienna, Austria, Feb 25, 34; US citizen; m 61, Eva; c Jon & Kate. *Educ:* Univ Chicago, AB, 52; Yale Univ, MD, 58. *Honors & Awards:* Holt Bk Prize, Yale Univ, 56; A E Bennett Award Psychiat Res, 66; First Prize Psychopharmacol, Am Psychol Asn, 71. *Prof Exp:* Intern med, Bronx Munic Hosp Ctr, Albert Einstein Col Med, 59-60; resident psychiat, Mass Ment Health Ctr, Boston, 60-62; clin assoc, NIMH, 62-64, career investr, 64-69; dir, Sleep Lab, Boston State Hosp, 64-80. *Concurrent Pos:* Am Cancer Soc fel, Gustave Roussy Res Inst, Univ Paris, 58-59; teaching fel, Harvard Med Sch, 60-61 & res fel, 61-62; consult, Mass Dept Prisons, 61-62; prin investr grants on sleep, 64-69, 66-72, 74-79, 79-82, 82-85 & 85- & grants on schizophrenia, 79-82; chmn clin res rev comt, Boston State Hosp, 67-76; lectr psychiat, Sch Med, Boston Univ, 70-; pvt pract, psychiat & sleep dis, 70-; consult, Panel Mem, Food & Drug Admin, 72-76; consult ed, Psychopharmacol, McLean J & assoc ed, Sem Psychiat; assoc dir sleep clinic, Peter Bent Brigham Hosp, 73-; fac mem, Boston Psychoanal Inst, 75-; dir, Sleep Dis Ctr, Newton-Wellesley Hosp, 84-; ed-in-chief, Dreaming. *Mem:* Fel Am Psychiat Asn; Sleep Res Soc; Soc Neurosci; fel Am Col Neuropsychopharmacol; Psychiat Res Soc; Asn Study Dreams (pres); AAAS. *Res:* Sleep; dreaming; sleep disorders; schizophrenia; mind-brain relationships; author of 8 books and over 280 scientific articles and abstracts. *Mailing Add:* 27 Clark St Newton MA 02159. *Fax:* 617-965-6548; *E-Mail:* ehdream@aol.com

HARTMANN, FORREST D, CONSERVATION. *Honors & Awards:* Oak Leaf Award, Nature Conserv, 93. *Mem:* Nature Conserv. *Mailing Add:* 430 Roblee Rd Baraboo WI 53913-1455

HARTMANN, FRANCIS XAVIER, neutrino physics, laser effects in nuclear systems, for more information see previous edition

HARTMANN, FREDERICK W, MATHEMATICS. *Current Pos:* From asst prof to assoc prof, 65-83, PROF MATH, VILLANOVA UNIV, 83-, CHMN DEPT, 81- *Personal Data:* b Repton, Ala, Mar 29, 40; m 67; c 2. *Educ:* Lehigh Univ, AB, 62, PhD(math), 68; Univ Pa, MA, 64. *Concurrent Pos:* Vis lectr, Univ Western Australia, 71. *Mem:* Am Math Soc. *Res:* Mathematical analysis, summability and complex function theory. *Mailing Add:* Dept Math Villanova Univ 800 Lancaster Ave Villanova PA 19085-1699

HARTMANN, GEORGE CHARLES, MYCOLOGY. *Current Pos:* Prof, 58-90, EMER PROF BIOL, RI COL, 90- *Personal Data:* b New Bedford, Mass, Mar 16, 27; m 49, Lorraine J; c Gregory P, Carol J & Jane A. *Educ:* Harvard Univ, AB, 50, MAT, 51; Univ RI, PhD(mycol), 63. *Concurrent Pos:* NSF sci fac fel bot, Univ Mich, 68-69. *Mem:* Sigma Xi; Mycol Soc Am. *Res:* Entomogenous fungi; fungal cytology. *Mailing Add:* 11 Powder Mill Lane Greenville RI 02828-2049

HARTMANN, GEORGE COLE, PHYSICS, ELECTROPHOTOGRAPHY. *Current Pos:* scientist electrophotog, Xerox Webster Res Ctr, 68-73, mgr imaging sci, 73-74 & Xerox Res Ctr Can, 74-78, mgr mat develop, 78-83, mgr process technol sect, 83-88, mgr technol strag, 88-93, PRIN, STRATEGY & INNOVATION, XEROX CORP RES & TECHNOL. *Personal Data:* b Exeter, NH, Mar 19, 40; m 65, Katharine Hanley; c Jonathan, Gregory & Stephanie. *Educ:* Mass Inst Technol, BS, 62, PhD(physics), 67. *Honors & Awards:* Charles Ives Award, Inst Sci & Technol, 93. *Prof Exp:* Res assoc elem particles, Mass Inst Technol & Stanford Linear Accelerator Ctr, 67-68. *Mem:* Am Phys Soc; Sigma Xi; Soc Imaging Sci & Technol. *Res:* Novel electrophotographic systems including photoactive-pigment electrophotography; photoconductivity and charge exchange phenomena at interfaces; xerographic systems and materials. *Mailing Add:* Xerox Wilson Ctr Technol W147 800 Phillips Rd Webster NY 14580

HARTMANN, GREGORY KEMENYI, PHYSICS. *Current Pos:* CONSULT MGT, HIST & MINE WARFARE, 73- *Personal Data:* b Buffalo, NY, May 25, 11; m 39; c 4. *Educ:* Calif Inst Technol, BS, 33; Oxford Univ, BA, 36, MA, 43; Brown Univ, PhD(physics), 39. *Honors & Awards:* Distinguished Civilian Serv Award, US Dept Navy, 45 & US Dept Defense, 58; Nat Civil Serv League Award, 60. *Prof Exp:* Asst physics, Brown Univ, 36-38; asst prof, Univ NH, 39-41; contract employee, Bur Ord, USN Dept, 41-42, physicist, 42-43, head res group appl explosives, 43-45, assoc chief explosives res div, Naval Ord Lab, 46-48, chief, 48-50, chief explosives res dept, 50-52, assoc tech dir res, 52-55, tech dir, White Oak, 55-73. *Concurrent Pos:* Tech dir, Bur Ord Instrumentation Group, Bikini Atom Bomb Tests, 46, Eninetok Atom Tests, 48 & 50; sr visitor, Dept Appl Math & Theoret Physics, Cambridge Univ, 64-65. *Mem:* Assoc mem Am Phys Soc; fel Acoust Soc Am; Fed Prof Asn (pres, 64). *Res:* Underwater acoustics; shock waves; explosives; instrumentation for blast and underwater explosions; weapon effects; administration of research and development; antisubmarine warfare; sea based deterrence. *Mailing Add:* 10701 Keswick St Box 317 Garrett Park MD 20896

HARTMANN, HANS S(IEGFRIED), CERAMICS. *Current Pos:* OWNER, MIND, BODY PRACT, WILMINGTON, 93- *Personal Data:* b Hohenleipisch, Ger, Feb 24, 31; US citizen; c 2. *Educ:* Clausthal Tech Univ, Dipl Ing, 57; Mass Inst Technol, ScD(ceramics), 64. *Prof Exp:* Supvr customer serv lab, Kerabedarf KG, Ger, 57-59; res asst metall, Mass Inst Technol, 59-64; sr res scientist, Tech Ctr, Owens-Ill, Inc, 64-70, mgr ceramic technol, Electronics Div, 70-73; mem staff, Pioneering Res Lab, Du Pont Electronics, 73-82, res assoc, 83-93. *Mem:* Am Ceramic Soc; Int Soc Hybrid Microelectronics; Sigma Xi. *Res:* Glass and ceramic materials for packaging, interconnection and hermetic sealing of semiconductors and similar electronic devices; precision alumina ceramics; development of alumina fibers for reinforcement of ceramic and metal-matrix composites, fabrication technology and nondestructive evaluation; fiber reinforced metals. *Mailing Add:* 2303 Delaware Ave Wilmington DE 19806

HARTMANN, HEIDI IRMGARD VICTORIA, ECONOMICS. *Current Pos:* FOUNDER & DIR, INST WOMEN'S POLICY RES, 87- *Personal Data:* b Elizabeth, NJ, Aug 14, 45; m 79, John Varick Wells; c Jessica Lee (Cochran), Laura (Cameron) & Katherine Lina. *Educ:* Swarthmore Col, BA, 67; Yale Univ, MPhil, 72, PhD(econs), 74. *Hon Degrees:* LLD, Swarthmore Col, 95. *Prof Exp:* Comput programmer & researcher, City Planning Dept, City of New Haven, 69; actg instr, Yale Univ, 72-73; vis asst prof econs, New Sch Social Res, 74-76; sr res economist, Off Res, US Comn Civil Rights, 76-78; res assoc, Nat Acad Sci/Nat Res Coun, 78-80, assoc exec dir, Comn Behav & Soc Sci & Educ, 80-83, study dir, 84-86; Am Statist Asn-NSF census fel, US Bur Census, 86-87. *Concurrent Pos:* Lectr, Women's Studies Prog, George Washington Univ, 78, Dept Econ, Univ Md, 79; bd dirs, Nat Coun Res Women; vis scholar, A E Havens Ctr Study Social Struct & Social Change, Univ Wis-Madison, 87; dir, Women's Studies Prog & prof, Dept Sociol, Rutgers Univ, 88; MacArthur Found fel, 94. *Mem:* Am Econ Asn; Nat Women's Studies Asn; Union Radical Polit Econs. *Mailing Add:* Inst Women's Policy Res 1400 20th St NW Suite 104 Washington DC 20036-5906

HARTMANN, HENRIK ANTON, PATHOLOGY, NEUROPATHOLOGY. *Current Pos:* From asst prof to assoc prof, 54-68, PROF PATH, UNIV WIS-MADISON, 68- *Personal Data:* b Norway, Mar 20, 20; m 52, Anastatia Smith; c Lisa (Chilton), Tony, Jeni, Arne, & Signe. *Educ:* Univ Oslo, MD, 49. *Concurrent Pos:* Consult, neuropathologist, Vet Admin Hosp, Madison, Wis. *Mem:* Am Asn Path; Am Asn Neuropath; Int Soc Neurochem. *Res:* Cytology of nerve cells; cytochemistry of single cells; RNA and protein changes in aging neurons and environmental factors; RNA changes in amyotrophic lateral sclerosis; neurosciences; copper deficiency and control nervous system. *Mailing Add:* Dept Path Univ Wis Madison WI 53706

HARTMANN, HUDSON THOMAS, horticulture; deceased, see previous edition for last biography

HARTMANN, JUDITH BROWN, ADVANCED RECORDING TECHNOLOGY, CONDENSED MATTER PHYSICS. *Current Pos:* Sr physicist, 77-80, res scientist, 80-82, res supvr, 82-84, RES MGR, 3M, 84- *Personal Data:* b Corning, Iowa, Feb 26, 46. *Educ:* Iowa State Univ, BS, 67; Cornell Univ, PhD(physics), 74. *Mem:* Am Phys Soc; Sigma Xi. *Res:* Advanced recording technology; optical and magnetic thin film materials. *Mailing Add:* 3M Ctr Bldg 201 1C 30 St Paul MN 55144

HARTMANN, RICHARD W, PLANT BREEDING. *Current Pos:* RETIRED. *Personal Data:* b Jersey City, NJ, Jan 5, 35; m 65; c 1. *Educ:* Rutgers Univ, BA, 56; Va Polytech Inst, MS, 57; Univ Calif, Los Angeles, PhD(plant sci), 62. *Prof Exp:* NIH fel genetics, Univ Calif, Davis, 62-63; asst prof hort, Univ Hawaii, 63-70, assoc prof, 70- *Mem:* Am Soc Hort Sci; Soc Advan Breeding Res Asia & Oceania. *Res:* Plant breeding and genetics of vegetables in the tropics, especially beans and lettuce for root-knot nematode and tomato spotted wilt virus resistance. *Mailing Add:* 3761 Kumulani Pl Honolulu HI 96822

HARTMANN, ROBERT CARL, HEMATOLOGY. *Personal Data:* b Everett, Wash, July 23, 19; m 77; c 6. *Educ:* Johns Hopkins Univ, AB, 41, MD, 44; Am Bd Internal Med, dipl, 56. *Prof Exp:* Intern, Pa Hosp, Philadelphia, 44-45, sr resident med, 45-46; fel med, Div Hemat, Johns Hopkins Hosp, Baltimore, 48-49, asst resident, 49-50, USPHS fel, Div Hemat, Johns Hopkins Univ, 50-51, AEC fel, 51-52; from asst prof to prof med, Sch Med, Vanderbilt Univ, 52-74; PROF MED, SCH MED, UNIV SFLA, TAMPA, 74- *Concurrent Pos:* Asst vis physician, Outpatient Dept, Johns Hopkins Hosp, 48-49 & 50-52; from asst vis physician to vis physician, Outpatient Dept, Vanderbilt Univ Hosp, 52-74, hematologist in-chg, 52-74; consult hematologist, Vet Admin Hosp, Nashville, Tenn, 52-74 & George Hubbard Hosp & Meharry Med Col, 67-74; consult, Inst Nutrit Cent Am & Panama Anemia & Nutrit Surv, Guatemala, Cent Am, 64-68, subcom platelet-glass adhesion, Int Comt Haemostasis & Thrombosis, 66-70, hemat study sect, NIH, 67-71, nat nutrit surv, Nutrit Off, USPHS, 68-70 & hemophilia adv comt, Tenn Pub Health Dept, 73-74, adv coun, Nat Heart, Lung & Blood Inst, 80-84. *Mem:* Am Fedn Clin Res; Am Soc Clin Invest; Am Soc Hemat; Asn Am Physicians; Int Soc Hemat. *Res:* Blood coagulation; physiology of heparin; function of blood platelets; hemolytic anemias, endotoxin; hepatic venous thrombosis. *Mailing Add:* 3630 Little Rd Lutz FL 33549

HARTMANN, SVEN RICHARD, PHYSICS. *Current Pos:* from asst prof to assoc prof, 62-68, dir, 68-71, co-dir radiation lab, 71-76, PROF PHYSICS, COLUMBIA UNIV, 76- *Personal Data:* b New York, NY, Feb 22, 32; m. *Educ:* Union Col, NY, BS, 54; Univ Calif, Berkeley, PhD(physics), 61. *Honors & Awards:* R W Wood Prize, Am Opt Soc, 83. *Prof Exp:* Res physicist, Univ Calif, Berkeley, 61-62. *Concurrent Pos:* Sloan res fel, 63-; John Simon Gugenheim fel, 78. *Mem:* Fel Am Phys Soc; fel Am Optical Soc; Sigma Xi; AAAS. *Res:* Magnetic resonance and relaxation; spin and photon echoes; interaction between light and matter. *Mailing Add:* Physics Dept Columbia Univ 538 W 120th St New York NY 10027

HARTMANN, WILLIAM HERMAN, PATHOLOGY, SURGICAL PATHOLOGY. *Current Pos:* dir surg path, 71-73, PROF PATH & CHMN DEPT, SCH MED, VANDERBILT UNIV, 73- *Personal Data:* b New York, NY, Mar 13, 31; m 54; c 3. *Educ:* Syracuse Univ, BA, 51; State Univ NY, MD, 55. *Prof Exp:* From assoc to asst prof path, Johns Hopkins Univ, Baltimore, 62-67; prof, Sch Med, Univ Tenn, 68; assoc pathologist, El Camino Hosp, Mountain View, Calif, 68-71. *Concurrent Pos:* Exchange prof path, Cayetano-Heredia Sch Med, Lima, Peru, 65; consult, St Thomas Hosp, Nashville, 72- & Vet Admin Hosp, 73-; Nat Cancer Inst trainee, Mem Hosp, NY, 58-60. *Mem:* Int Acad Path; Am Soc Clin Path. *Res:* Breast cancer. *Mailing Add:* 5220 E Longboat Blvd 5401 W Kennedy Blvd Tampa FL 33615

HARTMANN, WILLIAM K, PLANETARY SCIENCE, PLANETARY ASTRONOMY. *Current Pos:* SR SCIENTIST, PLANETARY SCI INST, DIV SAN JUAN RES INST, 70- *Personal Data:* b New Kensington, Pa, June 6, 39; m 71, Gayle Harrison; c Amy. *Educ:* Pa State Univ, BS, 61; Univ Ariz, MS, 65, PhD(astron), 66. *Honors & Awards:* Nininger Meteorite Award, 65; Asteroid 3341 named in recognition of res. *Prof Exp:* Asst prof astron, Univ Ariz, 66-69; scientist, Ill Inst Technol, Res Inst, 69-70. *Concurrent Pos:* Co-investr, Mariner 9 Mars Mapping Mission, NASA, 69-72, Mars Observer, 92-93, Russ Mars Mission, 94-96, Mars Global Survr Mission, 96-; prin investr, co-investr & consult, Var NASA Progs, 71-88; consult, House Select Comt Assasinations, 79. *Mem:* Am Astron Soc; Meteoritical Soc; Int Astron Union. *Res:* Origin and evolution of planets; author of 3 textbooks in astronomy. *Mailing Add:* Planetary Sci Inst 620 N Sixth Ave Tucson AZ 85705

HARTMANN, WILLIAM MORRIS, PSYCHOACOUSTICS, ACOUSTICS. *Current Pos:* from asst prof to assoc prof, 68-77, PROF PHYSICS, MICH STATE UNIV, 77- *Personal Data:* b Elgin, Ill, July 28, 39; m 67, Christine Rein; c 2. *Educ:* Iowa State Univ, BS, 61; Oxford Univ, PhD(physics), 65. *Prof Exp:* Res fel solid state theory, Argonne Nat Lab, 65-68. *Concurrent Pos:* Vis scientist, Inst Res & Coord Acoust Mus, Paris, 81-86, actg dir Acoust, 82-83; NSF & NIH res grants; chmn, Tech Comt on Musical Acoust, Acoust Soc of Am, 80-84; working group 100, Nat Res Coun-CHABA, 87-88; assoc ed, Music Perception J, 88- *Mem:* Fel Acoust Soc Am; Am Phys Soc; Asn Res Otolaryngol; Soc Music Perception & Cognition. *Res:* Human pitch perception; human binaural hearing system; acoustic signal processing; theory of the electron-phonon interaction; disordered solids. *Mailing Add:* Dept Physics Mich State Univ East Lansing MI 48824-1116

HARTNER, WILLIAM CHRISTOPHER, TRANSPLANTATION IMMUNOLOGY, ANIMAL PHYSIOLOGY. *Current Pos:* asst prof biol, 75-82, STAFF SCIENTIST & LECTR, NORTHEASTERN UNIV, 83- *Personal Data:* b West Rock Hill, Pa, Dec 24, 39; m 64; c 2. *Educ:* Pa State Univ, BS, 63; Univ Mo, MA, 68, PhD(physiol), 71. *Prof Exp:* Trainee physiol, Univ Ill, Urbana-Champaign, 71-73, res assoc, 74; asst prof biol, Wright State Univ, 74-75. *Mem:* AAAS. *Res:* Temperature regulation during hibernation cycles; temperature regulation and cold acclimation; control of sleep-wakefulness; mechanisms of allograft prolongation after treatment with antilymphocyte serum and donor bone marrow. *Mailing Add:* Med Lab Sci 206 Mugar Bldg Northeastern Univ Boston MA 02115

HARTNETT, JAMES P(ATRICK), MECHANICAL ENGINEERING. *Current Pos:* prof energy eng & head dept, 65-74, DIR, ENERGY RESOURCES CTR, UNIV ILL, CHICAGO CIRCLE, 74- *Personal Data:* b Lynn, Mass, Mar 19, 24; m 45; c 5. *Educ:* Ill Inst Technol, BS, 47; Mass Inst Technol, MS, 48; Univ Calif, Berkeley, PhD(mech eng), 54. *Honors & Awards:* Mem Award, Heat Transfer Div, Am Soc Mech Engrs, 69; Prof Achievement Award, Ill Inst Technol, 77. *Prof Exp:* Engr, Aircraft Gas Turbine Div, Gen Elec Co, 48-49; res engr, Univ Calif, 50-61; from asst prof to prof mech eng, Univ Minn, 54-61; prof & chmn dept, Univ Del, 61-65. *Concurrent Pos:* Guggenheim fel & vis prof, Univ Tokyo, 60-61; Fulbright prof & lectr, Univ Alexandria, 61; consult, Seoul Nat Univ, 65, Rand Corp, Calif, Kaiser Eng Co, Calif & Asian Inst Technol, Bangkok, Thailand, 77; Nat Acad Sci exchange scientist, Rumania, 69; mem orgn comt, Int Centre Heat & Mass Transfer, Belgrade, Yugoslavia, 69-77; vis prof, Israel Inst Technol, 70; mem, Adv Comt USSR & Europe-Nat Acad Sci, 74-78, Ill Energy Resources Comn, 74- & Sci Coun Regional Centre Energy, Heat & Transfer Asia & Pac, 76-; co-ed, Int J Heat & Mass Transfer, Letters in Heat & Mass Transfer, Heat Transfer-Japanese Res & Previews Heat & Mass Transfer. *Mem:* Fel Am Soc Mech Engrs; Am Inst Aeronaut & Astronaut; Am Soc Eng Educ; Am Inst Chem Engrs; Sigma Xi. *Res:* Heat and mass transfer; fluid mechanics; energy policy. *Mailing Add:* Univ Ill Energy Resources Ctr 851 S Morgan St 12th Floor Chicago IL 60607

HARTNETT, JOHN (CONRAD), BIOCHEMISTRY, ENZYMOLOGY. *Current Pos:* From instr to assoc prof, St Michael's Col, 43-63, prof, 63-87, chmn dept, 68-74, EMER PROF BIOL, ST MICHAEL'S COL, 87- *Personal Data:* b Astoria, NY, Feb 2, 22; m 44; Irene LaFountain, c Mary, Donna, Johnette & John. *Educ:* St Michael's Col, Vt, BS, 43; Univ Vt, MS, 47, PhD(biochem), 63. *Concurrent Pos:* Res asst, Univ Vt, 61-62, abstractor, Chem Abstr, 65-75; Am Cancer Soc res grants, 65-66, 67-68; res, Shelburne Mus, Vt, 70, assoc trustee & mus lectr, 71; co-dir TV ser human sexuality, Vt, 71; mem & vchmn, Vt Develop Dis Planning & Adv Coun, 72-81; mem bd trustees, Vt United Cerebral Palsy, 75-78; mem prof adv bd, Vt Epilepsy Asn, 75-77; mem, Vt Archit Barriers Compliance Bd, 76-97 & Vt Adv Coun Spec Educ, 87-97; dir, Vt Asn Blind, 85-89, reviewer, AAAS Sci Books & Films, 87- *Mem:* Am Inst Biol Sci; Am Inst Hist Pharm; Inst Society, Ethics & Life Sci. *Res:* Isolation and characterization of an esterproteolytic porcine pancreatic enzyme; enzyme activity towards synthetic homopolypeptides; etiological agent in renal uremia; bacterial growth problems; history of pharmacy and therapeutics. *Mailing Add:* 9 Florida Ave Winooski VT 05404

HARTOCOLLIS, PETER, psychiatry, psychoanalysis, for more information see previous edition

HARTOP, WILLIAM LIONEL, JR, RESEARCH ADMINISTRATION. *Current Pos:* CONSULT, 85- *Personal Data:* b Derry, NH, Sept 21, 21; m 48, Janet Chapman; c Karen E, Laura L & Lisa G. *Educ:* Univ NH, BS, 44, MS, 48; Northwestern Univ, PhD(chem), 50. *Prof Exp:* Instr, Army Spec Training Prog, Univ NH, 43-44; sr res chemist, Abbott Labs, 50-57, head, Spec Proj Res Dept, 57-61, mgr, Mat Res Dept, 61-62, area mgr anal & mat res, 62-64, dir res & develop, Ross Labs Div, Ohio, 64-67; from asst dir to dir res, Ortho Pharmaceut Corp, 67-72, dir res planning, 72- & 72-83; vpres dir admin, Johnson & Johnson Biotech Ctr, LaJolla, Calif, 83-85. *Mem:* AAAS. *Res:* Pharmaceuticals; reproduction and contraception; nutritional products; materials research; biotechnology. *Mailing Add:* 142 Seney Dr Bernardsville NJ 07924

HARTOV, ALEXANDER, HEALTH PHYSICS. *Current Pos:* PRES, ALEX HARTOV CONSULT, 93-; RES ASST PROF, DARTMOUTH SCH MED, 95- *Personal Data:* b Fontainebleau, France, Aug 5, 57; US citizen. *Educ:* Northeastern Univ, BSEE, 84; Dartmouth Col, MSc, 88, PhD(biomed eng), 91. *Prof Exp:* Proj dir biomed eng, Daut Res Corp, 96-97. *Concurrent Pos:* Res asst prof, Thayer Sch Eng, Dartmouth Col, 96- *Mem:* Nam Hypothermia Soc; Am Asn Psysicists Med; Am Inst Physics. *Res:* Developing devices for application in medicine for diagnostic or therapeutic purposes. *Mailing Add:* 53 School St Lebanon NH 03766

HARTRAMPF, CARL ROERIG, JR, PLASTIC & RECONSTRUCTIVE SURGERY. *Current Pos:* CLIN PROF PLASTIC SURG, SCH MED, EMORY UNIV, 84- *Personal Data:* b Atlanta, Ga, Aug 5, 32; m 51, Patricia Crawford; c Valljeanne (Arader), Carl R III & Havalyn Ann (Hensley). *Educ:* Med Col Ga, MD, 56; Am Bd Surg, dipl; Am Bd Plastic Surg, dipl. *Honors & Awards:* James Barrett Brown Award, Am Asn Plastics Surgeons, 83; Presidential Award, Am Soc Plastic & Reconstructive Surgeons, 91; Medal of Honor, Am Col Surgeons, 94; Sci Achievement Award, AMA, 95; Distinguished Serv Award, Am Cancer Soc, 95. *Prof Exp:* Intern, Univ NC/ NC Mem Hosp, 56-57, resident gen surg, 57-61; resident plastic surg, Wash Univ/Barnes Hosp, 61-62; secy, Atlanta Plastic Surg, Pa, 68-94. *Concurrent Pos:* Staff, Northside Hosp, 63-, Scottish Rite Children's Med Ctr, 63-, St Joseph's Hosp, 63- *Mem:* Fel Am Col Surgeons; Am Cancer Soc; AMA; Am Asn Plastic Surgeons; Am Soc Plastic & Reconstruct Surgeons. *Mailing Add:* 3661 Tuxedo Rd NW Atlanta GA 30305-1060

HARTRANFT, GEORGE ROBERT, ORGANIC POLYMER CHEMISTRY. *Current Pos:* Res chemist, 59-78, res scientist, 78-83, SR RES SCIENTIST, ARMSTRONG WORLD IND INC, 83- *Personal Data:* b Leola, Pa, Mar 29, 33; m 52, Margaret E Plank; c Kathy J, Cynthia & Karen. *Educ:* Franklin & Marshall Col, BS, 54; Univ Del, PhD(org chem), 59. *Mem:* Am Chem Soc. *Res:* Condensation polymers; vinyl polymers; fiber dyeing and treatment; photopolymerization. *Mailing Add:* 1516 Springside Dr Lancaster PA 17603-6321

HARTROFT, PHYLLIS MERRITT, EXPERIMENTAL PATHOLOGY. *Current Pos:* RETIRED. *Personal Data:* b Detroit, Mich, Feb 1, 28; div. *Educ:* Univ Mich, BS, 49; Univ Toronto, MA, 51, PhD, 54. *Prof Exp:* Asst, Banting & Best Dept Med Res, Univ Toronto, 49-54; asst path, Sch Med, Wash Univ, 54-58, asst prof, 58-61; res assoc, Hosp for Sick Children, Toronto, 61-63; asst prof path, Ind Univ, 63-66; assoc prof path, Sch Med, Wash Univ, 66-84. *Mem:* AAAS; Am Asn Anat; NY Acad Sci; Am Soc Nephrology; Am Asn Lab Animal Sci; Am Asn Pathologists; Am Inst Nutrit; Int Acad Path. *Res:* Kidney, renal juxtaglomerular cells; renin; cardiovascular diseases; pollution biology; laboratory animal science. *Mailing Add:* 5516 Lancaster Rd Hebron OH 43025. *E-Mail:* pjmhar@nextek.net

HARTRUM, THOMAS CHARLES, DATABASE, COMPUTER PERFORMANCE EVALUATION. *Current Pos:* ASST PROF ELEC ENG, AIR FORCE INST TECHNOL, 80- *Personal Data:* b Cambridge, Ohio, May 19, 45; m 67; c 2. *Educ:* Ohio State Univ, BEE & MS, 69, PhD(elec eng), 73. *Prof Exp:* Elec engr, US Army Electronics Command, 71-75; elec engr, Aerospace Med Res Lab, 75-80. *Mem:* Inst Elec & Electronics Engrs; Asn Comput Mach. *Res:* Analog models of neurons and their application as new communication techniques; hardware for processing speech signals for recognition and hardware for synthesis of speech. *Mailing Add:* Dept Elec Eng Air Force Inst Technol AFIT/ENG 2950 P St Wright Patterson AFB OH 45433

HARTSAW, WILLIAM O, ENGINEERING MECHANICS. *Current Pos:* Instr eng, Univ Evansville, 46-52, from asst prof to prof, 52-85, head, Dept Eng, 58-60, dir, Sch Eng, 60-68, dean eng, 68-77, head, Dept Mech Eng, 77-85, distinguished prof, 85-92, DISTINGUISHED EMER PROF MECH ENG, UNIV EVANSVILLE, IND, 92- *Personal Data:* b Tell City, Ind, Oct 17, 21; m 46, Delma Stuckey; c Mark A. *Educ:* Purdue Univ, BS, 46, MS, 53; Univ Ill, PhD(theoret & appl mech), 66. *Honors & Awards:* Tech Achievement Award, Am Soc Mech Engrs, 79, Centennial Metal, 80, Distinguished Serv Award, 89, Region V Outstanding Fac Adv of the Yr, 92. *Concurrent Pos:* Lilly Found fel, 60; NSF fac fel, 60-62; mem, Buffalo Trace Coun, Boy Scouts of Am, 68-, mem coun, Big Bend Dist, 86-; mem Evansville Urban Transp adv comt, 75-; vchmn, Evansville Environ Protection Agency, 77-79; chmn, Evansville Sect, Am Soc Mech Engrs, 81-82, Nat Agenda Coord Deleg, 81-83, vpres, Region VI, 83-85, nat bd issues mgt, 86-, nat bd prof develop, 88- *Mem:* AAAS; Am Soc Mech Engrs; Am Soc Eng Educ; Am Soc Heat, Refrig & Air-Conditioning Engrs; Am Soc Testing Mat; Am Asn Univ Profs. *Res:* Stress analysis; photoelasticity; refrigeration; design; mechanics of solids; materials; the Peltier Effect; a low cycle fatigue strength investigation of a high strength steel; stress analysis of refrigerator door lower hinge relation between evaporator T. *Mailing Add:* 1407 Green Meadow Rd Evansville IN 47715-6055

HARTSFIELD, HENRY WARREN, JR, ASTRONAUTICS. *Current Pos:* mem support crew, Apollo 16, Skylabs 2, 3, 4 missions, pilot, ASTRONAUT, LYNDON B JOHNSON SPACE CTR, NASA, 69- *Personal Data:* b Birmingham, Ala, Nov 21, 33; m 57, Judy F Massey; c Judy L & Keely W. *Educ:* Auburn Univ, BS, 54; Duke Univ, 54-55; Air Force Inst Technol, 60-61; Univ Tenn, MS, 70. *Hon Degrees:* DSc, Auburn Univ, 86. *Honors & Awards:* Meritorious Serv Medal, DSM, NASA, 82, 88, Space Flight Medal, 82, 84, 85; Nat Geog White Space Trophy, 73. *Prof Exp:* Commdr 2nd lt, USAF, 55, adv through grades to colonel, 74, 53rd tactical squadron, Bitburg, Ger, 61-64, instr, Test Pilot Sch, Edwards AFB, 65-66, Manned Orbiting Lab, 66-69. *Concurrent Pos:* Dep dir, Flight Crew Oper Directorate, NASA, 87-89, dir, tech integration & analysis, Off Space Flight, 89-90, dep dir oper space sta projs, Marshall Space Flight Ctr, 90-91, mgr man-tended capability phase Space Sta, Freedom Prog, 91-; civilian astronaut, NASA. *Mem:* Soc Exp Test Pilots; Air Force Asn. *Mailing Add:* MTC Phase Mgr SSFP Code MS Lyndon B Johnson Space Ctr Houston TX 77058

HARTSFIELD, SANDEE MORRIS, VETERINARY ANESTHESIOLOGY. *Current Pos:* asst prof physiol, 73-74, assoc prof, 77-82, PROF VET ANESTHESIA, TEX A&M UNIV, 82- *Personal Data:* b Bryan, Tex, May 18, 48; m 72; c 2. *Educ:* Tex A&M Univ, BS, 70, DVM, 71; Mich State Univ, MS, 73. *Prof Exp:* Postdoctoral fel vet anesthesia, Mich State Univ, 71-73; asst prof, Univ Ill, 74-77. *Concurrent Pos:* Vis prof, Dept Vet Clin Med, Univ Ill, 84-85; chief, Sect Anesthesia, Vet Teaching Hosp, Tex A&M Univ, 86- *Mem:* Am Col Vet Anesthesiologists (pres, 84); Am Soc Vet Anesthesiol (pres, 81-82); Am Vet Med Asn; Am Animal Hosp Asn; Am Asn Vet Clinicians. *Res:* Use of and cardiopulmonary effects of anesthetics and adjuncts in various domestic and laboratory species. *Mailing Add:* 1822 Laura Lane College Station TX 77840

HARTSHORN, JOSEPH HAROLD, GLACIAL GEOLOGY, PHYSICAL GEOGRAPHY. *Current Pos:* from assoc prof to prof, 67-87, head dept, 70-77, EMER PROF GEOL, UNIV MASS, AMHERST, 87- *Personal Data:* b Cleveland, Ohio, June 23, 22; m 42, 80; c 2. *Educ:* Harvard Univ, BS, 47, MA, 50, PhD(geormphol), 55. *Prof Exp:* Geologist, US Geol Surv, 50-67. *Concurrent Pos:* Res geologist, US Geol Surv, 67- *Mem:* AAAS; Geol Soc Am; Arctic Inst NAm; Am Quaternary Asn; Nat Asn Geol Teachers. *Res:* Glacial geology in New England, especially proglacial lakes and landforms; geomorphology and engineering geology of the East Coast of Greenland; glacial geology of the Malaspina Glacier, Alaska; Pleistocene archaeology. *Mailing Add:* Dept Geol/Geog Univ Mass Amherst MA 01003

HARTSHORNE, ROBERT (ROBIN) COPE, ALGEBRAIC GEOMETRY. *Current Pos:* assoc prof, 72-74, PROF MATH, UNIV CALIF, BERKELEY, 74- *Personal Data:* b Boston, Mass, Mar 15, 38; m 69, Edith Churchill; c Jonathan (deceased), Benjamin & Joemy G. *Educ:* Harvard Univ, AB, 59; Princeton Univ, PhD(math), 63. *Honors & Awards:* Steele Prize, Am Math Soc, 79. *Prof Exp:* Jr fel, Harvard Univ, 63-66, from asst prof to assoc prof math, 66-72. *Concurrent Pos:* Vis prof, Tata Inst Fundamental Res, Bombay, 69-70 & Kyoto Univ, Japan, 75-76, 82-84; A P Sloan Found fel, 70-72. *Mem:* Am Math Soc. *Res:* Algebraic geometry. *Mailing Add:* Dept Math Univ Calif Berkeley CA 94720. *E-Mail:* robin@math.berkeley.edu

HARTSOUGH, LARRY DOWD, MATERIALS SCIENCE, THIN FILMS. *Current Pos:* MGR PVD SOURCE TECHNOL, VARIAN ASSOCS, THIN FILM SYSTS, 91- *Personal Data:* b Wadsworth, Ohio, Jan 23, 42; m 65, Carolyn S; c John. *Educ:* Univ Calif, Berkeley, BS, 65, MS, 67, PhD(mat sci), 71. *Prof Exp:* Res metallurgist, Optical Coating Lab, Inc, 71-75; res engr, Temescal Div, Airco Inc, 75-77; sr staff scientist, Ultek Div, Perkin-Elmer, Inc, 77-81; co-founder vpres eng & dir, Technol Gryphon Prod, 81-88; sr staff scientist & proj mgr, Gen Signal Thin Film Co, 88-90. *Concurrent Pos:* Co-chair, Phys Interfaces & Carriers Stand Comt, Semiconductor Equip & Mat Int. *Mem:* Am Vacuum Soc; Sigma Xi. *Res:* Synthesis of thin film materials and their characterization; development of new sputter-deposition sources, processes and systems. *Mailing Add:* 3007 Benvenue Berkeley CA 94705

HARTSOUGH, ROBERT RAY, COATINGS FORMULATION, CERAMIC & GLASS CHEMISTRY. *Current Pos:* chemist, 81-86, chief chemist, 86-89, TECH DIR DISPERSION CHEM, GRAPHITE PROD CORP, 89- *Personal Data:* b Salem, Ohio, Aug 11, 57; m 83, Patricia Koch; c Raymond J, Thomas W & Paula E. *Educ:* Youngstown State Univ, BS, 79, MS, 85, MBA, 90. *Prof Exp:* Teaching asst chem, Youngstown State Univ, 79-81. *Mem:* Am Chem Soc; Am Powdered Metal Inst. *Res:* Synthesis of a control release system for an anticancer drug; improving properties and stability of suspension and dispersion of forging and extrusion lubricants. *Mailing Add:* 4210 Nottingham Dr Youngstown OH 44511

HARTSOUGH, WALTER DOUGLAS, PARTICLE PHYSICS. *Current Pos:* Physicist, physics res, 46-50, accelerator res & develop, 50-54, Bevatron opers head, 54-73, group leader, 73, assoc dir div head, eng & tech serv div, 73-75, assoc dir div head, facil mgt & tech serv div, 75-76, dir off minority outreach prog, 87, EMER ASSOC DIR, UNIV CALIF, LAWRENCE BERKELEY LAB, 87-; ASSOC, NATIONWIDE TECHNOL INC, 87- *Personal Data:* b Merced, Calif, Sept 17, 24; m 45, Patricia Fain; c Linda, Marian, Joan & Michael. *Educ:* Univ Calif, AB, 44. *Concurrent Pos:* Mem, Joint Comt High Energy Physics, US-Peoples Repub China, 79-87; mem adv comt, White House, 85-89; Initiative Sci & Technol Adv Comm HBCV, 86-; mem, Initiative Sci & Technol Adv Comm HBCV, 86-87. *Res:* Particle physics research and high energy particle accelerator research and development; counter and cloud chamber techniques; design and construction of prototype neutral beam injection systems for tokamaks. *Mailing Add:* 649 Ironbark Circle Orinda CA 94563

HARTSTEIN, ALLAN MARK, SOLID STATE PHYSICS, SEMICONDUCTOR DEVICES. *Current Pos:* fel, 74-76, RES STAFF MEM PHYSICS, THOMAS J WATSON RES CTR, IBM CORP, 76- *Personal Data:* b New York, NY, Oct 5, 47; c 2. *Educ:* Calif Inst Technol, BS, 69; Univ Pa, PhD(physics), 73. *Prof Exp:* Asst instr, Univ Pa, 69-73. *Mem:* Am Inst Physics; fel Am Phys Soc; sr mem Inst Elec & Electronics Engrs. *Res:* Interface phenomena; metal oxide semiconductor structures; transport in inversion layers; tunneling; physics of disordered systems; low dimensional systems; neural networks; computer design. *Mailing Add:* IBM Thomas J Watson Res Ctr PO Box 218 Yorktown Heights NY 10598. *Fax:* 914-995-2141; *E-Mail:* hart@watson.ibm.com

HARTSTEIN, ARTHUR M, PHYSICAL CHEMISTRY, ANALYTICAL CHEMISTRY. *Current Pos:* PHYS CHEMIST MINING RES, US DEPT ENERGY, WASHINGTON, DC, 77- *Personal Data:* b Englewood, NJ, Nov 12, 40; m 64; c 2. *Educ:* Polytech Inst Brooklyn, BS, 62; Adelphi Univ, PhD(phys chem), 70. *Prof Exp:* Res scientist, Power Sources Div, Gulton Industs, 69-70; res chemist, Anal Res Lab, Pittsburgh Mining & Safety Res Ctr, US Bur Mines, 70-75, phys chemist mining res, US Bur Mines, Washington, DC, 75-77. *Mem:* Am Chem Soc. *Res:* Improving the nations energy picture by developing and demonstrating methods for obtaining oil from oil shale rock. *Mailing Add:* 13811 Dowlais Dr Rockville MD 20853

HARTSTIRN, WALTER, PLANT PATHOLOGY. *Current Pos:* RETIRED. *Personal Data:* b New York, NY, Apr 16, 28; m 54; c 3. *Educ:* Mont State Univ, BS, 51; Univ Wis, MS, 53; Ore State Col, PhD(plant path), 58. *Prof Exp:* Asst plant pathologist, Ill Natural Hist Surv, 58-77; asst prof plant path, Univ Ill, Urbana-Champaign, 73-77; mem staff anal chem, Ill Power Co, 81-87. *Mailing Add:* 907 E Burkwood Dr Urbana IL 61801

HARTSUCK, JEAN ANN, BIOCHEMISTRY, X-RAY CRYSTALLOGRAPHY. *Current Pos:* Asst prof, 70-74, ASSOC PROF BIOCHEM, UNIV OKLA, 74- *Personal Data:* b Enid, Okla, July 18, 39; m 62, James M; c Rebecca (Hulsey), Mary (Fleischli) & Katherine. *Educ:* Univ Okla, BS, 60; Radcliffe Col, AM, 62; Harvard Univ, PhD(chem), 64. *Concurrent Pos:* Asst mem, Okla Med Res Found, 70-73, assoc mem, 73-; NIH fel, Harvard Univ, 64-65; Career Develop Award, Okla Med Res Found, 71-76. *Mem:* Am Crystallog Asn; Am Chem Soc; Am Soc Biol Chem. *Res:* Mechanisms of activation and catalysis of pepsin and homologous enzymes; x-ray crystallography of aspartic proteinases. *Mailing Add:* Okla Med Res Found 825 NE 13th St Oklahoma City OK 73104. *Fax:* 405-271-7249

HARTT, WILLIAM HANDY, METALLURGICAL & MATERIALS ENGINEERING. *Current Pos:* From asst prof to assoc prof, 68-75, PROF OCEAN ENG, FLA ATLANTIC UNIV, 75- *Personal Data:* b Long Beach, Calif, Apr 28, 39; m 62; c 2. *Educ:* Va Polytech Inst, BS, 61; Univ Fla, PhD(metall eng), 66. *Res:* Physical and mechanical metallurgy; marine materials and corrosion; environmental cracking of materials. *Mailing Add:* Dept Ocean Eng Fla Atlantic Univ 777 Glades Rd Boca Raton FL 33431

HARTUNG, G(EORGE) HARLEY, EXERCISE PHYSIOLOGY, PREVENTIVE MEDICINE. *Current Pos:* PROF PHYSIOL, SCH MED, UNIV HAWAII, 87- *Personal Data:* b Houston, Tex, Dec 15, 33; m 67; c 3. *Educ:* Tex A&M Univ, BS, 56; NTex State Univ, MEd, 65; Univ Tex, Austin, PhD(exercise physiol), 70; Univ Tex Health Sci Ctr Houston, MS, 87. *Prof Exp:* Asst prof phys educ, Southeastern La State Univ, 69-70; asst prof, Cent Mo State Univ, 70-75; asst prof phys med, Baylor Col Med, 75-84, assoc prof med & phys med, 84-87. *Concurrent Pos:* Adj assoc prof, Sch Pub Health, Univ Tex Health Sci Ctr, 76-87, vis assoc prof, 82-86; consult, Rehab Med Serv, Vet Admin Med Ctr, Houston, 76-87; vis grad fac, Tex A&M Univ, 77-87; adj grad fac, Univ Houston, 79-87; adj prof, Sch Pub Health, Univ Hawaii, 96- *Mem:* Fel Am Col Sports Med; Am Heart Asn; Am Physiol Asn. *Res:* Exercise physiology, especially as it relates to plasma lipid levels, cardiovascular disease and environmental factors; role of exercise in preventive medicine; effect of alcohol on plasma lipids and lipoproteins. *Mailing Add:* Dept Cardiol Serv Tripler Army Med Ctr MCHK-DMC Honolulu HI 96859-5000

HARTUNG, JACK BURDAIR, SR, planetary sciences, geochronology, for more information see previous edition

HARTUNG, JOHN, DIGITAL SIGNAL PROCESSING, COMPUTER ARCHITECTURE. *Current Pos:* mem tech staff, AT&T Bell Labs, 80-84, Bell Commun Res, 84-85, Info Systs Lab, 85-86, supvr, Bell Labs, 86-90, MEM TECH STAFF & PRIN INVESTR, LUCENT TECHNOLOGIES, 90- *Personal Data:* b Passaic, NJ, Nov 24, 51; m 83; c 1. *Educ:* Stevens Inst Technol, BS, 73; Rutgers Univ, MS, 75 & 78, PhD(elec eng), 80. *Prof Exp:* Mem tech staff, David Sarnoff Res Ctr, RCA, 79-80; asst prof elec eng, Rutgers Univ, 79-80. *Mem:* Inst Elec & Electronics Engrs. *Res:* Digital signal processing; design and implementation of video coding algorithms and multiprocessor digital signal processing architectures. *Mailing Add:* 22 Red Hill Rd Warren Township NJ 07059

HARTUNG, JOHN DAVID, NEUROANESTHESIOLOGY, SOCIOBIOLOGY. *Current Pos:* Assoc prof, 81-94, ASSOC PROF ANESTHESIOL, HEALTH SCI CTR STATE UNIV NY, 94- *Personal Data:* b 1947; m 92, Renata Quartermaine; c Tirah L. *Educ:* Univ Pa, BA, 73; Harvard Univ, PhD(anthropol), 81. *Concurrent Pos:* Assoc ed, J Neurosurg Anesthesiol, 88- *Mem:* Am Soc Anesthesiol; Human Behav & Evolution Soc. *Res:* Neuroanesthesiology; evolutionary theory. *Mailing Add:* Dept Anesthesiol State Univ NY Health Sci 450 Clarkson Ave Brooklyn NY 11203. *E-Mail:* jhartung@netmail.hscbklyn.edu

HARTUNG, ROLF, ENVIRONMENTAL TOXICOLOGY. *Current Pos:* Lectr indust health, 64, from asst prof to assoc prof, 65-74, PROF ENVIRON TOXICOL & RES SCIENTIST, UNIV MICH, ANN ARBOR, 74- *Personal Data:* b Bremen, Ger, Mar 1, 35; US citizen; m 59, Kathryn S Fredricks; c Steven, James & Susan. *Educ:* Univ Mich, BS, 60, MWM, 62, PhD(wildlife mgt), 64; Am Bd Toxicol, dipl, 80. *Concurrent Pos:* Mem comt health effects water pollution, Int Joint Comn (US & Can); mem comt geochem & health effects & water qual criteria, Nat Acad Sci; chair, Comt Rediation of Irrigation Induced Water Qual, Nat Acad Sci & Comt Environ, Effects, Transport & Fate, US Environ Protection Agency, Sci Adv Bd; Comn Environ, Effects, Transport &. *Mem:* Wildlife Soc; Am Indust Hyg Asn; Soc Toxicol; Soc Environ Toxicol & Chem; Soc Risk Anal. *Res:* Effects of polluting oils on waterfowl; toxicity of aminoethanols; coactions between chlorinated hydrocarbon pesticides and aquatic pollutants; environmental dynamics of heavy metals; risk assessment. *Mailing Add:* Dept Environ & Indust Health Univ Mich Ann Arbor MI 48109-2029. *Fax:* 313-971-4180; *E-Mail:* thartung@umich.edu

HARTUNG, THEODORE EUGENE, FOOD SCIENCE. *Current Pos:* prof poultry, 65-74, dean, Agr Col, 74-88, ASSOC VCHMN, AGR & NATURAL RESOURCES, UNIV NEBR, 88- *Personal Data:* b Denver, Colo, Jan 28, 29; m 51; c 3. *Educ:* Colo State Univ, BS, 51, MS, 53; Purdue Univ, PhD(food tech), 62. *Prof Exp:* Instr poultry, Colo State Univ, 51-53, exten specialist, 53-61, assoc prof, 61-65. *Mem:* Inst Food Technol; Poultry Sci Asn; Sigma Xi. *Res:* Microbiological, chemical and physical changes of food subjected to storage and handling variations; nutrient composition of food and alteration in processing. *Mailing Add:* Dept Food Sci-FYH 143 Univ Nebr E Campus PO Box 830919 Lincoln NE 68583-0919

HARTUNIAN, RICHARD ARAM, AEROPHYSICS, REENTRY PHYSICS. *Current Pos:* prin dir, Aero Lab, Aerospace Corp, 60-68, gen mgr, Reentry Systs Div, 68-76, vpres, Space Launch Opers, 76-86, CONSULT, AEROSPACE CORP, 87- *Personal Data:* m 56, Ena Galdi; c Paul & Richard. *Educ:* Rensselaer Polytechnic Inst, BS, 51; Cornell Univ, MS, 54, PhD(aeronaut eng), 56. *Prof Exp:* Prin scientist, Cornell Aero Lab, 56-60. *Concurrent Pos:* Consult & adv, Defense Sci Bd, 72-82; assoc ed, J Defense Res, 77-79; adv & study chmn, Nat Res Coun, 78-95. *Mem:* Fel Am Inst Aeronaut & Astronaut. *Res:* High temperature gas dynamics, chemical kinetics and gas physics related to flows around reentry vehicles, emphasis on nonequilibrium heat transfer, ionization, high temperature transport properties and chemical luminescence. *Mailing Add:* 2714 Graysby Ave San Pedro CA 90732

HARTWELL, GEORGE E, CATALYSIS, ORGANOMETALLIC CHEMISTRY. *Current Pos:* group leader, 74-86, res assoc, 86-90, ASSOC SCIENTIST, DOW CHEM USA, 90- *Personal Data:* b Port Jervis, NY, Aug 1, 40; m 65, Ieva Ogrins; c Peter & Erik. *Educ:* Union Col, NY, BS, 62; Univ Ill, Urbana, MS, 64, PhD, 66. *Prof Exp:* From asst prof to assoc prof chem, Ind Univ, Bloomington, 66-74. *Concurrent Pos:* NATO fel, Imp Col, Univ London, 66-67. *Mem:* Am Chem Soc. *Res:* Homogeneous and supported homogeneous catalysis, especially reduction chemistry; metal clusters; heterogeneous catalysts; catalytic processes and research in developing heterogeneous and homogeneous catalysts. *Mailing Add:* Cent Res Bldg 1776 Dow Chem USA Midland MI 48674

HARTWELL, LELAND HARRISON, GENETICS. *Current Pos:* assoc prof, 68-73, PROF GENETICS, UNIV WASH, 73-, PRES, CANCER RES CTR, 97- *Personal Data:* b Los Angeles, Calif, Oct 30, 39; div; c 3. *Educ:* Calif Inst Technol, BS, 61; Mass Inst Technol, PhD(microbiol), 64. *Honors & Awards:* Eli Lilly Award in Microbiol & Immunol, Am Soc Microbiol, 74; Merit Award, NIH, 90; Hoffman LaRoche Mattia Award, 91; Gairdner Found Int Award, 92. *Prof Exp:* Nat Acad Sci-Nat Res Coun fel animal virol, Salk Inst Biol Studies, 64-65; from asst prof to assoc prof biochem, Univ Calif, Irvine, 65-68. *Concurrent Pos:* Sabbatical, Stanford Univ, 83, Fred Hutchinson Cancer Res Ctr, 84; Guggenheim awardee & Am Cancer Soc scholar, 83-84; res prof genetics, Am Cancer Soc, 90-; Am Acad Microbiol; Am Soc Cell Biol. *Mem:* Nat Acad Sci; AAAS; Am Soc Microbiol; Genetic Soc Am (pres, 91). *Res:* Genetic analysis of cell division and cell communication in yeast. *Mailing Add:* Cancer Res Ctr Univ Wash 1100 Fairview Ave PO Box 19024 LY-301 Seattle WA 98109-1024

HARTWICK, EARL BRIAN, FISHERIES ECOLOGY. *Current Pos:* asst prof, 75-83, ASSOC PROF MARINE BIOL, SIMON FRASER UNIV, 83- *Personal Data:* b Toronto, Ont, Feb 19, 42; m 64, Heather Kearns; c Chris, Mike & Sean. *Educ:* Univ Toronto, BSc, 66, MSc, 68; Univ BC, PhD(ecol), 73. *Prof Exp:* Asst prof pop ecol, Univ Guelph, 73-75. *Concurrent Pos:* Univ Diving Officer, Can Stand Asn. *Mem:* Can Asn Underwater Sci (pres, 90-92); Inst Fisheries Anal; Am Acad Underwater Sci; Undersea & Hyperbasic Med Soc. *Res:* Marine invertebrate ecology; biology and ecology of octopuses; population processes in marine environments; applied marine ecology. *Mailing Add:* Dept Biol Sci Simon Fraser Univ Burnaby BC V5A 1S6 Can. *Fax:* 604-291-3496; *E-Mail:* hartwick@sfu.ca

HARTWICK, FREDERICK DAVID ALFRED, ASTRONOMY. *Current Pos:* from asst prof to assoc prof, 68-78, PROF ASTRON, UNIV VICTORIA, BC, 78- *Personal Data:* b Arvida, Que, May 27, 41. *Educ:* McGill Univ, BEng, 62; Univ Toronto, MA, 64, PhD(astron), 66. *Prof Exp:* NATO vis fel, Princeton Univ, 66-67; NATO res fel, Mt Wilson & Palomar Observ & Calif Inst Technol, 67-68. *Concurrent Pos:* Steacie fel, 78-79. *Mem:* Royal Astron Soc Can; fel Royal Astron Soc; Am Astron Soc; Can Astron Soc; Int Astron Union. *Res:* Kinematics of galaxy halos; space distribution of quasors. *Mailing Add:* Dept Physics & Astron Univ Victoria Victoria BC V8W 2Y2 Can

HARTWICK, RICHARD ALLEN, biomedical analyses, for more information see previous edition

HARTWICK, THOMAS STANLEY, QUANTUM ELECTRONICS, SOLID STATE PHYSICS. *Current Pos:* MGT CONSULT, 95- *Personal Data:* b Vandalia, Ill, Mar 19, 34; m 61, Alberta E Lind; c 3. *Educ:* Univ Ill, BS, 56; Univ Calif, Los Angeles, MS, 58; Univ Southern Calif, PhD, 69. *Prof Exp:* Mem tech staff, Hughes Aircraft Co, 56-59, group leader spin wave excitation in ferrites, 59-61; sect mgr quantum electronics, Labs Div, Aerospace Corp, 61-63 & 65-73; dept head, 73-75, asst dir, Electronics Res Lab, 75-78; mgr, E-O Develop Labs, Hughes Aircraft Co, 78-83, mgr, E-O Res Ctr, TRW, 83-86, mgr, Microelectronics Ctr, 86-90, proj mgr, 90-95. *Concurrent Pos:* Mem bd dirs, Laser Tech Inc, 67-92 & 3D Tech Labs, 96-; consult mem, Adv Group Electron Devices, Dept Defense, 78-88; chmn, Working Group C, 88-93; chair bd dirs, Laser Tech Inc, 92-95. *Mem:* Am Phys Soc; Optical Soc Am. *Res:* Magnetic resonance in ferrites; molecular lasers; optical communications and optical properties of ferro electrics; laser heterodyne radiometry; far infrared lasers and applications; laser communications. *Mailing Add:* PO Box 10125 Torrance CA 90505. *Fax:* 310-378-1596

HARTWIG, CURTIS P, COMPUTER LANGUAGES & SOFTWARE SUPPORT TOOLS, DIGITAL CONTROL SYSTEMS. *Current Pos:* DEVELOP ENGR CONTROL SYST, LOCKHEED MARTIN, BIRMINGHAM, NY, 79- *Personal Data:* b Boston, Mass, July 13, 39; m 62, 86, Nancy A Markham; c Eric K & Karl W. *Educ:* Mass Inst Technol, SB & SM, 62, PhD(elec sci), 66. *Prof Exp:* Tech aide sta apparatus, Bell Tel Labs, Inc, 59-60, mil res, 60, sr tech aide solid state devices, 61-62; asst elec eng,

Mass Inst Technol, 62-66; res scientist, Raytheon Co, 64, sr res scientist microwave physics, Res Div, 66-74; staff scientist, Microwave Div, Sander Assoc, Inc, 75-76; adv engr, Fed Systs Div, IBM Corp, 76-77. *Res:* Electrical science; microwave magnetics; electromagnetic properties of matter with emphasis on application to microwave devices; exploration of phenomena in materials which may lead to new types of devices; investigating techniques for developing software for digital control systems. *Mailing Add:* Lockheed Martin Control Systs 600 Main St Johnson City NY 13790-1888. *E-Mail:* chartwig@worldnet.att.net

HARTWIG, JOHN, LEUKOCYTE MOTILITY. *Current Pos:* ASST PROF MED, MED SCH, HARVARD UNIV, 83-; ASST PROF BIOL, MASS GEN HOSP, 83-; ASSOC PROF MED, BRIGHAM-WOMEN'S HOSP, 91- *Personal Data:* b Marshall, Mich, Sept 19, 49. *Educ:* Harvard Univ, PhD(cell develop biol), 80. *Mailing Add:* Exp Med Div Brigham-Women's Hosp 221 Longwood Ave Boston MA 02115

HARTWIG, NATHAN LEROY, WEED SCIENCE, SOIL CONSERVATION. *Current Pos:* PROF WEED SCI, PA STATE UNIV, UNIVERSITY PARK, 69- *Personal Data:* b Monroe, Wis, Aug 10, 37; m 63, Elfriede Dietz; c Susan. *Educ:* Univ Wis-Madison, BS, 59, PhD(agron), 70; Univ Ariz, MS, 65. *Mem:* Am Soc Agron; Weed Sci Soc Am. *Res:* Methods of controlling annual and perennial weeds in no-tillage corn; cover crop management in agronomic crop rotations; use of crownvetch as a living mulch for min- and no-tillage crop production. *Mailing Add:* Dept Agron Pa State Univ University Park PA 16802. *Fax:* 814-863-7043; *E-Mail:* nlh@psu.edu

HARTWIG, ROBERT EDUARD, APPLIED MATHEMATICS. *Current Pos:* from asst prof to assoc prof, 68-79, PROF MATH, NC STATE UNIV, 79- *Personal Data:* b Soerabaja, Indonesia, Mar 21, 41; m 66, Ingrid U Kaldun; c Roland M & Kirsten E. *Educ:* Univ Adelaide, BSc, 62, Hons, 63, PhD(math), 66. *Prof Exp:* NSF res fel math physics, Cornell Univ, 66-68. *Mem:* Soc Indust & Appl Math; Math Asn Am. *Res:* Non-negative matrices; cryptography; linear algebra; matrices; asymptotics; generalized inverses. *Mailing Add:* Dept Math NC State Univ Raleigh NC 27695-8205

HARTY, MICHAEL, ANATOMY, ORTHOPEDIC SURGERY. *Current Pos:* vis lectr, 53-54, from asst prof to prof, 54-88, EMER PROF ANAT & ORTHOP SURG, SCH MED, UNIV PA, 88- *Personal Data:* b Waterford, Ireland, July 29, 12; m 54; c 2. *Educ:* Univ Dublin, MB, 37, MCh, 52; Cambridge Univ, MA, 47; FRCS. *Honors & Awards:* Lindback Award, 80. *Prof Exp:* Surgeon, Emergency Med Serv, London, 39-41; demonstr anat, Cambridge Univ, 42-44 & 46-47, lectr, 49-53. *Mem:* Am Asn Anat; Anat Soc Gt Brit & Ireland; Brit Med Asn. *Res:* Surgical and functional anatomy of the locomotor system. *Mailing Add:* Dept Anat Univ Penn Sch Med Philadelphia PA 19104

HARTZ, BILLY J, ENGINEERING MECHANICS, CIVIL ENGINEERING. *Current Pos:* From asst prof to prof, 55-82, EMER PROF CIVIL ENG, UNIV WASH, 82-; PRES, BILLY BOARDS, INC, 85- *Personal Data:* b Cavalier, NDak, July 9, 26; div; c 4. *Educ:* Univ Calif, Berkeley, BS, 52, MS, 54, PhD(civil eng), 55. *Concurrent Pos:* NSF sr fel, 63-64; NTH, Zurich, Switz, Trondheim, Norway, 81-82. *Mem:* Am Soc Civil Engrs. *Res:* Matrix methods in structural mechanics; dynamic stability of elastic systems; dynamic response of structures; elastic wave propagation; author of over 55 publications. *Mailing Add:* 4016 NE 110th St Seattle WA 98125

HARTZ, JOHN WILLIAM, NEOPLASMS OF BIOCHEMISTRY, HEMATOPATHOLOGY. *Current Pos:* ASST PROF PATH, BOWMAN GRAY SCH MED, 74- *Personal Data:* b Detroit, Mich. *Educ:* Albion Col, AB, 58; Harvard Med Sch, MD, 62; Univ Wis, PhD(physiol chem), 68. *Prof Exp:* Lieutenant, USN Chem Lab, Naval Med Res, 68-69; fel biochem, Univ Wis, 69-71; resident path, Univ Chicago Hosps & Clins, 71-74. *Mem:* Sigma Xi. *Res:* Redcell proteins; membrane chemistry of neoplasms; hematopathology. *Mailing Add:* 230 Flintshire Rd Winston-Salem NC 27104-2704

HARTZ, ROY EUGENE, ORGANIC POLYMER CHEMISTRY. *Current Pos:* res scientist, Textile & Fiber Div, Uniroyal, Inc, 71-76, tire cord res & develop mgr, 76-85, tech mgr, Tire Textiles, 87-91, tire cord & royal cord res & develop mgr, 85-91, OPERS QUAL ASSURANCE REINFORCEMENTS MGR, UNIROYAL GOODRICH TIRE CO, 91- *Personal Data:* b Duncannon, Pa, Apr 20, 40; m 65, Martha Vamos; c Jane. *Educ:* Pa State Univ, BS, 62; Univ Md, PhD(org chem), 67. *Prof Exp:* Chemist, US Bur Mines, 63; res chemist, Res & Develop Ctr, Wayne, NJ, 66-69, res scientist, 69-71. *Mem:* Am Chem Soc; Sigma Xi; Adhesion Soc. *Res:* Pyrolysis of allylamines; reactions of trifluoracetic acid with unsaturated compounds; free radical and anionic initiated polymerizations in the areas of block copolymers and polar monomers; adhesion; adhesion mechanism problems; pollution areas; new adhesive system. *Mailing Add:* 101 Linsbury Circle Columbia SC 29210

HARTZELL, CHARLES ROSS, III, BIOPHYSICAL CHEMISTRY, PHYSIOLOGICAL CHEMISTRY. *Current Pos:* sr res scientist, 78-80, DIR RES, ALFRED I DUPONT INST, NEMOUR FOUND, 80- *Personal Data:* b Butler, Pa, Aug 12, 41; m 63; c 2. *Educ:* Geneva Col, BSc, 63; Ind Univ, Bloomington, PhD(biochem), 67. *Prof Exp:* Fel & res assoc chem, Ind Univ, Bloomington, 67; res scientist, Div Protein Chem, Commonwealth Sci & Indust Res Orgn, Australia, 67-68; Nat Insts Gen Med Sci fel & res assoc, Inst Enzyme Res, Univ Wis, Madison, 68-70, asst res prof, 70-71; from asst prof to assoc prof biochem, Pa State Univ, 71-78. *Concurrent Pos:* Mem coun basic sci & estab investr, Am Heart Asn, 70-75. *Mem:* Biophys Soc; Am Chem Soc; Am Heart Asn; Am Soc Biochem & Molecular Biol; Am Soc Cell Biol. *Res:* Perinatal growth and development of skeletal and cardiac muscle; biochemistry of neurotransmitter synthesis, storage and release; enzyme activities and protein turnover of mammalian skeletal muscle regeneration in cell culture. *Mailing Add:* Alfred I DuPont Inst Res Dept PO Box 269 Wilmington DE 19899-0269. *Fax:* 302-651-6899

HARTZELL, KENNETH R, JR, LASER PHYSICS. *Current Pos:* ASST PROF PHYSICS, VILLANOVA UNIV, 83- *Personal Data:* b Philadelphia, Pa, June 15, 54. *Educ:* Villanova Univ, BS, 76; Drexel Univ, MS, 78 & PhD, 86. *Concurrent Pos:* Adj inst & asst prof, Drexel Univ, 78-86. *Mem:* Am Phys Soc; Am Asn Physics Teachers; Optical Soc Am; Inst Elec & Electronics Engrs. *Res:* Investigation of theoretical models of free electron lasers for the purpose of gain enhancement and improvement of outdoor power and efficiency. *Mailing Add:* 521 Mercer Rd Marion Station PA 19066

HARTZELL, THOMAS H, FOOD SCIENCE. *Current Pos:* CONSULT, 92- *Personal Data:* b Passaic, NJ, Dec 12, 32; m 56; c 2. *Educ:* Pa State Univ, BS, 56, MS, 57. *Prof Exp:* Anal chemist, Res Ctr, Nat Biscuit Co, 57-60; chief chemist, Minn Malting Co, 60-67, tech dir, 67-75, vpres prod & tech dir, 74-85; vpres qual control, Minn Grain Pearling Co, 70-83; vpres malting, Schreier Malting Co, 85-89, sr vpres & tech dir, 89-92. *Mem:* Master Brewers Asn Am; Am Chem Soc; Am Soc Brewing Chem; Am Asn Cereal Chem; Inst Food Technol; Am Malting Barley Asn. *Res:* Cereal chemistry; grain malting technology; food technology; new techniques in malting technology; process and product development in malting technology. *Mailing Add:* 1717 Pheasant Lane Sheboygan WI 53081-7724

HARTZEMA, ABRAHAM GIJSBERT, PHARMACOEPIDEMIOLOGY, PHARMACEUTICAL OUTCOMES RESEARCH. *Current Pos:* PROF & RES ASSOC, HEALTH SERV CTR, SCH PUB HEALTH & SCH PHARM, UNIV NC, CHAPEL HILL, 81-, DIR, CTR PHARMACEUT OUTCOMES RES. *Personal Data:* b The Hague, Neth, May 10, 47; m 84, Christine Roth. *Educ:* Univ Utrecht, BSc, 73; Univ Wash, MSPH, 78; Univ Minn, PhD(social pharm), 82. *Concurrent Pos:* Res assoc, Vet Admin, 82-86. *Mem:* Am Pub Health Asn; Am Pharm Asn; Am Asn Col Pharm; Int Pharm Fedn; Asn Health Serv; Am Asn Pharmaceut Scientists; Int Soc Pharmacoepidemiol. *Res:* Program evaluation; pharmaceutical services; pharmacoepidemiology; pharmaceutical outcomes research; practise guideline development. *Mailing Add:* 6617 Turkey Farm Rd Chapel Hill NC 27514. *Fax:* 919-966-8486; *E-Mail:* bhartzem.pharm@mhs.unc.edu

HARTZFELD, HOWARD ALEXANDER, ORGANIC CHEMISTRY. *Current Pos:* Res chemist, 53-62, develop engr, 62-75, sr patent develop chemist, 75-79, SR PATENT DEVELOP SPECIALIST, PHILLIPS PETROL CO, 79- *Personal Data:* b Bronaugh, Mo, Jan 7, 28; m 65; c 1. *Educ:* Pittsburg State Univ, AB, 49; Iowa State Univ, PhD(org chem), 53. *Concurrent Pos:* Adj prof, Okla State Univ, 56-57. *Mem:* Am Chem Soc. *Res:* Organosilicon chemistry; chemical constitution and plant hormone action; petrochemistry. *Mailing Add:* 1409 SE Meadowcrest Ct Bartlesville OK 74006-6023

HARTZLER, ALFRED JAMES, MILITARY OPERATIONS. *Current Pos:* chief opers anal div, 65-73, tech adv, 73-77, SR ANALYST OPERS ANALYSIS OFF, US ARMS CONTROL & DISARMAMENT AGENCY, 77- *Personal Data:* b Manhattan, Kans, Apr 17, 22; m 50; c 1. *Educ:* Univ Chicago, BS, 43, MS, 44, PhD(physics), 51. *Prof Exp:* Res physicist, Gen Elec Co, 45-46, Carnegie Inst Technol, 50-55 & Opers Eval Group, Mass Inst Technol, 55-62; scientist, Ctr for Naval Anal, Franklin Inst, 62-65. *Mem:* AAAS; Opers Res Soc Am. *Res:* Cosmic rays; nuclear physics; operations research; strategic and peace research. *Mailing Add:* 1250 S Washington St Apt 203 Alexandria VA 22314

HARTZLER, EVA RUTH, BIOCHEMISTRY. *Current Pos:* RETIRED. *Personal Data:* b Longreen, Md, Jan 24, 11. *Educ:* Juniata Col, BS, 32; Pa State Col, MS, 33, PhD(biochem), 50. *Prof Exp:* Asst vitamin A, Oberlin Col, 33-35; res technician, Mayo Clin, 35-37; instr gen chem, Juniata Col, 37-38; jr chemist B vitamins, Bur Home Econ, USDA, 38-41; jr res chemist, Parke, Davis Co, 41-43; assoc nutritionist, Univ Hawaii, 43-47; instr biochem, Pa State Col, 47-50; asst prof, Juniata Col, 50-57, prof, 57-76, emer prof chem, 76-89. *Mem:* AAAS; Am Chem Soc. *Res:* Vitamin A utilization, purification and oxidation; vitamin-content of foods and methods of assay; utilization of ascorbic acid; ascorbic acid and enzymes in frozen vegetables. *Mailing Add:* 301 Westminster Dr Apt 302 Huntington PA 16652

HARTZLER, HARRIS DALE, ORGANIC CHEMISTRY. *Current Pos:* RETIRED. *Personal Data:* b Ill, July 29, 32; m 55; c 3. *Educ:* Univ Chicago, BA, 53, MS, 54, PhD(chem), 57. *Prof Exp:* Instr, Univ Mich, 57-59; res chemist, E I Du Pont de Nemours & Co, Inc, 59-74, group leader, 74-76, res suprv, 76-79, res mgr, Cent Res Dept, 79-90. *Mem:* Am Chem Soc. *Res:* Synthetic organic chemistry. *Mailing Add:* 112 S Spring Valley Rd Wilmington DE 19807

HARTZLER, HARROD HAROLD, physics; deceased, see previous edition for last biography

HARTZLER, JON DAVID, ORGANIC POLYMER CHEMISTRY. *Current Pos:* Res chemist, Pioneering Res Lab, Textile Fibers Dept, 67-73, sr res chemist, 73-74, sr res chemist, Dacron Plant Tech, 74-77, sr res chemist, Indust Tech, 77-81, RES ASSOC, SPRUANCE RES LAB, TEXTILE FIBERS DEPT, E I DU PONT DE NEMOURS & CO, INC, 81- *Personal Data:* b Peoria, Ill, Oct 15, 41; m 67. *Educ:* Goshen Col, BA, 63; Univ Del, PhD(org chem), 68. *Mem:* Am Chem Soc. *Res:* Polymer chemistry and fiber technology. *Mailing Add:* 3222 Fortunes Ridge Rd Midlothian VA 23112-4653

HARTZOG, DAVID G(EORGE), CHEMICAL ENGINEERING, APPLIED MATHEMATICS. *Current Pos:* SR STAFF ENG, ASPEN TECHNOL, 95- *Personal Data:* b St Louis, Mo, June 23, 41. *Educ:* Wash Univ, BSChE, 63, DSc(chem eng), 68. *Prof Exp:* Staff engr, Air Prod & Chem, Inc, 70-73, systs analyst, 73-76, systs mgr environ eng, 76-81, systs mgr process dynamics & environ eng, 81-87, lead systs engr, 87-94; pres, DGH Assocs, 94-95. *Mem:* Am Inst Chem Engrs; Am Chem Soc. *Res:* Development of deterministic mathematical models and computer programs for the simulation and design of various chemical processes, especially biochemical reactors and fixed-bed, pressure-swing adsorption units; transport of atmospheric pollutants; LNG hazard analysis; mass transfer with chemical reaction and numerical analysis, particularly parameter estimation algorithms. *Mailing Add:* Aspen Technol 9896 Bissonnet Houston TX 77036

HARTZOG, JAMES VICTOR, PHYSICAL CHEMISTRY. *Current Pos:* Res chemist, 67-74, SR RES CHEMIST, DACRON RES LAB, E I DU PONT DE NEMOURS & CO, INC, 74- *Personal Data:* b Reevesville, SC, Dec 3, 37; m 65; c 2. *Educ:* Clemson Col, BSc, 61, PhD(chem), 67. *Mem:* Am Chem Soc. *Res:* Electrical properties of polymers; surface chemistry; adsorption; polymer structure. *Mailing Add:* 1707 Sabra Dr Kinston NC 28504

HARUKI, HIROSHI, MATHEMATICS. *Current Pos:* PROF MATH, UNIV WATERLOO, 66- *Personal Data:* b Tokyo, Japan, Feb 18, 18; m 50; c 2. *Educ:* Osaka Univ, MSc, 40, PhD(math), 65. *Prof Exp:* Prof math, Kobe Merchantile Marine Col, 41-45; prof, Osaka High Sch, 45-49; assoc prof, Osaka Univ, 49-66. *Mem:* Am Math Soc. *Res:* Functional equations for analytic functions; partial differential equations. *Mailing Add:* Dept Pure Math Univ Waterloo Waterloo ON N2L 3G1 Can

HARUN, JOSEPH STANLEY, CLINICAL RESEARCH. *Current Pos:* vpres & med dir, 73-74, sr vpres & med dir, Wallace Labs Div, 74-76, CORP VPRES, MED & SCI AFFAIRS, CARTER-WALLACE, INC, 76- *Personal Data:* b Shenandoah, Pa, Jan 3, 25; m 52; c 5. *Educ:* Mt St Mary Col, Md, BS, 51; Jefferson Med Col, MD, 55. *Prof Exp:* Staff physician, Merck Sharp & Dohme, 59-60; pvt practr dermat, Pa, 60-62; head, Sci Info Dept, McNeil Labs, Inc, 62-64; dir med serv, Wallace Labs, 64-66; med dir, Madison Labs Div, Ciba Pharmaceut Co, 66-69, exec dir regulatory affairs, Ciba-Geigy Pharmaceut Div, 69-72, vpres drug regulatory affairs, 72-73. *Concurrent Pos:* Mem, NJ State Panel Sci Adv, 81-83. *Mem:* Soc Invest Dermat; fel Am Acad Dermat; Int Acad Law & Sci; AMA; Int Soc Trop Dermat. *Mailing Add:* Roxiticus Rd Mendham NJ 07945-3103

HARUTA, KYOICHI, PHYSICS. *Current Pos:* Mem tech staff, 63-83, DISTINGUISHED MEM TECH STAFF, BELL LABS, 83- *Personal Data:* b Kamakura, Japan, Jan 3, 31; m 60; c 3. *Educ:* Colby Col, BA, 57; Mass Inst Technol, PhD(physics), 63. *Mem:* Am Phys Soc. *Res:* X-ray diffraction study of single crystals and polycrystalline materials; acoustic vibrations in bounded media; numerical analysis; computer applications; very-large-scale intergation process simulation; integrated circuit interconnect modeling. *Mailing Add:* Bell Labs 1247 S Cedar Crest Blvd Allentown PA 18103. *E-Mail:* haruta@bell-labs.com

HARVATH, LIANA, IMMUNOLOGY. *Current Pos:* CHIEF LAB CELLULAR HEMAT & SR INVESTR-MICROBIOLOGIST, DIV HEMAT, CTR BIOL EVAL & RES, FOOD & DRUG ADMIN, BETHESDA, MD, 83- *Personal Data:* b Saginaw, Mich, Apr 27, 51. *Educ:* Mich State Univ, BS, 73; Univ Ill, PhD(path), 76. *Prof Exp:* From instr to asst prof microbiol & immunol, Univ Ill Med Ctr, Chicago, 76-79, res asst prof, Dept Med, 79; sr staff fel, Nat Cancer Inst, NIH, 79-83. *Concurrent Pos:* Immunopath res assoc, West Side Vet Admin Med Ctr, Chicago, Ill, 76-79, grad res grand award, Univ Ill Med Ctr, Chicago, 76-77; young investr res grant, Nat Heart, Lung & Blood Inst, NIH, 77-79; vis scientist, Semmelweis Med Univ, Budapest, Hungary, 87; mem, Subcomt on Flow Cytometry, Nat Comt Clin Lab Stand, 87- *Mem:* Am Asn Immunologists; Am Fedn Clin Res; Am Soc Hemat. *Res:* Neutrophil chemotactic factors; regulation of neutrophil chemotaxis; quality control in flow cytometry. *Mailing Add:* Ctr Biol Eval & Res Hemat Dept Food & Drug Admin 8800 Rockville Pike Bldg 29 Rm 321 Bethesda MD 20892-0001. *Fax:* 301-402-2780

HARVEL, CHRISTOPHER ALVIN, ASTRONOMY. *Current Pos:* resident astronr, Int Ultraviolet Explor Observ, 78-81, ASTRONR, SPACE TELESCOPE SCI INST, COMPUT SCI CORP, 81- *Personal Data:* b Columbia, SC, Dec 7, 44. *Educ:* Georgetown Univ, BS, 67; Univ SFla, MA, 73; Univ Fla, PhD(astron), 74. *Prof Exp:* Fel, Univ Fla, 74-75; res assoc astron, Nat Res Coun/Nat Acad Sci, 75-77 & NASA, Johnson Space Ctr, 77-78. *Mem:* Am Astron Soc. *Res:* Photographic and electrographic studies of diffuse nebulae, star clusters and galaxies; radiative transfer in circumstellar material; spectrophotometry, including visual and ultraviolet. *Mailing Add:* 6161 Stevens Forest Rd Columbia MD 21045

HARVEY, A(LEXANDER), ELECTRICAL ENGINEERING. *Current Pos:* RETIRED. *Personal Data:* b Stirling, Scotland, Sept 19, 30; m 67; c 2. *Educ:* Glasgow Univ, BSc, 52; Univ NMex, MS, 74. *Prof Exp:* Engr, Can Gen Elec Co, 54-56; design engr, Atomic Energy Can, Ltd, 56-58, res officer, 58-70; mem staff, Los Alamos Sci Lab, Univ Calif, 70-78; mem staff, Swiss Inst Nuclear Res, 78-80; staff mem, Los Alamos Nat Lab, Univ Calif, 80-88; head, mech eng dept, SLAC, Stanford, Calif, 88-93. *Res:* In-reactor instrumentation; high temperature thermometry; radiation-hardened components, especially accelerator magnets; radiation effects and radiation hardening of components, especially electrical engineering accelerator magnets; ceramic vacuum chambers for accelerator particle beams. *Mailing Add:* 2409 Benjamin Dr Mountainview CA 94043

HARVEY, ABNER MCGEHEE, MEDICINE. *Current Pos:* Asst, 34-37, instr, 40-41, prof, 46-73, PROF MED, SCH MED, JOHNS HOPKINS UNIV, 73- *Personal Data:* b Little Rock, Ark, July 30, 11; m 41; c 4. *Educ:* Washington & Lee Univ, AB, 30; Johns Hopkins Univ, MD, 34. *Honors & Awards:* Kober Medal, Asn Am Physicians, 81. *Concurrent Pos:* Intern & asst resident, Johns Hopkins Hosp, 34-37, resident physician, 40-41, physician-in-chief, 46-73; asst prof, Vanderbilt Univ, 41-42; fel, Nat Inst Med Res, London, 37-39; fel, Johnson Found Biophys, 39-40. *Mem:* Am Soc Clin Invest (pres, 56); fel Am Acad Arts & Sci; Asn Am Physicians (pres, 68); Am Clin & Climat Asn (pres, 71); master Am Col Physicians; Am Philos Soc. *Res:* Neurophysiology; clinical therapeutics; history of medicine. *Mailing Add:* Dept Med Johns Hopkins Univ Sch Med Suite 7200 1830 E Monument St Baltimore MD 21205. *Fax:* 301-955-0430

HARVEY, ALAN ERIC, FORESTRY. *Current Pos:* PLANT PATHOLOGIST, US FOREST SERV, 65- *Personal Data:* b Pittsburgh, Pa, Aug 2, 38; m 60; c 3. *Educ:* Col Idaho, BS, 60; Univ Idaho, MS, 62; Wash State Univ, PhD(plant path), 68. *Honors & Awards:* Cert Merit, USDA, 87; Forest Serv Stewardship Award, 91. *Concurrent Pos:* Adj prof, Univ Idaho, 65-73 & 79-, Univ Mont, 74-79 & Mich Tech Univ, 78- *Mem:* AAAS; Am Phytopath Soc; Am Inst Biol Sci; Sigma Xi. *Res:* Host parasite physiology as a means of developing selective plant disease control agents; microbial nitrogen transformations; mycorrhizae and forest tree root diseases. *Mailing Add:* Forestry Sci Lab USDA 1221 S Main Moscow ID 83843

HARVEY, ALBERT BIGELOW, ELECTRONICS, OPTICAL ENGINEERING. *Current Pos:* PROG DIR, LIGHTWAVE TECHNOL & NEW TECHNOLOGIES, NSF, 85- *Personal Data:* b Methuen, Mass, Dec 14, 38; m 63; c 2. *Educ:* Lowell Tech Inst, BS, 60; Mass Inst Technol, SM, 64; Tufts Univ, PhD(phys chem), 66. *Prof Exp:* Head chem diag br, Naval Res Lab, 66-85. *Concurrent Pos:* Vis res assoc, Microwave Lab, Stanford Univ, 73-74; rotator, NSF, 85-86, permanent, 86- *Mem:* AAAS; Am Chem Soc; Soc Appl Spectros; Sigma Xi; Coblentz Soc. *Res:* Optical spectroscopy; lasers; photonics; optoelectronics; semiconductor physics; non linear processes. *Mailing Add:* 12300 Old Colony Dr Upper Marlboro MD 20772-5031

HARVEY, ALBERT RAYMOND, MATHEMATICS. *Current Pos:* from asst prof to prof & chmn dept, 49-56, EMER PROF MATH, SAN DIEGO STATE UNIV, 83- *Personal Data:* b Lewiston, Maine, Jan 12, 21; m 50; c 1. *Educ:* Bates Col, BS, 42; Harvard Univ, AM, 43, PhD(math), 47. *Prof Exp:* From instr to asst prof math, Univ NH, 46-48; res fel, Calif Inst Technol, 48-49. *Concurrent Pos:* Fulbright lectr, Univ Baghdad, 57-58; vis prof, Col Virgin Islands, 63. *Mem:* Am Math Soc; Math Asn Am. *Res:* Analysis; mean of a function of exponential type. *Mailing Add:* 2350 Calle De La Garza La Jolla CA 92037

HARVEY, ALEXANDER LOUIS, PHYSICS, POWER GENERATION & DISTRIBUTION. *Current Pos:* assoc prof, Queens Col, NY, 62-66, chmn dept, 67-70, prof, 67-89, EMER PROF PHYSICS, QUEENS COL, NY, 89- *Personal Data:* b New York, NY, Oct 10, 17; m 53. *Educ:* City Col New York, BEE, 40; Polytech Inst Brooklyn, PhD(physics), 59. *Prof Exp:* From instr to asst prof physics, Polytech Inst Brooklyn, 55-62. *Mem:* NY Acad Sci; fel Am Phys Soc; Am Asn Physics Teachers. *Res:* Special relativity; general relativity. *Mailing Add:* 2 Sutton Pl S 5A New York NY 10022. *E-Mail:* harvey@scires.acf.nyu.edu

HARVEY, BIRT, PEDIATRICS. *Current Pos:* EMER CLIN PROF PEDIAT, STANFORD & UNIV CALIF SAN FRANCISCO, 95- *Personal Data:* b Teheran, Iran, Nov 24, 28; m; c 5. *Educ:* Johns Hopkins Univ, BA, 52; NY Univ, MD, 52. *Concurrent Pos:* Sr fel, Inst Health, Policy Studies, Univ Calif, San Francisco. *Mem:* Inst Med-Nat Acad Sci; Am Acad Pediat (pres). *Res:* Child health policy; child health financing. *Mailing Add:* 101 Alma St Palo Alto CA 94301. *Fax:* 650-327-5901; *E-Mail:* birtharvey@aol.com

HARVEY, BRYAN LAURENCE, GENETICS, PLANT BREEDING. *Current Pos:* dir, Crop Develop Ctr, 83-94, head, Hort Sci, 94-99, PROF CROP SCI, UNIV SASK, 66- *Personal Data:* b Newport, Wales, Nov 1, 37; Can citizen; m 60, Eileen Pfeiffer; c James & Donald. *Educ:* Univ Sask, BSA, 60, MSc, 61; Univ Calif, Davis, PhD(genetics), 64. *Prof Exp:* Asst prof crop sci, Univ Guelph, 64-66. *Concurrent Pos:* Chmn, Prairie Regist Recommending Comt Grain, Expert Comt Plant Gene Resources, Genetics Group, Univ Sask, 77-81; vis prof crop sci, Univ Nairobi, 75; asst dean agr, Univ Sask, 80-83, head crop sci & plant ecol, 83-94; dir, SeCan, 89-94, chmn adv comt variety regist, 87-95. *Mem:* Fel Am Soc Agron; fel Crop Sci Soc Am; fel Agr Inst Can; Can Soc Agron; Master Brewers Am; Am Soc Brewing Chemists; Can Seed Growers Asn. *Res:* Salinity tolerance in barley; genetics and breeding of malting barley; sprouting resistance in cereals; tissue culture cyto-genetics. *Mailing Add:* Crop Sci Dept Univ Sask 51 Campus Dr Saskatoon SK S7N 5A8 Can. *Fax:* 306-966-8106; *E-Mail:* harvey@duke.usask.ca

HARVEY, CHARLES ARTHUR, CONTROL THEORY, MECHANICS. *Current Pos:* RETIRED. *Personal Data:* b Gering, Nebr, Aug 14, 29; m 52, Margaret R Stone; c Jenny B (Chay), Charles A Jr & Peter J. *Educ:* Nebr Wesleyan Univ, AB, 51; Univ Nebr, MA, 53; Univ Minn, PhD(math), 60. *Prof Exp:* Develop engr, Aero Div, Honeywell, Inc, Minneapolis, 55-57, sr res scientist, Res Dept, St Paul, 60-64, prin scientist, 64-65, res staff scientist, 65-69; sr resident res assoc, Marshall Space Flight Ctr, NASA, 69-71; res staff scientist, Systs & Res Ctr, Honeywell, Inc, 71-80, prin res staff scientist, 80-87; vis res fel, Elec Eng Dept, Univ Newcastle, Australia, 87-88; vis prof, Elec Eng Dept, Nat Univ Singapore, 88-89, 91-93; prof, Aerospace Eng & Meh Dept, Univ Minn, Minneapolis, 89-90. *Mem:* Inst Elec & Electronics Engrs; Am Math Soc; Soc Indust & Appl Math; Am Inst Aeronaut & Astronaut. *Res:* Ordinary differential equations and application to control theory. *Mailing Add:* 3843 Zenith Ave S Minneapolis MN 55410

HARVEY, CLARENCE CHARLES, (JR), CHEMISTRY. *Current Pos:* RETIRED. *Personal Data:* b Winona, Miss, June 29, 18; m 43; c 2. *Educ:* Univ Miss, BA, 39, MS, 41. *Prof Exp:* Develop chemist, Ethyl Corp, 41-46, corrosion chemist, 47- 50, develop assoc, 51-52, supvr, 53-57, mkt analyst, 57-64, mkt res mgr, 64-84. *Mem:* Am Chem Soc; Chem Mkt Res Asn (secy, 79-80). *Res:* Chemical market analysis; plastics development; corrosion. *Mailing Add:* 6168 Chandler Dr Baton Rouge LA 70808-5018

HARVEY, DOUGLAS J, METALLURGICAL ENGINEERING. *Current Pos:* CONSULT, CLINTON METALL SERV INC, 89- *Personal Data:* b Utica, Mich, Apr 25, 24; m 50; c 3. *Educ:* Mich State Univ, BS, 49, MA, 50, PhD(metall eng), 55. *Prof Exp:* Instr mech eng, Mich State Univ, 51-56; sr res metallurgist, Gen Motors Corp, 56-80, sr staff engr, Res Labs, 80-89. *Concurrent Pos:* Pres, Clinton Metal & Mech Eng Serv, Inc. *Mem:* Am Welding Soc; Am Soc Metals; Am Inst Mining, Metall & Petrol Engrs. *Res:* Physical metallurgy; cast metals; welding metallurgy; granted 21 patents. *Mailing Add:* 11185 Clinton River Sterling Heights MI 48313. *Fax:* 810-731-6605

HARVEY, DOUGLASS COATE, MECHANICAL ENGINEERING. *Current Pos:* RETIRED. *Personal Data:* b Batavia, NY, Aug 28, 17. *Educ:* Purdue Univ, BS & ME, 39. *Prof Exp:* Engr, Eastman Kodak, 39-82, dir corp prod mgt, 70-73, vpres & gen mgr, Apparatus Div, 73-77, exec vpres & gen mgr, 77-82; dir, Tex Instruments Inc, 82-89; consult, 82-94. *Concurrent Pos:* Mem, Indust Mgt Coun. *Mem:* Nat Acad Eng; Optical Soc Am. *Mailing Add:* 3155 E Ave Rochester NY 14618

HARVEY, EVERETT H, REAL TIME SYSTEMS. *Current Pos:* COMPUT SCIENTIST, LAWRENCE BERKELEY LAB, 78- *Educ:* Univ Ill, BS, 67; Univ Minn, PhD(physics), 71. *Prof Exp:* Res assoc, Univ Pa, 71-72; res assoc, Univ Wis, 72-78. *Concurrent Pos:* Consult, Gailep Asn, 85- *Mem:* Am Phys Soc. *Mailing Add:* One Cyclotron Rd 46A Berkeley CA 94720

HARVEY, F REESE, GEOMETRY & ANALYSIS. *Current Pos:* from asst prof to assoc prof, 68-73, PROF MATH, RICE UNIV, 73- *Personal Data:* b Atlantic Beach, Fla, Feb 7, 41; m 69, Linda; c 3. *Educ:* Carnegie-Mellon Univ, BS & MS, 63; Stanford Univ, PhD(math), 66. *Prof Exp:* Instr math, Univ Calif, Berkeley, 66-68. *Concurrent Pos:* Alfred P Sloan fel, 72-74; assoc ed, Ind Math J, 76-; mem, Nat Sci Comt Math, 80-83; mem bd govs, Inst Math & Appln, 81-83; mem bd trustees, Math Sci Res Inst, 83- *Mem:* Am Math Soc. *Res:* Complex analysis, partial differential equations and differential geometry. *Mailing Add:* Dept Math Rice Univ PO Box 1892 Houston TX 77001

HARVEY, FRANCES J, II, metallurgy, materials science, for more information see previous edition

HARVEY, GALE ALLEN, METEOR PHYSICS. *Current Pos:* PHYSICIST, LANGLEY RES CTR, NASA, 62- *Personal Data:* b New York, NY, Nov 17, 38; div; c 2. *Educ:* NMex State Univ, BS, 62; Va Polytech Inst, MS, 66. *Honors & Awards:* Spec Achievement Award, Langley Res Ctr, NASA, 74. *Res:* Directs and operates FTIR and mass spectroscopy lab for gas cell, optical filter characterization, and contamination analyses, develops contamination analysis programs for space flight hardware and thermal-vacuum test chambers; analyze and report data. *Mailing Add:* 2 Donald St Hampton VA 23669

HARVEY, GEORGE RANSON, ORGANIC CHEMISTRY, ATMOSPHERIC SCIENCES GENERAL. *Current Pos:* OCEANOGR, ATLANTIC OCEANOG & METEOROL LABS, NAT OCEANIC & ATMOSPHERIC ADMIN, US DEPT COM, 77- *Personal Data:* b Boston, Mass, Dec 30, 37; m 60; c 3. *Educ:* Boston Col, BS, 60; Mass Inst Technol, PhD(org chem), 64. *Prof Exp:* Sr res chemist, Monsanto Co, 64-69; asst scientist, Woods Hole Oceanog Inst, 70-72, assoc scientist, 72-77. *Mem:* Am Chem Soc; Oceanog Soc; Am Geophys Union. *Res:* Chemical oceanography; organic geochemistry; humic acid chemistry, atmospheric chemistry. *Mailing Add:* 8375 SW 161st St Miami FL 33157

HARVEY, JOHN, JR, TECHNICAL MANAGEMENT, ENVIRONMENTAL SCIENCES. *Current Pos:* RETIRED. *Personal Data:* b Philadelphia, Pa, July 7, 25; m 47; c 2. *Educ:* Univ Pa, AB, 49, MS, 51, PhD(org chem), 53. *Prof Exp:* Res assoc, E I du Pont de Nemours & Co Inc, 52-70, res chemist, 70-72, sr res chemist, Biochem Dept, 72-80, sr res assoc, Agr Prod Div, 80-85; pres, Greenleaf Environ Inc, 86-89. *Res:* Determination of structure of natural products; agricultural chemicals; metabolism of pesticides; environmental fate of pesticides. *Mailing Add:* 48 Ulverston Dr Kennett Square PA 19348-2044

HARVEY, JOHN ADRIANCE, PSYCHOPHARMACOLOGY, NEUROSCIENCE. *Current Pos:* PROF PHARMACOL, MED COL PA, 88- *Personal Data:* b New York, NY, Oct 14, 30; m 58; c 3. *Educ:* Univ Chicago, AB, 55, PhD(biopsychol), 59. *Honors & Awards:* Merit Award, NIMH, 88. *Prof Exp:* Res assoc biopsychol, Univ Chicago, 59-61, from asst prof to assoc prof psychol & pharmacol, 61-68; prof psychol & pharmacol, Univ Iowa, 68-88. *Concurrent Pos:* USPHS res scientist award, 69-74; mem neuropsychol res rev comt, NIMH, 70-74, mem preclin psychopharmacol res rev comt, 75-79; consult ed, J Comp & Physiol Psychol, 71-; regional ed pharmacol, Biochem & Behav, 72-; chmn, Biopsychol Res Rev Comt, NIH, 81-85; ed, J Pharmacol & Exp Therapeut, 91- *Mem:* AAAS; fel Am Psychol Asn (pres); Am Soc Pharmacol & Exp Therapeut; Soc Neurosci; Am Soc Neurochem; fel Am Col Neuropsychopharmacol. *Res:* Effects of lesions on drug action and on central biochemistry; effects of lesions, drugs and biochemical substrates on operant and respondent behavior; biological basis of learning. *Mailing Add:* Dept Pharmacol Med Col PA EPPI 3200 Henry Ave Philadelphia PA 19129-1137. *Fax:* 215-843-1515

HARVEY, JOHN ARTHUR, NUCLEAR PHYSICS. *Current Pos:* PHYSICIST, OAK RIDGE NAT LAB, 55- *Personal Data:* b Saskatoon, Sask, Dec 14, 21; US citizen; m 49; c 2. *Educ:* Queen's Univ, Ont, BSc, 45; Mass Inst Technol, PhD(physics), 50. *Prof Exp:* Physicist, Atomic Energy Can, Ltd, 45-46; asst, Mass Inst Technol, 46-50; assoc physicist, Brookhaven Nat Lab, 51-55. *Mem:* Am Phys Soc. *Res:* Neutron physics; neutron time-of-flight spectroscopy; electron linear accelerators. *Mailing Add:* Oak Ridge Nat Lab PO Box 2008-MS 6354 Oak Ridge TN 37831. *Fax:* 215-843-1515

HARVEY, JOHN COLLINS, INTERNAL MEDICINE, GERIATRICS. *Current Pos:* PROF MED, GEORGETOWN UNIV, 72- *Personal Data:* b Youngstown, Ohio, Sept 11, 23; m 49, Adele Dillon; c 5. *Educ:* Yale Univ, BS, 44; Johns Hopkins Univ, MD, 47; St Mary's Univ, PhD (theol), 88. *Hon Degrees:* LLD, Barry Univ, 92. *Prof Exp:* From asst to prof med, Johns Hopkins Univ, 47-72. *Concurrent Pos:* House officer & asst resident, Osler Med Serv, Johns Hopkins Hosp, 47-51, resident physician, 51-52, physician, 52-, dir med care clin, 54-57, dir med clins, 57-62, dir outpatient serv, 62-68; A Blaine Brower traveling fel from Am Col Physicians, Guys Hosp, Eng, 56. *Mem:* AAAS; Biophys Soc; master Am Col Physicians; Am Fedn Clin Res; Am Clin & Climat Asn; fel Am Pub Health Asn. *Res:* Diseases of muscle and muscle physiology; medical ethics. *Mailing Add:* 8629 Fenway Rd Bethesda MD 20817-2709

HARVEY, JOHN GROVER, MATHEMATICS, EDUCATION. *Current Pos:* assoc prof, 66-75, PROF MATH & MATH EDUC, UNIV WIS-MADISON, 75- *Personal Data:* b Waco, Tex, Aug 10, 34. *Educ:* Baylor Univ, BS, 55; Fla State Univ, MS, 57; Tulane Univ, PhD(math), 61. *Prof Exp:* From instr to asst prof math, Univ Ill, Urbana, 61-66. *Concurrent Pos:* Prin investr, Wis Res & Develop Ctr Cognitive Learning, Univ Wis-Madison, 68-78; co-ed, Am Math Monthly, 68-73; mem, Comt on Testing, Math Asn Am, 84-93, chair, 89-93; Killam vis Scholar, Univ Calgary, 85; co-dir, MAA Calculator-Based Placement Test Prog Proj, 86-, Teaching Math with Calculators Proj, 90-, Technol Intensive Calculus Advan Placement Proj, 91- *Mem:* Math Asn Am; Am Educ Res Asn; Am Math Soc; Nat Coun Teachers Math. *Res:* Mathematics education; uses of technologies in mathematics instruction and testing. *Mailing Add:* Dept Math Univ Wis Madison WI 53706-1388. *Fax:* 608-263-8891; *E-Mail:* harvey@math.wisc.edu

HARVEY, JOHN MARSHALL, plant pathology; deceased, see previous edition for last biography

HARVEY, JOHN W(ARREN), ASTROPHYSICS. *Current Pos:* ASTRONR, NAT SOLAR OBSERV, 84- *Personal Data:* b Los Angeles, Calif, Sept 13, 40; m 68, Karen Angle; c David. *Educ:* Univ Calif, BA, 63, MA, 64; Univ Colo, PhD(astrogeophys), 69. *Honors & Awards:* James Arthur lectr, Ctr Astrophys, 81; Medal for Exceptional Sci Achievement, NASA, 90; Antarctic mountain named in honor of, 96. *Prof Exp:* Asst astronr, Kitt Peak Nat Observ, 69-74, astronr, 74-83. *Concurrent Pos:* Mem, Solar Physics Working Group, Astron Surv Comt, Nat Acad Sci, 79-80 & Solar & Space Physics Comt, 81-84; chmn, Solar Physics Div, Am Astron Soc, 80-81; mem, Astron Adv Comt, NSF, 82-85; mem, Space & Earth Sci Adv Comt, NASA, 84-87; vpres, Comn 12, IAU, 85-88, pres, 89-91; mem, Solar Physics Comt, 87-88, Astron Surv Comt Solar Panel, Nat Acad Sci, 89-90. *Mem:* Int Astron Union; Am Astron Soc; Am Geophys Union; Inst Elec & Electronics Engrs. *Res:* Solar magnetic and velocity fields, photosphere, chromosphere, prominences and corona; stellar magnetic and velocity fields; helioseismology, instrumentation. *Mailing Add:* Nat Solar Observ PO Box 26732 Tucson AZ 85726. *Fax:* 520-318-8278; *E-Mail:* jharvey@noao.edu

HARVEY, JOHN WILCOX, HEALTH PHYSICS. *Current Pos:* SR HEALTH PHYSICIST, MCMASTER UNIV, 68- *Personal Data:* b Hamilton, Ont, June 27, 38; m 62; c 2. *Educ:* McMaster Univ, BSc, 60, PhD(nuclear chem), 65. *Prof Exp:* Res assoc nuclear chem, Mass Inst Technol, 65-66; asst prof chem, Univ Man, 66-67; radiation protection chemist, Mass Inst Technol, 67-68. *Concurrent Pos:* Spec lectr physics & eng physics, 75- *Mem:* Health Physics Soc; Can Radiation Protection Asn. *Res:* Dosimetry. *Mailing Add:* 32 Thorndale Crescent Hamilton ON L8S 3K2 Can

HARVEY, JOSEPH ELDON, ANATOMY, OTOLARYNGOLOGY. *Current Pos:* CONSULT, 92- *Personal Data:* b Pensacola, Fla, July 10, 27; m 52, Ames; c Michael Joseph, Anthony Gerard, Patrick Gerard, Annamaria Teresa, Barbara Jane, John Frances, Robert James & Susanne Mara. *Educ:*

Univ Calif, Berkeley, BS, 54, MA, 64, PhD(anat), 68. *Prof Exp:* Phys therapist, San Francisco Bd Educ, Calif, 54-65 & Providence Hosp, Oakland, 66-68; asst prof anat, Univ Calif, Berkeley, 68; asst prof anat & otolaryngol, Sch Med, Washington Univ, 68-72, assoc prof exp otolaryngol, 72-92. *Concurrent Pos:* Phys therapist, Shriner's Hosp for Crippled Children, San Francisco, 60-63. *Mem:* AAAS; Am Asn Anat; NY Acad Sci; Am Phys Ther Asn; Asn Res Otolaryngol. *Res:* Nerve regeneration; transplantation physiology; induced phonation; electromyography of laryngeal muscles; laryngeal physiology; transposition of extralaryngeal (super and infrahyoid) muscles to larynx to substitute for extirpated laryngeal muscles of phonation. *Mailing Add:* 1046 N Rock Hill Rd St Louis MO 63119

HARVEY, KENNETH C, TRAPPED ATOMS, LASER SPECTROSCOPY. *Current Pos:* ASSOC PROF, SOUTHERN METHODIST UNIV, DALLAS, 86- *Personal Data:* b Shreveport, La, Sept 3, 47. *Educ:* Duke Univ, BSc, 69; Stanford Univ, MSc, 70, PhD(physics), 75. *Honors & Awards:* IR 100 Award. *Prof Exp:* Res assoc physics, Univ Toronto, 75-77; physicist, Nat Bur Standards, 77-81; res scientist, Univ Mich, Ann Arbor, 81-86. *Mem:* Am Phys Soc; Optical Soc Am; AAAS; Sigma Xi. *Res:* Laser spectroscopy; trapped atoms; computers in physics. *Mailing Add:* 5657 Amesbury Apt No 1915 Dallas TX 75206-3077

HARVEY, LAWRENCE HARMON, COTTON BREEDING & PRODUCTION. *Current Pos:* EXTEN AGRONOMIST, CLEMSON UNIV, 66- *Personal Data:* b Jacksonville, Fla, Aug 6, 30; m 55; c 2. *Educ:* Univ Ga, BSA, 52, MS, 59, PhD(agron), 69. *Prof Exp:* Asst breeder, Greenwood Seed Co, 56-57; cotton breeder, DeKalb Agr Assoc, Inc, 57-64; dir res, Cotton Hybrid Res, Inc, 65-66. *Mem:* Crop Sci Soc Am; Agron Soc Am; Soil Sci Soc Am. *Res:* Conducting cotton tests-demonstrations on production problems. *Mailing Add:* 207 Lark Circle Clemson SC 29631-0359

HARVEY, MACK CREEDE, ANALYTICAL CHEMISTRY. *Current Pos:* res chemist, Shell Develop Co, 67-68, Inorg & Spectros Sect leader, 69-72, staff res chemist, 72-80, INORG ANALYSIS SECT HEAD, SHELL DEVELOP CO, 80-; SCIENTIST, VALCO INSTRUMENTS CO, 80- *Personal Data:* b Barnsdall, Okla, Dec 25, 29; m 55, 71, 76; c 2. *Educ:* Ind Univ, BS, 52, PhD(inorg chem), 56. *Prof Exp:* Res chemist, Celanese Chem Co, 56-58; sr res chemist, W R Grace & Co, 58-61; res chemist, El Paso Natural Gas Prod Co, 61-62, anal sect leader, 62-67. *Mem:* Am Chem Soc; Soc Appl Spectros. *Res:* Infrared, x-ray and nuclear magnetic resonance spectrometry; organic functional group analysis; phosphate chemistry; gel permeation chromatography; high performance liquid chromatography; characterization of plastics and elastomers. *Mailing Add:* 2331 Greyburn Lane Houston TX 77080

HARVEY, MALCOLM, THEORETICAL NUCLEAR PHYSICS. *Current Pos:* Nat Res Coun Can fel physics, Chalk River Nuclear Labs, Atomic Energy Can, Ltd, 61-62, from asst res officer to assoc res officer, 62-67, sr res officer, 67-89, dir physics, 89-96, EMER RESEARCHER, CHALK RIVER LABS, ATOMIC ENERGY CAN, LTD, 96- *Personal Data:* b London, Eng, Oct 9, 36; m 59, Patricia A Jarman; c Michael, Deborah & Rebecca. *Educ:* Univ Southampton, BSc, 58, PhD(appl math), 61. *Honors & Awards:* Michael Smith Award for Sci Prom, Govt Can; Sci Achievement Award, Can Nuclear Asn. *Concurrent Pos:* Ford Found fel physics, Niels Bohr Inst, Copenhagen, Denmark, 64-65; vis sr fel, Manchester Univ, 78; vis prof, State Univ NY, Stony Brook, 81; dir, Third Summer Inst Theoret Physics, Queens Univ, 85; chmn, Gordon Res Conf Nuclear Structure, 86; chmn, Sci Teacher's Seminars, 87-95, TASCC Workshop Heavy Ion Physics, Chalk River, 88. *Mem:* Fel Am Phys Soc; Can Asn Physicists; Inst Particle Physics; Can Nuclear Soc; fel Royal Soc Can. *Res:* Theoretical nuclear physics, particularly groups in the shell model; self-consistent field theory; foundations of the spherical shell model; hadronic quark structure and the nucleon-nucleon force; soliton models of the hadrons. *Mailing Add:* 2 Mountain View Crescent Box 851 Deep River ON K0J 1P0 Can. *E-Mail:* harveym@intranet.ca

HARVEY, MICHAEL JOHN, BOTANY, AGROSTOLOGY. *Current Pos:* RETIRED. *Personal Data:* b Doncaster, Eng, Dec 10, 35; m 65. *Educ:* Univ Durham, BSc, 58, PhD(bot), 62. *Prof Exp:* Dept Sci Indust Res fel bot, Univ Birmingham, 61-63; from asst prof to assoc prof bot, Dalhousie Univ, 63-77, assoc prof biol, 77-90. *Res:* Grasses of North America; chromosome studies associated with speciation and the origin of polyploids. *Mailing Add:* 5061 Sooke Rd Victoria BC V9C 4C3 Can

HARVEY, RALPH CLAYTON, VETERINARY MEDICINE, ANESTHESIOLOGY. *Current Pos:* ASSOC PROF VET ANESTHESIOL, UNIV TENN, 85- *Personal Data:* b Knoxville, Tenn, July 12, 52; m 74; c 1. *Educ:* Tenn Technol Univ, BS, 74; Univ Tenn, DVM, 81; Univ NC, Chapel Hill, MS, 81; Am Col Vet Anesthesiol, dipl, 87. *Prof Exp:* Geneticist, genetic toxicol, Nat Inst Environ Health Sci, 74-78; intern vet anesthesiol, Intensive-Care Unit, Cornell Univ, NY State Col Vet Med, 81-82, resident, 83-85; vet clin pract, Concord Vet Hosp, 82-83; fel anesthesiol & lab animal med, Cornell Univ Med Ctr, 83-84. *Concurrent Pos:* Exec Secy, Am Col Veterinary Anesthesiologists. *Mem:* Am Vet Med Asn; Am Asn Veterinary Clinicians; AAAS; Am Col Vet Anesthesiologists. *Res:* Veterinary and comparative anesthesiology; anesthesia and analgesia in biomedical research. *Mailing Add:* Dept Small Animal Clin Scis Univ Tenn PO Box 1071 Knoxville TN 37901-1071

HARVEY, RICHARD ALEXANDER, BIOCHEMISTRY. *Current Pos:* from asst prof to assoc prof, 66-78, PROF BIOCHEM, RUTGERS MED SCH, 78- *Personal Data:* b Salt Lake City, Utah, Nov 21, 36; m 58; c 2. *Educ:* Univ Utah, BS, 59, PhD(biochem), 64. *Prof Exp:* Fel, Inst Biophys & Biochem, Paris, 64-66. *Mem:* Sigma Xi. *Res:* Fluorescence polarization spectroscopy: transient-state kinetics of enzymes and other biological macromolecules; mechanism of biosynthesis of riboflavin. *Mailing Add:* 28 Barnfield Ct Upper Saddle River NJ 07458

HARVEY, RICHARD DAVID, MINERALOGY, PETROLOGY. *Current Pos:* From asst geologist to geologist, 60-95, EMER PROF GEOL, ILL STATE GEOL SURV, 95- *Personal Data:* b Evansville, Ind, Dec 30, 28; m 52; c 3. *Educ:* Ind Univ, BS, 56, AM, 58, PhD(geol), 60. *Mem:* Geol Soc Am; Mineral Soc Am; Geochem Soc. *Res:* Physical properties of rocks; economic geology. *Mailing Add:* 403 W Indiana Ave Urbana IL 61801

HARVEY, ROBERT GORDON, JR, WEED SCIENCE, AGRONOMY. *Current Pos:* From asst prof to assoc prof, 70-78, PROF AGRON, UNIV WIS-MADISON, 78- *Personal Data:* b Upland, Calif, Dec 10, 45; m 65; c 2. *Educ:* Wash State Univ, BS, 67, PhD(agron), 70. *Mem:* Weed Sci Soc Am; Agron Soc Am. *Res:* Physiology and biochemistry of herbicide action on crops and weeds; interactions between herbicides and soil constituents; weed control in field and sweet corn, alfalfa, canning peas, lupines and soybeans. *Mailing Add:* Dept Agron 373 Moore Hall Univ Wis 1575 Linden Dr Madison WI 53706-1514

HARVEY, ROBERT JOSEPH, ORGANIC CHEMISTRY. *Current Pos:* PRES, VENTU-TECH INT, INC, 85- *Personal Data:* b Staten Island, NY, Nov 3, 38; m 62; c 1. *Educ:* Wagner Col, BS, 61; NY Univ, PhD(org chem), 65. *Prof Exp:* Res chemist, Halcon Res & Develop Corp, 65-85. *Concurrent Pos:* Int Sales & Technol Transfer. *Mem:* Am Chem Soc; NY Acad Sci; Sigma Xi. *Res:* Orientation and reactivity in aromatic free radical substitution reactions; instrumental analysis; development of new processes; heterogeneous and homogeneous liquid phase oxidations; olefin dimerization; organometallic chemistry. *Mailing Add:* 3 Canterbury Lane New Milford NJ 07646

HARVEY, ROGER BRUCE, MYCOTOXIN EXPERTISE FOR FOOD ANIMALS, AVIAN MEDICINE KNOWLEDGE & EXPERTISE. *Current Pos:* RES TOXICOLOGIST, FOOD ANIMAL PROTECTION RES LAB, USDA, 85-; PROF TOXICOL, TEX A&M UNIV, 88- *Personal Data:* b Orange, Tex, July 9, 46; m 70, Anna B Young; c Leanne & Richard. *Educ:* Tex A&M Univ, BS, 68, DVM, 69, MS, 83. *Honors & Awards:* Dr Daniel E Salmon Award, Nat Asn Fed Veterinarians, 91; Southern Plains Area Early Career Scientist Award, USDA, 91. *Prof Exp:* Vet med officer, US Army, 69-73; pvt vet practr, Tickle Animal Hosp, 73-75; asst prof animal sci & physiol & reproduction, SW Tex State Univ, 74-75; exten poultry vet, Tex Agr Exten Serv, 75-78; dir tech serv, Agr-Bio Corp, 78-81; res assoc, Tex A&M Univ, 81-85. *Concurrent Pos:* Vet med officer, USAR, 76-, training officer, 994th Med Detachment, 90-; chmn, Toxic, Infectious, Miscellaneous Dis Comt, Am Asn Avian Pathologists, 91-94. *Mem:* Am Vet Med Asn; Am Asn Avian Pathologists; Am Acad Vet & Comp Toxicol; Am Asn Vet Lab Diagnosticians; World Poultry Vet Asn. *Res:* Characterize effects of mycotoxins to livestock and poultry and to develop methods to prevent or reduce toxic effects and residues in animals, feed and food; published over 150 articles. *Mailing Add:* USDA/Agr Res Serv/Food Animal Protection Res Lab 2881 F & B Rd College Station TX 77845. *Fax:* 409-260-9377

HARVEY, RONALD GILBERT, ORGANIC CHEMISTRY, CARCINOGENESIS. *Current Pos:* instr & res assoc, 60-61, from instr to assoc prof, 61-68, PROF ORG CHEM, BEN MAY INST, UNIV CHICAGO, 75- *Personal Data:* b Ottawa, Ont, Sept 9, 27; US citizen; m 52, Helene H Szpara; c Ronald E. *Educ:* Univ Calif, Los Angeles, AB, 52; Univ Chicago, MS, 55, PhD(chem), 60. *Honors & Awards:* Res Award, Int Soc Pure & Appl Chem, 95. *Prof Exp:* Proj leader org chem, Sinclair Res Labs, Ill, 56-58. *Concurrent Pos:* USPHS spec fel, Imp Col, Univ London, 63-64; consult, Nat Cancer Inst, Nat Inst Environ Health Sci, Am Cancer Soc, Israel Fedn Labor. *Mem:* AAAS; Am Chem Soc; Am Asn Cancer Res; Chem Soc Brit; Am Inst Chemists. *Res:* Polycyclic aromatic hydrocarbons; chemical carcinogenesis; metal ammonia reduction, novel synthetic methods; author of more than 400 scientific papers, two books and two patents. *Mailing Add:* Ben May Lab Univ Chicago 5841 S Maryland Ave Chicago IL 60637. *Fax:* 773-702-6260; *E-Mail:* rharvey@ben_may.bsd.uchicago.edu

HARVEY, ROSS BUSCHLEN, PHYSICAL CHEMISTRY, INFORMATION SCIENCE. *Current Pos:* RETIRED. *Personal Data:* b Regina, Sask, Mar 27, 17. *Educ:* Univ Sask, BSc, 35, MSc, 38; McGill Univ, PhD, 40. *Prof Exp:* Res chemist, Nat Res Coun Can, 40-41; mem, Dept Nat Defence, 47-68, asst dir res, Defence Res Estab, Suffield, 68-72, spec proj res, Defence Sci Info Serv, 72-77, head proj support off, 78-83. *Mem:* Am Chem Soc; Chem Inst Can; Sigma Xi. *Res:* Structure of gases by electron diffraction; airblast and shocks from chemical explosions; analysis of random processes; information analysis centres; energy research. *Mailing Add:* 340 Fourth Ave SW Medicine Hat AB T1A 4Z7 Can

HARVEY, STEPHEN CRAIG, PHYSICS. *Current Pos:* fel, 71-73, from asst prof to assoc prof, 73-86, PROF, UNIV ALA, BIRMINGHAM, 86- *Personal Data:* b Bakersfield, Calif, Apr 13, 40; m 87; c 1. *Educ:* Univ Calif, Berkeley, AB, 63; Dartmouth Col, PhD(physics), 71. *Prof Exp:* Engr, Aerojet Gen Corp, 63-65; volunteer, Peace Corps, 65-67. *Mem:* Biophys Soc; AAAS; Sigma Xi; Fedn Am Scientists; Am Soc Biol Chemists; Am Chem Soc; Am Phys Soc. *Res:* Dynamic aspects of the structure of biological macromolecules. *Mailing Add:* Dept Biochem Univ Ala Birmingham AL 35294-0005. *Fax:* 205-975-2547

HARVEY, STEWART CLYDE, PHARMACOLOGY. *Current Pos:* instr, Univ Utah, 49-50, asst res prof, 50-53, from assoc prof to prof, 53-88, EMER PROF PHARMACOL, COL MED, UNIV UTAH, 88- *Personal Data:* b Denver, Colo, Feb 16, 21; m 42, 65; c 2. *Educ:* Univ Colo, BA, 43; Univ Chicago, PhD(pharmacol), 48. *Prof Exp:* Asst chem & lab coordr, Univ Colo, 43-44, instr, 44-46; instr & dir pharmacol, Dent Sch, Univ Tex, 48-49. *Concurrent Pos:* Markle scholar, 52-57. *Mem:* Am Soc Pharmacol & Exp Therapeut; Sigma Xi. *Res:* Autonomic and cardiovascular pharmacology. *Mailing Add:* Dept Pharmacol Univ Utah Col Med Salt Lake City UT 84132-0001

HARVEY, THOMAS LARKIN, ENTOMOLOGY. *Current Pos:* asst entomologist, 54-57, from asst prof to assoc prof, 57-70, PROF ENTOM, AGR RES CTR, KANS STATE UNIV, 70- *Personal Data:* b Ulysses, Nebr, Jan 17, 26; m 52, Joan Schroeder; c Fred, Mark, Marilyn, Stephen, Paul, James & Barbara. *Educ:* Kans State Col, MS, 51; Okla State Univ, PhD(entom), 63. *Honors & Awards:* Entom Soc Am Agr Recognition Award for Res, 74. *Prof Exp:* Asst entomologist, NMex Col, 52-53. *Mem:* Entom Soc Am. *Res:* Host plant resistance to insects; medical and veterinary entomology. *Mailing Add:* Agr Res Ctr 1232 240th Ave Hays KS 67601. *Fax:* 785-623-4369; *E-Mail:* tharvey@oznet.ksu.edu

HARVEY, THOMAS STOLTZ, PATHOLOGY. *Current Pos:* RETIRED. *Personal Data:* b Louisville, Ky, Oct 10, 12; m 41; c 5. *Educ:* Yale Univ, BS, 34, MD, 41. *Prof Exp:* Pathologist, Meriden Hosp, Conn, 43-45; pathologist, Med Res Lab, Army Chem Corps, 45-47; instr path, Sch Med, Univ Pa, 48-50, asst dir, Wm Pepper Lab Clin Med, 50-52; dir labs, Princeton Hosp, 52-60; pathologist, Vet Admin Hosp, Lyons, NJ, 61-75; med dir, Statlabs, 75-80. *Concurrent Pos:* Consult, NJ Bd Med Examr, 56-61; dir, Princeton Med Labs, 60-64. *Mem:* Am Soc Clin Pathologists; Am Chem Soc; Asn Clin Scientists. *Res:* Role of liquid chromatography in the clinical lab; cytological, morphological changes produced by viruses. *Mailing Add:* 144 Pleasant Valley Rd Titusville NJ 08560-2103

HARVEY, WALTER ROBERT, ANIMAL BREEDING. *Current Pos:* prof, 64-87, EMER PROF DAIRY, ANIMAL & POULTRY SCI & GENETICS, OHIO STATE UNIV, 87- *Personal Data:* b Tucumcari, NMex, June 19, 19; m 40; c 3. *Educ:* Okla Agr & Mech Col, BS, 42; Iowa State Col, MS, 47, PhD, 49. *Honors & Awards:* Animal Breeding, Am Soc Animal Sci, 68, Morrison Award, 87. *Prof Exp:* Instr animal husb, Iowa State Col, 47-49; assoc prof dairy husb, Univ Idaho, 50-54; biometrician in chg livestock res staff, Biomet Serv, Agr Res Serv, USDA, 54-64. *Concurrent Pos:* Ed-in-chief, J Animal Sci, 73-76. *Mem:* Fel Am Soc Animal Sci; Am Dairy Sci Asn; Am Statist Asn; Biomet Soc; Sigma Xi. *Res:* Applied statistics. *Mailing Add:* 4255 Mumford Dr Columbus OH 43220

HARVEY, WALTER WILLIAM, EXTRACTIVE METALLURGY, ENERGY TECHNOLOGIES. *Current Pos:* CONSULT EXTRACTIVE METALL, CHEM PROCESS, ENERGY & ENVIRON TECHNOL, 79- *Personal Data:* b St John's, Nfld, Dec 18, 25; US citizen; div; c Ronald W, Valerie L & Gail M. *Educ:* Bowdoin Col, BA, 47; Mass Inst Technol, PhD(phys chem), 52. *Prof Exp:* Asst metall, Mass Inst Technol, 47-50; instr chem, Bowdoin Col, 50-51; from asst prof to assoc prof, St Lawrence Univ, 51-55, actg head dept, 53-55; asst prof, Williams Col, 55-56; mem res staff, Lincoln Lab, Mass Inst Technol, 56-63; staff scientist, Ledgemont Lab, Kennecott Copper Corp, 63-67; group leader chem & surface sci, 67-75; vpres & dir process develop, EIC Corp, 75-79. *Concurrent Pos:* Regional ed, Surface Sci, 63-68; guest lectr, Mass Inst Technol, 63 & 67; chmn, Boston Sect, Electrochem Soc, 64-65; local counr & rep to bd dirs, 65-68; vis res assoc, Nat Bur Stand, 69-70; chmn, electrolytic processes comt, Metall Soc Am Inst Mining, Metall & Petrol Engrs, 74-75 & 80-82, & hydrometallurgy subcomt, electrolytic technol adv comt, Dept Energy, 77-80; prin investr, NSF res grants, 77-78 & 82-83 & Navy res contract, 90-93. *Mem:* Am Chem Soc; fel Inst Mining & Metall London. *Res:* Surface properties and electrochemistry of semiconductors; physical chemistry of solid state; leaching chemistry of sulfide minerals; electrowinning and electrorefining; extractive metallurgy of manganese nodules, phosphorites, nickeliferous laterites and ilmenite and chromite ores; geothermal energy utilization; electrochemical energy storage; ocean hard minerals exploitation; circuit foil etching; gas desulfurization; electrolytic corrosion. *Mailing Add:* 46 Earl St Malden MA 02148-2411. *E-Mail:* fwsl20a@prodigy.com

HARVEY, WILLIAM HOMER, GENETICS OF CANCER, VIROLOGY. *Current Pos:* from asst prof to assoc prof biol, 72-82, PROF BIOL, EARLHAM COL, 82- *Personal Data:* b Sept 1, 39; m 62, Mary N Asher; c Brian O. *Educ:* Georgetown Col, Ky, BS, 61; Univ Cincinnati, MS, 65; Univ Tenn, Knoxville, PhD(develop plant physiol), 71. *Prof Exp:* Asst prof biol, Albion Col, 71-72. *Concurrent Pos:* Microbiol & sci curric consult, 93- *Mem:* Am Soc Microbiol; AAAS; Develop Soc; Sigma Xi. *Res:* Role of lymphokines in modulating secondary transduction mechanisms in transformed (tumor) cells. *Mailing Add:* Dept Biol Earlham Col Richmond IN 47374. *Fax:* 765-983-1497; *E-Mail:* billh@yang.earlham.edu

HARVEY, WILLIAM ROSS, AUTOMATED ANALYTICAL CHEMISTRY, PROCESS MONITORING. *Current Pos:* RETIRED. *Personal Data:* b Clarksville, Tenn, Apr 14, 30; m 53; c 4. *Educ:* Austin Peay State Col, BS, 52; Univ Richmond, MH, 83. *Prof Exp:* Chemist, Barrow-Agee Labs, 56-60, Chemetron Corp, 60-64; chemist & proj leader anal chem, Phillip Morris Res Ctr, 64-90. *Mem:* Am Chem Soc. *Res:* Analytical chemistry; automated analytical methods development; ion chromatography, high-performance liquid chromatography, ultra violet light spectroscopy; on stream process analysis; classical wet analytical chemistry. *Mailing Add:* RR 1 PO Box 189 Cumberland VA 23040

HARVILLE, DAVID ARTHUR, STATISTICS. *Current Pos:* RES STAFF MEM, MATH SCI DEPT, IBM TJ WATSON RES CTR, 95- *Personal Data:* b Cleveland, Ohio Sept 6, 40. *Educ:* Iowa State Univ, BS, 62; Cornell Univ, MS, 64, PhD(animal breeding), 65. *Prof Exp:* Res math statistician, Aerospace Res Labs, Wright-Patterson AFB, Ohio, 65-75; prof statist, Iowa State Univ, 75-95. *Concurrent Pos:* Assoc ed, Biomet, 71-76 & J Am Statist Asn, 83-85. *Mem:* Fel Am Statist Asn; fel Inst Math Statist; Biomet Soc; Int Statist Inst. *Res:* Development of improved statistical methodology for analyzing data sets on the basis of linear statistical models. *Mailing Add:* Math Sci Dept IBM T J Watson Res Ctr PO Box 218 Yorktown Heights NY 10598-0218. *E-Mail:* harville@watson.ibm.com

HARVILLE, JOHN PATRICK, FISHERIES MANAGEMENT. *Current Pos:* RETIRED. *Personal Data:* b Eureka, Calif, Jan 13, 18; m 39; c 2. *Educ:* San Jose State Col, AB, 40; Stanford Univ, MA, 50, PhD, 56. *Prof Exp:* Lab asst entom, Stanford Univ, 41; teacher pub sch, 41-45; instr biol, San Mateo Jr Col, 46-48; instr biol, San Jose State Col, 48-51, from asst prof to prof biol & sci educ, 51-71, dir, Moss Landing Marine Labs, 65-71; exec dir, Pac Marine Fisheries Comn, 71-83, consult, 83-84. *Mem:* Ecol Soc Am; Am Fisheries Soc; Am Inst Fisheries Res Biol. *Res:* Bionomics of the California oak moth; population dynamics; biology of fishes and fresh water insects; local fauna. *Mailing Add:* 2430 SW Boundary St Portland OR 97219

HARWELL, JEFFREY HARRY, APPLIED SURFACTANT SCIENCE, ENVIRONMENTAL REMEDIATION. *Current Pos:* From asst prof to assoc prof, 82-92, DIR, DEPT CHEM ENG, UNIV OKLA, 91-, PROF CHEM ENG, 92- *Personal Data:* b Big Spring, Tex, Feb 8, 52; m 73, Joyce A Smith; c Jeffrey, Charissa, Amy & Nathan. *Educ:* Tex A&M Univ, BA, 74, MS, 79; Western Conservative Baptist Sem, MDiv, 77; Tex A&M Univ, MS, 79; Univ Tex, Austin, PhD(chem eng), 83. *Honors & Awards:* Victor K LaMer Award, Colloid Div, Am Chem Soc, 84; Masua Honor Lectr, Mid-Am State Univs Asn, 87. *Concurrent Pos:* Pres, Surfactant Assocs, Inc, 87-; prog dir, Separations Prog, NSF, 88-89; Conoco/DuPont prof, 95. *Mem:* Am Inst Chem Engrs; Am Chem Soc. *Res:* Basic and applied surfactant science: surfactant-soil washing and surfactant-aquifer remediation, surface modification via polymerization in admicelles, the use of surfactants to create new adsorbents and studies of surfactant adsorption. *Mailing Add:* Dept Chem Eng Univ Okla Norman OK 73019-0628

HARWELL, KENNETH EDWIN, AEROSPACE ENGINEERING, PROPULSION. *Current Pos:* SR VPRES RES & ASSOC PROF, UNIV ALA, HUNTSVILLE, 89- *Personal Data:* b Kellyton, Ala, Nov 22, 36; m 68, Sharon Hilton; c Kathryn, Karen & Kenneth. *Educ:* Univ Ala, BS, 59; Calif Inst Technol, MS, 60, PhD(aeronaut), 63. *Honors & Awards:* Gen H H Arnold Res Award, Am Inst Aeronaut & Astronaut, 81, Toffoy Res Mgt Award. *Prof Exp:* Res asst aeronaut, Calif Inst Technol, 60-63; from assoc prof to prof aerospace eng, Auburn Univ, 63-76; dir, Gas Diagnostics Res Div, Unif Tenn, 76-82, prof aerospace & mech, Space Inst, 76-89, dean, 82-89. *Concurrent Pos:* Res initiation grant, Auburn Univ, 63-65; consult, Hayes Int Corp, 65-68; US Army Ballistic Res Lab, 69; USAF, AFB, Fla, 70-73; USN & US Army & Auburn Res & Eng Assocs, 76-; asst to dir, US Army Missile Res & Develop & Elec Eng Lab, Huntsville, 73-74; mem, US Army Missile Sci Adv Group, 74-77; spec asst to vpres & dean, Univ Tenn Space Inst, 80-81. *Mem:* Fel Am Inst Aeronaut & Astronaut; Am Soc Eng Educ; Am Soc Mech Engrs; Technol Transfer Soc. *Res:* Diagnostics; missile aerodynamics; exhaust plume gas dynamics; radiation; laser-gas interactions; laser velocimetry; laser scattering from particles. *Mailing Add:* 1916 Country Club Dr Tullahoma TN 37388-8897

HARWELL, KENNETH ELZER, INDUSTRIAL ORGANIC CHEMISTRY, POLYMER CHEMISTRY. *Current Pos:* RETIRED. *Personal Data:* b Hillsboro, Tex, Sept 11, 21; m 61. *Educ:* Baylor Univ, BS, 45; Univ Tex, MA, 47, PhD(org chem), 51. *Prof Exp:* Chemist, Spec Probs, Union Carbide Chem Corp, 47-48; res scientist, Tex Cotton Res Comt, 48-50; res chemist, Celanese Corp Am, 51; res chemist, Res Found, Tex A&M Univ, 52-54; sr res chemist, Jefferson Chem Co, 54-57; chief exec, Tex Fine Chem Co, 57-61; res chemist, Continental Oil Co, 61-65; sr res chemist, Gulf Res & Develop Co, 65-72; sr res chemist, Cook Paint & Varnish Co, 73-79; mgr, Merriam Chem Develop Co, 79-83. *Mem:* Am Chem Soc. *Res:* Organic synthesis; plastics technology; process development; electronics and instrumentation; synthesis of new monomers. *Mailing Add:* 1916 Country Club Dr Tullahoma TN 37388

HARWELL, MARK ALAN, SYSTEMS ECOLOGY, ECOLOGY. *Current Pos:* ASSOC PROF, UNIV MIAMI, 91-; CONSULT, 91- *Personal Data:* b Lewisburg, Tenn, Nov 25, 47; m 68; c 2. *Educ:* Emory Univ, BS, 69, PhD(ecol), 78. *Prof Exp:* Teaching asst, Emory Univ, 75-77; res asst & comput consult, Emory Univ & AGNS Nuclear Fuel Recycling Plant, 77-78; res scientist environ assessment, Water & Land Resources Dept, Wash, 78-80; consult environ, Cannon Beach, Ore, 80-81; assoc dir, Ecosyst Res Ctr, Cornell Univ, 81-91, dir, Global Environ Prog, 87-91. *Concurrent Pos:* Fel, NSF, 69-75 & Emory Univ, 76-77; mem sci adv bd, Environ Protection Agency. *Mem:* AAAS; Sigma Xi; Ecol Soc Am; Am Inst Biol Sci. *Res:* Ecosystem model of air pollutant effects on forests; cross-systems comparison of biogeochemical cycles; long term environmental consequences of nuclear waste disposal; indirect effects of nuclear war; global environment stresses; ecosystems modeling. *Mailing Add:* 1660 Tigertail Ave Miami FL 33133

HARWIT, MARTIN OTTO, ASTROPHYSICS, HISTORY OF ASTRONOMY. *Current Pos:* NSF fel, Cornell Univ, 61-62, res assoc astrophys, 62, from asst prof to prof astron, 62-87, chmn dept, 71-76, co-dir, Prog Hist & Philos Sci & Technol, 85-87, EMER PROF ASTRON,

CORNELL UNIV, 88-; DIR, NAT AIR & SPACE MUS, SMITHSONIAN INST, 87- *Personal Data:* b Prague, Czech, Mar 9, 31; US citizen; m 57, Marianne Mark; c Alex, Eric & Emily. *Educ:* Oberlin Col, BA, 51; Univ Mich, MA, 53; Mass Inst Technol, PhD(physics), 60. *Honors & Awards:* Alexander von Humboldt Award, WGer, 76. *Prof Exp:* Physicist, Univ Mich, 54-55; NATO fel, Cambridge Univ, 60-61. *Concurrent Pos:* Vis res assoc, E O Hulburt Space Ctr, 63-64; NSF res grant, 63-; Nat Acad Sci exchange visitor, Czech Acad Sci, 69-70; vpres, Spectral Imaging, Inc, 70-77; Alexander von Humboldt Found Sr US Scientist fel, 76-77; external mem, Max Planck Inst Radioastron, WGer, 79- *Mem:* Fel Am Phys Soc; Am Astron Soc; Royal Astron Soc; Soc Hist Technol; fel AAAS. *Res:* Galaxy and star formation: cosmic dust; comets; infrared optics and astronomy; rocket astronomy; science policy; history and philosophy in science; educational astronomy. *Mailing Add:* 511 H St SW Washington DC 20024. *Fax:* 202-357-2426

HARWOOD, CLARE THERESA, PHARMACOLOGY. *Current Pos:* RETIRED. *Personal Data:* b New Bedford, Mass, Apr 5, 20. *Educ:* Seton Hill Col, AB, 41; Georgetown Univ, MS, 52, PhD(pharmacol), 55. *Prof Exp:* Lab technician hemat, Goodyear Fabric Corp, Mass, 41-42; anal chemist, US Naval Torpedo Sta, RI, 42-45; asst chem, Syracuse Univ, 45-46; instr sci, Sch Nursing, Union Hosp, Mass, 47-48; biochemist neurochem, Med Labs, US Army Chem Ctr, Md, 48-51; neuroendocrinol, Walter Reed Army Inst Res, DC, 51-58 & clin neuropharmacol res ctr, NIMH, 58-61; chief, Pharmacol & Biochem Lab, Clin Res Inst & asst prof pharmacol, Med Sch, Georgetown Univ, 61-68, lectr, 56-61; chief div drug sci, Bur Narcotics & Dangerous Drugs, Drug Enforcement Admin, Dept Justice, 68-70, actg chief drug control div, 70-71, chief, Biol Res Br, 71-73, chief pharmacologist, 73-76; consult, 76-93. *Concurrent Pos:* Fac mem, Oblate Col, 76-94. *Mem:* Am Soc Pharmacol & Exp Therapeut; Am Chem Soc; Sigma Xi. *Res:* Central regulation of anterior pituitary activity. *Mailing Add:* 3506 Dunlop St Chevy Chase MD 20815

HARWOOD, COLIN FREDERICK, PHYSICAL CHEMISTRY, CHEMICAL ENGINEERING. *Current Pos:* ASST VPRES RES & DEVELOP FINE FILTRATION, PALL CORP, 77- *Personal Data:* b Manchester, Eng, July 17, 37; US citizen; m 58. *Educ:* London Univ, BSc, 63, PhD(phys chem), 69. *Prof Exp:* Sci teacher chem & physics, St John's Col, Nassau, 63-66; sci adv fine particles, ITT Res Inst, Chicago, 69-77. *Concurrent Pos:* Lectr, Ill Inst Technol, 69-71 & Ctr Prof Advan, 70-; mem, Powder Adv Ctr. *Mem:* Fine Particle Soc (secy, 77); AAAS. *Res:* Measurement and characterization of particulate properties; control of particulate emissions by filtration; development of novel monitoring concepts; development of new filter medium. *Mailing Add:* 5870 N Moccasin Trail Tucson AZ 85750-0801

HARWOOD, DAVID SMITH, GEOLOGY, PETROLOGY. *Current Pos:* GEOLOGIST, US GEOL SURV, 64- *Personal Data:* b Manchester, Vt, Jan 19, 36; m 58; c 2. *Educ:* Dartmouth Col, AB, 58; Harvard Univ, PhD(geol), 67. *Mem:* Mineral Soc Am; Geol Soc Am. *Res:* Geologic mapping of early Paleozoic metamorphic rocks in west-central Maine; tectonics of southwestern Berkshire Highlands, Massachusetts and Connecticut. *Mailing Add:* 210 Royal Palm Ave El Granada CA 94018

HARWOOD, HAROLD JAMES, POLYMER CHEMISTRY. *Current Pos:* from asst prof to assoc prof chem, 59-69, PROF POLYMER SCI & CHEM & RES ASSOC INST POLYMER SCI, UNIV AKRON, 69- *Personal Data:* b Streator, Ill, Mar 2, 31; m 52; c 3. *Educ:* Univ Akron, BS, 52; Yale Univ, PhD(org chem), 56. *Prof Exp:* Res chemist, Monsanto Chem Co, 55-59. *Concurrent Pos:* Res assoc, Inst Rubber Res, 59-69; consult, Chem Industs. *Mem:* Am Chem Soc. *Res:* Organic polymer chemistry; characterization of sequence distribution in copolymers; organophosphorus chemistry; synthesis and characterization of macromolecules; polymer reactivity; synthetic polypeptides. *Mailing Add:* Dept Polymer Sci Univ Akron 302 Buchtel Mall Akron OH 44325-0001

HARWOOD, HAROLD JAMES, JR, ENZYMOLOGY, CHOLESTEROL & POLYISOPRENOID METABOLISM. *Current Pos:* res scientist, 86-88, sr res scientist, 89-91, SR RES INVESTR, DEPT METAB DIS, PFIZER CENT RES, 91- *Personal Data:* b New Haven, Conn, July 27, 54; m 77, Janice K Gill; c Katryn R & William B. *Educ:* Univ Akron, BS, 76, BS, 77; Purdue Univ, PhD(biochem), 82. *Prof Exp:* Fel pharmacol, Univ Fla, Gainesville, 82-84, asst prof, Dept Med & Pharmacol, 84-86. *Concurrent Pos:* Prin investr, Am Cancer Soc, 83-84, Univ Fla, 85-87 & Nat Cancer Inst, 85-88; mem, Coun Basic Sci, Am Heart Asn. *Mem:* Am Chem Soc; Am Soc Biochem & Molecular Biol; Am Heart Asn; Am Fedn Clin Res; Protein Soc. *Res:* Enzymology of cholesterol, bile acid and nonsterol polyisoprenoid snythesis and metabolism; pharmacologic and physiological modulation of enzyme activity and concentration; metabolic regulation of enzyme activity and lipoprotein reception activity. *Mailing Add:* Pfizer Cent Res Ctr Eastern Point Rd Groton CT 06340. *Fax:* 860-441-4111; *E-Mail:* hardn_j_harwood@groton.pfizer.com

HARWOOD, IVAN RICHMOND, PEDIATRIC PULMONOLOGY. *Current Pos:* asst prof pediat, 71-78, dir pediat intensive care unit, 72-78, assoc adj prof, 78-86, CHIEF PULMONARY DIV, UNIV CALIF MED CTR, SAN DIEGO, 72-, PROF PEDIAT, 87- *Personal Data:* b Huntington, WVa, July 3, 39. *Educ:* Dartmouth Col, BA, 61; Univ WVa, MD, 65; Am Bd Pediat, cert. *Honors & Awards:* First Prize, Int Rehab Film Libr Competition, 80. *Prof Exp:* Intern pediat, Univ WVa Hosp, Morgantown, 65-66; resident pediat, Yale-New Haven Hosp, 66-68, sr resident outpatient dept, 68-69; chief pediat, USAF Hosp 3646, Del Rio, Tex, 68-70. *Concurrent Pos:* Fel pediat cardiol, Univ Calif, 70-71; co-dir, Cystic Fibrosis Ctr, San Diego, 72-73, dir, 73; mem, Cystic Fibrosis Young Adult Comn, Atlanta, 74-80, chmn, 76-80, Cystic Fibrosis Ctr Comn, 86-89, vchmn, 90-; mem, San Diego Co Tuberc Control Bd, 74-78; mem patient care rev comt & others, Univ Calif Med Ctr, 76-. *Mem:* Nat Cystic Fibrosis Found. *Mailing Add:* Cystic Fibrosis Ctr 3020 Chldns Way MC 5070 San Diego CA 92123-4282

HARWOOD, JULIUS J, METALLURGY, CERAMICS & COMPOSITES. *Current Pos:* PRES, HARWOOD CONSULTS, 87- *Personal Data:* b New York, NY, Dec 3, 18; m 41, 83, Naomi Beitner; c Dane L, Gail A (Katz), Caren L (Feldman) & Rochelle Upfal. *Educ:* City Col New York, BS, 39; Univ Md, MS, 53. *Hon Degrees:* DEng, Mich Tech Univ, 86. *Honors & Awards:* John H Shoemaker Award, Am Soc Metals, 77; Orton lectr, Am Ceramic Soc, 78. *Prof Exp:* Mat engr, US Naval Gun Factory, 40-46; metallurgist, Off Naval Res, 46-60, head, Metall Br, 53-60; mgr, Metall Dept, Sci Lab, Ford Motor Co, 60-69, mgr, Res Planning Eng & Res Staff, 69-71, dir, Mat Sci Lab, Eng & Res Staff, 71-83; prof eng, Wayne State Univ, 84; pres, Ovonic Synthetic Mat Co, 84-87. *Concurrent Pos:* Chmn, Gordon Res Conf Corrosion, 56; chmn, Corrosion Res Coun, Eng Found, 64-66; mem bd control, Mich Technol Univ, 66-86, chmn bd, 70-71 & 86-87; nat mat adv bd, Nat Acad Sci-Nat Res Coun; chmn, Vis Comt, Sch Eng, Rensselaer Polytech Inst; mem, Mat Adv Comt, Off Technol Assessment, US Cong; mem, Mat Adv Comt, Nat Sci Fedn, 74-76; mem, Mich Asn Gov Bds of Univs; adj prof, Wayne State Univ, 75-; chmn, Nat Mat Adv Bd, Nat Acad Sci-Nat Res Coun, 77-79; vpres, Metro Ctr High Tech, 84. *Mem:* Nat Acad Eng; Am Inst Mining, Metall & Petrol Engrs (pres, 76); fel Am Soc Metals; fel Metall Soc (pres, 73); fel AAAS; hon mem Am Inst Mining Metall & Petrol Engrs; Am Ceramic Soc. *Res:* Physical metallurgy; stress corrosion cracking; advanced materials, research management; technology transfer; materials policy and management; ceramics surface modification technology; commercialization of materials technology; matrix composites. *Mailing Add:* 5023 Pheasant Cove West Bloomfield MI 48323. *Fax:* 248-681-6747

HARWOOD, THOMAS RIEGEL, SURGICAL PATHOLOGY, IMMUNOHEMATOLOGY. *Current Pos:* from instr to asst prof, Sch Med, 56-73, clin assoc prof, Sch Med & Sch Dent, 73-90, EMER ASSOC PROF PATH, NORTHWESTERN UNIV, 90- *Personal Data:* b Knoxville, Tenn, Dec 9, 26; m 49, 76, Phyllis Bredthaker; c Joseph D, Thomas M & Shannon D. *Educ:* Georgetown Univ, BS, 49; Vanderbilt Univ, MD, 53; Am Bd Path, cert, 58. *Prof Exp:* Asst path, Sch Med, Vanderbilt Univ, 54-55; instr, Med Col Va, 55-56. *Concurrent Pos:* Borden Award undergrad res, 53; asst pathologist, Wesley Mem Hosp, Chicago, 58-59; assoc chief lab serv, Vet Admin Lakeside Med Ctr, 69-73, actg chief, 73-76 & 80-81; med dir, Blood Servs Chicago, 73-87; emer pathologist, Vet Admin Lakeside Med Ctr, 76-87 & Ref Path Labs, Inc, 90-; assoc attend staff, Northwestern Mem Hosp, Chicago, 80-90. *Mem:* Am Soc Invest Path; Am Soc Clin Pathologists; Am Asn Blood Banks; AMA; NY Acad Sci. *Res:* Neoplasia; Mallory bodies in liver disease; salivary gland disease; cardiovascular disease; blood banking and immunohematology. *Mailing Add:* 916 Williamsburg Village Dr Jackson TN 38305. *Fax:* 847-742-6804

HARWOOD, WILLIAM H, PHYSICAL CHEMISTRY. *Current Pos:* RETIRED. *Personal Data:* b San Antonio, Tex, Sept 14, 22; m 43; c 4. *Educ:* Trinity Univ, Tex, BS, 48; Univ Tex, MA, 49, PhD(chem), 54. *Prof Exp:* Res chemist, Continental Oil Co, 51-57, sr res chemist, 57-60, res assoc chem, 60-69; from asst prof to prof chem, Cameron Univ, 69-87. *Mem:* AAAS; fel Am Inst Chem; Soc Am Archaeol; Am Phys Soc; Am Chem Soc. *Res:* Organic electrochemistry; metallo-organic chemistry; specific heats; spectroscopy; physical chemistry of surface films; colloids, especially foams, emulsions, dispersions, solid lubricants; theoretical and experimental thermodynamics; chemical kinetics; archaeology of Oklahoma and the Southwest. *Mailing Add:* HC 2 Box 35A Medina TX 78055-9409

HARWOOD-NASH, DEREK CLIVE, pediatric radiology, pediatric neuroradiology; deceased, see previous edition for last biography

HARYETT, ROWLAND D, ORTHODONTICS. *Current Pos:* RETIRED. *Personal Data:* b Bancroft, Ont, Aug 18, 23; m 48; c 1. *Educ:* Univ Toronto, DDS, 51, MSD, 53; FRCD(C). *Prof Exp:* Assoc prof, Univ Alta, 57-68, dir div, 58-74, prof orthod, Fac Dent, 68-96. *Mem:* Am Asn Orthod; Can Dent Asn; fel Int Col Dent; Can Asn Orthodontists (pres, 81). *Res:* Studies on the treatment and psychologic effects of arresting thumb sucking in preschool and public school groups of chronic thumb suckers. *Mailing Add:* 9727 141st St Edmonton AB P5N 2M5 Can

HASAN, ABU RASHID, CHEMICAL ENGINEERING, PETROLEUM ENGINEERING. *Current Pos:* From asst prof to assoc prof, 79-90, PROF STOICH & KINETICS, UNIV NDAK, 90- *Personal Data:* b Bangladesh, May 25, 49; m 73; c 2. *Educ:* Bangladesh Univ Eng & Technol, BSc Eng, 72; Univ Waterloo, Ont, MASc, 75, PhD(chem), 79. *Concurrent Pos:* Assoc Western Univ, Idaho Nat Eng Lab, 87-88; Can Commonwealth fel, 73-73. *Mem:* Am Inst Chem Engrs; Soc Petrol Engrs; Sigma Xi. *Res:* Multiphase flow; production logging, slurry rheology; moisture removal from low-rank coal (steam drying of lignite, dewatering of peat by solvent extraction); alternatives to diesel fuel; pressure transient analysis in oil wells. *Mailing Add:* Chem Eng Univ NDak Box 7101 Grand Forks ND 58202

HASAN, MAZHAR, NUCLEAR PHYSICS, PLASMA PHYSICS. *Current Pos:* assoc prof, 61-67, PROF PHYSICS, NORTHERN ILL UNIV, 67- *Personal Data:* b India, May 20, 27; m 57; c 2. *Educ:* Aligarh Muslim Univ, India, BSc, 48, MSc, 50; Ill Inst Technol, PhD(nuclear physics), 59. *Prof Exp:* Lab instr, Aligarh Muslim Univ, India, 48-50; lectr physics, Forman Christian

Col, Pakistan, 50-51; lectr, Loyola Univ, Ill, 54; asst physicist biol sci, Chicago Univ, 54-55; instr math & physics, Northern Ill Univ, 55-56, asst prof physics, 58-60; instr, Univ Ill, 56-58; sr physicist, Res Div, Gen Dynamics/Electronics, 60-61. *Concurrent Pos:* Fulbright lectr, Univ Alexandria, 67-68, Tehran Pahlavi Univ & Gondishapour Univ, Iran, 68-69. *Mem:* Am Phys Soc; Am Asn Physics Teachers; Sci Res Soc Am; Sigma Xi (vpres, 64-65, pres elect, 65-66). *Res:* Nuclear reactions and nuclear structure; principal methods of mathematical physics; plasma physics; controlled thermonuclear fusion. *Mailing Add:* Dept Physics Northern Ill Univ De Kalb IL 60115

HASAN, SYED EQBAL, HAZARDOUS WASTE MANAGEMENT, GEOTECHNICS & ENVIRONMENTAL GEOLOGY. *Current Pos:* asst prof, 79-83, ASSOC PROF GEOL, UNIV MO, 84-, DIR CTR ENVIRON STUDIES, DEPT GEOSCI, 96- *Personal Data:* b Patna, India, Apr 15, 39; US citizen; m 68, Farrukh; c Danish, Zeenat & Zeba. *Educ:* Patna Univ, BS, 60; Rookee Univ, MS, 63; Purdue Univ, PhD(eng geol), 78. *Prof Exp:* Jr res fel geol, Rookee Univ, 63-64; jr geologist, Geol Surv India, 65-70, sr eng geologist, 70-73; res asst geol, Purdue Univ, 73-78. *Concurrent Pos:* Vis asst prof, Univ Ariz, 78-79, Mich Technol Univ, 78, Kuwait Univ, 85-86. *Mem:* Asn Eng Geologists; Int Asn Eng Geol; Sigma Xi; fel Geol Soc India; fel Geol Soc Am. *Res:* Environmental geology and geotechnics: waste management; development of underground space for human use and occupancy. *Mailing Add:* Dept Geosci Univ Mo 5100 Rockhill Rd Kansas City MO 64110-2499. *Fax:* 816-235-5535; *E-Mail:* shasan@cctr.umkc.edu

HASBROOK, ARTHUR F(ERDINAND), ELECTRONICS, COMPUTERS. *Current Pos:* TECH CONSULT, AHLEGRE LABS, 76- *Personal Data:* b Wichita, Kans, Jan 9, 13; m 43. *Prof Exp:* Seismic observer-operator, Petty Geophys Eng Co, Tex, 33-35; head, Elec Dept, Petty Labs, Inc, Petty Geophys Eng Co, 35-38, head gravity res, gravity survs, 38-42, in charge electronic surv & navig, 46-57, res supvr, 58-66, res assoc, 66-67, mem tech staff, 67-72; off, USAF Radio Lab, Wrightfield, Ohio, 42-46; mem advan tech staff, Geosource, Inc, 73-75. *Mem:* AAAS; sr mem Inst Elec & Electronics Engrs; Am Geophys Union. *Res:* Research and design of geophysical and exploration equipment; research and development of electronic surveying equipment; geophysical data processing and analysis. *Mailing Add:* 9590 Oakland Rd San Antonio TX 78240

HASCALL, GRETCHEN KATHARINE, cell biology, for more information see previous edition

HASCALL, VINCENT CHARLES, JR, BIOCHEMISTRY. *Current Pos:* STAFF, BIOMED ENG, CLEVELAND CLIN FOUND RES INST, 94- *Personal Data:* b Burwell, Nebr, May 26, 40; div; c 2. *Educ:* Calif Inst Technol, BS, 62; Rockefeller Univ, PhD(biol sci), 69. *Hon Degrees:* DMed Univ Lund, Sweden, 86. *Honors & Awards:* Karl Meyer Award, Soc Glycoconjugate Res, 92. *Prof Exp:* From asst prof to assoc prof biol chem & oral biol, Sch Dent, Univ Mich, Ann Arbor, 69-75; sr staff fel, Nat Inst Dent Res, NIH, 75-76, res chemist, 76-94, chief proteoglycan chem sect, 78-94. *Concurrent Pos:* Swed Med Coun vis scientist, Univ Lund, 73; mem, Pathobiol Study Sect, NIH, 76-80; foreign work study fel, Univ Monash, Australia, 81; mem res coun, Juv Diabetes Found, 84; chmn, Gordon Conf Proteoglycans, 86; vis prof biochem, Rush-Presby-St Lukes Med Ctr, 89- *Mem:* Am Soc Biol Chemists & Molecular Biologists; Orthop Res Soc; Am Soc Cell Biologists; NAm Soc Glycobiol (pres, 87); Sigma Xi. *Res:* Biochemistry and biophysics of proteoglycans and glycoproteins of connective tissues. *Mailing Add:* Cleveland Clin Found Biomed Eng WB3 9500 Euclid Ave Cleveland OH 44195-0001. *Fax:* 216-445-4383

HASCHEMEYER, AUDREY ELIZABETH VEAZIE, BIOCHEMISTRY, ENVIRONMENTAL PHYSIOLOGY. *Current Pos:* assoc prof biol sci, 69-74, PROF BIOL & BIOCHEM, HUNTER COL, 74-, CHMN, DEPT BIOL SCI, 80- *Personal Data:* b Chicago, Ill, Oct 31, 36; c 2. *Educ:* Univ Ill, Urbana, BS, 57; Univ Calif, Berkeley, PhD(phys chem), 61. *Prof Exp:* Res assoc biol, Mass Inst Technol, 61-64; asst biologist, Mass Gen Hosp, 65-69. *Concurrent Pos:* USPHS fel, Mass Inst Technol, 62-64; Helen Hay Whitney Found fel, Mass Gen Hosp, 65-67; assoc, Harvard Med Sch, 67-69; mem grad fac, City Univ New York, 69-; bd fel & associateships, Nat Res Coun, 74-76; Am Cancer Soc Res Scholar, King's Col, London, 76; univ comt res, 77-78; chief scientist, R/V Alpha Helix, Caribbean-Pac, 78; proj dir, US Antarctic Res Prog, 78-, chief scientist, US Coast Guard Cutter Polar Star, Ross Sea, 81; mem corp, Marine Biol Lab, Woods Hole; grants, NSF, 69-, NIH, 70-77 & NATO, 78- *Mem:* Am Physiol Soc; Am Soc Biol Chemists; Biophys Soc; fel AAAS; French Soc Biol Chemists. *Res:* Regulation of protein synthesis in higher organisms; cold adaptation of fish; mechanism of action of thyroid hormone; biological reaction rates in vivo. *Mailing Add:* 21 Glendon Rd Woods Hole MA 02543

HASCHKE, FERDINAND, PEDIATRIC NUTRITION. *Current Pos:* from asst prof to assoc prof, 81-88, PROF PEDIAT, UNIV VIENNA, 88- *Personal Data:* b Linz, Austria, Sept 16, 48; m 72; c 4. *Educ:* Univ Vienna, MD, 72; Austrian Bd Physicians, License Pediat, 78. *Honors & Awards:* Milupa Award, Pediat Soc WGer, 84; V Pirquet Award, Pediat Soc Austria, 86. *Prof Exp:* Asst prof pediat, Univ Vienna, 77-79; res fel nutrit, Univ Iowa, 79-80. *Concurrent Pos:* Lectr, dept nutrit, Univ Vienna, 86-; adv, dept toxicol, WHO/Euro Copenhagen, 85; vis prof, Allama Iqbal Med Col, Pakistan, 86. *Mem:* Am Soc Clin Nutrit; Am Inst Nutrit; Soc Pediat Res. *Res:* Pediatric nutrition, mainly infant nutrition; growth studies of infants; body composition; trace elements; environmental contamination. *Mailing Add:* Nestec Av Nestle 55 Vevey CH-1800 Switzerland. *Fax:* 43 662-4482-2604

HASCHKE, JOHN MAURICE, SOLID STATE CHEMISTRY, HIGH TEMPERATURE CHEMISTRY. *Current Pos:* MEM STAFF, LOS ALAMOS NAT LAB, NMEX, 89- *Personal Data:* b San Antonio, Tex, Aug 5, 41; m 68; c 2. *Educ:* Tex Tech Univ, BS, 64; Mich State Univ, PhD(inorg chem), 69. *Prof Exp:* Res assoc chem, Ariz State Univ, 69-70; asst prof chem, Univ Mich, Ann Arbor, 70-76; res chemist, Rockwell Int, Golden, Co, 77-89. *Mem:* AAAS; Am Chem Soc; Sigma Xi. *Res:* Vaporization and thermodynamics of solids; phase equilibria; nonstoichiometric compounds; hydrothermal equilibria and reactions; lanthanide actinide chemistry. *Mailing Add:* 1211 Big Rock Loop Los Alamos NM 87544-2852

HASCICEK, YUSUF SUAT, LOW & HIGH TEMPERATURE SUPERCONDUCTORS, MICROSTRUCTURE & LOW TEMPERATURE TRANSPORT CHARACTERIZATION OF MATERIALS. *Current Pos:* res assoc, 88-92, asst scholar scientist, 92-93, ASSOC SCHOLAR SCIENTIST, NAT HIGH MAGNETIC FIELD LAB, FLA STATE UNIV, 93- *Personal Data:* b Uluborlu-Isparta, Turkey, Mar 3, 55; m, Anse Kablan; c Eyyup Y, Ayse H, Abmet H & Omer F. *Educ:* Ankara Univ, BSc, 76, MSc, 78; Oxford Univ, UK, PhD(metall & mat sci), 83. *Prof Exp:* Asst lectr, Firat Univ, 76-78; fel, Oxford Univ, 84-85; from asst prof to assoc prof solid state physics, Erciyes Univ, Turkey, 85-88. *Concurrent Pos:* Vis fel Royal Soc, Oxford Univ, 87; vis assoc prof & NATO fel, Polytech Univ, NY, 88. *Mem:* Am Phys Soc; Minerals Metals & Mat Soc; Mat Res Soc; Am Soc Mat Int. *Res:* Processing, material and transport characterization of high temperature superconductivity materials; microstructural analysis; critical current density measurements as a function of temperature and magnetic field; strain tolerance of Jc; magnet design and technology by standard and innovative techniques (eg, laser processing). *Mailing Add:* Fla State Univ Nat Magnetic Field Lab 1800 E Paul Diroc Dr Tallahassee FL 32306. *Fax:* 850-644-0867; *E-Mail:* yusef@magnet.fsu.edu

HASDAL, JOHN ALLAN, NUCLEAR WEAPON EFFECTS, KINETIC ENERGY INTERCEPTOR LETHALITY. *Current Pos:* PRES, ENTERPRISE SOFTWARE CONSULT, INC, 89- *Personal Data:* b Oak Park, Ill, Mar 17, 42; m 88. *Educ:* Univ Denver, BS, 64, PhD(physics), 69. *Prof Exp:* Scientist, BDM Corp, 69-71; assoc physicist, Cornell Aeronaut Lab, 71-73; mem tech staff, Hughes Aircraft Co, 73-75; sr analyst, R/M Systs, Inc, 75-78, Sci & Eng Assocs, Inc, 82-85; staff scientist, Sci Appln Inc, 78-82; sr scientist, Phys Res, Inc, 85-89. *Mem:* Am Phys Soc. *Res:* Kinetic energy interceptor lethality in ballistic missile defense; computer code design; weapon systems operational reliability and maintainability; nuclear weapon effects; electronic circuit protection. *Mailing Add:* 220 41st St Downers Grove IL 60515

HASE, WILLIAM LOUIS, PHYSICAL CHEMISTRY, CHEMICAL KINETICS. *Current Pos:* from asst prof to assoc prof, 73-81, PROF CHEM, WAYNE STATE UNIV, 81- *Personal Data:* b Washington, Mo, Mar 22, 45; m 67, Betty F Criscuolo; c Heidi J. *Educ:* Univ Mo, Columbia, BS, 67; NMex State Univ, PhD(chem), 70. *Prof Exp:* Res assoc chem, NMex State Univ, 70-71 & Univ Calif, Irvine, 71-73. *Concurrent Pos:* Fel, NMex State Univ, 68-70; prin investr, Petrol Res Found, 73-76, 81-84 & 91-93, Res Corp, 74-76 & NSF, 75-; prog officer, NSF, 83-84. *Mem:* Fel Am Phys Soc; Am Chem Soc. *Res:* Computer simulation of chemical reactions; Monte Carlo trajectory studies of molecular dynamics; theories of chemical kinetics; co-author graduate text. *Mailing Add:* Dept Chem 335 Chem Wayne State Univ 5950 Cass Ave Detroit MI 48202. *Fax:* 313-577-8822; *E-Mail:* hase@sun.chem.wayne.edu

HASEGAWA, ICHIRO, ELECTRON MICROSCOPY. *Current Pos:* RETIRED. *Personal Data:* b Seattle, Wash, Aug 2, 15; m 46; c 2. *Educ:* Univ Wash, BS, 43. *Prof Exp:* From jr chemist to res chemist, Atlantic-Richfield Co, 44-65; res scientist, Philip Morris Inc, 65-69, sr scientist electron micros, 69-81. *Concurrent Pos:* Mem adv bd, Va State Lab Servs, 82-85. *Mem:* Am Chem Soc; AAAS. *Res:* Aerosol research; microstructure of materials utilizing electron microscopy and x-ray diffraction techniques. *Mailing Add:* 1911 Bellevue Ave Apt D510 Richmond VA 23227

HASEGAWA, JUNJI, dermatology, histochemistry, for more information see previous edition

HASEGAWA, RYUSUKE, SOLID STATE PHYSICS, METAL PHYSICS. *Current Pos:* DIR, MAGNETICS RES & FAR EAST BUS DEVELOP, ALLIED-SIGNAL INC, 92- *Personal Data:* b Nagoya, Japan, Feb 7, 40; m 67, Pamela; c Sergei & Linnea. *Educ:* Nagoya Univ, BEng, 62; Calif Inst Technol, MS, 68, PhD(mat sci), 69. *Honors & Awards:* Distinguished lectr, Inst Elec & Electronics Engrs Magnetics Soc, 90. *Prof Exp:* Res fel mat sci, Calif Inst Technol, 69-72; mem staff phys sci, Thomas J Watson Res Ctr, IBM Corp, 73-75; sr staff physicist, Nippon Amorphous Metals, 75-78, group leader, 78-80, res assoc, 80-84, sr res assoc, 84-85, vpres, 85-89, dir, Far East Opers, 85-89. *Concurrent Pos:* Fulbright Scholar, 64; co-chmn, Amorphous Magnetism Conf, 79, Annual Magnetism & Magnetic Mat Conf, 81, chairperson, Magnetics Soc Amorphous Magnetic Mat Tech Comt, Inst Elec & Electronics Engrs, 82-; adj prof, Univ Tokyo, 88-89. *Mem:* Am Phys Soc; fel Inst Elec & Electronics Engrs; Mat Res Soc. *Res:* Magnetism and electron transport properties of noncrystalline metallic solids; development of new amorphous alloys for electromagnetic and structural applications. *Mailing Add:* Amorphous Metals Eastman Rd Parsippany NJ 07054. *Fax:* 973-581-7718

HASEK, ROBERT HALL, ORGANIC CHEMISTRY, RESEARCH ADMIN. *Current Pos:* RETIRED. *Personal Data:* b State College, Pa, June 25, 18; m 42, 78, Maryann Heppert; c J Reed. *Educ:* Pa State Col, BS, 39; Univ Ill, PhD(org chem), 43. *Prof Exp:* Lab asst, Charles Lennig, Pa, 37, Eastman Kodak Co, NY, 39-40 & Gen Elec Co, 42; from res chemist to sr res chemist, Res Labs, Tenn Eastman Co, 43-55, from res assoc to sr res assoc, 55-63, res dir, Eastman Res AG, Switz, 63-67, head chem res div, 67-76, res fel, 76-78. *Mem:* Fel AAAS; Am Chem Soc. *Res:* Polymers; oxidized cellulose; oxo reaction; hydrogenation; ketenes. *Mailing Add:* 46 Grove Hill Rd Kingsport TN 37660

HASELEY, EDWARD ALBERT, PHYSICAL CHEMISTRY, POLYMER SCIENCE. *Current Pos:* From res chemist to sr res chemist, E I du Pont de Nemours & Co, Inc, 63-65, res supvr, 65-69, sr res chemist, Dacron Res Lab, 69-78, ORGN DEVELOP SPECIALIST, TEXTILE FIBERS DEPT, E I DU PONT DE NEMOURS & CO, INC, 78- *Personal Data:* b Cleveland, Ohio, Nov 23, 30; m 53; c 4. *Educ:* Kenyon Col, AB, 53; Ohio State Univ, PhD(phys chem), 56. *Mem:* Am Chem Soc; Sigma Xi. *Res:* Boron hydride chemistry; polyester fiber technology. *Mailing Add:* 107 Ivy Rd Grifton NC 28530

HASELKORN, ROBERT, GENETICS, DEVELOPMENT. *Current Pos:* from asst prof to assoc prof biophys, chem & biochem, 61-69, chmn, Dept Biophys, 69-84, F L PRITZKER DIST SERV PROF, DEPT MOLECULAR GENETICS & CELL BIOL, UNIV CHICAGO, 84- *Personal Data:* b New York, NY, Nov 7, 34; m 57; c 2. *Educ:* Princeton Univ, AB, 56; Harvard Univ, PhD(biochem), 59. *Honors & Awards:* Darbaker Prize, Bot Soc Am, 82; Gregor Mendel Medal, Acad Sci Czech Repub, 96. *Prof Exp:* Am Cancer Soc fel, Virus Res Unit, Agr Res Coun, Eng, 59-61. *Concurrent Pos:* Ed, Virology; chmn, Virol Study Sect, NIH, 78-80; Sackler fel, Tel Aviv Univ, 87; mem, Panel Sci Adv, Int Ctr Genetic Eng & Biotechnol, UNIDO, 84-94; mem, rec DNA adv comt, NIH, 91-95. *Mem:* Nat Acad Sci; Am Soc Biochem & Molecular Biol; Am Soc Microbiol; Int Soc Plant Molecular Biol (pres, 87-88); fel Am Acad Arts & Sci. *Res:* Nitrogen fixation in cyanobacteria and in photosynthetic bacteria; molecular genetics of prokaryotic differentiation; plant molecular biology. *Mailing Add:* Dept Molecular Genetics & Cell Biol Univ Chicago 920 E 58th St Chicago IL 60637. *Fax:* 773-702-3172; *E-Mail:* r haselkorn@uchicago.edu

HASELTINE, FLORENCE PAT, OBSTETRICS & GYNECOLOGY. *Current Pos:* DIR, CTR POP RES, NAT INST CHILD HEALTH & HUMAN DEVELOP, NIH, 85- *Personal Data:* b Philadelphia, Pa, Aug 17, 42; m 70; c 2. *Educ:* Univ Calif, BA, 64; Mass Inst Technol, PhD(biophys), 69; Albert Einstein Col Med, MD, 72. *Prof Exp:* From asst prof to assoc prof obstet & gynec, Yale Univ Sch Med, 76-85. *Concurrent Pos:* Consult, Pediat Endocrine Clin, 78-85 & Behav Med Clin, Yale Univ, 83-85. *Mem:* Inst Med-Nat Acad Sci; Am Fertil Soc; Soc Gynec Invest; Soc Study Reproduction; Soc Reproductive Endocrinologists; Endocrine Soc; Am Col Obstetricians & Gynecologists. *Res:* Human reproduction; biomedical research on problems of human fertility and infertility; development of safe and efficacious fertility regulating methods; evaluation of the medical effects and efficacy of contraceptive methods. *Mailing Add:* NIH 6100 Executive Blvd Rm 8N07 Bethesda MD 20892

HASELTON, GEORGE MONTGOMERY, GEOLOGY, GEOMORPHOLOGY. *Current Pos:* from asst prof to assoc prof, 67-78, PROF GEOL, CLEMSON UNIV, 78- *Personal Data:* b Worcester, Mass, Feb 28, 28; m 55; c 2. *Educ:* Colby Col, BA, 51; Univ Boston, MA, 58; Ohio State Univ, PhD(geol), 67. *Prof Exp:* Field geologist, Raw Mat Br, US AEC, Calif, 55-56; instr geol, Marietta Col, 58-61; res assoc, Inst Polar Studies, Ohio State Univ, 62-67. *Concurrent Pos:* Partic, Am Geol Inst Int field inst, Spain, 71; res & teaching, Tromso Univ, Norway, 76-77; vis prof, Ore State Univ, 81-83. *Mem:* Arctic Inst NAm; Geol Soc Am; Int Asn Quaternary Res; Int Qual Asn; Nat Asn Geol Teachers; Am Qual Asn. *Res:* Glacial geology and geomorphological studies and research in Antarctica, Alaska, the Canadian Arctic and New England; late Pleistocene and Holocene geology of Alaska and special areas in New England. *Mailing Add:* 164 Falling Springs Rd Central SC 29630

HASEMAN, JOSEPH FISH, METALLURGY. *Current Pos:* CONSULT, 75- *Personal Data:* b Columbia, Mo, June 12, 14; m 41, Truella Kyd; c 3. *Educ:* Univ Mo, AB, 36, PhD(soil chem), 43; Cornell Univ, MA, 38. *Prof Exp:* Lab asst geol, Cornell Univ, 36-37; lab instr, 37-38; jr geologist, Shell Oil Co, Tex, 38-40; res chemist, Tenn Valley Authority, 42-52; group leader, Minerals Separation Group, Foote Minerals Co, 52-56; prin res engr, Int Minerals & Chem Corp, 56-62; res scientist, Armour Agr Chem Co, Fla, 62-66; metallurgist, Agrico Chem Co, Pierce, Fl, 66-75. *Mem:* Sigma Xi. *Res:* Use of heavy minerals in studying soil origin and development; concentration of non-metallic ores by flotation; physical chemistry of phosphate fixation by clay minerals. *Mailing Add:* 1905 Camphor Dr Lakeland FL 33803

HASEMAN, JOSEPH KYD, LABORATORY ANIMAL CARCINOGENICITY STUDIES. *Current Pos:* RES MATH STATISTICIAN, NAT INST ENVIRON HEALTH SCI, 70- *Personal Data:* b July 20, 43; m 72, Janelle Hood; c David & Ashley. *Educ:* Davidson Col, BS, 65; Univ NC, PhD(biostatist), 70. *Honors & Awards:* Director's Award, NIH, 83. *Concurrent Pos:* Assoc ed, Biometrics, 79-84. *Mem:* Fel Am Statist Asn; Biomet Soc; Soc Toxicol; Genotoxicity & Environ Mutagen Soc. *Res:* Develop statistical methodology for and design, analyze and interpret results from long term rodent carcinogenicity studies; published 200 scientific papers. *Mailing Add:* Nat Inst Environ Health Sci PO Box 12233 Research Triangle Park NC 27709. *Fax:* 919-541-4311; *E-Mail:* haseman@fred.niehs.nih.gov

HASENFUS, HAROLD J(OSEPH), MECHANICAL ENGINEERING, ELECTRICAL ENGINEERING. *Current Pos:* head, Satellite Appln Div, Naval Weapons Lab, 60-61, tech dir, 61-86, EMER TECH DIR, US NAVAL SPACE SURVEILLANCE, 86- *Personal Data:* b New York, NY, Apr 9, 21; m 45; c 4. *Educ:* City Col New York, BS, 43; Va Polytech Inst, MS, 76, MS, 84. *Prof Exp:* Asst plutonium technol, Metall Lab, 45; proj engr, Fercleve Corp, Tenn, 45; res engr rockets, Ballistic Res Labs, Aberdeen Proving Ground, 46-52, chief, Rocket Br, 52-60. *Concurrent Pos:* US Army deleg, Tripartite Conf Armaments, Explosives & Propellants, US Dept Defense, Que, Can, 59, USN deleg, Tripartite Conf Artificial Earth Satellites, Bermuda, 71; consult, Missiles & Astronaut Div, Am Defense Preparedness Asn. *Mem:* AAAS; Am Soc Mech Engrs; Am Inst Aeronaut & Astronaut; Am Math Soc; Am Defense Preparedness Asn; Asn Comput Mach. *Res:* Stability and control of missiles and rockets; ignition and combustion in solid-fuel rockets; instrumentation for rocket research, including radio telemetry, optics and transducer development; satellite orbit theory and computation. *Mailing Add:* 311 Ingleside Dr Fredericksburg VA 22405-2344

HASH, JOHN H, BIOCHEMISTRY. *Current Pos:* asst prof, Vanderbilt Univ, 64-67, assoc prof, 67-70, actg chmn dept, 68-72, interim chmn dept, 87-90, PROF MICROBIOL, SCH MED, VANDERBILT UNIV, 70-, ASSOC DEAN BIOMED SCI, 76- *Personal Data:* b Ferrum, Va, Feb 23, 29; m 53, Mary A Boone; c Debra L, Susan R & Richard G. *Educ:* Roanoke Col, BS, 49; Va Polytech Inst, MS, 55, PhD (biochem), 57. *Prof Exp:* Res assoc biochem, Columbia Univ, 57-58; res biochemist, Lederle Labs, Am Cyanamid Corp, 58-64. *Mem:* AAAS; Am Soc Biol Chem; Am Chem Soc; Sigma Xi. *Res:* Enzymology; protein chemistry; carbohydrate metabolism. *Mailing Add:* Dept Microbiol Sch Med Vanderbilt Univ Nashville TN 37215-2402

HASHIM, GEORGE A, IMMUNOLOGY, BIOLOGY. *Current Pos:* ASSOC RES DIR, COUN TOBACCO RES, USA INC, NEW YORK, 93- *Personal Data:* b Damour, Lebanon, May 28, 31; m 62, Audrey E Mailhiot; c Laura E, Charles E & Sami G. *Educ:* Columbia Univ, MS, 63, PhD, 67. *Honors & Awards:* Andres Bello Orden, Govt Venezuela, 80. *Prof Exp:* Fel, Salk Inst, La Jolla, 67-69; dir biol res, Continental Res Inst, New York, 69-72; dir exp immunol, St Luke's-Roosevelt Hosp Ctr, 72-93. *Concurrent Pos:* assoc prof microbiol, Columbia Univ, 76-85, sr res scientist & scholar, 85-93, mem study sect, NIH, Bethesda, 84-89; NIH grants, NSF, 67- *Mem:* Am Soc Neurochem (treas, 86-92, pres, 93-); Am Asn Immunologists; Am Soc Biol Chemists & Molecular Biologists; Int Soc Neurochem; Sigma Xi. *Res:* Notable research in peptides therapy and multiple sclerosis; editor six books, several patents, author of several book chapters and contributed over 150 articles to professional journals. *Mailing Add:* 24 Barney Park Irvington NJ 10533

HASHIM, SAMI A, METABOLISM, NUTRITION. *Current Pos:* DIR, DIV METAB & NUTRIT, ST LUKE'S HOSP, 61-, ATTEND PHYSICIAN, 71- *Personal Data:* b Lebanon, Sept 21, 29; US citizen; m 56; c 2. *Educ:* Am Univ Beirut, BA, 50 MS, 52; Univ Buffalo Sch Med, MD, 55. *Prof Exp:* Intern & resident med, Peter Bent Brigham Hosp, Boston, 55-57; res fel, Dept Nutrit, Harvard Univ, 57-58, med & nutrit, St Luke's Hosp & Columbia Univ, 58-61. *Concurrent Pos:* Mem, Nutrit Study Sect, NIH, 68-72; Type Two Intervention Study Monitoring Comt, 73-82, prin investr, 71- *Mem:* Am Soc Clin Invest; Am Soc Clin Nutrit; Am Inst Nutrit; Am Soc Clin Res; AAAS. *Res:* Lipid metabolism and transport, mechanisms of lipid absorption; adipose tissue metabolism; gastric factors in obesity; development of non-caloric fats; methods of improving malnutrition. *Mailing Add:* Div Metab St Luke's Hosp Ctr 114th St & Amsterdam Ave New York NY 10025

HASHIMOTO, ANDREW G, BIOPROCESS ENGINEERING. *Current Pos:* prof & head, Bioresource Eng Dept, 86-95, ASSOC PROVOST ACAD AFFAIRS, ORE STATE UNIV, 95- *Personal Data:* b Wailuku, Hawaii, Aug 13, 44; m 67, Merle Eguchi; c Meri L, Noelle, Andrew R & Joel. *Educ:* Purdue Univ, BS, 66, MS, 68; Cornell Univ, PhD(agr eng), 72. *Prof Exp:* Res leader, USDA, 69-86. *Concurrent Pos:* Asst prof, Cornell Univ, 72-76; from assoc prof to prof, Univ Neb, 76-86; ed, Bioresource Technol, 86-; sci adv, Unisyn Biowaste Technol, 90- *Mem:* AAAS; Am Soc Agr Engrs; Am Soc Eng Educ; Int Asn Water Pollution Res & Control; Am Chem Soc; Inst Biol Eng. *Res:* Bioprocess engineering, bioconversion processes, waste management and remediation, anaerobic fermentation and biomass pretreatment technologies. *Mailing Add:* Ore State Univ Corvallis OR 97331-2152. *Fax:* 541-737-3033; *E-Mail:* hashimoa@ccmail.orst.edu

HASHIMOTO, KEN, ELECTRON MICROSCOPY, IMMUNOHISTOCHEMISTRY. *Current Pos:* PROF DERMAT & CHMN DEPT DERMAT & SYPHIL, WAYNE STATE UNIV, 80- *Personal Data:* b Niigata City, Japan, June 19, 31; US citizen; m 62; c 4. *Educ:* Niigata Univ Sch Med, MD, 55. *Prof Exp:* Res assoc, dept dermat, Tufts Univ, 63-65, asst prof, Sch Med, 65-68; from assoc prof to prof med & anat, Univ Tenn, Memphis, 68-77, dir dermatopath, 75-77; prof anat & dermat, dir dermat & chief dermat sect, Wright State Univ, 77-80. *Concurrent Pos:* Res & clin fel, Boston City Hosp, 63-64; med investr, Vet Admin career develop prog, Vet Admin Med Ctr, Memphis, 68-70, chief dermat sect & dir Electron Micros Lab, 70-77; Vet Admin rep mem, Path B Study Sect, NIH, USPHS, Dept Health, Educ & Welfare, 74-77; mem, biol & climate effects res task group, Environ Protection Agency, 76-77; chief, dept dermat, Harper-Grace Hosp & Detroit Receiving Hosp, 80- *Mem:* Am Soc Dermatopath (pres-elect, 86, pres, 86-87); Soc Investigative Dermat (vpres, 80-81); AAAS; Am Dermat Asn. *Res:* Dermatological oncology; structure and function of the skin; monoclonal antibodies related to the skin structures; cutaneous amyloidosis; cutaneous molecular biology. *Mailing Add:* Dept Dermat Wayne State Univ Detroit MI 48202

HASHIMOTO, PAULO HITONARI, CEREBROSPINAL FLUID ABSORPTION, ELECTRON MICROSCOPY. *Current Pos:* PROF ANAT & PATHOL, KOSHIEN UNIV, 93- *Personal Data:* b Amagasaki, Japan, Mar 23, 30; m 60, Maria E Inoue; c Joseph Y, Elizabeth K, Theresia H, Michael M & Augustino N. *Educ:* Osaka Univ, MD, 53, DMSc(med sci), 60. *Prof Exp:* From instr to prof anat, Med Sch, Osaka Univ, 57-93. *Concurrent Pos:* Fel anat, Harvard Med Sch, 63-65; counr, Japanese Asn Anatomists, 74-93. *Mem:* Am Asn Anatomists; Am Soc Cell Biol; Int Brain Res Orgn; AAAS. *Res:* Fine structure of the central nervous system; vascular fine structure of circumventricular organs in relation to venous absorption of the cerebrospinal fluid. *Mailing Add:* Koshien Univ 10-1 Momijigaoka Takarazwka Hyogo 665 Japan. *Fax:* 81-797-87-5666

HASHIN, ZVI, APPLIED MECHANICS, MATERIALS ENGINEERING. *Current Pos:* vis prof, Israel Inst Technol, 68-69, prof mat eng, 71-73, chmn dept, 73-77 & 79-81, PROF SOLID MECH, MAT & STRUCT, TEL AVIV UNIV, 73-, NATHAN CUMMINGS PROF MECHS SOLIDS, 80- *Personal Data:* b Danzig, June 24, 29; m 59, Tamara Milner; c Orna, Leor, Eran. *Educ:* Israel Inst Technol, BSc, 53, & MSc 55; DSc, Sorbonne, 57. *Hon Degrees:* Dr, Free Univ Brussels, Belg, 94. *Honors & Awards:* Landau Prize, 72; Medal Excellence, Ctr Composite Mat, Univ Del, 84; Eng Sci Medal, Soc Eng Sci, 89. *Prof Exp:* Lectr mech, Israel Inst Technol, 57-58, sr lectr, 58-59; res fel struct mech, Harvard Univ, 59-60; from assoc prof to prof eng mech, Univ Pa, 60-71. *Concurrent Pos:* Consult, Scott Paper Co, 61-62, Gen Elec Co, 62-66, Armstrong Cork Co, 65-66, Franklin Inst, 66-68 & Monsanto Res Corp, 66-67; sci adv, Mat Sci Corp, 70-; prof mat eng, Technion-Israel Inst Technol, 71-73; vis prof mat sci & eng, Univ Pa, 77-79, adj prof, 78-, vis prof, Dept Mech Eng & Appl Mech, 89-92; Israel deleg, Int Union Theoret & Appl Mech; co-chmn, Int Union Theoret Appl Mech Symp, Composite Mat, Blacksburg, Va, 82, Damage & Fatigue Symp, Haifa & Tel Aviv, Israel, 85; distinguished lectr, Univ Del, 85; mem, Cong Comt, Int Union Theoret & Appl Mech, 88- *Mem:* Fel Am Soc Mech Engrs; Soc Rheology; Soc Eng Sci; Israel Soc Theoret & Appl Mech (pres, 76-93). *Res:* Mechanics of solids; heterogeneous media; composite materials; fatigue. *Mailing Add:* Dept Solid Mech Mat & Struct Fac Eng Tel Aviv Univ Tel Aviv Israel. *Fax:* 972-3-6429540; *E-Mail:* hashin@eng.tau.ac.il

HASHMALL, JOSEPH ALAN, SPACECRAFT ATTITUDE DETERMINATION, ATTITUDE SENSOR CALIBRATION. *Current Pos:* SR COMPUT SCIENTIST, COMPUT SCI CORP, 83- *Personal Data:* b New York, NY, Oct 15, 43; m 64; c 1. *Educ:* Univ Chicago, BS, 64; Univ Tex, Austin, PhD(chem), 69. *Honors & Awards:* Space Shuttle Orbiter Pres Award Tech Excellence; NASA Manned Flight Awareness Award. *Prof Exp:* Part-time instr chem, Huston-Tillotsen Col, 65-68; Swiss Nat Fund grant, Phys Chem Inst, Univ Basel, 69-70; NSF grant, Univ Calif, Berkeley, 71; asst prof chem, Georgetown Univ, 71-79; sr anal, RDS, Inc, 79-83. *Res:* Spacecraft ground support system development; development of sensor calibration algorithms. *Mailing Add:* 8116 Triple Crown Rd Bowie MD 20715-4535

HASINOFF, BRIAN BRENNEN, MEDICINAL CHEMISTRY, OXYGEN FREE RADICALS. *Current Pos:* PROF, FAC PHARM, UNIV MAN, WINNIPEG, 90- *Personal Data:* b Mannville, Alta, Nov 14, 44; m 70, Shelley Fishman; c Sam & Amy. *Educ:* Univ Alta, BSc, 66, PhD(chem), 70. *Prof Exp:* Res assoc chem, Univ Kent, Canterbury, 70-72; asst prof, Notre Dame Univ, Nelson, 73-75; from asst prof to prof chem & med, Mem Univ Nfld, 75-90. *Mem:* Am Chem Soc; Chem Inst Can; Am Asn Cancer. *Res:* Oxy radicals, drug induced oxy radical production, anthracyline cardioprotective agents; antioxidant drugs; topoisomerase II inhibitors; drug design. *Mailing Add:* Fac Pharm Univ Man Winnipeg MB R3T 2N2 Can. *Fax:* 204-275-7509; *E-Mail:* b_hasinoff@umanitoba.ca

HASKE, BERNARD JOSEPH, ORGANIC CHEMISTRY. *Current Pos:* assoc prof, 67-71, PROF CHEM, DOWLING COL, 71- *Personal Data:* b Baltimore, Md, Nov 14, 30; m 58; c 6. *Educ:* Loyola Col, Md, BS, 52; Univ Va, MS, 55, PhD(chem), 59. *Prof Exp:* Asst prof chem, Wheeling Col, 58-61; assoc prof, Washington Col, 61-67. *Mem:* Am Chem Soc. *Res:* Structural and synthetic studies of organic complexing agents. *Mailing Add:* 24204 Drayton Landing Dr Worton MD 21678

HASKELL, BARRY G, ENGINEERING. *Current Pos:* HEAD, VISUAL COMMUN RES DEPT, AT&T BELL LABS, 87- *Personal Data:* m; c 2. *Educ:* Univ Calif, Berkeley, AB, 64, MS, 65 & PhD(elec eng), 68. *Prof Exp:* Res asst, Univ Calif Electronics Res Lab, 64-68. *Concurrent Pos:* Res asst, Lawrence Livermore Lab; Instr grad courses, Rutgers Univ, City Col New York & Columbia Univ. *Mem:* Sigma Xi; fel Inst Elec & Electronics Engrs. *Res:* Digital transmission and coding of images; videotelephone; satellite television transmission; medical imaging; digital image processing; author of over 30 publications and 20 patents. *Mailing Add:* Visual Commun Res AT&T Bell Labs HO-4C538 Holmdel NJ 07733

HASKELL, BETTY ECHTERNACH, NUTRITIONAL BIOCHEMISTRY. *Current Pos:* PROF NUTRIT, UNIV TEX, 78- *Personal Data:* b Lewiston, Idaho, June 1, 25. *Educ:* Univ Idaho, BA, 46; Univ Chicago, MA, 47; Univ Calif, Berkeley, BS, 56, PhD(nutrit), 64. *Prof Exp:* Asst prof nutrit, Univ Calif, Davis, 64-69; from assoc prof to prof nutrit, Univ Ill, Urbana, 69-78. *Concurrent Pos:* Vis prof, Med Br, Univ Tex, Galveston, 82. *Mem:* Am Inst Nutrit; Am Soc Biol Chemists; Am Chem Soc. *Res:* Vitamin metabolism; ascorbic acid. *Mailing Add:* 2312 Rundell Pl Austin TX 78704

HASKELL, CHARLES THOMSON, MATHEMATICS. *Current Pos:* from asst prof to assoc prof, 63-71, PROF MATH, CALIF STATE POLYTECH COL, SAN LUIS OBISPO, 71- *Personal Data:* b Wenatchee, Wash, Jan 27, 24; m 47; c 3. *Educ:* Univ Wash, BA, 46; Univ Ariz, MS, 61, PhD(math), 65. *Prof Exp:* Teacher, Churchill County High Sch, Nev, 46-48; trust clerk, Peoples Nat Bank, Wash, 48-49; teller & trust clerk, First Nat Bank Nev, 49-55, asst trust officer, 55-59; asst math, Univ Ariz, 60-63. *Mem:* Math Asn Am; Am Math Soc. *Res:* Analytic number theory. *Mailing Add:* PO Box 706 Newport OR 97365

HASKELL, DAVID ANDREW, PLANT MORPHOLOGY. *Current Pos:* RETIRED. *Personal Data:* b Lakewood, Ohio, Mar 26, 28; m 58; c 2. *Educ:* Ohio State Univ, BSc, 51; Purdue Univ, MS, 57, PhD(bot), 60. *Prof Exp:* From asst prof to assoc prof bot, Smith Col, 60-79, chmn dept, 65-75, prof biol sci, 79-90. *Mem:* AAAS; Bot Soc Am; Am Inst Biol Sci; Sigma Xi. *Res:* Developmental morphology of angiosperm embryos; origin, structure and growth of plant apical meristems. *Mailing Add:* Dept Biol Sci Smith Col Northampton MA 01063

HASKELL, THEODORE HERBERT, JR, NATURAL PRODUCTS CHEMISTRY, CARBOHYDRATE CHEMISTRY & STRUCTURAL CHEMISTRY. *Current Pos:* RETIRED. *Personal Data:* b Los Angeles, Calif, June 16, 21; m 47, Mary Now; c Peter, Nancy, Theodore III & Stephen. *Educ:* Dartmouth Col, AB, 43; Ohio State Univ, PhD(physiol chem), 49. *Prof Exp:* Res chemist, Winthrop Chem Co, 43-46; sect dir, Parke, Davis & Co, 49-81. *Concurrent Pos:* Instr bio-org chem, Univ Mich & instr med chem, Washtenaw Community Col; consult. *Mem:* Am Chem Soc; Japan Antibiotics Res Asn; NY Acad Sci. *Res:* Chemistry of antibiotics; natural products; author of over 62 chemical publications. *Mailing Add:* 2400 Indian Creek Blvd-W Apt E-115 Vero Beach FL 32966

HASKELL, VERNON CHARLES, PHYSICAL CHEMISTRY. *Current Pos:* RETIRED. *Personal Data:* b Can, June 20, 19; US citizen; m 46, Marjorie Ketchum; c Vernon (deceased), Amy & Sidney. *Educ:* Univ Sask, BEng, 44, MSc, 46; Columbia Univ, PhD(chem), 48. *Prof Exp:* Asst chem, Columbia Univ, 46-48; res chemist, E I du Pont de Neumours & Co, 48-51, develop supvr, 51-56, res assoc, 56-66, res fel, Polymer Prod Dept, 66-82. *Concurrent Pos:* Fel, Ctr Advan Eng Study, Mass Inst Technol, 69-70. *Mem:* AAAS; Am Chem Soc; Sigma Xi. *Res:* Reaction kinetics and mechanism; cellulose chemistry; moisture proof coatings; fine structure of regenerated cellulose; polymer chemistry; colloids. *Mailing Add:* 95 Burlwood Dr San Francisco CA 94127

HASKILL, JOHN STEPHEN, IMMUNOPATHOLOGY. *Current Pos:* ASSOC PROF OBSTET & GYNEC & BACT & IMMUNOLOGY, UNIV NC, CHAPEL HILL, 77- *Personal Data:* b Toronto, Ont, Nov 10, 39; m 65; c 3. *Educ:* Univ Toronto, BSc, 62, MA, 64, PhD(med biophys & radiobiol), 66. *Prof Exp:* Asst prof path, Queen's Univ, Ont, 69-72; assoc prof path, McGill Univ, 72-74; assoc prof path, Dept Basic & Clin Immunol & Microbiol, Med Univ SC, Charleston, 74-77. *Concurrent Pos:* Nat Cancer Inst Can res fel med biophys, Walter & Eliza Hall Inst, Melbourne, Australia, 66-68. *Mem:* Can Soc Immunol; Can Asn Path; Am Soc Exp Path. *Res:* Cellular immunology and cancer biology. *Mailing Add:* Dept Comprehensive Cancer Ctr Univ NC CB 7295 218 Lineberger Chapel Hill NC 27599-7295

HASKIN, HAROLD H, MARINE BIOLOGY. *Current Pos:* dir, Oyster Res Lab, 50-84, EMER PROF, NJ AGR EXP STA, 84- *Personal Data:* b Niagara Falls, NY, Jan 3, 15; m 42; c 5. *Educ:* Rutgers Univ, BSc, 36; Harvard Univ, MA, 38, PhD(biol), 41. *Prof Exp:* Asst, Oceanog Inst, Woods Hole, 46; from asst prof to assoc prof, Rutgers Univ, 46-58, prof zool, 58-84. *Concurrent Pos:* Mem corp, Bermuda Biol Sta, 38- *Mem:* AAAS; Am Soc Limnol & Oceanog; Sigma Xi; Soc Invert Path; Am Soc Zool; Nat Shellfisheries Asn. *Res:* Shellfish biology; estuarine ecology; invertebrate pathology and physiology; continuing in shellfish biology & pathology primarily with American oyster. *Mailing Add:* Rutgers Shellfish Res Lab 6959 Miller Ave Port Norris NJ 08327-3167

HASKIN, LARRY A, GEOCHEMISTRY. *Current Pos:* chmn dept, 76-90, prof chem & earth & planetary sci, 76-86, R E MORROW DISTINGUISHED UNIV PROF EARTH & PLANETARY SCI & PROF CHEM, WASHINGTON UNIV, 86- *Personal Data:* b Olathe, Kans, Aug 17, 34; m 63, Mary A Gehl; c Dierk A, Rachel L & Jean M. *Educ:* Baker Univ, BA, 55; Univ Kans, PhD(radiochem), 60. *Honors & Awards:* NASA Except Sci Achievement Medal, 71. *Prof Exp:* Asst prof chem, Ga Inst Technol, 59-60; from instr to prof, Univ Wis-Madison, 60-74; chief planetary & earth sci div, NASA Johnson Space Ctr, 73-76. *Concurrent Pos:* Consult, NASA Johnson Space Ctr, 70-73. *Mem:* AAAS; Am Chem Soc; Am Geophys Union; Geochem Soc; Meteoritical Soc. *Res:* Trace element geochemistry, especially rare earths; neutron activation analysis; lunar sample analysis; physical chemistry of trace ions in silicate liquids; raman spectrometry for mineral analysis. *Mailing Add:* EPSc Campus Box 1169 Washington Univ One Brookings Dr St Louis MO 63130-4899

HASKIN, MARVIN EDWARD, RADIOLOGY. *Current Pos:* res asst prof physiol & biophys, 69-71, PROF DIAG RADIOL & CHMN DEPT, HAHNEMANN MED COL & HOSP, 71- *Personal Data:* b Ardmore, Pa, May 28, 30; m 59; c 2. *Educ:* Temple Univ, BA, 51, MD, 55. *Prof Exp:* Chief radiologist, USAF Hosp, Andrews AFB, Washington, DC, 57-58; chief diag, Philadelphia Gen Hosp, Pa, 61-63; radiologist, Haverford Gen Hosp, Havertown, Pa, 63-69. *Concurrent Pos:* Res fel radiol, Philadelphia Gen Hosp, Pa, 59-60; instr, Sch Med, Temple Univ, 61-63; assoc radiol,

Hahnemann Med Col, 63-66, clin asst prof, 67- *Mem:* AAAS; fel Am Col Physicians; fel Am Col Radiol; Am Nat Standards Inst; Int Sci Orgn. *Res:* Biomedical engineering; computer applications in medicine. *Mailing Add:* Broad & Vine St Philadelphia PA 19102

HASKIN, MYRA RUTH SINGER, PHYSICAL MEDICINE & REHABILITATION. *Current Pos:* RETIRED. *Personal Data:* b Philadelphia, Pa, Feb 12, 35; m 58; c 2. *Educ:* Univ Pa, BA, 56; Temple Univ, MD, 60. *Prof Exp:* Intern, Presby Hosp, Philadelphia, Pa, 60-61; res & asst instr phys med & rehab, Hosp Univ Pa, 61-64; chief phys med & rehab, Albert Einstein Med Ctr, South Div, 64-65; asst prof, Sch Med, Temple Univ, 66-67; psychiatrist, Philadelphia Gen Hosp, 67, assoc phys med & rehab, Hosp & instr, Sch Med, Univ Pa, 67-80. *Concurrent Pos:* Fel physiol, Grad Sch Med, Univ Pa, 63-64; res psychiatrist, Temple-Moss Philco Biomed Eng Dept, 66. *Mem:* AMA; Am Cong Rehab Med; Am Med Women's Asn; Am Acad Phys Med & Rehab. *Res:* Electromyology; psychiatry. *Mailing Add:* 718 Sussex Rd Wynnewood PA 19196

HASKINS, ARTHUR L, JR, obstetrics & gynecology, for more information see previous edition

HASKINS, CARYL PARKER, GENETICS, PHYSIOLOGY. *Current Pos:* CONSULT, 35- *Personal Data:* b Schenectady, NY, Aug 12, 08; m 40. *Educ:* Yale Univ, PhB, 30; Harvard Univ, PhD(physiol), 35. *Hon Degrees:* ScD, Tufts Col, 51, Union Univ, NY & Northeastern Univ, 55, Yale Univ, 58, Hamilton Col, NY, 59, George Washington Univ, 63; LLD, Cincinnati Univ, Carnegie Inst Technol & Boston Col, 60, Washington & Jefferson Col, 61, Univ Del, 65 & Pace Univ, 75. *Honors & Awards:* Joseph Henry Medal, Smithsonian Inst. *Prof Exp:* Mem staff, Res Lab, Gen Elec Co, 31-35; dir, pres & chmn bd, Haskins Labs Inc, 35-55. *Concurrent Pos:* Dir, Schenectady Trust Co, 34-; res assoc, Mass Inst Technol, 35-45; res prof, Union Col, NY, 37-55; pres & dir, Nat Photocolor Corp, NY, 39-55; asst liaison officer, Nat Defense Comt-Off Sci Res & Develop, 40-42; sr liaison officer, 42-43; exec asst to chmn, Nat Defense Res Comt, 43-44, dep exec officer, 44-45; sci adv, Policy Coun, Army & Navy Joint Res & Develop Bd, 47-48; res & develop bd, Nat Mil Estab, 47-51; chmn, Adv Comt Spec Weapons, Secy Defense, 48-49, consult, 50-56; mem, Pres Sci Adv Comt, 55-59, consult, 59-70; trustee, Carnegie Inst, Wash, 49-, pres, 55-71, trustee, Carnegie Corp, NY, 55, chmn bd, 76-; trustee, Nat Geog Soc, Woods Hole, Mass; regent, World Wildlife, Smithsonian Inst; dir, Coun Foreign Rels, Yale Univ; counr, Am Philos Soc, 76-78 & 81-83. *Mem:* Nat Acad Sci; fel AAAS; Am Phys Soc; Entom Soc Am; Genetics Soc Am; Royal Soc Arts; Royal Entomol Soc; Entomol Soc Am; Nat Geog Soc; Sigma Xi (pres, 66-68); Biophys Soc; NY Acad Sci; Brit Asn Advan Sci; Am Acad Arts & Sci. *Res:* Mechanism of speciation and evolution; radiation biophysics; cellular physiology, especially nutritional requirements of microorganisms. *Mailing Add:* 22 Green Acre Lane Westport CT 06880-5027

HASKINS, EDWARD FREDERICK, BOTANY. *Current Pos:* from asst prof to assoc prof, 66-83, PROF BOT, UNIV WASH, 83- *Personal Data:* b Minneapolis, Minn, Apr 10, 37. *Educ:* Univ Minn, BA, 59, MS, 62, PhD(protozool), 65. *Prof Exp:* Instr bot, Univ Minn, 62; NSF fel electron micros, Biol Labs, Harvard Univ, 65-66. *Mem:* AAAS; Bot Soc Am; Mycol Soc Am; Am Soc Protozool; Am Soc Zool. *Res:* Developmental biology of the Myxomycetes; electron microscopy; microbial ecology. *Mailing Add:* Dept Bot Univ Wash Box 355325 Seattle WA 98195-0001

HASKINS, FRANCIS ARTHUR, PLANT BIOCHEMISTRY. *Current Pos:* asst agronomist, Univ Nebr-Lincoln, 53-55, from assoc prof to prof agron, 55-58, George Holmes prof agron, 67-88, EMER PROF, UNIV NEBR-LINCOLN, 88- *Personal Data:* b Omaha, Nebr, Aug 20, 22; m 51, Dorothy G Masters; c John A, Ann (Olney), Katherine J & William P. *Educ:* Univ Nebr, BSc, 43, MSc, 48; Calif Inst Technol, PhD(chem genetics), 51. *Prof Exp:* Res fel chem genetics, Calif Inst Technol, 51-52; res scientist, Univ Tex, 52-53. *Mem:* Fel AAAS; Genetics Soc Am; Am Soc Plant Physiol; fel Am Soc Agron; Phytochem Soc NAm; fel Crop Sci Soc Am. *Res:* Aromatic metabolism in neurospora; enzyme studies in maize; chemical genetics of Melilotus, sorghum and other forage species. *Mailing Add:* Dept Agron Univ Nebr Lincoln NE 68583-0915

HASKINS, JOSEPH RICHARD, NUCLEAR PHYSICS. *Current Pos:* from asst prof to assoc prof, 59-65, PROF PHYSICS & CHMN DEPT, GETTYSBURG COL, 65- *Personal Data:* b Wooster, Ohio, Mar 27, 26; m 54; c 4. *Educ:* Univ Tex, BS, 46; Ohio State Univ, PhD(physics), 52. *Prof Exp:* Res physicist, Ord Missile Lab, Res Lab, Redstone Arsenal, 54-59. *Concurrent Pos:* Asst prof, Univ Ala, 58-59. *Mem:* Am Phys Soc; Am Asn Physics Teachers. *Res:* Nuclear spectra; Mossbauer effect. *Mailing Add:* 153 S Hay St Gettysburg PA 17325

HASKINS, MARK, ANIMAL MODELS, METABOLIC DISEASE. *Current Pos:* From asst prof to assoc prof, 81-91, PROF, SCH VET MED, UNIV PA, 91- *Personal Data:* b Philadelphia, Pa, Dec 27, 44. *Educ:* Pa State Univ, BS, 66; Univ Pa, VMD, 69, PhD(path), 77; Drexel Univ, MS, 73. *Honors & Awards:* Ralston Purina Small Animal Res Award. *Mem:* Am Vet Med Asn; AAAS; Int Acad Path; Am Asn Pathologists; Am Soc Human Genetics. *Res:* Pathogenesis and therapy of animals models of human genetic disease. *Mailing Add:* Path Lab Univ Pa Sch Vet Med 3800 Spruce St Philadelphia PA 19104-6051. *Fax:* 215-898-0719

HASKINS, REGINALD HINTON, MYCOLOGY, MICROBIOLOGY. *Current Pos:* RETIRED. *Personal Data:* b North Bay, Ont, July 16, 16; m 49; c 3. *Educ:* Univ Western Ont, BA, 38, MA, 40; Harvard Univ, PhD(biol), 48. *Prof Exp:* Demonstr bot, Univ Western Ont, 38-40, sr demonstr, 45-46; tutor, Dunster House, Harvard Univ, 47-48; from asst res officer to sr res officer, Nat Res Coun Can, 48-67, head physiol & biochem of fungi sect, 56-67, prin res officer, 67-81, head microbial physiol & biochem, Prairie Regional Lab, 70-81. *Mem:* Bot Soc Am; Mycol Soc Am; Am Soc Plant Physiol; Can Soc Microbiol; Brit Mycol Soc. *Res:* Physiology of biochemistry of fungi; industrial mycological fermentations; taxonomy of fungi; sexual reproduction and ultrastructure of phycomycetes. *Mailing Add:* 222 Lake Crescent Saskatoon SK S7H 3A2 Can

HASLAM, JOHN LEE, PHARMACEUTICAL CHEMISTRY. *Current Pos:* RETIRED. *Personal Data:* b Salt Lake City, Utah, Jan 4, 39; m 66, Gale A Christiansen; c 2. *Educ:* Univ Utah, BA, 63, PhD(chem), 66. *Prof Exp:* NIH fel, Cornell Univ, 66-68; asst prof chem, Univ Kans, 68-73; assoc dir develop, Interx Res Corp, Subsid Merck & Co, Inc, 73-95. *Mem:* Sigma Xi; Am Chem Soc; Am Asn Pharmaceut Scientists. *Res:* Pharmaceutical research and product development. *Mailing Add:* 1560 N 1060th Rd Lawrence KS 66046

HASLANGER, MARTIN FREDERICK, MEDICINAL CHEMISTRY, RATIONAL DRUG DISCOVERY. *Current Pos:* assoc dir, 85-88, DIR CHEM, SCHERING-PLOUGH RES, 88- *Personal Data:* b Dayton, Ohio, Mar 27, 47; m 69; c 2. *Educ:* Denison Univ, BS, 69; Univ Mich, PhD(org chem), 74. *Prof Exp:* Postdoctoral fel chem, Dept Chem, Harvard Univ, 74-76; res investr chem, Squibb Inst Med Res, 76-80, sr res investr, 80-81, group leader, 81-85. *Concurrent Pos:* Res chemist, Eastman Kodak, 69-70; NIH fel, 74-76. *Mem:* Am Chem Soc; AAAS; NY Acad Sci; Am Heart Asn. *Res:* New drug discovery; design and synthesis of enzyme inhibitors and receptor antagonists; peptide mimetics; use of data and computational chemistry to design and optimize small molecule-large molecule interactions. *Mailing Add:* Lilly Res Lab Lilly Corp Ctr Indianapolis IN 46285

HASLEM, WILLIAM JOSHUA, TECHNICAL MANAGEMENT. *Current Pos:* Proj officer, Dugway Proving Ground, US Army, 60-72, opers analyst, Tank-Automotive Command, 72-75, tech dir, Cold Regions Test Ctr, 75-91, TECH DIR, DUGWAY PROVING GROUND, US ARMY, 91- *Personal Data:* b Roosevelt, Utah, Nov 28, 36; m 57; c 3. *Educ:* Univ Utah, BS, 60; Cent Mich Univ, MA, 74. *Concurrent Pos:* Instr, Univ Alaska, 77-85. *Mem:* Int Test & Eval Asn; Am Defense Preparedness Asn. *Res:* Test and evaluation of defense equipment. *Mailing Add:* 103 N Donlee Dr St George UT 84770-4537

HASLER, ARTHUR DAVIS, ZOOLOGY. *Current Pos:* from instr to assoc prof zool, Univ Wis-Madison, 37-48, dir inst ecol, 71-74, chmn dept zool, 53-54 & 55-57, dir lab limnol, 63-78, prof, 68-78, EMER PROF ZOOL, UNIV WIS-MADISON, 78- *Personal Data:* b Lehi, Utah, Jan 5, 08; m 32; c 6. *Educ:* Brigham Young Univ, AB, 32; Univ Wis-Madison, PhD(zool), 37. *Hon Degrees:* DSc, Mem Univ Nfld, 67, Miami Univ, Oxford, Ohio, 88. *Honors & Awards:* Award Excellence, Am Fisheries Soc, 77; Sea Grant Award, Sea Grant Asn, 80; Naumann-Thienemann Medal, Int Asn Ecol, 92; Outstanding Achievement Award, Am Inst Fisheries Res Biol, 93. *Prof Exp:* Asst biologist, US Fish Wildlife Serv, 35-37. *Concurrent Pos:* Mem adv comt biol, Off Naval Res, 51-54, hydrobiol comt, 52-58; Fulbright res scholar, Ger, 54-55; mem comt environ biol, NSF, 55-59, comt biol sta & facil, 55-60; Nat Acad Sci-Nat Res Coun, 55-59; comt educ & recruitment oceanog, Am Soc Limnol & Oceanog-Nat Acad Sci, 60; chmn, Int Cong Limnol, 62; scholar & exchange prof, Univ Helsinki, 63-64; convenor comt freshwater productivity, Int Biol Prog, Int Coun Sci Union, 66-67; mem US Nat Comt, Int Union Biol Sci & US Comt Int Biol Prog, Nat Acad Sci-Nat Res Coun. *Mem:* Nat Acad Sci; AAAS; Am Soc Limnol & Oceanog (vpres, 47, pres, 51); Ecol Soc Am (pres, 61); Int Asn Ecol (pres, 67-74); Am Soc Zool (pres, 71); Royal Neth Acad Sci; Soc Zool Bot Fennica. *Res:* General and experimental limnology; migration of fishes; sense of smell in orientation to parent stream; sun-orientation in fishes; radioisotopes in hydrobiology. *Mailing Add:* Ctr Limnol 680 N Park St Univ Wis Madison WI 53706

HASLER, ARTHUR FREDERICK, METEOROLOGY. *Current Pos:* RES METEOROLOGIST, GODDARD SPACE FLIGHT CTR, NASA, 74- *Personal Data:* b Madison, Wis, Aug 21, 40; m 65; c 4. *Educ:* Univ Wis, BS, 63, MS, 65, PhD(meteorol), 71. *Prof Exp:* Res asst satellite meteorol, Univ Wis, 63-71; sr scientist, Nat Ctr Atmospheric Res, 71-74. *Concurrent Pos:* Vis researcher, Dynamic Meteorol Lab, Paris, 75-76; mem, COSPAR Working Group VI, Panel A Weather & Climate, 63-79. *Mem:* Am Meteorol Soc. *Res:* Extraction of meteorological parameters from geostationary satellite data; in situ verification of the parameters using aircraft; dynamical studies of severe storms and tropical cloud clusters using geostationary satellite data; stereoscopy using geosynchronous satellites; synthetic stereo using multichannel radiometric data. *Mailing Add:* Code 912 Goddard Lab Atmospheres Goddard Space Flight Ctr Greenbelt MD 20771

HASLER, MARILYN JEAN, REPRODUCTIVE PHYSIOLOGY. *Current Pos:* ADMIN ASST, EM TRAN INC, 86- *Personal Data:* b Chicago, Ill, July 3, 43; m 69; c 2. *Educ:* Swarthmore Col, BA, 65; Tulane Univ La, MS, 67; Univ Mo-Columbia, PhD(zool), 70. *Prof Exp:* Ford Found fel reproductive endocrinol & NIH fel, Univ Ill, Urbana, 72-74; qual control chemist & develop chemist, Micromedic Diagnostics, Inc, 74-78; vis asst prof biol, Franklin & Marshall Col & Lancaster Gen Hosp, 78-79; coordr assoc sci degree prog, 79-86. *Mem:* Am Soc Zool; Soc Study Reproduction; Sigma Xi. *Res:* Reproductive physiology and behavior of mammals. *Mailing Add:* 651 Eastside Dr Landisville PA 17538

HASLETT, JAMES WILLIAM, ELECTRONICS, SOLID STATE PHYSICS. *Current Pos:* CONSULT, 91- *Personal Data:* b North Battleford, Sask, Sept 27, 44; m 70, Kay Burton. *Educ:* Univ Sask, BS, 66; Univ Calgary, MS, 68, PhD(elec eng), 70. *Prof Exp:* From assoc prof to prof, Univ Calgary, 70-86, head, Dept Elec Eng, 86-97. *Mem:* Inst Elec & Electronics Engrs. *Res:* Electrical characteristics and noise in solid state devices and circuits; design and construction of instrumentation for oilfield exploration and oilwell testing; high temperature analog and digital very large scale integration. *Mailing Add:* Dept Elec Eng Univ Calgary Calgary AB T2N 1N4 Can. *Fax:* 403-282-6855; *E-Mail:* haslett@enel.ucalgary.ca

HASLING, JILL FREEMAN, MARINE METEOROLOGY, TROPICAL METEOROLOGY. *Current Pos:* dir opers, 87-90, DIR, WEATHER RES CTR, 90- *Personal Data:* b Bryan, Tex, June 8, 52; m 73, David P; c Jacquelyn C. *Educ:* Univ St Thomas, BA, 75. *Prof Exp:* Vpres meteorol, Inst Storm Res, 74-87. *Mem:* Am Meteorol Soc; Nat Coun Indust Meteorologists; AAAS. *Res:* Mechanics of hurricanes, hurricane waves, currents and storm surges; hurricane awareness; mitigation of damage and loss of life; real-time marine weather forecasting programs to aid in world-wide forecast. *Mailing Add:* Weather Res Ctr 3227 Audley Houston TX 77098. *Fax:* 713-528-3538; *E-Mail:* wrc@phoenix.net

HASLUND, R L, AERO-OPTICS. *Current Pos:* SR PRIN ENG, BOEING AEROSPACE, 64- *Personal Data:* b Brattleboro, Vt, Oct 3, 32; m 57; c 2. *Educ:* Univ Vt, BA, 54; Pa State Univ, MS, 56, PhD(physics), 61. *Mem:* Am Phys Soc; Am Inst Aeronaut & Astronaut. *Res:* Working on developing the technical base for aero-optics. *Mailing Add:* 8345 Avalon Dr Mercer Island WA 98040

HASPEL, MARTIN VICTOR, HYBRIDOMA RESEARCH, CANCER RESEARCH. *Current Pos:* DIR, HYBRIDOMA RES & DEVELOP, BIONETICS RES, 82- *Personal Data:* b New York, NY, Aug 24, 45; m 67, Linda Strachman; c 1. *Educ:* Yeshiva Univ, BA, 67; Pa State Univ, PhD(microbiol), 74. *Honors & Awards:* C B Thornton Adv Technol Award, Litton Industs, 84. *Prof Exp:* Fel virol, Col Med, Pa State Univ, 74-75; fel immunopath, Scripps Clin Res Found, 75-77, asst mem, 77-80; sr staff fel immunol, NIH, 80-82. *Concurrent Pos:* Adj assoc prof, Dept Microbiol, Col Med, Univ Md, 84-87, adj prof, 89-92. *Mem:* Am Soc Microbiol; Sigma Xi; Am Asn Neuropathologists; Am Asn Immunologists; Am Asn Cancer Res; Am Soc Invest Path. *Res:* Development of human monoclonal antibodies for cancer diagnosis and therapy; molecular basis of mechanisms of viral diseases; therapy of infectious diseases. *Mailing Add:* Per Immune Inc 1330 Piccard Dr Rockville MD 20850-4373

HASS, ALVIN A, PLASTICS & CHEMICAL ENGINEERING. *Current Pos:* RETIRED. *Personal Data:* b New York, NY, Apr 5, 28; m 58, Norma S Grasken; c Jamie & Lorelei. *Educ:* Polytech Inst Brooklyn, BChE, 49. *Prof Exp:* Plastics technologist, US Army Plastics Lab, Picatinny Arsenal, 49-54; mgr mat develop, Polymer Chem Div, W R Grace & Co, NJ, 56-63, asst dir tech serv, 63-66; mgr, appln res, Chemplex Co, Rolling Meadows, 66-86; mgr tech serv, USI Chem, 87. *Mem:* Soc Plastics Engrs. *Res:* Plastic mold and product design; coloring and compounding of polyolefin polymers for specific end uses; injection and blow molding and thermoforming of polyolefin polymers. *Mailing Add:* 908 Willow Lane Sleepy Hollow IL 60118

HASS, GEORG, OPTICAL PHYSICS, SOLID STATE PHYSICS. *Current Pos:* RETIRED. *Personal Data:* b Hanau, Ger, Aug 8, 13; US citizen; wid. *Educ:* Inst Tech Danzig, Ger, Dr rer tech (physics), 37, Dr habil, 43. *Honors & Awards:* Army Res Develop Achievement Award, 61 & 69; Sky Lab Achievement Award, 74; Welch Award, Am Vacuum Soc, 78; Frederic Ives Medal, Optical Soc Am, 81. *Prof Exp:* Res asst physics, Inst Tech Danzig, Ger, 36-43, asst prof, 43-45; consult, US Army Eng Res & Develop Labs, Va, 46-52, chief, Physics Res Sect, 52-54, supvry physicist & chief, Physics Res Lab, 54-65, dir, Physics Res Tech Area, Night Vision Lab, Electronic Command, 65-71; consult, US Army Night Vision Lab, Goddard Space Flight Ctr, NASA & US Naval Res Lab, 71-80. *Concurrent Pos:* Mem bd dirs, Optical Soc Am, 62-65. *Mem:* Am Phys Soc; Optical Soc Am; Am Vacuum Soc. *Res:* Optical properties of metals; oxidation phenomena of metal surfaces; electron diffraction; structure and behavior of evaporated films; temperature control of satellites. *Mailing Add:* 7728 Lee Ave Alexandria VA 22308

HASS, GEORGE MARVIN, PATHOLOGY. *Current Pos:* chmn, Dept Path, Rush-Presby-St Lukes Med Ctr, 46-75, prof path & head dept, Rush Med Col, 71-75, EMER PROF PATH, RUSH-PRESBY-ST LUKES MED CTR, 75- *Personal Data:* b Tingley, Iowa, Apr 29, 07; m 42; c 5. *Educ:* Harvard Univ, MD, 29. *Prof Exp:* Instr path, Harvard Med Sch, 30-39, assoc, 39; asst prof, Med Col, Cornell Univ, 39-42. *Concurrent Pos:* Prof path, Univ Ill, 46-71. *Mem:* Am Soc Exp Path; Am Asn Path & Bact; Int Acad Hist Sci; Sigma Xi. *Res:* Rickettsial diseases; aircraft accidents and safety; histochemistry; general pathology. *Mailing Add:* 53 S Lombard Ave Lombard IL 60148

HASS, GEORGE MICHAEL, biochemistry, for more information see previous edition

HASS, JAMES RONALD, ANALYTICAL CHEMISTRY, ENVIRONMENTAL HEALTH. *Current Pos:* PRES, TRIANGLE LAB, 84- *Personal Data:* b Statesville, NC, Sept 17, 45; m 65. *Educ:* Appalachian State Univ, BA, 67; Univ NC, Chapel Hill, PhD(analytical chem), 72. *Prof Exp:* Res fel chem, Univ Warwick, 72-73; asst prof, NC State Univ, 73-74; chem staff fel, Nat Inst Environ Health Sci, 74-78, res chemist, 78-84. *Concurrent Pos:* Adj asst prof environ sci & eng, Univ NC, 75-83, adj assoc prof environ sci, engr & chem, 83- *Mem:* Am Chem Soc; Am Soc Mass Spectrometry; Source Eval Soc; NY Acad Sci; Air & Waste Mgt Soc; Tech Asn Pulp & Paper Indust. *Res:* Chemical ionization mass spectrometry using novel reagent gases; application of gas chromatography and mass spectrometry in environmental and health problems; development of new gas chromatography and mass spectrometry techniques; development and application of field desorption mass spectrometry. *Mailing Add:* PO Box 13485 Research Triangle Park NC 27709. *Fax:* 919-493-1193; *E-Mail:* rhass@sphvax.sph.unc.edu

HASS, KENNETH PHILIP, METALLURGICAL ENGINEERING. *Current Pos:* RETIRED. *Personal Data:* b Minneapolis, Minn, Sept 17, 34; m 60; c 2. *Educ:* Univ Minn, BS, 56, MS, 59. *Honors & Awards:* Ironmaking Merit Award, Am Inst Mech Engrs. *Prof Exp:* Trainee, Nat Steel Corp, 59, res engr, Res & Develop Dept, 59-61, sr res engr, 61-63, supvr raw mat, 63-74, supvr process metal, 74-84, supvr chem & coal res, 84-85, mgr prod & process, tech, 85-93, mgr tech coord, 93- *Mem:* Am Inst Mining, Metall & Petrol Engrs; Am Soc Metals; Am Soc Testing & Mat; Asn Iron & Steel Engrs. *Res:* Agglomeration and beneficiation of ironbearing materials; coal and coke technology; direct reduction processes; ironmaking; economic evaluation of process metallurgy processes; steelmaking. *Mailing Add:* 2 Fairway Hill Weirton WV 26062-9679. *Fax:* 219-273-7368

HASS, LOUIS F, BIOCHEMISTRY. *Current Pos:* assoc prof biol chem, 68-88, EMER PROF, MILTON S HERSHEY MED CTR, PA STATE UNIV, 88- *Personal Data:* b Scranton, Pa, Aug 23, 26; m 60; c 3. *Educ:* Univ Scranton, BS, 50; Bucknell Univ, MS, 54; Duke Univ, PhD(biochem), 59. *Prof Exp:* Chemist, Armstrong Cork Co, 52-55; Nat Inst Cancer fel, Univ Minn, 59-61; chemist, NIH, 61-63; asst prof, Sch Med, State Univ NY, Buffalo, 63-68. *Concurrent Pos:* Prof & hon vis fel, Univ Aberdeen, Scotland, 80-81. *Mem:* Am Chem Soc; Am Soc Biol Chemists; Biochem Soc UK. *Res:* Correlation of enzyme structure and function; physicochemical characterization of native and modified proteins; mechanisms of enzyme action; erythrocyte metabolism. *Mailing Add:* RR 1 Box 282-C Centre PA 16828-9719

HASS, MARVIN, SOLID STATE PHYSICS. *Current Pos:* CONSULT, 82- *Personal Data:* b New York, NY, June 5, 30. *Educ:* City Col New York, BS, 50; Syracuse Univ, MS, 51; Univ Mich, PhD(physics), 55. *Prof Exp:* Asst chem, Syracuse Univ, 50-52 & Univ Mich, 52-53; physicist, US Naval Res Lab, 55-82. *Concurrent Pos:* Vis prof, Univ Nebr, 70. *Mem:* Fel Am Phys Soc. *Res:* Light scattering; infrared spectroscopy; lattice vibrations. *Mailing Add:* 309 Yoakum Pkwy Apt 605 Alexandria VA 22304-3923

HASS, MICHAEL A, CRIMINOLOGY, DNA ANALYSIS. *Current Pos:* FORENSIC DNA SPECIALIST, METRO-DADE POLICE DEPT, CRIME LAB BUR, MIAMI, FLA, 89- *Personal Data:* b St Louis, Mo, Oct 3, 50. *Educ:* Washington Univ, BA, 72; St Louis Univ, PhD(biochem), 78. *Prof Exp:* NIH res fel, Pulmonary Div, Sch Med, Univ Miami, 78-81, res asst prof, 81-89. *Concurrent Pos:* Prin investr, Fla Lung Asn, 82-83 & Am Lung Asn, 83-85. *Mem:* Am Soc Biochem & Molecular Biol; AAAS. *Res:* Forensic DNA fingerprinting; molecular biology; protein purification and characterization; regulation of metabolism; characterization of antibody specificity and use in immunoassays; mechanisms of oxidant injury and superoxide dismutase regulation; author of 18 technical publications. *Mailing Add:* Crime Lab Bur Metro-Dade Police Dept 9105 NW 25th St Miami FL 33172. *Fax:* 305-471-2025

HASS, ROBERT HENRY, FUEL TECHNOLOGY, PETROLEUM ENGINEERING. *Current Pos:* RETIRED. *Personal Data:* b Columbus, Ohio, Apr 30, 22; m 49; c 2. *Educ:* Purdue Univ, BSc, 43; Case Inst Technol, MSc, 49, PhD(chem eng), 54. *Prof Exp:* Chem engr, B F Goodrich Res, 43-47; instr, Case Inst Technol, 48-54; chem engr, Union Oil Co, Calif, 54- *Mem:* Am Inst Chem Engrs; Am Chem Soc; Instrument Soc Am; AAAS. *Res:* Development of new catalysts and processes useful in petroleum refining and environmental pollution control; hydrogen sulfide recovery and abatement; flue gas treating. *Mailing Add:* 3507 Sunnywood Dr Fullerton CA 92835-1664

HASS, WILLIAM K, MEDICINE, NEUROLOGY. *Current Pos:* asst prof, 60-64, assoc prof, 65-71, PROF NEUROL, SCH MED, NY UNIV, 71- *Personal Data:* b Detroit, Mich, Nov 20, 29; m 53; c 3. *Educ:* Kenyon Col, AB, 50; Univ Mich, MD, 54. *Prof Exp:* Fel neurol, Neurol Inst, Columbia Univ, 59-60, asst neurol, 60. *Concurrent Pos:* Mem exec comt, Nat Joint Study Extracranial Arterial Occlusion, 65-68; mem exec comt, Stroke Coun, Am Heart Asn, 68-, mem publ comt, 71-75, vchmn & chmn, Stroke Coun, 76-80; spec consult to dir, Nat Inst Neurol Dis & Stroke, 70-74; ed, Current Concepts Cerebrovasc Dis-Stoke, 71-75; mem bd trustees, Princeton Conf Cerebrovasc Dis, 78- *Mem:* Fel Am Acad Neurol; Asn Res Nerv & Ment Dis; Am Neurol Asn (vpres, 79-80); fel NY Acad Med; Harvey Soc. *Res:* Cerebral blood flow and metabolism; cerebrovascular disease; clinical mass spectrometry. *Mailing Add:* 530 First Ave New York NY 10016-6402

HASSAN, AFTAB SYED, BIOENGINEERING & BIOMECHANICS, PROBLEM-BASED MEDICAL EDUCATION. *Current Pos:* VPRES ACAD DEVEL, WILLIAMS & WILKINS EDUC SERV, 94- *Personal Data:* b Lahore, Pakistan, Apr 20, 52. *Educ:* Eng Univ Lahore, Pakistan, BSc Eng, 73; George Washington Univ, MS, 77, Dr Sci, 82; Columbia Pac Univ, PhD(water resources & hydraul), 85. *Prof Exp:* Chmn math & sci, Emerson

Prep Inst, 79-89; asst prof, George Washington Univ, 80-85; dir sci & educ res, Betz Publ Co, 91-94. *Concurrent Pos:* Res assoc fish physiol, Chesapeake Bay Tidewater Admin, 79-88; Acad Coord, Georgetown Univ, Med Sch, 81-89. *Mem:* Am Soc Civil Engrs; Nat Soc Prof Engrs; Am Soc Eng Educ; Nat Asn Prof Educrs; Nat Sci Teachers Asn; Nat Asn Develop Educrs; AAAS; Am Meteorol Soc; Am Soc Testing & Mat; Comput & Biomed Res Soc. *Res:* Biophysics and biotechnology; allied health education. *Mailing Add:* Metro Academic Res 4401-A Connecticut Ave NW No 291 Washington DC 20008

HASSAN, ASLAM SULTAN, BILE & METABOLISM. *Current Pos:* ASST PROF PHYSIOL, UNIV ILL, 82- *Educ:* Univ Ore, PhD(physiol), 79. *Mailing Add:* Dept Vet Biosci Univ Ill 2001 S Lincoln Ave Urbana IL 61801-6178

HASSAN, AWATIF E, SOIL-MACHINE SYSTEMS, MACHINE DESIGN & EQUIPMENT DEVELOPMENT. *Current Pos:* assoc prof, 75-80, PROF FORESTRY BIOL AGR ENG, NC STATE UNIV, 80- *Personal Data:* b Alexandria, Egypt, Dec 11, 37; US citizen; div; c 2. *Educ:* Univ Alexandria, Egypt, BS, 59; Univ Calif, Davis, MS, 64, PhD(eng), 68. *Prof Exp:* Asst prof mech eng, Cairo High Polytech Inst, 68-71; asst prof agr eng, Univ Alexandria, 71-73; asst prof agr & forest eng, Univ Maine, 74-75. *Concurrent Pos:* Fel, McGill Univ, Que, Can, 72-74; fac adv, Soc Women Engrs, 74-75; assoc ed, J Terra Mech, Int Soc Terrain-Vehicle Systs, 84-; vis prof, Land Tech Univ, Ger Nat Inst Agr Eng, 85-86; co-chair, Coun Forest Eng, 89-90. *Mem:* Am Soc Agr Engrs; Int Soc Terrain-Vehicle Systs; Coun Forest Eng; Int Union Forestry Res Orgn; Soc Women Engrs. *Res:* Design and development of all terrain vehicles, semi-automatic tree planter, precision seeder and several other devices; 2 patents; effect of machine traffic on soil physical and mechanical properties and vehicle instrumentation and capabilities under extremely wet conditions; tested several high flotation tires used in forestry and agriculture in England. *Mailing Add:* 3513 Morningside Dr Raleigh NC 27607

HASSAN, HASSAN AHMAD, AERONAUTICAL ENGINEERING. *Current Pos:* PROF AERONAUT ENG, NC STATE UNIV, RALEIGH, 62- *Personal Data:* b Tamra, Palestine, Feb 26, 31; m 58; c 2. *Educ:* Univ London, BSc, 52; Univ Ill, Urbana, MS, 53, PhD(aeronaut eng), 56. *Honors & Awards:* Western Elec Fund Award, Am Soc Eng Educ, 74; Charles Russ Mem Award, Am Soc Mech Engrs, 77; Alcoa Found Distinguished Award, 87,. *Prof Exp:* Res assoc, Univ Ill, Urbana, 53-55, instr aeronaut eng, 55-56; sr lectr mech eng, Univ Raghdad, Baghdad, Iraq, 56-59; from assoc prof to prof aeronaut eng, Va Polytech Inst, 59-62. *Concurrent Pos:* Aerodyn engr, Douglas Aircraft Co, 61; aerospace technologist, NASA, 62; consult, Douglas Aircraft Co, 62-64, Kaman Nuclear, 63-64, Res Triangle Inst, 64-65, Defense Atomic Support Agency, 70-71 & Forge Aerospace, Inc, 73-74; contractor, Langley Res Ctr, NASA, 79- *Mem:* Am Inst Aeronaut & Astronaut; Am Phys Soc; Sigma Xi. *Res:* Computational fluid dynamics; reacting flows; hypersonic aerodynamics; direct simulation Monte Carlo methods; transition and turbulence modeling. *Mailing Add:* Dept Mech & Aerospace Eng NC State Univ PO Box 7910 Raleigh NC 27695-7910

HASSAN, HOSNI MOUSTAFA, MOLECULAR BIOLOGY OF ANTIOXIDANT ENZYMES, NATURAL PRODUCTS MUTAGENICITY. *Current Pos:* from assoc prof to prof microbiol, toxicol & food sci, 80-91, PROF BIOCHEM MICROBIOL, TOXICOL & FOOD SCI, NC STATE UNIV, 92-, HEAD, MICROBIOL DEPT, 93- *Personal Data:* b Alexandria, Egypt, Sept 3, 37; US citizen; m 92, Linda C McDonald; c Jehan, Suzanne & Nora. *Educ:* Univ Ain Shams, Egypt, BSc, 59; Univ Calif, Davis, PhD(microbiol), 67. *Prof Exp:* From asst to assoc prof microbiol & food sci, Univ Alexandria, Egypt, 68-72; vis prof, McGill Univ, Montreal, 72-74; res assoc biochem, Med Ctr, Duke Univ, 75-79; assoc prof microbiol, McGill Univ, Montreal, 79-80. *Concurrent Pos:* Sci consult, Nat Res Coun, Egypt, 68-72; asst microbiologist, Univ Maine, 74-75; Fulbright sr res scholar, Paris, France, 87-88. *Mem:* Am Soc Biol Chemists; Am Soc Microbiol; NY Acad Sci; Sigma Xi; fel Am Inst Chemists. *Res:* Toxicity and the mutagenicity of oxygen free radicals and the protective roles of superoxide dismutases and catalases; regulation of the biosynthesis of superoxide dismutase and catalases; antioxidants. *Mailing Add:* Dept Microbiol NC State Univ PO Box 7615 Raleigh NC 27695-7615. *Fax:* 919-515-7867; *E-Mail:* hmhassan@mbio.ncsu.edu

HASSAN, MOHAMMAD ZIA, MANAGEMENT SCIENCES. *Current Pos:* from instr to assoc prof indust eng, 60-77, assoc prof & chmn, Dept Mgt Sci, 77-83, PROF MGT SCI & INDUST MGT & DEAN, STUART SCH BUS, ILL INST TECHNOL, 83- *Personal Data:* b Gurgaon, Brit India, Apr 2, 33; m 59; c 3. *Educ:* Punjab Univ, BSc, 54; Ill Inst Technol, MS, 58, PhD(indust eng), 65. *Prof Exp:* Indust engr, Dukane Corp, Ill, 56-58; sr indust engr, Webcor, Inc, Ill, 58-59, dir indust eng, 59-60. *Concurrent Pos:* Consult, Webcor, Inc, 60-62, Warwick Electronics, Inc, 62-74, H K Porter & Co, Inc, 65-67, Stand Kollsman Indust, Inc, Melrose Park, Ill, 67, Hamilton Indust, Chicago, 69-71, GRI Inc, Chicago, 74-75, Comput Peripheral Inc, Mich, 75-76, BRK Electronics, 78, 83, 85, UN Develop Prog, 81 & Fibre Craft Mat Corp, 82, Am Generator & Armature, 86-87, Kable News, 88- *Mem:* Inst Mgr Sci; Sigma Xi; fel Am Soc Qual Control. *Res:* Strategic planning; organizational effectiveness; productivity and quality management. *Mailing Add:* 5633 S Woodlawn Chicago IL 60637-1622

HASSAN, WILLIAM EPHRIAM, JR, PHYTOCHEMISTRY, PHARMACOLOGY. *Current Pos:* RETIRED. *Personal Data:* b Brockton, Mass, Oct 13, 23; m 51, Rosette T Amodeo; c William R & Thomas E (deceased). *Educ:* Mass Col Pharm, BS, 45, MS, 47, PhD(pharmacol), 51; Suffolk Univ, LLB, 65. *Prof Exp:* Asst pharmacog & biol, Mass Col Pharm, 47-49, instr, 49-51, asst prof, 51-55; from asst dir to dir, Peter Bent Brigham Hosp, 67-76; exec vpres, Brigham Women's Hosp, 80-82, vpres & gen counsel, 82-86. *Concurrent Pos:* Consult, Mass Col Pharm, 51-, prof lectr, 55-67, adj prof, 67-, trustee, 72-, vchmn bd trustees, 75-; pharmacist-in-chief, Peter Bent Brigham Hosp, 52-55; vpres admin, Affiliated Hosps Ctr Inc, 76-78, exec vpres, 78-80. *Mem:* Fel Am Col Hosp Adminr; Am Soc Hosp Pharmacists; Am Soc Law & Med; Am Pharmaceut Asn. *Res:* Complete study of anatomy, chemistry and pharmacology of six plants in the genus Asclepias; anatomical and chemical study of Indian belladonna and the camphor basil plant; study of various fractions of licorice for electrolytic activity in the adrenalectomized rat. *Mailing Add:* 18 Joseph Rd Newton MA 02160

HASSE, RAYMOND WILLIAM, JR, UNDERWATER ACOUSTICS, COMPUTER MODELING. *Current Pos:* FAC MEM, THAMES VALLEY STATE TECH COL, 81- *Personal Data:* b Detroit, Mich, Aug 7, 24; m 50; c 3. *Educ:* Mass Inst Technol, BS, 47; Univ Conn, MS, 58. *Honors & Awards:* Naval Underwater Sound Lab Sci Achievement Award, 69. *Prof Exp:* Prog officer acoust & oceanog, Naval Underwater Systs Ctr, New London, Conn, 49-53, electronic scientist, 55-59, head acoust res br, 59-62, head, Acoust Res Div, 62-66, head ocean sci div, 66-71, asst dir sonar res, 71-76, head, Spec Projs Dept, 76-81. *Concurrent Pos:* Res dir, Tudor Hill Lab, Bermuda Res Detachment, 60- *Mem:* Fel Acoust Soc Am. *Res:* Environmental systems and technology; deep ocean engineering; acoustic propagation loss and backscatter; ocean noise. *Mailing Add:* Thames Valley State Tech Col 574 New London Turnpike Norwich CT 06360

HASSELGREN, PER-OLOF J, SURGERY, BIOCHEMISTRY. *Current Pos:* asst prof, 87-89, ASSOC PROF SURG, UNIV CINCINNATI, 89- *Personal Data:* b Mulndal, Sweden, May 4, 47; m 70; c 2. *Educ:* Univ Goteborg, MD, 73, PhD(surg), 79. *Prof Exp:* From asst prof to assoc prof surg, Univ Goteborg, 79-84; res clin fel, Dept Surg, Univ Cincinnati, 84-86; assoc prof, Univ Lund, Sweden, 86-87. *Mem:* AMA; Swed Med Asn; Asn Acad Surg; Surg Infection Soc; Soc Univ Surgeons; fel Am Col Surgeons. *Res:* Protein metabolism in liver and skeletal muscle during sepsis shock and ischemia. *Mailing Add:* 7705 Anwenasa Lane Cincinnati OH 45243

HASSELKUS, EDWARD R, ORNAMENTAL HORTICULTURE. *Current Pos:* Res asst hort, Univ Wis-Madison, 57-61, proj asst, 61, asst prof hort, 61-64, from asst prof to assoc prof hort & land archit, 64-74, PROF HORT & LAND ARCHIT, UNIV WIS-MADISON, 74-, EXTEN HORTICULTURIST, 65- *Personal Data:* b Dousman, Wis, July 18, 32; m 60, Betty Risteen; c Jane C & John E. *Educ:* Univ Wis, BS, 54, MS, 58, PhD(hort & plant physiol), 62. *Honors & Awards:* L C Chadwick Award. *Mem:* Am Hort Soc; Am Soc Hort Sci; Am Asn Bot Gardens & Arboreta; Int Lilac Soc; Am Conifer Soc; Int Ornam Crabapple Soc; Magnolia Soc; Am Soc Landscape Architects. *Res:* Landscape plants; evaluation of woody ornamental plants. *Mailing Add:* 746 Miami Pass Madison WI 53711. *Fax:* 608-262-4743

HASSELL, CLINTON ALTON, BETA RADIOGRAPHY, ARCHAEOLOGY. *Current Pos:* lectr math, physics & chem, 82-85, instr chem, 85-91, LECTR CHEM & ARCHAEOL, BAYLOR UNIV, 92- *Personal Data:* b Seagraves, Tex, Oct 26, 45; m 68, Patricia Berryhill; c Clint & Sharina. *Educ:* Baylor Univ, BS, 69; Tex A&M Univ, PhD(chem), 75. *Prof Exp:* Welsh Found res fel, Cyclotron Inst, Tex A&M Univ, 75-76, lectr, 76-79, asst first year prog dir, Tex A&M Univ, 77-82. *Concurrent Pos:* Instr nuclear power plant technicians, 81-82. *Mem:* Am Chem Soc; Clay Minerals Soc. *Res:* Supplemental materials and large program coordination in chemical education; writing, problem solving for general chemistry; liberal arts chemistry; beta radiography of water marks in antique books; cleaning of antique copper coins. *Mailing Add:* Dept Chem Baylor Univ Waco TX 76706

HASSELL, JOHN ALLEN, PHYSICAL CHEMISTRY, VOCATIONAL REHABILITATION. *Current Pos:* VOC REHAB COMPUT CONSULT, 89- *Personal Data:* b Erie, Pa, July 27, 37; m 59; c 2. *Educ:* Pa State Univ, BS, 59; Carnegie Inst Technol, MS, 65, PhD(phys chem), 66. *Honors & Awards:* IR-100 Award. *Prof Exp:* Res asst heterogeneous catalysis, Mellon Inst Indust Res, Pa, 59-62; sr chemist, Tex US Chem Co, 65-68; sr res chemist, Battelle Mem Inst-Columbus, 68-90. *Concurrent Pos:* Voice input disabled chem students, ECU, Greenville, NC, 81-82, instr, 82. *Mem:* Am Chem Soc. *Res:* Adsorption and kinetics on metals and solid hydrocarbons; Langmuir film balance studies; solution and melt rheology with Weissenberg rheogonimeter on polymer systems; molecular characterization; process development and control; development of microcomputer acquisition and analysis of polymer molecular characteristics(GPC) and polymer rheology; microcomputer use in modeling solution and molecular properties of predicting useful life of materials; product properties and service life predictions of polymers, using rheological measurements and analysis; computer modelling of diffusion and rheological processes; software development of voice entry computer to aid handicapped students perform chemistry laboratory courses; development of computer analysis of gel permeation chromatography and thermoanalysis including graphic analysis; computer applications in rehabilitation technology for vision and physical disabilities; interfacing of adaptive equipment and technology to microcomputer through mainframe applications. *Mailing Add:* 2229 Northwest Blvd Columbus OH 43221

HASSELL, JOHN ROBERT, DEVELOPMENTAL BIOLOGY, BIOCHEMISTRY. *Current Pos:* PROF OPHTHAL, UNIV PITTSBURGH SCH MED, 88- *Personal Data:* b Cambridge, Mass, Oct 27, 43. *Educ:* Cent Conn State Col, BA, 66; Univ Conn, PhD(develop biol & biochem), 72. *Prof*

Exp: Investr develop biol & birth defects, Lab Biol Struct, NIH, 72-88. *Res:* Biochemical mechanisms regulating early embryonic growth; embryo nutrition; effects of pharmacological drugs on development; chick embryo culture; cytochemistry. *Mailing Add:* Dept Ophthamol Univ Pittsburgh Sch Med Eye & Ear Inst 203 Lothrop St Rm 915 Pittsburgh PA 15213-2588. Fax: 412-647-5880

HASSELL, THOMAS MICHAEL, dental research, pathology, for more information see previous edition

HASSELMAN, DIDERICUS PETRUS HERMANNUS, MATERIALS SCIENCE, THERMOPHYSICS. *Current Pos:* WHITTEMORE PROF MAT ENG, VA POLYTECH INST & STATE UNIV, 77-, PROF ENG SCI & MECH, 93- *Personal Data:* b The Hague, Neth, Aug 1, 31; US citizen; m 67. *Educ:* Queen's Univ Ont, BSc, 57; Univ BC, MASc, 60; Univ Calif, Berkeley, PhD(ceramic eng), 66. *Honors & Awards:* John Jeppson Gold Medal; Humboldt Prize, Int Acad Ceramics. *Prof Exp:* Physicist, Carborundum Co, 60-62; res asst, Lawrence Radiation Lab, Univ Calif, 62-66; sr ceramist, Stanford Res Inst, 66-67; sr res assoc, Mat Res Ctr, Allied Chem Corp, 68-70; prof metall & mat sci & dir, Ceramics Res Lab, Lehigh Univ, 70-76; mgr, Mont MHD Inst, Butte, Mont, 76-77. *Mem:* Am Ceramic Soc; Am Carbon Soc; Soc Eng Sci; fel Int Thermal Conductivity Conf; Mat Res Soc; Soc Eng Sci; Acad Mech. *Res:* Physical properties of high-temperature materials; elasticity; strength; creep; thermo-elastic fracture; crack growth and propagation; static and cyclic fatigue of single-phase and composite glasses and ceramics; thermophysical properties. *Mailing Add:* 601 Rainbow Ridge Dr Blacksburg VA 24060

HASSELMANN, KLAUS FERDINAND, METEOROLOGY. *Current Pos:* DIR, MAX PLANCK INST METEOROL, HAMBURG, 75-, GER CLIMATE COMPUT CTR, 88- *Personal Data:* b Hamburg, Ger, Oct 25, 31; m 57, Susanne Barthe; c Meike, Knut & Annette. *Educ:* Univ Gottingen, PhD, 57. *Honors & Awards:* Carl Christiansen Commemorative Award, 63; James B Macelwane Award, Am Geophys Union, 64; Sverdrup Medal, Am Meteorol Union, 71; Belfotop-Eurosense Award, Remote Sensing Soc, 81; Nansen Polar Bear Award, 93; Robertson Mem Lectr, Nat Acad Sci, 90. *Prof Exp:* from asst prof to assoc prof, Univ Calif, 61-64; lectr, Univ Hamburg, 64-66, prof, 66-69, dept dir & prof, 69-72, prof & managing dir, 72-75. *Concurrent Pos:* Doherty prof, Woods Hole Oceanog Inst, Mass, 70. *Mailing Add:* Fliederstieg 5 23863 Kayhude Germany

HASSELMEYER, EILEEN GRACE, PERINATAL BIOLOGY. *Current Pos:* RETIRED. *Personal Data:* b Brooklyn, NY, May 23, 24. *Educ:* NY Univ, BS, 54, MA, 56, PhD(nursing sci, human develop), 63. *Prof Exp:* Head nurse, Children's Med Serv, Bellevue Hosp, NY Univ, 46-50, supvr, 50-56; consult, Div Nursing, USPHS, 56-59, spec asst prematurity, Nat Inst Child Health & Human Develop, 63-67, actg dir, Perinatal Biol & Infant Mortality Prog, 67-68; Annie Goodrich prof perinatal res, Sch Nursing, Yale Univ, 68-69; dir, Perinatal Biol & Infant Mortality Prog, Nat Inst Child Health & Human Develop, 69-74 & 81-89, chief, Pregnancy & Infancy Br, 74-79; assoc dir sci rev, USPHS, 79, asst surg gen, 81; exec dir, Fed Col Nursing Task Force, Uniform Servs Health Sci, 89-92. *Concurrent Pos:* Lectr, Sch Nursing, Med Br, Univ Tex, Galveston, 53; NIH spec fel, NY Univ, 62-63; Am Nurses Found res grant, 62-64; vis prof, Univ BC, 66-71; Sigma Theta Tau res grant, 68; Yale fac res develop grant, 69; maternal & child health grant, Univ Conn, 69-70. *Mem:* Am Pedriat Soc. *Res:* Nursing science; relationship between early and later development for low birth weight infants; indices of fetal and neonatal maturation; influence of nursing care upon survival of high risk newborns; sudden infant death syndrome. *Mailing Add:* 8901 Paddock Lane Potomac MD 20854

HASSERT, G(EORGE) LEE, JR, PHYSIOLOGY, PHARMACOLOGY. *Current Pos:* RETIRED. *Personal Data:* b Passaic, NJ, Dec 15, 20; m 44, Judith Harper; c Sarah W & Deborah A. *Educ:* Rutgers Univ, BS, 43, PhD(physiol, biochem), 63. *Prof Exp:* Sr res scientist, Pharmacol Sect, E R Squibb & Sons, Inc, 46-70, sr res investr, 70-72, sect head, Dept Toxicol, Squibb Inst Med Res, 72-77, admin mgr qual control, 77-87. *Mem:* NY Acad Sci. *Mailing Add:* 21 Sylvan Ave Metuchen NJ 08840

HASSIALIS, MENELAOS D(IMITRI), mineral economics, nuclear engineering; deceased, see previous edition for last biography

HASSINGER, MARY COLLEEN, LASER SPECTROSCOPY. *Current Pos:* ASST PROF ANALYTICAL CHEM, VITERBO COL, 83- *Personal Data:* b Minneapolis, Minn, Mar 3, 53; m 80. *Educ:* Univ Minn, Duluth, BS, 75; Purdue Univ, MS, 79, PhD(analytical chem), 83. *Concurrent Pos:* Vis asst prof, Purdue Univ, 85; prin investr, NSF Col Sci Instrumentation Prog, 85-87. *Mem:* Am Chem Soc; Soc Appl Spectros. *Res:* Develop and test two-laser instruments for fundamental studies in molecular spectroscopy and combustion diagnostics; measurement of two-photon absorption spectra of metal chelate complexes in solution. *Mailing Add:* Dept Chem Viterbo Col 815 S Ninth St La Crosse WI 54601-8802

HASSLER, CRAIG REINHOLD, PHYSIOLOGY, BIOMATERIALS. *Current Pos:* physiologist, 70-74, sr physiologist, 74-80, RES LEADER, COLUMBUS LABS, BATTELLE MEM INST, 80- *Personal Data:* b Chicago, Ill, Mar 19, 42; m 69; c 2. *Educ:* Northwestern Univ, Evanston, BA, 63; Depauw Univ, MA, 66; Loyola Univ, Chicago, PhD(physiol), 69. *Prof Exp:* Instr physiol, Sch Med, Loyola Univ, 69-70. *Concurrent Pos:* Prin investr, Battelle Inst, 71-73 & NIH, 74- *Mem:* Am Physiol Soc; Inst Elec & Electronics Engrs; Biomat Soc; Orthop Res Soc. *Res:* Basic understanding of hard tissue; the use of biomaterials to replace hard tissue; tooth replacement systems; electrical augmentation of bone formation; cardiovascular toxicology; toxicology of biomaterials; Pharmacodynamics. *Mailing Add:* Dept Pharmacol & Toxicol Battelle Mem Inst 505 King Ave Columbus OH 43201-2693. Fax: 614-424-5263

HASSLER, F(RANCIS) J(EFFERSON), AGRICULTURAL ENGINEERING. *Current Pos:* from res asst prof to res assoc prof agr eng, NC State Univ, 50-54, in chg grad studies, 53-61, prof, 54-61, REYNOLDS PROF BIOL & AGR ENG & HEAD DEPT, NC STATE UNIV, 61- *Personal Data:* b Cooper Hill, Mo, Aug 2, 21; m 42; c 5. *Educ:* Univ Mo, BS, 46; Mich State Col, MS, 48, PhD(agr eng), 50. *Prof Exp:* Asst, Mich State Col, 46-47, instr, 47-48, asst, 48-50. *Mem:* AAAS; Am Soc Agr Engrs; Am Soc Eng Educ; Sigma Xi. *Res:* Frost control with infrared; fundamentals of tobacco curing; bulk curing of tobacco; patents. *Mailing Add:* Dept Biol & Agr Eng NC State Univ PO Box 7625 Raleigh NC 27695

HASSLER, THOMAS J, FISHERIES, FRESH WATER ECOLOGY. *Current Pos:* ASST LEADER, CALIF COOP FISHERY RES UNIT, FISH & WILDLIFE SERV, HUMBOLDT STATE UNIV, 73-, NAT BIOL SURV, 94- *Personal Data:* b McCook, Nebr, Jan 6, 34; m 56; c 4. *Educ:* Univ Nebr, BS, 57; Utah State Univ, MS, 60, PhD(fishery biol), 65. *Prof Exp:* Fishery biologist, NCent Reservoirs Invest, US Fish & Wildlife Serv, 64-72. *Mem:* Am Fisheries Soc; Am Inst Fishery Res Biol. *Res:* Reservoir fisheries management; toxicology; ecology of anadronous salmonids; fishery management. *Mailing Add:* Fisheries Humboldt State Univ 1 Harps St Arcata CA 95521-8229

HASSLER, WILLIAM WOODS, ANALYTICAL CHEMISTRY, ORGANIC CHEMISTRY. *Current Pos:* RETIRED. *Personal Data:* b Clearfield, Pa, Sept 6, 17; m 41; c 3. *Educ:* Juniata Col, BS, 39; Univ Pa, MS, 41, PhD(chem), 51. *Prof Exp:* Asst chem, Univ Pa, 39-42; res chemist plastics, Rohm & Haas Co, Pa, 42-46; asst prof chem, Drexel Inst, 46-51; prof & head dept, Beaver Col, 51-63; dean, Sch Lib Arts, Ind Univ, Pa, 63-69, pres, Univ, 69-75; pres, Wesley Col, 75-77. *Concurrent Pos:* Consult, Houdry Process Corp, 52-, Smith Kline & French, 54-, Harris D McKinney Co, 57, Selas Corp & Capital Systs, 60-; lectr, Eastern Baptist Col, 56-61. *Mem:* Am Chem Soc; fel Am Inst Chemists. *Res:* Technical writing and communication; potentiometric study of reactions between cupric salts and various bases; taste and odor control in water purification; synthesis of ion exchange resins; inorganic analytical chemistry. *Mailing Add:* 448 N Branddock St Winchester VA 22601-3922

HASSNER, ALFRED, STEREO CHEMISTRY, HETEROCYCLES. *Current Pos:* PROF CHEM, BAR-ILAN UNIV, RAMAT-GAN, 84- *Personal Data:* b Czernowitz, Romania, Nov 11, 30; US citizen; m 57, Cyd; c 2. *Educ:* Univ Technol Vienna, BS, 52; Univ Nebr, MS, 54, PhD(chem), 56. *Honors & Awards:* Fulbright Sr Award, 83; Nat Res Coun Award, 92. *Prof Exp:* Res chemist, E I du Pont de Nemours & Co, Inc, 54; postdoctoral fel chem, Harvard Univ, 56-57; from asst prof to prof, Univ Colo, Boulder, 57-75; leading prof, State Univ NY, Binghamton, 75-84. *Concurrent Pos:* Hon res assoc, Harvard Univ, 66; vis scientist, Swiss Fed Inst Technol, 67; vis prof, Weizmann Inst, 69, 72, Univ Wurzburg, 71, Univ Lyons, 80, Kyshu Tech Univ, 85, & Univ Calif, Berkeley, 89; consult, Univ Colo Med Sch, Chem Phys Eng Corp, Med Chem Panel, NIH, NSF-URP Panels, 3M Corp & SKB, Univ Nijmegen, 95; Humbolt fel, 71, NIH spec fel, 72-73, Lady Davis fel, 79 & Meyerhoff fel, 81. *Mem:* Am Chem Soc; Royal Soc Chem; Ger Chem Soc; ISR Chem Soc (pres, 94). *Res:* Synthesis and stereochemistry of organic nitrogen compounds; stereospecific additions to olefins; synthesis and reactions of nitrogen heterocycles; steroids; azides; design of new synthetic reactions; stereoselective cycloadditions; potential anticancer agents. *Mailing Add:* Dept Chem Bar-Ilan Univ Ramat-Gan 52900 Israel. Fax: 972-3-535-1250; E-Mail: hassna@gefen.cc.biu.ac.il

HASSOLD, GREGORY NAHMEN, MATERIALS PHYSICS. *Current Pos:* asst prof, 89-93, ASSOC PROF PHYSICS, GMI ENG & MGT INST, 93- *Personal Data:* b Oakland, Calif, Dec 12, 56; m 87, Noralynn Caduff; c Jacob & Laura. *Educ:* Harvey Mudd Col, BS, 79, Univ Colo, MS, 81, PhD(physics), 85. *Prof Exp:* Res asst fel, Harvard Univ, 86-87 & Univ Mich, 87-89. *Mem:* Am Phys Soc; Am Asn Physics Teachers; Sigma Xi. *Res:* Computer simulation of materials physics. *Mailing Add:* GMI Eng & Mgt Inst 1700 W Third Ave Flint MI 48504. E-Mail: ghassold@baby.gmi.edu

HASSOLD, TERRY JON, human cytogenetics, for more information see previous edition

HASSON, DENNIS FRANCIS, MATERIALS SCIENCE, MECHANICAL ENGINEERING. *Current Pos:* PROF MECH ENG, US NAVAL ACAD, 73- *Personal Data:* b Baltimore, Md, June 1, 34; m 61; c 2. *Educ:* Johns Hopkins Univ, BES, 55; Va Polytech Inst, MS, 58; Univ Md, College Park, PhD(chem eng), 70. *Prof Exp:* Aerospace res engr, Langley Res Ctr, NASA, 55-59, Proj Mercury, 59-60; appl physics lab, Johns Hopkins Univ, 60-61; aerospace technologist, Goddard Space Flight Ctr, NASA, 61-67; instr mech eng, Univ Md, College Park, 69-71, fel, 71; assoc prof mech eng, Univ DC, 71-73. *Concurrent Pos:* Consult, Comsat Labs, Md, 70-71, David Taylor Naval Ship Res & Develop Ctr & White Oak Lab, Naval Surface & Weapons Ctr; lectr, Univ Southern Calif, 76- & Cath Univ Am, 78- *Mem:* Am Soc Mech Engrs; Am Soc Metals; Am Inst Mining, Metall & Petrol Engrs; Sigma Xi. *Res:* Fracture mechanics and stress corrosion cracking of marine materials, corrosion fatigue; welding, fractography; mechanical and fracture behavior of metal, ceramic and polymer matrix composite materials; relaxation processes and mechanical properties of bone materials. *Mailing Add:* 20 East St Annapolis MD 21401-1708

HASSON, JACK, PATHOLOGY. *Current Pos:* ASSOC PROF PATH, UNIV CONN. *Personal Data:* Jan 26, 25; m 48, Margo Wolf; c Kenneth & Perry. *Educ:* City Col New York, BS, 47; State Univ NY, MD. *Honors & Awards:* Henry Moses Res Prize, 57. *Prof Exp:* Chief, Dept Path, Mt Sinai Hosp. *Mem:* Am Acad Path; Can Acad Path. *Res:* Autopsy as an audit of medical diagnostics; causes of avoidable and unavoidable diagnostic errors; clinicopathologic correlative case studes. *Mailing Add:* Dept Anat Path Univ Conn Health Ctr Farmington CT 06030. *Fax:* 860-679-4334

HASSOUN, GHAZI QASIM, THEORETICAL PHYSICS. *Current Pos:* ASSOC PROF PHYSICS, NDAK STATE UNIV, 66- *Personal Data:* b Haifa, Palestine, June 21, 35; US citizen; m 58. *Educ:* Am Univ Beirut, BS, 56; Univ Minn, Minneapolis, MS, 59, PhD(physics), 63. *Prof Exp:* Res assoc theoret physics, Univ Mich, 63-65; asst prof physics, Alfred Univ, 65-66. *Mem:* Am Phys Soc; Am Asn Physics Teachers; Sigma Xi. *Res:* Quantum field theory; elementary particles; electromagnetic theory; physics education. *Mailing Add:* 3720 Fairway Rd Fargo ND 58102-1279

HASSOUN, MOHAMAD HUSSEIN, ARTIFICIAL NEURAL SYSTEMS, MACHINE INTELLIGENCE. *Current Pos:* asst prof, 87-91, ASSOC PROF, ELEC & COMPUTE ENG DEPT, WAYNE STATE UNIV, 91- *Personal Data:* b Gazieh, Lebanon, Jan 1, 61; m; c 1. *Educ:* Wayne State Univ, BS, 81, MS, 82, PhD(elec eng), 86. *Prof Exp:* Res assoc, Digital Optics Inc, 86-87. *Concurrent Pos:* NSF res initiation award, 88 & presidential young investr award, 90-95; consult, Digital Optics Inc, 87-88, Federated Monetary Inc, 90; assoc ed, Inst Elec & Electronics Engrs Trans Neural Networks, 91-. *Mem:* Soc Photo-Optical Instrumentation Engrs; Int Neural Networks Soc; Inst Elec & Electronics Engrs; Am Soc Eng Educ; Sigma Xi. *Res:* Massively parallel, highly interconnected, and collective computations; artificial neural networks; learning machines; associative memories; photonic computing; search and optimization utilizing highly parallel architectures; genetic algorithms search and optimization; author of numerous publications; one US patent. *Mailing Add:* Dept Elec & Comput Eng Wayne State Univ 3100 Eng Bldg Detroit MI 48202

HAST, MALCOLM HOWARD, ANATOMY, PHYSIOLOGY. *Current Pos:* assoc prof, 69-74, PROF OTOLARYNGOL-HEAD & NECK SURG, MED SCH, NORTHWESTERN UNIV, CHICAGO, 74-, PROF CELL, MOLECULAR & STRUCT BIOL (ANAT), MED SCH, 77-, DIR RES, 69-, PROF BASIC & BEHAV SCI, DENT SCH, 90- *Personal Data:* b New York, NY, May 28, 31; m 53, Adele Krongelb; c David & Howard. *Educ:* Brooklyn Col, BA, 53; Ohio State Univ, MA, 58, PhD, 61; Inst Biol UK, C Biol, Fl Biol, 91. *Honors & Awards:* Gould Int Award, 71; Arnott Dem, Royal Col Surgeons, Eng, 85. *Prof Exp:* Instr, Univ Iowa, 61-63, res asst prof otolaryngol & maxillofacial surg, Col Med, 65-69. *Concurrent Pos:* NIH fel otolaryngol, Univ Iowa, 63-65; NIH res grants, 64-75, 78-84, 95-; assoc staff, Northwestern Mem Hosp, 69-; mem bd dirs, Ill Soc Med Res, 73-78; NSF res grant, 75-77; guest scientist, Max Planck Inst, Munich, 76; NATO sr fel sci, Oxford Univ, 78; vis prof, Royal Col Surgeons, Eng, 80-86, Univ Edinburgh, 87; guest sci zool, Forshunginstitut U Mus Koenig, 88; NEH grants, 95. *Mem:* Fel AAAS; fel Am Speech & Hearing Asn; Am Asn Hist Med; Am Physiol Soc; fel Inst Biol UK; fel Linnean Soc London; fel Royal Soc Med; Anat Soc Gt Brit & Ireland; Am Asn Anatomists; Am Asn Clin Anatomists; Am Soc Mammalogists; Sigma Xi. *Res:* Neuromuscular physiology and embryology of the larynx; comparative anatomy of larynx; human anatomy; history of medicine. *Mailing Add:* Dept Otolaryngol-Head & Neck Surg Northwestern Univ Med Sch Chicago IL 60611. *Fax:* 312-503-1616

HASTENRATH, STEFAN LUDWIG, METEOROLOGY, CLIMATOLOGY. *Current Pos:* assoc prof, 67-70, PROF METEOROL, UNIV WIS-MADISON, 70- *Personal Data:* b Budapest, Hungary, July 10, 34. *Educ:* Univ Bonn, Dr. *Prof Exp:* Asst prof meteorol, Univ Cologne, 59-60; chief, Climat Div, Nat Meteorol Serv, El Salvador, Cent Am, 60-63; proj assoc meteorol, Univ Wis-Madison, 63-65; assoc prof, Univ Wis, Milwaukee, 65-67. *Concurrent Pos:* Vis prof, Univ Witwatersrand, 71; World Meteorol Orgn/UN Develop Prog prof & head, Dept Meteorol, Univ Nairobi, Kenya, 73-74. *Mem:* Am Meteorol Soc; Ger Meteorol Soc; Meteorol Soc Japan; Royal Meteorol Soc; Int Glaciol Soc; Soc Brasil Meteorol. *Res:* Climate; tropics; glaciers. *Mailing Add:* Dept Meteorol Univ Wis Madison WI 53706

HASTERLIK, ROBERT JOSEPH, MEDICINE. *Current Pos:* CONSULT, 81- *Personal Data:* b Chicago, Ill, Mar 17, 15. *Educ:* Univ Chicago, SB, 34; Rush Med Sch, MD, 38; Am Bd Internal Med, dipl. *Prof Exp:* Clin asst, Med Sch, Northwestern Univ, 47-48; from asst prof to prof med, Univ Chicago, 48-70; clin prof, Univ Calif, San Diego, 70-72; prof med, Sch Med, Univ Southern Calif, 73-75; dir, Regional Cancer Control Prog, Cancer Ctr, Hawaii, 77-78; assoc dir, La Jolla Cancer Res Found, 79-81. *Concurrent Pos:* Jr attend physician, Evanston Hosp, 47-48; dir, Health Serv Div, Argonne Nat Lab, US AEC, 48-53; sr scientist, Div Biol & Med Res, 50-53, consult, 53-70; assoc dir, Argonne Cancer Res Hosp, 52-63; vpres, Enviro-Med, Inc, 70-73; assoc dir, Los Angeles Co-Univ Southern Calif Cancer Ctr, 73-75; assoc dir, Cancer Ctr Hawaii & dir, Comn Cancer Control Prog Hawaii, 77-78; mem, Ill Legis Comn Atomic Energy; mem, Radiation Protection Adv Coun, State Ill; mem, Subcomt 14, Nat Comt Radiation Protection, 71-77; mem, Nat Coun Radiation Protection & Measurements; mem res comt, Zool Soc San Diego, 79-87; bd trustees, Rush-Presby-St Luke's Med Ctr, 83- *Mem:* Fel AAAS; Radiol Soc NAm; Radiation Res Soc; fel Am Col Physicians. *Res:* Radiation effects and studies on radium poisoning; biological and biochemical effects of total body irradiation; planning studies of cancer research and treatment facilities and delivery of health services. *Mailing Add:* 7722 Ludington Place La Jolla CA 92037

HASTIE, JOHN WILLIAM, SPECTROSCOPY, CHEMICAL PHYSICS. *Current Pos:* RES CHEMIST, NAT INST STANDARDS & TECHNOL, 69- *Personal Data:* b Ilford, Eng, Mar 29, 41; US citizen; m 66, Hilary Asten; c 2. *Educ:* Univ Tasmania, BS, 63, PhD, 67. *Hon Degrees:* DSc, Univ Tasmania, 73. *Honors & Awards:* Indust Res-100 Award, 80. *Prof Exp:* Fel chem, Rice Univ, 66-69. *Mem:* Am Chem Soc; Soc Appl Spectros; Am Ceramic Soc; Int Union Pure & Appl Chem; Mat Res Soc. *Res:* Thermochemical properties of inorganic materials, ie, refractory solids, molten salts and slags, vapors and gases, at high temperatures; thermodynamics; kinetics and spectroscopy of high temperature vapors; chemistry of flames, inhibition and combustion; chemistry of thin film deposition. *Mailing Add:* 19405 Farber Ct Gaithersburg MD 20879

HASTINGS, ALAN MATTHEW, POPULATION BIOLOGY, MODELS IN ECOLOGY & GENETICS. *Current Pos:* From asst prof to assoc prof math & environ studies, 79-85, PROF & CHAIR ENVIRON STUDIES, UNIV CALIF, 85- *Personal Data:* b Riverhead, NY, Aug 27, 53. *Educ:* Cornell Univ, BA, 73, MS, 75, PhD(appl math), 77. *Res:* Investigating the dynamics of models in population ecology and genetics particularly emphasizing the role of spatial and age structure; work uses the tools of modern dynamical systems and includes studies of the roles of chaos. *Mailing Add:* Div Environ Studies Univ Calif Davis CA 95616. *E-Mail:* amhastings@ucdavis.edu

HASTINGS, DAVID FRANK, PHYSIOLOGY, BIOPHYSICS. *Personal Data:* b Rochester, NY, Dec 25, 45; m 68; c 3. *Educ:* Swarthmore Col, BA, 68; Duke Univ, PhD(physiol), 75. *Prof Exp:* Res assoc biophys, Inst Physiol, Univ Aarhus, 75-76; res assoc biochem, Duke Univ, 76-78; asst prof physiol, Univ SDak, 78-85. *Concurrent Pos:* Res assoc, Nat Res Serv Award from Gen Med Sci, NIH, 75-77; res scientist, Marine Biomed Ctr, Duke Univ, 81. *Mem:* Biophys Soc; Sigma Xi; AAAS; Am Phys Soc; NY Acad Sci. *Res:* Structure and functional mechanisms of membrane transport and their regulation. *Mailing Add:* 24009 Broad Dell Way Newhall CA 91321

HASTINGS, EARL L, MINING GEOLOGY. *Current Pos:* PRES, HASTINGS MINING CORP, 80- *Personal Data:* b Hampton, Va, June 15, 28; m 51; c 2. *Educ:* Univ Ala, BS, 53; Univ Mich, MS, 54. *Prof Exp:* Res mineralogist, Int Minerals & Chem Corp, 55; geologist, Geol Surv Ala, 56-61; consult geologist, 61-65; vpres mining, R E Wilson Mining Co, 65-68; pres, Eufaula Bauxite Mining Co, 68-73; pres, Spec Minerals Corp, 74-75; opers mgr, Eufaula Minerals, Div Combustion Eng, 76-78. *Res:* Economic geology; mineralogy. *Mailing Add:* PO Box 7 Troy AL 36081

HASTINGS, ELLSWORTH (BERNARD), ENTOMOLOGY. *Current Pos:* asst, Exp Sta, 37-39, from asst prof to prof, 49-77, EMER PROF ENTOM, MONT STATE UNIV, 77- *Personal Data:* b Billings, Mont, Aug 9, 10; m 35; c 3. *Educ:* Mont State Col, BS, 34, MS, 39. *Prof Exp:* Field supvr, Farm Security Admin, Mont, 34-37. *Mem:* Entom Soc Am. *Res:* Biology and physiology of Mormon cricket; various species of grasshoppers; sugarbeet webworm; codling moth; absorption of fumigants by grain and grain products; alfalfa weevil and animal ecology. *Mailing Add:* 416 S Sixth Ave Bozeman MT 59715

HASTINGS, FELTON LEO, INSECT TOXICOLOGY. *Current Pos:* res entomologist, 68-69, SUPVRY RES ENTOMOLOGIST, SOUTHEASTERN FOREST EXP STA, US FOREST SERV, 69- *Personal Data:* b Port Arthur, Tex, Jan 15, 38; m 61. *Educ:* Auburn Univ, BS, 60, MS, 62; NC State Univ, PhD(entom), 67. *Prof Exp:* Nat Inst Environ Health Sci res grant biochem, NC State Univ, 67-68. *Mem:* Am Chem Soc; Entom Soc Am. *Res:* Develop state, effective and selective chemicals for controlling destructive forest insect populations; determine strategies which minimize adverse effects on parasites, predators and other non-target organisms. *Mailing Add:* 111 Dublin Woods Dr Cary NC 27513

HASTINGS, HAROLD MORRIS, MATHEMATICAL BIOLOGY. *Current Pos:* assoc prof, 75-81, chmn dept, 85-90 & 93-96, assoc dean, Hofstra Col, 90-93, PROF MATH, HOFSTRA UNIV, 81- *Personal Data:* b Dayton, Ohio, Nov 21, 46; m 68; c 2. *Educ:* Yale Univ, BS, 67; Princeton Univ, MA, 69, PhD(math), 72. *Prof Exp:* From instr to asst prof math, Hofstra Univ, 68-74; vis assoc prof, State Univ NY, Binghamton, 74-75. *Concurrent Pos:* NSF grant, 77-79 & 81-83 & Woodrow Wilson grant, 80; lectr, Univ Ga, 78-79; consult comput models, 80-; NASA grant, 85-89; founder, Hastings Saalboch Assocs Inc, 83-96; consult, Long Island Jewish Med Ctr, 94- *Mem:* Am Math Soc; Asn Comput Mach; NY Acad Sci. *Res:* Stability theory of dynamical systems and applications to mathematical ecology; mathematical physiology; patentee in computerized medical monitoring and ultrasound imaging. *Mailing Add:* Hofstra Univ Dept Math Hempstead NY 11550. *Fax:* 516-463-5790; *E-Mail:* mathmh@hofstra.edu

HASTINGS, IAN JAMES, NUCLEAR FUEL. *Current Pos:* res off, Chalk River Labs, AECL Res, 68-79, head, fuel properties & behav group, 79-88, mgr, Fusion Blanket Prof, 86-91, mgr, Fuel Mat Br, 88-91, exec asst, pres & chief exec officer, 91-92, sr dir technol, 93-95, SR DIR STRATEGIC INITIATIVES, AECL, 95- *Personal Data:* b Brisbane, Australia, July 21, 43; m 68, Lyndell D Cox; c David & Caitlin. *Educ:* Univ Queensland, BSc, 64, PhD(metall), 68. *Prof Exp:* Lectr, Queensland Inst Technol, 66-68. *Mem:* Fel Australian Inst Mining & Metall; fel Am Ceramic Soc; Am Nuclear Soc; Can Nuclear Soc. *Res:* Irradiation effects in nuclear fuels; fission gas effects; fuel fabrication and design; computer modelling fuel performance; advanced fuel cycles; fusion breeder blanket materials and strategic planning. *Mailing Add:* AECL 2251 Speakman Dr Mississauga ON L5K 1B2 Can. *Fax:* 905-403-7318; *E-Mail:* hastingsi@aecl.ca

HASTINGS, JAMES MICHAEL, HUMAN PHYSIOLOGY, PATHOPHYSIOLOGY. *Current Pos:* PROF BIOL, DICKINSON STATE UNIV, 84- *Personal Data:* b Poplar Bluff, Mo, Feb 13, 47. *Educ:* Col of the Ozarks, BS, 69; SW Mo State Univ, MA, 73; Univ Ark, PhD(immunol), 81. *Prof Exp:* Fac, Cottey Col, Nev, Mo, 80-83; asst prof biol, Mo Southern State Col, 83-84. *Mem:* Sigma Xi; Am Soc Microbiol. *Res:* Human physiology and pathophysiology educator. *Mailing Add:* Dept Biol Dickinson State Univ Dickinson ND 58601. *Fax:* 701-225-0526; *E-Mail:* mike_hastings@dsu1.dsu.nodak.edu

HASTINGS, JOHN WOODLAND, BIOLUMINESCENCE, BIOLOGICAL RHYTHMS. *Current Pos:* PROF BIOL, HARVARD UNIV, 66-, MASTER N HOUSE, 76-, PAUL C MANGELSBERG PROF NATURAL HIST, 87- *Personal Data:* b Salisbury, Md, Mar 24, 27; m 53, Hanna Machlup; c Jennifer, David, Laura & Karen. *Educ:* Swarthmore Col, BA, 47; Princeton Univ, MA, 50, PhD(biol), 51. *Hon Degrees:* MA, Harvard Univ, 66. *Honors & Awards:* Yamada Found Award, 86; Alexander von Humboldt Prize, 79. *Prof Exp:* Instr natural sci, Col Cevenol, Le Chambonsur-Lignon, France, 47-48; AEC fel biol sci, Johns Hopkins Univ, 51-53; from instr to asst prof, Northwestern Univ, 53-57; from asst prof to prof biochem, Univ Ill, Urbana, 57-66. *Concurrent Pos:* Asst instr, Princeton Univ, 48-51; vis lectr, Univ Sheffield, 61-62; instr, Physiol Training Prog, Marine Biol Lab, Woods Hole, Mass, 61-62, dir course, 62-66; mem, Panel Molecular Biol, NSF, 63-66, Div Biol & Sci Adv Comt, 68-71, chmn, 70-71; mem, Comt Postdoctoral Fels Chem, Nat Acad Sci, 65-68, Comt Photobiol, 65-72; mem, Space Biol Subcomt, NASA, 66-70, mem, Biochem Training Comt, Nat Inst Gen Med Sci, 68-72; mem, Int Adv Comt, Red Sea Marine Res Sta, Eilat, Israel, 68-; NIH fel, Inst Phys Biochem, Paris, 72-73, Guggenheim fel, 65-66; vis prof, Rockefeller Univ, 65-66, Nat Inst Basic Biol, Okaza, Japan, 86 & Univ Konstaz, Ger, 79-88, Univ Munich, Ger, 93. *Mem:* AAAS; Am Soc Microbiol; Soc Res Biol Rhythms; Am Soc Biol Chemists; Int Soc Bioluminescence & Chemiluminescence (pres, 94-98); Am Soc Photobiol. *Res:* Marine biology, especially microorganisms; biochemical mechanism of bioluminescence and its biological roles; studies concerning molecular mechanisms of circadian daily rhythms; biological clocks. *Mailing Add:* 16 Divinity Ave Harvard Univ Cambridge MA 02138. *Fax:* 617-495-9300; *E-Mail:* hastings@fas.harvard.edu

HASTINGS, JULIUS MITCHELL, SOLID STATE CHEMISTRY. *Current Pos:* chemist, 47-89, CONSULT, BROOKHAVEN NAT LAB, 89- *Personal Data:* b New York, NY, Aug 24, 20; m 43; c Harold M, Jerome B & Alan M. *Educ:* NY Univ, AB, 40; Cornell Univ, PhD(phys chem), 45. *Prof Exp:* Sr physicist, Monsanto Chem Co, Ohio, 45-47. *Mem:* Fel Am Phys Soc. *Res:* Neutron scattering; critical phenomena. *Mailing Add:* 65 Ketcham Ave Patchogue NY 11772

HASTINGS, MARYAM SHAYEGAN, COMPUTER SCIENCE, TOPOLOGY. *Current Pos:* chair, Dept Math, Comput Sci & Info Systs, 85-86, 89-91 & 92-94, MATH & COMPUT SCI, MARYMOUNT COL, 82- *Personal Data:* m, William; c Iraj, Ramin & Shirin. *Educ:* Fairleigh Dickson Univ, BA, 64, MS, 87; Univ Mich, MA, 69; Univ Toledo, PhD(math), 75. *Prof Exp:* Sr tech asst, Bell Telephone Labs, 67-68; asst prof math, St Peters Col, 75-78, William Paterson Col, 78-82. *Concurrent Pos:* Lectr women & math, Marymount Col, 82-94. *Mem:* Math Asn Am; Am Math Soc; Asn Women Math. *Res:* Categorical topology; nearness spaces; mathematics of the computer screen and implemented programs in C. *Mailing Add:* Dept Math & Comput Sci Marymount Col Tarrytown NY 10591

HASTINGS, ROBERT CLYDE, LEPROSY. *Current Pos:* CHIEF PHARMACOL RES DEPT, NAT HANSEN'S DIS CTR, 71-, CHIEF LAB RES BR, 83- *Personal Data:* b Tenn, Apr 23, 38; m 81; c 3. *Educ:* Univ Tenn, Memphis, MD, 62; Tulane Univ, PhD(pharmacol), 71. *Concurrent Pos:* Ed, Int J Leprosy, 79-; adj prof pharmacol & clin prof med, Tulane Med Ctr, 83- *Mem:* Int Leprosy Asn; Am Soc Pharmacol & Exp Therapeut; Am Soc Clin Pharmacol & Therapeut; Am Soc Microbiol; AAAS. *Res:* Growth of M Leprae in athymic mice; growth of M Leprae in armadillos for the supply of lepromin and bacilli; microbiology, biochemistry, pathology, pharmacology and immunology of leprosy. *Mailing Add:* Lab Res Br GWNHDC La State Univ PO Box 25072 Baton Rouge LA 70894

HASTINGS, ROBERT WAYNE, ICHTHYOLOGY, MARINE BIOLOGY. *Current Pos:* PROF, DEPT BIOL, SOUTHEASTERN LA UNIV, 88- & DIR, TURTLE COVE ENVIRON RES STA, 84- *Personal Data:* b Memphis, Tenn, Nov 24, 43; m 69, Diana J Allen; c Kimberly M & Rachel L. *Educ:* Univ Fla, BS, 65; Fla State Univ, MS, 67, PhD(biol), 72. *Prof Exp:* From asst prof to assoc prof zool, Rutgers Univ, 72-88. *Mem:* Am Soc Ichthyologists & Herpetologists; Estuarine Res Fedn; Gulf Estuarine Res Soc; Org Biol Field Sta. *Res:* Ecology and distribution of fishes; microhabitat selection in fishes; estuarine ecology; environmental science; wetlands ecology; alligator biology. *Mailing Add:* Turtle Cove Environ Res Sta Southeastern La Univ PO Box 585 Hammond LA 70402. *Fax:* 504-549-5008; *E-Mail:* bhastings@selu.edu

HASTINGS, STUART, MATHEMATICS. *Current Pos:* PROF MATH, UNIV PITTSBURGH, 87- *Personal Data:* b Glen Cove, NY, May 12, 37; m 64; c 1. *Educ:* Brown Univ, ScB, 59; Mass Inst Technol, PhD(math), 64. *Prof Exp:* Asst prof math, Case Western Res Univ, 64-70; from assoc prof to prof math, State Univ NY, Buffalo, 70-87. *Mem:* Am Math Soc; Soc Indust & Appl Math; Math Asn Am. *Res:* Nonlinear differential equations from science and engineering. *Mailing Add:* Dept Math Univ Pittsburgh Pittsburgh PA 15260-4114

HASTREITER, ALOIS RUDOLF, PEDIATRIC CARDIOLOGY. *Current Pos:* PROF PEDIAT CARDIOL, UNIV ILL COL MED, 70-, HEAD, DIV PEDIAT CARDIOL, 89- *Personal Data:* b Rio de Janeiro, Brazil, Mar 22, 27; m 58, Louise Lear; c Roberta. *Educ:* Univ Brazil, MD, 54; Am Bd Pediat, dipl & cert cardiol, 61. *Prof Exp:* Intern, St Luke's Hosp, New Bedford, Mass, 55-56; pediat resident, Philadelphia Gen Hosp, 56-59; instr pediat cardiol, Children's Mem Hosp, Chicago, 61-63; asst prof pediat cardiol, Univ & dir, Cardiovasc Lab, Univ Hosp, 63-67, assoc prof, 67-70, dir sect pediat cardiol, 67-82. *Concurrent Pos:* Fel pediat cardiol, Children's Mem Hosp, Chicago, 59-61; instr, Northwestern Univ, 61-63; dir, Cardiovasc Lab, Cook Co Children's Hosp, Ill, 63-67. *Mem:* Fel Am Acad Pediat; fel Am Col Cardiol; Am Heart Asn; Asn Advan Med Instrumentation; Am Pediat Soc. *Res:* Digitalis, antiarrhythmics. *Mailing Add:* 3649 Whirlaway Dr Northbrook IL 60062. *Fax:* 312-413-1526

HASTY, DAVID LONG, CELL BIOLOGY, HYBRIDOMA RESEARCH. *Current Pos:* asst prof, 77-83, ASSOC PROF ANAT, UNIV TENN CTR HEALTH SCI, 83- *Personal Data:* b Atlanta, Ga, Sept 1, 47. *Educ:* Carson-Newman Col, BS, 69; Univ Tenn, PhD(anat), 74. *Prof Exp:* Fel anat, Harvard Med Sch, 74-77. *Mem:* Am Soc Cell Biol; Am Soc Develop Biol; NY Acad Sci; AAAS; Sigma Xi. *Res:* Analyzing the role of fibronectin and other extracellular macromolecule in development; adherence of bacteria to oral epithelial cells and other tissue. *Mailing Add:* Dept Anat & Neurobiol Univ Tenn Col Med 800 Madison Ave Memphis TN 38163-0001. *Fax:* 901-577-7273

HASTY, NOEL MARION, ORGANIC CHEMISTRY. *Current Pos:* res chemist, Elastomer Chem Dept, 73-79, sr res chemist, Polymer Prod Dept, 79-83, RES ASSOC, E I DU PONT DE NEMOURS & CO, INC, 83- *Personal Data:* b Los Angeles, Calif, Oct 22, 44; m 94, Mary A Mitchell; c Bettina & Benjamin. *Educ:* Univ Southern Calif, BS, 66; Univ Wis-Madison, PhD(org chem), 71. *Prof Exp:* Res asst org chem, Univ Calif, Riverside, 70-72; instr, Wesleyan Univ, 72-73. *Mem:* Am Chem Soc. *Res:* Polyurethane elastomers; polyesters; thermoplastic elastomers; spandex fibers. *Mailing Add:* 149 Mercer Mill Rd Landenberg PA 19350. *Fax:* 302-999-2922

HASTY, ROBERT ARMISTEAD, analytical chemistry, industrial chemistry, for more information see previous edition

HASTY, TURNER ELIAH, PHYSICS. *Current Pos:* RETIRED. *Personal Data:* b Linden, Ala, June 18, 31; m 59; c 2. *Educ:* Univ Ala, BS, 53, MS, 56, PhD(physics), 59. *Prof Exp:* Instr, Univ Ala, 58-59; mem tech staff, Tex Instruments, 59-69, mgr, Microwave Physics Br, 69-73, dir, Advan Technol Lab, 73-75, dir, Semiconductor Res & Eng Labs, 75-80, mgr complementaty metal-oxide semiconductor develop, 80-83, eng mgr, Semi-Custom Design Div, 83-87; mem mgt team, Sematech, 87, exec vpres & chief oper officer, 89-91; prof physics, Univ Tex, 91-94. *Concurrent Pos:* Consult mem, Adv Group Electron Devices, 73-79. *Mem:* Am Phys Soc; Sigma Xi. *Res:* Solid state physics; hot electron transport; Gunn effect; Impatt diodes; microwave engineering; complementary metal-oxide semiconductors. *Mailing Add:* 3775 Northaven Rd Dallas TX 75229

HATCH, ALBERT JEROLD, NUCLEAR STRUCTURE, PLASMA PHYSICS. *Current Pos:* RETIRED. *Personal Data:* b Little Rock, Ill, Apr 23, 16; m 46, Helen C Glenn; c Cecilia, Rebecca & David (deceased). *Educ:* Univ Ill, BS, 39, MS, 47. *Prof Exp:* Asst physics, Univ Ill, 43-47; instr & asst physicist, NMex State Univ, 47-49, asst prof & assoc physicist, 49-56; assoc physicist, Argonne Nat Lab, 56-72, physicist, 72-73, asst dir, Physics Div, 73-81; lectr, Roosevelt Univ, 82-92. *Concurrent Pos:* Lectr, Ill Inst Technol, 63-71; consult, Ultek Corp, Calif, 63-64; lectr, DePaul Univ, 80-81; instr, Triton Col, 82-83, Moraine Valley Community Col, 82-90. *Mem:* Fel Am Phys Soc; Sigma Xi. *Res:* High-frequency breakdown and gaseous discharges; controlled thermonuclear processes; electromagnetic levitation; nuclear structure; elementary particle physics. *Mailing Add:* 5460 S Cornell Ave Chicago IL 60615

HATCH, CHARLES ELDRIDGE, III, ORGANIC CHEMISTRY, TECHNICAL MANAGEMENT. *Current Pos:* From res chemist to sr res assoc, 80-81, mgr process res group, Agr Chem Group, 81-88, DIR PROCESS & FORMULATIONS, RES & DEVELOP, FMC CORP, 88- *Personal Data:* b Richmond, Va, Sept 30, 48; m 76; c 2. *Educ:* Old Dominion Univ, BS, 71; Johns Hopkins Univ, MS, 73, PhD(org chem), 75. *Mem:* Am Chem Soc; Sigma Xi. *Res:* Organic photochemistry with synthetic utility resulting in a novel route to several unusual penicillin analogs; carbamoyl fluoride approach to carbamate insecticides; asymmetric synthesis of pyrethroid insecticides; transition metal catalyzed coupling of Grignard reagents to produce substituted biphenyls. *Mailing Add:* 284 Wargo Rd Pennington NJ 08534-1825

HATCH, DORIAN MAURICE, THEORETICAL PHYSICS, SOLID STATE PHYSICS. *Current Pos:* from asst prof to assoc prof, 68-80, PROF PHYSICS, BRIGHAM YOUNG UNIV, 80- *Personal Data:* b Burley, Idaho, Sept 25, 40; m 60; c 5. *Educ:* Utah State Univ, BS, 62; State Univ NY, Stony Brook, MA, 66, PhD(physics), 68. *Prof Exp:* Vis prof physics, State Univ NY, Farmingdale, 68. *Concurrent Pos:* Fac res fel, Brigham Young Univ, 69-70; vis prof physics, Fed Inst Technol, Zurich, Switz, 72, 73, Univ Del, Newark, 80 & 81, Univ Wash, Seattle, 90. *Mem:* Sigma Xi; Am Phys Soc. *Res:* Inequivalent representations in field theory and the removal of cutoffs; field theory applied to solid state physics; second quantization of parastatistics; logic of quantum mechanics; phase transitions in solids, renormalization group; group theory. *Mailing Add:* Dept Physics & Astron 175 ESC Brigham Young Univ Provo UT 84602

HATCH, EASTMAN NIBLEY, NUCLEAR PHYSICS. *Current Pos:* prof, Utah State Univ, 69-89, head, Dept Physics, 72-74, dean, Sch Grad Studies, 74-79, EMER PROF PHYSICS, UTAH STATE UNIV, 89- *Personal Data:* b Salt Lake City, Utah, June 14, 27; m 52; c 3. *Educ:* Stanford Univ, BS, 50; Calif Inst Technol, PhD(nuclear physics), 56. *Prof Exp:* Asst physics, Calif Inst Technol, 54-56, res fel, 56-57; res assoc, Brookhaven Nat Lab, 57-58; sci liaison officer, Sci & Tech Unit, USN, Ger, 58-60; guest physicist, Heidelberg, 60-61; from assoc prof to prof physics, Iowa State Univ, 61-69, sr physicist, 66-69, asst dean grad col, 67-69. *Concurrent Pos:* Vis prof phys, Univ Freiburg, WGer, 79-80, Univ Cologne, WGer, 87. *Mem:* Fel Am Phys Soc; Sigma Xi; Am Asn Physics Teachers. *Res:* Precision gamma ray spectroscopy with bent crystal spectrometers; measurement of nuclear life-times. *Mailing Add:* Dept Physics UMC 4415 Utah State Univ Logan UT 84322-4415. *Fax:* 435-750-2492

HATCH, FREDERICK TASKER, TOXICOLOGY, FOOD SCIENCE. *Current Pos:* biochemist, Lawrence Livermore Nat Lab, 65-73, sect leader cell biol & mutagenesis, 73-80, asst assoc dir, Biomed & Environ Res Prog, 80-87, CONSULT, LAWRENCE LIVERMORE NAT LAB, UNIV CALIF, 87- *Personal Data:* b Boston, Mass, Aug 27, 24; m 46, Virginia Weeks; c Daniel, Daphne, Deborah & Douglas. *Educ:* Dartmouth Col, AB, 44; Harvard Univ, MD, 48; Mass Inst Technol, PhD, 60. *Prof Exp:* Intern med, Roosevelt Hosp, NY, 48-49; res fel & instr res serv, Goldwater Mem Hosp, Columbia Univ, 49-52; assoc med, Harvard Med Sch, 60-65. *Concurrent Pos:* Asst physician, Mass Gen Hosp, 60-65; investr, Am Heart Asn, 60-65; consult, Vet Admin Hosp, Livermore, Calif, 70-80; mem, Lipid Metab Adv Comt, Nat Heart & Lung Inst, NIH, 72-76, Human Subjects Inst Rev Bd, 74-87, chmn, 83-87, Animal Res Comt, 79-87 & Lab Safety Comt, 82-87; chmn, Melanoma Invest Task Group, 84-87. *Mem:* Am Heart Asn; Am Chem Soc; Am Soc Biochem & Molecular Biol; Environ Mutagen Soc; Am Inst Chemists. *Res:* Food mutagens; genetic toxicology; satellite DNAs, chromosome structure; chemical mutagenesis; tritium metabolism; quantitative lipoprotein electrophoresis; nutrition, genetics and lipoproteins in cardiovascular disease; chemical taxonomy of proteins. *Mailing Add:* 27 Pease Rd Meredith NH 03253-5506. *E-Mail:* fhatch@northstar.dartmouth.edu

HATCH, GARY EPHRAIM, TOXICOLOGY, NUCLEAR CHEMISTRY. *Current Pos:* RES PHARMACOLOGIST, INHALATION TOXICOL DIV, HEALTH EFFECTS RES LAB, US ENVIRON PROTECTION AGENCY, 79- *Personal Data:* b Provo, Utah, Sept 28, 47; m 72; c 6. *Educ:* Brigham Young Univ, BS, 72, MS, 74; Univ Utah, PhD(pharmacol), 77. *Honors & Awards:* Sci & Technol Achievement Award, US Environ Protection Agency, 82 & 83. *Prof Exp:* Res assoc, Dept Pharmacol & Med, Duke Univ, 77-79. *Concurrent Pos:* Proj officer, numerous extramural coop agreements, US Environ Protection Agency, 80-; prin investr, US Army Interagency Agreement, 84- & Innovative Res award, US Environ Protection Agency, 85- *Mem:* Am Soc Pharmacol & Exp Therapeut. *Res:* Inhalation toxicology of indoor and outdoor air pollutants in animals and extrapolation of results to human risk assessment; dosimetry of inhaled substances; oxygen-18 analysis in tissues; measurement of tissue oxidation and natural protective agents found in tissues. *Mailing Add:* Toxicol Br Environ Protection Agency MD-82 ERC Research Triangle Park NC 27711-0001. *Fax:* 919-541-0026

HATCH, JOHN PHILLIP, PSYCHOPHYSIOLOGY, BEHAVIORAL MEDICINE. *Current Pos:* res instr, 79-81, asst prof, 81-84, ASSOC PROF PSYCHIAT, UNIV TEX HEALTH SCI CTR, SAN ANTONIO, 84-, ASSOC PROF DENT, 87- *Personal Data:* b Highland Park, Ill, May 18, 46; m 69; c 2. *Educ:* Bradley Univ, BS, 68, MA, 72; Univ Tex, Arlington, PhD(psychol), 77. *Prof Exp:* Res fel psychol, State Univ NY, Stony Brook, 77-79. *Concurrent Pos:* Chmn, Task Force Comt, Biofeedback Soc Am, 83-87; grant reveiwer, Psychobiol Prog, NSF, 85-86; consult, Johnson Space Ctr, NASA, 86-87; bd dir, Asn Appl Psychophysiol, 88- *Mem:* Sigma Xi; Soc Psychophysiol Res; Am Asn Dent Res; Am Psychol Asn; Asn Appl Psychophysiol Biofeedback. *Res:* Investigating the psychological and physiological mechanisms that underlie stress related disorders including headache, hypertension, and sexual dysfunction. *Mailing Add:* Dept Psychiat Univ Tex Health Sci Ctr 7703 Floyd Curl Dr San Antonio TX 78284-7792

HATCH, MELVIN (JAY), POLYMER CHEMISTRY. *Current Pos:* assoc prof, 66-73, PROF CHEM, NMEX INST MINING & TECHNOL, 73- *Personal Data:* b Winslow, Ariz, Oct 20, 26; m 58, Martha Stewart; c Catherine, James (deceased) & Patricia. *Educ:* Univ Ariz, BS, 48; Univ Calif, Los Angeles, PhD(chem), 52. *Prof Exp:* Chemist, Dow Chem Co, 52-56, proj leader, 56-58, assoc scientist, 58-66. *Concurrent Pos:* Consult, Dow Chem Co, 66-88, Dionex Corp, 88- *Mem:* Am Chem Soc; fel Am Inst Chemists. *Res:* Ion exchange and ion retardation resins; water soluble polyelectrolytes; sulfonium compounds; halonium compounds; organic reaction mechanisms. *Mailing Add:* 1217 Apache Dr Socorro NM 87801

HATCH, RANDOLPH THOMAS, CHEMICAL ENGINEERING, BIOCHEMICAL ENGINEERING. *Current Pos:* PRES, AASTON, INC, 91- *Personal Data:* b Milwaukee, Wis, Apr 27, 45; m 68, Jacqueline; c Geoffrey R, Meredith K & Stephen T. *Educ:* Univ Calif, Berkeley, BS, 67; Mass Inst Technol, MS, 69, PhD(biochem eng), 73. *Prof Exp:* From asst prof to assoc prof chem eng, Univ Md, 72-84; dir fermentation & biochem eng, Biotechnica Int, 84-91. *Concurrent Pos:* Traineeship, NIH, 67-72; prog dir, NSF, 77-78, prin investr, NSF grant, 76-84. *Mem:* Am Soc Microbiol; Am Inst Chem Engrs; Am Chem Soc. *Res:* Biochemical engineering; membrane separations; reverse osmosis; fermentation technology; oxygen transfer computer control; mixed cultures; recombinant DNA products and processes. *Mailing Add:* 12 Falmouth Rd Wellesley MA 02181-1239. *Fax:* 781-239-0455

HATCH, RICHARD C, PHYSICAL CHEMISTRY. *Current Pos:* from asst prof to assoc prof, 62-74, PROF CHEM, MUHLENBERG COL, 74- *Personal Data:* b Aug 20, 36; US citizen; m 62; c 1. *Educ:* Brown Univ, BS, 58; Univ NH, PhD(chem), 63. *Prof Exp:* Asst chem, Univ NH, 59-62. *Mem:* Am Chem Soc. *Res:* Chemical kinetics; mechanisms of oxidation; reduction reactions in aqueous and nonaqueous media; radiation chemistry. *Mailing Add:* Dean Fac Muhlenberg Col 2400 W Chew St Allentown PA 18104-5564

HATCH, ROBERT ALCHIN, MINERALOGY. *Current Pos:* RETIRED. *Personal Data:* b Kalamazoo, Mich, Feb 20, 14; m 42; c 3. *Educ:* Univ Mich, BS, 37, MS, 38, ScD(mineral), 42. *Prof Exp:* Res microscopist & phys chemist, Corning Glass Works, NY, 42-47; mineralogist, Electrotech Lab, US Bur Mines, 47-50, leader, Synthetic Mineral sect, 50-55; sr chemist, 3M Co, 55-62, supvr, High Temp Mat Res, 62-65, mgr, 65-79. *Mem:* Fel Mineral Soc Am; fel Am Ceramic Soc. *Res:* Phase equilibria of silicate systems; silicate crystal chemistry; mineral synthesis; ceramics; synthetic mica. *Mailing Add:* 2223 Maple Lane E St Paul MN 55109

HATCH, ROGER CONANT, PHARMACOLOGY, TOXICOLOGY. *Current Pos:* assoc prof & supvr, 73-79, prof toxicol, Diag Assistance Lab, Col Vet Med, 79-80, SOIL & WATER CONSERV, UNIV GA, 80-, PROF TOXICOL & PHARMACOL, DEPT VET PHYSIOL & PHARMACOL, 82- *Personal Data:* b St Joseph, Mich, Jan 23, 35; m 56; c 2. *Educ:* Mich State Univ, BS, 57, DVM, 59; Purdue Univ, MS, 64, PhD(pharmacol), 66. *Prof Exp:* Practr vet med, Berwyn Animal Hosp, Ill, 59-60; US Army Vet Corps, 60-62; instr vet pharmacol & toxicol, Purdue Univ, 62-66; assoc prof pharmacol, Ont Vet Col, Univ Guelph, 66-73, sect head pharmacol, 67-70, supvr, Toxicol Testing Lab, 66-68, assoc prof, 70-73. *Mem:* Am Acad Vet & Comp Toxicol; Soc Toxicol; Am Acad Vet Pharmacol & Therapeut; NY Acad Sci. *Res:* Veterinary pharmacology and toxicology; therapy and antidotes for poisoning in companion and farm animals; pathologic changes in poisoned animals; poison effects on biochemical functions; poison levels in tissues; poisonous plants and plant poisons; biology; medicines. *Mailing Add:* 2385 White Rd Conyers GA 30207

HATCH, SCOTT ALEXANDER, ANIMAL POPULATION ECOLOGY, SEABIRD ECOLOGY. *Current Pos:* SUPVRY WILDLIFE BIOLOGIST, NAT BIOL SURV, 85- *Personal Data:* b Everett, Wash, June 7, 52; m 74, Martha A Laughlin; c Kyle & Megan. *Educ:* Univ Wash, BS, 75; Univ Alaska, MS, 79; Univ Calif, Berkeley, PhD(zool), 85. *Prof Exp:* Res wildlife biologist, Off Biol Serv, US Fish & Wildlife Serv, 78-81, Alaska Field Sta, Denver Wildlife Res Ctr, 81-85. *Mem:* Am Ornithologists' Union; Brit Ornithologists' Union; Cooper Ornith Soc; Asn Field Ornithologists; Wilson Ornith Soc. *Mailing Add:* 1101 E Tudor Rd Anchorage AK 99503. *Fax:* 907-786-3636; *E-Mail:* r8afwrc@mail.fws.gov

HATCH, STEPHAN LAVOR, SYSTEMATIC BOTANY. *Current Pos:* from asst prof & cur to assoc prof & cur, 79-90, PROF & CUR, S M TRACY HERBARIUM, DEPT RANGELAND ECOL & MGT, TEX A&M UNIV, 90- *Personal Data:* b Logan, Utah, July 22, 45; m 67, Nora L Cooper; c 7. *Educ:* Utah State Univ, BS, 70, MS, 72; Tex A&M Univ, PhD(range sci), 75. *Prof Exp:* Asst prof range sci, Tex A&M Univ, 74-75, fel, 75-76; asst prof, NMex State Univ, 76-79. *Mem:* Am Soc Plant Taxonomists; Southwestern Asn Naturalists. *Res:* Grass taxonomy and systematics: Schizachyrium; Sporobolus; Digitaria; Pennisetum and Cenchrus; grass flora of New Mexico; grasses of Texas; Carex. *Mailing Add:* Dept Rangeland Ecol & Mgt Tex A&M Univ College Station TX 77843-2126. *Fax:* 409-845-6430; *E-Mail:* shatch@tamu.edu

HATCHARD, WILLIAM REGINALD, POLYMER CHEMISTRY. *Current Pos:* res chemist, Cent Res Dept, 45-63 & Textile Fibers Dept, 63-69, RES ASSOC, EXP STA, TEXTILE FIBERS DEPT, E I DU PONT DE NEMOURS & CO, 69- *Personal Data:* b Sheerness, Eng, Oct 20, 19; nat US; m 44; c 3. *Educ:* Univ Portland, BS, 41; Univ Ill, PhD(org chem), 44. *Prof Exp:* Lab instr gen chem, Univ Portland, 40-41; asst, Univ Ill, 41-43, res chemist, 43-45; res chemist, Off Sci Res & Develop, Mass Inst Technol, 45. *Mem:* Am Chem Soc. *Res:* Free radicals; high energy radiation reactions; isothiazole chemistry; adhesives. *Mailing Add:* 120 Meriden Pl Hockessin DE 19707-1702

HATCHER, CHARLES RICHARD, PHYSICS. *Current Pos:* mgr, Exp Physics Dept, Santa Barbara Div, Los Alamos Sci Lab, 61-66, dir res & develop, 66-69, gen mgr, Los Alamos Div, 69-72, prog exec, Los Alamos Div EG&G, Inc, 72-77, STAFF MEM, LOS ALAMOS SCI LAB, 77- *Personal Data:* b Paris, Tex, June 3, 32; m 60; c 2. *Educ:* Univ Tex, BS, 53, PhD(physics), 58. *Prof Exp:* Scientist, Univ Tex, 58; sr physicist, Lawrence Radiation Lab, 58-61. *Concurrent Pos:* Cost free expert, Assigned Int Atomic Energy Agency, Vienna, Austria, 79 & 84-86. *Res:* Positron annihilation and positronium formation in organic liquids; high speed electronics instrumentation directed toward atomic weapons testing; nondestructive assay instrumentation for safeguarding special nuclear material. *Mailing Add:* Los Alamos Sci Lab PO Box 1553 Los Alamos NM 87545

HATCHER, HERBERT JOHN, BIOCHEMISTRY, ORGANIC CHEMISTRY. *Current Pos:* CONSULT, 90- *Personal Data:* b Minneapolis, Minn, Dec 18, 26; m 52, 86, Louise Fritsche; c Dennis M, Steven C, Roger D, Mark A, Susan D & Laura J. *Educ:* Univ Minn, BA, 53, MS, 64, PhD(microbiol), 66. *Prof Exp:* Asst microbiologist, Glen Lake Sanatorium, Minneapolis, Minn, 53-56; microbiologist, Vet Admin Hosp, Wilmington, Del, 56-57; Smith Kline & French Labs, 57-61 & Clinton Corn Processing Co Div, Stand Brands, Inc, Iowa, 66-67; microbiologist, Econ Lab, Inc, 67-73, mgr int prod develop, 73-77, scientist, 77-78, mgr, Fermentation Res, 80-84; sr res scientist, EG&G, Idaho, 84-90; co-owner, B/CG Consult Serv, Inc, 90-91. *Res:* Production of microbiological products, such as enzymes, organic acids and antibiotics; physiological studies on microorganisms; detergents; pulp and paper germicides; interaction of microorganisms with petroleum using gas chromatography/mass spectroscopy analytical techniques. *Mailing Add:* 13761 Horizon View Rd McCall ID 83638

HATCHER, ROBERT DEAN, JR, STRUCTURAL GEOLOGY & TECTONICS, GEOLOGY OF RADIOACTIVE WASTE MANAGEMENT. *Current Pos:* DISTINGUISHED SCIENTIST, OAK RIDGE NAT LAB, UNIV TENN, 86- *Personal Data:* b Madison, Tenn, Oct 22, 40; m 65; c 2. *Educ:* Vanderbilt Univ, BA, 61, MS, 62; Univ Tenn, PhD(geol), 65. *Honors & Awards:* Distinguished Serv Award, Geol Soc Am, 88. *Prof Exp:* Geologist, Humble Oil & Ref Co, 65-66; from asst prof to prof geol, Clemson Univ, 66-78; prof, Fla State Univ, 78-80 & Univ SC, 80-86. *Concurrent Pos:* Ed, Geol Soc Am Bull, 81-88. *Mem:* AAAS; Geol Soc Am (pres, 93); Am Geophys Union; Geol Asn Can; Am Asn Petrol Geologists; Sigma Xi; Am Geol Inst (pres, 96). *Res:* Structural geology; regional tectonics; regional geophysics; stratigraphy in medium to high grade metamorphic rocks; evolution of mountain chains; radioactive waste management; engineering geology. *Mailing Add:* Dept Geol Sci Univ Tenn Knoxville TN 37996-1410. *Fax:* 423-974-9326; *E-Mail:* bobmap@utk.edu

HATCHER, ROBERT DOUGLAS, SOLID STATE PHYSICS. *Current Pos:* RETIRED. *Personal Data:* b St John's, Nfld, June 26, 24; nat US; m 51, Helen Schober; c Robert, Brian, Peter & Christopher. *Educ:* Dalhousie Univ, BSc, 45, MSc, 47; Yale Univ, MS, 48, PhD(physics), 49. *Prof Exp:* From instr to assoc prof physics, NY Univ, 49-62; prof physics, Queen's Col, NY, 62-91. *Concurrent Pos:* Vis res assoc, Brookhaven Nat Labs, 57-58, consult, 58-; vis res assoc, Atomic Energy Res Estab, Harwell, Eng, 69-70; guest scientist, Kernforschungsanlage, Julich, WGer, 76-77, Univ Munich, 83, Univ Trento, 84 & Univ Amsterdam, 84. *Mem:* Fel Am Inst Physics. *Res:* Proton-proton scattering; relativistic equations of elementary particles; echelette diffraction gratings; far infra properties of alkali halides; defects in alkali halide crystals, ionic crystals, metals and superconductors. *Mailing Add:* 8 Winchester Lane Huntington NY 11743. *E-Mail:* hatcher@bnl.gov

HATCHER, VICTOR BERNARD, BIOCHEMISTRY, CELL BIOLOGY. *Current Pos:* from asst prof to assoc prof, 73-88, PROF, ALBERT EINSTEIN COL MED, 88-, PROF BIOCHEM, 91- *Personal Data:* b Ormstown, Que, Apr 1, 43; m 66; c 2. *Educ:* Bishop's Univ, BSc, 64; McGill Univ, MSc, 66, PhD(biochem), 69. *Prof Exp:* Res asst immunol, Univ Helsinki, 69-70; res assoc biol chem, Harvard Med Sch, Mass Gen Hosp, 70-73. *Mem:* Am Fedn Clin Res; Harvey Soc; NY Acad Sci; Soc Complex Carbohydrates; Sigma Xi; Fedn Am Soc Exp Biol. *Res:* Structure and function of human endothelial cells; bacterial interaction with human endothelial cells. *Mailing Add:* Albert Einstein Col Med 111 E 210th St Bronx NY 10467-2401. *Fax:* 718-547-2626; *E-Mail:* hatcher@aecom.yu.edu

HATCHER, WILLIAM JULIAN, JR, CHEMICAL ENGINEERING. *Current Pos:* RETIRED. *Personal Data:* b Augusta, Ga, July 21, 35; m 58, 85; c 3. *Educ:* Ga Inst Technol, BChE, 57; La State Univ, Baton Rouge, MSChE, 64, PhD(chem eng), 68. *Prof Exp:* Res engr, Esso Res Labs, Humble Oil & Ref Co, 60-66, sr res engr, 68-69; res assoc chem eng, La State Univ, Baton Rouge, 66-68; from asst prof to prof chem eng, Univ Ala, Tuscaloosa, 69-76, head dept, 73-83, actg dean, Col Eng, 81-83, actg head, Dept Comput Sci, 90- *Concurrent Pos:* Prof engr, State Ala, 71-; chmn, State Hazardous Waste Adv Comt, 78-82; adj fac, USMC Command Staff Col, 78-84. *Mem:* Am Inst Chem Engrs; Am Inst Chemists. *Res:* Chemical reactor design; chemical kinetics; transport phenomena; catalysis. *Mailing Add:* 6 Buena Vista Tuscaloosa AL 35404

HATCHER, WILLIAM S, MATHEMATICAL LOGIC. *Current Pos:* assoc prof, 68-72, PROF MATH, LAVAL UNIV, 72- *Personal Data:* b Charlotte, NC, Sept 20, 35; m 59; c 3. *Educ:* Vanderbilt Univ, BA, 57, MAT, 58; Univ Neuchatel, Dr es Sc(math), 64. *Prof Exp:* Res assoc, Univ Neuchatel, 61-64, prof charge de cours, 65; assoc prof math, Univ Toledo, 65-68. *Concurrent Pos:* Invited prof EPFL, Lausanne, Switz, 72-73. *Mem:* Asn Symbolic Logic; Am Math Soc; Math Asn Am. *Res:* Universal algebra; category theory; logic; computer science. *Mailing Add:* Univ Laval Quebec PQ G1K 7P4 Can

HATCHETT, JIMMY HOWELL, ENTOMOLOGY. *Current Pos:* MEM STAFF, DEPT ENTOM, KANS STATE UNIV, 75- *Personal Data:* b Mangum, Okla, June 2, 35; m 57; c 2. *Educ:* Okla State Univ, BS, 59, MS, 61; Purdue Univ, PhD(entom), 69. *Prof Exp:* Res entomologist, Agr Res Serv, USDA, 61-81. *Mem:* Entom Soc Am; Am Soc Agron; Sigma Xi. *Res:* Development of wheat varieties resistant to the Hessian fly; genetics of Hessian fly biotypes; biology, ecology and control of wheat insects. *Mailing Add:* 1509 Highland Dr Manhattan KS 66503

HATEFI, YOUSSEF, BIOCHEMISTRY. *Current Pos:* PROF IN RESIDENCE BIOCHEM, UNIV CALIF, SAN DIEGO, 67- *Personal Data:* b Tehran, Iran, Aug 9, 29; m 61; c 2. *Educ:* Davis & Elkins Col, BSc, 52; Univ Wash, PhD(biochem), 56. *Honors & Awards:* Sci Medal Honor, Ministry of Educ, Iran, 52. *Prof Exp:* Asst prof biochem, Inst Enzyme Res, Univ Wis, 59-61; assoc prof & head dept, Pahlavi Univ, Iran, 61-63, prof, provost & dept chancellor, 64-66. *Concurrent Pos:* Assoc mem, Scripps Clin & Res Found, 63-64 & 66-67, mem, 67-; vis prof, Sch Med, Univ Calif, San Francisco, 66, & Univ Wash, 69; ed, Arch Biochem & Biophys, 69-74; adv ed, Bioenergetics, 70-; vis prof, Univ Stockholm, 71. *Mem:* Am Soc Biol Chem; Biophys Soc; Am Chem Soc. *Res:* One-carbon metabolism; electron transport; oxidative phosphorylation; structure and function of biological membranes; mechanisms of enzyme action; water structure in biology. *Mailing Add:* Div Biochem Dept Molecular & Exp Med Scripps Res Inst 10550 N Torrey Pines Rd La Jolla CA 92037-1092. *Fax:* 619-784-2054

HATFIELD, CRAIG, GEOLOGY. *Current Pos:* From asst prof to assoc prof, 64-74, PROF GEOL, UNIV TOLEDO, 74- *Personal Data:* b Greenfield, Ind, Jan 24, 35; m 62. *Educ:* Univ Ind, BS, 57, MA, 61, PhD(geol), 64. *Res:* Richmondian stratigraphy and paleoecology in Indiana and Kentucky; upper Cretaceous stratigraphy and paleoecology in Kansas; Devonian stratigraphy in Michigan and Ohio. *Mailing Add:* Dept Geol Univ Toledo 2801 W Bancroft St Toledo OH 43606-3328

HATFIELD, DOLPH LEE, MOLECULAR BIOLOGY. *Current Pos:* RES BIOLOGIST, NAT CANCER INST, 68- *Personal Data:* b El Paso, Tex, Oct 3, 37; m 58, 83; c 3. *Educ:* Univ Tex, BA, 58, MA, 60, PhD(biol, Chem), 62. *Prof Exp:* Fel protein chem, Duke Univ, 62-64; Am Cancer Soc fel protein synthesis, NIH, 64-66; Nat Cancer Inst spec fel bact genetics, Pasteur Inst, Paris, 66-67. *Concurrent Pos:* USPHS fel, 63. *Mem:* Am Soc Biol Chem. *Res:* Transcriptional and translational control mechanisms of protein biosynthesis. *Mailing Add:* Nat Cancer Inst NIH Bldg 37 Rm 3C23 Bethesda MD 20892-4255. *Fax:* 301-496-0734

HATFIELD, EFTON EVERETT, ANIMAL NUTRITION, PHYSIOLOGY. *Current Pos:* from instr to assoc prof, 54-70, prof, 70-78, EMER PROF ANIMAL SCI, UNIV ILL, URBANA, 78- *Personal Data:* b Mindenmines, Mo, Jan 25, 19; m 42; c 3. *Educ:* Univ Ark, BS, 42; Okla Agr & Mech Col, MS, 49; Univ Ill, PhD(nutrit), 55. *Prof Exp:* Instr animal indust, Univ Ark, 46-47; asst prof animal husb, Panhandle Agr & Mech Col, 49-51. *Concurrent Pos:* Res partic, Oak Ridge Inst Nuclear Studies, 62. *Mem:* AAAS; Am Soc Animal Sci; Poultry Sci Asn; Am Inst Nutrit; Am Dairy Sci Asn. *Res:* Nonprotein nitrogen in animal nutrition; energy-protein relationships; vitamin and mineral nutriton; effect of antibiotics and certain drugs on nutrition and health; amino acid nutrition of ruminants. *Mailing Add:* 2015 Oak Hill Springdale AR 72764

HATFIELD, G WESLEY, BIOCHEMISTRY, MICROBIOLOGY. *Current Pos:* From asst prof to assoc prof, 70-78, PROF MICROBIOL, COL MED, UNIV CALIF, IRVINE, 78-, DIR, GENE RES & BIOTECHNOL PROG, 83- *Personal Data:* b Avant, Okla, Aug 2, 40; m 59; c 2. *Educ:* Univ Calif, Santa Barbara, BS, 64; Purdue Univ, PhD(molecular biol), 68. *Honors & Awards:* Eli Lilly Res Award Microbiol & Immunol, Am Soc Microbiol, 75. *Concurrent Pos:* NIH fel, Duke Univ, 68-70; Am Cancer Soc, NIH & NSF grants, Univ Calif, Irvine, 70-; USPHS career develop award, 71-76; IPA vis scientist, Lab Biochem, Nat Cancer Inst, 80-81; founder, dir, vpres res & chief scientist, Am Biogenetics Corp, Irvine, Calif, 83- *Mem:* AAAS; Am Soc Microbiol; Soc Exp Biol & Med. *Res:* Molecular mechanisms of biological control systems; interrelationships of tRNA and gene expression in bacteria and cultured animal cells; recombinant DNA and gene cloning; biotechnology. *Mailing Add:* Dept Microbiol B240 Med Sci I Univ Calif Col Med Irvine CA 92717-4025. *Fax:* 714-856-8598

HATFIELD, JERRY LEE, ENVIRONMENTAL PHYSICS, SOIL-PLANT-ATMOSPHERE INTERACTIONS. *Current Pos:* vis scientist, Water Conserv Lab, USDA-Agr Res Serv, 82, res plant physiologist, 83-86, res leader, 85-89, LAB DIR, NAT SOIL TILTH LAB, USDA-AGR RES SERV, AMES, IOWA, 89- *Personal Data:* b Wamego, Kans, May 1, 49; m 68, Patricia J Reigle; c Mark E & Andrew J. *Educ:* Kans State Univ, BS, 71; Univ Ky, MS, 72; Iowa State Univ, PhD(agr climat), 75. *Prof Exp:* From asst prof to assoc prof biometeorol, Univ Calif, 75-83. *Concurrent Pos:* Prin investr, grants, USDA, NASA, Dept Energy, NSF & Off Water Res & Technol, 76-; chmn, Div A-3, Am Soc Agron, 80 & Prog Comt, Agr & Forest Meteorol Soc, 81; tech ed, Agron J, Am Soc Agron, 81-89, ed, 90-; ed, Advan Soil Sci, 90- & Sustainable Agr Systs, 94. *Mem:* Fel Am Soc Agron; Crop Sci Soc Am; fel Soil Sci Soc Am; Am Meteorol Soc; Am Geophys Union; hon mem Indian Agrometeorol Soc. *Res:* Quantification of the water use rates by agricultural systems and the development of management techniques that will enhance water availability and reduce environmental impact. *Mailing Add:* 2702 Pierce Ave Ames IA 50010

HATFIELD, JOHN DEMPSEY, PHYSICAL CHEMISTRY, APPLIED MATHEMATICS. *Current Pos:* CONSULT, 81- *Personal Data:* b Sneedville, Tenn, Aug 18, 19; m 43, Mary W Hollingsworth; c Betty, Mary W, John & Kemper. *Educ:* Univ Tenn, BA, 38, MS, 39; Purdue Univ, PhD(agr chem), 42. *Honors & Awards:* Charles H Stone Award, 77. *Prof Exp:* Control chemist, E I du Pont de Nemours & Co, 39; asst animal nutrit, Purdue Univ, 40-41, asst chemist, 41-42; res chemist, Tenn Valley Authority, 43-81. *Mem:* Am Chem Soc. *Res:* Thermodynamics of solutions; diffusion; electrolytic equilibria; complexes in solution; polyphosphate chemistry; corrosion; design and analysis of tests; statistics and regression analysis; sulfur dioxide chemistry. *Mailing Add:* 1224 Sorrento Rd Florence AL 35630-5934

HATFIELD, LYNN LAMAR, INSULATORS, PULSED POWER PHYSICS. *Current Pos:* from asst prof to assoc prof, 68-86, PROF PHYSICS, TEX TECH UNIV, 86-, DIR ENG PHYSICS, 79- *Personal Data:* b Kansas City, Mo, July 6, 37; m 56; c 3. *Educ:* Ark Polytech Col, BS, 60; Univ Ark, MS, 64, PhD(physics), 66. *Prof Exp:* Instr physics, Little Rock Univ, 60-62; res assoc, Rice Univ, 66-68. *Mem:* Am Phys Soc; Inst Elec & Electronics Engrs; Dielectrics & Elec Insulation Soc. *Res:* Atomic physics applied to pulsed power; surface effects on insulators and metals used in spark gaps; control of spark gaps and discharges used as switches in high voltage systems. *Mailing Add:* Dept Physics Tex Tech Univ PO Box 41051 Lubbock TX 79409-1051. *Fax:* 806-742-1281

HATFIELD, MARCUS RANKIN, electrochemistry; deceased, see previous edition for last biography

HATFIELD, WILLIAM E, inorganic chemistry; deceased, see previous edition for last biography

HATHAWAY, BRUCE A, ORGANIC NON-LINEAR OPTICAL MATERIALS, STRUCTURE ACTIVITY RELATIONSHIPS OF PHARMACEUTICALS. *Current Pos:* ASSOC PROF CHEM, SOUTHEAST MO STATE UNIV, 88- *Personal Data:* b San Diego, Calif, Oct 2, 54; m 81, Ruth Ann Schmidt. *Educ:* Univ Tex, Austin, BS, 76; Purdue Univ, PhD(med chem), 80. *Prof Exp:* Postdoctoral res asst, Pomono Col, 80-82; asst prof chem, Southeast Mo State Univ, 82-88. *Concurrent Pos:* Jove res fel, Marshall Space Flight Ctr, NASA, 93. *Mem:* Am Chem Soc. *Res:* Preparation of novel organic non-linear optical materials and analgesic compounds; design of organic laboratory experiments which promote critical thinking and reasoning. *Mailing Add:* 1810 Georgia Cape Girardeau MO 63701

HATHAWAY, CHARLES EDWARD, PHYSICS. *Current Pos:* CHANCELLOR, UNIV ARK, 95- *Personal Data:* b Corpus Christi, Tex, Feb 29, 36; m 75; c 3. *Educ:* Tex A&M Univ, BS, 58; Univ Okla, PhD(physics), 65. *Prof Exp:* Jr prof physicist, US Naval Ord Test Sta, 58-59; res asst physics, Res Inst, Univ Okla, 59-65; from asst prof to prof physics, Kans State Univ, 66-81, head dept, 71-81; dean sci & math, Univ Tex, San Antonio, 81-86; vpres acad affairs, Wright State Univ, 86-95. *Concurrent Pos:* Dir, Moiser Inc. *Mem:* Am Phys Soc; Optical Soc Am; AAAS; Am Asn Physics Teachers. *Res:* Light scattering in gases, liquids and solids; infrared spectroscopy; lattice dynamics; physics education. *Mailing Add:* 2801 University Little Rock AR 72204

HATHAWAY, DAVID HENRY, GEOPHYSICAL FLUID DYNAMICS. *Current Pos:* SCIENTIST, MARSHALL SPACE FLIGHT CTR, NASA, 84- *Personal Data:* b Bangor, Maine, Aug 29, 51; m 73, Janet Baril; c Adam & Kimberly. *Educ:* Univ Mass, Amherst, BS, 73; Univ Colo, Boulder, MS, 75, PhD(astrophys), 79. *Prof Exp:* Teaching asst physics, Univ Colo, Boulder, 73-75; res asst, Sacramento Peak Observ, 75, res assoc, 81-82; res asst, Lab Atmospheric & Space Physics, 75-76 & Dept Astrogeophys, Univ Colo, 76-79; fel, Advan Study Prog, Nat Ctr Atmospheric Res, 79-81; asst astron, Nat Solar Observ, 82-84. *Mem:* Am Astron Soc; Int Astron Union; Sigma Xi. *Res:* Fluid flows in the sun, stars and planets, including small scale turbulence, large scale convection, global circulation and magnetohydrodynamical dynamos. *Mailing Add:* 1903 Helmsdale Circle SE Huntsville AL 35803-1765. *Fax:* 205-544-5862; *E-Mail:* hathaway@ssl.msfc.nasa.gov

HATHAWAY, DAVID ROGER, MEDICAL EDUCATION. *Current Pos:* EXEC DIR, CARDIOVASC PHARMACOL, BRISTOL MYERS SQUIBB PHARMACEUT RES INST. *Personal Data:* b Lafayette, Ind, Jan 8, 48; m 74, Elaine M Green; c Julia E & Alison S. *Educ:* Ind Univ, AB, 70, MD, 75; Am Bd Internal Med, dipl. *Prof Exp:* Intern, Ind Univ Med Ctr, 75-76, resident, 76-77, chief resident, 79-80, from asst prof to prof, 80; chief, Cardiovasc Div & dir, Krannert Inst Cardiol, 90- *Concurrent Pos:* Clin asst, Nat Heart Lung & Blood Inst, NIH, Bethesda, 76-77; lt comdr, USPHS, 77-79. *Mem:* Fel Am Col Cardiol; Am Fedn Clin Res (pres, 87-88); Am Soc Clin Invest; Asn Am Physicians (secy, 91); Asn Univ Cardiologists. *Res:* Patents for composition and method for delivery of drugs; methods for preventing restenosis following reconfiguration of body vessels. *Mailing Add:* Bristol Myers Squibb Pharmaceut Res Inst PO Box 4000 Princeton NJ 08543-4000

HATHAWAY, GARY MICHAEL, purification of immunoglobulins, for more information see previous edition

HATHAWAY, ROBERT J, CARBOHYDRATE CHEMISTRY, BIOCHEMISTRY. *Current Pos:* RETIRED. *Personal Data:* b Glendive, Mont, Dec 2, 21; m 45; c 6. *Educ:* Univ Ill, BS, 43; Mich State Univ, PhD(chem), 51. *Prof Exp:* Chemist res & develop, Abbott Lab, 43-46 & Miles Lab, 51-57; sr res chemist, A E Staley Co, 57-83. *Mem:* Am Chem Soc; Am Asn Cereal Chemists; Tech Asn Pulp & Paper Indust; Sigma Xi; AAAS. *Res:* Organic reactions of starch; rheology; application to papermaking, coating, textiles, detergents and other specialties; chemicals from saccharides, cellulose and renewable resources through organic and enzymatic reactions. *Mailing Add:* 2515 Ill Circle Decatur IL 62526

HATHAWAY, RONALD PHILIP, PARASITOLOGY. *Current Pos:* asst prof, 70-78, ASSOC PROF BIOL, COLO COL, 78- *Personal Data:* b Denver, Colo, Aug 22, 43; m 63; c 2. *Educ:* Ft Lewis Col, BS, 65; Univ NMex, MS, 66; Univ Ill, Urbana, PhD(zool), 70. *Prof Exp:* Asst biol, Univ NMex, 64-66; asst zool, Univ Ill, 66-70. *Mem:* Am Soc Parasitol. *Res:* Ultrastructural studies of parasitic helminthes; reproductive physiology of trematodes. *Mailing Add:* Dept Biol Colo Col 14 E Cachela Poudre Colorado Springs CO 80903-3243

HATHAWAY, SUSAN JANE, ORGANIC CHEMISTRY. *Current Pos:* CHEMIST, EASTMAN GELATINE CORP. *Personal Data:* b Potsdam, NY, Aug 8, 50. *Educ:* State Univ NY, Potsdam, BA, 71, MA, 73; Univ NH, PhD(chem), 78. *Prof Exp:* Asst prof chem, Gettysburg Col, 78-; staff mem, Gen Elec Res & Develop Ctr, Schenectady, NY. *Mem:* Am Chem Soc. *Res:* Stereochemistry; asymmetric synthesis, in particular asymmetric homogeneous hydrogenation. *Mailing Add:* Eastman Gelatine Corp 227 Washington St Peabody MA 01960-6973

HATHAWAY, WILFRED BOSTOCK, biology, taxonomic botany; deceased, see previous edition for last biography

HATHCOCK, BOBBY RAY, AGRICULTURE, PLANT BREEDING. *Current Pos:* ASST PROF AGRON, UNIV TENN, MARTIN, 71- *Personal Data:* b Ripley, Tenn, Aug 29, 42; m 64; c 2. *Educ:* Univ Tenn, Martin, BS, 64; Univ Tenn, Knoxville, MS, 66; Tex A&M Univ, PhD(plant breeding), 70. *Mem:* Am Soc Agron; Soil Conserv Soc Am; Crop Sci Soc Am. *Res:* Grain and forage crops. *Mailing Add:* Dept Agr Univ Tenn Martin TN 38238-0001

HATHCOCK, JOHN NATHAN, NUTRITION, TOXICOLOGY. *Current Pos:* chief, Exp Nutrit Br, 85-92, mgr, Diet-Toxicity Interactions Prog, 87-92, DIR, DIV SCI & APPL TECHNOL, FOOD & DRUG ADMIN, 92- *Personal Data:* b Marshville, NC, Aug 13, 40; m 59, Susan Maske; c 2. *Educ:* NC State Univ, BS, 62, MS, 64; Cornell Univ, PhD(animal nutrit), 67. *Prof Exp:* Res assoc biochem, Sch Med, St Louis Univ, 67-69; asst prof, Cornell Univ-Univ Philippines Exchange Prog, 69-71; asst prof biochem & biophys, Iowa State Univ, 71-72; asst prof nutrit, Div Biol Sci, Pa State Univ, 72-73; from assoc prof to prof, Iowa State Univ, 73-85. *Mem:* Am Inst Nutrit; Soc Toxicol; Am Soc Clin Nutrit; Inst Food Technologists. *Res:* Nutritional toxicology; nutrient toxicities; safety of natural anticarcinogens in foods; diet-cancer relationships. *Mailing Add:* Nutrit & Regulatory Sci 1300 19th St NW Washington DC 20036-1609. *Fax:* 202-872-9594; *E-Mail:* jxh@fdacfsan.bitnet

HATHCOX, KYLE LEE, SOLID STATE PHYSICS. *Current Pos:* PROF PHYSICS, UNION UNIV, 92- *Personal Data:* b Gilmer, Tex, Feb 22, 43; m 66, Sandra; c Susie, Alan & Paton. *Educ:* NTex State Univ, BS, 65, MS, 68, PhD(physics), 72. *Prof Exp:* Instr physics, NTex State Univ, 72-73; instr physics & math, Tarrant Community Col, 72-74; assoc prof physics, Union Univ, 74-88, chmn, Chem/Physics Dept, 80-88; prof & chmn, Sci Math Div, Gordon Col, 88-91. *Mem:* Am Asn Physics Teachers; Am Chem Soc; Nat Sci Teachers Asn. *Res:* Solid state, transport properties and stress studies on III-V materials. *Mailing Add:* Physics Dept Union Univ Jackson TN 38305. *Fax:* 901-661-5175; *E-Mail:* khathcox@buster.uv.edu

HATHEWAY, ALLEN WAYNE, HAZARDOUS WASTE CLEANUP, ENGINEERING GEOLOGY. *Current Pos:* PROF GEOL ENG, UNIV MO, ROLLA, 81- *Personal Data:* b Los Angeles, Calif, Sept 30, 37; m 90, Diane Rydel Anderson; c Shannon (Younger), Brian & Steven. *Educ:* Univ Calif, Los Angeles, AB, 61; Univ Ariz, MS, 66, PhD(geol eng), 71. *Honors & Awards:* Daniel W Mead Prize, Am Soc Civil Engrs, 75; E B Burwell Mem Award, Geol Soc Am, 81; F T Johnston Award, Asn Eng Geologists, 95. *Prof Exp:* Res assoc, Lunar & Planetary Lab, Univ Ariz, 66-69; staff engr, Law Eng Co, Los Angeles, 69-71; proj engr, Geotech Br, US Forest Serv, 71-72; sr proj engr, Woodward-Clyde Consult, 72-74; proj geologist, Shannon & Wilson, Inc, San Francisco, 74-76; vpres & chief engr, Haley & Aldrich, Inc, Cambridge, Mass, 76-81. *Concurrent Pos:* Colonel, CEngrs, US Army Res, 61-91; adj asst prof civil eng, Univ Southern Calif, 71-74; adj assoc prof geol, Boston Univ, 79-81; chmn, Eng Geol Div, Geol Soc Am, 80; US Nat Comt, Eng Geol, 80-81 & 85-86, Tunneling Technol, 83-86; chmn, Eng Geol Div, Geol Soc Am, 80; mem, US Nat Res Coun Bd Earth Sci, 87-90. *Mem:* Fel Geol Soc Am; Asn Eng Geologists (pres, 85); fel Am Soc Civil Engrs; Am Inst Mining, Metal & Petrol Engrs; Soc Am Mil Engrs; Am Geophys Union. *Res:* Waste management facility siting and design; remediation of treatment of uncontrolled waste disposal sites; remediation of former manufactured gas plants; seismic risk assessment; tunnels and underground construction; urban geology in reconstruction of cities. *Mailing Add:* 10256 Stoltz Dr Rolla MO 65401-0000. *Fax:* 573-341-6935; *E-Mail:* hatheway@umr.edu

HATHEWAY, CHARLES LOUIS, MICROBIOLOGY, PUBLIC HEALTH. *Current Pos:* adj assoc prof, Dept Parasitol & Lab Pract, 80-88, RES CHIEF, BOTULISM LAB, DIV BACT DIS, CTR INFECT DIS, CTRS DIS CONTROL, UNIV NC, 75- *Personal Data:* b Barberton, Ohio, July 27, 32; m 60; c 2. *Educ:* Ohio State Univ, BSc, 57, MSc, 61, PhD(dairy sci & immunogenetics), 64. *Prof Exp:* Res assoc immunochem, Evanston Hosp, Ill, 64-65; res supvr blood derivatives res, div labs, Mich Dept Health, 65-67; asst prof vet surg & med, Mich State Univ, 67-69; biochemist blood vaccines, Mich Dept Pub Health, 69-75. *Concurrent Pos:* Training fel, Med Sch, Northwestern Univ, 64-65. *Mem:* Am Soc Microbiol; Sigma Xi. *Res:* Genetics, serology and immunochemistry of blood group antigens; biologic products from blood; cancer research; bacterial vaccines and toxoids; botulism, clostridial foodborne illnesses; diagnostic procedures; epidemiology. *Mailing Add:* 1880 NE Mt Royal Dr Atlanta GA 30329-2515

HATHEWAY, RICHARD BRACKETT, GEOLOGY, PETROLOGY. *Current Pos:* from asst prof to assoc prof, 68-87, CHAIR, DEPT GEOL SCI, STATE UNIV COL, GENESEO, 87- *Personal Data:* b Melrose, Mass, Oct 27, 39; m 63; c 3. *Educ:* Bowdoin Col, BA, 61; Univ Mo, Columbia, MA, 64; Cornell Univ, PhD(geol), 69. *Prof Exp:* Teaching asst geol, Univ Mo, Columbia, 62-64 & Cornell Univ, 64-68. *Concurrent Pos:* NSF grant, Basin & Range Field Conf, 69; State Univ NY Res Found grant, 70-71 & 74; NATO Advan Study Inst Grant, 72. *Mem:* Mineral Soc Am; Sigma Xi; Geol Soc Am. *Res:* Igneous and metamorphic petrology including origin and significance of mylonites. *Mailing Add:* Dept Geol Sci State Univ NY Col 223 Green Bldg Geneseo NY 14454

HATHEWAY, WILLIAM HOWELL, BOTANY. *Current Pos:* assoc prof, 69-75, PROF FORESTRY, UNIV WASH, 75- *Personal Data:* b Hartford, Conn, Nov 28, 23; m 53; c 3. *Educ:* Chicago Univ, BS, 48, MS, 51; Harvard Univ, PhD(biol), 56. *Prof Exp:* Botanist, Atoll Res Proj, Pac Sci Bd, Nat Res Coun, 52; asst statistician, Field Staff Agr, Rockefeller Found, Colombia, 56-60, assoc statistician, Mex, 61-64; exec dir, Orgn Trop Studies, Costa Rica, 64-65; botanist, Trop Sci Ctr, 65-68. *Concurrent Pos:* Collab bot, Smithsonian Inst, 65- *Mem:* AAAS; Ecol Soc; Soc Study Evolution; Sigma Xi. *Res:* Quantitative ecology; tropical forestry; economic botany. *Mailing Add:* 7615 E Mercer Way Mercer Island WA 98040-5822

HATSELL, CHARLES PROCTOR, ELECTRICAL ENGINEERING. *Current Pos:* CHIEF SCIENTIST, AEROSPACE MED DIRECTORATE, ARMSTRONG LAB, BROOKS AFB, TEX. *Personal Data:* b Alexandria, Va, Sept 18, 44; m 67. *Educ:* Va Polytech Inst, BS, 67; Duke Univ, MS, 68, PhD(elec eng), 70. *Prof Exp:* Res asst, Adaptive Signal Detection Lab, Duke Univ, 69-70, res assoc, 70; asst prof elec eng, USAF Inst Technol, 70-76; res aerospace med physician, Med Crew Technol, USAF Sch Aerospace, 76-; chief med, USAF Aeromed Res Lab, Wright Patterson AFB, Dayton, Ohio. *Mem:* Inst Elec & Electronics Engrs. *Res:* Signal processing, information theory; biomedical sciences. *Mailing Add:* Biodynamic Res Corp 9901 IH 10 W Suite 1000 San Antonio TX 78230

HATSOPOULOS, GEORGE NICHOLAS, THERMODYNAMICS. *Current Pos:* pres, 58-96, FOUNDER & CHIEF EXEC OFFICER, THERMO ELECTRON CORP, 56- *Personal Data:* b Athens, Greece, Jan 7, 27; US citizen; m 59, Daphne; c Nicholas & Marina. *Educ:* Mass Inst Technol, BS, 49, MS, 50, ME, 54, ScD(mech eng), 56. *Hon Degrees:* DSc, NJ Inst Technol, 82, Adelphi Univ, 94; LHD, Univ Lowell, 91. *Honors & Awards:* Golden Plate Award, Acad Am Achievement, 61; Award Appreciation, Int Inst Energy Conserv, 89; John Frite Medal, 96; Nat Pub Serv Award, Int Hellenic Inst, 96; Heinz Award, 96. *Prof Exp:* From instr to assoc prof mech eng, Mass Inst Technol, 54-62, sr lectr, 62-90. *Concurrent Pos:* Bd dirs, Tappan Co, 67-80; US rep to liaison group on thermionic elec power generation, Europ Nuclear Energy Agency, 66-; dir, Rebuild Am, 88-90, Mass Ctr Excellence, 88-91, Inst Res Econ of Taxcition, 90-92, Bolt Beranek & Newman Inc, 90-96; trustee, Boston Mus Sci, 90-93, overseer, 93-96. *Mem:* Fel Nat Acad Eng; fel Inst Elec & Electronics Engrs; fel Am Inst Aeronaut & Astronaut; fel Am Soc Mech Engrs; fel Am Acad Arts & Sci; Am Soc Eng Educ; Sigma Xi. *Res:* Thermodynamics; direct energy conversion; author of over 60 technical publications; granted 5 patents on direct energy conversion. *Mailing Add:* Thermo Electron Corp 81 Wyman St PO Box 9046 Waltham MA 02254-9046

HATTAN, DAVID GENE, PHARMACOLOGY, TOXICOLOGY. *Current Pos:* TOXICOLOGIST FOOD ADDITIVES, FOOD & DRUG ADMIN, FOOD ADDITIVES EVAL, BUR FOODS, 78- *Personal Data:* b Independence, Kans, Feb 21, 42; m 67; c 1. *Educ:* Univ Kans, BS, 65; Ohio State Univ, PhD(pharmacol), 73. *Prof Exp:* Pharmacist, Indian Health Div, USPHS, 65-68; asst prof pharmacol, Sch Pharm, Univ Md, 73-78. *Mem:* AAAS; Acad Pharmaceut Sci; Am Col Toxicol. *Res:* Behavioral and electrophysiological correlates of alcohol in animals; temperature regulation. *Mailing Add:* 5126 Beaverbrook Rd Columbia MD 21044

HATTEMER, JIMMIE RAY, COMPUTER SCIENCE. *Current Pos:* from asst prof to assoc prof, 66-81, PROF COMPUT SCI, SOUTHERN ILL UNIV, 81- *Personal Data:* b St Louis, Mo, Jan 4, 39; m 60; c 2. *Educ:* Washington Univ, AB, 59, AM, 63, PhD(math), 64. *Prof Exp:* Instr math, Princeton Univ, 64-66. *Mem:* Asn Comput Mach; Inst Elec & Electronics Engrs Comput Soc. *Res:* Local boundary behavior of solutions to certain partial differential equations. *Mailing Add:* Dept Comput Sci Southern Ill Univ Edwardsville IL 62026

HATTEN, BETTY ARLENE, MEDICAL MICROBIOLOGY, IMMUNOLOGY. *Current Pos:* RETIRED. *Personal Data:* b Oxford, Kans, Dec 14, 29. *Educ:* Drury Col, BA, 52; Univ Tex Southwestern Med Sch Dallas, MA, 62, PhD(microbiol), 65. *Prof Exp:* USPHS training grant microbiol, Univ Tex Southwestern Med Sch Dallas, 65-66, from instr to asst prof microbiol, 68-73; asst prof basic health & biol sci, Southwestern Med Ctr, NTex State Univ, 73-80; chair, Dept Clin Lab Sci, Univ Okla, 83-90, assoc prof clin lab sci & dir, Med Technol Prog, Okla City Health Sci Ctr, 80-92. *Concurrent Pos:* Res dir, Med Res Found Tex grant, 67-68; prin investr, Nat Inst Allergy & Infectious Dis grant, 69-72. *Mem:* Am Soc Microbiol. *Res:* Animal reactions to Klebsiella antigens; ultrastructure, viability, filterability, reverting ability, antigenicity, toxicity, and pathogenicity of Brucella L-forms; immune capabilities of bats and their response to bacteriophage X 174; antigenic characterization of the mycoplasmas; age-related and leukemia-related changes in immune capabilities of mice. *Mailing Add:* 608A MaryLee Lane Edmond OK 73034

HATTERSLEY-SMITH, GEOFFREY FRANCIS, TOPONYMY, POLAR HISTORY. *Current Pos:* RETIRED. *Personal Data:* b London, Eng, Apr 22, 23; UK & Can citizen; m 55, Maria Kefallinou; c Kara M & Fiona A. *Educ:* Oxford Univ, MA, 51, DPhil(geol), 56. *Honors & Awards:* Royal Geog Soc Founder's Medal, 66. *Prof Exp:* Base leader glaciol, Falkland Islands Dependencies Surv, 48-50; defence sci staff officer geophys, Defence Res Bd Can, 51-71; head geotech, Defence Res Estab Ottawa, 71-73; prin sci officer, Brit Antarctic Surv, 73-91. *Concurrent Pos:* Mem assoc comt geod & geophys & chmn subcomt glaciers, Nat Res Coun Can, 59-66, mem assoc comt meteorites, 63-73; gov, Arctic Inst NAm, 63-66; secy, Antarctic Place Names Comt, UK, 75-91. *Mem:* Fel Arctic Inst NAm; fel Royal Geog Soc; fel Royal Soc Can. *Res:* Glaciology and glacial history of northern Ellesmere Island, Northwest Territories; toponymy of Antarctic; mountaineering. *Mailing Add:* Crossways Cranbrook TN17 2AG England

HATTIN, DONALD EDWARD, GEOLOGY. *Current Pos:* from asst prof to prof, 54-95, EMER PROF GEOL, IND UNIV, BLOOMINGTON, 95- *Personal Data:* b Cohasset, Mass, Nov 16, 28; m 50, Marjorie Elizabeth Macy; c Sandra Jane, Ronald Scott & Donna Jean. *Educ:* Univ Mass, BS, 50; Univ Kans, MS, 52, PhD(geol), 54. *Prof Exp:* Asst instr geol, Univ Kans, 50-52, instr, 53-54. *Concurrent Pos:* NSF sci fac fel, Univ Reading, 69, Univ Tex, Arlington, 78; grants, NSF, 75-77, 87-90 & Am Chem Soc, 78-80, 84-86; vis prof, Ernst-Moritz-Arndt-Univ, Greifswald, GDR, 85. *Mem:* Geol Soc Am; Soc Econ Paleontologists & Mineralogists; Am Asn Petrol Geologists; Paleont Soc. *Res:* Regional stratigraphy; depositional environments; paleontology of Upper Cretaceous formations in the US Western Interior region; paleoecology; petrology of chalk. *Mailing Add:* Dept Geol Sci Ind Univ Bloomington IN 47405. *E-Mail:* hattin@indiana.edu

HATTIS, DALE B, QUANTITATIVE RISK ASSESSMENT, PHARMACOKINETIC & PHARMACODYNAMIC MODELING. *Current Pos:* RES ASSOC PROF, CTR TECHNOL, ENVIRON & DEVELOP, CLARK UNIV, 90- *Personal Data:* b Santa Monica, Calif, Oct 31, 46; m 80, Kathleen Creed; c 1. *Educ:* Univ Calif, Berkeley, BA, 67; Stanford Univ, PhD(genetics), 74. *Prof Exp:* Sr res assoc, Complex Systs Inst, Case Western Res Univ, 73-74; res assoc, Ctr Policy Alternatives, Mass Inst Technol, 75-81, prin res assoc, Ctr Technol, Policy & Indust Develop, 81-90. *Concurrent Pos:* Vis sr lectr, Prog Social Ecol, Univ Calif, Irvine, 86. *Mem:* Soc Risk Anal; AAAS. *Res:* Quantitative risk assessment for both cancer and non-cancer effects; pharmacokinetic modeling; human interindividual variability, interspecies comparison and Monte Carlo simulation analysis of uncertainties. *Mailing Add:* 20 Wellington St Arlington MA 02174

HATTMAN, STANLEY, MICROBIOLOGY, VIROLOGY. *Current Pos:* from asst prof to assoc prof, 74-81, PROF BIOL, UNIV ROCHESTER, 81- *Personal Data:* b Brooklyn, NY, July 19, 38; m 63; c 3. *Educ:* City Col New York, BS, 60; Mass Inst Technol, PhD(microbiol), 65. *Prof Exp:* Helen Hay Whitney Found fel, 65-68. *Concurrent Pos:* Prin investr, USPHS, 68-71 & 72-91 & Am Cancer Soc, 69-70; Res Career Develop Award, NIH, 72-76. *Mem:* Am Soc Biol Chemists; Am Soc Microbiol. *Res:* Genetics and biochemistry of DNA-modification and restriction; regulation of gene expression. *Mailing Add:* Dept Biol Univ Rochester Wilson Blvd Rochester NY 14627-0001. *Fax:* 716-275-2070

HATTON, GLENN IRWIN, NEUROPHYSIOLOGY, NEUROENDOCRINOLOGY. *Current Pos:* PROF & CHAIR NEUROSCI, UNIV CALIF, RIVERSIDE. *Personal Data:* b Chicago, Ill, Dec 12, 34; m 54, Patricia J Dougherty; c 5. *Educ:* North Cent Col, BA, 60; Univ Ill, MA, 62, PhD(physiol psychol), 64. *Prof Exp:* From asst prof to prof psychol, Mich State Univ, 65-91, prof physiol, 84-91. *Concurrent Pos:* NIH res career develop award, 70-75; prin investr res grants, Nat Inst Neurol, Commun Dis & Stroke, 70-; neurobiol adv panel, NSF, 74-77; dir, Neurosci Prog, Mich State Univ, 78-; assoc ed, Brain Res Bull, 80-; prin investr, 81-; Fogart sr Int fel, 82-83; sr res scholar, Univ Cambridge, UK, 82-83; mem, Neurol Disorders Prog, Proj Rev Comt B, Nat Inst Neurol, Commun Dis & Stroke, 84-88, chmn, 86-88; Jacob Javits neurosci investr award, 86 & 93; Guggenheim fel, Cambridge, UK, 89-90. *Mem:* Soc Neurosci; Am Asn Anatomists; Am Physiol Soc; Soc Gen Physiologists; fel AAAS. *Res:* Neurophysiology, neuroanatomy and immunocytochemistry of neuropeptide-containing cells of the hypothalamus of the brain. *Mailing Add:* Dept Neurosci Univ Calif Riverside CA 92521-0146. *E-Mail:* glenn.hatton@ucr.edu

HATTON, JOHN VICTOR, WOOD PULPING, FOREST PRODUCTS. *Current Pos:* RETIRED. *Personal Data:* b Yorkshire, Eng, Apr 9, 34; m 61, Doreen L Roberts; c Stephen, Paul & Amanda. *Educ:* Oxford Univ, BA, 59, MA & DPhil, 61. *Honors & Awards:* Pulp Manufacture Div Award, Tech Asn Pulp & Paper Indust, 83, Johann Richter Prize, 83; Weldon Medal, Can Pulp & Paper Asn, 90, Douglas Akack Award, 91. *Prof Exp:* Fel chem, Nat Res Coun Can, 61-63; scientist org chem, Domtar Ltd, 64-65; head pulp bleaching pulp & paper, BC Res Coun, 65-67; res scientist fiber prod, Western Forest Prod Lab, 67-80, head, Wood Pulping Sect, 76-80; prin scientist & head, Resource Eval Sect, Paprican, 80-97. *Concurrent Pos:* Consult to pulp & paper indust. *Mem:* Can Pulp & Paper Asn; fel Tech Asn Pulp & Paper Indust; fel Chem Inst Can; Int Union Forest Res Org; Poplar Coun Can. *Res:* Complete tree utilization; chip quality; outside chip storage; process control; fibre resources for conversion to pulp; use of low quality materials in pulping; second-growth forests; forest genetics. *Mailing Add:* 3337 Quesnel Dr Vancouver BC V6S 1Z7 Can

HATTON, THURMAN TIMBROOK, JR, HORTICULTURE, POST HARVEST PLANT PHYSIOLOGY. *Current Pos:* CONSULT, POSTHARVEST PHYSIOL FRUITS & VEGETABLES, 89- *Personal Data:* b Bartow, Fla, Feb 4, 22; m 47, Marilyn Memory; c Mary, Nina, Alexa & Michele. *Educ:* Univ Fla, BS, 43, MS, 49; Wash State Univ, PhD, 53. *Prof Exp:* Asst plant physiol, Univ Fla, 48-49; asst prof hort & chmn dept, Col Agr & Mech Arts, Univ PR, 49-50; instr, Wash State Univ, 50-53; exten hort specialist, NC State Col, 53-55; invests leader mkt qual res, Agr Res Serv, USDA, 55-72, res leader, 72-89. *Concurrent Pos:* Sr horticulturist in chg, Mkt Qual & Transp Res, USDA, 55-64, invests leader, Subtrop & Trop Fruits Invest, 64-68, invests leader, SE Citrus & Veg Invests, 68-72; prof, Fruit Crops Dept, Univ Fla, 72-89. *Mem:* Fel Am Soc Hort Sci (pres); Int Hort Soc; Int Soc Citricult; Sigma Xi; Interam Soc Trop Hort. *Res:* Tropical horticulture and plant physiology; post-harvest studies of fruits and vegetables, particularly maturity, storage, handling and transportation; quarantine treatment research. *Mailing Add:* PO Box 660068 Chuluota FL 32766-0068

HATTORI, TOSHIAKI, NEUROCYTOLOGY. *Current Pos:* ASST PROF, DEPT ANAT, UNIV TORONTO, 78- *Personal Data:* b Japan, Dec 17, 31; m 69; c 1. *Educ:* Kyoto Univ, MS, 59, PhD, 76; Mie Univ, Japan, MD, 67. *Prof Exp:* Instr, Dept Physiol, Fac Med, Mie Univ, 59-62, lectr, 62-67; res assoc biochem, Ore State Univ, 67-70; res assoc neurol sci, Dept Psychiat, Univ BC, 70-78. *Mem:* Sigma Xi; Soc Neurosci; Am Asn Anat; AAAS. *Res:* Functional neuroanatomy of the extrapyramidal system of rodents by combined technique of electron microscopic autoradiography and immunohistochemistry. *Mailing Add:* Dept Anat Med Sci Bldg Univ Toronto Toronto ON M5S 1A8 Can

HATZAKIS, MICHAEL, RESEARCH ADMINISTRATION. *Current Pos:* DIR, MICROELECTRONICS INST DEMOCRITES, GREECE, 88- *Personal Data:* b Charia, Crete, Greece, Jan 1, 28; nat US. *Educ:* NY Univ, BSEE, 64, MSEE, 67. *Honors & Awards:* Cledo Brunetti Award, Inst Elec & Electronics Engrs, 87. *Prof Exp:* Technician, Radio Eng Labs, Long Island City, New York, NY, 58-61; technician, IBM TJ Watson Res Ctr, Yorktown Heights, NY, 61-67, staff mem, 67-76, mgr, 76-88, fel, 88-91. *Concurrent Pos:* Vis prof, Microelectronics Inst, Nat Res Ctr, Athens, Greece. *Mem:* Nat Acad Eng; Inst Elec & Electronics Engrs; Am Vacuum Soc; Electrochem Soc; Mat Res Soc. *Res:* Lithographic material, tools and processes; early development of electron beams for device fabrication; development of polymethyl methacrylate resist; lift-off metallization process; first micron and sub-micron sized bipolar and field effect transistors; photo and electron resists and processes; scanning electron microscopy; author of various publications; granted 19 patents. *Mailing Add:* Microelectronics Inst NCSR Demokritos PO Box 60228s Athens 153-10A Aghia Paraskevi Greece. *Fax:* 301-651-1723

HATZENBUHLER, DOUGLAS ALBERT, pharmaceutical formulation, physical chemistry, for more information see previous edition

HATZIOS, KRITON KLEANTHIS, PLANT PHYSIOLOGY, HERBICIDE TECHNOLOGY. *Current Pos:* from asst prof to assoc prof, 79-88, PROF PLANT PHYSIOL, VA POLYTECH INST & STATE UNIV, 88- *Personal Data:* b Florina, Greece, Aug 6, 49; US citizen; m 79; c 2. *Educ:* Aristotelian Univ, Thessaloniki, Greece, BS, 72; Mich State Univ, MS, 77, PhD(plant physiol), 79. *Honors & Awards:* Res Award, Agr Honor Soc, 85; Outstanding Young Scientist Award, Weed Sci Soc Am, 86, Outstanding Res Award, 94. *Prof Exp:* Res asst plant physiol, Mich State Univ, 76-79. *Mem:* Am Soc Plant Physiologists; AAAS; Weed Sci Soc Am; Am Chem Soc; Am Soc Photobiol; Scand Soc Plant Physiologists. *Res:* Mechanisms of action of herbicides and other plant growth regulators; metabolism of herbicides in higher plants; chemical and genetic manipulation of crop tolerance to herbicides; interactions of herbicides with other agrochemicals. *Mailing Add:* Dept Plant Path Va Tech Blacksburg VA 24061-0330

HAUBEIN, ALBERT HOWARD, organic chemistry; deceased, see previous edition for last biography

HAUBER, JANET ELAINE, MATERIALS COMPATIBILITY. *Current Pos:* Metallurgist, Lawrence Livermore Nat Lab, 70-74, sect leader, 74-76, dep div leader, 76-86, dep assoc dept head, 86-87, ENGR AT LARGE, LAWRENCE LIVERMORE NAT LAB, 87- *Personal Data:* b Milwaukee, Wis, July 21, 37; m 74. *Educ:* Marquette Univ, BS, 65; Stanford Univ, MS, 67, PhD(mat sci), 70. *Mem:* Soc Women Engrs; Nat Asn Female Execs. *Res:* Automation of engineering record retrieval. *Mailing Add:* 3285 Monika Lane Hayward CA 94541

HAUBRICH, DEAN ROBERT, PHARMACOLOGY, NEUROCHEMISTRY. *Current Pos:* DIR PROJ PLANNING & MGT, BRISTOL MYERS SQUIBB, 91- *Personal Data:* b Pittsburgh, Pa, Jan 4, 43; m 64, Margaret Kovac; c Laura & Matthew. *Educ:* Bethany Col, WVa, BS, 64; Purdue Univ, MS, 66, PhD(pharmacol), 69. *Prof Exp:* Res assoc pharmacol toxicol, NIH, 69-71; res investr pharmacol & neurochem, 71-73, sr res investr, Squibb Inst Med Res, 74-76; res fel, Merck Inst Therapeut Res, West Point, Pa, 76-81, sect head neuropsychopharmacol, 81-86; dir pharmacol, Sterling Drug, 86-89; sr dir biol sci, Rhone-Poulanc Rorer, 89-91. *Concurrent Pos:* Vis lectr neurochem, Princeton Univ, 72- *Mem:* Am Soc Pharmacol & Exp Therapeut; Soc Neurosci; AAAS. *Res:* Biochemical mechanisms of drug action; biochemical control of neurotransmitter metabolism; project planning and management. *Mailing Add:* Bristol-Myers Squibb Co 5 Research Pkwy PO Box 5100 Wallingford CT 06492-7660. *Fax:* 203-284-7832; *E-Mail:* dean_r_haubrich@ccmail.bms.com

HAUBRICH, ROBERT RICE, BIOLOGY. *Current Pos:* from asst prof to prof, 62-88, EMER PROF BIOL, DENISON UNIV, 88- *Personal Data:* b Claremont, NH, May 4, 23. *Educ:* Mich State Univ, BS, 49, MS, 52; Univ Fla, PhD(biol, psychol), 57. *Prof Exp:* Asst prof biol, ECarolina Col, 57-61 & Oberlin Col, 61-62. *Mem:* AAAS; Sigma Xi; NY Acad Sci; Int Soc Hist, Philos & Social Studies Biol. *Res:* Relationships among aggression, hierarchical behavior and learning ability in the South African frog; behavior, development and population analysis of the topminnow; conceptual structure of biology. *Mailing Add:* Dept Biol Denison Univ Granville OH 43023

HAUCK, FREDERICK ALEXANDER, NUCLEAR SCIENCE. *Current Pos:* RETIRED. *Personal Data:* b Dec 28, 1894. *Honors & Awards:* Haley Space Flight Award, Am Inst Aeronaut & Astronaut, 89. *Prof Exp:* Chmn bd, Max Wocher & Son Co, 15-37; pres, Transvaal Mining Co, Continental Mineral Processing, 48. *Mailing Add:* 3401 Carew Towers Cincinnati OH 45202

HAUCK, GEORGE F(REDERICK) W(OLFGANG), CIVIL ENGINEERING HISTORY, STRUCTURAL ENGINEERING. *Current Pos:* assoc prof civil eng, 75-88, exec dir, Coord Eng Prog, 91-92, PROF, UNIV MO, COLUMBIA, 88-, DIR, CIVIL ENG DEPT, 91- *Personal Data:* b Kassel, Ger, Sept 7, 32; US citizen; m 56, 74, Susan J Fershee; c 4. *Educ:* Okla State Univ, BArchE, 59, MArchE, 60; Northwestern Univ, PhD(struct eng), 64. *Honors & Awards:* Harry S Truman Award, 86. *Prof Exp:* Res asst soil mech, Okla Exp Sta, 58-59; designer struct eng, Am Bridge Div, US Steel Corp, 59-60; res asst, Northwestern Tech Inst, 60-63; prof civil eng & chmn dept, Tri-State Univ, 63-75. *Mem:* Am Soc Civil Engrs; Am Soc Eng Educ; Soc Hist Tech; Am Soc Testing & Mat. *Res:* Structural mechanics; stability of columns and frames; history of civil engineering; technological history; forensic engineering. *Mailing Add:* 5724 McGee St Kansas City MO 64113

HAUDENSCHILD, CHRISTIAN C, PATHOLOGY, CYTOLOGY. *Current Pos:* from asst prof to assoc prof, 79-82, PROF PATH, SCH MED, BOSTON UNIV, 82- *Personal Data:* b St Gallen, Switz, May 5, 39. *Educ:* Swiss Fed Inst Technol, Zurich, Switz, 59; Univ Basel, Switz, MD, 68; Am Bd Path, cert anat path, 77. *Prof Exp:* Res fel exp med, F Hoffman-LaRoche, Basel, Switz, 68-69, res assoc, 69-72; res assoc surg & path, Children's Hosp Med Ctr, Boston, 73-75; jr res asst path, Boston City Hosp, 74-75, sr res asst, 75-76; assoc pathologist, Malloryt Inst Path, Boston, 77. *Concurrent Pos:* Clin instr path, Harvard Med Sch, 76-80; consult pathologist, Boston Veterans Admin Hosp, 78-; mem, ad hoc study sects, NIH, Nat Heart Lung & Blood Inst, 80-; mem, Coun Arteriosclerosis, prog comt, Am Heart Asn, 83-84; hon consult prof, Fac med, Univ Siena, Italy, 85-; prin invest endothelium, Nat Heart Lung & Blood Inst grant, 79-; fel, Coun Arteriosclerosis, Am Heart Asn. *Mem:* Am Heart Asn; Am Soc Cell Biol; Am Asn Pathologists; Int Acad Path; AAAS; AMA. *Res:* Endothelium: motility and related functions; cardiovascular disease: structure and function of vascular cells in diabetes, hypertension, and vascularization of tumors; pathology; cell biology. *Mailing Add:* Holland Lab Am Red Cross 15601 Crabbs Br Way Rockville MD 20855. *Fax:* 301-738-0879

HAUEISEN, DONALD CARL, OPTICAL PHYSICS, LASERS. *Current Pos:* asst prof, 77-80, ASSOC PROF PHYSICS, PAC LUTHERAN UNIV, 80- *Personal Data:* b Columbus, Ohio, June 14, 45; m 68; c 2. *Educ:* Col Wooster, BA, 67; Cornell Univ, PhD(physics), 72. *Prof Exp:* Asst prof physics, Univ Dallas, 72-75; res assoc physics, Cornell Univ, 75-77. *Mem:* Am Phys Soc; Am Asn Physics Teachers; Astron Soc Pac. *Res:* Nonlinear optical effects. *Mailing Add:* Dept Eng Pac Lutheran Univ Tacoma WA 98447

HAUENSTEIN, JACK DAVID, POLYMER CHEMISTRY, PHYSICAL CHEMISTRY. *Current Pos:* Sr res chemist, Goodyear Tire & Rubber Co, 55-60, proj leader olefin plastics, 60-64, prof leader polyesters, 64-65, SECT HEAD POLYESTERS, GOODYEAR TIRE & RUBBER CO, 65- *Personal Data:* b Oskaloosa, Iowa, June 10, 29; m 50; c 3. *Educ:* Iowa Univ, BA, 50, PhD(phys chem), 55. *Mem:* AAAS; Am Chem Soc; Sigma Xi. *Res:* Synthesis and characterization of polymers, especially on condensation polymers; ethylene terephthalate based plastics and fibers. *Mailing Add:* RR1 Tracy IA 50256

HAUER, ALLAN A, PHYSICS. *Current Pos:* staff scientist, Inertial Fusion Prog, Los Alamos Nat Lab, 78-85, assoc group leader, Inertial Fusion & Laser Matter Interaction Exp Group, 85- 90, prog mgr, Inertial Fusion Exp, 89-91 & 93-94, CHIEF SCIENTIST, INERTIAL FUSION PROG, LOS ALAMOS NAT LAB, 94- *Personal Data:* m, Wendy Gardner; c Laurel A & Kevin B. *Educ:* Cornell Univ, BS & MS, 68; Univ Rochester, PhD(optics & appl physics), 76. *Prof Exp:* Res scientist, Optics & Quantum Electronics, United Technologies Corp, 68-72; res & teaching asst fel, Univ Rochester, 73-76, res assoc fel, 76-78. *Mem:* Fel Am Phys Soc. *Res:* Inertial fusion; plasma spectroscopy; laser matter interaction. *Mailing Add:* Los Alamos Nat Lab MS E554 Los Alamos NM 87545. *E-Mail:* hauer@lanl.gov

HAUFLER, CHRISTOPHER HARDIN, PLANT BIOSYSTEMATICS, PTERIDOLOGY. *Current Pos:* ASSOC PROF & CHAIRPERSON BOT DEPT, UNIV KANS, 79- *Personal Data:* b Niskayuna, NY, Apr 20, 50. *Educ:* Hiram Col, BA, 72; Ind Univ, MS, 74, PhD(bot), 77. *Prof Exp:* Fel, Gray Herbarium Harvard Univ, 77-78 & Mo Bot Garden, 78-79. *Mem:* AAAS; Am Soc Plant Taxonomists; Int Asn Pteridologists; Soc Study Evolution; Am Inst Biol Sci. *Res:* Application of data from such diverse sources as micromorphology, karyotype analysis, enzyme variability, and flavonoid biochemistry in examining patterns and processes of speciation in plants, especially ferns. *Mailing Add:* Dept Bot Univ Kans Lawrence KS 66045-0001

HAUFLER, JONATHAN B, HABITAT MANAGEMENT. *Current Pos:* MGR, WILDLIFE & ECOL, BOISE CASCADE CORP, 93- *Personal Data:* b Schenectady, NY, July 29, 52. *Educ:* Univ NH, BS, 74; Va Polytech Inst & State Univ, MS, 76; Colo State Univ, PhD(wildlife biol), 79. *Prof Exp:* From asst prof to prof wildlife ecol, Mich State Univ, 91-93. *Mem:* Wildlife Soc. *Res:* Wildlife responses to habitat manipulations; ecosystem management; forestry and wildlife relationships. *Mailing Add:* Boise Cascade Corp PO Box 50 Boise ID 83728. *E-Mail:* shaufler@aol.com

HAUG, ARTHUR JOHN, CHEMISTRY, FORESTRY. *Current Pos:* RETIRED. *Personal Data:* b Milwaukee, Wis, Sept 27, 19; m 53, Winifred A Scott; c 5. *Educ:* Marquette Univ, BS, 41; Lawrence Col, MS, 43, PhD(pulp & paper chem & eng), 47. *Prof Exp:* Lab asst, Hummel & Downing Co, Wis, 42; supvr, Tenn Eastman Corp, Tenn, 44-45; asst, Scott Paper Co, 43, process control engr, 47-48, tech dir, 49-50, supt, Paper Mill, 51-52, prod mgr, 53-58, mgr, Paper Mill, Wash, 58-60, prod serv, Pa, 60-65, plant mgr, Paper Mill, NY, 65-67, gen mgr, NE Opers, Me, 67-68, div vpres, 68-78; pres & chief exec officer, Forster Mfg Co, Inc, Wilton, Maine, 78-86. *Mem:* Tech Asn Pulp & Paper Indust. *Res:* Pulp and paper problems: chemical structure and information on guar mannogalactan; alkaline hypochlorite oxidation of guar mannogalactan with respect to certain variables. *Mailing Add:* 25188 Marion Ave A-106 Punta Gorda FL 33950. *Fax:* 941-639-4030; *E-Mail:* bhaug@juno.com

HAUG, EDWARD J, JR, MECHANICAL DESIGN, APPLIED MATHEMATICS. *Current Pos:* prof mech eng, Univ Iowa, 76-81, prof, 81-90, dir, Ctr for Comput Aided Design, 81-95, CARVER DISTINGUISHED PROF MECH ENG, UNIV IOWA, 90- *Personal Data:* b Bonne Terre, Mo, Sept 15, 40; div; c 1. *Educ:* Univ Mo, Rolla, BS, 62; Kans

State Univ, MS, 64, PhD(appl mech), 66. *Honors & Awards:* Colwell Award, Soc Automotive Engrs, 89; Computerworld-Smithsonian Award, 89; Design Automation Award, Am Soc Mech Engrs, 91, Machine Design Award, 93. *Prof Exp:* Mech engr, Systs Anal Directorate, Hq, US Army Weapons Command, 66-69, chief, 69-71, chief systs res eng, 71-73; chief concepts & technol eng, US Army Armament Command, 73-76. *Concurrent Pos:* Adj asst prof, Univ Iowa, 68-71, adj assoc prof, 71-75, adj prof, 75-76. *Mem:* Am Soc Mech Engrs; Sigma Xi. *Res:* Development of methods for mechanism and machine dynamics; ground vehicle driving simulation. *Mailing Add:* Col Eng Univ Iowa Iowa City IA 52242

HAUGAARD, NIELS, BIOCHEMISTRY, PHARMACOLOGY. *Current Pos:* Instr res med, Sch Med, Univ Pa, 49-51, assoc, 51-52, asst prof physiol chem, 52-53, from asst prof to prof, 54-87, EMER PROF, SCH MED, UNIV PA, 87-, INVESTR UROL RES, 87- *Personal Data:* b Copenhagen, Denmark, Feb 25, 20; US citizen; wid; c David & Lisa. *Educ:* Swarthmore Col, AB, 42; Univ Pa, PhD, 49. *Concurrent Pos:* Guggenheim Found fel, Carlsberg Lab, Denmark, 52; Commonwealth Found fel, Amsterdam, 65-66; mem, Exp Cardiovasc Sci Study Sect, NIH, 78-82; vis prof, Univ Oslo, 84; mem adv bd, Molecular & Cellular Biochem, 91- *Mem:* Am Soc Biol Chem; Am Soc Pharmacol & Exp Therapeut. *Res:* Intermediary metabolism; mechanism of hormone and drug action; carbohydrate metabolism; oxygen toxicity; bladder metabolism. *Mailing Add:* Hosp Univ Pa 3400 Spruce St Philadelphia PA 19104

HAUGE, PAUL STEPHEN, GEOPHYSICS. *Current Pos:* GEOPHYSICIST, CONOCO INC, 88- *Personal Data:* b Brookings, SDak, May 1, 45; m 67; c 4. *Educ:* SDak State Univ, BS, 67; Iowa State Univ, PhD(nuclear physics), 71. *Prof Exp:* NDEA fel & asst, Dept Physics, Iowa State Univ, 67-71; Nat Acad Sci-Nat Res Coun res assoc nuclear physics, Aerospace Res Lab, Wright-Patterson AFB, 71-72; res assoc, Cyclotron Dept, Mich State Univ, 72-74; geophysicist, Exxon Prod Res Co, 74-81; geophysicist, Phillips Petrol Co, 81-88. *Mem:* Soc Explor Geophys; Am Phys Soc. *Res:* Theoretical investigation of numerical methods for analyzing seismic data. *Mailing Add:* 9851 Meadow Glen Lane Apt 68 Houston TX 74042

HAUGEN, DAVID ALLEN, ENZYMOLOGY, CHEMICAL CARCINOGENESIS. *Current Pos:* asst biochemist, 75-81, BIOCHEMIST, BIOL ENVIRON & MED RES DIV, ARGONNE NAT LAB, 81- *Personal Data:* b Ft Dodge, Iowa, Nov 28, 45; m 67, Karen Jacobson; c Kristine & Ingrid. *Educ:* Augsburg Col, BA, 67; Univ Wis-Madison, PhD(biochem), 73. *Prof Exp:* Scholar, Dept Biol Chem, Univ Mich, 73-75, lectr biochem, 75. *Concurrent Pos:* NIH fel, Univ Mich, 73-75; vis scientist, Dept Biochem & Biophysics, Univ Hawaii, 77. *Mem:* Am Chem Soc; Am Soc Biochem & Molecular Biol. *Res:* Metabolism of drugs and carcinogens, especially the enzymology of monooxygenases; formation and fate of reactive metabolites, analysis of environmental exposure to carcinogens; environment, safety and health protection in research facilities. *Mailing Add:* Energy Environ & Biol Res Bldg 202 Argonne Nat Lab 9700 S Cass Ave Argonne IL 60439-4833

HAUGEN, ROBERT KENNETH, INDUSTRIAL & MANUFACTURING ENGINEERING. *Current Pos:* instnl prod mgr, 87-93, DIR RES & DEVELOP, INT SALES, ST CHARLES MFG, 93- *Personal Data:* b Detroit, Mich, July 12, 47; m 85, Talitha Glossbrenner; c Robert F. *Educ:* Univ Ill, Urbana-Champaign, BS, 69, MS, 73, PhD(sci educ), 78. *Prof Exp:* Chemist, Lawrence Livermore Labs, 68-69; analytical chemist, Tri-Met Sanitary Dist Sludge Proj, 70-74; assoc dir environ educ, Technol & Environ Proj, LaSalle, Ill, 74-84; instr physics, math & chem, Kishwaukee Col, Malta, Ill, 85-87. *Concurrent Pos:* Instr chem, Univ High Sch Gifted, 70-74; subcomt chmn, Am Soc Testing & Mat, 88-91; chief consult, Glogon Eng, 90-91. *Mem:* Am Soc Testing & Mat; Am Chem Soc; Am Soc Heating, Refrig & Air Conditioning Engrs. *Res:* Fume hood testing and product development, including flow pattern, containment studies, baffle arrangements, velocity alarms, and associated technologies. *Mailing Add:* 21 Clyde Ave Jamestown NY 14701. *Fax:* 630-584-3992

HAUGH, C(LARENCE) GENE, AGRICULTURAL & AQUACULTURE ENGINEERING. *Current Pos:* chmn, Dept Agr Eng, 79-86, PROF, DEPT BIOL SYSTS ENG, VA POLYTECH INST & STATE UNIV, 86- *Personal Data:* b Spring Mills, Pa, Oct 11, 36; m 62, Patricia A Breon; c Amy E, Jennifer L (Ulsh) & Mitchell B. *Educ:* Pa State Univ, BS, 58; Univ Ill, MS, 59; Purdue Univ, PhD(agr eng), 64. *Honors & Awards:* Young Researcher Award, Am Soc Agr Engrs, 76. *Prof Exp:* Instr agr eng, Purdue Univ, 61-64; asst prof, Univ Fla, 64-65; from asst prof to prof agr eng, Purdue Univ, 65-79. *Concurrent Pos:* Regist prof engr, State of Fla, 64-; lead analyst, World Food & Nutrit Study, Nat Acad Sci, 76-77; mem, Eng Accreditation Comn, Accredition Bd Eng & Technol, 85-90. *Mem:* Fel Am Soc Agr Engrs; Inst Food Tech; sr mem Nat Soc Prof Engrs; Am Soc Heating, Refrig & Air-Conditioning Engrs. *Res:* Heat and mass transfer; physical properties of biological materials; food processing; food losses; multimedia use in instruction; ultrasonics in determining internal qualities of products; aquaculture production. *Mailing Add:* Dept Biol Systs Eng Va Polytech Inst & State Univ Blacksburg VA 24061. *Fax:* 540-231-3199; *E-Mail:* haugh@vtvm1.cc.vt.edu

HAUGH, EUGENE (FREDERICK), PHYSICAL CHEMISTRY, PHOTOGRAPHIC SCIENCE. *Current Pos:* RETIRED. *Personal Data:* b Reedsburg, Wis, Mar 23, 29; m 57; c 4. *Educ:* Univ Wis, BS, 51, PhD(phys chem), 54. *Prof Exp:* From res chemist to sr res chemist, E I du Pont de Nemours & Co, 54-63, res supvr, 63-73, res mgr, 73-85, sr res fel, Imaging Systs Dept, 85-88. *Mem:* Soc Imaging Sci & Technol. *Res:* Photographic chemistry and theory. *Mailing Add:* 6164 Country Club Way Sarasota FL 34243

HAUGH, LARRY DOUGLAS, APPLIED STATISTICS, QUALITY CONTROL. *Current Pos:* from asst prof to prof, 75-90, DIR, STATIST PROG, UNIV VT, 90- & PROF ORTHOP & REHAB, 90- *Personal Data:* b Gary, Ind, June 11, 44; m 66, Jane A Booher; c Wendi A, Joshua D & Jeremy A. *Educ:* Wabash Col, BA, 66; Univ Wis-Madison, MA, 67, MS, 70, PhD(statist), 72. *Prof Exp:* Asst prof statist, Univ Fla, 72-75. *Concurrent Pos:* Acad assoc, IBM, Burlington, 78-81; statistician, Shell Res, Amsterdam, 81-82; mem bd dirs, Time Series Anal & Forecasting Soc, 81-85; lectr indust short courses; consult statist; assoc ed, Technometrics, 81-86; vis prof statist, Univ Tenn, 89-90; chair, Qual & Productivity Sect, Am Statist Asn, 93; assoc ed, J Am Statist Asn, 96- *Mem:* Am Statist Asn; Royal Statist Soc; Int Asn Statist Comput; Vint Biometric Soc; sr mem Am Soc Qual Control; Int Statist Inst. *Res:* Time series analysis with cross correlation identification; extremal value estimation via censoring and truncation; reliability estimation via the renewal function statistical process control; medical statistics; low back pain. *Mailing Add:* Statist Prog Univ Vt 16 Colchester Ave Burlington VT 05401-1455. *Fax:* 802-656-2552

HAUGHEY, FRANCIS JAMES, health physics, for more information see previous edition

HAUGHT, ALAN F, PLASMA PHYSICS. *Current Pos:* From res scientist to sr res scientist plasma physics, 62-64, from prin scientist to sr prin scientist, 64-74, MGR FUSION RES LAB, UNITED TECHNOL CORP, 74- *Personal Data:* b Buckhannon, WVa, Nov 5, 36; m 59; c 4. *Educ:* Amherst Col, AB, 58; Princeton Univ, MA, 60, PhD(physics), 62. *Mem:* Am Phys Soc; Sigma Xi. *Res:* Shock tube studies of thermal ionization rates; plasmas produced by high-intensity laser beam interaction with matter; magnetic field containment of high temperature plasmas. *Mailing Add:* 39 Fox Den Rd Glastonbury CT 06033

HAUGHTON, GEOFFREY, IMMUNOGENETICS, IMMUNOLOGY. *Current Pos:* from asst prof to assoc prof, 66-71, PROF IMMUNOL & GENETICS, SCH MED, UNIV NC, CHAPEL HILL, 71- *Personal Data:* b Leeds, Eng, June 10, 32; m 65; c 1. *Educ:* Univ Southampton, BSc, 55, PhD(bact enzymol), 58. *Prof Exp:* Demonstr physiol & biochem, Univ Southampton, 55-58; sr sci officer, Microbiol Res Estab, Eng, 61-64; vis scientist, Karolinska Inst, Sweden, 64-65. *Concurrent Pos:* Civil Serv sr res fel microbiol, Microbiol Res Estab, Eng, 58-61; Int Union Control Cancer Eleanor Roosevelt res fel, 64-65; USPHS res career develop award, 68; res asst, Royal South Hants Hosp, Eng, 55-58. *Mem:* Transplantation Soc; Am Asn Cancer Res; Am Asn Immunol. *Res:* Transplantation immunology and genetics; tumor immunobiology; basic immunology. *Mailing Add:* Dept Microbiol & Immunol Univ NC Med Sch CB No 7290 Chapel Hill NC 27599-7290. *Fax:* 919-962-8103

HAUGHTON, JAMES GRAY, PUBLIC HEALTH ADMINISTRATION. *Current Pos:* MED DIR, PUB HEALTH PROGS & SERVS, DEPT HEALTH SERVS, LOS ANGELES CO, 96- *Personal Data:* b Panama, Repub Panama, Mar 30, 25; US citizen; div; c 2. *Educ:* Pac Union Col, BA, 47; Loma Linda Univ, MD, 50; Columbia Univ, MPH, 62; Am Bd Prev Med, dipl, 68. *Hon Degrees:* DSc, Chicago Med Sch-Univ Health Sci, 71. *Honors & Awards:* Dr Mary McLeod Bethune Award of Merit, Nat Coun Negro Women, 72; Humanitarian Award, Nat Asn Health Serv Exec, 72; Mathew B Rosenhaus Lectr, Am Pub Health Asn, 74. *Prof Exp:* Intern, Unity Hosp, Brooklyn, 49-50, fel gen surg, 51-55; USNR Med Corps, 56-58; child health clinician, NY Health Dept, 58-60, resident pub health physician, 60-62; dir med care, 63-65, exec dir, Med Care Serv, 65-66; first dep comnr, NY Dept Hosps, 66; first dep adminr, Health Serv Admin, NY, 66-70; exec dir, Health & Hosps Gov Comn, Chicago, Ill, 70-79; assoc prof, Dept Community Health & Prev Med, Northwestern Univ, 77-80; exec vpres, Charles R Drew Postgrad Med Sch, 80-83, vpres finance & admin, 82-83; dir, City Houston Health Dept, 83-87; med dir, King/Drew Med Ctr, Los Angeles, 87-93. *Concurrent Pos:* Pvt pract, Obstet & Abdominal Surg, 52-66; dep med welfare adminr, New York City Welfare Dept, 63-65; med welfare adminr & coordr welfare serv, NY Hosp Dept, 65-66; adj asst prof admin med, Sch Pub Health & Admin Med, Columbia Univ, 63-70; lectr pub health, Sch Med, Yale Univ, 64-65; non-resident lectr med care orgn, Sch Pub Health, Univ Mich, 66-79; lectr admin health serv, Dept Polit Sci, Roosevelt Univ, 70-72; fac mem, Interagency Inst Fed Health Care Exec, 70-82; adj prof, Carnegie Mellon Univ, 77-78 & Univ Tex Health Sci Ctr, Houston, 84-87; bd dirs, Alan Gutmacher Res Inst, 85-91; AIDS consult, Reg Ministry Pub Health, Spain, 86; mem, AIDS Servs Prog, Robert Wood Johnson Found, 86-91, AIDS Prev Prog, 87-91, Substance Abuse Coverage Study Comt, Inst Med-Nat Acad Sci, 88-90, Comt Future Struct Vet Admin Med Care, 90-91, Study Co-Admin Serv/Res Progs NIH & Alcohol, Drug Abuse & Ment Health Admin, 90-91; prof med, Univ Calif, Los Angeles, 87; prof, Dept Family Med, Drew Univ Med & Sci, 87, assoc dean, 89-93; sr investr, Digestive Dis Ctr, 87-91. *Mem:* Inst Med-Nat Acad Sci; fel Am Pub Health Asn; fel Am Col Prev Med; fel NY Acad Sci; fel Royal Soc Health; AMA; Nat Med Asn. *Mailing Add:* Dept Health Servs 313 N Figueroa St Suite 806 Los Angeles CA 90012. *Fax:* 213-481-9853; *E-Mail:* jhaughton@dhs.co.la.ca.us

HAUGHTON, KENNETH E, MECHANICAL ENGINEERING. *Current Pos:* CONSULT, 92- *Personal Data:* b Myrtle Point, Ore, Jan 8, 28. *Educ:* Univ Calif, Berkeley, BS, 52, PhD(mech eng), 64; Iowa State Col, MS, 55. *Prof Exp:* Design engr, Gen Elec Co, 52-53; instr eng graphics, Iowa State Col, 53-56; instr eng mech, Cornell Univ, 56-57; res engr, IBM Corp, San Jose, Calif, 57-77, prod develop engr, 80-82, dir, Eng Lab, Lexington, Ky, 77-80; dean eng, Univ Santa Clara, 80-89; vpres eng, Da Vinci Graphics, 90-92. *Mem:* Nat Acad Eng; Am Soc Eng Educ; Am Soc Mech Eng. *Mailing Add:* 16200 Kennedy Rd Los Gatos CA 95032. *E-Mail:* vknr60a@prodigy.com

HAUGHTON, VICTOR MELLET, RADIOLOGY. *Current Pos:* PROF RADIOL, MED COL WIS, 81-, CHIEF NEURORADIOL RES, 82- *Personal Data:* b Willimantic, Conn, July 9, 39; m 65; c 3. *Educ:* Harvard Col, Mass, BA, 61; Yale Univ Med Sch, MD, 67. *Prof Exp:* Instr radiol, Harvard Med Sch, Mass, 73; clin instr radiol, Tufts Univ, 73; radiologist, Peter Bent Brigham Boston & Beth Israel Hosp, 73; consult radiol, Vet Admin Hosp, Boston, 73 & Vet Admin Hosp Milwaukee, 74-81. *Concurrent Pos:* Asst prof, Radiol Med Col Wis, 74; radiologist & chief neuroradiol, Milwaukee Co Med Complex, 74; int travel fel, NIH, Oslo, Norway, 80; mem, Sci Exhib Comt, Radiol Soc NAm, 85-; mem, Comt Magnetic Ressonance Appln, Comn Magnetic Resonance, 87-88; mem, Res Overview Comt, Am Soc Neuroradiol, 87-88; mem, Radiopharmaceut Drug Adv Comt, Food & Drug Admin, Dept Health & Human Serv, 88- *Mem:* Radiol Soc NAm; Am Col Radiol; Am Soc Neuroradiol; Asn Univ Radiologist. *Res:* Development of functional imaging to diagnose caues of back pain; applications of magnetic resonance spectroscopy and functional magnetic resonance imaging to surgical planning and to diagnosis of neuropsychiatric disorders. *Mailing Add:* 8700 W Wisconsin Ave Milwaukee WI 53226

HAUGLAND, RICHARD PAUL, ORGANIC CHEMISTRY, BIOPHYSICS. *Current Pos:* PRES, MOLECULAR PROBES, INC, 75- *Personal Data:* b Huron, SDak, July 17, 43; m 72, Rosaria; c Alex & Marina. *Educ:* Hamline Univ, BS, 65; Stanford Univ, PhD(chem), 70. *Prof Exp:* Chemist, Syntex Corp, 69; asst prof chem, Hamline Univ, 75-78. *Concurrent Pos:* Fel Cardiovasc Res Inst, Univ Calif, San Francisco, 72-74, NIH fel, 74-75. *Mem:* Biophys Soc; Am Chem Soc; Int Soc Anal Cytol; Am Soc Cell Biol. *Res:* Fluorescent probes, spectroscopy, organic syntheses, protein and membrane structure, cell biology. *Mailing Add:* Molecular Probes Inc 4849 Pitchford Ave Eugene OR 97402

HAUGSJAA, PAUL O, ATOMIC & MOLECULAR PHYSICS. *Current Pos:* Mem tech staff, Explor Res Lab, 69-81, res mgr, Lighting Technol Ctr, 81-82, RES MGR, COMPONENTS RES LAB, GTE LABS, INC, 82- *Personal Data:* b Las Vegas, Nev, Apr 3, 42; m 65; c 3. *Educ:* Concordia Col, Moorhead, Minn, BS, 64; Univ Denver, PhD(physics), 69. *Honors & Awards:* Leslie H Warner Award, 84 & 92. *Mem:* Am Phys Soc, Sigma Xi; Inst Elec & Electronics Engrs; Int Soc Hybrid Microelectronics; Electrochem Soc; Am Vacuum Soc. *Res:* Solid state device design and development; semiconductor devices development; collisional and radiative processes pertinent to gaseous electronics and plasma processes; seismic and reproductive acoustics; semiconductor device design and process development; transportation control; electrochemical kinetics; microwave transmission effects; charge storage and piezo electric effects; electrodeless lighting and bioeffects of light and microwaves; high speed integrated circuit development; heterostructural epitaxy of III-V materials; design and fabrication of integrated optical and optoelectronic circuits; optics. *Mailing Add:* 23 Taylor Rd Acton MA 01720-5447

HAUK, PETER, PHYSICAL CHEMISTRY. *Current Pos:* CONSULT, 84- *Personal Data:* b Dallas, Tex, Jan 19, 37; m 58; c 4. *Educ:* Univ Md, BS, 58; Carnegie Inst Technol, MS, 61, PhD(chem), 63. *Prof Exp:* Nat Acad Sci-Nat Res Coun fel chem, Calif Inst Technol, 63-64, NSF fel, 64-65, res fel, 65; res chemist, Beckman Instruments Inc, 65-66; sr res chemist, Bell & Howell Res Lab, 66-75; prin res scientist, Newport Res Corp, 74-84. *Mem:* Am Chem Soc; Am Phys Soc. *Res:* Quantum chemical modeling of small molecules and molecular electronic interactions, electrochemical sensors, photoconductor processes; optics and electro-optics instrumentation. *Mailing Add:* 10181 Beverly Dr Huntington Beach CA 92646-7199

HAUN, CHARLES KENNETH, ANATOMY, NEUROSCIENCES. *Current Pos:* asst prof, 62-68, ASSOC PROF ANAT, SCH MED, UNIV SOUTHERN CALIF, 68- *Personal Data:* b Los Angeles, Calif, June 13, 30; m 56, Yoshi Iwase; c 3. *Educ:* Pomona Col, BA, 52; Univ Calif, Los Angeles, PhD(anat), 60. *Prof Exp:* From instr to asst prof anat, Hahnemann Med Col, 59-62. *Mem:* Am Asn Anat; Int Soc Neuroendocrinol; Soc Neurosci. *Res:* Neuro-endocrine regulation; neuroanatomy; reproduction; integration of anterior and posterior pituitary secretion; acupuncture-mechanisms; the role of thyrotropin-releasing hormon (TRH), along with other neuro-peptides and transmitters in control of spinal motoneurons; the application of TRH and analogs as antispasticity agents. *Mailing Add:* Dept Anat & Cell Biol Sch Med Univ Southern Calif Los Angeles CA 90033. *Fax:* 215-342-3158; *E-Mail:* chaun@hsc.usc.edu

HAUN, J(AMES) W(ILLIAM), CHEMICAL ENGINEERING, REGULATORY MANAGEMENT. *Current Pos:* RETIRED. *Personal Data:* b Birmingham, Ala, Sept 8, 24; m 46, Lucia Land; c James W, Lucy, Daniel & Robert. *Educ:* Univ Tex, BS, 46, MS, 48, PhD(chem eng & chem), 50. *Prof Exp:* Instr chem eng, Univ Tex, 48-49; res engr, Plastics Div, Monsanto Chem Co, 50-56, res group leader, 56; head, Dept Chem Eng, Cent Res Labs, Gen Mills Inc, 56-60, dir, Phys Res, 60-63, dir & vpres corp eng, 63-75, vpres eng policy, 75-85, consult, 85-86. *Concurrent Pos:* Mem, Environ Qual Comt, Nat Asn Mfrs, 69-85; mem, Food Indust Adv Comt, Dept Energy, 78-81; mem comn environ, US Chamber Com, 78-84; mem sci Adv Bd, Environ Protection Agency, 82-90, consult, 90-93. *Mem:* Fel Am Inst Chem Engrs; Sigma Xi. *Res:* Applications of advanced engineering technology to food processing; environmental engineering; interaction between technology and public policy. *Mailing Add:* 6912 E Fish Lake Rd Minneapolis MN 55369

HAUN, JOHN DANIEL, PETROLEUM GEOLOGY. *Current Pos:* from asst prof to prof, 55-85, EMER PROF GEOL, COLO SCH MINES, 85- *Personal Data:* b Old Hickory, Tenn, Mar 7, 21; m 42, Lois Culbertson. *Educ:* Berea Col, AB, 48; Univ Wyo, MA, 49, PhD(geol), 53. *Honors & Awards:* Distinguished Serv Award, Am Asn Petrol Geologists, 73, Sidney Powers Mem Award, 95; Ben H Parker Mem Award, Am Inst Prof Geologists, 83; Halliburton Award, Colo Sch Mines, 85; Ian Campbell Medal 88; Mines Medal, 95; William B Heroy Jr Award, Am Geol Inst, 96. *Prof Exp:* Dir geol res, Petrol Res Co, 52-55. *Concurrent Pos:* Mem consult firm, Barlow & Haun, Inc, 57-90; ed, J Am Asn Petrol Geologists, 67-71; mem comt explor, Am Petrol Inst, 71-73, 78-88; US rep, Int Comt Petrol Reserves Classification, UN, 76-77; consult, Off Technol Assessment, US Cong, 76-80; comnr, Colo Oil & Gas Conserv Comn, 77-87, chmn, 85-87; mem, energy resources comt, Interstate Oil Compact Comn, 78-96 & Nat Petrol Coun, 79-90; mem, US Nat Comt Geol, 82-89, chmn, 85-87. *Mem:* Am Inst Prof Geologists (pres, 76); fel Geol Soc Am; hon mem Am Asn Petrol Geologists (pres-elect, 78-79, pres, 79-80); Soc Econ Paleontologists & Mineralogists; Sigma Xi; Am Geol Inst (pres, 81-82). *Res:* Cretaceous stratigraphy; regional structural geology; migration and accumulation of petroleum; methods of estimating undiscovered petroleum resources; hydrodynamics in petroleum migration and entrapment. *Mailing Add:* 1238 County Rd 23 Evergreen CO 80439

HAUN, JOSEPH RHODES, PLANT PHYSIOLOGY. *Current Pos:* prof hort, 65-84, EMER PROF, CLEMSON UNIV, 84- *Personal Data:* b Edinburgh, Va, May 13, 22; m 45; c 5. *Educ:* Berea Col, AB, 46; Univ Md, MS, 50, PhD(plant physiol), 51. *Prof Exp:* Res plant physiologist, E I du Pont de Nemours & Co, 51-58; horticulturist, New Crops Res Br, USDA, 58-61, invests leader, 61-64; tech dir, Cherry Hill Trust, Ga, 64-65; agr consult crop prod analysis__, 65. *Mem:* AAAS; Soc Econ Bot; Am Soc Plant Physiol; Am Soc Hort Sci; Am Soc Agronomists. *Res:* Influence of environmental factors on plant growth; crop production analysis. *Mailing Add:* 296 Jones Cove Rd Asheville NC 28805

HAUN, RANDY S, MOLECULAR BIOLOGY. *Current Pos:* PRES, MOLECULAR SOFTWARE, INC, 85-; STAFF FEL, NAT HEART LUNG & BLOOD INST, NIH, 89- *Personal Data:* b Ft Carson, Colo, Mar 14, 56. *Educ:* Univ Iowa, BS, 78; Purdue Univ, PhD(biochem), 88. *Prof Exp:* Res chemist, Uniformed Serv Univ Health Sci, Bethesda, Md, 79-82; res asst, Dept Biochem, Purdue Univ, 82-88, teaching asst, 84, fel, 89. *Mem:* Assoc mem Am Soc Biochem & Molecular Biol. *Res:* Cholecystokinin gene expression; cloning and expression of protein-tyrosine-phosphatase. *Mailing Add:* Dept Biochem Molecular Biol Univ Ark Med Sch Slot 516 4301 W Markham Little Rock AR 72205-7199. *Fax:* 501-686-8169

HAUN, ROBERT DEE, JR, ATOMIC & MOLECULAR PHYSICS. *Current Pos:* RETIRED. *Personal Data:* b Lexington, Ky, Apr 3, 30; m 53, 77; c 3. *Educ:* Univ Ky, BS, 52; Mass Inst Technol, PhD(physics), 57. *Prof Exp:* Asst physics, Mass Inst Technol, 53-57; res physicist, Westinghouse Elec Corp, 57-59, fel physicist, 59-62, sect mgr, 62-63, mgr quantum electronics res & develop, 63-69, dir appl physics & math res, 69-74, mgr, Appl Sci Div, 74-81, dir indust prod res & develop, 81-83, res dir, energy & adv technol, 83-84, res dir, Bus Unit Technol Progs, 84-87, dep chief scientist, 87-91. *Mem:* Am Phys Soc; Inst Elec & Electronics Engrs; Optical Soc Am; fel AAAS. *Res:* Lasers; quantum electronics; parametric amplification; ferromagnetic resonance; atomic frequency standards; atomic beam magnetic resonance spectroscopy. *Mailing Add:* 3008 Hidden Treasure Dr Las Vegas NV 89134

HAUNERLAND, NORBERT HEINRICH, LIPID BIOCHEMISTRY, INSECT BIOCHEMISTRY. *Current Pos:* asst prof, 89-93, ASSOC PROF BIOCHEM, SIMON FRASER UNIV, 93- *Personal Data:* b Essen, WGer, Feb 23, 55; m 88, Jutta Rickers; c Sven & Bengt. *Educ:* Univ Munster, Ger, dipl chem, 80, PhD(biochem), 82. *Honors & Awards:* H P Kaufmann Award, Deutsche Gesellschaft Fur Fettwissenschaft, 82; Young Chemist Award, Agrochem Div, Am Chem Soc, 88. *Prof Exp:* Assoc insect physiol, Cornell Univ, 82-84; res assoc insect biochem, Univ Ariz, 84-86, res asst prof, 87-89. *Mem:* Entom Soc Am; Am Chem Soc; Can Fedn Biol Sci; Gesellschaft Fur Biol Chem; Ger Soc Chem. *Res:* Lipid transport and metabolism in insects; structure and function of lipoproteins; intracellular fatty acid binding proteins and receptors; insects as biochemical model systems; storage protein uptake and metabolism. *Mailing Add:* Dept Biol Simon Fraser Univ Burnaby BC V5A 1S6 Can. *Fax:* 604-291-3496; *E-Mail:* norbert__haunerland@sfu.ca

HAUNOLD, ALFRED, PLANT GENETICS, CYTOLOGY. *Current Pos:* RETIRED. *Personal Data:* b Hollabrunn, Austria, Oct 7, 29; US citizen; m 59, Mary F; c Christopher, Monica, Michelle, Julie, Karl, Erik & Jennifer. *Educ:* State Univ Agr & Forestry, Austria, Dipl Ing, 51, Dr Agr, 52; Univ Nebr, PhD(plant breeding & genetics), 60. *Prof Exp:* Res assoc plant breeding, State Univ Agr & Forestry, Austria, 52-53; revision sect, Agr Bd Lower Austria & Vienna, 54-55; asst agron, Univ Nebr, 55-60, asst prof corn genetics & starch biochem, 60-64; prof analyst, Sci Info Exchange, Smithsonian Inst, 64-65; res plant geneticist, Agr Res Serv, USDA, Ore State Univ, 65-95. *Concurrent Pos:* Mem sci comn, Int Hop Prod Bur; mem, Hop Res Coun, 83; USDA collab, Ore State Univ, 95- *Mem:* Crop Sci Soc Am; Am Soc Brewing Chemists. *Res:* Wheat genetics and breeding; corn genetics and starch biochemistry as related to starch biosynthesis; breeding, genetics and cytogenetics of hops. *Mailing Add:* USA Crop Sci Bldg 425 Ore State Univ Corvallis OR 97331-3002. *Fax:* 541-737-1334

HAUPT, CLIFFORD A, ENVIRONMENTAL ANALYSIS & REGULATIONS. *Current Pos:* CHIEF, ENVIRON AFFAIRS PROG, US GEOL SURV, 88- *Personal Data:* b Brooklyn, NY, Nov 3, 40. *Educ:* NY Univ, MS, 66, MS, 72. *Prof Exp:* Propulsion engr, Grumman Airspace Corp,

63-68, McDonald Douglas, 68-71; environ proj mgr, Nuclear Regulatory Comn, 75-80. *Mem:* Am Inst Chem Engrs; Am Wastwater Asn; Air & Waste Mgt Asn. *Mailing Add:* US Geol Surv 423 Nat Cent Reston VA 22092. *Fax:* 703-648-4530; *E-Mail:* cahaupt@usgs.gov

HAUPT, L(EWIS) M(CDOWELL), JR, electrical engineering; deceased, see previous edition for last biography

HAUPT, RALPH FREEMAN, astronomy; deceased, see previous edition for last biography

HAUPT, RANDY LARRY, ELECTRICAL ENGINEERING. *Current Pos:* dir res, Elec Eng Dept, 90-91, CHIEF, COMMUN DIV, ELEC ENG DEPT, USAF, 91-; ASSOC PROF, USAF ACAD, 91- *Personal Data:* b Johnstown, Pa, Aug 11, 56; m 79, Sue E Slagle; c Bonny A & Amy J. *Educ:* USAF Acad, BSEE, 78; Western New Eng Col, MS, 81; Northeastern Univ, MSEE, 83; Univ Mich, PhD(elec eng), 87. *Honors & Awards:* USAF Res & Develop Award, 83 & 87; Frank J Seiler Award for Res Excellence, 90 & 92; Founder's Gold Medal, 93. *Prof Exp:* Proj engr, OTH-B Radar Electronic Syst Div, USAF, Hanscom AFB, Mass, 78-80, res engr microwave antennas, Rome Air Develop Ctr, 80-84; from instr to asst prof, USAF Acad, Colo, 87-91. *Concurrent Pos:* Res grantee, Rome Air Develop Ctr, 88-90, Frank J Seiler Res Lab, 90-, Cray Res Inc, 91-93, Phillips Lab, 92-; vis res engr, Los Alamos Nat Lab, 92. *Mem:* Inst Elec & Electronics Engrs; Am Soc Eng Educ; Appl Comput Electromagnetics Soc. *Res:* Electromagnetics, scattering, antennas, electro-optics, numerical methods, chaos theory, radar systems eng, communication systems. *Mailing Add:* 19420 Doewood Dr Monument CO 80132

HAUPTMAN, HERBERT AARON, X-RAY CRYSTALLOGRAPHY. *Current Pos:* mathematician, Hauptman-Woodward Med Res Inst, 70-72, res dir, 72-87, vpres, 72-85, PRES, HAUPTMAN-WOODWARD MED RES INST, 86-; RES PROF BIOPHYS SCI, STATE UNIV NY, BUFFALO, 70-, RES PROF COMPUT SCI, 91- *Personal Data:* b New York, NY, Feb 14, 17; m 40, Edith Citrynell; c Barbara & Carol (Fullerton). *Educ:* City Col New York, BS, 37; Columbia Univ, MA, 39; Univ Md, PhD(math), 55. *Hon Degrees:* Univ Md, 85; DSc, City Col New York, 86, D'Youville Col, 89, Bar-Ilan Univ, Israel, 90, Columbia Univ, 90, Tech Univ Lodz, 92, Queens Univ, Can, 93; DChem, Univ Parma, Italy, 89 & Niagara Univ, 96. *Honors & Awards:* Nobel Prize in Chem (co-recipient), 85; Schoellkopf Award, Am Chem Soc, 86; Patterson Award, 84. *Prof Exp:* Statistician, Census Bur, 40-42; radar instr, USAF, 42-43 & 46-47; physicist, Naval Res Lab, 47-61, mathematician, 62-70. *Concurrent Pos:* Lectr, Univ Md, 56-70. *Mem:* Nat Acad Sci; Endocrine Soc; Am Crystallog Asn; Math Asn Am; Am Math Soc; Am Phys Soc. *Res:* Phase problem in x-ray crystallography; mathematical basis underlying the direct methods of x-ray crystallography for the determination of crystal and molecular structures using the technique of x-ray diffraction. *Mailing Add:* Hauptman-Woodward Med Res Inst 73 High St Buffalo NY 41203. *Fax:* 716-852-6086; *E-Mail:* hauptman@hwi.buffalo.edu

HAUPTMAN, STEPHEN PHILLIP, IMMUNOLOGY, HEMATOLOGY. *Current Pos:* PROF MED, THOMAS JEFFERSON UNIV, 84- *Educ:* Col Osteop Med & Surg, DO, 68. *Mailing Add:* Thomas Jefferson Univ Philadelphia PA 19107

HAUPTMANN, RANDAL MARK, plant tissue culture, cryopreservation, for more information see previous edition

HAUPTSCHEIN, MURRAY, ORGANIC CHEMISTRY, RESEARCH ADMINISTRATION. *Current Pos:* CONSULT, 83- *Personal Data:* b New York, NY, Mar 15, 23; m 47; c 2. *Educ:* City Col New York, BS, 43; Duke Univ, PhD(chem), 50. *Honors & Awards:* Am Chem Soc Award, 62. *Prof Exp:* Res chemist, Manhattan Proj, SAM Labs, Columbia Univ, 43-45; res chemist, Carbide & Carbon Chem Corp, 45-46; asst, Duke Univ, 46-47; res assoc, Res Inst, Temple Univ, 50-52, dir org chem res, 52-55; sr res chemist & proj leader, Pennwalt Corp, 55-57, group leader, 57-63, dir, Org Res Dept, 63-73, assoc mgr res & develop, 73-74, mgr cent res develop, 74-79, mgr res & develop, 79-83. *Concurrent Pos:* Chmn, Gordon Res Conf Fluorine Chem, 65; mem, Exec Comt Div Fluorine Chem, Am Chem Soc, 67-69 & 72-74; pres, Res Mgt Group Philadelphia, 78; mem comt, Nat Am Chem Soc Corp Assocs, 78-80; mem, Indust Res Inst, 79- *Mem:* Am Chem Soc; Sigma Xi. *Res:* Organic synthesis; fluorine chemistry; polymerizations; lubricants; plastics; stain repellent finishes; surfactants for fire-fighting foams; sulfur chemistry; additives for plastics and rubber; pesticide and pharmaceutical research. *Mailing Add:* 129 Acacia Dr Unit 309 Indianhead Park La Grange IL 60525-9036

HAURANI, FARID I, MEDICINE. *Current Pos:* From asst to assoc prof, 57-74, PROF MED, JEFFERSON MED COL HOSP, 74- *Personal Data:* b Gaza, Palestine, May 28, 28; US citizen. *Educ:* Am Univ, Beirut, BA, 49, MD, 53. *Concurrent Pos:* Nat Cancer Inst res grants. *Mem:* Am Soc Hemat; Am Col Physicians; Sigma Xi. *Res:* Anemia of defective iron reutilization; metabolites and anti-metabolite and folate coenzymes in the stimulated lymphocyte and the leukemic cell. *Mailing Add:* 1015 Walnut St Philadelphia PA 19107-5005

HAURY, LOREN RICHARD, BIOLOGICAL OCEANOGRAPHY. *Current Pos:* from asst to assoc res oceanogr, 78-88, RES OCEANOGR, SCRIPPS INST, 88- *Personal Data:* b Tucson, Ariz, June 25, 39. *Educ:* Yale Univ, BE, 62; Univ Calif, San Diego, PhD(biol oceanog), 73. *Prof Exp:* Investr, Woods Hole Oceanog Inst, 74-76, asst scientist, 76-78. *Mem:* Am Soc Limnol & Oceanog; AAAS; Am Geophys Union. *Res:* Zooplankton ecology. *Mailing Add:* Marine Life Res Group Scripps Inst Oceanog La Jolla CA 92093-0218

HAUS, HERMANN A(NTON), ELECTRICAL ENGINEERING. *Current Pos:* asst, 51-53, from instr to prof, 53-87, INST PROF, MASS INST TECHNOL, 87- *Personal Data:* b Ljubljana, Yugoslavia, Aug 8, 25; nat US; m 52; c 4. *Educ:* Union Col NY, BSc, 49; Rensselaer Polytech Inst, MEE, 51; Mass Inst Technol, ScD(elec eng), 54. *Hon Degrees:* Dr, Union Col, Schenectady, NY, Tech Univ, Vienna Austria, Univ Ghent, Belgium. *Honors & Awards:* Quantum Electronics & Applns Soc Award, Inst Elec & Electronics Engrs, 84, Educ Medal, 91; C H Townes Award, Am Optical Soc, 87; Frederic Ives Medal, Optical Soc Am, 94; Pres Nat Sci Medal, 95; Ludwig Wittgenstein-Pres Award, Austrian Govt, 97. *Prof Exp:* Instr elec eng, Rensselaer Polytech Inst, 49-51. *Concurrent Pos:* Consult, Sylvania Elec Prod Corp, 53-56 & Raytheon Mfg Co, 56-; Guggenheim fel, Vienna Tech Univ, 59-60; Fulbright scholar, Vienna Tech Univ, 85. *Mem:* Nat Acad Sci; Nat Acad Eng; Am Phys Soc; fel Am Acad Arts & Sci; fel Inst Elec & Electronics Engrs; Sigma Xi. *Res:* Noise in electron devices; circuit theory of linear noisy networks; fluctuation phenomena; electromagnetic theory and microwaves; electron dynamics; quantum electronics; author or co-author of 5 books and over 280 journal articles. *Mailing Add:* Dept Elec Eng Mass Inst Technol Cambridge MA 02139. *Fax:* 617-253-9611

HAUS, JOSEPH WENDEL, QUANTUM FLUCTUATIONS & DIFFRACTION IN OPTICAL WAVE PROPAGATION, ELECTROMAGNETICALLY ENHANCED OPTICAL NONLINEAR RESPONSE. *Current Pos:* ASSOC PROF PHYSICS, RENSSELAER POLYTECH INST, 85- *Personal Data:* b Cleveland, Ohio, Dec 21, 48; m 70, Jean T Ehrbar; c 6. *Educ:* John Carroll Univ, BS, 71, MS, 72; Cath Univ Am, PhD(physics), 75. *Prof Exp:* Res assoc, Nat Bur Stand, 75-77; vis scientist, Kernforschungsanlage-Juelich, 77-78; scientist asst physics, Universitaet Essen, 78-83; res assoc, US Army Missile Command, 83-85. *Concurrent Pos:* Consult, US Army Missile Command, 83-91 & Dove Electronics, 86-87; Hitachi Ltd quantum mats chair, Univ Tokyo, 91-92. *Mem:* Optical Soc Am. *Res:* Theoretical research in quantum optics, nonlinear optics and diffusion in disordered materials. *Mailing Add:* Physics Dept Rensselaer Polytech Inst Troy NY 12181. *Fax:* 518-276-6680; *E-Mail:* hausjj@rpi.edu

HAUS, THILO ENOCH, AGRONOMY. *Current Pos:* Asst prof genetics & asst agronomist, 45-56, assoc prof & assoc agronomist, 56-62, PROF GENETICS & AGRONOMIST, COLO STATE UNIV, 62- *Personal Data:* b Rochester, Wis, Aug 16, 18; m 45; c 2. *Educ:* Univ Wis, BS, 41, MS, 45; Purdue Univ, PhD, 55. *Mem:* Am Soc Agron; Genetics Soc Am; Am Genetic Asn; Sigma Xi. *Res:* Small grain genetics and breeding. *Mailing Add:* 410 Buckeye St Ft Collins CO 80524

HAUSBERGER, FRANZ X, ANATOMY, PHYSIOLOGY. *Current Pos:* from asst prof to prof, 50-76, EMER PROF ANAT, JEFFERSON MED COL, 76- *Personal Data:* b Muhldorf, Ger, Feb, 8, 08; m 49; c 2. *Educ:* Univ Munich, MD, 35. *Prof Exp:* Resident med, Gertrauden Hosp, Berlin, Ger, 36-39; head, Internal Div, Salem Hosp, Koeslin, 39-47; head, Endocrine Div, Univ Hosp, Erlangen, 47-48. *Mem:* AAAS; Am Physiol Soc; Endocrine Soc; Am Diabetes Asn; Am Asn Anat. *Res:* Adipose tissue physiology and metabolism; obesity; fat embolism; gross anatomy. *Mailing Add:* Dept Analytical Sci Temple Univ Sch Dent 3223 N Broad St Philadelphia PA 19140-5096

HAUSCH, H GEORGE, dentistry administration, for more information see previous edition

HAUSCH, WALTER RICHARD, RUBBER CHEMISTRY. *Current Pos:* RETIRED. *Personal Data:* b Akron, Ohio, Oct 26, 17; m 43, Ann McKinniss; c 4. *Educ:* Univ Akron, BS, 40; Univ Cincinnati, MS, 42; Purdue Univ, PhD(org chem), 46. *Prof Exp:* Chemist, Gen Metals Powder Corp, Ohio, 40; asst chem, Univ Cincinnati, 40-41; res chemist, Columbia Chem Div, Pittsburgh Plate Glass Co, Ohio, 41-42; asst chem, Purdue Univ, 42-43; res chemist, J T Baker Chem Co, NJ, 45-47; res chemist, Firestone Tire & Rubber Co, 47-59, head, Adhesives Dept, 59-66, plant mgr, Permalastic Prod Co Div, 66-69, sr res chemist, Firestone Synthetic Rubber & Latex Co, 69-71, res assoc, 71-78, sr res assoc, Cent Res Lab, Firestone Tire & Rubber Co, 78-82. *Mem:* Am Chem Soc; Adhesion Soc. *Res:* Chlorination; fluorination; preparation of certain organic fluorides; silica pigments; polyurethane rubbers and adhesives. *Mailing Add:* 327 Caladonia Ave Akron OH 44333-5711

HAUSCHILD, ANDREAS H W, BACTERIOLOGY, FOOD MICROBIOLOGY. *Current Pos:* RETIRED. *Personal Data:* b Wense, Ger, Oct 13, 29; Can citizen; m 59; c 3. *Educ:* Univ Mainz, Dipl, 54; Univ Toronto, MA, 57; Queen's Univ, PhD(plant biochem), 62. *Prof Exp:* Teacher high schs, Ger, 54-56; res asst bact, Connaught Med Res Labs, Univ Toronto, 57-59; lectr, Queen's Univ, 60-61; res assoc, Connaught Med Res Labs, Univ Toronto, 63-65; res scientist, Microbiol Div, Food & Drug Directorate, Health Protection Br, 65-71, head, Bact Ecol Sect, Dept Nat Health & Welfare Can, 71-89. *Concurrent Pos:* Chmn, Can Botulism Ref Ctr, 74-; consult, Pan Am Health Orgn, 74-75, Int Comn Microbiol Spec Foods, 74-77, Int Stand Orgn, 77-79, Can Int Develop Agency, 82. *Mem:* Am Soc Microbiol; Can Soc Microbiol; Can Inst Food Sci & Technol. *Res:* Toxins of food-borne microorganisms; bacterial food ecology with particular reference to the control of clostridium botulinum in foods. *Mailing Add:* 5686 Sernbank Rd Stittsville ON K2S 1S3 Can

HAUSCHKA, STEPHEN D, DEVELOPMENTAL BIOLOGY, NEUROBIOLOGY. *Current Pos:* Fel, 66-67, from asst prof to assoc prof, 67-80, PROF BIOCHEM, UNIV WASH, 74- *Personal Data:* b Philadelphia, Pa, Apr 18, 40; m 64; c 2. *Educ:* Amherst Col, BA, 62; Johns Hopkins Univ, PhD(biol), 66. *Concurrent Pos:* Res career develop award, NIH, 73-77; mem, Cell Biol Sect, NIH, 75-76, Develop Biol Study Sect, NSF, 77-78, Sci Adv Comt, Muscular Dystrophy Asn, 90-; assoc ed, J Develop Biol, 87 & J Growth Factors, 88- *Mem:* Soc Develop Biol; Am Soc Cell Biol; Am Soc Biol Chemists; Am Soc Microbiol. *Res:* Mechanisms of gene regulation during skeletal and heart muscle development; cell lineage analysis of vertebrate; use of muscle gene regulatory casettes for gene therapy. *Mailing Add:* Dept Biochem Univ Wash Seattle WA 98105. Fax: 206-685-1792

HAUSDOERFFER, WILLIAM H, MATHEMATICS. *Current Pos:* RETIRED. *Personal Data:* b Weehawken, NJ, May 26, 13; m 39, Rosemary Canning; c William G. *Educ:* Trenton State Col, BS, 36; Columbia Univ, MA, 39; Rutgers Univ, EdD(math educ), 50. *Prof Exp:* Teacher elem sch, NJ, 36-40; demonstration teacher math, Trenton State Col, 40-42, from instr to asst prof astron & physics, 46-52, assoc prof math, 52-56, chmn dept, 56-74, prof math, 57-79. *Mem:* Nat Coun Teachers Math; Math Asn Am. *Res:* Differential equations. *Mailing Add:* 116 Woolsey Ct Pennington NJ 08534

HAUSE, NORMAN LAURANCE, ORGANIC & POLYMER CHEMISTRY. *Current Pos:* RETIRED. *Personal Data:* b Ft Lupton, Colo, July 26, 22; m 46, Marjorie Clinton; c 3. *Educ:* Univ Colo, AB, 47, PhD(chem), 50. *Prof Exp:* Asst, Univ Colo, 47; res chemist, Electrochem Dept, E I du Pont de Nemours & Co, Inc, 50-56, res supvr, Exp Sta, 56-60, lab mgr, 60-65, lab dir, Chestnut Run Lab, 65-70, lab dir & mgr polymer res sect, 70-72, res mgr polymer div, Plastic Prod & Resins Dept, 72-79, tech mgr, Ethylene Polymers Div, Polymer Prod Dept, 79-82. *Mem:* Am Chem Soc; Sigma Xi. *Res:* Mechanisms of dehydrohalogenation reactions; furfural chemistry; Diels-Alder reactions; polymers; adhesives; polymeric coatings, plasticizers and modifiers; plastics; thermoplastic elastomers. *Mailing Add:* 35 Hy-View Lane Sedona AZ 86336

HAUSEN, JUTTA, ALGEBRA. *Current Pos:* from asst prof to assoc prof, 68-77, PROF MATH, UNIV HOUSTON, 77- *Personal Data:* b Berlin, Ger, Jan 6, 43. *Educ:* Univ Frankfurt, Dipl Math & PhD(math), 67. *Prof Exp:* Fel, NMex State Univ, 67-68. *Concurrent Pos:* Prin investr res grant, NSF res grant, 72; assoc managing ed, Houston J Math, 74-80, ed, 80-90; res enabling grants & fac develop grants, Univ Houston. *Mem:* Am Math Soc. *Res:* Abelian groups. *Mailing Add:* Dept Math Univ Houston University Park Houston TX 77204-3476

HAUSENBUILLER, ROBERT LEE, SOILS, CHEMISTRY. *Current Pos:* RETIRED. *Personal Data:* b St Joseph, Mo, Sept 20, 18; m 41; c 2. *Educ:* Colo State Univ, BS, 41; Wash State Univ, MS, 48, PhD(soil sci), 51. *Honors & Awards:* Teaching Award, R M Wade Found, 64. *Prof Exp:* Asst soil scientist, Irrig Exp Sta, Wash State Univ, 51-56, asst prof soils, Univ Inter-Col Exchange Team, Univ Panjab, W Pakistan, 56-58, asst soil scientist, Irrig Exp Sta, 58-60, from assoc prof to prof soils, 60-83. *Res:* Soil fertility. *Mailing Add:* NE 1015 B Pullman WA 99163

HAUSER, EDWARD J P, biological sciences; deceased, see previous edition for last biography

HAUSER, EDWARD RUSSELL, PHYSICAL CHEMISTRY, COATINGS CHEMISTRY. *Current Pos:* Sr res chemist, 3M Co, 68-76, res specialist, Bldg Serv & Cleaning Prod Div, 76-85 & Protective Prod Div, 85-93, RES SPECIALIST, SPECIALTY CHEM DIV, 3M, 93- *Personal Data:* b Newark, NJ, July 15, 42; wid; c William & Frederick. *Educ:* Macalester Col, BA, 64; Case Western Res Univ, PhD(phys chem), 69. *Mem:* Am Chem Soc. *Res:* Nucleation of liquids; properties of nonaqueous dispersions with emphasis on the mechanism of surface potential; nonwoven web, fiber production and characterization; polymer crystallization phenomena; blown microfiber production and process; latex coating formulation; concrete forming release agents. *Mailing Add:* 1140 37th St Hudson WI 54016

HAUSER, FRANK MARION, ANTHRACYCLINE ANTIBIOTICS. *Current Pos:* PROF, STATE UNIV NY, ALBANY, 86- *Personal Data:* b Washington, DC, July 31, 43; m 65; c 2. *Educ:* Univ NC, BS, 65, PhD(org chem), 69. *Prof Exp:* Fel, Iowa State Univ, 69-70; fel, Res Triangle Inst, 70-71, chemist, 71-74; from assoc prof to prof, Ore Grad Inst, 74-86. *Concurrent Pos:* Res career develop award, NIH, 78-83. *Mem:* Am Chem Soc. *Res:* Total synthesis of biologically important natural products. *Mailing Add:* Dept Chem State Univ NY Rm CH 122 1400 Washington Ave Albany NY 12222

HAUSER, GEORGE, NEUROCHEMISTRY, LIPID METABOLISM. *Current Pos:* from res assoc to sr res assoc biol chem, 55-85, prof psychiat, biochem & neurosci, 85-93, EMER PROF PSYCHIAT, BIOCHEM & NEUROSCI, HARVARD MED SCH, 93- *Personal Data:* b Vienna, Austria, Dec 13, 22; nat US; m 55, Louise J Russo. *Educ:* Ohio State Univ, BS, 49; Harvard Univ, PhD(biochem), 55. *Concurrent Pos:* USPHS fel, 55-57; from asst biochemist to assoc biochemist, McLean Hosp, 57-78, biochemist, 78-93, sr biochemist, 93-; NIH grants, 65-93; NSF grant, 80-82; interim dir, Ralph Lowell Labs, 83-93; mem coun, Am Soc Neurochem, 83-87; dep chief ed, J Neurochem, 86-92; consult, NSF, Initial Rev Groups, NIH. *Mem:* Am Soc Biochem & Molecular Biol; Brit Biochem Soc; Am & Int Soc Neurochem; Soc Neurosci; Soc Glycoconjugates; fel Japanese Soc Prom Sci. *Res:* Metabolism of the nervous system; carbohydrate and lipid synthesis and function; properties of biological membranes; effects of drugs and cell surface receptor activation on phospholipid metabolism and signal transmission; protein kinase C; second messenger generation and function; signal transmission. *Mailing Add:* Ralph Lowell Labs McLean Hosp Belmont MA 02178-9106. Fax: 617-855-3745; E-Mail: ghauser@warren.med.harvard.edu

HAUSER, JOHN REID, SEMICONDUCTOR DEVICES, MICROELECTRONICS. *Current Pos:* from asst prof to assoc prof, 66-72, PROF ELEC ENG, NC STATE UNIV, 72- *Personal Data:* b Mocksville, NC, Sept 19, 38; m 62, Ann Covington; c John Jr, James & Daniel. *Educ:* NC State Univ, BS, 60; Duke Univ, MS, 62, PhD(elec eng), 64. *Honors & Awards:* Western Elec Fund Award, Am Soc Elec Engrs, 75. *Prof Exp:* Mem tech staff, Bell Tel Labs, 60-62; res engr, Res Triangle Inst, 63-66. *Concurrent Pos:* Vpres, Microelectronics Ctr, NC, 81-82. *Mem:* Fel Inst Elec & Electronics Engrs; Am Phys Soc. *Res:* Solid state electronic materials and devices; microelectronic fabrication techniques; electronic properties of devices and materials. *Mailing Add:* 432 Daniels Hall NC State Univ Raleigh NC 27695

HAUSER, MARC DAVID, COGNITIVE NEUROSCIENCE, BEHAVIORAL ECOLOGY. *Current Pos:* ASST PROF BIOANTHROP & PSYCHOL, HARVARD UNIV, 92- *Personal Data:* b Boston, Mass, Oct 25, 59. *Educ:* Bucknell Univ, BS, 81; Univ Calif, Los Angeles, PhD(biol anthrop), 87. *Honors & Awards:* Young Investr Award, NSF, 93. *Prof Exp:* Fel, Univ Mich, 87-88, Rockefeller Univ, 88-89, Univ Calif, Davis, 89-92. *Concurrent Pos:* Asst ed, Am J Primatology, 89; mem tech comt, Animal Bioacoust, 90. *Mem:* Animal Behav Soc; Acoust Soc Am. *Res:* Investigate the role of each hemisphere of the brain in the perception and production of non-human primate facial and vocal expressions; to contribute to understanding of the evolution of human language. *Mailing Add:* Dept Anthrop Harvard Univ Peabody Mus Cambridge MA 02138-3800

HAUSER, MARTIN, POLYMER CHEMISTRY. *Current Pos:* sr res & analytical chemist, Loctite Corp, 68-70, mgr, technol, 70-75, vpres res & develop, 75-81, vpres environ health & safety, 81-87, VPRES NEW BUS DEVELOP NAM, LOCTITE CORP, 87- *Personal Data:* b Berlin, Ger, Jan 6, 34; US citizen; m 55; c 3. *Educ:* Union Col, BS, 55; Univ Buffalo, MA, 58, PhD(org chem), 60. *Prof Exp:* Chemist, Stein-Hall, Inc, 55-56; res chemist, Am Cyanamid Co, 60-66, sr res chemist, 66-68. *Mem:* Am Chem Soc. *Res:* Heterocyclic synthesis and properties of hetero-atom polymers; polyester chemistry; anaerobic adhesives; cyanoacrylate adhesives. *Mailing Add:* Loctite Corp 1001 Trout Brook Crossing Rocky Hill CT 06067-3910

HAUSER, MICHAEL GEORGE, SPACE INFRARED ASTRONOMY & COSMOLOGY. *Current Pos:* head, Infrared Astron Group, Lab High Energy Astrophys, Goddard Space Flight Ctr, 74-77, head, Infrared Astrophys Sect, 77-85, head, Infrared Astrophyshys Br, Lab Extraterrestrial Physics, 85-87, assoc chief, Lab Astron & Solar Physics, 87-88, CHIEF, LAB ASTRON & SOLAR PHYSICS, GODDARD SPACE FLIGHT CTR, 88- *Personal Data:* b Chicago, Ill, Dec 3, 39; m 60, 81, Deanna S Goering; c Karen C (deceased), Gerald P, Lisa Grove, Amy (Canby) & Beth Grove. *Educ:* Cornell Univ, BEP, 62; Calif Inst Technol, PhD(physics), 67. *Honors & Awards:* Except Sci Achievement Medal, NASA, 84 & 91, Pub Serv Group Achievement Award, 84. *Prof Exp:* Res assoc physics, Princeton Univ, 67, instr, 67-70, asst prof, 70-72; sr res fel physics, Calif Inst Technol, 72-74. *Concurrent Pos:* Mem sci working group, Infrared Astron Satellite, 75-88; prin investr, Cosmic Background Explorer Mission, 76-; adj prof astron, Univ Md. *Mem:* AAAS; fel Am Phys Soc; Am Astron Soc; Sigma Xi; Int Astron Union. *Res:* Far infrared astronomy of galactic and extragalactic objects and diffuse cosmic infrared radiation; physics of cosmic infrared sources; sensitive detectors for submillimeter and millimeter wavelength radiation. *Mailing Add:* Space Telescope Sci Inc 3700 San Martin Dr Baltimore MD 21218

HAUSER, RAY LOUIS, MATERIALS ENGINEERING, CHEMICAL ENGINEERING. *Current Pos:* partner & res dir, 61-89, DIR & SR SCIENTIST, HAUSER LABS, 90- *Personal Data:* b Litchfield, Ill, Apr 16, 27; m 51, Consuelo Minnich; c 4. *Educ:* Univ Ill, Urbana, BS, 50; Yale Univ, MEng, 52; Univ Colo, PhD(chem eng), 57. *Prof Exp:* Sr engr, Conn Hard Rubber Co, 51-52; mem res staff, Univ Colo, 55-57; group engr, Martin Co, Colo, 57-58, unit head mat eng, 58-59, staff engr, 59-61. *Concurrent Pos:* Vis lectr, Univ Colo, 57-66. *Mem:* Fel AAAS; Soc Plastics Engrs; Am Inst Chem Engrs; Am Soc Test & Mat. *Res:* Applied research and development with plastics, adhesives, coatings and products; development of ultrasonic bonding techniques; medical applications and instrumentation with polymeric materials; forensic science and products liability testimony. *Mailing Add:* Hauser Inc 5555 Airport Blvd Boulder CO 80301

HAUSER, RICHARD SCOTT, ECOLOGY. *Current Pos:* RETIRED. *Personal Data:* b Chile, Mar 15, 19; US citizen; m 44; c 5. *Educ:* Oberlin Col, AB, 41; Mich State Univ, MS, 47, PhD(bot), 53. *Prof Exp:* From instr to assoc prof biol, State Univ NY Albany, 48-63, prof, 63-82. *Res:* Biogeography. *Mailing Add:* 245 McCormack Rd Slingerlands NY 12159-9320

HAUSER, ROLLAND KEITH, METEOROLOGY. *Current Pos:* From asst prof to assoc prof, 67-75, chmn, Dept Geol & Phys Sci, 70-72, PROF GEOSCI, CALIF STATE UNIV, CHICO, 75- *Personal Data:* b Marshalltown, Iowa, Aug 30, 37; m 63; c 3. *Educ:* Iowa State Univ, BS, 60; Univ Chicago, SM, 64, PhD(geophys sci), 67. *Honors & Awards:* Clean Air Award, Lung Asn. *Concurrent Pos:* Vis res prof, Environ Field Sta, Royal Mil Col Sci, Eng, 75; res meteorologist, Upper Air Br, Nat Meteorol Ctr, Marlow Heights, Md, 76; dir, Aerospace Educ Serv Proj, NASA, 76-78; tech dir, Nowcasting, Inc, Chico, Ca, 80-85; tech consult, Software Illus, Inc, Pleasant

Hills, Calif, 84-85; sci consult, Weather Network, Inc, Sunnyvale, Calif, 85-87; meteorol consult, USDA Forest Serv, 85-, Nat Oceanic & Atmospheric Admin, 86, US Dept Defense, Atmospheric Res Lab, 87-88, Sonoma Technol Inc, Santa Rosa, Calif, 89-91 & Aerovironment Inc, Monrovia, Calif, 90-91; chair, Unidata McIdas Broadcast Eval Comt, 87-88; mem, Comn Learning Resources & Instrnl Technol, Calif State Univ, 92-; fac sabbatical res appointment, Dept Energy, 93-94. *Mem:* Am Meteorol Soc; Am Geophys Union; AAAS; Am Asn State Climatologists; Coun Agr Sci & Technol; Int Air & Waste Mgt Asn. *Res:* Television presentation of subject matter; weather services via microcomputers; agricultural meteorology; air pollution meteorology; meteorology field studies. *Mailing Add:* Geo Sci Calif State Univ Chico 101 Orange St Chico CA 95929-0001

HAUSER, VICTOR LA VERN, AGRICULTURAL ENGINEERING, APPLIED MATHEMATICS. *Current Pos:* res engr water conserv, 57-70, res engr water qual, 70-76, RES ENGR WATER CONSERV, USDA, 76- *Personal Data:* b Hitchcock, Okla, July 1, 29; m 58; c 2. *Educ:* Okla State Univ, BS, 52; Univ Calif, Davis, MS, 57; Tex A&M Univ, PhD(agr eng), 73. *Prof Exp:* Asst prof agr eng, Tex Tech Univ, 57. *Concurrent Pos:* Adv water qual, Nat Acad Sci, 70-72. *Mem:* Fel Am Soc Agr Engrs; Am Soc Civil Engrs; Am Geophys Union; Soc Range Mgt; Soil Conserv Soc. *Res:* Hydrology; dryland water conservation; ground water recharge; water quality; irrigation; range and grassland management. *Mailing Add:* PO Box 781207 San Antonio TX 78278

HAUSER, WILLARD ALLEN, NEUROEPIDEMIOLOGY, ELECTROENCEPHALOGRAPHY. *Current Pos:* assoc prof neurol, 78-81, assoc prof neurol & epidemiol, 81-84, PROF NEUROL & EPIDEMIOL, COLUMBIA UNIV, 84- *Personal Data:* b Cleveland, Ohio, Mar 6, 37; div; c 3. *Educ:* Case Western Res Univ, AB, 58; St Louis Univ, MD, 62. *Prof Exp:* Resident neurol, Northwestern Univ, 63-66; staff neurologist, US Army, 66-68; res asst, Mayo Clin, 68-69, res assoc epidemiol, 69-70; from asst prof to assoc prof neurol, Univ Minn, 70-78. *Concurrent Pos:* Spec proj assoc, Dept Epidemiol, Mayo Clin, 70-86, sr vis scientist, 86-; examr, Am Bd Qual Electroencephal, 71- & Am Bd Psychiat & Neurol, 76-80; co-investr, Epidemiol & Genetics Sect Comprehensive Epilepsy Prog, State Minn, 75-; consult, Biomet & Epidemiol Br, 76-77 & Nat Adv Bd Epilepsy, 78-81; NATO fel, CNR, Italy, 91-92. *Mem:* Am Acad Neurol; Am EEG Soc; Soc Epidemiol Res; Am Epilepsy Soc; Am Neurol Soc; Am Epidemiol Soc. *Res:* Epidemiology of neurologic diseases. *Mailing Add:* G H Sergievsky Ctr 630 W 168th St New York NY 10032-3702

HAUSER, WILLIAM JOSEPH, FISH BIOLOGY, VERTEBRATE ZOOLOGY. *Current Pos:* REGIONAL BIOLOGIST-COOK INLET & PRINCE WILLIAM SOUND ALASKA DEPT FISH & GAME, DIV FISHERIES REHAB, ENHANCEMENT & DEVELOP, 80- *Personal Data:* b Davenport, Iowa, Aug 4, 42; m 69. *Educ:* Univ Wis-Madison, BS, 65; Mont State Univ, MS, 68; Univ Maine, Orono, PhD(zool), 73. *Prof Exp:* Asst res biologist, Univ Calif, Riverside, 73-77; mem staff, San Francisco Regional Lab, Nalco Environ Sci, 77-78, fisheries sect head, Hazelton Environ Sci, 78-80. *Mem:* Am Fisheries Soc; AAAS; Sigma Xi. *Res:* Biolgoical control of aquatic weeds in irrigation systems in the lower Colorado River basin by fish, especially Tilapia zillii. *Mailing Add:* 3621 Hazen Circle Anchorage AK 99502-2371

HAUSER, WILLIAM P, PHOTOGRAPHIC CHEMISTRY. *Current Pos:* REGISTERED PATENT AGENT, BRENEMAN, GEORGES & KRIKELIS, PA, 91- *Personal Data:* b Cincinnati, Ohio, Apr, 28, 34; m 66; c 3. *Educ:* Univ Notre Dame, BS, 56; Univ Rochester, PhD(phys chem), 61. *Prof Exp:* Aerospace technologist, Goddard Space Flight Ctr, NASA, 61-62; fel, Radiation Lab, Mellon Inst, 62-63; fel, Univ Notre Dame, 63-66; mem staff, E I du Pont de Nemours & Co Inc, 66-72, sr patent chemist, 72-81, patent assoc, Photo Prod Dept, 81-91. *Mem:* Am Chem Soc; Sigma Xi. *Res:* Thermal reaction kinetics; chemistry of upper atmosphere; radiation chemistry of gases; electron impact phenomena. *Mailing Add:* 129 Marlbrook Way Kennett Square PA 19348-1719

HAUSFATER, GLENN, PRIMATE BEHAVIOR. *Current Pos:* PROF BIOL, UNIV MO, 83- *Personal Data:* b St Louis, Mo, Feb 10, 47. *Educ:* Northwestern Univ, BA, 70; Univ Chicago, PhD(evolutionary biol), 74. *Prof Exp:* Asst prof psychol & biol, Univ Va, 73-77; assoc prof neurobiol & behav, Cornell Univ, 78-83. *Concurrent Pos:* Co-dir, Longitudinal Study Amboseli Baboons, Kenya, 74-83; prin investr grants, Nat Sci Found, 74-; assoc ed, Am J Primatol, Am J Phys Anthropol, The Behav & Brain Sci & Behav Ecol Sociobiol, 77-; dir, Liddell Lab Animal Behav, Cornell Univ, 78-82; bd dir, NCountry Inst Nat Philos; res career develop award, Nat Inst Child Health & Human Develop, 76-81; Lady Davis vis prof, Inst Life Sci, Hebrew Univ Jerusalem, Israel. *Mem:* Am Soc Primatologists; Animal Behav Soc; AAAS; Int Primatol Soc; East Africa Wildlife Soc. *Res:* Evolutionary causes and consequences of group-living in animals, especially nonhuman primates; dominance and aggression in primates; behavioral factors in the transmission of parasites and diseases. *Mailing Add:* 1842 N Burling Chicago IL 60614

HAUSLER, CARL LOUIS, ANIMAL SCIENCE, REPRODUCTIVE PHYSIOLOGY. *Current Pos:* Asst prof, 70-77, ASSOC PROF REPRODUCTIVE PHYSIOL, SOUTHERN ILL UNIV, CARBONDALE, 77- *Personal Data:* b Schenectady, NY, Aug 18, 41. *Educ:* Univ Vt, BS, 63, MS, 65; Purdue Univ, PhD(reproductive physiol), 70. *Concurrent Pos:* Educ specialist, Food & Agr Orgn, Southern Ill Univ, 70-72; consult, 75, Port, 82-84 & Liberia, 84. *Mem:* Am Soc Animal Sci; Am Dairy Sci Asn; Soc Study Reproduction; AAAS; Sigma Xi. *Res:* Reproductive physiology applied to increased efficiency of animal production; inducing ovulation in lactating sows; estrus detection in cattle; breeding management. *Mailing Add:* Animal Sci Southern Ill Univ Carbondale IL 62901-4399

HAUSLER, RUDOLF H, CORROSION, PETROLEUM CHEMISTRY. *Current Pos:* PRES, CORRO-CONSULTA CORP, 96- *Personal Data:* b Zurich, Switz, Apr 9, 34; US citizen; m 72, Barbara Corsan; c Natasha. *Educ:* Swiss Fed Inst Tech, MS, 58, PhD(chem), 61. *Honors & Awards:* Tech Achievement Award, Nat Asn Corrosion Engrs, 89; Plenary lectr, Singapore, 89, Italy, 90, Bahrain, 91. *Prof Exp:* Proj leader, Battelle Mem Inst, Switz, 61-63; res scientist, Universal Oil Prod Co, 63-67, assoc res coordr, 67-72, res assoc, 72-76; tech dir, Gordon Lab, Inc, Great Bend, Kans, 76-78; sr res chemist, Petrolite Corp, 79-82, prin investr, 82-86, res fel, 86-90; res assoc, Mobil Res & Develop Corp, 90-96. *Concurrent Pos:* Lectr, Ill Inst Technol, 75-76, Univ Aachen, Ger, Univ Ferrara, Italy & Univ Manchester, Eng, 85. *Mem:* Am Chem Soc; Electrochem Soc; Nat Asn Corrosion Engrs; Am Soc Metals; Soc Petrol Engrs. *Res:* Technology of nickel-cadmium batteries; organic electrochemistry; electrocatalysis; corrosion and corrosion inhibition in chemical process industry; crude oil production chemicals; industrial heat transfer; anti-foulants; corrosion inhibitors for oil and gas production; corrosion inhibition in chemical cleaning of nuclear steam generators; author of 3 books and 46 publications. *Mailing Add:* 7804 Pencross Lane Dallas TX 75248

HAUSLER, WILLIAM JOHN, JR, PUBLIC HEALTH ADMINISTRATION. *Current Pos:* after asst dir, Iowa State Hyg Lab, 59-65, PROF PREV MED & ENVIRON HEALTH, COLS MED, UNIV IOWA, 90-, PROF ORAL PATH, COL DENT, 90- *Personal Data:* b Kansas City, Kans, Aug 31, 26; m 49; c Cheryl K, K Randall, Eric R & Mark C. *Educ:* Univ Kans, AB, 51, MA, 53, PhD(bact), 58; Am Bd Med Microbiol, dipl. *Honors & Awards:* Henry Albert Award. *Prof Exp:* Asst instr bact, Univ Kans, 51-57; asst sanit, Kans State Bd Health, 57-58. *Concurrent Pos:* From asst prof to assoc prof hyg & prev med, Univ Iowa, 59-90, assoc prof oral path, 66-90; WHO consult to Iran, 69, China, 90 & Western Pac, UNDP-India; comnr, Iowa Air Pollution Control Comn; ed, Stand Methods for Exam Dairy Prods; dir, Iowa State Hyg Lab, Univ Iowa, 65-95, emer dir, 95-; lectr, Hebei Med Col, China, 87- *Mem:* Am Soc Microbiol; fel Am Pub Health Asn; Sigma Xi; fel Am Acad Microbiol; NY Acad Sci; AAAS. *Res:* Public health microbiology; physical-microbiological methods; Brucellosis; AIDS. *Mailing Add:* State Hyg Lab Univ Iowa Iowa City IA 52242. *Fax:* 319-335-4600; *E-Mail:* william-hausler@uiowa.edu

HAUSMAN, ARTHUR HERBERT, ELECTROMAGNETISM. *Current Pos:* RETIRED. *Personal Data:* b Chicago, Ill, Nov 24, 23; m 46; c 3. *Educ:* Univ Tex, BSEE, 44; Harvard, SM, 48. *Prof Exp:* Vpres res, Ampex Corp, 60-63, opers, 63-65, group vpres, 65-67, exec vpres, 67-71, pres & chief exec officer, 71-83, chmn bd, 81-87. *Concurrent Pos:* Lectr, Dept Appl Math, Univ Tex, 42-44; chmn, Tech Adv Comt, Dept Com, 73-75; mem vis comt, Dept Math, Mass Inst Technol, 83-86; mem, Pres Export Coun, 84-88, chmn, Export Admin Sub-Comt, 84-88; consult pvt indust & US Govt, 88- *Mem:* Inst Elec & Electronics Engrs. *Res:* Magnetic materials, magnetic tape and magnetic tape/disk recording; electromagnetic wave propagation in the radio high frequency spectrum. *Mailing Add:* 55 Flood Circle Atherton CA 94027

HAUSMAN, GARY J, FAT CELL DIFFERENTIATION & DEVELOPMENT. *Current Pos:* RES PHYSIOLOGIST, RICHARD RUSSELL RES CTR, USDA, 81- *Personal Data:* b Carol, Iowa, Dec 4, 48. *Educ:* Univ Wis-Madison, PhD(animal sci), 77. *Mem:* Am Soc Animal Sci; Am Inst Nutrit. *Mailing Add:* Richard B Russell Res Ctr USDA ARS PO Box 5677 Athens GA 30613-0001

HAUSMAN, HERSHEL J, NUCLEAR PHYSICS. *Current Pos:* from asst prof to prof, 52-89, supvr, Van De Graaff Lab, 62-89, EMER PROF PHYSICS, OHIO STATE UNIV, 89- *Personal Data:* b Pittsburgh, Pa, Aug 19, 23; m 50, Korene Brenner; c Herbert A, Sally Z & William B. *Educ:* Carnegie Inst Technol, BS, 48, MS, 49; Univ Pittsburgh, PhD(physics), 52. *Prof Exp:* Instr physics, Univ Pittsburgh, 49-50, res assoc, 50-52. *Concurrent Pos:* USAID consult, India, 64, 65. *Mem:* Fel Am Phys Soc; Am Asn Physics Teachers. *Res:* Nuclear scattering problems; nuclear reaction mechanisms; nuclear capture reactions. *Mailing Add:* Dept Physics Ohio State Univ 174 W 18th Ave Columbus OH 43212

HAUSMAN, ROBERT, pathology; deceased, see previous edition for last biography

HAUSMAN, ROBERT EDWARD, CELL-CELL INTERACTIONS & SIGNALING. *Current Pos:* asst prof, 78-87, ASSOC PROF DEVELOP BIOL & DIR GRAD STUDIES BIOL, DEPT BIOL, BOSTON UNIV, 87- *Personal Data:* b New York, NY, Feb 15, 47; m 87, Barbara S Wood; c Edward. *Educ:* Case Western Res Univ, AB, 69, MA, 69; Northwestern Univ, PhD(biol), 71. *Prof Exp:* Fel develop biol, Dept Biol, Univ Chicago, 71-74, res assoc, Comt Develop Biol, 74-78. *Concurrent Pos:* Investr, Cancer Ctr, Univ Chicago, 76-78; mem, Interdept Biochem Prog, Boston Univ, 78- *Mem:* AAAS; Asn Res Vision & Ophthal; Int Soc Develop Biologists; Soc Neurosci; Soc Develop Biol; Am Soc Cell Biol. *Res:* Control of gene expression during embryonic development especially of nerve and muscle; specific interest in the roles of cell-cell signaling and cell interactions in such gene control. *Mailing Add:* Biol Dept Boston Univ 5 Cummington St Boston MA 02215-2425. *Fax:* 617-353-6390

HAUSMAN, STEVEN J, IMMUNOGENETICS, CELL BIOLOGY. *Current Pos:* DEP DIR, NAT INST ARTHRITIS, MUSCULO SKELETAL & SKIN DIS, 90- *Personal Data:* b Philadelphia, Pa, May 20, 45. *Educ:* Univ Pa, BA, 67, MS, 68, PhD(biol), 72. *Prof Exp:* Assoc, Inst Cancer Res, 72-75; staff fel, Nat Inst Aging, NIH, 75-77; from spec asst to assoc dir, Nat Inst Arthritis,

Metab & Digestive Dis, 77-78; prog dir, Arthritis Ctr, Nat Inst Arthritis Diabetes, Digestive & Kidney Dis, 78-87, dep dir, extramural activ, 86-90. *Concurrent Pos:* Fel, Children's Hosp Pa, 75. *Mem:* AAAS; Am Asn Immunologists; Am Chem Soc; Am Soc Cell Biol; Tissue Cult Asn. *Mailing Add:* PO Box 3819 Gaithersburg MD 20885. *E-Mail:* nsh@cu.nih.gov

HAUSMAN, WARREN H, PRODUCTION & OPERATIONS MANAGEMENT. *Current Pos:* chmn, 82-92, PROF, DEPT INDUST ENG & ENG MGT, STANFORD UNIV, 77- *Personal Data:* m; c 2. *Educ:* Yale Univ, BA, 61; Mass Inst Technol, PhD(indust mgt), 66. *Prof Exp:* From asst prof to assoc prof, Grad Sch Bus & Pub Admin, Cornell Univ, 65-70; assoc prof, Sloan Sch Mgt, Mass Inst Technol, 70-73; from assoc prof to prof, Grad Sch Mgt, Univ Rochester, 73-77. *Concurrent Pos:* Consult var corp & bus, 62-; vis prof, Inst Admin Gestion, Univ Cath Louvain, Belg, 81; vis scholar, Europ Inst Advan Studies Mgt, Brussels, Belg, 81; author var publ; adv panel mem, Decision, Risk & Mgt Sci Progs, NSF, 87-90. *Mem:* Inst Mgt Sci; Inst Indust Engrs; Opers Res Soc Am. *Res:* Productions and operations management. *Mailing Add:* Dept Indust Eng & Eng Mgt Terman 350 Stanford Univ Stanford CA 94305

HAUSMAN, WILLIAM, PSYCHIATRY, SCIENCE EDUCATION. *Current Pos:* RETIRED. *Personal Data:* b Brooklyn, NY, July 25, 25; m 47, Lillian M Fuerst; c Steven, Peter, Clifford & Linda (Johnson). *Educ:* Washington Univ, MD, 47; Am Bd Neurol & Psychiat, dipl, 53. *Prof Exp:* Instr, Med Sch, Univ Pa, 50-52; chief, Psychiat Serv, Letterman Gen Hosp, US Army, 61-62, chief, Behav Sci Res Br, Off Surgeon Gen, 62-65, dep dir, Div Neuropsychiat, Walter Reed Army Inst, 65-66, assoc prof psychiat, Student Ment Health Serv & dir, Curriculum Options Study, Sch Med, Johns Hopkins Univ, 66-69; prof psychiat, Univ Minn, Minneapolis, 69-87, chmn dept, 69-80. *Concurrent Pos:* Mem res coun, US Army, 65-66; dir group rels conf, A K Rice Inst, 66-, mem bd dir, 67-74, pres bd, 70-73; mem fac, Wash Sch Psychiat, 67-69; consult, Univ Man, Winnipeg, 75-76 & Levinson Inst, 75- *Mem:* AAAS; fel Am Psychiat Asn; Int Asn Social Psychiat; fel Am Col Psychiat. *Res:* Selection and adaptation; group process; concepts basic to social psychiatry; psychiatric education. *Mailing Add:* 3785 Ranch Crest Dr Reno NV 89509

HAUSMANN, ERNEST, BIOCHEMISTRY. *Current Pos:* assoc prof, 66-70, PROF ORAL BIOL, STATE UNIV NY, BUFFALO, 70-, ASST DEAN, SCH DENT, 66- *Personal Data:* b Heidelberg, Ger, June 19, 29; US citizen; m 51; c 4. *Educ:* NY Univ, BA, 51; Harvard Univ, DMD, 56; Univ Rochester, PhD(biochem), 60. *Prof Exp:* Nat Inst Dent Res fel, 57-59; asst prof pharmacol, State Univ NY, Buffalo, 60-64; assoc prof periodont, Univ Ky, 64-66. *Concurrent Pos:* Nat Inst Dent Res career develop award, 61-66. *Mem:* Int Asn Dent Res. *Res:* Dental research; collagen; calcium metabolism. *Mailing Add:* 82 High Park Blvd Amherst NY 14226

HAUSMANN, WERNER KARL, SEPARATION TECHNIQUES. *Current Pos:* CONSULT QUAL ASSURANCE & ANALYTIC RES & DEVELOP, QUAL-EX CO, 85- *Personal Data:* b Edigheim, Ger, Mar 9, 21; US citizen; m 49, Helen Vas; c Gregory. *Educ:* Swiss Fed Inst Technol, MS, 45, DSc, 47. *Prof Exp:* Res fel biochem, Univ London, Eng, 47-48; res assoc, Rockefeller Inst Med Res, 49-57; group leader antibiotics res, Lederle Labs, 57-66; assoc dir qual control, Ayerst Labs, 66-71; dir, Stuart Pharmaceut, 71-74; corp dir qual assurance & analytical res & develop, Adria Labs, 74-84. *Concurrent Pos:* Lectr, Am Mgt Asn, 68. *Mem:* Fel Am Soc Qual Control; fel Am Inst Chemists; fel Royal Soc Chem; Am Soc Biol Chemists; Acad Pharmaceut Sci; Am Chem Soc; fel NY Acad Sci; fel AAAS; fel Chem Soc London. *Res:* Analytical chemistry; pharmaceutical compounds as such and in dosage forms and biological fluids; purification, isolation and structure determination of biologically active compounds; new antibiotics; high performance liquid chromatography. *Mailing Add:* 4332 Post Rd San Diego CA 92117

HAUSNER, MELVIN, GEOMETRY, COMBINATORICS. *Current Pos:* assoc prof, Washington Sq Col, NY Univ, 60-66, actg chmn dept, 65-66, chmn dept, 70-73, PROF MATH, WASHINGTON SQ COL, NY UNIV, 66- *Personal Data:* b USA, Apr 11, 28; m, Frieda Plotkin; c 2. *Educ:* Brooklyn Col, BSc, 48; Princeton Univ, MA, 49, PhD(math), 51. *Prof Exp:* Res mathematician, Rand Corp, 51-52; instr math, Brooklyn Col, 52-53, 55-56; asst prof, Stevens Inst Technol, 56-60. *Concurrent Pos:* Ed, Encycl Am. *Mem:* Am Math Soc; Math Asn Am. *Res:* Geometry and combinatorics. *Mailing Add:* Dept Math NY Univ 251 Mercer St New York NY 10012

HAUSPURG, ARTHUR, POWER SYSTEMS, ULTRAHIGH VOLTAGE TRANSMISSION SYSTEMS. *Current Pos:* RETIRED. *Personal Data:* b New York, NY, 1925. *Educ:* Columbia Univ, BS, 45, MS, 47. *Prof Exp:* Chmn & chief exec officer, Consolidated Edison Co, 82-90. *Mem:* Nat Acad Eng; fel Inst Elec & Electronics Engrs. *Mailing Add:* 4 Irving Place New York NY 10003. *Fax:* 212-460-1252

HAUSRATH, ALAN RICHARD, QUALITATIVE THEORY OF DIFFERENTIAL EQUATIONS, PERIODIC SOLUTIONS OF DIFFERENTIAL EQUATIONS. *Current Pos:* PROF MATH, BOISE STATE UNIV, 76- *Personal Data:* b E Cleveland, Ohio, Sept 12, 45; m 71, Anne Stites; c Elisabeth, Katherine & Daniel. *Educ:* Mass Inst Technol, ScB, 67; Brown Univ, PhD(appl math), 72; Wash State Univ, MEd, 77. *Prof Exp:* Asst prof math, Univ Pittsburgh, 71-76. *Concurrent Pos:* Vis prof, Univ Andes, Venezuela, 78-79; vis scholar, Univ Chile, 86. *Mem:* Am Math Soc; Math Asn Am. *Res:* Qualitative theory of differential equations; differential equations arising as models of biological systems; differential equations with infinite delay. *Mailing Add:* Dept Math & Comput Sci Boise Univ Boise ID 83725-0001. *Fax:* 208-334-3684; *E-Mail:* hausrath@math.idbsu.edu

HAUSSER, JACK W, ORGANIC CHEMISTRY. *Current Pos:* from asst prof to assoc prof, 62-72, chmn dept, 72-75, PROF CHEM, DUQUESNE UNIV, 72- *Personal Data:* b Cleveland, Ohio, Jan 6, 35; m 59; c 3. *Educ:* Case Western Res Univ, BS, 56; Univ Ill, PhD(org chem), 60. *Prof Exp:* Res assoc org chem, Iowa State Univ, 60-62. *Mem:* AAAS; Am Chem Soc; Sigma Xi. *Res:* Mechanisms of organic reactions; chemistry of small ring compounds; solvolytic displacement reactions. *Mailing Add:* Dept Chem Duquesne Univ Pittsburgh PA 15219

HAUSSER, OTTO FRIEDRICH, NUCLEAR PHYSICS. *Current Pos:* PROF PHYSICS, SIMON FRASER UNIV, BURNABY, BC, 83- *Personal Data:* b Schwabach, WGer, Dec 9, 37; c 2. *Educ:* Univ Erlangen, dipl, 62, PhD(physics), 64. *Prof Exp:* NATO fel, Oxford Univ, 64-66; Nat Res Coun Can fel, Chalk River Nuclear Labs, Atomic Energy Can Ltd, 66-67, res officer, 67-83. *Mem:* Fel Am Phys Soc; Can Asn Physicists. *Res:* Hyperfine interactions; weak interactions; nuclear moments; intermediate energy physics; polarized targets; nucleon structure; spin physics. *Mailing Add:* TRIUMF 4004 Wesbrook Mall Vancouver BC V6T 2A3 Can

HAUSSLEIN, ROBERT WILLIAM, CHEMICAL ENGINEERING. *Current Pos:* VPRES, HYPERIAN CATALYSIS INT. *Personal Data:* b New York, NY, Sept 17, 37; m 60; c 3. *Educ:* Mass Inst Technol, SB, 58, PhD(chem eng), 65. *Prof Exp:* Asst prof chem eng, Mass Inst Technol, 65-66; asst dir res, Amicon Corp, 66-71; from res group leader to sr res group leader, Polaroid Corp, 71-77, mgr photosysts, 77-80, sr res lab mgr, 80-88. *Concurrent Pos:* Ford fel, Mass Inst Technol, 65-66. *Mem:* Electrochem Soc. *Res:* Photographic chemistry; coating technology; colloid technology. *Mailing Add:* 20 Slocum Rd Lexington MA 02173

HAUSSLING, HENRY JACOB, FLUID DYNAMICS. *Current Pos:* MATHEMATICIAN FLUID DYNAMICS, DAVID W TAYLOR NAVAL SHIP RES & DEVELOP CTR, 68- *Personal Data:* b Newark, NJ, June 18, 45; m 68; c 7. *Educ:* Mass Inst Technol, BS, 67; Univ Md, PhD(meteorol), 74. *Mem:* Sigma Xi. *Res:* The use of numerical methods for solving partial differential equations; computational fluid dynamics; numerical ship hydrodynamics. *Mailing Add:* 13325 Norsire Lane Lovettsville VA 20180-9015

HAUSSMANN, ULRICH GUNTHER, STOCHASTIC OPTIMAL CONTROL, FILTERING THEORY. *Current Pos:* Fel & res assoc, 70, from asst prof to assoc prof, 70-82, PROF MATH, UNIV BC, 82- *Personal Data:* Can citizen. *Educ:* Univ Toronto, BSc, 66; Brown Univ, PhD(appl math), 70. *Concurrent Pos:* Vis prof, Univ Grenoble, 75-76, Univ Paris, 83 & Univ Provence, 84. *Mem:* Soc Indust & Appl Math. *Res:* Optimal control of stochastic systems, non-linear filtering theory, theory of diffusions. *Mailing Add:* Dept Math Univ BC 1984 Mathematics Rd No 121 Vancouver BC V6T 1Z2 Can

HAUST, M DARIA, PATHOLOGY, PEDIATRICS. *Current Pos:* assoc prof, 67-68, PROF PATH, UNIV WESTERN ONT, 68-, PROF PEDIAT, 72-, PROF OBSTET & GYNEC, 77- *Personal Data:* Can citizen; m; c 2. *Educ:* Queen's Univ, Ont, MSc, 59. *Honors & Awards:* Alexander von Humboldt & Distinguished Serv Award, 82; Serv Award, Am Heart Asn, 86; William Boyd lectr, Can Asn Pathologists, 90. *Prof Exp:* From asst prof to assoc prof path, Queen's Univ, Ont, 60-67. *Concurrent Pos:* Res assoc, Ont Heart Found, 60-63, sr res assoc, 63-71; mem coun arteriosclerosis, Am Heart Asn, 65-68; vis scientist, Oxford Univ, 72-73; mem educ comt, Intl Acad Path, 69-72, coun, 70-73; task force & rec secy, Int Atherosclerosis Soc, 76-78, chmn, Vomy Vondy, 77-79; coordr, Adv Expert Panel Pediat Path, Int Pediat Asn, 80-87. *Mem:* Am Asn Path & Bact; Am Soc Exp Path; Can Asn Path; Int Acad Path; Int Atherosclerosis Soc (secy-treas, 78-85, treas, 85-); Int Pediat Asn; Am Heart Asn; Int Acad Path. *Res:* Basic structural and biochemical nature of fibrous connective tissue in health and disease, especially inborn errors of metabolism, selected collagen diseases and atherosclerosis; obstetrics and gynecology. *Mailing Add:* Dept Path Univ Western Ont London ON N6A 5C1 Can

HAUSTEIN, PETER EUGENE, NUCLEAR STRUCTURE. *Current Pos:* assoc chemist, Brookhaven Nat Lab, NY, 75-78, chemist, 78-90, asst chmn Chem Dept, 88-90, assoc chmn, 90-95, SR CHEMIST, BROOKHAVEN NAT LAB, NY, 90- *Personal Data:* b Detroit, Mich, Jan 17, 44. *Educ:* Univ Calif, BS, 66; Iowa State Univ, MS & PhD(nuclear chem), 70. *Prof Exp:* Fel nuclear chem, Brookhaven Nat Lab, 70-72; asst prof chem, Yale Univ, 72-75. *Concurrent Pos:* Vis scientist, Lawrence Berkeley Nat Lab, 79, 89-90 & 97, Europ Coun Nuclear Res, 83-84; comt Nuclear & Radiochem Nat Acad Sci, 80-85; chmn, Div Nuclear Chem, Am Chem Soc, 97. *Mem:* Am Chem Soc; Am Phys Soc; Sigma Xi. *Res:* Nuclear structure and reaction studies; nuclear resonance spectroscopy; relativistic heavy-ion reactions; production and use of radioactie beams. *Mailing Add:* Dept Chem Brookhaven Nat Lab Bldg 555A Upton NY 11973-5000. *Fax:* 516-282-5815; *E-Mail:* haustein@bnldag.ags.bnl.gov

HAUSWIRTH, WILLIAM WALTER, GENE TRANSMISSION, GENE EXPRESSION. *Current Pos:* from asst prof to assoc prof, 76-85, PROF MOLECULAR GENETICS, COL MED, UNIV FLA, 85-, RYBACZKI-BALLARD PROF MOLECULAR GENETICS, 86- *Personal Data:* b San Francisco, Calif, Jan 1, 45. *Educ:* Stanford Univ, BS, 66; Ore State Univ, PhD(chem), 71. *Prof Exp:* Asst prof biochem, Johns Hopkins Univ, 74-75. *Concurrent Pos:* Mem, Molecular Biol Study Sect, NIH, 86- *Mem:* Am Chem Soc; Am Soc Biol Chemists; Am Soc Microbiol; Sigma Xi; Int Soc Plant Molecular Biol. *Res:* Animal and plant mitochondrial DNA molecular biology; transmission genetics; evolution; developmental biology. *Mailing Add:* Dept Med Microbiol Univ Fla Col Med PO Box J-266 Gainesville FL 32610. *Fax:* 352-392-3062

HAUT, ARTHUR, HEMATOLOGY, INTERNAL MEDICINE. *Current Pos:* assoc prof, 63-67, head, Sect Hemat, 63-72, PROF MED, MED CTR, UNIV ARK, LITTLE ROCK, 67-, DIR, DIV HEMAT & ONCOL, 72- *Personal Data:* b New York, NY, Oct 1, 27; m 53; c 4. *Educ:* Columbia Univ, AB, 46, MD, 50; Am Bd Internal Med, dipl, 57. *Prof Exp:* Instr med, Col Med, Univ Utah, 57-60, asst prof, 60-63. *Concurrent Pos:* Teaching fel med, Harvard Med Sch, 52-53; Am Cancer Soc fel, Col Med, Univ Utah, 53-55; Markle scholar acad med, 59-64; consult hemat, Surgeon Gen, US Army, Europe, 55-57 & Little Rock Vet Hosp, Ark, 63-; mem, Hemat study sect, NIH, 67-71; mem, Hemat Test Comt, Am Bd Internal Med, 70-73; mem, Merit Rev Bd Hemat, Vet Admin, 74- *Mem:* Am Fedn Clin Res; fel Am Col Physicians; Am Soc Hemat. *Res:* Chemotherapy of leukemia; erythrocytic nonhemoglobin proteins; cancer chemotherapy. *Mailing Add:* 4301 W Markham St Little Rock AR 72205-7101

HAUTALA, RICHARD ROY, ORGANIC CHEMISTRY, PHOTOCHEMISTRY. *Current Pos:* asst prof chem, 72-78, ASSOC PROF, UNIV GA, 78-; DISCOVER-DEPT CHEM RES DIV, AM CYANAMID CO. *Personal Data:* b Rock Springs, Wyo, July 12, 43; m 75. *Educ:* Colo Col, BS, 65; Northwestern Univ, PhD(org chem), 69. *Prof Exp:* Instr chem, Northwestern Univ, 69-70; res assoc, Columbia Univ, 70-72. *Concurrent Pos:* Vis staff, Los Alamos Nat Labs, Univ Calif, 78- *Mem:* Am Chem Soc; Inter-Am Photochem Soc; The Chem Soc. *Res:* Mechanistic organic photochemistry; catalysis by molecular organization; properties of Micelles; time-resolved spectroscopy; energy transfer mechanisms; solar energy storage; surface properties. *Mailing Add:* Wilson Art International 2400 Wilson Place Temple TX 76504

HAUTH, WILLARD ELLSWORTH, III, MATERIALS TECHNOLOGY FOR THERMAL MANAGEMENT, CERAMIC REINFORCEMENTS AND CERAMIC MATRIX COMPOSITES. *Current Pos:* DIR TECHNOL, REX ROTO CORP, 92- *Personal Data:* b Boston, Mass, May 20, 48; m 83, Pamela S Matheny; c Grant M & Stefanie L. *Educ:* Alfred Univ, BS, 70, MS, 74. *Honors & Awards:* Schwartzwalder-PACE Award, Nat Inst Ceramic Engrs, 83. *Prof Exp:* Ceramic engr, Babcock & Wilcox Co, 70-74 & Corning Glass Works, 74-75; res scientist, Los Alamos Nat Lab, 75-80; pres ceramics, Mat Technol Assocs, 77-80; res scientist, Battelle Mem Inst, 80-83; mgr, Mat Div, Dow Corning Corp, 83-89; sr vpres res, develop & eng, Advan Refractory Technologies, 89-92. *Concurrent Pos:* Gov, Am Asn Eng Soc, 84-86; comt mem, Nat Mat Adv Bd, 84-87; tech reviewer, Am Ceramic Soc, 84-90; comt mem, Mat Tech Adv Comt, US Dept Com, 86-90. *Mem:* Nat Inst Ceramic Engrs (secy/treas, 81, vpres, 82, pres-elect, 83, pres, 84); fel Am Ceramic Soc. *Res:* Applied development of oxide and non-oxide ceramic materials; fabrication technologies and advanced product forms, including chemically-derived ceramics, ceramic matrix composites and high-performance ceramic powders and composite reinforcements. *Mailing Add:* 321 N Court St Howell MI 48843

HAUXWELL, DONALD LAWRENCE, FOREST SOILS, AGROFORESTRY. *Current Pos:* From asst prof to prof soil sci, Humboldt State Univ, 66-76, NSF instnl grant, 69, prog leader natural resources, Sch Natural Resources, 70-73, dept chmn, Natural Resources Planning & Interpretation, 91-95, PROF NATURAL RESOURCES, HUMBOLDT STATE UNIV, 76- *Personal Data:* b Indianola, Nebr, June 25, 38; m 62; c 2. *Educ:* Univ Idaho, BS, 60, PhD(forest soils), 67. *Concurrent Pos:* Soil conservationist, US Soil Conserv Serv, 68; US Forest Serv admin study, Calif State Univ, Humboldt, 72-73; soil scientist, Bur Land Mgt, 79-80; vis prof, Univ Idaho, 75-76, NC State Univ, 83, Egerton Univ, Kenya, 89-90; chmn, Calif Forest Soils Coun, 94-96. *Mem:* Am Registry Prof Agron, Soils & Crop Sci; Am Soc Agron; Soil Sci Soc Am. *Res:* Tissue analysis in the management of soil nitrogen in a Douglas-fir seedling nursery; soils associated with various sagebrush species in Idaho; soil treatment to enhance erosion control vegetation on forest road cutbanks; moisture and temperature regimes of forest soils; agroforestry & soil fertility. *Mailing Add:* Dept Rangeland Resources & Wildland Soils Humboldt State Univ Arcata CA 95521. *Fax:* 707-826-4145; *E-Mail:* dlh2@axe.humboldt.edu

HAUXWELL, GERALD DEAN, COMPETITOR ASSESSMENT, MATHEMATICS. *Current Pos:* res engr, Sontara Develop, Pioneering Res Lab, 64-68, res assoc, Nomex & Kevlar Develop, Spruance Res Lab, 80-84, MGR, TECHNOL ASSESSMENT-FIBERS INDUST, E I DUPONT DE NEMOURS & CO, INC, 84- *Personal Data:* b Indianola, Nebr, Sept 24, 35; m 64, Ingrid Postner. *Educ:* Univ Colo, BS, 58; Univ Idaho, MS, 60; Ore State Univ, PhD(chem eng), 71. *Prof Exp:* Design engr, Atomic Power Equip Dept, Gen Elec Co, 62-64. *Concurrent Pos:* Res fel, Dow Chem Co, 68-70 & Shell Oil Co, 70-71; pvt consult var sponsoring orgn, 74-; adj prof, Va Commonwealth Univ, 75-, Univ Va, 77- & Va State Univ, 80-; bd dirs, Soc Competitor Intel Profs, 92-95, Conf Bd Coun Competitive Anal, 94- *Mem:* Am Inst Chem Engrs; Nat Soc Prof Engrs; Am Chem Soc; Tech Asn Paper Pulp Ind; Soc Competitor Intel Profs. *Res:* Heat, mass and momentum transfer; related to oxygen absorption, industrial processes, environmental control and energy conservation; expertise in competitor assessment including database construction competitive strategy development. *Mailing Add:* 11400 Edenberry Dr Richmond VA 23236-4032. *Fax:* 804-383-5014; *E-Mail:* hauxwehgd@spoc.dnet.dupont.com

HAUXWELL, RONALD EARL, ORGANIC CHEMISTRY, BIOCHEMISTRY. *Current Pos:* MEM STAFF, CORDOVA CHEM CO, 80- *Personal Data:* b Flint, Mich, May 19, 46; m 68; c 3. *Educ:* Western Mich Univ, BA, 69, MA, 71. *Prof Exp:* Res chemist, Burdick & Jackson Labs, Subsid Hoffmann-La Roche, Inc, 71-72, prod mgr org chem, 72-80. *Concurrent Pos:* Mem fac, Dept Chem, Muskegon Community Col, 78- *Mem:* Am Chem Soc. *Res:* Synthesis of phosphorescent enzyme inhibitors for use in structure elucidation; innovative drug synthesis and production process improvement and maximization. *Mailing Add:* PO Box 5240 North Muskegon MI 49445-0240

HAVA, MILOS, CLINICAL PHARMACOLOGY. *Current Pos:* CLIN PROF DIAG IMAGING, TEMPLE UNIV, 80- *Personal Data:* b Prague, Czech, Oct 15, 27; m 51, Maria Kovac; c Nadia. *Educ:* Charles Univ, MD, 52, PhD(pharmacol), 55, Educ Coun Foreign Med Grads, cert, 74. *Honors & Awards:* Res Award, Czech Acad Sci, 56. *Prof Exp:* Sr res worker pharmacol, Czech Acad Sci, 55-58; head dept, Res Inst Pharm & Biochem, 58-68; from asst prof to assoc prof, Med Sch, Univ Kans, 68-73; assoc prof, Peoria Sch Med, Med Col, Univ Ill, 73-75; asst med dir, Marion Labs, Inc, 75-79; med dir, Wallace Labs, 79-80, exec dir clin drug develop, 80-82; med dir, Wyeth Int, 82-87, dir clin develop, Wyeth-Ayerst, 87- *Concurrent Pos:* Consult, Czech Ministry Health, 58-68 & Ill Valley Ment Health Asn, 74-75; adj prof, Med Sch, Univ Kans, 77-80. *Mem:* AMA; AAAS; Am Soc Pharmacol & Exp Therapeut; Am Soc Clin Pharm Therapeut. *Res:* Clinical research and drug evaluation; pharmacology of gastrointestinal smooth muscle; pharmacology of steroids. *Mailing Add:* 126 South St Philadelphia PA 19147-2419

HAVAS, HELGA FRANCIS, MICROBIOLOGY, CANCER RESEARCH. *Current Pos:* from asst prof to prof 59-90, EMER PROF MICROBIOL, SCH MED, TEMPLE UNIV, 90-, ACTG CHAIR, DEPT MICROBIOL & IMMUNOL. *Personal Data:* b Vienna, Austria, Nov 26, 15; US citizen; m, Peter; c Eva & Steven. *Educ:* Columbia Univ, MA, 44; Lehigh Univ, PhD(bact), 50. *Prof Exp:* Res chemist, Sch Nutrit, Cornell Univ, 45-46; res fel chemother, Inst Cancer Res, 50-51, res assoc, 51-63. *Concurrent Pos:* USPHS fel, NIH, 64-66, career develop award, 66-70. *Mem:* Am Asn Cancer Res; Am Asn Immunol. *Res:* Role of suppressive factors and suppressor cells in tumor-induced immunosuppression; immunochemistry of carcinogen-protein conjugates; oncolytic and immunochemical properties of polysaccharides and bacterial toxins; tolerance to hapten conjugates; immunochemical aspects of tolerance; effect of carrier on anti-hapten response; mechanism of immunosuppression by plasmacytomas to hapten-conjugates and pneumococcal polysaccharides; immunomodulation by bacterial vaccine in tumor bearing host; immunotherapy with bacterial vaccine phase I study. *Mailing Add:* Dept Microbiol & Immunol Temple Univ & Health Sci Campus Broad & Ontario Philadelphia PA 19140

HAVAS, PETER, THEORY OF RELATIVITY. *Current Pos:* prof, 65-81, EMER PROF PHYSICS, TEMPLE UNIV, 81- *Personal Data:* b Budapest, Hungary, Mar 29, 16; US citizen; m, Helga F Hollerine; c Eva C & Steven W. *Educ:* Vienna Tech Univ, Absolutorium, 38; Columbia Univ, PhD(physics), 44. *Prof Exp:* Lectr physics, Columbia Univ, 41-45; instr, Cornell Univ, 45-46; from asst prof to prof, Lehigh Univ, 46-65. *Concurrent Pos:* Res fel, Inst de Physique Atomique, Lyon, France, 38-41; mem, Argonne Nat Lab, 58; Guggenheim Mem Found fel & mem, Inst Adv Study, 53-54; vis prof, Univ Gottingen, 73; adj prof, Univ Pa, 81-87, Utah State Univ, 81-90. *Mem:* Fel AAAS; Am Phys Soc; Soc Gen Relativity & Gravitation. *Res:* Theory of radiation; elementary particle theory; mathematical physics; history of physics; theory of relativity; foundation problems. *Mailing Add:* Dept Physics Temple Univ Broad & Montgomery Philadelphia PA 19122. *Fax:* 215-204-5652

HAVEL, HENRY ACKEN, BIOPHYSICS. *Current Pos:* res scientist, 90-95, SR RES SCIENTIST, BIOPHARMACEUTICAL DEVELOP, ELI LILLY & CO, 96- *Personal Data:* b Palmerton, Pa, May 23, 54; m 80, Mary Stickelmeyer. *Educ:* Univ Rochester, BS, 76; Univ Minn, PhD(phys chem), 81. *Prof Exp:* Scientist, Control Develop, Upjohn Co, 81-83, res scientist, Spectros Develop, 83-90, qual assurance consult, Specif Develop, 90. *Mem:* AAAS; Am Chem Soc; Biophys Soc; Coblentz Soc. *Res:* Biophysical characterization of proteins; protein structure and dynamics; protein and peptide aggregation; protein folding; antigen-antibody binding reactions. *Mailing Add:* Eli Lilly & Co Lilly Corp Ctr Indianapolis IN 46285-0835. *Fax:* 317-277-0833; *E-Mail:* hah@lilly.com

HAVEL, JAMES JOSEPH, ORGANIC CHEMISTRY. *Current Pos:* TECH MGR ANALYTICAL SCI, DOW CHEM CO, 80- *Personal Data:* b Urbana, Ill, July 22, 47; m 69; c 2. *Educ:* Lewis Univ, BA, 68; Pa State Univ, PhD(chem), 72. *Prof Exp:* Asst prof chem, Rice Univ, 72-77; asst prof chem, Pa State Univ, University Park, 77-80. *Mem:* Am Chem Soc; Sigma Xi. *Res:* Reactions of atomic species with organic compounds; reactive organic intermediates; organometallic chemistry. *Mailing Add:* 2501 Munford Dr Fallston MD 21047

HAVEL, RICHARD JOSEPH, MEDICINE. *Current Pos:* from asst prof to assoc prof, 56-64, PROF MED, SCH MED, UNIV CALIF, SAN FRANCISCO, 64-, DIR, CARDIOVASC RES INST, 73- *Personal Data:* b Seattle, Wash, Feb 20, 25; m 47; c 4. *Educ:* Reed Col, BA, 46; Univ Ore, MS & MD, 49. *Honors & Awards:* Theobald Smith Award, AAAS, 60; Eli Lilly Res Lectr, 74; Higgins Mem Lectr, Ore Regional Primate Res Ctr, 77; George Lyman Duff Lectr, Am Heart Asn, 84, Sci Coun Distinguished Achievement Award, 91; Arthur Scott Mem Lectr, Reed Col, 86; Rufus Cole Lectr, Rockefeller Univ, 86; Walter Cannon Lectr, Am Physiol Soc, 86; Gunnar Birke Lectr, Huddinge Hosp, 88; Bristol-Myers Squibb Award for Distinguished Achievement Nutrit Res, 89; Sci Achievement Award, Nat Coun Atherosclerosis & Hypertension, 91; Merck Frost Can Distinguished Lectr, Univ Alta, 91; McCollum Award, Am Soc Clin Nutrit, 93. *Prof Exp:* Asst biochem, Med Sch, Univ Ore, 45-49; from intern to resident physician, NY Hosp, 49-53; instr med, Med Col, Cornell Univ, 52-53; clin assoc, Nat Heart Inst, 53-64, res assoc, 54-56. *Concurrent Pos:* Estab investr, Am Heart Asn, 59-61, chmn coun arteriosclerosis, 77-79; assoc dir, Cardiovasc Res Inst, 61-73, dir, 73; spec res fel, USPHS, Stockholm, 62-63; chief, Metab Div, Dept Med, Univ Calif, 67-; dir, Specialized Ctr Res Arteriosclerosis, 70-; ed, J Lipid Res, 72-75; mem, var tasks forces & bds, 75- *Mem:* Nat Acad Sci; Inst Med-Nat Acad Sci; Am Physiol Soc; Am Soc Clin Invest; Am Fedn Clin Res (pres-elect, 64-65, pres, 65-66); Asn Am Physicians; fel AAAS; Am Acad Arts Sci; Am Soc Study Arteriosclerosis; Am Heart Asn; Sigma Xi; fel Am Inst Nutrit. *Res:* Intermediary and lipoprotein metabolism; apolipoproteins; lipid metabolism. *Mailing Add:* PO Box 1791 Ross CA 94957-1791

HAVEMEYER, RUTH NAOMI, PHARMACY, PROJECT MANAGEMENT. *Current Pos:* group leader, 66-72, mgr prod develop, 72-80, DIR, RES ADMIN, SYNTEX CORP, 80- *Personal Data:* b New York, NY, July 28, 32; m 68. *Educ:* Columbia Univ, BS, 53; Purdue Univ, MS, 55; Univ Wis, PhD(pharm), 60. *Prof Exp:* Res pharmacist, Nepera Chem Co, NY, 55-56; sr res scientist, Squibb Inst Med Res, 60-66. *Mem:* Fel AAAS; Am Asn Pharmaceut Sci; Sigma Xi. *Res:* Vitamin stability; chemical kinetics in pharmaceutical systems; biopharmaceutics. *Mailing Add:* 440 Cesano Ct Suite 301 Palo Alto CA 94306-4454

HAVEN, DEXTER STEARNS, FISH BIOLOGY. *Current Pos:* RETIRED. *Personal Data:* b Chicago, Ill, Nov 2, 18; m 51; c 1. *Educ:* RI State Col, BS, 42, MS, 48. *Prof Exp:* From asst biologist to sr biologist, Va Inst Marine Sci, 49-68, assoc prof, 74-77, head, Dept Appl Biol, 68-84; prof marine sci, Col William & Mary, Gloucester Pt, Va, 77-84. *Mem:* Ecol Soc Am; Nat Shellfisheries Asn. *Res:* Fisheries biology; ecology of oysters and biodeposition. *Mailing Add:* 130 Lafayette Rd Yorktown VA 23690

HAVENER, ROBERT D, INTERNATIONAL AGRICULTURAL DEVELOPMENT. *Current Pos:* PRES & CHIEF EXEC OFFICER, WINROCK INT INST AGR DEVELOP, 85- *Personal Data:* b London, Ohio, July 24, 30; c 1. *Educ:* Ohio State Univ, BS, 52, MSc, 58; Harvard Univ, MPA, 72. *Hon Degrees:* LLD, Univ Ark. *Honors & Awards:* Distinguished Serv Award, Am Agr Ed Asn. *Prof Exp:* Chmn, Coop Exten Serv, Ohio State Univ, 54-61; dist gen mgr, Ohio Farm Bur Coops, 61-63; merchandising mgr, Sugardale Provision Co, 63-64; agr prog officer, Ford Found, 66-78, prog adv, Pakistan, 66-71, dir, Arid Lands Agr Develop Prog, Lebanon, 72-76, prog develop officer, Int Ctr Agr Res Dry Areas, Mid East, 75-76, prog adv, Asia & Pac Region, 76-78; dir gen, Int Maize & Wheat Improv Ctr, Mex, 78-85. *Concurrent Pos:* Vis guest lectr, Am Univ Beirut, 75-76; mem bd trustees, Int Ctr Agr Res Dry Areas, Beirut, 76-78, Int Rice Res Inst, Manila, 77-78, Int Agr Develop Serv, 80-85 & Honduras Agr Res Found, 84-85; mem bd trustees-ex officio, Int Maize & Wheat Improv Ctr, Mex, 78-85; mem, Nat Planning Asn Food & Agr Coun. *Mem:* Fel AAAS; Am Agr Econ Asn. *Res:* Agricultural development issues; development of agricultural production programs. *Mailing Add:* 662 Ivy Lane Solvang CA 93463

HAVENOR, KAY CHARLES, GEOLOGY. *Current Pos:* CONSULT GEOLOGIST, EXPLOR & FIELD RES, 62- *Personal Data:* b Denver, Colo, Aug 16, 31; div; c 6. *Educ:* Colo Col, BS, 57; Univ Ariz, MS, 58. *Prof Exp:* Geologist, Pure Oil Co, 58-62. *Mem:* Am Asn Petrol Geol; fel Geol Soc Am; Am Inst Prof Geol. *Res:* Regional and local geology; petroleum and economic geology; groundwater; geohydrology of West Texas, New Mexico and Arizona. *Mailing Add:* 904 Moore Ave Roswell NM 88201-1144

HAVENS, JAMES MERYLE, meteorology, climatology, for more information see previous edition

HAVENS, JERRY ARNOLD, FIRE RESEARCH, RISK ASSESSMENT. *Current Pos:* asst prof, 70-75, assoc prof, 75-79, PROF, UNIV ARK, FAYETTEVILLE, 79- *Personal Data:* b Lonoke, Ark, Nov 24, 39; m 61; c 2. *Educ:* Univ Ark, BS, 62; Univ Colo, MS, 62; Univ Okla, PhD(chem eng), 69. *Prof Exp:* Proj engr, Procter & Gamble Co, 62-65; res engr, Res Inst, Univ Okla, 69-70. *Mem:* Am Soc Testing & Mat; Am Inst Chem Engrs; Am Asn Eng Educ; Sigma Xi. *Res:* Fire and explosion risk assessment; irreversible thermodynamics. *Mailing Add:* 809 Lighton Trl Fayetteville AR 72701-4439

HAVENS, LESTON LAYCOCK, PSYCHIATRY. *Current Pos:* from instr to assoc clin prof, 58-70, PROF PSYCHIAT, HARVARD MED SCH, 71- *Personal Data:* b Brooklyn, NY, July 31, 24; m 73, Susan E Miller; c Christopher, Jennifer, Sarah & Emily. *Educ:* Williams Col, Mass, BA, 47; Cornell Univ, MD, 52; Am Bd Psychiat & Neurol, dipl, 59. *Hon Degrees:* MA, Harvard Univ, 85; LHD, Mass Sch Prof Psychol, 93. *Honors & Awards:* Bennett Award, Soc Biol Psychiat, 58; McCurdy Prize, Mass Soc Res Psychiat; HC Solomon Award, Mass Mental Health Ctr, 77; Benjamin Rush Award, Am Psychiat Asn, 95. *Prof Exp:* Intern & asst resident med, NY Hosp, 52-54; resident psychiat, Boston Psychopath Hosp, 54-57, chief serv, 57-58. *Concurrent Pos:* Examr, Am Bd Psychiat & Neurol, 59; sr psychiatrist, Mass Ment Health Ctr, Boston Psychopath Hosp, 59-64, prin psychiatrist, 64-; chief psychiat consult, Mass Rehab Comn; Carnegie vis prof humanities, Mass Inst Technol, 68; H B Williams traveling prof, Psychiat Soc Australia & NZ, 75; prin psychiatrist, Cambridge Hosp, 84-, dir residency training, 87-96, dir educ, 96- *Mem:* Am Psychiat Asn; AAAS. *Res:* Schizophrenic psychopathology; perceptual processes; properties of psychiatric drugs; history of psychiatric ideas; methods of schools. *Mailing Add:* 151 Brattle St Cambridge MA 02138

HAVENS, TIMOTHY JOHN, SUPERCONDUCTING MAGNET DESIGN, MAGNETIC RESONANCE IMAGING. *Current Pos:* SR ENGR, GEN ELEC MED SYSTS, 90- *Personal Data:* b Bismark, NDak, Feb 1, 56; m, Janine Ley; c Garrett, Stanley & Luke. *Educ:* Eckerd Col, BS, 80; Col William & Mary, MS, 81, PhD(physics), 85. *Prof Exp:* Asst prof physics, Francis Marion Univ, 85-90. *Concurrent Pos:* Res fel, Oak Ridge Nat Lab, 79; res fel, Med Univ SC, 86; Fed Educ Econ Security Act, Higher Educ Coop Demonstration grant, 88-89; grantee, NSF, 90-91. *Res:* Develop superconducting magnets for use in magnetic resonance imaging systems; granted 4 patents. *Mailing Add:* 1208 Madison Ave Florence SC 29501

HAVENS, WILLIAM WESTERFIELD, JR, NUCLEAR PHYSICS. *Current Pos:* From asst to prof, Columbia Univ, 40-85, dir, Div Nuclear Sci & Eng, 61-85, dir, Energy Res Ctr, 76-85, RES SCIENTIST, COLUMBIA UNIV, 41-, EMER PROF PHYSICS, 85- *Personal Data:* b New York, NY, Mar 31, 20; m 44, Aldine Morris; c Nancy E (Hasty) & Cynthia (Gosline). *Educ:* City Col New York, BS, 39; Columbia Univ, MA, 41, PhD(physics), 46. *Concurrent Pos:* NSF sr fel, 59-60; mem, Nuclear Cross Sect Adv Group, AEC. *Mem:* AAAS (vpres, 67-68); fel Am Phys Soc (dep secy, exec secy, 85-90, emer exec secy, 91-); Sigma Xi; Am Asn Physics Teachers. *Res:* Electronics; neutron spectroscopy; meson physics; electronuclear accelerators. *Mailing Add:* 219 Palisade Ave Dobbs Ferry NY 10522

HAVENSTEIN, GERALD B, ANIMAL GENETICS. *Current Pos:* HEAD, DEPT POULTRY SCI, NC STATE UNIV, 89- *Personal Data:* b Manhattan, Kans, Sept 2, 39; m 63; c 2. *Educ:* Kans State Univ, BS, 61; Univ Wis, MS, 65, PhD(genetics), 66. *Prof Exp:* Instr genetics, Univ Wis, 66-67; geneticist, H & N Inc, 67-86; chmn, Dept Poultry Sci, Ohio State Univ, 86-89. *Mem:* World Poultry Sci Asn; Poultry Sci Asn; Am Inst Biol Sci; Am Asn Univ Prof. *Res:* Quantitative genetics and animal breeding. *Mailing Add:* Dept Poultry Sci NC State Univ PO Box 7608 Raleigh NC 27695-7608

HAVER, WILLIAM EMERY, TOPOLOGY. *Current Pos:* ASSOC PROF MATH SCI & CHMN DEPT, VA COMMONWEALTH UNIV, 77- *Personal Data:* b Somerville, NJ, Sept 19, 42; m 67; c 2. *Educ:* Bates Col, BS, 64; Rutgers Univ, MS, 67; State Univ NY Binghamton, PhD(math), 70. *Prof Exp:* Instr math, Bates Col, 67-68; from asst prof to assoc prof, Univ Tenn, Knoxville, 70-77. *Concurrent Pos:* Mem staff, Inst Advan Studies, 75-76. *Mem:* Am Math Soc; Math Asn Am. *Res:* Infinite dimensional topology with particular emphasis on the study of spaces of homeomorphisms on manifolds, cellular mappings and absolute neighborhood retracts. *Mailing Add:* Dept Math Sci Va Commonwealth Univ Richmond VA 23284-2014

HAVER KAMP, JENNIFER, ENVIRONMENTAL SCIENCES. *Current Pos:* ASST US TRADE REP, ENVIRON NATURAL RESOURCES, 95- *Personal Data:* b May 8, 57. *Educ:* Yale Univ, JD. *Mailing Add:* USTR 600 17th St NW Rm 415 Washington DC 20508

HAVERS, JOHN ALAN, CIVIL ENGINEERING. *Current Pos:* RETIRED. *Personal Data:* b Broadview, Sask, May 15, 25; m 76; c 2. *Educ:* Univ Sask, BSCE, 47; Purdue Univ, MSCE, 52, PhD(civil eng, soil mech), 56. *Prof Exp:* Resident engr, Sask Dept Hwy & Transp, Can, 47-49, supv engr, 49-51, prin design engr, 52-53; res engr, Purdue Univ, 53-56; dir eng & assoc partner, Harland Bartholomew & Assocs, Hawaii, 56-62; res engr, IIT Res Inst, 62-64, sr res engr, 64-65; prof civil eng, Purdue Univ, 65-86, head, Div Construct Eng, 80-86. *Concurrent Pos:* Indust consult, 65- *Mem:* Am Soc Civil Engrs; Eng Inst Can. *Res:* Engineering management; construction engineering and management; systems engineering. *Mailing Add:* 1930 Ashbrook Dr W Tucson AZ 85704

HAVERTY, MICHAEL IRVING, INSECT ECOLOGY. *Current Pos:* RES ENTOMOLOGIST, USDA FOREST SERV, 75- *Personal Data:* b Fresno, Calif, Oct 24, 46; m 68; c 1. *Educ:* Univ Calif, Davis, BS, 68; Univ Ariz, MS, 70, PhD(entom), 74. *Prof Exp:* Res assoc entom, Univ Ariz, 73-75. *Mem:* Sigma Xi; AAAS; Int Union Study Social Insects; Entom Soc Am; Ecol Soc Am. *Res:* Ecology of subterranean termites, especially the influence of physical and biological parameters on flight, foraging behavior, caste composition and nutrition. *Mailing Add:* 941 Carol Lane Lafayette CA 94549

HAVERTZ, DAVID S, MEDICAL ENTOMOLOGY, ECOLOGY. *Current Pos:* asst prof, 65-68, PROF ZOOL & DIR, CTR ENVIRON STUDIES, WEBER STATE COL, 68- *Personal Data:* b Salt Lake City, Utah, Feb 4, 31; m 57; c 4. *Educ:* Univ Utah, BS, 56, MS, 57, PhD(invert zool), 62. *Prof Exp:* Parasitologist epidemiol lab, USAF, Tex, 62-65. *Mem:* Am Mosquito Control Asn. *Res:* Nematode distribution; mosquito ecology and resistance to insecticides; seasonal distribution of Triatoma Reduviidae; brime fly ecology. *Mailing Add:* Dept Zool Weber State Univ 3750 Harrison Blvd Ogden UT 84408-0001

HAVILAND, JAMES WEST, MEDICINE, INTERNAL MEDICINE. *Current Pos:* RETIRED. *Personal Data:* b Glenns Falls, NY, 1911. *Educ:* Johns Hopkins Univ, MD, 36. *Prof Exp:* Intern med, Johns Hopkins Hosp, 36-37, intern pediat, 37, asst resident pediat, 37-38; asst resident med, New Haven Hosp, 38-39; attend staff physician, Swed Doctors Hosp, Harilos View Hosp, Univ Hosp, Seattle; clin prof med, Sch Med, Univ Wash, emer assoc dean clin affairs, 42-46. *Mem:* Inst Med-Nat Acad Sci; Am Med Asn. *Mailing Add:* 8208 SE 30th St Mercer Island WA 98040

HAVILAND, JOHN KENNETH, AEROSPACE ENGINEERING. *Current Pos:* RETIRED. *Personal Data:* b Mt Kisco, NY, Jan 19, 21; m 43; c 5. *Educ:* Univ London, BSc, 46; Mass Inst Technol, PhD(astronaut & aeronaut eng), 61. *Prof Exp:* Stress analyst, Bristol Aeroplane Co, Ltd, 46-47; jr res officer, Struct Lab, Nat Res Coun Can, 47-48; group leader struct & adv design, Canadair Ltd, 48-51; group supvr dynamics, Chance-Vought Corp, 51-58; res staff mem, Mass Inst Technol, 59-61; teaching asst aeronaut & astronaut, 60-61; sr tech engr, Astronaut Div, Ling-Temco Vought, 61-64, mgr, Struct & Mat Sect, 64-67; prof aerospace eng, Univ Va, 67-92. *Concurrent Pos:* Dir Div Space Sci, Va Assoc Res Ctr, 67-69. *Mem:* Assoc fel Am Inst Aeronaut & Astronaut. *Res:* Aerospace dynamics and flutter; acoustics; applications of Monte Carlo methods. *Mailing Add:* 210 Willow Brook Rd Earlysville VA 22936

HAVILAND, MERRILL L, FUEL TECHNOLOGY & PETROLEUM ENGINEERING. *Current Pos:* AUTOMOTIVE DEVELOP SPECIALIST, EXXON CHEM CO, 87- *Personal Data:* b Ridgeville, Ind, Jan 31, 33; m 52, Phyllis Bisel; c Lynn, Mark & Jonathan. *Educ:* Purdue Univ, BS, 54, MS, 56. *Honors & Awards:* Henry Ford Mem Award, 61. *Prof Exp:* From jr res engr to sr res engr, Gen Motors Corp, 56-76, dept res engr, res BS, 76-86, res assessment mgr, 86-87. *Concurrent Pos:* Mem staff, Mech Eng Sch, Wayne State Univ, 58-61. *Mem:* Soc Automotive Engrs; Soc Tribiol & Lubrication Engrs; Sigma Xi. *Res:* Measurement of flame and end gas temperatures in automotive engines and jet engine combustors; lubrication of sliding systems; power transmission fluids; vehicle fuel economy improvement; marketing automotive lubricant additives. *Mailing Add:* 1432 Bates Birmingham MI 48009

HAVILAND, ROBERT P(AUL), ELECTRICAL ENGINEERING, ENVIRONMENTAL SCIENCES. *Current Pos:* CHIEF ENGR, MINILAB INSTRUMENTS CO, 73- *Personal Data:* b Cleveland, Ohio, Oct 18, 13; m 37, Opal Dorf; c Kay, Jean & Jon R. *Educ:* Mo Sch Mines, BS, 39. *Prof Exp:* Res engr, Schlumberger Well Surv Corp, 39-42; engr, Gen Elec Co, 47-72. *Concurrent Pos:* Mem, Test Equip Group, Res & Develop Bd, 51; mem spec comt space technol, Nat Adv Comt Aeronaut, 58; mem comt sci & arts, Franklin Inst, 59-; mem US deleg, Int Radio Consult Comt & Int Telecommun Union; mem commun adv sub-comt, NASA, 68-73; mem, Fed Commun Comn/World Admin Radio Conf Adv Comt, 74. *Mem:* Fel Am Astronaut Soc; fel Inst Elec & Electronics Engrs; assoc fel Am Inst Aeronaut & Astronaut; fel Brit Interplanetary Soc. *Res:* Astronautics; space vehicles; communications and electronics; author of 15 books; granted 6 patents. *Mailing Add:* Minilab Instruments Co PO Box 21086 Daytona Beach FL 32121-1086. *E-Mail:* bobh@america.com

HAVIR, EVELYN A, PLANT PHYSIOLOGY. *Current Pos:* RES ASSOC, CONN AGR EXP STA, 64- *Personal Data:* b Scranton, Pa, Sept 5, 33; m 74. *Educ:* Beaver Col, BA, 55; Temple Univ, MA, 57; Cornell Univ, PhD(biochem), 62. *Prof Exp:* Asst biochemist, Pub Health Res Inst, NY, 62-64. *Mem:* Am Asn Biol Chemists; Am Soc Plant Physiologists. *Res:* Enzyme mechanisms; enzymology; regulation of photorespiration. *Mailing Add:* Dept Biochem Conn Agr Exp Sta PO Box 1106 New Haven CT 06504-1106

HAVIS, JOHN RALPH, HORTICULTURE. *Current Pos:* RETIRED. *Personal Data:* b Roaring Springs, Tex, Sept 5, 20; m 49; c 3. *Educ:* Tex Tech Col, BS, 42; Cornell Univ, MS, 47, PhD(veg crops), 49. *Prof Exp:* Asst, NY State Col Agr, Cornell Univ, 46-49; assoc prof hort, Va Polytech Inst, 49-51; horticulturist, Inter-Am Inst Agr Sci, 51-54; head, Waltham Field Sta, Univ Mass, 54-61, prof plant physiol, 61-85. *Mem:* Soc Hort Sci; Int Plant Propagation Soc. *Res:* Physiology of woody ornamentals. *Mailing Add:* 229 Dolomite Dr Colorado Springs CO 80919

HAVLEN, ROBERT J, GALACTIC STRUCTURE, STAR CLUSTERS. *Current Pos:* EXEC DIR, ASTRON SOC PAC, 93- *Personal Data:* b Utica, NY, Sept 16, 43; m 67; c 2. *Educ:* Univ Rochester, BS, 65; Univ Ariz, PhD(astron), 70. *Prof Exp:* Staff astronr, Europ Southern Observ, 70-77; vis lectr, Univ Va, 77-79; asst to dir, Nat Radio Astron Observ, 79-87, head observ servs, 87-93. *Mem:* Am Astron Soc; Int Astron Union. *Res:* Promote astronomy. *Mailing Add:* Astron Soc Pac 390 Ashton Ave San Francisco CA 94131

HAVLICEK, STEPHEN, ORGANIC & WATER CHEMISTRY. *Current Pos:* VPRES, CENT COAST ANALYTICAL SERV, 84- *Personal Data:* b Englewood, NJ, Aug 19, 41; m 61; c 3. *Educ:* Hope Col, AB, 63; Wayne State Univ, PhD(chem), 67. *Prof Exp:* Fel marine natural prods chem, Univ Hawaii, 67-70; asst prof chem, Bemidji State Col, 70-71; sr res chemist, Campbell Soup Co, 71-76; sr res scientist, Ga Inst Technol, 76-80; tech dir, Brown & Caldwell, 80-84. *Mem:* AAAS; Am Chem Soc; Inst Food Technologists; Am Water Works Asn; Air Pollution Control Asn. *Res:* Trace organic chemicals in wastewaters, surface waters and drinking water; structural elucidation by instrumental methods; environmental problems, particularly those related to public health; energy; waste product utilization. *Mailing Add:* 31110 Avenida Buena Suerte Temecula CA 92591

HAVLICK, SPENSER WOODWORTH, NATURAL HAZARDS & URBANIZATION IMPACTS, URBAN PLANNING BASED ON ECOLOGICAL PRINCIPLES. *Current Pos:* dean, Col Environ Design, 85-88, PROF ENVIRON DESIGN, UNIV COLO, 74- *Personal Data:* b Oak Park, Ill, June 21, 35; m 58; c 3. *Educ:* Beloit Col, BA, 57; Univ Colo, MS, 61; Univ Mich, PhD(environ planning), 67. *Prof Exp:* Asst prof natural resources, Univ Mich, 67-73. *Concurrent Pos:* Ed, J Ekistics, Athens, Greece, 72-; prof geog, Nat Taiwan Univ, Taipei, 90-91. *Mem:* AAAS; Am Planning Asn; Sigma Xi; Inst Behav Sci. *Res:* Urbanization and impacts on natural ecosystems including natural hazard mitigation. *Mailing Add:* Col Archit Univ Colo PO Box 1 Boulder CO 80309-0001

HAVNER, KERRY S(HUFORD), SOLID MECHANICS, MATERIALS SCIENCE. *Current Pos:* assoc prof, 68-75, PROF CIVIL ENG, NC STATE UNIV, 75-, PROF MAT SCI & ENG, 82- *Personal Data:* b Huntington, WVa, Feb 20, 34; m 54, Roberta Lee Rider; c Karen (Smith), Clark & Kris. *Educ:* Okla State Univ, BS, 55, MS, 56, PhD(appl mech), 59. *Honors & Awards:* Alco Found Distinguished Eng Res Award, 82. *Prof Exp:* Assoc engr, Douglas Aircraft Co, Okla, 56; from instr to asst prof civil eng, Okla State Univ, 57-62; sr stress & vibration engr, Aires Mfg Div, Garrett Corp, Ariz, 62-63; sect chief solid mech res, Douglas Missile & Space Systs Div, McDonnell Douglas Corp, Calif, 63-68. *Concurrent Pos:* Am Inst Steel Construct scholar, 51-55; lectr, Univ Southern Calif, 65-68; sr vis, Dept Appl Math & Theoret Physics, Univ Cambridge, 81 & 89; vis fel, Clare Hall, Cambridge, Eng, 81 & 89; chmn, Comt Inelastic Behav, 81-83; chmn, Eng Mech Div, Am Soc Civil Engrs, 87-88 & chmn, Civil Eng Res Found Res Awards Comt, 91-94; NSF res grants theoret plasticity metal, 71-85, 87-90, 91-94 & 94-98. *Mem:* Fel Am Acad Mech; fel Am Soc Civil Engrs; Am Soc Mech Engrs; Soc Eng Sci; Soc Indust Appl Math. *Res:* Mechanics of materials with emphasis on theoretical plasticity of metals; crystal plasticity. *Mailing Add:* NC State Univ Dept Civil Eng PO Box 7098 Raleigh NC 27695. *Fax:* 919-515-7908

HAVRAN, WENDY LYNN, IMMUNOLOGY. *Current Pos:* asst prof, 91-95, ASSOC PROF, DEPT IMMUNOL, SCRIPPS RES INST, LA JOLLA, CALIF, 95-, FAC, STROHM INFLAMMATORY BOWEL DIS CTR, SCRIPPS CLIN, 95- *Personal Data:* b Houston, Tex, Sept 1, 55. *Educ:* Duke Univ, BS, 77; Univ Chicago, PhD(immunol), 86. *Prof Exp:* Sr res technician, Dept Med, Div Hemat, Duke Univ Med Ctr, 77-80, res analyst, Dept Microbiol & Immunol, 80-82; fel, Cancer Res Lab, Univ Calif, Berkeley, 86-92. *Concurrent Pos:* NIH grants, 91-; Lucille P Markey scholar biomed sci, 89-96. *Mem:* Am Asn Immunologists. *Res:* Immunology; development, specificity and function of epithelial T lymphocytes. *Mailing Add:* Scripps Res Inst Dept Immunol 10550 N Torrey Pines Rd La Jolla CA 92037-1093. *Fax:* 619-784-8805; *E-Mail:* havran@scripps.edu

HAWBECKER, BYRON L, ORGANIC CHEMISTRY. *Current Pos:* DEAN, COL ARTS & SCI, 92- *Personal Data:* b Freeport, Ill, Oct 2, 35; m 61, Luxmore; c Denise (Sutherland) & Melissa (Miller). *Educ:* Manchester Col, BA, 57; Univ Ariz, MS, 62; Kent State Univ, PhD(org chem), 68. *Prof Exp:* Res chemist, Ethyl Corp, Mich, 57; A E Staley Mfg Co, Ill, 58, 62-63; asst prof chem, Monmouth Col, 61-62; from instr to assoc prof, Ohio Northern Univ, 63-78, prof chem & chmn dept, 78-92. *Concurrent Pos:* Cent Ohio Heart Asn supvr undergrad res students, 65-70, 71-; ed consult, Houghton-Mifflin Co, Boston & W B Saunders Co, Philadelphia, West Publishing Co, Amesbury, Mass; consult, BF Goodrich Tire & Rubber Co; fel, NSF, DuPont & Continental Oil. *Mem:* Am Chem Soc; Sigma Xi. *Res:* Chemical education; organic synthesis, particularly heterocycles of potential biological activity; molecular rearrangements; organic reaction mechanisms. *Mailing Add:* Col Arts & Sci Ohio Northern Univ Ada OH 45810. *Fax:* 419-772-2622; *E-Mail:* b-hawbecker@onu.edu

HAWES, ROBERT OSCAR, POULTRY BREEDING & AQUACULTURE GENETICS. *Current Pos:* assoc prof, 78-93, DEPT CHAIR, UNIV MAINE, ORONO, 92-, PROF ANIMAL SCI, 93- *Personal Data:* b Bangor, Maine, Jan 4, 35; m 58, Alice McKinstry; c Robert D, Steven W, Joel E & Ethan J. *Educ:* Univ Maine, BS, 56; Univ Mass, MS, 58; Pa State Univ, PhD(poultry genetics), 62. *Prof Exp:* From asst prof to assoc prof animal sci, MacDonald Col, McGill Univ, 62-71; geneticist & physiologist, Res Dept, Hy-Line Int, Des Moines, 71-78. *Mem:* Poultry Sci Asn; Am Genetics Asn; World Poultry Soc Asn; Int Asn Genetics Aquacult; Nat Shellfish Asn. *Res:* Selection for improved growth rate in the American oyster (Crassostrea virginica). *Mailing Add:* Dept Animal Vet Sci & Aquatic Sci 340 Hitchner Hall Univ Maine Orono ME 04469

HAWIGER, JACK JACEK, HEMATOLOGY, LABORATORY MEDICINE. *Current Pos:* assoc prof, 83-85, PROF MED, HARVARD MED SCH, 85- *Personal Data:* b Cracow, Poland, May 30, 38; US citizen; div; c 2. *Educ:* Copernicus Sch Med, MD, 62; Nat Inst Hyg, PhD(med microbiol), 67. *Hon Degrees:* MA, Harvard Univ. *Honors & Awards:* Sci Coun Award, Polish Ministry Health & Social Welfare, 67; Edward Kowalski Mem Award & lectr, Int Cong Thrombosis & Haemostasis, 85. *Prof Exp:* Instr microbiol med, Nat Inst Hyg, Warsaw, 66-67; res assoc med, Vanderbilt Univ Sch Med, 67-69, asst prof, 69-74, assoc prof, 74-78, assoc prof path, 75-78; prof med, Boston Univ, 78-79; prof path & med, Vanderbilt Univ Sch Med, 79-82. *Concurrent Pos:* Prin investr, Pub Health Serv res grants, NIH, 73-; res & educ assoc, Nashville Vet Hosp, 74-75; dir, Hemostasis & Thrombosis Lab, Vanderbilt Univ Hosp, 75-78; vis assoc prof, Univ Calif, San Diego, 77; chief, Hemostasis Sect, Boston Vet Admin Med Ctr, 78-79; lectr, Tufts Univ Sch Med, 79-80; dir, Div Exp Med, New Eng Deaconess Hosp, Boston, 83-; mem, Nat Adv Comt, Commonwealth Fund Fel Prog, 83-; mem, Hemat Study Sect, NIH, 83-87; chmn, Subcomt Platelets, Am Soc Hemat, 87-88, Coun Thrombosis, Am Heart Asn, 87-89. *Mem:* Asn Am Physicians; Am Soc Clin Invest; Am Asn Pathologists; Am Soc Hematol; Infectious Dis Soc Am; Am Soc Biochem & Molecular Biol. *Res:* Mechanism of formation and prevention of blood clots; regulation of platelet receptors for adhesive molecules; pathobiology of thrombosis; interactions of biological agents and immune complexes with platelets and the vessel wall. *Mailing Add:* Dept Microbiol & Immunol Vanderbilt Univ A-5321 Med Ctr N Nashville TN 37232-2363

HAWIRKO, ROMA ZENOVEA, microbiology, for more information see previous edition

HAWK, WILLIAM ANDREW, THYROID, BOWEL DISEASES. *Current Pos:* RETIRED. *Educ:* Univ Pa, MD. *Prof Exp:* Sr consult, Dept Path, Cleveland Clin Found, 83-89. *Mailing Add:* 9500 Euclid Ave Cleveland OH 44195-0001

HAWKE, SCOTT DRANSFIELD, PHYSIOLOGICAL ECOLOGY. *Current Pos:* From asst prof to assoc prof, 71-82, PROF BIOL, WILLAMETTE UNIV, 82- *Personal Data:* b Gary, Ind, May 30, 42; m 70; c 1. *Educ:* San Diego State Univ, BS, 64; Univ BC, MS, 66; Univ Calif, Riverside, PhD(biol), 70. *Concurrent Pos:* Instr, Ore State Corrections, 77-; adj fac, Am Col Naturopathic Med, 81- *Mem:* Am Inst Biol Sci; Am Soc Zoologists; AAAS. *Res:* Physiology and morphology of insect sense organs. *Mailing Add:* Dept Biol Willamette Univ 900 State St Salem OR 97301-3930

HAWKES, JOYCE W, MARINE BIOLOGY. *Current Pos:* FISHERIES RES BIOLOGIST CELL BIO, NORTHWEST & ALASKA FISHERIES RES CTR, 76- *Personal Data:* b Portland, Ore. *Educ:* Lewis & Clark Col, BA, 61; Wake Forest Univ, MA, 65; Pa State Univ, PhD(biophys), 71. *Honors & Awards:* Spec Achievement Award, Dept Com, 77. *Prof Exp:* Asst scientist cell biol, Ore Regional Primate Res Ctr, 71-76. *Concurrent Pos:* NIH fel, Ore Regional Primate Res Ctr, 71-75; affil assoc prof, Univ Wash, 78-; reviewer for grants, NSF, 78-; prin investr contracts, Environ Protection Agency, 77- *Mem:* Soc Cell Biol; Soc Invert Path; Am Soc Zool; Int Pigment Cell Soc; fel AAAS. *Res:* Ultrastructure and cell biology of the effects of environmental contaminants on marine organisms. *Mailing Add:* 16236 SE 24th St Bellevue WA 98008-5408

HAWKES, ROBERT LEWIS, METEOR PHYSICS, ATMOSPHERIC SCIENCE. *Current Pos:* asst prof phys educ, 80-86, assoc prof physics, 86-94, PROF PHYSICS, MT ALLISON UNIV, 94- *Personal Data:* b Moncton, NB, Sept 12, 51; m; c 2. *Educ:* Mt Allison Univ, BSc, 72; BEd, 78; Univ Western Ont, MSc, 74; PhD(physics), 79. *Prof Exp:* Teacher sci & math, Pub Sch NB, 78-80. *Mem:* Am Astron Soc; Can Astron Soc; fel Royal Astron Soc. *Res:* Development of optical observing systems for faint meteors; numerical modeling of ablation of meteoroids in planetary atmospheres. *Mailing Add:* Physics Dept Mt Allison Univ Sackville NB E0A 3C0 Can

HAWKES, STEPHEN J, ANALYTICAL CHEMISTRY, CHEMICAL EDUCATION. *Current Pos:* from assoc prof to prof, 68-93, EMER PROF CHEM, ORE STATE UNIV, 93- *Personal Data:* b London, Eng, May 30, 28; m 65, Pamela Johnson; c Eric & Logan. *Educ:* Univ London, BSc, 51, PhD(phys org chem), 63. *Prof Exp:* Lectr & res assoc chem, Univ Utah, 63-64; from asst prof to assoc prof, Brigham Young Univ, 64-68. *Concurrent Pos:* Vis prof, Inter Am Univ PR, 94. *Mem:* Am Chem Soc. *Res:* Variation of gas chromatographic retention indices with column conditions; defining curriculum of introductory chemistry. *Mailing Add:* Chem Dept Ore State Univ Corvallis OR 97331-4003. *Fax:* 541-737-2062; *E-Mail:* hawkess@ccmail.orst.edu

HAWKES, SUSAN PATRICIA, CYTOLOGY. *Current Pos:* ASSOC ADJ PROF, UNIV CALIF, SAN FRANCISCO, 85- *Personal Data:* b May 23, 46; Brit citizen. *Educ:* Queen Mary Col, London Univ, Eng, BSc, 69, PhD(virol), 72. *Prof Exp:* Res asst, Dept Tissue Immunol, London Hosp Med Col, 73; fel, Univ Calif, Berkeley, 74-76; staff scientist, Lab Chem Biodynamics, 76-78; assoc prof, Mich Molecular Inst, 78-85. *Concurrent Pos:* Vis researcher, Tumor Immunol Lab, St Louis Hosp, Paris, 73; fel, Am Asn Univ Women, 74-75 & Elsa Pardee Found, 75-; adj asst prof, Mich State Univ, 78-85. *Mem:* Am Soc Cell Biol. *Res:* Cell-extracellular matrix interactions; oncogenic transformation; metalloproteinases and their inhibitors; antisense oligodeoxynucleotides as potential therapeutic agents. *Mailing Add:* Dept Pharm Univ Calif 513 Parnassus Ave San Francisco CA 94143-0446

HAWKES, WAYNE CHRISTIAN, PROTEIN CHEMISTRY, NUTRITIONAL BIOCHEMISTRY. *Current Pos:* RES CHEMIST, WESTERN HUMAN NUTRIT RES CTR, AGR RES SERV, USDA, 84- *Personal Data:* b Oakland, Calif, Apr 23, 51; m 85. *Educ:* Univ Calif, Berkeley, BS, 74; Univ Calif, Davis, PhD(biochem), 80. *Prof Exp:* Prod supvr, Medi Physics, Roche, 72-76; res asst, Dept Food Sci & Technol, Univ Calif, Davis, 76-80, res biochemist, 80-84. *Mem:* AAAS; Am Chem Soc; Am Inst Nutrit; Fedn Am Socs Exp Biol. *Res:* Identify, purify, characterize and deduce the biological functions of human selenocysteine containing proteins; metabolic bases of the human selenium requirement. *Mailing Add:* Western Human Nutrit Res Ctr USDA PO Box 29997 San Francisco CA 94129-0602. *Fax:* 415-556-1432

HAWKING, STEPHEN W, ASTRONOMY, GRAVITATIONAL PHYSICS. *Current Pos:* Res stud appl math & theoret physics, Univ Cambridge, 62-65, res fel, 65-69, res asst astron, 72-73 & appl math & theoret physics, 73-74, prof gravitational physics, 77, LUCASIAN PROF MATH, UNIV CAMBRIDGE, 79- *Personal Data:* b Jan 8, 42; m 65, 95, Elaine Mason. *Hon Degrees:* DSc, Univ Oxford, 78, Univ Chicago, 81, Notre Dame Univ, 82, Priceton Univ, 82, NY Univ, 82, Leicester Univ, 82, Univ Leeds, 87, Univ Newcastle, 87, Tufts Univ, 89, Yale Univ, 89, Univ Cambridge, 89, Harvard Univ, 90. *Honors & Awards:* Eddington Medal, Royal Astron Soc, 75, Gold Medal, 85; Dannie Heinemann Prize, Am Inst Physics & Am Phys Soc,76; Maxwell Medal, Inst Physics, 76; Hughes Medal, Royal Soc, 76; Einstein Award, Strauss Found, 78; Albert Einstein Medal, Switz, 79; Wolf Found Prize, 88; Encycl Britannica Award, 89. *Concurrent Pos:* Fel, Cambridge Univ, 69-77, prof fel, 77; Sherman Fairchild distinguished scholar, Calif Inst Technol, 74-75; hon fel, Oxford Univ, 77, Univ Manchester Inst Sci & Technol, 90. *Mem:* Foreign hon mem Am Acad Arts & Sci; foreign mem Am Philos Soc; Pontifical Acad Sci; fel Royal Soc. *Res:* Applied mathematics and theoretical physics. *Mailing Add:* Dept Appl Math & Theoret Physics Cambridge Univ Cambridge CB3 9EW England

HAWKINS, A(LBERT) W(ILLIAM), CHEMICAL ENGINEERING. *Current Pos:* RETIRED. *Personal Data:* b Portland, Ore, July 3, 12; m 36; c 2. *Educ:* Univ Wash, Seattle, BS, 35, PhD(chem), 41. *Prof Exp:* Instr chem eng, Kans State Col, 40-41; develop chem engr, E I du Pont de Nemours & Co, Inc, 41-51, tech asst, Res Div, Explosives Dept, Del, 51-61, sect head appl math, Eastern Lab, NJ, 61-68, sr systs analyst, 68-70, sr res chem engr planning & eval, 70-71, sr res chem engr, Polymer Intermediates Dept, 72-80. *Concurrent Pos:* Vis prof, Univ Va, 67-68. *Mem:* Am Chem Soc; Am Inst Chem Engrs. *Res:* Planning and technical and economic evaluation for research guidance. *Mailing Add:* 13 Crosslands Dr Kenneth Square PA 19348

HAWKINS, BRUCE, HANDICAPPED COMPUTER AIDS. *Current Pos:* from asst prof to prof, 61-93, EMER PROF, PHYSICS, SMITH COL, 93- *Personal Data:* b Rochester, NY, Sept 8, 30; m 57; c 2. *Educ:* Amherst Col, BA, 51; Princeton Univ, PhD(physics), 54. *Prof Exp:* NSF fel physics, Swiss Fed Inst Technol, 54-55; instr, Yale Univ, 55-57; asst prof, Oberlin Col, 57-61. *Mem:* AAAS; Am Phys Soc; Am Asn Physics Teachers; Asn Comput Mach. *Res:* Computer data acquisition in the teaching laboratory. *Mailing Add:* Dept Physics Smith Col Northampton MA 01063-0001

HAWKINS, C MORTON, BIOSTATISTICS. *Current Pos:* from asst prof to assoc prof, 69-77, PROF BIOMET, UNIV TEX SCH PUB HEALTH, HOUSTON, 77-, ASSOC DEAN RES, 87- *Personal Data:* b Memphis, Tex, Jan 17, 38; m 61. *Educ:* Univ Okla, BS, 60; Univ Mich, MPH, 62; Tulane Univ, ScD(biostatist), 69. *Honors & Awards:* Albert Lasker Spec Pub Health Award, 80. *Prof Exp:* Statistician, Nat Inst Neurol Dis, NIH, 62-66; res assoc biostatist, Sch Pub Health, Tulane Univ, 66-69. *Concurrent Pos:* Mem, Opers Comt, Vet Admin, 73- *Mem:* Am Statist Asn; Biomet Soc; Am Pub Health Asn; Am Heart Asn. *Res:* Hypertension; cooperative clinic trial; propranolol heart trial; hypertension detection and followup program; systolic hypertension in the elderly program. *Mailing Add:* 4954 Yarwell Dr Houston TX 77096

HAWKINS, CHARLES EDWARD, PLASMA PHYSICS, ASTROPHYSICS. *Current Pos:* assoc prof, 80-86, PROF PHYSICS, NORTHERN KY UNIV, 86-, DIR, ACAD COMPUT, 88- *Personal Data:* b Pontiac, Mich, Nov 29, 41; m 64, 83, Barbara B Bonney; c Robert E, Rachael E & Elyse M. *Educ:* Greenville Col, AB, 64; Dartmouth Col, PhD, 71. *Prof Exp:* Asst prof physics, Spring Arbor Col, 69-74, assoc prof, 74-80. *Concurrent Pos:* Mem staff, NASA Lewis Res Ctr, 79-81. *Mem:* AAAS; Am Phys Soc; Am Asn Physics Teachers. *Res:* Plasma waves and instabilities; applications of plasma physics to astrophysical problems; spacecraft propulsion. *Mailing Add:* Dept Phys Northern Ky Univ Highland Heights KY 41099-6127. *Fax:* 606-572-5566; *E-Mail:* hawkins@nkuvax.edu

HAWKINS, DANIEL BALLOU, GEOCHEMISTRY. *Current Pos:* assoc prof, Univ Alaska, 67-71, head, Dept Geol, 72-75, head, Solid Earth Sci Prog, 75-76, actg dir, Grad Progs, 85-86, prof geol & chem, 85-90, prof geochem, Inst Water Resources, 71-90, EMER PROF GEOL & CHEM, UNIV ALASKA, 90-; HYDROLOGIST, US GEOL SURV, 90- *Personal Data:* b Dillon, Mont, Jan 24, 34; m 54, 73; c 3. *Educ:* Mont State Col, BSc, 56, MSc, 57; Pa State Univ, PhD(geochem), 61. *Prof Exp:* Analytical chemist, US Geol Surv, 57-58; geochemist, Waste Mgt Br, US Atomic Energy Comn, Idaho, 61-67. *Concurrent Pos:* Consult, J R Simplot Co, Idaho, 62-65, Geochem Serv, 72- & Los Alamos Sci Lab, 75-80. *Mem:* AAAS; Geochem Soc; Mineral Soc Am; Int Asn Math Geol; Int Asn Geochem & Cosmochem. *Res:* Mineral synthesis and hydrothermal alteration of rocks; radioactive waste disposal and ion-exchange studies; geochemical prospecting; environmental geochemistry of arsenic and other trace metals; study of Alaskan zeolites; hydrology and water resources; geochemistry of watersheds; statistical applications to geology. *Mailing Add:* Geol Dept Univ Alaska Fairbanks AK 99775

HAWKINS, DAVID A, MUSCLE MECHANICS. *Current Pos:* ASST PROF, UNIV CALIF, DAVIS, 92- *Personal Data:* b Burlingame, Calif, May 2, 61; m 91, Keri Somers; c Jennifer & William. *Educ:* Calif Polytech Inst, BS, 83; Univ Calif, San Diego, MS, 85; Univ Calif, Davis, PhD(biomed), 91. *Mem:* Am Soc Biomed; Am Col Sports Med; Am Soc Gravitation & Space Biol. *Res:* Gross human movement analysis and optimization; muscle-tendor performance and adaptation. *Mailing Add:* Dept Exercise Sci Hickey Gym Rm 275 Univ Calif Davis CA 95616. *Fax:* 530-752-6681; *E-Mail:* dahawkins@ucdavis.edu

HAWKINS, DAVID GEOFFREY, IMMUNOLOGY. *Current Pos:* PROF & CHMN MED & CONSULT, AFFIL HOSP, MEM UNIV NFLD, 80- *Personal Data:* b St John's, Nfld, June 21, 37. *Educ:* Mem Univ Nfld, dipl, 55; Dalhousie Univ, MD, 60. *Prof Exp:* From asst prof to prof med, Montreal Gen Hosp, McGill Univ, 68-80, dir, Div Rheumatol, 71-80, sr physician, 74-80, RES ASSOC IMMUNOL, MED CLIN, MONTREAL GEN HOSP, MCGILL UNIV, 68- *Concurrent Pos:* Royal Col Physicians & Surgeons Can fel internal med, 64; res fel exp path, Scripps Clin & Res Found, 65-67, res fel allergy, immunol & rheumatol, 67-68; Med Res Coun Can scholar, 68-73; consult physician, Montreal Children's Hosp, 80. *Mem:* Am Rheumatism Asn; Am Fedn Clin Res; Can Soc Immunol; Can Fedn Biol Sci; Can Soc Clin Invest. *Res:* Mechanisms of immunologic tissue injury; role of neutrophilic leukocytes in inflammatory response; immune complex diseases; anti-flammatory agents. *Mailing Add:* Dept Med Mem Univ Nfld Fac Med Prince Philip Dr St John's NF A1B 3V6 Can

HAWKINS, DAVID ROGER, RUMINANT NUTRITION. *Current Pos:* From asst prof to assoc prof, 69-78, PROF ANIMAL SCI, MICH STATE UNIV, 78- *Personal Data:* b Springfield, Ohio, Apr 10, 41; m 67; c 2. *Educ:* Ohio State Univ, BSc, 63, MSc, 65; Mich State Univ, PhD(animal husb), 69. *Mem:* Am Soc Animal Sci. *Res:* Ruminant nutrition; live animal growth, composition and evaluation. *Mailing Add:* 102 Anthony Hall Animal Sci Mich State Univ East Lansing MI 48824-1225

HAWKINS, DAVID ROLLO, SR, PSYCHIATRY, SCIENCE EDUCATION. *Current Pos:* PROF PSYCHIATRY, UNIV ILL, 90-; CLIN PROF PSYCHIAT, UNIV NC, CHAPEL HILL, 92- *Personal Data:* b Springfield, Mass, Sept 22, 23; m 46; Elizabeth G Wilson; c David R Jr, Robert W, John B & William A. *Educ:* Amherst Col, BA, 45; Univ Rochester, MD, 46. *Honors & Awards:* Pioneer Award, Asn Psychophysiol Study of Sleep, 77. *Prof Exp:* Intern, Strong Mem Hosp, Rochester, 46-48; capt, MC US Army, 48-50; Commonwealth Fund fel psychiat & med, Univ Rochester, 50-52; from instr to prof psychiat, Univ NC Sch Med, 52-67; prof & chmn, Dept Psychiat, Univ Va Sch Med, 67-77, alumni prof psychiat, 67-79, assoc dean, 69-70; psychiatrist-in-chief, Univ Va Hosp, 67-77; prof psychiat, Pritzker Sch Med, Univ Chicago, 79-90; dir, Liaison & Consult Serv, Dept Psychiat, Michael Reese Hosp, Chicago, 79-87, chmn, 87-92; prof psychiatry, Univ Ill, 90- *Concurrent Pos:* Assoc attend physician, NC Mem Hosp, Chapel Hill, 52-62, attend physician, 62-67; consult, Watts Hosp, Durham, 52-67, Vet Admin Hosp, Fayetteville, 56-67, Eastern State Hosp, Williamsburg, 71-, Vet Admin Hosp, Salem, 69-79; mem, Small Grants Comt, NIMH, 58-62, Nursing Res Study Sect, NIH, 65-67, Gov Comn Mental, Indigent & Geriatric Patients, 68- 72, Res Eval Comt, Va Dept Ment Hyg & Hosps, 70-73, Behav Sci Test Comt, Nat Bd Med Examiners, 70-73; spec res fel, Inst Psychiat, Univ London, 63-64; Fogarty int res fel, 76-77, US-USSR & Romania health exch fel, 78. *Mem:* Fel Am Col Psychoanalysts (treas, 89-91, pres, 93); fel Am Psychiat Asn; Am Psychosomatic Soc; AMA; Asn Am Med Col; Am Psychoanalytic Asn; AAAS; Sigma Xi. *Mailing Add:* 405 Deming Rd Chapel Hill NC 27514. *Fax:* 919-933-5722

HAWKINS, GEORGE ELLIOTT, JR, DAIRY NUTRITION. *Current Pos:* from asst prof to prof, 52-82, EMER PROF DAIRY SCI, AUBURN UNIV, 82- *Personal Data:* b Princeton, Ky, July 26, 19; m 46; c 1. *Educ:* Western Ky State Univ, BS, 41; Univ Ga, MS, 47; NC State Univ, PhD, 52. *Honors & Awards:* Honors Award, Am Dairy Sci Asn, 81. *Prof Exp:* Instr animal husb, Univ Ga, 48, asst prof dairy husb, 48-49; asst nutrit, NC State Col, 49-51. *Mem:* Am Soc Animal Sci; Am Dairy Sci Asn; Am Inst Nutrition. *Res:* Metabolism of volatile fatty acids by ruminants; role of saliva in ruminant nutrition; trace minerals in calf nutrition; calf management; pasture and harvested forage utilization; lipid metabolism; feeding management of dairy cattle; protein and gossypol in dairy cattle nutrition. *Mailing Add:* 601 Auburn Dr Auburn AL 36830-5549

HAWKINS, GERALD STANLEY, ASTRONOMY. *Current Pos:* RETIRED. *Personal Data:* b Gt Yarmouth, Eng, Apr 20, 28; US citizen; m 79, Julia M Dobson. *Educ:* London Univ, BSc, 49; Manchester Univ, PhD(physics), 52, DSc, 63. *Honors & Awards:* Arthur S Flemming Award, 65. *Prof Exp:* Astronr, Harvard-Smithsonian Observ, Cambridge, Mass, 54-74; prof astron, Boston Univ, 57-69; dean, Dickinson Col, Pa, 69-71; sci adv & ed, US Info Agency, 75-89. *Concurrent Pos:* Researcher, Boston Univ. *Mem:* Int Astron Union. *Res:* Astronomy of Stonehenge and other ancient sites; archaeoastronomy; meteors; mathematics of crop circle patterns. *Mailing Add:* Cosmos Club 2121 Mass Ave NW PO Box 1 Washington DC 20008

HAWKINS, GILBERT ALLAN, SOLID STATE PHYSICS. *Current Pos:* RES PHYSICIST, PHYSICS DIV, EASTMAN KODAK CO, 75- *Personal Data:* b Wichita, Kans, Dec 10, 46; m 69. *Educ:* Stanford Univ, BS, 69; Mass Inst Technol, PhD(physics), 73. *Prof Exp:* Miller fel basic res, Univ Calif, Berkeley, 73-75. *Mem:* Am Phys Soc; Am Inst Physics. *Res:* Magnetic and optical properties of thin films; superconductivity; dielectric properties, electrical conduction in polymer films; cooperative phenomena. *Mailing Add:* Eastman Kodak Co Bldg 81 Kodak Park Rochester NY 14650

HAWKINS, ISAAC KINNEY, RESTORATIVE DENTISTRY, HUMAN ANATOMY. *Current Pos:* ASST PROF ANAT & ORAL BIOL, MED COL GA, 69-, ASST PROF ORAL REHAB DENT, 73- *Personal Data:* b Johnson Co, Ark, Jan 17, 37; c 1. *Educ:* Univ Tex, BA, 58; Univ Tex Dent Br Houston, DDS, 62; Colo State Univ, PhD(anat), 69. *Concurrent Pos:* Pvt pract dent, 64-65 & 72- *Mem:* Asn Am Dentists; Aerospace Med Asn; Am Acad Oral Med. *Res:* Inert gases and their morphophysiologic and histochemical effects; in vivo effects on argentum amalgam; in vivo cavosurface margin leakage studies; neuroscience; science education; technical management. *Mailing Add:* PO Box 3225 Augusta GA 30914-3225

HAWKINS, JAMES WILBUR, JR, GEOLOGY. *Current Pos:* vis asst prof, 65-66, from asst prof to assoc prof, 66-76, PROF GEOL, SCRIPPS INST OCEANOG, UNIV CALIF, SAN DIEGO, 76- *Personal Data:* b Westerly, RI, Sept 10, 32; m 59; c 1. *Educ:* Univ Conn, BA, 54; Univ Wash, Seattle, MS, 60, PhD(geol), 63. *Honors & Awards:* Newcomb-Cleveland Award, AAAS, 80. *Prof Exp:* Jr scientist glaciol, Int Geophys Year Prog, Univ Wash, Seattle, 57-58, asst geol, 59-63, asst prof, 64-65; asst prof, Univ Alaska, 63-64. *Concurrent Pos:* NSF instnl grant, Univ Alaska & Geol Soc Am Penrose bequest, 64; NSF grants, 66, 67, 69 & 71-78. *Mem:* Fel Geol Soc Am; Am Mineral Soc. *Res:* Petrology, geochemistry and tectonics of island arcs, oceanic ridges and their remnants in fold mountain belts of continental margins. *Mailing Add:* Univ Calif San Diego 9500 Gilman Dr La Jolla CA 92093-5003

HAWKINS, JOSEPH ELMER, SPECIAL SENSES, PHYSIOLOGICAL. *Current Pos:* prof physiol acoust & chmn, Grad Prog, 63-84, EMER PROF OTOLARYNGOL, MED SCH, UNIV MICH, 84- *Personal Data:* b Waco, Tex, Mar 4, 14; m 39, Jane E Daddow; c Richard S, Peter D, James, William S & Priscilla A (Leach). *Educ:* Baylor Univ, AB, 33; Oxford Univ, BA, 37, MA, 66, DSc, 79; Harvard Univ, PhD(med sci), 41. *Honors & Awards:* Award of Merit Asn Res Otolaryngol, 85. *Prof Exp:* Instr, Harvard Med Sch, 41-45; asst investr, Nat Defense Res Comt Proj, Harvard Univ, 41-43, spec res assoc sci, Res & Develop Off Psychoacoust Lab, 43-45; asst prof physiol, Bowman Gray Sch Med, 45-46; res assoc & head, Dept Neurophysiol, Merck Inst Therapeut Res, 46-56; assoc prof otolaryngol, Sch Med, NY Univ, 56-63. *Concurrent Pos:* USPHS spec fel, Univ Goteborg, 61-63; Commun Dis Res Training Comt, Nat Inst Neurol Dis & Stroke, 65-69, mem, Study Sect Sensory Dis, NIH, Commun Sci Study Sect 75-79; chercheur etranger, Lab Audiol Exp, Univ Bordeaux II, 78; vis distinguished prof biol, Baylor Univ, 85-93; Humboldt Award fel, Univ Wurzburg, 91. *Mem:* Asn Res Otolaryngol; Am Physiol Soc; assoc mem Am Otol Soc; fel Acoust Soc Am; fel AAAS. *Res:* Anatomy, physiology and experimental pathology of auditory and vestibular systems; medical history otolaryngology, neurology; effects of noise, ototoxic drugs and aging on inner ear. *Mailing Add:* Kresge Hearing Res Inst Univ Mich Med Sch Ann Arbor MI 48109-0506. *Fax:* 313-764-0014; *E-Mail:* joseph.hawkins@um.cc.umich.edu

HAWKINS, MICHAEL JOHN, DRUG RESEARCH. *Current Pos:* head, Biol Eval Sect, 84-88, CHIEF, INVESTIGATIONAL DRUG BR, CANCER THER EVAL PROG, DIV CANCER TREATMENT, NAT CANCER INST, 88- *Personal Data:* b Cleveland, Ohio, Mar 24, 47. *Educ:* Washington & Lee Univ, BA, 69; Univ Va, MD, 76; Am Bd Internal Med, cert, 79, cert oncol, 81. *Prof Exp:* Intern, Dept Internal Med, Univ Wis Hosp, 76-77, resident, 77-79, fel med oncol, Wis Clin Cancer Ctr, 79-81, res assoc, Dept Human Oncol, 81-82, from instr to asst prof, 82-84. *Concurrent Pos:* Clin fel, Am Cancer Soc, 79-81. *Mem:* Am Col Physicians; AAAS; Am Soc Clin Oncol. *Res:* Cancer therapy; internal medicine; oncology. *Mailing Add:* Five Eldwick Ct Potomac MD 20854

HAWKINS, MORRIS, JR, SOMATIC CELL GENETICS, NEUROGENETICS. *Current Pos:* asst to dean, 82-89, ASSOC PROF MICROBIOL, HOWARD UNIV COL MED, 78-, SPEC ASST TO DEAN, 93- *Personal Data:* b Shreveport, La, Feb 13, 44. *Educ:* Southern Univ, BS, 65; Howard Univ, MS, 69, PhD(genetics), 71. *Prof Exp:* Tech asst life sci, Nat Res Coun, Nat Acad Sci, 69; lectr zool, Howard Univ, 69-70; prof asst neurobiol, Div Biol & Med Sci, NSF, 71; assoc prof & chmn, Dept Biol, WVa State Col, 71-75; vis assoc prof human genetics, Sch Med, Yale Univ, 75-78. *Concurrent Pos:* Sci fac fel, WVa Univ, 74; consult, Inst Serv Educ, 74-75; NSF sci fac fel, 75-76; sci fac fel, Nat Inst Gen Med Sci, 76-78. *Mem:* Soc Neurosci; Sigma Xi; Nat Inst Sci; Am Soc Human Genetics; Am Soc Cell Biol; Am Soc Microbiol. *Res:* Biochemical and genetic analysis of enzymes involved in neurotransmitter metabolism; using techniques of cell culture, biochemistry, immunochemistry, and somatic cell genetics and molecular biology techniques to determine the chromosomal location of human genes; factors controlling the expression and regulation of genes; human molecular genetics, isolation and characterization of DNA polymorphisms; genetic linkage analysis. *Mailing Add:* Dept Microbiol Col Med Howard Univ Washington DC 20059. *Fax:* 202-806-4508; *E-Mail:* mhawkinsjr@fac.howard.edu

HAWKINS, NEIL MIDDLETON, STRUCTURAL ENGINEERING. *Current Pos:* PROF & HEAD CIVIL ENG, UNIV ILL, 91- *Personal Data:* b Sydney, Australia, Jan 31, 35; m 61; c 2. *Educ:* Univ Sydney, BS, 55, BE, 57; Univ Ill, MS, 59, PhD(civil eng), 61. *Honors & Awards:* Edward Noyes Prize, Inst Engrs, Australia, 65; Wason Medal, Am Concrete Inst, 68; Reese Award, Am Concrete Inst, 76, 80 & 91 & Am Soc Civil Engrs, 79; T Y Lin Award, Am Soc Civil Engrs, 89. *Prof Exp:* Lectr & sr lectr struct, Univ Sydney, Australia, 61-68; prof & chmn civil eng, Univ Wash, 78-87, prof struct eng, 88-91, assoc dean res, 87-91. *Concurrent Pos:* Design engr, Portland Cement Asn, 66-67; consult, Boeing Aircraft Co, Post-Tensioning Inst, Precast/Prestressed Concrete Inst, USN & Bethlehem Steel Co; prin investr, NSF, 69- *Mem:* Am Concrete Inst; Am Soc Civil Engrs; Earthquake Eng Res Inst; Masonry Soc. *Res:* Strength and behavior of reinforced, precast, prestressed and composite steel and concrete structures with particular emphasis on their dynamic loading response. *Mailing Add:* 2229 Newmark Civil Eng Lab Univ Ill Urbana IL 61801

HAWKINS, RICHARD ALBERT, PHYSIOLOGY, BIOCHEMISTRY. *Current Pos:* prof & chmn physiol, 88-93, EXEC VPRES ACAD AFFAIRS & CHIEF ACAD OFFICER, FINCH UNIV HEALTH SCI, CHICAGO MED SCH, 93- *Personal Data:* b Greenwich, Conn, Mar 27, 40; m 64, Enriqueta Elias; c Richard A & Paul A. *Educ:* San Diego State Univ, BS, 63; Harvard Univ, PhD(physiol), 69. *Hon Degrees:* LHD, Univ Phoenix, 94. *Honors & Awards:* Morris Parker Meritorious Res Award, 92. *Prof Exp:* Instr biol, San Diego State Univ, 63-64; res asst biochem, Scripps Metab Clin, 64; fel, Oxford Univ, 69-71; staff fel neurochem, NIMH, 71-73, sr staff fel, 73-74; chief phys sci, Bur Med Devices, Food & Drug Admin, 74-76; assoc prof physiol, NY Univ, 76-77; prof physiol, Dept Anesthesia & Physiol & chief, Div Anesthesia & Metab Res, Hershey Med Ctr, Pa State Univ, 77-88. *Concurrent Pos:* Parker B Francis investr; hon prof, Univ Valencia, 89. *Mem:* Am Physiol Soc; Biochem Soc; Soc Neurosci; Am Soc Neurochem. *Res:* Cellular physiology-biochemistry with special emphasis on the study of brain metabolism and physiology. *Mailing Add:* Finch Univ Health Sci/Chicago Med Sch 3333 Green Bay Rd North Chicago IL 60064. *Fax:* 847-578-3404; *E-Mail:* exvpacdmc@mis.finchcms.edu

HAWKINS, RICHARD HOLMES, HYDROLOGY, WATERSHED SCIENCE. *Current Pos:* PROF & PROG LEADER WATERSHED SCI, SCH RENEWABLE NATURAL RESOURCES, UNIV ARIZ, 88- *Personal Data:* b St Louis, Mo, Dec 16, 34; m 59; c 3. *Educ:* Univ Mo, Columbia, BS, 57, BS, 59; Colo State Univ, MS, 61, PhD(watershed mgt), 68. *Prof Exp:* Forester, US Forest Serv, 59-60; assoc engr, State Calif Dept Water Resources, 61-66; instr watershed mgt, Colo State Univ, Ft Collins, 67-68; asst dir, Water Resources Ctr, State Univ NY, 68-71; assoc prof, Utah State Univ, 71-80, prof watershed sci, 80-88. *Concurrent Pos:* NDEA fel, Colo State Univ, 66-68; assoc prof forest engr, State Univ NY Col Forestry, Syracuse, 69-71; hydrologist, USDA, Agr Res Serv, Tucson, 77-78, 85; vis prof, Sch Renewable Natural Resources, Univ Ariz, 77-78; hydrologist, USDA, Agr Res Serv, Beltsville, Md, 84-85; distinguished vis scientist, US Environ Protection Agency, Corvallis, Ore, 86-88; prof engr, Calif & NY; prof hydrologist, Am Inst Hydrol. *Mem:* AAAS; Am Soc Civil Eng; Am Water Resources Asn; Am Geophys Union; Asn Univ Watershed Sci; Sigma Xi; Am Inst Hydrol. *Res:* Small watershed hydrology, processes and water quality; watershed modeling and applied hydrology; runoff, erosion; sedimentation; land use effects. *Mailing Add:* SRNR Univ Ariz 1600 E Univ Blvd Tucson AZ 85721-0001

HAWKINS, RICHARD HORACE, MANAGEMENT RADIOACTIVE WASTE. *Current Pos:* RETIRED. *Personal Data:* b Columbia, Mo, Nov 6, 22; m 53; c 2. *Educ:* Univ Mo, BS, 47, MS, 50; Texas A&M Univ, PhD(mineral), 60. *Prof Exp:* Assoc agronomist, Clemson Univ, 50-55; staff chemist, Savannah River Plant, E I du Pont de Nemours & Co, 60-89. *Mem:* Soil Sci Soc Am; Clay Minerals Soc. *Res:* Soil mineralogy applied to improved radioactive waste management. *Mailing Add:* 1027 Clark Rd Aiken SC 29803

HAWKINS, RICHARD THOMAS, ORGANIC CHEMISTRY. *Current Pos:* RETIRED. *Personal Data:* b Provo, Utah, Sept 9, 29; m 55, Marie Littleford; c Vance, Alice & Nancy. *Educ:* Brigham Young Univ, BA, 51; Univ Ill, PhD(org chem), 59. *Prof Exp:* Res chemist, Phillips Petrol Co, 51-54; Nat Petrochem Corp, 57; fel, Univ Ill, 59; from assoc prof to prof chem, Brigham Young Univ, 59-95, chmn dept, 71-74. *Concurrent Pos:* Vis prof, Du Pont, 65-66 & Phillips Petrol Co, 74-75 & 80. *Mem:* Am Chem Soc. *Res:* Synthesis of calixarenes and organoboron compounds; polymer chemistry. *Mailing Add:* Dept Chem Brigham Young Univ Provo UT 84602. *Fax:* 801-378-5474

HAWKINS, ROBERT C, ENGINEERING, GAS TURBINE TECHNOLOGY. *Current Pos:* RETIRED. *Prof Exp:* Gen mgr, Advan Technol Oper, Lynn Prod Div, Gen Elec, 88, consult, 88-90. *Mem:* Nat Acad Eng. *Mailing Add:* 570 Ocean Dr Apt 601 Juno Beach FL 33408

HAWKINS, ROBERT DRAKE, NEUROPHYSIOLOGY, EXPERIMENTAL PSYCHOLOGY. *Current Pos:* res fel, 75-79, staff assoc, 79-82, ASST PROF, CTR NEUROBIOL & BEHAV, COLUMBIA UNIV, 82-; RES SCIENTIST, NY STATE PSYCHIAT INST, 83- *Personal Data:* b Washington, DC, May 2, 46. *Educ:* Stanford Univ, BA, 68; Univ Calif, San Diego, MA, 69, PhD(psychol), 73. *Prof Exp:* Res assoc psychol, Univ Calif, San Diego, 74; res fel, Nat Ctr Sci Res, Gif-sur-Yvette, France, 74-75. *Mem:* AAAS; Soc Neurosci. *Res:* Neural basis of behavior, neural mechanisms of sensitization and classical conditioning in Aplysia California. *Mailing Add:* Ctr Neurobiol & Behavior Columbia Univ 722 W 168th St New York NY 10032

HAWKINS, THEO M, PUBLIC HEALTH. *Current Pos:* RETIRED. *Personal Data:* b Frederick, Okla, Mar 7, 28; m 48; c 3. *Educ:* Univ Calif, Berkeley, BS, 50, MPH, 58, DPH, 64. *Prof Exp:* Pub health lab dir, Sonoma Co Health Dept Calif, 50-55; assoc pub health, Univ Calif, Berkeley, 55-62; microbiologist, Ctr Dis Control, USPHS, 64-69, chief, Bacteriol Training Br, 69-86, training consult, 87-89, proj mgr, Nat Lab Training Network Proj, 89-93. *Mem:* Am Soc Microbiol; Am Pub Health Asn. *Res:* Microbiology. *Mailing Add:* 2220 Winding Way Tucker GA 30084

HAWKINS, THOMAS WILLIAM, JR, MATHEMATICS, HISTORY OF SCIENCE. *Current Pos:* assoc prof, 72-80, PROF MATH, BOSTON UNIV, 80- *Personal Data:* b Flushing, NY, Jan 10, 38; m 59; c 3. *Educ:* Houghton Col, BA, 59; Univ Rochester, MS, 61; Univ Wis, PhD(hist math), 68. *Prof Exp:* From instr to asst prof math, Swarthmore Col, 66-72. *Concurrent Pos:* Am Coun Learned Socs fel, Swiss Fed Inst Technol, 69-70; vis assoc prof, Yale Univ, 75; assoc ed, Historia Mathematica, 75-; vis scholar, Harvard Univ, 80-81. *Mem:* Hist Sci Soc; Am Math Soc. *Res:* History of mathematics, especially in 19th century; development of modern integration theory; history of group representation theory; history of matrix theory, lie groups and algebras. *Mailing Add:* Dept Math Boston Univ 111 Cummington St Boston MA 02215

HAWKINS, W(ILLIAM) BRUCE, SOFTWARE DEVELOPMENT, VIOLIN ACOUSTICS. *Current Pos:* from asst prof to assoc prof, 61-87, PROF PHYSICS, SMITH COL, 87- *Personal Data:* b Rochester, NY, Sept 8, 30; m 57; c 2. *Educ:* Amherst Col, BA, 51; Princeton Univ, PhD(physics), 54. *Prof Exp:* Instr physics, Yale Univ, 55-57; asst prof, Oberlin Col, 57-61. *Mem:* Am Phys Soc; Am Asn Physics Teachers; AAAS; Asn Comput Mach. *Res:* Data acquisition software for introductory laboratories; software for teaching upper level physics courses; violin acoustics. *Mailing Add:* Dept Physics Smith Col Northampton MA 01063

HAWKINS, WILLIAM M(ADISON), JR, NUCLEAR ENGINEERING, MECHANICAL ENGINEERING. *Current Pos:* vpres, 69-76, PRES, NUTEC, INC, 76- *Personal Data:* b Hannibal, Mo, Aug 7, 09; m 38; c 3. *Educ:* Harvard Univ, AB, 31, MSE, 33; Chrysler Inst Eng, MME, 35. *Prof Exp:* Res engr, Chrysler Corp, 34-42; proj engr, Continental Aviation & Eng Corp, 42-44; exp engr, Packard Motor Car Co, 44-48; res engr, chief engr & mgr res & develop, ACF Indust, Inc, 48-59; mgr res develop, Atomic Energy Div, Allis-Chalmers Mfg Co, 59-63, appln eng, 63-69. *Mem:* Am Nuclear Soc. *Res:* Peaceful applications of nuclear energy. *Mailing Add:* 9414 Thrush Lane Potomac MD 20854

HAWKINS, WILLIAM MAX, ECONOMIC GEOLOGY, MINERALOGY. *Current Pos:* from asst prof to assoc prof, 63-69, chmn dept, 64-77, PROF GEOL, STATE UNIV NY COL CORTLAND, 69-, CHMN DEPT, 80- *Personal Data:* b Brokenhead, Man, May 19, 26; m 55; c 2. *Educ:* Queen's Univ, BSc, 60; McGill Univ, MSc, 58, PhD(geol), 60. *Prof Exp:* Instr geol, Lawrence Col, 61-63. *Concurrent Pos:* State Univ NY Res Found grant-in-aid, 67. *Mem:* Geol Asn Can; Geochem Soc; Nat Asn Geol Teachers; Can Inst Mining & Metall; Spectros Soc Can. *Res:* Spectrochemical studies of wall rock alterations around sulfide ore deposits; significance of trace elements in ore deposits. *Mailing Add:* 38 Sweetland Rd Apt 3 Cortland NY 13045

HAWKINS, WILLIS M(OORE), AERONAUTICAL ENGINEERING. *Current Pos:* corp sr vpres, Lockheed Corp, 66-74, dir, 72-80, corp sr vpres & pres, Calif Co, 76-79, sr vpres aircraft, Lockheed Aircraft Corp, 79-80, SR ADV, LOCKHEED CORP, 80- *Personal Data:* b Kansas City, Mo, Dec 1, 13; wid, Anita Stanfil; c Nancy Gay (Bostick), Willis M III & James Walter. *Educ:* Univ Mich, BS, 37. *Hon Degrees:* DEng, Univ Mich, 65; DSc, Ill Col, 66. *Honors & Awards:* NASA Distinguished Civilian Serv Medal; Founders lectr, Nat Acad Eng; Nat Medal Sci, 88; Gardner lectr, Mass Inst Technol, 91. *Prof Exp:* Struct designer, fighter aircraft, Lockheed Aircraft Corp, 37-40 & preliminary design investr, 40-41, supvr, wind tunnel test group, 41, mgr, Preliminary Design Dept, 41-47, dir, Preliminary Design Div, 47-52, dir, Preliminary Design, Missiles & Space Div, 52-53, dir eng, 54-57, asst gen mgr, 57-60, vpres & gen mgr, Space Div, 60-62, vpres sci & eng, 62-63; asst secy, res & develop, US Army, 63-66. *Concurrent Pos:* Vis lectr, Univ Calif, Los Angeles; chmn, Aerospace Safety Adv Panel & mem adv coun, NASA; dir, Wackenhut Corp & Avemco. *Mem:* Nat Acad Eng; fel Royal Aeronaut Soc; hon fel Am Inst Aeronaut & Astronaut. *Res:* Research and development direction; weapon system management; system design and analysis; development. *Mailing Add:* 21931 Burbank Blvd No 35 Woodland Hills CA 91367. *Fax:* 818-888-5776

HAWKINSON, JON ERIC, BIOCHEMICAL PHARMACOLOGY. *Current Pos:* GROUP LEADER, COCENSYS INC, 92- *Personal Data:* b Renton, Wash, Aug 4, 57; m 86, Ann Nishita; c James & Ava. *Educ:* Univ Calif, Davis, PhD(pharmacol & toxicol), 87. *Prof Exp:* Specialist, Univ Calif, Berkeley, 87-92. *Mem:* Soc Neurosci; Am Soc Pharmacol & Exp Therapeut. *Res:* Target selection and screening of biochemical targets for drug discovery. *Mailing Add:* CoCensys Inc 213 Technology Dr Irvine CA 92618. *Fax:* 714-753-6151; *E-Mail:* jhawkinson@cocensys.com

HAWKINSON, STUART WINFIELD, CRYSTALLOGRAPHY, BIOCHEMISTRY. *Current Pos:* ENGR SOFTWARE APPLN, FLOATING POINT SYSTS INC, PORTLAND, 80- *Personal Data:* b Harris, Minn, Feb 3, 43; m 65; c 2. *Educ:* Wash State Univ, BS, 65; Univ Chicago, PhD(chem physics), 68. *Prof Exp:* USPHS fel, Dept Anat, Univ Chicago, 69; Univ Tenn investr, Biol Div, Oak Ridge Nat Lab, 69-71; asst prof biochem, Univ Tenn, Knoxville, 72-77, assoc prof, 77-80. *Concurrent Pos:* Guest scientist, Oak Ridge Nat Lab, 76- *Mem:* Am Chem Soc; Am Crystallog Asn. *Res:* X-ray crystallographic study of proteins, nucleic acids and interacting drugs. *Mailing Add:* 6695 SW 203rd St Beaverton OR 97007

HAWKRIDGE, FRED MARTIN, ANALYTICAL CHEMISTRY. *Current Pos:* from asst prof to assoc prof, 76-81, PROF CHEM, VA COMMONWEALTH UNIV, 81- *Personal Data:* b Ft Gordon, Ga, June 20, 44; m 69; c 2. *Educ:* Univ Ga, BS, 66; Univ Ky, PhD(chem), 71. *Prof Exp:* Fel analytical chem, Case Western Res Univ & Ohio State Univ, 71-72; asst prof chem, Univ Southern Miss, 72-76. *Concurrent Pos:* Vis prof, Univ Del, 81-82; prog officer, Chem Div, NSF, 89-90. *Mem:* Am Chem Soc; AAAS; Sigma Xi; Electrochem Soc; Soc Electroanalytical Chem; fel Japan Soc Prom Sci. *Res:* Heterogeneous electron transfer properties of biological molecules; biological molecule electron transfer mechanisms; trace organic analyses. *Mailing Add:* Dept Chem Va Commonwealth Univ Richmond VA 23284

HAWKS, BYRON LOVEJOY, OBSTETRICS & GYNECOLOGY. *Current Pos:* asoc prof, Univ Ark, Little Rock, 63-71, actg chmn dept, 69-71, prof, 71-78, EMER PROF OBSTET & GYNEC, SCH MED, UNIV ARK, LITTLE ROCK, 78- *Personal Data:* b New York, Nov 23, 09; m 41; c 3. *Educ:* Duke Univ, BA, 36; NY Univ, MD, 39; Am Bd Obstet & Gynec, dipl, 56. *Prof Exp:* Asst chief obstet & gynec, US Naval Hosps, Portsmouth, Va, 49-50, chief, Port Lyautey, Morocco, 50-52 & US Marine Hosp, Cherry Point, NC, 52-54; asst chief, US Naval Hosps, San Diego, Calif, 54-57, chief, Yokuska, Japan, 57-59 & Great Lakes, Ill, 59-63. *Concurrent Pos:* Commandants rep, US Navy, 64-; dir, State Ark Maternity & Infant Care Proj, 65-78; assoc dir, Ark State Dept Health, 78- *Mem:* Fel Am Col Obstet & Gynec. *Res:* Preinvasive carcinoma of cervix uteri; origin, disposal and prognostic potential of amniotic fluid; operative obstetrics. *Mailing Add:* 105 N Plaza Dr Little Rock AR 72205

HAWKS, GEORGE H, III, ORGANIC CHEMISTRY. *Current Pos:* RES ASSOC, EASTMAN KODAK RES LABS, 70- *Personal Data:* b Rochester, NY, Sept 5, 38; m 63; c 1. *Educ:* Princeton Univ, AB, 64, MS, 67, PhD(chem), 68. *Prof Exp:* Alexander von Humboldt stipend, Univ Munich, Ger, 68-70. *Mem:* AAAS; Am Chem Soc; Sigma Xi. *Res:* Synthesis and manipulation of reactive intermediates; synthesis of di-substituted sulfur ylides. *Mailing Add:* 63 Southern Pkwy Rochester NY 14618

HAWKS, KEITH HAROLD, MECHANICAL ENGINEERING. *Current Pos:* Asst prof, 69-76, ASSOC PROF MECH ENG, PURDUE UNIV, 76- *Personal Data:* b New Castle, Ind, Nov 9, 41; m 62; c 3. *Educ:* Purdue Univ, BS, 64, MS, 66, PhD(mech eng), 69. *Mem:* Am Soc Mech Engrs; Am Soc Eng Educ. *Res:* Power systems; cryogenics; thermal design; mathematical modeling. *Mailing Add:* Sch Mech Eng Purdue Univ West Lafayette IN 47907

HAWKSLEY, OSCAR, ECOLOGY, QUATERNARY PALEONTOLOGY. *Current Pos:* RETIRED. *Personal Data:* b Kingston, NY, June 30, 20; m 61, Dorothy D; c John & Derek. *Educ:* Principia Col, BS, 42; Cornell Univ, MS, 47, PhD, 50. *Prof Exp:* From asst prof to assoc prof, Cent Mo State Col, 47-56, prof biol, 56-79. *Mem:* Fel Nat Speleol Soc (vpres, 57-58). *Res:* Behavior and ecology of vertebrates; speleology; Pleistocene ecology. *Mailing Add:* 1104 S Holden Warrensburg MO 64093

HAWLEY, JOHN WILLIAM, ENVIRONMENTAL GEOLOGY, GEOMORPHOLOGY. *Current Pos:* SR ENVIRON GEOLOGIST & MGR ALBUQUERQUE OFF, NMEX BUR MINES & MINERAL RESOURCES, 77- *Personal Data:* b Evansville, Ind, Oct 7, 32; m 61, Diane Bandyk; c Glynis (Albrecht), Charles P & George M. *Educ:* Hanover Col, BA, 54; Univ Ill, PhD(geol), 62. *Honors & Awards:* Kirk Bryan Award, Geol Soc Am, 83; Cert Merit Arid Lands Res, AAAS-SWARM. *Prof Exp:* Geologist, Nev State Dept Conserv & Natural Resources, 59-61; geologist, Ground-Water Br, US Geol Surv, 61; geologist, Soil Conserv Serv, USDA, 62-77. *Concurrent Pos:* Adj prof geol NMex Tech, 80-; collabr, Pueblo Office Environ Protection, All Indian Pueblo Coun. *Mem:* Fel AAAS; fel Geol Soc Am; Am Quaternary Assoc; Am Inst Prof Geologists; Sigma Xi. *Res:* Geology and hydrogeology of Cenozoic deposits in the Basin and Range and southern Great Plains provinces; geomorphology and environmental geology of New Mexico; hazardous-waste management in arid regions. *Mailing Add:* 2808 Cent SE Albuquerque NM 87106. *Fax:* 505-255-5253; *E-Mail:* rease@admin.nmt.edu

HAWLEY, MARTIN C, CHEMICAL ENGINEERING. *Current Pos:* From asst prof to assoc prof, 64-75, PROF CHEM ENG, MICH STATE UNIV, 75- *Personal Data:* b Adrian, Mich, Sept 24, 39; m 59; c 1. *Educ:* Mich State Univ, BS, 61, PhD(chem eng), 64. *Honors & Awards:* Chem Engr Award, Am Inst Chem Engrs, 76. *Mem:* Am Inst Chem Engrs; Am Soc Eng Educ; Am Chem Soc; Sigma Xi. *Res:* Scale up of liquid-solid chromatographic columns; study of axial dispersion in packed beds. *Mailing Add:* 144 Lexington Ave Lansing MI 48823-4623

HAWLEY, MERLE DALE, ANALYTICAL CHEMISTRY. *Current Pos:* asst prof, 66-70, assoc prof, 70-76, PROF ANALYTICAL CHEM, KANS STATE UNIV, 76- *Personal Data:* b Olin, Iowa, Apr 19, 39; m 59; c 3. *Educ:* Northern Iowa Univ, BA, 60, MA, 62; Univ Kans, PhD(chem), 65. *Prof Exp:* Res chemist, Dow Chem Co, 65-66. *Mem:* Am Chem Soc; Electrochem Soc; Soc Electroanalytical Chem. *Res:* Electroanalytical chemistry; electrode processes of organic compounds. *Mailing Add:* 1609 Beechwood Terr Manhattan KS 66502-2310

HAWLEY, NATHAN, SEDIMENT TRANSPORT, PHYSICAL LIMNOLOGY. *Current Pos:* OCEANOGR, GREAT LAKES ENVIRON RES LAB, 82- *Personal Data:* b Camden, NJ, Jan 26, 49. *Educ:* Univ Chicago, BS, 71, MS, 76; Mass Inst Technol, PhD(geol), 78. *Prof Exp:* Asst prof geol, Univ Va, 78-79; res scientist, Univ Mich, 79-82. *Res:* Physical and chemical processes involved in the deposition, transport and erosion of cohesive sediments. *Mailing Add:* 2205 Commonwealth Blvd Ann Arbor MI 48105. *Fax:* 313-741-2055; *E-Mail:* hawley@glerl.noaa.gov

HAWLEY, ROBERT JOHN, CLINICAL MICROBIOLOGY, INFECTIOUS DISEASES. *Current Pos:* MEM STAFF, US ARMY MED RES INST INFECTIOUS DIS, 88- *Personal Data:* b Astoria, NY, July 13, 40; m 76, Evelyn M Downs; c Pamela A, Karen D & Eileen D. *Educ:* Pa Mil Col, BS, 62; Cath Univ Am, MS, 66; Col Med & Dent NJ, PhD(microbiol), 74. *Prof Exp:* Diag virol asst, Sch Med, WVa Univ, 62-64; chief, Bacteriol Sect, 249th Gen Hosp, APO San Francisco, 67-70; fel, Sch Med, Georgetown Univ, 74-75, instr to asst prof microbiol, 75-81; dir microbiol immunol, Holy Cross Hosp, Silver Spring, Md, 81-82; instr, Univ Md, College Park, 82-85; US Army Med Materiel Develop Active, 85-88. *Concurrent Pos:* Res microbiologist, NIH & Nat Inst Dent Res, 77-79. *Mem:* Am Soc Microbiol; Am Biol Safety Asn; NY Acad Sci. *Res:* Biological safety; rapid identification methods. *Mailing Add:* MCMR-UIZ-S USAMRIID Ft Detrick Frederick MD 21702-5011. *Fax:* 301-619-4768; *E-Mail:* dr._robert_hawley@detrick.army.mil

HAWORTH, DANIEL THOMAS, INORGANIC CHEMISTRY. *Current Pos:* from asst prof to assoc prof, 60-68, PROF CHEM, MARQUETTE UNIV, 68- *Personal Data:* b Fond du Lac, Wis, June 27, 28; m 52, Mary K Hormuth; c Daniel G, M Judith & Steven T. *Educ:* Univ Wis, Oshkosh, BS, 50; Marquette Univ, MS, 52; St Louis Univ, PhD(chem), 59. *Prof Exp:* Res chemist, Allis-Chalmers Mfg Co, 58-60. *Concurrent Pos:* Chem, Bur of Ships, 52-53. *Mem:* Am Chem Soc; Sigma Xi; NY Acad Sci. *Res:* Boron hydrides and related compounds; inorganic syntheses; high vacuum techniques; thin-layer and high pressure liquid chromatography; nuclear magnetic resonance spectroscopy; chemical sensors. *Mailing Add:* Dept Chem Marquette Univ PO Box 1881 Milwaukee WI 53201-1881. *Fax:* 414-288-7066; *E-Mail:* 6064haworthd@vms.csd.mu.edu

HAWORTH, JAMES C, PEDIATRICS. *Current Pos:* from asst prof to assoc prof, Univ Man, 63-70, prof pediat & human genetics, 70-94, head dept, 79-85, EMER PROF, DEPT PEDIAT & CHILD HEALTH, UNIV MAN, 94- *Personal Data:* b Gosforth, Eng, May 29, 23; m 51, Eleanor M Bowser; c 4. *Educ:* Univ Birmingham, MB, ChB, 45, MD, 60. *Honors & Awards:* Teddy Award, Children's Hosp Res Found, 85. *Prof Exp:* Walter Myers traveling studentship, Univ Birmingham, 45; house physician med, Gen Hosp, Birmingham, Eng, 46; house physician pediat, Children's Hosp, 46-47; registr, Alder Hey Hosp, Liverpool, 51-52; sr registr, Children's Hosp, Sheffield, 53-57; pediatrician, Winnipeg Clin, Man, 57-64. *Concurrent Pos:* House physician, Hosp Sick Children, London, 51; pediatrician, Winnipeg Children's Hosp, 57-93; consult pediat staff, St Beniface Gen Hosp, 74-93. *Mem:* Soc Pediat Res; Am Pediat Soc; Can Pediat Soc; fel Am Acad Pediat; fel Royal Col Physicians Can; hon fel Can Col Med Genetics; fel Royal Col Physicians (London). *Res:* Metabolic diseases and nutrition in infants and children. *Mailing Add:* Dept Pediat & Child Health Childrens Hosp 840 Sherbrook St Winnipeg MB R3A 1S1 Can. *Fax:* 204-787-1419, 787-4807

HAWORTH, RICHARD THOMAS, MARINE GEOPHYSICS, DEEP GEOLOGY. *Current Pos:* DIR GEN, SEDIMENTARY & MARINE GEOSCI, GEOL SURV CAN, 90- *Personal Data:* b Wirksworth, Eng, May 24, 44; m 69, Wilma McLaren; c Neil & Mark. *Educ:* Univ Durham, BSc, 65; Cambridge Univ, PhD(geophys), 68. *Prof Exp:* Res scientist, Atlantic Geosci Ctr, Beford Inst Oceonog, Geol Surv Can, 68-83; chief geophysicist, Brit Geol Surv, 83-90. *Concurrent Pos:* Res Coun Can, 69-74; Brit Nat Comt for Geodesy & Geophys, 84-; mem, Brit Nat Lithosphere Comt, 84-; hon lectr, Nottingham Univ, 85- *Mem:* Am Geol Inst; fel Geol Asn Can; Can Geophys Union; Am Geophys Union; fel Geol Soc London; fel Royal Astron Soc. *Res:* Marine geological and geophysical surveys of the continental shelves and oceanic areas; geological and geophysical correlations of Appalachian/Caledonide structures and their offshore subsurface extension; hydrocarbons, climate change, environmental geology, law of the sea. *Mailing Add:* Geol Surv Can 601 Booth St Ottawa ON K1A 0E8 Can. *Fax:* 613-996-6575; *E-Mail:* haworth@gsc.nrcan.gc.ca

HAWORTH, W(ILLIAM) LANCELOT, MATERIALS SCIENCE, METALLURGY. *Current Pos:* prog dir, Mat Res Group, 84-85, prog dir, Mat Res Lab, 85-93, PROG DIR, MAT RES SCI & ENG CTR, NSF, 93- *Personal Data:* b Rossendale, Eng, May 18, 41; m 68, Letitia Wells; c Cristina & James L. *Educ:* Univ Liverpool, BSc, 62; Univ Alta, MSc, 64; Yale Univ, MS, 66, MPhil, 68, PhD(mat sci), 69. *Prof Exp:* Res assoc metall, Univ Ill, 69-71; from asst prof to prof metall eng, Wayne State Univ, 72-85. *Concurrent Pos:* Mem, Res Inst Eng Sci, Wayne State Univ, 75-85, assoc chmn, Dept Metall Eng, 75-85; sr staff mem, Cent Solar Energy Res Corp, Mich Energy & Resource Res Asn, 77-78, vpres, 78-79; assoc prog dir, Metall Prog, NSF, 82-83. *Mem:* AAAS; Metall Soc; Am Phys Soc; Mat Res Soc. *Res:* Plastic deformation, fatigue and fracture of materials; research administration in materials science and condensed matter sciences. *Mailing Add:* 2349 Chestnut St Falls Church VA 22043. *Fax:* 703-306-0515; *E-Mail:* lhaworth@nsf.gov

HAWROT, EDWARD, NICOTINIC ACETYLCHOLINE RECEPTOR STRUCTURE & FUNCTION, ALPHA-NEUROTOXIN STRUCTURE & FUNCTION. *Current Pos:* PROF MED SCI, BROWN UNIV, 90-, CHMN, SECT MOLECULAR & BIOCHEM PHARMACOL, 90- *Personal Data:* b Hamburg, Ger, Aug 18, 48; US citizen; m 89, Diane Lipscomb; c Kathryn, James, Jacquelyn & Aimee. *Educ:* Univ Detroit, AB, 70; Harvard Univ, PhD(biochem), 76. *Prof Exp:* Helen Hay Whitney fel, Harvard Univ, 76-79; asst prof pharmacol, Yale Univ, 80-86, assoc prof, 86-90. *Concurrent Pos:* Vis assoc prof, Univ Calif, San Francisco, 89. *Mem:* AAAS; Soc Neurosci; Am Soc Biol Chem & Molecular Biol; NY Acad Sci; Protein Soc; Biophys Soc; Am Soc Pharmacol & Exp Therapeut. *Res:* Structure-function analysis of receptor-ligand interactions. *Mailing Add:* Brown Univ PO Box G Providence RI 02912-0001. *Fax:* 401-863-1595; *E-Mail:* edward_hawrot@brown.edu

HAWRYLEWICZ, ERVIN J, NEUROENDOCRINOLOGY, NUTRITION. *Current Pos:* CHMN DEPT RES & DIR RES, MERCY HOSP & MED CTR, 69-; PROF BIOCHEM, COL BASIC MED SCI, UNIV ILL, 75- *Personal Data:* b Chicago, Ill. *Educ:* Ill Inst Technol, BS, 50, MS, 53, PhD(biochem), 60. *Prof Exp:* Asst biochemist, Armour Pharmaceut Labs, 50-53; from asst chemist to assoc chemist, IIT Res Inst, 53-58, res biochemist, 58-61, mgr, Life Sci Div, 61-63, asst dir div, 63-69. *Concurrent Pos:* Mem res comt & chmn, Mercy Hosp Med Ctr, 69-; mem, Am Cancer Soc Res Comt, 73-78; chmn, Cancer Prevention Comt, vpres, Am Cancer Soc, Ill Div, 84-; mem, Inst Rev Bd, Ill Cancer Coun, 80- *Mem:* AAAS; Am Soc Neurochem; Sigma Xi; Am Inst Nutrit; Soc Neurosci. *Res:* Neonatal development with emphasis on brain as affected by malnutrition; enzyme alterations in breast tissue as a function of tumor growth; effect of diet on neuroendocrine system and breast tumors; mechanisms of disease process at subcellular level. *Mailing Add:* Dept Res Mercy Hosp & Med Ctr Stevenson Expwy King Dr Chicago IL 60616

HAWRYLKO, EUGENIA ANNA, CELLULAR & TUMOR IMMUNOLOGY, ALLERGY. *Current Pos:* CLIN ASST ATTEND, DEPT MED, BELLEVUE HOSP, 81- *Personal Data:* b New York, NY, Feb 7, 42; m 74, Raymond J Aab; c Allison & Elizabeth. *Educ:* Vassar Col, AB, 62; NY Univ, MD, 66; Am Bd Allergy & Immunol, dipl, 79. *Prof Exp:* Intern & resident internal med, Bellevue Hosp, 66-68; res fel med, Harvard Med Sch, Peter Bent Brigham Hosp, 68-69; res fel & asst mem cellular immunol, Trudeau Inst, 69-74; res assoc cellular immunobiol, Sloan-Kettering Inst, 74-75, assoc, 75-81. *Concurrent Pos:* Fac res award, Am Cancer Soc, 76-81; clin fel allergy & immunol, NY Hosp Cornell Med Ctr, 78-80; mem, Am Cancer Soc Adv Comt, 78-82; part time instr clin med, Dept Med, NY Med Ctr, 81-; chief, Allergy & Immunol Labs, Dept Allergy & Immunol, Long Island Col Hosp, 82-88, chief develop immunol, 85-88; exec comt, NY Allergy & Immunol Soc, 93- *Mem:* Am Asn Immunologists; Am Acad Allergy, Asthma & Immunol; AAAS; NY Acad Sci; Am Col Allergists. *Res:* Cell mediated mechanisms in antitumor immunity, delayed type hypersensitivity and allergy. *Mailing Add:* Dept Med NY Univ Sch Med 924 W End Ave No 43 New York NY 10025-3540. *Fax:* 212-222-4982; *E-Mail:* hawrylkoe@aol.com

HAWRYLUK, ANDREW MICHAEL, ELECTRICAL ENGINEERING. *Current Pos:* scientist, 83-89, group leader, 89-93, DEP PROG LEADER, ADV MICROTECH PROG, LAWRENCE LIVERMORE NAT LAB, 93- *Personal Data:* b Brooklyn, NY, May 24, 54; m 77; c 2. *Educ:* Mass Inst Technol, BS, 76, MS, 77, PhD(elec eng), 81. *Honors & Awards:* I R 100 Award, 86, 87, 88, 89, 90; Award of Excellence, Dept Energy, 86. *Prof Exp:* Res assoc, Univ Fla, 81-83. *Res:* Microfabrication technology; semiconductor devices; semiconductor fabrication; artificial human vision. *Mailing Add:* Ultratech Stepper 3050 Zanker Rd San Jose CA 95134

HAWRYLUK, RICHARD JANUSZ, PLASMA PHYSICS, SOLID STATE PHYSICS. *Current Pos:* Res assoc plasma physics, Princeton Univ, 74-75, staff physicist, 75-79, res physicist, 79-83, head, Tokamak Fusion Test Reactor Oper Div, 86, Tokamak Fusion Test Reactor, 91 & Tokamak Confinement Sys Dept, 94, PRIN RES PHYSICIST, PLASMA PHYSICS LAB, PRINCETON UNIV, 83-, DEP PROJ MGR, 91- *Personal Data:* b Mansfield, Eng, June 7, 50; US citizen; m 76; c 2. *Educ:* Mass Inst Technol, SB & MS, 72, PhD(physics), 74. *Honors & Awards:* Excellence Plasma Physics Award, Am Phys Soc, 88; Distinguished Assoc Award, US Dept Energy, 95. *Concurrent Pos:* Consult, Lincoln Lab, Mass Inst Technol, 70-73 & 80. *Mem:* Fel Am Phys Soc. *Res:* Plasma confinement and heating in toroidal confinement devices as part of the fusion program; microcircuit fabrication, electron beam lithography. *Mailing Add:* Plasma Physics Lab PO Box 451 Princeton NJ 08540. *Fax:* 609-243-3248

HAWRYSH, ZENIA JEAN, FOOD SCIENCE. *Current Pos:* from assoc prof to prof, Dept Foods & Nutrit, Fac Home Econ, 71-92, chmn, 80-92, PROF, DEPT AGR, FOOD SCI & NUTRIT, UNIV ALTA, 93- *Personal Data:* b Edmonton, Alta, Nov 4, 38. *Educ:* Univ Alta, BSc, 59; Mich State Univ, MS, 60, PhD(food sci), 70. *Prof Exp:* From lectr to asst prof, Sch Home Econ, Univ Alta, 60-66; fel food sci, Mich State Univ, 66-68, res asst, 68-70. *Concurrent Pos:* Mem, Can Comt Meats, 76-77; Can Sensory Adv Comt, Int Stand Orgn. *Mem:* Can Inst Food Sci & Technol; Inst Food Technologists; Am Dietetic Asn; Am Oil Chem Soc; Am Meat Sci Asn; Chemoreceptor Sci Asn. *Res:* Subjective (sensory) and objective (instrumental, chemical) evaluations of the eating quality characteristics of muscle foods (beef, pork, fish) and canola oils and canola oil products; foods for food service operations and for special diets; sensory methodology; taste perception measurements. *Mailing Add:* Agr Food & Nutrit Sci Dept Univ Alta Edmonton AB T6G 2P5 Can. *Fax:* 403-492-8914

HAWS, BYRON AUSTIN, AGRICULTURE, ECONOMIC ENTOMOLOGY. *Current Pos:* RETIRED. *Personal Data:* b Vernal, Utah, July 1, 21; m 45; c 4. *Educ:* Utah State Agr Col, BS, 48, MS, 49; Iowa State Col, PhD(zool, entom), 55. *Prof Exp:* Res fel entom, Univ Minn, 52-57; assoc prof, Utah State Univ, 57-71, dir int progs, 65-68, prof entom, 71-93, asst to pres, Latin Am Affairs, 64-93. *Concurrent Pos:* Chief party, Utah State Univ Tech Assistance Team, Bolivia, 68-71; consult, Honduran export stas, cocaine studies in Bolivia, African bees & bee industs in Ecuador. *Mem:* Entom Soc Am; Soc Range Mgt; Am Registry Prof Entomologists; Sigma Xi. *Res:* Range entomology; legume seed production, pollination and injurious insects. *Mailing Add:* 1646 E 1185 N Logan UT 84341-3036

HAWTHORNE, DONALD CLAIR, MICROBIOLOGY, GENETICS. *Current Pos:* res instr, Univ Wash, 59-65, res assoc prof, 65-70, prof, 70-83, EMER PROF GENETICS, UNIV WASH, 83- *Personal Data:* b Olympia, Wash, Jan 23, 26. *Educ:* Univ Wash, Seattle, BS, 50, MS, 53, PhD(microbiol), 55. *Prof Exp:* Asst microbiol, Univ Wash, 52-55; NSF res fel microbial genetics, Calif Inst Technol, 56; USPHS res fel, Gen Physiol Lab, Nat Ctr Sci Res, Ministry Ed, France, 57-58. *Concurrent Pos:* USPHS spec fel, France, 68; assoc prof, Univ Paris VI, 79. *Mem:* Genetics Soc Am. *Res:* Genetics of yeast; tetrad analysis; gene interactions; mutant characterization. *Mailing Add:* 2321 NE 55th St Seattle WA 98105

HAWTHORNE, FRANK CHRISTOPHER, CRYSTALLOGRAPHY, MINERALOGY. *Current Pos:* Fel, 73-75, RES ASSOC GEOL, UNIV MAN, 75-, PROF, 84- *Personal Data:* b Bristol, Eng, Jan 8, 46; m 70; c 2. *Educ:* Univ London, BSc Hons, 68, Royal Sch Mines, ARSM, 68; McMaster Univ, PhD(geol), 73. *Honors & Awards:* Hawley Medal, Mineral Asn Can, 84, 93; Past-Pres Medal, Geol Asn Can, 91, Logan Medal,; Willet G Miller Medal, Royal Soc Can, 93; Schluberger Medal, Mineral Asn Gt Brit, 95. *Mem:* Mineral Asn Can; Mineral Soc Am; Am Geophys Union; Am Crystallog Asn; fel Royal Soc Can. *Res:* Structure and chemistry of amphiboles and pyroxenes, hierarchical architecture of inorganic crystal structures; spectroscopy of minerals. *Mailing Add:* Dept Geol Sci Univ Man Winnipeg MB R3T 2N2 Can. *Fax:* 204-261-7581

HAWTHORNE, MARION FREDERICK, ORGANIC CHEMISTRY, ORGANOMETALLIC CHEMISTRY. *Current Pos:* PROF CHEM, UNIV CALIF, LOS ANGELES, 69- *Personal Data:* b Ft Scott, Kans, Aug 24, 28; m 51, 77, Diana Razzaia; c Cynthia & Candace. *Educ:* Pomona Col, BA, 49; Univ Calif, Los Angeles, PhD(chem), 53. *Hon Degrees:* DSc, Pomona Col, 74; PhD, Uppsala Univ, 92. *Honors & Awards:* McCoy Award, 73; Award Inorg Chem, Am Chem Soc, 74, Tolman Medal, 86, Distinguished Achievements Boron Sci Award, 88, Distinguished Serv to Inorg Chem, 88; Wooley Lectr, Ga Inst Technol, 69; Frontiers Sci Lectr, Wayne State Univ, 74; Reilly Lectr, Notre Dame, 74; Castle Lectr Chem, Univ SFla, 86; Gooch-Stephens Lectr, Baylor Univ, 91; Bailer Medal, 91; Polyhedron Medal & Prize, 93; Chem Pioneer Award, Am Inst Chemists, 94; Robert Welch Found Lectr, 95; Boomer Lectr, Univ Alta, 96; Award for Polyhedral Borane Chem, Imeboron Int Comt on Boran Chem, 96; Award Chem Sci, Nat Acad Sci, 97. *Prof Exp:* Res assoc, Iowa State Col, 53-54; sr res chemist, Redstone Arsenal Div, Rohm & Haas Co, Ala, 54-55, head, Metallo-Org Chem Group, 56-60, lab head, Pa, 61; prof chem, Univ Calif, Riverside, 62-68. *Concurrent Pos:* Vis lectr, Harvard Univ, 60, Sloan fel, 66, vis prof, 68; spec lectr, Queen Mary Col, Univ London, 63; Corn Prod lectr, Pa State Univ, 68; 3M Co lectr, Univ Minn, 69; ed, Inorg Chem J, Am Chem Soc, 69-; consult, Union Carbide Corp, 70-76, McMillan Sci Assoc, 72-, Adv Res Proj Agency, US Dept Defense, 74-76, Intelcom Radio Technol Corp, 75-76 & Vacuum Atmospheres Corp, 75-77; mem, Mat Res Coun, Dept Defense, 73-77; vis prof, Univ Tex, Austin, 74; distinguished scientist lectureship, Mich State Univ, 74; chmn, Gordon Res Conf Inorg Chem, 74; mem chem, Kaysen Panel, Nat Acad Sci, 75-77; rev panel, Stanford Synchrotron Radiation Proj, 75-77 & Nat Acad Sci US-Soviet Sci Exchange, 75-78; consult, Army Sci Adv Panel, 75-78; mem, USAF Sci Adv Bd, 79-86, bd Army Sci & Technol, Nat Res Coun, 86-90; consult, Callery Chem Co, 85-90, Xoma Inc, 87- & Ionix Corp, 94-; Humboldt sr scientist res award, 90-95. *Mem:* Nat Acad Sci; fel AAAS; Am Acad Arts & Sci; NY Acad Sci; Am Chem Soc; Chem Soc London; Int Soc Neutron Capture Ther (pres, 96); Sigma Xi; corresp mem Gottingen Acad Sci. *Res:* Organometallic and inorganic chemistry; synthesis, structural and mechanism studies with boron hydrides, carboranes and their transition metal derivatives; application of organometallic and inorganic chemistry to immunology and pharmacology; cancer diagnosis and therapy with boron neutron capture. *Mailing Add:* 3415 Green Vista Dr Encino CA 91436-4011. *Fax:* 818-784-7883

HAWTHORNE, ROBERT MONTGOMERY, JR, ORGANIC CHEMISTRY, HISTORY OF CHEMISTRY. *Current Pos:* CONSULT/AUTH, 91- *Personal Data:* b Akron, Ohio, Nov 1, 29; m 55, Judith Parker; c Kelvin, Christopher, David & Margaret. *Educ:* Columbia Univ, BS, 56; Rutgers Univ, PhD(org chem), 63; Univ Notre Dame, MA, 78. *Prof Exp:* Chemist, Nat Starch & Chem Co, 56-59 & Am Cyanamid Co, NJ, 59-60; teaching asst chem, Rutgers Univ, 60-61, instr, 61-63; teacher, Marlboro Col, 63-68; from asst prof to assoc prof chem, NCent Campus, Purdue Univ, 68-81; chmn, Environ Sci Ctr, Unity Col, 81-83 & 89-90, dean fac, 82-85, prof, 86-91. *Concurrent Pos:* Lectr, Bloomfield Col, 62-63; chem consult, Manley Bros, 79-80; secy, Maine Sect, Am Chem Soc, 82-84, chmn-elect, 88-89, chmn, 90-91, chmn/secy-treas, Div Hist Chem, 76-80; bd trustees, Marlboro Col, 94-; chmn elect, Green Mountain Sec, Am Chem Soc, 96-97. *Mem:* AAAS; Am Chem Soc; Hist Sci Soc; Soc Hist Alchemy & Chem; fel Am Inst Chemists; Soc Hist Technol. *Res:* Chemical history, particularly the nineteenth century. *Mailing Add:* PO Box 38 Marlboro VT 05344

HAWTHORNE, VICTOR MORRISON, PSYCHIATRIC EPIDEMIOLOGY. *Current Pos:* Sr lectr, 66-78, SR RES FEL EPIDEMIOL, UNIV GLASGOW, 78-; HON DIR, ROYAL COL PHYSICIANS EDINBURGH EDUC, ASST, RES DEPT, DIABETES REGISTRY, 89- *Personal Data:* b Glasgow, Scotland, June 19, 21; m 48; c 3. *Educ:* Univ Glasgow, MD, 62; FRCP(G), 73, FFPHM, 89, FRCP, 87. *Concurrent Pos:* Consult chest med, Western Regional Hosp Bd, 66-78; chmn, EDC Study Sect, NIH, 80-84; chmn, Kidney Dis Comt, Dept Health, State of Mich, 80-; Victor M Hawthorne res fel award prog; prof epidemiol & chmn dept, Sch Pub Health, Univ Mich, 78-87, emer prof, 90. *Mem:* Fel Am Col Epidemiol; Soc Epidemiol Res; Am Epidemiol Asn. *Res:* Epidemiological studies in west of Scotland and Tecumseh, Michigan of cardio-respiratory, diabetic, hypertensive, osteoarthritic & nutritional diseases; studies of screening for microalbuminuria in insulin-treated diabetes in Royal College of Physicians of Edinburgh, Diabetes Registry. *Mailing Add:* Dept Epidemiol Sch Pub Health Univ Mich 109 Observ St Ann Arbor MI 48109-2029

HAWTHORNE, WILLIAM (REDE), AEROSPACE & MECHANICAL ENGINEERING. *Current Pos:* master, 68-83, FEL, CHURCHILL COL, CAMBRIDGE, 83- *Personal Data:* b May 22, 13; m 39, Barbara Runkle; c 3. *Educ:* Trinity Col, Cambridge Univ, Mass Inst Technol. *Honors & Awards:* Royal Medal, Royal Soc, 82; R Tom Sawyer Award, Am Soc Mech Engrs, 92. *Prof Exp:* Develop engr, Babcock & Wilcox Ltd, 37-39; sci officer, Royal Aircraft Estab, 40-44; mem, Brit Air Command, Washington, 44; dep dir engine res, Ministry Supply, 45; assoc prof mech eng, Mass Inst Technol, 46, George Westinghouse prof, 48-51, Jerome C Hunsaker prof aerospace eng, 55-56; Hopkinson & ICI prof appl thermodyn, Univ Cambridge, 51-80, head, Dept Eng, 68-73. *Concurrent Pos:* Chmn, Home Off Sci Adv Coun, 67-76, Adv Coun Energy Conserv, 74-79; dir, Cummings Engine Co, Inc, 74-86, Dracone Develop Ltd, bd govs, Westminster Sch, 75-76. *Mem:* Foreign assoc Nat Acad Sci; foreign assoc Nat Acad Eng; fel Royal Soc; fel Am Inst Aeronaut & Astronaut; fel Royal Acad Eng; fel Am Soc Mech Engrs. *Mailing Add:* Dept Aeronaut Mass Inst Technol 77 Massachusetts Ave Rm 31-267 Cambridge MA 02139

HAWTON, MARGARET H, BIOLOGICAL PHYSICS, CHEMICAL PHYSICS. *Current Pos:* ASSOC PROF, LAKEHEAD UNIV, 66- *Personal Data:* b Jan 26, 42; div. *Educ:* Univ New Brunswick, HBSc, 64, MSc, 66; Univ Waterloo, PhD (physics), 81. *Mem:* Am Phys Soc. *Res:* Applications for biological materials, rocks and semiconductora; transport in and polarization of heterogeneous materials and interfaces. *Mailing Add:* Lakehead Univ Postal Sta P Thunder Bay ON D7B 5E1 Can

HAXBY, B(ERNARD) V(AN LOAN), ELECTRICAL ENGINEERING. *Current Pos:* From instr to asst prof, 49-60, from assoc prof elec eng & assoc head dept to prof & assoc head, 60-88, EMER PROF ELEC ENG, UNIV MINN, MINNEAPOLIS, 88- *Personal Data:* b Minneapolis, Minn, Nov 30, 21; m 44; c 4. *Educ:* Univ Minn, Minneapolis, BEE, 48, MS, 49, PhD(elec eng), 57. *Mem:* AAAS; Inst Elec & Electronics Engrs; Sigma Xi. *Res:* Physical electronics; microwave circuits. *Mailing Add:* Elec Eng Dept Univ Minn 4-174 Elec Eng CSCI Bldg 200 Union St SE Minneapolis MN 55455

HAXHIU, MUSA A, MEDICINE, RESPIRATION PHYSIOLOGY. *Current Pos:* vis prof, 87-90, PROF MED, CASE WESTERN RES UNIV, CLEVELAND, OHIO, 92- *Personal Data:* b Peje, Yugoslavia, Mar 15, 39; m 64; Radmila Novakovic; c Lendita, Monika & Gjergi. *Educ:* Univ Belgrade Med Sch, MD, 63; Univ Zagreb, PhD(med), 73. *Prof Exp:* Vis scientist, Postgrad Med Sch, London, Eng, 73; dean, Med Fac, Univ Prishtina, Yugoslavia, 73-75; prof clin physiol, 83-87; vis lectr, Univ Pa, Philadelphia, 75-76; pres, Acad Scis & Arts of Kosova, 90-92. *Concurrent Pos:* Vis scientist, Cardiovasc Res Inst, Med Sch, San Francisco, 87 & Dept Pharmacol, Univ Health Sci, Bethesda, Md, 89-90. *Mem:* NY Acad Sci; Yugoslav Physiol Soc (pres, 78-80); Am Physiol Soc; Soc Neurosci; AAAS. *Res:* Integrative aspects of the neuronal control of upper airway and chest wall muscles activity in health and disease; brain peptides and peptidergic pathways controlling airway tone and secretion; air pollution and chronic pulmonary diseases. *Mailing Add:* Case Western Res Univ 2074 Abington Rd Cleveland OH 44106. *Fax:* 216-844-3226

HAXO, FRANCIS THEODORE, OCEANOGRAPHY. *Current Pos:* from asst prof to assoc prof, Scripps Inst Oceanog, Univ Calif, San Diego, 52-63, chmn, Dept Marine Biol, 60-65, chmn, Marine Biol Res Div, 60-65 & 70-77, prof marine biol, 63-68, EMER PROF MARINE BIOL, SCRIPPS INST OCEANOG, UNIV CALIF, SAN DIEGO, 88- *Personal Data:* b Grand Forks, NDak, Mar 9, 21; m 47, 61; c 5. *Educ:* Univ NDak, BA, 41; Stanford Univ, PhD(biol), 47. *Prof Exp:* Asst biol, Univ NDak, 40-41; asst biol, Stanford Univ, 41-44, actg instr, 43, res assoc, Hopkins Marine Sta, 46-47; asst, Calif Inst Technol, 46; instr plant physiol, Johns Hopkins Univ, 47-48, asst prof, 49-52. *Concurrent Pos:* Instr, Marine Biol Lab, Woods Hole, 59-63 & 70; mem vis fac, Univ Calif, Berkeley, 57 & Univ Wash, 63; US Nat Comn Int Biol Prog, 66; pres's sci adv comt, Oceanog & Marine Biol, 66. *Mem:* Fel AAAS; Phycol Soc Am; Int Phycol Soc; Am Soc Photobiologists. *Res:* Algal physiology; photosynthesis; plant pigments. *Mailing Add:* 6381 Castejon Dr La Jolla CA 92037

HAXO, HENRY EMILE, JR, RUBBER CHEMISTRY, PLASTICS CHEMISTRY. *Current Pos:* PRES, MATRECON, INC, 73- *Personal Data:* b Missoula, Mont, Aug 20, 18; m 44; c 4. *Educ:* Univ NDak, BA, 38; Yale Univ, PhD(phys chem), 41. *Prof Exp:* Res chemist, Res Ctr, US Rubber Co, 41-42 & 46-67 & Uniroyal Inc, 67-72; assoc dir res, Mat Res & Develop Div, Woodward-Lundgren Assocs, 72-73. *Concurrent Pos:* Consult, Army-Navy Munitions Bd, 51. *Mem:* AAAS; Am Chem Soc; NY Acad Sci; Soc Plastics Engrs; Am Soc Testing & Mat. *Res:* Hazardous waste management; asphalt technology; molecular spectroscopy; polymerization, dienes and vinyls; evaluation and physics of synthetic rubbers; polymer-to-polymer adhesion; filler reinforcement of rubber; permeability of polymers to gases and liquids. *Mailing Add:* 700 Camino Ricardo Moraga CA 94556

HAXTON, WICK CHRISTOPHER, THEORETICAL PHYSICS. *Current Pos:* MEM STAFF, DEPT PHYSICS, UNIV WASH, SEATTLE. *Personal Data:* b Santa Cruz, Calif, Aug 21, 49; m 75; c 2. *Educ:* Univ Calif, Santa Cruz, BA, 71; Stanford Univ, BS, 73, PhD(physics), 75. *Prof Exp:* Res assoc, Universitat Mainz, 75-77; res assoc, 77-79, Jr Oppenheimer fel, Los Alamos Nat Lab, 79-; asst prof physics, Purdue Univ, 80- *Mem:* Am Phys Soc. *Res:* Nuclear and particle physics; theory of weak and electromagnetic interactions; astrophysics. *Mailing Add:* Dept Physics FM15 Univ Wash PO Box 351560 Seattle WA 98195

HAY, ALLAN STUART, ORGANIC CHEMISTRY, POLYMER CHEMISTRY. *Current Pos:* PROF POLYMER CHEM, MCGILL UNIV, 87- *Personal Data:* b Edmonton, Alta, Can, July 23, 29; m 56, Janet Keck; c Randall S, Bruce A, Lauren E & Susan C. *Educ:* Univ Alta, BSc, 50, MSc, 52; Univ Ill, PhD(chem), 55. *Hon Degrees:* DSc, Univ Alta, 87. *Honors & Awards:* Int Gold Medal, Soc Plastics Eng, 75; Carothers Award, 85; Chem Pioneer Award, Am Inst Chemists, 85. *Prof Exp:* Instr, Univ Alta, 50-52; org chemist, Gen Elec Co, 55-68, mgr, Chem Lab, Res & Develop Ctr, 68-80, res & develop mgr, Chem Labs, 80- *Mem:* Am Chem Soc; Royal Soc Chem; fel NY Acad Sci; fel Royal Soc London. *Res:* Homogenous catalytic oxidations; oxidative coupling reactions; organic and polymer synthesis. *Mailing Add:* Dept Chem McGill Univ 801 Sherbrooke St W Montreal PQ H3A 2K6 Can. *E-Mail:* ch19@musica.mcgill.ca

HAY, DONALD IAN, BIOCHEMISTRY. *Current Pos:* from asst staff mem to assoc staff mem, 65-79, SR STAFF MEM BIOCHEM, FORSYTH DENT CTR, BOSTON, 79-, ASSOC DIR, INST RES, 91-, INTERIM DIR, 96- *Personal Data:* b Peterborough, Eng, Nov 5, 33; m 68, Valerie Butterworth; c Ian M. *Educ:* London Univ, BSc, 59, PhD(biochem), 72. *Prof Exp:* Res scientist chem, Unilever Res Labs, Colworth House, Bedford, Eng, 59-65. *Concurrent Pos:* Asst clin prof, Harvard Sch Dent Med, 76-83, assoc clin prof, 83- *Mem:* AAAS; Am Chem Soc; Royal Soc Chem; Int Asn Dent Res. *Res:* Oral biochemistry; salivary protein structure and function; biochemical mechanisms of dental disease. *Mailing Add:* Forsyth Dent Ctr 140 Fenway Boston MA 02115. *Fax:* 617-262-4021; *E-Mail:* dihay@harvarda.harvard.edu

HAY, DONALD ROBERT, OPERATIONS RESEARCH, RESEARCH MANAGEMENT. *Current Pos:* PRES, TEKTREND INT, INC, 73- *Personal Data:* b Ottawa, Ont, Apr 1, 39; m 61, Claudette R; c John, Andrew, Joel, Peter & Thomas. *Educ:* McGill Univ, BEng, 61; Cornell Univ, MS, 64, PhD(mat sci), 66. *Prof Exp:* From asst prof to assoc prof metall eng, Drexel Univ, 66-72; invited prof, Ecole Poytechnique, 72-74, dir, Technol Ctr Develop, 74-79, dir, Indust Innovation Ctr, 79-81; tech dir, Hydrobien Ind Coun, 81-87. *Concurrent Pos:* Adj prof comput sci, Concordia Univ, 81- & mining eng, McGill Univ, 90- *Mem:* Am Soc Metals; Am Soc Nondestructive Testing; Sigma Xi; Am Soc Testing & Mat. *Res:* Fracture mechanics; pattern recognition; non-destructive testing; acoustic emission; systems and reliability engineering; neural networks; artificial intelligence. *Mailing Add:* Tektrend Int Inc Y113 A St Regis Blvd Montreal PQ H9B 2M9 Can. *Fax:* 514-333-7371

HAY, ELIZABETH DEXTER, CELL BIOLOGY, EMBRYOLOGY. *Current Pos:* asst prof, Harvard Med Sch, 60-64, Louise Foote Pfeiffer assoc prof embryol, 64-69, chmn, Dept Anat, 75-93, LOUISE FOOTE PFEIFFER PROF EMBRYOL, HARVARD MED SCH, 69-, PROF CELL BIOL, 93- *Personal Data:* b St Augustine, Fla, Apr 2, 27. *Educ:* Smith Col, AB, 48; Johns Hopkins Univ, MD, 52. *Hon Degrees:* DSc, Smith Col, 73, Trinity Col, 89 & Johns Hopkins Univ, Md, 90. *Honors & Awards:* Alcon Award for Vision Res, 88; E B Wilson Medal, Am Soc Cell Biol, 89; Excellence in Sci Award, Fedn Am Socs Exp Biol, 90; Henry Gray Award, Am Asn Anat, 92. *Prof Exp:* Intern, Osler Serv Hosp, Johns Hopkins Univ, 52-53, instr anat, Sch Med, 53-56, asst prof, 56-57; asst prof, Med Col, Cornell Univ, 57-60. *Concurrent Pos:* Mem cell biol study sect, NIH, 65-69; ed-in-chief, Develop Biol, 71-75; mem, Bd Sci Counrs, Nat Inst Child Health Human Develop, 71-76, Nat Inst Dent Res, 83-86 & Nat Inst Environ Health Sci, 90-93; mem, Nat Adv Coun, Nat Inst Gen Med Sci, 78-81; mem, adv coun, Johns Hopkins Sch Med, 82- *Mem:* Nat Acad Sci; Am Asn Anat (pres, 81-82); Am Soc Cell Biol (pres, 76-77); Soc Develop Biol (pres, 73-74); Int Soc Develop Biologists. *Res:* Origin of cells in amphibian limb regeneration; fine structure of dedifferentiating and differentiating tissues; autoradiographic studies of protein and nucleic acid synthesis in embryos and regenerates; fine structure of developing muscle, cartilage, skin and eye; collagen synthesis by epithelium; tissue interaction in the developing cornea; immunohistochemistry of collagen; gene expression during epithelial-mesenchymal transformation; mechanism of fibroblast migration; extracellular matrix cell interaction. *Mailing Add:* Harvard Med Sch Boston MA 02115. *Fax:* 617-432-0407; *E-Mail:* ehay@warren.med.harvard.edu

HAY, GEORGE EDWARD, MATHEMATICS. *Current Pos:* from instr to assoc prof, Univ Mich, Ann Arbor, 40-56, chmn, Dept Math, 57-67, assoc dean, Grad Sch, 67-76, PROF MATH, UNIV MICH, ANN ARBOR, 56- *Personal Data:* b Durham, Ont, June 11, 14; nat US; m 43; c 3. *Educ:* Univ Toronto, BA, 35, MA, 36, PhD(appl math), 39. *Prof Exp:* Instr math, Ill Inst Technol, 39-40. *Mem:* Am Math Soc; Soc Indust & Appl Math; Indust Math Soc; Math Asn Am; London Math Soc; Sigma Xi. *Res:* Mathematical theory of elasticity; mechanics; method of images applied to the problem of torsion; equilibrium of a thin compressible membrane. *Mailing Add:* 1714 Morton Ave Ann Arbor MI 48104-4522

HAY, GEORGE WILLIAM, CARBOHYDRATE CHEMISTRY. *Current Pos:* asst prof, 63-68, assoc dir, Carbohydrate Res Inst, 77-85, ASSOC PROF CHEM, QUEEN'S UNIV, ONT, 68- *Personal Data:* b Winnipeg, Man, May 19, 29; m 55, Jeanann D Becker; c Kathryn A & George F. *Educ:* Univ Man, BSc, 51, MSc, 52; Univ Minn, PhD(biochem), 59. *Prof Exp:* Civilian biochemist in chg, Serol Sect, Western Regional Crime Detection Lab, Royal Can Mounted Police, 52-55; fel enzymol, Nat Res Coun Can, 59-60 & biochem, Univ Minn, 60-63. *Concurrent Pos:* Vis prof, Inst Forestry, Univ Rural Rio De Janeiro, 79; chair, Undergrad Studies, Dept Chem, Queen's Univ, 92. *Mem:* Am Chem Soc; Chem Inst Can. *Res:* Carbohydrate chemistry; polysaccharide chemistry and polysaccharidases; synthetic sweeteners; synthesis of sugars with S or N in the ring; synthesis of radiopharmaceuticals; carbohydrates of soil; targetted drug delivery. *Mailing Add:* Dept Chem Queen's Univ Kingston ON K7L 3N6 Can. *Fax:* 613-545-6669

HAY, IAN LESLIE, POLYMER PHYSICS, ELECTRON MICROSCOPY. *Current Pos:* RES ASSOC, CELANESE RES CO, 68- *Personal Data:* b London, Eng, Dec 6, 34; m 64; c 3. *Educ:* Univ London, BSc, 57; Bristol Univ, PhD(physics), 68. *Prof Exp:* Res asst semiconductor physics, Assoc Elec Industs, 57-63. *Mem:* Brit Inst Physics & Phys Soc; Am Phys Soc. *Res:* Morphological characterization of solid polymers; relationships between processing, morphology and properties of polymers. *Mailing Add:* 129 Sorrento Dr Moore SC 29369

HAY, JAMES ROBERT, WEED SCIENCE. *Current Pos:* RETIRED. *Personal Data:* b Can, Oct 19, 25; m 74; c 2. *Educ:* Ont Agr Col, Guelph, BSA, 49; SDak State Col, MS, 51; Harvard Univ, PhD(plant physiol), 55. *Prof Exp:* Res officer weed control, Plant Res Inst, Can Dept Agr, 55- 62, dir, Exp Farm, 62-68, dir, Res Sta, 68-90. *Concurrent Pos:* Chmn, Can Weed Comt, 69-78. *Mem:* Fel Weed Sci Soc Am (pres, 79); Agr Inst Can; Can Soc Agron; Can Soc Pest Mgt (pres, 78). *Res:* Weed control. *Mailing Add:* 238 Christopher Crescent Saskatoon SK S7J 3R6 Can

HAY, PETER MARSLAND, INDUSTRIAL CHEMISTRY. *Current Pos:* RETIRED. *Personal Data:* b Ft Riley, Kans, Oct 5, 21; m 52; c 1. *Educ:* Antioch Col, BS, 44; Ohio State Univ, PhD(org chem), 51. *Prof Exp:* Asst instr chem, Ohio State Univ, 46-51; res chemist, Olin Mathieson Chem Corp, 52-56, res group leader, 56-59; group leader prod appln, Celanese Plastics Co, 59-63; group leader prod develop, J P Stevens & Co, 63-67; chem develop mgr, Colors & Chem Div, Sandoz-Wander, Inc, 67-72; mgr environ affairs, Colors & Chem Div, Sandoz Inc, East Hanover, 72-84; mem, Gov Sci Adv Comt, NJ, 80-87. *Concurrent Pos:* Independent consult, 85-; pres, ARIA Chem Serv, 85-; secy coun, Asn Consult Chemists & Chemical Engrs, NY, NY. *Mem:* NY Acad Sci; AAAS; Am Chem Soc. *Res:* Polymer physical chemistry; emulsion polymerization; physical properties of plastics; textile chemistry; environmental and toxicological properties of industrial chemicals. *Mailing Add:* 24 Bedford Rd Summit NJ 07901

HAY, PHILIP JEFFREY, THEORETICAL CHEMISTRY. *Current Pos:* staff mem chem, 74-81, group leader, Theoret Chem Group, 81-88 STAFF MEM, LOS ALAMOS SCI LAB, 88- *Personal Data:* b Philadelphia, Pa, Oct 4, 45; m 66; c 2. *Educ:* Franklin & Marshall Col, Lancaster, Pa, 67; Calif Inst Technol, Pasadena, PhD(chem), 72. *Prof Exp:* Res fel chem, Battelle Inst, Columbus, Ohio, 71-73 & Cornell Univ, Ithaca, NY, 73-74. *Mem:* Am Chem Soc; AAAS. *Res:* Electronic structure of molecules; potential energy surfaces; effective core potential; relativistic effects; excited states; transition-metal; actinide compounds; simulation of materials. *Mailing Add:* Los Alamos Sci Lab T12 Mail Stop B268 Los Alamos NM 87545

HAY, RICHARD LE ROY, SEDIMENTARY PETROLOGY. *Current Pos:* RALPH E GRIU PROF GEOL, UNIV ILL, URBANA, 83- *Personal Data:* b Goshen, Ind, Apr 29, 26; m 73; c 2. *Educ:* Northwestern Univ, BS, 47, MS, 49; Princeton Univ, PhD(geol). 52. *Honors & Awards:* Kirk Bryan Award, Geol Soc Am; Arnold Guyot Mem Award, Nat Geog Soc. *Prof Exp:* Geologist, US Geol Surv, 48-49, 52 & 54-55; asst prof geol, La State Univ, 55-57; from asst prof to prof geol, Univ Calif, Berkeley, 57-83. *Mem:* Geol Soc Am; Soc Econ Paleontologists & Mineralogists; Clay Mineral Soc. *Res:* Clay mineralogy, zeolites; silicate diagenesis; archeologic geology in northern Tanzania. *Mailing Add:* 5 Carriage Way Champaign IL 61821

HAY, ROBERT E, ECONOMIC GEOLOGY. *Current Pos:* asst prof, 66-70, assoc prof, 70-77, PROF GEOL, STATE UNIV NY COL CORTLAND, 78- *Personal Data:* b Kingston, Ont, Sept 3, 31; m 62; c 1. *Educ:* Queen's Univ, Ont, BSc, 58; McGill Univ, MSc, 59, PhD(geol), 64. *Prof Exp:* Tech off geologist, Geol Surv Can, 59-61; instr geol, Queen's Univ, Ont, 61-63; party chief geologist, Steep Rock Iron Mines, Ltd, 63; assoc prof geol, Catawba Col, 63-66. *Mem:* Geol Soc Am. *Res:* Igneous and metamorphic geology; mapping on Canadian Shield; Huronian stratigraphy. *Mailing Add:* Dept Geol State Univ NY PO Box 2000 Cortland NY 13045-0900

HAY, ROBERT J, CELL PHYSIOLOGY, DEVELOPMENTAL BIOLOGY. *Current Pos:* res assoc 75-76, HEAD, CELL CULT DEPT, AM TYPE CULT COLLECTION, 76- *Personal Data:* b Winnipeg, Man, Jan 23, 38; m 59; c 2. *Educ:* Univ Man, BSc, 60, MSc, 61; Glasgow Univ, PhD(biochem), 65. *Prof Exp:* Mem staff geront, Vet Admin, 64-67; develop biol, Carnegie Inst, 67-70; from asst prof to assoc prof biol sci, Wright State Univ, 70-75. *Mem:* Am Soc Cell Biol; Soc Exp Biol Med; Am Tissue Cult Asn; AAAS; Soc In-Vitro Biol (pres, 96-98). *Res:* Cellular biology of aging; mechanisms governing compensatory hyperplasia and hypertrophy; differentiated cells in culture; cell standardization and banking for distribution. *Mailing Add:* Cell Cult Dept ATCC 12301 Parklawn Dr Rockville MD 20852. *Fax:* 301-770-1848

HAY, RUSSELL EARL, JR, AGRONOMY, PLANT PHYSIOLOGY. *Current Pos:* RETIRED. *Personal Data:* b Dayton, Ohio, Jan 5, 18; m 43, Patricia Aull; c Nancy, Susan & Katherine. *Educ:* Miami Univ, AB, 40; Univ Nebr, MS, 42; Univ Ill, PhD(agron), 48. *Prof Exp:* Asst bot, Miami Univ, 38-40, Univ Nebr, 41; spec asst soil fertil, Univ Ill, 46-48; plant physiologist, Biol Labs, Chem Corps, Camp Detrick, 48-50; asst supvr agr res, Battelle Mem Inst, 50-53; plant physiologist, C F Kettering Found, 53-55; assoc dir res found, Ohio State Univ, 55-67; dir res develop, Wright State Univ, 67-76. *Mem:* AAAS; Am Chem Soc; Am Inst Biol Sci; Am Soc Plant Physiol; Am Soc Agron; Sigma Xi. *Res:* Nitrogen metabolism; plant growth regulators; research management; university development. *Mailing Add:* 1003 Scotia Village Laurinburg NC 28352-8528

HAY, WILLIAM WALTER, CIVIL ENGINEERING. *Current Pos:* from asst prof to prof, 47-77, EMER PROF RWY CIVIL ENG, UNIV ILL, URBANA, 77- *Personal Data:* b Bay City, Mich, Dec 10, 08; m 43; c 2. *Educ:* Carnegie Inst Technol, BS, 31, MgtEngr, 48; Univ Ill, MS, 48, PhD, 56. *Prof Exp:* From track supvr to proj engr, RR Co, Pa, NY, Iowa, Wis & Alaska, 34-47. *Concurrent Pos:* Engr & supt, Maintenance of Way, Europ Theater Opers, 43-45, chief engr, Korea RR, 45-46 & Transp Co, 43-46; consult, rail & track res, var US & Can rwy, 50-; Knappen Tippets Abbett Co, NY, 51, Govts Southern Rhodesia & Mozambique, 52-58, SAfrica, 55, Sangamon Co Planning Comn, Ill, 58-59. Northwestern Univ, 59-62 & Harland Bartholomew & Assocs; mem, Ill Prof Engrs Exam Comt, 59-69; adv panel, Res, Nat Res Coun; consult, CVG Ferromimera Orinoco, Venezuela, 76, Royal Comn on BC Rwy, 77-78 & Can Pac Consult Servs, 77-; annual short courses in railway eng, 75- *Mem:* Hon mem Am Rwy Eng Asn; hon mem Roadmasters & Maintenance of Way Asn Am. *Res:* Effects of weather on construction, maintenance and operation of transport agencies; conservation of transportation resources; engineering costs for track and roadway maintenance especially materials, lateral stability and economics of ballast studies. *Mailing Add:* Dept Civil Eng 310 Eng Hall Univ Ill 1308 W Green St Fribourg Switzerland

HAY, WILLIAM WINN, SEDIMENTARY MASS BALANCE, PALEOCEANOGRAPHY. *Current Pos:* dir mus, 82-87, PROF GEOL, UNIV COLO, 82- *Personal Data:* b Dallas, Tex, Oct 12, 34. *Educ:* Southern Methodist Univ, BS, 55; Univ Ill, Urbana, MS, 58; Stanford Univ, PhD(geol), 60. *Honors & Awards:* Francis P Shepard Medal, Soc Econ Paleontologists & Mineralogists, 81; Alexander von Humboldt Sr Scientist Award, 91. *Prof Exp:* From asst prof to prof geol, Univ Ill, Urbana, 60-73; prof geol & geophys, Rosenstiel Sch Marine & Atmospheric Sci, Univ Miami, 68-82, dean, 76-80. *Concurrent Pos:* Hon fel, Univ Col, Univ London, 72-; pres, Joint Oceanog Inst, 79-82; fel, Coop Inst Res Environ Sci, 82; adj prof, Rosenstiel Sch Marine & Atmospheric Sci, Univ Miami, 82-; Gast prof, Geomar, Christian-Albrechts Univ, Kiel, Ger, 90-; F C Donders prof, Univ Utrecht, Neth, 93. *Mem:* Geol Soc Am; Int Nannoplankton Asn; Swiss Geol Soc; Soc Econ Paleontologists & Mineralogists (pres, 87-88); Am Geophys Union. *Res:* Paleoceanography; paleoclimatology; exogene and endogene dynamics of the earths erosion sedimentation system; taxonomy and biostratigraphy of calcareous nannofossils. *Mailing Add:* Univ Colo Campus Box 218 Boulder CO 80309

HAYA, KATSUJI, SUBLETHAL EFFECTS, INTERMEDIARY METABOLISM. *Current Pos:* RES SCIENTIST BIOCHEM & TOXICOL, DEPT FISHERIES & OCEANS, GOVT CAN, ST ANDREWS, 78- *Personal Data:* b Ashcroft, BC, Nov 22, 43; m 69; c 3. *Educ:* Univ BC, BSP, 67, PhD(pharm & med chem), 73. *Prof Exp:* Fel drug metab, Dept Pharm, Chelsea Col, Univ London, 73-76; res assoc toxicol, Dept Pharm & Toxicol, Univ Kans, 76-78. *Concurrent Pos:* Can rep, Intergovt Oceanog Comn, Food & Agr Orgn, Intergovt Panel Harmful Algal Blooms. *Mem:* Soc Environ Toxicol & Chem; Soc Toxicol Can; NY Acad Sci. *Res:* Biochemical toxicology; biochemical and physiological responses of aquatic animals to sublethal concentrations of xenobiotics (pollutants); occurence, source and effects of natural marine toxins in the aquatic biosphere. *Mailing Add:* Dept Fisheries & Oceans Biol Sta St Andrews NB E0G 2X0 Can. *Fax:* 506-529-5862; *E-Mail:* haya@sta.dfo.ca

HAYAKAWA, KAN-ICHI, FOOD ENGINEERING. *Current Pos:* From asst prof to prof food sci, 64-82, DISTINGUISHED PROF FOOD ENG, RUTGERS UNIV, 82- *Personal Data:* b Shibukawa, Japan, Aug 12, 31; m 67, Setsuko Maekawa. *Educ:* Tokyo Univ Fisheries, BS, 55; Rutgers Univ, PhD(food sci), 64. *Concurrent Pos:* Invited lectr, Univ Campinas, Brazil, 72 & 73 & 94, Nat Taiwan Univ, Taipei, 82, WUXI Inst Light Indust, China, 86 & Tokyo Univ Fisheries, 92; prin investr, 64- *Mem:* AAAS; fel Inst Food Technol; Am Inst Chem Eng; Am Soc Heat, Refrig & Air-Conditioning Eng; Am Soc Agr Eng. *Res:* Biochemical engineering analysis of thermal processing of food; heat and/or mass transfer in food with hygro & thermo physical changes. *Mailing Add:* 631 Lake Dr Princeton NJ 08540-5634

HAYASAKA, STEVEN S, MARINE MICROBIOLOGY. *Current Pos:* asst prof, 75-80, ASSOC PROF MICROBIOL, CLEMENSON UNIV, 80- *Personal Data:* b Philadelphia, Pa, Feb 9, 47; m 72; c 2. *Educ:* Pa State Univ, BS, 69; Ore State Univ, MS, 72, PhD(microbiol), 75. *Prof Exp:* Res assoc microbiol, Ore State Univ, 75. *Mem:* Sigma Xi; Am Soc Microbiol. *Res:* Effect and interaction of marine environmental parameters on growth and function of marine bacteria; microbiology of seagrasses; diseases of maricultured animals. *Mailing Add:* Dept Microbiol Clemson Univ Clemson SC 29632-0001

HAYASHI, FUMIHIKO, PLANT PHYSIOLOGY. *Current Pos:* RETIRED. *Personal Data:* b Tokyo, Japan, Mar 28, 30; US citizen; m 70; c 3. *Educ:* Univ Kagoshima, BS, 55; Univ Tokyo, PhD(agr biochem), 65. *Honors & Awards:* Herman Flash Found Award. *Prof Exp:* Fel, Dept Veg Crops, Univ Calif, Davis, 60-63; lectr, Dept Agrobiol, Univ Tokyo, 63-66; sr biochemist, Woodard Res Corp, 68-70; leader, Plant Studies Criteria & Eval Div, US Environ Protection Agency, Washington, DC, 72-77, sr environ biochem, Hazard Eval Div, Off Pesticide Progs, 77-81, sr environ biochem, Health & Environ Rev Div, Off Toxic Substances, 81-97. *Concurrent Pos:* Environ Protection Agency rep, Man & Biosphere Prog, UNESCO; scholar, NIH & Ministry Educ, Japan. *Mem:* Am Chem Soc; Am Soc Hort Sci; Am Soc Plant Physiologists; Weed Sci Soc Am; NY Acad Sci; Sigma Xi. *Res:* Phytotoxicity caused by pesticide and toxic substance application on crop plants, and biochemical mode-of-action of herbicides and plant growth regulators. *Mailing Add:* 6421 Berkshire Dr Alexandria VA 22310. *Fax:* 703-960-4358

HAYASHI, IZUMI, cell biology, developmental biology; deceased, see previous edition for last biography

HAYASHI, JAMES AKIRA, BIOCHEMISTRY, TOXICOLOGY. *Current Pos:* asst dean instr, 75-79, PROF BIOCHEM, MED COL, RUSH UNIV, 71-; SR BIOCHEMIST, PRESBY-ST LUKE'S HOSP, 61- *Personal Data:* b Alameda, Calif, Dec 18, 26; m 55; c William, Karl & Vivian. *Educ:* Northern Ill State Teachers Col, BS, 48; Univ Wis, MS, 53, PhD(biochem), 56. *Prof Exp:* From res assoc to prof biochem, Univ Ill Col Med, 55-71. *Mem:* Am Chem Soc; Am Soc Biol Chem; Sigma Xi. *Res:* Cell walls; bacterial enzymes. *Mailing Add:* Dept Biochem Rush Med Col Chicago IL 60612

HAYASHI, MASAO, CELL BIOLOGY, SCIENCE POLICY. *Current Pos:* ASSOC PROF CELL BIOL, DEPT BIOL, OCHANOMIZU UNIV, 85- *Personal Data:* b Yokohama, Japan, Jan 4, 47; m 72, Kazuko. *Educ:* Saitama Univ, BSci, 69; Nagoya Univ, PhD(molecular biol), 74. *Prof Exp:* Asst prof biochem, Inst Biol Sci, Univ Tsukuba, 76-85. *Concurrent Pos:* Res fel, Lab Molecular Biol, Nat Cancer Inst, NIH, 80-83; counr, Japanese Soc Cell Biol, 87-; ed, Cell Struct & Function, 91- *Mem:* Am Soc Cell Biol; Japanese Soc

Cell Biol; Japanese Soc Biochem. *Res:* Cell adhesion and extracellular matrix, especially on a cell-adhesive glycoprotein vitronectin; transmembrane control of cellular activities by adhesive-proteins and extracellular matrix. *Mailing Add:* Dept Biol Ochanomizu Univ Bunkyo-ku Tokyo 112 Japan. *Fax:* 81-3-5978-5365; *E-Mail:* masa@fs.cc.ocha.ac.jp

HAYASHI, TERU, PHYSIOLOGY, CELL PHYSIOLOGY. *Current Pos:* EMER TRUSTEE, MARINE BIOL LAB, 81- *Personal Data:* b Atlantic City, NJ, Feb 12, 14; m 43, 70; c 4. *Educ:* Ursinus Col, BS, 38; Univ Mo, PhD(cell physiol), 43. *Prof Exp:* Instr physics, US Army Air Force, 43-44; instr zool, Univ Mo, 44-45, res assoc, 45-46; instr, Columbia Univ, 46-47, from asst prof to prof, 47-67, chmn dept, 62-67; prof, Biol & Chem Dept, Ill Inst Technol, 67-79; sr scientist, Papanicolaou Cancer Res Inst, 80-84. *Concurrent Pos:* Guggenheim & Fulbright fels, Denmark, 54-55; trustee, Marine Biol Lab, Woods Hole, 60-; vis prof, Japan Soc Adv Sci, Japan, 74-75; Fulbright fel Ger, 75; Humboldt Award, Ger, 79. *Mem:* AAAS; Soc Gen Physiol (pres, 62); Am Physiol Soc; Biophys Soc; Am Soc Cell Biol. *Res:* Cell physiology; physiology and biochemistry of muscle. *Mailing Add:* 7105 SW 112th Pl Miami FL 33173-1971

HAYASHI, TERUO TERRY, MEDICINE, BIOCHEMISTRY. *Current Pos:* chmn, 74-88, PROF OBSTET & GYNEC, SCH MED, UNIV PITTSBURGH, 65- *Personal Data:* b Sacramento, Calif, July 23, 21; m 53, Ursula Promann; c William, Peter, James, Ann & Robert. *Educ:* Temple Univ, AB, 44, MD, 48, MS, 54. *Prof Exp:* From instr to assoc prof obstet & gynec, Sch Med, Temple Univ, 54-65. *Concurrent Pos:* NIH grant, 59-; mem, Study Sect Human Embryol & Develop, NIH, 64-68; mem, Vomt Perinatal NBol & Infant Mortality Br, Nat Inst Child Health & Human Develop, 70-74, ad hoc consult comt, Maternal & Child Health Res, 74-, subcomt, Res Training, 78-82. *Mem:* Soc Gynec Invest (secy-treas, 65-71, pres, 71-72); Am Soc Biol Chemists. *Res:* Placental metabolism; nucleic acid metabolism of human placenta. *Mailing Add:* 146 Woodshire Rd Pittsburgh PA 15215-1714. *Fax:* 412-641-1133

HAYASHI, YOSHIKAZU, DYNAMIC METEOROLOGY. *Current Pos:* Res assoc, 72-75, mem res staff dynamic meteorol, 75-76, RES METEOROLOGIST, GEOPHYS FLUID DYNAMICS LAB, PRINCETON UNIV, 76- *Personal Data:* b Tokyo, Japan, Feb 9, 43; m 74. *Educ:* Univ Tokyo, BSc, 67, MSc, 69, PhD(geophys), 72. *Mem:* Meteorol Soc Japan; Am Meteorol Soc. *Res:* Space-time spectral analysis; dynamics of atmospheric waves simulated by a general circulation model. *Mailing Add:* 46 Perry Dr West Trenton NJ 08628

HAYASHIDA, TETSUO, anatomy, endocrinology; deceased, see previous edition for last biography

HAYAT, M A, BIOLOGY. *Current Pos:* assoc prof, 71-77, PROF BIOL, KEAN COL, 78- *Personal Data:* b Iran, Jan 31, 38. *Educ:* Univ Sind, Pakistan, BS, 56; Univ Tex, MA, 59; Ind Univ, PhD, 62. *Prof Exp:* Asst prof biol, Loyola Univ Chicago, 62-63, NDak State Univ, 63-67 & Univ Dayton, 67-71. *Concurrent Pos:* Res grants, NSF, Heart Inst & Am Philos Soc. *Mem:* Am Inst Biol Sci; Electron Micros Soc Am. *Res:* Principles and techniques of electron microscopy; practical methods for electron microscopy; biological scanning electron microscopy; positive staining for electron microscopy; fixation for electron microscopy. *Mailing Add:* 646 Mountain Ave Berkeley Heights NJ 07922

HAYBRON, RONALD M, PHYSICS. *Current Pos:* asst prof, 68-71, asst dean, Col Arts & Sci, 74-77, ASSOC PROF PHYSICS, CLEVELAND STATE UNIV, 71- *Personal Data:* b Zanesville, Ohio, June 6, 34; m 60; c 2. *Educ:* Case Western Res Univ, BS, 56, MS, 58, PhD(physics), 61. *Prof Exp:* Res assoc physics, Mich State Univ, 61-63, asst prof res physics, 63-65; mem staff, Oak Ridge Nat Lab, 65-68. *Concurrent Pos:* Adj assoc prof, Okla State Univ, NASA aerospace specialist, 81- *Mem:* AAAS; Am Phys Soc. *Res:* Scattering of electrons by nuclei; nuclear reactions produced by protons, deuterons and alphas, especially direct reaction domain, particularly at high energy; structure of nuclei as related to scattering properties. *Mailing Add:* Dept Physics Cleveland State Univ Euclid Ave Cleveland OH 44115

HAYCOCK, DEAN A, NEUROBIOLOGY. *Current Pos:* WRITER, BURTON PRESS, 93- *Personal Data:* b Atlantic City, NJ, Mar 20, 52. *Educ:* Brown Univ, AB, 76, PhD(neurobiol), 85. *Prof Exp:* Lab res asst, Neurobiol Sect, Brown Univ, 78-81; fel, Rockefeller Univ, 85-87, res assoc, Lab Molecular & Cellular Neurobiol, 87; sr res biologist, Dept Pharmacol, Sterling Res Group, 87-90, sr res investr, Dept Neurosci, 90-93. *Concurrent Pos:* Res training fel, Nat Res Serv Award, NIMH, 87. *Mem:* Am Soc Pharmacol & Exp Therapeut; Soc Neurosci; Am Soc Neurochem; Int Soc Neurochem. *Res:* Neuropharmacology of mental disorders; synaptic transmission. *Mailing Add:* PO Box 310 Salem NY 12865

HAYCOCK, JOHN WINTHROP, BIOCHEMISTRY, NEUROCHEMISTRY. *Current Pos:* ASSOC PROF, DEPT BIOCHEM, LA STATE UNIV MED CTR NEW ORLEANS, 86- *Personal Data:* b Washington, DC, Jan 16, 49. *Educ:* Mich State Univ, BS(physiol) & BS(psychol), 71; Univ Calif, Irvine, PhD(biol sci), 75. *Prof Exp:* Res assoc neurochem, Dept Psychobiol, Univ Calif, Irvine, 75-76, Riverside, 76-77, Irvine, 77-78; instr, Dept Neurobiol & Anat, Univ Tex Med Sch, 78-83; res assoc, Rockefeller Univ, 83-86. *Mem:* Soc Neurosci; Am Soc Neurochem; Am Soc Biol Chem Molecular Biol. *Res:* Regulation of cutecholamine metabolism, tyrosine hydroxyluse; phosphoxylation; schizophrenia. *Mailing Add:* Dept Biochem & Molecular Biol La State Univ Med Ctr 1100 Florida Ave New Orleans LA 70119-2799. *Fax:* 504-942-8175

HAYDEN, EDGAR C(LAY), RADIOLOCATION, RADIO PROPAGATION. *Current Pos:* INST SCIENTIST, SOUTHWEST RES INST, 73- *Personal Data:* b Wooster, Ohio, Aug 23, 22; m 51, Dora S Miller; c Elizabeth, Carl & Timothy. *Educ:* Ohio State Univ, BEE, 43; Univ Ill, MS, 52, PhD(elec eng), 58. *Honors & Awards:* Spec Achievement Award, US Dept Com, 74. *Prof Exp:* Res engr, Columbia Broadcasting Syst, 43-46; res asst, Univ Ill, 46-52, from res assoc to assoc prof radio propagation, 52-67; consult ionospheric telecommun, Inst Telecommun Sci, Environ Sci Serv Admin, US Dept Com, 67-70, consult radio telecommun, Off Telecommun, 70-73. *Mem:* Am Inst Elec & Electronics Engrs; Am Geophys Union; AAAS. *Res:* Propagation of radio waves through the ionosphere, and use of such information in the radiolocation process; antennas and antenna arrays; radiolocation systems. *Mailing Add:* Southwest Res Inst 6220 Culebra Rd PO Drawer 28510 San Antonio TX 78228. *E-Mail:* ehayden@swri.edu

HAYDEN, HOWARD CORWIN, ATOMIC PHYSICS. *Current Pos:* fel, 67-68, asst prof, 68-76, ASSOC PROF PHYSICS, UNIV CONN, 76- *Personal Data:* b Pueblo, Colo, June 20, 40; m 83; c 2. *Educ:* Univ Denver, BS, 62, MS, 64, PhD(physics), 67. *Prof Exp:* Res asst physics, Univ Denver, 63-67. *Mem:* Am Asn Physics Teachers; Am Phys Soc. *Res:* Atomic collisions; cross-section measurements of low energy charge transfer and ionization processes; energy loss measurements in inelastic scattering experiments; ion implantation; beam-foil spectroscopy; x-ray angular distributions. *Mailing Add:* Dept Physics U46 Univ Conn 2152 Hillside Rd Storrs CT 06269

HAYDEN, JESS, JR, ANATOMY, ANESTHESIOLOGY. *Current Pos:* AT EXECUAIDE, 94- *Personal Data:* b Eugene, Ore; div; c 4. *Educ:* Univ Ore, DMD, 47; Univ Mich, MS, 55; Loma Linda Univ, PhD(anat), 62; Am Bd Pediat Dent, dipl, 58. *Prof Exp:* Dentist pvt pract, Eugene, Ore, 47-51; instr pedodontics, Sch Dent, Loma Linda Univ, 55-57, asst prof oral surg, 57-60, asst prof, Anesthesia Sect, 60-62, from asst prof to assoc prof anat, Sch Med, 62-66; prof dent, coordr res & assoc dean, Col Dent, Univ Iowa, 66-74, prof pedodontics, 74-76; clin prof surg dent, Col Dent, Univ Colo Med Ctr, Denver, 76-80, clin asst prof anesthesiol, Col Med, 80-85; capt, Dent Corp, Dept Anesthesiol & Clin Invest Dept, USNR, San Diego, 90-92; prof cellbiol & anat, Ore Health Sci Univ, 94. *Concurrent Pos:* Am Scand Found travel grant-in-aid fel, 63; Fulbright-Hays vis prof, Royal Dent Col, Aarhus, 63-64; spec res fel, Nat Inst Dent Res, 57-60 & 73; pvt pract dent, 79-90; Am Asn Dent Educ Scholar, 91. *Mem:* Fel AAAS; Am Dent Asn; fel Am Col Dent; Sigma Xi; fel Am Dent Soc Anesthesiol; Am Asn Clin Anatomists. *Res:* Pathways and chronology of human tooth innervation by laboratory and clinical investigation; neuroanatomical-physiological correlates of sedation, local and general anesthesia in dentistry. *Mailing Add:* Execuaide Dept JH PO Box 2276 Van Nuys CA 91404. *Fax:* 818-780-9093

HAYDEN, MICHAEL, PHYSICS. *Current Pos:* asst prof, 91-95, DIR, GRAD PROG APPL PHYSICS, UNIV MD, BALTIMORE, 93-, ASSOC PROF PHYSICS, 95- *Personal Data:* b St Louis, Mo, May 25, 55. *Educ:* US Naval Acad, BS, 78; Univ Calif, Davis, MA, 84, PhD(physics), 87. *Prof Exp:* US Naval officer, 78-83; prin physicist, Unisys Defense Systs, St Paul, 87-91. *Concurrent Pos:* Lectr, Dept Physics, Macalester Col, 90; sr faculty fel, Am Soc Eng Educ, 92; fel, NSF, 93-; Fel, US Naval Acad & Martin Marietta Labs, 93; Cottrell Scholar Award, Res Corp, 94. *Mem:* Am Phys Soc; Am Chem Soc; Optical Soc Am. *Res:* Awarded 3 patents; author of numerous articles. *Mailing Add:* Dept Physics Univ Md 5401 Wilkens Ave Baltimore MD 21228

HAYDEN, MICHAEL V, INTELLIGENCE. *Current Pos:* USAF, 67-, analyst & briefer, Hq Strategic Air Command, Offutt AFB, Nebr, 70-72, chief, Current Intel Div, Hq Eighth Air Force, Anderson AFB, Guam, 72-75, acad instr & commandment cadets, Res Officer Training Corps, St Michael's Col, Vt, 75-79, chief intel 51st tactical fighter win, Osan AFB, Kora, 80-82, air attache, US Embassy, Sofia, People's Repub Bulgaria, 84-86, polit-mil affairs officer, Strategy Div, Hq, Washington, DC, 86-89, dir defense policy & arms control, Nat Security Coun, Washington, DC, 89-91, chief secy staff group, Off Secy Air Force, Hq, Washington, DC, 91-93, dir intel directorate, Hq US Europ Command, Ger, 93-95, spec asst to comndr, Hq Air Intel Agency, Kelly AFB, Tex, 95-96, COMNDR, AIR INTEL AGENCY & DIR, JOINT COMMAND & CONTROL WARFARE CTR, USAF, KELLY AFB, TEX, 96- *Personal Data:* m, Jeanine Carrier; c Margaret, Michael & Liam. *Educ:* Duquesne Univ, BA, 67, MA, 69. *Res:* Air and space intelligence; weapons monitoring. *Mailing Add:* Off Pub Affairs HQ Air Intel Agency 102 Hall Blvd Suite 234 San Antonio TX 78243-7036

HAYDEN, RICHARD AMHERST, HORTICULTURE, POMOLOGY. *Current Pos:* from assoc prof to prof, 66-94, EMER PROF HORT, PURDUE UNIV, 94- *Personal Data:* b Wooster, Ohio, June 14, 28; m 55; c 4. *Educ:* Ohio State Univ, BSc, 52, PhD, 56. *Honors & Awards:* Stark Award, Am Soc Hort Sci, 71. *Prof Exp:* Asst horticulturist, Agr Exp Sta, Univ Ga, 56-66. *Mem:* Am Soc Hort Sci; Am Pomol Soc; Int Dwarf Fruit Tree Asn. *Res:* High density fruit production systems, apple and peach rootstocks pruning and training; strawberry production systems, varieties; peach tree longevity, tree fruit production and related studies. *Mailing Add:* 1165 Dept Hort Purdue Univ West Lafayette IN 47907-1165

HAYDEN, RICHARD JOHN, PHYSICS. *Current Pos:* from asst prof to assoc prof, 49-58, PROF PHYSICS, UNIV MONT, 58- *Personal Data:* b Whitefish, Mont, Feb 25, 22; m 48. *Educ:* Oberlin Col, AB, 43; Univ Chicago, MS & PhD(physics), 48. *Prof Exp:* Jr physicist, Metall Lab, Univ Chicago, 43-46; assoc physicist, Argonne Nat Lab, 48-49 & 50-55. *Mem:* Fel Am Phys Soc. *Res:* Mass spectroscopy; radioactivity measurements; mass spectrographic mass assignment of radioactive isotopes; radiogenic geological dating by argon-potassium method. *Mailing Add:* 618 Crestline Dr Missoula MT 59803

HAYDEN, THOMAS DAY, MATERIALS SCIENCE. *Current Pos:* RES ASSOC, W R GRACE & CO, 78- *Personal Data:* b Boston, Mass, Oct 23, 44; m 78; c 2. *Educ:* Bates Col, BS, 66; Boston Univ, PhD(chem), 76. *Prof Exp:* Res scientist, Martin Marietta Labs, 77-78. *Concurrent Pos:* Lectr, Eastern Nazarene Col, 75. *Mem:* Am Chem Soc; Am Ceramic Soc; Am Crystallog Asn; Sigma Xi; Mat Res Soc; Transportation Res Bd. *Res:* Chemical and physical reactions of portland cement hydration; experimental design methods for the development of chemical additives which control, modify or accelerate these hydration reactions and thereby extend the technical usefulness of concrete as a building material. *Mailing Add:* 8 Everell Rd Winchester MA 01890-3902

HAYDEN, THOMAS LEE, MATHEMATICS. *Current Pos:* asst prof, 63-65, assoc prof, 65-77, PROF MATH, UNIV KY, 78- *Personal Data:* b Abilene, Tex, Feb 8, 32; m 57; c 1. *Educ:* Univ Tex, BS, 54, PhD(math), 61. *Prof Exp:* Asst prof math, Univ Ky, 61-62; vis mem, US Army Math Res Ctr, Univ Wis, 62-63. *Concurrent Pos:* Consult biomath, Oak Ridge Nat Labs. *Mem:* Soc Indust & Appl Math. *Res:* Distance matrices; linear algebra; non-linear optimization. *Mailing Add:* Dept Math Univ Ky Patterson Off Tower 825 Lexington KY 40506-0027

HAYDEN-WING, LARRY DEAN, WILDLIFE ECOLOGY. *Current Pos:* DIR, HAYDEN-WING ASSOC, ENVIRON CONSULT, 80- *Personal Data:* b Webster City, Iowa, Aug 13, 35; m; c 3. *Educ:* Univ Idaho, BS, 58, MS, 62, PhD(forestry), 70. *Prof Exp:* Res biologist, Wash State Univ, 62-65; asst prof zool & entom, Iowa State Univ, 69-72, assoc prof wildlife ecol, 72-77; assoc prof wildlife ecol, Univ Wyo, 77-78; dir, Wildlife Div, Land Inventory & Develop Inc, 78-80. *Mem:* Wildlife Soc; EAfrican Wildlife Soc. *Res:* Wild ungulate ecology and management; wildlife-habitat relationships; mechanisms controlling the selection of plants by grazing herbivores; conservation of African wildlife; environmental impacts and mitigation of energy extraction activities; other natural resource perterbations. *Mailing Add:* 1443 Haydenwing Lane Laramie WY 82070

HAYDOCK, PAUL VINCENT, GENE EXPRESSION. *Current Pos:* RES ASSOC, UNIV WASH, 83- *Educ:* Purdue Univ, PhD(biochem), 83. *Res:* Epithelial differentiation. *Mailing Add:* Microprobe Corp 1725 220th St SE No 104 Bothell WA 98021-0001. *Fax:* 425-486-8336

HAYDON, GEORGE WILLIAM, RADIO ENGINEERING. *Current Pos:* radio consult, Cent Radio Propagation Lab, 59-65, RADIO CONSULT, INST TELECOMMUN SCI, OFF TELECOMMUN, DEPT COM, 65- *Personal Data:* b Alma Center, Wis, July 10, 14; m 44, Thelma Groome. *Prof Exp:* Engr, Dept Army, 42-54, scientist, Off Chief Signal, 54-59. *Concurrent Pos:* Mem, Int Radio Consult Comts Ionospheric Propagation, 48-68 & Space Systs, 62-68; US deleg, Int Telecommun Radio Conf, 59 & Int Telecommun Aeronaut Radio Conf, 64 & 66. *Mem:* Inst Elec & Electronics Engrs; Sigma Xi; Int Union Radio Sci. *Res:* Radio spectrum utilization; prediction of performance of high frequency radio circuits using sky waves; international agreements concerning radio usage; selection of frequencies for satellite communication systems. *Mailing Add:* 350 Ponca Pl No 379 Boulder CO 80303-3828

HAYDU, JUAN B, TECHNOLOGY MANAGEMENT. *Current Pos:* VPRES TECHNOL, SUBSID ASARCO INC, ENTHONE INC, 62- *Personal Data:* b Budapest, Hungary, Apr 26, 30; US citizen; m 55; c 2. *Educ:* Univ Buenos Aires, ing, Ar, PhD(chem), 56; New Haven Univ, MBA, 79. *Honors & Awards:* Heussner Award, Am Electroplaters' Soc, 65. *Mem:* Am Chem Soc; Electrochem Soc; Am Electroplaters' & Surface Finishers Soc. *Res:* Electronic chemicals; corrosion; protection of materials. *Mailing Add:* 373 Old Silo Rd Orange CT 06477

HAYDUK, WALTER, CHEMICAL ENGINEERING. *Current Pos:* RETIRED. *Personal Data:* b Beauvallon, Alta, Sept 1, 31; m 85, Beverly Popyk; c 3. *Educ:* Univ BC, BA, 54, MA, 56, PhD(chem eng), 64. *Prof Exp:* Process engr, Polymer Corp Ltd, Ont, 55-61, tech supvr, Rubber Dept, 64-66; from asst prof to prof chem eng, Univ Ottawa, 66-96. *Concurrent Pos:* Chem Inst Can fel, 78. *Mem:* Can Soc Chem Eng; Can Asn Prof Engrs Ont. *Res:* Solubilities and diffusivities of gases in liquids; solar energy related studies; emulsion polymerization. *Mailing Add:* Dept Chem Eng Univ Ottawa 161 Louis Pasteur Ottawa ON K1N 6N5 Can. *Fax:* 613-564-9856

HAYE, KEITH R, developmental biology, molecular cell biology, for more information see previous edition

HAYEK, DEAN HARRISON, PHYSIOLOGY, EDUCATION ADMINISTRATION. *Current Pos:* asst dean, 70-78, ASSOC PROF PHYSIOL, SCH MED, ECAROLINA UNIV, 70-, ASSOC DEAN, 78- *Personal Data:* b Waukesha, Wis, Jan 1, 31; m 55; c 3. *Educ:* Univ Wis, BS, 54; Univ Tenn, MS, 60, PhD(radiation biol), 64. *Prof Exp:* Instr physiol, Med Col Va, 64-65, asst prof, 65-70. *Res:* Medical education. *Mailing Add:* 3008 Fern Dr Greenville NC 27858

HAYEK, LEE-ANN COLLINS, APPLIED STATISTICS. *Current Pos:* CHIEF MATH STATISTICIAN, SMITHSONIAN INST, 73- *Personal Data:* b Boston, Mass, Dec, 27, 44; m 70; c 4. *Educ:* Emmanuel Col, BS, 65; Catholic Univ Am, MS, 67; Univ Md, PhD(statist), 78. *Prof Exp:* Math analyst, Physics Res Div, Cambridge Res Labs, USAF, 62-65; chief analyst, Blue Cross Western Pa, 67-68; chief statistician, Consolidated Nat Gas Serv Co, 68-69; prof math & statist, Beaver Col, 69-73. *Concurrent Pos:* Lectr math & statist, Point Park Col, 67-71; consult, EEO Serv, 79-80, Justice Dept, Civil Rights Div, 81; res adj, Sch Med, Georgetown Univ, 81-84. *Mem:* Am Statist Asn; Biomet Soc; Am Educ Res Asn; Psychomet Soc; Inst Math Statist; Royal Statist Soc. *Res:* Development of statistical and mathematical models and research methodology; mathematical and statistical research activities published as solutions to problems of concern in paleontology, biological sciences, anthropology, nutrition and education. *Mailing Add:* Rm E 116 MRC 136 Mus Nat Hist Smithsonian Inst Washington DC 20560

HAYEK, MASON, TEXTILE & PAPER CHEMICALS, TECHNICAL WRITING. *Current Pos:* RETIRED. *Personal Data:* b St Paul, Minn, Mar 28, 20; m 44, Doris B; c Winifred. *Educ:* Univ Minn, BChem, 41; Ind Univ, MA, 43, PhD(org chem), 47. *Prof Exp:* Control chemist, Joseph E Seagram & Sons, Inc, 41-42, res chemist, 43-45; asst org chem, Ind Univ, 46-47; res chemist, E I du Pont de Nemours & Co, 47-51, group leader, 51-63, res assoc, 63-82. *Concurrent Pos:* Consult, 82-87; tech writing consult, 84-90. *Mem:* Am Chem Soc. *Res:* Chemical auxiliaries including antistats, surfactants and fluorochemicals for textiles, plastics and paper; product development; market development and writing; organic chemistry. *Mailing Add:* 113 Rockingham Dr Wilmington DE 19803

HAYEK, SABIH I, ENGINEERING MECHANICS, ACOUSTICS. *Current Pos:* From asst prof to prof, Pa State Univ, 65-92, scientist, Appl Res Lab, 65-70, head, Vibration & Radiation Group, 70-83, assoc dir, Res Ctr Acoust & Vibration, 86-90, DISTINGUISHED PROF ENG MECH, PA STATE UNIV, 92-, DIR, ACTIVE VIBRATION CONTROL LAB, 90- *Personal Data:* b Baghdad, Iraq, Mar 25, 38; US citizen; m 60, Guler Aksus; c Emil & Dina. *Educ:* Robert Col, Istanbul, BSc, 59, MSc, 60; Columbia Univ, DEngSc, 65. *Concurrent Pos:* Sr vis fel, Inst Sound Vibration, Univ Southhampton, Eng, 72; sr scientist, Naval Ocean Systs Ctr, San Diego, 80-81; guest prof, Tokyo Inst Technol, 92; vis prof, INSA, Lyon, France, 93-92. *Mem:* Fel Acoust Soc Am; fel Am Soc Mech Engrs; Inst Noise Control; Sigma Xi; founding mem Acad Mech; Soc Eng Sci. *Res:* Acoustic radiation from structures; acoustic properties of composite materials; acoustic theory of diffraction and scattering; noise barriers; machinery noise; active vibration control. *Mailing Add:* Dept Eng Sci & Mech Pa State Univ University Park PA 16802. *Fax:* 814-863-7967; *E-Mail:* sihesm@engr.psu.edu

HAYES, ALICE BOURKE, BOTANY. *Current Pos:* EXEC VPRES, PROVOST & PROF BIOL, ST LOUIS UNIV, 89- *Personal Data:* b Chicago, Ill, Dec 31, 37; wid. *Educ:* Mundelein Col, BS, 59; Univ Ill, Urbana, MS, 60; Northwestern Univ, PhD(biol), 71. *Prof Exp:* Lab asst bot, Univ Ill, 59-60; microbiologist, Munic Tuberc Sanitarium, Chicago, 60-62; from instr to prof natural sci, Loyola Univ, Chicago, 62-88, dept chairperson, 68-69 & 71-77, dean, 77-80, assoc acad vpres, 80-86, vpres acad affairs, 87-89. *Concurrent Pos:* NSF fel, Northwestern Univ, 69-71; mem, Proposal Develop & Proj Team, Inst Renewal Through Improv Teaching, HEW, 76-78, adv panels, NSF, 77-81 & Space Biol Prog, NASA, 80-84; NASA res grant, 80-84. *Mem:* Am Inst Biol Sci; Am Soc Plant Physiologists; Bot Soc Am; AAAS; Sigma Xi; Am Asn Univ Profs; Am Asn Univ Women; Am Coun Educ; Am Soc Gravitational & Space Biol. *Res:* Morphogenesis; planar form and plagiotropism of the leaf blade and sporulation in imperfect fungi. *Mailing Add:* Pres Off Univ San Diego 5998 Alcala Park San Diego CA 92110

HAYES, ANDREW WALLACE, II, PHARMACOLOGY, TOXICOLOGY. *Current Pos:* assoc prof, 75-76, prog dir, Training Prog Toxicol, 77-80, PROF PHARMACOL & TOXICOL, UNIV MISS MED CTR, 76-; VPRES, CORP PROD INTEGRITY, GILLETTE CO, 92-; PROF PHARMACOL & TOXICOL, BOWMAN GRAY SCH MED, 92- *Personal Data:* b Corning, Ark, Aug 21, 39; m 63, Sandra Smith; c Andrew W III, Helen C & Benjamin B. *Educ:* Emory Univ, AB, 61; Auburn Univ, MS, 64, PhD(biochem), 67; dipl, Am Bd Toxicol. *Prof Exp:* Res assoc biochem, Vanderbilt Univ, 66-68, from asst prof to assoc prof microbiol, 68-71; prof microbiol, Univ Ala, 75; group dir & corp toxicologist, RJR Nabisco, Inc, 84-87, vpres & corp toxicologist, 87-92. *Concurrent Pos:* USPHS fel, 67-69; adj prof, Univ Ala, 75- & Duke Univ, 85-; res prof, Tex A&M Univ, 79-, Temple Univ, 81-84; dir toxicol res, Rohm & Haas, 80-84; ed, Toxicol & Appl Pharmacol, 81-, Comments Toxicol, 85-; Res Career Develop Award, NIH, 74; NATO sr fel, 77; res prof, Med Col Va, 87-; adj prof, Bowman Gray Sch Med, Wake Forest Univ, 93- *Mem:* Am Soc Microbiol; Soc Toxicol; Am Inst Nutrit; Am Chem Soc; Am Soc Pharmacol & Exp Therapeut; Am Col Toxicol. *Res:* Carcinogenicity, teratogenecity and mode of action of mycotoxins; food safety; general toxicology. *Mailing Add:* Corp Prod Integrity Gillette Co Prudential Tower Bldg Boston MA 02199. *Fax:* 617-421-7360; *E-Mail:* a.wallace_hayes@gillette.com

HAYES, CAROL J, BIOLOGICAL RHYTHMS. *Current Pos:* from instr to assoc prof, 65-80, PROF BIOL, ST JOSEPHS COL, NY, 80-, CHMN DEPT, 76- *Personal Data:* b New York, NY, Dec 13, 40. *Educ:* St Joseph Col, NY, BA, 61; NY Univ, PhD(physiol), 75. *Prof Exp:* Res asst immunol, Col Med, Cornell Univ, 64-65. *Concurrent Pos:* Adj asst prof, Medgar Evers Col, City Univ New York, 70- *Mem:* Sigma Xi; AAAS; NY Acad Sci. *Res:* The effects of chemicals on rhythmic processes in vertebrates. *Mailing Add:* Dept Biol St Josephs Col 245 Clinton Ave Brooklyn NY 11205-3602

HAYES, CHARLES AMOS, JR, MATHEMATICS. *Current Pos:* from asst prof to prof, 47-78, chmn dept, 59-64, EMER PROF MATH, UNIV CALIF, DAVIS, 78- *Personal Data:* b Winnipeg, Man, Apr 9, 16; nat US; m 42; c 2. *Educ:* Univ Calif, AB, 37, MA, 38, PhD(math), 42. *Prof Exp:* Instr math, Univ Calif, Berkeley, 46-47. *Mem:* Am Math Soc; Math Asn Am; Sigma Xi. *Res:* Theory of functions of real variables; boundary value problems for elliptic systems of linear partial differential equations; theory of differentiation and integration of set functions. *Mailing Add:* 302 11th St Davis CA 95616-2010

HAYES, CHARLES FRANKLIN, PHYSICS. *Current Pos:* Asst prof physics, 67-74, assoc prof, 74-79, PROF PHYSICS & ASTRON, UNIV HAWAII, 79-, CHMN DEPT, 85-, ASSOC DEAN, 90- *Personal Data:* b Huntington, WVa, Nov 7, 41; div; c 2. *Educ:* Wheaton Col, BA, 63; WVa Univ, MS, 65, PhD, 67. *Mem:* Am Phys Soc; Illum Eng Soc. *Res:* Acoustics; entomology. *Mailing Add:* Dept Physics Univ Hawaii 2505 Correa Rd Honolulu HI 96822

HAYES, CLAUDE Q C, ELECTRO STATICS. *Current Pos:* CONSULT, SCI & TECHNOL, 81- *Personal Data:* b New York, Nov 15, 45. *Educ:* Columbia Univ, AB, 71, MBA, 73; Western State Law Sch, JD, 78. *Prof Exp:* Design, sales & mgt, Cyberton Eng, 72-75; instr phys sci & bus law, City Col, 76-79, instr phys sci & chem, bus law, phys geog & geol, Miramar Col, 76-82, instr phys sci, Nat Univ, 80-81; sr systs analyst, Gen Dynamics/Western Data Systs & specif analyst, Convair Div, 79-80. *Concurrent Pos:* Consult, Hitech & Inforama, Paris, France & USN, 82; instr phys sci & phys geog, San Diego Community Col Dist & Mira Costa Col, 85-90; adj asst prof phys chem, San Diego State Univ, 86; adj prof int bus mgt, Grad Sch, Univ Redlands, 86-88; defense contractor/consult, Defense Nuclear Agency, NOSC, Defense Advan Res Proj Agency, Strategic Defense Initiative Orgn, USAF, US Army & Ballistic Missile Orgn, 86- *Mem:* AAAS; sr mem Am Inst Aeronaut & Astronaut; NY Acad Sci; Am Chem Soc. *Res:* Endothermies; physical chemistry; author of various publications. *Mailing Add:* Hayes & Assocs 3737 Third Ave No 308 San Diego CA 92103

HAYES, DALLAS T, PHYSICS, MATHEMATICS. *Current Pos:* RES PHYSICIST, AIR FORCE CAMBRIDGE RES CTR, 67- *Personal Data:* b Easton, Md, Aug 15, 31; m 60; c 3. *Educ:* Mass Inst Technol, SB, 54; Univ Gottingen, dipl physics, 61, Dr rer nat(physics), 62. *Prof Exp:* Physicist systs eng, Lincoln Lab, Mass, 56-57; staff scientist plasma physics, Res & Adv Develop Div, Avco Corp, 63-67. *Mem:* AAAS; Am Phys Soc. *Res:* Many body problem as applied to nuclear physics; transport properties of dense plasmas; wave propagation in plasma; turbulent media. *Mailing Add:* 583 Peakham Rd Sudbury MA 01776-2237

HAYES, DAVID RYAN, NUMBER THEORY. *Current Pos:* assoc prof, 67-72, dept head, 91-94, PROF MATH, UNIV MASS, AMHERST, 72- *Personal Data:* b Raleigh, NC, July 14, 37; div; c Robert, Christopher & Jonathan. *Educ:* Duke Univ, AB, 59, PhD(math), 63. *Prof Exp:* From asst prof to assoc prof math, Univ Tenn, 63-67. *Concurrent Pos:* NSF fel, 66; vis prof, Oxford Univ, 74-75, Harvard Univ, 81, Univ Calif, San Diego, 83, Imp Col, London, 89, Univ Vt, 96. *Mem:* Am Math Soc; Math Asn Am. *Res:* Algebraic and analytic number theory; Drinfeld modules; Stark's conjectures. *Mailing Add:* Dept Math Univ Mass Amherst MA 01003

HAYES, DAVID WAYNE, OCEANOGRAPHY, CHEMISTRY. *Current Pos:* STAFF OCEANOGR, SAVANNAH RIVER LAB, E I DU PONT DE NEMOURS & CO, INC, 66- *Personal Data:* b Mineola, Tex, Nov 26, 36; m 59; c 2. *Educ:* NTex State Univ, BS, 61, MS, 63; Tex A&M Univ, PhD(oceanog), 66. *Mem:* Am Geophys Union; Am Chem Soc; Am Soc Limnol & Oceanog; Geochem Soc. *Res:* Marine chemistry; diffusion of natural waters; coastal oceanography; radiochemistry; model development for natural water systems. *Mailing Add:* PO Box 2253 Aiken SC 29801-2253

HAYES, DENNIS E, MARINE GEOLOGY, GEOPHYSICS. *Current Pos:* Res assoc, Columbia Univ, 66-70, assoc prof marine geophys, 74-77, assoc dir, 78-81, SR RES SCIENTIST, LAMONT-DOHERTY GEOL OBSERV, COLUMBIA UNIV, 71-, PROF GEOPHYS, 84-, CHMN, DEPT GEOL SCI, 89-, DEPT DIR, 93- *Personal Data:* b Saint Joseph, Mo, Oct 03, 38; m 78, Leslie Price; c Jennifer, Katharine, Elizabeth & Elan. *Educ:* Univ Kans, BSE, 61; Columbia Univ, PhD(marine geophys), 66. *Concurrent Pos:* NSF fel, 61-65; Guggenheim fel, 80-81. *Mem:* Fel Am Geophys Union; fel Soc Explor Geophysicists; fel Geol Soc Am; Am Asn Petrol Geologists; Sigma Xi. *Res:* Studies of the structure and evolution of the seafloor and subseafloor - especially the mid-ocean ridge system, continental margins, and marginal seas; many activities have focused on the circum-Antarctic seas. *Mailing Add:* Lamont-Doherty Earth Observ Columbia Univ Palisades NY 10964. *E-Mail:* Omnet: d.hayes

HAYES, DONALD CHARLES, PHARMACOLOGY, BIOCHEMISTRY. *Current Pos:* RETIRED. *Personal Data:* b Oakland City, Ind, June 29, 32; m 55; c 4. *Educ:* Ind Univ, BS, 58. *Prof Exp:* Sr scientist, Mead Johnson & Co, Bristol-Myers Co, 58-87. *Mem:* Am Chem Soc; AAAS. *Res:* Natural products isolation; tissue culture; lysosomes; protein chemistry; enzyme separations; lipid metabolism; cardiovascular pharmacology. *Mailing Add:* 18601 Old Princeton Rd Evansville IN 47711-9116

HAYES, DONALD H, PHYSIOLOGY, GENETICS. *Current Pos:* Assoc prof zool, 62-77, ASSOC PROF BIOL, SOUTHEASTERN LA UNIV, 78- *Personal Data:* b Washington, DC, Apr 13, 37; m 64; c 2. *Educ:* Univ Mo, BA, 59, MA, 62; La State Univ, PhD(zool), 68. *Mem:* Am Inst Biol Sci; AAAS. *Res:* Molecular physiology and genetics; history of biology, especially genetics. *Mailing Add:* Biol Sci Southeastern La Univ 500 Western Ave Hammond LA 70402-0001

HAYES, DONALD M, internal medicine, occupational medicine, for more information see previous edition

HAYES, DONALD SCOTT, ASTRONOMY, SCIENCE EDUCATION. *Current Pos:* INSTR ASTRON, PIMA COMMUNITY COL, 91- *Personal Data:* b Los Angeles, Calif, Oct 7, 39; m 83. *Educ:* Pomona Col, BA, 61; Univ Calif, Los Angeles, MS, 66, PhD(astron), 67. *Prof Exp:* Asst prof astron, Rensselaer Polytech Inst, 67-75; vis assoc prof physics, Ariz State Univ, 75-79; asst support scientist, Kitt Peak Nat Observ, 79-86; astronr, Fairborn Observ, 86-91. *Concurrent Pos:* Vis scientist, Mt Hopkins Observ, Smithsonian Inst, 74-75; mem, Inst Space Observations, 86- *Mem:* Int Astron Union; Am Astron Soc; Am Asn Physics Teachers. *Mailing Add:* 5348 Camino de la Culebra Tucson AZ 85750

HAYES, DORA KRUSE, BIOCHEMISTRY. *Current Pos:* res biochemist, 65-76, chief, Chem Biophys Control Lab, 76-79, RES LEADER, LIVESTOCK INSECTS LAB, USDA, 79- *Personal Data:* b Kindred, NDak, June 19, 31; m 53; c 2. *Educ:* Hamline Univ, BS, 52; Univ Wis, MS, 53; Univ Minn, PhD(biochem), 61. *Prof Exp:* Chemist, Gen Mills, Inc, Minn, 53-54; jr scientist, Univ Minn, 54-57, teaching asst, 57-61; biochemist, Dugway Proving Ground, 61-62, res biochemist, 62-65. *Concurrent Pos:* Abstractor, Chem Abstr, 61-74; equal employment officer, Fed Women's Prog Coord, Agr Res Serv, USDA, 74-77 & arranger res leaders mgt; mgt leader, ISC, 75 & 89; sabbatical, Pharmacol Dept, Johns Hopkins Univ, 85. *Mem:* AAAS; Am Chem Soc; Am Entom Soc; Am Soc Biol Chem; life mem Int Soc Chronobiology; Sigma Xi. *Res:* Insect chronobiology; insect biochemistry; membrane transport; Pasteurella tularensis metabolism; bacterial spore metabolism; biological aspects of aerosols; insect diapause; receptors; peptides. *Mailing Add:* 9105 Shasta Ct Fairfax VA 22031

HAYES, EARL T, METALLURGY. *Current Pos:* RETIRED. *Personal Data:* b Wallace, Idaho, Apr 1, 12; m 35; c 3. *Educ:* Univ Idaho, BS, 35, MS, 36; Univ Md, PhD(chem eng), 40. *Hon Degrees:* DSc, Univ Idaho, 71. *Prof Exp:* Mine leaser, Mullan, Idaho, 36-38; metallurgist, US Bur Mines, Utah, 40-48, chief, Phys Metall Br, Ore, 48-56, asst chief metallurgist, Washington, DC, 56-57, chief metallurgist, 57-62; asst dir mat, off dir, defense res & eng, US Dept Defense, 62-66; dep dir, US Bur Mines, 67-70, actg dir, 68 & 70, chief scientist, 70-73; consult, Mat Assocs, 74-78. *Mem:* Fel Am Soc Metals; Am Inst Mining, Metall & Petrol Engrs. *Res:* Metallurgy of zirconium, titanium, chromium and manganese metals and alloys; high purity and refractory metals; metallurgy and materials research and development programming direction, administration and management. *Mailing Add:* 517 Gilmore Dr Silver Spring MD 20901

HAYES, EDWARD FRANCIS, QUANTUM CHEMISTRY. *Current Pos:* VPRES RES, OHIO STATE UNIV, 91-, PROF CHEM, 91- *Personal Data:* b Baltimore, Md, Sept 8, 41; m 64, Ann Burt; c Elizabeth, Emily & Frank. *Educ:* Univ Rochester, BS, 63; Johns Hopkins Univ, MA, 65, PhD(chem), 66. *Honors & Awards:* Distinguished Serv Award, NSF, 85; Meritorious Exec Award, US Govt, 86. *Prof Exp:* Res asst chem, IBM, 62; res assoc chem, Univ Rochester, 63; grad fel chem, Johns Hopkins Univ, 64-67; fel chem, Princeton Univ, 67-68; prof chem, Rice Univ, 68-78; prog officer, NSF, 75-76, sect head, Chem Div, 76-80, dir, 82-83 & 85-87, controller, 83-85; budget analyst, Exec Off Pres, 80-82; assoc provost & vpres info systs, Rice Univ, 87-89, vpres grad studies, Res & Info Systs, 89-91. *Concurrent Pos:* Lectr, Georgetown Univ, 79-80; pres, Ohio State Univ Res Found, 91- *Mem:* Am Chem Soc; fel Am Phys Soc; fel AAAS; Sigma Xi. *Res:* Quantum theory of molecular structure; application of electronic computers in quantum chemistry; molecular potential functions and intermolecular interactions; scattering theory. *Mailing Add:* 208 Bricker Hall 190 N Oval Mall Columbus OH 43210-1321. *E-Mail:* ehayes@osu.edu

HAYES, EDWARD J(AMES), mechanical engineering, for more information see previous edition

HAYES, EVERETT RUSSELL, ANATOMY. *Current Pos:* from assoc prof to prof, 57-85, EMER PROF ANAT, STATE UNIV NY, BUFFALO, 85- *Personal Data:* b Pomeroy, Ohio, Feb 5, 17; m 46, Nancy Padan; c Anne, Alan & Kevin. *Educ:* Ohio Univ, AB, 38; Ohio State Univ, PhD(anat), 47. *Prof Exp:* Instr anat, Univ Buffalo, 45-48; from asst prof to assoc prof, Ohio State Univ, 48-57. *Mem:* Histochem Soc; Am Soc Zool; Am Asn Anat; Am Soc Cell Biol; Biol Stain Comn. *Res:* Plasmalogens; comparative histology and histochemistry. *Mailing Add:* 6599 Bear Ridge Rd Lockport NY 14094-9212

HAYES, GEORGE J, NEUROSURGERY. *Current Pos:* RETIRED. *Personal Data:* b Washington, DC, 1918. *Educ:* Johns Hopkins Univ, MD, 43; Am Bd Neurol Surg, dipl, 52. *Prof Exp:* Intern, Johns Hopkins Hosp, 44; fel neurosurg, Lahey Clin Boston, 44-46; chief, Neurosurg Serv, Walter Reed Gen Hosp, Washington, DC, 47-49, 50-51 & 55-66; fel neurosurg, Duke Hosp, 49-50; chief, Neurosurg Serv, Brooke Army Hosp, Ft Sam Houston, Tex, 53-55; dir prof serv, Off Serv Gen, Dept Army, 66-74. *Concurrent Pos:* Prin dep asst secy defense health & environ, Off Secy Defense, 71-74; clin prof neurosurg, George Washington Univ. *Mem:* Inst Med-Nat Acad Sci; AMA; Am Asn Neurol Surgeons; Am Col Surgeons. *Mailing Add:* 303 Skyhill Rd Alexandria VA 22314

HAYES, J SCOTT, cardio-vascular homodynamics, cardiovascular pharmacology, for more information see previous edition

HAYES, JANAN MARY, CHEMICAL EDUCATION, HISTORY OF SCIENCE. *Current Pos:* asst dean instr, 89-90, vpres instr, 91-92, PROF CHEM, MERCED COL, 93- *Personal Data:* b Los Angeles, Calif, Dec 10, 42. *Educ:* Ore State Univ, BS, 64, MS, 65; Brigham Young Univ, PhD(inorg

& analytical chem), 71. *Prof Exp:* Instr chem, Fortuna Union High Sch, 65-67; assoc prof chem, Am River Col, 71-81; asst dean sci & agr, Cosumnes River Col, 81-89. *Concurrent Pos:* Consult, Sumar Corp, 75-81; NSF proj dir sci educ, Am River Col, 78-79. *Mem:* Am Chem Soc; Sigma Xi. *Res:* Multicultural concerns in teaching science; science education for elementary teachers; chemical education for an informed public. *Mailing Add:* Merced Col 3600 M St Merced CA 95384

HAYES, JEFFREY CHARLES, metal reagents & catalysts, for more information see previous edition

HAYES, JEREMIAH FRANCIS, COMPUTER COMMUNICATIONS, COMMUNICATION THEORY. *Current Pos:* PROF ELEC & COMPUT ENG & CHMN DEPT, CONCORDIA UNIV, 84- *Personal Data:* b New York, NY, July 8, 34; m 62, Florence Perrella; c Mary, Ann, Jeremiah & Martin. *Educ:* Manhattan Col, BEE, 56; NY Univ, MS, 61; Univ Calif, Berkeley, PhD(elec eng), 66. *Honors & Awards:* Spec Acknowledgement, Inst Elec & Electronics Engrs Info Theory Group, 82; Can Award Telecomm Res, 96. *Prof Exp:* Mem tech staff, Bell Labs, 56-60; res engr, Electronics Res Labs, 60-62; actg instr elec eng, Univ Calif, 62-66; asst prof, Purdue Univ, 66-69; mem tech staff, Bell Labs, 69-78; assoc prof elec eng, McGill Univ, 78-84. *Concurrent Pos:* Tech rep, Int Telegraph & Tel Consult Comt, Int Telecom Union, 72-78; adj prof, Polytech Inst NY, 76-78; ed comput communications, Trans Commun, Inst Elec & Electronics Engrs, 81- *Mem:* Fel Inst Elec & Electronics Engrs. *Res:* Computer communications with special emphasis on local area networks; application of informaton theory to computer communications; source encoding; communication theory; author of computer communication network (1984) and data communication principles. *Mailing Add:* Dept Elec & Comput Eng Concordia Univ Montreal PQ H3G 1M8 Can

HAYES, JOHN A, PULMONARY DISEASE. *Current Pos:* PROF PATH, SCH MED, BOSTON UNIV, 76-, ASSOC CHMN PATH, 80-; LAB DIR LAB SERV, VET ADMIN MED CTR, 84- *Personal Data:* b Maesteg, Wales, July 16, 29. *Educ:* Univ Bristol, MD, 56, PhD(path), 68. *Mem:* Am Asn Pathologists; Int Acad Pathologists; Royal Col Path. *Res:* Toxic lung disease. *Mailing Add:* 150 South Huntington Ave Lab Serv Vet Admin Med Ctr Boston MA 02130-4893. *Fax:* 617-278-4476

HAYES, JOHN BERNARD, GEOLOGY, MINERALOGY. *Current Pos:* RETIRED. *Personal Data:* b Omaha, Nebr, Nov 30, 34; m 61; c 2. *Educ:* Iowa State Univ, BS, 56, MS, 57; Univ Wis, PhD(geol), 61. *Prof Exp:* From instr to assoc prof geol, Univ Iowa, 60-68; sr res geologist, Denver Res Ctr, Marathon Oil Co, 68-86. *Concurrent Pos:* Mineral consult, Iowa Geol Surv, 62-68; vis prof geol, Univ Colo, 73 & Colo Sch Mines, 76; lectr, Am Asn Petrol Geol Schs, 78-85. *Mem:* Geol Soc Am; Soc Econ Paleont & Mineral; Clay Minerals Soc (pres, 77-78); Am Asn Petrol Geol. *Res:* Sedimentary petrology and mineralogy, especially clay mineralogy and sandstone petrology; x-ray diffraction and crystallography; sedimentary basin analysis; Alaska and California geology. *Mailing Add:* 1517 W Briarwood Ave Littleton CO 80120

HAYES, JOHN MICHAEL, BIOGEOCHEMISTRY, MASS SPECTROMETRY. *Current Pos:* SR SCIENTIST, DEPT GEOL & GEOPHYS & DIR, NAT OCEAN SCI ACCELERATOR MASS SPECTROMETRY FACIL, WOODS HOLE OCEANOG INST, 96-; PROF PRACT BIOGEOCHEM, DEPT EARTH PLANETARY SCI, HARVARD UNIV, 97- *Personal Data:* b Seattle, Wash, Sept 6, 40; m 62, Janice M Boeke; c 3. *Educ:* Iowa State Univ, SB, 62; Mass Inst Technol, PhD(analytical chem), 66. *Honors & Awards:* Urey Medal, Europ Asn Geochem, 97. *Prof Exp:* Res assoc cosmochem, Enrico Fermi Inst, Univ Chicago, 66; sr scientist, Ames Res Ctr, NASA, 67-68; NATO fel org chem, Org Geochem Res Unit, Bristol, Eng, 69; from asst prof to prof chem & geol, Ind Univ, Bloomington, 70-84, prof, 84-90, distinguished prof biogeochem, 90-96, chmn, geol sci, 94-96. *Concurrent Pos:* Ed, Geochimica et Cosmochimica Acta, 71-74; consult, Hq, NASA, 71-79; mem, Precambrian Paleobiol Res Group, Univ Calif, Los Angeles, 79-80; Guggenheim fel, 87-88. *Mem:* Geochem Soc; Am Soc Mass Spectrometry; Am Geophys Union. *Res:* Natural chemistry of the isotopes of the volatile elements; development of relevant new techniques. *Mailing Add:* Nat Ocean Scis Accelerator Mass Spectrometry Fac Woods Hole Oceangraphy Inst Woods Hole Bloomington MA 02543-1539. *Fax:* 508-457-2183; *E-Mail:* jhayes@whoi.edu

HAYES, JOHN TERRENCE, ORTHOPEDIC SURGERY. *Current Pos:* RETIRED. *Personal Data:* b Howard City, Mich, Dec 8, 28; m 95, Marilyn Miele; c Brian, John M, Catherine, Karen, Colleen, John Jr, Anne & Laurie. *Educ:* Univ Mich, BS, 47, MD, 51. *Prof Exp:* Instr surg, Univ Mich, 56-58, from asst prof to assoc prof, 58-66; prof orthop surg & chief dept orthop surg & rehab, Bowman Gray Sch Med, 66-72. *Concurrent Pos:* Chief, Orthop Surg Serv, Wayne Co Gen Hosp, Eloise, 56-66; attend surgeon, US Vet Hosp, Ann Arbor, 56-66; fel ABC Traveling, 63; res fel, March of Dimes. *Mem:* Am Med Asn; Am Col Surg; Am Acad Orthop Surg. *Res:* Bone growth and repair; infectious diseases of bones and joints; orthopaedic implications of myelodysplasia (spina bifida). *Mailing Add:* 1342 Westgate Center Dr Winston-Salem NC 27103-2933. *Fax:* 919-760-3516

HAYES, JOHN THOMPSON, INSECT ECOLOGY, MINORITY SCIENCE EDUCATION. *Current Pos:* dir, Pre-Prof Sci Progs, Paine Col, 79-84 & 85-87, coordr, biol dept, 73-74 & 79, chairperson Div Natural Sci Math, 75-78, dir, Text Skills Develop Ctr, 87-90, BIOL FAC, PAINE COL, 69-, DIR PRE-PROF SCI PROGS & CHAIRPERSON, DIV NATURAL SCI MATH, 90- *Personal Data:* b Newton, Mass, Sept 10, 40; m 65, 80; c 3. *Educ:* Amherst Col, BA, 62; Cornell Univ, MS, 66, PhD(insect ecol), 68. *Prof Exp:* NIH fel, Savannah River Ecol Lab, Univ Ga, 67-69, US AEC res assoc, 69-73. *Concurrent Pos:* NIH Extramural Assoc, 78-79; mgr comput based educ, Med Col Ga, 84-85. *Mem:* Asn Educ Commun & Technol; Sigma Xi; NY Acad Sci. *Res:* Insect ecology; federal agencies and historically black institutions; plant succession; microcomputers in education; affective aspects of educational success and personal health. *Mailing Add:* Biol Dept Paine Col 1235 15th St Augusta GA 30910-2799

HAYES, JOHN WILLIAM, BIOCHEMISTRY, SOLAR PHYSICS. *Current Pos:* dean fac, 85-89, PROF CHEM, MARLBORO COL, 73-, DEAN FAC, 95- *Personal Data:* b Johnstown, Pa, Sept 8, 44; m 67, Joanne McNeil; c Stefanie & Andrew. *Educ:* Ill Benedictine Col, BS, 66; Purdue Univ, PhD(biochem), 71. *Prof Exp:* Fel & res assoc biol, Johns Hopkins Univ, 71-73. *Concurrent Pos:* Assoc ed & book rev ed, Passive Solar J, 81-86 & ed-in-chief, Progress in Passive Solar Energy, 82-84; mem bd dirs, Am Solar Energy Soc, 81-84, secy, 83, vchmn, 84. *Mem:* Am Chem Soc; AAAS; Int Solar Energy Soc; Am Solar Energy Soc (secy, 83). *Res:* Solar heating of buildings. *Mailing Add:* Marlboro Col Marlboro VT 05344. *Fax:* 802-257-4154; *E-Mail:* jhayes@marlboro.edu

HAYES, JOHNNIE RAY, NUTRITIONAL BIOCHEMISTRY. *Current Pos:* MASTER TOXICOLOGIST, RJR NABISCO, INC, 85- *Personal Data:* b Winston-Salem, NC, June 18, 42; m 64; c 1. *Educ:* Pfeiffer Col, BS, 66; Appalachian State Univ, MS, 68; Va Polytech Inst & State Univ, PhD(biochem), 73. *Prof Exp:* Res assoc biochem, Va Polytech Inst & State Univ, 73-75; sr res assoc nutrit biochem, Cornell Univ, 75-80; asst prof, Dept Pharmacol, Med Col Va, 80-85. *Mem:* Am Chem Soc; AAAS; Am Inst Biol Sci; Sigma Xi; Soc Toxicol. *Res:* Microsomal metabolism of carcinogens; interactions between dietary insufficiencies and metabolism of foreign compounds; mode of action of the hepatocarcinogen aflatoxin. *Mailing Add:* PO Box 1487 Winston-Salem NC 27102-1487. *Fax:* 910-741-1468

HAYES, JOSEPH EDWARD, JR, BIOCHEMISTRY, RESEARCH ADMINISTRATION. *Current Pos:* RETIRED. *Personal Data:* b El Dorado, Ark, Nov 9, 27; m 61; c 2. *Educ:* Univ Wash, AB, 48, MA, 50, PhD(biochem), 53. *Prof Exp:* Res fel biophys, Univ Pa, 53-54; biochemist, Walter Reed Army Inst, Res, 54-57; biochemist, Nat Heart Inst, NIH, 57-65, scientist adminstr, Extramural Prog, Res Grants Br, 65-69, Nat Ctr Health Serv Res & Develop, 70-71, exec secy, Hemat Study Sect, Div Res Grants, 71-80. *Mem:* AAAS; Am Chem Soc. *Res:* Mechanisms of enzymic reactions; fluorescence and phosphorescence phenomena; general hematology. *Mailing Add:* 11017 Madison St Kensington MD 20895

HAYES, KENNETH CRONISE, NUTRITIONAL PATHOLOGY. *Current Pos:* chmn, 87-90, PROF BIOL, BRANDEIS UNIV, 83-, DIR, FOSTER BIOMED RES LAB, 83- *Personal Data:* b San Francisco, Calif, Sept 24, 39; m 61; c 2. *Educ:* Wesleyan Univ, BA, 61; Cornell Univ, DVM, 65; Univ Conn, PhD(nutrit path), 68. *Prof Exp:* NIH res fel nutrit path, Harvard Univ, 68-69, res assoc, 69-70, from asst prof to assoc prof nutrit, Sch Pub Health, 70-83, chmn, Nutrit Div, New Eng Regional Primate Res Ctr, 78-83. *Concurrent Pos:* NIH career develop grant, Sch Pub Health, Harvard Univ, 72-77; mem, Nutrit Study Sect, NIH, 74-78 & Human Nutrit Adv Coun, USDA, 84-88; mem, Arteriosclerosis Coun, Am Heart Asn. *Mem:* rm Inst Nutrit; Am Soc Clin Nutrit; Int Acad Path; Soc Exp Biol & Med; Am Heart Asn. *Res:* Nutritional regulation of serum lipids and associated ultrastructure of atherogenesis in nonhuman primates; taurine and bile acid metabolism; diet and gallstones. *Mailing Add:* Foster Biomed Res Lab Brandeis Univ Waltham MA 02254. *Fax:* 781-736-2054

HAYES, KIRBY MAXWELL, food technology; deceased, see previous edition for last biography

HAYES, MARK ALLAN, SURGERY. *Current Pos:* from assoc prof to prof, 52-80, EMER PROF SURG, SCH MED, YALE UNIV, 80- *Personal Data:* b Bay City, Mich, Oct 19, 14; m 48; c 1. *Educ:* Univ Mich, AB, 37, MD, 40, PhD(anat), 48, MS, 51. *Hon Degrees:* MA, Yale Univ. *Prof Exp:* From intern to resident surg, Univ Mich Hosp, 40-43, instr anat, Med Sch, 46-48, instr surg, Univ Hosp & res assoc, AEC Lab, 49-51, asst prof surg, 51-52. *Concurrent Pos:* Kellogg fel, Univ Mich. *Mem:* Sigma Xi. *Res:* Gastrointestinal surgery; surgical anatomy; surgical metabolism and endocrinology. *Mailing Add:* 163 Ridgewood Ave North Haven CT 06473-4442

HAYES, MURRAY LAWRENCE, MARINE FISHERIES, OCEANOGRAPHY. *Current Pos:* CONSULT FISHERIES SCIENTIST, 86- *Personal Data:* b Ft Collins, Colo, July 17, 29; m 52; c 6. *Educ:* Univ Colo, BA, 51; Colo State Univ, MS, 57, PhD(zool), 59. *Prof Exp:* Fishery res biologist, US Bur Com Fisheries, Juneau, Alaska, 59-62, lab dir, Tech Lab, 62-70, assoc regional dir fisheries res, 70-71, dir, Kodiak Lab, 71-73; coordr energy related res, Nat Marine Fish Serv, Seattle, Wash, 73-77, dir resource assessment, 77-86. *Concurrent Pos:* Mem, Sci & Tech Comt, Pac Fisheries Coun, 76-86; affil prof, Univ Wash, Sch Fisheries, 79-; assoc ed, Am Fisheries Soc, 82-84. *Mem:* Am Fisheries Soc; Am Inst Fisheries Res Biol; Sigma Xi. *Res:* Composition, distribution, abundance and condition of commercial fish stocks of eastern North Pacific; king crab biology; commercial crustaceans; fisheries management; performance of commercial fishing gear; fisheries management analysis. *Mailing Add:* 20145 25th Ave NW Shoreline WA 98177-2451

HAYES, RAYMOND L, JR, ANATOMY, EMBRYOLOGY. *Current Pos:* CHMN DEPT ANAT, HOWARD UNIV SCH MED, 88- *Personal Data:* b Washington, DC, Feb 1, 38; m 61; c 3. *Educ:* Amherst Col, AB, 59; Univ Mich, MS, 61, PhD(anat), 63. *Prof Exp:* Instr anat, Harvard Med Sch, 63-65; asst prof, Sch Med, Univ Pittsburgh, 65-69, assoc prof anat & Cell Biol, 69-88. *Mem:* AAAS; Am Asn Anatomists; Tissue Cult Asn. *Res:* Application of in vitro techniques to problems of embryogenesis; myological organogenesis; differentiation of embryonic duodenum as affected by cortisone; reaggregation of dissociated embryonic cells. *Mailing Add:* Dept Anat & Cell Biol Howard Univ Sch Med 520 W St NW Washington DC 20059. *Fax:* 202-806-5212

HAYES, ROBERT ARTHUR, ORGANIC CHEMISTRY. *Current Pos:* RETIRED. *Personal Data:* b Kendallville, Ind, June 29, 20; m 46; c 1. *Educ:* Col Wooster, BA, 42; Univ Md, PhD(org chem), 48. *Prof Exp:* Asst chem, Univ Md, 42-44, res chemist, 46-48; chemist, Bur Entom & Plant Quarantine, USDA, Md, 44-45; res assoc, Allegheny Ballistics Lab, Md, 45; chemist, Firestone Tire & Rubber Co, 48-65, group leader plastics res, 65-67, mgr plastics & fibers res, 67-75, res assoc, 75-81, sr res assoc, 81-84. *Mem:* Am Chem Soc. *Res:* High polymers. *Mailing Add:* 2980 Cedar Hill Rd Cuyahoga Falls OH 44223-1239

HAYES, ROBERT E, CHEMISTRY. *Current Pos:* RETIRED. *Personal Data:* b Wilkes-Barre, Pa, Oct 1, 28. *Educ:* Union Col, BS; Univ Ill, PhD(food technol), 55, Mich Inst Technol, SM, 69. *Prof Exp:* Emer prof, Div Nat Sci, Olivet Nazarene Univ, Ill, 70-93. *Concurrent Pos:* Fulbright scholar, Nat Coun Sci Res, 95-96. *Mailing Add:* Olivet Nazarene Univ PO Box 595 Kankakee IL 60901

HAYES, ROBERT GREEN, PHYSICAL CHEMISTRY. *Current Pos:* From instr to assoc prof, 61-74, PROF CHEM, UNIV NOTRE DAME, 74- *Personal Data:* b Philadelphia, Pa, Oct 23, 36; m 60, Linda Joyce Shumaker; c Kevin, Brian, Amy, Derek & Sarah. *Educ:* Univ Pittsburgh, BS, 58; Univ Calif, Berkeley, PhD(phys chem), 62. *Mem:* AAAS; Am Chem Soc. *Res:* Experimental molecular structure and dynamics, primarily utilizing photoelectron spectroscopy. *Mailing Add:* 1909 Peachtree Lane South Bend IN 46617. *Fax:* 219-631-6652; *E-Mail:* hayes.1@nd.edu

HAYES, ROBERT M, WEED SCIENCE, ECOLOGY. *Current Pos:* PROF PLANT & SOIL SCI, UNIV TENN, 78- *Personal Data:* b Parsons, Tenn, Aug 7, 45; m 73, Kathryn Morris; c Shondra, Nathan & Nicholas. *Educ:* Univ Tenn, BS, 68; Univ Ill, PhD(agron), 74. *Prof Exp:* Asst prof agron, Univ Ky, 74-78. *Mem:* Weed Sci Soc Am; Am Soc Agron. *Res:* Development of effective weed control systems for soil and energy conserving methods of crop production; crop-weed ecosystems and their interactions; biology of individual weed species. *Mailing Add:* 605 Airways Blvd Jackson TN 38301. *Fax:* 901-425- 4729

HAYES, ROBERT MAYO, MATHEMATICS, INFORMATION SCIENCE. *Current Pos:* dean, Grad Sch Libr Serv, 74-89, prof, 64-90, EMER PROF SCH LIBR SERV, UNIV CALIF, LOS ANGELES, 90- *Personal Data:* b New York, NY, Dec 3, 26; m 52, Alice Peters; c Robert D. *Educ:* Univ Calif, Los Angeles, BA, 47, MA, 49, PhD(math), 52. *Honors & Awards:* Award Merit Am Soc Info Sci. *Prof Exp:* Mathematician, Nat Bur Stand, 49-52; res mathematician, Hughes Aircraft Co, 52-53; appln specialist, Nat Cash Register Co, 53-55; head, Bus Systs Dept, Res Labs, Magnavox Co, 55-59; vpres & sci dir, Electrada Corp, 59-64; pres, Adv Info Systs, Inc, 61-64. *Concurrent Pos:* Dir, Inst Library Res, Univ Calif, 64-70; vpres, Becker & Hayes, Inc, 70-73, 93- *Mem:* AAAS (vpres); Am Math Soc; Asn Comput Mach; Am Soc Info Sci (pres, 63). *Res:* Hilbert space; numerical analysis; data processing systems. *Mailing Add:* 3943 Woodfield Dr Sherman Oaks CA 91403. *E-Mail:* rhayes@ucla.edu

HAYES, RUSSELL E, ELECTRICAL ENGINEERING. *Current Pos:* PROF ELEC ENG, UNIV COLO, 63- *Personal Data:* b Wichita, Kans, Nov 14, 35; m 57, 83; c 4. *Educ:* Univ Kans, BS, 58, MS, 59; Stanford Univ, PhD(elec eng), 63. *Concurrent Pos:* Vis asst prof, Cornell Univ, 66-67. *Mem:* Inst Elec & Electronics Engrs. *Res:* Physics of semiconductor materials and devices. *Mailing Add:* Dept Elec & Comput Eng Univ Colo Boulder CO 80309-0425

HAYES, SHELDON P, immunology, bacteriology; deceased, see previous edition for last biography

HAYES, TERENCE JAMES, IMMUNOLOGY, PATHOLOGY. *Current Pos:* sr scientist parasitol, Hoffmann-La Roche Inc, 71-74, asst res group chief chemother & parasitol, Animal Health Res Dept, 74-78, res group chief, 78-86, res leader, Dept Toxicol & Path, 86-89, DIR INVESTIGATIVE TOXICOL, DEPT TOXICOL & PATH, HOFFMANN-LA ROCHE INC, 89- *Personal Data:* b Weehawken, NJ, Feb 25, 41; m 68; c 2. *Educ:* Univ Scranton, BS, 62; Univ Pa, VMD, 66, PhD(parasitol), 70; Am Bd Toxicol, cert, 80. *Prof Exp:* Res fel, Lab Parasitol, Univ Pa, 66-70. *Mem:* Am Vet Med Asn; Am Asn Vet Parasitologists; Soc Toxicol; Am Asn Immunologist. *Res:* Toxicologic, immunological and pathologic effects of drugs and cytokines in laboratory animals. *Mailing Add:* 525 Park St Montclair NJ 07043

HAYES, THOMAS B, HYDRAULIC & HYDROELECTRIC UTILITY SYSTEMS. *Current Pos:* RETIRED. *Educ:* Ore State Univ, BS; Mass Inst Technol, SM. *Prof Exp:* Founding partner & consult, CH2M Hill, Inc, 46-77. *Concurrent Pos:* Mem & past pres, State Ore Bd Eng Examiners; mem, Gov Alt Energy Develop Comn. *Mem:* Fel Am Soc Mech Engrs; fel Inst Elec & Electronics Engrs; Nat Soc Prof Engrs. *Res:* Effects of HVDC power transmission on buried structures; hydraulic systems; inventor developer of FLOmatcher scheme; conduit entrances and pumping station arrangements. *Mailing Add:* Ch2M Hill Inc PO Box 428 Corvallis OR 97333

HAYES, THOMAS G, HISTOLOGY, CYTOGENETICS. *Current Pos:* from instr to assoc prof, 65-78, PROF ANAT & ORAL BIOL, OHIO STATE UNIV, 78- *Personal Data:* b Canonsburg, Pa, July 3, 36; m 65, Sylvia Oprita; c Thomas M. *Educ:* Washington & Jefferson Col, BA, 58; Case Western Res Univ, MA, 60; Ohio State Univ, PhD(anat), 65. *Prof Exp:* Grad asst biol, Case Western Res Univ, 58-60. *Concurrent Pos:* Fel, Tissue Cult Div, Nat Cancer Inst, 67. *Mem:* Am Asn Anat; Sigma Xi. *Res:* Cytogenetic and teratogenic effects of anticonvulsant drugs. *Mailing Add:* Dept Cell Biol Neurobiol/Anat Ohio State Univ Col Med 4058 Graves Hall 333 W Tenth Ave Columbus OH 43210. *Fax:* 614-292-7659

HAYES, THOMAS JAY, III, CIVIL ENGINEERING. *Current Pos:* RETIRED. *Personal Data:* b Omaha, Nebr, Aug 26, 14; m 42, Jean Pedley; c Helen (Attride) & Barbara (Beddow). *Educ:* US Mil Acad, BS, 36; Mass Inst Technol, MS, 39, Engr, 40. *Honors & Awards:* George W Goethals Medal, Soc Am Mil Engrs, 61. *Prof Exp:* Engr officer, US, Greenland, Bahamas, Can & Alaska, CEngrs, US Army, 36-43, mem fac & asst commandant, Eng Sch, Ft Belvoir, Va, 44-45, eng liaison officer & asst mil attache, London, Eng, 46-49, asst eng comnr, Washington DC govt, 49-52, dist engr, Little Rock, Ark, 52-53 & Omaha, 53-57, engr, I Corps, Korea, 58-59, chief, Los Angeles Field Off, Off Chief Engrs, 59-60, vcomdr & comdr, CEngrs Ballistic Missile Construct Off, Los Angeles, 60-62, asst chief engrs NASA support & dep dir mil construct for space progs, Off Chief Engrs, 62-64, dir topography & mil eng, 64-67, comdr, SAtlantic Div, CE, Atlanta, Ga, 67-69; pres, Int Eng Co, Inc, 69-79, chmn, 79-80; dir, Burke Co, 79-87. *Concurrent Pos:* Mem, Permanent Int Asn Navig Cong, 51-80, US Comt Large Dams, 53-80; mem fed exec bd, Bd Engrs Rivers & Harbors, Coastal Eng Res Bd, 67-69; vchmn, SE Basin Inter Agency Comn, 67-69; pres, Cia Int de Ingenieria, Santiago, Chile, Asuncion, Paraguay, 69-80, & Int Eng Co, Kinshasa, Zaire, Cent Africa, 72-80; vpres, Morrison-Knudson Co, Inc, Boise, Idaho, 71-76; dir, Int Road Fedn, 78-79; consult, 80-88. *Mem:* Nat Acad Eng; fel Am Soc Civil Engrs; Soc Am Mil Engrs; Am Pub Works Asn. *Res:* Engineering experience in connection with projects in 60 countries plus the Arctic and Antarctic. *Mailing Add:* 2646 Chestnut St San Francisco CA 94123

HAYES, THOMAS L, BIOPHYSICS. *Current Pos:* BIOPHYSICIST, DONNER LAB & LAWRENCE BERKELEY LAB, UNIV CALIF, 55-, DEP DIR, DONNER LAB, 80- *Personal Data:* b Oakland, Calif, Sept 12, 27; m 52; c 5. *Educ:* Univ Calif, Berkeley, AB, 49, PhD(biophys), 55. *Concurrent Pos:* Adj prof biophysics, Univ Calif, Berkeley, 59- *Mem:* AAAS; Biophys Soc; Electron Micros Soc Am. *Res:* Scanning electron microscopy. *Mailing Add:* 6666 Colton Blvd Oakland CA 94611

HAYES, TIMOTHY MITCHELL, SOLID STATE PHYSICS. *Current Pos:* chair, 89-92, PROF PHYSICS, RENSSELAER POLYTECH INST, 89- *Personal Data:* b Springfield, Mass, Nov 1, 41; m 62, Linn Spencer; c Andrew & Michael. *Educ:* Bowdoin Col, BA, 63; Harvard Univ, AM, 65, PhD(appl physics), 68. *Prof Exp:* Res assoc, Stanford Univ, 67-69; scientist, Palo Alto Res Ctr, Xerox Corp, 69-70, mem res staff, 70-86; prof physics, Colo Sch Mines, 86-89. *Concurrent Pos:* Vis scientist, Atomic Energy Res Estab, Harwell, UK, 70; sr vis fel sci & eng res coun, Leicester Univ, UK, 81-82. *Mem:* Am Phys Soc. *Res:* Electron states in solids, especially eigenstates, cohesive energy, effects of disorder; thermal and electronic transport in disordered solids; atomic-scale structure of materials, and its relationship to electronic properties; x-ray absorption spectroscopy. *Mailing Add:* Physics Dept Rensselaer Polytech Inst Troy NY 12180-3590. *Fax:* 518-276-6680; *E-Mail:* thayes@rpi.edu

HAYES, WILBUR FRANK, ZOOLOGY. *Current Pos:* asst prof, 67-71, ASSOC PROF BIOL, WILKES COL, 71- *Personal Data:* b Rhinelander, Wis, Nov 10, 36; div; c Lynn, Robert, Dana, Richard, Gary & Kevin. *Educ:* Colby Col, BA, 59; Lehigh Univ, MS, 61, PhD(biol), 65. *Prof Exp:* Asst biol, Lehigh Univ, 60-65; Nat Inst Gen Med Sci res fel & lectr biol, Yale Univ, 65-67. *Concurrent Pos:* Vis assoc prof, Northeastern Univ, 87-88. *Mem:* Soc Integrative & Comp Biol; Sigma Xi; Micros Soc Am. *Res:* Comparative physiology of arthropod sense organs, especially proprioceptors and chemoreceptors in Limulus. *Mailing Add:* Dept Biol Stark Learning Ctr Wilkes Univ Wilkes-Barre PA 18766. *E-Mail:* whayes@wilkes1.wilkes.edu

HAYES, WILLIS B, GEOLOGY, COMPUTER-ASSISTED INSTRUCTION. *Current Pos:* assoc zool, 73-76, RES ASSOC GEOL, UNIV GA, 77- *Personal Data:* b Long Beach, Calif, Aug 23, 42; div. *Educ:* Stanford Univ, BA, 63; Scripps Inst Oceanog, PhD(oceanog), 69. *Prof Exp:* Res ecologist, marine ecol, Inst Marine Resources, 69-70; asst prof biol, Am Univ Beirut, 70-73. *Concurrent Pos:* Vis asst prof biol, Univ Victoria, 75. *Mem:* Nat Asn Geol Teachers; AAAS. *Res:* Geological modeling; geostatistics; computer-assisted instruction. *Mailing Add:* Rte 4 Box 4052 Danielsville GA 30633

HAYFLICK, LEONARD, CELL BIOLOGY, GERONTOLOGY. *Current Pos:* PROF ANAT, UNIV CALIF, SCH MED, DEPT ANAT, 88- *Personal Data:* b Philadelphia, Pa, May 20, 28; m 55; c 5. *Educ:* Univ Pa, BA, 51, MS, 53, PhD(med microbiol & chem), 56. *Honors & Awards:* Brookdale Award, Geront Soc Am, 80; Robert W Kleemeier Award, Geront Soc Am, 82-83; Leadership Award, Am Fedn Aging Res, 83; Pres Award, Int Orgn

Mycoplasmology, 84; Samuel Roberts Noble Res Award, 84; Stuart Mudd Mem Award lectr, 85; Sandoz Prize Gerontol, Int Asn Gerontol, 91. *Prof Exp:* Asst bact, Merck Sharp & Dohme, Inc, 51-52; asst instr med microbiol, Univ Pa, 55-56, asst prof, 65-68; assoc med microbiol & mem staff, Wistar Inst Anat & Biol, 58-68; prof med microbiol, Sch Med, Stanford Univ, 68-76; sr res cell biologist, Children's Hosp Med Ctr, Bruce Lyon Mem Res Lab, Oakland, Calif, 76-81; prof zool, immunol & microbiol, Ctr Geront Studies, Univ Fla, 81-88. *Concurrent Pos:* Vis scientist, Weizmann Inst Sci, Rehovoth, Israel, 80; ed-in-chief, Exp Geront, 85-; hon mem, Tissue Cult Asn, 89; hon lectr, Univ Brescia & Univ Parma, Italy, 91; vis prof, Kurume Univ Med Sch, Japan, 92-, Oita Med Univ, Oita, Japan, 93-; academician, Ukrainian Acad Med Sci, 95. *Mem:* Fel AAAS; Am Soc Microbiol; Tissue Cult Asn (vpres); Am Soc Cell Biol; fel Geront Soc (vpres). *Res:* Gerontology; cell culture; human diploid cell strains; viral oncogenesis; mycoplasmas; vaccine development. *Mailing Add:* Univ Calif San Francisco 36991 Greencroft Close PO Box 89 The Sea Ranch CA 95497. *Fax:* 707-785-3809; *E-Mail:* hayflick.leonard@gene.com

HAYGARTH, JOHN CHARLES, MATERIALS SCIENCE. *Current Pos:* sr res scientist, Teledyne Wah Chang, Albany, Ore, 70-79, chief process engr, 79-80, prin res scientist, 80-84, DIR RES & DEVELOP, TELEDYNE WAH CHANG, ALBANY, ORE, 85- *Personal Data:* b Keighley, Yorks, Sept 4, 40; US citizen; m 75. *Educ:* Univ Leeds, BSc, 62, PhD(phys chem), 65. *Prof Exp:* Res geophysicist, Inst Geophysics, Univ Calif, Los Angeles, 65-68; res scientist, E I du Pont de Nemours & Co, Inc, 68-69; res geophysicist, Inst Geophysics, Univ Calif, Los Angeles, 69-70. *Mem:* Am Chem Soc; Am Inst Mining Metall & Petrol Engrs; AAAS; Am Ceramics Soc; Vacuum Soc. *Res:* Extractive metallurgy of group IVA, VA and VIA metals; halide chemistry of groups III, IV, V and VI; chemical thermodynamics; material properties of metals and refractory hard materials; solar energy materials. *Mailing Add:* 37699 Govier Pl Corvallis OR 97330-9317

HAYGOOD, MARGO GENEVIEVE, CONTRACT RESEARCH, MARINE MICROBIOLOGY. *Current Pos:* sci officer admin, 85-88, asst prof, 88-, ASSOC PROF, OFF NAVAL RES, UNIV CALIF, SAN DIEGO. *Personal Data:* b Chicago, Ill, Oct 20, 54; m 82. *Educ:* Harvard Univ, BA, 76; Scripps Inst Oceanog, Univ Calif, San Diego, PhD(marine biol), 84. *Prof Exp:* Sr res fel, Univ Wash, 84-85. *Concurrent Pos:* Mem adv comt to dir, NIH, 76; Monbusho scholar, Univ Tokyo, 79-80; assoc res scientist, Johns Hopkins Univ & Chesapeake Bay Inst, 85-88. *Mem:* Am Soc Microbiol. *Res:* Marine microbiology; microbial physiology; molecular genetics; iron regulation of bacterial bioluminescence; molecular biology of bacterial symbiosis; genetics of methylotrophic bacteria. *Mailing Add:* Scripps Inst Oceanog MBRD A-002 Univ Calif La Jolla CA 92093-0202

HAYGREEN, JOHN G, WOOD TECHNOLOGY. *Current Pos:* ASSOC DEAN, SCH FORESTRY, AUBURN UNIV, 86- *Personal Data:* b Champaign, Ill, Oct 10, 30; m 52; c 2. *Educ:* Iowa State Univ, BS, 52; Mich State Univ, MS, 58, PhD(forest prod), 61. *Prof Exp:* Asst prof forest prod, Mich State Univ, 58-61; asst prof, Colo State Univ, 61-63; from assoc prof to prof forest prod, Univ Minn, St Paul, 63-86, head dept, Col Forestry, 71-84. *Concurrent Pos:* Consult, Wood Sci Serv; dir, Viking Eng & Develop. *Mem:* Soc Wood Sci & Tech (pres, 69); Forest Prod Res Soc (pres, 77-78); Am Soc Test & Mat; Brit Inst Wood Sci; Soc Am Foresters; fel Int Acad Wood Sci. *Res:* Wood mechanics; mechanical behavior of fiber and particle products; applications to building design; author of 50 papers on wood utilization. *Mailing Add:* 38 Dogwood Trail Dadeville AL 36853

HAYLES, WILLIAM JOSEPH, PHYSICAL CHEMISTRY, INORGANIC CHEMISTRY. *Current Pos:* RETIRED. *Personal Data:* b Dunellen, NJ, Jan 10, 27; m 48; c 3. *Educ:* Wesleyan Univ, BA, 50; Iowa State Univ, PhD(phys chem), 59. *Prof Exp:* From asst prof to assoc prof chem, Rochester Inst Technol, 54-64, prof, 64-80; mem staff, AT&T Bell Labs, 80-94. *Concurrent Pos:* Vis prof, Mich State Univ, 69-70. *Mem:* Am Chem Soc. *Res:* Applications of computers in chemical instrumentation. *Mailing Add:* 29 Lake Park Dr Piscataway NJ 08854-5123

HAYMAKER, RICHARD WEBB, THEORETICAL PHYSICS. *Current Pos:* asst prof, 71-76, assoc prof, 76-82, PROF PHYSICS, LA STATE UNIV, BATON ROUGE, 82- *Personal Data:* b San Francisco, Calif, Feb 13, 40; m 70; c 2. *Educ:* Carleton Col, BA, 61; Univ Calif, Berkeley, PhD(physics), 67. *Prof Exp:* Asst res physicist, Univ Calif, Santa Barbara, 67-69, lectr physics, 69; instr & res assoc, Cornell Univ, 69-70, actg asst prof, 70-71. *Concurrent Pos:* Vis staff mem, Los Alamos Sci Lab, NMex, 77-78; vis scientist, KEK Nat Lab, Tsukuba, Japan, 85, Tata Inst, Bombay, India, 86. *Mem:* Am Phys Soc. *Res:* Theoretical physics; study of elementary particle dynamics and symmetries. *Mailing Add:* Dept Physics & Astron La State Univ Baton Rouge LA 70803

HAYMAN, ALAN CONRAD, liquid chromatography, for more information see previous edition

HAYMAN, SELMA, ENZYMOLOGY. *Current Pos:* ATTY, 86- *Personal Data:* b New York, NY, May 18, 31. *Educ:* Antioch Col, BS, 53; Univ Wis, MS, 56, PhD(biochem), 61; Widener Univ Sch Law, JD, 86. *Prof Exp:* Proj asst, Univ Wis, 57-61; res fel ophthal biochem, Howe Lab, Harvard Med Sch, 61-65; res assoc, Inst Cancer Res, 65-73; res assoc chem, Univ Del, 73-83. *Mem:* AAAS. *Res:* Isolation and characterization of enzymes; study of enzyme active sites; study of relationship of enzyme structure to function. *Mailing Add:* 32 Rose Circle Newark DE 19711. *Fax:* 302-888-7716

HAYMES, ROBERT C, ASTROPHYSICS. *Current Pos:* from asst prof to assoc prof, 64-72, chmn dept, 82-87, PROF SPACE PHYSICS & ASTRON, RICE UNIV, 72- *Personal Data:* b New York, NY, July 3, 31; m 65, Jamie Buswell; c Douglas, Lisa & Nancy. *Educ:* NY Univ, BA, 52, MS, 53, PhD(physics), 59. *Honors & Awards:* Humboldt Award, Alexander von Humboldt Soc, 76. *Prof Exp:* Asst, NY Univ, 52-58, from instr to asst prof physics, 58-62; res fel, Jet Propulsion Lab, Calif Inst Technol, 62-64. *Concurrent Pos:* Prin investr, var res grants, 65-; chmn, Adv Panel Sci Ballooning, Univ Corp Atmospheric Res, 72-74; assoc, Baker Col, 78-82,; master, Will Rice Col, 82-87; secy-treas, High Energy Astrophys Div, Am Astron Soc, 87-90; chief scientist, Astrophys Div, NASA Hq, Washington, DC, 88-90; master, Brown Col, 93-; bd dirs, Tex Space Grant Consortium, 93- *Mem:* Am Astron Soc; Int Astron Union; Am Asn Univ Professors; Sigma Xi. *Res:* Cosmic rays; gamma ray astronomy; conducts measurements of nuclear gamma rays from various cosmic and atmospheric sources; cosmic ray neutrons. *Mailing Add:* Space Physics & Astron Dept Rice Univ Houston TX 77251-1892. *Fax:* 713-285-5143; *E-Mail:* rhaymes@spacvax.rice.edu

HAYMET, ANTHONY DOUGLAS-JOHN, STATISTICAL MECHANICS, THEORY OF LIQUIDS. *Current Pos:* ASST PROF CHEM, UNIV SYDNEY, 91- *Personal Data:* b Sydney, Australia, Feb 5, 56. *Educ:* Sydney Univ, BSc, 78, DSc, 97; Univ Chicago, PhD(chem), 81. *Honors & Awards:* Distinguished Young Chemist Award, Fedn Asian Chem Socs; Antarctic Sci Medal, US Navy. *Prof Exp:* Res fel physics, Harvard Univ, 81-83; asst prof chem, Univ Calif, Berkeley, 83-88 & Univ Utah, 88-91. *Concurrent Pos:* Presidential Young Investr Award, NSF, 85-90; Alfred P Sloan res fel, 86. *Mem:* Am Chem Soc; Am Phys Soc; Royal Australian Chem Inst. *Res:* Theoretical physical chemistry; theory and applications of statistical mechanics and quantum mechanics; proton transfer in solution; melting, freezing, glass formation nucleation and crystal growth; theory of liquids, liquid crystals and plastic crystals. *Mailing Add:* Dept Chem Univ Sydney Sydney NSW 2006 Australia

HAYMOND, HERMAN RALPH, MEDICAL IMAGING MAGNETIC RESONANCE IMAGING & SPECTROSCOPY. *Current Pos:* from asst prof to assoc prof, 55-68, PROF RADIOL, SCH MED, UNIV SOUTHERN CALIF, 68- *Personal Data:* b Salt Lake City, Utah, Aug 29, 24; m 49, Patricia Hindley; c Charles, Janice, Robert, Patricia, Philip & Elizabeth. *Educ:* Univ Calif, AB, 44, PhD(biophys), 55. *Prof Exp:* Physicist, Radiation Lab, Univ Calif, 47-55. *Concurrent Pos:* Radiation physicist, Los Angeles Co-Univ Southern Calif Med Ctr, 55-70, head radiation physicist, 70-74, head med radiation physicist, 74-86. *Mem:* Radiol Soc NAm; Inst Elec & Electronics Engrs; Am Chem Soc; Am Asn Physicists Med. *Res:* Radiologic physics; medical imaging; magnetic resonance imaging and spectroscopy. *Mailing Add:* Sch Med PO Box 304 Univ Southern Calif 1200 N State St Los Angeles CA 90033

HAYMORE, BARRY LANT, ORGANOMETALLIC CHEMISTRY, HOMOGENEOUS CATALYSIS. *Current Pos:* sr res scientist, 80-90, SCI FEL, CORP RES LABS, MONSANTO CO, ST LOUIS, MO, 90- *Personal Data:* b Melbourne, Australia, Nov 1, 45; US citizen; m 69, Shirley McCain; c 7. *Educ:* Univ Ariz, BSc, 68; Brigham Young Univ, MSc, 70; Northwestern Univ, PhD(inorg chem), 74. *Prof Exp:* Asst prof inorg chem, Ind Univ, Bloomington, 75-80. *Mem:* Am Chem Soc; Sigma Xi. *Res:* Coordination chemistry and reactions of pi-bonded nitrogen containing ligands; mechanisms of homogeneous catalysts; chemistry and structures of macrocyclic ligands; interactions of proteins with transition metal ions; inorganic and bioinorganic. *Mailing Add:* 13384 Walfield Lane St Louis MO 63141. *Fax:* 314-694-5953

HAYN, CARL HUGO, PHYSICS. *Current Pos:* from instr to assoc prof, 55-74, PROF PHYSICS, UNIV SANTA CLARA, 74- *Personal Data:* b Los Angeles, Calif, July 13, 16. *Educ:* Gonzaga Univ, AB, 39, AM, 40; Alma Col, STL, 48; St Louis Univ, PhD(physics), 55. *Prof Exp:* Teacher pvt sch, Calif, 40-43; instr physics, Loyola Univ, Calif, 43-44. *Mem:* Am Asn Physics Teachers. *Res:* Solid state; photoconductivity and photoemission; nuclear spectroscopy. *Mailing Add:* Dept Physics Univ Santa Clara Santa Clara CA 95053-0315

HAYNE, DON WILLIAM, BIOMETRICS. *Current Pos:* tech dir, 62-81, EMER PROF, SOUTHEASTERN COOP FISH & GAME STATIST PROJ, INST STATIST & PROF ZOOL & STATIST, NC STATE UNIV, 81- *Personal Data:* b Elgin, Ill, Apr 27, 11; m 60; c 3. *Educ:* Kalamazoo Col, AB, 32; Univ Mich, MA, 33, PhD(zool), 37. *Prof Exp:* Asst mus zool & lab vert genetics, Univ Mich, 33-37; asst econ vert zool, Agr Exp Sta, Mich State Col, 37-45, from asst prof to assoc prof zool, 45-57; biometrician, Inst Fisheries Res, State Dept Conserv, Mich, 57-60; staff biometrician, Br Wildlife Res, US Fish & Wildlife Serv, 60-62. *Concurrent Pos:* Fel, Univ Chicago, 53-54. *Mem:* AAAS; Am Soc Mammal; Wildlife Soc; Ecol Soc Am; Am Fisheries Soc; Sigma Xi. *Res:* Quantitative ecology; fish and wildlife statistics; pesticide ecology; variation of the oldfield mouse in northwestern Florida. *Mailing Add:* 151 Carol Woods 750 Weaver Dairy Rd Chapel Hill NC 27514-1440

HAYNES, BARTON F, RHEUMATOLOGY, CLINICAL IMMUNOLOGY. *Current Pos:* fac, 80-87, chief, Div Rheumat, Allergy & Clin Immunol, 87-95, FREDERIC M HANES PROF & CHAIR, DEPT MED, DUKE UNIV, 95- *Personal Data:* b Tenn. *Educ:* Univ Tenn, BS; Baylor Univ, MD. *Honors & Awards:* Lee C Howley Sr Prizer, Arthritis Found, 95. *Prof Exp:* Researcher, Nat Inst Allergy & Infectious Dis, NIH, 75-80. *Concurrent Pos:* Dir, Duke Univ Arthritis Ctr; co-dir, Duke Human Vaccine Inst. *Mem:* Inst Med-Nat Acad Sci. *Res:* Human t-cells in immune system development; host response to infectious agents; t-cell involvement in development of autoimmune and inflammatory syndromes. *Mailing Add:* Dept Med Duke Univ 1102 Hosp N Box 3703 Med Ctr Durham NC 27710

HAYNES, BOYD W, JR, SURGERY. *Current Pos:* from asst prof to assoc prof, 53-66, chmn, Div Trauma Surg, 72-82, DIR, BURN UNIT, MED COL VA, COMMONWEALTH UNIV, 54-, PROF SURG, 66- *Personal Data:* b Brandenburg, Ky, July 5, 17; m 55; c 6. *Educ:* Univ Louisville, AB, 38, MD, 41; Am Bd Surg, dipl. *Prof Exp:* Instr surg, Med Col Va, 48-49; asst prof, Baylor Col Med, 50-53. *Mem:* Fel Am Col Surg; Am Surg Asn; Soc Univ Surg; Am Asn Surg of Trauma; Am Burn Asn (past pres); Int Soc Burn Injury; Int Soc Surg; Surg Infection Soc. *Res:* Treatment of burns; author of 77 publications on burns and trauma. *Mailing Add:* 751 J Clyde Morris Blvd Newport News VA 23601

HAYNES, CALEB VANCE, JR, QUATERNARY GEOLOGY, RADIOCARBON DATING. *Current Pos:* PROF GEOL & ANTHROP, UNIV ARIZ, 74- *Personal Data:* b Spokane, Wash, Feb 29, 28; m 54; c 1. *Educ:* Colo Sch Mines, Geol Engr, 56; Univ Ariz, PhD(geol), 65. *Honors & Awards:* Roald Fryxell Award, 78; Archaeol Geol Award, Geol Soc Am, 84. *Prof Exp:* Sr engr, Am Inst Res, 56-59 & Martin Co, 60-62; asst prof geochronol, Univ Ariz, 65-68; from assoc prof to prof geol, Southern Methodist Univ, 68-74. *Concurrent Pos:* Consult, Nat Geog Soc, 62-; Guggenheim fel, 80-81; Smithsonian sr postdoctoral fel, 87. *Mem:* Nat Acad Sci; Am Quaternary Asn (pres, 76-78); fel AAAS; fel Geol Soc Am; Soc Am Archaeol; Sigma Xi. *Res:* Pleistocene geology; Paleo-Indian archaeology; lunar geology; geochronology of late Quaternary time; shuttle imaging radar and geomorphology of the eastern Sahara, Egypt and Sudan; archaeological geology of Custer Battlefield National Monument. *Mailing Add:* Dept Anthrop Univ Ariz Tucson AZ 85721

HAYNES, DEAN L, PLANT PROTECTION, POPULATION DYNAMICS. *Current Pos:* from asst prof to assoc prof, 66-74, EMER PROF ENTOM, MICH STATE UNIV, 74- *Personal Data:* b Mich, Sept 27, 32; m 56; c 3. *Educ:* Mich State Univ, BS, 54, MS, 57, PhD(entom), 60. *Prof Exp:* Forest biologist, Can Dept Forestry, 60-65; asst prof entom, NDak State Univ, 65-66. *Res:* Population ecology of insect pests of agriculture crops; design and management of environmental systems for pest control; pest management and the analysis of agroecosystems. *Mailing Add:* Dept Entom 243 Nat Sci Bldg Mich State Univ East Lansing MI 48824

HAYNES, DOUGLAS MARTIN, OBSTETRICS & GYNECOLOGY. *Current Pos:* assoc prof, Sch Med, Univ Louisville, 55-57, chmn dept, 57-69, interim dean, 69-70, dean 70-72, PROF OBSTET & GYNEC, SCH MED, UNIV LOUISVILLE, 57- *Personal Data:* b New York, NY, Jan 25, 22; m 61; c 2. *Educ:* Southern Methodist Univ, BA & BS, 43; Univ Tex, MD, 46; Am Bd Obstet & Gynec, dipl. *Prof Exp:* Asst prof obstet & gynec, Univ Tex Southwestern Med Sch, 52-55. *Mem:* Fel Am Col Obstet & Gynec; fel AMA; fel Am Gynec & Obstet Soc; Am Col Surgeons. *Res:* Experimental abruptio placentae in the rabbit; uterine blood volume; medical complications of pregnancy; cesarean hysterectomy. *Mailing Add:* Univ Louisville Sch Med ACB 550 S Jackson St Louisville KY 40292-1622

HAYNES, DUNCAN HAROLD, DRUG-CALCIUM INTERACTION, SUSTAINED-RELEASE DRUG DELIVERY. *Current Pos:* from asst prof to assoc prof, 73-82, PROF PHARMACOL, SCH MED, UNIV MIAMI, 82- *Personal Data:* b Owosso, Mich, June 27, 45; m 74, Gisela Busche; c Norman, Karl & Ellen. *Educ:* Butler Univ, BS, 66; Univ Pa, PhD(molecular biol), 70. *Prof Exp:* Fel biophys, Max-Planck Inst, Gottingen, Fed Repub Ger, 70-73. *Concurrent Pos:* Consult, 79-; vis prof, Inst Path, Univ Hamburg, Fed Repub Ger, 85; pres, Pharma-Logic, Inc, 85- *Mem:* Biophys Soc; Am Soc Pharmacol & Exp Therapeut; Soc Gen Pharmacologists; Soc Clin Invest; fel Am Col Clin Pharmacol; Am Physiol Soc. *Res:* Calcium signalling and handling in the human blood platelet; use of calcium channel blocking drugs as anti-platelet drugs in thrombosis; inventor of the patented phospholipid-coated microdroplet and microcrystal serving as injectable delivery system for water-insoluble drugs; commercial development. *Mailing Add:* Dept Pharmacol Univ Miami Sch Med PO Box 016189 Miami FL 33101-6189. *Fax:* 305-243-4555

HAYNES, EMANUEL, AERONAUTICAL & ASTRONAUTICAL ENGINEERING. *Current Pos:* RETIRED. *Personal Data:* b New York, NY, Oct 17, 16; m 42; c 3. *Educ:* City Col New York, BME, 37; Polytech Inst Brooklyn, MME, 40. *Prof Exp:* Sales engr, Niagara Mach & Tool Works, 37-39; jr naval architect, Philadelphia Naval Shipyard, 39-40; chief eng draftsman, NY Naval Shipyard, 40-43; mech engr, Franque A Dickins, Inc, 43-45; Bur Ships, USN, 45-46 & Off Naval Res, 46-51; physicist, Off Chief of Ord, US Army, 51-52; dep dir aeronaut sci, Off Sci Res, USAF, 52-59; prog mgr, Adv Res Projs Agency, Dept Defense, 59-64; dir, Adv Planning Div, Off Naval Res, 64-66; sr staff assoc, Nat Sci Found, 69-80; consult, Nat Acad Sci, George Washington Univ, 80-83. *Concurrent Pos:* Mem, Panel Hydrol, Res & Develop Bd, Dept Defense, 49-51; mem, Subcomt Internal Flow, Nat Adv Comt Aeronaut, 51; fluid mech, 55-59; asst secy defense, Interserv Comn Shock & Vibration, 56-59; chmn coord reps mech, Dir Defense Res & Eng, 56-59. *Res:* Fluid mechanics; aerodynamics; aeroelasticity; structures; propulsion; research management. *Mailing Add:* 6404 Earlham Dr Bethesda MD 20817

HAYNES, EMMIT HOWARD, ANIMAL NUTRITION. *Current Pos:* RETIRED. *Personal Data:* b Irvington, Ky, Sept 21, 26. *Educ:* Univ Ky, BSA, 51, MSA, 53; Cornell Univ, PhD(animal nutrit), 59. *Prof Exp:* Asst prof animal husb & exten specialist, Iowa State Univ, 56-59, from assoc prof to prof animal sci, 59-88, leader resident instr, 59-88. *Mem:* Am Soc Animal Sci. *Res:* Ruminant nutrition. *Mailing Add:* 12415 Nassau Lane Louisville KY 40243

HAYNES, GEORGE RUFUS, SYNTHETIC ORGANIC CHEMISTRY. *Current Pos:* Chemist, Agr Res Div, 56-63, group leader synthesis vet drugs & pharmaceut, 63-68, SUPVR ORG CHEM, SHELL DEVELOP CO, 68- *Personal Data:* b Nashville, Ark, Oct 30, 28; m 57; c 4. *Educ:* Ark State Teachers Col, BS, 50; Univ Ark, MS, 51; Univ Tex, PhD(org chem), 57. *Mem:* Am Chem Soc; Am Inst Chemists. *Res:* Divalent organosulphur compounds and their activity as nematocides and fungicides; synthesis of human and veterinary drugs; synthesis of animal growth improvers; scale-up synthesis of development materials. *Mailing Add:* 11706 Gardenglen Dr Houston TX 77070-2808

HAYNES, HENRY WILLIAM, JR, CHEMICAL ENGINEERING. *Current Pos:* prof, 82-86, PROF & HEAD CHEM ENG, UNIV WYO, 86- *Personal Data:* b Memphis, Tenn, Aug 15, 42; m 67, Linda Goodnight; c Laura, Patricia, Scott, Rebecca & Pamela. *Educ:* Univ Miss, BS, 64; Univ Colo, MS, 66, PhD(chem eng), 69. *Prof Exp:* Res engr synthetic fuels, Esso Res & Eng Co, 68-71; assoc prof, 71-80, prof chem eng, Univ Miss, 80-82. *Mem:* Am Inst Chem Eng; Am Chem Soc. *Res:* Chemical reaction engineering, heterogeneous catalysis, synthetic fuels; trona solution mining. *Mailing Add:* Dept Chem Eng Univ Wyo Laramie WY 82071. *Fax:* 307-766-6777; *E-Mail:* haynes@uwyo.edu

HAYNES, JAMES MITCHELL, AQUATIC ECOLOGY. *Current Pos:* asst prof, 89-83, ASSOC PROF BIOL, STATE UNIV NY, BROCKPORT, 84- *Personal Data:* b Forest Grove, Ore, May 8, 51; m 73. *Educ:* Carleton Col, BA, 73; Univ Minn, MS, 75, PhD(ecol), 78. *Prof Exp:* Res fel ecosyst, Battelle Pac NW Lab, 75-77. *Concurrent Pos:* Prin investr grants, 78- *Mem:* Am Fisheries Soc; Ecol Soc Am; Int Asn Great Lakes Res. *Res:* Aquatic ecology salmonid ecology, biotelemetry and impacts of coastal development. *Mailing Add:* Dept Biol Sci State Univ NY Brockport NY 14420

HAYNES, JOEL M, MECHANICAL ENGINEERING. *Current Pos:* COMBUSTION RES ENGR. *Educ:* Stanford Univ, BS, 90; Mass Inst Technol, MS, 93, PhD, 96. *Honors & Awards:* Gas Turbine Award, Am Soc Mech Engrs, 95. *Mem:* Am Soc Mech Engrs. *Res:* Research and developmennt in combustion issues related to gas turbines and gas appliances. *Mailing Add:* One Research Circle K1-ES209 Niskayuna NY 12309. *E-Mail:* haynes@crd.ge.com

HAYNES, JOHN J, civil & highway engineering; deceased, see previous edition for last biography

HAYNES, JOHN KERMIT, CELL BIOLOGY, DEVELOPMENTAL BIOLOGY. *Current Pos:* assoc prof, 78-79, PROF & DIR HEALTH PROFESSIONS PROG, MOREHOUSE COL, 79-, DAVID PACKARD ENDOWED CHAIR SCI, 85- *Personal Data:* b Monroe, La, Oct 30, 43; m 69. *Educ:* Morehouse Col, BS, 64; Brown Univ, PhD(develop biol), 70. *Prof Exp:* Asst prof molecular med, Meharry Med Col, 73-78. *Concurrent Pos:* Res fel molecular biol, Brown Univ, 70-71; vis res prof, 90-91; adj prof, 93-; res assoc biochem, Mass Inst Technol, 71-73. *Mem:* AAAS; Am Soc Cell Biol; Am Chem Soc; NY Acad Sci. *Res:* Molecular and cellular aspects of sickle cell disease; structure of cell membranes; cell volume regulation. *Mailing Add:* Dept Biol Morehouse Col Atlanta GA 30314. *Fax:* 404-522-0564; *E-Mail:* haynesjk@mhous2.auc.edu

HAYNES, JOHN LENNEIS, DRUG DELIVERY, FLOW CYTOMETRY. *Current Pos:* CONSULT, O'DONNELL GROUP, 93- *Personal Data:* b Washington, DC, Mar 25, 34; m 55, Alice M Sandi; c John L IV, Susan M (Belt) & Cathy A (Page). *Educ:* Cornell Univ, BEE, 56; Stanford Univ, MSEE, 58; Cornell Univ, MSEE, 89. *Honors & Awards:* Grand Award, Circuit Design, Electronic Equip Eng, 60. *Prof Exp:* Res engr, SRI Int, 56-61; chief engr, Pac Commun & Electronics, 62-65; BD Electronics Lab, 65-77, gen mgr, 77-79; assoc prin, Becton Dickinson Res Ctr, 79-92. *Mem:* Sr mem Inst Elec & Electronics Engrs; Asn Advan Med Instrumentation. *Res:* Health care device and instrument research and development; high performance particle analysis and sorting; electrically-assisted transdermal drug delivery; computer-aided engineering analysis in non-Newtonian systems; specification development; granted 20 US patents. *Mailing Add:* 107 Tweed Pl Chapel Hill NC 27514-6534. *E-Mail:* jhaynesnc@aol.com

HAYNES, KATHLEEN GALANTE, POTATO VARIETAL DEVELOPMENT, STATISTICAL GENETICS. *Current Pos:* RES GENETICIST, USDA AGR RES SERV, 87- *Personal Data:* b Oswego, NY, May 10, 56; m 79, Frank L; c Kathleen E & Benjamin F. *Educ:* LeMoyne Col, BS, 78; NC State Univ, MS, 81, MS, 85, PhD(plant breeding), 86. *Mem:* Potato Asn Am; Biomet Soc; Am Soc Hort Sci; Am Genetic Asn; Crop Sci Soc Am. *Res:* Potato breeding, varietal development, disease resistance breeding, quantitative genetics, statistical genetics. *Mailing Add:* USDA Agr Res Serv Bldg 010A Rm 312 Beltsville MD 20705. *Fax:* 301-504-5555; *E-Mail:* khaynes@asrr.arsusda.gov

HAYNES, LEROY WILBUR, ORGANIC CHEMISTRY. *Current Pos:* From instr to assoc prof, 61-74, PROF CHEM, COL WOOSTER, 74- *Personal Data:* b Queens, NY, Jan 31, 34; m 58; c 2. *Educ:* Drew Univ, BA, 56; Univ Ill, Urbana, PhD(org chem), 61. *Concurrent Pos:* NSF exten grant, 66-68; Am Chem Soc-Petrol Res Found grant, 70-71; NSF res grant, 76-77. *Mem:* Am Chem Soc; Sigma Xi. *Res:* Synthesis and reactions of various heterocyclic systems; isolation and characterization of natural products. *Mailing Add:* Dept Chem Col Wooster Wooster OH 44691. *Fax:* 330-263-2386; *E-Mail:* haynes@acs.wooster.edu

HAYNES, M ALFRED, PREVENTIVE MEDICINE. *Current Pos:* CONSULT, 86- *Personal Data:* b Guyana, SAm, Nov 17, 21; m 51, Hazel Edgcombe; c Theresa (Law). *Educ:* Down State Med Sch, MD, 54; Harvard Univ, MPH, 63. *Honors & Awards:* Champion of Prevention, Ctr Dis Control. *Prof Exp:* Asst prof pre med, Univ Vt, 64-69; prof, Drew Med Sch, assoc dean, Community Med, 74-77; pres & dean, Drew-Meharry-Morehouse Cancer Consortium Ctr, 79-86, dir, 86-90. *Concurrent Pos:* Mem, US Task Force Pre Health Serv, 85-; chmn, Steering Count, Nat Cancer Res Network, 86-; mem, Comt Health & Human Rights, Inst Med, 86-90. *Mem:* Inst Med-Nat Acad Sci; AAAS. *Res:* Published numerous articles in various journals. *Mailing Add:* 29249 Firthridge Rd Rancho Palos Verdes CA 90275. Fax: 310-541-5339; *E-Mail:* ahaynes@msn.com

HAYNES, MARTHA PATRICIA, EXTRAGALACTIC & SPECTRAL LINE RADIO ASTRONOMY. *Current Pos:* assoc prof, 81-91, PROF, DEPT ASTRON, CORNELL UNIV, 91- *Personal Data:* b Boston, Mass, April 24, 51. *Educ:* Wellesley Col, Mass, BA, 73; Ind Univ, MA, 75, PhD(astron), 78. *Prof Exp:* Fel res assoc, Nat Astron & Ionosphere Ctr, Arecibo Observ, 78-80; asst scientist & asst dir, Green Banks Opers, Nat Radio Astron Observ, WVa, 81- *Mem:* Am Astron Soc; Sigma Xi; Int Astron Union; Int Union Radio Sci; NY Acad Sci; AAAS. *Res:* Space distribution of galaxies and the effect of intergalactic environment on the gas content of galaxies, primarily via the 21 centimeter line of neutral hydrogen. *Mailing Add:* Dept Astron Space Sci Bldg Cornell Univ Ithaca NY 14853

HAYNES, MUNRO K, MAGNETIC RECORDING, MAGNETO-OPTIC RECORDING. *Current Pos:* RETIRED. *Personal Data:* b Elmira, NY, Dec 10, 23. *Educ:* Univ Rochester, BS, 47; Univ Ill, MS, 48, PhD(elec eng), 50. *Prof Exp:* Res assoc, IBM, Tucson, Ariz, 50-60, mem tech staff, mgr res planning staff, dir eng planning & dir storage technol, 60-71, res eng, 71-78, res scientist, 78-88. *Mem:* Fel Inst Elec & Electronics Engrs; Sigma Xi. *Res:* Magnetic and magneto-optic media; recording techniques for digital information storage; media evaluation; channel characterization; coding; test methods. *Mailing Add:* 3311 E Terra Alta Blvd Tucson AZ 85716-4517

HAYNES, N BRUCE, VETERINARY MEDICINE. *Current Pos:* RETIRED. *Personal Data:* b Ossining, NY, Sept 26, 26; m 46, F Elisabeth Harper; c Beth A (Giroux) & Robert B. *Educ:* Baldwin-Wallace Col, BS, 48; Cornell Univ, DVM, 52. *Prof Exp:* Pvt pract, 52-64; exten vet, NY State Col Vet Med, Cornell Univ, 65-79, assoc prof vet sci, 67-79; vet consult, 79-87. *Concurrent Pos:* Chmn bd dirs, Cornell Vet, Inc, 72-77; dir continuing educ, NY State Col Vet Med, 76-79. *Mem:* Am Vet Med Asn; Am Asn Vet Clinicians; Am Asn Bovine Practr; US Animal Health Asn. *Res:* Cattle diseases and nutrition. *Mailing Add:* Cottage Rd PO Box 9 Winthrop ME 04364-0009

HAYNES, RALPH EDWARDS, pediatrics, medical microbiology; deceased, see previous edition for last biography

HAYNES, ROBERT BRIAN, CLINICAL EPIDEMIOLOGY, MEDICAL INFORMATION. *Current Pos:* from asst prof to assoc prof, 77-85, dir, Prog Educ Develop, 81-87, PROF CLIN & EPIDEMIOL & MED, MCMASTER UNIV, 85-, CHIEF, HEALTH INFO RES UNIT, 87- *Personal Data:* b Calgary, Alta, Mar 1, 47; m 75; c 2. *Educ:* Univ Alta, BSc, 71, MD, 71; McMaster Univ, MSc, 73 & PhD(med sci), 75. *Honors & Awards:* Young Invest Award, Can Hypertension Soc, 80; Nat Health Scientist Award, Nat Health Res & Develop Prog, Can, 87. *Prof Exp:* Resident internal med, Toronto Gen Hosp, 71-72 & 75-76; registr internal med & hon lectr clin epidemiol, St Thomas Hosp, 76-77. *Concurrent Pos:* Vis prof med, Univ Toronto, 84-85; chmn, Ad Hoc Working Group Patient Compliance, US Nat Heart, Lung & Blood Inst, 84-85; nat health scientist, Nat Health Res & Develop Prog, Health & Welfare Can, 87- *Mem:* Am Fed Clin Res; fel Am Heart Asn; Can Soc Clin Invest; Can Hypertension Soc(secy & treas, 85-88, pres, 88-89); Acad Behav Med Res. *Res:* Clinical trials of treatment for vascular disorders such as stroke and hypertension; development and testing of information systems designed to reduce the gap between knowledge and practice in health care. *Mailing Add:* Dept Clin Epidemiol & Biostatics McMaster Univ Med Ctr 1200 Main St W Hamilton ON L8N 3Z5 Can

HAYNES, ROBERT C, limnology, for more information see previous edition

HAYNES, ROBERT CLARK, JR, PHARMACOLOGY. *Current Pos:* PROF PHARMACOL, SCH MED, UNIV VA, 69- *Personal Data:* b Springfield, Mo, Aug 17, 25; m 53; c 3. *Educ:* Washington Univ, MD, 48; Harvard Univ, PhD(biochem), 53. *Prof Exp:* Biochemist, Worcester Found Exp Biol, 51-53; from sr instr to assoc prof pharmacol, Western Res Univ, 54-69. *Mem:* AAAS; Endocrine Soc; Am Soc Pharmacol & Exp Therapeut; Am Soc Biol Chem. *Res:* Mechanism of action of hormones. *Mailing Add:* 2005 Pine Top Rd Charlottesville VA 29903-1232

HAYNES, ROBERT HALL, DNA REPAIR, MUTAGENESIS. *Current Pos:* chmn dept, 68-73, PROF BIOL, YORK UNIV, ONT, 68-, DISTINGUISHED RES PROF, 86- *Personal Data:* b London, Ont, Aug 27, 31; m 54, 66, Jane Banfield; c Mark, Geoffrey & Paul. *Educ:* Western Ont Univ, BSc, 53, PhD(biophys), 57. *Hon Degrees:* DSc, Univ Man, 95, Univ Western Ont, 97. *Honors & Awards:* Ann Res Award, Environ Mutagen Soc, 84; Gold Medal, Biol Coun Can, 84; Flavelle Medal, Royal Soc Can, 88; Presidential Citation, Genetics Soc Can, 89; Officer of Order, Can, 90; Award of Excellence, Genetics Soc Can, 93. *Prof Exp:* Brit Empire Cancer Campaign fel physics, St Bartholomew's Hosp Med Col, Univ London, 57-58; from instr to asst prof biophys, Univ Chicago, 59-64; assoc prof biophys & med physics, Univ Calif, Berkeley, 64-68. *Concurrent Pos:* Mem, Subcomt Radiobiol, Nat Acad Sci-Nat Res Coun, 63-73; biophysicist, Lawrence Berkeley Lab, 64-68; assoc prof, Dept Instrnl Biol, Univ Calif, Berkeley, 66-68; mem exp adv comt, Atomic Energy Can Ltd, 69-72, tech adv, Comt Nuclear Fuel Waste Mgt, 79-83; exchange visitor, USSR Acad Sci, 72, Japan Soc Prom Sci, Kyoto, 79 & Acad Sinica, Beijing, China, 80; Brit Coun Asn Commonwealth Univ exchange fel, Bot Sch, Oxford Univ, 73; vis fel molecular biophys, Yale Univ, 74-75; bd mem, Nat Res Coun Can, 75-82; chmn, Ministerial Adv Comt Environ Mutagenesis, Can Dept Nat Health & Welfare, 78-85; assoc fel & mem res coun, Can Inst Advan Res, 82-87; mem, Int Comm Protection Against Environ Mutagens & Carcinogens, 87-93; pres, Int Cong Genetics, Toronto, 88; pres, Int Asn Environ Mutagen Socs, 89-93; festschrift in mutation res, 93. *Mem:* Fel AAAS; Genetics Soc Can (vpres, 81-82, pres, 83-85); Genetics Soc Am; Environ Mutagen Soc; fel Royal Soc Can (pres, 95-97); Indian Sci Cong Asn; assoc fel Third World Acad Sci; foreign mem Pakistan Acad Sci. *Res:* Molecular biology; radiation genetics; environmental mutagenesis; photobiology; DNA repair; blood rheology; radiological physics; yeast genetics; mathematical analysis of mutagen dose-response relations; deoxynucleotide metabolism; exobiology and ecopoieses. *Mailing Add:* Dept Biol York Univ Toronto ON M3J 1P3 Can. Fax: 416-650-8002

HAYNES, ROBERT RALPH, PLANT TAXONOMY. *Current Pos:* from asst prof to assoc prof, 76-85, PROF BIOL, UNIV ALA, 85- *Personal Data:* b Minden, La, Feb 24, 45; m 67, Elizabeth Zappa; c Charles & Roxann. *Educ:* La Polytech Inst, BS, 67; Univ Southwestern La, MS, 69; Ohio State Univ, PhD(bot), 73. *Prof Exp:* Spec lectr bot, Ohio State Univ, 73-74; asst prof biol, La State Univ, Shreveport, 74-76. *Mem:* Am Soc Plant Taxonomists; Int Asn Plant Taxonomists; Bot Soc Am; Linnean Soc London. *Res:* Revisionary and phytogeographical investigations of the Alismatidae with special interests in the genera Potamogeton, Najas, Sagittaria, and Echinodorus. *Mailing Add:* Dept Biol Univ Ala Tuscaloosa AL 35487-0344. Fax: 205-348-1786; *E-Mail:* rhaynes@biology.as.ua.edu

HAYNES, RONNIE J, WILDLIFE ECOLOGY. *Current Pos:* ENVIRON SPECIALIST, US FISH & WILDLIFE SERV, 79- *Personal Data:* b Trumann, Ark, May 12, 44; m 66; c 3. *Educ:* Ark State Univ, BS, 66; Univ Ark, MS, 69; Southern Ill Univ, Carbondale, PhD(zool), 76. *Prof Exp:* Teacher biol & physiol, Merritt Island High Sch, Fla, 68-70; researcher ecol mined lands, Coop Wildlife Res Lab, Southern Ill Univ, Carbondale, 75-76; res assoc environ sci-terrestrial, Oak Ridge Nat Lab, Union Carbide Corp, 76-79. *Mem:* Sigma Xi; Wildlife Soc; Nat Wildlife Fedn; Soc Wetland Scientists; Ecol Soc; Am Soc Surface Mining & Reclamation. *Res:* Reclamation of mined lands such as surface and underground; plant succession and utilization of mined lands by wildlife; habitat evaluation methods; restoration ecology. *Mailing Add:* US Fish & Wildlife Serv US Dept Interior 1875 Century Blvd Suite 200 Atlanta GA 30345. Fax: 404-679-7081

HAYNES, SHERWOOD KIMBALL, physics; deceased, see previous edition for last biography

HAYNES, SIMON JOHN, ECONOMIC GEOLOGY, STRUCTURE. *Current Pos:* from asst prof to assoc prof, 74-89, PROF GEOL, BROCK UNIV, 89-, CHAIR & VCHMN COUN, 90- *Personal Data:* b Chelmsford, Eng, Jan 1, 44; Can citizen; m 71; c 4. *Educ:* Manchester Univ, Eng, BSc, 65; Carleton Univ, MSc, 69; Queen's Univ, Ont, PhD(geol), 75. *Honors & Awards:* World Decoration Excellence Medallion, Am Biol Inst, 89. *Prof Exp:* Asst geol, Carleton Univ, 65-68 & Queen's Univ, Ont, 68-72; asst prof, Pahlavi Univ, Iran, 72-74. *Concurrent Pos:* Consult asbestos, Magcobar Iran Ltd & Fars & Khuzestan Cement Co, 73-74, chloride in cement, St Lawrence Seaway Authority, 76, copper, Nat Iranian Copper Industs, Corp, 76-78, uranium, Golden Goose Mine Ltd, 78-80, Madawaska Mines Ltd, 79 & silver-lead-zinc Ngate Explor Ltd, 80- 82, gold deposits, NS Dept Mines & Energy, 82-84, Geol Surv Can, 84-85; vis scientist, Nanjing Univ, China, 86; gypsum deposits, Ont Min Northern Develop & Mines, 86-90; gold deposits, S China, China Nat Non-Ferrous Metal Corp, China, 87-89; D Bell & Assoc, 87-90; mem, chair res comt, Geol Soc, China Inland Mission. *Mem:* Fel Geol Asn Can; Mineral Asn Can; fel Soc Econ Geologists; AAAS; Can Inst Mining & Metall. *Res:* Processes of ore deposit formation; plate tectonics and metallogenesis; regional structure; gold deposits; gypsum deposits; crushed stone aggregates. *Mailing Add:* Dept Earth Sci Brock Univ Merritville Hwy St Catharines ON L2S 3A1 Can

HAYNES, SUZANNE G, SOCIAL EPIDEMIOLOGY, GERONTOLOGY. *Current Pos:* PROJ COORDR, COMMUNITY SURVEILLANCE CARDIOVASC DIS, SOUTHWESTERN US, 81-; CHIEF, HEALTH PROM SCI BR, NAT CANCER INST, 87- *Personal Data:* b Huntington Park, Calif; c 1. *Educ:* Univ Tenn, Knoxville, BA, 69; Univ Tex, Austin, MA, 70; Univ Tex, Sch Pub Health, Houston, MPH, 72; Univ NC, Chapel Hill, PhD(epidemiol), 75. *Honors & Awards:* Dix Award, Nat Ctr Health Statist, 88; Ctr Dis Control Statist Award, 89. *Prof Exp:* Res economist, Mayor's Manpower Planning Coun, Houston, 70-71; res assoc epidemiol, Univ NC, Chapel Hill, 74-76; epidemiologist, Nat Heart, Lung & Blood Inst, 75-80; res asst prof epidemiol, Univ NC, Chapel Hill, 80-84; chief, Med Statist Br, Nat Ctr Health Statist, Nat Cancer Inst, 84-87. *Concurrent Pos:* Ed, J Gerontol, 78-81; mem, Biomet & Epidemiol Contract Rev Comt, Nat Cancer Inst, 79-83, exec comt, Am Heart Asn Coun Epidemiol, 82-85 & adv comt, Western Ctr Behav & Prev Med, 80-87; consult, Epidemiol Br, Nat Heart, Lung & Blood Inst, 80-; estab investr, Am Heart Asn, 82-84; exec comt, Soc Epidemiol Res, 84-87; pres, Nat Ctr Health Statist Womens Coun, 86; Cardiovasc Working Group chair, Carter Ctr Closing Gap Proj, 86-87; mem, Gov Coun, Am Pub Health Asn, 87-89 & 90-92; NIH rep, Dept Health & Human Serv, 89-90. *Mem:* Fel Acad Behav Med; fel Am Col Epidemiol; fel

Soc Behav Med; fel Am Heart Asn. *Res:* Epidemiology of coronary heart diease; type A behavior and risk factors among women; social, psychological, functional characteristics of aging; cancer prevention and control research in smoking, nutrition and breast cancer screening; cardiovasculary epidemiology; cancer epidemiology. *Mailing Add:* 12330 Shadetree Lane Laurel MD 20708

HAYNES, TONY EUGENE, RADIATION EFFECT IN SEMICONDUCTORS, CRYSTALLIZATION IN AMORPHOUS SOLIDS. *Current Pos:* MEM RES STAFF, SOLID STATE DIV, OAK RIDGE NAT LAB, 87- *Personal Data:* b Concord, NC, Sept 8, 60; m 83. *Educ:* Wake Forest Univ, BS, 82; Univ NC, Chapel Hill, PhD(physics), 87. *Prof Exp:* Fel, Particle-Solid Interactions Div, Sandia Nat Lab, 85-86. *Mem:* Am Phys Soc; Mat Res Soc. *Res:* Materials modification by ion beams; direct ion beam deposition of thin films; ion implantation; radiation damage in semiconductors; ion beam analysis; solid-phase recrystallization. *Mailing Add:* Oak Ridge Nat Lab Bldg 3003-MS6048 PO Box 2008 Oak Ridge TN 37831-6048

HAYNES, WILLIAM MILLER, ANALYTICAL CHEMISTRY. *Current Pos:* RETIRED. *Personal Data:* b Bartlesville, Okla, July 26, 36; m 56; c 4. *Educ:* Okla State Univ, BA, 59, PhD(chem), 66. *Prof Exp:* Asst prof chem, Southeast Mo State Col, 65-68; sr res group leader, Environ Anal Sci Ctr, Monsanto Co, 77-80, mgr process technol, 80-85, dir, Anal Sci Ctr, 85-97. *Mem:* Am Indust Hyg Asn; Am Soc Testing & Mat; Am Chem Soc. *Res:* Polarographic analysis; ion selective electrodes; industrial hygiene sampling and analysis. *Mailing Add:* 14 Wools Hill Dr St Charles MO 63303. *Fax:* 314-694-7545

HAYNES, WILLIAM P, CHEMICAL ENGINEERING. *Current Pos:* DIV MGR, US DEPT ENERGY, 76- *Personal Data:* b Omaha, Nebr, Apr 7, 21; m 43; c 2. *Educ:* Univ Pittsburgh, BS, 42, MS, 51. *Prof Exp:* Chem engr, Bur Mines, US Dept Interior, 45-49, supvry chem res engr, 59-76. *Mem:* Am Inst Chem Engrs; Am Chem Soc; Catalyst Soc. *Res:* Catalytic conversion of synthesis gas to substitute natural gas and liquid hydrocarbon; production of hydrogen by steam-iron reaction; hot carbonate gas absorption process; coal gasification; processes for removal of sulfur oxides from flue gases. *Mailing Add:* 2345 Orlando Pl Pittsburgh PA 15235

HAYNIE, FRED HOLLIS, CORROSION SCIENCE, ENGINEERING ECONOMICS. *Current Pos:* CONSULT, 92- *Personal Data:* b Anniston, Ala, Feb 8, 32; m 55, Betty J Davis; c Christie L (Shook), Diana J (Ayscue), Steven G & Virginia B. *Educ:* Auburn Univ, BS, 54, MS, 59; Ohio State Univ, MS, 67. *Honors & Awards:* Sam Tour Award, Am Soc Testing & Mat. *Prof Exp:* Aviator, US Navy, 54-57; chief chem metall eng, Naval Air Mat Ctr, 61-64; sr chem eng, Battelle Mem Inst, 64-69; supvr environ eng, US Environ Protection Agency, 69-90. *Concurrent Pos:* Capt, Naval Air Res, 64-81. *Res:* Determining the effects of air pollution and acid deposition on man-made materials. *Mailing Add:* 300 Oakridge Rd Cary NC 27511

HAYNIE, THOMAS POWELL, III, NUCLEAR MEDICINE. *Current Pos:* assoc prof med, M D Anderson Hosp & Tumor Inst, Univ Tex, 65-75, prof med, Syst Cancer Ctr, 75-88, James E Anderson prof nuclear med, 88-95, EMER PROF, M D ANDERSON CANCER CTR, UNIV TEX, 95- *Personal Data:* b Hearne, Tex, Aug 9, 32; m 56, Bette Flossel; c David, Amy & Sue. *Educ:* Baylor Univ, MD, 56. *Honors & Awards:* Gold Medal Award, Am Col Nuclear Med, 97. *Prof Exp:* Intern med, Univ Mich Hosp, 56-57, resident internal med, 57-60, instr, Med Sch, Univ, 60-62, asst prof, 62; asst prof, Med Br, Univ Tex, 62-65. *Concurrent Pos:* Tech expert, Int Atomic Energy Agency, Morocco, 64; consult, Wilford Hall USAF Hosp, Tex, 67- & Johnson Space Ctr, NASA, 68-93; consult, Los Alamos Nat Labs; prof med & physiol, Univ Tex Grad Sch & Baylor Col; ed-in-chief, J Nuclear Med, 85-89. *Mem:* AMA; fel Am Col Physicians; Soc Nuclear Med; Am Col Nuclear Med; Radiol Soc Am; Am Thyroid Asn; Sigma Xi. *Res:* Radioactive nuclides in medicine; applications of radionuclide imaging in cancer; radioisotope therapy of cancer. *Mailing Add:* 1515 Holcombe Blvd Houston TX 77030. *Fax:* 713-792-0812; *E-Mail:* thaynie@rpimail.mdacc.tmc.edu

HAYON, ELIE M, PHOTOCHEMISTRY, RADIATION CHEMISTRY. *Current Pos:* DEAN GRAD STUDIES & RES & PROF CHEM, QUEEN'S COL, CITY UNIV NEW YORK, 78- *Personal Data:* b Cairo, Egypt, May 15, 32; m 82, Nina Mokady; c Rona. *Educ:* Univ Strathclyde, Glasgow, BSc, 54; Univ Durham, PhD(phys chem), 57. *Prof Exp:* Brit Empire res fel, King's Col, Eng, 57-58; res chemist, Brookhaven Nat Lab, 58-60; sr mem, Phys Chem Dept, Churchill Col, Cambridge Univ, 60-62; res scientist, French Atomic Energy Comt, France, 63-65; head, Phys Chem Lab, US Army Natick Labs, 66-75. *Concurrent Pos:* Adj prof, Brandeis Univ, 67-75; vis prof, Hebrew Univ, Jerusalem, 72-73. *Mem:* Am Chem Soc; Royal Soc Chem; Am Soc Photobiol; Biophys Soc; NY Acad Sci. *Res:* Fast-reaction studies of the mechanism and dynamics of chemical and biological reactions; laser spectroscopy; photophysics; chemistry of excited states; free radical chemistry; electron transfer process; free radical aspects of auto-oxidation. *Mailing Add:* 6 Einstein St Ra'anana Israel. *Fax:* 917-9-741-7586

HAYRE, HARBHAJAN SINGH, BIOMEDICAL ENGINEERING, FITNESS-FOR DUTY. *Current Pos:* CHIEF ENGR CEIE SPECS INC, 63-; PRES, IMPAIRMENT MEASURES, INC, 94- *Personal Data:* b Littran, India, July 12, 29; US citizen; m 57, Santosh; c Lali, Paul & Sheila. *Educ:* Punjab Univ, India, BA, 49; Univ Calif, Berkeley, BS, 52, MS, 54; Univ NMex, DSc, 62. *Honors & Awards:* Hon Consul of India, Govt India, 77; Centennial Medal, Inst Elec & Electronics Engrs, 84. *Prof Exp:* Asst, Univ Calif, Berkeley, 52-53; elec engr, Niagara Mohawk Power Corp, 53-55; exchange elec engr, Nordsjaellands Elektricitets Og, Sporvejs & Hamburgische Electricitata, Werkes, 55; proj engr, Stand Vacuum Oil Co, India, 56-57; instr elec eng, Univ NMex, 57-58, res assoc, 60-62; assoc prof, New Bedford Inst Technol, 58-60; prof elec eng, Univ Houston, 65-94, chmn grad fac, Cullen Col Eng, 67-68, dir, Wave Propagation Labs, Dept Elec Eng, 67-92, mem & chmn, Univ Governance Comt, 70-72. *Concurrent Pos:* Asst prof & lectr, Univ Buffalo, 54-55; sr engr, Curtiss-Wright Corp, NMex, 61; mem, Comn 2, US Nat Comt, Int Sci Radio Union, 62-; assoc prof, Kans State Univ, 62-65; consult, US Naval Res Lab, DC, 64-71; mem, Undergrad Res Panel, Nat Sci Found, 67-68; accreditation team elec eng, Eng Coun on Prof Develop, 70-73; vpres & dir res & develop, Specific Offshore Equip Co, Tex, 70-72; Presby coordr, Proj Equality, Tex; chmn, Tex Intersoc Legis Adv Comn, 77- & Houston Sect, Inst Elec & Electronics Engrs, 78-79; gen chmn, 1980 Nat Telecommun Conf, 77-80; hon consult India, Govt India, 77-83; Pres Tex Fac Asn, 90-91. *Mem:* Acoustic Soc Am; sr mem Inst Elec & Electronics Engrs; Am Soc Eng Educ; Am Astron Soc; sr mem Instrument Soc Am; Am Col Forensic Examr. *Res:* Pattern recognition; wave prop; engineering forensics; sensors-instrumentation; non-destructive testing; biomedical; communications; speech; fitness for duty. *Mailing Add:* PO Box 19756 Houston TX 77224-9756. *E-Mail:* santz@aol.com

HAY-ROE, HUGH, GEOLOGY. *Current Pos:* SR ADV TO PRES, ENERGY WORLD TRADE INC, HOUSTON, 91- *Personal Data:* b Edmonton, Can, Dec 7, 28; nat US; m 54; c 3. *Educ:* Univ Alta, BSc, 49; Univ Tex, MA, 52, PhD(geol), 58. *Prof Exp:* Asst gen mgr & geol supvr, Belco Petrol Corp, Lima, Peru, 68-71, asst vpres, NY, 71-74, vpres explor, Lima, Peru, 74-76; far east explor mgr, Superior Oil Co, Calgary, 76-78, gen mgr, Dominican Opers, Santo Domingo, 78-80; consult petrol geol, Global Energy Oper, Houston, 80-91. *Concurrent Pos:* Sr assoc & mgr, Murray & Assocs Int, Kingwood, Tex. *Mem:* Am Asn Petrol Geologists; fel Geol Soc Am; Am Inst Prof Geologists; fel Geol Asn Can. *Res:* Petroleum geology; oil reservoirs. *Mailing Add:* 1606 Burning Tree Rd Humble TX 77339-3922. *Fax:* 713-651-7879

HAYRY, PEKKA JUHA, TRANSPLANTATION SURGERY, CANCER. *Current Pos:* asst prof immunol, 70-79, DIR, TRANSPLANTATION LAB, UNIV HELSINKI, 76-, PROF TRANSPLANTATION SURG & IMMUNOL, 79-; DOC-IN-CHIEF, HELSINKI UNIV HOSP, 88- *Personal Data:* b Vihti, Finland, Dec 13, 39; div; c Valtteri. *Educ:* Univ Helsinki, MD, 65, ScD(exp path), 66. *Hon Degrees:* Mb, Finnish Acad Sci Sci & Lett, 89. *Honors & Awards:* Matti Ayrapaa Prize, Finnish Med Soc, 88; Medix Prize Biosci, 94. *Prof Exp:* Fel, Wistar Inst, Philadelphia, Pa, 67-70. *Concurrent Pos:* Resident surg, Helsinki Univ Hosp, 70-73, assoc chief surg, Dept IV Surg, 73-79; asst prof surg & transplantation surg, Univ Oulu, 74-80; vis prof, Univ Rene Descartes, France, 74, Dept Surg & Immunol, Duke Univ & Chapel Hill, 77 & Dept Med & Surg, Univ Adalaide, SAustralia, 81. *Mem:* Am Soc Transplant Surgeons; Am Asn Imunologists; Transplantation Soc; Int Soc Nephrol; Int Soc Heart Transplantation. *Res:* Tumor immunology. *Mailing Add:* Univ Helsinki Transplantation Lab PO Box 21 Helsinki 00014 Finland

HAYS, BYRON G, ORGANIC CHEMISTRY, PIGMENT CHEMISTRY. *Current Pos:* SR RES ASSOC, ENGELHARD CORP, 92- *Personal Data:* b Kansas City, Mo, Jan 1, 37; m 62; c 1. *Educ:* Wichita State Univ, BS, 58; Mass Inst Technol, PhD(phys org chem), 64. *Honors & Awards:* Super Varnish & Drier Co lectr, Nat Asn Printing Ink Mfrs, 90. *Prof Exp:* Res chemist, Esso Res & Eng Co, 64-66 & Interchem Co, 66-69; mgr, Prod Develop, Porvair Ltd, 69-71; res assoc, Inmont Co, 72-76, mgr prod develop & tech mgr, 77-86; res & develop dir spec projs, BASF Corp, 86-91. *Mem:* Am Chem Soc; Tech Asn Graphic Arts. *Res:* Organic pigments; surface treatments; surfactants; dispersants; dispersions; printing inks; disperse dyes; ultraviolet-cure coatings and inks; synthetic leather; polyurethanes and resins. *Mailing Add:* Englehard Corp 23800 Mercantile Rd Beachwood OH 44122-5908. *Fax:* 216-464-5780

HAYS, DAN ANDREW, PHYSICS. *Current Pos:* prin scientist physics, 68-96, RES FEL, XEROX CORP, 96- *Personal Data:* b Dallas Ctr, Iowa, July 12, 39; m 64, Judith Delp; c Andrew & David. *Educ:* Iowa State Univ, BS, 61; Rutgers Univ, MS, 63, PhD(physics), 66. *Honors & Awards:* IS&T Carlson Award, 91. *Prof Exp:* Fel physics, Univ Pittsburgh, 66-68. *Concurrent Pos:* RCA fel, 64-66, Andrew Mellon fel, 66-68. *Mem:* Am Phys Soc; Electrostatics Soc Am; fel Soc Imaging Sci & Technol; Am Chem Soc. *Res:* Contact electrification studies of insulating materials, electrostatic properties of small particles, characteristics of xerographic development systems. *Mailing Add:* Xerox Corp 114-22D 800 Phillips Rd Webster NY 14580. *Fax:* 716-265-5666; *E-Mail:* dan__hays@wb.xerox.com

HAYS, DANIEL MAUGER, PEDIATRIC SURGERY. *Current Pos:* clin assoc prof, Univ Southern Calif, 64-66, assoc prof, 66-73, prof surg, 73-81, PROF SURG & PEDIAT, SCH MED, UNIV SOUTHERN CALIF, 80- *Personal Data:* b Reading, Pa, Mar 9, 19; m 51; c 4. *Educ:* Stanford Univ, AB, 41; Cornell Univ, MD, 44. *Prof Exp:* Asst surg, Harvard Univ, 45-46; asst, Med Col, Cornell Univ, 50-51; from clin instr to clin assoc prof, Univ Calif, Los Angeles, 55-64. *Concurrent Pos:* Investr, NIH grant, Clin Res Ctr, Children's Hosp, Los Angeles, 61-64; prin investr, NIH grant, 65-; prin investr cancer training grant, 67-; consult, Univ Calif, Los Angeles, 54-64; clin prof, Am Cancer Soc, 84- *Mem:* Am Col Surg; Am Acad Pediat. *Res:* Hepatic regeneration; pediatric oncology; pediatric surgery; cancer: late effects; cancer survivors: economic problems. *Mailing Add:* Los Angeles Children's Hospital 4650 Sunset Blvd Los Angeles CA 90027-0016

HAYS, DONALD BROOKS, entomology, for more information see previous edition

HAYS, DONALD F(RANK), MECHANICAL ENGINEERING, ENGINEERING MECHANICS. *Current Pos:* RETIRED. *Personal Data:* b Portland, Ore, Mar 29, 29; m 55, Alice Morrow; c Audrey, Kenneth & Linda. *Educ:* Ore State Univ, BS, 51, MS, 52. *Honors & Awards:* Centennial Medallions, Am Soc Mech Engrs, 80; Mayo D Hersey Award, Am Soc Mech Engrs, 83. *Prof Exp:* Sr res engr, Res Lab, Gen Motors, 52-62, asst dept head, Mech Develop Dept, 62-75, asst dept head, Engr Mech Dept, 75-79, head, Mech Res Dept, 79-83, head, Fluid Mech Dept, 83-89. *Concurrent Pos:* Tech ed, J Lubrication Technol, Am Soc Mech Engrs, 74-80; mem, Am Soc Lubrication Handbk Adv Bd. *Mem:* Soc Tribologists & Lubrication Engrs; fel Am Soc Mech Engrs; Soc Automotive Engrs. *Res:* Hydrodynamics; mechanics; applied mathematics; fluid film bearings; seals; mensuration; fluid mechanics. *Mailing Add:* 639 Alpine Ct Rochester Hills MI 48309

HAYS, DONALD R, organic chemistry; deceased, see previous edition for last biography

HAYS, ELIZABETH TEUBER, PHYSIOLOGY, ZOOLOGY. *Current Pos:* ASSOC PROF BIOL, NAZARETH COL, ROCHESTER, 78-, CHMN DEPT, 79- *Personal Data:* b Greenport, NY, Apr 29, 40; m 67; c 2. *Educ:* Keuka Col, BA, 62; Univ Md, PhD(zool), 68. *Prof Exp:* Assoc physiol, Univ Rochester, 70-72, asst prof, 72-78. *Concurrent Pos:* Res asst, Nat Resources Inst, Univ Md, 65-67; fel, Duke Univ, 67-69; fel, Univ Rochester, 69-70. *Mem:* AAAS; Biophys Soc; Am Physiol Soc; Nat Sci Teachers Asn; Soc Col Sci Teachers. *Res:* Membrane transport; muscle physiology; bioenergetics; muscle metabolism. *Mailing Add:* Sch Nat & Health Sci Barry Univ 1130 NE Second Ave Miami Shores FL 33161-6695. *Fax:* 305-899-3845

HAYS, ESTHER FINCHER, ONCOLOGY, HEMATOLOGY. *Current Pos:* from instr to assoc prof med, Sch Med, Univ Calif, 55-72, from asst to assoc res physician, Lab Nuclear Med & Radiation Biol, 57-72, PROF MED, SCH MED & RES PHYSICIAN, LAB NUCLEAR MED & RADIATION BIOL, UNIV CALIF, LOS ANGELES, 72-, EMER DEAN MED, 93- *Personal Data:* b Lexington, Ky, Apr 18, 27; m 51, Daniel; c Sarah, Jonathan, Elizabeth & Margaret. *Educ:* Cornell Univ, AB, 48, MD, 51. *Prof Exp:* Intern med, New York Hosp, 51-52, asst resident, 52-54. *Mem:* Am Asn Cancer Res; Am Soc Hemat; Am Col Physicians; Int Soc Exp Hemat. *Res:* Studies of human immunodeficiency virus in the human thymus in vitro. *Mailing Add:* Deans Off Univ Calif Sch Med Los Angeles CA 90024. *Fax:* 310-206-5046; *E-Mail:* danhays@pc.net

HAYS, GEORGE E(DGAR), CHEMICAL ENGINEERING. *Current Pos:* RETIRED. *Personal Data:* b Alton, Ill, Apr 25, 21; m 46; c 12. *Educ:* Blackburn Col, AB, 41; Univ Iowa, BS, 43. *Prof Exp:* Chem engr, Phillips Petrol Co, 43-51, sr engr, 51-55, supvr fundamental eng, 56-58, mgr, Advan Eng Sect, 59-60, chem eng assoc, Res & Develop Dept, 61-68, sr eng assoc, 68-85. *Concurrent Pos:* Secy & treas, Washington Co Elder Care, Inc, 87- *Mem:* Am Chem Soc; fel Am Inst Chem Engrs. *Res:* Process engineering and economic evaluation: natural gas, petroleum and petro-chemicals technology; low temperature gas processing; fractionation; phase equilibrium; separations and rate processes; analysis and elimination of technical and economic process risk. *Mailing Add:* 1909 SE Moonlight Dr Bartlesville OK 74006

HAYS, HORACE ALBENNIE, MAMMALOGY. *Current Pos:* RETIRED. *Personal Data:* b Kisatchie, La, Nov 25, 14; m 43; c 1. *Educ:* Northwestern State Univ, La, AB, 36; La State Univ, MS, 41; Univ Okla, PhD, 54. *Prof Exp:* Teacher, Pub Schs, La, 37-42; from voc adv to chief, Guid Ctr, US Vet Admin, Lake Charles, La, 46-47; asst prof biol, Centenary Col, 47-51; from assoc prof to emer prof, Pittsburg State Univ, 54-96. *Mem:* Am Inst Biol Sci; Am Soc Mammal; Sigma Xi. *Res:* Mammalian ecology; vertebrate zoology; distribution and movement of small mammals; effect of microclimate on distribution of small mammals; bat research. *Mailing Add:* 1408 S Olive St Pittsburg KS 66762

HAYS, JAMES D, GEOLOGY. *Current Pos:* RES ASSOC, LAMONT-DOHERTY GEOL OBSERV, 65-; DIR, DEEP-SEA CORE LAB, 67-; PROF GEOL, COLUMBIA UNIV, 74- *Personal Data:* b Johnstown, NY, Dec 26, 33; m 65. *Educ:* Harvard Univ, AB, 56; Ohio State Univ, MS, 60; Columbia Univ, PhD(geol), 64. *Prof Exp:* From asst prof to assoc prof geol, Columbia Univ, 67-74; res assoc, Am Mus Natural Hist, 70-; exec dir, Climap Proj, 71-77. *Mem:* Sigma Xi; AAAS; Geol Soc Am; Am Geophys Union. *Res:* Radiolarian extinctions and magnetic reversals; deep-sea sediment research; paleo climatic research. *Mailing Add:* Geol Columbia Univ 2960 Broadway New York NY 10027-6902

HAYS, JAMES FRED, PETROLOGY, GEOPHYSICS. *Current Pos:* dir, Div Earth Sci, 82-87 & 89-90, sci adv, 87-89, 90-91, DIR, DIV EARTH SCI, NSF. *Personal Data:* b Little Rock, Ark, July 10, 33; m 56, Diane Huntoon; c Lee (Romano). *Educ:* Columbia Univ, AB, 54; Calif Inst Technol, MS, 61; Harvard Univ, PhD(geol), 66. *Prof Exp:* Geologist, US Geol Surv, 61; guest investr, Carnegie Inst Geophys Lab, 65; from asst prof to prof geol, Harvard Univ, 66-82, chmn, Dept Geol Sci, 81-82. *Concurrent Pos:* Mem, Lunar Sample Anal Planning Team, NASA Johnson Space Ctr, 74-76; chmn, Lunar & Planetary Rev Panel, 79-81; assoc ed, J Geophys Res, 78-80, 83-85; mem, Sci Adv Bd, Mt St Helens Nat Volcanic Monument, 83-87; vis prof chem & geol, Ariz State Univ, 77-79; counr, Geol Soc Am, 88-91, AAAS, 89-92; mem, Space Grant Rev Panel, NASA, 92- *Mem:* Fel Geol Soc Am; Am Geophys Union; fel Mineral Soc Am; Am Ornithologists Union; fel AAAS; Sigma Xi. *Res:* Experimental petrology; phase equilibria in silicates at high pressures and high temperatures; kinetics of crystallization; interior of the earth, moon and planets; principal investigator of Apollo lunar samples. *Mailing Add:* 7245 Earlys Rd Warrenton VA 22186. *Fax:* 703-306-0382; *E-Mail:* jhays@nsf.gov

HAYS, JOHN BRUCE, MOLECULAR GENETICS, DNA BIOCHEMISTRY. *Current Pos:* dept head, 87-90, PROF, DEPT AGR CHEM, ORE STATE UNIV, CORVALLIS, 87- *Personal Data:* b Springfield, Ill, June 21, 37; m 61, Judith Gumm; c Elinor, Stephen & Laura. *Educ:* Univ NMex, BS, 60; Univ Calif, San Diego, PhD(chem), 68. *Prof Exp:* Fel biol, Johns Hopkins Univ, 69-72; asst prof chem, Univ Md, Baltimore Co, 72-77, assoc prof chem, 77-82, prof, 82-87. *Mem:* Am Soc Biochem & Molecular Biol; Genetics Soc Am; Am Soc Microbiol; Environ Mutagenesis Soc. *Res:* Biochemistry and genetics of recombination, mutagenesis and DNA repair in bacteria, plants and amphibian eggs. *Mailing Add:* Dept Agr Chem Ore State Univ AGLS1007 Corvallis OR 97331-7301. *Fax:* 541-737-0497; *E-Mail:* haysj@bcc.orst.edu

HAYS, JOHN THOMAS, ORGANIC CHEMISTRY, INFORMATION SCIENCE. *Current Pos:* Res chemist, Exp Sta, Hercules Inc, 42-43, asst group leader, 43-45, tech asst to dir res, 45-49, spec asst, 49-51, mgr, Scouting Res Div, 51-53, tech asst to dir, Exp Sta, 53-56, sr res chemist, Exp Sta, 56-81, SR RES CHEMIST, RES CTR, HERCULES INC, 81- *Personal Data:* b Ozark, Mo, Nov 25, 14; m 43; c 2. *Educ:* Mont State Col, BS, 35; Oxford Univ, BA & BSc, 38; Calif Inst Technol, PhD(org chem), 42. *Res:* Carbohydrates; amino acids; pyridine compounds; polymers; synthetic rubber; rosin derivatives; nitrogen chemicals; ureaform fertilizers; technical information. *Mailing Add:* 209 Sterling Ave New Castle DE 19720-4729

HAYS, PAUL B, AEROSPACE ENGINEERING, ATMOSPHERIC OCEANICS & SPACE SCIENCE. *Current Pos:* asst res, Univ Mich, 59-63, assoc res engr, 63-66, from asst prof to assoc prof aerospace eng, 67-75, assoc prof atmospheric & oceanic sci, 72-75, dir, Space Physics Res Lab, 84-89, chmn, Dept Atmospheric, Oceanic & Space Sci, 91-92, PROF AEROSPACE ENG & ATMOSPHERIC, OCEANIC & SPACE SCI, UNIV MICH, 75- *Personal Data:* b Battle Creek, Mich, May 25, 35; c 3. *Educ:* Univ Mich, BS, 58, MS, 60, PhD(aerospace eng), 64. *Prof Exp:* Assoc engr, Douglas Aircraft, 58-59. *Concurrent Pos:* NATO postdoctoral fel, Queen's Univ, Belfast, 65-66, sr res fel, 66-67; mem, Comt Upper Atmosphere, Am Meteorol Soc, 72-78; mem, Working Group II, Inter-Union Comn Solar-Terrestrial Physics, 73-; mem, Comt Solar & Space Physics, Nat Acad Sci, 78-83; pres, PBH Consult Inc, 81- *Mem:* Sigma Xi; fel Am Geophys Union. *Mailing Add:* Space Physics Res Lab Univ Mich 2455 Haywood St Ann Arbor MI 48109 2143

HAYS, RICHARD MORTIMER, RENAL DISEASES. *Current Pos:* PROF MED, ALBERT EINSTEIN COL MED, 73-, DIR, DIV NEPHROL, 79- *Personal Data:* b Far Rockaway, NY, July 1, 27. *Educ:* Columbia Univ, MD, 54. *Mailing Add:* Dept Med Albert Einstein Col Med 1300 Morris Park Ave Bronx NY 10461-1975. *Fax:* 718-824-2765

HAYS, RUTH LANIER, ENDOCRINOLOGY, HISTOLOGY. *Current Pos:* From asst prof to assoc prof physiol, 65-81, PROF ZOOL, CLEMSON UNIV, 81- *Personal Data:* b Cartersville, Ga, July 22, 40; m 65, Sidney B; c Shanon A & Anna L. *Educ:* Berea Col, BA, 62; Auburn Univ, PhD(physiol), 66. *Mem:* Sigma Xi; Human Anat & Physiol Soc; Asn Int Med Studies; Am Soc Zool. *Res:* Endocrinology; neuroendocrinology; reproductive physiology; enterochromaffin cells; age changes in mammals; seasonal variations; disease state; nutritional state. *Mailing Add:* Dept Biol Sci Clemson Univ Long Hall PO Box 341903 Clemson SC 29634-1903. *Fax:* 864-656-0435; *E-Mail:* hruth@clemson.edu

HAYS, SIDNEY BROOKS, ENTOMOLOGY, ANIMAL PHYSIOLOGY. *Current Pos:* from asst prof to assoc prof entom res, 64-72, HEAD DEPT ENTOM, CLEMSON UNIV, 69-, PROF, 72- *Personal Data:* b Arab, Ala, May 31, 31; m 65, Ruth Lanier; c Shanon A & Anna L. *Educ:* Auburn Univ, BS, 53, MS, 58; Clemson Univ, PhD(entom), 62. *Honors & Awards:* Sigma Xi Res Award, Auburn Univ, 60; Hatch Act Res Award, Clemson Univ, 89. *Prof Exp:* Asst entom, Auburn Univ, 58-60; asst entomologist, Univ Ga, 62-63; asst prof entom, Auburn Univ, 63-64. *Mem:* Am Entom Soc; Entom Soc Am. *Res:* Economic entomology; insect physiology of reproduction; insect ecology. *Mailing Add:* 324 Waldrop Stone Rd Central SC 29630

HAYS, VIRGIL WILFORD, ANIMAL NUTRITION. *Current Pos:* prof, 67-90, dept chair, 74-90, SCOVILL DISTINGUISHED PROF ANIMAL NUTRIT, UNIV KY, 90- *Personal Data:* b Waurika, Okla, Oct 1, 28; m 52; c 3. *Educ:* Okla State Univ, BS, 54; Iowa State Univ, PhD(animal nutrit), 58. *Honors & Awards:* Am Feed Mfr Nutrit Award, Am Soc Animal Sci, 74, Distinguished Serv Award, 90. *Prof Exp:* From asst prof to prof animal nutrit, Iowa State Univ, 58-67, asst dir, Agr & Home Econ Exp Sta, 66-67. *Mem:* AAAS; Am Soc Animal Sci (pres, 78-79); Am Instr Nutrit; Am Dairy Sci Asn; Poultry Sci Asn; Coun Agr Sci & Tech (pres, 89-90); Am Registry Prof Animal Scientists (pres, 85-86). *Res:* Nutrition; minerals; amino acids; drugs; hormones. *Mailing Add:* Dept Animal Sci Univ Ky 1809 Bimini Rd Lexington KY 40502-2839. *Fax:* 606-323-1027

HAYS, WILLIAM HENRY, GEOLOGY. *Current Pos:* RETIRED. *Personal Data:* b Livingston, Mont, Mar 15, 22; m 61; c 2. *Educ:* Stanford Univ, BS, 48; Yale Univ, MS, 50, PhD(geol), 58. *Prof Exp:* Geologist, US Geol Surv, 58-85. *Mem:* Fel Geol Soc Am. *Res:* Geologic hazards; stratigraphy; structural geology. *Mailing Add:* 55 S Flower St Lakewood CO 80226

HAYSLETT, JOHN P, PHYSIOLOGY. *Current Pos:* From instr to assoc prof, 67-77, PROF MED & PEDIAT, SCH MED, YALE UNIV, 77- *Personal Data:* b Greenwich, Conn, Jan 6, 35; m 60; c 2. *Educ:* Col Holy Cross, AB, 56; Cornell Univ, MD, 60. *Concurrent Pos:* Res fel metab, Sch Med, Yale

Univ, 65-67; estab investr, Am Heart Asn, 71-76. *Mem:* Am Fedn Clin; Am Soc Nephrology; Am Soc Clin Invest; Am Physiol Soc; Am Col Physicians. *Res:* Clinical problems in renal disease; mechanisms for the renal control of sodium readsorption. *Mailing Add:* Dept Med Yale Univ Sch Med 333 Cedar St LMP 2073 New Haven CT 06510-8056

HAYT, WILLIAM H(ART), JR, ELECTRICAL ENGINEERING. *Current Pos:* From asst prof to assoc prof, Purdue Univ, 48-58, head, Sch Elec Eng, 62-65, asst to vpres acad affairs, 65-73, prof, 58-86, EMER PROF ELEC ENG, PURDUE UNIV, 86- *Personal Data:* b Wilmette, Ill, July 1, 20; m 46; c 3. *Educ:* Purdue Univ, BS, 42, MS, 48; Univ Ill, PhD(elec eng), 54. *Concurrent Pos:* Consult, Martin Co, Colo, 57-59, IBM Corp, 61-63 & Midwest Appl Sci Corp, 63-67; auth. *Mem:* Am Soc Eng Educ; fel Inst Elec & Electronics Engrs. *Mailing Add:* Purdue Univ Elec Eng Bldg West Lafayette IN 47907

HAYTER, JOHN BINGLEY, COLLOIDAL STRUCTURE, NEUTRON OPTICS. *Current Pos:* SR RES STAFF MEM, SOLID STATE DIV, OAK RIDGE NAT LAB, 84- *Personal Data:* b Auckland, NZ, Nov 27, 45; m 70; c 3. *Educ:* Univ Sydney, Australia, BSc Hons, 66, PhD(chem phys), 70. *Honors & Awards:* Inventor's Award, Martin Marietta Energy Syst, Inc, 88; R&D 100 Award, Res & Develop Mag, 89. *Prof Exp:* Res assoc phys chem, Univ Oxford, UK, 71-73; staff scientist, Inst Laue-Langevin, France, 73-84. *Concurrent Pos:* Sci dir, Advan Neutron Source Proj, Oak Ridge Nat Lab, 90- *Mem:* Am Phys Soc; Mat Res Soc. *Res:* Theoretical and experimental investigations of complex fluids and colloidal systems, primarily by neutron scattering; development of neutron optical techniques for surface studies. *Mailing Add:* Oak Ridge Nat Lab-FEDC MS 8218 PO Box 2009 Oak Ridge TN 37831

HAYTER, ROY G, INDUSTRIAL CHEMISTRY. *Personal Data:* b Bristol, Eng, May 23, 32; m 57; c 3. *Educ:* Bristol Univ, BSc, 52, PhD(chem), 55. *Prof Exp:* Fel inorg chem, Cornell Univ, 55-57; tech officer chem, Imp Chem Industs, Ltd, Eng, 57-60; fel, Mellon Inst, 60-63; chemist, Shell Develop Co, Calif, 63-68, res supv, 68-70, res dir, Shell Develop Co, Houston, Tex, 70-72, venture mgr, Shell Chem Co, 72-76; mgr, Plastics Dept, Shell Develop Co, 76-83, mgr, Polymer Systs Res & Develop Dept, 83-89; sr consult, SRI Int, 89-90. *Mem:* Am Chem Soc; Chem Soc; Soc Plastic Engrs. *Res:* Coordination, organometallic and polymer chemistry. *Mailing Add:* 1691 Yale St Mountain View CA 94040-3645

HAYTER, WALTER R, JR, ELECTRICAL ENGINEERING. *Current Pos:* Design engr, Westinghouse Elec Corp, 45-56, supv engr, 56-57, eng sect mgr, 57-70, SR ENGR, WESTINGHOUSE ELEC CORP, 70- *Personal Data:* b Stamford, Conn, Mar 9, 23; m 45; c 5. *Educ:* Univ Conn, BS, 44; Stevens Inst Technol, MS, 50. *Honors & Awards:* Westinghouse Most Meritorious Patent Award, 55. *Mem:* Inst Elec & Electronics Engrs. *Res:* Microwave tubes and devices; power tubes and vacuum interrupters. *Mailing Add:* 512 Underwood Ave Elmira NY 14905

HAYTHORNTHWAITE, ROBERT M(ORPHET), ENGINEERING MECHANICS, CIVIL ENGINEERING. *Current Pos:* dean, Col Eng Technol, 79-81, prof, 79-96, EMER PROF ENG SCI, TEMPLE UNIV, 97- *Personal Data:* b Whitley Bay, Eng, May 5, 22; m 52, Mary Swift; c Richard, Jennifer, Susan & Sheila. *Educ:* Univ Durham, BSc, 42; Univ London, PhD(eng), 52; Brown Univ, ScM, 53. *Honors & Awards:* Walter L Huber Civil Eng Res Prize, 63. *Prof Exp:* Jr sci off, Bldg Res Sta, Eng, 42-46; sci off, Dept Sci & Indust Res, 46-47; lectr civil eng, Univ Sheffield, 47-53; from instr to assoc prof eng, Brown Univ, 53-59; prof eng sci, Univ Mich, Ann Arbor, 59-67; head, Dept Eng Mech, Pa State Univ, 67-74, prof, 67-79. *Concurrent Pos:* Mem res comt, Column Res Coun, 56-64; chmn, Ed Comt, Nat Cong Appl Mech, 58; consult, Land Locomotion Res Br, Ord Corps, US Army, 60-69; ed, Mechanics, 71-72 & 89- *Mem:* Am Soc Civil Engrs; Am Soc Mech Engrs; Am Soc Eng Educ; Am Acad Mech (pres, 69-71). *Res:* Mechanics of solids; framed structures, plates and shells; theory of plasticity; soil mechanics. *Mailing Add:* Dept Civil Eng Temple Univ 084-53 Philadelphia PA 19122

HAYTON, WILLIAM LEROY, PHARMACOKINETICS, DRUG ABSORPTION. *Current Pos:* CHMN & PROF PHARMACEUT & PHARMACEUT CHEM DEPT, OHIO STATE UNIV, 90- *Personal Data:* b Mt Vernon, Wash, June 16, 44; m 67; c 2. *Educ:* Univ Wash, BS, 67; State Univ NY Buffalo, PhD(pharmaceut), 71. *Prof Exp:* From asst prof to prof pharm, Wash State Univ, 71-90, chmn, Grad Prog Pharmacol-Toxicol, 82-90. *Mem:* Am Asn Pharmaceut Sci; Am Soc Pharmacol & Exp Therapeut; AAAS; Sigma Xi; Soc Toxicol. *Res:* Kinetics of drug absorption, distribution, and elimination; intestinal permeability and xenobiotic accumulation by fish. *Mailing Add:* Col Pharm Ohio State Univ 500 W 12th Ave Columbus OH 43210-1291. *Fax:* 614-292-7766; *E-Mail:* hayton.1@osu.edu

HAYWARD, ANTHONY R, PEDIATRIC IMMUNOLOGY, IMMUNODEFICIENCY. *Current Pos:* PROF PEDIAT, MICROBIOL & IMMUNOL, UNIV COLO HEALTH SCI CTR, 84- *Educ:* Univ London, MD, 67, PhD(immunol), 74. *Mailing Add:* Dept Pediat B-140 Univ Colo Health Sci Ctr 4200 E Ninth Ave Denver CO 80262-0001. *Fax:* 303-270-4892

HAYWARD, BRUCE JOLLIFFE, ZOOLOGY. *Current Pos:* From asst prof to assoc prof, 61-75, PROF BIOL SCI, WESTERN NMEX UNIV, 75- *Personal Data:* b Pine Island, Minn, Apr 13, 28. *Educ:* Univ Minn, BS, 50; Univ Mich, MS, 52; Univ Ariz, PhD(zool), 61. *Mem:* Am Soc Mammal. *Res:* Natural history studies of bats in southwestern United States, Central America and South America. *Mailing Add:* Dept Natural Sci Western NMex Univ Silver City NM 88062

HAYWARD, CHARLES LYNN, ANIMAL ECOLOGY. *Current Pos:* RETIRED. *Personal Data:* b Paris, Idaho, July 16, 03; m 30; c 2. *Educ:* Brigham Young Univ, BS, 27, MS, 31; Univ Ill, PhD(animal ecol), 42. *Prof Exp:* From instr to emer prof zool, Brigham Young Univ, 31-82, chmn, Dept Zool, 58-61, cur life sci, Mus, 69-74. *Concurrent Pos:* Asst, Univ Ill, 38-39. *Mem:* Fel AAAS; Ecol Soc Am; Am Ornith Union; Cooper Ornith Soc. *Res:* Birds and mammals of Utah. *Mailing Add:* 959 Cedar Ave Provo UT 84604

HAYWARD, EVANS VAUGHAN, PHYSICS. *Current Pos:* RETIRED. *Personal Data:* b Camp Dix, NJ, Feb 17, 22; m 47, Raymond W; c Ariel. *Educ:* Smith Col, BA, 42; Univ Calif, MA, 45, PhD(physics), 47. *Honors & Awards:* Gold Medal, US Dept Com, 71; Federal Women's Award Winner, 75. *Prof Exp:* Physicist, Radiation Lab, Univ Calif, 47-50 & Nat Bur Stand, 50-90; physicist, Duke Univ, 90-92. *Concurrent Pos:* Guggenheim fel, Nordic Inst Theoret Atomic Physics, Denmark, 61-62; guest prof, Inst Nuclear Physics, Univ Frankfurt, 66; Sir Thomas Lyle fel, Univ Melbourne, 69; mem, Gen Adv Comt, US Atomic Energy Comn, 72-75, chmn, 74-75; mem, Md Gov Sci Adv Coun, 72-84; vis prof physics, Univ Toronto, 75, Duke Univ, 87; guest prof exp physics, Max Planck Inst, Mainz, Ger, 82-86; chmn, Div Nuclear Physics, Am Phys Soc, 83-84; sr vis scientist, Nuclear Physics Lab, Oxford, UK, 85-86; vis scientist, Physics Inst, Univ Lund, Sweden, 88-92; mem, Argonne Univ Asn Spec Comt Medium Energy Electron Accelerator, 82-84; mem bd trustees, Southern Univ Res Asn, 82-87. *Mem:* Fel Am Phys Soc. *Res:* Interactions of high energy radiations with matter; photonuclear reactions; electrodisintegration. *Mailing Add:* 8400 Westmont Ct Bethesda MD 20817. *E-Mail:* ehay@enh.nist.gov

HAYWARD, JAMES LLOYD, BEHAVIORAL ECOLOGY, PALEOBIOLOGY. *Current Pos:* PROF BIOL, ANDREWS UNIV, 86- *Personal Data:* b Melrose, Mass, Sept 30, 48; m 74, Cheryl Kirkpatrick; c Shanna M. *Educ:* Walla Walla Col, BS, 72; Andrews Univ, MA, 75; Wash State Univ, PhD(zool), 82. *Prof Exp:* Instr biol, Andrews Univ, 75-76, Southwestern Union Col, 76-77, Walla Walla Col, 80-81; from asst prof to assoc prof biol, Union Col, 81-86. *Concurrent Pos:* Vis prof biol, Walla Walla Col Marine Sta, 77, 79, 83 & 85. *Mem:* AAAS; Am Ornithologists Union; Sigma Xi. *Res:* Visual communication; temporal and spatial patterning of behavior; factors influencing fossilization of bird and dinosaur eggs; community ecology. *Mailing Add:* Dept Biol Andrews Univ Berrien Springs MI 49104. *Fax:* 616-471-6911; *E-Mail:* hayward@orion.cc.andrews.edu

HAYWARD, JAMES ROGERS, ORAL SURGERY. *Current Pos:* RETIRED. *Personal Data:* b Detroit, Mich, Dec 16, 20; m 43; c 3. *Educ:* Univ Mich, BS, 41, DDS, 44, MS, 46; Am Bd Oral Surg, dipl, 49. *Prof Exp:* Instr oral surg, W K Kellogg Found Inst, 47-50, assoc prof, 52-55, dir, Sect Oral Surg, Univ Hosp, 52, prof oral surg & chmn dept, W K Kellogg Found Inst, Univ Mich, Ann Arbor, 56- & prof dent & dent in surg, 78-, emer prof dent, oral & maxillofacial surg & surg, Sch Med. *Concurrent Pos:* Consult, Ann Arbor Vet Admin Hosp, 53-; ed, J Oral Surg. *Mem:* Am Soc Oral Surg; fel Am Col Dent; fel Am Col Oral Path. *Res:* Local anesthesia; jaw fractures; cleft lip and palate; tumors of mouth and jaw region. *Mailing Add:* 249 Second St Bonita Springs FL 34134

HAYWARD, JOHN S, ENVIRONMENTAL PHYSIOLOGY, AEROSPACE MEDICINE. *Current Pos:* RETIRED. *Personal Data:* b Vancouver, BC, Feb 14, 37; m 61; c 3. *Educ:* Univ BC, BSc, 58, PhD(zool), 64. *Prof Exp:* Exp officer animal physiol, Div Wildlife Res, Commonwealth Sci & Indust Res Orgn, Australia, 58-61; NATO fel, 64-65; asst prof zool, Univ Alta, 65-69; asst prof zool, Univ Victoria, 69-70, assoc prof, 70-78, prof biol, 79- *Mem:* Can Physiol Soc. *Res:* Physiological responses to cold; thermogenic mechanisms; brown fat and nonshivering heat production; man in cold water and cold air, his physiological responses and survival techniques; treatment of hypothermia. *Mailing Add:* Dept Biol Univ Victoria PO Box 1700 Victoria BC V8W 2Y2 Can

HAYWARD, JOHN T(UCKER), PHYSICS, AERONAUTICAL ENGINEERING. *Current Pos:* PRES, HAYWARD ASSOCS, 73- *Personal Data:* b New York, NY, Nov 15, 10; m 32; c 5. *Educ:* US Naval Acad, BS, 30; Univ Portland, DSc, 65. *Honors & Awards:* Robert D Conrad Sci Award, Secy Navy. *Prof Exp:* Asst chief engr, Instruments Naval Aircraft Factory, 39-40, test pilot, Test Ctr, 40, exp officer, Manhattan Dist, Calif Inst Technol, 44-46, head plans & opers, Atomic Warfare Armed Forces, Sandia AFB, 48-49 & Group Atomic Capability Aircraft Carriers, 49-51, dir, Weapons Res Div, Atomic Energy Comn, 51-53, comdr & tech dir, Naval Ord Lab, 54-56, dep chief naval opers res & develop, 56-62, comdr, Carrier Div 2, Flagship USS Enterprise, 62-63, comdr antisubmarine warfare forces Pac, 63-66; pres, Naval War Col, Newport, 66-68; vpres, Int, Gen Dynamics Corp, 68-73. *Concurrent Pos:* Consult, Lawrence Livermore Lab & Gen Dynamics, 73-, Charles Stark Draper Lab, Inc; bd dir, Hertz Found. *Mem:* AAAS; Am Inst Aeronaut & Astronaut; Am Phys Soc; Newcomen Soc NAm; fel Royal Aero Soc. *Res:* Aeronautics; ordnance engineering, especially modern underwater weapons; application of the atom to its official use by the Navy. *Mailing Add:* 3 Barclay Sq Newport RI 02840

HAYWARD, LLOYL DOUGLAS, PHYSICAL ORGANIC CHEMISTRY. *Current Pos:* RETIRED. *Personal Data:* b Cupar, Sask, June 10, 19; m 45; c 2. *Educ:* Univ Sask, BA, 43; McGill Univ, PhD(chem), 49. *Prof Exp:* Lectr analytical chem, Khaki Univ Can, Eng, 45-46; lectr, Sir George Williams Col, 47-48; sessional lectr org chem, McGill Univ, 49-50; asst prof chem, Regina Col, 50-51; from asst prof to prof org chem, Univ BC, 51-84. *Concurrent Pos:* Guest prof, Inst Phys Chem, Univ Uppsala, 64-65; consult, Ives Lab, 79-84, Syndel Lab, 80-, DH Stereochem, 80-; founder of Vol Prog, Do-It-Yourself Chem Exp in Elem Sch, 86. *Mem:* NY Acad Sci; fel Chem Inst Can; Royal Chem Soc. *Res:* Induced optical activity; circular dichroism studies; chemistry and pharmacology of the nitrate esters. *Mailing Add:* 2041 W 29th Ave Vancouver BC V6J 2Z9 Can

HAYWARD, OLIVER THOMAS, GEOLOGY. *Current Pos:* from asst prof to assoc prof, 55-71, PROF GEOL, BAYLOR UNIV, 71- *Personal Data:* b Las Cruces, NMex, Sept 26, 21; m 46; c 3. *Educ:* Univ Kans, BS, 45; Stanford Univ, MS, 51; Univ Wis, PhD(geol), 57. *Prof Exp:* Explor geologist, Phillips Venezuelan Oil Co, 45-50, consult, 50-53; area geologist, Calif Co, La, 53-55. *Concurrent Pos:* Dir, Coun Ed Geol Sci, Am Geol Inst, 64-65. *Mem:* Geol Soc Am; Nat Asn Geol Teachers (pres, 80); Am Asn Petrol Geologists. *Res:* Geomorphic evolution in Central Texas; drainage history Eastward drainage American Southwest; Central Texas; sedimentary geology; structural geology of sedimentary rocks; landscape evolution in central Texas. *Mailing Add:* 7820 Tallahassee Rd Waco TX 76712

HAYWARD, RAYMOND (W)EBSTER, NUCLEAR PHYSICS, ASTROPHYSICS. *Current Pos:* RETIRED. *Personal Data:* b Omaha, Nebr, July 28, 21; m 47; c 2. *Educ:* Iowa State Col, BS, 43; Univ Calif, PhD(physics), 50. *Honors & Awards:* John Price Wetherill Medal, Franklin Inst, 66; Gold Medal, US Dept Com, 58. *Prof Exp:* Electronic scientist, US Naval Res Lab, 43-45; physicist, Nat Bur Stand, 50-86, emer quest, physics. *Concurrent Pos:* Prof, Univ Md, 61-83. *Mem:* Fel Am Phys Soc. *Res:* Electromagnetic and weak interactions; relativistic quantum mechanics; Lagrangian field theory; gravitation interaction; quantum gravity. *Mailing Add:* 8400 Westmont Ct Bethesda MD 20817

HAYWARD, THOMAS DOYLE, EXPERIMENTAL NUCLEAR PHYSICS, GENERAL PHYSICS. *Current Pos:* SR PRIN ENGR, BOEING AEROSPACE, 83- *Personal Data:* b Hood River, Ore, June 19, 40; m 62; c 2. *Educ:* Univ Wash, BS, 62, PhD(physics), 69. *Prof Exp:* Fel nuclear physics, Duke Univ, 69-72, from instr to asst prof, 70-72; mem staff, Los Alamos Sci Lab, Univ Calif, 72-80, asst group leader physics, 74-76, alt group leader, 77-78, group leader accelerator technol, 78-80; sr scientist, Sci Appln Int Corp, 80-83. *Mem:* Am Phys Soc. *Res:* Negative ion beam generation, acceleration, and high energy negative ion beam stripping processes related to stripping injection into storage rings; granted one patent; accelerators for newtron radiography; hyperconducting accelerator development; free electron laser development; radio frequency quadrupols accelerator development. *Mailing Add:* 5409 Norpoint Way NE Tacoma WA 98422-4239

HAYWOOD, ANNE MOWBRAY, VIROLOGY, MEMBRANE CHEMISTRY. *Current Pos:* ASSOC PROF PEDIAT MED & MICROBIOL, MED SCH, UNIV ROCHESTER, 77- *Personal Data:* b Baltimore, Md, Feb 5, 35. *Educ:* Bryn Mawr, BA, 55; Harvard Univ, MD, 59; Am Bd Pediat, dipl, 81. *Prof Exp:* Res fel biol, Calif Inst Technol, 60-61 & 62-64; res fel biochem, Columbia Univ, 61-62; asst prof microbiol, Med Sch, Northwest Univ, 64-66; asst prof microbiol, Sch Med, Yale Univ, 66-73, resident pediat, 74-75; infectious dis fel, Univ Wash, 75-76 & Vanderbilt Univ, 76-77. *Concurrent Pos:* Am Cancer Soc fel, 60-62; vis asst prof, Rockefeller Univ, 71-72; vis scientist, Inst Animal Physiol, Cambridge, 72-74; Nat Inst Health spec fel, 71-73; Europ Molecular Biol Orgn fel, 73-74; vis assoc prof, Univ Calif Davis, 86; vis scientist, Univ Zurich, 87; Fogarty Sr Int Fel, 87. *Mem:* Am Soc Biochem & Molecular Biol; Biophys Soc; Infectious Dis Soc Am. *Res:* Biochemistry of viruses; host-virus interaction; viral entry, virus receptors, viral persistence; membranes; infectious diseases; pediatrics. *Mailing Add:* Dept Pediat Univ Rochester PO Box 777 Med Ctr 601 Elmwood Ave Rochester NY 14642. *Fax:* 716-273-1079; *E-Mail:* ahyw@ uhura.cc.rochester.edu

HAYWOOD, FREDERICK F, HEALTH PHYSICS, TECHNICAL WRITING. *Current Pos:* prog dir, 89-90, PRIN SCIENTIST, RADIAN CORP, 90- *Personal Data:* b Lumberton, NC, Sept 26, 36; m 85, Sally L Ledbetter. *Educ:* Lynchburg Col, BS, 58; Vanderbilt Univ, MS, 64. *Prof Exp:* Health physicist, Oak Ridge Nat Lab, 59-72, res staff mem, 72-75, proj mgr, 75-81; proj mgr, Eberline Analytical Corp, 81-85, tech dir, 85-89. *Concurrent Pos:* Consult, Int Atomic Energy Agency, 70-79; appointee, Subcomt Radiation Shielding, Adv Comt Civil Defense, Nat Acad Sci, 73-75. *Mem:* Am Nuclear Soc; Int Radiation Protection Asn; Health Physics Soc. *Res:* Direct planning and execution of radiological and chemical investigations at hazardous waste sites; evaluates field data to characterize contaminant boundaries; identifies principal pathways to humans; assesses potential health effects and recommends measures to mitigate human exposure. *Mailing Add:* 128 Westview Lane Oak Ridge TN 37830. *Fax:* 423-483-9061; *E-Mail:* frederick___haywood@radian.com

HAYWOOD, H CARL, COGNITIVE EDUCATION, MENTAL RETARDATION. *Current Pos:* prof neurol, 71-94, EMER PROF PSYCHOL & NEUROL, VANDERBILT UNIV, 94-; PROF PSYCHOL & DEAN, GRAD SCH EDUC & PSYCHOL, TOURO COL, NY. *Personal Data:* b Taylor County, Ga, July 2, 31; m 51, 93, Dona June; c Carlton, Terence, Elizabeth & Kristin. *Educ:* San Diego State Col, BA, 56, MA, 57; Univ Ill, PhD(psychol), 61. *Honors & Awards:* Nat Leadership Award, Am Asn Ment Deficiency, 85, R Res Award, 89; Edgar A Doll Award, Am Psychol Assoc, 88. *Prof Exp:* Psychologist, US Vet Admin, 61-62; prof psychol, George Peabody Col, 62-93. *Concurrent Pos:* Vis prof psychiat, Univ Toronto, 65-66; ed, Am J Ment Deficiency, 69-79; dir, Ment Retardation Res Training Prog, 68-73, Inst Ment Retardation & Intellectual Develop, George Peabody Col, 70-73, John F Kennedy Ctr, Peabody Col/Vanderbilt Univ, 71-83; presidential appointee, Nat Adv Child Health & Human Develop Coun, NIH, 84-88. *Mem:* Inst Med-Nat Acad Sci; Am Psychol Assoc; Am Asn Mental Deficiency (pres, 80-81); Soc Res in Child Develop; Psychonomic Soc; Int Asn Cognitive Educ (pres, 88-92). *Res:* Psychological research on mental retardation and intellectual development, individual differences in motivation to learn and achieve, and development and modifiability of cognitive processes; psychoeducational assessment and cognitive approaches to psychotherapy. *Mailing Add:* 402 Abbey Ct Brentwood TN 37027. *Fax:* 212-627-9144; *E-Mail:* haywoohc@vuctrvax.edu

HAYWOOD, L JULIAN, INTERNAL MEDICINE, CARDIOLOGY. *Current Pos:* from asst prof to assoc prof, Univ Southern Calif, 63-76, dir, Coronary Care Unit, Med Ctr, 66-84, dir, Comprehensive Sickle Cell Ctr, 72-91, PROF, SCH MED, UNIV SOUTHERN CALIF, LOS ANGELES, 76-; CLIN PROF MED, LOMA LINDA UNIV, 82- *Personal Data:* b Reidsville, NC, Apr 13, 27; m 52, Virginia E Paige; c 1. *Educ:* Hampton Inst, BS, 48; Howard Univ, MD, 52. *Honors & Awards:* Russell Award, Am Heart Asn, 88, Award Merit, Heart of Gold; Walter H Booker Award, Asn Black Cardiologists; Laureate Award, Am Col Physicians. *Prof Exp:* Asst prof, Loma Linda Univ, 61-73, assoc clin prof med, 73-82. *Concurrent Pos:* Fel cardiol, White Mem Hosp, 59-61; mem consult staff, White Mem Hosp, 61-; sr consult cardiol, Vet Admin Hosp, Long Beach, Calif, 61-70; Am Col Physicians traveling fel, Oxford Univ, 63; sr physician, LAC & Univ Southern Calif Med Ctr, 66-; consult, White Mem Hosp & St Vincent's Hosp, 68-, Calif State Div Indust Accidents & Health Resources Admin, USPHS; consult, Calif State Div Indust Accidents; fel, Coun Clin Cardiol, Epidemiol & Arteriosclerosis, Am Heart Asn past pres, greater Los Angeles Affil; consult, Health Resources Admin, USPHS; mem bd dirs & pres, Sickle Cell Dis Res Found; mem rev comt, Nat Heart, Lung & Blood Inst; mem, Epidemiol Bd, Armed Forces. *Mem:* Fel AAAS; Am Fedn Clin Res; NY Acad Sci; fel Am Col Physicians; fel Am Col Cardiol; Am Heart Asn; fel Coun Epidemiol; Coun Arteriosclerosis; Coun Clin Cardiol; Int Soc Hypertension in Blacks; Asn Black Cardiologists; Asn Acad Minority Physicians. *Res:* Cardiovascular disease; cardiovascular aspects of sickle cell anemia including coronary artery disease; biomedical and computer applications; hypertension and health access. *Mailing Add:* Univ Southern Calif Med Ctr 1200 N State St PO Box 305 Los Angeles CA 90033

HAYWOOD, THEODORE J, MEDICINE, ALLERGY. *Current Pos:* assoc prof, 70-84, ADJ ASSOC PROF MICROBIOL & IMMUNOL, BAYLOR COL MED, 70-, CLIN ASSOC PROF PEDIAT, 77- *Personal Data:* b Monroe, NC, Feb 13, 29; m 59; c 3. *Educ:* The Citadel, BS, 48; Vanderbilt Univ, MD, 52; Am Bd Allergy & Immunol, cert. *Prof Exp:* Asst pediat, Washington Univ, 52-53; teaching asst, Univ London, 53-54; asst, Tulane Univ, 54-55 & Harvard Univ, 55; assoc, McGovern Allergy Clin, 58-74. *Concurrent Pos:* House physician, Hosp Sick Children, London, Eng, 53-54; resident pediat, Charity Hosp, La, Tulane Univ, 54-55; clin assoc prof pediat allergy, Baylor Col Med, 77- *Mem:* Fel Am Col Allergists; fel Am Acad Allergy; fel Am Acad Pediat; fel Acad Psychosom Med; Sigma Xi. *Res:* Immunology of hypersensitivity; psychophysiology of allergic disease; hypothalamus and autonomic nervous system in allergic disease; insect and drug hypersensitivity; longitudinal studies on relationship of bacterial infections in asthma. *Mailing Add:* 4710 Bellaire Blvd Suite 200 Houston TX 77401

HAYWORTH, CURTIS B, CHEMICAL ENGINEERING. *Current Pos:* VAL ENG, US TREAS, 75- *Personal Data:* b Vienna, Austria, Dec 1, 20; US citizen; wid; c Steven & Karen. *Educ:* City Col New York, BChE, 44; NY Univ, MChE, 47, ScD(chem eng), 49, PE 49. *Prof Exp:* Lab asst, Gen Chem Div, Allied Chem Corp, 44-45, analyst, 45, tech supvr lab, 45-48, res chem engr, 48-53, asst mgr develop res, 53-54, asst dir, 54-58, dir, 58-61, asst tech dir, 61-63, asst dir, Cent Res Lab, 63-67, sr res tech assoc, Corp Res & Develop, 67-70; vpres, World Patent Develop Corp, 70-71, pres, 71-75. *Mem:* Am Chem Soc; Am Inst Chem Engrs; Sigma Xi. *Res:* Chemical engineering unit processes and economics; liquid-liquid extraction; numerous US and foreign patents. *Mailing Add:* PO Box 1447 Morristown NJ 07962

HAZARD, EVAN BRANDAO, MAMMALOGY, SCIENCE WRITING. *Current Pos:* From asst prof to prof biol, 58-94, head, Div Sci & Math, 69-71, EMER PROF BIOL, BEMIDJI STATE UNIV, 94- *Personal Data:* b Montclair, NJ, Nov 17, 29; m 52, Elaine J Willis; c Brian, Stuart & Kathryn. *Educ:* Cornell Univ, BS, 51; Univ Mich, MA, 55, PhD(zool), 60. *Concurrent Pos:* Mem, Minn Writing Proj, 82-84; sci-writing & ed consult, 83-; reviewer, Choice, 83- *Mem:* AAAS; Am Inst Biol Sci; Am Soc Mammal; Soc Study Evolution; Nat Asn Biol Teachers; Asn Religion & Intellectual Life. *Res:* Geographic distribution of Minnesota mammals; evolution and faith; vertebrate evolution; writing for biology majors and across-the-curriculum. *Mailing Add:* Dept Biol Bemidji State Univ 1500 Birchmond Ave NE Bemidji MN 56601-2699

HAZARD, HERBERT RAY, MECHANICAL ENGINEERING, FUEL TECHNOLOGY. *Current Pos:* PRES, HERBERT R HAZARD, INC, 84- *Personal Data:* b Johnson City, NY, Aug 4, 17; m 42, Ellen C Wedvik; c Christopher W, Bruce D & Carol (Babka). *Educ:* Pa State Univ, BS, 39. *Prof Exp:* Student engr, Babcock & Wilcox Co, NY, 39-40, analytical engr, 40-44; proj engr, Bendix Aviation Co, NY, 44-45; res engr, Battelle Mem Inst, 45-48, asst supvr, 48-53, asst div chief, 53-60, div chief, 60-62, fel, 62-76, prin mech engr, 76-81; consult, 82-83. *Concurrent Pos:* Lectr, Univ Mich, 53, 55 & 58; chair, Gas Turbine Power Div, Am Soc Mech Engrs, 59. *Mem:* Fel Am Soc Mech Engrs. *Res:* Combustion; heat transfer; fluid dynamics; gas turbines; nuclear reactors; deep-sea diving; low-emission combustion; advanced power generating concepts; boiler slagging and fouling; synthetic liquid fuels. *Mailing Add:* 2770 North Star Rd Columbus OH 43221-2960

HAZARD, JOHN BEACH, pathology; deceased, see previous edition for last biography

HAZARD, KATHARINE ELIZABETH, mathematics; deceased, see previous edition for last biography

HAZEL, CHARLES RICHARD, AQUATIC ECOLOGY, ENVIRONMENTAL IMPACT ANALYSIS. *Current Pos:* RETIRED. *Personal Data:* b Indianapolis, Ind, May 19, 29; m 51, Doris Pierre; c Charlotte, Roberta & Suzanne. *Educ:* Humboldt State Univ, BS, 60, MS, 63; Ore State Univ, PhD(fish biol), 69. *Prof Exp:* Res assoc water qual, Humboldt State Univ, 62-63; assoc water qual biol, Calif Dept Fish & Game, 63-64; teaching asst fisheries, Ore State Univ, 64-67; lab dir water qual, Calif Dept Fish & Game, 67-71; consult environ scientist, Jones & Stokes Assocs, Inc, 71-73, vpres environ consult, 73-82, pres, 83-90. *Concurrent Pos:* Phoenix Field Comt, USAF, Sacramento Co, 47-56. *Mem:* Am Fisheries Soc; Ecol Soc Am; Water Pollution Control Fedn; Asn Environ Prof; Sigma Xi. *Res:* Aquatic ecology in reference to resource planning, management and policy for decisions in the use of streams, lakes, and estuaries. *Mailing Add:* PO Box 126 Dallas OR 97338

HAZEL, JEFFREY RONALD, COMPARATIVE PHYSIOLOGY, CELL PHYSIOLOGY. *Current Pos:* from asst prof to assoc prof, 75-84, PROF ZOOL, ARIZ STATE UNIV, 84- *Personal Data:* b Youngstown, Ohio, Mar 4, 45; m 66; c 2. *Educ:* Col Wooster, BA, 67; Univ Ill, Urbana, MS, 69, PhD(physiol), 71. *Prof Exp:* Asst prof zool, Univ Nebr, Lincoln, 71-75. *Concurrent Pos:* Prin investr, NSF grant, 73-75, 76-92. *Mem:* Fel AAAS; Am Physiol Soc; Am Soc Zool; Am Chem Soc. *Res:* Mechanisms of thermal adaptation in poikilotherms; lipid metabolism, membrane structure and function in cold-blooded animals. *Mailing Add:* Dept Zool Ariz State Univ Tempe AZ 85281

HAZEL, JOSEPH ERNEST, BIOSTRATIGRAPHY, MICROPALEONTOLOGY. *Current Pos:* CAMPANILE PROF GEOL, LA STATE UNIV, 86- *Personal Data:* b Caruthersville, Mo, July 7, 33; m 56, Marilyn M Pata; c Joseph, James & Jonathan. *Educ:* Univ Mo, BA, 56, MA, 60; La State Univ, PhD(paleont), 63. *Prof Exp:* NSF fel, Mus Comp Zool, Harvard Univ, 63-64; chief, Br Paleontol & Stratig, US Geol Surv, 73-78, res geologist, 64-83; res assoc, Amoco Prod Co, 83-86. *Concurrent Pos:* Assoc prof lectr, George Washington Univ, 67-78. *Mem:* Geol Soc Am; Sigma Xi; Brit Micropaleont Soc; Soc Econ Paleontologists & Mineralogists; NAm Micropaleont Soc. *Res:* Mesozoic and cenolic biostratigraphy and stratigraphy, particularly of the Atlantic and Gulf Coastal Plain of the United States and Jamaica; quantitative techniques in tiostratigraphy and biogeography; micropalecritology. *Mailing Add:* Dept Geol & Geophys La State Univ Baton Rouge LA 70803-0001. *Fax:* 504-388-2302; *E-Mail:* glhazel@lsuvm.edu

HAZELBAUER, GERALD LEE, MEMBRANE BIOLOGY, BACTERIAL BEHAVIOR. *Current Pos:* assoc scientist biochem, Wash State Univ, 81-82, assoc prof, 82-85, actg chair, 89-90, PROF BIOCHEM, WASH STATE UNIV, 85-, CHAIR, 94-, DIR, BIOTECHNOL TRAINING PROG. *Personal Data:* b Chicago, Ill, Sept 27, 44; m 70, Linda L Randall. *Educ:* Williams Col, BA, 66; Case Western Res Univ, MS, 68; Univ Wis-Madison, PhD(genetics), 71. *Prof Exp:* Fel, Univ Wis-Madison, 71-72 & Inst Pasteur, Paris, 71-73; res fel molecular biol, Univ Uppsala, 73-75, asst prof, 75-81. *Concurrent Pos:* Fel, NSF, 71-72 & Muscular Dystrophy Asn Am, 72-73; res fel, Alfred P Sloan Found, 73-75; fac res award, Am Cancer Soc, 85-90. *Mem:* Am Soc Biol Chem; Am Soc Mirobiol; Protein Soc; fel Am Acad Microbiol. *Res:* Molecular biology of bacterial chemotaxis with emphasis on membrane proteins; characterization of receptors and signal transduction proteins; covalent protein modifications involved in sensory adaptation. *Mailing Add:* Biochem & Biophys Dept Wash State Univ Pullman WA 99164-4660

HAZELRIG, JANE, MODELING BIOLOGICAL SYSTEMS, SIMULATION. *Current Pos:* instr math, 67-77, from asst prof to assoc prof biomath, 77-82, ASST PROF PHYSIOL & BIOPHYS, UNIV ALA, BIRMINGHAM, 79-, ASSOC PROF BIOSTAT & BIOMATH, 82- *Personal Data:* b Chattanooga, Tenn, May 29, 37; m 58; c 2. *Educ:* Univ Ala, BS, 58; Univ Minn, MS, 65; Univ Ala, Birmingham, PhD(biophys sci), 76. *Prof Exp:* Assoc physicist, Southern Res Inst, 58-62; biophys technician, Mayo Clin, 62-67; fel biophys, Mayo Grad Sch Med, Univ Minn, 64-65. *Concurrent Pos:* Fac mem, Interdisciplinary Grad Prog Biophys Sci, Univ Ala, Birmingham, 79- *Mem:* Sigma Xi; Biomed Soc; AAAS; Soc Indust Appl Math. *Res:* Formulating, testing (via optimization methodology) and modifying mathematical models of biological systems to facilitate the testing of hypotheses and the design of experiments. *Mailing Add:* Dept Biomath Univ Sta Univ Ala Sch Med 1717 Seventh Ave S Birmingham AL 35294-0001

HAZELRIGG, GEORGE ARTHUR, JR, RESEARCH GRANT ADMINISTRATION. *Current Pos:* sr policy analyst, prog dir & dep div dir, 82-91, SR ADV, TECHNOL INTEGRATION, DIV DESIGN, MANUFACTURE & INDUST INNOVATION, NSF, 91- *Personal Data:* b Summit, NJ, Oct 28, 39; m 68, Lauretta B Powell; c George A III & Geoffrey A. *Educ:* NJ Inst Technol, BS, 61, MS, 63; Princeton Univ, MA, 66, MSE, 68, PhD(aerospace eng), 69. *Honors & Awards:* Outstanding Contrib to Aerospace Eng, Am Inst Aeronaut & Astronaut, 69. *Prof Exp:* Engr, Curtiss-Wright Corp, 61-63; instr, NJ Inst Technol, 62-63; engr, Jet Propulsion Lab, 66-67; staff scientist, Gen Dynamics, 68-71; res staff mem, Princeton Univ, 71-75; dir syst eng, Econ, Inc, 76-82. *Concurrent Pos:* Assoc ed, J Spacecraft & Rockets, 77-82; consult, Mathamatica, Inc, 71-73; Princeton Univ, 76-84, Econ, Inc, 82-84, Princeton Synergetics, 84-; chair, Emerging Technol Comt, Am Soc Mech Engrs, 89-; vis prof, Ajou Univ, 93. *Mem:* Am Inst Aeronaut & Astronaut; Am Soc Eng Educ; Inst Elec & Electronics Engrs; Am Soc Mech Engrs. *Res:* Development of the field of microelectromechanical systems. *Mailing Add:* NSF ECS Div Rm 1151 Washington DC 20550. *Fax:* 703-306-0298; *E-Mail:* ghazelri@nsf.gov

HAZELTINE, BARRETT, ELECTRICAL ENGINEERING, ENGINEERING MANAGEMENT. *Current Pos:* From asst prof to assoc prof, Brown Univ, 59-71, asst dean col, 61-63 & 67-72, assoc dean col, 72-93, PROF ELEC ENG, BROWN UNIV, 71- *Personal Data:* b Paris, France, Nov 7, 31; US citizen; m 56, Mary F Fenn; c Michael, Alice & Patricia. *Educ:* Princeton Univ, BSE, 53, MSE, 57; Univ Mich, PhD(elec eng), 62. *Hon Degrees:* ScD, State Univ NY, Stony Brook, 88. *Honors & Awards:* Fulbright lectr, Malawi, 89, Batswana, 93. *Concurrent Pos:* Asst to mgr, Adv Develop Lab, Space & Info Systs Div, Raytheon Co, 64-65; sr lectr, Univ Zambia, 70, vis prof, 76; mem, Adv Comt Nuclear Power, Pub Utilities Comn, State RI, 77-, NJ Dept Higher Educ & Coun for Understanding Technol in Human Affairs; vis prof, Univ Malaw, 81, 84, 89; trustee, Stevens Inst Technol; Robert Foster Cherry chair distinguished teaching, Baylor Univ, 91-92. *Mem:* Inst Elec & Electronics Engrs; Sigma Xi; Am Soc Eng Educ. *Res:* Engineering management; switching theory; appropriate technology. *Mailing Add:* Dept Eng Brown Univ Eng George St Cor Hope Providence RI 02912. *Fax:* 406-863-1157; *E-Mail:* hazeltine@brownvm.edu

HAZELTINE, JAMES EZRA, JR, PHYSICAL CHEMISTRY. *Current Pos:* RETIRED. *Personal Data:* b Warren, Pa, Sept 3, 16; m 89, Marjorie Greene; c James, Glenna & Rachel. *Educ:* Lafayette Col, BS, 37; Franklin & Marshall Col, MS, 50. *Prof Exp:* Asst mgr, Surface Coatings Dept, Armstrong Cork Co, 47-53, mgr, Plastic Flooring Res Dept, 53-59, asst dir, Div Res, 59-61, asst dir res, 61-70, vpres & dir res, Res & Develop Ctr, 70-81. *Mem:* Am Chem Soc; Am Inst Chemists. *Res:* Research direction and administration. *Mailing Add:* 611 Crestgate Pl Millersville PA 17515

HAZELTINE, RICHARD DEIMEL, PLASMA PHYSICS. *Current Pos:* res scientist theoret physics, 71-86, PROF PHYSICS, UNIV TEX, 86-, DIR, INST FUSION STUDIES, 91- *Personal Data:* b Jersey City, NJ, June 12, 42; m 64, Cheryl Pickett; c Richard E & Susannah E. *Educ:* Harvard Col, AB, 64; Univ Mich, MS, 66, PhD(physics), 68. *Prof Exp:* Lectr physics, Univ Mich, 69; vis mem, Inst Advan Study, 69-71; asst dir, Inst Fusion Studies, 82-86, actg dir, 87-88. *Concurrent Pos:* Fel comt, Div Plasma Physics, Am Phys Soc, 84 & 88; Simon Ramo Award Comt, Am Phys Soc, 86; rev panel, Magnetic Fusion Sci Fel Prog; adv comt, Fusion Energy Postdoctoral Res & Prof Dev Progs; consult, Austin Res Assocs, Los Alamos Nat Lab, GA Technol, Sci Applns Inc. *Mem:* Fel Am Phys Soc; AAAS; Sigma Xi. *Res:* Theoretical plasma physics, as applied to the problem of controlled fusion. *Mailing Add:* Inst Fusion Studies Univ Tex Rm 11 218 Austin TX 78712. *Fax:* 512-471-6715; *E-Mail:* rdh@hagar.ph.utexas.edu

HAZELTON, BONNI JANE, HUMAN RHABDOMYOSARCOMA, TUBULIAN EXPRESSION. *Current Pos:* DIR LAB SERV, ST JUDE CHILDREN'S RES HOSP, 85- *Educ:* Syracuse Univ, PhD(biol), 79. *Mailing Add:* Response Oncol Inc 1775 Moriah Woods Blvd Memphis TN 38117

HAZELTON, RUSSELL FRANK, CHEMICAL ENGINEERING. *Current Pos:* RETIRED. *Personal Data:* b Detroit, Mich, Apr 1, 14; m 41; c 3. *Educ:* Wayne State Univ, BS, 35; Univ Mich, MS, 37, PhD(chem eng), 43. *Prof Exp:* Asst chemist, Kimberly-Clark Corp, NY, 37-38, Wis, 38-39; asst chem engr, Solvay Process Co, Va, 41-45; chem engr, Dow Chem Co, 45-48; assoc prof chem eng, NC State Col, 48-52; chem engr & process consult develop, Agr Div, Allied Chem Corp, 52-67; prof chem eng, W Va Inst Technol, 67-82. *Mem:* Am Chem Soc; Am Inst Chem Engrs; Am Soc Eng Educ; Sigma Xi. *Res:* Design of chemical processes and plants; ethanolamines; distillation steps in phenol and chlorobenzene manufacture; chlorine from salt and nitric acid; melamine crystal from urea. *Mailing Add:* PO Box 364 Charlton Heights WV 25040-0364

HAZELWOOD, DONALD HILL, ZOOLOGY. *Current Pos:* RETIRED. *Personal Data:* b La Crosse, Wis, May 27, 31; m 54, 71; c 2. *Educ:* Univ Wis, BS, 53, MS, 54; Wash State Univ, PhD(zool), 61. *Prof Exp:* From asst prof to assoc prof zool, Univ Mo, Columbia, 61-92. *Concurrent Pos:* NIH res grant, 62-66; US CEngrs contract, 73-81. *Mem:* Am Soc Limnol & Oceanog. *Res:* Invertebrate zoology. *Mailing Add:* 4609 W Georgetown Dr Columbia MO 65203

HAZELWOOD, R(OBERT) NICHOLS, ENVIRONMENTAL AUDITING, RISK ASSESSMENT. *Current Pos:* distinguished tech assoc, 81-93, EMER & CONSULT IT CORP, 93- *Personal Data:* b Milwaukee, Wis, Jan 22, 28; m 58, Carol Weinert; c James, Arthur & Daniel. *Educ:* Haverford

Col, AB, 49; Marquette Univ, MS, 52; Univ Calif, Berkeley, PhD(biophys), 57. *Prof Exp:* Sect head chem, Line Mat Co Div, McGraw-Edison, Inc, 50-54; instr gen sci, Calif Col Arts & Crafts, 55-56; staff mem, Opers Res Group, Arthur D Little, Inc, 56-63; chief scientist, Hq, US Strike Command, 63-66; tech mgr, Data Systs Div, Litton Industs, Inc, 67-70; sr mem staff, Los Angeles Tech Serv Corp, 71-74; vpres & dir, Socio-Econ Systs, Inc, 75-77; chief scientist, Global Marine Develop, Inc, 78-81. *Concurrent Pos:* Assoc, Sch Med, Marquette Univ, 49-54; dir, Drake Steel Supply Co, 60-64; teacher, Hazardous Mats Prog, Univ Calif, Irvine Exten, 84-; bd ed, Environ Mgt, 87-; regist environ assessor, REA #137, Calif, 87-; dir, Air & Waste Mgt Asn, 87-90; bd ed, J Air & Waste Mgt Asn, 89-92; pres & bd trustees, Inst Prof Environ Pract, 93- *Mem:* Fel AAAS; fel Air & Waste Mgt Asn (vpres, 89-90); Soc Risk Analysis; Environ Auditing Roundtable. *Res:* Macromolecules; bellometrics; risk assessment; environmental impact analysis; energy systems; waste disposal; environmental carcinogenesis; air pollution; fate and transport of pollutants. *Mailing Add:* 18861 Via Messina Irvine CA 92612. *Fax:* 714-854-5123

HAZELWOOD, ROBERT LEONARD, ENDOCRINOLOGY. *Current Pos:* assoc prof biol, 63-71, PROF PHYSIOL, UNIV HOUSTON, 71- *Personal Data:* b Oakland, Calif, July 11, 27; m 55. *Educ:* Univ Calif, MA, 53, PhD(physiol), 58. *Prof Exp:* From instr to asst prof physiol, Sch Med, Boston Univ, 58-63. *Mem:* Soc Exp Biol & Med; Am Physiol Soc; Endocrinol Soc; Am Diabetes Assoc. *Res:* Comparative studies of carbohydrate metabolism; hormonal control of growth and metabolism; regulation of pancreatic endocrine secretion; pituitary-pancreatic interrelationships. *Mailing Add:* Dept Biol Univ Houston Houston TX 77204-5513. *Fax:* 713-743-2636

HAZEN, ANNETTE, physiology, nutrition, for more information see previous edition

HAZEN, GARY ALAN, ELECTRICAL ENGINEERING. *Current Pos:* Sr develop engr design, 75-80, DEVELOP PROJ ENGR DESIGN, SCHLUMBERGER WELL SERV, 80- *Personal Data:* b Mobile, Ala, July 18, 50; m 76. *Educ:* Univ S Ala, BS, 73, Ga Inst Technol, MS, 74. *Mem:* Inst Elec & Electronics Engrs. *Res:* Hostile environment electronics; communication electronics. *Mailing Add:* Schlumberger Technol Corp PO Box 2175 Houston TX 77252

HAZEN, GEORGE GUSTAVE, ORGANIC CHEMISTRY. *Current Pos:* sr chemist process develop, Merck & Co, Inc, 51-57, sect leader, 57-64, sect leader proc res, 64-69, mgr, 69-80, ASSOC DIR, MERCK & CO, INC, 80- *Personal Data:* b Ft Benton, Mont, Jan 1, 23; m 48; c 6. *Educ:* Mont State Col, BS, 44; Univ Mich, MS, 48, PhD, 51. *Prof Exp:* Instr org chem, Univ Mich, 49-51. *Mem:* Am Chem Soc; NY Acad Sci. *Res:* Steroids; polyhydric alcohols; substituted pyridines; development of complex organic and biosynthetic processes. *Mailing Add:* 205 Water St Perth Amboy NJ 08861-4426

HAZEN, MARTHA L(OCKE), ASTRONOMY. *Current Pos:* res fel, 57-69 & 60-69, lectr, 83-92, CUR ASTRON PHOTOGS, COL OBSERV, HARVARD UNIV, 69- *Personal Data:* b Cambridge, Mass, July 15, 31; m 91, Douglas B McHenry; c John L & Hilary (Ward). *Educ:* Mt Holyoke Col, AB, 53; Univ Mich, MA, 55, PhD(astron), 58. *Prof Exp:* Instr astron, Mt Holyoke Col, 57-59; lectr & res assoc, Univ Mich, 59-60. *Concurrent Pos:* Lectr, Wellesley Col, 61-63 & 66-67; adj assoc prof, Boston Univ, 79. *Mem:* Am Astron Soc; Int Astron Union; fel AAAS; Astron Soc Pac. *Res:* Photometry; globular clusters; variable stars. *Mailing Add:* Harvard Col Observ Harvard Univ 60 Garden St Cambridge MA 02138. *Fax:* 617-496-8016

HAZEN, RICHARD R(AY), ELECTRICAL ENGINEERING, NOISE ANALYSIS. *Current Pos:* RETIRED. *Personal Data:* b Zanesville, Ohio, Aug 26, 25; m 50, Patricia Jones; c Richard A & Lisa L. *Educ:* Univ Dayton, BEE, 53; Univ Cincinnati, MSEE, 62. *Prof Exp:* From instr to assoc prof, Univ Dayton, 53-71, chmn, Dept Electronic Eng Technol, 58-86, prof elec technol, 71-86, emer prof, 87. *Concurrent Pos:* Chmn, Eng Technol Comt, Engrs Coun Prof Develop, 74-75; prin investr, electro-mech devices, Air Forces Logistics Command, 81-; fel, Accreditation Bd Eng & Technol, 88. *Mem:* Am Soc Eng Educ; Inst Elec & Electronics Engrs; Armed Forces Commun & Electronics Asn. *Res:* Environmental noise; analysis and design. *Mailing Add:* 9672 Ferry Rd Dayton OH 45458

HAZEN, ROBERT MILLER, MINERALOGY & CRYSTAL CHEMISTRY, SCIENTIFIC LITERACY. *Current Pos:* RES FEL & MEM STAFF, GEOPHYS LAB, CARNEGIE INST WASHINGTON, 76-; ROBINSON PROF, GEORGE MASON UNIV, 89- *Personal Data:* b Rockville Centre, NY, Nov 1, 48; m 69; c 2. *Educ:* Mass Inst Technol, BA & SM, 71; Harvard Univ, PhD(mineral), 75. *Honors & Awards:* Mineral Soc Am Award; Ipatief Prize, Am Chem Soc; Deems Taylor Award. *Prof Exp:* NATO fel mineral, Cambridge Univ, 75-76. *Concurrent Pos:* Auth var publ. *Mem:* Mineral Soc Am; Am Geophys Union; Sigma Xi; Am Chem Soc; AAAS. *Res:* Development of high-pressure and high-temperature single crystal x-ray diffraction techniques; relationships between science and society; high pressure organic synthesis; origin of life. *Mailing Add:* Carnegie Inst Washington 5251 Broad Branch Rd NW Washington DC 20015-1305. *Fax:* 202-686-2419; *E-Mail:* hazen@gl.ciw.edu

HAZEN, TERRY CLYDE, AQUATIC ECOLOGY, PARASITOLOGY. *Current Pos:* fel scientist, 89-95, MGR BIOTECH, WESTINGHOUSE SAVANNAH RIVER CO, 94- *Personal Data:* b Pontiac, Mich, Feb 7, 51; m 72; c 2. *Educ:* Mich State Univ, BS, 73, MS, 74; Wake Forest Univ, PhD(parasite ecol), 78. *Honors & Awards:* George Westinghouse Gold Signature Award, 89, 90, 93, 94 & 95; Res & Develop 100 Award, 95-96. *Prof Exp:* Res assoc biol, Wake Forest Univ, 75-79; from asst prof to prof, Univ PR, 79-88; res scientist, E I du Pont de Nemours & Co Inc, 87-89. *Concurrent Pos:* Adj prof marine sci, Univ PR, Mayagaez, 80-88 & adj prof biol, Univ SC, Columbia, 88-; adj prof, Utah State Univ. *Mem:* Ecol Soc Am; Sigma Xi; AAAS; Am Soc Parasitol; Am Soc Microbiol; Am Acad Microbiol. *Res:* Bioremediation, environmental biotechnology, microbial ecology, fish pathology and computer applications; survival, activity and distribution of bacteria in fresh and marine waters; effect of physical, chemical and biological factors on bacteria in natural and polluted systems, and mathematical models that describe those relationships. *Mailing Add:* Environ Biotech Sect Savannah River Tech Ctr Aiken SC 29808-0001

HAZEN, WAYNE ESKETT, PHYSICS. *Current Pos:* from asst prof to prof, 47-84, EMER PROF PHYSICS, UNIV MICH, ANN ARBOR, 84- *Personal Data:* b Three Rivers, Mich, Feb 8, 14; m 39; c 4. *Educ:* Mass Inst Technol, BS, 36; Univ Calif, PhD(physics), 41. *Prof Exp:* From instr to asst prof physics, Univ Calif, 41-47. *Concurrent Pos:* Guggenheim fel, Mass Inst Technol, 47 & Imp Col, Univ London, 54; Fulbright scholar, Polytech Sch, Univ Paris, 53-54; Smith-Mundt prof, Am Univ Beirut, 58-59; researcher, Univ Hong Kong, High Energy Physics Inst, Beijing & Cosmic Ray Inst, Univ Tokyo. *Mem:* Fel Am Phys Soc. *Res:* Cosmic-ray air showers. *Mailing Add:* Dept Physics Univ Mich Ann Arbor MI 48103

HAZEN, WILLIAM EUGENE, ANIMAL ECOLOGY. *Current Pos:* from asst prof to assoc prof, 62-68, PROF BIOL, SAN DIEGO STATE UNIV, 68- *Personal Data:* b Canton, NY, June 4, 25. *Educ:* St Lawrence Univ, BS, 47; Univ Mich, MA, 48, PhD(zool), 54. *Prof Exp:* From instr to asst prof biol, Univ Chicago, 53-62. *Concurrent Pos:* Prog dir, Ecosystem Studies, NSF, 72 & 73. *Mem:* Ecol Soc Am; Am Soc Limnol & Oceanog; Brit Ecol Soc. *Res:* Biology of aquatic invertebrates; ecology of temporary ponds. *Mailing Add:* 4173 Hilldale Rd San Diego CA 92116

HAZEYAMA, YUJI, PHYSIOLOGY. *Current Pos:* PRES, MYU PUBL GROUP, 87- *Personal Data:* b Tokyo, Aug 5, 43; m 82. *Educ:* Musah Inst Technol, Tokyo, BS, 66, MS, 69; Univ Calif, Berkeley, PhD(elec eng & comput sci), 75. *Prof Exp:* Fel physiol, Univ Mich, 75-78; res fel, Childrens Hosp Northern Calif, Oakland, 78-80; asst prof chem, Lehigh Univ, 80-82; gen mgr, Ed Serv, Elsevier Sci Publ, Japan, 83-87. *Mem:* AAAS; Inst Elec & Electronics Engrs. *Res:* Identification of plasma borne vasconstruction which is closely related to the genesis of basal vascular tone; biomedical instrumentation (measurement of intracranial pressure). *Mailing Add:* MYU KK 5-19-11 Sendagi Tokyo 113 Japan

HAZI, ANDREW UDVAR, ATOMIC & MOLECULAR PHYSICS. *Current Pos:* physicist, Laser Prog, Lawrence Livermore Nat Lab, Univ Calif, 76-81, Chem Dept, 81-84, group leader, Physics Dept, 84-89, leader, High Temperature Physics Div, 89-94, SPEC ASST, PHYSICS ASSOC DIV, LAWRENCE LIVERMORE NAT LAB, UNIV CALIF, 94- *Personal Data:* b Budapest, Hungary, Sept 28, 41; US citizen. *Educ:* Univ Calif, Los Angeles, BS, 64; Univ Chicago, PhD(chem physics), 67. *Prof Exp:* Res assoc chem, Univ Southern Calif, 67-68; asst prof, Univ Calif, Los Angeles, 68-75; lectr, Calif Polytech State Univ, San Luis Obispo, 75-76. *Concurrent Pos:* Fel, Air Force Off Sci Res, 67-68; consult, McDonald-Douglas, 68 & McMillan Assocs, 74-75; comt, Nat Acad Sci/Nat Res Coun Atomic Molecular & Optical Scis, 87-92, physics, Dept Energy Basic Energy Sci, 89, Nat Acad Sci/Nat Res Coun, Assessment Nat Inst Sci & Technol, 92-96. *Mem:* Fel Am Phys Soc. *Res:* Electron scattering theory; electro-collisions with atoms, molecules and ions resonance phenomena in collisions; fundamental processes in gas lasers and plasmas, atomic x-ray lasers, atomic processes in high temperature plasmas. *Mailing Add:* Lawrence Livermore Lab L-051 Univ Calif PO Box 808 Livermore CA 94550. *Fax:* 510-422-9523; *E-Mail:* hazil@llnl.gov

HAZLEGROVE, LEVEN S, PHYSICO CHEMISTRY, BIOCHEMISTRY & IMMUNOLOGY. *Current Pos:* EXEC DIR, ALA ACAD SCI, 90- *Personal Data:* b Birmingham, Ala, Dec 1, 24; m 51, Anne Hinely; c Sarah L (Stepleton), Lee A (Darden) & Jane L. *Educ:* Howard Col, BS, 47; Emory Univ, MS, 49; Univ Ala, PhD(chem), 65. *Prof Exp:* Lab instr chem, Emory Univ, 48-49; asst prof & athletic dir, WGa Col, 49-56; res chemist, Food & Drug Admin, 56-57; asst prof chem, Howard Col, 57-63; res assoc biophys chem, Med Ctr, Univ Ala, 63-65; assoc prof, Samford Univ, 65-67, head dept, 78-84, prof chem, 67-90. *Concurrent Pos:* Instr, Exten Div, Univ Ga, Rome, 52-56; Ford Found lectr, WGa Col, 55-56; sr Danforth Assoc, 60-; NIH fel, 63-64; NSF fel, 63-65; vis prof, Med Ctr, Univ Ala, 65-, USAID, Univ Dacca & Rajshahi Univ, E Pakistan, 67-69, Anhui Univ, Wuhu, China & Dacca Univ, Bangladesh; chmn & trustee, Gorgas Scholarship Found, 76-; vis bioenergy ambassador, People-to-People, China, 85. *Mem:* AAAS; Am Chem Soc; Sigma Xi; Am Indust Hyg Asn. *Res:* Electrodeposition manganese using mercury cathode; spray residues on foods; polydispersity of hyaluronic acid, molecular weight determination by light scattering; computer program for molecular weight determinations; bio-polymers; gel-electrophoresis; macromolecular biochemistry; immunochemistry. *Mailing Add:* 208 Rockaway Rd Birmingham AL 35209-6626. *Fax:* 205-934-2543

HAZLEHURST, DAVID ANTHONY, INORGANIC CHEMISTRY, POLYMER CHEMISTRY. *Current Pos:* RETIRED. *Personal Data:* b Chester, Eng, Dec 9, 30; m 60, June Beresford; c Timothy & Naomi. *Educ:* Univ Liverpool, BSc, 52, PhD(inorg phys chem), 55. *Prof Exp:* Res fel inorg chem, Univ Tex, 55-56; res chemist, Carrington Res Lab, Shell Chem Co, Eng, 58-63; res chemist, E I du Pont de Nemours & Co, Inc, 63-66, sr res chemist, 66-67, supvr, 67-69, sr supvr nylon prod develop, 69-82, qual systs coordr, Nylon Textile, 82-83, sr res assoc, Nylon Indust, 83-93. *Mem:* Am Chem Soc. *Res:* Polymer chemistry; product development in plastics, textile fibers and foamed materials. *Mailing Add:* 102 N Plum St Richmond VA 23220. *E-Mail:* dhazlehu@atlas.vcu.edu

HAZLETT, DAVID RICHARD, pulmonary physiology, for more information see previous edition

HAZLETT, ROBERT NEIL, PHYSICAL ORGANIC CHEMISTRY, HYDROCARBON FUELS. *Current Pos:* FUEL CONSULT, ALEXANDRIA, VA, 88- *Personal Data:* b Sterling, Kans, Oct 4, 24; m 53, Margaret Shriver; c Heather & Douglas. *Educ:* Sterling Col, BS, 47; Univ Kans, PhD(chem), 50. *Hon Degrees:* ScD, Sterling Col, 70. *Prof Exp:* Instr chem, St Ambrose Col, 50-51; chemist, Fuels Br, US Naval Res Lab, Washington, DC, 51-71, head, Fuels Sect, Chem Dynamics Br, 72-76, head, Fuels Sect, Navy Technol Ctr for Safety & Survivability, Chem Div, 76-87. *Concurrent Pos:* Vis scientist, Mat Res Labs, Melbourne, Australia, 84-85. *Mem:* Am Chem Soc; Sigma Xi. *Res:* Jet aircraft fuels; hydrocarbon oxidation; fuel stability; separation of water from fuels; liquid rocket fuels; synthetic fuels; alternate energy sources; shale oil; shale derived fuels; diesel fuel; marine fuels. *Mailing Add:* 5205 Chippewa Pl Alexandria VA 22312-2023

HAZLEWOOD, CARLTON FRANK, PHYSIOLOGY, BIOPHYSICS. *Current Pos:* dir grad studies, Dept Physiol, 78-86, PROF PHYSIOL & PEDIAT, BAYLOR COL MED, 77- *Personal Data:* b Perrin, Tex, July 25, 35; m 56, Geraldine Boker; c Carlton F Jr, Karen Denise H (Cunningham) & Terri Lynn H (Woolard). *Educ:* Tex A&M Univ, BS, 57; Univ Tenn, PhD(physiol, anat), 62. *Hon Degrees:* Dr, Univ Med Sch, Pecs, Hungary. *Prof Exp:* Res physiologist, Children's Clin Res Ctr, 67-78; from instr to assoc prof physiol & pediat, 64-76. *Concurrent Pos:* Fel med, Sch Med, Johns Hopkins Univ, 62-64; consult, Westinghouse Elec Corp, 62-64; mem, Expert Comt Sci Coop Bur Eur & NAm Reg (UNESCO), 83-89; sr res assoc, Dept Physics, Rice Univ, 70-75, adj assoc prof physics, 75-78, prof, 78-; hon pres, Melius Found. *Mem:* AAAS; Biophys Soc; Soc Magnetic Resonance Imaging; Am Physiol Soc. *Res:* Mechanism of action of insulin; muscular dystrophy; ion accumulation in muscle; growth and development of muscle; physical state of ions and water in living tissues, cells and subcellular organelles; role of water in health and disease; in vivo nuclear magnetic resonance scanning; scanning tunneling microscopy. *Mailing Add:* 4714 O'Meara Houston TX 77035. *Fax:* 713-798-3475; *E-Mail:* carltonh@bcm.tmc.edu

HAZLEWOOD, DONALD GENE, NUMBER THEORY. *Current Pos:* asst prof, 71-77, ASSOC PROF MATH & COMPUT SCI, SOUTHWEST TEX STATE UNIV, 71- *Personal Data:* b Abilene, Tex. *Educ:* Univ Tex, Austin, BA, 63; Syracuse Univ, MS, 66, MA, 69, PhD(math), 71. *Prof Exp:* Sec teacher math, Independent Sch Dists, Tex, NMex & NY, 62-67. *Mem:* Am Math Soc; Math Asn Am; Sigma Xi. *Res:* Elementary methods in analytic number theory. *Mailing Add:* 1950 FM 1978 San Marcos TX 78666-1530

HAZUDA, DARIA JEAN, EXPERIMENTAL BIOLOGY. *Current Pos:* SR RES BIOCHEMIST, DEPT VIRUS & CELL BIOL, MERCK SHARP & DOHME, WEST POINT, PA, 89- *Educ:* Rutgers Univ, BA, 81; State Univ NY, Stony Brook, PhD(biochem), 86. *Prof Exp:* Grad teaching asst, State Univ NY, 81-83, grad res asst, 83-86; fel, Dept Molecular Genetics, Smith, Kline & French, Swedeland, Pa, 86-89. *Mem:* Am Soc Biochem & Molecular Biol; Protein Soc; Sigma Xi. *Res:* Author of numerous publications. *Mailing Add:* Dept 800 Merck Sharp & Dohme WP16-101 West Point PA 19486. *Fax:* 215-652-0994

HAZY, ANDREW CHRISTOPHER, ORGANIC CHEMISTRY. *Current Pos:* photochem, Horizons Res Inc, 69-71, gen mgr, Photohorizons, 71-75, vpres mfg, 76-79, VPRES TECHNOL, METALPHOTO DIV, HORIZONS INC, 79- *Personal Data:* b Windber, Pa, Sept 10, 38; m79, Carol Leap. *Educ:* St Vincent Col, BS, 59; Univ Notre Dame, PhD(org chem), 65. *Prof Exp:* Instr chem, St Vincent Col, 59-61; sr res chemist, Olin Corp, 64-68, group leader res chem, 68-69. *Mem:* Am Chem Soc; Soc Photog Sci & Eng. *Res:* Organic chemistry, especially related to photographic systems. *Mailing Add:* Horizons Inc 18531 S Miles Rd Cleveland OH 44128-4237

HAZZARD, DEWITT GEORGE, BIOCHEMISTRY, RESOURCE MANAGEMENT. *Current Pos:* DIR, CELL BIOL & ANIMAL MODELS PROGS, NAT INST AGING, NIH, 82-, HEAD, BIOL RESOURCES & RESOURCE DEVELOP PROG & BIOMED RES & CLIN MED, 85- *Personal Data:* b Scranton, Pa, May 23, 32; m 53; c 5. *Educ:* Pa State Univ, BS, 54, MS, 57; Univ Conn, PhD(animal nutrit), 63. *Honors & Awards:* Comnr's Special Citation, Food & Drug Admin, 81. *Prof Exp:* Res asst vitamin A res, Animal Nutrit Sect, Dept Animal Industs, Univ Conn, 57-62; biochemist, Nutrit Sect, Div Radiol Health, 62-63; chemist, Radiochem Sect, USPHS, 63-66, chemist, Physiol-Biophys Sect, Radiation Bio-Effects Prog, Nat Ctr Radiol Health, Rockville, 66-69, chief, Metab Studies Sect, Bur Radiol Health, Div Biol Effects, 69-72, dir, Off Extramural Res, Bur Radiol Health, Food & Drug Admin, USPHS, 78-82. *Concurrent Pos:* Exec secy, Radiol Health Res & Training Grant Rev Comt, Bur Radiol Health, FDA, 72-73, grants officer, 72-78. *Res:* Direct extramural programs in cell biology and animal models; development as related to understanding the aging process; direct development of biological and animal resources for use in aging research. *Mailing Add:* 2505 Seibel Dr Silver Spring MD 20905. *Fax:* 301-402-0010; *E-Mail:* dh35h@nih.gov

HAZZARD, WILLIAM RUSSELL, METABOLISM. *Current Pos:* PROF & CHAIR INTERNAL MED, BOWMAN GRAY SCH MED, WAKE FOREST UNIV, 86- *Personal Data:* b Ann Arbor, Mich, Sept 5, 36; m 61; c 4. *Educ:* Cornell Univ, AB, 58, MD, 62. *Prof Exp:* Intern med, NY Hosp, 62-63; res fel metab, Sch Med, Vet Admin Hosp, Seattle, 65-66, resident med, 66-67, res assoc, 69-70, from instr to asst prof, 69-73, clin investr, 70-71; dep dir, Northwest Lipid Res Clin, Univ Wash, 70-73, investr metab, Howard Hughes Med Inst, Sch Med, 71-, dir & assoc prof metab, 73-77, prof med & assoc dir, Northwest Lipid Res Clin, 77-, chief, Div Geront & Geriat Med, 78- *Concurrent Pos:* Fel, Coun Arteriosclerosis, Am Heart Asn, 74-; mem, Adv Bd, Wash-Alaska Regional Med Prog, 75- *Mem:* Inst Med-Nat Acad Sci; Sigma Xi; Am Fedn Clin Res; Am Diabetes Asn; Am Soc Clin Invest. *Res:* Epidemiological, clinical and biochemical investigation of hyperlipidemia in man with emphasis upon endocrinological and genetic aspects and relationship to atherosclerosis in man and animal models. *Mailing Add:* Bowman Gray Sch Med Wake Forest Univ Medical Center Blvd Winston-Salem NC 27157. *E-Mail:* nwoolard@bgsm.edu

HE, BIN, BIOELECTRIC PHENOMENA, BIOELECTRIC IMAGING CARDIAC & NEURAL PHYSIOLOGY. *Current Pos:* fel, 89-91, RES SCIENTIST, MASS INST TECHNOL, 91- *Personal Data:* b Wenchou, Zhejiang, China, Aug 14, 57; m 86, Wenjing Ye; c Eric J. *Educ:* Zhejiang Univ, BSc, 81; Tokyo Inst Technol, MSc, 85, PhD(bioelec eng), 88. *Honors & Awards:* Young Investr Award, NAm Soc Pacing & Electrophysiol, 92; TEJIMA Prize Outstanding PhD Thesis, TEJIMA Found, 89; Fuji TV Prize, Fuji TV, 87. *Prof Exp:* Vis scholar, Tokyo Inst Technol, 88-89. *Concurrent Pos:* Clin res ctr affil, Mass Inst Technol, 91-, prin investr, 92-; tech reviewer, Inst Elec & Electronics Engrs, 92-, Annals Biomed Eng, 93-, Comput Biol & Med, 93-; invited examr, PhD Thesis, Tel Avivi Univ, 93. *Mem:* Biomed Eng Soc; Am Heart Asn; Inst Elec & Electronics Engrs. *Res:* Bioelectric phenomena; cardiac and neural imaging and inverse problems; electrocardiology; electroencephalography; mathematical and computer modeling of biological systems; biomedical signal processing and bioinstrumentation; electrophysiology. *Mailing Add:* Univ Calif Berkeley Pines Group Berkeley CA 94720. *Fax:* 617-253-3019; *E-Mail:* bhe@mit.edu

HE, GUO-WEI, CARDIAC SURGICAL RESEARCH, VASCULAR BIOLOGY. *Current Pos:* DIR CARDIOVASC RES, STARR ACAD CTR, ST VINCENT HOSP, 94-; PROF & CHAIR CARDIOTHORACIC SURG, UNIV HONG KONG, 95- *Personal Data:* m 75, Cheng-Qin Yang; c Yang-Hui. *Educ:* Anhui Med Col, China, MD, 69; Peking Union Med Col, MMSc, 82; Monash Univ, Australia, PhD(surg/pharamacol), 88. *Prof Exp:* Cardiac surgeon, Fulvai Hosp, Beijing, 82-84; surg fel, Royal Children's Hosp, Melbourne, 84-85, St Vincent & Epworth Hosp, 85-88; res fel, Baker Med Res Inst, Melbourne, Australia, 86-88; res scientist & sr registr, Dept Pharmacol & Cardiothoracic Surg Univ, Royal Alfred Hosp, Univ Sydney, Australia, 89-90; vis scientist, Hosp Sick Children, 90-92; dir cardiovasc res, Cardiothoracic Surg Assocs NTex, 92-94. *Concurrent Pos:* Mem bd dirs, Med Col, Xia Men Univ, China, 96; vis prof, Great Wall Hosp, Beijing, 96. *Mem:* Soc Thoracic Surgs; Am Physiol Soc; Am Heart Asn; Int Soc Heart Res. *Res:* Cardiac surgery and cardiovascular system; physiology; cell biology; pharmacology and clinical research. *Mailing Add:* St Vincent Hosp No 240 9155 SW Barnes Rd Portland OR 97225

HE, XI, ECOSYSTEM ECOLOGY, LIMNOLOGY. *Current Pos:* FISHERIES BIOLOGIST, MASS DIV MARINE FISHERIES, 96- *Educ:* Shanghai Fisheries Col, BS, 82; Univ Wis-Madison, MS, 86, PhD(oceanog & limnol), 90. *Prof Exp:* Asst res scientist, St Norbert Col, 91-94; assoc res, Univ Hawaii, 94-96. *Mem:* Am Fisheries Soc; Ecol Soc Am. *Res:* Lake ecosystem ecology; fisheries ecology; limnology predator-prey interactions. *Mailing Add:* 30 Emerson Ave Gloucester MA 01930. *E-Mail:* xhe@state.ma.us

HE, YUDONG, PARTICLE & NUCLEAR ASTROPHYSICS, COSMOLOGY. *Current Pos:* res assoc, 89-93, res assoc, Space Sci Lab, 93-95, RES ASSOC FEL, PHYSICS DEPT, UNIV CALIF, BERKELEY, 93- *Personal Data:* b Lijiang, Yunnan, China, Nov 12, 61; US citizen; m, Liwei Li; c Katherine B & A Daniel. *Educ:* Yunnan Univ, BA, 82, MS, 86; Univ Calif, Berkeley, PhD(astrophys), 93. *Prof Exp:* Asst prof, Dali Med Univ, 82-83; res assoc, Yunnan Univ, 84-86, lectr, 86-87; res assoc, Inst High Energy Physics, Acad Sinica, Beijing, 87-89. *Concurrent Pos:* Postdoctoral scientist, Lawrence Berkeley Nat Lab, 95- *Mem:* Am Phys Soc. *Res:* Experimental high energy astrophysics, high energy cosmic-ray physics; relativistic heavy-ion physics; experimental cosmology; nuclear tracks and radiation effects in solids. *Mailing Add:* Physics Dept Univ Calif Berkeley CA 94720. *Fax:* 510-643-8497; *E-Mail:* yudong@physics.berkeley.edu

HEACOCK, CRAIG S, BIOCHEMISTRY. *Current Pos:* sr res chemist biochem, 87-89, PRIN RES SCIENTIST ANALYTICAL CHEM, CYTOGEN CORP, PRINCETON, NJ, 84- *Educ:* Univ Wash, Seattle, BS, 76; Colo State Univ, Ft Collins, PhD(biochem cell & molecular biol), 83. *Prof Exp:* Fac biochem, Colo State Univ, Ft Collins, 81-83; sr instr exp therapeut, Cancer Ctr, Univ Rochester, 83-87. *Res:* Author of numerous publications. *Mailing Add:* 53 Yarmouth Lane Downingtown PA 19335

HEACOCK, E(ARL) LARRY, ELECTRICAL ENGINEERING. *Current Pos:* dir systs develop, 76-85, DIR, SATELLITE OPERS, NAT OCEANIC & ATMOSPHERIC ADMIN, 85- *Personal Data:* b Tuscola, Ill, Jan 27, 35; m 56, Nancy L Voelkel; c Gregory L, Kent A & Christopher C. *Educ:* Univ Ill, BSEE, 57, MSEE, 66. *Prof Exp:* Engr, Ill Bell Tel Co, Springfield, 57-62; res engr, Environ Sci Servs Admin, 62-69; systs engr, Europ Space Agency, Holland, 70-72, meteosat proj mgr, Toulouse, France, 72-76. *Mem:* Fel Brit Interplanetary Soc; Am Inst Aeronaut & Astronaut; Am Astron Soc (pres, 89-90). *Res:* Weather satellite systems, data and environmental applications. *Mailing Add:* 363 Kingsberry Dr Annapolis MD 21401

HEACOCK, RICHARD RALPH, geophysics, magnetospheric physics, for more information see previous edition

HEACOCK, RONALD A, RESEARCH FUNDING, HEALTH RESEARCH POLICY. *Current Pos:* RETIRED. *Personal Data:* b London, Eng, Apr 14, 28; Can citizen; m 51; c 3. *Educ:* Univ London, BSc, 49, PhD(org chem), 52, DSc(org chem, biochem), 65. *Prof Exp:* Sci officer, Explosive Res & Develop Estab, UK, 51-54; res fel org chem, Nat Res Coun Can, 54-56; sr sci officer, Wye Col, Univ London, 56-57; chief res biochemist, Psychiat Res Unit, Univ Sask Hosp, 57-65; sr res officer & head, Physiol Chem Sect, Atlantic Regional Lab, Nat Res Coun Can, 65-74; dir, Contrib & Awards Div & res prog directorate, Health Prog Br, Dept Nat Health & Welfare, Can, 74-80, dir gen res progs, Health Serv & Prom Br, 80-92; vis prof, Univ Alta, Can, 92-93. *Concurrent Pos:* Lectr, Northampton Eng Col, London, 50-54; sessional lectr, Univ Sask, 58-64; assoc prof grad studies, Dalhousie Univ, 65-72; assoc mem, Med Res Coun Can, 80-90; mem, Nat Cancer Inst Can, 85-92. *Mem:* Fel Can Inst Chem; fel Royal Soc Chem. *Res:* Explosives chemistry; chemistry of heterocyclic organic compounds, including alkaloids; chemistry and biochemistry related to brain function; chemistry of biologically important substances; paper and thin-layer chromatography; gas chromatography; mass spectrometry; research programs administration; research proposal selection; research priority development. *Mailing Add:* 531 Brierwood Ave Ottawa ON K2A 2H4 Can

HEACOX, WILLIAM DALE, ASTRONOMY, MATHEMATICS. *Current Pos:* at NATURAL SCI DIV, UNIV HAWAII, HILO. *Personal Data:* b Pipestone, Minn, Mar 26, 42; m 66. *Educ:* Whitman Col, BA, 64; Wash State Univ, MA, 72; Univ Hawaii, MS, 75, PhD(astron), 77. *Prof Exp:* Res assoc, Nat Acad Sci & Nat Res Coun, Goddard Space Flight Ctr, NASA, 77-78; res assoc astron, Lunar & Planetary Lab, Univ Ariz, 78- *Mem:* Am Astron Soc; Astron Soc Pac; Soc Indust & Appl Math; Brit Interplanetary Soc. *Res:* Stellar atmospheres; extrasolar planetary systems; numerical smoothing; splines. *Mailing Add:* Kaiwiki Rd Hilo HI 96720

HEAD, CHARLES EVERETT, ATOMIC SPECTROSCOPY, PARTICLE THEORY. *Current Pos:* From asst prof to assoc prof, 65-73, PROF PHYSICS, UNIV NEW ORLEANS, 73- *Personal Data:* b Ark, Sept 6, 41; m 62; c 3. *Educ:* Univ Ark, Fayetteville, BS, 63, PhD(physics), 65. *Concurrent Pos:* Consult, Wadsworth Publ Co, 76- *Mem:* Am Phys Soc; Optical Soc Am; Am Asn Physics Teachers. *Res:* Measurement of radiative lifetimes of excited states of neutral and ionized atoms and molecules; accelerator-based atomic and molecular physics; fundamental particle structure; laser spectroscopy. *Mailing Add:* Dept Physics Univ New Orleans PO Box 1362 New Orleans LA 70148

HEAD, H HERBERT, DAIRY SCIENCE. *Current Pos:* asst prof, 63-71, ASSOC PROF DAIRY SCI, UNIV FLA, 71- *Personal Data:* b Jersey City, NJ, Oct 28, 35; m 60; c 4. *Educ:* Rutgers Univ, BS, 57, MS, 59; Univ Md, PhD(animal physiol), 63. *Prof Exp:* Asst dairy sci, Rutgers Univ, 57-59 & Univ Md, 59-63. *Mem:* Am Dairy Sci Asn; Am Soc Animal Sci. *Res:* Ruminant metabolism studies; metabolic regulation imposed by insulin growth hormone; bovine fetal growth patterns; factors affecting insulin secretion in the ruminant; hormonal requirements and mechanisms for lactogenesis and maintenance of lactation; induced lactation. *Mailing Add:* Dept Dairy Sci Univ Fla PO Box 110920 Gainesville FL 32611-0920

HEAD, JAMES WILLIAM, III, STRATIGRAPHY, PLANETARY GEOLOGY. *Current Pos:* asst prof, 73-74, assoc prof, 74-, PROF GEOL SCI, BROWN UNIV, 80- *Personal Data:* b Richmond, Va, Aug 4, 41; c 2. *Educ:* Washington & Lee Univ, BS, 64; Brown Univ, PhD(geol), 69. *Honors & Awards:* Medal, NASA, 71. *Prof Exp:* Geologist, Bellcomm, Inc, 68-73. *Concurrent Pos:* Interim dir, Lunar Sci Inst, Houston, Tex, 73-74; chmn, NASA Solar Syst Explor Mgt Coun, 86- *Mem:* AAAS; fel Geol Soc Am; fel Am Geophys Union; Am Asn Petrol Geol; Am Astron Soc; fel Meteorol Soc. *Res:* Geology, volcanology and tectonics of planetology surfaces; comparative planetology. *Mailing Add:* Dept Geol Sci Brown Univ Providence RI 02912

HEAD, MARTHA E MOORE, OCEAN ACOUSTICS, ATOMIC SPECTROSCOPY. *Current Pos:* adj assoc prof, 80-89, ADJ PROF PHYSICS, UNIV NEW ORLEANS, 89- *Personal Data:* b Little Rock, Ark, Dec 3, 41; m 62; c 3. *Educ:* Univ Ark, BS, 63, MS, 64; Tulane Univ, PhD(physics), 69. *Prof Exp:* Asst prof physics & math, Southern Univ, New Orleans, 69-73; assoc prof physics, West Tex State Univ, 73-79. *Concurrent Pos:* Manuscript reviewer & consult, Wadsworth Publ Co, 76-; mem staff, Acoust Div, Naval Oceanog Off, 83- *Mem:* Am Phys Soc; Optical Soc Am; Acoustical Soc Am. *Res:* Fundamental particle structure calculations; acoustic modeling; determination of mean lifetimes of excited electronic states of atoms. *Mailing Add:* Univ New Orleans Dept Physics Sci Bldg Rm 1021 Lake Front New Orleans LA 70148

HEAD, RONALD ALAN, CHEMISTRY. *Current Pos:* RETIRED. *Personal Data:* b Birmingham, Ala, May 12, 30; m 55, Dorothy Sheppard; c Laurie & Anne. *Educ:* Birmingham-Southern Col, BS, 52; Univ Ala, MA, 57; Univ of the Pac, PhD(chem), 64. *Prof Exp:* Teacher chem, Pensacola Jr Col, 57-65; chmn, Dept Phys Sci, Okaloosa-Walton Community Col, 65-88, chmn, Math Sci Div, 88-90. *Mem:* AAAS; Am Chem Soc; fel Am Inst Chem; Int Union Pure & Appl Chem. *Res:* Chemical education; inorganic halfwave potentials in liquid ammonia. *Mailing Add:* 403 Jame St Valparaiso FL 32580-1115

HEAD, THOMAS JAMES, MATHEMATICS. *Current Pos:* PROF MATH SCI, STATE UNIV NY, BINGHAMTON, 88- *Personal Data:* b Tonkawa, Okla, Jan 6, 34; m 69, Eileen Fay Siegal; c 4. *Educ:* Univ Okla, BS, 54, MA, 55; Univ Kans, PhD(math), 62. *Prof Exp:* Instr math, Univ Okla, 56-57 & Washburn Univ, 59-61; asst prof, Iowa State Univ, 62-65; prof math, Univ Alaska, 65-88. *Concurrent Pos:* Vis res prof, NMex State Univ, 70-71; vis prof, Univ Tex, El Paso, 72-74 & Calif Polytech State Univ, San Luis Obispo, 75; vis prof math sci, Rice Univ, 75-76; prog dir, Theoret Comput Sci, NSF, Washington, DC, 85-87. *Mem:* AAAS; Europ Asn Theoret Comput Sci; Am Math Soc; Asn Comput Mach. *Res:* Theoretical computer science; abstract algebra; computation with biomolecules. *Mailing Add:* Dept Math Sci State Univ NY Binghamton NY 13902-6000. *Fax:* 607-777-2450; *E-Mail:* tom@math.binghamton.edu

HEAD-GORDON, MARTIN PAUL, MOLECULAR ORBITAL THEORY, GAS-SURFACE INTERACTIONS. *Current Pos:* ASST PROF CHEM, UNIV CALIF, BERKELEY, 92- *Personal Data:* b Canberra, Australia, Mar 17, 62; m 85; c 1. *Educ:* Monash Univ, BSc, 83, MSc, 85; Carnegie-Mellon Univ, PhD(chem), 89. *Prof Exp:* Researcher, AT&T Bell Labs, 89-92. *Mem:* Am Chem Soc; Am Phys Soc; AAAS. *Res:* Theoretical chemistry, including quantum chemistry and the development of molecular orbital theory, with application to problems in surface science and molecular structure and properties. *Mailing Add:* Dept Chem Univ Calif Berkeley CA 94720-0001

HEAD-GORDON, TERESA LYN, BIOPHYSICS, PHYSICAL CHEMISTRY. *Current Pos:* RES, AT&T BELL LABS, 90- *Personal Data:* b Akron, Ohio, Sept 28, 60; m 85; c 1. *Educ:* Case Western Res Univ, BS, 83; Carnegie-Mellon Univ, PhD(chem), 89. *Prof Exp:* Res, Rutgers Univ, 89-90. *Concurrent Pos:* Consult, Pittsburgh Supercomput Ctr, 87-88. *Mem:* Am Chem Soc; Am Phys Soc; AAAS. *Res:* Theoretical methods applied to biopolymers and oligopeptides; heatbath modelling; electrostatics and dielectrics; neural networks; ab initio methods; research on protein folding. *Mailing Add:* 100 Ventura Ave Albany CA 94706-2529

HEADINGS, VERLE EMERY, MEDICINE, HUMAN GENETICS. *Current Pos:* From asst prof to assoc prof, 69-78, MED GENETICIST, HOWARD UNIV, 69-, PROF PEDIAT, COL MED, 78-, PROF GENETICS & HUMAN GENETICS, 80- *Personal Data:* b Hubbard, Ore, July 14, 35; m 62; c 3. *Educ:* Goshen Col, BA, 58; Univ Mich, Ann Arbor, MS, 62, MD, 64, PhD(human genetics), 70. *Concurrent Pos:* Div grad studies, Genetics & Human Genetics, 73- *Mem:* NY Acad Sci; Am Soc Human Genetics; Sigma Xi. *Res:* Psychological aspects of genetic disorders; newborn genetic screening; heritable variation in red cell adhesion factors. *Mailing Add:* 520 W St NW Box 75 Washington DC 20059. *Fax:* 202-865-4558

HEADINGTON, JOHN TERRENCE, PATHOLOGY. *Current Pos:* asst resident path, Med Sch, Univ Mich, Ann Arbor, 58-59, resident, 59-60, from jr clin asst to assoc prof, 60-71, PROF PATH, MED SCH, UNIV MICH, ANN ARBOR, 71-, PROF DERMAT, 77- *Personal Data:* b Grand Rapids, Mich, June 15, 30; m 57; c 2. *Educ:* Univ Mich, BA, 52, MD, 57. *Prof Exp:* Intern, Virginia Mason Hosp, 57-58. *Mem:* AAAS; Int Acad Path. *Res:* Dermatopathology; geographic pathology. *Mailing Add:* Dept Path Univ Mich 1500 E Medical Ctr Dr Ann Arbor MI 48109-0999

HEADLEE, RAYMOND, PSYCHIATRY, PSYCHOLOGY. *Current Pos:* from asst prof to prof, 58-62, chmn dept, 63-70, PROF PSYCHIAT, MED COL WIS, 62- *Personal Data:* b Shelby Co, Ind, July 27, 17; m 41; c 3. *Educ:* Ind Univ, Bloomington, AB, 39, AM, 41; Ind Univ, Indianapolis, MD, 44; Am Bd Psychiat & Neurol, dipl & cert psychiat, 51. *Honors & Awards:* Cert of Honor, Am Bd Psychiat & Neurol, 70. *Prof Exp:* Intern, St Elizabeth's Hosp, Washington, DC, 44-45; resident psychiat, 45; resident, Milwaukee Psychiat Hosp, 47-48. *Concurrent Pos:* Pvt pract psychiat & psychoanalysis, 47-; prof psychol, Marquette Univ, 65-77. *Mem:* Am Med Asn; fel Am Psychiat Asn; fel Am Col Psychiat; fel Am Col Psychoanalysts; Am Psychol Asn. *Res:* Experimental and in vivo research into the nature of charisma. *Mailing Add:* 1055 Legion PO Box 125 Elm Grove WI 53122-0125

HEADLEY, ALLAN DAVE, PHYSICAL ORGANIC CHEMISTRY. *Current Pos:* ASST PROF CHEM, TEX TECH UNIV, 89- *Personal Data:* b Jamaica, May 10, 55; m 87; c 1. *Educ:* Columbia Union Col, BA, 76; Howard Univ, PhD(chem), 82. *Prof Exp:* Chem, Univ Calif, Irvine, 82-83; lectr chem, 87-89; lectr chem, Univ WIndies, Mona, 83-87. *Concurrent Pos:* Vis prof, Univ Calif, Irvine, 87. *Mem:* Am Chem Soc. *Res:* Analysis of structural effects on proton-transfer reactions in the gas phase; solvation effects on the reactivity and solubility of amino acids and other molecules of biological interest. *Mailing Add:* Chem & Biochem Dept Tex Tech Univ Lubbock TX 79409-1061

HEADLEY, JOSEPH CHARLES, NATURAL RESOURCE ECONOMICS, PRODUCTION ECONOMICS. *Current Pos:* RETIRED. *Personal Data:* b Terre Haute, Ill, June 23, 30; m 64; c 2. *Educ:* Univ Ill, BS, 52, MS, 55; Purdue Univ, PhD(agr econ), 60. *Prof Exp:* Asst agr economist farm mgt, Univ Ariz, 55-57; grad asst, Purdue Univ, 57-59; assoc specialist, Univ Calif, Davis, 59-60; asst prof farm mgt, Univ Ill, 60-66; from assoc prof to prof econ, Univ Mo, 66-89; prof & head agr policy, Univ Ark, 89-96. *Concurrent Pos:* Vis scholar, Resources for the Future, 65-66; vis prof, Norweg Agr Univ, 72, Swed Agr Univ, 72-73, Danish Agr & Vet Univ, 73. *Mem:* Am Agr Econ Asn. *Res:* Economics of controlling agricultural pests; developed an economic interpretation of the economic threshold for initiating pest control. *Mailing Add:* 1311 Bradshaw Columbia MO 65203

HEADLEY, ROBERT N, CARDIOLOGY. *Current Pos:* instr, Bowman Gray Sch Med, 63-64, asst prof internal med, 64-68, assoc prof, 68-74, chief, Prof Serv, 76-81, assoc chief, Prof Serv, 81-82, actg dir, Cardiol Sect, 81-84, PROF INTERNAL MED, BOWMAN GRAY SCH MED, 74- *Personal Data:* b Boyd, Md, Mar 29, 32; m 55; c 4. *Educ:* Univ Md, BS, 54, MD, 56. *Prof Exp:* Intern med, Univ Va Hosp, 56-57; asst resident, NC Baptist Hosp, 61-62, resident, 62-63. *Concurrent Pos:* Fel cardiol, Bowman Gray Sch Med, 57-58, trainee cardiovasc dis, 60-61; Am Col Physicians Meade-Johnson scholar, 62-63; consult biomed aspects of landing impact, USAF, 60-61; attend physician, Vet Admin Regional Off, 62-63, consult, 71-; dir, Outpatient Serv, NC Baptist Hosp, 63-72, dir, Cardiac Care Unit, 71-80; consult Div Regional Med Prog, USPHS, 68-69; consult, Coronary Care Units, NC Med Care Comn, 68-69; dir, Heart Dis Div, NC Regional Med Prog, 69-72; dir, Dist Med Consult, Voc Rehab Admin. *Mem:* Fel Am Col Physicians; fel Am Col Cardiol. *Res:* Feasibility of the establishment of coronary care units in small community hospitals; system for specially equipped coronary care ambulances in a rural community. *Mailing Add:* Bowman Gray Sch Med Winston-Salem NC 27103

HEADLEY, VELMER BENTLEY, MATHEMATICS, PARTIAL DIFFERENTIAL EQUATIONS. *Current Pos:* asst prof, Brock Univ, 68-73, chmn dept, 81-84, assoc prof, 73-88, PROF MATH, BROCK UNIV, 88- *Personal Data:* b Barbados, WI, Sept 7, 34; m 65; c 2. *Educ:* Univ Col WI & Univ London, BSc, 62; Univ BC, MA, 66, PhD(math), 68. *Prof Exp:* Asst lectr math, Univ WI, 62-63. *Mem:* Am Math Soc; Math Asn Am; Can Math Soc. *Res:* Oscillation theory of ordinary and partial differential equations; turning-point problems; Gronwall-Bellman-Wendroff inequalities; approximation theory. *Mailing Add:* Dept Math Brock Univ St Catharines ON L2S 3A1 Can

HEADRICK, RANDALL L, ELECTRONIC MATERIALS, SURFACES & INTERFACES. *Current Pos:* STAFF SCIENTIST, CORNELL HIGH ENERGY SYNCHROTRON SOURCE, 90- *Personal Data:* b Lawrence, Kans, Apr 6, 60. *Educ:* Carnegie-Mellon Univ, BS, 82; Univ Pa, PhD(mat sci), 88. *Prof Exp:* Mem tech staff, AT&T Bell Labs, 88-90. *Concurrent Pos:* Consult, AT&T Bell Labs, 91- *Mem:* Am Vacuum Soc; Mat Res Soc; Am Phys Soc. *Res:* Surfaces and interfaces of semiconductors and metals and the growth of crystalline films of these materials; use of x-rays produced by synchrotron radiation to study structure of artificially grown thin films. *Mailing Add:* Cornell High Energy Synchrotron Source Cornell Univ, 2nd Fl Wilson Lab Ithaca NY 14853

HEADY, HAROLD FRANKLIN, PLANT ECOLOGY, RANGE SCIENCE & MANAGEMENT. *Current Pos:* RETIRED. *Personal Data:* b Buhl, Idaho, Mar 29, 16; m 40, 82; c 2. *Educ:* Univ Idaho, BS, 38; Syracuse Univ, MS, 40; Univ Nebr, PhD, 49. *Honors & Awards:* Renner Award, 80; Berkeley Citation, Univ Calif, Berkeley. *Prof Exp:* Teaching asst, NY State Col Forestry, Syracuse Univ, 38-40; range conservationist, Soil Conserv Serv, USDA, 41; asst prof plant ecol, NY State Col Forestry, Syracuse Univ, 42; asst prof range mgt, Col & Exp Sta, Mont State Col, 42-47; assoc prof, Agr & Mech Col Tex, 47-51; asst prof & asst plant ecologist, Univ Calif, Berkeley, 51-56, assoc prof & assoc plant ecologist, 56-62, prof forestry & plant ecologist, Exp Sta, 62-84, dean, Col Natural Resources, 74-77, asst vpres, Agr & Univ Serv & assoc dir, Agr Exp Sta, 77-80. *Concurrent Pos:* Fulbright res scholar, 58-59 & 66; Guggenheim fel, 58-59; consult range mgt, Food & Agr Orgn, Saudi Arabia, 62 & Malawi, 70-71; consult, Ralph M Parsons Co, 65. *Mem:* Soc Range Mgt (secy-treas, 47, pres, 80). *Res:* Utilization of forage by livestock; methods of sampling grassland; grassland ecology; range management; international rangeland conservation. *Mailing Add:* 1864 Capistrano Ave Berkeley CA 94707

HEADY, JUDITH E, DEVELOPMENTAL BIOLOGY, SCIENCE EDUCATION. *Current Pos:* asst prof, 74-79, ASSOC PROF BIOL, UNIV MICH, 79- *Personal Data:* b Cedar Rapids, Iowa, Dec 11, 39; c 2. *Educ:* Cornell Col, BA, 62; Univ Iowa, MS, 63; Univ Colo, PhD(develop biol), 70. *Prof Exp:* Res technician, Med Ctr, Univ Colo, 64-66, res assoc, 70-74. *Concurrent Pos:* Jr investr, Woods Hole Marine Biol Labs, 74; investr, Friday Harbor Labs, 76; vis asst prof biochem, Med Ctr, Univ Colo, 77; sabbatical res, Univ Minn, St Paul, 80-81; vis assoc prof biol, Univ Colo, Boulder, 83; vis res scientist, Marine Biol Lab, Woods Hole, Mass, 87-88; NSF distinguished vis prof biol & NSF fel, Univ Wis- LaCrosse, 95-96. *Mem:* Soc Develop Biol; Soc Col Sci Teachers; AAAS; Am Asn Higher Educ; Nat Sci Teachers Asn. *Res:* Writing for non-specialist audience on cancer, development, women in science; science education in areas of curricular/ course reform. *Mailing Add:* Dept Natural Sci Univ Mich 4901 Evergreen Rd Dearborn MI 48128. *Fax:* 313-593-4937; *E-Mail:* jheady@ umich.edu

HEAGARTY, MARGARET CAROLINE, PEDIATRICS. *Current Pos:* DIR PEDIAT, HARLEM HOSP CTR, 78-; PROF PEDIAT, COL PHYSICIANS & SURGEONS, COLUMBIA UNIV, 78- *Personal Data:* b Charleston, WVa, Sept 8, 34. *Educ:* Seton Hill Col, BA, 57; WVa Sch Med, BS, 59; Univ Pa, MD, 61. *Prof Exp:* Rotating intern, Philadelphia Gen Hosp, 61-62; resident pediat, St Christopher's Hosp Children, 62-64; res fel, Sch Med, Harvard Univ, 64-66, asst dir family health care, 66-68; assoc, Beth Israel Hosp, Boston, 67-69; dir ambulatory pediat care, NY Hosp, Cornell Univ, 69-78. *Concurrent Pos:* Fel med, Children's Hosp Med Ctr, Boston, 64-66; fel, Robert Wood Johnson Found, 75; consult, HEW, Nat Ctr Health Serv Res, 78-82 & 79-80; mem, Gov Coun, Inst Med-Nat Acad Sci. *Mem:* Inst Med-Nat Acad Sci; Soc Pediat Res; Am Pediat Asn; Am Acad Pediat; Am Pub Health Asn; Ambulatory Pediat Asn. *Mailing Add:* Dept Pediat Harlem Hosp Ctr 506 Lenox Ave New York NY 10037. *Fax:* 212-939-4015

HEAGLE, ALLEN STREETER, PLANT PATHOLOGY. *Current Pos:* RES PLANT PATHOLOGIST, USDA, 68- *Personal Data:* b Stanley, Wis, Apr 20, 38; m 60; c 2. *Educ:* Hamline Univ, BS, 60; St Cloud State Univ, MEd, 64; Univ Minn, PhD(plant path), 68. *Honors & Awards:* Agr Res Serv Outstanding Res Award, USDA, 80. *Mem:* Am Phytopath Soc. *Res:* Effects of air pollution on agronomic crops yield; effects of air pollution on parasitism of plants by fungi. *Mailing Add:* 1216 Scott Pl Cary NC 27511

HEAGLER, JOHN B(AY), JR, CIVIL ENGINEERING. *Current Pos:* RETIRED. *Personal Data:* b Cape Girardeau, Mo, Sept 8, 24; m 46; c 3. *Educ:* Univ Mo, BS, 51, MS, 54. *Prof Exp:* Instr appl mech, Mo Sch Mines, Univ Mo, Rolla, 51-55, from asst prof to prof civil eng, 55-67, prof civil eng, 67- *Res:* Soil mechanics, stabilization and foundations. *Mailing Add:* 1812 Independence Rolla MO 65401

HEAGY, FRED CLARK, NUCLEAR MEDICINE. *Current Pos:* clin prof, 78-85, PROF EMER NUCLEAR MED & DIAG RADIOL, UNIV WESTERN ONT, 85- *Personal Data:* b Stratford, Ont, Mar 17, 19; m 43, Margaret J McDonald; c 8. *Educ:* Univ Western Ont, MD, 43, MSc, 47, PhD(biochem & bact), 50; FRCP(C), 76. *Prof Exp:* Res assoc biochem, Glasgow Univ, 50-52; biochemist, London Clin, Ont Cancer Treatment & Res Found, 55-71, sr physician, 71-80; teaching staff nuclear med & diag radiol, Victoria Hosp, London, 80-84. *Concurrent Pos:* Nuffield Found Dom traveling fel, 50-51; Brit Empire Cancer Campaign exchange fel, 51-52; sr med res fel, Nat Res Coun Can, 52-55; asst prof biochem & therapeut radiol, Univ Western Ont, 61-70, assoc prof, 70-78; mem, Exec Coun, Adv Comt, Clin Uses of Radioisotopes, Dept Nat Health & Welfare, Can, 61-71, chmn, 71-73; mem teaching staff, Victoria Hosp, London; consult nuclear med, St Joseph's Hosp & Univ Western Ont Hosp; mem, Bd Govrs, Toronto Inst Med Technol, 74-77; hon staff, Victoria Hosp, 84- *Mem:* AAAS; Can Physiol Soc; Can Asn Nuclear Med (pres, 77-79); Am Soc Biol Chemists; Soc Nuclear Med. *Res:* Magnesium and temperature regulation; bacteriophage; nucleic acids; thyroid; cancer. *Mailing Add:* 1037 Brough St London ON N6A 3N5 Can

HEALD, CHARLES WILLIAM, DAIRY SCIENCE, CYTOLOGY. *Current Pos:* PROF, DEPT DAIRY & ANIMAL SCI, PA STATE UNIV, 81- *Personal Data:* b West Grove, Pa, May 1, 42; m 61; Judith L Walter; c Evan B & Elizabeth A. *Educ:* Pa State Univ, BS, 64; Univ NH, MS, 66; Va Polytech Inst & State Univ, PhD(dairy sci), 69. *Prof Exp:* Res assoc dairy sci, Va Polytech Inst & State Univ, 69-71, from asst prof to assoc prof, 71-81. *Concurrent Pos:* Interim dept head, Dairy & Animal Sci Exten, 87-90, coordr, 90-93. *Mem:* Am Dairy Sci Asn; Am Soc Animal Sci; AAAS; Nat Mastitis Coun. *Res:* Teach the use of farm management records and advise farm advisors and consultants; development of dairy farm record management systems using computer decision aids. *Mailing Add:* Dept Dairy & Animal Sci Pa State Univ 324 Henning Bldg University Park PA 16802

HEALD, EMERSON FRANCIS, PHYSICAL CHEMISTRY. *Current Pos:* from asst prof to assoc prof, 64-74, PROF CHEM, THIEL COL, 74- *Personal Data:* b Newport, RI, Dec 8, 34; m 59; c 3. *Educ:* Univ RI, BS, 56; Univ Hawaii, PhD(phys chem), 61. *Prof Exp:* From instr to asst prof, Univ Hawaii, 60-62; res assoc geochem, Pa State Univ, 62-64. *Concurrent Pos:* Vis res fel chem, Victoria Univ, Wellington, 68-69; vis fel chem, Western Australian Inst Technol, 7S-76. *Mem:* AAAS; Am Chem Soc; Sigma Xi. *Res:* Use of computers in chemical education; interfacing computers and laboratory instruments; solid-source mass spectrometry. *Mailing Add:* 88 Chambers Ave Greenville PA 16125-1771. *Fax:* 412-589-2021

HEALD, FELIX PIERPONT, JR, MEDICINE, PEDIATRICS. *Current Pos:* PROF PEDIAT & HEAD, DIV ADOLESCENT MED, SCH MED, UNIV MD, BALTIMORE CITY, 70- *Personal Data:* b Philadelphia, Pa, Dec 3, 21; m 48; c 5. *Educ:* Colo Col, AB, 46; Univ Pa, MD, 46. *Prof Exp:* Instr pediat, Harvard Med Sch, 53-59; asst prof, Sch Med, Georgetown Univ, 60-63, assoc prof, 63-66; prof & chmn dept, Sch Med, George Washington Univ, 67-70. *Concurrent Pos:* Mem staff adolescent med, Children's Med Ctr, Boston, 52-59; chief adolescent med, Children's Hosp, Washington, DC, 60-70. *Mem:* Soc Pediat Res; Am Acad Pediat; Soc Res Child Develop. *Res:* Adolescent medicine; physiological, metabolic and nutritional aspects of adolescence. *Mailing Add:* Univ Med Hosp 22 S Green St Baltimore MD 21201

HEALD, MARK AIKEN, ELECTROMAGNETIC THEORY, PLASMA PHYSICS. *Current Pos:* from asst prof to prof, Swarthmore Col, 59-92, chmn dept, 68-78, EMER PROF PHYSICS, SWARTHMORE COL, 92- *Personal Data:* b Princeton, NJ, Jan 27, 29; m 52, Jane Dewey; c Kathryn, John & Charles. *Educ:* Oberlin Col, 50; Yale Univ, MS, 51, PhD(exp physics), 54.

Prof Exp: Res staff mem microwave diagnostics, Proj Matterhorn, Plasma Physics Lab, Princeton Univ, 54-59. *Concurrent Pos:* Tech deleg, UN Conf Peaceful Uses of Atomic Energy, Geneva, 58; NSF fac fel, Culham Lab, UK Atomic Energy Authority, 63-64; NSF sci fac fel, Plasma Physics Lab, Princeton, 69-70, vis res physicist, 74-75; vis scientist, Nat Magnet Lab, Mass Inst Technol, 78-79. *Mem:* Am Phys Soc; Am Asn Physics Teachers; Fedn Am Sci; Sigma Xi. *Res:* Plasma physics; microwave diagnostics of plasmas; RF heating; author. *Mailing Add:* Dept Physics & Astron Swarthmore Col Swarthmore PA 19081-1397. *E-Mail:* mheald1@swarthmore.edu

HEALD, MILTON TIDD, SEDIMENTARY PETROLOGY. *Current Pos:* From instr to prof 48-84, EMER PROF GEOL, WVA UNIV, 84- *Personal Data:* b Woburn, Mass, Feb 19, 19; m 41, Doris Ethier; c Sandra S (Simmons), Cynthia J (Patton) & Marcia A (McGlothlin). *Educ:* Wesleyan Univ, AB, 40; Harvard Univ, AM, 47, PhD(geol), 49. *Mem:* Fel Geol Soc Am; Soc Econ Paleont & Mineral; Am Asn Petrol Geol; Nat Asn Geol Teachers (vpres, 58). *Res:* Diagenesis of clastic sediments. *Mailing Add:* Dept Geol WVa Univ Morgantown WV 26506

HEALD, WALTER ROLAND, SOIL CHEMISTRY. *Current Pos:* RETIRED. *Personal Data:* b Denver, Colo, Oct 27, 20; m 48; c 2. *Educ:* Colo State Univ, BS, 47; State Col Wash, MS, 49; Purdue Univ, PhD(soils), 54. *Prof Exp:* Assoc prof agron, Colo Agr & Mech Col, 49-51; soil scientist, Plant Indust Sta, USDA, 53-70, res invest leader, Water Qual Mgt Invest, Northeast Br, Soil & Water Conserv Res Div, Agr Res Serv, 71-72, location & res leader, Plant, Soil & Water Lab, 72-74, res soil scientist, Northeast Watershed Res Ctr, Sci & Educ Admin-Agr Res, 74-81. *Mem:* Am Soc Agron. *Res:* Effect of land use on the quality of ground and surface waters. *Mailing Add:* 18 W Forest Feezor St Vail AZ 85641

HEALEY, ANTHONY J, UNDERWATER ROBOTICS, CONTROL SYSTEMS. *Current Pos:* chmn, Mech Eng Dept, 86-92, PROF MECH ENG, NAVAL POSTGRAD SCH, MONTEREY, CALIF, 86- *Personal Data:* b London, Eng, Sept 10, 40; m 60, Mina McKay; c Anthony, JoAnna & Vicki. *Educ:* Univ London, BSc, 61; Univ Sheffield, PhD(mech eng), 66. *Honors & Awards:* Dedicated Service Award, Am Soc Mech Engrs, 94. *Prof Exp:* Engr, Bristol Aircraft, 61-63 & Gen Elec Co, 66-67; asst prof mech eng, Pa State Univ, 67-71; assoc prof mech eng, Univ Tex, Austin, 71-74, prof, 74-81; proj mgr, Brown & Root, Inc, 81-86. *Concurrent Pos:* Asst vis prof, Mass Inst Technol, 70; consult, gov & indust. *Mem:* Fel Am Soc Mech Engrs; Inst Elec & Electronics Engrs. *Res:* Fluidic control systems and components modeling; fluid power control; system dynamics; finite element; structural dynamics; pipelines; offshore vessels, moorings; underwater robotics; vehicle dynamics; artificial intelligence; control systems. *Mailing Add:* 1109 Circle Rd Pebble Beach CA 93953. *Fax:* 408-656-2238; *E-Mail:* healey@me.nps.navy.mil

HEALEY, CHRIS M, EARTH SCIENCE. *Honors & Awards:* Julian Boldy Mem Award, Can Inst Mining & Metall, 90. *Mailing Add:* c/o Can Inst Mining & Metall 3400 de Maisonneuve Blvd W Montreal PQ H3Z 3B8 Can

HEALEY, FRANK HENRY, PHYSICAL CHEMISTRY. *Current Pos:* RETIRED. *Personal Data:* b Worcester, Mass, Oct 5, 24; m 48; c 3. *Educ:* Clark Univ, AB, 47, PhD(chem), 49. *Prof Exp:* From instr to asst prof chem, Lehigh Univ, 49-56; sect chief physics & phys chem, Lever Bros Co, 56-58, sect chief detergent process develop, 58-60, dir res & develop, 60-64, vpres res & develop, 64-73, res vpres, 73-88, mem bd dirs, 68-88. *Concurrent Pos:* Mem bd dirs, Indust Res Inst, 70-79, pres, 78. *Mem:* Asn Res Dirs; Sigma Xi. *Res:* Surface chemistry; soap and detergent product and processing development. *Mailing Add:* 255 W Ridgewood Ave Ridgewood NJ 07450

HEALEY, MARK CALVIN, PRODUCTION & USE OF MONOCLONAL ANTIBODIES, SUBUNIT VACCINE DEVELOPMENT FOR SELECT ANIMAL DISEASES. *Current Pos:* res asst prof, 81-83, from asst prof to assoc prof, 83-91, PROF & ASST HEAD VET SCI, UTAH STATE UNIV, 91- *Personal Data:* b Salt Lake City, Utah, Mar 7, 47; m 69; c 3. *Educ:* Univ Utah, BS, 71, MS, 73; Purdue Univ, PhD(immunoparasitol), 76; Miss State Univ, DVM, 81. *Prof Exp:* Teaching fel, Univ Utah, 70-73; grad instr parasitol, Purdue Univ, 73-76; instr parasitol, Tex A&M Univ, 76-77; resident parasitol, Miss State Univ, 78-81. *Mem:* Am Soc Parasitologists; Am Asn Vet Parasitologists; Am Vet Med Asn; Am Soc Microbiol; Conf Res Workers Animal Dis. *Res:* Immunoparasitology; developing subunit vaccines against avian coccidiosis (Eimeria tenella), cryptosporidiosis (Cryptosporidium parvum) and ram lamb epididymitis (Actinobacillus seminis and Haemophilus somnus). *Mailing Add:* Biol Dept Utah State Univ Logan UT 84322-0001

HEALEY, MICHAEL CHARLES, POPULATION ECOLOGY, FISHERIES ECOLOGY. *Current Pos:* DIR, WESTWATER RES CTR, UNIV BC, 90- *Personal Data:* b Prince Rupert, BC, Mar 31, 42. *Educ:* Univ BC, BSc, 64, MSc, 66; Aberdeen Univ, PhD(natural hist), 69. *Prof Exp:* Nat Res Coun Can fel, Pac Biol Sta, Dept Fisheries & Oceans, 69-70, res scientist, Dept Environ, Freshwater Inst, Winnipeg, 70-74, res scientist & prog leader, Pac Biol Sta, 74-90. *Concurrent Pos:* Sr fel, Marine Policy & Ocean Mgt Prog, Woods Hole, Oceanog Inst, Mass, 82-83; chmn bd dir, Rawson Acad Aquatic Sci, 82-85, dir, 82-89; vis scientist, Univ BC, 88-89. *Mem:* Int Asn Theoret & Appl Limnol; Am Fisheries Soc; Pac Fishery Biologists (pres, 80-81); Rawson Acad Aquatic Sci. *Res:* Factors which influence the numbers of animals in natural populations and evolution of life history strategies; resource management strategy and application of decision analytic technology to resource management planning. *Mailing Add:* Westwater Res Ctr Univ BC Vancouver BC V6T 1W5 Can

HEALEY, PATRICK LEONARD, DEVELOPMENTAL & CELLULAR BIOLOGY. *Current Pos:* asst prof, Univ Calif, Irvine, 66-72, assoc dean sch, 67-69 & 70-72, acad asst to vpres, 72-75, ASSOC PROF BIOL SCI, UNIV CALIF, IRVINE, 72-, EXEC ASSOC DEAN, SCH BIOL SCI, 80- *Personal Data:* b Long Beach, Calif, Feb 20, 36; m 62; c 2. *Educ:* Univ Calif, Berkeley, AB, 60, PhD(bot), 64. *Prof Exp:* USPHS trainee & res assoc develop biol, Brown Univ, 64-65, asst prof biol sci, 65-66. *Mem:* AAAS; Am Soc Plant Physiologists; Bot Soc Am; Am Soc Cell Biol. *Res:* Cellular and histological changes in the shoot apex accompanying floral induction; ultrastructural and histochemical differentiation and development of plant secretory cells. *Mailing Add:* Dept Develop & Cell Biol Univ Calif Irvine CA 92717-0001

HEALY, BERNADINE P, CARDIOLOGY. *Current Pos:* DEAN, COL MED, OHIO STATE UNIV, 95- *Personal Data:* b New York, NY. *Educ:* Harvard Univ, MD, 70. *Prof Exp:* Dir, Coronary Care Unit, prof med & asst dean, postdoctoral progs & fac develop, Sch Med, Johns Hopkins Univ, 77-84; dep dir, Off Sci & Technol Policy, White House, 84-85; chmn, Res Inst, Cleveland Clin Found, 85-91; dir, NIH, 91-93. *Concurrent Pos:* Chmn, White House Cabinet Working Group Biotechnol & exec secy, Panel Health Univs, White House Sci Coun; mem adv groups, Coun Nat Heart, Lung & Blood Inst, Nat Cancer Inst & White House Working Group Health Policy & Econ; bd dirs, Am Heart Asn, 83-; bd overseers, Harvard Col, 89-; chmn, Pub Policy Comt, Am Fedn Clin Res; bd gov, Am Col Cardiol; mem, adv comt to dir, NIH, White House Sci Coun, Life Sci Strategic Planning Study Comt, NASA & Spec Med Adv Comt, Dept Vet Affairs; chmn adv panel, US Cong; vchmn, Pres Coun Advisors Sci & Technol; chair, Adv Panel Basic Res, Off Technol Assessment. *Mem:* Inst Med-Nat Acad Sci; Am Fedn Clin Res (pres, 83-84); Am Heart Asn (pres, 88-89). *Res:* Cardiovascular research and medicine; neurobiology; immunology; cancer; artificial organs; atherosclerosis; musculoskeletal disorders; molecular biology. *Mailing Add:* Col Med Ohio State Univ 370 W Ninth Ave Rm 258 Meilings Hall Columbus OH 43210. *Fax:* 216-292-1301; *E-Mail:* healy.21@osu.edu

HEALY, GEORGE RICHARD, PARASITOLOGY. *Current Pos:* RETIRED. *Personal Data:* b Springfield, Mass, Oct 30, 24; m 52; c 2. *Educ:* Providence Col, BS, 49; Univ Ky, MS, 52; Rice Inst, PhD(parasitol), 56. *Prof Exp:* Asst zool, Univ Ky, 49-51; investr dove dis, Ky Fish & Game Div, 51-52; asst biol, Rice Inst, 52-54; parasitologist & chief, Protozoan Dis Br, Parasitic Dis Div, Ctr Dis Control, USPHS, 57-87; adj prof pharmacol, Sch Med, Emory Univ, 60-92. *Mem:* Am Soc Parasitol; Am Soc Trop Med & Hyg; Sigma Xi; AAAS; Am Soc Microbiol. *Res:* Amebiasis; Babesiosis; Amebic meningoencephalitis; host-parasite relationships; protozoan and helminthic zoonoses. *Mailing Add:* 905 Vistavia Circle Decatur GA 30033

HEALY, GEORGE W(ILLIAM), METALLURGY. *Current Pos:* res prof, 74-80, ADJ PROF METALL, UNIV UTAH, 80- *Personal Data:* b Muhlan, Austria, May 18, 09; US citizen; m 41; c 6. *Educ:* Univ Paris, Cert de Math Gen, 30; Yale Univ, BS, 33. *Honors & Awards:* Hunt Award, Am Inst Mining, Metall & Petrol Engrs, 58. *Prof Exp:* Res metallurgist, Union Carbide Metals Co Div, Union Carbide Corp, 40-63; assoc prof metall, Pa State Univ, 63-74. *Concurrent Pos:* Int Hofmann Prize Consortium, Spec Prize, 80-81. *Mem:* Am Inst Mining, Metall & Petrol Engrs; Can Inst Metallurgists; Am Ceramic Soc. *Res:* Chemical metallurgy of steel, ferroalloys and non-ferrous metals. *Mailing Add:* 3258 Alta Hills Dr Sandy UT 84093

HEALY, JOHN H, GEOPHYSICS. *Current Pos:* res geophysicist, Colo, 61-68, RES GEOPHYSICIST, US GEOL SURV, CALIF, 68- *Personal Data:* b Chicago, Ill, Aug 7, 29; m 51; c 5. *Educ:* Mass Inst Technol, BS, 51; Calif Inst Technol, MS, 57, PhD(geophys), 61. *Prof Exp:* Physicist, Air Force Cambridge Res Ctr, 51-53; seismologist, Chevron Oil Co, 54-56; asst res geol, Calif Inst Technol, 56-61. *Mem:* Am Geophys Union; Soc Explor Geophys; Seismol Soc Am. *Res:* Crustal structure; earthquake seismology. *Mailing Add:* 306 Diablo Ct Palo Alto CA 94306

HEALY, JOHN JOSEPH, STATISTICAL ENGINEERING, DIMENSIONAL ANALYSIS. *Current Pos:* ENGR, MCDERMOTT INC CO, BABCOCK & WILCOX CO, 69-, SR ENGR, 76- *Personal Data:* b Vancouver, Wash, Apr 12, 43; m 70, Patricia Lenci; c Vicki L. *Educ:* Carnegie-Mellon Univ, BS, 65; George Washington Univ, MS, 78. *Prof Exp:* Prod engr, Elec Boat Div, Gen Dynamics Corp, 65-67; process engr, Combustion Eng Inc, 67-69. *Res:* Applied statistical inference; product dimensioning and tolerancing; cleanliness of nuclear components. *Mailing Add:* Babcock & Wilcox Co PO Box 785 MC 32 Lynchburg VA 24505. *Fax:* 804-522-5922

HEALY, MICHAEL L, OCEANOGRAPHY, ANALYTICAL CHEMISTRY. *Current Pos:* PRES, RAVEN SYSTS, SEATTLE, 84- *Personal Data:* b Pocatello, Idaho, Nov 17, 36; m 58; c 2. *Educ:* Ore State Univ, BS, 58, PhD(analytical chem), 65. *Prof Exp:* Prin oceanogr, Univ Wash, 65-84. *Mem:* Am Chem Soc; Sigma Xi; Am Soc Limnol & Oceanog; Sigma Xi. *Res:* Chemical oceanography; trace metal analysis; ocean nutrient analysis; coulometric methods; polarography. *Mailing Add:* 8506 NE 129th Pl Kirkland WA 98034

HEALY, PAUL WILLIAM, mathematics; deceased, see previous edition for last biography

HEALY, WILLIAM CARLETON, JR, MATHEMATICAL STATISTICS. *Current Pos:* RETIRED. *Personal Data:* b Rochester, NY, Feb 14, 25; m 49; c 3. *Educ:* Univ Mich, BSE, 48, MS, 49; Univ Ill, PhD(statist), 55. *Prof Exp:* Statistician, Gen Elec Co, 49-52; staff statistician, Ethyl Corp, Mich, 55-57, supvr math anal, 57-62; mgr, Opers Res Div, Marathon Oil Co, 62-69, Systs & Appln Div, 69-71 & Mgt Sci, 71-73, mgr comput sci, 73-89. *Mem:* Am Statist Asn; Asn Comput Mach. *Res:* Applied statistics; mathematical programming; operations research in petroleum industry; computing. *Mailing Add:* 5821 Laurel Pl Littleton CO 80123

HEALY, WILLIAM RYDER, EVOLUTIONARY ECOLOGY, HERPETOLOGY. *Current Pos:* From instr to assoc prof, 64-80, chmn dept, 76-81, PROF BIOL, COL HOLY CROSS, 80- *Personal Data:* b Lynn, Mass, May 10, 38; m 63; c 3. *Educ:* Boston Col, BS, 61; Univ Mich, Ann Arbor, MS, 63, PhD(zool), 66. *Mem:* AAAS; Am Soc Ichthyol & Herpet; Sigma Xi. *Res:* Population ecology of salamanders with emphasis on life history strategies. *Mailing Add:* Dept Biol Col Holy Cross Worcester MA 01610

HEANEY, DAVID PAUL, RUMINANT NUTRITION, INTENSIVE SHEEP MANAGEMENT. *Current Pos:* RETIRED. *Personal Data:* b Choteau, Mont, Dec 25, 27; m 52; c 1. *Educ:* Mont State Univ, BS, 51, MS, 56; Mich State Univ, PhD(animal nutrit), 60. *Honors & Awards:* Cert of Merit, Can Soc Animal Sci, 85. *Prof Exp:* Res scientist ruminant nutrit, Animal Res Ctr, Res Br, Agr Can, 60-89. *Res:* Feeding regimes, management regimes and nutritional requirements for artificially reared lambs and totally confined, intensively managed sheep. *Mailing Add:* 2383 Baseline Rd Ottawa ON K2C 0E2 Can

HEANEY, JAMES PATRICK, SANITARY ENGINEERING, OPERATIONS RESEARCH. *Current Pos:* RETIRED. *Personal Data:* b Chicago, Ill, Jan 12, 40; m 62; c 2. *Educ:* Ill Inst Technol, BS, 62; Northwestern Univ, MS, 65, PhD(civil eng), 68. *Prof Exp:* Engr trainee, Metro Sanit Dist, Chicago, 57-62; consult, Am Pub Works Asn, 67; sr res engr water resources, Pac Northwest Labs, Battelle Mem Inst, 67-68; from asst prof, Univ Fla, 68-80, prof environ eng sci & dir, Water Resources Res Ctr, 80-91. *Mem:* Am Water Works Asn. *Res:* Application of operations research and mathematical economics to problems in environmental engineering. *Mailing Add:* 7112 Old Post Rd Boulder CO 80301

HEANEY, LAWRENCE R, EVOLUTION, SYSTEMATICS. *Current Pos:* res fel, 86-88, asst cur, 88-91, ASSOC CUR, SMITHSONIAN INST, 91- *Personal Data:* b Dec 2, 52; m, Teresa Horton; c Benjamin. *Educ:* Univ Minn, BSci, 74; Univ Kans, PhD(biol), 79. *Prof Exp:* Asst prof biol & cur mammals, Univ Mich, 79-86. *Concurrent Pos:* Vis syst specialist, Field Mus Nat Hist, 81; res assoc, Smithsonian Inst, 88-; comt, Evolutionary Biol, 89-; hon res cur, 94- *Mem:* Am Soc Mammalogists; Soc Study Evolution; Soc Syst Biologists; Sigma Xi; Soc Conserv Biol; Wldlife Conserv Soc Phillippines. *Res:* Island biogeography, especially Southeast Asian mammals; speciation, approached through studies of hybridization; systematics of rodents and bats; conservation biology; ecology and evolution of biodiversity patterns. *Mailing Add:* Field Mus Natural Hist Div Mammals Roosevelt Rd at Lake Shore Dr Chicago IL 60605. *E-Mail:* heaney@fmppr.fmnh.org

HEANEY, ROBERT JOHN, ATMOSPHERIC CHEMISTRY, WATER CHEMISTRY. *Current Pos:* sr scientist, Res Ctr, Kennecott Copper Corp, 52-59, from actg dir to dir, Agr & Meteorol Res Dept, 59-64, agr & meteorol res engr, Qual Control Dept, 64-70, PROCESS CONTROL & ENVIRON ENGR, KENNECOTT COPPER CORP, 70- *Personal Data:* b East Rochester, NH, Aug 31, 22; m 46; c 4. *Educ:* Univ NH, BS, 43; Univ Colo, PhD, 50. *Prof Exp:* Jr chemist, Nat Bur Stand, 43-44, chemist, 46; chief chemist, Vitro Chem Co, 51-52. *Concurrent Pos:* Spec engr detachment, Manhattan Proj, Colo & Washington, DC, 44-46; mem, State Adv Comt Sci & Technol, 73-; pres, Great Salt Lake Health Planning Coun, 74- *Mem:* Am Chem Soc; Sigma Xi. *Res:* Biochemical effects of air contaminants on plants and animals; effects of water pollutants on humans and animals; effects of impurities on copper quality. *Mailing Add:* 1889 Wasatch Dr Salt Lake City UT 84108-3323

HEANEY, ROBERT PROULX, HUMAN BONE & CALCIUM METABOLISM. *Current Pos:* actg chmn, Dept Med, Creighton Univ, 60-61, chmn, 61-69, head, Endocrinol & Metab Sect, 69-71, vpres, Div Health Sci, 71-84, from asst prof to prof med, 57-84, JOHN A CREIGHTON UNIV PROF, CREIGHTON UNIV, 84- *Personal Data:* b Omaha, Nebr, Nov 10, 27; m 52; c 7. *Educ:* Creighton Univ, BS, 47, MD, 51. *Prof Exp:* Instr, Sch Med, Univ Okla, 54-55; clin instr, Sch Med, George Washington Univ, 55-57. *Concurrent Pos:* Chmn, Nat Inst Dent Res Spec Grants Rev, 82-86; mem, Nutrit Res Sci Adv Comt of Nat Dairy Coun, 86-89, chmn, 87-89; mem, Nat Osteoporosis Found, Sci Adv Comt, 86-91, bd dirs, 90; mem, Sci Adv Comt, Osteoporosis Found, 86. *Mem:* Fel Am Col Physicians; hon mem Am Dietetic Asn; Am Inst Nutrit; Am Soc Bone & Mineral Res; Cent Soc Clin Res. *Res:* Human bone and calcium metabolism; long term study of human osteoporosis; research and statistics for health professionals; author of over 200 scientific papers. *Mailing Add:* Creighton Univ 2500 California Plaza Omaha NE 68178

HEAPS, MELVIN GEORGE, PHYSICS, ATMOSPHERIC SCIENCES. *Current Pos:* INSTR, COMMUNITY COLS, 92- *Personal Data:* b Salt Lake City, Utah. *Educ:* Brigham Young Univ, BS, 67; Utah State Univ, PhD(physics), 72. *Prof Exp:* Res assoc physics, Univ Fla, 72-75; Nat Res Coun res assoc, US Army Ballistic Res Lab, 75-76; physicist, US Army Atmospheric Sci Lab, 76-90. *Mem:* Am Geophys Union; Sigma Xi. *Res:* Atmospheric effects on propagation and electro-optical sensors; smokes and obscurants; target detection. *Mailing Add:* 2136 W Knowles Circle Mesa AZ 85202-6440

HEARD, HARRY GORDON, PHYSICS, COMPUTER SCIENCE. *Current Pos:* SR SYSTS ENGR, LORAL AEROSPACE, 90- *Personal Data:* b Raines, Tenn, Sept 23, 22; m 47; c 2. *Educ:* Univ Calif, BS, 49, MS, 51. *Prof Exp:* Res engr, Lawrence Berkeley Labs, 51-59; chief engr, Levinthal Electronics Prod Inc, 59-60; vpres, Radiation Inc, 59-60, Energy Systs, Inc, 60-64 & HNU Systs Div, Ohio Steel, 64-68; pres, Resalab, Inc, 68-70; gen mgr, MBA Info Systs, 70-74; scientist, Inst Advan Comput, 75-77; dir, Technol Develop Calif, 78-88; sr systs designer & sr comput systs designer, Ford Aerospace, 88-90. *Concurrent Pos:* Dir, Intronex, Inc, Menlo Park, 75- *Mem:* Am Phys Soc; Inst Elec & Electronics Engrs; Optical Soc Am; Sigma Xi; Asn Comput Mach; Res Soc Am. *Res:* Optical data processing; cartographic systems; computer sciences; hollow-cathode lasers; quantum electronics; high vacuum physics; high voltage systems; satellite data systems; structure software systems design; class IX (super) computer system design; Lan-Wan design; computer simulation. *Mailing Add:* 50 Skywood Way Woodside CA 94062

HEARD, JOHN THIBAUT, JR, MICROBIAL PHYSIOLOGY. *Current Pos:* RES ASSOC, KIRKSVILLE COL OSTEOP MED, 78- *Personal Data:* b Houston, Tex, Sept 4, 40; m 81. *Educ:* Lamar State Col Technol, BS, 64; Sam Houston State Col, MS, 66; Univ Tex, Houston, PhD(biomed sci), 78. *Concurrent Pos:* Consult, Bio-Diesel Refiners Inc, Iowa, 81- *Mem:* Sigma Xi. *Res:* Biosynthesis and metabolism of nicotinamide adenine dinucleotide and its metabolites as a function of age or perturbations of the system under study. *Mailing Add:* RR 6 Kirksville MO 63501-9806

HEARD, WILLIAM HERMAN, MALACOLOGY. *Current Pos:* From instr to asst prof zool, 62-67, assoc prof, 67-80, PROF BIOL SCI, FLA STATE UNIV, 80- *Personal Data:* b Hart, Mich, Mar 4, 35; m 55; c 3. *Educ:* Univ Mich, BS, 57, MS, 59, PhD(zool), 63. *Mem:* Am Malacol Union; Am Micros Soc; Soc Syst Zool; Am Soc Zool; Ecol Soc Am. *Res:* Systematics, distribution and life histories of freshwater mollusks of North America. *Mailing Add:* Dept Biol Sci Fla State Univ 600 W College Ave Tallahassee FL 32306-1096

HEARING, VINCENT JOSEPH, JR, BIOCHEMISTRY, MOLECULAR BIOLOGY. *Current Pos:* Electron microscopist, NIH, 69-71, NIH fel, 71-72, sr staff fel biochem, 72-77, RES BIOLOGIST, NAT CANCER INST, NIH, 77- *Personal Data:* b Washington, DC, Aug 22, 45; m 68, Elizabeth D Brown; c Brian, Laura & David. *Educ:* Georgetown Univ, BS, 67; Cath Univ Am, PhD(cell biol), 71. *Honors & Awards:* Seiji Mem Award, 92; Vitiligo Res Award, 92; Takevchi Medal, 96. *Mem:* Am Soc Cell Biol; Am Asn Cancer Res; Sigma Xi; Am Soc Biochem & Molecular Biol; Soc Invest Dermat; Pan Am Soc Pigment Cell Res. *Res:* Control mechanisms involved in enzymology of melanin formation in mammals and aberrant proteins synthesized in the malignant melanocyte. *Mailing Add:* NIH Bldg 37 Rm 1B22 Bethesda MD 20892. *Fax:* 301-402-8787; *E-Mail:* hearingv@dc37a.nei.nih.gov

HEARN, ANTHONY CLEM, SYMBOLIC COMPUTATION. *Current Pos:* MEM TECH STAFF, RAND CORP, SANTA MONICA, 80- *Personal Data:* b Adelaide, Australia, April 13, 37; m 70; c 2. *Educ:* Univ Adelaide, BSc, 59; Cambridge Univ, PhD(theoret physics), 62. *Prof Exp:* Res assoc physics, Stanford Univ, 62-64; sr sci officer, Rutherford High Energy Lab, Eng, 64-65; asst prof physics, Stanford Univ, 65-69; from assoc prof to prof physics, Univ Utah, 69-78, adj prof elec eng, 71-78, prof comput sci & chmn dept, 73-80. *Concurrent Pos:* Vis scientist, Europ Ctr Nuclear Res, 62; Alfred P Sloan Found fel, 67-69; consult, Hewlett-Packard Co, 74-79 & Burroughs Corp, Detroit, 75-78. *Mem:* Am Phys Soc; Asn Comput Mach; Soc Indust & Appl Math. *Res:* Algebraic simplification; computational physics. *Mailing Add:* 451 23rd St Santa Monica CA 90402. *Fax:* 310-393-4818; *E-Mail:* hearn@rand.org

HEARN, BERNARD CARTER, JR, GEOLOGY. *Current Pos:* GEOLOGIST, US GEOL SURV, 57- *Personal Data:* b Baltimore, Md, Feb 8, 33; m 55; c 3. *Educ:* Wesleyan Univ, BA, 54; Johns Hopkins Univ, PhD(geol), 59. *Mem:* AAAS; Am Geophys Union; Geol Soc Am; Mineral Soc Am. *Res:* Structure and petrology of igneous rocks; kimberlites; geothermal volcanology. *Mailing Add:* MS 954 Nat Ctr Reston VA 20192. *Fax:* 703-648-6789

HEARN, CHARLES JACKSON, PLANT BREEDING. *Current Pos:* RETIRED. *Personal Data:* b Bellville, Ga, June 17, 36; m 58; c 3. *Educ:* Univ Ga, BSA, 57, MS, 59; Tex A&M Univ, PhD(plant breeding), 63. *Prof Exp:* Asst agronomist, Ga Coastal Plain Exp Sta, 57-58; res geneticist, USDA, 62-95, res leader, 85-95. *Concurrent Pos:* Res admin trainee, USDA, Beltsville, Md, 71-72, actg lab dir, 84; adj prof, Hort Sci Dept, Univ Fla, 79- *Mem:* Int Soc Citricult; Am Pomoyl Soc. *Res:* Breeding of citrus; citrus varieties; fruit breeding; fruit physiology; cytology of plants; development of improved varieties of oranges, grapefruit and tangerines. *Mailing Add:* 3311 Bellemeade Dr Valdosta GA 31605

HEARN, DAVID RUSSELL, ASTROPHYSICS. *Current Pos:* STAFF MEM, LINCOLN LAB, MASS INST TECHNOL, 84- *Personal Data:* b Tucson, Ariz, Jan 21, 42; m 77, Florence Oetjen. *Educ:* Calif Inst Technol, BS, 64; Harvard Univ, MA, 66, PhD(physics), 68. *Prof Exp:* Nat Acad Sci vis res assoc gamma-ray astron, Smithsonian Astrophys Observ, 68-70; res staff, Ctr

Space Res, Mass Inst Technol, 70-79; sr res physicist, Elscint, Inc, 79-80, physics group leader, 81-84. *Mem:* Am Phys Soc; Int Soc Optical Eng. *Res:* Analysis and publication of data from the soft x-ray telescope aboard the SAS-3 satellite, which was designed and built between 1970 and 1975; high energy laser system technology, adaptive optics, integrated optics and infrared imaging systems. *Mailing Add:* 18 Maurice Rd Wellesley MA 02181. *Fax:* 781-981-2213; *E-Mail:* drhearn@ll.mit.edu

HEARN, DWIGHT D, APPLIED MATHEMATICS. *Current Pos:* vis prof, 85-90, LECTR, DEPT COMPUT SCI, UNIV ILL, 90- *Personal Data:* b Detroit, Mich, Apr 30, 33. *Educ:* Wayne State Univ, BS, 62; Univ Mich, PhD(physics), 68. *Prof Exp:* Asst prof math & physics, Lawrence Inst Technol, 64-66; asst prof physics, Eastern Mich Univ, 66-68; res assoc & assoc instr, Univ Utah, 68-70; sr analyst, Lockheed Electronics Co, 70-72; sr scientist, Braddock, Dunn & McDonald, Inc, 72-73; assoc prof appl math & comput sci, Univ Southwestern La, 73-76; mem fac, Western Ill Univ, 76-80, chmn comput sci, 80-85. *Concurrent Pos:* Consult, Petrol Assocs, Inc, 75. *Mem:* Asn Comput Mech. *Res:* Applied mathematics; computer applications in artificial intelligence; heuristic programming; numerical analysis; computer uses in education; computer graphics. *Mailing Add:* Univ Ill 2225 Digital Comput Lab 1304 W Springfield Ave Urbana IL 61801

HEARN, HENRY JAMES, JR, microbiology, cancer, for more information see previous edition

HEARN, MICHAEL JOSEPH, ORGANIC CHEMISTRY. *Current Pos:* from asst prof to assoc prof, 77-90, PROF CHEM, WELLESLEY COL, 90- *Personal Data:* b Bangor, Maine, Mar 4, 49; m 91, Maureen Reilly; c Christopher Dues & Kathleen Dues. *Educ:* Rutgers Col, BA, 71; Yale Univ, MS, 73, MPhil, 75, PhD(org chem), 76. *Prof Exp:* Instr chem, Yale Univ, 76-77. *Concurrent Pos:* Assoc, Yale Univ, 76-77. *Mem:* Nat Sci Teachers Asn; Am Chem Soc; Sigma Xi; NY Acad Sci; fel Am Inst Chemists; Am Soc Microbio Coblentz Soc; Soc Appl Spectros; Coun Undergrad Res, Coun Near-Infrared Spectros. *Res:* Synthetic organic chemistry; new synthetic methods in the chemistry of hydrazines; synthesis and near-infrared spectra of anti-tuberculosis compounds. *Mailing Add:* Dept Chem Wellesley Col Wellesley MA 02181. *Fax:* 781 283 3642; *E Mail:* mhearn@lucy.wellesley.edu

HEARN, ROBERT HENDERSON, ELECTRONICS ENGINEERING, ENGINEERING MANAGEMENT. *Current Pos:* ENGR ELECTRONICS, NAVAL OCEAN SYST CTR, 76-, RES, DEVELOP, TECHNOL & ENG COMMAND CONTROL & OCEAN SURVEILLANCE CTR, 93- *Personal Data:* b Phoenix, Ariz, Apr 9, 40; m 62; c 2. *Educ:* Calif Inst Technol, BS, 62,. *Prof Exp:* Engr electronics, Naval Ord Test Sta, 63-70, Naval Undersea Res & Develop Lab, 70-71, Naval Undersea Warfare Ctr, 71-72 & Naval Undersea Ctr, 72-76. *Res:* Adaptive signal processing; ocean acoustics; real time acoustic simulation. *Mailing Add:* 6115 Radcliffe Dr San Diego CA 92122

HEARN, RUBY PURYEAR, MATERNAL HEALTH, HEALTH POLICY. *Current Pos:* prog officer, Robert Wood Johnson Found, 76-80, sr prog officer, 80, asst vpres, 80-82, vpres, 83-96, SR VPRES, ROBERT WOOD JOHNSON FOUND, 96- *Personal Data:* b Winston-Salem, NC, Apr 13, 40; m 61; c 2. *Educ:* Skidmore Col, BA, 60; Yale Grad Sch, MS, 64, PhD(biophys), 69. *Prof Exp:* Res assoc fel, Yale Univ, 68-69; dir, Content Devolup Health Show, Children's TV Workshop, Future Works Div, 72-76. *Concurrent Pos:* Mem, Adv Coun Tele-Commun Elderly, Mt Sinai Sch Med, NY, 74-76; bd trustees, Meharry Med Col, Nashville, Tenn, 81-86; bd overseers, Dartmouth Med Sch, Hanover, NH, 86-; mem, New York City Mayoral Child Health Comn, 88- *Mem:* Inst Med-Nat Acad Sci; AAAS; Soc Res & Child Develop; Ambulatory Pediat Asn. *Res:* Development of programs to improve the health and functioning of children and youth including programs to reduce infant mortality in isolated areas, consolidate health services for high-risk young people and develop methods for assessing and treating developmental failure. *Mailing Add:* Robert Wood Johnson Found PO Box 2316 Princeton NJ 08543-2316. *Fax:* 609-452-1865

HEARN, WALTER RUSSELL, BIOCHEMISTRY. *Current Pos:* RETIRED. *Personal Data:* b Shreveport, La, Feb 20, 26; m 47, 66, Virginia A Krauss; c Christine & Russell H. *Educ:* Rice Inst, BA, 48; Univ Ill, PhD(biochem), 51. *Prof Exp:* Instr biochem, Sch Med, Yale Univ, 51-52; instr biochem, Col Med, Baylor Univ, 52-54, asst prof, 54-55; asst prof chem, Iowa State Univ, 55-60, assoc prof biochem, 60-73; sci writer, Ed Am Sci Affil News, 69-93. *Concurrent Pos:* Am Inst Biol Sci vis biologist to cols, 61-66; res assoc, Univ Calif, Berkeley, 68-69; sr res fel, NIH, 68-69; vis assoc prof biochem, Univ Calif, Berkeley, 72-73; adj prof sci, New Col Berkeley, 78-93, prof sci & christianity, 93- *Mem:* Fel AAAS; Am Chem Soc; fel Am Sci Affil. *Res:* Isolation and characterization of natural products; chemistry and metabolism of amino acids, peptides and proteins; endocrinology; bacterial pigments; science education; science and religion. *Mailing Add:* 762 Arlington Ave Berkeley CA 94707-1634

HEARON, WILLIAM MONTGOMERY, BIOCHEMISTRY. *Current Pos:* RETIRED. *Personal Data:* b Kankakee, Ill, Feb 20, 14; m 44, Barbara Olsen; c Steve, Leigh & Hally. *Educ:* Univ Denver, BS, 35, MS, 37; Mass Inst Technol, PhD(org chem), 40. *Honors & Awards:* Com Develop Asn Honor Award, 65; Res & Develop Award, Tech Asn Pulp & Paper Indust, 75. *Prof Exp:* Asst chem, Univ Denver, 35-37; chemist, Eastman Kodak Co, 40-43; asst chief gas officer, Off Civilian Defense, Washington, DC, 43; asst prof chem, Mass Inst Technol, 46-47; dir, Basic Res Div, Cent Res Dept, Crown Zellerbach Corp, 47-49, asst dir res, 49-55, gen mgr, Chem Prod Div, 55-60, vpres res & develop, 60-67, mgt consult, 67-69; asst to vpres paper mgr, 69-77, dir chem opers, 77-79, consult, Boise Cascade Corp, 79-84. *Concurrent Pos:* Maj, Manhattan Dist CEngrs, US Army; mem vis comt, Col Forestry, Univ Wash; mem tech adv coun, Forest Prod Lab, Univ Calif & Indust Res Inst; res & develop award, Tech Asn Pulp & Paper Indust, 75. *Mem:* AAAS; Am Chem Soc; Am Forestry Asn; Forest Prod Res Soc; fel Tech Asn Pulp & Paper Indust. *Res:* Research and development; wood chemistry; paper technology. *Mailing Add:* 5337 SW 34th Pl Portland OR 97201-1124

HEARSEY, BRYAN VANDIVER, MATHEMATICS. *Current Pos:* asst prof, 71-77, assoc prof, 77-81, PROF MATH, LEBANON VALLEY COL, 81- *Personal Data:* b Bellingham, Wash, Aug 2, 42; m 65; c 1. *Educ:* Western Wash State Col, BA, 64; Wash State Univ, MA, 66, PhD(math), 68. *Prof Exp:* Teaching asst math, Wash State Univ, 64-68; asst prof, Univ Fla, 68-71. *Mem:* Am Math Soc; Math Asn Am; Soc Actuaries. *Res:* General topology, particularly the study of convergence spaces. *Mailing Add:* Dept Math Sci Lebanon Valley Col Annville PA 17003-0501

HEARST, JOHN EUGENE, BIOPHYSICAL CHEMISTRY. *Current Pos:* from asst prof to prof, 62-95, EMER PROF CHEM, UNIV CALIF, BERKELEY, 96- *Personal Data:* b Vienna, Austria, July 2, 35; US citizen; m 58, Jean Bankson; c 2. *Educ:* Yale Univ, BE, 57; Calif Inst Technol, PhD(chem & physics), 61. *Hon Degrees:* DSc, Lehigh Univ, 92. *Honors & Awards:* Robert A Welch Foundation lectr, 92-93; Research Award, Am Soc Photobiol, 94. *Prof Exp:* NSF res assoc chem, Dartmouth Col, 61-62; dir, Chem Biodynamics Div, Lawrence Berkeley Lab, 86-87 & 88-89, actg assoc dir, 86-87 & 88-89. *Concurrent Pos:* Exec ed, Anal Biochem, 77-82, Nucleic Acids Res, 90-93; dir, HRI Res, Inc, 78- & Steritech, Inc, 92-; founder & sr consult, Advan Genetics Res Inc, Oakland, Calif, 81-84; dir, Univ Northern Calif, 93-95; vpres, Cerus Corp, Concord, Calif, 96- *Mem:* AAAS; Am Chem Soc; Biophys Soc; Am Phys Soc; Am Soc Biol Chemists; Am Soc Photobiol (pres, 91-92). *Res:* Polymer statistics; physical chemistry of DNA, hydrodynamic properties of stiff chain macromolecules; psoralen photochemistry with nucleic acids; structure of nucleic acids in viruses, ribosomes and chromosomes; nucleic acid structure-function relationships; molecular genetics of photosynthetic processes. *Mailing Add:* Dept Chem Univ Calif Berkeley CA 94720

HEARST, JOSEPH R, GEOPHYSICAL WELL LOGGING. *Current Pos:* RETIRED. *Personal Data:* b Chicago, Ill, Sept 9, 31; m 57, Jean Frankel; c Edward, Marti & Dorothy. *Educ:* Reed Col, BA, 54; Mass Inst Technol, BS, 54; Boston Univ, MA, 55; Northwestern Univ, PhD(physics), 60. *Prof Exp:* Physicist, Lawrence Livermore Lab, Univ Calif, 59-94. *Concurrent Pos:* Fulbright award, Australia, 79; vis scientist, Brit Petrol Res Lab, 86. *Mem:* Soc Prof Well Log Analysts; Minerals & Geotech Logging Soc (vpres, 85-87, pres, 92-95). *Res:* Development of improved methods of well logging, especially nuclear logging and borehole gravimetry; quality control and computer programming for well log analysis. *Mailing Add:* 685 Glen Rd Danville CA 94526. *E-Mail:* hearst@ix.netcom.com

HEARST, PETER JACOB, ORGANIC CHEMISTRY. *Current Pos:* RES CHEMIST, NAVAL CIVIL ENG LAB, 50- *Personal Data:* b Stuttgart, Ger, Mar 31, 23; nat US; m 49; c 3. *Educ:* Harvard Univ, BS, 43; Stanford Univ, MS, 48, PhD(chem), 51. *Prof Exp:* Asst res chemist, Calif Res Corp, Stand Oil Co Calif, 43-48. *Mem:* AAAS; Am Chem Soc; Sigma Xi. *Res:* Pollution analysis and instrumentation; environmental chemistry; organic coatings and plastics degradation; chemical heat sources; electrical properties of materials. *Mailing Add:* 673 Devonshire Dr Oxnard CA 93030-4213

HEARTH, DONALD PAYNE, AERONAUTICAL ENGINEERING. *Current Pos:* RETIRED. *Personal Data:* b Fall River, Mass, Aug 13, 28; m 50; c 4. *Educ:* Northeastern Univ, BSME, 51; Fed Exec Inst, grad, 73. *Prof Exp:* Mem staff, NASA, 51-57; dept mgt, Marquardt Corp, Van Nuys, Calif, 57-62; mem staff, NASA, 62-67, dir planetary progs, Washington, DC, 67-70, dep dir, Goddard Space Flight Ctr, Greenbelt, Md, 70-75; dir, Langley Res Ctr, NASA, 75-; prof, Dept Eng, George Washington Univ, 75-85; prof eng, Univ Colo, 85-93. *Mem:* Nat Acad Eng; fel Am Astronaut Soc; Am Soc Pub Admin; fel Am Inst Aeronaut & Astronaut. *Mailing Add:* 127 Sycamore Pl Oberlin OH 44074

HEASELL, E(DWIN) L(OVELL), PHYSICS, ELECTRICAL ENGINEERING. *Current Pos:* assoc prof, 65-67, PROF ELEC ENG, UNIV WATERLOO, 67- *Personal Data:* b Bognor Regis, Eng, Jan 29, 31; m 52; c 2. *Educ:* Imp Col, Univ London, BSc, 54, ARCS, 54, PhD(physics), 57. *Prof Exp:* Physicist, A E I Res Lab, Eng, 57-59; lectr elec eng, Imp Col, Univ London, 59-65. *Mem:* Assoc Brit Inst Physics; Inst Elec & Electronics Engrs. *Res:* Ultrasonics and its applications to chemical structure determination; the properties of semiconductors, particularly the III-V compounds. *Mailing Add:* Elec & Comput Eng Dept Univ Waterloo Waterloo ON N2L 3G1 Can

HEASLEY, GENE, CHEMISTRY. *Current Pos:* From asst prof to assoc prof, 60-69, head dept, 75-80, PROF CHEM, BETHANY-NAZARENE COL, 69-, CHMN, DIV NATURAL SCI, 80- *Personal Data:* b Burnips, Mich, July 21, 32; m 55; c 4. *Educ:* Hope Col, AB, 55; Univ Kans, PhD(chem), 61. *Mem:* Am Chem Soc. *Res:* Mechanisms of reaction of halogens and alkyl hypohalites with conjugated dienes. *Mailing Add:* 6710 NW 33rd St Bethany OK 73008-3914

HEASLEY, VICTOR LEE, ORGANIC CHEMISTRY, BIOCHEMISTRY. *Current Pos:* PROF CHEM & HEAD DEPT, POINT LOMA COL, 63- *Personal Data:* b Burnips, Mich, Mar 30, 37; m 61, 83, Carol A Jacobs; c Victoria A, Thomas L, Sasha M & Eltran L. *Educ:* Hope Col, BA, 59; Univ Kans, PhD(org chem), 63. *Concurrent Pos:* Grants, Res Corp, Petrol Res Fund, Union Oil Co, NSF, US Geol Surv & NIH, 63-90. *Mem:* Am Chem Soc. *Res:* Addition of electrophiles to unsaturated hydrocarbons; author or co-author of 55 publications in the area of electrophilic additions. *Mailing Add:* Dept Chem Pt Loma Nazarene Col 3900 Lomaland Dr San Diego CA 92106-2810

HEASLIP, RICHARD JOSEPH, PULMONARY PHARMACOLOGY, ALLERGIC INFLAMMATION. *Current Pos:* sr scientist, Wyeth-Ayerst Res, 84-87, res scientist, 87-88, prin scientist, 89-90, RES FEL, WYETH-AYERST RES, 90- *Personal Data:* b New York, NY, Dec 7, 55. *Educ:* Univ Pa, BA, 77; Ohio State Univ, PhD(pharmacol), 82. *Prof Exp:* Fel, Univ Pa, 82-84. *Mem:* Am Soc Pharmacol & Exp Therapeut; Am Thoracic Soc; AAAS. *Res:* Pulmonary pharmacology; molecular pharmacological approaches to drug design; biochemical regulation of cellular reactivity; functional interaction of multiple drug-effector systems; cellular signal transduction; receptor pharmacology and physiology. *Mailing Add:* Wyeth-Ayerst Res PO Box 8299 Philadelphia PA 19101. *Fax:* 610-989-4568

HEASLIP, WILLIAM GRAHAM, INVERTEBRATE PALEONTOLOGY. *Current Pos:* assoc prof, 63-70, PROF GEOL, STATE UNIV NY, COL CORTLAND, 70- *Personal Data:* b Brooklyn, NY, Mar 26, 28; m 50; c 5. *Educ:* Columbia Univ, BS, 53, MA, 55, PhD, 63. *Prof Exp:* Lectr geol, Brooklyn Col, 57-58; instr, Hunter Col, 58-59; asst prof, Syracuse Univ, 59-63. *Concurrent Pos:* Mem, Paleont Res Inst. *Mem:* Paleont Soc. *Res:* Genus Venericardia evolution and taxonomy; Cenozoic mollusks; sexual dimorphism; bivalves. *Mailing Add:* 10 Abdallah Ave Cortland NY 13045

HEASTON, ROBERT JOSEPH, CHEMICAL ENGINEERING. *Current Pos:* MGR, GUIDE & CONTROL ANALYTICAL CTR, ILL INST TECH RES INST, CHICAGO, 87- *Personal Data:* b Kansas City, Kans, Mar 3, 31; m 56; c 3. *Educ:* Univ Ark, BS, 52, MS, 54; Ohio State Univ, PhD(chem eng), 64, Nat War Col, 75. *Prof Exp:* Sr proj engr, Propulsion Lab, Wright-Patterson AFB, Ohio, 55-58; prog mgr chem off, Adv Res Projs Agency, DC, 61-64; org chemist, Chem & Mat Br, Phys Sci Div, Off Chief Res & Develop, Hq, Dept Army, DC, 64-66, chief, Chem Br, Res & Develop Group, Europe, 66-70, chief, Technol Overview Team, Technol Div, 70-74, technol mgr weapon systs, Off Dep Chief Staff Res Develop & Acquisition, 75-87. *Concurrent Pos:* Mem, Solid & Liquid Subgroups, Interagency Chem Rocket Propulsion Group, 62-64; Solid Propellant Instability Comt, Dept Defense, 62-64; Army coord mem, Panel P-3 Org Mat, Subgroup P Mat, Tripartite Tech Coop Prog, 64-66, alt mem, panel O-2 Explosives & Panel O-3 Propellants, Subgroup O Ord, 65-66; alt mem, Interagency Adv Power Group, 65-66. *Mem:* AAAS. *Res:* Technical administration of government contracts in combustion, electrochemistry and organic chemistry; theoretical physics breakthroughs: redefined four fundamental forces, published the Heaston force, speed of light to fourth power divided by Newton's gravitational constant, and derived generic field theory. *Mailing Add:* Ill Inst Tech Res Inst GACIAC 10 W 35th St Chicago IL 60616-3703

HEATH, ALAN GARD, ECOTOXICOLOGY, COMPARATIVE PHYSIOLOGY. *Current Pos:* from asst prof to assoc prof zool, 64-97, PROF ZOOL, VA POLYTECH INST & STATE UNIV, 97- *Personal Data:* b Wichita, Kans, July 30, 35; m 61; c 2. *Educ:* San Jose State Col, BA, 58; Ore State Univ, MS, 61, PhD(physiol), 63. *Prof Exp:* Fishery res aide, US Fish & Wildlife Serv, 58; instr physiol, Ore State Univ, 62; NIH fel, 63-64. *Concurrent Pos:* Fed Water Qual Admin fel, 70; vis scholar, Univ Calif, Davis, 90-91. *Mem:* AAAS; Am Soc Zool; Soc Environ Toxicol Chem; Am Inst Biol Sci; Sigma Xi; Am Fisheries Soc. *Res:* Influence of environmental hypoxia or industrial pollutants on metabolism, cardiovascular and respiratory function of fish; physiological monitoring of pollution; temperature stress effects in fish; temperature and hypoxia effects on freshwater mussels. *Mailing Add:* Dept Biol Va Polytech Inst & State Univ Blacksburg VA 24061

HEATH, CARL E(RNEST), JR, CHEMICAL ENGINEERING. *Current Pos:* PRES, CORP TRANSFORMATIONS INT, 90- *Personal Data:* b Washington, DC, Jan 5, 30; m 54, Patricia Densford; c Alison, John & Julie. *Educ:* Johns Hopkins Univ, BE, 52; Univ Wis, PhD(appl reaction kinetics), 56. *Prof Exp:* Res engr, Process Res Div, Esso Res & Eng Co, 56-57, proj leader, 57-61, sect head, 61-66, govt res lab, 66-68, dir, 68-70, proj mgr, Exxon Enterprises, Inc, 70-77; res mgr, Esso Chem Res Ctr, 77-85; site mgr, Linden Tech Ctr, Exxon Chem, 85-90. *Concurrent Pos:* Consult, Govt Adv Panel on Fuel Cells, Off Sci & Tech, 63; mem, Panel on Electrically Powered Vehicles, Dept Com, 67- *Mem:* Am Chem Soc; Am Inst Chem Engrs; Sigma Xi. *Res:* Radiation chemistry and partial oxidation of hydrocarbons; chemical reactions in shock tubes; hydrocarbon fuel cells; electrocatalysis petroleum process research and development; fuel and lubricant additives. *Mailing Add:* 48 Hawthorne Pl Summit NJ 07901

HEATH, CLARK WRIGHT, JR, EPIDEMIOLOGY, INTERNAL MEDICINE. *Current Pos:* CONSULT, 85-; VPRES EPIDEMIOL & SURVEILLANCE RES, AM CANCER SOC, 88- *Personal Data:* b Leipzig, Ger, Jan 24, 33; US citizen; m 69, Janet Lee; c Thomas M, Andrew S & Mary D. *Educ:* Oberlin Col, AB, 54; Johns Hopkins Univ, MD, 58. *Prof Exp:* Intern internal med, Boston City Hosp & Harvard Med Sch, 58-60, resident, 62-63; dir, Chronic Dis Div, Ctr Environ Health, Ctr Dis Control, Atlanta, 65-85. *Concurrent Pos:* Fel hemat, Boston City Hosp & Tufts Univ, 63-65; Bureau of Preven Health Srv SC Dept Health & Environ Control, 85-88. *Mem:* Am Asn Cancer Res; Soc Epidemiol Res; Am Epidemiol Soc; Am Pub Health Asn; Am Col Epidemiol; AMA; AAAS. *Res:* Environmental health; cancer and birth defects epidemiology. *Mailing Add:* 1714 Vickers Circle Decatur GA 30030. *Fax:* 404-321-4669; *E-Mail:* cheath@cancer.org

HEATH, D(ONALD) P, CHEMICAL ENGINEERING. *Current Pos:* RETIRED. *Personal Data:* b Claytonville, Ill, Jan 8, 19; m 40, Marion Lewis; c 4. *Educ:* Purdue Univ, BS, 40. *Prof Exp:* Engr, Tech Serv Lab, Socony-Vacuum Oil Co, 40-45, res engr petrol fuels, Res & Develop Lab, 45-48, res assoc, 48-52; chief, Aviation Fuels Br, Petrol Admin Defense, US Dept Interior, 52-53; asst supvr petrol fuels develop, Res & Develop Lab, Socony Mobil Oil Co, 53-55, supvr petrol fuels appl res & develop, 55-63, mgr, Tech Serv Dept, Mobil Petrol Co, Inc, 63-65, mgr fuels, asphalt & spec prod, Tech Serv Dept, Mobil Int Oil Co, 65-74, coordr environ conserv, 74-81; consult, 81-91. *Concurrent Pos:* Mem, Refining Comt, Mil Petrol Adv Bd, 48-54 & Coord Res Coun, 54-63. *Mem:* Am Chem Soc; Soc Automotive Engrs. *Res:* Technology of petroleum fuels including motor and aviation gasoline, jet fuel, heating oil, kerosene, diesel and industrial fuels; fuel additives; motor gasoline performance correlations; stability of supersonic jet fuels. *Mailing Add:* 11 Euclid Ave Apt 5B Summit NJ 07901-2114

HEATH, DAVID CLAY, OPERATIONS RESEARCH. *Current Pos:* from asst prof to assoc prof, 75-88, PROF OPER RES, SCH OPERS RES, CORNELL UNIV, 88- *Personal Data:* b Oak Park, Ill, Dec 23, 42; m 64; c 3. *Educ:* Kalamazoo Col, BA, 64; Univ Ill, Urbana, MA, 65, PhD(math), 69. *Prof Exp:* Asst prof math, Univ Minn, Minneapolis, 69-75. *Concurrent Pos:* Researcher, US-France Exchange Scientists Prog, NSF & Ctr Nat Sci Res, France, 73-74; consult appl probability finance & mfg. *Mem:* Am Math Soc; Opers Res Soc. *Res:* Probability theory; stochastic processes; stochastic control; game theory. *Mailing Add:* 111 Burleigh Dr Ithaca NY 14850

HEATH, DWIGHT B(RALEY), DRUG & ALCOHOL USE & ITS OUTCOMES, DRUG & ALCOHOL POLICY. *Current Pos:* PROF ANTHROP, BROWN UNIV, 59- *Personal Data:* b Hartford, Conn, Nov 19, 30; m 55, Ann M Cooper; c David (deceased) & Alicia (deceased). *Educ:* Harvard Univ, BA, 52; Yale Univ, PhD(anthrop), 59. *Hon Degrees:* MA, Brown Univ, 62. *Concurrent Pos:* Chmn, Task Force Alcohol & Drugs, Am Anthrop Asn, 89-94. *Mem:* Am Anthrop Asn; Sigma Xi; AAAS; Soc Med Anthrop; Soc Appl Anthrop; Am Ethnol Soc. *Res:* Attempting to understand alcohol and drug use and sequelae (especially social and cultural) in cross-cultural perspective, throughout history. *Mailing Add:* 47 Barnes St Providence RI 02906. *Fax:* 401-863-7588, 351-5398

HEATH, EUGENE CARTMILL, PHARMACOLOGY, ANALYTICAL CHEMISTRY. *Current Pos:* DIR, ANALYTICAL SERV, HARRIS LABS, 80- *Personal Data:* b Elk City, Okla, Mar 2, 43; m 64; c 5. *Educ:* Univ Mo, BS, 65, MS, 68; Vanderbilt Univ, PhD(pharmacol), 72. *Prof Exp:* Fel, Vanderbilt Univ, 72-74, instr pharmacol, 74-75; sr scientist drug metab, Schering-Plough Corp, 75-80. *Concurrent Pos:* NIH fel, 72-74; chmn, North Jersey Mass Spectrometry Discussion, 78-80. *Mem:* Am Chem Soc; Am Soc Mass Spectrometry; Am Col Clin Pharmacol; Acad Pharmacuet Sci. *Res:* Pharmacology, drug metabolism and analytical chemistry. *Mailing Add:* Harris Labs 624 Peach St Lincoln NE 68503

HEATH, EVERETT, ANATOMY, REPRODUCTIVE BIOLOGY. *Current Pos:* RETIRED. *Personal Data:* b Boston, Mass, Jan 24, 35; m 57, Carla Wilson; c Christina K, Kathryn C & BabaTunji A. *Educ:* Swarthmore Col, BA, 58; Univ Pa, VMD, 62, PhD(anat), 69; Purdue Univ, MS, 64. *Prof Exp:* Instr vet anat, Purdue Univ, 62-64; lectr, Univ Ibadan, 64-66; res fel anat, Univ Pa, 66-69; asst prof vet anat, Univ Minn, St Paul, 69-74; sr lectr & actg head, Dept Vet Anat & Physiol, Univ Ibadan, 74-78; assoc prof, Univ Ill, Urbana, 78-87, adj prof, vet biosci, 87-94. *Concurrent Pos:* Pvt vet pract, home vet care, 87- *Mem:* Am Asn Vet Anat; World Asn Vet Anat. *Res:* Reproductive biology; veterinary anatomy. *Mailing Add:* 339 Sumpter St Lynchburg VA 24503

HEATH, G ROSS, GEOCHEMISTRY, MARINE GEOLOGY. *Current Pos:* PROF OCEANOG & DEAN, COL OCEANOG & FISHERY SCI, UNIV WASH, 84- *Personal Data:* b Adelaide, SAustralia, Mar 10, 39; m 72, Lorna M Sommerville; c Amanda & Alisa. *Educ:* Univ Adelaide, BSc, 60, Hons, 61; Univ Calif, San Diego, PhD(oceanog), 68. *Honors & Awards:* Fulbright Award, 63. *Prof Exp:* Geologist, SAustralian Geol Surv, 61-63; res asst oceanog, Scripps Inst Oceanog, Univ Calif, San Diego, 65-67; res assoc, Ore State Univ, 68-69, from asst prof to assoc prof oceanog, 69-75; from assoc prof to prof, Univ RI, 75-78; prof oceanog & dean, Col Oceanog, Ore State Univ, 78-84. *Concurrent Pos:* Mem, Ocean Sci Bd, Nat Acad Sci/Nat Res Coun, 76-79, Ocean Policy Comt, 81-83, Bd Radioactive Waste Mgt, 82-90, Bd Ocean Sci & Policy, 83-85, chair, 84-85, Geophys Res Forum, 84-85; lithologist, Deep-Sea Drilling Proj Leg 7 & co-chief scientist, Leg 16, 84; Comn Marine Biol, Int Union Geol Sci, 83-; vpres, Sci Comt Oceanic Res Int Coun Sci Unions, 84-90; mem bd, Oceans & Atmosphere, Nat Asn State Univ & Land-Grant Cols, 91- *Mem:* Fel Geol Soc Am; fel Am Geophys Union; fel AAAS; Clay Minerals Soc; Oceanog Soc. *Res:* Mineralogy and geochemistry of deep-sea sediments; processes of deep-sea sedimentation, paleoceanography; sub-seabed disposal of nuclear wastes; deep-sea manganese nodules; tectonics of South Atlantic and equatorial Pacific. *Mailing Add:* Monterey Bay Aquarium Res Inst 7700 Sand Holdt Rd PO Box 728 Moss Landing CA 95039. *Fax:* 206-543-6393; *E-Mail:* rheath@u.washington.edu

HEATH, GEORGE A(UGUSTINE), TEXTILE DYEING & FINISHING, ENVIRONMENTAL REGULATIONS. *Current Pos:* PRES & CHIEF EXEC OFFICER, BOWCHEM CO, 94- *Personal Data:* b Concord, NH, June 10, 27; m 52, Therese M Brochu; c Paul W, Diane T (Madden-deceased), Michael J, Karen R (Poetzsch), Judith M (Ellers), Peter J, Mark F, David P J & Denise M (Sprankle). *Educ:* Univ NH, BS, 48. *Prof Exp:* Chemist textiles, Waumbec Dyeing & Finishing Co, NH, 49-51; res chemist dyestuffs, Geigy Dyestuffs Div, Geigy Chem Corp, NY, 51-56; lab mgr textiles, Ca-Vel Div, Collins & Aikman Corp, NC, 56-58, tech dir, 58-61, mgr dyeing & finishing, 61-63; dyeing engr fibers & platics, Enjay Div, Esso Res & Eng Co, Linden, NJ, 63-66; mgr, Dyeing Tech Dept, Vectra Corp, Odenton, MD, 66-80; mgr, Tech Serv Dept, Chevron Fibers Co, Odenton, Md, 80-82; Chem Eng, Office Toxic Substances, Environ Protection Agency, Wash, DC, 82-93; chem engr toxic substances, Environ Protection Agency, Wash, DC, 82-93, chief, chem eng br, Off Pollution Prev & Toxics, 93-94. *Mem:* Am Chem Soc; Am Asn Textile Chemists & Colorists; Tech Asn Pulp & Paper Indust. *Res:* Dyeing of experimental and commercial fibers; printing of textiles; introduction of new fibers into textile processing; environmental regulations relative to pulp, paper and paperboard. *Mailing Add:* 4 Elkwood Ct Catonsville MD 21228-2521

HEATH, GEORGE L, ENERGY CONVERSION, FORENSIC ENGINEERING. *Current Pos:* from instr to prof, 47-84, EMER PROF MECH ENG, UNIV TOLEDO, 84- *Personal Data:* b Toledo, Ohio, Feb 12, 24; m 49; c 3. *Educ:* Marquette Univ, BS, 45; Univ Mich, MS, 50. *Prof Exp:* Jr engr, Aircraft Eng Div, Packard Motorcar Co, 46-47. *Concurrent Pos:* NSF sci fac fel, 62-63. *Mem:* Am Soc Mech Engrs; Am Soc Eng Educ; Nat Soc Prof Eng; Org Spare Part Equip. *Res:* Energy conversion; instrumentation and controls. *Mailing Add:* 1644 Park Ridge Lane Toledo OH 43614

HEATH, GORDON GLENN, OPTOMETRY, PHYSIOLOGY. *Current Pos:* from asst prof to assoc prof, 55-64, dean, Sch Optom, 70-88, PROF OPTOM, IND UNIV, BLOOMINGTON, 64- *Personal Data:* b Sultan, Wash, Sept 22, 22; m 54, Dorothy Faulkner; c Raymond, Kathleen, Douglass, Debra & Lauren. *Educ:* Los Angeles Col Optom, BS, 50, OD, 51; Univ Calif, Berkeley, MS, 54, PhD, 60. *Prof Exp:* Am Optom Found fel, Univ Calif, 52-55. *Concurrent Pos:* Consult, Nat Bd Examrs Optom, 55, 57, 59 & 61 & Mo Comn Higher Educ, 69-70; assoc res physiol opticist, Univ Calif, Berkeley, 62-64, vis prof, 67-68; res consult, Surgeon Gen, US Army, 64-79; mem comt on vision, Nat Res Coun-Nat Acad Sci, 64-71; mem, Nat Adv Coun Health Professions, 67-71; Nat Adv Eye Coun, 77-80 & Policy Adv Group, Nat Surv Visual Impairment & Causes, Nat Eye Inst, 80-84; mem, Nat Adv Eye Coun, 77-80; consult dean, Univ Mo, St Louis, 78-80. *Mem:* AAAS; Am Acad Optom (pres-elect, 81-82, pres, 83-84); Optical Soc Am; Asn Schs & Cols Optom (pres, 63-65). *Res:* Physiological optics; color vision; accomodation and convergence; dark adaptation; electrophysiology of visual processes. *Mailing Add:* 1206 S Longwood Dr Bloomington IN 47401. *Fax:* 812-855-6616

HEATH, HARRISON DUANE, DEVELOPMENTAL BIOLOGY. *Current Pos:* from assoc prof to prof, 60-90, EMER PROF BIOL SCI, CALIF STATE UNIV, HAYWARD, 90- *Personal Data:* b Burlington, Wash, June 3, 23; m 56, Margaret Kirby; c Matthew & Erin. *Educ:* Stanford Univ, AB, 44, AM, 46, PhD(biol), 51. *Prof Exp:* Asst biol, Stanford Univ, 44-47 & 49-50; instr zool, Washington Univ, 51-52; Am Cancer Soc fel, Stanford Univ, 52-53; asst prof biol, Univ Fla, 53-54; asst res embryologist, Univ Calif, Los Angeles, 54-56; asst prof biol sci, Stanford Univ, 56-58; assoc prof zool, Univ Miami, 58-60. *Concurrent Pos:* Asst clin prof pediat, Sch Med, Univ Calif, Los Angeles, 55-56; fel, Washington Univ, 50-51. *Mem:* Am Soc Zool; Soc Develop Biol. *Res:* Experimental embryology; growth of transplanted amphibian organs; developmental phenomena in Hydra. *Mailing Add:* Dept Biol Sci Calif State Univ Hayward CA 94542

HEATH, IAN BRENT, CELL BIOLOGY, MYCOLOGY. *Current Pos:* from asst prof to assoc prof, 71-80, PROF BIOL, YORK UNIV, 80- *Personal Data:* b Winchester, Eng, Feb 4, 45; m 67, Michele Roy; c Lorraine. *Educ:* Univ London, BSc & ARCS, 66, PhD(anal cytol) & DIC, 69. *Honors & Awards:* Huxley Mem Medal, Imp Col, London, 79; Distinguished Mycologist Award, Mycol Soc Am, 96. *Prof Exp:* NSF fel, Univ Ga, 69-71. *Mem:* Mycol Soc Am; Soc Evolutionary Protistology (pres-elect, 81-83, pres, 83-85); Brit Soc Exp Biol; Can Soc Cell Biol (secy, 77-81, pres-elect, 81-82, pres, 82-83); Am Soc Cell Biol; hon mem Int Soc Evolutionary Protistology, 94; fel Royal Soc Can. *Res:* Cell ultrastructure; fungi; nuclear division; electron microscopy; morphogenesis; microtubules cytoskeleton meiosis. *Mailing Add:* Dept Biol York Univ North York ON M3J 1P3 Can. *Fax:* 416-736-5698; *E-Mail:* brent@yorku.ca

HEATH, JAMES EDWARD, ZOOLOGY, PHYSIOLOGY. *Current Pos:* from asst prof to prof, 64-95, head dept, 76-83, EMER PROF PHYSIOL, UNIV ILL, URBANA, 95-; VIS SCHOLAR, DEPT ZOOL, UNIV TEX, AUSTIN. *Personal Data:* b Evansville, Ind, May 3, 35; m 55; c 3. *Educ:* Univ Calif, Los Angeles, BA, 57, MA, 58, PhD(zool), 62. *Prof Exp:* Instr biol sci, Univ Calif, Santa Barbara, 61-62; NIH fel zool, Univ Calif, Los Angeles, 62-64. *Concurrent Pos:* Lectr, Calif Lutheran Col, 63-64; Am Midland Naturalist, 72-76; prof zool & chmn dept, Univ Fla, 74-75; co-ed, Physiol Zool & J Thermal Biol, 75-; vis prof biol, Univ Nac del Sur, Bahia Blanca, Arg, 82 & Univ La Plata, Arg, 82; Fulbright sr investr, Arg, 86-87. *Mem:* Am Physiol Soc; Am Soc Zool; Am Soc Ichthyol & Herpet; Ecol Soc Am; Soc Study Evolution; Sigma Xi. *Res:* Temperature regulation and energetics; circulatory physiology. *Mailing Add:* Rte 1 Box 217 Buchanan Dam TX 78609. *E-Mail:* jheath@tstar.net

HEATH, JAMES EUGENE, VETERINARY PATHOLOGY, LABORATORY ANIMAL ONCOLOGY. *Current Pos:* VET PATHOLOGIST LAB ANIMAL PATH, SOUTHERN RES INST, 81- *Personal Data:* b Duck Hill, Miss, Feb 7, 42; m 66; c 2. *Educ:* Auburn Univ, DVM, 66; Am Col Vet Pathologists, dipl. *Prof Exp:* Area Vet, Animal & Plant Health Inspection Serv, USDA, 66-67; pract vet, 67-70; vet diagnostician, Kord Animal Dis Lab, Tenn Dept Agr, 70-75; vet pathologist, Int Res & Develop Corp, 75-79; vet pathologist, Nat Ctr Toxicol Res, Food & Drug Admin & Univ Ark Med Sci, 79-81. *Concurrent Pos:* Lectr & consult lab animal path, Univ Ark Med Sci, 79-81; consult, Int Res & Develop Corp, 79-80. *Mem:* Am Vet Med Asn; Soc Toxicol Pathologists. *Res:* Safety assessment of a wide variety of drugs and chemicals via nonclinical toxicology experiments; toxicity studies of cancer chemotherapeutic agents; publications in lab animal oncology and toxicological pathology. *Mailing Add:* Southern Res Inst 2000 Ninth Ave S Birmingham AL 35255

HEATH, JAMES LEE, POULTRY SCIENCE, FOOD SCIENCE. *Current Pos:* From asst prof to assoc prof poultry prod technol, 70-80, assoc dean, Col Agr, 80-82, PROF POULTRY SCI, UNIV MD, COLLEGE PARK, 80- *Personal Data:* b Monroe, La, Dec 6, 39; m 60; c 1. *Educ:* La State Univ, BS, 63, MS, 68, PhD(prod technol), 70. *Honors & Awards:* Res Award, Poultry & Egg Inst Am. *Mem:* Poultry Sci Asn; Inst Food Technologists; Sigma Xi (secy, 76-77, pres, 77-78). *Res:* Chemistry and quality of poultry and egg products; development of new poultry products and processing techniques; physical changes in poultry and egg products. *Mailing Add:* Dept Poultry Sci Animal Sci Ctr Univ Md College Park MD 20742-0001

HEATH, JAMES R, CHEMISTRY. *Current Pos:* ASST PROF, DEPT CHEM, UNIV CALIF, LOS ANGELES. *Concurrent Pos:* Packard fel, David & Lucile Packard Found, 94. *Mailing Add:* Dept Chem Univ Calif 405 Hilgard Ave Los Angeles CA 90024-1301

HEATH, LARMAN JEFFERSON, MECHANICAL ENGINEERING. *Current Pos:* RETIRED. *Personal Data:* b Poughkeepsie, Ark, Dec 25, 16; m 41; c 3. *Educ:* Univ Okla, BSME, 40. *Prof Exp:* Draftsman, Oklahoma City Wilcox Pool Eng Asn, 40-42; engr, W Edmond Field Eng Asn, 45-47; jr petrol engr, Sohio Petrol Co, 47-48; engr, Witcher Field Eng Co, 48-49; self employed, 49-53; engr, Bur Mines, Dept Interior, US Dept Energy, 53-55, Bur Indian Affairs, 56-60 & Bur Mines, 60-65, proj leader petrol eng res, 65-77, proj leader, 77-79. *Mem:* Soc Petrol Engrs. *Res:* Permeability and fluid deliverability of oil and gas formations. *Mailing Add:* 515 SE Crestland Dr Bartlesville OK 74006

HEATH, LARRY FRANCIS, MATHEMATICAL ANALYSIS. *Current Pos:* Asst prof, 65-68, ASSOC PROF MATH, UNIV TEX, ARLINGTON, 68- *Personal Data:* b Independence, Kans, Apr 18, 38; m 64, Carolyn Paul; c Susan, Christine, Brenda & Gregory. *Educ:* Washburn Univ, BS, 60; Univ Kans, MS, 62, PhD(math), 65. *Mem:* Am Math Soc; Math Asn Am; Soc Indust & Appl Math; Sigma Xi; Asn Comput Mach. *Res:* Entire and meromorphic functions; complex analysis; computational geometry. *Mailing Add:* 1804 Park Hill Dr Arlington TX 76012-1922. *Fax:* 817-794-5802; *E-Mail:* b350lfh@utanat.uta.edu

HEATH, LENWOOD S, GRAPH ALGORITHMS, SYMBOLIC COMPUTATION. *Current Pos:* asst prof, 87-93, ASSOC PROF COMPUT SCI, VA POLYTECH INST & STATE UNIV, 93- *Personal Data:* b Greenville, NC, May 23, 53; m 84, Sheila Rodenhizer; c James F & Kaitlin C. *Educ:* Univ NC, Chapel Hill, BS, 75, PhD(comput sci), 85; Univ Chicago, MS, 76. *Prof Exp:* Software engr, Telex Terminal Commun, 77-81; instr appl math comput sci, Mass Inst Technol, 85-87. *Concurrent Pos:* Prin investr, NSF grant, 91-95. *Mem:* Asn Comput Mach; Inst Elec & Electronics Engrs Comput Soc; Inst Elec & Electronics Engrs; Soc Appl & Indust Math; Sigma Xi; Europ Asn Theoret Comput Sci. *Res:* Graph embeddings, both the traditional kind and more unusual embeddings based on, for example, stacks or queues; computational geometry; general combinatorial algorithms; computation for noncommutative algebra. *Mailing Add:* Dept Comput Sci Va Polytech Inst & State Univ Blacksburg VA 24061-0106. *E-Mail:* heath@cs.vt.edu

HEATH, MARTHA ELLEN, REGULATORY PHYSIOLOGY, THERMOREGULATORY PHYSIOLOGY. *Current Pos:* ASST RES PHYSIOLOGIST, COLUMBIA UNIV, 86- *Personal Data:* b Whittier, Calif, July 28, 52. *Educ:* Calif State Univ, BS, 73, MA, 75; Cambridge Univ, PhD(animal physiol), 79. *Prof Exp:* Fel, Columbia Univ, 79 & Yale Med Sch, 79-80; fel, Scripps Inst Oceanog, 80-83, asst res physiologist, 83-86. *Concurrent Pos:* Vis asst fel, John B Pierce Found Lab, 79-80; vis scholar, Justus-Liebig Univ, WGer, 85, Naval Med Res Inst, 86- *Mem:* Am Soc Mammalogists; Am Soc Ichthyologists & Herpetologists; AAAS; Am Physiol Soc. *Res:* Thermoregulatory mechanism of animals and man; central integrating and controlling mechanism of body temperature; autonomic nervous system. *Mailing Add:* Bio Diversity Res PO Box 22683 San Diego CA 92192-2683

HEATH, MICHELE CHRISTINE, PHYTOPATHOLOGY, ELECTRON MICROSCOPY. *Current Pos:* fel, Univ Toronto, 71-72, lectr, 72-73, from asst prof to assoc prof, 73-81, PROF BOT, UNIV TORONTO, 81- *Personal Data:* b Bournemouth, Eng, Sept 22, 45; m 67, I Brent; c Lorraine. *Educ:* Univ London, BS, 66, PhD(plant path) & DIC, 69. *Honors & Awards:* Huxley Mem Medal, 79; Gordon Green Award, 84. *Prof Exp:* Fel plant path, Univ Ga, 69-71. *Concurrent Pos:* Sr ed, J Physiol Molecular Plant Path, 82-89, Am Phytopath Soc Press, 88-91; Steacie Mem fel, 82. *Mem:* Am Soc Plant

Physiologists; fel Am Phytopath Soc; fel Can Phytopath Soc (pres, 95-96); Am Mycol Soc; fel, Royal Soc Can. *Res:* Cell biology of plant-parasite interactions; evolution and basis of plant-parasite specificity. *Mailing Add:* Dept Bot Univ Toronto Toronto ON M5S 1A1 Can. *Fax:* 416-978-5878; *E-Mail:* heath@botany.utoronto.ca

HEATH, MILAN JOHN, MEDICAL DEVICE RESEARCH & DEVELOPMENT. *Current Pos:* biomed engr, 84-90, DIR ENG & DEVELOP, ZINETICS MED, 90- *Personal Data:* b Walla Walla, Wash, Aug 26, 38; m 70, Joleen Klocke; c Joseph. *Educ:* Gonzaga Univ, BS, 60; Univ Wash, PhD(physical & biophys), 74. *Prof Exp:* Postdoctoral fel, Univ Calif, Los Angeles, 74-80; res assoc, Univ Utah, 80-86. *Res:* Ph and pressure-sensing catheters for gastroenterological applications. *Mailing Add:* 1384 E Michigan Ave Salt Lake City UT 84105

HEATH, RALPH CARR, GEOLOGY. *Current Pos:* CONSULT HYDROGEOLOGIST, 87- *Personal Data:* b La Grange, NC, July 10, 25; m 47, Martha Sandidge; c William C & Susan A. *Educ:* Univ NC, BS, 48. *Honors & Awards:* Meritorious Serv Award, US Dept Interior, 81; Commendation, Nat Water Well Asn, 82, Distinguished lectr Ground-Water Hydrol, 86; Distinguished Serv In Hydrogeol Award, Geol Soc Am, 86; Spec Award, Asn Ground-Water Scientists & Engrs, 88, Henry Darcy Distinguished lectr, 90; Founders Award, Am Inst Hydrol, 91. *Prof Exp:* Ground water geologist, US Geol Surv, Fla, 48-53, actg dist geologist, 53-55, geologist in charge, NY, 55-60, dist geologist, NY, Conn & RI, 60-65, dist chief, NY, 65-67, dist chief, NC, 67-81, staff hydrol, US Geol Surv, NC, 81-82. *Concurrent Pos:* Adj assoc prof geol, Rensselaer Polytech Inst, 64-67; chmn, Bd Regist, Am Inst Hydrol, 83-84, mem, 84-; adj prof civil eng, NC State Univ, 83-; lectr, Univ NC, 84, Duke Univ, 85- *Mem:* Fel Geol Soc Am; Nat Groundwater Asn; Am Inst Hydrol. *Res:* Selection and evaluation of waste-disposal sites, effect of land use on ground water, regional appraisals of ground-water resources, hydrology of barrier islands, evaluation and design of ground-water-level observation programs. *Mailing Add:* 4821 Kilkenny Pl Raleigh NC 27612

HEATH, ROBERT BRUCE, VETERINARY ANESTHESIOLOGY. *Current Pos:* RETIRED. *Personal Data:* b Billings, Mont, Oct 8, 36; m 62; c 4. *Educ:* Iowa State Univ, DVM, 62; Ohio State Univ, MSc, 67; Col Vet Anesthesia, Dipl, 72. *Prof Exp:* Instr vet surg, Ohio State Univ, 64-68; assoc prof vet anesthesia, Colo State Univ, 68-77, prof clin sci, 77-92; res consult, wildlife anesthesiol, State Alaska, 92- *Concurrent Pos:* Ed, Vet Anesthesiol, 74- *Mem:* Am Soc Vet Anesthesia (vpres, 73-74, pres, 76-77); Am Soc Vet Clinicians (pres, 75-77); Am Vet Med Asn. *Res:* The effects of anesthetic drugs in the domestic species of animals, especially inhalation vapors in the horse and intramuscular agents in the cat; epidurals in animals; comparative endotracheal intubation. *Mailing Add:* 4920 Crest Rd Ft Collins CO 80526

HEATH, ROBERT GALBRAITH, PSYCHIATRY, NEUROLOGY. *Current Pos:* chmn dept & chief psychiat & neurol serv, Tulane Univ, 49-80, prof psychiat & neurol, Sch Med, 49-85, Robert G Heath, MD prof psychiat & neurol, 85, EMER PROF PSYCHIAT & NEUROL, TULANE UNIV, 85- *Personal Data:* b Pittsburgh, Pa, May 9, 15; m 40; c 5. *Educ:* Univ Pittsburgh, BS, 37, MD, 38; Am Bd Psychiat & Neurol, dipl, 46; Columbia Univ, cert psychoanalysis & DMSc, 49. *Hon Degrees:* DSc, Tulane Univ, 85. *Honors & Awards:* Gold Medal Award, Soc Biol Psychiat, 72; Frieda Fromm-Reichmann Award, Am Acad Psychoanal, 74. *Prof Exp:* Intern, Mercy Hosp, Pittsburgh, 38-39; instr med, Univ Pittsburgh, 39-40; asst resident neurol, Neurol Inst, NY, 40-41, chief resident, 41-42; demonstr, Jefferson Med Col, 42-43; inst neurol, Col Physicians & Surgeons, Columbia Univ, 46-49. *Concurrent Pos:* Sr vis physician, Charity Hosp La, New Orleans, 49-; sr consult, Southeast La Hosp & E La State Hosp. *Mem:* Fel AAAS; fel Am Col Physicians; fel Am Psychiat Asn; fel Am Acad Neurol; Soc Biol Psychiat (sr vpres, 66-68, pres, 68-69). *Res:* Schizophrenia; biochemical physiologic aberrations; author or coauthor of over 425 scientific publications. *Mailing Add:* Dept Psychiat & Neurol Tulane Univ Sch Med 1430 Tulane Ave New Orleans LA 70112

HEATH, ROBERT GARDNER, SURVEY-EXPERIMENTAL DESIGN & ANALYTICAL METHOD EVALUATION, QUALITY ASSURANCE & CONTROL. *Current Pos:* BIOMET CONSULT, 86- *Personal Data:* b Detroit, Mich, June 15, 24; m 48, Elsye Nygard; c Barbara H (Coker) & Deborah H (Koonce). *Educ:* Univ Mich, BS, 51; Mich State Univ, MS, 61. *Honors & Awards:* Bronze Medal, US Environ Protection Agency; Cash Awards. *Prof Exp:* Wildlife res biologist, Mich DNR, 52-60, asst biometrician, 60-61; chief mail surv, Patuxent Wildlife Res Ctr, US Dept Interior, 61-63, ctr biometrician & chief, Toxicol Sect, 63-74; chief, Ecol Monitoring Br, Off Pesticide Progs, US Environ Protection Agency, 74-77, sr biometrician, Health Effects Br, 77-83, Design & Develop Br, Off Toxic Substances, 83-86. *Mem:* Biomet Soc. *Res:* National study of underground motor fuel tanks for leakage; human pesticide exposure and associated health effects; method validation and quality assurance for analytical methods; statistical design and analysis in environmental monitoring; avian toxicology. *Mailing Add:* 13318 Gable Village Dr San Antonio TX 78231

HEATH, ROBERT LOUIS, BIOPHYSICS, PLANT PHYSIOLOGY. *Current Pos:* lectr, Univ Calif, Riverside, 69-70, asst prof, 70-73, asst biologist, 69-73, assoc biologist, 73-79, ASSOC PROF PHOTOSYNTHESIS, UNIV CALIF, RIVERSIDE, 73-, PROF PLANT PHYSIOL, 79-, PLANT PHYSIOLOGIST & BIOPHYSICIST, 79-, ASSOC DEAN, COL NAT & AGR SCI, 79- *Personal Data:* b Hermosa Beach, Calif, Feb 27, 40; m 66; c 3. *Educ:* Calif Inst Technol, BSc, 61; Univ Mich, Ann Arbor, MSc, 63; Univ Calif, Berkeley, PhD(biophys), 67. *Prof Exp:* Asst physicist, Bell & Howell Res Ctr, Calif, 61-62; res assoc photosynthesis, Brookhaven Nat Lab, 67-69. *Mem:* Biophys Soc; Am Bot Soc; Am Soc Plant Physiol. *Res:* Membrane alterations by oxidants (air and water pollutants and radiation products) resulting in disruption of cellular ionic and metabolic homostasis; ionic control of photosynthesis. *Mailing Add:* Dept Bot & Plant Sci Univ Calif Riverside CA 92521-0124

HEATH, ROBERT THORNTON, AQUATIC MICROBIAL ECOLOGY. *Current Pos:* from asst prof to assoc prof, 70-86, PROF BIOL SCI, KENT STATE UNIV, 87-; DIR, WATER RESOURCES RES INST, 93- *Personal Data:* b Chicago, Ill, Mar 12, 42; m 80, Elizabeth Buchanan; c David E & Tara L (Edward). *Educ:* Univ Mich, Ann Arbor, BS, 63; Univ Southern Calif, PhD(biophys), 68. *Prof Exp:* NIH fel, Calif Inst Technol, 68-70. *Concurrent Pos:* Vis asst prof, Inst Ecol, Univ Ga, 75-76; vis scientist, Great Lakes Environ Res Lab, Nat Oceanic & Atmospheric Admin, Ann Arbor, 92-93. *Mem:* AAAS; Am Physiol Soc; Ecol Soc Am; Am Soc Limnol & Oceanog; Am Soc Microbiol; Coop Inst Limnol & Ecosyst Res. *Res:* General system theory applied to ecosystem biology; computer simulation of model systems; holistic investigation of laboratory ecosystems; Great Lakes coastal wetlands; phosphorus dynamics in freshwater ecosystems; microbiol ecology; carbon dynamics in freshwater plankton. *Mailing Add:* Dept Biol Sci Kent State Univ Kent OH 44242. *Fax:* 330-672-3713; *E-Mail:* rheath@phoenix.kent.edu

HEATH, ROBERT WINSHIP, MATHEMATICS. *Current Pos:* NSF res grant, 71-72, PROF MATH, UNIV PITTSBURGH, 70- *Personal Data:* b Durham, NC, May 14, 33; m 55; c 2. *Educ:* Univ NC, BS, 53, PhD(math), 59. *Prof Exp:* Asst math, Univ NC, 54 & 56-58; instr, Woman's Col NC, 58-60; from asst prof to assoc prof, Univ Ga, 60-65, NSF res grant, 64; prof, Ariz State Univ, 65-70, NSF res grant, 66-69. *Concurrent Pos:* Vis assoc prof, Ariz State Univ, 64-65; vis lectr, Univ Wash, 67-69; Bucknell Univ, 71, State Univ NY, 72, Univ NC, Greensboro, 75; vis scholar, Oxford Univ, 86-87. *Mem:* Am Math Soc; Math Asn Am; Math Soc Belg; London Math Soc; Norweg Math Soc. *Res:* General topology; abstract spaces, especially metrization and generalizations of metric spaces; product topologies; ordered topological spaces; continuous selections and set-valued functions; topological groups homogeneous spaces. *Mailing Add:* Dept Math Thackeray Hall 308 Univ Pittsburgh Pittsburgh PA 15260

HEATH, ROY ELMER, INORGANIC CHEMISTRY. *Current Pos:* DEAN, SCH GRAD STUDIES & DIR RES & DEVELOP, NORTHERN MICH UNIV, 75-, PROF CHEM, 80- *Personal Data:* b Hastings, Mich, Feb 6, 15; m 39; c 2. *Educ:* Albion Col, AB, 36; Western Res Univ, PhD(inorg chem), 40. *Prof Exp:* Lectr chem, Western Res Univ, 39-40; instr, Univ Wis, 40-42; mgr mkt res, Mich Alkali Co, Mich, 42-43; res supvr, Manhattan Proj, Univ Chicago, 43-44; mgr mkt res, Wyandotte Chem Corp, 44-45, mgr, Indust, Railroad & Aircraft Div, 45-52; from assoc prof to prof chem, Mich Col Mining & Technol, 53-60; prof, Northern Mich Univ, 60-66, res coordr, 60-66, head dept, 65-66, dir res & develop, 65-66; dir res & develop, Bd Regents, Wis State Univ Syst, 66-74 & Univ Wis, Oshkosh, 74-75. *Mem:* Am Chem Soc. *Res:* Chemistry of less familiar element fluorides. *Mailing Add:* 9726 W Stagecoach Ct Sun City AZ 85373-1127

HEATH, RUSSELL LA VERNE, NUCLEAR PHYSICS, GAMMA-RAY SPECTROSCOPY. *Current Pos:* mem staff, 76-80, mgr, Physics Div, 80-84, SR SCI FEL, PHYSICS DIV, IDAHO NAT ENG LAB, 84- *Personal Data:* b Denver, Colo, June 13, 26; m 49, Edna Neel; c Deborah & Robert. *Educ:* Colo State Univ, BS, 49; Vanderbilt Univ, MS, 56. *Hon Degrees:* DSc, Colo State Univ, 84. *Honors & Awards:* Radiation Indust Award, 82. *Prof Exp:* Asst physics, Rutgers Univ, 49-50; sr health physicist, Am Cyanamid Co, 51-53, physicist, 53-60, chief, Physics Sect, Reactor Phys Br, 60-66, mgr, Nuclear Physics Br, 66-76. *Concurrent Pos:* Mem bd ed, Nuclear Instr & Methods, 70-84; mem, Comt Nuclear Sci, Nat Acad Sci, 72- & US Nuclear Data Comt, 75-80; mem, US Nuclear Data Comt, 75-80; mgr, Physics Div, EG&G, 76-84, lab sci fel, 84- *Mem:* Fel Am Phys Soc; fel Am Nuclear Soc; Inst Elec & Electronics Engrs. *Res:* Nuclear structure physics; gamma-ray spectrometry; development of electronic instrumentation for nuclear research; nuclear level schemes; solid state detectors; development of field-effect low-noise preamplifiers for nuclear spectroscopy; application of on-line computer systems to experimental nuclear physics; nuclear decay data compilation; nuclear safeguards research; development of measurement systems for nuclear medicine and space science. *Mailing Add:* Idaho Nat Eng Lab PO Box 1625 Idaho Falls ID 83403-1625. *Fax:* 208-526-2814; *E-Mail:* rlh2@ihel.gov

HEATH, TIMOTHY DOUGLAS, CELL BIOLOGY, DRUG DELIVERY. *Current Pos:* asst prof, 85-90, ASSOC PROF PHARMACEUT, SCH PHARM, UNIV WIS-MADISON, 90- *Personal Data:* b 52; UK citizen. *Educ:* Univ London, UK, BSc, 73, PhD(biochem), 76. *Prof Exp:* Asst res biochemist, Cancer Res Inst, Univ Calif, San Francisco, 81-85. *Mem:* Asn Res Vision & Ophthal. *Res:* Liposome research; drug targeting. *Mailing Add:* 6031 Old Middleton Rd Madison WI 53705

HEATHCOCK, CLAYTON HOWELL, SYNTHETIC ORGANIC CHEMISTRY. *Current Pos:* from asst prof to assoc prof, 64-75, Miller res prof, 82, 91, PROF ORG CHEM, UNIV CALIF, BERKELEY, 75- *Personal Data:* b San Antonio, Tex, July 21, 36; m 57, 80; c 4. *Educ:* Abilene Christian Col, BSc, 58; Univ Colo, PhD(chem), 63. *Honors & Awards:* Alexander von Humboldt US Sr Scientist Award, 78; Ernest Guenther Award, Am Chem Soc, 86; Creative Work in Org Synthesis Award, Am Chem Soc, 90; A C Cope Scholar, Am Chem Soc, 90. *Prof Exp:* Supvr chem tests, Champion Paper & Fibre Co, 58-60; NSF fel, Columbia Univ, 63-64. *Concurrent Pos:* Sloan Found fel, 67-69; chmn, Med Chem Study Sect, NIH, 82-84 & Div Org Chem, Am Chem Soc, 85; ed-in-chief, Org Synthesis, 85-86, J Org Chem, 88-

Mem: Nat Acad Sci; Royal Soc Chem; fel AAAS; Am Chem Soc. Res: Chemistry of natural products; total synthesis of steroids, terpenes, alkaloids and polyketides; development of new synthetic methodology; stereochemistry. Mailing Add: Dept Chem Univ Calif Berkeley CA 94720

HEATHER, JAMES BRIAN, SYNTHETIC ORGANIC CHEMISTRY. Current Pos: MGR RES INFO SYSTS, ZENECA AGR PRODS, 89- Personal Data: b Glendale, Calif, July 24, 44. Educ: Univ Calif, Los Angeles, BS, 67; Univ Wis-Madison, PhD(org chem), 72. Prof Exp: Res assoc natural prod synthesis, Sch Pharm, Univ Wis-Madison, 72-74; res scientist chem process res & develop, Upjohn Co, 74-79; gen mgr, USANCO, 79-80; sr res chemist, Process Res, Stauffer Chem Co, 80-89. Res: New synthetic methods and reagents; chemical process design. Mailing Add: Zeneca Agr Prods 1200 S 47th St Richmond CA 94804-0023

HEATHERLY, HENRY EDWARD, MATHEMATICS. Current Pos: from asst prof to assoc prof, 68-76, DISTINGUISHED PROF MATH, UNIV SOUTHWESTERN LA, 76- Personal Data: b Galveston, Tex, Dec 22, 36; m 56, May Huggins. Educ: Tex A&M Univ, BA, 60, MS, 62, PhD(math), 68. Honors & Awards: Arco Res Award, 93. Prof Exp: Instr math, Tex A&M Univ, 63-68. Concurrent Pos: Consult, Indian Inst Technol, India, 73-74; vis assoc prof, Texas A&M Univ, 76; distinguished prof, Univ Southwestern La, 76; NASA res fel, 80; consult, Madurai Univ, 81, Bar Ilan Univ, 82. Mem: Am Math Soc; Sigma Xi; London Math Soc. Res: Near-rings; ring theory; operational calculus; applications to difference equations; general algebraic systems; applications of integral and discrete transforms. Mailing Add: 529 Alonda Dr Lafayette LA 70503

HEATHERLY, LARRY G, WATER RELATIONS PLANT RESEARCH, CROPPING SYSTEMS RESEARCH. Current Pos: RES AGRONOMIST, AGR RES SERV, USDA, 75- Personal Data: b Union City, Tenn, Sept 17, 46; m, Elizabeth L Jackson; c Lorry, Kelly & Eric. Educ: Univ Tenn, BS, 68, MS, 72; Univ Mo, PhD(agron), 75. Honors & Awards: Team Res Award, Am Soybean Asn, 91. Concurrent Pos: Assoc ed, Crop Sci, Crop Sci Soc Am, 84-85, tech ed, 86-88. Mem: Fel Am Soc Agron; fel Crop Sci Soc Am; Soil Sci Soc Am; Sigma Xi. Res: Conservation tillage; crop water relations; cropping systems irrigation management for crops and economics of weed control; irrigation; tillage inputs for agricultural crops. Mailing Add: 513 W Second St Leland MS 38756-0343

HEATON, CHARLES DANIEL, ORGANIC CHEMISTRY. Current Pos: assoc prof, 64-74, PROF CHEM, NORTHERN ARIZ UNIV, 74- Personal Data: b Detroit, Mich, Feb 5, 21; m 48; c 3. Educ: Univ Calif, Los Angeles, BA, 41; Stanford Univ, PhD(chem), 50. Prof Exp: Asst chem, Stanford Univ, 42-47; instr, Univ Wyo, 48-51; res chemist, Calif Res Corp Div, Stand Oil Co Calif, 51-60; assoc prof chem, Cent Mo State Col, 60-64. Mem: Am Chem Soc; Sigma Xi. Res: Natural pigments; stereoisomerism. Mailing Add: Northern Ariz Univ PO Box 5698 Flagstaff AZ 86011-0001

HEATON, H THOMPSON, II, DOSIMETRY, RADIATION MEASUREMENT. Current Pos: CHIEF, RADIATION METROL BR, DIV ELECTRONICS & COMP SCI, FOOD & DRUG ADMIN, 90- Personal Data: b Bridgeport, Conn, Mar 30, 38. Educ: Colgate Univ, BA, 60; Univ Md, MS, 64. Prof Exp: Nuclear physicist, Neutron Physics Sect, Nat Inst Stand & Technol, 64-74, Integral Neutron Physics Sect, 74-74, Off Radiation Measurement, 75-90. Concurrent Pos: Mem, Am Nat Stand Inst, Irradiator Safety Subcomt, 78-90, mem, Equip Non Med Radiation Appln, 84-, sub comt electron microscopes, 84-86, secy, 84-86; tech expert, Conf Radiation Cont Prog Dirs, State Lab Accreditation Prog, 82-90, Radiation Measurements Comt, 83-90, High Energy Accelerators, Fed Resource Person, 76-; Fed Drug Admin rep, Coun Ionizing Radiation Measurements & Stand, 90-, mem, Sci & Technol Comt, 91-, chair, Med Sub Comt, 92-; US rep, Int Electrotech Comn, 91- Mem: Am Phys Soc; Am Assoc Physicists Med. Res: Author of over 50 publications; calibrating mammography instruments, calibration protocols, calibration laboratory program management, calibrating x-ray diagnostic instruments; radiation dosimetry (x-ray, gamma ray, betta, neutron), radiation metrology, research in ionizing radiation measurements; setting up secondary level calibration laboratories; quality assurance/quality control technology; uncertainty analysis procedures; neutron cross section measurements (differential & integral); computer applications for data gathering/analysis; use of industrial controllers for automating calibration equipment. Mailing Add: HFZ 143 12720 Twinbrook Pkwy Rockville MD 20852. Fax: 301-443-9101

HEATON, HOWARD S(PRING), MECHANICAL ENGINEERING. Current Pos: from asst prof to assoc prof, 63-77, PROF MECH ENG, BRIGHAM YOUNG UNIV, 77- Personal Data: b Kaysville, Utah, May 24, 35; m 57; c 5. Educ: Univ Southern Calif, BE, 57; Stanford Univ, MS, 59, PhD(heat transfer), 63. Prof Exp: Sr thermodynamicist, Lockheed Missiles & Space Co, 57-59; sr develop engr, Hercules Powder Co, 62-63. Mem: Am Soc Mech Engrs; Soc Automotive Engr; Sigma Xi. Res: Heat transfer and fluid mechanics. Mailing Add: 766 E 3750 N Provo UT 84604-4763

HEATON, LEROY, PHYSICS. Current Pos: RETIRED. Personal Data: b Holden, Mo, June 25, 24; m 50, Mary M Moon; c Lee A, Mary J, Nancy B & Julia M. Educ: William Jewell Col, AB, 48; Univ Okla, MS, 50; Univ Mo, PhD(physics), 54. Prof Exp: Asst physics, Univ Okla, 48-50; instr, Univ Mo, 50-52; from asst physicist to assoc physicist, Argonne Nat Lab, 54-70; coordr physics & astron, Parkland Col, 70-89. Concurrent Pos: Vis scientist, Ames Lab, Iowa State Univ, 68-69; adj prof, S F Austin State Univ, 78-79. Mem: AAAS; Am Phys Soc; Sigma Xi; Am Crystallog Asn; Am Asn Physics Teachers. Res: Solid state physics; x-ray and neutron diffraction; structure of solids and liquids; magnetic structures. Mailing Add: 2202 Glen Oak Dr 61821 Champaign IL 61820

HEATON, MARIA MALACHOWSKI, QUANTUM CHEMISTRY. Current Pos: asst prof, 72-77, ASSOC PROF CHEM, NMEX STATE UNIV, 77- Personal Data: b Shreveport, La, Nov 1, 32; m 57; c 2. Educ: Chestnut Hill Col, BS, 53; Univ Vt, PhD(chem), 69. Prof Exp: Res chemist, Eastern Lab, E I du Pont de Nemours & Co, Inc, 53-58; res assoc appl math, Queen's Univ Belfast, 69-70; res assoc chem, Johns Hopkins Univ, 70-72. Mem: Am Chem Soc; Am Phys Soc. Res: Atomic and molecular structure via self-consistant-field and configuration-interaction methods; atomic and molecular properties calculations; classical and variational approaches to scattering theory. Mailing Add: Chem NMex State Univ PO Box 30001 Las Cruces NM 88003-8801

HEATON, MARIETA BARROW, NEUROEMBRYOLOGY. Current Pos: from assoc prof, 75-88, PROF NEUROSCI, COL MED, UNIV FLA, 88- Personal Data: b Hazard, Ky. Educ: Fla State Univ, BS, 66; NC State Univ, PhD(psychol), 71. Prof Exp: Fel neuroembryol, Res Div, NC Dept Ment Health, 70-72, res assoc, 72-75. Mem: AAAS; Soc Neurosci. Res: Trophic & tropic factors critical in the development of the nervous systems; mechanisms of nervous system development; fetal alcohol syndrome. Mailing Add: Dept Neurosci Col Med Univ Fla Box 100244 Gainesville FL 32610-0244. Fax: 352-392-8347

HEATON, RICHARD CLAWSON, ANALYTICAL CHEMISTRY. Current Pos: mem staff chem, Los Alamos Sci Lab, 73, MEM STAFF, LOS ALAMOS NAT LAB, UNIV CALIF, 79- Personal Data: b Danville, Ill, July 18, 46; m 70; c 3. Educ: Univ Mich, Ann Arbor, BS, 68; Univ Ill, Urbana, MS, 71, PhD(chem), 73. Prof Exp: Res chemist, Hercules Inc, 73-79. Mem: AAAS. Res: Applied chemical research; actinide chemistry; process analytical chemistry. Mailing Add: 223 Rover Blvd Los Alamos NM 87544-3561

HEATON, WILLIAM ANDREW LAMBERT, HAEMATOLOGY. Current Pos: CLIN PROF LAB MED, UNIV CALIF, SAN FRANCISCO, 93- Personal Data: b London, Eng, Nov 30, 47; m 71, Isobel Priestley; c Edward & Olivia. Educ: Dublin Univ, BA, 69, MB, 71, MA, 72; Univ Cape Town, MMed, 76, Col Med SAfrica, FF(path), 76; Am Bd Path, dipl & cert clin path, 81, blood banking, 83; Royal Col Path, 91. Prof Exp: Intern med surg, Sir Patrick Duns Hosp, Dublin, 71-72; casualty officer accidents, Lancaster Royal Infirmary, 72; registr path, Groote Schuur Hosp, Univ Cape Town Med Sch, 72-76; dir haematol, Red Cross Hosp, 76-77; fel blood bank, Washington Univ Med Sch, 77-78; assoc dir, Blood Bank, Barnes Hosp, 78-79; dir, Mid Atlantic Region Am Red Cross Blood Serv, 79-92, sr prin officer, Area II, 92-93. Concurrent Pos: Med officer haematopathologist, Red Cross War Mem Childrens Hosp, 76-77; fel, Mo-Ill Regional Red Cross Blood Serv, 77-78, asst prof internal med & path, 78-79; from asst prof to assoc prof path, Eastern Va Med Sch, 79-93; pres, Irwin Mem Blood Ctrs, 93- Mem: Am Asn Blood Banks; Am Soc Haematol; Am Asn Clin Path; Int Soc Hemat; Int Soc Blood Bank; Amcol Physician Execs. Res: Platelet kinetics and platelet immunology; red blood cell preservation and hereditary defects in red blood cell metabolism; techniques of radio isotopic blood kinetic measurements; prolonged platelet storage and platelet storage solutions. Mailing Add: 2411 Green St San Francisco CA 94123. Fax: 415-921-6184

HEATWOLE, HAROLD FRANKLIN, HERPETOLOGY, BIOGEOGRAPHY. Current Pos: dept head, 91-96, PROF, DEPT ZOOL, NC STATE UNIV, 91- Personal Data: b Waynesboro, Va, Dec 2, 34; m 55, Audry Yoder; c Eric K & Miguel A. Educ: Goshen Col, BA, 55; Univ Mich, MS, 58, PhD(zool), 60; Univ NEng, DSc, 81; Univ Queensland, Australia, PhD(bot), 87. Prof Exp: Instr zool, Univ Mich, 59-60; from asst prof to assoc prof vert zool, Univ PR, 60-66; sr lectr comp physiol, Univ NEng, Australia, 66-71, assoc prof, 71-91. Concurrent Pos: Ed, Australian J Ecol, 85-87 & Amphibian Biol, 92- Mem: Am Soc Ichthyologists & Herpetologists; fel Explorers Club; Ecol Soc Am; Asn Trop Biol; Australian Coral Reef Soc (pres, 82-83); Ecol Soc Australia; Australian Soc Herpetologists (pres, 77-78). Res: Ecology and physiology of reptiles and amphibians; ecology of ants; community ecology of islands; deserts and the Antarctic; predator-prey relationships, especially between venomous snakes and their prey. Mailing Add: Dept Zool NC State Univ Raleigh NC 27695-7617. Fax: 919-515-5327

HEAVNER, JAMES E, NEUROPHARMACOLOGY, ANESTHESIA RESEARCH. Current Pos: assoc prof, 83-87, PROF ANESTHESIOL & PHYS & DIR ANESTHESIOL RES, TEX TECH UNIV HEALTH SCI CTR, 87- Personal Data: b Cumberland, Md, Apr 25, 44; m 67, Betsey Clark; c Benjamin D, Kori R & Matthew J. Educ: Univ Ga, DVM, 68; Univ Wash, PhD(pharmacol), 71. Honors & Awards: Hildegard Doerenkamp/Gerhard Zbinden Stiftung Spec Award, Mgt Chronic Pain In Lab Animals, 88. Prof Exp: From asst prof to assoc prof anesthesiol, Med Sch, Univ Wash, 71-80; vis scientist neurophysiol, Dept Physiol, Univ Edinburgh, 78; br chief pharmacol & toxicol, Div Vet Med Res, Bur Vet Med, Food & Drug Admin, 80-82. Concurrent Pos: NIH special fel, 71-74; reviewer, Am J Vet Res, Sci, J Pharm Exp Therapeuts, Anesthesiol & J Am Vet Med Asn, 72-; prin investr grants, NIH, 73-80; assoc ed, Vet Anesthesia, 74-78; consult, Green Lake Animal Hosp, Seattle, 74-80; vis prof, Sch Med, Univ Calif, Irvine & Mich State Univ, 76; relief vet, Univ Wash, 76-77; vis prof vet med, Dept Physics & Biophys, Colo State Univ, 79; adj prof pharm, Va-Md Regional Col Vet Med, 80-82; Am-Scandinavian Found fel studies, Finland, 86; Fulbright sr fel studies, Finland, 86. Mem: Am Soc Pharmacol & Exp Therapeuts; Int Asn Study Pain; Soc Neurosci; Am Col Vet Anesthesia; AAAS. Res: Applied research in toxicology and pharmacology; development of new methodology for the evaluation of chemicals, drugs, and other toxins; human and veterinarian anesthesiology. Mailing Add: Dept Anesthesiol Tex Tech Univ Health Sci Ctr 3601 4th St Lubbock TX 79430. E-Mail: anejeh@ttuhsc.edu

HEBARD, ARTHUR FOSTER, LOW TEMPERATURE PHYSICS. *Current Pos:* MEM TECH STAFF PHYSICS, BELL TEL LABS, 72- *Personal Data:* b New York, NY, Mar 2, 40; m 68, Caroline Gale; c Joanne, Andrew, Alastair & Heather. *Educ:* Yale Univ, BA, 62; Stanford Univ, MS, 64, PhD(physics), 70. *Prof Exp:* Res assoc physics, High Energy Physics Lab, Stanford Univ, 70-72. *Mem:* Fel Am Phys Soc; Am Inst Physics; AAAS; Sigma Xi. *Res:* Low temperature properties of thin films; fullerenes and doped fullerenes; Josephson effect; phase transitions in superconducting films; disordered superconductors; reactive ion beam sputter deposited thin films; high Tc superconductors; thin-film dielectrics. *Mailing Add:* Dept Physics Univ Fla Box 118440 Gainesville FL 32611-8440. *E-Mail:* afh@clockwise.att.com

HEBB, MAURICE F, JR, ELECTRICAL ENGINEERING. *Current Pos:* Engr, Fla Power Corp, 51-61, chief syst planning engr, 61-64, chief engr elec eng, 64-67, vpres eng, 67-71, VPRES SYST RES & DEVELOP DEPT, FLA POWER CORP, 71- *Personal Data:* b Tampa, Fla, Oct 19, 24; c 4. *Educ:* Univ Fla, BEE, 51. *Concurrent Pos:* Mem, Syst & Equip Comt, Edison Elec Inst, 62-65 & Coord Area Planning Comt, 65-69; Tech Adv Comt, Nat Elec Reliability Coun, 69-; Chmn, Tech Adv Comt, Southeastern Elec Reliability Coun, 69. *Mem:* Inst Elec & Electronics Engrs. *Res:* Electrical power system coordination with reference to reliability; management activities of utility system engineering; power option. *Mailing Add:* 6330 Bahama Shores Dr S St Petersburg FL 33705

HEBBARD, FREDERICK WORTHMAN, OPTOMETRY, PHYSIOLOGICAL OPTICS. *Current Pos:* from asst prof to prof, Ohio State Univ, 57-90, assoc dir, Sch Optom, 62-66, dir, 66-68, dean, Col Optom, 68-88, EMER PROF PHYSIOL OPTICS & OPTOM, OHIO STATE UNIV, 90- *Personal Data:* b Eureka, Utah, Aug 6, 23. *Educ:* Univ Calif, Berkeley, BS, 49, MS, 51, PhD(physiol optics), 57. *Honors & Awards:* Sigma Xi. *Prof Exp:* Asst optom, Univ Calif, Berkeley, 49, clin instr, 50-56. *Concurrent Pos:* Dir, Nat Bd Examr Optom, 64-74, vpres, 70-72, pres, 72-74; consult, USPHS, 66-70; mem, Armed Forces Vision Comt, Nat Res Coun, 67- *Mem:* Fel Am Acad Optom; Optical Soc Am; Am Optom Asn; Asn Schs & Cols Optom (vpres, 61-63, secy-treas, 75-79). *Res:* Binocular vision; accommodation and convergence; eye movements; clinical optometry; physiological optics; illumination; vision in aeronautics and space science. *Mailing Add:* 2100 Haverford Rd Columbus OH 43220

HEBBEL, ROBERT P, MEDICINE. *Current Pos:* From asst prof to assoc prof, 79-88, PROF MED, UNIV MINN, 88- *Mailing Add:* Univ Minn PO Box 480 420 Delaware St Minneapolis MN 55455-0374

HEBBEN, NANCY, NEUROPSYCHOLOGY, PAIN. *Current Pos:* NEUROPHYSIOLOGIST, MCLEAN HOSP, BELMONT, MASS, 82- *Personal Data:* b Detroit, Mich. *Educ:* Wayne State Univ, BA, 75, MA, 77, PhD(clin psychol), 79. *Prof Exp:* Intern neuropsychol, Boston Vet Admin Med Ctr, 78-79; res fel & res affil, Clin Res Ctr, Mass Inst Technol, 79-82. *Concurrent Pos:* Consult psychol, Mass Gen Hosp, 78-79, neuropsychol, Vet Admin Med Ctr, West Roxbury, 79-80; NIH nat res serv award, 79-82; consult, Peter Bent Brigham Hosp, Boston, Mass, 80-82; lectr, Brandeis Univ, 81; instr, Harvard Univ, 85. *Mem:* Sigma Xi; Am Psychol Asn; Int Neuropsychol Soc. *Res:* Effect of psychiatric surgery on the perception and report of pain and on the perception and expression of emotion; neuropsychological pattern associated with DSM-III psychiatric disorders. *Mailing Add:* Dept Neuropsychol McLean Hosp 115 Mill St Belmont MA 02178

HEBBORN, PETER, BIOCHEMICAL PHARMACOLOGY. *Current Pos:* vpres res & develop, 78-87, CONSULT, OWEN LABS, FT WORTH, 87-; ASSOC DIR, CIRD, VALBONNE, FRANCE, 87- *Personal Data:* b Leigh, Eng, Mar 6, 32; m 54; c 3. *Educ:* Univ London, BSc, 52, PhD(cancer chemother), 55. *Prof Exp:* Sr pharmacologist, Res Dept, Boots Pure Drug Co, 58-62; from asst prof to prof biochem pharmacol, Sch Pharm, State Univ NY, Buffalo, 62-78. *Concurrent Pos:* Vpres res & develop, Westwood Pharmaceut, Buffalo, 71-78. *Mem:* Am Cancer Soc; Am Soc Pharmacol & Exp Therapeut; Soc Invest Dermat; Am Acad Dermat; Skin Pharmacol Soc. *Res:* Cancer chemotherapy; hormone antagonists; cutaneous pharmacology. *Mailing Add:* CIRD GALDERMA Sophia Antipolis 06565 Valbonne France. *Fax:* 33-93-95-70-71

HEBDA, RICHARD JOSEPH, PALYNOLOGY, ETHNOBOTANY. *Current Pos:* HEAD, BOT & EARTH HIST, ROYAL BC MUS, 86- *Personal Data:* b Hamilton, Ont, Apr 6, 50; m 85, Elaine Whitmore; c Nicholas J R & Christopher F G. *Educ:* McMaster Univ, BSc, 73; Univ BC, PhD(bot), 77. *Prof Exp:* Asst prof biol & earth sci, Univ Waterloo, 77-80; asst cur archaeol, BC Prov Mus, 80-86. *Concurrent Pos:* Adj prof biol, Univ Victoria, 83-, Cent Earth & Ocean Res & Sch Earth & Ocean Scis, 90- *Mem:* Can Bot Asn (vpres 87-88); Geol Asn Can (pres, 93-94); Can Asn Palynologists (pres, 82); Am Quaternary Asn; Am Asn Stratig Palynologists. *Res:* Relationship between human cultural evolution and environmental history; changing landforms (sea level change); vegetation and climate in the late quaternary of British Columbia and Central America. *Mailing Add:* Bot Unit Royal BC Mus Victoria BC V8V 1X4 Can

HEBEL, JOHN RICHARD, BIOSTATISTICS. *Current Pos:* Asst prof, Univ Md, 66-72, assoc prof biostatist, Sch Med, 72-80, assoc prof, 80-, PROF, DEPT EPIDEMIOL & PREV MED, UNIV MD. *Personal Data:* b Lancaster, Pa, Oct 7, 35; m 66; c 2. *Educ:* Va Polytech Inst & State Univ, BS, 62, PhD(statist), 66. *Concurrent Pos:* Consult, Bur Biostatist, Baltimore City Health Dept, 67-72; hon res fel, Univ Birmingham, Eng, 74. *Mem:* Soc Epidemiol Res. *Res:* Epidemiologic methodology, specifically in the areas of perinatal investigation and hypertensive disease. *Mailing Add:* Prev Med Univ Md Sch Med 655 W Baltimore St Baltimore MD 21201-1559

HEBEL, LOUIS CHARLES, EXPERIMENTAL PHYSICS. *Current Pos:* mgr, Phys & Chem Sci Lab, 73-76, mgr res planning, 76-90, MGR TECHNOL EVAL, XEROX CORP, 90- *Personal Data:* b Oak Park, Ill, Oct 1, 30; m 53; c 3. *Educ:* DePauw Univ, BA, 52; Univ Ill, MS, 54, PhD(physics), 57. *Prof Exp:* Asst, Univ Ill, 52-58; res physicist, Bell Tel Labs, Inc, 58-65, dept head reentry & plasma physics, 65-68; dir phys res, Sandia Labs, 68-73. *Mem:* Fel Am Phys Soc. *Res:* Electronics in solids; magnetic resonance. *Mailing Add:* Xerox Parc 3333 Coyote Hill Rd Palo Alto CA 94304. *E-Mail:* hebel@parc.xerox.com

HEBELER, HENRY K, AERONAUTICAL & ASTRONAUTICAL ENGINEERING, STRUCTURAL ENGINEERING. *Current Pos:* RETIRED. *Personal Data:* b St Louis, Mo, Aug 12, 33; m 78; c 2. *Educ:* Mass Inst Technol, SB, 56, AerE, 56, MS, 70. *Prof Exp:* Struct engr, Boeing Co, 56-57; pres energy, Boeing Engr & Construct Co, 75-80, missiles & space, Boeing Aerospace Co, 80-85 & electronics, Boeing Electronics So, 85-87, corp vpres planning, Boeing Co, 87-89. *Concurrent Pos:* Lectr, Col Tech, 60; mem, Bd Gov, Mass Inst Technol Sloan Sch, 74-78, House Rep, Fusion Col Cemt, 76-78, Tech Adv Bd, Dept Com, 80-84, bd vis, Defense Systs Mgt, 80-84, Sci Adv Bd, Dept Energy, 84-86 & Consult Crit Mat, Dept Interior, 86- *Mem:* Fel Am Inst Aeronaut & Astronaut. *Res:* Two patents. *Mailing Add:* 24600 140th Ave SE Kent WA 98042

HEBER, DAVID, ENDOCRINOLOGY, PHYSIOLOGY. *Current Pos:* resident, 74-75, res assoc, 75-78, ASST PROF MED, HARBOR GEN HOSP, LOS ANGELES MED CTR, UNIV CALIF, LOS ANGELES, 78- *Personal Data:* b Celle, Ger, Apr 26, 48; US citizen; m 70; c 1. *Educ:* Univ Calif, Los Angeles, BS, 69, PhD(physiol), 78; Harvard Med Sch, MD, 73. *Prof Exp:* Intern, Beth Israel Hosp, Boston, 73-74. *Concurrent Pos:* NIH fel, 75-77. *Mem:* Endocrine Soc; Am Fed Clin Res; Am Col Physicians. *Res:* Control of protein metabolism in disease states; gonadotropin releasing hormone receptor physiology. *Mailing Add:* Dept Med Div Clin Nutrit 1000 Veterans Ave Univ Calif AL-57 Rehab Ctr Los Angeles CA 90024-2704. *Fax:* 301-206-5264

HEBERGER, JOHN M, PHYSICAL CHEMISTRY. *Current Pos:* staff res chemist, Am Hoechst Corp, 79-82, RES ASSOC, AM HOECHST CELANESE CORP, 82- *Personal Data:* b Rochester, NY, Apr 23, 44; m 69; c 3. *Educ:* St John Fisher Col, BS, 66; Rensselaer Polytech Inst, PhD(phys chem), 71. *Prof Exp:* Sr res & develop chemist, Celanese Plastics Co, 70-78, staff res chemist, 78-79. *Mem:* Am Chem Soc. *Res:* Surface-adhesion properties of polyester film; surface modification; coatings technology; diazo microfilm; drafting film; photographic film, video tape, computer tape, floppy disks, films. *Mailing Add:* 938 River Rd Greer SC 29651-8333

HEBERLE, JUERGEN, PHYSICS. *Current Pos:* assoc prof, 68-89, EMER PROF PHYSICS, STATE UNIV NY, BUFFALO, 89- *Personal Data:* b Koenigsberg, Ger, May 9, 25; nat US; m 57; c 2. *Educ:* Swarthmore Col, AB, 44; Columbia Univ, PhD(physics), 55. *Prof Exp:* Res asst, La State Univ, 46-47; aeronaut res scientist, Nat Adv Comt Aeronaut, 48-49; res asst, Columbia Univ, 49-55; instr physics, Yale Univ, 56-57; assoc physicist, Argonne Nat Lab, 57-65; assoc prof physics, Clark Univ, 65-67. *Concurrent Pos:* Vis prof, Univ Wash, 65, Phys Lab, Univ Groningen, 66 & Physics Fac, Freiburg, Ger, 74-75; vis prof, Munich Tech Univ, 67-68. *Mem:* Am Phys Soc; Am Asn Physics Teachers. *Res:* Hydrogen atom; Moessbauer spectroscopy; molecular structure; superconducting magnets; classical electrodynamics. *Mailing Add:* 54 High Park Blvd Buffalo NY 14226

HEBERLEIN, DOUGLAS G(ARAVEL), RESEARCH ADMINISTRATION, INDUSTRIAL CHEMISTRY. *Current Pos:* RETIRED. *Personal Data:* b Portage, Wis, Dec 6, 16; m 38, Helene Zodtner; c Diane H (Briggle) & Dorene E (West). *Educ:* Univ Wis, BS, 38. *Prof Exp:* Analytical chemist, Res Dept, Continental Can Co, 39-41, res chemist, 42-52; dept supt, Rocky Flats Plant, Dow Chem Co, 52-60, sect asst supt, 60-62, supt plutonium chem, 62, supt mfg tech, 62-67, patent officer, 67-75; patent officer, Rocky Flats Plant, Rockwell Int, 75-82. *Mem:* AAAS; Am Chem Soc; Am Nuclear Soc; Sigma Xi; fel Am Inst Chem. *Res:* Uranium, plutonium and food chemistry; process equipment design; vitamin chemistry with emphasis on methods of analysis; storage of dehydrated foods. *Mailing Add:* 2070 Neher Lane Boulder CO 80304-1606

HEBERLEIN, GARY T, MOLECULAR BIOLOGY, RESEARCH ADMINISTRATION. *Current Pos:* VPRES RES, DEAN, GRAD SCH & PROF BIOL SCI, WAYNE STATE UNIV, DETROIT, 85- *Personal Data:* b Milwaukee, Wis, Apr 11, 39; m 87, Martha W Tack; c Wendy A, Edward G, Jason W, Jarrod S. *Educ:* Ohio Wesleyan Univ, AB, 61; Northwestern Univ, MS, 63, PhD(plant physiol, microbiol), 65. *Honors & Awards:* Distinguished Young Scientist Award, Sigma Xi, 71. *Prof Exp:* Jane Coffin Childs Mem Fund Med Res fel microbiol, Ghent, Belg, 66-67; asst prof microbiol & plant physiol, NY Univ, 67-70, assoc prof biol, 70-72, chmn dept, 71-72; assoc prof, Univ Mo, St Louis, 72-75, chmn dept, 73-75 & 76-80; prof biol, Bowling Green State Univ, 76-86, dean, Grad Col & vprovost res, 80-85. *Concurrent Pos:* Jane Coffin Childs Mem Fund res grant, 67-60; NIH res grants, 63-92, NSF grants, 76-82, Food & Drug Admin, 76-77; chair, Am Soc Microbiol Found, 89-92. *Mem:* AAAS; Am Soc Microbiol; Sigma Xi; Soc Res Adminrs; Am Asn Higher Educ. *Res:* Mechanism by which bacteria induce plant tumors; genetics and biochemistry of crown gall tumor induction by Agrobactrium tumefaciens; genetic engineering of crop plants. *Mailing Add:* 35280 Spring Hill Rd Farmington MI 48331. *Fax:* 313-577-3626; *E-Mail:* gheberle@cms.cc.wayne.edu

HEBERLEIN, JOACHIM VIKTOR RUDOLF, ARC TECHNOLOGY, PLASMA CHEMISTRY. *Current Pos:* assoc prof, 89-94, PROF, DEPT MECH ENG, UNIV MINN, 94- *Personal Data:* b Berlin, Ger, Aug 19, 39; US citizen; m 70, Yuko Ninomiya; c Andrea & Markus. *Educ:* Univ Stuttgart, Ger, Diplom, Physics, 66; Univ Minn, PhD(mech eng), 75. *Honors & Awards:* Rosemount Instrumentation Award, Rosemount Inc, 74. *Prof Exp:* Res fel, Heat Transfer Lab, Univ Minn, 67-75; sr engr arc res, Westinghouse Elec Corp, 75-79, mgr lamp res, 80-82, mgr plasma res, Res & Develop Ctr, 82-89, mgr nuclear & radiation technol, 84-89. *Concurrent Pos:* Mem, Subcomt Plasma Chem, Int Union Pure & Appl Chem, 84-94, chmn, 92-93, Titular mem, Int Union Pure & Appl Chem, Phys Chem Div, 93-97; mem panel plasma processing, NRC, 90-91. *Mem:* Inst Elec & Electronics Engrs; Am Phys Soc; Mat Res Soc; Sigma Xi; AAAS. *Res:* Arc research; plasma heat transfer; electrode effects; vacuum arcs; plasma chemistry; thermal plasma chemical vapor deposition; plasma waste treatment. *Mailing Add:* Dept Mech Eng Univ Minn 111 Church St SE Minneapolis MN 55455. *Fax:* 612-624-1398

HEBERLING, JACK WAUGH, JR, ORGANIC CHEMISTRY. *Current Pos:* RETIRED. *Personal Data:* b Chicago, Ill, Apr 22, 28; m 59, Yvonne Wiest. *Educ:* Univ Ill, BS, 50; Univ Minn, PhD(org chem), 54. *Prof Exp:* Asst, Univ Minn, 50-53; res chemist, E I du Pont de Nemours Co, 54-59, patient liaison, Jackson Lab, Org Chem Dept, 59-77, patents & licensing, 78-85. *Mem:* Fel AAAS; Sigma Xi. *Res:* Sulfur and fluorine compounds; patents. *Mailing Add:* 422 Cypress Way E Naples FL 34110-1108. *E-Mail:* jheberling@naplesnet.com

HEBERLING, RICHARD LEON, VIROLOGY, HUMAN & SIMIAN DIAGNOSTIC VIROLOGY. *Current Pos:* VPRES & TECH DIR, VIRUS REF LAB INC, 88-; PRES, VIRATEST INT INC, 96- *Personal Data:* b Mt Penn, Pa, May 5, 26; m 58, 90, Patricia A Zunker; c Linda (Boyd), Lisa (Williams) & Susan. *Educ:* Albright Col, BS, 49; Univ Pa, MS, 53; Pa State Univ, PhD(bact), 57. *Prof Exp:* Res assoc microbiol, Sch Med, Univ Pittsburgh, 57-65; res microbiologist, Cancer Virol Sect, Nat Cancer Inst, 65-67; actg chmn, Virol Dept, Southwest Found Biomed Res, 67-70, assoc found scientist, 70-75, found scientist, Virol Dept, Div Microbiol & Infectious Dis, 75 88. *Concurrent Pos:* Consult, J Med Primate, NIH, Dept Justice. *Mem:* AAAS. *Res:* Simian viruses; human viruses; viral diagnostics. *Mailing Add:* Virus Ref Lab Inc 7540 Louis Pasteur San Antonio TX 78229-4018. *Fax:* 210-614-7355

HEBERT, ALVIN JOSEPH, COSMOCHEMISTRY, QUANTUM GRAVITY. *Current Pos:* PRES & FOUNDER, AM ELECTROSCI FOUND, 88-; SUBSTITUTE TEACHER, TORRANCE UNIFIED SCH DIST, 89- *Personal Data:* b Los Angeles, Calif, Sept 15, 32; div; c James Scott & Cheryl Marie. *Educ:* Univ Calif, Los Angeles, BS, 59; Univ Calif, Berkeley, PhD(phys chem), 63. *Prof Exp:* Fel, Lawrence Berkeley Lab, Univ Calif, 62-64, sr staff mem, 64-77; process engr & sr staff scientist, Altus Corp, 80-81; tech writer, Kaiser Electronics, 81-82. *Concurrent Pos:* Consult, Geol & Geophys Dept, Argon Dating Lab, Univ Calif, 77; prin investr, Earthtronics, 85 & Am Electrosci Industs, 86-87; adj fac chem, El Camino Col, Torrance, Calif, 89-90. *Mem:* Sigma Xi; AAAS; Am Phys Soc. *Res:* Gravity; quantized gravity; fundamental physical constants; nature's preclusion of "black-holes"; gamma ray bursters; quasars; supernovac as a consequence for "wanna be" "black-holes"; Einstein's gravitational redshift and Mach's principle united in terms of the Sommerfeld fine structure constant provide quantized gravity and explain observed stellar and galactic phenomena. *Mailing Add:* 1639 1/2 Cabrillo Ave No 42 Torrance CA 90501

HEBERT, DANIEL NORMOND, CELL BIOLOGY. *Current Pos:* FEL, YALE UNIV SCH MED, 92- *Personal Data:* b Corning, NY, May 6, 62; m 91, Leah Kelly. *Educ:* Univ NH, BA, 84; Univ Mass Med Sch, PhD(biochem & molecular biol), 91. *Mem:* Am Soc Cell Biol; AAAS. *Res:* Folding and maturation of viral membrane glycoprotein in the endoplasmic reticulum. *Mailing Add:* Dept Cellular Biol Yale Univ Sch Med 333 Cedar St PO Box 208002 New Haven CT 06520-8002. *Fax:* 203-785-7226

HEBERT, GERARD ROSAIRE, PHYSICS. *Current Pos:* from assoc prof to prof, 65-90, sr researcher, 90-, EMER PROF PHYSICS, YORK UNIV, 90- *Personal Data:* b South Lancaster, Ont, Sept 29, 24. *Educ:* Univ Ottawa, Can, BSc, 45; Univ BC, MSc(physics) & Cath Univ, MSc(math), 56; Univ Western Ont, PhD(physics), 60. *Honors & Awards:* Gov Gen Silver Medal, 45. *Prof Exp:* Sr demonstr physics, Univ Ottawa, Can, 45-46, lectr physics & math, 50-53; teacher high sch, 47-50; asst prof physics, St Francis Xavier Univ, 60-64 & Univ Western Ont, 64-65. *Mem:* Can Asn Physicists. *Res:* Properties of superfluid liquid helium; some properties of the nine point hyperbola; intensity measurements of diatomic molecular species of astrophysical interest; remote sensing. *Mailing Add:* 84 Wilkinson Ct Creg Quay ON K0C 1E0 Can

HEBERT, JOEL J, FAILURE ANALYSIS, FORENSIC ENGINEERING. *Current Pos:* SR MG ENGR, FAILURE ANALYSIS, 96- *Personal Data:* b Melville, La, June 23, 39; m; m 68, Beverly A Crow; c Joseph & Genevieve. *Educ:* La Polytech Inst, BSME, 61; Ohio State Univ, MSc, 62; Southern Methodist Univ, PhD, 70. *Honors & Awards:* R C Baker Found Award. *Prof Exp:* Construct engr, Calif Co, La, 62-64; aerothermodyn engr, Gen Dynamics, Tex, 66-67; instr mech eng, Southern Methodist Univ, 64-69; asst prof, Rice Univ, 69-74; sr mech engr, Fluor Corp, 74-77, Western Geophys Co, 78-80, Tiodyne Inc, 87-90; sect mgr, Schlumberger Technol Corp, 80-86; eng mgr, Ch & A Corp, 91-96. *Mem:* Am Soc Mech Engrs; Sigma Xi; Am Soc Safety Engrs. *Res:* Heat transfer; thermodynamics; energy conversion; seismic energy systems; mechanical safety. *Mailing Add:* 1802 Misty Hill Lane Kingwood TX 77345. *Fax:* 713-358-2517

HEBERT, NORMAND CLAUDE, ELECTROANALYTICAL CHEMISTRY. *Current Pos:* PRES, MICROELECTRODES INC, 70- *Personal Data:* b Bedford, Que, Jan 8, 30; US citizen; m 53, Therese; c Michele, Marc, Daniel & Suzanne. *Educ:* St Anselm's Col, AB, 53; Univ Detroit, MS, 58; Purdue Univ, PhD(inorg chem), 61. *Prof Exp:* Chemist, Res Labs, Ethyl Corp, 56-57; res chemist, Res & Develop Div, Corning Glass Works, 61-70. *Concurrent Pos:* Invited prof, Sch Med, Univ Sherbrooke, 67-72; adj prof, Univ Tex Med Br, Galveston, 73-83. *Mem:* AAAS; Am Chem Soc; Chem Soc France; Sigma Xi. *Res:* Chemistry of alkylboranes, metal carbonyls, benzene and cyclopentadienyl complexes; electrochemistry of glassy materials; hydrogen ion and ion-selective microelectrodes. *Mailing Add:* Wood Circle Goffstown NH 03045-3045

HEBERT, PAUL DAVID NEIL, TOXICOLOGY. *Current Pos:* PROF & CHAIR, DEPT ZOOL, UNIV GUELPH, 90- *Personal Data:* b Kingston, Ont, May 6, 47; m 70, Judith Clay; c Brianne C. *Educ:* Queens Univ, BSc, 69; Cambridge Univ, PhD(genetics), 73. *Prof Exp:* Prof, Dept Biol, Univ Windsor, 76-90. *Concurrent Pos:* Dir, Great Lakes Inst, 87-90; mem, Environ Hypersensitivity, Ministry Health, 90-92, Longterm Ecol Res, Can Fedn Biol Soc, 92-93. *Mem:* Fel Royal Soc Can. *Res:* Examines the nature and extent of genetic diversity in aquatic organisms; effort is particularly directed toward the analysis of breeding system diversity, species invasions, systematics and impacts of exposure to contaminants. *Mailing Add:* Univ Guelph Dept Zool Guelph ON N1G 2W1 Can. *Fax:* 519-767-1656, 253-4232 Ext 3598; *E-Mail:* phebert@uoguelph.ca

HEBERT, TEDDY T, PLANT PATHOLOGY. *Current Pos:* Res asst prof, 45-54, from assoc prof to prof, 54-80, EMER PROF PLANT PATH, EXP STA, NC STATE UNIV, 80- *Personal Data:* b Lafayette, La, Nov 24, 14; m 89; c 4. *Educ:* Univ Southwest La, BS, 38; La State Univ, MS, 39; NC State Univ, PhD(plant path), 46. *Concurrent Pos:* Fulbright lectr plant virol, Egypt, 63; consult, USAID Agr Prog, Peru, 67-72, & Africa, 72-84. *Mem:* Am Phytopath Soc. *Res:* Control of diseases on cereal crops; virus diseases on other crops. *Mailing Add:* 804 Ellynn Dr Cary NC 27511-4619

HECHEMY, KARIM E, MICROBIAL PHYSIOLOGY. *Current Pos:* DIR, DIAG IMMUNOL, NY STATE DEPT HEALTH, 71- *Personal Data:* b El Mansourah, Egypt, Dec 4, 38; US citizen; m 65; c 2. *Educ:* Cairo Univ, BSc, 60; Mass Col Pharm, MS, 65, PhD(microbiol), 68. *Prof Exp:* Trainee, Sch Med, Univ Pa, 68-71. *Concurrent Pos:* Dir, Diag Immunol, David Axelrod Inst. *Mem:* Am Soc Microbiol. *Res:* Physiology of growth of bacterial cell in relation to phospholipid biosynthesis. *Mailing Add:* David Axelrod Inst Pub Health NY State Dept Health Wadsworth Ctr Labs & Res PO Box 22002 Albany NY 12201-2002

HECHENBLEIKNER, INGENUIN ALBIN, ORGANIC CHEMISTRY. *Current Pos:* RETIRED. *Personal Data:* b Innsbruck, Austria, Jan 4, 11; nat US; m 42, Caroline Ward; c Bertha, Caroline, Peter & Paul. *Educ:* Davidson Col, BS, 32; Mass Inst Technol, PhD(chem), 38. *Prof Exp:* Res chemist, Am Cyanamid Corp, 37-55; res dir, Shea Chem Corp, 55-58; res dir, Carlisle Chem Works, Inc, 58-63, vpres, 63-70, bd dirs, 65-70; pres, Brookfield Chem Inc, 71-83. *Mem:* AAAS; Am Chem Soc; NY Acad Sci. *Res:* Organic insecticides; sodium alkyls; nitrogen and phosphorus organic compounds; vinyl stabilizers; chemical additives; organometallic compounds; plastic additives including antioxidants; exploratory chemistry on novel phosphorus compounds; photochemistry. *Mailing Add:* 12115 Quail Ridge Rd Land O Lakes FL 34639

HECHLER, STEPHEN HERMAN, MATHEMATICAL LOGIC, TOPOLOGY. *Current Pos:* from asst prof to assoc prof, 73-78, PROF MATH, QUEENS COL, NY, 78- *Personal Data:* b New York, NY, June 7, 39; m 69, Sandra Sherman; c Howard & Miriam. *Educ:* Calif Inst Technol, BS, 61; Univ Calif, Berkeley, MA, 64, PhD(math), 67. *Prof Exp:* Asst prof math, Case Western Res Univ, 67-73. *Mem:* Asn Symbolic Logic; Am Math Soc; Math Asn Am. *Res:* Applications of set theory to combinatorial and topological structures, particularly the study of various models of set theory with the aim of proving that certain statements can be neither proven nor disproven from the axioms of set theory. *Mailing Add:* 9 Greendale Lane East Northport NY 11731

HECHT, ADOLPH, BOTANY. *Current Pos:* from asst prof to prof, 47-79, chmn dept, 55-70, EMER PROF BOT, WASH STATE UNIV, 79- *Personal Data:* b Chicago, Ill, July 25, 14; m 42; c 2. *Educ:* Univ Chicago, BS, 36, MS, 37; Ind Univ, PhD(bot), 42. *Prof Exp:* Asst, Northwestern Rocky Mountain Forest & Range Exp Sta, US Forest Serv, 37-38; asst, Ind Univ, 38-42; instr bot, Univ Chicago, 46-47. *Concurrent Pos:* Mem, Comt Examiners for Advan Biol Exam, Grad Record Exam, 65-70; ed, Plant Sci Bull, Bot Soc Am, 65-71; mem, Comn Undergrad Educ Biol Sci, 66-69; NIH spec fel, 68; ed, Northwest Sci, 76-79. *Mem:* Bot Soc Am; Am Inst Biol Sci. *Res:* Cytology of Rudbeckia and of Sarracenia; cytogenetics of Oenothera; physiology of genetic self-incompatibility in plants; warm water treatments of Oenothera styles to reduce the incompatability reaction and find out what changes have occurred in the stylar tissues. *Mailing Add:* 1409 Blvd Park Lacey WA 98503-2523

HECHT, CHARLES EDWARD, STATISTICAL MECHANICS. *Current Pos:* from assoc prof to prof, 67-93, EMER PROF CHEM, HUNTER COL, 94- *Personal Data:* b Brooklyn, NY, June 26, 30; m 55, Mary Iorio; c Evelyn, Richard, Gregory & Dianne. *Educ:* Mass Inst Technol, SB, 52; Univ Chicago, MS, 54, PhD(phys chem), 56. *Prof Exp:* Res assoc, US Naval Res Lab, Univ Wis, 56-57; NSF res fel, Univ Amsterdam, 57-58; res assoc, Enrico Fermi Inst Nuclear Studies, Univ Chicago, 58-60; asst prof chem, Am Univ, Beirut,

60-63; from asst prof to assoc prof, Brooklyn Col, 63-67. *Concurrent Pos:* Vis prof physics, Delft Technol Univ, Neth, 78. *Mem:* Sigma Xi; Am Phys Soc. *Res:* Statistical mechanics and quantum mechanics applied especially to the many body problem; phase transitions; applications of fractal geometry; renormalization group transformations. *Mailing Add:* 1801 Ave N Brooklyn NY 11230

HECHT, ELIZABETH ANNE, MEDICAL SCIENCES. *Current Pos:* RETIRED. *Personal Data:* b Spokane, Wash, June 23, 39; m 60; c 3. *Educ:* Boston Univ, BA, 61; Harvard Univ, EdM, 62; Univ Calif, Los Angeles, MA, 74, PhD(psychol), 80. *Honors & Awards:* Danforth Award, Danforth Found, 57. *Prof Exp:* Guest lectr, Dept Psychol, Univ Calif, Los Angeles, 84, asst prof res ser, Dept Psychiat, 80-92. *Mem:* AAAS; Am Psychol Asn; NY Acad Sci. *Res:* Effects of marijuana on cognition; tobacco cessation; depressed (and anxious) womens' cogniting; factors contributing to drug and alcohol abuse among teenagers. *Mailing Add:* 311 Amalfi Dr Santa Monica CA 90402

HECHT, EUGENE, PHYSICS. *Current Pos:* NASA fel, 67, from asst prof to assoc prof, 67-78, PROF PHYSICS, ADELPHI UNIV, 78- *Personal Data:* b New York, NY, Dec 2, 38; m 60; c 3. *Educ:* NY Univ, BS, 60; Rutgers Univ, MS, 63; Adelphi Univ, PhD(physics), 67. *Prof Exp:* Physicist, Astro Electronics Div, RCA Corp, 60-63. *Mem:* Am Phys Soc. *Res:* Low temperature solid state physics; optics. *Mailing Add:* Dept Physics Adelphi Univ Garden City NY 11530

HECHT, FREDERICK, GENETICS, PEDIATRICS. *Current Pos:* PRES, HECHT ASSOCS, 89- *Personal Data:* b Baltimore, Md, July 11, 30; m 77, Barbara Kaiser; c Frederick M, Matthew W, Maude B, Tabias O, Kerrie K (McCaw) & Brian S (McCaw). *Educ:* Dartmouth Col, BA, 52; Univ Rochester, MD, 60. *Honors & Awards:* Ross Pediat Res Award. *Prof Exp:* Pediat intern & resident, Strong Mem Hosp, 60-62; from asst prof to prof pediat, med genetics & perinatal med, Med Sch, Univ Ore, 65-78; pres, Southwest Biomed Res Inst & Dir, Genetics Ctr, 78-89. *Concurrent Pos:* Res fel med genetics, Univ Wash, 62-64, Nat Inst Child Health, Genetics & Pediat spec fel, 64-65; Nat Inst Child Health & Human Develop spec res fel, Genetics Unit, Mass Gen Hosp; Royal Soc Med traveling fel, Gt Brit, 71-72; vis assoc prof pediat, Harvard Med Sch; adj prof zool, Ariz State Univ, 78-; adj prof pediat, Univ Ariz Health Sci Ctr, 80-81; mem pediat staff, Ariz Childrens Hosp, St Josephs Hosp, Good Samaritan Hosp & Desert Samaritan Hosp; mem med staff, Maricopa County Hosp; vis prof med genetics, Med Sch, Univ Nice, France, 92-95. *Mem:* Am Soc Human Genetics; Am Pediat Soc; Am Fedn Clin Res; Soc Pediat Res; Am Acad Pediat; Am Soc Pediat Hemat & Oncol; AAAS. *Res:* Medical genetics including cancer genetics and dysmorphology congenital malformations and technology including internet publishing and information transfer. *Mailing Add:* 4134 McGirts Blvd Jacksonville FL 32210-4362. *Fax:* 904-384-5136; *E-Mail:* tbhecht@aol.com

HECHT, GERALD, INDUSTRIAL PHARMACY, BIOPHARMACEUTICS. *Current Pos:* sect head, Alcon Labs Inc, 65-72, dir pharmaceut sci, 72-79, dir res & develop, 80-83, DIR PHARMACEUT SCI, ALCON LABS INC, 83- *Personal Data:* b St Louis, Mo, Aug 26, 34; m 53; c 3. *Educ:* St Louis Col Pharm, BS, 55, MS, 57; Purdue Univ, PhD(indust pharm, bionucleonics), 65. *Honors & Awards:* Bristol Award, Infectious Dis Soc Am, 55. *Prof Exp:* Chemist, Sigma Chem Co, Mo, 57-59; sr scientist pharmaceut prod develop, Mead Johnson & Co, Ind, 59-63. *Mem:* AAAS; NY Acad Sci; Am Pharmaceut Asn; Acad Pharmaceut Sci; Sigma Xi; Am Asn Pharmaceut Sci. *Res:* Pharmacodynamic properties of drugs as influenced by dosage form design; stabilization of pharmaceutical products and development of new dosage forms. *Mailing Add:* 6201 Wheaton Dr Ft Worth TX 76133

HECHT, HARRY GEORGE, PHYSICAL CHEMISTRY. *Current Pos:* head dept, 73-80, PROF CHEM, SDAK STATE UNIV, 73- *Personal Data:* b Powell, Wyo, May 6, 36; m 59; c 3. *Educ:* Brigham Young Univ, BS, 58, MS, 59; Univ Utah, PhD(phys chem), 61. *Prof Exp:* Asst, Argonne Nat Lab, 61-62; asst prof chem, Tex Tech Col, 62-66; mem staff, Los Alamos Sci Lab, 66-73. *Concurrent Pos:* Fulbright res grant, Commonwealth Sci & Indust Res Orgn, Australia, 65-66; Alexander von Humboldt-Stiftung fel, Univ Tubingen, 71-72; consult, Los Alamos Nat Lab, 73-78; fac res leave, Argonne Nat Lab, 83-84; exchange prof, People's Repub China, 88. *Mem:* Sigma Xi; Am Chem Soc. *Res:* Theoretical and experimental molecular structure and valence studies; actinide spectroscopy, reflectance spectroscopy, surface studies and photochemistry. *Mailing Add:* Dept Chem SDak State Univ PO Box 2202 Brookings SD 57007

HECHT, HERBERT, COMPUTER SCIENCE, CONTROL SYSTEMS. *Current Pos:* PRES, SOHAR INC, LOS ANGELES, 78- *Personal Data:* b Frankfort, Ger, Mar 6, 22; nat US; m 45, Esther Iuducan; c 2. *Educ:* City Col New York, BEE; Polytech Inst Brooklyn, MEE, 49; Univ Calif, Los Angeles, PhD(eng), 67. *Prof Exp:* Engr, Mat Lab, NY Naval Shipyard, 46-48; proj engr, Flight Control Systs, Sperry Gyroscope Co, 48-53, eng sect head, Servo Syst Develop Div, 53-55, dept head, Helicopter Flight Controls, 55-58; eng supvr, Light Aircraft Dept, Sperry Phoenix Co Div, Sperry Rand Corp, 58-62; sr staff engr, Aerospace Corp, 62-64, head, Electromech Dept, 64-70, dir, Comput & Guid Technol Progs, 70-77. *Concurrent Pos:* Lectr, Univ Calif, Los Angeles Exten. *Mem:* Inst Elec & Electronics Engrs; AAAS; Asn Comput Mach. *Res:* Space vehicle systems; computer design; software and hardware reliability; economics of reliability; fault tolerant computing. *Mailing Add:* 150 N Almont Beverly Hills CA 90211. *Fax:* 213-653-3624; *E-Mail:* herb@sohar.socal.com

HECHT, J(AMES) L(EE), CHEMICAL ENGINEERING. *Current Pos:* ADJ PROF & DIR, PROJ STUDY AM FUTURE, UNIV DEL, 86- *Personal Data:* b New York, NY, Dec 21, 26; m 53; c 2. *Educ:* Cornell Univ, BChE, 49; Ga Inst Technol, MS, 51; Yale Univ, PhD(chem eng), 55. *Honors & Awards:* Pub Serv Award, US Dept Interior. *Prof Exp:* Res engr, Film Dept, Yerkes Lab, E I du Pont de Nemours & Co, Inc, 53-59, res supvr, 59-68, res assoc, 68-70, Spruance Res & Develop Lab, 70-76, Plastic Prod & Resins Dept, 76-84, sr res assoc, 84-85. *Mem:* Am Chem Soc; Sigma Xi. *Res:* US and USSR cooperation. *Mailing Add:* 111 S Spring Valley Rd Wilmington DE 19807-2448

HECHT, MAX KNOBLER, VERTEBRATE BIOLOGY. *Current Pos:* from instr to assoc prof, 52-65, PROF BIOL, QUEENS COL, NY, 65- *Personal Data:* b New York, NY, Feb 15, 25; m 47; c 3. *Educ:* Cornell Univ, BS, 44, MS, 47, PhD, 52. *Prof Exp:* Lectr biol, Hunter Col, 48-51. *Concurrent Pos:* Res assoc, Dept Vert Paleont, Am Mus Natural Hist, 58- *Mem:* Soc Study Evolution; Am Soc Ichthyol & Herpet; Am Soc Naturalists; Soc Vert Paleont; Soc Syst Zool. *Res:* Paleontology and morphology of recent orders of reptiles and amphibians; biogeography; vertebrate systematics and phylogeny. *Mailing Add:* Dept Biol City Univ NY Queens Col 6530 Kissena Blvd Flushing NY 11367-1575

HECHT, MYRON J, FAULT TOLERANT COMPUTING, RELIABILITY ENGINEERING. *Current Pos:* VPRES, SOHAR INC, 80- *Personal Data:* b Oceanside, NY, May 11, 54; m 85; c 3. *Educ:* Univ Calif, Los Angeles, BS, 75, MS, 76, MBA, 82. *Prof Exp:* Assoc engr, Westinghouse, 76-78; staff scientist, Sci Appln Int Corp, 78-80. *Concurrent Pos:* Instr, Santa Monica Col, 87-88. *Mem:* Inst Elec & Electronics Engrs Comput Soc. *Res:* Development of techniques for dependable computing including fault tolerance, verification and validation, reliability prediction, safety analysis, and failure analysis. *Mailing Add:* Sohar Inc 8421 Wilshire Suite 201 Beverly Hills CA 90211. *Fax:* 213-653-3624

HECHT, NORMAN B, MOLECULAR BIOLOGY. *Current Pos:* from asst prof to assoc prof, 70-83, PROF BIOL, TUFTS UNIV, 83- *Personal Data:* b Newark, NJ, Dec 14, 40; m 68, Mary A Regnier; c David & Rachelle. *Educ:* Rensselaer Polytech Inst, BS, 62; Univ Ill, PhD(microbiol), 67. *Prof Exp:* Fel biol, Univ Calif, San Diego, 67-70. *Concurrent Pos:* USPHS-NIH res grant, 71-74, 76-79, 79-82, 80-83, 83-86, 85-88, 86-91, 87-92; past mem, Clin Sci Study Sect, NIH, steering comt, task force methods regulation of male fertility, WHO; mem, Reproductive Biol Study Sect, NIH. *Mem:* AAAS; Am Soc Cell Biol; Soc Study Reproduction; Am Soc Andrology. *Res:* Biochemistry of meiosis and mitosis; chromosome structure and cellular differentiation; molecular biology of mammalian spermatogenesis, regulation of DNA and RNA synthesis. *Mailing Add:* Dept Biol Tufts Univ Medford MA 02155. *Fax:* 617-627-3805; *E-Mail:* nhecht@pearl.tufts.edu

HECHT, RALPH J, MATERIALS SCIENCE ENGINEERING. *Current Pos:* Supvr coding develop & processing, 70-89, mgr fiber & intermetallic technol, 89-90, MGR HIGH SPEED CIVIL TRANSP MAT, PRATT & WHITNEY, 90- *Personal Data:* b St Louis, Mo, Nov 10, 42. *Educ:* Univ Mo, Rolla, BS, 64; Iowa State Univ, MS, 66. *Mem:* Am Soc Metals. *Mailing Add:* 130 Bowsprit Dr North Palm Beach FL 33408

HECHT, RALPH MARTIN, DEVELOPMENTAL GENETICS, MOLECULAR BIOLOGY. *Current Pos:* asst prof, Dept Biophys Sci, 77-83, prog dir, Develop Biol Prog, NSF, 87-88, ASSOC PROF DEVELOP GENETICS, DEPT BIOCHEM & BIOPHYS SCI, UNIV HOUSTON, 83- *Personal Data:* b New York, NY, Feb 28, 43; div; c 2. *Educ:* Washington Square Col, NY Univ, BS, 67; Univ Edinburgh, dipl animal genetics, 68, PhD(nucleic acids), 71. *Prof Exp:* Fel chromosome struct, Dept Biophys & Genetics, 72-76, fel develop genetics, Dept Molecular Develop & Cellular Biol, 76-77. *Concurrent Pos:* NIH fel, 76-77, grant, 78-81. *Mem:* AAAS; Am Soc Cell Biol; Am Soc Biol Chem. *Res:* Biochemical and genetic studies of developing systems and cell-cycle genes. *Mailing Add:* Dept Biochem & Biophys Sci Univ Houston 4800 Calhoun HSC 402 Houston TX 77204-5513. *Fax:* 713-743-8351

HECHT, SIDNEY MICHAEL, CHEMISTRY, BIOLOGICAL CHEMISTRY. *Current Pos:* JOHN W MALLET PROF CHEM & PROF BIOL, UNIV VA, 78- *Personal Data:* b New York, NY, July 27, 44; m 66. *Educ:* Univ Rochester, AB, 66; Univ Ill, PhD(chem), 70. *Honors & Awards:* Cope Scholar Award, Am Clin Soc, 96. *Prof Exp:* USPHS fel, Univ Wis, 70-71; from asst prof to assoc prof, Mass Inst Technol, 71-79. *Concurrent Pos:* Alfred P Sloan res fel, 75-79; NIH res career develop award, 75-80; John Simon Guggenheim fel, 77-78; Pres preclin res & develop, Smithkline Lab, 81-83, clin res & develop, 83-86, distinguished fel, 86-87. *Mem:* AAAS; Am Chem Soc; Royal Soc Chem; Am Soc Biol Chemists; Sigma Xi. *Res:* Site-specific transfer RNA modifications; synthesis of bleomycin; isolation of biologically active natural products. *Mailing Add:* Dept Chem/Biol Chem Bldg 388 Univ Va Charlottesville VA 22901

HECHT, STEPHEN SAMUEL, ORGANIC CHEMISTRY, CHEMICAL CARCINOGENESIS. *Current Pos:* WALLIN PROF CANCER PREV, CANCER CTR, UNIV MINN, 96- *Personal Data:* b Newark, NJ, Dec 10, 42; m 68, 91, Sharon E Murphy; c Charlotte. *Educ:* Duke Univ, BS, 64; Mass Inst Technol, PhD(org chem), 68. *Prof Exp:* NIH trainee chem, Mass Inst Technol, 68-69; asst prof chem, Haverford Col, 69-71; Nat Res Coun fel, Eastern Mkt & Nutrit Res Div, Agr Res Serv, 71-72; head, Sect Org Chem, Div Environ Carcinogenesis, Naylor Dana Inst Dis Prev, Am Health Found, 73-80, chief, Div Chem Carcinogenesis, 80-96, dir res, 87-96. *Concurrent Pos:*

Nat Cancer Inst res career develop award, 75; lectr, Am Chem Soc Short Courses, 79-83; mem, Chem Path Study Sect, NIH, 81-85; assoc ed, Cancer Res, 81-; outstanding investr grant, Nat Cancer Inst, 87-, bd sci counr, 89-95; mem, Res Comt, Health Effects Inst, 91-95. *Mem:* Am Chem Soc; Am Asn Cancer Res; AAAS; Am Soc Prev Oncol. *Res:* Human uptake and metabolism of environmental carcinogens; mechanism of chemical carcinogenesis; chemoprevention of cancer. *Mailing Add:* Univ Minn Cancer Ctr Minneapolis MN 55455. *Fax:* 612-626-5135; *E-Mail:* hecht002@gold.umn.tc.edu

HECHT, TOBY T, TUMOR IMMUNOTHERAPY. *Current Pos:* PROG DIR, BIOL RESOURCES BR, DEVELOP THERAPEUT PROG, NAT CANCER INST-FREDERICK CANCER RES & DEVELOP CTR, 87- *Personal Data:* b Apr 7, 47; m 69, Barry Hecht; c Spencer & Jonathan. *Educ:* Cornell Univ, BS, 67; Albert Einstein Col Med, PhD, 73. *Prof Exp:* Asst prof, Univ Md, 83-87. *Concurrent Pos:* Fel, Yale Univ, 75. *Mem:* Am Asn Immunologists. *Mailing Add:* Biol Resources Br-Biol Response Modifiers Prog DCT NCI-FCRDC PO Box B Bldg 1052 Rm 253 Frederick MD 21702-1201. *E-Mail:* hecht@ncifcrf.gov

HECHT, WILLIAM F, ELECTRICAL ENGINEERING. *Current Pos:* Engr, Pa Power & Light Co, 64-68, proj engr, 68-72, sr proj engr, 72-75, mgr distrib planning, 75-76, exec dir corp energy planning coun, 76-78, mgr systs planning, 78-84, vpres systs power, 84-87, vpres mkt, 87-90, exec vpres, 90-93, CHIEF EXEC OFFICER, CHMN & PRES, PA POWER & LIGHT CO, 93- *Educ:* Lehigh Univ, BSEE, 64, MSEE, 70. *Mailing Add:* Pa Power & Light Co 2 Ninth St Allentown PA 18101-1179

HECHTER, OSCAR MILTON, PHYSIOLOGY, CELL BIOLOGY. *Current Pos:* Nathan Smith Davis prof physiol & chmn dept, 70-78, prof physiol, 78-87, EMER PROF PHYSIOL & CELL, MOLECULAR & STRUCT BIOL, MED SCH, NORTHWESTERN UNIV, CHICAGO, 87- *Personal Data:* b Chicago, Ill, Sept 29, 16; m 40, Gertrude Horowitz; c Michael. *Educ:* Univ Chicago, BS, 38; Univ Southern Calif, MS, 42, PhD(biochem), 43. *Honors & Awards:* Ciba Award, Endocrine Soc, 50. *Prof Exp:* Asst, Dept Metab & Endocrinol, Michael Reese Hosp, Chicago, 32-37, res assoc, 37-40; res assoc, Cedars Lebanon Hosp, Los Angeles, 40-44; sr scientist, Worcester Found Exp Biol, 44-66; mem, Inst Biomed Res, 66 70. *Concurrent Pos:* Res assoc prof physiol, Boston Univ, 51-58; consult, Schenley Pharmaceut, Inc, 56-58 & Ayerst Labs, 58-66; vis prof biol, Brandeis Univ, 61-62; prof lectr, Dept Physiol, Univ Chicago, 66-70; pres, Group For Study Biol & Social Behav, 75-80; mem sci adv, Worcester Found Exp Biol, 68-73, Lab Reproductive Biol, Univ NC, 69-73, Elan Pharmaceut Res Corp, 81-83 & Progenics, Inc, 84-92. *Mem:* Fel Am Acad Arts & Sci. *Res:* Endocrinology; mechanisms of hormone action; biological information systems. *Mailing Add:* 3730 N Lakeshore Dr Chicago IL 60613

HECK, FRED CARL, VIROLOGY. *Current Pos:* RETIRED. *Personal Data:* b Wilkes-Barre, Pa, Nov 1, 30; m 52; c 3. *Educ:* Tex A&M Univ, BS, 59, MS, 62; Univ Tex, PhD(microbiol), 65. *Prof Exp:* Instr microbiol, Sch Vet Med, Tex A&M Univ, 59-62; asst res microbiologist, Parke, Davis & Co, 65-69; from assoc prof to prof vet microbiol, parsitol & vet pub health, Tex A&M Univ, 80-90. *Mem:* Am Soc Microbiol. *Res:* Animal virology immunology and electron microscopy; immunotheraphy of neoplastic disease. *Mailing Add:* 3803 Craig St Bryan TX 77801

HECK, HENRY D'ARCY, BIOCHEMICAL TOXICOLOGY, TOXICOKINETICS. *Current Pos:* scientist, 77-85, SR SCIENTIST, CHEM INDUST INST TOXICOL, 85- *Personal Data:* b Bryn Mawr, Pa, Apr 18, 39; m 84, Mercedes Casandva; c Katherin (Troy), Julia, John Schmitz & Lara (King). *Educ:* Princeton Univ, AB, 62; Northwestern Univ, PhD(chem), 66. *Honors & Awards:* Frank Blood Award, Soc Toxicol, 83. *Prof Exp:* Fel chem, Max-Planck Inst Phys Chem, 66-68; asst prof chem, Univ Calif, Berkeley, 68-72; scientist, Stanford Res Inst, 73-77. *Concurrent Pos:* Adj assoc prof, Duke Univ & Univ NC, Chapel Hill; advisor, Fed & Int Agencies, 83-; ed-in-chief, Fundamental & Appl Toxicol, 91-97. *Mem:* Am Chem Soc; AAAS; Soc Toxicol. *Res:* Inhalation toxicology; carcinogenesis; molecular dosimetry; endocrine toxicology. *Mailing Add:* Chem Indust Inst Toxicol PO Box 12137 Research Triangle Park NC 27709. *Fax:* 919-541-9015

HECK, JAMES VIRGIL, ANTIBIOTICS & CARBOHYDRATE CHEMISTRY, MEDICINAL & NATURAL PRODUCT CHEMISTRY. *Current Pos:* Sr res chemist, 76-82, from asst dir to sr dir synthetic chem, 82-92, EXEC DIR, MED CHEM & NATURAL PRODUCTS CHEM, MERCK, SHARP & DOHME RES LABS, 92- *Personal Data:* b Louisville, Ky, Mar 14, 52; m 72, Paula Zarrella; c 1. *Educ:* Bellarmine Col, BA, 72; Harvard Univ, MA, 74, PhD(org chem), 76. *Mem:* Am Chem Soc; AAAS; Am Soc Microbiol. *Res:* Drug design & synthesis, with a particular interest in the antibiotic and endocrinology fields. *Mailing Add:* Merck Res Lab PO Box 2000 Rahway NJ 07065. *Fax:* 732-594-4773; *E-Mail:* jim_heck@merck.com

HECK, JONATHAN DANIEL, GENETIC TOXICOLOGY. *Current Pos:* Biologist, 76-78, toxicologist, 84-85, MGR LIFE SCI, LORILLARD, INC, 86- *Personal Data:* b Vienna, Austria, July 28, 52; US citizen; m 81; c 1. *Educ:* Univ NC, Greensboro, BA, 75; Univ Tex Health Sci Ctr, Houston, PhD(pharmacol & toxicol), 83; Am Bd Toxicol, dipl, 87. *Mem:* Soc Toxicol; Environ Mutagen Soc; Am Col Toxicol; Genetic Toxicol Asn; AAAS. *Res:* Carcinogenesis; DNA damage and repair; inhalation toxicology; application of in vitro mammalian cell culture methodologies in toxicology. *Mailing Add:* 513 Woodvale Dr Greensboro NC 27410

HECK, JOSEPH GERARD, bacteriology, for more information see previous edition

HECK, MARGARET MATHILDE SOPHIE, EMBRYOLOGY. *Current Pos:* POSTDOCTORAL TRAINING MOLECULAR GENETICS, DEPT EMBRYOL, CARNEGIE INST WASHINGTON, BALTIMORE, MD, 88- *Personal Data:* b Munich, WGer, May 5, 59; US citizen; m 88. *Educ:* State Univ NY, Plattsburg, BA, 81; Johns Hopkins Univ, PhD(cell biol), 88. *Prof Exp:* Lab instr biol, State Univ NY, Plattsburg, 81, teaching asst, 82; lab instr cell & tissues, Sch Med, Johns Hopkins Univ, 84-87. *Concurrent Pos:* Jane Coffin Childs Mem Fund med res, 88-91. *Mem:* Am Soc Cell Biol. *Mailing Add:* Univ Edinburgh Mayfield Rd Swann Bldg KB Edinburgh EH9 3JR Scotland. *Fax:* 44 131 6508650

HECK, OSCAR BENJAMIN, PARASITOLOGY. *Current Pos:* asst prof, 61-69, ASSOC PROF ZOOL, OHIO UNIV, 69- *Personal Data:* b Bartlesville, Okla, Jan 13, 27; m 51. *Educ:* Univ Kans, AB, 49, MA, 51; State Col Wash, PhD(zool), 58. *Prof Exp:* Asst prof biol, Coe Col, 56-61. *Mem:* Am Soc Parasitol; Soc Syst Zool. *Res:* Cestodes of waterfowl. *Mailing Add:* Biol Sci Ohio Univ Athens OH 45701-2979

HECK, RICHARD FRED, ORGANIC CHEMISTRY. *Current Pos:* RETIRED. *Personal Data:* b Springfield, Mass, Aug 15, 31. *Educ:* Univ Calif, Los Angeles, BS, 52, PhD(org chem), 54. *Prof Exp:* Fel chem, Eidgenoische Tech Hoch, 55-56 & Univ Calif, Los Angeles, 56-57; res chemist, Hercules Inc, 57-71; prof chem, Univ Del, 71- *Res:* Organometallic chemistry, homogeneous catalysis, reaction mechanisms. *Mailing Add:* Golden Gate East 6160 28th Ave Naples FL 33999

HECK, RONALD MARSHALL, CHEMICAL ENGINEERING, ENVIRONMENTAL CATALYSIS. *Current Pos:* sr res chem engr, Engelhard Corp, 72-76, sect head chem process develop, 76-84, mgr, Catalytic Eng & Technol Syst Dept, 85-86, group leader, Environ Catalyst Res & Develop, 86-93, sr develop assoc, 93-95, RES MGR, ENGELHARD CORP, 95- *Personal Data:* b Baltimore, Md, Sept 23, 43; m 90, Barbara Thompson; c Ron, Kimberly & Teresa. *Educ:* Univ Md, BSc, 65, PhD(chem eng), 69. *Prof Exp:* Res chem engr catalysis, Celanese Chem Co, 69-72. *Mem:* Am Inst Chem Eng; Am Chem Soc; Soc Automotive Eng; Catalysis Soc; Air & Waste Mgt Asn. *Res:* Catalysis, reaction kinetics and chemical reaction engineering; general research and development in chemical engineering; fluid dynamics and mass transfer; process development and scale up; development and design of catalytic air pollution control equipment; automotive catalyst; air pollution control catalysts; environmental catalysis. *Mailing Add:* Engelhard Corp 101 Wood Iselin NJ 08830-0770. *Fax:* 732-205-5300; *E-Mail:* ron.heck@engelhard.com

HECK, WALTER WEBB, GROWTH & DEVELOPMENT, AIR POLLUTION EFFECTS. *Current Pos:* res plant physiologist, Taft Sanit Eng Ctr, USDA, 63-68, leader, Coop Air Pollution Prog, Plant Sci Res Div, Agr Res Serv, assigned to Div Ecol Res, Environ Protection Agency, 68-72, res leader Air Qual Prog, SAtlantic Area, 72-91, supvry plant physiologist, ARS, USDA, 91-95, COLLABR ARS, USDA, 95- *Personal Data:* b Columbus, Ohio, May 28, 26; m 59, Corinne Schillar; c 5. *Educ:* Ohio State Univ, BS, 47; Univ Tenn, MS, 50; Univ Ill, PhD, 54. *Honors & Awards:* Frank A Chambers Award, Air Pollution Control Asn, 81. *Prof Exp:* Teacher, Pub Schs, Ohio, 47-48; asst bot, Univ Tenn, 48-50; teacher, Pub Schs, Ohio, 50-51; asst bot, Univ Ill, 52-54, res biochem, 54-55; from asst prof to assoc prof biol, Ferris Inst, 55-59; assoc prof plant physiol, Tex A&M Univ, 59-63. *Concurrent Pos:* Prof, 72-95, emer prof bot, NC State Univ, 95- *Mem:* AAAS; fel Air Waste Mgt Asn; Bot Soc Am; Am Soc Plant Physiol; Am Inst Biol Sci; Sigma Xi. *Res:* Physiological and biochemical effects of air pollutants on plants of horticultural and agronomic importance, using controlled growth chambers, greenhouses and field chambers; develop a biological indicator monitoring program for Terestrial ecosystems; assess effects of ozone on terrestrial ecosystems of the SE. *Mailing Add:* 1509 Varsity Dr NC State Univ Raleigh NC 27606. *Fax:* 919-515-3593; *E-Mail:* walt_hech@ncsu.edu

HECKATHORN, HARRY MERVIN, III, ASTRONOMY, ELECTROOPTICS. *Current Pos:* ASTROPHYSICIST, ASTROPHYS SECT, SPACE SCI DIV, US NAVAL RES LAB, 78-, DIR BALLISTIC MISSILE DEFENCE, 92- *Personal Data:* b Warren, Ohio, Aug 30, 44; m 68; c 2. *Educ:* Carleton Col, BA, 66; Northwestern Univ, Ill, MS, 71, PhD(astrophys), 71. *Prof Exp:* Nat Res Coun res associateship, Astrophys Sect, Manned Spacecraft Ctr, NASA, 70-72; res associateship phys, Univ Houston, 72-74; prin scientist, Physics Dept, Lockheed Electronics Co, Johnson Space Ctr, NASA, 74-75; res scientist, Physics Dept, Johns Hopkins Univ, 76-77. *Mem:* Am Astron Soc; Soc Photo-Optical Instrumentation Engrs; Sigma Xi. *Res:* Space astronomy (unvisible to visible); galactic and extragalactic astronomy; photometry; spectroscopy; image intensification and electrography; microphotometry and computerized data analysis and display. *Mailing Add:* 19 N Garfield St Arlington VA 22201

HECKEL, DAVID G, BIOLOGICAL SCIENCES. *Current Pos:* ASSOC PROF BIOL SCI, CLEMSON UNIV. *Concurrent Pos:* Fulbright grantee biol sci, Commonwealth Sci & Indust Res Orgn, Canberra, Australia, 96-97. *Res:* Insect geomics; developing a genetic linkage map for the Australian cotton bollworm Helicoverpa armigera. *Mailing Add:* Dept Biol Sci Clemson Univ Clemson SC 29634

HECKEL, EDGAR, PHYSICAL CHEMISTRY. *Current Pos:* dir IWL, WGer, 80-87, group dir, LGA Bavaria, 89-91, div dir, 92-93, managing dir, USADD (Dresden), 93-95, DIR, INGENIEURBUERO UMWELTSCHUTZ, 88-, GROUP LEADER, LGA BAVARIA, 95- *Personal Data:* b Plauen, Ger, July 13, 36; m 62, Renate Jagla; c Detlef & Birgit. *Educ:* Tech Univ Berlin, BS, 58,

MS, 62, PhD(chem eng), 64. *Prof Exp:* Res assoc radiation chem, Hahn-Meitner Inst Nuclear Res, Ger, 64-66; fel chem, Univ Fla, 66-67; from asst prof to assoc prof, ECarolina Univ, 67-76, prof, 76-80. *Mem:* Am Chem Soc. *Res:* Chemical kinetics of reactions of free radicals and or ions formed by ionizing radiation in fluorocarbons or fluorocarbon-hydrocarbon mixtures; environmental research; mass spectrometry and analytical chemistry. *Mailing Add:* Ingenieurbuero Umweltschutz Asternweg 34 51143 Cologne Germany. *Fax:* 49-911-358598; *E-Mail:* qwhk@gw.lga.de

HECKEL, PHILIP HENRY, GEOLOGY. *Current Pos:* assoc prof, 71-78, PROF GEOL, UNIV IOWA, 78- *Personal Data:* b Rochester, NY, Nov 24, 38; m 69; c 2. *Educ:* Amherst Col, BA, 60; Rice Univ, PhD(geol), 66. *Prof Exp:* Geologist, Kans Geol Surv, Univ Kans, 65-67, res assoc, 67-71. *Concurrent Pos:* Vis prof, Wichita State Univ, 68-71; res assoc, Kans Geol Surv, 71- *Mem:* Soc Econ Paleont & Mineral. *Res:* Sedimentary geology; stratigraphy; carbonate petrography; paleoecology. *Mailing Add:* Dept Geol Univ Iowa Iowa City IA 52242-1000

HECKEL, RICHARD W(AYNE), PHYSICAL METALLURGY. *Current Pos:* prof, 76-96, EMER PROF METALL & MATS ENG, MICH TECHNOL UNIV, 96- *Personal Data:* b Pittsburgh, Pa, Jan 25, 34; m 59, Peggy A Simmons; c Scott A & Laura A (Rowe). *Educ:* Carnegie Mellon Univ, BS, 55, MS, 58, PhD, 59. *Honors & Awards:* Bradley Stoughton Young Teacher Award, Am Soc Metals Int, 69; Mich Technol Univ Res Award, 85. *Prof Exp:* Sr res metallurgist, Eng Res Lab, Exp Sta, E I du Pont de Nemours & Co, Inc, 59-63; assoc prof metall eng, Drexel Univ, 63-68, prof, 68-72; prof metall & mat sci & head dept, Carnegie-Mellon Univ, 72-76. *Concurrent Pos:* With SChina Inst Technol, Guangzhou, 84; with US Dept Energy, 87-90. *Mem:* Fel Am Soc Metals Int; Minerals Metals & Mat Soc; Am Soc Eng Educ. *Res:* Oxidation; diffusion phenomena; powder metallurgy; composite materials; coatings; trends in engineering education statistical. *Mailing Add:* Mich Technol Univ Houghton MI 49931. *Fax:* 906-487-2934; *E-Mail:* rheckel@up.net, heckel@mtu.edu

HECKELSBERG, LOUIS FRED, physical chemistry, for more information see previous edition

HECKER, ART L, NUTRITION. *Current Pos:* VPRES, RES & DEVELOP, ROSS LABS, DIV ABBOTT LABS & DIR MED NUTRIT RES, ROSS LABS, 80- *Personal Data:* b Forsyth, Mont, Mar 15, 44; m 67, Judy Larson; c Brett J & Kari D. *Educ:* Mont State Univ, BS, 66, MS, 68; Colo State Univ, PhD(nutrit biochem), 72. *Concurrent Pos:* Prof exercise physiol, Ohio State Univ, 85-90. *Mem:* Fel Am col Sports Med; Am Inst Nutrit. *Mailing Add:* vpres res & develop Ross Labs, Div Abbot Labs 625 Cleveland Ave Columbus OH 43215-1724

HECKER, GEORGE ERNST, HYDRAULICS, FLUID MECHANICS. *Current Pos:* PRES, ALDEN RES LAB, INC, 86- *Personal Data:* b Hamburg, Ger, Sept 10, 39; US citizen; m 62; c 2. *Educ:* Yale Univ, BS, 61; Mass Inst Technol, MS, 62. *Honors & Awards:* Centennial Medal, Am Soc Mech Engrs. *Prof Exp:* Res engr hydraul, Tenn Valley Authority, 62-68; sr engr, Stone & Webster Eng Corp, 68-70; asst dir & asst prof, 71-75, dir, Alden Res Labs, Worcester Polytech Inst & Res Prof Civil Eng, 75-86. *Concurrent Pos:* Chmn, exec comt, Hydraul Div, Am Soc Civil Engrs, 80-84. *Mem:* Am Soc Civil Engrs; Int Asn Hydraul Res; Sigma Xi. *Res:* Hydraulic structures; mixing and dispersion; stratified flow; thermal discharges; closed conduit flow. *Mailing Add:* Alden Res Lab Inc 30 Shrewsbury St Holden MA 01520. *Fax:* 508-829-5939

HECKER, RICHARD JACOB, PLANT BREEDING. *Current Pos:* RETIRED. *Personal Data:* b Miles City, Mont, Mar 26, 28; m 58; c 4. *Educ:* Mont State Col, BS, 58; Colo State Univ, PhD(plant genetics), 64. *Honors & Awards:* Merit Success Award, Am Soc Sugar Beet Technol. *Prof Exp:* Res geneticist, Crops Res Lab, USDA, Colo, 59-64, Calif, 64-65, res geneticist & res leader, Colo State Univ, 65-92. *Mem:* Fel Am Soc Agron; Am Soc Sugar Beet Technol; fel Crop Sci Soc Am. *Res:* Genetics of chemical and quality characters and disease resistance in sugar beets, also breeding methodology and population genetics. *Mailing Add:* 1100 Morgan St Ft Collins CO 80524

HECKER, SIEGFRIED STEPHEN, METALLURGY, MECHANICS. *Current Pos:* supvr chem mat sci, Los Alamos Nat Lab, 73-80, assoc div leader, 80-81, dep div leader, 81-83, actg chmn, Ctr Mat Sci, 81-83, div leader, 83-85, chmn, Ctr Mat Sci, 85-86, DIR, LOS ALAMOS NAT LAB, 86- *Personal Data:* b Tomasow, Poland, Oct 2, 43; US citizen; m 65; c 4. *Educ:* Case Western Res Univ, BS, 65, MS, 67, PhD(metall), 68. *Hon Degrees:* DSC, Col Santa Fe. *Honors & Awards:* Marcus Grossman Young Auth Award, Am Soc Metals, 76; E O Lawrence Award, 84; James O Douglas Gold Medal Award, 90; Appl Mech Div Award, Am Soc Mech Engrs, 94. *Prof Exp:* Appointee metall, Los Alamos Sci Lab, 68-70; sr res metallurgist, Phys Dept, Gen Motors Corp Res Labs, 70-73. *Concurrent Pos:* Bd Regents, Univ NMex; bd mem, Carrie Tingley Hosp; mem, Nat Comn Superconductivity; keynote lectr, Am Soc Mech Engrs, 94; plenary speaker, Mat Res Soc, 94. *Mem:* Nat Acad Eng; Am Inst Mining, Metall & Petrol Engrs; Metall Soc; fel Am Soc Metals; Sigma Xi; Mat Res Soc; hon mem Am Ceramics Soc. *Res:* Nuclear materials; high temperature and high strain rate behavior; metal-matrix fiber composite materials; plastic behavior of metals and materials; sheet metal formability. *Mailing Add:* PO Box 1663 MS A100 Los Alamos Nat Lab Los Alamos NM 87545. *Fax:* 505-667-2997; *E-Mail:* sh@lanl.gov

HECKERMAN, RAYMOND OTTO, VERTEBRATE MORPHOLOGY, CYTOLOGY. *Current Pos:* assoc prof anat, physiol & biol, Miami-Dade Jr Col, 64-65, from assoc prof to prof biol, 65-87, dir, Div Natural Sci, 65-87, EMER PROF BIOL, MIAMI-DADE JR COL, 87- *Personal Data:* b Rochester, Pa, Sept 16, 24; m 47; c 8. *Educ:* Geneva Col, BS, 47; Univ Pittsburgh, MS, 49, PhD(zool), 55. *Prof Exp:* Asst zool, Duquesne Univ, 47-49, lectr, 49-50, instr zool & embryol, 50-55, asst prof zool, embryol & genetics, 55-58, assoc prof, 58-59; assoc prof & chmn div, Quincy Col, 59-64. *Mem:* Inst Environ Sci; Sigma Xi. *Res:* Environmental control technology and general education man and environment; cytology and biochemistry of cell differentiation; reticuloendothelial response to infection. *Mailing Add:* 3741 NW 108th Ct Gainesville FL 32606-4941

HECKERT, DAVID CLINTON, RESEARCH ADMINISTRATION, BEHAVIORAL PHARMACOLOGY. *Current Pos:* res chemist, Miami Valley Labs, Procter & Gamble, 66-74, sect head, Ivorydale Tech Ctr, 74-77, sect head, Winton Hill Tech Ctr, 77-80, SECT HEAD, MIAMI VALLEY LABS, PROCTER & GAMBLE, 80- *Personal Data:* b Daily, WVa, Dec 31, 39; m 64; c 2. *Educ:* Manchester Col, BS, 61; Ohio State Univ, PhD(org chem), 65. *Prof Exp:* Res assoc org photochem, Iowa State Univ, 65-66. *Mem:* Am Chem Soc; Asn Chemoreception Sci; Soc Study Intake Behav. *Res:* Food chemistry; behavioral pharmacology. *Mailing Add:* 3561 Kehr Rd Oxford OH 45056-9286

HECKLER, GEORGE EARL, PHYSICAL CHEMISTRY. *Current Pos:* from asst prof to prof chem, 56-63, chmn dept, 61-83, EMER PROF CHEM, IDAHO STATE UNIV, 88- *Personal Data:* b Marietta, Ohio, Dec 20, 20; m 45; c 4. *Educ:* Marietta Col, BA, 47; Univ Wis, PhD(chem), 52. *Prof Exp:* Res chemist, E I du Pont de Nemours & Co, 52-56. *Mem:* AAAS; Am Chem Soc; Sigma Xi. *Res:* Sensitized photo-decomposition of aqueous organic acid solutions; electrical conductivity of solutions. *Mailing Add:* 529 S Seventh Ave Pocatello ID 83201-5834

HECKLY, ROBERT JOSEPH, MICROBIOLOGY. *Current Pos:* from asst res bacteriologist to assoc res bacteriologist, Naval Biol Lab, 51-62, asst dir, Naval Biomed Res Lab, 70-75, assoc dir, Naval Biosci Lab, 75-82, RES BACTERIOLOGIST, NAVAL BIOL LAB, 62- *Personal Data:* b Santa Barbara, Calif, May 6, 20; m 44; c 2. *Educ:* Univ Calif, AB, 42; Univ Wis, MS, 49, PhD(bact), 51. *Prof Exp:* Biochemist, Camp Detrick, Md, 43-47. *Concurrent Pos:* Biochemist, USDA, Denmark, 52-53. *Mem:* AAAS; Am Chem Soc; Am Acad Microbiol; Am Soc Microbiol; Soc Cryobiol; Sigma Xi. *Res:* Lyophilization and preservation of microorganisms; chemistry and immunology of anthrax and tubercle bacilli; Pseudomonas pseudomallei and botulinum toxins; microbial degradation of wastes. *Mailing Add:* 1156 Oxford St Berkeley CA 94707-2624

HECKMAN, CAROL A, ELECTRON MICROSCOPY, IMAGE ANALYSIS. *Current Pos:* ASSOC PROF CELL BIOL, BOWLING GREEN STATE UNIV, 82- *Personal Data:* b E Stroudsburg, Pa, Oct 18, 44. *Educ:* Beloit Col, BA, 66; Univ Mass, PhD(cell biol), 72. *Prof Exp:* Res assoc biochem, Sch Med, Yale Univ, 73-75; staff mem, Oak Ridge Nat Lab, Union Carbide Corp, 75-82. *Concurrent Pos:* Lectr cell biol, Grad Sch Biomed Sci, Univ Tenn, Oak Ridge, 76-80, adj assoc prof, 80-82; mem, NSF adv comt cell biol, 77-80; Int Cancer Res Technol Transfer fel, Int Union Against Cancer, 80, Heritage Found fel, Alta, Can, 82; dir, Electron Micros Facil, Bowling Green State Univ, 82-; guest fel, Uppsala Univ, 88-89. *Mem:* AAAS; Am Soc Cell Biol; Electron Micros Soc Am; Sigma Xi; Tissue Cult Asn. *Res:* Cell shape and adhesion mechanisms; cell responses to inducers of differentiation and growth; spatial signals modulating cell cycle. *Mailing Add:* EM Facil Bowling Green State Univ Bowling Green OH 43403-0212. *Fax:* 419-372-2024

HECKMAN, HARRY HUGHES, NUCLEAR PHYSICS. *Current Pos:* PHYSICIST, LAWRENCE BERKELEY LAB, UNIV CALIF, 53- *Personal Data:* b Long Beach, Calif, Nov 25, 23; m 54; c 2. *Educ:* Univ Calif, PhD(physics), 53. *Concurrent Pos:* Consult, Los Alamos Sci Lab, 59-60. *Mem:* Am Phys Soc; Am Geophys Union. *Res:* High energy physics; geomagnetically trapped radiation. *Mailing Add:* 144 Hill Rd Berkeley CA 94708

HECKMAN, RICHARD AINSWORTH, SANITARY & ENVIRONMENTAL ENGINEERING, NUCLEAR CHEMICAL ENGINEERING. *Current Pos:* DIV DIR, HAZARDOUS WASTE MGT, NATIONWIDE TECH INC, 90- *Personal Data:* b Phoenix, Ariz, July 15, 29; m 50; c 2. *Educ:* Univ Calif, Berkeley, BS, 50. *Prof Exp:* Chem engr, Radiation Lab, Univ Calif, Berkeley, 50-51 & Calif Res & Develop Co, Stand Oil Calif, 51-53; chem engr, Lawrence Livermore Nat Lab, Univ Calif, 53-61, group leader, 61-64, sect leader, 64-68, assoc div leader, 68-74, containment scientist, 74-76, prog leader, 76-78, energy policy analyst, Atomic Vapor Laser Isotope Separation Prog, 83-84, prog engr Hazardous Waste Mgt, 84-86, proj leader, Hazardous Waste Minimization, 86-90. *Mem:* Am Nuclear Soc; AAAS; NY Acad Sci; Am Inst Chem Engrs; Am Chem Soc; Acad Hazardous Mat Mgt; fel Am Inst Chemists. *Res:* Systems studies on impacts of national energy policy on energy technologies; system studies on alternative waste management systems for the nuclear fuel cycle; process research on new technologies for hazardous waste minimization treatment and disposal. *Mailing Add:* 5683 Greenridge Rd Castro Valley CA 94552-2625

HECKMAN, RICHARD COOPER, PHYSICS. *Current Pos:* RETIRED. *Personal Data:* b Richmond, Ind, Mar 28, 28; m 55; c 3. *Educ:* Antioch Col, BS, 51; Duke Univ, MA, 53, PhD(physics), 56. *Prof Exp:* Res physicist, Charles F Kettering Found, 55-61; staff mem, Sandia Corp, 61-65, div supv, 65-87. *Concurrent Pos:* Consult, G & C Merriam Co, 57-62; from asst prof to assoc prof, Antioch Col, 56-61. *Mem:* Am Phys Soc; Sigma Xi. *Res:* Electronics engineering; thermal physics; solid state physics; atomic and molecular physics. *Mailing Add:* 7408 Pickard Ave Albuquerque NM 87110

HECKMAN, ROBERT ARTHUR, ORGANIC CHEMISTRY, ANALYTIC CHEMISTRY. *Current Pos:* Res chemist, 65-80, proj mgr appl res & develop, 80-83, SR RES & DEVELOP, R J REYNOLDS INDUST, 83- *Personal Data:* b Dobbs Ferry, NY, Sept 4, 37; m 63; c 2. *Educ:* Ga Inst Technol, 59, PhD(org chem), 65. *Mem:* Am Chem Soc; Am Inst Chemists; Sigma Xi. *Res:* Synthetic organic chemistry; isolation and characterization of natural products; medicinal, flavor and agricultural chemistry; trace organic analysis; development of analytical methods. *Mailing Add:* 847 Wellington Rd Winston Salem NC 27106-5514

HECKMAN, TIMOTHY MARTIN, EXTRAGALACTIC ASTRONOMY. *Current Pos:* PROF PHYSICS & ASTRON, JOHNS HOPKINS UNIV, BALTIMORE, 89- *Personal Data:* b Toledo, Ohio, Oct 11, 51; m 78, Joanne Orsini; c David D & Steven K. *Educ:* Harvard Univ, BA, 73; Univ Wash, PhD(astron), 78. *Prof Exp:* Res fel, Leiden Observ, Leiden Univ, Neth, 78-80; Bart Bok res fel, Steward Observ, Univ Ariz, 80-82; from asst prof to assoc prof astron, Astron Prog, Univ Md, 82-89. *Concurrent Pos:* Vis prof, Dept Physics & Astron, Johns Hopkins Univ, 84-85; chmn, Users Comt, K H Peak Nat Observ, 85-89. *Mem:* Am Astron Soc; Int Astron Union. *Res:* Observational studies of starburst galaxies, active galactic nuclei, quasars, and their environments; observational extragalactic astronomy. *Mailing Add:* Dept Physics & Astron Johns Hopkins Univ 34th & Charles Baltimore MD 21218

HECKMANN, RICHARD ANDERSON, PARASITOLOGY. *Current Pos:* assoc prof, 72-78, PROF ZOOL, BRIGHAM YOUNG UNIV, 78- *Personal Data:* b Salt Lake City, Utah, Dec 7, 31; m 62, Karen Olson; c Lisa, Nancy, Amy, Adam & Camille. *Educ:* Utah State Univ, BS, 54, MS, 58; Mont State Univ, PhD(zool), 70. *Prof Exp:* Instr biol, Contra Costa Col, 62-67; lectr, Fresno State Col, 70-71, asst prof & NSF res grant, 70-72. *Concurrent Pos:* Instr, Fresno City Col, 70-71. *Mem:* Am Soc Parasitologists; Soc Protozoologists; Am Fisheries Soc; Wildlife Dis Asn; World Maricult Soc. *Res:* Diseases of fishes; ultrastructure of fish and mammalian tissue; host-parasite relationships; taxonomy and control of fish parasites; free living and parasitic ciliated protozoa; blood parasites of birds; aquaculture and mariculture. *Mailing Add:* Dept Zool Brigham Young Univ Provo UT 84602. *Fax:* 801-378-7499, 378-7423; *E-Mail:* heckmanr@acdi.byu.edu

HECKROTTE, CARLTON, physiological ecology, herpetology, for more information see previous edition

HECKSCHER, STEVENS, FUNCTIONAL ANALYSIS, MATHEMATICAL ECOLOGY. *Current Pos:* NATURALIST & CONSERV BIOLOGIST, NATURAL LANDS TRUST, 81- *Personal Data:* b Philadelphia, Pa, Aug 21, 30; m 52; c 5. *Educ:* Harvard Univ, AB, 52, AM, 54, PhD(math), 60. *Prof Exp:* Instr math, Rutgers Univ, 59-60; from instr to prof, Swarthmore Col, 60-80. *Concurrent Pos:* NSF fac fel, Cambridge Univ, 66-67. *Mem:* Soc Conserv Biol; NY Acad Sci; AAAS. *Res:* Functional analysis, including Banach and topological vector spaces, especially spaces of measurable functions; applications of functional analysis, plant ecology, ecological management, mathematical ecology; conservation biology. *Mailing Add:* 10 Ridley Dr Wallingford PA 19086. *Fax:* 610-353-0517

HECKY, ROBERT EUGENE, LIMNOLOGY, PALEOLIMNOLOGY. *Current Pos:* RES SCIENTIST LIMNOL, DEPT FISHERIES & OCEANS, FRESH WATER INST, 73- *Personal Data:* b Akron, Ohio, June 21, 44. *Educ:* Kent State Univ, BS, 66; Duke Univ, PhD(zool), 71. *Prof Exp:* Fel & res assoc paleoecol, Woods Hole Oceanog Inst, 72-73. *Mem:* Am Soc Limnol & Oceanog; Int Asn Theoret & Appl Limnol; AAAS. *Res:* Description and quantification of the effects of man's use of land and water on aquatic ecosystems; reservoir ecology; limnology and paleolimnology of the African Great Lakes; phytoplankton ecology; biogeochemistry of silicon. *Mailing Add:* CCIW/NWRI 867 Lakeshore Rd PO Box 5050 Burlington ON L7R 4A6 Can

HECTOR, DAVID LAWRENCE, APPLIED MATHEMATICS, FLUID DYNAMICS. *Current Pos:* staff mem, 82-87, mgr, Soft Eng, 87-90, MGR, RES & DEVELOP, MELCO INDUSTS, 90- *Personal Data:* b Royal Oak, Mich, Apr 12, 39; m 61; c 2. *Educ:* Northwestern Univ, Ill, BSSE, 62, PhD(mech eng), 66. *Prof Exp:* Asst prof, Univ Denver, 66-70, assoc prof math, 70-80; mem staff, Stearns-Roger Eng, 80-82. *Mem:* AAAS; Soc Indust & Appl Math. *Res:* Asymptotic methods; partial differential equations; computer applications in mathematics education; computer solutions of differential equations. *Mailing Add:* Crestride Corp 6909 S Holly Cir Suite 310 Englewood CO 80112

HECTOR, MINA FISHER, BIOCHEMISTRY. *Current Pos:* ASST PROF CHEM, CALIF STATE UNIV, CHICO, 75- *Personal Data:* b Oak Park, Ill, Oct 15, 47; m 75; c 1. *Educ:* Lake Forest Col, BA, 69; Univ Colo, Boulder, PhD(chem), 75. *Prof Exp:* Teacher, Chicago Bd Educ, 69-70. *Concurrent Pos:* Investr, Univ Found, Calif State Univ, 76- *Mem:* Am Chem Soc; Am Soc Microbiol; Int Union Biochem. *Res:* Biodegradation of petroleum products and plant neoplastic natural products. *Mailing Add:* Dept Chem Calif State Univ 101 Orange St Chico CA 95929-0001

HEDAYAT, A SAMAD, MATHEMATICS, STATISTICS. *Current Pos:* PROF STATIST, UNIV ILL, CHICAGO, 74- *Personal Data:* b Jahrom, Iran, July 11, 37; m 70; c 2. *Educ:* Univ Tehran, BS, 61, MS, 62; Cornell Univ, MS, 66, PhD(statist), 69. *Prof Exp:* Jr statistician, Inst Econ Res, Tehran, 60-64; asst prof statist, Cornell Univ, 69-72; assoc prof, Fla State Univ, 72-74; res scientist, Ctr Drug Eval & Res, FDA, 89-90. *Concurrent Pos:* Instr, Univ Tehran, 62-64; vis asst prof, Mich State Univ, 69, Univ Guelph, 70 & Univ Calif, Berkeley, 80-81; NSF res grant, 70, 74, 75 & 93-; Air Force Off Sci Res grants, 72-92; assoc ed, Inst Math Statist, 73-80; bd mem, Commun Statist; coord ed, J Statist Planning & Inference; assoc ed, Am J Statist Asn, 93-; found sr scholar, Univ Ill. *Mem:* Fel Inst Math Statist; fel Am Statist Asn; Int Statist Inst. *Res:* Theory of linear models; theory and construction of F-square designs; sum composition of orthogonal Latin square designs; successive experiment designs; multi-stage experiments; balanced designs; fractional factorial designs; optimal experimental designs; survey designs; statistical inference; repeated measurements designs; environmental statistics; medical statistics. *Mailing Add:* Dept Math Statist & Comput Sci MC/249 Univ Ill 851 S Morgan St Chicago IL 60607-3041. *Fax:* 312-996-4426; *E-Mail:* u29132@uicvm.uic.edu

HEDBERG, JAMES D, PETROLEUM EXPLORATION. *Current Pos:* RES PROF, ENERGY & GEOSCI INST, UNIV UTAH, 95- *Personal Data:* b Maracaibo, Venezuela, Feb 18, 36; US citizen; m 59, Nancy Marshall; c Randi, Linda, Kristy & Laura. *Educ:* Pa State Univ, BS, 58; Stanford Univ, MS, 61; Princeton Univ, PhD(geol), 68. *Prof Exp:* Geol mgr, SE Asia Div, ESSO Explor Inc, 69-74, explor mgr, Int Div, 74-75, div mgr, SE Asia Div, 84-86; div mgr, SE Div, Exxon Co, 75-76, geol supvr prod, 76-77, dist mgr, SE Dist, 77-78, geol mgr, SE Dist, 78-81, mgr new ventures, Exxon Co Int, 86-92, mgr technol, Exxon Explor Co, 92-93, mgr explor technol, Exxon Corp, 93-94; vpres & dir explor, ESSO Norway, 81-84. *Concurrent Pos:* Crosby prof, Mass Inst Technol, 75. *Mem:* Am Asn Petrol Geologists. *Res:* Identification and evaluation of petroleum exploration and production opportunities worldwide. *Mailing Add:* 20127 Chateau Bend Dr Houston TX 77450

HEDBERG, KAREN K, MONOCLONAL ANTIBODIES, IMMUNO FLUORESCENTS *Current Pos:* RES ASSOC, INST MOLECULAR BIOL, UNIV ORE, 84- *Educ:* Univ Ore, PhD(biol). *Mailing Add:* Inst Molecular Biol Univ Ore Eugene OR 97403. *Fax:* 541-346-4643

HEDBERG, KENNETH WAYNE, PHYSICAL CHEMISTRY. *Current Pos:* from asst prof to assoc prof, 56-65, prof, 65-87, EMER PROF CHEM, ORE STATE UNIV, 87- *Personal Data:* b Portland, Ore, Feb 2, 20; m 54, Lise Smedvik; c Erik & Katrina. *Educ:* Ore State Col, BS, 43; Calif Inst Technol, PhD(chem), 48. *Hon Degrees:* Dr Phil, Univ Trondheim, Norway, 92. *Prof Exp:* Noyes fel chem, Calif Inst Technol, 48-49, res fel, 49-52, sr res fel, 53-56; Guggenheim & Fulbright fel, Univ Norway, 52-53. *Concurrent Pos:* Sloan fel, 56-60; Royal Norweg Coun Sci & Indust res fel, 62-63; res prof, Royal Norweg Coun Sci & Humanities, 69-70; chmn, Div Chem Physics, Am Phys Soc, 72-73; mem, Comn Electron Diffraction, Int Union Crystallog, 75-84; sr vis res fel, Univ Reading, England, 76-77; Norweg Marshal Plan fel, 82-83. *Mem:* Norweg Acad Sci & Lett; Sigma Xi; fel Am Phys Soc; Am Chem Soc; fel AAAS; Royal Norweg Soc Sci 2 Leh. *Res:* Electron diffraction in vapor state; molecular structure. *Mailing Add:* Dept Chem Ore State Univ Corvallis OR 97331. *E-Mail:* hedbergk@ucs.orst.edu

HEDBERG, MARGUERITE ZEIGEL, MATHEMATICS. *Current Pos:* adj prof, 46-49, assoc prof, 49-76, EMER ASSOC PROF MATH, UNIV SC, 76- *Personal Data:* b Kirksville, Mo, Aug 27, 07; m 36. *Educ:* Delta State Teachers Col, BS, 28; Univ Mo, MA, 29, PhD(math), 32. *Prof Exp:* Asst prof math, Delta State Teachers Col, 31-32; from asst prof to prof, Lander Col, 32-36; teacher, Baylor Univ, 38-40; prof & actg head dept, Delta State Teachers Col, 42-43; asst prof, Univ Ga, 43-44. *Mem:* Math Asn Am; Sigma Xi. *Res:* Geometry; invariant properties of a two-dimensional surface in hyperspace. *Mailing Add:* 738 Poinsettia St Columbia SC 29205

HEDDE, RICHARD DUANE, ANIMAL NUTRITION. *Current Pos:* mgr nutrit res, Smith Kline Animal Health, 78-81, mgr nutrit & microbiol res, 81-84, dir pre clin res, 84-89, VPRES, PHARMACEUT DEVELOP, SMITH KLINE BEECHAM ANIMAL HEALTH, 89- *Personal Data:* b Grand Forks, NDak, Dec 5, 45; m 71; c 5. *Educ:* NDak State Univ, BS, 67, MS, 69; Colo State Univ, PhD(animal nutrit), 73. *Prof Exp:* Rumen physiologist, Syntex Res, 73-76, feedlot nutritionist, 76-78. *Mem:* Am Soc Animal Sci; Am Dairy Sci Asn; Sigma Xi; Am Inst Nutrit. *Res:* Function of microbial fermentation with emphasis on improving the utilization of protein and energy by gastrointestinal microorganisms and subsequently by the host animal; discovery of therapeutic antibiotics for livestock; development of active animal health research compounds for FDA and EEC registration. *Mailing Add:* Pfizer Central Res Eastern Point Rd Groton CT 06340

HEDDEN, GREGORY DEXTER, ORGANIC CHEMISTRY, METEOROLOGY. *Current Pos:* RETIRED. *Personal Data:* b Louisville, Ky, Sept 13, 19; m 50, Genevieve Groves; c Thomas D & James J. *Educ:* Univ Chicago, BS, 42, MS, 50, PhD(org chem), 51. *Honors & Awards:* New Prod Award, Indust Res, 63; Award of Hon, Underwater Mining Inst, 81. *Prof Exp:* Chemist & asst to dir opers res, Inst Air Weapons Res, Univ Chicago, 51-54; res chemist org chem res & develop, E I du Pont de Nemours & Co, 54-59; tech dir, Trionics Corp, 59-62; pres & tech dir, Madison Res & Develop Labs, Inc, 62-66; prof environ resources & dir, State Tech Serv & Sea Grant Adv Serv, Exten Div, Univ Wis-Madison, 66-83; dir, Radiation Measurements Inc, Middleton, Wis, 83-89. *Concurrent Pos:* Consult, Active Corps Execs, Small Bus Admin, 84-87; pres, Gregory D Hedden & Assoc Ltd, Madison,

Wis, 87-; dir, John R Cameron Med Physics Found, Madison, Wis, 87-89. *Mem:* Fel AAAS; fel Am Inst Chemists; Int Asn Great Lakes Res; Am Chem Soc; Technol Transfer Soc. *Res:* Ultraviolet spectroscopy; marine resources; organometallics; dielectric fluids; meteorology; operations research; thermoluminescence radiation dosimetry; information retrieval. *Mailing Add:* 4410 Travis Terr Madison WI 53711-2922

HEDDEN, KENNETH FORSYTHE, MATHEMATICAL MODELING, ENVIRONMENTAL ASSESSMENT. *Current Pos:* environ engr, Environ Compliance Div, 88-94, ENVIRON CHEMIST, ROBINS ENG & SCI LAB, WARNER ROBINS AIR LOGISTICS CTR, ROBINS AFB, GA, 94- *Personal Data:* b Glendale, Calif, Aug 13, 41; m 63, 90, Suzanne Whitlock; c Randolph, Stephen & William. *Educ:* Univ Calif, Berkeley, BS, 63; Univ Calif, Davis, PhD(microbiol), 68; Univ Ga, Athens, MPA, 80. *Prof Exp:* USPHS fel microbial biochem, Sch Med, Tufts Univ, 69-70; Res assoc, Purdue Univ, West Lafayette, 70-72; bacteriologist-lab supt, Anheuser-Busch, Inc, Ind, 72-75; sanit engr, US Army Environ Hyg Agency, 75-78; sanit engr, Environ Res Lab, Athens, Ga, US Environ Protection Agency, 78-83, chem engr, Environ Monitoring Systs Lab, 83-88. *Mem:* Air & Waste Mgt Asn; Sigma Xi; Soc Indust Microbiol; Conf Fed Environ Engrs. *Res:* Kinetics of growth of individual cells; phospholipid metabolism in bacteria and in vitro protein synthesis; multimedia mathematical modeling of fate and transport of toxic substances. *Mailing Add:* 1736 Hwy 49 Ft Valley GA 31030-9233. *Fax:* 912-926-1276; *E-Mail:* drshed@accucom.net

HEDDEN, OWEN F, MECHANICAL ENGINEERING, NUCLEAR ENGINEERING. *Current Pos:* CONSULT ENGR. *Honors & Awards:* Bernard F Langer Nuclear Codes & Stand Award, Am Soc Mech Engrs, 94. *Mailing Add:* 3110 Phelps Rd West Suffield CT 06093-3021

HEDDLE, JOHN A M, CYTOGENETICS, RADIOBIOLOGY. *Current Pos:* assoc prof, 71-76, PROF BIOL, ATKINSON COL, YORK UNIV, 76- *Personal Data:* b Oakville, Ont, Nov 9, 38; m 62, Judith G McArthur; c Robert M & Catharine M. *Educ:* Univ Toronto, BSc, 61; Univ Tenn, PhD(radiation biol), 64. *Honors & Awards:* Elizabeth Goldschmidt Mem lectr, Hebrew Univ, Jerusalem, 88. *Prof Exp:* Res asst, Univ Tenn, 61-62; James Picker Found fel radiol res, Oak Ridge Nat Lab, 64-65 & Med Res Coun Radiobiol Res Unit, Eng, 65-66; asst res cytogeneticist, Lab Radiobiol, Univ Calif, San Francisco, 66-67, from asst prof to assoc prof radiol in residence, 67-71. *Concurrent Pos:* Head genetics, Cell Mutation Unit, Univ Sussex, 77-78 & Toronto Br, Ludwig Inst Cancer Res, 81-84; prof med & biophy, Univ Toronto, 81-84; NAm ed, Mutagenesis, 86-93; Institut Curie, Paris, 87-88, Lawrence Livermore Lab, 93-94. *Mem:* Environ Mutagen Soc (vpres & pres-elect, 85-86, pres, 86-87); Genetics Soc Can (vpres, 89-91, pres, 91-93); Can Soc Toxicol; Fed Can Biol Soc. *Res:* Chromosome aberrations induced by radiations or chemicals; chromosome structure; environmental mutagenesis; human chromosome breakage syndromes; carcinogenesis; Somatic mutation. *Mailing Add:* Dept Biol York Univ 4700 Keele St Toronto ON M3J 1P3 Can. *Fax:* 416-736-5698; *E-Mail:* fs300505@sol.yorku.ca

HEDDLESON, MILFORD RAYNORD, SOIL CHEMISTRY, CONSERVATION. *Current Pos:* from asst prof to prof, 62-72, COORDR ENVIRON AFFAIRS, PA STATE UNIV, UNIVERSITY PARK, 72- *Personal Data:* b Caldwell, Ohio, Dec 20, 21; m 45; c 2. *Educ:* Ohio State Univ, BS, 51, MS, 54, PhD, 57. *Prof Exp:* From asst to asst prof agron, Ohio State Univ, 53-62. *Mem:* Am Soc Agron; Soil Sci Soc Am; Soil Conserv Soc Am. *Res:* Land use; waste disposal; micro-nutrients. *Mailing Add:* 311 Waring Ave State College PA 16801

HEDDLESTON, KENNETH LUTHER, MICROBIOLOGY. *Current Pos:* RETIRED. *Personal Data:* b New Matamoras, Ohio, Dec 1, 16; m 45; c 2. *Educ:* Univ Md, BS, 51. *Prof Exp:* Bacteriologist, USDA, 51-53, vet bacteriologist, Animal Dis & Parasite Res Div, 53-59, sr res microbiologist, Nat Animal Dis Lab, 59-61, prin res microbiologist & proj leader, Animal Dis & Parasite Res Div, Nat Animal Dis Lab, 61- *Concurrent Pos:* Consult, Nat Acad Sci-Nat Res Coun. *Mem:* Fel AAAS; Am Soc Microbiol; Conf Res Workers Animal Dis; Am Col Vet Microbiol; Am Asn Avian Pathologists. *Res:* Pasteurella and their significance in animals. *Mailing Add:* 19 Johns Circle Lakeview AR 72642

HEDENBURG, JOHN FREDERICK, ORGANIC CHEMISTRY. *Current Pos:* from res chemist to sr res chemist, 58-69, SECT SUPVR, GULF RES & DEVELOP CO, 70- *Personal Data:* b Pittsburgh, Pa, Oct 23, 24; m 46; c 3. *Educ:* Univ Pittsburgh, BS, 48, MS, 52, PhD(chem), 58. *Prof Exp:* Asst petrol, Mellon Inst, 48-50, fel insecticides, 50-58. *Mem:* AAAS; Am Chem Soc; Soc Automotive Engrs. *Res:* Automotive fuels and lubricants; synthetic lubricants. *Mailing Add:* 189 Woodshire Dr Pittsburgh PA 15215-1730

HEDGCOCK, FREDERICK THOMAS, PHYSICS. *Current Pos:* RETIRED. *Personal Data:* b Toronto, Ont, May 18, 24; m 57; c 1. *Educ:* Univ Man, BSc, 49; Univ Western Ont, MSc, 50, PhD, 54. *Prof Exp:* Lectr physics, Royal Mil Col Can, 50-52; Nat Res Coun Can res fel, 54-56; from asst prof to assoc prof physics, Univ Ottawa, 56-61; group leader, Franklin Inst Philadelphia, 61-64; prof physics, McGill Univ, 64- *Res:* Low temperature and solid state physics; magnetic and electrical properties of metals, alloys and semiconductors. *Mailing Add:* RR 1 Bath ON K0H 1G0 Can

HEDGCOTH, CHARLIE, JR, BIOCHEMISTRY. *Current Pos:* From asst prof to assoc prof, 65-76, PROF BIOCHEM, KANS STATE UNIV, 76- *Personal Data:* b Graham, Tex, Jan 29, 36; m 56, Barbara A Graham; c Kelli Michelle, Kimberly & Charles Michael. *Educ:* Univ Tex, BS, 61; Univ Tex, PhD(chem), 65. *Concurrent Pos:* Vis assoc prof biochem, Univ BC, 75; NATO sr fel, 75; res grantee, NIH, NSF, USDA & Am Cancer Soc. *Mem:* Am Chem Soc; Am Soc Biol Chemists; AAAS. *Res:* Transfer RNA; differences in tRNA from normal and virus-transformed mammalian cells; aminoacyl-tRNA synthetases; characterization of genes for plant storage proteins; plant mitochondrial DNA; wheat cytoplasmic male sterility. *Mailing Add:* Dept Biochem Kans State Univ Willard Hall Manhattan KS 66506-3702. *Fax:* 785-532-7278; *E-Mail:* cxhedg@ksu.ksu.edu

HEDGE, GEORGE ALBERT, PHYSIOLOGY. *Current Pos:* prof & chmn physiol, 77-90, ASSOC DEAN RES, WVA UNIV MED CTR, MORGANTOWN, 90- *Personal Data:* b St Louis, Mo, June 7, 39; m 63; c 2. *Educ:* Univ Mo, BS, 61, MA, 63; Stanford Univ, PhD(physiol), 66. *Prof Exp:* Assoc prof physiol, Col Med, Univ Ariz, 68-77. *Concurrent Pos:* NIH res fel physiol, Fac Med, Univ Utrecht, 66-68; prog dir, NIH training grant; USPHS & NSF res grants. *Mem:* Endocrine Soc; Am Physiol Soc; Am Thyroid Asn; Int Soc Neuroendocrinol. *Res:* Neural and endocrine regulation of thyroid secretion and blood flow. *Mailing Add:* Off Assoc Dean Res WVa Univ Med Ctr PO Box 9104 Morgantown WV 26506-9104. *Fax:* 304-293-7038

HEDGECOCK, DENNIS, POPULATION, EVOLUTIONARY GENETICS. *Current Pos:* Res geneticist, Aquacult Proj, Bodega Marine Lab, 74-78, from asst prof to assoc prof, 78-91, PROF, DEPT ANIMAL SCI, UNIV CALIF, DAVIS, 91- *Personal Data:* b Torrance, Calif, Apr 23, 49; m 88. *Educ:* St Mary's Col, Calif, BS, 70; Univ Calif, Davis, PhD(genetics), 74. *Concurrent Pos:* Fulbright-Hayes researcher, Univ Belgrade, Yugoslavia, 76 & 82. *Mem:* Am Genetics Soc; Genetic Soc Am; Soc Study Evolution; fel AAAS; Am Soc Naturalists; Nat Shellfisheries Asn; Sigma Xi. *Res:* Population, evolutionary and quantitative genetics of marine organisms, particularly those having aquacultural or fisheries importance. *Mailing Add:* Bodega Marine Lab Univ Calif PO Box 247 Bodega Bay CA 94923-0247

HEDGECOCK, LE ROY DARIEN, AUDIOLOGY, SPEECH PATHOLOGY. *Current Pos:* RETIRED. *Personal Data:* b Roy, NMex, Mar 7, 13; m 41; c 3. *Educ:* Colo State Col Educ, MA, 39; Univ Wis, PhD, 49. *Prof Exp:* Teacher speech & lip reading, Ind State Sch for Deaf, 36-38 & NJ Sch for Deaf, 38-43; supvr speech clin, Univ Wis, 43-44; instr & speech clinician, Ind Univ, 44-46; asst prof & sr speech clinician, Univ Minn, 46-49; consult audiologist, Mayo Clin, Mayo Grad Sch Med, Univ Minn, 49-69, assoc prof audiol, 69-78. *Mem:* Am Speech & Hearing Asn; Speech Commun Asn. *Res:* Selection and fitting of hearing aids; hearing therapy; clinical psychology; physics of sound. *Mailing Add:* 121 NE 14th St Rochester MN 55906

HEDGECOCK, NIGEL EDWARD, SOLID STATE PHYSICS. *Current Pos:* asst prof, 61-65, ASSOC PROF PHYSICS, UNIV WINDSOR, 65- *Personal Data:* b Birmingham, Eng, June 2, 34; Can citizen; m 61; c 1. *Educ:* Univ BC, BA, 54, MA, 56; McMaster Univ, PhD(physics), 59. *Prof Exp:* Res asst, Max Planck Inst Chem, WGer, 59-61. *Mem:* Can Asn Physicists. *Res:* Electron spin resonance of transition ion impurities in crystals. *Mailing Add:* Dept Physics Univ Windsor Windsor ON N9B 3P4 Can

HEDGEPETH, JOHN M(ILLS), AEROSPACE ENGINEERING, APPLIED MATHEMATICS. *Current Pos:* PRES, DIGISIM CORP, 83- *Personal Data:* b Southern Pines, NC, June 29, 26; m 48, 76, 84, Linda Lenoir Mulack; c 3. *Educ:* Washington Univ, BS, 47 & 48; Va Polytech Inst, MS, 58; Harvard Univ, PhD(appl math), 62. *Prof Exp:* Res engr, Nat Adv Comt Aeronaut, 48-52, head, Dynamics & Aeroelasticity Div, 52-57, struct mech, 57-60; dept mgr struct & mat, Martin Marietta Corp, 61-63, dept dir eng & res, 63-67, vpres, Astro Res Corp, 67-72, pres, 72-83. *Concurrent Pos:* Instr, Hampton Grad Exten, Univ Va, 50-60; adj prof, Martin Exten, Drexel Inst Technol, 61-67; mem, Space Systs & Technol Adv Comt, NASA, 78-87; Aeronaut & Space Eng Bd, Nat Res Coun, 90-96. *Mem:* Nat Acad Eng; Int Aerospace Acad; fel Am Inst Aeronaut & Astronaut. *Res:* Structures and aeroelasticity; magnetohydrodynamics; large space systems; deployable space structures. *Mailing Add:* 202 E Pedregosa Santa Barbara CA 93101

HEDGES, DOROTHEA HUSEBY, biochemistry, enzymology; deceased, see previous edition for last biography

HEDGES, HARRY G, ELECTRICAL ENGINEERING. *Current Pos:* RETIRED. *Personal Data:* b Lansing, Mich, Oct 7, 23; m 44, Kamla King; c Susan & Martha. *Educ:* Mich State Univ, BS, 49, PhD(elec eng), 60; Univ Mich, MS, 54. *Prof Exp:* Electronics engr, Wright Air Develop Ctr, 49-51; res assoc, Willow Run Res Ctr, Univ Mich, 51-54; from instr to assoc prof elec eng, Mich State Univ, 54-69, prof & chmn, Dept Comput Sci, 69-84, prog dir, NSF, 84-88, head, Off Cross Disciplinary Activ, 88-92. *Mem:* Inst Elec & Electronics Engrs Comput Soc; Asn Comput Mach. *Res:* General system theory, including analysis, design and optimization; power system economic studies; general computer science; computing education. *Mailing Add:* Comput & Info Sci Dir Off Cross Disciplinary Act V NSF Arlington VA 22230

HEDGES, JOHN IVAN, GEOCHEMISTRY. *Current Pos:* res asst prof, 77-80, ASST PROF OCEANOG, UNIV WASH, 80- *Personal Data:* b Radnor, Ohio, Feb 10, 46; m 73; c 2. *Educ:* Capital Univ, BS, 68; Univ Tex, PhD(chem), 75. *Prof Exp:* Fel, Carnegie Geophys Lab, 75-77. *Mem:* Geochem Soc; AAAS. *Res:* Origin, pathways and fates of organic substances in marine and fresh water environments with emphasis on the geochemistries of lignins, carbohydrates, and humic substances. *Mailing Add:* Sch Oceanog WB-10 Univ Wash 3900 Seventh Ave NE Seattle WA 98195-0001

HEDGES, RICHARD MARION, PHYSICAL CHEMISTRY. *Current Pos:* from asst prof to assoc prof, 60-67, PROF CHEM, TEX A&M UNIV, 67- *Personal Data:* b Dallas, Tex, May 27, 27; m 49; c 3. *Educ:* Southern Methodist Univ, BS, 50; Iowa State Univ, PhD(phys chem), 55. *Prof Exp:* Asst chem, Iowa State Univ, 50-55; from assoc to instr, Univ Tex, 55-60. *Mem:* Am Phys Soc; Am Chem Soc. *Res:* Molecular spectroscopy and molecular quantum mechanics. *Mailing Add:* Dept Chem Tex A&M Univ College Station TX 77840

HEDGES, THOMAS REED, JR, OPHTHALMOLOGY. *Current Pos:* from asst prof to assoc prof, 57-72, PROF OPHTHAL, SCH MED, UNIV PA, 72-, ASST CHIEF OPHTHAL, 67- *Personal Data:* b Sandusky, Ohio, Oct 19, 23; m 46; c 3. *Educ:* Ohio State Univ, AB, 44; Cornell Univ, MD, 47; Univ Pa, MMedSci, 51. *Prof Exp:* Chief ophthal, Beaumont Army Hosp, El Paso, Tex, 52-54. *Concurrent Pos:* Fel neurol, Cleveland Clin, 48-49; fel neuro-ophthal, Wilmer Inst, Johns Hopkins Univ, 49-50; chief ophthal, Burlington Co Hosp, Mt Holly, 58- & Pa Hosp, 72-; sr consult ophthal, Philadelphia Gen Hosp, 67- *Mem:* Am Acad Ophthal & Otolaryngol; fel Am Col Surg; Am Ophthal Asn. *Res:* Neuro-ophthalmology; headache. *Mailing Add:* 714 E Main Morristown NJ 08057

HEDGLIN, WALTER L, pharmaceutical development, for more information see previous edition

HEDIN, ALAN EDGAR, ATMOSPHERIC PHYSICS, AERONOMY. *Current Pos:* SPACE SCIENTIST, GODDARD SPACE FLIGHT CTR, NASA, 67- *Personal Data:* b St Paul, Minn, Dec 24, 35; m 69; c 1. *Educ:* Univ Minn, BS, 58, MS, 61, PhD(physics), 66. *Prof Exp:* Mem tech staff, Bellcommun, Inc, 66-67. *Mem:* Am Geophys Union; Sigma Xi; Am Inst Aeronaut & Astronaut. *Res:* Structure and variations of the upper atmosphere. *Mailing Add:* 47 Shaw Ave Silver Spring MD 20904

HEDIN, DAVID ROBERT, ELEMENTARY PARTICLE PHYSICS. *Current Pos:* from asst prof to assoc prof, 87-95, PROF, PHYSICS DEPT, NORTHERN ILL UNIV, 95- *Personal Data:* b Chicago, Ill, Nov 11, 54; m 82; c 1. *Educ:* Southern Ill Univ, BS, 75; Univ Wis, PhD(physics), 80. *Prof Exp:* Res assoc, Physics Dept, State Univ NY, Stony Brook, 81-86. *Mem:* Am Phys Soc. *Res:* Experimental high energy physics; construction of a detector which studies 2 TeV protein-antiproton collisions. *Mailing Add:* Physics Dept Northern Ill Univ Faraday Hall Dekalb IL 60115

HEDIN, PAUL A, NATURAL PRODUCTS, PHEROMONES. *Current Pos:* RES CHEMIST, CROP SCI RES LAB, USDA, 62- *Personal Data:* b Maple Plain, Minn, July 9, 26; m 51, Inna Johns; c Deborah, Mark, Holly, Stuart, Rebecca & Dale. *Educ:* Univ Minn, BA, 48, BS, 50, MS, 53, PhD(biol chem), 58. *Honors & Awards:* Outstanding Chemist, Am Chem Soc, 75; Super Serv Honor Award, USDA, 75. *Prof Exp:* Chemist, Food & Container Inst, US Army, 58-60, head, Biochem Lab, 60-62. *Concurrent Pos:* Adj prof, Miss State Univ, 63-; fel, Div Pest Chem, Am Chem Soc, 78. *Mem:* Am Chem Soc. *Res:* Identification of biologically active agents in crop plants including host plant resistance factors; pheromones; insect and plant growth regulators; vitamins; insect hormone; chemistry of host plant resistance to pests. *Mailing Add:* 202 Arrow Dr Starkville MS 39759. *Fax:* 601-323-0915

HEDLEY, MARK ALLEN, NUMERICAL MODELLING OF AIR QUALITY, NUMERICAL WEATHER PREDICTION. *Current Pos:* RES OFFICER, NAT RES COUN, 93- *Personal Data:* b Ottawa, Ont, Dec 28, 59; m 87, Kathleen Lawryuik; c Jasmine & Sarah. *Educ:* Univ BC, BSc, 82; McGill Univ, dipl, 83, MSc, 86, PhD(metereol), 91. *Prof Exp:* Res assoc, Univ Toronto, 91-93. *Mem:* Am Geophys Union. *Res:* Modelling air quality in regions with complex geography. *Mailing Add:* Inst Chem Process & Environ Technol Nat Res Coun Ottawa ON K1A 0R6 Can. *Fax:* 613-952-1275; *E-Mail:* mark.hedley@nc.ca

HEDLEY, WILLIAM H(ENBY), PROCESS DEVELOPMENT. *Current Pos:* SR ENG SPECIALIST, EG&G MOUND APPL TECHNOLOGIES, 88- *Personal Data:* b St Louis, Mo, June 11, 30; m 57, Denise M Coyle; c Charles W, Kathleen (Ryerson), Davin W & Claire C. *Educ:* Washington Univ, BSc, 53, DSc(chem eng), 57. *Prof Exp:* Develop engr, Uranium Div, Mallinckrodt Chem Works, 56-61; res chem engr, Monsanto Res Corp, 61-63, sr res chem engr, 63-65, res group leader phys chem & eng, 65-67, res mgr, 67-69, dir res, Monsanto Environ-Chem Systs, 69-72, mgr, 72-83, sr res eng specialist, 83-88. *Concurrent Pos:* Adj prof, Dept Chem Eng, Univ Dayton, 85-89. *Mem:* Fel Am Inst Chem Engrs; Sigma Xi. *Res:* Process developement (tritium control, uranium processing, pollution abatement studies); prediction and measurement of physical properties of compounds; applied physical chemistry; materials development; gas transport (flow and diffusion through fine capillaries). *Mailing Add:* 3424 Lenox Dr Dayton OH 45429-1512

HEDLEY-WHYTE, ELIZABETH TESSA, NEUROPATHOLOGY, CELL BIOLOGY. *Current Pos:* from asst prof to assoc prof neuropath, 70-78, assoc prof path, 78-91, PROF PATH, HARVARD MED SCH, 91-; NEUROPATHOLOGIST, MASS GEN HOSP, 84- *Personal Data:* b London, Eng, Jan 17, 37; m 59, John. *Educ:* Univ Durham, MB & BS, 60; Am Bd Path, dipl, 66, neuropath dipl, 73; Univ Newcastle Tyne, MD, 76. *Prof Exp:* Neuropathologist, Children's Hosp Med Ctr, 73-77. *Concurrent Pos:* Consult, Neurol Dis Prog-Proj Rev Comt, NIH & USPH, 76-81, chmn, 79-81; mem bd adv, Harvard Med Sch, 76-88, fac coun, 88-91; consult, Children's Hosp Med Ctr, 77-; pathologist, New Eng Deaconess Hosp, 77-81; assoc neuropathologist, Mass Gen Hosp, 81-84, pathol training prog dir, 85-, dir neuropath, 89- *Mem:* Am Soc Cell Biol; Soc Neurosci; Am Asn Pathologists; Soc Pediat Res; Am Asn Neuropathologists (vpres, 90-91); Am Soc Exp Path. *Res:* Developmental neurobiology; electron microscopy; brain tumors; Alzheimers disease. *Mailing Add:* Neuropath Lab Warren 3 Mass Gen Hosp 14 Fruit St Boston MA 02114-2696. *Fax:* 617-726-7474

HEDLEY-WHYTE, JOHN, ANESTHESIOLOGY, PHYSIOLOGY. *Current Pos:* from asst to prof, 61-76, DAVID S SHERIDAN PROF ANESTHESIA & RESPIRATORY THER, HARVARD UNIV, 76-, PROF, DEPT HEALTH POLICY & MGT, HARVARD SCH PUB HEALTH, 88- *Personal Data:* b Newcastle-on-Tyne, Eng, Nov 25, 33; US citizen; m 59, Tessa. *Educ:* Cambridge Univ, BA, 55, MB, 58, MA, 59, MD, 72. *Hon Degrees:* AM, Harvard Univ, 67. *Honors & Awards:* Litchfield lectr, Oxford Univ, 71; Bishop lectr, NY Anesthesia; Egan lectr, Am Soc Respiratory Ther, 78. *Prof Exp:* House physician, St Bartholomew's Hosp, 58-59, house surgeon & resident anesthetist, 59-60, chief resident, 60; resident anesthesia, Mass Gen Hosp, 60-61, chief resident, 61-62. *Concurrent Pos:* Sec to Fac Med, Harvard Univ; chmn, Comt Ventilators, Int Stand Inst & Am Nat Stand Inst, 67-; anesthetist-in-chief, Beth Israel Hosp, Boston, Mass, 67-87. *Mem:* Am Physiol Soc; Asn Univ Anesthetists; Am Soc Anesthesiol; Int Anesthesia Res Soc; Am Col Physicians; Am Soc Testing & Mat. *Res:* Interaction between gases and proteins; chemistry of lung; effect of anesthetics on macromolecules; management of respiratory failure; high resolution electron microscopic radioautography; cold preservation of tissues for scanning electron microscopy. *Mailing Add:* Harvard Sch Pub Health 1400 VFW Pkwy Boston MA 02132-4927

HEDLIN, CHARLES P(ETER), MECHANICAL ENGINEERING. *Current Pos:* at HEDLIN CONSULT, INC, 88- *Personal Data:* b Renown, Sask, Can, Apr 18, 27; m 51; c 6. *Educ:* Univ Sask, BSc, 50; Univ Minn, MSc, 52; Univ Toronto, PhD(mech eng), 57. *Prof Exp:* Assoc prof eng, Ont Agr Col, 52-60; res officer, Inst Res Construct, Prairie Regional Sta, Nat Res Coun, 60-75, officer-in-chg, 75-88. *Mem:* Fel Am Soc Heating, Refrig & Air Conditioning Engrs. *Res:* Properties of moist materials; humidity measurement; field performance of thermal insulations; energy consumption in buildings; heating and air conditioning; heat and mass transfer. *Mailing Add:* Hedlin Consult Inc 26 Weir Crescent Saskatoon SK S7H 3A9 Can

HEDLIN, ROBERT ARTHUR, SOILS. *Current Pos:* RETIRED. *Personal Data:* b Saskatoon, Sask, Jan 5, 21; c 3. *Educ:* Univ Sask, BSA, 45; Univ Alta, MS, 47; Univ Wis, PhD(soils), 50. *Prof Exp:* From asst prof to prof soils, Univ Man, 50-86. *Mem:* Soil Sci Soc Am; Am Soc Agron; Agr Inst Can. *Res:* Soil fertility. *Mailing Add:* 910 Riverwood Ave Winnipeg MB R3T 1L1 Can

HEDLUND, GUSTAV ARNOLD, mathematics; deceased, see previous edition for last biography

HEDLUND, JAMES HOWARD, MATHEMATICS, STATISTICS. *Current Pos:* math statistician, US Dept Transp, 76-87, chief, Math Anal Div, 82-87, dir, driver & pedestrian res, 87-90, dir, Alcohol & State Progs, Nat Hwy Traffic Safety Admin, 90-95, ASSOC ADMIN, TRAFFIC SAFETY PROGS, US DEPT TRANSP, 95- *Personal Data:* b Ithaca, NY, July 24, 41; m 64; c 2. *Educ:* Cornell Univ, BA, 63; Univ Mich, Ann Arbor, MA, 65, PhD(math), 68. *Prof Exp:* Asst prof math, Univ Mass, Amherst, 68-74 & Smith Col, 74-76. *Mem:* Am Math Soc; Am Statist Asn; Math Asn Am. *Res:* Traffic safety; applied statistics. *Mailing Add:* Nat Hwy Traffic Safety Admin NTS-01 400 Seventh St SW Washington DC 20590. *Fax:* 202-366-1755; *E-Mail:* jhedlund@nhtsa.dot.gov

HEDLUND, JAMES L, COMPUTER APPLICATIONS IN MENTAL HEALTH. *Current Pos:* prof psychiat, 71-90, dir, Mo Inst Psychiat, 80-90, EMER PROF PSYCHIAT, UNIV MO, COLUMBIA, 91- *Personal Data:* b Los Angeles, Calif, Aug 1, 28; m 50, Doris Martinsen; c Ann (Lane) & Carey E. *Educ:* State Univ Iowa, BA, 50, MA, 51, PhD(clin psychol), 53. *Prof Exp:* Instr psychol, US Army Med Field Serv Sch, 54-55; chief clin psychol, US Army Hosp, Frankfurt, Ger, 56-59; dir clin psychol, Intern Training, Walter Reed Army Med Ctr, 59-63; psychol consult, Off US Army Surgeon Gen, 63-66; chief, Biomed Stress Res Div, US Army Med Res & Develop Command, 66-69; dir, comput support in mil psychiat, Walter Reed Army Med Ctr, 69-71. *Concurrent Pos:* Mem exec coun, Nat Acad Sci-Nat Res Coun Comt on Hearing, Bioacoust, Biomech, 66-69; mem exec coun, Armed Forces Comt on Vision, 66-69; surgeon gen rep, Behav Sci Study Sect, NIMH, 66-69, & Army Human Factors Adv Comt, 66-69. *Mem:* Am Psychol Asn. *Res:* Research and development of computer applications in mental health, including sophisticated clinical data collection instruments, clinical prediction models, assessment instruments involving expert systems technology, and empirical research associated with large state-wide patient data base. *Mailing Add:* 820 Pacific Ave Cayucos CA 93940

HEDLUND, LAURENCE WILLIAM, MICROSCOPIC IMAGING, MAGNET RESONANCE IMAGING. *Current Pos:* asst prof, 78-89, ASSOC PROF, DUKE UNIV MED CTR, 90- *Personal Data:* b Detroit, Mich, Mar 16, 37; m 65; c 4. *Educ:* Wayne State Univ, BS, 60; Univ Pittsburgh, PhD(animal physiol), 68. *Prof Exp:* Asst prof, Univ Missouri, 70-78. *Mem:* Am Thoracic Soc; Am Asn Lab Animal Sci; Radiol Soc NAm; Soc Magnetic Resonance Imaging; Soc Magnetic Resonance Med; Asn Univ Radiologists. *Res:* Development of ventilation anesthesia and physiological motioning methods for magnetic resonance microscopy of small animals; evaluation analysis of toxic injury and tumorigenesis in lungs, liver, and kidney with magnetic resonance imaging. *Mailing Add:* 2439 Tilghman Circle Chapel Hill NC 27514-6817

HEDLUND, RICHARD WARREN, GEOLOGY, PALYNOLOGY. *Current Pos:* sr res scientist, Amoco Prod Co, 71-74, staff res scientist & res group supvr, 74-82, spec res assoc, Geol Res Div, 82-92, GEOL CONSULT, AMOCO PROD CO, 92- *Personal Data:* b Lowell, Mass, Dec 11, 35; m 60, Donita D Mendenhall; c Richard W Jr, Phillip R & Karl E. *Educ:* Univ Mass, BSc, 57; Univ Okla, MSc, 60, PhD(geol), 63. *Honors & Awards:* Distinguished Serv Award, Am Asn Stratig Palynologists, 83. *Prof Exp:* Sr res scientist, Geol Res Div, Pan Am Petrol Corp, 62-68; proj supvr, Prod Res Ctr, Geol Sci Group, Atlantic-Richfield Co, 68-71. *Mem:* Soc Econ Paleontologists & Mineralogists; Am Asn Stratig Palynologists (pres, 74-75). *Res:* Mesozoic and Tertiary palynology. *Mailing Add:* 6923 S Knoxville Ave Tulsa OK 74136

HEDLUND, RONALD DAVID, RESEARCH DEVELOPMENT, MANAGEMENT OF CAMPUS-WIDE RESEARCH. *Current Pos:* VPROVOST RES, UNIV RI, 89- *Personal Data:* b Joliet, Ill, June 16, 41; m 64, Ellen L Parrish; c Karen M & David P. *Educ:* Augustana Col, Ill, BA, 63, Univ Iowa, MA, 64, PhD(polit sci), 67. *Prof Exp:* From asst prof to prof polit sci, Univ Wis, Milwaukee, 67-89, assoc dean, Grad Sch, 80-89. *Concurrent Pos:* Prin investr, Nat Conf State Legis Leaders & NSF, 66-67, NSF, 77-78 & 84-89 & Ford Found, 85-87; managing partner, Wis Pub Opinion & Mkt Res, 76-89; co-chair resource, Network RI Partnership Sci & Technol, 90- *Mem:* Nat Coun Univ Res Adminr; Soc Res Adminr; Am Polit Sci Asn; Southern Polit Sci Asn. *Res:* Effects of structural and organizational changes in state legislatures sought by studying system-level performance variables, policy output data, and individual-level perceptions. *Mailing Add:* 401 Oakwoods Dr Wakefield RI 02879

HEDMAN, DALE E, INSULATION COORDINATION. *Current Pos:* CONSULT, 87- *Personal Data:* b Albert City, Iowa, Aug 22, 35; m 62, Shirley Bertolino; c Eric, Karen & Chris. *Educ:* Univ Nebr, BS, 58, MS, 60. *Prof Exp:* Engr, Gen Elec Co, 60-69; prin engr, Power Technol, Inc, 69-76, treas, 76-83, vpres, 83-87. *Concurrent Pos:* Bd dir, Power Technol, Inc, 69-88, Pond Hill Homes, 82-, Empire Info Serv, 87-91; secy, Tech Comt, 37; bd trustees, Ellis Hosp, 93- *Mem:* Fel Inst Elec & Electronics Engrs; Int Elec Comn; Int Conf on Large High Voltage Elec Systs. *Res:* Specialized in the general area of electric power system insulation coordination having worked on major projects including the ITAIPU hydro project in Brazil; propagation on three phase lines. *Mailing Add:* Power Technol Inc PO Box 1058 Schenectady NY 12301. *Fax:* 518-346-2777

HEDMAN, FRITZ ALGOT, PHYSICAL CHEMISTRY. *Current Pos:* CONSULT, AIR POLLUTION CONTROL, INC, BALTIMORE, 72- *Personal Data:* b Arnas, Sweden, Sept 10, 06; nat US; m 36; c 1. *Educ:* State Col Wash, BS, 31, BA, 33, PhD(chem), 34. *Prof Exp:* Chemist, Exp Sta, State Col Wash, 34-36; jr seafood inspector, Food & Drug Admin, USDA, 36-37; refrig engr, Servel, Inc, Ind, 37-40; res chemist, Am Viscose Corp, 40-49; chemist & phys scientist, Chem Corps, Dept Army, 49-62; design specialist, Fairchild Stratos Corp, 62-63; consult analyst, Gen Elec Co, 63-64; nuclear physicist, Defense Commun Agency, Nat Mil Command Systs, 64-67; opers res analyst, USPHS Hosp, 67-72. *Mem:* AAAS; NY Acad Sci; Am Chem Soc. *Res:* Interfacial tension of mercury and hydrocarbon interfaces; military aerosols; radiological defense. *Mailing Add:* 7503 Wells Blvd Hyattsville MD 20783-1923

HEDMAN, STEPHEN CLIFFORD, GENETICS, MOLECULAR BIOLOGY. *Current Pos:* asst prof biol, 68-72, assoc prof biol & biochem, 72-90, PROF BIOL & BIOCHEM/MOLECULAR BIOL, UNIV MINN, DULUTH, 90-, ASSOC GRAD SCH DEAN, 90-, ASSOC VCHANCELLOR, 94- *Personal Data:* b Duluth, Minn, Apr 13, 41; m 66; c 3. *Educ:* Univ Minn, BA, 63; Stanford Univ, PhD(genetics), 68. *Prof Exp:* NIH fel, Univ Minn, St Paul, 68. *Concurrent Pos:* NIH res grant, 69-72; NSF grant, 85-88. *Mem:* Genetics Soc Am; Sigma Xi. *Res:* Mitochondrial biochemistry; cytoplasmic inheritance in Neurospora crassa; chromosome staining and identification; fish cytogenetics. *Mailing Add:* Dept Biol/ Biochem Univ Minn 2400 Oakland Ave Duluth MN 55812

HEDRICH, LOREN WESLEY, MEDICINAL & ORGANIC CHEMISTRY. *Current Pos:* SR RES CHEMIST, GULF OIL CHEM CO, CHEVRON CORP, 72- *Personal Data:* b Nampa, Idaho, Dec 10, 29; m 56; c 3. *Educ:* Idaho State Univ, BS, 52, MS, 64; Univ Kans, PhD(med chem), 69. *Prof Exp:* Res chemist, Gulf Res & Develop Co, 68-72. *Mem:* Am Chem Soc; AAAS; Sigma Xi. *Res:* Design and synthesis of pharmaceutically and agriculturally active chemicals. *Mailing Add:* 3202 Redwood Lake Dr Kingwood TX 77345-1127

HEDRICK, ANN VALERIE, MATE CHOICE, GENETICS OF BEHAVIOR. *Current Pos:* ASST PROF, REED COL, 93- *Personal Data:* b Washington, DC, Sept 28, 55. *Educ:* Univ Va, BA, 77; Univ Calif, MS, 84, PhD(zool), 87. *Prof Exp:* NIH fel ethol, Univ Tenn, 87-89; NATO fel, Simon Fraser Univ, 89-91; fel, Ctr Insect Sci, Univ Ariz, 91-92. *Mem:* Animal Behav Soc; Soc Study Evolution; Int Soc Behav Ecol; Int Soc Neuroethol; Sigma Xi. *Res:* How female animals choose their mates and whether they choose mates for particular genetic traits; the evolution of anti-predator and foraging behavior. *Mailing Add:* Dept Biol Reed Col 3203 SE Woodstock Portland OR 97202-8138. *Fax:* 503-777-7773; *E-Mail:* ahedrick@reed.edu

HEDRICK, CLYDE LEWIS, JR, PLASMA PHYSICS. *Current Pos:* MEM STAFF PLASMA PHYSICS, OAK RIDGE NAT LAB, 70- *Personal Data:* b Los Angeles, Calif, Oct 14, 39; m 63; c 2. *Educ:* Univ Calif, Los Angeles, BA, 62, MS, 65, PhD(plasma physics), 70. *Prof Exp:* Physicist, US Naval Ord Test Sta, Pasadena, 63-65. *Mem:* Am Phys Soc. *Res:* Magnetic equilibria; macroscopic stability; particle orbits; transport coefficients; fluid and kinetic models of transport and energy balance. *Mailing Add:* 144 Montana Ave Oak Ridge TN 37830

HEDRICK, GEORGE ELLWOOD, III, COMPUTER SCIENCE. *Current Pos:* asst prof, 70-74, assoc prof, 74-79, PROF COMPUT SCI, OKLA STATE UNIV, 80- *Personal Data:* b Columbus, Ohio, Apr 22, 43; m 76; c 4. *Educ:* Adams State Col, BA, 64; Iowa State Univ, MS, 68, PhD(comput sci), 70. *Prof Exp:* Programmer, Kaman Nuclear, 64-65; mathematician, US Army Air Defense Command, 65-66; sr systs analyst, Ames Lab, 70. *Concurrent Pos:* Prof math, Univ Nottingham, Gt Brit, 79. *Mem:* Asn Comput Mach; Math Asn Am. *Res:* Programming languages; operating systems; data structures. *Mailing Add:* Dept Comput & Info Sci MS 219 Okla State Univ Stillwater OK 74078

HEDRICK, HAROLD BURDETTE, ANIMAL HUSBANDRY. *Current Pos:* From instr to prof, 54-93, EMER PROF, FOOD SCI & NUTRIT DEPT, UNIV MO, COLUMBIA, 90- *Personal Data:* b Sinks Grove, WVa, May 11, 24; m 48, Virginia; c David A & Thomas E. *Educ:* WVa Univ, BS, 51; Univ Mo, MS, 55, PhD(animal husb), 57. *Honors & Awards:* Meats Res Award, Am Soc Animal Sci, 80; R C Pollock Award, Am Meat Sci Asn, 90. *Mem:* Am Soc Animal Sci; Inst Food Technologists; Am Meat Sci Asn. *Res:* Meat science; food science. *Mailing Add:* 902 Westover St Columbia MO 65203

HEDRICK, HAROLD G, ENVIRONMENTAL MICROBIOLOGY. *Current Pos:* RETIRED. *Personal Data:* b Youngstown, Ohio, Nov 15, 24; m; c 3. *Educ:* Centre Col, AB, 50; Marshall Col, MA, 52, WVa Univ, PhD(agr microbiol), 57. *Prof Exp:* Instr sci, St Mary's Sch Nursing, 52-53; asst, WVa Univ, 53-55, instr agr bact, 55-57; plant pathologist, USDA, 57-58; dir microbiol res, Woodard Res Corp, 58-61; proj res scientist, Appl Sci Labs, Gen Dynamics, Ft Worth, 61-69; prof, La Tech Univ, 69-87. *Concurrent Pos:* Fulbright award. *Mem:* AAAS; Am Soc Microbiol; Soc Indust Microbiol; Sigma Xi. *Res:* Environmental microbiology. *Mailing Add:* 807 Sandy Lane Ruston LA 71270

HEDRICK, IRA GRANT, AEROSPACE TECHNOLOGY. *Current Pos:* RETIRED. *Personal Data:* b Kansas City, Mo, Feb 10, 13; m 34, 93, Tina Weindorf; c Ira G III & J Karl. *Educ:* Univ Ark, Fayetteville, BS, 36; Princeton Univ, CE, 37. *Honors & Awards:* Spirit of St Louis Award, Am Soc Mech Engrs, 67; Sylvanus Albert Reed Award, Am Inst Aeronaut & Astronaut, 71. *Prof Exp:* Designer, Waddell & Hardesty, Consult Engrs, 37-42; chief struct engr, Eritrean Proj, Johnson, Drake & Piper, 42-43; struct engr, US Army Eng Dept, 43; proj stress analyst, Grumman Aircraft Eng Corp, 43-46, chief of struct, 46-57, chief tech engr, 57-63, vpres eng, 63-70, sr vpres & dir tech opers, 70-73, sr vpres & dir advan systs technol, 73-75, sr vpres & presidential asst corp technol, 75-80, sr mgt consult, 80-94. *Concurrent Pos:* Mem vis comt, Dept Physics, Lehigh Univ, 66-74; Dept Aeronaut & Astronaut, Mass Inst Technol, 67-73; mem, Res & Technol Adv Coun & chmn, Res & Technol Adv Comt Mat & Struct, NASA, 71-77; mem, Aeronaut & Space Eng Bd, Nat Res Coun, 77-81; mem, USAF Sci Adv Bd, 76-84, NASA Aerospace Safety Adv Panel, 79-84. *Mem:* Nat Acad Eng; hon fel Am Inst Aeronaut & Astronaut. *Res:* Aerospace structures and materials. *Mailing Add:* 11 Riviera Ct Great River NY 11739

HEDRICK, JACK LEGRANDE, CHROMATOGRAPHY. *Current Pos:* from instr to assoc prof, 63-73, PROF CHEM, ELIZABETHTOWN COL, 73- *Personal Data:* b Glen Rock, Pa, July 23, 37; m 60, Doris Hostetter; c Joseph L & Robert B. *Educ:* Elizabethtown Col, BS, 59; Univ. Pittsburgh, MS, 62. *Prof Exp:* Instr chem, Albright Col, 62-63. *Mem:* AAAS; Sigma Xi; Am Chem Soc. *Res:* Chromatography. *Mailing Add:* Elizabethtown Col One Alpha Dr Elizabethtown PA 17022-2298

HEDRICK, JERRY LEO, GAMETE BIOLOGY, FERTILIZATION. *Current Pos:* from asst prof to assoc prof, 65-74, PROF BIOCHEM, UNIV CALIF, DAVIS, 74- *Personal Data:* b Knoxville, Iowa, Mar 11, 36; m 57, Karel J Harper; c Michael L, Kerry L, Benjamin A & Kimberly A. *Educ:* Iowa State Univ, BS, 58; Univ Wis, PhD(physiol chem), 61. *Prof Exp:* Res assoc physiol chem, Univ Wis, 61-62; res assoc biochem, Univ Wash, 62-65. *Concurrent Pos:* NIH fel, 62-64; sabbatical, Cambridge Univ & Guggenheim Found fel, 71-72; sabbatical, Hokkaido Univ, Sapporo, Japan, 85-86 & 89; vis scientist, Mitsubishi-Kasei Inst Life Sci, Japan, 89. *Mem:* AAAS; Am Chem Soc; Am Soc Biol Chemists; Soc Study Reproduction; Sigma Xi; Am Soc Cell Biol. *Res:* Structure-function relations of proteins and glycoproteins; molecular & cellular biology of fertilization. *Mailing Add:* Sect Molecular & Cellular Biol Univ Calif Davis CA 95616-8755. *Fax:* 530-752-3085; *E-Mail:* jlhedrick@ucdavis.edu

HEDRICK, PHILIP WILLIAM, GENETICS. *Current Pos:* PROF ZOOL, ARIZ STATE UNIV, 94- *Personal Data:* b Nov 21, 42; US citizen; m 65; c 2. *Educ:* Hanover Col, BA, 64; Univ Minn, MS, 66, PhD(genetics), 69. *Prof Exp:* Fel genetics, Univ Chicago, 68-69; asst prof systs & ecol, Univ Kans, 69-73, assoc prof genetics, 73-76, assoc prof syst & ecol, 76-87; prof biol, Pa State Univ, 87-94. *Mem:* Genetics Soc Am; Am Soc Nat; Soc Study Evolution. *Res:* Population and quantitative genetics; population ecology and competition in drosophila. *Mailing Add:* Dept Zool Ariz State Univ PO Box 871501 Tempe AZ 85287-1501

HEDRICK, RONALD PAUL, VIROLOGY. *Current Pos:* PROF INFECTIOUS DIS FISH, DEPT MED & EPIDEMIOL SCH VET MED, UNIV CALIF, DAVIS, 82- *Personal Data:* b Tacoma, Wash, Aug 2, 50; m 73; c 2. *Educ:* Ore State Univ, BS, 75, PhD(microbiol), 80; Univ Ore, BS, 76. *Honors & Awards:* Beechum Res Excellence Award, Pres Fish Health Sect, AFS, 88. *Mem:* Sigma Xi; Am Soc Microbiol; Soc Gen Microbiol; Europ Asn Fish Pathologists; Am Fish Soc; Fish Health Soc. *Res:* Study of infectious diseases of fish and shellfish and their detection, prevention and treatment. *Mailing Add:* Dept Med Vet Med Univ Calif Davis CA 95616

HEDRICK, ROSS MELVIN, ORGANIC CHEMISTRY. *Current Pos:* RETIRED. *Personal Data:* b West Salem, Ill, Apr 27, 21; m 49; c 3. *Educ:* Univ Ill, BS, 43; Ind Univ, AM, 44, PhD(org chem), 47. *Prof Exp:* Res chemist, Monsanto Co, 47-52, res group leader, 52-63, proj mgr & scientist, 63-69, sr sci fel, 69-72, distinguished sci fel, 72-86. *Mem:* AAAS; Am Chem Soc. *Res:* Organic fluorine compounds; isoflavones; herbicides; synthetic soil conditioners; polyelectrolytes; condensation polymers; ionic polymerization; reinforced plastics; block copolymers; metal/plastic laminates; nylon block copolymer reaction injection molding. *Mailing Add:* 300 Chasselle Lane St Louis MO 63141-7335

HEDRICK, THEODORE ISAAC, FOOD SCIENCE. *Current Pos:* RETIRED. *Personal Data:* b Polson, Mont, Sept 11, 12; m 42; c 2. *Educ:* Mont State Univ, BS, 35, MS, 37; Iowa State Univ, PhD(dairy bact), 41. *Honors & Awards:* USDA Merit Award, 55; Dairy Res Award, Am Dairy Sci Asn, 72. *Prof Exp:* From asst to instr dairy indust, Mont State Univ, 35-39; asst prof, Iowa State Univ, 42-44; dir labs, North Star Dairy, 46-49; nat qual coordr & chemist chg, Dairy & Poultry Labs, Dairy Div, Agr Mkt Serv, USDA, 49-56; from assoc prof dairy to prof, Mich State Univ, 56-78, plant mgr, 56-67, emer prof food sci, 79-88. *Concurrent Pos:* Mem, Bd Dirs, Am Dairy Sci Asn, 73-76; food technol consult, Mich State Univ Int Progs Indonesia & Brazil, 75-78; consult packaging, UN Food & Agr Orgn, 79. *Mem:* AAAS; Am Dairy Sci Asn; Inst Food Technologists; Int Asn Milk, Food & Environ Sanit. *Res:* Drying of milk products, ultra high temperature sterilization and aseptic packaging; new dairy foods and processes; airborne microbiology. *Mailing Add:* 1546 Sherman St SE Grand Rapids MI 49506

HEDSTROM, GERALD WALTER, MATHEMATICS. *Current Pos:* MATHEMATICIAN, LAWRENCE LIVERMORE LAB, 77- *Personal Data:* b Kenosha, Wis, July 31, 33; m 57; c 1. *Educ:* Univ Wis, BS, 55, MS, 56, PhD(math), 59. *Prof Exp:* From instr to asst prof math, Univ Mich, Ann Arbor, 59-68; from assoc prof to prof math, Case Western Res Univ, 68-77. *Mem:* Am Math Soc; Soc Indust & Appl Math. *Res:* Numerican analysis. *Mailing Add:* Lawrence Livermore Nat Lab PO Box 808 Livermore CA 94550-0808

HEDSTROM, JOHN RICHARD, MATHEMATICS, INTELLIGENT SYSTEMS. *Current Pos:* SOFTWARE SYSTS ENGR, TEX INST, 83- *Personal Data:* b Kansas City, Kans, Oct 14, 37; m 67; c 1. *Educ:* Univ Kans, BA, 59, MA, 66, PhD(algebra), 70; Southern Methodist Univ, MS, 90. *Prof Exp:* Assoc prof math, Univ NC, Charlotte, 70-83, assoc prof comput sci, 81-83. *Concurrent Pos:* Vis prof, Comput Sci Dept, Univ NC Chapel Hill, 80-81. *Mem:* Inst Elec & Electronics Engrs; Math Asn Am. *Res:* Pseudo-valuation domains; signal processing Ada Compiler; Ada-OODB Interface. *Mailing Add:* Texas Instruments 6550 Chase Oaks Dr MS 8935 Plano TX 75043

HEDTKE, JAMES LEE, AQUATIC TOXICOLOGY, FISH PHYSIOLOGY. *Current Pos:* ASSOC PROF PHARMACOL, ORE HEALTH SCI UNIV, 80- *Personal Data:* b Clintonville, Wis, Nov 22, 43; m 65; c 1. *Educ:* Univ Wis, Oshkosh, BS, 67; Univ Minn, PhD(pharmacol), 73. *Prof Exp:* Res assoc, Ore State Univ, 73-74 & 76-77, NIH res assoc, 74- 76, asst prof fisheries, 78-82. *Concurrent Pos:* Consult, Ore State Bd Dent Examr, 78-82 & Wash State Bd Dent Examr, 81-82; asst prof pharmacol, Ore Health Sci Univ, 77-80; staff mem, St Vincent's Hosp, 86- *Mem:* Sigma Xi. *Res:* Aquatic toxicology; comparative physiology and pharmacology with emphasis on the cardiovascular system of fish; interaction of aquatic toxicants. *Mailing Add:* 7341 NW Summit View Dr Portland OR 97229

HEE, CHRISTOPHER EDWARD, MATHEMATICS, CHEMICAL ENGINEERING. *Current Pos:* lectr, 69-70, from asst prof to assoc prof, 70-95, PROF MATH, EASTERN MICH UNIV, 95- *Personal Data:* b Olean, NY, Oct 2, 39; m 63, Joanne Smith; c Christine, Cynthia & Cheryl. *Educ:* Univ Detroit, BChE, 61; Univ Notre Dame, PhD(math), 71. *Prof Exp:* Eng aide, Air Preheater Corp, 58-61; teacher, Penn Yan Cent Sch, NY, 63-64. *Mem:* Math Asn Am. *Res:* Algebraic topology; Steenrod algebra; characteristic classes; relations over Steenrod algebra between characteristic classes; mathematical modeling; catastrophe theory. *Mailing Add:* Dept Math Eastern Mich Univ Ypsilanti MI 48197. *E-Mail:* mth___hee@emuvax.emich.edu

HEEB, MARY JO, REGULATION OF COAGULATION ENZYMES, PROSTATE SPECIFIC ANTIGEN. *Current Pos:* fel, 83-88, sci assoc, 88-92, ASST MEM, SCRIPPS RES INST, 92- *Personal Data:* b Lousville, Ky, Sept 20, 42; div; c Angela, Randall, Derek & Cynthia. *Educ:* Univ Fla, BS, 66, MS, 68; Georgetown Univ, PhD(biochem), 83. *Honors & Awards:* Wilhelm Turk Prize, Austrian Soc Hemat & Oncol, 86. *Prof Exp:* Res asst biochem, Univ Fla, 68-69; res asst pharm, Univ Miami, 69-70; res asst functional biol, Univ Miami Marine Sci, 70-71; teacher algebra, Hoggard High Sch, 71-72; instr, Univ NC, Wilmington, 73-75; group leader, Hazleton Labs, 75-78 & 81-83. *Concurrent Pos:* Consult, US Off Saline Water Res, 72-73. *Mem:* Int Soc Thrombosis & Hemostasis; Am Soc Biochem & Molecular Biol; Am Heart Asn; AAAS. *Res:* Study of interactions and regulation of coagulation proteins and their inhibitors, interactions of prostate specific antigen with inhibitors, carbohydrate-lectin interactions, enzymes; protease inhibitors. *Mailing Add:* 10550 N Torrey Pines Rd La Jolla CA 92037. *Fax:* 619-784-2243; *E-Mail:* heeb@scripps.edu

HEEBNER, CHARLES FREDERICK, PLANT PHYSIOLOGY, FORESTRY. *Current Pos:* RETIRED. *Personal Data:* b Norwich, Conn, Apr 30, 38; m 59, Beverly C Banks; c Kelli (Arden). *Educ:* Univ Conn, BA, 60, MS, 63; Wash State Univ, PhD(bot), 70. *Prof Exp:* Plant physiologist, Forest-Animal Unit, Bur Sport Fisheries & Wildlife, US Fish & Wildlife Serv, 68-74; res assoc, Western Wash Res & Ext Ctr, Wash State Univ, 75-76; natural resource res technician, State Dept Natural Resources, Olympia, 77-83. *Mem:* Sigma Xi; Am Soc Plant Physiologists. *Res:* Forest tree physiology and its relation to animal damage; soil biochemistry; forest genetics; Douglas-fir seed physiology. *Mailing Add:* 5503 110th Ave SW Olympia WA 98502-9220

HEEBNER, DAVID RICHARD, SCIENCE ADMINISTRATION, TECHNICAL MANAGEMENT. *Current Pos:* RETIRED. *Personal Data:* b Hackensack, NJ, Feb 27, 27; m 50; c 4. *Educ:* Newark Col Eng, BSEE, 50; Univ Southern Calif, MSEE, 55. *Prof Exp:* Systs engr, Hughes Aircraft Co, 53-60; consult, Nat Acad Sci, 60-61; mgr, Navy Systs Lab, Hughes Aircraft Co, 61-68; asst dir, Off Secy Defense, 68-70, dep dir defense res & eng, 70-75; vchmn bd & exec vpres, Sci Applns Int Corp, 75-93. *Concurrent Pos:* Mem, Defense Sci Bd, 87-90, Naval Studies Bd, Nat Acad Sci, 79-82; chmn, Naval Res Adv Comt, 82-86, mem, 86-87; vchmn, Defense Sci Bd, 93-; chmn, Nat Acad Sci, Naval Studies Bd. *Mem:* Asn Unmanned Vehicle Systs (pres, 76-77); fel Inst Elec & Electronics Engrs. *Res:* Conceived initial design and led team that built the first successful towed line-array sonar, a breakthrough leading to important developments in surface and submarine surveillance systems; development of a display system that was the first use of integrated circuits in the US Navy. *Mailing Add:* Sci Applns Inc 1710 Goodridge Dr PO Box 1303 McLean VA 22102

HEED, JOSEPH JAMES, MATHEMATICS. *Current Pos:* from asst prof to assoc prof, 62-74, head dept, 68-78, PROF MATH, NORWICH UNIV, 74- *Personal Data:* b New York, NY, Sept 22, 31; m 57; c 3. *Educ:* Us Mil Acad, BS, 54; St John's Univ, NY, MS, 61; Univ Nancy, DSc(math), 65. *Prof Exp:* Instr math, St Joseph's Col, NY, 58-60 & St John's Univ, NY, 60-62. *Mailing Add:* Dept Math Norwich Univ S Main St Northfield VT 05663

HEED, WILLIAM BATTLES, ZOOLOGY. *Current Pos:* from asst prof to prof genetics, 58-80, prof 80-94, EMER PROF, ECOL & EVOLUTIONARY BIOL, UNIV ARIZ, 94- *Personal Data:* b West Chester, Pa, June 9, 26; m 54; c 3. *Educ:* Pa State Univ, BS, 50; Univ Tex, MS, 52, PhD(zool), 55. *Prof Exp:* Res assoc genetics, Univ Tex, 55-56; instr, Univ Pa, 56-58. *Concurrent Pos:* Prog dir, Syst Biol, Ecol & Pop Biol Sect, Biol & Med Sci Div, NSF, 75-76. *Mem:* AAAS; Am Soc Naturalists (vpres, 78); Soc Study Evolution; Genetics Soc Am; Sigma Xi. *Res:* Evolutionary genetics; population biology of Drosophila. *Mailing Add:* Dept Ecol & Evol Biol Univ Ariz PO Box 210088 Tucson AZ 85721

HEEDE, BURCHARD HEINRICH, WATERSHED MANAGEMENT, EARTH SCIENCES. *Current Pos:* RETIRED. *Personal Data:* b Riga, Latvia, Dec 3, 18; nat US; m 44; c 3. *Educ:* Univ Gottingen, BS, 47, MF, 49; Colo State Univ, PhD(watershed resources), 67. *Prof Exp:* Res forester, Watershed Mgt, US Forest Serv, 68-73, prin hydraul eng, 74-77, res hydrologist, Rocky Mt Forest & Range Exp Sta, 78-93. *Concurrent Pos:* Forestry off, Food & Agr Orgn, UN, Greece, 68-70. *Mem:* Am Geophys Union; Sigma Xi; Int Asn Hydrol Sci. *Res:* Hydrology; hydraulics; erosion control; fluvial geomorphology; development of gully control systems; dynamics of stream systems, interactions between streams and stream-side forests, overland flow and sediment delivery from forests and wood lands. *Mailing Add:* 5629 S Marine Dr Tempe AZ 85283

HEEGER, ALAN J, POLYMERCHEMISTRY. *Current Pos:* PROF MAT, UNIV CALIF, SANTA BARBARA, 82-, PROF PHYSICS, 84-, DIR, INST POLYMERS & ORG SOLIDS, 82- *Personal Data:* b Sioux City, Iowa, Jan 22, 36; m 57; c 2. *Educ:* Univ Nebr, BS, 53; Univ Calif, PhD(physics), 61. *Hon Degrees:* MA, Univ Pa, 71; DSc, Univ de Mons-Hainart, Belgium, 93; Dr, Linskuping Univ, Sweden, 96. *Honors & Awards:* Oliver Buckley Prize Solid State Physics, 83; John Scott Award & Medal, 89; Balzan Prize Sci New Mat, 95. *Prof Exp:* Res assoc physics, Univ Calif, 61-62; from asst prof to assoc prof, Dept Physics, Univ Pa, Philadelphia, 62-67, prof physics, 67-82, dir, Lab Res Struct Matter, 74-81, actg vprovost res, 81-82. *Concurrent Pos:* Sloan Found fel, 63-66; Guggenheim fel & vis prof, Univ Geneva, 68-69; bd trustees, Aspen Ctr for Physics, 73-76. *Mem:* Fel Am Phys Soc; Am Chem Soc. *Res:* Fundamental physics of materials synthesized by chemical techniques; one-dimensional solids. *Mailing Add:* Dept Physics Univ Calif Santa Barbara CA 93106

HEEKS, R(OBERT) E(UGENE), CHEMICAL ENGINEERING, MATERIALS SCIENCE. *Current Pos:* RETIRED. *Personal Data:* b Rochester, NY, Jan 19, 28; m 55, Shirley Stam; c Leslie, Robert, Mark, Kathleen & Elizabeth. *Educ:* Univ Rochester, AB, 52, MS, 54, PhD(chem eng), 57. *Prof Exp:* Res assoc rheol, Univ Rochester, 54-55; processing engr photog papers & films, Xerox Corp, 55-60, sr chemist, 60-62, scientist, 62-66, mgr res & eng subsect, 66-73, mgr photoreceptor eng, 73-77, mgr mfg develop eng, 77-87. *Concurrent Pos:* Consult, Robert Christian, Inc, 78-84. *Mem:* Am Chem Soc; Am Inst Chem Engrs; Soc Photog Sci & Eng; Sigma Xi. *Res:* Photographic emulsion; process engineering of photo products plant; rheology of suspensions; cellulose chemistry as related to properties of paper; selenium and organic photoreceptors; coating technology. *Mailing Add:* 3538 W Lake Rd Canandaigua NY 14424

HEELIS, RODERICK ANTONY, IONOSPHERIC DYNAMICS. *Current Pos:* RES SCIENTIST SPACE PHYSICS, UNIV TEX, DALLAS, 73- *Personal Data:* b Luton, Eng, June 13, 48; m 69. *Educ:* Univ Sheffield, BSc, 69, PhD(math), 73. *Concurrent Pos:* Prin investr, Dynamics Explorer Mission, NASA, 76- *Mem:* Am Geophys Union. *Res:* Studies of neutral and charged particle dynamics in the upper atmospheres of the earth and planets; design and operation of satellite borne instrumentation for obtaining experimental data. *Mailing Add:* 7424 Stoney Point Dr Plano TX 75025

HEENAN, WILLIAM A, CHEMICAL ENGINEERING, PROCESS CONTROL. *Current Pos:* prof, 75-80, PROF, TEX A&M, KINGSVILLE, 82-, DEPT CHMN, CHEM ENG, 93- *Personal Data:* b Lansdale, Pa, Apr 17, 41; m 86; c 2. *Educ:* Univ Detroit, BChE, 64, MS, 67, DEng(chem eng), 69. *Prof Exp:* Coop engr, Ford Motor Co, 62-64; process engr, Monsanto Co, 64-67; res engr, Atomic Power Develop Assocs, 67-69; prof chem eng, Univ PR, 69-75; engr mgt, Celanese Chem Corp, 80-82. *Concurrent Pos:* Consult, Occidental Chem Corp, Pavillion, Lyondell, Ancus Chem Co. *Mem:* Am Inst Chem Engrs; Am Chem Soc. *Res:* Fuel and control rod design for liquid metal fast breeder reactor; chemical processing of products from the sea, agar production; computation of chemical equilibria and chemical process optimization; computer process control, error detection & data reconciliation. *Mailing Add:* Dept Chem Eng Tex A&M Univ Kingsville TX 78363. *Fax:* 512-595-2106; *E-Mail:* kfwahoo@taimvsi

HEER, CLIFFORD V, LASERS, QUANTUM OPTICS. *Current Pos:* from asst prof to prof physics, 49-90, PROJ SUPVR, UNIV RES FOUND, OHIO STATE UNIV, 55-, EMER PROF PHYSICS, 90- *Personal Data:* b Archbold, Ohio, May 31, 20; m 49, Esther J Leonard; c Barbara, Deborah & Daniel. *Educ:* Ohio State Univ, BSc, 42, PhD(physics), 49. *Honors & Awards:* William A Fowler Award, 90. *Prof Exp:* Mem Signal Corps, US Army, 42-46. *Concurrent Pos:* Consult, Ramo-Wooldridge Corp, 56-58, Space Tech Labs, 58-65, Honeywell, Inc, 64-65, TRW Inc, 65-70 & Army Res Off, 70-71. *Mem:* Fel Am Phys Soc. *Res:* Low temperature solid state physics; laser physics; physics related to space technology; laser gyro. *Mailing Add:* Dept Physics Ohio State Univ 174 W 18th Ave Columbus OH 43210

HEER, EWALD, SYSTEMS ENGINEERING, ENGINEERING PHYSICS. *Current Pos:* PRES, HEER ASSOCS INC, 84- *Personal Data:* b Friedensfeld, Ger, July 28, 30; US citizen; m 52, Hannelore Oehlers; c Thomas & Eric. *Educ:* Univ Hamburg, CE, 53; City Col New York, BS, 59; Columbia Univ, MS, 60, CE, 62; Hannover Tech Univ, DESc, 64. *Prof Exp:* Engr struct, Hinz Architects, Ger, 51-54, Dixon & Evans, Can, 54-55 & Hewitt-Robins, Inc, NY, 56-59; sr res eng, Paul Weidlinger Consult Engrs, 60-64; tech specialist struct dynamics, MacDonnell Aircraft Corp, 64-65; scientist, Space Sci Lab, Gen Elec Co, 65-66, res group leader struct mech, 66; supvr struct & dynamics res, Jet Propulsion Lab, Calif Inst Technol, 66-70; prog mgr, Lunar Explor Off, NASA Hq, 70-71; mgr, Advan Tech Studies off, Jet Propulsion Lab, Calif Inst Technol, 71-77, dir, autonomous systs & space mech, 77-84. *Concurrent Pos:* Lectr, Univ Hamburg, 63, Pa State Univ, 65-66, Univ Southern Calif, 69 & Univ Calif, Los Angeles, 69; adj prof indust & systs eng, Univ Southern Calif, 73-84; ed robotics, Mechanisms & Mach Theory J, 74-; dir, Inst Technoecon Systs, Univ Southern Calif, 78-84; prof indust & systs eng, Univ Southern Calif, 78-84; chmn, Comput Eng Div, Am Soc Mech Engrs, 84. *Mem:* Am Soc Civil Engrs; fel Am Soc Mech Engrs; assoc fel Am Inst Aeronaut & Astronaut; NY Acad Sci; Inst Elec & Electronics Engrs; Opers Res Soc Am; Am Asn Artificial Intel. *Res:* Aerospace engineering systems; automation; engineering design; cybernetics; man-machine systems; robotics; machine intelligence. *Mailing Add:* 5329 Crown Ave La Canada CA 91011-2807

HEEREMA, NICKOLAS, MATHEMATICS. *Current Pos:* RETIRED. *Personal Data:* b Hospers, Iowa, Oct 5, 22; m 47; c 4. *Educ:* Univ Mich, BS, 44; Univ Tenn, MS, 49, PhD, 51. *Prof Exp:* Res engr, Union Carbide Chem Co, 46-48; prof math, Fla State Univ, 51- *Concurrent Pos:* NSF grants, 60-71. *Mem:* Am Math Soc; Math Asn Am. *Res:* Pure mathematics; group theory; ring theory. *Mailing Add:* 3204 Enterprise Dr Tallahassee FL 32312

HEEREMA, RUURD HERRE, mineral engineering, for more information see previous edition

HEEREN, JAMES KENNETH, ORGANIC CHEMISTRY. *Current Pos:* asst prof, 62-67, ASSOC PROF CHEM, TRINITY COL, CONN, 67- *Personal Data:* b Fitchburg, Mass, Mar 22, 29; m 56. *Educ:* Tufts Univ, BS, 51, MS, 52; Mass Inst Technol, PhD(chem), 60. *Prof Exp:* Chemist, Am Cyanamid Co, 54-56, res chemist, 60-61; fel chem, Sch Advan Study, Mass Inst Technol, 61-62. *Concurrent Pos:* Guest prof, Univ Heidelberg, Ger, 69. *Mem:* Am Inst Chem; Am Chem Soc. *Res:* Epoxide reactions; organometallic compounds. *Mailing Add:* Trinity Col 93 Valley View Dr Wethersfield CT 06109

HEERMANN, DALE F(RANK), AGRICULTURAL ENGINEERING, IRRIGATION. *Current Pos:* AGR ENGR, AGR RES SERV, USDA, 68- *Personal Data:* b Scribner, Nebr, Mar 2, 37; m 57, Betty Tuchenhagen; c Sara, Philip & Laura. *Educ:* Univ Nebr, BS, 59; Colo State Univ, MS, 64, PhD(agr eng), 68. *Honors & Awards:* Man of the Year, Irrig Asn. *Mem:* Fel Am Soc Agr Engrs; Am Soc Agron; Soil Sci Soc Am; Irrig Asn; US Comt Irrig & Drainage; Soil & Water Conserv Soc. *Res:* Irrigation management; sprinkler and surface irrigation design; soil-plant-water relationships. *Mailing Add:* Agr Res Serv USDA Colo State Univ Foothills Campus Ft Collins CO 80523. *Fax:* 970-491-8247; *E-Mail:* dale@lily.aerc.colostate.edu

HEERMANN, RUBEN MARTIN, PLANT BREEDING. *Current Pos:* RETIRED. *Personal Data:* b Pilger, Nebr, July 18, 21; m 44; c 3. *Educ:* Univ Nebr, BSc, 43, MSc, 48; Univ Minn, PhD(plant genetics), 54. *Prof Exp:* Res agronomist, Bur Plant Indust, Soils & Agr Eng, USDA, 48-53, res agronomist, Cereal Crops Br, Agr Res Serv, 53-56, prin agronomist, Coop State Res Serv, 56-70; assoc dir res, NY State Col Agr & Life Sci & assoc dir, Agr Exp Sta, Cornell Univ, 70-76; asst dir, Dakotas-Alaska Area, Agr Res Serv, USDA, Fargo, 76-80, assoc dir, 80-82, prog analyst, NCent Regional Off, Peoria, 82-84. *Mem:* Fel AAAS; Crop Sci Soc Am; Am Soc Agron. *Res:* Field crops; breeding and genetics of tetraploid wheats; research administration. *Mailing Add:* 739 W Wonderview Dr Dunlap IL 61525

HEESCH, CHERYL MILLER, NEURAL CONTROL OF CIRCULATION, CARDIOVASCULAR PHYSIOLOGY. *Current Pos:* ASST PROF CARDIOVASC PHYSIOL, DEPT PHYSIOL, OHIO STATE UNIV, 90- *Personal Data:* b Kermit, Tex, Dec 28, 48. *Educ:* NMex State Univ, BS, 71; Univ Tex, San Antonio, PhD(pharmacol), 81. *Prof Exp:* Researcher, Col Med, Cardiovasc Ctr, Univ Iowa, 81-83, res scientist, 83-84; asst prof neurophysiol, Dept Physiol & Biophys, La State Univ Med Ctr, Shreveport, 84-85; asst res prof cardiovasc physiol, Dept Physiol & Biophys, Univ Ky, 85-90. *Concurrent Pos:* Prin investr, NIH grants, 84- & Am Heart Asn grant-in-aid, 84-87; ad-hoc grant reviewer, NIH, 87, 89 & 90; mem, Cardiovasc Res Study Comt, Am Heart Asn, 90- *Mem:* Fel Am Heart Asn; Am Physiol Soc (secy, 87-91); Soc Neurosci. *Res:* Neural control of the circulation in hypertension and in pregnancy; central nervous system mechanisms involved in cardiovascular reflex control of the circulation. *Mailing Add:* Dept Physiol Ohio State Univ 302 Hamilton 1645 Neil Ave Columbus OH 43210. *Fax:* 614-292-4888

HEESCHEN, DAVID SUTPHIN, RADIO ASTRONOMY. *Current Pos:* RETIRED. *Personal Data:* b Davenport, Iowa, Mar 12, 26; m 50, Eloise St Clair; c 3. *Educ:* Univ Ill, BS, 49; Harvard Univ, PhD(astron), 55. *Hon Degrees:* ScD, WVa Inst Technol, 74, NMex Inst Mining & Technol, 89. *Honors & Awards:* Distinguished Pub Serv Award, NSF, 80; Alexander Von Humboldt Sr Scientist Award, 85; Jansky Lectr, 93. *Prof Exp:* Instr astron, Wesleyan Univ, 54-55; lectr, Harvard Univ, 55-56; astronr, Nat Radio Astron Observ, 56-58, chmn, Astron Dept, 58-62, dir, 62-78, sr scientist, 77-92; res prof, Univ Va, 80-93. *Concurrent Pos:* Consult, NASA, 61, 68-72, 75 & Max-Planck Inst Radioastron, 69-76; assoc ed, Astron J, 69-72; pres, Comn 40, Int Astron Union, 70-73. *Mem:* Nat Acad Sci; Am Acad Arts & Sci; Am Philos Soc; Int Astron Union (vpres, 76-82); Am Astron Soc (vpres, 69-71, pres, 80-82). *Res:* Radio astronomy; galactic structure; extragalactic studies. *Mailing Add:* Nat Radio Astron Observ Edgemont Rd Charlottesville VA 22901

HEESCHEN, JERRY PARKER, PHYSICAL CHEMISTRY, NUCLEAR MAGNETIC RESONANCE. *Current Pos:* Res chemist, 58-63, sr res chemist, 63-75, RES ASSOC, DOW CHEM CO, 75- *Personal Data:* b Apr 14, 32; US citizen; m 56; c 3. *Educ:* Western Res Univ, BS, 53; Univ Ill, PhD(phys chem), 59. *Mem:* AAAS; Am Chem Soc; Sci Res Soc Am. *Res:* Nuclear magnetic resonance; molecular structure studies by spectroscopic techniques; molecular configuration and conformation; chemical analysis. *Mailing Add:* 309 Meadow Lane Midland MI 48640

HEESTAND, GLENN MARTIN, ATOMIC PHYSICS. *Current Pos:* PHYSICIST, LAWRENCE LIVERMORE NAT LAB, 82-, SEC LEADER, LIVERMORE NAT LAB, 88- *Personal Data:* b Canton, Ohio, June 17, 42; m 74, Marily Weire; c Greg. *Educ:* Case Inst Technol, BS, 64; Univ Wis, MS, 66, PhD(physics), 69. *Prof Exp:* Res assoc physics, Aarhus Univ, Denmark, 69-70; res assoc, Univ Wis, Madison, 70-72; asst prof, Univ Wis-Superior, 72-74; eng physicist, Exxon Nuclear Inc, 75-81, Oak Ridge, 81-82. *Mem:* AAAS; Am Phys Soc; Sigma Xi. *Res:* Development of laser isotope separation on industrial scale. *Mailing Add:* 2412 Via De Los Milagros Pleasanton CA 94566

HEETDERKS, WILLIAM JOHN, NEURAL PROSTHESIS. *Current Pos:* MED OFFICER NEURAL PROSTHESES, NIH, 86- *Personal Data:* b Grand Rapids, Mich, Feb 15, 48; m 69; c 5. *Educ:* Univ Mich, BSEE, 71 PhD(bioeng), 75; Univ Miami, MD, 83. *Prof Exp:* From asst prof to assoc prof elec eng, Cornell Univ, 76-83; med resident internal med, Butterworth Hosp, 83-86. *Mem:* Inst Elec & Electronics Engrs; Am Col Physicians. *Res:* Promote the development of techniques to selectively record & stimulate small groups of neurons for the purpose of rehabilitation of neurologically impaired individuals. *Mailing Add:* 2120 Hermitage Ave Silver Spring MD 20902

HEFFELFINGER, CARL JOHN, POLYMER PHYSICS. *Current Pos:* CHIEF CONSULT, INDUST FILMS CONSULT, INC, 85- *Personal Data:* b Rochester, NY, Aug 9, 24; m 50, Lois Arnold; c 3. *Educ:* Univ Buffalo, AB, 50, PhD(chem), 53. *Honors & Awards:* Lavoisier Medal. *Prof Exp:* Asst chem, Univ Buffalo, 50-51; res chemist, E I du Pont de Nemours & Co, Inc, 52-59, staff scientist, 59-65, res assoc, Film Dept, 65-80, res fel, Polymer Prod Dept, 80-85. *Mem:* Sigma Xi. *Res:* Kinetics of addition polymerization; polymer structure. *Mailing Add:* 124 Walnut Circle Pine Knoll Shores NC 28512

HEFFERLIN, RAY (ALDEN), PERIODIC CHARTS FOR MOLECULES. *Current Pos:* PROF PHYSICS & HEAD DEPT, SOUTHERN COL, 55- *Personal Data:* b Paris, France, May 2, 29; US citizen; m 54, Inelda E Phillips; c Lorelei, Heidi, Melissa & Jennifer. *Educ:* Pac Union Col, BA, 51; Calif Inst Technol, PhD(physics), 55. *Hon Degrees:* DSc, Andrews Univ, 93. *Concurrent Pos:* Nat Acad Sci exchange scholar to USSR, 78-79 & 81; vis prof, Univ Denver, 84-85. *Mem:* Am Phys Soc; Russ Chem Soc; Am Chem Soc; Europ Phys Soc. *Res:* Representations of periodic law for molecules based on tabulated data; systematics of molecules; theoretical formulations of periodic systems of small molecules. *Mailing Add:* Dept Physics Southern Adventist Univ Collegedale TN 37315-0370. *Fax:* 423-238-3001; *E-Mail:* hefferln@southern.edu

HEFFERNAN, GERALD R, METALLURGY. *Current Pos:* pres, 70-86, chmn, 87-90, DIR, CO-STEEL INC, 90- *Personal Data:* b Edmonton, Alta, July 12, 19. *Educ:* Univ Toronto, BaSc, 43. *Hon Degrees:* LLD, Queens Univ, 79. *Honors & Awards:* Noranda Award, Can Inst Mining & Metall, 75; Benjamin F Fairless Award, Am Inst Mining, Metall & Petrol Engrs, 83; Gold Medal, Asn Prof Engrs, 85; Bessemer Gold Medal Award, Inst Metals, 89. *Prof Exp:* Staff mem, Dept Metall, Univ BC, 45-46; metallurgist & asst gen mgr, Westland Iron & Steel Foundries, 46-48; supt, Western Can Steel, 48-54; managing dir, secy & vpres, Premier Steel Mills Ltd, 54-62; pres, Lake Ont Steel Co Ltd, 63-70. *Concurrent Pos:* Dir, Lake Ont Steel Co, Sheerness Steel Co plc, Raritan River Steel Co, Chaparral Steel Co, Tex Indust Inc, Corod Indust Inc, Harbour Petrol Co Ltd, Can Inst Advan Res, Roy L Merchant Group Inc, Nat Rubber Co Ltd & Innovations Found, Univ Toronto; vchmn, Can Inst Advan Res. *Mem:* Fel Am Soc Metals; Iron & Steel Soc; fel Can Inst Mining & Metall. *Res:* Metallurgy of steelmaking; commercial application of continuous casting; ferrous metallurgy. *Mailing Add:* 22 St Clair Ave E Suite 1700 Toronto ON M4T 2S3 Can

HEFFERNAN, LAUREL GRACE, MOLECULAR BIOLOGY. *Current Pos:* PROF BIOL SCI, CALIF STATE UNIV, SACRAMENTO, 86-, CHAIR, BIOL SCI, 96- *Personal Data:* b San Francisco, Calif, Sept 22, 45. *Educ:* San Francisco State Univ, BA, 68; Univ Calif, Santa Barbara, PhD(biol), 75. *Prof Exp:* NIH trainee genetics, Stanford Univ, 74-77; adj asst prof microbiol, Univ Calif, Los Angeles, 77-86. *Mem:* Sigma Xi; Am Soc Microbiol; AAAS. *Res:* Genic regulation in procaryotic organisms and their viruses. *Mailing Add:* Dept Biol Sci Calif State Univ 6000 J St Sacramento CA 95819-2694

HEFFERREN, JOHN JAMES, CHEMISTRY. *Current Pos:* PRES, ODONTEX, INC, 87-; ADJ PROF PHARM CHEM, UNIV KANS, 87-, RES PROF, CTR BIOMED RES, 89- *Personal Data:* b Chicago, Ill, Aug 12, 28; m 65. *Educ:* Loyola Univ, BS, 50; Univ Wis, MS, 52, PhD(pharmaceut chem), 54. *Prof Exp:* Chemist, AMA, 53-59; dir, Div Chem, Coun Dent Therapeut, Am Dent Asn, 59-66, dir, Div Biochem, 66-75, dir, Res Inst, 75-85; assoc biochem med & dent schs, Northwestern Univ, 66-80, coordr pres dent, 77-80, prof oral biol, 80-86; pres, J J Hefferren Resources Inc, 85- *Concurrent Pos:* Am Fedn Pharmaceut Educ fel, 50-53; lectr, Sch Pharm, Univ Mich, 74- *Mem:* Am Chem Soc; Am Pharmaceut Asn; AAAS; Int Asn Dent Res; Europ Orgn Caries Res; Am Acad Periodont. *Res:* Organic medicinal and bioanalytical organic chemistry; laboratory, pre-clinical and clinical studies to assess the potential of foods, dentifrices and other oral hygiene agents in humans and companion animals. *Mailing Add:* 3030 Campfire Dr Lawrence KS 66049

HEFFES, HARRY, ELECTRICAL ENGINEERING. *Current Pos:* PROF & DEPT HEAD, ELEC ENG & COMPUT SCI, STEVENS INST TECHNOL, HOBOKEN, NJ, 90-91. *Personal Data:* b Atlantic City, NJ, Sept 1, 39; div; c 2. *Educ:* City Col New York, BEE, 62; NY Univ, MEE, 64, PhD(elec eng), 68. *Honors & Awards:* S O Rice Award, Inst Elec & Electronics Engrs, 87. *Prof Exp:* Mem tech staff, AT&T Bell Labs, 62-89. *Mem:* Fel Inst Elec & Electronics Engrs; Opers Res Soc Am; Asn Comput Mach; Soc Indust & Appl Math. *Res:* Teletraffic and queueing theory; modeling and analysis of teletraffic systems. *Mailing Add:* Dept Elec Eng & Comput Sci Stevens Inst Technol Castle Point on the Hudson Hoboken NJ 07030

HEFFLEY, JAMES D, DIET & FOOD SUPPLEMENTS. *Current Pos:* DIR, NUTRIT COUN SERV, 74- *Personal Data:* b Ethel, Tex, Jan 12, 41; m 63, Betty E Dozier; c James M, Jon R, David D, Sara E & Anna C. *Educ:* Abilene Christian Univ, BS, 64; Univ Tex Austin, PhD(chem), 70. *Prof Exp:* Res asst, Clayton Found Biochem Inst, 65-70, res assoc, 70-74. *Concurrent Pos:* Consult, Tex Sch Blind, 72-74; lab dir, Ctr Better Health, 84-87. *Mem:* Int Acad Nutrit & Prev Med; Int Am Asn Clin Nutrit. *Res:* Effects of alcohol on amino acid metabolism and on assessing total nutrient value of single foods; writing on uses of food supplements and dietary manipulation to uncover food intolerance. *Mailing Add:* 3913 Medical Pkwy No 101 Austin TX 78756

HEFFNER, REID RUSSELL, JR, PATHOLOGY, NEUROPATHOLOGY. *Current Pos:* assoc prof, 74-84, PROF PATH, SCH MED, STATE UNIV NY, BUFFALO, 84-, ASSOC CHAIR DEPT, 85- *Personal Data:* b Philadelphia, Pa, Apr 16, 38; m 65; c 2. *Educ:* Yale Univ, BA, 60, MD, 65. *Prof Exp:* Instr path, Yale Sch Med, 68-69 & Cornell Sch Med, 69-70; neuropathologist, Armed Forces Inst Path, 70-72, chief, Neuromuscular Div, 72-74. *Concurrent Pos:* NIH fel neuropath, 68-69; consult, Vet Admin Hosp, Buffalo, NY, 75-, Roswell Park Mem Inst, 76- & Millard Fillmore Hosp, 76-; dir, Dept Path, Erie Co Med Ctr, Buffalo, 79- *Mem:* Am Acad Neurol; Am Asn Neuropathologists; Am Soc Clin Pathologists; Int Acad Path; Soc Neurosci. *Res:* Neuromuscular disease; muscular dystrophy. *Mailing Add:* Dept Path 204 Farber Hall Buffalo NY 14214

HEFFNER, ROBERT H, MAGNETISM & SUPERCONDUCTIVITY, TECHNICAL MANAGEMENT & RESEARCH ADMINISTRATION. *Current Pos:* fel, Los Alamos Nat Lab, 74-78, dep group leader appl group, 82-85, group leader condensed matter physics, 85-92, STAFF MEM, LOS ALAMOS NAT LAB, 92- *Personal Data:* b Washington, DC, Dec 17, 42; m 70, Paula S Zemliak; c Ryan A & Leanna R. *Educ:* Miami Univ, Ohio, BS, 64; Univ Wash, PhD(nuclear physics), 73. *Prof Exp:* Teaching asst physics, Miami Univ, Ohio, 64-65. *Concurrent Pos:* Chair, Subcomt Muon Sources for Solid State Res, Nat Res Coun, 83. *Mem:* Am Phys Soc. *Res:* Magnetic and superconducting properties of novel materials using magnetic resonance and neutron scattering techniques; nuclear structure and nuclear reactions with pions and protons. *Mailing Add:* MS K764 Los Alamos Nat Lab Los Alamos NM 87545. *Fax:* 505-665-7652; *E-Mail:* heffner_robert_h@lanl.gov

HEFFNER, THOMAS G, PSYCHOPHARMACOLOGY, ANTIPSYCHOTICS. *Current Pos:* group leader, 83-86, sr group leader, 86-90, SECT DIR, WARNER-LAMBERT-PARKE-DAVIS, 90- *Personal Data:* b Salem, Ohio, Sept 20, 49. *Educ:* Univ Pittsburgh, BS, 71, PhD(psychobiol), 76. *Prof Exp:* Teaching asst biol, Univ Pittsburgh, 71-74, teaching fel physiol, 74-76; NIMH fel pharmacol, Univ Chicago, 76-79, res asst prof, 79-83. *Concurrent Pos:* Lectr psychopharmacol, Pritzker Sch Med, Univ Chicago, 79-83; prin investr, Brain Res Found grant, Chicago, 81-83; co-prin investr, NIMH grant, 79-83; investr, Nat Inst Neurol Commun Dis & Stroke grant, 79-83. *Mem:* Am Soc Pharmacol & Exp Therapeut; Soc Neurosci; Am Psychol Asn. *Res:* Psychopharmacology; development and discovery of novel drugs to treat psychiatric disorders; etiology of central nervous system disorders; neurochemical basis of drug action; role of neurochemical changes accompanying environmental or behavioral stimuli in drug action. *Mailing Add:* Dept Pharmacol Warner-Lambert-Parke-Davis 2800 Plymouth Rd Ann Arbor MI 48105-2430. *Fax:* 313-998-4538

HEFFRON, PETER JOHN, INDUSTRIAL ORGANIC & SYNTHETIC ORGANIC CHEMISTRY. *Current Pos:* process chemist, Dyes, 82-83, sr res chemist, 83-88, GROUP LEADER, PROCESS RES & DEVELOP DYES, MORTON INT INC, 88- *Personal Data:* b Flushing, NY, Oct 2, 43; wid; c Margaret A. *Educ:* St Francis Xavier Univ, BS, 65; State Univ NY, Binghamton, MA, 67; State Univ NY, Stony Brook, PhD(org chem), 72. *Prof Exp:* Res fel entom, Univ Ky, 72-73; group leader, Dyes, Am Cyanamid Co, 73-82. *Mem:* Am Chem Soc; AAAS. *Res:* Novel synthetic routes in organic chemistry; process development in synthesis of chemical intermediates and dyes; stereochemistry and stereochemically controlled reactions. *Mailing Add:* 43 Capner St Flemington NJ 08822-1313

HEFFTER, JEROME L, METEOROLOGY. *Current Pos:* RES METEOROLOGIST, AIR RESOURCES LAB, NAT OCEANIC & ATMOSPHERIC ADMIN, 60- *Educ:* Univ Minn, BS, 55; Mass Inst Technol, MS, 60. *Mem:* Am Meteorol Soc. *Res:* Atmospheric transport and dispersion of pollutants with emphasis on volcanic ash. *Mailing Add:* NOAA-Air Resources Lab R/E/AR SSMC3-Rm 3151 1315 East West Hwy Silver Spring MD 20910

HEFLE, SUSAN LYNN, FOOD ALLERGY. *Current Pos:* Res specialist, 83-85, RES ASSOC, UNIV WIS-MADISON MED SCH, 91- *Personal Data:* b Milwaukee, Wis, Oct 23, 59. *Educ:* Univ Wis-Madison, BS, 82, MS, 87, PhD(food toxicol), 91. *Concurrent Pos:* Fel, Univ Wis Med Sch, 91- *Mem:* Am Acad Allergy & Immunol; Inst Food Technologists; Am Soc Microbiol. *Res:* Allergenic proteins in legumes, seafood, and molds; isolation and characterization of allergenic proteins biochemically and on a molecular level. *Mailing Add:* 4334 G St Lincoln NE 68506. *E-Mail:* hefle@macc.wisc.edu

HEFLEY, ALTA JEAN, ANALYTICAL CHEMISTRY, FOOD CHEMISTRY. *Current Pos:* ANALYTICAL CHEMIST, MILES LABS, 74- *Personal Data:* b Rifle, Colo, Jan 5, 41. *Educ:* Colo State Univ, BS, 63; Iowa State Univ, MS, 65, PhD(analytical chem), 67. *Prof Exp:* From asst prof to assoc prof chem, Mundelein Col, 67-74. *Mem:* Am Chem Soc; Sigma Xi; Inst Food Technologists. *Mailing Add:* 421 E Orchard Lane Arlington Heights IL 60005-2659

HEFLICH, ROBERT HENRY, MUTAGENESIS, CARCINOGENESIS. *Current Pos:* RES MICROBIOLOGIST MUTAGENESIS RES, DIV GENETIC TOXICOL, NAT CTR TOXICOL RES, 79- *Personal Data:* b Cairo, NY, Nov 10, 46; m 71. *Educ:* Rutgers Univ, BA, 68, MS, 70, PhD(microbiol), 76. *Prof Exp:* Res asst oral microbiol, Letterman Army Inst Res, Calif, 70-72; res assoc mutagenesis res, Carcinogenesis Lab, Mich State Univ, 76-79. *Mem:* Am Soc Microbiol; Sigma Xi; Environ Mutagen Soc. *Res:* Mechanisms of the induction of genotoxic events in cultural mammalian cells and bacteria by physical and chemical toxicants. *Mailing Add:* Div Genetic Toxicol HFT 120 Nat Ctr Toxicol Res Jefferson AR 72079

HEFLIN, JAMES RANDOLPH, PHYSICS, NONLINEAR OPTICS. *Current Pos:* ASST PROF PHYSICS, VA POLYTECH & STATE UNIV, 92- *Personal Data:* b Washington, DC, Mar 24, 63. *Educ:* Col William & Mary, BS, 84; Univ Pa, PhD(physics), 90. *Honors & Awards:* Cottrell scholar award, Res Corp, 95. *Prof Exp:* Postdoctoral fel, Univ Pa, 90-92. *Mailing Add:* Dept Physics Va Polytech & State Univ Blacksburg VA 24061. *Fax:* 540-231-7511; *E-Mail:* rheflin@vt.edu

HEFLINGER, LEE OPERT, APPLIED MATHEMATICS, EXPERIMENTAL PHYSICS. *Current Pos:* mathematician, 64-77, SR SCIENTIST, TRW SYSTS GROUP, 77- *Personal Data:* b Pasadena, Calif, May 23, 27; m 49; c 2. *Educ:* San Jose Col, BA, 50; Univ Calif, MA, 52, PhD(math), 56. *Prof Exp:* Asst, Univ Calif, 52-56; mathematician, Thompson-Ramo-Wooldridge, Inc, 56-58, Space Tech Labs, Inc, Los Angeles, 58-60 & Gen Tech Corp, 60-64. *Mem:* Am Math Soc; Am Phys Soc; Sigma Xi. *Res:* Asymptotic expansions; numerical analysis; experimental plasma research; pulsed laser holography. *Mailing Add:* 5001 Paseo de Pablo Torrance CA 90505-6628

HEFNER, LLOYD LEE, INTERNAL MEDICINE. *Current Pos:* RETIRED. *Personal Data:* b Bradenton, Fla, Nov 19, 23; c 4. *Educ:* Vanderbilt Univ, BA, 46, MD, 49. *Prof Exp:* Intern, Vanderbilt Univ Hosp, 49-50, fel psychiat, 50-51; resident internal med, Univ Ala, Birmingham, 53-55, fel cardiovasc dis, 55-56, from instr to prof med, 56-69, Ala heart prof cardiovasc res, 69-80, prof med, physiol & biophys, 80-88. *Concurrent Pos:* Estab investr, Am Heart Asn, 60-65, chmn, Coun Basic Sci, 70-72, mem, Coun Clin Cardiol, 70- *Mem:* Am Fedn Clin Res; Am Col Physicians; AMA; Am Heart Asn; Sigma Xi. *Res:* Biophysics of ventricular contraction. *Mailing Add:* 2835 Berwick Rd Birmingham AL 35213

HEFTI, FRANZ F, NEUROLOGY. *Current Pos:* PROF, ANDRUS GERONT CTR, UNIV SOUTHERN CALIF, LOS ANGELES, 89- *Personal Data:* b Zurich, Switz, Dec 22, 47; m 74; c 2. *Educ:* Univ Zurich, Switz, MS, 72, PhD(biol), 76. *Honors & Awards:* Robert Bing Prize, 90. *Prof Exp:* Res asst pharmacol, Univ Zurich, 74-77; res assoc neuroendocrinol, Mass Inst Technol, 78-80; res assoc neurobiol, Max Planck Inst, Munich, 81-82; head res lab pharmacol, Sandoz Ltd, Switz, 82-85; assoc prof pharmacol, Dept Neurol, Univ Miami, Fla, 85-89. *Concurrent Pos:* Parkinson res scholar, Nat Parkinson Found, 88; James E Birren Prof, 90. *Mem:* Soc Neurosci; Int Soc Neurochem; Europ Neurosci Asn; Swiss Soc Pharmacol & Toxicol. *Res:* Basic research relevant to human neurodegenerative diseases, in particular Parkinson's and Alzheimer's disease, role of trophic factors and hormones in these diseases. *Mailing Add:* Merck Sharp & Dohme Res Labs Terlings Park Harlow Essex England

HEFTMANN, ERICH, BIOCHEMISTRY, CHROMATOGRAPHY. *Current Pos:* ED, J CHROMATOGRAPHY SYMP VOLS, 83- *Personal Data:* b Vienna, Austria, Mar 9, 18; nat US; m 42, 68, Brigitte Sander; c Rex, Lisa & Erica. *Educ:* NY Univ, BA, 42; Univ Rochester, PhD(biochem), 47; Am Bd Clin Chem, dipl. *Honors & Awards:* Humboldt Award, 75. *Prof Exp:* Instr chem, Univ Md, 43-44; asst biochem & pharmacol, Univ Rochester, 44-47; biochemist & dir labs, Diabetes Sect, USPHS, 47-48, biochemist, Nat Cancer Inst, 48-50 & Nat Inst Arthritis & Metab Dis, 50-63, res leader, Western Regional Res Ctr, Agr Res Sci & Educ Admin, USDA, 63-83. *Concurrent Pos:* Lectr, Grad Sch, USDA, 54-62 & Georgetown Univ, 60; res fel, Calif Inst Technol, 59 & 61-64, res assoc, 64-69; vis assoc prof, Univ Southern Calif, 65-70. *Mem:* Fel AAAS; Am Soc Biol Chemists; Am Chem Soc. *Res:* Lipids; screening method for blood glucose; biochemistry of steroids; chromatography; plant biochemistry. *Mailing Add:* PO Box 928 Orinda CA 94563

HEGARTY, PATRICK VINCENT, NUTRITION. *Current Pos:* at DEPT HUMAN DEVELOP & CONSUMER SCI, UNIV HOUSTON. *Personal Data:* b Cork, Ireland, July 19, 39; m 67; c 2. *Educ:* Univ Col, Cork, BSc, 61, MSc, 63; Univ London, PhD(human nutrit), 66; Univ Col, Dublin, BA, 70. *Prof Exp:* From res officer to sr res officer muscle biol, Agr Inst, Dublin, Ireland, 66-70; fel, Univ Minn, St Paul, 70-72, assoc prof, 72-76, prof human nutrit, 76- *Mem:* Am Inst Nutrit; Brit Nutrit Soc; Inst Food Technologists. *Res:* Morphological and biochemical changes during various dietary deficiencies, and the subsequent rehabilitation in skeletal muscles, adipose tissue and bones. *Mailing Add:* Dept Food Sci & Human Nutrit Mich State Univ 204 Food Sci East Lansing MI 48824-0001. *Fax:* 517-432-1492

HEGE, E K, ASTRONOMY. *Current Pos:* MEM STAFF, STEWARD OBSERV, UNIV ARIZ. *Mailing Add:* Steward Observ Univ Ariz Tucson AZ 85721-0001

HEGEDUS, L LOUIS, CHEMICAL ENGINEERING, SPECIALTY CHEMICALS. *Current Pos:* VPRES RES & DEVELOP, ELF ATOCHEM NAM INC, KING OF PRUSSIA, PA. *Personal Data:* b Budapest, Hungary, Apr 13, 41; m 68, Eva Brem; c Caroline & Monica. *Educ:* Tech Univ Budapest, MS, 64; Univ Calif, Berkeley, PhD (chem eng), 72. *Hon Degrees:* Dr H C, Tech Univ, Budapest, 91. *Honors & Awards:* Allan P Colburn lectr, Univ Del, 75, J A Gerster lectr, 88; B F Dodge lectr, Yale Univ, 88; R H Wilhelm Award, Am Inst Chem Eng, 88; D M Mason lectr, Stanford Univ, 91; Regents' lectr, Univ Calif, Los Angeles, 91; Warren K Lewis Lectr, Mass Inst Technol, 94. *Prof Exp:* Group leader qual control, Daimler-ben, AG, Mannheim, WGer, 56-68; res engr process develop, Res Inst Org Chem Indust, Budapest, 64-65; res supvr catalysis & kinetics, Gen Motors Res Lab, 72-80; dir, W R Grace & Co, Columbia, Md, 80-84, vpres res, 84-96. *Concurrent Pos:* Consult ed, Am Inst Chem Engrs J, 85-88; gov bd, Coun Chem Res, 87-90; bd chem sci & technol, Nat Res Coun, 90-94; adv bd mem, Berkeley, Princeton, Wis & Northwestern Univs, UCLA; chmn, Coun Chem Res, 93-94; comn Phys Sci, Math & Applns, Nat Res Coun, 95- *Mem:* Nat Acad Eng; Am Chem Soc; NAm Catalysis Soc; Mat Res Soc; fel Am Inst Chem Eng. *Res:* Specialty chemicals; applied catalysis; mathematical modeling; design and preparation of catalysts; process research; emission control; environmental science and technology; chemical reaction engineering. *Mailing Add:* 6625 Paxton Rd North Bethesda MD 20852. *Fax:* 610-878-6200

HEGEDUS, LOUIS STEVENSON, ORGANIC CHEMISTRY, ORGANOMETALLIC CHEMISTRY. *Current Pos:* from asst prof to assoc prof, 71-79, PROF CHEM, COLO STATE UNIV, 79- *Personal Data:* b Cleveland, Ohio, May 6, 43; m 67. *Educ:* Pa State Univ, BS, 65; Harvard Univ, AM, 66, PhD(org chem), 70. *Prof Exp:* NIH fel org chem, Stanford Univ, 70-71. *Concurrent Pos:* Assoc ed, J Am Chem Soc, 87- *Mem:* Am Chem Soc. *Res:* Organic synthetic methods involving transition metal organometallic intermediates; homogeneous catalysis. *Mailing Add:* Dept Chem Colo State Univ Ft Collins CO 80523-0002. *Fax:* 970-491-5610

HEGEDUS, STEVEN SCOTT, SOLAR CELL DEVICE PHYSICS. *Current Pos:* RES ASSOC, INST ENERGY CONVERSION, UNIV DEL, 82- *Personal Data:* b Cleveland, Ohio, May 26, 55; m; c 2. *Educ:* Case Western Res Univ, BS, 77; Cornell Univ, MS, 81; Univ Del, PhD, 90. *Prof Exp:* Engr, IBM Corp, 77-82. *Mem:* Am Phys Soc; Union Concerned Scientist. *Res:* Developing low cost photo voltaic solar cells and studying amorphous silicon and CdTe devices. *Mailing Add:* Inst Energy Conversion Univ Del Newark DE 19711

HEGELE, ROBERT A, ENDOCRINOLOGY & METABOLISM, ATHEROSCLEROSIS RESEARCH. *Current Pos:* ASSOC PROF MED & STAFF PHYSICIAN, DIV ENDOCRINOL & METAB, UNIV TORONTO, 89- *Personal Data:* b Toronto, Ont, Nov 21, 57; m 87; c 2. *Educ:* Univ Toronto, MD, 81; FRCPC, 85 & 87. *Honors & Awards:* McDonald Award, Heart & Stroke Found, Can, 90; Doupe Award, Royal Col Physicians & Surgeons, Can, 90. *Prof Exp:* Resident internal med, Univ Toronto, 81-84, fel endocrinol, 84-85; res fel genetics, Rockefeller Univ, 85-87 & Howard Hughes Med Inst, Univ Utah, 87-89. *Concurrent Pos:* Staff doctor, St Michael's Hosp, Toronto, 89-; res scholar, Heart & Stroke Found, Can, 90- *Mem:* Am Heart Asn; Am Fedn Clin Res; Am Soc Human Genetics; Am Col Nutrit; fel Royal Col Physicians & Surgeons. *Res:* Genomic basis of biochemical abnormalities predisposing to premature cardiovascular disease. *Mailing Add:* 30 Bond St Toronto ON M5B 1W8 Can

HEGEMAN, GEORGE D, MICROBIOLOGY, BIOCHEMISTRY. *Current Pos:* assoc prof, 72-78, head, microbiol Prog, 84-89, PROF MICROBIOL, IND UNIV, BLOOMINGTON, 78- *Personal Data:* b Glen Cove, NY, Aug 31, 38; m 61, Sally Lofgren; c Susan & Adrian. *Educ:* Harvard Univ, AB, 60; Univ Calif, Berkeley, PhD(comp biochem), 65. *Prof Exp:* Instr bact, Univ Calif, Berkeley, 65; NIH fel, Lab Enzym, Nat Ctr Sci Res, Gif-sur-Yvette, France, 65-66; asst prof bact, Univ Calif, Berkeley, 66-72. *Concurrent Pos:* Pres, Monroe Co Bd Health; sr fel, Inst Cellular & Molecular Biol, Ind Univ. *Mem:* AAAS; Am Soc Microbiol; Am Soc Biol Chem; Am Acad Microbiol; Soc Indust Microbiol; Am Acad Microbiol. *Res:* Biology and chemistry of bacteria; enzymology and regulation of enzyme synthesis; bacterial physiology, genetics and biochemistry, especially the comparative control of catabolism in bacteria and evolution of catabolic pathways. *Mailing Add:* Dept Biol Jordan Hall 142 Ind Univ Bloomington IN 47405. *Fax:* 812-855-6705; *E-Mail:* ghegeman@bio.indiana.edu

HEGENAUER, JACK C, BIOINORGANIC CHEMISTRY. *Current Pos:* Fel, 70-72, asst res biologist, 72-77, ASSOC RES BIOLOGIST, UNIV CALIF, SAN DIEGO, 77- *Personal Data:* b Bay City, Mich, Nov, 26, 39; m 60; c 3. *Educ:* Univ Mich, BS, 61, MS, 68, PhD(zool), 70. *Mem:* Am Inst Nutrit; Am Col Toxicol; Int Asn Bioinorg Scientists; Soc Develop Biol; Sigma Xi. *Res:* Human and animal trace element nutrition; metabolism of trace elements (iron, copper, zinc and manganese); physical chemistry of metalloproteins (ferritin, transferrin, phosphoproteins); trace element fortification of foods; epidemiology of human trace element deficiencies. *Mailing Add:* Int Calif Corp 533 Madison Ave Prescott AZ 86301

HEGER, JAMES J, PHYSICAL METALLURGY & PROCESSING. *Current Pos:* RETIRED. *Personal Data:* b Jenkinstown, Pa, Feb 9, 18. *Educ:* Carnegie Inst Technol, BS, 40 MS, 48. *Prof Exp:* Chief staff engr stainless steel & metal processing, US Steel Res, 70-80. *Concurrent Pos:* Mem, Boiler & Pressure Vessel Code, Am Soc Mech Engrs. *Mem:* Am Soc Metals; Am Inst Mining Metall & Petrol Engrs; Nat Asn Corrosion Engrs; Am Soc Testing & Mat; Am Soc Mech Engrs. *Mailing Add:* 2610 Strathmore Lane Bethel PA 15102

HEGGERS, JOHN PAUL, MICROBIOLOGY, IMMUNOLOGY. *Current Pos:* PROG SURG, UNIV TEX MED BR, 88-; DIR CLIN MICROBIOL, SHRINERS BURN INST, 88- *Personal Data:* b Brooklyn, NY, Feb 8, 33; m 77; c 6. *Educ:* Mont State Univ, BA, 58; Univ Md, MSc, 65; Wash State Univ, PhD(microbiol), 72; Am Bd Bioanalysis, dipl. *Honors & Awards:* Fisher Award, Am Med Technol, 68; Lambert Award, Warner-Lambert, 73; Award Basic Sci Res, Am Soc Plastic & Reconstructive Surgeons, 79; Robert B Lindberg Award, Am Burn Asn, 86; Dr Stanley Reitman Mem Award, Int Soc Clin Lab Technol, 87. *Prof Exp:* Asst to dir, Armed Forces Inst Path, 73-74; asst chief, Clin Invest Serv, Madigan Army Med Ctr, 74-77; assoc prof, Univ Chicago, 77-80, prof, Dept Surg, 80-83, res assoc, plastic & reconstructive surg & dir res & labs, Burn Ctr, 77-83; prof surg, Univ Health Ctr, Wayne State Univ, 83-88. *Concurrent Pos:* Assoc prof, Univ Chicago, 77-80, prof, dept surg & res assoc, Plastic & Reconstructive Surg, 77-83; assoc lab dir, Moross Clin Lab, Detroit, 84-88. *Mem:* Plastic Surg Res Coun; Am Burn Asn; Nat Registry Microbiologists; Sigma Xi; Am Soc Med Technologists; Soc Exp Biol & Med; Univ Asn Emergency Med. *Res:* Pathophysiology of dermal ischemia; burn and surgical wound sepsis. *Mailing Add:* Shriners Burns Inst 610 Texas Ave Galveston TX 77550-2706

HEGGESTAD, CARL B, ANATOMY. *Current Pos:* RETIRED. *Personal Data:* b Starbuck, Minn, July 19, 30; m 53; c 3. *Educ:* Univ Minn, Minneapolis, BA, 52, MD, 57, PhD(anat), 60. *Prof Exp:* From instr to prof anat, Univ Minn, Minneapolis, 59- *Concurrent Pos:* Consult, Med Electronic Indust. *Mem:* AAAS; Am Asn Anat; Asn Am Med Cols. *Res:* Fetal endocrinology; placental permeability. *Mailing Add:* 1258 NE Skywood Lane Minneapolis MN 55432

HEGGESTAD, HOWARD EDWIN, PHYTOPATHOLOGY. *Current Pos:* RETIRED. *Personal Data:* b Stoughton, Wis, July 24, 15; m 39, Dolores Andersen; c Arnold, Margot & David. *Educ:* Univ Wis, PhB, 40, PhD(genetics, plant path), 44. *Honors & Awards:* Res Award Tobacco Breeding & Path, 61; Res Award, Am Soc Hort Sci, 73; Res Award, Environ Protection Agency, 84. *Prof Exp:* Asst hort, Univ Wis, 38-44, instr, 44-46; from asst agronomist to agronomist, Bur Plant Indust, Soils & Agr Eng, Tobacco Exp Sta, USDA, Tenn, 46-55, agronomist, Field Crops Res Br, Agr Res Serv, 54-55, sr agronomist & breeder, Plant Indust Sta, 55-57, prin agronomist, 57-64, prin pathologist, 64, leader, Tobacco Breeding & Dis Invests, 64-66, chief, Air Pollution Lab, 66-75, plant pathologist, Plant Stress Lab, Sci & Educ Admin, Plant Physiol Inst, 75-84. *Concurrent Pos:* Consult, Elec Power Res Inst, Palo Alto, Calif, 79-; Biol Sci Collabr, USDA Agr Res Serv, 90-91. *Mem:* AAAS; Am Phytopath Soc; Am Inst Biol Sci; Air Pollution Control Asn. *Res:* Tobacco breeding; tobacco diseases; tobacco production; plant injury from air pollutants; effects of air pollutants, especially ozone and sulfur dioxide, singularly and in combinations, on crop productivity; technology for minimizing losses such as the identification of tolerant cultivars; interaction soil moisture stress and ozone stress on yields of soybean cultivars under field and greenhouse conditions. *Mailing Add:* 1317 Roby Rd Stoughton WI 53589. *E-Mail:* hheggestad@aol.com

HEGGIE, ROBERT, ORGANIC CHEMISTRY. *Current Pos:* CONSULT, 71- *Personal Data:* b Glasgow, Scotland, Jan 19, 09; nat US; m 39, Florence T Sokovich; c Patricia H & Frances J. *Educ:* Mass Inst Technol, SB, 33, PhD(org chem), 36. *Prof Exp:* From asst to res assoc chem, Mass Inst Technol, 33-39; chemist & dir res & develop, Am Chicle Co Div, Warner-Lambert Pharmaceut Co, 39-57, vpres, 57-61, exec vpres, 61-70; vpres appl sci, Warner-Lambert Res Inst, 62-65, vpres consumer prod res, 65-69, vpres tech develop & control, 69-70. *Mem:* AAAS; Am Chem Soc; Am Inst Chemists; Soc Chem Indust. *Res:* Asymmetric synthesis; reaction rates; vitamin chemistry; high polymers; chemistry of flavors. *Mailing Add:* 3570 S Ocean Blvd Palm Beach FL 33480

HEGGIE, ROBERT MURRAY, ORGANIC CHEMISTRY. *Current Pos:* RETIRED. *Personal Data:* b Paisley, Scotland, Mar 14, 27; Can citizen; m 51, Norah Davidson; c 4. *Educ:* Univ Glasgow, BSc, 48, PhD(org chem), 51. *Prof Exp:* Fel chem, Nat Res Coun Can, 51-53, Univ Sask, 53-54 & Univ Ottawa, 54-55; sci officer, Defence Res Bd Can, 55-74 & Dept Nat Defence, Can, 74-75; chief, Defence Res Estab Suffield, 75-79, chief, Defence & Civil Inst Environ Med, 79-84, chief, Defence Res Estab Ottawa, 84-86; assoc chief res & develop, Dept Nat Defence, Can, 86-90. *Mem:* Fel Chem Inst Can; Royal Soc Chem. *Res:* Chemistry and toxicology of biologically active materials. *Mailing Add:* 2839 Flannery Dr Ottawa ON K1V 9S8 Can

HEGGTVEIT, HALVOR ALEXANDER, PATHOLOGY. *Current Pos:* prof, 82-96, EMER PROF PATH FAC HEALTH SCI, MCMASTER UNIV, 97-; HON MED STAFF, HAMILTON HEALTH SCI CORP, 97- *Personal Data:* b Montreal, PQ, Mar 3, 33; m 60; c 2. *Educ:* Univ Ottawa, MD, 57; Am Bd Path, dipl, 62; FRCP(C); FRCPath. *Honors & Awards:* Carveth Sci Award, Can Asn Pathol, 67. *Prof Exp:* Resident, Down State Med Ctr, State Univ NY & Kings Co Hosp, 59-61, instr, Med Ctr, 61-62; from lectr to prof path fac med, Univ Ottawa, 62-82, actg head dept, 73-75; pathologist, Ottawa Civic Hosp, 75-82. *Concurrent Pos:* Fel path, Univ Ottawa & Ottawa Gen Hosp, Ont, 57-59; pathologist, Ottawa Gen Hosp, 62-75, actg dir labs, 73-75; regional pathologist, Ont Atty Gen Dept, 63-82; sr res fel, Ont Heart Found, 66-70; dep registr, Med Coun Can, 67-71; res assoc, Ont Heart Found, 70-78; co-registr, Registry for Tissue Reactions to Drugs, 70-76; mem, Tis Subcomt, Can Heart Found, 70-73; consult pathologist, Nat Defense Med Ctr, Fed Food & Drug Directorate, Ottawa, Children's Hosp of Eastern Ont, Ottawa Gen Hosp & Nat Res Coun Can; adv, Sect Cardiovasc Dis, WHO; mem coun, Can Asn Pathologists, 75-78; pathologist, Chedoke-McMaster & Hamilton Gen Hosps, Hamilton, Ont, 82-96. *Mem:* Fel Am Col Cardiol; Int Acad Path; fel Am Soc Clin Path; fel Col Am Path; Soc Cardiovasc Path; Can Asn Pathologists. *Res:* Cardiovascular pathology and electron microscopy of myocardium. *Mailing Add:* Dept Path McMaster Univ Med Ctr 1200 Main St W Hamilton ON L8N 3Z5 Can

HEGLUND, NORMAN C, muscle physiology, for more information see previous edition

HEGMANN, JOSEPH PAUL, QUANTITATIVE GENETICS. *Current Pos:* From asst prof to prof, 73-85, EMER PROF ZOOL, UNIV IOWA, 85- *Personal Data:* b Kansas City, Mo, Sept 26, 40; m 60; c 3. *Educ:* Univ Ill, BS, 62, MS, 66, PhD(quant genetics), 68. *Mem:* AAAS; Soc Multivariate Exp Psychol; Genetics Soc Am; Am Genetic Asn; Sigma Xi. *Res:* Behavioral genetics; genetic variation affecting differences in complexly varying behaviors in laboratory and wild populations of rodents and insects. *Mailing Add:* 2110 Yucca Ave Ainsworth IA 52201-9240

HEGRE, CARMAN STANFORD, BIOCHEMISTRY. *Current Pos:* supvry res prog coordr, Nat Marine Water Qual Lab, 66-80, ENVIRON SCIENTIST, ENVIRON RES LAB, ENVIRON PROTECTION AGENCY, 80- *Personal Data:* b Columbus, Mont, Dec 5, 37; m 59; c 3. *Educ:* Va Polytech Inst, BS, 59, MS, 61, PhD(biochem), 63. *Prof Exp:* Res assoc & fel pharmacol, Western Res Univ, 63-66. *Concurrent Pos:* Mem group experts, sci aspects of marine pollution, UN, 73- *Mem:* AAAS; Am Chem Soc; Am Soc Limnol & Oceanog; Water Pollution Control Fedn. *Res:* Enzymology; non-photosynthetic carbon dioxide fixation; physiology, toxicology and intermediary metabolism of marine plankton. *Mailing Add:* 38 Whitehorn Dr Kingston RI 02881

HEGRE, ORION DONALD, anatomy, tissue culture, for more information see previous edition

HEGSTED, DAVID MARK, NUTRITION, BIOCHEMISTRY. *Current Pos:* EMER PROF NUTRIT, NEW ENG REGIONAL PRIMATE RES CTR, 82- *Personal Data:* b Rexburg, Idaho, Mar 25, 14; m 42; c 2. *Educ:* Univ Idaho, BS, 36; Univ Wis, MS, 38, PhD(biochem), 40. *Hon Degrees:* AM, Harvard Univ, 62; DSc, Univ Idaho, 86. *Honors & Awards:* Osborne-Mendel Award, Am Inst Nutrit, 65; Conrad Elvejhem Award, Am Inst Nutrit, 79; Eleanor Naylor Dana Award, Am Health Found, 80; Bristol-Myers Squibb Award, 93. *Prof Exp:* Asst biochem, Univ Wis, 36-41; res chemist, Abbott Labs, 41-42; from instr to prof, nutrit, Sch Pub Health, Harvard Univ, 42-78; adminr, Human Nutrit Ctr, USDA, 78-82. *Concurrent Pos:* Nutrit consult, Columbian Govt, 46 & Inst Inter-Am Affairs, Peru, 50; chmn food & nutrit bd, Nat Acad Sci-Nat Res Coun; mem var exp comts, WHO & Food & Agr Orgn, UN, 60-; ed, Nutrit Revs, 68-78. *Mem:* Nat Acad Sci; AAAS; hon mem Am Dietetic Asn; Am Chem Soc; Am Inst Nutrit (pres, 72-73). *Res:* Comparative nutrition; protein and calorie requirements; calcium requirements and metabolism; iron metabolism; nutrition problems of under-developed areas; experimental atherosclerosis. *Mailing Add:* One Pine Hill Dr Southborough MA 01772. *Fax:* 508-460-1209

HEGSTED, MAREN, MINERAL METABOLISM, INTERNATIONAL NUTRITION. *Current Pos:* ASSOC PROF NUTRIT, LA STATE UNIV, 80- *Personal Data:* b Salt Lake City, Utah, Sept 16, 50. *Educ:* Univ Utah, BS, 73; Univ Wis-Madison, MS, 78, PhD(nutrit), 80. *Prof Exp:* Vol nutrit, Peace Corps, ACTION, 73-75. *Concurrent Pos:* Consult, AID, 84; sect head, Human Nutrit & Food Sect, Human Ecol, La State Univ, 83- *Mem:* Am Inst Nutrit; Inst Food Technologists; Asn Women Develop. *Res:* Diet, exercise and bone density; rice bran and blood cholesterol; trace and ultratrace elements including zinc, copper and boron. *Mailing Add:* Sch Human Ecol La State Univ Baton Rouge LA 70803-0001. *Fax:* 504-388-2697

HEGSTROM, ROGER ALLEN, THEORETICAL CHEMISTRY. *Current Pos:* from asst prof to assoc prof, 69-80, PROF CHEM, WAKE FOREST UNIV, 80- *Personal Data:* b New Ulm, Minn, July 28, 41; m 67. *Educ:* St Olaf Col, BA, 63; Harvard Univ, AM, 64, PhD(chem), 68. *Prof Exp:* Res assoc chem, Nat Res Coun-Nat Bur Stand, 68-69. *Concurrent Pos:* Guggenheim fel, 78-79; sr vis fel, Oxford Univ, 78-79 & Univ Mich, 82; vis prof, Univ Ill, 90. *Mem:* Am Phys Soc; Am Chem Soc; Sigma Xi. *Res:* Electromagnetic and weak interactions in atoms and molecules; quantum mechanics. *Mailing Add:* Dept Chem Wake Forest Univ Winston-Salem NC 27109. *Fax:* 910-759-4656; *E-Mail:* hegstrom@wfu.edu

HEGYELI, RUTH I E J, CARDIOVASCULAR DISEASES & CANCER. *Current Pos:* asst dir int relations, 76-86, ASSOC DIR INT RELATIONS, OFF OF DIR, NAT HEART, LUNG & BLOOD INST, 87- *Personal Data:* b Stockholm, Sweden, Aug 14, 31; US citizen; wid. *Educ:* Univ Toronto, BA, 58, MD, 62. *Honors & Awards:* Super Serv Award, Dept HEW; Ger Friendship Award, 88; Copernicus Award, 88. *Prof Exp:* Res assoc anat, Univ Toronto, 59; intern med, Queen Charlotte Gen Hosp, Can, 61 & Toronto Gen Hosp, 62-63; res assoc tissue cult, Inst Muscle Res, Woods Hole, Mass, 63-65; head, Tissue Cult Lab, Battelle Mem Inst, 65-67, sr res pathologist & head, Cell Biol Lab, 67-69; med officer artificial heart res, Nat Heart Inst, 69-71 & prog planning, Off of Dir, 71-73, chief prog planning, Prog Develop & Eval Br, 73-76, actg dir, Off Prog Planning & Eval, 75-76. *Concurrent Pos:* Sr invest, res projs, NIH, 65-69; ed, J Soviet Res Cardiovasc Dis, 79-85; mem, Sci Adv Bd, Giovanni Lorenzini Found, 82-; mem bd dirs, Coun Geriat Cardiol, 88- *Mem:* NY Acad Sci; Am Soc Artificial Internal Organs; Coun Epidemiol & Prev; Acad Med Toronto Can. *Res:* Cancer; cardiovascular diseases; heart, lung and blood diseases. *Mailing Add:* 24301 Hanson Ct Gaithersburg MD 20882. *Fax:* 301-253-1602, 496-2734; *E-Mail:* hegyelir@nih.gov

HEGYI, DENNIS, ASTROPHYSICS. *Current Pos:* from asst prof to assoc prof, 75-86, PROF, DEPT PHYSICS, UNIV MICH, ANN ARBOR, 86- *Personal Data:* b Reading, Pa, Dec 23, 42; c Aron & Alex. *Educ:* Mass Inst Technol, BS, 63; Princeton Univ, PhD(physics), 68. *Prof Exp:* Nat Res Coun resident res assoc astrophys, Goddard Inst Space Studies, NASA, 68-70; staff mem, Dept Physics & Astron, Boston Univ, 70-73; asst prof, Bartol Res Found, 73-75. *Concurrent Pos:* Indust consult, sensor design. *Mem:* Am Phys Soc; Am Astron Soc. *Res:* Primordial helium and deuterium, cosmic blockbody radiation, maximum mass of neutron stars, galactic halos; cosmological dark matter. *Mailing Add:* 1708 Morton Ave Ann Arbor MI 48104

HEGYVARY, CSABA, PSYCHIATRY. *Current Pos:* asst prof, Rush Univ, 70-72, assoc prof cardiol, 75-78, prof internal med, 78-86, attend psychiat, 84, ASSOC PROF PHYSIOL, MED SCH, RUSH UNIV, 72- *Personal Data:* b Debrecen, Hungary, Feb 14, 38; US citizen; m 71, Sue Thomas; c Idiko & Adrian. *Educ:* Med Univ Budapest, MD, 62; Hungarian Stat Exam Bd, cert, 66; Am Bd Psychiat & Neurol, 85. *Honors & Awards:* Brainard Award, 76, 83. *Prof Exp:* Asst prof pathophysiol, Inst Pathophysiol, Med Univ Budapest, 62-66; res assoc virol, Krankenhaus Isar, Munich, 66-67; res assoc physiol, Med Sch, Vanderbilt Univ, 67-70. *Mem:* Biophys Soc; Physiol Soc; Sigma Xi; AAAS; Am Psychiat Asn. *Res:* Mechanism of ion-transport across cell membranes, mode of action of digitalis-glycosides on the heart; experimental induction of cardiac hypertrophy. *Mailing Add:* 901 Boren No 1020 Seattle WA 98104

HEGYVARY, SUE THOMAS, MEDICAL SOCIOLOGY, HEALTH SYSTEMS MANAGEMENT. *Current Pos:* asst prof nursing & social, Rush Univ, 72-74, assoc prof mednursing & chairperson dept, 74-77, asst prof social, Rush Univ Med Col, 77-80, PROF NURSING, ASSOC VPRES & ASSOC DEAN NURSING, COL NURSING, RUSH UNIV, RUSHY-PRESBY-ST LUKE'S MED CTR, 77- ASSOC PROF SOCIAL, MED COL, RUSH UNIV, 80- *Personal Data:* b Dry Ridge, Ky, Nov 28, 43; m 71; c 2. *Educ:* Univ Ky, BSN, 65; Emory Univ, MN, 66; Vanderbilt Univ, PhD(sociol), 74. *Prof Exp:* Staff nurse, Univ Ky Med Ctr, 65; instr med-surg nursing, Col Nursing, Univ Fla, 66-67, asst prof & chmn dept, 67-69. *Concurrent Pos:* Consult, Vet Admin Hosp, Miami, Fla, 68-69 & Student Health Coalition, Vanderbilt Univ, 71; investr, HEW contract, Rush-Presby-St Luke's Med Ctr Chicago, 72-; sci staff, Nat Hosp Inst, Neth, 79-80. *Mem:* Am Sociol Asn; Am Nurses' Asn; Am Acad Nursing. *Res:* Assessment of the quality of patient care and the influence of organizational, demographic and professional variables on the quality of care. *Mailing Add:* Dean/Dir Nursing Univ Wash 3900 Seventh Ave NE Seattle WA 98195-0001

HEHRE, EDWARD JAMES, ENZYMOLOGY, CARBOHYDRATE CHEMISTRY. *Current Pos:* head dept, 56-78, prof, 56-78, EMER PROF MICROBIOL & IMMUNOL, ALBERT EINSTEIN COL MED, 78- *Personal Data:* b New York, NY, Dec 14, 12; m 38, Florence D Baker; c Edward J Jr, Elizabeth J & Warren J. *Educ:* Cornell Univ, BA, 34, MD, 37. *Honors & Awards:* John Fogarty Sr Int Res Fel, NIH, 88; Medal of Merit, Japan Soc Starch Sci, 89. *Prof Exp:* Intern path, New York Hosp, 37-38; from asst to assoc prof bact & immunol, Med Col, Cornell Univ, 38-56. *Concurrent Pos:* John Simon Guggenheim fel, 64-65; vis prof, Grad Fac Sci, Tokyo Kyoiku Univ, 64-65 & Shizouka Univ, 71, Res Inst Food Sci, Kyoto Univ, 94; John Polachek fel, 70-71; vis researcher, Osaka Munic Tech Res Inst, 98. *Mem:* Am Chem Soc; Am Soc Biochem & Molecular Biol. *Res:* Enzymic synthesis of polysaccharides; glycosyl transfer concept; glycosyl-proton interchange basis of unified class of glycosylases; use of nonglycosidic substrates to gain new understanding of stereochemical behavior of glycosylases. *Mailing Add:* Dept Microbiol & Immunol Albert Einstein Col Med New York NY 10461

HEHRE, EDWARD JAMES, JR, PHYCOLOGY, PLANT TAXONOMY. *Current Pos:* CONSULT MARINE BIOL, UNIV AZORES, 78-; CONSULT, JACKSON LAB, UNIV NH. *Personal Data:* b New York, NY, Feb 22, 40; m 63; c 2. *Educ:* New Eng Col, BS, 63; Univ NH, PhD(bot), 69. *Prof Exp:* Asst prof bot, Southampton Col, Long Island Univ, 69-77; mem fac bot, Univ NH, 77-78. *Mem:* Phycol Soc Am; Int Phycol Soc. *Res:* Occurrence, distribution, seasonality and reproductive periodicity of marine red algae in New Hampshire; algal and vascular plant flora of Gardiners Island, New York; floristic studies and ecology of marine algae of New Hampshire; marine flora of Azores Islands. *Mailing Add:* 26 Park St South Berwick ME 03908

HEIBA, EL-AHMADI IBRAHIM, ORGANIC & PHYSICAL ORGANIC CHEMISTRY. *Current Pos:* RETIRED. *Personal Data:* b Egypt, May 7, 26; m 55; c 2. *Educ:* Alexandria Univ, BSc, 48; Univ London, PhD, 52. *Prof Exp:* Asst prof, Univ Cairo, 52-54; sr res chemist, Sch Pharm, Univ London, 54-55; fel & supvr radiation chem, Phoenix Mem Lab, Univ Mich, 55-58; sr radiation chemist, Arthur D Little, Inc, Mass, 58-62; dir chem res, Mobil Res & Develop Corp, 69-75; dir crop chem res, Mobil Chem Co, 75-82; consult, World Bank, 82-89. *Mem:* Am Chem Soc. *Res:* Free radicals chemistry and reaction mechanisms; chemical factor influencing plant photosynthesis and crop productivity; homogeneous and heterogeneous catalysis. *Mailing Add:* 11 Balsam Lane Princeton NJ 08540. *E-Mail:* el_ahmadiheiba1628@worldnet.att.net

HEIBERG, ELVIN R, III, CIVIL ENGINEERING, CONSTRUCTION. *Current Pos:* PRES, HEIBERG ASN, 94- *Personal Data:* b Hawaii, Mar 2, 32. *Educ:* Mass Inst Technol, MS, 58; George Washington Univ, MA, 61, MS, 71. *Mem:* Nat Acad Eng. *Mailing Add:* 10715 Harley Rd Mason Neck VA 22079. *Fax:* 703-550-1783; *E-Mail:* 103076.3327@compuserve.com

HEIBERGER, PHILIP, PHYSICAL CHEMISTRY, ORGANIC CHEMISTRY. *Current Pos:* RETIRED. *Personal Data:* b New York, NY, Mar 15, 19; m 42; c 3. *Educ:* Polytech Inst Brooklyn, BSc, 39; Cornell Univ, MA, 41; Univ Tex, PhD(org chem), 53. *Prof Exp:* Asst, Cornell Univ, 39-41; chemist, Colgate-Palmolive Co, 41-42; group leader, Ralph L Evans Assoc, 42-46; chemist new prod develop, Interchem Corp, 47-49; chemist thermoplastics & lacquers, Atlas Powder Co, 49-51; res scientist, Univ Tex, 51-53; group leader oil & resin develop, Nat Lead Co, 53-57; res chemist, E I du Pont de Nemours & Co, Inc, 57-66, develop specialist, 66-70, licensing coordr, 71-74, mgr technol licensing, 74-76, res assoc, 76-83. *Concurrent Pos:* Engr, Kellex Corp, 45; trustee, 74-76, pres, Paint Res Inst, 76-78; vol exec, Int Exec Serv Corp, 84 - *Mem:* Am Chem Soc. *Res:* Synthetic latices; condensation resins; organic coatings; utilization of drying oils; industrial paint systems; dispersion techniques; organic reaction mechanisms. *Mailing Add:* 8460 Limekiln Pike No 1113 Wyncote PA 19095-2612

HEIBLUM, MORDEHAI, MOLECULAR BEAM EPITAXY GROWTH OF III-V SEMI-CONDUCTORS, BALLISTIC TRANSPORT OF CHARGED CARRIERS IN SOLIDS. *Current Pos:* PROF, DEPT PHYSICS, WEIZMANN INST SCI, ISRAEL, 90- *Personal Data:* b Tel Aviv, Israel, May 25, 47; US citizen; m 70; c 4. *Educ:* Israeli Inst Technol, BSc, 73; Carnegie Mellon Univ, MSc, 74; Univ Calif, Berkeley, PhD(elec eng), 78. *Prof Exp:* Res staff mem, IBM, T J Watson Res Ctr, 78-86, res staff mem & group mgr, 86-90. *Mem:* Fel Inst Elec & Electronics Engrs; fel Am Physics Soc; Am Vacuum Soc. *Res:* In the physics and invention of new ultra fast devices, based primarily on III-V semi-conductor compounds. *Mailing Add:* Weizmann Inst Sci Sub Micron Semiconductor Ctr Dept Condensed Matter Phys Rehovot 76100 Israel

HEICHEL, GARY HAROLD, CROP PHYSIOLOGY, PLANT ECOLOGY. *Current Pos:* head, Dept Agron, 90-95, interim head, Dept Plant Path, 94-95, HEAD, DEPT CROP SCI, UNIV ILL, URBANA, 95- *Personal Data:* b Park Falls, Wis, Nov 9, 40; m 88, Iris Fehl. *Educ:* Iowa State Univ, BS, 62; Cornell Univ, MS, 64, PhD(agron), 68. *Honors & Awards:* Outstanding Scientist of Yr, USDA-Agr Res Serv, 86; Merit Cert, Am Forage Grassland Coun, 86; Crop Sci Res Award, Crop Sci Soc Am, 87. *Prof Exp:* Asst agron, Cornell Univ, 62-64, 66-68 & Univ Philippines-Cornell Univ Grad Educ Prog, 64-66; asst crop physiologist, 68-73, assoc plant physiologist, 73-76, plant physiologist, Conn Agr Exp Sta, 76; plant physiologist, USDA-Agr Res Serv, 76-90; adj prof, Univ Minn, 76-90. *Concurrent Pos:* Prog mgr, USDA Competitive Grants Off, 81; mem, Energy Eng Bd, Nat Res Coun, 83-87; consult ed, Am Scientist, 83-90; ed-in chief, Am Soc Agron, 88-90; mem, bd trustees, Am Soc Plant Physiol, 88-90; Kellogg fel, Food Agr Policy, Resources Future, 89. *Mem:* Am Soc Agron (pres, 97-98); Crop Sci Soc Am (pres-elect, 90-91, pres, 91-92); Am Soc Plant Physiologists; Am Forage & Grassland Coun; Sigma Xi; Crop Sci Soc Am; fel AAAS. *Res:* Symbiotic nitrogen fixation; photosynthesis; productivity of forage legumes; nitrogen cycling; physiology; physiological, morphogenetic and environmental limitations to forage yield; energy use in agriculture ecosystems. *Mailing Add:* Dept Crop Sci Univ Ill 1102 S Goodwin Ave AW-101 Urbana IL 61801-4798

HEICHELHEIM, HUBERT REED, CHEMICAL ENGINEERING. *Current Pos:* RETIRED. *Personal Data:* b McAlester, Okla, Jan 5, 31; m 56, Janis B Pesek; c George, Kenneth E, June M, Paul A, Karl W, Stephen J, Anna L & Judith B. *Educ:* Univ Notre Dame, BS, 53, MS, 56; Univ Tex, PhD(chem eng), 62. *Prof Exp:* Asst prof to assoc prof, Tex Tech Univ, 61-80, asst chmn chem eng, 80-96. *Concurrent Pos:* Process engr, Phillips Petrol & Suntide Refining; Gastdozent, Fachhchschule Wilhelmshaven, Ger. *Res:* Volumetric behavior and thermodynamic properties of gases. *Mailing Add:* Dept Chem Eng Tex Tech Univ Lubbock TX 79406. *E-Mail:* heich@coe1.coe.ttu.edu

HEICKLEN, JULIAN PHILLIP, ATMOSPHERIC CHEMISTRY. *Current Pos:* assoc prof, 67-71, PROF CHEM, PA STATE UNIV, UNIVERSITY PARK, 71-, MEM TECH STAFF, CTR AIR ENVIRON STUDIES & IONOSPHERE RES LAB, 67- *Personal Data:* b Rochester, NY, Mar 9, 32; m 59; c 3. *Educ:* Cornell Univ, BChE, 54; Univ Rochester, PhD(chem), 58. *Honors & Awards:* Am Chem Soc Award, Creative Advan Environ Sci & Technol, 84; Boris Pregel Award Appl Sci & Technol, NY Acad Sci, 84; Frank A Chambers Award, Air Pollution Control Asn, 85. *Prof Exp:* Res fel chem, Univ Minn, 59-60 & Univ Calif, 60-62; mem tech staff, Aerospace Corp, 62-65, mgr, Pyrolytic Mat & Kinetics Sect, 65-67. *Concurrent Pos:* Sigma Xi regional lectr, 71-72; consult, Panel Biol Effects Hydrocarbon Air Pollutants, Nat Res Coun, 72; vis prof, Hebrew Univ Jerusalem, 73-74; pres, Heicklen Assocs, 77- *Mem:* Fel AAAS; Am Chem Soc; fel Am Phys Soc; Royal Soc Chem; fel NY Acad Sci. *Res:* Photochemistry; reaction kinetics; vibrational spectroscopy; gerontology; carcinogenesis; mutogenesis; photochemistry; combustion chemistry. *Mailing Add:* 2008 Park Forest Ave State College PA 16803

HEID, ROLAND LEO, PHYSICS. *Current Pos:* From instr to asst prof math, St Vincent Col, 50-54, chmn dept, 50-54, from assoc prof to prof physics, 54-85, chmn dept, 54-68 & 72-84, EMER PROF, ST VINCENT COL, 85- *Personal Data:* b Erie, Pa, July 7, 14. *Educ:* St Vincent Col, AB, 37; Johns Hopkins Univ, PhD(physics), 50. *Mem:* Am Phys Soc; Optical Soc Am; Am Asn Physics Teachers. *Res:* Spectroscopy; optics. *Mailing Add:* Dept Physics St Vincent Col Latrobe PA 15650

HEIDBREDER, GLENN R, ELECTRICAL ENGINEERING. *Current Pos:* RETIRED. *Personal Data:* b Gerald, Mo, July 22, 29; div; c 1. *Educ:* Yale Univ, BE, 51, MEng, 56, DEng(elec eng), 59. *Prof Exp:* Instr elec eng, Yale Univ, 57-59; mem tech staff, Space Tech Labs, 59-62 & Aerospace Corp, 62-63 & 65-67; from asst prof to assoc prof elec eng, Univ Calif, Santa Barbara, 67-91. *Concurrent Pos:* Lectr, Univ Calif, Los Angeles, 60-63; sr scientist, Tech Serv Corp, 70-71. *Mem:* Inst Elec & Electronics Engrs. *Res:* Radar systems; communications theory; radio propagation in random media. *Mailing Add:* 11509 Hemingway Dr Reston VA 22094

HEIDCAMP, WILLIAM H, DEVELOPMENTAL BIOLOGY, CELL BIOLOGY. *Current Pos:* asst prof, 73-80, PROF BIOL, GUSTAVUS ADOLPHUS COL, 80-, CHMN DEPT, 78- *Personal Data:* b Saugerties, NY, Oct 26, 44; m 66; c 2. *Educ:* Siena Col NY, BS, 66; Univ Pittsburgh, PhD(biol), 71. *Prof Exp:* Instr biol, Carlow Col, 68-69, Carnegie-Mellon Univ, 69-71, Concordia Univ, 71-73. *Concurrent Pos:* Fel, Montreal Cancer Inst, 71-73; res fel, Dept Path, Univ Montreal, 73-74. *Mem:* AAAS; Am Inst Biol Sci; Nat Sci Teachers Asn; Sigma Xi. *Res:* Interaction of cation metabolism and Em expression of neoplasia. *Mailing Add:* Biol Dept Gustavus Adolphus Col St Peter MN 56082. *Fax:* 507-933-7041

HEIDEGER, WILLIAM J(OSEPH), CHEMICAL ENGINEERING, MASS TRANSFER. *Current Pos:* From asst prof to assoc prof, 57-70, PROF CHEM ENG, UNIV WASH, 70- *Personal Data:* b Beaver, Pa, Sept 17, 32; m 58; c 3. *Educ:* Carnegie Inst Technol, BS, 54; Princeton Univ, MSE, 56, PhD(chem eng), 59. *Concurrent Pos:* Consult, Puget Sound Div, Pac Corp, 63; Atomic Energy Comn fel, 67. *Mem:* Am Inst Chem Engrs; Am Chem Soc; Am Soc Eng Educ. *Res:* Mass transfer and interfacial phenomena; biological mass transfer. *Mailing Add:* 2514 Fifth Ave W Seattle WA 98119

HEIDELBAUGH, NORMAN DALE, FOOD TOXICOLOGY, PUBLIC HEALTH. *Current Pos:* prof, Food Sci & Technol, 76-90, DIR, FOOD SAFETY PROG DEVELOP, TEX A&M UNIV, 90- *Personal Data:* b Philadelphia, Pa, July 29, 27; m 63; c 3. *Educ:* Univ Pa, VMD, 54; Tulane Univ, MPH, 58; Mass Inst Technol, MS, 63, PhD(food sci), 70. *Honors & Awards:* Underwood-Prescott Award, 74. *Prof Exp:* Vet food technologist, USAF, 54-62; food technologist, Nat Acad Sci-USAF Mission, Arg, 63-64, vet officer & lectr food sci, USAF Sch Aerospace Med, 64-67, chief food sci, NASA Manned Spacecraft Ctr, Houston, 70-74, mgr, USAF Food Res & Develop Prog, US Army Natick Lab, 74-76. *Mem:* Am Vet Med Asn; Inst Food Technol. *Res:* Food science and technology; food safety; public health; food and drug law; nutrition under stress conditions; veterinary medicine; zoonoses control; food deterioration effects on health. *Mailing Add:* 1110 Langford St College Station TX 77840

HEIDELBERGER, PHILIP, DISCRETE EVENT SIMULATION. *Current Pos:* RES STAFF MEM, THOMAS J WATSON RES CTR, IBM, 78- *Personal Data:* b Madison, Wis, Nov 25, 51. *Educ:* Oberlin Col, BA, 74; Stanford Univ, PhD(opers res), 78. *Concurrent Pos:* Assoc ed, Opers Res, 82-90; prog chmn, 1989 Winter Simulation Conf, 89; area ed, Asn Comput Mach Trans on Comput Simulation, 90-, Asn Comput Mach Sigmetrics/ Performance Conf, 92; mem, Int Fedn Info Processing Working Group. *Mem:* Fel Asn Comput Mach; fel Inst Elec & Electronics Engrs; Opers Res Soc Am. *Res:* Discrete event simulation, including efficient simulation techniques and algorithms; probabilistic aspects of simulations. *Mailing Add:* Thomas J Watson Res Ctr IBM PO Box 704 Yorktown Heights NY 10598

HEIDEMANN, STEVEN RICHARD, CELL & DEVELOPMENTAL BIOLOGY, NEUROSCIENCE. *Current Pos:* asst prof, 78-82, assoc prof physiol & biol sci prog, 82-87, PROF, DEPT PHYSIOL, MICROBIOL & PUB HEALTH, MICH STATE UNIV, 87- *Personal Data:* b New York, NY, Sept 9, 49; m 73; c 2. *Educ:* State Univ NY, Stony Brook, BS, 71; Princeton Univ, MA, 73, PhD(biol), 76. *Prof Exp:* Res assoc cell biol, Dept Molecular, Cellular & Develop Biol, Univ Colo, 77-78. *Concurrent Pos:* NSF fel, 77-78; Res Career Develop Award, NIH, 81-86. *Mem:* Am Soc Cell Biol; Am Physiol Soc. *Res:* Cytomechanics of neural development. *Mailing Add:* Dept Physiol 219 Giltner Hall Mich State Univ East Lansing MI 48824. *Fax:* 517-355-5125; *E-Mail:* heidemann@psl.msu.edu

HEIDENREICH, CHARLES JOHN, ANIMAL HUSBANDRY. *Current Pos:* RETIRED. *Personal Data:* b Berwyn, Ill, Nov 27, 27; m 51; c 1. *Educ:* Univ Ill, BS, 51; SDak State Col, MS, 52; Univ Mo, PhD(animal physiol), 57. *Prof Exp:* Asst animal husb, SDak State Col, 51-52; from asst to instr animal sci, Univ Mo, 53-56; from asst prof to assoc prof animal physiol, Purdue Univ, 56-66; from assoc prof to prof animal sci, Univ Wis, Platteville, 66-90. *Concurrent Pos:* Consult livestock & feed mfg indust. *Mem:* Am Soc Animal Sci; Am Reg Prof Animal Sci. *Res:* Animal physiology, especially environmental effects upon productive efficiency of meat producing animals; non-ruminant Nutrit. *Mailing Add:* 202 Broadmoor Dr Fredricksburg TX 78624

HEIDENREICH, R D, PARTICLE PHYSICS. *Current Pos:* RETIRED. *Personal Data:* b Cuyahoga Falls, Ohio, Nov 22, 16. *Educ:* Case Univ, BS, 38, MS, 40. *Prof Exp:* Res scientist, AT&T Bell Labs. *Mem:* Am Phys Soc. *Mailing Add:* 4223 Quince Ct Boulder CO 80301

HEIDER, SHIRLEY (SCOTT) A(MBORN), MECHANICAL ENGINEERING. *Current Pos:* RETIRED. *Personal Data:* b West Salem, Wis, Apr 11, 12; m 49, Ruth Salisbury; c 1. *Educ:* Univ Wis, BS, 34. *Prof Exp:* Res & develop engr, Trane Co, 34-41; engr naval archit, Bur Ships, US Dept Navy, 41-46; underwriting supvr, Fed Housing Admin, 46-47; partner, Stem & Heider Co, 47-49; consult engr, Wilberding Co, Inc, 49-51; res engr, Bldg Res Adv Bd, Nat Acad Sci, 51-57, Fed Housing Admin, 57-64 & NSF, 64-72; gen engr, Dept Housing & Urban Develop, 72-80. *Concurrent Pos:* Ed consult, Nat Bur Stand, 80-82. *Mem:* Nat Soc Prof Engrs; Am Soc Testing & Mat. *Res:* Research facilities; building research; mechanical and electrical equipment; building materials and components. *Mailing Add:* 403 Russell Ave Apt G-5 Gaithersburg MD 20877-2811

HEIDGER, PAUL MCCLAY, JR, ANATOMY. *Current Pos:* assoc prof, 74-80, PROF ANAT, MED SCH, UNIV IOWA, 80- *Personal Data:* b St Johnsbury, Vt, Sept 13, 41; m 67; c 2. *Educ:* Univ Northern Colo, AB, 63; Tulane Univ, PhD(anat), 67. *Prof Exp:* NIH res fel anat, Harvard Med Sch, 67-69; from asst prof to assoc prof, Med Sch, Tulane Univ, 69-74. *Concurrent Pos:* NIH res grant, Med Sch, Tulane Univ, 71-74; NIH res contract, Med Sch, Univ Iowa, 74-76; NIH res grant, 78- *Mem:* Am Asn Anatomists; Electron Micros Soc Am; Soc Study Reproduction; Sigma Xi. *Res:* Cytochemistry and fine structure of reproductive system; tissue culture of normal and malignant prostate gland; electron microscopy of bacterial L-forms. *Mailing Add:* Dept Anat Univ Iowa Col Med Iowa City IA 52242

HEIDNER, ROBERT HUBBARD, ANALYTICAL CHEMISTRY. *Current Pos:* RETIRED. *Personal Data:* b Holyoke, Mass, Mar 14, 19; m 44, Ernestine Adams; c Karen (Ward), Sue A (Shelley) & Cynthia L (Elcan). *Educ:* Hamilton Col, BS, 40, MA, 42. *Prof Exp:* Asst chem, Hamilton Col, 40-42; res chemist, Monsanto Chem Co, Ohio, 42-45 & Mass, 45-52; res chemist, Chemstrand Corp, 52-55, group leader, Wet Methods Analysis Group, Res Ctr, Ala, 55-60; analysis group leader, Chemstrand Res Ctr, Inc, 60-68; supvr analysis & test methods develop, Monsanto Textiles Co, 68-78, supvr, Analysis & Control Lab, Tech Ctr, 78-80, supvr, Control Lab Stand, 80-82. *Mem:* Am Chem Soc. *Res:* Analytical chemistry of organic monomers, intermediates, high polymers and chemical fibers; wet methods; ultraviolet, visible and infrared spectroscopy; atomic absorption; tristimulus colorimetry; polymer and fiber characterization techniques. *Mailing Add:* 6 Sea Swallow Terr Ormond Beach FL 32176-2238

HEIDRICK, LEE E, PLANT PATHOLOGY. *Current Pos:* RETIRED. *Personal Data:* b Little Valley, NY, June 23, 21; m 52, Esther Lisdell. *Educ:* Cornell Univ, BS, 43, MS, 51; WVa Univ, PhD(plant path), 61. *Prof Exp:* Res assoc plant path, Rockefeller Found, Mex, 51-52; plant pathologist, Colombia, 52-63; res specialist, Chevron Chem Co, 63-84. *Mem:* AAAS; Potato Asn Am; Am Phytopath Soc; Sigma Xi. *Res:* Development of agricultural research in Latin America; organization, administration and training of agricultural technical workers; agricultural fungicides. *Mailing Add:* 100 Winthrop Dr Ithaca NY 14850-1733

HEIDRICK, MARGARET LOUISE, BIOCHEMISTRY, IMMUNOLOGY. *Current Pos:* asst prof, 73-78, ASSOC PROF BIOCHEM, UNIV NEBR MED CTR, OMAHA, 78- *Personal Data:* b Beloit, Kans, June 23, 38. *Educ:* Marymount Col, BS, 59; Univ Mo, 64; Univ Nebr, MS, 68, PhD(biochem), 70. *Prof Exp:* Chemist, US Fed Food & Drug Admin, Kansas City, Mo, 59-61; res technologist, Eppley Inst Cancer Res, Omaha, Nebr, 64-68. *Concurrent Pos:* NIH fel, Oak Ridge Nat Lab, 70-72; NIH staff fel, Geront Res Ctr, Baltimore, Md, 72-73; mem, Nat Adv Coun, Nat Inst Allergy & Infectious Dis, 75-77. *Mem:* Am Asn Immunologists; Am Soc Cell Biologists; fel Geront Soc. *Res:* Cancer; aging of immune system; cytochrome P-450 isozymes. *Mailing Add:* 600 S 42nd St Univ Nebr Col Med Omaha NE 68198-4525. *Fax:* 402-559-6650; *E-Mail:* mlheidri@mail.unmc.edu

HEIDT, GARY A, MAMMALOGY. *Current Pos:* from asst prof to assoc prof, 70-79, PROF BIOL & DIR, BASIC ANIMAL SERV UNIT, UNIV ARK, LITTLE ROCK, 79- *Personal Data:* b South Bend, Ind, May 20, 42; m 97, Suzanne Belcher; c Deborah, Scott & Nora. *Educ:* Manchester Col, BS, 64; Mich State Univ, MS, 68, PhD(zool), 69. *Honors & Awards:* Robert L Packard Outstanding Educ Award, Southwestern Asn Naturalists, 92. *Prof Exp:* Asst prof biol sci, Mich State Univ, 69-70. *Concurrent Pos:* Chmn bd dirs, Little Rock Mus Sci & Hist, 74-75; adj grad fac, Memphis State Univ, 80-; adj prof biol, NTex Univ, 93-, Univ Ark, Fayetteville. *Mem:* Am Soc Mammal; Wildlife Soc; Am Asn Lab Animal Sci; Wildlife Dis Asn. *Res:* Disease, ecological and behavioral interactions of mammals; primarily dealing with carnivores and rodents. *Mailing Add:* Dept Biol Univ Ark Little Rock AR 72204. *Fax:* 870-569-3271; *E-Mail:* gaheidt@ualr.edu

HEIFETZ, CARL LOUIS, BACTERIOLOGY, CHEMOTHERAPY. *Current Pos:* CONSULT, MICRODOC CONSULT INC, 92- *Personal Data:* b Somerville, NJ, Mar 9, 35; m 59; c 2. *Educ:* Univ Md, BS, 57, MS, 60, PhD(microbiol), 65. *Prof Exp:* Asst microbiol, Univ Md, 57-58, from asst to instr pharmacol, 58-64; assoc res bacteriologist, Microbiol Dept, Res Div, Parke Davis & Co, 64-68; res microbiologist, 68-71, res assoc, Div Res & Develop, 71-78, sr res assoc, 78-83, sect dir, 83-89, dir, Parke-Davis Pharmaceut Res Div, Warner Lambert Co, 83-92. *Concurrent Pos:* Res trainee dent microbiol, 62-64; adj prof & clin prof, Eastern Mich Univ; lectr, Sch Pub Health & Sch Pharm, Univ Mich, biol, Marquette Univ; chair-elect, Div A, Am Soc Microbiol, 90-, counr, 90- *Mem:* AAAS; Am Soc Microbiol; Brit Soc Antimicrobiol Chemother; Int Am Soc Chemother; fel Am Acad Microbiol. *Res:* Staphylococcal physiology and bacteriophages; antibacterial chemotherapy; immunomodulation; mechanism of action/toxicity of quinolones; bacterial mutations (Ames Test). *Mailing Add:* 3693 Siena Lane Palm Harbor FL 34685

HEIFETZ, JONATHAN, BIOMETRICS, ECOLOGY. *Current Pos:* FISHERY RES BIOLOGIST, AUKE BAY LAB, NAT MARINE FISHERIES SERV, 82- *Personal Data:* b Long Branch, NJ, June 28, 56; m 88, Carin J Smolin; c Lia G & Marc H. *Educ:* Emory Univ, BS, 78; Humboldt State Univ, MS, 82; Univ Alaska, PhD, 96. *Mem:* Am Fisheries Soc; Am Inst Fisheries Res Biologists. *Res:* Provide analyses and assessments of population dynamics of Alaskan groundfish; develop experimental designs, computer models, prepare manuscripts and conduct field studies. *Mailing Add:* 11305 Glacier Hwy Juneau AK 99801. *Fax:* 907-789-6094; *E-Mail:* jon.heifetz@noaa.gov

HEIFETZ, MILTON DAVID, NEUROSURGERY. *Current Pos:* RETIRED. *Personal Data:* b Hartford, Conn, Feb 7, 21; m 43, Betsy; c Laurence, Daniel, Ronnie & Deborah. *Educ:* Univ Ill, BS, 41, MD, 45; Am Bd Neurosurg, dipl, 55. *Prof Exp:* From instr to asst prof, 53-72, assoc prof neurosurg, Sch Med, Loma Linda Univ, 73- *Concurrent Pos:* Mem neurosurg staff, Cedars-Sinai & Med Ctr, Los Angeles; clin prof neurosurg, Sch Med, Univ Southern Calif; vis prof, Harvard Med Sch; adj prof law (ethics), Boston Col Law Sch. *Mem:* Cong Neurol Surg; assoc Am Acad Neurologists; Am Asn Neurol Surgeons. *Res:* Stereotactic radiosurgery; instrumentation design. *Mailing Add:* 704 N Bedford Dr Beverly Hills CA 90210. *Fax:* 310-273-1710

HEIFFER, MELVIN HAROLD, PHYSIOLOGY, PHARMACOLOGY. *Current Pos:* pharmacologist, Dept Med Chem, 56-66, CHIEF DEPT PHARMACOL, WALTER REED ARMY INST RES, 66- *Personal Data:* b Norfolk, Va, Sept 30, 27. *Educ:* Col William & Mary, BS, 49; George Washington Univ, MS, 51, PhD(physiol), 53. *Prof Exp:* Lab asst physiol, Sch Med, George Washington Univ, 51-52, asst, 52-53, fel, 53-54, asst res prof, 54-56. *Mem:* Am Soc Pharmacol & Exp Therapeut; fel Am Col Clin Pharmacol; Soc Exp Biol & Med; Radiation Res Soc; NY Acad Sci; Sigma Xi. *Res:* Drug development; autonomic pharmacology; radioprotectants; adrenergic mechanisms; antimalarials. *Mailing Add:* Dept Pharmacol Walter Reed Army Inst Res Washington DC 20307-5100. *Fax:* 301-427-6569

HEIGOLD, PAUL C, GROUNDWATER GEOLOGY. *Current Pos:* asst geophysicist, 62-74, ASSOC GEOPHYSICIST, ILL STATE GEOL SURV, 74- *Personal Data:* b St Louis, Mo, Apr 9, 36; m 67. *Educ:* St Louis Univ, BS, 57, MS, 61; Univ Ill, Urbana, MS, 64, PhD(geol), 69. *Prof Exp:* Geophysicist, Carter Oil Co, Okla, 57-58 & Desert Res Inst, Nev, 62. *Concurrent Pos:* Mem, Ill-Princeton Univ Archeol Exped, Morgantina, Sicily, 70. *Mem:* Am Geophys Union. *Res:* Shallow exploration and detailed gravity surveying of the entire state of Illinois; theoretical ground-water flow system analysis. *Mailing Add:* 2001 Melrose Dr Champaign IL 61820

HEIKEN, GRANT HARVEY, GEOLOGY, PLANETOLOGY. *Current Pos:* GEOLOGIST VOLCANOLOGY, LOS ALAMOS NAT LAB, UNIV CALIF, 75- *Personal Data:* b Monticello, Iowa, Oct 11, 42; m 67. *Educ:* Univ Calif, Berkeley, BA, 64; Univ Tex, Austin, MA, 66; Univ Calif, Santa Barbara, PhD(geol), 72. *Honors & Awards:* Cert Spec Commend, Geol Soc Am, 73; Cert Commend, Johnson Space Ctr, NASA, 74. *Prof Exp:* Geologist planetology, Johnson Space Ctr, NASA, 69-75. *Concurrent Pos:* Mem, Lunar Sample Preliminary Exam Teams, Apollo, 69-72; mem, Visual Observations Team, Skylab, 73. *Mem:* Geol Soc Am; Int Asn Volcanology & Chem Earth's Interior; Sigma Xi; Brit Interplanetary Soc. *Res:* Volcanology and igneous petrology; eruption phenomena and sources for geothermal energy; origins and utilization of pyroclastic rocks; planetology, in particular the formation of planetary regoliths and volcanic phenomena. *Mailing Add:* 119 Piedra Loop Los Alamos NM 87544

HEIKKENEN, HERMAN JOHN, FOREST ENTOMOLOGY. *Current Pos:* ASSOC PROF FOREST ENTOM, VA POLYTECH INST & STATE UNIV, 67- *Personal Data:* b Detroit, Mich, June 20, 30; m 52; c 2. *Educ:* Univ Mich, BSF, 53, MF, 57, PhD(forestry), 63. *Prof Exp:* Res asst forest entom, Weyerhaeuser Co, 57; entomologist, Lake States Forest Exp Sta, US Forest Serv, 58-61, proj leader forest entom, Southeastern Forest Exp Sta, 61-62; asst prof, Univ Wash, 62-67. *Mem:* AAAS; Soc Am Foresters; Entom Soc Am; Sigma Xi. *Res:* Host relations and interactions with insect pests. *Mailing Add:* 802 Preston Ave Blacksburg VA 24060-5138

HEIKKILA, JOHN J, MOLECULAR BIOLOGY. *Current Pos:* ASST PROF BIOL, UNIV WATERLOO, 84- *Personal Data:* b Alharma, Finland, Nov 22, 50. *Educ:* Toronto Univ, PhD(zool), 80. *Mailing Add:* Dept Biol Univ Waterloo Waterloo ON N2L 3G1 Can. *Fax:* 519-746-0614

HEIKKILA, WALTER JOHN, SPACE PHYSICS. *Current Pos:* from assoc prof to prof, Southwest Ctr Advan Studies, 63-68, PROF PHYSICS, UNIV TEX, DALLAS, 68- *Personal Data:* b South Porcupine, Ont, Feb 22, 28; div; c 2. *Educ:* Univ Toronto, BASc, 50, PhD(low temperature physics), 54. *Prof Exp:* Group leader tropospheric physics, Radio Physics Lab, Defence Res Bd, Ottawa, Ont, 54-58, sect leader, Rocket Sect, 58-63. *Concurrent Pos:* Adj prof elec eng, Southern Methodist Univ, 64-72; mem US comn four, Int Sci Radio Union; mem working group four, Comt Space Res. *Mem:* Am Geophys Union; Can Asn Physicists; Int Asn Geomagnetism & Aeronomy. *Res:* Rocket and satellite research on ionospheric, auroral and magnetospheric phenomena, especially soft particle fluxes on ISIS-1 and 2 satellites and laboratory studies of plasma probes; problems of population growth. *Mailing Add:* 2704 Canyon Valley Dr Richardson TX 75080

HEIKKINEN, DALE WILLIAM, NUCLEAR PHYSICS. *Current Pos:* SR PHYSICIST NUCLEAR PHYSICS, LAWRENCE LIVERMORE LAB, 68- *Personal Data:* b Virginia, Minn, Nov 14, 38; m 59; c 2. *Educ:* Univ Minn, Duluth, BA, 60; Univ Iowa, MS, 62, PhD(physics), 65. *Prof Exp:* Res assoc nuclear physics, Stanford Univ, 65-68. *Concurrent Pos:* Vis scholar, Stanford Univ, 70-71; vis assoc prof, Univ Jyvaskyla, 72-73. *Mem:* Am Phys Soc; Am Nuclear Soc. *Res:* Basic and applied research in nuclear physics. *Mailing Add:* L-397 Lawrence Livermore Lab UCL PO Box 808 Livermore CA 94550

HEIKKINEN, DONALD D, MATHEMATICS. *Current Pos:* assoc prof math, Northern Mich Univ, 68-71, dir, NSF In-Serv Inst, 68-69, head, Dept Math, 68-73, chmn Acad Senate, 73-74, dean Arts & Sci, 74-89, PROF MATH, NORTHERN MICH UNIV, 68- *Personal Data:* b Ramsay, Mich, Sept 10, 32; m 56; c 1. *Educ:* Univ Mich, BA, 58, MA, 60, PhD(math educ), 64. *Prof Exp:* Teacher, Lee M Thurston High Sch, 58-59; asst prof math, Eastern Mich Univ, 60-61; res asst math educ, Univ Mich, 61-62; assoc prof math, Northern Iowa Univ, 63-68, assoc dir, NSF Summer Inst, 65-67. *Concurrent Pos:* Math ed, Sch Sci & Math, 63-74. *Res:* Factors related to acceleration in the study of mathematics. *Mailing Add:* 1011 Tenth St Lillington NC 27546

HEIKKINEN, HENRY WENDELL, CHEMICAL EDUCATION, CHEMISTRY. *Current Pos:* dir, Math & Sci Teaching Ctr, 86-92, PROF CHEM, UNIV NORTHERN COLO, 86-, CO-DIR, 94- *Personal Data:* b Minneapolis, Minn, May 18, 35; m 64, 93, Catherine Chetney; c Susan & Henry. *Educ:* Yale Univ, BEng, 56; Columbia Univ, MA, 62; Univ Md, PhD(chem educ), 73. *Prof Exp:* Food engr res & develop, Gen Mills, Inc, 56-61; teacher chem, Richfield Pub Schs, Minn, 63-69; teaching assoc chem, Univ Md, College Park, 69-70, from instr to assoc prof chem, 70-86. *Concurrent Pos:* Adv Bd mem, Chem Mag, Am Chem Soc, 72-76 & Sci Teacher, Nat Sci Teachers Asn, 74-77; chief ed, ChemCom, 84-92; secy, educ sect, AAAS, 92-96, chair, 96-97. *Mem:* Am Chem Soc; Nat Asn Res Sci Teaching; AAAS; Nat Sci Teachers Asn; Sigma Xi; fel Finnish Chem Soc. *Res:* Teaching methods; curriculum development; evaluation at secondary and university levels. *Mailing Add:* 2163 Buena Vista Dr Greeley CO 80631. *Fax:* 970-351-1269

HEIL, JOHN F, JR, CHEMICAL ENGINEERING. *Current Pos:* RETIRED. *Personal Data:* b San Francisco, Calif, Feb 29, 36. *Educ:* Univ Calif, Berkeley, BS, 57, PhD(chem eng), 65. *Prof Exp:* Mgr, Prod Develop Sect, Western Res Ctr, Stauffer Chem Co, 57, 76, mgr energy resources, Wyo, 76-79, dir planning, Agr Chem Div, 79-81, corp prod dir, AG/Drug Intermediates, 81-83, corp prod dir, Agr Chem Intermediates, 83-85, dir, 85-87; dir, Western Res Ctr, ICI Americas Inc, 87-91. *Mem:* Am Chem Soc; Am Inst Chem Engrs. *Res:* Thermodynamics of phase equilibria. *Mailing Add:* 16 Kinross Dr San Rafael CA 94901-2420

HEIL, RICHARD WENDELL, BIO-REMEDIATION OF TOXIC ORGANIC SEDIMENTS, TRANSMISSION OF VISCOUS SLURRIES. *Current Pos:* ASSOC, KUDRNA & ASSOCS, LTD, 91- *Personal Data:* b Chicago, Ill, Mar 16, 26; m 47, Jane Olinger; c Nancy J, R Douglas & Margaret (Usery). *Educ:* Univ Ill, BS, 48. *Prof Exp:* Mining engr, US Steel Corp, 48-55; struct designer, Hazelet & Erdal, Consult Engrs, 55-58; struct engr, Metrop Water Recl Dist Greater Chicago, 58-64, prin civil engr, 64-70 & 71-79, asst chief engr, 70-71, engr treatment opers, 79-88; sr environ engr, HNTB Architects, Engrs & Planners, 88-91. *Concurrent Pos:* Vpres, Arthur S Darr & Assocs, 62-78, Kucaba & Heil Assocs, 64-66; prin, R W Heil, Struct Engr, 78-; mem archit adv bd, Clarendon Hills, 83-96. *Mem:* Fel Am Soc Civil Engrs; Water Environ Fedn. *Res:* Environmental and structural engineering; utilization of remediated sediments; three US patents for wastewater treatment. *Mailing Add:* 30 Arthur Ave Clarendon Hills IL 60514. *Fax:* 630-969-3122

HEIL, ROBERT DEAN, SOIL CONSERVATION. *Current Pos:* assoc prof soil surv, conserv & mgt, 70-77, EXEC DIR, AGRON STA, COLO STATE UNIV, 77- *Personal Data:* b White Butte, SDak, Aug 14, 32; m 59; c 7. *Educ:* SDak State Univ, BS, 60, MS, 64, PhD(soil sci), 72. *Prof Exp:* Soil scientist soil fertil, SDak State Univ, 60-61; soil scientist soil surv, Soil Conserv Serv, USDA, 61-63; soil scientist soil fertil & mgt, SDak State Univ, 63-65; soils exten assoc prof, Colo State Univ, 65-69; soil scientist remote sensing, SDak State Remote Sensing Inst, 69-70. *Concurrent Pos:* Soil scientist, Cameron Consult Engr, 71-72, Wallace, McHary & Todd Assoc, 72, Meehen Environ Eng, 72-73 & Jones, Jones & Humkins, Attys Law, 73. *Mem:* Soil Sci Soc Am; Soil Conserv Soc Am; Am Soc Agron; Sigma Xi. *Res:* Determining the behavior and suitability of soils for application of soils data to land use and environmental planning. *Mailing Add:* 937 Chippewa Ct Ft Collins CO 80525-1568

HEIL, WOLFGANG HEINRICH, TOPOLOGY. *Current Pos:* from asst prof to assoc prof, 70-83, PROF MATH, FLA STATE UNIV, 83- *Personal Data:* b Frankfurt, Ger, Nov 3, 40; m 66, Christel T Lehrmann; c Stephan R & Christopher P. *Educ:* Univ Frankfurt, vordiplom, 63, diplom, 67; Rice Univ, MA & PhD(math), 70. *Prof Exp:* Instr math, Rice Univ, 69-70. *Concurrent Pos:* Vis prof, Univ Ljubljana, Yugoslavia, 77-78, J W Goethe Univ, Frankfurt, WGer, 80-81, 88 & 93, F W Alexander Univ, Erlangen, WGer, 81, 84-85, Portland State Univ, Ore, 95. *Mem:* Am Math Soc. *Res:* Topology of 3-manifolds. *Mailing Add:* Dept Math Fla State Univ Tallahassee FL 32306. *E-Mail:* heil@gauss.math.fsu.edu

HEILENDAY, FRANK W (TOD), OPERATIONS RESEARCH, AIR DEFENSE. *Current Pos:* CONSULT, 84- *Personal Data:* b Jersey City, NJ, Dec 31, 27; m 51, Joan Braudmeyer. *Educ:* Mass Inst Technol, BS & MS, 49. *Prof Exp:* Aerophys engr, Convair Div, Gen Dynamics Corp, Tex, 49-51, sr dynamics engr, Calif, 53-55; assoc flight test engr, Cornell Aeronaut Lab, NY, 51-53; chief opers analysis, Hq 8th Air Force, Westover AFB, Mass, 55-65, chief, Syst Eval Div, Sci & Res, Hq Strategic Air Command, Offutt AFB, 66-84. *Concurrent Pos:* Adj prof, George Washington Univ; consult, RAND Corp. *Mem:* Mil Opers Res Soc; Asn Old Crows. *Res:* Systems analysis studies on aircraft offensive and defensive avionics requirements. *Mailing Add:* 720 Sherman St NW Olympia WA 98502-8801

HEILES, CARL, INTERSTELLAR MATTER, RADIO ASTRONOMY. *Current Pos:* PROF ASTRON, UNIV CALIF, BERKELEY, 66- *Personal Data:* b Toledo, Ohio, Sept 22, 39; c 2. *Educ:* Cornell Univ, BEng, 62; Princeton Univ, PhD(astrophys), 66. *Honors & Awards:* Heineman Prize, Am Phys Soc, 89. *Concurrent Pos:* Res astronr, Cornell Univ, 69-70; vis prof, Sci & Med Univ Grenoble, France, 83; vis fel, Joint Inst Lab Astrophys, Univ Colo, Boulder, 90. *Mem:* Nat Acad Sci; Am Astron Soc; Int Astron Union; Int Sci Radio Union; Astron Soc Pac. *Res:* Diffuse interstellar matter with concentration on atomic hydrogen; radio astronomy. *Mailing Add:* Astron Dept Univ Calif Berkeley CA 94720

HEILMAN, ALAN SMITH, BOTANY. *Current Pos:* from instr to asst prof, 60-70, ASSOC PROF BOT, UNIV TENN, 70- *Personal Data:* b Pittsburgh, Pa, Dec 23, 27. *Educ:* Univ Pittsburgh, BS, 49, MS, 51; Ohio State Univ, PhD(bot), 60. *Prof Exp:* Asst bot, Univ Pittsburgh, 49-52; asst bot, Ohio State Univ, 52-56, asst instr, 55-57, instr, 57, tech asst, 57-60. *Mem:* AAAS; Bot Soc Am; Sigma Xi. *Res:* Developmental floral and pollen morphology; pollination; microtechnique; scientific photography. *Mailing Add:* Dept Bot Univ Tenn 1345 Circle Park Knoxville TN 37996-0001

HEILMAN, CAROL A, RESPIRATORY RESEARCH. *Current Pos:* prog officer, Influenza & Viral Respiratory Dis, NIH, 86-88, actg chief, 88-89, chief, Respiratory Dis Br, Nat Inst Allergy & Infectious Dis, 89-, ASSOC DIR, DIV AIDS, NIH. *Educ:* Boston Univ, BA, 72; Rutgers Univ, MS, 76, PhD(microbiol), 79. *Prof Exp:* Asst scientist, Hoffman-La Roche, 73-74; res assoc, Nat Cancer Inst, 78-81, sr staff fel, 81-86. *Concurrent Pos:* Grad teaching fel, Rutgers Med Sch, 76-85; mem, Childcare Comt, NIH; rep, Women's Adv Comt, NIAID, EEO Comt, HCFA Influenza Demon Proj, NIH; reviewer, J Nat Cancer Inst & J Infectious Dis; mem, Step Comt. *Mem:* Am Soc Microbiol; Am Soc Virol; Int Soc Antiviral Res; AAAS. *Res:* Influenza research; acute viral respiratory diseases; Reyes Syndrome; infectious disease of the elderly; regulation of gene expression during differentiation and neoplastic transformation; author of numerous technical publications. *Mailing Add:* Nat Inst Allergy & Infectious Dis Div AIDS NIH Solar Bldg Rm 2A16 6003 Executive Blvd Bethesda MD 20892-7620. *Fax:* 301-496-8030

HEILMAN, PAUL E, FOREST NUTRITION, BIOMASS PRODUCTION. *Current Pos:* exten specialist hort, 67-69, FOREST SCIENTIST, WESTERN WASH RES & EXTEN CTR, WASH STATE UNIV, 69- *Personal Data:* b Seattle, Wash, Feb 13, 31; m 91, Rosemary Manning; c Rebecca (Hall) & Jeffrey H. *Educ:* Ore State Univ, BS, 57; Univ Wash, PhD(forestry), 61. *Prof Exp:* Instr agr, Skagit Valley Col, 61-63; asst horticulturist, Wash State Univ, 63-64; assoc prof forest soils res, Univ Alaska, 64-67. *Mem:* Soc Am Foresters; Am Soc Agron; Soil Sci Soc Am; Sigma Xi. *Res:* Plant productivity in relationship to soils and fertility; ecology; nitrogen nutrition of forests and sustainability; maximizing production of intensive plantations of populus hybrids for pulp and energy. *Mailing Add:* Natural Resource Wash State Univ One SE Stadium Way Pullman WA 99164-0001

HEILMAN, RICHARD DEAN, CARDIOVASCULAR PHARMACOLOGY, QUALITY ASSURANCE. *Current Pos:* DIR SCI & MED INFO, PHARMACO LSR, 87- *Personal Data:* b Sparta, Wis, Sept 8, 37; m 67, Patricia G Arendt; c Heidi, Daniel, Sara & Benjamin. *Educ:* Wis State Univ, La Crosse, BS, 59; Marquette Univ, PhD(pharmacol), 69. *Prof Exp:* From assoc scientist to scientist, Ortho Pharmaceut Corp, 69-73, group leader pharmaceut, 73-77; group leader pharmacol, Diamond Shamrock Corp, 77-80; sect head cardiovasc res, G D Searle & Co, 80-84; vpres res & develop, Amaric Corp, 85-87. *Mem:* Am Chem Soc; Inflammation Res Asn; Cardiovasc Pharmacol Discussion Group; Am Soc Pharmacol & Exp Therapeut; Am Col Clin Pharmacol; Am Soc Qual Assurance. *Res:* Interactions of the autonomic nervous system and the reproductive endocrine hormones in regulation of oviducal egg transport; effect of androgen on aggressive behavior; pharmacology of narcotic antagonists; cardiovascular and central nervous system toxicology of vehicles; clinical development of new drugs. *Mailing Add:* Pharmaco LSR 1301 Arronimink Circle Austin TX 78746-6303. *Fax:* 512-326-7725

HEILMAN, WARREN EMANUEL, GLOBAL CLIMATE CHANGE RESEARCH, ATMOSPHERIC MESOSCALE MODELING OF WILDLAND FIRE EPISODES. *Current Pos:* RES METEOROLOGIST, N CENT FOREST EXP STA, USDA FOREST SERV, 90-, PROJ LEADER, 92- *Personal Data:* b Eureka, SDak, Mar 9, 57; m 88, Tamara Joachim; c Lauren & Madison. *Educ:* SDak State Univ, BS, 79; Iowa State Univ, MS, 84, PhD(meteorol), 88. *Prof Exp:* Teaching asst physics, SDak State Univ, 79; res asst, Argonne Nat Lab, 80; teaching asst physics & meteorol, Iowa State Univ, 80-84, instr meteorol, 84-85, res asst, 85-88; res scientist, Comput Sci Corp, 88-89. *Concurrent Pos:* Mem, Fire Res Syst Comt, USDA Forest Serv, 92-, Nat Climate Scenario Task Force, 93-94, Ecosyst Mgt Res Comt, 93-94. *Mem:* Am Meteorol Soc; Nat Fire Protection Asn. *Res:* Relationship of large-scale atmospheric processes to mesoscale weather events that can have a direct impact on wildland fires; development of regional climate scenarios. *Mailing Add:* 5530 Strawberry Ln Haslett MI 48840. *Fax:* 517-355-5121

HEILMAN, WILLIAM JOSEPH, SYNTHETIC LUBRICANTS, POLYMER SYNTHESIS. *Current Pos:* dir res div, 83-86, sr scientist, 86-94, VPRES ADVAN TECHNOL, PENNZOIL PROD CO, 94- *Personal Data:* b Pittsburgh, Pa, Aug 31, 30; m 57, Charlotte Andrews; c Terry L, Christine & Eric. *Educ:* Univ Pittsburgh, BS, 52; State Univ NY, Syracuse, MS, 56; Tex Tech Col, PhD(physorg chem), 62. *Prof Exp:* Chemist, Res Ctr, Koppers Co, 52-54; from res chemist to sr res chemist, Gulf Oil Chem Co, 62-72, res assoc, Gulf Res & Develop Corp, 72-76, sect supvr, 76-81, dir polymer catalysis res, 81-83. *Mem:* Am Chem Soc; Soc Tribologists & Lubrication Engrs; Soc Automotive Engrs. *Res:* Free radical chemistry; mechanistic organic chemistry; polymer chemistry; synthetic lubricants. *Mailing Add:* 14826 La Quinta Lane Houston TX 77079-4506

HEILMAN, WILLIAM PAUL, MEDICINAL CHEMISTRY, PHARMACOLOGY. *Current Pos:* DIR TECH ACQUISITION, AM CYANAMID, 86- *Personal Data:* b Cheyenne, Wyo, Jan 7, 48; m 72; c 1. *Educ:* Muskingum Col, BS, 70; Ohio State Univ, MS, 72, PhD(med chem), 74; Case Western Res Univ, MBA, 79. *Prof Exp:* Mgr new bus develop, Diamond Shamrock Corp, 78-81; mgr licensing, FMC Corp, 81-86. *Concurrent Pos:* Res fel, NIH, 71-74, Eidgenossische Technische Hochschule, Zurich, 74-75. *Mem:* Am Chem Soc; Licensing Execs Soc; Asn Univ Technol Mgr. *Res:* Design, synthesis and biological evaluation of hypolipemic agents, antihypertensive agents, anti-inflammatory agents, antiarrhythmic agents and analgetic agents. *Mailing Add:* Am Cyanamid Co Agr Res & Develop PO Box 400 Princeton NJ 08540

HEILMEIER, GEORGE HARRY, SOLID STATE ELECTRONICS. *Current Pos:* pres & chief exec officer, 91-96, CHMN, BELLCORE, 96- *Personal Data:* b Philadelphia, Pa, May 22, 36; m 61; c 1. *Educ:* Univ Pa, BSEE, 58; Princeton Univ, MSE, 60, MA, 61, PhD(physics, elec eng), 62. *Hon Degrees:* DSc, Stevens Inst Technol, 95, Israel Inst Technol. *Honors & Awards:* David Sarnoff Award, Inst Elec & Electronics Engrs, 68, Phillips Award, 85, Founders Medal, 86, Medal of Honor, 97; IR-100 Award, 68 & 69; Commun & Comput Prize, Japan, 90; Nat Medal of Sci, 91; Founders Award, Nat Acad Eng, 92; Indust Res Inst Medal, 93. *Prof Exp:* Res scientist, RCA Labs, Inc, 58-66, head solid state & liquid state device res, David Sarnoff Res Ctr, 66-69, dir device concepts res, 69-70; White House fel, spec asst to Secy Defense, 70-71; asst dir defense res & eng electronics, Dept Defense, 71-75; dir, Defense Advan Res Proj Agency, 75-77; vpres, Tex Instruments, Inc, 77-78, vpres corp res, develop, eng & stategic planning, 78-83, sr vpres & chief tech officer, 83-91. *Concurrent Pos:* Bd dir, TRW, Mitre Corp, Compaq Comput Corp, ADP. *Mem:* Nat Acad Eng; fel Inst Elec & Electronics Engrs; Am Acad Arts & Sci. *Res:* Low noise microwave amplifiers; solid state harmonic generation; organic semiconductors; thin film devices; liquid crystals; electro-optics, integrated circuits; computer science; artificial intelligence. *Mailing Add:* Bell Commun Res 445 South St Morristown NJ 07960-6438

HEILWEIL, ISRAEL JOEL, PHYSICAL CHEMISTRY. *Current Pos:* sr res chemist, Mobil Oil Corp, 60-68, RES ASSOC, CENT RES LAB, MOBIL OIL RES & DEVELOP CORP, 68- *Personal Data:* b Poland, May 23, 24; nat US; m 48; c 3. *Educ:* City Col New York, BS, 48; Ohio State Univ, MS, 51, PhD(phys chem), 54. *Prof Exp:* Chemist, Res Ctr, Texaco, Inc, 54-60. *Mem:* Am Chem Soc; Soc Petrol Engrs. *Res:* Physical chemistry and theology of polymers and surfactants; oil recovery and liquid deep well drilling fluids; coal/water dispersions as fuels; oil and gasoline additives; petro-proteins; gel permeation chromatography; light scattering; surface phenomena. *Mailing Add:* 47 Linwood Circle Princeton NJ 08540-3623

HEIM, LYLE RAYMOND, IMMUNOLOGY, MICROBIOLOGY. *Current Pos:* RETIRED. *Personal Data:* b Lignite, NDak, Apr 30, 33; m 57; c 3. *Educ:* Univ Minn, Minneapolis, BA, 63, MS, 66, PhD(immunol, microbiol), 69. *Prof Exp:* USPHS fel infectious dis, Baylor Col Med, 69-71, USPHS fel exp biol & instr immunol, 71-72; clin asst prof lab med, Med Col Wis, 72-78; assoc prof & dir res, Dept Pediat, Sch Med, Tex Tech Univ, 78-83; dir, Pharmaceut Med Writing Dept, Bristol-Myers Co, 84-93; dir, Publ Med Commons, Hybrid Group, Div Hamilton Carver & Lee Inc, 94- *Concurrent Pos:* Ed-in-chief, Exp Hemat, 70-83; clin immunologist, Columbia Hosp, 72-78. *Mem:* AAAS; Coun Biol Ed; Am Soc Microbiol; Int Soc Exp Hemat; Am Med Writers Asn. *Res:* Transplantation immunology; pediatric immunology; cancer immunology; experimental hematology. *Mailing Add:* 4512 Somers Ave North Little Rock AR 72116

HEIM, WERNER GEORGE, HUMAN GENETICS, VERTEBRATE EMBRYOLOGY. *Current Pos:* prof, 67-94, EMER PROF BIOL, COLO COL, 94- *Personal Data:* b Mulheim an der Ruhr, Ger, Apr 7, 29; nat US; m 61, 73; c Elise, Lynn, Susan & David. *Educ:* Univ Calif, Los Angeles, BA, 50, MA, 52, PhD, 54. *Prof Exp:* Jr res zoologist, Col Agr, Univ Calif, Los Angeles, 54-56; instr biol, Brown Univ, 56-57; from asst prof to assoc prof, Wayne State Univ, 57-67. *Concurrent Pos:* Assoc ed, Am Biol Teacher, 70-74; vis prof biophys & genetics, Sch Med, Univ Colo, 78 & 86; chmn, Dept Biol, Colo Col, 71-76 & 86-89; consult geneticist, Div Genetics, Children's Hosp, Denver. *Mem:* Fel AAAS; Am Soc Zool; Soc Develop Biol; Int Soc Develop Biologists; Nat Soc Genetic Coun; Am Soc Human Genetics. *Res:* Methodology of karyotyping relation between maternal proteins and embryonic development. *Mailing Add:* Dept Biol Colo Col 14 E Cache La Poudre Colorado Springs CO 80903-3294

HEIMAN, DONALD EUGENE, CONDENSED MATTER PHYSICS, OPTICS. *Current Pos:* MEM STAFF, FRANCIS BITTER MAGNET LAB, MASS INST TECHNOL, 81- *Personal Data:* b Los Angeles, Calif, Nov 4, 47. *Educ:* Calif State Univ, Los Angeles, BS, 67; Univ Calif, Irvine, PhD(physics), 75. *Prof Exp:* Res assoc physics, Univ Southern Calif, 75-80. *Mem:* Fel Am Phys Soc; Mat Res Soc. *Res:* Optics and nonlinear optics as applied to condensed matter physics, with emphasis on semiconductors and materials science. *Mailing Add:* Francis Bitter Magnet Lab Mass Inst Technol Cambridge MA 02139

HEIMAN, MARK LOUIS, ENDOCRINOLOGY, NEUROENDOCRINOLOGY. *Current Pos:* sr scientist, 87-90, res scientist, 90-96, SR RES SCIENTIST, ELI LILLY & CO, 96-; PHYSIOL, MED SCH, IND UNIV, 87- *Personal Data:* b Fort Belvoir, Va, Oct 9, 52; m 81, Sharon Spears; c Justin & Mary J. *Educ:* Univ New Orleans, BA, 74; La State Univ, PhD(physiol), 78. *Prof Exp:* Teaching asst physiol, Med Ctr, La State Univ, 76-78; res assoc physiol, Med Sch, Ind Univ, 78-82; asst prof med, Med Sch, Tulane Univ, 82-86. *Mem:* AAAS; Endocrine Soc; Am Diabetes Asn. *Res:* Regulation of anterior pituitary hormone receptors; regulation of hypothalamic-hypophysial-growth axis; neuroendocrine control of blood glucose; metabolic endocrinology of obesity. *Mailing Add:* Lilly Res Lab Corp Ctr Drop 0540 Indianapolis IN 46285. *Fax:* 317-276-9574; *E-Mail:* heiman_mark_1@lilly.com

HEIMANN, PETER AARON, STATISTICS, QUALITY CONTROL. *Current Pos:* MEM TECH STAFF, BELL LABS, 80- *Personal Data:* b New York, NY, Dec 6, 49; m 72; c 2. *Educ:* City Col NY, BS, 71; Univ Md, MS, 73, PhD(physics), 77. *Prof Exp:* Grad res asst physics, Dept Physics, Univ Md, 74-77; staff scientist, Singer Co, Kearfott Div, 78-80. *Mem:* Am Phys Soc; Am Soc Qual Control. *Res:* Statistical, quality control and process improvement, as applied to manufacturing and service industries. *Mailing Add:* Bell Labs Rm 7C-104 Whippany Rd Whippany NJ 07981

HEIMANN, ROBERT L, PLASTIC & CABLE DESIGN, THERMOPLASTIC COMPOSITES & FAILURE ANALYSIS. *Current Pos:* MGR RES & DEVELOP, SR STAFF ENGR & RES & DEVELOPMENT GEN MGR, ORSCHELN CO, 77- *Personal Data:* b St Louis, Mo, Dec 7, 46; m 67, Donna Winner; c Daniel, Debra, Douglas, Denise & Dale. *Educ:* Univ Idaho, BSME, 71. *Honors & Awards:* Best New Prod Award, Nat Soc Prof Engrs, 88; Arch T Colwell Award, Soc Automotive Engrs, 89. *Prof Exp:* Designer aircraft & spacecraft, McDonnell-Douglas, 66-72; eng mgr prod design, Narragansett, 75-77. *Concurrent Pos:* Guest lectr, Univ Mo, Rolla, 90-94 & Columbia Col, 93. *Mem:* Soc Automotive Engrs. *Res:* Plastic and ceramic coatings; seal and lube designs for automotive and industrial parking brake, transhift, and release cables; ceramic coatings for corrosion protection on rebar, prestressed and bridge stay cables; composite cables; smart materials. *Mailing Add:* 1 Circle Dr Moberly MO 65270. *Fax:* 660-269-4510

HEIMBACH, DAVID M, SURGERY. *Current Pos:* PROG SURG, UNIV WASH, 74-, DIR, BURN CTR, HARBORVIEW. *Mailing Add:* Dept Surg ZA-16 Harborview Med Ctr 325 Ninth Ave Seattle WA 98104-2499

HEIMBACH, RICHARD DEAN, AEROSPACE MEDICINE, RADIATION BIOLOGY. *Current Pos:* assoc dir, 82-89, DIR, HYPERBARIC MED DEPT, SOUTHWEST TEX METHODIST HOSP, 89- *Personal Data:* b Chicago, Ill, Apr 5, 35; m 58, Jacquelin Williams; c Leah, Mike, Marah, Karen, Rebekah & Sarah. *Educ:* Univ Chicago, AB, 56, BS, 57, MD, 60; NY Univ, PhD(radiation biol), 67; Harvard Univ, MPH, 72. *Prof Exp:* Chief, outpatient clin, Ellsworth AFB Hosp, 62-63, adv radiation biol, Kirtland AFB, 67-71; chief med opers aerospace med, USAF Sch Aerospace Med, 74-79, chief hyperbaric med div, 79-82. *Concurrent Pos:* Vis prof, Univ NMex, 69-71; vis fac, Grad Sch, Tex A&M Univ, 77-; consult, USAF Surgeon Gen, 79- *Mem:* Fel Aerospace Med Asn; fel Royal Soc Health; fel Am Col Prev Med; Undersea Med Soc (vpres, 84-88, pres, 88); AMA; fel Royal Soc Med. *Res:* Effects of hyperbaric oxygen in reversing underlying pathology associated with radiation therapy; effects of pressure changes on pulmonary physiology. *Mailing Add:* 4499 Medical Dr Sublevel 2 San Antonio TX 78258-6824

HEIMBECKER, RAYMOND OLIVER, EXPERIMENTAL SURGERY, CARDIOVASCULAR SURGERY. *Current Pos:* prof, 73-88, EMER PROF SURG, UNIV WESTERN ONT, 88-; SR SURGEON MED ASN, BAHAMAS. *Personal Data:* b Calgary, Alta, Nov 29, 22; m 50, Kathleen Jensen; c Raymond, Kathleen, Harry, Anita & Constance. *Educ:* Univ Sask, BA, 44; Univ Toronto, MD, 47, MA, 48, MS, 55; FRCS(C), 55; FACS 59, FACCP, 67, FACC 69. *Honors & Awards:* George Armstrong Peters Award, 50; Lister Award, 55; Gold Medal, Royal Col Surgeons Can, 67; Res & Teaching Award, Rose Found India, 76; Gordon Murray Mem Lectr, Univ Toronto, 81; Medal Jeddah, Saudi Arabia, 83; P K Sen Mem Lectr, Bombay, India, 85; Wilfred Bigelow Lectr, Royal Col Physicians & Surgeons, Can, 85; Conrad Lam Lectr, Henry Ford Hosp, 86. *Prof Exp:* Res assoc, Ont Heart Found, 55-70, sr res assoc surg, 70-88. *Concurrent Pos:* Chief cardiothoracic surg, Univ Hosp, London, 73-88; examr, Royal Col Physicians & Surgeons Can; Hon mem, Beijing Heart Inst, 85, Can Med Asn, 86. *Mem:* Fel Am Col Surg; fel Am Asn Thoracic Surg; Int Cardiovasc Soc; Am Surg Asn; Can Soc Microcirc (pres, 71); hon mem Can Soc Cardiovasc & Thoracic Surgeons; hon mem Can Med Asn. *Res:* Cardiovascular physiology; experimental cardiovascular surgery; Third World surgery. *Mailing Add:* RR 1 Collingwood ON L9Y 3Y9 Can. *Fax:* 705-445-9649

HEIMBERG, MURRAY, PHARMACOLOGY, BIOCHEMISTRY. *Current Pos:* prof pharmacol, chmn, Dept Pharmacol & prof med, 81-96, Van Vleet prof, 86-96, DISTINGUISHED PROF, CTR HEALTH SCI, UNIV TENN, MEMPHIS, 96- *Personal Data:* b Brooklyn, NJ, Jan 5, 25; m 47, 64, Anna L Knox; c Richard G, Steven A, Larry M & David S. *Educ:* Cornell Univ, BS, 48, MNS, 49; Duke Univ, PhD(biochem), 52; Vanderbilt Univ, MD, 59. *Honors & Awards:* Sigma Xi Outstanding Res Award, 93. *Prof Exp:* NIH res fel biol chem, Wash Univ, 52-54; res assoc, Sch Med, Vanderbilt Univ, 54-59, from asst prof to prof pharmacol, 59-74, asst prof med, 71-74; prof pharmacol, chmn, Dept Pharmacol & prof med, Sch Med, Univ Mo, Columbia, 74-80. *Concurrent Pos:* Lederle Med Fac award, 59-62; estab investr, Am Heart Asn, 62-67; fel, Coun Arteriosclerosis & Basic Sci, Am Heart Asn; mem, Univ Tenn Med Group, dir, Lipid Metab Clin. *Mem:* Am Soc Pharmacol & Exp Therapeut; Am Col Clin Pharmacol; Endocrine Soc; fel AAAS; Am Soc Biol Chem & Molecular Biol; Am Soc Study Liver Dis; Sigma Xi; Am Oil Chem Soc; Am Heart Asn; Am Diabetes Asn. *Res:* Hormonal and substrate regulation of lipid/lipoprotein metabolism; lipid absorption and transport; interrelationships between carbohydrate and lipid metabolism; biosynthesis of proteins; enzymatic oxidation of sulfur compounds; endocrinology; atherosclerosis; hyperlipidemias and hyperlipoproteinemia; regulation of hepatic lipid metabolism; mechanisms of hepatotoxicity; hepatic metabolism of drugs; endocrinology. *Mailing Add:* Depts Pharmacol & Med Univ Tenn-Memphis Health Sci Ctr 874 Union Ave Memphis TN 38163. *Fax:* 901-448-7300; *E-Mail:* mheimberg@utmem1.utmem.edu

HEIMBROOK, MARGARET ELLEN, ENVIRONMENTAL MICROBIOLOGY. *Current Pos:* asst prof zool, 74-78, assoc prof biol, 78-84, PROF BIOL & MICROBIOL, UNIV NORTHERN COLO, 84- *Personal Data:* b Bethlehem, Pa, Mar 16, 42. *Educ:* Muskingum Col, BS, 64; Lehigh Univ, MA, 66; Univ Wis-Madison, MS, 69; Colo State Univ, PhD(microbiol), 74. *Prof Exp:* Instr zool & bacteriol, Univ Wis-Marshfield, 67-70. *Concurrent Pos:* Bact water qual specialist consult, Weld Lab, 88- *Mem:* Am Soc Microbiol; AAAS; Sigma Xi. *Res:* Diverse natural environments for bacteria in biogeochemical cycling of elements; microbial taxonomy and infection of Caulobacter crescantus with bacteriophage 0C65. *Mailing Add:* 6505 N County Rd 3 Ft Collins CO 80524. *Fax:* 970-351-2335; *E-Mail:* meheimb@bentley.univnorthco.edu

HEIMER, EDGAR P, biology, for more information see previous edition

HEIMER, NORMAN EUGENE, organic chemistry, for more information see previous edition

HEIMER, RALPH, BIOCHEMISTRY. *Current Pos:* prof, 67-90, EMER PROF BIOCHEM, MED COL, THOMAS JEFFERSON UNIV, 90- *Personal Data:* b Vienna, Austria, Nov 4, 21; US citizen; m 43, 74, Phyllis Sampson; c Robert & Paul. *Educ:* City Col New York, BS, 48; Columbia Univ, AM, 51, PhD(biochem), 57. *Prof Exp:* Asst prof biochem, Hosp Spec Surg, Med Col, Cornell Univ, 56-62; assoc prof biochem, NJ Col Med, 63-66. *Concurrent Pos:* NIH res awards, 59-76 & 80-86; sr investr, Arthritis Found, 63-67; Am Cancer Soc res awards, 68-70; res awards, Eastern Pa Chap, Arthritis Found, 87 & 88; ed, Matrix Biol, 95- *Mem:* Am Rheumatism Asn; Am Soc Biol Chemists; Am Asn Immunologists; Sigma Xi; Int Soc Matrix Biol. *Res:* Chemistry of glycosaminoglycans; immunochemistry; tumor immunology; technology of glycosaminoglan and proteoglycan detection; polyacrylamide gel electrophoresis and electrotransblot technology. *Mailing Add:* Ctr Gene Ther Allegheny Univ Health Sci Mailstop 421 Philadelphia PA 19102. *Fax:* 215-762-7408; *E-Mail:* heimer@allegheny.edu

HEIMERL, JOSEPH MARK, COMBUSTION MODELLING, CHEMICAL KINETICS. *Current Pos:* sr scientist exp aeronomy, 70-74, sr scientist modelling aeronomy, 74-78, SR SCIENTIST MODELLING COMBUSTION, BALLISTIC RES LAB, 78- *Personal Data:* b Woodbury, NJ, Feb 25, 40; m 68; c 2. *Educ:* St Joseph's Col, BS, 62; Univ Pittsburgh, PhD(physics), 68. *Prof Exp:* Res assoc spectros, Ames Ctr, NASA, 68-70. *Concurrent Pos:* Nat Res Coun res assoc, Ames Ctr, NASA, 68-70. *Mem:* Combustion Inst; Am Phys Soc. *Res:* Flame inhibition; muzzle flash suppression; flame modelling; elementary gas phase chemical kinetics; aeronomy modelling; D-region ion chemistry; ion molecule reactions. *Mailing Add:* 108 Paradise Dr Havre De Grace MD 21078

HEIMLICH, HENRY JAY, CLINICAL SCIENCE, SURGERY. *Current Pos:* ASSOC CLIN PROF SURG, UNIV CINCINNATI COL MED, 69- *Personal Data:* b Wilmington, Del, Feb 3, 20; m 51, Jane Murray; c Philip, Peter, Janet & Elizabeth. *Educ:* Cornell Univ, BA, 41, MD, 43; Am Bd Surg, dipl; Am Bd Thoracic Surg, dipl. *Hon Degrees:* DSc, Wilmington Col, 81, Adelphi Univ, 82, Rider Col, 83. *Honors & Awards:* Lasker Award for Pub Serv, Lasker Found, 84. *Prof Exp:* Intern, Boston City Hosp, 44; resident, Vet Admin Hosp, Bronx, 46-47; Mt Sinai Hosp, 47-48, Bellevue Hosp, 48-49, Triboro Hosp, New York, 49-50; attending surgeon, Div Surg, Montefiore Hosp, 50-69; dir surg, Jewish Hosp, Cincinnati, 69-77; prof advan clin sci, Xavier Univ, 77-99. *Concurrent Pos:* Pres, Heimlich Inst; mem, Pres Nat Cancer Found, 63-68; Pres Comn Heart Dis, Cancer & Stroke, 65. *Mem:* Fel Am Col Surgeons; fel Am Col Chest Physicians; fel Am Col Gastroenterol; Soc Thoracic Surgeons; AMA; Soc Surg Alimentary Tract; Am Gastroenterol Asn; Pan-Am Med Asn. *Res:* Developer of Heimlich operation (reversed gastric tube esophagoplasty) for replacement of esophagus; inventor Heimlich chest drain valve; developer Heimlich maneuver. *Mailing Add:* 2368 Victory Pkwy Cincinnati OH 45206-2804

HEIMLICH, RICHARD ALLEN, GEOLOGY. *Current Pos:* From instr to assoc prof, 61-70, chmn, Dept Geol, 76-92, PROF GEOL, KENT STATE UNIV, 70- *Personal Data:* b Elizabeth, NJ, Aug 8, 32; m 61, Charlee Marcus; c John & Steven. *Educ:* Rutgers Univ, BS, 54; Yale Univ, MS, 55, PhD(petrol), 59. *Concurrent Pos:* Res grants, NSF, Los Alamos Nat Lab & US Dept Educ. *Mem:* Fel Geol Soc Am; Am Inst Prof Geologists. *Res:* Igneous and metamorphic petrology. *Mailing Add:* Dept Geol Kent State Univ Kent OH 44242. *Fax:* 330-672-7949; *E-Mail:* rhelmlic@kentvm.kent.edu

HEIMSCH, CHARLES W, PLANT ANATOMY, MORPHOLOGY. *Current Pos:* chmn dept, 59-77, prof, 59-80, EMER PROF BOT, MIAMI UNIV, 80- *Personal Data:* b Dayton, Ohio, May 4, 14; m 74, Evah Jo Smith; c Richard, Carolyn & Alan. *Educ:* Miami Univ, Ohio, AB, 36; Harvard Univ, MA, 39, PhD(bot), 41. *Honors & Awards:* Merit Award, Bot Soc Am. *Prof Exp:* Asst biol, Harvard Univ, 36-37 & 39-40, tech asst wood collection, 38-39, asst biol, Radcliffe Col, 37-38; Sheldon traveling fel from Harvard Univ, Univ Calif, 41-42; instr bot, Swarthmore Col, 42-46; asst prof biol, Amherst Col, 46-47; from asst to prof, Univ Tex, 47-59. *Concurrent Pos:* Res assoc, Plant Res Inst, Univ Tex, 47-50, anatomist, 50-59; ed, Am J Bot, Bot Soc Am, 65-69; sr fel, NATO, 73; prog dir, Bot Soc Am, 77-80. *Mem:* AAAS; Bot Soc Am (treas, 63-64, vpres, 71, pres, 72); Torrey Bot Club; Am Inst Biol Sci; Asn Trop Biol; Int Asn Wood Anatomists. *Res:* Wood anatomy; developmental anatomy of roots. *Mailing Add:* 316 Pearson Hall (Bot) Miami Univ Oxford OH 45056

HEIMSCH, RICHARD CHARLES, FOOD MICROBIOLOGY, FERMENTATION TECHNOLOGY. *Current Pos:* from asst prof to assoc prof bact, 72-83, asst dir agr res, 86-90, PROF BACT, UNIV IDAHO, 83-, ASSOC DIR AGR RES, 90- *Personal Data:* b Philadelphia, Pa, Dec 20, 42; m 65, K Prudence Ray; c Elizabeth H, Kathleen H & Hilary L. *Educ:* Miami Univ, BA, 65; Univ Wis, MS, 71, PhD(bact), 73. *Prof Exp:* Instr microbiol, Ore State Univ, 71-72. *Concurrent Pos:* Interim head, Dept Bact & Biochem, Univ Idaho, 90-92. *Mem:* Am Soc Microbiol; AAAS; Sigma Xi; Inst Food Technologists; Soc Indust Microbiol. *Res:* Discovery, detection and control of microbial toxins in the food chain; production of single-cell protein and biochemicals by bioconversion of agricultural and industrial wastes; food borne disease hazards; microbial biotechnology. *Mailing Add:* 213 N Howard St Moscow ID 83843. *Fax:* 208-885-6654

HEIN, DALE ARTHUR, WILDLIFE MANAGEMENT, VERTEBRATE ECOLOGY. *Current Pos:* assoc prof, 68-77, PROF WILDLIFE BIOL, COLO STATE UNIV, 77- *Personal Data:* b Redmond, Ore, Apr 21, 33; m 65. *Educ:* Ore State Univ, BS, 59; Iowa State Univ, MS, 62, PhD(wildlife mgt), 65. *Prof Exp:* Asst prof biol, Wake Forest Univ, 65-68. *Mem:* AAAS; Wildlife Soc; Wilson Ornith Soc; Am Ornith Union; Am Inst Biol Sci; Sigma Xi. *Res:* Vertebrate ecology; population dynamics and habitat management, especially research applicable to management of wildlife. *Mailing Add:* Dept Fish & Wildlife Biol Colo State Univ Ft Collins CO 80523-0001

HEIN, DAVID WILLIAM, PHARMACOGENETICS, CHEMICAL CARCINOGENESIS. *Current Pos:* PROF & CHAIR PHARMACOL, UNIV NDAK SCH MED, 89- *Personal Data:* b Faith, SDak, Aug 17, 55; m 78, Korla Raab; c Joshua & Jacob. *Educ:* Univ Wis-Eau Claire, BS, 77; Univ Mich, PhD(pharmacol), 82. *Honors & Awards:* Thomas J Clifford Fac Achievement Award Excellence in Res, Univ NDak. *Prof Exp:* From asst prof to prof pharmacol, Morehouse Sch Med, 82-89, actg chair, 83-85, chmn, 85-89, prog dir res, 86-89. *Concurrent Pos:* Grad fac, Atlanta Univ, 83-89; prin investr, Nat Cancer Inst grant, NIH, 83-, Div Res Resources grant, 87-89; adj asst prof, Sch Med, Emory Univ, 86-89; adj assoc prof, Ga State Univ, 89-; peer reviewer, Nat Cancer Inst Study Sect, 90-92; deleg, US Pharmacopeial Conv, 91- *Mem:* Am Asn Cancer Res; Am Soc Pharmacol & Exp Therapeut; Asn Med Sch Pharmacol; Int Soc Study Xenobiotics; Sigma Xi. *Res:* Studies to understand and predict genetic predisposition to cancer and other toxicities following exposures to drugs and environmental chemicals. *Mailing Add:* Dept Pharmacol & Toxicol Univ NDak Sch Med 501 N Columbia Rd Grand Forks ND 58202-9037. *Fax:* 701-777-6124; *E-Mail:* david.hein@medicine.und.nodak.edu

HEIN, JAMES R, GEOLOGY, MARINE MINERAL DEPOSITS. *Current Pos:* GEOLOGIST, US GEOL SURV MARINE & COASTAL GEOL, 73- *Personal Data:* b Santa Barbara, Calif, Mar 15, 47; c Lanee T & Tasha R. *Educ:* Ore State Univ, BS, 69; Univ Calif, Santa Cruz, PhD(earth sci), 73. *Prof Exp:* Lectr earth sci prin, Univ Calif, Santa Cruz, 72-73 & 80. *Concurrent Pos:* Res geologist, Nat Res Coun, 74-75; int group leader, Int Geol Correlation Proj, UNESCO, 76-86 & 91-96; convenor, Penrose Conf, Geol Soc Am, 78; convenor, Int Conf Siliceous Deposits, Japan, 81, Yugoslavia, 86, Marine Mineral Deposits, Hawaii, 90, Marine Mining Develop task force, US Minerals Mgt Serv, 84; ed, Elsevier, 83, Van Nostrand Reinhold, 87, Springer-Verlag, 89, Geol Soc, London, 97, Elsevier, 97; guest scientist, Japanese Nat Oil Corp, 85, Chinese Ministry Petrol & Marine Geol, 86, Indian Ministry oceanog 86, Korean Ocean Res & Develop Inst, 88, 90 & 97, Ger Res Cruises, 84, 85 & 86; expert witness, US Cong Comt Deep Sea Mining, 86; leader, USA-USSR Prog Geochem Marine Sediments, 88-94, USA-Korea Prog Marine Mineral Deposits, 88-94; marine geol panel, USA-Japan prog Nat Res, 88-; assoc ed, Geo-Marine Letters, 90-, Marine Geol, 95- *Mem:* AAAS; fel Geol Soc Am; Am Geophys Union; Oceanog Soc; fel Soc Econ Geologists; Geochem Soc. *Res:* Marine geology, low temperature geochemistry, authigenic mineralogy, clay mineralogy, field geology, siliceous and calcareous deposits, ore deposits at constructive and destructive plate boundaries, island arcs, marine ferromanganese deposits; seamounts, marine mineral deposits. *Mailing Add:* US Geol Surv MS 999 345 Middlefield Rd Menlo Park CA 94025. *Fax:* 650-354-3191; *E-Mail:* jhein@octopus.wr.usgs.gov

HEIN, JOHN WILLIAM, DENTISTRY. *Current Pos:* RETIRED. *Personal Data:* b Chester, Mass, Sept 29, 20; m 44. *Educ:* Am Int Col, BS, 41; Tufts Col, DMD, 44; Univ Rochester, PhD(pharm), 52. *Hon Degrees:* AM, Harvard Univ, 62; DSc, Am Int Col, 79. *Prof Exp:* Instr oral path, Dent Sch, Tufts Col, 43-44; instr, Univ Rochester, 51-53, asst prof dent res & chmn dept dent & dent res, 52-55; dent dir, Colgate-Palmolive Co, 55-59; prof prev dent, lectr pharmacol & dean, Sch Dent Med, Tufts Univ, 59-62; prof dent, Sch Dent Med, Harvard Univ, 62-69; dir, Forsyth Dent Ctr, 62-92. *Concurrent Pos:* Instr anat & physiol, Eastman Sch Dent Hyg, 50-55 & dent res, 53-55; assoc res specialist, Bur Biol Res, Rutgers Univ, 55-59. *Mem:* AAAS; Am Dent Asn; Int Asn Dent Res; Int Col Dentists (pres, 83-84); Sigma Xi; hon mem Royal Soc Med. *Res:* Chemical therapy for dental caries prevention; oral hygiene; experimental caries in Syrian Hamster; clinical studies of dental caries and periodontal disease. *Mailing Add:* 3 Bridge St PO Box 156 Medfield MA 02052-1539

HEIN, PETER LEO, JR, PSYCHIATRY. *Current Pos:* PROF PSYCHIAT & DIR RESIDENCY TRAINING, MED CTR, WVA UNIV, 71-, PROF BEHAV MED, 80- *Personal Data:* b Chicago, Ill, Feb 12, 30. *Educ:* Georgetown Univ, BS, 51, MD, 55; Am Bd Psychiat & Neurol, dipl, 62. *Prof Exp:* Intern psychiat, Univ Chicago Clins, 55-56; resident, DC Gen Hosp, 56-57; chief open ward serv & outpatient dept, Sheppard AFB Hosp, Wichita Falls, Tex, 57-59; resident, Med Ctr, Georgetown Univ, 59-61; from instr to assoc prof, Duke Univ, 61-71, mem, Steering Comt Post Doctoral Res Training Prog, 65-71, head psychophysiol lab, Clin Res Unit Comt & Human Experimentation Comt, 68-71. *Concurrent Pos:* Res fel, Duke Univ, 61-63; clin investr, Vet Admin Hosp, Durham, NC, 63-65. *Mem:* Am Psychiat Asn; Soc Psychophysiol Res; Am Electroencephalog Soc. *Res:* Electroencephalography; psychophysiology. *Mailing Add:* Dept Psychiat WVa Univ Hosp Morgantown WV 26506

HEIN, R(OWLAND) F(RANK), CHEMICAL ENGINEERING. *Current Pos:* RETIRED. *Personal Data:* b Minneapolis, Minn, Aug 5, 23; m 47, Edna Burrill; c Leland, Karen & Andrea. *Educ:* Univ Minn, BChE, 44, PhD(chem eng), 52. *Prof Exp:* Res engr, E I du Pont de Nemours & Co, 52-60, res supvr, 60-77, res assoc, 78-82. *Mem:* AAAS; Am Chem Soc; Am Inst Chem Engrs. *Res:* Mass transfer; process development; reactor design. *Mailing Add:* Box 603 Mendenhall PA 19357-0603

HEIN, RICHARD EARL, CHEMISTRY. *Current Pos:* gen mgr res & develop, H J Heinz Co, 73-77, gen mgr res & qual assurance, Tomato Prod & Condiments Div, 77-81, gen mgr Res & Qual Assurance, 81-83, SPEC TECH CONSULT, HEINZ USA DIV, H J HEINZ CO, 83- *Personal Data:* b Erie, Ill, May 25, 19; m 44; c 4. *Educ:* Univ Iowa, BS, 42; Iowa State Univ, PhD(chem), 50. *Prof Exp:* Jr chemist, Manhattan Metall Proj, AEC, Iowa State Univ, 42-50; from asst prof to assoc prof chem, Kans State Col, 50-57; admin fel, Mellon Inst, 57-65; mgr food res, H J Heinz Co, 65-71, sr mgr prod res & develop, 71-73. *Concurrent Pos:* Int Exec Service Corp, 83. *Mem:* AAAS; Am Chem Soc; Inst Food Technologists. *Res:* Fission product and hot-atom chemistry; application of tracers to biochemical problems; physical aspects of food technology; rheology of suspensions; gas chromatography; food product development. *Mailing Add:* 2104 Mazatlan Rd Punta Gorda FL 33983-2633

HEIN, RICHARD WILLIAM, INDUSTRIAL ORGANIC CHEMISTRY, COATINGS. *Current Pos:* MGR, MOONEY CHEMICALS, INC, 84- *Personal Data:* b Cleveland, Ohio, Nov 29, 34; m 58, Ruth Gersten Berger; c John, Jane & David. *Educ:* Capital Univ, BS, 56; Case Inst Technol, MS, 58, PhD(org chem), 61. *Prof Exp:* Chemist, Escambia Chem Corp, 61-68; develop scientist, BF Goodrich Chem Co, 68-73, tech mgr, 73-80, sr res & develop assoc, 80-84. *Mem:* Am Chem Soc. *Res:* Petrochemicals; monomer synthesis; oxidations; heterogeneous catalysis; separation processes; water treatment; wood preservatives; coatings; general catalysis. *Mailing Add:* 51 Nantucket Dr Hudson OH 44236. *Fax:* 216-781-6632; *E-Mail:* dhein@omgin.com

HEIN, ROSEMARY RUTH, DEVELOPMENTAL ANATOMY, DEVELOPMENTAL BIOLOGY. *Current Pos:* PROF BIOL & CHMN DIV NATURAL SCI & MATH, ST MARY'S COL, MD, 77- *Personal Data:* b Chicago, Ill, Sept 12, 24. *Educ:* Carleton Col, BA, 46; George Washington Univ, MS, 51; Northwestern Univ, PhD(biol), 54. *Prof Exp:* Biologist, Nat Cancer Inst, NIH, 46-50; assoc prof anat, physiol & embryol, Keuka Col, 54-62; assoc prof anat & biol, Winthrop Col, 62-65; assoc prof anat & embryol, 65-67, actg dean, 72-73, prof anat & embryol, Upsala Col, 67-77. *Mem:* Am Soc Zool; Am Inst Biol Sci; Sigma Xi. *Res:* Nutritional effects of cancer; developmental physiology; regeneration. *Mailing Add:* Continuing Educ St Mary's Col St Mary's City MD 20686-9999

HEIN, WARREN WALTER, NUCLEAR PHYSICS. *Current Pos:* assoc prof, 79-84, PROF PHYSICS, SDAK STATE UNIV, 84-; PROF PHYSICS, NORTHERN STATE COL, 79- *Personal Data:* b Plymouth, Wis, May 13, 44; m 65, 85; c 4. *Educ:* Wis State Univ-Whitewater, BS, 66; Iowa State Univ, PhD(nuclear physics), 70. *Prof Exp:* From asst prof to assoc prof, Northern State Col, 70-79. *Mem:* Am Asn Physics Teachers; Sigma Xi; Am Soc Eng Educ; Optical Soc Am. *Res:* Optics; alignment of large x-ray optical systems; low level radioactivity of groundwater; remote sensing of soil moisture. *Mailing Add:* PO Box 2209 SDak State Univ Brookings SD 57007

HEINBERG, MILTON, PHYSICS, OPERATIONS RESEARCH. *Current Pos:* CONSULT, DEPT ENERGY, 90- *Personal Data:* b Birmingham, Ala, Apr 3, 28; m 56, Mary A Dinges; c Cynthia & Leslie. *Educ:* Oberlin Col, AB, 52; Univ Pittsburgh, PhD(physics), 56. *Prof Exp:* Res assoc physics, Univ Pittsburgh, 56-57 & Cornell Univ, 57-59; exp physicist, Lawrence Livermore Lab, Univ Calif, 59-71; sr scientist, Nuclear Defense Res Corp, Albuquerque, 71-73; staff scientist, RCA Corp, 73-74; sr test & eval scientist, EG & G Co, Albuquerque, 74-75; sr scientist, Dikewood Corp, Albuquerque, NMex, 75-76; staff mem, Los Alamos Nat Lab, 76-90. *Mem:* Am Phys Soc. *Res:* Positron annihilation; beta decay; high energy nuclear physics; high speed weapon diagnostics; military operational tests and evaluations; nuclear materials safeguards and security; classification. *Mailing Add:* 8416 Harron Valley Ct Gaithersburg MD 20879

HEINDEL, NED DUANE, ORGANIC CHEMISTRY, MEDICINAL CHEMISTRY. *Current Pos:* from asst prof to prof chem, 66-76, H S BUNN CHAIR PROF, LEHIGH UNIV, 76- *Personal Data:* b Red Lion, Pa, Sept 4, 37; m 59, Linda Heefner. *Educ:* Lebanon Valley Col, BS, 59; Univ Del, MS, 61, PhD(org chem), 63. *Hon Degrees:* DSc, Lebanon Valley Col, 85, Albright Col, 93. *Honors & Awards:* Cancer Res Achievement Award, Brady Cancer Res Found, 89. *Prof Exp:* From asst to instr chem, Univ Del, 61-62; NSF fel, Princeton Univ, 63-64; asst prof, Marshall Univ, 64-66. *Concurrent Pos:* Benedum Found fac fel, Marshall Univ, 65; grants, Petrol Res Fund, 64-65, Res Corp, 64-66, Sigma Xi Res Fund, 65, US Army, 66-72, NIH, 66-, Milheim Fund for Cancer Res, 73-74 & 81-84, Am Cancer Soc, 75-78 & Pardee Fund, 75-77 & 81-84; asst prof, Univ Ohio, 65; adj assoc prof nuclear med, Hahnemann Univ, 73-84, adj prof, 85-; dir div biol chem & biophys, Ctr Health Sci, Lehigh Univ, 73-80, Ctr Health Sci, 80-87; trustee, Keystone Jr Col, LaPlume, Pa, 75-88 & Ctr Hist Chem, Philadelphia, 82-; dir, Am Chem Soc, 85-, pres, 94; trustee, Coun Chem Res, Washington DC, 95- *Mem:* Am Asn Pharmaceut Scientists; Am Chem Soc (pres, 94); Soc Nuclear Med. *Res:* Heterocyclic and medicinal syntheses; history of chemistry; nuclear medicine and diagnostic radioactive pharmaceuticals; anti-tumor compounds and central nervous system depressants; monoclonal antibody drug conjugates. *Mailing Add:* Dept Chem Lehigh Univ Bethlehem PA 18015. *E-Mail:* ndh0@lehigh.edu

HEINDL, CLIFFORD JOSEPH, NUCLEAR PHYSICS. *Current Pos:* res specialist physics, 59-61, group supvr nuclear physics, 61-65, tech mgr res, 65-78, DEP, DIV MGR SCI, JET PROPULSION LAB, CALIF INST TECHNOL, 78- *Personal Data:* b Chicago, Ill, Feb 4, 26. *Educ:* Northwestern Univ, BS, 47, MS, 48; Columbia Univ, AM, 50 & PhD(physics), 59. *Prof Exp:* Physicist, Bendix Aviation Corp, 53-54; asst sect chief, Babcock & Wilcox Co, 56-58. *Mem:* Am Phys Soc; Am Nuclear Soc; Health Physics Soc; Am Inst Aeronaut & Astronaut. *Res:* Reactor physics. *Mailing Add:* 179 Mockingbird Lane South Pasadena CA 91030

HEINDSMANN, T(HEODORE) E(DWARD), MARINE SCIENCES, ACOUSTICS. *Current Pos:* MANAGING DIR & CONSULT, RIS ASSOCS, 91- *Personal Data:* b Aug 2, 25; US citizen; m 49; c 3. *Educ:* Rensselaer Polytech Inst, BEE, 44; Univ Calif, Berkeley, MS, 50. *Prof Exp:* Electronic scientist, Navy Underwater Sound Lab, Conn, 45-47, sect head acoust res, 49-55; res engr, inst transp & traffic, microwave lab, Univ Calif, Berkeley, 47-49; res specialist, tech staff, Boeing Co, 55-58, antisubmarine prog chief, 58-61, space tech mgr, 61-64, sr tech mgr, AWACS staff, 64-84, sr tech mgr, Acousts & ASW Systs, 84-90. *Concurrent Pos:* Sr lectr & ed, Ocean Tech Ser, 65-68; gen chmn, Int Ocean Eng Conf, 80, adv comt, 81, 89. *Mem:* AAAS; Acoust Soc Am; Inst Elec & Electronics Engrs; Marine Technol Soc; Ocean Eng Soc. *Res:* Propagation and reception of acoustic and electromagnetic energy; classification of signal and background sources; instrumentation for remote sensing; bioacoustics. *Mailing Add:* 18003 Westside Hwy SW Vashon WA 98070-4433

HEINE, GEORGE WINFIELD, III, SIMULATED ANNEALING, GEOSPATIAL ANALYSIS. *Current Pos:* MATH ANALYST, BUR LAND MGT, 84- *Personal Data:* b Oakland, Calif, Sept 22, 49; m 87. *Educ:* Reed Col, BA, 71; Univ Colo, MS, 89, PhD, 94. *Mem:* Soc Indust & Appl Math; Math Asn Am; Am Statist Asn. *Res:* Investigating necessary and sufficient conditions for effectiveness of simulated annealing and other combinational optimization algorithms; developing provably correct polygon overlay software for use in geographic information systems. *Mailing Add:* 200 Sunset Lane Pueblo CO 81005. *E-Mail:* gheine@mathnmaps.com

HEINE, HAROLD WARREN, ORGANIC CHEMISTRY, O-QUINONE MONOIMIDES. *Current Pos:* from asst prof to assoc prof, Bucknell Univ, 48-53, chair, 70-86, Bucknell presidential prof, 72-78, prof chem, 54-93, DIR, MA DEGREE PROG CHEM, BUCKNELL UNIV, 93- *Personal Data:* b Highland Park, NJ, Sept 14, 22; m 53, Marjorie Boote; c Katharine, Elizabeth & Eric. *Educ:* Rutgers Univ, BS, 44, PhD(org chem), 48. *Honors & Awards:* Harbison Prize for Distinguished Teaching & Res, Danforth Found, 70; Catalyst Award, Chem Mfrs Asn, 80; Res Award, Am Chem Soc, 87. *Prof Exp:* Asst, Rutgers Univ, 47-48. *Concurrent Pos:* Res chemist, Dow Chem Co, 56-57; NSF sr fac fel, Ger, 61-62; consult to Surgeon Gen, 65-; vis prof, Univ Heidelberg, 69-70 & Univ Auckland, NZ, 86; pres, Chem Div, Coun Undergrad Res, 88-90. *Mem:* Am Chem Soc. *Res:* Bromoamides; chlorohydrins; ethylenimines; kinetics; chemistry of diaziridines and cycloadditions; nitrones; benzodiazepines; o-quinone monoimides. *Mailing Add:* Dept Chem Bucknell Univ Lewisburg PA 17837

HEINE, MELVIN WAYNE, OBSTETRICS & GYNECOLOGY, ENDOCRINOLOGY. *Current Pos:* PROF & CHMN DEPT OBSTET & GYNEC, TEX TECH SCH MED, 77- *Personal Data:* b Ellendale, NDak, Mar 21, 33; m 58; c 2. *Educ:* Duke Univ, MD, 58. *Prof Exp:* Intern med, Med Col Va, 58-59; asst resident obstet & gynec, Teaching Hosp, Univ Fla, 59-61, chief resident & instr, 61-62, asst prof, Col Med, 63-64, asst prof & dir endocrinol, 66-70; prof obstet & gynec & chief endocrine serv, Col Med, Univ Ariz, 70-77. *Concurrent Pos:* Fel, Worcester Found Exp Biol, 62-63; Ford Found grant, Univ Fla & Univ Ariz, 67-70; Fed Drug Admin grant. *Mem:* Am Fertil Soc; Int Soc Res Reproduction; AMA; Am Col Obstet & Gynec; Am Gynec Club. *Res:* Gynecologic endocrinology; female infertility; contraception; fetal endocrinology; menopause. *Mailing Add:* Univ Ariz Health Sci Ctr Obstet/ Gynec 1501 N Campbell Tucson AZ 85724-0001

HEINE, RICHARD W, metallurgical engineering, for more information see previous edition

HEINE, URSULA INGRID, CYTOLOGY, BIOLOGY. *Current Pos:* RETIRED. *Personal Data:* b Berlin, Ger, Feb 19, 26. *Educ:* Univ Berlin, MS, 50, PhD(biol), 53. *Prof Exp:* Assoc, Inst Cancer Res, Ger Acad Sci, 50-59; assoc, Med Ctr, Duke Univ, 59-68; microbiologist, Nat Cancer Inst, 68-71, head, Ultrastruc Studies Sect, 71-91. *Mem:* AAAS; Electron Micros Soc Am; Am Asn Cancer Res; Am Soc Cell Biol. *Res:* Electron microscopic studies on tumor viruses and their relation to the host cell, as well as the response of nontransformed cells to chemical carcinogens. *Mailing Add:* 18712 Willow Grove Rd PO Box 97 Olney MD 20832-0097

HEINEKEN, FREDERICK GEORGE, CHEMICAL ENGINEERING. *Current Pos:* PROG DIR, NSF, 85- *Personal Data:* b Chicago, Ill, Oct 22, 39; div; c Chris. *Educ:* Northwestern Univ, BSChE, 62; Univ Minn, PhD(chem eng), 66. *Prof Exp:* Sr res chem engr, Monsanto Co, St Louis, 66-72; instr, Univ Colo, 75-76; sr proj eng, Cobe Labs, Inc, 76-78, dept eng 78-81, ther scientist, 81-85. *Concurrent Pos:* Fel, Univ Colo Med Ctr, 72-74, Young Pulmonary res investr, 74-76. *Mem:* Am Chem Soc; AAAS; Am Inst Chem Engrs; Am Soc Artificial Internal Organs; Asn Advan Med Instrumentation. *Res:* Mathematical aspects of enzyme kinetics; oxygen transfer; microbial enzyme synthesis; continuous fermentation; membrane separation techniques; enzyme recovery techniques; blood gas exchange; artificial kidney design; kidney machine design; physiological modelling of dialysis patients. *Mailing Add:* NSF 4201 Wilson Blvd Arlington VA 22230. *Fax:* 703-306-0312; *E-Mail:* fheineke@nsf.gov

HEINEMAN, FREDERICK W, BIOENERGETICS, CARDIOVASCULAR PHYSIOLOGY. *Current Pos:* med res fel, NIH, 86-89, SR RES INVESTR, LAB CARDIAC ENERGETICS, NAT HEART, LUNG & BLOOD INST, NIH, 89- *Educ:* Mich State Univ, BS, 73, MS, 76; Univ Toronto, PhD(physiol), 83; Wayne State Univ, MD, 84. *Prof Exp:* Internal med resident, Wayne State Univ, 84-86. *Concurrent Pos:* Mem, Basic Sci Coun, Am Heart Asn. *Mem:* Am Physiol Soc; AAAS; Am Heart Asn. *Res:* Investigations of myocardial supply/demand and energy metabolism. *Mailing Add:* NHLBI Lab Cardiac Energet Bldg 1 Rm B3-07 NIH Bethesda MD 20892-0001. *Fax:* 301-402-0334; *E-Mail:* fosh@helix.nih.gov

HEINEMAN, WILLIAM RICHARD, ANALYTICAL CHEMISTRY, ELECTROCHEMISTRY. *Current Pos:* from asst prof to prof chem, 72-80, DISTINGUISHED PROF, UNIV CINCINNATI, 88- *Personal Data:* b Lubbock, Tex, Oct 15, 42; m 69, Linda Harkins; c David & John. *Educ:* Tex Tech Univ, BS, 64; Univ NC, Chapel Hill, PhD(chem), 68. *Honors & Awards:* Sr Humboldt Award, 89. *Prof Exp:* Res chemist, Hercules, 68-70; res assoc chem, Case Western Res Univ, 70-71, Ohio State Univ, 71-72. *Concurrent Pos:* Ed, Cintacs, Cincinnati Sect, Am Chem Soc, 74-75, secy, 75-76, first vchmn & chmn elect, 76-77, chmn, 77-78, trustee, 78-81 & counr, 84-91; sci adv, Food & Drug Admin, 75-80; treas, Div Analytical Chem, Am Chem Soc, 83-85; mem bd dirs, Soc Electroanal Chem, 84-90, chmn, 84-85. *Mem:* Am Chem Soc; Electrochem Soc; Sigma Xi; Soc Electroanal Chem (pres, 84-85); Am Asn Clin Chem; AAAS. *Res:* Analytical chemistry; electroanalytical chemistry; optically transparent thin layer electrodes; bioelectrochemistry; immunoassay by electrochemical techniques; polymer modified electrodes. *Mailing Add:* Dept Chem Univ Cincinnati Cincinnati OH 45221-0001. *Fax:* 513-556-9239

HEINEMANN, HEINZ, PHYSICAL CHEMISTRY. *Current Pos:* sr scientist, 78-94, DISTINGUISHED SCIENTIST, LAWRENCE BERKELEY LAB, UNIV CALIF, BERKELEY, 94- *Personal Data:* b Berlin, Ger, Aug 21, 13; nat US; m 48; c 2. *Educ:* Univ & Tech Hochschule, Berlin, Ger, BS, 35; Univ Basel, PhD(chem), 37. *Honors & Awards:* E V Murphree Medallist, Am Chem Soc, 71; E J Houdry Award, Catalysis Soc NAm, 75; H Lowry Award, US Dept Energy, 93. *Prof Exp:* Chief res chemist, Rodessa Oil & Ref Corp, 38-39; res chemist, Danziger Oil & Refining, 39-41; res fel, Carnegie Inst Technol, 41; lab supvr, Attapulgus Clay Co, 41-48; sect chief process res, Houdry Process Corp, 48-57; asst to vpres res & develop & assoc dir res, M W Kellogg Co, 57-61, mgr, 61-67, dir chem & eng res, 67-69; sr res assoc, Cent Res Lab, Mobil Res & Develop Corp, 69-70, mgr catalysis res, 70-76, mgr res contracts, 76-78. *Concurrent Pos:* Pres, Int Cong Catalysis, 56-60; mem, Coun Sci Res, Spain, 64-; lectr chem eng, Univ Calif, Berkeley, 79- *Mem:* Nat Acad Eng; Am Chem Soc; fel Am Inst Chemists; fel Royal Soc; Catalysis Soc NAm. *Res:* Catalysis; petroleum processing; coal conversion and synthetic fuels; clays and adsorbents; carbohydrate to hydrocarbon conversion. *Mailing Add:* 4600 Conn Ave Apt 206 Washington DC 20008

HEINEMANN, RICHARD LESLIE, CYTOGENETICS. *Current Pos:* RETIRED. *Personal Data:* b Jan 14, 31; US citizen; m 64, Mary Perry; c Anne. *Educ:* Champlain Col, NY, BA, 53; Univ Rochester, MS, 58; Med Col Va, PhD(biol & genetics), 68. *Prof Exp:* From asst prof to prof biol, Longwood Col, 63-91, emer prof, 91. *Mem:* Soc Study Evolution; Sigma Xi. *Res:* Genetics, cytogenetics and evolution of the sex determining mechanisms in arrhenotokous parthenogenetic species. *Mailing Add:* Rte 4 Box 1535 Farmville VA 23901. *Fax:* 804-395-2652

HEINEMANN, WILTON WALTER, ANIMAL NUTRITION. *Current Pos:* NUTRIT CONSULT, 86; TEXTBK WRITER, 87- *Personal Data:* b Ritzville, Wash, Mar 9, 20; m 80, Lois Jackson; c Allen H, Maureen (McCuen) & Lisa (Freund). *Educ:* Wash State Univ, BS, 42, MS, 45; Ore State Univ, PhD(animal nutrit), 54. *Prof Exp:* Exten agt & asst co agt, Kittitas Co, 42-43; asst animal husb, Irrig Exp Sta, Wash State Univ, 43-45, asst animal husbandman, 45-54, assoc animal scientist animal nutrit, 54-61, prof animal nutrit & animal scientist, 61-85. *Concurrent Pos:* Consult, Bur Sport Fisheries, US Dept Interior, 60-70 & Battelle Mem Inst, 72-; lectr, Polish Acad Sci, Krakow, 79, Japanese Farm Coops, Japan & Korean Farm Coops, Korea, 83.

Mem: Fel AAAS; fel Am Soc Animal Sci; Am Forage & Grassland Coun; Sigma Xi; Int Grassland Cong. *Res:* Vitamins in pork production; soil-plant-animal relationships; irrigated pastures; forage utilization by ruminants; net energy and metabolism research with ruminants; energy, metabolism and feeding research on industrial and other by-products and wastes. *Mailing Add:* 4406 Terrace Heights Dr Yakima WA 98901

HEINEN, JAMES ALBIN, DIGITAL SIGNAL PROCESSING, SPEECH PROCESSING. *Current Pos:* Lectr elec eng, Marquette Univ, 67-68, from asst prof to assoc prof 69-80, grad adminr, 71-73, chmn dept, 73-76, dir grad studies, 87-95, PROF, ELEC & COMP ENG, MARQUETTE UNIV, 80-, DIR SIGNAL PROCESSING RES CTR, 90- *Personal Data:* b Milwaukee, Wis, June 23, 43. *Educ:* Marquette Univ, BEE, 64, MS, 67, PhD(elec eng), 69. *Mem:* Inst Elec & Electronics Engrs; Am Soc Eng Educ. *Res:* Digital signal processing; speech processing; analysis and design of digital filters; stability and analysis of control systems. *Mailing Add:* Marquette Univ PO Box 1881 Milwaukee WI 53201-1881

HEINEN, JOEL THOMAS, CONSERVATION BIOLOGY, NATIONAL PARK & NATURE RESERVE MANAGEMENT. *Current Pos:* ASST PROF ENVIRON STUDIES, FLA INT UNIV, 93-, ADJ ASST PROF BIOL, 94- *Personal Data:* b Buffalo, NY, Mar 9, 58. *Educ:* Univ Mich, BS, 79, PhD(natural resources), 92; Va Tech, MS, 82; Ohio State Univ, MS, 84. *Prof Exp:* Lectr, Inst Forestry, Tribhuvan Univ, Nepal, 84-87, Sch Natural Resources, Univ Mich, 92-93. *Concurrent Pos:* Res prin investr, Dept Nat Parks & Wildlife Conserv, Kosi Tappu Wildlife Res, Nepal, 86-87; lectr, Biol Sta, Univ Mich, 90-; res assoc, Found Res Econ & Environ, 93. *Mem:* Sigma Xi; NY Acad Sci; Soc Conserv Biol; Asn Trop Biol; AAAS; Ecol Soc Am; Am Soc Ichthyologists & Herpetologists. *Res:* Applied ecology and conservation biology, especially design and management of nature reserves, large mammal conservation, and ecology of reptiles and amphibians; some restoration ecology. *Mailing Add:* Dept Environ Studies Fla Int Univ Miami FL 33199-0001. *Fax:* 305-348-3772

HEINER, DOUGLAS C, PEDIATRICS, ALLERGY. *Current Pos:* PROF PEDIAT, MED SCH, UNIV CALIF, LOS ANGELES, 69- *Personal Data:* b Salt Lake City, Utah, July 27, 25; m 46, Joy L Wiest; c Susan, Craig, Joe, Marianne, James, David, Drew, Carolee & Pauli. *Educ:* Idaho State Col, BS, 46; Univ Pa, MD, 50; McGill Univ, PhD(immunol), 69; Am Bd Pediat, dipl allergy, immunol & cardiol. *Honors & Awards:* Western Soc Pediat Res & Ross Labs Res Award, 61. *Prof Exp:* Intern, Hosp Univ Pa, 50-51; resident, Boston Children's Med Ctr, 53-55, res fel cardiol, 55-56; from instr to asst prof pediat, Univ Ark, 56-59, actg head dept, 57-58; from asst prof to assoc prof, Col Med, Univ Utah, 60-69; dir, Div Immunol & Allergy, Dept Pediat, Harbor Univ Calif Med Ctr, 69-94. *Concurrent Pos:* Asst, Harvard Med Sch, 54-55; USPHS spec res fel, Royal Victoria Hosp, 66-69; vis prof, Univ Bern, Inst Clin Immunol, Switz, 78-79; res assoc, Div Biol, Cal Tech, 89-90; Fogarty Int Fel, 78-79. *Mem:* Am Acad Allergy & Immunol; Am Acad Pediat; Am Asn Immunologists; Soc Pediat Res; Am Pediat Soc; Am Col Allergy & Immunol. *Res:* Pediatric allergy and immunology; IgE; IgD; food sensitivity; pulmonary hemosiderosis; celiac disease; pediatric AIDS; immunology; immune deficiency disorders. *Mailing Add:* Provo Allergy & Immunol Clin 3909 Foothills Dr Provo UT 84604. *Fax:* 310-212-7140

HEINER, TERRY CHARLES, BOTANY, FORESTRY. *Current Pos:* from asst prof to assoc prof, 70-87, PROF BIOL SCI, WESTERN NMEX UNIV, 87-, CHMN, DEPT NATURAL SCI, 94- *Personal Data:* b Smoot, Wyo, Feb 1, 41; m 66, JoAnn Bridge; c 3. *Educ:* Utah State Univ, BS, 66; Ore State Univ, MS, 67; Iowa State Univ, PhD(bot), 70. *Concurrent Pos:* Adv, NMex Environ Inst, 71-75. *Mem:* Bot Soc Am. *Res:* Plant competition, population ecology. *Mailing Add:* Dept Natural Sci Western NMex Univ PO Box 680 Silver City NM 88062

HEINES, THOMAS SAMUEL, COMPUTER SCIENCE, CHEMICAL ENGINEERING. *Current Pos:* from assoc prof to prof, 65-85, chmn, 85-95, EMER PROF COMPUT SCI, CLEVELAND STATE UNIV, 95- *Personal Data:* b Grand Rapids, Mich, Oct 20, 27; m 51; c 2. *Educ:* Univ Mich, Ann Arbor, BSE, 49, MSE, 50, PhD(chem eng), 54. *Prof Exp:* Res engr, Union Carbide Corp, 54-57; res assoc chem eng, Nat Distillers, 57-65. *Mem:* Asn Comput Mach; Inst Elec & Electronics Engrs. *Res:* Computer linguistics; simulation; modeling; control. *Mailing Add:* CIS Dept Cleveland State Univ Euclid at 24th Cleveland OH 44115

HEINICKE, HERBERT RAYMOND, FOOD SCIENCE & TECHNOLOGY. *Current Pos:* TECH CONSULT, PET FOOD, HUMAN & AUTOGENOUS EXTRUSION, 71- *Personal Data:* b Elgin, Ill, June 7, 27; m 55, Janet Hart; c Peter, John, Mary, Mark & Sarah. *Educ:* Northwestern Univ, BS, 49; Univ Wis, MS, 52, PhD(biochem), 55. *Prof Exp:* Res assoc leukemia, Med Sch, Univ Wis, 55-56; proj leader cat food nutrit, Res Labs, Quaker Oats Co, 56-59, proj leader pet food nutrit, 59-62, mgr, 62-67, mgr pet food nutrit & eval, 67-71. *Mem:* Fel AAAS; Inst Food Technologists; Asn Vitamin Chemists (pres, 71-72). *Res:* Cat and dog nutrition; care of cats and dogs as laboratory animals; pet food technology and evaluation; human nutrition; environmental sciences; technology assessment; patentee in field. *Mailing Add:* 1302 W Boston Ave Indianola IN 50125. *Fax:* 515-961-8903

HEINICKE, PETER HART, DATA ACQUISITION SOFTWARE, SIMULATION SOFTWARE. *Current Pos:* PRES, PRECISION COMPUT METHODS INC, 89- *Personal Data:* b Madison, Wis, Mar 26, 56. *Educ:* Washington Univ, BA, 77, MA, 77; Princeton Univ, MA, 79; Ill Inst Technol, MS, 85. *Prof Exp:* Engr, Int Harvester Corp, 80; systs analyst, Fermi Nat Lab, 80-89. *Concurrent Pos:* Consult, Comp Method, Inc, 79-89. *Mem:* Asn Comput Mach; Am Phys Soc. *Res:* Design and implimation of VME data acquisition systems which will read out KMAC using Motorola 68,000 and which will feed into vax. *Mailing Add:* Precision Comput Methods Inc 517 Elm Ave Geneva IL 60134

HEINICKE, RALPH MARTIN, ALKALOIDS. *Current Pos:* CHMN, BIOTECHNOL RESOURCES INC, 87- *Personal Data:* b Hickory, NC, Sept 3, 14; m 44; c 1. *Educ:* Cornell Univ, BS, 36; Univ Minn, PhD(biochem), 50. *Prof Exp:* Agr chemist, Shell Oil Co, 39-42; biochemist, Pineapple Res Inst, 50-55; dir chem & food res, Dole Co, 55-71, dir chem & food res, Jintan Dole Co, 64-70; mem tech staff, Kuakini Med Res Inst, 71-72; dir chem & new prod res, Aresco, 80-84; tech pharmacol consult, Jintan Dolph Co, 74-87; vpres res & develop, BCC Systs, Inc, 85-87. *Concurrent Pos:* Assoc fac mem, Univ Hawaii, 50-; consult, Drug & Food Co. *Mem:* AAAS; Am Chem Soc; Am Inst Chemists; Inst Food Technologists. *Res:* Role of proteases in animal and plant physiology; biosynthesis of alkaloids in plants, people and microorganisms and the physiological role of xeronine and the xeronine system in cells; waste water treatment. *Mailing Add:* 1124 Rostrevor Circle Louisville KY 40205

HEINIG, HANS PAUL, MATHEMATICS. *Current Pos:* From asst prof to prof, 65-96, EMER PROF MATH, MCMASTER UNIV, 96- *Personal Data:* b Dortmund, Ger, June 30, 31; Can citizen; m 60, Fumiyo Kinoshita; c Nina & Nicola. *Educ:* McMaster Univ, BS, 61; Univ Western Ont, MA, 62; Univ Toronto, PhD(math), 65. *Mem:* Am Math Soc; Math Asn Am. *Res:* Classical analysis; Laplace and Fourier transforms; Banach spaces; linear operators and interpolation in Orlicz spaces; functions of bounded mean oscillation; weighted inequalities. *Mailing Add:* Dept Math McMaster Univ Hamilton ON L8S 4K1 Can. *Fax:* 905-522-0935; *E-Mail:* heinig@mcmail.cis.mcmaster.ca

HEINIGER, HANS-JORG, CELL BIOLOGY. *Current Pos:* PRES & CHIEF EXEC OFFICER, CENT LAB, BLOOD TRANSFUSION SERV, 88- *Personal Data:* b Burgdorf, Switz, Aug 30, 38; m 62; c 2. *Educ:* Univ Geneva, BA, 59; Univ Bern, MA, 61, DVM, 65. *Honors & Awards:* Edward A Stein Award, Univ Bern, 64. *Prof Exp:* Asst prof neuropath, Inst Comp Neurol, Sch Vet Med, Univ Bern, 64, asst prof histochem, Inst path, Sch Med, 64-67; staff scientist & head, Lab Cell Biol, Inst Med, Nuclear Res Ctr, Julich, WGer, 67-70; vis scientist, 70-72, staff scientist cell biol, 72-80, dir animal resources, 81-83, sr staff scientist, Jackson Lab, 80-88. *Concurrent Pos:* Res collabr, Swiss Inst Exp Cancer Res, 67- & Brookhaven Nat Lab, Upton, NY, 74-; coop prof zool, Univ Maine, Orono, 1981; mem gov bd, Int Coun Lab Animal Sci. *Mem:* Soc Exp Med & Biol; Swiss Soc Molecular Biol; Soc Nuclear Med; Int Union Against Cancer; Am Asn Lab Animal Practitioners; Am Asn Immunologists; Fedn Am Socs Exp Biol; Int Soc Blood Transfusion. *Res:* Function of lipids, especially cholesterol in mammalian cell membranes. *Mailing Add:* Hema Sure Inc 140 Locke Dr Marlboro MA 01752-7230. *Fax:* 504-485-6045

HEININGER, CLARENCE GEORGE, JR, PHYSICAL CHEMISTRY, ANALYTICAL CHEMISTRY. *Current Pos:* from asst prof to assoc prof, St John Fisher Col, 58-64, chmn, 65-70 & 79-90, dean fac & instr, 69-72, prof, 64-91, EMER PROF CHEM, ST JOHN FISHER COL, 91- *Personal Data:* b Rochester, NY, July 30, 28; m 52, Katherine Kress; c Joseph, Laurence, Ann, Ellen & Peter. *Educ:* Villanova Univ, BS, 50; Univ Rochester, PhD(phys chem), 54. *Prof Exp:* Asst chem, Princeton Univ, 53-55; asst prof chem, Villanova Univ, 55-58. *Concurrent Pos:* Sect ed, Chem Abstr, 61-69; vis prof, Univ Lyon, France, 67-68 & Univ Del, 82-83. *Mem:* Am Chem Soc; Sigma Xi. *Mailing Add:* 2048 Five Mile Line Rd Penfield NY 14526

HEININGER, S(AMUEL) ALLEN, ORGANIC CHEMISTRY. *Current Pos:* RETIRED. *Personal Data:* b New Britain, Conn, June 13, 25; wid; c Janet, Kathryn, Kenneth & Keith. *Educ:* Oberlin Col, BA, 48; Carnegie Inst Technol, MS, 51, DSc, 52. *Hon Degrees:* DBA, Adrian Col, 84. *Prof Exp:* Asst, Carnegie Inst Technol, 48-51; res chemist, Cent Res Dept, Monsanto Co, 52-56, group leader, 56-58, proj mgr, Develop Dept, 58-59, sect mgr, 59-64, dir develop, 65-68, dir food & fine chem bus group, Org Chem Div, 68-71, dir corp plans & develop, 71-74, gen mgr, Plasticizers Div, 74-76, dir corp res, 76-77, vpres res & develop, 77-79, vpres technol develop, 79-80, vpres corp plans & bus develop, 80-84, corp vpres res planning, 84-90. *Concurrent Pos:* Mem, Indust Res Inst, 76-90, vis comt sponsored res, MIT, 80, dir, 83-85, Nat Technol Medal Select Comt, 84-90, vpres, 85-86, pres elect, 86-87, pres, 87-88; US/Mexico Found Sci, Bd Gov, 93-97. *Mem:* Am Chem Soc (pres elect, 90, pres, 91); Sigma Xi; Com Develop Asn; Chem Mkt Res Asn; NY Acad Sci; fel AAAS. *Res:* Acrylonitrile chemistry; sulfenyl chlorides; organophosphorus; petrochemicals; food acidulants; sweeteners; food ingredients; drug intermediates; flavors and fragrances. *Mailing Add:* 11110 Hermitage Hill St Louis MO 63131-3323. *Fax:* 314-726-4666; *E-Mail:* alh@xtrn.org

HEINIS, JULIUS LEO, HORTICULTURE & BOTANY. *Current Pos:* from assoc prof to prof, 67-93, EMER PROF BOT, FLA A&M UNIV, 93- *Personal Data:* b Liestal, Switz, Oct 2, 26; nat US; m 52, Margareta; c James, Andrea, Steven & Sandra. *Educ:* Swiss Fed Inst Technol, IngAgr, 51; Ore State Col, PhD, 54. *Prof Exp:* Asst, NY Exp Sta, Geneva, 51; plant pathologist, Ore Dept Agr, 54-60; asst prof plant path, Citrus Ctr, Tex Col Arts & Indust, 61-62; asst prof biol, Concord Col, 62-65; assoc prof, Quincy Col, 65-67. *Concurrent Pos:* Consult, trop fruit. *Mem:* AAAS; Am Inst Biol Sci; Am Soc Microbiol; Caribbean Food Crops Soc. *Res:* Peanut proteins; tree fruit diseases; tropical fruit; online computering. *Mailing Add:* 1924 E Indian Head Dr Tallahassee FL 32301. *E-Mail:* jheinis@mailer.fsu.edu

HEINISCH, ROGER PAUL, OPTICS, PHYSICS. *Current Pos:* prin res scientist, Honeywell Inc, 68-73, dir res, 78-79, dir, 80-81, vpres, 81-85, vpres, Mil Avionics, 85-87, vpres corp, 88-90, SR PRIN RES SCIENTIST, SYSTS & RES CTR, HONEYWELL INC, 73-, MGR, OPTICS TECHNOL PROGS, BALLISTIC MISSILE DEFENSE ADVAN TECHNOL CTR, 75-, VPRES ALLIANT TECHNOL, 90- *Personal Data:* b St Paul, Minn, May 17, 38; m 4; c 3. *Educ:* Marquette Univ, BS, 60, MS, 64; Purdue Univ, PhD, 68. *Prof Exp:* Instr, Purdue Univ, 64-65; res assoc, Argonne Nat Lab, 66-68. *Mem:* Am Soc Mech Eng; Am Inst Aeronaut & Astronaut; Optical Soc Am; Sigma Xi. *Res:* Optics and radiative transfer with efforts split between theoretical and experimental work; fluid mechanics. *Mailing Add:* 23630 Olinda Trail N Scandia MN 55073

HEINKE, CLARENCE HENRY, mathematics education; deceased, see previous edition for last biography

HEINKE, GERHARD WILLIAM, environmental engineering, municipal engineering, for more information see previous edition

HEINLE, DONALD ROGER, ECOLOGY, PHYSIOLOGY. *Current Pos:* MGR, ENVIRON SCI, CH2M HILL, INC, NORTHWEST, 80- *Personal Data:* b New Salem, NDak. *Educ:* Univ Wash, BS, 59; Univ Md, MS, 65, PhD(zool), 69. *Prof Exp:* Biologist, Fisheries Res Inst, Univ Wash, 59-60; res asst to assoc prof ecol, Chesapeake Biol Lab, Univ MD, 69-80. *Mem:* Am Soc Limnol & Oceanog; Estuarine Res Fedn. *Res:* Ecology of zooplankton, cycling of materials in estuaries, food chains, effects of pollutants, fisheries; water quality. *Mailing Add:* 10630 181st Ave NE Redmond WA 98052

HEINLE, PRESTON JOSEPH, organic chemistry, for more information see previous edition

HEINMILLER, ROBERT H, JR, PHYSICS, OCEANOGRAPHY. *Current Pos:* VPRES, OMNET INC, 82- *Personal Data:* b Cleveland, Ohio, Dec 17, 40; m 78, Susan Kathleen Kubany; c Patricia Minsk. *Educ:* Mass Inst Technol, BS, 62. *Honors & Awards:* Ocean Sci Award, Am Geophys Union, 94. *Prof Exp:* Res specialist, Woods Hole Oceanog Inst, 62-76; res asst, Mass Inst Technol, 76-82. *Mem:* AAAS; Am Geophys Union; Oceanog Soc; Am Soc Limnol & Oceanog. *Res:* Deep sea oceanographic mooring technology. *Mailing Add:* PO Box 1284 Staunton VA 24402-1284

HEINO, WALDEN LEO, INORGANIC CHEMISTRY. *Current Pos:* asst prof, 64-73, ASSOC PROF CHEM, LUTHER COL, IOWA, 73- *Personal Data:* b Eveleth, Minn, Apr 13, 30; m 53; c 3. *Educ:* Univ Minn, BS, 53, PhD(inorg chem), 57. *Prof Exp:* Res chemist, E I du Pont de Nemours & Co, Niagara Falls, 57-63; res chemist, Wilmington, 63-64. *Mem:* Am Chem Soc. *Res:* Coordination chemistry; non-aqueous systems. *Mailing Add:* 12005 River Rd Grand Rapids MN 55744

HEINOLD, ROBERT H, CHEMICAL ENGINEERING. *Current Pos:* TECH DIR, A SCHULMAN, INC, AKRON, OH, 79- *Personal Data:* b East Orange, NJ, June 28, 31; m 56; c 3. *Educ:* Lafayette Col, Easton, Pa, ChE, 53. *Prof Exp:* Var, Hercules Inc, Wilmington, Del, 53-79. *Res:* Chemicals; aerospace; plastics; modification of polypropylene to broaden its structural and environmental capabilities. *Mailing Add:* 3824 Chickasaw Trail Uniontown OH 44685

HEINRICH, BERND, PHYSIOLOGY, ECOLOGY. *Current Pos:* PROF ZOOL, UNIV VT, BURLINGTON, 80- *Personal Data:* b Ger, Apr 19, 40; US citizen; m 68; c 2. *Educ:* Univ Maine, BA, 64, MS, 66; Univ Calif, Los Angeles, PhD(zool), 70. *Honors & Awards:* Von Humboldt Prize. *Prof Exp:* Fel zool, Univ Calif, Los Angeles, 70-71; from asst prof to prof entom, Univ Calif, Berkeley, 71-80. *Mem:* Fel AAAS; Am Soc Zool; Am Ornith Soc; Ecol Soc Am. *Res:* Physiology of temperature regulation in insects; ecology and energetics of foragers. *Mailing Add:* Dept Biol Univ Vt Burlington VT 05405

HEINRICH, GERHARD, ENDOCRINOLOGY. *Current Pos:* instr med, 80-, ASST PROF, SCH MED, HARVARD UNIV. *Personal Data:* b Lauban, Ger. *Educ:* Oberlin Col, Ohio, BA, 66; Case Western Res Univ, MD, 74. *Prof Exp:* Instr med, Univ Wis-Madison, 78-79. *Mem:* AAAS; Soc Neurosci. *Res:* Regulation of Nerve Growth Factor Gene Expression, and role of neurotrophic factors in neurodegenerative disease (Alzheimer's) and therapeutic applications. *Mailing Add:* Dept Med & Biochem Boston Univ Med Sch Evans 6 88 E Newton St Boston MA 02118. *Fax:* 617-638-6009

HEINRICH, JANET, NURSING RESEARCH. *Current Pos:* DIR, AM ACAD NURSING. *Prof Exp:* Dep dir & Dir Div Extramural Progs, Nat Ctr Nursing Res, NIH, 85. *Mailing Add:* Am Acad Nursing 600 Maryland Ave SW Suite 100 Washington DC 20024-2571

HEINRICH, KURT FRANCIS JOSEPH, ANALYTICAL CHEMISTRY. *Current Pos:* RETIRED. *Personal Data:* b Vienna, Austria, May 31, 21; US citizen; m 56; c 2. *Educ:* Univ Buenos Aires, Dr Chem, 48. *Prof Exp:* Chemist, Nat Lead Co, Arg, 41-42, A S W Borinski, 42-46 & E Teubal, 46-50; sect chief indust chem, E Lix Klett & Co, 50-56; chemist, E I du Pont de Nemours & Co, 56-64; chemist, Spectrochem Anal Sect, Nat Bur Standards, 64-71, sect chief, Microanal Sect, Anal Chem Div, 71-82, chief, Off Int Rels, 82-89; *Concurrent Pos:* From lab instr to chief lab instr, Univ Buenos Aires, 48-56; lectr, Univ Del, 63-64 & Phila Col Pharm, 64. *Mem:* Am Chem Soc; Am Soc Appl Spectros; Electron Probe Anal Soc Am (pres, 69). *Res:* Inorganic analytical chemistry; trace analysis; x-ray spectrometry as an analytical tool; electron probe microanalysis. *Mailing Add:* 804 Blossom Dr Rockville MD 20850

HEINRICH, MAX ALFRED, JR, PHARMACOLOGY. *Current Pos:* exec secy career develop rev br, NIH, 63-65, head res career sect, Nat Inst Gen Med Sci, 65-74, SCIENTIST ADMINR, MANPOWER BR, DIV HEART & VASCULAR DIS, NAT HEART, LUNG & BLOOD INST, 74- *Personal Data:* b Elmira, NY, May 22, 24; m 49; c 4. *Educ:* Philadelphia Col Pharm, BS, 47, MS, 48; Jefferson Med Col, PhD(pharmacol), 53. *Prof Exp:* Instr physiol & pharmacol, Philadelphia Col Pharm, 48-50; instr pharmacol, Jefferson Med Col, 50-52; asst prof, Med Sch, Univ SDak, 52-59; from assoc prof to prof & head dept, NDak State Univ, 60-63. *Mem:* AAAS; Am Soc Pharmacol & Exp Therapeut; NY Acad Sci. *Res:* Central nervous system; toxicology; pulmonary pharmacology. *Mailing Add:* 5755 Box Elder Ct Frederick MD 21701-7139

HEINRICH, R(AYMOND) L(AWRENCE), CHEMICAL ENGINEERING. *Current Pos:* CONSULT, 77- *Personal Data:* b Galveston, Tex, Nov 1, 11; m 44; c 5. *Educ:* Rice Univ, BS, 35. *Prof Exp:* Chemist, Humble Oil & Refining Co, 42-43, res chemist, 43-54, res chem engr, 54-57, sr res chem engr, 57-65; sr res chem engr, Esso Res & Eng Co, 65-71; pres, Eng Res Assoc, 71-77. *Mem:* Am Chem Soc. *Res:* Separation processes; polymerization; hydrogenation; oxidation; petrochemicals production, applications and economics; organic acids, alcohols and polyols; aromatic condensation products; coal conversion to fuels and chemicals; plant start up and operation; design and implementation of research programs; air and water pollution control. *Mailing Add:* 112 Lakewood Baytown TX 77520-1510

HEINRICHS, DONALD FREDERICK, GEOPHYSICS, OCEANOGRAPHY. *Current Pos:* prog mgr submarine geol & geophysics, 75-85, HEAD, OCEANOG CTR & FAC SECT, NSF, 85- *Personal Data:* b Shafter, Calif, Nov 8, 38; m 62, Jean Smutny; c Thomas & Steven. *Educ:* Stanford Univ, BS, 60, PhD(geophys), 66. *Prof Exp:* Res asst geophys, Stanford Univ, 61-66; instr physics, Menlo Col, 64-66; asst prof geophys oceanog, Ore State Univ, 66-75. *Concurrent Pos:* Mem staff, Off Naval Res, Arlington, Va, 74-75. *Mem:* Am Geophys Union; Soc Explor Geophys; Geol Soc Am; Marine Technol Soc. *Res:* Paleomagnetics; marine magnetics; marine and land gravity. *Mailing Add:* 8321 Riverside Rd Alexandria VA 22308. *Fax:* 703-306-0390; *E-Mail:* dheinric@nsf.gov

HEINRICHS, W LEROY, biochemistry, obstetrics & gynecology, for more information see previous edition

HEINRIKSON, ROBERT L, PROTEIN CHEMISTRY. *Current Pos:* DISTINGUISHED SR SCIENTIST, PHARMACEUT UPJOHN CO, 85- *Personal Data:* b Sioux City, Iowa, Dec 31, 35; m 63; c 2. *Educ:* Augustana Col, Rock Island, Ill, BA, 58; Univ Chicago, PhD(biochem), 63. *Prof Exp:* Res assoc protein chem, Rockefeller Univ, New York, 63-65; NATO postdoctoral, Lab Molecular Biol, Med Res Coun, Cambridge, Eng, 65-66; from asst prof to prof biochem, Univ Chicago, 66-85. *Concurrent Pos:* Ed, J Protein Chem, 75- & J Biol Chem, 88-93 & 95-; *Mem:* Sigma Xi; Protein Soc. *Res:* Relationship between protein structure and function; protein chemistry and enzymology. *Mailing Add:* Biochem Pharmaceut Upjohn Co Kalamazoo MI 49001. *Fax:* 616-833-1488

HEINS, ALBERT EDWARD, mathematics; deceased, see previous edition for last biography

HEINS, CONRAD F, ORGANIC POLYMER CHEMISTRY, RENEWABLE ENERGY TECHNOLOGY. *Current Pos:* DIV HEAD SCI & TECHNOL, JORDAN COL, CEDAR SPRINGS, MICH, 80-, PROF, 87- *Personal Data:* b Kolar, India, Apr 25, 39; US citizen; m 65, Alison; c Sylvia & Katherine. *Educ:* Drew Univ, AB, 59; Univ Ill, MS, 61, PhD(org chem), 62. *Prof Exp:* NSF fel, Cornell Univ, 62-64; org chemist, E I du Pont de Nemours & Co, Inc, 64-68; res scientist & adj prof, Denver Res Inst, Univ Denver, 68-75; head, Sci Dept, Scattergood Sch, West Branch, Iowa, 75-80. *Mem:* Am Solar Energy Soc; Int Solar Energy Soc. *Res:* Thermoplastic polymer composites; polymer concretes; technology transfer and solar technology; applied research in the alternative energy field with a focus on photovoltaics. *Mailing Add:* 3000 E Cedar Valley Rd Traverse City MI 49684. *Fax:* 616-784-0998

HEINS, DAVID CARL, ICHTHYOLOGY, AQUATIC BIOLOGY. *Current Pos:* from asst prof to assoc prof biol, 82-93, from asst dean to assoc dean, 82-97, PROF BIOL, TULANE UNIV, 93- *Personal Data:* b Orlando, Fla, Jan 17, 48; m 83, Elizabeth Day. *Educ:* Univ Cent Fla, BA, 70; Miss State Univ, MS, 72; Tulane Univ, PhD(biol), 79. *Honors & Awards:* George Henry Penn Mem Award. *Prof Exp:* Asst prof biol, Millsaps Col, 78-82. *Mem:* Am Soc Ichthyologists & Herpetologists; Sigma Xi; Soc Study Evolution. *Res:* Investigation of life-history patterns of fresh-water fishes inhabiting streams of the northern Gulf coastal plain and of threespine stickleback in Alaska. *Mailing Add:* Dept Ecol Evolution & Org Biol Tulane Univ New Orleans LA 70118

HEINS, MAURICE HASKELL, MATHEMATICAL ANALYSIS. *Current Pos:* distinguished prof complex anal, 74-86, EMER PROF MATH, UNIV MD, COL PARK, 87- *Personal Data:* b Boston, Mass, Nov 19, 15; m 40, Hadassah Wagman; c Samuel D & Sulamith H. *Educ:* Harvard Univ, AB, 37, AM, 39, PhD(math), 40. *Hon Degrees:* AM, Brown Univ, 47. *Prof Exp:* Instr & tutor math, Harvard Univ, 39-40; asst, Inst Advan Study, 40-42; asst prof math, Ill Inst Technol, 42-44; mathematician, Off Chief Ord, US Army, 44-45; from actg asst prof to prof math, Brown Univ, 45-58; prof math, Univ Ill, Urbana, 58-74. *Concurrent Pos:* Pres fel, Brown & Fulbright res fel, Univ Paris, 52-53; vis prof, Univ Calif, Berkeley, 63-64; exchange prof, Univ Paris VI, 79; emer prof math, Univ Ill, Urbana, 74- *Mem:* Am Math Soc; fel Am Acad Arts & Sci; London Math Soc; Sigma Xi. *Res:* Functions of a complex variable; conformal mapping; Riemann surfaces. *Mailing Add:* 3304 Winnett Rd Chevy Chase MD 20815-3202

HEINSELMAN, MIRON L, FOREST ECOLOGY. *Current Pos:* CONSULT, 74- *Personal Data:* b Duluth, Minn, Feb 7, 20; m 42; c 2. *Educ:* Univ Minn, BA, 42, BS, 48, MF, 51, PhD(forest ecol), 61. *Prof Exp:* Res forester silvicult, Lake States Forest Exp Sta, US Forest Serv, 48-61, forest ecologist, 61-69, forest ecologist, NCent Forest Exp Sta, 69-74. *Concurrent Pos:* Adj prof ecol & behav biol, Dept Ecol & Behav Biol, Univ Minn, St Paul, 74- *Mem:* AAAS; Soc Am Foresters; Ecol Soc Am; Am Inst Biol Sci. *Res:* Peatlands ecology, including factors affecting growth of trees on peatlands; peatland genesis and development; factors controlling floristics and vegetation development; patterned organic terrain; silviculture of Picea mariana on peatlands; natural role of fire in northern conifer forest ecosystems. *Mailing Add:* 1783 Lindig St St Paul MN 55113

HEINSOHN, ROBERT J(ENNINGS), MECHANICAL ENGINEERING. *Current Pos:* from asst prof to assoc prof, 63-70, PROF MECH ENG, PA STATE UNIV, 70- *Personal Data:* b Brooklyn, NY, Aug 28, 32; m 55; c 2. *Educ:* Rensselaer Polytech Inst, BSME, 54; Mass Inst Technol, SMME, 55; Mich State Univ, PhD(eng), 63. *Honors & Awards:* Ralph A Teetor Award, Soc Automotive Engrs, 67. *Prof Exp:* Analytical engr, Pratt & Whitney Aircraft, 54-59; instr eng, eve div, Johns Hopkins Univ, 56-58; instr mech eng, Mich State Univ, 58-63. *Concurrent Pos:* NSF fac fel, 62-63, res grants, 64-72; Environ Protection Agency Serv res grant, 67-77; Pub Health Serv grants, 78-84. *Mem:* Am Soc Mech Engrs; Air Pollution Control Asn; Am Soc Heating, Refrig & Air-Conditioning Engrs. *Res:* Control contaminants in workplace and out of doors; combustion; author of one book. *Mailing Add:* Dept Mech Eng Pa State Univ 140B Reber Bldg University Park PA 16802

HEINSTEIN, PETER, BIOCHEMISTRY. *Current Pos:* asst prof, 69-74, assoc prof biochem & chem, 74-83, PROF MED CHEM & BIOCHEM PROG, SCH PHARMACOL, PURDUE UNIV, WEST LAFAYETTE, 83- *Personal Data:* b Heidelberg, Ger, Apr 14, 35; US citizen; m 57; c 6. *Educ:* Strickhof Col, Switz, dipl agr, 54; NC State Univ, MS, 63, PhD(biochem), 67. *Prof Exp:* Res technician, dept animal nutrit, NC State Univ, 59-63; NIH fel, Univ Calif, Davis, 67-69. *Concurrent Pos:* Lederle fac res award, 71; sr Fulbright res fel 78-79. *Mem:* AAAS; Am Chem Soc; Am Soc Biol Chemists; Sigma Xi. *Res:* Biosynthesis of natural products; enzyme function and properties; signal transduction across plant cell membranes; mechanism of plant cell pathogen interaction. *Mailing Add:* Dept Med Chem Purdue Univ Sch Pharm West Lafayette IN 47907-1333. *Fax:* 765-494-6790

HEINTZ, EDWARD ALLEIN, ANALYTICAL CHEMISTRY, GRAPHITE TECHNOLOGY. *Current Pos:* INDEPENDENT CONSULT, CARBON & GRAPHITE TECH, 88-; RES PROF, STATE UNIV NY, BUFFALO, NY, 88- *Personal Data:* b Buffalo, NY, Apr 8, 31; m 56, Ruth Schulz; c Debra & Rebecca. *Educ:* Univ Buffalo, BA, 53; Mass Inst Technol, PhD(anal chem), 57. *Honors & Awards:* J F Schoellkopf Medal, Am Chem Soc, 80; George D Graffin Lectureship, Am Carbon Soc, 94. *Prof Exp:* Asst, Mass Inst Technol, 55-57; asst, Union Carbide Metals Co, 57-61; instr, Millard Fillmore Col, State Univ NY, Buffalo, 59-61; res chemist, Cornell Aeronaut Lab, 61-63, res supvr, 63-64; mgr carbon & graphite res, Res Lab, Airco Carbon, 64-70, mgr chem & phys measurement res, 70-71, mgr res, Carbon-Graphite Tech Dept, 71-88. *Concurrent Pos:* Guest mem, Northern Carbon Res Labs, Univ Newcastle-on-Tyne, Eng, 82 & 90; adj prof chem, Erie Community Col, Buffalo, NY, 92- *Mem:* Am Chem Soc; Am Carbon Soc; Combustion Inst; Am Sec Testing & Mat. *Res:* Reactions in non-aqueous solvents; electrodeposition of radioactive tracers; analytical chemistry of the less familiar transition elements; corrosion of graphite in aqueous solutions; gas phase reactions of graphite; carbon and graphite technology; microscopy of carbon and graphite. *Mailing Add:* Carbon & Graphite Technol 67 Red Oak Dr Buffalo NY 14221-2303. *Fax:* 716-835-4872

HEINTZ, ROGER LEWIS, BIOCHEMISTRY. *Current Pos:* assoc prof, 75-80, PROF CHEM, STATE UNIV NY, PLATTSBURGH, 80- *Personal Data:* b Jackson Center, Ohio, Mar 15, 37; m 62, Judith Fisher; c Claude R, Robert A, James S & Steven G. *Educ:* Ohio Northern Univ, BS, 59; Ohio State Univ, MS, 61; Univ Wis-Madison, PhD(biochem), 64. *Prof Exp:* NIH fel biochem, Univ Ky, 64-66, Am Heart Asn adv res fel, 66-68; assoc prof biochem, Iowa State Univ, 68-75. *Concurrent Pos:* NIH res grants, 67-68 & 68-75, 75-76 & 78-82; State Univ NY Res Found grant, 76 & 77, grant, 82. *Mem:* AAAS; Am Chem Soc; Am Soc Biol Chem; Sigma Xi. *Res:* Mechanism of action of thyroid hormone receptor; fluorescence/HPLC assays for neurotransmitters. *Mailing Add:* Dept Chem State Univ NY Plattsburgh NY 12901. *E-Mail:* heintzrl@splava.cc.plattsburgh.edu

HEINTZ, WULFF DIETER, ASTRONOMY. *Current Pos:* assoc prof, 69-73, chmn dept, 72-82, PROF ASTRON, SWARTHMORE COL, 73- *Personal Data:* b Wurzburg, Ger, June 3, 30; m 57; c 2. *Educ:* Univ Munich, Dr rer nat(astron), 53; Munich Tech Univ, Priv Doz, 67. *Prof Exp:* Res asst, Univ Munich Observ, 54-66, observator, 66-69. *Mem:* Int Astron Union; Royal Astron Soc; Am Astron Soc. *Res:* Double and multiple stars; positional astronomy. *Mailing Add:* Dept Physics & Astron Swarthnore Col 500 College Ave Swarthmore PA 19081

HEINTZELMAN, RICHARD WAYNE, ENVIRONMENTAL CHEMISTRY, METABOLISM. *Current Pos:* GROUP LEADER, METAB & ENVIRON FATE, RHONE-POULERC AGR CO, 87- *Personal Data:* b Danville, Pa, Feb 3, 47; m 67; c 2. *Educ:* Lycoming Col, BA, 70; Univ Va, PhD(org chem), 74. *Prof Exp:* Res assoc sulfur-nitrogen compounds, Fels Res Inst & Dept Chem, Temple Univ, 74-75; res chemist, Amchem Prod Inc, Subsid Union Carbide Corp, 75-77, group leader, synthesis group, 77-79; group leader, Synthesis Group, Union Carbide Agr Prod Co, Inc, 79-80, group leader metab & environ chem, 80-86. *Concurrent Pos:* NSF res fel, Univ Va, 72-74. *Mem:* Am Chem Soc; Asn Off Analytical Chemists. *Res:* Organic synthesis; heterocylces; sulfur-nitrogen compounds; herbicides; plant growth regulators; insecticides; environmental fate; metabolism; radiochemistry. *Mailing Add:* 104 Crimmons Circle Cary NC 27511

HEINY, ROBERT LOWELL, MATHEMATICAL STATISTICS. *Current Pos:* assoc prof, 68-77, PROF STATIST, UNIV NORTHERN COLO, 77- *Personal Data:* b Washington, DC, June 10, 42; m 64; c 3. *Educ:* Colo Col, BS, 64; Colo State Univ, MS, 66, PhD(statist), 68. *Mem:* Am Statist Asn. *Res:* Educational research; estimation; statistics education; stochastic processes. *Mailing Add:* 1617 27th Ave Ct Greeley CO 80631

HEINZ, DON J, PLANT BREEDING, CYTOGENETICS. *Current Pos:* assoc geneticist, 61-66, head dept genetics & path, 66-78, asst dir, 77-78, vpres & dir, 79-85, PRES & DIR, EXP STA, HAWAIIAN SUGAR PLANTERS ASN, 86- *Personal Data:* b Rexburg, Idaho, Oct 29, 31; m 56; c 6. *Educ:* Utah State Univ, BS, 58, MS, 59; Mich State Univ, PhD(farm crops), 61. *Concurrent Pos:* Affil mem, Grad Fac, Univ Hawaii, 63-; chmn germplasm comn, Int Soc Sugar Cane Technologists, 75-87; Pres Reagan's Coun Agr. *Mem:* Int Soc Sugar Cane Technologists; AAAS; Sigma Xi. *Res:* Sugarcane improvement; genetics; cytogenetics and disease control; agronomy; development of cell and tissue culture procedures in crop improvement. *Mailing Add:* 1647 W 1000 S Rexburg ID 83440

HEINZ, ERICH, PHYSIOLOGY, BIOPHYSICS. *Current Pos:* PROF DEPT PHYSIOL, MAX-PLANCK INST, FED REPUB GER. *Personal Data:* b Essex, Ger; US citizen. *Educ:* Univ Kiel, Ger, MD, 41, DrHabil, 49. *Prof Exp:* Assoc prof biochem, Med Sch, Tufts Univ, 55-58; res prof physiol, George Washington Univ, 58-59; prof biochem, T W Goethe Univ, Ger, 59-78; prof physiol & biophys, Med Sch, Cornell Univ, 78- *Concurrent Pos:* Res assoc biophys, Med Sch, Harvard Univ, 56-58; consult, Harvard Biophys Lab, 56-58; vis prof, Nat Heart Inst, NIH, 62 & Hunter Col, City Univ New York, 68; prin investr, NIH, 78-; sponsor comt, Int Conf Biol Membranes, 70- *Mem:* Am Soc Biol Chemists; Biophys Soc. *Res:* Biological membrane transport; electrolyte metabolism; amino acid transport; ion pumps. *Mailing Add:* Dept Physiol Max-Planck Inst Molecular Physiol Rheinlanddamm 201 44139 Dortmund Germany

HEINZ, OTTO, PHYSICS. *Current Pos:* assoc prof, 62-67, chmn dept, 67-73, PROF PHYSICS, NAVAL POSTGRAD SCH, 67- *Personal Data:* b Vienna, Austria, Sept 18, 24; nat US; m 48; c 3. *Educ:* Univ Calif, BA, 48, PhD(physics), 54. *Prof Exp:* Mem tech staff, Bell Tel Labs, 54-55; physicist, Stanford Res Inst, 55-70. *Mem:* Am Phys Soc; Am Geophys Union. *Res:* Geomagnetic fields in the sea and on the ocean floor. *Mailing Add:* Dept Physics Naval Postgrad Sch Code 0223 Monterey CA 93943

HEINZ, RICHARD MEADE, HIGH ENERGY PHYSICS, HIGH ENERGY ASTROPHYSICS. *Current Pos:* from asst prof to assoc prof, 66-72, PROF PHYSICS, IND UNIV, BLOOMINGTON, 72- *Personal Data:* b Toledo, Ohio, June 16, 39; div; c 2. *Educ:* Univ Toledo, BS, 61; Univ Mich, MS, 62, PhD(physics), 64. *Prof Exp:* Instr physics & res assoc, Univ Mich, 65; NSF fel, Europ Orgn Nuclear Res, Univ Geneva, 65-66. *Concurrent Pos:* Prog Off Elem Particle Physics, NSF, 80-82. *Mem:* Am Phys Soc. *Res:* Collaborator in MACRO (Monopole, Astrophysics, and Cosmic Ray Observatory) and MINDS (Main Injector Neutrino Oscillation Experiment). *Mailing Add:* Dept Physics Ind Univ Bloomington IN 47405. *Fax:* 812-855-5533; *E-Mail:* heinz@indiana.edu

HEINZ, TONY F, LASER SPECTROSCOPY, SURFACE SCIENCE. *Current Pos:* PROF PHYSICS & ELEC ENG, COLUMBIA UNIV, 95- *Personal Data:* b Palo Alto, Calif, Apr 30, 56. *Educ:* Stanford Univ, BS, 78; Univ Calif, Berkeley, PhD(physics), 82. *Honors & Awards:* Int Com Optics Prize, 95; A von Humboldt Res Award, 96. *Prof Exp:* NSF grad fel, 78-81; IBM fel, 82; res staff mem, IBM Thomas J Watson Res Ctr, 83-95. *Concurrent Pos:* Prog comt, CLEO, 86, IQEC, 87-88, 90 & QELS, 89, 91, 92, OSA ann meeting, 92, 94; prog chair, QELS, 93, gen chair, 95; ed, J Optical Soc Am B, 94-; chair, Optical Sci Div, Optical Soc Am, 96- *Mem:* Fel Am Phys Soc; Mats Res Soc; Optical Soc Am; Am Vacuum Soc. *Res:* Ultrafast spectroscopy; studies of surface dynamics using laser spectroscopic approaches. *Mailing Add:* Dept Physics Columbia Univ 538 W 120th St New York NY 10027. *Fax:* 212-854-1901

HEINZ, ULRICH WALTER, HEAVY-ION COLLISIONS. *Current Pos:* PROF PHYSICS, UNIV REGENSBURG, 87- *Personal Data:* b Ludwighafen, WGer, Apr 25, 55; m 80; c 3. *Educ:* J W Goethe Univ, Frankfurt, WGer, Dipl, 78, DPhil, 80, DHabil(physics), 84. *Honors & Awards:* Hess Prize, 88. *Prof Exp:* Res & teaching asst theoret physics, Inst Theoret Physics, J W Goethe Univ, Frankfurt, WGer, 78-80; teaching fel, Yale Univ, 80-82; res assoc, Inst Theoret Physics, JW Goethe Univ, 82-84; assoc physicist nuclear theory, Brookhaven Nat Lab, 84-87. *Concurrent Pos:* Vis asst prof, Vanderbilt Univ, Nashville, Tenn, 83-84; consult, Oak Ridge Nat Lab, 83-84; guest assoc physicist, Brookhaven Nat Lab, 87- *Mem:* Am Phys Soc; Deutsche Physikalische Ges. *Res:* Theory of heavy-ion collisions at low and high energy; positron creation in collisions between very heavy ions; quark-gluon plasma formation in relativistic nuclear collisions. *Mailing Add:* Inst Theoretishe Physik Univ Regensburg Postfach 101042 93040 Regensburg Germany

HEINZE, JOHN EDWARD, ENVIRONMENTAL FATE & EFFECTS, GENETIC TOXICOLOGY. *Current Pos:* RES MGR ENVIRON SAFETY, VISTA CHEM CO, 89- *Personal Data:* b Nov 3, 47; m 71, Rebecca J Williams; c Steven E. *Educ:* Okla Baptist Univ, BS, 70; Univ Ill, Urbana, PhD(microbiol), 75. *Prof Exp:* Res biologist, NIH, 75-77; sr microbiologist, Armour-Dial, Inc, 77-80; group leader, 80-83, res mgr, 83-89. *Concurrent Pos:* Chmn, Non-Animal Testing Subcomt, Soap & Detergent Asn, 90-92, Environ Fate & Effects Subcomt, 92. *Mem:* Soap & Detergent Asn. *Res:* Environmental fate and effect of commercial laundry detergents and ingredients, especially surfactants; biodegradation and aquatic toxicity. *Mailing Add:* Nat Press Bldg Washington DC 26045. *Fax:* 512-331-2387

HEINZE, WILLIAM DANIEL, SEISMIC MODELLING, INVERSE. *Current Pos:* OWNER, APPL GEOPHYS SOFTWARE, INC, 78- *Personal Data:* b St Louis, Mo, Apr 26, 48; m 77; c 3. *Educ:* Tex A&M Univ, BS, 70, MS, 72, PhD(geophysics), 77; Mass Inst Technol, MS, 73. *Prof Exp:* Instr geophysics, Tex A&M Univ, 75-77, res fel, 77-78; res fel geophysics, Dept Terrestrial Magnetism, Carnegie Inst, Washington, DC, 78-79. *Concurrent Pos:* Co-investr, Dept Geophys, Tex A&M Univ, 76-77, prin investr, 77-78. *Mem:* Am Geophys Union; Sigma Xi, Soc Explor Geophysicists. *Res:* Seismic modelling; image processing; rock deformation. *Mailing Add:* PO Box 218470 Houston TX 77218

HEIPLE, CLINTON R, PHYSICAL METALLURGY. *Current Pos:* METALL CONSULT, 92- *Personal Data:* b Tacoma, Wash, Nov 12, 39; div; c Robin & Penny. *Educ:* Stanford Univ, BS, 61; Univ Sheffield, MMet, 62; Univ Ill, Urbana, PhD(metall), 67. *Honors & Awards:* William Spraragen Award, Am Welding Soc, 83 & McKay-Helm Award, 87. *Prof Exp:* Fel, Sci Ctr, NAm Rockwell Corp, 67-68; res metallurgist, Rocky Flats Div, Dow Chem USA, 68-76; sr res specialist, Rocky Flats Plant, Rockwell Int, 76-79, assoc scientist, 79-89; assoc scientist, EG&G Rocky Flats, Rockwell Int, 90-92. *Concurrent Pos:* Fel, Acoust Emission Working Group, 90. *Mem:* Am Soc Metals; Am Welding Soc; Int Inst Welding. *Res:* Effect of impurities on shape of gas tungsten arc welds; dislocation sources of acoustic emission; beryllium; stainless steel; liquid metal embrittlement; mechanical testing. *Mailing Add:* 1785 Deer Valley Rd Boulder CO 80303

HEIPLE, LOREN RAY, SANITARY ENGINEERING. *Current Pos:* CONSULT, 84- *Personal Data:* b Oakwood, Ill, Apr 19, 18; m 44; c 2. *Educ:* Iowa State Univ, BS, 39, CE, 50; Harvard Univ, MS, 40; Stanford Univ, PhD, 67. *Prof Exp:* Serv & develop engr, Infilco, Inc, Ill, 40-41; jr sanit engr, Iowa Ord Plant, 41; instr, Iowa State Univ, 41-42, asst prof civil eng, 46-48; city engr, Boone, Iowa, 48-49; consult engr, Pub Admin Serv, Ill, 49-50 & Little Rock Wastewater Utility, 84-85; head civil eng, Univ Ark, Fayetteville, 50-71, dean, Col Eng, 71-79, prof civil eng, 79-84. *Concurrent Pos:* Consult, New Wonder World Encycl. *Mem:* Am Soc Civil Engrs; Am Soc Eng Educ; Nat Soc Prof Engrs; Water Pollution Control Fedn. *Res:* Sewage treatment processes; stream pollution and recovery; conservation of water resources, both surface and underground supplies. *Mailing Add:* 1492 Century Dr Fayetteville AR 72703

HEIRMAN, DONALD N, ELECTROMAGNETIC COMPATIBILITY, MEASUREMENT TECHNIQUES & STANDARDS. *Current Pos:* Mem tech staff, AT&T Bell Labs, 63-83, Am Bell, 83-84, supvr info systs, AT&T, 84-88, supvr, 88-91, mgr, 91-96, MGR, LUCENT TECHNOLOGIES, 96- *Personal Data:* b Mishawaka, Ind, Aug 16, 40; m 63, Lois M Smith. *Educ:* Purdue Univ, BSEE, 62, MSEE, 63. *Honors & Awards:* Lawrence G Cumming Award, Electromagnetic Compatibility Soc, Inst Elec & Electronics Engrs, 84 & Centennial Medal & Charles Proteus Steinmetz Award, 84. *Concurrent Pos:* Past pres, vpres, current mem bd dirs & dir tech servs, Electromagnetic Compatibility Soc, Inst Elec & Electronics Engrs, 74-; lectr, Ctr Prof Advan, East Brunswick, NJ, 77-, course dir, 87-; mem & chmn, Comt C63, subcomt 1, 3, 5, 6, 8, Am Nat Stand Inst, 81-; tech expert, US Deleg to Int Electrotechnical Comn, Int Spec Comt on Radio Interference, 85-; mem exec comt, US Nat Comt, Int Electrotechnical Comn, 95- *Mem:* Inst Elec & Electronics Engrs; Am Nat Stand Inst; Nat Asn Radio & Telecom Engrs; Electronics Industs Asn. *Res:* Accurate electromagnetic emission and immunity measurements; methods of measurement standards; test facility construction, calibration and improvements. *Mailing Add:* 143 Jumping Brook Rd Lincroft NJ 07738-1442. *Fax:* 732-530-5695; *E-Mail:* d.heirman@worldnet.att.net

HEIRTZLER, JAMES RANSOM, EARTH SCIENCES. *Current Pos:* geophysicist & head, Geol & Geomagnetism Br, 86-91, STAFF SCIENTIST GEOPHYS, NASA/GODDARD SPACE FLIGHT CTR, 91- *Personal Data:* b Baton Rouge, La, Sept 16, 25; m 91, K Nazarova. *Educ:* La State Univ, BS, 47, MS, 48; NY Univ, PhD(physics), 53. *Honors & Awards:* Microfossil named in honor, Pithonella heirtzleri, 72; Antartica feature named in honor, Heirtzler Ice Piedmont, 85; Otto Schmidt Medal, Inst Phys Earth, Moscow, 94. *Prof Exp:* Res assoc physics, La State Univ, 47-48; asst, NY Univ, 48-50, asst & instr, 50-53; asst prof, Am Univ, Beirut, 53-56; sr physicist, Gen Dynamics Corp, 56-60; res scientist, Lamont-Doherty Earth Observ, Columbia Univ, 60-64, sr res scientist, 64-67, dir, Hudson Lab, 67-69; chmn dept, Woods Hole Oceanog Inst, 69-76, sr scientist geol & geophys, 69-86. *Concurrent Pos:* Mem, JOIDES Planning Comt, 69-79, chmn, 78-79; US chief scientist, Proj Famous, 71-75; reporter, US Geodynamics Comt, 71-83; mem, US & NAm Magnetic Anomaly Map Comt, 75-83; dir sci res & sr adv to pres, Joint Oceanog Inst Inc, 79-80; pres-elect & pres, Am Geophys Union Sect on Geomagnetism & Paleomagnetism, 80-84; ed, J Reviews Geophys, 84-88; bd gov, Am Inst Physics, 90-93; spec hon session, Am Geophys Union, 95. *Mem:* Fel AAAS; fel Geol Soc Am; fel Am Geophys Union; Am Phys Soc; Int Asn Geomag & Aeronomy; Sigma Xi. *Res:* Geophysics; author of more than 140 publications. *Mailing Add:* NASA Goddard Space Flight Ctr Code 920 Greenbelt MD 20771. *Fax:* 301-286-1757; *E-Mail:* jamesh@ltpmail.gsfc.masa.gov

HEISE, EUGENE ROYCE, HISTOCOMPATIBILITY, IMMUNOGENETICS. *Current Pos:* asst prof, 69-74, ASSOC PROF MICROBIOL & IMMUNOL, BOWMAN GRAY SCH MED, WAKE FOREST UNIV, 74- *Personal Data:* b Hamlin, Kans, July 11, 32; m 62, Clara Muehlbaecher. *Educ:* Wittenberg Univ, BS, 56; Univ Iowa, MS, 60; Bowman Gray Sch Med, PhD(microbiol), 66. *Prof Exp:* Sr fel microbiol, Sch Med, Univ Wash, 66-69. *Concurrent Pos:* Chmn, Am Bd Histocompatibility & Immunogenetics, 84-90. *Mem:* Am Asn Immunologists; Am Soc Histocompatibility & Immunogenetics. *Res:* Immunogenetics; transplantation immunology; autoimmunity. *Mailing Add:* Dept Microbiol & Immunol Wake Forest Univ Bowman Gray Sch Med Med Park Blvd Winston-Salem NC 27157

HEISE, JOHN J, BIOLOGY, CHEMISTRY. *Current Pos:* ASSOC PROF BIOL, GA INST TECHNOL, 66- *Personal Data:* b Paoli, Ind, Feb 6, 31. *Educ:* Earlham Col, AB, 53; Washington Univ, PhD(bot), 62. *Prof Exp:* Phys sci aide, Radioisotope Unit, Vet Admin Hosp, Indianapolis, Ind, 53-54; asst bot, Washington Univ, 55-60; res assoc biol sci, Fla State Univ, 60-62; fel, C F Kettering Res Lab, 62-63; molecular pathologist, Abbott Labs, 63-65. *Mem:* AAAS; Am Chem Soc; Am Inst Biol Sci; Am Soc Photobiol; Sigma Xi. *Res:* Molecular and sub-molecular aspects of photosynthesis; enzyme processes and metabolism by the study of free radicals and transition elements; trace elements in the environment. *Mailing Add:* Sch Biol Ga Inst Technol Atlanta GA 30332-0001

HEISER, ARNOLD M, ASTRONOMY. *Current Pos:* ASSOC PROF PHYSICS & ASTRON, VANDERBILT UNIV, 65- *Personal Data:* b New York, NY, Feb 9, 33; m 64, Vivian Jacobs; c Naomi Alizabeth & David Alan. *Educ:* Ind Univ, AB, 54, AM, 57; Univ Chicago, PhD(astrophys), 61. *Honors & Awards:* H Shapley Vis Lectr. *Prof Exp:* Asst prof, A J Dyer Observ, 61-65, actg dir, 71-72, dir, 72-86. *Mem:* Am Astron Soc; Int Astron Union; Astronom Soc Pac; Sigma Xi. *Res:* Stellar photometry; galactic structure; variable stars. *Mailing Add:* A J Dyer Observ 1000 Oman Dr Brentwood TN 37027-4143

HEISER, CHARLES BIXLER, JR, BOTANY. *Current Pos:* from asst prof to prof, Ind Univ, Bloomington, 47-79, dir herbarium, 47-92, distinguished prof, 79-86, EMER DISTINGUISHED PROF BOT, IND UNIV, BLOOMINGTON, 86- *Personal Data:* b Cynthiana, Ind, Oct 5, 20; m 44, Dorothy Gaebler; c Lynn, Cynthia & Charles III. *Educ:* Wash Univ, AB, 43, MA, 44; Univ Calif, PhD(bot), 47. *Honors & Awards:* Gleason Award, NY Bot Garden, 69; Merit Award, Bot Soc Am, 72; Distinguished Econ Botanist, Soc Econ Bot, 84; Pustovoit Award, Int Sunflower Asn, 85; Asa Gray Award, Am Soc Plant Taxonomists, 88. *Prof Exp:* Instr bot, Wash Univ 44-45; botanist, Herbarium, Univ Calif, 45-46, assoc bot, Exp Sta, 46-47. *Concurrent Pos:* Guggenheim fel, 53; NSF sr fel, 62; vis prof, Univ Tex, 78. *Mem:* Nat Acad Sci; Bot Soc Am (pres, 80); Am Soc Plant Taxonomists (pres, 67); Soc Study Evolution (pres, 75); Soc Econ Bot (pres, 78). *Res:* Systematics; evolution; ethnobotany; cytogenetics; author of 5 books. *Mailing Add:* Dept Biol Ind Univ Bloomington IN 47405. *Fax:* 812-855-6705

HEISERMAN, GARY, EXPERIMENTAL BIOLOGY. *Prof Exp:* Postdoctoral fel cancer res, Cold Spring Harbor Lab, 90-91. *Mailing Add:* 269 Toho Trail PO Box 23547 Flagstaff AZ 86001

HEISEY, LOWELL VERNON, ORGANIC CHEMISTRY, SYNTHETIC ORGANIC & NATURAL PRODUCTS CHEMISTRY. *Current Pos:* RETIRED. *Personal Data:* b Ping Ting Chow, China, Oct 1, 19; m 45, Hazel Shavely; c Galen, Maylee (Samuels), Loren & Curtis. *Educ:* Manchester Col, AB, 41; Purdue Univ, MS, 44, PhD(org chem), 47. *Prof Exp:* Asst chem, Purdue Univ, 42-43; from asst prof to assoc prof, McPherson Col, 47-50; from assoc prof to prof chem, Bridgewater Col, 50-85; Fulbright lectr chem, Cuttington Univ Col, Liberia, 86-87. *Mem:* Am Chem Soc. *Res:* Organic synthesis; heterocyclic compounds; plant hormones; collecting native tropical herbal drugs. *Mailing Add:* 22 College Woods Dr Bridgewater VA 22812-9503

HEISEY, ROD MARTIN, ALLELOCHEMICAL INTERACTIONS OF PLANTS WITH OTHER PLANTS & MICROORGANISMS, INSECTS & BIOGEOCHEMICAL CYCLING OF PLANT NUTRIENTS. *Current Pos:* assoc prof, 90-97, PROF BIOL, PA STATE UNIV, 97- *Personal Data:* b

Lancaster, Pa, Feb 18, 50; m 86, Teresa Kish. *Educ:* Millersville State Col, BA, 72; Univ Conn, MS, 76; Univ Calif, Davis, MS, 79, PhD(ecol), 82. *Prof Exp:* Postdoctoral res assoc, Mich State Univ, 82-86; asst prof biol, Fordham Univ, 86-90. *Res:* Allelochemical interactions of plants with other plants in use of natural products as herbicides, insecticides and fungicides; biogeochemical cycling of nutrient elements, heavy metals and environmental pollutants. *Mailing Add:* 200 University Dr Schuylkill Haven PA 17972. *Fax:* 717-385-6232; *E-Mail:* rmhll@email.psu.edu

HEISEY, S(AMUEL) RICHARD, MEDICAL PHYSIOLOGY. *Current Pos:* assoc prof, 67-71, PROF PHYSIOL, MICH STATE UNIV, 71- *Personal Data:* b Elizabethtown, Pa, Oct 16, 28; m 58, Ann Leftridge; c David & Janet. *Educ:* Elizabethtown Col, BS, 51; Johns Hopkins Univ, ScD, 59. *Prof Exp:* Pharmacologist, Med Res Lab, Army Chem Ctr, Md, 53-56; res fel physiol, Harvard Med Sch, 59-60, from instr to assoc, 60-67. *Concurrent Pos:* Biol asst, Army Chem Ctr, Md; hon res fel, Univ Exeter, Eng, 85-86; Nat Inst Neurol Dis & Blindness career develop award, 68-72. *Mem:* Fel AAAS; Am Physiol Soc; Soc Exp Biol & Med; Soc Neurosci; Sigma Xi. *Res:* Comparative physiology of cerebrospinal fluid; respiratory control; acid-base physiology; cranial compliance; intercranial pressure. *Mailing Add:* Dept Physiol Mich State Univ East Lansing MI 48824-1101. *Fax:* 517-355-5125

HEISIG, CHARLES G(LADSTONE), CHEMICAL ENGINEERING. *Current Pos:* RETIRED. *Personal Data:* b Minneapolis, Minn, Feb 8, 24; m 60; c 4. *Educ:* Univ Minn, BS, 44; Univ Tex, MS, 48, PhD, 51. *Prof Exp:* Develop engr, Oak Ridge Nat Lab, 50-53 & Union Carbide Chem Co Div, Union Carbide Corp, 53-56; res engr, Eng Res Inst, Univ Mich, 56-57; proj mgr res, Taylor Instrument Co, Div Sybron Corp, 57-67, res specialist, 67-72, analysis systs specialist, Taylor Instruments Process Control, 72-83; sr engr, Eastman-Kodak Co, Rochester, NY, 84-90. *Concurrent Pos:* Consult engr, 83-84. *Mem:* Am Chem Soc; Instrument Soc Am. *Res:* Development of continuous measuring instruments and sampling systems for chemical process control systems. *Mailing Add:* Four Chapman Rd West Rush NY 14543-9423

HEISING, CAROLYN D, NUCLEAR ENGINEERING. *Current Pos:* PROF INDUST & NUCLEAR ENG, IOWA STATE UNIV, 93- *Educ:* Univ Calif, San Diego, BS, 74; Stanford Univ, MS, 75, PhD(mech eng), 78. *Honors & Awards:* Young Scholar Award, Am Asn Univ Women, 87; Spec Seminar Award, NSF, 81. *Prof Exp:* Asst prof nuclear eng, Mass Inst Technol, 80-84; prof indust eng, Northeastern Univ, 84-93. *Concurrent Pos:* Vis prof nuclear eng, Univ Fla, 90-91; mem bd dirs, Am Nuclear Soc, 92-98; plenary speaker, Obninsk Lab, Russia, 91, Europ Nuclear Conf, 94. *Res:* Reliability analysis; probability risk assessment; statistical quality control; total quality management; technology safety assessment; nuclear power plant safety; contributed articles to professional journals. *Mailing Add:* Iowa State Univ 110 B Engineering Annex Ames IA 50011. *Fax:* 515-294-3524; *E-Mail:* cheising@iastate.edu

HEISINGER, JAMES FREDRICK, TOXICOLOGY. *Current Pos:* assoc prof, 68-75, PROF BIOL, UNIV SDAK, 75-, ASSOC DEAN ARTS & SCI, 89- *Personal Data:* b Jefferson City, Mo, Nov 4, 35; m 61; c 2. *Educ:* Univ Mo, BS, 56, MA, 58, PhD(zool), 65. *Prof Exp:* Asst prof biol, physiol, Univ Mo, St Louis, 65-68. *Mem:* Ecol Soc Am; Sigma Xi; Am Inst Biol Sci; Soc Environ Toxicol & Chem. *Res:* Physiological adaptations of vertebrates to natural and man-made environmental conditions and aquatic toxicology. *Mailing Add:* Biol Univ SDak 414 E Clark St Vermillion SD 57069-2390

HEISLER, CHARLES RANKIN, biochemistry; deceased, see previous edition for last biography

HEISLER, JOSEPH PATRICK, MATHEMATICS. *Current Pos:* CONSULT, 81- *Personal Data:* b Decatur, Ill, Aug 9, 34. *Educ:* St Edward's Univ, BS, 56; Univ Notre Dame, MS, 59; Univ Mich, PhD(math), 65. *Prof Exp:* Teacher high schs, Ill, 56-58, Fla, 59-61 & Tex, 61-62; from asst prof to prof math, St Edward's Univ, 65-81. *Mem:* Math Asn Am; Am Math Soc. *Res:* Diophantine analysis; finite rings. *Mailing Add:* PO Box 10 Jemez Springs NM 87025-0070

HEISLER, RODNEY, RADIO ENGINEERING, GEOPHYSICS. *Current Pos:* asst prof, 70-77, PROF ENG, WALLA WALLA COL, 77- *Personal Data:* b Tamaqua, Pa, Jan 1, 42; m 64; c 3. *Educ:* Walla Walla Col, BSEE, 65; Wash State Univ, MSEE, 67, PhD(eng sci), 70. *Concurrent Pos:* Consult, Goddard Space Flight Ctr, NASA, 77-81. *Mem:* Inst Elec & Electronics Engrs; Am Soc Eng Educ. *Res:* Application of multidimensional Fourier transforms to paraboloidal reflecting antennas; multidimensional transform algorithms. *Mailing Add:* Dept Eng Walla Walla Col College Place WA 99324

HEIST, HERBERT ERNEST, ZOOLOGY. *Current Pos:* prin res scientist, Honeywell Res Ctr, 62-72, mgr, Chem Dept, Honeywell Corp Res Ctr, 72-77, DIR TECH ASSESSMENT & PLANNING, SCI & TECH, HONEYWELL CORP, 77- *Personal Data:* b Waverly, Iowa, Nov 30, 24; m 47; c 3. *Educ:* Wartburg Col, BA, 49; Univ Iowa, MA, 51, PhD(zool, bact), 57. *Prof Exp:* Bacteriologist, Wis State Hyg Lab, 54-59; assoc tech dir, Cancer Screening Dept, Alumni Res Found, Wis, 59-61; bacteriologist, Children's Med Ctr, 61-62. *Concurrent Pos:* Res assoc, Harvard Med Sch, 61-62. *Mem:* Am Soc Microbiol. *Res:* Medical bacteriology; cell biology. *Mailing Add:* 18800 Kingswood Terr Hopkins MN 55345

HEISTAD, DONALD DEAN, CARDIOVASCULAR DISEASES. *Current Pos:* from asst prof to assoc prof, 70-76, PROF, COL MED, UNIV IOWA, 76-, DIR, CTR AGING, 90-, DEP DIR, CARDIOVASC CTR, 94-, DIR, CARDIOVASCULAR DIS DIV, 95- *Personal Data:* b Chicago, Ill, Apr 2, 40; m 64, Sandra Jensen; c Dean & Wendy. *Educ:* Univ Chicago, MD, 63. *Honors & Awards:* Cecile Lehman Mayer Res Award, Am Col Chest Physicians, 73; Irving S Wright Award, Am Heart Asn, 76 & Harry Goldblatt Award, 80; Merck Int Award, Int Soc Hypertension, 94. *Prof Exp:* From intern to resident, Univ Chicago, 63-66; cardiovasc trainee, Univ Iowa, 66-67; res internist, US Army Res Inst Environ Med, 67-70. *Concurrent Pos:* Clin investr, Vet Admin Hosp, Iowa City, 71-74; traveling fel, Royal Soc Med Found, 73; res career develop award, Nat Heart & Lung Inst, 75-; chmn, Midwest Sect, Am Fed Clin Res, 77-81; med investr, Vet Admin Hosp, Iowa City, 78- *Mem:* Am Physiol Soc; Am Soc Pharmacol & Exp Therapeut (secy, 93-94, treas, 94-); Am Fed Clin Res (secy-treas, 77-81); Am Soc Clin Invest; Asn Am Physicians; Asn Univ Cardiologists. *Res:* Control of cerebral blood flow; vascular effects of atherosclerosis; gene therapy of blood vessels; endothelium. *Mailing Add:* Dept Med Univ Iowa Col Med Iowa City IA 52242. *Fax:* 319-353-6343

HEITKAMP, NORMAN DENIS, RESEARCH ADMINISTRATION, APPLIED STATISTICS. *Current Pos:* from res mathematician to sr res mathematician, Shell Develop Co, 79-85, supvr, 84-85, supvr/staff res mathematician, 85-87, res mgr statist, 87-90, TECH MGR QUAL ASSURANCE, SHELL MARTINEZ REFINING CO, 90- *Personal Data:* b Houston, Tex, Jan 3, 40; m 63; c 3. *Educ:* Univ Tex, BS, 61; Southwest Tex State Col, MA, 63; Tex A&M Univ, PhD(phys chem), 65. *Prof Exp:* Sr res chemist, Southwest Res Inst, 65-68; res chemist, Brown & Williamson Tobacco Corp, 68-70, area supvr, 70-78. *Mem:* Am Chem Soc; Am Statist Asn; Opers Res Soc Am. *Res:* Experimental design, linear models and regression analysis; multivariate analysis. *Mailing Add:* Shell Martinez Refining Co PO Box 711 Martinez CA 94553-1391

HEITKEMPER, MARGARET M, GASTROINTESTINAL PHYSIOLOGY. *Current Pos:* ASSOC PROF PHYSIOL, UNIV WASH, 81- *Personal Data:* b Longview, Wash, Aug 21, 51. *Educ:* Univ Ill, PhD(physiol & biophysics), 81. *Mem:* Am Physiol Soc; Am Geront Soc; Am Nurses Asn. *Mailing Add:* Nursing Univ Wash 3900 Seventh Ave NE Seattle WA 98195-0001

HEITMAN, HUBERT, JR, animal nutrition, environmental physiology; deceased, see previous edition for last biography

HEITMAN, RICHARD EDGAR, MANAGEMENT, PRODUCT DEVELOPMENT. *Current Pos:* mem prof staff opers res, Arthur D Little, Inc, 56 & 58-65, head, London Mgt Sci Group, Arthur D Little, Ltd, 65-69, sr div staff, Mgt Sci Div, 69-73, SR VPRES, ARTHUR D LITTLE, INC, 73- *Personal Data:* b Bronx, NY, Mar 30, 30; m 68; c 1. *Educ:* Mass Inst Technol, BS, 52; Princeton Univ, MS, 53, PhD(chem eng), 60. *Prof Exp:* Asst, Princeton Univ, 53-54. *Concurrent Pos:* Mem opers res Chem Corps, US Army, 54-55; dir, Multibank Financial Corp, 77-; gov bd mem, Asn Princeton Grad Alumni, 79- *Mem:* Oper Res Soc UK; Opers Res Soc Am; Am Inst Chem Engrs. *Res:* Application of technology to meet business and scientific needs; identification and promotion of market opportunities for new technology-based products; design, evaluation and implementation of automated systems. *Mailing Add:* 117 Hosmer St Acton MA 07120

HEITNER, CYRIL, WOOD CHEMISTRY, PHOTOCHEMISTRY. *Current Pos:* Nat Res Coun indust fel, Pulp & Paper Res Inst Can, 71-72, scientist, 72-88, sr scientist, 88-95, PRIN SCIENTIST, PULP & PAPER RES INST CAN, 95- *Personal Data:* b Montreal, Que, July 8, 41; m 66, Norma Toby; c 3. *Educ:* Sir George Williams Univ, BS, 63; Dalhousie Univ, MS, 66; McGill Univ, PhD(chem), 71. *Honors & Awards:* I H Weldon Medal, Can Pulp & Paper Asn, 81. *Mem:* Am Chem Soc; Can Pulp & Paper Asn; Tech Asn Pulp & Paper Indust; fel Chem Inst Can. *Res:* Modification of lignin, hemicellulose and cellulose in wood for the purpose of paper manufacture. *Mailing Add:* 4466 Glendale Pierrefonds PQ H9H 2L2 Can

HEITSCH, CHARLES WEYAND, INORGANIC CHEMISTRY. *Current Pos:* RETIRED. *Personal Data:* b Pontiac, Mich, July 5, 31; m 52, Leona C Mason; c Russell D, Carrie J, Grace M, Charles W & Irene A. *Educ:* Univ Mich, BS, 56, MS, 57, PhD(chem), 60. *Prof Exp:* Asst chem, Res Inst, Univ Mich, 55-59; instr inorg chem, Iowa State Univ, 59-63; res chemist, E I du Pont de Nemours & Co, Inc, 63-67; mem staff & sr res specialist, Monsanto Co, 67-85; instr, St Louis Community Col & Bellville Area Col, 86; asst chmn & res engr, Univ Mo, Rolla, 86-97. *Mem:* Am Chem Soc. *Res:* Synthetic and physical chemistry of inorganic and organometallic compounds; industrial process chemistry of inorganic and organo-phosphorous compounds. *Mailing Add:* HC 01 Box 66 Bourbon MO 65441

HEITSCH, JAMES LAWRENCE, FOLIATED MANIFOLDS. *Current Pos:* from asst prof to assoc prof, 73-85, PROF MATH, UNIV ILL, CHICAGO, 85- *Personal Data:* b Ypsilanti, Mich, July 15, 46; m 67, Lynn Bowser; c 2. *Educ:* Univ Ill, BS, 67; Univ Chicago, MS, 68, PhD(math), 71. *Prof Exp:* Lectr math, Univ Calif, Berkeley, 71-73, vis asst prof, Los Angeles, 73-74. *Concurrent Pos:* Consult, LaSalle State Securities, 72-75; vis assoc prof, Cath Pontifical Univ, Rio de Janeiro, 75-76 & Univ Lille, France, 81; vpres res, Burrito & Burrito, 80-84; Math Sci Res Inst, 84-85; mem math, Inst Advan Study, 82; fel, Japan Soc Promotion Sci, 86-87; vis prof, Univ Lyon, France, 89. *Mem:* Am Math Soc. *Res:* Analysis on foliated manifolds. *Mailing Add:* 1011 Dempster St Evanston IL 60201. *E-Mail:* u25483@uicvm.bitnet

HEITSCHMIDT, RODNEY KEITH, RANGE SCIENCE, RANGE MANAGEMENT. *Current Pos:* RES LEADER, FT KEOGH LIVESTOCK & RANGE RES LAB, USDA, AGR RES STA, 90- *Personal Data:* b Hays, Kans, Oct 28, 44; m 65; Judy S Thompson; c Jason K & Dustin L. *Educ:* Fort Hays State Univ, BS, 67, MS, 68; Colo State Univ, PhD(range sci), 77. *Honors & Awards:* Outstanding Achievement Award, Soc Range Mgt, 91. *Prof Exp:* Prof, Tex Agr Exp Sta, Tex A&M Univ, 77-90. *Concurrent Pos:* Mem, Coun Agri Sci & Technol. *Mem:* Soc Range Mgt; Ecol Soc Am; Am Inst Biol Sci; Am Soc Soil & Water Conserv. *Res:* Grazing management; quantifying impact of various livestock grazing tactics on rangeland ecosystems particularly primary productivity. *Mailing Add:* 1116 S Merriam Ave Miles City MT 59301

HEITZ, JAMES ROBERT, BIOCHEMISTRY, PHOTOBIOLOGY. *Current Pos:* from asst prof to assoc prof, 70-79, PROF BIOCHEM, MISS STATE UNIV, 79- *Personal Data:* b Louisville, Ky, Feb 22, 41; m 69, Ann Rothenhoefer; c Elizabeth, Catherine & Michael. *Educ:* Bellarmine Col, Ky, AB, 63; Univ Tenn, Knoxville, PhD(biochem), 67. *Prof Exp:* Res assoc biochem, Johns Hopkins Univ, 68-70. *Concurrent Pos:* Pres, Photodye Int, Inc, 93- *Mem:* Am Soc Biol Chem; Am Chem Soc. *Res:* Enzymology; photodynamic action; insect biochemistry; development of improved specific pesticides; xanthene dyes; photochemistry. *Mailing Add:* Miss State Univ PO Box 9650 Mississippi State MS 39762. *Fax:* 601-325-8664; *E-Mail:* jrheitz@ra.msstate.edu

HEIZER, KENNETH W, ELECTRICAL ENGINEERING. *Current Pos:* RETIRED. *Personal Data:* b Iola, Tex, Nov 21, 23; m 60; c 4. *Educ:* Southern Methodist Univ, BS, 50, MS, 51; Univ Ill, PhD(elec eng), 62. *Prof Exp:* From instr to assoc prof elec eng, Southern Methodist Univ, 51-60; instr, Univ Ill, 61-62; prof elec eng, Southern Methodist Univ, 62-92. *Concurrent Pos:* Consult, Tex Instruments Inc, 55-56, 57-58, 62-63 & 65 & Nat Data Processing Corp, 58-60. *Mem:* Inst Elec & Electronics Engrs; Am Soc Eng Educ; Sigma Xi. *Res:* Electric circuit theory. *Mailing Add:* Southern Methodist Univ Sea Caruth Bldg Dallas TX 75275

HEIZER, WILLIAM DAVID, MEDICAL SCIENCES. *Current Pos:* from asst prof to assoc prof, 70-78, PROF MED, UNIV NC, 78- *Personal Data:* b Rawlings, Va, Mar 23, 37; m 60; c 2. *Educ:* King Col, BA, 58; Johns Hopkins Univ, MD, 63. *Prof Exp:* Actg instr chem, King Col, 58-59; intern med, Johns Hopkins Univ, 63-64; asst resident, 64-65; clin assoc med, NIH, 65-67. *Concurrent Pos:* Career develop award, NIH, 72; res grant, NIH, 71, Nat Cancer Inst, 90; prof, Nutrit Dept, Sch Pub Health, 91-; mem bd dirs, Am Soc Parenteral & Enteral Nutrit, 91. *Mem:* Am Gastroenterol Asn; Am Soc Parenteral & Enteral Nutrit; Am Soc Clin Nutrit; Am Inst Nutrit. *Res:* Absorption of nutrients and drugs from various segments of the intestinal tract. *Mailing Add:* Digestive Dis & Nutrit CB No 7080 318 Burnett-Womack Bldg Univ NC Chapel Hill NC 27599-7080

HEJHAL, DENNIS ARNOLD, COMPLEX VARIABLE & NUMBER THEORY, SUPERCOMPUTING. *Current Pos:* PROF MATH, UNIV MINN, 78-; PROF MATH, UPPSALA UNIV, SWEDEN, 94- *Personal Data:* b Chicago, Ill, Dec 10, 48. *Educ:* Univ Chicago, BS, 70; Stanford Univ, PhD(math), 72. *Honors & Awards:* Goran Gustafsson Prize Math, Royal Swed Acad Sci, 97. *Prof Exp:* Asst instr math, Harvard Univ, 72-74; assoc prof, Columbia Univ, 74-78. *Concurrent Pos:* Fel, Sloan Found, 74-76, Minn Supercomput Inst, 85-; vis prof, Univ Calif, San Diego, 81, Chalmers Univ Technol, Sweden, 87, Princeton Univ, 93; mem, Inst Advan Study, Princeton, 83, 84, 85, 90 & 93. *Mem:* Am Math Soc; Math Asn Am; Swed Math Soc; Royal Soc Sci Sweden. *Res:* Complex variable; analytic number theory; trace formulas; supercomputers. *Mailing Add:* Sch Math Univ Minn Minneapolis MN 55455

HEJNA, WILLIAM FRANK, ORTHOPEDIC SURGERY. *Current Pos:* SR VPRES, RUSH PRESBY ST LUKES MED CTR, 76-; PROF ORTHOPEDIC SURG, RUSH MED COL, 76. *Personal Data:* b Chicago, Ill, May 13, 32; m 55; c 4. *Educ:* Grinnell Col, BA, 54, DSc, 74; Washington Univ, MD, 58; Am Bd Orthop Surg, dipl. *Hon Degrees:* DSc, Grinnell Col, 74. *Prof Exp:* Intern, Presby-St Luke's Hosp, 58-59; resident, Univ Ill Res & Educ Hosps, 59-63; dir electrolyography lab & coordr orthop clins & med student training, 63-70, asst chmn dept orthop surg, 65-70, assoc attend surgeon, 67-70, coordr hip clin & adult orthop clin, 68-70, secy staff, 69-71, assoc dean, Off Surg Sci & Serv, 70-73, dean, Rush Med Col & vpres med affairs, Med Ctr, 73-76. *Concurrent Pos:* Examr, Am Bd Orthop Surg, 69-72; sr attend surg, Dept Orthop Surg, Presby-St Luke's Hosp, 71-; pres, Coun Med Deans, State of Ill, 74-76; pres, Bioserv Corp & Bus Consult Inc; consult, Medicus Affil Inc & Whittaker Corp; chmn bd trustees, Ancor Orgn, Health Maintenance Orgn, 81- *Mem:* Fel Am Col Surgeons; fel Am Acad Orthop Surgeons; Am Asn Med Cols; Orthop Res Soc; Clin Orthop Soc; Sigma Xi. *Res:* Total hip replacement; cartilage studies in arthritis; chemonucleolysis; osteoporosis; sports medicine. *Mailing Add:* 321 N Delaplaine Riverside IL 60546-1853

HEJTMANCIK, JAMES FIELDING, MOLECULAR GENETICS OF INHERITED EYE DISEASES, MOLECULAR DIAGNOSTICS. *Current Pos:* med res assoc, Nat Inst Child Health & Develop, 80-83, MED OFFICER, NAT EYE INST, 91- *Personal Data:* b Galveston, Tex, Dec 24, 51. *Educ:* Rice Univ, BA, 79; Baylor Col Med, PhD(cell biol), 76, MD, 78. *Prof Exp:* Intern/resident, Duke Univ Med Ctr, 79-80. *Concurrent Pos:* Fel, Baylor Col Med, 84-85, asst prof, 85-91. *Mem:* Am Soc Human Genetics; Asn Res Vision & Ophthal. *Res:* Molecular genetics of inherited eye diseases with particular interests in positional cloning, molecular diagnostics and biology of the lens crystallins. *Mailing Add:* Bldg 6 Rm 2A 14 OGC5B/NEI Nat Inst Health 9000 Rockville Pike Bethesda MD 20892-0001. *Fax:* 301-496-1759; *E-Mail:* j3h@mge3.nei.nih.gov

HEJTMANCIK, MILTON R, INTERNAL MEDICINE, CARDIOLOGY. *Current Pos:* RETIRED. *Personal Data:* b Caldwell, Tex, Sept 27, 19; m 43, 76, Myrtle M McCormick; c Kelly (Erwin), Milton R Jr & Peggy L. *Educ:* Univ Tex, BS, 39, MD, 43; Am Bd Internal Med, dipl, 51; Am Bd Cardiovasc Dis, dipl, 63. *Honors & Awards:* Billings Gold Medal, AMA, 73; Titus Harris Distinguished Serv Award, 92. *Prof Exp:* Instr internal med, Univ Tex Med Br Galveston, 49-51, asst dir heart sta, 49-65, dir, Heart Sta, 49-65, dir heart clin, 49-80, asst prof internal med, 51-54, assoc prof, 54-65, prof internal med & dir heart sta, 65-80; prof internal med, Tex A&M Col Med, Temple, Tex, 81-82; cardiologist, Olin E Teague Vet Admin Hosp, Temple, Tex, 81-82; cardiologist, Beaumont Vet Admin Clin, 82-86. *Concurrent Pos:* Consult, St Mary's Infirmary, 51-80, Galveston County Mem Hosp, 53-80 & USPHS Hosp, 57-80; med adv, Bur Hearings & Appeals, Social Security Admin, 68-80; fel, Coun Clin Cardiol, Am Heart Asn. *Mem:* Am Heart Asn; fel Am Col Physicians; fel Am Col Chest Physicians; fel Am Col Cardiol; Am Fedn Clin Res. *Res:* Clinical cardiology, especially electrocardiography, vectorcardiography, echocardiography, arrhythmias of the heart, drug therapy of cardiac disorders. *Mailing Add:* 500 N Spruce St Hammond LA 70401

HEKAL, IHAB M, MATERIALS CHEMISTRY, PROCESS DEVELOPMENT. *Current Pos:* DIR ADVAN TECHNOL, CONTINENTAL GROUP, 78- *Personal Data:* b Cairo, Egypt, Oct 27, 38; US citizen; m 64; c 1. *Educ:* Univ Graz, Austria, BSc, 62, MSc, 64; Univ Hannover, Ger, PhD(phys chem), 66. *Prof Exp:* Scientist, Nat Res Ctr, Cairo, Egypt, 67-68; sr scientist, Contiental Can Co, Ill, 68-72, mgr surface chem, 72-76, consult process develop, 76-78. *Concurrent Pos:* Lectr chem, Roosevelt Univ, 70-71 & Hebrew Theol Col, 71-72. *Mem:* Am Chem Soc. *Res:* Coating material and process (wash coat for cans); compile recycling of aluminum treated chemicals with zeno effluent; composits (metals/minerals); oxygen Barries material for packaging; electro chemical process for oxygen removal from juices for shelf life improvement. *Mailing Add:* 121 Black Berry Dr Stamford CT 06903

HEKKER, ROELAND M T, MACHINE VISION, PATTERN RECOGNITION. *Current Pos:* vpres, 90-92, PRES, ENG PATTERN RECOGNITION, IMPACA TECHNOL CORP, 92- *Personal Data:* b Djakarta, Indonesia, Nov 25, 53; Neth citizen; m 76; c 2. *Educ:* Univ Technol Delft, Neth, BD, 77, MS, 79. *Prof Exp:* Optical syst design indust, Philips-Data Systs, 79-82; dept mgr optical disk technol, OSI Laser Magnetic Syst, 82-85; mem staff advan optical rec, Hewlett & Parkard Res Labs, 85; vpres eng optical signal processing, Global Holonetics Corp, 85-89. *Concurrent Pos:* Pres, ELA-Hi Tech Eng, 90- *Mem:* Int Soc Optical Eng; Soc Mfg Engrs; affil Inst Elec & Electronics Engrs. *Res:* Digital signal processing; pattern recognition; artificial neural nets and fuzzy logic as they apply to image processing; scientific visualization and machine vision. *Mailing Add:* Impact Tech 205 W Burlington Ave Fairfield IA 52556

HEKMAT, HAMID MOAYED, ANXIETY & FEAR, PAIN ETIOLOGY & INTERVENTION. *Current Pos:* PROF PSYCHOL, UNIV WIS-STEVENS POINT, 68- *Personal Data:* b Tehran, Iran, Aug 24, 40; US citizen; m 69; c 1. *Educ:* Huntingdon Col, BA, 64; Univ Southern Calif, PhD(psychol), 68. *Mem:* Am Psychol Asn; Asn Advan Behav Ther. *Res:* Etiology of phobias; management of anxiety disorders; treatment of cold pressor pain; psychological mechanism in arthritis and other chronic pain disorders. *Mailing Add:* Psychol Univ Wis 2100 Main St Stevens Point WI 54481-3871

HEKMATPANAH, JAVAD, NEUROSURGERY, NEUROLOGY. *Current Pos:* resident neurosurg, 61-63, instr & chief resident, 63-64, asst prof, 64-70, assoc prof, 70-75, PROF NEUROSURG, UNIV CHICAGO HOSPS, 75- *Personal Data:* b Isfahan, Iran, Mar 25, 34; m 59; c 3. *Educ:* Univ Tehran, MD, 56. *Prof Exp:* Intern, Mt Sinai Hosp, Chicago, 57-58; resident neurol, Univ Wis Hosp, 58-61. *Mem:* Am Col Surgeons; Am Asn Neurologists; Am Acad Neurol; Sigma Xi. *Res:* Cerebral circulation in trauma; brain tumors; multimodal therapy in man and viral induction in rats. *Mailing Add:* Univ Chicago Med Ctr 5841 S Maryland MC Chicago IL 60637-1470

HELANDER, DONALD P(ETER), PETROLEUM ENGINEERING. *Current Pos:* VPRES & CO-OWNER, BNJ OIL PROPERTIES INC, 81-; PRES, INT PETROL CONSULT INC, 77- *Personal Data:* b Milwaukee, Wis, May 26, 31; m 56; c 3. *Educ:* Univ Tulsa, BS, 57, MS, 60; Univ Okla, PhD(petrol eng), 65. *Prof Exp:* Jr field logging engr, Schlumberger Well Surv Corp, 57-58; instr petrol eng, Univ Tulsa, 58-62, asst prof, 65-66, asst dir info serv dept, 65-66, dir, 66-68, assoc prof & head dept, 68-77. *Concurrent Pos:* Teacher formation eval & reservoir eng, 65- *Mem:* Sigma Xi; Soc Prof Well Log Analysts; Soc Petrol Engr; Can Well Logging Soc. *Res:* Formation evaluation, especially electric, acoustic and radioactive well logging; oil and gas reservoir analysis; author. *Mailing Add:* 4124 E 98th St Tulsa OK 74137-4807

HELANDER, HERBERT DICK FERDINAND, CELL BIOLOGY, GASTROENTEROLOGY. *Current Pos:* SR RES ADV, ASTRA HAESSLE AB, MOLNDAL, SWEDEN, 84- *Personal Data:* b Lund, Sweden, Dec 7, 35; m 61, Kerstin Lindblom; c 3. *Educ:* Univ Goteborg, Sweden, BM, 56, PhD(anat), 62, MD, 63. *Prof Exp:* Asst prof anat, Univ Goteborg, Sweden, 63-65; prof anat, Univ Umea, Sweden, 66-84. *Concurrent Pos:* Vis asst prof, Dept Med, Univ Okla Med Ctr, 64-65; Fulbright scholar, 64-65; sr foreign scientist, NSF, 70; vis prof, Dept Physiol, Univ Ala Med Ctr, 70-72, Cardiovasc Res Inst, Univ Calif, San Francisco, 76, Dept Med, Univ Calif, Los Angeles, 83-; chmn, Dept Anat, Univ Umea, Sweden, 74-84; adj prof, Dept Anat, Univ Goteborg, Sweden, 85- *Mem:* Am Gastroenterol Asn; Am Soc Cell Biol; Am Soc Histotechnol. *Res:* Structure and function of the gastric mucosa; morphological studies of gastric acid secretion. *Mailing Add:* Astra Haessle AB Molndal 431 83 Sweden. *Fax:* 46-31-7763705

HELANDER, MARTIN ERIK GUSTAV, USER INTERFACE AUTOMATION. *Current Pos:* PROF MECH ENG & ERGONOMICS, LINKOPING UNIV TECHNOL, LINKOPING, SWEDEN, 96- *Personal Data:* b Uppsala, Sweden, May 13, 43; div; c 2. *Educ:* Chalmers Univ Technol, Gotenborg, Sweden, MS, 67, PhD(civil eng), 73; Lulea Univ, Sweden, PhD(eng psychol), 77. *Prof Exp:* Prof ergonomics, Lulea Univ, 75-83; assoc prof indust eng, Univ SFla, 83-85; assoc prof indust eng, State Univ NY, Buffalo, 85-96. *Concurrent Pos:* Sr scientist human factors, Canyon Res Group, 77-82; secy, TRB Comt on Vehicle Users Characteristics, Nat Res Coun, 79-; chmn, Tech Stand Comt, Human Factors Soc, 80-; vis prof, Va Tech, 82-83; US deleg, Int Ergonomics Asn, 85. *Mem:* Fel Human Factors Soc; fel Ergonomics Soc; Inst Indust Engrs; Robotics Int. *Res:* Human factors or ergonomics research in the areas of traffic safety and driver performance; office and industrial automation; human-computer interaction. *Mailing Add:* Dept Mech Eng Linkoping Univ Technol 58133 Linkoping Sweden

HELAVA, U(UNO) V(ILHO), photogrammetry, geodesy, for more information see previous edition

HELBERT, JAMES RAYMOND, BIOCHEMISTRY. *Current Pos:* RETIRED. *Personal Data:* b Miles City, Mont, Aug 4, 18; m 49; c 4. *Educ:* St John's Univ, Minn, AB, 47; Marquette Univ, MS, 58; Northwestern Univ, PhD(biochem), 63. *Prof Exp:* Chief chemist, Orthmann Labs, Inc, 47-51; res chemist, Red Star Yeast & Prod Co, 51-58; res biochemist, Geriat Res Proj, Vet Admin Hosp, 58-62, actg chief, 62-63; res assoc, Dept Hemat, Michael Reese Hosp & Med Ctr, 63-67; supvr biochem res, Miller Brewing Co, 67-76, mgr biochem res & admin, 76-85. *Mem:* Am Chem Soc; Am Statist Asn; fel Am Inst Chem. *Res:* Physical biochemistry; statistical design of experiments; fermentation; fermentation kinetics. *Mailing Add:* PO Box 47049 Chicago IL 60647-0049

HELBERT, JOHN N, RADIATION CHEMISTRY & POLYMER CHEMISTRY, INDUSTRIAL & MANUFACTURING ENGINEERING. *Current Pos:* processing engr, 80-85, mem tech staff, 84-90, SR MEM TECH STAFF, MOTOROLA, 90- *Personal Data:* b Wichita, Kans, Aug 3, 46; m 69, Roxie; c Derek & Tania. *Educ:* Ariz State Univ, BS, 68; Wayne State Univ, PhD(chem), 72; US Army Command & Gen Staff Col, MA, 87. *Prof Exp:* Res asst chem, Wayne State Univ, 69-72; res physicist, US Army Electronics Command, 72-75, res chemist, 75-80. *Mem:* Am Chem Soc; Sigma Xi; Electrochem Soc. *Res:* Radiation chemistry of polymers to include magnetic resonance investigations of polymer radicals; photolithography and resist processing engineering investigations; semiconductor process engineering. *Mailing Add:* Motorola COM1 W102 5005 E McDowell Rd Phoenix AZ 85008

HELBIG, HERBERT FREDERICK, ATOMIC PHYSICS. *Current Pos:* PHYSICIST, ROME LAB. *Personal Data:* b Bronx, NY, Jan 2, 34; m 57; c Florence Lucas. *Educ:* Yale Univ, AB, 56; Univ Conn, MS, 62, PhD(physics), 65. *Prof Exp:* from asst prof to prof physics, Clarkson Univ, 65-97, exec officer, 68-73, actg chmn, 84-85. *Concurrent Pos:* Consult, Lawrence Livermore Nat Lab, 79-81. *Mem:* Am Phys Soc; Sigma Xi; Am Vacuum Soc. *Res:* Ion-atom and ion-surface scattering experiments and simulations; atomic and solid state physics experiments and simulations. *Mailing Add:* Rome Laboratory/ERDR 525 Brooks Rd Rome NY 13441-4505. *E-Mail:* helbigh@rl.af.mil

HELBING, REINHARD KARL BODO, PHYSICS. *Current Pos:* PROF PHYSICS, UNIV WINDSOR, 72- *Personal Data:* b Stettin, Ger, June 1, 35; m 60; c 1. *Educ:* Univ Bonn, dipl, 61, Dr rer nat(physics), 66. *Prof Exp:* Asst physics, Inst Appl Physics, Univ Bonn, 62-68; assoc prof eng & appl sci, Univ Calif, Los Angeles, 69-72. *Concurrent Pos:* Staff scientist, Gen Dynamics/Convair, 66-69. *Mem:* Am Phys Soc; Ger Phys Soc; Europ Phys Soc; NY Acad Sci. *Res:* Properties of atoms and molecules investigated by applying molecular beams of thermal and higher energies; elastic and inelastic scattering; theoretical treatment of collision phenomena. *Mailing Add:* Dept Physics Univ Windsor Windsor ON N9B 3P4 Can

HELD, ABRAHAM ALBERT, MYCOLOGY. *Current Pos:* from asst prof to assoc prof, 71-82, PROF BIOL SCI, DEPT BIOL SCI, LEHMAN COL, CITY UNIV NEW YORK, 83-; MEM ADJ FAC, ROCKEFELLER UNIV, 71- *Personal Data:* b Vienna, Austria, Mar 27, 34; nat US; m 67. *Educ:* Hebrew Univ, Israel, MSc, 63, Univ Calif, Berkeley, PhD(microbiol), 67. *Prof Exp:* Guest investr parasitol, Rockefeller Univ, 67-70, res assoc, 70-71. *Mem:* Am Soc Microbiol. *Res:* Biology of aquatic phycomycetes; fungal nutrition and cultivation; biomedical terminology. *Mailing Add:* Dept Biol Sci Lehman Col City Univ NY 250 Bedford Park W Bronx NY 10468-1589

HELD, BEREL, OBSTETRICS & GYNECOLOGY. *Current Pos:* PROF OBSTET & GYNEC & CHMN DEPT, UNIV TEX MED SCH HOUSTON, 72- *Personal Data:* b Brooklyn, NY, Aug 31, 38; m 62; c 4. *Educ:* Tulane Univ, MD, 62. *Prof Exp:* From asst prof to assoc prof obstet & gynec, Col Med, Univ Fla, 68-72. *Concurrent Pos:* Fel path, Harvard Med Sch, 66; consult gynec, M D Anderson Hosp & Tumor Inst, 72-; chief obstet & gynec, Hermann Hosp, 72- *Mem:* Am Col Obstet & Gynec. *Res:* Perinatology. *Mailing Add:* Marshall Univ Huntington WV 25701

HELD, IRENE RITA, NEUROCHEMISTRY, NEUROSCIENCES. *Current Pos:* CHIEF NEUROSCI RES SECT, VET ADMIN HOSP, HINES, ILL, 72- *Personal Data:* b Milwaukee, Wis. *Educ:* Marquette Univ, BS, 55; Northwestern Univ, MS, 62, PhD(biochem), 65. *Prof Exp:* Res biochemist, Vet Admin Hosp, Downey, Ill, 65-72. *Concurrent Pos:* Instr biochem, Med Sch, Northwestern Univ, Chicago, 66-70, assoc, 70-74, asst prof pharmacol, Stritch Sch Med, Loyola Univ Chicago, 74-77 & assoc prof pharmacol & biochem, 77- *Mem:* Am Soc Neurochem; Soc Neurosci; AAAS; Res Soc Alcoholism. *Res:* Biochemical mechanisms in the neurotrophic relation between nerve and muscle; effect of ethanol exposure on muscle and brain proteins. *Mailing Add:* Chief Neurosci Hines Vet Hosp Hines IL 60141

HELD, ISAAC MEYER, GEOPHYSICAL FLUID DYNAMICS, CLIMATE DYNAMICS. *Current Pos:* METEOROLOGIST, GEOPHYS FLUID DYNAMICS LAB, NAT OCEANIC & ATMOSPHERIC ADMIN, PRINCETON UNIV, 78- *Personal Data:* b Ger Oct 23, 48; m 84; c 1. *Educ:* Univ Minn, BPhys, 69; State Univ Ny, Stony Brook, MA, 70; Princeton Univ, PhD, 76. *Honors & Awards:* Meisinger Award, Am Meteorol Soc, 87. *Prof Exp:* Res fel climate, Harvard Univ, 76-78. *Concurrent Pos:* Assoc ed, J Atmospheric Sci, 79-87; ed, J Atmospheric Sci, 87-90. *Mem:* Fel Am Meteorol Soc; Am Geophys Union. *Res:* Large-scale atmospheric dynamics; models of climatic sensitivity and variability; fluid dynamics. *Mailing Add:* Geophys Dynamics Lab Forrestal Village Rte 1 US Rte 1 Princeton NJ 08542

HELD, JOE R, PRIMATOLOGY, PARASITOLOGY. *Current Pos:* RETIRED. *Personal Data:* b Los Angeles, Calif, June 23, 31; m 56, Carolyn A Friderich; c Lisa (Doseff), Robert J, Lesle (Clark) & Teresa (Johnson). *Educ:* Univ Calif, Davis, BS, 53, DVM, 55; Tulane Univ, MPH, 59. *Honors & Awards:* James H Steele Award, World Vet Epidemiol Soc, 77; K F Meyer Award, Am Vet Epidemiol Soc, 82; Charles River Prize, Am Vet Med Asn, 84; XII Int Vet Cong Prize, Am Vet Med Asn, 89; J A McCallam Award, Asn Mil Surgeons, 90. *Prof Exp:* Vet epidemiologist, Commun Dis Ctr, 55-57; pvt pract, 57-58; asst chief rabies control unit, Vet Sect, Epidemiol Br, Commun Dis Ctr, 59-60, asst to sect chief, 60-61, asst to br chief, 61-62; sr vet officer, Primate Ctr Grant Admin, Animal Resources Br, NIH, 62-64, sr vet officer malaria res, Nat Inst Allergy & Infectious Dis, 64-67; vet epidemiologist, Pan Am Zoonoses Ctr, Arg, 67-69; chief vet res br, 69-72, dir, Div Res Serv, NIH, 72-84; dir, Pan Am Zoonoses Ctr, Pan Am Health Orgn, 84-87, coordr, Vet Pub Health Prog, 87-89; vpres primate opers, Charles River Labs, 89-90; admin dir, Biotechnol Group, Microbiol Assocs, 91-92. *Concurrent Pos:* Chief vet off, USPHS, 75-84. *Mem:* Am Vet Med Asn; hon mem Am Col Lab Animal Med; Am Soc Primates; Int Primate Soc; Nat Asn Fed Vet; Am Asn Lab Animal Sci; Am Col Epidemiol; Am Col Vet Prev Med; AAAS. *Res:* Primate malarias, particularly the exo-erythrocytic stages; brucellosis; infectious hepatitis; rabies; toxoplasmosis; dermatomycoses; zoonoses. *Mailing Add:* 1300 Crystal Dr No 505 Arlington VA 22202-3234. *Fax:* 703-416-0548; *E-Mail:* 76537.3136@compuserve.com

HELD, ROBERT PAUL, PHYSICAL CHEMISTRY, POLYMER CHEMISTRY. *Current Pos:* from res chemist to sr res chemist, 65-74, res assoc, 74-76, RES FEL, PRINTING & PUBL, E I DU PONT DE NEMOURS & CO, INC, 76- *Personal Data:* b Brooklyn, NY, Nov 18, 39; wid; c Howard, Richard & Corey. *Educ:* Queens Col, NY, BS, 59; Brooklyn Col, MA, 62; Univ Vt, PhD, 65. *Prof Exp:* Jr chemist, Kings Co Hosp, 59-60; chemist, Hempstead Gen Hosp, 60-62. *Mem:* Am Chem Soc; Soc For Imaging Science & Technol. *Res:* Thermodynamics of nonaqueous solutions; entropy correlations of electrolytic solutions; photosensitive imaging systems; gelatin interactions with silver halide crystals; photopolymer imaging systems; dispersions; emulsions; ink jet ink/media development. *Mailing Add:* Printing & Publ E I du Pont de Nemours & Co Inc PO Box 80293 Wilmington DE 19880-0293

HELD, WILLIAM ALLEN, BIOCHEMISTRY, MOLECULAR BIOLOGY. *Current Pos:* asst prof, 74-80, ASSOC PROF CELL & MOLECULAR BIOL, ROSWELL PARK MEM INST, 80-, SR CANCER RES SCIENTIST, 74- *Personal Data:* b West Bend, Wis, Nov 14, 40. *Educ:* Marquette Univ, BS, 62, MS, 65, PhD(biol), 69. *Prof Exp:* Fel biochem, genetics, Univ Wis, 69-74. *Concurrent Pos:* NIH fel, 69-71; NIH grants, 75-78 & 79-81. *Mem:* Am Soc Microbiol; NY Acad Sci; Am Soc Biol Chemists. *Res:* Regulation of gene expression and protein synthesis. *Mailing Add:* Dept Molecular & Cellular Biol Roswell Park Cancer Inst 666 Elm St Buffalo NY 14263-0001. *Fax:* 716-845-8169

HELDERMAN, J HAROLD, RENAL TRANSPLANTS, NEPHROLOGY. *Current Pos:* PROF MED, MICROBIOL & IMMUNOL & DIR VANDERBILT TRANSPLANT CTR, VANDERBILT UNIV, 89- *Personal Data:* b Newark, NJ, Feb 5, 45; m 67, Phyllis Koppel; c Alex, Ira & Roz. *Educ:* Univ Rochester, AB, 67; State Univ NY, Downstate Med Ctr, MD, 71. *Prof Exp:* From asst to assoc prof, Univ Tex, 77-83, dir kidney transplant comt, 83-87, dir organ transplant, 87-89; prof med, Univ Tex-Southwest, 85-89. *Concurrent Pos:* Prog chair, NAm Soc Dialysis & Transplant, 88-, Am Soc Transplant Physicians, 92-; assoc ed, J Am Soc Nephrology. *Mem:* Am Soc Clin Invest; Int Transplantation Soc; Am Asn Immunologist; Am Soc Nephrology; Am Diabetes Asn; Am Fedn Clin Res; Am Soc Transplant Physicians; NAm Soc Dialysis & Transplant; Geront Soc; Am Heart Asn. *Res:* Discover elements of lymphocyte activation with special reference to activation, molecules such as receptors toward manipulation for improved transplantation. *Mailing Add:* Dept Nephrol Vanderbilt Univ 1161 21st Ave S S 3223 MCN Nashville TN 37232-2372. *Fax:* 615-343-7156

HELDMAN, DENNIS RAY, FOOD ENGINEERING, FOOD SCIENCE & TECHNOLOGY. *Current Pos:* PRIN, WEINBERG CONSULT GROUP, INC, 91-; PROF FOOD PROCESS ENG, UNIV MO, 92-, CO-LEADER, FOODS, FEEDS & PROD RES CLUSTER, 92-, UNIT LEADER FOOD SCI & ENG, 94- *Personal Data:* b Findlay, Ohio, June 12, 38; m 56, 90, Louise A Campbell; c Cynthia A (Young), Candace L (Berger) & Craig S.

HELDMAN, [continued] Educ: Ohio State Univ, BS, 60, MS, 62; Mich State Univ, PhD(agr eng), 65. *Honors & Awards:* Food Engrs Award, Am Soc Agr Engrs, 81. *Prof Exp:* From instr to assoc prof agr eng & food sci, Mich State Univ, 65-71, prof agr eng, 71-84, chmn dept, 75-79, prof food eng, 79-84; vpres, Process Res & Develop, Campbell Inst Res & Technol, Campbell Soup Co, 84-88; exec vpres, Sci Affairs, Nat Food Processor Asn, 88-91. *Concurrent Pos:* Vis assoc prof, Univ Calif, Davis, 70 & vis prof, 80; ed, J Food Process Eng, 77-; consult ed, McGraw-Hill Publ Co, 80-90. *Mem:* Am Soc Agr Engrs; fel Inst Food Technol; Am Dairy Sci Asn; Inst Asn Milk, Food & Environ Sanit; Am Inst Chem Engrs; AAAS; Am Asn Cereal Chem. *Res:* Thermal, rheological and thermodynamic properties of processed foods; mathematical description of processes for food; thermal processing of food; air quality in food processing facilities; characteristics of microbial particles in enclosed spaces. *Mailing Add:* 5013 Cullen Ct Columbia MO 65203. *Fax:* 573-882-1115; *E-Mail:* aedennis@muscmail.missouri.edu

HELDMAN, JULIUS DAVID, PETROLEUM CHEMISTRY, ENERGY CONVERSION. *Current Pos:* CONSULT, 80-; DIR, SOLV-EX COPR, 82- *Personal Data:* b Cleveland, Ohio, May 9, 19; m 42, Gladys Medalie; c Carrie & Julie (Weiss). *Educ:* Univ Calif, Los Angeles, AB, 39, MA, 40; Stanford Univ, PhD(phys chem), 42. *Prof Exp:* Asst chem, Univ Calif, Los Angeles, 39-40 & Stanford Univ, 40-41; Nat Res fel, Univ Calif, 42-43, instr, 43-45; technologist, Shell Oil Co, San Francisco, 45-48, Wilmington, 48-49, chief res chemist, 49, tech adv, Houston, 49-51, chief res technologist, 51-53, sr technologist, 53-57, asst mgr mfg res, 57-61, mgr prod develop, 61-65, develop mgr petrochem div, Shell Chem Co, 65-69, vpres, Shell Develop Co, 69-80; pres, Cell Sci Ltd, 80-84. *Concurrent Pos:* Woodrow Wilson vis fel, 78-83. *Mem:* AAAS; Am Chem Soc; Am Inst Chem Eng; Sigma Xi. *Res:* Chemistry and technology of petroleum; solar energy; research administration; science policy; physical chemistry; semi-conductors; recovery of oil and minerals from tar sands. *Mailing Add:* 1002 Old Pecos Trail Santa Fe NM 87501

HELDMAN, MORRIS J, COLLOID CHEMISTRY, ACADEMIC ADMINISTRATION. *Current Pos:* pres, 68-76, EMER PRES, WEST LOS ANGELES COL, 76- *Personal Data:* b Cleveland, Ohio, June 18, 14; m 78; c 2. *Educ:* Univ Calif, Los Angeles, BA, 34, MA, 36; Univ Southern Calif, PhD(colloid chem), 47. *Prof Exp:* Asst chem, Univ Calif, Los Angeles, 35-36; city testing engr, Los Angeles, 36-37, teacher pub sch, Bd Educ, 37-42; asst, Univ Southern Calif, 42-44, lectr, 44; teacher, Los Angeles Pub Sch, Bd Educ, 44-46; instr chem & electronics, E Los Angeles Col, 46-57, asst dean, 57-62; head chemist, US Naval Ord Test Sta, Calif, 51-52; mem staff, Wichita Found Indust Res, 53; res engr, Hughes Aircraft Co, 56-57; dean, Los Angeles Metrop Col, 63-66; dean, Los Angeles Pierce Col, 66-68. *Concurrent Pos:* Educ consult, 70-83. *Mem:* AAAS; Am Chem Soc; Sigma Xi; fel AAAS. *Res:* Kinetics of inorganic reactions in solution; liquid crystals-phase studies; electrochemistry. *Mailing Add:* 5920 Hill Rd Culver City CA 90230-5445

HELDT, LLOYD A, METALLURGY. *Current Pos:* from asst prof to assoc prof, 61-69, head dept, 77-92, PROF METALL ENG, MICH TECHNOL UNIV, 69- *Personal Data:* b Evansville, Ind, July 27, 34; m 57, Patricia Metzdorf; c James & Dan. *Educ:* DePauw Univ, BA, 56; Ind Univ, MS, 58; Univ Pa, PhD(metall), 62. *Mem:* Am Inst Mining Metall & Petrol Engrs; Electrochem Soc; fel Am Soc Metals Int; Nat Asn Corrosion Engrs. *Res:* Corrosion; fracture; environment-sensitive mechanical properties; semiconducting materials; electrometallurgy. *Mailing Add:* Dept Metall & Mat Eng Mich Technol Univ Houghton MI 49931

HELDT, WALTER Z, ORGANIC CHEMISTRY, PHYSICAL CHEMISTRY. *Current Pos:* PRES, HOBSON TECHNOL CORP, 87- *Personal Data:* b Danzig, Poland, July 2, 28; nat US; m 56; c 3. *Educ:* Univ Heidelberg, Dipl chem, 49; Rutgers Univ, MS, 52, PhD(chem), 54; Univ Pa, MBA, 58. *Prof Exp:* Res, E I Du Pont de Nemours & Co, Inc, 53-81; pres & chmn bd, Helix Assocs, Inc, 81-89. *Concurrent Pos:* Gen partner, Helix Ltd Partnership, 81-89; chmn bd, RWJ Industs, Inc, 90- *Mem:* Am Chem Soc; Am Mkt Soc. *Res:* Reaction mechanisms; polymer intermediates; organic syntheses and catalysis; plastics composites; operations research; financial planning, licensing, acquisitions. *Mailing Add:* 106 Willow Spring Rd Wilmington DE 19807-2434

HELE, PRISCILLA, BIOCHEMISTRY. *Current Pos:* RETIRED. *Personal Data:* b Cambridge, Eng, Nov 22, 20. *Educ:* Cambridge Univ, BA, 41 & 42, MA & MB, BCh, 45, PhD(biochem), 50. *Prof Exp:* Williams-Waterman fel enzym, Univ Wis, 50-51; res assoc, Exp Radiopath Res Unit, Hammersmith Hosp, London, Eng, 54-57, independent investr sr staff, 58-62 & mem sci staff, Med Res Coun Gt Brit, 54-62; mem res unit chem path ment dis, Univ Birmingham, 62-64; sr scientist, Worcester Found Exp Biol, 64-78. *Mem:* AAAS; Am Soc Biol Chemists; Brit Biochem Soc; Brit Med Asn. *Res:* Enzymology; nucleic acids; amino acid activation; protein biosynthesis. *Mailing Add:* 40 Dennis Circle Northborough MA 01532

HELFAND, EUGENE, POLYMER THEORY, STATISTICAL MECHANICS. *Current Pos:* Mem tech staff chem, 58-83, DISTINGUISHED MEM TECH STAFF, BELL LABS, 83- *Personal Data:* b Brooklyn, NY, Jan 8, 34; m 57, Sondra Yoskowitz; c Robin H, Dawn A & Russ D. *Educ:* Polytech Inst Brooklyn, BS, 55; Yale Univ, MS, 57, PhD(chem), 58. *Honors & Awards:* High Polymer Physics Prize, Am Phys Soc, 89. *Concurrent Pos:* Adj prof, Yeshiva Univ, 60-62 & Polytech Inst Brooklyn, 64-65; John Simon Guggenheim fel, Stanford Univ, 69-70; chmn, Div High Polymer Physics, Am Phys Soc, 87-88. *Mem:* Am Phys Soc; Am Chem Soc; Soc Rheology. *Res:* Polymer theory, block copolymers, interfaces, rheology, shear induced effects, kinetics of conformational transitions. *Mailing Add:* AT&T Bell Labs 1A-361 600 Mountain Ave PO Box 636 Murray Hill NJ 07974-0636. *Fax:* 908-582-3958; *E-Mail:* geh@allwise.att.com

HELFER, HERMAN LAWRENCE, ASTRONOMY. *Current Pos:* from asst prof to prof physics & astron, 58-77, prof astron, 77-92, SR FAC ASSOC, DEPT PHYSICS & ASTRON, UNIV ROCHESTER & SR SCIENTIST, LAB LUSEN ENERGETICS, 86-, EMER PROF ASTRON, 93- *Personal Data:* b New York, NY, Nov 11, 29; m 56; c 4. *Educ:* Univ Chicago, PhB, 48, PhD(astron), 53. *Prof Exp:* Res fel radio astron, Carnegie Inst, 53-54 & 56-57; res assoc astron, Calif Inst Technol, 57-58. *Concurrent Pos:* Guggenheim Mem Found fel, 65-66. *Mem:* Am Astron Soc; Royal Astron Soc; Sigma Xi. *Res:* Radio astronomy; hydromagnetics; theoretical astrophysics; astronomical spectroscopy. *Mailing Add:* Dept Physics Univ Rochester Rochester NY 14627

HELFFERICH, FRIEDRICH G, CHEMICAL ENGINEERING. *Current Pos:* prof chem eng, 80-90, EMER PROF, PA STATE UNIV, 90- *Personal Data:* b Berlin, Ger, Aug 1, 22; wid; c Christiane (Wiese), Cornelia & Stefanie (Hailperin). *Educ:* Univ Hamburg, Ger, Vordipl chem, 49; dipl chem, 52; Univ Gottingen, Ger, Dr rer nat, 55. *Honors & Awards:* Cert Merit, Am Chem Soc, 67, Separation Sci & Technol Award, 87; Kurt Wohl Mem Lectr, Univ Del, 75; AT&T Found Award for Excellence in Instr Eng Students, Am Soc Eng Educ, 85. *Prof Exp:* Res asst, Max Planck Inst Phys Chem, Gottingen, Ger, 51-56, Mass Inst Technol, Cambridge, Mass, 54 & Calif Inst Technol, Pasadena, Calif, 56-58; supvr & sr staff res chemist, Shell Develop Co, Emeryville, Calif, & Houston, Tex, 58-59. *Concurrent Pos:* Vis scientist, Max Planck Inst Phys Chem, Gottingen, Ger, 58; lectr, Univ Calif, Berkeley, 62-63 & Am Inst Chem Engrs Today Ser, 82-; chmn, Gordon Res Conf Ion Exchange, 67; vis prof & lectr, Univ Tex, Austin, Univ Houston & Rice Univ, Houston, Tex, 80; founder & ed-in-chief, Reactive Polymers, 81-; fac mem, Sch Artificial Membranes, Warsaw, Coun Mutual Econ Assistance, Warsaw, 83- & Pa State Environ Eng Prog, 84-90; consult, Exxon Chem, Duracell Int, Raychem, 84-; fac consult, Pa State Instrnl Develop Prog, 85-86; vis prof, East China Univ Chem Technol, Shanghai, People's Repub China, 87. *Mem:* Fel Am Inst Chemists; fel Am Inst Chem Engrs; Int Membrane Soc. *Res:* Dynamics of multivariable systems; nonlinear wave propagation; reaction kinetics; ion exchange; nonlinear chromatography. *Mailing Add:* Dept Chem Eng Pa State Univ University Park PA 16802

HELFGOTT, CECIL, PHYSICAL CHEMISTRY, POLYMER CHEMISTRY. *Current Pos:* SR SCIENTIST, CHAMPION INT, 84- *Personal Data:* b Brooklyn, NY, Nov 29, 26; m 51; c 2. *Educ:* Brooklyn Col, BA, 49; Rutgers Univ, New Brunswick, PhD(phys chem), 68. *Prof Exp:* Res chemist, Am Cyanamid Co, 54-62 & Colgate Palmolive Co, 62-63; res asst, Rutgers Univ, 63-66; sr res chemist, Celanese Res Co, 66-70; sr res chemist, St Regis Paper Co, 70-77; sr staff chemist, 77-79, group leader, 79-83. *Mem:* Sigma Xi; Am Chem Soc; Tech Asn Pulp & Paper Indust. *Res:* Desalination membranes; polyelectrolytes; fibers; films; textile finishes; converted products, paper/plastics; surfactants. *Mailing Add:* 35 Eberling Dr New City NY 10956

HELFMAN, HOWARD N, mechanical engineering, for more information see previous edition

HELFRICH, CHARLES THOMAS, PALEONTOLOGY, STRATIGRAPHY. *Current Pos:* asst prof geol, 71-74, ASSOC PROF GEOL, EASTERN KY UNIV, 74- *Personal Data:* b Dallastown, Pa, Jan 25, 32; m 59; c 6. *Educ:* St Charles Sem, BA, 54; Villanova Univ, MS, 67; Va Polytech Inst & State Univ, PhD(geol), 72. *Prof Exp:* Teacher, York City Sch Dist, 57-67. *Mem:* Geol Soc Am. *Res:* Mid-Paleozoic conodont biostratigraphy of North America. *Mailing Add:* Geol Eastern Ky Univ 521 Lancaster Ave Richmond KY 40475-3100

HELFRICH, PHILIP, GEN MARINE SCIENCES, RESEARCH ADMINISTRATION. *Current Pos:* assoc dean, Res Training & Spec Progs, 76-80 DIV, MARINE BIOL, UNIV HAWAII, 80-, PROF ZOOL, 86- *Personal Data:* b San Francisco, Calif, June 22, 27; m 56; c 4. *Educ:* Univ Santa Clara, BS, 51; Univ Hawaii, PhD(zool), 58. *Prof Exp:* Asst marine biologist, Hawaii Inst Marine Biol, Univ Hawaii, 58-63, from asst dir to actg dir, 63-64, assoc marine biologist, 64-70, head, Aquacult Prog, 70-72; dir, Int Ctr Living Aquatic Res Mgt, 74-76. *Concurrent Pos:* Mem fac zool, 61-; consult, SPac Comn, 62; mem, French Polynesia Inst Med Res, 64-68; mem, US-Japan Coop Res Prog Marine Toxins, 66-69; bd dirs, Micronesia Found, 70-71; dir, Eniwetok Marine Biol Lab, Mid-Pac Marine Lab, Marshall Islands, 70-75, 80-86; mem, Christmas Island Artemia Res, 71; SSC, West Pac Fish Mgt Coun, 77-81, Gov's Marine Affairs Adv Coun, Hawaii, 77-, Aquacult Develop Coun, Hawaii; aquacult adv, Govt Thailand, 78-; coun chmn, Consortium Int Fisheries & Agr Develop, 81-; bd dir, Ctr Trop & Subtrop Aquacult, 87- *Mem:* AAAS; Ecol Soc Am; World Aquacult Soc. *Res:* Marine ecology; fisheries; aquaculture. *Mailing Add:* 45-274 Kokokahi Pl Kaneohe HI 96744

HELGASON, SIGURDUR, MATHEMATICS. *Current Pos:* from asst prof to assoc prof, 59-65, PROF MATH, MASS INST TECHNOL, 65- *Personal Data:* b Akureyri, Iceland, Sept 30, 27; m 57, Artie Gianopulos; c Thor H & Anna L. *Educ:* Univ Iceland, BS, 46; Univ Copenhagen, MS, 52; Princeton Univ, PhD, 54. *Hon Degrees:* Dr, Univ Iceland, 86, Univ Copenhagen, 88 & Uppsala Univ, 96. *Honors & Awards:* Steele Prize, Am Math Soc, 88; Major Knights Cross of Icelandic Falcon, 91. *Prof Exp:* Moore instr math, Mass Inst Technol, 54-56; Louis Block lectr, Univ Chicago, 57-59. *Concurrent Pos:* Vis asst prof, Columbia Univ, 59-60; mem, Inst Advan Study, 64-66, 74-75 & 83-84. *Mem:* Am Math Soc; Am Acad Arts & Sci; Royal Danish Acad Sci & Lett; Icelandic Acad Sci. *Res:* Geometric analysis on Lie groups and coset spaces; Fourier analysis and invariant differential operators. *Mailing Add:* Dept Math Mass Inst Technol Cambridge MA 02139. *Fax:* 617-253-4358; *E-Mail:* helgason@mit.edu

HELGESEN, ROBERT GORDON, INSECT ECOLOGY. *Current Pos:* DEAN, FOOD & NATURAL RESOURCES, UNIV MASS, 89- *Personal Data:* b Cleveland, Ohio, Oct 9, 42; m 64. *Educ:* Univ Mich, BS, 65; NDak State Univ, MS, 67; Mich State Univ, PhD(entom), 69. *Prof Exp:* Prof entom, Cornell Univ, 69-80; dept head entom, Kans State Univ, 80-89. *Mem:* AAAS; Entom Soc Am; Sigma Xi. *Res:* Insect ecology; insect pest management. *Mailing Add:* Natural Resources Univ Mass Amherst MA 01003-0002

HELGESON, HAROLD CHARLES, ORGANIC & INORGANIC REACTIONS IN GEOCHEMICAL PROCESSES. *Current Pos:* PROF GEOCHEM, UNIV CALIF, BERKELEY, 70- *Personal Data:* b Minneapolis, Minn, Nov 13, 31; m 56, 78, 86, France Damon; c Christopher, Kimberley & Broghan. *Educ:* Mich State Univ, BS, 53; Harvard Univ, PhD(geol), 62. *Honors & Awards:* Goldschmidt Medal Distinguished Res, Geochem Soc, 88. *Prof Exp:* Geologist, Tech Mine Consult Ltd, Can, 53-54 & Anglo Am Corp, SAfrica, 56-59; consult, BC & Alaska, 59; chemist, Shell Develop Co, Tex, 62-63, res chemist, 63-65; from asst prof to assoc prof geol, Northwestern Univ, 65-70. *Concurrent Pos:* Miller res prof, Univ Calif, Berkeley, 74-75; Guggenheim fel, 77-78. *Mem:* Am Chem Soc; Geochem Soc; fel Geol Soc Am; fel Mineral Soc Am; Europ Asn Geochem; Int Asn Geochem & Cosmochem; fel Royal Soc Chem. *Res:* High temperature solution chemistry; chemical thermodynamics; phase equilibria; inorganic, organic and biogeochemistry; application of the principles of physical chemistry and mathematics to geologic problems; chemical petrology; chemical kinetics and mass transfer in geochemical processes. *Mailing Add:* Dept Geol & Geophys Univ Calif Berkeley CA 94720

HELGESON, JOHN PAUL, PLANT PHYSIOLOGY. *Current Pos:* from asst prof to assoc prof plant, 66-75, PROF PLANT PATH & BOT, UNIV WIS-MADISON, 75-, RES PLANT PHYSIOLOGIST, PIONEERING RES LAB, AGR RES SERV, 66- *Personal Data:* b Barberton, Ohio, July 25, 35; m 57; c 3. *Educ:* Oberlin Col, AB, 57; Univ Wis, PhD(bot), 64. *Prof Exp:* NSF fel org chem, 64-66. *Concurrent Pos:* Prog mgr biol stress, USDA competitive grants, 82-83; vis scientist, Cellular Biol Lab, CNRA, Versailles, France, 85-86. *Mem:* AAAS; Am Phytopath; Am Soc Plant Physiol; Bot Soc Am. *Res:* Growth and development in plants; genetic modification of plants to obtain novel disease resistances; physiology of host-parasite interactions; use of plant tissue cultures for metabolic and host-parasite studies and to obtain modified crop plants. *Mailing Add:* Plant Path 284 Russell Lab Univ Wis 1630 Linden Dr Madison WI 53706-1520

HELIN, ELEANOR KAY, PLANETARY SCIENCE, GEOLOGY. *Current Pos:* Res asst meteorite statist, Jet Propulsion Lab, Calif Inst Technol, 60-61 & meteorite anal, 61-68, assoc scientist asteroid res & surv, 69-76, sr scientist asteroid surv & planetary sci, 76-79, mem prof staff, 79-80, MEM TECH STAFF, JET PROPULSION LAB, CALIF INST TECHNOL, 80- *Personal Data:* b Pasadena, Calif; c 1. *Mem:* Am Astron Soc; Int Astron Union; Meteoritical Soc. *Res:* Systematic surveys for planet-crossing asteroids; origin and history of earth-approaching asteroids; impact history of terrestrial planets; meteoritics. *Mailing Add:* Jet Propulsion Lab Calif Inst Technol 4800 Oak Grove Dr 183-501 Pasadena CA 91109

HELINSKI, DONALD RAYMOND, BIOCHEMISTRY, GENETICS. *Current Pos:* assoc prof, Univ Calif, San Diego, 65-70, chmn, 79-81, dir, Ctr Molecular Genetics, 84-85, PROF, DEPT BIOL, UNIV CALIF, SAN DIEGO, 70-, ASSOC DEAN NAT SCI, 94- *Personal Data:* b Baltimore, Md, July 7, 33; m 62, Patricia G Doherty; c Matthew & Maureen. *Educ:* Univ Md, BS, 54, MS, 56; Case Western Res Univ, PhD(biochem), 60. *Prof Exp:* USPHS fel biochem genetics, Stanford Univ, 60-62; asst prof, Dept Biol, Princeton Univ, 62-65. *Concurrent Pos:* USPHS career develop award, 68-73; mem, Recombinant DNA Adv Comt, NIH, 75-78; Guggenheim fel, 81-82; mem bd dirs, Coun Res Planning Biol Sci, 82-88; mem, Microbiol Physiol & Genetics Study Sect 2, Dept Health & Human Serv, NIH, 83-87; mem adv comt, Frederick Cancer Res Facil, 89-, Nat Cancer Inst-Frederick Cancer Res & Develop Ctr, 90-; actg dir, Systemwide Biotechnol Res & Educ Prog, Univ Calif, 90- *Mem:* Nat Acad Sci; Am Soc Biol Chem; fel AAAS; Genetics Soc Am; Am Soc Microbiol; Am Acad Arts & Sci. *Res:* Plasmids; DNA replication. *Mailing Add:* Ctr Molecular Genetics Univ Calif 9500 Gilman Dr La Jolla CA 92093

HELKE, CINDA JANE, NEUROPHARMACOLOGY, AUTONOMIC REGULATION. *Current Pos:* from asst prof to assoc prof, 80-88, PROF, UNIFORMED SERV UNIV HEALTH SCI, 88-, DIR NEUROSCI PROG, 93- *Personal Data:* b Waterloo, Iowa, Feb 27, 51; m 74, Joel Helkef. *Educ:* Creighton Univ, BS, 74; Georgetown Univ, PhD(pharmacol), 78. *Honors & Awards:* Deane N Calvert Award, Am Soc Pharmacol & Exp Therapeut, 78. *Prof Exp:* Staff fel neurosci, NIMH, NIH, 78-80. *Concurrent Pos:* Neurol BII Study Sect, NIH, 87-91; prin investr, NIH grants, 81- *Mem:* Soc Neurosci; Asn Women Sci; AAAS; Am Pharmacol & Exp Therapeut; Int Brain Res Orgn. *Res:* Using cellular and system neuropharmacologic and neuroanatomic approaches, aspects of chemical neurotransmission (transmitter localization and coexistence, plasticity in the adult animal, et cetera) in autonomic control systems. *Mailing Add:* Dept Pharmacol Uniformed Serv Univ Health Sci Bethesda MD 20814-4799. *Fax:* 301-295-3220; *E-Mail:* helke@usuhsb.usuhs.mil

HELLACK, JENNA JO, ZOOLOGY. *Current Pos:* PROF BIOL, CENT STATE UNIV, 77- *Personal Data:* b Ardmore, Okla, Apr 6, 45. *Educ:* ECent Univ, BS, 68; Okla State Univ, MS, 69, PhD(zool), 75. *Prof Exp:* Vis prof zool, Univ Okla, 75-76. *Mem:* Genetics Soc Am. *Res:* Evolutionary genetics; Drosophila population genetics. *Mailing Add:* Biol Univ Cent Okla 100 N University Dr Edmond OK 73034-5209

HELLE, JOHN HAROLD (JACK), FISH BIOLOGY. *Current Pos:* res biologist, Nat Oceanic & Atmospheric Admin, 70-95, PROG MGR OCEAN CARRYING CAPACITY RES, ALASKA FISHERIES SCI CTR, US DEPT COM, NAT MARINE FISHERIES SERV, 96- *Personal Data:* b Williston, NDak, Apr 26, 35; m 59, Marilyn Matthews; c Jeanmarie & Joanna. *Educ:* Univ Idaho, BS, 58, MS, 61; Ore State Univ, PhD(fisheries sci), 79. *Prof Exp:* Res biologist, Bur Com Fish, US Fish & Wildlife Serv, 60-70. *Concurrent Pos:* Hon fel, Dept Natural Hist, Univ Aberdeen, Scotland, 64. *Mem:* Am Inst Fishery Res Biologists (pres, 90-92); Am Fisheries Soc; AAAS; Sigma Xi. *Res:* Influence of environment and heredity on age and size at maturity; growth and survival of pacific salmon; genetic considerations in hatchery and wild populations; stock identification; effect of climate change on abundance of salmon in North Pacific Ocean. *Mailing Add:* Auke Bay Lab 11305 Glacier Hwy Juneau AK 99801

HELLEBUST, JOHAN ARNVID, ALGOLOGY. *Current Pos:* assoc prof, 69-73, PROF BOT, UNIV TORONTO, 73-, CHMN, 87- *Personal Data:* b Tysfjord, Norway, Mar 7, 33; Can citizen; m 58; c 3. *Educ:* Univ Toronto, BA, 58, MA, 59, PhD(plant physiol), 62. *Prof Exp:* Ford Found fel marine biol, Woods Hole Oceanog Inst, 62-63, asst scientist, 63-64; asst prof, Harvard Univ, 64-69. *Concurrent Pos:* Ed, J Phycol, 84-87. *Mem:* Am Soc Plant Physiol; Can Soc Plant Physiol; Phycol Soc Am. *Res:* Physiology, biochemistry and ecology of algae; heterotrophy, transport systems and osmoregulation. *Mailing Add:* Dept Bot Univ Toronto Toronto ON M5S 3B2 Can

HELLEINER, CHRISTOPHER WALTER, BIOCHEMISTRY. *Current Pos:* asst prof med biophys, Univ Toronto, 57-63, from asst prof to assoc prof, 63-65, head dept, 65-79, PROF BIOCHEM, DALHOUSIE UNIV, 65- *Personal Data:* b Vienna, Austria, Mar 21, 30; Can citizen; m 55; c 2. *Educ:* Univ Toronto, BA, 52, PhD(biochem), 55. *Prof Exp:* Nat Res Coun Can fel, Univ Oxford, 55-57. *Concurrent Pos:* Asst scientist, Ont Cancer Inst, Toronto, 57-63; Med Res Coun Can vis scientist award, Univ Glasgow, 69-70. *Mem:* Can Biochem Soc. *Res:* DNA chemistry and repair. *Mailing Add:* Dept Biochem Dalhousie Univ Halifax NS B3H 4H7 Can

HELLEMS, HARPER KEITH, CARDIOLOGY. *Current Pos:* PROF MED & CHMN DEPT, SCH MED, UNIV MISS, 65- *Personal Data:* b Sinks Grove, WVa, Mar 16, 20; m 73; c 3. *Educ:* Univ Va, MD, 43; Am Bd Internal Med, dipl, 52. *Prof Exp:* Intern, Montreal Gen Hosp, 44-45; asst med, Peter Bent Brigham Hosp, 46-48, sr asst resident, 49-50; from asst prof to prof, Col Med, Wayne State Univ, 50-60; prof med & dir div cardiovasc dis, NJ Col Med & Dent, 60-65. *Concurrent Pos:* Res fel med, Harvard Med Sch, 46-48, teaching fel, 49-50; asst resident, West Roxbury Vet Admin Hosp, 48-49; attend physician & dir med outpatient dept, City Detroit Receiving Hosp, 50-; consult, Dearborn Vet Admin Hosp, Vet Admin Regional Off, Detroit, 50- & Grace Hosp, 51; mem courtesy staff, Harper Hosp, 55, dir cardiovasc serv, Children's Hosp, Mich, 58; dir, White Cardiopulmonary Inst & attend physician, Berthold S Pollak Hosp Chest Dis, 60-65; mem cardiovasc study sect, NIH, 62-66; physician-in-chief, Med Ctr, Univ Miss, 65-; fel coun clin cardiol, Am Heart Asn. *Mem:* Am Soc Clin Invest; Cent Soc Clin Res; Am Asn Physicians; Am Clin & Climatol Soc; fel Am Col Cardiol. *Res:* Cardiovascular diseases, especially hemodynamics. *Mailing Add:* Dept Med Univ Miss Med Ctr 2500 N State St Jackson MS 39216-4505

HELLENTHAL, RONALD ALLEN, SYSTEMATICS, AQUATIC ECOLOGY. *Current Pos:* from vis asst prof to asst prof, 77-84, ASSOC PROF BIOL, DEPT BIOL SCI, UNIV NOTRE DAME, 84-, GILLEN DIR, ENVIRON RES CTR, 88- *Personal Data:* b Tucson, Ariz, June 9, 45; m 76. *Educ:* Los Angeles Valley Col, AA, 65; Calif State Univ, Northridge, BA, 67; Univ Minn, PhD(entom), 77. *Concurrent Pos:* Environ adv comt, Northern States Power Co, 70-71; Mem, Higher Educ Comt, Minn Educ Comput Consortium, 75-77; res assoc, Dept Entom, Fish & Wildlife, Univ Minn, St Paul, 78-80; dir, Biocomput Facil, Univ Notre Dame, 80- *Mem:* Sigma Xi; Entom Soc Am; NAm Benthological Soc; Am Soc Limnol & Oceanog; Soc Syst Zool; Water Pollution Control Fedn. *Res:* Host-parasite relationships; systematics and ecology of aquatic insects; assessment of environmental data; computerized systems for the automation of taxonomic and environmental data analyses. *Mailing Add:* PO Box 369 Univ Notre Dame Notre Dame IN 46556-0369

HELLER, ABRAHAM, MENTAL HEALTH, FORENSIC PSYCHIATRY. *Current Pos:* prof, 77-90, vchmn, 80-90, EMER PROF, DEPT PSYCHIAT & COMMUNITY MED, SCH MED, WRIGHT STATE UNIV, 90- *Personal Data:* b Calremont, NH, Mar 17, 17; m 57; c 1. *Educ:* Brandeis Univ, BA, 53; Boston Univ, MD, 57. *Prof Exp:* Intern, Gen Rose Mem Hosp, Denver, 57-58; resident psychiat, Med Ctr, Univ Colo, 58-61; from asst to assoc dir & chief in patient serv, Community Ment Health, Psychiat Serv, Denver Gen Hosp, 61-73; chief psychiat & dir, Community Ment Health, Newport Hosp, RI, 73-77. *Concurrent Pos:* Assoc clin prof, Sch Med, Brown Univ, 73-77. *Mem:* Fel Am Psychiat Asn; fel Am Orthopsychiat Asn; fel Am Asn Social Psychiat. *Res:* Forensic psychiatry studies on the right to treatment of forensic patients in psychiatric hospitals; impact of unemployment on mental and physical health. *Mailing Add:* Wright State Univ Dayton OH 45401

HELLER, ADAM, CHEMISTRY. *Current Pos:* ERNEST COCKRELL SR CHAIR & PROF CHEM ENG, CHEM & MAT SCI, UNIV TEX, AUSTIN, 88- *Personal Data:* b Cluj, Romania, June 25, 33; US citizen; m 56, Elana Grawshana; c Ephraim & Jonathan. *Educ:* Hebrew Univ, Jerusalem, Israel, MSc, 57, PhD, 61. *Hon Degrees:* Dr, Uppsala Univ, Swed, 91. *Honors & Awards:* Battery Res Award, Electrochem Soc, 78, David C Grahame Award, 88; Regents lectr, Univ Calif Los Angeles, 82, 84; Robert A Welch lectr, 86;

Raymond & Beverly Sackler Distinguished lectr, Tel Aviv Univ, 87; Vittorio de Nora Gold Medal, 88; Berkeley lectr Chem, Gly, 91; Chem Mat (DuPont) Award, Am Chem Soc, 94; Faraday Medal, Royal Chem Soc (UK), 96. *Prof Exp:* Mem staff, Weizman Inst, 55-56; French govt scholar, Univ Paris, 57-58; sr scientist, Res Ctr, Israel Atomic Energy Comn, 59-62; assoc, Univ Calif, Berkeley, 62-63; mem tech staff, Bell Labs, 63-64; res mgr explor res, GTE Labs, 64-75; mem tech staff, AT&T Bell Labs, 75-77, head, Electronics Mat Res Dept, 77-88. *Concurrent Pos:* Mem rev comt, Chem & Mat Res Div, Lawrence Berkeley Labs; mem adv bd, Solar Energy Res Inst; Case Centennial scholar, 80; guest prof, Col France, 82; div ed, J Electrochem Soc; bd gov, Ben Gurion Univ, Israel; prof engr, State Tex. *Mem:* Am Chem Soc; Am Phys Soc; Int Soc Electrochem; fel Electrochem Soc; fel AAAS. *Res:* Amperometric biosensors based on electrical connection of enzyme redox centers to electrodes and on photoelectrochemistry; photocatalytically self cleaning surfaces; electrical micro-engineering of enzymes; author of 200 publications in the fields; lithium batteries; liquid lasers; photoelectrochemical solar cells; biosensors; granted 40 patents. *Mailing Add:* Dept Chem Eng Univ Tex Austin TX 78712-1062. Fax: 512-471-8799; E-Mail: heller@che.utexas.edu

HELLER, AGNES S, ENGINEERING, STATISTICS. *Current Pos:* REALTOR, 89- *Personal Data:* b Hungary; US citizen; c 2. *Educ:* City Col NY, BBA, 54; Columbia Univ, MA, 63. *Prof Exp:* Res assoc eng, Columbia Univ, 57-67; instr math statist, Va Polytech Inst & State Univ, 67-74; prin engr statist & probabilistic methods, Babcock & Wilcox Co, 75-85; sr analyst, Eval Res Corp, 85-89. *Concurrent Pos:* Mem, Comt Pressure Vessel Res Coun, 78. *Mem:* Am Nuclear Soc; Sigma Xi. *Res:* Probabilistic methods and statistical analyses in energy related systems. *Mailing Add:* 4330 McDowell Ct Blacksburg VA 24060

HELLER, ALEX, MATHEMATICS. *Current Pos:* prof, 65-71, DISTINGUISHED PROF MATH, GRAD SCH, CITY UNIV NEW YORK, 71- *Personal Data:* b New York, NY, July 9, 25; m 56; c 1. *Educ:* Columbia Univ, AB, 47, PhD(math), 50. *Prof Exp:* Lectr math, Columbia Univ, 47-48, Nat Res Coun fel, 50-51; Benjamin Pierce instr, Harvard Univ, 52-54; from asst prof to prof, Univ Ill, 54-65. *Concurrent Pos:* Sloan Found fel, Univ Ill, 55-59; mem, Div Math Sci, Nat Acad Sci-Nat Res Coun, 65-67; managing ed, J Pure & Appl Algebra, 71-; assoc prof, Univ Paris VII, 79; vis prof, Milan, Italy, 84-95. *Mem:* Am Math Soc. *Res:* Algebraic topology; homological algebra; category theory; recursion theory. *Mailing Add:* City Univ New York Grad Sch 33 W 42nd St New York NY 10036-8099

HELLER, ALFRED, PHARMACOLOGY. *Current Pos:* Res assoc, 56-60, from asst prof to assoc prof, 60-73, chmn dept, 73-88, PROF PHARMACOL & PHYSIOL SCI, UNIV CHICAGO, 73- *Personal Data:* b Chicago, Ill, July 23, 30; m 56. *Educ:* Univ Ill, BS, 52; Univ Chicago, PhD(pharmacol), 56, MD, 60. *Concurrent Pos:* Mem, Nat Bd Med Examiners Pharmacol; nat adv med sci coun, NIH, 79- *Mem:* AAAS; Am Soc Pharmacol & Exp Therapeut; Am Soc Neurochem. *Res:* Neuropharmacology; neurochemical consequences of central nervous system lesions. *Mailing Add:* Dept Pharmacol & Physiol Sci Univ Chicago Abbott Hall 947 E 58th St Chicago IL 60637-1431. Fax: 773-702-3513

HELLER, BARBARA RUTH, ESTIMATION & STATISTICAL TESTS, STEREOLOGY. *Current Pos:* ASSOC PROF STATIST, PROBABILITY & MATH, ILL INST TECHNOL, 80- *Personal Data:* b Milwaukee, Wis, May 15, 31; m 56; c 1. *Educ:* Roosevelt Univ, BS, 53; Univ Chicago, MS, 65, PhD(statist), 79. *Mem:* Inst Math Statist; Am Statist Asn; Soc Indust & Appl Math; Am Math Soc; NY Acad Sci; Sigma Xi. *Res:* Characterization of probability distributions, goodness-of-fit test for the negative binomial distribution; use of the computer algebra program Macsyma for problems in statistics; symbolic manipulation programs on the computer; problems in stereology, cell counting and measuring. *Mailing Add:* Dept Math Ill Inst Technol Chicago IL 60616

HELLER, CHARLES O(TA), STRUCTURAL MECHANICS, COMPUTER SCIENCE. *Current Pos:* dir, Md Indust Partnerships, 86-89, DIR, DINGMAN CTR ENTREPRENEURSHIP, UNIV MD, 89- *Personal Data:* b Prague, Czech, Jan 25, 36; US citizen; m 59; c 1. *Educ:* Okla State Univ, BS, 59, MS, 60; Cath Univ Am, PhD(struct mech), 68. *Prof Exp:* Engr, Missiles & Space Systs Div, Douglas Aircraft Co, 60-62; mem tech staff, Bell Tel Labs, 62-63; assoc prof aerospace eng, US Naval Acad, 63-68; vpres, Bay Tech Assocs Inc, 68-69; pres, Cadcom Inc, 69-79, exec dir, Cadcom Div, 79-81, vpres corp develop, Mantech Int Corp, 82-83; pres, Intercad Corp, 84-86. *Concurrent Pos:* Lectr, Univ Calif, Los Angeles, 61-62; consult, US Naval Ship Res & Develop Lab, 64-66, Lockheed Electronics Co, 66-67, Hydrodyn Develop Corp, 66-68 & Head Ski Co, 67-68; partic & lectr, Nat Acad Sci Exchange Prog, 70. *Mem:* Am Soc Civil Engrs; Asn Comput Mach; Am Inst Aeronaut & Astronaut; Am Mgt Asn. *Res:* Computer-aided design of aerospace and marine vehicles; structural analysis of plates and shells; finite elements techniques; use of interactive time-shared computing in engineering education; computer graphics; applications in engineering design; entrepreneurship. *Mailing Add:* 1211 Hillcrest Rd Arnold MD 21012

HELLER, EDWARD LINCOLN, MECHANICAL ENGINEERING, MINING ENGINEERING. *Current Pos:* RETIRED. *Personal Data:* b Newark, NJ, Feb 12, 12; m 46, Irene Farrar; c Peter & Gregory. *Educ:* Lehigh Univ, BS, 34; Harvard Univ, MBA, 39. *Prof Exp:* Mining engr, Empire Zinc Co, 34-38; transp eng, Stand Oil Co, 39-41; chief test sect, QM Res & Develop, US Army, 41-42; chief qual control, QM Inspection Serv, 43-46; chief engr, McLaughlin Carr Assoc, 46-47; staff engr nuclear, Joint Cong Comt Atomic Energy, US Cong, 47-55; chief engr nuclear proj, H K Ferguson Div Morrison Knudsen, 56-59; regional mgr new prod, Gen Atomic Co, 59-75; consult energy, Res & Develop Div Gulf Oil Corp, 75-78; asst inspector gen, Dept Energy, US Govt, 78-82. *Concurrent Pos:* Mem, Ohio State Adv Bd Atomic Energy, 57-58, Atomic Energy Panel; Soc Naval Archit & Marine Eng, 64-65; res work, Eng & Indust Div, Smithsonian Mus, Washington DC, 83-97. *Mem:* Am Soc Mech Eng; Am Nuclear Soc; Marine Tech Soc. *Res:* Uranium ore deposits, process heat reactors, synthetic fuels from coal and oil shale; fusion reactors for electric power production, solar heat and power production, geothermal heat sources; history of hydro electric plants 1880's to WWI; history of stone blast furnaces. *Mailing Add:* 3517 Hamlet Pl Chevy Chase MD 20815

HELLER, ERIC JOHNSON, CHEMICAL PHYSICS, SEMICLASSICAL APPROXIMATIONS. *Current Pos:* PROF PHYSICS, HARVARD UNIV, 93- *Personal Data:* b Washington, DC, Jan 10, 46; m 79, Sharl; c Kyaa, Eric & Cassandra. *Educ:* Univ Minn, Minneapolis, BA, 68; Harvard Univ, PhD(chem physics), 73. *Prof Exp:* Res assoc chem physics, James Franck Inst, Univ Chicago, 73-75; from asst prof to prof chem, Univ Calif, Los Angeles, 75-84; prof physics, Dept Chem, Univ Wash, 84-94. *Concurrent Pos:* Sr scientist & dir, Inst Theoret Atomic & Molecular Physics, Harvard-Smithsonian Ctr Astrophys; Guggenheim fel, 92. *Mem:* Fel AAAS; fel Am Phys Soc; Am Chem Soc; Int Acad Quantum Molecular Sci. *Res:* Semiclassical theory of quantum mechanics with applications to atoms and molecules, mesoscopic systems and chaos; theoretical molecular spectroscopy; radiationless transitions; quantum mechanics of chaotic systems; scattering theory. *Mailing Add:* Dept Physics Harvard Univ Cambridge MA 02138. E-Mail: heller@physics.harvard.edu

HELLER, HORACE CRAIG, BIOLOGY, PHYSIOLOGY & NEUROPHYSIOLOGY. *Current Pos:* from asst prof to assoc prof, 72-83, Bing prof human biol, 86-93, PROF, STANFORD UNIV, 83-, LORRY LOKEY BUS WIRE PROF, 93- *Personal Data:* b Philadelphia, Pa, Aug 5, 43; m 70, Renu Anand; c Meer D. *Educ:* Ursinus Col, BS, 65; Yale Univ, MPhil, 67, PhD(biol), 70. *Prof Exp:* Fel physiol, Scripps Inst Oceanog, 70-72. *Mem:* Am Physiol Soc; Soc Res Biol Rhythms; Sleep Res Soc. *Res:* Neurobiology of sleep; circadian rhythms; hibernation; regulation of body temperature. *Mailing Add:* Dept Biol Sci Stanford Univ Stanford CA 94305-5020. Fax: 650-725-5356; E-Mail: ms.hch.@forsythe.stanford.edu

HELLER, IRVING HENRY, MEDICINE, NEUROLOGY. *Current Pos:* RETIRED. *Personal Data:* b Montreal, PQ, Mar 26, 26; m 48; c 2. *Educ:* McGill Univ, BS, 46, MD, CM, 50, MS, 54, PhD(neurochem), 62. *Prof Exp:* Asst prof neurol, McGill Univ, 60-72, assoc prof, 72-81, prof neurol & neurosurg, 81-95. *Concurrent Pos:* Neurologist, Montreal Neurol Hosp; sr neurologist, Royal Victoria Hosp; consult neurologist, Douglas Hosp & Queen Elizabeth Hosp. *Mem:* Am Acad Neurol; Can Neurol Soc. *Res:* Migraine. *Mailing Add:* Dept Neurol-Neurosurg Montreal Neurol Hosp 3801 University St Montreal PQ H3A 2B4 Can

HELLER, JACK, COMPUTER SCIENCE. *Current Pos:* PROF COMPUT SCI, STATE UNIV NY, STONY BROOK, 69- *Personal Data:* b US, Sept 11, 22; m 46; c 4. *Educ:* Polytech Inst Brooklyn, BA, 44, MA, 46, PhD(physics), 50. *Prof Exp:* Asst, Polytech Inst Brooklyn, 44-46; stress analyst, Repub Aviation Corp, 46; instr math, Newark Col Eng, 46-50; asst, Princeton Univ, 52; res scientist, Inst Math Sci, NY Univ, 53-61, assoc prof math, 61-64, prof math, dir Heights Acad Comput Facil & dir Inst Comput Res in Humanities, 65-69. *Mem:* Asn Comput Mach. *Res:* Applied mathematics; information retrieval; data base management systems; software systems. *Mailing Add:* Dept Comput Sci State Univ NY Stony Brook NY 11794

HELLER, JOHN HERBERT, medical physics, anthropology; deceased, see previous edition for last biography

HELLER, JOHN PHILIP, PHYSICS. *Current Pos:* SR SCIENTIST, PETROL RECOVERY RES CTR, NMEX TECH, 79- *Personal Data:* b Brooklyn, NY, Apr 15, 23; m 46; c 3. *Educ:* Queens Col, NY, BS, 44; Iowa State Univ, PhD(physics), 53. *Honors & Awards:* Enhanced Oil Recovery Pioneer, Soc Petrol Engrs. *Prof Exp:* Asst microwaves, Columbia Radiation Lab, 44; instr physics, Iowa State Univ, 50-53; sr res physicist, Socony-Mobil Oil Co, 53-61, res assoc, Field Res Lab, Mobil Res & Develop Corp, 61-79. *Mem:* Am Phys Soc; Sigma Xi; Soc Petrol Engrs; AAAS; Am Chem Soc; Am Inst Chem Engrs. *Res:* Spectroscopy; optics; low speed hydrodynamics and flow in porous media; instrumentation; dispersion and drying in porous media; computer control; petroleum production processes, especially enhanced oil recovery by carbon dioxide flooding; effects of both viscous and gravitationally induced frontal instabilities, and of permeability variability on displacement patterns in oil reservoirs and aquifers. *Mailing Add:* 509 NW Mesa Pl Socorro NM 87801-4492

HELLER, JORGE, ORGANIC & POLYMER CHEMISTRY, CONTROLLED DRUG RELEASE. *Current Pos:* PRIN SCIENTIST, ADVAN POLYMER SYSTS, 93- *Personal Data:* b Liberec, Czech, Aug 17, 27; m 55, 78; c Stephen E & David E. *Educ:* Univ Calif, BS, 52; Univ Wash, PhD(org chem), 57. *Honors & Awards:* Clemson Award, 90; Distinguished Serv Award, Controlled Release Soc. *Prof Exp:* Res chemist, Union Carbide Plastics Co, 57-59; sr polymer chemist, Stanford Res Inst, 59-67, mgr polymer chem dept, 67-70, dir phys sci, Alza Res, 70-74, dir polymer sci, 74-93. *Concurrent Pos:* Adj prof pharm, Univ Calif, San Francisco, 84-; adj prof, Univ Utah; affil prof, Univ Wash; docent abo akaden Finland. *Mem:* Fel Biomat Soc; Am Chem Soc; fel Am Asn Pharmaceut Scientists; Controlled Release Soc. *Res:* Synthesis of monomers and polymers; biomedical application of polymers; controlled drug release. *Mailing Add:* Advan Polymer Systs 3696 Haven Ave Redwood City CA 94063. Fax: 650-368-4470

HELLER, KENNETH JEFFREY, EXPERIMENTAL HIGH ENERGY PHYSICS. *Current Pos:* from asst prof to assoc prof, 78-86, PROF PHYSICS, UNIV MINN, 86- *Personal Data:* b Port of Spain, Trinidad, Nov 7, 43; m 72, Patricia Autry. *Educ:* Univ Calif, BA, 65; Univ Wash, PhD(physics), 73. *Prof Exp:* Res assoc & instr, Univ Mich, 72-78. *Concurrent Pos:* Fel, Univ Mich, 72-75; mem bd trustees, Univs Res Asn, 85-88; vis prof, Univ Utah, 85; prin investr, High Energy Physics, Univ Minn, 89- *Mem:* Am Phys Soc; Am Asn Physics Teachers. *Res:* High energy physics experiments; quark dynamics from strong interactions of hadrons, quark confinement from magnetic moments of baryons and their weak decay properties; muons from high energy interactions. *Mailing Add:* Sch Phys & Astron Univ Minn Minneapolis MN 55455

HELLER, LEON, NUCLEAR PHYSICS, FUNCTIONAL IMAGING OF THE BRAIN. *Current Pos:* Staff mem, 56-91, group leader, Medium Energy Physics Theory Group, 71-73, LAB ASSOC, BIOPHYS GROUP, LOS ALAMOS NAT LAB, 92- *Personal Data:* b New York, NY, Dec 16, 29; m 52, Rosalie Liebschutz; c Peter, Anthony & Jean. *Educ:* Brooklyn Col, BA, 51; Cornell Univ, PhD(physics), 57. *Concurrent Pos:* Vis asst prof, Case Inst Technol, 62-63; exchange scientist, AEC-UK Atomic Energy Authority, Harwell, 69-70; staff mem, Ctr Theoret Physics, Mass Inst Technol, 76-77; Fulbright sr scholar, Univ Adelaide, 85-86. *Mem:* Fel Am Phys Soc; AAAS. *Res:* Quark structure of hadrons; magnetoencephalography. *Mailing Add:* MS D454 Los Alamos Nat Lab Los Alamos NM 87545. *Fax:* 505-665-4507; *E-Mail:* heller@lawyer.lanl.gov

HELLER, LOIS JANE, MEDICAL PHYSIOLOGY. *Current Pos:* asst dean student affairs, 73-76, assoc prof, 72-89, PROF PHYSIOL, SCH MED, UNIV MINN, DULUTH, 89- *Personal Data:* b Detroit, Mich, Jan 4, 42; m 66, Robert; c John & Suzanne. *Educ:* Albion Col, BA, 64; Univ Mich, Ann Arbor, MS, 66; Univ Ill Med Ctr, Chicago, PhD(physiol), 70. *Prof Exp:* Asst prof physiol, Univ Ill Med Ctr, Chicago, 70-71. *Mem:* Am Physiol Soc; Sigma Xi; Am Heart Asn; Soc Exp Biol Med; Int Soc Heart Res. *Res:* Contractile properties and excitation processes in cardiac muscle and coronary vasculature as influenced by aging, hypertension and immediate hypersensitivity reactions. *Mailing Add:* Univ Minn Sch Med Med Sci Bldg Duluth MN 55812. *Fax:* 218-726-6356; *E-Mail:* lheller@d.umn.edu

HELLER, MARVIN W, PHYSICS. *Current Pos:* asst prof, 61-68, ASSOC PROF PHYSICS, COLO STATE UNIV, 68- *Personal Data:* b Grundy Center, Iowa, Oct 4, 26; m 53; c 3. *Educ:* Grinnell Col, BA, 51; Iowa State Univ, PhD(physics), 60. *Prof Exp:* Res assoc solid state physics, Iowa State Univ, 60-61. *Concurrent Pos:* Consult, Naval Res Lab, 69-71. *Mem:* Am Asn Physics Teachers. *Res:* Transport properties of semiconductors. *Mailing Add:* Dept Physics Colo State Univ Ft Collins CO 80523

HELLER, MELVIN S, MEDICINE, PSYCHIATRY. *Current Pos:* assoc prof, 63-67, CLIN PROF PSYCHIAT, SCH MED, TEMPLE UNIV, 67-, DIR DIV FORENSIC PSYCHIAT, 65- *Personal Data:* b Boston, Mass, Aug 11, 22; m 54; c 3. *Educ:* Tufts Univ, BS, 44, MS & MD, 48. *Prof Exp:* Intern surg, Beth Israel Hosp, 48-49; resident, Vet Admin Hosp, Newington, Conn, 49-50, resident psychiat, 50-51; staff psychiatrist, Fed Penitentiary, Ind, 51-53; resident psychiat, Sch Med, Yale Univ, 53-54; consult, Fed Bur Prisons, 58-59. *Concurrent Pos:* Fel, Child Study Ctr, Philadelphia, 54-56; lectr, Temple Univ, 57-, co-dir, Unit Law & Psychiat, 58-; dir psychiat, State Correctional Inst Philadelphia, 59-70; dir psychiat serv, Children's Aid Soc, 62-70; mem, Govr's Comn Comprehensive Ment Health Planning, Pa; mem, Nat Coun Juvenile Court Judges. *Mem:* Am Psychiat Asn; AMA. *Res:* Forensic psychiatry. *Mailing Add:* Two Schiller Ave Narberth PA 19072-1534

HELLER, MICHAEL, CARDIOVASCULAR RESEARCH, MEMBRANE & LIPID BIOCHEMISTRY. *Current Pos:* PROF PHARMACOL, NORTHWESTERN UNIV MED SCH, 89- *Personal Data:* b Berlin, Ger; m, Tova Aizenband; c Ori-Nathan. *Educ:* Hebrew Univ, Jerusalem, BS, MS & PhD(biochem). *Prof Exp:* From lectr to prof, Hebrew Univ, Hadassah Med Sch, 70-89, head lab myocardial res, 75-89, vchmn, Inst Biochem, 86-89. *Concurrent Pos:* Vis assoc prof & Castera fel, Univ Calif, Los Angeles Sch Med, 75-76; vis prof & Hoffman La Roche fel, Univ Bern, Switz, 81; Max Planck fel, Max Planck Inst Med Res, Heidelberg, 84-85; vis scientist, Roche Inst Molecular Biol, Nutley, NJ, 88-89; res fel, Abbott Labs, 89- *Mem:* Am Heart Asn; Am Soc Pharmacol & Exp Therapeut; Int Soc Heart Res; Int Soc Appl Cardiovasc Biol. *Res:* Lipid biochemistry and enzymology; membrane-bound enzymes and ion transport; cardiovascular biochemical pharmacology; mechanism of cardiac glycosides; cardiac ischemia, nitric oxide synthase-biochemical, pharmacologic, molecular-biological and drug discovery aspects. *Mailing Add:* PO Box 346 Lake Forest IL 60045

HELLER, MILTON DAVID, MEDICAL RESEARCH. *Current Pos:* RETIRED. *Personal Data:* b Newark, NJ, May 18, 21; m 46; c 4. *Educ:* Univ Mich, BS, 42, MS, 47, PhD(chem), 52. *Prof Exp:* Chemist, E I du Pont de Nemours & Co, 42; instr, Univ Mich, 50-51; chemist, Am Cyanamid Co, 51-74, ed & analyst, Lederle Labs Div, 74-77, clin study analyst, Med Res Div, 71-88, clin res assoc, 81-87. *Mem:* Am Chem Soc; Am Inst Chemists. *Res:* Natural product synthesis; steroid synthesis; pulmonary and allergy research; oncology research. *Mailing Add:* Seven Highview Ave New City NY 10956-2856

HELLER, PAUL, INTERNAL MEDICINE, HEMATOLOGY. *Current Pos:* clin asst prof, Univ Ill Med Ctr, 54-60, assoc prof, 60-63, chief hemat sect, Dept Med, 67-79, PROF MED, COL MED, UNIV ILL MED CTR, 63-, CONSULT HEMAT, 78-; PHYSICIAN & HEMATOLOGIST, VET ADMIN WESTSIDE HOSP, 54-, SR MED INVESTR, 69- *Personal Data:* b Komotau, Czech, Aug 8, 14; nat US; m 46, 88, Anna Corunberg; c Thomas A & Carol E. *Educ:* Ger Univ, Prague, MD, 38; Am Bd Internal Med, dipl. *Honors & Awards:* Middleton Award, 75; Ann Langer Award, Cancer Res, 80. *Prof Exp:* Demonstr biochem, Biochem Inst, Ger Univ, Prague, 35-37; resident pulmonary dis, Montefiore Hosp, 46-47; intern, Beth Israel Hosp, 47-48; clin instr med, Sch Med, George Washington Univ, 50-51; assoc, Col Med, Univ Nebr, 52-54. *Concurrent Pos:* Physician, Group Health Asn, 48-51 & Vet Admin, Nebr, 52-54; chief med serv, Vet Admin WestSide Hosp, 67-69; mem, Hemat Study Sect, NIH, 67-71. *Mem:* Am Soc Hemat; Am Fedn Clin Res; fel Am Col Physicians; Asn Am Immunologists; Asn Am Physicians. *Res:* Hemoglobinopathies; molecular biology of fetal hemoglobin. *Mailing Add:* 1522 Dobson St Evanston IL 60202-3720. *Fax:* 312-633-2129

HELLER, PAUL R, TURFGRASS, ORNAMENTAL HORTICULTURE. *Current Pos:* asst prof, 76-86, ASSOC PROF ENTOM EXTEN, DEPT ENTOM, PA STATE UNIV, 76- *Personal Data:* b Wooster, Ohio, May 11, 48. *Educ:* Malone Col, BA, 70; Ohio State Univ, MS, 72, PhD(entom), 76. *Prof Exp:* Res assoc entom, Dept Entom, Ohio Agr Res & Dev Ctr, 70-76; supvr pest mgt, Pest Mgt Consults, Inc, 76. *Concurrent Pos:* Consult, E C Geiger Supply Co, 78 & 81 & J T Baker Chem Co, 79-80; lectr, Pa Turfgrass Conf, 78-, Univ Md Turfgrass Conf, Mass Hort Cong, Univ Mass Turfgrass Conf, Pa State Christmas Tree Growers Asn & Dept Plant Sci, Univ Mass Turfgrass Winter Courge. *Mem:* Entom Soc Am; Am Registry Prof Entomologists. *Res:* Effect of nitrogen levels on piercing-sucking insects associated with turfgrass; effect of turfgrass fungicides on the latter pests; evaluation of entomgeneous nematodes to control turfgrass arthropods; evaluation of pesticides to control turfgrass arthropods. *Mailing Add:* 107 Ashwood Pl State College PA 16801

HELLER, ROBERT, JR, MATHEMATICS. *Current Pos:* ASSOC PROF, MISS STATE UNIV, 64- *Personal Data:* b San Angelo, Tex, June 13, 31; m 67; c 2. *Educ:* Univ Houston, BA, 50; Univ Tex, MA, 54, PhD(math), 58. *Prof Exp:* Instr math, Univ Tex, 53-58; asst prof, Univ Houston, 58-64. *Mem:* Am Math Soc; Math Asn Am. *Res:* Analysis; continued fractions. *Mailing Add:* 2413 Maple Dr Starkville MS 39759

HELLER, ROBERT A, ENGINEERING MECHANICS, CIVIL ENGINEERING. *Current Pos:* PROF ENG SCI & MECH, VA POLYTECH INST & STATE UNIV, 67- *Personal Data:* b Budapest, Hungary, Feb 12, 28; nat US; m 54; c 2. *Educ:* Columbia Univ, BS, 51, MS, 53, PhD(eng mech), 58. *Honors & Awards:* Western Elect Award, Am Soc Engr Educ. *Prof Exp:* Asst, Columbia Univ, 51-57, from instr to assoc prof civil eng, 57-65, assoc dir, Inst Study of Fatigue & Reliability, 65-67. *Concurrent Pos:* Consult, USAF, 72- & US Army, 75- *Mem:* assoc fel Am Inst Aeronaut & Astronaut; Soc Exp Stress Anal; Am Acad Mech; Am Soc Civil Engr. *Res:* Inelastic behavior of engineering materials and structures; fatigue and reliability; educational models and motion pictures; probabilistic mechanics. *Mailing Add:* Dept Eng Sci Va Polytech Inst & State Univ PO Box 0219 Blacksburg VA 24061

HELLER, ROBERT LEO, STRATIGRAPHY, PALEONTOLOGY. *Current Pos:* from asst prof to prof, Univ Minn, Duluth, 50-60, head dept, 52-69, dir earth sci curric proj, 62-65, from asst provost to provost, 65-85, chancellor, 85-87, PROF GEOL, UNIV MINN, DULUTH, 60-, EMER CHANCELLOR, 87- *Personal Data:* b Dubuque, Iowa, Apr 10, 19; m 46; c 3. *Educ:* Iowa State Col, BS, 42; Univ Mo, MS, 43, PhD(statig & paleont), 50. *Honors & Awards:* Neil A Miner Award, 65; Ian Campbell Medal, 85. *Prof Exp:* Geologist, US Geol Surv, 43-44. *Concurrent Pos:* Ed, Environ Times, 76-80; vchmn bd trustees, Am Geol Inst Found, 84-86, chmn, 86-; chmn bd dirs, Wolf Ridge Environ Learning Ctr, 90-; chmn, Coun Sci Soc Pres, 82-83. *Mem:* AAAS; Geol Soc Am; Am Asn Petrol Geologists; Nat Asn Geol Teachers (pres, 76-77); Am Geol Inst (pres, 78-79). *Res:* Lower Paleozoic stratigraphy and paleontology. *Mailing Add:* 320 Morley Pkwy Duluth MN 55803

HELLER, STEPHEN RICHARD, SPECTROSCOPY, CHEMICAL INFORMATION. *Current Pos:* RES SCIENTIST, AGR RES SERV, 84- *Personal Data:* b Manhattan, NY, Jan 5, 43; m 64, Rachelle Silverman; c Joshua, Adam & Matthew. *Educ:* State Univ NY Stony Brook, BS, 63; Georgetown Univ, PhD(chem), 67. *Honors & Awards:* Gold Medal, Environ Protection Agency. *Prof Exp:* Res chemist biophys dept, Div Nuclear Med, Walter Reed Army Inst Res, Walter Reed Army Med Ctr, 67-70; sr staff fel, NIH, 70-73; res chemist, enciron protection agency, 73-84. *Concurrent Pos:* Vis prof, Hebrew Univ, 81. *Mem:* AAAS; Am Chem Soc; Sigma Xi; Am Soc Mass Spectrometry. *Res:* Genome databases, spectroscopy datasets; chemical information systems. *Mailing Add:* Bldg 005 Rm 337 Beltsville MD 20705. *Fax:* 301-504-6231; *E-Mail:* srheller@gig.usda.gov

HELLER, STEVEN NELSON, FOOD SCIENCE. *Current Pos:* RES & DEVELOP DIR, GEN MILLS, 81- *Personal Data:* b Gettysburg, Pa, Nov 14, 50; m 76. *Educ:* Univ Md, BS, 72; Cornell Univ, MS, 75, PhD(food sci), 77. *Prof Exp:* Food technologist prof develop, Armour-Dial Co, 77-81. *Mem:* Inst Food Technol. *Res:* Development of new food products. *Mailing Add:* 1512 Hunter Dr Wayzata MN 55391

HELLER, WILLIAM MOHN, PHARMACY, DRUG INFORMATION & STANDARDS. *Current Pos:* RETIRED. *Personal Data:* b Orrville, Ohio, Mar 15, 26; m 50, Joanne E Teale; c Kathleen J (Spalding). *Educ:* Univ Toledo, BS, 49; Univ Md, MS, 51, PhD, 55. *Hon Degrees:* DSc, Philadelphia Col Pharm & Sci, 81, Univ Md, 87, Univ Ark, 88, Univ Toledo, 95. *Honors & Awards:* Whitney Lectr Award, Am Soc Hosp Pharmacists, 72; Remington Hon Medal, Am Pharmaceut Asn, 84; Distinguished Career Award, Drug Info Asn, 90; Distinguished Serv Profile Award, Am Found Pharmaceut Educ, 90. *Prof Exp:* Intern, Johns Hopkins Univ Hosp, 49-51; instr pharm, Univ Md, 53-54; asst prof, Sch Pharm, Univ Ark, Little Rock, 54-60, asst prof, Sch Med, 60-62, chief pharmacist, Univ Hosp, 54-66; dir, Dept Sci Serv, Am Soc Hosp Pharmacists, 66-68; exec dir designate, US Pharmacopeia, 68-70, exec dir, 70-90. *Concurrent Pos:* Pharmacist, Retail Stores, 50-53; dir, Am Hosp Formulary Serv, 55-62; chief investr drug systs res, Univ Ark, Little Rock, 62-66; vchmn, Nat Coun Patient Info & Educ; spec consult, Am Found Pharmaceut Educ. *Mem:* Fel AAAS; Am Soc Hosp Pharmacists; fel Am Pharmaceut Asn; Int Pharmaceut Fedn; Drug Info Asn; fel Acad Pharmaceut Sci; fel Am Asn Pharmaceut Scientists; Am Asn Cols Pharm. *Res:* Hospital pharmacy; pharmacy education; drug standards; drug info; medication errors. *Mailing Add:* 1408 Palm City Rd Stuart FL 34994-7118. *Fax:* 561-286-4542

HELLER, WILLIAM R, solid state physics, applied mathematics; deceased, see previous edition for last biography

HELLERMAN, HERBERT, COMPUTER SCIENCE, ELECTRICAL ENGINEERING. *Current Pos:* RETIRED. *Personal Data:* b Brooklyn, NY, July 8, 27; m 48; c 3. *Educ:* Purdue Univ, BSEE, 49; Syracuse Univ, PhD(elec eng), 55. *Prof Exp:* Electronic scientist, Wright Field, USAF, Ohio, 49; from instr to asst prof elec eng, Syracuse Univ, 49-57; assoc prof, Univ Del, 57-59; staff mem, Int Bus Mach Corp, 59-64, sr staff mem, systs res inst, 64-66, sr systs consult, systs develop div, 66-69; prof comput sci, Sch Advan Technol, State Univ NY, Binghamton, 69-77, chmn dept, 77; prin comput architect, Amdahl Corp, 77-84, consult, 84-92. *Mem:* Asn Comput Mach; Inst Elec & Electronics Engrs. *Res:* Computer system organization; education in computer systems; computer performance; software engineering. *Mailing Add:* 2716 Katrina Way Mountainview CA 94040

HELLERSTEIN, STANLEY, PEDIATRIC NEPHROLOGY, CLINICAL CHEMISTRY. *Current Pos:* PROF PEDIAT, SCH MED, UNIV MO-KANSAS CITY, 63- *Personal Data:* b Denver, Colo, Oct 3, 26; m 49; c 3. *Educ:* Univ Colo, BA, 48, MD, 52. *Concurrent Pos:* Physician clin chem, Children's Mercy Hosp, Kansas City, 63-; clin prof, Sch Med, Univ Kans, 65-; chief, Sect Pediat Nephrology, Children's Mercy Hosp, 80- *Res:* Fluid and electrolyte metabolism; red blood composition, alterations in disease states and with growth. *Mailing Add:* Children's Mercy Hosp 24th at Gillham Rd Kansas City MO 64108

HELLICKSON, MARTIN LEON, HVAC-FRUIT STORAGES. *Current Pos:* Asst prof, 75-80, ASSOC PROF AGR ENG, ORE STATE UNIV, 80- *Personal Data:* b Dickinson, NDak, April 6, 45; m 70, Beverley B Bryant; c Amy & Benjamin. *Educ:* NDak State Univ, BS, 68; SDak State Univ, MS, 72; Univ Minn, PhD(agr eng), 75. *Concurrent Pos:* Consult engr, Calif Law, 79-80, ground-source heat pumps, 85. *Mem:* Am Soc Agr Engrs; Sigma Xi. *Res:* Computer control of fruit storage refrigeration systems; energy conservation in fan-cycled fruit storages; postharvest preservation, storage and transportation of fresh fruits and vegtables. *Mailing Add:* 3120 Greenbriar Pl Corvallis OR 97330. *Fax:* 541-737-2082

HELLICKSON, MYLO A, AGRICULTURAL ENGINEERING. *Current Pos:* assoc prof, 69-78, PROF AGR ENG, SDAK STATE UNIV, 78-, HEAD DEPT, 82- *Personal Data:* b Dickinson, NDak, July 17, 42; m 64. *Educ:* NDak State Univ, BS, 64, MS, 66; WVa Univ, PhD(eng), 69. *Prof Exp:* Res asst, WVa Univ, 66-67, instr & res asst, 67-69. *Concurrent Pos:* Sr sabbatical leave, Los Alamos Sci Lab. *Mem:* Am Soc Agr Engrs; Am Soc Eng Educ; AAAS; Coun Agr Sci & Technol; Nat Soc Prof Engrs; Sigma Xi; Am Soc Heating, Refrig & Air Conditioning Engrs. *Res:* Structures and environment for livestock; energy use in agriculture and food production. *Mailing Add:* 2104 Olwein St Brookings SD 57006

HELLIER, THOMAS ROBERT, JR, AQUATIC BIOLOGY. *Current Pos:* from asst prof to assoc prof, 60-71, PROF BIOL, UNIV TEX, ARLINGTON, 71- *Personal Data:* b Ft Pierce, Fla, Dec 24, 28; m 52; c 3. *Educ:* Univ Fla, BA, 55, MS, 57; Univ Tex, PhD(zool, marine sci), 61. *Prof Exp:* Res scientist ecol, Inst Marine Sci, Univ Tex, 57-59. *Mem:* AAAS; Ecol Soc Am; Am Fisheries Soc; Am Soc Ichthyologists & Herpetologists; Am Soc Limnol & Oceanog. *Res:* Environmental relationships of fishes. *Mailing Add:* Dept Biol Box 19498 Univ Tex Arlington TX 76019. *Fax:* 817-272-2855; *E-Mail:* thellier@albert.uta.edu

HELLING, CHARLES SIVER, SOIL CHEMISTRY, PESTICIDE CHEMISTRY. *Current Pos:* res soil scientist, Natural Resources Inst, 67-89, RES SOIL SCIENTIST, PLANT SCI INST, AGR RES SERV, USDA, 89- *Personal Data:* b Madelia, Minn, Jan 9, 40; m 64, Sharon A Thormodson; c Michael. *Educ:* St Olaf Col, BA, 61; Univ Wis, MS, 63, PhD(soil chem), 66. *Prof Exp:* Res assoc agron, Cornell Univ, 65-67. *Mem:* Am Soc Agron; Soil Sci Soc Am; Weed Sci Soc Am; Am Chem Soc; Coun Agr Sci Technol. *Res:* Pesticide movement in soils; pesticide-soil adsorption mechanisms; soil organic chemistry; pesticide metabolism by soil microorganisms; cation exchange in soils; narcotic crop eradication. *Mailing Add:* 11307 Emack Rd Beltsville MD 20705-2351. *Fax:* 301-504-6491; *E-Mail:* chelling@asrr.arsusda.gov

HELLING, JOHN FREDERIC, ORGANOMETALLIC CHEMISTRY. *Current Pos:* from asst prof to assoc prof, 62-78, PROF CHEM, UNIV FLA, 78-, ASSOC CHMN CHEM, 92- *Personal Data:* b Madelia, Minn, June 4, 33; m 62, Judith Weiner; c Melanie & Bruce. *Educ:* St Olaf Col, BA, 55; Ohio State Univ, PhD(org chem), 60. *Prof Exp:* Res assoc chem, Mass Inst Technol, 60-61; asst prof, Mich State Univ, 61-62. *Concurrent Pos:* Nat counr, Am Chem Soc, 81-95. *Mem:* Am Chem Soc. *Res:* Metallocenes; bisarene complexes of transition metals; transition metal intermediates in organic syntheses. *Mailing Add:* Dept Chem Univ Fla Gainesville FL 32611-2046. *Fax:* 352-392-8758

HELLING, ROBERT BRUCE, GENETICS. *Current Pos:* asst prof, 65-70, ASSOC PROF BOT, UNIV MICH, ANN ARBOR, 70- *Personal Data:* b Madelia, Minn, Mar 21, 36; m 61; c 1. *Educ:* St Olaf Col, BA, 58; Univ Pittsburgh, MS, 50, PhD(bact), 63. *Prof Exp:* NSF fel microbial genetics, Karolinska Inst, 63-65. *Mem:* Genetics Soc Am; Am Soc Microbiol. *Res:* Microbial genetics; genetic control mechanisms. *Mailing Add:* 2014 Washtenaw Ave Ann Arbor MI 48104

HELLIWELL, ROBERT ARTHUR, RADIOSCIENCE, WAVE PROPAGATION. *Current Pos:* Actg instr elec eng, Stanford Univ, 42-43, instr, 43-44, res assoc, 44-46, actg asst prof, 46-50, from asst prof to assoc prof, 50-58, prof, 58-95, EMER PROF ELEC ENG, STANFORD UNIV, 95- *Personal Data:* b Red Wing, Minn, Sept 2, 20; m 42; c 4. *Educ:* Stanford Univ, AB, 42, MS, 43, EE, 44, PhD(elec eng), 48. *Honors & Awards:* Appleton Prize, Royal Soc London, 72. *Concurrent Pos:* Consult, Nat Bur Stand, Ionospheres & Radiophysics Sub-Comt Space Sci Steering Comt, NASA; mem comns & US nat comt, Int Union Radio Sci, chmn comn, 57-63; mem, Polar Res Bd Exec Comt, Nat Res Coun, 78-81. *Mem:* Nat Acad Sci; Am Geophys Union. *Res:* Whistlers and related ionospheric phenomena; ionospheric and magnetospheric research including plasma wave experiments in space physics; analysis of power line radiation effects; VLF wave amplification studies; HF and VLF direction-finding techniques; modification of the upper atmosphere. *Mailing Add:* Stanford Univ Starlab 325 Durand St Stanford CA 94305

HELLIWELL, THOMAS MCCAFFREE, THEORETICAL PHYSICS. *Current Pos:* Chair, Physics Dept, 81-89, fac chair, 90-93, PROF PHYSICS, HARVEY MUDD COL, 62-,. *Personal Data:* b Minneapolis, Minn, June 8, 36. *Educ:* Pomona Col, BA, 58; Calif Inst Technol, PhD(physics), 63. *Concurrent Pos:* NSF fac fel, Univ Md, 68-69 & Cambridge Univ, 75-76. *Mem:* AAAS; Am Asn Physics Teachers. *Res:* General relativity, including fundamental problems and applications to astrophysics. *Mailing Add:* Harvey Mudd Col Claremont CA 91711

HELLMAN, ALFRED, virology, cell physiology, for more information see previous edition

HELLMAN, FRANCES, SPECIFIC HEAT MEASUREMENT, THIN FILM GROWTH. *Current Pos:* ASST PROF PHYSICS, UNIV CALIF, SAN DIEGO, 87- *Personal Data:* b Gt Brit, Oct 28, 56; US citizen. *Educ:* Dartmouth Col, BA, 78; Stanford Univ, PhD(appl physics), 85. *Prof Exp:* Mem tech staff, AT&T Bell Labs, 85-87. *Concurrent Pos:* Assoc ed, J Mat Sci & Eng, 87-; prog & exec comt, Thin film div, Am Vacuum Soc. *Mem:* Am Phys Soc; Mat Res Soc. *Res:* Characterization and physical properties of novel solid materials in film form; primary experimental tool, vapor deposition chambers, a nultra-sensitive wide temperature and magnetic field range specific heat experiment; amorphous magnetic materials; epitaxial sillicides and superconductors. *Mailing Add:* Dept Physics 0319 Univ Calif San Diego 9500 Gilman Dr La Jolla CA 92093

HELLMAN, HENRY MARTIN, CHEMISTRY. *Current Pos:* RETIRED. *Personal Data:* b Norrfors, Sweden, July 4, 20; nat US; m 51. *Educ:* Ind Univ, BS, 43; Purdue Univ, MS, 45, PhD(org chem), 47. *Prof Exp:* Asst chem, Purdue Univ, 43-44; from instr to assoc prof, NY Univ, 47-69, from actg chmn to chmn dept, 64-73, prof chem, 69-90. *Mem:* Am Chem Soc. *Res:* Organic chemistry; mechanism of organic reactions; haloalkylation; organo-metallic compounds; oxidation reactions. *Mailing Add:* 20708 Colfax St Lowell IN 46356-9705

HELLMAN, KENNETH P, BIOCHEMISTRY, ENZYMOLOGY. *Current Pos:* from asst prof to assoc prof, Smith Col, 61-76, chmn, Chem Dept, 66-69, 78-81 & 85-88, dir, Biochem Prog, 81-95, PROF CHEM, SMITH COL, 76- *Personal Data:* b Baltimore, Md, July 28, 34; m 58; c Christopher & Gregory. *Educ:* Drew Univ, AB, 56; Mich State Univ, MS, 59, PhD(chem), 62. *Concurrent Pos:* Res assoc, Inst Biol Chem, Univ Rome, 69-70; vis res assoc, Microbiol Res Estab, Porton, Eng, 75-76, 78 & 82. *Mem:* Protein Soc; Am Chem Soc; Fedn Am Soc Exp Biol. *Res:* Enzyme mechanisms; protein structure and function. *Mailing Add:* Dept Chem Smith Col Northampton MA 01063. *Fax:* 413-585-3786

HELLMAN, MARTIN EDWARD, ELECTRICAL ENGINEERING. *Current Pos:* PROF ELEC ENG, STANFORD UNIV, 71- *Personal Data:* b New York, NY, Oct 2, 45; m 67; c 2. *Educ:* NY Univ, BE, 66; Stanford Univ, MS, 67, PhD(elec eng), 69. *Honors & Awards:* Donald G Fink Award, Inst Elec & Electronic Engrs, 81. *Prof Exp:* Mem staff, Thomas J Watson Res Ctr, IBM Corp, 68-69; asst prof elec eng, Mass Inst Technol, 69-71. *Concurrent Pos:* Vinton Hayes fel, 69-71. *Mem:* Inst Elec & Electronic Engrs; Inst Math Statist. *Res:* Information and communication theory; cryptography and data security; international security. *Mailing Add:* Elec Eng Dept Stanford Univ Durand 135 Palo Alto CA 94305

HELLMAN, NISON NORMAN, CHEMISTRY. *Current Pos:* VPRES & HEAD LAB, TRANSFORMER DESIGN INC OF MILWAUKEE, 69- *Personal Data:* b Milwaukee, Wis, May 19, 20; m 42; c 4. *Educ:* Univ Wis, BS & MS, 42, PhD, 43. *Prof Exp:* Asst chemist, Metall Lab, Univ Chicago, 43-45; chemist, Northern Regional Res Lab, Bur Agr & Indust Chem, USDA, 45-50, in chg phys chem group, Northern Utilization Res Br, 50-55; res chemist, Froedtert Malt Corp, 56-59, asst tech dir, 59-60; consult chemist, 60-69. *Mem:* AAAS; Am Chem Soc; Am Asn Cereal Chem; Inst Food Technologists. *Res:* X-ray diffraction; physical properties of colloidal systems; molecular characterization of biological polymers; synthetic and degradative enzymatic activities; foods development. *Mailing Add:* 2135 W Edward Lane Milwaukee WI 53209-2814

HELLMAN, SAMUEL, RADIOTHERAPY. *Current Pos:* dean, Biol Sci Div & Pritzker Sch Med & vpres, Met Ctr, 88-93, DISTINGUISHED SERV PROF, DEPT RADIATION & CELLULAR ONCOL, UNIV CHICAGO, 93- *Personal Data:* b New York, NY, July 23, 34; m 57; c 2. *Educ:* Allegheny Col, BS, 55; State Univ NY, MD, 59. *Hon Degrees:* MS, Harvard Univ, 68. *Prof Exp:* Fel radiother, Sch Med, Yale Univ, 62-64; fel, Inst Cancer Res & Royal Marsden Hosp, London, 65-66; asst prof radiol, Yale Univ, 66-68; assoc prof, Harvard Med Sch, 68-70, Fuller-Am Cancer Soc prof radiol & chmn, Dept Radiation Ther, 68-83; physician & chief, Mem Sloan Kettering Cancer Ctr, New York, 83-88. *Mem:* Radiation Res Soc; Am Soc Therapeut Radiol; Am Col Radiologists; Asn Univ Radiologists. *Res:* Cancer; radiation biology; cell kinetics; hematopoiesis. *Mailing Add:* Dept Radiation & Cellular Oncol 5758 S Maryland Ave MC9001 Chicago IL 60637. *Fax:* 773-702-4347

HELLMAN, WILLIAM S, PHYSICS. *Current Pos:* asst prof, 64-69, ASSOC PROF PHYSICS, BOSTON UNIV, 69- *Personal Data:* b Brooklyn, NY, May 14, 31; m 54; c 1. *Educ:* Brooklyn Col, BS, 53; Syracuse Univ, MS, 58, PhD(physics), 61. *Prof Exp:* Res assoc physics, US Naval Ord Lab, 62-64. *Concurrent Pos:* Nat Acad Sci res assoc, 62-64. *Mem:* Am Phys Soc; Sigma Xi. *Res:* Quantum field theory; elementary particle physics. *Mailing Add:* Dept Physics Boston Univ 590 Commonwealth Ave Boston MA 02215-2507

HELLMANN, MAX, SCIENCE ADMINISTRATION. *Current Pos:* CONSULT, 83- *Personal Data:* b Beroun, Czech, Nov 27, 19; nat US; m 57, Elizabeth Robitschek. *Educ:* Col Wooster, BA, 42; Univ Buffalo, MA, 47, PhD(chem), 50. *Honors & Awards:* Meritorious Serv Award, NSF, 81. *Prof Exp:* Instr chem, Univ Buffalo, 48-49; res fel radiochem, Univ NC, 49-51; res chemist, Nat Bur Standards, 51-60; proj dir, Int Sci Activ, NSF, 60-62, dep chief scientist, NSF/Rio, 62-64, prog dir, 64-68, head coop sci activ sect, Off Int Sci Activ, 68-69, head liaison staff, New Delhi, 69-71; mgr, Latin Am & Pac Sect, 71-76, dep dir, Div Int Prog, 76-81; dep dir, US-Israel Binational Sci Found, Jerusalem, 81-83. *Mem:* Fel AAAS. *Res:* Isotope effect studies on carbon-14; aromatic fluorine compounds; international science activities. *Mailing Add:* 1235 34th St NW Washington DC 20007

HELLMERS, HENRY, PLANT PHYSIOLOGY, HYDROLOGY & WATER RESOURCES. *Current Pos:* RETIRED. *Personal Data:* b Palmerton, Pa, Sept 5, 15; m 45; c 2. *Educ:* Pa State Univ, BS, 37, MS, 39; Univ Calif, Berkeley, PhD(plant physiol), 50. *Prof Exp:* Mem, New Eng Emergency Proj, US Forest Serv, 39-40; forestry inspector, Pa Turnpike Comn, 40-41; plant physiologist, Pac Southwest Forest & Range Exp Sta, US Forest Serv, 49-65; dir phytotron, Duke Univ, 65-79, prof bot, 65-83, prof forestry, 68-83. *Concurrent Pos:* Res fel, Calif Inst Technol, 50-55, sr res fel, 55-65; lectr, Pasadena City Col, 61-65; NZ sr res fel forestry, 73-74; vis prof, Japan Soc Prom Sci. *Mem:* Fel AAAS; Soc Am Foresters; Am Soc Plant Physiologists. *Res:* Metabolism of pine pollen; soil fertility of wildland areas; temperature and photoperiodic effects upon growth of grasses, shrubs and trees; long term effects on plants of elevated carbon dioxide concentrations. *Mailing Add:* Dept Bot Duke Univ Durham NC 27706

HELLMUTH, WALTER WILHELM, ORGANIC CHEMISTRY. *Current Pos:* Res chemist, 64-74, group leader res & technol, 74-79, GROUP LEADER ANALYSIS & TESTING, TEXACO INC, 79- *Personal Data:* b New York, NY, Nov 6, 38; m 61; c 3. *Educ:* Iona Col, BS, 60; Univ Conn, MS, 63, PhD(org chem), 65. *Mem:* Am Chem Soc. *Res:* Automotive lubricants and fuels, additives and new technology; bench test development; thermal analysis. *Mailing Add:* Texaco Res Ctr 12 Deerwood Dr Hopewell Junction NY 12533

HELLOU, JOCELYNE, HYDROCARBONS, CONTAMINANTS. *Current Pos:* Fel Natural Sci & Eng Res Coun Can, 85, res chemist, 86-90, RES SCIENTIST DEPT FISHERIES & OCEANS, NW ATLANTIC FISHERIES, 90- *Personal Data:* m 82, A E Hay; c Philip & Natasha. *Educ:* Univ Montreal, BS, 78; Univ BC, MS, 81, PhD(chem oceanog), 85. *Mem:* Chem Inst Can; Int Union Pure & Appl Chem; Soc Environ Toxicol & Chem; Int Soc Chem Ecol. *Res:* Fates of hydrocarbons and non-polar contaminants (as well as biogenic compounds) in marine organisms; bioaccumulation of free xenobiotics and in bile metabolites produced by fish; hydrocarbons present in petroleum sources and sediments. *Mailing Add:* Dept Fisheries & Oceans BIO PO Box 1006 St John's NF B2Y 4A2 Can

HELLSTROM, HAROLD RICHARD, EXPERIMENTAL BIOLOGY, PATHOLOGY. *Current Pos:* CHIEF, LAB SERV, VET ADMIN MED CTR, SYRACUSE, NY, 79-; PROF PATH, STATE UNIV NY, 79- *Personal Data:* b Marianna, Pa, Mar 22, 28; m 73, Martha Montag. *Educ:* Waynesburg Col, BS, 50; Univ Pittsburgh, MD, 52; Am Bd Path, cert anat path, 57, cert clin path, 60. *Prof Exp:* Teaching fel, Dept Path Sch Med, Univ Pittsburgh, 53-57, instr, 58, clin asst prof, 60-66, from asst prof to assoc prof path, 66-79, staff pathologist, Vet Admin Med Ctr, Pittsburgh, 57-70, chief lab serv, 70-79. *Concurrent Pos:* Staff pathologist, Vet Admin Hosp, Pittsburgh, 57-70, chief lab serv, 70-79. *Mem:* Col Am Pathologists; Am Soc Clin Path; AAAS; Int Acad Path; Am Asn Pathologists. *Res:* Multiple publications in pathology; developer of alternate paradigm to explain ischemic heart disease, the model asserts that symptoms in ischemic heart disease are due to primary spasm of resistance vessels. *Mailing Add:* 5035 Bridlepath Rd Fayetteville NY 13066-9741

HELLSTROM, INGEGERD ELISABET, IMMUNOLOGY. *Current Pos:* asst prof microbiol & nursing, Univ Wash, 66-69, res assoc microbiol, Bristol-Myers Squibb PRI, 69-72, PROF MICROBIOL & IMMUNOL, UNIV WASH, 72-, VPRES, IMMUNOL DIS, BRISTOL-MYERS SQUIBB PRI, 91- *Personal Data:* b Falun, Sweden, Jan 3, 32; m 60, Karl E; c 2. *Educ:* Karolinska Inst Med Sch, Sweden, lic med, 64, Dr Med, 66. *Honors & Awards:* Lucy Wortham James Award, Ewing Soc, 72; Pap Award, Papanicolaou Cancer Res Inst, 73; Nat Award, Am Cancer Soc, 74. *Prof Exp:* Res assoc tumor biol, Karolinska Inst Med Sch, 59-66. *Concurrent Pos:* Mem, Gen Assembly, Gen Motors Cancer Res Found; Humboldt Award, Bonn, 80. *Mem:* Am Asn Immunologists; Am Fedn Clin Res. *Res:* Experimental studies on the organism's immunological defense mechanisms to tumors. *Mailing Add:* Bristol-Myers Squibb Pharmaceut Res Inst 3005 First Ave Seattle WA 98121-1069. *Fax:* 206-727-3507

HELLSTROM, KARL ERIK LENNART, IMMUNOLOGY, ONCOLOGY. *Current Pos:* from assoc prof to prof path, 66-86, AFFIL PROF PATH, SCH MED, UNIV WASH, 87- *Personal Data:* b Stockholm, Sweden, Apr 16, 34; m 60; c Per & Katarina. *Educ:* Karolinska Inst, Sweden, MD, 64, PhD, 66. *Honors & Awards:* Lucy Wortham James Award, Ewing Soc, 72; Pap Award, Papanicolaou Cancer Res Inst, 73; Nat Award, Am Cancer Soc, 74; Knight Order Northern Star, 76; Humboldt Award, Sr Am Scientist, Bonn, Ger, 80. *Prof Exp:* Res assoc histol, Sch Med, Karolinska Inst, 54-57, res assoc tumor biol, 58-62, asst prof, 62-66. *Concurrent Pos:* Hutchinson Cancer Res Ctr, 75-83; lab dir, Oncogen, 83-85; vpres, Bristol-Myers Squibb Pharmaceut Res Inst, 85- *Mem:* AAAS; NY Acad Sci; Am Asn Cancer Res; Am Soc Exp Path; Fedn Am Socs Exp Biol; Sigma Xi. *Res:* Experimental studies on the organism's immunological defense mechanisms to tumors. *Mailing Add:* Bristol Myers Squibb Pharmaceut Res Inst 3005 First Ave Seattle WA 98121. *Fax:* 206-727-3607

HELLUMS, JESSE DAVID, CHEMICAL ENGINEERING, BIOENGINEERING & BIOMEDICAL ENGINEERING. *Current Pos:* from asst prof to assoc prof chem eng, Rice Univ, 60-68, dir biomed eng, 68-80, chmn dept, 70-76, dean eng, 80-88, PROF CHEM ENG, RICE UNIV, 68-, A J HARTSOOK PROF, 85- *Personal Data:* b Stamford, Tex, Aug 19, 29; m 57, Marilyn Biel; c Mark & Jay. *Educ:* Univ Tex, BS, 50, MS, 58; Univ Mich, PhD(chem eng), 61. *Honors & Awards:* Whitaker Lectr, Biomed Eng Soc, 93. *Prof Exp:* Process engr, Mobil Oil, Tex, 50-53; Lt, USAF, 53-56. *Concurrent Pos:* NSF sci fac fel, Cambridge & Edinburgh Univs, 67-68; adj prof med, Baylor Col Med, 70- & Univ Tex, 77-; vis prof, Imp Col, London, 73-74 & Univ TSU Kuba, Japan, 95; vis scholar, Univ Calif, San Diego, 88; spec vis prof, Tokyo Inst Technol, 89. *Mem:* Am Inst Chem Engrs; Am Chem Soc; AAAS; Am Soc Artificial Internal Organs; Microcirculation Soc; fel Am Inst Chem Engr; Biomed Eng Soc; fel Am Inst Med & Biol Eng. *Res:* Fluid mechanics; biomedical engineering; various aspects of chemical engineering in medicine and biology including tissue engineering, blood and vascular biology, and mass transport in the microcirculation. *Mailing Add:* Dept Chem Eng Rice Univ MS 142 6100 S Main St Houston TX 77005. *Fax:* 713-285-5353; *E-Mail:* jhellums@rice.edu

HELLWARTH, ROBERT WILLIS, MODERN OPTICS, LASERS. *Current Pos:* GEORGE PFLEGER PROF ELEC ENG & PHYSICS, UNIV SOUTHERN CALIF, 70- *Personal Data:* b Ann Arbor, Mich, Dec 10, 30; m 57, 86, Theresia deVroom; c Benjamin, Margaret, Thomas & William. *Educ:* Princeton Univ, BSE, 52; Oxford Univ, DPhil, 55. *Honors & Awards:* Charles Hard Tones Award, Optical Soc Am, 83; Quantum Elec Award, Inst Elec & Electronics Engrs, 85. *Prof Exp:* Mem tech staff, Hughes Res Labs, 55-65, sr staff physicist, 65-70. *Concurrent Pos:* Lectr, Calif Inst Technol, 55-66, Hughes fel, 55-56, sr res fel, 66-70; vis assoc prof, Univ Ill, 64-65; mgr, Theoret Studies Dept, Hughes Res Labs, 68-70; sr fel, NSF, Clarendon Lab, Oxford, Eng, 70-71; vis fel, St Peter's Col, 70-71; assoc ed, Inst Elec & Electronics Engrs J Quantum Electronics. *Mem:* Nat Acad Sci; Nat Acad Eng; fel Am Phys Soc; fel Inst Elec & Electronics Engrs; fel AAAS; fel Optical Soc Am. *Res:* Nonlinear optics; solid state physics; laser devices; physics of materials. *Mailing Add:* Dept Elec Eng & Physics Univ Southern Calif Los Angeles CA 90089-0484

HELLWEGE, HERBERT ELMORE, INORGANIC CHEMISTRY, CLINICAL CHEMISTRY. *Current Pos:* RETIRED. *Personal Data:* b Harsefeld, Ger, Mar 3, 21; US citizen; m 53; c 2. *Educ:* Univ Hamburg, DSc(chem), 53. *Prof Exp:* Asst geochem, Univ Hamburg, 51-53; chemist, Food Res Labs, NY, 53-54; prof chem, Rollins Col, 54-74, Archibald Granville Bush prof sci, 74-86, chmn pre-med comt, 76-86. *Concurrent Pos:* Consult, Radiation Incorp, 61-63; NSF fac fel, Gothenburg Univ, 64-65; lab dir, Louis C Herring & Co, 74- *Mem:* Am Chem Soc; Am Asn Bioanal. *Res:* Solvent extraction of metal chelates; coordination chemistry; trace elements in hair; trace elements in urinary calculi. *Mailing Add:* 1141 Banbury Trail Maitland FL 32751

HELLWIG, HELMUT WILHELM, TIME & FREQUENCY, QUANTUM ELECTRONICS. *Current Pos:* DEP ASST SECY SCI, TECHNOL & ENG, OFF SECY AIR FORCE ACQUISITION, ARLINGTON, VA, 96- *Personal Data:* b Berlin, Ger, May 7, 38; US citizen; m 60, Thekla; c Frank & Peter. *Educ:* Tech Univ Berlin, Dipl-Ing, 63, Dr-Ing, 66. *Hon Degrees:* Dr, Univ Besancon, 89. *Honors & Awards:* Sci Award, Dept Defense, Secy Army, 68; IR-100 Award, 76; E U Condon Award, Secy Com, 79. *Prof Exp:* Res physicist masers, Heinrich Hertz Inst, Berlin, 63-66, US Army Electronics Command, Ft Monmouth, NJ, 66-69 & Nat Bur Standards, Boulder, Colo, 69-74, sect chief atomic clocks, 74-79; pres & gen mgr atomic clocks & crystal oscillators, Frequency & Time Systs Inc, 79-86; vpres, Datum Inc, 83-86; assoc dir, Nat Bur Stands, Gaithersburg, 87-90; dir, Air Force Off Sci Res, Bolling AFB, Washington, DC, 90-96. *Concurrent Pos:* Mem, Int Radio Consult Comt, 72-; mem, US Nat Comt, Int Union Radio Sci, 74-, vchmn Comn A, 78-81, chmn, 81-83. *Mem:* Fel Inst Elec & Electronics Engrs; Am Phys Soc; Sigma Xi; Int Union Radio Sci. *Res:* Atomic clocks and frequency standards; atomic and molecular beams; masers; lasers; quantum electronics; time and frequency metrology. *Mailing Add:* 1919 S Eads St, Suite 100 Arlington VA 22202-3053. *Fax:* 703-602-4548; *E-Mail:* hellwigh@af.pentagon.mil

HELLWIG, L(ANGLEY) R(OBERTS), CHEMICAL ENGINEERING. *Current Pos:* RETIRED. *Personal Data:* b Beaumont, Tex, May 21, 28; m 51; c 1. *Educ:* Univ Tex, BS, 49, MS, 51, PhD(chem eng), 55. *Prof Exp:* Tech serv engr, Ethyl Corp, 54-55, develop engr, 55-56, spec coordr, 57-58; head eng sect, Res Div, Petrol Chem, Inc, 58-60; mgr planning dept, Cities Serv Res & Develop Co, 60-63; dir chem res dept, Columbian Carbon Co, 64-67; vpres & mgr res, Cities Serv Res & Develop Co, 67-69, mgr corp planning, Cities Serv Co, 69-72, vpres, Planning & Econ Div, 72-76, exec vpres & pres chem group, 76-79; pres & chief exec officer, Columbian Chem Co, 80-86. *Mem:* Am Inst Chem Engrs; Am Chem Soc; AAAS. *Res:* Process development; research planning; petroleum and petroleum-derived chemicals and polymers. *Mailing Add:* PO Box 2641 Athens TX 75751

HELLY, WALTER S, OPERATIONS RESEARCH. *Current Pos:* PROF OPERS RES, POLYTECH INST NY, 66- *Personal Data:* b Vienna, Austria, Aug 22, 30; US citizen; m 56; c 1. *Educ:* Cornell Univ, BA, 50; Univ Ill, MS, 51; Mass Inst Technol, PhD(physics), 60. *Prof Exp:* Sr engr mil control systs, Sylvania Elec Co, 54-56; sr engr commun & reconnaissance, Melpar, Inc, 56-59; mem tech staff tel traffic, Bell Tel Labs, 59-62; res engr traffic & gen opers res, Port NY Authority, 62-65; proj planner tel opers res, NY Tel Co, 65-66. *Mem:* Opers Res Soc Am; Inst Indust Engrs. *Res:* Single lane, network and queueing problems of vehicular traffic; congestion in telephone switching systems and networks; applications of operations research to urban areas. *Mailing Add:* 91 Cent Park W New York NY 10023

HELM, CHARLES GEORGE, soybean insect pest management, insect surveys, for more information see previous edition

HELM, DONALD CAIRNEY, GROUNDWATER HYDROLOGY, MECHANICS OF AQUIFER MOVEMENT. *Current Pos:* RES HYDROGEOLOGIST, WATER RESOURCES DIV, US GEOL SURV, 91-; RES HYDROGEOLOGIST, NEV BUR MINES, UNIV NEV, 92-, PROF GEOL, MACKAY SCH MINES, 92- *Personal Data:* b Yokohama, Japan, Mar 26, 37; US citizen; m 82, Karen Reed; c Rebecca B. *Educ:* Amherst Col, AB, 59; Hartford Sem Found, MDiv, 62; Univ Calif, Berkeley, MS, 70, PhD(civil eng), 74. *Prof Exp:* Asst rural develop India, Community Serv, Inc, 63-64; hydraul engr groundwater hydrol, 65-69, res hydrologist, Water Resources Div, US Geol Surv, 69-78, physicist, Earth Sci Div, Lawrence Livermore Nat Lab, Univ Calif, 78-84, group leader, Geohydrology & Environ Studies Group, 81-84; prin res scientist, Groundwater Mech's Div Geo-Mech's, Commonwealth Sci & Indust Res Orgn, 84-92; chief, Las Vegas Off, Nev Bur Mines & Geol, 89-93. *Concurrent Pos:* Instr, UNESCO Int Sem, Land Subsidence, Mexico City, 79; mem steering comt, Geothermal Subsidence Res Prog, US Dept Energy, 76-81; found mem, Bd Dirs, Ctr Study Theol & Natural Sci, Grad Theol Union, Berkeley, 81-84; vis scientist, State Elec Comn Victoria, Australia, 82-83; exchange scientist, Chinese Acad Sci, 88; mem comt, D-34 on waste disposal, Am Soc Testing & Mat, 81-83; vis scientist, Nev Bur Mines & Geol, 89-92, grad fac, Univ Nev, Reno, 90-; Samuel P Massie chair excellence, US Dept Energy, Morgan State Univ, 96- *Mem:* Am Geophys Union; Am Soc Civil Engr; Asn Eng Geologists; Int Nat Water Well Asn; Nat Soc Prof Engrs; Am Soc Testing & Mat; Int Asn Hydrogeologist; Int Asn Eng Geol; Int Soc Rock Mech; Int Soc Soil Mech & Found Eng; fel Geol Soc Am; AAAS; fel Inst Engrs Australia. *Res:* Geohydrology; underground waste migration; mechanics of aquifer systems; consolidation theory; land subsidence; response of granular skeleton to transient groundwater flow; flow through fractured rock. *Mailing Add:* Sch Eng Morgan State Univ Baltimore MD 21251

HELM, JAMES LEROY, plant breeding, genetics; deceased, see previous edition for last biography

HELM, RAYMOND E, DAIRY SCIENCE, NUTRITION. *Current Pos:* RETIRED. *Personal Data:* b West, Tex, Sept 11, 30; m 51; c 4. *Educ:* Tex A&M Univ, BS, 59, MS, 60, PhD(dairy sci), 70. *Prof Exp:* Instr dairy sci, Tex A&M Univ, 65-67; asst prof agr, SW Tex State Univ, 67-77, assoc prof, 77-85. *Mem:* Am Dairy Sci Asn. *Res:* Dairy production and nutrition. *Mailing Add:* PO Box 1314 San Marcos TX 78667

HELM, RICHARD H, HIGH ENERGY PARTICLE ACCELERATOR PHYSICS. *Current Pos:* STAFF MEM PHYSICS, STANFORD LINEAR ACCELERATOR CTR, 58- *Personal Data:* b National City, Calif, Aug 2, 22; m 49; c 2. *Educ:* Stanford Univ, AB, 47, MS, 50, PhD(physics), 56. *Prof Exp:* Staff mem physics, Univ Calif, Los Alamos Sci Lab, 56-58. *Mem:* Am Inst Physics; Sigma Xi. *Res:* Beam dynamics and beam transport design and analysis in high energy particle accelerators. *Mailing Add:* 334 Lincoln Ave Palo Alto CA 94301

HELM, ROBERT ALBERT, INTERNAL MEDICINE. *Current Pos:* RETIRED. *Personal Data:* b Cincinnati, Ohio, Mar 28, 21; m 59; c 1. *Educ:* Univ Cincinnati, BS, 42, MD, 45. *Prof Exp:* From instr to assoc prof med, Univ Cincinnati, 50-64, prof, 64-88. *Concurrent Pos:* Consult, Vet Admin Hosp, 58-88; mem coun clin cardiol & coun circulation, Am Heart Asn. *Mem:* Fel Am Col Cardiol; fel Am Col Physicians; Sigma Xi. *Res:* Cardiovascular disease with emphasis on electrocardiography. *Mailing Add:* 308 Warren Ave Cincinnati OH 45220

HELMAN, SANDY I, PHYSIOLOGY, BIOPHYSICS. *Current Pos:* from asst prof to assoc prof, 72-80, PROF, DEPT PHYSIOL & BIOPHYS, UNIV ILL, URBANA-CHAMPAIGN, 80- *Personal Data:* b Winnipeg, Man, May 30, 39; nat US. *Educ:* Univ Man, BSEE, 61; Drexel Inst Technol, MS, 62; Marquette Univ, PhD(physiol), 66. *Prof Exp:* Res assoc, Presby Hosp, Drexel Inst Technol, Pa, 61-62 & Vet Admin Hosp, Wis, 62-66; USPHS postdoctoral fel, Lab Kidney & Electrolyte Metab, NIH, Bethesda, Md, 66-69; from asst prof to assoc prof, Dept Physiol, Sch Med, Tulane Univ, La, 69-72. *Concurrent Pos:* Mem, Prog Adv Comt, Am Physiol Soc, 77-79; secy-treas, Membrane Biophys Group, Biophys Soc, 77-83. *Mem:* Am Physiol Soc; Am Soc Nephrology; Biophys Soc; Int Soc Nephrology; AAAS; Sigma Xi; Soc Gen Physiologists. *Mailing Add:* Dept Physiol & Biophys 524 Burrill Hall Univ Ill 407 S Goodwin Ave Urbana IL 61801-3796. *Fax:* 217-333-1133

HELMAN, WILLIAM PHILLIP, PHYSICAL CHEMISTRY. *Current Pos:* fel chem, 66-67, jr fel, 67-68, asst fac fel, 68-72, ASSOC PROF SPECIALIST, RADIATION LAB, UNIV NOTRE DAME, 72- *Personal Data:* b Grand Junction, Colo, Nov 2, 36. *Educ:* Calif Inst Technol, BS, 58, MS, 60; Univ Minn, PhD(phys chem), 64. *Prof Exp:* Res chemist, Jackson Lab, E I du Pont de Nemours & Co, Inc, 64-66. *Mem:* Am Phys Soc; Am Chem Soc. *Res:* Luminescence and reactions of excited organic molecules; pulse radiolysis. *Mailing Add:* 2741 Portland Lane South Bend IN 46635

HELMANN, JOHN DANIEL, TRANSCRIPTION, GENE REGULATION. *Current Pos:* ASST PROF, DEPT MICROBIOL, CORNELL UNIV, 90- *Personal Data:* b San Jose, Calif, May 24, 61. *Educ:* Univ Calif, Santa Cruz, BA(chem) & BA(biol), 82; Univ Calif, Berkeley, PhD(biochem), 87. *Honors & Awards:* Vector Young Investr Award, Am Soc Microbiol, 93. *Prof Exp:* Fel biol chem & molecular pharmacol, Harvard Med Sch, 87-90. *Mem:* AAAS; Am Soc Microbiol; Am Chem Soc. *Res:* Study subunit structure and function of Bacillus subtilis RNA polymerase with an emphasis on the sigma and delta subunits. *Mailing Add:* Sect Microbiol Wing Hall Cornell Univ Ithaca NY 14853-8101. *Fax:* 607-255-3904

HELMBERGER, DONALD V, PHYSICS, GEOPHYSICS. *Current Pos:* from asst prof to assoc prof, 70-79, PROF GEOPHYSICS, CALIF INST TECHNOL, 79- *Personal Data:* b Perham, Minn, Jan 23, 38. *Educ:* Univ Minn, BA, 62; Univ Calif, San Diego, MS, 65, PhD, 67. *Honors & Awards:* Lehman Medal, 97. *Prof Exp:* Res assoc, Dept Geol & Geophysics, Mass Inst Technol, 67-69; asst prof geophysics, Princeton Univ, 69. *Mem:* Fel Am Geophys Union; Soil Soc Am. *Res:* Modeling seismograms to estimate source properties or to determine earth structure; author or co-author of 160 publications. *Mailing Add:* Seismol Lab 252-21 Calif Inst Technol Pasadena CA 91125

HELMBOLD, ROBERT LAWSON, MODELLING MILITARY OPERATIONS, WEAPON SYSTEMS ANALYSIS. *Current Pos:* OPERS RES ANALYST, US ARMY CONCEPTS ANALYSIS AGENCY, 84- *Personal Data:* b Wilkinsburg, Pa, Nov 4, 31; m 57, Paula Crawford Shirey; c Elizabeth, David, Bruce & Eric. *Educ:* Carnegie Mellon Univ, BSc, 53, MSc, 54, PhD (math), 57. *Prof Exp:* Opers analyst, Combat Opers Res Group, 57-61, sr staff analyst, 62-65; math linguistician, Tech Opers Res Div, Tech Opers Inc, 65-66; sr eng specialist, Data Systs Div, Litton Indust, 67-69; assoc, Rand Corp, Santa Monica, 69-72; sr staff analyst Res & Develop Assocs, 72-80; opers res analyst, Naval Air Develop Ctr, 81-84. *Mem:* Inst Opers Res & Mgt Sci. *Res:* Quantitative analysis of historical combat data; modelling of complex military operations and weapon systems; statistics. *Mailing Add:* 4505 Avamere St Bethesda MD 20814. *Fax:* 301-295-1834; *E-Mail:* helmbold@erols.com

HELMER, JOHN, physics, electronics, for more information see previous edition

HELMER, RICHARD GUY, EVALUATION OF NUCLEAR STRUCTURE & DECAY DATA, EXPERIMENTAL NUCLEAR PHYSICS. *Current Pos:* sr scientist, Aeroject Nuclear Co, 71-76, prin scientist, EG&G Idaho Inc, 76-94, CONSULT SCIENTIST, LOCKHEED MARTIN IDAHO TECHNOL CO, 94- *Personal Data:* b Homer, Mich, Feb 19, 34; m 56, Mary J Scrivens; c Gary A & Carl W. *Educ:* Univ Mich, BS, 56, MS, 57, PhD(physics), 61. *Prof Exp:* Physicist, Phillips Petrol Co, 61-66; Idaho Nuclear Corp, 66-71. *Concurrent Pos:* Asst prof & collabr, Utah State Univ, 65-75; elected mem, Int Comt Radio Nuclide Metrology, 91- *Mem:*

AAAS; fel Am Phys Soc; Am Nuclear Soc; NY Acad Sci. *Res:* Decay schemes of radioactive nuclides; nuclear structure studies and precise gamma-ray and electron spectroscopy; evaluation of nuclear structure data. *Mailing Add:* Idaho Nat Eng Lab Lockheed Martin Idaho Technol Co Idaho Falls ID 83415-2114

HELMERICK, ROBERT HOWARD, PLANT BREEDING. *Current Pos:* SR PLANT BREEDER, HILLESHOG-MONOHY INST, 84- *Personal Data:* b Greybull, Wyo, Feb 25, 26; m 54; c 5. *Educ:* Univ Wyo, BS, 50 & MS, 54; Univ Nebr, PhD(genetics), 58. *Prof Exp:* Plant breeder, Am Crystal Sugar Co, 58-64; asst dir agr res, Holly Sugar Co, 64-80, dir, Holly Seed Div, 80-82; plant breeder, Great Western Sugar Co, 82-84. *Mem:* Am Soc Agron; Am Study Sugarbeet Technologists. *Res:* Development of sugar beet varieties for North America. *Mailing Add:* 2313 Corey St Longmont CO 80501

HELMERS, DONALD JACOB, MECHANICAL ENGINEERING. *Current Pos:* from instr to assoc prof, 48-64, PROF MECH ENG, TEX TECH UNIV, 65- *Personal Data:* b Quincy, Ill, Jan 8, 17; m 43; c 3. *Educ:* Tex Tech Col, BS, 48; Univ Mich, MS, 50; Tex A&M Univ, PhD(mech eng), 65. *Prof Exp:* Power plant engr, Ford Motor Co, 36-41; mem teaching staff, Ford Aircraft Sch, 41-43. *Concurrent Pos:* Consult, Hughes Aircraft Co. *Mem:* Am Soc Mech Engrs; Am Soc Eng Educ; Nat Soc Prof Engrs. *Res:* Fluid dynamics and heat transfer, especially the use of analog and digital computers for a model study. *Mailing Add:* 3815 43rd St Lubbock TX 79413

HELMHOLZ, AUGUST CARL, HIGH ENERGY PHYSICS. *Current Pos:* Physicist, Radiation Lab, Univ Calif, Berkeley, 40-42 & 46-58, physicist, Manhattan Proj, 43-46, from instr to assoc prof, Univ, 40-51, prof, 51-80, Chem Dept, 55-62, EMER PROF PHYSICS, UNIV CALIF, BERKELEY, 80-, PHYSICIST, LAWRENCE BERKELEY LAB, 58- *Personal Data:* b Evanston, Ill, May 24, 15; m 38, Elizabeth Little; c Chalan H (Colby), George L, Frederic V, Edith H (Roth). *Educ:* Harvard Univ, AB, 36; Univ Calif, PhD(physics), 40. *Hon Degrees:* ScD, Univ Strathclyde, 79. *Concurrent Pos:* Guggenheim fel, 62-63; with Europ Orgn Nuclear Res, 62-63; mem gov bd, Am Inst Physics, 64-66; vis sci prog, 66-71; Berkeley fel, 88- *Mem:* AAAS; Am Phys Soc; Am Asn Physics Teachers; Sigma Xi. *Res:* Nuclear reactions; nuclear physics; pion nucleon interactions; double beta decay. *Mailing Add:* 28 Crest Rd Lafayette CA 94549

HELMICK, LARRY SCOTT, ANALYTICAL CHEMISTRY, SCIENCE EDUCATION. *Current Pos:* PROF CHEM, CEDARVILLE COL, 68- *Personal Data:* b Traverse City, Mich, Nov 18, 41; m 62, Catherine L Walmsley; c John & Shannon. *Educ:* Cedarville Col, BS, 63; Ohio Univ, PhD(org chem), 68. *Concurrent Pos:* Fel, Univ Fla, 69-71 & 74-75, Univ Ill, 72-74; fac fel, NASA-Lewis Res Ctr, 80-87 & 90-93, fel, Nat Res Coun, 88-89. *Mem:* AAAS; Am Chem Soc; Creation Res Soc. *Res:* Base-catalyzed hydrogen-deuterium exchange in aromatic nitrogen heterocycles; synthesis, structure determination, reactivity and theoretical chemistry of nitrogen heterocycles; racemization of amino acids; rates of dripstone deposition; origin of optical activity; search for Noah's Ark; Meisenheimer Adducts; thermal stability of fuels and lubricants. *Mailing Add:* Dept Chem Cedarville Col PO Box 601 Cedarville OH 45314-0601. *Fax:* 937-766-7631; *E-Mail:* helmickl@cedarville.edu

HELMINGER, PAUL ANDREW, MOLECULAR SPECTROSCOPY. *Current Pos:* asst prof, 73-77, assoc prof, 77-81, PROF PHYSICS, UNIV S ALA, 81- *Personal Data:* b Mills Springs, NC, Sept 5, 41; m 64, Sammy Hodges; c Andrew G. *Educ:* NC State Univ, BS, 63; Duke Univ, PhD(physics), 69. *Prof Exp:* Teaching asst physics, Duke Univ, 63-64, res asst, 64-69, res assoc & instr, 69-73. *Concurrent Pos:* Sr res scientist, Duke Univ, 79-90; vis prof, Ohio State Univ, 91- *Mem:* Am Phys Soc; Sigma Xi; Am Asn Physics Teachers; Optical Soc Am. *Res:* Millimeter and submillimeter microwave spectroscopy of molecules of atmospheric significance; variable temperature pressure broadening studies. *Mailing Add:* Dept Physics Univ SAla Mobile AL 36688

HELMINIAK, THADDEUS EDMUND, CHEMISTRY. *Current Pos:* RES CHEMIST, POLYMER BR, AIR FORCE MAT LAB, WRIGHT-PATTERSON AFB, 64- *Personal Data:* b Chicago, Ill, Aug 11, 35; m 59; c 2. *Educ:* John Carroll Univ, BSNS, 57, MS, 59; Univ Akron, PhD(chem), 62. *Prof Exp:* Res chemist, Inst Rubber Res, Univ Akron, 60-62; Nat Acad Sci res fel polymer chem, aeronaut systs div, Wright-Patterson AFB, 62-63; res chemist, Res Inst, Univ Dayton, 63-64. *Concurrent Pos:* Adj prof, Univ Dayton, 73- *Mem:* Am Chem Soc. *Res:* Physics and physical chemistry of polymers; solution properties of macromolecules; physical property-molecular structure relationships. *Mailing Add:* 405 Orchard Dr Dayton OH 45419-1726

HELMKAMP, GEORGE KENNETH, ORGANIC CHEMISTRY. *Current Pos:* from instr to assoc prof, 53-65, chmn dept, 70-75, assoc dean, Col Nat & Agr Sci, 75-77, PROF CHEM, UNIV CALIF, RIVERSIDE, 65- *Personal Data:* b Nebr, Feb 24, 21; m 47; c 4. *Educ:* Wartburg Col, BA, 42; Claremont Cols, MA, 50; Calif Inst Technol, PhD(chem), 53. *Prof Exp:* Control chemist, Atmospheric Nitrogen Corp, 42-43; analyst, Wilshire Oil Co, 43-45; chemist, Socal Oil & Refining Co, 47-49; instr org chem, Pomona Col, 52-53. *Mem:* Am Chem Soc. *Res:* Synthesis and properties of small-ring systems; stereochemistry of the reaction of epoxides; interactions of purines and pyrimidines. *Mailing Add:* Dept Chem 027 Univ Calif Riverside CA 92521-0403

HELMKAMP, GEORGE MERLIN, JR, BIOCHEMISTRY. *Current Pos:* from asst prof to assoc prof, 75-86, PROF BIOCHEM, UNIV KANS MED CTR, 86- *Personal Data:* b Washington, DC, Nov 29, 43; m 67; c 2. *Educ:* Rensselaer Polytech Inst, BS, 65; Harvard Univ, PhD(biochem & molecular biol), 70. *Prof Exp:* Res chemist, US Army Inst Surg Res, 70-73; fel biochem, State Univ Utrecht, 73-75. *Mem:* Sigma Xi; AAAS; Am Soc Biochem Molecular Biol; Biophys Soc. *Res:* Lipid-protein interactions, especially in biological and artificial membranes; phospholipid transfer proteins and their mechanism of action; metabolism of phosphatidylinositol. *Mailing Add:* Dept Biochem & Molecular Biol Univ Kans Med Ctr 39th & Rainbow Kansas City KS 66160-7421. *Fax:* 913-588-7440

HELMREICH, ERNST J M, BIOCHEMISTRY. *Current Pos:* prof, 68-90, EMER PROF PHYSIOL CHEM & CHMN DEPT, MED SCH, WURZBURG UNIV, 90- *Personal Data:* b Munich, Ger, July 1, 22; nat US; m 49, Rosmarie Hartmann; c Irene & Ilka. *Educ:* Univ Munich & Erlangen, MD, 49. *Prof Exp:* Fel, Ger Res Coun, Munich Tech Univ, 49-53; Nat Acad Sci-Int Coop Admin foreign fel & privat docent, Med Sch, Univ Munich, 54-56; from asst prof to assoc prof biol chem, Med Sch, Wash Univ, 56-68. *Concurrent Pos:* Fogarty scholar in residence, NIH-FIC, Bethesda, Md, 93-94. *Mem:* Am Soc Biol Chem; Ger Chem Soc; Ger Soc Biol Chem (pres, 73-75); Am Chem Soc; Sigma Xi; Ger Acad Sci; Europ Molecular Biol Organ. *Res:* Regulation of enzymes on the level of cellular and molecular organization; signal transduction by hormones; role of pyridoxal-5'-P in glycogen phosphorylase. *Mailing Add:* Werner von Siemens-Str 97076 Wurzburg Germany. *Fax:* 49-931-201-3153

HELMS, BOYCE DEWAYNE, INDUSTRIAL CHEMISTRY, ANALYTICAL CHEMISTRY. *Current Pos:* plant chemist, 70-80, safety & health, 80-93, ENVIRON MGR, AIR PROD & CHEM INC, 93-; CONSULT, 80- *Personal Data:* b Tuckerman, Ark, June 27, 37; m 59; c 2. *Educ:* Harding Col, BS, 59; Univ Ark, MS, 62. *Prof Exp:* Chemist, Escambia Chem Corp, 62-67; chief chemist, Arkla Chem Corp, 67-70. *Mem:* Am Chem Soc. *Mailing Add:* 345 Grover Lane Benton KY 42025

HELMS, CARL WILBERT, ZOOLOGY, PHYSIOLOGICAL ECOLOGY. *Current Pos:* head dept, 75-87, PROF BIOL SCI, CLEMSON UNIV, 75- *Personal Data:* b New Brighton, Pa, May 26, 33; m 70, Doris Reitinger; c Katherine, Margaret, Thomas, Robert & Lindsey. *Educ:* Univ Colo, BA, 55; Harvard Univ, AM, 56, PhD(biol), 60. *Prof Exp:* From asst prof to assoc prof biol, Bucknell Univ, 60-68, chmn dept, 64-68; mem, Inst Ecol, Univ Ga, NSF sci fac fel zool, 66-67, assoc prof, 68-75, grad coordr, 69-75. *Concurrent Pos:* NIH grant, 62-65; health scientist adminr & grants assoc, NIH, 70-71. *Mem:* Fel AAAS; Am Ornith Union; Asn Appl Interactive Multimedia (pres, 93-94); Asn Educ Commun Technol; Asn Comput Mach. *Res:* Bioenergetics; annual cycles in birds; seasonal variations in fat and fatty acid reserves; seasonal variations in endocrine function; control of lipogenesis; migratory restlessness; proximate factors and migration; biometry; advanced technology in education. *Mailing Add:* Dept Biol Sci Clemson Univ 132 Long Hall Clemson SC 29634-1903. *Fax:* 864-656-0435; *E-Mail:* cwhelms@clemson.clemson.edu

HELMS, JOHN ANDREW, FORESTRY. *Current Pos:* lectr & assoc specialist, 64-65, asst prof forestry, 65-71, SILVICULTURIST, 65-, ASSOC PROF FORESTRY, UNIV CALIF, BERKELEY, 71-, ASST CHMN DEPT, 73- *Personal Data:* b Esperance, Western Australia, Sept 29, 31; m 60. *Educ:* Univ Sydney, BSc, 53; Univ Wash, MF, 60, PhD(silvicult), 63. *Prof Exp:* Forestry officer, Tasmanian Forestry Comn, 53-58; res assoc silviculture, Univ Wash, 63-64. *Res:* Tree physiology; growth of trees in relation to environment; evaluation of photosynthesis; transpiration and microclimate under field conditions. *Mailing Add:* Environ Sci Univ Calif Berkeley CA 94720-0001

HELMS, JOHN F, ORGANIC CHEMISTRY. *Current Pos:* RETIRED. *Personal Data:* b Neenah, Wis, Apr 7, 19; m 46, Betty B Beeson; c Thomas F & Mary E. *Educ:* Lawrence Col, BA, 41; Univ Wis, PhM, 43. *Prof Exp:* Asst, Univ Wis, 42-43; chemist, Am Can Co, 43-44 & 45-47; chemist, Marathon Corp, 47-53; group leader coatings, 53-57; group leader coatings, Am Can Co, 57-65; supvr formulations, 65-67; mgr lab serv, Packaging Tech Serv, 67-73, assoc dir lab serv, packaging res & develop, 73-80. *Mem:* Am Chem Soc; Tech Asn Pulp & Paper Indust; Am Soc Testing & Mat. *Res:* Protective and functional coatings and laminations for the food packaging industry. *Mailing Add:* 693 Congress Pl Neenah WI 54956

HELMS, LESTER LAVERNE, MATHEMATICS. *Current Pos:* from asst prof to assoc prof, 58-68, PROF MATH, UNIV ILL, URBANA, 68- *Personal Data:* b Peoria, Ill, Dec 29, 27; m 52; c 3. *Educ:* Bradley Univ, BS, 52; Purdue Univ, MS, 53, PhD, 56. *Prof Exp:* Mathematician, Convair Div, Gen Dynamics Corp, 55-57; asst prof math, Mich State Univ, 56-58. *Mem:* Am Math Soc; Inst Math Statist. *Res:* Differential equations and probability theory and their interrelations. *Mailing Add:* Dept Math Univ Ill 1409 W Green St Urbana IL 61801-2917

HELMS, THOMAS JOSEPH, INSECT PATHOLOGY, BIOLOGICAL CONTROL. *Current Pos:* asst dir, 88-94, ASSOC DIR, MISS AGR & FORESTRY EXP STA, 94- *Personal Data:* b St Louis, Mo, Dec 20, 39; m 58; c 4. *Educ:* Ark State Univ, BS, 62, MS, 63; Iowa State Univ, PhD(entom), 67. *Prof Exp:* Instr entom, Iowa State Univ, 66-67; from asst prof to assoc prof, Univ Nebr, 67-78, asst dean agr, 73-78; prod develop mgr, Monsanto Co, 78-81; prof entom & head dept, Miss State Univ, 81-88. *Concurrent Pos:* Chair, Sect F, Entom Soc Am, 85-86; pres, Miss Asn Regist Prof Entomologists, 87-88. *Mem:* Entom Soc Am. *Res:* Agriculture and forestry; insect pathology and biological control. *Mailing Add:* Southern Asn Exp Sta Dirs PO Box 9656 Mississippi State MS 39762

HELMS, WARD JULIAN, ELECTRICAL ENGINEERING, GEOPHYSICS. *Current Pos:* res assoc elec eng, 63-68, asst prof elec eng & geophys & NSF grant, Byrd Sta, Antarctica, 68-75, ASSOC PROF ELEC ENG & GEOPHYS, UNIV WASH, 75- *Personal Data:* b Everett, Wash, June 12, 38; m 64; c 3. *Educ:* Wash State Univ, BS, 60; Univ Wash, MS, 63, PhD(elec eng), 68. *Prof Exp:* Field engr, Stanford Univ, 61-63. *Concurrent Pos:* NASA grant, 71- *Mem:* Inst Elec & Electronics Engrs; Am Geophys Union; Sigma Xi. *Res:* Very low frequency sounding of the D region; electronic circuit design philosophy; radioscience. *Mailing Add:* Wash Univ Seattle Redmond WA 98195

HELMSEN, RALPH JOHN, BIOCHEMISTRY, OPHTHALMOLOGY. *Current Pos:* res chemist, Nat Eye Inst, 69-76, chief, Anterior Segment Disease Br, 75-88, res training & resources officer, 88-92, RES RESOURCES OFFICER, NAT EYE INST, 93- *Personal Data:* b St Louis, Mo, May 28, 32; m 65, Mary Vukelich; c Eric, Joseph & John. *Educ:* Wash Univ, AB, 53; Univ Mo, MS, 59; St Louis Univ, PhD(biochem), 66. *Prof Exp:* Staff fel ophthal chem, Nat Inst Neurol Dis & Blindness, 65-69. *Mem:* Am Chem Soc; Asn Res Vision & Ophthal. *Res:* Isolation and characterization of corneal antigens; macromolecules of vitreous body of eye; nutritional effects on ocular diseases. *Mailing Add:* 9602 Dewmar Lane Kensington MD 20895. *Fax:* 301-402-0528

HELMSTETTER, CHARLES E, MICROBIOLOGY. *Current Pos:* PROF & DIR CELL BIOL, FLA INST TECHNOL, 89- *Personal Data:* b Newark, NJ, Oct 18, 33; m 88, Wendy; c Charles, Michael & Lee. *Educ:* Johns Hopkins Univ, BA, 55; Univ Mich, MS, 56; Univ Chicago, MS, 57, PhD(biophys), 61. *Honors & Awards:* Selman A Waksman Award, 70. *Prof Exp:* Scientist molecular biol, NIH, 61-63; USPHS fel, Univ Inst Microbiol, Copenhagen, 63-64; assoc cancer res scientist, Roswell Park Mem Inst, 64-69, prin cancer res scientist, 69-74, dir cancer res & head dept biol, 74-89. *Concurrent Pos:* Nat Cancer Inst res grant, Roswell Park Mem Inst, 65-89; res asst prof, State Univ NY Buffalo, 65-70, res prof, 70-90; res prof, Niagara Univ, 68-89 & Canisius Col, 68-89. *Mem:* AAAS; Am Soc Microbiol; Am Soc Biol Chemists. *Res:* Cell growth and division; macromolecular synthesis; cell cycle. *Mailing Add:* Dept Biol Fla Inst Technol Melbourne FL 32901-6988. *Fax:* 407-952-1818; *E-Mail:* helmstetter@roo.fit.edu

HELMSWORTH, JAMES ALEXANDER, THORACIC SURGERY. *Current Pos:* from asst clin prof to assoc prof, 49-69, PROF SURG, UNIV CINCINNATI, 69-, DIR CARDIOVASC & THORACIC SURG, 70- *Personal Data:* b Jamestown, NDak, Mar 31, 15; m; c 3. *Educ:* Jamestown Col, BS, 35; Univ Pa, MD, 39. *Prof Exp:* Intern, Hosp Univ Pa, 39-41; surg resident, Cincinnati Gen Hosp, 41-44 & 47-49. *Concurrent Pos:* Mem attend staff, Cincinnati Gen Hosp, Christian R Holmes Hosp & Children's Hosp; assoc attend staff, Good Samaritan Hosp; surg consult, Vet Admin Hosp; consult thoracic surgeon, Bethesda Hosp & Shriners Burns Inst; prin investr, USPHS, Ohio State-Am Heart Asn & Southwestern Ohio Heart Asn res grants; mem, Am Bd Surg. *Mem:* Sr mem Am Asn Thoracic Surg; Am Col Cardiol; Am Col Surgeons; Am Heart Asn; Soc Vascular Surg. *Res:* Cardiac transplants; heterografts; homograft reconstruction; bronchography; counterpulsation with intra-aortic balloon in treatment of cardiogenic shock; deep hypothermia and circulatory arrest for intracardiac surgery in infants; use of aortic shunt in treatment of acute and chronic thoracic aneurysms. *Mailing Add:* Dept Surg Univ Cincinnati 231 Bethesda Ave Cincinnati OH 45267-0558

HELMUTH, HERMANN SIEGFRIED, PHYSICAL ANTHROPOLOGY, PRIMATOLOGY. *Current Pos:* asst prof, 68-71, assoc prof, 72-79, PROF PHYS ANTHROP, TRENT UNIV, 79- *Personal Data:* b Dresden, Germany, Mar 27, 39; m 64; c 2. *Educ:* Univ Kiel, Dr rer nat, 64, Dr habil(phys anthrop), 75. *Prof Exp:* Sci asst, Anthrop Inst, Kiel, WGer, 64-69. *Concurrent Pos:* Vis prof, Univ Guelph, 82-83. *Mem:* Ger Anthrop Soc; Can Asn Phys Anthrop. *Res:* Human osteology, evolution; anthropometry and human factors engineering; behavior of fossil man; evolution and creationism; Maya, Bavarian osteology. *Mailing Add:* Dept Anthrop Trent Univ Peterborough ON K9J 7B8 Can. *Fax:* 705-748-1613; *E-Mail:* hhelmuth@trentu.ca

HELQUIST, PAUL M, ORGANOMETALLIC CHEMISTRY. *Current Pos:* chmn, Dept Chem & Biochem, 88-93, PROF CHEM, UNIV NOTRE DAME, 84- *Personal Data:* b Duluth, Minn, Mar 5, 47; m 70, Christie M Wick; c 2. *Educ:* Univ Minn, BA, 69; Cornell Univ, MS, 71, PhD(org chem), 72. *Hon Degrees:* PhD, Univ Uppsala, Sweden, 88. *Prof Exp:* Teaching asst chem, Cornell Univ, 69-71, res asst, 71-72; fel, Harvard Univ, 73-74; from asst prof to prof, State Univ NY, Stony Brook, 74-86. *Concurrent Pos:* NSF fel chem, Cornell Univ, 69-72; instr synthetic org chem, Am Chem Soc, 81-; Bergquist fel, Am Scandinavian Found, 82. *Mem:* Am Chem Soc. *Res:* New Synthetic methods; applications of organometallic compounds in synthetic organic chemistry; total synthesis of biologically active compounds. *Mailing Add:* 17494 Stoney Pt Rd Granger IN 46530-7682

HELRICH, CARL SANFRID, JR, STATISTICAL MECHANICS, BIOPHYSICS. *Current Pos:* PROF & DEPT CHAIR PHYSICS BEGINNING & ADVAN PHYSICS & LAB, GOSHEN COL, 85- *Personal Data:* b Everett, Mass, Sept 12, 41; m 67, Betty J Weaver; c Carl S & David C. *Educ:* Case Inst Technol, BS, 63; Northwestern Univ, PhD(plasma physics), 69. *Prof Exp:* Asst prof statist mech plasma physics, Space Inst, Univ Tenn, 69-71; scientist res, Kernsforschungsanlage, Julich, 71-74; assoc prof & dept chair physics beginning & advan physics & lab, Bethel Col, Kansas, 76-85. *Concurrent Pos:* NASA/Am Soc Elec Eng fel res, Marshall Space Flight Ctr, 71; actg dir, Turner Lab, Goshen Col, 86-87, 88-89; consult Mat Sci, CTS Corp, 86; guest scientist, Kernforschungsanlage Julich, 82-83. *Mem:* Am Phys Soc; Sigma Xi; Coun Undergrad Res; NY Acad Sci; Fed Am Scientists. *Res:* Biological ion channels; bilayer studies; modelling; chaotic dynamics. *Mailing Add:* Dept Physics Goshen Col Goshen IN 46526. *E-Mail:* carlsh@goshen.edu

HELRICH, MARTIN, ANESTHESIOLOGY. *Current Pos:* prof anesthesiol & head dept, 56-87, EMER PROF, SCH MED, UNIV MD, BALTIMORE CITY, 87- *Personal Data:* b New York, NY, Mar 31, 22; m 50; c 2. *Educ:* Dickinson Col, BS, 46; Univ Pa, MD, 46. *Prof Exp:* Resident anesthesiol, NY Univ, 48-51; res assoc, Sch Med, Univ Pa, 53-54, asst prof, 55-56. *Concurrent Pos:* Consult, US Naval Med Ctr, Bethesda, Md, Walter Reed Army Med Ctr, Washington, DC, US Naval Med Ctr, Portsmouth, Va, Baltimore City Hosp; gov, Am Col Anesthesiologists, 71-74; dir, Am Bd Anesthesiol, 74-, secy-treas, 81-85, pres, 85-86. *Mem:* Am Soc Pharmacol & Exp Therapeut; AMA; Asn Univ Anesthetists; Am Soc Anesthesiol; Am Col Anesthesiologists. *Res:* Physiology and pharmacology of anesthesia. *Mailing Add:* 3507 Old Post Dr Baltimore MD 21208. *Fax:* 410-328-8538

HELSDON, JOHN H, JR, ATMOSPHERIC ELECTRICITY, NUMERICAL CLOUD MODELING. *Current Pos:* assoc prof meterol, 81-93, RES SCIENTIST, INST ATMOSPHERIC SCI, SDAK SCH MINES & TECHNOL, 79-, PROF METEOROL, 93-, CHMN, DEPT METEOROL, 94- *Personal Data:* b Buffalo, NY, Oct 29, 48; m 77, Dolores Matuszak; c Karen & Kristin. *Educ:* Trinity Col, BS, 70; State Univ NY, Albany, MS, 73, PhD(atmospheric sci), 79. *Prof Exp:* Res asst, Res Found, State Univ NY, 77-79. *Concurrent Pos:* Prin investr, NASA res grant, 84-86, NSF res grant, 84-97; mem, Comt Atmospheric Elec, Am Meteorol Soc, 86-88 & 90-92. *Mem:* Am Meteorol Soc; Am Geophys Union; Sigma Xi. *Res:* Numerical modeling of thunderstorm electrification and lightning in the context of multi dimensional cloud models with emphasis on determining which charge separation mechanisms are important. *Mailing Add:* Inst Atmospheric Sci SDak Sch Mines & Technol Rapid City SD 57701-3995. *Fax:* 605-394-6061; *E-Mail:* jhelsdon@lightning.ias.sdsmt.edu

HELSEL, ZANE ROGER, CROP SCIENCE, AGRONOMY. *Current Pos:* ASST PROF, DEPT AGRON, UNIV MO. *Personal Data:* b East Freedom, Pa, Mar 5, 49; m 78. *Educ:* Penn State Univ, BS, 71, MS, 73; Iowa State Univ PhD(agron), 77. *Prof Exp:* Res assoc, 73-75, instr agron, Iowa State Univ, 75-77; asst prof crop & soil sci, Mich State Univ, 77- *Mem:* Am Soc Agron; Crop Sci Soc Am; Am Soc Agr Eng. *Res:* Soybean production; forage quality and production; energy in agriculture. *Mailing Add:* Rutgers Corp Exten Cook Col Rm 111 Martin Hall Rutgers Univ PO Box 231 New Brunswick NJ 08903

HELSETH, DONALD LAWRENCE, JR, HEALTHCARE. *Current Pos:* sr info specialist, 89-90, info consult, 90-91, SCI COLLAB CONSULT, INFO RESOURCE CTR, BAXTER HEALTHCARE CORP, 91- *Personal Data:* b Corvallis, Ore, Sept 23, 53; m; c 2. *Educ:* Tex Christian Univ, Ft Worth, BS, 75; Northwestern Univ, PhD(biochem), 81. *Prof Exp:* Postdoctoral res fel, Dept Biochem, Rutgers Med Sch, Univ Med & Dent NJ, Piscataway, 81-82; postdoctoral res fel, Dent Sch, Northwestern Univ, 82-83, from instr to asst prof, 83-89. *Concurrent Pos:* Partic, Gordon Res Conf Collagen, 83; spec consult, Site Visit Team, Nat Inst Dent Res, 84; mem, Radiation Safety Comt, Northwestern Univ, 85-88 & Dent Coun, Dent Sch, 87-89; mem, Spec Grants Rev Comt, Nat Inst Dent Res, 87-91. *Mem:* AAAS; Am Chem Soc; Am Soc Biochem & Molecular Biol; Sigma Xi. *Mailing Add:* 810 Oakwood Ave Wilmette IL 60091-3318. *Fax:* 847-270-5381

HELSLEY, CHARLES EVERETT, GEOLOGY, GEOPHYSICS. *Current Pos:* PROF GEOL & GEOPHYS, UNIV HAWAII, MANOA, DIR, HAWAII INST GEOPHYS. *Personal Data:* b Oceanside, Calif, June 24, 34; m 55; c 4. *Educ:* Calif Inst Technol, BS, 56, MS, 57; Princeton Univ, PhD(geol), 60. *Prof Exp:* Asst prof geol, Calif Inst Technol, 60-62; asst prof, Case Western Res Univ, 62-63; from asst prof to assoc prof, Southwest Ctr for Advan Studies, Univ Tex, Dallas, 63-69, prof geosci, 69-76, assoc head, Geosci Div, 71-72, head, Geosci Prog & dir, Inst Geosci, 72-75. *Concurrent Pos:* Adj prof, Southern Methodist Univ, 63-76 & Univ Tex Marine Sci Inst, Galveston, 73-76. *Mem:* Geol Soc Am; Am Geophys Union. *Res:* Rock magnetism and paleomagnetism and their implications regarding continental drift; marine geophysics; magnetostratigraphy; geothermal resource exploration. *Mailing Add:* Geol & Geophys Univ Hawaii Manoa Honolulu HI 96822-2270

HELSLEY, GROVER CLEVELAND, ORGANIC CHEMISTRY, MEDICINAL CHEMISTRY. *Current Pos:* dir res, 70-72, vpres, 72-87, SR VPRES PHARMACEUT RES, HOECHST-ROUSSEL PHARMACEUT, INC, 87- *Personal Data:* b Strasburg, Va, Sept 26, 26; m 48; c 3. *Educ:* Shepherd Col, BS, 54; Univ Va, MS, 56, PhD(chem), 58. *Prof Exp:* Res chemist, E I du Pont de Nemours & Co Inc, 58-62 & A H Robins Co, 62-64, group leader, 64-68, assoc dir chem res, 68-70. *Mem:* Am Chem Soc; Sigma Xi. *Res:* Chemistry of heterocyclic compounds; fluoride displacement on aromatic rings. *Mailing Add:* PO Box 153 Rosemont NJ 08556-0053

HELSON, HENRY, HARMONIC ANALYSIS, FUNCTION THEORY. *Current Pos:* RETIRED. *Personal Data:* b Lawrence, Kans, June 2, 27; m 54, Ravenna Mathews; c David, Ravenna & Harold. *Educ:* Harvard Univ, AB, 47, PhD(math), 51. *Prof Exp:* Lectr math, Univ Uppsala, 50-51; instr, Yale Univ, 51-52, Jewett fel, 52-54, asst prof math, 54-55; from asst prof to prof, Univ Calif, Berkeley, 55-92. *Concurrent Pos:* Vis prof, France, Ghana, India & Sweden; mem, Inst for Advan Study, Princeton, 60. *Mem:* Am Math Soc. *Res:* Analyticity on compact abelian groups; prediction theory. *Mailing Add:* Dept Math Univ Calif Berkeley CA 94720-3840. *E-Mail:* helson@math.berkeley.edu

HELSON, LAWRENCE, ONCOLOGY, NEUROBIOLOGY. *Current Pos:* RETIRED. *Personal Data:* b New York, NY, Mar 21, 31; c 3. *Educ:* City Col New York, AB, 53; NY Univ, MS, 57; Univ Geneva, MD, 62; Am Bd Pediat, cert, 69. *Prof Exp:* Asst res & teaching, Dept Bact, Inst Med & Hyg, Univ Geneva, 62-63; instr path, New York City Community Col, 65-66; USPHS sr clin trainee, Mem Hosp, 67-68; from instr to assoc prof, Med Col, Cornell Univ, 68-86. *Concurrent Pos:* From clin asst pediatrician to assoc attend pediatrician, Mem Hosp, 68-74, attend pediatrician, 74-86; assoc, Sloan-Kettering Inst Cancer Res, 72-86. *Mem:* Harvey Soc; Am Soc Clin Oncol; fel Am Acad Pediat; Am Asn Cancer Res; Soc Pediat Res; Sigma Xi. *Res:* Clinical cancer, particularly pediatric; chemotherapy, neurobiology, specific tumors, neuroblastoma, neurosarcoma, neurofibroma; brain tumors; laboratory-nerve growth stimulating substance; tumor cell cyclic nucleotide effectors, phosphodiesterases; vitamins E, B6, C and cancer autologous bone marrow transplantation, catecholamine metabolism. *Mailing Add:* 10 Pondview Close Chappaqua NY 10514

HELSTROM, CARL WILHELM, APPLIED PHYSICS. *Current Pos:* prof, 66-91, EMER PROF ELEC ENG, UNIV CALIF, SAN DIEGO, 91- *Personal Data:* b Easton, Pa, Feb 22, 25; m 56, Barbro Dahlbom; c Lars & Stefan. *Educ:* Lehigh Univ, BS, 47; Calif Inst Technol, MS, 49, PhD(physics), 51. *Honors & Awards:* Centennial Medal, Inst Elec & Electronics Engrs, 84; Quantum Commun Award, 96. *Prof Exp:* Adv mathematician, Res Labs, Westinghouse Elec Corp, 51-66. *Concurrent Pos:* Lectr, Univ Calif, Los Angeles, 63-64; ed, Inst Elec & Electronics Engrs Trans Info Theory, 67-71. *Mem:* Fel Inst Elec & Electronics Engrs; fel Optical Soc Am. *Res:* Signal detection theory; optics; stochastic processes; communication theory. *Mailing Add:* Univ Calif 0407 La Jolla CA 92093-0407. *Fax:* 619-534-2486; *E-Mail:* helstrom@ucsd.edu

HELTEMES, EUGENE CASMIR, PHYSICS, MAGNETISM. *Current Pos:* sr res physicist, Cent Res Labs, Minn Mining & Mfg Co, 63-67, supvr, Instrumentation & Control Systs Eng Dept, 67-71, res specialist, 71-75, Lab Mgr, 75-83, SR RES SPECIALIST, 3M CO, 83- *Personal Data:* b St Cloud, Minn, Sept 26, 34; m 56; c 2. *Educ:* St John's Univ, Minn, BA, 56; Iowa State Univ, PhD(physics), 61. *Prof Exp:* Asst, Iowa State Univ, 56-57; asst, Ames Labs, AEC, 57-61. *Mem:* Am Phys Soc. *Res:* Low temperature physics; optics; solid state physics; instrumentation; magnetic properties. *Mailing Add:* 2537 Orchard Lane St Paul MN 55110

HELTNE, PAUL GREGORY, GROSS ANATOMY. *Current Pos:* DIR, CHICAGO ACAD SCI, 82- *Personal Data:* b Lake Mills, Iowa, July 4, 41; div; c 2. *Educ:* Luther Col, Iowa, BA, 62; Univ Chicago, PhD(primatology), 70. *Prof Exp:* Instr anat & biol, Univ Chicago, 70; asst prof anat, animal med & pathobiol, Johns Hopkins Univ, 70-79. *Concurrent Pos:* Consult, Sangamon State Univ, 70 & 71 & Dept Anat, Med Sch, Harvard Univ, 71; mem, Comt Conservation Nonhuman Primates, Ilar, Nat Res Coun, 72-75; assoc ed, Growth, 73-, assoc ed-in-chief, 78-87; planning coordr, Baltimore Zoo & Druid Hill Park, 74-76; consult, Pan Am Health Orgn, Bolivia, 75, Northern Colombia, 77 & Peru, 80-82. *Mem:* AAAS; Soc Study Evolution; Am Soc Primatologists; Int Primatological Soc; Sigma Xi. *Res:* Biology of South American primates; demography of New World primates; long term capture reproduction of Aotus, the owl monkey; physical anthropology of humans specifically Hottentots and XYY males, including their cytogenetics; evolution and ontogeny of form; morphology of genetic syndromes; population biology and ecology; sustained yield management of natural ecosystems. *Mailing Add:* Chicago Acad Sci 2060 N Clark St Chicago IL 60614-4712

HELTON, AUDUS WINZLE, PLANT PATHOLOGY. *Current Pos:* RETIRED. *Personal Data:* b Bethel, Okla, Oct 5, 22; m 45; c 5. *Educ:* Ohio Wesleyan Univ, BA, 47, MS, 48; Ore State Univ, PhD(plant path), 51. *Prof Exp:* From asst prof & asst plant pathologist to prof & plant pathologist, Univ Idaho, 51-86. *Mem:* AAAS; Am Phytopath Soc. *Res:* Tree fruit pathology. *Mailing Add:* HCR-85 Box 152-A Bonners Ferry ID 83805

HELTON, J WILLIAM, mathematics, electronics engineering, for more information see previous edition

HELTON, WALTER LEE, ECONOMIC GEOLOGY, STRATIGRAPHY. *Current Pos:* from asst prof to assoc prof, 66-77, PROF GEOL, TENN TECHNOL UNIV, 77-, CHMN DEPT, 68- *Personal Data:* b Sloans Valley, Ky, Nov 4, 33; m 58; c 2. *Educ:* Univ Ky, BS, 59, MS, 64; Univ Tenn, Knoxville, PhD(geol), 67. *Prof Exp:* Petrol geologist, Ferguson & Bosworth Oil Co, 59-61; econ geologist, Ky Geol Surv, 61-64. *Mem:* AAAS; Geol Soc Am; Nat Asn Geol Teachers. *Res:* Silurian and Devonian stratigraphy of Kentucky; geology of the Conasauga group of the southern Appalachians. *Mailing Add:* 964 Wyleswood Dr Cookeville TN 38501

HELWEG, OTTO JENNINGS, WATER RESOURCES PLANNING & MANAGEMENT, GROUND WATER HYDROLOGY. *Current Pos:* DEAN, COL ENG & ARCHIT, NDAK STATE UNIV, 96- *Personal Data:* b Kalamazoo, Mich, Feb 1, 36; m 64, Virginia M Caldwell; c Otto J II, Mark W & Steven J. *Educ:* US Naval Acad, BS, 58; Fuller Theol Sem, MDiv, 66; Univ Calif, Los Angeles, MS, 67; Colo State Univ, PhD(civil eng), 75. *Honors & Awards:* Nat Sci Award, Nat Water Well Asn, 83. *Prof Exp:* Officer, USN, 58-62; youth worker, Hollywood Presby Church, 62-66; missionary, United Presby Church, 67-73; from asst prof to assoc prof civil eng, Univ Calif, Davis, 75-79; dir, Dept Comput Systs, Calif Water Resources Ctr, 79, assoc dir, 80-82; prof, Tex A&M Univ, 83-87; prof & chmn, Univ Memphis, 88-95. *Concurrent Pos:* Consult, UN Develop Prog/UN Educ Sci & Cult Orgn, India, 79; pres, Helweg & assoc, 80-; ed, J Irrigation & Drainage, Am Soc Civil Engrs, 89-92. *Mem:* Fel Am Soc Civil Engrs; Am Geophys Union; Am Water Works Asn; Am Water Resources Asn; Am Soc Eng Educ; Asn Ground Water Scientists & Engrs. *Res:* Water resources systems; large scale optimization; well hydrology; municipal and industrial water supply. *Mailing Add:* Col Eng & Archit NDak State Univ Fargo ND 58105-5285. *Fax:* 701-231-7195; *E-Mail:* helweg@badlands.nodak.edu

HELWIG, HAROLD LAVERN, BIOCHEMISTRY. *Current Pos:* RETIRED. *Personal Data:* b Mendon, Mich, May 20, 17; m 44; c 3. *Educ:* Mich State Univ, BS, 39; Univ Calif, PhD(biochem), 52. *Prof Exp:* Res biochemist, Donner Lab Med Physics, Univ Calif, 51-53; prin scientist, Radioisotope Unit, Vet Admin Hosp, Calif, 53-56; chief air & indust hyg lab, Calif State Dept Pub Health, 56-63, chief cancer biochem lab, 63-66; independent consult chem, 66-78. *Mem:* AAAS; Am Chem Soc. *Res:* Trace element nutrition and intermediary metabolism; hematopoiesis and red blood cell dyscrasias; biochemical defects in alcoholism; radiochemical tracer techniques; chemistry and biological effects of air pollution; chemical carcinogenesis. *Mailing Add:* 442 Panoramic Way Berkeley CA 94704-2533

HELWIG, JAMES A, TECTONICS. *Current Pos:* GEOL CONSULT, 91- *Personal Data:* b Abington, Pa, Sept 25, 41; m 67; c 1. *Educ:* St Louis Univ, BS, 63; Columbia Univ, PhD(geol, stratig), 67. *Prof Exp:* Asst prof geol, Case Western Reserve Univ, 67-75; res geologist, Arco Oil & Gas Co, 75-80, dir tectonics res, 81-83, sr res adv, 83-85; sr consult, Schlumberger-Doll Res, 85-88; res scientist, Mobil Oil Res & Develop, 88-91. *Concurrent Pos:* Vis prof, Univ Vienna, 75; vis sr res assoc, Lamont-Doherty Geol Observ, 84. *Mem:* Am Asn Petrol Geologists; Geol Soc Am; Am Geophys Union. *Res:* Tectonics and stratigraphy of mountain belts and sedimentary basins; modeling of geological environments and processes. *Mailing Add:* 4508 Shady Hill Dr Dallas TX 75229

HELWIG, JOHN, JR, INTERNAL MEDICINE, CARDIOLOGY. *Current Pos:* clin assoc prof, 69-74, CLIN PROF MED, TEMPLE UNIV, 74-; CHIEF CARDIOL, GERMANTOWN HOSP, 65- *Personal Data:* b Philadelphia, Pa, Dec 10, 27, m, c 4. *Educ:* La Salle Col, AB, 50; Univ Pa, MD, 54; Am Bd Internal Med & Am Bd Cardiovasc Dis, dipl. *Prof Exp:* Intern, Univ Hosp, Univ Pa, 54-55, asst resident & asst instr surg, 55-56, resident & asst instr med, 56-57, fel cardiol & instr med, 57-59, asst prof med, Sch Med & assoc dir cardiovasc clin res ctr, Univ Hosp, 59-65. *Mem:* AAAS; AMA; fel Am Col Physicians; Am Col Cardiol. *Res:* Cardiovascular disease. *Mailing Add:* Cv Sect Germantown Hosp Philadelphia PA 19144

HELZ, GEORGE RUDOLPH, ENVIRONMENTAL GEOCHEMISTRY. *Current Pos:* From asst prof to assoc prof, 70-84, PROF CHEM, UNIV MD, COLLEGE PARK, 84-; DIR, MD WATER RESOURCES RES CTR, 90- *Personal Data:* b Silver Spring, Md, Mar 4, 42; m 70, Rosalind Tuthill; c Catherine. *Educ:* Princeton Univ, AB, 64; Pa State Univ, PhD(geochem), 71. *Concurrent Pos:* Mem disinfectants chem subcomt, Nat Acad Sci-Nat Res Coun, 78; vis prof, Stanford Univ, 83-84; AAAS environ fel, 88; chmn, geochem div, Am Chem Soc, 85; sr vis fel, Manchester Univ, UK, 89-90; pres, Geol Soc Washington, 96. *Mem:* Am Geophys Union; Geochem Soc (treas, 75-78); Geol Soc Am; Am Chem Soc; Soc Environ Toxicol Chem; Estuarine Res Fed. *Res:* Aqueous geochemistry; geochemistry of mineral deposits; environmental chemistry; fate of pollutants in estuaries. *Mailing Add:* Dept Chem & Biochem Univ Md College Park MD 20742. *Fax:* 301-314-9121; *E-Mail:* gh17@umail.umd.edu

HELZ, ROSALIND TUTHILL, PETROLOGY. *Current Pos:* Geologist, Exp Geochem & Mineral Br, 68-82 & Br Igneous & Geothermal Processes Br, 82-91, GEOLOGIST, LITHOSPHERIC PROCESSES BR, US GEOL SURV, 91- *Personal Data:* b Ames, Iowa, July 6, 44; m 70; c 1. *Educ:* Stanford Univ, BS, 65; Pa State Univ, MS, 68, PhD(geochem/mineral), 78. *Mem:* Mineral Soc Am; Geol Soc Am; Am Geophys Union. *Res:* Petrogenesis of basalts; petrology of the earth's mantle; chemistry of igneous rocks; mineralogy of igneous rocks; experimental determination of phase relations of igneous rocks. *Mailing Add:* US Geol Surv Sunrise Valley Dr Reston VA 20192

HELZER, GERRY A, ALGEBRA. *Current Pos:* Asst prof, 64-74, ASSOC PROF MATH, UNIV MD, COLLEGE PARK, 74- *Personal Data:* b Portland, Ore, Dec 7, 37; m 65. *Educ:* Portland State Col, BA, 59; Northwestern Univ, MA, 61, PhD(math, algebra), 64. *Mem:* Am Math Soc. *Res:* Linear algebra; numerical analysis. *Mailing Add:* Dept Math Univ Md College Park MD 20742-0001

HEM, JOHN DAVID, aqueous geochemistry, non-equilibrium thermodynamics; deceased, see previous edition for last biography

HEM, STANLEY L, PHYSICAL PHARMACY. *Current Pos:* from asst prof to assoc prof, 69-76, assoc dean grad sch, 85-87, PROF PHYS PHARM, SCH PHARM, PURDUE UNIV, 76-, ASST VPRES RES, 87- *Personal Data:* b New York, NY, Oct 5, 39; m 63; c 2. *Educ:* Rutgers Univ, BS, 61; Univ Conn, PhD(phys pharm), 66. *Honors & Awards:* Res Achievement Award in Pharmaceut Technol, Am Asn Pharmaceut Scientists, 91. *Prof Exp:* Sr res pharmacist, Wyeth Labs, Inc, 65-69. *Mem:* AAAS; fel Acad Pharmaceut Sci; Am Chem Soc; fel Am Asn Pharmaceut Scientists. *Res:* Suspensions; aluminum hydroxide chemistry. *Mailing Add:* Purdue Univ Sch Pharm Lafayette IN 47907

HEMAMI, HOOSHANG, ELECTRICAL ENGINEERING. *Current Pos:* res assoc, 65-66, asst prof, 66-70, assoc prof, 70-80, PROF ELEC ENG, OHIO STATE UNIV, 80- *Personal Data:* b Esfahan, Iran, Apr 9, 36; m 62; c 1. *Educ:* Univ Tehran, BS, 58; Mass Inst Technol, MS & EE, 62; Ohio State Univ, PhD(elec eng), 66. *Prof Exp:* Res asst elec eng, Mass Inst Technol, 62-63; sr res engr, Nat Cash Register Co, 63-64. *Mem:* Inst Elec & Electronics Engrs. *Res:* Pattern recognition; human locomotion; control and nonlinear systems. *Mailing Add:* Ohio State Univ 2015 Neil Ave Columbus OH 43210

HEMAN-ACKAH, SAMUEL MONIE, CHEMOTHERAPY, BIOPHARMACEUTICS. *Current Pos:* asst dean, 73-76, PROF PHARM & CHMN DEPT, HOWARD UNIV, 73- *Personal Data:* b Dunkwa, Ghana, Nov 16, 26; m; c 3. *Educ:* Nottingham Univ, BPharm, 54; Pharm Soc Gt Brit, MPS, 55; Univ London, PhD(pharmaceut), 65. *Prof Exp:* From lectr to sr lectr pharmaceut, Univ Sci & Technol, Kumasi, Ghana, 56-61, assoc prof & actg chmn dept, 65-69; res, Univ Fla, 69-71; assoc prof pharmaceut & asst dean, Fla A&M Univ, 72-73. *Mem:* Brit Pharmaceut Soc; Am Pharmaceut Asn; Acad Pharmaceut Sci; Am Soc Microbiol; Am Chem Soc; Sigma Xi. *Res:* Kinetics and mechanisms of action of drugs on microorganisms; cancer chemotherapy; bioavailability of drugs from multiphase dosage formulations; combined action of mutagenic carcinogens. *Mailing Add:* Dept Pharm Howard Univ 2400 Sixth St NW Washington DC 20059-0001

HEMANN, RAYMOND GLENN, DEFENSE & FOREIGN THREAT ANALYSES, AEROSPACE SYSTEMS ENGINEERING & ANALYSES. *Current Pos:* PRES & CHIEF EXEC OFFICER, ADVAN SYSTS RES INC, 89- *Personal Data:* b Cleveland, Ohio, Jan 24, 33; m 87, Pamela J Schaap; c James Edward & Carolyn Frances. *Educ:* Fla State Univ, BS, 57; Calif State Univ, Fullerton, MS, 70, MA, 72. *Prof Exp:* Res analyst, Fla State Rd Dept, 57-59; asst prog mgr, Mil Concepts Autonetics Div, Rockwell Int, 59-63, chief req anal, Autonetics Div, 64-70, dir future req, 82-86, dir threat anal, 86-89; asst prof opers res, US Naval Postgrad Sch, 63-64; mgr avionics design & anal, Lockheed-Calif Co, 70-72, prog develop mgr strategic systs, 76-80, mgr advan concepts, 80-82; gen mgr, Western Div, Arinc Res Inc, 72-76. *Concurrent Pos:* Instr quant methods, Calif State Univ, Fullerton, 64-70; consult, Nat Intel Coun, 82-89, Inst Defense Analyses, 89-, Dir Cent Intel, 92-95; Naval Studies Bd Panels Combat Networks, Future Naval Aviation & Navy-21, Nat Acad Sci, 85-92; adj fel, Ctr Strategic & Int Studies, 89-; instr systs eng, Indust Relations Ctr, Calif Inst Technol, 92-95; chmn, Indust Panels Labs Infrastruct Study, Off Secy Defense, 94-95; bd dirs, Fla State Univ Res Found, 94- *Mem:* Fel AAAS; assoc fel Am Inst Aeronaut & Astronaut; Asn Unmanned Vehicle Systs; Inst Elec & Electronics Engrs; Mil Opers Res Soc Am; Asn Old Crows. *Res:* Defense systems analyses and systems engineering; development of analytic techniques and methodologies for systems engineering, systems analysis and management information systems; national policy planning; intelligence analyses of foreign threat systems and science and technologies; strategic systems, command and control, avionics and management information systems. *Mailing Add:* 1215 Hartwood Point Dr Pasadena CA 91107

HEMBREE, GEORGE HUNT, PHYSICAL CHEMISTRY. *Current Pos:* RETIRED. *Personal Data:* b Richmond, Ky, Sept 2, 30; m 52, Betty Williams; c George, Elizabeth & Susan. *Educ:* Eastern Ky State Col, BS, 52; Ohio State Univ, PhD(chem), 58. *Prof Exp:* Asst chem, Ohio State Univ, 52-53, asst, Res Found, 55-57; from res chemist to sr res chemist, 58-64, res supvr, 65-68, res mgr, Parlin, NJ, 68-69 & 71-73 & Rochester, NY, 69-71, mkt mgr, Wilmington, Del, 73-74, lab dir, Photo Prod Dept, E I Du Pont de Nemours & Co, Inc, 74-88. *Mem:* Am Chem Soc. *Res:* Hydrocarbon oxidation; photographic systems. *Mailing Add:* 600 Whitby Dr Wilmington DE 19803

HEMBROUGH, FREDERICK B, CARDIOVASCULAR PHYSIOLOGY. *Current Pos:* from asst prof to assoc prof, 66-73, PROF PHYSIOL, IOWA STATE UNIV, 73- *Personal Data:* b Jacksonville, Ill, May 1, 24; m 47; c 3. *Educ:* Univ Ill, BS, 52, DVM, 54, MS, 63, PhD(physiol), 66. *Prof Exp:* Pvt pract vet med, 54-60; instr physiol, Univ Ill, 60-65. *Concurrent Pos:* NIH fel, 64-65; Iowa Heart Asn grant, 66-67; NIH grant geront studies, 71-73. *Mem:* Am Vet Med Soc; Am Physiol Soc; Am Soc Vet Physiol & Pharmacol; Sigma Xi. *Res:* Cardiovascular research, especially effects of starvation-refeeding and aging on the distensibility of the arterial system; effect of age on isolated canine papillary muscle function; effect of cardiac lesions on heart function. *Mailing Add:* Dept Physiol & Pharmacol Iowa State Univ Col Vet Med Ames IA 50010-0001

HEMBRY, FOSTER GLEN, ANIMAL NUTRITION. *Current Pos:* PROF & CHMN ANIMAL SCI, UNIV FLA, 90- *Personal Data:* b Decatur, Iowa, Jan 3, 41; m 64; c 2. *Educ:* Iowa State Univ, BS, 63; Univ Tenn, MS, 66; Univ Mo, PhD(animal nutrit), 69. *Prof Exp:* From asst prof to prof animal nutrit, La State Univ, 69-80, prof animal sci & assoc dean grad sch, 80-90. *Mem:* Am Soc Animal Sci. *Res:* Forage evaluation; protein metabolism; climatic-nutritional interrelationships; growth stimulants. *Mailing Add:* Dept Animal Sci Univ Fla PO Box 110910 Gainesville FL 32611-0910

HEMDAL, JOHN FREDERICK, ACOUSTICS. *Current Pos:* CONSULT, UNIV TOLEDO, 82- *Personal Data:* b Peru, Ind, July 29, 34; m 58; c 3. *Educ:* Purdue Univ, BSEE, 57, MSEE, 59, PhD(elec eng), 64. *Prof Exp:* Assoc engr, Appl Physics Lab, Johns Hopkins Univ, 57-58; instr elec eng, Purdue Univ, 58-64; res asst acoust, Univ Mich, Ann Arbor, 64-68, assoc res acoustician, 68-72; res acoustician, Environ Res Inst Mich, 72-74, head acoust & seismics, 74-77; consult, Hearing & Noise Assocs, 77-82. *Concurrent Pos:* Noise control consult, 75- *Mem:* Inst Elec & Electronics Engrs; Acoust Soc Am; Pattern Recognition Soc; Inst Noise Control Eng; Nat Soc Prof Eng. *Res:* Pattern recognition; automatic recognition of speech; acoustic phonetics; atmospheric acoustics; noise control; vibrations; signal processing; forensic engineering; electrical accident investigation. *Mailing Add:* 1211 Meanwell Rd Dundee MI 48131-9716

HEMENWAY, MARY-KAY MEACHAM, ASTRONOMY. *Current Pos:* lectr, 74-87, SR LECTR ASTRON, UNIV TEX, AUSTIN, 87- *Personal Data:* b Akron, Ohio, Nov 20, 43; m 68; c 2. *Educ:* Notre Dame Ohio, BS, 65; Univ Va, MA, 67, PhD(astron), 71. *Prof Exp:* Lectr physics, Mary Baldwin Col, 70-71 & astron, Univ Va Exten, 70-73. *Concurrent Pos:* Consult var sch dist & reg serv ctrs, 81- & Chautauqua Prog Col Sci Teachers, 85-89; reviewer, Choice, 82-; prin investr, NSF, 90-97; educ officer, Am Astron Soc, 91-97; res assoc, Univ Tex, Austin, 93-96. *Mem:* Am Astron Soc; Sigma Xi; Int Astron Union. *Res:* Astronomy education; astronomy laboratory activities; author of various publications. *Mailing Add:* 5710 Highland Hills Dr Austin TX 78731-4233. *Fax:* 512-471-6016; *E-Mail:* marykay@astro.as.utexas.edu

HEMILY, PHILIP WRIGHT, CRYSTALLOGRAPHY. *Current Pos:* sr prof officer, Off Int Affairs, 84-95, ADV, NAT ACAD SCI, 95- *Personal Data:* b Newaygo, Mich, June 2, 22; c 3. *Educ:* Univ Mich, BS, 47; Univ Paris, Dr, 53. *Honors & Awards:* Einstein Gold Medal, UNESCO, 91; Award Int Sci Cooperation, AAAS, 97. *Prof Exp:* Instr math, Auburn Univ, 47-49; res assoc crystallog res, Nat Sci Res Ctr, France, 55-57; prog dir, NSF, 57-61, dep head, Off Int Sci Activ, 61-65, sci attache, US Mission to Orgn Econ Coop & Develop, Paris, State Dept, 65-74; dep off dir, Bur Oceans & Int Environ & Sci Affairs, State Dept, 74-76; dep asst sect gen sci affairs, NATO, Brussels, Belg, 76-83. *Concurrent Pos:* Consult, Int Sci & Technol, State Dept, NATO, Stanford Res Inst, 83-85, Carnegie Comn Sci, Technol & Govt, 90-92. *Mem:* Fel AAAS; Am Crystallog Asn. *Res:* Inorganic crystal structure determinations at low temperatures by x-ray diffraction methods; science policy studies of international scientific organizations. *Mailing Add:* Off Int Affairs Nat Acad Sci Washington DC 20418. *Fax:* 202-334-2231

HEMING, BRUCE SWORD, ENTOMOLOGY, MORPHOLOGY DEVELOPMENT. *Current Pos:* From asst prof to assoc prof, 68-80, prof entom, 80-94, PROF BIOL, UNIV ALTA, 94- *Personal Data:* b Ithaca, NY, Dec 1, 39; Can citizen; m 76, Karin Elisabeth Van Baltum; c Arthur L & Steven A. *Educ:* Ont Agr Col, Univ Toronto, BSA, 63; NC State Univ, PhD(entom), 68. *Honors & Awards:* G Gordon Hewitt Award, Entom Soc Can, 76. *Mem:* AAAS; Can Soc Zoologists; Entom Soc Can; Entom Soc Am. *Res:* Insect structure, function, ontogeny and phylogeny; systematics and phylogeny of Thysanoptera. *Mailing Add:* Dept Biol Sci Univ Alta Edmonton AB T6G 2E9 Can. *Fax:* 403-492-1767

HEMINGHOUS, WILLIAM WAYNE, SR, MATERIALS & PROCESS PRODUCT DEVELOPMENT, FAILURE ANALYSIS AND PRODUCT IMPROVEMENT. *Current Pos:* dir mat eng mat sci, Thomson Saginaw Ball Screw Co, 88-92, DIR QUAL ASSURANCE & TECHNOL, THOMSON BAY CO, THOMSON INDUST, 92- *Personal Data:* b Mattoon, Ill, Nov 11, 45; m 70, Brenda Bauman; c Wayne, Lydia & John. *Educ:* Univ Ill, BS, 68; Purdue Univ, BS, 70; Ind Univ, BS, 83. *Prof Exp:* Exp metallurgist turbine engine metall, Allison Div, GMC, 68-79; pipe line metallurgist gas transmission indust, Tex Gas Transmission, 71-72; group leader reliability, Cummins Engine Co, 72-83; tech serv mgr metall qual assurance, Teledyne Continental Motors, Mobile, Ala, 83-86; sci lab mgr phy sci, Sverdrup Technol, Stennis Space Ctr, NASA, 86-88. *Concurrent Pos:* Sec adv, Kings Serv, Indianapolis, Ind, 78-81; customer qual assurance mgr, metall qual assurance, Consolidated Diesel Co, Cummins Engine Co, 81-83; inventor, Teledyne Continental Motors, Mobile, Ala, 83-86; prin investr plume diag, Sverdrup Technol, Stennis Space Ctr, NASA, 86-88; level III inspector, NDE Thomson Industs, 89-91, NDE instr, Thomson Sagmaw Ball Screw Co, 90-91; prog comt, Am Soc Metals, 90-91. *Mem:* Am Soc Metals; Soc Automotive Engrs; Am Soc Nondestructive Testing; Am Soc Testing & Mat; Am Soc Qual Control. *Res:* Advanced aerospace lubricant research and development; exploratory research in plume diagnostics of liquid fueled space shuttle engines; development and patent for nitrocarburization heat treatment of aircraft components; concept, development, and international patents on advanced turbo-compounded rotary aircraft engines; advanced materials and processes development for linear motion systems; specialist in high rate induction hardening and laser processing of materials. *Mailing Add:* 9681 Geddes Rd Saginaw MI 48609. *Fax:* 517-686-7920

HEMINGWAY, BRUCE SHERMAN, THERMODYNAMICS, CALORIMETRY. *Current Pos:* Asst chief, Br Igneous & Geothermal Processes, 86-91, chief, Br Lithospheric Processes, 91-95, GEOLOGIST, US GEOL SURV, 69-, CHIEF, NAT CTR THERMODYN DATA MINERALS, 88- *Personal Data:* b Chicago, Ill, Nov 19, 39; m 71, Carole Rogers; c Sean. *Educ:* Macalester Col, AB, 62; Univ Minn, MS, 65, PhD(geol & geophys), 71. *Concurrent Pos:* Mem, Conf Thermodyn & Nat Energy Probs, Nat Acad Sci, 74; mem, Panel Rock-Mech Res Requirements, Nat Res Coun & Nat Acad Sci, 79-81; vchmn & US nat rep, Working Group Thermodyn Natural Processes, IAGC, 83-; mem, CODATA Task Group Geothermodynamic data, 84-; chair, financial adv comt, Mineral Soc Am, 90-92. *Mem:* Geochem Soc; fel Mineral Soc Am. *Res:* Thermodynamic data measured and evaluated, used to test models in geologic and industrial processes and are provided in the form of a data base for use by others. *Mailing Add:* Nat Ctr Thermodyn Data Minerals US Geol Surv 955 Nat Ctr Reston VA 22092. *Fax:* 703-648-6032; *E-Mail:* bhemingw@usgs.gov

HEMINGWAY, GEORGE THOMSON, THEOLOGY. *Personal Data:* b Corvallis, Ore, Aug 23, 40; m 68, Jean A Potym; c Gillian C. *Educ:* San Diego State Univ, BS, 66, MS, 73. *Prof Exp:* Lectr practical oceanog, San Diego State Univ, 72-73; prof & chair biol, Fac Marine Sci, Autonomous Univ, Baja, Calif, 73-75; asst dir, Marine Life Res Group, Scripps Inst Oceanog, Univ Calif, San Diego, 78-93. *Concurrent Pos:* Adj prof biol, Fac Marine Sci, Autonomous Univ, Baja, Calif, 75-; coord, Calif Coop Ocean Fisheries Invest, 79-81, 85-88 & 91-, Interamericas Prog, Scripps Inst Oceanog, 79-, Tinker

Found, Latin Am Prog, Scripps Inst, 82-85; hon prof marine sci, Autonomous Univ, Baja, Calif. *Mem:* Am Soc Zool; Am Inst Biol Sci; AAAS; Western Soc Naturalists; Ctr Theol & Natural Sci; hon mem Mex Soc Oceanog. *Res:* Longterm, largescale study of the California current ecosystem, integrating its biology, chemistry and physics. *Mailing Add:* Scripps Inst Oceanog Univ Calif San Diego 9500 Gilman Dr La Jolla CA 92093-0227. *Fax:* 619-534-6500; *E-Mail:* ghemingway@ucsd.edu

HEMKEN, ROGER WAYNE, DAIRY NUTRITION. *Current Pos:* assoc prof, 70-72, PROF DAIRY HUSB, UNIV KY, 72-, DAIRY COMMODITY CHMN, 70- *Personal Data:* b Pontiac, Ill, Dec 9, 28; m 55; c 3. *Educ:* Univ Ill, BS, 50, MS, 54; Cornell Univ, PhD(dairy husb), 57. *Honors & Awards:* Am Feed Mfrs Award, Am Dairy Sci Asn, 74, Borden Award, 92. *Prof Exp:* From asst prof to prof dairy husb, Univ Md, 57-70. *Concurrent Pos:* Moormans Travel fel, Animal Nutrit Res, Nat Feed Ingredients Asn, 84; mem, Comt Animal Nutrit, Nat Acad Sci, 90-94. *Mem:* AAAS; Am Soc Animal Sci; Am Dairy Sci Asn; Am Inst Nutrit; Am Dairy Asn (vpres, 93-94, pres, 94-95). *Res:* Ruminant nutrition; nutritive evaluation of forages; mineral nutrition. *Mailing Add:* Dept Animal Sci Univ Ky 500 S Limestone St Lexington KY 40546-0001

HEMLEY, JOHN JULIAN, GEOCHEMISTRY, THERMODYNAMICS. *Current Pos:* RETIRED. *Personal Data:* b El Paso, Tex, Nov 8, 26; m 52, Virginia Jones; c Russel, Curt & Ginette. *Educ:* Tex Col Mines & Metall, BS, 49; Northwestern Univ, MS, 52; Univ Calif, Berkeley, PhD(geol), 58. *Honors & Awards:* Silver Medal, Soc Econ Geologist, 87. *Prof Exp:* Geologist, Calif Res Corp, Stand Oil Co Calif, 52-54 & US Geol Surv, 72-96; chief geochemist, Anaconda Co, 68-72. *Mem:* Soc Econ Geologists; Geol Soc Am; Geochem Soc; Am Mineral Soc; Am Geophys Union; AAAS. *Res:* Geochemistry; petrology; mineral genesis; aqueous chemistry and fields of stability of mineral phases characteristic of hydrothermal alteration and ore deposition. *Mailing Add:* US Geol Surv Reston VA 22092

HEMM, ROBERT VIRGIL, CHEMICAL ENGINEERING, TECHNICAL MANAGEMENT. *Current Pos:* RETIRED. *Personal Data:* b St Louis, Mo, June 20, 21; m 42, Barbara C Vollmer; c Barbara, Robert Jr & Ian. *Educ:* Wash Univ, BS, 42, DSc, 53; Auburn Univ, MBA, 72. *Prof Exp:* Sect chief packaging mat, USAF, 43-46, head packaging res, Mallinckrodt Chem Works, 46-51, proj engr, Power Plant Lab, 51-52, chief, Decontamination & Cleaning Sect, Mat Lab, 52-54, Protective Processes Br, 54-56, staff officer mat res & develop, 56-57, tech liaison officer, Foreign Technol Div, 57-61, res & develop dir hq, Res & Technol Div Air Force Systs Command, 62-66, res & develop staff engr, 66-68, chief, Technol Br, Sci & Technol Div, 68-70, chief sci & technol studies, Air War Col, 70-73, Commander European Off Aerospace Res & Develop Air Force Systs Command, 73-77; exec secy, Nat Mat Adv Bd, Nat Acad Sci, 77-82. *Concurrent Pos:* Substitute teacher sci, eng & math, Fairfax high schs Va, 83- *Mem:* Am Chem Soc; Sigma Xi. *Res:* Materials and techniques for packaging military equipment; packaging of chemicals; research and development of aerospace materials; management of defense research and development; technical information management; materials policy studies. *Mailing Add:* 8218 Dabney Ave Springfield VA 22152

HEMMENDINGER, ARTHUR, NUCLEAR PHYSICS, NEUTRON PHYSICS. *Current Pos:* RETIRED. *Personal Data:* b Bernardsville, NJ, July 11, 12; m 45, Margaret E Ross; c Ross, Anna & Dennis. *Educ:* Cornell Univ, AB, 33; Calif Inst Technol, PhD(physics), 37. *Prof Exp:* From instr to asst prof physics, Univ Okla, 37-41; physicist, Naval Ord Lab, Washington, DC, 41-44 & Metall Lab, Univ Chicago, 45; physicist, Los Alamos Sci Lab, 45-77; consult, Los Alamos Nat Lab, 77-80. *Mem:* Fel Am Phys Soc; AAAS. *Res:* Mass spectroscopy; underwater sound; instrumentation for nuclear physics; separation of the isotopes of potassium and rubidium and determination of naturally radioactive isotope; light particle reactions, especially those involving tritium and helium three; neutron and radiation physics; cross section measurements. *Mailing Add:* 1117 Sangre de Cristo St Santa Fe NM 87501-1055

HEMMENDINGER, HENRY, COLOR MEASUREMENT. *Current Pos:* partner, Davidson & Hemmendinger, 52-63, vpres, treas & dir color ctr, 63-70, DIR, HEMMENDINGER COLOR LAB, 70- *Personal Data:* b Bernardsville, NJ, Apr 1, 15; m 40; c David, Carol (Selikowitz) & Mark. *Educ:* Harvard Univ, AB, 35, AM, 37; Princeton Univ, PhD(astron), 39. *Honors & Awards:* Armin J Bruning Award, Fedn Socs Paint Technol, 66; Henry E Millson Award Invention, Am Asn Textile Chemists & Colorists, 88; Godlove Award, Inter-Soc Color Coun, 97. *Prof Exp:* Bausch & Lomb fel physics, Mass Inst Technol, 39-41; physicist, Inst Optics, Univ Rochester, 42-44; consult opers res group, USN, 44-45; physicist & group leader spectros, Cent Res Lab, Gen Aniline & Film Corp, Pa, 46-52. *Concurrent Pos:* Mem, Harvard-Mass Inst Technol Eclipse Exped, USSR, 36; chmn, US Nat Comt 1-3 Colorimetry, Int Comn Illumination, 77-79. *Mem:* Fel Optical Soc Am; Inter-Soc Color Coun. *Res:* Spectroscopy; solar physics; excitation conditions in light sources; operations research; spectrophotometry; luminescence; color and constitution; colorimetry; color standards. *Mailing Add:* Hemmendinger Color Lab 438 Wendover Dr Princeton NJ 08540. *Fax:* 609-497-3499

HEMMERLE, WILLIAM J, STATISTICS, COMPUTER SCIENCE. *Current Pos:* dir comput lab, Univ RI, 65-73, prof comput sci, 65-82, chmn dept comput sci & exp statist, 67-82, EMER PROF COMPUT SCI, UNIV RI, 82- *Personal Data:* b Des Plaines, Ill, May 8, 27; m 48; c 4. *Educ:* Univ Colo, BS, 50; Univ Wis, MS, 51; Iowa State Univ, PhD(math statist), 63. *Prof Exp:* Analyst, Nat Security Agency, DC, 51-55; asst mgr data processing ctr, mgr comput ctr & sr appl sci rep to fed govt, Int Bus Mach Corp, DC & NY, 55-60; from asst prof to assoc prof & head numerical anal prog group, Iowa State Univ, 60-65. *Concurrent Pos:* Consult, Nat Sch Agr Mex, 64; NSF grants, 64-; vis scientist, Inst Statist, Tex A&M Univ, 71-72; vis res prof, Dept Statist, NC State Univ, 78-79. *Mem:* Am Statist Asn. *Res:* Statistical computations. *Mailing Add:* 350 Ministerial Rd Wakefield RI 02882

HEMMES, DON E, CELL BIOLOGY, MYCOLOGY. *Current Pos:* PROF BIOL, UNIV HAWAII, HILO, 73-, CHMN NATURAL SCI DIV, 85- *Personal Data:* b Hampton, Iowa, Dec 28, 42; m 67, Helen Van Zanten; c Kimo & David. *Educ:* Cent Col, Iowa, BA, 65; Univ Hawaii, Honolulu, MS, 67, PhD(microbiol), 70. *Honors & Awards:* W H Weston Jr Award, Teaching Excellence, Mycol Soc Am. *Prof Exp:* Fel, Univ Zurich, Switz, 70-72 & Univ Calif, Riverside, 72-73. *Concurrent Pos:* Pac Island Minority Schs Biomed Res grant, 75. *Mem:* Sigma Xi; Mycol Soc Am. *Res:* Ultrastructural investigations of morphogenesis in fungi. *Mailing Add:* Biol Dept Univ Hawaii 200 W Kawili St Hilo HI 96720

HEMMES, PAUL RICHARD, CHEMICAL BATCH PROCESS DEVELOPMENT, TECHNOLOGY TRANSFER. *Current Pos:* staff scientist, 89-, VPRES OPERS, ENVIRON TEST SYSTS. *Personal Data:* b Staten Island, NY, June 14, 44; c 2. *Educ:* Clarkson Col, BS, 66; Polytechnic Inst Brooklyn, PhD(phys chem), 70. *Prof Exp:* Res assoc, Chem Dept, Univ Utah, 69-70; from asst prof to prof, Rutgers Univ, Newark, NJ, 70-81; supvr res & develop, Diag Div, Miles Labs, 81-85, dir process develop, 85-88, vpres mfg, Angenics Inc, 88-89. *Concurrent Pos:* Nat Acad Sci exchange visitor, USSR, 78 & 81; assoc ed, Microchem J, 85-88; consult, 89- *Res:* Application of medical diagnostic test technology to environmental tests; improving technology transfer between research and manufacturing, including batch chemical process development. *Mailing Add:* 4271 Norwalk Dr Apt X314 San Jose CA 95129

HEMMINGER, JOHN CHARLES, SURFACE CHEMISTRY. *Current Pos:* from asst prof to assoc prof, 78-87, PROF CHEM, UNIV CALIF, IRVINE, 87- *Personal Data:* b Lyons, NY, Apr 2, 49; m 78. *Educ:* Univ Calif, Irvine, AB, 71; Harvard Univ, PhD(chem physics), 76. *Honors & Awards:* Alfred P Sloan Res Award. *Prof Exp:* NSF fel, Univ Calif, Berkeley, 76-77, fel chem, 77-78. *Mem:* Am Chem Soc; Am Vacuum Soc. *Res:* Chemistry and physics of adsorbates on well characterized surfaces; molecular spectroscopy of chemisorbed species. *Mailing Add:* Dept Chem Univ Calif Irvine CA 92717

HEMMINGS, RAYMOND THOMAS, materials science & technology, materials chemistry, for more information see previous edition

HEMMINGSEN, BARBARA BRUFF, ENVIRONMENTAL MICROBIOLOGY. *Current Pos:* lectr, 73-77, from asst prof to assoc prof, 73-88, PROF MICROBIOL, SAN DIEGO STATE UNIV, 88- *Personal Data:* b Whittier, Calif, Mar 25, 41; m 67, Edvard Alfred; c Grete. *Educ:* Univ Calif, Berkeley, BA, 62, MA, 64; Univ Calif, San Diego, PhD(marine biol), 71. *Prof Exp:* Res microbiologist, Ames Res Ctr, NASA, 64-65; vis asst prof microbial ecol, Aarhus Univ, Denmark, 71-72. *Concurrent Pos:* Consult, hydrocarbon-degrading bacteria, 88- *Mem:* AAAS; Am Soc Microbiol; Sigma Xi; Soc Gen Microbiol; Soc Protozoologists. *Res:* Intracellular gas supersaturation tolerances; microbial ecology of the bioremediation of petroleum spills; methods for enumerating and stimulating the in situ growth of hydrocarbon-degrading bacteria. *Mailing Add:* Dept Biol San Diego State Univ San Diego CA 92182-4614. *E-Mail:* bhemming@sunstroke.sdsu.ed

HEMMINGSEN, EDVARD A(LFRED), ANIMAL PHYSIOLOGY. *Current Pos:* from jr res physiologist to assoc res physiologist, 60-77, RES PHYSIOLOGIST & LECTR PHYSIOL, UNIV CALIF, SAN DIEGO, 77- *Personal Data:* b Tromso, Norway, July 15, 32; m 67; c Grete A. *Educ:* Univ Oslo, Norway, MagSci, 58, DrPhil, 65. *Prof Exp:* Res fel physiol, Norweg Res Coun, 58-59; vis fel glaciol, Arctic Inst NAm, 59-60. *Concurrent Pos:* Vis prof physiol, Univ Aarhus, Denmark, 71-72. *Mem:* Am Physiol Soc; AAAS. *Res:* Diffusive transport of oxygen in animals; functions and properties of myoglobin; respiratory and cardiovascular functions in fishes; gas-water interactions at high pressures; gas bubble formation in animals. *Mailing Add:* Scripps Inst Oceanog A-004 La Jolla CA 92093-0204. *Fax:* 619-534-1305; *E-Mail:* ehemmingsen@ucsd.edu

HEMMINGSEN, ERIK, MATHEMATICS. *Current Pos:* from instr to prof, 47-87, chmn dept, 71-79, EMER PROF MATH, SYRACUSE UNIV, 88- *Personal Data:* b Espergaerde, Denmark, Sept 16, 17; nat US; m 46, Louise M Branson; c Carl E & Kirsten (Emigholz). *Educ:* Temple Univ, BS, 38; Univ Notre Dame, MS, 40; Univ Pa, PhD(math), 46. *Prof Exp:* Asst instr math, Univ Notre Dame, 39-41; asst instr, Univ Pa, 41-42; physicist, Naval Air Exp Sta, Philadelphia, 42-45; asst prof math, Univ Ga, 46-47. *Concurrent Pos:* Vis prof, Univ Trondheim, 65-66; chmn, Dept Math, Vanderbilt Univ, 69-70. *Mem:* Am Math Soc; Math Asn Am. *Res:* Topology; structure and design of gyroscopic aircraft flight instruments; theorems in dimension theory for normal Hausdorff spaces; plane homeomorphisms with equicontinuous iterates; light interior maps of n-manifolds on n-manifolds. *Mailing Add:* 101 Eton Lane Manlius NY 13144

HEMOND, CONRAD J(OSEPH), JR, CIVIL ENGINEERING, ACOUSTICS. *Current Pos:* chmn dept, 55-77, dir eng res, 68-71, PROF MECH ENG, UNIV HARTFORD, 55-, DEAN, 81- *Personal Data:* b Holyoke, Mass, June 8, 16; m 52; c 3. *Educ:* Univ Mass, BS, 38, MS, 46. *Prof Exp:* Asst city engr, Holyoke, Mass, 38-40; field engr, US Eng Dept, Westover Field, 40-43; instr physics, Rensselaer Polytech Inst, 43-45; asst prof,

Amherst Col, 45-50; proj engr, Bolt Beranek & Newman, 50-52 & Indust Sound Control, Inc, 52-55. *Concurrent Pos:* Mem, Noise Bldg Comt, Bldg Res Inst, 59, Membership Comt, 59-60; Nat Coun Acoust consult. *Mem:* Acoust Soc Am; Sigma Xi; Am Soc Mech Engrs; Am Soc Eng Educ. *Res:* Fluid flow; underwater sound; architectural acoustics; industrial noise control. *Mailing Add:* 3 Cricket Lane Simsbury CT 06070

HEMP, GENE WILLARD, APPLIED MECHANICS. *Current Pos:* from asst prof to assoc prof, Univ Fla, 67-76, asst vpres, 74-76, assoc vpres, 76-89, actg provost, 89-90, PROF ENG SCI & MECH, UNIV FLA, 76-, VPROVOST, 90- *Personal Data:* b Minneapolis, Minn, Dec 6, 38; m 60, Evelyn H Ploetz; c 2. *Educ:* Univ Minn, BS, 61, BSB, 62, MS, 63, PhD(eng mech), 67. *Prof Exp:* Res technol asst, Univ Minn, 59-63, instr, 63-64, vis lectr mech, 66-67. *Mem:* Am Soc Mech Engrs; Am Inst Aeronaut & Astronaut; Soc Eng Sci; Am Soc Eng Educ. *Res:* Nonlinear oscillations; biomechanics; dynamic material properties; analog simulation; vibrations of discrete and continuous media; rigid body dynamics. *Mailing Add:* 9909 NW 59th Pl Gainesville FL 32653

HEMPEL, FRANKLIN GLENN, RESPIRATION PHYSIOLOGY, SCIENCE ADMINISTRATION. *Current Pos:* DEP DIR, BASIC NEUROSCI, NIH, 88- *Personal Data:* b Gillett, Tex, Sept 22, 39; m 63; c 1. *Educ:* Univ Tex, Austin, BA, 64, MA, 66, PhD(zool), 69. *Prof Exp:* NIH fel, Med Ctr, Duke Univ, 70-72; Stapells fel, Univ Toronto, 72-73; asst prof physiol, Med Ctr, Duke Univ, 73-79; sci officer physiol prog, Off Naval Res, Arlington, Va, 81-88. *Concurrent Pos:* Actg chief, Lab Molecular Biol, Nat Inst Neurol Dis & Stroke. *Mem:* Am Physiol Soc. *Res:* Metabolism of retina; visual electrophysiology; oxygen toxicity; bioenergetics of central nervous system. *Mailing Add:* Basic Neurosci Labs NINDS NIH Bldg 36 Rm 5A05 Bethesda MD 20892-0001. *Fax:* 301-402-1566

HEMPEL, JOHN PAUL, TOPOLOGY. *Current Pos:* from asst prof to assoc prof, 64-75, PROF MATH, RICE UNIV, 75- *Personal Data:* b Salt Lake City, Utah, Oct 14, 35; m, Edith Froese-Gertzen; c Kristian J. *Educ:* Univ Utah, BS, 57; Univ Wis, MS, 59, PhD(math), 62. *Prof Exp:* Asst prof math, Fla State Univ, 62-63; mem, Inst Advan Study, 63-64. *Concurrent Pos:* Mem, Inst Advan Study, 71-72. *Mem:* Am Math Soc. *Res:* Topology of manifolds; positional properties of submanifolds; group theory; geometry; three-dimensional manifolds. *Mailing Add:* Dept Math Rice Univ PO Box 1892 Houston TX 77005. *Fax:* 713-285-5231; *E-Mail:* hempel@rice.edu

HEMPEL, JUDITH CATO, INORGANIC CHEMISTRY, THEORETICAL CHEMISTRY. *Current Pos:* SR SCI PROJ LEADER, BIO SYM TECH, 89- *Personal Data:* b Stephenville, Tex, Feb 16, 41; m 63; c 1. *Educ:* Univ Tex, Austin, BS, 62, MA, 65, PhD(chem), 67. *Prof Exp:* Fel chem, Univ Tex, Austin, 67-70; res assoc chem, Univ NC, Chapel Hill, 70-72; York Univ, 72-73 & Duke Univ, 73-75; vis asst prof chem, Wake Forest Univ, 75-76; asst prof, Univ NC, Greensboro, 76-77; asst prof chem, Swarthmore Col, 77-80; sr investr, Smith, Kline & French Labs, 80-89. *Mem:* Sigma Xi; Am Chem Soc. *Res:* Drug design. *Mailing Add:* UCSF Molecular Design Inst 513 Parnasisus Ave S-926 San Francisco CA 94143

HEMPERLY, JOHN JACOB, NEUROBIOLOGY. *Current Pos:* GROUP LEADER NEUROBIOL, BECTON DICKINSON RES CTR, 87- *Personal Data:* b Ft Belvoir, Va, Dec 22, 51; m 74; c 4. *Educ:* Ind Univ, BS, 73; Rockefeller Univ, PhD, 79. *Prof Exp:* Asst prof, Rockefeller Univ, 80-87. *Mem:* Soc Neurosci; Am Soc Biochem & Molecular Biol; Protein Soc; AAAS. *Res:* Structures and regulations of biomolecules involved in cell-cell adhesion in vertebrate tissues; human cell adhesion molecules, particularly their involvement in disease. *Mailing Add:* Becton Dickinson & Co Res Ctr PO Box 12016 Research Triangle Park NC 27709. *Fax:* 919-549-7572; *E-Mail:* hemperly@bdrc.bd.com

HEMPFLING, WALTER PAHL, MICROBIOLOGY. *Current Pos:* AT PHILLIP MORRIS RES CTR, RICHMOND, VA. *Personal Data:* b Cincinnati, Ohio, Mar 21, 38; m 60; c 2. *Educ:* Univ Cincinnati, BS, 59; Yale Univ, PhD(microbiol), 64. *Prof Exp:* NIH trainee phys biochem, Johnson Found, Univ Pa, 63-65, res assoc & Pa Plan scholar, 65-66; asst prof microbial biochem, Temple Univ, 66-68; assoc prof biol, Univ Rochester, 68-81, actg chmn biol, 79-80, prof & assoc chmn, 81-83. *Concurrent Pos:* Vis investr, Scripps Clin Res Inst, 78-79 & Gastprof, Univ Bonn, 79. *Mem:* Am Soc Biol & Molecular Biol. *Res:* Microbial and plant biochemistry. *Mailing Add:* Phillip Morris Res Ctr PO Box 26583 Richmond VA 23261-6583

HEMPHILL, ADLEY W(ALTON), CHEMICAL ENGINEERING. *Current Pos:* RETIRED. *Personal Data:* b Pittsburgh, Pa, Dec 19, 25; m 50; c 3. *Educ:* Grove City Col, BS, 47; Univ Pittsburgh, MS, 50. *Prof Exp:* Mem staff, Pittsburgh Coke & Chem Co, 49-50; process engr, W R Grace & Co, 51-54, mgr, 55-59, res coordr, 60-62, div tech serv, 62-64, mgr desiccants, 65-69, vpres, 69-76, pres, Davison Chem Div, 76-87. *Mem:* Am Chem Soc. *Res:* Chemical engineering and design of parathion and phthalate plasticizer units; engineering, design and operation of specialty catalyst facility and silica gel unit; natural gas treating, petroleum catalysis, dehydration and molecular sieve development. *Mailing Add:* 60 Woodenbridge Lane Pinehurst NC 28374

HEMPHILL, DELBERT DEAN, HORTICULTURE, ENVIRONMENTAL HEALTH. *Current Pos:* Asst hort, 40-42, 46-48, from asst prof to assoc prof, 48-58, PROF HORT, UNIV MO, COLUMBIA, 58- *Personal Data:* b Crane, Mo, Nov 8, 18; m 43; c 4. *Educ:* Univ Mo, Columbia, BS, 40, PhD(hort), 48. *Concurrent Pos:* Res Assoc, Environ Health, 64-; consult, Midwest Res Inst, 73- *Mem:* Fel AAAS; Am Soc Hort Sci; Soc Environ Geochem & Health (pres, 71-73); fel Weed Sci Soc Am; Am Pub Health Asn. *Res:* Phytohormones; effects of plant growth-regulating substances on plant growth and development; herbicides; effects of pesticides and trace metals on human health; pollution of environment by pesticides and toxic metals. *Mailing Add:* 703 NW 13th Ave Canby OR 97013-2724

HEMPHILL, LOUIS, SANITARY ENGINEERING, CHEMISTRY. *Current Pos:* RETIRED. *Personal Data:* b Gainesville, Tex, Jan 25, 27; m 51; c 2. *Educ:* NTex State Univ, BA, 49, MS, 51; Univ Mich, MPH, 51; Univ Mo, PhD(civil eng), 67. *Prof Exp:* Instr chem & biol, NTex State Univ, 49-51; instr chem, Sch Pub Health, Univ Mich, 51-53, res assoc environ health, 53-55; eng leader, Oak Ridge Nat Lab, 56-61; asst prof sanit eng, Okla State Univ, 61-64; instr, Univ Mo, Columbia, 64-67, assoc prof civil eng, 67- *Concurrent Pos:* Prin investr, Univ Mo Water Resources, 67-68. *Mem:* Am Water Works Asn; Water Pollution Control Fedn; Health Physics Soc; Am Chem Soc. *Res:* Instrumentation; nuclear wastes. *Mailing Add:* 1109 S Glenwood Ave Columbia MO 65203

HEMPLING, HAROLD GEORGE, PHYSIOLOGY. *Current Pos:* chmn dept, 71-87, PROF PHYSIOL, MED UNIV SC, 71- *Personal Data:* b Brooklyn, NY, May 21, 26; m 47; c 3. *Educ:* NY Univ, AB, 48; Oberlin Col, MA, 50; Princeton Univ, PhD(biol), 53. *Prof Exp:* Instr physiol, Sch Med, Univ Pa, 53-55, assoc, 55-57; from asst prof to assoc prof, Med Col, Cornell Univ, 57-71. *Mem:* Am Physiol Soc; Biophys Soc; Soc Gen Physiol. *Res:* Permeability of cell membranes; ion transport; electrolyte movements; volume regulation; computer modelling; computer assisted instruction. *Mailing Add:* Dept Physiol Med Univ SC 171 Ashley Ave Charleston SC 29425

HEMPSTEAD, CHARLES FRANCIS, EXPERIMENTAL PHYSICS, SOLID STATE PHYSICS. *Current Pos:* RETIRED. *Personal Data:* b Gloucester, Mass, May 15, 25; m 50; c 3. *Educ:* Northwestern Univ, BS, 49; Cornell Univ, PhD(physics), 55. *Prof Exp:* Mem staff, Electronics & Radio Res Dept, Bell Labs, 54-60, Quantum Electronics Res Dept, 60-65, Visual Systs Res Dept, 65-66 & Lab Measurements Dept, 66-69, supvr, Comput Aided Anal & Characterization Dept, 69-82 & Magnetics & Characterization Dept, 82-88, mgr, Built-In-Self-Test & Thermal Characterization Dept, 88-90. *Mem:* Inst Elec & Electronics Engrs. *Res:* Microwave spectroscopy and solid state masers; millimeter wave length backward wave oscillators; x-ray spectroscopy; superconductivity research; visual processes research. *Mailing Add:* 8 Sagamore Dr Andover MA 01810

HEMPSTEAD, J(EAN) C(HARLES), INDUSTRIAL ENGINEERING. *Current Pos:* prof, 64-76, EMER PROF INDUST ENG, IOWA STATE UNIV, 76- *Personal Data:* b Woden, Iowa, Aug 6, 04; m 28. *Educ:* Iowa State Univ, BS, 26; Univ Pa, MA, 30; Univ Iowa, CE, 42. *Prof Exp:* Instr math, Drexel Inst Technol, 27-30; instr gen eng, Iowa State Univ, 30-42 & 46-51; instr marine eng, US Naval Acad, 52-55; assoc prof math, USAF Acad, 55-64, fac exec officer, 60-63, dep head math, 63-64. *Mem:* Am Soc Eng Educ. *Res:* Mathematics of industrial property retirements; engineering valuation and depreciation. *Mailing Add:* 1801 20th St Ames IA 50010

HEMPSTEAD, ROBERT DOUGLAS, THIN FILM MAGNETIC DEVICES. *Current Pos:* CONSULT, 89- *Personal Data:* b Cincinnati, Ohio, Aug 20, 43; div; c Kenneth D & Cameron P. *Educ:* Mass Inst Technol, SB & SM, 65; Univ Ill, Urbana-Champaign, PhD(physics), 70. *Prof Exp:* Adv engr magnetic rec, Gen Prod Div, IBM Corp, 70-81; sr vpres eng & develop, Cybernex, 81-84, vpres res & develop, 84-86; vpres develop, Domain, 86-89. *Mem:* Inst Elec & Electronics Engrs. *Res:* Materials research, design, analysis and process development for thin film magnetic recording heads, magnetic recording media and magnetic bubbles. *Mailing Add:* Censtor Corp 530 Race St San Jose CA 95126

HEMSKY, JOSEPH WILLIAM, NUCLEAR PHYSICS. *Current Pos:* Asst prof, 66-70, ASSOC PROF PHYSICS, WRIGHT STATE UNIV, 70- *Personal Data:* b Cedar Rapids, Iowa, Oct 26, 36; m 64; c 1. *Educ:* Mo Sch Mines, BS, 58; Purdue Univ, PhD(physics), 67. *Mem:* Am Asn Physics Teachers. *Res:* Nuclear reactions. *Mailing Add:* Dept Physics Wright State Univ Colonel Glenn Hghwy Dayton OH 45435

HEMSWORTH, MARTIN C, ENGINEERING. *Current Pos:* RETIRED. *Personal Data:* b Waterloo, Iowa, June 3, 18. *Educ:* Univ Nebr, BSME, 40. *Prof Exp:* Engr, Test Facil Aircraft Engine Bus Group, Gen Elec Co, 40-48, mgr test facil, Evandale Plant, 48-52, engr, Mgt Engine Develop Dept, 52-80, chief engr, 80-85, sr consult engine design, Cincinnati, 85-87. *Mem:* Nat Acad Eng; fel Am Soc Mech Engrs; fel Soc Automotive Eng. *Mailing Add:* 648 Maple Trace Cincinnati OH 45246

HEMWALL, EDWIN LYMAN, cardiovascular, allergy, for more information see previous edition

HEN, JOHN, surface chemistry, for more information see previous edition

HENCH, DAVID LE ROY, ELECTRO-OPTICS DIGITAL SIGNAL PROCESSING. *Current Pos:* SR SCIENTIST, OPTICAL SCIS CO, PLACENTIA, CALIF, 83- *Personal Data:* b Cherokee, Iowa, May 19, 41; m 75; c 1. *Educ:* Iowa State Univ, BS, 63, MS, 65; Rice Univ, PhD(elec eng),

72. *Prof Exp:* Elec eng bio-instrumentation, NASA, Manned Space Craft Ctr, Houston, 65-66; res engr clin automation, Pulmonary Physiol Lab, Methodist Hosp, Houston, 71-75; mem tech staff, Image Res, Electron Res Ctr. Rockwell Int, Anaheim, 75-83. *Concurrent Pos:* NDEA fel, 67-69, PHS trainee, Rice Univ, Houston, 69-71. *Mem:* Inst Elec & Electronics Engrs. *Res:* Analysis and systems design of infrared systems used for target detection and of visible systems used for space object imaging. *Mailing Add:* 717 E Rainier Orange CA 92665-1329

HENCH, LARRY LEROY, MATERIALS SCIENCE ENGINEERING. *Current Pos:* asst prof ceramic & mat eng, Univ Fla, 64-68, assoc prof, Dept Metall & Mat Eng, 68-70, head prof ceramics, Dept Metall & Mat Eng, 70-72, prof & head ceramics div, Dept Mat Sci & Eng, 72-83, dir Biomed Eng Prog, 74-79, prof, Dept Mat Sci & Eng, 83-86, GRAD RES PROF, DEPT MAT SCI & ENG, UNIV FLA, 86-, DIR BIOGLASS RES CTR, 88- *Personal Data:* b Shelby, Ohio, Nov 21, 38; m 62, 80; c 2. *Educ:* Ohio State Univ, BCE, 61, PhD(ceramic eng), 64. *Honors & Awards:* Clemson Award, Soc Biomat; George Morey Award, Am Ceramic Soc, Whitewares Award, PACE Award; Scholes Lectr, Alfred Univ; Wedgewood Lectr, Wedgewood Found. *Prof Exp:* Res engr, Battelle Mem Inst, 64. *Concurrent Pos:* Consult, Holmes Co, Inc, 65-66, E I du Pont de Nemours & Co & Knox Glass, Inc, 66- & Phys Sci Br, Picatinny Arsenal, US Army, 69-; co-chmn, workshop on urolithiasis, Nat Res Coun; chmn, 7th Univ Conf Ceramic Res. *Mem:* Fel Am Ceramic Soc; Nat Inst Ceramic Engrs; Soc Biomat (secy-treas, 77-79, pres, 79); fel Brit Soc Glass Technol; Acad Ceramics; Mat Res Soc; Sigma Xi. *Res:* Materials engineering; structure and properties of glasses, bio-materials, radiation damage and glass-ceramics; electrical behavior of semiconducting glasses and oxides; dielectric and materials; nuclear waste disposal; sol-gel processing; optical materials; technology transfer theory; ethics of science, engineering & technology. *Mailing Add:* 3948 NW 23rd Circle Gainesville FL 32605

HENCH, MILES ELLSWORTH, MEDICAL MICROBIOLOGY. *Current Pos:* from asst prof to prof clin path & microbiol, Va Commonwealth Univ, 52-82, asst dean admis, 61-67, assoc dean admis, 67-82, dir alumni res, Sch Med, 83-84, EMER PROF CLIN PATH, MED COL, VA COMMONWEALTH UNIV, 82- *Personal Data:* b Minneapolis, Minn, Oct 28, 19; m 45; c Virginia E, Carol A (Valentine) & Thomas G. *Educ:* Lawrence Col, BS, 41; Univ Mich, MS, 49, PhD(bact), 52; Am Bd Med Microbiol, dipl. *Prof Exp:* Asst, Univ Mich, 49-52. *Mem:* AAAS; Am Asn Med Clins; Am Soc Microbiol. *Res:* Diagnostic microbiology; environmental sanitation. *Mailing Add:* 5201 Kimberwick Dr Glen Allen VA 23060

HENCHMAN, MICHAEL J, PHYSICAL CHEMISTRY. *Current Pos:* assoc prof, 67-86, PROF CHEM, BRANDEIS UNIV, 86- *Personal Data:* b London, Eng, Feb 28, 35; m 89, Katrina Gromt; c Anna & Sacha. *Educ:* Univ Cambridge, BA, 56, MA, 60; Yale Univ, MS, 58, PhD(chem), 61. *Honors & Awards:* Humboldt Prize, 91. *Prof Exp:* Asst lectr phys chem, Univ Leeds, 61-63, lectr, 63-67. *Mem:* Am Chem Soc. *Res:* Gas phase ion chemistry; kinetics and thermodynamics; chemistry and art. *Mailing Add:* Dept Chem Brandeis Univ Waltham MA 02254-9110. *Fax:* 781-736-2516; *E-Mail:* henchman@binah.cc.brandeis.edu

HENDEE, JOHN CLARE, FORESTRY. *Current Pos:* PROF & DEAN, WILDLIFE & RANGE SCI, COL FORESTRY, UNIV IDAHO, 85- *Personal Data:* b Duluth, Minn, Nov 12, 38; c 6. *Educ:* Mich State Univ, BS, 60; Ore State Univ, MF, 62; Univ Wash, PhD(forestry), 67. *Honors & Awards:* Nat Conserv Award, Am Motors, 74; Lifetime Achievement Award, Am Soc Pub Admin, 88. *Prof Exp:* Forester, Sinslaw Nat Forest, Us Forest Serv, 61-64, res scientist, Pac Southwest Forest Exp Sta, 64-65, Pac Northwest Forest Exp Sta, 65-76, legis coord forestry, Wash, 76-78, asst dir, Southeast Forest Exp Sta, 78-85. *Concurrent Pos:* Adj assoc prof, Univ Wash, 68-76; cong fel, Am Polit Sci Asn, 76-77. *Mem:* Soc Am Foresters; Soc Range Mgt; Wildlife Soc. *Res:* Author or co-author of one hundred articles reporting research results on human behavior aspects of natural resources; textbook written on wilderness management; forestry; wildlife in wilderness. *Mailing Add:* Wilderness Res Ctr Rm 18A Col Forestry Univ Idaho Moscow ID 43844-1144

HENDEE, WILIAM R, DIAGNOSTIC IMAGING, VISUAL PERCEPTION & COGNITION. *Current Pos:* SR ASSOC DEAN RES, VPRES TECHNOL & PROF RADIOL, BIOPHYS & RADIATION ONCOL, MED COL WIS, 91- *Personal Data:* b Owosso, Mich, Jan 1, 38; m 60, Jeannie Wesley; c Mikal, Shonn, Eric, Gareth, Gregory, Lara & Karel. *Educ:* Millsaps Col, BS, 59; Univ Tex, PhD(physics), 62. *Hon Degrees:* DSc Millsaps Col, 88. *Honors & Awards:* Wright Langham Mem lectr, Univ Ky, 91; Distinguished Serv Award, Am Acad Home Care Physicians, 91. *Prof Exp:* From asst prof to assoc prof physics, Millsaps Col, 62-64, assoc prof astron & physics & chmn dept, 64-65; NSF res fel, NMex Highlands Univ, 63; instr modern physics, Miss State Univ Ext, 63; AEC res fel, Rad Dosimetry Sect Health Physics Div, Oak Ridge Nat Lab, 64; from asst prof to prof radio, Univ Colo Med Ctr, 65-85, actg chmn, 76-78, chmn, Dept Radiol, 75-85; vpres sci & technol, Am Med Asn, 85-91; adj prof radiol, Northwestern Univ Sch Med, 85-91. *Concurrent Pos:* Dir, Nat Cancer Inst Cancer Control Projs, Southwestern Med Physics Ctr; consult ed, J Nuclear Med Technol; assoc ed, J Optical Eng & Int J Radiation Oncol, Biol & Physics; assoc ed, Med Progress Through Technol, 90- & Radiographics, 92-; Centennial Distinguished lectr, Millsaps Col, 90; consult ed, Am Inst Physics, 92-, vis scientist prog physcs, 92- *Mem:* Health Physics Soc; fel Am Asn Physicists Med; Soc Nuclear Med; Am Col Radiol; Soc Photo-Optical Instrument Eng; fel Am Inst Med & Biol Eng; Radiol Soc NAm; Am Roentgen Ray Soc. *Res:* Development of back projection computations from multiple projections for determination of attenuation coefficients for inhomogeneity connections in radiation therapy; optimization of pulse sequences (TE and TR) for soft tissue visualization in magnetic resonance imaging; principles of visual perception applied to interpretations of x-ray images; quality optimization of x-ray imaging parameters. *Mailing Add:* Med Col Wis 8701 Watertown Plank Rd Milwaukee WI 53226. *Fax:* 414-257-8464; *E-Mail:* whendee@its.mcw.edu

HENDEL, ALFRED Z, PHYSICS. *Current Pos:* vis asst prof, 59-64, assoc prof, 64-70, PROF PHYSICS, UNIV MICH, ANN ARBOR, 70- *Personal Data:* b Vienna, Austria, Oct 19, 16. *Educ:* Univ Vienna, dipl, 48; Univ Paris, DUniv, 55. *Prof Exp:* Prof physics, La Paz Univ, 45-56; res assoc, Princeton Univ, 57-58. *Concurrent Pos:* Assoc prof, Brazilian Ctr Physics Res, 52-56; res physicist, Polytech Sch, Paris, 54-55. *Res:* Cosmic rays; strange particles; air showers; electromagnetic interactions. *Mailing Add:* Dept Physics Univ Mich 738 Bennison 317B West Hall Ann Arbor MI 48109

HENDEL, HANS WILLIAM, MEASUREMENT OF FUSION REACTION RATES. *Current Pos:* RETIRED. *Personal Data:* b Woldenberg, Ger, Nov 27, 22; US citizen; m 53; c 3. *Educ:* Munich Tech Univ, BS, 46, MS, 49, PhD(physics), 53. *Prof Exp:* Physicist, AGFA Camera Works, 53-57; res physicist, US Army Eng Res & Develop Labs, Ft Monmouth, NJ, 57-61; mem tech staff, David Sarnoff Res Lab, RCA Corp, 61-89; vis prin physicist, Plasma Physics Lab, Princeton, Univ, 65-89. *Concurrent Pos:* Leader plasma & space physics, Astro-electronics Div, RCA Corp, 64-68. *Mem:* Fel Am Phys Soc; Sigma Xi. *Res:* Plasma waves and instabilities; fusion reaction products. *Mailing Add:* 214 Riverside Dr Princeton NJ 08540

HENDERLONG, PAUL ROBERT, FORAGE CROPS, CROPPING SYSTEMS. *Current Pos:* from assoc prof to prof, 68-95, EMER PROF AGRON, OHIO STATE UNIV, 95- *Personal Data:* b Marshallville, Ohio, Sept 9, 37; m 62, Mary Horn; c Jay P, Amy K & Lisa R. *Educ:* Ohio State Univ, BSc, 59, MSc, 61; Va Polytech Inst, PhD(physiol & biochem), 64. *Honors & Awards:* Alfred J Wright Award, 77. *Prof Exp:* Asst prof soil fertil, WVa Univ, 64-65, pasture & turfgrass res, 65-68. *Concurrent Pos:* Vis prof pasture agron, Makerere Univ, Uganda, 72-73; assoc ed, Agron J, 76-79; chmn, CSSA Div, C-3, 81; agron ed adv, Longman Publ Inc, 83-85; campus coordr, Int Progs Agr, 84-88. *Mem:* Am Soc Agron; Crop Sci Soc Am; Am Soc Plant Physiol; Weed Sci Soc Am; Am Forage Grassland Coun; Coun Agr Sci & Technol. *Res:* Legume and grass physiology; biochemistry and nutrition as related to crop production and utilization; cropping systems. *Mailing Add:* Dept Hort & Crop Sci Ohio State Univ 2021 Coffey Rd Columbus OH 43210-1086. *Fax:* 614-292-7162

HENDERSHOT, WILLIAM FRED, BIOCHEMISTRY. *Current Pos:* VPRES SCI AFFAIRS, TENNEX PHARM, MORTON GROVE, ILL, 93- *Personal Data:* b Dalton, Ga, Feb 21, 30; m 49; c 4. *Educ:* Ind Univ, BS, 54; Univ Wis, PhD(biochem), 59. *Prof Exp:* Asst chemist, Forest Prod Lab, USDA, 54-58, assoc biochemist, Northern Utilization Res & Develop Div, 58-62; sr res biochemist & sect head, Ames Res Labs Div, Miles Labs Inc, 62-67, mgr qual control develop, 67-68, dir qual control, Oper Serv Div, 68-70, dir corp qual assurance, vpres, Miles Labs Inc. *Mem:* AAAS; Pharmaceut Mfrs Asn; Am Chem Soc; Sigma Xi. *Res:* Diagnostic research; clinical enzymology; microbiological investigations; fermentation products; intermediary metabolism and enzymology; control systems; automation of analytical procedures; computerization of data acquisition. *Mailing Add:* 805 Garfield Ave Libertyville IL 60048

HENDERSHOTT, CHARLES HENRY, JR, HORTICULTURE. *Current Pos:* RETIRED. *Personal Data:* b Marked Tree, Ark, Oct 13, 23; m 44; c 5. *Educ:* Univ Ark, MS, 52; NC State Col, PhD(plant physiol), 59. *Prof Exp:* Jr horticulturist & instr hort, Univ Ark, 52-54, horticulturist, Mission to Panama, 54-57; from asst plant physiologist to assoc plant physiologist, Citrus Exp Sta, Fla Citrus Comn, 59-64 & Dept Fruit Crops, Univ Fla, 64-67; head dept & chmn div, Univ Ga, 67-74, prof hort, 74-79, head dept & chmn div, 79- *Mem:* Fel Am Soc Hort Sci; Am Soc Plant Physiol. *Res:* Horticultural physiology. *Mailing Add:* 155 Chinquapin Way Athens GA 30605

HENDERSON, ALEX, VERTEBRATE MORPHOLOGY, BIOLOGY. *Current Pos:* assoc prof sci, 55-57, chmn dept, 64-73, PROF BIOL, MILLERSVILLE STATE COL, 57- *Personal Data:* b Bicknell, Ind, July 2, 24; m 48; c 1. *Educ:* Pa State Univ, AB, 47, DEd, 57; Univ Wichita, MS, 49. *Prof Exp:* Operator, Rohm and Haas Chem Co, 43-44; pub sch teacher, Kans, 50-53; instr, Pa State Univ, 54-55. *Concurrent Pos:* Sci consult, Pa Dept Educ, 63-; mem, Pa Coun Educ Dept Pub Instr Col Eval Team, 63-; vis res prof, Glasgow, 65; pres, Environ Sci Res Assocs, Inc; biologist in residence, Marine Sci Consortium, 77-80; mem bd, Commonwealth Pa, Univ Biologists. *Mem:* Sigma Xi. *Res:* Morphology of Terrapene ornata; biology of Coenobita clypeatus; biology of Coregonus clupeoides; atlas of fisheries of Virginia eastern shore; scientific illustration. *Mailing Add:* 6 Leaf Park Lancaster PA 17603

HENDERSON, ARNOLD RICHARD, geology, for more information see previous edition

HENDERSON, BEAUFORD EARL, COMMUNICATION ENGINEERING. *Current Pos:* br chief eng, 72-83, DEP DIR, LISTER HILL NAT CTR BIOMED COMMUN, 83- *Personal Data:* b Dothan, Ala, June 26, 39; m 65; c 3. *Educ:* Newark Col Eng, BSEE, 61; Univ Southern Calif, MSEE, 68; Univ Calif, Los Angeles, MSE, 72. *Prof Exp:* Electronic officer radar, USAF, 61-64; engr elec, Bunker Ramo Corp, 64-65 & Hughes

Aircraft Co, 65-68; staff engr, Magnavox Res Labs, 68-72. *Mem:* Sr mem Inst Elec & Electronics Engrs. *Res:* Broadband communication systems and techniques related to the storage, transmission and display of video signals; image processing. *Mailing Add:* Dir Lister Hill Nat Ctr Biomed 8600 Rockville Pike Bethesda MD 20814. *E-Mail:* deh@lac.nlm.nih.gov

HENDERSON, BILLY JOE, ELECTROMAGNETISM. *Current Pos:* SPECIALIST ENG, BOEING SPACE CO, 78-; CONSULT, 88- *Personal Data:* b Texarkana, Tex, Aug 10, 37; m 67. *Educ:* NC State Col, BS, 59, MS, 62, MBA, 83; Univ Ga, PhD(physics), 67. *Prof Exp:* Nuclear engr, Aircraft Nuclear Propulsion Dept, Gen Elec Co, 59-60; asst prof physics, Univ Ga, 67-68; asst prof physics, Fla Technol Univ, 68-77. *Mem:* Sigma Xi. *Res:* Theory of direct nuclear reactions; analysis of nuclear reactions which proceed via compound nucleus formation; molecular vibrational energy levels; nuclear reactor analysis; bioelectric effects. *Mailing Add:* 1057 Summit E Seattle WA 98102

HENDERSON, BRIAN EDMOND, PREVENTIVE MEDICINE. *Current Pos:* from assoc prof to prof path, 70-78, prof prev med & dept chmn, 78-88, DIR, COMPREHENSIVE CANCER CTR, UNIV SOUTHERN CALIF, LOS ANGELES, 83- *Personal Data:* b San Francisco, Calif, June 27, 37; m 60, Judith A McDermott; c Sean, Marie, Sarah, Brian J & Michael. *Educ:* Univ Calif, Berkeley, BA, 58; Univ Chicago, MD, 62. *Honors & Awards:* Richard & Hinda Rosenthal Found Award, Am Asn Cancer Res, 87. *Prof Exp:* Resident, Mass Gen Hosp, Boston, 62-64; chief arbovirol, Ctr Dis Control, 69-70. *Concurrent Pos:* Consult, WHO, SPac Comn & US-Japan-Hawaii Cancer Prog; mem bd counrs, Nat Cancer Inst, 79-82; mem sci coun, Int Agency Res Cancer, 82-86; assoc ed, Cancer Res; distinguished scholar, Nat Acad Sci, China, 82. *Mem:* AAAS; Infectious Dis Soc Am; Am Epidemiol Soc. *Res:* Cancer. *Mailing Add:* Univ Southern Calif Norris Cancer Hosp 1441 E Lakeland Ave Los Angeles CA 90033-1039

HENDERSON, CHARLES B(ROOKE), CHEMICAL ENGINEERING. *Current Pos:* DIR, ARCTECH INC, 87- *Personal Data:* b Washington, DC, Mar 13, 29; m 54; c 3. *Educ:* Purdue Univ, BS, 50; Mass Inst Technol, SM, 52. *Prof Exp:* Chem engr, Altantic Res Corp, 54-57, head chem eng group, 57-59, dir, Chem Eng Div, 59-66, asst gen mgr, Propulsion Div, 66-71, dir res & technol, 71-75, vpres, 75-80, sr vpres, 80-88, corp dir, 77-90. *Mem:* Sigma Xi; Am Inst Aeronaut & Astronaut; Am Chem Soc. *Res:* Rocket propulsion; alternate fuels; thermodynamics; fluid dynamics; heat transfer; combustion. *Mailing Add:* 17189 Clarks Ridge Rd Leesburg VA 22075-9307

HENDERSON, COURTLAND M, CHEMICAL ENGINEERING. *Current Pos:* CONSULT, 83- *Personal Data:* b Sullivan, Ind, Sept 2, 15; m 40, Juanita Ford; c David, Sue & Mark. *Educ:* Purdue Univ, BChE, 40. *Prof Exp:* Chem engr, Columbian Enameling & Stamping Co, Ind, 40-44; res engr, Linde Co, div Union Carbide Corp, 44-52; res develop engr, Mallinckrodt Chem Works, 52-55; res engr, Uranium Plant, 55-56, tech supt, Uranium metal plant, 56-57; res group leader, Res & Eng Div, Monsanto Chem Co, 57-61, res mgr, 61-66, supvr, Mound Facil, 66-68, mgr prog planning & tech coordr nuclear opers, 68-76, mgr, Liaison-Coal Conversion Progs, Mound Facil, 76-79; pres, Site-Tac, Inc, 79-83. *Mem:* Am Chem Soc; Am Inst Chem Engrs. *Res:* Ultrahigh temperature chemical reactors; dispersion-strengthened metals; flame and arc-plasma research; thermoelectric materials and devices; radioisotopes; advanced coal conversion research and development; technical monitoring of engineering and plant design and construction of coal conversion demonstration plants; pressure sensitive adhesives; gaseous diffusion equipment design. *Mailing Add:* 5642 Cobblegate Dr Dayton OH 45449-2838

HENDERSON, D(ELBERT) W, IRRIGATION. *Current Pos:* RETIRED. *Personal Data:* b Colo, Apr 8, 19; m 45. *Educ:* Univ Ariz, BS, 46; Univ Calif, PhD(soil sci), 50. *Prof Exp:* Asst irrig, Univ Calif, Davis, 46-50, from instr & jr irrigationist to assoc prof & assoc irrigationist, 50-65, prof, 65-86, emer prof water sci & irrigationist, 86-88. *Res:* Soil physics; plant-soil-water relations; irrigation management. *Mailing Add:* 15037 Guadalupe Dr Rancho Murieta CA 95683

HENDERSON, DALE BARLOW, PLASMA PHYSICS. *Current Pos:* Mem staff controlled fusion, Thermonuclear Res, Los Alamos Nat Lab, 66-71, alt group leader, 72-75, group leader, 75-80, mem staff laser-fusion, 71-80, assoc div leader, Nuclear Explosive Physics, Appl Theoret Physics Div, 80-84, dep assoc dir, Theoret & Computative Physics, 84-85, chief scientist, Studies & Anal Div, 86-88, CHIEF SCIENTIST, COMPUT DIV, LOS ALAMOS NAT LAB, 88- *Personal Data:* b Tulsa, Okla, June 6, 41; m 64; c 4. *Educ:* Cornell Univ, BEngr Physics, 63, PhD(appl physics), 67. *Concurrent Pos:* Chief scientist SDI, Nat Test Bd, FY, 89. *Mem:* AAAS; Am Inst Astronaut & Aeronaut; Am Phys Soc. *Res:* Computer simulation; physics of nuclear weapons and related computer codes; laser-fusion; hydrodynamics; controlled fusion. *Mailing Add:* 723 Kris Ct Los Alamos NM 87544

HENDERSON, DAVID ANDREW, TUMOUR THEORY. *Current Pos:* staff scientist endocrinol, Dept Biochem Pharmacol, 82-89, HEAD, DEPT EXP ONCOL, SCHERING AG, 89- *Personal Data:* b Alyth, Scotland, Apr 9, 48; UK citizen; m 75, Lorraine A Erickson; c Kirsten A, Daniel A & Peter A. *Educ:* Univ Edinburgh, Scotland, BSc, 70; Vanderbilt Univ, PhD(molecular biol), 74. *Prof Exp:* Fel, Calif Inst Technol, Pasadena, 75-76; fel cell biol, Max Planck Inst Biophys Chem, Goettingen, Ger, 76-77, staff scientist, 77-82. *Mem:* Sigma Xi; NY Acad Sci; Am Soc Cell Biol; Endocrine Soc. *Res:* Growth control processes in normal and malignant cells, especially in endocrine dependent tumours; drug discovery and development of therapeutic agents for tumour therapy. *Mailing Add:* 15049 San Pablo Dr Richmond CA 94804-0099. *Fax:* 510-262-7844

HENDERSON, DAVID EDWARD, CHROMATOGRAPHY, MASS SPECTROMETRY. *Current Pos:* from asst prof to assoc prof, 77-84, PROF CHEM, DEPT CHEM, TRINITY COL, 88- *Personal Data:* b Richmond, Va, Sept 22, 46; m 72; c 2. *Educ:* St Andrews Presby Col, BA, 68; Univ Mass, PhD(chem), 75. *Prof Exp:* Res assoc chem, Univ Mass, 74-77. *Concurrent Pos:* Teaching assoc, Dept Chem, Mt Holyoke Col, 74-77; lectr consult, Ctr Prof Adv, 75- & Univ Mass, 77; consult examr, Charter Oak Col. *Mem:* Am Soc Mass Spectrometry; Sci Res Soc NAm; Sigma Xi; AAAS. *Res:* Low temperature high performance liquid chromatography of labile metal complexes and peptides; microbore high performance liquid chromatography of proteins; mass spectrometry of peptides and metal complexes; air pollution; lipid-carbohydrate thermal interactions. *Mailing Add:* Dept Chem Trinity Col Hartford CT 06106-3187

HENDERSON, DAVID MICHAEL, ELECTROOPTICS. *Current Pos:* sr proj eng, Hughes Aircraft Co, 74-76, sect head electrooptics, 76-81, dept mgr, 81-84, lab mgr, 84-89, dep div mgr, 89-96, DEP DIR ENG, HUGHES RES LAB, 96- *Personal Data:* b Zanesville, Ohio, May 14, 40; m 68; c 2. *Educ:* Miami Univ, AB, 62, MS, 64; Yale Univ, PhD(appl sci), 69. *Prof Exp:* Mem tech staff laser physics, Bell Lab, 69-74. *Concurrent Pos:* Yale Univ fel. *Mem:* Am Phys Soc; Inst Elec & Electronics Engrs. *Res:* Interaction of infrared radiation with materials for purposes of detection, imaging and modulation. *Mailing Add:* Hughes Aircraft Co EO/E1/A123 PO Box 902 El Segundo CA 90245

HENDERSON, DAVID WILSON, MATHEMATICS. *Current Pos:* asst prof, 66-68, assoc prof, 68-82, PROF, CORNELL UNIV, 82-, MEM FAC MATH, 66- *Personal Data:* b Walla Walla, Wash, Feb 23, 39; m 83; c 2. *Educ:* Swarthmore Col, BA, 61; Univ Wis, MS, 62, PhD(math), 64. *Prof Exp:* Mem math, Inst Advan Study, 64-66. *Concurrent Pos:* Alfred P Sloan res fel, 68-72; vis prof, Birzeit Univ, Jordan, 81; exchange scientist, Soviet Union & Poland, 70. *Mem:* Am Math Soc; Math Asn Am; Asn Women Math. *Res:* Basic geometry; geometric topology; meaning in mathematics; mathematics education. *Mailing Add:* Dept Math Cornell Univ White Hall Ithaca NY 14853-7901

HENDERSON, DONALD, SENSORY PSYCHOLOGY, SENSORY PHYSIOLOGY. *Current Pos:* MEM STAFF, STATE UNIV NEW YORK, BUFFALO, 87- *Personal Data:* b Hamilton, Ont, Oct 3, 38; m 63. *Educ:* Western Wash State Col, BA, 62; Univ Tex, Austin, PhD(psychol), 66. *Prof Exp:* Res assoc psychol, Radiobiol Labs, Univ Tex, 62-64 & Tracor, Inc, 64-66; res assoc physiol, Cent Inst Deaf, 66-68; asst prof otolaryngol, Upstate Med Ctr, State Univ NY, 68-80; mem staff, Callier Ctr Commun Disorders, 80-87. *Concurrent Pos:* Lectr, Univ Tex, 65-66, Wash Univ, 66-68 & Syracuse Univ, 69- *Mem:* AAAS; Acoust Soc Am; Am Speech & Hearing Asn. *Res:* Relation between sensory phenomena and the underlying physiological mechanisms, specifically how the auditory system reacts to various parameters of high intensity noise. *Mailing Add:* Commun Disorders State Univ NY 105 Park Hall Buffalo NY 14260-0001

HENDERSON, DONALD AINSLIE, PUBLIC HEALTH, EPIDEMIOLOGY. *Current Pos:* dean, 77-90, Edgar Berman Prof epidemiol & int health, 77-93, UNIV DISTINGUISHED SERV PROF, SCH HYG & PUB HEALTH, JOHNS HOPKINS UNIV, 93- *Personal Data:* b Cleveland, Ohio, Sept 7, 28; m 51, Nana Bragg; c Leigh, David & Douglas. *Educ:* Oberlin Col, BA, 50; Univ Rochester, MD, 54; Johns Hopkins Univ, MPH, 60. *Hon Degrees:* ScD, Univ Rochester, 77, Oberlin Col, 78, Univ Ill, 79, Univ Md, 80, Yale Univ, 86, Albany Med Col, 86 & Univ Mo, 92, LLD, Marietta Col, 78; MD, Universite de Geneve, 80, LHD, State Univ NY, 81, Johns Hopkins Univ, 94, Towson State Univ, 94. *Honors & Awards:* Indian Soc Malaria & Other Commun Dis Award, Govt India, 75; Ernst-Jung Preis fur Medizin, 76; Medal for Health, Govt India, 78; Pub Welfare Medal, Nat Acad Sci, 78; Joseph C Wilson Award Int Affairs, 78; George MacDonald Prize & Medal, London Sch Hygiene & Trop Med & Royal Soc Trop Med & Hygiene; James Bruce Award, Am Col Physicians, 78; Gairdner Found Int Award Merit, 83; Albert Schweitzer Int Prize Med, 85; Charles S Dana Found Award, 86; Nat Medal Sci, 86; Richard T Hewitt Award, Royal Soc Med, 86, Edward Jenner Medal, 96; Walter Reed Medal, Am Soc Trop Med & Hyg, 93; Sabin Gold Medal, Albert Sabin Found, 94; Oswaldo Cruz Gold Medal of Merit, Govt Brazil, 95. *Prof Exp:* Intern, Mary Imogene Bassett Hosp, 54-55, resident, 57-59; chief epidemic intel serv, Commun Dis Ctr, USPHS, 55-57, asst chief, Epidemiol Br, 60-61, chief, Surveillance Sect, 61-67; chief smallpox eradication, WHO, Geneva, 67-77. *Concurrent Pos:* Mem, Expert Adv Panel Virus Dis, WHO; chmn, Tech Adv Group Immunization-Pan Am Health Orgn; dep asst socy health, Dept Health & Human Serv; assoc dir life sci, Off Sci & Technol Policy, Exec Off of Pres, 91-93; dep asst secy for health, Dept Health & Human Serv, 93-95; bd trustees, Mary Imogene Bassett Hosp, NY. *Mem:* Inst Med-Nat Acad Sci; Am Epidemiol Soc; hon fel Am Acad Pediat; fel Royal Col Physicians; fel Am Col Epidemiol; fel Am Col Prev Med. *Res:* Infectious diseases; public health administration; educational administration. *Mailing Add:* Johns Hopkins Sch Hyg & Pub Health Hampton House Baltimore MD 21205. *Fax:* 410-889-6514; *E-Mail:* dhenders@phnet.sph.jhu.edu

HENDERSON, DONALD LEE, COMPUTER SCIENCES, DATA COMMUNICATIONS. *Current Pos:* RETIRED. *Personal Data:* b Holstein, Iowa, July 6, 33; c 2. *Educ:* Wayne State Col, BA, 58; Univ SDak, MA, 59; Okla State Univ, EdD(comput sci), 67. *Prof Exp:* Instr math, Mankato State Col, 59-62, asst registr & dir comput serv, 62-68, dir comput serv & chmn comput sci, 68-73; exec dir, Minn Educ Comput Consortium, 73-75; chmn comput sci, Mankato State Univ, 75-83, prof comput sci, 84- *Concurrent Pos:* Comt mem, Minn Governor's Comput Adv Comt, 75-83; chmn comput sci, Western Ky, 83-84. *Mem:* Asn Comput Mach; Asn Educ Data Systs. *Res:* Data communication curriculum development. *Mailing Add:* Dept Comput Sci Mankato State Univ Ellis Ave Mankato MN 56001

HENDERSON, DONALD MUNRO, MINERALOGY. *Current Pos:* from instr to prof, 48-89, EMER PROF GEOL, UNIV ILL, URBANA, 89- *Personal Data:* b Boston, Mass, Nov 8, 20; m 48; c 5. *Educ:* Brown Univ, AB, 43; Harvard Univ, AM, 46, PhD(geol), 50. *Prof Exp:* Geologist strategic minerals invests, US Geol Surv, 44-45. *Concurrent Pos:* Guggenheim fel, 58-59. *Mem:* Mineral Soc Am; Mineral Soc Gt Brit & Ireland; Norweg Geol Soc; Nat Asn Geol Teachers; Am Geophys Union. *Res:* Mineralogy; crystallography. *Mailing Add:* Univ Ill Urbana 1301 W Green St Urbana IL 61801-2919

HENDERSON, DOUGLAS J, THEORETICAL PHYSICS, THEORETICAL CHEMISTRY. *Current Pos:* PROF CHEM, BRIGHAM YOUNG UNIV, 95- *Personal Data:* b Calgary, Alta, July 28, 34; m 60, Rose M Steen-Nielssen; c Barbara, Dianne & Sharon. *Educ:* Univ BC, BA, 56; Univ Utah, PhD(physics), 61. *Honors & Awards:* IBM Outstanding Res Contrib Award, 73, 87. *Prof Exp:* Asst prof theoret physics, Univ Idaho, 61-62 & Ariz State Univ, 62-64; assoc prof, Univ Waterloo, 64-67, prof theoret physics & appl math, 67-69; res scientist, Res Lab, IBM Corp, 69-90, res scientist, IBM USI partnership, 90-95. *Concurrent Pos:* Alfred P Sloan Found fel, 64 & 66; Ian Potter Found fel & vis scientist, Chem Res Labs, Commonwealth Sci & Indust Res Orgn, Australia, 66-67; adj prof, Univ Waterloo, 69-; vis prof physics, Nat Univ La Plata, Arg, 73, Univ Guelph, 91; vis prof chem, Korea Advan Inst Sci, Seoul, 74; assoc ed, J Chem Physics, 74-76; Manuel Sandoval Vallarta distinguished vis prof physics, Universidad Autonoma Metropolitana Mex, 88, Juan de Oyarzabal distinguished vis prof physics, 93. *Mem:* Fel Am Phys Soc; Am Chem Soc; Math Asn Am; fel Brit Inst Physics; Can Asn Physicists; Sigma Xi; corresp mem Mex Nat Acad Sci. *Res:* Investigation of intermolecular forces and development of theory to use these potentials to calculate properties of matter, particularly in liquid state. *Mailing Add:* Dept Chem Brigham Young Univ Provo UT 84602. *Fax:* 801-378-5474; *E-Mail:* doug@huey.byu.edu

HENDERSON, DOUGLASS MILES, BIOSYSTEMATICS, BOTANY. *Current Pos:* from asst prof to assoc prof bot, 72-93, DIR HERBARIUM, UNIV IDAHO, 72-, PROF BOT, 93- *Personal Data:* b Long Beach, Calif, July 9, 38; m 71; c 3. *Educ:* Fresno State Col, BA, 65; Univ Wash, PhD(bot), 72. *Prof Exp:* Inspector food prod, Consumer & Mkt Serv, USDA, 65-67. *Concurrent Pos:* Managing ed, Syst Bot, Am Soc Plant Taxonomists, 84-89. *Mem:* Am Soc Plant Taxonomists; Int Asn Plant Taxonomists; Am Bot Soc. *Res:* Biosystematic studies in the genus Sisyrinchium and Idaho floristics; biology of rare and endangered species; praceal of Idaho. *Mailing Add:* Dept Biol Sci Univ Idaho 375 S Line St Moscow ID 83843-4140

HENDERSON, EARL ERWIN, MICROBIOLOGY, VIROLOGY. *Current Pos:* ASST PROF MICROBIOL, TEMPLE UNIV, 77- *Personal Data:* b Detroit, Mich, Aug 2, 46; c 2. *Educ:* Va Polytechnic Inst & State Univ, BS, 69; Univ Chicago, PhD(microbiol), 75. *Prof Exp:* Res specialist, Walter Reed Army Med Ctr, 70-71; fel pediat & epidemiol, Yale Univ, 75-77. *Concurrent Pos:* Special fel, Leukemia Soc Am, 78-80. *Mem:* Am Soc Microbiol; Sigma Xi. *Res:* Development and characterization of cell lines transformed by Epstein-Barr Virus. *Mailing Add:* Dept Microbiol Temple Univ Sch Med 3400 N Broad Philadelphia PA 19140-5104

HENDERSON, EDWARD GEORGE, BIOPHYSICS, PHARMACOLOGY. *Current Pos:* asst prof, 68-73, ASSOC PROF PHARMACOL, UNIV CONN HEALTH CTR, 73- *Personal Data:* b Bridgeport, Conn, Apr 6, 35; m 58; c 2. *Educ:* Univ Conn, BA, 61; Univ Md, PhD(biophys), 66. *Prof Exp:* Group leader radiochem, Wyeth Labs, 65-68. *Mem:* Biophys Soc; Am Soc Pharmacol & Exp Therapeut; Neurosci Soc. *Res:* Ion transport; electrophysiology; neurophysiology; membrane pharmacology. *Mailing Add:* Dept Pharmacol Univ Conn Sch Med 263 Farmington Ave Farmington CT 06030-0001

HENDERSON, EDWARD S, INTERNAL MEDICINE, ONCOLOGY. *Current Pos:* res prof med, 73-81, chief med oncol, 79-89, prof med, 81-, PROF MED, VET AFFAIRS, STATE WESTERN NY HEALTH CARE SYST UNIV NY, BUFFALO. *Personal Data:* b Ventura, Calif, July 19, 32; m 54, 70; c 5. *Educ:* Stanford Univ, BA, 53, MD, 56; Am Bd Internal Med, dipl, 64, cert med oncol, 74. *Prof Exp:* Intern, Los Angeles Co Gen Hosp, 56-57, resident med, 57-59; instr internal med & fel hemat, Sch Med, Univ Southern Calif, 59-61; clin assoc med oncol, Nat Cancer Inst, 61-64, sr investr pharm, 64-65, head leukemia serv, 65-71, actg chief, Hemat & Supportive Care Br, 71-73; chief, Dept Med, Roswell Park Mem Inst, 73-89. *Mem:* Am Fedn Clin Res; Am Soc Clin Oncol; Am Soc Hemat; Am Asn Cancer Res; Transplantation soc; fel Am Col Physician. *Res:* Clinical cancer chemotherapy; clinical oncology; pharmacology of cancer chemotherapeutic agents; complications of cancer therapy. *Mailing Add:* State Univ NY 3495 Bailey Ave Buffalo NY 14215-1199

HENDERSON, ELLEN JANE, CELL BIOLOGY, DEVELOPMENTAL BIOLOGY. *Current Pos:* from asst prof to assoc prof, 80-91, PROF BIOL, GEORGETOWN UNIV, 91- *Personal Data:* b Little Rock, Ark, Feb 16, 40. *Educ:* Purdue Univ, BS, 66, PhD(biochem), 71. *Prof Exp:* Jane Coffin Childs Mem Fund fel, Univ Edinburgh, 71-73, res staff molecular biol, 73-74; asst prof chem, Mass Inst Technol, 74-80. *Concurrent Pos:* Mem adv subcomt develop biol, NSF, 80-84; vis scientist, Imp Cancer Res Fund, London/Clare Hall Lab, 85 & 86; nat lectr, Sigma Xi, 87 & 88; mem bd trustees, Soc Develop Biol, 92- *Mem:* Am Soc Cell Biol; Soc Develop Biol; Sigma Xi; fel AAAS; Soc Glycobiol; Asn Women Sci. *Res:* Glycoprotein synthesis in Dictyostelium discoideum; structure-function relationships of glycoconjugates intercellular cohesion; intercellular cohesion. *Mailing Add:* Dept Biol Georgetown Univ Washington DC 20057-1028. *Fax:* 202-687-5662

HENDERSON, FLOYD M, REMOTE SENSING, LAND USE ANALYSIS. *Current Pos:* from asst prof to assoc prof, 73-85, PROF GEOG, STATE UNIV NY, ALBANY, 85-, ASSOC DEAN, COL SOCIAL & BEHAV SCI, 87- *Personal Data:* b Denison, Iowa, Feb 23, 46; m 68. *Educ:* Nebr Wesleyan Univ, BA, 68; Univ Kans, MA, 70, PhD(geog), 73. *Prof Exp:* Asst prof geog, San Diego State Univ, 72-73. *Concurrent Pos:* Co-dir, Geog Info Systs & Remote Sensing Lab, State Univ NY, Albany, 75-; vis asst prof, La State Univ, 77; vis scientist, Inst Bodenkultur, Vienna, Austria, 85. *Mem:* Am Soc Photogram & Remote Sensing; Int Soc Photogram & Remote Sensing; Inst Elec & Electronics Engrs; Soc NAm Cult Surv. *Res:* Effects of environmental modulation on imaging radar signal response; digital and contextual analysis of remote sensing imagery for terrain features. *Mailing Add:* Dept Geog State Univ NY Albany 1400 Washington Ave Albany NY 12222-1000. *Fax:* 518-442-4867; *E-Mail:* fmh06@css.albany.edu

HENDERSON, FREDERICK BRADLEY, III, geology, for more information see previous edition

HENDERSON, GARY BORGAR, BIOCHEMISTRY. *Current Pos:* Asst mem, 76-83, ASSOC MEM, SCRIPPS CLIN & RES FOUND, 83- *Personal Data:* b Seattle, Wash, Feb 8, 46; m 70; c 2. *Educ:* Univ Wash, BS, 68; Univ Calif, PhD(biochem), 73. *Mem:* Am Soc Biol Chemists; Am Asn Cancer Res; Am Soc Microbiol. *Res:* Mechanisms and components of transport systems for folate compounds, vitamins, and anions; antineoplastic drugs; drug uptake and delivery systems. *Mailing Add:* Dept Biochem Scripps Res Inst 10550 N Torrey Pines Rd NX6 La Jolla CA 92037-1027. *Fax:* 619-784-7981

HENDERSON, GARY LEE, PHARMACOLOGY. *Current Pos:* ASSOC PROF PHARMACOL, SCH MED, UNIV CALIF, DAVIS, 71- *Personal Data:* b Springfield, Mo, Dec 13, 38; m 60. *Educ:* Univ Calif, Berkeley, AB, 65; Univ Calif, Davis, PhD(comp pharmacol & toxicol), 69. *Prof Exp:* Asst res pharmacologist, Sch Med, Univ Calif, Los Angeles, 70-71. *Concurrent Pos:* USPHS scholar, Brain Res Inst, Ctr Health Sci, Sch Med, Univ Calif, Los Angeles, 69-70. *Mem:* AAAS; Am Chem Soc. *Res:* Drug metabolism and pharmacokinetics; development of methodology for micro-determination of drugs and their metabolites in biological fluids and tissues. *Mailing Add:* Dept Pharmacol Univ Calif Davis Sch Med Davis CA 95616-5224. *Fax:* 530-795-1115

HENDERSON, GEORGE ASA, THEORETICAL PHYSICS, ATOMIC, MODULAR & COMPUTATIONAL PHYSICS. *Current Pos:* from asst prof to assoc prof, 70-78, PROF PHYSICS, SOUTHERN ILL UNIV, EDWARDSVILLE, 78- *Personal Data:* b Charleston, WVa, Aug 22, 40; m 63; c 3. *Educ:* Georgetown Univ, BS, 62, MS, 67, PhD(physics), 70. *Prof Exp:* Res assoc quantum chem, Johns Hopkins Univ, 69-70. *Concurrent Pos:* Fac res partic, Argonne Nat Lab, 72-75; res assoc Univ NC, 75-76; fac fel NASA-Langley Res Ctr, 81; res, McDonnell Douglas Corp, 82-92. *Mem:* Am Phys Soc; Am Asn Physics Teachers; AAAS. *Res:* Computational models for lasers; density matrix theory; electronic properties of atoms and molecules; density fuctional theory. *Mailing Add:* Dept Physics Southern Ill Univ Edwardsville IL 62026-1654. *E-Mail:* ghender@sive.edu

HENDERSON, GEORGE EDWIN, AGRICULTURAL ENGINEERING. *Current Pos:* RETIRED. *Personal Data:* b Kenton, Ohio, Sept 10, 06; m 33; c 2. *Educ:* Ohio State Univ, BSAgr, 29. *Prof Exp:* Rural engr, Ohio Edison Power Co, 29-32 & Dayton Power & Light Co, 32-37; rural elec eng ed, Tenn Valley Authority, 37-39, head, Ed Sect, 39-41, asst chief, Ag Eng Div, 41-45, chief, 45-47, Agr Eng & Food Processing Div, 47-48; prof agr eng, Univ Ga, 49-73, emer prof, 73- *Concurrent Pos:* Exec dir, Am Asn Voc Instrnl Mat. *Mem:* Fel Am Soc Agr Engrs. *Res:* Rural electrification; structures and farm power. *Mailing Add:* 150 Valley Rd Athens GA 30606

HENDERSON, GEORGE I, TERATOLOGY, AGING. *Current Pos:* ASSOC PROF MED & PHARMACOL, UNIV TEX HEALTH SCI CTR, SAN ANTONIO, 82- *Personal Data:* b Indianapolis, Ind, July 2, 43. *Educ:* Vanderbilt Univ, PhD(pharmacol), 72. *Prof Exp:* Asst prof pharmacol, Vanderbilt Univ, 76-82. *Mem:* Teratology Soc; Am Soc Pharmacol & Exp Therapeut; Am Inst Nutrit; Sigma Xi; Res Soc Alcoholism. *Mailing Add:* Dept Pharmacol Univ Tex Health Sci Ctr 7703 Floyd Curl Dr San Antonio TX 78284-7878. *Fax:* 210-567-4654

HENDERSON, GEORGE RICHARD, ENZYMOLOGY, TRANSPORT. *Current Pos:* Instr, 76-77, ASST PROF PHARMACOL, MED COL OH, 77- *Personal Data:* b New York, NY, Oct 28, 45; m 77; c 1. *Educ:* St Lawrence Univ, BS, 67; Cornell Univ, PhD(pharmacol), 76. *Mem:* Sigma Xi. *Res:* Properties and functions of sodium. *Mailing Add:* Wyeth-Ayerst 170 Radnor Chester Rd St Davids PA 19087

HENDERSON, GERALD GORDON LEWIS, geology, for more information see previous edition

HENDERSON, GILES LEE, MOLECULAR SPECTROSCOPY, PHYSICAL CHEMISTRY. *Current Pos:* Assoc prof, 67-80, PROF CHEM, EASTERN ILL UNIV, 80- *Personal Data:* b Aberdeen, SDak, July 19, 43; m 62; c 2. *Educ:* Mont State Col, BS, 65, MS, 66; Ind Univ, PhD(chem physics), 73. *Res:* Spectroscopic studies of the properties and structures of van der Waals molecules. *Mailing Add:* Dept Chem Eastern Ill Univ Charleston IL 61920

HENDERSON, GREGORY WAYNE, ADVANCED MATERIALS FOR TACTICAL AIRCRAFT, DESIGN FOR ENVIRONMENTAL COMPLIANCE. *Current Pos:* MGR DESIGN, LOCKHEED TACTICAL AIRCRAFT SYSTS 95- *Personal Data:* b Bridgeport, Conn, Nov 30, 50; m 77, Marion Melnyk. *Educ:* Univ Conn, BS, 72; Okla State Univ, MS, 79. *Honors & Awards:* Outstanding Young Mem, Soc Automotive Engrs, 83. *Prof Exp:* Eng specialist, Ft Worth Div, Gen Dynamics, 80-86, eng chief, 87-91; fel & sr policy analyst, White House Sci Off, 86-87; mgr mat & processes, Lockheed Ft Worth Co, 91-94. *Concurrent Pos:* Chmn, Comt Mats, White House Fed Coord Coun Sci Eng & Technol, 86-87; mem, US Comt Foreign Invest, 87; co-organizer, White House Conf High Temp Superconductivity, 87; consult, White House Sci Off, 88; prof eng, State Bd Regist Prof Engrs, Austin, Tex, 93. *Mem:* Soc Automotive Engrs; fel Am Soc Mat Int. *Res:* Research, develop and application of state-of-the-art materials, processes and structures for advanced tactical military aircraft; source reduction of hazardous materials through innovative design changers. *Mailing Add:* MZ2860 PO Box 748 Ft Worth TX 76101

HENDERSON, H(OMAN) THURMAN, SOLID STATE ELECTRONICS & PHYSICS. *Current Pos:* assoc prof elec eng, 68-, DIR CTR MICROSENSORS & KARTALIA PROF ELEC ENG, UNIV CINCINNATI. *Personal Data:* b Berea, Ky, Dec 28, 32; m 54; c 3. *Educ:* Ind Inst Technol, BSEE, 58; Southern Methodist Univ, MSEE, 61, PhD(elec eng), 68; Harvard Univ, SM, 67. *Prof Exp:* Electronics engr & sr tech writer, Chance Vought Corp, 58-60; from instr to asst prof elec eng, Univ Tex, Arlington, 60-68. *Concurrent Pos:* Prin investr, NSF grant, 69-70, Inst Space Sci, Univ Cincinnati-NASA res grant, 70 & NASA res grant, 71-; mem bd sci adv, KDI Corp, 70. *Mem:* Am Soc Eng Educ; Am Phys Soc; Inst Elec & Electronics Engrs; Cryogenic Soc Am; Sigma Xi. *Res:* Electrical materials science, particularly the effects of radiation on the electrical properties of materials; high level injection in semi-insulators and the role of deep impurities in achieving unique volt-ampere characteristics and instabilities; microelectronics. *Mailing Add:* Dept Elec Eng PO Box 210030-Rm ERC 390 Univ Cincinnati Cincinnati OH 45221-0030

HENDERSON, HALA ZAWAWI, PEDODONTICS. *Current Pos:* RETIRED. *Personal Data:* b Karachi, Pakistan, July 11, 31; US citizen; m 61; c 1. *Educ:* Bombay Univ, BDS, 56; Ind Univ, MSD, 59, DDS, 70; Am Bd Pedodontics, dipl, 79. *Prof Exp:* Jr lectr dent, Govt Dent Col, Bombay Univ, 59-60; head, Dent Div, Sch Health Serv, Ministry Health, Kuwait, Arabia, 60-68; from asst prof to assoc prof, Ind Univ, 70-82, prof pedodontics, dent, 82-96. *Concurrent Pos:* Dent consult, Ministry Health, Sultanate, Oman, 81. *Mem:* Am Soc Dent Children; Am Dent Asn; Am Acad Pedodontics; Am Asn Dent Sch. *Res:* Clinical dentistry, including correlation between ankylosed teeth; use of chrome crowns on primary molars; diet counseling for the child patient. *Mailing Add:* 3239 Lincoln Ct Indianapolis IN 46208

HENDERSON, JAMES B(ROOKE), CHEMICAL ENGINEERING. *Current Pos:* RETIRED. *Personal Data:* b Washington, DC, Feb 26, 26; m 48; c 2. *Educ:* Purdue Univ, BS, 46, PhD(chem eng), 49. *Prof Exp:* Asst instr, Purdue Univ, 46-47, res assoc, 47-49; from technologist to gen mgr, Synthetic Rubber Div, Shell Chem Co, Houston, 49-66, indust, Chem Div, 66-70, vpres, 70-72, vpres, Shell Oil Co, 72-77, mkt coordr, Shell Int Petrol Co, 77-79, pres, Shell Chem Co & exec vpres & dir, Shell Oil Co, 79-85. *Mem:* Am Inst Chem Engrs; Am Chem Soc; Sigma Xi. *Mailing Add:* 11646 SE Plandome Dr Hobe Sound FL 33455

HENDERSON, JAMES HENRY MERIWETHER, PLANT PHYSIOLOGY, TISSUE CULUTRE. *Current Pos:* asst prof & res assoc plant physiol, Carver Res Found, Tuskegee Inst, 45-50, res assoc prof biol, 50-68, head dept, 57-68, dir res found, 68-75, chmn, Nat Sci Div, 68-96, dir, Minority Biomed Res Prog, 73-86, SR RES PROF BIOL, CARVER RES FOUND, TUSKEGEE INST, 75- *Personal Data:* b Falls Church, Va, Aug 10, 17; wid; c Edith E (Wimbish), Dena R (Sewell), James F & Edward B II. *Educ:* Howard Univ, BS, 39; Univ Wis, MPh, 40, PhD(plant physiol), 43. *Honors & Awards:* Distinguished Serv Award, Am Soc Plant Physiologists. *Prof Exp:* Jr chemist, Badger Ord Works, Wis, 42-43; asst pharmacol, Nat Defense Res Comt, Calif, 43-45. *Concurrent Pos:* Res fel, Kerckhoff Biol Labs, Calif Inst Technol, 48-50; NSF sr fac fel, Nat Ctr Sci Res, France, 61-62; comnr, Coun Undergrad Educ Biol Sci, 67-70; res biochem & cell cult, Hawaii Sugar Planters Ans, 74; vis scientist, Int Inst Trop Agr, 86. *Mem:* Fel AAAS; Am Soc Plant Physiol; Nat Inst Sci; Sigma Xi; Soc In Vitro Biol. *Res:* Tissue culture; auxin and plant growth regulator metabolism and physiology, including the mechanism of action; physiology of normal and abnormal plant tissues; gibberellins; regeneration of sweet potato plants in vitro. *Mailing Add:* Dept Biol Tuskegee Univ Tuskegee AL 36088

HENDERSON, JAMES MONROE, chemical engineering, process metallurgy; deceased, see previous edition for last biography

HENDERSON, JAMES STUART, PATHOLOGY, ONCOLOGY. *Current Pos:* PROF PATH, UNIV MANITOBA, 70- *Personal Data:* b Dundee, Scotland, May 26, 28; m 56; c 2. *Educ:* Univ St Andrews, MB, ChB, 51. *Prof Exp:* Intern med, Muhlenberg Hosp, Plainfield, 51-52; secondment, Atomic Bomb Casualty Comn, Hiroshima, 54; instr path, Duke Univ, 55-57; res assoc, Rockefeller Inst Med Res, 57-60; asst prof, Rockefeller Univ, 60-70. *Concurrent Pos:* Consult pathologist & dir exp path, Deer Lodge Vet Admin Hosp, Winnipeg, 70-83; consult pathologist, Health Sci Ctr, Winnipeg, 80 & St Boniface Hosp, 83. *Mem:* NY Acad Sci; Reticuloendothelial Soc; Am Asn Cancer Res; Am Asn Path & Bact; fel Royal Soc Med; Group Res Path Educ. *Res:* Cancer, especially co-factors which cause progression in certain mouse tumors; medical education, especially the use of interactive computer programs. *Mailing Add:* Dept Path Univ Manitoba Fac Med 770 Bannatyne Ave Winnipeg MB R3E 0W3 Can

HENDERSON, JOHN FREDERICK, PHYSICAL CHEMISTRY, POLYMER CHEMISTRY. *Current Pos:* MGR TECHNOL SCANNING & ASSESSMENT, NOVA CORP, ALTA, 90- *Personal Data:* b Montreal, Que, Apr 26, 33; m 61; c 2. *Educ:* McGill Univ, BSc, 54, PhD(phys chem), 58. *Prof Exp:* Fel, Nat Res Coun Can, 57-59; sr res chemist, Polymer Corp Ltd, 59-62, proj supvr exp res, 62-66, proj supvr resins, 67-69, mgr current prod res, 69-71; tech mgr emulsion polymers, Polysar Ltd, 71-73, tech develop mgr, 73-79, global prod mgr emulsion rubbers, 79-82, mgr technol scanning & assessment, 82-86, Polysar fel, 86-90. *Concurrent Pos:* Mem assoc comt high polymer res, Nat Res Coun Can, 68-69. *Mem:* Fel Chem Inst Can. *Res:* Chemical kinetics in gas and solution phases; sterospecific, anionic and free radical polymerization; polymer characterization. *Mailing Add:* 6942 Livingstone Dr SW Calgary AB Can

HENDERSON, JOHN WARREN, OPHTHALMOLOGY. *Current Pos:* From asst prof to assoc prof, Mayo Grad Sch Med, 47-67, chmn sect ophthal, Mayo Clin, 67-72, prof, 67-77, EMER PROF OPHTHAL, MAYO GRAD SCH MED, 77- *Personal Data:* b Nebr, Sept 11, 12; m 33; c 2. *Educ:* Univ Nebr, MA, 36, MD, 37; Univ Minn, MS, 43. *Mailing Add:* Mayo Clin Rochester MN 55905

HENDERSON, JOHN WOODWORTH, OPHTHALMOLOGY. *Current Pos:* From intern to resident, Univ Hosp, Univ Mich, Ann Arbor, 42-45, from instr to prof, Med Sch, 45-78, chmn dept, 68-78, EMER PROF OPHTHAL, MED SCH, UNIV MICH, ANN ARBOR, 78- *Personal Data:* b Clarinda, Iowa, Mar 8, 16; m 42, Joyce Hildebrandt; c John H & Louise W. *Educ:* Occidental Col, BA, 37; Northwestern Univ, MD & MS, 42; Am Bd Ophthal, dipl, 46; Univ Mich, PhD(neuro-ophthal), 48. *Mem:* Am Ophthal Soc (pres, 80); fel Am Acad Opthal; Asn Univ Profs Ophthal (pres, 76). *Res:* Neuro-ophthalmology; anatomical research in Macaca mulatta; human embryology; anatomical basis for certain reflex and automatic eye movements; ocular signs in brain tumor and in aneurysms; corneal disease and surgery. *Mailing Add:* 1358 Laurel View Dr Ann Arbor MI 48105

HENDERSON, LAVELL MERL, BIOCHEMISTRY. *Current Pos:* RETIRED. *Personal Data:* b Swan Lake, Idaho, Sept 9, 17; m 39, Maurine Criddle; c Janet, Jeanne & Linda. *Educ:* Utah State Univ, BS, 39; Univ Wis, MS, 41, PhD(biochem), 47. *Hon Degrees:* DSc, Utah State Univ, 74. *Honors & Awards:* Lalor Found Award, 55; Borden Award in Nutrit, 70. *Prof Exp:* Instr biochem, Univ Wis, 47-48; asst prof, Univ Ill, 48-57; prof & head dept, Okla State Univ, 57-63; head dept biochem, Univ Minn, St Paul, 63-74, prof, 63-84, assoc dean, Col Biol Sci, 78-84. *Mem:* AAAS; Am Chem Soc; Am Soc Biochem & Molecular Biol; Am Inst Nutrit; Am Soc Microbiol. *Res:* Metabolism of amino acids; amino acid assay; vitamin B complex in animal nutrition; tryptophan metabolism; niacin, carnitine and alkaloid biosynthesis; hydroxylysine metabolism. *Mailing Add:* 8612 Mt Majestic Rd Sandy UT 84093-1833

HENDERSON, LAWRENCE J, SOIL FERTILITY, SOIL CHEMISTRY. *Current Pos:* LAB DIR, MAT TESTING & CONSULT, MT VERNON, WASH, 90- *Personal Data:* b Oceanside, Calif, Aug 10, 52; m 73; c 5. *Educ:* Brigham Young Univ, BS, 77; Okla State Univ, MS, 80, PhD(soil sci), 83. *Prof Exp:* Soil Technologist, US Sugar Corp, 82-90. *Mem:* Am Soc Agronomy; Soil Sci Soc Am; Am Soc Sugarcane Technologists. *Res:* Conducting and evaluating fertility, irrigation and drainage and cultural studies for sugarcane on sand soils and histisols; supervision of routine soil and tissue analyses for sugarcane, pasture, citrus and corn production. *Mailing Add:* Mat Testing & Consult 1151 Knudson Rd Burlington WA 98233

HENDERSON, LINDA SHLATZ, BIOCHEMISTRY, ENDOCRINOLOGY. *Current Pos:* ASST DIR, CARDIOPULMONARY THERAPEUT UNIT, SMITHKLINE BEECHAM. *Personal Data:* b Johnson City, NY, Feb 21, 46; m 77; c Lauren & Kristen. *Educ:* St Lawrence Univ, BS, 67; Univ Rochester, PhD(biochem), 72. *Prof Exp:* Fel physiol, Mt Sinai Sch Med, 71-73, res assoc, 73-74; res assoc biochem, Med Sch, Univ Mass, 74-75; asst prof med & biochem, Sch Med, Univ Rochester, 75-77; asst prof biochem, Med Col Ohio, 77- *Concurrent Pos:* USPHS fel, 71-74; res assoc, Max Planck Inst Biophys, Frankfurt, 72-73; USPHS grants, 75-77 & 77- *Mem:* AAAS; Sigma Xi. *Res:* Effects of hormones and calcium on membrane structure and function; importance of membrane polarity in the kidney and small intestine with respect to hormone action; regulation of gastric secretion. *Mailing Add:* 9 Whitehall Acres Oxford PA 19363

HENDERSON, LOUIS E, BIOCHEMISTRY. *Current Pos:* SECT SUPVR, VIRAL PROTEIN LAB, PRI FT DETRICK, FREDERICK, MD, 89- *Personal Data:* b Rulo, Nebr, Jan 1, 34; m 71, Ulla Bjornros; c John. *Educ:* Univ Omaha, BA, 57; Univ Colo, PhD(biochem), 65. *Prof Exp:* NIH fel biochem, Harvard Univ, 65-68, mem tutorial bd, 66-68; Nobel vis scientist, Chalmers Univ Technol, Sweden, 69; mem staff, Sweden Indust Res Coun, 70-73; res assoc biochem & biophys, Yale Univ, 73-76; sr res scientist, Frederick Cancer Res Ctr, 76-89. *Concurrent Pos:* Adj prof, Univ Md, Baltimore; grad studies adv, Hood Col. *Mem:* AAAS; Am Chem Soc; NY Acad Sci. *Res:* Protein chemistry; radiation research; protein structure; vetrovirology; AIDS. *Mailing Add:* SAIC AIDS Vaccine Prog Frederick Cancer Res & Develop Ctr Frederick MD 21701. *Fax:* 301-846-5588; *E-Mail:* henderson@aupvx1.ncifcrf.gov

HENDERSON, MADELINE M BERRY, information resources management, application standards information systems, for more information see previous edition

HENDERSON, MAUREEN MCGRATH, EPIDEMIOLOGY. *Current Pos:* prof, Sch Dent, Univ Wash, 75-96, actg dean, 77, assoc vpres health sci, 79-81, dir, Pac Northwest Long-Term Care Ctr, 81-83, EMER PROF EPIDEMIOL & MED, UNIV WASH, 96- *Personal Data:* b Tynemouth, Eng, May 11, 26; nat US. *Educ:* Univ Durham, MB, BS, 49, DPH, 56. *Honors & Awards:* John A Snow Award, Am Pub Health Asn, 90. *Prof Exp:* Fel cancer epidemiol, Dept Path, St Bartholomew's Hosp & Med Sch, London, Eng, 56-58, clin epidemiologist, Med Res Coun Group Res on Atmospheric Pollution, 58-60; from instr to prof prev med, Sch Med, Univ Md, 60-75, chmn, Dept Social & Prev Med, 71-75. *Concurrent Pos:* Vis prof chronic dis, Sch Hyg & Pub Health, Johns Hopkins Univ, 68-69, assoc dir, Regional Med Prog, Epidemiol & Statist Ctr, 68-73, assoc epidemiol, 70-75; mem, Steering Comt, Social Security Res Studies, Inst Med-Nat Acad Sci, 74-76; mem, Panel Health Serv Res, Comt Study Nat Needs Biomed & Behav Res Personnel, Nat Acad Sci-Nat Res Coun, 74-76; chmn, Expert Panel Reserpine & Breast Cancer, Food & Drug Admin, 74-76; deleg, US-USSR Joint Working Group Epidemiol Cancer, 74-; mem, President's Biomed Res Panel with Interdisciplinary Cluster Epidemiol, Biostatics & Bioeng, 75; mem, Task Force Theory & Appln Prev Med Health Care Delivery, Fogarty Nat Ctr & Am Col Prev Med, 75; mem, Expert Comt Review Data Carcinogenicity Cyclamate, Nat Cancer Inst, 75-76; mem, Comt Impacts Stratospheric Change, Nat Res Coun, 75-; mem, Adverse Drug Effects Adv Panel, Off Technol Assessment, US Cong, 76; head, Cancer Prev Res Prog, Fred Hutchinson Cancer Res Ctr, 83-94, mem, 94- *Mem:* Inst Med-Nat Acad Sci; Am Epidemiol Soc (pres-elect, 89-90, pres, 90); Int Epidemiol Soc; Soc Epidemiol Res (pres, 69-70); Asn Teachers Prev Med (vpres, 70-72, pres, 72-73); Am Soc Prev Oncol; Am Asn Cancer Res; Am Col Epidemiol; Am Pub Health Asn; Royal Soc Med. *Res:* Health services research with emphasis on health manpower; adverse drug reaction; preventive services, clinical trials. *Mailing Add:* Cancer Prev Res Prog Fred Hutchinson Cancer Res Ctr 1124 Columbia St Seattle WA 98104

HENDERSON, MERLIN THEODORE, AGRONOMY. *Current Pos:* RETIRED. *Personal Data:* b Oakdale, La, Dec 5, 14; m 41; c 3. *Educ:* Southwestern La Inst, BS, 39; La State Univ, MA, 41; Univ Minn, PhD(plant genetics), 45. *Prof Exp:* Asst potato breeding, USDA, 39-41; instr & asst prof plant breeding, Univ Minn, 41-45; assoc prof agron, Pa State Col, 45-48; prof, 48-77, alumni prof agron, La State Univ, Baton Rouge, 77-80. *Concurrent Pos:* Agt, Regional Pasture Res Lab, Bur Plant Indust, Soils & Agr, USDA, Pa, 47-48. *Mem:* Am Soc Agron; Am Genetic Asn. *Res:* Potato breeding; barley breeding and genetics; breeding of forage plants; inheritance of reaction to leaf rust in barley; breeding and genetics of cotton; cytogenetics of rice; genetics of sugarcane. *Mailing Add:* 5538 Riverstone Dr Baton Rouge LA 70820

HENDERSON, METTA LOU, PHARMACY, PHARMACOLOGY. *Current Pos:* assoc prof, 78-85, PROF, COL PHARM, OHIO NORTHERN UNIV, 85-, ASSOC DEAN, PHARM STUDENT AFFAIRS, COL PHARM, 95- *Personal Data:* b Battle Creek, Mich, Sept 11, 38. *Educ:* Univ Ariz, BS, 61, MS, 66, PhD(pharm/educ), 78. *Honors & Awards:* Rufus A Lyman Award, Am Asn Cols Pharm, 84. *Prof Exp:* Dir pharm, Community Hosp Battle Creek, Mich, 66-73; asst prof, Sch Pharm, Ferris State Col, 74-76. *Concurrent Pos:* Asst to vpres acad affairs, Ohio Northern Univ, 80-84, chmn, Dept Pharm Proct, Col Pharm, 93-95, asst dean, Pharm Student Affairs, 95-97. *Mem:* Fel Am Found Pharmaceut Educ; Am Asn Cols Pharm; Am Pharmaceut Asn; Sigma Xi. *Res:* Women in pharmacy; pharmacy education; pharmacy practice; toxicology and pharmacology. *Mailing Add:* Col Pharm Ohio Northern Univ Ada OH 45810

HENDERSON, NANNETTE SMITH, PLANT PATHOLOGY. *Current Pos:* dir, Col Transfer Prog, 76-78, HEAD DIV MATH-SCI PUB SERV PROGS, VANCE-GRANVILLE COMMUNITY COL, 78- *Personal Data:* b Washington, DC, June 9, 46; m 69; c 2. *Educ:* Howard Univ, BS, 67, MS, 69; NC State Univ, PhD(plant path), 73. *Prof Exp:* Lab asst virol, Plant Indust Sta, 67; microbiologist, Walter Reed Army Hosp Med Res, 67-68; teaching asst biol, Howard Univ, 68-69; lab asst mycol, Forestry Res Sta, 69; asst prof plant path, NC State Univ, 73-76. *Mem:* Nat Educ Asn; Nat Sci Teachers Am. *Mailing Add:* Continuing Educ Vance-Granville Community Col PO Box 917 Henderson NC 27536-0917

HENDERSON, NORMAN LEO, PHYSICAL PHARMACY. *Current Pos:* CONSULT PHARMACEUT RES, 92- *Personal Data:* b Jersey City, NJ, Feb 18, 32; m 56; c 3. *Educ:* Rutgers Univ, BSc, 53; Temple Univ, MSc, 58, PhD(pharm), 62. *Prof Exp:* Proj leader pharmaceut res & develop, Lederle Labs Div, Am Cyanamid Co, 61-67, group leader tablet & powder technol, 67-72; dir pharmaceut develop, Hoechst-Rouseel Pharmaceuticals Inc, 72-84, dir pharmaceut res, 84-92. *Concurrent Pos:* Mem adv comt pharm, Rutgers Univ, 80-92; mem pharmaceut develop comt, Pharmaceut Mfrs Asn, 82-85. *Mem:* Am Pharmaceut Asn; Acad Pharmaceut Sci; AAAS; Sigma Xi. *Res:* Pharmaceutical dosage forms; research and development of new drug entities from pre-formulation studies through production; evaluation of formulation factors upon clinical efficacy of dosage forms; novel drug delivery systems. *Mailing Add:* Patriot Rd Gladstone NJ 07934

HENDERSON, RALPH JOSEPH, JR, BIOCHEMISTRY. *Current Pos:* asst prof, Sch Med, La State Univ, Shreveport, 71-76, assoc prof biochem, 76-92, assoc prof med, 92-94, ASST DEAN STUDENT AFFAIRS, SCH MED, LA STATE UNIV, SHREVEPORT, 93-, PROF MED, 94- *Personal Data:* b Galveston, Tex, Sept 21, 40; m 64, Nancy Henslee; c R Jonathan & Pamela N. *Educ:* Univ Tex, Austin, BS, 63; Univ Tex Med Br Galveston, PhD(biochem), 70. *Prof Exp:* Chemist, Jefferson Chem Co, 64-66; trainee biochem, Univ Tex Southwestern Med Sch Dallas & Vet Admin Hosp, Dallas, 70-71. *Mem:* Am Chem Soc; AAAS; Sigma Xi; Am Soc Biochem & Molecular Biol. *Res:* Nucleotide and nucleoside metabolism; effects of extracellular matrix on cells; cell biology. *Mailing Add:* Off Student Affairs La State Univ Sch Med Shreveport LA 71130. *Fax:* 318-675-5077

HENDERSON, RICHARD ELLIOTT LEE, MEDICINAL CHEMISTRY. *Current Pos:* ASSOC PATENT COUN, PATENT DEPT, BAYER CORP, 88- *Personal Data:* b Lincolnton, NC, Feb 17, 45; m 78, Mary Beth Van Curg. *Educ:* Univ NC, Chapel Hill, BS, 67; Univ Ill, Urbana-Champaign, PhD(org chem), 73; IIT Chicago-Kent, JD, 86. *Prof Exp:* Res investr chem & coord res, Develop Div, Corp Patent Dept & Patent Dept, G D Searle & Co, 73-87; Patent Dept, Merck & Co, 87. *Mem:* Am Chem Soc; Am Intellectual Property Law Asn. *Mailing Add:* 316 Dickson Ave Pittsburgh PA 15202

HENDERSON, RICHARD WAYNE, ORGANIC CHEMISTRY, PHYSICAL CHEMISTRY. *Current Pos:* STAFF MEM, SRL INC, 80- *Personal Data:* b Baton Rouge, La. *Educ:* La State Univ, BS, 66, PhD(org chem), 71. *Prof Exp:* Fel, Memphis State Univ, 71-72; assoc prof chem, Francis Marion Col, 72-80. *Mem:* Am Chem Soc; Am Acad Forensic Sci; Am Soc Testing & Mat; Nat Asn Fire Invest; Int Asn Arson Invest. *Res:* Polar effects in radical reactions; heavy metal chemistry; arson research; analysis for accelerant residues. *Mailing Add:* 3516 E Palmetto St Florence SC 29506

HENDERSON, ROBERT E, TURBOMACHINERY. *Current Pos:* Res asst, Appl Res Lab, 59-72, from assoc prof to prof, Mech Eng & Appl Res Lab, 72-91, EMER PROF, MECH ENG & APPL RES LAB, PA STATE UNIV, 91- *Personal Data:* b Olean, NY, Nov 1, 35; m 57, Annalee Rosenswie; c Gregory D, Michael E & Lori E. *Educ:* Penn State Univ, BS, 58, MS, 62; Cambridge Univ, PhD(mech eng), 73. *Concurrent Pos:* Underwater Comt, Am Inst Aeronaut & Astronaut, 66-69; Turbomach Comt, Am Soc Mech Engrs, 79-; head, Fluid Dynamics & Turbomach Dept, Appl Res Lab, Pa State Univ, 83-90, asst dir appl sci, 90-91. *Mem:* Fel Am Soc Mech Engrs; Am Soc Naval Engrs; assoc fel Am Inst Aeronaut & Astronaut. *Res:* Fluid dynamics of turbomachinery. *Mailing Add:* Noesis 4200 Wilson Blvd Suite 900 Arlington VA 22203-1800. *E-Mail:* reh@arlvax.arl.psu.edu

HENDERSON, ROBERT EDWARD, PHYSICS, ENGINEERING. *Current Pos:* DIR, SC RES AUTHORITY, 83- *Personal Data:* b Kokomo, Ind, Feb 28, 25; m 52; c 6. *Educ:* Carleton Col, BA, 49; Univ Mo, MA, 51, PhD(physics), 53. *Prof Exp:* Instr physics, Univ Mo, 51-53; exp engr, Allison Div, Gen Motors Co, 53-56, supvr appl physics, 56-58, res mgr applied sci, 58-66, mgr exp res, 66-69, dir res, 69-73; chmn sci adv bd, Ind Ctr Adv Res Inc, 70-83, exec dir, 73-78, pres, Ind Ctr Adv Res Inc, 78-82; pres, Technol Develop Corp, 82-83. *Concurrent Pos:* Mem comt on solar energy for heating & cooling of bldgs, Bldgs Res Adv Bd, Nat Acad Sci; adv, Aeronaut Systs Div, Div Adv Group, Dept Air Force; prof, Purdue Sch Engr & Technol, Ind; prof, dept radiol, Ind Univ Sch Med; adj prof, Ind Univ Sch Pub & Environ Affairs; pres, Ind Sci & Eng Found, 82. *Mem:* Fel Am Inst Aeronaut & Astronaut; Am Phys Soc; Solar Energy Soc; Sigma Xi. *Res:* Energy conversion research. *Mailing Add:* 225 Pebble Creek Rd Columbia SC 29223-3314

HENDERSON, ROBERT WESLEY, NUMISMATICS, PHOTOGRAPHY. *Current Pos:* assoc prof & assoc agronomist, Dept Farm Crops, 46-48, asst to dir agr exp sta, 47-53, asst dir agr exp sta, 53-76, EMER PROF AGRON CROP SCI, ORE STATE UNIV, 77- *Personal Data:* b Omaha, Nebr, Mar 31, 14; m 38; c 4. *Educ:* Ore State Univ, BS, 38; Cornell Univ & Univ Minn, PhD(plant genetics), 50. *Prof Exp:* Asst, Sherman Exp Sta, Moro, Ore, 38-41; asst plant breeding, Cornell Univ, 41-42; assoc geneticist, USDA, Univ Minn, 42-46. *Concurrent Pos:* Geneticist, USDA, 46-52; chief-of-party, Ore State Univ Adv Staff to Kasetsart Univ, Bangkok, 59-61; proprietor, Henderson Enterprises, 75- *Mem:* Fel AAAS; Sigma Xi. *Res:* Plant breeding, rubber plants, sugar beets, red clover and wheat. *Mailing Add:* 3732 NW Van Buren Corvallis OR 97330

HENDERSON, ROGENE FAULKNER, BIOCHEMISTRY. *Current Pos:* BIOCHEMIST & TOXICOLOGIST, LOVELACE ENVIRON & BIOMED RES INST, INC, 67- *Personal Data:* b Breckenridge, Tex, July 13, 33; m 57, Thomas R; c Tim, Edith & Lucy. *Educ:* Tex Christian Univ, BA, 55; Univ Tex, Austin, PhD(chem), 60; Am Bd Toxicol, dipl, 81. *Honors & Awards:* Frank Blood Award, Soc Toxicol, 89; Chancellors Distinguished lectr, Univ Calif, Irvine, 92. *Prof Exp:* NIH fel, Sch Med, Univ Ark, 60-62, res assoc biochem, 62-66. *Concurrent Pos:* Mem, NIH Toxicol Study Sect, 82-86; mem, Ed Bd Toxicol, 84-88, J Biochem Toxicol, 86-92 & Inhalation Toxicol, 88-; mem, Nat Res Coun/Nat Acad Sci Comts, Toxicol, 85-91, chair, Biol Markers, 86-88, Epidemiol Air Pollution, 84-85, Common Risk Assessment Methodology, 90-; mem, Burroughs Wellcome Adv Comt Toxicol, Scholar Award, 87-89; adj prof, Dept Vet Microbiol, Path & Public Health, Sch Vet Med; clin prof, Col Pharm, Univ NMex, 89-; mem, Assoc Western Univs Lab Adv Bd, 88-89; assoc ed, Toxicol Appl Pharmacol, 90-, J Exposure Anal & Environ Epidemiol, 91. *Mem:* NY Acad Sci; AAAS; Am Chem Soc; Soc Toxicol. *Res:* Early indicators of pulmonary toxicity; toxicokinetics of inhaled organic compounds; pathogenesis of noncancer diseases of respiratory tract. *Mailing Add:* 5609 Don Felipe Ct SW Albuquerque NM 87105-6765. *Fax:* 505-845-1198

HENDERSON, RUTH MCCLINTOCK, PHARMACOLOGY, PHYSIOLOGY. *Current Pos:* RETIRED. *Personal Data:* b St Paul, Minn, Apr 4, 25; m 61. *Educ:* Univ Minn, BS, 46, MS, 47, PhD(physiol), 56. *Prof Exp:* Sci teacher, Am Collegiate Inst, Turkey, 47-50; instr physiol, Univ Minn, 51-54, res fel, 54-55, instr, 55-57; physiologist, Nat Inst Arthritis & Metab Dis, 57-58, biochemist, 58-59; asst prof physiol, Sch Med, George Washington Univ, 59-63; asst prof physiol, Univ Alta, 63-66, from asst prof to prof pharmacol, 67-88. *Concurrent Pos:* Assoc, Sch Med, George Washington Univ, 57-59. *Mem:* AAAS; Pharmacol Soc Can; Micros Soc Can; Am Physiol Soc; Electron Micros Soc Am. *Res:* Measurement of total metabolism; electrochemistry of ion selective membranes; renal function; transport processes; ultrastructure of kidney and smooth muscle; actions of diuretics. *Mailing Add:* 9704 165th St Suite 61 Edmonton AB T5P 4W4 Can

HENDERSON, SHERI DAWN, radiation biophysics, radiation biology, for more information see previous edition

HENDERSON, THOMAS E, ADULT EDUCATION PROGRAMS. *Current Pos:* RETIRED. *Personal Data:* b Middletown, NY, Aug 17, 34; m 81; c 3. *Educ:* State Univ NY, New Paltz, BS, 58; Univ Albany, MS, 79. *Honors & Awards:* One Idea Ahead of Its Time Award, Atlantic Richfield, 74; Technol Today Award, 80. *Prof Exp:* Teacher IV, Dept Correctional Serv, NY State, 62-89; adj prof, Mercy Col, 79-92; adj prof, Sullivan Co Community Col, 91-94. *Concurrent Pos:* Founder & coordr, Solar Energy Proj, NY State Dept Corrections, 78-80. *Res:* Established first solar energy program in NY State Prison System. *Mailing Add:* 130 W Main St Middletown NY 10940

HENDERSON, THOMAS OTIS, BACTERIOLOGY, BIOCHEMISTRY. *Current Pos:* asst prof, 68-74, assoc prof, 74-80, PROF BIOCHEM, UNIV ILL COL MED, 80-, ASSOC DEAN ACAD PROG, 77- *Personal Data:* b Hickory, NC, Nov 17, 37; m 61, 70; c 5. *Educ:* Lenoir-Rhyne Col, BS, 61; NC State Univ, MS, 64, PhD(microbiol, nutrit biochem), 67. *Prof Exp:* Res technician chem, Tape Div, Shuford Mills, NC, 60-61. *Concurrent Pos:* NIH res fel, Univ Chicago, 66-68; NIH res grants, 70-76; Am Heart Asn grant, 74-77. *Mem:* AAAS; Am Soc Biol Chem; Am Soc Microbiol. *Res:* Regulation of fatty acid synthesis in bacteria; bacterial phospholipid metabolism; phosphonic acid chemistry and metabolism. *Mailing Add:* Dept Biochem M/C 536 Univ Ill Chicago A-312 CMWT Chicago IL 60612-7334. *Fax:* 312-413-0364

HENDERSON, THOMAS RANNEY, ORGANIC CHEMISTRY. *Current Pos:* RETIRED. *Personal Data:* b Orange, NJ, Apr 11, 41; m 63, 90, Virginia Going; c Meredith & Erica. *Educ:* Drew Univ, BA, 63; Rutgers Univ, PhD(org chem), 73. *Prof Exp:* Jr chemist, Hoffmann-La Roche Inc, 64-68; develop scientist III, Burroughs Wellcome Co, 74-77, develop scientist IV, 77-87, admin & tech serv mgr, 88- *Concurrent Pos:* Res assoc, Univ Ill, Urbana, 72-74. *Mem:* Am Chem Soc. *Res:* Development of new routes to pharmaceutically important compounds. *Mailing Add:* 400 S Boylan Ave Raleigh NC 27603

HENDERSON, THOMAS RICHARD, BIOCHEMISTRY. *Current Pos:* BIOCHEMIST, LOVELACE ENVIRON & BIOMED RES INST, INC, 66- *Personal Data:* b Edinburg, Tex, Aug 24, 32; m 57; c 3. *Educ:* Pan Am Col, BA, 53; Univ Tex, PhD(biochem), 60. *Prof Exp:* Instr biochem, Sch Med, Univ Ark, 60-63, asst prof, 63-66. *Concurrent Pos:* Asst prof chem, Univ Albuquerque, 84- *Mem:* AAAS; Am Chem Soc; Am Soc Biol Chemists. *Res:* Geochemistry; environmental chemistry; inhalation toxicology; mass spectrometry; chemistry and toxicology of combustion effluents; diesel exhaust analysis. *Mailing Add:* 5609 Don Felipe Ct SW Albuquerque NM 87105-6765

HENDERSON, ULYSSES VIRGIL, JR, ORGANIC CHEMISTRY. *Current Pos:* RETIRED. *Personal Data:* b Miami, Fla, July 15, 26; m 51; c 2. *Educ:* US Merchant Marine Acad, BS, 47; Ga Inst Technol, BS, 51, PhD(org chem), 54. *Prof Exp:* Res chemist, Stand Oil Co, Ind, 54; sr scientist, Exp Inc, 56-61; res chemist, Texaco Inc, 61-62, group leader, 62-65, asst supvr, 65-68, supvr fundamental & explor res, 68-71, supvr chem res, 71-72, supvr air & water conserv, 72-82, assoc dir, 82-87, dir, Environ Affairs, 88-91, gen mgr, Environ & Prod Safety, 91. *Mem:* AAAS; Am Chem Soc. *Res:* Reaction mechanisms; decomposition of monopropellants; high speed gas phase reactions; heterogeneous combustion; chemical vapor plating; petrochemical processes and products; solid and aqueous waste management for petroleum industry. *Mailing Add:* 8315 Houghton Pl Chesterfield VA 23832

HENDERSON, WARREN ROBERT, HORTICULTURE. *Current Pos:* asst prof, 59-67, ASSOC PROF HORT, NC STATE UNIV, 67- *Personal Data:* b Boston, Mass, May 5, 27. *Educ:* Univ NH, BS, 49; Harvard Univ, AM, 51; Ohio State Univ, PhD(hort), 59. *Honors & Awards:* L M Ware Award, 71. *Prof Exp:* Asst hort, Ohio State Univ, 54-59. *Mem:* Am Soc Hort Sci; Sigma Xi. *Res:* Tomato breeding and genetics; disease resistance breeding of cabbage, squash, and watermelon. *Mailing Add:* 2605 Sawmill Rd Raleigh NC 27613-1619

HENDERSON, WILLIAM ARTHUR, JR, ORGANIC CHEMISTRY. *Current Pos:* RETIRED. *Personal Data:* b Winthrop, Mass, Oct 5, 32; m 60; c 2. *Educ:* Harvard Univ, BA, 54; Yale Univ, MS, 56, PhD(org chem), 60. *Prof Exp:* From res chemist to sr res chemist, Am Cyanamid Co, 60-84, assoc res fel org chem, 84- *Mem:* Am Chem Soc; Geol Soc Am. *Res:* Chemistry of phosphines, cyclopolyphosphines, photochromic compounds and photochemistry; singlet oxygen; photostabilization of polymers; thermal and photostabilization of agricultural chemicals; photochemical methods of immunoassay, chiral synthesis of pharmaceuticals; synthesis of polyisocyanates. *Mailing Add:* 47 Robin Ridge Dr Madison CT 06443

HENDERSON, WILLIAM BOYD, CIVIL ENGINEERING. *Current Pos:* PRES, CHIEF EXEC OFFICER & CHIEF OPERS OFFICER, TRIDENT ENG ASSOCS, 83- *Personal Data:* b Elkton, Tenn, Apr 8, 28; m 53, Virginia D Ferguson; c William B II, Kimberly A & Karen B. *Educ:* Vanderbilt Univ, BCE, 50; Univ Pittsburgh, MEng, 59. *Prof Exp:* Eng mgr, Westinghouse Elec Corp, 54-74; pres, Buell Div, Envirotech Corp, 74-80; pres & chmn bd, Rettew Assocs Inc, 80-83. *Concurrent Pos:* Consult, Self-Air Pollution Equip, 79-83. *Res:* Nuclear power. *Mailing Add:* Trident Eng Assocs Inc 2010 Industrial Dr Annapolis MD 21401-1673

HENDERSON-ARZAPALO, ANNE PATRICIA, AQUACULTURE, FISHERIES SCIENCE. *Current Pos:* FISHERY BIOLOGIST, NAT BIOL SURV, 87- *Personal Data:* b New York, NY, Aug 17, 55; m 77, Alfred. *Educ:* State Univ NY, BS, 77; Tex A&M Univ, MS, 79, PhD(wildlife & fisheries sci), 83. *Prof Exp:* Res asst, Tex A&M Univ, 78-83; biologist, Tex Parks & Wildlife, 83-47. *Mem:* Am Fisheries Soc; Am Inst Fishery Res Biologist; World Aquacult Soc. *Res:* Reproduction and aquaculture production of tilopia, red drum, spotted seatrout, flounder, corvina, snook and striped bass. *Mailing Add:* Biol Resources Div Leetown Sci Ctr-Nat USGS Kearneysville WV 25430

HENDLER, EDWIN, HUMAN PHYSIOLOGY, AEROSPACE PHYSIOLOGY. *Current Pos:* RETIRED. *Personal Data:* b Philadelphia, Pa, Aug 29, 22; m 45; c 2. *Educ:* Pa State Univ, BS, 43; Univ Pa, MS, 56, PhD(physiol), 59. *Honors & Awards:* Paul Bert Award for Physiol Res, Aerospace Med Asn, 73; Prof Excellence Award, Life Scis & Biomed Engr Br, Aerospace Med Asn, 88. *Prof Exp:* Physicist, Aerospace Crew Equip Lab, Naval Air Eng Ctr, 46-49, head physiol sect, 50-52, head acceleration br, 52-55, supt med sci res div, 55-63, mgr life sci res group, 63-71, head appl physiol lab, Crew Systs Dept, 71-74, head, life sci res group, Aircraft & Crew Systs Directorate, Naval Air Develop Ctr, 75-81; consult, life sci, 81-91. *Concurrent Pos:* Assoc, Sch Med, Univ Pa, 60-63. *Mem:* Biophys Soc; fel Aerospace Med Asn; Am Physiol Soc; Sigma Xi. *Res:* Aerospace physiology; human engineering; acceleration effects; thermal physiology; temperature sensation; pulmonary physiology. *Mailing Add:* 8 Sandringham Pl Cherry Hill NJ 08003-1531

HENDLER, ERNESTO DANILO, INTERNAL MEDICINE, NETHROLOGY. *Current Pos:* from instr to asst prof, 68-76, ASSOC PROF MED, SCH MED, YALE UNIV, 76- *Personal Data:* b San Martin, Mendoza, Arg, Oct 24, 35; m 61; c 2. *Educ:* San Martin Nat Col, Arg, BS, 52; Univ Buenos Aires, MD, 60. *Hon Degrees:* Hon dipl, Univ Buenos Aires, 61. *Prof Exp:* Clin fel nephrology, Inst Med Res, Univ Buenos Aires, 64-66; intern med, Rivadavia Hosp, Buenos Aires, 61; resident internal med, Vet Admin Hosp, DC, 66-67; instr, Vet Admin Div, Sch Med, George Washington Univ, 67-68. *Concurrent Pos:* NIH res fel, 67-68; spec res fel, 68-70; staff physician, Med Serv, West Haven Vet Admin Hosp, Conn, 70-, assoc dir dialysis unit, 70-73, dir, 73- *Mem:* Am Soc Artificial Internal Organs; Int Soc Nephrol; Am Fedn Clin Res; Am Soc Nephrology. *Res:* Metabolic aspects of kidney function, especially regarding the active transport of sodium; treatment of acute and chronic renal failure. *Mailing Add:* Vet Admin Hosp Spring St West Haven CT 06516-1230

HENDLER, GORDON LEE, SYSTEMATICS, INVERTEBRATE ZOOLOGY. *Current Pos:* assoc cur, 85-90, CURATOR NATURAL HIST MUS, LOS ANGELES CO, 90-, HEAD, INVERT ZOOL SECT, 87-; RES ASSOC, SMITHSONIAN INST, 93- *Personal Data:* b New York, NY, Dec 11, 46; m 90, Florence H Nishida Okamoto; c Suzanne Ogawa, Elise (Myers), Brian Ogawa & Katy Nishida. *Educ:* Rutgers Univ, BA, 68; Univ Conn, PhD(zool), 73. *Prof Exp:* Fel, Woods Hole Oceanog Inst, 73-74; Walter Rathbone Bacon fel, Smithsonian Inst, 74-75, res marine biologist, Smithsonian Trop Res Inst, 75-78, marine biologist, Benthic Sect, Smithsonian Oceanog Sorting Ctr, 78-85. *Concurrent Pos:* Expeds, Smithsonian Philippines, 78 & research vessel Alpha Helix Moro, 79; field work Cent Am & Antartica, 81-85; res, submersible cruises, Caribbean & Eastern Pac, 82-96; adj assoc prof, Univ Southern Calif, 88- *Mem:* Sigma Xi; Soc Integrative & Comp Biol; Soc Syst Zool; AAAS; Western Soc Naturalists. *Res:* Systematics, ecology and behavior of echinoderms, primarily ophiuroids; curation of LACM echinoderm collection; study of bathyal Caribbean brittlestars with submersibles; brittlestar photoreception, reproduction, skeletal ontogeny, functional morphology. *Mailing Add:* Natural Hist Mus 900 Exposition Blvd Los Angeles CA 90007. *Fax:* 213-746-2999; *E-Mail:* hendler@bcf.usc.edu

HENDLER, JAMES A, COMPUTER SCIENCE. *Current Pos:* assoc prof, 86-92, ASSOC PROF, COMPUT SCI DEPT, UNIV MD, 86-, INST ADVAN COMP STUDIES, 87-, INST SYSTS RES, 88-, HEAD, PARALLEL UNDERSTANDING SYSTS LAB, 89-, HEAD, AUTONOMOUS MOBILE ROBOTICS LAB, 93- *Personal Data:* b Apr 2, 57; m, Gerry Horonit; c Sharon. *Educ:* Yale Univ, BS, 78; Southern Methodist Univ, MS; Brown Univ, ScM, 83, PhD(comput sci), 85. *Prof Exp:* Res programmer, Artificial Intel Proj, Yale Univ, 77-79; mem tech staff, Tex Instruments Inc, 79-82; teaching & res asst, Comput Sci Dept, Brown Univ, 83-85, lectr, 84. *Concurrent Pos:* Programmer, Bernard Screen Printing Corp, 76; vis scientist, Int Comput Sci Inst, Calif, 89, Australian Artificial Intel Inst, 91; guest researcher, Cognitive Neurosci Sect, Nat Inst, Neurolog Dis & Stroke, NIH, 91-; vis researcher, NEC Corp, Japan, 92; vis prof, Bar-Ilan Univ, Israel, 94; res fel, KISS Inst Practical Robotics, 94; Fulbright fel, 95; assoc ed, J Exp & Theoret AI & Connection Sci: An Int J Neural Network & PDP Res; mem, Defence Sci Study Group, Inst Defense Analysis, 96-97. *Mem:* AAAS; Am Asn Artificial Intel; Cognitive Sci Soc; Sigma Xi; NY Acad Sci. *Res:* Artificial intelligence; knowledge-based reasoning; robotics; contributed numerous articles to professional journals. *Mailing Add:* Univ Md College Park MD 20742. *Fax:* 301-405-6707

HENDLER, NELSON HOWARD, PSYCHIATRY, NEUROPHYSIOLOGY. *Current Pos:* From instr to asst prof psychiat, 75-82, psychiat consult, Chronic Pain Treat Ctr, 75-82, ASST PROF NEUROSURG IN PSYCHIAT, JOHNS HOPKINS HOSP, 75-; CLIN DIR, MENSANA CLIN, 78-; ASSOC PROF PHYSIOL, SCH DENT SURG, UNIV MD, 89- *Personal Data:* b New York, NY, Aug 15, 44; m 74, Lee Meyerhoff; c Sam, Alex, Lindsay & Josepha. *Educ:* Princeton Univ, BA, 66; Univ Md Sch Med, MD, 72, MS, 74. *Honors & Awards:* William Meninger

Award. *Concurrent Pos:* Dir med res, Reflex Sympathetic Dystrophy Asn, 85-; Falk fel, Comt Res & Develop, Am Psychiat Asn, 74-75. *Mem:* Am Asn Study Headache; AMA; Hans Selye Am Inst Stress (vpres, 83-); Pavlovian Soc; Am Pain Soc; Israeli Pain Soc; Am Psychiat Asn; Acad Psychosom Med; Int Asn Study Pain. *Res:* Research into chronic pain and testing to research the validity of chronic pain and the Mentana Clinic back pain test; author of 3 books, 21 chapters, and 45 articles. *Mailing Add:* Mensana Clin 1718 Greenspring Valley Rd Stevenson MD 21153. Fax: 410-653-2403

HENDLER, RICHARD WALLACE, BIOCHEMISTRY, BIOPHYSICS. *Current Pos:* BIOCHEMIST, NAT HEART & LUNG INST, 55-, HEAD SECT MEMBRANE ENZYMOL, LAB CELL BIOL, 75- *Personal Data:* b Philadelphia, Pa, Mar 3, 27; m 48; c 2. *Educ:* Pa State Univ, BS, 48; Univ Pa, MS, 49; Univ Calif, PhD(biochem), 52. *Prof Exp:* Asst biochem, Univ Calif, 50-52. *Concurrent Pos:* Fel, Nat Found Infantile Paralysis, Nat Heart Inst & NIH, 52-54; USPHS fel, Free Univ Brussels, 54-55. *Mem:* Am Soc Biol Chemists; Biophys Soc. *Res:* Role of cellular membranes in energy producing activities of cells. *Mailing Add:* Lab Cell Biol Nat Heart & Lung Inst Bethesda MD 20892. Fax: 301-402-1519; E-Mail: rwh@hwlix.nih.gov

HENDLEY, EDITH DI PASQUALE, NEUROSCIENCES. *Current Pos:* from assoc prof to prof, 73-94, EMER PROF PHYSIOL, MED COL, UNIV VT, 94- *Personal Data:* b New York, NY, Sept 5, 27; m 52, Daniel Dees; c Jane A, Joyce L & Paul D. *Educ:* Hunter Col, AB, 48; Ohio State Univ, MS, 50; Univ Ill, PhD(physiol), 54. *Prof Exp:* Instr physiol, Univ Chicago, 54-56; asst lectr, Univ Sheffield, 57-58; instr ophthal, Johns Hopkins Univ, 63-66; res assoc pharmacol & exp therapeut, 66-71; sr investr, Friends Med Sci Res Ctr, Inc, 72-73. *Mem:* Am Physiol Soc; Am Soc Pharmacol & Exp Therapeut; Soc Neurosci; Asn Women Sci; Sigma Xi; AAAS. *Res:* Neurochemical basis of behavior; biogenic amines in brain; inbred rat strains as models of human diseases: hypertension and hyperactivity. *Mailing Add:* Dept Molecular Physiol & Biophys Univ Vt Col Med Burlington VT 05405. Fax: 802-656-0747; *E-Mail:* hendley@salus.med.uvm.edu

HENDLEY, JOSEPH OWEN, PEDIATRICS. *Current Pos:* from asst prof to assoc prof, 70-82, PROF PEDIAT, SCH MED, UNIV VA, 82- *Personal Data:* b Chattanooga, Tenn, Aug 18, 37; c 4. *Educ:* Vanderbilt Univ, BA, 59; Univ Pa, MD, 63. *Prof Exp:* Intern pediat, Med Ctr, Duke Univ, 63-64, resident, 64-65; res fel pediat & prev med, Sch Med, Univ Va, 65-67; resident pediat, Med Ctr, Duke Univ, 64-65; res fel infectious dis, Harvard Sch Pub Health, 68-70. *Concurrent Pos:* Epidemic Intel Off, Dept Preventative Med, USPHS, Univ Va, 65-68. *Mem:* Am Soc Microbiol; Infectious Dis Soc Am; Am Acad Pediat; Am Epidemiol Soc; Soc Pediat Res. *Res:* Pediatric infectious disease; interruption of rhinovirus transmission; characterization of gonococcal capsule; mechanisms of human immunity to bordetella pertussis. *Mailing Add:* Univ Va Health Sci Ctr Box 386 Charlottesville VA 22902-0386

HENDLIN, DAVID, MICROBIOLOGY. *Current Pos:* RETIRED. *Personal Data:* b Harbin, China, Mar 8, 20; nat US; m 44, Ruth Maltz; c Susan(MooAllem) & Harriet. *Educ:* Brooklyn Col, NY, BA, 41; Iowa State Univ, MSc, 43; Rutgers Univ, PhD(microbiol), 49. *Prof Exp:* Res microbiologist, Merck Sharp & Dohme Res Lab, 43-48, head nutrit sect, 48-53, mgr microbiol dept, 53-56, asst dir, 56-67, dir bact labs, Merck Inst Therapeut Res, 67-69, dir basic microbiol, 69-74, sr dir develop microbiol, 74-81, exec adminr, Japan, 81-85, sr dir & sci liaison, 85-90. *Mem:* AAAS; Am Chem Soc; Am Soc Microbiol; fel NY Acad Sci; fel Am Acad Microbiol; Soc Gen Microbiol; Soc Ind Microbiol. *Res:* Antibiotics; production of chemicals by microorganisms; microbial nutrition; chemotherapy of bacterial infections. *Mailing Add:* Five Laurel Dr Springfield NJ 07081

HENDON, JOSEPH C, ORGANIC CHEMISTRY. *Current Pos:* CHEMIST, PB&S CHEM CO, 81- *Personal Data:* b Mayfield, Ky, July 19, 38; m 62; c 2. *Educ:* Murray State Univ, BS, 61; Univ Ky, PhD(org chem), 68. *Prof Exp:* Res chemist, Tenn Eastman Co, 67-69; from asst prof to assoc prof org chem, Murray State Univ, 69-74; CHMN, DEPT SCI & MATH, PIKEVILLE COL, 78- *Mem:* Am Chem Soc. *Res:* Synthesis and determination of carcinogenic activity of isoquinoline azo dyes related to butter yellow-synthesis of cationic dyes for use in dying fibers; environmental contaminents (air and water) monitoring associated with the development of a coal gasification plant. *Mailing Add:* 331 Old Orchard Lane Henderson KY 42420-4756

HENDREN, RICHARD WAYNE, BIOCHEMISTRY. *Current Pos:* DEPT HEAD, OLIGOMER DEVELOP, GLAXO RES INST, RESEARCH TRIANGLE PARK, NC, 92- *Personal Data:* b Salisbury, NC, June 24, 48; m 69, Anne Rhodes; c Katherine & Kristin. *Educ:* Univ NC, Chapel Hill, BS, 70; Harvard Univ, PhD(chem), 77. *Prof Exp:* Res scientist biochem, Corp Res Lab, Union Carbide Corp, 77-79; sr res biochemist, Chem & Life Sci Div, Res Triangle Inst, 79-87; lab head, Pharmaceut & Drug Delivery, AMGEN, Thousands Oaks, Calif, 87-92. *Mem:* Am Chem Soc; AAAS; Am Asn Pharmaceut Scientists; Controlled Release Soc. *Res:* Formulation and delivery of peptides proteins, oligo-and polynucleotides; antisense and gene therapy. *Mailing Add:* 105 Bastille Ct Cary NC 27511-6462

HENDREY, GEORGE RUMMENS, LIMNOLOGY, ECOLOGY. *Current Pos:* DIV HEAD, BIOSYSTS DIV, BROOKHAVEN NAT LAB, 77- *Personal Data:* b Seattle, Wash, Dec 9, 40; m 65; c 2. *Educ:* Univ Wash, BA, 66, MS, 70, PhD(aquatic biol), 73. *Prof Exp:* Assoc res engr chem, Boeing Co, 66-68; trainee, Pub Health Serv, 68-73; res assoc aquatic biol, Univ Wash, 70-73; res scientist limnol, Norweg Inst Water Res, Oslo, 73-76, tenure, 75; vis lectr & sr res assoc, Sect Ecol & Systs, Cornell Univ, 76-77. *Concurrent Pos:* Vis fel, Ctr Environ Res, Cornell Univ, 76-; adv, Int Joint Comn, 79-81; prin investr, Effects Acid Precipitation Crop Growth & Yield, US Environ Protection Agency & Northeastern Nat Environ Res Park, Dept Energy, 77-; consult, Environ Criteria Assessment Off, Environ Protection Agency, 79-81; mem, Biol Effects Gov Bd, NADP, 79-81, Environ Protection Agency Adminr Round Table, 83; expert witness, Environ Defense Fund, Scenic Hudson Inc, Hudson River Fisherman's Asn, 81, City of New York, Hudson River Found, State of Fla, 83-85; DOE Intragency Personnel Assignment, 84-88. *Mem:* Am Asn Limnol & Oceanog; Int Soc Limnol; Int Asn Theoret & Appl Limnol; Am Chem Soc; NY Acad Sci. *Res:* Aquatic biology; limnology; bioassay; acid and precipitation effects; geochemistry. *Mailing Add:* Biosysts Div Brookhaven Nat Lab Bldg 318 PO Box 5000 Upton NY 11973

HENDRICH, CHESTER EUGENE, PHYSIOLOGY, ENDOCRINOLOGY. *Current Pos:* assoc prof physiol & endocrinol, 73-77, PROF PHYSIOL, MED COL GA, 77- *Personal Data:* b Clinton, Mo, Jan 29, 35; m 59; c 3. *Educ:* Univ Mo-Columbia, AB, 59, MS, 61, PhD(endocrinol), 65. *Prof Exp:* Fel endocrinol, Emory Univ, 64-65 & Dartmouth Med Sch, 65-67; asst prof physiol & endocrinol, Col Med, Ohio State Univ, 67-73. *Mem:* Am Physiol Soc; Endocrine Soc; Soc Exp Biol & Med. *Res:* Effects of thyroid and parathyroid hormone on other maternal hormone secretions and fetal metabolism and development; effects of artificial atmospheres on the endocrine system. *Mailing Add:* Dept Physiol Med Col Ga Augusta GA 30912-3000

HENDRICK, LYNN DENSON, NUCLEAR PHYSICS, SCIENCE EDUCATION. *Current Pos:* PROF PHYSICS, FRANCIS MARION UNIV, 70- *Personal Data:* b Panama City, Fla, July 23, 37; m 62, Carlanna Lindamood; c Jeff & Andrew. *Educ:* Auburn Univ, BEP, 59, MS, 60; Univ SC, PhD(physics), 66. *Prof Exp:* Asst prof physics, Maryville Col, 61-62; res assoc, Univ SC, 66-67; assoc prof & head, Dept Phys Sci, Columbia Col, 67-70. *Concurrent Pos:* Chmn manpower & prof, Educ Comt, Health Physics Soc, 86-88; distinguished prof, Francis Marion Univ, 89. *Mem:* Am Asn Physics Teachers; Am Phys Soc; Sigma Xi; Health Physics Soc. *Res:* Nuclear spectroscopy; structure and decay schemes; accelerator based atomic physics. *Mailing Add:* Dept Physics Francis Marion Univ Florence SC 29501. E-Mail: hendrick@scarolina.fmarion.edu

HENDRICK, MICHAEL EZELL, ORGANIC CHEMISTRY. *Current Pos:* SR RES SCIENTIST ORG CHEM, PFIZER INC-CENT RES, 74- *Personal Data:* b Memphis, Tenn, July 31, 45; m 69; c 1. *Educ:* Southwestern, Memphis, BS, 67; Princeton Univ, AM, 69, PhD(chem), 71. *Prof Exp:* Res fel org chem, Ruhr Univ, Bochum, Ger, 71-73 & Stanford Univ, 73-74. *Concurrent Pos:* NIH fel, Stanford Univ, 74. *Mem:* Am Chem Soc. *Res:* Organic chemistry of odor and taste, especially sweeteners, odorants, and flavors. *Mailing Add:* 42 Pine Island Rd Groton CT 06340

HENDRICKER, DAVID GEORGE, INORGANIC CHEMISTRY. *Current Pos:* From asst prof to assoc prof, 65-74, PROF CHEM, OHIO UNIV, 74- *Personal Data:* b Aurora, Ill, Oct 14, 38; m 65. *Educ:* Northern Ill Univ, BS, 60; Iowa State Univ, MS, 63, PhD(inorg chem), 65. *Mem:* Am Chem Soc; Sigma Xi. *Res:* Metal carbonyl, phosphorus and aluminum hydride chemistry; coordination compounds; application of nuclear magnetic resonance and infrared spectroscopy to inorganic chemistry. *Mailing Add:* Dept Chem Ohio Univ Athens OH 45701

HENDRICKS, ALBERT CATES, AQUATIC BIOLOGY, AQUATIC TOXICOLOGY. *Current Pos:* prof biol, 71-80, ASSOC PROF ZOOL, VA POLYTECH INST & STATE UNIV, 80- *Personal Data:* b Beaumont, Tex, Dec 28, 37; m 67; c 3. *Educ:* Lamar Univ, BA, 63; NTex State Univ, MA, 66, PhD(biol), 70. *Prof Exp:* Hydrologist ecol, Tex Water Develop Bd, 70. *Mem:* Sigma Xi; Am Soc Limnol & Oceanol; Ecol Soc Am; NAm Benthol Soc. *Res:* Fate and effect of toxic chemicals in the aquatic environment; use of biomonitoring as early warning devices. *Mailing Add:* Biol Dept Va Polytech Inst & State Univ PO Box 0406 Blacksburg VA 24063-0001

HENDRICKS, CHARLES D(URRELL), JR, INERTIAL CONFINEMENT FUSION. *Current Pos:* PRIN INST SCIENTIST, INST PLASMA & FUSION RES, UNIV CALIF, LOS ANGELES. *Personal Data:* b Lewiston, Utah, Dec 5, 26; m 48; c 2. *Educ:* Utah State Univ, BS, 49; Univ Wis, MS, 51; Univ Utah, PhD(physics), 55. *Prof Exp:* Physicist, US Naval Ord Test Sta, 52 & Off Ord Res, 54; mem staff, Lincoln Lab, Mass Inst Technol, 55-56; from asst prof to prof elec eng, Univ Ill, Urbana, 56-80, emer prof, 80; dep assoc prog leader, AIT Flight Prog, Lawrence Livermore Nat Lab, Univ Calif, 88-90. *Concurrent Pos:* Consult, Lincoln Lab, Mass Inst Technol, 56-57, Ramo-Wooldridge Corp, 57-, Space Tech Labs, 62- & Xerox Corp, 63-, Rand Corp, 72-78, Exxon Res & Eng Ctr, 74-, Calif Inst Technol, 78-, Nuclear Eng Dept, Univ Wis, 79; assoc prog leader, laser fusion target fabrication, Lawrence Livermore Nat Lab, Univ Calif, 74-80, sr scientist, 80-88; pres, Int Microprod, Inc, 87-; chief scientist, W J Schafer Assoc. *Mem:* Fel Am Phys Soc; foreign fel Electrostatics Soc Japan; fel Inst Elec & Electronics Engrs; assoc fel Am Inst Aeronaut & Astronaut; Electrostatics Soc Am. *Res:* Research in inertial confinement fusion primarily in target fabrication for fusion experiments; plasma and small particle physics and electrostatic phenomena and processes. *Mailing Add:* 2817 Pardee Pl Livermore CA 94550

HENDRICKS, CHARLES HENNING, OBSTETRICS & GYNECOLOGY. *Current Pos:* RETIRED. *Personal Data:* b Traverse City, Mich, Oct 26, 17; m 42; c 5. *Educ:* Univ Mich, AB, 41, MD, 43; Am Bd Obstet & Gynec, dipl. *Honors & Awards:* Am Asn Obstet & Gynec Found Prize, 56. *Prof Exp:* Instr obstet & gynec, Ohio State Univ, 48-51, asst prof, 51-54; from assoc prof to prof, Case Western Res Univ, 54-68; Robert A Ross distinguished prof obstet & gynec & chmn dept, Sch Med, Univ NC, Chapel Hill, 68-90. *Mem:* AAAS; AMA; Am Gynec Soc; Am Asn Obstet & Gynec; Am Col Obstet & Gynec. *Res:* Physiology of pregnancy. *Mailing Add:* 102 Boulder Lane NC Mem Hosp Chapel Hill NC 27514

HENDRICKS, DAVID WARREN, SANITARY ENGINEERING. *Current Pos:* assoc prof, 70-82, PROF CIVIL ENG, COLO STATE UNIV, 82- *Personal Data:* b Springfield, Mo, Sept 10, 31; m 59, Betty A Omo; c Bridgette, Philip & Sara. *Educ:* Univ Calif, Berkeley, BS, 54; Utah State Univ, MS, 60; Univ Iowa, PhD(sanit eng), 65. *Prof Exp:* Jr civil engr, State Dept Water Res, Calif, 54; instr civil eng, Univ Idaho, 58-61, asst res prof, 61-62; from asst prof to assoc prof, Utah State Univ, 65-70. *Concurrent Pos:* Consult, Eimco Corp, Salt Lake City, 66-67, Pan Am Health Asn, 78, UNESCO, 78 & Yemen Govt, 80 & numerous others. *Mem:* Am Soc Civil Engrs; Water Pollution Control Fedn; Am Water Works Asn; Am Chem Soc; Asn Environ Eng Prof; Int Water Qual Asn; Int Water Supply Asn; Am Inst Chem Engrs. *Res:* Water resources; physical chemistry; hydraulic engineering; waste management systems; environmental interdisciplinary problems; filtration; adsorption; membranes. *Mailing Add:* 2306 Tanglewood Ft Collins CO 80525-1953. *Fax:* 970-491-8480

HENDRICKS, DELOY G, MINERAL METABOLISM, NUTRIENT BIOAVAILABILITY. *Current Pos:* Asst prof nutrit, dept nutrit, 67-72, assoc prof, 72-77, PROF NUTRIT & FOOD SCI, UTAH STATE UNIV, 77- *Personal Data:* b Pocatello, Idaho, Dec 18, 38; m 62, Cora J Wood; c Judy L, JaLee, Jolene, Janet S, Jerrae, Joy M & Clint E. *Educ:* Univ Idaho, BS, 61; Mich State Univ, PhD(animal nutrit), 67. *Concurrent Pos:* Vis scientist, Vet Admin Hosp, Baltimore, Md, 71; vis prof, USDA Human Nutrit Lab, Beltsville, Md, 80-81. *Mem:* Am Inst Nutrit. *Res:* Mineral metabolism and bioavailabiltiy; food storage and safety; nutritional status and behavior. *Mailing Add:* Dept Nutrit & Food Sci Utah State Univ Logan UT 84322-8700. *Fax:* 435-750-2379; *E-Mail:* deloyh@extsparc.agsci.usa.edu

HENDRICKS, DONOVAN EDWARD, ENTOMOLOGY, ECOLOGY. *Current Pos:* RETIRED. *Personal Data:* b Apr 8, 40; US citizen. *Educ:* Purdue Univ, Ind, BSc, 63, MSc, 65, Am Bd Entom, Cert. *Honors & Awards:* Merit Achievement Award for Develop Bioassay Syst, USDA, 75. *Prof Exp:* Res entomologist ecol & entom, Agr Res Serv, USDA, 66-95. *Mem:* Entom Soc Am; Am Registry Prof Entomologists. *Res:* Insect ecology and behavior in relation to field mating and migration of Lepidoptera; biophysics; insect detection systems; electronic insect detection; US patent for SODAR insect detection device. *Mailing Add:* Agr Res Serv USDA Box 346 Stoneville MS 38776-0346

HENDRICKS, GAVIN J, MECHANICAL ENGINEERING. *Current Pos:* MECH ENGR, UNITED TECHNOL RES CTR, EAST HARTFORD, CONN. *Honors & Awards:* Gas Turbine Award, Am Soc Mech Engrs, 95. *Mailing Add:* United Technol Res Ctr 411 Silver Lane Mail Stop 129-20 East Hartford CT 06108

HENDRICKS, GRANT WALSTEIN, petroleum chemistry; deceased, see previous edition for last biography

HENDRICKS, JAMES OWEN, ELASTOMERS, ADHESIVES. *Current Pos:* RETIRED. *Personal Data:* b Waynetown, Ind, Sept 3, 09; wid; c 3. *Educ:* Wabash Col, AB, 31; Univ Ill, PhD(phys chem), 36. *Honors & Awards:* Carlton Award, Minn Mining & Mfg Co, 73. *Prof Exp:* Teaching fel, Univ Calif, 31-32; chemist, Kendall Ref Co, Pa, 33-34; asst & fel, Univ Ill, 34-36; res chemist, Minn Mining & Mfg Co, 36-42, head colloid sect, Cent Res Dept, 42-47, from asst dir to assoc dir, 47-53, mgr res tape div, 53-66, sci liaison, 66-74. *Concurrent Pos:* Campbell fel award, Wabash Col. *Mem:* Am Chem Soc. *Res:* Elasticity of permanently tacky adhesives; specific adhesion of rubber adhesives; water dispersed adhesives; low adhesion surfaces. *Mailing Add:* 2292 Sixth St White Bear Lake Sta St Paul MN 55110

HENDRICKS, JAMES RICHARD, parasitology; deceased, see previous edition for last biography

HENDRICKS, JERRY DEAN, FISH BIOLOGY, FOOD TOXICOLOGY. *Current Pos:* res assoc, 75-78, from asst prof to assoc prof, 78-85, PROF HISTOPATHOL, ORE STATE UNIV, 85-, PROF, DEPT FOOD SCI, 80- *Personal Data:* b Atkinson, Nebr, July 7, 44; m 68, Barbara E May; c David, Timothy, Greta, Joanna & Michael. *Educ:* Colo State Univ, BS, 66, PhD(fishery biol), 71. *Prof Exp:* Fishery biologist histopathol, Nat Oceanic & Atmospheric Admin, Nat Marine Fisheries Serv, 71-72 & US Fish & Wildlife Serv, 73-74. *Mem:* Am Fisheries Soc; Am Asn Cancer Res; Sigma Xi. *Res:* Fish histology and histopathology; fish nutrition; carcinogenesis; food toxicology. *Mailing Add:* Dept Food Sci & Tech Ore State Univ 100 Wiegand Hall Corvallis OR 97331-6602. *Fax:* 541-737-6074

HENDRICKS, LAWRENCE JOSEPH, limnology, fisheries, for more information see previous edition

HENDRICKS, LEWIS T, FOREST PRODUCTS, MARKETING. *Current Pos:* assoc prof, 67-76, EXTEN SPECIALIST, UNIV MINN, 67-, PROF FOREST PROD, 76- *Personal Data:* b Rome, NY, July 3, 40; m 62; c 2. *Educ:* State Univ NY, BS, 61, MS, 63; Mich State Univ, PhD(econ, mkt), 67. *Prof Exp:* Teaching asst forest prod, Mich State Univ, 62-64; technologist, USDA, 64-67. *Concurrent Pos:* Consult, Wood Prods Indust; vis prof, Univ Wis-Madison, 85-86; spec assignment, Forest Prod Lab, USDA Forest Serv; coordr, Cold Climate Housing Info Ctr, Univ Minn, 87-89, dir, 89-90. *Mem:* Sigma Xi; Forest Prod Res Soc. *Res:* Veneer and plywood industry; wood finishing; wood preservation; moisture relationships; economics of woodburning; ice-dam prevention in residential housing; performance of wood in buildings. *Mailing Add:* Forest Prod 220 Kaufert Lab Univ Minn 2004 Folwell Ave St Paul MN 55108-6128

HENDRICKS, ROBERT WAYNE, MATERIALS SCIENCE, DIFFRACTION PHYSICS. *Current Pos:* PROF MAT SCI & ENG, VA POLYTECH INST & STATE UNIV, 86- *Personal Data:* b Trail, BC, Apr 30, 37; US citizen; m 58, Delores D Black; c James R & Karen M. *Educ:* Cornell Univ, BMetE, 59, PhD(phys metall), 64; Univ Tenn, MBA, 85. *Honors & Awards:* IR-100 Award, 77. *Prof Exp:* Res metallurgist & mem res staff, Oak Ridge Nat Lab, 64-81, assoc dir, Nat Ctr Small-Angle Scattering Res, 78-81; mgr specialty prods, Technol for Energy Corp, 81-85, chief scientist, 85-86. *Concurrent Pos:* Res assignment, Inst fur Festkorperforschung der Kernforschungsanlage, WGer, 72-73. *Mem:* Am Inst Mining, Metall & Petrol Engrs; fel AAAS; Am Crystallographic Asn; fel Am Phys Soc; Sigma Xi; Am Soc Metals Int; Mat Res Soc; Am Asn Physics Teachers; Am Soc Eng Educ. *Res:* Solid state physics; physical chemistry; x-ray diffraction; application of small-angle and high-angle diffuse x-ray and neutron scattering techniques to radiation damage and phase transformation problems in physical metallurgy and in structure of polymeric materials; determination of residual stresses in metals and ceramics and electronic materials by x-ray diffraction; research instrumentation; expert systems for materials research; residual stress. *Mailing Add:* 2904 Wakefield Dr Blacksburg VA 24060. *Fax:* 540-231-8919; *E-Mail:* robert.hendricks@vt.edu

HENDRICKS, ROBERT WILLIAM, PHYSICAL CHEMISTRY. *Current Pos:* RETIRED. *Personal Data:* b Mt Home, Idaho, June 2, 29; m 51, Carole Axworthy; c Todd, Anne & Jill. *Educ:* Univ Rochester, BS, 51; Brown Univ, PhD(chem), 56. *Prof Exp:* Res chemist, Exp Sta, Film Res Lab, E I du Pont de Nemours & Co, Inc, 55-60, res supvr, Circleville Res & Develop Lab, 60-64, develop supvr, Circleville Mylar Plant, 64-65, mgr, Develop Dept, 65-66, res supvr, Photo Prod Dept, 66-74, res mgr, 74-77, lab dir, Rochester Photo Prod Dept, 77-90. *Res:* Photographic products; magnetic recording; polymer chemistry; polymeric films and coatings. *Mailing Add:* 403 French Rd Rochester NY 14618. *E-Mail:* 71045.1222@compuserve.com

HENDRICKS, WALTER JAMES, mathematics, for more information see previous edition

HENDRICKSON, ADOLPH C(ARL), COMPUTER SCIENCE, INTELLIGENCE SYSTEMS. *Current Pos:* COMPUT SCIENTIST, COMPUT SCI CORP, 81- *Personal Data:* b Kearsarge, Mich, June 19, 27; m 51, Joanna Shaw-Eagle; c Philip & Kirsten. *Educ:* Mass Inst Technol, BS & MS, 52. *Prof Exp:* Res engr, analog missile simulation, Mass Inst Technol, 52-53; mathematician, digital comput prog, Remington Rand, Inc, 53-56; staff analyst, Gen Kinetics, Inc, 56-59; opers analyst, Res Anal Corp, 59-63; sr assoc, Planning Res Corp, 64-65; mem tech staff, Gen Res Corp, 66-68; pres, Hendrickson Corp, 68-81. *Mem:* Asn Comput Mach; Sigma Xi; Audubon Naturalist Soc. *Res:* Computer application to operations research; micro-analytic simulation and gaming; software systems; database design; requirement analysis. *Mailing Add:* 5014 Newport Ave Bethesda MD 20816

HENDRICKSON, ALFRED A, METALLURGY. *Current Pos:* RETIRED. *Personal Data:* b Lake Linden, Mich, May 18, 29; m 54; c 2. *Educ:* Mich Tech Univ, BS, 51; Columbia Univ, MS, 54; Northwestern Univ, PhD(metall), 60. *Prof Exp:* Metallurgist, FWD Corp, 51-52 & Ampco Metal Inc, 54-56; from asst prof to assoc prof, Mich State Univ, 56-70, forging indust prof metall eng, 70-78. *Concurrent Pos:* Lectr, Northwestern Univ, 54-58; hon res fel, Univ Birmingham, 70-71; Nat Sci Coun Prof, Nat Sun-Yat Sen Univ, 82. *Mem:* Am Soc Metals; Am Inst Mining, Metall & Petrol Engrs; Soc Mfg Engrs. *Res:* Strength of solids; metal processing; forging processes. *Mailing Add:* 1762 S Manitou Trail Lake Leelanau MI 49653

HENDRICKSON, ANITA ELIZABETH, DEVELOPMENTAL NEUROBIOLOGY. *Current Pos:* res instr biol struct, 65-67, from instr to assoc prof 67-81, PROF OPHTHAL, UNIV WASH, 81-, PROF BIOL STRUCT, 84-, CHAIR DEPT, 94- *Personal Data:* b LaCrosse, Wis, Feb 20, 36; m 57; c 3. *Educ:* Pac Luthern Col, BA, 57; Univ Wash, PhD(anat), 64. *Honors & Awards:* Dolly Green Scholar Res, Prevent Blindness, Inc, 81-82. *Prof Exp:* Instr anat, Northwestern Med Sch, 64-65. *Concurrent Pos:* Vis assoc prof, Dept Neuropath, Harvard Med Sch, 75-76; vis B study sect, Div Res Grants, NIH, 76-80; Wellcome fel, Neurochem Pharmacol Unit, Med Res Coun, Eng, 79; sci counr, NIMH, 81-84; invest ophthalmologist, vis scientist, J Neurosci; mem, nat coun, Soc Neurosci, 82-86; vis fel, Australian Res Coun, Univ Queensland, 93; trustee, Asn Res Vision & Opthal, 93-. *Mem:* Soc Neurosci; Asn Res Vision & Ophthal; Am Asn Anatomists; Int Soc Eye Res; fel AAAS. *Res:* Development of the visual system of primates with emphasis on the synaptic organization and identification of neurotransmitters in retina, thalamus and visual cortex; determination of developmental mechanisms controlling cell and regional specification in primate retina. *Mailing Add:* Dept Biostruct Univ Wash SM-20 Seattle WA 98195. *Fax:* 206-543-7524; *E-Mail:* anitah@u.wash.edu

HENDRICKSON, CHRIS THOMPSON, TRANSPORTATION ENGINEERING, GREEN DESIGN. *Current Pos:* From asst prof to assoc prof, 78-87, assoc dean, Carnegie Inst Technol, 91-96, PROF CIVIL ENG, CARNEGIE-MELLON UNIV, 87-, EDUC DIR, ENG DESIGN RES CTR, 89-, HEAD, DEPT CIVIL & ENVIRON ENG, 96-; PROF ENG, DUQUESNE LIGHT CO, 96- *Personal Data:* b Oakland, Calif, Mar 31, 50; m 77, Kathleen Devine; c Drew, Tommy & Peter. *Educ:* Stanford Univ, BS, MS, 73; Oxford Univ, BPhil, 75; Mass Inst Technol, PhD(civil eng), 78. *Honors & Awards:* Huber Res Award, Am Soc Civil Eng, 88. *Mem:* Opers Res Soc Am; Am Econ Asn; Am Soc Civil Eng; Trans Res Bd. *Res:* Engineering planning and management, including green design, estimation techniques, system performance, finance and computer applications. *Mailing Add:* Dept Civil & Environ Eng Schenley Park Pittsburgh PA 15213. *Fax:* 412-268-7813; *E-Mail:* cth@cmu.edu

HENDRICKSON, CONSTANCE MCRIGHT, BIOPHYSICAL CHEMISTRY, SURFACTANT CHEMISTRY. *Current Pos:* OWNER, ARKON CONSULTS, 83- *Personal Data:* b Baton Rouge, La, June 7, 49; m 71, William H; c David & Emily. *Educ:* La Polytech Univ, BS, 71; La State Univ, PhD(biochem), 75; Univ NTex, Med, 84. *Prof Exp:* Grad asst biochem, La State Univ, Baton Rouge, 71-75; NIH fel biophysics, Johns Hopkins Univ, 75-78; clin chem fel, Univ Ala Med Ctr, 78-79; asst prof, Tex Wesleyan Col, 80-81; chief chemist, Rockwood Systs Corp, 82-83. *Concurrent Pos:* Environ technol develop prog, Brookhaven Col, dir environ technol, 94- *Mem:* Sigma Xi; Am Chem Soc; fel Am Inst Chemists (pres elect, 96-97); NY Acad Sci. *Res:* Liposome and micelle formation; aqueous foam structure and formation; biological and artificial membrane and transport phenomena; specialty industrial cleaners. *Mailing Add:* PO Box 171087 Irving TX 75017. *Fax:* 972-254-1582; *E-Mail:* cmhendrickson@dcccd.edu

HENDRICKSON, DAVID NORMAN, INORGANIC CHEMISTRY. *Current Pos:* PROF CHEM, UNIV CALIF, SAN DIEGO, 88- *Personal Data:* b Minneapolis, Minn, Jan 1, 43; m 65; c 2. *Educ:* Univ Calif, Los Angeles, BS, 66, Berkeley, PhD(chem), 69. *Honors & Awards:* Humboldt Found Res Prize, 93. *Prof Exp:* From asst prof to prof chem, Univ Ill, Urbana, 70-88. *Concurrent Pos:* Fel, Calif Inst Technol, 69-70, Sloan Found & Jap Soc Prom Sci; Dreyfus teacher scholar. *Mem:* Am Chem Soc; Sigma Xi; AAAS. *Res:* Bioinorganic chemistry; mixed valence chemistry; electron transfer; superparamagnetism; ferrofluids; clay and zeolite supported catalysts; magnetic exchange interactions; molecular electronic devices. *Mailing Add:* Dept Chem Univ Calif San Diego La Jolla CA 92093-0506. *Fax:* 619-534-5383; *E-Mail:* dhendrichson@ucsd.edu

HENDRICKSON, DONALD ALLEN, MEDICAL MICROBIOLOGY, MICROBIAL ECOLOGY. *Current Pos:* PROF BIOL, BALL STATE UNIV, 70- *Personal Data:* b New Rockford, NDak, Feb 9, 42; m 66; c 2. *Educ:* Minot State Col, BS, 64; Colo State Univ, MS, 69, PhD(microbiol), 70. *Prof Exp:* Pub sch teacher sci & math, NDak, 64-66; asst microbiol, Colo State Univ, 69-70. *Concurrent Pos:* Adj prof microbiol, Sch Med, Ind Univ, 71-72; Am Soc Microbiol area adv & consult commun media. *Mem:* Am Soc Microbiol. *Res:* Alflatoxin and mycotoxin production on solid wastes; factors affecting slime formation by bacteria; biological indicators of water quality. *Mailing Add:* Dept Biol Ball State Univ Muncie IN 47306-0001

HENDRICKSON, FRANK R, RADIATION ONCOLOGY. *Current Pos:* RETIRED. *Personal Data:* b Springfield, Pa, Aug 3, 26; m 55, Joan Scott; c 4. *Educ:* Swarthmore Col, BA, 47; Jefferson Med Col, MD, 50; Am Bd Radiol, cert radiol & nuclear med, 55. *Prof Exp:* Intern, Jefferson Med Col Hosp, 50-51, resident radiol, 51-54; Am Cancer Soc fel, Univ Lund, 54-55 & Eng & Scand Therapeut Ctrs, 55-56; asst prof, Univ Ill, Chicago Circle, 56-64, assoc prof, 64-71; prof radiol, Univ Ill, 68-71; prof therapeut radiol, Rush Med Col, 71-94. *Concurrent Pos:* From asst radiologist to attend radiologist & dir sect radiation ther, Presby-St Luke's Hosp, Chicago, 56-94, safety radiol officer, Radioisotope Comt, 56-71, mem tumor comt, 56-94; pres, Nuclear Oncol Serv Corp, 71-95. *Mem:* Am Col Radiol; Am Soc Therapeut Radiol (pres, 77); Radiation Res Soc; Radiol Soc NAm; Radium Soc; Sigma Xi. *Res:* Clinical radiation oncology and radiation biology. *Mailing Add:* Gale Ave River Forest IL 60305

HENDRICKSON, HERBERT T, VERTEBRATE ZOOLOGY. *Current Pos:* asst prof, 68-74, ASSOC PROF BIOL, UNIV NC, GREENSBORO, 75- *Personal Data:* b Jersey City, NJ, Oct 13, 40; m 62, Sylvia H Dumont; c Jennifer & Thomas. *Educ:* Cornell Univ, BS, 62, PhD(vert zool), 66. *Prof Exp:* Instr biol, Yale Univ, 66-68. *Mem:* Am Ornith Union; Soc Syst Zool; Soc Study Evolution; Wilson Ornith Soc; Cooper Ornith Soc; Asn Field Ornithologists. *Res:* Population trends of wintering birds in North Carolina piedmont. *Mailing Add:* Dept Biol Univ NC 1000 Spring Garden St Greensboro NC 27412-0001. *Fax:* 910-334-5839; *E-Mail:* hendrick@goodall.uncg.edu

HENDRICKSON, HERMAN STEWART, II, BIOCHEMISTRY. *Current Pos:* asst prof, 68-73, assoc prof, 73-80, PROF CHEM, ST OLAF COL, 80- *Personal Data:* b Los Angeles, Calif, May 14, 37; m 60; c 3. *Educ:* Pomona Col, BA, 59; Univ Ill, PhD(chem), 62. *Prof Exp:* Res chemist, Univ Calif, Berkeley, 62-63 & Western Regional Res Lab, USDA, 63-65; asst prof biochem, Southwestern Med Sch, Univ Tex, 65-68. *Concurrent Pos:* Res assoc, State Univ Utrecht, 74-75; vis scholar, Univ Calif, San Diego, 82-83; res assoc, Univ Ore, 89-90. *Mem:* AAAS; Am Chem Soc; Am Soc Biochem & Molecular Biol; Protein Soc. *Res:* Phospholipases; surface chemistry of lipids; biomembranes; lipid-protein interactions. *Mailing Add:* Dept Chem Univ Wash PO Box 351700 Seattle WA 98195-1700. *Fax:* 206-685-8665; *E-Mail:* hend@stolaf.edu

HENDRICKSON, JAMES BRIGGS, INTELLIGENT SYSTEMS, SOFTWARE SYSTEMS. *Current Pos:* assoc prof, 63-66, PROF CHEM, BRANDEIS UNIV, 66- *Personal Data:* b Toledo, Ohio, Jan 3, 28; m 53; c 2. *Educ:* Calif Inst Technol, BS, 50; Harvard Univ, MA, 51, PhD, 55. *Prof Exp:* Nat Res Coun res fel, Univ London, 54-55; NIH res fel, Harvard Univ, 55-57; asst prof chem, Univ Calif, Los Angeles, 57-62. *Concurrent Pos:* Guggenheim fel, 64; Fulbright prof, Univ Cape Coast, Ghana, 74-76. *Mem:* Am Chem Soc; Royal Chem Soc; Ghana Sci Asn. *Res:* Computerized design of organic synthesis; design of new synthetic reactions; synthesis of natural products. *Mailing Add:* Dept Chem Brandeis Univ Waltham MA 02254-9110. *E-Mail:* jbh@j3n.chem.brandeiss.edu

HENDRICKSON, JOHN ALFRED, JR, BIOLOGICAL STATISTICS, STATISTICAL ECOLOGY. *Current Pos:* asst cur limnol, 69-77, assoc cur limnol & ecol, 77-82, RES ASSOC, ACAD NATURAL SCI, PHILADELPHIA, 83-, DIR COMP, 84- *Personal Data:* b San Francisco, Calif, June 2, 41; m 68; c 1. *Educ:* Univ San Francisco, BS, 63; Univ Kans, PhD(entom), 67. *Prof Exp:* Instr biol, Stanford Univ, 68-69. *Concurrent Pos:* Adj asst prof biol, Univ Pa, 70-76; adj lectr statist, Temple Univ, 83-85 & 88- *Mem:* Ecol Soc Am; Biomet Soc; Am Statist Asn; Soc Study Evolution; Soc Syst Zool; Sigma Xi. *Res:* Biological statistics, especially theoretical development and application of randomization tests for current questions in ecology/evolutionary biology. *Mailing Add:* Acad Natural Sci 19th St & The Parkway Philadelphia PA 19103-1195

HENDRICKSON, JOHN ROSCOE, VERTEBRATE ZOOLOGY, ECOLOGY. *Current Pos:* RETIRED. *Personal Data:* b Tipton, Iowa, Aug 26, 21; m 46; c 4. *Educ:* Univ Ariz, BSc, 44; Univ Calif, Berkeley, MA, 49, PhD(zool), 51. *Prof Exp:* Lectr zool, Univ Malaya, Singapore, 51-59; prof & head dept, Univ Malaya, Kuala Lumpur, 59-63; vchancellor, Inst Student Interchange, East-West Ctr, Univ Hawaii, 63-67; dir oceanic inst, Oceanic Found, Waimanalo, Hawaii, 67-69; prof biol, Univ Ariz, 69-76, prof ecol & evolutionary biol, 76-87. *Mem:* AAAS; Am Inst Biol Sci; Am Soc Ichthyol & Herpet; Zool Soc London; World Maricult Soc. *Res:* General tropical ecology; sea turtles; biological oceanography and ecology of Gulf of California; aquaculture, conservation and other activities applying basic biological knowledge to human impacts on ecosystems. *Mailing Add:* 4917 N Camino Arenoso Tucson AZ 85718

HENDRICKSON, LESTER ELLSWORTH, METALLURGY, PHYSICS. *Current Pos:* asst prof 68-73, fac res grant, 69-71, ASSOC PROF ENG SCI, ARIZ STATE UNIV, 73- *Personal Data:* b Republic, Mich, Nov 23, 41; m 67; c 2. *Educ:* Mich Technol Univ, BS, 63, MS, 64; Univ Ill, PhD(metall), 69. *Prof Exp:* Res asst metall, Mich Technol Univ, 63-64 & Univ Ill, 64-68. *Concurrent Pos:* Consult to legal profession; fac res grant, Ariz State Univ, 69-71. *Mem:* Am Soc Metals; Metall Soc. *Res:* Impurity; lattice defect interactions in high purity dilute alloys of aluminum; mechanical properties of semiconducting solids; failure analysis. *Mailing Add:* 2329 W El Moro Circle Mesa AZ 85202

HENDRICKSON, RICHARD A(LLAN), NUCLEAR ENGINEERING. *Current Pos:* Grad asst nuclear eng, Ames Lab, Atomic Energy Comn, Iowa State Univ, 60-62, jr engr, 62-64, from instr to assoc prof, 64-85, PROF NUCLEAR ENG & MGR, REACTOR OPERS & MAINTENANCE, IOWA STATE UNIV, 85- *Personal Data:* b Omaha, Nebr, Feb 1, 33; m 56; c 2. *Educ:* Iowa State Univ, BS, 55, MS, 62, PhD(nuclear eng), 66. *Honors & Awards:* Sigma Xi. *Mem:* Am Nuclear Soc; Am Soc Eng Educ. *Res:* Nuclear reactor engineering; reactor kinetics and noise analysis; radiation detection and measurement. *Mailing Add:* 132 24th St Ames IA 50010

HENDRICKSON, ROBERT MARK, JR, ENTOMOLOGY. *Current Pos:* RETIRED. *Personal Data:* b Corona, Calif, Jan 19, 38. *Educ:* Calif State Polytech Univ, Kellogg-Voorhis Campus, BS, 65; Univ Calif, Riverside, PhD(entom), 74. *Prof Exp:* Entomologist forage crops, Sci & Educ Admin-Agr Res, USDA, 74- *Concurrent Pos:* Adj asst prof, Univ Del, 75. *Mem:* Entom Soc Am; Int Orgn Biol Control. *Res:* Biological control of agromyzids on alfalfa. *Mailing Add:* PO Box 1035 Livingston MT 59047

HENDRICKSON, THOMAS JAMES, PHYSICS. *Current Pos:* asst prof, 60-63, assoc prof, 63-80, PROF PHYSICS, GETTYSBURG COL, 80- *Personal Data:* b Detroit, Mich, Mar 26, 26; m 61. *Educ:* Univ Mich, BS, 47, MS, 49; Iowa State Univ, PhD(physics), 56. *Prof Exp:* Instr physics, Mich Col Mining & Technol, 48-50; from instr to asst prof, Tufts Univ, 56-60. *Mem:* Sigma Xi. *Res:* Solid state physics; ferromagnetism; antiferromagnetism; order-disorder transformations in alloys; optic properties of solids. *Mailing Add:* 65 Confederate Dr Gettysburg PA 17325-8421

HENDRICKSON, TOM A(LLEN), NUCLEAR ENGINEERING. *Current Pos:* DIR NUCLEAR WASTE TECHNOL, EBASCO DIV, DIR SPEC PROJ, RAYTHEON ENGRS & CONSTRUCTORS, 93- *Personal Data:* b Los Angeles, Calif, Dec 25, 35; m 81, Anne M Church; c Holly M, Anne A & Andrew E. *Educ:* Harvard Col, AB, 57; Georgetown Univ, MS, 62. *Prof Exp:* Nuclear engr, Nuclear Power Div, USN Bur Ships, 57-64, chief, Submarine Fluid Systs Br, Naval Ship Systs Command, 64-72; from chief nuclear engr to dep dir eng, Burns & Roe Inc, 72-78, asst to pres, 78-80, vpres, 80-85; pres & chief exec officer, Proto-Technol Corp, A Kollmorgen Co, 85-87; prin dep asst secy nuclear energy, US Dept Energy, 90-91, dir, Off New Prod Reactors, 91-92, actg under secy, 92. *Concurrent Pos:* Dir, Gen Physics Corp, 77-85, Separative Work Unit Corp (SWUCO), 85-88 & Magnetic Bearings Inc, 88-90. *Mem:* Am Nuclear Soc; Am Soc Mech Engrs; Am Phys Soc. *Mailing Add:* 24 Mulders Lane Midland Park NJ 07432-1614

HENDRICKSON, WALDEMAR FORRSEL, HIGH LEVEL WASTE MANAGEMENT. *Current Pos:* CHEM ENGR, AEC-ERDA-DEPT ENERGY, 74- *Personal Data:* b Tobias, Nebr, June 7, 34; m 58, 84; c Jene D (Michaud) & Olaf K. *Educ:* Univ Idaho, BS, 56, MS, 58; Wash State Univ, MS, 64, PhD(eng sci), 71. *Prof Exp:* Chem engr, Hanford Atomic Prod Opers, Gen Elec Co, 57-58; asst nuclear engr, Wash State Univ, 60-71; scientist, Northwest Orgn Cols & Univs, 71; res physicist, US Navy Ord Lab, 72-74. *Concurrent Pos:* Asst, Nat Res Coun, 71-74; adj prof, Wash State Univ, Tri Cities, 86- *Mem:* Am Nuclear Soc; Health Physics Soc. *Res:* Electrochemical kinetics (oxidation of chloride ion) at electrode (carbon) with radiochemical absorbtion techniques; automated analysis of trace elements in sea water by neutron activation analysis using a large Californium source; nuclear fuel cycle (mixed oxide fuel fabrication and reprocessing). *Mailing Add:* Dept Energy Box 550 Richland WA 99352. *Fax:* 509-376-2002

HENDRICKSON, WAYNE ARTHUR, MOLECULAR BIOPHYSICS, STRUCTURAL BIOLOGY. *Current Pos:* PROF BIOCHEM & MOLECULAR BIOPHYS, COL PHYSICIANS & SURGEONS, COLUMBIA UNIV, 84-; INVESTR, HOWARD HUGHES MED INST, 86- *Personal Data:* b Spring Valley, Wis, Apr 25, 41; m 69; c Helen M & Igna M. *Educ:* Univ Wis-River Falls, BA, 63; Johns Hopkins Univ, PhD(biophys), 68. *Hon Degrees:* PhD, Uppsala Univ, 95. *Honors & Awards:* Navy Meritorious Civilian Serv Award, 78; A L Patterson Award, Am Crystallog Asn, 81; Fritz Lipmann Award, Am Soc Biochem & Molecular Biol, 91; Hugh Clark Distinguished Lectr, Univ Conn, 91; Harvey Lectr, 93; Coover Lectr, Iowa State Univ, 94; Aminoff Prize, Royal Swedish Acad Sci, 97; Christian B Anfinsen Award, Protein Soc, 97. *Prof Exp:* Res assoc, Johns Hopkins Univ, 68-69; Nat Res Coun postdoctoral res assoc, US Naval Res Lab, 69-71, res biophysicist, 71-84. *Concurrent Pos:* Mem, NSF Molecular Biol Adv Panel, 80-83 & Review Panel, Stanford Synchrotron Radiation Lab, 80-89; sr adv, Molecular Biophys Tech, Inc, 83-87; mem, Biophys Chem Study Sect, NIH, 86-89; consult, Molecular Structure Corp, 85-89, sci adv bd, Progenics Pharmaceut, 87-; assoc ed, J Molecular Biol, 87-; proposal rev panel, Cornell High Energy Synchrotron Source, 87-; mem, Biomed Adv Comt, Pittsburgh Supercomputing Ctr, 87-; mem, Proposal Eval Bd, Advan Photon Source, 89-; mem, Sci Policy Bd, Stanford Synchrotron Radiation Lab, 91- *Mem:* Nat Acad Sci; Biophys Soc; Am Crystallog Asn; Am Soc Biochem & Molecular Biol; fel AAAS. *Res:* Macromolecular structure and function; properties of specific proteins; principles of protein structure, dynamics and assembly; diffraction methods; crystallographic computing; synchrotron radiation. *Mailing Add:* Dept Biochem & Molecular Biophys Columbia Univ 630 W 168th St New York NY 10032

HENDRICKSON, WILLARD JAMES, PSYCHIATRY. *Current Pos:* Intern, Univ Hosp, 45-46, resident psychiat, Neuropsychiat Inst, 48-50, from instr to assoc prof, Univ, 50-72, PROF PSYCHIAT, UNIV MICH, ANN ARBOR, 72- *Personal Data:* b Battle Creek, Mich, Aug 23, 16; m 46; c 2. *Educ:* Calif Inst Technol, BS, 42; Univ Mich, MD, 45, MS, 53. *Concurrent Pos:* Consult Vet Admin Hosp, 53- *Mem:* Am Psychiat Asn. *Res:* Clinical investigation of methods of psychiatric treatment of adolescent patients. *Mailing Add:* Univ Hosp Ann Arbor MI 48109-0001

HENDRICKSON, YNGVE GUST, ORGANIC CHEMISTRY. *Current Pos:* RETIRED. *Personal Data:* b Virginia, Minn, Sept 3, 27; m 64; c 2. *Educ:* Mass Inst Technol, SB, 51; Univ Ill, PhD, 55. *Prof Exp:* Res chemist, Chevron Res Co, Chevron Corp, 55-64, sr res chemist, 64-69, sr res assoc, 69-86. *Mem:* Am Chem Soc; The Chem Soc. *Res:* Physical organic chemistry; study of mechanisms of organic reactions; composition of petroleum and its fractions; stability of distillate fuels; lubricating oil additives; lubricating oils and greases. *Mailing Add:* 8364 Kent Dr El Cerrito CA 94530-2548

HENDRICKX, ANDREW GEORGE, EMBRYOLOGY. *Current Pos:* assoc res physiologist, Calif Primate Res Ctr, 69-73, prof reproduction, Sch Vet Med, 73-78, RES PHYSIOLOGIST & PROF HUMAN ANAT, SCH MED, UNIV CALIF, DAVIS, 73-, DIR, CALIF PRIMATE RES CTR, 87- *Personal Data:* b Butler, Minn, July 14, 33; m 57; c 5. *Educ:* Concordia Col, BS, 59; Kans State Univ, MS, 61, PhD(zool), 63. *Prof Exp:* Asst prof zool, Southern Ill Univ, 63-64; embryologist, Southwest Found Res & Educ, Tex, 64-69. *Mem:* Am Asn Anat; Soc Study Reprod; Teratol Soc; Am Soc Primatologists. *Res:* Reproduction, embryology and teratology of primates, with emphasis on domestic breeding, developmental staging and effects of environmental agents on prenatal and postnatal development. *Mailing Add:* Calif Primate Res Ctr Univ of Calif Davis CA 95616

HENDRIE, DAVID LOWERY, PHYSICS. *Current Pos:* WITH DIV NUCLEAR PHYSICS, US DEPT ENERGY, 85- *Personal Data:* b St Louis, Mo, Sept 22, 32; m 56; c 2. *Educ:* Univ Wash, PhD(physics), 64. *Prof Exp:* Physicist, Lawrence Berkeley Lab, 64-73 & 80-85, dir, Cyclotron, 73-78; prof, Univ Md, 78-80. *Concurrent Pos:* Guggenheim fel, Saclay Nuclear Res Ctr, France, 71-72. *Mem:* Fel Am Phys Soc. *Res:* Nuclear reactions and structure. *Mailing Add:* ER-23 GTN US Dept Energy Washington DC 20585

HENDRIE, JOSEPH MALLAM, APPLIED PHYSICS, NUCLEAR ENGINEERING. *Current Pos:* SR SCIENTIST & CONSULT ENGR, BROOKHAVEN NAT LAB, 81- *Personal Data:* b Janesville, Wis, Mar 18, 25; m 49, Elaine Kostell; c Susan & Barbara. *Educ:* Case Inst Technol, BS, 50; Columbia Univ, PhD(physics), 57. *Honors & Awards:* E O Lawrence Award, Atomic Energy Comn. *Prof Exp:* Asst, Radiation Lab, Columbia Univ, 50-53, asst physics, 53-55; asst physicist reactor physics, Brookhaven Nat Lab, 55-57, assoc physicist, 57-60, proj chief engr high flux beam reactor, 58-65, actg head exp reactor physics div, 65-66, assoc head eng div, Dept Appl Sci, 66-70, proj mgr pulsed fast reactor proj, 67-70, sr physicist & head eng div, Dept Appl Sci, 71-72; dep dir licensing for tech rev, AEC, 72-74; chmn dept appl sci, Brookhaven Nat Lab, 75-77; chmn, US Nuclear Regulatory Comn, 77-81. *Concurrent Pos:* Consult, Columbia Radiation Safety Comt, 64-72, US Atomic Energy Comn & Nuclear Regulatory Comn, 74-75, US Gen Acct Off, 75-77, Elec Power Res Inst, 82 & various nuclear utilities, 81-; mem adv comt reactor safeguards, AEC, 66-72, chmn 70; US rep, Sr Adv Group Reactor Safety Standards, Int Atomic Energy Agency, 74-79; dir, Am Nuclear Soc, 76-77; mem, Appl Physics Div Vis Comt, Argonne Nat Lab, 76-77, Comt Mem, Nat Acad Eng, 80-83, Comt Int Coop Magnetic Fusion Nat Res Coun, 83-85, Adv Coun, Inst Nuclear Power Opers, 84-90, Adv Comt Enforcement Policy, US Nuclear Regulatory Comn, 84-85, Comt Res & Tech Planning, Am Soc Testing & Mat, 85-88, Reactor Safety & Anal Div Rev Comt, Argonne Nat Lab, 85-87; dir, Houston Indust Inc, 85-96, Houston Lighting & Power Co, 85-96, Syst Energy Resources Inc, 87-90 & Entergy Opers Inc, 90-95; mem, Spec Comt Integrated Fast Reactor, Univ Chicago, 87- *Mem:* Nat Acad Eng; fel Am Nuclear Soc (pres, 84-85); Nat Soc Prof Engrs; Am Concrete Inst; Inst Elec & Electronics Engrs; fel Am Soc Mech Engrs; Am Phys Soc. *Res:* Physics and engineering design of research reactors; safety of nuclear power reactors; structural analysis and design of reinforced and prestressed high-strength concrete; electrical power transmission. *Mailing Add:* 50 Bellport Lane Bellport NY 11713-2736

HENDRIKS, HERBERT EDWARD, GEOLOGY. *Current Pos:* from instr to prof, 47-83, WILLIAM HARMON NORTON EMER PROF GEOL, CORNELL COL, 83- *Personal Data:* b West Liberty, Iowa, Jan 23, 18; m 41; c 1. *Educ:* Cornell Col, BA, 40; Univ Iowa, MS, 42, PhD(geol), 49. *Prof Exp:* Field geologist, Lone Star Steel Co, Tex, 42-44; geologist, Sun Oil Co, Miss, 44-45; asst geol, Univ Iowa, 46-47. *Concurrent Pos:* Dir, Camp Norton Geol Field Camp, 50-52; field geologist, Ashland Oil & Refining Co, 52-56; consult, Shell Oil Co, 57-58. *Mem:* AAAS; Geol Soc Am; Paleont Soc; Nat Asn Geol Teachers; Sigma Xi. *Res:* Cambro-Ordovician stratigraphy; stratigraphy and structure of the Ozark Mountains and the Wind River Range; stratigraphy and structure of Big Snowy Mountains, Montana; geology of the Crooked Creek Area, Missouri. *Mailing Add:* 1650 Koehler Dr NW 153 Cedar Rapids IA 52405-1575

HENDRIX, C(HARLES) E(DMUND), SYSTEMS ENGINEERING. *Current Pos:* RETIRED. *Personal Data:* b Moberly, Mo, Mar 14, 24; m 46; c 3. *Educ:* Boston Univ, AB, 48; Univ Calif, Los Angeles, MS, 55, PhD(eng), 64. *Prof Exp:* Technician, Physics Lab, Tenn Eastman Corp, 46-47; mech designer, Polaroid Corp, 47; jr engr, Lab for Electronics Inc, 48-49 & Mo Res Lab Inc, 49-51; electronic scientist, Electronic Systs Br, US Naval Ord Test Sta, Calif, 51-56, head, Photophys Br, 56-57, staff consult, Instrument Develop Div, 59-62; biomed engr, Chem & Biol Div, Space-Gen Corp, 62-66, sr scientist, Ctr Res & Educ, 66-69; sr scientist, Telluron, 69-71; tech staff mgr, Hughes Aircraft Co, 71-88, lab chief scientist, 88-93. *Concurrent Pos:* Lectr, Univ Calif, 56. *Mem:* Sigma Xi. *Res:* Physical and biological instrumentation; simulation of neuron networks; analysis, simulation and optimization of complex physical systems; communication satellites design; millimeter wave propagation. *Mailing Add:* 833 Bienvenida Ave Pacific Palisades CA 90272-2310

HENDRIX, DONALD LOUIS, PLANT PHYSIOLOGY, ANALYTICAL CHEMISTRY. *Current Pos:* PLANT PHYSIOLOGIST, WESTERN COTTON RES LAB, AGR RES SERV, USDA, 81- *Personal Data:* b Snohomish, Wash, Aug 21, 42; m 65, Susan J Newlean; c 3. *Educ:* Cent Wash Univ, BA, 65; Wash State Univ, PhD(bot), 73. *Prof Exp:* Res assoc plant physiol, Purdue Univ, 74; asst prof biol, Univ Houston, 74-81. *Concurrent Pos:* Adj assoc prof bot, Ariz State Univ, 81-; fel, Orgn Econ Coop & Develop, 87; adj prof agron, Univ Ark, 93- *Mem:* Am Soc Plant Physiologists; Scand Soc Plant Physiologists; Sigma Xi; Crop Sci Soc Am. *Res:* Biophysics and biochemistry of metabolite transport; plant biochemistry; photosynthate translocation; natural product analysis; honeydew formation by phloem-feeding homoptera, especially whiteflies and aphids. *Mailing Add:* Western Cotton Res Lab USDA Agr Res Serv 4135 E Broadway Rd Phoenix AZ 85040. *Fax:* 602-379-4509; *E-Mail:* dhendrix@asrr.arsusda.gov

HENDRIX, FLOYD FULLER, JR, PLANT PATHOLOGY, SOIL MICROBIOLOGY. *Current Pos:* RETIRED. *Personal Data:* b Columbia, NC, Apr 18, 33; m 87, Rosemary Kron; c 3. *Educ:* NC State Univ, BS, 55, MS, 57; Univ Calif, Berkeley, PhD(plant path), 61. *Honors & Awards:* Campbell Award, Am Inst Biol Sci, 64; Cert Merit, US Forest Serv. *Prof Exp:* Plant pathologist, Southeastern Forest Exp Sta, US Forest Serv, 61-64; asst plant pathologist, Univ Ga, 65-68, from assoc prof to prof plant path, 68-95. *Mem:* Am Phytopath Soc; Mycol Soc Am. *Res:* Ecology of fungi in soil with particular emphasis on Fusarium Phytophthora and Pythium species, fomes annosus, taxonomy of the genus Pythium; diseases of apples and peaches. *Mailing Add:* 250 Red Fox Run Athens GA 30605. *Fax:* 706-542-4102; *E-Mail:* dppaat@uga.cc.uga.edu

HENDRIX, JAMES EASTON, POLYMER CHEMISTRY, ORGANIC CHEMISTRY. *Current Pos:* SR VPRES DEVELOP, CLARK-SCHWEBEL INC, 92- *Personal Data:* b Pensacola, Fla, Oct 31, 41; m 66, Linda R Akulick; c James, John & Deborah. *Educ:* Auburn Univ, BS, 66; Clemson Univ, MS, 68, PhD(chem), 70; Winthrop Col, MBA, 82. *Honors & Awards:* Super Serv Award Res, USDA, 72. *Prof Exp:* Res chemist, FMC Corp, 69-70; res fel, Nat Acad Sci-Nat Res Coun Southern Regional Labs, New Orleans, 70-72; res mgr, Milliken Res Corp, 72-75, dir develop, Milliken & Co, Inc, 75-78; dir res, Springs Indust Inc, 78-85, vpres res & develop, 85-92. *Mem:* Fiber Soc; Am Chem Soc; Am Asn Textile Chemists & Colorists. *Res:* Flame inhibition mechanisms; pyrolytic degradation of organic high polymers; high temperature reactions of organic phosphates; instrumental techniques for determining textile flammabilities; synthetic coatings for textile substrates; management. *Mailing Add:* 855 Quarter Round Rd Pacolet SC 29372

HENDRIX, JAMES HARVEY, JR, PLASTIC SURGERY. *Current Pos:* RETIRED. *Personal Data:* b Newbern, Tenn, Jan 22, 20; c 3. *Educ:* Univ Tenn, Knoxville, BS, 42; Univ Tenn, Memphis, MD, 43; Am Bd Plastic Surg, dipl. *Prof Exp:* Intern, Methodist Hosp, Memphis, Tenn, 44; resident surgeon, Univ Tex Med Br, Galveston, 47-50, instr surg, 50, resident gen surg & plastic surg, Univ Tex Med Br, Galveston & Baptist Mem Hosp, Memphis, 51; asst, Dept Surg, Univ Tenn, Memphis, 51-52; chief plastic surg, Univ Miss, Jackson, 55-72; chief plastic surg, Univ Tenn, Memphis, 72-78, prof surg, 72-91. *Concurrent Pos:* Pvt pract, Miss & Tenn, 51-; mem, Adv Coun Plastic & Maxillofacial Surg, Am Col Surgeons, 73-77, chmn, 75; mem bd, Am Bd Plastic Surg; mem, Plastic Surg Res Coun; consult plastic surg, Miss Crippled Children's Serv, Tenn Crippled Children's Serv, St Jude Children's Res Hosp & Vet Admin Hosp. *Mem:* Am Soc Plastic & Reconstruct Surgeons (pres, 73-74); Am Asn Plastic Surgeons; fel Am Col Surgeons; Am Cleft Palate Asn; Am Trauma Soc. *Res:* Healing of tendons in hands of monkeys; treatment of fractures of mandibular condyles with growth studies using piglets. *Mailing Add:* 910 Madison Ave Suite 525 Memphis TN 38103-3454

HENDRIX, JAMES LAURIS, CHEMICAL ENGINEERING, BIOENGINEERING. *Current Pos:* PROF CHEM ENG, COL ENG & TECHNOL, UNIV NEBR. *Personal Data:* b Omaha, Nebr, July 19, 43; m 65. *Educ:* Univ Nebr, BS, 66, MS, 68, PhD(chem eng), 69. *Prof Exp:* From asst prof to prof chem eng, Univ Nev, Reno, 69-92. *Mem:* Am Soc Chem. *Res:* Biological fuel cells. *Mailing Add:* Col Eng & Technol W181 Nebr Hall Univ Nebr Lincoln NE 68588-0501

HENDRIX, JAMES WILLIAM, MYCOLOGY, MYCORRHIZAL FUNGI. *Current Pos:* assoc prof, 67-73, PROF PLANT PATH, UNIV KY, 73- *Personal Data:* b Kinston, NC, Apr 18, 37; m 59, Janet Powell; c Donna H (Avery) & Keith W. *Educ:* NC State Univ, BS, 59, PhD(plant path), 63; Univ Ark, MS, 60. *Prof Exp:* NSF fel plant path & biochem, Univ Nebr, 63-64; res plant pathologist, Crops Res Div, Agr Res Serv, USDA, 64-67. *Concurrent Pos:* Vis assoc & NIH spec fel biol, Calif Inst Technol & City of Hope Med Ctr, 68-69. *Mem:* Am Phytopath Soc; Mycol Soc Am; Soil Ecol Soc; Soil Sci Soc Am. *Res:* Ecology of mycorrhizal fungi; ecology of soil-borne phytopathogenic fungi; soil productivity. *Mailing Add:* Dept Plant Path Univ Ky 500 S Limestone St Lexington KY 40506-0001. *Fax:* 606-323-1961

HENDRIX, JOHN EDWIN, PLANT PHYSIOLOGY. *Current Pos:* from asst prof to assoc prof bot, 67-89, PROF PLANT PATH, COLO STATE UNIV, 89- *Personal Data:* b Van Nuys, Calif, Aug 30, 30; m 54; c 2. *Educ:* Fresno State Col, BS, 56, AB, 60; Ohio State Univ, MS, 63, PhD(bot), 67. *Prof Exp:* Orchard foreman, Fresno State Col, 59-60; instr bot, Ohio State Univ, 65-67. *Mem:* AAAS; Am Soc Plant Physiol; Am Inst Biol Sci; Sigma Xi. *Res:* Phosphate uptake and transport in plants; stachyose synthesis and transport in plants; carbohydrate transport in plants; carbohydrate accumulation in developing grain; fructan metabolism. *Mailing Add:* Dept Biol & Plant Path Colo State Univ Ft Collins CO 80523

HENDRIX, JOHN WALTER, PLANT PATHOLOGY. *Current Pos:* RETIRED. *Personal Data:* b Quincy, Ill, Nov 20, 15; m 45; c 2. *Educ:* NC State Col, BS, 37; Yale Univ, MF, 40; Univ Minn, PhD(plant path), 48. *Prof Exp:* Asst plant pathologist, Tenn Agr Exp Sta, Univ Hawaii, 43-48, assoc plant pathologist, 48-52, head dept, 43-52; assoc prof & assoc plant pathologist, Agr Exp Sta, Wash State Univ, 52-58, actg head dept, 53-54 & 58-69, prof plant path & plant pathologist, 58-82. *Mem:* Am Phytopath Soc; Am Soc Hort Sci. *Res:* Phytopathology; breeding and genetics of tomatoes; plant diseases caused by atmospheric pollutants; cereal rusts. *Mailing Add:* 1010 NE Duncan Lane Pullman WA 99163

HENDRIX, JON RICHARD, HUMAN GENETICS EDUCATION, BIOETHICAL DECISION-MAKING EDUCATION. *Current Pos:* from asst prof to assoc prof, 77-80, DIR, HUMAN GENETICS & BIOETHICS LAB, BALL STATE UNIV, 73-, PROF BIOL, 80- *Personal Data:* b Passaic, NJ, May 4, 38; m 62, Janis R Rouhselange; c Margaret S (Spangler), Joann R (McKinney) & Amy T. *Educ:* Ind State Univ, BS, 60, MS, 63; Ball State Univ, EdD, 74. *Honors & Awards:* Whitinger lectr, 93. *Prof Exp:* Sci supvr & biol teacher, Sch Town Highland, 60-71; *Concurrent Pos:* Adj prof sci ed, Ind Univ, 68-70; prin investr genethics, NSF, 91-94. *Mem:* Nat Asn Biol Teachers; Nat Sci Teachers Asn; Sigma Xi; Soc Col Sci Teachers. *Res:* Improvement of teaching biology, human genetics and bioethical decision-making to secondary and higher education students and faculty. *Mailing Add:* 8800 Eucalyptus Muncie IN 47304. *Fax:* 765-285-1624; *E-Mail:* 01jrhendrix@leo.bsuuc.bsu.edu

HENDRIX, MARY J C, CELL BIOLOGY, CANCER BIOLOGY. *Current Pos:* assoc prof histol, 80-85, ASSOC PROF ANAT, UNIV ARIZ, 86- *Personal Data:* b La Jolla, Calif, Sept 19, 53. *Educ:* Shepherd Col, BS, 74; George Washington Univ, PhD(anat), 77. *Prof Exp:* Teaching asst gross anat, Harvard Univ, 78-80. *Concurrent Pos:* Comnr, Ariz Dis Control Res Comn, 86-; adj researcher path, Univ Calif, San Francisco, 81- *Mem:* Electron Micros Soc Am; AAAS; Am Soc Cell Biol; Soc Develop Biol; Am Asn Anatomists; Int Pigment Cell Soc. *Res:* The normal and abnormal interactions of cells with extracellular matrices; the remodeling of the extracellular matrices by cellular interactions during normal developmental events; the study of tumor cell degradation and modification of the extracellular matrices during transformation and metastasis. *Mailing Add:* Dept Anat Univ Iowa Col Med 51 Newton Rd 1-402 BSB Iowa City IA 52242-1109

HENDRIX, ROGER WALDEN, MOLECULAR BIOLOGY. *Current Pos:* asst prof microbiol, 73-78, assoc prof, 78-86, PROF, BIOL SCI, UNIV PITTSBURGH, 86- *Personal Data:* b San Francisco, Calif, July 7, 43; m 71. *Educ:* Calif Inst Technol, BS, 65; Harvard Univ, PhD(biochem & molecular biol), 70. *Prof Exp:* Fel biochem, Stanford Univ, 71-73. *Concurrent Pos:* Res Career Develop Award, NIH, 75. *Res:* Biochemistry and genetics of virus assembly, using bacteriophage lambda as a model system; role of protein processing, host factors, and catalytically acting proteins in assembly processes. *Mailing Add:* Dept Biol Sci A234 Langley Hall Univ Pittsburgh 4200 5th Ave Pittsburgh PA 15260-0001

HENDRIX, SHERMAN SAMUEL, MARINE PARASITOLOGY, HELMINTHOLOGY. *Current Pos:* Instr, Gettysburg Col, 64-70, from asst prof to assoc prof, 70-90, chmn dept, 85-90, PROF BIOL, GETTYSBURG COL, 90- *Personal Data:* b Bridgeport, Conn, June 1, 39; m 61, Carol Seibel; c Marc & Robin. *Educ:* Gettysburg Col, BA, 61; Fla State Univ, MS, 64; Univ Md, PhD(parasitol), 72. *Mem:* Am Soc Parasitologists; Am Malacol Union; Wildlife Dis Asn; Am Fisheries Soc. *Res:* Systematics, zoogeography and ecology of aspidogastrid trematodes and monogenea of fishes and mollusks. *Mailing Add:* Dept Biol Gettysburg Col 300 N Washington St Gettysburg PA 17325-1400. *Fax:* 717-337-6157

HENDRIX, THOMAS EUGENE, GEOLOGY. *Current Pos:* assoc prof, 78-80, PROF GEOL, GRAND VALLEY STATE COLS, 80- *Personal Data:* b Lancaster, Pa, Feb 6, 33; m 55; c 3. *Educ:* Franklin & Marshall Col, BS, 55; Univ Wis, MS, 57, PhD(geol), 60. *Prof Exp:* From instr to assoc prof geol, Ind Univ, Bloomington, 59-78, assoc dir geol field sta, 62-68. *Concurrent Pos:* Ed, J Geol Educ, 69-71. *Mem:* Geol Soc Am; Nat Asn Geol Teachers (pres, 73-74). *Res:* Structural geology of Precambrian metamorphic tectonites; laramide structures of southwestern Montana; Precambrian tectonites. *Mailing Add:* Dept Geol 125 Padnos Hall Grand Valley State Univ One Campus Dr Allendale MI 49401

HENDRIX, THOMAS RUSSELL, GASTROENTEROLOGY. *Current Pos:* PROF MED & GASTROENTEROL, JOHNS HOPKINS UNIV, 68- *Personal Data:* b Ft Ancient, Ohio, Oct 17, 20. *Educ:* Johns Hopkins Univ, MD, 51. *Mailing Add:* Dept Med Johns Hopkins Univ Sch Med Blalock 935 Baltimore MD 21287. *Fax:* 410-614-9612

HENDRON, ALFRED J, JR, GEOTECHNICAL & CIVIL ENGINEERING. *Current Pos:* CONSULT ENGR, 95- *Personal Data:* b Clifton, Ill, Oct 4, 37. *Educ:* Univ Ill, BS, 59, MS, 60, PhD(civil eng), 63. *Prof Exp:* From asst prof to assoc prof, Univ Ill, 65-70, prof civil eng, 70-95. *Mem:* Nat Acad Eng; Am Soc Civil Eng. *Mailing Add:* 4 College Park Ct PO Box 125 Savoy IL 61874. *Fax:* 217-351-8700

HENDRY, ANNE TERESA, MEDICAL MYCOLOGY. *Current Pos:* MICROBIOL DEPT, HAMILTON HEALTH SCI CORP, 75- *Personal Data:* b Hearst, Ont, Feb 29, 36; wid; c 1. *Educ:* Univ Toronto, BSA, 59; Univ Guelph, MSc, 66; Univ Western Ont, PhD(microbiol), 71. *Prof Exp:* Lab scientist, Ont Ministry Health, 59-64; teacher biol, Halton Co Sch Bd, 70-71; res assoc biochem, Med Fac, Univ Western Ont, 72-74; assoc prof microbiol, Med Sch, McMaster Univ, 75- *Concurrent Pos:* Clin microbiologist, Hamilton Gen Hosp, 75- *Mem:* Int Soc Human & Animal Mycol; Am Soc Microbiol; Can Asn Clin Microbiol Infectious Dis. *Res:* Auxotyping and physiological studies of Neisseria gonorrhoeae; aromatic amino acid biosynthesis and regulation in N gonorrhoeae. *Mailing Add:* Microbiol Dept Hamilton Gen Div Hamilton Civic Hosp 237 Barton St E Hamilton ON L8L 2X2 Can. *E-Mail:* hendrya@fhs.csu.mcmaster.ca

HENDRY, ARCHIBALD WAGSTAFF, ELEMENTARY PARTICLE PHYSICS. *Current Pos:* from asst prof to assoc prof, 69-77, assoc dean, 85-88, PROF THEORET PHYSICS, IND UNIV, 77- *Personal Data:* b Scotland, Nov 18, 36; m 64, Jeanette; c Diana, Andrew & Gordon. *Educ:* Glasgow Univ, BSc, 58, PhD(physics), 62. *Prof Exp:* Res assoc theoret physics, Univ Calif, San Diego, 62-64; sr sci officer, Rutherford High Energy Lab & Oxford Univ, 64-67; res asst prof, Univ Ill, Urbana, 67-69. *Concurrent Pos:* Guest prof, Univ Heidelberg, 67. *Mem:* Asn Am Univ Profs; Am Asn Physics Teachers. *Res:* Theoretical high energy physics; elementary particle physics. *Mailing Add:* Dept Physics Ind Univ Bloomington IN 47405. *Fax:* 812-855-5533; *E-Mail:* hendry@indiana.edu

HENDRY, GEORGE ORR, RADIO FREQUENCY SYSTEMS, MAGNET DESIGN. *Current Pos:* VPRES RES & DEVELOP, RDS, 86- *Personal Data:* b Oakland, Calif, June 23, 37. *Educ:* Univ Calif, Berkeley, BS, 60, MS, 63. *Prof Exp:* Proj engr, W M Brobeck & Assoc, 63-65; proj engr, the Cyclotron Corp, 65-69, vpres res & eng, 69-83; dir res & develop, CTI, 84-92. *Concurrent Pos:* Pres, Cyclotron Inc. *Res:* Development of positive and negative ion cyclotron particle accelerators and their associated targets and shielding. *Mailing Add:* 3104 Redwood Rd Napa CA 94558

HENDRY, HUGH EDWARD, geology; deceased, see previous edition for last biography

HENDRY, RICHARD ALLAN, BIOCHEMISTRY, ORGANIC BIOCHEMISTRY. *Current Pos:* assoc prof, 59-63, PROF CHEM, WESTMINSTER COL, PA, 63- *Personal Data:* b Santa Barbara, Calif, Oct 13, 29; m 63, Joanne R Peck; c Thomas & Jonathan. *Educ:* Univ Calif, Santa Barbara, BA, 51; Univ Pac, MA, 52; Baylor Univ, Col Med, PhD(biochem),

56. *Prof Exp:* Res assoc chem, Univ Ill, 56-57; asst prof, Tex Tech Col, 57-59. *Concurrent Pos:* Vis prof, Mich State Univ, 68-69 & 90-91; res assoc chem, Univ Ill, 80-81. *Mem:* Am Chem Soc; Am Sci Affil; Sigma Xi. *Res:* Chromatographic methods of analysis, amino acid chemistry; chemistry of antibiotics; history of chemistry; chemical education; chemistry of glycosphingolipids. *Mailing Add:* Dept Chem Westminster Col New Wilmington PA 16172-0001. *Fax:* 412-946-7171; *E-Mail:* hendryra@westminster.edu

HENEGHAN, JAMES BEYER, PHYSIOLOGY. *Current Pos:* From instr to assoc prof, 62-74, PROF PHYSIOL & SURG RES, LA STATE UNIV MED CTR, NEW ORLEANS, 74-, DIR GERMFREE LAB, 62- *Personal Data:* b La Porte, Ind, Feb 5, 35; m 59; c 2. *Educ:* Univ Notre Dame, BS, 57, PhD(physiol), 62. *Concurrent Pos:* Mem, NIH Proj Site Visit Comt, 67; chmn & ed, IV Int Symp Germfree Res, 72-73. *Mem:* AAAS; Am Physiol Soc; Am Soc Microbiol; Asn Gnotobiotics (vpres, 70-71, pres, 71-72); Soc Nuclear Med. *Res:* Gastrointestinal physiology and oncology; hemorrhagic shock; neonatal growth; application of gnotobiotic technology to hospital patient care; germfree animals. *Mailing Add:* Physiol La State Univ Sch Med 1542 Tulane Ave New Orleans LA 70112-2825

HENEIN, NAEIM A, ENGINE COMBUSTION, TRIBOLOGY. *Current Pos:* assoc prof, 70-76, PROF MECH ENG, WAYNE STATE UNIV, 76-, DIR, CTR AUTOMOTIVE RES, 80- *Personal Data:* b Egypt; US citizen; m, Naira S; c Michael. *Educ:* Cairo Univ, BSc, 49; Alexandria Univ, MSc, 52; Univ Mich, PhD(mech eng), 57. *Prof Exp:* From lectr to asst prof mech eng, Alexandria Univ, 57-65; vis assoc prof, Univ Mich, 65-70. *Concurrent Pos:* Consult, Nat Res Coun, Nat Acad Sci, 74, Dept Transp, Transp Syst Ctr, Cambridge Mass, 78-80, US Tank Automotive Command, Warren, Mich, 79-88, Environ Protection Agency, Washington, DC, 83-92, Gen Motors, Ford Motor Co, Eaton Corp, Outboard Marine Co & Honda NAm, 97. *Mem:* Fel Soc Automotive Engrs; Combustion Inst; Am Soc Mech Engrs; Sigma Xi; Soc Tribologists & Lubrication Engrs. *Res:* Internal combustion engines; autoignition; emissions; performance; fuel economy; electronic controls; friction and wear; cold starting phenomena. *Mailing Add:* Col Eng Wayne State Univ Detroit MI 48202. *Fax:* 313-577-8789; *E-Mail:* henein@mel.eng.wayne.edu

HENERY, JAMES DANIEL, INDUSTRIAL CHEMISTRY. *Current Pos:* MEM STAFF, EL PASO PROD CO, 80- *Personal Data:* b Forney, Tex, Sept 23, 40; m 71. *Educ:* Univ Tex, Austin, BS, 66, PhD(chem), 70. *Prof Exp:* Res chemist, Petro-Tex Chem Corp, 69-77, sr res chemist, 77-80. *Mem:* Am Chem Soc. *Res:* Synthesis of intermediates using inorganic and organometallic catalysts; preparation of petrochemical by gas phase catalysis. *Mailing Add:* 2034 Hidden Creek Dr Kingwood TX 77339

HENERY-LOGAN, KENNETH ROBERT, ORGANIC CHEMISTRY. *Current Pos:* from asst prof to assoc prof, 60-69, prof, 69-89, EMER PROF, CHEM, UNIV MD, COL PARK, 89- *Personal Data:* b Montreal, Que, July 7, 21; m 61, Mary Tompkins. *Educ:* McGill Univ, BSc, 42, PhD(org chem), 46. *Prof Exp:* Res assoc, Mass Inst Technol, 51-60. *Concurrent Pos:* Vis lectr, Boston Univ, 57-58; vis prof, Northeastern Univ, 80; fel org chem, Univ Chicago, 48-50. *Mem:* Am Chem Soc. *Res:* Synthesis and chemistry of compounds with potential anticancer activity. *Mailing Add:* 1400 Castle Blvd Apt 211 Silver Spring MD 20904-4605. *Fax:* 301-314-9121

HENEY, LYSLE JOSEPH, JR, CHEMICAL ENGINEERING, PHYSICAL CHEMISTRY. *Current Pos:* RETIRED. *Personal Data:* b Minneapolis, Minn, Oct 31, 23; m 46, Arthemise Wystrach; c Marsha L & Lysle J III. *Educ:* Univ Minn, Minneapolis, BChE, 45, PhD(chem eng, phys chem), 51. *Prof Exp:* Chem engr, Am Cyanamid Co, 51-85. *Mem:* Am Chem Soc; Am Inst Chem Engrs; Sigma Xi. *Res:* Measurement of surface area of solids; measurement of energy absorbed by solids during comminution; investigation of relationship between new surface and absorbed energy for comminution of solids; economic analysis and process designs of first-of-a-kind chemical plants, reactors, separations, recoveries and environmental controls. *Mailing Add:* 11 Mead Ave Middlesex NJ 08846-2340

HENGEHOLD, ROBERT LEO, SOLID STATE & OPTICAL PHYSICS. *Current Pos:* from instr to assoc prof, 61-73, PROF PHYSICS, USAF INST TECHNOL, 73-, HEAD, DEPT ENG PHYSICS, 83- *Personal Data:* b Cincinnati, Ohio, June 18, 36. *Educ:* Thomas More Col, AB, 56; Univ Cincinnati, MS, 60, PhD(physics), 65. *Mem:* Am Phys Soc; Am Asn Physics Teachers; Am Soc Eng Educ; Sigma Xi. *Res:* Optical properties of solids; electron interaction with solids and surfaces; laser diagnostics. *Mailing Add:* 5501 Red Coach Dr Dayton OH 45429. *Fax:* 937-255-2921; *E-Mail:* rhengeho@afit.af.mil

HENIKA, RICHARD GRANT, FOOD CHEMISTRY, FOOD SCIENCE. *Current Pos:* Chemist, Western Condensing Co, 43-44 & 46-50, proj leader res & develop, 50-53, foods sect head, 53-55, proj leader, Foremost Dairies, Inc, 55-64, group leader, 64-67, assoc dir res & develop, 67-74, MGR TECH SERV, TECH MGR DAIRY DIV & PATENT COORDR, FOREMOST FOODS CO, FOREMOST-MCKESSON, INC, 74- *Personal Data:* b Wauwatosa, Wis, Sept 19, 21; m 41; c 4. *Educ:* Lawrence Col, BA, 43. *Honors & Awards:* Co-recipient Indust Achievement Award, Inst Food Technol, 67. *Mem:* Inst Food Technol; Am Asn Cereal Chem; Am Chem Soc; Am Soc Bakery Eng; fel Am Inst Chem. *Res:* Development of new products and methods in bread baking, whipping agents and food proteins; research management. *Mailing Add:* 90 Stephanie Lane Alamo CA 94507-1994

HENINGER, GEORGE ROBERT, PSYCHIATRY. *Current Pos:* from asst prof to assoc prof, 66-76, PROF PSYCHIAT, SCH MED, YALE UNIV, 76- *Personal Data:* b Nov 15, 34; US citizen; m 57; c 4. *Educ:* Univ Utah, BS, 57, MD, 60; Am Bd Psychiat & Neurol, dipl. *Honors & Awards:* Wintrobe Award, 60; Anna Monica Award, 95. *Prof Exp:* Intern med, Boston City Hosp, 60-61; resident psychiat, Mass Ment Health Ctr, 61-64; clin assoc, NIMH, 64-65; prog specialist, Nat Clearinghouse Ment Health Info, 65-66. *Concurrent Pos:* Teaching fel psychiat, Harvard Univ, 61-64; consult, Conn Valley Hosp, 66-; prin investr, NIMH grants, 67, 70, 73, 76, 81, 86, 91 & 96. *Mem:* AAAS; fel Am Psychiat Asn; Soc Biol Psychiat; Psychiat Res Soc; Am Psychopath Soc; fel Am Col Neuropsychopharmacol. *Res:* Neuro pharmacology of antidepressant treatment; neuroimmunology of stress and behavior disorders. *Mailing Add:* Dept Psychiat 333 CMHC Yale Univ 34 Park St New Haven CT 06508

HENINGER, RICHARD WILFORD, PHYSIOLOGY, BIOCHEMISTRY. *Current Pos:* assoc prof zool, 66-71, PROF ZOOL, BRIGHAM YOUNG UNIV, 71- *Personal Data:* b Raymond, Alta, Sept 28, 31; m 55; c 2. *Educ:* Brigham Young Univ, BSc, 57; Okla State Univ, MSc, 59, PhD(physiol), 61. *Prof Exp:* Trainee endocrinol, Med Sch, Univ Wis-Madison, 61-62, asst prof physiol, 62-66. *Mem:* Endocrine Soc; Brit Soc Endocrinol; Am Physiol Soc. *Res:* Peripheral metabolism of thyroid hormones. *Mailing Add:* Dept Biol Brigham Young Univ Provo UT 84602-5250. *Fax:* 801-378-7499

HENINGER, RONALD LEE, FOREST MANAGEMENT. *Current Pos:* scientist III, Weyerhaeuser Co, 74-76, scientist IV silvicult, 76-81, actg mgr forestry res field sta, 81-83, MGR, ORE FORESTRY RES FIELD STA, WEYERHAESER CO, 83- *Personal Data:* b Waukegan, Ill, Dec 28, 44; m 68, Merle D George; c Robin L & Scott G. *Educ:* Mich Technol Univ, BSF, 68, MSF, 69; Mich State Univ, PhD(forest soils), 73. *Honors & Awards:* Researcher of Yr, Foresters Soc Am 96. *Prof Exp:* Instr silvicult, Mich State Univ, 73-74; forester, Dept State Hwys & Transp, Mich, 74. *Mem:* Soc Am Foresters; Soil Sci Soc Am; Sigma Xi; Am Soc Agron. *Res:* Development of science based silvicultural prescriptions that are environmentally and ecologically adapted; studies include plantation establishment, weed control, thinning, fertilization, forest soils and long-term site productivity. *Mailing Add:* 572 N 71st St Springfield OR 97478. *Fax:* 541-741-5589; *E-Mail:* heningr@wdni.com

HENINS, IVARS, PHYSICS. *Current Pos:* CONSULT, 90- *Personal Data:* b Pampali, Latvia, June 2, 33; US citizen; m 60, Marlene McClure; c Rita, Mark & Andrew. *Educ:* Friends Univ, BA, 55; Johns Hopkins Univ, PhD(physics), 61. *Prof Exp:* Instr physics, Johns Hopkins Univ, 61-62; staff mem, Los Alamos Sci Lab, Univ Calif, 62-90. *Mem:* Am Phys Soc; Am Vacuum Soc. *Res:* Plasma physics; controlled thermonuclear research; high altitude plasma phenomena; optical instrumentation. *Mailing Add:* 121 Monte Rey Dr N Los Alamos NM 87544

HENION, RICHARD S, ORGANIC CHEMISTRY. *Current Pos:* sr develop chemist, 68-80, TECH ASSOC, SYNTHETIC CHEM DIV, EASTMAN KODAK CO, 80- *Personal Data:* b Brockport, NY, Dec 14, 39; m 59; c 2. *Educ:* Alfred Univ, BA, 62; Syracuse Univ, PhD(org chem), 67. *Prof Exp:* Res assoc, Mass Inst Technol, 67-68. *Mem:* Am Chem Soc. *Res:* Organic syntheses; chemistry of heterocyclic compounds; reaction mechanisms; sulfur compounds. *Mailing Add:* 312 Gallup Rd Spencerport NY 14559

HENIS, JAY MYLS STUART, PHYSICAL CHEMISTRY, MEMBRANE & MEDIA. *Current Pos:* PRES, HENIS TECHNOL INC, 92- *Personal Data:* b New York, NY, July 9, 38; m 63; c 2. *Educ:* Alfred Univ, BA, 59; Syracuse Univ, PhD(phys chem), 64. *Honors & Awards:* Incheba Gold Medal, 80; Kirkpatric Award, 81; Soc Plastics Engr Award, 83; Award for Separating Sci & Technol, Am Chem Soc, 88. *Prof Exp:* Res assoc molecular beams, Brown Univ, 64-66; res specialist, Cent Res Dept, Monsanto Co, St Louis, 66-75, sci fel, 75-78, sr fel, 78, sr fel & dir, 80-92, res dir, 84. *Concurrent Pos:* Adj assoc prof chem, Washington Univ, St Louis, 73-84; adj prof chem eng, Washington Univ, St Louis, 92-; assoc dir, Membrane Technol & Commercialization, Topchiew Inst Petrochem Synthesis, Moscow, Russia, 93- & Membrane Sci, Los Alamos Nat Lab, 94- *Mem:* Am Chem Soc; Am Phys Soc. *Res:* Ion molecule reactions; mass and ion cyclotron resonance spectroscopy; molecular beams; discharges; reactions of exited intermediates; membrane separations; hollow fibers; diffusion; pollution control; energy utilization; hydrogen production and recovery; controlled delivery of proteins and peptides; cell culture devices and systems; ion exchange and affinity separations; chromatography; polymer and surface modification; tests and measaurements. *Mailing Add:* Henis Technol Inc 501 Marford Dr St Louis MO 63141-7506. *Fax:* 314-994-1932

HENISCH, HEINZ KURT, SOLID STATE PHYSICS, HISTORY OF PHOTOGRAPHY. *Current Pos:* prof appl physics, Pa State Univ, 63-70, prof physics, 63-89, assoc dir mat res lab, 69-75, prof, 73-89, res prof, 89-93, EMER PROF HIST PHOTOG, PA STATE UNIV, 93-, EMER PROF PHYSICS, 93- *Personal Data:* b Neudek, Apr 21, 22; m 60, Bridget Wilsher. *Educ:* Reading Univ, BSc, 42, PhD(physics), 49. *Hon Degrees:* DSc, Reading Univ, 78. *Prof Exp:* Jr sci officer physics, Royal Aircraft Estab, Eng, 42-46; lectr, Univ Reading, 48-63. *Concurrent Pos:* Vis scientist, Sylvania Elec Prod, Inc, NY, 55-56; consult, Mining & Chem Prod, UK, 57-63; ed, Int Ser of Monogr on Semiconductors, 57-68; consult, Eng Elec Valve Co, 58-63, Polaroid Corp, Mass, 63-67, Carborundum Corp, 67-75 & Energy Conversion Devices, 68-89; ed-in-chief, Mat Res Bull, 85-94; founder & ed, Hist of Photog, 87-90; guest cur exhibition, Photographic Experience, Palmer Mus Art, Pa State Univ, 88. *Mem:* Fel Am Phys Soc; fel Royal Photog Soc; fel Brit Inst Physics; fel Inst Arts & Humanistic Studies. *Res:* Semiconductors;

phosphors; electroluminescence; contact and surface phenomena; crystal growth; amorphous materials; history of photography; computational physics; author of 13 books. *Mailing Add:* 346 W Hillcrest Ave State College PA 16803

HENISZ, JERZY EMIL, PSYCHIATRY. *Current Pos:* res assoc, 70- 71, from asst prof to assoc prof, 71-85, CLIN ASSOC PROF PSYCHIAT, YALE UNIV, 85- *Personal Data:* b Warsaw, Poland, July 2, 37; m 62, Anna; c Witold. *Educ:* Acad Med, Warsaw, MD, 61, DrMedSci, 65. *Prof Exp:* Resident psychiat, Acad Med, Warsaw, 62-67, asst, 65-69. *Mem:* Polish Psychiat Asn; Am Psychiat Asn. *Res:* Social psychiatry; utilization and delivery of mental health services; evaluation of clinical services. *Mailing Add:* PO Box 1089 Sharon CT 06069

HENIZE, KARL GORDON, space debris, planetary nebulae; deceased, see previous edition for last biography

HENKART, PIERRE, IMMUNOLOGY, BIOCHEMISTRY. *Current Pos:* staff fel, 71-75, staff chemist, 75-80, SR INVESTR, NAT CANCER INST, 80- *Personal Data:* b New York, NY, Aug 28, 41. *Educ:* Rensselaer Polytech Inst, BS, 63; Harvard Univ, PhD(biochem & molecular biol), 68. *Prof Exp:* NIH fel biol, Univ Calif, San Diego, 68-70, res biologist, 70-71. *Mem:* Am Asn Immunolgists. *Res:* Mechanism of lymphocyte cytotoxicity. *Mailing Add:* NCI NIH Bldg 10 Rm 4B17 Bethesda MD 20892-1360

HENKE, BURTON LEHMAN, PHYSICS. *Current Pos:* sr scientist, 85-89, EMER SR STAFF SCIENTIST, LAWRENCE BERKELEY LAB, UNIV CALIF, BERKELEY, 89- *Personal Data:* b Ohio, Aug 27, 22; m 48, Wilma Lange; c Raymond & Thomas. *Educ:* Miami Univ, BA, 44; Calif Inst Technol, MS, 46, PhD(physics), 53. *Prof Exp:* From instr to prof physics, Pomona Col, 48-67; prof physics & astron, Univ Hawaii, 67-84. *Concurrent Pos:* Prin investr, Off Sci Res Grants, USAF, 54- & US Dept Energy grants, 76-87; Guggenheim fel, 56; Dept Energy grant, 76-87; consult X-Ray physics, govt & indust. *Mem:* Fel Am Phys Soc; Am Asn Physics Teachers; Am Asn Univ Professors; Sigma Xi; Am Astron Soc. *Res:* Low energy x-ray and electron physics. *Mailing Add:* 1200 Mira Mar No 921 Medford OR 97504. *Fax:* 541-857-7599

HENKE, MITCHELL C, HEAT TRANSFER-FOOD, AIR IMPINGEMENT. *Current Pos:* Elec engr, 71-80, supvr elec eng, 80-81, RES & DEVELOP MGR, LINCOLN FOOD SERV PROD, INC, 81- *Personal Data:* b Wausau, Wis, Sept 19, 49; m 71; c 2. *Educ:* Valparaiso Univ, BSEE, 71; Purdue Univ, MSE, 78. *Honors & Awards:* Doctorate Food Serv hon medallion, Nat Asn Food Equip Mfrs, 87. *Mem:* Soc Advan Food Serv Res (pres, 88-89); Inst Elec & Electronics Engrs; Inst Food Technologists; Nat Soc Prof Engrs; Int Microwave Power Inst. *Res:* Assess, develop and implement strategic, technology based new products; air impingement cooking technology to reduce cooking time and yet improving or maintaining cooking quality; heat transfer, air movement and control related to air impingement cooking; granted several patents; author of various publications. *Mailing Add:* 5208 Oak Chase Run Ft Wayne IN 46845

HENKE, RUSSELL W, MECHANICAL ENGINEERING, FLUID POWER. *Current Pos:* CONSULT, FLUID POWER CONSULTS INT & LAB FLUID POWER, 71- *Personal Data:* b Milwaukee, Wis, Apr 28, 24; m 47; c 2. *Educ:* Univ Wis, BS, 49, MS, 53, PME, 60. *Honors & Awards:* Prod Eng-Master Designer Award, 67 & Pascal Medal, 70, Fluid Power Soc; Distinguished Achievement Award, Fluid Power Soc, 89. *Prof Exp:* Proj engr, Heil Co, Wis, 50-52; chief res & develop engr, Badger Meter Mfg Co, 52-55; dir eng, Construct Equip Div, Am Marietta Corp, 55-57; consult engr, 57-60; dir fluid power res, Racine Hydraul & Mach, 60-62; prof mech eng & dir, Fluid Power Inst, Milwaukee Sch Eng, 62-68; exec vpres, Fluid Power Soc, 68-71. *Concurrent Pos:* Mem, US adv group to Int Standardization Orgn Tech Comt, 131; mem, Hydraul & Pneumatic Comt, Soc Automotive Engrs; mem, Fluid Power Stand Comt, Am Nat Standards Inst. *Mem:* Nat Asn Corrosion Engrs; Am Soc Eng Educ; Am Soc Mech Engrs; Am Soc Testing & Mat; fel Fluid Power Soc (vpres, 55-66, pres, 66-67); Soc Automotive Engrs. *Res:* Fluid power devices and systems; related instrumentation; hydraulics; pneumatics; controls. *Mailing Add:* 1000 Grandview Dr Elm Grove WI 53122-0106. *Fax:* 414-782-0410

HENKEL, ELMER THOMAS, PHYSICS, SCIENCE EDUCATION. *Current Pos:* assoc prof, 67-77, chmn dept, 69-73, PROF PHYSICS, WAGNER COL, 78-, DIR, WAGNER SOLAR ENERGY DEMONSTRATION PROJ, 76- *Personal Data:* b Toledo, Ohio, June 28, 36; m 62; c 3. *Educ:* Columbia Col, AB, 58; Univ Toledo, MEd, 63, MS & PhD(sci educ, physics), 65. *Prof Exp:* Asst prof physics, Southampton Col, Long Island Univ, 65-67. *Concurrent Pos:* Energy conserv consult, 87- *Mem:* Am Asn Physics Teachers; Int Solar Energy Soc. *Res:* Metallic friction, changes in the coefficient of friction due to variation in normal loads and relative velocity of surfaces; relationships between critical thinking abilities of students and instruction in physics; low energy nuclear physics; application of solar energy for the heating and cooling of commercial size buildings. *Mailing Add:* 86 Silver Lake Rd Staten Island NY 10301

HENKEL, JAMES GREGORY, MEDICINAL CHEMISTRY, ORGANIC CHEMISTRY. *Current Pos:* asst prof, 77-82, ASSOC PROF MED CHEM, UNIV CONN, 82-, ASSOC DEAN, GRAD SCH, 86- *Personal Data:* b Santa Monica, Calif, Nov 22, 45; m 70; c Kristin & Todd. *Educ:* Univ Calif, Los Angeles, BS, 67; Brown Univ, PhD(chem), 73. *Prof Exp:* Res specialist, Univ Minn, 72-74, asst prof med chem, 74-77. *Concurrent Pos:* Secy, Sect Teachers Chem, Am Asn Col Pharm, 83-86, chair-elect, 87-88, chair, 88-89. *Mem:* Am Chem Soc; Am Asn Col Pharm; Asn Develop Comput-Based Instruct. *Res:* Biological alkylations; synthesis of potential central nervous system active compounds; chemical toxicology; electronic data processing research applications. *Mailing Add:* 45 Hamilton Dr Manchester CT 06040

HENKEL, JOHN HARMON, THEORETICAL SOLID STATE PHYSICS. *Current Pos:* from asst prof to assoc prof, Univ Ga, 55-64, actg head, Dept Physics & Astron, 75-77, prof physics, 64-90, EMER PROF PHYSICS, UNIV GA, 90- *Personal Data:* b Kentwood, La, Aug 14, 24; m 48; c 5. *Educ:* Tulane Univ, BS, 47, MS, 48; Brown Univ, PhD(physics), 54. *Prof Exp:* Jr res technologist, Magnolia Petrol Co, 48-51, res technologist, Field Res Labs, 54-55; asst, Brown Univ, 51-54. *Concurrent Pos:* NSF fel, 59-60; Nat Res Coun sr res assoc, Aerospace Res Labs, Wright Patterson AFB, Ohio, prog mgr, Directorate Physics, Air Force Off Sci Res, 77-78. *Mem:* Fel AAAS; Am Phys Soc; Sigma Xi. *Res:* Theoretical solid state physics; electrical geophysical exploration; induced polarization; lattice dynamics; ferroelectricity; band calculations. *Mailing Add:* 395 Hampton Ct Athens GA 30605

HENKEL, RICHARD LUTHER, SCIENCE EDUCATION, ELECTRICAL ENGINEERING. *Current Pos:* RETIRED. *Personal Data:* b Toledo, Ohio, Mar 24, 21; m 47; c 3. *Educ:* Univ Toledo, BE, 43; Univ Wis, PhD(physics), 50. *Prof Exp:* Teaching asst, Univ Toledo, 40-43; res assoc radar res, Harvard Univ, 43-46; res asst nuclear physics, Univ Wis, 46-50; nuclear physics staff, Los Alamos Nat Lab, 50-55, group leader, 55-76. *Mem:* Fel Am Phys Soc. *Res:* Experimental research in neutron physics, primarily fission measurements. *Mailing Add:* PO Box 128 Pitkin CO 81241

HENKELS, WALTER HARVEY, SOLID STATE PHYSICS. *Current Pos:* RES STAFF MEM, RES DIV, IBM CORP, 71- *Personal Data:* b Philadelphia, Pa, Oct 10, 44; m 66; c 2. *Educ:* Lehigh Univ, BS, 66; Cornell Univ, PhD(appl physics), 74. *Mem:* Am Phys Soc; Inst Elec & Electronics Engrs; AAAS. *Res:* Feasibility of and application of Josephson junctions as logic and memory devices for use in computer hardware. *Mailing Add:* Thomas J Watson Res Ctr IBM Corp PO Box 218 Yorktown Heights NY 10598

HENKENS, ROBERT WILLIAM, BIOPHYSICAL CHEMISTRY, ENZYME TECHNOLOGY. *Current Pos:* asst prof, 69-73, ASSOC PROF CHEM, DUKE UNIV, 73- *Personal Data:* b Chicago, Ill. *Educ:* Univ Wash, BA, 58; Yale Univ, MS, 64, PhD(chem), 67. *Prof Exp:* Chemist, Gen Elec Co, 58-62; res fel, Harvard Univ, 68-69. *Concurrent Pos:* Chmn, Enzyme Technol Res Group, Inc, 84-; mem, NC Biomolecular Eng & Mat Applns Ctr, 84- *Mem:* Am Chem Soc; Sigma Xi. *Res:* Spectroscopic, kinetic and thermodynamic studies of proteins, especially metalloenzymes and enzyme catalysis. *Mailing Add:* Dept Chem Duke Univ Durham NC 27706

HENKER, FRED OSWALD, III, PSYCHIATRY. *Current Pos:* from instr to assoc prof, 58-74, PROF PSYCHIAT, MED CTR, UNIV ARK, LITTLE ROCK, 75-, CHIEF CONSULT SERV, 64- *Personal Data:* b Little Rock, Ark, Sept 20, 22; m 45; c 2. *Educ:* Univ Ark, BS, 44, MD, 45. *Prof Exp:* Chief psychiat, Vet Admin Hosp, Jackson, Miss, 57-58. *Concurrent Pos:* Clin instr, Univ Miss, 57-58. *Mem:* AMA; Am Psychiat Asn; Acad Psychosom Med (pres, 83-84); Int Col Psychosomatic Med. *Res:* Psychosomatic medicine. *Mailing Add:* 9 Belmont Dr Little Rock AR 72204

HENKIN, HYMAN, PHYSICAL CHEMISTRY. *Current Pos:* RETIRED. *Personal Data:* b New York, NY, Feb 2, 15; m 40; c 3. *Educ:* City Col New York, BS, 36; NY Univ, PhD(phys chem), 40. *Prof Exp:* Assoc chemist, US Bur Mines, 44; res mgr & sect head, Colgate-Palmolive Co, 44-63; dir res, Helene Curtis Industs, Inc, 63-80, vpres res & develop, 65-80. *Mem:* Am Chem Soc; Soc Cosmetic Chem. *Res:* Administration; cosmetics and toiletries. *Mailing Add:* Exeter E 2073 Boca Raton FL 33434-3699

HENKIN, JACK, ENZYMOLOGY, PROTEIN CHEMISTRY. *Current Pos:* sr biochemist, Phys Biochem Lab, Pharmaceut Prod Div, 84-87, SECT HEAD, THROMBOLYTICS DISCOVERY, ABBOTT LABS, 87- *Personal Data:* b Ger, Dec 23, 47; US citizen. *Educ:* City Col New York, BS, 69; Brandeis Univ, PhD(biochem), 75. *Prof Exp:* Res fel bio-org, Dept Chem, Harvard Univ, 74-77; asst prof biochem, Dept Biochem & Molecular Biol, Med Sch, Univ Tex, Houston, 77-84. *Concurrent Pos:* Adj asst prof, Chicago Med Sch, 85- *Mem:* Am Chem Soc; Am Soc Biol Chemists. *Res:* Protein structure and function applied to enzymes, hormones and receptors; design of metabolic inhibitors and peptinomimetics as drugs; photochemistry and drug delivery. *Mailing Add:* Bldg AP9 Rm 2124 Abbott Labs Abbott Park North Chicago IL 60034-3500. *Fax:* 847-937-4150

HENKIN, LEON (ALBERT), MATHEMATICAL LOGIC. *Current Pos:* from asst prof to prof math, 53-91, Univ Calif, Berkeley, from vchmn to chmn dept, 59-68, chmn, 83-85, prof educ, 83-91, EMER PROF MATH & EDUC, UNIV CALIF, BERKELEY, 91- *Personal Data:* b Brooklyn, NY, Apr 19, 21; m 50, Ginette Potvin; c Paul & Julian. *Educ:* Columbia Univ, AB, 41; Princeton Univ, MA, 42, PhD(math), 47. *Hon Degrees:* DSc, Univ Ill, 95. *Honors & Awards:* Chauvenet Prize, Math Asn Am, 64, Distinguished Serv Math Award, 90. *Prof Exp:* Mathematician, Kellex Corp, NY, 43-45 & Carbide & Carbon Chem Co, Tenn, 45-46; Fine Instr math, Princeton Univ, 47-48, Jewett fel, 48-49; from asst prof to assoc prof math, Univ Southern Calif, 49-53. *Concurrent Pos:* NSF grants, 52-; Fulbright res scholar, Neth,

54-55 & Israel, 79; vis prof, Dartmouth Col, 60-61; Guggenheim fel & mem, Inst Advan Study, 61-62; vis fel, All Souls Col, Oxford Univ, 68-69; vis scholar, Univ Colo, 75-76. Mem, US Nat Comt Hist & Philos Sci, 62-65, chmn comt logic & methodology sci, 62-64; mem coun, Conf Bd Math Sci, 63-64; prin investr, Community Teaching Fel Prog, Univ Calif, 69-75; vis scholar, Univ Paris VII, 87; distinguished vis prof, Mills Col, 90-95. Mem: Fel AAAS; Am Math Soc; Math Asn Am; Asn Symbolic Logic (vpres, 53-55, pres, 62-64). Res: Mathematical logic; algebra; mathematics education. Mailing Add: Dept Math Univ Calif Berkeley CA 94720-3840. E-Mail: henkin@math.berkeley.edu

HENKIN, ROBERT I, TASTE & SMELL DISORDERS, NEUROBIOLOGY. Current Pos: DIR, CTR MOLECULAR NUTRIT & SENSORY DIS, TASTE & SMELL CLIN, WASHINGTON, DC, 86- Personal Data: b Los Angeles, Calif, Oct 5, 30; c Amanda J, Michael J, David G, Joshua A, Elizabeth M & Hannah D. Educ: Univ Southern Calif, AB, 51; Univ Calif, Los Angeles, MA, 53, PhD(music, psychol), 56, MD, 59. Honors & Awards: Gill Mem lectr, 81; Dow Lectr Biochem, Bucknell Univ, 90. Prof Exp: Asst Music, Univ Calif, Los Angeles, 52-54; intern med, Univ Hosp, 59-60, resident, Jackson Mem Hosp, Miami, Fla, 60-61; res assoc, NIMH, 61-63; sr investr, Nat Heart & Lung Inst, 63-69, chief sect neuroendocrinol, 69-75; prof neurol, Med Ctr, Georgetown Univ, Washington, DC, 75-86. Concurrent Pos: Nat Kidney Dis Found traveling fel, 63; clin instr med, Hosp, Georgetown Univ, 64-67, asst clin prof, Sch Med, 67-75; consult, Gynec Endocrinol Clin, Lenox Hill Hosp, New York, 67-70; US Postal Serv, 74-, NIH, 75-, Hooker Chem Co, 76-77, ITT-Continental Baking Co, 76-80 & USDA, 78-, Lewis Howe Co, 79, Nat Geog Soc, 81-82, Bristol Myers Squibb, 85-86, Flornsynth, 86- , Wash Conf Zinc, 87- & Westport Pharmacol, 87-; mem sect renal dis, Coun Circulation, Am Heart Asn; chmn panel zinc, BEEP Comt, Nat Res Coun-Nat Acad Sci, 72-78; dir, Taste & Smell Clin, 75-; guest prof nutrit, Univ Ga, Athens, 83; Sigma Xi nat lectr, 84-86; dir & chief exec officer, Sialon Corp, 87- Mem: Biophys Soc; Am Fedn Clin Res; Endocrine Soc; Am Soc Clin Invest; Am Inst Nutrit; Sigma Xi; Am Col Nutrit. Res: Taste and olfaction, basic science and clinical disorders; nutrition; trace metal metabolism; steroid and sensory physiology; neuroendocrinology; psychology of music; United States and foreign patents; biochemistry and physiology of saliva and salivary proteins in diagnosis of systemic diseases and diseases of the oral cavity; diseases of saliva and nasal mucus. Mailing Add: 6601 Broxburn Dr Bethesda MD 20817

HENLE, JAMES MARSTON, COMBINATORIAL SET THEORY. Current Pos: from asst prof to assoc prof, 76-88, PROF MATH, SMITH COL, 88- Personal Data: b Washington, DC, Nov 13, 46; m 69; c 1. Educ: Dartmouth Col, AB, 68; Mass Inst Technol, PhD(math), 76. Prof Exp: Vis instr math, Peace Corps, Col Baguio, Univ Philippines, 68-70; teacher, Burgundy Farm Country Day Sch, 71-73. Concurrent Pos: Fulbright lectr, Univ Philippines, Quezon City, 80; co-prin investr, NSF grant, 84- Mem: Math Asn Am; Asn Symbolic Logic. Res: Models of set theory without the Axiom of Choice; models of the Axiom of Determinateness and infinite-exponent partition relations. Mailing Add: 105 Prospect St Northampton MA 01060

HENLEY, ERNEST J(USTUS), CHEMICAL ENGINEERING. Current Pos: PROF CHEM ENG, COL ENG, UNIV HOUSTON, 67- Personal Data: b Ger, Sept 30, 26; nat US; m 54; c 2. Educ: Univ Del, BS, 50; Columbia Univ, MS, 51, EngScD, 53. Prof Exp: Asst prof chem eng, Columbia Univ, 54-58; from assoc prof to prof, Stevens Inst Technol, 58-67. Concurrent Pos: Consult, Knolls Atomic Power Labs, 52-54, Am Cyanamid Co, 54-58 & E I du Pont de Nemours & Co, 78; dir, RAI res, 54-88, Procedyne Corp, 61-, Houston Glass Fabrication Corp, 71-81, Cache Corp, 75-86, Henley Int Inc, 76- & Continuous Learning Corp, 80-86; US deleg, Warsaw Conf, Int Atomic Energy Agency, 59; dir, US-Japanese Coop Sci Sem, Kyoto, 74; dir, NATO Advan Study Inst, Liverpool, 73, Sogesta, Italy, 78. Mem: Am Chem Soc; Am Nuclear Soc; Radiation Res Soc; Am Inst Chem Engrs. Res: Nuclear engineering; safety and reliability. Mailing Add: Dept Chem Eng Univ Houston Houston TX 77204

HENLEY, ERNEST MARK, THEORETICAL NUCLEAR PHYSICS. Current Pos: from asst prof to prof physics, Univ Wash, 54-95, chmn Univ Senate, 71-72, chmn dept, 74-77, dean, Col Arts Sci, 79-87, EMER PROF, UNIV WASH, 95- Personal Data: b Ger, June 10, 24; nat US; m 48, Elaine Dimitman; c M Bradford & Karen M. Educ: City Col New York, BEE, 44; Univ Calif, PHD(physics), 52. Honors & Awards: Sr Alexander Von Humboldt Award, 84; T W Bonner Award, Am Phys Soc, 89. Prof Exp: Elec engr, Airborne Instruments Lab, 46-48; elec engr, Microwave Lab, Univ Calif, 48-50, physicist, Radiation Lab, 50-51; assoc physics, Stanford Univ, 51-52; lectr, Columbia Univ, 52-54. Concurrent Pos: Jewett fel, Columbia Univ, 52-53; NSF sr fel, 58-59; consult, Los Alamos Sci Lab, 62-; Guggenheim Fel, 67-68; NATO sr fel, 76-77; exchange scientist to USSR, Nat Acad Sci, 77; chmn, Div Nuclear Physics, Am Phys Soc, 78-79, counr, 82-86; distinguished scholar to People's Rep China, 83; bd dir, Wash Technol Ctr, 83-87 & Pac Sci Ctr, 84-87; chair, Nuclear Sci Adv Comn, 86-89; chair, Physics Sect, AAAS, 89, bd trustees, Assoc Univs, 89-; dir, Inst Nuclear Theory, 90-91, assoc dir, 91-; managing ed, Int, JMod Physics E, 92- Mem: Nat Acad Sci; fel Am Phys Soc (vpres, pres-elect, pres, 90-92); fel AAAS; fel Am Acad Arts & Sci. Res: Theoretical nuclear and particle physics; symmetries. Mailing Add: Univ Wash Dept Physics Box 351560 Seattle WA 98195-1560. Fax: 206-685-0635; E-Mail: henley@phys.washington.edu

HENLEY, JOHN RAYMOND, DESIGN & TEST OF ELECTRO-OPTICAL DEVICES & SYSTEMS. Current Pos: DIR RES ELECTRO-OPTICS, MISSION RES CORP, 92- Personal Data: m 80, Maria E Baquiran; c Ashley & Jason. Educ: Univ Calif, San Diego, PhD(physics), 78. Prof Exp: Theoret physics group leader, Res & Develop Div, 82-91, prog mgr, Sensor Survivability Prog, Lockheed Missiles & Space Co, 86-87, chief scientist, LWIR Advan Technol Seeker, Res & Develop Div, 88-91. Concurrent Pos: Prin investr, Weapons Related Theoret Physics, Lockheed Res & Develop Div, 84-86, Nonlinear Signal Processing, 88-91, co-prin investr, Real-Time SAR Processing, 88. Mem: Am Phys Soc. Res: Photonics; advanced detector technology; advanced focal plane design and test; signal processing. Mailing Add: 1740 Split Oak Lane Colorado Springs CO 80919

HENLEY, KEITH STUART, GASTROENTEROLOGY. Current Pos: from instr to assoc prof, Med Sch, 54-68, physician-in-chg, sect gastroenterol, 73-81, PROF INTERNAL MED, MED CTR, UNIV MICH, ANN ARBOR, 68- Personal Data: b Hamburg, Ger, Feb 18, 24; nat US; m 59, Marcelle Marianne Picano; c Roy Hugh. Educ: Univ Durham, MB & BS, 48, MD, 57. Prof Exp: Physician, Newcastle Gen Hosp, 48; surgeon, Royal Victoria Infirmary, 49; physician, Postgrad Med Sch, Univ London, 50, registr internal med, 52-54. Concurrent Pos: Res career develop award, USPHS, 61-66. Mem: Am Gastroenterol Asn; Am Physiol Soc; fel Am Col Physicians; Am Fedn Clin Res; Brit Med Asn; Int Asn Study Liver. Res: Biochemical properties of liver gastroenterology; prostaglandins in liver transplantation; acute cellular rejection. Mailing Add: Dept Internal Med Univ Mich Hosps 3912F Taubman Ann Arbor MI 48109-0001

HENLEY, MELVIN BRENT, JR, PHYSICAL CHEMISTRY. Current Pos: Asst prof, 67-70, chair, 88-92, ASSOC PROF CHEM, MURRAY STATE UNIV, 70- Personal Data: b Hickory Valley, Tenn, Aug 25, 35; m 54; c Sonny, Stan, Stuart, Steve & Shane. Educ: Murray State Col, BS(physics, math, chem), 61; Univ Miss, Phd(chem), 64; Murray State Univ, MBA, 90. Concurrent Pos: Vchmn, Bd of Regents, Murray State Univ, 83-86. Mem: Am Chem Soc. Res: Catalytic effects on gas-phase dehydrohalogenations. Mailing Add: Dept Chem Murray State Univ Murray KY 42071

HENLEY, WALTER L, PEDIATRICS, IMMUNOLOGY. Current Pos: res fel pediat & virol, Mt Sinai Hosp, 53-56, chief resident, 56-57, from asst attend physician to assoc attend physician, 57-74, assoc prof, Sch Med, 66-74, ATTEND PHYSICIAN PEDIAT, MT SINAI HOSP, 74-, PROF, MT SINAI SCH MED, 74- Personal Data: b June 4, 22; US citizen; m, Edith Hertz; c Madeline & Elizabeth. Educ: Univ Calif, Los Angeles, BA, 47; Univ Pa, MD, 51. Prof Exp: Rotating intern, Univ Pa Hosp, 51-52; resident pediat, Bronx Hosp, NY, 52-53. Concurrent Pos: Instr, Col Physicians & Surgeons, Columbia Univ, 56-65; Am Cancer Soc fel immunochem, Rockefeller Univ, 66-68; Nat Soc Prev Blindness grants & Fight for Sight Inc grants, 69 & 77; USPHS grant, Mt Sinai Sch Med, 70-79, chief, Pediat Outpatient Dept, 68-73, res assoc prof ophthal, 77-; attend pediat, Beth Israel Med Ctr, 76- Mem: Am Acad Pediat; Am Soc Pediat; Harvey Soc; Am Asn Immunologists; Asn Res Vision & Ophthal. Res: Humoral and cellular immunology in pediatrics and ophthalmology; infectious diseases. Mailing Add: Dept Pediat Beth Israel Med Ctr First Ave & 16th St New York NY 10003. Fax: 212-420-4052

HENN, FRITZ ALBERT, NEUROPSYCHIATRY, NEUROCHEMISTRY. Current Pos: PROF PSYCHIAT & CHMN DEPT, STATE UNIV NY, STONY BROOK, 82- Personal Data: b Aldan, Pa, Mar 26, 41; m 64; c 2. Educ: Wesleyan Univ, Conn, BA, 63; Johns Hopkins Univ, Baltimore, PhD(biochem), 67; Univ Va, MD, 71. Prof Exp: Res scientist neurochem, Inst Neurobiol, Univ Goteborg, Sweden, 70-71; res psychiatrist, Wash Univ, St Louis, Mo, 71-74; from asst prof to prof psychiat, Sch Med, Univ Iowa, Iowa City, 74-82. Concurrent Pos: Falk fel, Am Psychiat Asn, 73; consult, Drug Enforcement Agency, 73-74; mem coun res & develop, Am Psychiat Asn, 73-74; dir, Inst Ment Health Res, State Univ NY, Stony Brook, 83- Mem: Int Soc Neurochem; Am Soc Neurochem; Am Psychiat Asn; Psychiat Res Soc; Am Psychopath Soc. Res: Study of neuronal modulation by glial cells through removing and metabolizing neurotransmitters and controlling ion movements; forensic psychiatry study of relationship between psychiatric illness and criminal activity; biology markers of schizophrenia. Mailing Add: HSC Sch Med-Psychiat Stony Brook NY 11790

HENNEBERGER, WALTER CARL, ELECTRODYNAMICS. Current Pos: from asst prof to assoc prof, 63-72, chmn dept, 74-75, PROF PHYSICS, SOUTHERN ILL UNIV, CARBONDALE, 72- Personal Data: b Bradley, Ill, Jan 17, 30; m 67; c 2. Educ: Purdue Univ, BS, 52, MS, 56; Univ Gottingen, Dr nat sci(physics), 59. Prof Exp: Res assoc physics, Univ Notre Dame, 59-60; asst prof, Fordham Univ, 60-62; scholar, Dublin Inst Advan Studies, 62-63. Concurrent Pos: Consult, US Army Missile Command, Redstone Arsenal, Ala, 75-76. Mem: Am Phys Soc; Am Asn Physics Teachers. Res: Quantum electrodynamics; interaction of laser beams with matter, Aharonov-Bohm effect. Mailing Add: 1516 W Taylor Dr Carbondale IL 62901

HENNEBERRY, RICHARD CHRISTOPHER, CELL PHYSIOLOGY IN NERVOUS SYSTEM. Current Pos: VIS PROF BIOL, WILLIAMS COL, 95- Personal Data: b Yonkers, NY, Nov 15, 37; m 59, Patricia Roderer; c 4. Educ: St Michael's Col, AB, 59; Univ Mass, Amherst, MS, 66, PhD(microbiol), 69. Honors & Awards: Dir's Award, NIH, 88; Outstanding Serv Medal, USPHS, 89. Prof Exp: Fel molecular biol, Yale Univ, 69-71; chief, Molecular Neurobiol Sect, Lab Molecular Biol, Nat Inst Neurol Dis & Stroke, 71-90; vpres & dir, neurosci prog, Conte Inst Environ Health, Pittsfield, Mass, 90-94. Concurrent Pos: Res consult, Dept Biol, Georgetown Univ, 78-80, Dept Physiol, George Wash Univ Sch Med, 79-90, Neurosci Prog, Williams Col, 93- Mem: AAAS; Sigma Xi; NY Acad Sci; Soc Neurosci. Res: Mechanisms of action of neurotransmitters in mammalian brain, with special emphasis on receptor-mediated neurotoxicity and role of perturbations of energy metabolism in excitatory amino acid neurotoxicity in the etiology of the neurodegenerative disorders. Mailing Add: 439 Shaker Ridge Dr Canaan NY 12029. E-Mail: rhennebe@williams.edu

HENNEBERRY, THOMAS JAMES, ENTOMOLOGY. *Current Pos:* Res entomologist & res leader, Western Region, 51-52 & 55-74, LAB DIR, WESTERN COTTON RES LAB, SCI & EDUC ADMIN-AGR RES, USDA, 74- *Personal Data:* b Milford, Mass, Feb 26, 29; m 51; c 4. *Educ:* Univ Mass, BS, 51; Univ Md, MS, 56, PhD, 60. *Honors & Awards:* Miles Cotton Res Award. *Mem:* Fel Entom Soc Am; Sigma Xi. *Res:* Insect and mite biology; radiation and chemosterilant research; cotton insect research. *Mailing Add:* Agr Res Serv 4135 E Broadway Phoenix AZ 85040

HENNEIKE, HENRY FRED, INORGANIC CHEMISTRY. *Current Pos:* ASSOC PROF INORG CHEM, GA STATE UNIV, 70- *Personal Data:* b Kankakee, Ill, Jan 27, 39; m 58; c 3. *Educ:* Univ Ill, BS, 63, PhD(chem), 67. *Prof Exp:* Asst prof inorg chem, Univ Minn, Minneapolis, 66-70. *Mem:* Am Chem Soc. *Res:* Lewis acid-base interactions in solution, hydrogen bonding and semi-empirical molecular orbital methods applied to inorganic systems. *Mailing Add:* 5815 Silver Ridge Dr Stone Mountain GA 30087-5799

HENNEKE, EDMUND GEORGE, II, MATERIALS SCIENCE, SOLID MECHANICS. *Current Pos:* from asst prof to assoc prof eng mech, 71-78, interim dean, Col Eng, 93-94, PROF ENG SCI & MECH, VA POLYTECH INST & STATE UNIV, 78-, HEAD, ENG SCI & MECH DEPT, 89- *Personal Data:* b Baltimore, Md, May 30, 41; m 63; c Christian & Samantha. *Educ:* Johns Hopkins Univ, BES, 63, MSE, 66, PhD(mech), 68. *Prof Exp:* Asst prof eng sci, Fla State Univ, 68-71. *Concurrent Pos:* Assoc tech ed, Mat Eval; bd dirs, Am Soc Nondestructive Testing, 87-89, 91-93,; chmn, Res Coun, 91-93. *Mem:* Acoust Soc Am; Am Soc Testing & Mat; Am Soc Nondestructive Testing. *Res:* Composite materials; wave propagation in anisotropic media; mechanical properties; non-destructive testing. *Mailing Add:* Dept Eng Sci & Mech Va Polytech Inst & State Univ Blacksburg VA 24061. *Fax:* 540-231-4574; *E-Mail:* henneke@vt.edu

HENNELLY, EDWARD JOSEPH, PHYSICAL CHEMISTRY, RADIOACTIVE WASTE PREPARATION & DISPOSAL. *Current Pos:* RETIRED. *Personal Data:* b Schenectady, NY, Mar 29, 23; m 46, Barbara Sheahan; c 5. *Educ:* Union Col, BS, 43; Princeton Univ, MA, 48, PhD(chem), 49. *Prof Exp:* Chemist, E I du Pont de Nemours & Co Inc, 49-51, reactor physicist, 52-55, sr res supvr, 55-67, res assoc, 67-79, prog coordr, 79-86. *Concurrent Pos:* Vchmn, SC Nuclear Adv Coun, 75-76, chmn, 76-79, mem, 93-94; mem, Coun Sci Soc Pres, 80-81. *Mem:* Am Chem Soc; fel Am Nuclear Soc (vpres/pres elec, 78-79 & pres, 79-80); Sigma Xi. *Res:* Reactor physics; radioisotope production and applications; nuclear fusion technology; nuclear cross sections; radioactive waste technology and disposal. *Mailing Add:* 638 Magnolia St SE Aiken SC 29801-4904

HENNEMAN, HAROLD ALBERT, ANIMAL HUSBANDRY. *Current Pos:* From asst prof to prof animal husb, Mich State Univ, 51-59, dir, Dept Short Courses, 59-66, prof, 66-85, EMER PROF ANIMAL HUSB, MICH STATE UNIV, 85- *Personal Data:* b Belmont, Wis, Nov 20, 18; m 46, Dolores O'Brien; c Linda (DeCelles). *Educ:* Univ Wis, BS, 40; Mich State Col, MS, 42, PhD(animal husb), 53. *Mem:* Fel Am Soc Animal Sci. *Res:* Animal physiology. *Mailing Add:* 1520 Greenview Ave East Lansing MI 48823

HENNEN, JOE FLEETWOOD, BOTANY, MYCOLOGY. *Current Pos:* PROF BOT & CUR ARTHUR HERBARIUM, PURDUE UNIV, 68- *Personal Data:* b Sherman, Tex, Jan 6, 28; m 54; c 1. *Educ:* Southern Methodist Univ, BS, 50; Purdue Univ, MS, 52, PhD, 54. *Prof Exp:* Asst bot, Purdue Univ, 50-54; asst plant pathologist, SDak State Col, 54-58; from assoc prof to prof bot, Ind State Univ, 58-68. *Concurrent Pos:* Vis prof, Biol Inst Sao Paulo, Brazil, 75-76. *Mem:* Mycol Soc Am; Am Phytopath Soc; Soc Plant Taxon. *Res:* Taxonomy of rust fungi; biosystematics of Uredinales of Neotropica. *Mailing Add:* Dept Bot Purdue Univ West Lafayette IN 47907-1968

HENNEN, SALLY, DEVELOPMENTAL BIOLOGY. *Current Pos:* asst prof, 69-72, ASSOC PROF BIOL, MARQUETTE UNIV, 72- *Personal Data:* b New Rochelle, NY, Apr 18, 35. *Educ:* Wellesley Col, BA, 57; Ind Univ, PhD(exp embryol), 62. *Prof Exp:* USPHS res fel, Inst Cancer Res, Pa, 62-63; USPHS res fel, Ind Univ, 63-64, res assoc zool, 64-66; NATO fel, Univ St Andrews, 66-67; res assoc zool, Ind Univ, 67-69. *Mem:* Soc Develop Biol; Am Soc Cell Biol; Int Soc Develop Biologists. *Res:* Nucleocytoplasmic interactions during development; developmental genetics and cytology. *Mailing Add:* Dept Biol Marquette Univ PO Box 1881 Milwaukee WI 53201-1881

HENNES, ROBERT G(RAHAM), civil engineering, for more information see previous edition

HENNESSEY, AUDREY KATHLEEN, MEDICAL INFORMATION SYSTEMS DESIGN, INDUSTRIAL SYSTEMS DESIGN. *Current Pos:* assoc prof comput sci, 82-86, ASSOC PROF INFO SYSTS, TEX TECH UNIV, 87-, DIR INST STUDIES ORGN AUTOMATION, 87- *Personal Data:* b Fairbanks, Alaska, Apr 4, 36; m 63, Gerard; c Brian M & Kathleen E. *Educ:* Stanford Univ, BA, 57; Univ Toronto, HSA(B), 68; Univ Lancaster, Eng, PhD(systs), 82. *Honors & Awards:* Halliburton Found Award Teaching & Res, 86; Distinguished Info Sci Award, Data Processing Mgt Asn, 92. *Prof Exp:* Systs anal, Northern Tel Co, Can, 62-63; pension admin, Mfr Life Ins, Toronto, 64-65; instr off systs, Adult Educ Ctr, Toronto, 65-68; lectr, Off Systs, Salford Col, UK, 68-70; sr lectr data processing, Manchester Polytech, UK, 70-80; lectr comput, Univ Manchester, UK, 80-82. *Concurrent Pos:* Prin investr & consult, Xerox Corp, 85-86, Tex Instruments, 82- & Tex Advan Technol, Prog, 88-94; vis lectr, Fed Law Enforcement Training Ctr, 85-88; prin investr, Systs Explor, 86-87; Am Nat Stand Inst X3VI Comt, Doc Interchange Stand, 87- *Mem:* Inst Elec & Electronics Engrs; Data Processing Mgt Asn; Asn Comput Mach; Soc Mfg Engrs. *Res:* Automated visual inspection; automated document interchange; data interchange and process protocols; knowledge bases systems; development of knowledge-based image analysis facilities for semiconductor inspection and military applications as well as a distributed database for tracking immunization of West Texas children. *Mailing Add:* Tex Tech Univ ISOA MS 2101 Col Bus Admin Tex Tech Univ Lubbock TX 79409-2101. *Fax:* 806-742-3466; *E-Mail:* odakh@ttuacs1.ttu.edu

HENNESSEY, JOHN P, JR, ANALYTICAL BIOCHEMISTRY, VACCINE DEVELOPMENT. *Current Pos:* sr res chemist, Merck Res Labs, 89-91, res fel, 92, assoc dir bio-anal res, 93-96, DIR BIOPROCESS & BIOANALYTICAL RES, MERCK RES LABS, 96- *Personal Data:* b Pensacola, Fla, Mar 31, 56; c Daniel P, Sarah C & Bryan M. *Educ:* Ore State Univ, BS, 78, PhD(biol Oceanog), 86. *Prof Exp:* Fel, Dept Pharmacol, Univ NC, 86-89. *Mem:* AAAS; Am Soc Biochem & Molecular Biol. *Res:* Biological, chemical and physical analysis of biological macromolecules including recombinant products, viruses, and semi-synthetic vaccine components. *Mailing Add:* Merck Res Labs WP44-I130 West Point PA 19486. *E-Mail:* hennessey@merck.com

HENNESSY, JOHN LEROY, COMPUTER SCIENCE. *Current Pos:* from asst prof to assoc prof, 77-86, PROF ELEC ENG & COMPUT SCI, STANFORD UNIV, 86- *Personal Data:* b New York, NY, Sept 22, 52; m 74; c 2. *Educ:* Villanova Univ, BE, 73; State Univ NY, MS, 75, PhD(comput sci), 77. *Prof Exp:* Prog consult, Computation Ctr, Villanova Univ, 71-73, instr intro prog, 72-73; res asst, instr & teaching asst, Comput Sci Dept, State Univ NY, 74-77. *Concurrent Pos:* Prin investr, NSF, 78-80, co-prin investr, TRW, 80-81, Off Naval Res, Lawrence Livermore Lab, 80-81, Defense Advan Res Proj Agency, 81-83 & 82-85; assoc ed, Inst Elec & Electronics Engrs Micro, 81-; chief scientist, MIPS Comput Systs, 84- *Mem:* Inst Elec & Electronics Engrs; Asn Comput Mach. *Res:* Programming languages and implementation: compilers for novel architectures and the design of protable, optimizing compilers; very-large-scale integration design systems and very-large-scale integration architectures, especially processor design. *Mailing Add:* Prof Gates Comput Sci Bldg Rm 308 Stanford Univ Stanford CA 94305

HENNEY, CHRISTOPHER SCOT, IMMUNOLOGY. *Current Pos:* EXEC VPRES & SCI DIR, ICOS CORP, BOTHELL, WASH, 89- *Personal Data:* b Sutton Coldfield, Eng, Feb 4, 41; m 64; c 2. *Educ:* Univ Birmingham, BSc, 62, PhD(exp path), 65, DSc, 73; ARIC, 64. *Honors & Awards:* Pinkham lectr, 90. *Prof Exp:* Fel, Dept Exp Path, Univ Birmingham, 65-66; fel immunol, Children's Asthma Res Inst, Denver, 66-68; immunologist, WHO, Geneva, 68-70; asst prof med, Med Sch, Johns Hopkins Univ, 70-73, assoc prof med & microbiol, 73-78; prof microbiol & immunol, Med Sch, Univ Wash, 78-82; sci dir, Immunex Corp, Seattle, 82-89. *Concurrent Pos:* WHO consult, Ibadan, Nigeria, 70; head prog basic immunol, Fred Hutchinson Cancer Res Ctr, Seattle, 78-; sci med lectr, Case Western Res, 80 & Univ Wash, 80; chmn, Immunol Adv Comt, Am Cancer Soc, 83; Res Career Develop Award, NIH, 72-77. *Mem:* Brit Soc Immunologists; Am Asn Immunologists; Transplantation Soc; Am Soc Exp Pathologists; Reticuloendothelial Soc. *Res:* Quantitation of the cell-mediated immune response; correlations between humoral and cellular immunity; lymphokines; immune regulation; inflammatory diseases. *Mailing Add:* Activated Cell Therapy Inc 291 N Bernardo Ave Mountain View CA 94043. *Fax:* 425-485-0885

HENNEY, DAGMAR RENATE, MATHEMATICS. *Current Pos:* asst prof, 65-70, ASSOC PROF MATH, GEORGE WASHINGTON UNIV, 70- *Personal Data:* b Berlin, Ger; US citizen; c Alan Jr. *Educ:* Univ Miami, BS, 54, MS, 56; Univ Md, PhD(math), 65. *Prof Exp:* Asst, Univ Miami, 54-56; instr math, Univ Md, 56-65. *Concurrent Pos:* Univ pres liaison, Capitol Hill. *Mem:* Hon mem Am Math Soc; Math Asn Am; Sigma Xi; Nat Asn Sci Writers; Austrian Math Asn. *Res:* Functional analysis, especially functional equations; author of numerous publications and books. *Mailing Add:* 6912 Prince Georges Ave Takoma Park MD 20912-5414

HENNEY, HENRY RUSSELL, JR, MOLECULAR BIOLOGY, GENETICS. *Current Pos:* from asst prof to assoc prof, 66-77, PROF BIOL, UNIV HOUSTON, 77- *Personal Data:* b Carnegie, Pa, Apr 3, 34; m 60; c 2. *Educ:* Univ Ariz, BS, 60, MS, 61; Univ Tex, PhD(microbiol), 65. *Honors & Awards:* Scholar award, Am Cancer Soc, 92. *Prof Exp:* Res assoc, Clayton Found Biochem Inst, Univ Tex, 64-66. *Mem:* AAAS; Am Soc Microbiol. *Res:* Molecular biology and differentiation of eukaryotic microbes, especially amoebae (Acanthamoeba). *Mailing Add:* Dept Biol Univ Houston 4800 Calhoun Rd Houston TX 77204-0001. *Fax:* 713-743-2636; *E-Mail:* biolb0@jetson.uh.edu

HENNEY, ROBERT CHARLES, ANALYTICAL CHEMISTRY. *Current Pos:* assoc prof, 64-70, PROF CHEM, MANKATO STATE UNIV, 70- *Personal Data:* b Dunlap, Iowa, June 3, 25; m 53; c 4. *Educ:* Colo State Col Educ, BA, 52; SDak State Univ, MNS, 59; Univ Nebr, MS, 62, PhD(chem), 66. *Prof Exp:* High sch teacher, Iowa, 54-58; high sch prin, Iowa, 59-60; instr chem, Northwest Mo State Col, 62-64. *Mem:* Am Chem Soc; Sigma Xi. *Res:* Polarographic behavior of complex ions. *Mailing Add:* 5 Southview Dr Mankato MN 56001

HENNIG, HARVEY, CHEMICAL ENGINEERING. *Current Pos:* RETIRED. *Personal Data:* b Brazil, SAm, July 11, 19; nat US; m 42; c 1. *Educ:* Stevens Inst Technol, ME, 41. *Prof Exp:* Jr res engr, Res Ctr, Pure Oil Co, Ill, 42, sr res engr, 43-59, sect suprv, 59-61, div dir, 61-65; sr eng assoc, Res Ctr, Unocal Corp, 65-67, supvr process eval, 67-84; consult, 84-85. *Mem:* Am Inst Chem Engrs. *Res:* Petrochemical and petroleum refining processes; butadiene manufacturing, carbon disulfide ex methane and sulfur; synthetic liquid fuels; process economics and design; alternate energy. *Mailing Add:* 880 Morningside Dr No M228 Fullerton CA 92635

HENNIGAN, ROBERT DWYER, ENVIRONMENTAL MANAGEMENT. *Current Pos:* dir grad prog environ sci, State Univ NY, 75-81; prof & chmn environ sci fac, 82-92, PROF POLICY & PROG AFFAIRS, SCH ENVIRON & RESOURCES MGT, STATE UNIV NY COL ENVIRON SCI & FORESTRY, 68-, PROF ENVIRON MGT, SCH ENVIRON & RESOURCES ENG, 81-, EMER PROF, 93- *Personal Data:* b Syracuse, NY, Sept 21, 25; m 50, Virginia Egan; c Robert Jr, Patricia, Joseph, Karen, Peter, William, Daniel & Christopher. *Educ:* Manhattan Col, BCE, 49; Syracuse Univ, MA, 64; Am Acad Environ Eng, dipl. *Honors & Awards:* Bedell Award, Water Pollution Control Fedn, 80. *Prof Exp:* Regional water pollution engr, NY State Dept Health, Syracuse Univ, 49-58, chief water pollution control sect, Albany, 58-60; prin engr, Div Munic Serv, NY State Off Local Govt, 60-65; asst comnr, Div Pure Waters, Dept Health & dir, Bur Water Resources, 65-67. *Concurrent Pos:* Lectr, Rennselaer Polytech Inst, 58-59; mem adv bd, Int Joint Comn US & Can, 65-67; alt mem, NY State Water Resources Comn, 65-67; dir, State Univ Water Resources Ctr, State Univ NY Col Forestry, Syracuse Univ, 67-71; consult, Fed Water Pollution Control Admin, 68, New York City Bd Water Supply, 68-69, Monroe County Pure Waters Agency, 69-70, US Army CEngrs, 70 & Dept Natural Resources, Wis, 70; exec dir, Temp State Comn Water Supply Needs Southeastern NY, 70-75; dir cent NY water qual mgt proj, 75-80; dir, Water Supply Source Protection Proj, NY State Dept Health, 79-81. *Mem:* Fel Am Soc Civil Engrs; Am Pub Health Asn; Am Water Resources Asn; Am Acad Environ Eng; Am Water Works Asn; Sigma Xi; Water Environ Fedn. *Res:* Water supply and water quality management; urban water resources; land use management and control; environmental management and control; water resources management. *Mailing Add:* 3882 Highland Ave Skaneateles NY 13152. *Fax:* 315-470-6915

HENNIGAR, GORDON ROSS, JR, PATHOLOGY. *Current Pos:* PROF PATH & CHMN DEPT, MED UNIV SC, 65- *Personal Data:* b Halifax, NC, Dec 16, 19; m 47; c 5. *Educ:* Dalhousie Univ, MD, 45. *Prof Exp:* Intern, Victoria Gen Hosp, NS, 44-45; asst path, Banting Inst & Dalhousie Univ, 45-46; intern, Union Mem Hosp, MD, 46-47; pathologist, South Baltimore Gen Hosp, 47-48; instr path, Sch Med, Johns Hopkins Univ, 48-50; assoc prof, Med Col Va, 50-57; prof, State Univ NY Downstate Med Ctr & dir labs, Kings County Hosp, 57-65. *Concurrent Pos:* Consult, Off Chief Med Examr, 52-57; consult, Vet Admin Hosp, Charleston, SC & US Naval Hosp. *Mem:* Soc Exp Path; fel Am Soc Clin Path; Am Col Physicians; fel Acad Forensic Sci; fel Int Acad Pathologists. *Res:* Chemical and drug reactions. *Mailing Add:* Dept Path Lab Med Med Univ SC 171 Ashley Ave Charleston SC 29425-0687

HENNIGER, JAMES PERRY, MATHEMATICS. *Current Pos:* asst prof, 67-74, ASSOC PROF MATH, TRENT UNIV, 74- *Personal Data:* b Smiths Falls, Ont, May 30, 38; m 63; c 3. *Educ:* McGill Univ, BSc, 60, MSc, 62, PhD(math), 65. *Prof Exp:* Nat Res Coun Can fel, 65-67. *Mem:* Can Math Cong; Am Math Soc; Math Asn Am. *Res:* erodic theorytems; dynamical systems; ergodic theory. *Mailing Add:* Dept Math Trent Univ Lady Eaton Col 1755 W Bank Dr Peterborough ON K9L 1Z6 Can. *E-Mail:* jhenniger@trentu.ca

HENNING, CARL DOUGLAS, MECHANICAL ENGINEERING, SUPERCONDUCTIVITY. *Current Pos:* dep proj mgr, 78-80, head, Mirror Fusion Prog Off, 81-86, PROG LEADER, FUSION TECHNOL, LAWRENCE LIVERMORE NAT LAB, 86- *Personal Data:* b Cleveland, Ohio, Feb 28, 39; m 62; c Kirsten & Lisa. *Educ:* Ohio Univ, BS, 61; Univ Mich, MS, 63, PhD(mech eng), 65. *Honors & Awards:* Lincoln Arc Welding Found Award, 71 & 80; Outstanding Tech Achievement Award, Am Nuclear Soc, 82. *Prof Exp:* Res engr, Lawrence Livermore Lab, 65-71, proj engr, Controlled Thermonuclear Fusion Res, 71-73; vpres, Intermagnetics Gen Corp, 73-75; chief magnetic systs, Magnetic Fusion Dept, US Dept Energy, 75-78. *Concurrent Pos:* Dep managing dir, Int Thermonuclear Exp Reactor; spec asst, Lab Admin, Pres Off, Univ Calif. *Mem:* Fel Am Nuclear Soc; Fusion Power Asn; Inst Elec & Electronics Engrs. *Res:* Heat transfer; cryogenics; superconducting magnets; magnetic field theory; magnetic fusion energy; lasers. *Mailing Add:* Lawrence Livermore Nat Lab PO Box 808 Livermore CA 94550. *Fax:* 510-422-4667; *E-Mail:* henning1@llnl.gov

HENNING, HARLEY BARRY, ELECTROOPTICS, MATHEMATICAL PHYSICS. *Current Pos:* ENG STAFF SPECIALIST, GDE SYSTS, INC, 93- *Personal Data:* b New York, NY, May 12, 31; m 61; c 3. *Educ:* Univ Mich, BS(elec eng) & BS(math), 53; Yale Univ, ME, 54; Harvard Univ, PhD(appl physics), 59. *Prof Exp:* Sr engr math physics, LFE Corp, 59-64; prin engr electrooptics, Raytheon Corp, 64-71; prin mem eng staff electronics & optics, RCA Corp, 71-72; res staff phys sci, Rand Corp, 72-76; res engr, Northrop Corp, 76-85; tech staff, Hughes Aircraft Corp, 85-88; eng staff specialist, Gen Dynamics, 88-93. *Concurrent Pos:* Lectr mech eng, Northeastern Univ, 67-68; ed reviewer, Inst Elec & Electronics Engrs, 72- *Mem:* Inst Elec & Electronics Engrs. *Res:* Electronics; lasers and holography; lidar, radar and sonar theory; probability theory and mathematical physics; systems analysis; signal processing and information theory; management systems and resource allocation. *Mailing Add:* 18229 Verano Dr Rancho Bernardo CA 92128

HENNING, LESTER ALLAN, CHEMICAL COATINGS. *Current Pos:* RETIRED. *Personal Data:* b Oak Park, Ill, Apr 3, 39; m 73; c 4. *Educ:* Wayne State Univ, BS, 64; Northwestern Univ, MBA, 70. *Prof Exp:* Sr chemist, W P Fuller Co, 65-66; group leader, Desoto, Inc, 66-68, chief chemist, 68-69, prod mgr, 70-72, tech mgr, 73-76, mgr, 77-78, dir res, 80-85, dir, Indust Res & Prod Develop, 79-90, dir qual excellence, 86-90. *Concurrent Pos:* Dir, Soc Mfr Engrs/Asn Finishing Processes, 78-82; lectr, Univ Wis, 82-83. *Mem:* Indust Res Inst; Soc Mfr Engrs/Asn Finishing Processes (vpres, 80-81); Nat Paint & Coatings Asn; Am Soc Qual Control. *Res:* Research and development of coatings and polymers; research computer operations. *Mailing Add:* 346 Sheridon Rd Winthrop Harbor IL 60096

HENNING, RUDOLF E, MICROWAVE ENGINEERING. *Current Pos:* prof & assoc dean col eng, 71-82, actg chmn elec eng, 86-87, PROF ELEC ENG, UNIV SFLA, 82- *Personal Data:* b Hamburg, Ger, Aug 3, 23; US citizen; m 61, Patricia A Miklas; c Patricia E (Irwin). *Educ:* Columbia Univ, BS, 43, MS, 47, DEngSc(elec eng), 54. *Honors & Awards:* Centennial Medal, Inst Elec & Electronics Engrs, 84, Citation Honor, 92. *Prof Exp:* Jr engr, Radio Receptor Co, 46; proj engr, Sperry Gyroscope Co Div, Sperry Rand Corp, 47-54, eng sect head, 54-58, chief engr, Sperry Microwave Electronics Div, 58-70; lectr elec eng & asst dean col eng, Univ SFla, 70-71; dept head eng sci, Naval Electronics Lab Ctr, San Diego, 71. *Concurrent Pos:* Consult, ANRO Eng Inc, 89-; mem, Microwave Theory & Tech Soc Admin Comt, Inst Elec & Electronics Engrs, 66-71, & chmn, 68; evaluator, Inst Elec & Electronics Engrs/ABET Prog, 88-93. *Mem:* Fel Inst Elec & Electronics Engrs; Am Soc Eng Educ; Nat Soc Prof Engrs; Sigma Xi; Soc Photo-Optical Instrumentation Engrs. *Res:* Microwave theory and techniques; high frequency instrumentation; electronic measurement techniques; interdisciplinary electronics; electronic sensing and detection techniques; microwave/optical systems. *Mailing Add:* Dept Elec Eng Univ SFla Tampa FL 33620. *Fax:* 813-974-5250; *E-Mail:* henning@ec.usf.edu

HENNING, SUSAN JUNE, GASTROENTEROLOGY, DEVELOPMENTAL BIOLOGY. *Current Pos:* PROF, BAYLOR COL MED, 89- *Personal Data:* b Griffith, Australia, June 6, 46; m 74, M Vikram Rao; c Justin, Colin & Mitchell. *Educ:* Univ Melbourne, BS, 67, PhD(biochem), 71. *Honors & Awards:* Merit Award, NIH, 89. *Prof Exp:* Fel develop biochem, Stanford Univ, 71-74 & Fels Res Inst, 74-75; asst prof biol, Temple Univ, 75-79; from assoc prof to prof biol, Univ Houston, 79-89. *Mem:* Endocrine Soc; Am Gastroenterol Asn; Soc Pediat Res; Soc Develop Biol; Soc Exp Biol Med; Sigma Xi. *Res:* Development of intestinal function in mammals, with emphasis on the changes that occur at weaning; hormonal and dietary regulation of these changes on a molecular level; gene transfer into intestinal epithelium. *Mailing Add:* Dept Pediat Baylor Col Med One Baylor Plaza Houston TX 77030. *Fax:* 713-770-3633

HENNING, WALTER FRIEDRICH, NUCLEAR PHYSICS. *Current Pos:* physicist, 76-81, sr physicist, 81-86, DIR PHYSICS DIV, ARGONNE NAT LAB, 91- *Personal Data:* b Bad Hersfeld, Ger, Jan 13, 39. *Educ:* Darmstadt Tech Univ, dipl, 66; Tech Univ Munich, PhD(physics), 68. *Prof Exp:* Asst prof physics, Tech Univ Munich, 68-76; prof physics, Univ Mainz, 86-91. *Mem:* Am Phys Soc; Ger Phys Soc. *Res:* Nuclear physics research with heavy and light ion induced reactions; nuclear instrumentation in heavy ion research. *Mailing Add:* Argonne Nat Lab 9700 S Cass Ave Bldg 203 Argonne IL 60439

HENNINGER, ANN LOUISE, PHYSIOLOGY. *Current Pos:* registr & dir spec prog, Wartburg Col, 83-85, assoc prof biol & registr, 85-89, assoc prof, 89-96, PROF BIOL & CHAIR DEPT, WARTBURG COL, 96- *Personal Data:* b Chambersburg, Pa, Apr 13, 46; m 73, Mark F Trax. *Educ:* Wilson Col, AB, 68; Univ Mich, PhD(physiol), 73. *Prof Exp:* Asst prof, Lebanon Valley Col, 73-81, assoc prof biol & dir continuing educ, 80-83. *Mem:* Am Physiol Soc; Nat Sci Teachers Asn; Sigma Xi; Soc Col Sci Teachers; Human Anat & Physiol Soc. *Res:* Baroreceptor control of heart rate; effect of diet on serum cholesterol and triglyceride levels. *Mailing Add:* Wartburg Col Waverly IA 50677. *Fax:* 319-352-8606; *E-Mail:* ahenninger@wartburg.edu

HENNINGER, ERNEST HERMAN, SCIENCE, TECHNOLOGY & SOCIETY. *Current Pos:* asst prof, 68-74, PROF PHYSICS, DEPAUW UNIV, 68-, PRE ENG ADV, 76- *Personal Data:* b Indianapolis, Ind, Dec 1, 32; m 59; c 2. *Educ:* Wabash Col, BA, 55; Harvard Univ, MAT, 56; Purdue Univ, MS, 62, PhD(physics), 66. *Prof Exp:* Instr physics, Purdue Univ, 56-59, asst, 59-66; res fel chem physics, Calif Inst Technol, 66-68. *Concurrent Pos:* Res metallic glasses, Oak Ridge Nat Lab, 81-82; pres, Ind Sect, Am Asn Physics Teachers, 85-86. *Mem:* Am Phys Soc; Am Soc Eng Educ; Am Asn Physics Teachers. *Mailing Add:* 51 Rd 43 S Greencastle IN 46135

HENNINGFIELD, MARY FRANCES, ENTERAL NUTRITION, IMMUNOLOGY. *Current Pos:* CLIN RES ASSOC, ROSS LABS, 89- *Personal Data:* b Burlington, Wis, Aug 15, 61. *Educ:* Univ Wis-Madison, BS, 83, MS, 86, PhD(nutrit sci), 88. *Prof Exp:* Postdoctorate, Temple Univ, 89. *Mem:* Am Inst Nutrit; Clin Immunol Soc. *Res:* Research of effects of enteral nutrition for trauma/intensive care unit patients. *Mailing Add:* 1263 Millstone Square Westerville OH 43081. *Fax:* 614-624-3705

HENNINGS, GEORGE, ENVIRONMENTAL BIOLOGY. *Current Pos:* from assoc prof to prof, 60-87, EMER PROF BIOL, KEAN COL NJ, 88- *Personal Data:* b Mt Vernon, NY, June 16, 22; m 68, Dorothy Grant. *Educ:* Montclair State Col, BA, 47, MA, 48; Columbia Univ, EdD(sci educ), 56; Rutgers Univ, MS, 68. *Prof Exp:* Pub sch teacher, NJ, 47-48 & NY, 48-52; asst prof sci, Ball State Teachers Col, 52-55; chmn dept, NJ High Sch, 55-60.

Mem: AAAS; Nat Sci Teachers Asn. *Res:* Science education; writer of teacher preparation books in science and social studies; freelance editor and writer of student study and test materials for textbooks, editor and reviewer children's science books. *Mailing Add:* 21 Flintlock Dr Warren NJ 07059

HENNINGS, HENRY, ONCOLOGY, CARCINOGENESIS. *Current Pos:* staff fel, 71-74, RES CHEMIST, NAT CANCER INST, 74- *Personal Data:* b Elyria, Ohio, June 30, 41; m 81, Marsha Higby; c William H. *Educ:* Ohio State Univ, BS, 63; Univ Wis, PhD(exp oncol), 68. *Prof Exp:* Wis Div Res, Am Cancer Soc res fel oncol, Univ Oslo, 68-70; res assoc, McArdle Lab, Univ Wis, 70. *Mem:* AAAS; Am Asn Cancer Res; Tissue Cult Asn. *Res:* Chemical carcinogenesis in mouse skin; epidermal cell culture; control of epidermal proliferation and differentiation; genetics of susceptibility to carcinogenesis. *Mailing Add:* Rm 3B26 Bldg 37 Nat Cancer Inst Bethesda MD 20892. *Fax:* 301-496-8709; *E-Mail:* henningh@dc37a.nci.nih.gov

HENNION, GEORGE FELIX, ORGANIC CHEMISTRY. *Current Pos:* RETIRED. *Personal Data:* b South Bend, Ind, Aug 23, 10; m 33; c 4. *Educ:* Univ Notre Dame, BS, 32, MSc, 33, PhD(org chem), 35. *Prof Exp:* Asst chem, Univ Notre Dame, 32-35; from instr to assoc prof, 35-45, dir res chem, 42-45, Nieuwland prof chem, 45-76. *Mem:* AAAS; Am Chem Soc. *Res:* Acetylene chemistry; medicinal agents; organoboron compounds; reaction mechanisms. *Mailing Add:* 1441 E LaSalle Ave South Bend IN 46617-3327

HENNIS, HENRY EMIL, ORGANIC CHEMISTRY. *Current Pos:* RETIRED. *Personal Data:* b Madelia, Minn, Oct 23, 25; m 51. *Educ:* Univ Minn, BCh, 50; Univ Mo, PhD(chem), 56. *Prof Exp:* Org chemist, Dow Chem Co, 56-57, proj leader, 57-63, group leader, 63-71, assoc scientist, 71-86. *Concurrent Pos:* Instr org chem, Cent Mich Univ, 64-69. *Mem:* AAAS; Am Chem Soc; Sigma Xi; NY Acad Sci. *Res:* Organic chemical syntheses; chemical reaction mechanisms; chemical process development. *Mailing Add:* 4959 W Baker Rd RFD 3 Coleman MI 48618-9364

HENNON, DAVID KENT, PEDIATRIC DENTISTRY, ORTHODONTICS. *Current Pos:* RETIRED. *Personal Data:* b Midland, Ind, Oct 20, 33; m 57, Clarice F Graves; c David B & Michael K. *Educ:* Ind Univ, AB, 57, DDS, 60, MSD, 75; Am Bd Pediat Dent, dipl, 80, cert orthod, 83. *Prof Exp:* USPHS fel, Ind Univ-Purdue Univ, 60-62; from asst prof to assoc prof prev dent, 62-74, assoc prof, 74-79, prof pediat dent, sch Dent, 79-88, prof orthod & pediat dent, 88-95. *Concurrent Pos:* Pediat dentist & orthodontist, Craniofacial Anomales Team. *Mem:* Am Dent Asn; Am Asn Orthodontists; Am Acad Pediat Dent; Am Soc Clin Hypn; Am Soc Dent Children; fel Am Col Dentists. *Res:* Orthodontic treatment and management of oral hygiene in these patients; craniofacial growth in cleft lip and palate patients and preventive dentistry, pediatric dentistry, orthodontics. *Mailing Add:* Sch Dent Ind Univ-Purdue Univ Indianapolis IN 46202-5186

HENNY, CHARLES JOSEPH, FIELD RISK ASSESSMENT, POPULATION STUDIES. *Current Pos:* LEADER, PAC NORTHWEST RES STA, US NAT BIOL SURV, CORVALLIS, ORE, 76- *Personal Data:* b Salem, Ore, Mar 20, 43; m 67; c 2. *Educ:* Ore State Univ, BS, 65, MS, 67, PhD(wildlife ecol), 71. *Prof Exp:* Res biologist, US Fish & Wildlife Serv, Laurel, Md, 70-74; leader forest environ studies, US Fish & Wildlife Serv, Denver, Colo, 74-76. *Concurrent Pos:* Vis prof, Ohio State Univ, 72; assoc prof, Ore State Univ, 76-87, prof, 87-; assoc ed, J Raptor Res, 90- *Mem:* Wildlife Soc; Am Ornithologists Union; Sigma Xi; Am Soc Mammalogists; Raptor Res Found. *Res:* Study environmental contaminants, pesticides, trace elements, industrial pollutants and their effects on natural populations of wildlife-primarily birds in the Pacific Northwest with special interest in birds of prey. *Mailing Add:* 884 NW Chipmunk Pl Corvallis OR 97333-3706

HENRICH, CHRISTOPHER JOHN, PURE MATHEMATICS. *Current Pos:* systs programmer, Perkin-Elmer Corp, 75-76, sr mem tech staff, 76-78, prin mem tech staff, 78-88, CONSULT MEM TECH STAFF, CONCURRENT COMPUTER CORP, 88- *Personal Data:* b Brooklyn, NY, Feb 16, 42. *Educ:* Princeton Univ, AB, 62; Harvard Univ, MA, 65, PhD(math), 68. *Prof Exp:* Instr math, Stevens Inst Technol, 66-67 & Fordham Univ, 67-68; Joseph Fells Ritt instr, Columbia Univ, 68-71; asst prof, Fordham Univ, 71-75. *Concurrent Pos:* Consult, Cornell Aeronaut Lab, 66-67. *Mem:* Am Math Soc; Math Asn Am; Asn Comput Mach. *Res:* Abstract analysis group representations; several complex variables; harmonic analysis; partial differential equations. *Mailing Add:* ITex Systems Inc 170 Patterson Ave Two Crescent Place Shrewsbury NJ 07701

HENRICH, CURTIS J, CELL BIOLOGY. *Current Pos:* SR SCIENTIST CELL BIOL, LIFE TECHNOL INC, 89- *Mailing Add:* Dept Cell Biol Life Technol Inc 8717 Grovemont Circle PO Box 6009 Gaithersburg MD 20877-4194. *Fax:* 301-948-8977

HENRICH, VICTOR E, SURFACE PHYSICS. *Current Pos:* PROF, DEPT APPL PHYSICS, YALE UNIV, 78- *Personal Data:* b Detroit, Mich, Oct 1, 39; m 67; c 2. *Educ:* Univ Mich, BSE, 61, MS, 62, PhD(physics), 67. *Hon Degrees:* MA, Yale Univ, 83. *Prof Exp:* Staff mem solid state physics, Lincoln Lab, Mass Inst Technol, 67-78. *Mem:* Fel Am Phys Soc; Am Vacuum Soc; Catalysis Soc; AAAS. *Res:* Electron spectroscopy; surface structure; surface physics; chemisorption; catalysis. *Mailing Add:* Dept Appl Physics Yale Univ PO Box 2157 New Haven CT 06520

HENRICH, WILLIAM LLOYD, NEPHROLOGY. *Current Pos:* chief med serv, 95-96, PROF MED, PROF PHYSIOL & MOLECULAR MED, PROF & CHMN, DEPT MED, MED COL OHIO, 95- *Personal Data:* b Aug 7, 47; m, Mary L Dennis; c John M & Emily K. *Educ:* Columbia Univ, AB, 68; Baylor Univ, MD, 72. *Honors & Awards:* Pres Award, Nat Kidney Found, 89 & 96, Distinguished Serv Award, 90. *Prof Exp:* Chief, Home Dialysis Unit, Vet Admin Med Ctr, Dallas, 78-81, chief Renal Serv, 78-83, assoc chief staff res & develop, 89-95; fac, Univ Tex Southwestern Med Sch, Dallas, 78-95. *Concurrent Pos:* Fel, Coun High Blood Pressure Res, Am Heart Asn; mem, Am Bd Int Med, Nephrology; chmn, Popular Med Comt, Nat Kidney Found, Pub Policy Comn, Health & Sci Affairs Comt; assoc prof med, Health Sci Ctr, Univ Tex, 83- *Mem:* Am Soc Clin Invest; Asn Am Physicians; Am Fedn Med Res; Am Clin & Climat Asn; fel Am Heart Asn. *Res:* Renin-angiotensin system; hemodynamics of dialysis patients; analgesics and kidney disease. *Mailing Add:* Med Col Ohio 3000 Arlington Ave PO Box 10008 Toledo OH 43699-0008. *Fax:* 419-382-0354; *E-Mail:* whenrich@aol.com

HENRICHS, PAUL MARK, PHYSICAL ORGANIC CHEMISTRY. *Current Pos:* FEL, NYCOMED INC, 93- *Personal Data:* b Roswell, NMex, June 18, 43; m 68; c 2. *Educ:* Rice Univ, BA, 65; Univ Calif, Los Angeles, PhD(org chem), 70. *Prof Exp:* Fel, Univ Basel, Switz, 70-71, Univ SC, 71-73; res assoc, Eastman Kodak Co, 73-90, Exxon Chem Co, 90-92. *Concurrent Pos:* Chair, Exp NMR Conf, 84. *Mem:* Am Chem Soc; Royal Chem Soc; Sigma Xi; Int Biomed Optics Soc. *Res:* Determination of structure and dynamics of dissolved and solid organic compounds and polymers, primarily with nuclear magnetic resonance. *Mailing Add:* 40 Stonehurst Ct Wayne PA 19087. *E-Mail:* mark.henrichs@americas.nycomed.com

HENRICHSEN, COLLEEN ANNETTE, HEALTH & SCIENCE PUBLIC INFORMATION. *Current Pos:* pub commun specialist, Warren Grant Magnuson Clin Ctr, NIH, 80-86, dep chief, 86-88, chief, Div Comput Res & Technol, 88-90, CHIEF, CLIN CTR COMMUN, WARREN GRANT MAGNUSON CLIN CTR, NIH, 90- *Educ:* Brigham Young Univ, BA, 73. *Prof Exp:* Pub info specialist, Cabinet Comt Opportunities Spanish Speaking People, 73-74; press aide, Rep Larry P McDonald, 75-78; pub commun specialist, Brigham Young Univ, 78-79; dir res, US Chamber Com, Washington, DC, 79-80. *Mailing Add:* Warren Grant Magnuson Clin Ctr 9000 Rockville Pike Bldg 10 Rm 1C255 Bethesda MD 20892-1170

HENRICI, CARL RESSLER, ELECTRONICS ENGINEERING. *Current Pos:* RETIRED. *Personal Data:* b Minneapolis, Minn, Sept 11, 15; m 40, Jill Kuntz. *Educ:* Univ Minn, BEE, 37. *Prof Exp:* Engr, Collins Radio Co, 40-55, dir res & develop, Staff Div, 56-57, dir mfg, Tex Mfg Div, 57-59, proj dir, Commun Systs, Alpha Corp, 59-62, asst dir, Spacecraft Systs Div, 62-71, eng admin staff, 72-73, prog mgr, Tactical Air Navig, Rockwell Int Corp, Collins Govt Avionics Div, 73-77, prog mgr, very high frequency commun, 77-81. *Mem:* Sigma Xi. *Res:* Electronic systems. *Mailing Add:* 304 Red Fox Rd SE Cedar Rapids IA 52403-2048

HENRICK, CLIVE ARTHUR, ORGANIC CHEMISTRY, SELECTIVE PESTICIDES. *Current Pos:* chief chemist, Zoecon Corp, 69-71, dir chem res, 71-87, DIR CHEM & ANALYTICAL RES, SANDOZ CROP PROTECTION, ZOECON RES INST, 88- *Personal Data:* b Big Bell, Australia, Jan 13, 41; m 95, Solita Abrera; c 3. *Educ:* Univ Western Australia, BSc Hons, 62, PhD(org chem), 65. *Prof Exp:* Queen Elizabeth II fel org chem, Univ Sydney, 65-67; fel org chem, Syntex Res, 67-68, sr chemist, 68-69. *Mem:* Royal Soc Chem; Am Chem Soc; AAAS; Weed Sci Soc Am. *Res:* Organic chemistry with emphasis on the synthesis of biologically active compounds useful for the selective control of insect and arachnid pests and of weeds; insect hormones and pheromones; herbicides. *Mailing Add:* 975 California Ave Palo Alto CA 94304-1104

HENRICKS, DONALD MAURICE, BIOCHEMISTRY, ENDOCRINOLOGY. *Current Pos:* assoc prof, 68-75, PROF BIOCHEM, CLEMSON UNIV, 75- *Personal Data:* b Quincy, Ill, Mar 13, 36; m 57; c 4. *Educ:* Univ Mo, BS, 57, PhD(biochem), 65; Purdue Univ, MS, 61. *Prof Exp:* Asst prof animal sci, Iowa State Univ, 65-68. *Concurrent Pos:* Consult, Syntex Res Corp, 73- *Mem:* Am Chem Soc; Am Physiol Soc; Am Soc Animal Sci; Endocrine Soc; Soc Study Reproduction. *Res:* Occurance and role of steroid hormones and gonadotropins in reproductive processes; determination of steroid residues by radioimmunoassay in mammalian tissues; bioassay and radioimmunoassay of gonadotropins. *Mailing Add:* Dept Vet & Animal Sci Clemson SC 29634

HENRICKSEN, THOMAS ALVA, GEOLOGY. *Current Pos:* SR GEOLOGIST, US BORAX & CHEM CORP, 77- *Personal Data:* b Marinette, Wis. *Educ:* Univ Wis-Oshkosh, BS, 69; Ore State Univ, PhD(geol), 74. *Prof Exp:* Geologist, Asarco, Inc, 74-77. *Mem:* Geol Soc Am; Am Inst Mining Metall & Petrol Engrs; Soc Econ Geol. *Res:* Planning and carrying out base and precious metal exploration programs in the Pacific Northwest. *Mailing Add:* 5812 E 25th St Spokane WA 99223

HENRICKSON, CHARLES HENRY, COLLEGE-HIGH SCHOOL CHEMISTRY INTERFACE. *Current Pos:* PROF CHEM, WESTERN KY UNIV, 68- *Personal Data:* b Cornell, Wis, Nov 27, 38; m 81; c 2. *Educ:* Univ Wis-Eau Claire, BS, 62; Univ Iowa, PhD(chem), 68. *Prof Exp:* Chemist, 3M Co, 62-64. *Concurrent Pos:* Lectr gen chem, Univ Ill, 76-77; mem, Comt Chem Health Professions, Am Chem Soc, 81-; res, Univ Calif, Berkeley, 86. *Mem:* Am Chem Soc; Sigma Xi. *Res:* Textbooks and laboratory manuals in general chemistry and health-related areas; computer-based instructional materials in general chemistry; computational chemistry; distonic ion reaction pathways. *Mailing Add:* Dept Chem Western Ky Univ Bowling Green KY 42101

HENRICKSON, EILER LEONARD, ECONOMIC GEOLOGY. *Current Pos:* PROF & CHMN, DEPT GEOL, COLO COL, 87- *Personal Data:* b Crosby, Minn, Apr 23, 20; m 78; c 4. *Educ:* Carleton Col, BA, 43; Univ Minn, PhD, 56. *Prof Exp:* Geologist, US Geol Surv, Calif, 43-44; instr geol, Carleton Col, 46-47 & Univ Minn, 47-48; from instr to asst prof, Carleton Col, 48-53; instr, Univ Minn, 53-54; from asst prof to prof, 54-70, Charles L Denison Prof Geol & Chmn Dept, Carleton Col, 70-87. *Concurrent Pos:* Consult, Jones & Laughlin Steel Co, 46-58, Fremont Mining Co, 58-61, C T Schjeldahl Co, 61-62, Bear Creek Mining Co, 65-66, Argonne Nat Lab, 66-75, Minn Messenia Exped, 66- & Exxon-Esso Eastern, 77-78; Fulbright res scholar, Greece, 69-70. *Mem:* AAAS; Mineral Soc Am; Soc Econ Geologists; Nat Asn Geol Teachers; Geol Soc Am; Sigma Xi. *Res:* Economic geology of metals; metamorphic geology; mineralogy and petrology; structural and field geology; trace element analysis of copper and bronze artifacts and copper and tin ores for correlation studies; adaptation of geochemistry and geophysics to archaeological studies; geology of Greece and Egypt. *Mailing Add:* Dept Geol Colo Col 14 E Cache La Poudre Colorado Springs CO 80903-3243

HENRICKSON, JAMES SOLBERG, PLANT TAXONOMY. *Current Pos:* From instr to assoc prof, 66-77, PROF BOT, CALIF STATE UNIV, LOS ANGELES, 77- *Personal Data:* b Eau Claire, Wis, Oct 15, 40; m, Maria Vela; c Jonathan & Kelsey R. *Educ:* Wis State Univ, Eau Claire, BS, 62; Claremont Grad Sch & Univ Ctr, MA, 64, PhD(bot), 68. *Concurrent Pos:* Dir, Independent Environ Consults. *Mem:* Int Asn Plant Taxon; Bot Soc Am; Am Asn Plant Taxon. *Res:* Flora of Chihuahuan-Mojavean deserts; plant anatomy; Toxonomy Woody Rosaceoe. *Mailing Add:* Dept Biol Calif State Univ Los Angeles CA 90032. *Fax:* 213-343-2097

HENRICKSON, ROBERT LEE, FOOD SCIENCE. *Current Pos:* RETIRED. *Personal Data:* b Hays, Kans, Jan 31, 20; m 42; c Cherlyn, Gary & Sondra. *Educ:* Kans State Col, BS, 47, MS, 49; Univ Mo, PhD(meat technol), 54. *Prof Exp:* Asst prof animal sci, Kans State Col, 47-49; assoc prof, WVa Univ, 49-51; asst prof, Univ Mo, 51-58; prof animal sci, Okla State Univ, 59- *Mem:* Inst Food Technologists; Am Meat Sci Asn; Am Soc Animal Sci. *Res:* Histochemical characteristics of muscle as a food; removal of glucose from pork; microbial flora in fresh pork sausage; characteristics of the bovine muscle fiber as influenced by prerigor boning, precooking, degeneration; development as an instrument for measuring the physical properties of a muscle fiber. *Mailing Add:* 704 W Hillcrest Ave Stillwater OK 74075-1309

HENRIE, THOMAS A, METALLURGY. *Current Pos:* RETIRED. *Personal Data:* b Sutherland, Utah, Feb 6, 23; m 43, Faye Davis; c Thomas D, Myrna J, Robert A, Jane, David & Janice. *Educ:* Brigham Young Univ, BS, 52; Univ Utah, PhD(metall), 55. *Honors & Awards:* Douglas Gold Medal, Am Inst Mech Engrs. *Prof Exp:* Res chemist titanium metall, Metals Res Labs, Union Carbide Corp, 55-58; supvry phys chemist, Fundamental Res, US Bur Mines, 58-60, supv res metallurgist, Reno Metall Ctr, 60-66, res dir, 66-70, dep dir mineral resources & environ develop, 70-86, assoc dir mineral & mat res & develop, 76-86. *Mem:* Electrochem Soc; Am Inst Mining, Metall & Petrol Engrs. *Res:* Physical chemistry of process metallurgy; fused salt reactions with reactive metals and the slag metal interfacial reactions. *Mailing Add:* 657 S 1050 E Orem UT 84058

HENRIKSEN, MELVIN, MATHEMATICS. *Current Pos:* chmn dept, 69-72, PROF MATH, HARVEY MUDD COL, 69- *Personal Data:* b New York, NY, Feb 23, 27; m 46, 64; c 3. *Educ:* City Col New York, BS, 48; Univ Wis, MS, 49, PhD(math), 51. *Prof Exp:* Asst math, Univ Wis, 48-50, instr, Exten Div, 50-51; asst prof, Univ Ala, 51-52; from instr to prof, Purdue Univ, 52-65; prof & head dept, Case Inst Technol, 65-68; res assoc, Univ Calif, Berkeley, 68-69. *Concurrent Pos:* Sloan fel, 56-58; mem, Inst Advan Study, Princeton Univ, 56-57 & 63-64; vis prof, Wayne State Univ, 60-61; res assoc math, Univ Man, 75-76; vis prof, Wesleyan Univ, 78-79, 82-83 & 86-87. *Mem:* Am Math Soc; Math Asn Am. *Res:* Algebra; ring theory; lattice-ordered rings; rings of continuous functions; general topology. *Mailing Add:* Dept Math Harvey Mudd Col Claremont CA 91711-5990

HENRIKSEN, RICHARD NORMAN, ASTROPHYSICS. *Current Pos:* PROF PHYSICS, QUEEN'S UNIV, KINGSTON, ONT, 78- *Personal Data:* b St John, NB, Dec 14, 40; m 62; c 3. *Educ:* McGill Univ, BSc, 62; Univ Manchester, PhD(astron), 65. *Prof Exp:* From asst prof to assoc prof physics, Queen's Univ, Kingston, Ont, 66-72; sr res fel astron, Astron Ctr, Univ Sussex, Eng, 72-73. *Concurrent Pos:* Nat Res Coun grant, 66-85; Alexander von Humboldt Found fel, 72-73 & 80-81; sr res assoc, Stanford, 80-81; chmn coun, Can Inst Theoret Physics, Univ Toronto, 83-85 & fel, 84-85, coun, 88-92; vis scientist Saclay-Meudan (France) 88-89. *Mem:* Can Astron Soc; Am Astron Soc; Int Astron Union. *Res:* Galactic structure and evolution; radio galaxies; gravitational collapse; x-ray sources and pulsars; relativistic astrophysics; cosmology. *Mailing Add:* Astron Group Dept Physics Queen's Univ Kingston ON K7L 3N6 Can

HENRIKSON, ERNEST HILMER, speech pathology, for more information see previous edition

HENRIKSON, FRANK W, RESEARCH EVALUATION, STRATEGIC PLANNING, TECHNOLOGY ASSESSMENT, MEASUREMENT & SENSING SYSTEM APPLICATIONS FOR PROCESSING SYSTEMS. *Current Pos:* assoc dir combat rations, 88-90, MGR IN-LINE SENSORS PROJ, 88-, ASSOC DIR DEVELOP & ADMIN, CTR ADVAN FOOD TECHNOL, COOK COL, RUTGERS UNIV, 90- *Personal Data:* b Brooklyn, NY, Oct 2, 35; m 64, Doris; c John & Karin. *Educ:* Polytechnic Univ Brooklyn, BME, 56; Stevens Inst Technol, MS, 60. *Prof Exp:* Sect head, Acoust, Mech & Mat Eng Exxon Res & Eng, 60-68, mgr, Mech & Mat Eng Lab, 60-78, mgr, Eng Res & Develop, 78-81, sr staff adv to vpres, Corp Res, 81-86; consult to mgt, Ayerst Pharmaceut Lab, Bell Atlantic Mobile Systs, Exxon Res & Eng, Round Valley Comput, Rutgers Univ, 86-88. *Concurrent Pos:* Invited speaker, Res & Develop Assoc, 91; Am Inst Baking-Sci Adv Coun, 92; NY Inst Food Technol, 93; mem new prod subcomt, Inst Food Technologists, 92- *Mem:* Inst Food Technologists; Am Soc Mech Engrs; Instrument Soc Am. *Res:* Research, development, management, stewardship and technology transfer of a major program in online sensing for measurement and control of food processing systems; administration of intellectual property protection. *Mailing Add:* Ctr Advan Food Tech Cook Col Rutgers Univ PO Box 231 New Brunswick NJ 08903. *Fax:* 732-932-8690; *E-Mail:* henrikson@aesop.rutgers.edu

HENRIKSON, KATHERINE POINTER, ENZYMOLOGY, STEROIDS. *Current Pos:* RES SCIENTIST, DIV LABS & RES, NY STATE HEALTH DEPT, 79- *Personal Data:* b Erie, Pa, Oct 4, 39; m 66; c 2. *Educ:* Univ Rochester, BA, 61; Harvard Univ, MA, 63, PhD(biol chem), 68. *Prof Exp:* Res scientist, Commonwealth Sci & Indust Res Orgn, 67-69; res assoc, Col Physicians & Surgeons, Columbia Univ, 70-71; adj asst prof biochem, Sch Dent, Fairleigh Dickinson Univ, 73-74. *Concurrent Pos:* Res assoc, Albany Med Col, 76-79, asst prof biochem, 79-93; lect biol, State Univ NY, Albany, 85; asst prof, NY State Univ, 86-92, assoc prof, Grad Sch Pub Health, 93-, adj assoc prof, 94- *Mem:* AAAS; Microbiol Soc; Sigma Xi; Endocrine Soc; Am Soc Biochem & Molecular Biol; Am Women Sci. *Res:* Role of thrombin in normal metastatic growth. *Mailing Add:* Wadworth Ctr Lab & Res Ny State Health Dept PO Box 509 Albany NY 12201-0509. *Fax:* 518-473-1505

HENRIKSON, RAY CHARLES, CELL BIOLOGY. *Current Pos:* assoc prof, 76-89, PROF ANAT, ALBANY MED COL, 89-, COORDR ANAT EDUC. *Personal Data:* b Worcester, Mass, May 22, 37; m 66, Katherine Pointer; c Charles & Andrew. *Educ:* Univ Mass, BSc, 59; Brown Univ, MSc, 61; Boston Univ, PhD(biol), 66. *Prof Exp:* Instr dermat, Sch Med, Boston Univ, 66-67; res scientist animal physiol, Commonwealth Sci & Indust Res Orgn, Sydney, Australia, 67-69; asst prof anat, Col Physicians & Surgeons, Columbia Univ, 69-76. *Mem:* AAAS; Am Soc Cell Biol; Am Asn Anatomists; Sigma Xi. *Res:* Ultrastructure of cutaneous cells and appendages; transport across epithelia; computer assisted instruction. *Mailing Add:* Anat (A-135) Albany Med Col Albany NY 12208. *Fax:* 518-262-5136

HENRIKSSON, THOMAS MARTIN, ANALYTICAL METHODS, BIOPHARMACEUTICALS. *Current Pos:* scientist, 91-92, PRIN SCIENTIST, CHIRON CORP, 92- *Personal Data:* b Kvistofta, Sweden, Dec 13, 51; US citizen; m 80, Diana Lander; c Sarah & Kristofer. *Educ:* Univ Lund, BS, 73, PhD(biochem), 82. *Prof Exp:* Fel, Univ Calif, Berkeley, 82-85; sr res chemist, Sclavo Inc, 85-88; res scientist, Athena Neurosci, 88-89; scientist, Cetus Corp, 89-91. *Mem:* Am Chem Soc; Am Asn Clin Chem; AAAS. *Res:* Analytical methods development (especially immunoassay and molecular biology) for biopharmaceutical products. *Mailing Add:* 4560 Horton St Emeryville CA 94608. *E-Mail:* thomas_henriksson@cc.chiron.com

HENRIQUEZ, THEODORE AURELIO, ACOUSTICS. *Current Pos:* CONSULT, 89- *Personal Data:* b Tampa, Fla, July 20, 34; m 56; c 6. *Educ:* Univ Tampa, BS, 55. *Prof Exp:* Physicist, Naval Underwater Explosion Res Div, 56-57; mathematician, Gen Elec Corp, 57-59; physicist, Underwater Sound Ref Lab, 59-71; sr consult, Naval Res Lab, Underwater Sound Ref Div, 71-89. *Mem:* Fel Acoust Soc Am. *Res:* Development of underwater electro-acoustic transducers. *Mailing Add:* 633 McArthur Dr Orlando FL 32839

HENRY, ALLAN FRANCIS, PHYSICS. *Current Pos:* prof, 69-95, EMER PROF NUCLEAR ENG, MASS INST TECHNOL, 95- *Personal Data:* b Philadelphia, Pa, Jan 12, 25. *Educ:* Yale Univ, BS, 45, MS, 47, PhD(physics), 50. *Prof Exp:* Mgr, Theoret Physics Sect, Bettis Atomic Power Lab, Westinghouse Elec Corp, 50-59, mgr, Reactor Theory Sect, 59-69. *Mem:* Nat Acad Eng; Am Nuclear Soc. *Res:* Molecular spectroscopy reactor theory. *Mailing Add:* Dept Nuclear Eng Mass Inst Technol Cambridge MA 02139

HENRY, ARNOLD WILLIAM, POLYMER SCIENCE. *Current Pos:* tech specialist & proj mgr, 76-93, PRIN SCIENTIST, XEROX CORP, 93- *Personal Data:* b Williamsport, Pa, June 16, 38; m 61, Frances Snider; c Debra & Staci. *Educ:* Cornell Univ, BChemE, 61; Princeton Univ, MScE, 62; Univ Akron, PhD(polymer sci), 67. *Prof Exp:* Assoc research scientist polymer res, Jet Propulsion Labs, 62-64; res scientist silicone rubber, Union Carbide Corp, 66-70; mgr res & develop elec insulation, Bishop Elec Div, Sola Basic Industs, 70-76. *Mem:* Am Chem Soc; Sigma Xi. *Res:* Optimization of electrical and physical properties of polymers; high temperature polymers; thermally conductive polymers; elastomers. *Mailing Add:* 43 Deer Creek Rd Pittsford NY 14534-4152

HENRY, BOYD (HERBERT), MATHEMATICS. *Current Pos:* from assoc prof to prof math, 77-91, DIR MATH & SCI RESOURCE CTR, COL IDAHO, 91- *Personal Data:* b Bronson, Iowa, Feb 19, 25; m 48, Eileen Larson; c Lois, Douglas, Ruth, Carol & Beth. *Educ:* Morningside Col, BS, 46; Univ Iowa, MS, 48. *Prof Exp:* Pub sch teacher, Iowa, 46-47; asst math, Univ Iowa, 47-48; from instr to asst prof, Parsons Col, 48-55; mem actuarial dept, Bankers Life Co, 55-57. *Concurrent Pos:* Dir, NSF In-Serv Inst, Col Idaho, 62-72, 77-80. *Mem:* Nat Coun Teachers Math. *Res:* Factoring of integers; audiovisual aids in mathematics; effective means of appealing to child's intuition in teaching mathematics. *Mailing Add:* Master Ctr Albertson Col Idaho Caldwell ID 83605. *Fax:* 208-454-2077; *E-Mail:* bhenry@acori.edu

HENRY, BRYAN ROGER, PHYSICAL CHEMISTRY. *Current Pos:* dept chair, 88-93, PROF PHYS CHEM, UNIV GUELPH, 87- *Personal Data:* b Vancouver, BC, Nov 14, 41; m 63, Vaile Tory; c Jennifer & Darrell. *Educ:* Univ BC, BSc, 63; Fla State Univ, PhD(phys chem), 67. *Honors & Awards:* Gerhard Herzberg Award, Spectros Can, 92. *Prof Exp:* Res asst, Fla State Univ, 64-66; Nat Res Coun Can fel, 68-69; from asst prof to prof physical chem, Univ Man, 69-86, head dept, 80-86. *Concurrent Pos:* Vis prof, Australian Nat Univ, 75-76, & Univ BC, 84-85; chair elect, Chem Inst Can. *Mem:* Fel Chem Inst Can; Can Soc Chem (pres, 92-93). *Res:* Theory of vibrational overtone intensity; intramolecular vibrational energy redistribution; overtone spectroscopy; intracavity laser photoacoustic spectroscopy; local mode description of highly vibrationally excited molecules. *Mailing Add:* Dept Chem & Biochem Univ Guelph Guelph ON N1G 2W1 Can. *Fax:* 519-766-1499; *E-Mail:* chmhenry@uoguelph.ca

HENRY, CHARLES H, SEMICONDUCTOR PHYSICS, SEMICONDUCTOR LASER. *Current Pos:* Dept head, 70-75, MEM TECH STAFF, SEMICONDUCTOR RES, BELL LABS, 65- *Personal Data:* b Chicago, Ill, May 6, 37; m 58; c 3. *Educ:* Univ Chicago, MS, 59; Univ Ill, Urbana, PhD(physics), 65. *Mem:* Am Phys Soc; fel, AAAS. *Res:* Semiconductor lasers and integrated optics and its application to optical communications. *Mailing Add:* 12515 Meadowood Dr Silver Spring MD 20904

HENRY, CHARLES STUART, ENTOMOLOGY. *Current Pos:* from asst prof to assoc prof, 75-85, PROF BIOL, UNIV CONN, 85- *Personal Data:* b Pittsfield, Mass, Mar 16, 46; m 70, 86, Julie J Goemer; c Cameron A, William H, Chandra W, Kenneth H, Zoe W & Brett H. *Educ:* Harvard Univ, BA, 68, PhD(biol), 73. *Prof Exp:* Asst prof biol sci, George Washington Univ, 73-75. *Mem:* Soc Study Evolution; Entom Soc Am. *Res:* Acoustical communication in lacewings of the family Chrysopidae (Neuroptera); mechanisms of speciation. *Mailing Add:* Dept Ecol & Evolutionary Biol Univ Conn Box U-43 75 Eagleville Rd Storrs CT 06269. *Fax:* 860-486-6364; *E-Mail:* chenry@uconnvm.uconn.edu

HENRY, CHRISTOPHER D, GEOLOGIC MAPPING, GEOCHRONOLOGY. *Current Pos:* RES GEOLOGIST, NEV BUR MINES & GEOL, UNIV NEV, 93- *Personal Data:* b Kansas City, Mo, Aug 21, 46; m 84, Jan Sloan; c Donelle. *Educ:* Calif Tech Univ, BS, 69; Univ Tex, Austin, MA, 72, PhD(geol), 75. *Prof Exp:* Res scientist, Bur Econ Geol, Univ Tex, 74-90, sr res scientist, 90-93. *Mem:* Fel Geol Soc Am; Am Geophys Union. *Res:* Investigation of magmatism, tectonism and mineralization through geologic mapping, geochemistry and geochronology. *Mailing Add:* Nev Bur Mines & Geol Univ Nev Reno NV 89557. *Fax:* 702-784-1709; *E-Mail:* chenry@nbmg.unr.edu

HENRY, CLAUDIA, CELLULAR IMMUNOLOGY. *Current Pos:* RETIRED. *Personal Data:* b Townsville, Australia, May 19, 31; c Cassis. *Educ:* Univ Queensland, BApplSci, 53, Hons, 54; Univ Pittsburgh, PhD, 62. *Prof Exp:* Demonstr microbiol, Univ Queensland, 53, instr biochem, 54; Am Asn Univ Women res fel virol, Univ Pittsburgh, 55-56, USPHS fel immunol, 63-64, asst prof, 65-66; res fel, Wellcome Res Labs, Eng, 56-58; Wellcome fel, Max Planck Inst Virus Res, Tubingen, Ger, 58; mem, Paul Ehrlich Inst, Ger, 66-67; res immunologist, Univ Calif, San Francisco, 68-72; adj assoc prof bact & immunol, Univ Calif, Berkeley, 72-82, adj prof, 82-88. *Concurrent Pos:* mem, Basel Inst Immunol, Switz, 79. *Mem:* Am Asn Immunologists. *Res:* Antibody formation and its control; expression and function of lymphocyte receptors, regulation of idiotype type expression. *Mailing Add:* Box 2951 State Line NV 89449

HENRY, DAVID P, II, PHARMACOLOGY, ENDOCRINOLOGY. *Current Pos:* clin pharmacologist res, 74-88, SR CLIN PHARMACOLOGIST RES, ELI LILLY & CO, 88- *Personal Data:* b Durham, NC, Aug 23, 42; m 75; c 3. *Educ:* Univ NC, BA, 64; Duke Univ, MD, 68. *Prof Exp:* Intern & resident med, Sch Med, Duke Univ, 68-70; res fel neuropharmacol, NIMH, 70-72; sr res fel med & endocrinol, Univ Wash, 72-74. *Concurrent Pos:* From asst prof to assoc prof, Sch Med, Ind Univ, 75-81, prof med and pharmacol, 81- *Mem:* Am Soc Clin Invest; Endocrine Soc; Am Soc Pharmacol & Exp Therapeut; Am Soc Clin Pharmacol & Therapeut; Cent Soc Clin Res; fel Am Col Physicians. *Res:* Neurochemistry; endocrinology; biogenicamine metabolism. *Mailing Add:* 2275 Wynnedale Rd Indianapolis IN 46208-3247

HENRY, DAVID WESTON, MEDICINAL CHEMISTRY. *Current Pos:* ASSOC DIR DRUG DISCOVERY, GREEN CANCER CTR, 90-; CONSULT, 91- *Personal Data:* b Los Angeles, Calif, Oct 13, 32; m 55; c 3. *Educ:* Univ Minn, BS, 54; Univ Calif, Los Angeles, PhD(org chem), 58. *Prof Exp:* NSF fel, Imp Col, Univ London, 59-60; sr org chemist, Merck Sharp & Dohme Res Labs, 60-64; sr org chemist, SRI Int, 64-70, dir, Dept Bio-Org Chem, Life Sci Res Div, 70-77; head, Dept Org Chem, Wellcome Res Lab, Burroughs Wellcome Co, 77-88; vpres & dir res, Agouron Pharmaceut Inc, 88-90. *Concurrent Pos:* Mem, Med Chem Adv Comt, Walter Reed Army Inst Res, 79-, chmn, 81-83; mem steering comt, WHO Sci Working Group on Filariasis, 77-79; mem, NIH Med Chem Study Sect A, 81-83. *Mem:* AAAS; Am Asn Cancer Res; Am Chem Soc; NY Acad Sci. *Res:* Synthetic organic chemistry; structure-activity relationships of chemotherapeutic agents; anti-parasitic drugs; anti-tumor drugs; computer assisted drug design. *Mailing Add:* 975 Olive Crest Dr Encinitas CA 92024-6828

HENRY, DONALD LEE, PHYSICS. *Current Pos:* ASST PROF PHYSICS, WILSON COL, 76-, COORD DIV NATURAL SCI & MATH, 79- *Personal Data:* b Akron, Ohio, Apr 24, 42. *Educ:* Ohio Univ, BS, 64; Johns Hopkins Univ, PhD(physics), 70. *Prof Exp:* Fel chem eng, Rice Univ, 70-74; asst prof & res assoc physics, McMaster Univ, 74-76. *Mem:* Am Phys Soc; Sigma Xi. *Res:* Studies of transport properties of fluids near the critical point. *Mailing Add:* Sch Natural & Soc Sci Shepherd Col Shepherdstown WV 25443

HENRY, DORA PRIAULX, SYSTEMATIC ZOOLOGY. *Current Pos:* res assoc oceanog & zool, 45-60, from res assoc prof to res prof oceanog, 60-87, EMER RES PROF OCEANOG, UNIV WASH, 87- *Personal Data:* b Maquoketa, Iowa, May 24, 04; m 26. *Educ:* Univ Calif, AB, 25, MA, 26, PhD(zool), 31. *Prof Exp:* Asst zool, Univ Calif, 25-26; res assoc oceanog & zool, Univ Wash, 32-42; asst oceanog, Hqs, Air Forces, US Dept Army, 42-43; assoc oceanogr, Hydrographic Off, US Dept Navy, 43-45, oceanogr, 45. *Mem:* Soc Syst Zool; Crustacean Soc. *Res:* Protozoan parasites of birds and mammals; amoebae of man; coccidiosis of the guinea pig; protozoan parasites of invertebrates; taxonomic study of barnacles. *Mailing Add:* 11031 Durland Ave NE Seattle WA 98125

HENRY, EGBERT WINSTON, PLANT PHYSIOLOGY. *Current Pos:* from asst prof to assoc prof, 74-85, PROF BIOL, OAKLAND UNIV, 85-, CHAN, 88- *Personal Data:* b New York, NY, Apr 28, 31; m 64. *Educ:* Queens Col, NY, BS, 53; Brooklyn Col, MA, 59; City Univ New York, PhD(biol), 72. *Prof Exp:* From instr to asst prof biol, Herbert L Lehman Col, City Univ New York, 71-74. *Concurrent Pos:* Grant-in-aid res, Sigma Xi. *Mem:* Am Soc Plant Physiologists; Scand Soc Plant Physiol; Japanese Soc Plant Physiologists; Sigma Xi. *Res:* Biochemical and histochemical localization of peroxidase enzymes in plant tissue, particularly abscission zone tissue; the effect of ethylene in inducing peroxidase enzymes in plant tissue; polyphenol oxidase activity and localization in chloroplasts. *Mailing Add:* 18034 Oak Dr Detroit MI 48221

HENRY, EUGENE W, ELECTRICAL ENGINEERING, COMPUTER ENGINEERING. *Current Pos:* assoc prof elec eng, Univ Notre Dame, 60-70, dir Eng Comput Lab, 68-81, scientist, Radiation Labs, 76-86, PROF ELEC ENG, UNIV NOTRE DAME, 70- *Personal Data:* b Wichita Falls, Tex, Dec 31, 32; m 55; c 6. *Educ:* Univ Notre Dame, BSEE, 54, MSEE, 55; Stanford Univ, PhD(elec eng), 60. *Prof Exp:* Proj engr, Wright Air Develop Ctr, Ohio, 55-57; develop engr, Sylvania Electronic Defense Lab, Calif, 57-60. *Concurrent Pos:* Consult, Keltec Indusrs, Va, 61-66; mem bd dir, Nat Electronics Conf, 62-63, trustee, 66-73; mem, Simulation Coun; NASA-Am Soc Eng Educ summer fac fel, Goddard Space Flight Ctr, 70-71. *Mem:* Asn Comput Mach; Inst Elec & Electronics Engrs; Am Soc Eng Educ; Soc Comput Simulation. *Res:* Electronic computers and automatic control systems. *Mailing Add:* 537 River Ave South Bend IN 46601-3253

HENRY, HAROLD ROBERT, CIVIL ENGINEERING, HYDROLOGY. *Current Pos:* RETIRED. *Personal Data:* b Stockbridge, Ga, June 2, 28; m 50; c 5. *Educ:* Ga Inst Technol, BCE, 48; Univ Iowa, MS, 50; Columbia Univ, PhD(civil eng), 60. *Honors & Awards:* Stevens Award, Am Soc Civil Engrs. *Prof Exp:* Instr math, Ga Inst Technol, 47-48, instr civil eng, 49-50; asst fluid mech, Univ Iowa, 48-49; lectr & asst, Columbia Univ, 50-53; civil engr, Ebasco Serv, NY, 53-54; from asst prof to assoc prof civil eng, Mich State Univ, 54-64; prof eng mech, Univ Ala, Tuscaloosa, 64-69, head dept, 69-84, prof civil eng, 69-90; consult hydrologist, 90- *Concurrent Pos:* Consult for numerous pvt & govt agencies; mem, Nat Adv Environ Health Sci Coun, 74-78; assoc ed, J Hydraul Eng, 85-91. *Mem:* Am Soc Civil Engrs; Am Soc Eng Educ; Am Geophys Union; Nat Soc Prof Engrs; Am Water Resources Asn; Am Soc Photogrammetry & Remote Sensing; Am Meteorol Soc; Am Water Resources Asn. *Res:* Flow in porous media; hydrology; waste migration in groundwater flow; coastal engineering; urban hydrology; hydrologic simulation; stochastic hydrology; real-time flood forecasting; use of radar in hydrology; use of satellite derived data in hydroligic forecasting. *Mailing Add:* 36 Glenn Springs Rd Travelers Rest SC 29690

HENRY, HARRY JAMES, BIOCHEMISTRY. *Current Pos:* RETIRED. *Personal Data:* b Kokomo, Ind, June 28, 17; m 40; c 3. *Educ:* Hanover Col, AB, 39. *Prof Exp:* Biochemist, Eli Lilly & Co, 39-48, head dept biochem preparations, 48-62, mgr assay & insulin control, 62-67, mgr biochem prod, 67-77, tech adv, 77-81. *Mem:* AAAS; Am Chem Soc; Asn Contamination Control. *Res:* Hormones; antibiotics; growth factors; glandular products. *Mailing Add:* 6060 Shawnee Trail Indianapolis IN 46220-5072

HENRY, HELEN L, ENDOCRINOLOGY. *Current Pos:* PROF BIOCHEM, UNIV CALIF, RIVERSIDE. *Personal Data:* b Fairborn, Ohio, Sept 21, 44; m 76; c 1. *Educ:* Wash Univ, PhD(biol), 70. *Honors & Awards:* Fuller Albright Award, Am Soc Bone Mineral Res, 84. *Mem:* Am Soc Bone Mineral Res; Endocrine Soc; Am Inst Nutrit; Am Soc Biochem & Molecular Biol; Am Women in Sci. *Res:* Hormonal regulation of calcium metabolism; cytochrome P-450 and steroid metabolism; gene structure and function. *Mailing Add:* Dept Biochem Univ Calif Riverside Riverside CA 92521-0001. *Fax:* 909-787-4784

HENRY, HERMAN LUTHER, JR, INDUSTRIAL ENGINEERING, COMPUTER SCIENCE. *Current Pos:* RETIRED. *Personal Data:* b Arcadia, La, Mar 6, 18; m 41, Eva Grissom; c Krista (Vernon) David M. *Educ:* La Polytech Inst, BS, 40; Ill Inst Technol, MS, 46. *Prof Exp:* Instr tech drawing, Ill Inst Technol, 42-46; from asst prof to assoc prof mech eng, La Polytech Inst, 46-51; proj engr power plants & elec distribution, Tex Div, Dow Chem Co, 51-55; assoc prof mech eng, La Tech Univ, 55-56, prof mech eng & head gen eng dept, 56-62, prof indust eng & head dept, 62-76, assoc dean eng, 76-83, prof indust, 83-85. *Mem:* Am Soc Eng Educ; Nat Soc Prof Engrs. *Res:* Engineering economy; guidance of freshman engineering students. *Mailing Add:* 2300 Hillside Rd Ruston LA 71270. *E-Mail:* henry@linknet.net

HENRY, HUGH FORT, RADIATION PROTECTION, NUCLEAR STRUCTURE. *Current Pos:* prof & chmn dept physics, 61-81, EMER PROF PHYSICS, DEPAUW UNIV, 81- *Personal Data:* b Emory, Va, Apr 25, 16; m 42; c 4. *Educ:* Emory & Henry Col, BS & BA, 36; Univ Va, MS, 38, PhD(physics), 40. *Prof Exp:* Prof, Emory & Henry Col, 38; prof physics & math, Col Ozarks, 40-41; from instr to assoc prof physics, Univ Ga, 41-49; head radiation hazards & safety dept, Carbide & Carbon Chems Co, 49-54, head safety fire & radiation control dept, Union Carbide Corp, 54-61. *Concurrent Pos:* US rep, Tech Comt 85, Int Standards Orgn, 58, 60 & 65; consult, US AEC, Union Carbide Nuclear Co, Goodyear Atomic Corp & Oolithic Limestone Corp; pres bd dirs, Cent States Univs, Inc, 67; vchmn radiation protection comt N-13, Am Nat Standards Inst. *Mem:* AAAS; Optical Soc Am; Am Phys Soc; Sigma Xi; Am Nuclear Soc. *Res:* Health physics; nuclear safety; electrical discharge in liquids. *Mailing Add:* 404 Linwood Dr Greencastle IN 46135-1137

HENRY, JAMES H(ERBERT), ELECTRICAL ENGINEERING. *Current Pos:* RETIRED. *Personal Data:* b Toronto, Ont, Oct 29, 22; nat US; m 49, Marion Dare Wetmore; c 3. *Educ:* Univ Toronto, BASc, 43; Mass Inst Technol, SM, 48. *Prof Exp:* Asst electronics, Mass Inst Technol, 46-47, instr elec eng, 47-48; opers analyst & div chief, Opers Res Off, Johns Hopkins Univ, 48-62; sr staff mem, Sci & Technol Div, Inst Defense Anal, 62-79, mem staff, Strategy, Forces & Resources Div, 79-87, mem staff, 87. *Concurrent Pos:* Consult, Off Civil Defense, 61, US Army Aviation, 65; mem, Explosive Tagging Tech Comt, Bur Alcohol, Tobacco & Firearms, Dept Treas, 72-; mem, Washington Opers Res/Mgt Sci Coun. *Mem:* Fel Opers Res Soc Am; Sigma Xi. *Res:* Operations research; air defense; tactical aviation; civil defense; protection technology; explosive detection technology; surveillance; air traffic controller training; satellite applications; enology and viticulture; technology assessment; military comparisons. *Mailing Add:* 43745 Drumcliff Rd Hollywood MD 20636

HENRY, JAMES PAGET, MEDICINE. *Current Pos:* prof physiol, 63-80, PROF PHYSIOL & BIOPHYS, SCH MED, UNIV SOUTHERN CALIF, 80- *Personal Data:* b Leipzig, Ger, July 12, 14; US citizen; m 38; c 3. *Educ:* Cambridge Univ, BA, 35, MA, 38, MD, 52; McGill Univ, MS, 42; Calif Inst Technol, PhD(exp med), 55. *Honors & Awards:* Arnold Tuttle Award, Aerospace Med Asn, 53; John Jeffries Award, Am Inst Aeronaut & Astronaut, 55; Carl Ludwig Medal, Ger Heart Asn, 76. *Prof Exp:* From asst prof to assoc prof physiol, Univ Southern Calif, 43-47; chief sect, Aeromed Lab, Wright Air Develop Ctr, Wright-Patterson AFB, 47-56; flight surgeon, USAF Med Corps, 56-63. *Concurrent Pos:* Panel mem, Res & Develop Bd, Environ Physiol, 49-53; mem, Behav Biol Panel, NASA, Am Inst Biol Sci, 62-65; nat consult, Surgeon Gen, USAF, 70-75; ed, Am Psychosom Soc, 72- *Mem:* Am Physiol Soc; fel Aerospace Med Asn; Am Inst Int Soc Hypertension; Am Psychosom Soc; fel Int Col Psychosom Med. *Res:* Aerospace physiology, acceleration and altitude; cardiovascular physiology, blood volume regulation; psychosocial stress, hypertension and pathophysiological changes in animals and man; role of the autonomic and endocrine systems in stress response. *Mailing Add:* Dept Psychiat Loma Linda Univ Sch Med Loma Linda CA 92350. *Fax:* 213-563-4924

HENRY, JOHN BERNARD, MEDICINE. *Current Pos:* OFC PRES UPSTATE MED CTR, SYRACUSE, NY. *Personal Data:* b Elmira, NY, Apr 26, 28; m 53; c 6. *Educ:* Cornell Univ, AB, 51; Univ Rochester, MD, 55. *Prof Exp:* Asst med, Wash Univ, 55-56; asst path, Col Physicians & Surgeons, Columbia Univ, 56-57, instr, 57-58; Nat Cancer Inst trainee, 58-60; asst prof path, Col Med, Univ Fla, 60-63, assoc prof, 63-64; prof path, State Univ NY Upstate Med Ctr, 64-79, dean, Col Health Related Prof, 70-77; dean, Sch Med, Georgetown Univ, 79- *Concurrent Pos:* Intern, Barnes Hosp, St Louis, 55-56; resident, Presby Hosp, NY, 56-58 & New Eng Deaconess Hosp, Boston, 58-60; teaching fel, Harvard Med Sch, 59-60; nat consult clin path, Surgeon Gen, USAF, 70-; pres, Am Asn Blood Banks, 70-71; pres, Am Bd Path, 76-77; pres, Am Blood Comn, 78-80. *Mem:* Am Chem Soc; Am Soc Exp Pathologists; Am Soc Clin Pathologists (vpres, 78-79); Col Am Pathologists (pres, 80-81); Int Soc Blood Transfusion. *Res:* Enzymology, especially serum enzymes of diagnostic value and localization at the tissue level; blood groups and immunohematology; clinical chemistry automation; medical education; health care delivery; HLA antigens and disease; transplantation immunopathology. *Mailing Add:* Dept Path State Univ Ny Health Sci Ctr Syracuse 750 E Adams St Syracuse NY 13210-2375. *Fax:* 315-464-5275

HENRY, JONATHAN FLAKE, water pollution control, environmental engineering, for more information see previous edition

HENRY, JOSEPH L, ANATOMY, DENTISTRY. *Current Pos:* assoc dean, 78-90, dean, 90-95, PROF & CHMN ORAL DIAG & RADIOL, SCH DENT MED, HARVARD UNIV, 76-, EMER ASSOC DEAN FAC AFFAIRS, 95- *Personal Data:* b New Orleans, La, May 2, 24; m 43; c Joseph H Jr, Leiloni, Ronald, Joan & Peter. *Educ:* Howard Univ, DDS, 46; Xavier Univ, BS, 48; Univ Ill, MS, 49, PhD(anat), 51. *Hon Degrees:* DHL, Ill Col Optom, 73; ScD, Xavier Univ, 75; MA, Harvard Univ, 79. *Prof Exp:* Instr oral med, Howard Univ, 46-48; extern, Res & Educ Hosps, Univ Ill, 49-51; assoc prof, Howard Univ, 51-53, supt clins, 53-65, prof oral med, 58-76, dir clins, 65-76, dean, Col Dent, 66-76. *Concurrent Pos:* Consult, Freedmen's Hosp, 51 & Crownsville State Hosp, 60; consult path, Vet Admin Hosp, 62; mem, Nat Comt Advan Educ, Am Asn Dent Schs, 65, White House Conf Int Coop, 65 & Conf Aid to Handicapped, 67; consult, St Elizabeth's Hosp, Washington, DC, 68; trustee, Community Group Health Found, Inc, Neighborhood Health Ctr, 68; mem, Nat Adv Comt Policy & Award of Scholar for Negroes to Study Dent, Am Fund Dent Educ, 68-69; consult, Nat Adv Comt Health Affairs, NIH, 69-72; dir, Pub Health & chmn, DC Task Force Dent Affairs, 70; mem, Bd External Visitors, Sch Dent Med, Harvard Univ, 70; mem, Nat Study Comn Optom Educ, 71, Dean's Comt, Mt Alto Vet Admin Hosp & DC Gen Hosp & Nat Steering Comt, Ann Am Conf Teachers Pract Admin; mem attend staff, Brigham & Women's Hosp, 80; chmn bd trustees, Illuni Col Optom, 81-86. *Mem:* Inst Med-Nat Acad Sci; fel Am Col Dent; Am Acad Periodont; Am Dent Asn; Int Asn Dent Res. *Res:* Colchicine; root resorption; periodontal diseases; cancer; hereditary dental diseases; dental education. *Mailing Add:* Dept Oral Diag & Radiol Harvard Sch Dent Med Boston MA 02115

HENRY, JOSEPH PATRICK, ASTROPHYSICS. *Current Pos:* dir 2.2m telescope, 84-87, assoc prof, 87-90, PROF, DEPT PHYSICS & ASTRON, UNIV HAWAII, 90- *Personal Data:* b Mojave, Calif, Apr 16, 47. *Educ:* La Salle Col, Pa, BA, 69; Univ Calif, Berkeley, PhD(physics), 74. *Prof Exp:* Physicist astrophys, Astrophys Observ, Smithsonian Inst, 74-81. *Concurrent Pos:* Prin investr, NASA & NSF Grants, 82-; consult, Patrick Henry & Assocs, 84-; Woodrow Wilson Fel, 69. *Mem:* Am Astron Soc. *Res:* Observations of clusters of galaxies and quasars at optical, infrared and x-ray wavelengths; imaging detector development. *Mailing Add:* Inst Astron 2680 Woodlawn Dr Honolulu HI 96822. *Fax:* 808-988-2790; *E-Mail:* henry@galileo.ifa.hawaii.edu

HENRY, KENNETH ALBIN, FISH BIOLOGY, STATISTICS. *Current Pos:* fishery biologist, Wash, 63, lab dir, NC, 63-69, FISHERY BIOLOGIST, RES, AFSC NAT MARINE FISHERIES SERV, 69- *Personal Data:* b Everett, Wash, July 10, 23; wid; c Chris, Karen & Lori. *Educ:* Univ Wash, BS, 49, PhD, 61; Iowa State Univ, MS, 52. *Honors & Awards:* Silver Medal, Dept Com, 83. *Prof Exp:* Fishery aide, Fish Comn Ore, 48, fishery biologist, 49-52, chg coastal rivers invest, 52-56 & Columbia River invest, 56; fishery biologist, Int Pac Salmon Fishery Comn, 56-62, chief biologist, 62-63. *Concurrent Pos:* Chmn, Pac Fish Mgt Coun Salmon Tech Team; mem, US/Can Salmon Treaty Tech Comts. *Mem:* Am Inst Fisher Res Biol. *Res:* Population dynamics; life history studies; migrations; scale patterns as a basis for racial identification of sockeye salmon; effect of various environmental factors on salmon production; fishery management. *Mailing Add:* Alaska Fisheries Ctr Bldg 4 7600 Sandpoint Way NE Seattle WA 98115. *Fax:* 206-526-6723; *E-Mail:* khenry@afsc.noaa.gov

HENRY, MARY GERARD, AQUATIC TOXICOLOGY, FISH BEHAVIORAL ECOLOGY. *Current Pos:* MINN COOP FISH & WILDLIFE RES UNIT. *Personal Data:* b Detroit, Mich, Aug 11, 54. *Educ:* Univ Detroit, BS, 75; Purdue Univ, MS, 78; Iowa State Univ, PhD(animal ecol), 84. *Prof Exp:* Fishery biologist, Columbia Nat Fishery Res Lab, US Fish & Wildlife Serv, 80-82, sect chief, 82-84, proj leader physiol & behav, Great Lakes Fishery Res Lab, 84- *Concurrent Pos:* Res assoc, Univ Mo, 82-; proj coordr, Energy Prod, Columbia Nat Fishery Res Lab, 83-84, Acid Rain, 84-85; vis scientist, US-USSR Sci Exchange, 84; adj prof, Mich State Univ, 85- *Mem:* Soc Environ Toxicol & Chem; Am Fisheries Soc; Sigma Xi; Int Asn Great Lakes Res; Am Soc Testing & Mat. *Res:* Impact of aquatic contaminants on fish; behavioral, physiological and toxicological assessments made to determine the ecological significance of metals, organochlorines, organophosphates, PCB's and fossil fuels on various species of warm water and cold water fish and invertebrates. *Mailing Add:* 6010 Washington Blvd Arlington VA 22205

HENRY, MYRON S, APPLIED MATHEMATICS. *Current Pos:* PROVOST, KENT STATE UNIV. *Personal Data:* b Logansport, Ind, Nov 13, 41; m 62; c 2. *Educ:* Ball State Univ, BS, 62; Colo State Univ, MS, 65, PhD(math), 68. *Prof Exp:* High sch teacher, Ind, 62-63; prof math, Mont State Univ, 68-80, actg dean, Col Lett & Sci, 78-79; prof math & dean, Col Arts & Sci, Cent Mich Univ, 80-87; vpres acad affairs, Old Dominion Univ, 87- *Concurrent Pos:* Vis assoc prof math, NC State Univ, 75-76; actg dean, Col Lett & Sci, Mont State Univ, 78-79; vis prof, Old Dominion Univ, 79-80. *Mem:* Am Math Soc; Math Asn Am; Soc Indust & Appl Math. *Res:* Approximation theory; numerical analysis; differential equations. *Mailing Add:* Acad & Student Affairs Provost Kent State Univ PO Box 5190 Kent OH 44242-0001

HENRY, NEIL WYLIE, MULTIVARIATE STATISTICS, DATA ANALYSIS. *Current Pos:* ASSOC PROF MATH & SOCIOL, VA COMMONWEALTH UNIV, 75- *Personal Data:* b Winchester, Mass, Nov 30, 37; m 64, Alice Depew; c Elizabeth. *Educ:* Wesleyan Univ, BA, 58; Dartmouth Col, MA, 60; Columbia Univ, PhD(math statist), 70. *Prof Exp:* Lectr & res assoc, Columbia Univ, 62-67; asst prof sociol, Cornell Univ, 67-73; sr staff statistician, Gary Income Maintenance Exp, Ind Univ, 73-75. *Concurrent Pos:* Assoc ed, Sociol Methods & Res, 71-, Am Sociol Rev, 72-75, J Am Statist Asn, 75-76 & J Educ Statist, 81- *Mem:* Am Statist Asn; Am Sociol Asn; Math Asn Am; Am Educ Res Asn. *Res:* Latent structure analysis and measurement theory; statistical design and analysis of evaluation research studies; statistical computing. *Mailing Add:* Sociol & Anthropol Va Commonwealth Univ 910 W Franklin St Richmond VA 23284-9004. *E-Mail:* nhenry@cabell.vcu.edu

HENRY, PATRICK M, ORGANOMETALLIC CHEMISTRY, CATALYSIS. *Current Pos:* CONSULT, 86. *Personal Data:* b Joliet, Ill, Sept 29, 28; m 56; c 3. *Educ:* De Paul Univ, BS, 51, MS, 53; Northwestern Univ, PhD(chem), 56. *Prof Exp:* Res chemist, Hercules Inc, 56-71; from assoc prof to prof chem, Univ Guelph, 71-81; prof & chmn chem, Loyola Univ, Chicago,

81-86, prof, 81-97. *Mem:* Am Chem Soc; Sigma Xi; fel Chem Inst Can. *Res:* Heterogeneous catalysis; physical chemistry of polymers; mechanism of metal ion catalysis, especially noble metals; environmental chemistry energy; asymmetric synthesis. *Mailing Add:* 3506 Greenwood Ave Wilmette IL 60091

HENRY, RAYMOND LEO, ANATOMY, PHYSIOLOGY. *Current Pos:* From instr to assoc prof, 61-73, actg chmn, 81-82, PROF PHYSIOL, SCH MED, WAYNE STATE UNIV, 73- *Personal Data:* b Shabbona, Ill, July 14, 30; m 53; c 4. *Educ:* Univ Ill, BS, 53, MS, 57; Med Col SC, PhD(anat), 61. *Mem:* Am Asn Anatomists; Microcirculatory Soc. *Res:* Rheology of blood in the microcirculatory system, especially mechanisms of genesis and lysis of intravascular thrombosis; erythrocyte and platelet function in the spleen. *Mailing Add:* 22473 Revere St Clair Shores MI 48080-1338

HENRY, RICHARD CONN, SPACE ASTRONOMY, COSMOLOGY. *Current Pos:* from asst prof to assoc prof, 68-77, PROF PHYSICS & ASTRON, JOHNS HOPKINS UNIV, 77-, DIR, MD SPACE GRANT CONSORTIUM, 89- *Personal Data:* b Toronto, Ont, Mar 7, 40; nat US; m 75, Rita Mahon; c George W & Mark W. *Educ:* Univ Toronto, BSc, 61, MA, 62; Princeton Univ, PhD(astron), 67. *Honors & Awards:* Gold Medal, Royal Astron Soc Can, 61. *Prof Exp:* Res assoc, Inst Advan Study, Princeton, 67; res appointee astrophys, Naval Res Lab, E O Hulburt Ctr Space Res, 67-69. *Concurrent Pos:* Lectr, Int Sch Space Sci, Cordoba, Arg, 69; res physicist, E O Hulburt Ctr Space Res, Naval Res Lab, 69-76; Alfred P Sloan res fel, 71-75; managing ed, Astrophys Lett, 75-77, ed-in-chief, 77-86; dep dir astrophys div, NASA Hq, 76-78. *Mem:* Fel AAAS; Am Astron Soc; fel Royal Astron Soc; Royal Astron Soc Can; Am Physical Soc. *Res:* Ultraviolet astronomy; abundances of the elements; cosmology. *Mailing Add:* Dept Physics & Astron Johns Hopkins Univ Baltimore MD 21218-2686. *Fax:* 410-516-4109; *E-Mail:* rch@pha.jhu.edu

HENRY, RICHARD JOSEPH, biochemistry; deceased, see previous edition for last biography

HENRY, RICHARD LYNN, INORGANIC CHEMISTRY, SOLID STATE CHEMISTRY. *Current Pos:* Res chemist, Code 6821, 75-90, SUPVRY RES CHEMIST SYNTHESIS & CRYSTAL GROWTH ELECTRON MAT, NAVAL RES LAB CODE 6870, 90- *Personal Data:* b Lewistown, Pa, May 30, 48; m 71, Loralee Omlor; c Stephen & Jonathan. *Educ:* Millersville State Col, BA, 72; Brown Univ, PhD(inorg chem), 76. *Mem:* Am Chem Soc; Am Asn Crystal Growth. *Res:* Synthesis, bulk crystal growth, epitaxial growth and solid state chemistry of semi-conductor compounds; thin film growth of oxide superconductors. *Mailing Add:* Naval Res Lab Code 6860 4555 Overlook Ave SW Washington DC 20375-5000

HENRY, RICHARD WARFIELD, PHYSICS. *Current Pos:* chmn dept, 70-80, pres & head dept, 80-84, PROF PHYSICS, BUCKNELL UNIV, 70- *Personal Data:* b New York, NY, Nov 23, 32; m 54; c 2. *Educ:* Union Univ, NY, BA, 54; Univ Ill MS, 56, PhD, 58. *Prof Exp:* Asst physics, Univ Ill, 54-56, asst prof, 58-59; from asst prof to assoc prof, Union Univ, NY, 59-70. *Concurrent Pos:* NSF fel, Calif Inst Technol, 63-64; vis assoc prof, Mass Inst Technol, 67-69. *Mem:* Am Phys Soc. *Res:* Optics; quantum electronics. *Mailing Add:* Dept Physics Bucknell Univ Lewisburg PA 17837

HENRY, ROBERT DAVID, PLANT MORPHOLOGY, FLORISTICS. *Current Pos:* asst prof, 60-64, ASSOC PROF BIOL SCI, WESTERN ILL UNIV, 65- *Personal Data:* b Columbus, Ohio, Aug 25, 27; m 75. *Educ:* Ohio State Univ, BS, 51, PhD(bot), 58; Univ Ill, MS, 53. *Prof Exp:* Asst bot, Univ Ill, 51-53; asst & asst instr, Ohio State Univ, 55-58; vis instr, Ohio Wesleyan, 58-59; asst prof, 59-60. *Mem:* AAAS; Bot Soc Am; Int Soc Plant Morphol; Am Soc Plant Taxon; Sigma Xi. *Res:* Vascular plant floristics of West Central Illinois; vascular plant morphology and anatomy. *Mailing Add:* RR 1 Macomb IL 61455

HENRY, ROBERT LEDYARD, PHYSICS. *Current Pos:* chmn dept, 56-86, prof, 56-89, EMER PROF PHYSICS, WABASH COL, 89- *Personal Data:* b New Ulm, Minn, July 4, 20; m 42, 93, Dolores Albers; c Dennis C, Carl F, Walter L, Lawrence R, James H & Rebecca A. *Educ:* Carleton Col, BA, 41; Johns Hopkins Univ, PhD(physics), 47. *Prof Exp:* Instr physics, Johns Hopkins Univ, 43-46; instr, Carleton Col, 46-48, asst prof, 48-52; assoc prof, Ripon Col, 52-55, prof, 55-56, chmn dept, 52-56. *Concurrent Pos:* Mem, exec bd, Am Asn Physics Teachers, 74-77. *Mem:* Am Phys Soc; Am Asn Physics Teachers; Optical Soc Am; Sigma Xi. *Res:* Nuclear magnetic resonance; x-ray diffraction. *Mailing Add:* 310 Crawford St Crawfordsville IN 47933-2702

HENRY, ROBERT R, CODE GENERATION FOR COMPILERS. *Current Pos:* ASST PROF COMPUT SCI, UNIV WASH, 84- *Personal Data:* b Pasadena, Calif, Oct 31, 55. *Educ:* Univ Calif, Davis, BS, 77, Berkeley, MS, 81, PhD(comput sci), 84. *Prof Exp:* Eng aid, Naval Weapon Ctr, 73-77; teaching assoc comput sci, Univ Calif, Berkeley, 77-78, res assoc, 78-84. *Concurrent Pos:* Prin investr comput sci, NSF, 85- *Mem:* Asn Comput Mach. *Res:* Compiler construction; retargetable compilers; machine dependent Graham-Glanville code generators; table driven tree pattern matchers; algorithm animation. *Mailing Add:* 10512 17th Ave NE Seattle WA 98125

HENRY, ROBERT WILLIAM, biological tissue preservation, plastination, for more information see previous edition

HENRY, ROGER P, MECHANICAL ENGINEERING. *Current Pos:* ENG, NATURAL RESOURCES CAN, 90- *Personal Data:* b Toronto, Ont, Apr 2, 38; m 63; c 2. *Educ:* Univ Toronto, BASc, 61, MASc, 64, PhD(mech eng), 68. *Honors & Awards:* Teetor Award, Soc Automotive Engrs, 70. *Prof Exp:* From asst prof to assoc prof, Univ Ottawa, 68-75; specialist engine training, Technol Res & Develop Br, Dept Pub Works Can, 75-79, specialist solar design, 79-81, chief, Tech Systs Secretariat, 81-86, CAD specialist, 86-90. *Concurrent Pos:* Ont Dept Univ Affairs grant, 68-69; Nat Res Coun operating grants, 68-75; Am Soc Mech Eng diesel & gas power grant, 69. *Mem:* Am Soc Mech Engrs; Soc Automotive Engrs. *Res:* Applied thermodynamics; pollution control; engine environmental problems; computer-aided-design in buildings; lighting design; building energy systems analysis; solar energy. *Mailing Add:* Technol-Solutions 64 Fuller St Ottawa ON K1Y 3R8 Can

HENRY, RONALD ALTON, MICROBIOLOGY, BIOCHEMISTRY. *Current Pos:* asst prof, 73-80, ASSOC PROF BIOL, ST JOHN'S UNIV, 80- *Personal Data:* b La Crosse, Wis, Oct 30, 40; c 2. *Educ:* Univ Wis, La Crosse, BS, 65; Univ Minn, Minneapolis, PhD(microbiol), 72. *Prof Exp:* Res asst, Dept Microbiol, Univ Minn, 65-71; res assoc, Diamond Lab Inc, 71-73. *Concurrent Pos:* Consult, Fromm Lab Inc, 74-78; res grant, Dr J E Salsbury Found, 74-78 & MacPherson Found, 78-79; sec chmn, Am Leptospirosis Res Conf Inc, 75 & 78. *Mem:* Am Soc Microbiol; AAAS. *Res:* Survival and maintenance of virulence of pathogenic bacteria outside the normal host; physiological differences between avirulent and virulent microorganisms; isoenzyme patterns and activity in aquatic animals at different temperatures. *Mailing Add:* Dept Biol St John's Univ PO Box 7155 Collegeville MN 56321-7155

HENRY, RONALD ANDREW, CHEMISTRY. *Current Pos:* sr chemist, US Naval Ord Test Sta, 47-53, head, Org Chem Br, 53-74, SR RES SCIENTIST, US NAVAL WEAPONS CTR, 74- *Personal Data:* b Yakima, Wash, Jan 26, 16; m 42; c 3. *Educ:* Univ Wash, BS, 38, PhD(chem), 42. *Prof Exp:* Res chemist, Procter & Gamble Co, 42-47. *Mem:* Am Chem Soc; Sigma Xi. *Res:* Chemistry of nitrogen compounds; chemiluminescence; tetrazole complexes; chemistry of explosives and propellants; dyes for lasers. *Mailing Add:* 329 Perdew Ave Ridgecrest CA 93555

HENRY, RONALD JAMES WHYTE, ATOMIC PHYSICS. *Current Pos:* VPRES ACAD AFFAIRS & PROF PHYSICS, AUBURN UNIV, 89-, PROVOST, 96- *Personal Data:* b Belfast, Ireland, Feb 5, 40; m 65; c 2. *Educ:* Queen's Univ, Belfast, BSc, 61, PhD(appl math), 64. *Prof Exp:* Asst lectr appl math, Queen's Univ, Belfast, 64-65; Nat Acad Sci-Nat Res Coun resident res fel physics, Goddard Space Flight Ctr, 65-66; asst physicist, Kitt Peak Nat Observ, Ariz, 66-69; assoc prof, La State Univ, Baton Rouge, 69-74, chmn, Dept Physics & Astron, 76-82, prof physics, 74-89, dean, Col Basic Sci, 82-89. *Mem:* Fel Am Phys Soc. *Res:* Atomic collision theory. *Mailing Add:* Dept Physics Ga State Univ Atlanta GA 30303

HENRY, SUSAN ARMSTRONG, MOLECULAR GENETICS OF YEAST, LIPID BIOCHEMISTRY. *Current Pos:* dept head biol sci, 87-91, PROF, DEPT BIOL SCI, CARNEGIE-MELLON UNIV, 87-, DEAN, MELLON COL SCI, 91- *Personal Data:* b Alexandria, Va, June 27, 46; m 68, Peter; c Rebecca & Joshua. *Educ:* Univ Md, BS, 68; Univ Calif, PhD(genetics), 71. *Prof Exp:* Fel molecular biol & genetics, Brandeis Univ, 71-72; from asst prof to assoc prof genetics & molecular biol, Albert Einstein Col Md, 72-82, dir, Grad Div, 83-87. *Concurrent Pos:* Prin investr, 72-; vis prof, Harvard Univ, 82-83; mem, Genetics Study Sect, NIH, 82-86 & Genetics Basis Dis Rev Comt, 89-; ed, Molecular & Cellular Biol, 82-86, Yeast, 86-; dir, Undergrad Biol Sci Educ Initiative, Howard Hughes Med Inst, 89-; co-dir, W M Keck Ctr Comput Biol, 92- *Mem:* Genetics Soc Am; Am Soc Biochem & Molecular Biol; Am Soc Microbiol; AAAS. *Res:* Genetic and molecular studies on the mechanism of regulation of synthesis of membrane phospholipids in bakers yeast, Saccharomyces cerevisiae; emphasis is on the role of inositol and choline-containing lipids in regulation and cell physiology. *Mailing Add:* Dept Biol Sci Carnegie-Mellon Univ 4400 Fifth Ave Pittsburgh PA 15213-2683. *Fax:* 412-268-3268

HENRY, SYDNEY MARK, MICROBIOLOGY, PHYSIOLOGY. *Current Pos:* PRES, WESTMINSTER SERV CLIN RES, INC, 90- *Personal Data:* b Brooklyn, NY, Dec 27, 30; m 53, Grace Donahoe; c Richard, James, Diane, Maureen & Kevin. *Educ:* St John's Univ, BS, 53, MS, 55; NY Univ, PhD(physiol), 61. *Honors & Awards:* Perry Bros Award, Soc Cosmetic Chemists, 77. *Prof Exp:* Res scientist, Boyce Thompson Inst Plant Res, NY, 55-64; head dept microbiol, Bristol-Myers Co, 64-73; mgr biol res, 73-84, mgr clin res personal care, 84-90. *Concurrent Pos:* NIH grants, 62, 63 & 64; lectr, Col Pharmaceut Sci, Columbia Univ, 70-74, adj asst prof, 74-78. *Mem:* Am Soc Microbiol; Am Chem Soc; fel Soc Cosmetic Chemist; fel Royal Soc Med. *Res:* Biochemistry and physiology of symbiotic relationships; sulfur metabolism; amino acid metabolism; insect nutrition; microbiology of scalp, skin, mouth; intermicrobial influences; chromatographic techniques; microbial spoilage and preservation; efficacy testing of deodorants and antiperspirants; research administration. *Mailing Add:* 183 William Cook Blvd Manahawkin NJ 08050-3543

HENRY, TIMOTHY JAMES, HEALTH SCIENCE ADMINISTRATION. *Current Pos:* HEALTH SCI ADMINR, BACT STUDY SECT, NIH, 87- *Personal Data:* b Doylestown, Ohio, Sept 21, 39; c 2. *Educ:* Kent State Univ, BS, 61; Univ Calif, Berkeley, MS, 64; Univ Wis-Madison, PhD(molecular biol), 69. *Prof Exp:* Fel molecular biol, Univ Pittsburgh, 68-70; Helen Hay Whitney fel, Friedrich-Miescher-Lab, Tubingen, WGer, 71-73; fel, Princeton Univ, 73; res assoc, Sloan-Kettering Inst, 74-76; cancer expert, Lab Molecular Biol, Nat Cancer Inst, 77-79; staff sci adv, molecular biol, 79-80, reviewing toxicologist, Bur Foods, Food & Drug Admin, 80-82; dir biol sci, Health Ind Mfg Asn, 82-85; assoc dir, Biol Instr Prog, NSF, 86. *Mem:* NY Acad Sci; Genetic Toxicol Asn; Fedn Am Scientists; AAAS; Am Soc Microbiol; Sigma Xi. *Res:* Identification and isolation of virus directed proteins made in vivo; electron microscopy of virus maturation and release; molecular biology of RNA tumor viruses; nucleic acid hybridization; recombinant DNA technology; short-term carcinogenesis/mutagenesis tests; genetic toxicology; risk assessment. *Mailing Add:* 6905 Wilson Lane Bethesda MD 20817. *E-Mail:* hry@drgpo.drg.nih.gov

HENRY, VERNON JAMES, JR, oceanography, geology, for more information see previous edition

HENRY, WALTER LESTER, JR, medicine, endocrinology, for more information see previous edition

HENRY, WARREN ELLIOTT, MAGNETISM & MEASUREMENT OF MAGNETIC PROPERTIES, DESIGN OF SCIENTIFIC EQUIPMENT. *Current Pos:* prof, 68-81, EMER PROF PHYSICS, HOWARD UNIV, 81- *Personal Data:* b Evergreen, Ala, Feb 18, 09; m 57, Jeanne Pearlson; c Eva R. *Educ:* Tuskagee, BS, 31; Atlanta Univ, MS, 37; Univ Chicago, PhD(phys chem), 41. *Hon Degrees:* DSc, Lehigh Univ, 83; LLD, Atlanta Univ, 85. *Prof Exp:* Prin, Escambia County Training Sch, 31-34; instr, Spelman Col, 34-36, Tuskagee, 36-38, physics & chem, 41-43, physics, Univ Chicago, 46-47; asst prof physics, Spelman Col, 43-46; Staff scientist, Radiation Lab, Mass Inst Technol, 43-46; prof physics, Morehouse Col, 47-48; physicist, US Naval Res Lab, 48-60; sr staff scientist, Lockheed Missle & Space Co, 60-69. *Concurrent Pos:* Chmn, Wash Chap, Fedn Am Scientist, 57; Consult, Lawrence Livermore Lab, 64-66; US Aid (Niger); mem, Int Comt Environ, 71, Am Phys Soc Comt, SAfrica. *Mem:* fel Am Phys Soc. *Res:* Magnetic properties of paramagnets, ferromagnetics, anti ferromagnetics, superconductors, semiconductors in high magnetic fields and at low temperatures. *Mailing Add:* Dept Physics Howard Univ PO Box 761 Washington DC 20006

HENRY, WILLIAM MELLINGER, ENVIRONMENTAL CHEMISTRY. *Current Pos:* RETIRED. *Personal Data:* b Westerville, Ohio, Apr 20, 18; m 49; c 3. *Educ:* Otterbein Col, AB, 40. *Prof Exp:* Lab technician, Repub Steel Corp, Ohio, 40-42; engr, Chrysler Corp, Ill, 42-45; from asst chief anal dept to chief anal spectros, Battelle-Columbus Labs, 45-63, chief Anal Chem Div, 63-71, chief Envrion & Mat Characterization Div, 71-73, proj mgr, 73-81. *Mem:* Am Soc Testing & Mat; Am Chem Soc; Am Acad Forensic Sci; Air Pollution Control Asn. *Res:* Technical direction and management of research and development for sampling and analysis of environmental pollutants; spectroscopy; metallurgy. *Mailing Add:* 2335 Arlington Columbus OH 43221

HENRY, ZACHARY ADOLPHUS, AGRICULTURAL PROCESS ENGINEERING, PHYSICAL PROPERTIES OF CELLULAR MATERIAL & CURING-DRYING. *Current Pos:* from asst prof to assoc prof, 61-82, PROF AGR ENG, UNIV TENN, KNOXVILLE, 82- *Personal Data:* b Stockbridge, Ga, Apr 25, 30; m 53, Norma R Taylor; c Zachary A Jr, Lydia C, Vera L, Nathan L & Stephan T. *Educ:* Univ Ga, BSAE, 51; Clemson Col, MSAE, 59; NC State Univ, PhD(agr eng), 62. *Prof Exp:* Construct engr, E I du Pont de Nemours & Co, Ga, 51-52; sales engr, Tri-State Culvert & Mfg Div, Fla Steel Corp, Ga, 55-57. *Mem:* AAAS; Am Phys Soc; Am Soc Eng Educ; Am Soc Naval Engrs; Am Soc Testing & Mat; Am Soc Agr Engrs. *Res:* Development of instruments and techniques for research on the physical properties of agricultural products; curing and drying agricultural products; materials handling; pneumatic conveying and systems engineering; waste management systems; mechanization for tobacco production. *Mailing Add:* Dept Agr Eng Univ Tenn Knoxville TN 37996-4500. *Fax:* 423-974-4514; *E-Mail:* zhenry@utk.edu

HENSCHEN, LAWRENCE JOSEPH, COMPUTER SCIENCE. *Current Pos:* PROF COMPUT SCI, NORTHWESTERN UNIV, 71- *Personal Data:* b Joliet, Ill, Oct 11, 44. *Educ:* Univ Ill, Urbana, BA, 66, MA, 68, PhD(math), 71. *Concurrent Pos:* Vis scientist, Argonne Nat Lab, 72-; vpres micro-comput appln, Hank's Pacing Bodies, 74-; vis scientist, Bell Labs, 80- *Mem:* Asn Comput Mach; Am Asn Artificial Intel. *Res:* Develop programs for digital computers that display intelligence; mathematical logic as a vehicle for implementing automated deduction in mathematics and other areas; logic and data bases. *Mailing Add:* Dept Comput Sci Northwestern Univ 2141 Sheridian Rd Evanston IL 60208

HENSEL, DALE ROBERT, SOIL FERTILITY. *Current Pos:* RETIRED. *Personal Data:* b Carmel, Ind, Sept 8, 31; m 54; c 4. *Educ:* Purdue Univ, BS, 53, MS, 58; Rutgers Univ, PhD(soil fertil), 60. *Prof Exp:* Asst prof & asst soils chemist, Agr Res Ctr, Univ Fla, 60-63, dir, 64-96. *Concurrent Pos:* Dir, Potato Asn Am, 84-87. *Mem:* Am Soc Agron; Soil Sci Soc Am; Potato Asn Am; Am Inst Chemists; Sigma Xi. *Res:* Pest management programs; soil fertility and soil management problems associated with sandy flatwood soils which includes irrigation and drainage of potatoes and cabbage. *Mailing Add:* 4241 Wicks Branch Rd St Augustine FL 32086

HENSEL, GUSTAV, MATHEMATICS. *Current Pos:* From instr to asst prof, 61-68, ASSOC PROF MATH, CATH UNIV AM, 69- *Personal Data:* b Sheboygan, Wis, Nov 11, 34; m 63; c 2. *Educ:* Cath Univ Am, AB, 57; Princeton Univ, PhD(math), 63. *Mem:* Am Math Soc; Math Asn Am; Asn Symbolic Logic. *Res:* Mathematical logic. *Mailing Add:* Dept Math Cath Univ Am Washington DC 20064-0001

HENSEL, JOHN CHARLES, PHYSICS OF SEMICONDUCTORS. *Current Pos:* DISTINGUISHED RES PROF, NJ INST TECHNOL, NEWARK, 90- *Personal Data:* b Pontiac, Mich, Dec 5, 30; m 58, Carolyn Bahle; c Katherine, Thomas, Ann-Elizabeth & Caroline. *Educ:* Univ Mich, BSE, 52, MS, 53, PhD(physics), 58. *Prof Exp:* Mem Tech Staff, Bell Labs, 58-90. *Mem:* Fel Am Phys Soc; Sigma Xi. *Mailing Add:* 6 Hillcrest Ave Summit NJ 07901

HENSENS, OTTO DERK, PHYSICAL BIOCHEMISTRY. *Current Pos:* SR INVESTR, NATURAL PROD CHEM, MERCK SHARPE & DOHME RES LABS, 74- *Personal Data:* b Zuidlaren, Holland, Nov 27, 40; Australian citizen; m 70. *Educ:* Univ NEng, Australia, BSc, 62, Hons, 63, PhD(org chem), 69. *Prof Exp:* Fel, Univ Hawaii, 68-70; res fel, Calif Inst Technol, 70-72; sr res fel, Oxford Univ, 72-74. *Mem:* Am Chem Soc. *Res:* Chemistry of natural products and elucidation of biosynthetic pathways, especially by Fourier transform nuclear magnetic resonance techniques. *Mailing Add:* RY 80Y-345 Merck Sharp & Dohme Res Labs Rahway NJ 07065-0900

HENSHAW, CLEMENT LONG, PHYSICS, SCIENCE EDUCATION. *Current Pos:* from instr to prof physics & chmn dept physics & astron, 36-73, EMER PROF PHYSICS, COLGATE UNIV, 73- *Personal Data:* b Pittsfield, Mass, Dec 18, 06; m 38; c 3. *Educ:* Union Univ, NY, BS, 28; Univ Mich, MA, 29; Yale Univ, PhD(physics), 36. *Prof Exp:* Instr physics, Lehigh Univ, 29-31; instr, Yale Univ, 31-33, asst, 33-34, instr, 35-36. *Concurrent Pos:* Consult, Col Entrance Exam Bd, 49-61; fac fel, Ford Fund Advan Educ, 52-53; vis prof, Univ Chicago, 56-57; consult, Educ Testing Serv, 63-72. *Mem:* Am Phys Soc; Am Asn Physics Teachers. *Res:* Evaluation in science education. *Mailing Add:* 7 Charles St Hamilton NY 13346

HENSHAW, ROBERT EUGENE, ENVIRONMENTAL ANALYSIS & PHYSIOLOGY. *Current Pos:* RETIRED. *Personal Data:* b New York, NY, July 27, 34; div; c 3. *Educ:* Ohio Wesleyan Univ, BA, 56; Univ Mich, MS, 58; Univ Iowa, PhD(physiol), 65. *Prof Exp:* Instr physiol, Univ Iowa, 63-65; asst prof biol, Carnegie-Mellon Univ, 65-68 & Pa State Univ, Univ Pk, 68-74; assoc environ analyst, NY State Environ Conserv, 74-82, environ mgt specialist, 82-, staff develop coordr, 89- *Concurrent Pos:* Adj prof, Rensselaer Polytech Inst, 85-86, State Univ NY, Albany, 86- *Res:* Methods of environmental decision making; physiology of acclimatization; energy metabolism; water balance; comparative environmental physiology; energetic and vascular adaptations of homeothermic and hibernating mammals. *Mailing Add:* 91 Louis Dr West Sand Lake NY 12196

HENSLER, DONALD H, SOLID STATE ELECTRONICS. *Current Pos:* MEM TECH STAFF, BELL LABS, 62- *Personal Data:* b Baltimore, Md, Mar 2, 33; m 54; c 3. *Educ:* Western Md Col, BA, 55; Dartmouth Col, MA, 57; Univ Wis, PhD(physics), 62. *Mem:* Am Phys Soc; Optical Soc Am; Sigma Xi. *Res:* Galvanomagnetic effects in thin vanadium dioxide films; deposition and structural effects on the metal-semiconductor transition in vanadium dioxide films; optical propagation in thin films of Ta-2O-5; x-ray diffraction in thin tantalum films; light scattering from fused aluminum oxide surfaces; metal oxide semiconductor, large scale memory design; reliability physics of semiconductor integrated circuits. *Mailing Add:* 417 Iroquois St Emmaus PA 18049-1718

HENSLER, JOSEPH RAYMOND, CHEMISTRY. *Current Pos:* Sect head, Glass Chem Lab, Bausch & Lomb, 54-60, head, Ceramics Res & Develop Labs, 60-65, dir mat res & develop, 65-68, dir, Cent Res Lab, 68-71, mgr, Glass & Mat Div, 71-77, MEM STAFF, MAT RES & DEVELOP, BAUSCH & LOMB, 77- *Personal Data:* b Pittsburgh, Pa, May 1, 24; m 56; c 3. *Educ:* Pa State Col, BS, 46, PhD(ceramics), 51. *Mem:* Am Chem Soc; fel Am Ceramic Soc; Am Crystallog Asn; Sigma Xi. *Res:* Ultraviolet transmission in glass; glass luminescence. *Mailing Add:* 415 Yarmouth Rd Rochester NY 14610-1453

HENSLER, RONALD FRED, SOIL FERTILITY, SOIL CHEMISTRY. *Current Pos:* asst prof soil chem, 71-77, ASSOC PROF SOIL SCI, UNIV WIS-STEVENS POINT, 77- *Personal Data:* b Watertown, Wis, Aug 15, 44; m 71. *Educ:* Univ Wis-Madison, BS, 66, MS, 68, PhD(soils), 70. *Prof Exp:* Proj assoc soils fertil, Univ Wis-Madison, 70-71. *Mem:* Am Soc Agron; Soil Sci Soc Am; Sigma Xi. *Res:* Effect of manure handling on crop yields, nutrient recovery, and runoff losses; movement of nitrogen and sulfur through soil profiles; soil and water contamination from sewage sludge disposal. *Mailing Add:* 1619 Carriage Lane Custer WI 54423

HENSLEY, DANNIE A, BIOLOGY. *Current Pos:* PROF MARINE SCI, UNIV PR, 80- *Personal Data:* b Upland, Calif, Oct 24, 44. *Educ:* Calif State Univ, Fullerton, BA, 68; Univ SFla, PhD(biol), 78. *Prof Exp:* Instr biol, Univ Tampa & Hillsborough Community Col, 72-73; Fla High Sch, 72-74; biologist, Marine Res Lab, Fla Dept Nat Res, 74-78; res assoc, Fla Atlantic Univ, 78-80. *Concurrent Pos:* Fulbright scholar, JLB Smith Inst Ichthyol, Grahamstown, SAfrica, 95-96. *Mem:* Soc Syst Biol; Sigma Xi; Fr Soc Ichthyol; Ichthyol Soc Japan; Am Inst Fishery Res Biologists; Am Soc Zoologists. *Mailing Add:* Dept Marine Sci Univ PR Mayaquez PR 00681. *Fax:* 787-899-5500; *E-Mail:* 72712.602@compuserve.com

HENSLEY, DOUGLAS AUSTIN, NUMBER THEORY. *Current Pos:* from asst prof to assoc prof, 77-89, PROF MATH, TEX A&M UNIV, 90- *Personal Data:* b New York, NY, Mar 25, 49; m 70; c 5. *Educ:* Univ Kans, BA, 70; Univ Minn, PhD(math), 74. *Prof Exp:* Vis lectr math, Univ Ill, Urbana, 74-76; mem, Inst Advan Study, Princeton Univ, 76. *Mem:* Am Math Soc. *Res:* Analytic number theory, inequalities; probabilistic number theory and related areas of analysis and probability which can be used to give asymptotic estimates of the density of numbers with a given multiplicative structure; fractal structure of continued fractions. *Mailing Add:* Dept Math Tex A&M Univ College Station TX 77843-1246

HENSLEY, EUGENE BENJAMIN, SOLID STATE PHYSICS. *Current Pos:* from asst prof to prof, 53-85, EMER PROF PHYSICS, UNIV MO, COLUMBIA, 85- *Personal Data:* b Augusta, WVa, Jan 6, 18; m 54. *Educ:* Cent Col, Mo, AB, 47; Univ Mo, Columbia, MA, 48, PhD(physics), 51. *Prof Exp:* Mem staff, Res Lab Electronics, Mass Inst Technol, 51-53. *Mem:* Am Phys Soc. *Res:* Color centers and electronic structure of alkaline earth chalogenides; thermionic and photoelectric emission; oxide coated cathodes. *Mailing Add:* 802 Greenwood Ct Columbia MO 65203

HENSLEY, JOHN COLEMAN, II, EXPERIMENTAL PATHOLOGY, COMPUTER-AIDED DIAGNOSTICS. *Current Pos:* SUPVRY VET MED OFFICER FOOD SAFETY, USDA, 89- *Personal Data:* b Jasper, Tex, May 31, 33; m 53, Tressie Rives; c John, Michael, Connie, Henry & April. *Educ:* Southwestern La Univ, BS, 58; Tex A&M Univ, DVM, 62. *Prof Exp:* Instr diag path, Tex A&M Univ, 62-63, fel vet path, 65-66; mgr prog res mammalian radiobiol, Los Alamos Sci Lab, Univ Calif, 63-65; dir, Environ Sci Labs, Gulf Southern Res Inst, 66-68, dir, Div Environ Eng, 68-69, prog dir defense & related progs, 69-71; chief, Biophys Lab & sci liaison officer, Animal & Plant Health Inspection Serv, USDA, 71-76; pres, Identronix, Inc, Santa Cruz, 76-80; chmn & chief exec officer, Teledata, Inc, 80-82; chmn, Exec Consults, 82-89. *Concurrent Pos:* Consult, Int Animal Exchange, 64- & Tex Agr Exp Sta, 65-66; NIH training grant, 65-66; consult, Behlen Mfg, Animal Conf Feeding, 65-66, US Agency Int Develop, Cent Am, 67-68. *Mem:* Am Vet Med Asn; assoc Am Col Lab Animal Med; Am Asn Lab Animal Sci; US Animal Health Asn; Int Geront Soc; NY Acad Sci. *Res:* Evaluation of the effects of adverse environmental stresses on the biological systems, especially the effects as seen in pathologic physiology and behavioral reaction; single cell diagnostic pathology; remote electronic temperature monitoring and animal identification; image enhancement; public health-food technology; artificial intelligence-medical diagnostics. *Mailing Add:* 235 Fellowship Church Loop Dubach LA 71235. *Fax:* 318-368-4249

HENSLEY, MARBLE JOHN, SR, TRANSPORTATION & TRAFFIC ENGINEERING. *Current Pos:* dir & mem exec comt, 92-96, DIR BUS DEVELOP, PIEDMONT OLSEN HENSLEY INC, 96- *Personal Data:* b Ball Ground, Ga, Nov 6, 22; m 48, Ruth Collins; c Carol (Hastey), Sandra (Wise), Kathlyn (MacFarlane) & Marble J Jr. *Educ:* Ga Inst Technol, BCE, 49. *Prof Exp:* Jr engr, Ga Hwy Dept, 49-50; asst traffic engr, Atlanta, Ga, 50-54; traffic engr, Chattanooga, 54-58, city coordr, 58-63; pres, Hensley-Schmidt Inc, 63-81, chief exec officer, 63-85, chmn, 72-92. *Concurrent Pos:* Pres, Hensley & Assocs Inc, 57-63; mem, Nat Comt Uniform Traffic Control Devices, 63-74; dir, Inter Fed Savings Bank, 81-92 & Am South Bank Tenn, 92-95. *Mem:* Fel Am Soc Civil Engrs; fel Am Consult Eng Coun; Inst Transp Engrs (secy, tres, vpres, 66-69, pres, 69-70). *Mailing Add:* 7028 Pauline Circle Chattanooga TN 37421. *Fax:* 423-756-7197

HENSLEY, SESS D, SUGARCANE PESTS INSECTS WEEDS & DISEASES. *Current Pos:* assoc prof entom, 61-67, prof, 67-76, AFFIL PROF ENTOM, LA STATE UNIV, BATON ROUGE, 67-; CONSULT, SUGARCANE CROP PROTECTION & PRODUCTION, SUGARCANE FIELD LAB, HOUMA, 85- *Personal Data:* b Smithville, Okla, Jan 18, 20; m 50; c 3. *Educ:* Okla State Univ, BS, 54, MS, 55, PhD, 60. *Prof Exp:* Entomologist, Sugar Cane Field Lab, Agr Res Serv, USDA, 57-61. *Concurrent Pos:* Res leader crop protection, Sugarcane Field Lab, Houma, 76-85. *Mem:* Entom Soc Am; Int Soc Sugar Cane Technol; Sigma Xi. *Res:* Pest management of insects attacking sugar cane. *Mailing Add:* 204 Pendleton Dr Houma LA 70360

HENSON, ANNA MIRIAM (MORGAN), NEUROBIOLOGY. *Current Pos:* instr, 75-78, from res asst prof to res assoc prof, 78-87, RES PROF DEPT SURG, DIV OTOLARYNGOL, SCH MED, UNIV NC, 87- *Personal Data:* b Springfield, Mo, Nov 7, 35; m 64, Odell Williams; c Phillip W. *Educ:* Park Col, AB, 57; Smith Col, MA, 59; Yale Univ, PhD(biol), 67. *Honors & Awards:* Claude Pepper Award. *Prof Exp:* Instr zool, Smith Col, 60-61; res assoc, Yale Univ, 67-74. *Concurrent Pos:* Fulbright scholar, Australia, 59-60. *Mem:* Sigma Xi; Assoc Res Otolaryngol. *Res:* Structural and functional correlates of hearing and biosonar; normal and pathological conditions in the inner ear; quantitative morphometry and three dimensional reconstruction (computer assisted) at light and electron microscopic levels of the inner ear; distribution of cells with contractile properties, using immunofluorescence techniques, and their role in hearing; efferent auditory system; magnetic resonance imaging microscopy of inner ear. *Mailing Add:* 317 Reade Rd Chapel Hill NC 27516. *E-Mail:* mmhenson@med.unc.edu

HENSON, BOB LONDES, PHYSICS, APPLIED MATHEMATICS. *Current Pos:* FROM ASST PROF TO PROF PHYSICS, UNIV MO-ST LOUIS, 66- *Personal Data:* b Pierce City, Mo, July 28, 35; m 60, Rayma L Hammer. *Educ:* Univ Mo, BS, 57, MS, 60; Wash Univ, PhD(physics), 64. *Prof Exp:* Res assoc physics, Wash Univ, 64; asst prof, Univ NDak, 64-66. *Mem:* AAAS; Am Phys Soc; Soc Indust & Appl Math; Am Math Soc; Sigma Xi. *Res:* Weakly ionized gases; ion transport phenomena; electrical corona discharges; fluid dynamics; mathematical modeling in physics; hydrology and biophysics; nonequilibrium and irreversible processes. *Mailing Add:* Dept Physics Univ Mo St Louis MO 63121. *Fax:* 314-516-6152; *E-Mail:* bhenson@newton.umsl.edu

HENSON, C WARD, MATHEMATICAL LOGIC. *Current Pos:* from asst prof to assoc prof, 75-81, PROF MATH, UNIV ILL, 81- *Personal Data:* b Worcester, Mass, Sept 25, 40; m 63, Faith Travis; c Julia R, Suzanne A & Claire V. *Educ:* Harvard Univ, AB, 62; Mass Inst Technol, PhD(math), 67. *Prof Exp:* Asst prof, Duke Univ, 67-74; assoc prof, NMex State Univ, 74-75. *Concurrent Pos:* Dept Chair, Univ Ill, 88-92; vis prof, Univ Wis-Madison, 79-80, RWTH Agchen, 85-86, Univ Tuebingen, 92-93. *Mem:* Am Math Soc; Asn Symbolic Logic (secy/treas, 82-); Math Asn Am; Europ Asn Theoret Comput Sci. *Res:* Model theory, nonstandard analysis, geometry of Banach spaces, and logical decision problems. *Mailing Add:* Dept Math Univ Ill 1409 W Green St Urbana IL 61801. *Fax:* 217-333-9576; *E-Mail:* henson@math.uiuc.edu

HENSON, CARL P, CLINICAL CHEMISTRY, HEMATOLOGY. *Current Pos:* sr mgr lab systs, 76-80, staff scientist, Systs Support, Coulter Diag Div, 80-84, MGR MKT RES, COULTER ELECTRONICS, INC, 84- *Personal Data:* b Buffalo, NY, Sept 14, 38. *Educ:* Bethany Col, WVa, BS, 60; Univ Wis-Madison, MS, 63, PhD(biochem), 66. *Prof Exp:* NSF fel, Ind Univ, 66-68; chemist, Xerox Med Diag Opers, 68, sect mgr, 68-69; dir & mgr automated reagents, Biodiagnostics, Inc, 70-71; mgr prod develop, Abbott Sci Prod Div, Abbot Labs, 70-73, mgr clin chem, Abbott Diag Div, 73-76. *Mem:* Am Chem Soc; Am Asn Clin Chem. *Res:* Enzyme kinetics, mechanisms and protein structure; formation of mitochondria; development of high quality analytical methodology and instruments for clinical chemistry; analytical instrument development. *Mailing Add:* Coulter Electronics Inc 11800 SW 147th Ave Bldg 4 Kendall FL 33196

HENSON, DONALD E, EARLY CANCERS. *Current Pos:* PROG DIR, NAT CANCER INST, NIH, 81- *Personal Data:* b St Louis, Mo, Mar 12, 35. *Educ:* St Louis Univ, MD, 62. *Mem:* Int Acad Path; Col Am Pathologists; Asn Pathologists. *Mailing Add:* 4616 Woodfield Rd Bethesda MD 20814-4044

HENSON, EARL BENNETTE, limnology; deceased, see previous edition for last biography

HENSON, JAMES BOND, VETERINARY PATHOLOGY, INTERNATIONAL DEVELOPMENT. *Current Pos:* assoc prof exp path, Wash State Univ, 65-68, chmn dept vet path, 68-74, dir res & grad educ, Col Vet Med, 73-74, dir gen, Int Lab Res on Animal Dis, 74-78, proj dir, Western Sudan Agr Res Proj, 79-84, PROF VET PATH, WASH STATE UNIV, 68-, DIR INT PROG DEVELOP, 78- *Personal Data:* b Colorado City, Tex, Nov 13, 33; m 56; c 3. *Educ:* Tex A&M Univ, BS, 56, DVM, 58, MS, 59; Wash State Univ, PhD(vet path), 64. *Honors & Awards:* Nancy Kay Dunkee Mem Award, 67. *Prof Exp:* Asst vet, Tex Agr Exp Sta, 58-60; NIH fel vet path, Wash State Univ, 60-62; assoc prof, Tex A&M Univ, 62-65. *Concurrent Pos:* NIH res career develop award, 65-; prof exp animal med, Univ Wash Col Med, Seattle, 71-74; dir gen, Int Lab Res Animal Dis, Nairobi, Kenya, 74-78; mem, Prog Res Training Trop Dis, WHO, 78-82; Int Educ & Develop, 78-; Strategic Planning Res Technol Transfer & Econ Develop, 78- *Mem:* Am Vet Med Asn; Am Soc Exp Pathologists; Am Soc Immunologists; Conf Res Workers Animal Dis; Am Col Vet Path. *Mailing Add:* Int Prog Develop Off PO Box 2684 CS Pullman WA 99165-2684. *Fax:* 509-335-1949

HENSON, JAMES WESLEY, PLANT PHYSIOLOGY, CELL BIOLOGY. *Current Pos:* from asst prof to assoc prof, 68-77, PROF BIOL, UNIV TENN, MARTIN, 77- *Personal Data:* b Pierce City, Mo, Dec 30, 29; m 53; c 3. *Educ:* Univ Mo, Columbia, BS, 51, MST, 63, PhD(bot), 68; Washington Univ, MA, 62. *Prof Exp:* Instr pub schs, Mo, 51-59, teacher, 59-65. *Concurrent Pos:* Res asst, Univ Mo, Columbia, 65-68. *Mem:* AAAS. *Res:* Hormonal control of plant growth and development; productivity of aquatic environments. *Mailing Add:* Biol Sci Univ Martin Martin TN 38238-0001

HENSON, JOSEPH LAWRENCE, ENTOMOLOGY, MICROBIOLOGY. *Current Pos:* from instr to prof biol, 57-65, chmn dept biol, 65-73, CHMN DIV NATURAL SCI, BOB JONES UNIV, 74- *Personal Data:* b Hollis, Okla, Aug 13, 32; m 53; c 2. *Educ:* Bob Jones Univ, BSc, 53; Clemson Univ, MSc, 63, PhD(entom), 65. *Prof Exp:* Chief chemist, Vanadium Corp Am, 53, chemist, 56-57. *Concurrent Pos:* Lectr, Univ SC, 64-65 & Clemson Univ, 65-67. *Mem:* AAAS; Am Sci Affil; Entom Soc Am. *Res:* Phytoplankton and zooplankton in sewage lagoons; the effect of apholate on the reproductive organs of face flies; plant pathology; medical entomology; parasitology. *Mailing Add:* Box 34621 Bob Jones Univ Greenville SC 29614

HENSON, MICHAEL CHRIS, PLACENTAL PHYSIOLOGY, ENDOCRINOLOGY OF PREGNANCY & MATERNAL-FETOPLACENTAL UNIT. *Current Pos:* ASST PROF OBSTET & GYNEC, SCH MED, TULANE UNIV, 92- *Personal Data:* b Somerville, Tenn, Mar 19, 54; m 80, Elizabeth Wilbourn; c Katherine, Rachel & Chris. *Educ:* Univ Tenn, Martin, BS, 76, Knoxville, MS 81; Univ Ark, Fayetteville, PhD(physiol), 85. *Prof Exp:* NIH postdoctoral fel perinatal endocrinol, Dept Physiol, Obstet & Gynec, Sch Med, Univ Md, 84-88, res asst prof, 88-92. *Concurrent Pos:* Adj asst prof physiol, Dept Physiol, Sch Med, Tulane Univ, 92-, dir, Sect Perinatal Res, Dept Obstet & Gynec, 92-; affil scientist, Tulane Regional Primate Res Ctr, 92- *Mem:* AAAS; Sigma Xi; Soc Study Reproduction; Endocrine Soc; Asn Profs Gynec & Obstet; Int Fedn Placental Asns. *Mailing Add:* Dept Obstet & Gynec Sch Med Tulane Univ 1430 Tulane Ave New Orleans LA 70112-2699

HENSON, O'DELL WILLIAMS, JR, ANATOMY, PHYSIOLOGY. *Current Pos:* PROF ANAT, SCH MED, UNIV NC, CHAPEL HILL, 74- *Personal Data:* b Kansas City, Mo, Jan 11, 34; m 64, Miriam Morgan; c Phillip. *Educ:* Univ Kans, BA, 57, MA, 60; Yale Univ, PhD(anat), 64. *Honors & Awards:* Alexander von Humboldt Award; Claude Pepper Award. *Prof Exp:* From instr to assoc prof anat, Sch Med, Yale Univ, 63-74. *Concurrent Pos:* Chmn, Comn Anat, State NC. *Mem:* Am Asn Anatomists; Asn Res Otolaryngol; AAAS; Sigma Xi. *Res:* Bio-sonar, particularly neurophysiological correlates of echolocation in bats; comparative anatomy; sensory physiology; magnetic resonance microscopy. *Mailing Add:* Dept Cell Biol & Anat Univ NC Sch Med Taylor Hall CB7090 Chapel Hill NC 27599. *Fax:* 919-966-1856; *E-Mail:* owh@med.unc.edu

HENSON, PAUL D, ORGANIC CHEMISTY, ENVIRONMENTAL SCIENCE & HEALTH. *Current Pos:* dir environ protection, 84-88, mgr hazardous mat protection, 88-91, DIR SAFETY & HAZARDOUS MAT, NORFOLK SOUTHERN CORP, 91- *Personal Data:* b Elliston, Va, Dec 25, 37; m 65; c 1. *Educ:* Roanoke Col, BS, 60; Va Polytech Inst & State Univ, MS, 62, PhD(org chem), 65. *Prof Exp:* From asst prof to assoc prof chem, Roanoke Col, 64-75, prof & chmn dept, 75-80; dir environ protection, Norfolk & Western Rwy Co, 80-84. *Concurrent Pos:* Pub Health Inst spec res fel, Princeton Univ, 68-69; res fel, Med Col Va, Va Commonwealth Univ, 75-76. *Mem:* Am Chem Soc; Sigma Xi; Water Pollution Control Fedn; AAAS; Am Rwy Eng Soc; Am Bd Indust Hyg. *Res:* Organophosphorus chemistry; cancer chemotherapy. *Mailing Add:* 6836 Trevilian Rd NE Roanoke VA 24019-6252

HENSON, PETER MITCHELL, IMMUNOLOGY, CELL BIOLOGY. *Current Pos:* dir res, Dept Pediat, 77-82, EXEC VPRES BIOMED AFFAIRS, NAT JEWISH CTR, 82-; PROF PATH & MED, UNIV COLO MED CTR, 77- *Personal Data:* b Eng, Aug 25, 40; m 62; c 2. *Educ:* Univ Edinburgh, BVM & S, 63, BSc, 64; Cambridge Univ, PhD(immunol), 67. *Prof Exp:* USPHS training grant, Scripps Clin & Res Found, 67-69, assoc, 69-72, assoc mem immunopath, 72-77. *Mem:* AAAS; Royal Col Vet Surg; Am Asn Immunologists; Am Soc Exp Pathologists; Reticuloendothelial Soc. *Res:* Mediation of tissue injury; activation of mediator cells and secretion of mediators; inflammation; complement. *Mailing Add:* Nat Jewish Ctr Immunol & Res Med 1400 Jackson St Denver CO 80206-2762. *Fax:* 303-398-1381

HENSON, RICHARD NELSON, PARASITOLOGY. *Current Pos:* from asst prof to assoc prof, 70-79, PROF INVERT ZOOL & PARASITOL, APPALACHIAN STATE UNIV, 79- *Personal Data:* b Asheville, NC, Mar 13, 41; m 66; c 2. *Educ:* Lamar State Univ, BS, 63; Tex A&M Univ, MS, 66, PhD(zool), 70. *Prof Exp:* Instr invert zool, Tex A&M Univ, 69-70. *Mem:* Am Soc Parasitol; Am Soc Zool. *Res:* Cestodes of elasmobranch fishes; veterinary and human parasites as they relate to various economic problems. *Mailing Add:* Dept Biol Appalachian State Univ One Appalachian State Boone NC 28608-0001

HENSON, W(ILEY) H(IX), JR, AGRICULTURAL ENGINEERING. *Current Pos:* Agr engr, Agr Eng Res Div, 56-61, res invest leader, 61-72, RES LEADER, SOUTHERN REGION, AGR RES SERV, USDA, 72-; ASSOC PROF AGR ENG, UNIV KY, 62-, GRAD FAC, 66- *Personal Data:* b Cohutta, Ga, June 7, 28; m 54; c 3. *Educ:* Univ Ga, BS, 52; NC State Univ, MS, 56, PhD(agr eng), 62. *Concurrent Pos:* Consult & prin investr, US Dept Energy, 75- *Mem:* Sigma Xi; Am Soc Agr Engrs. *Res:* Tobacco curing, including electronic methods of moisture measurement and control; investigation of mathematical models which relate the environmental factors to drying of foliar materials, such as tobacco leaves. *Mailing Add:* 3558 Spendthrift Lane Lexington KY 40517

HENSZ, RICHARD ALBERT, horticulture, for more information see previous edition

HENTEA, TOMA IOAN, SIGNAL PROCESSING, NEURAL NETWORKS & FUZZY LOGIC APPLICATIONS. *Current Pos:* from asst prof to assoc prof, 83-93, PROF ELEC & COMPUT ENG & HEAD, ENG DEPT, PURDUE UNIV, CALUMET, 94- *Personal Data:* m 71, Mariana Ignat; c Irina & Marius. *Educ:* Polytech Inst Timisoara, Romania, BS, 66; Univ Calif, MS, 75, PhD(elec eng & comput sci), 77. *Prof Exp:* Asst prof comput eng, Polytech Inst Timisoara, Romania, 77-82. *Concurrent Pos:* Fulbright scholar, US Govt-Romania Exchange Prog, 73-76; fac res grant, Argonne Nat Lab, 87; vis scientist grant, Advan Mat Inst JRC-Europe Union, 90-91. *Mem:* Inst Elec & Electronics Engrs; Comput Eng Soc; Am Soc Eng Educ. *Res:* Digital filter design for image processing applications; system design for industrial computed tomography; image processing application to fatigue testing of materials; neural networks and fuzzy logic for signal processing and control applications; image processing and fuzzy logic applications to steel industry. *Mailing Add:* Purdue Univ Calumet Hammond IN 46323-2094. *Fax:* 219-989-2898; *E-Mail:* hentea@calumet.purdue.edu

HENTGES, DAVID JOHN, MICROBIOLOGY, BIOCHEMISTRY. *Current Pos:* prof & chmn microbiol & immunol, Sch Med, 81-96, VPROVOST RES, DEAN GRAD SCH BIOMED SCIS & ASSOC DEAN BASIC SCI, HEALTH SCI CTR, TEX TECH UNIV, 96- *Personal Data:* b Le Mars, Iowa, Sept 18, 28; m 57, Kathleen E Mullan; c Stephen, Kathleen & Margaret. *Educ:* Univ Notre Dame, BS, 53; Loyola Univ, Ill, MS, 58, PhD(microbiol), 61. *Prof Exp:* Res assoc, La State Int Ctr Med Res & Training, Costa Rica, 62-64; from asst prof to assoc prof microbiol, Sch Med, Creighton Univ, 64-68; from assoc prof to prof microbiol, Sch Med, Univ Mo, Columbia, 68-81. *Concurrent Pos:* Contract, US Army Med Res & Command, 66-74 & Nat Cancer Inst, 73-76; Thrasher res fund, 86-89; fel, Am Acad Microbiol, 87-; regional ed, Microbiol Ecol Health & Dis, 87- *Mem:* Am Soc Microbiol; Asn Gnotobiotics; Sigma Xi; Soc Microbiol Ecol & Dis (pres, 87-89). *Res:* Enteric bacteriology; anaerobes; role of the intestinal flora in protection against disease. *Mailing Add:* Res & Grad Prog Health Sci Ctr Tex Tech Univ Lubbock TX 79430. *Fax:* 806-743-2656

HENTGES, JAMES FRANKLIN, JR, RUMINANT NUTRITION. *Current Pos:* RETIRED. *Personal Data:* b Perry, Okla, Feb 6, 25; m 46; c 3. *Educ:* Okla Agr & Mech Col, BS, 48; Univ Wis, MS, 50, PhD(animal husb & biochem), 52. *Prof Exp:* Asst biochem, Univ Wis, 48-51, instr animal husb, 51-52; asst prof & asst animal husbandman, Univ Fla, 52-56, assoc prof, 56-66, prof animal husb, 66- *Concurrent Pos:* Consult to Cuban Mission, Int Coop Admin, 57, US Feed Grains Coun, Venezuela, 84. *Mem:* Am Soc Animal Sci; Am Dairy Sci Asn; Am Inst Nutrit; Soc Range Mgt; Nat Cattlemen's Asn. *Mailing Add:* 550 NW 55th St Gainesville FL 32607

HENTGES, LYNNETTE S W, NUTRITION, PHYSIOLOGY. *Current Pos:* NUTRIT-RES CONSULT, 91- *Personal Data:* b Queens, NY, July 19, 57; m 84, Eric J; c Rachel & Margot. *Educ:* Cornell Univ, BS, 79; Iowa State Univ, MS, 81, PhD(nutrit physiol), 84. *Prof Exp:* Res data analyst, Dept Animal Sci, Cornell Univ, 77-79; grad res asst, Nutrit Physiol Sect, Iowa State Univ, 79-84; res assoc, Dept Foods & Nutrit, Univ Ga, 84-87; res scientist, Dept Nutrit, Health & Toxicol, Kraft, Inc, 87-88; nutrit res assoc, Nutrit Res & Tech Serv, Nat Dairy Coun, 88-91. *Mem:* Am Soc Nutrit Scis; Fedn Am Socs Exp Biol. *Res:* Dietary influences on cholesterol and lipoprotein metabolism; diet and chronic disease relationships; endocrine and dietary control of maternal and fetal lipid metabolism during gestation; effects of genetically-induced obesity on serum lipid metabolism. *Mailing Add:* Nutrit-Res Consult 5500 Woodland Ave West Des Moines IA 50266

HENTSCHEL, HILARY GEORGE, TURBULENCE DISORDER SYSTEMS. *Current Pos:* PROF, DEPT PHYSICS, EMORY UNIV, 90- *Personal Data:* b Tel Aviv, Israel, Jan 13, 51. *Educ:* Univ Col London, BSc, 73; Cambridge Univ, PhD(theoret chem), 78. *Prof Exp:* Prof physics, Cambridge Univ, 87-90. *Mem:* Royal Soc Chem; Am Phys Soc. *Mailing Add:* Emory Univ Atlanta GA 30322. *Fax:* 406-727-0873

HENTSCHEL, ROBERT A(DOLF) A(NDREW), METALLURGY. *Current Pos:* RETIRED. *Personal Data:* b New York, NY, Oct 1, 10; m 38; c 3. *Educ:* Mass Inst Technol, ScB, 33, ScD, 36. *Prof Exp:* Metallurgist, Remington Arms Co, Conn, 36-37, res supvr, 37-40, asst mgr res div, NY, 40-42, asst supt process eng & control, 42-44, eng supt tech div, 44-46; res supvr, E I du Pont de Nemours & Co, Inc, 46-47, res mgr, 47-59, prod develop mgr, 59-64, res mgr tech div, 64-75. *Res:* Metallurgy of arms, ammunition and cutlery; design of fire arms; manufacturing processes for fire arms, and rayon and plastic films; properties of and manufacturing processes for synthetic fibers and related products. *Mailing Add:* 3204 Swarthmore Rd Wilmington DE 19807

HENTZ, FORREST CLYDE, JR, INORGANIC CHEMISTRY, PHYSICAL CHEMISTRY. *Current Pos:* asst prof, 64-70, ASSOC PROF CHEM, NC STATE UNIV, 70-, DIR GEN CHEM, 68- *Personal Data:* b Mullins, SC, Aug 20, 33; m 58; c 3. *Educ:* Newberry Col, BS, 55; Univ NC, MA, 58, PhD(chem), 63. *Prof Exp:* From instr to asst prof chem, Randolph-Macon Woman's Col, 58-64. *Concurrent Pos:* Res grant, Water Resources Res Inst NC, 65-68; consult, Am Enka Corp, 64-65. *Mem:* AAAS; Am Chem Soc. *Res:* Hydrolysis and aggregation of metal and metalate ions; chemistry of basic salts, coordination chemistry of second and third-row transition metal ions. *Mailing Add:* 609 Angel Ct Raleigh NC 27606

HENTZEL, IRVIN ROY, MATHEMATICS. *Current Pos:* From asst prof to assoc prof, 68-79, PROF MATH, IOWA STATE UNIV, 79- *Personal Data:* b Burlington, Iowa, July 4, 43; m 70, Patricia Lee Carney; c 4. *Educ:* Univ Iowa, BA, 64, MA, 66, PhD(math), 68. *Concurrent Pos:* Res appointment, Iowa State Univ Sci & Humanities Res Inst, 74- *Mem:* Am Math Soc; Math Asn Am. *Res:* Algebra and ring theory; representation theory; computers in non-associative algebra. *Mailing Add:* Dept Math/400 Carver Hall Iowa State Univ Ames IA 50010-2066. *Fax:* 515-294-5454; *E-Mail:* hentzel@iastate.edu

HENYEY, FRANK S, FLUID DYNAMICS. *Current Pos:* PRIN PHYSICIST, UNIV WASH, 91- *Personal Data:* b Geneva, Wis, Aug 23, 42. *Educ:* Univ Calif, Berkeley, BS, 63; Calif Inst Technol, PhD(physics), 67. *Mem:* Am Phys Soc. *Mailing Add:* Appl Physics Lab HN10 1013 NE 40th St Seattle WA 98105

HENZEL, RICHARD PAUL, ORGANIC CHEMISTRY. *Current Pos:* RES ASSOC, EASTMAN KODAK CO RES LABS, 72- *Personal Data:* b Philadelphia, Pa, Jan 15, 45; m 68; c 2. *Educ:* Lebanon Valley Col, BS, 66; Bucknell Univ, MS, 68; Ohio State Univ, PhD(chem), 72. *Mem:* Am Chem Soc. *Res:* Quinone-hydroquinone chemistry; aromatic chemistry; intramolecular reactions; photographic chemistry. *Mailing Add:* 699 Ashdon Circle Webster NY 14580-9166

HENZL, MILAN RASTISLAV, medicine, endocrinology, for more information see previous edition

HENZLIK, RAYMOND EUGENE, PHYSIOLOGY, HEALTH SCIENCES. *Current Pos:* asst prof biol physiol, Ball State Univ, 62-63, assoc prof physiol, 63-68, radiol health officer, 67-68, Ctr Med Educ, 70-73, PROF PHYSIOL, BALL STATE UNIV, 68- *Personal Data:* b Casper, Wyo, Dec 26, 26; m 50, Wilma Bartels; c 2. *Educ:* Univ Nebr, BS, 48, MS, 52, PhD(zool), 60. *Prof Exp:* Teacher high schs, Nebr, 48-50; supvr biol, Univ Nebr, 52-53; teacher high sch, Nebr, 53-56; instr biol, Nebr Wesleyan Univ, 57-58; from instr to asst prof zool, Univ Nebr, 59-61. *Concurrent Pos:* NSF grants, Acad Year Inst, Cornell Univ, 61-62; consult, Nat Prescription Footwear Applicator's Asn, 62-, lectr pedorthosis mgt, 75-; res, US Radiobiol Lab, Beaufort, NC; res grants, AEC, PR Nuclear Ctr, 67; res grants, Argonne Nat Lab, Ill, 69, consult, Ctr Educ Affairs; fel physiol, Baylor Col Med, 70-71; mem staff, Ball State Europ Ctr Educ, 77-78; fel & vis prof physiol & pharmacol, Col Vet Med, Tex A&M Univ, 84-85. *Mem:* Sigma Xi; Nutrit Today Soc; AAAS; Ecol Soc Am. *Res:* Science education; animal ecology and zoogeography; radiation effects and radioisotopic tracer methodology; physiology-anatomy instructional material. *Mailing Add:* 5009 N Somerset Dr Muncie IN 47304-6501

HEPBURN, FRANK, NUTRITION. *Current Pos:* RETIRED. *Personal Data:* b Peoria, Ill, June 23, 22. *Educ:* Cornell Univ, MA, 48. *Prof Exp:* chief, Nutrit Data Res Br, Human Nutrit Info Serv, USDA, 77-87. *Mailing Add:* 923 Glyndon St SE Vienna VA 22180-5920

HEPBURN, JOHN, PHYSICS. *Current Pos:* PROF CHEM & PHYSICS, UNIV WATERLOO, ONT. *Personal Data:* Sandra Ingham; c Daniel, Monica & Joseph. *Educ:* Univ Waterloo, BSc, 76; Univ Toronto, PhD, 80. *Honors & Awards:* Rutherford Mem Medal in Physics, Royal Soc Can, 93. *Concurrent Pos:* A P Sloan Found fel, 88; Killam fel, 95. *Mem:* Am Phys Soc. *Res:* Laser chemistry and spectroscopy; threshhold photoionization spectroscopy; ZE&E spectroscopy. *Mailing Add:* Dept Chem Univ Waterloo Waterloo ON N6Z 3G1 Can. *Fax:* 519-746-0435; *E-Mail:* hepburn@watsci.uwaterloo.ca

HEPBURN, JOHN CHRISTOPHER, GEOCHEMISTRY OF METAMORPHIC ROCKS, TECTONICS. *Current Pos:* From instr to assoc prof geol, 71-89, chmn, Dept Geol & Geophys, 80-89, PROF GEOL, BOSTON COL, 89- *Personal Data:* b Glen Ridge, NJ, Nov 10, 42; m 71, Judith A Rehmer; c Sabrina K. *Educ:* Colgate Univ, AB, 64; Harvard Univ, AM, 65, PhD(geol), 72. *Mem:* Fel Geol Soc Am; Geochem Soc; fel AAAS; Am Geophys Union; fel Geol Soc (London). *Res:* Petrology of igneous and metamorphic rocks; geochemistry; structure and tectonics of the New England Appalachians. *Mailing Add:* 132 Stanley Rd Newton MA 02168

HEPBURN, JOHN DUNCAN, ACCELERATOR PHYSICS, COMPUTER CONTROL. *Current Pos:* CONSULT, HEPBURN CONSULT, 97- *Personal Data:* b Ganges, Can, Sept 29, 44; m 77; c 3. *Educ:* Univ BC, BSc, 65, MSc, 67; Univ Alta, PhD(elec eng), 73. *Prof Exp:* Asst res officer, Atomic Energy Can Ltd, 67-69, assoc res officer, 73-83, res officer, 83-85, sci admin officer, Res Group, 85-86, admin asst to vpres physics & health sci, 86-90, interim proj mgr, SNO Proj, 89-90, detector proj mgr, SNO Proj, 90-97. *Mem:* Can Asn Physicists. *Res:* High voltage techniques; direct current ion accelerators, electron guns, neutron generators, microprocessors and smart instruments; computer control of accelerator components; project management. *Mailing Add:* Hepburn Consult 44 Eden Point Dr Sudbury ON P3E 4B5 Can

HEPFINGER, NORBERT FRANCIS, ORGANIC CHEMISTRY, POLYMER CHEMISTRY. *Current Pos:* asst prof, 66-70, ASSOC PROF ORG CHEM, RENSSELAER POLYTECH INST, 70-, ASST CHMN, DEPT CHEM, 76- *Personal Data:* b Erie, Pa, Oct 4, 32; m 56; c 4. *Educ:* Gannon Col, BA, 54; Univ Pittsburgh, PhD(chem), 63. *Prof Exp:* Res chemist, Celanese Corp Am, 63-65; Nat Inst Gen Med Sci spec fel chem, Ill Inst Technol, 65-66. *Mem:* Am Chem Soc. *Res:* Additions of aromatic nitroso compounds to olefins; cationic polymerization of cyclic ethers; nuclear magnetic resonance spectroscopy. *Mailing Add:* Dept Chem Rensselaer Polytech Inst 110 Eighth St Troy NY 12180-3522

HEPLER, CHARLES DOUGLAS, PHARMACY, PHARMACY HEALTH CARE ADMINISTRATION. *Current Pos:* PROF & CHMN, DEPT PHARM HEALTH CARE ADMIN, COL PHARM, UNIV FLA, 88-; CO-DIR, DUBOW FAMILY CTR RES PHARMACEUT CARE, 93- *Personal Data:* b Newton, Mass, Dec 18, 38; m 61, Barbara Parks; c Melanie, Andrew & Heather. *Educ:* Univ Conn, BS, 60; Univ Iowa, MS, 65, PhD(pharm & socio-econ), 73. *Honors & Awards:* Achievement Award, Am Soc Hosp Pharmacists Res & Educ Found, 86, Res Award, 89; Parke-Davis Distinguished lectr, Ferris State Univ Col Pharm, 88; Res Achievement Award, Am Pharmaceut Asn, 91; Res Achievement Award, Am Asn Pharmaceut Scientists, 92. *Prof Exp:* Asst chief pharm serv, USPHS Indian Hosp, 61-63; clin res pharm, Univ Iowa, 64-65; assoc dir pharm serv, Duke Univ Med Ctr, 65-66, instr, 66-73, asst prof hosp pharm, Col Pharm, Univ Iowa, 73-80; assoc prof, Dept Pharm & Pharmaceut, Va Commonwealth Univ, 79-88. *Concurrent Pos:* Pharm educ consult, Vet Admin Hosp, Iowa City, 68-; bd dir, Iowa Soc Hosp Pharm, 73-76; ed bd, Drugs in Health Care, Am Soc Hosp Pharm Res & Educ Found, 74-75; chmn, Am Soc Hosp Pharm Coun Educ & Manpower, 83-84; ed, Pharm Mgt, 85- *Mem:* Am Soc Hosp Pharmacists; Am Asn Col Pharm; Am Pub Health Asn; Sigma Xi; AAAS; Am Pharmaceut Asn. *Res:* Professional health service delivery systems; drug prescribing behavior and drug utilization; prescribing and drug use process; sociology of pharmacy. *Mailing Add:* 6515 NW 54th Way Gainesville FL 32653. *Fax:* 904-392-7782; *E-Mail:* hepler.cop1@mail.health.ufl.edu

HEPLER, LOREN GEORGE, physical chemistry, water chemistry; deceased, see previous edition for last biography

HEPLER, OPAL ELSIE, pathology; deceased, see previous edition for last biography

HEPLER, PAUL RAYMOND, HORTICULTURE. *Current Pos:* Asst prof, 56-60, ASSOC PROF HORT, EXP STA, UNIV MAINE, ORONO, 60- *Personal Data:* b Dover, NH, Nov 27, 25; m 59; c 4. *Educ:* Mich State Univ, BS, 48; Univ Ill, MS, 50, PhD(hort), 56. *Concurrent Pos:* Res assoc, Mass Inst Technol, 59-60. *Mem:* Am Soc Sugar Beet Technol; Am Soc Hort Sci; Int Inst Sugar Beet Res. *Res:* Physiology and plant breeding of sugar beets, small fruits and vegetables. *Mailing Add:* 6 Chapel St Orono ME 04473

HEPLER, PETER KLOCK, CELL MOTILITY, CYTOMORPHOGENESIS. *Current Pos:* from assoc prof to prof, 77-89, RAY ETHAN TORREY PROF BOT, UNIV MASS, AMHERST, 89- *Personal Data:* b Dover, NH, Oct 29, 36; m 64; c 3. *Educ:* Univ NH, BA, 58; Univ Wis, PhD(bot), 64. *Honors & Awards:* Pelton Award, Bot Soc Am, 75. *Prof Exp:* Res parasitologist malaria res, Walter Reed Army Inst Res, 64-66; res fel, Harvard Univ, 66-67, lectr cell biol, 67-68, asst prof, 68-70; asst prof, Stanford Univ, 70-77. *Concurrent Pos:* Mem, Develop Biol Panel, NSF, 72-75; investr, Marine Biol Lab, Woods Hole, Mass, 78-; vis prof, Australian Nat Univ, Canberra, 81-82, Univ Siena, Siena, Italy, 85; dir, Plant Growth & Develop Panel, USDA, 86-87. *Mem:* Am Soc Cell Biol; Am Soc Plant Physiol; AAAS. *Res:* Formation, structure and function of the mitotic apparatus in dividing cells, with special reference to the role of calcium ions in the regulation of mitosis; the role of calcium ions as mediators of development in plant cells. *Mailing Add:* Bot Dept Morrill Sci Ctr Univ Mass Amherst MA 01003-0001. *Fax:* 413-545-3243

HEPLER, ROBERT S, ophthalmology, for more information see previous edition

HEPPA, DOUGLAS VAN, NUMERICAL ANALYSIS, NUMERICAL INTEGRATION TECHNIQUES. *Current Pos:* quant analyst, 76-80, assoc staff analyst, 80-81, COMPUT SPECIALIST, NY FIRE DEPT, 81- *Personal Data:* b Brooklyn, NY, May 26, 45; m 75. *Educ:* Polytech Inst, BS, 68, BS, 71, MS, 73 *Prof Exp:* Assoc engr, Submarine Signal Div, Raytheon Co, 68-70; systs engr, PRD Electronics, 70-71; mathematician, Underwater Sound Lab, USN, 71; asst comput engr, George Sharp-Marine Design, 72-73; programmer, New York Dept Social Servs, 75. *Concurrent Pos:* Pres, Algorithm Develop Co Inc, 85- *Mem:* Math Asn Am; Am Mgt Asn; Soc Indust & Appl Math; Asn Comput Mach; Inst Elec & Electronics Engrs; Am Math Soc. *Res:* Investigating new numerical techniques in both two and three dimensional numerical integration and modeling. *Mailing Add:* Arson Info Mgt Syst 49-51 Chambers St New York NY 10007

HEPPE, R RICHARD, AERONAUTICAL ENGINEERING. *Current Pos:* RETIRED. *Personal Data:* b Kansas City, Mo, Mar 4, 23; m 47; c 3. *Educ:* Stanford Univ, BS, 44, MS, 45; Calif Inst Technol, AE, 47. *Honors & Awards:* Slvanus Albert Reed Aeronaut Award, 87. *Prof Exp:* Vpres & gen mgr govt projs, Lockheed Corp, 74-79, vpres opers, 79-81, vpres & asst gen mgr adv develop projs, 81-84, vpres, 74-88, pres, Lockheed-Calif Co, 84-88. *Concurrent Pos:* Sr consult, Rand Corp. *Mem:* Nat Acad Eng; fel Am Inst Aeronaut & Astronaut; Sigma Xi. *Res:* Aerodynamics; dynamics and aircraft design. *Mailing Add:* 3153 Riley Rd Solvang CA 93463

HEPPEL, DAVID ELLIOTT, PEDIATRICS. *Current Pos:* chief, Child & Adolescent Primary Care Servs Br, 83-88, DIR, DIV MATERNAL INFANT CHILD & ADOLESCENT HEALTH, MATERNAL & CHILD HEALTH BUR, 88- *Personal Data:* b Washington, DC, Dec 14, 47; m, Jane Martin; c Jennifer Lynn. *Educ:* Wesleyan Univ, BA, 69; Univ Rochester, MD, 73. *Prof Exp:* off dir, Liaison Indian Affairs, Child & Family Servs Prog, NIMH, 78-80, assoc chief, Child Servs Sect, Div Mental Health Servs Progs, 80-81; dir, Indian Children's Prog, Off Mental Health Progs, Indian Health Serv, Health Resources & Servs Admin, 81-83. *Concurrent Pos:* Instr pediat, Johns Hopkins Med Inst, 78-81; staff app, John F Kennedy Inst, Johns Hopkins Hosp, 78-; mem, Interagency Task Force Presch Handicapped Children, HEW, 791. *Mem:* Soc Develop Pediat. *Res:* Concern for the welfare of this nation's children; trying to assure quality health maintenance services for children and adolescents and working to improve the health and safety of children in child care settings; collaboration of public health departments, private health care providers and buyers of health care to produce efficient community-based systems of health care to meet the variety of health needs of all citizens. *Mailing Add:* Div Maternal Child & Infant Health Rm 18A-39 Parklawn Bldg 5600 Fishers Lane Rockville MD 20857

HEPPEL, LEON ALMA, CELL BIOLOGY. *Current Pos:* prof, 67-92, EMER PROF BIOCHEM, CORNELL UNIV, 92- *Personal Data:* b Granger, Utah, Oct 20, 12; m 44; c 2. *Educ:* Univ Calif, BS, 33, PhD(biochem), 37, MD, 41. *Honors & Awards:* 3M Award Life Sci, Fedn Am Socs Exp Biol, 78. *Prof Exp:* From asst surgeon to surgeon, NIH, 42-51, sr surgeon, 51-57, med dir, 57-58, chief, Lab Biochem & Metab, Nat Inst Arthritis & Metab Dis, 58-67. *Concurrent Pos:* Guggenheim fel, 53 & 75; Fogarty fel, NIH, 80-82. *Mem:* Nat Acad Sci; Am Soc Biol Chemists; Am Chem Soc. *Res:* Study of growth factors and permeable agents in cultured mammalian cells. *Mailing Add:* Dept Biochem Wing Hall Rm 202 Cornell Univ Ithaca NY 14850

HEPPNER, FRANK HENRY, ORNITHOLOGY. *Current Pos:* from asst prof to prof, 69-85, prof, 80-85, HON PROF ZOOL, UNIV RI, 85- *Personal Data:* b San Francisco, Calif, Oct 21, 40; m, Marjorie Donohoe; c Michael. *Educ:* Univ Calif, Berkeley, AB, 62; San Francisco State Col, MA, 64; Univ Calif, Davis, PhD(zool), 67. *Prof Exp:* Res assoc zool, Univ Wash, 67-68, actg asst prof, 68-69. *Concurrent Pos:* Partic, Vis Biologists Prog, Am Inst Biol Sci; consult, Am Petrol Inst, Bur Land Mgt, 73-; Lilly Found fel, 79-80, Fulbright fel, 81-82; vis prof biol, Xavier Univ, 81-82, Univ NMex, 92 & sci educ, Univ Brunei Darussallam, 95-96; Am Assoc Col Nat Comt Biol Maj, 89-90; Fulbright fel, 95-96. *Mem:* Am Soc Zool; Am Ornith Union; Cooper Ornith Soc; Wilson Ornith Soc; Ecol Soc Am; fel Explorer's Club. *Res:* Mechanisms of flocking behavior in birds; population studies of coastal birds; bird aerodynamics. *Mailing Add:* Dept Biol Sci Univ RI Kingston RI 02881. *Fax:* 401-874-4256

HEPPNER, GLORIA HILL, IMMUNOLOGY, CANCER BIOLOGY & BREAST CANCER. *Current Pos:* sr vpres, 85-91, CHMN, DEPT IMMUNOL, MICH CANCER FOUND, 79-; ASSOC CHMN RES, DEPT INTERNAL MED, WAYNE STATE UNIV, 91-; DIR, BREAST CANCER PROG, MEYER L PRENTIS COMPREHENSIVE CANCER CTR, 91-; DEP DIR, KARMANOS CANCER INST, 95- *Personal Data:* b Great Falls, Mont, May 30, 40; div; c Michael. *Educ:* Univ Calif, Berkeley, BA, 62, MA, 64, PhD(bact, immunol), 67. *Prof Exp:* Asst prof biomed sci, Brown Univ, 69-75, assoc prof path, 75-79. *Concurrent Pos:* Damon Runyon fel path, Univ Wash, 67-69; chmn, Nat Bladder Cancer Working Group, 84-89; bd dir, Am Asn Cancer Res, 83-86; mem, exp therapeut, NIH Study Sect, 76-82, path B, 86-88; pres, Women Cancer Res, 89-90; mem, Bd Sci Counrs, NI Dent Res, 92- *Mem:* Am Asn Cancer Res; Am Asn Immunol; AAAS; Int Soc Differentiation (vpres, 90-92, pres, 92-). *Res:* Immune responses to tumors; mouse mammary tumors; tumor heterogeneity; tumor progression; breast cancer; preneoplasia. *Mailing Add:* Karmanos Cancer Inst 110 E Warren Ave Detroit MI 48201. *Fax:* 313-831-3564; *E-Mail:* heppnerg@kci.wayne.edu

HEPPNER, JAMES P, SPACE PHYSICS, GEOPHYSICS. *Current Pos:* SR STAFF ADV, HUGHES STX CORP, 90- *Personal Data:* b Winona, Minn, Aug 9, 27; m 55, Edith Summa; c 3. *Educ:* Univ Minn, BS, 48; Calif Inst Technol, MS, 50, PhD(geophys), 54. *Honors & Awards:* Except Sci Achievement Medal, NASA, John C Lindsay Mem Award, 83. *Prof Exp:* Res proj leader, Geophys Inst, Univ Alaska, 50-52; physicist, Naval Res Lab, 54-58, head electromagnetic fields sect, 58; head magnetic fields sect, Goddard Space Flight Ctr, NASA, Greenbelt, 59-60, asst head fields & particles br, 61-63, head fields & plasmas br, 63-69, assoc chief lab space physics, 69-74, head, Electrodynamics Br, 74-89; mgr space sci, BDM Int, 89-90. *Concurrent Pos:* Tech adv, Bilateral US-USSR Coop in Space, 62-; mem panel world magnetic surv, Geophys Res Bd, Nat Acad Sci, 62-; mem, Int Sci Radio Union; proj scientist, Orbiting Geophys Observ, 65-; discipline rep, Inter-Union Comn Solar Terrestrial Physics, 69- *Mem:* Fel Am Geophys Union. *Res:* Measurement of magnetic and electric fields in space; chemical release measurements of ionospheric winds; auroral physics. *Mailing Add:* 6201 Green Valley Rd New Market MD 21774

HEPPNER, JOHN BERNHARD, SYSTEMATIC ENTOMOLOGY. *Current Pos:* CUR LEPIDOPTERA, FLA STATE COLLECTION ARTHROPODS, 83- *Personal Data:* b Timmendorfer Strand, WGer, Nov 18, 47; US citizen; m 80, A Marina Garcia-Malpartida; c Vanessa. *Educ:* Univ Calif, Berkeley, BA, 70, BS, 72; Univ Fla, PhD(entom), 78. *Prof Exp:* Asst cur entom, Smithsonian Inst, 78-82. *Concurrent Pos:* NSF grants, 76-77, 82-85 & 87-89; exec dir, Asn Trop Lepidop, 89- *Mem:* Lepidop Soc; Royal Entom Soc London; Soc Europaea Lepidop; Asn Trop Lepidop; Am Inst Biol Sci. *Res:* Systematics of microlepidoptera, especially Glyphipterigidae, Choreutidae, Brachodidae, Immidae, Tortricidae and families in Copromorphoidea and Yponomeutoidea. *Mailing Add:* Fla State Collection Arthropods DPI FDACS PO Box 147100 Gainesville FL 32614-7100. *Fax:* 352-955-2301

HEPTINSTALL, ROBERT HODGSON, MEDICINE, PATHOLOGY. *Current Pos:* from assoc prof to prof, 62-69, Baxley Prof Path & Dir Dept, 69-88, DISTINGUISHED SERV PROF PATH, SCH MED, JOHNS HOPKINS UNIV, 88- *Personal Data:* b Keswick, Eng, July 22, 20; m 50, Ann Enright Porter; c Bridge, Gillian, Jonathans, James, Caroline & Christopher. *Educ:* Univ London, MB & BS, 44, MD, 48. *Honors & Awards:* Maude Abbott Lectr, Int Acad Path, 83; David M Home Award, Nat Kidney Found, 86; John P Peters Award, Am Soc Nephrol, 93. *Prof Exp:* Registr bact, Wright-Fleming Inst, Eng, 47; registr path, St Mary's Hosp, 47-49 & from jr lectr to sr lectr, 49-60; vis prof, Wash Univ, 60-62. *Concurrent Pos:* Med Res Coun Eli Lilly fel, Johns Hopkins Hosp, 54-55, pathologist, 62-69 & 88-, pathologist-in-chief, 69-88; consult, Path Study Sect, NIH, 63-71; ed, Lab Invest, 76-81. *Mem:* US-Can Acad Path; Am Soc Nephiology (pres, 72-73); Int Soc Nephrol, (vpres, 81-84). *Res:* Human and experimental arteriosclerosis; hypertension and renal disease in general. *Mailing Add:* Dept Path Johns Hopkins Hosp 600 N Wolfe St Baltimore MD 21205

HEPTON, ANTHONY, vegetable crops, for more information see previous edition

HEPWORTH, H(ARRY) KENT, MECHANICAL ENGINEERING. *Current Pos:* asst prof mech eng, 70-75, assoc prof mech eng, 75-81, PROF AREA COORDR MECH ENG, NORTHERN ARIZ UNIV, 76-, PROF ENG & TECHNOL, 81- *Personal Data:* b Phoenix, Ariz, Aug 14, 42; m 74; c 2. *Educ:* Okla State Univ, BS, 64; Ariz State Univ, MS, 66, PhD(eng), 70. *Prof Exp:* Res assoc fluid mech, Ariz State Univ, 69-70. *Concurrent Pos:* Consult, Aires Mfrs Co Calif, 79-84, Gen Dynamics Convair & Space Systs Div, 85- *Mem:* Am Soc Mech Engrs; assoc fel Am Inst Aeronaut & Astronaut; Am Soc Eng Educ; Sigma Xi. *Res:* Fluid mechanics with special emphasis in non-steady internal flows, thin film lubrication and vortex phenomenon; gas turbine engine operation; thermodynamics with specialty in cryogenics. *Mailing Add:* Mech Eng PO Box NAV Northern Ariz Univ Flagstaff AZ 86011

HEPWORTH, MALCOLM T(HOMAS), METALLURGY. *Current Pos:* sr res metallurgist, 75-79, SECT SUPVR, AMAX EXTRACTIVE RES & DEVELOP INC, 79-; PROF CIVIL & MINERAL ENG, UNIV MINN. *Personal Data:* b Singapore, Malaya, Oct 1, 32; nat US; m 57, Elouise Peck; c Allison, Marianna, Edward & Todd. *Educ:* Mass Inst Technol, BS, 54; Purdue Univ, PhD(metall), 58. *Prof Exp:* Asst, Purdue Univ, 54-58; asst prof metall eng, Colo Sch Mines, 58-61; assoc prof, Purdue Univ, 61-68; from assoc prof to prof metall & chmn, Univ Denver, 68-75. *Concurrent Pos:* Metallurgist, US Bur Mines, Nev, 68. *Mem:* Am Inst Mining, Metall & Petrol Engrs; fel Am Inst Chemists; Sigma Xi; Hazardous Material Control Res Inst. *Res:* Solid and hazardous waste processing and recovery; desulfurization of fuel gases via regenerable sorbents; pollution prevention via process modifications; alternate uses for waste products: oil sorbents from waste tire shreddings; granted 10 US patents. *Mailing Add:* Dept Civil Eng 500 Pillsbury Dr SE Minneapolis MN 55455-0220. *Fax:* 612-626-7750; *E-Mail:* hepwo001@maroon.tc.umn.edu

HERAKOVICH, CARL THOMAS, ENGINEERING MECHANICS. *Current Pos:* PROF APPL MECH & DIR APPL MECH PROG, UNIV VA, 87- *Personal Data:* b East Chicago, Ind, Aug 6, 37; m 60, Marlene Vukowich; c 4. *Educ:* Rose-Hulman Inst Technol, BS, 59; Univ Kans, MS, 62; Ill Inst Technol, PhD(mech), 68. *Prof Exp:* Asst prof civil eng, Rose-Hulman Inst Technol, 62-64; instr mech, Ill Inst Technol, 64-67; from asst prof to assoc prof eng mech, Va Polytech Inst & State Univ, 67-76, asst head dept, 71-72, prof eng sci & mech, 76-87. *Mem:* Fel Am Soc Civil Engrs; fel Am Soc Mech Engrs; Soc Exp Stress Anal; Am Soc Testing & Mat; Soc Eng Sci; Soc Advan Mat Process Eng; fel Am Acad Mech. *Res:* Mechanics of composite materials, theory and experiment. *Mailing Add:* Dept Civil Eng & Appl Mech Univ Va Charlottesville VA 22903. *Fax:* 804-982-2951; *E-Mail:* herak@virginia.edu

HERALD, CHERRY LOU, ORGANIC CHEMISTRY. *Current Pos:* sr res chemist natural prod isolation, Cancer Res Inst, Ariz State Univ, 74-83, asst to dir, 77-89, from assoc res prof to res prof, 81-89, RES PROF & ASSOC DIR, CANCER RES INST, ARIZ STATE UNIV, 89- *Personal Data:* b Beeville, Tex, Dec 23, 40; m 64, Delbert L Jr; c Heather A & Delbert L III. *Educ:* Ariz State Univ, BS, 62, MS, 65, PhD(org chem), 68. *Mem:* Am Chem Soc; Am Soc Pharmacog. *Res:* Isolation of potential antineoplastic agents from natural sources of plants, insects, marine animals. *Mailing Add:* 1324 W Seventh St Tempe AZ 85281

HERALD, DELBERT LEON, JR, NATURAL PRODUCTS CHEMISTRY. *Current Pos:* fac res assoc, Cancer Res Inst, Ariz State Univ, 73-80, from res chemist to sr res chemist, 80-84, asst res prof, 84-87, ASSOC RES PROF, CANCER RES INST, ARIZ STATE UNIV, 88- *Personal Data:* b Fondis, Colo, Oct 9, 41; m 64, Cherry L Bell; c Heather A & Delbert L III. *Educ:* Univ Colo, BA, 63; Ariz State Univ, PhD(org chem), 70. *Prof Exp:* Ga Forest Res Coun-NSF fel, 69-70, univ gen res grant, Univ Ga, 70-71; sea grant chem, Univ Okla, 71-73. *Mem:* Am Chem Soc; Am Soc Pharmacog. *Res:* Chemistry and reactions of epoxides; x-ray crystallography: isolation, synthesis and structure determination of antineoplastic drugs, particularly of plant and marine origin; computer assisted synthetic and structure analysis. *Mailing Add:* 1324 W Seventh St Tempe AZ 85281. *E-Mail:* dherald@asu.edu

HERB, JOHN A, SEMICONDUCTOR PHYSICS, CHEMICAL VAPOR DEPOSITION. *Current Pos:* DIR PROD DEVELOP, CRYSTALLUME. *Personal Data:* b Wauseon, Ohio, Dec 1, 46. *Educ:* Miami Univ, BS, 68; Univ Wash, MS, 69, PhD(physics), 74. *Prof Exp:* Teaching asst physics, Univ Wash, 68-70; res asst, Univ Wash, 70-74; res fel physics, Calif Inst Technol, 74-77; physicist, Optoelectronic Div, Hewlett Packard, 77-83; mat develop mgr, Microwave Prod Div, Gould Elect, 83-85, res & develop mgr, 85-88. *Concurrent Pos:* Physicist, Lawrence Livermore Lab, 69. *Mem:* Am Inst Physics; Mat Res Soc; Electrochem Soc; Inst Elec & Electronics Engrs. *Res:* Growth and properties of diamurd by chemical vapor deposition; device research and epitaxial growth of compound semiconductors. *Mailing Add:* Crystallume 3506 Bassett St Santa Clara CA 95054

HERB, RAYMOND GEORGE, physics; deceased, see previous edition for last biography

HERBACH, LEON HOWARD, STATISTICS, MATH. *Current Pos:* admin officer, Polytech Univ, 73-74, head dept, 74-78, prof opers res & syst anal, 73-77, PROF MATH & STATIST, POLYTECH UNIV, 78- *Personal Data:* b Brooklyn, NY, Jan 9, 23; m 48; c 2. *Educ:* Brooklyn Col, AB, 43; Columbia Univ, AM, 47, PhD(math statist), 57. *Prof Exp:* Instr math, Brooklyn Col, 46-50 & 51-53; lectr math & statist, Hunter Col, 50; from res assoc to sr res scientist, Res Div, Sch Eng, NY Univ, 53-62, lectr & adj asst prof indust eng, 56-57, adj asst prof math, 57-58, adj assoc prof, 58-61, adj assoc prof opers res, 61, from assoc prof to prof, 62-73. *Concurrent Pos:* Consult, Mus Natural Hist, 49-50; statist consult serv, Columbia Univ, 50-51, Radio Corp Am, 58, Am Power Jet Co, 62-, Naval Appl Sci Lab, 63-70, US Army, 76-77 & Mobil, 79-81; Inst Math Statist rep, Int Adv Comt Statist Nomenclature, Int Stand Orgn, 67-72; vis prof, Univ Grenoble, 68-69, Technion, 79 & Univ Lisbon, 80. *Mem:* Am Statist Asn; Inst Math Statist; Opers Res Soc Am; Int Statist Inst; Sigma Xi. *Res:* Reliability; probabilistic models and statistical inference as applied in engineering and physical science; analysis of variance; teaching statistics to engineers. *Mailing Add:* 136 Waverly Rd Scarsdale NY 10583

HERBEIN, JOSEPH HENRY, JR, RUMINANT NUTRITION, HEPATIC METABOLISM. *Current Pos:* asst prof, 78-84 ASSOC PROF ANIMAL NUTRIT, VA POLYTECH INST & STATE UNIV, 84- *Personal Data:* b Dec 16, 43; m 66, Sue Bortz; c Jennifer & Joel. *Educ:* Pa State Univ, BSc, 71,

MSc, 73, PhD(animal nutrit), 76. *Prof Exp:* Res assoc, Iowa State Univ, 76-78. *Mem:* Am Inst Nutrit; Am Dairy Sci Asn; Am Soc Animal Sci. *Res:* Nutritional and endocrine control of hepatic and mammary gland metabolism; lactation. *Mailing Add:* Dept Dairy Sci Va Polytech & State Univ Blacksburg VA 24061-0315. *Fax:* 540-231-5014

HERBEL, CARLTON HOMER, RANGE SCIENCE. *Current Pos:* res leader, Jornada Exp Range & tech adv range mgt, 72-87, RES RANGE SCIENTIST, JORNADA EXP STA, WESTERN REGION, SCI & EDUC ADMIN-AGR RES, USDA, 56-72 & 87- *Personal Data:* b San Antonio, Tex, June 2, 27; m 52, Carolene Callahan; c Belinda A (Fiedler) & Kurt C. *Educ:* Tex Col Arts & Indust, BS, 49; Kans State Univ, MS, 54, PhD(agron), 56. *Prof Exp:* Asst agronomist, Southwest Found Res, 49-50; asst, Kans State Univ, 53-56; agronomist, Southwest Found Res, 56. *Concurrent Pos:* Mem grad fac, NMex State Univ; mem range mgt task force, Great Plains Agr Coun, 74-78; mem directorate, US Man & Biosphere Prog Grazing Lands, 75-88. *Mem:* Soc Range Mgt; Am Soc Agron; Sigma Xi; fel AAAS. *Res:* Physiological effects of environment on range plants; microclimate; reseeding; brush control; grazing management; soil-plant-environment-animal relationships. *Mailing Add:* USDA Agr Res Serv Jornada Exp Range NMex State Univ PO Box 30003 Dept 3JER Las Cruces NM 88003-0003. *Fax:* 505-646-5889; *E-Mail:* vlaplant@nmsu.edu

HERBENER, GEORGE HENRY, QUANTITATIVE ELECTRON MICROSCOPY, IMMUNOCYTOCHEMISTRY. *Current Pos:* from instr to assoc prof, 68-89, PROF, SCH MED, UNIV LOUISVILLE, 89- *Personal Data:* b Watertown, Wis, Oct 19, 29. *Educ:* Wartburg Col, BA, 60; Univ Louisville, MS, 60, PhD(anat), 68. *Prof Exp:* Res biologist path, US Army Med Res Lab, Ft Knox, Ky, 63-67. *Mem:* Am Soc Cell Biol. *Res:* Immunocytochemical, cytochemical and stereological studies on protein secretion; cell biology. *Mailing Add:* Dept Anat Sci & Neurobiol Health Sci Ctr Univ Louisville Louisville KY 40292-0001. *Fax:* 502-852-6228; *E-Mail:* ghherb01@ulkyvm.louisville.edu

HERBENER, ROLAND EUGENE, ORGANIC CHEMISTRY. *Current Pos:* PROF CHEM & HEAD DEPT, IIILLSDALE COL, 61 *Personal Data:* b Wilmington, Del, Mar 5, 23; m 45; c 4. *Educ:* Western Mich Univ, AB, 48; Univ Del, MS, 52; Univ NH, MS, 62. *Prof Exp:* Teacher high sch, Mich, 48-61. *Concurrent Pos:* Mem, NSF Res Partic & Acad Year Exten for Col Chem Teachers, Ohio, 64-65, NSF sci fac fel, 66-67. *Mem:* Am Chem Soc. *Res:* Derivatives of 1, 2, 4-Triazine, its reactions; computer applications in chemistry and chemical education. *Mailing Add:* 9 W Hallett St Hillsdale MI 49242

HERBER, JOHN FREDERICK, ORGANIC CHEMISTRY. *Current Pos:* Res chemist, 60-65, res specialist, 65-66, group leader res & develop, 66-76, mgr res & develop, 76-79, technol mgr, process chem, Monsanto Flavor & Essence, Monsanto Chem Intermediates Co, 79-82, MGR RES & DEVELOP, MONSANTO INDUST CHEM CO, 83- *Personal Data:* b Ft Wayne, Ind, Mar 27, 33; m 55; c 4. *Educ:* Univ Notre Dame, BS, 55; Univ Pa, PhD(org chem), 60. *Mem:* Am Chem Soc. *Res:* Synthesis, process development and manufacture of chemical intermediates. *Mailing Add:* No 29 Crestwood Dr St Louis MO 63105-3072

HERBER, LAWRENCE JUSTIN, MINERALOGY, ENGINEERING GEOLOGY. *Current Pos:* Asst prof geol, 66-70, assoc prof physics & earth sci, 70-74, PROF GEOL, CALIF STATE POLYTECH UNIV, POMONA, 74- *Personal Data:* b Ft Wayne, Ind, Sept 5, 37; m 61, Lucy S Gonzales; c 6. *Educ:* St Joseph's Col, BA, 59; NMex Inst Mining & Technol, MS, 62; Univ Nev, PhD(geol), 68. *Concurrent Pos:* Consult geologist; earth sci coordr, 69-71. *Mem:* AAAS; Nat Asn Geol Teachers; Am Geol Inst; Inland Geol Soc. *Res:* Order and disorder in co-existing feldspars; Cucamonga fault; floatation-separation of feldspars from quartz; geology in land use and urban planning; erosion in granite monuments; failure mechanisms of large paleolandslides. *Mailing Add:* Dept Geol Sci Calif State Polytech Univ 3801 W Temple Ave Pomona CA 91768-2557

HERBER, RAYMOND, GASTROENTEROLOGY, BIOCHEMISTRY. *Current Pos:* instr, Sch Med, Loma Linda Univ, 63-64, asst prof, 66-72, assoc prof, 72-81, PROF INTERNAL MED, SCH MED, LOMA LINDA UNIV, 81- *Personal Data:* b Sattuck, Okla, Mar 1, 32; m 54; c 2. *Educ:* Union Col, Nebr, BA, 53; Loma Linda Univ, MD, 57; Am Bd Internal Med, dipl, 65. *Prof Exp:* Fel gastroenterol, Sch Med, Washington Univ, 64-66. *Mem:* Am Fedn Clin Res; Am Asn Study Liver Dis; fel Am Col Physicians; Am Gastroenterol Asn; Sigma Xi. *Res:* Pathogenesis and genetic considerations in disaccharidase deficiency in the human intestinal mucosa; bilirubin metabolism in the isolated rat liver. *Mailing Add:* 11561 Richardson St Loma Linda CA 92354-3439

HERBER, ROLFE H, CHEMICAL PHYSICS, SOLID STATE PHYSICS. *Current Pos:* from asst prof to assoc prof, 59-77, DISTINGUISHED PROF CHEM, RUTGERS UNIV, NEW BRUNSWICK, 77- *Personal Data:* b Ger, Mar 10, 27; nat US; m 54; c 3. *Educ:* Univ Calif, Los Angeles, BS, 49; Ore State Univ, PhD(phys chem), 52. *Prof Exp:* Res assoc chem, Mass Inst Technol, 52-55; asst prof, Univ Ill, 55-59. *Concurrent Pos:* NSF sr fel, 65-66; vis sr scientist, Ctr Nuclear Studies, Grenoble, France, 74; mem exec bd, Int Comt Application of Mossbauer Effect, 75-; Karl Taylor Compton prof physics, Technion, 81, 82; JSPS lectr, Japan, 78. *Mem:* Fel Am Phys Soc; Fel AAAS. *Res:* Nuclear chemistry; radiochemistry; Mossbauer effect; hot atom chemistry; FTIR low temp vibrational spectroscopy. *Mailing Add:* Dept Chem Rutgers Univ Busch Campus PO Box 939 Piscataway NJ 08855-0939

HERBERMAN, RONALD BRUCE, CANCER CENTER ADMINISTRATION, CANCER IMMUNOLOGY. *Current Pos:* DIR, PITTSBURGH CANCER INST, 85-; PROF MED & PATH, SCH MED, UNIV PITTSBURGH, 85- *Personal Data:* b Brooklyn, NY, Dec 26, 40; m 63; c Steve & Holly. *Educ:* NY Univ, BA, 60, MD, 64. *Hon Degrees:* MD, Univ Rome, 86. *Honors & Awards:* Lifetime Sci Award, Inst Advan Studies Immunol & Aging, 92. *Prof Exp:* Intern & asst resident med, Mass Gen Hosp, 64-66; clin assoc immunol, USPHS, 66-68; sr investr, Immunol Br, Nat Cancer Inst, NIH, 68-71, head, Cellular & Tumor Immunol Sect, Lab Cell Biol, 71-74, chief, Lab Immunodiag, 75-81 & Biol Therapeut Br, 81-85. *Concurrent Pos:* Sect ed, J Immunol, 74-77; assoc ed, Cancer Res, 75-, Clin Immunol & Immunopath, 78-, J Immunol Methods & Clin Immunol Ther, 80-, J Clin Immunol, 81- & J Nat Cancer Inst, 72-; actg assoc dir biol response prog, Nat Cancer Inst, NIH, 81-85, dir immunodiag contract prog, 72-76; mem, Immunol & Immunother Study Sect, Am Cancer Soc, 84-; mem, FDA rev panel diag tests, 79-83; mem, AIDS Clin Drug Develop Comt, Nat Inst Allergy & Infectious Dis, 86-; bd dirs, Am Asn Cancer Res, 87-90. *Mem:* Reticuloendothelial Soc (pres, 84); Am Soc Clin Invest; Am Asn Immunologists; Am Asn Cancer Res; Int Soc Interferon Res; fel Am Acad Microbiol; Clin Immunol Soc; Soc Biol Ther; Am Soc Clin Oncol. *Res:* Cancer immunology and immunotherapy; immunodiagnostic tests for cancer; natural killer cells characterization and in vivo role in resistance to cancer and AIDS. *Mailing Add:* Pittsburgh Cancer Inst 3471 Fifth Ave Suite 201 Pittsburgh PA 15213. *Fax:* 412-692-4665

HERBERT, DAMON CHARLES, ANATOMY, ENDOCRINOLOGY. *Current Pos:* Instr, Univ Tex Health Sci Ctr, 73-74, asst prof, 74-78, assoc prof, 78-95, PROF CELLULAR & STRUCT BIOL & INTERIM ASSOC DEAN STUDENT AFFAIRS, GRAD SCH BIOMED SCIS, UNIV TEX HEALTH SCI CTR, SAN ANTONIO, 95- *Personal Data:* b New York, NY, Apr 15, 45; m 67, Marjorie E Geoden; c Garrick T & Michelle L. *Educ:* Calif State Univ, Chico, AB, 67; Univ Calif, San Francisco, PhD(anat), 73. *Concurrent Pos:* Edith Claypole fel, Univ Calif, San Francisco, 70-72; res grants, NIH, 71-81, NSF, 82-85, March of Dimes, 86-91; assoc ed, The Anat Record, 78- *Mem:* Am Asn Anat; Soc Study Reproduction; Am Asn Dent Schs; AAAS; Sigma Xi. *Res:* Reproductive endocrinology; pituitary histophysiology; published over 200 scientific papers and abstracts. *Mailing Add:* Dept Cellular & Struct Biol Univ Tex Health Sci Ctr 7703 Floyd Curl Dr San Antonio TX 78284-7762. *E-Mail:* herbert@hthscsa.edu

HERBERT, FLOYD LEIGH, ASTROPHYSICS, GEOPHYSICS. *Current Pos:* Res assoc, Solar Syst Astrophys, 75-79, SR RES ASSOC, LUNAR & PLANETARY LAB, UNIV ARIZ, 79- *Personal Data:* b Orange, Calif, Apr 16, 42; m 92, Mary A Gilman. *Educ:* Calif Inst Technol, BS, 64; Univ Ariz, PhD(physics), 75. *Mem:* Am Astron Soc; Am Geophys Union; AAAS. *Res:* Origin and evolution of solar system bodies; planetary thermospheres, exospheres, magnetospheres; physics of the plasma interactions with planetary atmospheres, fields and surfaces. *Mailing Add:* Lunar & Planetary Lab W Gould-Simpson Bldg Univ Ariz Tucson AZ 85721. *Fax:* 520-621-8364; *E-Mail:* herbert@vega.lpl.arizona.edu

HERBERT, JACK DURNIN, BIOCHEMISTRY, NUTRITION. *Current Pos:* from instr to asst prof, 70-76, ASSOC PROF BIOCHEM, MED CTR, LA STATE UNIV, NEW ORLEANS, 76- *Personal Data:* b Hammond, La, Aug 2, 40; m 68; c 2. *Educ:* Southwestern Univ, Memphis, BA, 62; La State Univ, New Orleans, MS, 65, PhD(biochem), 67. *Prof Exp:* Instr pharmacol, Med Ctr, La State Univ, New Orleans, 67-68; tech dir clin chem, Cent Path Lab, Path Assocs New Orleans, 68-70. *Concurrent Pos:* Chief chemist, La Community Pesticide Study, 67-68; consult, Cent Path Lab, Path Assocs New Orleans, 70-72. *Mem:* Am Inst Nutrit; Am Soc Biol Chemists; NY Acad Sci. *Res:* Intermediary metabolism of amino acids; protein nutrition; role of carbonic anhydrase in intermediary metabolism. *Mailing Add:* Dept Biochem La State Univ Med Ctr 1100 Florida Ave New Orleans LA 70119-2714

HERBERT, MARC L, SOFTWARE ENGINEERING. *Current Pos:* SR ENGR, LOCKHEED MARTIN CORP, 82- *Personal Data:* b Kew Gardens, NY, Sept 2, 48; m 82, Judith Leichman; c 2. *Educ:* State Univ NY, BA, 69; Purdue Univ, MS, 71; Univ Pittsburgh, PhD(physics), 78. *Prof Exp:* Sr engr, Singer-Kearfott, 78-82. *Concurrent Pos:* Adj asst prof, William Paterson State Col, 80-81, Hofstra Univ, 82-85. *Mem:* Am Phys Soc; Inst Elec & Electronics Engrs. *Res:* Software engineering; computer aided software engineering; software testing; automated documentation; real-time systems. *Mailing Add:* 3450 Manchester Rd Wantagh NY 11793. *E-Mail:* herbert@turbo__system.gn.ramax.com

HERBERT, MICHAEL, BACTERIOLOGY, BIOCHEMISTRY. *Current Pos:* assoc prof, 63-67, PROF BIOL SCI, BLOOMSBURG STATE COL, 67- *Personal Data:* b Lansford, Pa, May 29, 28. *Educ:* Univ Md, BS, 53; Lehigh Univ, MS, 55, PhD(bact), 60. *Prof Exp:* Chemist, Lehigh Valley Coop Dairy, Pa, 53-55; instr bact, Univ Mass, 60-61; res assoc sanit eng, Johns Hopkins Univ, 61-63. *Mem:* AAAS; Am Soc Microbiol; Am Pub Health Asn. *Res:* Interaction of nitrated and halogenated phenols with amino acids; effect of phenols on bacteria and their reversal by amino acids; water pollution; environmental health; aquatic microbiology; dairy bacteriology. *Mailing Add:* Dept Biol Sci Bloomsburg Univ Bloomsburg PA 17815

HERBERT, MORLEY ALLEN, FUNCTIONAL ELECTRICAL STIMULATION. *Current Pos:* DIR RES, HUMANA ADVAN SURG INST, DALLAS, TEX, 88- *Personal Data:* b Toronto, Ont, July 7, 44; m 68; c 3. *Educ:* Univ Toronto, BSc, 66, MSc, 68, PhD(med biophys), 72. *Prof Exp:* Res assoc, Hosp Sick Children, 72-77, scientist, 77-81, from asst prof to assoc prof surg, 81-88; res assoc, Univ Toronto, 79-82, asst prof surg, 82-88, adj asst prof biomed eng, 83-88. *Concurrent Pos:* Consult, Dept Orthod, Univ Toronto, 83-88, Ont Ctr Crippled Children, 80-88 & Bur Med Devices, Govt Can, 84-85. *Mem:* Scoliosis Res Soc; NY Acad Sci; Can Med & Biol Eng Soc; Biomat Soc Can; Can Stand Asn. *Res:* Investigations of effect of electrical muscle and nerve stimulation on the body and its clinical application in areas of rehabilitation; electro-magnetic fields and growth. *Mailing Add:* 6320 Clear Ridge Dr Dallas TX 75248

HERBERT, STEPHEN AVEN, PETROLEUM CHEMISTRY, RESEARCH ADMINISTRATION. *Current Pos:* res chemist, Res Lab, Shell Oil Co, 52-54, technologist, Mfg Res Dept, NY, 54-57, group leader res lab, 57-60, spec engr prod appln dept, 61-64, mgr eastern region prod appl dept, 65-67, gen supt int lubricant corp, 67-69, mgr sales & tech develop lubricants, 69-70, mgr prod dept, MTM Res Lab, Ill, 70-71, mgr indust prod, Oil Prod Res & Develop Lab, Shell Develop Co, 71-74, mgr lubricants, 75-79, MGR FUELS & LUBRICANTS DEPT, OIL PROD RES & DEVELOP LAB, SHELL DEVELOP CO, 80- *Personal Data:* b Houston, Tex, July 1, 23; m 46; c 3. *Educ:* Pa State Univ, BS, 44, MS, 48; Purdue Univ, PhD(chem), 52. *Prof Exp:* Res assoc fuel technol, Mineral Indust Exp Sta, Pa State Univ, 44-45, 47-48; asst chem, Purdue Univ, 48-49. *Mem:* Am Chem Soc; fel Am Inst Chem; NY Acad Sci; Soc Automotive Engrs. *Res:* High pressure hydrogenation of coal; reaction of alkyl halides with silver salts free radical chemistry; polymers; lubricant research; rubber chemistry; all types of lubrication; electrochemical studies related to fuel cells and super batteries. *Mailing Add:* 3307 El Dorado Blvd Missouri City TX 77459-3013

HERBERT, THOMAS JAMES, BIOPHYSICS. *Current Pos:* asst prof, 74-79, ASSOC PROF BIOL, UNIV MIAMI, 80- *Personal Data:* b Seattle, Wash, Nov 3, 42; m 72; c 2. *Educ:* Mass Inst Technol, BS, 64; Johns Hopkins Univ, PhD(biophys), 70. *Prof Exp:* Fel biophys, Johns Hopkins Univ, 70-71 & Brown Univ, 71-72; res assoc biophys, Cornell Univ, 72-74. *Mem:* Biophys Soc; Am Chem Soc; Am Optical Soc; Sigma Xi. *Res:* Laser light scattering from muscle proteins cytoplasmic contractile systems; electro-optical methods applied to biological systems. *Mailing Add:* Biol Univ Miami PO Box 248106 Miami FL 33124-8106

HERBERT, THORWALD, NONLINEAR PHENOMENA, COMPUTATIONAL SCIENCE. *Current Pos:* PROF MECH & AEROSPACE ENG, OHIO STATE UNIV, 87- *Personal Data:* b Horba, Ger, July 13, 37; c 3. *Educ:* Univ Gottingen, Ger, dipl, 63; Univ Karlsruhe, Dr Eng, 74; Univ Stuttgart, Dr Eng, 78. *Prof Exp:* Res asst astrophys, Max-Planck Inst Physics, 58-59; res asst comput physics, AVA Gottingen, 59-63; res scientist, Max-Planck Inst Aeronomy, 63-66, Max-Planck Inst Fluid Mech, 66-67 & DFVLR-AVA Gottingen, 67-71; asst appl math, Univ Freiburg, 71-77; pvt docent aerospace eng, Univ Stuttgart, 77-80; prof eng sci, Va Polytech Inst & State Univ, 80-87. *Concurrent Pos:* Prin investr, NSWC, White Oak, Md, 81-82, Off Naval Res, 83-85, US Army, Aberdeen Proving Ground, 83- & Off Sci Res, Bolling AFB, 84-; consult, Batelle Res, Triangle Park, NC, 82 & ICASE, Hampton, Va, 87-90; pres, Dyna Flow, Inc, 90- *Mem:* Fel Am Phys Soc; Am Inst Aeronaut & Astronaut; Am Soc Mech Eng; Sigma Xi; Soc Eng Sci. *Res:* Fluid dynamics: hydrodynamic stability, laminar-turbulent transition, wave phenomena, steady and unsteady viscous flows, stratified, rotating, compressible and real gas flows; methods: analytical modeling and numerical simulation, diagnostic tools and visual methods for analysis of computational data. *Mailing Add:* Dynaflow Inc 3040 Riverside Dr Suite 109 PO Box 21319 Columbus OH 43221

HERBERT, VICTOR, MEDICINE. *Current Pos:* PROF MED, MT SINAI MED CTR, 85- *Personal Data:* b New York, NY, Feb 22, 27; m 53, 68; c Robert, Steven, Kathy, Alissa & Laura. *Educ:* Columbia Univ, BS, 48, MD, 52, JD, 74. *Honors & Awards:* McCollum Award, Am Soc Clin Nutrit, 72; Middleton Award, US Vet Admin, 78; Herman Award, Am Soc Clin Nutrit, 86; Dupont Award, Clin Ligand Assay Soc, 89; Van Slyke Award, Am Asn Clin Chem, 90. *Prof Exp:* Intern, Walter Reed Army Med Ctr, 52-53; jr asst resident med, Montefiore Hosp, NY, 54-55; asst hemat, Mt Sinai Hosp, 58-59; from instr med to asst prof, Harvard Med Sch, 59-64; assoc clin prof, Col Physicians & Surgeons, Columbia Univ, 64-70, clin prof med, 74-76; vchmn, Downstate Med Ctr, 76-80, prof med, State Univ NY Downstate Med Ctr, 76-84, attend physician, Univ Hosp, 76-84; chair med, Hahnemann Univ, 84-85. *Concurrent Pos:* Sr res fel hemat, Montefiore Hosp, NY, 57-58; res fel med, Albert Einstein Col Med, Yeshiva Univ, 55-57; res assoc, Thorndike Mem Lab, Boston City Hosp, 59-64; med consult, WHO, 62-; assoc dir hemat, Mt Sinai Hosp, 64-69, attend hematologist, 65-69, attend physician, 69-70; prof, Mt Sinai Sch Med, 66-70; chief hemat & nutrit lab, Vet Admin Bronx Hosp, 70-; chief med serv, Vet Admin Brooklyn Hosp, 76-77; clin prof path, Columbia Univ, 70-76; mem, Food & Nutrit Bd, Nat Acad Sci, 79-85; Vischer prof & chmn med, Hahnemann Univ, 84-85. *Mem:* Am Soc Clin Nutrit (pres, 80-81); Am Soc Clin Invest; Asn Am Physicians; Am Soc Hemat; Asn Prof Med. *Res:* Nature, diagnosis and treatment of nutritional anemias; mechanisms of absorption, transport, delivery, metabolism and excretion of nutrients; development of assays for vitamins, minerals and hormones. *Mailing Add:* 130 W Kingsbridge Rd Bronx NY 10468

HERBETTE, LEO G, DRUG-MEMBRANE INTERACTIONS, MEMBRANE STRUCTURE. *Current Pos:* Instr med, Univ Conn Health Ctr, 80-81, asst prof med, 81-86, asst prof biochem, 83-86, asst prof radiol, 86, DIR BIOMOLECULAR STRUCT ANALYSIS CTR, UNIV CONN HEALTH CTR, 84-, ASSOC PROF RADIOL, MED & BIOCHEM, 87-, HEAD BASIC RES, DEPT RADIOL, 87- *Personal Data:* b Derby, Conn, May 23, 53; m 76; c 3. *Educ:* Univ Conn, Storrs, BS, 75; Univ Pa, Philadelphia, PhD(biophys), 80. *Concurrent Pos:* Asst scientist, Brookhaven Nat Lab, Upton, NY, 80-86, sr scientist, 86-, chmn, Adv Comt, Partic Res Team, High Flux Beam Reactor, 89-; consult to major pharmaceut co, 81-; mem, High Flux Beam Reactor Prog Adv Comt, 90- *Mem:* Biophys Soc; Int Soc Heart Res; Am Soc Biol Chemists; Protein Soc; Am Crystallog Soc. *Res:* Structure of model and native biological membranes; understanding molecular mechanisms for the way drugs and toxins interact with cell membranes. *Mailing Add:* Biomolecular Struct Analysis Ctr Univ Conn Health Ctr Farmington CT 06032-2017. *Fax:* 860-679-1989

HERBICH, JOHN BRONISLAW, CIVIL ENGINEERING, PHYSICAL OCEANOGRAPHY. *Current Pos:* PROF COASTAL & OCEAN ENG, HYDRAUL ENG & FLUID MECH, TEX A&M UNIV, 67-, HEAD FLUID MECH DIV & DIR CTR DREDGING STUDIES, 70- *Personal Data:* b Warsaw, Poland, Sept 1, 22; US citizen; m 51; c 3. *Educ:* Univ Edinburgh, BSc, 49; Univ Minn, Minneapolis, MS, 53; Pa State Univ, PhD(civil eng), 63. *Honors & Awards:* Karl Emil Hilgard Hydraul Prize, Am Soc Civil Engrs, 66. *Prof Exp:* Field engr, John Laing & Son, Eng, 48; res engr coastal eng, Tech Univ Delft, 49-50; intermediate engr, Aluminum Co Can Ltd, 50-53; res fel hydromech, Univ Minn, 53-57; from asst prof to prof fluid mech & hydraul eng, Lehigh Univ, 57-67. *Concurrent Pos:* Consult hydraul engr, Bethlehem Steel Corp & Dragon Cement Co, 57-67 & Ellicott Mach Corp, Hale Fire Pump Co, Pekor Iron Works Inc & Pa Dept Hwys, 57-; Ford Found fel civil eng, Hydraul Lab, Pa State Univ, 63, NSF fac fel, 63; fel water resources, Utah State Univ, 66; consult ocean engr, Timewealth Corp, Chevron Oil Co & Ocean Pollution Control, Inc, 67- *Mem:* Am Soc Eng Educ; Am Soc Civil Engrs; Am Soc Oceanog; Int Asn Hydraul Res; World Dredging Asn; Sigma Xi. *Res:* Coastal engineering; dredging; wave mechanics; hydromechanics; physical oceanography. *Mailing Add:* 7310 Seawall Blvd Galveston TX 77551

HERBIG, GEORGE HOWARD, ASTRONOMY. *Current Pos:* ASTRONOMER, INST ASTRON, UNIV HAWAII, 87- *Personal Data:* b Wheeling, WVa, Jan 2, 20; m 43, 68; c 4. *Educ:* Univ Calif, Los Angeles, AB, 43; Univ Calif, PhD(astron), 48. *Honors & Awards:* Warner prize, Am Astron Soc, 55; Catherine Wolfe Bruce Gold Medal, Astron Soc Pac, 80; H N Russell Lectr, Am Astron Soc, 75; Petrie Prize, Can Astron Soc, 95. *Prof Exp:* Asst, Univ Calif, Santa Cruz, 44-46, jr astronr, 48-50, from asst astronr to astronr, 50-66, asst dir, 60-63, actg dir, 70-71, prof astron, Lick Observ, 66-87. *Concurrent Pos:* Nat Res Coun fel, Mt Wilson Observ, Carnegie Inst, Palomar Observ, Yerkes Observ, Chicago & McDonald Observ, Chicago-Tex, 48-49; vis prof, Yerkes Observ, Chicago, 59, Nat Univ Mex, 61 & Observ Paris, 65; NSF sr fel, 65; vis prof, Max Planck Inst Astron, 69, foreign sci mem, 71; nat lectr, Sigma Xi, 72-73. *Mem:* Nat Acad Sci; Am Acad Arts & Sci; corresp mem Royal Belg Soc Sci; Int Astron Union; Am Astron Soc. *Res:* Stellar and interstellar spectroscopy. *Mailing Add:* Inst Astron Univ Hawaii 2680 Woodlawn Dr Honolulu HI 96822. *Fax:* 808-956-9580; *E-Mail:* herbig@galileo.ifa.hawaii.edu

HERBISON, GERALD J, EXERCISE PHYSIOLOGY, MUSCLE DISEASE. *Current Pos:* PROD MED, THOMAS JEFFERSON COL, 76- *Personal Data:* b Cleveland, Ohio, Aug 28, 37. *Educ:* Loyola Univ, MD, 62. *Mem:* Fel Am Col Physicians; fel Am Acad Phys Med & Rehab. *Mailing Add:* 185 Woodstock Villanova PA 19085-1416

HERBLIN, WILLIAM FITTS, biochemistry, pharmacology, for more information see previous edition

HERBOLSHEIMER, GLENN, CHEMICAL ENGINEERING. *Current Pos:* RETIRED. *Personal Data:* b East Moline, Ill, Feb 13, 12; m 40; c 2. *Educ:* Univ Ill, BS, 37; Pa State Col, MS, 39, PhD(chem eng), 42. *Prof Exp:* Asst, Pa State Col, 37-43; process engr, Phillips Petrol Co, 43-49, sr develop engr, 49-76. *Mem:* Am Chem Soc; Am Inst Chem Engrs; Am Inst Chem. *Res:* Hydrocarbon oxidation; liquid-liquid solvent extraction of hydrocarbons; conversion of hydrocarbons to chemicals. *Mailing Add:* 1425 Shawnee Ave Bartlesville OK 74003

HERBRANDSON, HARRY FRED, ORGANIC CHEMISTRY. *Current Pos:* from asst prof to prof chem, 49-86, EMER PROF CHEM, RENSSELAER POLYTECH INST, 86- *Personal Data:* b Watertown, SDak, July 25, 21; m 46; c 3. *Educ:* Univ Minn, BChem, 42; Univ Ill, PhD(org chem), 45. *Prof Exp:* Asst org chem, Univ Ill, 42-44, asst antimalarial res, Comt Med Res & Off Sci Res & Develop, 44-45; res chemist, Nat Aniline Div, Allied Chem & Dye Corp, 45-46; Pittsburgh Plate Glass Co fel, Harvard Univ, 46-47; asst prof chem, Union Univ, NY, 47-49. *Concurrent Pos:* Consult, Robert G Allen Co, 53-55, IBM Corp, 62-66, J De Beer & Son, Inc, 81-82, NJ Dept Higher Educ, 82-83 & Dionex Corp, 83-85; vis lectr, Albany Med Col, 69-73. *Mem:* Fel AAAS; Am Chem Soc; Sigma Xi; Royal Soc Chem; NY Acad Sci. *Res:* Physical organic chemistry and organic reaction mechanisms; heterocyclic chemistry; organic-sulfur compounds. *Mailing Add:* 253 Walker St Lenox MA 01240

HERBST, ARTHUR LEE, MEDICINE. *Current Pos:* JOSEPH BOLIVAR DELEE PROF & CHMN, DEPT OBSTET & GYNEC, PRITZER SCH MED, UNIV CHICAGO, 76-, DISTINGUISHED SERV PROF, DIV BIOL SCI, 84- *Personal Data:* b New York, NY, Sept 14, 31. *Educ:* Harvard Univ, AB, 53, MD, 59; Am Bd Obstet & Gynec, dipl, 67, cert oncol, 74, recert, 83. *Honors & Awards:* Upjohn Award, Endocrine Soc, 62; Frances Stone Burns Award, Am Cancer Soc, 72; Found Prize, Am Asn Obstetricians & Gynecologists, 73; Frank Locke Lectr, Bowman Gray Univ, 77, Conrad Julian Lectr, Vanderbilt Univ, 80, Marlowe Lectr, Acad Med, Toronto, 81, John Rock Lectr, Univ Pa, 82, JPA Latour Lectr, McGill Univ, Can, 84, Coy L Lay Guest Prof Lectr, Univ SFla, 85, Alexander H & Dorothy Rosenthal Lectr, LI Jewish Med Ctr, State Univ NY, Stony Brook, 88, Warren Lang

Lectr, Jefferson Med Sch, Pa, 89, Richard E Hunter MD Lectr, Univ Mass, 91, Charles A Hunter Jr MD Lectr, Ind Univ, 92, John L McKelvey Lectr, Univ Minn, 94, Edgar L Makowski Lectr, Univ Colo, Denver, 94, Richard W Telinde's Lectr, Johns Hopkins Med Sch, 96; Daggett Harvey Award, Northwestern Univ Med Sch, Chicago, 89. *Prof Exp:* Intern surg, Mass Gen Hosp, 59-60, asst resident, 60-62; resident, Boston Lying-In Hosp & Free Hosp Women, 62-65; vis res worker, Clin Endocrinol Unit, Edinburgh, Scotland, 65; affiliated scientist, NE Reg Primate Res Ctr, 73-76. *Concurrent Pos:* Josiah Macy Jr teaching fel, Obstet & Gynec, Harvard Med Sch, 59-65, res fel, 65, instr & sr staff scientist, 65-76; asst-assoc vis surgeon, Mass Gen Hosp, 65-76; Esher Laneger Res Award, 85; dir, Am Bd Obstet & Gynec, 85-93, Div Gynec Oncol, 88-91, vpres, 89-90; foreign vis lectr, 66th annual meeting Korean Obstet & Gynec Soc, Seoul, 90, Mex Acad Surg, Mexico City, 91; guest speaker, Gordon Res Conf, Salve Regina Col, RI, 93. *Mem:* Inst Med-Nat Acad Sci; AAAS; fel Am Col Obstet & Gynec; fel Am Col Surgeons; Am Fertil Soc; Am Gynec Club; AMA; Asn Prof Obstet & Gynec; Endocrine Soc; Int Soc Study Reproduction; assoc mem Int Soc Gynec Path; Sigma Xi; Soc Endocrinol; Soc Gynec Oncologists; Soc Pelvic Surgeons; Am Gynec & Obstet Soc (pres elect, 96-97). *Mailing Add:* Dept Obstet & Gynec Univ Chicago Sch Med 5841 S Maryland Chicago IL 60637-1463

HERBST, EDWARD JOHN, BIOCHEMISTRY. *Current Pos:* RETIRED. *Personal Data:* b Jacksonport, Wis, Dec 14, 18; m 51; c 3. *Educ:* Univ Wis, BS, 43, MS, 44, PhD(biochem), 49. *Prof Exp:* From asst prof to assoc prof biochem, Med Sch, Univ Md, 49-62; chmn dept, Univ NH, 62-74, prof biochem, 74- *Mem:* Am Soc Biol Chem; Sigma Xi. *Res:* Identification of putrescine as a growth factor and continued investigations of the role of the new growth factor in the metabolism of microorganisms and other forms of life. *Mailing Add:* 183 Reservoir Rd Perryville MD 21903

HERBST, ERIC, MOLECULAR ASTRONOMY, MOLECULAR SPECTROSCOPY. *Current Pos:* PROF PHYSICS, OHIO STATE, 91-, PROF ASTRON, 92- *Personal Data:* b Brooklyn, NY, Jan 15, 46; m 72, Judith Strassman; c Elisabeth, Andrea & Seth. *Educ:* Univ Rochester, AB, 66; Harvard Univ, MA, 69, PhD(chem), 72. *Honors & Awards:* Sherman Fairchild Prize, Cal Tech; Max Planck Res Award, Alexander Von Humboldt Sr Award. *Prof Exp:* Res assoc chem, Harvard Univ, 72-73; res assoc lab astrophysics, Joint Inst Lab Astrophys, Univ Colo, 73-74; from asst prof to assoc prof chem, Col William & Mary, 74-80; from assoc prof to prof physics, Duke Univ, 80-91. *Concurrent Pos:* Prin investr, NSF & NASA grants, 79-; consult, NASA, 82-; mem, Comt Planetary Biol & Chem Evolution, Nat Acad Sci, 85-; Humboldt Sr Fel, 88-89; mem, astron adv com, NSF, 89-92. *Mem:* Am Astron Soc; Am Chem Soc; Am Phys Soc; Int Astron Union; Sigma Xi. *Res:* Molecular astrophysics: the development of molecular complexity throughout the universe; molecular spectroscopy, particularly gas phase molecular ions; chemical dynamics. *Mailing Add:* Dept Physics Ohio State Univ Columbus OH 43210-1106. *Fax:* 614-292-7557; *E-Mail:* herbst@ohstpy.mps.ohio-state.edu

HERBST, JAN FRANCIS, SOLID STATE PHYSICS. *Current Pos:* assoc sr res physicist, Gen Motors Res & Develop Ctr, 77-80, staff res physicist, 80-84, sr staff res scientist solid state physics, 85-93, PRIN RES SCIENTIST, GEN MOTORS RES & DEVELOP CTR, 93- *Personal Data:* b Tucson, Ariz, May 1, 47; m 82, Margaret M Priest; c Helen, John & Mary. *Educ:* Univ Pa, BA & MS, 68; Cornell Univ, PhD(physics), 74. *Honors & Awards:* John M Campbell Award, Gen Motors Res Labs, 83, Charles L McCuen Award, 87 & Kettering Award, 87; Int Prize New Mat, Am Phys Soc, 86. *Prof Exp:* Res assoc, Nat Bur Stand, 74-76; asst physicist, Brookhaven Nat Lab, 76-77. *Concurrent Pos:* Secy-treas, Div Condensed Matter Physics, Am Phys Soc, 85-90. *Mem:* Fel Am Phys Soc; Sigma Xi. *Res:* Physics of rare earth materials, especially magnetic and magnetostrictive properties. *Mailing Add:* Physics & Phys Chem Dept Gen Motors Res & Develop Ctr Mail Code 480-106-224 Warren MI 48090-9055. *E-Mail:* jherbst@gmr.com

HERBST, JOHN A, RESEARCH ADMINISTRATION. *Current Pos:* MEM STAFF, CALLAWAY CHEM CO, EXXON CORP. *Mailing Add:* 341 Barschall Dr Columbus GA 31904

HERBST, JOHN J, PEDIATRICS, GASTROENTEROLOGY. *Current Pos:* chair & prof, 85-91, PROF GASTROENTEROL, LA STATE UNIV MED CTR, 85- *Personal Data:* b Cincinnati, Ohio, July 18, 35; m 61, Diana Lobitz; c 2. *Educ:* Xavier Univ, BS, 57; St Louis Univ, MD, 61. *Prof Exp:* Intern pediat, Cincinnati Gen Hosp, 61-62; resident, 62-64; lt comdr, USPHS Indian Health Serv, Gallup, NMex, 64-66; fel, Stanford Med Ctr, 66-69; from asst prof to prof pediat, Univ Utah Med Ctr, 69-85. *Concurrent Pos:* Co-chmn, Nat Digestive Dis Comn, NIH, 77-78. *Mem:* Am Soc Pediat Gastroenterol (pres, 77-78); NAm Soc Pediat Gastroenterol Inc, (pres, 78-79); Am Gastroenterol Asn; Soc Pediat Res; Am Pediat Soc. *Res:* Development relationship to intestine and esophagus; esophageal function in children. *Mailing Add:* Dept Pediat Sect Gastroenterol La State Univ Med Ctr PO Box 33932 Shreveport LA 71130. *E-Mail:* jherbs@lsumc.edu

HERBST, MARK JOSEPH, LASER-PLASMA INTERACTIONS, PLASMA INSTABILITIES. *Current Pos:* RES PHYSICIST, US NAVAL RES LAB, 80- *Personal Data:* US citizen. *Educ:* Mass Inst Technol, BS, 73; Univ Calif, Los Angeles, PhD(elec eng), 79. *Prof Exp:* Asst res engr, Univ Calif, Los Angeles, 79; res scientist, Mission Res Corp, 79-80. *Concurrent Pos:* Cong fel, 85. *Mem:* Am Phys Soc; AAAS. *Res:* Laser-matter interaction and basic plasma physics relevant to laser-induced thermonuclear fusion. *Mailing Add:* 7709 Elgar St Springfield VA 22151-2515

HERBST, NOEL MARTIN, ELECTRICAL ENGINEERING. *Current Pos:* SOFTWARE DESIGNER, TANDEM COMPUTERS, 82- *Personal Data:* b New York, NY, Sept 10, 37; m 65. *Educ:* Cornell Univ, BSEE, 59, MSEE, 61, PhD(elec eng), 63. *Prof Exp:* Res staff mem, comput sci dept, IBM Res Ctr, 63-82. *Mem:* Asn Comput Mach. *Res:* Applications of computers to non-numeric data; pattern recognition; character recognition; artificial intelligence; large programming systems. *Mailing Add:* 20 Spiros Way Menlo Park CA 94025-5935

HERBST, RICHARD PETER, ALGOLOGY, FRESHWATER ECOLOGY. *Current Pos:* ENG ASSOC, EXXON CHEM CO. *Personal Data:* b Milwaukee, Wis, Nov 16, 40; m 65; c 1. *Educ:* Univ Wis, Milwaukee, BS, 64, MS, 66; Univ Pittsburgh, PhD(aquatic ecol), 69. *Prof Exp:* Asst bot, Univ Wis, Milwaukee, 64-66; asst prof biol, Univ Wis, Whitewater, 69-71; asst prof bot, Univ Wis, Waukesha, 71-78; mgr, Environ Measurements Div, Environ Res & Tech, Inc,. *Concurrent Pos:* Consult, Limnetics, Inc, 71-, assoc dir, Environ Res Div, 72-74; consult, Wis Elec Power Co, 72- & Rainbow Springs Trout Farm, Inc, 74- *Mem:* AAAS; Am Mgt Asn; Ecol Soc Am; Int Soc Petrol Indust Biologists; Am Soc Limnol & Oceanog. *Res:* Toxicology; ecology of aquatic systems; hazardous waste disposal and ground water problems; ecosystem planning and siting; wetlands. *Mailing Add:* 2704 S Wildwind Circle Woodlands TX 77380

HERBST, ROBERT TAYLOR, mathematics; deceased, see previous edition for last biography

HERBST, WILLIAM, ASTRONOMY. *Current Pos:* from asst prof to assoc prof astron, 78-90, PROF ASTRON, VAN VLECK OBSERV, WESLEYAN UNIV, 90- *Personal Data:* b Doylestown, Pa, Nov 12, 47; m 70; c 2. *Educ:* Princeton Univ, AB, 70; Univ Toronto, MSc, 72, PhD(astron), 74. *Prof Exp:* Lectr physics, York Univ, 74-76; fel astron, Carnegie Inst Washington, 76-78. *Mem:* Am Astron Soc; Int Astron Union; Sigma Xi. *Res:* Observational stellar astronomy; star associations and clusters; star formation; galactic structure. *Mailing Add:* Astron Dept Wesleyan Univ Middletown CT 06457-0001

HERBSTMAN, SHELDON, ORGANIC CHEMISTRY, FUEL & FUEL ADDITIVE TECHNOLOGY. *Current Pos:* sr chemist, Texaco Inc, 65-68, res chemist, 68-76, res assoc, 88-91, SR RES CHEMIST, BEACON RES LABS, TEXACO INC, 76-, SR RES ASSOC, 91- *Personal Data:* b New York, NY, June 15, 31; m 60, Bernita Rabiner; c 2. *Educ:* Brooklyn Col, BS, 54, MA, 59; NY Univ, PhD(chem), 63. *Prof Exp:* Sr res chemist, Eastern Res Ctr, Stauffer Chem Co, 61-65. *Mem:* Am Chem Soc; Soc Automotive Engrs. *Res:* Organometallic chemistry, especially Grignard reaction mechanisms; sulfur mustards and episulfides; petroleum chemistry; petroleum chemistry; chemistry of lubricant and fuel additives; investigation of petroleum process and catalyst systems; alcohol and ether chemistry and processing related to use in gasoline. *Mailing Add:* 2 Ferndale Rd New City NY 10956-2856

HERCULES, DAVID MICHAEL, ANALYTICAL CHEMISTRY. *Current Pos:* chmn dept, 80-89, PROF CHEM, UNIV PITTSBURGH, 76- *Personal Data:* b Somerset, Pa, Aug 10, 32; m 70; c 3. *Educ:* Juniata Col, BS, 54; Mass Inst Technol, PhD(analytical chem), 57. *Honors & Awards:* Lester W Strock Medal, Soc Appl Spectros, 81; Alexander von Humboldt Fel, 82; Fisher Nat Award Analytical Chem, Am Chem Soc, 86; Benedetti-Pichler Award, Am Microchem Soc, 87. *Prof Exp:* Asst chem, Mass Inst Technol, 54-57; asst prof, Lehigh Univ, 57-60; assoc prof, Juniata Col, 60-63; from asst prof to assoc prof, Mass Inst Technol, 63-69; from assoc prof to prof, Univ Ga, 69-76. *Concurrent Pos:* Mem, Vis Scientist Prog, NSF, 64-76; chmn, Gordon Conf Anal Chem, 66 & Gordon Conf Electron Spectros, 74; Guggenheim fel, 73-74; chmn, Div Analytical Chem, Am Chem Soc, 77-78; res chemist, Geol Div, US Dept Interior, 84-; mem, Appl Res Ctr, Univ Pittsburgh, 88-; task force, analytical chem, Am Chem Soc, 89. *Mem:* AAAS; Am Vacuum Soc; Am Chem Soc; Soc Appl Spectros; Mat Res Soc; Sigma Xi. *Res:* Analytical chemistry of surfaces; use of techniques like ESCA, Auger spectroscopy, ion scattering, FT infrared and Raman spectroscopy; types of investigations involve catalysts, polymers, biomedical materials, quantitative analysis, trace analysis and chemically modified surfaces; mass spectrometry of solids; use of pulsed layers and pulsed ion beams to study mass spectra of solids; emphasis on understanding volatilization/ionization mechanisms with main emphasis on mass spectrometry polymers; other types of materials include polymers, silicates, coordination compounds, carbohydrates and large biomolecules. *Mailing Add:* Dept Chem Vanderbilt Univ Nashville TN 37235. *Fax:* 615-343-7262; *E-Mail:* hercules@crtvax.vanderbilt.edu

HERCZFELD, PETER ROBERT, PHYSICS, ELECTRICAL ENGINEERING. *Current Pos:* from asst prof to assoc prof, 67-79, PROF ELEC ENG, DREXEL UNIV, 79- *Personal Data:* b Budapest, Hungary, Aug 9, 36; US citizen; m 66; c 2. *Educ:* Colo State Univ, BS, 61; Univ Minn, MS, 63, PhD(elec eng), 67. *Honors & Awards:* European Microwave Prize. *Prof Exp:* Teaching asst physics, Univ Minn, 61-63; res assoc & instr elec eng, 63-67. *Concurrent Pos:* Guest ed, joint issue, Trans on MTT & J Lightwave Technol. *Mem:* Am Phys Soc; fel Inst Elec & Electronics Engrs; Int Soc Optical Eng; Int Solar Energy Soc. *Res:* Fluctuation phenomena in solids; microwave studies in photoconductors; solid state properties of photodetectors; bioelectronics. *Mailing Add:* 7105 Green St Philadelphia PA 19119

HERCZOG, ANDREW, physical chemistry, materials science; deceased, see previous edition for last biography

HERCZYNSKI, ANDRZEJ, FLUID MECHANICS, MATHEMATICAL PHYSICS. *Current Pos:* PROF PHYSICS, BOSTON COL, 96- *Personal Data:* b Warsaw, Poland, Apr 29, 56. *Educ:* Warsaw Univ, MS, 80; Lehigh Univ, MS, 83, PhD(physics), 87. *Prof Exp:* Teaching asst physics, Lehigh Univ, 80-85, lectr math, 87; res assoc fluid dynamics, Univ Colo, Boulder, 87-90; asst to exec dir, Am Inst Physics, 90-96. *Mem:* Am Phys Soc; Soc Indust & Appl Math. *Res:* Mathematical modelling of continuum mechanical systems; eigenfunction expansions for elasto-dynamic problems; asymptotic models of heat and mass transfer in compressible fluids; kinetic theory using realistic intermolecular potential. *Mailing Add:* Dept Physics Boston Col 140 Commonwealth Ave Chestnut Hill MA 02167. *Fax:* 301-205-3133; *E-Mail:* ah3@aip.org

HERD, DARRELL GILBERT, ACTIVE FAULTS, GEOMORPHOLOGY. *Current Pos:* RES GEOLOGIST, US GEOL SURV, 74- *Personal Data:* b Logansport, Ind, Jan 13, 49. *Educ:* Ind Univ, AB, 71; Univ Wash, MS, 72, PhD(geol), 74. *Concurrent Pos:* Govt consult, Geosci Br, US Nuclear Regulatory Comn, 77- & US Army CEngrs, San Francisco District, 77-78. *Mem:* AAAS. *Res:* Neotectonics of the San Francisco Bay area; study of the active faults of central and northern coastal California; Sonoran earthquake of 1887; investigation of the earthquake tectonics of northern Mexico and southern Arizona. *Mailing Add:* 14 Oakdale Ct Sterling VA 20165

HERD, JAMES ALAN, PHYSIOLOGY. *Current Pos:* PROF MED, BAYLOR COL MED, 81- *Personal Data:* b Vancouver, BC, Feb 7, 32; US citizen; m 55; c 3. *Educ:* Univ BC, MD, 56. *Prof Exp:* Intern, Vancouver Gen Hosp, BC, 56-57, asst resident med, 57-58, assoc resident path, 58-59; asst resident med, Peter Bent Brigham Hosp, Boston, 62-63; from instr to assoc prof physiol, Harvard Med Sch, 63-74, assoc prof psychobiol, 74-81. *Concurrent Pos:* Life Ins Med Res Fund fel med, Harvard Med Sch, 59-60 & fel physiol, 60-61; Am Heart Asn Adv Res Fund fel, 61-62; Webster Underhill fel, 62-63; NIH res scientist develop grant, 69-; estab investr, Am Heart Asn, 63. *Mem:* AAAS; Am Physiol Soc; Sigma Xi. *Res:* Mammalian cardiovascular physiology and pathophysiology; renal blood flow and function; physiology of behavior; preventive cardiology. *Mailing Add:* Dept Med Baylor Col Med 6550 Fannin St MSSM 1153 Houston TX 77030. *Fax:* 713-798-3577

HERDA, HANS-HEINRICH WOLFGANG, ROCK FRACTURE GEOMETRY, FEVER CONCEPTS HISTORY & COMBINATORIAL GEOMETRY. *Current Pos:* PROF MATH, UNIV MASS, BOSTON, 82- *Personal Data:* b Berlin, Ger, July 6, 38; US citizen; m 62, Phyllis Goldman; c Annette, Joel & Rachel. *Educ:* Wayne State Univ, BA, 60, MA, 66, PhD(math), 68. *Prof Exp:* Math ed, Info Process J, Cambridge Commun, Mass, 65; asst prof math, Salem State Col, 66-68 & Tufts Univ, 68-70; from asst prof to prof math, Boston State Col, 70-82. *Concurrent Pos:* Vis scientist, Weizman Inst Sci, 78-79, 85-86; vis scientist, Dept Civil Eng, Mass Inst Technol, 82-87, res affil, 87-; invited foreign scholar, Col Eng, Kyoto Univ, Japan, 92-93. *Mem:* Am Math Soc; Math Asn Am. *Res:* Rock fracture geometry; history of concepts of fever; combinatorial geometry. *Mailing Add:* Dept Math Univ Mass Harbor Campus Boston MA 02125-3393. *E-Mail:* hans@cs.umb.edu

HERDENDORF, CHARLES EDWARD, III, DEEP OCEAN MARINE BIOLOGY, COASTAL WETLANDS & ESTUARIES. *Current Pos:* from assoc prof to prof geol & zool, 71-88, dir, Lake Erie Area Res, 71-88, PROF LIMNOL & OCEANOG, OHIO STATE UNIV, 71-, EMER PROF GEOL & ZOOL, 88- *Personal Data:* b Sheffield Lake, Ohio, Oct 2, 39; m 93, Ricki Crowl. *Educ:* Ohio Univ, BS, 61, MS, 63; Ohio State Univ, PhD(limnol & oceanog), 70. *Prof Exp:* Geologist, Div Shore Erosion, Ohio Dept Natural Resources, 60-61 & Div Geol Surv, 61-64, sect head, 64-71; dir res, Ctr Lake Erie Area Res, 71-87, Ohio Sea Grant Prog, 78-87. *Concurrent Pos:* Dir, F T Stone Hydrobiol Lab, 73-88 & Ohio Sea Grant Col Prog, 78-88; Mem, Nat Coastal Zone Mgt Comt, 73-79; vis prof earth Sci, Waikato Univ, Hamilton, NZ, 85-86; coastal oceanogr, NZ Water Qual Ctr, 85-87 & 91-93; oceanogr & marine archaeologist, Columbus-Am Discovery Group, 88- *Mem:* Int Asn Great Lakes Res (vpres, 80-81); Am Inst Prof Geologists; Nat Soc Prof Engrs; Am Soc Limnol & Oceanog; Am Fisheries Soc; UK Freshwater Biol Asn. *Res:* Aquatic and marine ecosystems, particularly the Great Lakes, New Zealand estuaries and deep ocean benthic communities; special interest in relationship of physical and biological oceanography to deep sea, marine archaeology; environmental impact studies on Lake Erie; physical oceanography, New Zealand estuaries; deep-sea benthic fauna; North Atlantic Ocean. *Mailing Add:* Dept Zool Ohio State Univ 1507 Cleveland Rd E Suite 410 Huron OH 44839. *Fax:* 419-433-3266; *E-Mail:* herdendorf.1@osu.edu

HERDKLOTZ, JOHN KEY, CHEMISTRY. *Current Pos:* group leader, Eval Labs, Celanese Fibers Mkt Co, 74-90, EXEC VPRES RES MFG, HOECHST ROUSSEL PHARMACEUT INC, HOECHST CELANESE CORP, 90-; PROD MGR CELANESE FIBERS, FIBERS INDUST INC, 85- *Personal Data:* b Rockford, Ill, Apr 23, 43; m 64; c 2. *Educ:* Rockford Col, BA, 65; Rice Univ, PhD(phys chem), 69. *Prof Exp:* Res assoc & fel phys chem, Rice Univ, 68-69; NIH fel lipid res, Baylor Col Med, 69-70; res chemist, Fibers Indust Inc, 70-74, res & develop mgr, 79-84. *Mem:* Am Chem Soc; Am Asn Textile Chemists & Colorists. *Res:* Crystal structure analysis of interesting organic molecules; solid state conformation of molecules of biological importance; structural characterization of man-made polymers; textile test methods. *Mailing Add:* PO Box 2337 Banner Elk NC 28604-2337

HERDKLOTZ, RICHARD JAMES, PHYSICAL CHEMISTRY. *Current Pos:* SR ENG PROJ MGR, FLUOR DANIEL ENG, 85- *Personal Data:* b Rockford, Ill, Dec 26, 40; m 63, Sharon Brough; c Jim, Jeff, Jana & Joe. *Educ:* Bob Jones Univ, BS, 63; Univ Tenn, PhD(phys chem), 70. *Prof Exp:* Instr phys sci & chem, 63-67, prof chem, Bob Jones Univ, 70-79, chmn dept, 72-79; proj engr, Universal Serv SC, 78-84; chem engr, Arce & Hendrix Eng, 85. *Concurrent Pos:* Mech engr, Piedmont Engrs, Architects & Planers, 73-78; vchmn, Greenville Co Coun, 85-; Monsanto fel; Oran fel. *Mem:* Sigma Xi; Am Chem Soc. *Res:* Thermodynamics of aqueous electrolyte solutions over wide ranges of temperature and concentration; mathematical treatment of experimental data; spontaneous precipitation from sea salt solutions; thermodynamic properties of sea water. *Mailing Add:* 424 Leyswood Dr Greenville SC 29615

HERDLE, LLOYD EMERSON, CELLULOSE CHEMISTRY. *Current Pos:* RETIRED. *Personal Data:* b Homerville, Ohio, Oct 6, 13; m 46, Rebecca Arnold; c William, Kenneth, Anne, Dorothy, Lee & Beth. *Educ:* Mt Union Col, BS, 34; Ohio State Univ, PhD(org chem), 37. *Prof Exp:* Res chemist, Procter & Gamble Co, Ohio, 37-41; cellulose res supvr, Eastman Kodak Co, 41-78. *Mem:* Am Chem Soc. *Res:* Cellulose; cellulose esters; vapor and sulfuric acid sorption by cellulose; cellulose crystallinity and swelling; pulping of wood; photographic paper; paper sizing; polymer solubility and plasticizers. *Mailing Add:* 315 Colebrook Dr Rochester NY 14617

HERDMAN, TERRY LEE, APPLIED MATHEMATICS. *Current Pos:* vis asst prof, 74-75, from asst prof to assoc prof, 75-88, PROF MATH, VA POLYTECH INST & STATE UNIV, 88- *Personal Data:* b LaCrosse, Kans, Dec 2, 45; m 63, Carol Littler; c Kirk, Darwin & Kimbra. *Educ:* Fort Hays State Univ, BS, 67; Univ Okla, MA, 70, PhD(math), 74. *Prof Exp:* Asst math, Univ Okla, 67-72, spec instr, 72-74. *Concurrent Pos:* Dir, Interdisciplinary Ctr Appl Math, Va Polytech Inst & State Univ, 87- *Mem:* Am Math Soc; Math Asn Am; Soc Indust & Appl Mat. *Res:* Functional differential equations; Volterra integral equations; differential equations; singular integral equations. *Mailing Add:* Dept Math Va Polytech Inst Blacksburg VA 24061-0123. *Fax:* 540-231-7079; *E-Mail:* herdman@icam.ut.edu

HERDT, ROBERT WILLIAM, AGRICULTURAL ECONOMICS. *Current Pos:* sr scientist, 86-87, DIR AGR SCI, ROCKEFELLER FOUND, 87- *Personal Data:* b New York, NY, 39. *Educ:* Cornell Univ, BS, 61, MS, 63; Univ Minn, PhD(agr econ), 69. *Prof Exp:* Asst agr econ, Cornell Univ, 61-62; training assoc farm mgt, Ford Found, New Delhi, India, 62-64; res asst agr econ, Univ Minn, 64-66; res asst, Rockefeller Found, India, 67-68; from asst prof to assoc prof agr econ, Univ Ill, Urbana, 69-75; agr economist & head agr econ dept, Int Rice Res Inst, 78-83; sci adv, Consultative Group Int Agr Res, World Bank, 83-86. *Concurrent Pos:* Agr economist, Int Rice Res Inst, Los Banos, Philippines, 73-78; adj prof, Agr Econ Dept, Cornell Univ, 81- *Mem:* Am Agr Econ Asn; Am Econ Asn; Int Asn Agr Econ; Indian Soc Agr Econ; fel AAAS. *Res:* Economics of agricultural development, with special interest in South and South East Asia and the role of technological change in development. *Mailing Add:* Rockefeller Found 420 Fifth Ave New York NY 10018-2702

HEREFORD, FRANK LOUCKS, JR, PHYSICS. *Current Pos:* RETIRED. *Personal Data:* b Lake Charles, La, July 18, 23; m 48; c 3. *Educ:* Univ Va, BA, 43; PhD(physics), 47. *Hon Degrees:* DSc, Fla Inst Technol, 74; LLD, Hampden-Sydney Col, 74. *Prof Exp:* Res assoc, Off Sci Res & Develop, 43-45; physicist, Bartol Res Found, Franklin Inst, 47-49; from assoc prof to prof physics, Univ Va, 49-66, dean, Grad Sch Arts & Sci, 62-65, univ vpres & provost, 65-71, Robert C Taylor prof, 66-, pres, 74-85. *Concurrent Pos:* Fulbright scholar, Univ Birmingham, 57-58; vis prof, Univ St Andrews, 71. *Mem:* AAAS; fel Am Phys Soc. *Res:* Luminescence of liquid helium; nuclear reactions; interactions of polarized neutrons; color vision. *Mailing Add:* 23 Parkview Dr Charlottesville VA 22901

HEREMANS, JOSEPH P, THERMAL CONDUCTIVITY, NARROW-GAP SEMICONDUCTORS. *Current Pos:* sr res scientist, 84-85, staff res scientist & group leader, 85-87, MGR ATOMICALLY ENG MAT & SR STAFF RES SCIENTIST, GEN MOTORS RES LABS, 87- *Personal Data:* b Leuven, Belg, Jan 8, 53; m 78; c 2. *Educ:* Cath Univ Louvain, Belg, MS, 75, PhD(appl physics), 78. *Honors & Awards:* Campbell Award, Gen Motors. *Prof Exp:* Researcher appl physics, Fonds Nat Res Sci, Belg, 78-83 & Cath Univ Louvain, 83-84. *Concurrent Pos:* Vis scientist, Francis Bitter Nat Magnet Lab, Mass Inst Technol, 80 & Ctr Mat Sci & Eng, 81, Inst Solid State Physics, Univ Tokyo, 82 & IV C Orsted Inst, Univ Copenagen, 83; mem, Panel Diluted Magnetic Semiconductors, Nat Res Coun, 89; vis prof, Cath Univ Louvain, 89- *Mem:* Fel Am Phys Soc; AAAS; Mat Res Soc. *Res:* Thermal and electrical transport in narrow-gap semiconductors IV-VI and III-V compounds, two dimensional systems; semimetals, graphite, intercalation compounds, carbon manotubes and group V semimetals, and superconductors; magnetic field sensors. *Mailing Add:* Dept Physics Gen Motors Res Labs 30500 Mound Rd PO Box 9055 Warren MI 48090. *Fax:* 810-986-3091; *E-Mail:* jhereman@cmsa.gmr.com

HERENDEEN, ROBERT ALBERT, ENERGY ANALYSIS. *Current Pos:* assoc prof scientist, 85-95, NAT RES & ENVIRON SCI, ILL NATURAL HIST SURV, 95- *Personal Data:* b Freeport, NY, Oct 18, 40; div; c Laurel & Paul. *Educ:* Rensselaer Polytech Inst, BS, 62; Cornell Univ, PhD(physics), 70. *Prof Exp:* Fel, Oak Ridge Nat Lab, 71-72; res asst prof, Ctr Adv Comput, Univ Ill, 72-75; fel, Tech Univ Norway, 75-77; res asst prof, Energy Res Group, Univ Ill, 77-81, asst prof, Dept Forestry, 81-85, assoc prof, Dept Urban & Regional Planning & Dept Ecol, Ethology & Evolution. *Mem:* Int Soc Ecol Modelling; Int Soc Ecol Econ. *Res:* Energy analysis; efficiency of energy and other resource use, environmental impacts of resource use; ecological modelling. *Mailing Add:* Ill Natural Hist Surv Champaign IL 61820. *Fax:* 217-333-6494; *E-Mail:* herendee@uiuc.edu

HERFORTH, ROBERT S, GENETICS. *Current Pos:* From asst prof to assoc prof, 67-84, PROF BIOL, AUGSBURG COL, 84- *Personal Data:* b Wahoo, Nebr, July 13, 39; m 70. *Educ:* Wartburg Col, BA, 60; Univ Nebr, MS, 63, PhD(genetics), 68. *Honors & Awards:* Harold Winfred Manter Prize, 68. *Mem:* AAAS; Sigma Xi. *Res:* Studies on hereditary viruses of Drosophila. *Mailing Add:* Dept Biol Augsburg Col 2211 Riverside Ave Minneapolis MN 55454-1351

HERGENRADER, GARY LEE, LIMNOLOGY, FISH BIOLOGY. *Current Pos:* From asst prof to assoc prof zool, Univ Nebr, 67-76, vchmn dept, 71-73, chmn sect organismic biol, 73-74, interim dir sch life sci, 74-75, prof zool, 76-81, HEAD & STATE FORESTER, DEPT FORESTRY FISHERIES & WILDLIFE, UNIV NEBR-LINCOLN, 81- *Personal Data:* b Scottsbluff, Nebr, Jan 18, 39; m 59, Phyllis Arnold; c Alan & Anne. *Educ:* Univ Nebr, BS, 61; Univ Wis, MS, 63, PhD(zool), 67. *Mem:* Am Fisheries Soc; Am Soc Limnol & Oceanog; Sigma Xi; Am Inst Fishery Res Biologists; Soc Am Foresters; Am Forestry Asn. *Res:* Biology of freshwater fishes; experimental and comparative limnology. *Mailing Add:* Forest Pi101 E Campus Univ Nebr PO Box 830814 Lincoln NE 68583-0814. *Fax:* 402-472-2964

HERGENROTHER, WILLIAM LEE, ORGANIC POLYMER CHEMISTRY. *Current Pos:* Res chemist, Firestone Tire & Rubber Co, 63-68, group leader, 68-73, res assoc, 73-79, sr res assoc, 79-88, SR RES ASSOC, BRIDGESTONE/FIRESTONE RES INC, 88- *Personal Data:* b Springfield, Ill, Oct 4, 38; m 64, Anne Egan; c Robert W, Michael L, John S, Paul J. *Educ:* Univ Notre Dame, BS, 60, PhD(chem), 63. *Mem:* Am Chem Soc; Sigma Xi; AAAS. *Res:* Synthesis, characterization and evaluation of polar-nonpolar block copolymers; mechanism and characterization cure of rubbers and thermosetting resins; synthesis of modified rubber and plastics, organic systhesis. *Mailing Add:* 195 Dorchester Rd Akron OH 44313-7806

HERGERT, HERBERT L, INFRARED SPECTROSCOPY. *Current Pos:* SR SCIENTIST, REPAP TECHNOL INC, 87- *Personal Data:* b Portland, Ore, Feb 20, 27; m 49, Lois M Lilly; c Lawrence A, Gregory K, David E & Daniel W. *Educ:* Reed Col, BA, 48; Ore State Col, MS, 51, PhD(chem), 54. *Honors & Awards:* First Tannin Chem Int Award, 89. *Prof Exp:* Res chemist, Ore Forest Prod Lab, 52-54; res chemist, Rayonier, Inc, 54-60, group leader, Res Div, 60-64, sect head, 64-69, res supvr, ITT Rayonier Inc, 69-70, asst dir res, 70-72, dir res & develop, 72-74, vpres & dir res & develop, 74-80, vpres & dir tech mkt, ITT Rayonier Inc, 80-87. *Concurrent Pos:* Consult forest prod. *Mem:* Am Chem Soc; Am Sci Affil; fel Tech Asn Pulp & Paper Indust; Phytochem Soc NAm; AAAS; Int Org Paleobot; fel Int Acad Wood Sci; Am Bot Soc. *Res:* Wood chemicals, extractives, lignin; infrared spectroscopy; paleobotany; cellulose derivatives; pulp and paper technology; textiles, plant taxonomy. *Mailing Add:* Repap Technol Inc 2650 Eisenhower Ave PO Box 766 Valley Forge PA 19482-0766. *Fax:* 610-630-0966

HERGET, CHARLES JOHN, ELECTRICAL ENGINEERING. *Current Pos:* ENGR, LAWRENCE LIVERMORE LAB, UNIV CALIF, 78- *Personal Data:* b Los Angeles, Calif, Dec 2, 37; m 64; c 2. *Educ:* Univ Calif, Los Angeles, BS, 59, MS, 64, PhD(eng), 67. *Prof Exp:* Mem tech staff, Hughes Aircraft Co, 59-64; res asst eng, Univ Calif, Los Angeles, 64-67; group head, Hughes Aircraft Co, 67-69; from asst prof to assoc prof elec eng, Iowa State Univ, 69-78. *Mem:* Inst Elec & Electronics Engrs. *Res:* Control systems theory; applied mathematics; system identification; process control. *Mailing Add:* 2714 Farnsworth Dr Livermore CA 94550

HERGET, WILLIAM F, GAS ANALYSIS BY FOURIER TRANSFER INFRARED SPECTROSCOPY. *Current Pos:* PRIN SCIENTIST, ENVIRON TECHNOLOGIES GROUP, 94- *Personal Data:* b Wheeling, WVa, Sept 29, 31; div; c 4. *Educ:* Univ Richmond, BS, 52; Vanderbilt Univ, MS, 55; Univ Tenn, PhD(physics), 62. *Honors & Awards:* Bronze Medal Award, Environ Protection Agency, 78. *Prof Exp:* From res asst to res assoc physics, Univ Tenn, 60-62; sr res physicist, Rocketdyne Div, Rockwell Int, 62-70; res physicist, Environ Res Ctr, Environ Protection Agency, 70-75, head spec tech group, 75-81; proj scientist, Nicolet Instrument Corp, 81-83, sr scientist, Radian Corp, 92-94. *Concurrent Pos:* Nicolet fel award, 83. *Mem:* Optical Soc Am; Air & Waste Mgt Asn; Coblentz Soc; Soc Automotive Engrs; Soc Appl Spectros. *Res:* Pressure induced spectral line broadening and shifts; infrared and ultraviolet characteristics of rocket exhaust radiation; remote sensing of air pollutants by spectroscopic methods; applications of Fourier transform infrared spectroscopy to gas analysis. *Mailing Add:* 43 Dawn Dr Linwood NJ 08221

HERGLOTZ, HERIBERT KARL JOSEF, PHYSICAL CHEMISTRY, X-RAY & POLYMER PHYSICS. *Current Pos:* RETIRED. *Personal Data:* b Dux, Czech, Dec 26, 19; m 42, Margit Guettner; c Helga, Harald, Heidemarie & Helen. *Educ:* Tech Univ Prague, MS, 44; Mining Acad, Freiberg, PhD(phys chem), 48; Vienna Tech Univ, x-ray physics, 55, PD. *Honors & Awards:* Herglotz Award, 89. *Prof Exp:* Asst phys chem, Mining Acad, Freiberg, 46-47, chief asst, 47-49; asst exp physics, Vienna Tech Univ, 49-55; physicist, Pigments Dept, E I du Pont de Nemours & Co, 56-59; sect head physics res, Chemie Linz AG, 59-61; sr res physicist, Eng Physics Lab, E I du Pont de Nemours & Co, Inc, 61-62, res assoc, 62-71, res fel, 71-84. *Concurrent Pos:* Asst, Charles Univ Prague, 44-55; consult, US Dept Army, 55-56; privat-dozent, Vienna Tech Univ, 55-62, extraordinary prof, 62-; trustee, Mt Cuba Astron Observ, 69-88; consult, Condux. *Mem:* Am Phys Soc; Austrian Phys Soc; Sigma Xi. *Res:* Polymer physics; x-ray diffraction and spectroscopy; astronomy; x-ray materials testing; electron spectroscopy for chemical analysis. *Mailing Add:* 2409 Hartley Pl Wilmington DE 19808-4258. *Fax:* 302-994-9253, 302-738-0161

HERIC, EUGENE LEROY, PHYSICAL CHEMISTRY. *Current Pos:* asst prof, 56-60, ASSOC PROF CHEM, UNIV GA, 60-, ASST DEAN GRAD SCH, 72- *Personal Data:* b Bellingham, Wash, Aug 30, 24; m 52; c 3. *Educ:* Univ Wash, BSChem, 48; Western Reserve Univ, MS, 50, PhD(chem), 52. *Prof Exp:* Res chemist, Shell Oil Co, 52-53; instr chem, Williams Col, 53-54; asst prof, Va Mil Inst, 54-56. *Mem:* Am Chem Soc. *Res:* Thermodynamics; thermochemistry; physical properties and heterogeneous equilibrium in binary and multicomponent systems; phase equilibrium. *Mailing Add:* 186 Catawba Ave Athens GA 30606-4304

HERIN, REGINALD AUGUSTUS, TOXICOLOGY, PHARMACOLOGY. *Current Pos:* RETIRED. *Personal Data:* b Jackson, Miss, June 17, 24; m 46; c 1. *Educ:* Colo State Univ, BS, 55, DVM, 58, MS, 59; Univ Minn, PhD, 66. *Prof Exp:* From instr to prof physiol, Colo State Univ, 59-68, prof pharmacol, 68-85. *Concurrent Pos:* NSF fel, Colo State Univ, 58-59; NIH spec fel, 65-66. *Mem:* AAAS; Am Vet Med Asn. *Res:* Toxicology, electroencephalography and neuropharmacology. *Mailing Add:* 980 N Mariott Ave Sequim WA 98382

HERING, ROBERT GUSTAVE, HEAT TRANSFER, FLUID MECHANICS. *Current Pos:* prof & chmn, 71-72, actg dean, 72-73, DEAN, COL ENG, UNIV IOWA, 73- *Personal Data:* b Chicago, Ill, Feb 18, 34; m 56; c 4. *Educ:* Univ Ill, BS, 56; Univ Southern Calif, MS, 58; Purdue Univ, PhD(mech eng), 61. *Prof Exp:* Res asst engr, Armour Res Found, 56; mem tech staff, Hughes Res & Develop Lab, 56-59; supvr, Allison Div Gen Motors, 60-61; from asst prof to prof mech eng, Univ Ill, 61-71. *Concurrent Pos:* Consult, Hughes Res & Develop Lab, 58-60 & Jet Propulsion Lab, 62-65; res adv, Argonne Nat Lab, 62; tech staff, Bell Tel Lab, 63; vis prof, Hokkaido Univ, Japan Soc Promotion Sci, 78; mem, Iowa Hwy Res Bd, Dept Transp, 71-; Fulbright res scholar, Univ Stutgart, WGer, 80-81. *Mem:* Am Soc Mech Eng; Am Inst Aeronaut & Astronaut; Am Soc Eng Educ. *Mailing Add:* Univ Iowa Col Engr Iowa City IA 52242

HERING, THOMAS M, orthopedics, for more information see previous edition

HERION, JOHN CARROLL, MEDICINE. *Current Pos:* from instr to assoc prof, 57-70, PROF MED, SCH MED, UNIV NC, CHAPEL HILL, 70- *Personal Data:* b Salisbury, NC, Sept 5, 27; m 53; c 5. *Educ:* Davidson Col, BS, 49; Harvard Univ, MD, 53. *Prof Exp:* Intern, NC Mem Hosp, 53-54 & from jr asst resident to sr asst resident med, 54-56. *Concurrent Pos:* Nat Heart Inst res fel, 56-57; USPHS grant & career res develop award, 62-72; fel, Am Col Phys, 73. *Mem:* AAAS; Am Fedn Clin Res; Am Soc Hemat; Am Soc Int Med; Am Soc Law & Med; Royal Soc Med. *Res:* Physiology of blood cells, especially kinetics of leukocytes, their role in production of fever and in hemostasis; control of production and differentiation of marrow progenitor cells. *Mailing Add:* Med Hemat Univ NC Sch Med Chapel Hill NC 27599-7005

HERITAGE, JONATHAN PAUL, MODERN OPTICS. *Current Pos:* STAFF MEM, LAWRENCE LIVERMORE NAT LAB, UNIV CALIF, 91- *Personal Data:* b Washington, DC, July 10, 44. *Educ:* Univ Calif, Berkeley, BS, 67, PhD(physics), 75; San Diego State Univ, MS, 70. *Prof Exp:* Res scientist, Bell Labs, 76-84; Bell Commun Res, 84-91. *Mem:* Fel Am Phys Soc; fel Inst Elec & Electronics Engrs; fel Optical Soc Am. *Mailing Add:* EEECS Dept UCD Bainer Hall Univ Calif Davis CA 95616

HERK, LEONARD FRANK, TECHNICAL CONTRACT PROMOTION. *Current Pos:* RETIRED. *Personal Data:* b Milwaukee, Wis, Apr 16, 31; m 53; c 2. *Educ:* Marquette Univ, BS, 53; State Univ NY, PhD(phys chem), 62. *Prof Exp:* Res chemist, E I du Pont de Nemours & Co, 53-55; phys sci specialist, US Army, Quartermaster R&E Ctr, 55-57; res specialist, 3M Co, 61-66, photo prods lab supvr, 66-71, pavement mark lab mgr, 71-74, prog mgr carbide prod, 74-79, bus opportunities mgr, New Ventures Div, 79-82; dir, Bus & Indust Develop Inst, Saginaw Valley State Univ, 82-88; dir, Detroit Off, Southwest Res Inst, 88-95. *Mem:* Soc Automotive Engrs; Soc Plastic Engrs. *Res:* Corporate contacts and team formation for major research and development contracts with Southwest Research Institute in the midwest. *Mailing Add:* 5566 Baker Rd Bridgeport MI 48722

HERKE, WILLIAM HERBERT, USE OF COASTAL MARSH AS NURSERY FOR MARINE-TRANSIENT FISHES & CRUSTACEANS, EFFECTS OF HUMAN PERTURBATIONS OF MARSH ON NURSERY. *Current Pos:* RETIRED. *Personal Data:* b Fonda, Iowa, Nov 27, 29; m 54, M Joan Farrell; c Kristin J (Gould), John M, David F & Scott W. *Educ:* Iowa State Univ, Ames, BS, 56, MS, 57; La State Univ, PhD(zool), 71. *Prof Exp:* Fishery biologist, Fla Game & Freshwater Fish Comn, 58-62 & US Fish & Wildlife Serv, 62-63; asst leader, US Fish & Wildlife Serv, 63-93; asst leader, La Coop Fish & Wildlife Res Unit, Nat Biol Surv, 93-94. *Concurrent Pos:* From staff to adj prof, Sch Forestry, Wildlife & Fisheries, La State Univ, 63- *Mem:* Am Fisheries Soc; fel Am Inst Fishery Res Biologists. *Res:* Life history and ecology of juvenile marine-transient (estuarine-dependent) fishes, shrimps and crabs while they use the Louisiana coastal marsh as a nursery; study the effects of man-made water-control structures, and other human-induced perturbations of the marsh, on nursery use by these organisms. *Mailing Add:* 555 Staring Lane Baton Rouge LA 70810-2602. *Fax:* 504-388-4144

HERKENHAM, MILES, NEUROANATOMY. *Current Pos:* CHIEF FUNCTIONAL NEUROANAT, NIMH, NIH, 90- *Personal Data:* b Yosemite Nat Park, Calif, May 2, 49. *Educ:* Northeastern Univ, PhD(physiol psychol), 75. *Mem:* Soc Neurosci. *Mailing Add:* Functional Neuroanat Br NIMH Bldg 36 Rm 2D15 Bethesda MD 20892. *Fax:* 301-402-2200; *E-Mail:* milesh@codon.nih.gov

HERKES, FRANK EDWARD, INDUSTRIAL ORGANIC CHEMISTRY & FINE CHEMICALS. *Current Pos:* sr res chemist, Exp Sta, 68-80, res assoc, Laplace, La, 80-88, sr res assoc, Exp Sta, 88-94, RES FEL, E I DU PONT DE NEMOURS & CO, INC, WILMINGTON, DEL, 94- *Personal Data:* b Chicago, Ill, July 2, 39; m 66, Mary; c Douglas, Joan & Diane. *Educ:* DePaul Univ, BS, 62; Univ Iowa, MS, 64, PhD(org chem), 66. *Prof Exp:* NSF fel, Harvard Univ, 66-68. *Mem:* Am Chem Soc; Org Reactions Catalysis Soc; NAm Catalysis Soc. *Res:* Aromatic diazonium chemistry; heterogeneous hydrogenation catalysts; raney catalysis; ring and nitrile reductions, reductive aminiation and alkylation; work in fiscner tropsen and zeolite catalysis. *Mailing Add:* 223 Charleston Dr Wilmington DE 19808. *E-Mail:* herkesfe@esvax.dnet.dupont.com

HERKSTROETER, WILLIAM G, PHOTOCHEMISTRY. *Current Pos:* SCIENTIST, UNIV ROCHESTER, 93- *Personal Data:* b St Louis, Mo, Nov 30, 38; m 67; c 2. *Educ:* Wesleyan Univ, BA, 60; Calif Inst Technol, PhD(chem), 66. *Prof Exp:* NSF fel, Univ Chicago, 65-66; sr res chemist, Eastman Kodak Co, 66-74, res assoc, 75-93. *Mem:* Inter-Am Photochem Soc; Europ Photochem Asn; Am Soc Photobiol. *Res:* Mechanisms of photochemical reactions; flash photolysis and transient absorption spectroscopy; luminescence spectroscopy. *Mailing Add:* Chem Dept Univ Rochester Rochester NY 14627-0216

HERLANDS, CHARLES WILLIAM, CATEGORY THEORY. *Current Pos:* Asst prof, 75-82, ASSOC PROF MATH, STOCKTON STATE COL, 82- *Personal Data:* US citizen. *Educ:* Stanford Univ, BS, 68; Univ Calif, San Diego, MA, 69; Univ Calif, Irvine, PhD(math), 73. *Mem:* Am Math Soc; Math Asn Am. *Res:* Category theory; homological algebra; triple cohomology; maps of triples. *Mailing Add:* Div Natural Sci & Math Richard Stockton Col NJ Pomona NJ 08240

HERLEY, PATRICK JAMES, SOLID STATE CHEMISTRY. *Current Pos:* res assoc physics, 65, GUEST SCIENTIST, BROOKHAVEN NAT LAB, 65-; PROF MAT SCI, STATE UNIV NY, STONY BROOK, 78- *Personal Data:* b Johannesburg, SAfrica, July 14, 34; m 60. *Educ:* Rhodes Univ, SAfrica, BSc, 56, Hons, 57, MSc, 58, PhD(chem), 60; Univ London, PhD(chem) & DIC, 64. *Hon Degrees:* DSc, Univ London, 82. *Prof Exp:* Fel, Univ Notre Dame, 64. *Concurrent Pos:* From asst prof to assoc prof mat sci, State Univ NY, Stony Brook, 71-78; sr vis fel chem dept, UK Sci & Eng Res Coun, Univ Cambridge, 87-88. *Mem:* The Chem Soc; Am Chem Soc. *Res:* Thermal and photolytic decomposition processes in pseudo-stable solids; x-ray topography of structural defects in inorganic single crystals; electron microscopy of metal hydrides. *Mailing Add:* Dept Mat Sci State Univ NY Stony Brook NY 11794-2275

HERLICZEK, SIEGFRIED H, ORGANIC POLYMER CHEMISTRY. *Current Pos:* sr res scientist, 70-78, DIR, PROD TECHNOL LAB, LIBBEY-OWENS-FORD CO, 78- *Personal Data:* b Breslau, Ger, June 17, 40; US citizen; m 67. *Educ:* Univ Mass, Amherst, BS, 63; Northeastern Univ, PhD(chem), 70. *Prof Exp:* Res chemist, Consumer Prod Corp, Union Carbide Corp, 63-64; asst, Northeastern Univ, 65-68. *Mem:* Am Chem Soc; Soc Plastic Eng; Soc Automotive Engrs. *Res:* Synthetic organic chemistry; studies on the mechanism of separation of diastereoisomeric compounds by gas-liquid chromatography; synthesis of polyurethane polymers; research and development of plastic film-glass laminates. *Mailing Add:* Libbey-Owens-Ford Co Tech Ctr 1701 E Broadway Toledo OH 43605

HERLIHY, JEREMIAH TIMOTHY, CARDIOVASCULAR, AGING. *Current Pos:* ASST PROF PHYSIOL, HEALTH & SCI CTR, UNIV TEX, SAN ANTONIO, 75- *Educ:* Univ Va, PhD(physiol), 72. *Mailing Add:* Dept Physiol Health & Sci Ctr Univ Tex 7703 Floyd Curl Dr San Antonio TX 78284-7756. *Fax:* 210-567-4410

HERLIN, MELVIN ARNOLD, PHYSICS. *Current Pos:* RETIRED. *Personal Data:* b Salt Lake City, Utah, 25, 23; m 43; c 2. *Educ:* Univ Utah, BS, 43; Mass Inst Technol, PhD(physics), 48. *Prof Exp:* Mem staff magnetron res, Radiation Lab, Mass Inst Technol, 43-45, res assoc microwave gaseous electronics, Res Lab Electronics & Dept Physics, 45-48, mem staff, 48-49, asst prof low temperature physics, 49-55, group leader, Lincoln Lab, Mass Inst Technol, 55-63, assoc div head, 63-70 & 78-79, div head, 71-78, asst to dir, 79-87. *Mem:* Am Inst Aeronaut & Astronaut; Am Phys Soc. *Res:* Microwave magnetrons; microwave gaseous electronics; low temperature physics; radar; reentry physics; data systems. *Mailing Add:* 25 Alsace St Laguna Niguel CA 92677

HERLINGER, ALBERT WILLIAM, INORGANIC CHEMISTRY. *Current Pos:* asst prof, 72-76, ASSOC PROF CHEM, LOYOLA UNIV, CHICAGO, 76- *Personal Data:* b Philadelphia, Pa, Nov 9, 43; c 2. *Educ:* Hobart Col, BS, 65; Pa State Univ, PhD(chem), 70. *Prof Exp:* Res assoc, Univ Ill, Urbana, 70-71; vis asst prof chem, Bucknell Univ, 71-72. *Concurrent Pos:* Vis scholar, Northwestern Univ, 72-75; vis scientist, Argonne Nat Lab, 96- *Mem:* Am Chem Soc; Sigma Xi. *Res:* Vibrational spectroscopy; inorganic and organometallic chemistry; transition metal cluster compounds; heavy element coordination chemistry; chemical separations. *Mailing Add:* Dept Chem Loyola Univ 6525 N Sheridan Rd Chicago IL 60626. *Fax:* 773-508-3086

HERLYN, DOROTHEE MARIA, TUMOR IMMUNOLOGY, TUMOR BIOLOGY. *Current Pos:* assoc scientist immunol, Wistar Inst, 76-79, assoc scientist tumor immunol, 79-81, res assoc, 81-85, asst prof, 85-91, ASSOC PROF TUMOR IMMUNOL, WISTAR INST, PHILADELPHIA, 91- *Personal Data:* b Seltmans, WGer, Apr 17, 45; m 70; c 2. *Educ:* Univ Munich, DVM, 70. *Prof Exp:* Res asst endocrinol, Inst Physiol, Freising Univ, Ger, 69-70; res asst immunol, Inst Physiol, Univ Munich, Ger, 71-76. *Mem:* Am Asn Immunologists; Am Asn Cancer Res. *Res:* Use of monoclonal anti-human anti-human tumor antibodies in localization and therapy of human tumors; approaches to immunotherapy of human cancer with anti-idiotypic antibodies. *Mailing Add:* Wistar Inst Anat & Biol 36th & Spruce St Philadelphia PA 19104-4268. *Fax:* 215-898-0980

HERM, RONALD RICHARD, CHEMICAL PHYSICS, INFRA-RED PHYSICS. *Current Pos:* dept head, Iran A Getting Labs, Aerospace Corp, 76-89, systs dir, Advan Orbital Systs Opers, 89-91, distinguished engr, Advan Progs Div, 91-95, DISTINGUISHED ENGR, SPACE BASED SURVEILLANCE DIV, AEROSPACE CORP, 95- *Personal Data:* b Louisville, Ky, Jan 18, 40; m 63, Maria I Florez; c Joseph & Charles. *Educ:* Univ Notre Dame, BS, 61; Harvard Univ, PhD(chem physics), 65. *Prof Exp:* Nat Acad Sci-Nat Res Coun & Air Force Off Sci Res fels photoionization, Univ Chicago, 65-66; asst prof chem, Univ Calif, Berkeley, 66-74; assoc prof, Iowa State Univ, 74-76. *Concurrent Pos:* Alfred P Sloan Found fel, 70-72. *Mem:* Am Chem Soc; Am Phys Soc. *Res:* Chemical kinetics; atomic and molecular collisions; infra-red signature phenomenology. *Mailing Add:* Aerospace Corp PO Box 92957 Los Angeles CA 90009. *Fax:* 310-336-2204; *E-Mail:* herm@aesosbsd.aero.org

HERMACH, FRANCIS L, ELECTRICAL MEASUREMENTS. *Current Pos:* INDEPENDENT CONSULT ELEC MEASUREMENTS, 72- *Personal Data:* b Bridgeport, Conn, Jan 8, 17; wid; c 2. *Educ:* George Washington Univ, BEE, 43. *Honors & Awards:* Silver Medal, US Dept Com, 54; Morris E Leeds & Centennial Awards, Inst Elec & Electronics Engrs, 76 & 84. *Prof Exp:* Elec engr, Nat Bur Stand, 39-63, chief, Elec Instruments Sect, 63-72. *Concurrent Pos:* Assoc dir, Metrol Div, Instrument Soc Am, 67-69. *Mem:* Fel Inst Elec & Electronics Engrs Instrumentation & Measurement Soc (pres, 68-69); fel Instrument Soc Am; Precision Measurements Asn. *Res:* Electrical instruments and measurements fundamental standards for ac voltage and current; hazards from static electricity. *Mailing Add:* 15101 Glade Dr No 3F Silver Spring MD 20906

HERMAN, BARBARA HELEN, neuropeptides, pediatric psychiatric disorders, for more information see previous edition

HERMAN, BENJAMIN MORRIS, METEOROLOGY & RADIATIVE TRANSFER, OPTICAL SCATTERING & REMOTE SENSING. *Current Pos:* res assoc, 59-64, from asst prof to assoc prof meteorol, 64-68, prof atmospheric sci, Inst Atmospheric Physics, 68-95, DEPT HEAD, UNIV ARIZ, 95- *Personal Data:* b Port Chester, NY, Aug 13, 29; m 54; c 3. *Educ:* NY Univ, BS, 51, MS, 54; Univ Ariz, PhD(meteorol), 64. *Prof Exp:* Weather officer, USAF, 51-57; res meteorologist severe storms, US Weather Bur, 57; assoc scientist physics, Res & Adv Develop Div, Avco, 57-59. *Mem:* Am Meteorol Soc; Am Geophys Union. *Res:* Radiative transfer through atmosphere; single and multiple scattering and polarization; remote sensing of atmosphere; influence of aerosols on radiative transfer; remote sensing from space. *Mailing Add:* Inst Atmospheric Physics Univ Ariz Tucson AZ 85721

HERMAN, BRIAN, CELL GROWTH, HYPOXIA. *Current Pos:* PROF CELL BIOL & ANAT, SCH MED, UNIV NC, 83- *Personal Data:* b Nov 3, 53; m, Deborah K Smith; c Lindsey. *Educ:* Univ Conn, Farmington, PhD(cell biol & biophys), 80. *Mem:* Am Soc Cell Biol; Biophys Soc; Am Soc Biochem & Molecular Biol; AAAS. *Res:* Abnormal cell growth in cancer and heart disease; hypoxic and ischemic injury; human papilloma virus and cervical cancer. *Mailing Add:* Dept Cell Biol & Anat Sch Med Univ NC 232 Taylor Hall CB No 7090 Chapel Hill NC 27599-7090. *Fax:* 919-966-1856; *E-Mail:* bhgf@med.unc.edu

HERMAN, CEIL ANN, ENDOCRINOLOGY, COMPARATIVE PHYSIOLOGY. *Current Pos:* from asst prof to assoc prof, 79-89, PROF, DEPT BIOL, NMEX STATE UNIV, 89- *Personal Data:* b New York, NY, Nov 12, 46; m 68. *Educ:* Carnegie-Mellon Univ, BS, 68; Duquesne Univ, MS, 69; Univ Mo, PhD(zool), 74. *Prof Exp:* Teaching asst zool, Duquesne Univ, 68-69; res asst, Univ Mo, 69-72, teach asst, 72-74, res assoc biochem, 74-76; res chemist physiology, Vet Admin Hosp, St Louis, 76-78; res assoc, Washington Univ, 78-79. *Mem:* Am Physiol Soc; Sigma Xi; Am Fedn Clin Res; fel AAAS. *Res:* Evolution of hormonal systems in non-mammalian vertebrates, with particular emphasis on synthesis and physiological actions of prostaglandins; interactions of hormones, with adenylate cyclase in plasma membranes of amphibians. *Mailing Add:* Dept Biol NMex State Univ Box 3AF Las Cruces NM 88003. *Fax:* 505-646-5665

HERMAN, CHESTER JOSEPH, LABORATORY INSTRUMENTS. *Current Pos:* PROF PATH, EMORY UNIV, 91- *Personal Data:* b Cincinnati, Ohio, Nov 24, 41; m 76, Gail Robertson Janes. *Educ:* Univ Rochester, MD & PhD(path), 70. *Honors & Awards:* Commendation Medal, USPHS, 78; Japanese Govt Award for Foreign Specialists, 78. *Prof Exp:* Chief, Quant Cytol, Nat Cancer Inst, Bethesda, Md, 75-79; assoc prof path, Cath Univ, Nijmegen, Holland, 79-83; pathologist, Lab Delft Hosps, Holland, 83-86; prof & chair path, Loyola Univ Chicago, 86-90. *Concurrent Pos:* Clin assoc, NIH, Bethesda, Md, 70-72, resident path, 72-76; vis scientist, Nat Cancer Ctr,

Tokyo, Japan, 78; dir path, Grady Hosp; assoc dir, Winship Cancer Ctr. *Mem:* Int Acad Pathologists; fel Col Am Pathologists; Int Soc Anal Cytol. *Res:* Application of new technology in laboratory and clinical medicine; new medical technology evaluation. *Mailing Add:* Dept Path Grady Mem Hosp Atlanta GA 30335

HERMAN, DANIEL FRANCIS, ORGANIC CHEMISTRY. *Current Pos:* CONSULT, POLYMER CHEM, 82- *Personal Data:* b Brooklyn, NY, Feb 19, 19; m 47; c 1. *Educ:* Purdue Univ, BS, 39, MS, 40; Pa State Univ, PhD(chem), 43. *Prof Exp:* Res chemist, Grosvenor Lab, 43-44; group leader, Publicker Indusis, Inc, 44-47; head, Org Res Dept, NL Indusis, Inc, 47-61, asst tech dir, Hightstown Cent Res Lab, 61-69, assoc dir res, Hightstown Cent Res Lab, 69-82. *Concurrent Pos:* Mem adv coun, plastics dept, Princeton Univ; Plenary lect, 5th Int Cellulose Cong. *Mem:* AAAS; Am Inst Chem; Am Chem Soc. *Res:* Locus controlled polymerization process for encapsulation of cellulose; glass fibers with polyolefins; organometallics; first synthesis of organotitanium compound; catalysts; paper technology; vehicles; polyelectrolytes; super absorbing polymers surface chemistry; gellants; paints; microviod coatings. *Mailing Add:* 39 Hemlock Circle Princeton NJ 08540

HERMAN, E(LVIN) E(UGENE), ELECTRONICS ENGINEERING. *Current Pos:* RETIRED. *Personal Data:* b Sigourney, Iowa, Mar 17, 21; m 45, Grace Eklund; c Jane A. *Educ:* Univ Iowa, BS, 42. *Honors & Awards:* Lawrence A Hyland Patent Award, Hughes Aircraft Co, 71. *Prof Exp:* Engr, Naval Res Lab, Washington, DC, 42-51; engr circuits group, Nat Bur Stand, Calif, 51-53; sr staff engr, Hughes Aircraft Co, 53-55, head, Radar Systs Dept, 55-58, mgr, Signal Processing & Display Lab, 58-68, asst mgr, Res & Develop Div, 63-70, tech dir, Radar Systs Group, 70-84. *Concurrent Pos:* Eng consult, 84- *Mem:* Sigma Xi; fel Inst Elec & Electronics Engrs. *Res:* Design and development of counter-countermeasures; display; signal processing; air-to-air and high resolution radar; granted 24 patents. *Mailing Add:* 1200 Lachman Lane Pacific Palisades CA 90272

HERMAN, ELIOT MARK, PLANT PHYSIOLOGY. *Current Pos:* PLANT PHYSIOLOGIST, AGR RES SERV, USDA, BELTSVILLE, MD, 85- *Personal Data:* b Boston, Mass, Sept 26, 52; c Debbie & Sarah. *Educ:* Univ Calif, Santa Barbara, BA, 73, MA, 75; Univ Calif, San Diego, PhD(biol), 80. *Prof Exp:* Res assoc, Calif Inst Technol, 80-81; assoc biochem, Univ Calif, Riverside, 81-83; asst res biochemist, 84. *Concurrent Pos:* Adj assoc prof bot, Univ Md, College Park, 90-; ed, Planta, 93- *Mem:* AAAS; Am Soc Plant Physiologists; Am Soc Biochem & Molecular Biol; Sigma Xi. *Res:* Ontogeny of seed oil and protein storage organelles using soybean and tobacco as model systems. *Mailing Add:* Plant Molecular Biol Lab USDA Agr Res Serv Bldg 006 Beltsville MD 20705. *Fax:* 301-504-5320; *E-Mail:* eherman@asrr.arsusda.gov

HERMAN, EUGENE ALEXANDER, MATHEMATICS. *Current Pos:* from asst prof to assoc prof, 65-74, PROF MATH, GRINNELL COL, 74- *Personal Data:* b Washington, DC, Apr 25, 37; m 63; c 2. *Educ:* Univ Chicago, BS, 59; Univ Calif, Berkeley, MA, 61, PhD(math), 64. *Prof Exp:* Instr math, Univ Calif, Berkeley, 64-65. *Concurrent Pos:* Alexander von Humboldt Found fel, Univ Hamburg, 67-68. *Mem:* Am Math Soc; Math Asn Am. *Res:* Educational computing; functional analysis. *Mailing Add:* Dept Math & Comput Sci Grinnell Col Grinnell IA 50112-0806

HERMAN, EUGENE H, CARDIOVASCULAR PHARMACOLOGY, CARDIOVASCULAR TOXICOLOGY. *Current Pos:* RES PHARMACOLOGIST, DIV RES & TESTING, CTR DRUG EVAL & RES, FOOD & DRUG ADMIN, 73- *Personal Data:* b Minneapolis, Minn, Mar 26, 36; m 58, Esther Cywan; c Alisa, Rachel, Elana & David. *Educ:* Univ Calif, Berkeley, AB, 59; Univ Calif, San Francisco, MS, 63, PhD(pharmacol), 65. *Honors & Awards:* Accommodation Medal, Pub Health Serv, 81, Outstanding Serv Medal, 89. *Prof Exp:* Res pharmacologist, Med Ctr, Univ Calif, San Francisco, 65; pharmacologist, Walter Reed Army Inst Res, 65-67; sr investr preclin pharmacol div, Cancer Chemother Dept, Microbiol Assocs, Inc, 67-73. *Mem:* Am Soc Pharmacol & Exp Therapeut; Soc Toxicol; Soc Exp Biol & Med; Am Asn Cancer Res. *Res:* Drug-induced alterations in the cardiovascular and pulmonary systems. *Mailing Add:* 511 New York Ave Takoma Park MD 20912-4119. *Fax:* 301-594-3037

HERMAN, FRANK, SOLID STATE PHYSICS, THEORETICAL PHYSICS. *Current Pos:* mgr, Large-Scale Sci Computations Dept, 69-72, RES PHYSICIST, IBM RES LAB, SAN JOSE, 72- *Personal Data:* b Brooklyn, NY, Mar 21, 26; m 53; c 3. *Educ:* Columbia Univ, BS, 45, MS, 49, PhD(physics), 53. *Prof Exp:* Instr elec eng, Cooper Union, 47-49; res physicist, David Sarnoff Res Ctr, Radio Corp Am, 49-61; sr consult scientist & head theoret chem, Lockheed Palo Alto Res Labs, 62-69. *Concurrent Pos:* RCA Labs award, 50,52 & 55; sci consult, Lawrence Radiation Lab, Livermore, 65-69; consult, NSF, 71; Alexander von Humboldt sr US scientist award, 85-88; vis scientist, Max Planck Inst Solid State Res, Stuttgart, WGer, 86; Nordita guest prof, Chalmers Univ, Gothenberg, Sweden, 77, 85. *Mem:* Fel Am Phys Soc; fel Inst Elec & Electronics Engrs; AAAS; Sigma Xi. *Res:* Theoretical solid state physics, especially band structure, space groups, lattice dynamics, alloys and disordered solids; atomic structure; exchange, correlation, relativistic effects; computational physics; theoretical chemistry; surface physics; organic solids; quantum chemistry; atomic and molecular physics; theory of superconductivity magnetism. *Mailing Add:* 15 Anderson Way Menlo Park CA 94025

HERMAN, FREDERICK LOUIS, MEMBRANE SEPARATION PROCESSES, ORGANIC CHEMISTRY. *Current Pos:* Res chemist, 75-79, contract develop mgr, 79-81, GROUP LEADER, AIR PROD & CHEM, 81- *Personal Data:* b Brooklyn, NY, Jan 8, 51. *Educ:* Brooklyn Col, BS, 71; Columbia Univ, PhD(chem), 75; Lehigh Univ, MBA, 81. *Mem:* Am Chem Soc. *Res:* Functional monomer-polymer chemistry; organofluorine chemistry; catalysis; nitration chemistry; separation science. *Mailing Add:* 232 Graham St Highland Park NJ 08904

HERMAN, GEORGE, SPEECH SCIENCE. *Current Pos:* RETIRED. *Personal Data:* b New York, NY, Apr 19, 22; m 46, Lee D & Linda Jo; c 2. *Educ:* Brooklyn Col, AB, 41; Univ Mich, MS, 43, PhD(speech), 52. *Prof Exp:* Asst prof speech, Wayne Univ, 46-52 & Univ Mich, 52-58; from asst prof to assoc prof speech, 58-71, vprovost, 71-75, prof speech, Bowling Green State Univ, 71-81; dir bus commun, Dacor Comput Systs, 81-83; col prof spec ed, NMex State Univ, 85-88. *Mem:* Acoust Soc Am. *Res:* Experimental phonetics. *Mailing Add:* 2861 Buena Vida Ct Las Cruces NM 88011-5056. *E-Mail:* lcgeorge@aol.com

HERMAN, HARVEY BRUCE, ANALYTICAL CHEMISTRY. *Current Pos:* assoc prof, 69-73, actg head, 81-82, PROF CHEM, UNIV NC, GREENSBORO, 73-, HEAD, 82- *Personal Data:* b Brooklyn, NY, Oct 15, 36; m 60; c 4. *Educ:* Polytech Inst Brooklyn, BS, 58. Syracuse Univ, PhD(anal chem), 64. *Prof Exp:* Asst prof chem, Univ Ga, 64-69. *Concurrent Pos:* Assoc ed, Compute Mag. *Mem:* AAAS; Am Chem Soc; Electrochem Soc; Sigma Xi. *Res:* Electroanalytical chemistry including chronopotentiometry polarography and coulometry; ion selective electrodes; adsorption and kinetics; instrumentation and computers. *Mailing Add:* Dept Chem Univ NC Greensboro NC 27412-0001

HERMAN, HERBERT, MATERIALS SCIENCE ENGINEERING, OCEAN ENGINEERING. *Current Pos:* assoc prof mat sci, 68-72, chmn, Dept Mat Sci, 74-80, LEADING PROF MAT SCI, STATE UNIV NY, STONY BROOK, 72-, PROF, MARINE SCI RES CTR, 80- *Personal Data:* b Brooklyn, NY, June 15, 34; m 63, Barbara Budin; c Daniel L. *Educ:* De Paul Univ, BS, 56; Northwestern Univ, MS, 58, PhD(metall), 61. *Prof Exp:* Fulbright fel metall, Univ Paris, 61-62; fel, Argonne Nat Lab, 62-63; asst prof, Univ Pa, 63-68. *Concurrent Pos:* Ford Found prof indust, Western Elec Eng Res Ctr, 67-68; mem undersea vehicle comt, Marine Technol Soc, 68; liaison scientist, London Br, US Off Naval Res, 75-76; guest scientist physics, Brookhaven Nat Lab, 76-, consult mat div, 78-; ed-in-chief, Mat Sci & Eng J & ed, Treatise Mat Sci & Eng Ser; chair, Thermal Spray Div, Am Soc Metals, 86-89. *Mem:* AAAS; fel Am Soc Metals; Am Welding Soc; Marine Technol Soc; Am Inst Mining, Metall & Petrol Engrs; fel Am Ceramic Soc; Am Soc Eng Educ; Mat Res Soc. *Res:* Thermal sprayed protective coatings and free standing structural components; intermetallic compounds; metal and ceramic matrix composites; ceramics; fuel cell processing; powder metallurgy; powder processing; corrosion protection of transportation and marine structures. *Mailing Add:* Dept Mat Sci & Eng State Univ NY Stony Brook NY 11794-2275. *Fax:* 516-632-8052

HERMAN, IRA MARC, CELL MOTILITY, MITOSIS & CYTOKINESIS. *Current Pos:* ASST PROF CELL BIOL & ANAT, SCH MED, TUFTS UNIV, 81- *Personal Data:* b New York, NY, June 9, 52. *Educ:* State Univ NY, Buffalo, BA, 74; Tulane Univ, PhD(cell biol), 78. *Prof Exp:* Teaching asst biol sci, Tulane Univ, 75-78; Muscular Dystrophy Asn fel, Med Sch, Johns Hopkins Univ, 78-81, lab instr histol, 79-81. *Concurrent Pos:* Estab Investigatorship Award, Am Heart Asn, 83-88. *Mem:* Am Soc Cell Biol; Sigma Xi. *Res:* Molecular mechanism utilized by non-muscle cells for powering cell locomotion, division and chromosome movement. *Mailing Add:* Dept Anat & Cell Biol Sch Med 136 Harrison Ave Tufts Univ Boston MA 02111-1800. *Fax:* 617-636-0445

HERMAN, IRVING PHILIP, LASER PHYSICS, CHEMICAL PHYSICS. *Current Pos:* STAFF PHYSICIST, LAWRENCE LIVERMORE LAB, 77- *Personal Data:* b Brooklyn, NY, Oct 18, 51; m 77. *Educ:* Mass Inst Technol, SB, 72, PhD(physics), 77. *Mem:* Am Phys Soc; Am Chem Soc. *Res:* Laser-initiated chemical reactions; laser spectroscopy; deuterium isotope separation; laser development. *Mailing Add:* Dept Appl Physics Columbia Univ 202 SW Mudd New York NY 10027

HERMAN, JAN ALEKSANDER, PHYSICAL CHEMISTRY. *Current Pos:* RETIRED. *Personal Data:* b Warszawa, Poland, Oct 4, 23; m 51. *Educ:* Cath Univ Louvain, Dr en Sc, 51. *Prof Exp:* With lab phys chem, Queen Elizabeth Med Found, Belg, 51-57; from asst prof to assoc prof, Laval Univ, 57-66, prof chem, 66- *Mem:* Am Chem Soc; Chem Inst Can; Faraday Soc. *Res:* Radiation and photochemistry; mass spectrometry. *Mailing Add:* 3754 Lecorbusier Quebec PQ G1W 4P4 Can

HERMAN, JEROME HERBERT, RHEUMATOLOGY, IMMUNOLOGY. *Current Pos:* from asst prof to assoc prof, 69-77, PROF MED IMMUNOL/CONNECTIVE TISSUE DIS, UNIV CINCINNATI MED CTR, 77-; ATTEND PHYSICIAN INTERNAL MED, UNIV HOSPS, 69- *Personal Data:* b Baltimore, Md, Dec 1, 34; m 62; c 3. *Educ:* Univ Md, BS, 58, MD, 60. *Prof Exp:* Intern/residency, Sinai Hosp, Baltimore, 60-62; residency internal med, Univ Colo Med Ctr, Denver, 62-64. *Concurrent Pos:* Fel rheumatol, Univ Colo Med Ctr, Denver, 64-66; fel immunol & rheumatol, Univ Tex Southwestern Med Sch, Dallas, 66-68; consult physician, Vet Admin Hosp, Cincinnati, 69-; Arthritis Found fel, 70-73. *Mem:* Am Col Rheumatol; Am Asn Immunol; Am Fedn Clin Res; Cent Soc Clin Res; NY Acad Sci. *Res:* Biochemistry/immunology of connective tissue diseases; immunobiology of cartilage; biophysical force modulation of connective tissue metabolism. *Mailing Add:* Med Col ML No 563 Univ Cincinnati 231 Bethesda Ave Cincinnati OH 45267

HERMAN, JOHN EDWARD, SOFTWARE SYSTEMS. *Current Pos:* asst prof, 66-74, ASSOC PROF COMPUT SCI, WESTERN MICH UNIV, 74- *Personal Data:* b Port Huron, Mich, June 6, 38; m 61; c 2. *Educ:* Univ Mich, BSE, 60, MSE, 61, MS, 63, PhD(physics, elec eng), 66. *Prof Exp:* Asst res engr, Cooley Res Lab, Univ Mich, 62-64, res asst electron magnetic resonance, Univ, 64-66. *Mem:* Asn Comput Mach; AAAS. *Res:* Use of computers in instruction; graphics. *Mailing Add:* 7705 MacArthur Lane Portage Kalamazoo MI 49002

HERMAN, LAWRENCE, CELL BIOLOGY, ELECTRON MICROSCOPY. *Current Pos:* RETIRED. *Personal Data:* b New York, NY, May 22, 24; m 61; c 2. *Educ:* NY Univ, BA, 47; Columbia Univ, MA, 48; Univ Chicago, PhD(zool), 56. *Prof Exp:* Instr biol, Olivet Col, 48-49; instr, Allegheny Col, 49-51; teaching asst, Univ Chicago, 55-56; res assoc path, Sch Med, Cornell Univ, 56-57; from asst prof to prof path, State Univ NY Downstate Med Ctr, 57-76; prof & chmn, NY Med Col, Valhalla, 76-85, prof, Dept Anat, 86-91. *Concurrent Pos:* NIH spec res fel, 68-69; Fulbright res scholar biophys, All-India Inst Med Sch, New Delhi, India, 75-76; Fogarty scholar, Dept Med Biochem, Cambridge Univ Sch Med, Eng, 78. *Mem:* Am Soc Cell Biol; Am Soc Exp Path; Am Soc Zool; Electron Micros Soc Am; Biophys Soc. *Res:* Mechanisms of secretion; comparative morphology of endocrine organs and muscle. *Mailing Add:* 7 Seneca Dr Chappaqua NY 10514

HERMAN, MARTIN, COMPUTER VISION. *Current Pos:* GROUP LEADER, NAT INST STANDS & TECHNOL, 85- *Personal Data:* b Tel-Aviv, Israel; US citizen; m 79. *Educ:* Cooper Union, BS, 72; Univ Md, MS, 77, PhD(comput sci), 79. *Prof Exp:* Tech info specialist, Prog Methods, Inc, 73; data syst analyst, NASA, 74-75; res assoc, Carnegie-Mellon Univ, 79-85. *Mem:* Asn Comput Mach; Am Asn Artificial Intel. *Res:* Artificial intelligence; computer vision and knowledge acquisition; automated computer acquisition of three-dimensional geometric descriptions from two-dimensional images of objects and scenes. *Mailing Add:* Nat Inst Stands & Technol Bldg 220 Rm B124 Gaithersburg MD 20899

HERMAN, MARVIN, METALLURGY. *Current Pos:* RETIRED. *Personal Data:* b New York, NY, Mar 2, 27; m 51; c 4. *Educ:* Drexel Inst, BS, 51; Univ Pa, MS, 53, PhD(metall), 65. *Prof Exp:* Develop engr metall, Westinghouse Elec Corp, 50-51; asst, Univ Pa, 51-55; lab mgr, Franklin Inst, 55-65; sect chief mat sci, Allison Div, Gen Motors Corp, 65-92. *Mem:* Sigma Xi; Am Inst Mining, Metall & Petrol Engrs; Am Soc Metals. *Res:* Sintering and mechanical behavior of metals; substructure in metals; purification of reactive metals; beryllium metallurgy; composite materials; ceramics; materials selection. *Mailing Add:* 1103 Fairway Dr Indianapolis IN 46260

HERMAN, MARY M, NEUROPATHOLOGY, PATHOLOGY. *Current Pos:* prof path & co dir, Div Neuropath, 81-92, SR STAFF SCIENTIST, NIH, UNIV VA, CHARLOTTESVILLE, 96-; SR STAFF SCIENTIST, CLIN BRAIN DIS BR, NIMH, 96- *Personal Data:* b Plymouth, Wis, July 26, 35; wid. *Educ:* Univ Wis, BS, 57, MD, 60; Am Bd Path, dipl, 67, cert neuropath, 68. *Honors & Awards:* Weil Award, Am Asn Neuropathologists, 74. *Prof Exp:* Intern, Mary Hitchcock Mem Hosp, Hanover, NH, 60-61; resident neurol, Wis Univ Hosps, 61-62; intern path, Yale Univ, 62-63, asst resident, 63-64; actg instr path, Stanford Univ, 66-67, from asst prof to assoc prof, 67-81; res assoc path, Yale Univ, 63-64; Nat Inst Neuropath, Div Neuropath, Univ Va Sch Med, 81-91; prof, Div Clin Path, Univ Va, 91-92; spec expert clin brain dis, Neuropath Sect, NIMH, 91-96. *Concurrent Pos:* USPHS fel, Wis Univ Hosps, 61-62 & fel path, Yale Univ, 63-64; Nat Inst Neurol Dis & Blindness spec fel neuropath, 64-65 & Stanford Univ, 65-66, spec fel, 66-67; Regents, Hazel Duling & Johnson Found scholar, Univ Wis; Mary Putnam Jacobi fel, Yale Univ; Nat Inst Neurol Dis & Blindness res develop award, Stanford Univ, 67-72, Merck fac develop award, 69; Nat Inst Neurol Dis & Stroke res grant, 69-72; vis asst prof, Albert Einstein Col Med, Bronx, NY, 71-72; co-prin investr, Nat Cancer Inst res grant, 71- & Nat Inst Neurol Dis & Stroke Training grant, 72-91; mem spec subcomt, Neurol Dis Prog Proj Rev Comt, Spinal Cord Injury Ctr, Nat Inst Neurol Dis & Stroke, 72-73, mem, Neurol Dis Prog Proj Rev Comt, 73-77; Nat Inst Alcohol Abuse & Alcoholism grant, 74-77; ad hoc mem, Path A Study Sect, NIH, 86-; consult, Lab Serv, VA Hosp, Salem, Va & Cent Va Training Ctr, Lynchburg, Va, 81-; mem med staff, Univ Va Hosps, 81-91; consult neuropath, DC Med Examr Off, 92-; assoc & mem med staff, DC Gen Hosp, 92-; neuropathologist, Stanley Found Brain Coll. *Mem:* AAAS; Am Soc Cell Biol; Soc Biol Psychiat; Soc Develop Biol; Int Soc Neuropath; Am Asn Pathologists; Int Acad Path; AMA; Am Soc Investigative Path; Soc Neurosci. *Res:* Aluminum neurotoxicity; neuropathology of mental illness; dementias. *Mailing Add:* Clin Brain Disorders Br NIMH Neurosci St Elizabeths Washington DC 20032. *Fax:* 202-373-6214

HERMAN, MICHAEL SCOTT, FILLED CONDUCTIVE ADHESIVES. *Current Pos:* RES & DEVELOP MGR, ENGINEERED POWDERS DIV, TECHNIC INC, 94- *Personal Data:* b Bangor, Maine, Oct 23, 64; m 96, Jodi Krom. *Educ:* Clarkson Univ, BS, 86; Univ Rochester, MS, 88, PhD(chem). *Prof Exp:* Res assoc, Univ Ariz, 92-93. *Mem:* Am Chem Soc; Int Miroelectrons & Packaging Soc. *Res:* New metal powders and flakes for filled conductive adhesives, inks and coatings. *Mailing Add:* 300 Park East Dr Woonsocket RI 02895. *Fax:* 401-769-2472

HERMAN, PAUL THEODORE, PHYSICS. *Current Pos:* physicist, Lawrence Radiation Lab, 68-71, PHYSICIST, LAWRENCE LIVERMORE LAB, 71- *Personal Data:* b Harrisburg, Pa, July 25, 39; m 57, Dolores Doll; c Julia. *Educ:* Muhlenberg Col, BS, 60; Lehigh Univ, MS, 62, PhD(physics), 66. *Prof Exp:* Res fel physics, Univ Md, College Park, 66-68. *Concurrent Pos:* NSF int travel grant, Neth, 67. *Mem:* Am Phys Soc. *Res:* Equilibrium and nonequilibrium statistical mechanics; nuclear weapons research; nonproliferation and arms control. *Mailing Add:* 2080 Pulsar Ave Livermore CA 94550. *Fax:* 510-422-6434; *E-Mail:* herman2@llnl.gov

HERMAN, RAY MICHAEL, SOLID STATE PHYSICS. *Current Pos:* MAGNAVOX, TORRANCE, CALIF. *Personal Data:* b Chicago, Ill, Oct 19, 49; m 74; c 1. *Educ:* Univ Ill, BS, 71, MS, 72, PhD(physics), 76. *Prof Exp:* Mem staff, Hughes Aircraft, 76- *Mem:* Inst Elec & Electronics Engrs. *Mailing Add:* Hughes Space & Commun Bldg 510 MS 5308 PO Box 92919 Los Angeles CA 90009

HERMAN, RICHARD GERALD, CATALYSIS, ENERGY CHEMICALS. *Current Pos:* res scientist I, 75-82, res scientist II, 82-89, PRIN RES SCIENTIST, ZETTLEMOYER CTR SURFACE STUDIES, LEHIGH UNIV, BETHLEHEM, PA, 89-, EXEC DIR, 95- *Personal Data:* b Springville, NY, Mar 11, 44; m, Helen L Ramer; c Richard, Sarah & Jonathan. *Educ:* State Univ NY Fredonia, BS, 66; Ohio Univ, PhD(chem), 72. *Prof Exp:* Res assoc, Dept Chem, Univ Lund, Sweden, 72-73 & Tex A&M Univ, Col Sta, 73-75. *Concurrent Pos:* Adj assoc prof, Dept Chem, Lehigh Univ, 80; ed, Catalytic Conversions Synthesis Gas & Alcohols to Chem, 84; interim dir Zettlemoyer Ctr Surface Studies, Lehigh Univ, 89; chmn, Lehigh Valley Sect, Am Chem Soc, 89, alt counr, 91-96. *Mem:* Am Chem Soc; Catalysis Soc NAm; Sigma Xi. *Res:* Synthesis of high octane alcohols and ethers from synthesis gas; preparation and characterization of inorganic catalysts; ion exchange; catalytic testing; selective methane oxidation; granted 4 patents and published 95 articles. *Mailing Add:* Lehigh Univ Sinclair Lab 7 Asa Dr Bethlehem PA 18015. *Fax:* 601-758-6555; *E-Mail:* rgh1@lehigh.edu

HERMAN, RICHARD HOWARD, MATHEMATICAL PHYSICS, OPERATOR ALGEBRAS. *Current Pos:* PROF MATH & DEAN COMPUT SCI, UNIV MD, 90- *Personal Data:* b Huntington, NY, Sept 4, 41; m 64; c 3. *Educ:* Stevens Inst Technol, BS, 63; Univ Md, College Park, PhD(math), 67. *Prof Exp:* Res assoc math physics, Univ Rochester, 66-68; asst prof math, Univ Calif, Los Angeles, 68-72; from assoc prof to prof math, Pa State Univ, University Park, 78-90. *Mem:* Am Math Soc. *Res:* Operator algebras. *Mailing Add:* Dean's Off 3400 A V Williams Bldg Univ Md College Park MD 20742-3281

HERMAN, ROBERT, civil engineering; deceased, see previous edition for last biography

HERMAN, ROGER MYERS, ATOMIC PHYSICS, MOLECULAR PHYSICS & OPTICAL PHYSICS. *Current Pos:* from asst prof to assoc prof, 64-68, PROF THEORET PHYSICS, PA STATE UNIV, UNIVERSITY PARK, 68- *Personal Data:* b Torrington, Conn, Dec 10, 34; m 58; c 3. *Educ:* Lehigh Univ, BS, 57; Yale Univ, MS, 59, PhD(physics), 63. *Prof Exp:* Mem tech staff, TRW Space Tech Labs, 62-64. *Concurrent Pos:* Consult, Phys Studies, Inc, 65-70; vis prof, Mem Univ St Johns, 73, Univ Guelph, Ont, 79, Univ Heidelberg, Ger, 80-81; US Sr Scientist Award, Alexander von Humboldt Found, Ger, 80-81; proj specialist, Chinese Ministry Educ, 85; distinguished vis prof, Nankai Univ, Peoples Repub China, 85; vis scholar, Univ Toronto, 87; consult, AMPAC Inc, 87-; vis scientist, Joint Inst Lab Astrophys, Boulder, Colo, 88; vis scholar, Lebeder Phys Inst, Moscow, Russia, 91; vis scientist, Cent Design Bur Specialized Instrumentation, Moscow, 91. *Mem:* Fel Am Phys Soc. *Res:* Theoretical aspects of atomic, molecular and optical physics; level shifts and spin relaxation in gases; molecular collisions and coherence relaxation; intramolecular physics; nonlinear optics; atom-surface interactions; liquid crystal studies; molecular hydrogen properties; classical and quantum optics; optical accelerators. *Mailing Add:* 104 Davey Lab Pa State Univ University Park PA 16802

HERMAN, SAMUEL SIDNEY, RESEARCH ADMINISTRATION. *Current Pos:* CONSULT, 84- *Personal Data:* b Boston, Mass, Oct 29, 17; m 54, Liselotte Vogt-Perl; c Hans O & Georg N. *Educ:* Harvard Univ, AB, 40; Loyola Univ, DDS, 44; Yale Univ, MPH, 48, PhD(pub health), 50. *Prof Exp:* Dent officer, US Dept Interior, 46-47; staff officer div pub health methods, USPHS, 49-50, chief dent resources planning br, 50-55, asst to chief dent off, 54-55; asst chief div med serv, Off Voc Rehab, US Dept HEW, 56-57, chief, 56-59, exec secy radiation study sect & dir Russian Sci Trans Prog, NIH, 59-61, prog coordr & head foreign grants & awards, Off Int Res, 61-63, dep asst comnr health & med affairs, & exec secy med study sect, Voc Rehab Admin, 63-64, spec asst to assoc dir, Nat Cancer Inst, 64-65, dep assoc dir grants & training, 65-67, assoc dir for extramural res, Nat Inst Environ Health Sci, 67-69, assoc dir for extramural progs, Nat Eye Inst, 69-71; assoc dean, Grad Sch, Temple Univ, 71-79, assoc vpres, Health Sci Campus, 71-84, assoc dean, Sch Med, 73-84. *Concurrent Pos:* Co-ed, Child Develop Abstr & Bibliog, Am Soc Res & Child Develop, 52-54; lectr, Sch Med, Howard Univ, 54-58; mem bd dirs, Nat Health Coun, 57-58; comt prosthetics educ & info, Nat Acad Sci-Nat Res Coun, 58-59, consult comn human resources, 74-; consult, Comt Rehab, Am Heart Asn, 58-59; tech adv, Alexander & Margaret Stewart Trust, 66-71; consult, Nat Eye Inst, 71-73, comt nat needs biomed & behav res personnel, Nat Acad Sci-Nat Res Coun, 74-85 & Lucille P Markey Charitable Trust, 84-; mem bd dirs, Federated Med Resources, 75-84, pres, 77-80, vpres, 80-81; adj prof, Sch Dent, Temple Univ, 71-84; mem bd dirs, Philadelphia Asn Clin Trials, 86-88, chmn human res bd, 81-; adv sci policy, Col Grad Studies, Thomas Jefferson Univ. *Mem:* AAAS; Am Pub Health Asn. *Res:* Science and public policy; biomedical research manpower analyses; research administration; ethics of human experimentation. *Mailing Add:* 4705 Chevy Chase Blvd Chevy Chase MD 20815-5341

HERMAN, SIDNEY SAMUEL, biological oceanography, for more information see previous edition

HERMAN, WARREN NEVIN, PHYSICS. *Current Pos:* SR TECH SPECIALIST NON-LINEAR OPTICAL POLYMERS, NAVAL AIR WARFARE CTR, PATUXENT RIVER, MD, 89- *Personal Data:* b Danville, Pa, Mar 10, 48; m 70; c 2. *Educ:* Bloomsburg State Col, BA, 70; Franklin & Marshall Col, MS, 72; Temple Univ, PhD(physics), 77. *Prof Exp:* Assoc prof physics, Spring Garden Col, 76-86; res engr, Gen Elec, 87-89. *Mem:* Am Phys Soc. *Res:* Classical relativistic theories of interacting particles; general relativity. *Mailing Add:* 1187 Golden West Way Lusby MD 20657

HERMAN, WILLIAM H, DIABETES, ENDOCRINOLOGY. *Current Pos:* asst prof internal med & obstet/gynec, 89-91, ASSOC PROF ENDOCRINOL & METAB, UNIV MICHIGAN, 95- *Personal Data:* b Bryn Mawr, Pa, Sept 17, 53. *Educ:* Yale Univ, BS, 75; Boston Univ, MD, 79; Univ Mich, MPH, 93. *Prof Exp:* Staff mem, Ctr Dis Control & Prev, 91-95. *Mem:* Am Diabetes Asn. *Mailing Add:* Univ Mich 3920 Taubman Ctr Box 0354 Ann Arbor MI 48109. Fax: 313-936-9240

HERMAN, WILLIAM S, ZOOLOGY. *Current Pos:* from asst prof to prof, Univ Minn, Minneapolis, 66-75, head, dept genetics & cell biol, 80-89, PROF CELL BIOL, UNIV MINN, ST PAUL, 75- *Personal Data:* b Seattle, Wash, Oct 12, 31; m 62; c 3. *Educ:* Portland State Univ, BS, 58; Northwestern Univ, MS, 60, PhD(zool), 64. *Prof Exp:* USPHS fel, 64-66. *Mem:* Am Soc Zool; AAAS. *Res:* Anthropod neuroendocrinology. *Mailing Add:* Genetics 250 Biol Sci Ctr Univ Minn 1445 Gortner Ave St Paul MN 55108-1095

HERMAN, ZELEK SEYMOUR, THEORETICAL CHEMISTRY & PHYSICS. *Current Pos:* res fel, 80-82, RES ASSOC CHEM & PHYSICS, LINUS PAULING INST, 82- *Personal Data:* b Denver, Colo, July 10, 45. *Educ:* Case Inst Technol, BS, 67; Univ Uppsala, Sweden, MS, 68, PhD(quantum chem), 75. *Prof Exp:* Res assoc, Dept Chem, Univ Denver, 77-78; scholar, Molecular Theory Lab, Dept Genetics, Med Ctr, Stanford Univ, 78-79 & Molecular Theory Lab, Rockefeller Univ, 79-80. *Concurrent Pos:* Fulbright distinguished prof, Rudjer Boskovic Inst, Zagreb, Yugoslavia, 85. *Mem:* Sigma Xi; Int Soc Quantum Biol. *Res:* Inorganic chemistry; spectroscopy; mathematical analysis; analytical chemistry; computer science; biostatistics. *Mailing Add:* 521 Del Medio Ave No 107 Mountain View CA 94040

HERMANCE, C(LARKE) E(DSON), AERONAUTICAL ENGINEERING. *Current Pos:* prof mech eng & chmn civil & mech eng dept, 82-91, PROF MECH ENG, UNIV VT, 91- *Personal Data:* b Windsor, Ont, Oct 6, 36; US citizen; m 63, Harriette Ottosor; c 3. *Educ:* Yale Univ, BEng, 58; Princeton Univ, PhD(aeronaut eng), 63. *Prof Exp:* Res assoc aeronaut eng, Princeton Univ, 63-64; res scientist, Aeronaut Res Inst Sweden, 64-65; from asst prof to prof mech eng, Univ Waterloo, 65-82. *Concurrent Pos:* Vis prof, Royal Inst Technol, Sweden, 71-72. *Mem:* Am Inst Aeronaut & Astronaut; Sigma Xi; Am Soc Mech Engrs. *Res:* Combustion and propulsions; ignition processes; heat transfer; gaseous fire hazards; mathematical modeling; aerothermochemistry; welding heat transfer; pyrotechnics. *Mailing Add:* Mech Eng Dept Univ Vt Burlington VT 05405-0516. Fax: 802-656-1929

HERMANCE, JOHN FRANCIS, ENVIRONMENTAL GEOPHYSICS, ELECTROMAGNETISM. *Current Pos:* from asst prof to assoc prof, 68-82, PROF GEOL SCI, BROWN UNIV, 82- *Personal Data:* b Kingston, NY, Jan 9, 39; div; c Scott & Travis. *Educ:* State Univ NY Col New Paltz, BSc, 61; Syracuse Univ, MSc, 64; Univ Toronto, PhD(physics), 67. *Prof Exp:* Res assoc geophys, Mass Inst Technol, 67-68. *Concurrent Pos:* Vis fac fel, Res Div, Phillips Petrol Co, 74; mem, Sci Adv Comt, Magma Energy Prog, Sandia Nat Labs, 74-81, 85-92; sr vis res assoc, Lamont-Doherty Geol Observ, 75-76; assoc ed, Environ Geol, 80-82 & Tectonophysics, 87-92; exec comt & bd dir, Deep Observ & Sampling Earth's Crust; mem, Thermal Regimes Panel, Continental Sci Drilling Comt, Nat Acad Sci, 80-85, chmn, 85-86; chmn, US Geodynamics Comt Task Group Mobilizing Nat Geomagnetic Initiative, Nat Res Coun/Nat Acad Sci, 90-93. *Mem:* Am Geophys Union; Soc Explor Geophys; Europ Asn Explor Geophys; Soc Eng & Environ Geophys; Nat Ground Water Asn. *Res:* Application of geophysical methods to environmental site assessments and ground water studies; characterization of fluids in the crust; regional and global studies of the earth's thermal regime; geophysical and far-field sensing experiments associated with continental scientific drilling. *Mailing Add:* Dept Geol Sci Brown Univ Providence RI 02912-1846. Fax: 401-863-2058; E-Mail: john_hermance@brown.edu

HERMANN, ALLEN MAX, SUPERCONDUCTIVITY, PHOTO-VOLTAICS. *Current Pos:* PROF PHYSICS, UNIV COLO, 90- *Personal Data:* b New Orleans, La, July 17, 38; m 79, Leonora Christopher; c Miriam, Mary, Neil & Scott. *Educ:* Loyola Univ, BS, 60; Univ Notre Dame, MS, 62; Tex A&M Univ, PhD(physics), 65. *Honors & Awards:* Distinguished Scientist Award, Am Asn Physics Teachers, 86. *Prof Exp:* Sr scientist, Jet Propulsion Lab, Calif Inst Technol, 65-67; from asst prof to prof physics, Tulane Univ, 67-81; task mgr, Solar Energy Res Inst, 80-85; tech mgr, Jet Propulsion Lab, Calif Inst Technol, 85-86; prof physics, Univ Ark, 86-88, distinguished prof, 88-90. *Concurrent Pos:* Consult, Meditronics Corp, 76-78; Cardiac Pacemakers Inc, 77-80, Lewis Res Ctr, NASA, 80, USAF, 80, Jet Propulsion Lab, 87, Ethyl Corp, 88, Radiation Monitoring Devices, 89-92, Superconducting Core Technologies Inc, 90, Boundless Corp, 96, Childsafe Int, 96. *Mem:* Fel Am Phys Soc; sr mem Inst Elec & Electronics Engrs; Mat Res Soc. *Res:* High temperature superconductors; new materials synthesis; characterization; thin-films; devices; thin-film photovoltaic materials and devices; batteries. *Mailing Add:* Dept Physics Univ Colo Campus Box 390 Boulder CO 80309-0390. Fax: 303-492-2998; E-Mail: allen.hermann@colorado.edu

HERMANN, EDWARD ROBERT, HEALTH ENGINEERING HYGIEOLOGY, TOXICOLOGY. *Current Pos:* prof occup & environ med, Med Ctr, Univ Ill, Chicago, 75-80, prof environ & occup health sci, 81-88, dir, Indust Hygiene Progs, 76-88, EMER PROF, SCH PUB HEALTH, UNIV ILL, CHICAGO, 88-; CONSULT, HERMANN ASSOCS, 63- *Personal Data:* b Newport, Ky, Oct 9, 20; m 46, Eleanor Hill; c Mary E, Carolyn B, Catherine J, Georgia A, Joseph F, Michael E & John E. *Educ:* Univ Ky, BS, 42, CE, 53; Mass Inst Technol, SM, 49; Univ Tex, PhD(eng/health sci), 57; Am Acad Environ Eng, dipl, 57; Am Acad Indust Hyg, dipl, 62. *Honors & Awards:* Harrison Prescott Eddy Medal, Water Pollution Control Fedn, 59; Resources Div Award, Am Water Works Asn, 60; Radebaugh Award, Cent States Water Pollution Control Asn, 76; Borden Found Award, Am Indust Hyg Asn, 88. *Prof Exp:* Jr engr, Tenn Valley Authority, 42; instr eng & physics, Univ Ky, 43-44; partner, Hermann Consult Engrs, 46-47; teaching asst, Mass Inst Technol, 47-48; asst sanit engr, US Atomic Energy Comn, Los Alamos, NMex, 49, pub health engr, 50-51, chief Health & Sanit Sect, 51-52, sanit engr, 52-53, chief sanit engr, 53-54; res engr, Univ Tex, 54-57; indust health engr, Humble Oil & Refining Co, 57-62; prof & assoc prof, Northwestern Univ, 63-75. *Concurrent Pos:* Pres, Bayshore Munic Utility Dist, 61-62; pvt pract consult engr, 63-, pres sci adv comt, Energy Study Group, 63-64 & Space Sci Bd, Panel Waste in Space, Nat Acad Sci, 65-67, Panel Spacecraft Solid & Liquid Wastes, 69-70. *Mem:* Fel AAAS; fel Am Indust Hyg Asn; life mem Water Environ Fedn; fel Am Soc Civil Engrs; fel Am Pub Health Asn; life mem Am Acad Environ Eng. *Res:* Establishment of thresholds, of health effects, development of scientific approaches to environmental standard setting; effects of noise on humans; measurement, evaluation and control of substances and energy releases of health significance; toxicity of cyanides, sulfides and heavy metals; heat stress, waste treatment. *Mailing Add:* 117 Church Rd Winnetka IL 60093. E-Mail: hygieology@aol.com

HERMANN, HENRY REMLEY, JR, insect morphology & behavior, for more information see previous edition

HERMANN, JOHN ALEXANDER, APPLIED CHEMISTRY. *Current Pos:* sr res engr, 56-63, chief spec proj, 63, sr res group leader chem, 64-67, asst mgr, Hobbs Potash Facil, 67-69, PROJ MGR, KERR MCGEE CORP, 69- *Personal Data:* b San Francisco, Calif, Nov 22, 21; m 49; c 3. *Educ:* NJ Inst Technol, BS, 42; Univ NMex, PhD(chem), 56. *Prof Exp:* Line supvr explosives, Hercules Powder Co, 42-43; res engr, Manhattan Proj, 44; staff mem, Los Alamos Sci Lab, 44-56. *Mem:* Am Chem Soc; Metall Soc. *Res:* Separation processes; precipitation and crystallization; coprecipitation, solvent extraction; extractive metallurgy of uranium, vanadium, lithium, molybdenum; potash, phosphate and fertilizer chemistry. *Mailing Add:* 320 NW 21st St Oklahoma City OK 73103-1923

HERMANN, RICHARD KARL, PLANT ECOLOGY. *Current Pos:* RETIRED. *Personal Data:* b Munich, Ger, Feb 16, 24; US citizen; m 48; c 1. *Educ:* Univ Munich, BS, 51; Yale Univ, MF, 56; Ore State Univ, PhD(plant ecol), 60. *Hon Degrees:* Dr forest, Georg-August Univ, Gottingen, 79. *Prof Exp:* Instr bot, Ore State Univ, 58-59; res assoc forest ecol, Ore Forest Res Ctr, Forest Protection & Conserv Comt, 59-61; from asst prof to prof forest ecol, Ore State Univ, 61-90. *Concurrent Pos:* Vis prof, Georg-August Univ, Goettingen, 82 & 89; chmn, Div I, Silvicult & Forest Environ, Int Union Forest Res Orgn, 82-86. *Mem:* Ecol Soc Am; Soc Am Foresters; Am Inst Biol Sci; corresp mem Ital Acad Forest Sci. *Res:* Ecology and physiology of tree roots. *Mailing Add:* 1511 SW Park Ave No 1002 Portland OR 97201

HERMANN, ROBERT J, SCIENCE & TECHNOLOGY. *Current Pos:* vpres systs technol, United Technol Corp, 82-84, vpres advan systs, 84-87, vpres, 87-92, SR VPRES SCI & TECHNOL, UNITED TECHNOL CORP, 92- *Educ:* Iowa State Univ, BS, MS, PhD(elec eng). *Prof Exp:* Prin dep asst secy defense, Nat Security Agency, 77-79, asst secy, USAF, 79-81, spec asst intel, 81-82. *Concurrent Pos:* Mem, Defense Sci Bd; chmn, Naval Studies Bd; mem, Indust Adv Group, Nat Soc Prof Engrs. *Mem:* Nat Acad Eng. *Res:* Development of technical resources. *Mailing Add:* United Technol Corp One Financial Plaza Hartford CT 06101

HERMANS, COLIN OLMSTED, INVERTEBRATE ZOOLOGY. *Current Pos:* from asst prof to assoc prof, 69-77, PROF BIOL, SONOMA STATE UNIV, 77- *Personal Data:* b Seattle, Wash, May 4, 36; m 58; c 3. *Educ:* Pomona Col, BA, 58; Univ Wash, MS, 64, PhD(zool), 66. *Prof Exp:* NATO fel zool, Univ Newcastle, 66-67; NIH fel, Univ Calif, Berkeley, 67-68, asst res zoologist, 68-69. *Concurrent Pos:* Alexander von Humboldt fel, Univ Gottingen, WGer, 75-76; vis prof, Univ Osnabruck, 85, Ariz State Univ, 88-89; treas, Western Soc Naturalists, 80-81. *Mem:* Fel AAAS; Am Soc Zool; Micros Soc Am; Int Asn Meiobenthologists; mem Western Soc Naturalists. *Res:* Polychaetous annelids; invertebrate photoreceptors; invertebrate adhesion; electron microscopy. *Mailing Add:* Dept Biol Sonoma State Univ 1801 E Cotati Ave Rohnert Park CA 94928-3613

HERMANS, HANS J, COMPUTER SCIENCE. *Current Pos:* staff consult, Univac Div, Sperry Rand Corp, 68-85, sr res scientist, 89-91, DIR, ADVAN CASE DEVELOP, UNISYS CORP, 91- *Personal Data:* b The Hague, Neth, Mar 21, 38; m 62, Ann Bloem; c Hans T, Mark A, Paul B & Erik M. *Educ:* Boston Col, BS, 60; Univ Notre Dame, PhD(chem), 67. *Prof Exp:* Assoc res scientist, Radiation Lab, Univ Notre Dame, 67-68. *Mem:* Am Chem Soc; Asn Comput Mach. *Res:* Microwave spectroscopy; object oriented repository technology. *Mailing Add:* 1611 Stephens Dr Wayne PA 19087. Fax: 610-783-7440

HERMANS, JAN JOSEPH, PHYSICAL CHEMISTRY. *Current Pos:* distinguished prof, 68-80, EMER PROF CHEM, UNIV NC, CHAPEL HILL, 80- *Personal Data:* b Leiden, Neth, Nov 1, 09; nat US; m; c 1. *Educ:* Univ Leiden, PhD(chem), 37. *Prof Exp:* Instr chem, Univ Leiden, 36-37, res assoc, Sch Pediat, 41-42, prof phys chem, 53-58; Ramsay Mem fel, Univ London, 38-39; res assoc, Wageningen, 40-41; res chemist, Inst Cellulose Res, Utrecht, Neth, 42-46; prof phys chem, Groningen Univ, 46-53; dir cellulose res inst, Col Forestry, State Univ NY, 58-61; sr staff scientist, Chemstrand Res Ctr, 61-68. *Concurrent Pos:* Rockefeller fel, Polytech Inst Brooklyn, 50-51; vis prof, Univ Toronto, 56 & Univ NC, Chapel Hill, 65-66. *Mem:* Am Chem Soc; NY Acad Sci; Royal Neth Chem Soc; Royal Neth Acad Sci. *Res:* Polymers. *Mailing Add:* 203 Wild Turkey Trail Chapel Hill NC 27516

HERMANS, PAUL E, INTERNAL MEDICINE, INFECTIOUS DISEASES. *Current Pos:* From instr internal med to assoc prof med, 63-76, chmn Div Infectious Dis, 73-83, PROF MED, MAYO SCH MED, UNIV MINN, 76- STAFF MEM, MAYO CLIN, 62- *Personal Data:* b Rotterdam, Neth, Oct 17, 27; US citizen; m 54; c 3. *Educ:* Univ Utrecht, MD, 57; Univ Minn, MS, 62. *Concurrent Pos:* Fel internal med, Mayo Clin, 58-61, asst to staff, 61-62, consult infectious dis, 62- *Mem:* Infectious Dis Soc Am; Med Mycol Soc Americas; Am Soc Microbiol; NY Acad Sci; Am Col Physicians. *Res:* Clinical immunology, especially immunologic deficiency diseases. *Mailing Add:* Mayo Clin 200 First St SW Rochester MN 55905-0001

HERMANSON, HARVEY PHILIP, AGRICULTURAL & FOOD CHEMISTRY. *Current Pos:* RETIRED. *Personal Data:* b Spring Valley, Minn, Oct 7, 32; m 55; c 1. *Educ:* Univ Minn, BS, 54, PhD(soils), 61; Cornell Univ, MS, 57. *Prof Exp:* Asst prof soil chem & asst agr chemist, Univ Idaho, 61-64; NIH trainee soil chem pesticide residues, Univ Calif, Riverside, 64-67, univ fel, 65-67; asst res prof agr chem, Rutgers Univ, 67-70; asst res prof chem, NC A&T State Univ, 70-71, assoc prof plant sci, 73-78. *Concurrent Pos:* Consult, Chevron Chem Co, 64-67. *Mem:* Am Soc Agron; Int Soc Soil Sci; Sigma Xi. *Res:* Soil chemistry to pesticides, especially insecticides; special techniques of regression statistics applied to soil fertility and chemistry; problems; soil fertility problems of peat soils; ecology of birdsfoot trefoil; disposal of effluent from septic tanks in problem soils; tobacco and pesticide research. *Mailing Add:* 1401 Whilden Pl Greensboro NC 27408

HERMANSON, JOHN CARL, SOLID STATE PHYSICS. *Current Pos:* from asst prof to assoc prof, 73-80, PROF PHYSICS, MONT STATE UNIV, 80-, PHYSICS DEPT HEAD, 90- *Personal Data:* b Stevens Point, Wis, June 2, 40; m 65; c 3. *Educ:* Mass Inst Technol, BS, 62; Univ Chicago, MS, 64, PhD(physics), 66. *Prof Exp:* Res assoc physics, Univ Ill, Urbana, 66-68; res fel, Miller Inst Basic Res Sci & Univ Calif, Berkeley, 68-69, res assoc, 69-70. *Concurrent Pos:* Theoret consult, Michelson Labs, China Lake, Calif, 73-77; vis prof, Univ Munich, Fed Repub Ger, 78-79. *Mem:* Am Phys Soc; Am Inst Physics. *Res:* Optical properties of solids; theory of excitons; electronic structure of solid surfaces; photoemission spectroscopy; dynamics of film growth on surfaces. *Mailing Add:* Dept Physics Mont State Univ Bozeman MT 59717. *Fax:* 406-994-4452; *E-Mail:* uphjh@msu.oscs.montana.edu

HERMANSON, RONALD ELDON, WATER RESOURCES, ANIMAL WASTE MANAGEMENT. *Current Pos:* EXTEN AGR ENGR WATER QUALITY & SOIL & WATER ENG, WASH STATE UNIV, 73- *Personal Data:* b Kiester, Minn, Mar 31, 33; m 55; c 3. *Educ:* Iowa State Univ, BS, 58, MS, 64, PhD(water resources), 67. *Prof Exp:* Staff engr water resources, Iowa Natural Resources Coun, 58-62; res assoc agr eng, Iowa State Univ, 62-64, fel water resources, 64-66; asst prof agr eng, Auburn Univ, 66-72. *Concurrent Pos:* Off Water Resources Res grant, 66-72; mem, USDA task force animal waste mgt, 68 & Environ Protection Agency task force fruit & veg waste guidelines, 74. *Mem:* Sigma Xi; Am Soc Agr Engrs. *Res:* Animal waste management especially to develop economical methods of handling animal waste that will avoid air, water and land pollution; control of groundwater contamination from agrichemicals. *Mailing Add:* Smith Agr Eng Bldg Rm 220 Wash State Univ Pullman WA 99164-6120

HERMENS, RICHARD ANTHONY, PHYSICAL CHEMISTRY. *Current Pos:* from asst prof to assoc prof, 66-70, PROF CHEM & CHMN DEPT, EASTERN ORE UNIV, 70- *Personal Data:* b Forest Grove, Ore, Nov 17, 35; m 61, Maxine Kinzer; c Leonard, Louise, Michael & Joyce. *Educ:* Pac Univ, BS, 57; Ore State Univ, MS, 60; Univ Idaho, PhD(phys chem), 63. *Prof Exp:* Instr chem, Univ Idaho, 62-63; asst prof, Millikin Univ, 63-66. *Concurrent Pos:* Consult, 80-86. *Mem:* Am Chem Soc; Sigma Xi. *Res:* Instrumental, polarographic and spectrophotometric analyses. *Mailing Add:* Dept Chem Eastern Ore Univ La Grande OR 97850. *Fax:* 541-962-3873; *E-Mail:* rhermens@eosc.osshe.edu

HERMES, HENRY, CONTROL THEORY. *Current Pos:* chmn dept math, 74-76, PROF MATH, UNIV COLO, BOULDER, 67- *Personal Data:* b Jersey City, NJ, July 24, 33; m 58, Imelda Wasinger; c Karen & Tanet. *Educ:* Montclair State Col, BA, 54; Univ NMex, MS, 59, PhD(math), 62. *Prof Exp:* Assoc res scientist, Martin Co, Colo, 61-64; asst prof appl math, Brown Univ, 64-66. *Concurrent Pos:* Assoc ed, J on Control, Soc Indust & Appl Math, 67-92 & Acta Applicandae Mathematicae, 83-92. *Mem:* Am Math Soc; Soc Indust & Appl Math. *Res:* Ordinary differential equations and control theory. *Mailing Add:* Dept Math Box 395 Univ Colo Boulder CO 80309-0395

HERMES, O DON, PETROLOGY, GEOCHEMISTRY. *Current Pos:* from asst prof to assoc prof, 68-78, PROF GEOL, UNIV RI, 78- *Personal Data:* b Brighton, Ill, Mar 13, 39; m 62; c 2. *Educ:* Washington Univ, AB, 61; Univ NC, Chapel Hill, MS, 63, PhD(geol), 66. *Prof Exp:* Fel, Univ Calif, Los Angeles, 66-68. *Mem:* Am Geophys Union; Geol Soc Am. *Res:* Igneous and metamorphic petrology; mineralogy; analytical chemistry. *Mailing Add:* Dept Geol Univ RI Kingston RI 02881

HERMODSON, MARK ALLEN, BIOCHEMISTRY. *Current Pos:* assoc prof, 77-80, PROF BIOCHEM, PURDUE UNIV, 80-, HEAD DEPT BIOCHEM, 81- *Personal Data:* b Crookston, Minn, Jan 30, 42; m 68, Susan Head; c Amy E & Gail S. *Educ:* St Olaf Col, BA, 64; Univ Wis, PhD(biochem), 68. *Prof Exp:* Fel biochem, Univ Wis, 68-69 & Univ Wash, 69-72; res asst prof med genetics, Univ Wash, 72-77. *Concurrent Pos:* Adj assoc prof biochem, Ind Univ Sch Med, 79-84, adj prof, 84- *Mem:* Am Soc Biol Chem; Protein Soc (pres, 91-93); AAAS. *Res:* Protein structure; amino acid sequencing; enzymology; membrane transport. *Mailing Add:* Dept Biochem Purdue Univ West Lafayette IN 47907. *Fax:* 765-494-7897; *E-Mail:* hermodson@aclcb.purdue.edu

HERMRECK, ARLO SCOTT, VASCULAR & GENERAL SURGERIES. *Current Pos:* PROF SURG, UNIV KANS MED CTR, 71- *Educ:* Univ Kans, PhD(physiol), 70. *Mailing Add:* Univ Kans Med Ctr 39th & Rainbow Kansas City KS 66160-7308. *Fax:* 913-588-7540

HERMSEN, RICHARD J, ELECTRICAL ENGINEERING. *Current Pos:* assoc prof, 67-72, chmn dept, 73-81, PROF ELECTRONICS, CALIF STATE POLYTECH UNIV, POMONA, 72- *Personal Data:* b Little Chute, Wis, Oct 20, 28; m 53. *Educ:* Univ Wis, BS, 59, MS, 60, PhD(nuclear eng), 63. *Prof Exp:* Design specialist, Gen Dynamics Corp, Calif, 63-65; mem tech staff, Aerospace Corp, 65-67. *Concurrent Pos:* Vis asst prof, Univ Redlands, 66-67. *Mem:* Inst Elec & Electronics Engrs. *Res:* Analytical aspects of automatic control systems; analog and digital communication systems; digital signal processing. *Mailing Add:* Elec & Electronics Eng Dept Calif State Poly Univ Pomona CA 91768

HERMSEN, ROBERT W, COMBUSTION RESEARCH. *Current Pos:* staff scientist res combustion kinetics, United Technologies Chem Systs, 61-70, sr staff scientist Phys Sci Lab, 70-71, mgr, 71-75, chief, kinetics & combustion res chem Systs Div 75-85, MGR COMBUSTION RES & DEVELOP, UNITED TECHNOLOGIES CHEM SYSTS DIV, 85- *Personal Data:* b Baker, Ore, Apr, 25, 34; m 57; c 4. *Educ:* Ore State Univ, BS, 56; Univ Calif, Berkeley, PhD(chem eng), 62. *Prof Exp:* Res engr, Titanium Metals Corp Am, 56-57. *Mem:* Combustion Inst; Am Inst Chem Engrs; Am Inst Aeronaut & Astronaut. *Res:* High temperature thermodynamics; chemical kinetics; combustion of metals; chemical propulsion; solid propellant combustion; production of sound from flames; coal gasification; two-phase flow in combustion systems; rocket motor performance; detonation hazards of rocket motors. *Mailing Add:* 3563 Evergreen Dr Palo Alto CA 94303-4425

HERMSMEIER, LEE F, AGRICULTURAL ENGINEERING. *Current Pos:* RETIRED. *Personal Data:* b Quincy, Ill, Aug 13, 17; m 49; c 3. *Educ:* Univ Minn, BS, 49; Iowa State Univ, MS, 50. *Prof Exp:* Area engr, Soil Conserv Serv, USDA, 50-56, res agr engr, Soil & Water Conserv Div, Agr Res Serv, Minn, 57-68, res agr engr, Agr Res Serv, Imp Vally Conserv Res Ctr, 68-83. *Concurrent Pos:* Mem, US Comt Irrig, Drainage & Flood Control; drainage consult, several foreign countries, Algeria, Cuba & Egypt, 73-81, Pakistan, 85; consult, 83- *Res:* Irrigation efficiencies and irrigation scheduling for arid lands; development of improved drainage methods and procedures; use of alternate materials for drainage of arid lands. *Mailing Add:* 352 J St Brawley CA 92227

HERMSMEYER, RALPH KENT, PHYSIOLOGY. *Current Pos:* PROF CELL & DEVELOP BIOL & MED, ORE HEALTH SCI UNIV, 88-; SR SCIENTIST, ORE REGIONAL PRIMATE RES CTR, 92- *Personal Data:* b Litchfield, Ill, Oct 13, 42; m 64, Warner; c Amanda. *Educ:* Univ Ill, AB, 64, MS, 66, PhD(physiol), 69. *Honors & Awards:* Katz Prize, Am Heart Asn, 75; Bowditch Award, Am Physiol Soc, 82. *Prof Exp:* Asst prof physiol & biophys, Univ Nebr Med Ctr, Omaha, 70-73; from asst prof to prof pharmacol, Col Med, Univ Iowa, 73-91; prof & chair physiol, Univ Nev, 86-87. *Concurrent Pos:* Nat Heart Inst fel, Sch Med, Univ Va, 68-70; Nebr Heart Asn res grant, Univ Nebr Med Ctr, Omaha, 71-73; USPHS res grant, 71-74; Iowa Heart Asn res grant, Univ Iowa, 73-75; USPHS res grant, 74-81; res cancer develop award, NIH, 75-80; mem circulation & high blood pressure coun, Am Heart Asn; Forgarty sr int fel to Switz, NIH, 84. *Mem:* Am Physiol Soc; Biophys Soc; Soc Gen Physiol; Am Soc Zool; Am Soc Pharmacol & Exp Therapeut. *Res:* Electrophysiology of vascular muscle and heart; hypertension; ca channels; coronary vasospasm. *Mailing Add:* Ore Regional Primate Res Ctr 505 NW 185th Ave Beaverton OR 97006. *Fax:* 503-690-5563; *E-Mail:* rkh@compuserve.com

HERN, THOMAS ALBERT, MATHEMATICS, COMPUTER GRAPHICS. *Current Pos:* From instr to prof, 69-92, PROF MATH, BOWLING GREEN STATE UNIV, 92-, PROF, 92- *Personal Data:* b Cincinnati, Ohio, Dec 23, 41. *Educ:* Univ Cincinnati, AB, 64; Ohio State Univ, MS, 66, PhD(math), 69. *Concurrent Pos:* Vis assoc prof, comput sci, Univ NC, Chapel Hill, 82-84; mem, Spec Interest Group Comput Graphics & Interactive Tech of Asn Comput Mach. *Mem:* Math Asn Am; Soc Indust & Appl Math. *Mailing Add:* Dept Math & Statist Bowling Green State Univ Bowling Green OH 43403. *Fax:* 419-372-6092; *E-Mail:* hern@bgsu.edu

HERNANDEZ, GONZALO J, OPTICS, ATMOSPHERIC PHYSICS. *Current Pos:* PROF, GRAD PROG GEOPHYS, UNIV WASH, 88- *Personal Data:* b San Jose, Costa Rica. *Educ:* Univ Notre Dame, BS, 58; Univ Rochester, PhD, 62. *Prof Exp:* Physicist, Air Force Cambridge Res Lab, 61-69; res scientist, Space Physics Res Lab, Univ Mich, 85-87; dir, Fritz Peak Observ, Nat Oceanic & Atmospheric Admin, 70-85, physicist, Environ Res Labs, 69-86. *Concurrent Pos:* Affil prof geophys, Univ Alaska. *Mem:* Am Geophys Union; Am Phys Soc; Optical Soc Am; Sigma Xi. *Res:* Upper atmosphere physics; high resolution spectroscopy; optical aeronomy. *Mailing Add:* 15545 65th Pl NE Bothell WA 98011-4327. *E-Mail:* hernandez@u.washington.edu

HERNANDEZ, JOHN PETER, CONDENSED MATTER PHYSICS. *Current Pos:* From instr to assoc prof, 66-77, PROF PHYSICS, UNIV NC, CHAPEL HILL, 77- *Personal Data:* b Madrid, Spain, Sept 6, 40; nat US; c 4. *Educ:* Manhattan Col, BEE, 62; Stanford Univ, MS, 63; Univ Rochester, PhD(optics), 67. *Concurrent Pos:* Sr Fulbright lectr, Univ Autonoma Madrid, 72-73; Kenan Res prof, Univ Oxford, 82-83; ministry sci sabbatical grantee, Univ Autonoma Madrid, 91-92, W R Kenau Jr res prof, 91-92, Quincentenary fel, 92, Nicolas Cabrera prof, 93. *Mem:* Am Phys Soc; Sigma Xi. *Res:* Theoretical condensed matter and chemical physics; electronic properties of disordered materials, insulator- metal & vapor-liquid transitions of metal-atom fluids. *Mailing Add:* Dept Physics Univ NC Chapel Hill NC 27599-3255. *Fax:* 919-962-0480; *E-Mail:* hernandz@physics.unc.edu

HERNANDEZ, JOHN W(HITLOCK), ENGINEERING, ENVIRONMENT. *Current Pos:* assoc prof sanit eng, 65-68, dean eng, 75-80, PROF CIVIL ENG, NMEX STATE UNIV, 68- *Personal Data:* b Albuquerque, NMex, Aug 17, 29; m 51, Frances Baker. *Educ:* Univ NMex, BS, 51; Purdue Univ, MS, 59; Harvard Univ, MS, 61, PhD(water resources), 65. *Prof Exp:* Asst engr dam design, State Game & Fish Dept, NMex, 54-55, engr waterworks design, State Engrs Off, 55-57, assoc engr, State Health Dept, 57-63. *Concurrent Pos:* Dep adminr, US Environ Protection Agency, 81-83; asst to state engr, NMex, 91-; vis prof, Malaysia, 86-87, Univ Auckland, 92; consult, Eng-Sci Inc, Bangkok, Kuwait, Beijing, 93. *Mem:* Am Soc Civil Engrs; Nat Soc Prof Engrs; Am Water Works Asn; Water Pollution Control Fedn; Am Acad Environ Eng; Sigma Xi. *Res:* Biological treatment of sanitary area waste waters; application of systems analysis technique to water resources development; development and application of water laws in New Mexico. *Mailing Add:* PO Box 3196 Las Cruces NM 88003. *Fax:* 505-827-6160

HERNANDEZ, JUAN ANTONIO, PATHOLOGY. *Current Pos:* CLIN ASST PROF PATH, COL MED & DENT NJ, NEWARK, 76-; ASSOC PATHOLOGIST, ST ELIZABETH HOSP, 76- *Personal Data:* b Holguin, Cuba, Sept 4, 29; US citizen; m 51; c 3. *Educ:* Inst Sec Teachings, Holguin, Cuba, BS, 18; Univ Havana, MD, 56; Am Bd Path, dipl, 64. *Prof Exp:* Intern, Ga Baptist Hosp, Atlanta, Ga, 58-59, trainee path, 59-61; res fel pulmonary path, Baptist Mem Hosp, Jacksonville, 63-76. *Mem:* Col Am Path; Am Soc Clin Path. *Res:* Pulmonary pathology; gross and microscopic morphology; pathogenesis of emphysema. *Mailing Add:* 7 Crest Circle South Orange NJ 07079-1307

HERNANDEZ, NORMA, SCIENCE ADMINISTRATION, HISTORY & PHILOSOPHY OF SCIENCE. *Current Pos:* full prof & dean, Col Educ, 74-80, ASST PROF MATH EDUC, UNIV TEX, EL PASO, 69-, PROF, 80- *Personal Data:* b El Paso, Tex, May 19, 34; m 54; c 4. *Educ:* Tex Western Col, BS, 54; Univ Tex, MS, 60, PhD(math educ), 70. *Prof Exp:* Instr math educ, Univ Tex, Austin, 66-69. *Concurrent Pos:* Founding pres, El Paso Coun, Teachers Math, 65-66; pres, Tex Coun Teachers Math, 68-69; mem, panel Labs & Ctrs, NIE, 78-80 & bd dir, Southwest Educ Develop Lab, Austin, Tex, 83- *Mem:* Nat Coun Teachers Math; Sch Sci & Math Asn; Math Asn Am. *Res:* Identification of teaching/learning strategies that will increase mathematical abilities for all children; factors affecting achievement of Mexican Americans. *Mailing Add:* Col Educ Univ Tex El Paso TX 79968

HERNANDEZ, TEME P, HORTICULTURE, PLANT BREEDING. *Current Pos:* RETIRED. *Personal Data:* b Lafayette, La, May 15, 19; m 56; c 3. *Educ:* La State Univ, BS, 40, MS, 42; Univ Wis, PhD(hort), 49. *Prof Exp:* Supt, Sweet Potato Res Ctr, La State Univ, Baton Rouge, 49-57, prof hort, 58-81. *Mem:* AAAS; Am Soc Hort Sci; Genetics Soc Am. *Res:* Breeding and testing of horticultural crops, including sweet potatoes and tomatoes. *Mailing Add:* 625 Kimbro Lane Baton Rouge LA 70808

HERNANDEZ, THOMAS, PHARMACOLOGY. *Current Pos:* RETIRED. *Personal Data:* b Lafayette, La, May 17, 14; m 43; c 4. *Educ:* La State Univ, BA, 36, MS, 38, MD, 47; Univ Iowa, PhD(zool), 42. *Prof Exp:* Asst surgeon, Marine Hosp, USPHS, New Orleans, 47-48; instr biochem, Sch Med, La State Univ, 48-49, asst prof, 49-51; sr asst surgeon, NIH, 51-53; from asst prof to prof biochem, La State Univ Med Ctr, New Orleans, 53-60, chmn dept, 60-76, prof pharmacol, 60-80, prof exp therapeut, 76-80. *Concurrent Pos:* Assoc mem, Armed Forces Epidemiol Bd Comn Malaria, 65. *Mem:* AAAS; Soc Exp Biol & Med; Am Physiol Soc; Am Soc Pharmacol & Exp Therapeut. *Res:* Endocrinology; antimalarial drugs; biochemical studies of cold blooded animals; fluid and electrolytes; carbohydrate and nitrogen metabolism. *Mailing Add:* 145 Saul Dr Duson LA 70529-9713

HERNANDEZ-AVILA, MANUEL LUIS, COASTAL PHYSICAL OCEANOGRAPHY, RESEARCH ADMINISTRATION. *Current Pos:* asst prof, Univ PR, Mayaguez, 74-77, dir, Dept Marine Sci, 78-91, dir sea grant prog, 80-95, dir MBRS-NIH Prog, 86-95, PROF PHYS OCEANOG, UNIV PR, MAYAGUEZ, 78-, DIR, RES & DEVELOP CTR. *Personal Data:* b Quebradillas, PR, Apr 15, 35; m 56, Evangelina Fradera. *Educ:* Univ PR, BS, 67, MS, 70; La State Univ, PhD(marine sci, phys oceanog), 74. *Prof Exp:* Res asst marine geol, Univ PR, Mayaguez, 67-69; res asst phys oceanog, Coastal Studies Inst, La State Univ, Baton Rouge, 70-73. *Mem:* Am Geophys Union; Sigma Xi; Marine Technol Soc; Am Meteorol Soc. *Res:* Coastal physical processes; estuarine dynamics; coral reefs dynamics. *Mailing Add:* Marine Sci Col Station Caam Res & Develop Ctr Univ PR Mayaquez PR 00681-5000. *E-Mail:* ma_hernandez@rwmac.upr.clu.edu

HERNDON, CHARLES HARBISON, ORTHOPEDIC SURGERY. *Current Pos:* instr, 47-49, asst prof & demonstr anat, 49-53, from assoc prof to prof clin orthop, 53-61, Rainbow prof, 61-82, EMER RAINBOW PROF ORTHOP SURG, SCH MED, CASE WESTERN RES UNIV, 85- *Personal Data:* b Dublin, Tex, Dec 12, 15; m 44; c 2. *Educ:* Univ Tex, BA; Harvard Univ, MD, 40; Am Bd Orthop Surg, dipl, 49. *Prof Exp:* Surg intern, Univ Hosps, Cleveland, 40-41; jr orthop surgeon, Am Hosp Brit, Oxford, Eng, 42; orthop resident, Hosp Spec Surg, New York, 46-47. *Concurrent Pos:* Beekmen fel orthop surg, Columbia Univ, 45-46; Bunts, Crile & Lower fel, Case Western Reserve Univ, 47-53; assoc orthop surgeon, Rainbow Hosp, 47-52, dir, Orthop Surg, 52-82; asst orthop surgeon, Univ Hosps, Cleveland, 47-53, dir, Dept Orthop, 53-82; consult orthopedist, Elyria Mem & Gates Mem Hosps, Elyria, Ohio, 48-59 & Vet Admin Hosp, 56-82; assoc orthopedist, Highland View Hosp, 53-82; mem, Skeletal Syst Comt, Nat Res Coun-Nat Acad Sci, 58-67, chmn, 62-67; mem, Am Bd Orthop Surg, 60-66, chmn, Exam Comt, 61-64, pres, 64-66; mem, Bd Trustees, J Bone & Joint Surg, 69-75; mem, Adv Bd, Ohio State Serv Crippled Children; assoc mem, Orthop Res & Educ Found. *Mem:* Clin Orthop Soc; Am Acad Orthop Surg (pres, 68-69); Am Col Surgeons (2nd vpres, 74); Orthop Res Soc (secy-treas, 54-55, pres, 57); Am Orthop Asn. *Res:* Problems related to bone transplantation and bone induction. *Mailing Add:* 13700 Shaker Blvd Apt 410 Cleveland OH 44120

HERNDON, CHARLES L(EE), FORENSIC ENGINEERING. *Current Pos:* from asst prof to prof, 65-84, chmn dept, 76-80, EMER PROF ENG SCI, MONT COL MINERAL SCI & TECHNOL, 84-, ADJ PROF, 90- *Personal Data:* b Grant City, Mo, Apr 19, 21; m 64; c 2. *Educ:* Univ Tex, BSME, 43, MSME, 57. *Honors & Awards:* Teetor Award, Soc Automotive Engrs, 75. *Prof Exp:* Liaison engr, Douglas Aircraft Co, Okla, 43-47; sales & design engr, Frigidaire Dept, Straus-Frank Co, Tex, 47-49; Air Conditioning Div, Alamo Lumber Co, 49-54 & Deansteel Prod, 54-56; asst prof eng & physics, San Antonio Col, 56-58; assoc prof eng, Evansville Col, 58-62; asst prof, Calif State Col Los Angeles, 62-65. *Concurrent Pos:* Instr, Univ Tex, 46-47; sr proj engr, US Naval Civil Eng Lab, Calif, 62-65; forensic engr, Herndon Assocs, 66- *Mem:* Am Soc Heating, Refrig & Air-Conditioning Engrs. *Res:* Air conditioning and refrigeration; solar energy; machine design; forensics. *Mailing Add:* Herndon & Assoc 1321 W Platinum Butte MT 59701-2125

HERNDON, DAVID N, SURGERY. *Current Pos:* CHIEF STAFF, SHRINERS BURN INST, 81- *Personal Data:* b Cleveland, Ohio, Feb 20, 50. *Educ:* Case Western Res Univ, MD, 74. *Mailing Add:* Shriners Burn Inst 815 Market St Galveston TX 77550-2725

HERNDON, JAMES HENRY, JR, DERMATOLOGY. *Current Pos:* Assoc prof internal med, 74-79, assoc clin prof dermat, 79-89, CLIN PROF DERMAT, UNIV TEX HEALTH SCI CTR, DALLAS, 89- *Personal Data:* b Dallas, Tex, June 2, 39; div; c Eleanor, Margaret & Emily. *Educ:* Univ Tex Southwestern Med Sch, MD, 63. *Concurrent Pos:* Consult dermat, Vet Admin Hosp, Dallas & Children's Med Ctr, 70-79, Presby Hosp, Dallas, 79-; USPHS res career develop award, 70-75. *Mem:* Soc Invest Dermat; Am Acad Dermat; Am Contact Dermatitis Soc; Am Soc Dermat Surg. *Res:* Pathogenesis of psoriasis, regulation of epidemial proliferation mechanisms of pruritus. *Mailing Add:* Perm Ctr 8230 Walnut Hill Lane Suite 500 Dallas TX 75231-4404

HERNDON, JAMES W, ORGANIC SYNTHESIS, ORGANOMETALLIC CHEMISTRY. *Current Pos:* ASST PROF, DEPT CHEM, UNIV MD, COLLEGE PARK, 85- *Personal Data:* b Greensboro, NC, Aug 3, 57; m 87. *Educ:* Univ NC, Greensboro, BS, 79; Princeton Univ, MA, 80, PhD(chem), 83. *Prof Exp:* NIH postdoctoral fel chem, Univ Wis-Madison, 83-85. *Mem:* Am Chem Soc. *Res:* Design of new reagents for use in organic synthesis and organometallic chemistry. *Mailing Add:* Dept Chem Univ Md College Park MD 20742-2021

HERNDON, ROBERT MCCULLOCH, NEUROLOGY, NEUROPATHOLOGY. *Current Pos:* PROF NEUROL, ORE HEALTH SCI UNIV, 88-; CHIEF NEUROL, GOOD SAMARITAN HOSP, 88- *Personal Data:* b Richmond, Va, May 29, 35; m 55, Kathryn E Stearns; c Robert M Jr, William D & Cynthia M. *Educ:* Univ Chicago, BA, 55; Univ Tenn, MD, 58. *Honors & Awards:* Arthur Weil Award, Am Asn Neuropath, 68 & 72 & Moore Award, Am Asn Neuropath, 83. *Prof Exp:* From intern to chief resident neurol, Detroit Receiving Hosp, 59-61; neurologist, USAF Hosp, Travis AFB, Calif, 63-64; chief neurol, 64-65; asst prof neurol, Med Sch, Stanford Univ, 66-69; assoc prof neurol, Med Sch, Johns Hopkins Univ, 69-77, prof & chmn, Ctr Brain Res & Neurol, Med Sch, Univ Rochester, 77-88. *Concurrent Pos:* Fel neuropath, Montreal Neurol Inst, 62-63; fel anat, Harvard Med Sch, 65-66; chief neurol, Palo Alto Vet Admin Hosp, 68-69. *Mem:* Am Asn Neuropath; Am Neurol Asn; Soc Exp Neuropath. *Res:* Electron microscopic studies of the normal cerebellum and of chemical and virus induced abnormalities; viral disease of the nervous system and multiple sclerosis; experimental neuropathology. *Mailing Add:* VAMC Dept Neurol 1500 E Woodfed Wilson Jackson MS 39216

HERNDON, ROY C, NUCLEAR PHYSICS, HAZARDOUS WASTE MANAGEMENT. *Current Pos:* DIR, CTR BIOMED & TOXICOL RES & WASTE MGT, FLA STATE UNIV, TALLAHASSEE, FLA, 80-; CO-DIR, CTR HUNGARIAN/AM ENVIRON RES, STUDIES & EXCHANGES. *Personal Data:* b Washington, DC, Sept 25, 34. *Educ:* Washington & Lee Univ, BS, 55; Univ Ill, MS, 58; Fla State Univ, PhD(nuclear physics), 62. *Prof Exp:* Physicist, Lawrence Livermore Lab, Calif, 62-67; assoc prof physics, Phys Oceanog Lab, Nova Univ, 68-71; prof physics & comput sci, 71-74. *Concurrent Pos:* Exec dir, Gov Hazardous Waste Policy Adv Coun; dir,

Southern Waste Info Exchange; vis prof physics, Fla State Univ, Tallahassee, 74-77, Univ Lausanne, Switz, 77, 79, 81, 84 & 90; hon prof, Tech Univ Budapest, Hungary, 92. *Mem:* Am Phys Soc; Sigma Xi; AAAS; NY Acad Sci; Am Inst Biol Sci; Nat Environ Training Asn. *Res:* Environmental research. *Mailing Add:* 232 Westminster Dr Tallahassee FL 32304-3519

HERNDON, WALTER ROGER, BOTANY. *Current Pos:* head dept bot, Univ Tenn, 61-64, assoc dean col lib arts, 64-67, asst vpres acad affairs, 67-68, assoc vchancellor acad affairs, 68-70, PROF BOT, UNIV TENN, KNOXVILLE, 61-, VCHANCELLOR ACAD AFFAIRS, 70- *Personal Data:* b Birmingham, Ala, Sept 7, 26; m 49; c 4. *Educ:* Univ Ala, BS, 47, MS, 48; Vanderbilt Univ, PhD(biol), 54. *Prof Exp:* Asst biol, Univ Ala, 47; asst, Vanderbilt Univ, 48-50; instr, Mid Tenn State Univ, 50-54, asst prof, 54-55; from asst prof to assoc prof, Univ Ala, 55-61. *Concurrent Pos:* Asst biol, Vanderbilt Univ, 53-54. *Mem:* AAAS; Am Bot Soc; Phycol Soc Am (secy-treas, 61-64, vpres, 64-65, pres, 66-); Int Phycol Soc; Sigma Xi. *Res:* Phycology; marine botany. *Mailing Add:* PO Box 2260 Stone Mountain GA 30086-2260

HERNDON, WILLIAM CECIL, PHYSICAL ORGANIC CHEMISTRY, ENVIROMENTAL CHEMISTRY. *Current Pos:* chmn Dept Chem, 72-82 & 89-95, dean Col Sci, 82-87, DUDLEY MEM PROF CHEM, UNIV TEX, EL PASO, 87- *Personal Data:* b El Paso, Tex, Aug 12, 32; m 56, Nancy R Fairbanks; c Matthew S & William R. *Educ:* Tex Western Col, BS, 54; Rice Univ, PhD(chem), 59. *Prof Exp:* Res chemist, Cent Res Div, Am Cyanamid Co, 58-61; asst prof chem, Univ Miss, 61-64; assoc prof, Fla Atlantic Univ, 64-66; from asst prof to prof, Tex Tech Univ, 66-72. *Concurrent Pos:* Consult, Bell Tel Labs, 65; prog dir chem dynamics, NSF, 75-76. *Mem:* Fel NY Acad Sci; Sigma Xi; AAAS; Am Chem Soc. *Res:* Theoretical organic chemistry; organic photochemistry; benzenoid hydrocarbon chemistry. *Mailing Add:* Dept Chem Univ Tex El Paso TX 79912. *Fax:* 915-747-5748; *E-Mail:* wherndon@utep.edu

HERNER, ALBERT ERWIN, ENVIRONMENTAL CHEMISTRY, DATABASE DEVELOPMENT. *Current Pos:* RES CHEMIST, ENVIRON CHEM LAB, USDA, BELTSVILLE, 89- *Personal Data:* b Brooklyn, NY, Jan 24, 31; div; c Philip, Sharon & Mary Beth. *Educ:* Union Col, Schenectady, BS, 52; NY Univ, MS, 54; Fla State Univ, PhD(biochem), 60. *Prof Exp:* Postdoctoral biochem, USPHS, 60-62; assoc chemist, Midwest Res Inst, 62-64; chemist, New Eng Nuclear Corp, 64-67; res assoc molecular biol, Beth Israel Hosp, Boston, 67-69; chief radiochem, Clin-Chem Labs, Boston, 69-72; dir, Herner Anal, Inc, 72-84; assoc dir, Bionetics-Metpath, 84-89. *Concurrent Pos:* Lectr chem, George Washington Univ, 87-90. *Mem:* Sigma Xi; NY Acad Sci; Am Asn Clin Chem; Am Chem Soc; Asn Off Anal Chemists. *Res:* Analysis of soil, water, and agricultural products for pesticides and other agricultural chemical and methodology development; organized pesticide properties database. *Mailing Add:* ARS NRI Environ Chem Lab USDA Beltsville MD 20705. *Fax:* 301-504-5048

HERNES, GUDMUND, SCIENCE ADMINISTRATION. *Current Pos:* PROF, UNIV OSLO, 89- *Personal Data:* b Mar 25, 41; c Stein. *Educ:* PhD(sociol), 71. *Prof Exp:* Prof, Univ Bergen, 71; fel, Behav Sci Ctr Advan Study, Palo Alto, Calif, 74-75; state secy, Planning Secretariat, 80-81; doctor, Univ Umea, 82; head res, Fafo Inc; minister, Church, Educ & Res, Norway. *Mem:* Norweg Acad Sci. *Res:* Contributed articles to professional journals. *Mailing Add:* Ministry Educ Res & Church Affairs Akersgt 42 POB 8119 DEP Oslo 0032 Norway

HERNQVIST, KARL GERHARD, QUANTUM ELECTRONICS, LASERS. *Current Pos:* RETIRED. *Personal Data:* b Boras, Sweden, Sept 19, 22; US citizen; m 48, Thyra Josefsson; c Lars, Tomas & Ingrid. *Educ:* Royal Inst Technol Sweden, EE, 45, PhD(electronics), 59. *Honors & Awards:* Indust Res-100 Award, 67; David Sarnoff Award, RCA Corp, 74 & 82. *Prof Exp:* Mem tech staff electronics, Res Inst Nat Defense Sweden, 46-52; fel electronics, RCA Labs, 52-86, David Sarnoff Res Ctr, 86-90. *Concurrent Pos:* Fel RCA Labs, 70. *Mem:* Sigma Xi; Am Phys Soc; fel Inst Elec & Electronics Engrs. *Res:* Gas lasers; optics; gaseous discharges; energy conversion; electron physics; display tubes. *Mailing Add:* 667 Lake Dr Princeton NJ 08540

HEROD, JAMES VICTOR, MATHEMATICAL ANALYSIS. *Current Pos:* From asst prof to assoc prof, 66-79, PROF MATH, SCH MATH, GA INST TECHNOL, 79- *Personal Data:* b Selma, Ala, May 4, 37; m 60; c 3. *Educ:* Univ Ala, BS, 59, MS, 60; Univ NC, Chapel Hill, PhD(math), 64. *Concurrent Pos:* Vis prof, US Mil Acad, 81-82. *Mem:* Am Math Soc; Math Asn Am; Am Asn Univ Professors. *Res:* Connections between operator equations, evolution systems and product integrals; product integral representation for generalized inverses of operators that are unbounded; nonlinear Boltzmann equations. *Mailing Add:* Sch Math Ga Inst Technol Atlanta GA 30332-0160

HEROLD, KEITH EVAN, HEAT & MASS TRANSFER, ABSORPTION HEAT PUMPS. *Current Pos:* asst prof, 87-93, ASSOC PROF, UNIV MD, 93- *Personal Data:* b Philadelphia, Pa, Apr 3, 53. *Educ:* Univ Akron, BS, 77; Ohio State Univ, MS, 79, PhD(mech eng), 85. *Prof Exp:* Res scientist, Battelle Mem Inst, 79-87. *Mem:* Am Soc Mech Engrs; Am Soc Heating Refrig & Air Conditioning Engrs. *Res:* Experimental and analytical investigation of coupled heat and mass transfer processes in absorption heat pump systems; development of more effective thermally motivated systems for heating, cooling, waste heat recovery and related applications. *Mailing Add:* 3504 Esquilin Terr Bowie MD 20716. *Fax:* 301-314-9477; *E-Mail:* herold@eng.umd.edu

HEROLD, RICHARD CARL, developmental biology, for more information see previous edition

HEROLD, ROBERT JOHNSTON, ORGANIC CHEMISTRY. *Current Pos:* RETIRED. *Personal Data:* b Hasbrouck Heights, NJ, Oct 7, 20; m 46; c 5. *Educ:* Temple Univ, AB, 42, MA, 50. *Prof Exp:* Analyst explosives, Gen Chem Co, 42-43; asst hydrocarbon chem, Magnolia Petrol Co, 43-46; instr anal chem, Southern Methodist Univ, 46; res chemist polymer chem, Socony Mobil Oil Co, 46-56; sr res chemist, Gen Tire & Rubber Co, 57-63, group leader rubber res, 63-71, res scientist, 71-84. *Mem:* Am Chem Soc; Sigma Xi. *Res:* Hydrocarbon reactions; hydrocarbon polymers; unsaturated polyesters; polyethers; polyurethanes; catalysis; development of catalyst systems for polymerization; synthesis of oligomeric polyethers and polyesters; investigations of curing conditions for polyurethane and for unsaturated polyesters. *Mailing Add:* 28944 Hubbard St No 116 Leesburg FL 34748

HERON, S DUNCAN, JR, GEOLOGY. *Current Pos:* From instr to assoc prof, 50-71, chmn dept, 68-78, PROF GEOL, DUKE UNIV, 71- *Personal Data:* b Jackson, Miss, Sept 18, 26; m 48; c 2. *Educ:* Univ SC, BS, 48, MS, 50; Univ NC, PhD, 58. *Concurrent Pos:* Geologist, SC State Develop Bd, 58-70; ed-in-chief, Southeastern Geol; assoc ed, Bull Geol Soc Am, 89-94. *Mem:* Geol Soc Am; Am Asn Petrol Geol; Sigma Xi; Soc Sedimentary Geol; Asn Earth Sci Ed (pres, 90). *Res:* Cretaceous and Tertiary stratigraphy of the Atlantic Coastal Plain; Pleistocene and Holocene barrier island development; clay mineralogy of Atlantic Coastal Plain sediments; nonmetallic economic and general geology. *Mailing Add:* Div Earth Sci Box 90277 Durham NC 27708-0227. *Fax:* 919-684-5321; *E-Mail:* heron@geo.duke.edu

HEROY, WILLIAM BAYARD, JR, GEOLOGY, GEOPHYSICS. *Current Pos:* RETIRED. *Personal Data:* b Washington, DC, Aug 13, 15; m 37, Dorothy Meincke; c Bayord P, David B, June C (Leverett) & Barbara A (Stock). *Educ:* Dartmouth Col, AB, 37; Princeton Univ, PhD(geol), 41; Harvard Univ, Advan Mgt Prog, 61. *Honors & Awards:* Campbell Medal, Am Geol Inst, 86; Distinguished Serv Award, Geol Soc Am, 90. *Prof Exp:* Asst geol, Princeton Univ, 39-41; from asst geologist to geologist field party, Tex Co, 41-45; geologist, Geotech Corp, 45-46, supvr, 46-50, vpres & dir, 50-59, exec vpres, 59-61, pres, 61-65, exec vpres, Teledyne Inc, 65-68, pres, Geotech Div, 65-67, group mgr, 67-68, asst to pres, Inc, 68-70; vpres-treas, Southern Methodist Univ, 70-76, prof, 70-76, emer prof geol sci, 81-82. *Concurrent Pos:* Pres, Inst Study Earth & Man, treas, 76-81, sr scientist, 81-; mem bd, Ft Burgwin Res Ctr. *Mem:* Fel Geol Soc Am (treas, 76-); Soc Explor Geophys; Am Inst Prof Geologists; Am Asn Petrol Geol (treas, 70-72); Am Geol Inst (pres, 69). *Res:* Geology of the Shell Canyon area; economic geological petroleum; geophysical prospecting; surface and structural geology; stratigraphy, sedimentation and seismology. *Mailing Add:* 20 Old Oak Ct Durham NC 27705-5644. *Fax:* 919-403-2316

HERPEL, COLEMAN, mathematics; deceased, see previous edition for last biography

HERR, DAVID GUY, STATISTICS, MATHEMATICS. *Current Pos:* asst prof, 73-78, ASSOC PROF MATH, UNIV NC, GREENSBORO, 78- *Personal Data:* b Abbington, Pa, Mar 12, 37; m 61; c 2. *Educ:* Ga Inst Technol, BEE, 59, MS, 61; Univ NC, Chapel Hill, PhD(statist), 67. *Prof Exp:* Instr math, Ga Inst Technol, 61-62; instr, Univ NC, Charlotte, 65-66, asst prof, 66-67; asst prof, Duke Univ, 67-73. *Concurrent Pos:* Statist consult, Western Elec, 79- *Mem:* Am Math Asn; Am Statist Asn; Math Asn Am; Inst Math Statist. *Res:* Linear models; unbalanced designs; coordinate-free or geometric approach. *Mailing Add:* Dept Math Univ NC Greensboro NC 27412-0001

HERR, DAVID WALTER, NEUROPHYSIOLOGY, NEUROCHEMISTRY. *Current Pos:* TOXICOLOGIST, US ENVIRON PROTECTION AGENCY, 90- *Personal Data:* b Lancaster, Pa, May 15, 57. *Educ:* Pa State Univ, BS, 79; NC State Univ, MS, 83; Univ NC, PhD(toxicol), 88. *Prof Exp:* Res assoc, Nat Res Coun-Environ Protection Agency, 88-90. *Mem:* Soc Toxicol; Soc Neurosci; Int Brain Res Orgn. *Res:* Assessing sensory toxicity of environmental compounds using neurophysiological techniques; investigative neuroanatomical and neurochemical generators of sensory evoked potentials. *Mailing Add:* MD-74B NHEERL/NTD-NPTB US Environ Protection Agency Durham NC 27711. *E-Mail:* herr.david@epamail.epa.gov

HERR, DONALD EDWARD, AGRONOMY. *Current Pos:* RETIRED. *Personal Data:* b Dec 23, 26; US citizen; m 54; c 2. *Educ:* Ohio State Univ, BS, 51, PhD(weed control, agron), 65; Mich State Univ, MS, 62. *Prof Exp:* Assoc exten agent, Ohio State Univ, 52-54, mgr res farm, Ohio Agr Res & Develop Ctr, 54-62, res asst weed control, 62-64; from instr to prof agron, Ohio State Univ, 64-90. *Concurrent Pos:* US AID adv, India, 69-70 & Somalia, 78. *Mem:* Am Soc Agron; Weed Sci Soc Am. *Res:* Movement and persistence of herbicides in soil; agronomic crop production. *Mailing Add:* 4454 Sussex Dr Columbus OH 43220

HERR, EARL BINKLEY, JR, BIOCHEMISTRY. *Current Pos:* sr biochemist, Eli Lilly & Co, 57-62, mgr antibiotic purification develop dept, 62-64, head pharmaceut res, 64-65, asst dir prod develop, 65, div dir antibiotics mfg & develop, 65-68, exec dir biochem & biol opers, 68-69, vpres, biochem & biol opers, 69-70, vpres res, develop & control, 70-74, pres, Lilly Res Labs, 74-86, EXEC VPRES, ELI LILLY & CO, 86- *Personal Data:* b Lancaster, Pa, Apr 14, 28; m 50; c 2. *Educ:* Franklin & Marshall Col, BS, 48; Univ Del, MS, 50, PhD(biochem), 53. *Hon Degrees:* DSc, Ind Univ. *Prof Exp:* AEC asst, Univ Del, 50-53; res fel, Cornell Univ, 53-55; res fel, Brookhaven Nat Lab, 55-57. *Concurrent Pos:* Bd dirs res comt, Eli Lilly & Co, 71- *Mem:* AAAS; Chem Soc; Am Chem Soc; Sigma Xi. *Res:* Enzyme mechanisms and purification; antibiotics; pharmaceutical research and development. *Mailing Add:* 12011 Eden Glen Dr Carmel IN 46033-4303

HERR, FRANK LEAMAN, JR, GEOCHEMISTRY, PHYSICAL CHEMISTRY. *Current Pos:* Nat Res Coun-Nat Acad Sci Res Assoc, 75-77, chemist, Ocean Sci Div, 77-80, CHEMIST, ENVIRON SCI DIV, NAVAL RES LAB, WASHINGTON, DC, 80- *Personal Data:* b Schenectady, NY, Feb 17, 48; m 70; c 2. *Educ:* Hamilton Col, BA, 70; Univ Md, PhD(chem), 75. *Mem:* Am Geophys Union. *Res:* Aqueous solution thermodynamics of the electrolyte and inorganic non-electrolyte constituents of seawater and natural waters; analysis of trace constituents in natural waters (gases, oxidants, organics) resulting from photochemical or interfacial phenomena. *Mailing Add:* 6431 Noble Dr McLean VA 22101

HERR, HARRY WALLACE, UROLOGY, ONCOLOGY. *Current Pos:* clin fel urol & oncol, 75-80, ASSOC ATTEN SURG, MEM SLOAN-KETTERING CANCER CTR, 80-; ASSOC PROF SURG & UROL, MED COL, CORNELL UNIV, 80- *Personal Data:* b St Louis, Mo, Oct 1, 43; m 65; c 3. *Educ:* Univ Calif, Davis, AB, 65; Univ Calif, Irvine, MD, 69; Am Bd Urol, dipl, 76. *Honors & Awards:* F C Valentine Award, NY Acad Med, 75; Meller Award, Mem Sloan-Kettering Cancer Ctr, 75. *Prof Exp:* Intern, Los Angeles County-Univ Southern Calif Med Ctr, 69-70; resident gen surg, Univ Calif, Irvine, 70-71 & urol, 71-74; res fel tumor immunol, Sloan-Kettering Inst Cancer Res, 74-76. *Concurrent Pos:* Fel surg, Cornell Univ Med Col, 75-76; clin fel, Am Cancer Soc, 75-76; assoc attend surgeon, New York Hosp, 80- *Mem:* AAAS; NY Acad Sci; Am Col Surgeons; Am Asn Cancer Res; Acad Appl Sci. *Res:* Clinical and laboratory investigation on genitourinary cancers. *Mailing Add:* Dept Surg Cornell Univ Med Col 1275 York Ave New York NY 10021

HERR, JOHN CHRISTIAN, PROTEIN SECRETION, REPRODUCTIVE IMMUNOLOGY. *Current Pos:* From asst prof to assoc prof, 81-90, DIR, LYMPHOCITE CULTURAL CTR, UNIV VA, 82-, PROF ANAT & CELL BIOL, 90- *Personal Data:* b Dubuque, Iowa, June 29, 48. *Educ:* Univ Iowa, PhD(anat & cell biol), 78. *Honors & Awards:* Munkigaard Award, Am Soc Reproductive Immunol, 95. *Mem:* Am Soc Cell Biol; Am Asn Anatomists; AAAS; Am Soc Reproductive Immunol; Soc Study Reproduction. *Res:* Molecular biology of human spermatogenesis; contraceptive vaccine development. *Mailing Add:* Dept Cell Biol Univ Va Charlottesville VA 22908. *Fax:* 804-982-3912

HERR, JOHN MERVIN, JR, PLANT EMBRYOLOGY. *Current Pos:* from asst prof to assoc prof, 59-69, PROF BIOL, UNIV SC, 69- *Personal Data:* b Charlottesville, Va, July 26, 30; m 52, 74, Lucrecia Linder; c 3. *Educ:* Univ Va, BA, 51, MA, 52; Univ NC, PhD(bot), 57. *Prof Exp:* Instr biol, Washington & Lee Univ, 52-54; Fulbright fel, India, 57-58; asst prof biol, Pfeiffer Col, 58-59. *Mem:* Bot Soc Am; Int Soc Plant Morphol. *Res:* Angiosperm embryology; progress in both descriptive experimental phases of angiosperm embryology. *Mailing Add:* Dept Biol Univ SC Columbia SC 29208. *Fax:* 803-777-4002; *E-Mail:* herr@biol.scarolina.edu

HERR, LEONARD JAY, SOIL MICROBIOLOGY, MYCOLOGY. *Current Pos:* from instr to prof, 56-95, EMER PROF PLANT PATH, OHIO AGR RES & DEVELOP CTR, OHIO STATE UNIV, 95- *Personal Data:* b Orville, Ohio, Dec 21, 28; m 54, Lucille Adelsberger; c Lynn, Karen & Melissa. *Educ:* Ohio State Univ, BSc, 52, MSc, 53, PhD(plant path), 56. *Mem:* Sigma Xi; Am Phytopath Soc; Am Asn Univ Prof. *Res:* Soil microbiology in relation of soil-borne plant pathogens; diseases of sugar beets and lettuce; biocontrol of rhizoctonia. *Mailing Add:* Dept Plant Path Ohio State Univ Ohio Agr Res & Develop Ctr Wooster OH 44691-4096. *Fax:* 216-263-3841

HERR, RICHARD BAESSLER, OBSERVATIONAL ASTRONOMY, VARIABLE STARS. *Current Pos:* Asst prof, 64-70, ASSOC PROF ASTRON, MT CUBA ASTRON OBSERV, UNIV DEL, 70- *Personal Data:* b Philadelphia, Pa, Mar 3, 36; m 58, Mary Dilling; c Daniel D. *Educ:* Franklin & Marshall Col, BS, 57; Univ Del, MS, 60; Case Inst Technol, PhD(astron), 65. *Mem:* Royal Astron Soc Can; Int Astron Union; Am Astron Soc. *Res:* Observational astrophysics; photoelectric photometry. *Mailing Add:* 913 Pickett Lane Newark DE 19711. *E-Mail:* herr@strauss.udel.edu

HERR, ROSS ROBERT, ORGANIC CHEMISTRY, REGULATORY AFFAIRS. *Current Pos:* res chemist, 56-66, mgr pesticide regulatory affairs, 66-77, EXEC DIR PHARMACEUT REGULATORY PRACT, UPJOHN CO, 77- *Personal Data:* b Chicago, Ill, Aug 11, 26; m 48; c 4. *Educ:* Univ Ill, BS, 47; Northwestern Univ, PhD(chem), 51. *Prof Exp:* Res chemist, Armour Labs, 51-56. *Mem:* Am Chem Soc. *Res:* Isolation and chemistry of antibiotics; natural products. *Mailing Add:* 7741 Kenmore Dr Apt 10 Portage MI 49024

HERREID, CLYDE F, II, COMPARATIVE & ECOLOGICAL PHYSIOLOGY. *Current Pos:* assoc prof, 68-82, PROF BIOL, STATE UNIV NY, BUFFALO, 82-, ACAD DIR HONORS PROF & DISTINGUISHED TEACHING PROF, 88- *Personal Data:* b Grand Forks, NDak, Apr 8, 34; m 57; c 2. *Educ:* Colo Col, BA, 56; Johns Hopkins Univ, MS, 59; Pa State Univ, PhD(zool), 61. *Prof Exp:* Asst ecol, Johns Hopkins Univ, 56-59; asst zool, Pa State Univ, 59-61; NIH fel marine biol, Inst Marine Sci, Univ Miami, 61; asst prof zool, Univ Alaska, 62-65 & Duke Univ, 65-67. *Concurrent Pos:* Vis prof biol, Univ Nairobi, 88-89. *Mem:* AAAS; Am Physiol Soc; Am Soc Zoologists (secy, 84-86); Nat Sci Teachers Asn. *Res:* Temperature regulation, metabolism and water balance in vertebrates; behavior and ecology of bats, crabs, frogs, sea cucumbers and snails; locomotion and energetics of invertebrates. *Mailing Add:* Dept Biol Sci State Univ NY Buffalo NY 14260. *Fax:* 716-645-2975; *E-Mail:* herreid@acsu.buffalo.edu

HERRELL, ASTOR Y, SCIENCE EDUCATION & ADMINISTRATION. *Current Pos:* PROF CHEM & CHMN DEPT, WINSTON-SALEM STATE UNIV, NC, 79- *Personal Data:* b Fork Ridge, Tenn, Feb 13, 35; m 60, Doris Smith; c Patricia F. *Educ:* Berea Col, Ky, BA, 57; Tuskegee Inst, MSEd, 61; Wayne State Univ, PhD(chem), 73. *Prof Exp:* Instr chem, Morristown Col, Tenn, 59-60 & St Augustine's Col, NC, 61-63; from asst prof to prof chem, Knoxville Col, Tenn, 63-79, chmn dept, 72-79. *Concurrent Pos:* At Sandia Labs, NMex, 74; mem fac, Lawrence Livermore Nat Lab, Univ Calif, Berkeley, 75; consult, Fisk Univ, Tenn, 77-83; fac res, Arnold Eng Ctr, Tenn, 85. *Mem:* Sigma Xi; Am Chem Soc. *Res:* Synthesis and energy; thermodynamic properties of materials. *Mailing Add:* 1735 Ardmore Rd Winston-Salem NC 27127-7508

HERRERO, FEDERICO ANTONIO, GEOPHYSICS, ATMOSPHERIC PHYSICS. *Current Pos:* ASTROPHYSICIST, GODDARD SPACE FLIGHT CTR, NASA, 81- *Personal Data:* b Santo Domingo, Dominican Repub, July 17, 41; US citizen; m 64; c 4. *Educ:* Spring Hill Col, BS, 63; Univ Fla, Gainesville, MS, 65, PhD(physics), 68. *Prof Exp:* Res assoc excitation collisions, Johns Hopkins Univ, 70-72; asst prof physics, Univ PR-Mayaguez, 72-75; assoc prof physics, Univ PR, Rio Piedras, 75-81, chmn, Dept & Lab Collisions, 77-81. *Concurrent Pos:* Scientist I, PR Nuclear Ctr, Mayaguez, 73-75; investr, NIH grant, 74-75; proj dir, NSF grant, 74-75; guest worker, Nat Astron & Ionosphere Ctr, PR, 75-; proj dir, Energy Domonst Lab, Dept Energy grant, 77-; prin investr, NSF grant, 78-80. *Mem:* Am Phys Soc; Am Geophys Union; AAAS. *Res:* Study of the dynamics of the earth's ionosphere with measurements of airglow and radar backscatter intensities; theoretical and experimental studies of vibrational excitation of diatomic molecules by ion impact. *Mailing Add:* 11420 Kedleston Rd Glenn Dale MD 20769

HERRETT, RICHARD ALLISON, BIOCHEMISTRY, PLANT PHYSIOLOGY. *Current Pos:* EXEC DIR, AGR RES INST, 94- *Personal Data:* b Buffalo, NY, Aug 4, 32; m 78, Joan Maurer; c Steven, Jeffrey, William & Maxwell. *Educ:* Rutgers Univ, BS, 54; Univ Minn, MS, 56, PhD(agr bot), 59. *Prof Exp:* Asst agron & plant genetics, Univ Minn, 54-56, asst plant path & bot, 56-58; Union Carbide Corp fel plant physiol, Boyce Thompson Inst Plant Res, Inc, 59-60; plant physiologist, Olefins Div, Union Carbide Corp, 60-67, dir biol res, 67-70; tech mgr, Agr Chem Div, ICI Americas Inc, 70-75, dir res & develop, 75-87, pres, Environ Agr Assoc, 87-92, pres, Environ Agr Assoc, 92-94. *Concurrent Pos:* Treas & mem exec bd, NC Biotechnol Ctr; bd mem, C V Riley Mem Found; mem bd dir, NC Biotech Ctr. *Mem:* Am Soc Plant Physiol; Am Chem Soc; Weed Sci Soc Am; AAAS; Agr Res Inst. *Res:* Chemical control of plant growth; differentiation and the mechanism of action of plant growth regulators; pesticide metabolism in plants; discovery, development and registration of reduced risk pesticides. *Mailing Add:* 23 Sonneborn Severna Park MD 21146. *Fax:* 301-530-7007

HERRICK, CLAUDE CUMMINGS, physical chemistry, for more information see previous edition

HERRICK, DAVID RAWLS, THEORETICAL CHEMISTRY. *Current Pos:* asst prof chem & assoc, 75-80, ASSOC PROF CHEM, INST THEORET SCI, UNIV ORE, 81- *Personal Data:* b Lafayette, Ind, May 9, 47; m 68; c 1. *Educ:* Univ Rochester, BS, 69; Yale Univ, PhD(chem), 73. *Prof Exp:* Fel chem physics, Bell Labs, 73-75. *Mem:* Am Phys Soc; Am Chem Soc. *Res:* Theoretical chemical physics; Lie algebraic descriptions of electron correlation; collisional and field induced Rydberg angular momentum transfer; decaying state resonances, multiply-excited atoms. *Mailing Add:* Dept Chem Univ Ore Eugene OR 97403

HERRICK, ELBERT CHARLES, HETEROGENEOUS CATALYSIS, POLLUTION PREVENTION. *Current Pos:* CONSULT CHEMIST & ENGR, 89- *Personal Data:* b Joliet, Mont, Oct 16, 19; m 43, 62, Doris Brock; c David, Dennis,Douglas & Donna M. *Educ:* Mont State Col, BS, 41; Princeton Univ, ChemE, 42; Mass Inst Technol, PhD(org chem), 49. *Prof Exp:* Res chem engr, Plastics Div, Monsanto Chem Co, 42; asst, Mass Inst Technol, 48-49; res chemist, E I du Pont de Nemours & Co, 49-54, Am Viscose Corp, 54-55 & Houdry Process Corp, 55-58; supvr chem res, Climax Molybdenum Co, Mich, 58-59; res chemist, Basic Res Div, Res & Eng Dept, Sun Oil Co, 59-61; sr res chemist, Dow Chem Co, 62-63; consult chemist, 63-64; sect head org res, Great Lakes Res Corp, 65-67; dir chem res, Escambia Chem Corp, 67-71; sr org chemist, Houdry Labs, Air Prod & Chem Inc, Marcus Hook, 71-77; environ systs scientist, Mitre Corp, McLean, Va, 77-88; sr scientist, Dynamac Corp, 88-89. *Mem:* AAAS; Am Chem Soc; Sigma Xi; Am Inst Chem Eng; NY Acad Sci. *Res:* Cyclooctatetraene derivatives; high pressure hydrogenation of carbon monoxide to polymethylene; polymerization of acetylene to monovinylacetylene; synthesis of peptides; catalytic synthesis of nitrogen heterocycles including the polyurethane catalyst, DABCO; carbene reaction; olefin polymerization by Ziegler type catalysts; preparation of dyeable polypropylene fibers; catalysts for toluenediamine synthesis; thermal decomposition of methyl carbamates to toluene diisocyanates; decontamination of nitroaromatic waste streams. *Mailing Add:* 5051 El Don Dr Apt 501 Rocklin CA 95677-4427

HERRICK, FRANKLIN WILLARD, ORGANIC CHEMISTRY. *Current Pos:* RETIRED. *Personal Data:* b Seattle, Wash, Dec 14, 22; m 45, Norma H McCarty; c Sidney J & Denise K. *Educ:* Willamette Univ, AB, 46; Mich State Univ, PhD(org chem), 50. *Prof Exp:* Asst anal chem, Mich State Univ, 46-47 & org chem, 47-49; chemist, Res Div, ITT Rayonier Res Ctr, 50-58, group leader, 58-63, sect leader, 63-69, res supvr, Olympic Res Div, 69-75, res assoc, 75-83, sr res assoc, 83-86. *Mem:* Am Chem Soc; Forest Prod Res Soc. *Res:* Synthesis of organic chemicals; chemistry of cellulose, lignin and bark; chemical grouting, soil stabilization; soil mechanics; forest genetics;

fermentation of wood carbohydrates or components; enzymatic hydrolysis of wood carbohydrates; cellulose derivatives; cellulose acetate; regenerated cellulose; microfibrillated cellulose; vanillin and derivatives. *Mailing Add:* 705 Holly Lane Shelton WA 98584-1316

HERRICK, GLENN ARTHUR, MOLECULAR BIOLOGY, BIOCHEMISTRY. *Current Pos:* ASSOC PROF CELLULAR VIRAL MOLECULAR BIOL, UNIV UTAH MED CTR, 77- *Personal Data:* b Mar 10, 45; US citizen. *Educ:* Col Wooster, BA, 67; Princeton Univ, MA, 70, PhD(biochem), 73. *Concurrent Pos:* Jane Coffin Childs fel, Boulder, Colo, 73-75, Nat Inst GMS fel, 75-77. *Res:* Eukaryotic genome; organization and function; somatic genome reorganization in ciliated protozoa, telomeres. *Mailing Add:* Dept Microbiol Univ Utah Sch Med 50 N Medical Dr Salt Lake City UT 84132-0001

HERRICK, JOHN BERNE, VETERINARY MEDICINE. *Current Pos:* RETIRED. *Personal Data:* b Sheffield, Iowa, Dec 18, 19; m 41; c 10. *Educ:* Iowa State Univ, BS, 41, DVM, 46, MS, 50. *Honors & Awards:* Distinguished Serv Award, USDA, 67; Borden Award, Am Vet Med Asn, 70; Am Asn Bovine Practr Award, 86; Am Vet Med Asn Award, 87. *Prof Exp:* With Voc Agr Inst, Iowa, 41-42; asst vet physiol, Iowa State Univ, 43-46; pvt pract, 46-47; in-chg artificial insemination, Iowa State Univ, 48-51, prof exten vet in-chg cattle, 51-80, prof vet clin serv, 80-83. *Concurrent Pos:* Consult, Nat Asn Artificial Breeding Indust; vpres, Pan Am Vet Cong, 68-70; animal health consult, 83- *Mem:* Am Vet Med Asn (pres, 69-70). *Res:* Reproductive disorders and diseases of cattle; organized educational programs on disease control. *Mailing Add:* 7807 N Calle Caballeros Paradise Valley AZ 85253

HERRICK, JOSEPH RAYMOND, mechanical engineering, for more information see previous edition

HERRICKS, EDWIN E, ENVIRONMENTAL BIOMONITORING, AQUATIC ECOLOGY. *Current Pos:* from asst prof to assoc prof, 75-91, PROF ENVIRON BIOL, UNIV ILL, URBANA-CHAMPAIGN, 91- *Personal Data:* b Axtell, Kans, Dec 24, 46; m 68; c 2. *Educ:* Univ Kans, BA, 68; Johns Hopkins Univ, MS, 70; Va Polytech Inst & State Univ, PhD(biol), 74. *Prof Exp:* Res assoc civil eng & instr agr eng, Va Polytech Inst & State Univ, 73; aquatic res biologist & field edologist, Union Carbide Corp, 73-75. *Concurrent Pos:* Res scientist, Rocky Mountain Biol Lab, Colo, 77; vis asst prof & assoc prof evolution & environ biol, Univ Pa, 79-82; vis fel, Johns Hopkins Univ, 83; Fulbright fel & distinguished prof, 89. *Mem:* Affil mem Am Soc Civil Engrs; Am Water Res Asn; Int Asn Water Pollution Res & Control; NAm Benthological Soc; Soc Environ Toxicol & Chem; Water Pollution Control Fedn. *Res:* Effects of contaminants and other environmental alterations on communities of organisms, including aquatic and terrestrial ecosystems; analysis of habitat factors which affect the ecological interactions; connections between engineering practice and environmental consequences; biological monitoring procedures for environmental decision-making. *Mailing Add:* Dept Ecol & Evolution Univ Ill 505 S Goodwin Ave Urbana IL 61801-3707

HERRIN, CHARLES SELBY, SR TECHNICAL WRITING IN SOFTWARE DEVELOPMENT. *Current Pos:* Software testing mgr, 86-93, SR TECH WRITER SOFTWARE DEVELOP, NOVELL INC, 93- *Personal Data:* b Mechanicsburg, Miss, May 16, 39; m 61; Vila J Williams; c Rebecca K (Wright), Michael J, ViAna R (Brower), Lauralie (Morales), Deena D (Pankratz), Daniel S, Thomas C, Jeannie M & TerriLyn. *Educ:* Brigham Young Univ, BS, 63, MS, 66; Ohio State Univ, PhD(entom), 69. *Prof Exp:* Res assoc entom, Univ Ga, 69-70; NSF res assoc biol, Ga Southern Col, 70-72; consult biostatist & comput data-base mgr, Res Div, Brigham Young Univ, 75-78, mus comput mgr & programmer, 78-83; systs programmer & cust support serv supvr, Code 3 Health Info systs, 3M Corp, 83-86. *Concurrent Pos:* Proj dir ectoparasites of African mammals, US Army (MR & D), Ctr Health & Environ Studies, Brigham Young Univ, 72-76. *Res:* Software testing; technical writing. *Mailing Add:* 920 W 1020 S Provo UT 84601. *E-Mail:* sherrin@novell.com

HERRIN, EUGENE THORNTON, JR, GEOPHYSICS. *Current Pos:* from asst prof to prof geol & geophys, 58-74, chmn dept, 71-74, Shuler-Foscue prof geol sci, 74-80, SHULER-FOSCUE EARTH SCI, SOUTHERN METHODIST UNIV, 80- *Personal Data:* b Dallas, Tex, Nov 19, 29; m 53; c 3. *Educ:* Southern Methodist Univ, BS, 51, MS, 53; Harvard Univ, PhD(geol, geophys), 58. *Honors & Awards:* Grove Karl Gilbert Award, 64. *Prof Exp:* Asst geophys, Harvard Univ, 53-55; instr geol, Southern Methodist Univ, 55-57; asst geophys, Harvard Univ, 57-58. *Concurrent Pos:* Fel, Carnegie Inst Washington, 64. *Mem:* Seismol Soc Am; fel Geol Soc Am; fel Am Geophys Union. *Res:* Experimental and theoretical seismology; problems of terrestrial heat flow and heat production; structural geology; experimental tectonics. *Mailing Add:* Southern Methodist Univ PO Box 750001 Southern Methodist Univ Dallas TX 75275-0001

HERRIN, MORELAND, CIVIL ENGINEERING. *Current Pos:* assoc prof mat, 58-63, PROF MAT, UNIV ILL, URBANA, 63- *Personal Data:* b Morris, Okla, Nov 14, 22; m 46; c 3. *Educ:* Okla State Univ, BSCE, 47, MSCE, 49; Purdue Univ, PhD(hwy mat), 54. *Honors & Awards:* Epstein Mem Award, 63. *Prof Exp:* Instr struct, Okla State Univ, 47-50; design engr, Hudgins, Thompson & Ball, Engrs, 50-51; from asst prof to assoc prof hwy eng, Okla State Univ, 54-58. *Concurrent Pos:* Comt chmn, Hwy Res Bd, 63-; pvt consult hwy mat. *Mem:* Asn Asphalt Paving Technol (pres, 80); Am Soc Eng Educ; Am Soc Civil Engrs. *Res:* Rheological behavior and failure mechanics of bituminous materials; durability and strength of stabilized materials. *Mailing Add:* 1414 W William St Champaign IL 61821

HERRING, CAREY REUBEN, MATHEMATICS EDUCATION. *Current Pos:* PROF MATH, CARSON-NEWMAN COL, 67-, CHMN, DEPT MATH, 94- *Personal Data:* b Tifton, Ga, Oct 4, 43; m 65; c 2. *Educ:* Carson-Newman Col, BS, 65; Samford Univ, MA, 67; Univ Tenn, EdD, 75. *Mem:* Nat Coun Teachers Math; Math Asn Am. *Mailing Add:* Dept Nat Sci Carson-Newman Col Russell Ave Jefferson City TN 37760. *E-Mail:* herring@chcacc.cn.edu

HERRING, H(UGH) JAMES, AERONAUTICAL ENGINEERING. *Current Pos:* PRES, DYNALYSIS OF PRINCETON, 70- *Personal Data:* b Boston, Mass, Aug 3, 39; m 60; c 3. *Educ:* Harvard Col, BA, 61, BS, 62; Princeton Univ, MA & MS, 66, PhD(aeronaut eng), 67. *Prof Exp:* Mem res staff, Dept Aerospace & Mech Sci, Princeton Univ, 67-76. *Concurrent Pos:* Assoc ed, J Fluids Eng, 78-81. *Mem:* AAAS; Sigma Xi; Am Inst Aeronaut & Astronaut (treas, 76-79); Am Soc Mech Engr. *Res:* Fluid mechanics and numerical simulation. *Mailing Add:* Eighteen Winfield Rd Princeton NJ 08540

HERRING, HAROLD KEITH, animal science, biochemistry, for more information see previous edition

HERRING, JACKSON REA, THEORETICAL PHYSICS, FLUIDS. *Current Pos:* SR SCIENTIST, NAT CTR ATMOSPHERIC RES, 72- *Personal Data:* b Ashland, Ky, Oct 2, 31; m 59, Betty Jean Pegram; c Peter R & Christopher J. *Educ:* Wake Forest Col, BS, 53; Univ NC, MA, 56, PhD(physics), 59. *Prof Exp:* Theoret physicist, Goddard Space Flight Ctr, NASA, 59-72. *Concurrent Pos:* Green scholar, Univ Calif, San Diego, 78; assoc ed, Physics Fluids, 86-91; assoc prof, Inst Mecanique Grenoble, 88; vis prof, Univ Pierre & Marie Curie, Paris, 95. *Mem:* Fel Am Phys Soc. *Res:* Nuclear structure; statistical physics; fluid turbulence theory. *Mailing Add:* 2581 Briarwood Dr Boulder CO 80303

HERRING, JOHN WESLEY, JR, ELECTRIC POWER SYSTEMS & CONTROLS. *Current Pos:* from assoc prof to prof, 67-92, EMER PROF ELEC ENG, MISS STATE UNIV, 92- *Personal Data:* b Brookhaven, Miss, Aug 8, 27; m 59, Frances L Coffman; c Jan, Jeannette & Wes. *Educ:* Miss State Univ, BSEE, 50; Univ Ariz, MSEE, 60, PhD(elec eng), 67. *Prof Exp:* Chief comput, Western Geophys Co Am, 50-52; engr, Miss Power Co, 52-57; instr elec eng, Miss State Univ, 57-58, asst prof, 59-63; instr, Univ Ariz, 66-67. *Concurrent Pos:* Res engr, US Army Missile Command, Huntsville, Ala. *Mem:* Inst Elec & Electronics Engrs; Am Soc Eng Educ. *Res:* Power system stability; nonlinear stability theory; design and analysis of control systems. *Mailing Add:* Dept Elec Eng Miss State Univ PO Drawer EE Mississippi State MS 39762

HERRING, RICHARD NORMAN, CHEMICAL ENGINEERING, CRYOGENICS. *Current Pos:* staff scientist, Ball Bros Res Corp, 68-72, mgr advan progs, 72-78, dir sci & applns exp, 78-79, exec vpres, 79-84, PRES, BALL AEROSPACE SYSTS DIV, 85- *Personal Data:* b Reading, Pa, Dec 25, 38; m 61; c 4. *Educ:* Lehigh Univ, BS, 60; Univ Colo, MS, 62, PhD(chem eng), 64. *Prof Exp:* Chem engr, Cryogenic Div, Nat Bur Stand, 60-64; res dir thermodyn, P-V-T Inc, 64-65; adv design engr cryogenics, Beech Aircraft Corp, 65-68. *Res:* Management of space experiments and spacecraft for astrophysics, earth applications and Department of Energy requirements. *Mailing Add:* Carthwatch PO Box 1235 MS BEB Broomfield CO 80038-1235

HERRING, SUSAN WELLER, ANATOMY. *Current Pos:* PROF ORTHOD & ADJ PROF ZOOL, UNIV WASH, SEATTLE, 90- *Personal Data:* b Pittsburgh, Pa, Mar 25, 47; m 95, Norman S Wolf. *Educ:* Univ Chicago, BS, 67, PhD(anat), 71. *Prof Exp:* From asst prof to assoc prof oral anat, Univ Ill, 72-86, prof oral anat & anat, 86-90. *Concurrent Pos:* NIH fel oral anat, Univ Ill Med Ctr, 71-72, Nat Inst Dent Res grants, 74-77, 82-; chmn, Div Vert Morphol, Am Soc Zool, 81-84; vis assoc prof biol sci, Univ Mich, 82; Muscular Dystrophy Asn grant, 82-83; Oral Biol & Med Study Sect, NIH, 86-89; NSF grant, 90-92. *Mem:* Fel AAAS; Am Soc Mammal; Am Soc Zool; Soc Vert Paleont; Am Asn Anat; Int Asn Dent Res; Int Soc Vert Morphol (pres, 94-97). *Res:* Functional mammalian anatomy; evolutionary biology; biomechanics. *Mailing Add:* Dept Orthod Univ Wash Box 357446 Seattle WA 98195. *Fax:* 206-685-8163; *E-Mail:* herring@u.washington.edu

HERRING, THOMAS, EARTH SCIENCE. *Current Pos:* Kerr-McGee assoc prof, 89-92, ASSOC PROF GEOPHYSICS, DEPT EARTH ATMOSPHERIC & PLANETARY SCI, MASS INST TECHNOL, 92- *Personal Data:* b Queensland, Australia, July 17, 55. *Educ:* Univ Queensland, BA, 76, M, 78; Mass Inst Technol, PhD(earth & planetary sci), 83. *Honors & Awards:* S E Reilly Prize in Surv, 75; Macelwane Medal, Am Geophys Union, 91; Bomford Prize, Int Asn Geod, 95. *Prof Exp:* Res assoc, Harvard Univ, 83-89. *Concurrent Pos:* Vis scientist, Div Nat Mapping, Australian Dept Energy & Resources, 86; mem, Geol Comt, Nat Acad Sci, 90-94, Appln Space-based Interferometry, Int Asn Geol, 92, Geodynamics Comt, Nat Acad Sci, 95-96, Gravity Measurements Space Comt, Nat Coun Bd Earth Sci, 96-97; chmn, Info Technol Comt, Am Geophys Union, 92-96, Comt Geod, Nat Acad Sci, 94-96, Comn Int Coord Space Tech Geod & Geodynamics, Proj Space Geodetic Data Combination, Int Asn Geod, 95-98; assoc ed, J Geophys Res, 89-92, actg geod ed, 91; co-chair, Measurement Tech & Technol Panel, NASA, 89. *Mem:* Fel Am Geophys Union (secy, 90-92); AAAS. *Res:* Very long baseline interferometry and global positioning system data to develop geophysically based models of changes in rotation of the Earth and global deformations; developing kinematic models of deformations in California and Central Asia; developing improved models and analysis systems for very long baslnine interferometry and global positioning system. *Mailing Add:* Mass Inst Technol 77 Massachusetts Ave Rm 54 618 Cambridge MA 02139

HERRING, WILLIAM BENJAMIN, INTERNAL MEDICINE. *Current Pos:* RETIRED. *Personal Data:* b Pender County, NC, July 16, 28; m 50; c 2. *Educ:* Wake Forest Col, BS, 49, MD, 53; Am Bd Internal Med, dipl, 63. *Prof Exp:* Asst resident internal med, Univ Va Hosp, 56-57, fel cardiol, 57-58, fel hemat, 58-59; res fel hemat, Sch Med, Univ NC, Chapel Hill, 61-63, from asst prof to assoc prof internal med, 63-78, chief med teaching serv, Moses H Cone Mem Hosp, 67-81, prof med, 78-94. *Mem:* Am Fedn Clin Res; Am Soc Hemat; fel Am Col Physicians. *Res:* Hematology. *Mailing Add:* 6212 Dryads Ct Browns Summit NC 27214

HERRING, WILLIAM CONYERS, THEORETICAL SOLID STATE PHYSICS. *Current Pos:* prof, 78-81, EMER PROF APPL PHYSICS, STANFORD UNIV, 81- *Personal Data:* b Scotia, NY, Nov 15, 14; m 46, Louise Preusch; c Lois M, Alan J, Brian C & Gordon R. *Educ:* Univ Kans, AB, 33; Princeton Univ, PhD(math physics), 37. *Honors & Awards:* Buckley Prize, Am Phys Soc, 59; Luck Award, Nat Acad Sci, 80; Von Hippel Award, Mat Res Soc, 80; Wolf Prize Physics, 85. *Prof Exp:* Nat Res Coun fel, Mass Inst Technol, 37-39; instr math & res assoc math physics, Princeton Univ, 39-40; instr physics, Univ Mo, 40-41; mem sci staff, Div War Res, Columbia Univ, 41-45; prof, Univ Tex, 46; mem tech staff, Bell Labs, 46-78. *Concurrent Pos:* Mem, Inst Advan Study, 52-53. *Mem:* Nat Acad Sci; AAAS; fel Am Phys Soc; fel Am Acad Arts & Sci; Am Soc Info Sci; Mat Res Soc. *Res:* Theory of solids; scientific communication. *Mailing Add:* Dept Appl Physics Stanford Univ Stanford CA 94305. *Fax:* 650-725-7509

HERRINGTON, KERMIT (DALE), chemistry; deceased, see previous edition for last biography

HERRINGTON, LEE PIERCE, FOREST METEOROLOGY, GEOGRAPHIC INFORMATION SYSTEMS. *Current Pos:* exec secy, Consortium Environ Forestry Studies & Coordr, Res & Grad Studies, Sch Forestry, PROF RESOURCE INFO MGT & DIR, LAB APPL GEOG INFO SYSTS, COL ENVIRON SCI & FORESTRY, STATE UNIV NY, 91- *Personal Data:* b New Haven, Conn, June 11, 33; m 55; c 4. *Educ:* Univ Maine, BS, 59; Yale Univ, MF, 60, PhD(forest meteorol), 64. *Prof Exp:* Sr meteorologist, Melpar, Inc, Westinghouse Air Brake Co, 64-65; from asst prof to prof meteorol, State Univ NY Col Environ Sci & Forestry, 65-78; urban forest res coordr, Northeast Forest Exp Sta, US Forest Serv, 78-79; vpres, Forestry Software Assocs, 81-83, pres, 84-92. *Mem:* Am Meteorol Soc; Am Forestry Asn; Sigma Xi; Soc Am Foresters; Am Soc Photogram & Remote Sensing; Urban & Regional Info Systs Asn. *Res:* Computer applications to forest management; expert systems for resources management; urban meteorology. *Mailing Add:* 113 Janet Dr Syracuse NY 13224. *E-Mail:* lpherrin@mailbox.syr.edu

HERRINTON, PAUL MATTHEW, PROCESS RESEARCH & DEVELOPMENT, ORGANIC SYNTHETIC METHODS. *Current Pos:* RES CHEMIST, UPJOHN CO, 86- *Personal Data:* b Detroit, Mich, Sept 21, 57. *Educ:* Wayne State Univ, BS, 79; Mich State Univ, MS, 82, PhD(chem), 84. *Prof Exp:* Postdoctoral fel, Univ Calif, Irvine, 85-86; asst prof, Nazareth Col, 90-91. *Mem:* Am Chem Soc; affil mem Int Union Pure & Appl Chem. *Res:* Identify and develop new reactions and processes used in manufacturing pharmaceuticals and fine chemicals; steroids; antibiotics. *Mailing Add:* Upjohn Co Unit 1500-91-2 Kalamazoo MI 49002-0199

HERRIOT, JOHN GEORGE, COMPUTER SCIENCE, NUMERICAL ANALYSIS. *Current Pos:* from instr to prof math, Stanford Univ, 42-61, instr eng, sci & mgt war training, 45, prof, 61-82, EMER PROF COMPUT SCI, STANFORD UNIV, 82- *Personal Data:* b Winnipeg, Man, Mar 7, 16; nat US; m 41, Sarah Tribble; c Robert, Jean, James & John. *Educ:* Univ Man, BSc, 37; Brown Univ, ScM, 38, PhD(math), 41. *Honors & Awards:* Fulbright lectr, Univ Grenoble, France, 62-63. *Prof Exp:* Instr math, Brown Univ, 39-41 & Yale Univ, 41-42. *Concurrent Pos:* Physicist, Ames Aeronaut Lab, Nat Adv Comt Aeronaut, Moffett Field, Calif, 44-46; guest prof, Math Inst, Tech Univ, Munich, Ger, 69-70; guest mem, Math Res Inst, Fed Inst Technol, Zurich, Switz, 76-77; guest prof math, Inst Tech Univ, Munich, Ger, 80. *Mem:* Am Math Soc; Math Asn Am; Asn Comput Mach; Soc Indust & Appl Math. *Res:* Multiple Fourier series; potential theory; numerical analysis; computing machines; spline fuctions; partial differential equations. *Mailing Add:* Comput Sci Dept Stanford Univ Stanford CA 94305-2140. *E-Mail:* herriot@sccm.stanford.edu

HERRIOTT, ARTHUR W, ORGANIC CHEMISTRY. *Current Pos:* assoc prof, 73-80, assoc dean, Col Arts & Sci, 76-90, PROF, FLA INT UNIV, 80-, DEAN, COL ARTS & SCI, 90-, PROF, 80- *Personal Data:* b New Brighton, Pa, June 17, 41; m 64; c 2. *Educ:* Col Wooster, BA, 63; Univ Fla, PhD(chem), 67. *Prof Exp:* NSF fel chem, Princeton Univ, 67-68; asst prof, State Univ NY Albany, 68-73. *Mem:* Am Chem Soc; AAAS. *Res:* Physical organic chemistry; catalysis mechanisms; organophosphorus chemistry. *Mailing Add:* Col Arts & Scis Fla Int Univ Miami FL 33199. *E-Mail:* herriott@fiu.edu

HERRIOTT, DONALD R, OPTICS, ELECTRICAL ENGINEERING. *Current Pos:* RETIRED. *Personal Data:* b Rochester, NY, Feb 2, 28; c 4. *Educ:* Duke Univ, BA, 49; Univ Rochester, MA, 51. *Honors & Awards:* Cledo Brunetti Award, Inst Elec & Electronics Engrs; Franhofer Medal, Optical Soc Am; Res Coun Patent Yr, 79; Edison Award, 86. *Prof Exp:* Mem sci bur, Bausch & Lomb Co, 49-56; mem staff, Res Dept, Bell Lab, 56-68, head, Dept, Lithographic Syst, 68-81; sr sci adv, Perkin-Elmer Corp, 81-90. *Mem:* Nat Acad Eng; fel Optical Soc Am (pres, 84); sr mem Inst Elec & Electronics Engrs. *Res:* Lasers-optics-interferometry-electron beams. *Mailing Add:* 1237 Isabel Dr Sanibel FL 33957

HERRIOTT, JON R, BIOCHEMISTRY, BIOPHYSICS. *Current Pos:* Sr fel, Dept Biol Struct, 67-69, asst prof biochem, 69-77, ASSOC PROF BIOCHEM, UNIV WASH, 77- *Personal Data:* b New York, NY, Apr 8, 37; m 61; c 3. *Educ:* Dartmouth Col, BA, 59; Johns Hopkins Univ, PhD(biophys), 67. *Res:* Protein structure; x-ray crystallography; structure-function relationships in macromolecules; proton nuclear magnetic resonance. *Mailing Add:* C/O 11759 Palatine Ave N Seattle WA 98133

HERRLINGER, STEPHEN PAUL, AIRCRAFT & MISSILE TESTING. *Current Pos:* chief of testing, ESC/ZJ, 94-95, PROG MGR, ESC/ZJ, USAF, HANSCOM AFB, 95- *Personal Data:* b Louiseville, Ky, Nov 23, 59; m 89, Julie Louise Nelson; c Kyle H. *Educ:* Univ Akron, BS, 81; USAF Inst Technol, BS, 85; Golden Gate Univ, MS, 89; Embry Riddle Aeronaut Univ, MAeroSc, 92. *Honors & Awards:* Spec Achievement Award, Int Test & Eval Asn, 94. *Prof Exp:* Res chemist, USAF Rocket Propulsion Lab, Edwards AFB, Calif, 81-83, aerodyn engr advan cruise missile, 4200 Test & Eval Squadron, 85-86, chief, Advan Cruise Missile Aerodyn Sect, 31st Test & Eval Squadron, 86-87, chief, Advan Cruise Missile Performance, Environ Sect, 87-89; proj mgr, E-9A Surveillance Aircraft Prog, 4484th Test Squadron, Tyndall AFB, Fla, 89-91, dir, Missile Scoring Flight Test, 91-92, dir, C-27A Oper Flight Test, 84th Test Squadron, 92-94. *Concurrent Pos:* Adj instr, Gulf Coast Community Col, Univ WFla, 91-94. *Res:* Patentee in field; contributed articles to professional journals. *Mailing Add:* 35 Shaw Circle Hanscom AFB MA 01731-2414

HERRMANN, CHRISTIAN, JR, CLINICAL NEUROLOGY. *Current Pos:* from asst prof to assoc prof, 54-69, PROF NEUROL MED, SCH MED, UNIV CALIF, LOS ANGELES, 69- *Personal Data:* b Lansing, Mich, Jan 25, 21. *Educ:* Univ Mich, AB, 42, MD, 44. *Prof Exp:* Asst neurol, Columbia Univ, 50-52, instr, 52-53. *Concurrent Pos:* USPHS res fel, Columbia Univ, 52-54, vis fel, 53-54. *Mem:* Asn Res Nervous & Ment Dis; Am Neurol Asn; Am Acad Neurol; Sigma Xi. *Res:* Neurological and neuromuscular disorders, especially myasthenia gravis. *Mailing Add:* Neurol/Reed Res Ctr Univ Calif 405 Milgard Ave Los Angeles CA 90095

HERRMANN, ERNEST CARL, JR, VIROLOGY. *Current Pos:* VPRES, MOBILAB INC, 75-, LAB DIR, 81- *Personal Data:* b Elkhart, Ind, Jan 1, 25; m 70; c 2. *Educ:* Univ Md, BS, 50, MS, 51, PhD(bact), 53. *Prof Exp:* Res assoc virol, Inst Microbiol, Rutgers Univ, 53-54; head virol sect, Chemother Dept, E R Squibb & Sons, 54-56; head virol lab, Biochem Dept, Res Div, Schering Corp, 56-61; assoc prof virol, Mayo Grad Sch Med, Univ Minn & head virol lab, Mayo Clin, 61-71; assoc prof microbiol, Univ Ill Col Med, Peoria, 71-87. *Concurrent Pos:* Consult, Am Med Asn, NIH, Am Bd Bioanal & various firms & insts. *Mem:* Int Soc Antiviral Res; Am Soc Microbiol; Pan-Am Soc Clin Virol. *Res:* Antiviral agents; relation of viruses to human diseases; diagnostic virology. *Mailing Add:* Mobilab Inc 5116 Big Hollow Rd Peoria IL 61615. *Fax:* 309-691-4513; *E-Mail:* ernestc@ix.netcom.com

HERRMANN, GEORGE, STRUCTURAL MECHANICS, STRUCTURAL ACOUSTICS. *Current Pos:* chmn, Div Appl Mech, 75-84, prof appl mech & civil eng, 70-91, chmn, Dept Appl Mech, 70-91, EMER PROF, STANFORD UNIV, 91- *Personal Data:* b USSR, Apr 19, 21; US citizen. *Educ:* Swiss Fed Inst Technol, Zurich, CE, 45, PhD(mech), 49. *Honors & Awards:* Centennial Medal, Am Soc Mech Engrs, 80; Theodore von Karman Medal, Am Soc Civil Engrs, 81; Silver Anniversary, Soc Eng Sci, 88; Distinguished Serv Award, Am Acad Mech, 89. *Prof Exp:* Asst prof mech, Ecole Polytech, Montreal, 49-50; from asst prof to assoc prof, Columbia Univ, 50-62; prof, Northwestern Univ, 62-70. *Concurrent Pos:* Sci liaison officer, Dept Navy, Off Naval Res Br Off, London, 60-61; consult, Off Sci Res, USAF, 57-71, 64-69, Eng Sci Div, US Army, Insect Repellent Res Inst, 70-80, Aerospace Corp, 72-76; adv eval panels, Grad Traineeship Progs, NSF, 64 & 65; res assoc, Lab Exp Surg, Swiss Res Inst, Davos, Switz, 69-70; co-organizer, Conf Continuum Mech Solids, Oberwolfach, Ger, 81, 83, 86 & 90; mem, Comt Recommendations, US Army Basic Sci Res, Nat Res Coun, 81-84. *Mem:* Nat Acad Eng; Am Soc Civil Engrs; hon mem Am Soc Mech Engrs; assoc fel Am Inst Aeronaut & Astronaut; Am Soc Eng Educ; Am Acad Mech; Acoust Soc Am; Biomed Eng Soc; Soc Appl Math & Mech; Int Soc Interaction Mech & Math. *Res:* Wave propagation; acoustoelasticity; composite materials dynamics; dynamic stability; dynamic fracture mechanics; conservation laws in continuum mechanics. *Mailing Add:* Dept Mech Eng Div Appl Mech Durand Bldg Stanford Univ Stanford CA 94305-4040

HERRMANN, HEINZ, CHEMICAL EMBRYOLOGY. *Current Pos:* RETIRED. *Personal Data:* b Vienna, Austria, Oct 17, 11; US citizen; m 47; c 1. *Educ:* Univ Vienna, MD, 36. *Prof Exp:* Res asst biochem, Univ Vienna, 32-36; Rask-Oerstedt fel tissue culture & protein chem, Carlsberg Labs, Carlsberg Found, 36-39; instr ophthal, Sch Med, Johns Hopkins Univ, 39-46; asst prof embryol, Yale Univ, 46-49; assoc prof pediat & head lab chem embryol, Sch Med, Univ Colo, 49-59; prof, Univ Conn, 59-79, emer prof biol, 79- *Concurrent Pos:* Corresp comt develop biol, Nat Acad Sci, 53-55; mem study sect morphogenesis & genetics, NIH, 55-58 & cell biol, 60-64; res prof, Am Cancer Soc, 60-80; vis prof NATO, Univ Milan, 71. *Mem:* Am Soc Cell Biol; Am Soc Biol Chem; Soc Develop Biol. *Res:* Molecular mechanisms of embryonic development, particularly control of protein synthesis; relationship of cell structure and function on the molecular level; author of several books and papers about cell biology, philosophy of biology and philosophy of science. *Mailing Add:* Prof Cell Biol 12 Sycamore Dr Storrs CT 06268-3125

HERRMANN, JOHN BELLOWS, MEDICINE, SURGERY, VASCULAR SURGERY. *Current Pos:* vchmn, Dept Surg, 83-96, PROF SURG, UNIV MASS MED SCH, WORCESTER, 72- *Personal Data:* b Cincinnati, Ohio, Nov 21, 32; m 60, Mary J Gaiser; c Christian L, Karen & Mark E. *Educ:* Dartmouth Col, AB, 54, cert med, 55; Harvard Med Sch, MD, 57; Am Bd Surg, dipl, 63. *Prof Exp:* Intern surg, Mass Gen Hosp, Boston, 57-58, resident, 58-62, clin asst, 64-65; resident surgeon, Walter Reed Army Inst Res, 62-64; from asst prof to assoc prof surg, Georgetown Univ, 65-72; chief of surg, Worcester City Hosp, 72-83. *Concurrent Pos:* Asst chief of surg, Vet Admin Hosp, Washington, DC, 65-72. *Mem:* AMA; fel Am Col Surg; Asn Acad Surg. *Res:* Experimental surgery; vascular physiology; wound healing; experimental pathology; surgical education. *Mailing Add:* Dept Surg Univ Mass Med Sch 55 Lake Ave N Worcester MA 01655

HERRMANN, KENNETH L, MEDICINE, VIROLOGY. *Current Pos:* RETIRED. *Personal Data:* b Cincinnati, Ohio, Nov 16, 34; m 59, Sara Evens; c 3. *Educ:* Dartmouth Col, AB, 56; Harvard Med Sch, MD, 59. *Prof Exp:* Rotating intern, Strong Mem Hosp, Med Ctr, Univ Rochester, 59-61, resident pediat, 61-62; med officer, Ctr Dis Control, USPHS, 62-93, dep dir, Div Viral & Rickettsial Dis, 85-93. *Concurrent Pos:* Asst chief resident pediat, Buffalo Children's Hosp, NY, 66-67. *Mem:* AMA; Sigma Xi; Am Soc Microbiol. *Res:* Methods of diagnostic virology; rubella virus infection. *Mailing Add:* 460 Chelsea Circle NE 1600 Clifton Rd NE Atlanta GA 30307

HERRMANN, KENNETH WALTER, PHYSICAL CHEMISTRY, SURFACE CHEMISTRY. *Current Pos:* RETIRED. *Personal Data:* b Chicago, Ill, Dec 13, 29; m 51; c 5. *Educ:* Valparaiso Univ, BA, 51; Iowa State Univ, PhD(rare earth phys properties), 55. *Prof Exp:* Res chemist, Procter & Gamble Co, 55-62, head, Surface Chem Sect, 62-66 & Oral Prods Res Sect, Winton Hill Tech Ctr, 66-68, assoc dir, Toilet Goods Prod Res, 68-72, assoc dir, Corp Res & Develop, Int Toilet Goods, 72-74, assoc dir, Tech Serv Dept, Bar Soap & Household Cleaning Prod Div, 74-81, mgr, Prod Safety & Regulatory Serv, Sharon Woods Tech Ctr, 81-90. *Mem:* Am Chem Soc; Int Asn Dent Res. *Res:* Physical-metallurgical properties of rare earth elements; modification of chemical, surface and mechanical properties of fibrous proteins; micellar, surface, adsorption and phase properties of surfactants; dental research; chemistry of biological systems; toxicology. *Mailing Add:* 830 Carini Lane Cincinnati OH 45218

HERRMANN, KLAUS MANFRED, BIOCHEMISTRY, MOLECULAR BIOLOGY. *Current Pos:* from asst prof to prof, 69-83, PROF BIOCHEM, PURDUE UNIV, 83- *Personal Data:* b Lingen, Ger, June 27, 37; m 70; c 2. *Educ:* Univ Munster, Diplomchem Vorexamen, 60; Univ Freiburg, Diplomchem Hauptexamen, 64, Dr rer nat(chem), 66. *Prof Exp:* German Res Found grants, Univ Freiburg, 66-67 & Stanford Univ, 67-68, res assoc, 68-69. *Concurrent Pos:* Chmn, Univ Senak, 85-86; asst dean, Grad Sch, 86-87. *Mem:* Am Soc Biol Chemists; Am Soc Plant Physiol. *Res:* Molecular genetics; allosteric enzymes. *Mailing Add:* Dept Biochem Purdue Univ West Lafayette IN 47907-1968

HERRMANN, LEO ANTHONY, GEOLOGY. *Current Pos:* RETIRED. *Personal Data:* b San Antonio, Fla, Oct 14, 25; m 47; c 4. *Educ:* Miami Univ, Ohio, BS, 47; Johns Hopkins Univ, PhD, 51. *Prof Exp:* Party chief geol & geophys, NJ Zinc Co, 51-53, resident geologist, 53-56; explor geologist, Magnolia Petrol Co Div, Socony Mobil Oil Co, Inc, 56-59; sr explor geologist, Mobil Oil Co Div, 59-66; assoc prof geol, La Tech Univ, 66-70, prof, 70-89, head, Dept Geosci, 72-89. *Concurrent Pos:* Asst geologist, Ga Geol Surv, 49-50; consult various industs, 66- *Mem:* Fel Geol Soc Am; Am Asn Petrol Geologists; Sigma Xi. *Res:* Exploration for petroleum; computer applications in exploration; subsurface stratigraphy. *Mailing Add:* 1402 St John Ave Ruston LA 71270

HERRMANN, LEONARD R(ALPH), CIVIL ENGINEERING, APPLIED MECHANICS. *Current Pos:* chmn, Civil Eng Dept, 72-76, PROF CIVIL ENG, UNIV CALIF, DAVIS, 65- *Personal Data:* b Quinn, SDak, Mar 21, 36; m 57, 88; c 2. *Educ:* Univ Calif, Berkeley, BS, 58, MS, 60, PhD(civil eng), 62. *Prof Exp:* Sr res engr, Aerojet-Gen Corp, 62-65. *Concurrent Pos:* Consult, Aerojet-Gen Corp, 65-, Thiokol Chem Corp, 67-69, Calif Dept Water Resources, 68-69 & Div Hwys, 69-, Lockheed Corp, 70, Sandia Corp, 71 & United Technol, 77. *Mem:* Am Soc Civil Engrs. *Res:* Structural mechanics; development and application of finite element procedure; material characterization. *Mailing Add:* Dept Civil Eng Univ Calif Davis CA 95616

HERRMANN, RAYMOND, NATURAL RESOURCES MANAGEMENT, WATERSHED SCIENCES. *Current Pos:* Hydrologist/geologist, Southeast Region, Nat Park Serv, 73-74, chief, Natural Sci Res Div, 74-79, chief, Air & Water Resources Div, 79-81, dir, Water Resources, Field Support Lab, 81-85, chief appl res br, Water Resources Div, 85-90, leader, Water Resources Coop Park Studies Unit, 90-93, NAT PARK SURV, NAT BIOL SURV, 93-96, WATERSHED RES USGS, 96- *Personal Data:* b Chicago, Ill, July 16, 41; m 65; c 2. *Educ:* Columbia Univ, BS, 68; Univ Wyo, MS, 72, PhD(geol), 72. *Honors & Awards:* Presidents Award Outstanding Serv, Am Water Resources Asn, 96. *Concurrent Pos:* Assoc fac, Colo State Univ, 81-; adj assoc prof, Univ Tenn, Knoxville, 80-82. *Mem:* Fel Am Water Resources Asn (vpres, 86, pres, 88); fel Geol Soc Am; AAAS; Sigma Xi; Am Geophys Union. *Res:* Study the effects of low level acid inputs on park streams and aquatic resources; technology assessment research as related to development of remote natural area monitoring and research; geologic and water resources research and applications directed towards solution of natural resources management problems; long term watershed/ecological investigations in parks and equivalent reserves in parks and equivalent reserves US/Russia bilateral research. *Mailing Add:* 927 Greenfields Ft Collins CO 80524. *E-Mail:* wrcpsu@lamar.colostate.edu

HERRMANN, ROBERT ARTHUR, NONSTANDARD LOGIC, NONSTANDARD MODELS. *Current Pos:* PROF MATH, US NAVAL ACAD, ANNAPOLIS, MD, 68- *Personal Data:* b Baltimore, Md, Apr 29, 34; m 69; c 3. *Educ:* Johns Hopkins Univ, BA, 63; Am Univ, MA, 68, PhD(math), 73. *Concurrent Pos:* Adv, US Cong, 68-; proin investr, US Naval Acad Res Coun, 76-; dir, Inst Math Philos, 80- *Mem:* Sigma Xi; Am Math Soc; Math Asn Am. *Res:* Mathematical philosophy; mathematical logic; nonstandard analysis; model theory; applied mathematics; general topology; philosophical and natural system models; author and coauther of over 150 articles and reports. *Mailing Add:* Math Dept US Naval Acad 572 Holloway Rd Annapolis MD 21402-5002. *E-Mail:* rah@nadn.navy.mil

HERRMANN, ROBERT BERNARD, SEISMOLOGY. *Current Pos:* from asst to assoc prof, 75-83, PROF GEOPHYS, ST LOUIS UNIV, 83- *Personal Data:* b Cincinnati, Ohio, Dec 22, 44; m; c 2. *Educ:* Xavier Univ, Ohio, BS, 67; St Louis Univ, PhD(geophys), 74. *Prof Exp:* Res assoc geophys, Coop Inst Res Environ Sci, Univ Colo, 74-75. *Mem:* Seismol Soc Am; Am Geophys Union; Soc Explor Geophysicists. *Res:* Transmission of elastic waves; prediction of ground motion due to local earthquakes. *Mailing Add:* Dept Earth Sci St Louis Univ 221 N Grand Blvd St Louis MO 63103-2006

HERRMANN, ROBERT LAWRENCE, BIOCHEMISTRY, BIOETHICS & SCIENCE EDUCATION. *Current Pos:* lectr, 81-82, exec dir, Am Sci Affil, 81-93, ADJ PROF CHEM, GORDON COL, 82-; PROG DIR, JOHN TEMPLETON FOUND, 90- *Personal Data:* b New York, NY, July 17, 28; m 50, Elizabeth A Cook; c Stephen, Karen, Holly & Anders. *Educ:* Purdue Univ, BS, 51; Mich State Univ, PhD(biochem), 56. *Honors & Awards:* Staley lectr, Gordon Col, 74, Stony Brook, 84, Eastern Col, 85, Trinity Col, 87. *Prof Exp:* Asst biochem, Mich State Univ, 52-56; res assoc, Mass Inst Technol, 58-59; from asst prof to assoc prof biochem, Sch Med, Boston Univ, 59-76; prof biochem & chmn dept, Schs Med & Dent, Oral Roberts Univ, 76-81, assoc dean biomed sci, 77-79. *Concurrent Pos:* Damon Runyon fel, Mass Inst Technol, 56-58; trustee, Barrington Col, 76-79, Templeton Found, 86-, Southeastern Mass Univ, 88-; chmn, Med Ethic Comn, Christian Med Soc, 76-83. *Mem:* Fel AAAS; Soc Health Human Values; fel Geront Soc; Am Soc Biol Chem; fel Am Sci Affil; Victoria Inst, Philos Soc Gt Brit; Sigma Xi. *Res:* Biochemical genetics; enzyme structure and mechanism; viral etiology of cancer; genetic mechanisms of aging. *Mailing Add:* Dept Chem Gordon Col 255 Grapevine Rd Wenham MA 01984. *Fax:* 978-524-3708; *E-Mail:* herrmann@gordonc.edu

HERRMANN, SCOTT JOSEPH, TRICHOPTERA & CHIRONOMIDAE, SYSTEMATICS & ECOLOGY. *Current Pos:* From asst prof to assoc prof, 68-77, PROF BIOL, UNIV SOUTHERN COLO, 77- *Personal Data:* b Chicago, Ill, Apr 6, 42; m 67; c 3. *Educ:* Northern Ill Univ, BS, 64; Univ Colo, PhD(zool), 68. *Mem:* Am Entom Soc; NAm Benthol Soc. *Res:* Chemical and physical limnology as applied to trace metal pollution; systematics and ecology of Trichoptera, Plecoptera and Chironomidae, especially in alpine environments. *Mailing Add:* Dept Biol Univ Southern Colo 2200 Bonforte Blvd Pueblo CO 81001-4901. *Fax:* 719-549-2732; *E-Mail:* herrmann@starburst.uscolo.edu

HERRMANN, STEVEN H, BIOCHEMISTRY, CELL BIOLOGY. *Current Pos:* AT DEPT CELL IMMUNOL, GENETICS INST. *Educ:* Wash Univ, PhD(biochem), 78. *Prof Exp:* Assoc prof path, Med Sch, Harvard Univ, 84- *Mailing Add:* Dept Cell Immunol Genetics Inst 87 Cambridge Park Dr Cambridge MA 02140-2387. *Fax:* 617-498-8878

HERRMANN, ULRICH OTTO, PHYSICS. *Current Pos:* from asst prof to assoc prof, 61-75, PROF PHYSICS, UNIV TEX, ARLINGTON, 75- *Personal Data:* b Schneidemuhl, Ger, Mar 27, 25; m 53; c 2. *Educ:* Univ Giessen, BS, 51, MS, 53, PhD(physics), 56. *Prof Exp:* Res physicist, Well Surv, Inc Div, Dresser Industs, 56-58; staff physicist, Jet Res Ctr, Inc, 58-61. *Mem:* AAAS; Am Asn Physics Teachers; Am Astronaut Soc. *Res:* Radioactive well logging; explosive shaped charges; crystal optics and colorimetry. *Mailing Add:* 913 Shady Oaks Ct Arlington TX 76012

HERRMANN, WALTER, CONSTITUTIVE EQUATIONS, WAVE PROPAGATION IN SOLIDS. *Current Pos:* RETIRED. *Personal Data:* b Johannesburg, SAfrica, May 2, 30; US citizen; m 54; c Peter F & Inga L. *Educ:* Univ Witwatersrand, BSc, 51, PhD(eng), 55. *Prof Exp:* Res engr, Aeroelastic & Struct Res Lab, Mass Inst Technol, 53-55, sr res engr, 57-59, aeronaut res engr, 59-64; lectr mech eng, Univ Cape Town, 55-57; div supvr, Sandia Corp, 64-67, dept mgr, 67-82, dir eng sci, Sandia Nat Labs, 82-90, sr fel, 90-93. *Mem:* Nat Acad Eng; Am Soc Mech Engrs; Am Phys Soc. *Res:* Transient compressible aerodynamics; shock tubes; hypervelocity impact; stress waves in solids; elastic-plastic shell response; constitutive equations. *Mailing Add:* 13800 Winterwood Way SE Albuquerque NM 87123-4345

HERRMANN, WALTER L, obstetrics & gynecology, for more information see previous edition

HERRMANNN, MARILYN MURDOCH, PUBLIC HEALTH, NURSING. *Current Pos:* instr community health nursing, 80-83, asst prof, Sch Nursing, 83-89, ASSOC DEAN UNDERGRAD PROG, SCH NURSING, LOMA LINDA UNIV, 89- *Personal Data:* b Gt Brit, Nov 9, 43; US citizen; m 65, Enoch Clifford; c Paul Clifford & Ruth Marie. *Educ:* Columbia Union Col, BS, 65; Loma Linda Univ, MS, 80; Claremont Grad Sch, PhD(educ), 92. *Prof Exp:* Pub Health Nurse, Floyd Co, Va, 66-68. *Mem:* Am Pub Health Asn. *Res:* Teenage parenting and self esteem; parenting competence. *Mailing Add:* PO Box 437 Loma Linda CA 92354

HERRMANNSFELDT, WILLIAM BERNARD, ELECTRON OPTICS, PARTICLE ACCELERATOR APPLICATIONS. *Current Pos:* MEM STAFF, STANFORD LINEAR ACCELERATOR CTR, 62- *Personal Data:* b Chicago, Ill, Apr 22, 31; m 54, Marcia Bowman; c Glen A & Paul W. *Educ:* Univ Educ: Miami Univ, Ohio, AB, 53; Univ Ill, MS, 55, PhD(physics), 58. *Prof Exp:* Mem staff, Los Alamos Sci Lab, 58-62. *Concurrent Pos:* Consult work in electron gun design, 65-; br chief, Am Eng Coun/Electronic Resources Develop Agency, 74-76; mem fusion policy adv comt, Dept Energy, 90; vchmn, Div Physics Beams, Am Phys Soc. *Mem:* Fel Am Phys Soc; AAAS. *Res:* Design and planning for high energy accelerators and storage rings; heavy ion accelerators for inertially confined fusions; computer modeling of charged particle beams; electron gun design; fusion energy. *Mailing Add:* 451 Patrick Way Los Alamos NM 94022

HERRNKIND, WILLIAM FRANK, ANIMAL BEHAVIOR, MARINE BIOLOGY. *Current Pos:* From asst prof to assoc prof, 67-80, PROF BIOL SCI, FLA STATE UNIV, 80- *Personal Data:* b Bayshore, NY, Oct 15, 40; m 62; c 2. *Educ:* State Univ NY Albany, BS, 61; Univ Miami, MS, 65, PhD(marine biol), 68. *Mem:* AAAS; Am Inst Biol Sci; Am Soc Zoologists; Animal Behav Soc; Sigma Xi. *Res:* Orientation of marine animals, especially crustaceans, the adaptive significance and functional mechanisms; ontogenetic development of orientational and related behavior. *Mailing Add:* Dept Biol Sci B-10 Unit I Fla State Univ Tallahassee FL 32306

HERRO, JOHN JOSEPH, SOFTWARE FOR EQUIPMENT FOR TELEPHONE OPERATORS, EDUCATIONAL SOFTWARE. *Current Pos:* PRES, SOFTWARE INNOVATIONS TECHNOL, 88-; SOFTWARE ANALYST, GOLDEN ENTERPRISES INC, 89- *Personal Data:* b Watertown, Wis, Oct 3, 45; m 72, Beverly Franz; c Carla, Brian & Emily. *Educ:* Ill Inst Technol, BS, 67, MS, 68, PhD(elec eng), 73. *Prof Exp:* Assoc engr, Ill Inst Technol Res Inst, 72-75; tech staff mem, Logicon Inc, 75-77; systs analyst, Cincinnati Electronics Corp, 77-78; sr software engr, Gen Elec Co, 78-86; staff software engr, Grumman Aerospace Corp, 86-88 & Harris Corp, 88-89. *Concurrent Pos:* Teacher & software eng ADA State Univ NY, Binhamton, 85 & Fla Inst Technol Melbourne, 88-89. *Mem:* Asn Comput Mach. *Res:* Written and published software to teach the ADA programming language; developing software for telephone operator equipment. *Mailing Add:* 1083 Mandarin Dr NE Palm Bay FL 32905-4706. *Fax:* 407-259-0027; *E-Mail:* johnherro@aol.com

HERROD, HENRY GRADY, IMMUNOLOGY, PEDIATRICS. *Current Pos:* PROF PEDIAT, UNIV MEMPHIS, 78- *Educ:* Univ Ala, MD, 72. *Mem:* Soc Pediat Res; Am Asn Immunologists; Am Acad Allergy Immunol. *Res:* Allergy immunology. *Mailing Add:* Le Bonheur Children's Med Ctr 850 Poplar Ave Memphis TN 38105

HERRON, DAVID KENT, MEDICINAL CHEMISTRY. *Current Pos:* sr chemist, 71-77, res scientist, 77-84, SR RES SCIENTIST, ELI LILLY & CO, 84- *Personal Data:* b Toledo, Ohio, Apr 30, 42; m 66, Helen Arnold; c Michael & Katherine. *Educ:* Carleton Col, BA, 64; Rockefeller Univ, PhD(life sci), 69. *Honors & Awards:* Indust Grand Challenge Award, Nat Ctr Supercomput Appln, 92. *Prof Exp:* Fel chem, Harvard Univ, 69-71. *Mem:* Am Chem Soc; AAAS; NY Acad Sci; Shock Soc; Asn Comput Mach; Molecular Graphics Soc Am. *Res:* Design and synthesis of new agents for the treatment of diseases; scientific applications of supercomputers. *Mailing Add:* 5945 Andover Rd Indianapolis IN 46220-5320. *Fax:* 317-276-1417; *E-Mail:* dkherron@lilly.com

HERRON, GEORGE M, soil science, for more information see previous edition

HERRON, ISOM H, FLUID MECHANICS, STABILITY THEORY. *Current Pos:* PROF, RENSSELAER POLYTECH INST, 91- *Personal Data:* b St Louis, Mo, Sept 8, 46; m 81; c 1. *Educ:* Mass Inst Technol, BS, 67; Johns Hopkins Univ, PhD(mechanics), 73. *Prof Exp:* Res fel appl math, Calif Inst Technol, 72-73; from asst prof to prof math, Howard Univ, 74-91. *Concurrent Pos:* Vis scholar & vis assoc prof, Northwestern Univ, 81-82; Ford Found postdoctoral fel, Nat Res Coun, 88-; vis res assoc, Univ Md, Inst Phys Sci & Technol, 88-89. *Mem:* Am Math Soc; Math Asn Am; Am Phys Soc; Soc Indust & Appl Math. *Res:* Applied mathematics; problems in fluids mechanics; stability of flows; ORR-Sommerfeld equation; spectral theory. *Mailing Add:* Dept Math Sci Rensselaer Polytech Inst Troy NY 12180-3590

HERRON, JAMES DUDLEY, SCIENCE EDUCATION, CHEMISTRY. *Current Pos:* CHAIR, DEPT PHYS SCI, MOREHEAD STATE UNIV, 94- *Personal Data:* b Providence, Ky, June 15, 36; m 56, Joyce Kincer; c D Keith & B Alan. *Educ:* Univ Ky, AB, 58; Univ NC, MS, 60; Fla State Univ, PhD(sci educ), 65. *Honors & Awards:* Catalyst of the Year, Chem Mfg Asn, 83. *Prof Exp:* Prof chem & educ, Purdue Univ, 77-91, head, Div Chem & Educ, 83-86, dir, Sch Math & Sci Ctr, 87-89, head, Dept Curric & Instr, 89-91. *Concurrent Pos:* Consult & ctr coordr, Intermediate Sci Curric Study, 66-72; training adv, Regional Educ Ctr Sci & Math, Penang, Malaysia, 72-73. *Mem:* Fel AAAS; Am Chem Soc; Nat Asn Res Sci Teaching; Nat Sci Teachers Asn; Asn Educ Teachers Sci. *Res:* Science curriculum development; techniques of evaluating science achievement; application of theories of cognitive psychology to teaching chemistry; problem solving; curriculum development. *Mailing Add:* 1576 Perkins St Morehead KY 40351-1689. *Fax:* 606-783-5002; *E-Mail:* d.herron@msuacad.morehead__st.edu

HERRON, JAMES WATT, BOTANY. *Current Pos:* from asst botanist to assoc botanist, 52-57, assoc prof hort & assoc horticulturist, 57-67, EXTEN PROF AGRON, AGR EXP STA, UNIV KY, 67- *Personal Data:* b Beaver, Pa, May 27, 20; m 43; c 2. *Educ:* Pa State Teachers Col, BS, 41; Cornell Univ, MS, 48, PhD(econ bot), 51. *Prof Exp:* Pub sch teacher, Pa, 41-44 & 45-47; instr econ bot, Cornell Univ, 51-52. *Mem:* Weed Sci Soc Am; Am Soc Hort Sci. *Res:* Weed control; agronomic crops, horticultural crops, turf and aquatic weeds; economic botany. *Mailing Add:* 278 Farmington Rd Lexington KY 40502

HERRON, JOHN THOMAS, PHYSICAL CHEMISTRY. *Current Pos:* Res chemist, 57-80, chief, Chem Kinetics Div, 80-84, DIR, CHEM KINETICS DATA CTR, NAT BUR STANDARDS, 84- *Personal Data:* b Winnipeg, Man, Jan 19, 31; US citizen; m 59; c 3. *Educ:* Univ Man, BSc, 53, MSc, 55; McGill Univ, PhD(chem), 57. *Mem:* AAAS; Am Chem Soc; Combustion Inst. *Res:* Application of mass spectrometry to the study of free radicals and gas kinetics; air pollution and combustion chemistry; data evaluation. *Mailing Add:* 19120 Roman Way Gaithersburg MD 20879

HERRON, MICHAEL MYRL, SEDIMENTARY GEOCHEMISTRY, GEOCHEMICAL WELL LOGGING. *Current Pos:* RES SCIENTIST, SCHLUMBERGER-DOLL RES, 82- *Personal Data:* b Chula Vista, Calif, Oct 12, 49; m 77; c 2. *Educ:* Univ Calif, San Diego, BA, 70; State Univ NY, PhD(geol sci), 80. *Prof Exp:* Res asst prof geol, State Univ NY, 80-82. *Mem:* Soc Prof Well Log Analysts; Soc Petrol Engrs; Am Asn Petrol Geologists. *Res:* Sedimentary geochemistry and geochemical well logging. *Mailing Add:* 21 Beaver Brook Rd Ridgefield CT 06877-0001

HERRON, NORMAN, ZEOLITE CHEMISTRY, CATALYSIS. *Current Pos:* RES ASSOC INORG CHEM, E I DUPONT DE NEMOURS & CO INC, CR&D, WILMINGTON, DEL, 83- *Personal Data:* b Newcastle-upon-Tyne, UK, July 14, 54; m 77; c 2. *Educ:* Univ Warwick, Coventry, UK, BSc, 75, PhD(chem), 78. *Prof Exp:* Teaching fel inorg chem, Ohio State Univ, Columbus, 79-81, sr res asst, 81-83. *Res:* Inorganic coordination chemistry; synthesis and characterization of novel homogeneous and solid state materials. *Mailing Add:* 408 Apple Rd Newark DE 19711

HERRUP, KARL, GENETICS. *Current Pos:* DIR DIV DEVELOP NEUROBIOL, E K SHRIVER CTR, 88-; PROF NEUROL & NEUROSCI, CASE WESTERN RES MED SCH, 92- *Personal Data:* b Pittsburgh, Pa, July 16, 48; c 3. *Educ:* Brandeis Univ, BA, 70; Stanford Univ, PhD(neurosci, biobehav sci), 75. *Prof Exp:* Res assoc neuropath, Harvard Med Sch, 74-78, res asst neurosci, Children's Hosp Med Ctr, 74-78; from asst prof to assoc prof human genetics, Med Sch, Yale Univ, 78-88; assoc prof neurol, Mass Gen Hosp, 88-92; assoc prof neurosci prog, Harvard Med Sch, 88-92. *Concurrent Pos:* Jane Coffin Childs Mem Fund Med Res fel, 74-76; Med Found fel, 76-78; fel, Dept Pharmacol, Bioctr, Univ Basel, 78; Andrew Mellon Found fel, 84; Cornelius Wiersma vis prof neurosci, Div Biol, Calif Tech, 86. *Mem:* Soc Neurosci; Soc Develop Biol. *Res:* Developmental genetics of the nervous system from the perspective of quantitative cell biology with emphasis on neurological mutants of cerebellar development, mutant-wild type chimeric mice and transgenic mice. *Mailing Add:* Case Western Res Med Sch Alzheimer Res Lab 10900 Euclid Ave Cleveland OH 44106. *Fax:* 216-368-3079; *E-Mail:* kxh@po.cwru.edu

HERSCHBACH, DUDLEY ROBERT, CHEMICAL PHYSICS. *Current Pos:* prof chem, Harvard Univ, 63-76, chmn chem physics prog, 64-77, chmn, Dept Chem, 77-80, mem, Fac Coun, 80-83, BAIRD PROF SCI, HARVARD UNIV, 76- *Personal Data:* b San Jose, Calif, June 18, 32; m 64, Georgene; c 2. *Educ:* Stanford Univ, BS, 54, MS, 55; Harvard Univ, AM, 56, PhD(chem physics), 58. *Hon Degrees:* DSc, Univ Toronto, 77, Cornell Col, 83, Framingham State, 89, Adelphi Univ, 90, Dartmouth Col, 92, Charles Univ, Prague, 93 & Univ Ill, 94. *Honors & Awards:* Nobel Prize, 86; Phillips Lectr, Haverford Col, 62; Pure Chem Prize, 65; Rollefson Lectr, Univ Calif, Berkeley, 69; Reilly Lectr, Univ Notre Dame, 69; Phillips Lectr, Univ Pittsburgh, 71; Gordon Lectr, Univ Toronto, 71; Spiers Medal, 76; Centenary Medal, 77; Pauling Medal, 78; Clark Mem Lectr, San Jose State Univ, 79; Clark Lectr, WVa Univ, 81; Flygare Lectr, Univ Ill, 88, Kaufman Lectr, Univ Pittsburgh, 89; Priestly Lectr, Pa State Univ, 90; Polanyi Medal, 81; Langmuir Prize, 83; Nat Medal of Sci, 91; Jaroslav Heyrovsky Medal, 92; Kosolapoff Award, 94; William Walker Prize, 94. *Prof Exp:* Jr fel chem, Harvard Univ, 57-59; from asst prof to assoc prof, Univ Calif, Berkeley, 59-63. *Concurrent Pos:* Alfred P Sloan res fel, 59-63; Falk-Plaut Lectr, Columbia Univ, 63; vis prof, Univ Gottingen, 63; Harvard lectr, Yale Univ, 64; Guggenheim fel, 68; vis fel, Joint Inst Lab Astrophys, Colo, 68-69; consult, Los Alamos Nat Lab & Aerodyne Corp, 74-; Fluorocarbon Res Panel, 74-86; Fairchild scholar, Calif Inst Technol, 76; assoc ed, J Phys Chem, 80-88; Exxon fac fel, 81-; trustee, Herschbach Fund Arts, 86- *Mem:* Nat Acad Sci; fel AAAS; fel Am Acad Arts & Sci; fel Am Phys Soc; Am Chem Soc; fel Royal Chem Soc; fel Am Philos Soc; Archimedes Soc; Sigma Xi. *Res:* Theory of molecular spectra, collision processes and electronic structure; molecular beam scattering; dynamics of chemical reactions; molecular beam studies of reaction stereodynamics; intermolecular forces in liquids; dimensional scaline approach to electronic structure. *Mailing Add:* Dept Chem & Chem Biol Harvard Univ 12 Oxford St Cambridge MA 02138

HERSCHLER, MICHAEL SAUL, EMBRYOLOGY, CYTOGENETICS. *Current Pos:* From asst prof to assoc prof biol, 64-80, PROF LIFE SCI, OTTERBEIN COL, 80- *Personal Data:* b New York, NY, July 22, 36; m 57; c 3. *Educ:* Cornell Univ, BS, 58; Ohio State Univ, MSc, 61, PhD(cytogenetics), 64. *Concurrent Pos:* NIH res grant, 66-69. *Res:* Cytogenetics of the genus anthurium. *Mailing Add:* Life & Earth Sci Otterbein Col Westerville OH 43081-2006

HERSCHMAN, HARVEY R, BIOLOGICAL CHEMISTRY, CELL BIOLOGY. *Current Pos:* from asst prof to assoc prof, 69-79, PROF BIOL CHEM, SCH MED, UNIV CALIF, LOS ANGELES, 79- *Personal Data:* b Cleveland, Ohio, June 21, 40; m 69. *Educ:* Rice Univ, BA, 62; Univ Calif, San Diego, PhD(cell biol), 67. *Concurrent Pos:* USPHS trainee, Brandeis Univ, 67-69; mem, Molecular Biol Inst, Univ Calif, Los Angeles, 69-, mem, Brain Res Inst, 70-; assoc dir, Lab Biomed & Environ Sci & dir basic res progs, Univ Calif, Los Angeles-Jonsson Comprehensive Cancer Ctr, 81- *Res:* Control of gene expression; regulation of cell division and cell cycle; mechanisms of carcinogenesis. *Mailing Add:* Dept Biochem Univ Calif Sch Med 10833 Le Conte Ave Los Angeles CA 90024-1300

HERSCHORN, MICHAEL, ANALYSIS, FUNCTIONAL ANALYSIS. *Current Pos:* Lectr, McGill Univ, 54-59, from asst prof to assoc prof, 59-79, assoc dean fac sci, 69-78, dean students, 78-82, chmn, dept math & statist, 82-88, PROF MATH, MCGILL UNIV, 79- *Personal Data:* b Montreal, Que, Apr 21, 33; m 54, 89; c 2. *Educ:* McGill Univ, BA, 53, MA, 56, PhD(math), 58. *Concurrent Pos:* Vis mem, Courant Inst Math Sci, NY Univ, 60-61. *Mem:* AAAS; Am Math Soc; Math Asn Am; Can Math Soc; Am Schs Oriental Res. *Res:* Uniqueness, stability and oscillation theorems for ordinary differential equations. *Mailing Add:* Dept Math & Statist McGill Univ 805 Sherbrooke St W Montreal PQ H3A 2K6 Can

HERSCOVICS, ANNETTE ANTOINETTE, BIOCHEMISTRY. *Current Pos:* assoc prof, Fac Med, 81-87, PROF, MCGILL CANCER CTR, DEPT MED & BIOCHEM, MCGILL UNIV, 87-, PROF, DEPT ONCOL, 92- *Personal Data:* b Paris, France, June 29, 38; c 1. *Educ:* McGill Univ, Montreal, BSc, 59, PhD(biochem), 63. *Prof Exp:* Res fel biochem, McGill-Montreal Gen Hosp Res Inst, 62-63; res fel biochem, Dept Anat, McGill Univ, 63-67, lectr, 67-69, asst prof, 69-71; res assoc biol chem, Harvard Univ Med Sch, 71-75, prin res assoc, 75-81. *Concurrent Pos:* Damon Runyon Mem Fund res fel, 62-63; vis fel biochem, Mass Gen Hosp, 71-74, asst biochemist, 74-81. *Mem:* Biochem Soc; Can Biochem Soc; Soc Complex Carbohydrates; Am Soc Biol Chemists; Am Soc Cell Biol. *Res:* Structure function and biosynthesis of complex carbohydrates in animal cells. *Mailing Add:* McGill Cancer Ctr 3655 Drummond St Montreal PQ H3G 1Y6 Can. *Fax:* 514-398-6769; *E-Mail:* annette@medcor.mcgill.ca

HERSCOWITZ, HERBERT BERNARD, IMMUNOLOGY, MICROBIOLOGY. *Current Pos:* PROF MICROBIOL, SCH MED, GEORGETOWN UNIV, 81- *Personal Data:* b Brooklyn, NY, June 19, 39; m 61, Ellen C Levine; c Robert, Stefanie & Andrew. *Educ:* Brooklyn Col, BS, 61; Long Island Univ, MS, 63; Hahnemann Univ, PhD(microbiol), 68. *Honors & Awards:* Reteculoendothelial Soc Award, 85. *Prof Exp:* Asst instr microbiol, Sch Dent Med, Univ Pa, 62-65; chief bacteriologist, Med Arts Labs, 65-66; from asst prof to assoc prof, Sch Med & Dent, 70-81. *Concurrent Pos:* USPHS fel immunol, Case Western Res Univ, 68-70; consult, Dynatech Labs-Cooke Eng, Coleman Assocs, Nat Geog Soc, Prentice-Hall Publishers, Westinghouse Elec Corp, Off Extramural Res & Training, NIH, Off Protection from Res Risks, NIH & Hybritech, Inc; guest worker, Lab Immunol, Nat Inst Allergy & Infectious Dis, 78-79; mem, Vincent T Lombardi Cancer Res Ctr, Georgetown Univ Med Ctr, 89-, Exp Immunol Study Sect, NIH, DRG, 89-93; chmn, Exp Immunol Study Sect, NIH, DRG, 90-93. *Mem:* AAAS; Reticuloendothelial Soc; Am Asn Immunol; Am Soc Microbiol; Sigma Xi. *Res:* Regulation of antibody formation; alveolar macrophage function; bone marrow transplantation in breast cancer. *Mailing Add:* Dept Microbiol & Immunol Georgetown Univ Sch Med Washington DC 20007. *Fax:* 202-687-1800; *E-Mail:* herscowh@medlib.georgetown.edu

HERSEY, STEPHEN J, PHYSIOLOGY. *Current Pos:* from asst prof to assoc prof, 70-79, PROF PHYSIOL, EMORY UNIV, 79-, DIR GRAD STUDIES, 74- *Personal Data:* b Buffalo, NY, Jan 17, 43; m 63; c 3. *Educ:* Cornell Univ, AB, 64; Duke Univ, PhD(physiol), 68. *Prof Exp:* Asst prof physiol, Duke Univ, 69-70. *Concurrent Pos:* NIH trainee, Duke Univ, 68-69, career develop award, 71-76. *Mem:* Am Physiol Soc. *Res:* Membrane transport; ion secretion; gastric acid secretion. *Mailing Add:* Dept Physiol Rm 362 Physiol Bldg Emory Univ Atlanta GA 30322-1100. *Fax:* 404-727-2648

HERSH, CHARLES K(ARRER), chemical engineering, for more information see previous edition

HERSH, EVAN MANUEL, IMMUNOLOGY, ONCOLOGY. *Current Pos:* from asst prof to assoc prof, 66-75, PROF MED, UNIV TEX M D ANDERSON HOSP & TUMOR INST, HOUSTON, 75- *Personal Data:* b New York, NY, Mar 18, 35; m 56; c 3. *Educ:* City Col New York, BS, 56; Columbia Univ, MD, 60. *Honors & Awards:* Ward Medal, City Col New York. *Prof Exp:* Intern med, St Luke's Hosp, NY, 60-61; resident, Stanford Univ, 61-62; clin assoc, Nat Cancer Inst, 62-65. *Concurrent Pos:* Am Cancer Soc fel, Stanford Univ, 65-66. *Mem:* Am Asn Cancer Res; AMA; Am Soc Clin Oncol; Am Soc Hemat; Am Asn Immunol. *Res:* Host defense mechanisms; cancer immunology and chemotherapy; immunosuppression; immunotherapy of cancer. *Mailing Add:* Ariz Cancer Ctr 1501 N Campbell Ave Tucson AZ 85724-0001. *Fax:* 520-626-2225

HERSH, HERBERT N, MATERIALS SCIENCE, TECHNICAL MANAGEMENT. *Current Pos:* RETIRED. *Personal Data:* b New York, NY, Feb 6, 23; m 48; c 3. *Educ:* Ohio State Univ, PhD(chem), 50. *Prof Exp:* Res scientist, Nat Adv Comt Aeronaut, 50-53; phys chemist, Zenith Radio Corp, 54-60, div chief, Res Dept, 60-78; prog mgr, Argonne Nat Lab, 78-85; consult, 86-87; coodr, US Environ Protection Agency, 88-95. *Mem:* Am Chem Soc; fel Am Phys Soc; Electrochem Soc; Tech Asn Pulp & Paper Indust. *Res:* Materials science; low temperature phenomena; coloration of ionic crystals; solid state diffusion; energy analysis; spectroscopy of solids; photochemistry; radiation damage; luminescence; image display; electrochemistry. *Mailing Add:* 706 W Buena Ave No 1W Chicago IL 60613

HERSH, JOHN FRANKLIN, METROLOGY. *Current Pos:* RETIRED. *Personal Data:* b Allentown, Pa, Mar 27, 20. *Educ:* Oberlin Col, AB, 41; Harvard Univ, MA, 42, PhD(appl physics), 57. *Prof Exp:* Res assoc underwater sound lab, Harvard Univ, 42-45, asst acoust res lab, 53-57; from instr to asst prof physics, Wellesley Col, 47-53; engr, Gen Radio Co, 57-80, mgr Eng Standards Lab, 80-85. *Res:* Applied physics; electrical impedance standards and measurements; electromechanical transducer analysis and measurement. *Mailing Add:* 225 Prairie St Concord MA 01742-2927

HERSH, LEROY S, SURFACE CHEMISTRY. *Current Pos:* from res chemist to sr res chemist, Corning Glass Works, 66-78, RES ASSOC CHEM, CORNING INC, 78- *Personal Data:* b New York, NY, Aug 15, 31; m 68, Anne Berthold; c Cliff & Ross. *Educ:* Polytech Inst Brooklyn, BChE, 53; Univ Chicago, PhD(chem), 64. *Prof Exp:* Tech specialist nuclear eng, Brookhaven Nat Lab, 53-54; instr chem, Barat Col, 58-59; USPHS fel, 64-66. *Mem:* Mat Res Soc; Sigma Xi; Am Chem Soc. *Res:* Surface chemistry; cell culture surface studies; development of novel cell culture surfaces. *Mailing Add:* Sullivan Park FR6 Corning Inc Corning NY 14831

HERSH, LOUIS BARRY, BIOCHEMISTRY. *Current Pos:* asst prof, 68-72, ASSOC PROF BIOCHEM, UNIV TEX HEALTH SCI CTR DALLAS, 72- *Personal Data:* b Baltimore, Md, Mar 28, 40; m 67; c 2. *Educ:* Drexel Inst, BSc, 62; Brandeis Univ, PhD(biochem), 67. *Prof Exp:* Fel biochem, Nat Heart Inst, 66-68. *Concurrent Pos:* NIH res grant, Univ Tex Health Sci Ctr Dallas, 69- *Mem:* Am Soc Biol Chem; Am Chem Soc. *Res:* Metabolism; flavin chemistry; enzymology. *Mailing Add:* Dept Biochem Univ Ky Med Ctr 800 Rose St MN 607 Med Ctr Lexington KY 40536-0084. *Fax:* 606-323-1037

HERSH, REUBEN, MATHEMATICAL ANALYSIS. *Current Pos:* from asst prof to assoc prof, 64-70, PROF MATH, UNIV NMEX, 70- *Personal Data:* b New York, NY, Dec 9, 27; m 49; c Daniel & Eva. *Educ:* Harvard Univ, BA, 46; NY Univ, MS, 60, PhD(math), 62. *Honors & Awards:* Chauvenet Prize, Math Asn Am, 75, Ford Prize, 95; Am Book Award, 82. *Prof Exp:* Asst ed, Sci Am Mag, 48-52; machinist, Varityper Corp, 55-57; asst prof math, Fairleigh Dickinson Univ, 62; instr, Stanford Univ, 62-64. *Concurrent Pos:* Vis mem, Courant Inst, NY Univ, 70-71; vis prof, Brown Univ, 79, Univ Calif, Berkeley, 79, Ctr Invest & Studies, Avanzadus, Mex, 73. *Mem:* Math Asn Am. *Res:* Differential equations; stochastic processes; operator theory; applied mathematics; philosophy of mathematics. *Mailing Add:* Dept Math Univ NMex Albuquerque NM 87131. *E-Mail:* rhersh@math.unm.edu

HERSH, ROBERT TWEED, BIOPHYSICS. *Current Pos:* chmn dept, 71-78, from asst prof to assoc prof, 58-67, PROF BIOCHEM, UNIV KANS, 67-, DIR, HUMAN BIOL, 85- *Personal Data:* b Cleveland, Ohio, Oct 22, 27; m 59; c 2. *Educ:* Columbia Univ, AB, 47, MA, 51; Univ Calif, PhD(biophys), 55. *Prof Exp:* USPHS fel, Univ Calif, 56; physicist cent res, E I du Pont de Nemours & Co, 57-58. *Concurrent Pos:* NIH career develop award, 60-70. *Mem:* AAAS; Biophys Soc; Am Acad Sci. *Res:* Physical biochemistry; properties of biological macromolecules; cell division; mathematical biology. *Mailing Add:* 3030 W Ninth St Lawrence KS 66049-4518

HERSH, SOLOMON PHILIP, FIBER & TEXTILE SCIENCE, STATIC ELECTRICITY. *Current Pos:* from assoc prof to prof textile technol, NC State Univ, 66-73, Charles A Cannon prof, 73-94, actg head, Dept Textile Mat & Mgt, 83-85, head, Dept Textile Eng & Sci, 85-88, dir grad progs, 88-94, EMER PROF TEXTILES, NC STATE UNIV, 94- *Personal Data:* b Winston-Salem, NC, Jan 14, 29; m 54, Rosalie Peskin; c Marla R Camille. *Educ:* NC State Col, BS, 49; Inst Textile Technol, MS, 51; Princeton Univ, MA, 53, PhD(phys chem), 54. *Honors & Awards:* O Max Gardner Award, Univ NC Syst, 79. *Prof Exp:* Res fel, Textile Res Inst, 51-54; res chemist, Res Dept, Union Carbide Chem Co, 54-62; sr res chemist, Chemstrand Res Ctr, Inc, 62-66. *Mem:* Am Chem Soc; Fiber Soc; Electrostatics Soc Am; Am Asn Textile Chem & Colorists; Am Asn Aerosol Res; Air & Waste Mgt Asn. *Res:* Cellulose chemistry; electrical properties of filaments; synthetic fibers; viscoelastic properties of polymers; cotton dust control; preservation of historic and artistic textiles; byssinosis; electrostatic phenomena; expert systems for cad; fiber fatigue; protection against toxic & biological agents. *Mailing Add:* NC State Univ Col Textiles Campus Box 8301 Raleigh NC 27695-8301. *Fax:* 919-515-6532; *E-Mail:* sol_hersh@ncsu.edu

HERSH, SYLVAN DAVID, CHEMISTRY. *Current Pos:* SR PROJ SCIENTIST, ITT CORP, 82- *Personal Data:* b Philadelphia, Pa, July 18, 40; m 61; c 2. *Educ:* Drexel Univ, BS, 62; Univ Del, PhD(chem), 69. *Prof Exp:* Res chemist, Am Viscose Div, FMC Corp, 69-76; mem staff, AM McGraw Lab, 76-82. *Mem:* Am Chem Soc. *Res:* Infrared and nuclear magnetic resonance spectroscopy to investigate composition of industrial unknowns; thin layer chromatographic separations and identifications; pharmaceutical analyses. *Mailing Add:* 2448 Desert Sands Dr Las Vegas NV 89103

HERSH, THEODORE, INTERNAL MEDICINE, GASTROENTEROLOGY. *Current Pos:* PROF MED, DEPT RES CLIN CARE, SCH MED, EMORY UNIV, 73- *Personal Data:* b May 27, 33; m, Rebecca Siman. *Educ:* Harvard Col, AB, 55; Columbia Univ, MD, 59. *Prof Exp:* Asst prof med, Yale Univ Sch Med, 65-69; assoc prof med, Baylor Col Med, 69-71. *Concurrent Pos:* Spec asst to clin dir, Emory Clin. *Mem:* Master Am Gastroenterol Asn; AMA; Am Col Gastroenterol; Am Asn Study Liver Dis. *Mailing Add:* Sch Med Emory Univ 1365 Clifton Rd NE Atlanta GA 30322. *Fax:* 404-841-6497

HERSHBERG, PHILIP I, MEDICAL ENGINEERING. *Current Pos:* DIR, DEERMONT MKT CTR. *Personal Data:* b Albany, NY, Aug 5, 35; m 58, Simon; c 3. *Educ:* Rensselaer Polytech Inst, BEE, 57; Yale Univ, MEE, 58; State Univ NY, MD, 66. *Prof Exp:* Res fel med, Harvard Sch Pub Health, 68-70, asst prof, 70-73; asst prof med, Med Sch, Boston Univ, 73-81; dir res, Neico Co, 81-83; vpres, Invocom, Inc, 83-85; staff physician, Richmond Mem Hosp, 87-89; assoc med dir, Worcester Co Hosp, 90-93. *Concurrent Pos:* Consult indust, 66-; asst med, Brigham Hosp, 68-73. *Mem:* Inst Elec & Electronics Engrs; Am Col Prev Med; Am Soc Internal Med. *Res:* Electronics in medicine. *Mailing Add:* Deermont Mkt Ctr 70 Walnut St Wellesley MA 02181. *Fax:* 781-239-8005; *E-Mail:* philhers@aol.com

HERSHBERGER, CHARLES LEE, MOLECULAR BIOLOGY. *Current Pos:* sr microbiologist, Eli Lilly Co, 76-80, res scientist, 81-86, sr res scientist, 87-94, GROUP LEADER, ELI LILY & CO, 88-, RES ADV, 95- *Personal Data:* b Louisville, Ill, May 1, 42; m 62, Marla K Kylander; c Marla D, C Douglas & Jaime L. *Educ:* Eureka Col, BS, 64; Univ Ill Col Med, PhD(biochem), 67. *Honors & Awards:* Sci Achievement Award, Am Soc Microbiol, 87, HM Powell Award, 91; Charles Thomas Award, Soc Indust Microbiol, 90. *Prof Exp:* Res assoc molecular biol, Univ Wis-Madison, 67-69; asst prof microbiol, Univ Ill, Urbana, 69-76. *Concurrent Pos:* USPHS-NIH trainee, Univ Wis-Madison, 67-68, Am Cancer Soc fel, 68-69. *Mem:* AAAS; Am Soc Biochem & Molecular Biol; Soc Indust Microbiol; Sigma Xi; Am Soc Microbiol. *Res:* Synthesis of nucleic acids; recombinant DNA; cellular regulatory mechanisms; cloned genes for peptide hormones and biosynthesis; cloned genes for industrial process enzymes. *Mailing Add:* Lilly Corp Ctr 3224 Eli Lilly & Co Indianapolis IN 46285. *Fax:* 317-276-5499; *E-Mail:* hershberger_charles_l@lilly.com

HERSHBERGER, TRUMAN VERNE, ANIMAL NUTRITION. *Current Pos:* instr animal sci, Ohio Agr Exp Sta, 51-55, asst prof animal nutrit, 55-60, res fel, 65-66, ASSOC PROF ANIMAL NUTRIT, PA STATE UNIV, 60- *Personal Data:* b Walnut Creek, Ohio, Oct 10, 27; m 49, Dorothy Steiner; c Timothy, Louise & Susan. *Educ:* Goshen Col, BA, 49; Ohio State Univ, MSc, 51, PhD(agr biochem), 55. *Prof Exp:* Asst natural sci, Goshen Col, 47-49; asst agr biochem, Ohio State Univ, 49-51. *Mem:* Fel AAAS; Am Inst Nutrit; Am Chem Soc; Am Soc Animal Sci; Am Sci Affil; NY Acad Sci. *Res:* Rumen physiology; energy metabolism, protein requirements; equine nutrition. *Mailing Add:* 257 Homan Ave State College PA 16801-6333

HERSHENOV, B(ERNARD), MICROWAVE ENGINEERING, ENERGY MANAGEMENT. *Current Pos:* CONSULT, 93- *Personal Data:* b New York, NY, Sept 22, 27; m 50, Miriam Gold; c Ruth (Basu). *Educ:* Univ Mich, BS, 50, MS, 52, PhD(elec eng), 59. *Honors & Awards:* Microwave Appln Award, Microwave Theory & Techniques Soc, Inst Elec & Enectronics Engrs, 92. *Prof Exp:* Assoc res engr, Univ Mich, Ann Arbor, 52-59; develop eng, GE Power Tube Div, Schenectady, NY, 59-60; mem tech staff, RCA, Tokyo, 60-68, head microwave integrated circuits, 68-72, dir res labs, 72-75, staff adv res labs, Princeton, NJ, 75-77, head, Energy Systs Group, 77-79, dir optoelectronics res lab, RCA Res Labs, 79-87, dir, Mkt Coord, 87-89, Dir, EAsia Bus Develop, David Sarnoff Res Ctr, Princeton, 89-93, sr adv, 94-95. *Concurrent Pos:* Co-adj staff mem math dept, Rutgers Univ, 64-66. *Mem:* Fel Inst Elec & Electronics Engrs. *Res:* Microwave ferrites and integrated circuits; millimeter wave devices; energy management; surface state physics; optoelectronics. *Mailing Add:* 22 Raleigh Rd Kendall Park NJ 08824

HERSHENOV, JOSEPH, MATHEMATICS. *Current Pos:* from asst prof to assoc prof, 62-76, chmn dept, 69-80, PROF MATH, QUEEN'S COL, NY, 77- *Personal Data:* b Brooklyn, NY, Mar 2, 35. *Educ:* Yeshiva Univ, BA, 55; Mass Inst Technol, SM, 57, PhD(math), 61. *Prof Exp:* From res asst to res assoc math, Mass Inst Technol, 55-62. *Mem:* Math Asn Am; Am Math Soc; Soc Indust & Appl Math. *Res:* Hydrodynamics stability theory; complex variables; numerical analysis. *Mailing Add:* Dept Math Queen's Col City Univ NY Flushing NY 11367-0904

HERSHENSON, BENJAMIN R, PHARMACOGNOSY, ACADEMIC ADMINISTRATION. *Current Pos:* From instr to asst prof pharmacog & bot, Mass Col Pharm, 64-71, assoc prof, 71-80, dir, Div Spec Prog, 74-78, asst dean, 78-81, dean admis, 81-83, dean admin, 83-88, PROF BIOL, MASS COL PHARM, 81-, DEAN COL & VPRES ACAD AFFAIRS, 88- *Personal Data:* b Boston, Mass, July 13, 40. *Educ:* Mass Col Pharm, BS, 62, MS, 64, PhD(pharm), 68. *Concurrent Pos:* Consult, Sch Nursing, Mass Gen Hosp, 68-, Pharmaceut Res Assocs, Inc, 68- & Mass Dept Educ; chmn, Coun Deans, Am Asn Col Pharm, 88-90. *Mem:* Am Asn Col Pharm; Am Pharmaceut Asn; Am Soc Allied Health Profession. *Res:* Natural products research, primarily phytochemical screening of West Indian plants, including extraction, isolation and characterization of active constituents. *Mailing Add:* 1317 A Catherine St Key West FL 33040

HERSHENSON, HERBERT MALCOLM, CHEMISTRY. *Current Pos:* VPRES, TURBINE COMPONENTS CORP, 86- *Personal Data:* b Brooklyn, NY, Feb 17, 29; m 53; c 3. *Educ:* Mass Inst Technol, BS, 49, PhD(anal chem), 52. *Prof Exp:* Asst, Mass Inst Technol, 49-51; asst prof chem, Univ Kans, 52 & Wesleyan Univ, 52-55; supvr anal chem, Aircraft Nuclear Engine Lab, Pratt & Whitney Aircraft Div, United Aircraft Corp, 55-57; group leader, Olin Mathieson Chem Corp, 58; asst tech dir, Baird-Atomic, Inc, 59-60; asst dir, Advan Mat Res & Develop Lab, 60-70, asst mgr, Mat Eng & Res Lab, Pratt & Whitney Aircraft Group, United Technologies Corp, 71-77; vpres & gen mgr, Coatings Technol Corp, 77-83. *Concurrent Pos:* Consult engr, Pratt & Whitney Aircraft Div, United Aircraft; adj assoc prof, Hartford Grad Ctr, Rensselaer Polytech Inst, 56-58; pres, Amity Group Investment Adv, 84- *Mem:* Am Chem Soc. *Res:* Chemical problems related to materials development; diffusion and plasma spray coatings. *Mailing Add:* 120 Peck Hill Rd Woodbridge CT 06525-1305

HERSHEY, ALLEN VINCENT, MATHEMATICAL PHYSICS, COMPUTER TYPOGRAPHY. *Current Pos:* contract employee, 39-43, physicist, 46-61, scientist, Naval Surface Weapons Ctr, Dahlgren, Va, 61-79, RES AFFIL, NAVAL POSTGRAD SCH, 79- *Personal Data:* b Kellogg, Idaho, Aug 15, 10; m 49, Eva J Griffith; c Dorothy E (Donhauser). *Educ:* Univ Calif, BS, 32, MA, 36, PhD(physics), 38. *Honors & Awards:* Ed Rosse Award, Comput Micrographic Technol Users Group, 78. *Prof Exp:* Res engr, Gen Elec Co, NY, 38-39. *Mem:* AAAS; Am Phys Soc. *Res:* Chemical kinetics; gaseous ionics; terminal ballistics; polycrystal plasticity; visual perception; ellipsoidal potentials; rational approximations; cartography and typography; computers and laser jet printers; fluid dynamics. *Mailing Add:* 722 Redwood Lane Pacific Grove CA 93950

HERSHEY, DANIEL, CHEMICAL ENGINEERING, SYSTEMS SCIENCE. *Current Pos:* from asst prof to assoc prof, 62-68, asst to pres, 73-76, PROF CHEM ENG, UNIV CINCINNATI, 68- *Personal Data:* b New York, NY, Feb 12, 31; m 65, Barbara D Hershey; c Michael & Andrea. *Educ:* Cooper Union, BS, 53; Univ Tenn, MS, 59, PhD(chem eng), 61. *Honors & Awards:* Clin Res Award, Bariatric Physicians, 89. *Prof Exp:* Chem engr, Pall Filtration Co, 53-54 & Merck, Sharpe & Dohme, 61-62. *Concurrent Pos:* NIH res grant, Univ Cincinnati, 64-69; Fulbright fel, 75 & 91; pres, Basal Tech, 92- *Mem:* Am Inst Chem Engrs; Soc Gen Systs Res; Am Asn Univ Profs; Am Aging Asn; Am Soc Bariatric Physicians. *Res:* Entropy analysis; living systems; corporations; restructuring of corporations; metabolic fitness analysis. *Mailing Add:* Dept Chem Eng Univ Cincinnati Cincinnati OH 45221-0171. *Fax:* 513-751-2723; *E-Mail:* daniel.hershey@uc.edu

HERSHEY, FALLS BACON, SURGERY. *Current Pos:* DIR VASCULAR SURG & DIR BLOOD FLOW LAB, ST JOHN'S MED CTR, ST LOUIS, 78- *Personal Data:* b Chicago, Ill, Aug 16, 18; m 45; c 4. *Educ:* Univ Ill, BS, 39; Harvard Med Sch, MD, 43. *Prof Exp:* Intern, Peter Bent Brigham Hosp, Mass, 43-44; intern, Mass Gen Hosp, 46-47, asst resident, 47-48 & 50-51, chief resident surg, East Surg Serv, 52; res assoc biol, Mass Inst Technol, 49-50; from instr to assoc prof surg, Sch Med, Wash Univ, 53-59, assoc prof clin surg, 59-64; prof surg, Chicago Med Sch, 64-66; chmn div surg & dir surg res, Michael Reese Hosp & Med Ctr, Univ Chicago, 64-66; assoc prof clin surg, Sch Med, Wash Univ, 66-77. *Concurrent Pos:* Fel, Nat Cancer Inst, 49-50; teaching fel, Harvard Med Sch, 52. *Mem:* Soc Univ Surg, Int Cardiovasc Soc; Am Col Surg; Sigma Xi. *Res:* Vascular surgery; cancer surgery; biochemical research in the enzymes of skin and cancer. *Mailing Add:* 11 Wydown Terr Clayton MO 63105-2217

HERSHEY, H GARLAND, GEOLOGY, HYDROLOGY. *Current Pos:* From geologist to state geologist, 36-69, EMER STATE GEOLOGIST, IOWA GEOL SURVEY, 69- *Personal Data:* b Quarryville, Pa, Oct 1, 05. *Educ:* Johns Hopkins Univ, BS, 29, PhD(geol), 36. *Concurrent Pos:* Chmn, Iowa Nat Resources Coun, 48-69; oil & gas adminr, State Iowa, 55-69; chmn, US Comt Int Hydrol Decade, 68-72; dir, Off Water Resource Res, US Dept Interior, 69-72. *Mem:* Fel Geol Soc Am. *Mailing Add:* 2423 Walden Rd Iowa City IA 52246

HERSHEY, HARRY CHENAULT, CHEMICAL ENGINEERING. *Current Pos:* res assoc, 66-67, from asst prof to prof, 67-96, EMER PROF CHEM ENG, OHIO STATE UNIV, 96- *Personal Data:* b Baton Rouge, La, Nov 10, 38; m 61; c 3. *Educ:* Univ Mo, Rolla, BS, 60, MS, 63, PhD(rheology), 65. *Prof Exp:* Assoc engr, Union Carbide Nuclear Co, 60-62; asst prof chem eng, Univ Mo, Rolla, 65-66. *Concurrent Pos:* Consult, Battelle Mem Inst, Sohio. *Mem:* Am Chem Soc; Am Inst Chem Engrs; Asn Comput Mach; Soc Rheology; Sigma Xi. *Res:* Fluid mechanics of viscoelastic fluids; dilute polymer solutions; mathematical methods in chemical engineering, especially statistics and numerical analysis; thermodynamics. *Mailing Add:* Dept Chem Eng Ohio State Univ 140 W 19th Ave Columbus OH 43210

HERSHEY, JOHN LANDIS, ASTRONOMY. *Current Pos:* COMPUT SCI CORP, SPACE TELESCOPE SCI INST, 89- *Personal Data:* b Lancaster, Pa, Sept 6, 35; m 60; c 3. *Educ:* Eastern Mennonite Col, AB, 58; Univ Va, MA, 66, PhD(astron), 69. *Prof Exp:* Res assoc astron, Sproul Observ, Swarthmore Col, 68-72, from asst prof to assoc prof, 72-80, actg dir, 80-81, astron, 83-85; astron, US Naval Observ, 82-89. *Concurrent Pos:* Vis assoc prof, Univ Md, 80-82. *Mem:* Am Astron Soc; Sigma Xi. *Res:* Long focus astronomy for determining distances, orbital motions and masses of stars; astrometric applications of CCD arrays; high precision measuring machines; long base line optical interferometry. *Mailing Add:* 9006 Sudbury Rd Silver Spring MD 20901

HERSHEY, JOHN WILLIAM BAKER, BIOCHEMISTRY, ORGANIC CHEMISTRY. *Current Pos:* asst prof to assoc prof, 70-78, PROF BIOL CHEM, UNIV CALIF, DAVIS, 78- *Personal Data:* b Lancaster, Pa, Jan 27, 34; m 60; c 2. *Educ:* Haverford Col, BA, 58; Rockefeller Inst, PhD(biochem), 63. *Prof Exp:* Jane Coffin Childs Mem Fund fel org chem, Cambridge Univ, 63-65; res biochemist, Huntington Labs, Mass Gen Hosp, 65-67; res fel, tutor & lectr, Harvard Univ, 67-70. *Mem:* Am Soc Biol Chemists; Sigma Xi. *Res:* Initiation of protein synthesis; translational control mechanisms; ribosome structure and function. *Mailing Add:* Dept Biol Chem Univ Calif Sch Med Davis CA 95616. *Fax:* 530-752-3516

HERSHEY, LINDA ANN, NEUROPHARMACOLOGY, CLINICAL PHARMACOLOGY. *Current Pos:* assoc prof, 86-94, PROF NEUROL & PHARMACOL, STATE UNIV NY BUFFALO, 94-, CHIEF NEUROL, BUFFALO VET ADMIN MED CTR, 86- *Personal Data:* b Marion, Ind, Jan 15, 47; m 76, Charles O; c Edward, William & Erin. *Educ:* Purdue Univ, BS,

68; Washington Univ, PhD(neurobiol), 73, MD, 75. *Prof Exp:* Intern med, St John's Mercy Hosp, St Louis, 75-76; resident neurol, Barnes Hosp, 76-78; fel & instr, Strong Mem Hosp, Rochester, NY, 78-80; asst prof neurol & clin pharmacol, Univ Hosp, Case Western Reserve Univ, Cleveland, 80-86. *Concurrent Pos:* Med adv, Comt Combat Huntington's Dis, 80-; chief, Div Neuropharmacol, Univ Hosp, Case Western Reserve Univ, Cleveland, 80-86, chmn, Pharm & Therapeut Comt, 81-86; prin investr, Tidopidine-Aspirin Stroke Study, Cleveland, 81-86 & Pergolide Study in Parkinson's Dis, 83-86; Andrew W Mellon Found scholar, 80-81; prin investr, Tacrine Study in Alzheimers Dis, Buffalo, 90-93, Clopidogrel Aspirin Stroke Study, 92-96, Melanieline Study in Alzheimers Dis, 96-98, Nat Acad Sci, 92-96, Aspirin Caratid Endarterectomy, 95-98. *Mem:* Soc Neurosci; fel Am Acad Neurol; Am Soc Clin Pharmacol & Therapeut; fel Am Neurol Asn; fel Am Heart Asn Stroke Coun; Movement Dis Soc. *Res:* Conduct clinical trials to test new medications or other treatments for patients with stroke, Parkinson's and Alzheimer's diseases; validate new diagnostic studies and endpoint measurements for patients with these three diseases. *Mailing Add:* 66 North Dr Buffalo NY 14226

HERSHEY, NATHAN, PUBLIC HEALTH EDUCATION. *Current Pos:* res assoc, 56-58, from asst prof to assoc prof, 58-68, PROF HEALTH LAW, SCH PUB HEALTH, UNIV PITTSBURGH, 68- *Personal Data:* b New York, NY, Apr 28, 30; m 58; c 2. *Educ:* NY Univ, AB, 50; Harvard Univ, LLB, 53. *Prof Exp:* Pvt pract law, NY, 55-56. *Concurrent Pos:* Mem, Secy's Comn Med Malpract, Legal Issues Adv Panel, HEW, 72, Pa Bd Med Educ, 74-80, Vision Serv Assocs, 76, bd dirs, Women's Health Serv, 76- & Comt Utilization Mgt Third Parties, Inst Med, 88-89; consult, Pa State Comt Pub Health & Welfare, 73-80; counr, Markel, Schafer & Means, Pittsburgh & Post & Schell, Philadelphia; Soc Hosp Attorneys Western Pa, 79. *Mem:* Inst Med-Nat Acad Sci; Am Pub Health Asn; Am Acad Hosp Attorneys (pres, 72). *Res:* Law affecting health services delivery; author of 150 technical publications. *Mailing Add:* Sch Pub Health MS 101 Univ Pittsburgh 207 C Tarran Hall Pittsburgh PA 15261. *Fax:* 412-624-5510

HERSHEY, ROBERT LEWIS, AIR POLLUTION CONTROL TECHNOLOGIES, RESEARCH PROGRAM APPRAISAL METHODOLOGIES. *Current Pos:* EXEC ENGR, O'DONNELL CONSULTING ENGRS, 88- *Personal Data:* b Chicago, Ill, Dec 18, 41. *Educ:* Tufts Univ, BS, 63; Mass Inst Technol, MS, 64; Cath Univ Am, PhD(eng), 73. *Honors & Awards:* Nat Capital Award for Prof Achievement Eng, DC Coun Eng & Archit Soc, 74. *Prof Exp:* Mem tech staff, Bell Tel Labs, 63-67; mgr acoust, Weston Instruments Inc, 67-68; sr scientist, Bolt Beranek & Newman, 68-71; mgr acoust progs, Booz Allen & Hamilton, 71-79; prog vpres, Sci Mgt Corp, 79-80, div vpres, 80-88. *Concurrent Pos:* Mem, Joint Bd Sci & Eng Ed, 72-78; nat secy, Prof Engrs in Indust Div, Nat Soc Prof Engrs, 73-75; secy, DC Prof Coun, 74, DC Prof Eng Regist Bd, 91-; mem, Coord Comt Productivity & Innovation, Am Asn Eng Soc, 84-88; sci policy analyst, George Bush Presidential Campaign, 88 & 92, Bob Dole Presidential Campaign, 96; consult, Energetics Inc, 88-89, Franklin Assocs, 89-90 & Parsons Power Group, 96- *Mem:* Nat Soc Prof Engrs; Am Soc Mech Engrs; Acoust Soc Am; Soc Mfg Engrs; AAAS. *Res:* Technologies for control of air toxics, flue gas desulfurization, and reduction of NOx; increased energy efficiency for industrial processes; automotive engine combustion; coal technologies for Eastern Europe; acoustics; statistical modeling of glass fractures under dynamic loading. *Mailing Add:* 1255 New Hampshire Ave NW Washington DC 20036. *Fax:* 202-429-1835; *E-Mail:* hershey@cpcug.org

HERSHEY, SOLOMON GEORGE, ANESTHESIOLOGY. *Current Pos:* PROF ANESTHESIOL, ALBERT EINSTEIN COL MED, 67-, DIR OFF CONTINUING MED EDUC, 71- *Personal Data:* b New York, NY, June 23, 14; m 41; c 1. *Educ:* City Col New York, BS, 34; NY Univ, MD, 39; Am Bd Anesthesiol, dipl. *Prof Exp:* Intern, Beth Israel Hosp, 39-41; resident anesthesiol, Bellevue Hosp, 42-44; instr anesthesia, Col Med, NY Univ, 45, asst clin prof anesthesiol, 46-50, clin prof, Post-Grad Med Sch, 50-63, prof, Med Ctr, 64-67, attend physician & assoc dir, Univ Hosp, 64-67. *Concurrent Pos:* Fel anesthesia, Col Med, NY Univ, 44; from asst vis anesthesiologist to assoc vis anesthesiologist, 45-59, vis anesthetist, 59-; attend anesthesiologist & chief serv, Beth Israel Hosp, 46-59, dir anesthesiol, 59-63, consult, 64-; res assoc, Washington Sq Col, 52-55; lectr, Univ London, 59; vis prof, Univ Calif, San Francisco, 63; mem comt shock, Nat Res Coun-Nat Acad Sci, 65-71; attend anesthesiologist, Bronx Munic Hosp Ctr, NY, 67-, Hosp Albert Einstein Col Med, 67- & Lincoln Hosp Med Ctr, 67-76; ed, Anesthesiol, Am Soc Anesthesiol, 63-72; mem consult panel, Nat Heart, Blood & Lung Inst, 77- *Mem:* Fel Am Col Anesthesiol; Am Asn Med Col; Asn Univ Anesthetists; fel Royal Soc Med; Soc Exp Biol & Med. *Res:* Physiology of circulation. *Mailing Add:* 750 Ladd Rd Bronx NY 10471-1204

HERSHFIELD, EARL S, INTERNAL MEDICINE. *Current Pos:* DIR, RESPIRATORY HOSP, WINNIPEG, 75- *Personal Data:* b Winnipeg, Man, May 17, 34; m 57; c 3. *Educ:* Univ Man, MD & BSc, 58; FRCP(C). *Prof Exp:* Asst physician, Cent Tuberc Clin, 64-67; from assoc med dir to med dir, D A Stewart Ctr, 68-73; from asst prof to assoc prof, Univ Man, 67-82, prof med, 82- *Concurrent Pos:* Asst physician, Health Sci Ctr, Manitoba, 66; chmn, Med Adv Comt, Man Lung Asn Div, Sanatorium Bd Man, 73-; med dir, Can Tuberc & Respiratory Dis Asn, 76-82. *Mem:* Am Thoracic Soc; assoc Am Col Physicians; fel Am Col Chest Physicians; Can Thoracic Soc. *Res:* Chest diseases. *Mailing Add:* 810 Sherbrook St Winnipeg MB R3A 1R8 Can

HERSHFIELD, MICHAEL STEVEN, BIOCHEMICAL GENETICS, RHEUMATOLOGY. *Current Pos:* asst prof med, 76-80, ASST PROF BIOCHEM, DIV RHEUMATIC & GENETIC DIS, DUKE UNIV, 76-, ASSOC PROF MED, 80- *Personal Data:* b Wilkes Barre, Pa, June 28, 42. *Educ:* Franklin & Marshall Col, AB, 63; Univ Pa, MD, 67. *Prof Exp:* Intern Med, Philadelphia Gen Hosp, 67-68; staff fel & sr staff fel biochem, NIH, 68-72; res fel genetics, Sch of Med, Univ Calif, San Diego, 72-74; resident internal med, 74-75, fel rheumatology, 75-76. *Concurrent Pos:* NIH res fel, 75-76; res grant, Nat Inst Arthritis & Metab Dis, NIH, 78-; Basil O'Connor res grant, Nat Found March Dimes, 77-; NIH career develop award, 78- *Mem:* Am Fedn Clin Res; Am Soc Clin Investr; Am Soc Biol Chem. *Res:* Human biochemical genetics; diseases of purine metabolism; immunodeficiency diseases; somatic cell genetics; nucleic acid metabolism; biological transmethylation. *Mailing Add:* Dept Med & Biochem Duke Univ Sch Med Box 3049-M Durham NC 27710-0001

HERSHFIELD, SELMAN P, SOLID STATE & THEORETICAL PHYSICS. *Current Pos:* ASST PROF PHYSICS, UNIV FLA, 92- *Personal Data:* b Washington, DC, Aug 24, 61. *Educ:* Univ Md, BS(math & physics), 83; Cornell Univ, PhD(physics), 89. *Prof Exp:* Postdoctoral researcher, Princeton Univ, 88-90 & Ohio Univ, 90-92. *Concurrent Pos:* Nat young investr award, NSF, 93; Cottrell scholar award, Res Corp, 95. *Mem:* Am Phys Soc; Am Asn Physics Teachers. *Mailing Add:* Univ Fla Dept Physics PO Box 118440 Gainesville FL 32611. *Fax:* 352-392-0524; *E-Mail:* selman@phys.ufl.edu

HERSHKOWITZ, NOAH, PHYSICS. *Current Pos:* asst prof to prof physics, 67-80, PROF PHYSICS &ASTRON, UNIV IOWA, 80- *Personal Data:* b Brooklyn, NY, Aug 16, 41; m 62; c 2. *Educ:* Union Col, NY, BS, 62; Johns Hopkins Univ, PhD(physics), 66. *Honors & Awards:* Merit Award, Inst Elec & Electronics Engrs, 87. *Prof Exp:* Instr physics, Johns Hopkins Univ, 66-67. *Concurrent Pos:* Irving Langmuir prof, Nuclear Eng & Eng Physics Dept, Inst Elec & Electronics Engrs; Dept Nuclear Eng, Univ Wis. *Mem:* Fel Am Phys Soc; Inst Elec & Electronics Engrs; Am Geophys Union; Am Vacuum Soc. *Res:* Experimental plasma physics; plasma etching; ICRF; tandem mirror physics; tokamak physics; basic plasma physics. *Mailing Add:* Dept Nuclear Eng Univ Wis 1500 Johnson Dr Madison WI 53706-1687

HERSHKOWITZ, ROBERT L, TEXTILE CHEMISTRY. *Current Pos:* SELF EMPLOYED. *Personal Data:* b New York, NY, Feb 11, 38; m 59; c 4. *Educ:* Brooklyn Col, AB, 57; Syracuse Univ, PhD(org chem), 64. *Prof Exp:* Res chemist, Textile Fibers Dept, E I Du Pont De Nemours & Co, Inc, 64-80. *Mem:* Am Chem Soc. *Res:* Organophosphorus chemistry; substitution reactions; polyamidation. *Mailing Add:* 2504 Bona Rd Wilmington DE 19810

HERSHMAN, JEROME MARSHALL, INTERNAL MEDICINE, ENDOCRINOLOGY. *Current Pos:* CHIEF ENDOCRINE SECT, WADSWORTH VET ADMIN HOSP, 72-; PROF MED, SCH MED, UNIV CALIF, LOS ANGELES, 72- *Personal Data:* b Chicago, Ill, July 20, 32; m 57, Fleurette Kram; c Daniel, Michael & Jeffrey. *Educ:* Northwestern Univ, BS, 52; Calif Inst Technol, MS, 53; Univ Ill, Chicago, MD, 57. *Prof Exp:* Clin investr, Vet Admin Res Hosp, 64-67; from asst prof to prof med, Univ Ala, Birmingham, 67-72. *Concurrent Pos:* Fel endocrinol, Tufts Univ-New Eng Med Ctr, 61-63; NIH & Vet Admin res grants, 64-96. *Mem:* Am Soc Clin Invest; Endocrine Soc; Am Thyroid Asn (pres); Am Fedn Clin Res; Am Col Physicians; Asn Am Physicians. *Res:* Control of thyroid function; thyroid physiology and disease; pituitary hormones. *Mailing Add:* Wadsworth Vet Admin Hosp 11301 Wilshire Blvd Los Angeles CA 90028. *Fax:* 310-268-4879; *E-Mail:* jhershmn@ucla.edu

HERSHNER, IVAN RAYMOND, JR, MATHEMATICS. *Current Pos:* RETIRED. *Personal Data:* b Lincoln, Nebr, Aug 24, 16; m 48; c 4. *Educ:* Univ Nebr, BS, 38, MA, 40; Harvard Univ, MA, 41, PhD(math), 47. *Prof Exp:* Asst math, Univ Nebr, 38-40; instr, Univ Chicago, 47-48; asst prof, Univ NC, 48-51; prof & chmn dept, Univ Vt, 53-56; consult, US Dept Army, 53-56, math adv, Chief Res & Develop, 56-58, chief phys sci div, Off Chief Res & Develop, 58-72, sci dir army res, 72-75, asst dir res progs, Off Dep Chief of Staff Res, Develop & Acquisition, 75-80; prof math, George Mason Univ, 80-87. *Concurrent Pos:* Mem appl math adv coun, Nat Bur Stand, 52-54. *Mem:* Am Math Soc; Math Asn Am. *Res:* Conformal mapping; complex variable analysis. *Mailing Add:* 5427 37th St N Arlington VA 22207-1314

HERSKOVITS, THEODORE TIBOR, PHYSICAL CHEMISTRY. *Current Pos:* assoc prof, 65-74, PROF CHEM, FORDHAM UNIV, 74- *Personal Data:* b Kosice, Czech, June 11, 28; US citizen; m, Ethel Gourse; c 2. *Educ:* City Col New York, BS, 55; Yale Univ, MS, 57, PhD, 60. *Prof Exp:* Fel chem, Purdue Univ, 59-61; res assoc biophys, Univ Chicago, 61-62; phys chemist, Agr Res Serv, USDA, 62-65. *Mem:* Am Chem Soc; Biophys Soc; Fedn Am Socs Exp Biol; Sigma Xi. *Res:* Macromolecular chemistry; proteins; nucleic acids. *Mailing Add:* 100 Bennet Ave No 6J New York NY 10033

HERSKOVITZ, THOMAS, ORGANOMETALLIC CHEMISTRY, BIOINORGANIC CHEMISTRY. *Current Pos:* RES CHEMIST, E I DU PONT DE NEMOURS & CO, INC, 73- *Personal Data:* b Budapest, Hungary, Apr 15, 47; US citizen; m 72. *Educ:* Case Western Res Univ, BS, 68; Mass Inst Technol, PhD(inorg chem), 73. *Mem:* Am Chem Soc. *Res:* Homogeneous catalysis; coordination chemistry of carbon dioxide. *Mailing Add:* 52 Rock Glen Rd Wynnewood PA 19096

HERSKOWITZ, GERALD JOSEPH, ELECTRICAL ENGINEERING. *Current Pos:* DIR, STEVENS ASSOCS, 75- *Personal Data:* b Brooklyn, NY, Feb 20, 36; m 59; c 3. *Educ:* Polytech Inst Brooklyn, BSEE, 57; Rutgers Univ, MSEE, 59; NY Univ, Eng ScD(elec eng), 63. *Prof Exp:* Mem res staff, RCA Labs, NJ, 57-59; mem tech staff, Bell Tel Labs, 63-65; prof elec eng, Stevens Inst Technol, 65-77. *Concurrent Pos:* Chmn, Arrangements Comt, Solid State

Circuits Conf, 65-67; consult, Bell Tel Labs, 65-, US Army, 65 & Lockheed Electronics Co, 65-; lectr, Univ Wis, 67 & Univ Mo, 67; ed, Design Automation Workshop, 69-71; vprog chmn, Int Comn Commun, 76. *Mem:* Inst Elec & Electronics Engrs. *Res:* Solid-state device and integrated circuit research; lasers; magnetic memory systems; microwaves; computers; optical communications; microprocessors. *Mailing Add:* Dept Fel Comput Sci Stevens Inst Technol Castle Point on Hudson Hoboken NJ 07030

HERSKOWITZ, IRA, MOLECULAR GENETICS. *Current Pos:* chmn dept, 90-95, PROF GENETICS & HEAD, DEPT BIOCHEM & BIOPHYS, DIV GENETICS, UNIV CALIF, SAN FRANCISCO, 81- *Personal Data:* b Brooklyn, NY, July 14, 46. *Educ:* Calif Inst Technol, BS, 67; Mass Inst Technol, PhD(microbiol), 71. *Honors & Awards:* Eli Lilly Award, Microbiol & Immunol, 83; Nat Acad Sci Award, Sci Reviewing, 85; Streisinger Lectr, 85; Genetics Soc Am Medal, 88; MacArthur Found Fel, 91; Mendel Lectr, 91; Bateson Lectr, 94. *Prof Exp:* Instr biol, Mass Inst Technol, 72; from asst prof to prof biol, Univ Ore, 72-81, assoc, Inst Molecular Biol, 72-81. *Concurrent Pos:* MacArthur Found fel, 88-; Mem, Sci Rev Bd Genetics, Howard Hughes Med Inst & Tularik, Inc, 92-96; counr, Am Soc Cell Biol, 96; bd sci counrs, Nat Cancer Inst, 96- *Mem:* Nat Acad Sci; Genetics Soc Am (pres, 85); Am Soc Microbiol; Am Acad Arts & Sci; Am Soc Cell Biol. *Res:* Control of gene expression in yeast; pathogen-host interactions; control of cell growth and cell polarity. *Mailing Add:* Dept Biochem & Biophys Univ Calif San Francisco CA 94143-0448. *Fax:* 415-476-0943; *E-Mail:* ira@cgl.ucsf.edu

HERSKOWITZ, IRWIN HERMAN, GENETICS. *Current Pos:* RETIRED. *Personal Data:* b New York, NY, Mar 18, 20; m 45; c 4. *Educ:* Brooklyn Col, AB, 40; Univ Mo, MA, 42; Columbia Univ, PhD(zool), 49. *Prof Exp:* Res assoc genetics & cancer, Sch Med, La State Univ, 48-49, instr anat, 49-51; res exec zool, Ind Univ, 51-57; from assoc prof to prof biol, St Louis Univ, 57-63; prof biol, Hunter Col, 63-85. *Mem:* Am Soc Naturalists; Am Soc Zoologists; Soc Human Genetics. *Res:* Point mutation; chromosomal breakage and rearrangement induced by chemicals and radiations; chromosome arrangement in sperm; salivary gland chromosome electron microscopy and histochemistry; homoeosis; tumors; Drosophila bibliography. *Mailing Add:* 3326 Arcara Way No 208 Lake Worth FL 33467

HERSON, DIANE S, MICROBIOLOGY. *Current Pos:* from asst prof to assoc prof biol sci, 68-74, ASSOC PROF, SCH LIFE & HEALTH SCI, UNIV DEL, 74- *Personal Data:* b New York, NY, Apr 23, 44; m 73; c 2. *Educ:* Cornell Univ, BS, 64; Rutgers Univ, MS, 66, PhD(bact), 68. *Prof Exp:* Res asst, Rutgers Univ, 64-66. *Concurrent Pos:* Consult. *Mem:* NY Acad Sci; Sigma Xi; AAAS; Am Soc Microbiol; Soc Indust Microbiol. *Res:* Microbial of drinking water; assessment of the viability and activity of microbes in the environment; biodegradation of toxic chemicals. *Mailing Add:* Biol Univ Del Newark DE 19717-0001

HERTEL, GEORGE ROBERT, COMPUTER APPLICATIONS. *Current Pos:* RETIRED. *Personal Data:* b Detroit, Mich, Apr 26, 34; m 63; c 3. *Educ:* Mich Technol Univ, BS, 56; Rensselaer Polytech Inst, MS, 58; Johns Hopkins Univ, PhD(phys chem), 64. *Prof Exp:* Honor prog trainee res & develop, Gen Elec Co, NY, 56-58, mass spectroscopist, Knolls Atomic Power Lab, 59-60, res chemist, Oak Ridge Nat Lab, 64-68; from asst prof to assoc prof chem, Fla Technol Univ, 68-76; prof chem, Univ Cent Fla, 76-90. *Mem:* Am Chem Soc. *Res:* Computer applications in chemistry lab; estimation methods in thermodynamics. *Mailing Add:* 28010 29th Rd Branford FL 32008

HERTELENDY, FRANK, REPRODUCTIVE PHYSIOLOGY. *Current Pos:* from asst prof to prof med, 71-80, assoc prof physiol, 71-76, PROF PHYSIOL, SCH MED, ST LOUIS UNIV, 76-, PROF OBSTET & GYNEC, 80- *Personal Data:* b Velikigaj, Yugoslavia, June 19, 31; m 62. *Educ:* Univ Budapest, BSc, 55; Univ Reading, PhD(physiol chem), 62. *Prof Exp:* Nat Res Coun Can fel, McGill Univ, 62-64; res scientist, Dept Life Sci, Monsanto Co, Mo, 64-71. *Concurrent Pos:* Asst prof, Univ Mo-St Louis, 70-71. *Mem:* Brit Biochem Soc; Endocrine Soc; Soc Study Reproduction; Soc Gynec Invest. *Res:* Reproductive physiology; mode of action of prostaglandins; regulation of ovarian steroidogenesis. *Mailing Add:* Dept Obstet-Gynec 1402 S Grand Blvd St Louis Univ Sch Med St Louis MO 63104-1004

HERTER, FREDERIC P, SURGERY. *Current Pos:* From instr to assoc prof surg, Columbia Univ, 54-69, asst prof clin surg, 60-61, actg chmn dept, 69-71, prof, 69-72, AUCHINCLOSS PROF SURG, COLUMBIA UNIV, 72-, VCHMN DEPT, 71- *Personal Data:* b Brooklyn, NY, Nov 12, 20; m 42; c 3. *Educ:* Harvard Univ, MD, 44; Am Bd Surg, dipl, 51. *Honors & Awards:* Distinguished Ser Award, Col Physicians & Surgeons, Columbia Univ, 92. *Concurrent Pos:* Health Res Coun New York investr, 61-; trustee, Mary Jonogene Bassett Hosp, 65-; dir surg, Francis Delafield Hosp, NY, 66-69; assoc attend surgeon, Presby Hosp & attend surgeon, 69-, actg dir surg serv, 69-71, dep dir surg serv, 71-; consult, St Luke's Hosp, 74- & Goldwater Mem Hosp; trustee, Am Univ Beirut, 77-, chmn bd trustees, 85-87, pres, 87-93, emer pres, 93- *Mem:* Am Col Surg; Am Surg Asn; Am Soc Clin Oncol; Int Surg Soc; AMA. *Res:* Surgical aspects of gastrointestinal tract cancer; cancer chemotherapy; surgical application. *Mailing Add:* 784 Park Ave New York NY 10021

HERTH, KAYE ANN, GERONTOLOGY, THANTOLOGY. *Current Pos:* PROF & CHAIR, DEPT NURSING, GA SOUTHERN UNIV, 93- *Personal Data:* b Oak Park, Ill; m 71, Leonard A; c Wendy J & Randy S. *Educ:* Northern Ill Univ, BS, 68; Univ Minn, MS, 73; Tex Woman's Univ, PhD(nursing), 87. *Prof Exp:* Asst prof nursing, ETenn State Univ, 73-78, Univ Tex, Houston, 78-85 & Univ Okla, Tulsa, 86-88; assoc chair & assoc prof, Northern Ill Univ, 88-93. *Concurrent Pos:* Distinguished lectr, Sigma Theta Tau Int, 91-; mem, Ga League Nursing, 93- *Mem:* Fel Am Acad Nursing. *Res:* Exploring hope, humor, and grief in those individuals with a chronic or terminal illness and the impact on their family/significant others; quantitative and qualitative research methodology, as well as instrument development and testing; instruments to measure hope have been translated into six foreign languages. *Mailing Add:* PO Box 2536 Statesboro GA 30459. *Fax:* 912-681-5455; *E-Mail:* kherth@gsums2.cc.qasou.edu

HERTING, DAVID CLAIR, NUTRITIONAL BIOCHEMISTRY, ANALYTICAL CHEMISTRY. *Current Pos:* RETIRED. *Personal Data:* b Pottstown, Pa, Sept 29, 28; m 52, Martha Schaeffer; c David, Kenneth, Philip & Carl. *Educ:* Pa State Univ, BS, 50; Univ Wis, MS, 52, PhD(biochem), 54. *Honors & Awards:* Glycerine Producers Asn Basic Res Award, 60. *Prof Exp:* Res biochemist, Distillation Prod Industs, 54-58, sr res biochemist, 58-63, res assoc, 63-71; res assoc, Health & Nutrit Div, Tenn Eastman Co, 71-76, sr res assoc, 76-88; adj prof, Dept Surg, E Tenn State Univ, 87-92. *Concurrent Pos:* Mem bd vis, Sch Appl Sci & Technol, E Tenn State Univ, 86-89. *Mem:* Fel AAAS; Am Chem Soc; Am Inst Nutrit; fel Am Inst Chemists; Sigma Xi. *Res:* Nutrition, metabolism, toxicology and analysis of fats, fat-soluble vitamins, sterols and carotenoids; physiological disposition of antibiotics, coating agents, fungistats and other materials useful in animal science and agriculture; endocrinology of animal production; growth promoters for monogastric animals. *Mailing Add:* 120 Tall Pines Lane Johnson City TN 37601

HERTING, ROBERT LESLIE, INTERNAL MEDICINE, CLINICAL PHARMACOLOGY. *Current Pos:* VPRES, CLIN RES, G D SEARLE, 80- *Personal Data:* b Aurora, Ill, Jan 26, 29; m 54, Claireen Molzan; c Robert L Jr. *Educ:* Univ Ill, BS, 50, MD, 54; Ill Inst Technol, MS, 61, PhD(biol), 70; Am Bd Internal Med, dipl, 69. *Prof Exp:* Clin investr, 57-63, clin pharmacologist, 63-68, med dir pharmaceut prod div, 68-69, dir exp med, 69-71, vpres exp med, 71-73, vpres clin res & develop, Abbott Labs, 73-77, vpres corp med res, Schering-Plough, 77-80. *Concurrent Pos:* From clin asst to clin asst prof, Univ Ill Col Med, 57-71, clin assoc prof, 71-77; from assoc attend physician to attend physician, Cook County Hosp, Chicago, 63-73; assoc prof, Cook County Grad Sch Med, 66-69, prof, 69-77; consult, Ill Cent Hosp, Chicago, 67-77. *Mem:* AAAS; Am Fedn Clin Res; AMA; Am Soc Microbiol; fel Am Col Physicians. *Res:* Clinical pharmacology of the cardiovascular system; central nervous system drugs; antimicrobial agents; appetite suppressants; enzymology of quanine deaminase. *Mailing Add:* 1281 N Northwest Hwy Park Ridge IL 60068-1662. *Fax:* 847-982-8720; *E-Mail:* rlhert@searle.monsanto.com

HERTL, WILLIAM, PHYSICAL CHEMISTRY. *Current Pos:* SR RES ASSOC, CORNING INC, 63- *Personal Data:* b Philadelphia, Pa, July 2, 32; m 64; c 2. *Educ:* Univ Pa, BS, 54; Cambridge Univ, PhD(chem), 62. *Prof Exp:* Res chemist, Ciba, Ag, Switz, 62-63. *Concurrent Pos:* Prof, Univ of the Andes, Venezuela, 70-71; vis scientist, Cornell Univ, 87. *Mem:* Am Chem Soc; Royal Soc Chem; Mat Res Soc; Am Phys Soc; Bohmische Phys Soc. *Res:* Kinetics of heterogeneous reactions and infrared spectroscopy; clinical chemistry; bio-chemistry; surface chemistry; rheology; electrochemistry; ceramics; heterogeneous catalysis; ion beam implantation. *Mailing Add:* Res & Develop Lab Corning Inc Corning NY 14831

HERTLEIN, FRED, III, INDUSTRIAL HYGIENE, ANALYTICAL CHEMISTRY. *Current Pos:* PRES, INDUST ANALYTICAL LAB, INC, 78- *Personal Data:* b San Francisco, Calif, Oct 17, 33; div; c Fritz, Hans, Lisa M & Gretel M. *Educ:* Univ Nev, Reno, BS, 56; Am Bd Indust Hyg, cert, 72. *Prof Exp:* Grad asst chem, Dept Chem, Univ Hawaii, 56-58; oceanog chemist, US Dept Interior, Fish & Wildlife Serv, Pac Oceanic Fishery Invest, 57-59; radiochemist, Pearl Harbor Naval Shipyard Med Dept, Indust Hyg Div, 59-62, indust hygienist, 62-72; indust hyg prog mgr, US Naval Regional Med Clin, Indust Hyg Br, Hawaii, 72-78. *Concurrent Pos:* Pres, Fred Hertlein & Assoc Environ Consult, 70-78; lab dir & indust hyg dir, Indust Anal Lab, 78-; tech book reviewer, Am Indust Hyg Asn, 76-80; chmn hyperbarics comt, Am Conf Govt Indust Hyg, 64-71; mem, Occup Safety & Health Comt, Am Inst Chemists; asst clin prof, Univ Hawaii, Sch Pub Health, 74-; licensed lab dir, Hawaii State Dept Health, 73-84; cert AHERA inspector, mgt planner & asbestos abatement supvr, 87-; vpres & bd dir, Synthetic Technol Corp, 84-95; bd dir, Combined Technologies Inc, 87-; vpres & bd dir, Tech Experts Inc, 92- *Mem:* Am Indust Hyg Asn; Am Acad Indust Hyg; Am Chem Soc; Am Inst Chem. *Res:* Atmospheric sampling and analysis of a wide variety of gases, vapors, dusts, mists and fumes in the occupational environment; evaluation of physical, chemical and biological stressors in occupational environments, noise, ionizing and nonionizing radiation, heat, humidity and pressure. *Mailing Add:* Indust Anal Lab Inc 3615 Harding Ave Suite 304 Honolulu HI 96816. *Fax:* 808-735-0047

HERTLER, WALTER RAYMOND, ORGANIC CHEMISTRY. *Current Pos:* RETIRED. *Personal Data:* b Philadelphia, Pa, Apr 10, 33; m 61; c 2. *Educ:* Univ Pa, AB, 55; Univ Ill, PhD, 58. *Prof Exp:* Sr res fel, E I Du Pont de Nemours & Co, Inc, 58-95. *Mem:* Am Chem Soc; Sigma Xi. *Res:* Polymer chemistry. *Mailing Add:* 1375 Parkersville Rd Kennett Square PA 19348

HERTSGAARD, DORIS M FISHER, MATHEMATICAL STATISTICS. *Current Pos:* From instr to assoc prof, 64-81, PROF MATH, NDAK STATE UNIV, 81- *Personal Data:* b Mandan, NDak, Feb 14, 39; c 2. *Educ:* Univ NDak, BA, 60; NDak State Univ, MS, 64; Univ Iowa, PhD(statist), 72. *Concurrent Pos:* Bd dir, Asn Women Math Educ. *Mem:* Am Statist Asn; Sigma Xi; Nat Coun Teachers Math; Asn Women Math. *Res:* Testing procedures for asymmetric distributions, specifically with adaptive procedures. *Mailing Add:* 2615 River Moorehead ND 56560

HERTWECK, GERALD, SYSTEMS ENGINEERING, TECHNICAL MANAGEMENT. *Current Pos:* opers res analyst, Opers Res & Systs Anal Off, 71-79, asst Army Combat Food Serv Syst, 79-80, spec asst Dept Defense Food Prog, US Army Natick Res & Develop Labs, 80-83, CHIEF, FOOD EQUIP & SYSTS DIV, FOOD ENG DIR, US ARMY NATICK RES, DEVELOP & ENG CTR, 83- *Personal Data:* b Evansville, Ind, Sept 19, 34; m 56; c 3. *Educ:* Southern Ill Univ, BA, 59; Northeastern Univ, MS, 70; Univ Mass, PhD, 76. *Prof Exp:* Mathematician & physicist, US Naval Weapons Lab, 59-62, supvry opers res analyst, 62-65; fel scientist, Advan Studies Group, Westinghouse Elec Corp, Waltham, 66-71. *Concurrent Pos:* Naval res assoc, Inst Naval Studies, Ctr Naval Anal, 65-66; lectr sch mgt, Boston, 77-79. *Mem:* Opers Res Soc Am; Sigma Xi. *Res:* Military food service systems and operations. *Mailing Add:* 907C Ridgefield Circle Clinton MA 01510

HERTWIG, WALDEMAR R, CHEMICAL ENGINEERING. *Current Pos:* RETIRED. *Personal Data:* b San Francisco, Calif, Sept 28, 20; m 46, Ruth Hull; c Thomas A & Elizabeth A (Thiel). *Educ:* Columbia Univ, BS, 42, ChE, 43. *Prof Exp:* Chem engr, Stand Oil Co Ind, Am Oil Co, 43-51, sect leader, Pilot Plant Div, Res Dept, 51-61, res assoc, process econ div, 61-80. *Mem:* Am Chem Soc; Am Inst Chem Engrs. *Res:* Development and economics of petroleum process and synthetic fuels. *Mailing Add:* 8575 Costa Verde Blvd Apt 1406 San Diego CA 92122-1145

HERTZ, DAVID BENDEL, OPERATIONS ANALYSIS. *Current Pos:* DISTINGUISHED PROF, ART INTEL, UNIV MIAMI, 83- *Personal Data:* b Yoakum, Tex, Mar 25, 19; m 41; c 2. *Educ:* Columbia Univ, BA, 39, BS, 40, PhD(indust eng), 49; US Navy Postgrad Sch, MS, 44; NY Univ, JD, 80. *Honors & Awards:* George S Kimmbel Award, Opers Res Soc, 81. *Prof Exp:* Prod engr, Radio Corp Am, 40-41; asst dir eng res, Celanese Corp, 45-49; from asst prof to assoc prof indust eng, Columbia Univ, 49-54; mgr opers res, Popular Merchandise Co, 54-56; prin, opers res, Arthur Andersen & Co, 57-61; dir, McKinsey & Co, Inc, 62-83. *Concurrent Pos:* Lectr, Columbia Univ, 48-49, 55-83; grant, Columbia Coun, 70-71; mem sci adv coun, Picatinny Arsenal, 50-55; consult, Nat Res Coun, 51-52; dir proj team res, Off Naval Res, 51-53; dir eng, Plastics Div, Celanese Corp, 53-54; trustee, Columbia Univ, 77-83 & Columbia Univ Press, 74-; tech anal dir, Adv Panel, Nat Bur Stand, chmn, 73-77; chmn bd gov, 77-83, Opportunity Fund Corp, 67-; vis prof, Grad Sch Bus Studies, Univ London, 77-82; adj prof, Grad Sch Bus, Columbia Univ, 77-83; mem exec comt minority enterprise, President's Adv Coun; publs ed, Opers Res Soc, pres, 74-75; Nat Acad Sci liaison subcomt, Int Inst Systs Anal, 84-85; vis prof, Univ Vienna, 86-87. *Mem:* Fel AAAS; Int Fedn Opers Res Soc (pres, 76-79); NY Acad Sci (secy, 52-54); Opers Res Soc Am (pres, 70-73); Inst Mgt Sci (vpres, 56-63, pres, 64-65). *Res:* Applications of management science, systems analysis and operations research; systems engineering; computer systems. *Mailing Add:* Intelligent Syst Res Inst Univ Miami PO Box 248235 Coral Gables FL 33124

HERTZ, ELLEN SHAPIRO, CATEGORICAL ANALYSIS. *Current Pos:* MATH STATISTICIAN, NAT HWY TRAFFIC SAFETY ADMIN, 88- *Personal Data:* b New York, NY, Apr 5, 37. *Educ:* City Col NY, BS, 58; Columbia Univ, AM, 60, PhD(math), 70. *Prof Exp:* Lectr math, City Col NY, 66-68; opers res analyst, US Dept Defense, 79-83. *Mem:* Am Statist Asn; Math Asn Am. *Res:* Statistical analysis in highway safety issues. *Mailing Add:* 5565 Columbia Pike No 205 Arlington VA 22204. *Fax:* 202-366-7078; *E-Mail:* ehertz@nhtsa.dot.gov

HERTZ, HARRY STEVEN, QUALITY MANAGEMENT, ANALYTICAL CHEMISTRY. *Current Pos:* dir, Ctr Analytica Chem, Nat Inst Stand & Technol, 83-91, dir, Chem Sci & Technol Lab, 91-92, dep dir, Qual Progs, 92-96, DIR, NAT QUAL PROG, NAT INST STAND & TECHNOL, 96- *Personal Data:* b New York, NY, Feb 25, 47; m 69, Francine Turkowitz; c Matthew Adam & Joshua Lee. *Educ:* Polytech Inst Brooklyn, BS, 67; Mass Inst Technol, PhD(org chem), 71. *Honors & Awards:* Bronze Medal, US Dept Com, 81, Silver Medal, 86; Arthur S Flemming Award Outstanding Fed Serv, 86. *Prof Exp:* Alexander von Humboldt fel biochem, Univ Munich, 71-73; res chemist, Nat Bur Stand, 73-78, chief org analytical chem, Div Analytical Chem, 78-83. *Concurrent Pos:* Secy, Nat Comt Clin Lab Stand, 83-84, pres-elect, 84-86, pres, 86-88; mem, Health & Environ Res Adv Comn, Dept Energy, 84-88; mem adv comt, Health & Human Serv Good Mfg Pract, 88-89. *Mem:* Am Chem Soc; Sigma Xi; Am Soc Mass Spectrometry (secy, 83-85); fel AAAS. *Res:* Quality management and industrial competitiveness; roles of quality assurance and accuracy in chemical measurement programs and systems; organic mass spectrometry; health measurements. *Mailing Add:* Nat Qual Prog Nat Inst Stand & Technol Gaithersburg MD 20899. *Fax:* 301-948-3716; *E-Mail:* harry.hertz@nist.gov

HERTZ, JOHN ATLEE, statistical physics, for more information see previous edition

HERTZ, LEONARD B, HORTICULTURE. *Current Pos:* horticulturist, 67-80, PROF HORT, UNIV MINN, ST PAUL, 80- *Personal Data:* b South Milwaukee, Wis, Nov 26, 24; m 50; c 4. *Educ:* Univ Wis, BS, 49, MS, 50, PhD(agron), 56. *Prof Exp:* Conservationist, Soil Conserv Serv, USDA, 50-53; agronomist, Kans State Univ, 56-61; res biologist, Niagara Chem Div, FMC Corp, 61-67. *Mem:* Weed Sci Soc Am; Am Soc Hort Sci. *Res:* Weed control in fruit crops; culture of fruit crops. *Mailing Add:* 426 Woodhill Dr St Paul MN 55113

HERTZ, PAUL ERIC, ECOLOGY. *Current Pos:* from asst prof to assoc prof, 79-92, PROF, BARNARD COL, COLUMBIA UNIV, 92- *Personal Data:* b Brooklyn, NY, July 8, 51. *Educ:* Stanford Univ, BS, 72; Harvard Univ, AM, 73, PhD(biol), 77. *Prof Exp:* Fel biol, Dalhousie Univ, 77-79. *Concurrent Pos:* Res assoc zool, Univ Wash, 80-81; res assoc, Inst Evolution, Univ Haifa, Israel, 80; vis Scientist Entomol, NC State Univ, 87-88; vis Res Prof Biol, Univ Antwers, 93-94. *Mem:* Am Soc Zoologists; Soc Study Evolution; Ecol Soc Am; Am Soc Naturalists. *Res:* Strategies of adaptation in reptiles; thermal biology and physiological ecology of reptiles; structure of reptile communities. *Mailing Add:* Dept Biol Sci Barnard Col 3009 Broadway New York NY 10027-6598. *E-Mail:* phertz@barnard.columbia.edu

HERTZ, ROY, ENDOCRINOLOGY, REPRODUCTION. *Current Pos:* res prof, 73-84, EMER PROF PHARMACOL, OBSTET & GYNEC, MED CTR, GEORGE WASHINGTON UNIV, WASHINGTON, DC, 84-; EMER SCIENTIST, NAT INST CHILD HEALTH & HUMAN DEVELOP, NIH, BETHESDA, MD, 89- *Personal Data:* b Cleveland, Ohio, June 19, 09; m 34, 62; c 2. *Educ:* Univ Wis, AB, 30, PhD(physiol), 33, MD, 39; Johns Hopkins Univ, MPH, 41. *Hon Degrees:* DSc, Univ Wis, 86. *Honors & Awards:* Anne Frankel Rosenthal Mem Award for cancer res, AAAS, 57; Distinguished Serv Award, Am Col Obstetricians & Gynecologists, 75; Twenty-fifth Medal, Barren Found, 85; Axel Munthe Found Medallion, 85. *Prof Exp:* Asst zool, Univ Wis, 30-34; instr pharmacol, Med Sch, Howard Univ, 34-35; intern, Wis Gen Hosp, 39-40; res officer, USPHS, 41-47, endocrinologist, chmn, Endocrinol Sect & mem, Study Sect Endocrinol & Metab, Nat Cancer Inst, 47-65; sci dir, Nat Inst Child Health & Develop, 65-66; prof obstet & gynec, Sch Med, George Washington Univ, 66-67; dir, Reproduction Res Br, Nat Inst Child Health & Develop, 67-69; sr physician & assoc dir, Biomed Div, Pop Coun, Rockefeller Univ, 69-72; prof obstet & gynec & med, NY Med Col, 72-73. *Concurrent Pos:* Mem, Endocrinol & Metab Study Sect, NIH, 47-55, lectr, 61, adj scientist, Nat Inst Child Health & Human Develop, Bethesda, MD, 87-89; chmn, Panel Endocrinol, Nat Res Coun, 53-56; chmn, Adv Comt Ther, Am Cancer Soc, 56-59, Res Adv Coun, 59-62; mem coun, Endocrine Soc, 59-62; cancer res award, Int Col Surgeons, 69; mem, Int Comt Contraceptive Res, 71-; med res award, Lasker Found, 72. *Mem:* Nat Acad Sci; fel Am Col Physicians; hon fel Am Asn Obstet & Gynec; Endocrine Soc (vpres, 60-61); Soc Exp Biol & Med; Sigma Xi; AAAS; Am Physiol Soc; AMA; Fedn Clin Invest. *Res:* Endocrinology; reproduction; cancer; metabolism; nutrition; author or co-author of over 130 publications. *Mailing Add:* 25006 Half Paine Point Rd Hollywood MD 20636

HERTZBERG, ABRAHAM, AERODYNAMICS, HEAT TRANSFER. *Current Pos:* prof, Dept Aeronaut & Astronaut & dir, Aerospace & Energetics Res Prog, 65-93, EMER PROF, DEPT AERONAUT & ASTRONAUT, UNIV WASH, 93- *Personal Data:* b New York, NY, July 8, 22; m 50, Ruth; c 3. *Educ:* Va Polytech Inst, BS, 43; Cornell Univ, MS, 49. *Honors & Awards:* Paul Vieille lectr, 69 & 89; Minta-Martin lectr, Univ Md, 75; Dryden Medal Award, Am Inst Aeronaut & Astronaut, Plasma Dynamics & Laser Award, 92; Irv Glass Mem lectr, 96. *Prof Exp:* Engr, Cornell Aeronaut Lab, 49-57, asst head, Aerodyn Res Dept, 57-59, head, 59-65. *Concurrent Pos:* Vis lectr, Chinese Acad Sci, 83 & 88. *Mem:* Nat Acad Eng; fel Am Inst Aeronaut & Astronaut; Am Phys Soc; Am Asn Univ Profs; Int Acad Astronaut. *Res:* Energy conversion; propulsion; high powered lasers; fusion; advanced energy conversion techniques and concepts; laser applications; space laser concepts; high energy gas dynamics, gas physics as related to lasers phenomenon; reentry phenomena. *Mailing Add:* Aerospace & Energetics Res Prog Box 352250 Univ Wash Seattle WA 98195

HERTZBERG, RICHARD WARREN, MECHANICAL METALLURGY. *Current Pos:* res assoc metall, 64-65, prof, 65-78, NJ ZINC PROF METALL & MAT SCI, LEHIGH UNIV, 78-, DIR MECH BEHAV LAB, MAT RES CTR, 65-, CHAIRPERSON, 87- *Personal Data:* b New York, NY, Aug 17, 37; m 61; c 2. *Educ:* City Col New York, BME, 60; Mass Inst Technol, MMet, 61; Lehigh Univ, PhD(metall eng), 65. *Honors & Awards:* William Woodside Mem lectr, Am Soc Metals, 78. *Prof Exp:* Res asst metall, Mass Inst Technol, 60-61; assoc res scientist, Res Labs, United Aircraft Corp, 61-64. *Concurrent Pos:* Vpres, Del Res Corp, 70-73; consult to numerous corp; Libsch Res Award, 84. *Mem:* fel Am Soc Metals; Am Inst Mining, Metall & Petrol Engrs; Am Soc Testing & Mat. *Res:* Deformation and fracture of materials; special efforts related to fatigue crack propagation of metals and polymers; mechanical response of unidirectionally solidified eutectic composites; fractography and failure analysis. *Mailing Add:* Dept Mat Sci & Eng Lehigh Univ Whitaker Lab, 5 E Packer Ave Bethlehem PA 18015

HERTZENBERG, ELLIOT PAUL, INORGANIC CHEMISTRY. *Current Pos:* SR RES FEL, PQ CORP, 72- *Personal Data:* b Brooklyn, NY, Oct 4, 38; m 68, Virginia L; c 2. *Educ:* Hofstra Univ, BS, 60; Adelphi Univ, MS, 65; Univ Ill, Urbana, PhD(inorg chem), 69. *Prof Exp:* Chemist, Fairchild Camera & Instrument Corp, 60-65; asst chem, Univ Ill, 65-69; res chemist, Pigment Dept, E I Du Pont de Nemours & Co, Inc, 69-72. *Concurrent Pos:* Mem, comt D-32, Am Soc Testing & Mat. *Mem:* Am Chem Soc. *Res:* Coordination chemistry; solid phase reactions of coordination compounds; industrial inorganic chemistry; silica gels, zeolites. *Mailing Add:* 2420 Graydon Rd Chatham Wilmington DE 19803

HERTZIG, DAVID, ALGEBRA. *Current Pos:* chmn dept math, 70-76, PROF MATH, UNIV MIAMI, 70- *Personal Data:* b Brooklyn, NY, Dec 15, 32; div; c 4. *Educ:* Cornell Univ, BA, 53; Univ Chicago, PhD(math), 57; Univ Miami, JD, 78. *Prof Exp:* Vis mem, Sch Math, Inst Advan Study, 57; asst prof math, Cornell Univ, 58-61; vis asst prof, Princeton Univ, 61-62; assoc prof, Purdue Univ, 62-70. *Concurrent Pos:* Consult, Inst Defense Anal, 62-71. *Mem:* Math Asn Am; Am Math Soc; Math Soc France. *Res:* Algebraic geometry; algebraic groups. *Mailing Add:* Dept Math/Comput Sci Univ Miami Univ Sta PO Box 249085 Coral Gables FL 33124

HERTZLER, BARRY LEE, AGING PREDICTIONS FOR SOLID ROCKET MOTORS. *Current Pos:* res scientist plasma chem, 75-81, MAT SCIENTIST, PALO ALTO RES LAB, LOCKHEED MISSILES & SPACE CO, INC, 81- *Personal Data:* b Elizabethtown, Pa, May 5, 47; div. *Educ:* Elizabethtown Col, BS, 68; Princeton Univ, MS, 70, PhD(phys chem), 74. *Prof Exp:* Grad res asst reaction mech, Dept Chem, Princeton Univ, 69-74; res assoc, Emory Univ, Atlanta, 74-75. *Concurrent Pos:* Chmn, Joint Army-Navy-NASA, Air Force Serv Life Panel. *Mem:* Am Chem Soc; Am Inst Aeronaut & Astronaut. *Res:* Aging of materials-polymers; solid rocket motors. *Mailing Add:* Lockheed Martin Advan Technol Ctr 3251 Hanover St Orgn V1-50 Bldg 204 Palo Alto CA 94304

HERTZLER, DONALD VINCENT, POLYMER CHEMISTRY. *Current Pos:* from asst prof to assoc prof, 69-84, PROF CHEM, SOUTHWESTERN OKLA STATE UNIV, 84- *Personal Data:* b Cherokee, Okla, June 7, 38; m 63; c 2. *Educ:* Northwestern State Col, Okla, BS, 60; Okla State Univ, MS, 65, PhD(chem), 69. *Prof Exp:* From instr to asst prof chem, Panhandle State Col, 63-66. *Concurrent Pos:* NSF fac sci fel, 65-67 & 81-82. *Mem:* Am Chem Soc; Am Asn Univ Professors. *Res:* Synthetic organic chemistry; polymer chemistry. *Mailing Add:* 513 N Arizona Weatherford OK 73096-5710

HERTZLER, EMANUEL CASSEL, PHYSIOLOGY. *Current Pos:* RETIRED. *Personal Data:* b Norristown, Pa, Jan 7, 17; m 42; c 3. *Educ:* Goshen Col, BA, 38; Univ Mich, MA, 40, PhD(zool), 51. *Prof Exp:* From asst prof to prof biol, Kent State Univ, 46-60; spec fel neurophysiol, NIH, Wash Univ, 60-61; assoc prof, Univ Mich, Dearborn, 61-62, chmn math & sci div, 63-67, chmn dept natural sci, 71-73, prof, 62-82, assoc dean acad affairs, 73-82, emer prof biol, 83- *Concurrent Pos:* Prof zool, Univ Mich, Ann Arbor, 62-82. *Mem:* AAAS; Am Soc Zool. *Res:* Pigmentation; bioelectric potentials; neurophysiology; sympathetic nervous system; serotonin and blocking agents; bioengineering; biotelemetry. *Mailing Add:* 1404 Pennbrook Cresent Apt 6 Goshen IN 46526

HERUM, FLOYD L(YLE), AGRICULTURAL ENGINEERING, GRAIN PROCESSING & STORAGE. *Current Pos:* prof, 64-87, EMER PROF AGR ENG, OHIO STATE UNIV, 87- *Personal Data:* b Dolliver, Iowa, Mar 2, 28; m 52, Melva Highland; c 3. *Educ:* Iowa State Univ, BS, 53, MS, 54; Purdue Univ, PhD(agr eng), 64. *Prof Exp:* Res assoc agr eng, Iowa State Univ, 54-55; Int Coop Admin contract specialist for Univ Ariz in Iraq, 55-57; asst prof, Univ Ill, 57-63. *Mem:* Am Soc Agr Engrs. *Res:* Measurement of physical properties of agricultural products for evaluating natural quality and effects of harvesting, handling and storage parameters, design of grain processing and storage systems. *Mailing Add:* 1580 Pemberton Dr Columbus OH 43221

HERWALD, SEYMOUR W(ILLIS), AUTOMATIC CONTROL SYSTEMS, ELECTRONICS. *Current Pos:* RETIRED. *Personal Data:* b Cleveland, Ohio, Jan 17, 17; m 41; c 3. *Educ:* Case Inst Technol, BS, 38; Univ Pittsburgh, MS, 40, PhD(math), 44. *Prof Exp:* Cent engr, Westinghouse Elec Corp, 39-46, spec prod engr, 46-47, mgr, Develop Sect, 47-51, mgr, Eng Dept, Air Arm Div, 51-56, mgr, Air Arm Div, 56-59, vpres res, 59-62, vpres, Electronic Components & Specialty Prod Group, 62-68, vpres eng, 68-70, vpres eng & develop, 70-77, vpres serv, 77-79. *Concurrent Pos:* Mem, Air Force Sci Adv Bd, 56-71; consult, NASA, 60-64, NSF, 74-76; consult, 79-85. *Mem:* Nat Acad Eng; Sigma Xi; Am Soc Mech Engrs; Inst Elec & Electronics Engrs (pres, 68); Am Inst Aeronaut & Astronaut. *Res:* Design servomechanisms; feedback control systems design; autopilots; airborne radar directed fire control systems. *Mailing Add:* 122 Lakeshore Dr North Palm Beach FL 33408

HERWIG, LLOYD OTTO, ENGINEERING PHYSICS, MATERIALS SCIENCE ENGINEERING. *Current Pos:* solar div sci adv & sr int specialist, 77-80, chief scientist, 81-83, PROG MGR, PHOTOVOLTAIC DIV, DEPT ENERGY, 83- *Personal Data:* b West Union, Iowa, Nov 4, 21; m 49; c 5. *Educ:* Luther Col, Iowa, BA, 43; Univ Iowa, MS, 47; Iowa State Univ, PhD, 53. *Prof Exp:* Asst physics, Univ Iowa, 43-44 & 46-47, jr physicist, Weapon Res & Develop, 44-46; instr physics, Iowa State Univ, 47-50, asst physics, 50-53, res assoc, 53-54; sr scientist & supvr, Naval Reactors Proj, Bettis Lab, Westinghouse Elec Corp, 54-58, mgr, High Temperature Test Reactor Facil, 58-61; sr res scientist, Res Labs, United Technol Corp, Conn, 61-64; staff assoc, Div Inst Progs, NSF, 64-70, prog mgr, Advan Technol Appln Div, 71-73, dir, Advan Solar Energy Res & Technol, 73-75; sci adv & actg dep dir, Solar Energy Div, Energy Res & Develop Admin, 75-77. *Concurrent Pos:* US deleg to UN Conf New & Renewable Energy Resources, 81. *Mem:* Int Solar Energy Soc; AAAS; Am Phys Soc; Sigma Xi; Inst Elec & Electronics Engrs. *Res:* Optical stimulated emission; solar energy research and development in solar heating and cooling, biomass for fuels, solar thermal, photovoltaic, wind and ocean thermal systems; nuclear and atomic physics; particle ionization phenomena; reactor neutron physics, nuclear reactor analysis, accelerators and electronic instrumentation; solar energy research and development; applied mathematics. *Mailing Add:* 2309 N Stafford St Arlington VA 22207

HERWITZ, PAUL STANLEY, MATHEMATICS, STATISTICS. *Current Pos:* mathematician, IBM Corp, Armonk, 55-59, mgr mach oriented prog, 59-63, adv prog develop, 63, sr mem tech staff to dir res, 63-64, tech asst to dir exp comput & prog, 64-65, prog dir prog resources, 65-74, mem develop staff, IBM Corp, Poughkeepsie, 74-77, MATHEMATICIAN, CORP STAFF, IBM CORP, ARMONK, 77- *Personal Data:* b Cincinnati, Ohio, June 10, 23; m 49; c 2. *Educ:* Univ Cincinnati, AB, 48, MA, 50; Univ NC, PhD(math), 54. *Prof Exp:* Res assoc, Inst Coop Res, Johns Hopkins Univ, 53-55. *Mem:* Am Statist Asn; Am Math Soc; Math Asn Am; Sigma Xi. *Res:* Computer systems planning, organization, systems programming; problems inherent in programming as a profession; problems of the programming development process. *Mailing Add:* 4 Lakeview Ave W Cortland & Manor Peekskill NY 10566-6416

HERZ, ARTHUR H, SURFACE CHEMISTRY. *Current Pos:* Res Chemist, 53-89, CONSULT, RES LAB, EASTMAN KODAK CO, 90- *Personal Data:* b Ger, Feb 11, 21; nat US; m 47; c 4. *Educ:* Univ Rochester, BS, 50, PhD(chem), 53. *Mem:* Am Chem Soc; Soc Imaging Sci & Technol; Royal Photog Soc. *Res:* Correlation of structure of compounds and their effect on properties of silver halides. *Mailing Add:* 1020 Park Ave Rochester NY 14610

HERZ, CARL SAMUEL, mathematics; deceased, see previous edition for last biography

HERZ, FRITZ, BIOCHEMISTRY, CELL BIOLOGY. *Current Pos:* ASSOC PROF PATH, ALBERT EINSTEIN COL MED, YESHIVA UNIV, 73-; HEAD, DIV TISSUE CULT, DEPT PATH, MONTEFIORE MED CTR, 73- *Personal Data:* b Heilbronn, Ger, July 16, 30; US citizen; m 66, Vona R Uern; c Eric N & Lisa S. *Educ:* Univ Guayaquil, Chemist, 54, PhD(biochem), 55. *Prof Exp:* Assoc head dept tuberc, Nat Inst Hyg, Ecuador, 55-57; from res asst to res assoc, Sinai Hosp, 62-67; assoc dir pediat res, 67-73; asst prof pediat, Sch Med, Johns Hopkins Univ, 70-73. *Concurrent Pos:* Humboldt res fel org chem, Tech Univ Berlin & Humboldt res fel microbiol, Free Univ Berlin, 57-59; USPHS res fel pediat res, Sinai Hosp, 60-62. *Mem:* Am Chem Soc; Am Soc Biochem & Molecular Biol. *Res:* Biochemistry of cultured cells; regulation of enzyme synthesis; tumor marker analysis. *Mailing Add:* Tissue Cult Div 45 Dora Lane New Rochelle NY 10804-1005. Fax: 718-515-5315

HERZ, JACK L, PHYSICAL ORGANIC CHEMISTRY. *Current Pos:* PRES & CHIEF EXEC OFFICER, SEA-SOURCE TECHNOL INC, 94- *Personal Data:* b Frankfurt, Ger, July 10, 38; US citizen; m 64; c 2. *Educ:* City Col New York, BS, 60; Cornell Univ, PhD(org chem), 64. *Honors & Awards:* Medal, Am Inst Chemists, 60. *Prof Exp:* Sr res chemist, Cent Res Labs, Allied Chem Corp, 64-67; group leader, Cowles Chem Co, 67-68; sr res chemist, Stauffer Chem Co, 68-72, asst to dir, Eastern Res Ctr, 72-74, sr bus analyst corp planning & develop, 74-76, mgr corp develop, 76-77, bus dir, Whey Proteins, 77-81, dir formulated food syst, 81-83, corp prod dir, 83-85; pres & chief exec officer, Deltown Chemurgic Corp, 86-94. *Concurrent Pos:* NIH fel, 60-64; adj assoc prof chem, Hunter Col, 74-76. *Mem:* Am Chem Soc; Am Soc Lubrication Engrs; Inst Food Technologists. *Res:* Structure-properties relationships; flammability properties of organic compounds; organic reactions and polymerization kinetics and mechanisms; lubrication technology; food technology; whey processing; whey derived proteins; food science and technology; chemical marketing; research management; general management. *Mailing Add:* 35 November Trail Weston CT 06883

HERZ, MARVIN IRA, PSYCHIATRY. *Current Pos:* DIR, MENT HEALTH SERVS RES & LONG TERM CARE PROG, DEPT PSYCHIAT, PROF PSYCHIAT, SCH MED & DENT, UNIV ROCHESTER, 91- *Personal Data:* b New York, NY, Dec 24, 27; m 52, Beatrice Mittelman; c Joan, Suzanne & Joseph. *Educ:* Univ Mich, BA, 49; Yale Univ, MS, 51, Chicago Med Sch, MD, 55; Columbia Univ, cert psychoanal, 68; Am Bd Psychiat & Neurol, dipl. *Honors & Awards:* PIA Found Prize, Am Psychiat Asn, 88; Stanley Dean Award, Res in Schizophrenia, Am Col Psychiatrists, 93; Award Psychiat Res, World Asn Psychosocial Rehab/US Br, 94, Sci Distinction Award, 95. *Prof Exp:* Intern, Univ Ill Res & Educ Hosps, 55-56; residency, Michael Reese Hosp, Chicago, 56-59; dir inpatient serv, Div Psychiat, Montefiore Hosp, NY, 61-63; dir, Day Hosp & asst prof psychiat, Albert Einstein Col Med, 63-65; assoc in psychiat, Col Physicians & Surgeons, Columbia Univ, 65-72, assoc prof clin psychiat, 72-77, assoc prof clin psychiat, 72-77; prof psychiat, Emory Univ, 77-78; prof psychiat & chmn dept, State Univ NY, Buffalo, 78-91. *Concurrent Pos:* Ward admin to dir, Community Serv, NY State Psychiat Inst, 65-77; dir, 68-72, actg clin dir, 75-76; educ consult, Nat Inst Heart & Lung Dis, 75-78; consult, Task Panel of President's Comn Ment Illness, 77; med dir & dir res, Ga Ment Health Inst, 77-78; consult, Psychiat Educ Br, NIMH, 78-; consult psychiat, Vet Admin Med Ctr, 78-; dir, Psychiat Dept, Buffalo Gen Hosp, 78-91; dir psychiat, Erie Co Med Ctr, 78-91; chmn, Psychiat Adv Comt, NY Off Ment Health, 80-87; mem, Spec Rev Comn, NIMH, 81, Psychosocial Res Rev Comt, 81-85; chmn, comt educ, Am Col Psychiatrists, 87-90; sr sci adv/dir, NIMH, 89-91; bd regents, Am Col Psychol, 90-93; chair res comt, World Asn Psychosocial Rehab, US Br, 92-; chair workgroup, Develop Pract Guidelines Treatment Schizophrenia, Am Psychiat Asn, 92- *Mem:* Fel Am Psychiat Asn; World Fedn Ment Health; fel Am Psychopath Asn; Am Col Psychiatrists (pres, 97-98); Am Col Psychoanalysts (pres elect 97-98); fel Am Col Ment Health Admin; fel Asn Clin Psychosocial Res (pres, 93-). *Res:* Efficacy of psychiatric treatments; clinical research and services in schizophrenia; social and community psychiatry; delivery of mental health services. *Mailing Add:* Strong Ties Univ Rochester Med Ctr 1650 Elmwood Ave Rochester NY 14620. Fax: 716-244-7053; *E-Mail:* mherz@strongties.urmc.rochester.edu

HERZ, MATTHEW LAWRENCE, PHYSICAL ORGANIC CHEMISTRY. *Current Pos:* Res chemist, US Army Natick Labs, 69-77, oper res analyst, 77-81, supvry opers res analyst, Res & Develop Command, 81-84, chief, Phys Sci Div, 84-88, dir technol, Res & Develop Ctr, 88-94, DIR, ADVAN CONCEPTS, US ARMY NATICK LABS, 94- *Personal Data:* b Newport, RI, Dec 18, 41; m 65, Elise Krull; c Harold & Ellen. *Educ:* Tufts Univ, BS, 63; Univ RI, PhD(phys org chem), 69; Boston Col, MBA, 78. *Concurrent Pos:* Instr, Metropolitan Col, Boston Univ, 69-70 & Boston Col, 78-81. *Mem:* Am Chem Soc; Sigma Xi. *Res:* Mechanistic organic chemistry; laser photochemistry, photophysical studies, polymers; mathematical modeling; operations research. *Mailing Add:* 20 Swanson Rd Framingham MA 01701. *E-Mail:* mherz@natick.emhi.army.mil

HERZ, NORMAN, ARCHAEOLOGICAL GEOLOGY. *Current Pos:* head, Dept Geol, Univ Ga, 70-78, prof geol, 70-94, dir, Ctr Archaeol Sci, 84-94, actg head, 90-94, EMER PROF GEOL, UNIV GA, 94- *Personal Data:* b New York, NY, Apr 12, 23; m 93, Christine M Suite; c David S, Jonathan A & Sara J. *Educ:* City Col New York, BS, 43; Johns Hopkins Univ, PhD(geol), 50. *Honors & Awards:* Pomerance Award Archaeol, Archaeol Inst Am, 95. *Prof Exp:* Fulbright Act res scholar, Am Sch Classical Studies, Greece, 51-52; geologist, US Geol Surv, 52-85. *Concurrent Pos:* Geologist, Conn Geol & Natural Hist Surv, 50-51 & AID, US Geol Surv, 56-64; vis prof, Univ Sao Paulo, 62-64, George Washington Univ, 69, Univ Orleans, France, 83; exchange scientist, Nat Acad Sci, Romania, 71 & 73, Bulgaria, 76; Am Sch Classical Studies, Athens, Greece, 95 & 96. *Mem:* AAAS; Geol Soc Am; Sigma Xi; Soc Archaeol Sci; Geol Soc Brazil; foreign mem Brazilian Acad Sci. *Res:* Economic geology; archaeological geology; classical Greek and Roman marble provenance signatures; stable isotopic geochemistry applied to archaeology. *Mailing Add:* Dept Geol Univ Ga Athens GA 30602. *Fax:* 706-542-2425; *E-Mail:* normherz@uga.cc.uga.edu

HERZ, WERNER, ORGANIC CHEMISTRY. *Current Pos:* from asst prof to prof chem, 49-87, R O LAWTON DISTINGUISHED PROF CHEM, FLA STATE UNIV, 87- *Personal Data:* b Stuttgart, Ger, Feb 12, 21; nat US; m 45, Marcia Lucile King; c 4. *Educ:* Univ Colo, BA, 43, MA, 45, PhD(org chem), 47. *Honors & Awards:* Fla Award, Am Chem Soc, 65. *Prof Exp:* Instr math, Univ Colo, 45-47; Am Cyanamid fel, Univ Ill, 47-49. *Concurrent Pos:* Mem chem panel, Cancer Chemother Nat Serv Ctr, Nat Cancer Inst, 59-62, consult, 62-65, mem chemother study sect, NIH, 62-66, mem med chem study sect, 70-74; adv panel chem, NSF, 61-64; sr ed, J Org Chem, Am Chem Soc, 63-89; ed, Fortschritte der Chemie Organischer Naturstoffe, 69-; vis prof, Univ Munster, 70. *Mem:* Am Chem Soc; Royal Soc Chem. *Res:* Isolation and structure of natural products; terpene chemistry; molecular rearrangements; chemotaxonomy of Compositae; antitumor substances. *Mailing Add:* Dept Chem Fla State Univ Tallahassee FL 32306-1096. *Fax:* 850-644-8281

HERZBERG, GERHARD, MOLECULAR SPECTROSCOPY. *Current Pos:* dir, Div Physics, Nat Res Coun Can, 49-55, Div Pure Physics, 55-69, distinguished res scientist, 69-94, EMER DISTINGUISHED RES SCIENTIST, NAT RES COUN CAN, 94- *Personal Data:* b Hamburg, Ger, Dec 25, 04; Can citizen; m 29, 72; c 2. *Educ:* Darmstadt Tech Univ, Dipl Ing, 27, Dr Ing(physics), 28. *Hon Degrees:* Various from US & foreign univs. *Honors & Awards:* Nobel Prize Chem, 71; Tory Medal, Royal Soc Can, 53; Gold Medal, Can Asn Physicists, 57; Companion, Order of Can, 68; Willard Gibbs Medal, Am Chem Soc, 69; Faraday Medal, The Chem Soc, 70; Linus Pauling Medal, Am Chem Soc, 71; Royal Medal, Royal Soc, 71. *Prof Exp:* Privatdozent & asst, Darmstadt Tech Univ, 30-35; res prof physics, Univ Sask, 35-45; prof spectros, Yerkes Observ, Chicago, 45-49. *Mem:* Foreign assoc Nat Acad Sci; hon foreign mem Am Acad Arts & Sci; foreign mem Am Philos Soc; centennial foreign fel Am Chem Soc; fel Am Phys Soc; fel Royal Soc London. *Res:* Atomic and molecular spectroscopy; structure of atoms and molecules; astrophysics. *Mailing Add:* Steacie Inst Molecular Sci Nat Res Coun Can Ottawa ON K1A 0R6 Can

HERZENBERG, ARVID, THEORETICAL PHYSICS. *Current Pos:* prof eng & appl sci, 69-80, PROF APPL PHYSICS, YALE UNIV, 80-, PROF PHYSICS, 90- *Personal Data:* b Vienna, Austria, Apr 16, 25; m 49, Marjorie Swift; c Catherine, Anne & Stephen. *Educ:* Victoria Univ Manchester, BSc, 49, PhD(physics), 52, DSc(physics), 64. *Prof Exp:* Asst lectr physics, Victoria Univ Manchester, 52-55, lectr, 55-58, sr lectr, 58-64, reader, 64-69. *Mem:* Am Phys Soc; Inst Physics London. *Res:* Theoretical physics of atoms and molecules; theory of electron collisions with atoms, molecules, surfaces and in solids. *Mailing Add:* Appl Physics Yale Univ New Haven CT 06520

HERZENBERG, CAROLINE STUART LITTLEJOHN, APPLIED PHYSICS. *Current Pos:* PHYSICIST, ARGONNE NAT LAB, 77- *Personal Data:* b East Orange, NJ, Mar 25, 32; m 61, Leonardo; c Karen A & Catherine (Stuart). *Educ:* Mass Inst Technol, SB, 53; Univ Chicago, MS, 55, PhD(physics), 58. *Hon Degrees:* DSc, State Univ NY, 91. *Prof Exp:* Res assoc nuclear physics, Univ Chicago, 58-59 & Argonne Nat Lab, 59-61; asst prof physics, Ill Inst Technol, 61-67, Res Corp grant, 63-64; res physicist, IIT Res Inst, 67-70, sr physicist, 70-71; consult, 71-72; vis assoc prof physics, Univ Ill Med Ctr, 72-74; consult, 74-75; lectr physics, Calif State Univ, Fresno, 75-76. *Concurrent Pos:* Consult, Argonne Nat Lab, 61-62, delegate-at-large, Fedn Am Scientists, 64-65; prin investr, NASA Apollo Lunar Sample Anal Prog, 67-71; TV producer-host, Freeport Cablevision Inc, 74-75; past pres & mem exec bd, Asn Women Sci, 90-92; distinguished vis prof, State Univ NY, Plattsburgh, 91. *Mem:* Fel AAAS; fel Am Phys Soc; fel Asn Women Sci (secy, 82-84, pres elect, 86-88, pres, 88-90); Fedn Am Scientists; Sigma Xi. *Res:* Low energy experimental nuclear physics; Mossbauer effect studies; lunar sample analysis; nuclear analysis methods; instrumentation development; fossil energy utilization technology; radioactive isotope applications; nuclear radiation physics; history of science; technological emergency preparedness. *Mailing Add:* Dis Div Bldg 900 Argonne Nat Lab Argonne IL 60439-4817. *Fax:* 630-252-3379; *E-Mail:* herzenbc@anl.gov

HERZENBERG, LEONARD ARTHUR, IMMUNOLOGY, GENETICS. *Current Pos:* From asst prof to assoc prof, 59-69, PROF GENETICS, STANFORD UNIV, 69- *Personal Data:* b Brooklyn, NY, Nov 5, 31; m 53; c 4. *Educ:* Brooklyn Col, BA, 52; Calif Inst Technol, PhD(biochem), 56. *Concurrent Pos:* Am Cancer Soc fel, Pasteur Inst, Paris, 55-57; mem, Genetics Study Sect, NIH; mem, Comt Pub Affairs, Am Asn Immunologists, 93-96. *Mem:* Nat Acad Sci; fel AAAS; Genetics Soc Am; Am Asn Immunologists; fel Soc Anal Cytol; Soc Develop Biol; Am Acad Microbiol. *Res:* Genetics of mammalian cells; immunogenetics; genetics of immunoglobulins; membrane proteins; cellular immunology; mechanism of antibody formation; cell separation; genetics of immune response; molecular biology; flourescence activated cell sorting. *Mailing Add:* Dept Genetics Stanford Univ Med Ctr Stanford CA 94305-5125

HERZFELD, CHARLES MARIA, PHYSICS ENGINEERING. *Current Pos:* CONSULT, 92- *Personal Data:* b Vienna, Austria, June 29, 25; nat US; m 90, Shannon Stock; c Charles C, Thomas A & Paul V. *Educ:* Cath Univ, BChE, 45; Univ Chicago, PhD(phys chem), 51. *Honors & Awards:* Flemming Award, 63. *Prof Exp:* Lectr, Univ Chicago, 46-47 & DePaul Univ, 48-50; physicist, Ballistic Res Lab, Aberdeen Proving Ground, 51-53 & US Naval Res Lab, 53-55; consult to chief, Heat & Power Div, Nat Bur Stand, 55-56, actg asst chief, 56-57, chief, Heat Div, 57-61, assoc dir, 61; dir ballistic missile defense, Adv Res Projs Agency, US Dept Defense, 61-63, dep dir, 63-65, dir, 65-67; tech dir, ITT Corp Defense Space Group, ITT Corp, 67-75, tech dir, ITT Aerospace, Electronics, Components & Energy Group, 75-77, tech dir, ITT Telecommun & Electronics Group-NA, 78-79, dir res, 79-85, vpres, 81-85; vchmn, Aetna, Jacobs Ramo Technol Ventures, 85-90; dir, Defense Res & Eng, Dept Defense, 90-91; sr consult, Off Sci & Technol Policy, Whitehouse, Washington, DC, 91-92. *Concurrent Pos:* Lectr, Univ Md, 53-57, prof, 57-61; mem, Brookings Inst Fifth Conf Career Execs Fed Govt, 58, Defense Sci Bd, 68-82; consult, USN & Nat Security Coun; chief, Naval Opers Exec Panel, Defense Policy Bd, 83-90; bd dirs, Westronix, 85-, chmn, 85-90; bd dirs, T Cell Sci, Coordn Technol, Inc, Memorexi, 87-90. *Mem:* Fel Am Phys Soc; Int Inst Strategic Studies (London); Coun Foreign Rels; fel AAAS. *Res:* Heterogeneous catalysis; theory of interior ballistics; magnetism and spectra of solids; trapped radicals; group theory; missile defense; strategy; arms control; technology management. *Mailing Add:* 1531 Live Oak Dr Silver Spring MD 20910. *Fax:* 301-587-2636; *E-Mail:* cmhssbon@aol.com

HERZFELD, JUDITH, PROTEINS. *Current Pos:* assoc prof, 85-90, PROF BIOPHYS CHEM, BRANDEIS UNIV, 90-, CHAIRPERSON, DEPT CHEM, 95- *Personal Data:* b Guayaquil, Ecuador, Jan 12, 48; US citizen; m 74; c 2. *Educ:* Barnard Col, AB, 67; Mass Inst Technol, PhD(chem physics), 72; Harvard Univ, MPP, 73. *Honors & Awards:* NSF Fac Award for Women Scientists & Engrs, 91. *Prof Exp:* Asst prof chem, Amherst Col, 73-74; res assoc, Sch Med, Harvard Univ, 74-75, lectr biophys, 75-76, asst prof, 76-83, assoc prof physiol & biophys, 83-85. *Concurrent Pos:* Exec comt mem-at-large, Div Biol Physics, Am Phys Soc, 88-91; coun mem, Biophys Soc, 89-93 & mem exec bd, 90-92; mem, Biophys Chem Study Sect, NIH, 89-93, prog chmn, 93-94. *Mem:* Am Chem Soc; Biophys Soc; fel Am Phys Soc; Am Soc Biochem & Molecular Biol; NY Acad Sci; AAAS. *Res:* Phase behavior of self-assembling systems; structure and function of membrane transport systems; cooperativity in oligomeric proteins. *Mailing Add:* Dept Chem Brandeis Univ Waltham MA 02254-9110. *Fax:* 781-736-2516

HERZFELD, VALERIUS E, ELECTRICAL ENGINEERING, EDUCATION ADMINISTRATION. *Current Pos:* RETIRED. *Personal Data:* b Weyauwega, Wis, Mar 1, 21; m 49; c 2. *Educ:* Univ Wis, BS, 49, MS, 51, PhD(elec eng), 53. *Prof Exp:* Elec engr, Broadcast Eng, Wis, 48; field engr, Ill Northern Utilities Co, 49-50; res asst, Univ Wis, 50-53; elec engr, Remington Rand, Univac, 53-54, proj engr, Sperry Rand Corp, 54-56, supvr engr, 56-58, mgr spec prod develop, 59-60, mgr tele-control dept, 60-61, mgr eng & tele-systs, 61, mgr indust control comput, 61-62, dir com eng, Univac, 62-64, mgr com opers, 64, vpres res & eng, Data Processing Div, 64-68, vpres prod develop, 68-71, vpres bus planning & develop, 71-81; asst dean, grad bus & prof admin sci, St Joseph's Univ, 81-89. *Mem:* Inst Elec & Electronics Engrs; Sigma Xi. *Res:* Computer peripherals and systems; textbook and management science. *Mailing Add:* St Joseph's Univ 5600 City Ave Philadelphia PA 19131

HERZIG, DAVID JACOB, PHARMACOLOGY. *Current Pos:* sr scientist immunopharmacol, Warner Lambert Res Inst, 68-75, sr res assoc, 75-77, dir immunopharmacol, 77-81, sr dir sci develop licensing, 81-94, VPRES DRUG DEVELOP, WARNER LAMBERT-PARKE DAVIS, 94- *Personal Data:* b Cleveland, Ohio, Dec 13, 36; m 62; c Michael, Pamela, Roberta & Karen. *Educ:* Oberlin Col, BA, 58; Univ Cincinnati, PhD(chem), 63. *Prof Exp:* Vis scientist protein chem, Lab Chem Biol, Nat Inst Arthritis & Metab Dis, NIH, 63-65, staff fel, Lab Gen & Comp Biochem, NIMH, 65-67; sr res assoc neurochem, Dept Psychiat, Sch Med, NY Univ, 67-68. *Concurrent Pos:* Damon Runyon fel, Lab Chem Biol, Nat Inst Arthritis & Metab Dis, NIH, 63-65; instr, NIH Grad Prog, 65-67. *Mem:* Am Acad Allergy & Immunol; Am Soc Pharmacol & Exp Therapeut; AAAS; Sigma Xi; Am Diabetes Asn. *Res:* Pharmacological control of the immune response; new therapies for allergies and immune diseases; control of bronchoconstriction; pulmonary diseases; develop new therapies for diabetes. *Mailing Add:* Parke-Davis Pharmaceut Res 2800 Plymouth Rd Ann Arbor MI 48105. *Fax:* 313-996-7962; *E-Mail:* herzigd@aa.wl.com

HERZLICH, HAROLD JOEL, TIRE SAFETY & RELIABILITY, OPTIMIZATION OF CHEMICAL & STRUCTURAL SYSTEMS USED IN TIRES. *Current Pos:* CONSULT ENGR TIRE SAFETY, HERZLICH CONSULT, 90-; PRES, ELASPHALT CORP, 90-; TECH ED, RUBBER & PLASTICS NEWS, 90- *Personal Data:* b Brooklyn, NY, Aug 1, 34; m 57, Carol; c 2. *Educ:* NY Univ, BChE, 56. *Prof Exp:* Engr, Tires Mfg, Goodyear Tire & Rubber, 56-57; chemist, tires res & develop, Armstrong Rubber Co, 58-62, mgr, 62-85; dir, Tire Safety, Pirelli Armstrong Tire, 88-90. *Concurrent Pos:* Dir, Connect Rubber Group, 58-62, treas, 62-64, vchmn, 65 & chmn, 66; treas, Rubber Div, Am Chem Soc, 78-81, chmn-elect, 81 & chmn, 82; chmn, Elastomed, 83; tire indust lectr, Clemson Univ, SC; chmn, Int Tire Expos & Conf, 93- *Mem:* hon mem Am Chem Soc; Am Soc Testing & Mat; Am Acad Forensic Sci; Soc Automotive Engrs; AAAS. *Res:* Pioneered usage of silanes, antiozonants, adhesion promoters, polybutadiene rubber, ethylene propylene rubber, halobutyl rubber and hypalon rubber in tires; aging, adhesion and fracture resistance of chemical/polymer systems in tires; optimization of tire manufacturing processes; inyracarcass pressurization; granted one patent; author of various publication. *Mailing Add:* 8908 Desert Mound Dr Las Vegas NV 89134-8801. *Fax:* 702-255-1104

HERZLINGER, GEORGE ARTHUR, BIOPHYSICS, BIOENGINEERING. *Current Pos:* PRES, BELMONT INSTRUMENT CORP, 80- *Personal Data:* b Newark, NJ, June 16, 43; m 66; c 2. *Educ:* Mass Inst Technol, SB, 65, PhD(physics), 71. *Prof Exp:* Instr, Dept Physics, Mass Inst Technol, 71-72; sr scientist med group, Avco-Everett Res Lab Inc, Everett, Mass, 72-80. *Mem:* Am Heart Asn. *Res:* New methods for monitoring cardiovascular function; cardiac assist devices; cardiac simulation; applications of fluid control systems to medicine. *Mailing Add:* 560 Concord Ave Belmont MA 02178

HERZOG, BERTRAM, ENGINEERING MECHANICS. *Current Pos:* DIR, CTR INFO TECHNOL INTEGRATION, UNIV MICH, ANN ARBOR, 87-, DIR, RES SYSTS, 90- *Personal Data:* b Offenburg, Ger, Feb 28, 29; US citizen; m 50, 71; c 3. *Educ:* Case Inst Technol, BS, 49, MS, 55; Univ Mich, PhD(eng mech), 61. *Prof Exp:* Struct engr, Dalton-Dalton Assocs, 52-53; instr eng mech, Case Inst Technol, 53-54, res assoc Proj Doanbrook, 54-55; from instr to assoc prof, Univ Mich, 55-63; mgr eng methods, Ford Motor Co, 63-65, adv comput systs planning, 65; from assoc prof to prof indust eng, Univ Mich, Ann Arbor, 65-75; dir, Univ Comput Ctr, Univ Colo, Boulder, 76-79, prof elec eng & comput sci, 76-81; pres, Herzog Assocs, Inc, 79-87. *Concurrent Pos:* Consult, Gen Elec Co, 47 & Builders Struct Steel Co, 61; consult, Res Tire Proj, Univ Mich, 61-63; consult, Bendix Systs Div, 62 & Boeing Co, 62; vis fac mem, Boeing Aircraft Co, Seattle, Wash, 62; nat lectr, Asn Comput Mach, 65-74; dir, Mich Educ Res & Info Triad, Inc, 68-74; assoc ed, Comput Graphics & Image Processing, Res J, 72-78 & Comput & Graphics, 74-; vis staff mem, Los Alamos Nat Lab, 76-83. *Mem:* Am Soc Mech Engrs; Am Soc Civil Engrs; Asn Comput Mach; Sigma Xi. *Res:* Computer networks, especially as applied to needs of educational institutions; computer graphics as an interactive man-computer communication mechanism for computer-aided design and other activities. *Mailing Add:* 16 Haverhill Ct Ann Arbor MI 48105-1407

HERZOG, BEVERLY LEAH, HYDROLOGY. *Current Pos:* from asst hydrogeologist to assoc hydrogeologist, 80-90, SR HYDROGEOLOGIST & HEAD, GROUNDWATER RESOURCES & PROTECTION SECT, ILL STATE GEOL SURV, 90- *Personal Data:* b Fond du Lac, Wis, Aug 27, 54; m 79, Craig Cutbirth. *Educ:* Univ Wis, BS, 76; Stanford Univ, MS, 78. *Prof Exp:* Asst hydrogeologist, Donahue & Assoc, 77, Camp Dresser & McKee, 78-79. *Concurrent Pos:* Instr, Groundwater Contamination Mgt, Asn Groundwater Sci & Eng, 92; instr, environ sampling, Environ Educ & Enterprises, 94. *Mem:* Asn Groundwater Sci & Eng; Am Geophys Union; Am Inst Prof Geologists; Am Soc Test Mat; Sigma Xi. *Res:* Groundwater resources and their protection; characterizing fluid flow and developing sampling techniques for wells finished in relatively impermeable deposits. *Mailing Add:* Ill State Geol Sur 615 E Peabody Dr Champaign IL 61820-6918. *Fax:* 217-244-2785; *E-Mail:* herzog@geoservisgs.uiuc.edu

HERZOG, DAVID PAUL, IMMUNOCHEMISTRY, BIOCHEMISTRY. *Current Pos:* VPRES OPERS, OHMICRON CORP, 88- *Personal Data:* b Detroit, Mich, Oct 19, 49; m 72, Kathleen Shull; c Matthew & Gregory. *Educ:* Mich State Univ, BS, 71; Univ Notre Dame, PhD(microbiol), 81. *Prof Exp:* Asst res scientist, Ames Co, Div Miles Labs Inc, 71-72, supvr, 72-78, mgr immunol & microbiol, 78-80; mgr res, Micromedic Systs, Rohn & Haas Co, 81-85; mgr res & develop, ICN Micromedic Systs, 85-88. *Mem:* Asn Official Anal Chemists; Am Chem Soc; Sigma Xi; Am Asn Clin Chemists; NY Acad Sci; Am Soc Microbiol. *Res:* Development of immunochemical methods for the detection and measurement of agricultural and environmental chemicals. *Mailing Add:* 999 Liberty Lane Warrington PA 18976. *Fax:* 215-860-7156; *E-Mail:* 72530.2033@compuserve.com

HERZOG, EMIL RUDOLPH, ASTRONOMY. *Current Pos:* RETIRED. *Personal Data:* b Basel, Switz, Mar 18, 17; nat US; m 46; c 1. *Educ:* Univ Basel, PhD, 46. *Prof Exp:* Teacher math, physics & astron, Athenaeum, Basel, Switz, 46-49, 51-56; res scientist, Extra Galactic, Calif Inst Technol, 49-51, 56-68; prof math, Calif State Polytech Univ, Pomona, 68-85, chmn dept, 73-77. *Concurrent Pos:* Vis assoc prof, Univ Southern Calif, 63-71. *Mem:* AAAS; Am Astron Soc; Swiss Math Soc; Am Math Soc; Math Asn Am. *Res:* Galaxies; novae and supernovae; celestial mechanics; theory of numbers; complex variables. *Mailing Add:* 580 S Rancho Simi Dr Covina CA 91724

HERZOG, FRITZ, MATHEMATICS. *Current Pos:* from asst prof to prof, 43-73, EMER PROF MATH, MICH STATE UNIV, 73- *Personal Data:* b Posen, Ger, Dec 6, 02; nat US; m 37. *Educ:* Columbia Univ, PhD(math), 35. *Prof Exp:* Res assoc elec eng, Cornell Univ, 37-39, instr math, 38-43. *Concurrent Pos:* Vis assoc prof, Wash Univ, 48; vis assoc prof, Univ Mich, 49-50, vis prof, 56 & 62; NSF res grant, 63-64; Sigma Xi sr res award, Mich State Univ, 69. *Mem:* Am Math Soc; Math Asn Am. *Res:* Functions of a complex variable; power series; boundary behavior; number theory. *Mailing Add:* Dept Math Mich State Univ East Lansing MI 48824

HERZOG, GERALD B(ERNARD), ELECTRICAL ENGINEERING. *Current Pos:* GEN MGR, DATA GENERAL, SUNNYVALE, CALIF. *Personal Data:* b Minneapolis, Minn, Aug 19, 27; m 47; c 4. *Educ:* Univ Minn, BSEE, 50, MSEE, 51. *Prof Exp:* Res engr transistor TV circuits, RCA Corp, 51-54, res engr color TV reproducers, 54-57, res engr & group leader high speed comput, 57-67, dir process res & develop lab, 67-71, dir digital res lab, 71-72, sr vpres technol ctrs, David Sarnoff Res Ctr, 72-79; dir eng, Consumer Prod Group, Tex Instruments, 79- *Mem:* Fel Inst Elec & Electronics Engrs. *Res:* Application of new semiconductor devices to the fields of digital logic and memory, including semiconductor memories; calculators, speaking products, home computers. *Mailing Add:* 1452 Graywood Dr San Jose CA 95129

HERZOG, GREGORY F, NUCLEAR CHEMISTRY, METEORITES. *Current Pos:* from asst to assoc prof, 71-85, PROF CHEM, RUTGERS UNIV, 85- *Personal Data:* b New York, NY, Apr 14, 44. *Educ:* Cornell Univ, BA, 64; Columbia Univ, MA, 65, PhD(chem), 69. *Prof Exp:* Res assoc chem, Univ Chicago, 69-71. *Concurrent Pos:* Prin investtr, NASA, 80-97, mem, Meteorite Working Group, 88-91, LPGRP, 90-93. *Mem:* AAAS; Am Geophys Union; Meteoritical Soc. *Res:* Isotopic abundances in meteorites; cosmic ray interactions in meteorites; accelerator mass spectrometry. *Mailing Add:* Dept Chem Rutgers Univ New Brunswick NJ 08903

HERZOG, HAROLD ALBERT, JR, HERPRETOLOGY, EXPERIMENTAL PSYCHOLOGY. *Current Pos:* PROF PSYCHOL, WESTERN CAROLINA UNIV, 86- *Personal Data:* b Miami, Fla, June 13, 46; m 74, Mary J Ronan; c Adam, Elizabeth & Kathrine. *Educ:* Am Univ Beirut, BA, 68; Univ Tenn, MA, 74, PhD(psychol), 79. *Prof Exp:* Prof psychol, Mars Hill Col, 74-86. *Concurrent Pos:* Vis prof psychol, Univ Tenn, 85-86. *Mem:* AAAS; Animal Behav Soc; Sigma Xi; Int Soc Anthrozool. *Res:* Studies of behavior development in reptiles, human-animal interactions and ethical decision-making. *Mailing Add:* 105 Gudger Hill Rd Cullowhee NC 28723. *Fax:* 704-227-7388; *E-Mail:* herzog@wcuvax1.bitnet

HERZOG, HERSHEL LEON, CHEMISTRY. *Current Pos:* PRES, L & H HERZOG ASSOCS, INC, 83- *Personal Data:* b Brooklyn, NY, May 4, 24; m 48, Levonna Horwin; c Daniel, Barbara & Laura. *Educ:* Univ Ill, BS, 44; Univ Southern Calif, MS, 47, PhD(org chem), 50. *Prof Exp:* Org chemist, E R Squibb & Sons, 44-45; chemist nat prod, Schering Corp, 50-58, mgr process res, 58-64, mgr natural prod res, 64-67, dir chem develop, 67-70, dir chem & microbiol develop, 70-73, dir chem res & develop, 73-75, vpres develop, '75-77, sr vpres, develop opers, 77-82. *Concurrent Pos:* Adj prof chem, Stevens Inst Technol, 73-82; fel, Drew Univ, 83-95; consult, Drexel Burnham Lambert, 83-85, E I du Pont de Nemours, 83-88, Merrill Lynch, 85-, People Repub China, 86-91, Vimrx Pharmaceut, 91-94 & Taro Pharmaceut, USA, 91- *Mem:* Am Chem Soc; Am Soc Microbiol. *Res:* Steroid chemistry; antibiotics; natural products; microbiological transformations. *Mailing Add:* PO Box 8199 Glen Ridge NJ 07028

HERZOG, JAMES HERMAN, ELECTRICAL ENGINEERING, COMPUTER SCIENCE. *Current Pos:* assoc prof elec eng, 67-70, ASSOC PROF ELEC & COMPUT ENG, ORE STATE UNIV, 70- *Personal Data:* b Chicago, Ill, Nov 28, 39; m 62. *Educ:* Northwestern Univ, BS, 62; Univ Mich, MS, 63, PhD(elec eng), 67. *Prof Exp:* Res asst man-mach systs, Univ Mich, 65-67. *Mem:* Inst Elec & Electronics Engrs. *Res:* Real-time systems; digital systems; robotics. *Mailing Add:* Dept Elec & Comput Eng Ore State Univ Corvallis OR 97331

HERZOG, JOHN ORLANDO, MATHEMATICS. *Current Pos:* assoc prof, Pac Lutheran Univ, 67-72, chmn, Math Dept, 68-74, 83-84 & 91-92, chmn, Div Natural Sci, 75-81, dean, 84-90, PROF MATH, PAC LUTHERAN UNIV, 72- *Personal Data:* b Ulen, Minn, Apr 6, 35; m 91, Colleen S Bone; c Barbara, Michael, Jane, Kathleen & Daniel. *Educ:* Concordia Col, Moorhead, Minn, BA, 57; Univ Nebr, MA, 59, PhD(math), 63. *Prof Exp:* Instr math, Univ Nebr, 59-61; asst prof, Idaho State Univ, 63-67. *Concurrent Pos:* NSF In-serv Inst grant, 66-67 & 68-72; energy educ grants, 79, 82 & 85; vis scholar, Univ Canterbury, NZ, 91 & 93. *Mem:* Am Math Soc; Math Asn Am; Nat Coun Teachers Math. *Res:* Mathematical analysis. *Mailing Add:* Dept Math Pac Lutheran Univ Tacoma WA 98447

HERZOG, KARL A, PHARMACEUTICAL RESEARCH & DEVELOPMENT, QUALITY ASSURANCE CONTROL. *Current Pos:* RETIRED. *Personal Data:* b Philadelphia, Pa, May 2, 40; m 73; c 3. *Educ:* Gettysburg Col, BA, 62; Philadelphia Col Pharm, BSc, 67; Univ Conn, PhD(pharmaceut), 71. *Prof Exp:* Sr pharmaceutical chemist, Smith, Kline & French Labs, 71-77; qual control mgr, Merck, Sharp & Dohme, 77-83; mgr & dir corp qual assurance, SmithKline Beecham Corp, 83-89. *Mem:* Am Pharmaceut Asn; Acad Pharmaceut Sci; Am Chem Soc. *Res:* Drug transfer through polymeric membranes; application of physical chemical principles to pharmaceutical systems during preformulation, product development and pilot scale-up; quality control service to computer-controlled, continuous-process film coated tablet and parenteral antibiotic manufacturing and packaging operations; quality control; corporate quality assurance in the health care industry. *Mailing Add:* 2005 Spring Valley Rd Landsdale PA 19446

HERZOG, LEONARD FREDERICK, II, APPLIED PHYSIOLOGY. *Current Pos:* PROF APPL PHYSIOL, NOLL CTR PHYSIOL RES, PA STATE UNIV, 94- *Personal Data:* b Syracuse, NY, June 17, 26; m 55, Elisabeth J Moffitt; c L Frederick, Heather E & Clayton E M. *Educ:* Calif Inst Technol, BS, 46; Mass Inst Technol, PhD(nuclear geophys & econ geol), 52. *Honors & Awards:* Pres E Award, 62; Free Enterprise Assoc Award, 64. *Prof Exp:* Asst metall, Mass Inst Technol, 48-49, asst geol, 51-52, res assoc geol & geophys & dir, Mass Spectrometry Labs, 52-56, prof geophys & geochem, Pa State Univ, 56-67; chmn & pres, Nuclide Corp, 54-87; mgr tech opers, measurement & analysis systs, 87-92. *Concurrent Pos:* Vis scientist, Dept

Terrestrial Magnetism, Carnegie Inst, 51-52; mem, Comt Isotopic Measurements Stand, US AEC; consult, 52-67 & 87-; pres, HoPar, In, 62-64; pres & dir, Sci Ctr Inc, 69; vis prof, Pa State Univ, 92-94. *Mem:* Am Soc Mass Spectros; Geol Soc Am; Am Soc Testing & Mat; Am Phys Soc; Meteoritical Soc; Planetary Soc; Am Chem Soc. *Res:* Development of automated mass spectrometer systems for new applications, such as determining elemental and isotopic compositions of rocks, meteorites, materials, and gases; isotopic-label studies in vivo in physiology etc; systems for implanting ions and atoms, and for the analysis of surfaces by cathodoluminescence; implementing group-interactive, computer-cum-WW Web-based systems to scaffold knowledge building. *Mailing Add:* 443 Waring Ave State College PA 16801. *Fax:* 814-865-4602

HERZOG, RICHARD (FRANZ KARL), PHYSICS. *Current Pos:* RETIRED. *Personal Data:* b Vienna, Austria, Mar 13, 11; nat US. *Educ:* Univ Vienna, PhD, 33. *Prof Exp:* From asst prof to assoc prof physics, Univ Vienna, 39-53; br chief, Air Force Cambridge Res Ctr, 53-58; sci dep dir, Space Sci Lab, GCA Corp, 58-66, chief scientist space sci opers, 66-73; prof physics & astron, Univ Southern Miss, 73-77. *Res:* Mass spectroscopy; electron optics; vacuum technique. *Mailing Add:* 9221 W Broward Blvd No 2304 Plantation FL 33324

HERZYK, DANUTA JADWIGA, IMMUNOTOXICOLOGY, BIOLOGICAL, DRUG DEVELOPMENT. *Current Pos:* sr assoc investr, 92-94, SR INVESTR, SMITHKLINE BEECHAM PHARM RES & DEVELOP, 94- *Personal Data:* b Zbtorgja, Poland, Oct 13, 54; wid. *Educ:* Med Univ Wroclaw, Poland, MS, 78, PhD(pharmaceut sci), 84. *Prof Exp:* Res asst prof, Med Univ Wroclaw, Poland, 84-85; postdoctoral researcher, Dept Microbiol & Immunol, Ohio State Univ, 85-86, res assoc, Dept Internal Med, 86-92. *Mem:* Am Fedn Med Res; Am Asn Immunologists. *Res:* Evaluation of new immunoactive compounds in preclinical phase of drug development; characterization of potential effects of new drugs on the immune system at the functional and molecular level, using in-vitro, ex vivo and invivo systems, with a focus on effects on host defense against infections. *Mailing Add:* 450 Freedom View PO Box 574 Valley Forge PA 19481. *Fax:* 610-270-7504; *E-Mail:* danuta.j.herzyk@sbphrd.com

HESKETH, HOWARD E, CHEMICAL ENGINEERING. *Current Pos:* PROF ENG, SOUTHERN ILL UNIV, 66-6- *Personal Data:* b Erie, Pa, Feb 24, 31; m 55; c 5. *Educ:* Pa State Univ, BS & MS, 53, PhD(chem eng), 68; Environ Eng Intersoc, dipl. *Honors & Awards:* L A Ripperton Award Outstanding Educr, Air & Waste Mgt Asn, 86; Stanley Kappe Award Outstanding Serv, Am Acad Environ Engrs, 88. *Prof Exp:* Sr chem engr, E I du Pont de Nemours & Co, Inc, 53-60; supvr high purity chems, Beryllium Corp, 60-63; proj coordr, Western Elec Corp, 63; asst prof chem eng, Pa State Univ, 65; scientist, Kutztown State Col, 63-66. *Concurrent Pos:* External examr, chem eng grad studies, Univ Windsor & Univ Waterloo, Can; consult air pollution control, 66- *Mem:* Nat Soc Prof Engrs; Am Inst Chem Engrs; Am Chem Soc; Am Soc Mech Engrs; Am Acad Environ Engrs. *Res:* Air pollution control; atomization devices, especially Venturi wet scrubber for both particulate and gaseous air pollution removal; fluidization related to material handling and combustion related to air pollution control and hazardous waste management. *Mailing Add:* RR4 Carbondale IL 62901. *Fax:* 618-453-7455

HESKETH, J D, PLANT PHYSIOLOGY, PLANT ECOLOGY & AGRONOMY. *Current Pos:* adj prof & plant physiologist, Miss State Univ, 68-71, NC State Univ, 71-73 & Miss State Univ, 73-78, PROF PLANT PHYSIOL & PLANT PHYSIOLOGIST, UNIV ILL, USDA, 78- *Personal Data:* b Sebec, Maine, Mar 12, 35; m 63, Susan Fahr; c 3. *Educ:* Univ Maine, BS, 56; Cornell Univ, MS, 58, PhD(crop ecol), 61. *Prof Exp:* Fel crop physiol, Conn Agr Exp Sta, 61-63; asst plant breeder, Univ Ariz, 63-65; plant physiologist, Div Plant Indust, Commonwealth Sci & Indust Res Orgn, Australia, 65-68. *Mem:* Am Hort Soc. *Res:* Leaf and canopy photosynthetic rates; carbon budgets; crop productivity; crop yield prediction; crop modeling. *Mailing Add:* 190 EMRL 1201 W Gregory Urbana IL 61801-3838

HESP, B, medicinal chemistry, for more information see previous edition

HESPENHEIDE, HENRY AUGUST, III, TROPICAL ECOLOGY, TAXONOMY. *Current Pos:* from asst prof to assoc prof, 73-94, PROF BIOL, UNIV CALIF, LOS ANGELES, 94- *Personal Data:* b Norfolk, Va, Dec 3, 42; m 76; c 2. *Educ:* Duke Univ, BSc, 64; Univ Pa, PhD(pop biol), 69. *Prof Exp:* Smithsonian fel, Smithsonian Trop Res Inst, 69-70; asst prof ecol, Univ Conn, 70-73. *Concurrent Pos:* Bd dirs, Orgn Trop Studies. *Mem:* Asn Trop Biol; Am Ornith Union; Entom Soc Am; Int Soc Hymenopterists; Coleopterists Soc. *Res:* Ecology of birds and insects, especially biodiversity, resource use and predation; taxonomy and ecology of leaf-mining beetles (Buprestidae and Curculonidae); taxonomy of Lepanthes (Orchidaceae); mimicry; ecology of extrafloral nectaries. *Mailing Add:* Dept Biol Univ Calif Los Angeles CA 90095-1606. *Fax:* 310-206-3987; *E-Mail:* henryh@biology.lifesci.ucla.edu

HESS, ADRIEN LEROY, mathematics education; deceased, see previous edition for last biography

HESS, ALLAN DUANE, CELLULAR IMMUNOLOGY. *Current Pos:* ASST PROF ONCOL & IMMUNOL, ONCOL CTR SCH MED, JOHNS HOPKINS UNIV, 78- *Educ:* Univ Ill, PhD(path & immunol), 76. *Res:* Bone marrow transplantation; immunosuppression. *Mailing Add:* Oncol Ctr Sch Med Johns Hopkins Univ 600 N Wolfe St Rm 3-127 Baltimore MD 21287-8985. *Fax:* 410-955-1969

HESS, ARTHUR, NEUROSCIENCES. *Current Pos:* PROF NEUROSCI & CELL BIOL, RW JOHNSON MED SCH, Univ Med & Dent NJ, 84- *Personal Data:* b New York, NY, Feb 19, 27; m 53; c 2. *Educ:* Univ Ark, BS, 46, MS, 47; Univ London, PhD(anat), 49, DSc, 59. *Prof Exp:* From instr to asst prof anat, Sch Med, Wash Univ, 51-61; assoc prof physiol, Col Med, Univ Utah, 61-67; prof & chmn, Anat Dept, Rutgers Med Sch, 67-84. *Mem:* Soc Neurosci; Am Asn Anat. *Res:* Neuroanatomy; neurohistology; neurophysiology. *Mailing Add:* Dept Anat UMDNJ-RW Johnson Med Sch 675 Hoes Lane Piscataway NJ 08854

HESS, BERNARD ANDES, JR, ORGANIC CHEMISTRY. *Current Pos:* from asst prof to assoc prof, 68-80, chmn dept, 82-94, PROF CHEM, VANDERBILT UNIV, 80- *Personal Data:* b Wilmington, Del, Apr 20, 40; m 63; c 2. *Educ:* Williams Col, BA, 62; Yale Univ, MS, 63, PhD(org chem), 66. *Prof Exp:* NIH fel org chem, Univ Ore, 66-68. *Concurrent Pos:* Am Chem Soc Petrol Res Fund starter grant, 68-70; Nat Acad Sci Exchange fel, Czech Acad Sci, Prague, 73-74. *Mem:* Am Chem Soc. *Res:* Physical organic chemistry. *Mailing Add:* 7332 Stevenson Ctr PO Box 1822 Sta B Nashville TN 37235

HESS, CARROLL V, AGRICULTURAL ECONOMICS. *Current Pos:* RETIRED. *Personal Data:* b Waynesboro, Pa, Jan 14, 23; m 49; c 4. *Educ:* Pa State Univ, BS, 47; Iowa State Univ, MS, 48, PhD(agr econ), 53. *Prof Exp:* Instr agr econ, Pa State Univ, 47-48, asst prof, 50-54; assoc prof, Southern Ill Univ, 54-56; agr economist, Prod Econ Res Div, Econ Res Serv, USDA, Cornell Univ, 56-59; prof agr econ, Univ Minn, 59-66; dean, Col Agr & assoc dir, Agr Exp Sta, Kans State Univ, 66-80, prof agr econ, 81. *Mem:* Am Agr Econ Asn; Sigma Xi. *Res:* Factors influencing the decision-making processes of farmers; agricultural adjustment analysis of representative farm situations; marketing efficiency studies. *Mailing Add:* 2104 Blue Hills Rd Manhattan KS 66502

HESS, CECIL F, ENGINEERING. *Current Pos:* DIR ENG, METROLASER, 88- *Personal Data:* b Sosua, Dominican Repub, Apr 29, 49; m 68, Josefina E Acosta; c Rachel & Karen. *Educ:* Cath Univ Mother & Teacher, Dominican Repub, BS; Univ Calif, Berkeley, MS, 73, PhD, 79. *Prof Exp:* Sr scientist, Spectron Develop Labs, Inc, 79-88. *Res:* Laser-based particle sizing system. *Mailing Add:* Metrolaser 18006 Skypark Circle Suite 108 Irvine CA 92614-5428

HESS, CHARLES, HORTICULTURE, PLANT PHYSIOLOGY. *Current Pos:* dean, Col Agr & Environ Sci, 75-89, PROF, UNIV CALIF, DAVIS, 91-, DIR, INT PROGS, 92- *Personal Data:* b Paterson, NJ, Dec 20, 31; m 53, Eva L Goldschmidt; c Mary, Carol, Nancy, John & Peter. *Educ:* Rutgers Univ, BS, 53; Cornell Univ, MS, 54, PhD(plant physiol, hort), 57. *Hon Degrees:* Dr Agr, Purdue Univ, 83; DSc, Delaware Valley, Col, 92. *Honors & Awards:* Int Plant Propagators Soc Award, 63; Norman Jay Coleman Award, 67; Jackson Dawson Mem Medal, 71. *Prof Exp:* From asst prof to prof hort, Purdue Univ, 58-66; res prof & chmn, Dept Hort & Forestry, Rutgers Univ, 66-70, dir, NJ Agr Exp Sta & assoc dean col agr & environ sci, 70, actg dean, 71-72, dean, Cook Col, 72-75; asst secy, Sci & Educ, US Dept Agr, 89-91. *Concurrent Pos:* Int ed, Int Plant Propagators Soc, 62-72; pres, West Lafayette Community Sch Bd, 64-65; consult, AID, 65 & Off Technol Assessment, 77-; mem, Nat Sci Bd, 82, 88 & 92-, vchmn, 84-88; mem bd dirs, Int Serv Nat Agr Res, 92- & Asian Veg Res & Develop Ctr, 94- *Mem:* Am Soc Plant Physiologists; fel Am Soc Hort Sci (pres elect, 71, pres, 72); Int Plant Propagators Soc (pres, 70); fel AAAS; Sigma Xi. *Res:* Physiology of the initiation of roots in stem cuttings and isolation of naturally occurring fungistatic inhibitors. *Mailing Add:* Dept Environ Hort Col Agr & Environ Sci Univ Calif Davis CA 95616. *Fax:* 530-752-1196; *E-Mail:* cehess@ucdavis.edu

HESS, CHARLES THOMAS, NUCLEAR PHYSICS. *Current Pos:* assoc prof, 69-83, PROF PHYSICS, UNIV MAINE, 83- *Personal Data:* b Cincinnati, Ohio, Nov 21, 40; m 65, Anne L Hess; c Samuel T. *Educ:* Wabash Col, BA, 62; Ohio Univ, PhD(nuclear physics), 67. *Prof Exp:* Fels, Ohio Univ, 67-68 & Fla State Univ, 68-69. *Concurrent Pos:* Fels, Univ Tex, Sch Pub Health, Houston, 81. *Mem:* AAAS; Am Asn Physics Teachers; Am Phys Soc; Am Nuclear Soc; Health Physics Soc. *Res:* Theoretical models of odd-odd deformed nuclei; environmental radioactivity; radon in water and air; lead 210 dating of sediment. *Mailing Add:* Dept Physics Univ Maine Orono ME 04469. *Fax:* 207-581-3410

HESS, DAVID CLARENCE, PHYSICS. *Current Pos:* RETIRED. *Personal Data:* b USA, Oct 30, 16; m 41; c 3. *Educ:* Univ Denver, BS, 37; Univ Chicago, PhD(physics), 49. *Prof Exp:* Asst, Univ Chicago, 40-42; physicist, Ballistic Res Lab, Aberdeen Proving Grounds, 42-46; physicist, Argonne Nat Lab, 46-77. *Concurrent Pos:* Guest investr, Max Planck Inst Chem, Mainz, Germany, 62-63; assoc ed, Appl Physics Lett & J Appl Physics, 70-83. *Mem:* Inst Elec & Electronics Engrs. *Res:* Mass spectroscopy; cosmology; ion optics applied to surface studies. *Mailing Add:* 4425 Oakwood Downers Grove IL 60515-2712

HESS, DAVID FILBERT, GEOLOGY, PETROLOGY. *Current Pos:* INDUST MINERAL & PETROL CONSULT & ED, 91-; PROF GEOL, WESTERN ILL UNIV, 95- *Personal Data:* b Lebanon, Pa, Aug 17, 40; m, Linda Nelson; c Jeffrey & Bryan. *Educ:* Franklin & Marshall Col, AB, 62; Ind Univ, MA, 64, PhD, 67. *Prof Exp:* Asst prof to assoc prof geol, Western Ill Univ, 66-95. *Mem:* Geol Soc Am; Friends of Mineral; Mineral Soc Am; Nat Asn Geol Teachers. *Res:* Metamorphic petrology; mineralogy and geochemistry; Precambrian geology; earth science education; geologic and biogeographic factors in the distribution of Rhopalocera (butterflies); groundwater geology; Caribbean mollusks. *Mailing Add:* Dept Geol Western Ill Univ Macomb IL 61455. *E-Mail:* df-hess@wiv.edu

HESS, DELBERT COY, agronomy, for more information see previous edition

HESS, DENNIS WILLIAM, ELECTRONIC & PHOTONIC MATERIALS, PLASMA CHEMISTRY. *Personal Data:* b Reading, Pa, Mar 1, 47; m 68, Patricia Weidner; c Amy H (Fulmer) & Sarah Elizabeth. *Educ:* Albright Col, BS, 68; Lehigh Univ, MS, 70, PhD(phys chem), 73. *Honors & Awards:* Callinan Award, Electrochem Soc, 93. *Prof Exp:* Mem res staff, Fairchild Semiconductor, 73-77; from asst prof to prof chem eng, Univ Calif, Berkeley, 77-91; prof chem eng & chmn dept, Lehigh Univ, 91-96. *Concurrent Pos:* Div ed, J Electrochem Soc, 78-90; consult, var integrated circuit & semiconductor equip mfg cos, 78-; asst dean, Col Chem, Univ Calif, Berkeley, 82-87, actg vchmn, Dept Chem Eng, 88, vchmn, 89-91; assoc ed, Chem Mat, 88-; chmn, Gordon Conf Chem Electronic Mat, 88. *Mem:* AAAS; Am Chem Soc; Am Inst Chem Engrs; fel Electrochem Soc (pres, 96-97); Sigma Xi. *Res:* Science and technology of thin film formation and etching techniques; design of thin film materials for specific applications; chemistry and physics of glow discharges, plasmas, used in thin film processing and surface modification. *Mailing Add:* Sch Chem Ga Inst Technol 778 Atlantic Dr Atlanta GA 30332. *E-Mail:* dennis.hess@che.gatech.edu

HESS, DEXTER WINFIELD, PLANT TAXONOMY & HISTORICAL PLANT RESEARCH, FOOD PRODUCT FORMULATIONS. *Current Pos:* CONSULT, HIST BOT, 87- *Personal Data:* b Rome, Ga, Aug 1, 27; m 56; c 3. *Educ:* Duke Univ, AB, 52, MA, 53; Univ Colo, PhD, 59. *Prof Exp:* Asst biol, Univ Colo, 53-56; researcher ecol, Inst Arctic Alpine Res, Univ Colo, 56-59; teacher bot & bact, Otero Jr Col, 59-83, chmn dept sci & math, 71-77, dean fac & acad instruct, 77-83; mgr, Qual Assurance Labs, Western Food Prod Co Inc, 83-87. *Concurrent Pos:* Partic, Inst Desert Biol, Ariz State Univ, 69 & Inst Radiation Biol, Tex Woman's Univ, 70; guest lectr, Univ Denver, 71 & Univ Colo & Colo State Univ, 84 & 85. *Mem:* AAAS. *Res:* Compiling local flora of Southeastern Colorado; historical changes to local flora in Southeastern Colorado. *Mailing Add:* 2202 Santa Fe La Junta CO 81050

HESS, EARL HOLLINGER, AGRICULTURAL CHEMISTRY, ENVIRONMENTAL CHEMISTRY. *Current Pos:* CHMN BD, MOUNTAIN STATES ANALYTICAL, INC, 86- *Personal Data:* b Lancaster, Pa, June 16, 28; m 51; c 3. *Educ:* Franklin & Marshall Col, BS, 52; Univ Ill, PhD(org chem), 55. *Honors & Awards:* Spec Serv Citation, Am Coun Independent Labs, 79, Roger W Truesdail Award Outstanding Serv, 83. *Prof Exp:* Asst chem, Univ Ill, 52-54; asst prof, Franklin & Marshall Col, 55-57; proj leader & org res chemist, Res Lab, Gen Cigar Co, Inc, 57-61; pres & chief exec officer, Lancaster Labs Inc, 61-95. *Concurrent Pos:* Pres, Am Coun Independent Labs, 84-86, co-chmn, Pub Relations Comt, 89-90; treas & mem bd dirs, Commwealth Found; assets, Inst Global Ethics, Res Inst Small Emerging Bus. *Mem:* Am Asn Lab Accreditation; AAAS; Am Chem Soc; Am Soc Testing & Mat; NY Acad Sci; Sigma Xi; hon mem Am Coun Independent Labs. *Res:* Agricultural and environmental chemistry and biology, including structure-biological activity relationships; agricultural and industrial by-product recovery and utilization; industrial waste treatability; agricultural by product cetiliation (now referred to a recycling) with laten contributions in analytical science. *Mailing Add:* 2435 New Holland Pike Lancaster PA 17601

HESS, EUGENE LYLE, BIOCHEMISTRY. *Current Pos:* RETIRED. *Personal Data:* b Superior, Wis, May 14, 14; m 41, Lila Huhtala; c Gretchen (Gage) & Jennifer (Asher). *Educ:* Univ Minn, BCh, 38; Univ Wis, MS, 42, PhD(chem), 47. *Prof Exp:* Asst prof mil sci & tactics, Univ Minn, 40-42; res assoc, Univ Wis, 47-48; res assoc, Rheumatic Fever Res Inst, Northwestern Univ, 48-57; sr scientist, Worcester Found Exp Biol, 57-65; prog dir metab biol, NSF, 65-66, head molecular biol sect, 66-70, sr staff assoc, Off Asst Dir Res, 70-71; exec dir, Fedn Am Socs Exp Biol, 71-79. *Concurrent Pos:* Affil prof, Clark Univ, 61-65; adv comt, NSF, 76-80 & Nat Res Coun, 71-79; bd trustees, Biosis, 76-81, treas, 78-81. *Mem:* AAAS; Am Chem Soc; Am Soc Biol Chem; Biophys Soc; Am Hort Soc. *Res:* Ultracentrifugation; moving boundary electrophoresis; light scattering; proteins; nucleic acids. *Mailing Add:* 655 Willow Valley Sq L104 Lancaster PA 17602-4873

HESS, EVELYN V, INTERNAL MEDICINE, IMMUNOLOGY. *Current Pos:* assoc prof, Col Med & dir div immunol & connective tissue dis, 64-69, dir div immunol, 69-95, McDONALD PROF MED & DIR DIV IMMUNOL, MED CTR, UNIV CINCINNATI, 69- *Personal Data:* b Dublin, Ireland, Nov 8, 26; US citizen; m 54, Michael Howett. *Educ:* Univ Dublin, MB, BCh & BAO, 49, MD, 80. *Hon Degrees:* MD, Univ Del Nord, Columbia, 87. *Honors & Awards:* Oscar Schmidt Award, Univ Cincinnati; Award for Excellence, Arthritis Found; Distinguisehd Rheumatologist Award, Am Col Rheumatology. *Prof Exp:* Registr med, Rheumatic Dis Unit, Royal Free Hosp & Med Sch, 56-57; from instr to asst prof internal med, Univ Tex Southwestern Med Sch, 60-64. *Concurrent Pos:* Empire Rheumatism Coun traveling fel, 58-59; attend physician, Vet Admin Hosp & Parkland Mem Hosp, Dallas, Tex, 61-64; sr investr, Arthritis & Rheumatism Found, 63-68; mem bd gov, Arthritis Found, 67-70; attend physician, Univ Hosps & Vet Admin Hosp; consult physician, Childrens Hosp, Cincinnati. *Mem:* Fel Am Acad Allergy & Immunol; fel Am Col Physicians; fel AAAS; Am Soc Nephrology; Cent Soc Clin Res; Am Asn Immunol; hon mem Italian Soc Rheumatism; hon mem Peruvian Soc Rheumatol; hon mem Japanese Soc Clin Immunol; Am Rheumatism Soc (vpres, 82-83); master Am Col Rheumatol. *Res:* Immunologic drug reactions; immunology of rheumatic diseases; AIDS and related diseases; tolerance mechanisms; computers in medicine. *Mailing Add:* Univ Cincinnati Med Ctr Rm 7562 Cincinnati OH 45267. *Fax:* 513-558-3799

HESS, F DAN, CELL BIOLOGY, ELECTRON MICROSCOPY. *Current Pos:* dir biol & biochem res, Sandoz Crop Protection, 86-94, vpres res, Sandoz Agro, Inc, 95-96, VPRES RES, NOVARTIS CROP PROTECTION, 97- *Personal Data:* b Tacoma, Wash, Mar 22, 46. *Educ:* Mich State Univ, BS, 69; Univ Calif, Davis, MS, 73, PhD(plant physiol), 75. *Honors & Awards:* Outstanding Young Researcher Award, Weed Sci Soc Am, 85; Staniforth lectr, Iowa State Univ, 96. *Prof Exp:* Asst prof bot & weed sci, Colo State Univ, 75-76; from asst prof to assoc prof plant physiol & weed sci, Purdue Univ, 76-86. *Concurrent Pos:* Assoc ed, Weed Sci, 85-88, abstract ed, 90-92; bd dirs, Weed Sci Soc Am, 93-95. *Mem:* Am Soc Plant Physiologists; Electron Microscope Soc Am; fel Weed Sci Soc Am (vpres, 96, pres-elect, 97). *Res:* Mechanism of action of herbicides; physiological and cell biological effects of herbicides; analytical electron microscopy of plant tissue; absorption and translocation of postemergence herbicides; plant cuticle development. *Mailing Add:* Novartis Crop Protection Res Div 975 California Ave Palo Alto CA 94304-1104. *Fax:* 650-857-1125; *E-Mail:* hess@sandog.com

HESS, GEORGE BURNS, LOW TEMPERATURE PHYSICS, PHYSISORPTION. *Current Pos:* from asst prof to assoc prof, 68-88, PROF PHYSICS, UNIV VA, 88- *Personal Data:* b Princeton, NJ, Sept 17, 36; m 65, Blanche Isobe; c Harry & Frank. *Educ:* Princeton Univ, BA, 58; Stanford Univ, PhD(physics), 67. *Prof Exp:* Res assoc, Stanford Univ, 67-68. *Concurrent Pos:* Vis assoc prof, Univ Wash, 79-80; vis prof, Pa State Univ, 94-95. *Mem:* Am Phys Soc. *Res:* Surface physics; superfluid helium; fluid dynamics; study of multilayer physisorption by ellipsometry and other techniques. *Mailing Add:* Dept Physics Univ Va Charlottesville VA 22901. *Fax:* 804-924-4576

HESS, GEORGE G, ORGANIC CHEMISTRY OF GROUNDWATER. *Current Pos:* asst prof, 65-70, chmn, Chem Dept, 84-88, ASSOC PROF CHEM, WRIGHT STATE UNIV, 70-, chmn. *Personal Data:* b Collingswood, NJ, Jan 4, 38; m 62, Sylvia Middlekauff; c Heidi (Senbel) & Jonathan. *Educ:* Juniata Col, BS, 59; Pa State Univ, PhD(chem), 64. *Prof Exp:* Res assoc chem, Pa State Univ, 64-65. *Concurrent Pos:* Consult, gas chromatography & mass spectrometry technol, Monsanto Res Corp, Dayton, 80-85; vis scientist, USEPA-ERL, Athens, Ga, 90-91. *Mem:* Am Chem Soc; Am Asn Univ Professors. *Res:* Analyses of organics in water and sediments in multidisciplinary projects. *Mailing Add:* Dept Chem Wright State Univ Dayton OH 45435. *Fax:* 513-873-3301

HESS, GEORGE J, MANUFACTURING ENGINEERING. *Current Pos:* VPRES PLANNING, INGERSOLL MILLING MACH CO, 81- *Educ:* Univ Wis, BS. *Mem:* Nat Acad Eng; fel Soc Mfg Engrs; Inst Elec & Electronics Engrs. *Mailing Add:* Ingersoll Milling Mach Co 707 Fulton Ave Rockford IL 61103. *Fax:* 815-987-6725; *E-Mail:* gjh@ingersoll.com

HESS, GEORGE PAUL, BIOPHYSICAL CHEMISTRY, BIOCHEMISTRY. *Current Pos:* From instr to assoc prof biochem, 55-64, prof chem, 64-66, PROF BIOCHEM & MOLECULAR BIOL, CORNELL UNIV, 66- *Personal Data:* b Vienna, Austria, Nov 18, 26; nat US; m 53, 80, Susan Hess; c 4. *Educ:* Univ Calif, AB, 49, PhD(biochem), 53. *Honors & Awards:* Alexander von Humboldt Award, 82; Naito lectr, Japan Found, 88. *Prof Exp:* Nat Found Infantile Paralysis fel chem, Mass Inst Technol, 53-55. *Concurrent Pos:* Guggenheim fel & sr Fulbright grantee, Max Planck Inst Phys Chem, Ger, 62-63; vis prof, Johnson Found, Univ, Pa, 64-65; Fulbright selectee, 66-67; NIH spec fel, Med Res Coun Lab Molecular Biol & fel, Churchill Col, 69-70; mem numerous adv panels, NIH; mem ed bd, Fedn Am Socs Exp Biol 72-76; adv panel mem, NSF, 77- *Mem:* Nat Acad Sci; Am Biophys Soc; Am Soc Biol Chem; Soc Neurosci; fel AAAS; Am Chem Soc; Protein Soc. *Res:* Development and use of laser-pulse photolysis techniques for studying chemical kinetic mechanisms of reactions on the surface of single cells in the microsecond time region. *Mailing Add:* Sect Biochem Molecular & Cell Biol Cornell Univ 216 Biotechnol Bldg Ithaca NY 14853-2703. *Fax:* 607-255-2428; *E-Mail:* gph2@cornell.edu

HESS, HANS-JURGEN ERNST, ORGANIC CHEMISTRY. *Current Pos:* res chemist, Pfizer Inc, 59-64, res supvr, 64-67, sect mgr, 67-71, asst dir to exec dir, 71-84, SSR EXEC DIR, MED CHEM RES, CENT RES, PFIZER, INC, 84- *Personal Data:* b Helmstedt, Ger, June 20, 30; m 64; c 2. *Educ:* Brunswick Tech Univ, dipl, 55, Dr rer nat(org chem), 57. *Prof Exp:* Fel org chem, Univ Va, 57-58 & Univ Ill, 58-59. *Concurrent Pos:* Ed-in-chief, annual reports in Med Chem, 79-84. *Mem:* Am Chem Soc; Soc Ger Chem; NY Acad Sci. *Res:* Peptides; cardiovascular-renal-pulmonary-gastrointestinal drugs; prostaglandins, antibodies, anti-inflammatory drugs, natural products, chemistry. *Mailing Add:* Jericho Dr Old Lyme CT 06371

HESS, HELEN HOPE, BIOCHEMISTRY, NEUROPATHOLOGY. *Current Pos:* res med officer, Biochem Sect, Lab Vision Res, 71-79 & 81-85, med res officer, Clin Br, Sect Retinal & Occular Tissue Dis, 79-81, RES MED OFFICER, OFF SCI DIR, NAT EYE INST, NIH, 86- *Personal Data:* b Clarksburg, WVa, Aug 26, 23. *Educ:* WVa Univ, BA, 46, BS, 48; Harvard Med Sch, MD, 51. *Prof Exp:* Instr anat, WVa Univ, 49-50; asst in neuropath, McLean Hosp, Mass, 53-56, from asst neuropathologist to assoc neuropathologist, 56-71; asst in neuropath, Harvard Med Sch, 53-56, instr, 56-59, res assoc, 59-69, prin res assoc, 69-70, assoc prof neuropath & neurochem, 70-71; prof neurol & biochem, Med Sch, George Washington Univ, 71-75. *Concurrent Pos:* USPHS fel neurochem, Res Lab, McLean Hosp, Mass, 51-53; mem, Neurol Study Sect, NIH, 73-75. *Mem:* Fel AAAS; Asn Res Vision Ophthal; Am Soc Neurochem; Am Chem Soc; Int Soc Neurochem; Am Asn Neuropathologists. *Res:* Neurochemistry and neuropathology of retina and brain; cerebral cortex; photoreceptor, neuronal and glial membranes; correlation of histological structure, biochemical composition and metabolic activity in nervous tissues, normal and diseased; cataracts in retinal degenerations, genetic and toxic in origin; nutritional prevention in Royal College of Surgeons rats; methylnitrosourea as an agent causing cataracts with retinal degeneration. *Mailing Add:* Off Sci Dir Bldg 9 Rm 1E-118 NIH-Nat Eye Inst Bethesda MD 20892

HESS, HOWARD M, power generation & distribution; deceased, see previous edition for last biography

HESS, JOHN BERGER, ECOLOGY, GENETICS. *Current Pos:* PROF BIOL, CENT MO STATE UNIV, 69- *Personal Data:* b Dayton, Ohio, Apr 4, 42; c 1. *Educ:* Wheaton Col, BS, 64; Southern Ill Univ, MS, 66; Colo State Univ, PhD(zool), 70. *Mem:* Sigma Xi; AAAS; Soc Study Amphibians & Reptiles; Biol Photog Asn. *Res:* Genetics of natural populations, particularly the influence of environmental conditions on composition of the gene pool. *Mailing Add:* Dept Biol Cent Mo State Univ Warrensburg MO 64093

HESS, JOHN LLOYD, METABOLIC REGULATION, OXIDATIVE STRESS. *Current Pos:* asst prof, 67-74, assoc prof biochem & nutrit, 75-92, PROF BIOCHEM, VA POLYTECH INST & STATE UNIV, 93- *Personal Data:* b Landisville, Pa, Nov 25, 39; m 66, Ann Ulland; c David A, Jonathan A, Carrie M & Steven R. *Educ:* Franklin & Marshall Col, BA, 61; Univ Del, MS, 63; Mich State Univ, PhD(biochem), 66. *Prof Exp:* Res assoc biochem, Mich State Univ, 66; res biochemist, Scripps Inst, Univ Calif, 66-67. *Concurrent Pos:* Res Corp NY res grant, 68-69; NIH res grant, 72-, USDA Coop State Res Serv, 73-76, Environ Protection Agency, 85-90 & USDA Forest Serv, 90; dir, Va Jr Acad Sci, 75-78; fel, Dept Plant Biol, Carnegie Inst Washington, 78-79. *Mem:* Am Chem Soc; Am Soc Plant Physiol; Am Soc Biochem & Molecular Biol; Sigma Xi; Asn Res Vision & Ophthal. *Res:* Investigations in plant metabolism in response to oxidative stress and cold temperature stress; enzyme regulation; mechanisms of cataract formation in rat lens; intercellular transport and cellular compartmentation. *Mailing Add:* Dept Biochem & Anaerobic Microbiol Va Polytech Inst & State Univ Blacksburg VA 24061-0308. *Fax:* 540-231-9070; *E-Mail:* jlhess@vt.edu

HESS, JOHN MONROE CONVERSE, PHYSICAL CHEMISTRY. *Current Pos:* assoc prof, 63-65, chmn sci div, 65-69, chmn dept chem, 69-85, PROF CHEM, NORTH ADAMS STATE COL,65- *Personal Data:* b Sunbury, Pa, Nov 22, 31; m 55, 75, Donna Denelli; c 2. *Educ:* Pa State Univ, BS, 53; Univ Maine, MS, 55, PhD(phys chem), 61. *Prof Exp:* Asst chemist, Maine Tech Exp Sta, Univ Maine, 55-56, instr chem, 56-62; sr chemist, Sprague Res Ctr, Sprague Elec Co, Mass, 62-63. *Mem:* Sigma Xi; Am Chem Soc. *Res:* Thermodynamics and determination of formation constants for complex association in electrolytes; molten salts and concentrated aqueous solutions of electrolytes. *Mailing Add:* 128 Thornliebank Rd Williamstown MA 01267-2765

HESS, JOHN WARREN, HYDROGEOCHEMISTRY, ISOTOPE HYDROLOGY. *Current Pos:* Asst res prof, Water Resources Ctr, Univ Nev Syst, 74-78, assoc res prof, hydrogeochem, 78-86, dir, Isotope Lab, 81-87, dep exec dir, 87-89, RES PROF, DESERT RES INST, WATER RESOURCES CTR, UNIV NEV SYST, 86-, EXEC DIR, 89-, VPRES, ACAD AFFAIRS, 95- *Personal Data:* b Lancaster, Pa, May 6, 47; m 71, Letitia J Schrantz; c Nathan J & Joshua K. *Educ:* Pa State Univ, BS, 69, PhD(geol, hydrogeol), 74. *Concurrent Pos:* Chmn, Res Adv Comt, Nat Speleol Soc, 77-84; res fel, Scottish Univ Res & Reactor Ctr, 80-81; prof, Univ Nev, Las Vegas, 81-92; mem, IAH Karst Comn, 90-; bd chmn, Karst Waters Inst, 93-; chair, Hydrogiol Div, Geol Soc Am, 95-96. *Mem:* Am Geophys Union; fel Geol Soc Am; Nat Speleol Soc; Sigma Xi; Geochem Soc; Int Asn Hydrogeologists. *Res:* Hydrogeologic, isotopic, hydrogeochemical, and geophysical research pertaining to carbonate rock terrains, unsaturated zones and groundwater monitoring. *Mailing Add:* 7205 Fury Lane Las Vegas NV 89128. *Fax:* 702-895-0496; *E-Mail:* jack@snsc.dri.edu

HESS, JOSEPH W, JR, MEDICAL EDUCATION, GERIATRIC MEDICINE. *Current Pos:* div chief, Family Med, 88-93, assoc chmn, 93-95, PROF, DEPT FAMILY & PREV MED, UNIV UTAH, 93- *Personal Data:* b Farmington, Utah, June 7, 26; m 53, Jean Stallwood; c 6. *Educ:* Utah State Univ, BS, 53; Univ Utah, MD, 56; Univ Ill, Urbana, MEd(med), 68. *Prof Exp:* From instr to assoc prof internal med, Sch Med, Wayne State Univ, 60-72, chief, Sect Rheumatol, 65-68, dir educ serv & res, 68-74, prof family med & chmn dept, 74-88. *Concurrent Pos:* NSF fel, 60-61; guest worker, Nat Inst Arthritis & Metab Dis, 65; mem, Med Adv Comt, Nat Myasthenia Gravis Found, 66-67; consult, WHO, 70-; mem, Nat Rev Comt, Regional Med Progs, 70-73. *Mem:* Am Col Physicians; Am Educ Res Asn; Asn Am Med Cols; Am Acad Family Physicians; Soc Teachers Family Med. *Res:* Muscles and connective tissue metabolism; methods for improving the assessment of student and physician performance and for improving the effectiveness of the learning environment in undergraduate medical education; nutrition in the elderly; osteoporosis prevention. *Mailing Add:* Dept Med Univ Utah Salt Lake City UT 48202

HESS, KARL, SOLID STATE ELECTRONICS. *Current Pos:* assoc dir, Beckman Inst, 87-90, PROF ELEC ENG, UNIV ILL, URBANA-CHAMPAIGN, 80-, SWANLUND CHAIR, 96- *Personal Data:* b Trumau, Austria, June 20, 45; US citizen; m 67, Sylvia Horvath; c Ursula & Karl III. *Educ:* Univ Vienna, Austria, PhD(energy relaxation, semiconductors), 70. *Honors & Awards:* J J Ebers Award, Electron Devices Soc, Inst Elec & Electronics Engrs; D Sarnoff Field Award, Inst Elec & Electronics Engrs. *Prof Exp:* Dozent, Univ Vienna, 77-80. *Concurrent Pos:* Vis assoc prof, Coord Sci Lab, Univ Ill, Urbana-Champaign, 77-80; adj prof, Supercomput Appln, Univ Ill, 88-; consult, US Army, Ft Momouth, Naval Res Lab, Siemens, Ger, Gould, Chicago; Fulbright fel, 73-74. *Mem:* Fel Inst Elec & Electronics Engrs; fel Am Phys Soc; fel AAAS. *Res:* Semiconductor physics; hot electrons; electronic transport in semiconductor heterolayers; nanostructure physics; simulation of quantum well laser diooles; computational electronics. *Mailing Add:* Univ Ill Beckman Inst 405 N Matthews Urbana IL 61801. *Fax:* 217-244-4333; *E-Mail:* k-hess@uiuc.edu

HESS, LAVERNE DERRYL, PHYSICAL CHEMISTRY, ELECTRONIC & PHOTONIC MATERIALS. *Current Pos:* PROG DIR, NSF, 89- *Personal Data:* b Stockton, Ill, Oct 28, 33; m 56, Dawne McDermott; c Donald, Patti, Susan, Daniel, Bart & Jennifer. *Educ:* Univ Calif, Riverside, BA, 61, PhD(phys chem), 65. *Prof Exp:* Sr scientist, Hughes Res Labs, 65-89. *Mem:* Mat Res Soc. *Res:* Photochemistry; chemical lasers; chemical kinetics-relaxation phenomena; nonlinear optics; excimer lasers; laser annealing; laser-induced epitaxy; liquid crystal light valves; superconductivity. *Mailing Add:* NSF 4201 Wilson Blvd Rm 1065 Arlington VA 22230

HESS, LAWRENCE GEORGE, SYNTHETIC ORGANIC CHEMISTRY. *Current Pos:* RETIRED. *Personal Data:* b Humboldt, Kans, Feb 25, 16; m 43, 86; c 3. *Educ:* Univ Notre Dame, BS, 38, MS, 39, PhD(org chem), 41. *Prof Exp:* Asst, Univ Notre Dame, 38-41; chemist, Res & Develop Dept, Union Carbide Corp, 41-71, develop scientist chem & plastics, 71-78. *Mem:* Am Chem Soc. *Res:* Process development. *Mailing Add:* 1578 Kanawha Blvd E Charleston WV 25311

HESS, LINDSAY LAROY, MATHEMATICAL MODELING, COMPUTER SIMULATION. *Current Pos:* VPRES ACAD AFFAIRS, MONT TECH, 83- *Personal Data:* b Great Falls, Mont, Apr 30, 40; m 77; c 6. *Educ:* Mont State Univ, BS, 62, MS, 65; Univ Ill, MA, 67; Ohio Univ, PhD(physics), 71. *Prof Exp:* Res physicist, ERDA, 74-76; asst prof elec eng, Univ NDak, 76-77; assoc prof math & physics, Carroll Col, Mont, 77-83. *Concurrent Pos:* NSF fel, Univ Ill, 64-67; NDEA fel, Ohio Univ, 68-71; educ consult, Indians Into Med, 73-74; dir, Mont Sci Talent Search, 86-88; pres, Mont Sect, Am Asn Physics Teachers, 86-87 & Mont Acad Sci, 87-88. *Mem:* Sigma Xi; Am Asn Physics Teachers. *Res:* Applied modeling of systems; math and science education. *Mailing Add:* Dept Eng Sci Mont Tech Univ Butte MT 59701

HESS, MARILYN E, PHARMACOLOGY. *Current Pos:* Asst pharmacol, Univ Pa, 49-50, asst instr physiol & from asst instr pharmacol to asst prof, 52-68, assoc prof, 68-76, PROF PHARMACOL, SCH MED, UNIV PA, 76- *Personal Data:* b Erie, Pa, Dec 31, 24. *Educ:* Villa Maria Col, BS, 46; Univ Pa, MS, 49, PhD(pharmacol), 57, MS Ed, 85. *Honors & Awards:* Lindback Award. *Concurrent Pos:* Am Heart Asn res fel, 60-62, estab investr, 62-67, mem, Coun Basic Sci; NIH career develop award, 67-72; vis scientist, Mario Negri Inst Pharmacol, Italy, 70-71. *Mem:* AAAS; Am Soc Pharmacol & Exp Therapeut; NY Acad Sci. *Res:* Circulatory and respiratory reflexes; effect of antiarrhythmic drugs on carbohydrate metabolism of heart muscle; toxic actions of oxygen; effect of sympathomimetic amines on phosphorylase activity in heart muscle; influence of hormones on cardiac function and metabolism; female hormones and urinery bladder function. *Mailing Add:* Dept Pharmacol 6084 Univ Pa Sch Med Philadelphia PA 19104-6084. *Fax:* 215-573-2236; *E-Mail:* hess@pharm.med.upenn.edu

HESS, MICHAEL L, MEDICINE. *Current Pos:* PROF & CHMN, DIV CARDIOPULMONARY LAB & RES, VA MED COL, 91- *Personal Data:* b Philipsburg, Pa, Aug 10, 42. *Educ:* Pittsburgh Univ, MD, 68. *Mailing Add:* Dept Med Va Med Col Box 281 Richmond VA 23298

HESS, PATRICK HENRY, RESEARCH MANAGEMENT, ENHANCED OIL RECOVERY. *Current Pos:* res chemist to sr res chemist, Chevron Res Co, 60-69, SR RES ASSOC, CHEVRON OIL FIELD RES CO, 69- *Personal Data:* b Albia, Iowa, Aug 6, 31; m 59, Ann Marie Malone; c Michelle, Maria, Margaret, Catherine & John. *Educ:* Univ Iowa, BS, 53; Univ Nebr, MS, 58, PhD(org chem), 60. *Prof Exp:* Chemist, State Hyg Labs, Iowa, 53-54; asst, Univ Nebr, 56-58. *Mem:* Am Chem Soc; Soc Petrol Engrs. *Res:* Chemical flooding for enhanced oil recovery; control of sand and water associated with petroleum production; addition and condensation polymers; furans, polyesters, epoxys, acrylics; mechanisms of organic elimination reactions. *Mailing Add:* 12463 Jeremiah Dr Auburn CA 95603-9051. *E-Mail:* pathess@neworld.net

HESS, PAUL C, PETROLOGY, GEOCHEMISTRY. *Current Pos:* From asst prof to assoc prof, 68-80, chmn dept, 80-84, PROF GEOL, BROWN UNIV, 80- *Personal Data:* b Sanremo, Italy, July 2, 40; US citizen; m 63; c 3. *Educ:* Tufts Univ, AB, 63; Harvard Univ, MS, 65, PhD(geol), 69. *Concurrent Pos:* Assoc ed, Geochem Cosmochem Act, 83-; series ed, Cambridge Press, 86- *Mem:* Mineral Soc Am; Geochem Soc. *Res:* Metamorphic petrology; solution theory of silicate melts and glasses; phase equilibria of solids and fluids; planetary petrology. and geochemistry. *Mailing Add:* Dept Geol Sci Brown Univ Brown Sta Providence RI 02912-9100

HESS, R(ONALD) A(NDREW), AEROSPACE ENGINEERING. *Current Pos:* assoc prof, 82-84, PROF MECH & AERON ENG, UNIV CALIF, DAVIS, 84- *Personal Data:* b Norwalk, Ohio, Mar 12, 42; m 67, Connaught A; c Christian & Catherine. *Educ:* Univ Cincinnati, BS, 65, MS, 67, PhD(aerospace eng), 70. *Prof Exp:* Asst prof aeronaut, Naval Postgrad Sch, 70-76; res scientist, Ames Res Ctr, NASA, 76-82. *Concurrent Pos:* Assoc ed,

J Aircraft, 77-, Inst Elec & Electronics Engrs, Trans on Syst, Man & Cybernet, 80- *Mem:* Assoc fel Am Inst Aeronaut & Astronaut; Sigma Xi; sr mem Inst Elec Electronics Engrs; Am Helicopter Soc. *Res:* Manual control theory; man-machine systems; automatic control systems; vehicle handling qualities. *Mailing Add:* Dept Mech & Aeron Eng Univ Calif Davis CA 95616. *Fax:* 916-762-4158; *E-Mail:* hess@poppy.engr.ucdavis.edu

HESS, RICHARD WILLIAM, INORGANIC PIGMENT CHEMISTRY. *Current Pos:* Res chemist, E I Du Pont de Nemours & Co, Inc, 71-73, tech supvr res & develop, Pigments Dept, 74-76, prod mgr ferric chloride, 76-79, res mgr white pigment & mineral prods, C&P Dept, 79-93, RES MGR TECH PLANNING NYLON BUS, E I DU PONT DE NEMOURS & CO INC, 93- *Personal Data:* b Rochester, NY, Nov 18, 44; m 67. *Educ:* Kalamazoo Col, BA, 66; Univ Wis-Madison, PhD(inorg chem), 71. *Mem:* Am Chem Soc. *Res:* Inorganic pigments. *Mailing Add:* 103 North Rd Wilmington DE 19809

HESS, ROBERT L(AWRENCE), ENGINEERING MECHANICS. *Current Pos:* asst prof eng mech, chem & metall eng, Univ Mich, Ann Arbor, 52-54, assoc prof eng mech, 54-58, asst dir, Willow Run Labs, 58-60, prof eng mech, 58-80, PROF APPL MECH, UNIV MICH, ANN ARBOR, 80-, ASSOC DIR INST SCI & TECHNOL, 60-, DIR HWY SAFETY RES INST, 67- *Personal Data:* b Orange, NJ, Sept 29, 24; m 45; c 3. *Educ:* Univ Mich, BSE(eng math) & BSE(eng mech), 45, MS, 48, PhD(mech eng). 50. *Prof Exp:* Instr eng mech, Univ Mich, 46-49; mem tech staff, Bell Tel Labs, 49-52. *Concurrent Pos:* Consult, US Army Sci Adv Bd, 75- *Mem:* Sigma Xi. *Res:* Electron tube envelopes; glass structure; stress analysis; design of magnetrons and transistors; computer modeling of automobile braking; handling and crash reconstruction. *Mailing Add:* 2629 Danbury Lane Ann Arbor MI 48103-2216

HESS, RONALD EUGENE, ORGANIC CHEMISTRY. *Current Pos:* from asst prof to assoc prof, 66-83, PROF CHEM, URSINUS COL, 83- *Personal Data:* b Lock Haven, Pa, Nov 22, 38; m 61; c 2. *Educ:* Lock Haven State Col, BS, 60; Cornell Univ, PhD(org chem), 67. *Prof Exp:* Teacher high sch, Pa, 60-62. *Concurrent Pos:* Premed adv, Ursinus Col, 81- *Mem:* Am Chem Soc; Sigma Xi; Nat Asn Adv to Health Prof. *Res:* Dimerization and trimerization of aldoketenes; preparation and chemistry of small-ring carbocyclic ketones, especially cyclobutanones; nuclear magnetic resonance spectroscopy of organometallic compounds. *Mailing Add:* Dept Chem Ursinus Col Collegeville PA 19426

HESS, WENDELL WAYNE, INORGANIC CHEMISTRY. *Current Pos:* from asst prof to assoc prof, 63-71, prof, 71-90, DEAN, ILL WESLEYAN UNIV, 76-, EMER PROF CHEM & PROVOST, 90- *Personal Data:* b Sweetwater,Tex, Jan 1, 35; m 55; c 2. *Educ:* McMurry Col, BA, 57; Univ Kans, PhD(inorg chem), 63. *Prof Exp:* Chemist rocket fuel, Phillips Petrol Co, 57-58, reactor engr atomic energy, 58-59. *Mem:* AAAS; Am Chem Soc; Sigma Xi. *Res:* Reactions of inorganic free radicals, particularly those concerning the halogen and pseudohalogen compounds; coordination compounds. *Mailing Add:* 309 Highland Ave Normal IL 61761-3652

HESS, WILFORD MOSER (BILL), BOTANY, PLANT PATHOLOGY. *Current Pos:* from asst prof to assoc prof bot, 62-71, chmn, Dept Bot & Range Sci, 57-96, PROF BOT, BRIGHAM YOUNG UNIV,71-, DIR, ELECTRON OPTICS LAB, 78- *Personal Data:* b Clifton, Idaho, Feb 18, 34; m 54, Carlene B Falkenburg; c Carl Z & Carla A. *Educ:* Brigham Young Univ, BS, 57; Ore State Univ, MS, 60, PhD(plant path), 62. *Concurrent Pos:* NSF fel, Cell Res Inst, Univ Tex, 64-65; NIH fel, Swiss Fed Inst Technol, 66-67; NSF grants, 67-79, 87-; NIH career develop award, 69-74; USDA grant, 72-74. *Mem:* AAAS; Am Phytopath Soc; Am Bot Soc; Mycol Soc Am; Micros Soc Am; Am Soc Econ Bot; Sigma Xi. *Res:* Fungus and host ultrastructure and interaction; ultrastructure and biochemistry of fungus spores; x-ray microanalysis of fungal spores and interaction; morphological and chemical studies of hair. *Mailing Add:* 129 W1DB Dept Bot & Range Sci Brigham Young Univ Provo UT 84602. *Fax:* 801-378-7499; *E-Mail:* wilford_hess@byu.edu

HESS, WILMOT NORTON, NUCLEAR PHYSICS. *Current Pos:* RETIRED. *Personal Data:* b Oberlin, Ohio, Oct 16, 26; m 50; c 3. *Educ:* Columbia Univ, BE, 46; Oberlin Col, MA, 49; Univ Calif, PhD(physics), 54. *Hon Degrees:* DSc, Oberlin Col, 70. *Prof Exp:* Instr physics, Mohawk Valley Community Col, 46-47 & Oberlin Col, 49-50; physicist, Lawrence Radiation Lab, Univ Calif, 54-61; chief, Theoret Div, Goddard Space Flight Ctr, 61-67; dir sci & appln directorate, Manned Spacecraft Ctr, NASA, Tex, 67-69; dir, Environ Res Labs, Environ Sci Serv Admin, Colo, 69-71 & Nat Oceanic & Atmospheric Admin, 71-80; dir, Nat Ctr Atmospheric Res, NSF, 80-86; assoc dir, US Dept Energy, Washington, DC, 86-87, dir high energy & nuclear physics res, 87-93, assoc dir, Off Energy Res, 93-96. *Mem:* Nat Acad Eng; Am Meteorol Soc; Am Geophys Union; Am Phys Soc. *Res:* High energy nuclear physics; neutron scattering; cosmic ray neutrons; production of Van Allen radiation belt. *Mailing Add:* 1620 Le Roy Ave Berkeley CA 94709

HESSE, CHRISTIAN AUGUST, MINERAL PROJECT EVALUATION & CONCEPTUAL DESIGN, SHAFT CONSULTATION SERVICES. *Current Pos:* CONSULT, 74-; PRIN, HESSE ASSOC, 91- *Personal Data:* b Chemnitz, Ger; US citizen; m 64, Brenda N Rigby; c Rob C & Bruce W. *Educ:* Univ Toronto, BASc, 48. *Prof Exp:* Asst layout engr, Inco Ltd, Sudbury, Can, 49-52; construct engr & proj engr, Perini-Walsh, Niagara Falls, Ont & Perini Lt, 52-55; field engr, Pluton Uranium Mines & Aries Copper Mines, 55-56; instr mining eng, Univ Toronto, Can 56-57; chief engr & planning engr, Stanleigh Uranium Mines, Elliot Lake, Ont, 57-60; field construct engr, Johnson-Perini-Kiewit, Toronto, Can, 60-61; sr mining engr, mine engr & staff engr, US Borax, Carlsbad, NM, 61-64, prin engr, US Borax & Chem Corp, Los Angeles, 69-70, mgr mining develop, 72-74, chief engr & proj dir major plant expansion, 74-77, proj dir, Boric Acid Plant, 77-81, vpres eng, 77-90, vpres mining develop, 84-90; opers mgr & shaft & mine supt, Allan Potash Mines, Sask, 64-69; managing dir & proj mgr, Yorkshire Potash Ltd, London, Eng, 70-71; pres & gen mgr, APM Opers, Ltd, 74. *Concurrent Pos:* Deleg, 7th Commonwealth Mining Cong, Southern Africa, 61; vpres & proj mgr, Quartz Hill Proj, Alaska, 81-90; proj dir & chmn Mgt Comt, Trinity Silver Mine, Nev, 87-90. *Mem:* Soc Mining Metall & Explor; Can Inst Mining & Metall; fel Inst Mining & Metall; NW Mining Asn; Prospectors & Developers Asn Can. *Res:* Submarine tailings disposal. *Mailing Add:* 2701 Lake Hollywood Dr Los Angeles CA 90068-1629. *Fax:* 213-463-8851

HESSE, M(AX) H(ARRY), electrical engineering; deceased, see previous edition for last biography

HESSE, REINHARD, SEDIMENTOLOGY, MARINE GEOLOGY. *Current Pos:* RETIRED. *Personal Data:* b Halle, Ger, Mar 9, 36; wid. *Educ:* Univ Gottingen, Vordipl, 57; Munich Tech Univ, diplom, 61, Dr rer nat, 64, Habilitation, 69. *Honors & Awards:* Hermann Credner Award, Ger Geol Soc, 71. *Prof Exp:* Prof res assoc sedimentol & marine geol, Munich Tech Univ, 64-68, asst prof, 69; from asst prof to prof geol, McGill Univ, 69-96. *Concurrent Pos:* Pvt docent, Munich Tech Univ, 69-95; hon prof, Ludwig Maximilian's Univ, Munich, 95- *Mem:* Geol Soc Am; Swiss Geol Soc; Ger Geol Soc; Soc Econ Paleontologists & Mineralogists; Int Asn Geol Chem & Cosmochem; Geol Soc London. *Res:* Clastic sediments, diagenesis, processes and environments of deposition, turbidites, pelagic sediments, glaciomarine sediments; continental margin evolution; marine geology-Labrador Sea; sedimentary petrography and geochemistry; clay mineralogy. *Mailing Add:* Dept Earth & Planetary Sci McGill Univ 3450 University St Montreal PQ H3A 2A7 Can. *Fax:* 514-398-4680; *E-Mail:* rein_h@geosci.lan.mcgill.ca

HESSE, WALTER HERMAN, agronomy, for more information see previous edition

HESSE, WALTER J(OHN), SOLAR ENERGY, TRANSPORTATION SYSTEMS. *Current Pos:* PRES & CHIEF EXEC OFFICER, ENTECH, INC, 83- *Personal Data:* b St Louis, Mo, Apr 4, 23; m 47, 75; c 5. *Educ:* Purdue Univ, BSME, 44, MSME, 49, PhD, 51. *Prof Exp:* Instr, Purdue Univ, 46-49; chief eng, Test Pilot Training Div, Naval Air Test Ctr, Md, 49-56; mgr adv systs eng, Chance Vought Aircraft Corp, 56-60; prog dir, Nucleonic Systs, LTV Aerospace Corp, 60-64, Adv Missile Systs, 64-65, vpres & dir, Vertical Short Takeoff & Landing Progs, 65-69, vpres plans & requirements, Vought Aeronaut Div, 69-71, vpres, Transp Progs, 71-73; vpres, Advan Transp Syst Div, Rohr Industs, 73-77; vpres & gen mgr, Energy Technol Ctr, E Systs, Inc, 77-83. *Concurrent Pos:* Vis prof, Univ Md, 49-56; lectr, Southern Methodist Univ, 56-57; consult, Adv Panel Aeronaut, US Dept Defense; mem panel sci & technol, Comt Sci & Astronaut, US House of Rep, 63- *Mem:* Solar Energy Indust Asn; Sigma Xi. *Res:* Aeronautics; solar energy. *Mailing Add:* 847 Wolfcreek Rd Valley View TX 76272

HESSEL, ALEXANDER, PHYSICS. *Current Pos:* res assoc, Microwave Res Inst, 57-60, from asst prof to assoc prof, 60-67, EMER PROF ELEC ENG, POLYTECH UNIV, 88- *Personal Data:* b Vienna, Austria, Oct 19, 16; US citizen; m 49; c 2. *Educ:* Hebrew Univ, Israel, MSc, 44; Polytech Inst Brooklyn, DEE, 60. *Prof Exp:* Engr, Broadcasting Sta, Israel, 45-48; res scientist, Israeli Ministry Defense, 48-51, head microwave group, 53-56. *Concurrent Pos:* Mem US comn B, URSI, Int Sci Radio Union. *Mem:* Fel Inst Elec & Electronics Engrs; Sigma Xi. *Res:* Electromagnetics; antennas; phased arrays; conformal arrays. *Mailing Add:* 2128 E Fourteenth St Brooklyn NY 11229-4325

HESSEL, DONALD WESLEY, CLINICAL CHEMISTRY, TOXICOLOGY. *Current Pos:* RETIRED. *Personal Data:* b Menomonie, Wis, May 12, 22; m 52, Myrtle L Schwandt; c Donald A & Paul A. *Educ:* Union Col, Nebr, BA, 49; Univ Wis, MS, 51; Univ Calif, Los Angeles, PhD, 57. *Prof Exp:* Res chemist cancer, White Mem Hosp, 51-52; asst gen chem, Qual Anal & Org Chem, Univ Calif, Los Angeles, 52-56; res assoc chem marine biotoxins, Loma Linda Univ, 56-59; res chemist, World Life Res Inst, 59-61; mem staff, Bio Labs, Loma Linda Univ Med Ctr & Fac Med Lab, 61-80, mem staff, 80-91. *Mem:* Am Chem Soc. *Res:* Development of new analytical methods and the application of new instrumental techniques to clinical chemistry and forensic toxicology. *Mailing Add:* 22854 Minona Dr Grand Terrace CA 92324-5162

HESSEL, KENNETH RAY, OPTICS. *Current Pos:* SUPVR LASERS & OPTICS, SANDIA LABS, 69- *Personal Data:* b West, Tex, Dec 16, 39. *Educ:* Univ Tex, BS, 65, MS, 66, PhD(elec eng), 69. *Mem:* Inst Electronics & Elec Engrs; Optical Soc Am. *Res:* Laser applications; noise limitations of optical systems; coherent and incoherent optical processing; fiber optics; electro-optics. *Mailing Add:* 12113 Prospect Ave NE Albuquerque NM 87112

HESSEL, MERRILL, MOLECULAR PHYSICS, LASERS. *Current Pos:* DEP GEN MGR, NAT INITIATE PROD DATA EXCHANGE, 91- *Personal Data:* b Brooklyn, NY, Nov 25, 33; div, Elizabeth J Clark; c 2. *Educ:* Cornell Univ, BChE, 56; Columbia Univ, MA, 62, PhD(physics), 65. *Honors & Awards:* Bronze Medal, Dept Com, 80, Silver Medal, 93. *Prof Exp:* Engr, Savannah River Plant, E I du Pont de Nemours & Co, 56-59; res physicist, Columbia Univ, 65-68; from asst prof to assoc prof physics, Fordham Univ,

68-74; sect chief, Nat Inst Stand & Technol, 74-78, chief laser spectros sect, 76-78, chief molecular spectros div, 78-82, dep dir, Ctr Chem Eng, 82-86, info technol adv to NBS dir, 88-89, asst to dir, 89-91. *Concurrent Pos:* Vis scientist, Quantum Electronics Div, Nat Bur Stand, 73-74; pres exchange exec, The Boeing Co, 86-88, info technol adv, 86-87. *Mem:* AAAS; Am Phys Soc; Am Chem Soc; Sigma Xi; Am Inst Chem Engrs. *Res:* Molecular beams and spectroscopy; molecular and heat pipe spectroscopy as applied to lasers and laser processes; computing and computers; manufactoring research and technology. *Mailing Add:* 8113 Whirlwind Ct Nat Inst Stand & Technol Gaithersburg MD 20882. *Fax:* 301-926-8730; *E-Mail:* hessel@nist.gov

HESSELINK, LAMBERTUS, NON-LINEAR OPTICS, IMAGE PROCESSING, INFORMATION SCIENCE. *Current Pos:* from asst prof to assoc prof, 80-90, PROF, ELEC ENG DEPT & AERONAUT/ASTRONAUT DEPT, STANFORD UNIV, 90- *Personal Data:* b Enschede, Neth, Dec, 48. *Educ:* Twente Inst Technol, BS(med eng), 70, BS(appl physics), 71; Calif Inst Technol, MS, 72, PhD(appl mech & appl physics), 77. *Prof Exp:* Res fel fluid mech, Grad Aeronaut Lab, Calif Inst Technol, 77-79, instr appl physics, 78-80. *Concurrent Pos:* Consult, Space & Commun Group, Hughes Aircraft Co, 78-88, Microelectronics Corp, Visulux Corp, NSF, VSL Corp, Phys Optics Corp, Air Force, 80-88; invited lectr, Von Karman Inst, Brussels, Belg, 84 & 86, Int Sch Quantum Electronics, Erice, Italy, 88; mem adv panel, NSF, 87-88, mem sci adv bd, 88-90; assoc ed, J Appl Sci Res, 87-90; chief exec officer, Optitek, Inc. *Mem:* Sigma Xi; Am Phys Soc; fel Optical Soc Am; Int Soc Optical Eng; Am Inst Aeronaut & Astronaut; Dutch Acad Sci. *Res:* Non-linear optics, holographic data storage, photorefractives and optical processors; application of new image processing techniques to optical diagnostics and visualization of scientific data; author of over 160 articles and papers. *Mailing Add:* Elec Eng Dept Stanford Univ Durand Bldg Rm 377 Stanford CA 94305

HESSELTINE, CLIFFORD WILLIAM, MYCOLOGY. *Current Pos:* RETIRED. *Personal Data:* b Brighton, Iowa, Apr 4, 17; m 41; c 4. *Educ:* Univ Iowa, BA, 40; Univ Wis, PhD, 50. *Honors & Awards:* Ciba-Geigy Microbiol Award, 76; Pasteur Award, 78; Thom Award, 80. *Prof Exp:* Res mycologist, Lederle Labs, Am Cyanamid Co, 48-53; prin microbiologist in-chg cult, Collection Group, Northern Utilization Res Br, USDA, 53-67, chief, Fermentation Lab, Northern Regional Res Lab, Agr Res Serv, 67-86. *Concurrent Pos:* Mycol Soc Am rep, Nat Res Coun; chmn, US Toxic Microorganisms Panel, Joint US-Japan Coop Develop & Utilization Natural Resources. *Mem:* AAAS; assoc Mycol Soc Am (pres, 63-64); assoc Int Soc Plant Path; assoc Torrey Bot Club; Soc Indust Microbiol (pres, 58); Brit Mycol Soc; Soc Appl Bacteriologists; Japanese Mycol Soc. *Res:* Soil fungi; taxonomy of mucorales and actinomycetes; maintenance of culture collections; mycotoxins; fungus food and industrial fermentations. *Mailing Add:* 5407 N Isabell Ave Peoria IL 61614

HESSELTINE, WILBUR R, DAIRY HUSBANDRY. *Current Pos:* from assoc prof to prof, 59-80, EMER PROF DAIRY, UNIV DEL, 80- *Personal Data:* b Malone, NY, Sept 14, 19; m 47; c 4. *Educ:* Cornell Univ, BS, 47; Univ Conn, MS, 52; Univ Wis, PhD(dairy), 59. *Prof Exp:* Asst county agr agent dairy, Allegany County Exten Serv. 47-49; asst prof, Univ Conn, 49-59. *Mem:* Am Dairy Sci Asn. *Res:* Dairy production. *Mailing Add:* Hart Rd Smyrna DE 19977

HESSEMER, ROBERT A(NDREW), JR, ELECTRICAL ENGINEERING. *Current Pos:* RETIRED. *Personal Data:* b Montesano, Wash, June 20, 23; m 51; c 2. *Educ:* Univ Wash, BS, 47; Stanford Univ, MS, 48, PhD(elec eng), 53. *Prof Exp:* From instr to asst prof elec eng, Univ NMex, 48-55; prof elec eng, Univ Ariz, 55-82. *Concurrent Pos:* Res assoc, Stanford Univ, 50-51; consult, Sandia Corp, 53-55, RCA Corp, 57-59, Bell Aerosysts Co, 62-65 & Electro Tech Anal Corp, 66-70. *Mem:* Am Soc Eng Educ; Inst Elec & Electronics Engrs. *Res:* Passive non-invasive temperature measurement of the interior of a body using acoustic or electromagnetic thermal noise spectra of the body. *Mailing Add:* Dept Elec Eng Univ Ariz Tucson AZ 85614

HESSER, JAMES EDWARD, ASTROPHYSICS, MOLECULAR SPECTROSCOPY. *Current Pos:* assoc res officer, 77-80, assoc dir, 84-86, SR RES OFFICER, DOMINION ASTROPHYS OBSERV, NAT RES COUN CAN, 80-, DIR, 86- *Personal Data:* b Wichita, Kans, June 23, 41; m 63, Betty Hinsdale; c Nadja, Rebecca & Gillian. *Educ:* Univ Kans, BA, 63; Princeton Univ, MA, 65, PhD(molecular & atomic physics), 66. *Honors & Awards:* Northcutt Lectr, Royal Astron Soc Can, 81. *Prof Exp:* Res asst atomic & molecular physics, Princeton Univ, 63-66, res assoc observational astrophys & lab spectros, 66-68; jr astronr, Cerro Tololo Interam Observ, 68-69, asst astronr, 69-71, asst dir, 72-74, assoc astronr, 71-77. *Concurrent Pos:* Vis prof astron, Univ Chile, Santiago, 74; mem, bd dirs, Astron Soc Pac, 81-88, assoc comt astron, 83-89, assoc comt space res, 84-89, chmn, Joint Subcomt Space Astron, 84-89; counr, Am Astron Soc, 84-87; adj prof physics & astron, Univ Victoria, 87- *Mem:* Am Astron Soc (vpres, 91-94); Int Astron Union; Can Astron Soc; Astron Soc Pac (vpres, pres, 85-88); assoc mem Royal Astron Soc. *Res:* Determination of atomic and molecular oscillator strengths in the ultraviolet; power spectrum analysis of ultrashort period variable stars; precision photometry of globular and galactic clusters; K-line photometry of A stars; spectroscopy of galactic halo stars; analysis of globular clusters in extragalactic systems; interstellar lines in the carina nebula; development of instrumentation for space astronomy. *Mailing Add:* 1874 Ventura Way Victoria BC V8N 1R3 Can. *Fax:* 250-363-6970; *E-Mail:* james.hesser@hia.nrc.ca

HESSINGER, DAVID ALWYN, CELL BIOLOGY, TOXINOLOGY. *Current Pos:* ASSOC PROF PHYSIOL & PHARMACOL, SCH MED, LOMA LINDA UNIV, CALIF, 78- *Personal Data:* b Niagara Falls, NY, May 28, 42; m 69; c 3. *Educ:* Kenyon Col, BA, 64; Univ Miami, PhD(cell biol), 70. *Prof Exp:* Fel biophys, Sch Med, Univ Miami, 70-71 & immunobiol, Univ Calif, Irvine, 71-73; asst prof biol, Univ SFla, 73-78. *Mem:* AAAS; Sigma Xi; Am Soc Cell Biol; Int Soc Toxicol. *Res:* Mechanism of action of protein toxins from nematocysts on the structure and function of biological membranes; nematocyst structure, function and cnidocyte control of nematocyst discharge. *Mailing Add:* Dept Physiol Pharmacol Sch Med Loma Linda Univ Loma Linda CA 92350. *Fax:* 909-478-4119

HESSLER, JACK RONALD, LABORATORY ANIMAL MEDICINE, PHYSIOLOGY. *Current Pos:* ASSOC PROF PHYSIOL & DIR ANIMAL RESOURCE DIV, CTR HEALTH SCI, UNIV TENN, 75-; CHIEF VET MED UNIT, VET ADMIN MED CTR, 75- *Personal Data:* b St Louis, Mo, Oct 31, 39; m 62; c 3. *Educ:* Univ Mo, Columbia, BS & DVM, 63; Univ Fla, MS, 68; Am Col Lab Animal Med, dipl, 69. *Prof Exp:* Captain Vet Corp, US Army, 63-65; USPHS fel comp med, Univ Fla, 65-68, from asst prof to assoc prof, 68-75. *Concurrent Pos:* Consult, Am Asn Accreditation Lab Animal Care, 70-81, mem coun accreditation, 81-; pres, Asn Vet Admin Veterinary Med Officers, 85- *Mem:* Am Asn Lab Animal Med; Am Vet Med Asn; Am Physiol Soc; Asn Am Vet Med Col. *Res:* Perinatal physiology; respiration physiology; pulmonary circulation; diseases of laboratory animals and animal models of human disease; control of the research animal's environment. *Mailing Add:* Dept Vet Affairs 810 Vermont Ave NW Washington DC 20420-0001

HESSLER, JAN PAUL, CHEMICAL PHYSICS, PHYSICAL CHEMISTRY. *Current Pos:* vis scientist chem physics, 75-78, asst scientist chem physics, 78-81, PHYSICIST, CHEM DIV, ARGONNE NAT LAB, 81- *Personal Data:* b Detroit, Mich, Jan 13, 44; m 68, Nancy Ruth Loebe. *Educ:* Kalamazoo Col, BA, 65; Mich State Univ, PhD(physics), 71. *Prof Exp:* Res assoc chem phys, Enrico Fermi Inst, Dept Chem, Univ Chicago, 71-73; instr physics, Queen's Univ, 73-75. *Mem:* Am Phys Soc; Optical Soc Am; Inst Elec & Electronics Engrs; Sigma Xi; AAAS. *Res:* Experimental studies of high-temperature chemical kinetics; combustion modeling; data analysis and reduction; laser spectroscopy of reactive species. *Mailing Add:* 4728 Middaugh Downers Grove IL 60515. *Fax:* 630-252-4470; *E-Mail:* hessler@anlchm.chm.anl.gov

HESSLER, ROBERT RAYMOND, ZOOLOGY. *Current Pos:* from assoc prof to prof zool, 69-80, PROF BIOL OCEANOG, SCRIPPS INST OCEANOG, UNIV CALIF, SAN DIEGO, 80- *Personal Data:* b Chicago, Ill, Nov 22, 32; m 54. *Educ:* Univ Chicago, AB, 53, BS, 55, PhD(invert paleont), 60. *Prof Exp:* Assoc scientist, Dept Biol, Woods Hole Oceanog Inst, 60-69. *Res:* Arthropod morphology and evolution, especially in Crustacea; taxonomy of Isopod; deep-sea benthic ecology. *Mailing Add:* Scripps Inst Oceanog Univ Calif San Diego 9500 Gilman Dr La Jolla CA 92093-0202

HESSLEY, RITA KATHLEEN, ORGANIC CHEMISTRY, ANALYTICAL CHEMISTRY. *Current Pos:* HEAD, DEPT CHEM & LIFE SCI, ROSE HULMAN INST TECHNOL, 96- *Personal Data:* b Warren, Pa, Dec 6, 46. *Educ:* Univ Mo-Rolla, PhD(chem), 74. *Prof Exp:* Asst prof chem, Tenn Tech Univ, 74-77; res assoc, Univ Tex, Arlington, 77-79 & Oak Ridge Nat Lab, 79-81; assoc prof, Western Ky Univ, 81-87, prof chem, 87-96. *Mem:* Am Chem Soc; Sigma Xi. *Res:* Redox reaction kinetics; structural studies and depolymerization processes for coal. *Mailing Add:* Dept Chem Rose-Hulman Inst Technol 5500 Wabash Ave Terre Haute IN 47803-3999

HESTENES, DAVID, THEORETICAL PHYSICS. *Current Pos:* asst prof, 66-69, assoc prof, 69-76, PROF PHYSICS, ARIZ STATE UNIV, 76- *Personal Data:* b Chicago, Ill, May 21, 33; m 54, Nancy Shinkoethe; c 5. *Educ:* Pac Lutheran Univ, BA, 54; Univ Calif, Los Angeles, MA, 58, PhD(physics), 63. *Honors & Awards:* Fulbright, England, 88. *Prof Exp:* Res assoc physics, Univ Calif, Los Angeles, 63-64; NSF fel, Palmer Phys Lab, Princeton Univ, 64-66. *Mem:* Am Phys Soc; Am Asn Physics Teachers; AAAS; Int Neural Network Soc; Soc Neurosci. *Res:* Relativity; quantum electrodynamics; neural networks; physics education. *Mailing Add:* Dept Physics Ariz State Univ Tempe AZ 85287

HESTER, DONALD L, ELECTRICAL ENGINEERING. *Current Pos:* RETIRED. *Personal Data:* b Stanley, NC, Mar 28, 34; m 58; c 2. *Educ:* NC State Col, BSEE, 61; Univ NMex, MSEE, 63; Duke Univ, PhD(nonlinear oscillator theory), 67. *Prof Exp:* Staff mem, Sandia Corp, NMex, 61-64; asst prof elec eng, Va Polytech Inst, 66-68; mem tech staff, Bell Tel Labs, 68-77; pres, Micro Comput Systs, Inc, 77- *Res:* Microcomputers; telephone loop plant testing. *Mailing Add:* 1295 Old Salem Rd Kernersville NC 27284

HESTER, JACKSON BOLING, JR, MEDICINAL CHEMISTRY, ORGANIC SYNTHESIS. *Current Pos:* RES SCIENTIST CHEM, UPJOHN CO, 60- *Personal Data:* b Norfolk, Va, Sept 28, 33; m 60, Judith S Graves; c Michael E & Matthew R. *Educ:* Mass Inst Technol, SB, 55; Univ Wis, PhD(org chem), 60. *Honors & Awards:* UpJohn Award, 72, 88; PMA Discoveries Award, 89. *Mem:* Am Chem Soc; AAAS. *Res:* Heterocyclic organic chemistry; pharmaceutical chemistry, including indoles and alkaloids; chemistry of benzodiazepines which have antianxiety activity; chemistry of medicinal agents in central nervous system and cardiovascular areas. *Mailing Add:* 9219 E ML Ave Galesburg MI 49053

HESTER, JOHN NELSON, CHEMICAL ENGINEERING. *Current Pos:* RETIRED. *Personal Data:* b Washington, DC, Dec 1, 30. *Educ:* Tri-State Col, BS, 58; Mich State Univ, MS, 59; Univ Calif, Davis, PhD(appl math), 71. *Prof Exp:* Eng supvr fluid dynamics, Aerojet-Gen Corp, 60-69; assoc prof mech eng, Calif State Univ, Sacramento, 69-74, prof, 74-95. *Concurrent Pos:* Consult, Alternative Energy Co, 79-, Calif Energy Comn, 79-, Agroset Tech Systs Co, 84- *Mem:* Am Chem Soc; Am Inst Chem Engrs; Am Soc Eng Educ. *Res:* Thermodynamics; chemical kinetics; waste product energy conversion and thermal destruction of hazardous wastes. *Mailing Add:* 8854 Ridge Hill Ct Orangeville CA 95662

HESTER, LAWRENCE LAMAR, JR, OBSTETRICS & GYNECOLOGY. *Current Pos:* RETIRED. *Personal Data:* b Anderson, SC, May 23, 20; m 47; c 4. *Educ:* The Citadel, BS, 41; Med Col SC, MD, 44. *Hon Degrees:* Dsc, The Citadel, 80. *Prof Exp:* prof obstet & gynec & chmn dept, Med Univ SC, 56-84. *Mem:* Am Col Obstet & Gynec; Am Asn Obstet & Gynec; Am Gynec Club. *Res:* Chemotherapy of gynecological cancer and the diagnosis and treatment of fetal distress. *Mailing Add:* 78 Elm Ct Highlands NC 28741

HESTER, NORMAN ERIC, ENVIRONMENTAL CHEMISTRY, ORGANIC CHEMISTRY. *Current Pos:* TECH DIR, TRUESDAIL LABS, 83- *Personal Data:* b Niangua, Mo, Dec 16, 46; m 73, Sylvia J Hurt; c Jenay A, Yvette J & Trinity M. *Educ:* Calif State Univ, BS, 68; Univ Calif, Riverside, MS, 71, PhD(org chem), 72. *Prof Exp:* Chemist air pollution, Statewide Air Pollution Res Ctr, Univ Calif, Riverside, 72-74; air qual chemist, US Environ Protection Agency, 74-77; mem tech staff environ chem, Environ Monitoring & Serv Ctr, Rockwell Int Corp, 77-80; group head, Environ Res, Occidental Res Corp, 80-83. *Mem:* Am Chem Soc; Am Soc Testing & Mat. *Res:* Development of procedures for the collection and analysis of trace levels of environmental pollutants. *Mailing Add:* Truesdail Labs Inc 14201 Franklin Ave Tustin CA 92680. *Fax:* 714-730-6462

HESTER, RICHARD KELLY, PHARMACOLOGY, PHYSIOLOGY. *Current Pos:* asst prof, 79-85, ASSOC PROF, DEPT MED PHARMACOL, COL MED, TEX A&M UNIV, 85-, INVESTR, MICROCIRCULATION RES INST, 81- *Personal Data:* b Austin, Tex, July 30, 47; m 79; c 2. *Educ:* Austin Col, BA, 69; Health Sci Ctr, Univ Tex, San Antonio, PhD(pharmacol), 75. *Prof Exp:* From instr to asst prof, Dept Pharmacol, Health Sci Ctr, Univ Tex, Dallas, 77-79. *Concurrent Pos:* USPHS fel & Am Heart Asn fel, Sch Med, Univ Miami, 75-76; res fel, Health Sci Ctr, Univ Tex, Dallas, 76-77; vis res assoc, Dept Pharmacol, John A Burns Sch Med, Univ Hawaii, Honolulu, 78-79; young investr res grant, Nat Heart, Lung & Blood Inst, 80-84; teaching consult, Dept Pharmacol, Sch Med, Tex Tech Univ Health Sci Ctr, Lubbock, Tex, 85-86. *Mem:* AAAS; Am Heart Asn; Sigma Xi; Western Pharmacol Soc; Am Soc Pharmacol & Exp Therapeut; Microcirculatory Soc. *Res:* Excitation/contraction (relaxation) coupling in vascular smooth muscle; correlation of calcium kinetics with tension development and-or relaxation; receptor-mediated calcium ion entry; microvascular physiology and pharmacology. *Mailing Add:* Tex A&M Univ Col Med Reynolds Med Bldg College Station TX 77843-1114

HESTER, ROBERT LESLIE, MICROCIRCULATION, OXYGEN DELIVERY. *Current Pos:* ASST PROF CARDIOVASC PHYSIOL, UNIV MISS, 85- *Personal Data:* b Sept 12, 53; m; c 1. *Educ:* Univ Miss, PhD(physiol), 82. *Mem:* Am Phys Soc; Microcirculatory Soc; Biomed Eng Soc. *Mailing Add:* Dept Physiol Univ Miss Med Ctr 2500 N State St Jackson MS 39216-4505

HESTERBERG, GENE ARTHUR, FOREST PATHOLOGY. *Current Pos:* RETIRED. *Personal Data:* b Cincinnati, Ohio, Aug 30, 18; m 41; c 2. *Educ:* Purdue Univ, BS, 41; Univ Mich, MS, 47, PhD, 56. *Prof Exp:* Biologist, State Dept Conserv, Mich, 47-48; prof forestry, Mich Technol Univ, 48-81; head dept, 67-81. *Concurrent Pos:* Collabr, Lake States Forest Exp Sta, US Forest Serv. *Mem:* Soc Am Foresters; Wilson Ornith Soc. *Res:* Pathology in forest practice. *Mailing Add:* 119 Chippawa Trail Dollar Bay MI 49922

HESTERBERG, THOMAS WILLIAM, CARCINOGENESIS. *Current Pos:* CONSULT, 88-; MGR PROD STEWARDSHIP. *Personal Data:* b Tucson, Ariz, Mar 16, 50; m 71; c 2. *Educ:* Univ Calif, Los Angeles, BA & MA; Univ Calif, Davis, PhD(pharmacol/toxicol), 81. *Prof Exp:* Fel cancer res, Nat Inst Environ Health Sci, 81-84; scientist, Chem Indust Inst Toxicol, 84-88. *Mem:* Am Asn Cancer Res; Soc Toxicol. *Res:* Direct the testing of man-made fibers and other particulates using animal inhalation models; study the mechanisms of chemical carcinogenesis using cell culture models. *Mailing Add:* Health Safety & Environ Dept Johns Manville Corp PO Box 625005 Littleton CO 80162

HESTON, LEONARD L, PSYCHIATRY, GENETICS. *Current Pos:* assoc prof, 70-74, dir, Psychiat Res Unit, 77-80, PROF PSYCIAT, UNIV WASH, SEATTLE, 74- *Personal Data:* b Burns, Ore, Dec 16, 30; m 66; c Steven, William, Dearina, Gwendolyn, Barbara & Ardis. *Educ:* Univ Ore, BS, 55, MD, 61. *Honors & Awards:* Dobzhansky Award, Behav Genetics Asn; Paul Hoch Award, Am Psychopath Asn. *Prof Exp:* Intern med, Bernalillo County-Indian Hosp, 61-62; resident psychiat, Med Sch, Univ Ore, 62-65; guest worker, Psychiat Genetics Res Unit, Med Res Coun, London, 65-66; asst prof psychiat, Univ Iowa, 66-70. *Concurrent Pos:* Spec fel, NIMH, 65-66; mem epidemiol studies rev comt, NIMH, Nat Adv Coun, Nat Inst Drug Abuse. *Mem:* AMA; Am Eugenics Soc; Am Psychopath Asn; Am Soc Human Genetics. *Res:* Genetics of psychiatric and neurological disorders; genetics of normal behavior; medical history. *Mailing Add:* Dept Psychiat Univ Wash Seattle WA 98195. *Fax:* 360-260-3139; *E-Mail:* hestonl@u.washington.edu

HESTON, WILLIAM MAY, JR, PHYSICAL CHEMISTRY. *Current Pos:* CONSULT, 90- *Personal Data:* b Toledo, Ohio, Nov 2, 22; m 50, Marian C Watt; c Mary, Elizabeth, Katherine & Richard. *Educ:* Ohio State Univ, BSc, 43; Princeton Univ, MA, 48, PhD(phys chem), 49. *Prof Exp:* Asst, Princeton Univ, 46-48; res chemist, E I du Pont de Nemours & Co, 49-51; res physicist, Argonne Nat Lab, 51-52, staff scientist, Del, 52-53; res supvr, Radiochem Eng, Savannah River Lab, 53-54, personnel supvr tech placement, 54-55; tech asst to lab dir, Employee Rels Dept, 55-58, placement rep, 58-59; dir, Univ Off Res & Assoc Chem, Case Western Res Univ, 59-63, vpres res, 63-64, vpres student serv, 64-66, vprovost & assoc dean arts & sci, 66-67, vpres, Univ Plans & Progs, 67-69; vpres, Hofstra Univ, 69-73; assoc provost, NY Inst Technol, 77-78, dean, 83-88, dir, Ctr Natural Sci, 78-88, Pro Life Sci, 81-90. *Concurrent Pos:* Mem prog-proj comt, Nat Inst Dent Res, 64-68; AID consult, Govt India, 65; vis prof, Univ Mysore, 65; consult grad chem prog develop, NSF, 65-68, instnl sci develop prog, 68-70; trustee, Laurel Sch Girls, Shaker Heights, 67-69; AMD Res Found, 77-78; consult sci develop prog, Cleveland Pub Schs, 67-69; spec consult to dir, Nat Inst Dent Res, 68-70, mem dent res insts & spec progs adv comt, 70-74; mem bd adv, Heald, Hobson & Co, 69-70; mem sci adv comt, Nassau Co Police Dept, 70-72; exec dir, Nassau Higher Educ Consortium, 73-75 & Long Island Regional; Adv Coun Higher Educ, 75-76; consult, Nat Inst Gen Med Sci, 76-80, Standford Res Inst, 81-84 & Nat Can Inst, 81-90. *Mem:* Fel AAAS; Sigma Xi. *Res:* Microwave adsorption; molecular structure; inorganic polymers; ion exchange; chemical problems associated with nuclear reactor operation; colloids; comprehensive postsecondary continuing education plan. *Mailing Add:* 47 Hilton Ave Garden City NY 11530-4427

HETENYI, GEZA JOSEPH, MEDICAL PHYSIOLOGY. *Current Pos:* prof physiol & head dept, Univ Ottawa, 70-79, vdean, Fac Health Sci, 79-86, dir, Acad Affairs Heart Inst, 92-94, EMER PROF, UNIV OTTAWA, 92- *Personal Data:* b Budapest, Hungary, Sept 26, 23; m 47. *Educ:* Univ Budapest, MD, 47; Univ Toronto, PhD, 60; FRCP(C), 87. *Honors & Awards:* Jancso Medal, Szent Gyorgy Med Univ, Szeged, Hungary, 88; Sarazin Prize, Can Physiol Soc, 96. *Prof Exp:* Lectr, Med Sch, Univ Szeged, 47-51, asst prof, 51-56; res assoc physiol, Charles H Best Inst, Univ Toronto, 57-60, from asst prof to prof, 70-79; sci adv to pres, Med Res Coun Can, 86-92. *Concurrent Pos:* Bd dir, Can Diabetic Asn, 92-95. *Mem:* Am Physiol Soc; Can Physiol Soc (vpres, 75-76, pres, 76-77). *Res:* Physiology of carbohydrate metabolism; glucose; control of blood sugar level; tracer methods; mathematical modeling. *Mailing Add:* Dept Physiol Univ Ottawa Ottawa ON K1H 8M5 Can

HETERICK, ROBERT CARY, JR, COMPUTER SCIENCE, STRUCTURAL ENGINEERING. *Current Pos:* PRES & CHIEF EXEC OFFICER, EDUCOM, 93- *Personal Data:* b Washington, DC, Apr 9, 36; m 61; c 4. *Educ:* Va Polytech Inst, BS, 59, MS, 61, PhD(eng), 68. *Prof Exp:* From instr to assoc prof civil eng, Va Polytech Inst & State Univ 59-68, dir comput ctr, 68-74, prof bldg construction & chmn dept, Col Archit, 75-, dir Design Automation Lab, 75-93. *Concurrent Pos:* Consult, Hayes, Seay, Mattern & Mattern, 61-68; mem, Va Adv Coun Educ Data Processing, 68-; pres, Commonwealth Comput Consults, Inc, 70-75; consult, Gov Va Mgt Study, 70-71; lectr, IBM Corp, 71-; consult, Penton Learning Systs Inc, 77- *Mem:* Nat Soc Prof Engrs; Am Soc Civil Engrs; Am Soc Eng Educ; Am Inst Constructors. *Res:* Effect of management information systems on organizational structure; computer-aided design. *Mailing Add:* EDUCOM 1112 16th St NW Washington DC 20036. *Fax:* 202-872-4318

HETHCOTE, HERBERT WAYNE, MATHEMATICAL EPIDEMIOLOGY. *Current Pos:* From asst prof to assoc prof, 69-79, PROF MATH, UNIV IOWA, 79- *Personal Data:* b Villisca, Iowa, Nov 18, 41; m, Leslie B Marshall; c 2. *Educ:* Univ Colo, BS, 64; Univ Mich, MS, 65, PhD(math), 68. *Concurrent Pos:* Boettcher Found scholar, 59-64; NSF fel, 64-66; grantee, NSF, 68, NIH, 77-80, Ctrs Dis Control, 76, 80, 87-91 & 94-95; vis mathematician, M D Anderson Hosp & Tumor Inst, 74-75 & NIH, 80-81; vis assoc prof, Ore State Univ, 77-78. *Mem:* Am Math Soc; Math Asn Am; Soc Indust & Appl Math; Soc Math Biol. *Res:* Mathematical analysis of models for the spread of infectious diseases; modeling the transmission and control of specific diseases such as measles, rubella, influenza and gonorrhea; using models to study HIV transmission and AIDS, for the Centers for Disease Control. *Mailing Add:* Dept Math Univ Iowa City Iowa City IA 52242-1466. *Fax:* 319-335-0627; *E-Mail:* herbert-hethcote@uiowa.edu

HETHERINGTON, DONALD WORDSWORTH, BETA SPECTROSCOPY, NEUTRINO MASS. *Current Pos:* RES ASST, APPL PHYSICS, UNIV MONTREAL, 87- *Personal Data:* b Montreal, Can, Feb 27, 45; m 68; c 2. *Educ:* Univ Toronto, BASc, 67, MSc, 68; McGill Univ, PhD(nuclear physics), 85. *Prof Exp:* Lectr physics, Ahmach Bello Univ, Nigeria, 68-70; engr, Canatom Ltd, Montreal, Can, 70-71; teacher physics, Vanier Col, 71-82; res fel, Atomic Energy Can, Ltd, 84-86. *Mem:* Can Asn Physicists. *Res:* Low energy nuclear physics; beta spectroscopy; measurement of spectral shapes to study weak magnetism and neutrino mass. *Mailing Add:* 4019 Melrose Montreal PQ H4A 2S5 Can

HETNARSKI, RICHARD BOZYSLAW, MECHANICS, APPLIED MATHEMATICS. *Current Pos:* distinguished vis prof, 70-71, prof, 71-92, JAMES E GLEASON PROF MECH ENG, ROCHESTER INST TECHNOL, 92- *Personal Data:* b Stopnica, Poland, May 31, 28; nat US; m 60, Leokadia E Lalak; c Adam & Eve. *Educ:* Gdansk Tech Univ, MSc, 52; Warsaw Univ, MSc, 60; Polish Acad Sci, Dr Tech Sci, 64. *Prof Exp:* Teaching asst math, Gdansk Tech Univ, 50-51; designer, Design Bur Diesel Engines, Warsaw, 52-54; res scientist, Inst Aircraft Res, 55-59 & Polish Acad Sci, 59-69; vis assoc prof theoret & appl mech, Cornell Univ, 69-70. *Concurrent Pos:* Polish Acad Sci fel, Columbia Univ, 64-65; res fel, Northwestern Univ, 65; ed-in-chief, J Thermal Stresses, 78-; Am Soc Eng Educ fel, Lewis Res Ctr,

NASA, 79; lectr, Int Ctr Mech Sci, Udine, Italy, 79; aeronaut engr, NASA Lewis Res Ctr, 79-80; ed, Thermal Stress Handbk; vis prof, Univ Paderborn, Ger. *Mem:* Am Acad Mechanics; Am Soc Eng Educ; fel Am Soc Mech Engrs. *Res:* Theory of elasticity, thermoelasticity; vibrations, stress analysis; integral transforms; mechanical design. *Mailing Add:* Dept Mech Eng Rochester Inst Technol Rochester NY 14623. *Fax:* 716-475-7710; *E-Mail:* 632hetna@rit.edu

HETRICK, BARBARA ANN, MYCORRHIZAL FUNGI, SOIL MICROBIOLOGY. *Current Pos:* ASSOC PROF, DEPT BIOL, UNIV NORTHERN IOWA, 95- *Personal Data:* b San Francisco, Calif, Sept 10, 51; m 83; c 1. *Educ:* Ohio Wesleyan Univ, BA, 73; Wash State Univ, MS, 75; Ore State Univ, PhD(plant path), 78. *Prof Exp:* Fel, Univ Calif, Riverside, 78-80; assoc prof plant path, Kans State Univ, 80-95. *Concurrent Pos:* Consult, Lehigh Univ, 82-83. *Mem:* Am Phytopath Soc; Sigma Xi; Mycol Soc Am. *Res:* Ecology of vesicular-arbuscular mycorrhizal fungi and their potential for commercialization; use of these fungi to retard drought stress or to stimulate plant growth in infertile soils. *Mailing Add:* Dept Biol Univ Northern Iowa Cedar Falls IA 50614-0001

HETRICK, DAVID LEROY, NUCLEAR SAFETY. *Current Pos:* prof nuclear & energy eng, 63-92, EMER PROF, UNIV ARIZ, 92- *Personal Data:* b Scranton, Pa, Jan 26, 27; m 48, Margaret Wetsel; c Carol, Nancy & Amy. *Educ:* Rensselaer Polytech Inst, BS, 47, MS, 50; Univ Calif, Los Angeles, PhD(physics), 54. *Prof Exp:* Instr physics, Rensselaer Polytech Inst, 47-50; physicist, Rockwell Int, 50-59; pvt consult, 59; mem tech staff, Systs Labs Div, Electronic Specialty Co, 59-60; assoc prof physics, Calif State Univ Northridge, 60-63. *Concurrent Pos:* Admin judge, US Nuclear Regulatory Comm, 72-; consult, Los Alamos Nat Lab, 90- *Mem:* AAAS; Am Nuclear Soc; Am Phys Soc; Soc Comput Simulation. *Res:* Dynamics and safety of nuclear reactors and fuel processing systems; applied mathematics; pulsed reactors; nuclear criticality safety. *Mailing Add:* Aeospace & Mech Eng Bldg 119 Univ Ariz Tucson AZ 85721

HETRICK, FRANK M, VIROLOGY. *Current Pos:* from asst microbiol to assoc prof virol, 58-68, actg chmn, 68-69 & 75-76, PROF VIROL, UNIV MD, 68-, CHMN, 89- *Personal Data:* b York, Pa, Aug 28, 32; m 54; c 5. *Educ:* Mich State Univ, BS, 54; Univ Md, MS, 60, PhD(microbiol), 62. *Prof Exp:* Microbiologist, Mich Dept Health, 56-58. *Concurrent Pos:* Int work, Egypt, Brazil, Japan & China; Sea Grant Prog, 77-; Am Soc Microbiol Found lectr, 84-85. *Mem:* AAAS; Am Soc Microbiol; Tissue Cult Asn; fel Am Acad Microbiol; Am Fisheries Soc; Am Inst Biol Sci. *Res:* Viral and bacterial diseases of marine and freshwater fish; developmental and comparative immunology; oncogene activation and tumor development in fish. *Mailing Add:* Gudelsky Vet Ctr 106 Avrum College Park MD 20742

HETRICK, JOHN HENRY, dairy technology; deceased, see previous edition for last biography

HETRICK, LAWRENCE ANDREW, entomology, forestry; deceased, see previous edition for last biography

HETTCHE, LEROY RAYMOND, MATERIALS SCIENCE, SOLID MECHANICS. *Current Pos:* DIR, APPL RES LAB & PROF ENG RES, PA STATE UNIV, 81- *Personal Data:* b Baltimore, Md, Mar 24, 38; m 65; c 3. *Educ:* Bucknell Univ, BS, 61; Carnegie-Mellon Univ, MS, 63, PhD(civil eng), 65. *Prof Exp:* Asst prof civil eng, Rutgers Univ, 64-66; Nat Res Coun res assoc, Nat Bur Stand, 66-68; struct engr, Naval Res Lab, 68-71, phys scientist, 71-74, supt, Mat Sci & Tech Div, 74-81. *Mem:* Acoust Soc Am; Am Soc Test & Mat; Am Soc Mech Engrs. *Res:* Response of materials to pulsed radiation heating; dynamic plasticity; stress wave analysis; fracture mechanics; impact testing; numerical analysis. *Mailing Add:* 219 Morningside Circle State Col PA 16803

HETTINGER, DEBORAH D R, TEMPERATURE REGULATION BIOENERGETICS. *Current Pos:* ASST PROF BIOL & CHEM, TEX LUTHERAN COL, 80- *Educ:* Univ Calif, PhD(physiol & biochem), 80. *Mailing Add:* Dept Biol Tex Lutheran Col 1000 W Court St Seguin TX 78155-9480

HETTINGER, WILLIAM PETER, JR, physical chemistry, catalysis, for more information see previous edition

HETTMANSPERGER, THOMAS PHILIP, STATISTICS. *Current Pos:* Assoc prof, 67-76, head dept, 88-90, PROF STATIST, PA STATE UNIV, UNIVERSITY PARK, 76-,. *Personal Data:* b Wabash, Ind, Aug 30, 39; m 61; c 3. *Educ:* Ind Univ, BA, 61; Univ Iowa, MS, 65, PhD(statist), 67. *Concurrent Pos:* Assoc ed, Am Statistician, 72-73 & J Am Statist Asn, 78-80, 88-91, J Nonparametric Statist, 90-, J Educ Statist, 89-, ed bd comn statist, 87-; NSF fac fel, 74-75; res assoc, dept statist, Univ Calif, Berkeley, 74-75; vis assoc prof, dept statist, Princeton Univ, 76-77; bd dir, Am Statist Asn, 83; vis fel, dept statist, Univ Melbourne & Univ Latrobe, 84-85; vis prof, Univ Bern, 90; Walter Scott vis prof, Univ New SWales, 90. *Mem:* Fel Inst Math Statist; fel Am Statist Asn; Psychomet Soc. *Res:* Nonparametric statistics and robustness. *Mailing Add:* 246 E Hamilton Ave State College PA 16801

HETZEL, DONALD STANFORD, ORGANIC CHEMISTRY. *Current Pos:* RETIRED. *Personal Data:* b Philadelphia, Pa, July 1, 41. *Educ:* Ohio Wesleyan Univ, BA, 63; Univ Ill, MS, 65, PhD(org chem), 68. *Prof Exp:* Res chemist, Chem Div, Pfizer, Inc, 67-72; dir licensing health care prods, 72-74; dir corp res, Howmedia, Inc, 74-76, vpres corp res, 76-81; vpres corp res, Becton Dickinson & Co, 81-96. *Mem:* Am Chem Soc; Soc Biomat Res; NY Acad Sci. *Res:* Organic synthesis; biomedical polymers; technology evaluation and aquisition; research management; strategic planning. *Mailing Add:* Hetzel Group Bean River Rd Pine Plains NY 12567

HETZEL, HOWARD ROY, invertebrate zoology; deceased, see previous edition for last biography

HETZEL, RICHARD ERNEST, CONTROL SYSTEM & INSTRUMENT ENGINEERING. *Current Pos:* CONSULT, CONTROL SYST ENG, 88- *Personal Data:* b New York, NY, 1935. *Educ:* Stevens Inst Technol, BS, 56. *Prof Exp:* Serv engr, Repub Flow Meters Co, 56-59; mem qual control dept, Tech Mat Corp, 61-65; sr instrument engr, Crawford & Russell Inc, 65-69; sr instrument engr, Stauffer Chem Co, 69-88. *Mem:* Sr mem, Instrument Soc Am. *Mailing Add:* 200 G High Point Dr Hartsdale NY 10530-1139

HETZLER, BRUCE EDWARD, PHYSIOLOGICAL PSYCHOLOGY, NEUROPHARMACOLOGY. *Current Pos:* From instr to assoc prof, 76-89, PROF PSYCHOL, LAWRENCE UNIV, 89- *Personal Data:* b St Louis, Mo, Oct 18, 48; c 2. *Educ:* DePauw Univ, BA, 70; Northwestern Univ, MA, 73, PhD(psychol), 78. *Concurrent Pos:* Res psychologist, Neurotoxicol Div, US Environ Protection Agency, 83-84; dir, Lawrence Univ London Centre, London, 87-88. *Mem:* AAAS; Soc Neurosci; Int Soc Biomed Res Alcoholism. *Res:* Behavioral electrophysiology; operant control of neural events; pharmacological effects on evoked brain activity; hypothermia. *Mailing Add:* Dept Psychol Lawrence Univ Main Campus 115 S Drew St Appleton WI 54911-5732

HETZLER, MORRIS CLIFFORD, JR, SOLID STATE PHYSICS. *Current Pos:* Asst prof, 64-73, ASSOC PROF PHYSICS, UNIV TENN, CHATTANOOGA, 73- *Personal Data:* b Chattanooga, Tenn, Nov 1, 37; m 65; c 2. *Educ:* Univ Chattanooga, AB, 59; Vanderbilt Univ, PhD(physics), 70. *Mem:* Am Phys Soc; Am Asn Physics Teachers; Sigma Xi. *Res:* Experimental investigation of dielectric properties of insulators as functions of temperature and of externally applied fields. *Mailing Add:* 3359 Northbrook Dr Atlanta GA 30340

HEUBERGER, OSCAR, ORGANIC CHEMISTRY. *Current Pos:* RETIRED. *Personal Data:* b Berne, Switz, May 30, 24; nat US; m 55; c 2. *Educ:* Swiss Fed Inst Technol, PhD(chem), 49. *Honors & Awards:* Silver Medal, Swiss Fed Inst Technol, 50. *Prof Exp:* Instr, Swiss Fed Inst Technol, 48-50; fel, Imp Col, London, 50-51; res chemist, E I du Pont de Nemours & Co, Inc, 51-74, lab dir textile fibers dept, 74-83, mgr res & develop, 83-85. *Mem:* Am Chem Soc. *Res:* Polymer chemistry; textile fibers; textile technology. *Mailing Add:* 250 Pantops Mountain Rd No 21 Charlottesville VA 22911

HEUCHLING, THEODORE P, ELECTRICAL ENGINEERING. *Current Pos:* sect head eng sci, Arthur D Little, Inc, 59-68, vpres, 65-85, head eng div, 68-74, corp tech staff, 74-85, pres, Arthur D Little Enterprises, Inc, 86-91, SR VPRES, ARTHUR D LITTLE, INC, 85- *Personal Data:* b Chicago, Ill, June 24, 25; m 49, 77, Patricia Curley; c Donna, Theodore J, Paul, Claire, Ann & Clifford. *Educ:* Mass Inst Technol, SB, 46, SM, 48. *Prof Exp:* Res asst elec eng, Servomech Lab, Mass Inst Technol, 46-48, staff mem, 48-51; proj engr & sect head comput controls, Ultrasonic Corp, 51-55; vpres & chief eng, Feedback Controls, Inc, 55-59. *Concurrent Pos:* Consult environ mgt & energy resources. *Mem:* Sr mem Inst Elec & Electronics Engrs; Am Inst Aeronaut & Astronaut. *Res:* Feedback controls; analog computers; instrumentation. *Mailing Add:* Arthur D Little Inc 20 Acorn Park Winchester MA 01890

HEUER, ANN ELIZABETH, MICROBIOLOGY, IMMUNOLOGY. *Current Pos:* assoc prof, 68-74, prof biol sci, 74-89, EMER PROF BIOL SCI, CALIF STATE UNIV, HAYWARD, 89- *Personal Data:* b Irvington, NJ, Oct 11, 30. *Educ:* Rutgers Univ, BS, 52, MS, 54, PhD(bact), 62. *Prof Exp:* Instr bact, Douglass Col, Rutgers Univ, 54-57; res asst microbiol, Inst Microbiol, 57-59; instr bact, Douglass Col, 58-59; instr bact, Vassar Col, 59-60; res assoc, Inst Microbiol, Douglass Col, Rutgers Univ, 60-62; USPHS fel immunol, Univ Milan, 62-63; res assoc, Inst Microbiol, Douglass Col, Rutgers Univ, 64; asst prof microbiol, Carnegie Inst Technol, 64-68. *Mem:* Am Soc Microbiol. *Res:* Bacterial population dynamics; genetic control of pigment synthesis in Serratia; immune response and mechanism of enhancement. *Mailing Add:* Dept Biol Sci Calif State Univ 25800 Carlos Bee Blvd Hayward CA 94542-3000

HEUER, ARTHUR HAROLD, CERAMICS. *Current Pos:* asst prof metall, Case Western Res Univ, 67-70, from assoc prof to prof ceramics, 70-85, dir, Mat Res Lab, 77-80, KYOCERA PROF CERAMICS, CASE WESTERN RES UNIV, 85- *Personal Data:* b New York, NY, Apr 29, 36; m 56; c 3. *Educ:* City Col New York, BS, 56; Univ Leeds, PhD(ceramics), 66, DSc, 77. *Honors & Awards:* Ross Coffin Purdy Award, Am Ceramic Soc, 81. *Prof Exp:* Res chemist, Electronics Div, Ind Gen Corp, 56-60; res engr, Electron Tube Div, Bendix Corp, 60-61; res asst ceramics, Univ Leeds, 61-65; staff scientist, Space Systs Div, Avco Corp, 65-67. *Concurrent Pos:* Chmn, Ceramics Gordon Conf, 72; ed, J Am Ceramic Soc, 88-90; external sci mem, Max

Planck Inst Metall forschung, 90- *Mem:* Nat Acad Eng; Am Inst Mining, Metall & Petrol Engrs; fel Am Ceramic Soc; fel Inst Physics UK; AAAS; Am Ceramic Soc. *Res:* Physical ceramics; mechanical properties; study of phase transformation and diffusion-controlled processes; transmission electron microscopy of ceramics; magnetic properties; fracture mechanics; properties of ceramics; electron microscopy of rock and minerals; displacive phase transformations in oxides and silicates; solid-state precipitation in ceramics and minerals; fracture mechanics and deformation behavior in single crystal and poly-crystalline ceramics; oxidation of non-oxide ceramics; transformation toughening; author of over 200 publications. *Mailing Add:* Mat Sci & Eng Case Western Res Univ 10900 Euclid Ave Cleveland OH 44106

HEUER, CHARLES VERNON, MATHEMATICS. *Current Pos:* assoc prof & chmn dept, 66-73, PROF MATH, CONCORDIA COL, MOORHEAD, MINN, 73- *Personal Data:* b Bertha, Minn, Apr 27, 37; m 57; c 4. *Educ:* Concordia Col, Moorhead, Minn, BA, 58; Univ Nebr, MA, 60, PhD(math), 63. *Prof Exp:* Asst prof math, Univ Mo-Columbia, 63-66. *Concurrent Pos:* Hon fel, Univ Wis-Madison, 74. *Mem:* Am Math Soc; Math Asn Am. *Res:* Group theory; algebraic theory of semigroups. *Mailing Add:* Dept Math Concordia Col Moorhead MN 56560

HEUER, GERALD ARTHUR, THEORY OF GAMES, ANALYSIS & FUNCTIONAL ANALYSIS. *Current Pos:* from instr to prof, 56-88, Sigurd & Pauline Prestegaard Mundhjeld prof math, 88-95, EMER PROF MATH & MATHEMATICIAN IN RESIDENCE, CONCORDIA COL, 95- *Personal Data:* b Bertha, Minn, Aug 31, 30; m 54, Jeanette Knedel; c Paul, Karl, Ruth & Otto. *Educ:* Concordia Col, Moorhead, Minn, BA, 51; Univ Nebr, MA, 53; Univ Minn, PhD(math), 58. *Prof Exp:* Asst, Univ Nebr, 51-53 & Univ Minn, 53-55; instr math, Hamline Univ, 55-56. *Concurrent Pos:* Vis asst prof, Univ Nebr, 60-61; consult, Control Data Corp, 60-63; res assoc math, Univ Calif, Berkeley, 66-67; vis mathematician, Math Inst, Cologne Univ, Ger, 73-74; vis prof math, Wash State Univ, 80-81; vis prof, Institut fur Statistik und Opers Res, Graz Univ, Austria, 87-88, 90, 94; leader Am team, Int Math Olympiad, 88-90. *Mem:* Am Math Soc; Math Asn Am; Deut Math Ver Ger; Austrian Math Soc. *Res:* Theory of 2-person games; probability; real analysis. *Mailing Add:* Dept Math Concordia Col Moorhead MN 56562. *Fax:* 218-299-4308; *E-Mail:* heuer@cord.edu

HEUSCH, CLEMENS AUGUST, ELEMENTARY PARTICLE PHYSICS, PARTICLE DETECTION. *Current Pos:* PROF PHYSICS, UNIV CALIF, SANTA CRUZ, 69- *Personal Data:* b Aachen, Ger, Apr 19, 32; m 68, Karin von Gilgenheimb; c Marina & Bettina. *Educ:* Aachen Tech Univ, dipl physics, 55; Munich Tech Univ, Dr rer nat, 59. *Honors & Awards:* Fulbright Award, Bowdoin Col, 51-52; Humboldt Prize, 91. *Prof Exp:* Res asst neutron physics, Munich Tech Univ, 56-59; proj supvr semiconductor physics, AEG Res Labs, Frankfurt, Ger, 60-61; res assoc high energy physics, Deutsch Elektronen-Synchtron, Hamburg, 61-63; res fel, Calif Inst Technol, 63-65, sr res fel, 65-67, assoc prof physics, 67-69. *Concurrent Pos:* Fulbright Award, Bowdoin Col, 51-52; consult, AEG, Frankfurt, 56-62; vis prof & vis assoc, Calif Inst Technol, 70-72; vis Prof, Max Planck Inst Physics, Ger, 74; vis prof, Univ Munich, 74-75 & 90-91 Univ Aachen, 80 & Academia Sinica, Beijing, 87; vis scientist European Ctr Nuclear Res, Switz, 74-75 & 83- *Mem:* Am Phys Soc. *Res:* Electron-positron annihilation studies; nuclear instrumentation; interactions of leptons and photons with nucleons at high energies; flavor conservation in elementary particle interactions; search for heavy neutrinos electron colliders at very high energies. *Mailing Add:* 553 Ravenscourt Rd Burlingame CA 94010. *Fax:* 650-926-4905

HEUSCHELE, ANN, AQUATIC BIOLOGY. *Current Pos:* MEM BIOL FAC, NORMANDALE COMMUNITY COL, 70- *Personal Data:* b Cadillac, Mich, Sept 5, 38; m 64; c 2. *Educ:* Univ Mich, BS & MS, 60; Univ Minn, PhD(zool), 68. *Prof Exp:* Instr biol, Canisius Col, 61-64; asst prof, Carleton Col, 68-69. *Mem:* Asn Women Sci; NAm Benthological Soc; Ecol Soc Am. *Res:* Lake Superior benthos; invertebrate biology; aquatic ecology; biology of women. *Mailing Add:* Dept Biol Normandale Community Col Bloomington MN 55431

HEUSCHELE, WERNER PAUL, VETERINARY VIROLOGY, PREVENTIVE MEDICINE. *Current Pos:* lab dir, 82-, RES SCIENTIST, SAN DIEGO ZOO. *Personal Data:* b Ludwigsburg, Ger, Aug 28, 29; US citizen; m 53; c 6. *Educ:* Univ Calif, Davis, AB, 52, DVM, 56; Univ Wis-Madison, PhD(vet sci), 69. *Prof Exp:* Vet & mgr hosp & lab, Zool Soc San Diego, 56-61; vet res officer, USDA, Plum Island Animal Dis Lab, 61-70; assoc prof microbiol, Col Vet Med, Kans State Univ, 70-71; head virol, Jensen-Salsbery Labs, 71-76; assoc prof, Dept Vet Prev Med, Col Vet Med, Ohio State Univ, 76-78, prof, 78-82. *Concurrent Pos:* Resident trainee vet path, Armed Forces Inst Path, 66-69. *Mem:* Am Vet Med Asn; US Animal Health Asn; Conf Res Workers Animal Dis; Wildlife Dis Asn. *Res:* Foreign animal diseases, especially African swine fever; bovine and equine viral diseases. *Mailing Add:* San Diego Zoo 2920 Zoo Dr San Diego CA 92101-1693

HEUSER, EVA T, PEDIATRICS, PATHOLOGY. *Current Pos:* asst prof med, 64-76, ASST PROF PATH, UNIV SOUTHERN CALIF, 76-; DEP MED EXAMR, LOS ANGELES COUNTY, 80- *Personal Data:* b Warsaw, Poland, Nov 8, 32; US citizen; c 2. *Educ:* Queen's Univ, Ont, MD, CM, 56. *Prof Exp:* Assoc pathologist, Children's Hosp, Los Angeles, 64-80. *Mem:* Int Acad Path. *Res:* Pediatric forensic pathology. *Mailing Add:* Coroners Off 1104 N Mission Rd Los Angeles CA 90033-1017

HEUSER, GUNNAR, HEADACHE & PAIN MEDICINE. *Current Pos:* MED DIR, BEVERLY HILLS HEADACHE & PAIN MED GROUP, 75-; PVT PRACT, LOS ANGELES, CALIF, 82- *Personal Data:* b Hamburg, Ger, July 17, 27. *Educ:* Cologne Univ, Ger, MD, 52; Univ Montreal, PhD(exp med & surg), 57. *Prof Exp:* Asst Clin Prof Med, Univ Calif, Los Angeles, 70- *Concurrent Pos:* Med dir, Environ Med Res & Info Ctr. *Mem:* Fel Am Col Physicians. *Mailing Add:* Dept Med Univ Calif-Los Angeles 323 S Moorpark Rd Thousand Oaks CA 91361

HEUSINKVELD, MYRON ELLIS, PHYSICS. *Current Pos:* RETIRED. *Personal Data:* b Hull, Iowa, Aug 3, 21; m 53; c 3. *Educ:* Iowa State Col, BS, 43; Univ Minn, PhD(physics), 51. *Prof Exp:* Elec engr, US Naval Res lab, Washington, DC, 44-47; physicist, Lawrence Livermore Lab, Univ Calif, 51-83. *Mem:* AAAS; Am Phys Soc; Soc Eng Sci; Am Geophys Union. *Res:* Nuclear physics; particle accelerator development; shock and other transient stress experimentation. *Mailing Add:* 3875 Pestana Way Livermore CA 94550

HEUSNER, ALFRED AUGUST, BASAL METABOLISM & BODY SIZE, CIRCADIAN & SEASONAL RHYTHMS. *Current Pos:* PROF PHYSIOL, SCH VET MED, UNIV CALIF, DAVIS, 67- *Educ:* Univ Strasbourg, France, ScD, 63. *Mailing Add:* 819 Malaga Ave Davis CA 95616

HEUSSER, CALVIN JOHN, BOTANY. *Current Pos:* assoc prof dept biol & geol, 67-71, prof biol, 71-91, EMER PROF BIOL, NY UNIV, 91- *Personal Data:* b North Bergen, NJ, Sept 10, 24; m 47, Linda Esslinger; c Eric & Kristin. *Educ:* Rutgers Univ, BS, 47, MS, 49; Ore State Col, PhD, 52. *Honors & Awards:* David Livingstone Centenary Medal, Am Geog Soc, 87. *Prof Exp:* Seessel fel, Yale Univ, 52-53; res assoc, Am Geog Soc, 53-67, adminr, Juneau Ice Field Proj, 53-59. *Concurrent Pos:* Guggenheim & Fulbright fel, Chile, 62-63; assoc ed, Torrey Bot Club, 71-77, pres, 75-76; fel, Clare Hall, Univ Cambridge, 86-. *Mem:* AAAS; Ecol Soc Am; Torrey Bot Club; Am Asn Stratig Palynologists; Sigma Xi. *Res:* Quaternary palynology of western North America and southern Chile and Argentina; paleoecological employing fossil pollen and spores and radiometric dating techniques in stratigraphic settings to trace vegetation and climate during the quaternary as a basis for paleoclimatic theory. *Mailing Add:* Clinton Woods Tuxedo NY 10987

HEUSSER, LINDA OLGA, QUATERNARY PALEOCLIMATOLOGY. *Current Pos:* RES SCIENTIST, LAMONT-DOHERTY GEOL OBSERV, COLUMBIA UNIV, 78- *Personal Data:* b Sharon, Pa, Apr 12, 32; m 70, Calvin John; c Faith, Ben, H.W. III, & Eric. *Educ:* Wellesley Col, BA, 54; Columbia Univ, MA, 66; NY Univ, PhD(geol), 71. *Prof Exp:* Lectr geol, Iona Col, 65; asst prof, Orange Co City Col, 75; geologist, US Geol Surv, 78-82; sr res scientist, NY Univ, 87-90. *Concurrent Pos:* Sr res scientist, NY Univ, 70-81. *Mem:* Geol Soc Am; AAAS; Am Geophys Union; Quaternary Res Asn; Am Quaternary Res Asn. *Res:* Marine palynology; analysis of pollen from North Pacific, North and South Atlantic to reconstruct vegetational and climate history of Northeast Asia. *Mailing Add:* 100 Clinton Rd Tuxedo NY 10987. *E-Mail:* heusser@lamont.ldgo.columbia.edu

HEUSTIS, ALBERT EDWARD, PUBLIC HEALTH ADMINISTRATION. *Current Pos:* HEALTH PROGS CONSULT, 71- *Personal Data:* b Fitchburg, Mass, Apr 22, 13; m 36; c 5. *Educ:* Univ Mich, AB, 33, MD, 36; Johns Hopkins Univ, PM MPH, 42. *Hon Degrees:* LLD, Mich State Univ, 55. *Honors & Awards:* Cert Appreciation, Nat Found Infantile Paralysis, 54; Citation Merit Serv, US Civil Defense Coun, 63; McCormack Award, Asn State & Territorial Health Officers, 63. *Prof Exp:* From asst dir to dir, Monroe County Health Dept, 42-45; dir, Branch County Health Dept, 45-48 & Branch County Community Hosp, 46-48; comnr, State Dept Health, Mich, 48-67; prog coordr, Mich Asn Regional Med Progs, 67-71. *Mem:* Am Pub Health Asn; AMA; Asn State & Territorial Health Officers; hon fel Am Col Chest Physicians. *Res:* Most effective and least expensive application of knowledge to build better health for the individual, the family and the community. *Mailing Add:* 12321 Hoffman Rd Three Rivers MI 49093-9543

HEUVERS, KONRAD JOHN, FUNCTIONAL EQUATIONS & LINEAR ALGEBRA. *Current Pos:* From asst prof to assoc prof, 69-82, PROF MATH, MICH TECHNOL UNIV, 82- *Personal Data:* b Stockton, Calif, Mar 15, 40; m 67, Barbara Michna; c Joseph & Kristina. *Educ:* Stanford Univ, BS, 62, MS, 64; Ohio State Univ, PhD(math), 69. *Mem:* Am Math Soc; Math Asn Am; Sigma Xi; Ger Math Union; Austrian Math Soc; Soc Indust & Appl Math. *Res:* Functional equations; linear algebra; combinatorics and finite mathematics. *Mailing Add:* Dept Math Mich Technol Univ Houghton MI 49931-1295. *Fax:* 906-487-3133; *E-Mail:* kheuvers@mtu.edu

HEUZE, FRANCOIS E, GEOLOGICAL ENGINEERING, ROCK MECHANICS. *Current Pos:* HEAD, GEOTECH GROUP & MGR, UNCONVENTIONAL GAS PROG, LAWRENCE LIVERMORE NAT LAB, 79- *Personal Data:* b Oran, Algeria, Dec 3, 41; US citizen; m 72; c 2. *Educ:* Nat Sch Mines, France, MSc, 64; Univ Calif, Berkeley, MSc(civil eng), 67, D Eng(geol eng), 70. *Honors & Awards:* Publs Bd Award, Soc Mining Eng of AIME, 82; Case Histories Award, US Nat Comt Rock Mech/Nat Res Coun, 86. *Prof Exp:* Asst res specialist, Univ Calif, Berkeley, 67-70, asst res engr, 70-75, lectr, 70-75; assoc prof civil eng, Univ Colo, 75-79. *Concurrent Pos:* Consult geol eng & rock mech, 72-; app mem, Geotech Bd Nat Res Coun/Nat Acad Sci, 87. *Mem:* Fel Am Soc Civil Eng; Soc Mining Engrs; Int Soc Rock Mech; Eng & Sci Soc France; Am Soc Testing Mat. *Res:* Analysis and design of rock structures; foundations; tunnels; slopes; mines; gas recovery; hydraulic fracturing; dynamic ground motion; cratering; penetration; subsidence. *Mailing Add:* 859 Redwood Dr Danville CA 94506-2184

HEVERAN, JOHN EDWARD, ANALYTICAL CHEMISTRY. *Current Pos:* DIR, METPATH, 88- *Personal Data:* b New York, NY, Aug 7, 38; m 59; c 2. *Educ:* Manhattan Col, BS, 60; Purdue Univ, MS, 62, PhD(chem), 65; Am Bd Clin Chem, dipl, 77. *Honors & Awards:* Cert Honor, Am Asn Clin Chem, 87. *Prof Exp:* Proj chemist, Am Cyanamid Co, 65-66; sr chemist, Hoffmann-La Roche Inc, 66-67, group leader, 67-68, mgr anal res, 68-73, res group chief to sr res group chief, 73-80; dir res & develop, Gen Diag Div, Warner Lambert Co, 80-82; managing dir, Heveran & Assocs, Inc, 82-88; tech dir, Lab Serv Inc, 83-88. *Concurrent Pos:* Adj assoc prof, Univ Med & Dent, NJ. *Mem:* Am Chem Soc; Am Asn Clin Chem; NY Acad Sci; Sigma Xi. *Res:* Pharmaceutical analysis; clinical chemistry; immunochemistry; diagnostic immunology; toxicology. *Mailing Add:* 6 Caryn Pl Fairfield NJ 07006-1802

HEVNER, ALAN RAYMOND, DATABASE SYSTEMS, INFORMATION SYSTEMS DEVELOPMENT. *Current Pos:* PROF INFO SYSTS, UNIV MD, 81- *Personal Data:* b Marion, Ind, Dec 9, 50; m 85, Susan Nichols; c Caitlin M. *Educ:* Purdue Univ, BS, 73, MS, 76, PhD(comput sci), 79. *Prof Exp:* Asst prof comput sci, Univ Minn, 79-81. *Concurrent Pos:* Consult, Honeywell, Inc, 80-85, IBM, 85- & MCI, 90- *Mem:* Asn Comput Mach; Inst Elec & Electronics Engrs Comput Soc; Opers Res Soc Am. *Res:* Database systems design; distributed database systems; systems engineering; information systems analysis and design. *Mailing Add:* 15703 Cheston Ct Tampa FL 33647. *Fax:* 301-314-9157; *E-Mail:* ahevner@bmgtmail.umd.edu

HEW, CHOY-LEONG, BIOCHEMISTRY. *Current Pos:* PROF BIOCHEM, UNIV TORONTO, 83-; SR SCIENTIST, HOSP SICK CHILDREN, 83- *Personal Data:* b Ipoh, Malaysia, Mar 10, 42; m 68. *Educ:* Nanyang Univ, BSc, 63; Simon Fraser Univ, MSc, 66; Univ BC, PhD(biochem), 70. *Honors & Awards:* Fraser Award, Atlantic Prov Inter Univs Coun Soc, Can. *Prof Exp:* Res assoc biochem, Yale Univ, 70-72; C H Best fel, Univ Toronto, 73-74; from asst prof to prof biochem, Mem Univ Nfld, 74-82. *Mem:* Can Biochem Soc; Am Soc Biol Chemists; NY Acad Sci; AAAS. *Res:* Proteins structure and function; biosynthesis and regulation of peptide hormones in marine organisms; structure and biosynthesis of antifreeze proteins; hydroxylation of collagen. *Mailing Add:* Banting Inst Univ Toronto 100 College St Rm 351 Toronto ON M5G 1L5 Can

HEWER, GARY ARTHUR, APPLIED MATHEMATICS, SYSTEMS SCIENCE. *Current Pos:* MATHEMATICIAN, NAVAL WEAPONS CTR, CHINA LAKE, 68- *Personal Data:* b Mitchell, SDak, Aug 11, 40; m 69. *Educ:* Yankton Col, BA, 62; Wash State Univ, MA, 64, PhD(math), 68. *Mem:* Soc Indust & Appl Math; Sigma Xi. *Res:* Controllability and stabilizability of control systems; general theory of Riccati equations; numerical solutions of linear and quadratic matrix equations; applied stochastic process theory; robust kalman filtering; radar signature analysis. *Mailing Add:* 636 Las Flores Ridgecrest CA 93555-3404

HEWES, RALPH ALLAN, SOLID STATE PHYSICS. *Current Pos:* RES PHYSICIST, GEN ELEC CO, 66- *Personal Data:* b Columbus, Ohio, July 4, 39; m 62; c 2. *Educ:* Case Inst Technol, BS, 61; Univ Ill, MS, 63, PhD(physics), 66. *Prof Exp:* Res assoc physics, Univ Ill, 66. *Mem:* Am Phys Soc; Sigma Xi. *Res:* Radiation damage in semiconductors; energy transfer; luminescence of solids. *Mailing Add:* 39 Velina Dr Burnt Hills NY 12027-9416

HEWETSON, JOHN FRANCIS, VIROLOGY, IMMUNOLOGY. *Current Pos:* CHIEF, DEPT IMMUNOTHER & DIAG, US ARMY MED RES INST INFECTIOUS DIS, FREDERICK, MD, 81- *Personal Data:* b Chicago, Ill, July 3, 39; m 64, 83, Pamela Warwick; c Peter & Kathryn. *Educ:* Pa State Univ, BS, 61; Fla State Univ, MS, 65; Rutgers Univ, PhD(virol & microbiol), 69. *Prof Exp:* Asst prof biol, Newark State Col, 65-66; res assoc, Univ Pa, 71-72, asst prof virol, 72-76; assoc prof microbiol, Med Col Pa, 77-81. *Concurrent Pos:* Damon Runyon Fund fel tumor biol, Karolinska Inst, Sweden, 69-71; res assoc, Children's Hosp, Philadelphia, 71-72; scholar, Leukemia Soc Am, 75-80. *Mem:* AAAS; Am Soc Microbiol; Int Soc Toxinol. *Res:* Virology and immunology of tumors; cellular immune response associated with neoplasia; immunological response to low molecular weight toxins. *Mailing Add:* 126 Kline Blvd Frederick MD 21701. *Fax:* 301-619-2348; *E-Mail:* hewetson@ftdetrck-riid1.army.mil

HEWETT, DENNIS W, NUMERICAL SIMULATION PLASMA & PARTICLE ACCELERATORS, MAGNETIC & INERTIAL CONFINEMENT FUSION. *Current Pos:* STAFF MEM, LAWRENCE LIVERMORE LABS, 83- *Personal Data:* b Girard, Kans, Sept 17, 47; m; c 2. *Educ:* Pittsburgh State Univ, BS, 69; Univ Kans, PhD(plasma physics), 73. *Prof Exp:* Staff physicist, Los Alamos Nat Lab, 73-78, assoc group leader, 78-82; assoc group leader, Plasma Fusion Ctr, Mass Inst Technol, 82-83. *Mem:* Am Physiol Soc; Am Geophys Union. *Res:* Investigating microscopic properties of magnetic reconnection by numerical simulation and numerical investigation of particle acceleration, especially physics of high current heavy ion beams. *Mailing Add:* L-418 Lawrence Livermore Nat Lab PO Box 5508 Livermore CA 94550

HEWETT, JAMES VEITH, ORGANIC CHEMISTRY. *Current Pos:* PVT INVESTR, 83-; CONSULT, CONDUX, 90- *Personal Data:* b Broken Bow, Nebr, July 25, 21; m 50, Kathryn Kirby; c Ernest Kirby & Kathryn Anne. *Educ:* Univ Nebr, BS, 43; Univ Purdue, MS, 48, PhD(chem), 50. *Prof Exp:* Chemist, Phillips Petrol Co, 43-46; asst chem, 46-48, fel, Purdue Univ, 48-50; chemist, E I du Pont de Nemours & Co, Inc, 50-53, group supvr, 53-55, from supvr to res assoc, 55-83. *Mem:* Am Chem Soc. *Res:* Acrylic, spandex and high temperature fiber technology; process economics; process and product modeling; open end spinning of staple fibers; time series analysis and modeling. *Mailing Add:* 1211 Keesling Ave Waynesboro VA 22980-5217

HEWETT, JOANNE LEA, ELECTROWEAK PHENOMENOLOGY. *Current Pos:* ASST PROF, STANFORD LINEAR ACCELERATOR CTR, 94- *Personal Data:* b Boulder, Colo, Mar 15, 60; m 85, Thomas Rizzo. *Educ:* Iowa State Univ, BS, 82; Univ Calif, Irvine, MS, 84, Iowa State Univ PhD, 88. *Prof Exp:* Teaching asst physics, Iowa State Univ, 82-83 & Univ Calif, Irvine, 83-84; res asst physics, Ames Lab, Iowa State Univ, 84-88; asst prof physics, Univ Wis-Madison, 88-91; asst physicist, Argonne Nat Lab, 91-94. *Mem:* Am Women Sci; Am Phys Soc. *Res:* Theoretical high energy physics: composite models, fermion masses, extended electroweak theories, grand unified theories and superstring theories. *Mailing Add:* Theory Group MS 81 Stanford Linear Accelerator Ctr PO Box 4349 Stanford CA 94309. *E-Mail:* hewett@slac.stanford.edu

HEWETT, JOHN EARL, STATISTICS. *Current Pos:* from asst prof to assoc prof, 65-78, PROF STATIST, UNIV MO, COLUMBIA, 78- *Personal Data:* b Fairfield, Iowa, Feb 20, 37; m 60; c 3. *Educ:* Parsons Col, BS, 58; Univ Iowa, MS, 62, PhD(math), 65. *Prof Exp:* Teacher math, Monroe Community High Sch, 58-60; lectr, Univ Iowa, 65. *Concurrent Pos:* Consult, Harry S Truman Mem Vet Hosp, 73- *Mem:* Fel Am Statist Asn; Inst Math Statist; Biomet Soc. *Res:* Statistical distribution theory; regression; hypothesis testing; prediction. *Mailing Add:* 1410 Overhill Rd Columbia MO 65203

HEWETT, LIONEL DONNELL, SOLAR PHYSICS. *Current Pos:* From asst prof to assoc prof, 64-77, PROF PHYSICS, TEX A&I UNIV, 77-, CHMN, PHYSICS DEPT, 85- *Personal Data:* b Cleburne, Tex, July 20, 38; m 70; c 2. *Educ:* Tex A&I Univ, BS, 60; Univ Mo-Rolla, PhD(eng physics), 65. *Mem:* Am Asn Physics Teachers. *Res:* Physics teaching techniques. *Mailing Add:* Dept Physics Tex A&M Univ 700 University Blvd Kingsville TX 78363-8203

HEWETT-EMMETT, DAVID, HUMAN MOLECULAR GENETICS, MOLECULAR EVOLUTION. *Current Pos:* ASSOC PROF GENETICS, UNIV TEX HEALTH SCI CTR, 84-, DIR, GRAD SCH PROG GENETICS, 92- *Personal Data:* b Bromley, Eng, June 2, 46; m 87, Maureen E Goode. *Educ:* Univ Cambridge, Eng, BA(Hons), 68; Univ London, MSc, 69, PhD(biochem), 73. *Prof Exp:* Asst res scientist human genetics, Univ Mich, 79-84. *Mem:* Am Soc Humam Genetics; Am Soc Biochem & Molecular Biol; Int Soc Molecular Evolution; Soc Molecular Biol & Evolution. *Res:* Human genetics; molecular evolution; medical sciences. *Mailing Add:* Univ Tex Houston Health Sci Ctr Genetics Ctr PO Box 20334 Houston TX 77225-0334. *Fax:* 713-792-4615

HEWGILL, DENTON ELWOOD, MATHEMATICS. *Current Pos:* asst prof, 69-80, ASSOC PROF MATH, UNIV VICTORIA, 80- *Personal Data:* b Collingwood, Ont, Feb 11, 40; m 64; c 2. *Educ:* Univ BC, BSc, 63, PhD(math), 66. *Prof Exp:* Res assoc & fel math, Univ BC, 66-67; Nat Res Coun Can fel, NY Univ, 67-69. *Res:* Singular elliptic partial differential equations; mathematical analysis; fluid dynamics; numerical analysis of partial differential equations. *Mailing Add:* Dept Math Univ Victoria Victoria BC V8W 2Y2 Can. *Fax:* 520-721-8962

HEWINS, ROGER HERBERT, MINERALOGY, PETROLOGY. *Current Pos:* from asst prof to assoc prof, 75-85, PROF MINERAL & PETROL, RUTGERS UNIV, 85- *Personal Data:* b Farnham, Eng, Nov 29, 40; US citizen; m 63; c 2. *Educ:* Aberdeen Univ, BSc, 62; Univ Toronto, PhD(geol), 71. *Prof Exp:* Geologist, Geol Surv Brit Guiana, 63-65 & Falconbridge Nickel Mines Ltd, 65-67; teaching asst mineral, Univ Toronto, 67-71, lectr, 71-72; res assoc lunar petrol, Lehigh Univ, 72-75. *Concurrent Pos:* Res assoc, Am Mus Natural Hist, NY, 76-; abstractor mineral abstracts, London, 80-; prin investr, grants on metal & silicates in meteorites, NASA. *Mem:* Meteoritical Soc; Geol Asn Can; Mineral Asn Can; Mineral Soc Am. *Res:* Thermal and collisional history of parent bodies of igneous meteorites; dynamic crystallization experiments on chondrule compositions; microprobe analysis of minerals; petrology of mafic igneous rocks; geothermometry. *Mailing Add:* Dept Geol Sci Rutgers Univ New Brunswick NJ 08903

HEWISH, ANTONY, RADIOASTRONOMY. *Current Pos:* EMER PROF, CAVENDISH LABS, 90- *Personal Data:* b Fowey, Cornwall, Eng, May 11, 24. *Educ:* Kings Col, Caius Col. *Honors & Awards:* Nobel Prize in Physics, 74; Hamilton Prize, 51; Eddington Medal, Royal Astron Soc, 68. *Prof Exp:* Asst dir res, Gonville & Caius Col, 53-61; reader radio astron, Univ Cambridge, 69-71; dir, Mullard Radio Astron Observ, 82-90. *Mem:* Am Acad Arts & Sci; Indian Nat Sci Acad. *Mailing Add:* Cavendish Labs Mattingley Rd Cambridge CB3 0HE England

HEWITSON, WALTER MILTON, PLANT MORPHOLOGY. *Current Pos:* from asst prof to assoc prof, 70-77, PROF BIOL, BRIDGEWATER STATE COL, 77- *Personal Data:* b Neptune, NJ, Dec 21, 33; m 71. *Educ:* Miami Univ, Ohio, AB, 56; Cornell Univ, MS, 59; Wash Univ, St Louis, PhD(plant morphol), 62. *Prof Exp:* Instr bot, Miami Univ, Ohio, 58-59 & Parsons Col, 62-63; asst prof, Southern Ill Univ, 63-65 & Univ Pac, 65-70. *Concurrent Pos:* Res fel, Highlands Biol Sta, NC, 63-73; consulting work, wetlands delineations & replicatious. *Mem:* Bot Soc Am; Torrey Bot Club. *Res:* Comparative morphology of lower vascular plants. *Mailing Add:* Biol Sci Bridgewater State Col 131 Summer St Bridgewater MA 02324-2699

HEWITT, ALLAN A, PLANT PHYSIOLOGY. *Current Pos:* RETIRED. *Personal Data:* b Sacramento, Calif, Mar 1, 34; m 55; c 2. *Educ:* Univ Calif, BS, 55, MS, 57; Univ Md, PhD(hort), 62. *Honors & Awards:* Joseph H Gourley Award, 60. *Prof Exp:* Res horticulturist, Crops Res Div, USDA, 62-64; asst res pomologist, Univ Calif, Davis, 64-68; from assoc prof to prof pomol, Calif State Univ, 70-92. *Mem:* Am Soc Hort Sci; Am Soc Plant Physiol. *Res:* Nitrogen uptake and nitrogen-carbohydrate relationships in deciduous fruits; pistachio research. *Mailing Add:* 1702 E Stuart Ave Fresno CA 93710

HEWITT, ANDREW, PESTICIDE APPLICATION TECHNOLOGY, SPRAY DRIFT RESEARCH. *Current Pos:* APPLN TECHNOLOGIST, STEWART AGR RES, 93- *Personal Data:* b Saffron Walden, Essex, Eng, Apr 14, 64. *Educ:* Sheffield Univ, UK, BS, 85; Cranfield Inst Technol, MS, 87; London Univ, PhD(pesticide appln), 91. *Prof Exp:* Res scientist, Dole Fruit Co, Costa Rica, 87-88; res specialist, Imp Col, UK, 88-91; appln technologists, NMex State Univ, 91-93. *Concurrent Pos:* Chmn, Agr Sprays Comt, Inst Liquid Atomization & Sprays Systs, 92-; comt mem, Pesticides & Particle Size Measurement, Am Soc Testing & Mat. *Mem:* Inst Liquid Atomization & Sprays Systs; Am Soc Testing & Mat. *Res:* Spray drift; atomization of pesticides and spray drift; physical properties. *Mailing Add:* Stewart Agr Res Servs Inc Box 509 Macon MO 63552. *Fax:* 660-762-4295

HEWITT, ANTHONY VICTOR, ASTRONOMY. *Current Pos:* AT HUGHES MISSILE SYSTS, 94- *Personal Data:* b Witney, Eng, Feb 2, 43; m 65. *Educ:* Oxford Univ, BA, 64, DPhil(astron), 67. *Prof Exp:* Astron, Flagstaff Sta, US Naval Observ, 67-83; at Loral Electronic Systs, 83-85; at Gen Elec, 85-93. *Mem:* Am Astron Soc; Int Astron Union; Int Soc Optical Instrumentation Engrs. *Res:* Application of image tubes to astronomy; development and use of the navy electronic camera; real-time data processing; image analysis; optical and infra-red sensors. *Mailing Add:* 4021 N Cerro de Falcon Tucson AZ 85718

HEWITT, ARTHUR TYL, SURFACE PROTEOGLYCANS, GLYCOPROTEINS. *Current Pos:* ASST PROF OPHTHAL, WYNN CTR RETINAL DEGENERATION, WILMER INST, JOHNS HOPKINS MED SCH, 82- *Educ:* Emory Univ, PhD(develop biol), 78. *Res:* Cell surface properties. *Mailing Add:* NICHD NIH 6100 Bldg Rm 4B01 Bethesda MD 20892-0001

HEWITT, CHARLES HAYDEN, GEOLOGY, MINERALOGY. *Current Pos:* MGR MINING SYNTHETIC FUELS DIV, EXXON PROD RES CO, HOUSTON, TEX, 80- *Personal Data:* b Butte, Mont, May 18, 29; m 54; c 2. *Educ:* Mont Sch Mines, BS, 51; Univ Mich, MS, 53, PhD(mineral), 57. *Prof Exp:* Asst, Eng Res Inst, Univ Mich, 51-53; sr res geologist, Denver Res Ctr, Marathon Oil Co, Ohio, 56-57, assoc res dir, 67-74, coord mgr prod explor, Ohio, 74-76, vpres minerals, 77-80. *Mem:* Fel Geol Soc Am; Soc Econ Paleontologists & Mineralogists; Am Asn Petrol Geol; Soc Petrol Eng; Sigma Xi. *Res:* Petrology and petrography of sandstones; geologic characteristics of petroleum reservoirs; petroleum exploration and production; mineral exploration and production. *Mailing Add:* 13903 Calmont Dr Houston TX 77070-2401

HEWITT, DAVID, medical statistics, for more information see previous edition

HEWITT, EDWIN, MATHEMATICS. *Current Pos:* from asst prof to assoc prof, 48-54, PROF MATH, UNIV WASH, 54- *Personal Data:* b Everett, Wash, Jan 20, 20; m 44, 64; c 2. *Educ:* Harvard Univ, AB, 40, MA, 41, PhD(math), 42. *Honors & Awards:* Sr US Sci Award, Alexander Von Humboldt Found. *Prof Exp:* Instr, Harvard Univ, 42-43; opers analyst, USAF, 43-45; Guggenheim fel, Inst Adv Study & Princeton Univ, 45-46; asst prof math, Bryn Mawr Col, 46-47; lectr, Univ Chicago, 47-48. *Concurrent Pos:* Vis prof, Univ Uppsala, 51-52, Univ Hokkaido, 82 & Univ Alaska, 83; Guggenheim fel, Inst Adv Study, 55-56; mem, Div Math, Nat Res Coun, 57-65; vis res assoc, Yale Univ, 59; vis prof, Australian Nat Univ, 63, vis res assoc, 70; vis scholar, Steklov Inst, Moscow, 69-70 & Univ New S Wales, 80, 82, & 84; ed, Pac J Math; vis scholar, Steklov Inst, Moscow, 73 & 76; comt mem, US Nat Comt Math, 74-77; Alexander Von Humboldt Found fel, Ger, 75-76; fac lectr, Univ Wash, 81. *Mem:* Am Math Soc; Math Asn Am. *Res:* Harmonic analysis on groups, measure theory, number theory. *Mailing Add:* 5624 56th Ave NE Seattle WA 98105-2163

HEWITT, FREDERICK GEORGE, PHYSICS. *Current Pos:* RES DIR, ORFIELD ASSOC, 88- *Personal Data:* b Aurora, Ill, Apr 4, 29; m 54, Carol Mary Shukle; c Kevin, John, Ann, Jeanne & Martin. *Educ:* St Procopius Col, BS, 51; Univ Notre Dame, PhD(physics), 58. *Prof Exp:* Asst prof physics, Col St Thomas, 57-61; sr staff scientist, Unisys Corp, 61-88. *Concurrent Pos:* Asst, Univ Notre Dame, 58. *Res:* Optics; polymer physics; acoustics; magnetics; visibility; lighting. *Mailing Add:* 545 Chapel Lane Eagan MN 55121

HEWITT, HUDY C, JR, measurements, thermal science; deceased, see previous edition for last biography

HEWITT, JACQUELINE N, ASTRONOMY, ASTROPHYSICS. *Current Pos:* Asst prof, 89-94, ASSOC PROF PHYSICS, MASS INST TECHNOL, 94- *Educ:* Bryn Mawr Col, AB, 80; Mass Inst Technol, PhD, 86. *Honors & Awards:* Henry G Booker Prize, Int Union Radio Sci, 93; Marie Goeppart-Mayer Award, Am Phys Soc, 95. *Mem:* Am Astron Soc; corresp mem Int Union Radio Sci. *Mailing Add:* Dept Physics Mass Inst Technol Cambridge MA 02139

HEWITT, KENNETH, GEOGRAPHY, GEOMORPHOLOGY. *Current Pos:* univ prof res, 88-89, PROF, DEPT GEOG, WILFRID LAURIER UNIV, WATERLOO, 76-, COLO REGIONS RES CTR, 88-, BD MEM RES ASSOC. *Personal Data:* Mar 8, 36; m, Fanda Azhar; c 4. *Educ:* Cambridge Univ, BA, 61, MA, 63; Univ London, PhD, 67. *Prof Exp:* Lectr geog, City of London Col, 63-66, Sidney Webb Col Educ, 63-66; fel & lectr, Univ Toronto, 67-69, asst prof, 69-71, assoc prof, Dept Geog & Inst Environ Sci & Eng, 71-73; chmn & prof, Dept Human Ecol & Soc Sci, Rutgers Univ, 73-76. *Concurrent Pos:* Res fel, Emergency Measures Orgn, 67-69; assoc, Natural Hazards Res Proj, Toronto-Chicago-Clark Univ, 67-72; consult, Disaster Div, UNESCO, 72; BC Hydro Int, 91; grantee, Can Coun, 76, Soc Sci & Humanities Res Coun Can, 80, 81, 85, 87-90 & 90-91, Int Develop Res Ctr, 84, 87 & 89-90, World Meteorol Orgn Forecasting Proj, 87; adv, Pakistan Sci Found, 75; mem, Subcomt Glaciers, Nat Res Coun, 85; dir, Ctr Hazards & Develop Res, Wilfrid Laurier Univ, 85-87; prin investr, Himalaya, 85-88; consult, Disaster Mgt Comt, Commonwealth Sci Coun, 88-89; distinguished vis prof, Univ BC, 89; guest prof, Geograph Inst, Univ Koln, Ger, 92-93. *Mem:* Can Asn Geogr; Am Asn Geogrs; AAAS. *Res:* Regional ecology; geomorphology of high mountain regions, especially Kardecium Himalaya, natural hazardous and disasters. *Mailing Add:* Dept Geog Wilfrid Laurier Univ 75 University Ave W Waterloo ON N2L 3C5 Can

HEWITT, PHILIP COOPER, GEOLOGY, PALEONTOLOGY. *Current Pos:* chmn dept geol & earth sci, 67-74, coordr, Fac Sci, 68-70, PROF GEOL & EARTH SCI, STATE UNIV NY COL BROCKPORT, 67- *Personal Data:* b Boston, Mass, Sept 28, 25; div; c 4. *Educ:* Harvard Univ, AB, 49; Univ Tenn, MS, 53; Cornell Univ, PhD(paleont, stratig), 58. *Prof Exp:* Assoc prof geol, Union Col, NY, 56-67, chmn dept, 60-67. *Concurrent Pos:* NSF grant, Int Field Inst, Am Geol Inst, Paris Basin, 65. *Mem:* Geol Soc Am; Paleont Soc; Am Asn Geol Teachers (vpres, 64-65, pres, 65-66). *Res:* Foraminifera; stratigraphy and sedimentology; Taconic geology; sedimentologic and paleontologic environmental studies. *Mailing Add:* Dept Geol & Earth Sci State Univ NY Col 350 New Campus Dr Brockport NY 14420-2915

HEWITT, ROBERT LEE, THORACIC SURGERY, CARDIOVASCULAR SURGERY. *Current Pos:* Intern surg, Charity Hosp of La, 59-60, resident, 60-63, instr surg, 64-65, instr thoracic surg, 65-66, from asst prof to prof surg, 68-76, chief cardiac surg, 70-76, CLIN PROF SURG, SCH MED, TULANE UNIV, 76- *Personal Data:* b Paducah, Ky, Nov 2, 34; m 59; c 4. *Educ:* Tulane Univ, MD, 59; Am Bd Surg, cert; Am Bd Thoracic Surg, cert. *Concurrent Pos:* Fel cardiovasc surg, Sch Med, Tulane Univ, 63-64; chief resident, Charity Hosp of La, 64-66, mem vis staff, 68-; consult, Keesler AFB Hosp, 68-; mem staff, Southern Baptist Hosp, Touro Infirmary & Tulane Univ Hosp, New Orleans; bd gov, Tulane Med Ctr; bd dir, Tulane Univ Hosp. *Mem:* Am Col Surg; Int Cardiovasc Soc; Am Asn Thoracic Surg; Soc Thoracic Surg; Soc Vascular Surg. *Res:* Cardiovascular research and surgery. *Mailing Add:* Dept Surg SL22 Tulane Med Ctr 1430 Tulane Ave New Orleans LA 70112

HEWITT, ROBERT T, PSYCHIATRY. *Current Pos:* CONSULT NIMH, 75- *Personal Data:* b Roth, NDak, June 28, 09; m 37; c 3. *Educ:* Univ Minn, BM & MD, 38; Am Bd Neurol & Psychiat, dipl, 47; Johns Hopkins Univ, MPH, 48. *Prof Exp:* Intern, USPHS Hosp, Stapleton, NY, 37-38; resident psychiat, Ellis Island, NY & Lexington, Ky, 38-41, from asst clin dir to clin dir, Lexington, KY, 41-45, clin dir, Ft Worth, Tex, 45-49; dir, Phoenix Ment Health Ctr, Ariz, 49-52; asst dir clin ctr, NIH, 52-55, chief hosp consult serv, NIMH, 55-61; dir ment health prog, Western Interstate Comn Higher Educ, Univ Colo, 61-64; chief dep dir, Calif State Dept Ment Hyg, 64-73; field rep, Accreditation Coun Psychiat Facil, Joint Comn Accreditation Hosps, 73-77. *Mem:* Fel Am Psychiat Asn; AMA. *Res:* Administration of mental health programs. *Mailing Add:* 1617 Gary Way Carmichael CA 95608-5931

HEWITT, ROGER R, BIOCHEMISTRY. *Current Pos:* actg dean, 78-79, MEM GRAD FAC, UNIV TEX GRAD SCH BIOMED SCI HOUSTON, 67-, ASSOC DEAN, 79-; PROF BIOL, UNIV TEX MD ANDERSON HOSP & TUMOR INST HOUSTON, 77- *Personal Data:* b Portland, Ore, Nov 27, 37; div; c 4. *Educ:* Willamette Univ, BA, 59; Univ Rochester, MS, 60, PhD(radiation biol), 63. *Prof Exp:* USPHS res trainee radiobiol, Univ Tex M D Anderson Hosp & Tumor Inst, Houston, 63-65, Am Cancer Soc fel, 65-67, from asst prof to assoc prof, 67-77. *Concurrent Pos:* Mem, NIH Chem Path Study Sect, 78-81. *Mem:* Radiation Res Soc; Biophys Soc; Am Soc Cell Biol; Am Soc Photobiol; Am Soc Biol Chem. *Res:* Ultraviolet light effects on DNA replication; roles of dexyribonucleases in DNA metabolism; identification of chemical carcinogens. *Mailing Add:* 2415 White Oak Dr Houston TX 77009

HEWITT, SUZANNE M, PUBLIC HEALTH COMMUNICATIONS, SCIENCE ADMINISTRATION. *Current Pos:* tech pubs writer/ed, 89-91, SUPVR TECH WRITER/ED, COUN BIOL ED, CTR DIS CONTROL & PREV, 91- *Personal Data:* b Fairmont, WVa, Nov 13, 37. *Educ:* Fairmont State Col, BA, 73; Univ Ga, MPA, 92. *Prof Exp:* Supvr & social worker, WVa Dept Human Servs, Fairmont, 66-75, asst dir, Div Communs, dir policy clearinghouse & mgt eval, Charleston, 75-88. *Mailing Add:* Ctr Dis Control & Prev 1600 Clifton Rd MS-C08 Atlanta GA 30333

HEWITT, WILLIAM BORIGHT, PHYTOPATHOLOGY. *Current Pos:* RETIRED. *Personal Data:* b Fayetteville, Ark, July 17, 08; m 34. *Educ:* Univ Calif, BS, 33, MS, 34, PhD(plant path), 36. *Honors & Awards:* Ruth Allen Award, Am Phytopath Soc, 74. *Prof Exp:* Plant pathologist, Agr Exp Sta, Univ Calif, Davis, 37-68, chmn, Dept Plant Path, 68-69, from instr & jr plant pathologist to prof, 73-74, emer prof plant path, 74. *Concurrent Pos:* Pres, Int Coun Study Viruses & Virus Dis Grapevine. *Mem:* Fel Am Phytopath Soc (pres, 62); Ital Acad Vines & Wines; Ital Soc Phytopath. *Res:* Disease of grapevines; ecology and epidemiology of fungi associated with post harvest rots of grapes; viruses that infect grapevines; transmission and survival of soil-borne viruses. *Mailing Add:* 102 Turn Again Pl Sequim WA 98382

HEWLETT, ERIK L, BACTERIAL TOXINS. *Current Pos:* from asst prof to assoc prof pharmacol, 80-87, assoc prof med, 80-85, PROF MED, SCH MED, UNIV VA, 85-, PROF PHARMACOL, 87- *Personal Data:* b Memphis, Tenn, Nov 10, 46; m, Jane Wilson Berie; c John A, Christopher E & Susannah J. *Educ:* Westminster Col, BA, 68; Johns Hopkins Univ, MD, 72. *Prof Exp:* Intern med, Cornell Med Ctr, NY Hosp, 72-73, resident, 73-74; clin assoc, NIH, 74-78; asst prof med, Sch Med, Case Western Res Univ, 78-80. *Concurrent Pos:* Head, Div Clin Pharmacol, Sch Med, Univ Va, 84-, dean res, 92-; mem, Pertussis Task Force, Nat Inst Allergy & Infectious Dis, NIH, 89- *Mem:* Am Fedn Clin Res; Am Soc Trop Med & Hyg; Am Soc Clin Invest; fel Infectious Dis Soc Am; Am Soc Microbiol. *Res:* Structure and mechanism of action of bacterial toxins; adenylate cyclase toxin, a virulence factor of Bordetella pertussis. *Mailing Add:* Sch Med Univ Va Box 419 Charlottesville VA 22908. *Fax:* 804-982-0874, 982-3830; *E-Mail:* eh2u@virginia.edu

HEWLETT, JOHN DAVID, FOREST HYDROLOGY, WATER RESOURCES. *Current Pos:* RETIRED. *Personal Data:* b Philadelphia, Pa, Mar 29, 22; m 50; c 2. *Educ:* State Univ NY, Col Forestry, Syracuse Univ, BS, 49, MS, 56; Duke Univ, PhD(plant physiol), 62. *Prof Exp:* Res forester, Southeastern Forest Exp Sta, Forest Serv, USDA, 56-59, res ctr leader, Coweeta Hydrol Lab, 59-64; assoc prof, Sch Forest Resources, Univ Ga, 64-70, prof forest hydrol, 70-84. *Concurrent Pos:* Panel mem, Comt Water Resources Res, Off Sci & Technol, 65; Univ Ga del, Univs Coun Water Resources, 65-; mem work group, Rep & Exp basins, US Nat Comt, Int Hydrol Decade, Nat Acad Sci-Nat Res Coun, 69-75; consult, SAfrican countries, 70; Food & Agr Orgn specialist, USSR, 70; ollasidnal consult land-moe & water. *Mem:* AAAS; Am Geophys Union; Sigma Xi; Int Asn Sci Hydrol; Am Water Resources Asn. *Res:* Runoff and evapo-transpiration from forests, clarifying the role of plant and soil in the water cycle; originator of variable source area concept in hydrology; authority on small water shed experimentation and forest-water relations. *Mailing Add:* 360 Ashton Dr Athens GA 30606-1622

HEWLETT, MARTINEZ JOSEPH, MOLECULAR BIOLOGY, VIROLOGY. *Current Pos:* asst prof cellular & develop biol, ASSOC PROF MOLECULAR & CELLULAR BIOL & BIOCHEM, UNIV ARIZ, TUCSON, 82- *Personal Data:* b Los Angeles, Calif, Dec 6, 42; m 66; c 1. *Educ:* Univ Southern Calif, BA, 64; Univ Ariz, PhD(biochem), 73. *Prof Exp:* Res biochemist, Vet Admin Hosp, Sepulveda, Calif, 64-69; fel virol, Ctr Cancer Res, Mass Inst Technol, 73-76. *Concurrent Pos:* mem, Virol Study Sect, NIH, 80-84; fac res award, 82-86, Fogarty Sr Int fel, Am Cancer Soc, 86-87; mem, Neurol Dis Problem Proj Review B Comt, NIH. *Mem:* Am Soc Microbiol; AAAS; Am Soc Virol. *Res:* Structure and function of viral nucleic acids with emphasis on the RNA of bunyaviruses; structure of enveloped viruses. *Mailing Add:* Dept Molecular & Cellular Biol Univ Ariz 1600 E University Blvd Tucson AZ 85721-0001

HEWSON, EDGAR WENDELL, METEOROLOGY. *Current Pos:* prof physics, 68-69, chmn dept atmospheric sci, Sch Sci, 69-76, prof atmospheric sci, 76-81, EMER PROF ATMOSPHERIC SCI, ORE STATE UNIV, 81- *Personal Data:* b Amherst, NS, July 12, 10; nat US; m 35; c 2. *Educ:* Mt Allison Univ, BA, 32; Dalhousie Univ, MA, 33; Univ Toronto, MA, 35; Univ London, PhD(meteorol), 37, DIC, 37. *Honors & Awards:* Am Meteorol Soc Award, 69; Buchan Prize, Royal Meteorol Soc, 39; Am Wind Power Asn Award, 83. *Prof Exp:* Res meteorologist, Meteorol Serv Can, 38-47, asst controller training & res serv, 47-48; proj dir, Mass Inst Technol, 48-53; lectr meteorol, Univ Mich, 53-54, prof, 54-68, res physicist, Eng Res Inst, 53-54. *Concurrent Pos:* Hon spec lectr, Univ Toronto, 38-41 & 48; consult meteorologist, Consol Mining & Smelting Co Can, Ltd, 39-40, US Bur Mines, 39-40 & 45-46 & Bendix Aviation Corp, 58-59; ed, Monogr, Am Meteorol Soc, 47-57; mem comt climat, Nat Acad Sci, 57-61; trustee, Univ Corp Atmospheric Res, 59-68; ed, Environ Sci Monogr, Acad Press. *Mem:* Am Geophys Union; fel Am Meteorol Soc; fel Royal Meteorol Soc. *Res:* Atmospheric thermodynamics and radiation; meteorological aspects of atmospheric pollution; atmospheric diffusion in transitional states; mountain and valley winds; industrial and engineering meteorology; meteorological aspects of wind and solar power. *Mailing Add:* 1770 Avenida del Mundo No 1604 Coronado CA 92118-3060

HEWSTON, JOHN G, WILDLIFE CONSERVATION, FISH MANAGEMENT. *Current Pos:* asst prof wildlife, Humboldt State Univ, 66-70, assoc prof natural resources, 70-77, prof, 77-88, EMER PROF RESOURCE PLANNING & INTERPRETATION, HUMBOLDT STATE UNIV, 88- *Personal Data:* b Roy, Wash, Aug 21, 23; m 55; c 3. *Educ:* Pac Lutheran Col, BA, 50; Ore State Univ, MS, 55; Utah State Univ, PhD(fisheries), 66. *Prof Exp:* Mem, Staff Game Farm, Ore & Wash Game Depts, 48-52; res biologist, Ore Fish Comn, 52 & Wash Dept Fish, 53; dist biologist, NDak Game & Fish Dept, 53-55, div chief info & ed, 55-62; res biologist, Coop Fish Unit, Utah State Univ, 62-66. *Mem:* Wildlife Soc; Conserv Educ Asn (pres, 81-85); Western Interpreters Asn. *Res:* Artificial propagation of Northern Pike eggs; role of fishery in establishment of recreational-use patterns in a new reservoir; natural resource management, interpretation and conservation education. *Mailing Add:* 333 Fickle Hill Rd Arcata CA 95521

HEXTER, ROBERT MAURICE, SPECTROSCOPY. *Current Pos:* chmn dept, 69-75, actg dir, Ctr Microelectronic & Info Sci, 81-83, PROF CHEM, UNIV MINN, MINNEAPOLIS, 69- *Personal Data:* b Atlanta, Ga, Oct 15, 25; m 48; c 3. *Educ:* Univ Minn, AB, 48; Columbia Univ, AM, 50, PhD(chem), 52. *Prof Exp:* Asst, Univ Minn, 48 & chem, Columbia Univ, 48-50, lectr, 51-52; from instr to asst prof chem, Cornell Univ, 52-57; sr fel fundamental res, Mellon Inst, 57-69, prof chem, Carnegie-Mellon Univ, 67-69. *Concurrent Pos:* Vis prof, Fla State Univ, 60; Guggenheim fel, 61-62; Fulbright res scholar, 61-62; vis prof Israel Inst Technol, 61-62; adj prof, Carnegie Inst Technol, 65-67; consult, 3M Co, 75-77 & IBM Co, 77-; mem bd, Control Data Corp & North Star Res Inst, 81-; co-dir, NSF Regional Instrumentation Facil Surface Anal, 79- *Mem:* Am Chem Soc; Am Phys Soc. *Res:* Infrared spectroscopy at very low temperatures; theoretical and experimental studies of intermolecular forces in molecular crystals; very rapid chemical reactions by rapid scanning infrared spectroscopy; critical point analysis in molecular crystals by use of modulation spectroscopy; fluorescence and raman probes of metal surface-adsorbed molecule interactions. *Mailing Add:* 3620 Phillips Pkwy Minneapolis MN 55455

HEXTER, WILLIAM MICHAEL, BIOLOGY, GENETICS. *Current Pos:* from instr to prof, 53-77, EDWARD SHARKUESS PROF BIOL, AMHERST COL, 77- *Personal Data:* b Canton, Ohio, Aug 10, 27; m 50; c 3. *Educ:* Univ Calif, AB, 49, MA, 51, PhD(zool), 53. *Prof Exp:* Asst zool, Univ Calif, 50-53. *Concurrent Pos:* NSF sci fac fel, 63-64; lectr, 71-72; lectr, AAAS, 71-72. *Mem:* AAAS; Genetics Soc Am; Am Soc Zoologists; Sigma Xi. *Res:* Genetics of Drosophila. *Mailing Add:* Dept Biol Amherst Col Amherst MA 01002

HEXUM, TERRY DONALD, PHARMACOLOGY. *Current Pos:* from asst prof to assoc prof, 71-92, PROF PHARMACOL, UNIV NEBR MED CTR, 92- *Personal Data:* b Appleton, Wis, July 20, 41; m 66; c 3. *Educ:* Univ Wis, River Falls, BS, 63; Univ Kans, PhD(biochem), 68. *Honors & Awards:* Int Travel Award, Am Soc Pharmacol & Exp Therapeut; Golden Apple Award, Am Med Students Asn, 77 & 80. *Prof Exp:* Teaching asst biochem, Univ Kans, 63-65, res asst, 65-68; NIH fel pharmacol, Univ Wis-Madison, 68-71. *Concurrent Pos:* Pharmacologist, Ctr Ment Retardation, Univ Nebr Med Ctr, 71-74; vis scientist, Nat Inst Mental Health, 79-80; vis scientist, Univ Calif, San Diego, 89-90. *Mem:* Sigma Xi; Soc Neurosci; AAAS; Am Soc Pharmacol & Exp Therapeut; Am Soc Neurochem. *Res:* Opiate peptides in adrenal junction, hypertension; role of catechalameres in membrane function; adrenergic receptor mechanisms; autonomic pharmacology; neuropeptide. *Mailing Add:* Pharmacol Med Sch Univ Nebr 600 S 42nd St Omaha NE 68198-6260

HEY, JOHN ANTHONY, PULMONARY PHARMACOLOGY & PHYSIOLOGY, NEUROPHARMACOLOGY. *Current Pos:* sr scientist, 88-90, ASSOC PRIN SCIENTIST ALLERGY & PULMONARY PHARMACOL, SCHERING-PLOUGH RES, 90- *Personal Data:* b New York, NY, Sept 7, 59. *Educ:* Univ Okla, PhD(pharmacol), 86. *Prof Exp:* Postdoctoral fel ocular pharmacol, Dean McGee Eye Inst, 86-88. *Concurrent Pos:* Adj asst prof pharmacol, Rutgers Univ, Newark, 88- *Mem:* Am Soc Pharmacol & Exp Therapeut; Soc Neurosci; NY Acad Sci; Sigma Xi. *Res:* Studies of mechanisms of allergic disease, autonomic control of pulmonary function and its role in airway disease; Histamine-3 receptor mechanisms in vivo; models of asthma and pulmonary pharmacology; autonomic pharmacology. *Mailing Add:* Dept Allergy Schering Plough Res 2015 Galloping Hill Rd Kenilworth NJ 07033

HEY, RICHARD N, COMPUTER GRAPHICS, MARINE GEOPHYSICS. *Current Pos:* res geophysicist, 75-81, PROF GEOPHYSICS, HAWAII INST GEOPHYSICS, UNIV HAWAII, 86- *Personal Data:* b Lebanon, Tenn, June 2, 47. *Educ:* Calif Inst Technol, BS, 69; Princeton Univ, PhD(geophysics), 75. *Prof Exp:* Res assoc, Marine Sci Inst, Univ Tex, 74-75; from asst to assoc res geophysicist, Scripps Inst Oceanog, Univ Calif, San Diego, 81-86. *Concurrent Pos:* Mem, Oceanog Review Panel, NSF, 79, Crustal Geodynamics Review Panel, NASA, 80- & Int Lithosphere Proj, Working Group 6, 81-; adj lectr, Scripps Inst Oceanog, 83-90. *Mem:* Am Geophys Union; Geol Soc Am; AAAS. *Res:* Investigation of the plate tectonic history of the Earth; development of the propagating rift hypothesis; investigations of microplate tectonics. *Mailing Add:* Hawaii Inst Geophysics & Planetology Univ Hawaii 2525 Correa Rd Honolulu HI 96822. *Fax:* 808-956-3188; *E-Mail:* hey@soest.hawaii.edu

HEYBACH, JOHN PETER, ENDOCRINE PHYSIOLOGY, BEHAVIORAL PHYSIOLOGY. *Current Pos:* ASST GEN MGR, NUTRASWEET AG, ZUG, SWITZ, 89- *Personal Data:* b Chicago, Ill, Sept 25, 50; m 71; c 2. *Educ:* Northern Ill Univ, BA, 72, MA, 74, PhD(psychol), 76; Kellogg Grad Sch Bus Admin, Northwestern Univ, 88. *Prof Exp:* Nat Acad Sci/Nat Res Coun fel, Biomed Res Div, Ames Res Ctr, NASA, 76-78; res assoc, Dept Physiol & Pharmacol, Bowman Gray Med Sch, 78-79; res specialist nutrit & physiol, Cent Res Div, Gen Foods Corp, White Plains, NY, 79-85; dir sci affairs, G D Searle & Co, Nutrasweet Group, 85-87; dir, Nutrasweet Co, 87-89. *Concurrent Pos:* Partic, workshop methods assessing food & nutrient intake, Nat Acad Sci, 84. *Mem:* Endocrine Soc; Soc Neurosci; Inst Food Technologists; Am Inst Nutrit. *Res:* Neuroendocrine physiology and regulation of endocrine stress responses; central nervous system and behavioral; regulation of body weight and food intake; regulation of sensory systems; human food intake and selection; human nutrition status; body weight regulation. *Mailing Add:* The NutraSweet Co 1751 Lake Cook Rd Deerfield IL 60015

HEYBORNE, ROBERT L(INFORD), electrical engineering, engineering education; deceased, see previous edition for last biography

HEYD, ALLEN, PHARMACEUTICS. *Current Pos:* ASSOC DIR MED RES, MILES PHARMACEUT, 80- *Personal Data:* b Leola, SDak, May 27, 35; m 58; c 1. *Educ:* Columbia Univ, BS, 62, MS, 65; Purdue Univ, PhD(indust & phys pharm), Purdue 68. *Prof Exp:* Asst prof pharm, Sch Pharm, Univ Conn, 68-70; sr pharmaceut scientist, Vick Div Res & Develop, 70-72, group leader,

72-78, sect head oral hyg, 78-80. *Mem:* Am Pharmaceut Asn; Acad Pharmaceut Sci; Asn Clin Pharmacol. *Res:* Dissolution of macromolecules and their application in pharmaceutical dosage forms; study of formulation and manufacturing parameters affecting oral hygiene dosage forms. *Mailing Add:* 8 Three Seasons Ct Norwalk CT 06851

HEYD, CHARLES E, ORGANIC CHEMISTRY. *Current Pos:* MGR MKT & MKT RES, AMOCO CONTAINER CO, 78- *Personal Data:* b Detroit, Mich, Mar 3, 28; m 50; c 2. *Educ:* Univ Detroit, BS, 50, MS, 52; Mich State Univ, PhD(org chem), 56. *Prof Exp:* Res chemist, E I du Pont de Nemours & Co, Inc, 56-60; res supvr, Avisun Corp, 60-69; coordr packaging & fabricated prods depts, Res & Develop Dept, Amoco Chem Corp, 69-73, mgr com develop, Plastic Prods Div, Chicago, 73-75, sr proj mgr, Packaging Div, 75-78. *Mem:* Am Chem Soc; Soc Plastics Eng; Brit Plastics Inst. *Res:* Development of polyolefin resins for fiber and film applications; development of polyolefin stabilizer systems and formulations; industrial applications for new synthetic fibers produced by unique methods. *Mailing Add:* 520 Brook Hollow Circle Marietta GA 30067

HEYD, WILLIAM ERNST, MEDICINAL CHEMISTRY, ORGANIC CHEMISTRY. *Current Pos:* res chemist org med chem, Upjohn Co, 73-78, sr staff scientist, 78-86, contracts assoc dir, 86-89, SR ACQUISITIONS REV MGR, UPJOHN CO, 89- *Personal Data:* b Cleveland, Ohio, Oct 2, 45; m 68; c Geoffrey W & Cynthia A. *Educ:* Princeton Univ, AB, 67; Case Western Res Univ, PhD(org chem), 72. *Prof Exp:* Fel, Univ Saarland, 71-72 & Ohio State Univ, 72-73. *Mem:* Am Chem Soc; AAAS; Licensing Execs Soc. *Res:* Patent liaison specialist; interest in a wide variety of intellectual property agreements and licensing. *Mailing Add:* Pharmcia & Upjohn 9273-24-322 301 Henrietta St Kalamazoo MI 49001. *Fax:* 616-385-7207

HEYDA, DONALD WILLIAM, PHYSICS, NUCLEAR MEDICINE. *Current Pos:* Sr scientist, 74-76, MGR ENG NUCLEAR MED, NUCLEAR DIV, BAIRD CORP, 76- *Personal Data:* b Chicago, Ill, Apr 11, 46; m 72. *Educ:* Univ Ill, Urbana, BS, 68; Harvard Univ, AM, 70, PhD(physics), 76. *Mem:* Am Phys Soc; AAAS; Soc Nuclear Med. *Res:* Nuclear medicine imaging devices; computer processing in cardiology and nuclear medicine. *Mailing Add:* 378 Davis Rd Bedford MA 01730

HEYDANEK, MENARD GEORGE, JR, FOOD CHEMISTRY. *Current Pos:* mgr flavor technol, 71-84, sr mgr tech & new bus develop, 84-86, DIR, GOLDEN GRAIN RES & DEVELOP, QUAKER OATS CO, 86- *Personal Data:* b Chicago, Ill, Sept 19, 42; m 64; c 2. *Educ:* Northern Ill Univ, BS, 64; Utah State Univ, MS, 66; Northwestern Univ, PhD(chem), 68. *Prof Exp:* Res chemist, Kraftco Corp, 68-71. *Concurrent Pos:* Instr, Ill Inst Technol, 75. *Mem:* Am Chem Soc; Inst Food Technologists; Am Asn Cereal Chem. *Res:* Application of chemical instrumentation to flavor studies and correlation of flavor chemistry with organoleptic properties of foods. *Mailing Add:* 4 Jane Ct Hawthorn Woods Lake Zurich IL 60047-9292

HEYDARI, SHAHRYAR, ONLINE EDUCATION, WEB CONFERENCING IN EDUCATION. *Current Pos:* PROF MATH & DEPT CHAIR, PIEDMONT COL, 93- *Personal Data:* m 91, Mahnaz Asoudeh; c Maryam. *Educ:* Univ SC, BS, 82, MS, 84; Fla State Univ, PhD(math), 92. *Honors & Awards:* Golden Coin Award, Amirkabir Univ, 96. *Prof Exp:* Vis prof math, Fla State Univ, 92-93; asst prof math, Univ Tehran, 93-94. *Concurrent Pos:* Vis prof math, Amirkabir Univ & Shahid Beheshti Univ, 93-94. *Mem:* Am Math Soc; Math Asn Am; Iranian Math Soc. *Res:* Study of zeta regularized products and their applications in special functions theory; use of technology and internet in teaching mathematics and statistics. *Mailing Add:* 2272 Morning Dew Pl Lawrenceville GA 30244. *Fax:* 706-776-2811; *E-Mail:* shahryar.heydari@piedmont.edu

HEYDEGGER, H(ELMUT) ROLAND, PHYSICAL CHEMISTRY, ANALYTICAL CHEMISTRY. *Current Pos:* from asst prof to assoc prof, Purdue Univ, Calumet, 70-81, dept head, 79-95, actg dean, 83-84, PROF CHEM, PURDUE UNIV, CALUMET, 81- *Personal Data:* b Philadelphia, Pa, Dec 3, 35. *Educ:* Queens Col, NY, BS, 56; Univ Ark, Fayetteville, MS, 58; Univ Chicago, PhD(chem), 68. *Prof Exp:* Phys chemist, Petrol Res Ctr, US Bur Mines Okla, 58; instr chem, Prairie State Col, 61-62; from res assoc to sr res assoc, Enrico Fermi Inst, Univ Chicago, 68-88. *Concurrent Pos:* Consult, Argonne Nat Lab, 73-74; vis fel, Res Sch Earth Sci, Australian Nat Univ, 76-77, 84 & 90; vis staff mem, Los Alamos Sci Lab, Univ Calif, 78-85; Nat Res Coun sr fel, NASA Johnson Space Ctr, 85; vis scholar, Lab Astrophys Space Res, Univ Chicago, 95. *Mem:* Am Chem Soc; Am Phys Soc; Am Geophys Union; Geochem Soc; Meteoritical Soc; Int Asn Geochem. *Res:* Applications of nuclear and radiochemistry in geochemistry, cosmochemistry, physical and analytical chemistry; cosmic ray and solar particle induced nuclear reactions; activation analysis; isotopic anomalies in the early solar system. *Mailing Add:* Dept Chem Physics Purdue Univ Calumet Hammond IN 46323-2094

HEYDEMANN, PETER LUDWIG MARTIN, PHYSICS, NEUROPHYSIOLOGY. *Current Pos:* DIR, TECHNOL SERV, NAT INST STAND & TECHNOL, 93- *Personal Data:* b Gottingen, Ger, Nov 10, 28; US citizen; m 58; c 2. *Educ:* Univ Gottingen, PhD(physics), 58. *Honors & Awards:* IR-100 Award. *Prof Exp:* Asst prof physics, Univ Gottingen, 57-61, asst to dir, 61-64; physicist, Nat Bur Stand, 64-70, chief, Pressure & Vacuum Sect, 70-78, prog analyst, 78-80, dir, Ctr Chem Physics, 80-81, assoc dir, 80-86; dir, Ctr Basic Stand, Indust Technol Serv, 86-87, dep dir, 87-88; sci counr, US Embassy, New Delhi, 88-93. *Concurrent Pos:* Assoc mem, Comn Thermodyn, Int Union Pure & Appl Chem, 70-; mem, Indo-US Subcomn, Sci & Technol, 75- *Mem:* Am Soc Mech Engrs; Am Phys Soc; Sigma Xi. *Res:* Physics of polymer, mechanical and dielectric properties; high pressure technology, ultrasonics, pressure and vacuum measurements, solid and liquid states at very high pressures; manometry; neurology of the auditory system; chemistry; science administration; program analysis; budget preparation; chemical physics; interferometry. *Mailing Add:* Technol Serv Nat Inst Stand & Technol Gaithersburg MD 20899. *Fax:* 301-975-2183; *E-Mail:* peter.heydemann@nist.gov

HEYDENBURG, N P, NUCLEAR PHYSICS. *Current Pos:* RETIRED. *Personal Data:* b Big Rapid, Mich, June 8, 08. *Educ:* Univ Olivet, Mich, BS; State Univ Iowa, MS, PhD(physics). *Prof Exp:* Res scientist, Carnegie Inst, Washington, 34-61; fac, Dept Physics, Fla State Univ, 61-74. *Mem:* Fel Am Phys Soc. *Mailing Add:* 4140 Covenant Lane Tallahassee FL 32308

HEYDING, ROBERT DONALD, SOLID STATE CHEMISTRY. *Current Pos:* prof inorg chem, 62-, head dept, 76-, EMER PROF, QUEEN'S UNIV, ONT. *Personal Data:* b Regina, Sask, July 25, 25; m 47; c 3. *Educ:* Univ Sask, BE, 47, MSc, 49; McGill Univ, PhD(chem), 51. *Prof Exp:* Nat Res Coun Can fel, 51-53 & State Univ Leiden, 53-54; res officer inorg chem, Div Appl chem, Nat Res Coun Can, 54-61. *Mem:* Chem Inst Can. *Res:* Solid state inorganic chemistry; properties of compounds formed by transition metals and the elements of groups VA and VIA. *Mailing Add:* Dept Chem Queen's Univ Kingston ON K7L 3N6 Can

HEYDRICK, FRED PAINTER, MICROBIOLOGY, SCIENCE ADMINISTRATION. *Current Pos:* PRES, BIO REV INC, 89- *Personal Data:* b Clearfield, Pa, Jan 30, 34; m 78, Margaret Eaton; c Stanley, Sharon, David, Douglas & Max. *Educ:* Juniata Col, BS, 55; Univ NH, MS, 61; Pa State Univ, PhD(microbiol), 67. *Prof Exp:* Microbiologist, US Army Biol Labs, Ft Detrick, 61-71; health sci adminr, Nat Heart, Lung & Blood Inst, 71-89. *Mem:* Sigma Xi. *Res:* Isolation and characterization of viruses; lipids of host cells and virus progeny; management of research grant and contract review groups; management of evaluation and advisory panels in biotechnology and biomedical research. *Mailing Add:* 6813 Sunnybrook Dr Frederick MD 21702

HEYDT, GERALD THOMAS, ELECTRICAL ENGINEERING. *Current Pos:* DIR, CTR ADVAN CONTROL ENERGY & POWER SYSTS, ARIZ STATE UNIV, 93- *Personal Data:* b New York, NY, Oct 1, 43. *Educ:* Cooper Union, BS, 65; Purdue Univ, MS, 67, PhD(elec eng), 70. *Honors & Awards:* Power Eng Educr Yr, Inst Elec & Electronics Engrs, 94. *Prof Exp:* Elec engr, US AEC, 65-66 & EG&G Inc, 66-67; assoc prof elec eng, Purdue Univ, 65-94. *Concurrent Pos:* Inst, Am Elec Power Co, 70-72 & Politecnica Nacional, Quitto, 77; NSF grant, 73-75; consult, Peabody Coal co, 74-76, Westmoreland Coal Co, 74-76, US Army, 74-78; US Dept Energy grant, 76-80. *Mem:* Nat Acad Eng; Sigma Xi. *Res:* Electric power engineering; reliability of power systems. *Mailing Add:* Ariz State Univ PO Box 875706 Tempe AZ 85287. *Fax:* 602-965-0745; *E-Mail:* heydt@enuxsa.eas.asu.edu

HEYERDAHL, EUGENE GERHARDT, FISHERIES BIOLOGY, DATA MANAGEMENT. *Current Pos:* fishery biologist, 71-76, NE REGIONAL DATA BASE ADMINR, NAT MARINE FISHERIES SERV, NAT OCEANIC & ATMOSPHERIC ADMIN, US DEPT COM, 77- *Personal Data:* b Williston, NDak, Feb 11, 40; m 60; c 3. *Educ:* Luther Col, Iowa, BA, 62; Univ Minn, St Paul, PhD(fisheries biol), 68. *Prof Exp:* Res assoc fisheries, Univ Minn, St Paul, 68-71. *Mem:* Sigma Xi; Am Inst Fish Res Biol. *Res:* Regional data management coordination, including technical supervision of computer systems development and implementation, and equipment procurement and installation. *Mailing Add:* 86 Vidal Ave East Falmouth MA 02536

HEYERDAHL, THOR, ANTHROPOLOGY. *Current Pos:* ORGANIZER, MUSEO BRUNING ARCHEOL PROJ, TUCUME, 88-, TENERIFE, 90- *Personal Data:* b Larvik, Norway, Oct 6, 14; m 36, 49, Yvonne Dedekam-Simonsen; c Thor, Bjorn, Anette, Mariarf & Bettina. *Educ:* Larvik Col, Realartium, 33. *Hon Degrees:* PhD, Oslo Univ, 61. *Honors & Awards:* Retzius Medal, Royal Swed Anthrop & Geog Soc, 50, Vega Gold Medal, 62; Mungo Park Medal, Royal Scottish Geog Soc, 51; Patron's Gold Medal, Royal Geog Soc, 64; co-recipient, Int Pahlavi Environ Prize, UN, 78. *Prof Exp:* Researcher, Ethnol Collection & Primitive Man, Polynesia & BC, 37-40, Andes Region, 54; leader & organizer, Exped, Kon-Tiki, 47, Galapogos Islands, 52, Easter Island & East Pacific, 55-56, Ra, 69-70, Tigris, 77-78, Maldives Islands, 82-84 & Easter Island, 86-88; doc film producer, Kon-Tiki, 51 & Galapogos, 55. *Concurrent Pos:* Founder & bd mem, Kon-Tiki Museum, Oslo; trustee, World Wildlife Fund Int. *Mem:* Fel NY Acad Sci; Belg Anthrop & Geog Soc; hon mem Norweg Geog Soc; World Asn World Federalists; Worldview Int; Brazilian Anthrop & Geog Soc; Peruvian Anthrop & Geog Soc; Russian Anthrop & Geog Soc; hon mem Swed Anthrop & Geog Soc; Norweg Acad Sci. *Res:* Author of many books on expeditions. *Mailing Add:* Colla Micheri Laigueglia 17020 Italy

HEYING, THEODORE LOUIS, ORGANIC CHEMISTRY, RESEARCH ADMINISTRATION. *Current Pos:* VPRES, GEM BIOMED, INC, 90- *Personal Data:* b Baltimore, MD, Oct 19, 27; m 52, Patricia Worthington; c Theodore Jr & Maria T (Evans). *Educ:* Loyola Col, Md, BS, 48; Col of the Holy Cross, MS, 49; Univ Md, PhD(chem), 54. *Prof Exp:* Res chemist, Olin Corp, 53-58, sr res chemist, 58-59, chem proj leader, 59-60; chief synthesis sect, United Tech Corp, 60-63; proj mgr, Olin Corp, 60-63, sect mgr, 63-64, tech dir, 65- 70, mgr spec prod, 70-72, tech dir, 72-74, dir res, 74-82, dir int technol, 82-86; consult, 87-90. *Mem:* Am Chem Soc; Sigma Xi; Inst Food Technologists. *Res:* Inorganic, organometallic and polymer chemistry. *Mailing Add:* 60 Clintonville Rd Northford CT 06472. *Fax:* 203-484-7319

HEYL, ALLEN VAN, JR, GEOLOGY, GEOPHYSICS. *Current Pos:* GEOL CONSULT, 90- *Personal Data:* b Allentown, Pa, Apr 4, 18; m 48, Maxine Hawke; c Nancy (Swaintek) & Allen D. *Educ:* Pa State Univ, BS, 41; Princeton Univ, PhD(geol), 50. *Honors & Awards:* Interior Dept Meritorious Award; Thayer-Lindley Distinguished Lectr, Soc Econ Geologists, 85-86. *Prof Exp:* Field geologist, Nfld Geol Surv, Field Seasons, 37-40, proj chief, 42; asst mineral, Princeton Univ, 42-43; geologist, Md, Wis, DC, US Geol Surv, Denver, 68-90. *Concurrent Pos:* Chmn, Int Asn Genesis Ore Deposits; silver, lead, zinc resource specialist, US Geol Surv; chmn, Soc of Econ Geologists, Int Exchange Lectr Comt; ivited lectr, Grad Col, Beijing Univ Geol Sci; consult geol; invited lead lectr, Int Asn Genesis Ore Deposits, Beijing, China, 94. *Mem:* Fel Mineral Soc Am; fel Geol Soc Am; fel Soc Econ Geologists; fel Brit Inst Mining & Metall. *Res:* Geochemistry and geology of Mississippi Valley mineral deposits; geology of eastern states mineral deposits; oxidized sulfide deposits and lead, zinc, silver resources of United States; geology and ore deposits of Southern NMex and West; basement structure and earthquake geology of USA. *Mailing Add:* PO Box 1052 Evergreen CO 80437-1052

HEYL, GEORGE RICHARD, geology, economic geology & geophysics; deceased, see previous edition for last biography

HEYMAN, ALBERT, INTERNAL MEDICINE, NEUROLOGY. *Current Pos:* from assoc prof to prof med, 53-77, PROF NEUROL, SCH MED, DUKE UNIV, 77- *Personal Data:* b Baltimore, Md, May 30, 16; m 42; c 2. *Educ:* Univ Md, BS, 36, MD, 40; Am Bd Internal Med, dipl; Am Bd Psychiat & Neurol, dipl, 61. *Prof Exp:* Intern, Baltimore City Hosps, 40-41; med intern, Grady Mem Hosp, Emory Univ, 41-42, asst resident med, 42-43, from asst to asst prof med, Sch Med, 43-53. *Concurrent Pos:* Fel, WHO, 51; travel award, NSF, 57; pub health physician, State Dept Pub Health, Ga, 43-53; chief neurol sect, Vet Admin Hosp, Durham, NC, 54-69; mem subcomt venereal dis, Nat Res Coun, 50-53; mem comt cerebral vascular dis, USPHS, 55. *Mem:* Am Soc Clin Invest; Am Fedn Clin Res. *Res:* Cerebrovascular disease; cerebral circulation. *Mailing Add:* Duke Univ Med Ctr Box 3203 Durham NC 27710

HEYMAN, DUANE ALLAN, ORGANIC CHEMISTRY, POLYMER CHEMISTRY. *Current Pos:* SR CHEMIST POLYMER CHEM, BASF WYANDOTTE CORP, 78- *Personal Data:* b Toledo, Ohio, June 11, 41; m 68; c 1. *Educ:* Case Inst Technol, BS, 63; Univ Calif, Berkeley, PhD(org chem), 68. *Prof Exp:* Asst prof chem, Whitman Col, 68-69; chemist org chem, Owens-Ill, Toledo, 69-74; sr chemist, Sherwin-Williams Chem, 74-78. *Concurrent Pos:* Chemist org chem, Battelle-Northwest, 69. *Mem:* Am Chem Soc; Am Inst Chem; Sigma Xi. *Res:* Synthetic aspects of urethane chemicals, block and graft copolymers, aromatic nitrogen heterocycles, silicon-carbon multiple bonded systems and organothallium chemistry. *Mailing Add:* BASF Wyandotte Corp 1419 Biddle Ave Wyandotte MI 48192

HEYMAN, JOSEPH SAUL, ULTRASONICS, PHYSICS. *Current Pos:* res leader ultrasonics, Lab Ultrasonics, NASA-Langley Res Ctr, 71-81, head, Mats Characterization Instrumentation Group, Instrument Res Div, 81-87, head, Nondestructive Eval Sci Br, 87-93, mgr, nondestructive eval res prog, dep dir Technol Applns Group, 93-95, DIR TECHNOL APPLNS GROUP, NASA-LANGLEY RES CTR, 96- *Personal Data:* b New Bedford, Mass, Nov 4, 43; m 68, Berna Levine; c Laura Dawn. *Educ:* Northeastern Univ, BA, 68; Wash Univ, MA, 71, PhD(physics), 75. *Honors & Awards:* Arthur S Fleming Award, 81, IR-100 Award, 74, 76, 78 & 81. *Prof Exp:* Coop student physics, NASA Langley Res Ctr, 64-68, aerospace technologist, 68-69; teaching asst, Wash Univ, 69-70, res asst, 70-71. *Concurrent Pos:* Adj prof physics, Col William & Mary, Williamsburg, Va, 79-; Comnr Hampton Rds Sanit Dist (vchmn, 89-). *Mem:* Am Phys Soc; Inst Elec & Electronics Engrs; Sigma Xi. *Res:* Physics of ultrasonic propagation in materials and application to the development of a better understanding and measurement of materials; author and coauthor of over 120 publications; granted over 24 patents. *Mailing Add:* 130 Indian Springs Rd Williamsburg VA 23185. *Fax:* 757-864-8088; *E-Mail:* j.s.heyman@larc.nasa.gov

HEYMAN, KARL, ORGANIC CHEMISTRY. *Current Pos:* pres, 51-68, CHMN BD, MONA INDUST, INC, 68- *Personal Data:* b Elberfeld, Ger, July 30, 04; nat US; m 41. *Educ:* Univ Freiburg, BA, 25; Univ Munich, MA, 27, PhD, 29. *Prof Exp:* Asst, Rockefeller Inst Med Res, 29-30; asst patent law, Eng, 31; res chemist dyestuffs, I G Farbenindust, Ger, 33-36; res chemist rubber thread, Filatex Corp, NJ & Va, 37-38; group leader vinyon synthetic fibers, Am Viscose Corp, Pa, 39-43; chief chemist textile chem specialties, Kearny Mfg Co, NJ, 43-51. *Mem:* AAAS; Am Chem Soc; Am Asn Textile Chemists & Colorists; Am Inst Chemists. *Res:* Surface active agents; dyestuffs; synthetic fibers; rubber and elastomers; corrosion inhibitors. *Mailing Add:* MONA Indust Inc 76 E 24th St Paterson NJ 07524

HEYMAN, LAUREL ELAINE, INORGANIC CHEMISTRY, TECHNICAL MATHEMATICS. *Current Pos:* assoc prof, 72-80, PROF CHEM, OWENS TECH COL, 80- *Personal Data:* b West Elizabeth, Pa, Jan 2, 41; m 68; c 1. *Educ:* Mt Union Col, BS, 62; Case Inst Technol, PhD(inorg chem), 66. *Prof Exp:* Asst prof chem, Eastern Wash State Col, 66-69; vis lectr, Bowling Green State Univ, 70; vis prof, Defiance Col, 70-72. *Mem:* Am Chem Soc. *Res:* Coordination compounds; synthesis and physical properties, particularly Schiff base complexes of multidentate ligands and their characterization by spectroscopic methods. *Mailing Add:* 1902 S Raisinville Rd Monroe MI 48161-9704

HEYMAN, LOUIS, petroleum geology; deceased, see previous edition for last biography

HEYMAN, MELVIN BERNARD, PEDIATRIC GASTROENTEROLOGY. *Current Pos:* asst prof, 81-88, assoc prof, 88-94, CHIEF PEDIAT GASTROENTEROL & NUTRIT, UNIV CALIF, SAN FRANCISCO, 90-, PROF, PEDIAT, 94- *Personal Data:* b San Francisco, Calif, Mar 24, 50; m 88, Jody E Switky. *Educ:* Univ Calif, Berkeley, BA, 72; Univ Calif, Los Angeles, MD, 76, MPH, 81; Am Bd Pediat, dipl. *Prof Exp:* From intern to resident, Los Angeles Co-Univ Southern Calif Med Ctr, 76-79; fel, Univ Calif, Los Angeles, 79-81. *Concurrent Pos:* Mem consult staff, San Francisco Gen Hosp, Oakland Childrens Hosp, Sonoma Co Med Ctr, Natividad Med Ctr & Scenic Gen Hosp; grantee, Childrens Liver Found, 84-85; John Tung grantee, Am Cancer Soc, 85-89; sabbatical leave, Human Nutrit Res Ctr on Aging, Tufts Univ, Boston, Dept Nutrit, Mass Inst Technol, Cambridge, 89. *Mem:* Am Gastroenterol Asn; Am Soc Gastrointestinal Endoscopy; Am Inst Nutrit; Am Soc Parenteral & Enteral Nutrit; Cancer Cytol Found Am; NAM Soc Pediat Gastroenterol & Nutrit. *Res:* Pediatric gastroenterology and nutrition. *Mailing Add:* Dept Pediat 500 Parnassus Mu 4 E Univ Calif PO Box 0136 San Francisco CA 94143-0136. *Fax:* 415-476-1343; *E-Mail:* mheyman@peds.ucsf.edu

HEYMANN, DIETER, ASTRONOMY, GEOLOGY. *Current Pos:* assoc prof, 66-77, PROF GEOL & SPACE SCI, RICE UNIV, 77- *Personal Data:* b Mannheim, Ger, Aug 4, 27; m 58; c 3. *Educ:* Univ Amsterdam, PhD(chem), 58. *Prof Exp:* Jr scientist, Found Fundamental Res Matter Lab, Neth, 54-59, sr scientist, 61-63; res assoc chem, Brookhaven Nat Lab, 59-61; res asst meteorites, Enrico Fermi Inst Nuclear Studies, Univ Chicago, 63-66. *Res:* Isotope separation; thermal diffusion; meteorites and planets, particularly mass spectrometry; lunar samples. *Mailing Add:* 3009 Lafayette St Houston TX 77005

HEYMANN, HILDEGARDE, SENSORY SCIENCE, FLAVOR CHEMISTRY. *Current Pos:* ASSOC PROF SENSORY SCI, UNIV MO, 86- *Personal Data:* b Pretoria, Transvaal, SAfrica, Apr 14, 56. *Educ:* Univ Stellenbosch, SAfrica, BSc, 77; Univ Calif, Davis, MS, 80, PhD(agr & environ chem), 86. *Prof Exp:* Researcher, Rupert Int, SAfrica, 78-79; res scientist, Stellenbosch Farmers Winery, SAfrica, 80-81. *Mem:* Inst Food Technologists; Am Soc Testing & Mat. *Res:* Sensory methodology involving food and non-food products; wine sensory evaluation; flavor chemistry. *Mailing Add:* 122 Eckles Hall Univ Mo Food Sci Columbia MO 65211-0001. *Fax:* 573-882-0596; *E-Mail:* hheymann@showme.missouri.edu

HEYMANN, MICHAEL ALEXANDER, PEDIATRICS, CARDIOLOGY. *Current Pos:* asst clin prof, 67-69, asst prof in residence, 69-73, assoc prof in residence pediat, 73-74, assoc prof 74-78, PROF PEDIAT & OBSTET, GYNEC & REPRODUCTIVE SCI, UNIV CALIF, SAN FRANCISCO, 78- *Personal Data:* b Johannesburg, SAfrica, Feb 24, 37; m 63; c 1. *Educ:* Univ Witwatersrand, Johannesburg, MB & BCh, 59. *Honors & Awards:* Young Investr Award, Am Acad Pediat, 68; Res Career Develop Award, Nat Inst Child Health & Human Develop, 69. *Prof Exp:* House surgeon & physician, Johannesburg Gen Hosp, 60; sr house physician pediat, Transvaal Mem Hosp Children, 61; resident & chief resident pediat, Albert Einstein Col Med, 62-64. *Concurrent Pos:* Res fel, Albert Einstein Col Med, 64-66; res fel, Cardiovasc Res Inst, Univ Calif, San Francisco, 66-67, assoc staff mem, 69-76, sr staff mem, 76-; mem exam comt, Am Bd Neonatal-perinatal Med, 76- *Mem:* Am Acad Pediat; Am Heart Asn; Am Pediat Soc; Soc Gynec Invest; Soc Pediat Res. *Res:* Fetal and perinatal cardio-pulmonary physiology. *Mailing Add:* Pediat Univ Calif Med Sch 513 Parnassus Ave San Francisco CA 94122-2722

HEYMSFIELD, ANDREW JOEL, ATMOSPHERIC SCIENCES, METEOROLOGY. *Current Pos:* SCIENTIST CLOUD PHYSICS, NAT CTR ATMOSPHERIC RES, 75- *Personal Data:* b Brooklyn, NY, June 12, 47; m 75. *Educ:* State Univ NY, Fredonia, BA, 69; Univ Chicago, MA, 70, PhD(meteorol), 73. *Prof Exp:* Scientist cloud physics, Meteorol Res Inc, 73-75. *Concurrent Pos:* Adv Comt Field Observ Facil, Nat Ctr Atmospheric Sci, 78-81; pres, Cloud Physics Comt, Am Meteorol Soc, 86-88; mem, Int Cloud Physics Comt, 89. *Mem:* Am Meteorol Soc. *Res:* Area of cloud physics, specifically cirrus clouds, climate and hail research; precipitation initiation processes; cloud dynamics. *Mailing Add:* 2895 Vassar Dr Boulder CO 80303

HEYMSFIELD, GERALD M, RADAR METEOROLOGY, MESOMETEOROLOGY. *Current Pos:* METEOROLOGIST, GODDARD SPACE FLIGHT CTR, NASA, 79- *Personal Data:* b Queens, NY, Nov 15, 49; m 82; c 2. *Educ:* State Univ NY, Fredonia, BA, 71; Univ Chicago, MA, 72; Univ Okla, PhD(meteorol), 76. *Prof Exp:* Res assoc radar meteorol, Univ Chicago, 76- *Mem:* Am Meteorol Soc. *Res:* Severe storm dynamics, winter cyclonic storm wind and precipitation structure; satellite and radar meteorology; development of weather radars for the NASA high-altitude aircraft. *Mailing Add:* NASA Goddard Space Flight Ctr Code 912 Greenbelt MD 20771. *Fax:* 301-286-1762; *E-Mail:* heymsfie@carmen.gsfc.nasa.gov

HEYMSFIELD, STEVEN B, INTERNAL MEDICINE. *Current Pos:* ASSOC PROF MED, EMORY UNIV HOSP, 79-, ASSOC PROF MED, COLUMBIA UNIV COL PHYSICIANS & SURGEONS, NY 86- *Personal Data:* b New York, July 15, 44; m 85, Beverly Goss; c Chelsey & Jill. *Educ:* Mt Sinai Sch Med, MD, 71. *Concurrent Pos:* Dep dir, NY Obesity Res Ctr. *Mem:* Am Fedn Clin Res; Am Soc Clin Nutrit; Am Heart Asn; Am Soc Parenteral & Enteral Nutrit. *Res:* Obesity; nutrition support; body composition. *Mailing Add:* St Luke's Roosevelt Hosp Columbia Univ Sch Med 411 W 114th St New York NY 10025

HEYN, ARNO HARRY ALBERT, ANALYTICAL CHEMISTRY. *Current Pos:* from instr to prof, 47-84, EMER PROF CHEM, BOSTON UNIV, 84- *Personal Data:* b Breslau, Ger, Oct 6, 18; US citizen; m 42, Helen Pielemeier; c Evan, Margaret & Robert. *Educ:* Univ Mich, BS, 40, MS, 41, PhD(analytical chem), 44. *Honors & Awards:* Henry A Hill Award, Northeastern Sect, Am Chem Soc, 86. *Prof Exp:* Exp chemist, Sun Oil Co, Pa, 44-47. *Concurrent Pos:* Sci adv, US Food & Drug Admin, Boston Dist, 67-72; vis scientist, Kernforschungszentrum Karlsruhe, 73, 80-82; chmn, Const & Bylaws Comt, Am Chem Soc, 83-85 & Coun Policy Comt, 86-91; ed, Nucleus, Am Chem Soc, 89- *Mem:* Fel AAAS; Am Chem Soc; Am Asn Univ Prof. *Res:* Physical methods of analysis; photochemical methods in analysis; environmental analysis. *Mailing Add:* 21 Alexander Rd Newton MA 02161. *Fax:* 617-527-2032

HEYNE, ELMER GEORGE, AGRONOMY. *Current Pos:* agron agt, Div Cereal Crops & Dis, Exp Sta, Kansas State Univ, 36-38, from jr agronomist to agronomist, 38-56, prof agron, 47-82, prof plant breeding, 57-82, EMER PROF, KANS STATE UNIV, 82- *Personal Data:* b Wisner, Nebr, Apr 4, 12; m 38; c 4. *Educ:* Univ Nebr, BSc, 35; Kans State Col, MSc, 38; Univ Minn, PhD, 52. *Honors & Awards:* Dekalb-Pfizer Crop Sci Distinguished Career Award, Crop Sci Soc Am; Agron Achievement Award, Am Soc Agron. *Prof Exp:* Jr agronomist, Soil Conserv Serv, USDA, Tex, 35-36. *Mem:* Fel AAAS; fel Am Soc Agron; Genetics Soc Am; Am Phytopath Soc; Am Genetic Asn; fel Crop Sci Soc Am. *Res:* Plant breeding and genetics of wheat, oats and barley; disease and insect resistance; quality and yield. *Mailing Add:* 918 Ratone St Manhattan KS 66502

HEYNEMAN, DONALD, PARASITOLOGY, EDUCATION ADMINISTRATION. *Current Pos:* assoc res parasitologist & assoc prof parasitol, Univ Calif, San Francisco, 62-68, res parasitologist, Hooper Found, 68-77, asst dir, 70-77, actg chmn, Dept Epidemiol & Int Health, 75-78, PROF PARASITOL, MED CTR, UNIV CALIF, SAN FRANCISCO, 68- *Personal Data:* b San Francisco, Calif, Feb 18, 25; m 71; c 5. *Educ:* Harvard Univ, AB, 50; Rice Inst, MA, 52, PhD, 54. *Prof Exp:* Asst biol, Rice Inst, 52-54; from instr to asst prof zool, Univ Calif, Los Angeles, 54-59; head dept parasitol, US Naval Med Res Unit, Cairo, 60-62. *Concurrent Pos:* Resident coordr, Int Ctr Med Res & Training, Inst Med Res, Kuala Lumpur, Malaysia, 64-66; assoc prof, Med Ctr, Univ Calif, San Francisco, 65-68; consult-rapporteur, WHO Traveling Sem Leishmaniasis USSR, 67, consult, US Navy Med Res Unit 3, Cairo, Egypt, 67-88; mem, Adv Sci Bd, Gorgas Mem Inst, 67-91; vis prof parasitol, Univ Toronto, 71; vis biologist, Am Inst Biol Sci, 71-74; mem, Trop Med & Parasitol Study Sect, Nat Inst Allergy & Infectious Dis, NIH, 73-76; external examr trop med & parasitol, State La Bd Regents, La State Univ, 78; mem, UN Develop Prog/WHO Joint Schistosomiasis Control Proj Rev Mission, Ghana, 78; mem, Addis Ababa Univ,Univ Calif, San Francisco, Trop Dis Surv, Southwest Ethiopia, 81; consult, WHO, UN Develop Prog & Agency Int Develop; external examr, Sch Biol Sci, Univ Nebr, Lincoln, 86; chair, Joint Med Prog, dir, Health & Med Sci & assoc dean, Sch Pub Health, Univ Calif, Berkeley, 87-91. *Mem:* Sigma Xi; Am Soc Parasitol (pres, 82-83); Soc Protozool; Am Micros Soc; Am Soc Trop Med & Hyg. *Res:* Parasite immunology and host-parasite studies; epidemiology; evolution and systematics of helminths; biological control of trematode infections in snail hosts; disease impact of development in Third World. *Mailing Add:* Intl Health Univ Calif Med Sch 513 Parnassus Ave San Francisco CA 94122-2722

HEYNER, SUSAN, CELLULAR PROLIFERATION & DEVELOPMENT. *Current Pos:* PROF, UNIV PA, 90-, DIR IN VITRO FERTIL & ANDROLOGY LAB, MED CTR, 90- *Personal Data:* b Hemel Hempstead, UK, Jan 21, 36; m 63; c 2. *Educ:* Univ Southampton, BSc, 57; Univ London, PhD(physiol), 60. *Honors & Awards:* Res Career Develop Award, NIH, 78. *Prof Exp:* Res fel, Royal Col Surgeons Eng, 61-63; res assoc, Univ Pa, 64-69; from asst prof to prof, Philadelphia Col Pharm & Sci, 69-85; prof, Sch Med, Temple Univ, 85-90. *Concurrent Pos:* Mem, HED Study Sect, 75-79, REB Study Sect, NIH, 81-85; assoc ed, Contraception, 82-; bd mem, Soc Develop Biol, 83-85; assoc ed, Molecular Reprod & Develop, 91- *Mem:* Am Soc Cell Biol; AAAS; Soc Develop Biol; Soc Study Reproduction. *Res:* Underlying early mammalian development; intrinsic and extrinsic factors that govern cellular proliferation and development. *Mailing Add:* Dept Obstet & Gynec 311A Univ Pa Med Ctr 36th Hamilton Walk Philadelphia PA 19104-6080

HEYNICK, LOUIS NORMAN, PHYSICS, MATHEMATICS. *Current Pos:* RETIRED. *Personal Data:* b Brooklyn, NY, Mar 17, 19; m 41, Yetta Milstein; c Carla (Garrett) & Mitchell. *Educ:* Brooklyn Col, BS, 40; Columbia Univ, MA, 48. *Prof Exp:* Asst chief electron physics sect, US Naval Appl Sci Lab, 47-56; chief mat & processing, US Army Electronics Command, 56-59, res team leader, 59-63; mgr phys electronics, SRI Int, 63-73, staff scientist, 73-84. *Concurrent Pos:* Assoc ed, Trans Electron Devices, Inst Elec & Electronics Engrs, 69-77, comt man & radiation, 78-; consult, 85-; consult, Inst Elec & Electronics Engrs, stand coord comt 28, 85- *Mem:* Am Phys Soc; Sigma Xi; Inst Elec & Electronics Engrs; Int Microwave Power Inst; Bioelectromagnetics Soc. *Res:* Electron device research and development; imaging and display devices; biological effects of radiation; electron optics and lithography; microwave devices; sensors and instrumentation. *Mailing Add:* 833 Richardson Ct Palo Alto CA 94303

HEYS, JOHN RICHARD, ORGANIC RADIOCHEMICAL SYNTHESIS, RADIOCHEMISTRY. *Current Pos:* sr investr, 83-87, asst dir, 87-91, ASSOC DIR, SYNTHETIC CHEM DEPT, SMITH KLINE & FRENCH LABS, 91- *Personal Data:* b Dayton, Ohio, Oct 15, 47; m 75, Anna E Bury; c Stuart L. *Educ:* DePauw Univ, BA, 69; Stanford Univ, PhD(org chem), 76. *Prof Exp:* Assoc org chem, Dept Chem, Yale Univ, 76; assoc chemist, Midwest Res Inst, Kansas City, 77-78, sr radiochemist & prog mgr, org & radiosynthesis, 78-83. *Mem:* Am Chem Soc; AAAS; Int Union Pure & Appl Chem; Int Isotope Soc. *Res:* Organic synthesis of isotopically labeled compounds; development of synthetic methods for isotopically labeled compounds of medicinal and biological interest; catalysis of hydrogen isotope exchange; peptide labeling methods. *Mailing Add:* Smith Kline Beecham Pharmaceut 709 Swedeland Rd PO Box 1539 Mail Stop UW2830 King of Prussia PA 19406. *E-Mail:* j_richard_heys@sbphrd.com

HEYSE, STEPHEN P, PREVENTIVE MEDICINE, PUBLIC HEALTH ADMINISTRATION. *Current Pos:* spec asst dis prev & tech assessment, Nat Inst Diabetes, Digestive & Kidney Dis, 82-87, sci officer, Diabetes Control & Complications Trial, 83-87, DIR, OFF DIS PREV, EPIDEMIOL & CLIN APPLN, NAT INST ARTHRITIS, MUSCULOSKELETAL & SKIN DIS, NIH, 87- *Personal Data:* b New York, NY, May 1, 48; m, Christine Aufricht; c Eric, Jennifer & Michael. *Educ:* Univ NC, BA, 70; State Univ NY Upstate Med Ctr, MD, 74; Johns Hopkins Univ, MPH, 78. *Prof Exp:* Health sci analyst, Nat Ctr Health Care Technol, Off Asst Secy Health, 80-82. *Mem:* Am Col Rheumatology. *Res:* Epidemiologic studies and clinical trials in arthritis and musculoskeletal and skin diseases; antibiotic treatment of rheumatoid arthritis; osteoporosis and related fractures. *Mailing Add:* 307 Warrenton Dr Silver Spring MD 20904. *Fax:* 301-480-6069

HEYSSEL, ROBERT M, HEMATOLOGY, NUCLEAR MEDICINE. *Current Pos:* pres, 86-92, EMER PRES, JOHNS HOPKINS HEALTH SYST, 92- *Personal Data:* b Jamestown, Mo, June 19, 28; m 55, Maria McDaniel; c Jim, Lisa, Bob, Kurt & Rerri. *Educ:* Univ Mo, BS, 51; St Louis Univ, MD, 53. *Hon Degrees:* DSc, St Louis Univ, 85; LHD, Johns Hopkins Univ, 92. *Prof Exp:* Intern, St Louis Univ, 53-54; asst resident, Vet Admin Hosp, St Louis, 54-55, Barnes Hosp, 55-56; sr asst, Surgeon Sta, Atomic Bomb Casualty Comm, USPHS, 56-58; fel hemat, Sch Med Washington Univ, 58-59; from instr to assoc prof med, Vanderbilt Univ, 59-68; from assoc prof to prof med, Sch Med Johns Hopkins Univ, 68-92. *Concurrent Pos:* Consult radiation, Tenn Dept Pub Health, 54; asst dir, Radioisotope Ctr, Vanderbilt Univ Hosp, 59-61, dir, 62-68; dir, Div Nuclear Med & Biophys, Dept Med, Vanderbilt Sch Med, 62-68; mem, Expert Panel, Int Atomic Energy Agency, Vienna, 65; res consult, Oak Ridge Assoc Univ, 67, chmn, Med Prog Rev Comt, 70-71; assoc dean, Johns Hopkins Univ, Sch Med & physician & dir, Outpatient Serv & Off Health Care Prog, Johns Hopkins Hosp, 68-72; chmn, Health Serv Adv Comt, Asn Am Med Col, 71-74, Comt Emergency Med Serv, NAS, 73-76 & controlling supply short term gen hosp beds study, 75-76, Asn Am Med Col, 83-84, Commonwealth Fund Task Force Acad Health Ctr, 83-; mem, Liaison Comt Grad Med Educ, 74-77, Gen Assembly, Asn Am Med Col, 74-80, adv comt, Subcomt Health Ways & Means, US House Rep, 74-78, Coun Teaching Hosp Admin Bd, Asn Am Med Col, 75-79; pres, Johns Hopkins Hosp, 83-86 & 88-92, trustee, 83-92; bd dir, Fair Lanes Inc, 84-87, Greater Baltimore Comt, 86-89, Signet Bank, 86-, Monsato, 88-; bd trustees, St Louis Univ, 89-91. *Mem:* Nat Acad Sci; Inst Med-Nat Acad Sci; AAAS; Am Soc Hemat; Am Fedn Clin Res; fel Am Col Physicians; Asn Am Physicians; Sigma Xi; Reticuloendothelial Soc; fel Int Soc Hemat. *Res:* Radiation induced leukemia; epidemiology; thrombocyte kinetics; serotonin metabolism; vitamin B-12 absorption, turnover and requirements; human whole body counting; iron metabolism; health services research; author of over 50 publications. *Mailing Add:* Off Pres Johns Hopkins Health Syst Johns Hopkins Hosp RD 5 4 Canal Lane Seaford DE 19973

HEYTLER, PETER GEORGE, BIOCHEMISTRY. *Current Pos:* RETIRED. *Personal Data:* b Prague, Czech, Apr 24, 30; nat US; m 50; c 3. *Educ:* Cornell Univ, BA, 50, MS, 52, PhD(biochem), 56. *Prof Exp:* Chemist, Lederle Labs, Am Cyanamid Corp, 52-54; asst, Cornell Univ, 54-56; biochemist, Cent Res Dept, E I du Pont de Nemours & Co, Inc, 56-61, res supvr, 61-86, res assoc, 86-90; sr res assoc, Dupont Merck Pharmaceut Co, 90-92. *Mem:* Am Soc Biol Chem; AAAS. *Res:* Bioenergetics; membrane biochemistry; endocytosis; neurochemistry. *Mailing Add:* 2509 Duncan Rd Wilmington DE 19808-4609. *E-Mail:* heytler@udel.edu

HEYWOOD, JOHN BENJAMIN, MECHANICAL ENGINEERING. *Current Pos:* from asst prof to prof mech eng, 76-89, LEADERS FOR MFG PROF, MASS INST TECHNOL, 89-, DIR, SLOAN AUTOMOTIVE LAB, 72-, SUN JAE PROF MECH ENG, 92- *Personal Data:* b Sidcup, Eng, Jan 11, 38; m 61; c James, Stephen & Benjamin. *Educ:* Cambridge Univ, BA, 60, ScD, 84; Mass Inst Technol, SM, 62, PhD(mech eng), 65. *Honors & Awards:* Ayreton Premium Award, Brit Inst Elec Engrs, 69; Ralph R Teetor Award, Soc Automotive Engrs, 71, Arch T Colwell Merit Award, 73, 81 & 89, Fel, 82, Horning Mem Award, 84; Freeman Scholar, Am Soc Mech Engrs, 86, Soichiro Honda Lectr, 90; Nat Award Advan Motor Vehicle Res & Develop, US Dept Transp, 96. *Prof Exp:* Res assoc mech eng, Mass Inst Technol, 64-65; res officer, Cent Elec Generating Bd, UK, 65-67, group leader, Leatherhead, 67-68. *Concurrent Pos:* Lectr, Northeastern Univ, 63-65; consult, Avco Systs Div, Bendix, Ford Motor Co, Jaguar Cars, Nat Acad Sci, Mobil Res & Develop Corp and var others. *Mem:* Assoc fel Am Inst Aeronaut & Astronaut; fel Brit Inst Mech Engrs; Combustion Inst; Am Soc Mech Engrs; fel Soc Automotive Engrs. *Res:* Internal combustion engines; combustion; power generation; thermodynamics. *Mailing Add:* Dept Mech Eng Rm 3-340 77 Massachusetts Ave Cambridge MA 02139. *Fax:* 617-253-5981

HEYWOOD, PETER, CELL BIOLOGY, PHYCOLOGY. *Current Pos:* asst prof, Brown Univ, 74-78, assoc prof, 78-88, assoc dean, 80-81, PROF BIOL, BROWN UNIV, 88- *Personal Data:* b Manchester, UK, Apr 1, 43. *Educ:* London Univ, BSc, 64, PhD(bot), 68. *Honors & Awards:* Nat Sci Teacher Asn. *Prof Exp:* Maria Moors Cabot res fel bot, Harvard Univ, 68-70; asst prof microbiol, Sch Med, Yale Univ, 70-74. *Mem:* Nat Sci Teachers Asn; Bot Soc Am; Brit Phycol Soc; Sigma Xi; Phycol Soc Am. *Res:* Botany; nuclear cytology of eukaryotic microorganisms; evolution of eukaryotic microorganisms; development of the inner ear. *Mailing Add:* Div Biol & Med Sci Brown Univ Providence RI 02912-0001

HEYWOOD, STUART MACKENZIE, MOLECULAR BIOLOGY, BIOCHEMISTRY. *Current Pos:* from asst prof to assoc prof, 67-73, PROF CELL BIOL, UNIV CONN, 73-, HEAD, SECT CELL BIOL & GENETICS, 74-, HEAD, DEPT MOLECULAR & CELL BIOL, 85- *Personal Data:* b Concord, Mass, Oct 15, 34; m 58; c 2. *Educ:* Univ Mass, BS, 57; Syracuse Univ, PhD(biochem), 65. *Prof Exp:* Am Heart Asn fel molecular biol, Mass Inst Technol, 65-66, NIH fel, 66-67. *Concurrent Pos:* NIH res grant, 67- & career develop award, 70- *Mem:* Biophys Soc; Am Soc Cell Biol; Am Soc Biol Chem. *Res:* Protein synthesis in higher organisms; transcription and translational controls during differentiation; ribonucleic acid metabolism. *Mailing Add:* Fort Rachel Marina Mystic CT 06355

HIATT, ANDREW JACKSON, PLANT PHYSIOLOGY, AGRONOMY. *Current Pos:* From asst prof to assoc prof, 60-67, chmn Dept Agron, 69-88, PROF AGRON, UNIV KY, 67-, ASSOC DEAN ADMIN, 88- *Personal Data:* b Wildie, Ky, Apr 14, 32; m 54, Elaine Parrett; c William A & Alison P (Smith). *Educ:* Univ Ky, BS, 53, MS, 57; NC State Univ, PhD(plant physiol), 60. *Concurrent Pos:* Mem coun, Agr Sci & Technol; res award, Univ Ky, 65, fac-alumni res award, 66. *Mem:* Am Soc Plant Physiol; fel Am Soc Agron; Soil Sci Soc Am; Crop Sci Soc Am. *Res:* Investigations of role of ions in metabolism of plants, mechanism of absorption of salts by cells and translocation of ions by plants. *Mailing Add:* 3114 Montavesta Rd Lexington KY 40502

HIATT, CASPAR WISTAR, III, BIOPHYSICAL CHEMISTRY. *Current Pos:* DIR, TECHSCAN LABS, 77- *Personal Data:* b Lakewood, Ohio, Sept 23, 19; m 52; c 4. *Educ:* Case Western Reserve Univ, BS, 42, PhD(immunochem), 48. *Prof Exp:* Res chemist, Stand Oil Co, Ohio, 42-43; asst, Inst Path, Cleveland, 46-48; Merck fel natural sci, Rockefeller Inst, 48-50; chief vet chem, Army Med Serv Grad Sch, Walter Reed Med Ctr, 50-56; biochemist, Viral Prod Lab, Div Biol Stand, NIH, 56-60, chief lab biochem & biophys, 60-67; prof chem & chmn dept, Fla Atlantic Univ, 67-68; chmn dept, Univ Tex Health Sci Ctr, San Antonio, 68-77, prof, 77-79. *Mem:* AAAS; Am Chem Soc; NY Acad Sci; Am Soc Photobiol. *Res:* Chemical factors in immunity; physical properties of viruses; ultracentrifugation; extraction of spirochetal antigens; kinetics of inactivation of viruses. *Mailing Add:* 861 Cumberstone Rd Harwood MD 20776-9560

HIATT, HAROLD, PSYCHIATRY. *Current Pos:* RETIRED. *Personal Data:* b Wilmington, Ohio, Oct 15, 21; m 62; c 3. *Educ:* Wilmington Col, BS, 43; Univ Cincinnati, MD, 46. *Prof Exp:* Rotating internship, Cincinnati Gen Hosp, 46-47; from jr resident to chief resident, Dept Psychiat, Univ Cincinnati, 49-52, from instr to asst prof psychiat, 52-64, assoc clin prof, 64-68; assoc prof, Univ Cinncinnati, 68-74, prof psychiat, 74- *Concurrent Pos:* Attend psychiatrist & clinician, Cincinnati Gen Hosp Dept Psychiat; chief psychiat serv, Vet Admin Hosp, Cincinnati, 54-74; mem admin comt, Cincinnati Col Med, 64-71; mem bd, Cincinnati Ment Health Asn, 66-72; coordr psychol curric, Dept Psychiat, Univ Cincinnati, 66-68; pres, Cincinnati Soc Neurol & Psychiat, 67-68; mem bd, Marjorie P Lee Home Aged, 67-70; mem prog comt, Cincinnati Acad Med, 68; mem, Bd Cancer Control Coun, Pub Health Fedn, 68-74; asst ed, Cincinnati Col Med Alumni Bull, 71. *Mem:* AMA; Am Psychiat Asn; Am Col Psychiat. *Res:* Geriatrics; psychotherapy. *Mailing Add:* 2353 Bedford Ave Cincinnati OH 45208

HIATT, HOWARD HAYM, INTERNAL MEDICINE, PUBLIC HEALTH. *Current Pos:* instr & assoc to asst prof med, Harvard Univ, 55-63, Herman L Blumgart prof, 63-72, dean, Sch Pub Health, 72-84, PROF MED, HARVARD UNIV, 72- *Personal Data:* b Patchogue, NY, July 22, 25; m 47; c 3. *Educ:* Harvard Univ, MD, 48. *Hon Degrees:* DSc, Northeastern Univ & Mass Col Pharm. *Prof Exp:* Investr, Nat Inst Arthritis & Metab Dis, 53-55. *Concurrent Pos:* Res fel med, Med Col, Cornell Univ & NY Hosp, 51-53; assoc med, Beth Israel Hosp, 55-63, physician-in-chief, 63-72; Am Cancer Soc res scholar, 58-59; Lederle med fac award, 59-62; Commonwealth Fund travel fel, Pasteur Inst, Paris, 60-61; vis scientist, Imp Cancer Res Fund Lab, London, 69-70. *Mem:* Inst Med-Nat Acad Sci; Am Soc Biol Chem; Am Soc Clin Invest; AAAS; Asn Am Physicians. *Res:* Research in social medicine. *Mailing Add:* Dept Med Brigham & Woman's Hosp Boston MA 02115. *Fax:* 617-732-5344; *E-Mail:* hhiatt@bics.bwh.harvard.edu

HIATT, JAMES LEE, ADMINISTRATION, ANATOMICAL SCIENCES & EDUCATION. *Current Pos:* res assoc, 67-72, from instr to asst prof, 72-76, ASSOC PROF ANAT, DENT SCH, UNIV MD, BALTIMORE, 76- *Personal Data:* b Lebanon, Ind, July 25, 34; m 54; c 3. *Educ:* Ball State Univ, BS, 59, MS, 68; Univ Md, PhD(anat), 73. *Prof Exp:* Teacher biol, Wendell Wilkie High Sch, Elwood, Ind, 59-67. *Concurrent Pos:* Consult, US Army Inst Dent Res, Walter Reed Army Med Ctr, Washington, DC, 82-; Oral Surg, Johns Hopkins Hosp; Dent Corp, Ft Meade Army Med Ctr. *Mem:* Int Asn Dent Res; Am Asn Dent Res; Am Asn Anatomists. *Res:* Craniofacial development in rodents related to teratogenic effects on development; tooth development in mammals; craniofacial development in trisomic mice; CAI development; 3-D computer reconstruction. *Mailing Add:* Dept Anat Dent Sch Univ Md 666 W Baltimore St Baltimore MD 21201. *Fax:* 410-706-3028

HIATT, NORMAN ARTHUR, POLYMER CHEMISTRY, ORGANIC CHEMISTRY. *Current Pos:* CONSULT, CHEM, PLASTICS & PACKAGING FIELDS, 87- *Personal Data:* b Worcester, Mass, Nov 22, 37; m 65, Barbara Weininger; c Adrienne & Eric. *Educ:* Worcester Polytech Inst, BS, 59; Lowell Technol Inst, PhD(org polymer chem), 68. *Prof Exp:* Engr plastics develop, Gen Dynamics Corp, 59-60 & AVCO Corp, 60-62; res scientist polymer res & develop, Uniroyal Inc, 69-73, sr group leader rubber res & develop, 73-74; sr res engr develop high temperature plastics, Norton Co, 74-76; res assoc heat transfer labs, Therimage Prod Div, Dennison Mfg Co, 76-78, res sect head heat transfer labels & indust crepe, 78-81, mgr tech develop heat transfer labels, 81-87. *Concurrent Pos:* Res fel, Univ Louvain, Belg, 68-69. *Mem:* Am Chem Soc; Soc Plastics Engrs. *Res:* Photochromic polymers; organo-sulfur polymers; polyurethanes; high-temperature polymers; adhesives; coating; printing technology. *Mailing Add:* 763 Waverly St Framingham MA 01701. *Fax:* 508-872-2252

HIATT, ROBERT BURRITT, SURGERY, PHYSIOLOGY. *Personal Data:* b Wilmington, Ohio, Apr 30, 17. *Educ:* Wilmington Col, Ohio, BA, 38; Univ Cincinnati, MD, 42; Am Bd Surg, dipl. *Prof Exp:* From intern to resident, Columbia-Presby Med Ctr, 42-46; asst surg, Col Physicians & Surgeons,l Columbia Univ, 46-50, instr, 50-56, asst prof clin surg, 56-61, from assoc prof to prof surg, 61-83, dir undergrad surg teaching, 62-68. *Concurrent Pos:* Asst attend surgeon,l Babies & Bellevue Hosps, New York, 46-50; asst attend surgeon, Presby Hosp, New York, 50-56, assoc attend, 56-62, chief, West Surg Serv, 62-68; dir surg, Shiraz Med Ctr, Iran, 54-56; NIH career develop award, 61-66, grant, 64-66; New York City Health Res Coun grant, 64-66; pres, Coherin Res Found, 80- *Mem:* Fel Am Col Surgeons; AMA; Pan-Am Med Asn; Am Surg Asn. *Res:* Intestinal physiology; abdominal surgery. *Mailing Add:* Rt 128 Dresden ME 04342

HIBBARD, MALCOLM JACKMAN, GEOLOGY. *Current Pos:* From asst prof to assoc prof, 62-73, PROF GEOL, MACKAY SCH MINES, UNIV NEV, RENO, 73- *Personal Data:* b Rockport, Mass, Feb 20, 36; m 83, Terrie Nault; c Dorothea, Monique, Anita & Hillary. *Educ:* Dartmouth Col, BA, 58; Univ Wash, MS, 60, PhD(geol), 62. *Mem:* Geol Soc Am. *Res:* Igneous and metamorphic petrology. *Mailing Add:* Dept Geol Univ Nev Reno NV 89557-0001

HIBBARD, WALTER ROLLO, JR, MATERIALS SCIENCE, ENERGY. *Current Pos:* RETIRED. *Personal Data:* b Bridgeport, Conn, Jan 20, 18; m 42, 72, Louise A Brembeck; c Douglas, Lawrence & Diana. *Educ:* Wesleyan Univ, AB, 39; Yale Univ, DEng(metall), 42. *Hon Degrees:* LLD, Mich Technol Univ, 66; DEng, Mont Col Mineral Technol, 68. *Honors & Awards:* Raymond Award, 50; Douglas Medal, Am Inst Mining, Metall & Petrol Engrs, 67; Mineral Econ Award, 83. *Prof Exp:* From asst to assoc prof metall, Yale Univ, 46-51; res assoc & mgr metals & ceramics, Gen Elec Res Lab, 51-65; dir, Bur of Mines, US Dept of Interior, 65-68; vpres res & develop tech serv, Owens Corning Fiberglas, 68-74; Energy Res & Develop Off, Fed Energy Admin, 74; emer prof eng, Va Polytech Inst & State Univ, 74-88. *Concurrent Pos:* Bd dir, Norton Co, Mass, 72-88; chmn, Mat Adv Bd, Nat Res Coun, 63-65 & Bldg Adv Bd, 75-76; ed, Mat & Soc, 75-88; emer dir, Va Ctr for Coal & Energy Res, 77-88. *Mem:* Nat Acad Eng; fel Am Ceramic Soc; fel Am Soc Metals; fel Am Acad Arts & Sci; Am Inst Mining, Metall & Petrol Engrs (pres, 67); fel Metall Soc; distinguished mem Soc Mining Engrs. *Res:* Materials, energy, environment, mineral processing, mineral economics. *Mailing Add:* 1403 Highland Circle Blacksburg VA 24060-5624

HIBBELER, RUSSELL CHARLES, ENGINEERING MECHANICS, NUCLEAR ENGINEERING. *Current Pos:* PROF, UNIV SOUTHWESTERN LA, 77- *Personal Data:* b Evanston, Ill, Jan 18, 44; m 74, Cornelie G Ruighauer; c Mary A. *Educ:* Univ Ill, Urbana, BS, 65, MS, 66; Northwestern Univ, PhD(theoret & appl mech), 68. *Honors & Awards:* AMCO Teaching Excellence Award. *Prof Exp:* Mem staff, Argonne Nat Lab, 68-70 & Youngstown State Univ, 69-72; instr, Ill Inst Technol, 72-73; asst prof, Union Col, 73-76. *Concurrent Pos:* Pres, March Eng, Inc, 81- *Mem:* Am Soc Eng Educ; Am Soc Civil Engrs; Am Soc Mech Engrs. *Res:* Thermal and creep problems in nuclear reactor components; problems in the theory of vibrations and theory of elasticity. *Mailing Add:* 149 Shannon Rd Lafayette LA 70503

HIBBEN, CRAIG RITTENHOUSE, PLANT PATHOLOGY. *Current Pos:* RETIRED. *Personal Data:* b Montclair, NJ, May 25, 30; m 58; c 2. *Educ:* Pa State Univ, BS, 53; Cornell Univ, MS, 59, PhD(plant path), 62. *Prof Exp:* Researcher plant path, Kitchawan Res Lab, Brooklyn Bot Garden, 62-92. *Concurrent Pos:* Mem, Int Shade Tree Conf. *Mem:* Am Phytopath Soc; Sigma Xi. *Res:* Forest and ornamental tree diseases, especially virus infection and air pollution injury; diebacks of forest tree species. *Mailing Add:* 2132 Gerrard Ct Yorktown Heights NY 10598

HIBBERT, LARRY EUGENE, PARASITOLOGY, PROTOZOOLOGY. *Current Pos:* PROF BIOL, RICKS COL, 69-, DEPT HEAD, 72- *Personal Data:* b LaGrande, Ore, May 17, 37; m 59; c 7. *Educ:* Eastern Ore Col, BS, 62; Utah State Univ, MS, 67, PhD(zool), 69. *Concurrent Pos:* Vis asst prof, Univ Utah, 68-69. *Mem:* Sigma Xi; Soc Protozoologists; Am Inst Biol Sci; Human Anat & Physiol Soc. *Res:* Excystation of bovine coocidia, both invitro, and comparing their stimuli for excystation with other mammalian coocidia. *Mailing Add:* Biol Sci Ricks Col 525 S Center St Rexburg ID 83460-0001

HIBBITS, JAMES OLIVER, JR, ANALYTICAL CHEMISTRY. *Current Pos:* CONSULT, 90-; EXEC VPRES, COAL RESOURCE RECOVERY CO, 92- *Personal Data:* b St Louis, Mo, Oct 27, 24; m 47, Virginia A Starkey; c James O III, Lynne C & Kari A. *Educ:* St Louis Univ, BS, 50, MS, 52. *Honors & Awards:* Tech Excellence, Gen Elec, 65. *Prof Exp:* Assoc chemist, Union Carbide Nuclear Corp, 51-55; chemist, Mallinckrodt Chem Works, 55-56; sr chemist aircraft nuclear propulsion, Gen Elec Co, 56-60, prin chemist, 60-64, mgr anal chem, Nuclear Mat & Propulsion Oper, Ohio, 64-70; mgr anal chem, Owens-Ill Inc, Toledo, 70-73, mgr, Chem & Phys Testing Dept, 73-87; pres, Monarch Anal Labs, 87-90. *Concurrent Pos:* Bd dirs, Eitel Inst Silicate Res, 87- *Mem:* Am Chem Soc. *Res:* Analytical inorganic chemistry; analytical chemistry of the rare earths, uranium and less familiar elements; specific reactions obtained by liquid-liquid extraction and semi-specific reagents; potentiometry and other phases of electro-analytical chemistry; gas chromatography. *Mailing Add:* 4555 Crestview Dr Sylvania OH 43560. *E-Mail:* jim.hib@juno.com

HIBBS, ANDREW D, LOW-TEMPERATURE PHYSICS, SUPERCONDUCTIVITY INSTRUMENTATION. *Current Pos:* res physicist, 89-92, DIR RES, QUANTUM MAGNETICS, 92- *Educ:* Cambridge Univ, Eng, MA, 85, PhD(physics), 89. *Honors & Awards:* R&D 100 Award, 92. *Prof Exp:* Res assoc, Nat Ctr Superconductivity, 87-89. *Concurrent Pos:* Prin investr, Army Elec Tech Lab, 91. *Mem:* Cryog Soc Am. *Res:* Designed and developed custom built cryogenic instrumentation for magnetic imaging; design and develop ultrasensitive magnetic instrumentations for fundamental research and practical fielded applications; high temperature superconductivity. *Mailing Add:* Quantum Magnetics Inc 7740 Kenamar Ct San Diego CA 92121-2425

HIBBS, CLAIR MAURICE, VETERINARY PATHOLOGY, MICROBIOLOGY. *Current Pos:* RETIRED. *Personal Data:* b Lucerne, Mo, Oct 10, 23; m 46; c 2. *Educ:* Univ Mo, BS, 49, DVM, 53; Kans State Univ, MS, 62, PhD(path), 65. *Honors & Awards:* Rotary Paul Harris Award, 88. *Prof Exp:* Technician, Univ Mo, 50-52 & pvt pract, 53-60; res assoc, Kans State Univ, 60-62, instr parasitol, 62-63 & diag lab, 63-65, from asst prof to assoc prof path, 65-; from assoc prof to prof, N Platte Agr Exp Sta, Univ Nebr, Lincoln, 73-90; dir, NMex Vet Diag Serv, 79-90. *Concurrent Pos:* Consult pathologist, Chemagro Corp, 67-69; Agr Res Serv, USDA coop agreement, Kans State Univ, 69-; Mark Morris Animal Found fel; pres, Western Vet Conf, 97- *Mem:* Conf Res Workers Animal Dis; Am Asn Vet Lab Diagnosticians; Am Asn Bovine Practitioners. *Res:* Infectious diseases, anomalies and related pathology. *Mailing Add:* 1172 Edgewater Lane Lynden WA 98264

HIBBS, JOHN BURNHAM, MACROPHAGE PHYSIOLOGY. *Current Pos:* PROF MED, COL MED, UNIV UTAH, 80- *Educ:* Univ Pittsburgh, MD, 62. *Mailing Add:* Div Infectious Dis Ctr Univ Utah Sch Med Salt Lake City UT 84132-0001. *Fax:* 801-585-3377

HIBBS, RICHARD GUYTHAL, HISTOLOGY. *Current Pos:* RETIRED. *Personal Data:* b Winner, SDak, Feb 17, 22; m 46; c 3. *Educ:* Univ SDak, BA, 50; Univ Minn, PhD(anat), 55. *Honors & Awards:* Gold Award, Am Acad Dermat, 59. *Prof Exp:* From asst to instr anat, Univ Minn, 51-55; from instr to prof, Tulane Univ, 55-75; prof anat, Sch Med, La State Univ, Shreveport, 75-87, head dept, 77-87. *Mem:* Am Asn Anat; Am Soc Cell Biol. *Res:* Electron microscopy and histochemistry of the cardiovascular system. *Mailing Add:* 6231 S Lakeshore Dr Shreveport LA 71119

HIBBS, ROBERT A, CHEMISTRY, BACTERIOLOGY. *Current Pos:* PROF CHEM, BOISE STATE UNIV, 71- *Personal Data:* b Cocoa, Fla, Sept 9, 23; m 52; c 6. *Educ:* Univ Fla, BSA, 47, MS, 48; Wash State Univ, PhD, 51. *Prof Exp:* Asst, Univ Fla, 47-48 & Wash State Univ, 48-51; qual control supvr, Darigold Farms, Wash, 51-54; asst prof dairy sci, Univ Idaho, 54-61; dir, Hibbs Labs, 61- *Concurrent Pos:* From asst prof to assoc prof phys sci, Boise State Col, 65-71. *Res:* Food technology; quality improvement in processing food products; new product development. *Mailing Add:* 15 Mesa Vista Dr Boise ID 83705

HIBBS, ROGER FRANKLIN, CHEMISTRY. *Current Pos:* RETIRED. *Personal Data:* b St Louis, Mo, Jan 28, 21; m 45; c 8. *Educ:* Eastern Ill State Teachers Col, Charleston, BEd, 43. *Prof Exp:* Jr chemist anal chem, Tenn Eastman Corp, 43-44, lab supvr mass spectrometry, 44-47, lab dept supt, 47; lab dept supt, Carbide & Carbon Chem Co, 47-52, lab div head chem & phys measurements, Union Carbide Corp, 52-54, supt, Process Div, 54-58, supt, Tech Div, Union Carbide Nuclear Co Div, 58-62 from plant mgr to vpres, Nuclear Div, 62-70, pres, Nuclear Div, 70-84. *Mem:* AAAS; Am Chem Soc; Am Nuclear Soc. *Res:* Mass spectrometry. *Mailing Add:* Sugar Grove Valley Rd Harriman TN 37748

HIBLER, CHARLES PHILLIP, ZOOLOGY, BIOCHEMISTRY. *Current Pos:* RETIRED. *Personal Data:* b Austin, Tex, Aug 19, 30; m 53; c 4. *Educ:* NMex State Univ, BS, 56; Utah State Univ, MS, 59; Colo State Univ, PhD(zool), 63. *Prof Exp:* Res scientist, Animal Dis & Parasite Res Div, USDA, 62-65; prof parasitol, Col Vet Med, Colo State Univ, 65-87, dir, Wild Animal Dis Ctr, 71-87. *Mem:* Am Soc Parasitologists; Wildlife Dis Asn. *Res:* Biology of parasitic nematodes, especially the Filarioidea. *Mailing Add:* 12000 Rist Canyon Rd Bellvue CO 80512-6404

HIBLER, WILLIAM DAVID, III, SEA ICE DYNAMICS, GLACIOLOGY. *Current Pos:* RES PROF ENG, THAYER SCHOOL ENG, DARTMOUTH COL, 86- *Personal Data:* b Brunswick, Mo, Feb 8, 43; m 65; c 2. *Educ:* Univ Mo Columbia, BS, 65; Cornell Univ, PhD(physics), 69. *Prof Exp:* Vis asst prof physics, Univ Cincinnati, 69-70; res physicist glaciol, US Army Cold Regions Res & Eng Lab, 70-86. *Concurrent Pos:* Vis fel, Geophys Fluid Dynamics Prog, Princeton Univ, 76-78 & 81-82; mem, Global Atmospheric Res Prog Polar Subprog Panel, Nat Acad Sci, 77-79, Glaciol Subcomt, Polar Res Bd, 85-88; vis scientist, Max Planck Inst Meteorol, Hamburg, Fed Repub Ger, 84-85. *Mem:* Am Geophys Union; Int Glaciol Soc; Am Meteorol Soc; Sigma Xi. *Res:* Large scale numerical modeling of sea ice and ice covered oceans; geophysical scale ice mechanics. *Mailing Add:* Thayer Sch Eng Dartmouth Col Box 8000 Hanover NH 03755-8000

HICHAR, JOSEPH KENNETH, PHYSIOLOGY, ZOOLOGY. *Current Pos:* dean col arts & sci, State Univ NY, 70-72, dean fac natural sci, 72-75, prof, 70-85, EMER PROF BIOL, STATE UNIV NY, BUFFALO, 85- *Personal Data:* b Allentown, Pa, Aug 5, 28; m 55, Barbara J Gill; c Joseph K II & Mark N. *Educ:* Univ Pittsburgh, BS, 50; Pa State Univ, MS, 52; Harvard Univ, PhD(biol), 58. *Prof Exp:* Mgr sales promotion, Everson Elec Co, 50; investr, Liberty Mutual Ins Co, 50-51; asst, Pa State Univ, 51-52; asst prof biol, Moravian Col Women, 52-53; from asst prof to assoc prof, State Univ NY Col, Brockport, 53-55; teaching res fel, Harvard Univ, 55-58; asst prof zool, Ohio Wesleyan Univ, 58-60; from assoc prof to prof biol, Parsons Col, 60-65, dean grad sch, 61, dean col, 61-62, dean fac sci, 62-64; prof biol, dean col & vpres acad affairs, Hiram Scott Col, 65-70. *Concurrent Pos:* NIH res grantee, 60-65; Fulbright prof, Univ Ceylon, 63-64; admin dean, Hiram Scott Col, 65-66, vpres acad affairs, 66-70; NSF grantee, Int Conf Med Electronics, Paris, 59 & biomed eng, Univ Vt, 60; Nat Acad Sci-Nat Res Coun grantee, Int Cong biophysics, Stockholm & Moscow, 61; NIH grantee, Int Conf Med Electronics & Biol Eng, Tokyo, 65; US Off Educ grant newer mediated learning syts, Univ Nebr, 68-69. *Mem:* Fel AAAS; Am Soc Zool; Biophys Soc; Sigma Xi; NY Acad Sci; Am Inst Biol Sci. *Res:* Neurophysiology, electrophysiology and neuropharmacology of crustaceans; developed techniques of pulse height analysis of the electrical activity in the central nervous system and demonstrated effects of various drugs on specific nerve cells; neuro-electrophysiology; neurohormones; behavior; peripheral nervous system; isolated nerves. *Mailing Add:* 219 Cotuit Rd Sandwich MA 02563

HICKENBOTTOM, JOHN POWELL, BIOCHEMISTRY. *Current Pos:* ASSOC PROF BIOL, D'YOUVILLE COL, BUFFALO, NY, 80- *Personal Data:* b Burns, Ore, Apr 12, 38; m 68; c 2. *Educ:* Idaho State Univ, BS, 60; Univ Wash, PhD(biochem), 67. *Prof Exp:* From asst prof to assoc prof pharmacol & biochem, Sch Pharm, Univ Miss, 69-80. *Concurrent Pos:* Nat Heart Inst fel, Dept Pharm, Sch Med, Emory Univ, 67-69. *Mem:* NY Acad Sci; Am Chem Soc; Sigma Xi. *Res:* Mechanisms of hormonal control of glycogen metabolism in muscle and liver; effects of chlorinated hydrocarbons on hepatic glycogen metabolism in mammals and marine animals. *Mailing Add:* 17 Townsend Pl Athens OH 45701

HICKERNELL, FRED SLOCUM, ACOUSTICAL & OPTICAL MICROELECTRONICS. *Current Pos:* MEM TECH STAFF, MOTOROLA SPACE & SYSTS TECHNOL GROUP, 60- *Personal Data:* b Phoenix, Ariz, Jan 16, 32; m 54, Thresa Kerr; c Fred, Diana, Robert & Thomas. *Educ:* Ariz State Univ, BA, 53, MS, 59, PhD(physics), 66. *Honors & Awards:* Eng Achievement, Inst Elec & Electronics Engrs, 69; Tech Achievement, NASA, 74; Achievement Award, Inst Elec & Electronics Engrs Ultrasonics, Ferroelectrics & Frequency Contol Soc, 95. *Prof Exp:* Instr physics, Ariz State Univ, 57-58; engr math, Goodyear Aerospace, 58-60. *Concurrent Pos:* Fac assoc, Dept Math, Ariz State Univ, 81-83; vis prof, Univ Ariz, 85-87, adj prof, 87-; Dan Noble fel, Motorola Inc, 87. *Mem:* Am Phys Soc; Am Meteorol Soc; fel Inst Elec & Electronics Engrs; fel Am Sci Affil; Sigma Xi; Am Vacuum Soc. *Res:* Microwave acoustics and integrated optics; bulk and surface acoustic wave materials and devices; integrated acousto-optic devices; microwave ferrites; vacuum thin films; silicon microelectronic circuits. *Mailing Add:* Motorola Space & Syst Technol Group 8201 E McDowell Rd Scottsdale AZ 85252. *E-Mail:* f.hickernell@ieee.org

HICKERNELL, GARY L, FOOD CHEMISTRY, AGRICULTURAL & FOOD CHEMISTRY. *Current Pos:* ASST PROF, KEUKA COL, 90- *Personal Data:* b Meadville, Pa, Sept 30, 42; m 65; c 2. *Educ:* Allegheny Col, BS, 64; Univ Wash, PhD(org chem), 68. *Prof Exp:* Sr chemist coffee res, Gen Foods Corp, 68-88; vis asst prof, Vassar Col, 88-90. *Mem:* AAAS; Am Chem Soc; Inst Food Technologists. *Res:* Natural products structural elucidation, especially papuanic acid; chemistry of coffee, particularly with regards to its effect on flavor; quantitative structure-activity relationship regarding sweetness, bitterness; cereal chemistry and flavor. *Mailing Add:* 12 Terrich Ct Ossining NY 10562-3708

HICKERNELL, ROBERT K, OPTOELECTRONICS. *Current Pos:* GROUP LEADER, OPTOELECTRON MFG, NAT INST STAND & TECHNOL, 94- *Personal Data:* b July 31, 59. *Educ:* Univ Ariz, PhD(optical sci), 87. *Mem:* Optical Soc Am; Am Physicists Soc. *Mailing Add:* Nat Inst Stand & Technol 815-04 324 Broadway Boulder CO 30303. *E-Mail:* bobhick@boulder.nist.gov

HICKEY, ANTHONY JAMES, PHARMACEUTICAL AEROSOL SCIENCE, DRUG DELIVERY SYSTEMS. *Current Pos:* ASSOC PROF PHARMACEUT, UNIV NC, 93- *Personal Data:* b Hereford, UK, Nov 3, 55; m 88, Lesley Marson; c Helen R & Ruth A. *Educ:* Portsmouth Polytech, BSc, 77; Univ Birmingham, UK, MSc, 80; Univ Aston, Birmingham, PhD(pharmaceut), 85. *Hon Degrees:* MIBiol, C Biol, Inst Biol, Gt Brit, 87. *Honors & Awards:* Young Investr Pharm & Pharmaceut Technol, Am Asn Pharmaceut Scientists, 90. *Prof Exp:* Exp biologist, Toxicol Labs Ltd, 77-79; fel, Univ Ky Col Pharm, 84-86, res scientist, 86-88; asst prof pharmaceut, Univ Ill, Chicago, 88-92. *Concurrent Pos:* Res asst prof med, Univ Ill, Chicago, 90-93, assoc prof pharmaceut, 92-93, affil ctr pharmaceut biotechnol, 92-93, assoc prof bioeng, 93. *Mem:* Am Asn Pharmaceut Scientists; Am Chem Soc; Am Asn Aerosol Res; Controlled Release Soc; Int Soc Aerosols Med; Int Asn Colloid & Interface Scientists. *Res:* Manufacture, characterization and administration of microparticulate drug delivery systems, particularly in the form of aerosols for inhalation. *Mailing Add:* Univ NC Sch Pharm Beard Hall CB 7360 Chapel Hill NC 27599-7360

HICKEY, BARBARA MARY, PHYSICAL OCEANOGRAPHY. *Current Pos:* Res asst prof, 73-80, RES ASSOC PROF PHYS OCEANOG, UNIV WASH, 80- *Personal Data:* b Toronto, Ont, June 7, 45. *Educ:* Univ Toronto, BSc, 67; Univ Calif, San Diego, MS, 69, PhD(phys oceanog), 75. *Mem:* Am Geophys Union. *Res:* Physical oceanography of the Washington-Oregon continental shelf and slope regions; dynamics of Eastern Boundary Current Systems; dynamics of topographic effects in coastal areas; sediment transport. *Mailing Add:* Sch Oceanog WB-10 Univ Wash 3900 Seventh Ave NE Seattle WA 98195-0001

HICKEY, DONAL, POPULATION GENETICS, EVOLUTIONARY THEORY. *Current Pos:* from asst prof to assoc prof, 81-88, PROF GENETICS & EVOLUTION, UNIV OTTAWA, 88- *Personal Data:* b Co Kerry, Ireland, July 13, 48. *Educ:* Nat Univ Ireland, BSc, 70; Harvard Univ, PhD(biol), 77. *Honors & Awards:* Assoc Fel, Can Inst Advan Res. *Prof Exp:* Asst prof genetics, Brock Univ, 78-81. *Mem:* Genetics Soc Am; Genetics Soc Can; Soc Study Evolution; Am Soc Naturalists; AAAS. *Res:* Gene regulation in eukaryotes; biochemical genetics of drosophila populations; population genetics and evolutionary theory; importance of regulatory gene polymorphisms in adaptive evolution; evolution of eukaryotic genome structure. *Mailing Add:* Dept Biol Univ Ottawa Ottawa ON K1N 6N5 Can. *E-Mail:* hicsb@acadvm1.uottawa.ca

HICKEY, JIMMY RAY, LAPLACE TRANSFORM, DIFFERENTIAL EQUATION. *Current Pos:* PROF MATH, BAYLOR UNIV, 59- *Personal Data:* b Hallsville, Tex, Feb 12, 29; m; c 2. *Educ:* ETex State Univ, BS, 53; Baylor Univ, MA, 59; Univ Tex, Austin, PhD(math), 71. *Prof Exp:* Instr math, Talco High Sch, 53-55; seismologist, Shell Oil Co, 55-57. *Mem:* Math Asn Am; Soc Indust & Appl Math. *Res:* Operational calculus for generalized functions; the theory of distributions, generalized transforms and solution of differential equations using generalized functions. *Mailing Add:* RR2 Waco TX 76706

HICKEY, JOSEPH JAMES, wildlife ecology; deceased, see previous edition for last biography

HICKEY, KENNETH DYER, PLANT PATHOLOGY. *Current Pos:* PROF PLANT PATH & SCIENTIST-IN-CHG, FRUIT RES LAB, PA STATE UNIV, 76- *Personal Data:* b Sparta, Tenn, Mar 4, 33; m 60, Patricia A Heckenluber; c Deborah A (Murray), Benjamin D & Beth I (Hocker). *Educ:* Tenn Polytech Univ, BS, 55; Pa State Univ, MS, 58, PhD(plant path), 60. *Prof Exp:* Asst, Pa State Univ, 55-60; asst prof plant path & exten plant pathologist, Cornell Univ, 60-66; assoc prof plant path & res fruit pathologist, Va Polytech Inst & State Univ, 66-76. *Mem:* Am Phytopath Soc; Int Phytopath Soc; Sigma Xi. *Res:* Development of disease control programs including evaluation of fungicides and bioagents for control of fruit diseases. *Mailing Add:* Fruit Res Ext Ctr Box 309 Biglerville PA 17307. *Fax:* 717-677-4112; *E-Mail:* kdh4@psu.edu

HICKEY, LEO JOSEPH, GEOLOGY, PALEOBOTANY. *Current Pos:* dir, Yale Peabody Mus, 82-87, PROF, DEPT GEOL & BIOL, YALE UNIV, 82- *Personal Data:* b Philadelphia, Pa, Apr 26, 40; m 68, Judith McKendry; c Geoffrey A, Damian M & Jason A. *Educ:* Villanova Univ, BS, 62; Princeton Univ, MA, 64, PhD(geol), 67. *Hon Degrees:* MPhil, Yale Univ, 83. *Honors & Awards:* All-Cong Lectr, Thirteenth Int Bot Cong, Sydney, 81; H A Gleason Award, NY Bot Garden, 78. *Prof Exp:* Nat Acad Sci res assoc, Smithsonian Inst, 66-69, assoc cur, 69-80, cur, 80-82. *Concurrent Pos:* Counr, Yellowstone Bighorn Res Asn, 73-79 & 85-, vpres, 79-81, pres, 81-83 & past pres, 83-85; chmn, Exhibits Comt, Nat Mus Nat Hist, 73-75, chmn-elect & treas, Senate Scientists; mem, Smithsonian Inst Trop Biol Steering Comt, 77-79; assoc ed, Paleobiol, 80-83, 87-90; trustee, Sheffield Sci Sch, Yale Univ, 82-87; sci adv bd, Sci Mus Conn, 84-87; sci adv comt, Yale Press, 85-86, publ comt, 88-91. *Mem:* AAAS; Geol Soc Am; Bot Soc Am; Paleont Soc; Am Geol Inst. *Res:* Early flowering plant evolution; late Cretaceous and early Tertiary paleobotanical and stratigraphic studies of the Rocky Mountains and Arctic; application of leaf architecture to angiosperm phylogeny and systematics. *Mailing Add:* Geol & Geophysics Yale Univ PO Box 208109 New Haven CT 06520-8109. *Fax:* 203-432-3134; *E-Mail:* hleo@yalevm.ycc.yale.edu

HICKEY, RICHARD JAMES, BIOCHEMISTRY, HUMAN ECOLOGY. *Current Pos:* RETIRED. *Personal Data:* b Rock Island, Ill, Sept 18, 13; m 41; c 4. *Educ:* Univ Ill, BS, 35; Iowa State Univ, PhD(biophys chem), 41. *Prof Exp:* Asst chem, Univ Buffalo, 35-36 & Iowa State Univ, 36-41; res microbiol chemist, Com Solvents Corp, 41-53; sr res biochemist, Inst Coop Res, Univ Pa, 53-58; Res & Develop Dept, Com Solvents Corp, 58-63; sr res investr, Inst Environ Studies, Wharton Sch, 68-71, sr res investr, Mgt & Behav Sci Ctr, 71-74, sr res investr, Dept Statist, 75-86. *Mem:* AAAS; Am Chem Soc; NY Acad Sci. *Res:* Air pollution and health; theoretical biology; evolutionary biology; psychobiology; complex biological systems analysis; genetics; ethology; population biology; environmental mutagens and mutagenesis; biological senescence; etiologies of chronic diseases; cancer; cardiovascular diseases; birth defects; statistics; radiation biology; radiation hormesis; human epidemiology; scientific malpractices. *Mailing Add:* 43 E Clearfield Rd Havertown PA 19083-1401

HICKEY, ROBERT CORNELIUS, medicine, for more information see previous edition

HICKEY, ROBERT JOSEPH, DNA REPLICATION, MOLECULAR CLONING. *Current Pos:* ASST PROF PHARMACOL, SCH MED, UNIV MD, 89- *Personal Data:* b Jamaica, NY; m 81. *Educ:* Queens Col, BA, 72; City Univ New York, PhM, 79, PhD(biochem), 79. *Prof Exp:* Fel molecular biol, Albert Einstein Col Med, 80-85; res assoc, Worcester Found, 85-86, sr res assoc biochem, 86-89. *Concurrent Pos:* Adj asst prof molecular & cell biol, Univ Md, 89-, pharmacol & exp therapeut, 89-, oncol, 90- & toxicol, 91- *Mem:* AAAS; Am Asn Cancer Res; Sigma Xi. *Res:* Activity, function and assembly of a human cell multiprotein DNA replication complex in normal and neoplastic cells; molecular cloning and biochemical analysis of transporters for neurotransmitters; effects of heavy metals and organic toxins on DNA replication in human cells. *Mailing Add:* Dept Pharmacol Sch Med Univ Md 685 W Baltimore St Baltimore MD 21201

HICKEY, ROGER, EXPERIMENTAL PHYSICS. *Current Pos:* From asst prof to assoc prof, Hartwick Col, 69-82, chmn, Sci Div, 77-79 & 84-86, chmn dept, 75-91, PROF PHYSICS, HARTWICK COL, 82- *Personal Data:* b Troy, NY, June 8, 42; wid, Paula Williamson; c Sharon & Kevin (deceased). *Educ:* Siena Col, NY, BS, 64; Clarkson Col Technol, MS, 67, PhD(physics), 70. *Concurrent Pos:* Nat counr, Soc Physics Students, 73-74. *Mem:* Am Phys Soc; Am Asn Physics Teachers. *Res:* Computers in physics education, chaos. *Mailing Add:* Dept Physics Hartwick Col Oneonta NY 13820. *Fax:* 607-431-4374; *E-Mail:* hickeyr@hartwick.edu

HICKEY, WILLIAM AUGUST, ENTOMOLOGY, GENETICS. *Current Pos:* RETIRED. *Personal Data:* b Stroudsburg, Pa, June 24, 36; m 57, Barbara Stachowiak; c William Jr, Timothy, Sandra & Kristina J. *Educ:* King's Col, BS, 57; Univ Notre Dame, MS, 59, PhD(biol), 65. *Hon Degrees:* LLD, Univ Notre Dame, 95. *Honors & Awards:* President's Medal, Saint Mary's Col, 85. *Prof Exp:* Asst biol, Univ Notre Dame, 57-59; from instr to prof biol & chmn dept, St Mary's Col, Ind, 59-72, vpres acad affairs, 72-74, actg pres, 74-75 & 85-86, vpres & dean fac, 75-85, pres, St Mary's Col, Ind, 86-97. *Concurrent Pos:* Res assoc, Mosquito Genetics Proj, Univ Notre Dame, 59-62; Entom Soc Am travel grant, Int Cong Entom, London, 64. *Mem:* AAAS; Am Asn Higher Educ; Entom Soc Am; Am Inst Biol Sci; Sigma Xi; Am Coun Educ; Asn Am Cols. *Res:* Culicidae; transmission genetics, population genetics and genetics of sex ratios in Aedes aegypti. *Mailing Add:* 51263 Lake Pointe Ct Granger IN 46530. *Fax:* 219-284-4800; *E-Mail:* hickey@saintmarys.edu

HICKIE, ROBERT ALLAN, MOLECULAR BIOLOGY, CANCER RESEARCH. *Current Pos:* from asst prof to assoc prof, 66-76, PROF PHARMACOL, FAC MED, UNIV SASK, 76- *Personal Data:* b Melville, Sask, Aug 29, 36; m 59, Doreen; c David, Pave, Colleen & Mark. *Educ:* Univ Sask, BSc, 58, MSc, 60; Univ Toronto, PhD(pharmacol), 65. *Prof Exp:* Lectr pharmacol, Univ Toronto, 65-66. *Concurrent Pos:* Nat Cancer Inst fel, Univ Toronto & Univ Sask, 65-69; Med Res Coun Can fel, Univ Sask, 69- *Mem:* Am Asn Cancer Res; Pharmacol Soc Can; AAAS; NY Acad Sci. *Res:* Cell membranes; cyclic nucleotides; cancer chemotherapy; calmodulin; cell growth regulation. *Mailing Add:* Dept Pharmacol Univ Sask Health Sci Bldg Saskatoon SK S7N 0W0 Can. *Fax:* 306-966-6220; *E-Mail:* hickie@skyfox.u.sask.ca

HICKMAN, ALBERT PEET, INELASTIC SCATTERING PROCESSES, OPTICAL PROCESSES IN GASES. *Current Pos:* PROF PHYSICS, LEHIGH UNIV, 94- *Personal Data:* b Knoxville, Tenn, Oct 19, 47; m 85; c 1. *Educ:* Rice Univ, BA, 69, MA, 71, PhD(physics), 73. *Prof Exp:* Physicist, Molecular Physics Lab, SRI Int, 73-94. *Concurrent Pos:* Vis scientist, Serv Atomic Physics, Ctr Nuclear Study, Saclay, France, 80-81; Sch Physics, Univ Kaiserslautern, Ger, 92-93. *Mem:* Fel Am Phys Soc; Am Geophys Union; Sigma Xi. *Res:* Development of theoretical and computational models for atomic and molecular collision processes; theory of Rydberg atom collisions and fine-structure-changing collisions. *Mailing Add:* Dept Physics Lehigh Univ 16 Memorial Dr Bethlehem PA 18015. *E-Mail:* aph2@lehigh.edu

HICKMAN, CAROLE STENTZ, PALEOBIOLOGY, MALACOLOGY. *Current Pos:* from asst prof to assoc prof, 77-85, PROF PALEONT, UNIV CALIF, BERKELEY, 85- *Personal Data:* b LaSalle, Ill, Jan 5, 42; m 64. *Educ:* Oberlin Col, BA, 64; Univ Ore, MS, 68; Stanford Univ, PhD(geol), 75. *Prof Exp:* Adj res assoc biol, Swarthmore Col, 70-77. *Concurrent Pos:* Consult, US Geol Surv, 73- & NSF, 81-84; vis invest, Dept Paleobiol, Smithsonian Inst, 75-76; res assoc, Dept Malacol, Acad Natural Sci Philadelphia, 76-77; NSF grants, 77- *Mem:* Paleont Soc; Paleont Res Inst; Am Malacol Union; AAAS; Soc Econ Paleontologists & Mineralogists. *Res:* Systematics, evolution and historical zoogeography of Cenozoic marine mollusks; age, origin and evolution deep-water mollusk faunas; functional morphology of gastropod radulae; systematics and ecology of deep-water limpets. *Mailing Add:* Dept Integrative Biol Univ Calif Berkeley CA 94720-3410

HICKMAN, CLEVELAND PENDLETON, JR, ZOOLOGY. *Current Pos:* assoc prof, 67-69, PROF ZOOL, WASHINGTON & LEE UNIV, 69- *Personal Data:* b Greencastle, Ind, Oct 29, 28; m 50, Rae Rickenbacher; c Andrew R & Diane (Liss). *Educ:* DePauw Univ, AB, 50; Univ NH, MS, 53; Univ BC, PhD(zool), 58. *Prof Exp:* Fishery res, Univ Wash, Seattle, 54-55; asst zool, Univ BC, 55-58; from asst prof to assoc prof, Univ Alta, 58-67. *Concurrent Pos:* Vis researcher, Duke Univ Marine Lab, 65-66, Univ Uppsala, Sweden, 72-73; vis prof, Univ Oxford, 78 & 83. *Mem:* AAAS; Am Soc Zool. *Res:* Systematics of marine invertebrates of the Galapagos Islands; kidney function in fish with emphasis on glomerular permeability. *Mailing Add:* Dept Biol Washington & Lee Univ Lexington VA 24450-9904. *Fax:* 540-463-8012; *E-Mail:* hickman.c@wlu.edu

HICKMAN, EUGENE, SR, PHARMACEUTICS. *Current Pos:* assoc prof, 59-74, PROF PHARMACEUT, TEX SOUTHERN UNIV, 74- *Personal Data:* b DeRidder, La, Nov 28, 28; m 52; c 3. *Educ:* Tex Southern Univ, BS, 52; Univ Tex, MS, 55; Univ Iowa, PhD(pharm), 59. *Prof Exp:* Asst, Univ Iowa, 56-59. *Mem:* Am Pharmaceut Asn. *Res:* Synthesis and testing of organic compounds for their possible application as anti-fungal agents. *Mailing Add:* Dept Pharmaceut Tex Southern Univ 3100 Cleburne St Houston TX 77004-4501

HICKMAN, HOWARD MINOR, ORGANIC CHEMISTRY. *Current Pos:* PRES, HICKMAN ASSOCS, 88- *Personal Data:* b Sept 6, 25; US citizen; m 52; c 3. *Educ:* Southwestern Col, AB, 48; Kans State Univ, MS, 49; Univ Ill, PhD(food technol), 53. *Prof Exp:* Res chemist, Archer-Daniels-Midland Co, 53-60; res chemist, Gustin-Bacon Mfg Co, 60-62; mgr reinforced plastics res, 62-68; dir res & develop, Clark-Schwebel Fiberglass, 68-69; group leader chem spec, Ashland Chem Co, 69-79; sect mgr, Sherex Chem Co, 79-80, res admin, 81-87. *Mem:* Am Chem Soc; Sigma Xi; AAAS. *Res:* Glass fiber reinforced plastics; fatty chemicals; antioxidants; chemical specialties; fuel, lube oil additives, environmental. *Mailing Add:* 596 Whitney Ave Worthington OH 43085-2436

HICKMAN, JAMES BLAKE, physical chemistry; deceased, see previous edition for last biography

HICKMAN, JAMES CHARLES, ACTUARIAL MATHEMATICS, STATISTICS. *Current Pos:* dean, Sch Bus, 85-90, prof, 72-93, EMER PROF BUS-STATIST & EMER DEAN, UNIV WIS-MADISON, 93- *Personal Data:* b Indianola, Iowa, Aug 27, 27; m 50, Margaret W; c Charles W, Donald R & Barhara J. *Educ:* Simpson Col, BA, 50; Univ Iowa, MS, 52, PhD(math), 61. *Honors & Awards:* Halmstad Prize for actuarial res, 81 & 84. *Prof Exp:* Actuarial asst, Bankers Life Co, Des Moines, 52-57; from instr math to prof statist, Univ Iowa, 57-72. *Concurrent Pos:* Consult, Panel Consults, Financial Probs Soc Security, Cong Res Serv, 75-76; mem, Med Malpract Comt, Wis Legis, 76, Acturial Stand Bd, 85-92. *Mem:* Fel Soc Actuaries(vpres, 75-77); assoc Casualty Actuarial Soc; Am Acad Actuaries; Am Statist Asn; Math Asn Am; Am Risk & Ins Asn. *Res:* Mortality estimation and projection; pension funding models under dynamic economic and demographic conditions. *Mailing Add:* Sch Bus Univ Wis 975 University Ave Madison WI 53706

HICKMAN, JAMES JOSEPH, PHOTOCHEMISTRY. *Current Pos:* Res chemist, E I DuPont de Nemours & Co, Inc, 67-70, res chem & tech rep, 70-73, suprvr customer serv, 73-76, prog mgr new prod, 76-78, eastern sales mgr, Riston Div, Photoprod Dept, 78-80, Europ sales mgr, 80-83, SALES DIR, AM RISTON DIV, E I DUPONT DE NEMOURS & CO, INC, 83- *Personal Data:* b Medford, Mass, Aug 30, 42; m 64; c 2. *Educ:* Tufts Univ, BS, 64; Univ Notre Dame, PhD(phys org chem), 68. *Mem:* Am Chem Soc; Sigma Xi; Am Electroplaters Soc; Inst Printed Circuits. *Res:* New photo polymers for extrusion into film form. *Mailing Add:* 7749 Willow Point Dr Falls Church VA 22042-7534

HICKMAN, JOHN ROY, ENVIRONMENTAL HEALTH. *Current Pos:* sci adv, Div Toxicol, Food Adv Bur, Food & Drug Directorate, Ottawa, Can, 67-74; chief planning & eval, Health Protection Br, 74-75, dir, Bur Chem Hazards, Environ Health Directorate, 75-79, DIR GEN, ENVIRON HEALTH DIRECTORATE, HEALTH & WELFARE, OTTAWA, CAN, 79- *Personal Data:* b Wellington, Eng, Apr 19, 34; m 64, Christine Elkington; c Sarah & Christopher. *Educ:* Univ London, BPharm, 53; Univ Aston, ACT, 55; Univ Birmingham, MSc, 56. *Honors & Awards:* NSF Environ Leadership Award. *Prof Exp:* Asst pharm, Queen Elizabeth Hosp, Birmingham, Eng, 53-54; asst toxicol, Univ Birmingham, 54-57; sci officer, Wantage Res Lab, Atomic Energy Auth, Harwell, 57-60, sr sci officer, 60-67. *Concurrent Pos:* Consult, Food & Agr Orgn, UN, Rome, 62-64; guest lectr, Food & Agr Orgn-Int Atomic Energy Agency, Sofia, Bulgaria, 68, Bangkok, Thailand & Bombay, India, 71; consult, WHO, Geneva, 68-69, Int Atomic Energy Agency, Vienna, 70 & Europ Nuclear Energy Agency, Orgn Econ Coop & Develop, 70; proj leader, Int Food Irradiation Proj, WGer, 71-74; consult, WHO, 74, Int Atomic Energy Agency, Rio de Janeiro, 75 & WHO, Copenhagen, 78; temp adv, UN Environ Prog, 79-82; pres, Intergovt forum chem safety, 97- *Res:* Health effects of environmental contaminants; industrial health; product safety. *Mailing Add:* Environ Health Directorate Health Protection Br Ottawa ON K1A 0L2 Can. Fax: 613-952-2206; E-Mail: roy_hickman@inet.hwc.ca

HICKMAN, MICHAEL, PHYCOLOGY, PALEOLIMNOLOGY. *Current Pos:* from asst prof to assoc prof, 70-81, PROF BOT, UNIV ALTA, 81- *Personal Data:* b Evesham, Eng, May 10, 43; m 68; c 2. *Educ:* Univ Western Ont, BSc, 66; Bristol Univ, PhD(biol), 70. *Prof Exp:* Res asst bot, Bristol Univ, 66-70. *Mem:* Can Bot Asn; Brit Phycol Soc; Brit Freshwater Biol Asn; Brit Ecol Soc; Phycol Soc Am. *Res:* Palaeolimnology, effects of holoceneclimate change upon Western Canadian lakes, particularly those of central Alberta and alpine and subalpine lakes of British Columbia; interpretations and reconstructions based upon pollen, diatom, chrysophyte stomato cyst, pigment and inoreanic geochemical analyses. *Mailing Add:* Biol Scis Univ Alta Edmonton AB T6G 2E9 Can

HICKMAN, ROY D, STATISTICS. *Current Pos:* instr educ, Iowa State Univ, 64-66, assoc statist, 66-67, from asst prof to assoc prof, 67-76, PROF STATIST, IOWA STATE UNIV, 76- *Personal Data:* b Kress, Tex, Sept 12, 32; m 55; c 2. *Educ:* Tex A&M Univ, BS, 54, MEd, 60; Iowa State Univ, PhD(educ), 67. *Prof Exp:* Foreign area training adv, Tex A&M Univ, 58-62, asst registr, 62-63. *Mem:* Am Statist Asn; Am Agr Econ Asn; Biomet Soc. *Res:* Research design and analysis of research projects in the social sciences; operational aspects of surveys; statistical methods. *Mailing Add:* 215 Store Ridge Dr Kerrville TX 70828

HICKMAN, ROY SCOTT, AEROSPACE & MECHANICAL ENGINEERING. *Current Pos:* CONSULT, 94- *Personal Data:* b Ponca City, Okla, Apr 13, 34; m 55; c Scott N, David J, Lisa R & Linda R. *Educ:* Univ Calif, BS, 57, PhD(mech eng), 62. *Prof Exp:* Mech engr, Lawrence Radiation Lab, Univ Calif, 57-60; sr res engr, Jet Propulsion Lab, Calif Inst Technol, 61-62; sr res scientist, Heliodyne Corp, 62-64; from asst prof to assoc prof aerospace eng, Univ Southern Calif, 64-68; assoc prof mech eng, Univ Calif, Santa Barbara, 68-77, prof mech & environ eng, 77-94. *Concurrent Pos:* Lectr, Univ Calif, Los Angeles, 62-63; consult, Aerophys Lab, Douglas Aircraft Co, 65-75. *Mem:* Nat Soc Prof Engrs; Am Soc Mech Engrs; Nat Acad Forensic Engrs; Soc Automotive Engrs. *Res:* Rarefied gas dynamics; heat transfer; spacecraft temperature control; cryogenics; Raman spectroscopy; electron beam; shock tubes; gas dynamics; accident analysis. *Mailing Add:* 921 E Rancho Rd Santa Barbara CA 93108. *E-Mail:* rscott@silcom.com

HICKMAN, WARREN DAVID, MATHEMATICS EDUCATION. *Current Pos:* PROF MATH & CHAIR DEPT, WESTMINSTER COL, 68- *Personal Data:* b Pittsburgh, Pa, Aug 20, 41; m 65; c 3. *Educ:* Capital Univ, Columbus, BS, 63; Case Western Univ, Cleveland, PhD(math), 74. *Mem:* Am Math Soc; Math Asn Am; Nat Coun Teachers Math. *Res:* Mathematics education; why past mathematics reforms have not succeeded; geometry; using the computer in teaching calculus. *Mailing Add:* Dept Math Westminster Col Box 14 Market St New Wilmington PA 16172-0001

HICKMOTT, THOMAS WARD, PHYSICS. *Current Pos:* RETIRED. *Personal Data:* b Kalamazoo, Mich, May 1, 29; m 59; c Donald D, Andrew J, Nancy A & Peter W. *Educ:* Yale Univ, BS, 50; Northwestern Univ, PhD(chem physics), 54. *Prof Exp:* Phys chemist, Res & Develop Ctr, Gen Elec Co, 54-66; phys chemist, IBM Components Div, IBM Corp, 66-70, Thomas J Watson Res Ctr, 70-92. *Mem:* Am Phys Soc. *Res:* Surface chemistry; gas-metal interactions; semiconductor surfaces; conduction in oxide films; properties of sputtered insulator films; semiconductor physics. *Mailing Add:* 2263 Preisman Dr Schenectady NY 12309

HICKNER, RICHARD ALLAN, ORGANIC POLYMER CHEMISTRY. *Current Pos:* From res chemist to sr res chemist, Dow Chem Co USA, 58-67, group leader, Designed Prod Dept, 67-72, develop specialist, 72-81, RES ASSOC, DOW CHEM CO USA, 81- *Personal Data:* b Baudette, Minn, June 29, 32; m 56; c 7. *Educ:* St John's Univ, Minn, BA, 54; Purdue Univ, MS, 56, PhD(org chem), 58. *Mem:* Am Chem Soc. *Res:* Heterocyclic vinyl compounds and their reactions; reactions of urea with polyamines and alkanolamines; urethane coatings; thermoset adhesives; organosulfur chemistry; radiation cure of coatings, printing inks and adhesives. *Mailing Add:* 119 Bougainvillea St Lake Jackson TX 77566

HICKOK, LESLIE GEORGE, MUTATION SELECTION, PLANT GENETICS. *Current Pos:* from asst prof to assoc prof, 79-86, PROF BOT, UNIV TENN, 86- *Personal Data:* b Schenectady, NY, July 15, 46; m 67; c 1. *Educ:* Murray State Univ, BA, 69; Ohio Univ, MS, 71; Univ Mass, PhD(bot), 75. *Prof Exp:* Asst prof bot, Miss State Univ, 74-78. *Mem:* Am Soc Plant Physiologists; AAAS; Sigma Xi; Am Fern Soc. *Res:* Genetics and cytogenetics; mutation induction and selection; stress physiology; teaching biology. *Mailing Add:* Dept Bot Univ Tenn Knoxville TN 37996-0003. *E-Mail:* lhickok@utk.edu

HICKOK, ROBERT BAKER, HYDROLOGY & WATER RESOURCES. *Current Pos:* RETIRED. *Personal Data:* b Ypsilanti, Mich, Apr 18, 10; m 32; c 2. *Educ:* Mich State Univ, BS, 32. *Prof Exp:* Jr engr soil erosion control, civilian conserv corps, State Dept Agr, Wis, 33-34; asst engr, soil conserv serv, USDA, 34-35, assoc res engr, 35-37, suprvr, soil & water res, coop with Purdue Univ, 37-52, watershed hydrol res, southwestern region, 52-56; proj engr, Holmes & Narver, Inc, 56-60; air res & develop command, Ballistic Missiles Div, US Dept Air Force, 60-61; dir watershed eng res, southwest br, soil & water conserv res div, Agr Res Serv, USDA, 62-68; consult land & water resources develop & mgt, 68-83. *Concurrent Pos:* US Comt, Int Comm Irrig, Drainage & Flood Control; mem, Southwest Inter-Agency Comn River Basin Planning. *Mem:* AAAS; Am Soc Agr Engrs; Am Soc Civil Engrs; Soil & Water Conserv Soc; Sigma Xi. *Res:* Soil and water resources; development planning research; facilities site selection; management. *Mailing Add:* 8290 Coleman St Riverside CA 92504

HICKOK, ROBERT L, JR, PLASMA DIAGNOSTICS. *Current Pos:* FROM ASSOC PROF TO PROF ELECTROPHYS, RENSSELAER POLYTECH INST, 71- *Personal Data:* b Schenectady, NY, Feb 25, 29; m 49; c 3. *Educ:* Rensselaer Polytech Inst, BS, 51, PhD(physics), 56; Dartmouth Col, MA, 53. *Honors & Awards:* Fel, Am Phys Soc; fel, Inst Elec & Electronics Engrs. *Prof Exp:* Fel, Yale Univ, 56-58; res assoc, Mobil Res & Develop Corp, 58-71. *Mem:* Am Phys Soc; Inst Elec & Electronics Engrs; Nuclear & Plasma Sci Soc; Sigma Xi. *Res:* Plasma and nuclear physics; development of controlled thermonuclear fusion energy source. *Mailing Add:* Electrophys Div Rensselaer Polytech Inst Troy NY 12181

HICKOK, ROBERT LEE, physical chemistry, materials science, for more information see previous edition

HICKS, ARTHUR M, ORGANIC CHEMISTRY. *Current Pos:* from assoc prof to prof chem, 50-86, chmn, Div Sci & Math, 66-86, EMER PROF CHEM, LA GRANGE COL, 86- *Personal Data:* b Atlanta, Ga, Nov 29, 17; m 43, Catherine Werner; c Claude Bernard, Frank Sharp, Joseph Eugene &

Sue Meredith. *Educ:* Emory Univ, AB, 40, MS, 41; Auburn Univ, PhD(org chem), 65. *Prof Exp:* Asst, Emory Univ, 39-41 & Rutgers Univ, 41-43; chemist, Johnson & Johnson, 43-45 & Graton & Knight Co, 45-50. *Mem:* Am Chem Soc. *Res:* Organic synthesis. *Mailing Add:* 302 Park Ave La Grange GA 30240-3032

HICKS, BRUCE BOUNDY, ATMOSPHERIC PHYSICS. *Current Pos:* dir, Atmospheric Turbulence & Diffusion Div, Oak Ridge, Tenn, 81-90, DIR AIR RESOURCES LAB, NAT OCEANIC & ATMOSPHERIC ADMIN, SILVER SPRING, MD, 90- *Personal Data:* b Melbourne, Australia, June 24, 40; m 66; c 2. *Educ:* Univ Tasmania, BS, 62; Melbourne Univ, MS, 68. *Honors & Awards:* David Syme Res Award, Univ Melbourne, 72. *Prof Exp:* Exp officer atmospheric physics, Div Meteorol Physics, Commonwealth Sci & Indust Res Orgn, 62-68, from res scientist to sr res scientist, 68-73; meteorologist, Argonne Nat Lab, 73-76, sect head atmospheric physics, Radiol & Environ Res Div, 76-81. *Concurrent Pos:* Vis res assoc, Biol & Med Res Div, 65-66 & Radiol Physics Div, Argonne Nat Lab, 70-71; chmn, Task Group Atmospheric Chem, Nat Acid Precipitation Assessment Prog, 85- *Mem:* Royal Meteorol Soc; Am Meteorol Soc; Am Geophys Union. *Res:* Micrometeorology; air-surface exchange; planetary boundary layer studies; air quality. *Mailing Add:* 2416 Artesian Lane Bowie MD 20716

HICKS, CHARLES ROBERT, APPLIED STATISTICS. *Current Pos:* RETIRED. *Personal Data:* b Syracuse, NY, Apr 7, 20; m 42; c 3. *Educ:* Syracuse Univ, AB, 42, MS, 44, PhD(educ), 53. *Honors & Awards:* Brumbaugh Award, Am Soc Qual Control, 57. *Prof Exp:* Asst physics, Syracuse Univ, 42-44; qual control engr, Eastman Kodak, 44-46; instr math & educ, Syracuse Univ, 46-53; asst prof math, Purdue Univ, West Lafayette, 53-57, assoc prof math & statist, 57-60, asst dean, Sch Sci Educ & Humanitites, 60-64, head, Educ Dept, 64-74, dir teacher educ, 70-74, prof educ, 70-90, prof statist, 74-90. *Mem:* Fel Am Soc Qual Control (vpres, 69-71); Am Statist Asn; Comp & Int Educ Soc; Biomet Soc. *Res:* Quality control. *Mailing Add:* 2741 N Salisbury St West Lafayette IN 47906

HICKS, DALE R, PLANT BREEDING, STATISTICS. *Current Pos:* from asst prof to assoc prof, 68-76, PROF AGRON, UNIV MINN, ST PAUL, 76-, EXTEN AGRONOMIST, 68- *Personal Data:* b Odin, Ill, Oct 10, 38; m 60; c 3. *Educ:* Univ Ill, BS, 60, MS, 66, PhD(agron), 68. *Prof Exp:* Asst farm adv, Univ Ill, 64-65, teaching asst statist, 66-68. *Mem:* Fel Am Soc Agron; Crop Sci Soc Am. *Res:* Growth regulator effects on yield; genotypes and yield of both corn and soybeans; production practices and maximum yield. *Mailing Add:* 3590 Snelling Ave N St Paul MN 55112

HICKS, DARRELL LEE, RIGOROUS APPLIED & COMPUTATIONAL MATHEMATICS, COMPUTATIONAL SCIENCE. *Current Pos:* dir, Ctr Exp Comput, 87-88, PROF MATH SCI, MICH TECH UNIV, 83- *Personal Data:* b Clovis, NMex, July 3, 37; m 79, 85, Lorie M Liebrock; c April L & Jason C. *Educ:* Univ NMex, BS, 61, PhD(math), 69. *Prof Exp:* Mathematician, Air Force Weapons Labs, 62-69 & Sandia Labs, 69-81; prof math, Univ Colo, Denver, 81-83. *Concurrent Pos:* Consult, Idaho Nat Eng Labs, 82-87, KMS Fusion Inc, Ann Arbor, 83-88 & Sandia Nat Labs, 91-; assoc ed, J Appl Math & Comput, 85; vis scholar, NSF, Res Parallel Comput, Rice Univ, Houston, Tex, 89-90; consult, Liebroch-Hicks Res, 94- *Mem:* Math Asn Am; Am Math Soc; Soc Indust & Appl Math; Am Phys Soc; Am Statist Asn; Sigma Xi; Am Acad Mech; Am Nuclear Soc; Asn Comput Mach; Int Asn Math & Comput Modelling; Int Asn Math & Comput Simulation; Int Soc Sci & Tech Develop; Soc Comput Simulation. *Res:* Analysis of the equations of material dynamics; rigorous applied mathematical and computational sciences; mathematical modelling; serial and parallel algorithms for material dynamics. *Mailing Add:* Dept Sci Mich Tech Univ Houghton MI 49931. *Fax:* 906-337-5817; *E-Mail:* dlhicks@math.mtu.edu

HICKS, DAVID L, PHYSIOLOGICAL ECOLOGY, ORNITHOLOGY. *Current Pos:* PROF BIOL, WHITWORTH COL, WASH, 67- *Personal Data:* b Alliance, Ohio, July 20, 35; m 56; c 3. *Educ:* Cascade Col, BA, 56; Univ Ga, MS, 65, PhD(zool), 67. *Mem:* Ecol Soc Am; Am Ornithologists Union; Cooper Ornith Soc. *Res:* Physiological effects and ecological significance of depletion and utilization of adipose tissue in migrating passerine birds. *Mailing Add:* Dept Biol Whitworth Col 300 W Hawthorne Rd Spokane WA 99251-0001

HICKS, DONALD GAIL, ANALYTICAL CHEMISTRY, INORGANIC CHEMISTRY. *Current Pos:* ASSOC PROF CHEM, GA STATE UNIV, 65- *Personal Data:* b Quanah, Tex, Feb 11, 34; m 55; c 2. *Educ:* Murray State Univ, BS, 55; Univ Ky, MS, 58; Univ Tenn, PhD(analytical chem), 65. *Prof Exp:* Asst prof chem, The Citadel, 58-59 & Murray State Univ, 59-65. *Mem:* AAAS; Am Chem Soc; fel Am Inst Chemists; Nat Sci Teachers Asn; Soc Appl Spectros. *Res:* Atomic absorption and emission flame spectrophotometry; trisubstituted group V element coordination compounds; solvent extraction; cyclic group V element ligands; mechanism of decomposition in flames. *Mailing Add:* Dept Chem Ga State Univ 33 Gilmer St SE Atlanta GA 30303-3083

HICKS, EDWARD JAMES, immunology, preventive medicine, for more information see previous edition

HICKS, ELIJA MAXIE, JR, ORGANIC POLYMER CHEMISTRY. *Current Pos:* RETIRED. *Personal Data:* b Florence, SC, Aug 26, 20; m 44, Joanne Sly; c Elija J & Joanne (Robblee). *Educ:* Furman Univ, BS, 41; Princeton Univ, MS, 43, PhD(chem), 44. *Hon Degrees:* LLD, Furman Univ, 77. *Prof Exp:* Res chemist, E I du Pont De Nemours & Co, Inc, Va, 44-47, res supvr, 47-50, tech supvt, NY, 50-53, mfg supvt, Va, 53-57, tech serv mgr, 57-59, orlon tech dir, 59-72, dir, Nylon Mfg Div, Textile Fibers Dept, 72-73, dir, Int Develop & Opers Div, 73-76, dir manufacture, Textile Fibers Dept, 76-81. *Concurrent Pos:* Consult, 81-90. *Mem:* Fel AAAS; Am Chem Soc; NY Acad Sci; fel Textile Inst London. *Res:* Steroid synthesis; cellulose chemistry; synthetic fiber technology. *Mailing Add:* 4777 Ringwood Meadows The Meadows Sarasota FL 34235-7728

HICKS, ELLIS ARDEN, ZOOLOGY. *Current Pos:* RETIRED. *Personal Data:* b Lamoni, Iowa, Feb 12, 15; m 46; c 1. *Educ:* Iowa State Col, BS, 38, MS, 40, PhD(econ zool), 47. *Prof Exp:* Exten asst wildlife conserv, Iowa State Univ, 38-41, exten assoc, 46, from instr to prof zool & entom, 47-76, prof zool, 76-81. *Res:* Arthropod fauna of bird nests; insect-mite symbioses, acarology. *Mailing Add:* 3012 Woodland St Ames IA 50014. *Fax:* 515-292-2431

HICKS, GARLAND FISHER, JR, MICROBIOLOGY. *Current Pos:* ASSOC PROF BIOL, VALPARAISO UNIV, 74- *Personal Data:* b Southampton, NY, Nov 19, 45; m 67. *Educ:* St Lawrence Univ, BS, 67; Mich State Univ, PhD(microbiol), 75. *Mem:* Am Soc Microbiol. *Res:* Chestnut canker disease; natural areas of west Tennessee. *Mailing Add:* Dept Biol Valparaiso Univ Valparaiso IN 46383-6493

HICKS, HAROLD E(UGENE), CHEMICAL ENGINEERING. *Current Pos:* RETIRED. *Personal Data:* b Minneapolis, Minn, Jan 20, 19; m 41, 90, Virginia Calvin; c Barbara A (Young), Charlotte A (Silvia), David H & Douglas E. *Educ:* Univ Minn, BChE, 41. *Prof Exp:* Res chemist, Hercules Powder Co, 41-54, oper supvr, Hercules, Inc, 54-57, safety supvr, 57-62, resin supvr, 62-64, plant supt, 64-66, plant mgr, 66-81. *Concurrent Pos:* Tech adv, Dawood Hercules Chem Ltd, Pakistan, 76-78. *Mem:* Am Chem Soc; Am Inst Chem Engrs. *Res:* Ammoniation; chlorination; hydrogenation; polymerization; hydrogen manufacture; industrial health and safety; labor relations; plant management. *Mailing Add:* 133 Shore Rush Dr St Simons Island GA 31522. *Fax:* 912-638-6700

HICKS, HARRY GROSS, nuclear chemistry; deceased, see previous edition for last biography

HICKS, HERALINE ELAINE, craniofacial biology, teratology, for more information see previous edition

HICKS, JACKSON EARL, WASTEWATER TREATMENT, INCINERATION. *Current Pos:* chemist, Tenn Eastman Co, 67-69, sr chemist, Acid Div, Anal Develop Lab, 69-70, sr chemist & dir, Serv Anal Lab, 70-76, dept supt, Water & Waste Treatment Dept, 76-93, DIR, HEALTH SAFETY & ENVIRON SERV DIV, TENN EASTMAN DIV, EASTMAN CHEM CO, 93- *Personal Data:* b Fruitland Park, Fla, Dec 12, 34; m 58, Nancy Bennett; c Margaret E. *Educ:* Erskine Col, BA, 58; Univ Va, MS, 60; Ga Inst Technol, PhD(anal chem), 67. *Prof Exp:* Chemist, WVa Pulp & Paper Co, Va, 60-63. *Mem:* Am Soc Testing & Mat; Am Chem Soc; Sigma Xi. *Res:* Application of organic complexing reagents to analytical chemistry, especially photometric titrations, atomic absorption spectrophotometry, gas chromatography and spectrophotometric methods; analytical application of infrared spectroscopy; analytical aspects of air and water pollution; biological wastewater treatment; waste disposal; waste minimization; quality management. *Mailing Add:* 2416 E Stone Dr Kingsport TN 37660. *Fax:* 423-224-7254

HICKS, JANICE MARIE, LASER METHODS IN CHEMISTRY, SURFACES. *Current Pos:* CLARE BOOTH LUCE ASST PROF CHEM, GEORGETOWN UNIV, 89- *Personal Data:* b Baltimore, Md, July 28, 58. *Educ:* Bryn Mawr Col, AB, 80; Columbia Univ, MS, 82, MPhil, 85, PhD(chem), 86. *Prof Exp:* Teaching fel, Dept Chem & Physics, Univ Pa, 86-89. *Mem:* Am Chem Soc; Am Phys Soc; Am Geophys Soc; Asn Women Sci. *Res:* Interested in the structure of chemical environments, especially surfaces and liquids; application of lasers in surface chemistry; ice surface chemistry; chirality. *Mailing Add:* Dept Chem Georgetown Univ 1421 37th St NW Washington DC 20057-0001. *Fax:* 202-687-6209; *E-Mail:* jhicks@guvax.georgetown.edu

HICKS, JIMMIE LEE, ADMINISTRATION. *Current Pos:* assoc dean, Clin Rotations, 83-92, PROF PHYSIOL, COL OSTEOP MED, PAC, 83-, ASSOC DEAN BASIC SCI, 92- *Personal Data:* b 1936; m, Shirley A Roll; c Lori Lee & James John. *Educ:* Colo State Univ, PhD(physiol-biophys), 71. *Prof Exp:* From asst prof to assoc prof physiol, Univ Health Sci, Col Osteop Med, Kansas City, 71-83. *Concurrent Pos:* Instr Biol, Col St Thomas, St Paul, Minn, 63-67. *Mem:* Am Physiol Soc. *Res:* Environmental physiology with emphasis on altitudinal and temperature adaptations. *Mailing Add:* Western Univ Health Sci Col Osteopathic Med Col Plaza Pomona CA 91766-1889

HICKS, JOCELYN MURIEL, LABORATORY MEDICINE, PATHOLOGY. *Current Pos:* from asst prof to assoc prof, 72-81, PROF, GEORGE WASHINGTON UNIV MED CTR, 81-; CHILDRENS HOSP NAT MED CTR, WASHINGTON, 90-, DIR CLIN SUPPORT SERV. *Personal Data:* b Leamington Spa, Warwickshire, Eng, Aug 17, 37; m 59, 73, Melvin Blecher. *Educ:* Univ London, BS, 59, MSc, 62; Georgetown Univ, PhD, 71. *Honors & Awards:* Joseph H Roe Award, Am Asn Clin Chem, 76, Bernard Gerulat Mem Award, 83, Fisher Award, 84, Van Slyke Award, 88, Miriam Reiner Award, 91 & Outstanding Contrib to Clin Chem Award, 93;

Kone Award, Asn Clin Biochemists, 87. *Prof Exp:* Dir clin chem, Childrens Hosp Nat Med Ctr, Washington, 71-75, chmn, Dept Lab Med, 75-90. *Concurrent Pos:* Clin affil, Cath Univ Am, 82-; mem prof staff, Hosp Sick Children, Washington, 84-; consult, Eastman Kodak Co & Miles Diagnostics. *Mem:* Am Asn Clin Chem; Acad Clin Lab Physicians & Scientists. *Res:* Clinical chemistry. *Mailing Add:* Childrens Nat Med Ctr 111 Michigan Ave NW Washington DC 20010

HICKS, JOHN W, III, AGRICULTURAL ECONOMICS. *Current Pos:* from asst prof to assoc prof, 50-60, exec asst to pres, 55-82, actg pres, 82-83, sr pres, 83-87, PROF AGR ECON, PURDUE UNIV, WEST LAFAYETTE, 60- *Personal Data:* b Sydney, Australia, Dec 2, 21; US citizen; m 47; c 8. *Educ:* Mass State Col, BS, 46; Purdue Univ, MS, 48, PhD(agr econ), 50. *Hon Degrees:* DEd, Vincennes Univ, 84. *Prof Exp:* Instr agr econ, Univ Mass, 46-47. *Concurrent Pos:* Dir, Ind Comn State Tax & Financing Policy, 53-55; dir, Comt Inst Coop, Coun of 10 & Univ Chicago, 60-62; chmn, Ind Post High Sch Study Comn, 61-63; secy, Bd Trustees, Purdue Univ, Lafayette, 72-73; actg comnr voc & tech educ, State of Ind, 87. *Mem:* Am Agr Econ Asn; Sigma Xi. *Res:* Political economy; higher education. *Mailing Add:* 132 Mohican Ct West Lafayette IN 47906

HICKS, KENNETH WARD, CHEMICAL KINETICS, BIOINORGANIC REACTIONS. *Current Pos:* PROF & DEPT HEAD PHYS CHEM, NORFOLK STATE UNIV, 94- *Personal Data:* b Cleveland, Ohio, Sept 5, 40; m 71, Beverly A Pettigrew; c Nedra & Kevin. *Educ:* Miami Univ, BA, 62, MS, 64; Howard Univ, PhD(phys chem), 69. *Prof Exp:* Postdoctoral assoc, Univ Calif, San Diego, 68-70; From asst prof to prof chem, Eastern Mich Univ, 70-85; prof, NC A&T State Univ, 86-94. *Concurrent Pos:* Vis assoc prof, Univ Utah, 77-78 & Battelle Nat Lab, 89; staff assoc, NSF, 81-82; consult, NIH, NIGMS, MARC, 82-87. *Mem:* Am Chem Soc; Nat Asn Black Chemists & Chem Engrs; Sigma Xi. *Res:* Oxidation of dimeric Mo(V) complexes by MnO4, VO2 and Ce(IV); prep and kinetics of bioinorganic dimeric Mo(V) model complexes. *Mailing Add:* Dept Chem Norfold State Univ Norfolk VA 23504

HICKS, KEVIN B, CARBOHYDRATE CHEMISTRY, CARBOHYDRATE BIOCHEMISTRY *Current Pos:* res chemist, 80-85, LEAD SCIENTIST, PLANT SCI RES, EASTERN REGIONAL RES CTR, USDA, 85- *Personal Data:* b Ironton, Mo, Apr 3, 52; m 78. *Educ:* Univ Mo, BS, 74, MS, 76, PhD(biochem), 79. *Prof Exp:* Assoc res fel, Dairy Res Found, 79-80. *Concurrent Pos:* Mem exec comt, Div Carbohydrate Chem, Am Chem Soc, 83, exec secy, 85- *Mem:* Am Chem Soc (secy, 84-85); AAAS. *Res:* Chemistry and biochemistry of carbohydrates; conversion of known carbohydrates into new and potentially useful forms; new analytical methods especially helpful for evaluation, separation and identification of sugars and related bio-molecules; preparative of biomolecules. *Mailing Add:* Eastern Regional Res Ctr 600 E Mermaid Lane Wyndmoor PA 19038

HICKS, PATRICIA FAIN, BIOLOGICAL CHEMISTRY, COMMUNICATION SCIENCE. *Current Pos:* RETIRED. *Personal Data:* b Brownwood, Tex, Dec 16, 27; m 66. *Educ:* Univ Tex, BA, 47; Tex Tech Col, MS, 51, PhD(biol chem), 53. *Prof Exp:* Anal chemist, Mallinckrodt, Inc, 48-50; mem staff mass spectrometry, Los Alamos Sci Lab, 53-55; asst prof chem, Tex Tech Col, 55-57; tech ed, Mallinckrodt Inc, 57-70, sr res assoc, 70-71, asst to dir pub rels, 71-82, dir pub rels, 82-89. *Concurrent Pos:* Robert Welch Found grant, Houston, Tex, 56-57. *Mem:* Am Chem Soc; Sigma Xi. *Res:* Fine chemicals; technical writing. *Mailing Add:* 12930 Ferntop Lane St Louis MO 63141-6135. *E-Mail:* osceo@inlink.com

HICKS, ROBERT EUGENE, neuropsychology, psychopharmacology, for more information see previous edition

HICKS, ROSS S, PLASMA PHYSICS. *Current Pos:* PROF, DEPT PHYSICS, UNIV MASS, 81- *Personal Data:* b Melbourne, Australia, Oct 21, 45. *Educ:* Univ Australia, BS, 68, MS, 72. *Mem:* Am Phys Soc. *Mailing Add:* Dept Physics Univ Mass Amherst MA 01003. *Fax:* 413-545-4884

HICKS, SAMUEL PENDLETON, NEUROPATHOLOGY. *Current Pos:* PROF PATH, SCH MED, UNIV MICH, ANN ARBOR, 62- *Personal Data:* b Bryn Athyn, Pa, Nov 21, 13; m 41; c 2. *Educ:* Univ Pa, AB, 36, MD, 40. *Honors & Awards:* Max Weinstein Award, Cerebral Palsy, 51. *Prof Exp:* Assoc prof path, Sch Med, Georgetown Univ, 47-48; pathologist, New Eng Deaconess Hosp, 48-62; assoc prof path, Harvard Med Sch, 52-62. *Concurrent Pos:* Head dept path & consult neuropathologist, Nat Naval Med Ctr, 47-48; pathologist-in-chief, Peter Bent Brigham Hosp, Boston, 50-51. *Mem:* Am Asn Neuropathologists; AMA; Am Acad Neurol; Soc Neurosci; Am Soc Human Genetics. *Res:* Environmental and genetic factors in morphologic and functional development of nervous system; neuropathology; radiobiology. *Mailing Add:* Univ Mich Med Ctr Ann Arbor MI 48109-0602

HICKS, SONJA ELAINE, BIOCHEMISTRY. *Current Pos:* asst prof, Wellesley Col, 68-74, dir molecular biol prog, 70-74, chmn dept, 74-77, ASSOC PROF CHEM, WELLESLEY COL, 74- *Personal Data:* b Machiasport, Maine, May 25, 40. *Educ:* Univ Maine, BS, 62; Univ Mich, PhD(biochem), 66. *Prof Exp:* Fel biochem, Woods Hole Oceanog Inst, 66-67; res assoc, Mass Inst Technol, 67-68. *Concurrent Pos:* Asst prof pediat, Harvard Med Sch, 71-73; res scientist biochem, Mass Gen Hosp, 71-73; chmn, Premed Adv Comt, Wellesley Col, 73- *Mem:* Sigma Xi. *Res:* Studies of biochemical effects of prostaglandins on membrane structure and function; development of new biochemical clinical tests. *Mailing Add:* Dept Chem Wellesley Col Wellesley MA 02181-8203

HICKS, STEACY DOPP, PHYSICAL OCEANOGRAPHY, TIDES & SEA LEVEL. *Current Pos:* RETIRED. *Personal Data:* b Detroit, Mich, Apr 19, 25; m 48, Lynn Gray; c Stephen, Carol (Greene) & Beth (Oden). *Educ:* Univ Calif, Los Angeles, BA, 50; Scripps Inst Oceanog, MS, 52. *Honors & Awards:* Silver Medal Res Phys Oceanog, US Dept Com. *Prof Exp:* From instr to asst prof phys oceanog, Univ RI, 52-62; phys oceanogr, Nat Ocean Surv, Nat Oceanic & Atmospheric Admin, 62-65 & 71-90, chief, Oceanog Div, 65-70, chief, Oceanog Res Group, 70-71. *Concurrent Pos:* Sci fel, US Dept Com, 64-65; assoc prof lectr oceanog, George Washington Univ, 66-90; US Naval War Col, 69-70. *Res:* Physical oceanography; tides and sea level variations. *Mailing Add:* 20510 Falcons Landing Circle No 1305 Sterling VA 20165-7502

HICKS, T PHILIP, SENSORY NEUROPHARMACOLOGY, NEUROPHYSIOLOGY. *Current Pos:* from asst prof to assoc prof med physiol, Sch Med, 81-88, ASSOC PROF FAC ARTS & SCI, UNIV NC, GREENSBORO, 88- *Personal Data:* b Fredericton, NB, Dec 30, 52; m 75; c 1. *Educ:* Carleton Univ, BA, 73; Dalhousie Univ, BSc, 76; Univ BC, PhD(physiol), 79. *Prof Exp:* Fel, neurobiol, Max Planck Inst Biophys Chem, 79-81; fel, vision res, Inst Equilibrium Res, Gifu Univ, Japan, 81. *Mem:* Can Physiol Soc; Can Fedn Biol Soc; AAAS; Int Brain Res Orgn; Soc Neurosci; Brit Physiol Soc. *Res:* Characterization by pharmacological techniques and neurochemical methods of receptors for endogenous synaptic transmitters in ascending sensory pathways, and studies of their physiological roles using electrophysiological procedures. *Mailing Add:* Psychol Univ NC 1000 Spring Garden Greensboro NC 27412-0001

HICKS, TROY L, MATHEMATICS. *Current Pos:* from asst prof to assoc prof, 67-78, PROF MATH, UNIV MO, ROLLA, 78- *Personal Data:* b Pampa, Tex, Sept 30, 32; m 55; c 2. *Educ:* Southwest Mo State Col, BS, 57; Univ Mo, Columbia, MEd, 60; Univ Kans, MA, 61; Univ Cincinnati, PhD(math), 65. *Honors & Awards:* Cert Meritorious Serv, Math Asn Am, 88. *Prof Exp:* Teacher, Rural Sch, Mo, 49-53; asst prof math, Col Sch of the Ozarks, 57-60; instr, Univ Cincinnati, 61-65; assoc prof, Ill State Univ, 65-67. *Mem:* Am Math Soc; Math Asn Am; Am Asn Univ Prof; Sigma Xi. *Res:* Topology and functional analysis. *Mailing Add:* Dept Math Univ Mo Rolla MO 65401-0249

HICKS, WILLIAM B(RUCE), CHEMICAL ENGINEERING. *Current Pos:* Res chem engr, Cent Res Dept, Ohio, 46-51, proj specialist, Org Div, Develop Dept, Mo, 51-56, develop mgr, 56-65, dir, Int Org Chem, Europe, 69-71, dir growth, Int Div, 70-73, dir, Int Planning & Admin, 73-79, DIR, PROCESS CHEM & PHOSPHORUS, MONSANTO CO, 79- *Personal Data:* b Washington Court House, Ohio, May 9, 25; m 47; c 2. *Educ:* Univ Ill, BS, 45. *Mem:* Am Chem Soc; Soc Plastics Indust; Com Develop Asn. *Res:* Polymers; plastics; surface coatings; adhesives; paper chemistry; commercial chemical development. *Mailing Add:* 114 Augusta St Simons Island GA 31522-2437

HICKSON, DONALD ANDREW, SURFACE CHEMISTRY, PETROLEUM CHEMISTRY. *Current Pos:* RETIRED. *Personal Data:* b Windsor, Ont, July 28, 31; m 74; c 5. *Educ:* Wayne State Univ, BS, 53; Iowa State Univ, PhD(phys chem), 58. *Prof Exp:* Chemist, Ames Lab, AEC, Chevron Res Co, 52-58, res chemist catalysis, Calif Res Corp, 58-65, Chevron Res Co, 65-70, sr res assoc, Chevron Oil Field Res Co, 72-75, sr res assoc, 75-86; consult, W R Grace Co, 87-88 & Leybold Mat Inc, 89-93. *Concurrent Pos:* Tech training consult, vacuum metall, Soc Petrol Chemists, trainer; teaching credentials, San Francisco State Univ, sci & math, 90, instr credentials chem, math, 90. *Mem:* Am Chem Soc; Clays & Clay Mineral Soc; Int Zeolite Asn; Asn Supv & Curric Develop; Am Soc Training & Develop. *Res:* Electrochemical phenomena at interphases; electrophillic properties and structure of mixed-oxide catalysts; infrared spectroscopy of solids and gas-solid interactions; petroleum processing catalysis; in-situ processing of carbonaceous materials and assisted recovery methods; hydrocarbon catalyst and zeolite catalyst preparation, formulation and evaluation; aerogal, synthetic clay synthesis and application; electron-beam vacuum metallurgy. *Mailing Add:* 189 Carlisle Way Benicia CA 94510-1615

HICKSON, JAMES FORBES, protein metabolism, sports nutrition; deceased, see previous edition for last biography

HICKSON, JOHN LEFEVER, SUGAR CHEMISTRY. *Current Pos:* RETIRED. *Personal Data:* b Milford, NH, June 17, 16; m 38, 71, Doris I McFadden; c Carolyn J (Brown), Janet S (Mueller) & Linda D (Barns). *Educ:* Ohio Wesleyan Univ, BA, 37; Purdue Univ, MS, 52, PhD(biochem), 53. *Prof Exp:* Chemist, Nat Aniline Div, Allied Chem & Dye Corp, 38-46; asst prof chem, Kans Wesleyan Univ, 46-48; chemist, Ind State Chemist's Labs, 48-50; Corn Industs fel, 50-53; asst to pres, Int Sugar Res Found, Inc, 53-60, vpres & sci dir, 60-68, vpres & dir res, 68-71; sr assoc, Sidney M Cantor Assocs, Inc, 71; sci dir, Cigar Res Coun, 71-75, consult, Int Sugar Res Found, Inc, 74-77. *Mem:* Emer mem Am Chem Soc; hon mem Am Inst Chem (pres, 66-67). *Res:* Chemical, physical, physiological and food technological properties of sugars and oligosaccharides as well as pleasure and health aspects of cigar smoking. *Mailing Add:* 1045 Linn-Hipsher Rd Marion OH 43302-8224

HIDA, GEORGE T, COMBUSTION SYNTHESIS, MECHANICAL ALLOYING. *Current Pos:* chief res scientist, 88-91, DIR TECHNOL, BENCHMARK STRUCT CERAMICS, 91- *Personal Data:* m 75, Rodica Silvia; c Sven & Sever. *Educ:* Polytech Inst Bucharest, BS, 69, MS, 70; Univ Bucharest, MS, 72; Technion Israel Inst Technol, PhD(sci technol), 87. *Prof Exp:* Mfg eng glass technol, Kinescope Tubes Plant, Bucharest, 70-73; sr res scientist fine ceramics, Res Inst Electrotech Indust, 73-82; sr scientist non-oxide ceramics, Israel Inst Ceramics & Silicates, 82-86, asst prof mat sci & engr technol, 86-87; res assoc prof combustion synthetics, State Univ NY, 87-88. *Mem:* NY Acad Sci. *Res:* Development of high performance, reliable ceramic materials and energy saving technologies to synthesize these and process the powders to high performance structures. *Mailing Add:* 235 Aero Dr Cheektowaga NY 14225. *Fax:* 716-565-1064

HIDALGO, HENRY, FLUID MECHANICS, AEROSPACE SCIENCE. *Current Pos:* MEM TECH STAFF, ROCKWELL INT CORP, 84- *Personal Data:* b Ecuador, Sept 1, 22; US citizen; m 47; c 4. *Educ:* Tri-State Col, BS, 49; Mass Inst Technol, MS, 51. *Prof Exp:* Res engr, United Aircraft Res Lab, United Aircraft Corp, 51-54; tech engr, Small Engine Dept, Gen Elec Co, 54-56; sr engr, Avco-Everett Res Lab, Avco Corp, 56-60, prin engr, 60-62; prin engr, Heliodyne Corp, 62-64; staff mem, Inst Defense Anal, 64-81; mgr advan technol & mission anal, Advan Systs Div, Gould Advan Technol Ctr, 81-84. *Concurrent Pos:* Consult, Univ Mich & Stanford Res Inst, 62 & Atomics Int Div, NAm Rockwell Corp, 63-64. *Mem:* Assoc fel Am Inst Aeronaut & Astronaut. *Res:* Ballistic missile defense technology and systems; air to air warfare technology and systems; naval warfare technology and system; directed energy technology and advanced space systems; aeronautical and astronautical engineering. *Mailing Add:* 3750 N Woodrow St Arlington VA 22207

HIDORE, JOHN J, PHYSICAL GEOGRAPHY, CLIMATOLOGY. *Current Pos:* dept head, 80-87, PROF GEOG, UNIV NC, GREENSBORO, 80- *Personal Data:* b Cedar Falls, Iowa, July 6, 32; m 96, Suzanne Cole; c John W & Jill Helen. *Educ:* Univ Northern Iowa, BA, 54; Univ Iowa, MA, 58, PhD(geog), 60. *Prof Exp:* Instr geog, Univ Wis, 60-62; assoc prof, Okla State Univ, 62-66; from assoc prof to prof geog, Ind Univ, Bloomington, 66-80, chmn dept, 68-71. *Concurrent Pos:* Vis prof, Cent Wash State Col, 65, 69 & 73, Univ Ife, Nigeria, 71-72, Univ Khartoum, Sudan, 74-75 & Ben Gurion Univ Negev, 78. *Mem:* Asn Am Geog; Am Meteorol Soc; Sigma Xi; Am Geog Soc. *Res:* Hydroclimatology; climatology. *Mailing Add:* Dept Geog Univ NC Greensboro NC 27412. *Fax:* 910-334-5864; *E-Mail:* hidorej@durkheim.uncg.edu

HIDU, HERBERT, MARINE ECOLOGY. *Current Pos:* RETIRED. *Personal Data:* b Bridgeport, Conn, Dec 18, 31; m 57; c 3. *Educ:* Univ Conn, BS, 58; Pa State Univ, MS, 60; Rutgers Univ, PhD(zool), 67. *Prof Exp:* Fisheries res biologist, Biol Lab, US Bur Com Fisheries, Conn, 60-63; asst res prof, Chesapeake Biol Lab, Univ Md, Solomons, 67-70; asst prof oceanog & zool, Ira C Darling Ctr, Univ Maine, Walpole, 70-74, assoc prof oceanog, 74-91. *Concurrent Pos:* Proj coordr, Nat Park Serv grant, Univ Md, 69-70; prin investr, NSF grant, Univ Maine, 71-72 & 80-82, proj coordr, Sea Grant Coherent Areas Award, 71-78. *Mem:* Nat Shellfisheries Asn (pres, 80-81); Atlantic Estuarine Res Soc; New Eng Estuarine Res Soc. *Res:* Marine shellfish biology and ecology, especially the ecology and physiology of recruitment in bivalve mollusks; shellfish mariculture. *Mailing Add:* Old Sheepscot Rd Wiscasset ME 04578

HIDY, GEORGE MARTEL, PHYSICAL CHEMISTRY, CHEMICAL ENGINEERING. *Current Pos:* VPRES, ENVIRON DIV, ELEC POWER RES INST, 87- *Personal Data:* b Kingman, Ariz, Jan 5, 35; m 58, 90, Doris Schubert; c Anne, Adrienne & John. *Educ:* Columbia Univ, AB, 56, BS, 57; Princeton Univ, MSE, 58; Johns Hopkins Univ, DEng, 62. *Prof Exp:* Res engr, Miami Valley Labs, Procter & Gamble Co, 58-59; prog head aerosol physics & fluid dynamics, Nat Ctr Atmospheric Res, 62-67, asst head, Dept Chem & Microphys, Lab Atmospheric Sci, 67-68; staff scientist, Sci Ctr, NAm Rockwell Corp, 68-70, group leader, Atmospheric Sci, 70-73, dir air qual res & monitoring, 73-74; gen mgr, Environ Chem Ctr, Environ Res & Technol Inc, 74-81, vpres, 74-84, chief scientist, 81-84; pres, Desert Res Inst, 84-87. *Concurrent Pos:* Sr res fel environ eng, Calif Inst Technol, 69-73; sci adv bd, Welded Electronic Packaging Asn, 81-; prof eng, Univ Nev Las Vegas, 84-87. *Mem:* Fel AAAS; Am Phys Soc; Am Chem Soc; Am Meteorol Soc; Am Geophys Soc; Air Pollution Control Asn; Am Asn Aerosol Res; Am Inst Chem Eng. *Res:* Aerosol physics and chemistry; atmospheric chemistry; air-sea interaction; fluid dynamics; environmental science. *Mailing Add:* 1104 Altadena Ryse Birmingham AL 35242

HIDY, PHIL HARTER, MICROBIAL BIOCHEMISTRY. *Current Pos:* RETIRED. *Personal Data:* b North Manchester, Ind, Feb 11, 15; m 39; c 2. *Educ:* Ind Univ, BS, 38, AM, 42, PhD(chem), 44. *Prof Exp:* Chemist, Inland Steel Co, 39-40; asst prof biochem, Col Med, Baylor Univ, 43-47; res biochemist, Com Solvents Corp, 47-53, group leader biochem, 53-76, mgr microbiol res, Int Minerals & Chem Corp, 76-79. *Mem:* Am Chem Soc. *Res:* Carbohydrate metabolism; antibiotics; organic chemistry; physiology; effect of different starches and starch degradation products on the activity of potato phosphorylase; fermentation biochemistry. *Mailing Add:* 1120 E Davis Dr Apt 628 Terre Haute IN 47802-4065

HIEBER, THOMAS EUGENE, BIOCHEMISTRY. *Current Pos:* VPRES, MDH LAB. *Personal Data:* b Dayton, Ohio, Aug 6, 36; m 64; c 2. *Educ:* Univ Dayton, BS, 59; Univ Cincinnati, MS, 63; St Thomas Inst, PhD(biochem), 72. *Prof Exp:* Chemist cancer & heart res, Miami Valley Hosp, 59-60; asst org chem, Univ Cincinnati, 61-63; chemist res & develop, MC/B Mfg Chemists, 63-74; tech dir drug prod res & develop, Sperti Drug Co, 75- *Mem:* Am Chem Soc. *Res:* Antihemolytic drugs, such as adrenochrome semicarbazone and over the counter drugs containing salicylic acid and methyl salicylate. *Mailing Add:* 4764 Clevesdale Dr Cincinnati OH 45238

HIEBERT, ALLEN G, ANALYTICAL CHEMISTRY. *Current Pos:* PROF CHEM, TABOR COL, 84- *Personal Data:* b Goessel, Kans, Oct 17, 41; m 63, Lois Frantz; c 2. *Educ:* Tabor Col, BA, 63; Univ Ill, Urbana, MS, 65, PhD(chem), 67. *Prof Exp:* Postdoctoral res chem, Mich State Univ, 67-68; prof chem, Knox Col, 68-84. *Concurrent Pos:* Vis prof, Univ Ill, Urbana, 72, Univ Ariz, Tucson, 77-78, Univ Kans, 91-92. *Mem:* Am Chem Soc. *Res:* Electroanalytical methods applied to trace analysis, primarily metal ions in the environment. *Mailing Add:* Tabor Col Hillsboro KS 67063-9513. *Fax:* 316-947-2607

HIEBERT, ERNEST, VIROLOGY, PLANT PATHOLOGY. *Current Pos:* From asst prof to assoc prof, 69-81, PROF VIROL, UNIV FLA, 81- *Personal Data:* b Rosenfeld, Man, May 28, 41; m 64; c 1. *Educ:* Univ Man, BSA, 64; Purdue Univ, MS, 67, PhD(plant virol), 69. *Honors & Awards:* Ruth Allen Award, Am Phytopath Soc, 92. *Concurrent Pos:* NSF grants, 72-74, 75-78, 78-79 & 84-87, USDA, 82-85 & 84-87, BARD, 85-88; vis scientist, Agr Can, Vancouver, 77-78, Inst Molecular & Cellular Biol, Strassbourg, France, 86. *Mem:* Am Phytopath Soc; Can Phytopath Soc; Am Soc Virol; Int Soc Plant Molecular Biol; Soc Gen Microbiol. *Res:* Molecular biology of plant viruses and their nonstructural proteins; cloning of viral genomes. *Mailing Add:* Univ Fla Plant Path Dept PO Box 110680 Gainesville FL 32611-0680. *Fax:* 904-392-6532; *E-Mail:* ehi@ifasgnv

HIEBERT, ERWIN NICK, HISTORY OF SCIENCE. *Current Pos:* chmn dept, 77-84, prof, 70-90, EMER PROF HIST SCI, HARVARD UNIV, 90- *Personal Data:* b Waldheim, Sask, May 27, 19; US citizen; m 43; c 3. *Educ:* Bethel Col, Kans, AB, 41; Univ Kans, AM, 43; Univ Chicago, MS, 49; Univ Wis, PhD(chem & hist sci), 54. *Prof Exp:* Res chemist, Manhattan Proj, Stand Oil Co, 43-46, Inst Metals, Univ Chicago, 47-50; asst prof chem, San Francisco State Col, 52-54; instr hist sci, Harvard Univ, 55-57; from asst prof to prof, Univ Wis-Madison, 57-70. *Concurrent Pos:* Fulbright lectr, Max Planck Inst Physics, Gottingen, 54-55; vis prof, Univ Tubingen, 65; vis scholar, Sch Hist Studies, Inst Advan Study, Princeton, 61-62 & 68-69; fel Churchill Col, Cambridge Univ, 84-85; vis prof, Univ Minn, 87. *Mem:* Fel AAAS; Sigma Xi; Hist Sci Soc; fel Am Acad Arts & Sci; Am Phys Soc; fel Acad Int d Hist des Sci; Czech Soc Hist Sci & Technol. *Res:* History of physical sciences since 1800. *Mailing Add:* Widener Libr 172 Harvard Univ Cambridge MA 02138. *Fax:* 617-495-3344

HIEBERT, GORDON LEE, physical chemistry, for more information see previous edition

HIEBERT, JOHN COVELL, NUCLEAR PHYSICS. *Current Pos:* from asst prof to assoc prof, 65-74, PROF PHYSICS, TEX A&M UNIV, 74- *Personal Data:* b Mt Lake, Minn, Aug 18, 34; m 62, Doris Hodgson; c Helen & Susan. *Educ:* Harvard Univ, AB, 56; Yale Univ, MS, 60, PhD(physics), 64. *Prof Exp:* AEC spec fel, Oak Ridge Nat Lab, 63-65. *Concurrent Pos:* Guest scientist, Kernfoschungszentrum, Karlsruhe, Fed Repub Ger, 81-82. *Mem:* Am Phys Soc; Am Asn Physics Teachers. *Res:* Few particle problems in nuclear physics using neutron beams. *Mailing Add:* Physics Dept Tex A&M Univ College Station TX 77843-4242. *E-Mail:* jch@phys.tamu.edu

HIEBLE, J PAUL, CARDIOVASCULAR PHARMACOLOGY. *Current Pos:* Asst dir, 82-84, res fel pharmacol, 84-90, SR RES FEL, SMITHKLINE BEECHAM PHARMACEUT, 91- *Personal Data:* b Lansing, Mich, Jan 13, 48; m 85; c 1. *Educ:* N Tex State Univ, PhD(org chem), 71; Univ Tex Med Br, PhD(pharmacol), 77. *Mem:* Am Chem Soc; Sigma Xi; Am Soc Pharmacol & Exp Therapeut. *Res:* Adrenergic pharmacology, specifically on the role of adrenergic and dopaminergic receptors in neurotransmission and in maintenance of smooth muscle tone; neuromodulators and co-transmitters. *Mailing Add:* Dept Pharmacol Smith Kline Beecham Pharmaceut PO Box 1539 L510 King of Prussia PA 19406-0939

HIEFTJE, GARY MARTIN, ANALYTICAL CHEMISTRY. *Current Pos:* from asst prof to prof anal chem 69-85, assoc chmn dept chem, 78-80, DISTINGUISHED PROF ANAL CHEM, IND UNIV, BLOOMINGTON, 85- *Personal Data:* b Zeeland, Mich, Oct 1, 42. *Educ:* Hope Col, AB, 64; Univ Ill, PhD(anal chem), 69. *Honors & Awards:* Can Test Award, Chem Ins Can, 79; Anachem Award, 84; Meggars Award, Soc Appl Spectros, 84; Lester W Strock Medal, 84; Chem Instrumentation Award, Am Chem Soc, 85; Pittsburgh Anal Chem Award, 86; Theophilus Redwood Award, Royal Soc Chem, 86; Anal Chem Award, Am Chem Soc, 87; Tracy M Sonneborn Award, Indiana Univ, 87. *Prof Exp:* Res asst phys chem, Ill State Geol Surv, 64-65. *Concurrent Pos:* Consult, Lawrence Livermore Lab, 70-, Upjohn Co, 79-, Los Alamos Nat Lab, 83-, Am Cyanamid, 84-, LECO, 87-; sr fel, Sci & Eng Res Coun, Eng, 83. *Mem:* Am Chem Soc; Soc Appl Spectros; Optical Soc Am; Sigma Xi; fel AAAS. *Res:* Basic mechanisms in atomic emission, absorption and fluorescence flame spectrometric analysis; development of flame methods of analysis; computer interfacing and control in analysis; chemical instrumentation; correlation spectroscopy. *Mailing Add:* Dept Chem Ind Univ Bloomington IN 47405

HIEL, CLEMENT, MULTIDISCIPLINARY DESIGN & ANALYSIS. *Current Pos:* DESIGN SPECIALIST ADVAN COMPOSITES, NASA AMES RES CTR, 87- *Personal Data:* m 83, Hilde Van Dun; c Lynn & Tom. *Educ:* Antwerp Inst Technol, BS 74; Univ Brussels, MS, 78, PhD(mech eng), 83. *Prof Exp:* Fel, Nat Res Coun, 83-84, NATO, 86; assoc prof design, Univ Brussels, 83-87. *Concurrent Pos:* vis prof, Univ Brussels, 87-; prin investr, NASA, 87-; adj prof, Univ Brussels, 87- *Mem:* Soc Advan Mat & Processing Eng; Am Soc Testing & Mat; Am Inst Aeronaut & Astronaut. *Res:* Development of multidisciplinary design and analysis methods for advanced composite materials and the practical implementation thereof; to develop relevant joint projects for students to work with industry. *Mailing Add:* 680 Elmbridge Dr San Jose CA 95129

HIELSCHER, FRANK HENNING, ELECTRICAL ENGINEERING. *Current Pos:* from asst prof to assoc prof elec eng, 71-84, PROF COMPUT SCI & ELEC ENG, LEHIGH UNIV, 84- *Personal Data:* b Jeserig, Ger, Dec 8, 38; US citizen. *Educ:* Drexel Univ, BSEE, 61; Univ Denver, MSEE, 63; Univ Ill, Urbana, PhD(elec eng), 66. *Prof Exp:* Res assoc, Univ Ill, Urbana, 66-67; mem tech staff, Sprague Elec Co, 67-70. *Mem:* Sr mem Inst Elec & Electronics Engrs. *Res:* Semiconductor device modeling; design automation and testing; design of analog and digital integrated circuits. *Mailing Add:* Dept Comput Sci & Elec Eng Lehigh Univ Bethlehem PA 18015

HIEMENZ, PAUL C, PHYSICAL CHEMISTRY, COLLOID CHEMISTRY. *Current Pos:* from asst prof to assoc prof, 65-73, PROF CHEM, CALIF STATE POLYTECH UNIV, POMONA, 73- *Personal Data:* b Los Angeles, Calif, June 23, 36. *Educ:* Loyola Univ, BS, 58; Univ Southern Calif, PhD(chem), 64. *Prof Exp:* Res chemist, Dow Chem Co, 64-65. *Concurrent Pos:* Developer & admin, Minority Sci Prog; outstanding adv, Nat Acad Advan Asn. *Mem:* AAAS; Am Chem Soc; Sigma Xi; Nat Sci Teachers Asn. *Res:* Colloid, surface and polymer chemistry; chemical education; minority education. *Mailing Add:* 121 S Hollenbeck Ave Covina CA 91723

HIENZ, ROBERT DOUGLAS, SENSORY PSYCHOLOGY, BEHAVIORAL PHARMACOLOGY. *Current Pos:* asst prof behav biol, 75-82, RES ASSOC BIOMED ENGR, JOHNS HOPKINS MED SCH, 73-, ASSOC PROF BEHAV BIOL, 82- *Personal Data:* b Detroit, Mich, Dec 21, 44; m 67, Kathryn Westphal; c Erick & Nicholas. *Educ:* Univ Mich, BA, 67; Western Mich Univ, MA, 68; Univ NC, Chapel Hill, PhD(exp psychol), 71. *Prof Exp:* Fel psychol, Univ NC, Chapel Hill, 68-69, res asst, 69-70, teaching fel, 70-71; fel neurophysiol, Med Sch, Univ Wash, 71-73. *Concurrent Pos:* mem, Col Prob Drug Dependence. *Mem:* AAAS; Acoust Soc Am; Asn Res Otolaryngol; Behav Pharmacol Soc; Behav Toxicol Soc. *Res:* Animal psychophysics; audition; neurophysiology of audition; behavioral pharmacology. *Mailing Add:* Behav Biol Res Ctr Hopkins Bayview Res Campus 5510 Nathan Shock Dr Suite 3000 Baltimore MD 21224-6823. *E-Mail:* bhienz@bpru.uucp.jhu.edu

HIERGEIST, FRANZ XAVIER, MATHEMATICAL ANALYSIS. *Current Pos:* From asst prof to prof math, 64-82, assoc chmn dept, 75-82, PROF COMPUTE SCI, WVA UNIV, 82- *Personal Data:* b Pittsburgh, Pa, July 31, 38; m 61; c 3. *Educ:* Univ Pittsburgh, BS, 59, PhD(math), 64. *Mem:* Math Asn Am; Asn Comput Mach. *Res:* Compiler design and programming languages; mathematics of computer science. *Mailing Add:* Dept Comput Sci & Statist WVa Univ Box 6330 Morgantown WV 26506

HIERHOLZER, JOHN CHARLES, MEDICAL VIROLOGY, BIOCHEMISTRY. *Current Pos:* RETIRED. *Personal Data:* b Gravenhurst, Ont, July 1, 38; US citizen; m 67, Connie McArthur; c Jack, Karl & Mike. *Educ:* Spring Hill Col, BS, 60; Univ Fla, MS, 62; Univ Md, PhD(microbiol), 66. *Prof Exp:* Microbiologist, Blood Antigen Pioneering Res Lab, Agr Res Ctr, USDA, 63-66; supvry res microbiologist, Virol Div, Ctr Dis Control, USPHS, 66-94. *Concurrent Pos:* Consult, Fernbank Sci Ctr, Atlanta, 75-94; vis fel, Fac Med, Univ Newcastle, Australia, 83-84; consult, diag prods. *Mem:* AAAS; Am Soc Microbiol; Am Chem Soc; NY Acad Sci; Sigma Xi; Am Soc Virol. *Res:* Anaerobic cellulolytic bacteria; erthrocyte antigens; respiratory viruses; purification of viral antigens; laboratory diagnosis of respiratory virus infection; automated serological techniques; immunogenetics; immunology of viral infections; viral serology; viral conjunctivitis and pneumonia. *Mailing Add:* 1874 Fisher Trail NE Atlanta GA 30345

HIERL, PETER MARSTON, CHEMICAL KINETICS. *Current Pos:* from asst prof to assoc prof, 69-81, PROF CHEM, UNIV KANS, 81-, ASSOC CHMN, CHEM DEPT, 87- *Personal Data:* b Brooklyn, NY, May 17, 41; m 65; c 5. *Educ:* Mass Inst Technol, BS, 63; Rice Univ, PhD(phys chem), 67. *Prof Exp:* Res assoc chem, Yale Univ, 67, Univ Colo, 67-69. *Mem:* AAAS; Am Chem Soc; Am Phys Soc; Am Soc Mass Spectrometry. *Res:* Mass spectrometry; electron impact phenomena; ion-molecule reactions; molecular beam studies of reactive scattering. *Mailing Add:* Dept Chem Univ Kans Lawrence KS 66045-0001

HIESERMAN, CLARENCE EDWARD, CHEMISTRY. *Current Pos:* plant mgr textiles div, Monsanto Co, Ala, 66-72, PLANT MGR, MONSANTO TEXTILES CO, PENSACOLA, FLA, 72- *Personal Data:* b Iowa Park, Tex, Jan 15, 17; m 42; c 3. *Educ:* Tex Tech Col, BS, 37; Mich State Univ, MS, 39. *Prof Exp:* Res chemist, Celanese Corp Am, 42-47, mfg supt, 47-49, sect head res & develop, 49-51, supt res, Amcelle Plant, 51-52; sr res chemist, Chemstrand Co, 52-54, group leader res & develop, 54-55, sect head pilot plants, 55-57, sr sect head, 57-58, mgr acrilan develop, 58-61 & mgr acrilan mfg, 61-66. *Mem:* Am Chem Soc. *Res:* Dyestuff and other organic chemical syntheses and identifications; polymer synthesis and spinning of chemical fibers; manufacturing processes in the field of cellulose acetate, polyamide, polyester and acrylic chemical fibers. *Mailing Add:* 212 N Cliff Dr Gulf Breeze FL 32561-4440

HIESTAND, EVERETT NELSON, PHYSICAL PHARMACY, PHARMACEUTICS. *Current Pos:* RETIRED. *Personal Data:* b Hancock Co, Ohio, Aug 17, 20; m 53, Margie L Corwin; c Nelson E & Carolyn K. *Educ:* Bluffton Col, AB, 42; Ohio State Univ, PhD(phys chem), 50. *Honors & Awards:* Ebert Prize, Am Pharmaceut Asn, 78; Indust Pharmaceut Technol Award, Am Pharmaceut Asn, 82. *Prof Exp:* Asst prof chem, SDak State Col, 49-51; prin chemist, Battelle Mem Inst, 51-55; sr res scientist, Upjohn Co, 55-90. *Concurrent Pos:* Lectr, Univ Mich, 65-66, adj prof, 67-92. *Mem:* Am Chem Soc; fel Am Asn Pharmaceut Scientists; fel AAAS; fel Acad Pharmaceut Sci. *Res:* Suspensions; solid dosage forms; compaction physics; micromeretics; rheology; powder technology. *Mailing Add:* 11 378 East G Ave Galesburg MI 49053

HIETANEN-MAKELA, ANNA (MARTTA), GEOLOGY. *Current Pos:* GEOLOGIST, US GEOL SURV, 49- *Personal Data:* b Isokyro, Finland, Apr 10, 09; US citizen; m 46; c 1. *Educ:* Univ Helsinki, MS, 33, PhD(geol), 38. *Prof Exp:* Instr geol & mineral, Univ Helsinki, 36-46, docent, 44-46; instr mineral, Stanford Univ, 46-47; asst prof geol, Univ Ore, 48-49. *Concurrent Pos:* Collins fel, Bryn Mawr Col, 38-39; Finnish Govt fel, Johns Hopkins Univ, 39-40. *Mem:* Fel AAAS; fel Geol Soc Am; fel Mineral Soc Am; Am Geophys Union; Geochem Soc. *Res:* Petrology; structural geology; petrofabrics; rock forming minerals; metamorphism and metasomatism. *Mailing Add:* 1134 Palo Alto Ave Palo Alto CA 94301

HIETBRINK, BERNARD EDWARD, drug metabolism, enzyme activity, for more information see previous edition

HIETBRINK, EARL HENRY, APPLIED MATHEMATICS. *Current Pos:* RETIRED. *Personal Data:* b Firth, Nebr, Apr 28, 30; m 52; c 3. *Educ:* Cent Col, Iowa, BA, 51; Univ Nebr, MA, 56. *Prof Exp:* Sr mathematician, Res Dept, Allison Div, Gen Motors Corp, Ind, 56-67, survry res engr, Gen Motors Res Labs, 67-87. *Concurrent Pos:* Adj prof math, 87-90. *Mem:* Soc Automotive Engrs; Math Asn Am; Electrochem Soc. *Res:* Advanced battery and fuel cell systems for vehicular applications; direct conversion of energy to electricity by electrochemical power systems. *Mailing Add:* Castle Ridge Fairfield Bay AR 72088

HIGA, HARRY HIROSHI, MEDICAL MICROBIOLOGY. *Current Pos:* RETIRED. *Educ:* Univ Hawaii, AB, 40; Univ Southern Calif, MS, 46; Syracuse Univ, PhD(microbiol), 54. *Prof Exp:* Fel microbiol chem & res assoc microbiol, Purdue Univ, 54-56; microbiologist, USDA, 56-59, biochemist, 59-61; res assoc biochem, Univ Hawaii, 61-64, asst agr biochemist, 64-65; tech dir, Pac Labs, Inc, 66-67; microbiologist, Hawaii State Dept Health, 67- *Concurrent Pos:* Res assoc, Chem Corps, Dept Army, 54-56. *Mem:* AAAS; Am Chem Soc; Am Soc Microbiol. *Res:* Zoonoses, especially rodent plague, typhus and leptospirosis surveillances, detection, isolation and identification of causative organisms; biochemistry, especially enzymology and nucleic acids. *Mailing Add:* 98-346 Puahoku Pl Aiea HI 96701

HIGA, LESLIE HIDEYASU, ORAL PATHOLOGY. *Current Pos:* PROF ORAL SURG & ORAL PATH & DIAG, COL DENT, UNIV IOWA, 65- *Personal Data:* b Hawi, Hawaii, Oct 8, 25; m 61; c 3. *Educ:* Grinnell Col, BA, 53; Univ Mo, Kansas City, DDS, 60; Univ Chicago, MS, 67; Am Bd Oral Path, dipl, 72. *Prof Exp:* Fel dent, Zoller Dent Clin, Univ Chicago, 60-65. *Concurrent Pos:* Fel Am Acad Oral Path, 65; consult, Vet Admin Hosp, Iowa City, Iowa, 73. *Mem:* Am Acad Oral Path; Int Asn Dent Res; Am Dent Asn; AAAS. *Res:* Pain control. *Mailing Add:* 11 Gilmore Ct Iowa City IA 52246

HIGA, WALTER HIROICHI, APPLIED PHYSICS, ELECTRICAL ENGINEERING. *Current Pos:* RETIRED. *Personal Data:* b Maui, Hawaii, Sept 21, 19; m 46; c 3. *Educ:* Tri-State Col, BS, 42; Univ Cincinnati, MS, 47, PhD(physics), 49. *Prof Exp:* Instr physics, Seattle Univ, 49-50; res engr electronics, NAm Aviation, 50-54; res scientist appl physics, Jet Propulsion Lab, 54-80. *Mem:* Sr mem Inst Elec & Electronics Engrs; Cryogenic Soc Am; Am Phys Soc; fel Inst Advan Eng. *Res:* Quantum electronics and cryogenic refrigeration technology. *Mailing Add:* 600 Tamarac Dr Pasadena CA 91105

HIGASHIYAMA, TADAYOSHI, BIOCHEMISTRY, ENDOCRINOLOGY. *Current Pos:* RES SCIENTIST ENDOCRINE BIOCHEM, MED FOUND BUFFALO, 77- *Personal Data:* b Osaka, Japan, Mar 24, 33; m 59; c 1. *Educ:* Osaka Univ, Japan, BS, 58, MS, 60, PhD(biochem), 65. *Prof Exp:* Asst prof inorg biochem, Osaka Univ, Japan, 66-75; res asst prof biochem, State Univ NY, Buffalo, 73-77. *Res:* Isolation and purification of cytochrome P-450-containing enzymes related to steroid hormone biosynthesis; study of topography of hormone action and biosynthesis. *Mailing Add:* Med Found Buffalo 73 High St Buffalo NY 14203-1196. *Fax:* 716-852-4846

HIGDEM, ROGER LEON, ADMINISTRATION. *Current Pos:* From asst prof to assoc prof, 59-71, chmn dept, 71-73, PROF MATH, COL IDAHO, 71-, CHMN DIV NATURAL SCI, 73-; PROF & CHAIR MATH, ALBERTSON COL IDAHO, 90- *Personal Data:* b Fosston, Minn, Nov 20, 33; m 58, Mary Simmet; c Dane. *Educ:* Univ NDak, BS, 55, MS, 59; Ore State Univ, PhD(math), 70. *Concurrent Pos:* Acad vpres, Col of Idaho, 81-83. *Res:* Additive number theory; instructional materials writer. *Mailing Add:* 724 S 20th Caldwell ID 83605. *Fax:* 208-454-2077; *E-Mail:* rhigdem@stimpy.edu

HIGERD, THOMAS BRADEN, MICROBIAL PHYSIOLOGY, IMMUNOLOGY. *Current Pos:* asst prof, 72-79, ASSOC PROF MICROBIOL & IMMUNOL, MED UNIV SC, 79-, ASSOC DEAN, RESOURCE PLANNING, COL MED, 90- *Personal Data:* b Pittsburgh, Pa, July 1, 42; m 64; c 2. *Educ:* Washington & Jefferson Col, BA, 64; Wayne State Univ, PhD(med microbiol), 69. *Prof Exp:* Am Cancer Soc Dernham jr fel oncol, Scripps Clin & Res Found, 69-72. *Concurrent Pos:* Intermittent fac appointee, Nat Marine Fisheries Serv & Nat Oceanic & Atmospheric Admin, 80-86. *Mem:* Am Soc Microbiol; Int Asn Dent Res. *Res:* Microbial physiology, metabolism and genetics, characteristics of pyocin, a Pseudomonas bacteriocin; role of proteolytic enzymes in sporulation and genetics of Bacillus subtilis; bacterial modulators of the immune response; dental research; ciguatera seafood poisoning. *Mailing Add:* Microbiol & Immunol Med Univ SC 171 Ashley Ave Charleston SC 29425-0001

HIGGINBOTHAM, ROBERT DAVID, MICROBIOLOGY. *Current Pos:* prof microbiol, Med Sch, Univ Louisville, 67-80, actg chmn dept, 70-72, prof microbiol & immunol, 80-91, EMER PROF MICROBIOL & IMMUNOL, MED SCH, UNIV LOUISVILLE, 91- *Personal Data:* b Salt Lake City, Utah, Mar 15, 21; m 46; c 2. *Educ:* Univ Utah, BA, 49, MS, 50, PhD(bact), 55. *Prof Exp:* Asst bact, Univ Utah, 50-53, res assoc anat, 53-55, res instr, 55-57, instr, 57-58; from asst prof to prof microbiol, Med Br, Univ Tex, 58-67. *Concurrent Pos:* Lederle med fac award, 57-60. *Mem:* AAAS; Am Soc Microbiol; Am Asn Immunologists; Am Soc Exp Path: Reticuloendothelial Soc. *Res:* Mast cells; bacterial endotoxins; viruses; immunology; virology; connective tissue function and resistance with regard to cells and endogenous secretions. *Mailing Add:* 4017 Ashridge Dr Louisville KY 40241

HIGGINS, BRIAN GAVIN, FLUID MECHANICS OF COATING FLOWS, LANGMIER-BLODGETT FILMS. *Current Pos:* from asst prof to assoc prof, 83-90, PROF CHEM ENG, UNIV CALIF, DAVIS, 90- *Personal Data:* b Umtata, Transkei, SAfrica, July 24, 48; div; c 1. *Educ:* Univ Witwatersrand, Johannesburg, SAfrica, BSc, 72, MSc, 75; Univ Minn, PhD(chem), 80. *Prof Exp:* Res asst, Inst Paper Chem, 80-82, res assoc, 82-83. *Concurrent Pos:* Actg chmn, Dept Chem Eng, 88-90, chmn, 90- *Mem:* Am Inst Chem Engrs; Am Phys Soc. *Res:* Fluid mechanics of coating flows; interfacial mechanics; hydrodynamic stability of thin films; Langmier-Blodgett films for nonlinear optics. *Mailing Add:* Dept Chem Eng Univ Calif Davis CA 95616

HIGGINS, CHARLES GRAHAM, GROUNDWATER & HILLSLOPE GEOMORPHOLOGY. *Current Pos:* from asst prof to prof, 51-90, EMER PROF GEOL, UNIV CALIF, DAVIS, 90- *Personal Data:* b Oak Park, Ill, Nov 18, 25; m 74, Rosalie Darleen Davis; c Kimberley F (Tolley) & Lesley V. *Hon Degrees:* Univ Chicago, SB, 46, SM, 47; Univ Calif, Berkeley, PhD(geol), 50. *Honors & Awards:* E B Burnell, Jr, Mem Award, Eng Geol Div, Geol Soc, 95. *Prof Exp:* Asst, Dept Geol Sci, Univ Calif, Berkeley, 48-49; instr geol, Univ Mich, 50-51. *Mem:* Fel Geol Soc Am; Sigma Xi; Brit Geomorphol Res Group; Am Quaternary Asn. *Res:* Geomorphology; coastal geology; geomorphic theory; origin and significance of tiered slopes and other microrelief features; development of drainage networks and landforms by subsurface outflow and sapping; subsurface physical environments in beaches. *Mailing Add:* PO Box 1727 Carmel Valley CA 93924-1727. *Fax:* 530-752-0951

HIGGINS, DOROTHY MARIE, COORDINATION CHEMISTRY, SOLUTION EQUILIBRIA. *Personal Data:* b Lawrence, Mass, May 1, 30. *Educ:* Emmanuel Col, BA, 51; Cath Univ Am, MS, 61; Boston Col, PhD(inorg & org chem), 66. *Prof Exp:* Teacher high sch, Mass, 54-58; instr anal org chem, Emmanuel Col, Mass, 66, assoc prof inorg phys chem; 66-87, chmn dept chem, 69-77, res assoc chem, 75-87; div chmn math, sci & technol, Roxbury Community Col, 86-90. *Concurrent Pos:* Partic, Chautague Course interfacing microcomput & lab instrumentation, NSF, 81-82; mem, Extramural Assoc Prog, NIH, 84; educ consult, high schs & cols, Japan, 86. *Mem:* Am Chem Soc; Nat Sci Teachers Asn; Sigma Xi. *Res:* Investigation of equilibria involved in the formation of mixed ligand chelates of indium (III); transition metal complexes of tameta 3HBr. *Mailing Add:* 581 Highland Ave No 4 Waterbury CT 06708. *Fax:* 203-575-9691; *E-Mail:* dmh@mail.teikyopost.edu

HIGGINS, E ARNOLD, RESPIRATORY PHYSIOLOGY. *Current Pos:* RETIRED. *Personal Data:* b Norman, Okla, May 5, 30. *Educ:* Univ Okla, PhD(physiol), 65. *Prof Exp:* Supvr, Survival Res Unit, Civil Aeromed Inst, 82- *Mem:* Fel Aerospace Med Asn; Am Physiol Soc. *Mailing Add:* 3805 Cedarbrook Dr Norman OK 73072

HIGGINS, EDWIN STANLEY, BIOCHEMISTRY. *Current Pos:* RETIRED. *Personal Data:* b New York, NY, Mar 12, 25; m 58; c 3. *Educ:* Alfred Univ, BA, 52; Syracuse Univ, PhD(biochem), 56. *Prof Exp:* Asst physiol, anat & biol, Alfred Univ, 51-52; from asst prof to prof biochem & molecular biophys, Med Col Va, 56-91, from asst to dean, Sch Basic Health Sci, 85-91. *Concurrent Pos:* Dir biochem res, Bur Alcohol Studies & Rehab, Va State Health Dept, 59-73; vis lectr, Univ Ctr Va, Inc, 60-67; mem, Int Cong Alcohol & Alcoholism, 68. *Mem:* AAAS; Am Chem Soc; Soc Exp Biol & Med; Am Soc Cell Biol; Am Inst Nutrit. *Res:* Biochemistry of mitochondrial functions and changes accompanying hepatotoxicities and tissue regeneration; brain metabolism; alcohol metabolism and toxic mechanisms; fungal metabolism. *Mailing Add:* 5928 Old Orchard Rd Richmond VA 23227

HIGGINS, FREDERICK B(ENJAMIN), JR, SANITARY ENGINEERING. *Current Pos:* assoc prof civil & environ eng technol & chmn dept, Temple Univ, 73-78, prof environ eng, 73-78, dean, Col Eng & Archit, 81-89, PROF ENG, TEMPLE UNIV, 89- *Personal Data:* b Portsmouth, Va, Sept 28, 36; m 58; c 2. *Educ:* Ga Inst Technol, BCE, 58, MSSE, 60, PhD(sanit eng), 64. *Prof Exp:* Sanit engr water pollution control, Environ Hyg Agency, US Army, 63-65, asst for air pollution eng serv directorate, 65-66, chief, Air Pollution Eng Div, 66-67; proj engr, Roy F Weston, Inc, Pa, 67-68, proj mgr, 68-69; asst prof environ eng, Drexel Univ, 69-73. *Mem:* AAAS; Am Soc Civil Engrs; Am Soc Eng Educ. *Res:* Radiological hygiene; air and water pollution; solid wastes. *Mailing Add:* 12th & Norris St Philadelphia PA 19122

HIGGINS, GEORGE A, JR, SURGERY. *Current Pos:* CHIEF SURG SERV, VET ADMIN HOSP, WASHINGTON, DC, 60- *Personal Data:* b Wichita, Kans, Mar 30, 17; m 45; c 5. *Educ:* Univ NMex, BS, 38; Harvard Univ, MD, 42; Am Bd Surg, dipl; Am Bd Thoracic Surg, dipl. *Prof Exp:* Intern surg, Boston City Hosp, 42-43; resident, Mt Alto Hosp, 46-49; chief surg serv, Vet Admin Hosp, Wichita, 49-52; chief surg serv, Vet Admin Hosp, Kansas City, Mo, 52-60. *Concurrent Pos:* Instr, George Washington Univ, 48-50, clin prof, Sch Med, 60-; instr, Georgetown Univ, 49-60, clin prof, Sch Med, 60-68, prof, 68-; from asst prof to prof, Med Sch, Univ Kans, 52-60. *Mem:* Western Surg Asn; Am Col Surg; Am Surg Asn. *Res:* Clinical surgery. *Mailing Add:* Santa Barbara Cottage Hosp Santa Barbara CA 93102

HIGGINS, IAN T, EPIDEMIOLOGY. *Current Pos:* prof community health serv & adult health & aging unit, 67-70, prof epidemiol, 67-85, prof environ & indust health, 70-85, EMER PROF EPIDEMIOL, ENVIRON & INDUST HEALTH, UNIV MICH, ANN ARBOR, 85- *Personal Data:* b Edinburgh, Scotland, Mar 12, 19; m 64. *Educ:* Univ London, MB, BS, 46, MD, 51. *Prof Exp:* Resident med officer, Royal Nat Hosp, Ventnor, Eng, 43-44; house physician & receiving officer, London Hosp, 44-45; house physician, Hosp Sick Children, 45-46; house surgeon, Norfolk & Norwich Hosp, 46-47; resident med officer, 47-48; sr registr chest clin, Grimsby County Borough, 48-49; resident physician, Mont Hall, Switz, 50-53; sr registr, Cambridge Chest Clin, 53; mem, Sci Staff, Pneumoconiosis Res Unit, Med Res Coun, 53-56, asst dir, Epidemiol Res Unit, 62-63; prof chronic dis epidemiol, Grad Sch Pub Health, Univ Pittsburgh, 63-67. *Concurrent Pos:* Wander scholar & registr, Children's Dept, Westminster Hosp, Eng, 45-46; actg physician in chg, Cotswold Sanatorium, Cranham, 62; consult, Div Occup Health, USPHS & Epidemiol Br, Commun Dis Ctr, Ga, 65-66; fel coun arteriosclerosis & fel coun epidemiol, Am Heart Asn. *Mem:* Am Epidemiol Soc; fel Brit Thoracic Soc. *Res:* Epidemiology of chronic diseases, especially pneumoconiosis and chronic non-specific respiratory disease; effects of occupation and tobacco smoking on heart and lung conditions. *Mailing Add:* 252 Indian River Pl Ann Arbor MI 48104

HIGGINS, IRWIN RAYMOND, ion exchange, electrochemistry; deceased, see previous edition for last biography

HIGGINS, JAMES JACOB, STATISTICS. *Current Pos:* dept head, 90-95, PROF STATIST, KANS STATE UNIV, 80- *Personal Data:* b Canton, Ill, Oct 31, 43; m 67; c 2. *Educ:* Univ Ill, BS, 65; Ill State Univ, MS, 67; Univ Mo, Columbia, PhD(statist), 70. *Prof Exp:* Asst prof math, Univ Mo, Rolla, 70-74; from asst prof to assoc prof math, Univ SFla, 74-80. *Mem:* Am Statist Asn; Inst Math Statist; Math Asn Am. *Res:* Reliability theory; classical and Bayesian estimation theory; statistical modelling; nonparametric statistics. *Mailing Add:* Dept Statist Kans State Univ Manhattan KS 66506-2602. *E-Mail:* jhiggins@ksu.edu

HIGGINS, JAMES THOMAS, JR, INTERNAL MEDICINE, PHYSIOLOGY. *Current Pos:* CHIEF MED SERV, ALBANY VET ADMIN MED CTR & PROF MED, ALBANY MED COL, 87- *Personal Data:* b Columbia, SC, July 13, 34; m 56; c 4. *Educ:* Duke Univ, Durham, BS, 59, MD, 59. *Prof Exp:* Intern, Duke Univ Hosp, 59-60; fel, Dept Med, Duke Univ, 60-61; investr, Nat Heart Inst, Bethesda, 61-63; resident, Yale-New Haven Hosp, 63-65; clin investr, Vet Admin Hosp, Conn, 65-67; instr med, Yale Univ, 65-66, asst prof, 66-67; from asst prof to prof, Ind Univ, Indianapolis, 67-76, prof med & chief nephrol, Med Col Ohio, 76-87. *Concurrent Pos:* Nat Heart Inst career develop award, 69-74; dir, Specialized Ctr Res in Hypertension, Sch Med, Ind Univ, Indianapolis, 71-76. *Mem:* Am Physiol Soc; Am Soc Nephrology; Cent Soc Clin Res; Endocrine Soc; fel Am Col Physicians. *Res:* Renal physiology; control of water and electrolyte balance; membrane physiology; causes and treatment of hypertension. *Mailing Add:* Med Service III Vet Admin Med Ctr 113 Holland Ave Albany NY 12208. *Fax:* 518-462 0268

HIGGINS, JAMES VICTOR, HUMAN GENETICS. *Current Pos:* Asst prof zool, 61-70, PROF ZOOL & HUMAN DEVELOP, MICH STATE UNIV, 70- *Personal Data:* b Sandusky, Ohio, Jan 24, 33; m 53; c 3. *Educ:* Mich State Univ, BS, 54; Univ Minn, MS, 58, PhD(zool), 61. *Mem:* AAAS; Am Soc Human Genetics; Am Eugenics Soc; Am Genetic Asn; Am Asn Ment Deficiency; Sigma Xi. *Res:* Gene action in relation to mental retardation; population frequency and biochemical variation. *Mailing Add:* 2035 Wilshire Dr SE Grand Rapids MI 49506

HIGGINS, JAMES WOODROW, GEOLOGY. *Current Pos:* RETIRED. *Personal Data:* b Seaman, Ohio, Feb 5, 21; m 44; c 2. *Educ:* Miami Univ, AB, 43; Univ Chicago, PhD(geol), 47. *Prof Exp:* Asst geol, Miami Univ, 40-42 & Univ Chicago, 45-47; geologist & geophysicist, Standard Oil Co, Calif, 47-53, area geologist, 53-55, dist geologist, 55-58, geologist, Staff of Vpres Oil Field Res, Calif Res Corp, 58-61, dist geologist, Alaskan Dist, Standard Oil Co Calif, 61-65, financial analyst, Comptroller's Dept, 65-68, sr geologist, 68-77. *Concurrent Pos:* Instr, Exten Serv, Univ Calif, 49. *Mem:* Geol Soc Am; Am Asn Petrol Geol. *Res:* Petroleum exploration; investment analysis. *Mailing Add:* 12225 Lakeshore SE Auburn CA 95602

HIGGINS, JERRY MITCHELL, SPEECH PATHOLOGY. *Current Pos:* RETIRED. *Personal Data:* b St Louis, Mo, Oct 28, 30; m 56; c 2. *Educ:* Asbury Col, BA, 56; Univ Iowa, MA, 65; Mich State Univ, PhD(speech path), 71. *Prof Exp:* Asst prof speech path & dir, Speech & Lang Clin, Med Ctr, Univ Ala, Birmingham, 71-74; assoc prof, Asbury Col, 74-78; asst prof, Mich State Univ, 78-82; exec vpres, Prentke Rumich Co, Wooster, Ohio, 86-92. *Mem:* Am Speech & Hearing Asn. *Res:* Development of a more versatile electro-larynx; modification of nasality in the deaf. *Mailing Add:* 4585 Marlbourogh Rd Okemos MI 48864

HIGGINS, JOHN CLAYBORN, MATHEMATICS, COMPUTER SCIENCE. *Current Pos:* from instr to assoc prof, 62-74, PROF MATH, BRIGHAM YOUNG UNIV, 74- *Personal Data:* b Logan, Utah, June 14, 34; m 61, Seiko Takeda; c Ann, Ellen & Michael. *Educ:* Brigham Young Univ, BA, 58, MA, 60; Univ Calif, Davis, PhD(math), 66. *Prof Exp:* Instr math, Church Col Hawaii, 60-62. *Concurrent Pos:* NSF sci fac fel, 65-66; vis prof, Shimane Univ Matsue, Japan, 76. *Mem:* Am Math Soc; Soc Indust & Appl Math; Math Asn Am. *Res:* Semigroups; topological semigroups; category theory; recursive functions; automata; formal languages; scryptography. *Mailing Add:* Brigham Young Univ 3374 TMCB Provo UT 84602. *Fax:* 801-378-2800; *E-Mail:* higgins@ca.byu.edu

HIGGINS, JOHN J, SEMI-CONDUCTOR DEVICES. *Current Pos:* ENGR SCIENTIST, IBM CORP, 82- *Personal Data:* b Norfolk, Va, Nov 20, 43. *Educ:* NC State Univ, BS, 66; Mich State Univ, PhD(physics), 72, MS, 82. *Prof Exp:* Res assoc, Mich State Univ, 77-82. *Mem:* Am Phys Soc; Inst Elec & Electronics Engrs. *Mailing Add:* 19 Forest Rd Essex Junction VT 05452

HIGGINS, JOSEPH JOHN, BIOPHYSICS. *Current Pos:* res assoc, Johnson Found, 61-63, asst prof biophys, 63-67, chmn biophys grad group, 67-77, assoc prof biophys, 67-80, ASSOC PROF BIOPHYS & BIOCHEM, UNIV PA, 80- *Personal Data:* b Philadelphia, Pa, Jan 26, 32; m 56; c 5. *Educ:* Univ Pa, BA, 54, PhD(physics), 59; Harvard Univ, MA, 55. *Prof Exp:* Asst analogue comput, Johnson Found, Univ Pa, 49-59, asst digital comput, 56-59, lectr reaction kinetics & med math, Univ, 56; USPHS fel, Free Univ Brussels, Inst Phys Chem, Univ Copenhagen & Quantum Chem Group, Univ Uppsala, 59-61. *Concurrent Pos:* NIH career develop award, 70- *Mem:* AAAS; Am Phys Soc; Biophys Soc; NY Acad Sci. *Res:* Chemical and cellular kinetics; irreversible thermodynamics; electronic analogue and digital computers. *Mailing Add:* Biochem & Biophysics Univ Pa Col Med Philadelphia PA 19104

HIGGINS, LARRY CHARLES, plant taxonomy, plant morphology, for more information see previous edition

HIGGINS, LINDEN ELIZABETH, DEVELOPMENTAL & BEHAVIORAL PLASTICITY, ARACHNOLOGY. *Current Pos:* lectr introductory biol, 92, RES ASSOC, UNIV TEX, AUSTIN, 93- *Personal Data:* b Durham, NC, Jan 21, 58. *Educ:* Univ Chicago, BA, 80, MS, 82; Univ Tex, Austin, PhD(zool-ecol), 88. *Prof Exp:* Vis researcher, Ctr Ecol, Nat Univ Mex, 88-90, class C researcher, 90-91. *Concurrent Pos:* Fel, Orgn Am States, 88-90. *Mem:* Am Arachnological Soc; Ecol Soc Am; Animal Behav Soc; Sigma Xi. *Res:* Physiological underpinnings of apparent trade-offs between behavior and growth in juvenile spiders, expressed as changes in web size and growth rates. *Mailing Add:* Dept Zool Univ Tex Austin TX 78712. *Fax:* 512-471-9651; *E-Mail:* higgins@cpease.zo.utexas.edu

HIGGINS, MICHAEL LEE, MICROBIOLOGY, BIOCHEMISTRY. *Current Pos:* from asst prof to assoc prof, 68-78, PROF MICROBIOL, SCH MED, TEMPLE UNIV, 78- *Personal Data:* b Ft Worth, Tex, Sept 2, 40. *Educ:* Univ NTex, BA, 63, MS, 64; Rutgers Univ, PhD(microbiol), 68. *Honors & Awards:* Rutgers Microbiol Res Award, 68. *Prof Exp:* Vis investr mycol, Rutgers Univ, 64-65. *Concurrent Pos:* Chmn, Ultrastruct Div, Am Soc Microbiol, 86. *Mem:* Am Soc Microbiol. *Res:* Physiology and ultrastructure of procaryote organisms. *Mailing Add:* Dept Microbiol Temple Univ Sch Med 3400 N Broad St Philadelphia PA 19140-5104

HIGGINS, MILLICENT WILLIAMS PAYNE, MEDICINE, EPIDEMIOLOGY. *Current Pos:* ASSOC DIR EPIDEMIOL & BIOMETRY, NAT HEART, LUNG & BLOOD INST, NIH, 84- *Personal Data:* b Halifax, Eng, Mar 5, 28; m 64; c 2. *Educ:* Univ Durham, MB & BS, 51, DPH, 56, MD, 59. *Prof Exp:* Trainee asst to Dr A B Follows, York, Eng, 51-52; casualty officer, Nottingham Children's Hosp, 52-53; intern med, Royal Victoria Hosp, Montreal, Que, 53-54; sr house officer, Newcastle Gen Hosp, Eng, 54-56; res asst pediat, Durham Univ, 56-58; med officer, Gateshead Health Dept, Eng, 58-59; res assoc epidemiol, Univ Mich, 59-62, asst prof, 63-64; asst prof, Univ Pittsburgh, 64-67; from assoc prof to prof epidemiol, Sch Pub Health, Univ Mich, Ann Arbor, 67-85, dir, Prog Gen Epidemiol 73-85, prof internal med, 82-85. *Concurrent Pos:* Fel, Coun Epidemiol, Am Heart Asn; mem adv coun, Nat Heart & Lung Inst. *Mem:* Am Thoracic Soc; Soc Epidemiol Res; Brit Med Asn; hon fel Am Col Chest Physicians; fel Am Col Epidemiol. *Res:* Epidemiological studies of chronic diseases, especially chronic respiratory diseases; diabetes, hypertension and coronary disease; relationships between pregnancy and childbirth and health and disease. *Mailing Add:* 252 Indian River Pl Ann Arbor MI 48104-1825

HIGGINS, N PATRICK, DNA ENZYMOLOGY, GENE TRANSPOSITION. *Current Pos:* ASSOC PROF BIOCHEM, UNIV ALA, BIRMINGHAM, 83- *Personal Data:* b Wichita, Kans, Mar 17, 46; m 69; c 3. *Educ:* Wichita State Univ, BS, 68, MS, 69; Univ Chicago, PhD(microbiol), 76. *Prof Exp:* Asst prof biochem, Univ Wyo, 79-83. *Mem:* Am Soc Microbiol; AAAS; Am Soc Biol Chem. *Res:* Genetic recombination and DNA transposition in bacteria; understanding how purified proteins interact with their DNA substrates. *Mailing Add:* Dept Biochem Univ Ala Birmingham AL 35294-2170. *Fax:* 205-934-5955

HIGGINS, PAUL DANIEL, physiological ecology, botany; deceased, see previous edition for last biography

HIGGINS, RICHARD J, SOLID STATE PHYSICS. *Current Pos:* PROF ELEC ENG, GA INST TECHNOL, 87-, DIR, MICROELECTRON RES CTR, 88- *Personal Data:* b Winchester, Mass, May 15, 39; m 65; c 2. *Educ:* Mass Inst Technol, BS, 60; Northwestern Univ, PhD(mat sci), 65. *Prof Exp:* Mem staff phys chem, Fundamental Res Lab, US Steel Corp, 60; from asst prof to prof physics, Univ Ore, 65-87. *Concurrent Pos:* Vis prof, Univ Islamabad & consult, Ford Found, Pakistan, 71; consult & resident vis, Bell Labs, Murray Hill, NJ, 72-73; prog chmn, Int Conf on Electron Lifetimes in Metals, 74; vis researcher, Nat Magnet Lab, Mass Inst Technol & consult analog devices, 83-85. *Mem:* Am Phys Soc; Fedn Am Sci; Inst Elec & Electronics Engrs; Am Asn Univ Profs; Sigma Xi. *Res:* Experimental study of the electronic structure of metals, alloys and semiconductors; Fermi surface measurements; electronic instrumentation; application of mini-computers and microcomputers in scientific research. *Mailing Add:* Microelectron Res Ctr Ga Inst Technol Atlanta GA 30332-0269. *E-Mail:* richard.higgins@mirc.gatech.edu

HIGGINS, ROBERT ARTHUR, ELECTRONICS ENGINEERING, SOFTWARE SYSTEMS & OPTOELECTRONICS. *Current Pos:* prof, 85-95, EMER PROF ELEC ENG, ST CLOUD STATE UNIV, 95- *Personal Data:* b Watertown, SDak, Sept 5, 24; m 58, Barbara Fagerlie; c Patricia, Daniel & Steven. *Educ:* Univ Minn, Minneapolis, BEE, 48; Univ Wis-Madison, MS, 64; Univ Mo, Columbia, PhD(elec eng), 69. *Prof Exp:* Engr, Schlumberger Well Surv Corp, Tex, 48-57; sr res technologist, Mobil Res & Develop Corp, 58-61; sr res engr, United Aircraft Res Labs, Conn, 65; staff specialist, Remote Sensing Inst, 69-71; asst prof elec eng, SDak State Univ, 69-74, assoc dir, Eng Exp Sta, 73-77, prof elec eng, 74-77; consult, Control Data Corp, 77-80; prin engr, Sperry Univac, 81-86. *Concurrent Pos:* US Dept Interior Off Water Resources res grant, SDak State Univ, 71-74; consult, Lawrence Livermore Lab, 71-73 & USAF Off Sci Res, 76; proj dir, NSF, 73-76 & 88-89; prof elec eng, SDak State Univ, 77-79; consult, NCR Comten, 88-89, FMC, 90-91 & Ontrack Comput Systs, 93-97. *Mem:* Inst Elec & Electronics Engrs; Sigma Xi. *Res:* Adaptive system theory; data communications; nonlinear system identification; instrumentation; memory systems; computer architecture; electromagnetic compatibility; magneto optics; power electronics; magneto optics; optoelectronics. *Mailing Add:* 11260 Windrow Dr Eden Prairie MN 55344. *Fax:* 612-949-4139; *E-Mail:* higgins@kanga.stcloud.msus.edu

HIGGINS, ROBERT H, STEREOCHEMISTRY, SPECTROSCOPY. *Current Pos:* asst prof, Fayetteville State Univ, 76-79, coordr, 79-85, assoc prof chem, 82-95, PROF CHEM, FAYETTEVILLE STATE UNIV, 95- *Personal Data:* b Warren, Ohio, Dec 9, 42; div; c Jamie L (Clark), John David, Chi Ae (Yu) & Yong Hyon. *Educ:* Ohio Univ, BS, 65, MS 67; Univ Nebr, PhD(org chem), 71. *Prof Exp:* Instr chem, Doane Col, 68-70; res fel, Univ Nebr, 71-72; res chemist, Dorsey Labs, 72-74; res fel, Univ Colo, 74-75; asst prof chem, Metrop State Col, 76. *Concurrent Pos:* Dow fel, Univ Nebr, 68; consult, Am Inst Res, 84-87; prin investr, NIH, 85-93 & 94; consult, NIH & Ga State Univ, 95- *Mem:* Sigma Xi; Am Chem Soc; Coun Undergrad Res. *Res:* Synthesis, stereochemistry and reactions of l-alkylazetidinols, particularly as applicable to a new route of beta-adrenolytics and anti-tumor drugs; molecular modeling and quantum calculations on organic chemicals and reaction transition states and/or intermediates. *Mailing Add:* Rte 20 Box 1254 Fayetteville NC 28306. *Fax:* 910-486-1083; *E-Mail:* higgins@chi1.uncfsu.edu

HIGGINS, ROBERT PRICE, INVERTEBRATE ZOOLOGY. *Current Pos:* oceanogr, Smithsonian Inst, 68-69, dir, Mediter Marine Sorting Ctr, Tunisia, 69-71, dir oceanog & limnol prog, 71-74, actg dir, Int Environ Sci Prog, 74, sr zoologist, 74-78, cur, 78-93, EMER RES SCIENTIST, DEPT INVERT ZOOL, SMITHSONIAN INST, 93- *Personal Data:* b Denver, Colo, Oct 8, 32; m 54, Gwendolyn Litherland; c Kent E & Kim A. *Educ:* Univ Colo, BA, 56, MA, 58; Duke Univ, PhD(zool), 61. *Hon Degrees:* DSc, Univ Copenhagen, 93. *Prof Exp:* From asst prof to assoc prof biol, Wake Forest Univ, 61-68; resident systematist, Systs-Ecol Prog, Marine Biol Lab, Woods Hole, 68; assoc prof & dir marine prog, Boston Univ, 68. *Concurrent Pos:* Mem, Int Indian Ocean Exped, 64; NSF grants syst biol, 64, 68; mem adv comt, Smithsonian Oceanog Sorting Ctr, 64-69; NASA grant, 65; mem, SE Pac Biol Oceanog Prog, 66; consult zoologist, Smithsonian Inst, 66-68; assoc ed trans, Am Micros Soc, 66-93; res assoc, Baruch Inst Marine Biol & Coastal Res, 75-; adj prof biol, W Carolina Univ, Cullowhee, 90-, ETenn State Univ, Jonhson City, 93-94; adj res prof biol, Asheville, 94-; distinguished adj prof biol, Univ NC, Charlotte, 93-94; mem bd dirs, NC Acad Sci, 96- *Mem:* Soc Integrative Comp Zool; Am Micros Soc (vpres, 76, pres, 79); Int Asn Meiobenthologists (chmn, 80-81); Biol Soc Wash. *Res:* Systematics, life history and ecology of meiobenthic and bryophilic invertebrates, especially Kinorhyncha Loricifera Priapulida and Tardigrada. *Mailing Add:* 2 Pond Lane Asheville NC 28804. *Fax:* 704-254-0319; *E-Mail:* rphiggins@unca.campus.mci.net

HIGGINS, TERRY JAY, T-CELL ACTIVATION, CARBOHYDRATE ANTIGENS-LIGANDS. *Current Pos:* sr res investr, 88-90, prin res investr immunopharmacol, 90-91, FEL, STERLING DRUG, INC, 91- *Personal Data:* b Napa, Calif, July 22, 47; m 71; c 4. *Educ:* Univ Calif, Davis, BS, 70; Harvard Univ, PhD(immunol), 76. *Prof Exp:* Res asst biochem, Univ Calif, Davis, 70-71; fel immunol, Australian Nat Univ, 77-79, res fel, 79-80; asst prof microbiol, Sch Med, Univ Pa, 81-87. *Mem:* NY Acad Sci; Am Asn Immunologists; Complex Carbohydrate Soc; AAAS. *Res:* Basic molecular mechanisms of T cell, B cell and macrophage activation and effector function to discover ways of immunomodulating the host response to self-antigens (autoimmunity/inflammation) and transplants. *Mailing Add:* Appoilon Inc 1 Great Valley Pkwy Suite 30 1250 S Collegeville Rd Malvern PA 19355-1423

HIGGINS, THEODORE PARKER, MATHEMATICS. *Current Pos:* MEM STAFF MATH, SCI RES LABS, BOEING AIRPLANE CO, 58- *Personal Data:* b Houston, Tex, Jan 18, 20; m 48; c 1. *Educ:* Agr & Mech Col, Tex, BS, 40; Univ Tex, MS, 53, PhD(math), 55. *Prof Exp:* Geophysicist, Carter Oil Co, Okla, 40-50; instr math, Univ Tex, 52-55; res specialist, Boeing Airplane Co, Wash, 55-58; sr scientist, Dalmo Victor Co, Calif, 58. *Mem:* Am Math Soc; Soc Indust & Appl Math; Math Asn Am; Sigma Xi. *Res:* Applications of techniques of applied mathematics to problems in electromagnetic theory. *Mailing Add:* 4222 Mercerwood Dr Mercer Island WA 98040-4245

HIGGINS, THOMAS ERNEST, ENVIRONMENTAL ENGINEERING, CIVIL ENGINEERING. *Current Pos:* ASST PROF ENVIRON ENG, DEPT CIVIL ENG, ARIZ STATE UNIV, 77- *Personal Data:* b Plattsburgh, NY, Aug 24, 48; m 68; c 1. *Educ:* Univ Notre Dame, BS, 70, MS, 73, PhD(environ health eng), 75. *Prof Exp:* Proj engr environ eng, Harza Eng Co, 75-77. *Concurrent Pos:* Consult & environ engr, Ten-Ech Environ Consult, 70-74; partner, Higgins Eng, 74-75; teaching asst, Dept Civil Eng, Notre Dame, 73-75; res grant, Eng Found, New York, 78-79; USAF, 80-82; res fel, USAF, 80 & US Dept Eng, 81. *Mem:* Am Chem Soc; Am Soc Civil Eng; Am Water Works Asn; Water Pollution Control Fedn; Am Acad Environ Eng. *Res:* Physiochemical treatment of water and wastewater; water chemistry; design of water and wastewater treatment systems; wastewater reuse; movement of heavy metals in soil systems; treatment of metal plating wastewaters; treatment of shale oil process waste waters. *Mailing Add:* Texaco Eng Div 4800 Fournace Pl Bellaire TX 77401

HIGGINS, THOMAS JAMES, ELECTRICAL ENGINEERING. *Current Pos:* prof, 48-82, EMER PROF, ELEC ENG, UNIV WIS-MADISON, 82- *Personal Data:* b Charlottesville, Va, July 4, 11; m 42, 76; c 2. *Educ:* Cornell Univ, EE, 32, MA, 37; Purdue Univ, PhD(elec eng), 41. *Honors & Awards:* Westinghouse Award, Am Soc Eng Educ, 54; Eckman Award, Instrument Soc Am, 64; Donald P Eckman Sr Mem Distinguished Activ Educ Award, Instrument Soc Am, 64; Centennial Medal, Inst Elec & Electronics Engrs, 82. *Prof Exp:* Instr math, Auburn Collegiate Ctr, NY, 33-34; plant engr, Agfa Ansco Corp, 34-35; instr elec eng, Wyomissing Polytech Inst, 35-37; instr, Purdue Univ, 37-41; asst prof, Tulane Univ, 41-42; from assoc prof to prof, Ill Inst Technol, 42-48. *Concurrent Pos:* Consult elec engr. *Mem:* Nat Soc Prof Engrs; fel Am Soc Eng Educ; fel Instrument Soc Am; fel Inst Elec & Electronics Engrs; Tensor Soc (vpres, 64-86); Sigma Xi; fel AAAS. *Res:* Electric circuit theory; applied elasticity; electromagnetic theory; servomechanism and automatic control theory; power systems engineering; electric machine theory; nuclear reactor control theory. *Mailing Add:* 12 Pin Oak Trail Madison WI 53717

HIGGINS, VERNA JESSIE, PLANT PATHOLOGY. *Current Pos:* From asst prof to assoc prof, 69-81, PROF PLANT PATH, UNIV TORONTO, 81-, CHAIR, 92- *Personal Data:* b Brookvale, NS, Feb 11, 43. *Educ:* Acadia Univ, BS, 64; Cornell Univ, MS, 66, PhD(plant path), 69. *Mem:* Am Phytopath Soc; Can Phytopath Soc; Am Soc Plant Physiol. *Res:* Physiological plant pathology; physiology of host-parasite interactions; mechanisms by which plants actively resist infection and response of fungi to such resistance mechanisms. *Mailing Add:* Dept Bot Univ Toronto 25 Willcocks St Toronto ON M5S 3B2 Can. *Fax:* 416-978-5878; *E-Mail:* higgins@botany.utoronto.ca

HIGGINS, W(ILLIAM) F(RANCIS), ELECTRICAL ENGINEERING. *Current Pos:* staff eng, 68-77, GROUP LEADER, MITRE CORP, BEDFORD, 77- *Personal Data:* b Boston, Mass, Sept 2, 20; m 48; c 2. *Educ:* Univ Mass, BS, 50, MS, 53. *Prof Exp:* Engr, Vitro Corp Am, 50-52; instr elec eng, Univ Mass, 52-53 & Brown Univ, 53-55; engr, Sylvania Elec Prod, Inc, Gen Tel & Electronics Corp, 55-60; mem staff, Mass Inst Technol, 60-64 & Sylvania Elec Prod, Inc, Gen Tel & Electronics Corp, 64-68. *Mem:* Inst Elec & Electronics Engrs. *Res:* Statistical communications and systems engineering. *Mailing Add:* H&K Assoc 10 Highgate Rd Wayland MA 01778

HIGGINS, WILLIAM JOSEPH, COMPARATIVE PHYSIOLOGY. *Current Pos:* Asst prof, 73-77, ASSOC PROF ZOOL, UNIV MD, COLLEGE PARK, 77-, ASSOC DEAN, COLS AGR & LIFE SCI, 90- *Personal Data:* b Lakewood, Ohio, May 13, 47; m; c 3. *Educ:* Boston Col, BS, 69; Fla State Univ, PhD(physiol), 73. *Mem:* Am Soc Zoologists; Sigma Xi. *Res:* Cyclic nucleotide control of contractility and membrane permeability of molluscan muscles; cyclic nucleotide regulation of cell growth and division. *Mailing Add:* Dept Zool Univ MD College Park MD 20742-0001

HIGGINSON, GEORGE W, JR, CHEMICAL ENGINEERING. *Current Pos:* RETIRED. *Personal Data:* b Philadelphia, Pa, Oct 6, 23; m 47; c 3. *Educ:* Univ Pa, BS, 43, MS, 48. *Prof Exp:* Chem engr, Bakelite Corp, NY, 43-44; asst instr chem, Univ Pa, 46-47; chem engr, Firestone Plastics Co, Pa, 47-51; develop supvr, Attapulgus Clay Co, NJ, 51-52; process develop engr, Houdry Process & Chem Co Div, Pa, 52-54, asst plant mgr, Paulsboro, NJ, 54-56, plant mgr, 56-68, mgr mfg & mfg serv, 68-69, dir catalyst sales, 69-71, mgr catalyst sales, 71-74, proj mgr, 74-76, sales mgr, Catalytic, Inc, Subsidiary, Air Prods & Chem, Inc, 76-81. *Mem:* Am Chem Soc; Am Inst Chem Engrs. *Res:* Chemical production and sales management. *Mailing Add:* 22 Chadwyn Dr Palermo NJ 08230

HIGGINSON, JOHN, pathology, environmental carcinogenesis, for more information see previous edition

HIGGS, LLOYD ALBERT, RADIO ASTRONOMY. *Current Pos:* DIR, DOMINION RADIO ASTROPHYS OBSERV, BC, 81-, PRIN RES OFFICER, 96- *Personal Data:* b Moncton, NB, June 21, 37; m 66; c 3. *Educ:* Univ NB, BSc, 58; Oxford Univ, DPhil, 61. *Prof Exp:* Asst res officer, Radio Astron Sect, Nat Res Coun Can, 61-67, assoc res officer astrophys, 67-74, sr res officer, Herzberg Inst Astrophys, 75-81. *Concurrent Pos:* Sci civil servant, Observ, State Univ Leiden, 64-65; ed, J Royal Astron Soc Can, 76-80. *Mem:* Am Astron Soc; Royal Astron Soc Can (pres, 88-); Royal Astron Soc; Can Astron Soc (vpres, 88-). *Res:* Physics of interstellar medium, diffuse nebulae; astronomical automation and data processing. *Mailing Add:* Dominion Radio Astrophys Observ Nat Res Coun Can Box 248 Penticton BC V2A 6K3 Can

HIGGS, ROBERT HUGHES, GEOMAGNETICS. *Current Pos:* RETIRED. *Personal Data:* b Morgantown, WVa, July 29, 32; m 57, Marcia J Buchanan; c Kathi, Steven & Lori. *Educ:* Pa State Univ, BS, 54; Univ Ariz, 58. *Honors & Awards:* Navy Civilian Meritorious Serv Award & Medal, 77. *Prof Exp:* Navy officer, instr & supvr explosive ord disposal, 54-57; geophysicist, US Naval Oceanog Off, 58-63, head, Magnetics Div, Marine Br, 63-74, dir, Magnetics Div, 74-76, phys sci adminr & dir, Hydrographic Dept, 76-86, sci & tech dir, 85-86, dir, Geophys Dept, 86-87, geophys & mgt consult, 87-90. *Concurrent Pos:* Mem, Soc Explor Geophysicists Comt for Nat Magnetic Anomaly Map, 75-81 & NAm Magnetic Anomaly Map Comt, Geol Soc Am. *Mem:* Am Geophys Union; Soc Explor Geophysicists; Geol Soc Am; Sigma Xi; Archaeol Inst Am; Nat Speleol Soc. *Res:* Application of geomagnetic survey data to navigation and antisubmarine warfare problems; geological interpretation of geomagnetic data; geomagnetic temporal variation studies; geophysics and hydrographic surveying. *Mailing Add:* 3031 Oak Hill Rd Sevierville TN 37862-7584

HIGGS, ROGER L, CROP BREEDING, GENETICS. *Current Pos:* Assoc prof, 66-77, PROF AGRON, UNIV WIS-PLATTEVILLE, 77- *Personal Data:* b Trivoli, Ill, Apr 10, 38; m 62; c 2. *Educ:* Univ Ill, BS, 60, MS, 61; Iowa State Univ, PhD(crop breeding), 66. *Mem:* Am Forage & Grassland Coun; Am Soc Agron; Crop Sci Soc Am; Soil Conserv Soc Am. *Res:* Corn breeding and hybrid evaluation; crop sequence; alfalfa fertilization; corn cultural experiments; agricultural mathematics. *Mailing Add:* Agr Univ Wis One University Plaza Platteville WI 53818-3099

HIGH, LEE RAWDON, JR, GEOLOGY. *Current Pos:* CONSULT GEOLOGIST, MOBIL EXPLOR & PROD SERV INC, 78- *Personal Data:* b Pine Bluff, Ark, Feb 6, 41; c 3. *Educ:* Princeton Univ, AB, 63; Rice Univ, PhD(geol), 67. *Prof Exp:* Instr geol, Univ Nebr, 66-67; asst prof, 67-72, assoc prof geol, Oberlin Col, 72-78. *Concurrent Pos:* Petrol Res Fund res grants, 67-69 & 71-; Res Corp res grant, 70-71. *Mem:* Am Asn Petrol Geol; Geol Soc Am; Soc Econ Paleont & Mineral. *Res:* Environmental interpretation of sedimentary rocks; lacustrine rocks; recent coastal sediments; sedimentary structures; Triassic stratigraphy; environmental and archaeological geology; regional geology. *Mailing Add:* 2129 Winslow Dr Plano TX 75023

HIGHET, ROBERT JOHN, ORGANIC CHEMISTRY. *Current Pos:* CHEMIST, NAT HEART, LUNG & BLOOD INST, 54- *Personal Data:* b Springfield, Ill, Oct 6, 25; m 55; c 3. *Educ:* Univ Ill, BS, 50; Univ Wis, PhD(chem), 54. *Prof Exp:* Chemist, E I du Pont de Nemours & Co, Inc, 52. *Concurrent Pos:* Am Cancer Soc res fel, Swiss Fed Inst Technol, 57-58. *Mem:* Am Chem Soc; The Chem Soc; NY Acad Sci. *Res:* Alkaloids of the Amaryllidaceae and Cassia species; nuclear magnetic resonance and mass spectrometry. *Mailing Add:* 6004 Anniston Rd Bethesda MD 20817

HIGHLAND, HENRY ARTHUR, ECONOMIC ENTOMOLOGY. *Current Pos:* ENTOMOLOGIST, USDA, 57- *Personal Data:* b Patchogue, NY, July 17, 24; m 51; c 4. *Educ:* Washington Col, BS, 50; Univ Md, MS, 55, PhD, 57. *Prof Exp:* Biol aide, NIH, 50-51 & USDA, 51-53; asst, Univ Md, 53-57. *Mem:* Am Asn Cereal Chem; Entom Soc Am. *Res:* House fly attractants and baits; biology and control of insects affecting ornamental plants; stored-product insects; insect resistant food packaging. *Mailing Add:* 424 E Macon St Savannah GA 31401

HIGHLAND, VIRGIL LEE, physics; deceased, see previous edition for last biography

HIGHLANDER-BULTEMA, SARAH KATHERINE, BACTERIAL GENE EXPRESSION, BACTERIAL GENETICS. *Current Pos:* ASST PROF MICROBIOL & IMMUNOL, BAYLOR COL MED, 90- *Personal Data:* b Kalamazoo, Mich, Aug 7, 56; m 84, Stephen. *Educ:* Univ Mich, BS, 78; NY Univ, MS, 84, PhD(microbiol), 85. *Prof Exp:* Res asst, Upjohn Co, 78-81; res fel, Univ Tex Med Sch, Houston, 85-90. *Mem:* Am Soc Microbiol; Asn Women Sci. *Res:* Study of protein-DNA interactions involved in transcriptional regulation of virulence genes in Pasteurella nacmolytica; examining amino acid transport in this organism. *Mailing Add:* Dept Microbiol Baylor Col Med One Baylor Plaza Houston TX 77030-3411. *E-Mail:* sarahh@bcm.tmc.edu

HIGHLANDS, MATTHEW EDWARD, BACTERIOLOGY, FOOD SCIENCE. *Current Pos:* assoc food technologist, Agr Exp Sta, Maine, 47-68, head, Dept Food Sci, 55-68, prof food technol, 55-70, EMER PROF FOOD SCI, UNIV MAINE, ORONO, 70- *Personal Data:* b Huntington, Ind, June 19, 05; m 31. *Educ:* Univ Maine, AB, 28; Mass Inst Technol, SM, 34; Univ Mass, PhD, 51. *Prof Exp:* Asst microbiol, Mass Inst Technol, 28-29, 32-34, res assoc, 35; assoc bacteriologist, Frigidaire Corp, Div, Gen Motors Corp, Ohio, 29-32; bacteriologist & food technologist, Palo Prod Co, PR, 34-35;

from instr to asst prof bact, Univ Maine, 35-42; mgr res & processing, Friend Bro, Inc, Mass, 46; prod mgr, Lange Canning Corp, Wis, 47. *Concurrent Pos:* Dir, Food & Container Assocs, 58-60. *Mem:* Am Soc Microbiol; Inst Food Tech; Am Inst Chem Eng. *Res:* Freezing of fruits; potato product development; canning technology; dehydration of vegetables; technology of processed fisheries products. *Mailing Add:* 111 Forest Ave Orono ME 04473

HIGHLEY, TERRY L, FOREST PRODUCTS PATHOLOGY, WOODS DECAY. *Current Pos:* PLANT PATHOLOGIST, US FOREST PROD LAB, 67-; WOOD DETERIORIZATION CONSULT, HIGHLEY CONSULT, 97- *Personal Data:* b Anamosa, Iowa, July 3, 40; m 67, Barbara McKnight; c Christopher & Stephanie. *Educ:* Iowa State Univ, BS, 62; Ore State Univ, MS, 64, PhD(plant path), 67. *Honors & Awards:* Annual Colley Lectr Award, Am Wood Preservers Asn, 89. *Concurrent Pos:* Res plant pathologist, Forest Prod Labs, US Forest Serv, 67-86, supvry res plant pathologist, 86-97; co-ed, Mat Organism, 92- *Mem:* Int Res Group Wood Preserv; Am Phytopath Soc. *Res:* Forest products pathology; fungal hydrolytic enzymes; natural durability of wood; nontoxic methods of improving durability of wood; deterioration of wood in the marine environment; applied studies in diagnosis of wood decay and remedial treatments. *Mailing Add:* 1 Gifford Pinchot Dr Madison WI 53705. *E-Mail:* 75164.3371@compuserve.com

HIGHSMITH, PHILLIP E, physics, for more information see previous edition

HIGHSMITH, RAYMOND C, INTERTIDAL ECOLOGY, CORAL REEF ECOLOGY. *Current Pos:* PROF MARINE SCI, INST MARINE SCI, UNIV ALASKA, FAIRBANKS, 83-; DIR, WEST COAST NAT UNDERSEA RES CTR, 90- *Personal Data:* b State Center, Iowa, July 8, 41. *Educ:* Univ Iowa, BA, 72; Univ Wash, PhD(zool), 79. *Prof Exp:* Fel, Smithsonian Inst, 79-81, Univ Wash, 81-83. *Res:* Ecology of benthic communities. *Mailing Add:* Inst Marine Sci Univ Alaska PO Box 757220 Fairbanks AK 99775-7220

HIGHSMITH, ROBERT F, BASIC SCIENCE RESEARCH, CELL CULTURE. *Current Pos:* PROF PHYSIOL & BIOPHYS, COL MED, UNIV CINCINNATI, 75- *Personal Data:* b June 22, 45; m 67; c 2. *Educ:* Univ Cincinnati, PhD(physiol), 72. *Prof Exp:* Fel biophys, Harvard Med Sch, 72-74. *Concurrent Pos:* Consult & prin investr, NIH; mem comt, Soc Exp Biol & Med. *Mem:* Am Physiol Soc; Int Soc Thrombosis/Hemostasis; Soc Exp Biol & Med; AAAS. *Res:* Intercellular communication in the blood vessel wall; endothelial cell-vascular smooth muscle coupling; ion channels. *Mailing Add:* Physiol & Biophys Univ Cincinnati Med Col 231 Bethesda Ave PO Box 670576 Cincinnati OH 45267-0576. *Fax:* 513-558-2639

HIGHSMITH, RONALD EARL, POLYMER FLOCCULANTS, POLYELECTROLYTES. *Current Pos:* DIR RES & DEVELOP, DOW CHEM CO, RICHMOND, VA, 91-; AT ALLIED. *Personal Data:* b Olney, Ill, Feb 2 39; m 63; c 2. *Educ:* Eastern Ill Univ, BS, 63; Univ Fla, PhD(chem), 68. *Prof Exp:* Fel & lectr, Chem Dept, Univ Pa, 68-69; chemist, Carborundum Co, Niagara Falls, NY, 69-72, proj mgr, 72-77, new prod mgr, Knoxville Tenn, 77-78; gen mgr, Micron Chem Co, Knoxville, Tenn, 78-80; dir res & develop water treat polymers, Allied-Signal Inc, Syracuse, NY, 80-88; dir res & develop, Polypure Inc, 88-91. *Res:* Water purification; water pollution control; sludge dewatering equipment; polymer flocculants; polymer hydrogels; microbial polysaccharides; mechanisms of polymer flocculation; synthesis of polymer flocculants; colloid chemistry. *Mailing Add:* 9100 Avocet Ct Chesterfield VA 23838

HIGHSTEIN, STEPHEN MORRIS, ANIMAL PHYSIOLOGY. *Current Pos:* PROF OTOLARYNGOL, ANAT & NEUROBIOL, WASH UNIV, ST LOUIS, 83- *Personal Data:* b Baltimore, Md, Aug 23, 39; m 69; c 2. *Educ:* Rensselaer Polytech Inst, BS, 61; Med Sch, Univ Md, MD, 65, Univ Tokyo, PhD(physiol), 76. *Prof Exp:* Intern med, Maimonides Hosp, NY, 65-66; resident med, Mt Sinai Hosp, NY, 66-69; fel physiol, Fac Med, Univ Tokyo, 69-72; asst prof neurol, Mt Sinai Hosp, NY, 73-74; from asst prof to prof neurosci, Albert Einstein Col Med, NY, 74-83. *Concurrent Pos:* Fel, Nat Inst Neruol, Commun Disorders & Stroke; scholar, New York Health Coun Career Scientist, 73-75, NIH Res Career Develop Award, 75-80; chair, Nat Acad Res Study Sect; mem, Soc Neurosci Prog Comt & Panel NIH/NINDS Nat Strategic Res Plan. *Mem:* Soc Neurosci; Am Physiol Soc; Int Brain Res Orgn. *Res:* Structure function studies of the central vestibular and oculomotor systems using intracellular recording and staining; cellular basis of responses of the peripheral vestibular apparatus including efferent control, using intracellular recording and staining, molecular techniques. *Mailing Add:* Dept Anat & Otol & Neurobiol Wash Univ Med 660 S Euclid Ave Box 8115 St Louis MO 63110

HIGHT, DONALD WAYNE, MATHEMATICS. *Current Pos:* assoc prof, 62-67, PROF MATH, PITTSBURG STATE UNIV, 67- *Personal Data:* b Neodesha, Kans, Aug 23, 31; m 51; c 2. *Educ:* Kans State Col Pittsburg, BS, 53; Okla State Univ, MS, 58, EdD(math educ), 61. *Prof Exp:* Teacher high schs, Kans, 53, 55-57, 58-60; asst prof math, Ark State Col, 61-62. *Concurrent Pos:* NSF sci fac fel, Univ Mass, 67-68; dir, Am Asn Col Teachers Educ, 71-74; mem adv coun, Assoc Orgns for Teacher Educ, 70. *Mem:* Math Asn Am. *Res:* Mathematics education and participation in accreditation of teacher education by learned societies and academic organizations. *Mailing Add:* RR2 Pittsburg KS 66762

HIGHT, ROBERT, SOLID STATE PHYSICS. *Current Pos:* RETIRED. *Personal Data:* b Springfield, Mo, Mar 16, 30; m 62. *Educ:* Southwest Mo State Col, BS, 55; Univ Mo, MS, 59, PhD(physics), 62. *Prof Exp:* Assoc physicist, Midwest Res Inst, 61-62; asst prof physics, Kans State Col Pittsburg, 62-65; from asst prof to assoc prof, Univ Mo, St Louis, 65-91. *Mem:* Am Phys Soc; Am Asn Physics Teachers. *Res:* Debye-Waller characteristics of II-VI and III-V compounds. *Mailing Add:* 13101 Dartagnan St St Louis MO 69141

HIGHTON, RICHARD, HERPETOLOGY. *Current Pos:* From asst prof to assoc prof, 56-73, PROF ZOOL, UNIV MD, COLLEGE PARK, 73- *Personal Data:* b Chicago, Ill, Dec 24, 27; m 50; c 4. *Educ:* NY Univ, AB, 50; Univ Fla, MS, 53, PhD(biol), 56. *Mem:* Fel AAAS; Am Soc Naturalists; Soc Study Evolution; Genetics Soc Am; Am Soc Ichthyologists & Herpetologists (pres, 76); Soc Syst Zool; Ecol Soc Am. *Res:* Evolution; population genetics; systematics; life history of salamanders. *Mailing Add:* Dept Zool Univ Md College Park MD 20742

HIGHTOWER, COLLIN JAMES, NUMBER THEORY. *Current Pos:* Asst prof, Boulder, 65-72, vchmn in charge Denver Ctr, 67-69, math chmn, 72-76, PROF MATH, UNIV COLO, DENVER, 72- *Personal Data:* b Liverpool, Eng, Aug 12, 36; US citizen; m 65; c 2. *Educ:* Univ Ark, BS, 58; Tulane Univ, PhD(math), 63. *Mem:* Math Asn Am; Am Math Soc. *Res:* Geometry of numbers. *Mailing Add:* 1720 Shallot Circle LaFayette CO 80026

HIGHTOWER, DAN, VETERINARY NUCLEAR MEDICINE. *Current Pos:* assoc prof, 66-72, PROF VET PHYSIOL & PHARMACOL, TEX A&M UNIV, 72- *Personal Data:* b Eastland, Tex, Oct 15, 25; m 51. *Educ:* Tex A&M Univ, DVM, 46; NC State Univ, MS, 61. *Prof Exp:* Vet officer, Vet Corps, US Army, 46-56, radiation planning officer, Qm Radiation Planning Agency, 57-59, chief reactor sect, Walter Reed Army Inst Res, 61-63 & Dept Biophys, 63-66. *Mem:* AAAS; Am Vet Med Asn; Radiation Res Soc; Soc Nuclear Med. *Res:* Biological effects of particulate radiations; neutrons, use of radioisotopes in biology and medicine and applications of activation analysis to biology and medicine. *Mailing Add:* Dept Vet Physiol & Pharmacol Tex A&M Univ College Station TX 77843-4466

HIGHTOWER, FELDA, surgery, for more information see previous edition

HIGHTOWER, JAMES K, OBJECT ORIENTED PROGRAMMING LANGUAGES & METHODS. *Current Pos:* assoc dir, Comput & Commun Resources, Calif State Univ, 76-90, adminr, Spec Proj, 91-94, prof develop leave, 93-94, dir acad comput, 90-91, PROF MGT SCI/INFO SYSTS, CALIF STATE UNIV, FULLERTON, 94- *Personal Data:* b Kalamazoo, Mich, Mar 22, 37; m 57, Sharon J Wiley; c Matthew W & Elizabeth (Putrino). *Educ:* Kalamazoo Col, AB, 58; Claremont Grad Sch, MA, 67, PhD(econ), 70. *Prof Exp:* Nat Defense Emergency Authorization fel, 60-63; asst prof math & econ, Univ Richmond, 64-67; asst prof econ, Calif State Polytech Univ, Pomona, 67-68; assoc dean, Grad Prog, Calif State Univ, Fullerton, 70-73, assoc prof quant methods, 69-76. *Concurrent Pos:* Lectr, Claremont Grad Sch, 67-69 & 73-; adj prof comput sci, Calif State Univ, Dominguez Hills, 83-87, Fullerton, 88-90. *Mem:* Asn Comput Mach; Inst Elec & Electronics Engrs; NY Acad Sci; Econometric Soc. *Res:* Object oriented programming languages and methods. *Mailing Add:* Dept Mgt Sci/Info Systs Calif State Univ Fullerton CA 92634-9480. *Fax:* 909-624-0641; *E-Mail:* hightower@acm.org, hightower@acm.org

HIGHTOWER, JESSE ROBERT, CHEMICAL ENGINEERING. *Current Pos:* Staff mem process develop, Oak Ridge Nat Lab, 64-74, prog mgr, 74-76, sect head process res & develop, Martin Marietta Energy Systs, Inc, 76-88, ASSOC DIV DIR, RADIO CHEM PROC, OAK RIDGE NAT LAB, 88- *Personal Data:* b Cleveland, Tenn, Apr 9, 39; m 61; c 1. *Educ:* Univ Miss, BS, 61; Tulane Univ, MS, 63, PhD(chem eng), 64. *Mem:* Am Inst Chem Engrs; AAAS. *Res:* Nuclear fuel processing development; development of fossil fuel conversion technology; chemical engineering research and development. *Mailing Add:* 104 Scenic Dr Oak Ridge TN 37830

HIGHTOWER, JOE W(ALTER), PHYSICAL CHEMISTRY, CHEMICAL ENGINEERING. *Current Pos:* assoc prof chem eng, 67-71, PROF CHEM ENG, RICE UNIV, 71- *Personal Data:* b Morrilton, Ark, Sept 14, 36; m 80, Ann Grekel; c Amy M. *Educ:* Harding Col, BS, 59; Johns Hopkins Univ, MS, 61, PhD(catalysis), 63. *Honors & Awards:* Nat Petrol Chem Award, Am Chem Soc, 73; Jefferson Prize, 83. *Prof Exp:* NSF fel catalysis, Queen's Univ, Belfast, 63-64; Gulf fel, Mellon Inst, 64-67. *Concurrent Pos:* Res grants, Petrol Res Fund & NASA, 68-70, NSF, 69-71, Welch Found, 69-72 & Baroid Div grant, NL Industs, 71-75; consult, Exxon Res & Eng, 68-71, Chevron Oil Field Res Co, 72-76, several Nat Res Coun panels on auto emission control catalysts, 72-77, Monsanto Co, 74- & Catalytica Assocs, 74-85; founder & pres, Human Resources Develop Found, 68-; chmn, Gordon Res Conf Catalysis, 73; chmn adv bd, Petrol Res Found, 82-92; pres, Dow Chem, 84-86. *Mem:* Am Chem Soc; Catalysis Soc; Am Inst Chem Engrs; Southwest Catalysis Soc (pres, 68-70); Sigma Xi. *Res:* Heterogeneous catalysis, mainly with the use of isotopic tracers to study reaction mechanisms. *Mailing Add:* Dept Chem Eng MS-362 Rice Univ 6100 Main St Houston TX 77005-1892. *Fax:* 713-285-5478; *E-Mail:* jhigh@rice.edu

HIGHTOWER, KENNETH RALPH, biophysics, for more information see previous edition

HIGHTOWER, LAWRENCE EDWARD, BIOCHEMISTRY, MOLECULAR BIOLOGY. *Current Pos:* from asst prof to assoc prof, 75-85, PROF BIOL, UNIV CONN, 85- *Personal Data:* b Fresno, Calif, June 2, 46; m 70; c 1. *Educ:* Hampden-Sydney Col, BS, 68; Harvard Univ, PhD(biochem), 74. *Prof Exp:* Instr microbiol, Med Sch, Univ Mass, 74-75. *Concurrent Pos:* Cell biol adv panel, NSF, 81-84. *Mem:* Am Soc Microbiol; Am Soc Cell Biol; AAAS; Protein Soc; Soc Molecular Biol & Evolution; Soc Environ Toxicol & Chem. *Res:* Molecular and cell biology of environmental stress responses; the heat shock response in mammalian, avian, and fish cells. *Mailing Add:* Dept Molecular & Cell Biol Univ Conn Storrs CT 06269-3044. *Fax:* 860-486-1784

HIGHTOWER, NICHOLAS CARR, JR, physiology; deceased, see previous edition for last biography

HIGINBOTHAM, WILLIAM ALFRED, arms control; deceased, see previous edition for last biography

HIGLEY, LEON GEORGE, ARTHROPOD & PLANT STRESS RELATIONSHIPS, PEST MANAGEMENT THEORY. *Current Pos:* ASST PROF, UNIV NEBR, 89- *Personal Data:* b Sacramento, Calif, Mar 7, 58; m 81; c 1. *Educ:* Cornell Univ, BA, 80; Iowa State Univ, MS, 84, PhD(entom & crop physiol), 88. *Honors & Awards:* J H Comstock Award, Entom Soc Am. *Prof Exp:* Temp asst prof, Iowa State Univ, 88-89. *Mem:* Entom Soc Am; Crop Sci Soc; Am Agron Soc. *Res:* Plant physiological responses to biotic stress; arthropod and plant stress interactions; photosynthetic responses to injury; pest management theory; soybean entomology; insect ecology. *Mailing Add:* 202 Plant Indust Bldg Univ Nebr Lincoln NE 68583-0816

HIGMAN, DONALD GORDON, MATHEMATICS. *Current Pos:* from asst prof to assoc prof, 57-63, PROF MATH, UNIV MICH, ANN ARBOR, 63- *Personal Data:* b Vancouver, BC, Sept 20, 28; m 49; c 3. *Educ:* Univ BC, BA, 49; Univ Ill, MA, 50, PhD(math), 52. *Prof Exp:* Nat Res Coun fel, 52-54; assoc prof math, Univ Mont, 54-57. *Concurrent Pos:* Vis prof, Univ Frankfurt, 62-63. *Res:* Group theory. *Mailing Add:* Dept Math Univ Mich Ann Arbor MI 48109

HIGMAN, HENRY BOOTH, NEUROCHEMISTRY, PHARMACOLOGY. *Current Pos:* PROF NEUROL & CHMN DEPT, SCH MED, UNIV PITTSBURGH, 68- *Personal Data:* b Millington, Md, Mar 17, 27; m 52; c 4. *Educ:* St John's Col, BA, 50; Univ Md, MD, 55. *Prof Exp:* Intern, Del Hosp, Wilmington, 55-56; resident, Dept Neurol, La State Univ, 56-59; instr neurol, Univ, 62-64; from asst prof to assoc prof, Univ Ill, 64-67. *Concurrent Pos:* NIH spec training fel neurochem, Col Physicians & Surgeons, Columbia Univ, 59-62; NIH grant, 64-68; res career develop award, 66-68; mem, Neurol Sci Res Training Comt, Nat Inst Neurol Dis & Blindness, 67-71. *Mem:* Am Acad Neurol; Am Neurol Asn; assoc Am Asn Neuropath; Int Soc Neurochem. *Res:* Molecular mechanism of cholinergic transmission; ion flux in excitable membranes. *Mailing Add:* Dept Neurol Sch Med Univ Pittsburgh Pittsburgh PA 15261

HIGMAN, JAMES B, FISHERIES. *Current Pos:* fishery biologist, Inst Marine Sci, 59-67, RES SCIENTIST, ROSENSTIEL SCH MARINE & ATMOSPHERIC SCI, UNIV MIAMI, 67-, EXEC DIR, GULF & CARIBBEAN FISHERIES INST, 59- *Personal Data:* b Millington, Md, Feb 22, 22; m 49; c 4. *Educ:* Western Md Col, AB, 43; Univ Miami, MS, 65. *Prof Exp:* Fishery biologist, Marine Lab, Univ Miami, 50-56; fisheries methods & equip specialist, US Fish & Wildlife Serv, Fla & Washington, DC, 56-59. *Mem:* Am Fisheries Soc; Am Inst Fishery Res Biol. *Res:* Fisheries. *Mailing Add:* 5891 SW 49th St Miami FL 33155

HIGUCHI, HIROSHI, FLUID MECHANICS. *Current Pos:* assoc prof, 89-96, PROF DEPT MECH & AEROSPACE ENG, SYRACUSE UNIV, 96- *Personal Data:* b Japan. *Educ:* Univ Tokyo, BS, 70; Calif Inst Technol, MS, 71, PhD(aeronaut), 77. *Honors & Awards:* Space Act Award, NASA, 88. *Prof Exp:* Res assoc, Nat Res Coun, NASA Ames, 76-77; res scientist, Dynamics Technol, 77-80; sr res assoc, Univ Santa Clara, 80-81; res assoc asst prof, Univ Minn, 81-89. *Concurrent Pos:* Prin investr, NASA Ames Res Ctr, 76-81; mem, Nat Parachute Technol Coun, 90- *Mem:* Assoc fel Am Inst Aeronaut & Astronaut; Am Soc Mech Engrs; Am Phys Soc. *Res:* Bluff body aerodynamics; vortex interactions; turbulent boundary layers and wakes; hydroacoustics. *Mailing Add:* Dept Mech & Aerospace Eng Syracuse Univ Syracuse NY 13244-1240

HIGUCHI, WILLIAM IYEO, PHARMACEUTICAL CHEMISTRY. *Current Pos:* from assoc prof to prof pharm, 62-76, PROF DENT, UNIV MICH, ANN ARBOR, 66-, ALBERT B PRESCOTT PROF PHARM, 76-; AT PHARMACEUT DEPT, COL PHARM, UNIV UTAH. *Personal Data:* b San Jose, Calif, Mar 16, 31; m 56; c 4. *Educ:* San Jose State Col, AB, 52; Univ Calif, PhD(chem), 57. *Honors & Awards:* Ebert Prize, Am Pharmaceut Asn, 68 & 70, Res Achievement Award Phys Pharm, 70. *Prof Exp:* Proj assoc phys pharm, Univ Wis, 56-58; res chemist phys chem, Calif Res Corp, 58-59; asst prof phys pharm, Univ Wis, 59-62. *Concurrent Pos:* Mem dent training comt, Nat Inst Dent Res. *Mem:* AAAS; Am Chem Soc; Am Pharmaceut Asn; fel Acad Pharmaceut Sci; Am Asn Dent Res; Sigma Xi. *Res:* Physical pharmaceutical chemistry; thermodynamic and kinetic behavior of polyphase systems; nucleation kinetics; dissolution phenomena; adsorption and surface properties; colloids, emulsions and suspensions; solubilization phenomena in aqueous and nonaqueous systems; enamel demineralization mechanisms. *Mailing Add:* Pharmaceut Dept Col Pharm Univ Utah Salt Lake City UT 84112-1102

HIHARA, LLOYD HIROMI, CORROSION, MECHANICAL BEHAVIOR OF MATERIALS. *Current Pos:* ASST PROF MECH ENG, UNIV HAWAII, MANOA, 89- *Personal Data:* b Honolulu, Hawaii, Oct 29, 61. *Educ:* Univ Hawaii, Manoa, BS, 83; Mass Inst Technol, SM, 85, PhD(mat sci & eng), 89. *Concurrent Pos:* Prin investr, NSF, 90- & TRW grant, 93-94; Am Soc Mech Engrs outstanding fac award, Univ Hawaii, 90; presidential young investr award, NSF, 90. *Mem:* Nat Asn Corrosion Engrs; Electrochem Soc; Metall Soc; Am Soc Mech Engrs; Sigma Xi; Am Water Work Asn. *Res:* Corrosion studies of: metal-matrix composites, ceramic films on metal substrates, and copper. *Mailing Add:* 718 Hoomoe St Pearl City HI 96782-2949. *Fax:* 808-956-2373

HIHARA-ENDO, LINDA MASAE, WATER RESOURCES. *Current Pos:* CHIEF OPERS BR, PAC OCEAN DIV, US ARMY CORPS ENGRS, 94- *Personal Data:* b Honolulu, Hawaii, May 10, 56; m 85, Howard K Endo; c Ashley M, Nicole S & Sara E. *Educ:* Univ Hawaii, BS, 78; Univ Calif, Berkeley, MS, 79, PhD(civil eng), 84. *Prof Exp:* Hydraul engr, US Army CEngrs Pac Ocean Div, 84-90, chief, Environ Br, 90-91, actg chief, Environ Div, 91-92; asst prof civil eng, Univ Hawaii, Manoa, 92-94. *Concurrent Pos:* Asst prof, Water Resources Res Ctr, Univ Hawaii, 93-94. *Mem:* Am Soc Civil Engrs; Am Water Works Asn; Water Environ Fedn. *Res:* Studies of chemical migration in the vadose zone; nutrient biogeochemistry and water stability. *Mailing Add:* 98-1860 E Kaahumanu St Pearl City HI 96782. *Fax:* 808-438-4060; *E-Mail:* linda.hihara-endo@pod01.usace.army.mil

HIKIDA, ROBERT SEIICHI, EXPERIMENTAL MORPHOLOGY, HISTOLOGY. *Current Pos:* asst prof, 69-73, assoc prof, 73-77, PROF ZOOL, OHIO UNIV, 77-, PROF MICROANAT, COL OSTEOP MED, 91- *Personal Data:* b Long Beach, Calif, June 3, 41; m 64, Geraldine Karen Oki; c Stephen M. *Educ:* Univ Ill, BS, 63, MS, 65, PhD(zool), 67. *Prof Exp:* Nat Inst Neurol Dis & Blindness res assoc biol, Columbia Univ, 67-69. *Concurrent Pos:* Assoc ed, Anatomical Record, 80- *Mem:* Am Col Sports Med; Am Asn Anat; Am Soc Cell Biol. *Res:* Nucleo-cytoplasmic relations in muscle; maintenance of skeletal muscle integrity; regeneration, neurotrophism, development; ultrastructure, histochemistry and histology; adaptations of human muscle to activity; aging changes in muscle. *Mailing Add:* Dept Biol Sci Ohio Univ Athens OH 45701-2979. *Fax:* 740-593-0300; *E-Mail:* hikida@ouvaxa.cats.ohiou.edu

HILAL, SADEK K, RADIOLOGY. *Current Pos:* from asst prof to assoc prof, 63-69, PROF RADIOL, COL PHYSICIANS & SURGEONS, COLUMBIA UNIV, 69-, DIR NEURORADIOL, 75- *Personal Data:* b Cairo, Egypt, Mar 11, 30; US citizen; m 64; c 4. *Educ:* Univ Cairo, MD, 55; Univ Minn, PhD(radiol), 66. *Honors & Awards:* Gold Medal, Asn Univ Radiologists, 62. *Prof Exp:* Resident radiation ther, Mem Ctr Cancer & Allied Dis, 57-58; resident radiodiag, Univ Minn, 59-61. *Concurrent Pos:* Res grants diag & therapeut radiol & radiologist training grant; assoc ed, Invest Radiol & Child's Brain; chmn, Int Symp Small Vessel Angiography; consult, Study Sect, NIH & Am Bd Radiol. *Mem:* Am Roentgen Ray Soc; Am Col Radiol; Asn Univ Radiologists; Radiol Soc NAm; Am Soc Neuroradiol (pres, 77-78). *Res:* Neuroradiology radiodiagnosis; cerebral blood flow and angiography; methodology; radiographic image improvement; exploration of the small intracranial vessels in man with a magnetic catheter and the conduction of interventional procedures; toxicity of radiographic contrast media; developed the fourth generation computed tomography scanner. *Mailing Add:* 710 W 168th St New York NY 10032-2603. *Fax:* 212-305-5718

HILBERG, ALBERT WILLIAM, PATHOLOGY. *Current Pos:* RETIRED. *Personal Data:* b Michigan City, Ind, Apr 5, 22; m 43, Rosemary Kross; c Jeffrey, Eric, David, Kristin & Susan. *Educ:* Elmhurst Col, BS, 44; Ind Univ, MD, 46. *Hon Degrees:* DSc, Elmhurst Col, 61. *Prof Exp:* Intern, Evangel Hosp, Chicago, 46-47; from asst to instr path, Sch Med, Univ Iowa, 49-51; pathologist, Lab Path, Nat Cancer Inst, 52-57, head cytodiag serv, Dept Path Anat, 53-57, path consult, Field Invests & Demonstrations Br & head cytol sect, 57-62; chief radiopath div, Armed Forces Inst Path, 62-65; dep chief res br, Div Radiol Health, USPHS, MD, 65-67, chief pop studies prog, Nat Ctr Radiol Health, 67-68; prof assoc, Div Med Sci, Nat Acad Sci-Nat Res Coun, 68-79. *Concurrent Pos:* Fel, Hosp for Joint Dis, NY, 51-52. *Mem:* Am Asn Path & Bact; emer fel Col Am Path; emer fel Am Soc Clin Path; emer mem Soc Nuclear Med; NY Acad Sci; emer mem Int Acad Path. *Res:* Long-term effects of ionizing radiation induction; histogenesis and morphology of bone tumors; exfoliative cytology. *Mailing Add:* 12512 Davan Dr Silver Spring MD 20904

HILBERT, ROBERT S, OPTICS. *Current Pos:* SR VPRES ENG, OPTICAL RES ASSOCS, INC, 75- *Personal Data:* b Washington, DC, Apr 29, 41; m 66; c 2. *Educ:* Univ Rochester, BS, 62, MS, 64. *Prof Exp:* Fel, Inst Optics, Univ Rochester, 62; engr, Itek Corp, 63-65, suprv, 65-67, asst mgr, 67-69, mgr, 69-74, dir, 74-75. *Concurrent Pos:* Lectr, Grad Sch Eng, Northeastern Univ, 67-69. *Mem:* Optical Soc Am; Soc Photo-Optical Instrumentation Engrs. *Res:* Development of new optical products or systems from conception through early production; development of new concepts and designs for optical systems; optical design for a broad variety of fabricated optics. *Mailing Add:* Optical Res Assocs Inc 3280 E Foothill Blvd Pasadena CA 91107

HILBERT, STEPHEN L, CARDIOPULMINOLOGY, PEDIATRICS. *Current Pos:* res pathologist, 76-96, MED OFFICER, CTR DEVICES & RADIOL HEALTH, FOOD & DRUG ADMIN, 96- *Personal Data:* b Hanover, Pa, Apr 27, 47. *Educ:* Univ Md, BS, 71, MS, 74, PhD(path), 76; Georgetown Univ, MD, 96. *Concurrent Pos:* Mem, Thrombosis Coun & Cardiothoracic & Vascular Surg Coun, Am Heart Asn. *Mem:* Soc Biomat; Am Heart Asn. *Mailing Add:* Ctr Devices & Radiol Health Food & Drug Admin 12200 Wilkins Ave Rockville MD 20852. *Fax:* 301-827-3935

HILBERT, STEPHEN RUSSELL, NUMERICAL ANALYSIS, MATHEMATICS. *Current Pos:* Asst prof, 69-74, ASSOC PROF MATH, ITHACA COL, 74- *Personal Data:* b Brooklyn, NY, Dec 27, 42. *Educ:* Univ Notre Dame, BS, 64; Univ Md, College Park, PhD(math), 69. *Mem:* Am Math Soc; Math Asn Am; Soc Indust & Appl Math. *Res:* Galerkin methods; approximation theory. *Mailing Add:* Dept Math Ithaca Col Ithaca NY 14853-5901

HILBORN, DAVID ALAN, BIOCHEMISTRY. *Current Pos:* RES CHEMIST, EASTMAN KODAK CO, 81- *Personal Data:* b Norristown, Pa, Apr 14, 45; m 68; c 2. *Educ:* Lafayette Col, BS, 67; Cornell Univ, PhD(chem), 73. *Prof Exp:* NIH fel cell biol, Salk Inst Biol Studies, 72-74; asst prof chem, Rochester Inst Technol, 74-79, assoc prof, 79-80. *Mem:* Sigma Xi; Am Chem Soc. *Res:* Isolation and characterization of plant lectins; molecular basis of growth regulatory mechanisms in mammalian cells. *Mailing Add:* Ten Southern Hills Circle Henrietta NY 14467

HILBORN, ROBERT CLARENCE, ATOMIC PHYSICS, LASERS. *Current Pos:* PROF PHYSICS, AMHERST COL, 86-, LISA & AMANDA CROSS PROF PHYSICS, 92- *Personal Data:* b Norristown, Pa, June 24, 43; m 70; c Stephen & Kurt. *Educ:* Lehigh Univ, BA, 66; Harvard Univ, MA, 67, PhD(physics), 71. *Hon Degrees:* MA, Amherst Col, 87. *Prof Exp:* Res assoc physics, State Univ NY, Stony Brook, 71-72, lectr, 72-73; from asst prof to prof physics, Oberlin Col, 73-86. *Concurrent Pos:* Vis researcher, Univ Calif, Santa Barbara, 79-80; consult, Gilford Instrument Labs, 81-83; lectr, Taiyuan Univ Tech, Shanxi, People's Repub China, 84; vis prof, Ga Inst Technol, 94. *Mem:* Sigma Xi; Am Asn Physics Teachers (vpres, 94, pres, 96, past-pres, 97); Am Phys Soc. *Res:* Tunable dye lasers; atomic and molecular spectroscopy; Hanle effect and level-crossing experiments; molecular beam experiments; non-linear dynamics. *Mailing Add:* Dept Physics Amherst Col Amherst MA 01002. *E-Mail:* rchilborn@amherst.edu

HILBURN, JOHN L, ELECTROMAGNETICS. *Current Pos:* PRES, MICROCOMPUT SYSTS, INC, 76- *Personal Data:* b Mobile, Ala, June 7, 38; m 61; c 2. *Educ:* Auburn Univ, BEP, 62, MSEE, 64, PhD(elec eng), 67. *Prof Exp:* Engr, Irby & Rester Eng Co, Ala, 56-62; asst elec eng, Auburn Univ, 62-64, instr, 64-67; from asst prof to prof elec eng, La State Univ, Baton Rouge, 67-80. *Mem:* Inst Elec & Electronics Engrs. *Res:* Microcomputers and microcomputer-based industrial instrumentation; antenna and microwave engineering; electromagnetic fields. *Mailing Add:* 1212 Baird Dr Baton Rouge LA 70808

HILD, WALTER J, anatomy; deceased, see previous edition for last biography

HILDE, THOMAS WAYNE CLARK, MARINE GEOPHYSICS, PLATE TECTONICS. *Current Pos:* DIR GEODYNAMICS RES INST & PROF GEOPHYSICS MARINE GEOPHYSICS, TEX A&M UNIV, 77- *Personal Data:* b Stanley, NDak, May 4, 38; m 59; Diane; c Tom & Christine. *Educ:* San Diego State Univ, BA, 63; Univ Tokyo, DSc, 73. *Prof Exp:* Res asst marine geol, Scripps Inst Oceanog, Univ Calif, San Diego, 59-67; oceanogr marine geol & geophysics, US Naval Oceanog Off, 67-70; adv oceanog marine sci, Govt Taiwan, Repub China, 70-73; vis marine geophysicist, Earthquake Res Inst, Univ Tokyo, 73; sr marine geologist & geophysicist, UN, Bangkok, Thailand, 74-76. *Concurrent Pos:* Mem, Western Pac Working Group Inter-Union Comn Geodynamics, 74-80, Ocean Crustal Dynamics Comt, JOI, Inc, 78-81, Gulf Coast Working Group, US Geodynamics Comn, 79-; ed, Western Pac Final Report, Inter-Union Comn Geodynamics, 79-; chmn, oceanic lithosphere working group 4, Int Comn Lithosphere. *Mem:* AAAS; Am Geophys Union; Geol Soc Am. *Res:* Marine geophysics and tectonic evolution of the western Pacific marginal seas; origin and evolution of the Pacific Ocean basin; studies of convergence, subduction and the geodynamics of trench-arc-back arc systems; plate tectonics. *Mailing Add:* 2515 Oak Circle Bryan TX 77802. *Fax:* 409-845-3138

HILDEBOLT, WILLIAM MORTON, FOOD TECHNOLOGY. *Current Pos:* PRES, NATURE'S SELECT PREMIUM TURF SERV, INC, 92. *Personal Data:* b Richmond, Ind, Dec 7, 43; m 64, Sandra Oafler; c William H & Joseph R. *Educ:* Ohio State Univ, BS, 66, MS, 67, PhD(food technol), 69. *Prof Exp:* Teaching assoc food technol, Ohio State Univ, 66-69; from res technologist to sr res technologist, Campbell Soup Co, 69-72, sr res scientist, 72-74, mgr prod develop, 74-77, dir, 77-79, vpres prod technol, 79-83, vpres prod develop, 83-84, vpres int res & develop, 84-85; vpres res & develop, R J Reynolds Tobacco, 85-92. *Concurrent Pos:* Mem bd dirs, Ohio State Univ Res Found, 86-; vchmn & mem bd dirs, Res & Develop Assoc for Mil Food & Packaging Systs, Inc; Nat Acad Sci & Eng partic, Seminar Post-Harvest Food Losses Fruits & Veg, China State Sci & Technol Comn, 84. *Mem:* Sigma Xi; Inst Food Technologists. *Mailing Add:* 3410 Baron Rd Winston Salem NC 27106. *Fax:* 910-768-5280

HILDEBRAND, ADOLF J, ANALYTIC NUMBER THEORY, PROBABILISTIC NUMBER THEORY. *Current Pos:* From asst prof to assoc prof, 86-91, PROF MATH, UNIV ILL, URBANA, 91- *Personal Data:* b Leutkirch, WGer, Nov 25, 56. *Educ:* Univ Freiburg, PhD(math), 83. *Concurrent Pos:* Vis mem math, Inst Advan Study, Princeton, NJ, 90-91; assoc ed, J Number Theory, 90-, Ill J Math, 90- *Mem:* Am Math Soc. *Res:* Problems in number theory such as the distribution of prime numbers or other special sets of integers; questions at the interface between number theory and other areas of mathematics such as analysis, combinatorics and probability theory. *Mailing Add:* Dept Math Univ Ill Urbana IL 61801

HILDEBRAND, BERNARD, FUNDING UNIVERSITY RESEARCH, INTERNATIONAL COOPERATIVE RESEARCH. *Current Pos:* CONSULT, SOUTHEASTERN UNIVS RES ASN, 89- *Personal Data:* b New York, NY, Jan 23, 24; m 50, Ruth Levy; c Deborah & Joanne. *Educ:* Brooklyn Col, BA, 44; Univ Ill, MS, 46; Rensselaer Polytech Inst, PhD(physics), 53. *Prof Exp:* Res asst radar res & develop, Columbia Radiation Lab, Columbia Univ, 44-45; instr & res asst physics, Rensselaer Polytech Inst, 46-52; radiation det engr res & develop, Westinghouse Elec Corp, 52; consult cosmic rays, US Naval Res Lab, 52-60; from asst to assoc prof physics, Worcester Polytech Inst, 53-60; res physicist, US Naval Res Lab, 60-65; physicist high energy physics, AEC, 65-68, chief, Physics Res, Div High Energy Physics, Energy Res & Develop Admin, Dept Energy, 69-88. *Concurrent Pos:* Exec secy, High Energy Physics Adv Panel, 69-76, US-USSR Joint Coord Comt on Fundamental Properties of Matter, 76-88, US-Japan Comt on High Energy Physics, 79-88. *Mem:* Fel Am Phys Soc; Hist Sci Soc; Fedn Am Scientists; Sigma Xi. *Res:* Intergalactic matter path from cosmic ray nuclei transformations; international cooperative emulsion flight studies of ultra high energy jets; funding high energy physics research; high energy physics achievements; continuous electron beam accelerator facility and SSC particle physics in southeastern United States. *Mailing Add:* 7002 Tilden Lane Rockville MD 20852

HILDEBRAND, BERNARD PERCY, OPTICS, ULTRASOUND. *Current Pos:* sr res scientist, Pac Northwest Labs, Battelle Mem Inst, 67-69, mgr, Phys Measurements Sect, 69-71, sr staff engr, 71-89, LEAD SCIENTIST, PAC NORTHWEST LABS, BATTELLE MEM INST, 89- *Personal Data:* b Emerson, Man, May 5, 30; US citizen; m 52; c 2. *Educ:* Univ BC, BASc, 54, MASc, 56; Univ Mich, PhD(elec eng), 67. *Prof Exp:* Electronics engr, Canadair, Ltd, 55-59; sr electronics engr, Hallamore Electronics Co, 59-60; mem tech staff undersea warfare, Hughes Aircraft Co, 60-61; res assoc radar & optics, Inst Sci & Technol, Univ Mich, 61-63, assoc res engr, 63-67. *Concurrent Pos:* Affil prof, Univ Wash, Wash State Univ & Ore State Univ, 69-; Battelle res fel, Battelle Seattle Res Ctr, Wash, 70. *Mem:* Optical Soc Am; Inst Elec & Electronics Engrs; Am Inst Ultrasound Med; Soc Explor Geophysicists. *Res:* Random processes; application of communications and systems technology to the physical sciences such as optics, ultrasonic imaging and seismology; biological effects of ultrasound; digital processing of ultrasonic and television images. *Mailing Add:* Battelle Mem Inst Pac Northwest Labs MS K5-26 Box 999 Battelle Blvd Richland WA 99352

HILDEBRAND, CARL EDGAR, BIOCHEMISTRY, BIOPHYSICS. *Current Pos:* Appointee res, 71-72, actg dep group leader, 81-82, mem staff res, 72-84, DEP GROUP LEADER, LOS ALAMOS NAT LAB, 84- *Personal Data:* b Gettysburg, Pa, June 3, 44; m 66; c 1. *Educ:* Gettysburg Col, BA, 66; Pa State Univ, MS, 68, PhD(biophys), 70. *Concurrent Pos:* Mem Nat Inst Child Health & Human Develop, NIH, 83-84. *Mem:* Am Soc Biochem & Molecular Biol; Am Soc Human Genetics; Am Soc Cell Biol; AAAS. *Res:* Regulation of gene structure and activity; chromosome organization; human genome physical mapping; US patent, on nucleic acid isolation. *Mailing Add:* Genetics Group Los Alamos Nat Lab MS886 Los Alamos NM 87545. *Fax:* 505-667-0851

HILDEBRAND, DAVID KENT, STATISTICS, OPERATIONS RESEARCH. *Current Pos:* Lectr, 65-66, from asst prof to assoc prof, 66-77, PROF STATIST, UNIV PA, 77- *Personal Data:* b Minneapolis, Minn, June 24, 40; m 64; c 2. *Educ:* Carleton Col, BA, 62; Carnegie Inst Technol, MS, 65, PhD(statist), 67. *Hon Degrees:* MA, Univ Pa, 71. *Concurrent Pos:* Vis asst prof statist, Carnegie-Mellon Univ, 70-71. *Mem:* Inst Math Statist; Am Statist Asn. *Res:* Methods for analyzing qualitative data, arising in social science problems. *Mailing Add:* Dept Statist Univ Pa Wharton Sch 3620 Locust Walk Philadelphia PA 19104-6302

HILDEBRAND, DONALD CLAIR, phytobacteriology, for more information see previous edition

HILDEBRAND, FRANCIS BEGNAUD, MATHEMATICS. *Current Pos:* RETIRED. *Personal Data:* b Washington, Pa, Sept 1, 15; m 43; c Susan, Robert & Jean. *Educ:* Washington & Jefferson Col, BS, 36, MA, 38; Mass Inst Technol, PhD(math), 40. *Hon Degrees:* ScD, Washington & Jefferson Col, 69. *Prof Exp:* From instr to prof math, Mass Inst Technol, 40-84, staff mem, Radiation Lab, 42-47. *Mem:* Am Math Soc; Math Asn Am. *Res:* Integral equations; aerodynamics; theory of elasticity; numerical analysis. *Mailing Add:* Seven Bucknell Rd Wellesley MA 02181

HILDEBRAND, HENRY H, MARINE BIOLOGY. *Current Pos:* ASSOC PROF BIOL, TEX A&I UNIV, 73- *Personal Data:* b Greensburg, Kans, Aug 19, 22. *Educ:* Univ Kans, BA, 46; McGill Univ, MS, 48; Univ Tex, PhD(zool), 54. *Prof Exp:* Asst eastern Arctic investr, Can Fish Res Bd, 47-48; aquatic biologist, US Fish & Wildlife Serv, Bering Sea & NPac, 49; res scientist, Inst Marine Sci, Tex, 53-56; prof marine biol, Univ Corpus Christi, 57-73. *Mem:* Am Soc Ichthyologists & Herpetologists; Am Soc Mammal; Soc Vert Paleont; Arctic Inst NAm; Sigma Xi. *Res:* Arctic fishes; natural history of Gulf of Mexico fishes and shrimp; pesticides; fish-eating birds. *Mailing Add:* 413 Millbrook Corpus Christi TX 78418-3942

HILDEBRAND, JOHN G(RANT), NEUROBIOLOGY, NEUROETHOLOGY. *Current Pos:* ASSOC BEHAV BIOL, MUS COMP ZOOL, HARVARD UNIV, 80-; PROF BIOCHEM, ENTOM, MOLECULAR & CELLULAR BIOL, UNIV ARIZONA, 85-, DIR, ARIZONA RES LABS, DIV NEUROBIOL, 85-, REGENT'S PROF NEUROBIOL, 89- *Personal Data:* b Boston, Mass, Mar 26, 42; m 82, Gail

D Burd. *Educ:* Harvard Univ, AB, 64; Rockefeller Univ, PhD(biochem), 69. *Honors & Awards:* Givaudan lectr, Asn Chemoreception Sci, 85; Lang lectr, Marine Biol Lab, Woods Hole, 85; Javits Award, NIH, 86; Merit Award, NIH, 86; Spencer Mem lectr, Univ BC, 90; R H Wright Award Olfactory Res, 90; Max Planck Res Award, Alexander von Humboldt-Stiftung, 90; King Solomon Lectr, Hebrew Univ, Jerusalem, 95; K D Roeder Mem Lectr, Tufts Univ, 95; Felix Snatschi Lectr, Univ Zurich,, 95; Founders Mem Award, Entomol Soc Am, 97. *Prof Exp:* From instr to asst prof, Harvard Med Sch, 70-77, tutor biochem sci, 70-80, assoc prof neurobiol, 77-80, prof biolsci, Columbia Univ, 80-85. *Concurrent Pos:* Teaching fel neurobiol, Harvard Med Sch, 69-70; Helen Hay Whitney Found res fel, 69-72; trustee, Rockefeller Univ, 70-73; estab investr, Am Heart Asn, 72-75; A P Sloan res fel, 73-75; mem, NSF adv panel neurobiol, 74-77, Dana Alliance Brain Initiatives, 93-; prog comt, Soc Neurosci, 78-83; dir, Neurobiol course, 80-84, trustee Marine Biol Lab, Woods Hole, 81-89; regents prof, Univ Ariz, 89-; sci counr, Zool Sta, Naples, Italy, 96- *Mem:* Int Soc Neurobiol (pres, 95-98); Soc Integrative & Comp Biol (pres, 98); Am Soc Biochem & Molecular Biol; Asn Chemoreception Scis; Soc Neurosci (treas, 93-94); fel Royal Entom Soc (UK). *Res:* Chemical aspects of synaptic transmission; physiology and anatomy of chemical senses; developmental neurobiology; behavior and biology of arthropods; chemical ecology of insect-plant interactions. *Mailing Add:* Ariz Res Labs Div Neurobiol 611 Gould-Simpson Bldg Univ Ariz PO Box 21077 Tucson AZ 85721-0077. *Fax:* 520-621-8282; *E-Mail:* jgh@ neurobio.arizona.edu

HILDEBRAND, MILTON, VERTEBRATE MORPHOLOGY. *Current Pos:* Lectr, zool, Univ Calif, Davis, 48-52, from asst prof to assoc prof, 52-61, chmn col lett & sci, 67-69, EMER PROF ZOOL, UNIV CALIF, DAVIS, 86- *Personal Data:* b Philadelphia, Pa, June 15, 18; m 43, Viola Memmler; c Ross, Kern & Joan (Sowada). *Educ:* Univ Calif, AB, 40, MA, 48, PhD(zool), 51. *Mem:* Soc Evolution Integrative Biol; Am Soc Mammal; AAAS. *Res:* Analysis of vertebrate locomotion; bone-muscle systems; effective university teaching; morphology of fossorial mammals. *Mailing Add:* 30 Parkside Dr Davis CA 95616

HILDEBRAND, ROGER HENRY, ASTRONOMY. *Current Pos:* from asst prof to assoc prof physics, Univ Chicago, 52-60, dir inst, 65-68, dean col, 69-73, chmn, Dept Astron & Astrophys, 84-88, PROF PHYSICS, ENRICO FERMI INST & DEPT PHYSICS, UNIV CHICAGO, 60-, PROF ASTRON & ASTROPHYS, 78-, SAMUEL K ALLISON DISTINGUISHED SERV PROF, 85- *Personal Data:* b Berkeley, Calif, May 1, 22; m 44, Jane Beedle; c Peter, Alice, Kathryn & Daniel. *Educ:* Univ Calif, Berkeley, AB, 47, PhD(physics), 51. *Prof Exp:* Physicist, Radiation Lab, Univ Calif, 42-51. *Concurrent Pos:* Assoc lab dir high energy physics, Argonne Nat Lab, 58-64, actg dir, 59-64; chmn, Sci Policy Comt, Stanford Linear Accelerator Ctr, 62-66; Guggenheim fel, Univ Calif, Berkeley, 68-69; chmn, Rev Comt US Medium Energy Sci, AEC-NSF, 74, Airbone Astron Users Group, 83-84, Sloan fel, 75, consult, Group Strotospheric Observ Infrared Astron, Ames Res Ctr, NASA, 85-89; mem, Comt Space Astron & Astrophys Space Sci Bd, 87-90; mem, Astron & Astrophys Surv Comt, Nat Acad Sci, Panel Infrared Astron, 89-90; mem, Sci & Tech Adv Comt Submillimeter Array, Smithsonian Astrophys Observ, 89-; mem, Observ Vis Comt, Asn Univs Res Astron, 93-96, chmn, 95 & 96. *Mem:* Fel Am Phys Soc; Am Astron Soc; Int Aston Union; fel AAAS. *Res:* Neutron scattering; conservation of isospin in particle production; bubble chamber development; muon capture and decay; electronic component of primary cosmic radiation; kaon decay; infrared and submillimeter astronomy photometry and polarimetry; properties of interstellar material; magnetic fields in interstellar clouds; dust and magnetic fields in the interstellar medium; properties of the galactic center. *Mailing Add:* Enrico Fermi Inst Univ Chicago Chicago IL 60637. *Fax:* 773-702-8212; *E-Mail:* roger@oddjob.uchicago.edu

HILDEBRAND, STEPHEN GEORGE, AQUATIC ECOLOGY. *Current Pos:* Res assoc environ impacts nuclear plants, Oak Ridge Nat Lab, 73-74, res assoc mercury & trace elements in aquatic systs, 74-76, res staff mem & group leader environ impacts energy technol, 76-78, res staff mem & group leader environ res, 78-80, mgr environ impacts prog, 81-85, head, Environ Anal Sect, 85-89, head, Ecosyst Studies Sect, 90-91, assoc dir, Environ Sci Div, 91-93, DIR, ENVIRON SCI DIV, OAK RIDGE NAT LAB, 94- *Personal Data:* b Reedsburg, Wis, Apr 14, 44; m 69, Gail Ziegel; c Jessica & Eric. *Educ:* Wabash Col, BA, 66; Univ Mich, MS, 69, PhD(fisheries), 73. *Concurrent Pos:* Adv, Inst Ecol & Nat Comn Water Qual, 73-74; adj fac, Univ Tenn, 84-; mem, Assessment & Policy Task Group, Nat Acid Precipitation Assessment Prog, 84-86, CEQ/NSF Panel Ecol Res, 85, UNESCO Int Hydrol Prog, 86- *Mem:* Ecol Soc Am; Am Fisheries Soc; fel AAAS; Sigma Xi. *Res:* Aquatic ecology; structure and function of aquatic ecosystems; stream invertebrates; environmental assessment of stress on aquatic systems; environmental risk assessment; science administration. *Mailing Add:* Environ Sci Div PO Box 2008 Oak Ridge TN 37831-6037

HILDEBRANDT, ALVIN FRANK, solar energy, low temperature physics; deceased, see previous edition for last biography

HILDEBRANDT, JACOB, respiratory physiology, for more information see previous edition

HILDEBRANDT, PAUL KNUD, PATHOLOGY. *Current Pos:* VPRES & SR PATHOLOGIST, PATHCO, INC, 85- *Personal Data:* b Lamar, Colo, Nov 18, 33; m 53, Eleanor J Jacob; c John H, Kristie K, Jerry S & Lori L. *Educ:* Colo A&M Col, BS, 55; Colo State Univ, DVM, 59; Am Col Vet Pathologists, dipl, 68. *Prof Exp:* Vet clinician, Ft Detrick, 59-62; vet path resident, Armed Forces Inst Path, 62-64, asst chief, Dept Vet Path, 64-65; vet pathologist, Navy Med Res Unit No 3, Cairo, 65-67; chief, Dept Vet Path, Walter Reed Army Inst Res, 67-71, dir, Div Path, 71-78; staff vet pathologist, US Army Bioeng Res & Develop Lab, Ft Detrick, Md, 78-80; vet pathologist, Tracor Jitco, Inc, 80-85. *Concurrent Pos:* Chmn, Case of Month Prog, Am Col Vet Pathologists, 72-78; consult vet path, Surgeon Gen, 72-80, Dept Path, Litton Bionetics Inc, 74-78, USDA, 78-80; mem, Coun Res, Am Vet Med Asn, exec bd. *Mem:* Am Vet Med Asn; Am Col Vet Pathologists (pres); Fedn Am Soc Exp Biol; Soc Trop Med & Hyg; Soc Trop Vet Med. *Res:* Veterinary pathology; radiation injury; pathophysiology of host-parasite relationships; toxicologic pathology. *Mailing Add:* Pathco Inc Hyatt Park II 10075 Tyler Pl No 16 Ijamsville MD 21754

HILDEBRANDT, THEODORE WARE, MATHEMATICS, COMPUTER SCIENCE. *Current Pos:* dir, Acad Comput Ctr, 76-86, prof, 76-93, EMER PROF MATH, UNIV NC, GREENSBORO, 93- *Personal Data:* b Ann Arbor, Mich, Dec 8, 22; m 53, 62; c 5. *Educ:* Univ Mich, AB, 42, AM, 47, PhD(math), 56; Mass Inst Technol, SM, 51. *Prof Exp:* Asst physics, Univ Mich, 43-44; design engr, Electronic Comput Proj, Inst Advan Study, Princeton, NJ, 47-48; asst math, Mass Inst Technol, 48-51; assoc scientist, Oak Ridge Inst Nuclear Studies, 56-57; from asst prof to prof math, Ohio State Univ, 57-68, assoc chmn comput & info sci, 67-68; prof comput sci & dir, Comput Ctr, Kans State Univ, 68-69; head comput facil, Nat Ctr Atmospheric Res, Colo, 69-73, consult, 73-74; expert consult, Inst Telecommun Sci, US Dept Com, 74-75. *Concurrent Pos:* Asst dir, Comput Ctr, Ohio State Univ, 57-66, actg chmn, Div Comput Sci, 66-67. *Mem:* Am Math Soc; Math Asn Am; Asn Comput Mach. *Res:* Numerical analysis; computing machines; mathematical programming; data communication; micro processors. *Mailing Add:* 1109 Pebble Dr Greensboro NC 27410-4539

HILDEBRANDT, THOMAS HENRY, APPLIED PATTERN RECOGNITION, NEURAL NETWORK LEARNING THEORY. *Current Pos:* ADJ ASST PROF ELEC ENG & COMPUT SCI, LEHIGH UNIV, 91- *Personal Data:* b Columbus, Ohio, May 9, 59; m 90, Adair D Dingle; c Brian H & Eleanor H. *Educ:* Univ Colo, BS(comp sci) & BS(elec eng), 80; NC State Univ, MS, 86, PhD(comp eng), 91. *Prof Exp:* Design engr, Gen Elec Co, 80-85; contract programmer, Self Employed, 86-89. *Concurrent Pos:* Tech translr & ed, Script Tech Div, John Wiley & Sons, 89-92; pres, Triplex Software Co, 93- *Mem:* Inst Elec & Electronics Engrs; Int Neural Network Soc. *Res:* Development of new models and training algorithms for environmentally adaptive pattern recognition systems; modification of these for computational modelling of biological neural systems. *Mailing Add:* Elec Eng & Comput Sci Dept Lehigh Univ Packard Labs Bldg 19 Rm 304 Bethlehem PA 18015-1718. *Fax:* 610-758-6279; *E-Mail:* thildebr@athos.eecs.lehigh.edu

HILDEBRANDT, WAYNE ARTHUR, ELECTROANALYTICAL CHEMISTRY. *Current Pos:* asst prof, 75-83, ASSOC PROF CHEM, NORTHERN ARIZ UNIV, 83-, ASST DEAN, 88- *Personal Data:* b Tacoma, Wash, June 11, 47; div. *Educ:* Univ Wash, BS, 69; Wash State Univ, PhD(chem), 74. *Prof Exp:* Asst prof chem, Univ Mich, Flint, 74-75. *Mem:* Am Chem Soc. *Res:* Development and characterization of new ion selective electrodes and new data manipulation techniques for their use; computer automation and interfacing techniques for use with ion selective electrodes. *Mailing Add:* 501 W Santa Fe Ave No 18 Flagstaff AZ 86001

HILDEBRANT, JOHN A, ALGEBRA, TOPOLOGY. *Current Pos:* asst prof, 66-71, ASSOC PROF MATH, LA STATE UNIV, BATON ROUGE, 71-, PROF. *Personal Data:* b Aug 8, 39; US citizen; m 64; c 1. *Educ:* Univ Okla, BS, 57; Univ Tenn, MA, 64, PhD(topological algebra), 65. *Prof Exp:* Asst prof math, Univ Tenn, 66. *Mem:* Am Math Soc. *Res:* Topological algebra; compact divisible topological semigroups. *Mailing Add:* 544 Seyburn Dr Baton Rouge LA 70808

HILDEMAN, GREGORY JOHN, MATERIALS SCIENCE, METALLURGY. *Current Pos:* sr scientist alloy res, Aluminum Co Am, 77-81, staff scientist, 81-85, sect head, 85-87, DIV MGR, ALUMINUM CO AM, 87- *Personal Data:* b Milwaukee, Wis, May 16, 47; m 70, Joy A Christensen; c Christopher & Douglas. *Educ:* Univ Wis, Madison, BS, 70; Univ Wis, Milwaukee, MS, 74; Mass Inst Technol, DSc(metall), 78. *Prof Exp:* Sr develop engr process develop, Allen-Bradley Co, 70-74. *Mem:* Fel Am Soc Metals Int; Minerals Metals & Mats Soc; Sigma Xi. *Res:* Development of new aluminum powder metallurgy alloys by rapid solidification processes. *Mailing Add:* 3108 Treeline Dr Murrysville PA 15668-1568

HILDEN, SHIRLEY ANN, CELL PHYSIOLOGY. *Current Pos:* HEALTH ADMIN, NIH, BETHESDA, MD, 95- *Personal Data:* b Montevideo, Minn, July 2, 40. *Educ:* St Olaf Col, BA, 62; Stanford Univ, MA & PhD(biol), 69. *Prof Exp:* Asst prof biol, Univ Idaho, 70-71; res assoc physiol, Med Sch, Univ Wis-Madison, 72-76; mem staff, Nat Inst Aging, 76-95. *Concurrent Pos:* Am Asn Univ Women fel, Hokkaido Univ, 69-70. *Mem:* AAAS; Biophys Soc; Am Soc Cell Biologists. *Res:* Ionic regulation in protozoa; membrane physiology. *Mailing Add:* Div Res Grants NIH 6701 Rockledge Dr Rm 4218 MSC 7814 Bethesda MD 20892-7814

HILDERBRAND, DAVID CURTIS, CHEMISTRY, ATOMIC SPECTROSCOPY. *Current Pos:* from asst prof to assoc prof, 74-83, head dept, 80-93, PROF CHEM, SDAK STATE UNIV, 83-, DIR INT PROGS, 88-, DIR, SIOUX FALLS PROGS, 93-, ACTG DEAN GRAD SCH. *Personal Data:* b California, Mo, Apr 1, 46; m 69, Julie Vaughn; c Grant & Lucas. *Educ:* SW Baptist Univ, BA, 67; Univ Mo, Columbia, MA, 69, PhD(chem), 71. *Prof Exp:* Instr res, Dept Obstet & Gynec, Sch Med, Univ

Mo, 71-74. *Concurrent Pos:* Bd cur, SW Baptist Univ, 81-84; mem bd regents, Bethel Col, 89-94; mem bd dirs, Arid Land Consortium, Asn Int Educ Adminr. *Mem:* Am Chem Soc; Sigma Xi; Asn Int Educ Adminr. *Res:* Method development for analyses using flame and flameless atomic spectroscopy including sample preparation and interpretation of chemical processes occuring in high temperature flame and flameless systems; educational administration; science education. *Mailing Add:* 132 S Dakota Ave Sioux Falls SD 57104. *Fax:* 605-339-6561; *E-Mail:* hilderbd@sdstate.edu

HILDERBRANDT, RICHARD L, MOLECULAR SIMULATIONS & COMPUTATIONAL CHEMISTRY. *Current Pos:* PROG DIR THEORET & COMPUTATIONAL CHEM, NSF, 87- *Personal Data:* b Sellersville, Pa, Dec 31, 42; m 64, Joan; c Ami & Brian. *Educ:* Pa State Univ, BS, 64; Cornell Univ, PhD(phys chem), 69. *Prof Exp:* Sr staff scientist, San Diego Supercomput Ctr, 85-87. *Concurrent Pos:* Prof phys chem, NDak State Univ, 72-85; consult, Sterling Drugs Inc, 87- *Mem:* Am Chem Soc. *Res:* Structural chemistry by gas phase electron diffraction; molecular simulations; quantitative structure property relationships. *Mailing Add:* 1512 Roundleaf Ct Reston VA 20190. *E-Mail:* rhilderb@nsf.gov

HILDING, STEPHEN R, MATHEMATICS. *Current Pos:* assoc prof, 65-68, chmn dept, 68-72, PROF MATH, GUSTAVUS ADOLPHUS COL, 68- *Personal Data:* b Duluth, Minn, Aug 5, 36; m 58, Arlene Anderson; c Mark, Gregory, Jonathan & Elena. *Educ:* Gustavus Adolphus Col, BA, 58; Kans State Univ, MS, 60; Univ Mich, DEd, 65. *Prof Exp:* Instr math, NDak State Univ, 60-61, Mankato State Col, 61-62 & Univ Mich, 64-65. *Concurrent Pos:* Assoc math, Univ Minn, 74-75. *Mem:* Am Math Soc; Math Asn Am. *Res:* Functional analysis; Banach algebras. *Mailing Add:* Dept Math Gustavus Adolphus Col St Peter MN 56082. *E-Mail:* hilding@nic.gac.edu

HILDNER, ERNEST GOTTHOLD, III, SOLAR PHYSICS. *Current Pos:* vis scientist, 85-86, DIR, SPACE ENVIRON LAB, NAT OCEANIC & ATMOSPHERIC ADMIN, 86- *Personal Data:* b Jacksonville, Ill, Jan 23, 40; m 68; c 2. *Educ:* Wesleyan Univ, BA, 61; Univ Colo, MA, 64, PhD(physics), 71. *Prof Exp:* Fel, Nat Ctr Atmospheric Res, 71-72, scientist, 72-80; br chief, Marshall Space Flight Ctr, NASA, 80-85. *Mem:* Int Astron Union; Am Astron Soc; Am Geophys Union; AAAS; Sigma Xi. *Res:* Solar coronal physics; magnetohydrodynamics; interplanetary medium; solar wind; solar cosmic rays; solar radio bursts. *Mailing Add:* Space Environ Lab Nat Oceanic & Atmospheric Admin 325 Broadway Boulder CO 80303

HILDRETH, EDWARD WESLEY, III, GEOLOGY, VOLCANOLOGY. *Current Pos:* GEOLOGIST, US GEOL SURV, 77- *Personal Data:* b Mass, Aug 17, 38; m 82, Gail Mahood. *Educ:* Harvard Col, BA, 61, Univ Calif, Berkeley, PhD, 77. *Honors & Awards:* Distinguished Bradley Lectr, 83; N L Bowen Award, Am Geophys Union. *Prof Exp:* Naturalist, Nat Park Serv, 66-71; instr, Univ Calif, Berkeley, 73-75. *Concurrent Pos:* G K Gilbert fel, US Geol Soc, 83-85; assoc ed, J Geophys Res, 84-86; Geol Rev Chile, 87- & Bull Volcanol, 91-; prin investr, NSF, Cent Chile, 91-93. *Mem:* Fel Geol Soc Am; fel Am Geophys Union; Int Asn Volcanol & Chem Earths Interior. *Res:* Field-based process-oriented research on how volcanoes work; calderas, ignimbrites and stratovolcanoes in Alaska, Chile, Washington and California. *Mailing Add:* US Geol Surv Volcano Hazards Team MS-910 345 Middlefield Rd Menlo Park CA 94025

HILDRETH, EUGENE AUGUSTUS, INTERNAL MEDICINE & IMMUNOLOGY. *Current Pos:* asst instr med, Hosp Univ Pa, 48-53, instr med, 53-54, chief allergy & immunol, 53-69, assoc prof med, 54-55, from asst to assoc prof, 55-69, assoc dean, Sch Med, 64-67, prof, 72-95, EMER PROF CLIN MED, HOSP UNIV PA, 95- *Personal Data:* b St Paul, Minn, Mar 11, 24; m 46, Dorothy Myers; c Jeffrey, William, Anne & Katherine. *Educ:* Washington & Jefferson Col, BS, 43; Univ Va, MD, 47; Am Bd Internal Med, dipl, 54; Am Bd Allergy & Immunol, dipl, 64. *Honors & Awards:* Alfred Stengal Award, Am Col Physicians, 94. *Prof Exp:* Intern, Johns Hopkins Hosp, 47-48; dir, Dept Med, Reading Hosp & Med Ctr, 69-89. *Concurrent Pos:* Res fel, USPHS, Univ Pa, 49-51; chief resident med, Hosp Univ Pa, 53-54; consult, Vet Admin, Philadelphia, 54-76; Markle scholar, 58-63; consult med, Wernersville State Hosp; mem, Adv Comt Reactions Drugs, Nat Acad Sci, 67-69; mem, Nat Adv Comt, Int Medic Alert Found, 67-; mem, Am Bd Internal Med, 68-80, chmn, 81-82, chmn, Specialty Bd Allergy & Immunol, 69-71; founding comt, Am Bd Allergy & Immunol, 70-71, chmn med, 71-72; consult med, Wernersville State Hosp, 72-80; consult, Annals Internal Med; chmn, Federated Coun Internal Med, 81-82; lectr bioethics, Hosp Asn Pa, 84-85 & Darmouth-Hitchcock Med Ctr, 84, Univ NMex, 86; chmn bd, Am Col Physicians, 89-91; lectr & dir, St Joseph Col & Albright Col. *Mem:* Inst Med-Nat Acad Sci; master Am Col Physicians (pres, 91-92); Am Acad Allergy; NY Acad Sci; AAAS; Fedn Am Soc Exp Biol; Am Bd Internal Med; Am Bd Allergy & Immunol; Am Clin & Climatologic Asn; Peripathetic Soc; Royal Soc Med. *Res:* Diseases of antigen-antibody interaction; lipid metabolism; nephrology; biothetics; health care reform. *Mailing Add:* RR 3 Box 3960 Mohnton PA 19540-9265

HILDRETH, MICHAEL B, PARASITOLOGY, CELL BIOLOGY. *Current Pos:* asst prof, Dept Biol & Microbiol, 87-91, accoc prof, 91-97, PROF PARASITOL,SDAK STATE UNIV, 97- *Personal Data:* b Bisbee, Ariz, Apr 5, 55; m 79, Marilyn Molitor; c Michele L & Matthew A. *Educ:* Westmar Col, BA, 77; Tulane Univ, PhD(biol), 83. *Prof Exp:* Teaching & res assoc hist, Sch Vet Med, Univ Wis, 83-86, lectr histol, 86-87. *Concurrent Pos:* vis prof, Sch Vet Med, Univ Wis, 86; prin investr, NIH Area grant, 90-92. *Mem:* Am Soc Parasitologists; Am Soc Trop Med & Hyg; Am Asn Vet Parasitologists. *Res:* Molecular and immunological methods for parasite diagnosis; resistance of cestode membranes to digestion; biocontrol of grasshoppers; stress on parasite loads; epidemiology of echinococcus multiocularis. *Mailing Add:* Dept Biol & Microbiol SDak State Univ Brookings SD 57007. *Fax:* 605-688-5624; *E-Mail:* hildretm@mg.sdstate.edu

HILDRETH, PHILIP ELWIN, GENETICS. *Current Pos:* chmn, Dept Biol, 67-74, chmn, Div Math & Natural Sci, 68-70, dean, Col Sci & Math, 70-74, DISTINGUISHED PROF BIOL, UNIV NC, CHARLOTTE, 67-, VCHANCELLOR ACAD AFFAIRS, 74- *Personal Data:* b Marlboro, NH, Jan 14, 23; m 52; c 3. *Educ:* Dartmouth Col, AB, 47; Univ Calif, MA, 50, PhD(zool), 55. *Prof Exp:* Biologist, Radiation Lab, Univ Calif, 51-56; asst prof biol, Long Beach State Col, 56-59; biologist, Radiation Lab, Univ Calif, Berkeley, 59-67, consult, 58-59. *Mem:* AAAS; Genetics Soc Am; Am Inst Biol Sci; Sigma Xi. *Res:* Lethal production in Drosophila melanogaster; spontaneous and induced lethal mutation rates; developmental genetics. *Mailing Add:* 6001 Landmark Dr Charlotte NC 28226

HILDRETH, ROBERT CLAIRE, plant pathology, for more information see previous edition

HILE, MAHLON MALCOLM SCHALLIG, CROP PHYSIOLOGY, VEGETABLE CROPS. *Current Pos:* PROF VEG CROPS, CALIF STATE UNIV, FRESNO, 77- *Personal Data:* b Sacramento, Calif, Feb 17, 46. *Educ:* Chico State Col, BA, 68; Calif State Univ, Chico, MS, 73; Ore State Univ, PhD(crop physiol), 76. *Prof Exp:* Crop physiologist, Cel Pril Indust Inc, 76-77. *Mem:* Am Soc Agron; Crop Sci Soc Am; Sigma Xi. *Res:* Physiological factors affecting adaptability, production, quality and cultural management of crop plants. *Mailing Add:* Plant Sci Calif State Univ 2415 E San Ramon Fresno CA 93740-8033

HILEMAN, ANDREW R, POWER SYSTEMS, TRANSIENT LIGHTING. *Current Pos:* Staff, 51-68, ADV ENGR, WESTINGHOUSE CORP, 68- *Personal Data:* b New Bethlehem, Pa, Aug 28, 26. *Educ:* Lehigh Univ, BSEE, 51; Univ Pittsburgh, MSEE, 54. *Concurrent Pos:* Lamme fel, Westinghouse Elec Corp, 66-67; chmn, Inst Elec & Electronics Engrs Surge Protective Devices, 64-66, Am Nat Standards Inst, 70-86. *Mem:* Fel Inst Elec & Electronics Engrs. *Mailing Add:* 109 Overlook Circle Monroeville PA 15146

HILEMAN, ORVILLE EDWIN, JR, ANALYTICAL CHEMISTRY. *Current Pos:* from asst prof to assoc prof, 64-81, PROF CHEM, MCMASTER UNIV, 81- *Personal Data:* b Celina, Ohio, Dec 23, 36; div; c 2. *Educ:* Bowling Green State Univ, BScEd, 58; Case Inst Technol, PhD(chem), 64. *Prof Exp:* Teacher high sch, Ohio, 58-60. *Concurrent Pos:* Consult, Peabody Holmes Ltd, 74-82, Radian Corp & Gas Res Inst, 85- *Mem:* Chem Inst Can; Am Chem Soc; Sigma Xi. *Res:* Fundamental studies on nucleation and coprecipitation from solution and on mesophase transformations in lyotropic liquid crystalline systems; liquid redox desulfurization systems; electron transfer processes. *Mailing Add:* Dept Chem McMaster Univ Hamilton ON L8S 4M1 Can

HILEMAN, ROBERT E, ORGANIC CHEMISTRY. *Current Pos:* RETIRED. *Personal Data:* b Bloomsburg, Pa, Aug 16, 29; m 86, Marjorie M Minard; c William, Lynn (Barr), Judy (Gummerson), Karen & Marcia (Vickers). *Educ:* Bloomsburg Univ, BS, 51; Rutgers Univ, BS, 56; Univ Minn, PhD(org chem), 60. *Prof Exp:* From sr chemist to res chemist, 60-69, group leader, 69-80, technologist, 80-85, sr technologist, Beacon Res Lab, Texaco Inc, 85-87. *Concurrent Pos:* Fuel consult, 87- *Mem:* Am Soc Testing & Mat; Sigma Xi. *Res:* Mechanisms of organic chemistry; fuel properties; synthesis of fuel additives; fuel quality; fuel specifications; automobile exhaust emissions; gasoline blending; fuel additives; fuel manufacture; fuel marketing; fuel distribution. *Mailing Add:* 29 Bates Lane Wallkill NY 12589

HILEMAN, STANLEY MICHAEL, REGULATION OF LUTEINIZING HORMONE-RELEASING HORMONE BY TESTOSTERONE IN MALES, PHOTOPERIODIC CONTROL OF REPRODUCTION. *Current Pos:* NIH fel, 91-92, RES ASSOC, UNIV ILL, 92- *Personal Data:* b Wheeling, WVa, Sept 9, 63; m 85, Patricia; c Stephen & Mark. *Educ:* WVa Univ, BS, 85; Univ Ky, MS, 88, PhD(animal sci), 91. *Concurrent Pos:* Fel, USDA, 95-97; vis asst prof, 97- *Mem:* Am Soc Animal Sci; AAAS; Soc Study Reproduction; Soc Study Fertil. *Res:* Investigation of the neural mechanisms whereby testosterone regulates release of luteinizing hormone-releasing hormone in the male; neural centers involved in photoperiodic regulation of reproduction, mechanisms whereby nutrition influences reproduction. *Mailing Add:* Univ Ill Col Vet Med 2001 S Lincoln Ave Urbana IL 61801. *Fax:* 217-333-4628; *E-Mail:* shileman@uiuc.edu

HILER, EDWARD ALLAN, AGRICULTURAL ENGINEERING. *Current Pos:* from asst prof to prof agr eng, Tex A&M Univ, 66-68, head dept, 74-88, dept chancellor acad prog planning & res, 89-92, VCHANCELLOR & DEAN, AGR & LIFE SCIS & DIR TEX AGR EXP STA, TEX A&M UNIV, 92- *Personal Data:* b Hamilton, Ohio, May 14, 39; m 60, Patricia Burke; c Karen, Rick & Scott. *Educ:* Ohio State Univ, BS & MS, 63, PhD(agr eng), 66. *Prof Exp:* Res asst agr eng, Ohio State Univ, 62-63, instr, 63-64 & 65-66. *Concurrent Pos:* Consult. *Mem:* Fel AAAS; Am Soc Agr Engrs; Am Soc Eng Educ; Nat Soc Prof Engrs; Am Geophys Union; Sigma Xi. *Res:* Irrigation and drainage design criteria; water use efficiency; energy conservation; biomass utilization; liquid fuels from agricultural crops. *Mailing Add:* Agr Prog Tex A&M Univ College Station TX 77843-2142

HILES, MAURICE, THE USE OF POLYMERS IN THE CONTAINMENT OF MECHANICALLY INDUCED VIBRATION, CONVERSION OF CELLULOSE WASTE. *Current Pos:* CONSULT, 83-; PRES TECHNOL 2000 INC, 86- *Personal Data:* b London, Eng, Oct 14, 36; m 60; c Sara J. *Educ:* Oxford Univ, BA, 57; London Univ, BSc, 59, MSc, 65, PhD, 69. *Honors & Awards:* C W Swank Award, 91; John W Hyatt Award, 92. *Prof*

Exp: Res chemist org, Procter & Gamble, 65-68; training mgr, Thorn Elec Industs, 68-72; pres polymer res, Advan Polymer Technol, 72-81; prof biomat sci, Univ Akron, 81-83. *Concurrent Pos:* Consult, BTR Indust, 74-88, Brit Technol Group & Ministry Defence, 76-81. *Mem:* Chartered Chemist, fel Royal Soc of Chem; fel Am Inst Chem; Am Col Sports Med; Am Asn Orthop Med; Aerospace Med Asn; Plastics & Rubber Inst. *Res:* Development and formulation of Lurex and Abraflex; development and formulation of visco-elastomers; sorbothane, sarathon, SIN4 and SIN6; the development of simultaneous interpenetrating; network (SIN) technology. *Mailing Add:* 37 Starboard Circle Forest Cove Akron OH 44319. *Fax:* 216-645-9179

HILES, RICHARD ALLEN, BIOCHEMISTRY, TOXICOLOGY. *Current Pos:* MGR PHARMACOL & TOXICOL, FUJI SAWA, 91- *Personal Data:* b Asheville, NC, Aug 31, 43; m 66. *Educ:* Clemson Univ, BS, 65; Mich State Univ, PhD(biochem), 70. *Prof Exp:* Fel, Gortner Lab, Univ Minn, St Paul, 70-71; toxicologist, Procter & Gamble Co, 71-78; vpres toxicol, Springborn Inst Biores, 78-86; prog mgr, Hazleton Labs, Madison, Wis, 86-91. *Concurrent Pos:* Adj prof, Ohio Northern Univ, 80- *Mem:* Am Chem Soc; AAAS; Soc Toxicol; Soc Cosmetic Chemists. *Res:* Metabolism of natural and man-made compounds in animals; biochemical toxicology of metabolism and pharmacokinetics. *Mailing Add:* 222 Maggies Rd Clarks Summit PA 18411

HILF, RUSSELL, BIOCHEMISTRY, ENDOCRINE ONCOLOGY. *Current Pos:* actg chair, 80-82, PROF BIOCHEM, UNIV ROCHESTER, 69-, INTERIM DIR BASIC SCI, CANCER CTR, 93- *Personal Data:* b Brooklyn, NY, Aug 13, 31; m 55, Beverly S Polak; c Elise R, Merrill J & Lawrence M. *Educ:* City Col New York, BS, 52; Rutgers Univ, MS, 53, PhD(biochem), 55. *Prof Exp:* Head biochem lab, QM Food & Container Inst, 58-59; head cancer endocrine sect, Squibb Inst Med Res, Olin Mathieson Chem Corp, 59-69. *Concurrent Pos:* Mem, Breast Cancer Task Force, Nat Cancer Inst, 76-80, Merit Review Bd Oncol, Vet Admin, 80-83 & Sci Adv Bd, Univ Wis Cancer Ctr, 81-84; Reproduction Endocrinol Study Sect, NIH, 86-89; mem, Biochem Chem Carcinogen Adv Comt & Biochem Endocrinol Adv Comt, Am Cancer Soc, 87-92 & Sci Adv Panel, Am Inst Cancer Res, 90-; Wellcome vis prof, 94. *Mem:* Fel AAAS; Am Soc Biol Chemists; Am Asn Cancer Res; Endocrine Soc; fel NY Acad Sci; Am Soc Photobiol. *Res:* Biochemistry and metabolism of tumors and normal tissue; response of target tissue to hormones; photodynamic therapy of tumors. *Mailing Add:* Dept Biochem Univ Rochester Med Ctr Box 607 Rochester NY 14642. *Fax:* 716-271-2683

HILFER, SAUL ROBERT, ORGANOGENESIS, CELL CULTURE. *Current Pos:* from asst prof to assoc prof, 61-74, PROF BIOL, TEMPLE UNIV, 74- *Personal Data:* b Quakertown, Pa, June 12, 31; m 59; c 3. *Educ:* Queens Col, BS, 54; Amherst Col, MA, 55; Yale Univ, PhD(zool), 60. *Prof Exp:* NIH trainee anat, Harvard Med Sch, 59-60, fel, 60-61. *Mem:* Int Soc Develop Biol; Am Soc Cell Biol; Soc Develop Biol. *Res:* Control of cell shape and cell-matrix interactions during early embryonic development; morphogenetic movements during organogenesis; role of extracellular matrix in differentiation of organs; control of shape changes during organ formation; role of cytoskeleton. *Mailing Add:* Dept Biol Temple Univ Philadelphia PA 19122. *Fax:* 215-204-6646; *E-Mail:* shilfer@thunder.ocis.temple.edu

HILFERTY, FRANK JOSEPH, BRYOLOGY. *Current Pos:* RETIRED. *Personal Data:* b Medway, Mass, July 1, 20. *Educ:* Bridgewater State Col, BS, 42; Cornell Univ, PhD(biol), 52. *Prof Exp:* Instr pub sch, Mass, 42-46; asst prof biol, Univ Maine, 46-52; assoc prof biol, Salem State Col, 52-54; chmn, Dept Biol Sci, Bridgewater State Col, 54-65, commonwealth prof bot, 54-81, dir, Div Sci & Math, 65-78, dean, Grad Sch, 65-81. *Concurrent Pos:* NSF grant, Inst Bot, Cornell Univ, 56; NSF fac & res fels, Gray Herbarium, Harvard Univ, 59-60. *Mem:* Sigma Xi. *Res:* Taxonomy of New England mosses and vascular plants; teaching biology at the college level. *Mailing Add:* 20 Aspen Dr Bridgewater MA 02324

HILFIKER, FRANKLIN ROBERTS, ORGANIC CHEMISTRY. *Current Pos:* res chemist, 70-73, SUPVR, JACKSON LAB, E I DU PONT DE NEMOURS & CO, INC, 73-, TECH SERV SUPVR, CHESTNUT RUN, 78-, TECH SERV CONSULT, 80- *Personal Data:* b Warsaw, NY, June 7, 43; m 67, Jean Harper; c David, Julie & Peter. *Educ:* Univ Rochester, BS, 65; State Univ NY Buffalo, PhD(org chem), 69. *Prof Exp:* Turner fel chem, Rice Univ, 69-70. *Concurrent Pos:* Prod mgr, Ciba-Geigy Corp, 87-89, Int Mkt dir, 89-94. *Mem:* Am Chem Soc. *Res:* Dye chemistry; natural products chemistry; pigment chemistry. *Mailing Add:* 103 Venus Dr Newark DE 19711. *Fax:* 302-998-2934

HILGAR, ARTHUR GILBERT, MEDICAL RESEARCH, MEDICAL ADMINISTRATION. *Current Pos:* RETIRED. *Personal Data:* b Butler Co, Pa, Dec 21, 26; m 66, Elizabeth Neale; c Mary E & Rachel E. *Educ:* Eastern Nazarene Col, AB, 50. *Prof Exp:* Biologist, Bur Entom & Plant Quarantine, USDA, 52-53; Path Lab, Nat Cancer Inst, 53-56, Endocrinol Sect, Cancer Chemother Nat Serv Ctr, 56-61; head, Biol Activities Hormones Sect, Endocrine Eval Br, Nat Cancer Inst, 61-67; dir data mgt, Mason Res Inst, Mass, 67-71; from asst dir to assoc dir, Nat Bladder Cancer Prog, St Vincent Hosp, 71-84; sci adminr, Organ Systs Coord Ctr, Roswell Park Mem Inst, 84-89; consult, 89-90. *Mem:* Am Asn Cancer Res. *Res:* Cancer research administration; endocrine bioassays; experimental designs and data evaluation. *Mailing Add:* 4 Cricket Lane Worcester MA 01602

HILGARD, HENRY ROHRS, CELLULAR IMMUNOLOGY. *Current Pos:* PROF BIOL, UNIV CALIF, SANTA CRUZ, 67- *Educ:* Stanford Univ, MD, 62; Univ Minn, PhD(microbiol), 70. *Res:* Graft-versus-host reactions. *Mailing Add:* 710 Highland Ave Santa Cruz CA 95060-2008

HILGER, ANTHONY EDWARD, MEDICAL MYCOLOGY, MYCOLOGY. *Current Pos:* asst prof, 80-84, ASSOC PROF MED TECHNOL, UNIV NC, CHAPEL HILL, 84- *Personal Data:* b Louisville, Ky, Aug 1, 44; m 69; c 1. *Educ:* Bellarmine Col, BA, 67; Univ SC, MS, 69, PhD(mycol), 74. *Prof Exp:* Instr biol, Univ SC, 68-69; biologist asst, Letterman Army Inst Res, 70-71; asst prof biol, Presby Col, 73-75; asst prof microbiol, Univ Health Sci, Chicago Med Sch, 75-80. *Mem:* Int Soc Human & Animal Mycol; Am Soc Microbiol; Med Mycol Soc Am; Am Soc Clin Path. *Res:* Fungal susceptibility testing. *Mailing Add:* Dept Med Allied Health Prof Div Clin Lab Sci Univ NC Med Sch CB 7145 Med Sch Wing E Chapel Hill NC 27599-7145

HILGER, JAMES EUGENE, IMAGE PROCESSING, PATTERN RECOGNITION. *Current Pos:* ELECTRONICS ENGR, CTR NIGHT VISION, 89- *Personal Data:* b Wilmington, Del. *Educ:* Salisbury State Univ, BS, 85; Univ Tenn, MS, 88. *Prof Exp:* Teaching asst, Elec Eng Lab, Univ Tenn, 86-87; res asst, Oak Ridge Nat Lab, 87-89. *Res:* Developing high speed processors in miniaturized packages for image processing applications. *Mailing Add:* 13737 Mahoney Dr Woodbridge VA 22193

HILIBRAND, J(ACK), ELECTRICAL ENGINEERING. *Current Pos:* PRIN ENGR, MICROELECTRONICS ASSOCS, 91- *Personal Data:* b New York, NY, Sept 15, 30; m 56, Thelma C Leeberg; c Laurence E, Deborah A & Alan S. *Educ:* City Col New York, BEE, 51; Mass Inst Technol, ScD(elec eng), 56. *Prof Exp:* Mem tech staff, labs, Radio Corp Am, 56-60, mgr advan devices, Solid State Div, 60-62, mgr indust transistor design, 62-65, mgr indust semiconductor eng, 65-66; opers mgr transistors & semiconductors, Transitron Electronics Corp, 66; mgr integrated circuit technol, Solid State Div, RCA Corp, 67-68; mgr digital integrated circuit design, 68-69, mgr advan projs, 69-70, mgr adv mat & processes, 70-71, staff tech adv, Govt Systs Div, 71-81, mgr, integrated circuit planning, 81-85; prin staff scientist, GE Aerospace, 85-90. *Concurrent Pos:* Lectr, grad sch technol, City Col NY, 57-59. *Mem:* Fel Inst Elec & Electronics Engrs; Am Inst Physics; Sigma Xi. *Res:* Integrated circuit design, development and applications; techniques for very large scale integration; complementary metal-oxide semiconductor technology; bulk and SOS technology; very large scale integration packaging. *Mailing Add:* 1037 Owl Lane Suite 200B Cherry Hill NJ 08003-2934

HILKER, DORIS M, NUTRITION, BIOCHEMISTRY. *Current Pos:* RETIRED. *Personal Data:* b Aurora, Ind, Dec 23, 23. *Educ:* Univ Chicago, BS, 49; Loyola Univ, MS, 55; Tulane Univ, PhD(biochem), 58. *Prof Exp:* Res biochemist, Vet Admin Ctr, WVa, 59-60; asst prof nutrit & chmn dept, Univ Hawaii, 60-68, assoc prof food & nutrit sci, 68-75, prof, 75- *Mem:* Am Chem Soc; Inst Food Technol; NY Acad Sci. *Res:* Toxic and deleterious substances in food; bioavailability of nutrients. *Mailing Add:* 115 Lakeview Dr Lexington TN 38351

HILKER, HARRY VAN DER VEER, JR, PHYSICS. *Current Pos:* CONSULT, 75- *Personal Data:* b Hamilton, Ohio, June 19, 25; m 47, Norma Harris; c Don D, Laura & Caryl. *Educ:* Kalamazoo Col, AB, 47. *Prof Exp:* Advert asst, Atlas Press Co, 47-48; assoc ed, Modern Photog, 48-51; physicist, US Naval Ord Test Sta, 51-52, missile proj engr, 52-54, sr physicist, 54-55, res scientist, 55-59, consult, 59-61; vpres, Decision Control, Inc, 61-67 & Varian Data Mach, Inc, 67-70; pres, Accra-Point Arrays, 70-75. *Mem:* Sigma Xi; Inst Elec & Electronics Engrs. *Res:* Applied physics; sequential machines; logic design and switching theory; digital computer systems; electronics; missile test instrumentation; analog-digital techniques; robotic control systems; design of high-speed data processors. *Mailing Add:* 1118 Pescador Dr Newport Beach CA 92660

HILL, ALBERT G, communications; deceased, see previous edition for last biography

HILL, ALFRED, JR, MEDICAL ENTOMOLOGY. *Current Pos:* From instr to asst prof, 52-62, PROF BIOL, A&T STATE UNIV, NC, 62- *Personal Data:* b Henderson, Tex, Feb 17, 19; m 47; c Lionel G, Charles A, Kelley J, Sharon D & Courtney B. *Educ:* Prairie View Agr & Mech Col, BS, 47; Colo State Univ, MS, 51; Kans State Univ, PhD(entom), 62. *Mem:* Entom Soc Am. *Res:* Systemic insecticides for control of insect pests on plants and on animals. *Mailing Add:* Dept Biol A&T State Univ 1601 E Market St Greensboro NC 27401-3209

HILL, ANDREW, PALEOANTHROPOLOGY, PALEOECOLOGY & PALEOENVIRONMENTS. *Current Pos:* from asst prof to assoc prof, 85-92, PROF ANTHROP, YALE UNIV, 92- *Personal Data:* b Huthwaite, Notts, Eng, May 6, 46. *Educ:* Reading Univ, BSc, 67; London Univ, PhD(geol), 75. *Hon Degrees:* MA, Yale Univ, 92. *Prof Exp:* Res officer, Nat Mus Kenya, 75-77; res fel, Int Louis Leakey Mem Inst African Prehist, 77-80, admin dir, 80-81; res assoc, Dept Anthrop, Harvard Univ, 81-85. *Concurrent Pos:* Res assoc, Peabody Mus Anthrop, Harvard Univ, 81-85, fac affil, 89-92, cur anthrop, 92-; dir, Baringo Paleont Res Proj, 85- *Mem:* Am Asn Phys Anthropologists. *Res:* Human evolution and behavior in the context of changing mammalian communities and environments; origin of hominidae and genus Homo; taphonomy and archaeozoology. *Mailing Add:* Dept Anthrop Yale Univ PO Box 208277 New Haven CT 06520-8277. *Fax:* 203-432-3669; *E-Mail:* ahill@yalevm.cis.yale.edu

HILL, ANN GERTRUDE, INORGANIC CHEMISTRY, COMPUTER SCIENCES. *Current Pos:* prof chem, Ursuline Col, 46-52, head dept, 52-88, chmn, Div Natural Sci, 77-85, dir Comput Ctr, 81-88, PROF COMPUT SCI, URSULINE COL, 88- *Personal Data:* b Cleveland, Ohio, Mar 15, 22. *Educ:* Ursuline Col, BS, 44; Univ Notre Dame, MS, 52, PhD, 57. *Prof Exp:* Teacher, Villa Angela Acad, 44-46. *Concurrent Pos:* Res assoc, Atomic Energy Comn, Univ Notre Dame, 55-57. *Mem:* Am Chem Soc. *Res:* Absorption spectra of coordination compounds; ligand exchange on ion exchange resins. *Mailing Add:* 2550 Lander Rd Pepper Pike OH 44124

HILL, ANNLIA PAGANINI, PUBLIC HEALTH & EPIDEMIOLOGY, BIOMETRICS-BIOSTATISTICS. *Current Pos:* instr community med & pub health, 76-77, asst prof, family & prev med, 77-82, assoc prof, 82-89, PROF PREV MED, UNIV SOUTHERN CALIF, 90- *Personal Data:* b San Mateo, Calif, Aug 22, 46; m 72, Merton E III. *Educ:* Univ Calif Los Angeles, BA, 68, MS, 70, PhD(biostatist), 74. *Prof Exp:* Fel ment retardation, Univ Calif, Los Angeles, 74-76. *Concurrent Pos:* Statist consult, HEAR Found, 72-73; data coordr, Univ Southern Calif Comprehensive Cancer Ctr, 76-77; prin investr, Nat Cancer Inst, 85- *Mem:* Am Statist Asn; Soc Epidemiol Res. *Res:* Prospective cohort study designed to measure the risks and benefits of menopausal estrogen replacement therapy in terms of incident disease and mortality and to evaluate the effects of other health-related practices in older adults; case-control study to study the effect of infection/inflammation on stroke risk; case-control study to investigate the effects of hormone replacement therapy on breast cancer risk; clinical trial of estrogen replacement therapy in treatment of Alzheimer's disease. *Mailing Add:* Dept Prev Med Univ Southern Calif Sch Med 1721 Griffin Ave No 200 Los Angeles CA 90033

HILL, ARCHIBOLD G, PROCESS CONTROL. *Current Pos:* ASSOC PROF CHEM ENG, UNIV SOUTHWESTERN LA, 86- *Personal Data:* b Louisville, Ky, Jan 5, 50; m 87; c 2. *Educ:* Univ Louisville, MEng, 73; La Tech Univ, PhD(chem eng), 80. *Prof Exp:* Res assoc chem eng, La Tech Univ, 77-80; asst prof chem eng, Okla State Univ, 80-86. *Mem:* Am Inst Chem Engrs; Instrument Soc Am; Int Ozone Asn; Sigma Xi; Am Soc Eng Educ; Soc Indust & Appl Math. *Res:* Process instrumentation and control; process identification; adaptive control; control of multivariable processes. *Mailing Add:* Dept Chem Eng Univ SWestern La Box 44130 Lafayette LA 70504-4130

HILL, ARCHIE CLYDE, AIR POLLUTION EFFECTS. *Current Pos:* RETIRED. *Personal Data:* b Salt Lake City, Utah, July 18, 22; m 46, 82; c 8. *Educ:* Brigham Young Univ, BS, 50; Rutgers Univ, PhD(soil chem), 52. *Prof Exp:* Plant physiologist, Monsanto Chem Co, 52-54; supvr agr res & technol, Columbia-Geneva Steel Div, US Steel Corp, 54-64; assoc res prof bot, Univ Utah, 64-75, prof biol, 75-90, dir, Environ Studies Lab, Res Inst, 85-90. *Res:* Air pollution effects on plants, acid rain and visibility; soil and plant relationships; trace elements; herbicides. *Mailing Add:* 310 S 1500 E Pleasant Grove UT 84062

HILL, ARTHUR JOSEPH, JR, ORGANIC CHEMISTRY. *Current Pos:* Res chemist, 44-53, sr res supvr, 53-60, sr res chemist, 60-74, STAFF CHEMIST, E I DU PONT DE NEMOURS & CO, INC. 74- *Personal Data:* b New Haven, Conn, Oct 24, 18; m 44; c 4. *Educ:* Yale Univ, BS, 41, PhD(org chem), 44. *Mem:* Fel AAAS; Am Chem Soc; Am Nuclear Soc; fel Am Inst Chem; Sigma Xi. *Res:* Organic syntheses; chemotherapeutics; design, development and operation of facilities for research work with radioactive materials; decontamination of equipment and processing of radioactive waste products; fire prevention and protection in atomic energy facilities. *Mailing Add:* PO Box 42 Aiken SC 29802-0042

HILL, ARTHUR S, CHEMICAL ENGINEERING, POLYMER ENGINEERING. *Current Pos:* sr proj leader med prod, 75-80, SR RES ASSOC & ASST MGR, JOHNSON & JOHNSON MED RES CTR, 80- *Personal Data:* b McKeesport, Pa, Apr 7, 41; m 64; c 3. *Educ:* Mass Inst Technol, SB, 63; Princeton Univ, MSE, 64, PhD(chem eng), 68. *Prof Exp:* Res engr polymers, Harry Diamond Lab, Washington, DC, 67-69; res engr plastics, Exp Sta, E I du Pont de Nemours & Co Inc, Wilmington, Del, 69-75. *Concurrent Pos:* Adj asst prof, Philadelphia Col Textiles & Sci, 71-73. *Mem:* Am Chem Soc; Soc Plastics Engrs; Adhesion Soc. *Res:* Pressure sensitive adhesives, rheology and processing. *Mailing Add:* 6619 Nantucket Lane Arlington TX 76017

HILL, ARTHUR THOMAS, POULTRY HUSBANDRY, PHYSIOLOGY & GENETICS. *Current Pos:* CAN EXEC SERV OVERSEAS VOLUNTEER, 80- *Personal Data:* b Carman, Man, Jan 15, 20; m 48, Newcombe; c David, Barbara, Ren, Patricia & Donald. *Educ:* Univ Man, BSA, 43; Univ BC, MSA, 47; Tex A&M Univ, PhD(animal genetics), 64. *Prof Exp:* Instr poultry, Univ Sask, 47-48; geneticist, Can Dept Agr, Ottawa, 49-53 & Dereen Poultry Farm Ltd, Sardis, 53-54; poultry farmer, 54-56; mem, Poultry Mgt Animal Sect, Res Sta, Agassiz, BC, Can Dept Agr, 56-79. *Concurrent Pos:* Transfer, Poultry Res Centre, Edinburgh, Scotland, 72-73; broiler prod proj, Peru, 81, Agr Educ Panama, 84; secy-treas, BC Div, Can Feed Indust, 81-88; goose prod & mkt, Guatemala, 86; duck prod & mkt, Trinidad & Can Exec Servs, 88. *Mem:* Poultry Sci Asn; World Poultry Sci Asn; Agr Inst Can. *Res:* Population stress factors affecting the performance of laying and broiler stock and the quality of the resultant eggs and meat. *Mailing Add:* 5410 Huston Rd Chilliwack BC V4Z 1E5 Can

HILL, BENNY JOE, PHYSICS. *Current Pos:* asst prof & head dept, 64-66, PROF & HEAD DEPT PHYSICS, SOUTHWESTERN OKLA STATE UNIV, 68- *Personal Data:* b Cordell, Okla, Feb 20, 35; m 53; c 4. *Educ:* Okla State Univ, BS, 57; Tex A&M Univ, PhD(physics), 69. *Prof Exp:* Res asst physics, Los Alamos Sci Lab, 57-59; instr, Southwestern Okla State Univ, 59-60; mem staff, Los Alamos Sci Lab, 60-64. *Concurrent Pos:* Res assoc, Theoret Physics Group, Tex A&M Univ, 66-68; vis staff mem, Los Alamos Sci Lab, 69; prin staff mem, The BDM Corp, 84- *Mem:* Am Phys Soc; Am Asn Physics Teachers. *Res:* Theoretical physics; nuclear physics; computers in physics education; plasma physics; electromagnetics. *Mailing Add:* BDM Corp 1801 Randolph SE Albuquerque NM 87106

HILL, BERNARD DALE, PESTICIDE SCIENCE, MODELING. *Current Pos:* RES SCIENTIST PESTICIDE RESIDUE CHEM, AGR CAN, 78- *Personal Data:* b Brandon, Man, Aug 10, 48; m 73. *Educ:* Brandon Univ, BSc, 69; Univ Man, MSc, 74, PhD(pesticide biochem), 78. *Prof Exp:* Res assoc pesticide biochem, Univ Man, 77. *Mem:* Am Chem Soc. *Res:* Determination of the fate, persistence and environmental acceptability of pesticides; residue data for new insecticides on soils and crops. *Mailing Add:* Agr Can Res Sta PO Box 3000 Main Lethbridge AB T1J 4B1 Can

HILL, BRIAN, CERAMICS. *Current Pos:* RETIRED. *Personal Data:* b Carmarthen, Wales, May 11, 38; m 62; c 2. *Educ:* Univ Wales, BSc, 58; Univ London, PhD(ceramics) & DIC, 63. *Prof Exp:* Res engr, E I du Pont de Nemours & Co, Inc, 63-67; asst prof, Drexel Inst Technol, 67-69; res metallurgist, Paul D Merica Res Labs, Int Nickel Co, Inc, 69-78; sales mgr, Zircar Prods, Inc, 78-80; res mgr, Brush Wellman Inc, 80- *Mem:* Am Ceramic Soc; Nat Inst Ceramic Engrs; Brit Inst Metals; Int Soc Hybrid Microelectronics. *Res:* Properties of alumina; processing of ceramics; electronic ceramics. *Mailing Add:* Brush Wellman Inc 17876 St Clair Ave Cleveland OH 44110

HILL, BRIAN KELLOGG, REFLECTIVE MATERIALS, OPTICAL SYSTEMS. *Current Pos:* Sr res chemist, 3M Co, 69-74, supvr, Nuclear Med Dept, 74-76, supvr, New Prod Traffic Control Mat, 76-80, mgr, New Bus Develop, 80-89, lab mgr, Energy Control Prods, 83-89, TECH DIR, COM OFF, SUPPLY DIV, 3M CO, 89- *Personal Data:* b Boise, Idaho, July 11, 43; m 65. *Educ:* Univ Idaho, BS, 65; Mont State Univ, PhD(chem), 69. *Res:* Photo and thermal chemistry of transition metals; catalytic activity of transition metal complexes; development of nuclear diagnostic pharmaceuticals; development of products for new business opportunities in reflective materials; large scale imaging; optical material for controlling energy. *Mailing Add:* 8821 82nd St Ct S Cottage Grove MN 55016

HILL, BRUCE COLMAN, BIOMEDICAL ENGINEERING, BIOPHYSICS. *Current Pos:* SR INVESTR BIOENG, PALO ALTO MED FOUND RES INST, 78- *Personal Data:* b Houston, Tex, Jan 24, 48. *Educ:* Rice Univ, BA, 69; Stanford Univ, MS, 72, PhD(appl physics), 77. *Concurrent Pos:* Consult, Vets Admin Hosp, Palo Alto, 78-82. *Mem:* Biophys Soc. *Res:* Interferometric measurements of axon structural changes; biomedical instrumentation for blood flow measurements; electro-optical system design for eardrum displacement measurements; optical measurements of action potential propagation in cardiac tissue. *Mailing Add:* Kaiser Hosp 99 Montecillo Rd San Rafael CA 94720

HILL, BRUCE M, STATISTICS. *Current Pos:* Lectr bio-statist, 60-61, from asst prof to prof math, 61-70, PROF STATIST, UNIV MICH, ANN ARBOR, 70- *Personal Data:* b Chicago, Ill, Mar 13, 35; m 58; c Alec, Russell & Gregory. *Educ:* Univ Chicago, BS, 56; Stanford Univ, MS, 58, PhD(statist), 61. *Concurrent Pos:* Consult var indust firms, 61-81; vis assoc prof, Harvard Univ, 64-65; vis prof, Univ Lancaster, UK, 68-69, Univ Utah, 79, Univ Milan, Italy, 89 & Univ Rome, Italy, 89; prin investr, NSF grants, 81-85; pres, Ann Arbor Chap, Am Statist Asn, 86-; USAF, 87-88. *Mem:* Fel Inst Math Statist; fel Am Statist Asn; Am Math Asn; Int Statist Asn. *Res:* Statistical theory and applications to science and industry; Bayesian inference and decision-making; subjective probability models; Zipf's law. *Mailing Add:* Dept Statist Univ Mich Ann Arbor MI 48109. *E-Mail:* bruce_m_hill@um.cc.umich.edu

HILL, CARL MCCLELLAN, ORGANIC CHEMISTRY. *Current Pos:* RETIRED. *Personal Data:* b Norfolk, Va, July 27, 07; m 27, 70; c 2. *Educ:* Hampton Inst, BS, 31; Cornell Univ, MS, 35, PhD(org chem), 41. *Hon Degrees:* LLD, Univ Ky; DSc, East Ky Univ, 75. *Honors & Awards:* Col Chem Teachers Award, Mfg Chemists Asn, 62. *Prof Exp:* Instr, High Sch, Hampton Inst, 31-39, asst prof chem, 39-40, prin, Lab Sch, 40-41; assoc prof chem, Agr & Tech Univ NC, 41-44; head dept, Tenn State Univ, 44-52, prof, 44-62, chmn dept, 52-58, dean fac & sch arts & sci, 58-62; prof chem & pres, Ky State Univ, 62-75; pres, Hampton Inst, 76-78. *Concurrent Pos:* Gen Educ Bd fel; Rosenwald fel. *Mem:* Fel Am Chem Soc; fel Nat Inst Sci (pres, 46); fel Am Inst Chemists; Sigma Xi. *Res:* Organic chemical research with ketenes, aliphatic, alicyclic and arylunsaturated ethers and Grignard reagents, quality levels of fruits and vegetables; low temperature treatment of soft coals; aryloxy acids and plant hormones; lithium aluminum hydride reduction studies of dimetric ketenes. *Mailing Add:* 431 Elizabeth Lake Dr Hampton VA 23369

HILL, CATHERINE L, PERSONNEL & BUDGET ALLOCATION, AGREEMENTS. *Current Pos:* ASST CHIEF HYDROLOGIST OPERS, US GEOL SURV, VA, 95- *Personal Data:* b Ohio, June 20, 51. *Educ:* Am Univ, BS, 73; Duke Univ, MCM, 89. *Mailing Add:* US Geol Surv MS 441 Nat Ctr Reston VA 22092. *E-Mail:* clhill@usgs.gov

HILL, CHARLES EARL, FAMILY MEDICINE. *Current Pos:* asst dir, 72-75, EXEC DIR FAMILY PRACT PROG, SCH MED, UNIV MD, BALTIMORE, 75-, MEM FAC FAMILY MED, 72-, DIR, FAMILY PRACT RESIDENT PROG, 78- *Personal Data:* b Baltimore, Md, July 12, 35; m 57; c 4. *Educ:* Loyola Col, Md, BSc, 56; Univ Md, Baltimore, MD, 60. *Prof Exp:* Intern, St Agnes Hosp, Baltimore, 60-61; pvt pract, 61-62 & 64-72; consult, Md House Correction, Jessup, 68-72. *Concurrent Pos:* Consult, Resident Asst Prog, 80-86; mem, Accreditation Rev Comt, ACCME, 87- *Mem:* Soc Teachers Family Med; Asn Am Med Cols. *Res:* Color vision testing; family practice library. *Mailing Add:* Dept Family Med Univ Md Sch Med 295 Paca St Baltimore MD 21201

HILL, CHARLES GRAHAM, JR, CHEMICAL ENGINEERING, FOOD ENGINEERING-KINETICS-CATALYSIS. *Current Pos:* from asst prof to assoc prof, 67-76, chmn, Dept Chem Eng, 89-92, PROF CHEM ENG, UNIV WIS-MADISON, 76-, PROF FOOD SCI, 89-, SOBOTA PROF CHEM ENG, 95- *Personal Data:* b Elmira, NY, July 28, 37; m 64, Katharine Koon; c Elizabeth, Deborah & Cynthia. *Educ:* Mass Inst Technol, SB, 59, SM, 60, ScD(chem eng), 64. *Prof Exp:* Asst prof chem eng, Mass Inst Technol, 64-65. *Concurrent Pos:* Consult, Arthur D Little, Inc, 63-65, Joseph Schlitz Brewing Co, 73-76 & Tomah Prod, 76 & Nat Bur Stand, 79-87; Ford Found fel eng, 64-65. *Mem:* Fel Am Inst Chem Engrs; Am Chem Soc; Inst Food Technologists. *Res:* Chemical kinetics; catalysis; reverse osmosis and membrane separation processes; thermodynamics; laser Raman spectroscopy; photocatalysis; ceramic membrane technology; immobilized enzyme reactors; composite wood products. *Mailing Add:* Dept Chem Eng Univ Wis Madison WI 53706

HILL, CHARLES HORACE, JR, NUTRITION, BIOCHEMISTRY. *Current Pos:* assoc prof poultry nutrit, 52-70, PROF POULTRY SCI, NC STATE UNIV, 70- *Personal Data:* b Indianapolis, Ind, Aug 2, 21; m 48; c 2. *Educ:* Colo Agr & Mech Col, BS, 48; Cornell Univ, MS, 49, PhD, 51. *Prof Exp:* Asst chemist biochem & nutrit, Univ Nebr, 51-52. *Mem:* Am Chem Soc; Poultry Sci Asn. *Res:* Unidentified factors and role of antibiotics in poultry nutrition; nutrition in resistance to disease; inhibition of growth due to unheated soybean meal; bacterial nutrition. *Mailing Add:* Dept Poultry Sci NC State Univ Box 7608 Raleigh NC 27695-0001. *Fax:* 919-515-2625

HILL, CHARLES WHITACRE, BIOCHEMISTRY, GENETICS. *Current Pos:* From asst prof to assoc prof, 68-81, PROF BIOCHEM & MOLECULAR BIOL, HERSHEY MED CTR, PA STATE UNIV, 81- *Personal Data:* b Danville, Va, Mar 6, 40; m 62, Sylverlyn Barksdale; c Richard & Andrew. *Educ:* Univ Va, BS, 62; Univ Wis, PhD(biochem), 67. *Concurrent Pos:* NSF fel biochem, Stanford Univ, 66-68. *Mem:* Am Soc Microbiol; Genetics Soc Am; Am Soc Biochem & Molecular Biol; AAAS. *Res:* Genetics and biochemistry of transfer RNA; chromosomal rearrangement; microbial evolution. *Mailing Add:* Dept Biochem & Molecular Biol Pa State Univ Hershey Med Ctr PO Box 850 Hershey PA 17033-0850. *Fax:* 717-531-7072; *E-Mail:* chill@cor____mail.biochem.hmc.psu.edu

HILL, CHRISTOPHER T, ELEMENTARY PARTICLE PHYSICS. *Current Pos:* fel, Fermi Nat Accelerator Lab, 79-81, assoc scientist physics, 81-85, scientist I, 85-89, SCIENTIST II, FERMI NAT ACCELERATOR LAB, 89- *Personal Data:* b Neenah, Wis, June 19, 51; div; c Katherine & Graham. *Educ:* Mass Inst Technol, BS & MS, 72; Calif Inst Technol, PhD(physics), 77. *Prof Exp:* Fel physics, Univ Chicago, 77-79. *Concurrent Pos:* CERN assoc, 87-88; vis scholar, Univ Chicago, 88-; prof, Univ Chicago, 96- *Mem:* Fel Am Phys Soc. *Res:* Problems of high energy theoretical physics including construction of realistic grand unified field theories and theory of electroweak symmetry breaking. *Mailing Add:* Theory Group MS 106 Fermilab PO Box 500 Batavia IL 60510

HILL, CHRISTOPHER THOMAS, CHEMICAL ENGINEERING, POLICY ANALYSIS. *Current Pos:* SR POLICY ANALYST, RAND, 93- *Personal Data:* b Clarksburg, WVa, Aug 29, 42; m 65, Sheila Poleselli. *Educ:* Ill Inst Technol, BS, 64; Univ Wis-Madison, MS, 66, PhD(chem eng), 69. *Prof Exp:* Res engr, Uniroyal, Inc, NJ, 68-70; from asst prof to assoc prof chem eng, Washington Univ, 70-76, assoc prof technol & human affairs, 76-78; sr res assoc, Ctr Policy Alternatives, Mass Inst Technol, 78-83; sr specialist sci & tech policy, Libr Cong, 83-90; exec dir mgr forum, Nat Acad Eng & Sci, 90-93. *Mem:* Fel AAAS; Am Inst Chem Engrs; Am Chem Soc; Am Economics Asn; Asn Pub Policy Anal & Mgt. *Res:* Policy analysis; technological innovation and assessment; manufacturing, energy, resources and environment; government regulation; chemical industry; multiphase rheology. *Mailing Add:* Inst Pub Policy MS-3C6 George Mason Univ Fairfax VA 20037. *Fax:* 202-452-8377; *E-Mail:* chill@wash.rand.org

HILL, CLIFF OTIS, PHYSICAL CHEMISTRY, PHOTOCHEMISTRY. *Current Pos:* SR RES CHEMIST, EASTMAN KODAK CO, 69- *Personal Data:* b Glendale, Calif, Sept 10, 41; m 64; c 2. *Educ:* Wichita State Univ, BS, 64, MS, 65; Ari State Univ, PhD(phys chem), 69. *Mem:* Am Chem Soc. *Res:* GaAs integrated circuit design; Photochemistry of transition metal complexes; theoretical studies of luminescence and luminescence quenching. *Mailing Add:* 1254 Old Farm Circle Webster NY 14580

HILL, CRAIG LIVINGSTON, CHEMISTRY. *Current Pos:* assoc prof, 83-88, prof, Dept Chem, 88-90, GOODRICH C WHITE PROF CHEM, EMORY UNIV, 96-; ADJ PROF, GA INST TECHNOL, 95- *Personal Data:* b Pomona, Calif, Feb 24, 49; m, Linda S Ross. *Educ:* Univ Calif, San Diego, BA, 71; Mass Inst Technol, PhD(chem), 75. *Honors & Awards:* Charles H Stone Award, Am Chem Soc, 92; Sr award, Alexander Von Humboldt Found, 94; Albert E Levy Sci Res Award, Sigma Xi, 96; Nat Group Honor Award for excellence in Res, USDA, 96. *Prof Exp:* Fel, Stanford Univ, 77; asst prof, Univ Calif, Berkeley, 77-83. *Concurrent Pos:* NSF grantee, 84-; NIH fel, 86-; Army Res Off grantee, 87-; ed, New J Chem, 89- & Alkane Functionalization J, 89; consult, Interox Int, 89-93, ARCO Chem Co, 87-92, Johnson Matthey, 89-93, Allied-Signal, 90-94, Clorox Corp, 93- Avid Therapeut Inc, 94- & Sandoz-Agro, 96-; evaluator, NSF Mat Sci & Eng Ctr, 96-, NSF panel geochem & biochem, 96- *Mem:* Am Chem Soc; Royal Soc Chem; AAAS; Int Union Pure & Appl Chem; NY Acad Sci; Electrochem Soc; Sigma Xi. *Res:* Multitasking, combinatorial optimization and intelligence; catalysis of technologically and environmentally significant process; biology and chemistry of clusters and large molecules; granted several patents; author of 145 publications. *Mailing Add:* Dept Chem Emory Univ 1515 Pierce Dr Atlanta GA 30322

HILL, DALE EUGENE, PHYSICS, DEFECTS SILICON. *Current Pos:* Res physicist, 58-70, SCI FEL, MONSANTO CO, 70- *Personal Data:* b Struthers, Ohio, Mar 1, 31; m 53; c 3. *Educ:* Case Inst Technol, BS, 53; Purdue Univ, MS, 55, PhD(physics), 59. *Honors & Awards:* IR 100 Award, 84. *Mem:* AAAS; Am Phys Soc; Sigma Xi. *Res:* Semiconductor physics, especially process induced defects in silicon wafers, also electrical, optical and luminescence properties of III-V compound semiconductors; light emitting devices. *Mailing Add:* 940 Wood Ave St Louis MO 63122-2828

HILL, DAVID ALLAN, ELECTROMAGNETICS, ANTENNAS. *Current Pos:* ELECTRONICS ENGR, NAT INST STAND & TECHNOL, 82- *Personal Data:* b Cleveland, Ohio, Apr 21, 42; m 71, Elaine C Dempsey. *Educ:* Ohio Univ, BS, 64, MS, 66; Ohio State Univ, PhD(elec eng), 70. *Prof Exp:* Vis fel, Coop Inst Res Environ Sci, 70-71; electronics engr, Inst Telecommun Sci, 71-82. *Concurrent Pos:* Adj prof, Univ Colo, 79-; ed, Inst Elec & Electronics Engrs Trans Geosci & Remote Sensing, 80-84 & Inst Elec & Electronics Engrs Trans Antennas & Propagation, 86-89. *Mem:* Fel Inst Elec & Electronics Engrs; Int Union Radio Sci; fel Electromagnetics Acad. *Res:* Electromagnetic theory with applications to antennas, propagation, electromagnetic compatibility, and remote sensing; author of more than 100 publications. *Mailing Add:* Nat Inst Stand & Technol 325 Broadway Boulder CO 80303

HILL, DAVID BYRNE, MATHEMATICS, STATISTICS. *Current Pos:* from asst prof to assoc prof math & community med, 69-78, dir, Acad Comput Ctr, 66-74, PROF & CHMN DEPT COMPUTER SCI, UNIV VT, 74-, PROF SURG, 78- *Personal Data:* b Brooklyn, NY, Nov 3, 38; m 60; c 4. *Educ:* Stevens Inst Technol, ME, 60, MS, 61, PhD(math), 63. *Prof Exp:* Instr math, Stevens Inst Technol, 63-64; USPHS fel biomath, Stanford Univ, 64-65. *Concurrent Pos:* Consult, Vt Dept Taxes, 65-, Health Serv & Ment Health Admin, 69-, NSF, 69- & NIH, 71-; vpres, Geomet Inc, 72-74. *Mem:* Am Math Soc; Am Inst Math Statist; Asn Comput Mach. *Res:* Computer architecture. *Mailing Add:* 111 E Shore N Grand Isle VT 05458

HILL, DAVID EASTON, SOIL SCIENCE. *Current Pos:* Asst soil scientist, 57-60, assoc, 61-80, SOIL SCIENTIST, CONN AGR EXP STA, 80- *Personal Data:* b Orange, NJ, Apr 26, 29; m 57; c 3. *Educ:* Rutgers Univ, BS, 52, PhD(soil sci), 58. *Mem:* Am Soc Agron. *Res:* Soil morphology and genesis; land classification and survey; soil survey interpretations; horticulture. *Mailing Add:* 146 Wildcat Rd Madison CT 06443. *Fax:* 203-789-7232

HILL, DAVID G, MEDICAL PHYSICS, HIGH ENERGY PHYSICS. *Current Pos:* MGR, CTR RES & DEVELOP, SIEMENS CORP, 82- *Personal Data:* b Tarentum, Pa, Dec 1, 37; m 61; c 2. *Educ:* Carnegie Inst Technol, BS, 59, MS, 60, PhD(physics), 64. *Prof Exp:* Physicist, Brookhaven Nat Lab, 64-72; asst prof, Univ Md, College Park, 72-76; develop scientist, Pfizer Med Systs, 76-82. *Mem:* Am Phys Soc; Am Asn Phys Med. *Res:* High energy hadron physics; development of x-ray computerized axial tomographic scanners. *Mailing Add:* c/o Imatron 389 Oyster Point Blvd South San Francisco CA 94080

HILL, DAVID LAWRENCE, NUCLEAR PHYSICS, INSTRUMENTATION. *Current Pos:* PRES, HARBOR RES CORP, 78-, VALUTRON NV, 80-, PATENT ENFORCEMENT FUND, INC, 90- *Personal Data:* b Booneville, Miss, Nov 11, 19; m 50; c 7. *Educ:* Calif Inst Technol, BS, 42; Princeton Univ, PhD(nuclear physics), 51. *Prof Exp:* Asst, Metall Lab, Chicago, 42-43; jr physicist, 43-44; assoc physicist & group leader, Argonne Nat Lab, 44-46; from asst prof to assoc prof physics, Vanderbilt Univ, 49-54; group leader, Los Alamos Sci Lab, 54-58, consult theoret physics, 58-59; pres Southport Comput, Inc, 73-80. *Concurrent Pos:* Consult, Los Alamos Sci Lab, 52-54; mem fel panel, Nat Res Coun, 54. *Mem:* AAAS; Fedn Am Scientists (chmn, 53-54); fel Am Phys Soc; Inst Elec & Electronics Engrs. *Res:* Nanosecond pulse generators; 100 and 200 megacycle logic systems and counters; instrumentation; fission theory; nuclear structure; relation of nuclear shapes to transition rates and energy levels. *Mailing Add:* 1095 Sasco Hill Rd Fairfield CT 06430-6346

HILL, DAVID PAUL, GEOPHYSICS. *Current Pos:* Geophysicist, Crustal Studies Br, US Geol Surv, 59-64 & Hawaiian Volcano Observ, 64-66, geophysicist, Off Earthquake Studies, 71-78, chief, Seismol Br, 78-82, CHIEF SCIENTIST, LONG VALLEY CALDERA STUDIES, US GEOL SURV, 83- *Personal Data:* b Livingston, Mont, June 18, 35; m 61, Ann Rivers; c 1. *Educ:* San Jose State Col, BS, 58; Colo Sch Mines, MS, 61; Calif Inst Technol, PhD(geophys), 71. *Honors & Awards:* Meritorious Serv Award, Dept

Interior. *Concurrent Pos:* Assoc ed, J Geophys Res, 85-88. *Mem:* AAAS; fel Am Geophys Union; Seismol Soc Am. *Res:* Elastic wave propagation with applications to earth structure and earthquake studies; application of geophysical methods to the study of earthquake and volcanic processes. *Mailing Add:* 3794 Redwood Circle Palo Alto CA 94306

HILL, DAVID THOMAS, AGRICULTURAL WASTE UTILIZATION, ENERGY PRODUCTION. *Current Pos:* assoc prof, 79-86, ALUMNI PROF AGR ENG, AUBURN UNIV, 86- *Personal Data:* b Griffin, Ga, Oct 11, 47; m 67, Linda Burns; c Heather A, Erin E & Joel T. *Educ:* Univ Ga, BSAE, 70, MS, 71; Clemson Univ, PhD(agr eng), 75. *Honors & Awards:* Nat Young Researcher, Am Soc Agr Engrs, 85. *Prof Exp:* Instr agr eng, Clemson Univ, 73-75; asst prof agr eng, Univ Fla, 75-79. *Mem:* Am Soc Agr Engrs; Nat Soc Prof Engrs; Am Soc Eng Educ; Sigma Xi. *Res:* Energy recovery from agricultural wastes through anaerobic fermentation; novel utilization systems development and design refinement of animal waste systems. *Mailing Add:* Agr Eng Dept Auburn Univ Auburn AL 36849-5417. *Fax:* 334-844-3530; *E-Mail:* dhill@eng.auburn.edu

HILL, DAVID W(ILLIAM), GROUNDWATER GEOCHEMISTRY, HAZARDOUS WASTE SITE ANALYSIS. *Current Pos:* Res sanit engr, Fed Water Pollution Control Admin, Environ Protection Agency, 66-71; supv sanit engr, 71-83, environ engr, Southeast Water Lab, 83-86, ENVIRON ENGR, ENVIRON PROTECTION AGENCY, GROUNDWATER BR, 86- *Personal Data:* b Orange, NJ, Sept 24, 36; m 60, Nina Huchingson; c Jeffrey, Abigail & Daniel. *Educ:* Cornell Univ, AB, 58; Stanford Univ, MS, 63, PhD(sanit eng), 66. *Honors & Awards:* Spec Achievement Award, Environ Protection Agency, 88 & 89; Notable Achievement Award, Environ Protection Agency, 90, 92-96. *Mem:* Am Geophys Union. *Res:* Anaerobic degradation of pesticides; waste treatment and characterization; environmental monitoring; remote sensing; environmental assessments; groundwater contamination. *Mailing Add:* Water Mgt Div Region 4 Environ Protection Agency 100 Alabama St SW Atlanta GA 30303-3104. *Fax:* 770-562-9224

HILL, DEREK LEONARD, physical chemistry, electrochemistry; deceased, see previous edition for last biography

HILL, DONALD GARDNER, GEOLOGY, GEOPHYSICS. *Current Pos:* Res geophysicist, Chevron Oil Field Res Co, 69-78, sr geophysicist, Chevron Resources Co, 78-81, SR DEVELOP GEOLOGIST, CHEVRON OVERSEAS PETROL, INC, STAND OIL CO CALIF, 94- *Personal Data:* b Lansing, Mich, May 17, 41; m 65; c 1. *Educ:* Mich State Univ, BS, 63, PhD(geol, geophys), 69. *Mem:* Am Geophys Union; Soc Explor Geophys; Soc Petrol Eng; Europ Asn Explor Geophys; Soc Prof Well Log Analysists. *Res:* Petrophysics; well log analysis; seismic interpretation research; mining geophysics and geothermal research. *Mailing Add:* 1012 Hillerdale Ct Walnut Creek CA 94596

HILL, DONALD LOUIS, animal physiology; deceased, see previous edition for last biography

HILL, DONALD LYNCH, BIOCHEMICAL PHARMACOLOGY, CANCER. *Current Pos:* sr biochemist, Southern Res Inst, 65-71, head, Membrane Biochem Sect, 71-76, assoc dir, 84-85, head, Biochem Pharmacol Div, 76-85, dir, 86-90, vpres, Biochem Res, 90-93, DISTINGUISHED SCIENTIST, SOUTHERN RES INST, 94- *Personal Data:* b Decherd, Tenn, June 24, 37; m 60, Elaine Martin; c John, Gerald & Stephen. *Educ:* Mid Tenn State Col, BS, 60; Vanderbilt Univ, PhD(biochem), 64. *Prof Exp:* Res asst, Univ Calif, 64-65. *Concurrent Pos:* Assoc adj prof pharmacol, Univ Ala, Birmingham, 77- *Mem:* AAAS; Am Asn Biol Chem; Am Asn Cancer Res; Soc Toxicol. *Res:* Dispostion metabolism and sites of action of antitumor agents and carcinogens; prevention of cancer. *Mailing Add:* Southern Res Inst PO Box 55305 Birmingham AL 35255-5305. *Fax:* 205-581-2877

HILL, DONALD P, PATHOLOGY. *Current Pos:* From asst prof to assoc prof, 60-70, actg chmn dept, 78-79, PROF PATH, UNIV OTTAWA, 70- *Personal Data:* b Orillia, Ont, Nov 9, 29; m 54; c 8. *Educ:* Univ Ottawa, MD, 54. *Concurrent Pos:* Res fel, Ont Cancer Treatment & Res Found, 59-64; fel cytol, Mem Hosp, NY, 60; pathologist, Ottawa Gen Hosp, 58-, assoc dir labs, 69-75, dir, 75-79; asst registr tumor path, Can Tumor Registry, 60-66, assoc registr, 67-73, actg registr, 73-76; asst, Can Asn Path, 65-73; mem assoc comt dent res, Nat Res Coun Can, 65-67. *Mem:* Can Asn Pathologists (secy-treas, 73-76, vpres, 76-77, pres-elect, 77-78, pres, 78-79); Can Soc Forensic Sci (vpres, 70-, pres, 71). *Res:* Exfoliative cytology; tumor, forensic and anatomic pathology. *Mailing Add:* 515 San Laurent Blvd Apt 113 Ottawa ON K1K 3X5 Can

HILL, DOUGLAS WAYNE, MEDICAL MICROBIOLOGY. *Current Pos:* ADJ PROF, UNIV CALIF, 87- *Personal Data:* b Bountiful, Utah, Aug 6, 27; m 50; c 2. *Educ:* Univ Utah, BS, 50, MS, 52, PhD(bact), 59. *Prof Exp:* Asst mycol, Univ Utah, 50-52, res assoc virol, 53-55, instr, 55-70, assoc prof microbiol, 70-87. *Concurrent Pos:* Consult, US Army Chem Corps, 59. *Mem:* Am Soc Microbiol; Reticuloendothelial Soc. *Res:* Experimental immunology of viral and mycotic diseases. *Mailing Add:* 2196 San Anseline Ave Long Beach CA 90815

HILL, DOYLE EUGENE, BIOCHEMISTRY, CLINICAL CHEMISTRY. *Current Pos:* res chemist, Res Labs, Eastman Kodak Co, 74-79, supvr med prod eval, 79-89, mgr, Strategic Resources, Clin Prod Div, 89-91, GEN MGR & VPRES IMMONODIAG STRATEGIC RESOURCES, EASTMAN KODAK CO, 92- *Personal Data:* b Anthony, Kans, Oct 15, 46; m 85, Ruth M Ibach; c Kyle, Todd, Taylor, Michael, Matthew & Jennifer. *Educ:* Northwestern Okla State Univ, BS, 68; Okla State Univ, PhD(biochem), 72. *Prof Exp:* NIH fel biochem, Cornell Univ, 73-74. *Mem:* Sigma Xi; Am Chem Soc; AAAS; Am Asn Clin Chem. *Res:* Enzyme kinetics in solution and diffusion limited situations; physical chemistry of enzymes to delineate structure-function problems; use of enzymes for analytical determinations; in vitro diagnostic product development. *Mailing Add:* 350 Stafford Way Rochester NY 14626-1666

HILL, EDDIE P, BOTANY, MYCOLOGY. *Current Pos:* from asst prof to assoc prof, 64-76, PROF BIOL, MACALESTER COL, 75- *Personal Data:* b Allen, Nebr, June 9, 30; m 59; c 2. *Educ:* Nebr State Teachers Col, Wayne, BA, 52; Colo State Col, MA, 57; Univ Nebr, PhD(bot), 62. *Prof Exp:* Res assoc bot, Univ Mich, 62-64. *Mem:* AAAS; Am Soc Microbiol. *Res:* Fungal physiology; spore dormancy; growth and development. *Mailing Add:* Dept Biol Macalester Col 1600 Grand Ave St Paul MN 55105-1801

HILL, EDWARD C, obstetrics & gynecology, for more information see previous edition

HILL, EDWARD T, MATHEMATICS. *Current Pos:* asst prof math, 69-75, actg dean, 75-76, PROF MATH, CORNELL COL, 78- *Personal Data:* b Minneapolis, Minn, Mar 1, 38; m 64; c 2. *Educ:* Luther Col, Iowa, BA, 63; Vanderbilt Univ, MA, 65, PhD(math), 68. *Prof Exp:* Asst prof math, Calif Lutheran Col, 67-69. *Mem:* Sigma Xi; AAAS; Math Asn Am. *Res:* Modular group rings of p-groups. *Mailing Add:* 600 First St W Mt Vernon IA 52314

HILL, ELGIN ALEXANDER, PHYSICAL ORGANIC CHEMISTRY, ORGANOMETALLIC COMPOUNDS. *Current Pos:* chmn dept, 70-72, from asst prof to assoc prof, 66-80, PROF ORG CHEM, UNIV WIS-MILWAUKEE, 80- *Personal Data:* b Pittsburgh, Pa, May 16, 35; m 58; c 3. *Educ:* Allegheny Col, BS, 57; Calif Inst Technol, PhD(chem), 61. *Prof Exp:* NSF fel, Pa State Univ, 60-61; asst prof org chem, Univ Minn, Minneapolis, 61-66. *Mem:* Am Chem Soc. *Res:* Physical organic chemistry; organometallic structure and rearrangements; structure and reactivity correlations; isotope effects; free radical rearrangements. *Mailing Add:* 4203 N Ardmore Ave Milwaukee WI 53211

HILL, ELWOOD FAYETTE, WILDLIFE TOXICOLOGY. *Current Pos:* LEADER, WILDLIFE TOXICOL GROUP & RES TOXICOLOGIST, PATUXENT WILDLIFE RES CTR, NAT BIOL SURV, MD, 69-; ADJ PROF, PROG TOXICOL, UNIV MD, 90- *Personal Data:* b Tonopah, Nev, Feb 18, 39; m 63, Vicki Rebrook; c Margo, Michael & Maureen. *Educ:* San Jose State Univ, BA, 61; Univ Md, MS, 72, PhD(avian physiol/toxicol), 81. *Prof Exp:* Wildlife mgr II, Nev Fish & Game Dept, 61-66; wildlife biologist, Tech Develop Labs, US Pub Health Serv, Fla, 66-69. *Mem:* Soc Environ Toxicol & Chem; Sigma Xi; Wildlife Soc; AAAS; Soc Toxicol; Ecol Soc Am. *Res:* Effects of environmental contaminants on wild vertebrates; emphasis on biochemical indicators of toxicity, development of wildlife testing protocols and assessment of mine effluent and pesticide hazard to wildlife. *Mailing Add:* 605 E St Louis Ave Las Vegas NV 89104

HILL, ERIC STANLEY, PHYSICAL CHEMISTRY. *Current Pos:* RETIRED. *Personal Data:* b Liverpool, Eng, Feb 12, 25; m 55; c 3. *Educ:* Univ Liverpool, BS, 50, PhD(phys chem), 55. *Prof Exp:* Res chemist, Imp Chem Industs, Eng, 53-56, sect head man made fibers, 56-58, qual control mgr, 58-60; asst tech dir, Fiber Industs, Inc, 60-67, mfg tech dir, 67-70, tech dir, 70-, vpres, 71- *Concurrent Pos:* Consult, Montefibres, Milan, Italy, 84-86. *Res:* Nylon and polyester fibers including new products and development of new design data for new plant facilities. *Mailing Add:* 3953 Abingdon Rd Charlotte NC 28211

HILL, ERNEST E(LWOOD), NUCLEAR ENGINEERING. *Current Pos:* PRES, HILL ASSOCS, 82- *Personal Data:* b Oakland, Calif, May 15, 22; m 42, Bettejean Schaegelen; c 3. *Educ:* Univ Calif, BS, 43, MS, 59. *Prof Exp:* Design engr, Daco Develop Co, 46-47; indust engr & prod supt, Fed Pac Elec Co, 47-55; supvr opers res reactor, Lawrence Radiation Lab, Univ Calif, 55-64; chief, reactor safety br, San Francisco Opers Off, AEC, 64-67; head safety systs anal group, Lawrence Livermore Lab, Univ Calif, 67-74, assoc div leader, Nuclear Test Eng div, 74-77, div leader, Magnetic Fusion Eng Div, 77-82. *Concurrent Pos:* Admin judge, Atomic Safety Licensing Bd, Panel Nuclear Regulatory Comn, 73- *Mem:* Am Nuclear Soc. *Res:* Nuclear engineering and reactor operation; nuclear safety; human factors engineering; probabilistic risk assessment. *Mailing Add:* 210 Montego Dr Danville CA 94526. *Fax:* 510-743-8429

HILL, FLOYD ISOM, MECHANICAL ENGINEERING. *Current Pos:* RETIRED. *Personal Data:* b Memphis, Tenn, Aug 10, 21; m 43; c 3. *Educ:* Univ Tenn, BS, 43; Johns Hopkins Univ, MS, 52. *Prof Exp:* Analyst, Pratt & Whitney Aircraft Div, United Aircraft Corp, 43-45; ord engr recoil systs anal, US Army Ballistic Res Labs, 46-49, sect head weapons systs anal, 49-51, br chief, 51-55; sr engr, Opers Res, Inc, 56-57; assoc dir oper testing, Tech Opers, Inc, 57-58; prin engr combat surveillance, Cornell Aeronaut Lab, Inc, 58-60, dep dir, 60-62, head, Wash Projs Dept, 62-71; consult, 71- *Mem:* AAAS; Opers Res Soc Am; NY Acad Sci; Sigma Xi. *Res:* Analysis of unsteady compressible flow of liquid; mathematical analysis of ground warfare; design and analysis of operational field tests and war games. *Mailing Add:* 6338 Cross Woods Dr Falls Church VA 22044

HILL, FRANK B(RUCE), PHOTOREACTOR ENGINEERING. *Current Pos:* assoc chem engr, Nuclear Eng Dept, 54-57, supvr, Processing Sect, 57-58, proj chem engr, 58-61, chem engr, 61-62, supvr radiation chem eng, Dept Appl Sci, 62-72, prin investr environ sci, Dept Appl Sci, 72-75, prin investr chem eng sci, Dept Energy & Environ, 75-80, GROUP LEADER SEPARATION SCI & TECHNOL, BROOKHAVEN NAT LAB, 80- *Personal Data:* b Washington, DC, Aug 9, 24; m 49; c 3. *Educ:* Cath Univ, BChE, 49; Princeton Univ, PhD(chem eng), 59. *Prof Exp:* Instr chem eng, Princeton Univ, 52-53, asst, 53-54. *Concurrent Pos:* Adj res prof & consult, NJ Inst Technol, 73-; adj prof chem eng, NC State Univ, 73-75; adj prof nuclear eng, Polytechnic Inst NY, 79. *Mem:* Am Chem Soc; Am Inst Chem Engrs. *Res:* Separation of industrial gases, isotopes, biological substances, hazardous wastes; engineering of photochemical and radiation chemical reactors; modelling of acid rain production; emission of biogenic atmospheric sulfur compounds. *Mailing Add:* 9227 41st Way N Pinellas Park FL 34666

HILL, FRANKLIN D, BIOCHEMISTRY. *Current Pos:* assoc prof, 63-65, PROF CHEM, GRAMBLING STATE UNIV, 65- *Personal Data:* b Boley, Okla, May 15, 33; m 55; c 3. *Educ:* Langston Univ, BS, 56; Iowa State Univ, MS, 58, PhD(biochem), 60. *Prof Exp:* Prof chem, Langston Univ, 60-62; assoc biochem, Iowa State Univ, 62-63. *Mem:* Am Chem Soc; Am Oil Chem Soc. *Res:* Autoxidation and metabolism of lipids. *Mailing Add:* Dept Chem Grambling State Univ 99 S Main St Grambling LA 71245-3099

HILL, FREDERICK BURNS, JR, FLUORINE CHEMISTRY, POLYMER CHEMISTRY. *Current Pos:* RETIRED. *Personal Data:* b Portsmouth, Va, Aug 2, 13; m 45; c 3. *Educ:* Col William & Mary, BS, 34; Univ Va, PhD(org chem), 40. *Prof Exp:* Chemist, Corn Prod Refining Co, Ill, 34-36; res chemist, Org Chem Dept, Jackson Lab, E I du Pont de Nemours & Co, Inc, 40-55, Tech Sales Serv, Freon Prod Div, 55-61, mkt assoc, 61-69, mgr blowing agt develop, 69-71, sales mgr blowing agents, 71-76. *Mem:* Am Chem Soc; Sigma Xi. *Res:* Elastomers; resins; fluorocarbons. *Mailing Add:* 1904 Greenbriar Dr Wilmington DE 19810

HILL, FREDERICK CONRAD, VERTEBRATE ZOOLOGY, ARCHAEOZOOLOGY. *Current Pos:* PROF ZOOL, BLOOMSBURG UNIV, PA, 75- *Personal Data:* b Waukegan, Ill, Apr 6, 43; m 75; c 3. *Educ:* Ill State Univ, BS, 65, MS, 70; Univ Louisville, PhD(biol), 75. *Prof Exp:* Instr biol, Jefferson Col, 67-70. *Mem:* Sigma Xi; Am Malacol Union; Soc Am Archaeol. *Res:* Archaeozoology; fish and mollusc remains. *Mailing Add:* Dept Biol & Health Sci Bloomsburg Univ 400 E Second St Bloomsburg PA 17815-1399

HILL, FREDRIC WILLIAM, NUTRITION OF DOMESTIC & LABORATORY ANIMALS, AGRICULTURAL & FOOD CHEMISTRY. *Current Pos:* prof & chmn, Dept Poultry Husb, Univ Calif, Davis, 59-65, assoc dean, Col Agr, 65-66, chmn, Dept Nutrit, 65-73, assoc dean res & int prog, 76-80, PROF NUTRIT, UNIV CALIF, DAVIS, 65- *Personal Data:* b Erie, Pa, Sept 2, 18; m 44, Charlotte Gummoe; c Linda C, James F & Dana E. *Educ:* Pa State Univ, BS, 39, MS, 40; Cornell Univ, PhD(animal nutrit), 44. *Honors & Awards:* Res Prize, Poultry Sci Asn, 57; Nutrit Res Award, Am Feed Mfrs Asn, 58; Newman Mem Int Res Award, 59; Borden Award, 61. *Prof Exp:* Asst poultry husb, Pa State Univ, 39-40 & Cornell Univ, 40-43; head, Nutrit Div, Res Labs, Western Condensing Co, 44-48; assoc prof animal nutrit & poultry husb, Cornell Univ, 48-53, prof, 53-59. *Concurrent Pos:* Mem, Animal Nutrit Subcomt on Hormonal Relationships & Applns, Nat Res Coun, 53, Animal Nutrit Subcomt on Poultry Nutrit, 53-74 & Food & Nutrit Bd, 75-78; mem, Task Force Livestock Res, USDA; comnr, Calif Poultry Improvement Comn, 59-65; lectr, Univ Nottingham, Eng, 63; deleg, World Conf Animal Prod, Rome, 63; Guggenheim fel, Nat Inst Med Res, London & Hebrew Univ, 66-67; vis scientist, Hebrew Univ, Jerusalem, 67, USDA, 75 & US Food & Drug Admin, 75 & 88; ed, J Nutrit, 69-79; mem, USAID-Nat Acad Sci Sem on Protein Foods, Bangkok, Thailand, 70 & US Info Agency Sem on Food, Pop & Energy, Philippines, SVietnam, Malaysia, Indonesia, Japan, India & Bangladesh, 74-75; fel, Japan Soc Prom Sci, 74-75; consult, Nat Inst Agron Res, France, 82; alumni fel, Pa State Univ, 83; plenary lectr, Int Cong Asian-Australasian Animal Prod Socs, Seoul, Korea, 85. *Mem:* Fel AAAS; Am Chem Soc; fel Poultry Sci Asn; Am Soc Animal Sci; fel Am Inst Nutrit; Nutrit Soc Gt Brit. *Res:* Experimental nutrition, especially energetics, energy values of foods, quantitative nutrient requirements; nutritional properties of fats; carbohydrates; nutritional priorities in national and world food production; nutrition of poultry, laboratory species. *Mailing Add:* Dept Nutrit Univ Calif Davis CA 95616. *E-Mail:* fwhill@ucdavis.edu

HILL, FREDRICK J, ELECTRICAL ENGINEERING. *Current Pos:* assoc prof, 63-70, PROF ELEC ENG, UNIV ARIZ, 70- *Personal Data:* b Las Vegas, Nev, Sept 2, 36; m 57; c 3. *Educ:* Univ Utah, BS, 58, MS, 60, PhD(elec eng), 63. *Prof Exp:* Teaching asst elec eng, Univ Utah, 58-61. *Concurrent Pos:* Consult, Motorola Integrated Circuits Ctr, Rockwell Microelectronics & Gen Instrument Res & Develop; mem, Int Working Group on a consensus hardware description lang, 75- *Mem:* Inst Elec & Electronics Engrs. *Res:* Test sequence generation for sequential circuits; hardware description languages. *Mailing Add:* Dept Elec Eng Univ Ariz Tucson AZ 85721

HILL, GALE BARTHOLOMEW, MICROBIOLOGY, INFECTIOUS DISEASES. *Current Pos:* USPHS fel, Dept Microbiol, Med Sch, Duke Univ, 66-67, res assoc microbiol & immunol, Med Ctr, 66-71, assoc radiol, Div Radiol, 67-72, instr microbiol, 71-73, asst prof radiol, 72-73, asst prof obstet & gynec, 73-78, ASST PROF MICROBIOL, MED CTR, DUKE UNIV, 73-, ASSOC PROF OBSTET & GYNEC, 78-, DIR DIV ANAEROBIC MICROBIOL, 75- *Personal Data:* b Atlanta, Ga, Sept 20, 36. *Educ:* Fla State Univ, BS, 60; Duke Univ, PhD(microbiol), 66. *Mem:* Am Soc Microbiol; Infectious Dis Soc Obstet & Gynec; AAAS; Sigma Xi. *Res:* Infectious diseases primarily anaerobic bacterial infections and pathogenesis; anaerobic infections in obstetrics and gynecology; therapeutic agents for infection and evaluation in animal models. *Mailing Add:* Dept Reproductive Biol Box 3172 Duke Univ Med Ctr Durham NC 27710

HILL, GARY MARTIN, RUMINANT NUTRITION, ANIMAL SCIENCE. *Current Pos:* asst prof, 83-87, ASSOC PROF, ANIMAL SCI DEPT, COASTAL PLAIN STA, TIFTON, GA, 87- *Personal Data:* b Hendersonville, NC, Nov 11, 46; m 68; c 3. *Educ:* Clemson Univ, BS, 69; Univ Kent, MS, 74, PhD(animal sci), 77. *Honors & Awards:* Merit Cert, Am Forage & Grassland Coun, 90. *Prof Exp:* Res asst animal sci, Univ Kent, 72-77; asst prof animal sci, 77-80, assoc prof, La State Univ, 80-83. *Mem:* Am Soc Animal Sci; Am Dairy Sci Asn; Am Forage & Grassland Coun; Sigma Xi; Am Registry Prof Animal Scientists. *Res:* Ruminant nutrition as it affects preweaning and postweaning beef animals; forage utilization by ruminants and forage management systems. *Mailing Add:* 2815 Teresa Dr Tifton GA 31794

HILL, GEORGE CARVER, PARASITOLOGY, BIOCHEMISTRY. *Current Pos:* ASSOC PROF, DIV BIOMED SCI, MEHARRY MED COL. *Personal Data:* b Moorestown, NJ, Feb 19, 39; m 65; c 2. *Educ:* Rutgers Univ, BA, 61; Howard Univ, MS, 63; NY Univ, PhD(biol), 67. *Prof Exp:* NIH fel, Med Ctr, Univ Ky, 67-69; res investr biochem parasitol, Squibb Inst Med Res, 69-71; NIH spec res fel, Molteno Inst, Univ Cambridge, 71-73; mem staff, Squibb Inst Med Res, 73-77; assoc prof path, Colo State Univ, Ft Collins, 77- *Concurrent Pos:* Dept Army res grant, 67-68. *Mem:* Soc Protozoologists; Am Soc Microbiol. *Res:* Purification and properties of Trypanosomatid cytochromes C; characterization of electron transport systems in Trypanosomatids; ultrastructure and function of mitochondria in Trypanosomatids. *Mailing Add:* Div Biomed Sci Meharry Med Col 1005 D B Todd Jr Blvd Nashville TN 37208-3599. *Fax:* 615-321-4694

HILL, GEORGE JAMES, SURGERY, CANCER. *Current Pos:* CLIN PROF SURG, UNIFORMED SERVS UNIV HEALTH SCIS, BETHESDA, MD, 89- *Personal Data:* b Cedar Rapids, Iowa, Oct 7, 32; m 60, Helene Zimmermann; c James, David, Sarah & Helena. *Educ:* Yale Univ, AB, 53; Harvard Med Sch, MD, 57. *Honors & Awards:* Lederle Med Fac Award, 67-70; Gorgas Medal, Asn Mil Surgeons US, 91; Edwards Medal, Am Asn Cancer Educ, 94. *Prof Exp:* Clin assoc med, NIH, Bethesda, Md, 61-63; instr surg, Univ Colo Sch Med, 66-67, from asst prof to assoc prof, 67-73; prof, Wash Univ Sch Med, 73-76, Surg & Chmn Dept, Marshall Univ Sch Med, 76-81; prof surg & dir oncol, NJ Med Sch, Univ Med & Dent, NJ, 81-96, Am Cancer Soc prof clin oncol, 89-92, prof prev med & community health, 91-96. *Concurrent Pos:* Jr fac fel, Am Cancer Soc, 70-73; vis prof, Univ Saigon, Repub Vietnam, 72-73; chief surg, St Louis City Hosp, 73-76; assoc dean clin affairs, Marshall Univ Sch Med, 76-78; chmn, Nat Cancer Inst Clin Cancer Educ Comt, 78-80; pres, Am Cancer Soc, WVa Div, 80-81; pres, Am Cancer Asn, Cancer Educ, 85-86; pres, Am Cancer Soc, NJ Div, 87-88; vis fel, Molecular Biol, Princeton Univ, 88; dir at large, Am Cancer Soc Nat Bd, 89-96; mem bd trustees, Sterling Col, Craftsbury Common, Vt, 90-96; actg pres, Sterling Col, 96. *Mem:* Am Asn Cancer Res; fel Am Col Surgeons; Soc Surg Oncol; Soc Univ Surgeons; Sigma Xi; Royal Soci Med; Am Asn Cancer Educ; hon mem Am Cancer Soc. *Res:* Cancer research, surgery; chemotherapy; immunotherapy; radiation therapy; cancer education-new programs, trials and evaluation; medical education programs in developing countries and rural America; history of medicine and health. *Mailing Add:* 3 Silver Spring Rd West Orange NJ 07052. *Fax:* 973-736-0758; *E-Mail:* gjhill@pegasus.rutgers.edu

HILL, GEORGE RICHARD, CHEMISTRY, FUEL SCIENCE. *Current Pos:* envirotech prof chem eng, 77-87, EMER PROF, UNIV UTAH, 87- *Personal Data:* b Ogden, Utah, Nov 24, 21; m 41, Melba Parker; c G Richard IV, Margaret (Nielson), Robert P, Carolyn (Allen), Susan (Mann), Nancy (Bauman) & David P. *Educ:* Brigham Young Univ, AB, 42; Cornell Univ, PhD(inorg chem), 46. *Hon Degrees:* Brighan Young Univ, DSc, 80. *Honors & Awards:* Henry H Storch Award, 71. *Prof Exp:* Asst chem, Cornell Univ, 42-43, instr, 43-46; from instr to prof, Univ Utah, 46-72; dir, US Off Coal Res, 72-73; dir, Fossil Fuel Dept, Elec Power Res Inst, 73-77. *Concurrent Pos:* Head dept fuel technol, Univ Utah, 53-60, chmn dept fuels eng, 60-66, dean, Col Mines & Mineral Indust, 65-72; consult, NSF, 60-; mem comt mineral sci & technol, Nat Res Coun; mem coal sci team, Europ Econ Community Group, 67 & 71; mem comt mineral resources, Nat Asn State Univs & Land-Grant Cols, 70-; chmn, Gordon Res Conf Coal Sci, 71; mem, Energy Res & Develop Admin-FE Gen Tech Adv Comt, 73-; mem bd energy studies, Nat Acad Sci-Nat Acad Eng, 74-76; mem bd mineral & energy resources, Nat Res Coun, 76- *Mem:* Nat Acad Eng; fel Am Inst Chem; Am Inst Mining, Metall & Petrol Eng; Sigma Xi; Am Chem Soc. *Res:* Kinetics of coal conversion reactions and in situ production of shale oil. *Mailing Add:* 241 Vine St 1203 W Salt Lake City UT 84103

HILL, GIDEON D, AGRONOMY, WEED SCIENCE. *Current Pos:* CONSULT, 87- *Personal Data:* b Winston-Salem, NC, Nov 2, 22; m 47; c 2. *Educ:* Berea Col, BS, 48; NC State Col, MS, 51; Ohio State Univ, PhD(agron), 53. *Prof Exp:* Instr agron, NC State Col, 49-50; res supvr agr chem, 53-65, prod develop mgr, 65-68, mgr prod develop, 68-78, assoc div biol res, Exp Sta, E I Du Pont De Nemours & Co, 78-87. *Mem:* Hon mem Weed Sci Soc Am. *Res:* Weed control in tobacco plant beds with methyl bromide, allyl alcohol and uramon plus cyanamide; control of Canada thistle with various herbicides and adjuvants; role of soil factors in pre-emergence weed control in economic crops; herbicides; insecticides; fungicide; agricultural chemicals. *Mailing Add:* 6634 North Seedlescone Dr Fresno CA 93711

HILL, GRETCHEN MYERS, COPPER, ZINC. *Current Pos:* ASSOC PROF NUTRIT, DEPT ANIMAL SCI, MICH STATE UNIV, 93- *Personal Data:* b July 28, 42; c 1. *Educ:* Mich State Univ, PhD(nutrit), 81. *Prof Exp:* Asst prof clin nutrit & nutrit sci, Community Health & Nutrit Prog, Univ Mich, 84-86; asst prof, Univ Mo, 86-88, assoc prof, Dept Human Nutrit, 88-93. *Concurrent Pos:* Supvr res nutrit, Community Health & Nutrit Prog, Mich State, 84- *Mem:* Am Inst Nutrit; Am Soc Clin Nutrit. *Res:* Copper and factors affecting its metabolism; impact of breakfast in dietary adequacy. *Mailing Add:* Mich State Univ 2209 Anthony Hall East Lansing MI 48824-1225. *E-Mail:* hillgre@pilot.msu.edu

HILL, HAMILTON STANTON, MINERALOGY. *Current Pos:* Prof, 35-72, EMER PROF GEOL & MINERAL, PASADENA CITY COL, 72- *Personal Data:* b Brookline, Mass, Jan 19, 11; m 36, Mary; c Roger & Catherine. *Educ:* Pomona Col, BA, 33; Claremont Grad Sch, MA, 40. *Honors & Awards:* Neil Miner Award, Nat Asn Geol Teachers, 71. *Concurrent Pos:* Cur minerals, Calif Inst Technol, 79-88. *Mem:* Fel Geol Soc Am; Mineral Soc Am; Mineral Soc Gt Brit & Ireland; fel Geol Soc, London. *Res:* History of geological sciences; development of early geologic ideas. *Mailing Add:* 2661 Bowring Dr Altadena CA 91001

HILL, HARRY RAYMOND, PEDIATRICS, PATHOLOGY. *Current Pos:* asst prof, 74-76, ASSOC PROF PEDIAT & PATH, UNIV UTAH, 76- *Personal Data:* b Slidell, La, Dec 18, 41; m 66; c 2. *Educ:* Baylor Col Med, MD, 66. *Honors & Awards:* Outstanding Young Investr, Western Soc Pediat Res, 80. *Prof Exp:* Intern, Grady Mem Hosp, Emory Univ, 66-67; epidemic intel serv officer, Ctr Dis Control, USPHS, 67-69; resident pediat, Univ Wash, 69-71; fel infectious dis, Univ Minn, 71-73, from instr to asst prof pediat, 73-74. *Concurrent Pos:* Investr, Howard Hughes Med Inst, 75, prof path & pediat, 81. *Mem:* Soc Pediat Res; Am Fedn Clin Res; Reticuloendothelial Soc; Am Soc Microbiol; Western Soc Clin Res. *Res:* The role of cyclic nucleotides and pharmacologic agents in regulating the host defense mechanism; host defense mechanisms in group B streptococcal infection. *Mailing Add:* Dept Path Univ Utah Col Med Salt Lake City UT 84132-0001. *Fax:* 801-581-4517

HILL, HELENE ZIMMERMANN, CANCER BIOLOGY, GENETICS. *Current Pos:* PROF & HEAD CANCER SECT, DEPT RADIOL, NJ MED SCH, 81-, PROF MICROBIOL & MOLECULAR GENETICS, 81-, PROF BIOCHEM & MOLECULAR BIOL, 91- *Personal Data:* b Philadelphia, Pa, Apr 10, 29; m 60, George J; c James W, David H, Sarah & Helena (Rundall). *Educ:* Smith Col, AB, 50; Brandeis Univ, PhD(biol), 64. *Prof Exp:* Instr biol, Brandeis Univ, 63-64; from instr biophys to asst prof biophys & genetics, Med Ctr, Univ Colo, Denver, 67-72; assoc prof radiol, Sch Med, Wash Univ, 73-76; from assoc prof to prof biochem, Sch Med, Marshall Univ, 76-81. *Concurrent Pos:* Fel, Harvard Med Sch, 64-66; NIH fels, 64-68; prin investr, NIH grant, 71-75; adj assoc prof biol, Wash Univ; prin investr, NIH grant, 92- *Mem:* Int Soc Pigment Cell Res; Am Soc Photobiol; Radiation Res Soc; Am Asn Cancer Res; AAAS; Sigma Xi; Asn Women Sci. *Res:* Role of melanin in the caroinogenesis of melanoma; radiation response of melanoma; role of autocrine growth factors in the therapeutic responses of melanoma. *Mailing Add:* 3 Silver Spring Rd West Orange NJ 07052-4317. *Fax:* 973-972-5592; *E-Mail:* hill@umdnj.edu

HILL, HENRY ALLEN, ASTROPHYSICS, OPTICS & NUCLEAR STRUCTURE. *Current Pos:* PROF PHYSICS, UNIV ARIZ, 66- *Personal Data:* b Port Arthur, Tex, Nov 25, 33; m 54, Ethel L Eplin; c Henry A Jr, Pamela L & Kimberly R. *Educ:* Univ Houston, BS, 53; Univ Minn, MS, 56, PhD(nuclear physics), 57. *Hon Degrees:* MA, Wesleyan Univ, 66. *Prof Exp:* Res assoc physics, Princeton Univ, 57-58, from instr to asst prof physics, 58-64; from assoc prof to prof, Wesleyan Univ, 64-74; chmn dept, 69-71. *Concurrent Pos:* Sloan fel, 66-68; chmn bd, Zetetic Inst, 92- *Mem:* Fel Am Phys Soc; Am Astron Soc; Royal Astron Soc; Optical Soc Am; Int Astron Union; AAAS. *Res:* Major research in experimental relativity and the solar interior via the study of global oscillations of the sun. *Mailing Add:* Dept Physics Univ Ariz Tucson AZ 85721. *Fax:* 520-621-4721; *E-Mail:* hhill@sclera.physics.arizona.edu

HILL, HERBERT HENDERSON, JR, ANALYTICAL CHEMISTRY, CHROMATOGRAPHY. *Current Pos:* From asst prof to assoc prof, 76-85, PROF CHEM, WASH STATE UNIV, 85- *Personal Data:* b Helena, Ark, Nov 25, 45; m 68; c 2. *Educ:* Rhodes Col, Memphis, BS, 70; Univ Mo, Columbia, MS, 73; Dalhousie Univ, NS, PhD(chem), 75. *Honors & Awards:* Keene P Dimick Award Chromatography, 89. *Concurrent Pos:* Killam fel, 73-74, Japan Soc for Prom Sci fel, 83-84; dir, Off Grant & Res Develop, Wash State Univ, 85-87; vis prof, Univ Byreath, Ger, 93. *Mem:* Am Chem Soc. *Res:* Over 100 research publications in environmental chemistry and instrumentation for chemical analysis; chromatography; mass spectrometry; ion mobility spectrometry. *Mailing Add:* Wash State Univ Chem Dept Fulmer AN23 Pullman WA 99164-4630

HILL, HERBERT HEWETT, MECHANICAL ENGINEERING. *Current Pos:* PRES, RES ENGRS, INC, 68- *Personal Data:* b Tampa, Fla, Aug 31, 33; m 55. *Educ:* Ga Inst Technol, BSME, 55, MSME, 61; NC State Univ, PhD, 69. *Prof Exp:* Engr, Lockheed Aircraft Corp, 59-61; res engr, Astra, Inc, NC, 62; systs analyst, Res Triangle Inst, 63-67. *Mem:* Nat Soc Prof Engrs. *Res:* Vehicle and traffic research; kinematics of accident reconstruction; mechanical machine design; vibrational and stress analysis. *Mailing Add:* Res Engrs Inc 8821 Midway West Rd Raleigh NC 27613

HILL, HUBERT MACK, SYSTEMS ANALYSIS, APPLIED STATISTICS. *Current Pos:* RETIRED. *Personal Data:* b Sheridan, Mich, Aug 3, 18; m 44; c 4. *Educ:* Alma Col, BS, 40; Univ Conn, MS, 42; Purdue Univ, PhD(org chem), 47. *Prof Exp:* Asst chem, Univ Conn, 40-42; Bristol res fel, Purdue Univ, 42-46; Bristol res assoc, Ohio State Univ, 46-47; sr chemist, Tenn Eastman Co, Eastman Kodak Co, 47-58, sr mathematician, 58-65, consult, 65-81; consult, Innovative Problem Solving, 81-90. *Concurrent Pos:* Vis prof, Alma Col, Mich, 82. *Mem:* Am Chem Soc; fel Am Soc Qual Control. *Res:* Design of experiments; quality control; information systems; systems planning; problem solving strategies; statistics. *Mailing Add:* 1225 Buchelew Dr Kingsport TN 37663-9404

HILL, JACK DOUGLAS, ELECTRICAL ENGINEERING, MATHEMATICS. *Current Pos:* sect mgr, 82-84, mgr, Electronics Dept, 84-86, SR PROG MGR, BATTELLE MEM INST, 86- *Personal Data:* b Fort Frances, Ont, Nov 28, 37; m 59, Margaret A McCarthy; c 2. *Educ:* Univ Man, BSc, 59, MS, 60; Purdue Univ, PhD(elec eng), 65. *Prof Exp:* Sci officer, Defence Res Bd Can, Ottawa, 60-61; instr & res engr, Purdue Univ, 61-64; mem tech staff, Bellcomm Inc, 64-65. *Mem:* Am Defense Preparedness Asn; Inst Elec & Electronics Engrs; Armed Forces Commun & Electronics Asn; Asn Old Crows. *Res:* Development and application of system methodologies for planning, managing and assessing complex interdisciplinary research programs in both social and engineering sciences; basic research in optimization, modeling, technology assessment and management. *Mailing Add:* Battelle Columbus Lab 505 King Ave Columbus OH 43201

HILL, JACK FILSON, POULTRY BREEDING, GENETICS. *Current Pos:* RETIRED. *Personal Data:* b Hamilton, Mo, Feb 23, 26; m 49; c 6. *Educ:* Univ Mo, BS, 49, MS, 50; Iowa State Univ, PhD(poultry breeding), 57. *Honors & Awards:* Gold Cup, Flour Adv Bd, UK, 66. *Prof Exp:* Geneticist, Hy-Line Poultry Farms, 50-59; vpres & dir res, Babcock Industs, 59-76 & Colonial Poultry Farms, 76-80; consult geneticist, Tatum Farms, 81-82; consult geneticist, H & N, Inc, 82-85; consult, Tatom Farms, 85-92. *Concurrent Pos:* Geneticist, Tokai Breeding Farms Ltd, 77-84. *Mem:* Fel AAAS; Poultry Sci Asn; World Poultry Sci Asn; Sigma Xi. *Res:* Development and improvement of commercial egg laying crosses of chickens by hybridization. *Mailing Add:* 1910 Hidden Valley Dr Pleasant Hill MO 64080-1914

HILL, JAMES CARROLL, MICROBIOLOGY, BACTERIOLOGY. *Current Pos:* RETIRED. *Personal Data:* b Manila, Ark, June 30, 41; div. *Educ:* Ark State Col, BS, 62; Univ Ark, MS, 65, PhD(microbiol), 67. *Prof Exp:* Bacteriologist, Naval Biol Lab, Naval Supply Ctr, US Navy, 67-69, microbiologist, Naval Med Res Inst, Nat Naval Med Ctr, 69-74; bact vaccines prog officer, Develop & Applications Br, Nat Inst Allergy & Infectious Dis, 74-83, assoc dir, Intramoral Res Prog, 83-84, asst to dir, 84-87, dep dir, 87- *Mem:* Am Soc Microbiol; Infectious Dis Soc Am; Sigma Xi; Am Venereal Dis Asn; Sigma Xi. *Res:* Pigment production by Aspergillis species and Pseudomonas species; serology and antigenicity of Neisseria meningitidis, physiology and basic biology of the Neisseria; science administration. *Mailing Add:* Nat Inst Allergy & Infect Dis-NIH Bldg 31-Rm 7A03 Bethesda MD 20892-0031

HILL, JAMES EDWARD, BUILDING RESEARCH. *Current Pos:* mech engr thermal eng, Nat Bur Stand, 72-77, leader, Thermal Solar Group, Ctr Bldg Technol, 78-80, chief, Bldg Equip Div, 80-86, CHIEF, BLDG ENVIRON DIV, CTR BLDG TECHNOL, NAT BUR STAND, 86- *Personal Data:* b Bluefield, WVa, Jan 19, 42; m 63; c 3. *Educ:* Va Polytech Inst, BS, 63; Ga Inst Technol, MS, 66, PhD(mech eng), 68. *Honors & Awards:* Dept Com Spec Achievement Award, 74; Crosby Field Award, Am Soc Heating, Refrig & Air-Conditioning Engrs, 75; Dept Com Silver Medal, 76. *Prof Exp:* Res asst, Ga Inst Technol, 63-67; engr, Mission Planning & Anal Div, Manned Spacecraft Ctr, NASA, 67-68; aerospace res engr, Air Force Dynamics Lab, 68-69; asst prof mech eng, Univ Md, College Park, 69-72. *Mem:* Am Soc Mech Engrs; Am Soc Heating, Refrig, & Air-Conditioning Engrs. *Res:* Air-conditioning; refrigeration; solar heating and cooling of buildings. *Mailing Add:* Nist Bldg 226 Rm B 306 Gaithersburg MD 20899

HILL, JAMES LAFE, ENGINEERING MECHANICS, MECHANICAL ENGINEERING. *Current Pos:* Assoc prof, 63-76, PROF ENG MECH, UNIV ALA, 76- *Personal Data:* b Clinton, Okla, Feb 23, 37; m 61, 85, Marion Neill. *Educ:* Univ Okla, BS, 59; Univ Ill, MS, 62, PhD(theoret & appl mech), 63. *Honors & Awards:* AT&T Found Award, 85. *Mem:* Am Soc Mech Engrs; Am Soc Eng Educ; Am Acad Mech; Sigma Xi. *Res:* FEM; expert systems; CAD; dynamics; vibrations; solid mechanics. *Mailing Add:* 5201 Northwood Lake Dr W Northport AL 35476

HILL, JAMES LESLIE, BEHAVIORAL BIOLOGY. *Current Pos:* vis assoc unit res behav systs, NIMH, 77-84, expert consult, comp studies of brain & behav, 84-85, BIOSTATISTICIAN, CLIN SCI LAB, NIMH, 85- *Personal Data:* b Calgary, Alta, June 11, 40; m 66; c 2. *Educ:* Univ Alta, Calgary, BSc, 63, MSc, 66; Mich State Univ, PhD(zool), 70. *Prof Exp:* Asst prof biol, Richmond Col, City Univ New York, 70-75; sr res assoc zool, Mich State Univ, 75-77, Dept Biomech, 76-77. *Concurrent Pos:* Statist consult, Lamar Res Group, 74-75. *Mem:* AAAS. *Res:* Social behavior of mammals as a regulator of spacing patterns, resource utilization, mate selection and gene flow within and between populations. *Mailing Add:* Med Develop Div NIDA Rm 11-A-55 Parklawn NIMH Bldg 10 Rm 3D41 Rockville MD 20857

HILL, JAMES MILTON, BIOLOGICAL CHEMISTRY. *Current Pos:* PROF OPHTHAL, PHARMACOL & MICROBIOL, LA STATE UNIV EYE CTR, 85- *Personal Data:* b Pascagoula, Miss, Feb 20, 44; m 68; c 2. *Educ:* Spring Hill Col, BS, 64; Univ Miss, MS, 67; Baylor Col Med, PhD(pharmacol), 71. *Prof Exp:* Res asst microbiol, Univ Miss Sch Med, 67; fel biochem, Harvard Med Sch, 71-73; from asst prof to assoc prof biol, microbiol & pharmacol, Med Col Ga, 73-85. *Concurrent Pos:* NIH fel, 71-73; NSF grant, 73-; Am Lung Asn fel, 77-; consult, Warner-Lambert/Parke-Davis & Co, 76- & Burton-Parsons & Co, Inc, 78-; Nat Inst Dent Res fel, 78-; grant, Nat Eye Inst, 79- *Mem:* Am Soc Cell Biol; Am Asn Cancer Res; Am Soc Microbiol; Soc Exp Biol & Med; Asn Res Ophthal & Visual Sci. *Res:* Herpes virus forms of infections; antiviral chemotherapy; iontophoresis for drug delivery; pathogenesis of bacterial keratitis. *Mailing Add:* Dept Ophthal La State Univ Eye Ctr 2020 Gravier St Suite B New Orleans LA 70112-2234. *Fax:* 504-568-4210; *E-Mail:* jhill@lsumc.edu

HILL, JAMES STEWART, electromagnetic compatibility, electromagnetic environment; deceased, see previous edition for last biography

HILL, JAMES WAGY, ORGANIC CHEMISTRY, ANALYTICAL CHEMISTRY. *Current Pos:* asst prof, 74-, PROF CHEM, PANHANDLE STATE UNIV, 88- *Personal Data:* b Southgate, Calif, Apr 7, 42; m 70. *Educ:* Kans State Teachers Col, BS, 63; Southern Ill Univ, MS, 66, PhD(chem), 68. *Prof Exp:* Asst prof chem, Emporia Kans State Col, 68-74. *Mem:* Am Chem Soc. *Res:* Mercury in minerals by atomic absorption spectroscopy; superpure gold and superpure silver. *Mailing Add:* Dept Chem Panhandle State Univ Goodwell OK 73939

HILL, JANE VIRGINIA FOSTER, PLANT MORPHOGENESIS & FUNCTION. *Current Pos:* vol plant physiologist, Forest Physiol Lab, 80-82, VOL PLANT PHYSIOLOGIST, CLIMATE STRESS LAB, USDA BARC-W, BELTSVILLE, MD, 83- *Personal Data:* b Portland, Ore, Apr 15, 46; m 71. *Educ:* Carleton Col, BA, 68; George Washington Univ, MS, 76, PhD(bot), 80. *Prof Exp:* Botanist, Water Resources Div, US Geol Surv, Reston, Va, 78-80. *Mem:* Sigma Xi; Bot Soc Am. *Res:* Study of functional and developmental plant anatomy (structure and morphogenesis) with special reference to trees; identification of environmental and endogenous factors which influence and direct the course of wood-cell differentiation. *Mailing Add:* 8211 Hawthorne Rd Bethesda MD 20817

HILL, JESSE KING, ASTRONOMY. *Current Pos:* analyst astron, Systs & Appl Sci Corp, 78-86, ST SYSTS CORP, 86-; CHIEF SCIENTIST, HUGHES STX, 90- *Personal Data:* b Billings, Mont, Dec 31, 47. *Educ:* Stanford Univ, BS, 70; Univ Calif, Berkeley, MA, 71, PhD(astron), 75. *Prof Exp:* Res assoc astron, Nat Radio Astron Observ, 75-78. *Mem:* Am Astron Soc. *Res:* Interstellar gas dynamics; observation of interstellar absorption lines; ultraviolet astronomy; galaxies; globular clusters. *Mailing Add:* 6206 87th Ave Hyattsville MD 20784

HILL, JIM T, METABOLISM, BIOCHEMISTRY. *Current Pos:* VPRES, SPEC PRODS GROUP, SRS INT, 97- *Personal Data:* b Cushing, Okla, Apr 27, 39; m 63, Linda Archer; c 3. *Educ:* Abilene Christian Univ, BS, 61; Univ Tenn, MS, 64, PhD(biochem), 68. *Prof Exp:* Sr res scientist, E R Squibb & Sons, 68-69; sr res biochemist, Lakeside Labs, 69-75; sr res specialist, Monsanto Co, 75-78; dir chem, Hazleton Labs Am Inc, 78-80; mgr toxicol, Phelps Dodge Corp, 80-81; dir sci affairs, Chem Spec Mfr Asn, 81-86, dir, Pesticide Ingredient Rev Prog, 86-97. *Mem:* Am Chem Soc; Environ Mutagen Soc; Sigma Xi; Am Soc Pharmacol & Exp Therapeut; Am Col Toxicol; Soc Toxicol. *Res:* Biochemical pharmacology; chemical carcinogenesis; microbial fermentation of hydrocarbons; development of analytical techniques for identification of biological products; environmental and mammalian safety, toxicology and metabolism. *Mailing Add:* 2477 Freetown Dr Reston VA 22091-2527. *Fax:* 703-620-3116; *E-Mail:* jimthill@srsinternational.com

HILL, JOHN CAMPBELL, SOLID STATE PHYSICS. *Personal Data:* b Detroit, Mich, May 30, 38; div; c 3. *Educ:* Wayne State Univ, BS, 60; Yale Univ, MS, 61, PhD(far infrared spectros), 66. *Prof Exp:* Res asst, Yale Univ, 62-66; from assoc sr res physicist to sr res physicist, Gen Motors Res Lab, 66-73, supvry res physicist, 73-77, dept res scientist, 77-79, asst dept head, 79-87, prin res scientist, 87-91. *Mem:* Am Phys Soc; Sigma Xi. *Res:* Infrared spectroscopy of crystalline solids; infrared diode laser spectroscopy of gases; tungsten-halogen light bulb technology; light emitting diodes; metal physics, metal deformation; combustion physics. *Mailing Add:* 33 Devonshire Rd Pleasant Ridge MI 48069-1209

HILL, JOHN CHRISTIAN, NUCLEAR PHYSICS, HEAVY ION PHYSICS. *Current Pos:* from asst prof to assoc prof, 75-81, PROF PHYSICS, IOWA STATE UNIV, 81- *Personal Data:* b Blacksburg, Va, Apr 13, 36; m 67; c 1. *Educ:* Davidson Col, BS, 57; Purdue Univ, MS, 62, PhD(physics), 66. *Prof Exp:* Fel physics, Univ Mich, 66-68; asst prof, Tex A&M Univ, 68-75. *Concurrent Pos:* Res assoc, Univ Mich, 66-68; res grant, Robert A Welch Found, 69-75 & NSF, 74-78; prog dir, Ames Lab, 77-; vis scientist, KFA J06lich, WGer, 80-81. *Mem:* Am Phys Soc; Am Chem Soc; AAAS; Sigma Xi. *Res:* Structured neutron-rich fission products using the mass separator Tristan search for new isotopes; electromagnetic dissociation processes with relativistic heavy ions at the Bevalac, AGS & CERN-SPS accelerators. *Mailing Add:* Dept Physics Iowa State Univ Ames IA 50011m

HILL, JOHN DONALD, VETERINARY MEDICINE, CARDIOLOGY. *Current Pos:* RETIRED. *Personal Data:* b Santa Monica, Calif, Dec 5, 30. *Educ:* Wash State Univ, BS, 58, DVM, 60; Univ Pa, MMS, 67. *Prof Exp:* Pvt pract, Calif, 60-62; instr med & surg, Sch Vet Med, Univ Calif, Davis, 62-63; instr cardiol, Univ Pa, 63-64, Nat Heart Inst fel, 64-67, asst prof med & USPHS fel physiol, 67-68; assoc scientist, Ore Regional Primate Res Ctr, 68-76, asst prof med, Med Sch, Ore Health Sci Univ, 68-; scientist, Ore Regional Primate Res Ctr, 76-88, chmn, Dept Surg, 68-88. *Mem:* AAAS; Am Heart Asn; Am Vet Med Asn. *Res:* Experimental surgery; comparative cardiology; electrocardiography; experimental surgery in nonhuman primates; electrophysiology and cardiovascular physiology of spontaneous heart diseases in dogs; cardiovascular physiology in monkeys including pregnant animals; fetal surgery in monkeys. *Mailing Add:* 160 NW 11th Ave Canby OR 97013

HILL, JOHN HAMON MASSEY, ORGANIC CHEMISTRY. *Current Pos:* assoc prof, 61-66, PROF CHEM, HOBART & WILLIAM SMITH COLS, 66-, CHMN DEPT, 69- *Personal Data:* b Belfast, Northern Ireland, June 12, 32; m 60. *Educ:* Queen's Univ, Belfast, BSc, 53, PhD(org chem), 56. *Prof Exp:* Fel org chem, Univ Munich, 56-57; res assoc, Johns Hopkins Univ, 57-59; res chemist, Du Pont of Can, 59-60; lectr chem, Royal Mil Col, Ont, 60-61. *Concurrent Pos:* F G Cottrell res grant, 63-65. *Mem:* Am Chem Soc. *Res:* Nucleophilic heteroaromatic substitution; novel heteroaromatic compounds; chemiluminescence; carbanion rearrangements. *Mailing Add:* Chem Hobart & William Smith Col 300 Pulteney St Geneva NY 14456-3304

HILL, JOHN JOSEPH, physics, for more information see previous edition

HILL, JOHN LEDYARD, WOOD SCIENCE & TECHNOLOGY. *Current Pos:* RETIRED. *Personal Data:* b El Paso, Tex, Aug 11, 19; m 44; c 3. *Educ:* Colo State Univ, BS, 42; Yale Univ, MS, 47, DFor, 54. *Honors & Awards:* Wood Award, Forest Prod Res Soc, 49. *Prof Exp:* Instr wood technol, Mich State Univ, 50-55; prof, Auburn Univ, 56-58; wood technologist, Nat Lumber Mfrs Asn, Washington, DC, 58-64; assoc prof forest resources, Univ NH, 64-70, prof wood sci & technol, 70-89. *Mem:* Soc Wood Sci & Technol; Forest Prod Res Soc; Am Soc Testing & Mat; Sigma Xi. *Res:* Relation of tree growth to wood quality; drying stress analysis and automatic dry kiln control. *Mailing Add:* 3 Chesley Dr Durham NH 03824

HILL, JOHN MAYES, JR, BIOCHEMISTRY. *Current Pos:* asst prof, 71-74, ASSOC PROF FOOD SCI & NUTRIT, BRIGHAM YOUNG UNIV, 71- *Personal Data:* b San Antonio, Tex, Mar 4, 38; c 1. *Educ:* Rice Univ, BA, 61, PhD(biol), 65. *Prof Exp:* USPHS res fel, Univ Calif, Los Angeles, 65-66; asst prof chem & genetics, Wash State Univ, 66-70, asst prof genetics, 70-71. *Mem:* AAAS; Genetics Soc Am. *Res:* Genetic control and metabolic regulation of cells, especially regulatory enzymes in the metabolic pathways which supply energy to the cell. *Mailing Add:* Food Serv & Nutrit Brigham Young Univ 475 Widlo Provo UT 84602-1049

HILL, JOHN ROGER, COLON & RECTAL SURGERY. *Current Pos:* RETIRED. *Personal Data:* b Reinersville, Ohio, Mar 5, 12; m 37; c 3. *Educ:* Ohio State Univ, AB, 33, MD, 36; Univ Minn, MS, 41. *Prof Exp:* Mem staff, Sect Proctol, Mayo Med Sch, Univ Minn, 46-77, assoc prof, 65-70, sr consult, Sect Proctol, 67-77, prof proctol, 71-77. *Concurrent Pos:* Ed-in-chief, Dis Colon & Rectum, 67-87. *Mem:* Fel Am Proctol Soc; fel Am Col Surgeons; Am Gastroenterol Asn. *Res:* Colloid adenocarcinoma; polypoid lesions of the terminal portion of the colon; annular rectal structure resulting from internal fistula in ano; abscesses, fistulas and pain in the anorectal region; anorectal rings in infancy; multiple polyposis; infections and sinuses other than fistulas in the perianal region; ulceration of the rectum and colon; physiology of the large intestine. *Mailing Add:* 1010 SW Tenth St Rochester MN 55902

HILL, JOHN WILLIAM, ORGANIC CHEMISTRY. *Current Pos:* from asst prof to assoc prof, 63-69, chmn dept, 70-72 & 74-84, PROF CHEM, UNIV WIS-RIVER FALLS, 69- *Personal Data:* b Decherd, Tenn, Aug 20, 33; m 56, Ina Maddux; c Cynthia & Donald. *Educ:* Mid Tenn State Col, BS, 57; Univ Ark, PhD(org chem), 60. *Honors & Awards:* Robert C Brasted Award Outstanding Col Teaching, Am Chem Soc, 89. *Prof Exp:* Asst prof chem, Northeast La State Col, 60-63. *Concurrent Pos:* Vis prof, Univ Ariz, 71 & Cornell Univ, 81, Murray State Univ, 90. *Mem:* Am Chem Soc; AAAS; Soc Chem Indust; Nat Sci Teachers Asn; fel Am Inst Chemists. *Res:* Organic sytheses using phase transfer catalysts; author: Introductory Chemistry books. *Mailing Add:* 532 N Seventh St River Falls WI 54022. *Fax:* 715-425-4487

HILL, JOSEPH MACGLASHAN, PATHOLOGY. *Current Pos:* RETIRED. *Personal Data:* b Buffalo, NY, Mar 26, 05; m 33; c 5. *Educ:* Univ Buffalo, BS & MD, 28; Am Bd Path, dipl, 37. *Hon Degrees:* Dr, Univ Guadalajara, 44; DSc, Baylor Univ, 45. *Honors & Awards:* Marchman Award, AMA, 47; Res Medal, Southern Med Asn, 57. *Prof Exp:* Assoc pathologist, Buffalo City Hosp, 31-32; asst prof path, Col Med, Univ Okla, 32-33; from asst prof to assoc prof path, Baylor Col Dent, 34-43, prof, 45-69, dean, Grad Res Inst, 48-68, dir labs, Baylor Univ Hosp, 34-59, chief hemat sect, 54-71; exec dir, Wadley Insts Molecular Med, 69-76, pres, 76-77, dir res & chmn, 77-84. *Concurrent Pos:* Instr, Sch Med, Univ Buffalo, 29-32, asst, 31-32; dir, Buchanan Blood, Plasma & Serum Ctr, Dallas, 43-44; prof clin path, Univ Tex Southwestern Med Sch Dallas, 43-51, clin prof path, 57-; hon prof, Univ Guadalajara, 44-; consult, Brooks Gen Hosp, San Antonio, 57-; dir, Wadley Insts Molecular Med, 51-69; res consult, Baylor Univ Med Ctr, 59-; exec comt bd trustees, Wadley Insts Molecular Med, 77- *Mem:* AAAS; fel Am Col Physicians; fel Col Am Path; fel Int Soc Hemat (pres, 48-49); Am Soc Clin Oncol. *Res:* Immuno-hematology; desiccation of plasma from frozen state; blood coagulation and leukemia. *Mailing Add:* 4339 Shady Hill Dr Dallas TX 75229-2852

HILL, JOSEPH PAUL, GENETICS, EPIDEMIOLOGY. *Current Pos:* asst prof, 78-84, ASSOC PROF PLANT PATH & WEED SCI, COLO STATE UNIV, 84- *Personal Data:* b Colver, Pa, Feb 5, 47; m 69; c 1. *Educ:* Pa State Univ, BS, 69, MA, 75, PhD(plant path), 79. *Prof Exp:* Res aide, Dept Plant Path, Pa State Univ, 73-78. *Mem:* Am Soc Agron; Am Phytopath Soc. *Res:* Diseases of cereals; genetics of host parasite interactions; fungal genetics; epidemiology; population genetics. *Mailing Add:* Dept Plant Path Colo State Univ Ft Collins CO 80523-0001

HILL, KENNETH RICHARD, PESTICIDE RESIDUE ANALYSIS. *Current Pos:* RETIRED. *Personal Data:* b Hillsboro, Ill, May 12, 30; m 55, Carole S Sandling; c Christy J (Draper) & Carter R. *Educ:* Purdue Univ, BS, 52, MS, 58, PhD(org chem), 61. *Honors & Awards:* Bronze Medallion, Organizing Comt, Third Int Cong Pesticide Chem, Helsinki, Finland, 74; Engraved Silver Teaspoon, Sci Prog Comt, Fourth Int Cong Pesticide Chem, Zurich, 78. *Prof Exp:* Chemist, Pitman-Moore Co Div, Dow Chem Co, 54-56; staff scientist org electrochem, P R Mallory & Co, Inc, 61-67; supvry chemist, Agr Res Serv, USDA, 67-73, res leader, Anal Chem Lab, Agr Environ Qual Inst, 73-89; sr sci fel, EPL/BIO-Anal Serv, Inc, 89-91. *Concurrent Pos:* Mem, Terminal Pesticide Residues Comn, Int Union Pure & Appl Chem, 68-77, secy, 68-73, chmn, 73-75; mem, Food & Agr Orgn-WHO Joint Meeting Pesticide Residue, 70-73 & 78-83, vchmn, 71-73, chmn, 72 & 82; co-organizer & chmn workshop, Fourth Int Cong Pesticide Chem, Int Union Pure & Appl Chem, 78 & chmn, Comt Instrumental Methods & Data Handling, Asn Off Analytical Chemists, 83-87; vchmn, Pilot Secretariat No 17 Int Orgn Legal Metrol, 88-89; invited lectr, residue anal & int regulations, Training Course Control Environ Contaminants in Food, Food & Agr Orgn, UN Environ Prog, Mysore, India, 78, 79, Int Course Prin & Methods Modern Toxicol, Belgirate, Italy, 79 & World Bank, Regional Training Prog on Qual Control of Pesticide Formulations, Gurgaon, India, 88; consult, AID, Islamabad, Pakistan, 80. *Mem:* NY Acad Sci; AAAS; Am Chem Soc; Sigma Xi. *Res:* Develop methods of analysis for pesticide chemicals and their residues; new instrumentation for residue analysis. *Mailing Add:* 5540 Sandview Dr Pensacola FL 32507

HILL, KENNETH WAYNE, ATOMIC SPECTROSCOPY, ATOMIC PHYSICS. *Current Pos:* physicist, 78-86, PRIN RES PHYSICIST, PRINCETON PLASMA PHYSICS LAB, 87- *Personal Data:* b Winston-Salem, NC, Apr 23, 45; m 66, Mary Clinkscales; c Kenneth W Jr & Lisa R. *Educ:* Drexel Inst Technol, BS, 68; Univ NC, MS, 69, PhD(physics), 74. *Prof Exp:* Instr physics, Surry Community Col, 69-71; Nat Res Coun resident res assoc atomic collision & x-ray spectros, Naval Res Lab, 74-76; physicist, Fusion Energy Div, Oak Ridge Nat Lab, 76-78. *Concurrent Pos:* Mem tech steering comt, Nat Laser Users Facil, Lab Laser Energetics, Univ Rochester, 89-92. *Mem:* Am Phys Soc. *Res:* Study of ion-atom collision physics and atomic structure by x-ray and vacuum-ultraviolet spectroscopy of ion beam-target interactions and of plasmas; physics studies and design of x-ray diagnostics for Tokamak Fusion Test Reactor; plasma diagnostics; modeling of x-ray and XUV emission from magnetic fusion plasmas. *Mailing Add:* 2651 Princeton Pike Lawrenceville NJ 08648. *Fax:* 609-243-2418; *E-Mail:* hill@pppl.gov

HILL, L(OUIS) LEIGHTON, PEDIATRICS, NEPHROLOGY. *Current Pos:* resident pediat, Affil Hosps, 55-57, from instr to assoc prof, 59-71, PROF PEDIAT, BAYLOR COL MED, 71-, ASST DEAN ADMIS. *Personal Data:* b Baton Rouge, La, Dec 19, 28; wid; c Melanie (Pierce), Laurie (Hierrez) & Courtney (Hill). *Educ:* La State Univ, MD, 52. *Prof Exp:* Intern med, Brooke Army Hosp, San Antonio, 52-53. *Concurrent Pos:* Res fel metab & renalogy, Baylor Col Med, 57-58; res fel metab & renalogy, Case Western Res Univ, 58-59; head, Renal & Metab Serv Clins, Tex Children's Hosp, 60-94; pres, Southern Soc Pediat Res, 67; chairperson, Nephrology Sect, Am Acad Pediat, 89-91. *Mem:* Soc Pediat Res; Am Soc Nephrol; Am Diabetes Asn; Am Fedn Clin Res; Am Pediat Soc Res; Am Acad Pediat; hon mem Pediat Asn Mex. *Res:* Water and electrolyte metabolism; renal diseases. *Mailing Add:* Dept Pediat Baylor Col Med Houston TX 77030

HILL, LEMMUEL LEROY, NUCLEAR PHYSICS. *Current Pos:* Physicist, US Naval Ord Lab, Naval Surface Warfare Ctr, 59-62, res physicist, 62-64, supvry res physicist, 64-68, supvry physicist, 68-74, sci adv to comdr, US Naval Surface Fleet, Atlantic, 74-75, head radiation div, 75-76, head res dept, 76-78, head weapon systs dept, 78-80, tech dir, Off Naval Technol, 80-84, dir, 84-89, DIR, SCI & TECHNOL DIV, INST DEFENSE ANALYSIS, NAVAL SURFACE WARFARE CTR, 89- *Personal Data:* b Ithaca, NY, Mar 17, 33; m 60, Suzanne Kennedy; c 4. *Educ:* Rensselaer Polytech Inst, BS, 59; Cath Univ Am, PhD(physics), 67. *Mem:* Am Phys Soc. *Res:* Plasma, reentry, theoretical nuclear physics and nuclear weapon effects; electromagnetics; electrooptics; research administration. *Mailing Add:* 12307 Keel Turn Bowie MD 20715

HILL, LOREN GILBERT, ICHTHYOLOGY, ECOLOGY. *Current Pos:* from asst prof to assoc prof zool, 66-75, asst dir, Biol Sta, 67-69, dir, Biol Sta, 69-74, PROF ZOOL & DIR BIOL SURV, UNIV OKLA, 75-, CHMN, DEPT ZOOL, 80- *Personal Data:* b Tulia, Tex, Mar 23, 40; m 61; c 2. *Educ:* WTex State Univ, BS, 61; Univ Ark, MS, 63; Univ Louisville, PhD(ichthyol), 66. *Prof Exp:* Instr zool, Catherine Spalding Col, 65-66. *Concurrent Pos:* Pres, Southwestern Asn Naturalists, 77-79. *Mem:* Am Fisheries Soc; Am Soc Ichthyologists & Herpetologists. *Res:* Organismic responses of fishes to water quality parameters. *Mailing Add:* Dept Zool Univ Okla Main Campus 900 Asp Ave Norman OK 73019-4050

HILL, LOREN WALLACE, POLYMER CHEMISTRY. *Current Pos:* sci fel, Monsanto Co, 80-86, SR FEL, 86- *Personal Data:* b New Leipzig, NDak, May 1, 39; m 62, Norma Carlson; c Richard & Stacey. *Educ:* NDak State Univ, BS, 61; Pa State Univ, PhD(phys chem), 65. *Honors & Awards:* Mattilleo Lectr, Fedn Soc Coatings Technol, 91. *Prof Exp:* From asst prof to prof phys chem, NDak State Univ, 65-71, prof polymers & coatings, 71-80. *Concurrent Pos:* Chmn, Gordon Res Conf Coatings & Films, 85; adj prof, NDak State Univ, 87- *Mem:* Am Chem Soc; Sigma Xi; Fedn Soc Coatings Technol. *Res:* Polymer chemistry; weathering of industrial coatings; water soluble coatings; adhesion; kinetics; catalysis; surface chemistry. *Mailing Add:* Monsanto Co 730 Worcester St Springfield MA 01151

HILL, LOUIS A, JR, CIVIL & STRUCTURAL ENGINEERING. *Current Pos:* CONSULT, 88- *Personal Data:* b Okemah, Okla, May 18, 27; m 50; c 3. *Educ:* Okla State Univ, BA, 49, BSCE, 54, MSCE, 55; Case Inst Technol, PhD(civil struct eng), 65. *Prof Exp:* Engr struct & hwy, Lee Hendrix consult, 55-57; struct engr, Hudgins, Thompson, Ball & Assoc, 57-58; from asst prof to assoc prof struct eng, Ariz State Univ, 58-70, chmn, Dept Civil Eng, 74-81, prof struct eng, 70- *Concurrent Pos:* Dean eng, Univ Akron, Ohio, 81, assoc vpres, res & grad studies, 88. *Mem:* Nat Soc Prof Engrs; Am Soc Civil Engrs; Am Soc Eng Educ; Sigma Xi. *Res:* Application of electronic computers to structural engineering problems, especially automated optimum cost design; integrated approach to study of structural engineering. *Mailing Add:* 3208 N 81st Pl Scottsdale AZ 85251-5800

HILL, LYNN MICHAEL, PLANT SCIENCES. *Current Pos:* from asst prof to assoc prof, 72-78, prof, 78-92, CHMN, BIOL DEPT, BRIDGEWATER COL, 81-, H G M JOPSON PROF BIOL, 92- *Personal Data:* b Washington, DC, Aug 12, 41; m 69; c 2. *Educ:* Ala Col, BS, 63; Tenn Technol Univ, MS, 65; Univ NH, PhD(plant sci), 72. *Prof Exp:* Instr biol, Univ Tenn, Martin, 66-69. *Mem:* AAAS; Bot Soc Am; Int Asn Plant Taxon & Nomenclature. *Res:* Chromosome numbers of angiosperms. *Mailing Add:* Dept Biol Bridgewater Col 402 E College St Bridgewater VA 22812-1511

HILL, MARION ELZIE, ORGANIC CHEMISTRY. *Current Pos:* sr res chemist, 60-61, mgr synthesis res, 62-65, chmn synthesis res dept, 65-67, dir org & polymer chem div, 67-68, dir chem lab, 68-84, SR SCI ADV, STANFORD RES INST, 84- *Personal Data:* b Pawnee, Okla, Jan 18, 20; m 45; c 3. *Educ:* Univ Ore, BA, 48, MA, 50. *Prof Exp:* Res assoc phys chem, Nat Bur Standards, 49-51; sr res assoc org chem, Naval Ord Lab, 51-60. *Mem:* Am Chem Soc; AAAS; Sigma Xi. *Res:* Organic reaction mechanisms; synthesis; catalysis of alcohol reactions; reactions in sulfuric acid; explosives; propellants; fluorine chemistry. *Mailing Add:* 4270 Pomona Ave Palo Alto CA 94306-4337

HILL, MARQUITA K, RESEARCH ADMINISTRATION, WOOD & PULPING CHEMISTRY. *Current Pos:* instr, 78-79, prog develop specialist, 79-81, ASSOC RES PROF, DEPT CHEM ENG, UNIV MAINE, 81- *Personal Data:* b Hickory, NC, Dec 18, 38; m 76; c 1. *Educ:* Mich State Univ, BA, 60; Univ Calif, Davis, PhD(biochem), 66. *Prof Exp:* Assoc fel, Univ Calif, Los Angeles, 66-68; from asst prof to assoc prof biochem, Va Polytech Inst, 68-77. *Concurrent Pos:* Prin investr, Dept Energy contract, Univ Maine, 84-87. *Mem:* Fedn Am Soc Exp Biol; Am Chem Soc; Tech Asn Pulp & Paper Indust. *Res:* Ultrafiltration of industrial streams, especially of kraft black liquor; wood and pulping chemistry; utilization of biomass. *Mailing Add:* 207 Jenness Hall Univ Maine Orono ME 04469-5737

HILL, MARTHA ADELE, ANALYTICAL CHEMISTRY, BIOCHEMICAL ENGINEERING. *Current Pos:* RETIRED. *Personal Data:* b London, Ont, Apr 13, 22; nat Can. *Educ:* Wheaton Col, BS, 43; Rutgers Univ, MSc, 45; Univ Toronto, PhD(chem), 49. *Prof Exp:* Asst chem, Wheaton Col, 42-43 & NJ Col Women, Rutgers Univ, 43-45; demonstr, Univ Toronto, 45-48; res chemist, Eastman Kodak Co, 49-57, res assoc, 57-64; res assoc, Univ Western Ont, 73-80; consult, Univ Tex, El Paso, 81, Univ Western Ont, 82. *Concurrent Pos:* Exec asst, VI Int Fermentation Symp, 78-80. *Mem:* Am Chem Soc. *Res:* Study of biodegradation of sulfite mill waste for pollution control of pulp and paper industry; chemical literature searches; photographic chemistry. *Mailing Add:* 103 Wychwood Court London ON N6G 1S6 Can

HILL, MARVIN FRANCIS, ANATOMY, PHYSIOLOGY. *Current Pos:* RETIRED. *Personal Data:* b Missoula, Mont, Feb 4, 25; m 55; c 4. *Educ:* Ore State Col, BS, 49, MS, 51, PhD, 55. *Prof Exp:* Lectr anat, Ore State Col, 54-55; lectr, Univ Heidelberg, 55; instr, Med Sch, Tulane Univ, 56-58; from asst prof to assoc prof anat, Sch Med, Creighton Univ, 58-70, prof, Sch Dent, 70-90. *Mem:* AAAS; Am Asn Anatomists; Soc Exp Biol & Med; Soc Cryobiol. *Res:* Gross neuro-anatomy; developmental histochemistry; regeneration in mammals; histochemical calcium stains. *Mailing Add:* 3406 S 91st St Omaha NE 68124

HILL, MARY RAE, GEOMORPHOLOGY. *Current Pos:* RETIRED. *Personal Data:* b Great Falls, Mont, Sept 2, 23. *Educ:* Univ Colo, BA, 44; San Francisco State Univ, MA, 70. *Prof Exp:* From geol aide to geologist & geol data officer, Calif Div Mines & Geol, 49-75; info officer, US Geol Surv, Menlo Park, 75-79. *Concurrent Pos:* Ed, Calif Geol, 53-74; adj prof, San Francisco State Univ, 79- *Mem:* Asn Earth Sci Ed (vpres, 73, pres, 74). *Res:* Environmental geology; shore processes; cinematography as an earth science tool; science for the layman. *Mailing Add:* Rte 7 Box 124-MU Santa Fe NM 87505. *Fax:* 505-984-8119

HILL, MASON LOWELL, GEOLOGY. *Current Pos:* RETIRED. *Personal Data:* b Pomona, Calif, Jan 17, 04; m 42; c 5. *Educ:* Pomona Col, AB, 26; Claremont Col, AM, 29; Univ Wis, PhD, 32. *Hon Degrees:* ScD, Pomona Col, 71. *Prof Exp:* Geologist, Shell Oil Co, 27-28, 29-30; instr geol, Coalinga Jr Col, Calif, 33-35; geologist, Shell Oil Co, 35-37 & Richfield Oil Co, 37-65, explor mgr, Int Div, Atlantic Richfield Co, 65-70; res assoc, Univ Calif, Los Angeles, 70-73; instr geol, Univ Calif, Irvine, 73- *Concurrent Pos:* Consult geologist, 70-79. *Mem:* Fel Geol Soc Am; Am Asn Petrol Geologists (pres, 62-63); Asn Eng Geologists. *Res:* Structural geology and petroleum; seismic hazards, fault tectonics and faulting in California. *Mailing Add:* 14067 E Summit Dr Whittier CA 90602

HILL, MAX W, NUCLEAR PHYSICS. *Current Pos:* RETIRED. *Personal Data:* b Payson, Utah, May 20, 30; m 54; c 7. *Educ:* Brigham Young Univ, BA, 54; Univ Calif, Berkeley, PhD(nuclear chem), 59. *Prof Exp:* From asst prof to assoc prof physics, Brigham Young Univ, 58-68, prof, 68-92, asst dept chmn, 79-92. *Concurrent Pos:* Res asst chem, Univ Calif, Berkeley, 55-58; res scientist, Gen Elec Co & Pac Northwest Labs, Battelle Mem Inst, 64-65. *Res:* Nuclear spectroscopy; trace element analysis of environmental samples. *Mailing Add:* 1745 Lambert Lane Provo UT 84604

HILL, MERTON EARLE, III, EARTH SCIENCES, PALEONTOLOGY. *Current Pos:* SR RES MICROPALEONTOLOGIST, UNION SCI & TECHNOL DIV, UNION OIL CO OF CALIF, 79- *Personal Data:* b Long Beach, Calif, Oct 17, 47; m 72. *Educ:* Univ Redlands, BS, 69; Univ Calif, Los Angeles, PhD(geol), 75. *Prof Exp:* Asst prof geol, Calif State Univ, 76-79. *Concurrent Pos:* Lectr geol, Santa Monica Col, 75-76; lectr paleont, Univ Southern Calif, 76-; explor res geologist, 79- *Mem:* Int Nannofossil Asn. *Res:* Calcareous nannofossil (coccolith) biostratigraphy of the North Sea, North Africa, Ecuador, Colombia, Western Interior of the United States, and Gulf of Mexico. *Mailing Add:* 1091 Gaviota Dr Laguna Beach CA 92651

HILL, ORVILLE FARROW, NUCLEAR FUEL CYCLE. *Current Pos:* CONSULT NUCLEAR FUEL CYCLE, 84- *Personal Data:* b Decatur, Ill, Jan 6, 19; m 44, Alta L Meeker; c Diane L, James M & Barbara J. *Educ:* Millikin Univ, BS, 40; Univ Ill, MS, 41, PhD(inorg chem), 48. *Hon Degrees:* DSc, Millikin Univ, 63. *Honors & Awards:* Richland Sect Award, Am Chem Soc, 82. *Prof Exp:* Res chemist, Manhattan Dist, 42-46; res chemist, Hanford Atomic Prod Opers, Gen Elec Co, Richland, Wash, 48-49, mgr chem res, 50-53, mgr plant processes, 53-56, mgr chem develop, 56-64, prin chem engr, 65-66; staff scientist, Pac Northwest Labs, Battelle Mem Inst, 64-65; prin chem engr, Isochem, Inc, 66-67 & Atlantic Richfield Hanford Opers, Atlantic Richfield Co, Wa, 67-77; staff engr, Pac Northwest Lab, Battle Mem Inst, 77-84. *Concurrent Pos:* Engr-on-loan, AEC Combined Oper Planning, Tenn, 67-69, Div Regulation, 72-74; vis prof environ chem, Prairie View A&M, Tex, 69-70. *Mem:* Am Chem Soc; Am Nuclear Soc; fel Am Inst Chem Engrs. *Res:* Chemistry of the nuclear fuel cycle; science and engineering of spent fuel reprocessing and nuclear waste management; environmental surveys and impact statements. *Mailing Add:* 240 Southmoreland Pl Decatur IL 62521

HILL, PATRICK ARTHUR, ECONOMIC GEOLOGY, ENVIRONMENTAL GEOLOGY. *Current Pos:* lectr, Carlton Univ, 53-54, Geol Dept, 53-59, from asst prof to prof, 54-87, ADJ PROF GEOL, CARLTON UNIV, 87- *Personal Data:* b Calcutta, India, Jan 8, 22; m 56, Susanne Putnam Richards; c Patrick & Declak. *Educ:* Univ London, BSc, 48; Columbia Univ, PhD(geol), 57. *Honors & Awards:* Michel Donaldson Award, 83. *Prof Exp:* Instr geol, Brooklyn Col, 50-51; instr phys & hist geol, Wellesley Col, 51-52. *Concurrent Pos:* Consult, govt & indust agencies, 43-; vis res prof, Univ Tasmania, 60-61; visitor, Univ Reading, 67 & Bristol Univ, 71; res assoc, Univ Ireland, Cork, 86- *Mem:* Fel Royal Geog Soc; Prehist Soc; fel Royal Soc Antiquaries Ireland. *Res:* Archaeological and applied geology; coal geology; medical geology; text appraiser/reviewer. *Mailing Add:* Dept Geol Carleton Univ Ottawa ON K1S 5B6 Can. *Fax:* 613-730-1970

HILL, PAUL DANIEL, MATHEMATICS. *Current Pos:* PROF MATH, AUBURN UNIV, 75- *Personal Data:* b Dadeville, Ala, May 8, 33; m 58, Betty Mayton; c Steven P, John M & Jennifer. *Educ:* Auburn Univ, BS, 56, MS, 58, PhD(math), 60. *Prof Exp:* NSF fel math, Inst Advan Study, 60-61; asst prof, Auburn Univ, 61-63; assoc prof, Emory Univ, 63-65; prof, Univ Houston, 65-68; prof math, Fla State Univ, 68-75. *Concurrent Pos:* Distinguished Grad Fac lectr, Auburn Univ. *Mem:* Am Math Soc; Math Asn Am. *Res:* Semigroups, groups and group algebras. *Mailing Add:* Dept Math Auburn Univ Auburn AL 36849-5307. *E-Mail:* hillpad@mail.auburn.edu

HILL, PERCY HOLMES, ERGONOMICS, CONSUMER PRODUCT RESEARCH & DEVELOPMENT. *Current Pos:* prof, 48-83, EMER PROF ENG DESIGN, TUFTS UNIV, 83-; PRES, APPL ERGONOMICS CO, 76- *Personal Data:* b Norfolk, Va, Feb 19, 23; m 46; c 2. *Educ:* Rensselaer Polytech Inst, BME, 44; Harvard Univ, SM, 51. *Honors & Awards:* Oppenheimer Award Design Graphics, Am Soc Eng Educ, 68, Distinguished Serv Award, 72; Fred Merrifield Award, Am Soc Eng Educ, 82. *Prof Exp:* Instr eng & math, Va Polytech Inst, 46-48. *Concurrent Pos:* Dir & prin investr, Biodent Eng Res, Tufts Univ, 64-70, chmn comt decision & policy making, 77-81; pres, Stratford Labs, Inc, 82-; mem bd dirs, Am Soc Eng Educ, 85-87; vpres res & develop, Powell Technol Prod, 89- *Mem:* Am Soc Eng Educ; Human Factors Soc. *Res:* Author of 9 textbooks in area of descriptive geometry, engineering graphics, kinematics and creative problem solving; holder of 6 patents in the area of dental health. *Mailing Add:* East Shore Dr Silver Lake NH 03875

HILL, PHILIP G(RAHAM), MECHANICAL ENGINEERING. *Current Pos:* head dept, 78-83, PROF MECH ENG, UNIV BC, 76- *Personal Data:* b Vancouver, BC, July 18, 32; m 59. *Educ:* Queen's Univ, Ont, BSc, 53; Univ Birmingham, MSc, 55; Mass Inst Technol, ScD, 58. *Prof Exp:* From asst prof to prof mech eng, Queen's Univ, 68-73; Commonwealth vis prof, Univ Sheffield, Cambridge, 73-74; prof, Queen's Univ, 74-75. *Concurrent Pos:* Guggenheim fel, 62-63; consult, various indust co. *Mem:* Fluid mechanics; propulsion; power. *Mailing Add:* Dept Mech Eng Univ BC 2075 Wesbrook Pl Vancouver BC V6T 1Z1 Can. *Fax:* 604-822-2403

HILL, RAY ALLEN, CELL BIOLOGY, PLANT ANATOMY. *Current Pos:* SCI TEACHER, LOWELL COL PREP SCH, SAN FRANCISCO, 86- *Personal Data:* b Houston, Tex, Sept 16, 42. *Educ:* Howard Univ, BS, 64, MS, 65; Univ Calif, PhD(bot), 77. *Prof Exp:* Instr bot, Southern Univ, 65-66 & Howard Univ, 66-75; assoc prof, Fisk Univ, 77-80; assoc prof bot, Col Baltimore, 80-82; assoc prof biol, Morgan State Univ, 82-85. *Concurrent Pos:* NSF fac fel, Fac Sci Develop Prog, NSF, 74-75; vis scientist, Environ Protection Agency, 78, Nat Aeronautics & Space Admin, 79 & Lawrence Berkeley Lab, 80; panelist, Comprehensive Assistance to Undergrad Sci, NSF, 79 & Instrnl Sci Equip Prog, 81; vis scholar, Stanford Univ & Asn Marine Eng Sch Res Facil, NASA, 83-84; vis res assoc prof, Univ Calif, San Francisco, 85; lectr, Calif State Univ, Hayward, 87; vis prof, bot & plant path, Purdue Univ, 89-91; adj prof, Santa Rosa Jr Col, 93; fel, NSF, 74-75, jr fac fel Howard Univ, 74-75 & diss fel, Ford Found, 75-76. *Mem:* Inst Med-Nat Acad Sci; Bot Soc Am; NY Acad Sci; AAAS. *Res:* Ultrastructure and histochemistry of ovules in cotton; developmental approach through maturation and senescence; transformation studies; alternative gene splicing; botony-phytopathology; cytology; molecular biology. *Mailing Add:* 8751 Fehler Lane Cotati CA 94931

HILL, REBA MICHELS, pediatrics, neonatology; deceased, see previous edition for last biography

HILL, RICHARD A, CHEMICAL ENGINEERING. *Current Pos:* RETIRED. *Personal Data:* b Springfield, Ohio, Aug 14, 32; m 56; c 3. *Educ:* Univ Fla, BSPh, 56, MS, 58, BChE & PhD(pharm), 60. *Prof Exp:* Sr res pharmacist, Squibb Inst Med Res, 60-64, res supvr, 64-67, mgr res eng, 67-69, dir res eng, 69-71, dir eng & tech servs, 71-75, dir tech admin, 75-76; dir develop, Norwich Eaton Pharmaceut, 76-78, vpres develop, 78-80, vpres res & develop, 80-84, vpres prod develop-int, 84-90. *Concurrent Pos:* Fel, Am Found Pharmaceut Educ & NSF. *Mem:* Am Pharmaceut Asn; Sigma Xi; Am Soc Hosp Pharmacists. *Res:* Directing research and development; new product development, licensing and acquisition, computer systems, statistical services, corporate management committee, international liaison. *Mailing Add:* 100 Village Del Prado Way St Augustine FL 32084

HILL, RICHARD C(ONRAD), MECHANICAL ENGINEERING. *Current Pos:* RETIRED. *Personal Data:* b Schenectady, NY, Oct 15, 18; m 44; c 5. *Educ:* Syracuse Univ, BS, 41. *Prof Exp:* Engr gas turbine, Gen Elec Co, 41-46; prof mech eng, Univ Maine, Orono, 46-92, actg dean col technol, 67-69, dir dept indust coop, 69-92. *Mem:* Am Soc Eng Educ; Am Soc Mech Engrs; Am Soc Heating, Refrig & Air Conditioning Engrs. *Res:* Thermodynamics; steam and gas turbines; compressible fluid flow. *Mailing Add:* 501 College Rd Orono ME 04469

HILL, RICHARD KEITH, ORGANIC CHEMISTRY. *Current Pos:* actg head dept, 69-71, 77-78, PROF CHEM, UNIV GA, 68- *Personal Data:* b Erie, Pa, June 1, 28; m 54; c 4. *Educ:* Pa State Univ, BS, 49; Harvard Univ, MA, 50, PhD(chem), 54. *Prof Exp:* From instr to assoc prof chem, Princeton Univ, 53-68. *Concurrent Pos:* Consult, Schering Corp, 56-57; Sloan Found fel, 61-65; res assoc, Textile Res Inst, 64-68; NSF sr fel, 65-66; mem, Med Chem Study Sect, NIH, 68-72; mem chem panel, Sr Fulbright-Hays Prog, 70-73; consult, Burroughs Wellcome Co, 74-77; NATO sr fel sci, NSF, 76; mem adv bd, Petrol Res Fund, 80-85. *Mem:* Fel AAAS; Am Chem Soc; Royal Soc Chem; Am Soc Pharmacog. *Res:* Organic natural products; stereochemistry; molecular rearrangements; synthesis. *Mailing Add:* Dept Chem Univ Ga Athens GA 30602

HILL, RICHARD M, PHYSIOLOGICAL OPTICS. *Current Pos:* assoc prof, 64-68, PROF PHYSIOL OPTICS & BIOPHYS, COL OPTOM, OHIO STATE UNIV, 68-, ASSOC DEAN, COL OPTOM, 78- *Personal Data:* b San Francisco, Calif, Dec 16, 34; m 57; c 1. *Educ:* Univ Calif, Berkeley, BS, 57, MOpt, 58, PhD(physiol optics), 61. *Prof Exp:* Clin instr optom, Univ Calif, Berkeley, 58-61, asst prof physiol optics, 61-64. *Mem:* Fel AAAS; Am Physiol Soc; Sigma Xi. *Res:* Neurophysiology of visual system; single cell responses of visual pathways and gas exchange properties of cornea. *Mailing Add:* 1601 Lafayette Dr Upper Arlington OH 43220-3868

HILL, RICHARD NORMAN, ENVIRONMENTAL HEALTH, GENETICS. *Current Pos:* mem staff, Off Asst Admin, 76-80, SR SCI ADV, PREV, PESTICIDES & TOXIC SUBSTANCES, US ENVIRON PROTECTION AGENCY, WASHINGTON, DC, 80- *Personal Data:* b Stockton, Calif, May 30, 37; m 61; c 2. *Educ:* Johns Hopkins Univ, BA, 59; Univ Minn, MD, 67, PhD(genetics), 68. *Prof Exp:* Asst prof pharmacol & genetics, Hershey Med Ctr, Pa State Univ, 69-76. *Concurrent Pos:* NIH fel biol, Univ Colo, 67-69. *Res:* Behavior of cells at the molecular level using tissue culture; biochemical toxicology; cytogenetics. *Mailing Add:* US Environ Protection Agency (7101) Washington DC 20460. *Fax:* 202-260-1847

HILL, RICHARD PETER, RADIATION BIOLOGY, TUMOR BIOLOGY. *Current Pos:* MEM STAFF, RES DIV, ONT CANCER INST, TORONTO, 73-; PROF, DEPT MED BIOPHYS, UNIV TORONTO, 79- *Personal Data:* b Belfast, Northern Ireland, Dec 27, 42; m 66; c 3. *Educ:* Oxford Univ, Eng, BA, 64; London Univ, PhD(radiation biol), 67. *Prof Exp:* Staff biophys dept, Inst Cancer Res, London, 71-73. *Concurrent Pos:* Fel radiol res, James Picker Found, 67-71. *Mem:* Radiation Res Soc; Am Asn Cancer Res; Metastasis Res Soc. *Res:* Radiation biology and tumor biology in their application to the treatment of cancer; mechanisms of metastasis and tumor progression. *Mailing Add:* Res Div Ont Cancer Inst Toronto ON M5G 2M9 Can. *Fax:* 416-946-2984

HILL, RICHARD WILLIAM, NUCLEAR PHYSICS, RESEARCH ADMINISTRATION. *Current Pos:* RETIRED. *Personal Data:* b Paterson, NJ, Mar 5, 25; m 48, Lois Eliezer; c Mark, Raymond & Bruce. *Educ:* NY Univ, BS, 48; Univ Wis, MS, 49, PhD(physics), 53. *Prof Exp:* Res physicist, Res Labs, Westinghouse Elec Corp, 53-58; physicist, Lawrence Livermore Lab, Univ Calif, 58-88; consult in-situ coal gasification, 88-87. *Mem:* Am Phys Soc. *Res:* In-situ coal gasification. *Mailing Add:* 1945 Heidelberg Livermore CA 94550

HILL, RICHARD WILLIAM, COMPARATIVE PHYSIOLOGY, ENVIRONMENTAL BIOLOGY & SULFUR BIOGEOCHEMISTRY. *Current Pos:* PROF ZOOL, MICH STATE UNIV, 82-, ASSOC CHAIR ZOOL, 96- *Personal Data:* b Philadelphia, Pa, July 11, 42; m 68, Susan Douglas; c 2. *Educ:* Univ Del, BA, 64; Univ Mich, Ann Arbor, AM, 66, PhD(zool), 70. *Prof Exp:* Lectr zool, Univ Mich, Ann Arbor, 69-70; asst prof biol sci, Univ Del, 70-72; from asst prof to assoc prof, 72-82, cur living vert, The Mus, 72-96. *Concurrent Pos:* Guest investr, Woods Hole Oceanog Ins, 90-96. *Mem:* Fel AAAS; Am Soc Mammal; Sigma Xi; Soc Int Comp Biol; Am Soc Limnol Oceanog. *Res:* Physiological ecology; mammalian and avian thermoregulation; ontogeny of thermoregulation; energetics; metabolism of sulfur in marine organisms; sulfur biogeochemistry. *Mailing Add:* Dept Zool Mich State Univ 203 Natural Sci East Lansing MI 48824-1115. *E-Mail:* hillr@pilot.msu.edu

HILL, ROBERT, PHYSIOLOGY, BIOCHEMISTRY. *Current Pos:* PRES, HILL RES ASSOCS, INC, 85- *Personal Data:* b New York, NY, Apr 6, 22; m 51; c 3. *Educ:* Univ Calif, AB, 49, PhD(physiol), 53. *Prof Exp:* Assoc res physiologist, Univ Calif, 53-58; pres & sci dir, Diablo Labs, Inc 58-64; pres & sci dir, Hill Res Inst, 64-65; mgr toxicol & path, Syntex Corp, 65-69, dir dept toxicol, 69-77, asst dir, Inst Clin Med, 73-77, dir toxicol & path, 77-81, vpres & dir, Inst Toxicol Sci, 81-85. *Concurrent Pos:* Advan res fel, Am Heart Asn, 58-60; abstractor, Chem Abstr, 59-60; vis prof environ toxicol, Univ Calif, Santa Cruz, 77-78; expert toxicol & pharmacol, French Minister Health, 78; adj prof toxicol, San Jose State Univ, 81-85. *Mem:* Sigma Xi; Am Physiol Soc; Soc Toxicol; Environ Mutagenesis Soc; Europ Soc Toxicol. *Res:* Endocrines; nutrition; intermediary metabolism; toxicology. *Mailing Add:* 150 Robin Way Los Gatos CA 95031-5642

HILL, ROBERT BENJAMIN, COMPARATIVE PHYSIOLOGY. *Current Pos:* assoc prof, 68-75, PROF ZOOL, UNIV RI, 75- *Personal Data:* b New York, NY, July 23, 30; m 65, Isako Murai; c Andrew & Evan. *Educ:* Tufts Univ, SB, 52; Harvard Univ, PhD(biol), 57. *Prof Exp:* Instr zool, Univ Maine, 56-59; USPHS fel, Dept Zool, Glasgow Univ, 59-61; from instr to asst prof physiol, Med Sch, Dartmouth Col, 61-68. *Concurrent Pos:* Corp mem, Bermuda Biol Sta. *Mem:* Fel AAAS; Am Soc Zoologists; Soc Exp Biol; Am Physiol Soc; Soc Neurosci; Marine Biol Asn UK. *Res:* Neurohumoral transmission in invertebrates; nervous control of molluscan hearts; active state ionic pumps and excitation-contraction coupling in molluscan muscle. *Mailing Add:* Dept Biol Sci Univ RI Kingston RI 02881

HILL, ROBERT D, AGRICULTURAL BIOCHEMISTRY. *Current Pos:* from asst prof to assoc prof, 67-77, PROF PLANT SCI, UNIV MAN, 77- *Personal Data:* b Winnipeg, Man, Feb 23, 37; m 59; c 2. *Educ:* Univ Man, BSc, 58, MSc, 63, PhD(biochem), 65. *Prof Exp:* Res asst chem, plant sci dept, Univ Man, 59-63; fel biochem, Univ Calif, Los Angeles, 65-67. *Mem:* Can Soc Plant Physiologists; Can Biochem Soc; Am Soc Plant Physiol; Am Asn Cereal Chemists. *Res:* Carbohydrates in cereal grains; germination physiology. *Mailing Add:* Dean's Off Facil Agr & Food Scis Univ Man Winnipeg MB R3T 2N2 Can

HILL, ROBERT DICKSON, PHYSICS. *Current Pos:* CONSULT PHYSICIST, 66-; RES PHYSICIST, UNIV CALIF, SANTA BARBARA, 78- *Personal Data:* b Melbourne, Australia, July 3, 13; m 42, Judith A Fowler; c Robert B. *Educ:* Cambridge Univ, 37-38; Univ Ill, 38-39; Univ Melbourne, DSc, 46. *Prof Exp:* Sr lectr physics, Univ Melbourne, 41-47; from asst prof to prof physics, Univ Ill, Urbana, 47-65. *Concurrent Pos:* Fulbright sr fel, 60; Guggenheim fel, 61. *Mem:* Fel Am Phys Soc; fel Int Soc Study Origin Life. *Mailing Add:* 612 Alston Rd Santa Barbara CA 93108. *E-Mail:* hillite@msn.com

HILL, ROBERT F, nuclear & chemical engineering, for more information see previous edition

HILL, ROBERT GEORGE, JR, HORTICULTURE. *Current Pos:* From asst prof to prof, 50-60, assoc chmn dept, 70-83, EMER PROF HORT, OHIO STATE UNIV & OHIO AGR RES DEVELOP CTR, 83- *Personal Data:* b Silver Spring, Md, Jan 11, 22; m 48; c 2. *Educ:* Univ Md, BS, 43, MS, 48, PhD(hort), 50. *Mem:* Fel Am Soc Hort Sci; Am Soc Plant Physiol; Weed Sci Soc Am; Am Pomol Soc. *Res:* Stone and small fruit cultural practices; cultivar evaluation; chemical weed control. *Mailing Add:* 473 E Beverly Rd Wooster OH 44691

HILL, ROBERT JAMES, biochemistry, for more information see previous edition

HILL, ROBERT JOE, MATHEMATICS. *Current Pos:* ASSOC PROF MATH, PURDUE UNIV, CALUMET CAMPUS, 70- *Personal Data:* b Tipton, Ind, Feb 25, 30; m 53; c 3. *Educ:* Auburn Univ, BS, 57, MS, 58; Univ Ala, PhD, 70. *Prof Exp:* Mem staff, NASA, 60-70. *Res:* Linear algebra. *Mailing Add:* 74 Seldom Seen Rd Bradford Woods PA 15015

HILL, ROBERT LEE, PROTEIN CHEMISTRY, ENZYME CHEMISTRY. *Current Pos:* from assoc prof to prof, 61-74, chmn dept, 69-94, J B DUKE PROF BIOCHEM, MED CTR, DUKE UNIV, 74- *Personal Data:* b Kansas City, Mo, June 8, 28; m 48; c 4. *Educ:* Univ Kans, AB, 49, MA, 51, PhD(biochem), 54. *Prof Exp:* Asst instr biochem, Univ Kans, 49-51, instr, 51-53; instr, Col Med, Univ Utah, 56-57, asst res prof, 57-60, assoc prof, 60-61. *Concurrent Pos:* Consult, Biochem Training Comt, Nat Inst Gen Med Sci, 66-69; mem, Biochem Training Comt, NIH, 66-69, chmn, 67-69, mem, Physiol Chem Study Sect, 69-73, chmn, 70-73; mem, Biochem Test Comt, 66-70, chmn, 68-70, Nat Bd Med Examr, 68-; mem bd, Fedn Am Socs Exp Biol, 71-74. *Mem:* Nat Acad Sci; Inst Med-Nat Acad Sci; AAAS; Am Soc Biol Chemists (secy, 72-75, pres, 76-77); fel Am Acad Arts & Sci. *Res:* Structural aspects of protein chemistry; mechanism of action of enzyme. *Mailing Add:* Dept Biochem Med Ctr Duke Univ Durham NC 27710. *E-Mail:* hill@bchem.biochem.duke.edu

HILL, ROBERT MATHEW, BIOCHEMISTRY. *Current Pos:* RETIRED. *Personal Data:* b Caledonia, Minn, Mar 21, 22; m 46, Mariana Byrne; c Jerome M, Joseph F, Mathew D & Owen R. *Educ:* St Mary's Col, Minn, BS, 44; Univ Minn, MS, 54, PhD(agr biochem), 55. *Prof Exp:* Instr chem & math, St Mary's Col, Minn, 46-47; from asst to instr agr biochem, Univ Minn, 47-55; from asst biochemist to assoc biochemist, Univ Nebr, 55-60, asst prof chem, 56-60, assoc prof biochem, 60-87. *Res:* Chemical and physical properties of proteins; analysis of biochemical materials. *Mailing Add:* 308 S 54th Lincoln NE 68510

HILL, ROBERT MATTESON, PHYSICS, ATOMIC & MOLECULAR PHYSICS. *Current Pos:* mem staff, 70-83, SR SCI ADV, STANFORD RES INST INT, 83- *Personal Data:* b New York, NY, Sept 20, 26; m 47, April Blackburn; c Leigh, Barbara, Katherine & David. *Educ:* Cornell Univ, AB, 49; Duke Univ, PhD(physics), 53. *Prof Exp:* Physicist, Sylvania Elec Prod Inc, Gen Tel & Electronics Corp, 53-63 & Lockheed Res Lab, 63-70. *Concurrent Pos:* Prog officer, NSF, 80-81. *Mem:* AAAS; fel Am Phys Soc; NY Acad Sci; Sigma Xi. *Res:* Gaseous electronics; plasma physics; ferroelectricity; echos in ferri and anti-ferri magnetic resonance and in electron cyclotron resonance; high n Rydberg atoms, kinetics of laser media; chemical physics. *Mailing Add:* Stanford Res Inst 333 Ravenwood Ave PN071 Menlo Park CA 94025

HILL, ROBERT NYDEN, THEORETICAL PHYSICS. *Current Pos:* from asst prof to assoc prof, 64-73, PROF PHYSICS, UNIV DEL, 73- *Personal Data:* b Evanston, Ill, Mar 5, 35; m 62, JoAnne Kirmis; c Lauren. *Educ:* Carleton Col, BA, 56; Yale Univ, MS, 57, PhD(physics), 62. *Prof Exp:* NSF fel physics, Princeton Univ, 62-63 & Yale Univ, 64. *Mem:* Am Phys Soc. *Res:* Mathematical physics of atoms and molecules; eigenvalue estimation; relativistic classical particle dynamics; miscellaneous theoretical physics. *Mailing Add:* 40 Lynn Dr Newark DE 19711. *Fax:* 302-831-1637; *E-Mail:* gab00689@udelvm.udel.edu

HILL, ROBERT WILLIAM, POLYMER CHEMISTRY. *Current Pos:* RETIRED. *Personal Data:* b Chicago, Ill, Dec 13, 27; m 51; c 4. *Educ:* Augustana Col, BA, 50; Univ Ill, PhD(chem), 54. *Prof Exp:* Res chemist, Spencer Chem Div, Gulf Oil Corp, 54-59, group leader, Gulf Res & Develop Co, 59-68, sect supvr, 68-75, mgr Polymer Res, Gulf Oil Chem Co, 76-83. *Mem:* Am Chem Soc; Sigma Xi; The Chem Soc; AAAS. *Res:* Organometallic chemistry; coordination polymerization; polyolefins; surface coatings; aminoplast and phenolic resins; polyamides; aromatic polymers; composites. *Mailing Add:* 423 Green Park Dr Houston TX 77079-2301

HILL, ROGER W(ARREN), CHEMICAL ENGINEERING. *Current Pos:* RETIRED. *Personal Data:* b Fruitdale, SDak, June 11, 19; m 45. *Educ:* SDak Sch Mines & Technol, BS, 42; Va Polytech Inst, MS, 48. *Prof Exp:* Shift supvr, Hercules Powder Co, 42-43; foreman prod opers, Tenn Eastman Corp, 43-44; asst chem eng, Va Polytech Inst, 46-47; engr, Cent Res Labs, Gen Aniline & Film Corp, 47-52; res engr, Calif Res Corp, 52-59; sr chemist, Iranian Oil Ref Corp, 59-61; group supvr polymer process res, Chevron Res Corp, 62-69, admin asst to vpres, 69-72, prod specialist, 72-73, sr res engr, 73-83. *Mem:* AAAS; Am Chem Soc; Am Inst Chem Engrs. *Res:* Process research and development; polyolefin polymerization and petrochemical manufacturing processes. *Mailing Add:* 775 Deercroft Dr Blacksburg VA 24060-0270

HILL, ROLLA B, JR, pathology, developmental biology; deceased, see previous edition for last biography

HILL, RONALD AMES, PHOTOMETRICS & OPTICAL DEVELOPMENT. *Current Pos:* RETIRED. *Personal Data:* b Caro, Mich, June 19, 34; div; c 2. *Educ:* Mich State Univ, BS, 57, MS, 58, PhD(molecular struct), 63. *Prof Exp:* Staff mem plasma spectros, Sandia Labs, 63-69, supvr exp aerophys, 69-77, staff mem laser applns & spectros, 77-79, staff mem neutron devices, 79-87, supvr photom & optical develop, 87-94. *Mem:* Am Phys Soc; Optical Soc Am. *Res:* High resolution infrared spectroscopy and molecular structure; time resolved plasma spectroscopy; plasma diagnostics; raman spectroscopy; optical devices. *Mailing Add:* 7313 Gladden Ave NE Albuquerque NM 87110

HILL, RONALD STEWART, endocrinology, cell biology, for more information see previous edition

HILL, RUSSELL JOHN, PHYSICAL CHEMISTRY, HIGH TEMPERATURE CHEMISTRY. *Current Pos:* DIR, BOC COATING TECHNOL, 86- *Personal Data:* b Ilford, Eng, May 7, 34; US citizen; m 58; c 3. *Educ:* Univ Wales, BSc, 56; Univ London, PhD(phys chem) & DIC, 59. *Prof Exp:* Sci officer, UK Atomic Energy Res Estab, 59-62; adv develop engr, Radio Corp Am, 62-65; actg sect chief metals res, Space Systs Div, Avco Corp, Mass, 65-71; asst dir res, High Vacuum Int, Berkeley, 71-73, dir res, 73-76, vpres temescal, 76-86. *Concurrent Pos:* Lectr, West Ham Col Technol, Eng, 59-61 & Ctr Continuing Educ, Northeastern Univ, 67-69. *Mem:* Am Ceramic Soc; Am Soc Metals; Am Vacuum Soc. *Res:* Metals and ceramic materials science; surface chemistry; ultra-high vacuum technology. *Mailing Add:* 8502 Buckingham Dr El Cerrito CA 94530

HILL, SAMUEL RICHARDSON, JR, INTERNAL MEDICINE. *Current Pos:* from asst prof to assoc prof med, Univ Ala, Birmingham, 54-62, dir, Metab & Endocrine Sect, 54-62, dean, Med Col, 62-68, prof med, 62-94, vpres health affairs & dir, Med Ctr, 68-77, pres, 77-87, distinguished prof, 87-93, DISTINGUISHED EMER PROF, UNIV ALA, BIRMINGHAM, 94- *Personal Data:* b Greensboro, NC, May 19, 23; m 50, Janet Redman; c Susan (Lindley), Samuel Richardson III, Elizabeth (Humphreys) & Margaret (Cohn). *Educ:* Duke Univ, BA, 43; Wake Forest Univ, MD, 46; Am Bd Internal Med, cert, 54. *Hon Degrees:* DSc, Univ Ala, 75, Wake Forest Univ, 79. *Prof Exp:* Intern med, Peter Bent Brigham Hosp, Boston, 47-48, asst resident, 48-49, asst, 49-50; instr, Bowman Gray Sch Med, 50-51; asst, Peter Bent Brigham Hosp, Boston, 53-54. *Concurrent Pos:* Teaching fel, Harvard Med Sch, 48-49, Dazian Med Found fel, 49-50; chief resident, NC Baptist Hosp, 50-51; asst, Harvard Med Sch, 53-54; chief, Metab Sect, Birmingham Vet Admin Hosp, 54-57; dir, Metab & Endocrine Sect, Med Col Ala, 57-62; dir, Syst Med Educ Prog, Univ Ala, 72-79, mem bd dirs, various & comts; Coun Sci Affairs, AMA, 76-78. *Mem:* Inst Med-Nat Acad Sci; Endocrine Soc; Am Diabetes Asn; Am Thyroid Asn; fel Am Col Physicians; Am Fedn Clin Res (pres, 61-62); Am Soc Internal Med; fel AAAS; Am Asn Clin Endocrinologists; AMA; Sigma Xi; Am Clin & Climat Asn; fel NY Acad Sci; Royal Soc Med; Soc Exp Biol & Med. *Res:* Metabolic and endocrine diseases. *Mailing Add:* Univ Ala at Birmingham UAB Sta Birmingham AL 35294. *Fax:* 205-934-9977; *E-Mail:* pfrench@uab.edu

HILL, SHIRLEY ANN, mathematics education, for more information see previous edition

HILL, SHIRLEY YARDE, psychophysiology, for more information see previous edition

HILL, STEPHEN JAMES, GEOPHYSICS, ASTROPHYSICS. *Current Pos:* staff geophysicist, 80-90, MGR, CONOCO INC, 90- *Personal Data:* b Des Moines, Iowa, July 20, 43; m 65; c 2. *Educ:* Iowa State Univ, BS, 65; Univ Colo, PhD(physics, astrophys), 71. *Prof Exp:* From asst prof to assoc prof astrophys, Mich State Univ, 71-78; assoc geophysicist, Continental Oil Corp, 78-80. *Mem:* Soc Explor Geophys. *Res:* Seismic migration theory; hydrodynamics in variable stars; numerical seismic reduction techniques; computer automation in optical telescopes; seismic data reduction to modeling. *Mailing Add:* Conoco Inc Ponca City OK 74601

HILL, STUART BAXTER, ECOLOGY, ENTOMOLOGY. *Current Pos:* Nat Res Coun Can res assoc entom, 69-72, lectr, 72-73, asst prof, 73-79, ASSOC PROF ENTOM, MACDONALD COL, MCGILL UNIV, 79- *Personal Data:* b Aylesbury, Eng, Apr 11, 43; m 63, 66; c 2. *Educ:* Univ Wales, Swansea, BSc, 65; Univ WI, Trinidad, PhD(ecol), 69. *Honors & Awards:* Queen's Silver Jubilee Medal, 77. *Prof Exp:* Demonstr zool, Univ WI, Trinidad, 65-67 & Univ Reading, 67-69. *Mem:* Brit Ecol Soc; Entom Soc Can. *Res:* Orchard pest management; tropical cave ecology; ecological agriculture; soil mite ecology, taxonomy, extraction and effects of agricultural and forestry practices on them; food policy and agroecosystem design. *Mailing Add:* Dept Entom Macdonald Campus McGill Univ 21,111 Lakeshore Ste Anne de Bellevue PQ H9X 1C0 Can

HILL, SUSAN DOUGLAS, EFFECTS OF ENVIRONMENT ON DEVELOPMENT, REGENERATION. *Current Pos:* ASST PROF, DEPT ZOOL, MICH STATE UNIV, 81- *Personal Data:* b Toronto, Ont, Can, Sept 4, 40; m 68, Richard W; c David & Christine. *Educ:* Queen's Univ, Kingston, Ont, Can, BSc, 63; Univ Mich, Ann Arbor, MS, 65, PhD(zool), 69. *Prof Exp:* Fel, Dept Anat, Univ Mich, 69-70; asst prof, Dept Health Sci, Univ Del, 70-72; res assoc, Dept Zool, Mich State Univ, 73-81; instr, Lansing Community Col, 79-80. *Concurrent Pos:* Mem, Bermuda Biol Sta, 70- & Marine Biol Lab, 87-; prin investr, Marine Biol Lab, Woods Hole, 83, 86-88 & 90-96. *Mem:* Soc Develop Biol; Am Soc Zoologists; Sigma Xi. *Res:* Regeneration in polychaete worms; effects of tail loss and regeneration on fitness; effects of extremely low frequency electromagnetic fields on embryological development; endogenous currents in wound healing and regeneration effects of environment on development. *Mailing Add:* Dept Zool Mich State Univ East Lansing MI 48824. *Fax:* 517-432-2789, 336-2789; *E-Mail:* hillss@pilot.msu.edu

HILL, TERRELL LESLIE, BIOPHYSICS, PHYSICAL BIOCHEMISTRY. *Current Pos:* res chemist, 71-88, EMER SCIENTIST, LAB MOLECULAR BIOL, NAT INST ARTHRITIS, METAB & DIGESTIVE DIS, 88- *Personal Data:* b Oakland, Calif, Dec 19, 17; m 42, Laura Gano; c Julie, Carolynn & Ernest. *Educ:* Univ Calif, Berkeley, AB, 38, PhD(chem), 42. *Honors & Awards:* Flemming Award, US Govt, 54; Kendall Award, Am Chem Soc, 69. *Prof Exp:* Instr chem, Western Reserve Univ, 42-44; res chemist, Radiation Lab, Univ Calif, 44-45; res assoc, Univ Rochester, 45-46, asst prof chem, 46-49; chemist, Naval Med Res Inst, 49-57; prof chem, Univ Ore, 57-67 & Univ Calif, Santa Cruz, 67-71, vchancellor sci, 68-69. *Concurrent Pos:* Guggenheim fel, Yale Univ, 52-53; Sloan fel, 58-62; adj prof, 77-88, emer prof, Univ Calif, Santa Cruz, 88- *Mem:* Nat Acad Sci; Am Chem Soc; Biophys Soc. *Res:* Thermodynamics; statistical mechanics; biophysics; physical biochemistry. *Mailing Add:* 433 Logan St Santa Cruz CA 95062

HILL, THOMAS WESTFALL, PLANETARY MAGNETOSPHERES. *Current Pos:* res assoc space physics, 72-74, sr res assoc, 74-76, asst prof, 76-80, assoc res scientist, 80-85, sr res scientist, 86-90, DISTINGUISHED FAC FEL, RICE UNIV, 90- *Personal Data:* b Olean, NY, July 28, 45; m 76, Patricia Reiff; c Andrea, Adam & Amelia. *Educ:* Rice Univ, BA, 67, MS, 71, PhD(space sci), 73. *Honors & Awards:* James B Macelwane Award, Am Geophys Union, 80. *Concurrent Pos:* Mem, Upper Atmosphere Panel, Nat Res Coun, 74-77; resident res assoc, Nat Oceanic & Atmospheric Admin, 75-76; assoc ed, J Geophys Res, 78-80 & Geophys Res Lett, 83-88; consult, Southwest Res Inst, 79; mem, Associateship Panel, Nat Res Coun, 84-89, Steering Comt Geospace Environ Modeling Prog, NSF, 89-92; mem, Mgt Opers Working Group, NASA, 89-91 & Space Physics Sub Comt, 91-94. *Mem:* Fel Am Geophys Union; Int Asn Geomagnetism & Aeronomy; AAAS. *Res:* Theoretical research in space plasma physics, particularly solar-wind interactions with the terrestrial magnetosphere and the dynamics of rapidly rotating planetary and astrophysical magnetospheres. *Mailing Add:* Space Physics & Astron Dept Rice Univ Houston TX 77005-1892. *E-Mail:* hill@rice.edu

HILL, TREVOR BRUCE, ORGANIC CHEMISTRY. *Current Pos:* assoc prof org chem, 63-71, PROF CHEM, COL WILLIAM & MARY, 71- *Personal Data:* b St Catharines, Ont, May 23, 28; m 48, Shirley M Jackson. *Educ:* Univ Alta, BSc, 52; Cornell Univ, PhD(chem), 58. *Prof Exp:* Res chemist, E I du Pont de Nemours & Co, Inc, 57-63. *Mem:* Am Chem Soc. *Res:* Synthesis of polynuclear aromatic hydrocarbons; organic coatings. *Mailing Add:* 228 Longhill Rd Williamsburg VA 23185-2702

HILL, VICTOR ERNST, IV, GROUP THEORY, HISTORY MATHEMATICS. *Current Pos:* From asst prof to assoc prof, 66-78, prof, 78-89, THOMAS T READ PROF MATH, WILLIAMS COL, 89- *Personal Data:* b Pittsburgh, Pa, Nov 3, 39; div; c Victoria & Christopher. *Educ:* Carnegie-Mellon Univ, BS, 61; Univ Wis, MA, 62; Univ Ore, PhD(math), 66. *Concurrent Pos:* Vis prof, Ga Tech, 88 & 91-92. *Mem:* Soc Lit & Sci; Math Asn Am; Sigma Xi. *Res:* History of mathematics; mathematics and musicc. *Mailing Add:* Dept Math Williams Col Williamstown MA 01267. *Fax:* 413-597-4116; *E-Mail:* vhill@williams.edu

HILL, WALTER ANDREW, AGRONOMY, HORTICULTURE. *Current Pos:* from asst prof to assoc prof, 78-84, adminr, Coop Ext Prog, 87-91, PROF PLANT & SOIL SCI, TUSKEGEE UNIV, 84-, DIR AGR EXP STA, 86-, DEAN, SCH AGR & HOME ECON, 87- *Personal Data:* b New Brunswick, NJ, Aug 9, 46; m 84, Jill Harris; c Shaka, Asia & Osei. *Educ:* Lake Forest Col, BA, 68; Univ Chicago, MAT, 70; Univ Ariz, MS, 73; Univ Ill, Urbana, PhD(soil chem & fertil), 78. *Honors & Awards:* Distinguished Serv Award, Carver Plant & Soil Sci Club, 82; Russell Brown Distinguished Sci Res Award, Sigma Xi, 91. *Prof Exp:* Res asst chem, Lake Forest Col, 67-68; teacher chem, Chicago, 69-71; res asst soil chem/fertil, Univ Ariz, 71-73; irrig/fertil specialist, Univ Ariz Exp Sta, 73-74; res asst soil chem & fertil, Univ Ill, 74-77, teaching asst soils, 76-77; res asst soil chem /fertil, Univ Ill, 74-77. *Concurrent Pos:* Dean, Res Dir & Exten Adminr, Tuskegee Univ, 87-; prin investr, USDA, Coop State Res Serv, 79-, Sweet Potato Plant Environ Relationship, 85-91, USAID, 86-, Environ Technol & Waste Mgt, Dept Environ, 90-; bd trustees, Lake Forest Col; bd dir, Agr Satellite Corp, 90-93; mem, Nat Res Coun Comt Syst Ag & Environ in the Tropics, 90-93; sci liaison officer, Asian Veg Res & Develop Ctr, 89-93; consult, USAID/Univ Md-ES & Ark Comn Higher Educ; chmn, Prof Agr Workers Conf, 88- & Int Symp Sweet Potato Tech 21st Centennial, 91; counr, Int Soc Trop Root Corps, 85-88; vis scientist, Purdue Univ, 82, Int Inst Trop Agr, 85 & NASA, 87; Kellogg fel, NCFAP/RFF, 88; dir, Ctr Food Prod, Processing & Waste Mgt, NASA, 91-; mem, Panel Biolnitrogen Fixation, Nat Res Coun, 92- *Mem:* Soil Sci Soc Am; fel Am Soc Agron; Crop Sci Soc Am; Int Soc Trop Root Crops; Am Soc Hort Sci; Sigma Xi; Am Soc Gravitational & Space Biol. *Res:* Administers interdisciplinary research teams and teaching faculty in agriculture, food, environment, rural development and forestry; uses the sweet potato as a model crop to assess plant- microbiol-soil-nutrient-water interactions and crop production for controlled ecological life support systems for space missions. *Mailing Add:* Sch Agr & Home Econs Campbell Hall Tuskegee Univ Tuskegee AL 36088. *Fax:* 334-727-8493

HILL, WALTER EDWARD, JR, geochemistry; deceased, see previous edition for last biography

HILL, WALTER ENSIGN, BIOPHYSICS, BIOCHEMISTRY. *Current Pos:* from asst prof to assoc prof, 69-77, assoc dean grad sch, 78-79, PROF CHEM, UNIV MONT, 77- *Personal Data:* b Bottineau, NDak, July 25, 37; m 61; c 7. *Educ:* Brigham Young Univ, BS, 61; Univ Wis, MS, 64, PhD(biophys), 67. *Prof Exp:* Res assoc biochem & biophys, Ore State Univ, 67-69. *Concurrent Pos:* NIH career develop award, 72-77; prog dir, NSF, 89-90. *Mem:* Biophys Soc; Am Soc Biol Chem; fel AAAS; Am Soc Microbiol. *Res:* Probing structure and function of ribosomes using short complementary DNA oligonucleotides; physical study of ribosomes and other macromolecules using analytical utlracentrifugation, density measurements, diffusion measurements and viscometry. *Mailing Add:* Div Biol Sci Univ Mont Missoula MT 59812-1002

HILL, WALTER ERNEST, genetic methods for detecting pathogenic foodborne microorganisms, molecular subtyping of bacteria, for more information see previous edition

HILL, WILLIAM JOSEPH, STATISTICS. *Current Pos:* dir, Math & Simulation Sci Dept, 89-91, qual officer res & technol, 92-94, RES FEL, ALLIED SIGNAL INC, 95- *Personal Data:* b St Catharines, Ont, Jan 20, 40; m 62, Barbara Heaton; c Catherine & Cheryl. *Educ:* Princeton Univ, BSE, 63; Univ Wis, MS, 64, PhD(statist), 66. *Honors & Awards:* William G Hunter Award, Am Soc Qual Control, 88, Shewhart Medal, 90. *Prof Exp:* Sr engr, Allied Corp, 66-72, mgr math sci, 73-84, dir, Ctr Appl Math, 84-89; Emerson Elec & Wis distinguished prof indust eng, Univ Wis, 90-92, dir, Ctr Qual & Productivity Improv, 91-92. *Concurrent Pos:* Adj assoc prof, State Univ NY, Buffalo, 74-77; mem, Epidemiol Subcomt, Chem Indust Inst Toxicol, 78-80; chair, Gordon Conf on Statists, 80; vchair, Continuing Educ Adv Comt, Am Statist Asn, 81-84, mem bd dirs, 83, UN Environ Programme Comt on the Sci Assessment Stratospheric Ozone, 89, steering comt, Network for the Detection of Stratospheric Change, 90- *Mem:* Fel Am Statist Asn; Am Soc Qual Control; fel AAAS. *Res:* Design and analysis of experiments for model discrimination, parameter estimation and chemical process improvement; time series analysis of environmental data; probability analysis in epidemiological and occupational health studies; statistical process control and quality improvement. *Mailing Add:* Allied Signal Inc 20 Peabody St Buffalo NY 14210. *Fax:* 716-827-6373

HILL, WILLIAM T, GEOLOGY. *Current Pos:* CONSULT, 90- *Personal Data:* b Covington, Ky, Apr 8, 25; m 50; c 3. *Educ:* Univ Tenn, BA, 50, MS, 51, PhD, 71. *Prof Exp:* Geologist, Am Zinc Co, 51-53; teaching asst geol, Univ Tenn, 53-55; geologist, Tenn Div Geol, 55-56; explor supt, B H Putnam & Assocs, 56-59; geologist I, NJ Zinc Co, Jefferson City, Tenn, 59-60, res geologist, Treadway, 60-65, distr geologist, 65-66, asst to mgr, 66-69, asst to div mgr mines, 69-70, proj mgr, 70-74, mgr, Elmwood Mine, 76-79, pres, 79-84; assoc, Condor Mine Mgt, 84-85; state geologist, Tenn, 85-90. *Concurrent Pos:* Dir, Enuex Mineracao, Brazil, 74-76. *Mem:* Soc Econ Geol; Am Inst Mining, Metall & Petrol Eng. *Res:* Minerals exploration; mine and production planning; geological research. *Mailing Add:* 100 Jackson Lane Hendersonville TN 37075-4007

HILLAIRE-MARCEL, CLAUDE, ISOTOPIC GEOCHEMISTRY, QUATERNARY GEOLOGY. *Current Pos:* dir, Dept Earth Sci, 82-84, PROF GEOL, UNIV QUE, MONTREAL, 69-, CHAIR ENVIRON SCI, 90- *Personal Data:* b Salies de Bearn, France, April 1, 44; m 75, Anne de Vernal; c Adrien. *Educ:* Univ Paris at the Sorbonne, France, LLSci, 67, DES, 67; Univ Pierre & Marie Curie, Paris, DSci, 79. *Honors & Awards:* Michel-Jurdant Prize, Can Asn Advan Sci. *Concurrent Pos:* prof, Ctr Nat Res Sci, France, 80; assoc prof, Univ Orsay, Paris, 81-96; head, Geotop Res Ctr, 81-89. *Mem:* Soc Geol France; Geol Soc Am; Chem Soc; fel Royal Soc Can; Geol Asn Can. *Res:* Environmental isotopes; paleoceanography; paleohydrology; paleoclimatology; biogeochemistry; natural isotopes in life science. *Mailing Add:* GEOTOP-UQAM C P 8888 Succ Centre-ville Montreal PQ H3C 3P8 Can. *Fax:* 514-987-4634

HILLAKER, HARRY J, ENGINEERING. *Current Pos:* AEROSPACE CONSULT. *Personal Data:* b Flint, Mich, May 9, 19. *Educ:* Univ Mich, AE. *Honors & Awards:* Aircraft Design Award, Am Inst Aeronaut & Astronaut. *Prof Exp:* Vpres & dep prog dir, F-16 Gen Dynamics, Ft Worth. *Concurrent Pos:* Mem, sci adv bd & adv group, Aeronaut Systs Div, USAF; chmn, Aerospace Vehicles Panel. *Mem:* Nat Acad Eng; Am Inst Aeronaut & Astronaut. *Res:* Aircraft design and technologies. *Mailing Add:* 4001 Shannon Dr Ft Worth TX 76116

HILLAM, BRUCE PARKS, MATHEMATICAL ANALYSIS. *Current Pos:* asst prof, 73-77, assoc prof math & comput sci, 77-81, assoc prof comput sci, 81-83, PROF & CHAIR, DEPT COMPUT SCI, CALIF STATE POLYTECH UNIV, POMONA, 83- *Personal Data:* b Salt Lake City, Utah, May 23, 45. *Educ:* Univ Calif, Riverside, BA, 68, MA, 69, PhD(math), 73. *Prof Exp:* Asst prof math, Univ Calif, Riverside, 73. *Mem:* Soc Indust & Appl Math; Math Asn Am; Asn Comput Mach; AAAS. *Res:* Existence of fixed point solutions of functional equations with applications to modeling and simulation on computers. *Mailing Add:* Dept Comput Sci Calif State Polytech Univ Pomona CA 91768

HILLAM, KENNETH L, MATHEMATICS. *Current Pos:* from instr to assoc prof, 57-69, PROF MATH, BRIGHAM YOUNG UNIV, 69-, CHMN DEPT, 63- *Personal Data:* b Salt Lake City, Utah, July 15, 27; m 50; c 3. *Educ:* Univ Utah, BS, 49, MS, 56; Univ Colo, PhD(math), 62. *Prof Exp:* Instr appl math, Univ Colo, 56-57. *Mem:* Am Math Soc; Math Asn Am. *Res:* Complex analysis; convergence criteria for continued fractions; real variables. *Mailing Add:* 11017 S Surrey Dr Covered Bridge Canyon Spanish Fork UT 84660

HILLAR, MARIAN, BIOCHEMISTRY, MOLECULAR BIOLOGY. *Current Pos:* from asst prof to assoc prof, 71-81, PROF BIOCHEM, TEX SOUTHERN UNIV, 81- *Personal Data:* b Bydgoszcz, Poland, Mar 22, 38; US citizen; m 70, Janett; c Anne M & Christopher J. *Educ:* Univ Med Sch, Gdansk, Poland, MD, 62, PhD(biochem), 66. *Prof Exp:* Instr biochem, Univ Med Sch, Gdansk, Poland, 58-62, asst prof, 62-69; res assoc, Baylor Col Med, 69-70. *Concurrent Pos:* NIH fel, Nat Cancer Inst, 72-84; Fulbright award, 80; prof, Ponce Sch Med, PR, 86- *Mem:* Biophys Soc; Biochem Soc London; AAAS; Inst Relig Age Sci; Polish Inst Arts & Sci Am; Soc Advan Am Philos. *Res:* Control of bioenergetic reactions in mitochondria; mechanisms of control of gene expression by endogenous peptides associated with chromatin and poly(A)-MRNA; philosophy in XVI and XVII centuries; socinianism; origin of christianity. *Mailing Add:* 9330 Bankside Houston TX 77031. *Fax:* 713-713-7132

HILLARD, CECILIA JANE, DRUG ABUSE, NEUROCHEMISTRY. *Current Pos:* Asst prof, 85-93, ASSOC PROF PHARMACOL, MED COL WIS, 93- *Personal Data:* b Dec 22, 54; m 80, Douglas H; c Christopher, Matthew & Jennifer. *Educ:* Med Col Wis, PhD(pharmacol), 83. *Mem:* Soc Neurosci; Am Soc Pharmacol & Exp Therapeut. *Mailing Add:* Med Col Wis 8701 Watertown Plank Rd Milwaukee WI 53226-4801. *Fax:* 414-266-8460

HILLCOAT, BRIAN LESLIE, CANCER CHEMOTHERAPY. *Current Pos:* MED SERV ADV, DEPT COMMUN SERV & HEALTH, DRUG EVAL BR, 89-; HEAD, EVAL UNIT 4, DRUG EVAL BR, COMMONWEALTH DEPT HEALTH & FAMILY SERVS, 90- *Personal Data:* b Rockhampton, Australia, July 26, 32; m 57; c 4. *Educ:* Univ Queensland, MB, BS, 55, BSc, 62, MD, 63; Australian Nat Univ, PhD(biochem), 65. *Prof Exp:* USPHS fel biochem pharmacol, Sch Med, Yale Univ, 65-67, asst prof, 67-68; from assoc prof to prof biochem, McMaster Univ, 68-78; exp, Nat Cancer Inst, NIH, 78; head, Solid Tumor Chemother Unit, Cancer Inst, Melbourne, 78-84, prof cancer med, 84-89. *Concurrent Pos:* Vis prof med, Yale Univ, 75; Nuffield travelling fel, 75; outpatient physician, Cancer Clin, Henderson Hosp, 75-78. *Mem:* AAAS; Clin Oncol Soc Australia; NY Acad Sci; Am Soc Clin Oncol; Am Asn Cancer Res. *Res:* Mechanism of action of drugs that interact with DNA; effects of anticancer drugs on gene expression. *Mailing Add:* Drug Eval Br Therapeut Goods Admin PO Box 100 Woden ACT 2606 Australia. *Fax:* 61-6-289-7724

HILLDRUP, DAVID J, MATHEMATICS, OPERATIONS RESEARCH. *Current Pos:* RETIRED. *Personal Data:* b Manchester, Eng, Apr 5, 36. *Educ:* Univ London, BSc, 59, MSc, 60; Univ Hawaii, MBA, 73; Laurentian Univ, BA, 75. *Prof Exp:* Head, Dept Appl Math, NManchester Grammar Sch, 59-61; asst prof math, Bishop's Univ, 61-65; assoc prof com, Laurentian Univ, 65-, dir, Sch Com & Admin & dean, Fac Prof Schs, 78-81. *Mem:* Opers Res Soc Am; Can Opers Res Soc; Inst Mgt Sci. *Res:* Inventory, forecasting and queueing models. *Mailing Add:* Sch Com Laurentian Univ Ramsey Lake Rd Sudbury ON P3E 2C6 Can

HILLE, BERTIL, PHYSIOLOGY, BIOPHYSICS. *Current Pos:* from asst prof to assoc prof, 68-74, PROF PHYSIOL & BIOPHYS, UNIV WASH, 74- *Personal Data:* b New Haven, Conn, Oct 10, 40; m 64, Merrill Burr; c Erik & Trygve. *Educ:* Yale Univ, BS, 62; Rockefeller Univ, PhD(life sci), 67. *Honors & Awards:* Sr Scientist Award, Alexander von Humboldt Found, 75-76; Bristol-Myers Squibb Award, Neurosci Res, 90. *Prof Exp:* Helen Hay Whitney fel physiol, Cambridge Univ & Agr Res Coun Inst Animal Physiol, Babraham, 67-68. *Concurrent Pos:* Biophys Soc Counr, 77-79; vis prof, Univ Saarland, Fed Repub Ger, NIH, Physiol Study Sect, 80-84; Neurosci res prog assoc, 85- *Mem:* Nat Acad Sci; Biophys Soc; Soc Gen Physiologists; Soc Neurosci; fel AAAS. *Res:* Permeability changes in axon and muscle membranes; conduction of nervous impulses; ionic channels of excitable membranes; neurotransmitters and second messengers; calcium and exocytosis; neuroendocrinology. *Mailing Add:* Dept Physiol & Biophys Box 357290 Univ Wash Seattle WA 98195

HILLE, KENNETH R, LIMNOLOGY, AQUATIC TOXICOLOGY. *Current Pos:* assoc prof biol, 69-81, ASSOC PROF BIOL & CHMN NATURAL & SOCIAL SCI, FIRELANDS COL, BOWLING GREEN STATE UNIV, 81- *Personal Data:* b New York, NY, Sept 16, 27; m 56; c 2. *Educ:* Wagner Col, BS, 52; Bowling Green State Univ, MA, 56; Ohio State Univ, PhD(aquatic ecol), 69. *Prof Exp:* Instr, Fremont City Schs, 54-65. *Mem:* Am Soc Limnol & Oceanog; Am Fisheries Soc; Sigma Xi. *Res:* Toxicity of chlorinated hydrocarbons, as dieldrin, to fish; toxicity of surfactants, as detergents to fish; stream macro-invertebrate community structure; water quality criteria of streams. *Mailing Add:* 8809 Frailey Rd Huron OH 44839-9752

HILLE, MERRILL BURR, EMBRYOLOGY. *Current Pos:* ASSOC PROF ZOOL, UNIV WASH, SEATTLE, 76- *Personal Data:* b Feb 15, 39; m; c 2. *Educ:* Rockefeller Univ, PhD(life sci), 65. *Mem:* Soc Develop Biol; Am Soc Cell Biol. *Res:* Translational control in eggs; embryos of Echinoderms; cell adhesion during gastrulation. *Mailing Add:* Dept Zool NJ-15 Univ Wash Seattle WA 98195-0001

HILLEGAS, WILLIAM JOSEPH, MATERIALS SCIENCE, BIOENGINEERING & VACUUM TECHNOLOGY. *Current Pos:* VPRES, CHIEF TECH OFFICER, DIR & CO-FOUNDER, SOLOHILL ENG INC, 84- *Personal Data:* b Quakertown, Pa, Aug 31, 37; m 82, Kathleen Branson; c Lisa L, Gregory C, William J, Sara E (Hawley) & Jennifer A (Hawley). *Educ:* Drexel Inst Technol, BSChE, 60; Northwestern Univ, MS, 67, PhD(mat sci), 68. *Prof Exp:* Jr engr, Lansdale Div, Philco Corp, 60-61, engr, 61-63; assoc scientist, Res Div, Xerox Corp, 68-69, scientist, 69-78; res scientist, KMS Fusion Inc, 78-85. *Concurrent Pos:* Prin investr, Small Bus Innovative Res Phase I & II; Nat Cancer Inst res awards, 84-98; res fund grants, Mich State, 87-90. *Mem:* Tissue Cult Asn; AAAS; NY Acad Sci; Tissue Eng Soc. *Res:* Bioengineering process development for large scale cell cultures; fabrication of inertial fusion targets; materials process technologies associated with semiconducting and amorphous photoreceptive materials; physics of defects in solids; thin film vacuum technologies; published 25 refereed journal articles and granted 5 patents. *Mailing Add:* SoloHill Labs Inc 4220 Varsity Dr Ann Arbor MI 48108. *Fax:* 313-973-3029; *E-Mail:* solohill@ic.net

HILLEL, DANIEL, SOIL & ENVIRONMENTAL PHYSICS, HYDROLOGY. *Current Pos:* prof, 77-94, EMER PROF SOIL PHYSICS & HYDROL, UNIV MASS, 94- *Personal Data:* b Los Angeles, Calif, Sept 13, 30; m 84, Michal Artzy; c Adi, Ron, Sari, Ori & Shira. *Educ:* Univ Ga, BS, 50; Rutgers Univ, MS, 51; Hebrew Univ, PhD(soil physics), 58. *Hon Degrees:* DSc, Guelph Univ, 92, Ohio State Univ, 95. *Honors & Awards:* Award for Excellence in Publ in Earth Sci, Am Asn Publishers, 92; Distinguished Achievement Award, Soil Sci Soc Am, 95. *Prof Exp:* Soil survr, Soil Conserv Serv, Israel, 51-52; founding mem, Kibbutz Sde-Boker, Negev, Israel, 52-55; adv land develop, Govt Burma, 56-58; res fel soil physics, Univ Calif, 59-61; head, Soil Technol Div, Agr Res Ctr, Rehovot, Israel, 61-65; prof & head soil & water sci, Hebrew Univ, Jerusalem, 66-74; vis prof soil physics, Tex A&M Univ, 74-75; vis prof environ sci, Univ Va, 75-77. *Concurrent Pos:* consult water conserv, Govt Calif, 79-80; prin investr, NSF Res Projs, 79-83 & 86-89; irrig consult, World Bank, 82-97, environ sci adv, 87-, USAID, Govt Egypt, 84; ed, Advan in Irrig, 82-; res consult, Commonwealth Sci & Indust Res Orgn, Australia, 84; consult ed, Soil Sci & Hydrol Processes, 84-; vis prof, Israel Inst Technol, 82-84 & Haifa Univ, 85-86; nat lectr, Sigma Xi Sci Hon Soc, 87-89; Guggenheim res award, 93; consult, UN Food & Agr Orgn, 95-97; consult, Govt Nepal, 96-97. *Mem:* Fel Soil Sci Soc Am; fel Am Soc Agron; Am Geophys Union; fel AAAS; Am Soc Agr Engrs; Int Soil Sci Soc (vpres, 64-68 & 82-86). *Res:* Soil-water dynamics; soil-plant-water relations; the water regime of natural habitats and agricultural fields; irrigation efficiency; drainage; water conservation; land reclamation; environmental physics; pollution control; mathematical modeling and field measurements of hydrological processes; author of over 200 scientific papers and of 16 books in soil and environmental physics. *Mailing Add:* Univ Mass 11 Stockbridge Hall Amherst MA 01003

HILLEMAN, MAURICE RALPH, VIROLOGY, VACCINOLOGY. *Current Pos:* from dir to exec dir virus & cell biol res, Merck Inst Therapeut Res, Merck & Co, Inc, 57-71, dir virus & cell biol res & vpres, Merck Sharp & Dohme Res Labs, 70-78, vpres, 72-78, sr vpres, 78, DIR, MERCK INST THERAPEUT RES, MERCK SHARP & DOHME RES LAB, 84- *Personal Data:* b Miles City, Mont, Aug 30, 19; m 43, 63, Lorraine Witmer; c Jeryl L & Kirsten J. *Educ:* Mont State Univ, BS, 41; Univ Chicago, PhD(microbiol & virol), 44. *Hon Degrees:* DSc, Mont State Col, 66, Univ Md, 68, Univ Leuven, 83 & Washington & Jefferson Col, 92. *Honors & Awards:* Howard Taylor Ricketts Prize, 45; Flemming Award, 56; Golden Plate Award, Am Acad Achievement, 75; 19th Graugnard Lectr, Tulane Univ, 78; Howard Taylor Ricketts Award, 83; Albert Lasker Med Res Award, 83; Sci Achievement Award, AMA, 83; Jos E Smadel Award, Infectious Dis Soc, 84; Richard Hinda Rosenthal Found Award, 84; Albert B Sabin Medal, 88; Nat Medal Sci, Pres US, 88; Robert Koch Gold Medal, 89; Order of St Agatha, Govt San Marine, 90; John Herr Musser Lectr, Tulane Univ, 69. *Prof Exp:* Asst bacteriologist, Univ Chicago, 42-44; res assoc virus labs, E R Squibb & Sons, NJ, 44-47, chief, Virus Dept, 47-48; chief, Respiratory & Virus Res & Diag Sect, Army Med Serv Grad Sch, Walter Reed Army Med Ctr, 48-56, asst chief lab affairs, 53-56, chief respiratory dis, Walter Reed Army Inst Res, 56-57. *Concurrent Pos:* Vis instr, Rutgers Univ, 47; vis investr, Rockefeller Inst Med Res, 51; mem, Expert Adv Panel Virus Dis, WHO, 52-, Expert Comt Influenza, 52, Respiratory Dis, 58, Sci Group Measles Vaccine Studies, 63, Sci Group Measles Vaccine Studies, 63, Sci Group Viruses & Cancer, 64, Sci Group Virus Vaccines, 65, investr animal models for res immunity cancer, 73, mem, Sci Group Immunol Adjuvants, 75 & Study Group Cerebrospinal Meningitis Control, 75; vis prof, Univ Md, 53-57; mem, Study Sect Microbiol & Immunol, Grants-in-Aid Prog, USPHS, 53-61, spec consult, Panel Respiratory Dis, 60-64; assoc mem, Comn Influenza, US Armed Forces Epidemiol Bd, 55-58 & Comn Respiratory Dis, 56-58; consult, Surgeon Gen, US Army, 58-63; mem, Primate Study Group, Nat Cancer Inst, 64-70, Working Group Immunol & Epidemiol, Spec Virus Cancer Prog, 69-70; adj prof virol pediat, Sch Med, Univ Pa & consult, Children's Hosp, Philadelphia, 68-; mem, Permanent Sect Microbiol Stand, Int Asn Microbiol Socs; mem, Coun Anal & Proj, Am Cancer Soc, 71-76 75 & Study Group Cerevrospinal Meningitis Control, 75; trustee, Merck Inst Therapeut Res, 76-; mem, Coun Div Biol Sci & Pritzger Sch Med, Univ Chicago, 77-; mem, Overseas Med Res Labs Comt, US Dept Defense, 80; mem, Prev & Control Viral Dis Res Briefing Panel, Inst Med-Mat Acad Sci, 86, Comt Nat Strategy Acquired Immune Deficiency Syndrome, 86-; mem bd sci dir, Jos Stokes Res, Univ Pa, 86-; mem bd dir, Nat Found Infectious Dis, 87-; mem, Molecular Immun & Vaccine Develop Panel, Nat Task Force, NIH, 92-, Human Immunodeficiency Virus Res & Develop Vaccine Working Group, Nat Inst Allergy & Infectious Dis, 92-, Blue Ribbon Panel Vaccine Res, Nat Inst Allergy & Infectious Dis, 93; mem, AIDS Vaccine Design & Eval Group, Nat Inst Allergy & Infectious Dis, NIH, 95-; mem, Comt Russ-US Collab on Biol Weapons Control, Nat Acad Sci, 96- *Mem:* Nat Acad Sci; Inst Med-Nat Acad Sci; hon foreign mem Russian Acad Biotech; fel Am Acad Microbiol; foreign mem Nat Acad Pharm France; Am Acad Arts & Scis; Infect Dis Soc Am. *Res:* Medical virology, especially adenoviruses, S40, Rhinoviruses, influenza, psittacosis-lymphogranuloma venereum group, poliomyelitis, measles and carcinogenic viruses; virus in cancer and immunology in cancer; epidemiology and preventive medicine; interferon and host resistance, chemotherapy in viral infections; viral vaccines and immunologic adjuvants. *Mailing Add:* Merck Inst Therapeut Res Merck Res Lab West Point PA 19486. *Fax:* 215-652-2154

HILLER, DALE MURRAY, PHYSICAL CHEMISTRY. *Current Pos:* INDEPENDENT CONSULT, 90- *Personal Data:* b Chicago, Ill, Oct 13, 24; wid; c Karen, Margaret, Steven & Eric. *Educ:* Univ Nebr, BSEE, 47; Miami Univ, AB, 48; Iowa State Col, PhD(chem), 52. *Prof Exp:* Res chemist, Pigments Dept, E I Du Pont de Nemours & Co, Inc, 52-65, sr res chemist, Photo Dept, 65-69, 72-77, qual control supvr, 69-72, res assoc, Electronics Dept, 77-90. *Mem:* Am Chem Soc; Inst Elec & Electronics Engrs; Sigma Xi. *Res:* Photofission of thorium; titanium dioxide pigments; extractive metallurgy; photographic film; magnetic tape. *Mailing Add:* Cokesbury Village Apts 726 Loveville Rd Hockessin DE 19707-1501. *Fax:* 302-239-4320; *E-Mail:* dmhfed@aol.com

HILLER, FREDERICK CHARLES, MEDICINE. *Current Pos:* from asst prof to assoc prof, dept med, 75-83, assoc prof, dept pharmacol, 82-83, PROF MED & INTERDISCIPLINARY TOXICOL, UNIV ARK MED SCI, 83-, MED DIR, RESPIRATORY THER DEPT, 80-, SLEEP DIS CTR & MED & INTENSIVE CARE UNIT, 84-, DIR, DIV PULMONARY & CRIT CARE MED, 85- *Personal Data:* b Kansas City, Kans, Jan 30, 42; m 65; c 4. *Educ:* Univ Kans, Lawrence, AB, 64, Kansas City, MD, 68. *Prof Exp:* Intern, Med Ctr, Univ Kans, Kansas City, 68-69, resident internal med, 71-73, fel, 73-75; captain, Med Corps, US Army Res, 69-71. *Concurrent Pos:* Dir, pulmonary function lab, Univ Ark Med Sci, 75-; chest consult, Ark State Health Dept, 75-; consult, Little Rock Vet Admin Med Ctr, 75-; med adv, Ark State Respiratory Ther Asn, 81-; chief, Pulmonary & Critical Care Med Div, Univ Ark Med Sci & Little Rock Vet Admin Med Ctr, 85- *Mem:* Am Thoracic Soc; fel Am Col Chest Physicians; Am Fedn Clin Res; Sigma Xi. *Res:* Aerosol physical properties, deposition in respiratory tract; drug absorbtion from the respiratory rack. *Mailing Add:* Pulmonary Div Slot 555 Univ Ark Med Sci 4301 W Markham Little Rock AR 72205-7101

HILLER, FREDERICK W, INORGANIC CHEMISTRY, PHYSICAL CHEMISTRY. *Current Pos:* RETIRED. *Personal Data:* b Melstone, Mont, Feb 28, 27; m 56, 77; c 3. *Educ:* Ore State Univ, BS, 50, PhD(inorg chem), 67. *Prof Exp:* Instr chem, SDak State Col, 56-57, Idaho State Col, 57-64 & Ore State Univ, 64-66; from asst prof to prof, Calif State Univ, Chico, 66-92, chmn dept, 80-83. *Mem:* AAAS; Am Chem Soc; Sigma Xi. *Res:* Inorganic kinetics and reaction mechanisms. *Mailing Add:* 1901 Dayton Rd Space 97 Chico CA 95928

HILLER, JACOB MOSES, NEUROPHARMACOLOGY. *Current Pos:* from asst res scientist to assoc res scientist med, 70-74, res asst prof med, 74-80, RES ASSOC PROF PSYCHIAT, MED CTR, NY UNIV, 80- *Personal Data:* b New York, NY, Dec 12, 39; m 65; c 3. *Educ:* City Col New York, BS, 61; NY Univ, MS, 67, PhD(biol), 70. *Prof Exp:* From asst res scientist to res scientist biol, Grad Sch Art & Sci, NY Univ, 69-70. *Concurrent Pos:* Prin investr grant, Nat Inst Aging, 89-92; Ad Hoc Grant Reviewer, Nat Inst Drug Abuse. *Mem:* AAAS; Am Soc Microbiol; Sigma Xi; NY Acad Sci. *Res:* Molecular basis of the pharmacological effects of narcotics, including analgesia and development of tolerance and physical dependence; localization, solubilization and purification of stereospecific opiate receptors in animal and human brain. *Mailing Add:* Dept Psychiat NY Univ Med Ctr New York NY 10016. *Fax:* 212-263-5591

HILLER, LARRY KEITH, HORTICULTURE, VEGETABLE CROPS. *Current Pos:* asst prof & asst hort, 73-79, ASSOC PROF & ASSOC HORT, WASH STATE UNIV, 79- *Personal Data:* b Morning Sun, Iowa, Apr 28, 41; m 63; c 2. *Educ:* Iowa State Univ, BS, 63, MS, 64; Cornell Univ, PhD(veg crops), 74. *Prof Exp:* Tech adv, Iowa State, USAID Prog, Uruguay, 64-67; res asst, Cornell Univ, 68-73. *Concurrent Pos:* Kellogg Found Nat Fel Prog, 80-83; consult veg, Ecuador, Peru & Columbia, 79-82. *Mem:* Am Soc Hort Sci; Am Soc Plant Physiologists; Coun Agr Sci & Technol; Potato Asn Am; Weed Sci Soc Am. *Res:* Production practices, physiological tuber disorders and quality factors affecting fresh market and processing grades of Washington potatoes; production and quality factors in irrigated vegetable crops. *Mailing Add:* Hort & Landscape Archit Dept Wash State Univ Pullman WA 99164-6414. *Fax:* 509-335-8690; *E-Mail:* hillerl@wsu.edu

HILLER, ROBERT ELLIS, OPERATIONS RESEARCH. *Current Pos:* RETIRED. *Personal Data:* b Traveler's Rest, SC, Dec 14, 27; m 52, Carolyn Thomas; c Douglas & Page. *Educ:* Clemson Col, BS, 50; NC State Col, MS, 53; Univ NC, PhD(physics), 56. *Prof Exp:* Asst, NC State Col, 51-53; instr physics, Univ NC, 53-56, asst prof & res assoc, 56-57; opers analyst, USAF, Europe, 57-61, chief opers analyst, Pac Air Forces, 61-87. *Mem:* Opers Res Soc Am. *Res:* Mathematics. *Mailing Add:* 44-404 Kaneohe Bay Dr Kaneohe HI 96744

HILLERS, JOE KARL, GENETICS, ANIMAL SCIENCE. *Current Pos:* From asst prof to assoc prof, 71-82, PROF ANIMAL SCI, WASH STATE UNIV, 82- *Personal Data:* b Centerville, Iowa, July 20, 38; m 63; c 2. *Educ:* NW Mo State Col, BA, 60; Iowa State Univ, MS, 62, PhD(animal breeding), 65. *Mem:* Am Dairy Sci Asn; Am Soc Animal Sci. *Res:* Selection programs and computer systems analysis of livestock production traits, particularly dairy. *Mailing Add:* Dept Animal Sci Clark Hall 116 Wash State Univ Pullman WA 99163. *Fax:* 509-335-1082; *E-Mail:* hillerjo@wsu.edu

HILLERT, MATS H, PHASE TRANFORMATIONS, THERMODYNAMICS. *Current Pos:* EMER PROF, DEPT MAT SCI & ENG, DIV PHYS METALL, ROYAL INST TECHNOL, 90- *Personal Data:* b Goteborg, Sweden, Nov 28, 24. *Educ:* Chalmers Tech Univ, BSc, 47; Mass Inst Technol, DSci, 56. *Mem:* Nat Acad Eng. *Res:* Establishing computerized thermodynamic/kinetic systems to predict complex multi-component phase relationships. *Mailing Add:* Dept Mat Sci Royal Inst Technol Brinellv 23 Stockholm S100-44 Sweden

HILLERY, HERBERT VINCENT, ART CONSERVATION, BAMBOO RESEARCH. *Current Pos:* MEM STAFF, HILLERY ENTERPRISES, 78- *Personal Data:* b Lima, Ohio, Dec 8, 24; m 56, 90, Patricia Martin; c Vincent & Nathan. *Educ:* Oberlin Col, AB, 47. *Prof Exp:* Mem staff acoust, 50-67, spec res assoc acoust, Appl Res Lab, Univ Tex, Austin, 67-78. *Concurrent Pos:* NSF res grant, 72- *Mem:* Am Bamboo Soc; assoc mem Am Inst Conserv; Sigma Xi. *Res:* Art conservation & restoration; research on bamboo agriculture for Texas; noise vibration in solids; organic adhesives. *Mailing Add:* 1909 Richcreek Rd Austin TX 78757

HILLERY, PAUL STUART, FEDERAL DRUG REGULATIONS, DRUG ABUSE RESEARCH. *Current Pos:* CHEMIST & PROJ OFFICER, NAT INST DRUG ABUSE, 92- *Personal Data:* b Morristown, NJ, June 19, 41; m 69; c 3. *Educ:* Johns Hopkins Univ, BA, 63; Univ Va, PhD(phys org chem), 68. *Prof Exp:* Lab instr, Univ Va, 63-65; res assoc, Inst Environ Med, NY Univ, 69-70; res chemist, Biochem Mech Sect, Nat Inst Arthritis, Metab & Digestive Dis, NIH, 71-77; chemist, Div Oncol & Radiopharmaceut Drug Prod, Food & Drug Admin, Ctr Drug Eval & Res, 78-89, reviewing chemist, Pilot Drug Eval Staff, 89-92. *Concurrent Pos:* Vis scientist, Lab Analytical Chem, Nat Cancer Inst, NIH, 79-80 & Lab Med Chem, Nat Inst Diabetes, Digestive & Kidney Dis, 81- *Mem:* Am Chem Soc, Org Div, Med Chem Div. *Res:* Intramolecular catalysis; solution kinetics and reaction mechanisms; heterocyclic synthesis; PCP/sigma ligands. *Mailing Add:* Nat Inst Drug Abuse Rm 10A-19 Parklawn Bldg 5600 Fishers Lane Rockville MD 20857. *Fax:* 301-594-6043; *E-Mail:* ph44x@nih.gov

HILLIARD, JOHN ROY, JR, ENTOMOLOGY. *Current Pos:* assoc prof, 68-71, PROF BIOL, SAM HOUSTON STATE UNIV, 72- *Personal Data:* b Irving, Tex, Feb 7, 24; m 50, Evelyn J Herzog; c James R & Richard A. *Educ:* Trinity Col, Tex, BA, 47; Univ Colo, MA, 51; Univ Tex, PhD(zool), 59. *Prof Exp:* Instr, Trinity Col, Tex, 48-51; prof, McMurry Col, 51. *Mem:* Sigma Xi; Entom Soc Am; Southwestern Entom Soc; Orthopterists Soc. *Res:* Ecology and taxonomy of Orthopterous insects; systematics of the eggs and egg pods of grasshoppers. *Mailing Add:* Biol Sci Sam Houston State Univ Huntsville TX 77341-1001

HILLIARD, RONNIE LEWIS, PHYSICS. *Current Pos:* PRES, OPTOMECHANICS RES, INC, 81- *Personal Data:* b Havre, Mont, July 17, 37; div; c 3. *Educ:* Whitman Col, BA, 59; Univ Sask, PhD(physics), 64. *Prof Exp:* Res asst, Steward Observ, Univ Ariz, 64-66, asst prof astron & asst astronr, 66-70, res assoc instrumentation, 70-80. *Mem:* Int Astron Union. *Res:* Design and development of systems and techniques for astronomical optical instrumentation. *Mailing Add:* PO Box 87 Vail AZ 85641

HILLIARD, ROY C, CHEMISTRY. *Current Pos:* Chemist, 53-65, supvr flavor res, 65-72, asst mgr prod develop div, 72-75, mgr prod develop div, 75-87, DIR RES, LIGGETT & MYERS TOBACCO CO, 88- *Personal Data:* b Middlesex, NC, May 19, 31; m 57; c 2. *Educ:* Duke Univ, AB, 53. *Mem:* Inst Food Technologists. *Res:* Flavor chemistry of tobacco and related products; panel evaluation of tobacco products; organoleptic chemistry. *Mailing Add:* 3612 Randolph Rd Durham NC 27705-5349

HILLIARD, STEPHEN DALE, EMBRYOLOGY, PHYSIOLOGY. *Current Pos:* PROF BIOL, BALDWIN-WALLACE COL, 72- *Personal Data:* b Greenfield, Ohio, May 30, 39; m 62; c 3. *Educ:* Univ Cincinnati, BS, 64, MS, 66, PhD(physiol), 68. *Prof Exp:* Technician, Gastric Lab, Cincinnati Gen Hosp, Univ Cincinnati, 58-65; lectr biol, Univ Cincinnati, 67-68; from asst prof to assoc prof, Col of the Virgin Islands, 68-72. *Mem:* Soc Develop Biol; Nat Soc Teachers Asn; Am Inst Biol Sci; Sigma Xi. *Res:* Development and electron microscopy. *Mailing Add:* 32611 Carriage Lane Avon Lake OH 44012-1636

HILLIER, FREDERICK STANTON, OPERATIONS RESEARCH. *Current Pos:* From asst prof to assoc prof indust eng, 61-68, PROF OPERS RES, STANFORD UNIV, 68- *Personal Data:* b Aberdeen, Wash, Mar 4, 36; m 58; c 3. *Educ:* Stanford Univ, BS, 58, MS, 59, PhD(indust eng), 61. *Concurrent Pos:* Vis asst prof, Cornell Univ, 62-63; Inst Mgt Sci-Off Naval Res grant, Stanford Univ, 65-66; vis prof, Carnegie-Mellon Univ, 69-70 & Tech Univ Denmark, 76-77; Erskine fel, Univ Canterbury, NZ, 89. *Mem:* Opers Res Soc Am (treas, 74-76); Inst Mgt Sci (vpres, 81-84); Am Inst Indust Eng; Math Prog Soc. *Res:* Queueing theory; mathematical programming; capital budgeting; textbooks in operations research. *Mailing Add:* Dept Opers Res Stanford Univ Stanford CA 94035

HILLIER, JAMES, PHYSICS, RESEARCH ADMINISTRATION. *Current Pos:* CONSULT, 78- *Personal Data:* b Brantford, Ont, Aug 22, 15; nat US; wid; c James R & William W. *Educ:* Univ Toronto, BA, 37, MA, 38, PhD(physics), 41. *Hon Degrees:* Univ Toronto, DSc, 78, NJ Inst Technol, 81. *Honors & Awards:* Albert Lasker Award, Am Pub Health Asn, 60; David Sarnoff Award, Inst Elec & Electronics Engrs, 67, Founders Medal, 81; IRI Medal, Indust Res Inst, 75; Nat Inventors Hall Fame, 80; Common Wealth Award Laureate, 80. *Prof Exp:* Demonstr physics, Univ Toronto, 37-39, asst, Banting Inst, 40; res engr, labs, Radio Corp Am, 40-53; dir res dept, Melpar, Inc, Westinghouse Air Brake Co, 53-54; admin engr, res & eng, RCA Corp, 54-55, chief engr, commercial electronic prod, 55-57, gen mgr, labs, 57-58, vpres, 58-68, vpres, res eng, 68-69, exec vpres res eng, 69-76, exec vpres & sr scientist, 76-78. *Concurrent Pos:* Assoc, Sloan Kettering Inst, 49-51; vis lectr, dept biol, Princeton Univ, 51-53, chmn adv coun, dept elec eng, 65-69; pres, Indust Reactor Labs, 64-65. Mem, indust adv comt, NASA, 62-64, gov bd, Am Inst Physics, 62-65 & Gov NJ Higher Educ Study Comt, 63-64; pres, Indust Res Inst, 63-64; mem comm tech adv bd, US Dept Comm, 64-70; mem adv coun, Col Eng, Cornell Univ, 65-; mem joint consult comt, Acad Sci Res & Technol, Egypt & Nat Acad Sci, 77-85. *Mem:* Nat Acad Eng; fel AAAS; fel Am Phys Soc; Electron Micros Soc Am (vpres, 44, pres, 45); fel Inst Elec & Electronics Engrs; Indust Res Inst (pres, 63). *Res:* Electron microscopy; instrumentation and applications; electron diffraction, instrumentation and applications; electronic methods of microanalysis; biophysics; research management. *Mailing Add:* 22 Arreton Rd Princeton NJ 08540-1402

HILLIER, RICHARD DAVID, ECOLOGY, BOTANY. *Current Pos:* asst prof, 71-76, ASSOC PROF BIOL, UNIV WIS-STEVENS POINT, 76- *Personal Data:* b Boulder, Colo, Sept 3, 38; m 67; c 1. *Educ:* Haverford Col, AB, 60; Duke Univ, PhD(bot), 70. *Prof Exp:* Asst prof biol, Erskine Col, 69-71. *Mem:* Ecol Soc Am; Am Inst Biol Sci; Sigma Xi. *Res:* Plant microenvironments and physiological ecology; vegetation of central Wisconsin; alpine plant distribution. *Mailing Add:* Dept Biol Univ Wis 2100 Main St Stevens Point WI 54481-3871

HILLIG, KURT WALTER, II, MOLECULAR SPECTROSCOPY. *Current Pos:* Postdoctoral scholar, 81-83, ASST RES SCIENTIST, UNIV MICH, 83- *Personal Data:* b Schenectady, NY, Sept 12, 54; m 81. *Educ:* Union Col, NY, BS, 75; Univ Mich, Ann Arbor, MS, 79, PhD(chem), 81. *Concurrent Pos:* Fac fel, NASA/Am Soc Eng Educ/Jet Propulsion Lab, 83 & 84. *Mem:* Am Chem Soc. *Res:* Microwave and millimeter wave spectroscopy to study molecular structures and hyperfine interactions in molecular spectra; instrumentation development for molecular beam; pulsed fourier transform microwave spectroscopy. *Mailing Add:* Dept Chem Univ Mich Ann Arbor MI 48109

HILLIG, WILLIAM BRUNO, CERAMIC MATRIX COMPOSITES, HIGH TEMPERATURE MATERIALS. *Current Pos:* CONSULT & RES PROF MAT ENG, RENSSELAER POLYTECHNIC INST, 90- *Personal Data:* b Detroit, Mich, Oct 3, 24; m 49, Beth E Cook; c Beth C (McKeen), Kurt W II & Karl W. *Educ:* Univ Mich, BS, 44, MS, 48, PhD(phys chem), 54. *Honors & Awards:* S B Meyer Award, Am Ceramic Soc, 63. *Prof Exp:* Res asst inorg mat, Mass Inst Technol, 44-47; instr chem, Univ Mich, 49-52; scientist phys chem, Gen Elec Res & Develop Ctr, 53-63, liaison scientist mat, 63-65, scientist phys chem, 65-69, mgr composites, 69-80, scientist phys chem, 80-90. *Concurrent Pos:* Mem bd assessment, Nat Bur Stand Progs, Mat Sci, 81-87; vol, Tech Assistance, 59-; mem, Assessment Team, Japanese Composite Technol, 90. *Mem:* Fel Am Ceramic Soc; fel AAAS; Am Chem Soc; NY Acad Sci. *Res:* Theory of strength and fracture of materials; ceramic composites; impact phenomena; solidification; kinetics of phase transformations; vitreous state; high temperature materials and coatings; solar reflector devices; magnetochemistry. *Mailing Add:* Rensselaer Polytechnic Inst Troy NY 12180-3590. *Fax:* 518-276-8554; *E-Mail:* hilliw@rpi.edu

HILLIKER, DAVID LEE, PROGRAMMING. *Current Pos:* RETIRED. *Personal Data:* b Los Angeles, Calif, Sept 1, 35. *Educ:* Univ Calif, Los Angeles, AB, 59, MA & PhD(math), 65. *Prof Exp:* Asst prof math, Univ Calif, Irvine, 66-68; Pa State Univ, 68-70; assoc prof, Cleveland State Univ, 70-75; mem staff comput sci, Calif State Univ, Fullerton, 77-79; mem staff math, Univ Calif, Los Angeles, 79-81; mem staff comput sci, Calif State Univ, Dominguez Hills, 81-84; mem staff, Long Beach, 84-89; mem staff comput sci, Calif State Univ, Los Angeles, 90-91. *Concurrent Pos:* NSF grant, 68-69. *Mem:* Am Math Soc; Math Asn Am; Asn Comput Mach. *Res:* Diophantine equations; transcendental numbers; analytic number theory. *Mailing Add:* 2415 Fordham Dr Costa Mesa CA 92626

HILLIS, ARGYE BRIGGS, MEDICAL STATISTICS. *Current Pos:* asst prof, 82-84, ASSOC PROF MED MICROBIOL & IMMUNOL STATIST, TEX A&M UNIV, 84- *Personal Data:* b Borger, Tex, July 27, 33; m 52; c 3. *Educ:* Towson State Col, BS, 68; Johns Hopkins Univ, PhD(biostatist), 74. *Prof Exp:* Asst prof social & prev med, Univ Md, 74-78; asst prof ophthal & statist, Johns Hopkins Univ, 78-83. *Concurrent Pos:* Prin investr, NIH, 78-82 & 88-; ad hoc consult, Nat Eye Inst, NIH, 78; mem panel, NIH Consensus Conf, 88; chmn Biostatist Comt Intraocular Lenses, Food & Drug Admin, 80-82; mem Coun Epidemiol, Am Diabetes Asn; mem, Vision Res Rev Comt, Nat Eye Inst, NIHV, 89-90. *Mem:* Am Statist Asn; Biometrics Soc; Asn Res Vision & Ophthal; Am Pub Health Asn; Soc Clin Trials. *Res:* Design, organize and coordinate collaborative clinical trials, primarily in ophthalmology; clinically oriented research in collaboration with physicians; develop statistical methodology for these studies; mathematical modeling of disease processes and epidemiological phenomena. *Mailing Add:* Dept Stats Tex A&M Univ College Station TX 77843-0100

HILLIS, DAVID MARK, EVOLUTION, SYSTEMATICS. *Current Pos:* from asst prof to assoc prof zool, 85-91, ALFRED W ROARK CENTENNIAL PROF, UNIV TEX, AUSTIN, 91- *Personal Data:* b Copenhagen, Denmark, Dec 21, 58; US citizen; m 80, Ann M Mackie; c Ereckson B & Jonathan D. *Educ:* Baylor Univ, BS, 80; Univ Kans, MA, 83, MPh, 84, PhD(biol sci), 85. *Honors & Awards:* NSF presidential young investr award, 87. *Prof Exp:* Asst prof biol, Univ Miami, 85-87. *Concurrent Pos:* Mem, adv panel, Nat Biol Res Ctr Prog, NSF, 87-88, adv panel, Res Training Groups Prog, 90-91 & Species Survival Comn, World Conserv Union, 90-; ed, Syst Zool, 89-92. *Mem:* Soc Syst Zoologists; Am Soc Ichthyologists & Herpetologists; Soc Study Evolution; AAAS; Herpetologists League; Am Malacological Union. *Res:* Molecular aspects of evolutionary biology; phylogenetic analysis; molecular mechanisms of evolution; systematic theory. *Mailing Add:* Dept Zool Tex Univ Austin TX 78712-1026. *Fax:* 512-471-9651; *E-Mail:* hillis@bull.zo.utexas.edu

HILLIS, LLEWELLYA, coral reefs, molecular evolution, for more information see previous edition

HILLIS, WILLIAM DANIEL, SR, VIROLOGY, NEPHROLOGY. *Current Pos:* prof & chmn biol, 82-86, exec vpres, 85-89, VPRES STUDENT LIFE, BAYLOR UNIV, 89-, CORNELIA MARSHALL SMITH DISTINGUISHED PROF BIOL, 95- *Personal Data:* b Paris, Ark, June 12, 33; m 52, Argye Briggs; c W Daniel Jr, David M & Argye E (Trupe). *Educ:* Baylor Univ, BS, 53; Johns Hopkins Univ, MD, 57. *Honors & Awards:* Louis

Livingston Seaman Prize, Asn Mil Surgeons US. *Prof Exp:* Intern internal med, Johns Hopkins Hosp, Baltimore, Md, 57-58; virologist, USAF Sch Aerospace Med, 60-61, chief epidemiol, Air Force Epidemiol Lab, Lackland AFB, Tex, 62-65; assoc prof pathobiol, Sch Hyg, 68-82, Sch Med, Johns Hopkins Univ, from asst prof to assoc prof med, Sch Med, 72-82. *Concurrent Pos:* Fel pathobiol, Sch Hyg, Johns Hopkins Univ, 58-60; vis scientist, State Serum Inst, Copenhagen, Denmark, 58-60, Yerkes Labs Primate Biol, Orange Park, Fla, 61-62 & Delta Regional Primate Res Ctr, Tulane Univ, 64-65; chief virol, Johns Hopkins Univ Ctr for Med Res & Training, Calcutta, India, 68-70, resident coordr, 70; resident renology, Johns Hopkins Hosp, Baltimore, 71-72, dir Outpatient Dept, Clin Res Ctr, 73-82. *Mem:* AAAS; Am Soc Microbiol; Aerospace Med Asn; Soc Exp Biol & Med; NY Acad Sci; Sigma Xi; Am Asn Immunol. *Res:* Epidemiology of virus infections of man and animals; in vitro growth and characterization of viruses; serological and immunological aspects of virus infections; pathology of renal diseases of man; clinical aspects of hemodialysis and transplantation. *Mailing Add:* Baylor Univ PO Box 97016 Waco TX 76798-7016. *Fax:* 254-755-3843; *E-Mail:* william_hillis@baylor.edu

HILLMAN, ABRAHAM P, MATHEMATICS. *Current Pos:* assoc prof, 65-67, PROF MATH, UNIV NMEX, 67- *Personal Data:* b Brooklyn, NY, Dec 18, 18; m 55. *Educ:* Brooklyn Col, BA, 39, MA, 40; Princeton Univ, PhD(math), 50. *Prof Exp:* Asst mathematician, Nat Bur Stand, 41-43, mathematician, 45-48; asst, Princeton Univ, 43-44, instr, 44-45; instr, Columbia Univ, 50-56, asst prof, Wash State Univ, 56-57; from asst prof to assoc prof, Univ Santa Clara, 57-65. *Mem:* Math Asn Am; Am Math Soc; Fibonacci Asn. *Res:* Differential algebra; combinatorial analysis. *Mailing Add:* 709 Solano Dr SE Albuquerque NM 87108-3382

HILLMAN, DEAN ELOF, NEUROBIOLOGY. *Current Pos:* PROF PHYSIOL, SCH MED, NY UNIV, 76- *Personal Data:* b Shell Lake, Wis, Nov 26, 36; m 59; c 3. *Educ:* Gustavus Adolphus Col, BS, 59; Univ NDak, MS, 62, PhD(anat), 64. *Prof Exp:* NIH fel, Marquette Univ, 64-65; asst prof anat, Sch Med, Wayne State Univ, 65; asst mem neurobiol, Inst Biomed Res, AMA, 67-70; from assoc prof to prof physiol & biophys, Univ Iowa, 70-76. *Concurrent Pos:* Mem study sect neurol B, NIH, 71-75. *Mem:* Soc Neurosci; AAAS; Am Asn Anatomists; NY Acad Sci. *Res:* Neuronal form; components and connections of the cerebellum and vestibular system studied by use of Golgi impregnations, electron microscopy, degeneration techniques and three dimensional reconstruction. *Mailing Add:* Dept Physiol NY Univ Sch Med 550 First Ave New York NY 10016. *Fax:* 212-263-9462

HILLMAN, DONALD, DAIRY NUTRITION & ECONOMICS, ANIMALS. *Current Pos:* 4-H Club Agent Genesee Co, Mich State Univ, 53-55, exten dairy spe cialist, 55-82, prof dairy, 59-82, EMER PROF ANIMAL SCI, MICH STATE UNIV, 82-; pvt consult res & sales, 82- *Personal Data:* b Deckerville, Mich, Jan 10, 29; m 51, Mary A Richardson; c Donald L, Louis R, Richard L, Mary Lea (Schwaner), Christine M (Lacroix), Ann M (Flood) & Lisa M (Rolka). *Educ:* Mich State Univ, BS, 51, MS, 56, PhD(dairy), 59. *Honors & Awards:* Super Serv Award, USDA, 74. *Prof Exp:* Instr voc agr, Pub Schs, Mich, 51-53. *Concurrent Pos:* Consult, Dairy Prod & Econs, 82- *Mem:* Am Dairy Sci Asn; Am Soc Animal Sci. *Res:* Feed preservation, processing and feeding value; nutrient requirements for growth and milk production, computer ration formulation; cattle feeding and management; fluoride and iodide toxicities; animal waste management and odor control; agricultural education; effects of electrical stress on cattle; dairy farm economics and loss estimation expert witness. *Mailing Add:* 750 Berkshire Lane East Lansing MI 48823-2745. *Fax:* 517-351-1944

HILLMAN, DONALD ARTHUR, pediatrics, endocrinology, for more information see previous edition

HILLMAN, ELIZABETH S, PEDIATRICS, TOXICOLOGY. *Current Pos:* PROF PEDIAT, MEM UNIV, ST JOHNS, NFLD, 76- *Personal Data:* b Ont; m 55; c 5. *Educ:* Univ Western Ont, MD, 51. *Prof Exp:* Dir ambulatory pediat, Montreal Children's Hosp, 57-69, dir poison ctr, 58-69; asst prof pediat, McGill Univ, 60-69; sr lectr, Univ Nairobi, 69-71; assoc prof pediat, McGill Univ, 71-74; dir, Ambulatory Pediat & Poison Ctr, Montreal Children's Hosp, 71-74; sr lectr pediat, Univ Nairobi, Kenya, 74-76. *Concurrent Pos:* Pres, Med Coun Can, 81-82. *Mem:* Can Paediat Soc; Am Acad Pediat. *Res:* Community pediatrics; prevention of poisoning. *Mailing Add:* Ctr Int Health & Develop Dept Med, Univ Ottawa 501 Smyth Ont NF K1H 8L6 Can

HILLMAN, GILBERT R, NEUROPHARMACOLOGY, BIOCHEMISTRY. *Current Pos:* assoc prof, 76-85, assoc dir acad comput, 89-96, PROF PHARMACOL, UNIV TEX MED BR, GALVESTON, 85- *Personal Data:* b New Haven, Conn, May 1, 43; m 65, Rachel Read; c Laura. *Educ:* Harvard Univ, BA, 65; Yale Univ, PhD(pharmacol), 69. *Prof Exp:* Conn Heart Asn fel, Yale Univ, 69-70; instr, Brown Univ, 70-71, asst prof med sci, 71-76. *Concurrent Pos:* Res grants, NIH & Dept Defense. *Mem:* AAAS; Am Soc Pharmacol & Exp Therapeut; NY Acad Sci; Inst Elec & Electronics Engrs. *Res:* Pharmacology of synapses; computer applications in histochemistry; computer image analysis. *Mailing Add:* Dept Pharmacol Univ Tex Med Br Galveston TX 77555-1031

HILLMAN, MANNY, ORGANOMETALLIC & NUCLEAR CHEMISTRY. *Current Pos:* RETIRED. *Personal Data:* b St Louis, Mo, Nov 8, 28; m 53, Ruth Bender; c David & Ben. *Educ:* Brooklyn Col, AB, 49; Wash Univ, PhD(chem), 53. *Prof Exp:* Instr chem, Brooklyn Col, 49-50; asst, Wash Univ, 50-52, instr, 53; res fel, Wayne State Univ, 55-56; sr res chemist, Olin Mathieson Chem Co, 56-59; chemist, Brookhaven Nat Lab, 59-62, group leader, 62-86, consult, 86-88. *Concurrent Pos:* Asst, Brookhaven Nat Lab, 51; Nat Acad Sci exchange fel, US & Hungary, 74; adj prof, Southampton Col, 74-; vis prof, Weizmann Inst Sci, 75-76; adj prof, State Univ NY, Binghamton, 81-86. *Mem:* Sigma Xi; AAAS. *Res:* Metallocene chemistry; organic chemical reactions; chemistry of boranes; numerical analysis; nuclear structure and reactions; hot atom chemistry. *Mailing Add:* 22 Bayview Ave Blue Point NY 11715

HILLMAN, RALPH, GENETICS, CELL BIOLOGY & DEVELOPMENT. *Current Pos:* from asst prof to assoc prof, 60-71, chmn dept, 64-67 & 85-88, PROF BIOL, TEMPLE UNIV, 71- *Personal Data:* b Bridgeport, Conn, Apr 9, 29; m 60, Nina Williams; c Tara L. *Educ:* Stanford Univ, BA, 51; Yale Univ, PhD, 57. *Prof Exp:* Asst zool, Yale Univ, 51-56; instr, Univ Conn, 56-57; instr biol, Univ Pa, 57-60. *Concurrent Pos:* Vis scientist, Univ Sussex, 70. *Mem:* Genetics Soc Am; Am Soc Zool; Sigma Xi; fel AAAS; Am Soc Cell Biol. *Res:* Developmental and physiological genetics of drosophila; phenotypic expression at the cellular and morphological level of polygenic systems affecting protein synthesis; neurochemical control of development. *Mailing Add:* Dept Biol Temple Univ Philadelphia PA 19122. *Fax:* 215-204-6646; *E-Mail:* rhillman@thunder.ocis.temple.edu

HILLMAN, RICHARD EPHRAIM, METABOLISM, MEDICAL GENETICS. *Current Pos:* PROF CHILD HEALTH & BIOCHEM & DIR METAB GENETICS, UNIV MO, COLUMBIA, 87- *Personal Data:* b Pawtucket, RI, Oct 6, 40; m 70, Laura Smith; c 6. *Educ:* Brown Univ, AB, 62; Yale Univ, MD, 65; Am Bd Pediat, dipl, 71. *Prof Exp:* Fel genetics & metab, Yale Univ, 67-69; staff pediat, metab & genetics, Nat Naval Med Ctr, 69-71; from asst prof to assoc prof pediat, Sch Med Wash Univ, 71-78, assoc prof genetics, 78-81, dir, Endocrinol & Metab, 79-85, prof pediat, 78-87, prof genetics, 81-87, dir genetics, 85-87. *Concurrent Pos:* Dir, Metab Screening Labs, St Louis Children's Hosp, 71-87. *Mem:* Soc Pediat Res; Am Acad Pediat; Am Soc Human Genetics; Am Soc Clin Invest; Soc Inherited Metab Disorders (pres-elect, 81, pres, 82). *Res:* Study of metabolism of amino acids by cultured cells. *Mailing Add:* Dept Child Health Univ Mo One Hosp Dr Columbia MO 65212

HILLMAN, ROBERT B, VETERINARY MEDICINE & LARGE ANIMAL REPRODUCTION, VETERINARY ACUPUNCTURE. *Current Pos:* med intern large animal med, ambulatory clin, NY State Vet Col, Cornell Univ, 58-60, Nat Inst Allergy & Infectious Dis res fel, 60-61, from asst prof to assoc prof large animal med, 61-71, SR CLINICIAN, NY STATE VET COL, CORNELL UNIV, 71- *Personal Data:* b Hancock, NY, Jan 23, 30; m 64, Beverly Brink; c Denley, Alison & Robert. *Educ:* Syracuse Univ, BA, 51; Cornell Univ, DVM, 55, MS, 61. *Prof Exp:* US Army, Vet Corp, 55-57; pvt & mixed pract, NY, 57-58. *Mem:* Am Vet Med Asn; NY Acad Sci; Am Asn Equine Practr; Am Asn Bovine Practr; Am Asn Small Ruminant Practr; Int Vet Acupuncture Soc. *Res:* Bovine mycotic abortion; plant poisonings in large animals; artificial insemination in mares; cyclic and seasonal changes in hormone levels in mare; bovine fetal serology; induction of parturition in mares; vet acupuncture. *Mailing Add:* NY State Vet Col Cornell Univ Ithaca NY 14850. *Fax:* 607-253-3056; *E-Mail:* rbh7@cornell.edu

HILLMAN, ROBERT EDWARD, PATHOLOGY. *Current Pos:* sr marine biologist, 65-68, sr res scientist, 68-90, RES LEADER, BATTELLE MEM INST, 90- *Personal Data:* b Brooklyn, NY, Nov 5, 33; div; c Jennifer A & Stephanie J. *Educ:* Hofstra Univ, BA, 55, MA, 58; Univ Del, PhD(zool), 62. *Prof Exp:* Assoc invert zool, Marine Biol Lab, Univ Del, 61-62; res assoc shellfish genetics, Natural Resources Inst, Univ Md, 62-64, res asst prof, 64-65. *Concurrent Pos:* NSF grant, Univ Md, 64-66; ed, Proc Nat Shellfisheries Asn, 75-80, J Shellfish Res, 80-82. *Mem:* AAAS; Am Soc Zoologists; Soc Invert Path; Nat Shellfisheries Asn (vpres, 83-84, pres-elect, 84-85, pres, 85-86); Am Fisheries Soc; Sigma Xi. *Res:* Genetics, histology, histochemistry and histopathology of marine invertebrates; oceanography and estuarine ecology. *Mailing Add:* Battelle Mem Inst 397 Washington St Duxbury MA 02332-4505. *Fax:* 781-934-2124

HILLMAN, STANLEY SEVERIN, COMPARATIVE PHYSIOLOGY, PHYSIOLOGICAL ECOLOGY. *Current Pos:* from asst prof to assoc prof, 77-85, PROF BIOL, PORTLAND STATE UNIV, 85- *Personal Data:* b Chicago, Ill, Feb 4, 48; m 76, Deborah Duffield; c 2. *Educ:* Calif State Univ, Fullerton, BA, 70, MA, 72; Univ Calif, Los Angeles, PhD(biol), 77. *Prof Exp:* Lectr biol, Univ Calif, Riverside, 76-77. *Mem:* Am Soc Ichthyologists & Herpetologists; Am Physiol Soc; Am Soc Zoologists; Herpetologists League. *Res:* Cardiovascular consequences of hyperosmolality and hypovolemia; physiology of activity metabolism in lower vertebrates. *Mailing Add:* Dept Biol Portland State Univ PO Box 751 Portland OR 97207-0751. *Fax:* 503-725-4751

HILLNER, EDWARD, METALLURGICAL CHEMISTRY, METALLURGICAL ENGINEERING. *Current Pos:* RETIRED. *Personal Data:* b Bronx, NY, Apr 1, 29; m 51, Beatrice Bizoff; c David Scott & Elaine (Lau). *Educ:* City Col New York, BS, 51; NY Univ, MS, 53, PhD(chem), 55. *Prof Exp:* From metall engr to sr metall engr, Westinghouse Elec Corp, 57-71, fel engr, 71-82, adv engr, Bettis Atomic Power Div, 82-92. *Concurrent Pos:* Consult, Elec Power Res Inst, 78-80 & Westinghouse Elec Corp, 96. *Mem:* Nat Asn Corrosion Engrs. *Res:* High temperature oxidation and corrosion of refractory metals and plant materials. *Mailing Add:* 322 Cavan Dr Pittsburgh PA 15236. *E-Mail:* ehillner@aol.com

HILLOOWALA, RUMY ARDESHIR, ANATOMY & HISTORY ANATOMY, PHYSICAL ANTHROPOLOGY. *Current Pos:* from instr to asst prof, 70-75, ASSOC PROF ANAT, WVA UNIV, 75- *Personal Data:* b Surat, India, Dec 20, 35; m 65, Julianne Stauffer; c Franak & Yasmin. *Educ:* Univ Bombay, BDent Surg, 60; Univ Pa; Howard Univ, MS, 65; Univ Ala, Birmingham, PhD(anat), 70. *Prof Exp:* Intern oral surg, Goculdas Tejpal Hosp, Bombay, 60; resident anesthesiol, George Washington Univ Hosp, 61-62; scientist, Bionetics Res Labs, 64-66; instr anat, Med Ctr, Univ Ala, Birmingham, 66-69. *Mem:* Am Asn Anat; Am Asn Phys Anthrop; Int Primatological Soc; Am Asn Hist Med; Smithsonian Inst; Int Soc Hist Med. *Res:* Evolution and phylogeny in relation to human anatomy; primate anatomy; cranio-facial development (post-natal) in fossil man, apes and modern human; history of anatomy especially in relation to Renaissance art; XVIII century anatomical wax models. *Mailing Add:* Dept Anat WVa Univ Med Ctr Morgantown WV 26506. *Fax:* 304-293-8159

HILLS, CLAUDE HIBBARD, FOOD SCIENCE. *Current Pos:* RETIRED. *Personal Data:* b Kirksville, Mo, June 21, 12; m 40, Signe L Haughom; c Andrew W, Robert C (deceased), Thomas E & James H. *Educ:* Northeast Mo State Teachers Col, BS, 33; Univ Mo, MA, 35; Univ Minn, PhD(agr biochem), 37. *Honors & Awards:* Superior Serv Award, US Dept Agr, 67. *Prof Exp:* Asst horticulturist, Univ Mo, 34-35; asst biochemist, Univ Minn, 36-37; res chemist, Borden Co, NY, 37-38; Hormel res fel, Univ Minn, 38-40; assoc chemist, protein div, Bur Agr Chem & Eng, 41-42 & Bur Agr & Indust Chem, Sci & Educ Admin, Agr Res, USDA, 42-45, chemist, 45-53, chemist, Eastern Regional Res Lab, 53-77, head fruit prod sect, 48-73, head maple syrup sect, 73-77. *Mem:* Am Chem Soc; Am Soc Hort Sci; assoc mem NAm Maple Syrup Coun; Inst Food Technologists. *Res:* Tobacco mosaic virus; amylases of barley; milk solids in baked products; meat processing; pectin; fruit products; maple syrup. *Mailing Add:* 510 E Valley Green Rd Flourtown PA 19031

HILLS, FRANCIS ALLAN, URANIUM GEOCHEMISTRY, PETROLOGY GRANITE. *Current Pos:* GEOLOGIST, US GEOL SURV, DENVER, COLO, 75- *Personal Data:* b Charleston, SC, Aug 17, 34; m 62, Sonia Mehech; c Mark, Robert & Valerie. *Educ:* Univ NC, BS, 56; Yale Univ, PhD(geol), 65. *Prof Exp:* Res fel geol, Univ Minn, 62-65; res staff geologist, Yale Univ, 65-68; asst prof geol, State Univ NY Buffalo, 68-75. *Mem:* AAAS; Geol Soc Am. *Res:* Uranium in Precambrian rocks; geochronology and tectonics of Proterozolc-Archean boundary; origin of Anorthosite-syenite; uranium and gold in Precambrian conglomerate; geochemistry of granite; geochronology; strontium isotopes in evaporite rocks. *Mailing Add:* 3850 Hoyt St Wheat Ridge CO 80033

HILLS, HOWARD KENT, SPACE SCIENCE. *Current Pos:* SR SCIENTIST, SIGMA DATA SERV CORP, 78-; CHIEF SCIENTIST, HUGHES STX, 86- *Personal Data:* b Mt Pleasant, Iowa, Sept 21, 38; m 60; c 3. *Educ:* Univ Iowa, BA, 61, MS, 64, PhD(space physics), 67. *Prof Exp:* Asst prof physics, Iowa Wesleyan Col, 67-68; res assoc, Rice Univ, 68-71, sr res assoc space sci, 71-78. *Mem:* Am Geophys Union. *Res:* Particles and fields in the earth's magnetosphere, in interplanetary space and in the lunar surface environment. *Mailing Add:* 7003 Kingfisher Lane Lanham MD 20706

HILLS, JACK GILBERT, THEORETICAL ASTROPHYSICS. *Current Pos:* actg group leader, Theoret Astrophys Group, 91-96, MEM STAFF, LOS ALAMOS NAT LAB, 81-, DEP GROUP LEADER, 83- *Personal Data:* b Keflavik, Iceland, May 15, 43; US citizen; m 86, Cynthia L Zeller; c Erica A. *Educ:* Univ Kans, AB, 66, MA, 67; Univ Mich, Ann Arbor, MS, 67, PhD(astron), 69. *Prof Exp:* From instr to asst prof astron, Univ Mich, Ann Arbor, 69-76; asst prof, Univ Ill, Urbana, 76-77; from assoc prof astron-astrophys to prof physics & astron, Mich State Univ, East Lansing, 77-83. *Mem:* Am Astron Soc; Royal Astron Soc; Int Astron Union; fel Am Phys Soc. *Res:* Stellar dynamics; quasi-stellar objects; earth-crossing asteroids and comets. *Mailing Add:* Los Alamos Nat Lab PO Box 1663 Mail Stop B288 Los Alamos NM 87545. *Fax:* 505-665-4055; *E-Mail:* jgh@agn.lanl.gov

HILLS, JOHN MOORE, GEOLOGY. *Current Pos:* RETIRED. *Personal Data:* b Oak Park, Ill, Mar 15, 10; c 3. *Educ:* Lafayette Col, BS, 31; Univ Chicago, PhD(geol), 34. *Prof Exp:* Asst geologist, Amerada Petrol Corp, 34-41; prof, Univ Tex, El Paso, 67-80; consult geologist, 41-; emer prof geol, Univ Tex, El Paso, 80-84. *Concurrent Pos:* Vis lectr, Univ Tex, 59-60; partner, Penn, Hills & Turner, Consult Geologists, 67- *Mem:* fel Geol Soc Am; Am Inst Mining, Metall & Petrol Engrs; hon mem Am Asn Petrol Geologists; Sigma Xi. *Res:* Permian stratigraphy; oil field structure; microscopic examination of well cuttings; petroleum geology; oil and gas property exploration and appraisal; structural geology of West Texas and New Mexico. *Mailing Add:* 1575 Belvidere St El Paso TX 79912

HILLS, LEONARD VINCENT, GEOLOGY. *Current Pos:* asst prof to assoc prof, 66-74, PROF GEOL, UNIV CALGARY, 74- *Personal Data:* b Judah, Alta, Jan 3, 33; m 59; c 2. *Educ:* Univ BC, BSc, 60, MSc, 62; Univ Alta, PhD, 65. *Prof Exp:* Explor palynologist, Shell Can, 65-66. *Concurrent Pos:* Ed, Arctic, Jour of Arctic Inst NAm; co-ed, Arctic Profiles, 88-; adj res scientist, Tyrrell Mus Palaeont, 88-; adj prof, fac environ design, Univ Calgary. *Mem:* Can Soc Petrol Geologists (pres, 79); Am Asn Stratig Palynologists; fel Arctic Inst NAm. *Res:* Devonian-Tertiary-Pleistocene palynology; stratigraphy. *Mailing Add:* Dept Geol & Geophys Univ Calgary 2500 University Dr Calgary AB T2N 1N4 Can

HILLS, LORAN C, BIOCHEMISTRY. *Current Pos:* from instr to assoc prof, 61-70, dir, Med Lab Technician Prog, 71-81, PROF CHEM, DAKOTA WESLEYAN UNIV, 70-, HEAD DEPT, 65-, HEAD, NAT SCI DIV, 70-, DIR, COMPUT SCI PROG, 81- *Personal Data:* b Oacoma, NDak, May 15, 25; m 47; c 3. *Educ:* Black Hills State Col, BS, 50; Stanford Univ, MA, 58; SDak State Univ, 63-64. *Prof Exp:* Teacher, high schs, Wyo, 50-51, SDak, 51-61. *Mem:* Sigma Xi. *Res:* Selenium metabolism. *Mailing Add:* 1313 E Fifth Ave Mitchell SD 57301

HILLS, STANLEY, ELECTROCHEMISTRY. *Current Pos:* RETIRED. *Personal Data:* b New York, NY, June 4, 30; m 53, 88, Anne A Pinkowitz; c Kevin A & Karen B (Brown). *Educ:* City Col New York, BS, 52; Duke Univ, MA, 54, PhD(phys chem), 56. *Prof Exp:* Res electrochemist, Reynolds Metals Co, 55-56 & Yardney Elec Co, 56-61; instr chem, City Col New York, 58-60; head, silver cadmium lab, Elec Storage Battery Co, 61-66, head basic develop chem, 66-69; sr electrochemist, Switchgear Bus Div, Gen Elec Co, 69-83, process develop engr, Space Systs Div, 83-92. *Concurrent Pos:* Co-adj assoc prof chem, Rutgers Univ, 71-74. *Mem:* Am Chem Soc; Electrochem Soc; Sigma Xi. *Res:* Plating processes; corrosion studies; pollution control; electrodeposition of alloys and organic polymers; battery electrode processes; battery active materials development. *Mailing Add:* 1224 Heartwood Dr Cherry Hill NJ 08003. *E-Mail:* stannhills@msn.com

HILLSMAN, MATTHEW JEROME, PHYSICS, ADMINISTRATIVE MANAGEMENT. *Current Pos:* ARCHAEOLOGIST, PHYSICIST & MUS CUR, BLACKWATER DRAW MUS, EASTERN NMEX UNIV, 92- *Personal Data:* b Crucible, Pa, Oct 1, 35; div; c Carl Eric & Ian Higham. *Educ:* Pa State Univ, BS, 61; Eastern NMex Univ, MA, 92. *Prof Exp:* Physicist optical systs, Naval Underwater Sound Lab, Conn, 61-67; physicist & bio-instrumentation technologist biomed measurements & instrumentation systs technol, Electronics Res Ctr, NASA, 67-70; physicist & admin mgr, Optical Systs & Admin Mgt, Naval Underwater Systs Ctr, Conn, 71-85. *Concurrent Pos:* Physicist & consult biomed systs, 69-71. *Mem:* AAAS; Optical Soc Am; Am Inst Physics; Soc Am Archaeol. *Res:* Optical/spectroscopic characterization of cherts and related lithics and ceramics; submarine optical and electromagnetic communication systems, including near infrared communications, low light level telescopes and television, periscopes and radio communications. *Mailing Add:* PO Box 2886 Eastern NMex Univ Portales NM 88130. *E-Mail:* hillsman@ziavms.enmu.edu

HILLSON, CHARLES JAMES, PLANT ANATOMY, PLANT MORPHOLOGY. *Current Pos:* From instr to prof bot, Buckhout Lab, 53-89, EMER PROF BOT, MUELLER LAB, PA STATE UNIV, 89- *Personal Data:* b Monroeville, Ohio, Dec 18, 26; m 58, Patricia Fulmer; c Carolyn. *Educ:* Bowling Green State Univ, BS(educ) & BS(biol), 50; Univ Miami, MS, 52; Pa State Univ, PhD(bot), 57. *Mem:* AAAS; Bot Soc Am; Phycol Soc Am; Int Oceanog Found. *Res:* Developmental anatomy; morphology, particularly the phylogenetic specialization of vascular tissue; morphology of lower plants. *Mailing Add:* 128 W Doris Ave State College PA 16801-5921

HILLSTROM, WARREN WILLIAM, SURFACE CHEMISTRY, COMBUSTION CHEMISTRY. *Current Pos:* TEAM LEADER, US ARMY RES LAB, 92- *Personal Data:* b Chicago, Ill, July 29, 35; m 63. *Educ:* Earlham Col, BA, 58; Univ Cincinnati, PhD(org chem), 63. *Prof Exp:* Asst proj chemist, Am Oil Co, 63-64, develop chemist, Amoco Chem Corp, 64-68; proj leader, Ballistic Res Lab, 68-92. *Mem:* Am Chem Soc; Sigma Xi; Am Defense Preparedness Asn. *Res:* High temperature metal oxidation; solid-solid reactions; lubricant additives; liquid surface effects; liquid pool fires; explosive formulation. *Mailing Add:* 808 Stiles Ct Joppa MD 21085-1321

HILLYARD, IRA WILLIAM, TOXICOLOGY, TERATOLOGY. *Current Pos:* assoc prof & dir, poison control & drug info, Idaho Drug Info & Regional Poison Control Ctr, 77-79, dean Col Pharm, 79-86, PROF PHARMACOL & TOXICOL, COL PHARM, IDAHO STATE UNIV, 79- *Personal Data:* b Richmond, Utah, Mar 23, 24; m 70; c 3. *Educ:* Idaho State Col, Pocatello, BS, 49; Univ Nebr, Lincoln, MS, 51; St Louis Univ, PhD(pharmacol), 57. *Prof Exp:* Instr, Col Pharm, Univ Nebr, 49-51; dir, Pharm Serv, US Naval Hosp, Oakland, Calif, 51-53; instr, pharmacol dept, Med Sch, St Louis Univ, 53-57; sr pharmacologist, dept pharmacol, Mead Johnson & Co, 57-59; sr res assoc, dept pharmacol, Warner-Lambert Res Inst, 59-69; assoc prof pharmacol, Col Pharm, Idaho State Univ, 69-73; dir, Pharmacol & Toxicol Res, ICN Pharmaceut, Inc, Irvine, Calif, 73-77. *Concurrent Pos:* Continuing ed lectr, Am Optom Asn, 70-77; sci rev, Drug Interaction Panel, Am Pharmaceut Asn, 73-76; consult, ICN Pharmaceut, Inc, Irvine, Calif, 78-80, Pennwalt Corp, Rochester, NY, 79-82. *Mem:* Am Soc Pharmacol & Exp Therapeut; NY Acad Sci; Am Pharmaceut; Am Asn Col Pharm; Am Acad Pharmaceut Sci. *Res:* Assessment of adverse effects caused by maternal drug-taking on the developing embryo or surviving newborn; terato logic evaluations of commonly used and abused-over-the counter and social drugs. *Mailing Add:* 2750 Mt Borah Pl Pocatello ID 83201-0001

HILLYARD, STANLEY DONALD, EPITHELIAL TRANSPORT. *Current Pos:* ASSOC PROF BIOL, UNIV NEV, 76- *Educ:* Univ Calif, Riverside, PhD(biol), 74. *Res:* Changes in the ionic channels in cell membranes of amphibian skin during metamorphosis. *Mailing Add:* Dept Biol Sci Univ Nev Las Vegas 4505 Maryland Pkwy Las Vegas NV 89154-4004. *Fax:* 702-895-3956

HILLYARD, STEVEN ALLEN, NEUROPSYCHOLOGY. *Current Pos:* From asst prof to assoc prof, 71-80, PROF NEUROSCI, UNIV CALIF, SAN DIEGO, 80- *Personal Data:* b Long Beach, Calif, Oct 8, 42; m 66; c 2. *Educ:* Calif Inst Technol, BS, 64; Yale Univ, PhD(psychol), 68. *Concurrent Pos:* USPHS grant neurosci, Univ Calif, San Diego, 68-70; consult, NIH, NSF & study sect, NIMH. *Mem:* Fel AAAS; Soc Neurosci. *Res:* Brain electrophysiology and behavior; perception and information processing. *Mailing Add:* Dept Neurosci M-008 Univ Calif San Diego Med Sch 9500 Gilman Dr La Jolla CA 92093-5003

HILLYER, GEORGE VANZANDT, IMMUNOLOGY & PARASITOLOGY, PATHOLOGY & MICROBIOLOGY. *Current Pos:* From asst prof to prof parasitol & immunol, Univ PR, 72-80, assoc prof path, 76-80, prof parasitol immunol, 80-87, prof & chmn, Dept Biol, Col Natural Sci, 81-87, PROF PATH & LAB MED, MED SCI CAMPUS, UNIV PR, SAN JUAN, 80-, ASSOC DEAN BIOMED SCI & DIR GRAD STUDIES, SCH MED, 95- *Personal Data:* b Santurce, PR, Dec 8, 43; US citizen; m 68, Josilina Glomez; c 2. *Educ:* Univ PR, BS, 67; Univ Chicago, PhD(parasite immunol), 72. *Honors & Awards:* Henry Baldwin Ward Medal, Am Soc Parasitologists, 82; Bailey K Ashford Award, Am Soc Trop Med & Hyg, 86; Carrion Award, Soc Microbiol PR. *Concurrent Pos:* Sr scientist (ad honorem), PR Nuclear Ctr, 72-; consult immunologist, parasitologist, Vet Admin Ctr, San Juan, PR, 73-, Div Res Resources, NIH, 75- & Trop Med & Parasitol Study Sect, NIH, 80-85; dir training prog, Fac Nat Sci, Univ PR, Rio Piedras, 74-; adj assoc prof trop med & parasitol, Sch Pub Health & Trop Med, Tulane Univ, 79-81, prof, 81-; James W McLaughlin vis prof, Univ Tex Med Br, Galveston, 85; Rockefeller Found fel, Dept Path, Univ Cambridge, Eng, 85; dir parasitic dis res prog, PR, 85-, Lab Parasite Immunol & Path, 87-; mem, Microbiol & Infectious Dis Rev Comt, NIH-NIAID, 89-93, mem rev res, 93-97; pres, Caribbean Div, AAAS, 90-91; post-doctorate res fel, Howard Hughes Med Inst Physicians Res Panel, 90-91. *Mem:* Am Asn Immunologists; Am Soc Parasitologists; Am Soc Trop Med & Hyg; fel Royal Soc Trop Med & Hyg; Am Soc Microbiol; Soc Exp Biol & Med; Soc Microbiol PR (pres, 79-80); (Soc Allergy & Immunol PR (pres, 87-91); Sigma Xi; fel AAAS; fel Am Acad Microbiol. *Res:* Immunology and molecular biology of parasitic infections; AIDS. *Mailing Add:* Himalaya 254 Monterrey Urb Rio Piedras PR 00926. *Fax:* 787-751-9210; *E-Mail:* g_hillger@rcmaca.upr.clu.edu

HILLYER, IRVIN GEORGE, HORTICULTURE. *Current Pos:* RETIRED. *Personal Data:* b Thief River Falls, Minn, Dec 1, 27. *Educ:* NDak Agr Col, BS, 51; Univ Idaho, MS, 53; Mich State Univ, PhD(hort), 56. *Prof Exp:* Asst hort, Mich State Univ, 53-56; from asst prof to prof agr, Southern Ill Univ, Carbondale, 56-94. *Mem:* Am Soc Hort Sci; Am Soc Plant Physiol. *Res:* Physiology of vegetable crops; growth regulators and their effects on flowering and fruiting of plants. *Mailing Add:* RR 2 1032 Koonce Rd Murphysboro IL 62966

HILMAS, DUANE EUGENE, RADIATION BIOLOGY, VETERINARY MEDICINE. *Current Pos:* DIR HEALTH EFFECTS, ROCKY FLATS ENVIRON TECHNOL SITE, 91- *Personal Data:* b Virginia, Minn, Jan 6, 38; m 61, Barbara L Heldman; c Gregory E, Kenneth D, Arie T, Corey J & Natalie L. *Educ:* Univ Minn, BS, 59, DVM, 61; Univ NC, MSPH, 64; Colo State Univ, PhD(radiation biol), 72; Am Bd Vet Pub Health, dipl, 75. *Honors & Awards:* Army Commendation Medal, US Army Labs, 66; Army Commendation Medal First Oak Leaf Cluster, US Army Med Res & Develop Command, 69; Meritorious Serv Medal, US Army Res Inst Infectious Dis, 77; Legion of Merit, US Army Med Res & Develop Command, 85. *Prof Exp:* Vet pract, Cloquet, Minn, 61-62; asst vet, Martin Army Hosp, Ft Benning, Ga, 62-63; asst food irradiation, Natick Labs, US Army, 64-66, asst chief, Med Res Div, Med Res & Develop Command, 66-69, chief, Animal Assessment Div, Med Res Inst Infectious Dis, 72-77, chief, Off Irradiated Food, 77-79, res mgr, Med Defense Against Chem Agents, Med Res & Develop Command, 79-82, chief, Drug Assessment Div, Med Res Inst Chem Defense, 82-83, dir & comdr, 83-85; sr prog mgr, Biol & Chem Tech Ctr, Battelle, 85-91. *Concurrent Pos:* Consult radiobiol, Surg Gen, Dept Army, 75-; clin asst prof, Hershey Med Ctr, Pa State Univ, 76-79; Army Med Dept Liaison Radiation Study Sect, NIH, 78-85. *Mem:* Am Vet Med Asn; Sigma Xi; Health Physics Soc; Radiation Res Soc; Soc Exp Biol & Med; Risk Assessment Soc. *Res:* Radiation oncology and experimental therapy; in vivo and in vitro immunobiology; antiviral chemotherapy and combined therapy modalities; radiation and infection; comparative toxicologic assessments in experimental animals; chemical agent pretreatment, therapy and protection; toxicology. *Mailing Add:* 7523 Estate Circle Niwot CO 80503. *Fax:* 303-966-2873

HILPMAN, PAUL LORENZ, GENERAL ENVIRONMENTAL SCIENCES. *Current Pos:* prof, 74-91, EMER PROF GEOSCI, UNIV MO, KANSAS CITY, 91- *Personal Data:* b New York, NY, Feb 3, 32; m, Carol Stempfly; c 5. *Educ:* Brown Univ, AB, 54; Univ Kans, AM, 56, PhD, 59. *Prof Exp:* Geologist, Oil & Gas Div, State Geol Surv Kans, 55-62, div head, 62-65, sect chief environ geol, 65-74; assoc prof geol, Univ Kans, 70-74. *Concurrent Pos:* Consult, 15- *Mem:* Fel Geol Soc Am; Am Inst Prof Geologists; Asn Eng Geologists. *Res:* Engineering and environmental geology; urban planning; foundation damage. *Mailing Add:* Geosci Dept Univ Mo 5100 Rock Hill Rd Kansas City MO 64110. *Fax:* 816-587-9980; *E-Mail:* philpman@umkc.edu

HILSENHOFF, WILLIAM LEROY, ENTOMOLOGY, AQUATIC INSECTS. *Current Pos:* Proj assoc entom, 57-60, from asst prof to assoc prof, 60-72, PROF ENTOM, UNIV WIS-MADISON, 72- *Personal Data:* b Madison, Wis, July 13, 29; m 52, Jane L Sylvan; c Leslie, Linda & Ronald. *Educ:* Univ Wis, BS, 51, MS, 52, PhD(entom), 57. *Mem:* Entom Soc Am; NAm Benthological Soc; Coleopterists Soc. *Res:* Biology, ecology and taxonomy of aquatic insects and their use as indicators of water quality. *Mailing Add:* 33 S Eau Claire Ave Madison WI 53705

HILSINGER, HAROLD W, THEORETICAL PHYSICS. *Current Pos:* asst prof, 62-67, ASSOC PROF PHYSICS, WORCESTER POLYTECH INST, 67- *Personal Data:* b Midland, Mich, May 31, 32; m 75. *Educ:* Univ Mich, BS, 54; Univ Conn, MS, 57, PhD(physics), 64. *Prof Exp:* Asst instr physics, Univ Conn, 57-59. *Res:* Theory of relativity and philosophy of physics. *Mailing Add:* Dept Physics Worcester Polytech Inst 100 Institute Rd Worcester MA 01609

HILST, ARVIN RUDOLPH, AGRONOMY. *Current Pos:* instr, Purdue Univ, 49-54, from asst prof to assoc prof, 55-61, asst head dept agron, 66-69, PROF AGRON, PURDUE UNIV, 61-, DIR RESIDENT INSTR & ASSOC DEAN SCH AGR, 69- *Personal Data:* b Manito, Ill, June 14, 24; m 44; c 2. *Educ:* Univ Ill, BS, 46, MS, 49; Purdue Univ, PhD, 55. *Prof Exp:* Asst, Univ Ill, 48. *Mem:* Am Soc Agron. *Res:* Herbicides; morphology. *Mailing Add:* 502 Emilie Dr West Lafayette IN 47906

HILST, GLENN RUDOLPH, METEOROLOGY. *Current Pos:* CONSULT, 87- *Personal Data:* b Meade, Kans, May 1, 23; m 86, Zenobia Ratchford; c Randolph, Elizabeth & Katherine. *Educ:* Mass Inst Technol, SB, 48, SM, 49; Univ Chicago, PhD(meteor), 57. *Honors & Awards:* Charles Franklin Brooks Award, Am Meteorol Soc, 73. *Prof Exp:* Asst radar meteorol, Mass Inst Technol, 48-49; res meteorologist, Gen Elec Co, 49-52, mgr atmospheric physics, Wash, 54-60; assoc meteorologist, Argonne Nat Lab, 52-54; asst dir weather systs div, Travelers Ins Co, 60, vpres, Travelers Res Ctr, Inc, 61-68, exec vpres, Travelers Res Corp, 68-70; vpres environ res, Aeronaut Res Assocs of Princeton, Inc, 70-75; chief scientist, The Res Corp of New Eng, 75-77; sr mem tech staff, Elec Power Res Inst, 77-80, prog mgr environ physics & chem, 80-87; sr sci advisor, Battelle Pac Northwest Labs, 90-93; mem, Res Adv Coun, Physics Dept, Gonzaga Univ, 90- *Concurrent Pos:* Spec consult to surgeon gen, USPHS, 61; consult, NIH, 63-; mem, Conn Air Pollution Comn, 67-69; mem, US Nat Comt, Int Biol Prog, 67-70; chmn ad hoc comt, Global Network Environ Monitoring; mem environ sci adv comt, NSF, 68-69, chmn, 70; study dir, Nat Acad Sci, 70, mem, Monitoring Panel, Comt Int Environ Progs, 74-77; vis scientist, Am Meteorol Soc, 70; mem, Nat Acid Precipitation Assessment Prog, ORB, 89- *Mem:* Fel AAAS; fel Am Meteorol Soc; fel Explorers Club. *Res:* Atmospheric turbulence and diffusion; earth-air exchange phenomena; micrometeorology; physical radar meteorology; environmental effects of atmosphere and hydrologic phenomena. *Mailing Add:* W 1404 Country Club Ct Spokane WA 99218-2964

HILT, RICHARD LEIGHTON, PHYSICS. *Current Pos:* from asst prof to assoc prof, 64-80, PROF PHYSICS, COLO COL, 80- *Personal Data:* b Detroit, Mich, Apr 3, 36; m 65, Sandra Ness. *Educ:* Oberlin Col, AB, 58; Univ NC, PhD(physics), 64. *Prof Exp:* Asst prof physics, NC State Univ, 63-64. *Mem:* Am Asn Physics Teachers; Am Geophys Union; Sigma Xi. *Res:* Geophysics. *Mailing Add:* 2260 Mesa Rd Colorado Springs CO 80904. *Fax:* 719-389-6929; *E-Mail:* dhilt@cc.colorado.edu

HILTBOLD, ARTHUR EDWARD, JR, SOIL MICROBIOLOGY. *Current Pos:* assoc prof agron, 55-68, PROF AGRON & SOILS, AUBURN UNIV, 68- *Personal Data:* b Brooklyn, NY, Apr 24, 25; m 49; c 3. *Educ:* Cornell Univ, BS, 48, PhD, 55; Iowa State Col, MS, 50. *Prof Exp:* Asst agron, Iowa State Col, 48-50; instr, Cornell Univ, 50-54. *Concurrent Pos:* Assoc ed, Agron J; reviewer, Weed Sci; assoc, Soil Microbiologist, 55- *Mem:* Am Soc Agron; Soil Sci Soc Am; Weed Sci Soc Am; Am Peanut Res & Educ Soc. *Res:* Microbiological transformations of nitrogen in soils; movement and persistence of herbicides in soil; nitrogen fixation in soybeans and peanuts. *Mailing Add:* 730 Hollon Ave Auburn AL 36830

HILTERMAN, FRED JOHN, EXPLORATION GEOPHYSICS. *Current Pos:* ASSOC PROF GEOPHYS, UNIV HOUSTON, 73- *Personal Data:* b Pittsburgh, Pa, Aug 30, 41; m 61; c 2. *Educ:* Colo Sch Mines, Prof Engr, 63, PhD(geophys), 70. *Prof Exp:* Engr, Geophys Serv Ctr, Mobil Oil Corp, 63-66, assoc geophysicist, Explor Serv Ctr, 70-72, activ leader, Field Res Lab, 72-73. *Concurrent Pos:* Consult res, GeoQuest Int, Ltd, 74-, educ, Prof Geophys Inc; assoc ed, Soc Explor Geophysicists, 75- *Mem:* Soc Explor Geophysicists; Europ Asn Explor Geophysicists; Sigma Xi. *Res:* Application of wave propagation models to seismic exploration data processing techniques and interpretational techniques. *Mailing Add:* Geophys Develop Corp 8401 Westheimer Suite 150 Houston TX 77063-2707

HILTIBRAN, ROBERT COMEGYS, BIOCHEMISTRY. *Current Pos:* ASSOC PROF AGRON, UNIV ILL, URBANA, 69- *Personal Data:* b Urbana, Ohio, Sept 24, 20; m 45, Lois Armstrong; c Robert G, Cheryl M & Karen K. *Educ:* Denison Univ, BS, 48; Univ Kans, MS, 51, PhD(biochem), 54. *Prof Exp:* Instr biochem, Med Sch, Northwestern Univ, 53-55; Herman Frasch Found fel protein chem, Dept Agr Biochem, Ohio State Univ, 55-57; assoc biochemist, ILL Natural Hist Surv, 57-69, biochemist, aquatic biol sect, 69-82. *Concurrent Pos:* Res biochemist, Vet Admin Hosp, Hines, Ill, 53-55. *Mem:* Am Chem Soc; Weed Sci Soc Am; Sigma Xi; Am Inst Biol Sci; hon mem N Cent Weed Sci Soc; Aquatic Plant Mgt Soc. *Res:* Fish; enzymes of fish liver; aquatic weed control; biochemistry of brain tissue; isolation and characterization of natural products; water pollution and its effect; biochemical effects of pollutants on fish. *Mailing Add:* 608 E Washington St Urbana IL 61801

HILTON, ASHLEY STEWART, ANALYTICAL CHEMISTRY. *Current Pos:* res scientist, Firestone Tire & Rubber Co, 70-80, sr res scientist, 80-87, ASSOC SCIENTIST, BRIDGESTONE/FIRESTONE, INC, AKRON, 87- *Personal Data:* b St Marys, Pa, Apr 28, 40; m 62, Sharon Podmenik; c A

Stewart Jr & Scott A. *Educ:* Pa State Univ, BS, 62; Ohio State Univ, PhD(analytical chem), 68. *Prof Exp:* Res scientist, Aerospace Res Labs, USAF, 67-70. *Mem:* Am Chem Soc. *Res:* Application of mass spectrometry, high performance liquid chromatography, gas chromatography and other instrumental analytical techniques to research in polymer chemistry. *Mailing Add:* 7431 Shadyview NW Massillon OH 44646

HILTON, DONALD FREDERICK JAMES, INSECT ECOLOGY, BEHAVIORAL ECOLOGY. *Current Pos:* from asst prof to assoc prof, 73-85, PROF ZOOL, BISHOP'S UNIV, 85- *Personal Data:* b Calgary, Alta, May 9, 44; m 66; c 2. *Educ:* Univ Alta, BSc, 65, PhD(parasitol), 71; Univ Kans, MA, 67; Univ London, DIC, 72; Simon Fraser Univ, MAg. *Prof Exp:* Bacteriologist, Royal Alexandria Hosp, 67-68; NATO fel med entom, Imperial Col, Univ London, 71-73. *Mem:* Animal Behav Soc; Soc Conserv Biol; Can Nature Fedn; Int Soc Behav Ecol; Royal Entom Soc London; Flora & Fauna Preserv Soc. *Res:* Behavioral ecology of insects, especially reproductive behavior. *Mailing Add:* Dept Biol Sci Bishop's Univ Lennoxville PQ J1M 1Z7 Can

HILTON, FREDERICK KELKER, ZOOLOGY. *Current Pos:* from instr to assoc prof, 58-74, PROF ANAT, SCH MED, UNIV LOUISVILLE, 74- *Personal Data:* b Harrisburg, Pa, Feb 8, 26; m 50; c 4. *Educ:* Cornell Univ, BS, 50; Johns Hopkins Univ, DSc(ecol), 58. *Prof Exp:* Asst pathobiol, Johns Hopkins Univ, 55-58. *Mem:* Am Asn Anatomists; Soc Study Reproduction; Animal Behav Soc. *Res:* Biochemistry and endocrinology of animal behavior; physiology and endocrinology of reproduction. *Mailing Add:* Dept Anat Univ Louisville Sch Med 2301 S Third St Louisville KY 40292-0001

HILTON, H WAYNE, ORGANIC CHEMISTRY. *Current Pos:* RETIRED. *Personal Data:* b Salt Lake City, Utah, Aug 24, 23; m 48. *Educ:* Univ Utah, BA, 49; Ohio State Univ, PhD(org chem), 52. *Prof Exp:* Res chemist high polymers, Visking Corp, 52-55; Prin chemist, Exp Sta, Hawaiian Sugar Planter's Asn, 55-76, head, Dept Crop Sci, 76-88. *Concurrent Pos:* Consult, 88- *Mem:* Am Chem Soc; AAAS; Am Soc Agron; Weed Sci Soc. *Res:* Carbohydrates; vinyl high polymers; agricultural chemicals. *Mailing Add:* 378 Hema Plane Honolulu HI 96821-1835

HILTON, HORACE GILL, STATISTICS. *Current Pos:* From asst prof to assoc prof, 62-75, chmn dept, 69-80, PROF STATIST, BRIGHAM YOUNG UNIV, 75- *Personal Data:* b Delta, Utah, June 28, 32; m 56; c 9. *Educ:* Brigham Young Univ, BS, 57; NC State Univ, MS, 60, PhD, 63. *Concurrent Pos:* Nat Res Coun fel, 68-69. *Mem:* Am Statist Asn; Biomet Soc. *Res:* Design and analysis of scientific experiments. *Mailing Add:* Dept Statist Brigham Young Univ Provo UT 84602-1044

HILTON, JAMES GORTON, PHARMACOLOGY. *Current Pos:* RETIRED. *Personal Data:* b Baltimore, Md, Sept 21, 23; m 46; c 2. *Educ:* Va Polytech Inst, BS, 47; Univ Tenn, MS, 52, PhD(pharmacol), 54. *Prof Exp:* Res assoc pharmacol, Univ Va, 48-50; from actg asst prof to assoc prof, Univ Miss, 53-58; assoc prof, Sch Med, Marquette Univ, 59-61; from assoc prof to prof pharmacol, Univ Tex Med Br Galveston, 61-93, actg chmn, 79-82; chief pharmacol, Shriners Burn Inst, 76-93. *Concurrent Pos:* Fulbright res scholar, Biol Ctr, Gulbenkian Inst Sci, Portugal, 68-69; Fulbright lectr, Univ San Agustin, Peru, 59; mem pharmacol & endocrinol fel rev comt, NIH, 64-67; mem comt persistent pesticides, Nat Acad Sci, 67-69; consult, Environ Protection Agency, 70-72. *Mem:* AAAS; Am Physiol Soc; Am Soc Pharmacol & Exp Therapeut; Am Heart Asn; Am Burn Asn. *Res:* Sympathetic ganglion transmission; factors regulating vascular permeability; cardiovascular changes after thermal injury. *Mailing Add:* 2626 Gerol Ct Galveston TX 77551

HILTON, JOHN L, PLASMA PHYSICS. *Current Pos:* ADJ PROF, DEPT STATIST, BRIGHAM YOUNG UNIV, PROVO, UTAH, 86- *Personal Data:* b Woodruff, Ariz, May 25, 27; m 50; c 8. *Educ:* Brigham Young Univ, BA, 52. *Prof Exp:* Proj engr, Sandia Corp, NMex, 52-57; dept head, Aerojet-Gen Nucleonics Div, Gen Tire & Rubber Co, 57-70; proj engr, Cyclotron Corp, 70-84; consult, Univ Pa & Fox Chase Cancer Ctr, 84-86; staff physicist, Physics Int Co, 86-88. *Mem:* AAAS; Am Phys Soc. *Res:* Ion sources; accelerators; statistical studies of word patterns. *Mailing Add:* 604 Sagewood Ave Provo UT 84604

HILTON, MARY ANDERSON, BIOCHEMISTRY. *Current Pos:* from instr to asst prof, 63-73, ASSOC PROF BIOCHEM, SCH MED, UNIV LOUISVILLE, 74- *Personal Data:* b State College, Pa, July 6, 26; m 50; c 4. *Educ:* Pa State Col, BS, 47; Cornell Univ, PhD(biochem), 51. *Prof Exp:* Asst biochem, Cornell Univ, 47-50; asst med, Johns Hopkins Univ, 51-55, instr chem, Hosp Sch Nursing, 57-58. *Res:* Cell biology; amino acid metabolism. *Mailing Add:* Health Sci Ctr 604A Univ Louisville Sch Med Louisville KY 40292-0001. Fax: 502-852-6222

HILTON, PETER JOHN, MATHEMATICS. *Current Pos:* DISTINGUISHED EMER PROF, DEPT MATH SCI, STATE UNIV NY, BINGHAMTON. *Personal Data:* b London, Eng, Apr 7, 23; m 49, Meg; c Nicholas & Timothy. *Educ:* Oxford Univ, MA & DPhil, 50; Cambridge Univ, PhD(topology), 52. *Hon Degrees:* DHum, NMich Univ, 77; DSc, Mem Univ, 83; DSc, Autonomous Univ Barcelona, 89. *Honors & Awards:* Silver Medal, Univ Helsinki, 75; Centenary Medal, John Carroll Univ, 85. *Prof Exp:* Prof math, Cornell Univ, 62-71 & Univ Wash, 71-73; Beaumont Univ Prof Math, Case Western Res Univ, 73-82. *Concurrent Pos:* Co-chmn, Cambridge Conf Sch Math, 65; fel, Battelle Res Ctr, Seattle, 71-; chmn, US Comn Math Instr, 71-74; chmn comt appl math training, Nat Res Coun, 77-; corresp mem, Brazil Acad Sci, 79; distinguished prof, Dept Math, Univ Cent Fla, Orlando, 94- *Mem:* Am Math Soc; London Math Soc; Royal Statist Soc; hon mem Math Soc Belg; Math Asn Am (first vpres, 78-80); Can Math Soc. *Res:* Algebraic topology; homological algebra; category theory; group theory. *Mailing Add:* Dept Math Sci State Univ NY Binghamton NY 13902-6000

HILTON, RAY, PHYSICAL CHEMISTRY. *Current Pos:* SR SCIENTIST, PHYS SCI RES LAB, TEX INSTRUMENTS INC, 60-, MGR INFRARED GLASS LAB, ELECTROOPTICS DIV, 74- *Personal Data:* b Houston, Tex, Sept 3, 30; m 51; c 4. *Educ:* Tex A&M Univ, BS, 53, MS, 57, PhD(chem), 59. *Prof Exp:* Anal chemist, Sinclair Oil & Refining Co, 55-56; res engr, Prod Res Div, Humble Oil & Refining Co, 59-60. *Mem:* Soc Appl Spectros; Optical Soc Am. *Res:* Optical properties of solids, especially semiconductors; solid state chemistry of chalcogen based infrared transmitting glasses; infrared optical materials and electrooptic devices. *Mailing Add:* 505 Park Lane Richardson TX 75081

HILTON, WALLACE ATWOOD, physics; deceased, see previous edition for last biography

HILTUNEN, JARL KALERVO, FRESH WATER ECOLOGY. *Current Pos:* RETIRED. *Personal Data:* b Sault Ste Marie, Mich, Apr 14, 33. *Educ:* Wayne State Univ, BA, 59, teaching cert, 62. *Prof Exp:* Fishery biologist, Great Lakes Fishery Lab, US Fish & Wildlife Serv, Ann Arbor, Mich, 62-85. *Res:* Vascular flora and benthic invertebrate fauna of the St Lawrence Great Lakes region. *Mailing Add:* 8723 E Northshore Dr Sault Ste Marie MI 49783

HILTY, JAMES WILLARD, PLANT PATHOLOGY. *Current Pos:* From asst prof to assoc prof, 65-76, PROF PLANT PATH, UNIV TENN, KNOXVILLE, 76- *Personal Data:* b Wadsworth, Ohio, Oct 11, 36; m 59, Harriette C Heninger; c Ellen & James. *Educ:* Ohio State Univ, BSc, 58, MSc, 60, PhD(plant path), 64. *Mem:* Am Phytopath Soc; Sigma Xi. *Res:* Diseases of field crops; vegetable crops. *Mailing Add:* Entom & Plant Path Univ Tenn 1345 Circle Park Knoxville TN 37996-0001

HILTZ, ARNOLD AUBREY, PHYSICAL CHEMISTRY. *Current Pos:* sr scientist, Reentry Systs Dept, 66-79, mgr mat appln, Space Systs Div, 79-87, ASTRO SPACE DIV, GEN ELEC CO, KING OF PRUSSIA, 87- *Personal Data:* b PEI, July 31, 24; nat US; m 46; c 2. *Educ:* Acadia Univ, BS, 47; McGill Univ, PhD(chem), 52. *Prof Exp:* Defense res sci officer, Defense Res Bd Can, 51-53; res chemist, Am Viscose Corp, 53-59, group leader, 59-60, group leader, Avisun Corp, 60-65; res chemist, Cent Res Lab, Borden Chem Co, 65-66. *Res:* Determination of polymer properties; effects of molecular structure on properties; thermal protection for re-entry vehicles; materials and materials applications for satellites. *Mailing Add:* 524 Cedar Lane Swarthmore PA 19081

HILU, KHIDIR WANNI, PLANT SYSTEMATICS & EVOLUTION, CROP EVOLUTION. *Current Pos:* ASSOC PROF BOT, VA POLYTECH INST & STATE UNIV, 81- *Personal Data:* b Baghdad, Iraq, Jan 1, 46; m 77; c 2. *Educ:* Univ Baghdad, BS, 66, MS, 71; Univ Ill, PhD(bot), 76. *Prof Exp:* Asst prof bot, Okla City Univ, 77-78; res assoc biosysts, Univ Calif, Riverside, 78-79, Univ Ill, 79-81. *Concurrent Pos:* NSF travel grant, 81; assoc curator, Crop Evolution Lab herbarium; consult, UN Int Bd Plant Genetic Resources. *Mem:* Bot Soc Am; Int Asn Plant Taxon; AAAS; Am Soc Naturalists; Soc Econ Bot; Am Soc Plant Taxonomists; Int Soc Plant Molecular Biol. *Res:* Biosystematic and evolution of higher plants in general and grasses in particular with emphasis on using molecular approaches; origin, evolution and systematics of domesticated plants; genetics of morphological characters and macroevolution in flowering plants. *Mailing Add:* Dept Biol Va Polytech Inst & State Univ PO Box 0406 Blacksburg VA 24063-0001

HIME, WILLIAM GENE, ANALYTICAL CHEMISTRY. *Current Pos:* PRIN, WISS, JANNEY, ELSINER ASSOCS, 84- *Personal Data:* b Dayton, Ohio, Dec 31, 25; m 50, Nancy Price; c Carolyn, Lisa & Sandra. *Educ:* Heidelberg Col, BS, 48. *Prof Exp:* Assoc res chemist, Portland Cement Asn, 51-54; asst prof chem, La Polytech Inst, 54-55; res chemist, Portland Cement Asn, 55-58, supvr analytical chem, 58-66, mgr, chem & petrog res sect, 66-71; vpres, Erlin, Hime Assocs, 71-84. *Mem:* Am Soc Testing & Mat; Am Chem Soc; Soc Appl Spectros; Am Concrete Inst; Nat Asn Corrosion Engrs. *Res:* Silicate analysis; infrared, flame and x-ray emission spectroscopy; x-ray diffraction analyses; cement and concrete chemistry; corrosion chemistry. *Mailing Add:* 2701 Fontana Dr Glenview IL 60025-4707. Fax: 847-291-5189

HIMEL, CHESTER MORA, BIOPHYSICS, ENTOMOLOGY. *Current Pos:* RETIRED. *Personal Data:* b Des Plaines, Ill, Mar 10, 16; m 43; c 2. *Educ:* Univ Chicago, BS, 38; Univ Ill, PhD(org chem), 42. *Prof Exp:* Chemist, ammonia dept, E I du Pont de Nemours & Co, 42; asst group leader, Barrett Div, Allied Chem Corp, 42-44; group leader, Phillips Petrol Co, 44-49; dir org div, Stanford Res Inst, 49-65; res prof entom, Univ Ga, 65-86. *Concurrent Pos:* Fel, Intra-Sci Res Found. *Mem:* Am Chem Soc; Entom Soc Am. *Res:* Fluorescence spectroscopy; molecular fluorescence; cholinergic transmission and receptor sites; fluorescent substrate analogs; narcotic receptors; insect biochemistry; insecticides; agricultural physics and biology; controlled release pesticide systems; pesticide spray physics. *Mailing Add:* 2005 E View Dr Sun City Center FL 33573-5498

HIMELICK, EUGENE BRYSON, PLANT PATHOLOGY, RESEARCH & CONSULTANT ON URBAN & FOREST TREE DISEASES. *Current Pos:* prof, 72-88, EMER PROF PLANT PATH, UNIV ILL, URBANA, 88-, EMER PLANT PATHOLOGIST, ILL NATURAL HIST SURV, 88-, RES ASSOC, MORTON ARBORITUM, 88- *Personal Data:* b Summitville, Ind, Feb 11, 26; m 51, Elizabeth Oyler; c David E, Kirk J & Douglas N. *Educ:* Ball State Univ, BS, 50; Purdue Univ, MS, 52; Univ Ill, PhD(plant path), 59. *Prof Exp:* From asst plant pathologist to assoc plant pathologist, Ill Natural Hist Surv, 52-65, plant pathologist, 65-88. *Concurrent Pos:* Exec dir, Int Soc Arboricult, 69-79; assoc ed, Plant Dis Reporter, USDA, 77-79 & Plant Dis, Am Phytopath Soc, 79-81 & ed, Int Wood Collectors Soc, 83-86; pvt consult, 88- *Mem:* Am Phytopath Soc; Am Soc Consult Arborists (pres, 95); hon mem Int Soc Arboricult; Sigma Xi; Int Wood Collector Soc (pres, 90-92). *Res:* Forest and shade tree diseases; urban tree maintenance and selection; field research on vascular disease of trees, fertilization of trees, transplanting trees; published over 300 research and extension publications. *Mailing Add:* 601 Burkwood Ct E Urbana IL 61801. *E-Mail:* ghimelick@worldnet.att.net

HIMES, CRAIG L, BIOLOGY. *Current Pos:* RETIRED. *Personal Data:* b Homestead Park, Pa, June 11, 27; m 61; c 1. *Educ:* Clarion State Col, BSEd, 49; Univ Pittsburgh, MS, 57, PhD(biol & higher educ), 71. *Prof Exp:* Teacher sci & biol, SButler Co Joint Schs, 49-57; teacher biol, Butler Area Sr High Sch, 57-58 & Am Dependent Sch, Orleans, France, 58-60; res asst, Univ Pittsburgh, 60-61; emer prof, Bloomsburg Univ, 61-83, chmn, Bloomsburg State Col, 73-79,. *Concurrent Pos:* Reviewing textbk manuscripts in biol & human sexuality. *Res:* Freshwater biology; limnology and pollution. *Mailing Add:* 13 E Park St Bloomsburg PA 17815

HIMES, FRANK LAWRENCE, SOIL CHEMISTRY. *Current Pos:* from asst prof to prof, 57-92, asst chmn, 85-88, EMER PROF AGRON, OHIO STATE UNIV, 92- *Personal Data:* b Crawfordsville, Ind, July 30, 27; m 51, Dorothy L Hostetler; c Laura (Lafferty), Caroline D & Glenn S. *Educ:* Wabash Col, AB, 49; Purdue Univ, MS, 51, PhD(soil fertil), 56. *Prof Exp:* Asst prof agron, Mid Tenn State Col, 56-57. *Concurrent Pos:* Res assignment, Rothamsted Exp Sta, Harpenden, Eng, 66 & Dept Chem, Univ Birmingham, Eng, 81. *Mem:* Fel Soil Sci Soc Am; fel Am Soc Agron; Am Chem Soc; Sigma Xi; Int Soil Sci Soc; Soil Sci Soc Am; Am Soc Agron; Int Humic Substance Soc. *Res:* Fertility; movement and availability of essential elements for growth which form chelates with organic compounds found in soil. *Mailing Add:* 2749 Eastcleft Dr Columbus OH 43221-1707

HIMES, JAMES ALBERT, VETERINARY PHARMACOLOGY, VETERINARY PHYSIOLOGY. *Current Pos:* from asst pharmacologist to pharmacologist, Univ Fla, 65-90, dir vet med educ, 75-77, assocs dean student activ, Col Vet Med, 77-90, EMER PROF, UNIV FLA, 90- *Personal Data:* b Lucas, Ohio, Aug 12, 19; m 73; c 2. *Educ:* Muskingum Col, BS, 41; Univ Pa, VMD, 50; Cornell Univ, PhD(physiol), 65. *Prof Exp:* Asst zool, Univ Nebr, 41-42, 46; NIH trainee physiol & pharmacol, NY State Vet Col, Cornell Univ, 62-65. *Mem:* AAAS; Am Vet Med Asn; Am Soc Vet Physiol & Pharmacol. *Res:* Plasma cholinesterase; bile flow and related liver physiology; hepatic metabolism of drugs and enzyme induction. *Mailing Add:* 3716 SW 30th Terr No 41C Gainesville FL 32608

HIMES, JOHN HARTER, MATERNAL & CHILD HEALTH, CHILD GROWTH & NUTRITION. *Current Pos:* ASSOC PROF/PROF, SCH PUB HEALTH, UNIV MINN, 87-, DIR NUTRIT COORD CTR, DIV EPIDEMIOL, 95- *Personal Data:* b Salt Lake City, Utah, July 25, 47; m 72; c Rachel, Matthew & Sarah. *Educ:* Ariz State Univ, BS, 71; Univ Tex, Austin, PhD(human biol), 75; Harvard Univ, MPH, 82. *Honors & Awards:* Nathalie Masse Mem Prize, Int Childrens's Ctr, 80. *Prof Exp:* Res scientist, Fels Res Inst, 76-79; asst prof pediat, Sch Med, Wright State Univ, 77-79; proj dir, Abt Assocs, Inc, 79-82; assoc prof health & nutrit sci, Brooklyn Col, City Univ NY, 82-87. *Concurrent Pos:* Vis scientist, Inst Nutrit Cent Am & Panama, 73-74; bk rev ed, Human Biol, 78-81; NIH trainee, Harvard Sch Pub Health, 80-82. *Mem:* Am Soc Clin Nutrit; Human Biol Coun; Am Pub Health Asn; Soc Study Human Biol; Am Asn Phys Anthropologists; Int Asn Human Auxology; Am Soc Nutrit Sci. *Res:* Physical growth and nutrition of children; anthropometry; anthropometric assessment of nutritional status assessment of dietary intake; body composition; subcutaneous fat; obesity; analysis of serial data; nutritional epidemiology. *Mailing Add:* Div Epidemiol Univ Minn 1300 S Second St Suite 300 Minneapolis MN 55454. *Fax:* 612-624-9328; *E-Mail:* himes@epivax.epi.umn.edu

HIMES, MARION, biology, cytology, for more information see previous edition

HIMES, RICHARD H, BIOCHEMISTRY. *Current Pos:* from asst prof to assoc prof, 63-71, chmn dept, 78-84, PROF BIOCHEM, UNIV KANS, 71- *Personal Data:* b Philadelphia, Pa, July 2, 35; m 59; c 3. *Educ:* Univ Pa, AB, 56; Univ Calif, Berkeley, PhD(biochem), 61. *Prof Exp:* NIH fel, 61-63. *Mem:* AAAS; Am Chem Soc; Am Soc Biochem & Molecular Biol; Am Soc Cell Biol. *Res:* Structure and function of proteins. *Mailing Add:* Dept Biochem Univ Kans Lawrence KS 66045-2106. *Fax:* 785-867-5321

HIMMEL, LEON, ELECTRICAL ENGINEERING, MANAGEMENT. *Current Pos:* From engr to pres, avionics, prod assurance & value eng, Fed Labs, Int Tel & Tel Corp, 42-67, pres, Avionics Div, 67-70, ASST TO PRES, INT TEL & TEL CORP, 70-, DIR CAPITAL ASSETS, 88-, DIR MIS, 90- *Personal Data:* b Mount Vernon, NY, Jan 24, 21; m 45; c 1. *Educ:* City Col New York, BEE, 42. *Concurrent Pos:* Mgt consult, eng, info systs, commun & financial. *Mem:* Fel Inst Elec & Electronics Engrs. *Res:* Instrument landing and radio navigation, antisubmarine warfare, range instrumentation and simulation; electronic defense, countermeasures and reconnaissance; communications. *Mailing Add:* Himmel Assocs 39 Club Rd Upper Montclair NJ 07043

HIMMELBERG, CHARLES JOHN, TOPOLOGY, MATHEMATICAL ANALYSIS. *Current Pos:* From asst prof to assoc prof, 59-65, PROF MATH, UNIV KANS, 68-, CHMN DEPT, 78- *Personal Data:* b North Kansas City, Mo, Nov 12, 31; m; c 5. *Educ:* Rockhurst Col, BS, 52; Univ Notre Dame, MS, 54, PhD(math), 57. *Concurrent Pos:* Assoc analyst, Midwest Res Inst, 57-59; vis prof, Inst Math, Univ Florence, 75. *Mem:* Am Math Soc; Math Asn Am; Sigma Xi. *Res:* Generalized differential equations; set-valued functions; stochastic decision theory and fixed point theory. *Mailing Add:* Dept Math Univ Kans Lawrence KS 66045-2142

HIMMELBERG, GLEN RAY, PETROLOGY. *Current Pos:* assoc prof, 69-73, PROF GEOL, UNIV MO, COLUMBIA, 73- *Personal Data:* b Glasgow, Mo, Oct 31, 37; m 57; c 3. *Educ:* Tex Tech Col, BS, 59, MS, 60; Univ Minn, PhD(geol), 65. *Prof Exp:* Geologist, US Geol Surv, 65-69. *Mem:* Mineral Soc Am; Am Geophys Union; Geol Soc Am. *Res:* Studies of phase equilibrium of coexisting minerals in igneous and metamorphic rocks to determine the physical and chemical environment of crystallization. *Mailing Add:* Dept Geol Univ Mo 101 Geol Bldg Columbia MO 65211-0002

HIMMELBLAU, DAVID M(AUTNER), CHEMICAL ENGINEERING. *Current Pos:* PROF, UNIV TEX, AUSTIN, 57- *Personal Data:* b Chicago, Ill, Aug 29, 23; m 48, Betty Hartman; c Andrew & Margaret. *Educ:* Mass Inst Technol, BS, 47; Northwestern Univ, MBA, 50; Univ Wash, Seattle, MS, 56, PhD, 57. *Prof Exp:* Instr chem eng, Univ Wash, Seattle, 55-57. *Concurrent Pos:* Pres, Cache Corp, 78-80; pres, Ramad Corp, 79- *Mem:* Am Chem Soc; Am Inst Chem Engrs; Sigma Xi. *Res:* Fault detection; optimization; process analysis and simulation. *Mailing Add:* Dept Chem Eng Univ Tex Austin TX 78712

HIMMELSBACH, CLIFTON KECK, PHARMACOLOGY. *Current Pos:* assoc dean, Schs Med & Dent, Georgetown Univ, 65-77, prof, 66-77, adminr sponsored progs, 71-72, EMER PROF COMMUNITY MED & PHARMACOL, GEORGETOWN UNIV, 77- *Personal Data:* b Philadelphia, Pa, Mar 17, 07; m 28, 61; c 2. *Educ:* Univ Va, MD, 31. *Honors & Awards:* Meritorious Serv Award, USPHS, 65; Nathan B Eddy Mem Award, 87. *Prof Exp:* Intern, USPHS Hosp, New Orleans, La, 31-32; clin researcher drug addiction, Kans, 33-34; Mass, 34-35, Ky, 35-44; clin researcher, NIH, 44, off voc rehab, 45-46, fed employee, Health Div, 47, med officer chg outpatient clin, 48-53, asst chief, Div hosps, 53-54, chief, 54-57, dir spec prog, Div Res Grants, 57-59, assoc dir, Clin Ctr, 59-65. *Concurrent Pos:* Fel pharmacol, Western Reserve Univ, 33; mem bd dirs, Washington Home, Iona House Sr Serv Ctr, Am Cancer Soc, Retired Officers Asn; mem bd dirs, Acad Med of Washington DC, pres, 90-91. *Mem:* Fel AMA; fel Am Col Physicians; Am Hosp Asn; Sigma Xi. *Res:* Addiction; opiates in man; control of hospital-acquired infections; human experimentation; hospice care. *Mailing Add:* 3731 Harrison St NW Washington DC 20015

HIMMELSTEIN, SYDNEY, ELECTRICAL ENGINEERING. *Current Pos:* dir eng, 60-80, PRES, S HIMMELSTEIN & CO, 80- *Personal Data:* b New York, NY, Oct 1, 27; m 66. *Educ:* NY Univ, BEE, 47. *Prof Exp:* Proj engr, US Naval Ord Lab, 47-50; chief, Vehicular Equip Sect, Eng Res & Develop Labs, 50-56; exec engr, Res Labs, Cook Elec Co, 56-57, tech dir, Data Stor Div, 57-60. *Concurrent Pos:* Lectr, Cath Univ Am, 52-53; pres, Electronic Applications, Inc, 53-56. *Mem:* Inst Elec & Electronics Engrs; Audio Eng Soc; Nat Soc Prof Engrs. *Res:* Magnetic recording systems and computer peripheral equipment; design and manufacture of control and monitoring systems for rotating machinery. *Mailing Add:* 2490 Pembroke Ave Hoffman Estates IL 60195

HIMMS-HAGEN, JEAN, BIOCHEMISTRY, METABOLISM. *Current Pos:* assoc prof, Univ Ottawa, 67-71, actg chmn dept, 75-77, 88, chmn dept, 77-82, PROF BIOCHEM, UNIV OTTAWA, 71- *Personal Data:* b Oxford, Eng, Dec 18, 33; m 56, Paul; c Anna & Nina. *Educ:* Univ London, BSc, 55; Oxford Univ, DPhil(pharmacol), 58. *Honors & Awards:* Bond Award, Am Oil Chemists Soc, 72; Ayerst Award, Can Biochem Soc, 73. *Prof Exp:* Fel biochem, Med Sch, Univ Harvard, 58-59; asst prof physiol, Univ Man, 59-64; asst prof biochem, Queen's Univ, Ont, 64-67. *Concurrent Pos:* Assoc, Med Res Coun, Can, 66-77, mem, 70-75. *Mem:* Fel Royal Soc Can; Am Soc Pharmacol & Exp Therapeut; Brit Biochem Soc; Am Inst Nutrit; Am Physiol Soc; Can Biochem Soc. *Res:* Brown adipose tissue metabolism; disordered brown adipose tissue metabolism in obesity. *Mailing Add:* Dept Biochem Univ Ottawa Ottawa ON K1H 8M5 Can

HIMOE, ALBERT, BIOCHEMISTRY. *Current Pos:* RETIRED. *Personal Data:* b Albany, Calif, Oct 23, 38. *Educ:* Reed Col, BA, 59; Univ Chicago, PhD(chem), 64. *Prof Exp:* Asst prof biochem, Baylor Col Med, 67-75; res assoc agron, Univ Ill, 76-77. *Concurrent Pos:* Fel biochem, Cornell Univ, 64-67. *Mem:* Asn Comput Mach; Am Chem Soc. *Res:* History of chemistry, atheism and science in the 18th century. *Mailing Add:* 811 Oakland Ave Urbana IL 61801

HIMPSEL, FRANZ J, SOLID STATE PHYSICS, TECHNICAL MANAGEMENT. *Current Pos:* PROF PHYSICS, UNIV WIS, 95- *Personal Data:* b Rosenheim, Ger, Oct 30, 49; m 80; c 2. *Educ:* Munich Univ, PhD(physics), 76. *Honors & Awards:* Peter Mark Award, Am Vacuum Soc, 85. *Prof Exp:* Mem res staff, IBM Res Div, 80-95. *Concurrent Pos:* Vis prof,

Univ Munich, 84-85; sr mgr surface sci, IBM Res, 85-89. *Mem:* Fel Am Phys Soc; Am Vacuum Soc. *Res:* Surface science, using photoelectron spectroscopy with synchrotron radiation and inverse photoemission. *Mailing Add:* 6618 Sutton Rd Madison WI 53711

HINATA, SATOSHI, PLASMA ASTROPHYSICS, SOLAR PHYSICS. *Current Pos:* CONSULT. *Personal Data:* b Tokyo, Japan, Aug 6, 44; m 69; c 3. *Educ:* Univ Tokyo, BE, 67; Univ Ill, MS, 69, PhD(physics), 73. *Prof Exp:* Res assoc, Univ Ill, 73-74; res fel, Harvard Univ, 74-76; res instr, Yale Univ, 76-78; res scientist, Solar Nat Observ, 78-80. *Mem:* Am Astron Soc. *Res:* Plasma astrophysics of stars and sun; nonlinear dynamos of solar type stars; stellar atmosphere & magnetic field. *Mailing Add:* Dept Physics Auburn Univ Auburn AL 36849-3501

HINCHEN, JOHN J(OSEPH), PHYSICAL & LASER CHEMISTRY. *Current Pos:* MEM STAFF, UNITED TECH RES CTR, 64- *Personal Data:* b North Bergen, NJ, Sept 18, 26; m 53; c 2. *Educ:* Seton Hall Univ, BS, 50; Rensselaer Polytech Inst, PhD(phys chem), 62. *Prof Exp:* Chemist, Wright Aeronaut Corp, 50-51 & Gen Elec Co, 54-59; fel & res assoc phys chem Rensselaer Polytech Inst, 62-63; res scientist, United Technol Corp, 63-64, sr res scientist. *Concurrent Pos:* Consult, Kearfott Div, Gen Precision Inc, 60-61; adj prof, Univ Hartford, 75-85. *Mem:* Am Chem Soc; Am Phys Soc; Sigma Xi. *Res:* Gas-solid absorption; molecular beam studies of heterogeneous catalysis; kinetics; laser chemistry, laser spectroscopy, development of chemical lasers; laser studies of excited state lifetimes. *Mailing Add:* 56 Jean Rd Manchester CT 06040-4566

HINCHMAN, RAY RICHARD, PLANT ECOLOGY, PHYTOREMEDIATION. *Current Pos:* Sci asst plant physiol & morphol, Argonne Nat Lab, 64-70, appointee, 71-74, staff scientist plant ecol & environ biol, 74 & dep dir, land reclamation prog, 77-82, PROJ LEADER & PRIN INVESTR & PLANT PHYSIOLOGIST, ENERGY SYSTS DIV, ARGONNE NAT LAB, 82- *Personal Data:* b Chicago, Ill, Aug 20, 37; m 63, Carline A Schwegler; c Carrie R & Timothy K. *Educ:* Univ Ill, Urbana, BS, 61; Univ Wash, MS, 64; Univ Chicago, PhD(bot), 71. *Concurrent Pos:* Adv, Argonne Nat Lab, Northern Ill Univ, 75-83, prin investr, reclamation & revegetation of disturbed land, 79-; consult, Utah State Univ, 80-83; conf chmn, Soc Ecol Restoration, 90. *Mem:* Bot Soc Am; Am Soc Plant Physiologists; AAAS; Sigma Xi; Soc Ecol Restoration. *Res:* Rehabilitation and revegetation of disturbed land in the US, Germany and Nepal; phytoremediation; environmental fate of hazardous wastes in soils and vegetation; environmental impact assessment; effects of pollutants on plants; gravity sensing mechanisms in plants; ultrastructure of plant plastids; plant morphology; plant and algal physiology; hydroponics. *Mailing Add:* Energy Systs Div Argonne Nat Lab Bldg 362 Argonne IL 60439-4815. *Fax:* 620-252-6407; *E-Mail:* hinchman@anl.gov

HINCK, LAWRENCE WILSON, MICROBIOLOGY, PARASITOLOGY. *Current Pos:* Prof biol, 69-93, PROF MICROBIOL, ARK STATE UNIV, 93- *Personal Data:* b Cape Girardeau, Mo, Dec 12, 40; m 64, Carol J Ahrens; c Cheryl L & Laura J (Howard). *Educ:* Southeast Mo State Univ, BS, 63; Med Ctr, Univ Mo, MS, 65; Med Ctr, Univ Okla, PhD(parasitol), 71. *Concurrent Pos:* Consult microbiol, Helena Chem Co, 74-, Foremost Dairy, 76, Joseph A Coors Brewing Co, 84 & Emerson Electric Co, 90- *Mem:* Am Soc Microbiol; Am Soc Parasitologists; Sigma Xi; Nat Asn Adv Health Professions. *Res:* Physiology of infection mechanisms of nematodes; bacterial and parasitic infections of catfish; trypanosomes of wild mammals; influence of fever on acquired immunity; lyme disease in Arkansas; mobility of gliding bacteria; naegleria fowleri in Arkansas. *Mailing Add:* Dept Biol Sci Ark State Univ Box 1561 State University AR 72467

HINCK, VINCENT C, RADIOLOGY. *Current Pos:* PROF RADIOL, BAYLOR COL MED, 73- *Personal Data:* b New York, NY, Feb 7, 26; m 59; c 1. *Educ:* Cornell Univ, AB, 48; New York Med Col, MD, 53; Am Bd Radiol, dipl. *Prof Exp:* Intern, Grace-New Haven Community Hosp, Conn, 53-54; resident radiol, Hosp St Raphael, New Haven, 54-56; chief resident, Med Sch Hosps, Univ Ore, 56-57, from instr to prof, 57-69; prof radiol & head div diag radiol, Med Ctr, Univ Wis-Madison, 69-73. *Mem:* Fel Am Col Radiol. *Res:* Neuroradiology; radiographic measurement criteria for diagnosis of intraspinal tumor and spinal canal stenosis; femorocerebral angiographic technic. *Mailing Add:* Dept Radiol Baylor Col Med Houston TX 77030

HINCKLEY, ALDEN DEXTER, APPLIED ECOLOGY. *Current Pos:* CONSULT ECOLOGIST, 95- *Personal Data:* b New York, NY, Nov 2, 31; m 59; c 5. *Educ:* Harvard Univ, AB, 53; Univ Hawaii, MS, 56, PhD, 60. *Prof Exp:* Entomologist, Fiji, 60-63, ecologist, Apia, WSamoa, 64-67; vis ecologist, Biol Dept, Brookhaven Nat Lab, 67-70; assoc prof environ sci, Univ Va, 70-74, asst dean, Col Arts & Sci, 73-74; assoc dir, Inst Ecol, 74-76, actg dir, 77; tech staff, Mitre Corp, 78; sr ecologist, Gen Res Corp, 79-81; environ protection specialist, Off Res & Develop, Environ Protection Agency, 82, Off Solid Waste, 83-86, ecologist, Off Policy Analysis, 87-94. *Mem:* Am Inst Biol Sci; Ecol Soc Am; AAAS. *Res:* Application of ecological principles to the management of renewable resources; ecological risk assessment; ecological effects of rapid climate change; value of biodiversity. *Mailing Add:* 5604 Bloomfield Dr No 102 Alexandria VA 22312. *E-Mail:* dhinckley@igc.apc.org

HINCKLEY, CONRAD CUTLER, PHYSICAL CHEMISTRY. *Current Pos:* from asst prof to assoc prof, 66-76, PROF CHEM, SOUTHERN ILL UNIV, CARBONDALE, 76- *Personal Data:* b Ft Worth, Tex, May 8, 34; m 56; c 2. *Educ:* NTex State Univ, BS, 59, MS, 60; Univ Tex, PhD(chem), 64. *Honors & Awards:* Kaplan Res Award. *Prof Exp:* Fel chem, Univ Tex, 64-66. *Concurrent Pos:* Fel, A P Sloan Found, 73. *Mem:* AAAS; Am Chem Soc; Chem Soc London; Sigma Xi. *Res:* Applications of lanthanide shift reagents in nuclear magnetic resonance spectroscopy; inorganic chemistry; osmium chemistry; coal chemistry. *Mailing Add:* 907 S Valley Rd Carbondale IL 62901-2420

HIND, ALFRED THOMAS, JR, mathematics, for more information see previous edition

HIND, GEOFFREY, BIOCHEMISTRY, PLANT PHYSIOLOGY. *Current Pos:* res assoc, Brookhaven Nat Lab, 64-65, assoc plant physiologist, 65-67, plant physiologist, 67-78, actg chmn, 77-78, dep chmn, 78-87, chmn, Biol Dept, 87-90, SR BIOCHEMIST, BROOKHAVEN NAT LAB, 78- *Personal Data:* b Bolton, Eng, Apr 7, 37. *Educ:* Cambridge Univ, BA, 58; Univ London, PhD(biochem), 61. *Prof Exp:* Res assoc biol, McCollum-Pratt Inst, Johns Hopkins Univ, 61-64. *Mem:* Am Soc Plant Physiol; Am Soc Biol Chem; Am Soc Photobiol; Biophys Soc. *Res:* Photosynthetic electron transport; ion transport and phosphorylation in higher plants; plant protein kinases and phosphatases. *Mailing Add:* Biol Dept Brookhaven Nat Lab Upton NY 11973-5000. *Fax:* 516-344-3407; *E-Mail:* hind@bnl.gov

HIND, JOSEPH EDWARD, AUDITORY NEUROPHYSIOLOGY, PHYSIOLOGICAL ACOUSTICS. *Current Pos:* proj assoc, Dept Neurophysiol & Psychiat Inst, Univ Wis-Madison, 54-56, from asst prof to assoc prof physiol & neurophysiol, 56-64, prof, 64-94, chmn dept, 73-88, EMER PROF, NEUROPHYSIOL, UNIV WIS-MADISON, 94- *Personal Data:* b Chicago, Ill, Apr 2, 23; m 47, Ruth Lueders; c David, Thomas & Susan (Kronen). *Educ:* Ill Inst Technol, BS, 44; Univ Chicago, PhD(psychol), 52. *Prof Exp:* Asst mfg engr, Western Elec Co, Ill, 44-45; radio engr, Naval Res Lab, 45-46; asst otolaryngol & physiol acoust, Univ Chicago, 47-53; res assoc auditory electrophysiol, Cent Inst Deaf, Mo, 53-54. *Concurrent Pos:* Mem, NIH Commun Sci Study Sect, 62-66 & Comput & Biomath Sci Study Sect, 69-73; trustee, Beltone Inst Hearing Res, 63-86. *Mem:* AAAS; fel Acoust Soc Am; Soc Neurosci; Int Brain Res Orgn; Asn Res Otolaryngol. *Res:* Auditory neurophysiology, especially the acoustical and neural mechanisms of sound localization; electrophysiological and electroacoustical instrumentation, including computer techniques for processing physiological data. *Mailing Add:* Dept Neurophysiol Univ Wis Med Sch 1300 University Ave Madison WI 53706-1532. *Fax:* 608-265-3500; *E-Mail:* hind@neurophys.wisc.edu

HINDAL, DALE FRANK, PLANT PATHOLOGY, MYCOLOGY. *Current Pos:* Fel plant path, 73-75, asst prof mycol, 76-81, ASSOC PROF MYCOL & ASSOC MYCOLOGIST, WVA UNIV, 81- *Personal Data:* b Ladysmith, Wis, May 18, 38; m 65; c 1. *Educ:* Univ Wis, Eau Claire, BS, 67; Iowa State Univ, PhD(plant path), 73. *Mem:* Am Phytopath Soc; Am Mycol Soc; Sigma Xi. *Res:* Host parasite interaction of woody plant wilt disease; fungus physiology; mycoparasite relationships. *Mailing Add:* 416 Lawnview Dr Morgantown WV 26505

HINDER, RONALD ALBERT, SURGERY. *Current Pos:* assoc prof, 87-91, PROF SURG, CREIGHTON UNIV, 91- *Personal Data:* b Johannesburg, SAfrica, Jan 14, 42; Swiss citizen; m 68, Philla; c Ingrid, Paul & Lisa. *Educ:* Witwatersrand Univ, MB Bch, 65, PhD(surg), 76. *Prof Exp:* Lectr surg, Witwatersrand Univ, 70-82, assoc prof, 82-87. *Concurrent Pos:* Harry E Stuckenhoff endowed prof, 93- *Mem:* Am Col Surgeons; Cent Surg Asn; Am Gastroenterol Asn; Soc Surg Alimentary Tract; Western Surg Asn. *Res:* Foregut physiology and pathophysiology; gastroesophageal and duodenogastric reflex. *Mailing Add:* Surg Dept Creighton Univ Sch Med 2500 California St Omaha NE 68178-0001

HINDERSINN, RAYMOND RICHARD, ORGANIC POLYMER CHEMISTRY. *Current Pos:* CONSULT, 81- *Personal Data:* b Central Falls, RI, July 24, 18; m 44; c 1. *Educ:* Brown Univ, ScB, 49; Univ Wis, PhD(org chem), 54. *Honors & Awards:* Schoellkopf Medal, Am Chem Soc, 82. *Prof Exp:* Res chemist, Merck & Co, Inc, 49-51; res chemist, Hooker Chem Corp, 54-58, res supvr polymer chem, 58-68, supvr polymer testing & eval, 68-70, res coordr, 70-73, mgr polymer res, Hooker Chems & Plastics Corp, 73-75, mgr polymer appln & test, 75-78, sr scientist polymer res, 78-81. *Concurrent Pos:* Mem ad hoc comt on fire safety aspects of polymeric materials, Nat Mat Adv Bd-Nat Acad Sci, 72-78; consult polymer indust, 81- *Mem:* Am Chem Soc; Soc Plastic Eng; Sigma Xi. *Res:* Polymer synthesis; polymer testing and evaluation; organophosphorous chemistry; polymer fire retardance and fire retardant mechanisms; unsaturated polyesters; polyurethane foams; engineering thermoplastics. *Mailing Add:* 4288 Lower River Rd Youngstown NY 14174

HINDLE, BROOKE, EARLY AMERICAN SCIENCE & TECHNOLOGY. *Current Pos:* dir Nat Mus Hist & Technol, 74-78, sr historian, 78-85, EMER HISTORIAN, US NAT MUS AM HIST, SMITHSONIAN INST, 85- *Personal Data:* b Drexel Hill, Pa, Sept 28, 18; m 43, Helen Morris; c Margaret H (Hazen) & Donald M. *Educ:* Brown Univ, BA, 40; Univ Pa, MA, 42, PhD(hist), 49. *Honors & Awards:* Anson Phelps lectr, NY Univ, 79; Fel's Award Medal, Early Am Industs Asn, 83; Leonardo Da Vinci Medal, Soc Hist Technol, 84. *Prof Exp:* Asst hist, Univ Pa, 41-42 & 45-48; res assoc hist, Inst Early Am Hist & Cult, 48-50; from assoc prof to prof hist, NY Univ, 50-74, chmn dept hist, Univ Col, 65-67, dean, 67-69, head dept, 70-74. *Concurrent Pos:* Lectr hist, Col William & Mary, 48-50, Northwestern Univ, 50; sr res scholar, Eleutherian Mills-Hagley Found, 69-70; Killian vis prof hist sci & technol, Mass Inst Technol, 71-72; lectr, NY State Hist Asn, Cooperstown, 80; vis prof hist technol, Univ Central Fla, 81; distinguished vis prof hist technol, Univ Del, 82. *Mem:* Fel AAAS; Soc Hist Technol (vpres,

77-80, pres, 81-82); Soc Indust Archaeol; Hist Sci Soc (secy, 58-60); Am Philos Soc; Int Acad Hist Sci. *Res:* American technology and science from the Revolutionary to the Ante-bellum era; internal and external history; creativity in technology. *Mailing Add:* 415 Russell Ave No 808 Gaithersburg MD 20877-2841

HINDLE, MARGUERITA C, DYEING, FINISHING. *Current Pos:* TEXTILE CONSULT, TCE CONSULT SERVS, 88- *Personal Data:* b Providence, RI, Nov 26, 28; m 50, Robinson J. *Educ:* Univ RI, BS, 49. *Hon Degrees:* DSc, Univ RI, 93. *Honors & Awards:* Chapin Award, Am Asn Textile Chemists & Colorists, 93. *Prof Exp:* Lab technician, Kenyon Indust, 50-60, chief chemist, 60-70, dir res, 70, vpres res & develop, 78-88. *Concurrent Pos:* Lectr, Clemson Univ, NC State Univ, Univ Puget Sound, Wash State Univ & Univ Mass, 70-90, Swed Textile Mfrs Inst, 85; vis prof, Univ RI, 70-; chair, Environ Preserv Comt, Am Textile Mfrs Inst, 82-83. *Mem:* Am Asn Textile Chemists & Colorists (vpres, 78-80, pres, 87-88); Am Textile Mfrs Inst; Indust Fabrics Asn Int. *Res:* New product and process development for textile wt process manufacturing. *Mailing Add:* 15 Bellerose Dr Westerly RI 02891. *Fax:* 401-348-8310

HINDMAN, EDWARD EVANS, ATMOSPHERIC SCIENCES. *Current Pos:* ASSOC PROF, EARTH & PLANETARY SCI, CITY COL, CITY UNIV NY, 88- *Personal Data:* b Los Angeles, Calif, Sept 26, 42; div; c 3. *Educ:* Univ Utah, BSc, 65; Colo State Univ, MSc, 67; Univ Wash, PhD(atmos sci), 75. *Honors & Awards:* Father J B Macelwane Award, Am Meteorol Soc, 66. *Prof Exp:* Res meteorologist, Navy Weather Res Facil, 67-71, actg head phys meteor and weather modification br, 70-71; head plans, anal & reports sect, Naval Weapons Ctr, 71-74, head atmospheric interactions sect, 74-79; res assoc atmos sci, Colo State Univ, 79-88. *Concurrent Pos:* Naval Weapons Ctr fel, Univ Wash, 72-74; vis prof, US Naval Acad, 84-87, Drexel Univ, 88. *Mem:* Am Meteorol Soc; Royal Meteorol Soc; Am Geophys Union; Int Tech & Sci Orgn Soaring Flight. *Res:* Micro-structure of winter snowstorms, hurricanes and fogs; impact of industrial effluents on rainfall; physical, chemical, optical properties of clouds. *Mailing Add:* 195 Ft Lee Rd Apt 2E Leonia NJ 07605

HINDMAN, JOSEPH LEE, PLANT MORPHOLOGY, DEVELOPMENTAL ANATOMY. *Current Pos:* prof & chmn prog gen biol, 70-81, DIR ADV, WASH STATE UNIV, 81- *Personal Data:* b Baker, Ore, Dec 24, 33; m 55, Sharon McCord; c Jeffrey L, Kathryn M, Nancy L & James P. *Educ:* Harvard Univ, AB, 56; Univ Ore, MA, 58, PhD(plant morphol), 62. *Prof Exp:* Asst prof biol, La State Univ, New Orleans, 61-63 & State Univ NY Buffalo, 63-67; assoc prof bot, Univ Ga, 67-70. *Mem:* Bot Soc Am; Am Inst Biol Sci; Sigma Xi. *Res:* Floral morphogenesis; culture of floral buds in vitro. *Mailing Add:* SALC Wash State Univ Pullman WA 99164-1064

HINDMARSH, KENNETH WAYNE, PHARMACY. *Current Pos:* fac, 71-79, asst dean, 87-92, PROF, COL PHARM, UNIV SASK, 79-; DEAN, FAC PHARM, UNIV MAN, 92- *Personal Data:* b Grandview, MB, Aug 13, 41; m 66, Lois I Dies; c Carla A & Ryan J. *Educ:* Univ Sask, Can, BSP, 64, MSc, 65; Univ Alta, PhD, 70. *Prof Exp:* Staff pharmacist, Univ Hosp Saskatoon, 65-66; lectr, Univ Sask, 66-67; toxicologist, Royal Can Mounted Police, Regina, Sask, 70-71. *Concurrent Pos:* Med Res Coun vis prof, Man, 79, vis scientist, 81. *Mem:* Can Soc Forensic Sci (pres, 84); Asn Fac Pharm Can (pres, 77-78); Soc Toxicol Can; Can Pharm Asn; Nat Inst Nutrit; Int Asn Forensic Sci. *Mailing Add:* Fac Pharm Univ Man Winnipeg MB R3T 2N2 Can

HINDS, DAVID STEWART, PHYSIOLOGICAL ECOLOGY. *Current Pos:* from asst prof to assoc prof, 86-88, PROF BIOL, CALIF STATE UNIV, BAKERSFIELD, 76-, CHMN, DEPT BIOL, 86-88 & 95- *Personal Data:* b LaJolla, Calif, Dec 3, 39; m, E Annette Halper; c Michael Shaw, Jeffrey Wayne & Patrick Halper. *Educ:* Pomona Col, BA, 62; Univ Ariz, MS, 64, PhD(zool), 69. *Prof Exp:* Res assoc physiol ecol, Duke Univ, 64 & Univ Ariz, 69-70. *Concurrent Pos:* Fulbright sr scholar, Flinders Univ, SAustralia, 85-86, vis prof, 85-86 & 90; vis researcher, Dept Ecol & Evolutionary Biol, Univ Calif, Irvine, 80-82. *Mem:* Am Inst Biol Sci; AAAS; Ecol Soc Am; Am Asn Biol Sci; Nat Asn Biol Teachers. *Res:* Adjustment of physiology of vertebrates in response to the changing environment; seasonal changes in thermoregulation of vertebrates and their energy exchange in the natural microclimate. *Mailing Add:* Dept Biol Calif State Univ Bakersfield CA 93311-1099

HINDS, FRANK CROSSMAN, ANIMAL NUTRITION. *Current Pos:* PROF & HEAD, DEPT ANIMAL SCI, UNIV WYO, 80- *Personal Data:* b Sioux Falls, SDak, Nov 30, 30; m 53; c 3. *Educ:* Ill State Norm Univ, BS, 52; Univ Ill, MS, 57, PhD(animal sci), 59. *Prof Exp:* Asst animal sci, Univ Ill, Urbana, 55-59, asst prof to prof, 59-80, res assoc animal nutrit, Dixon Springs Exp Sta, 59-80. *Mem:* AAAS; Am Soc Animal Sci; Soc Range Mgt. *Res:* Nutrition and reproductive physiology of ruminants, especially the influence of anabolic agents on ruminants and factors related to utilization of forages by ruminants. *Mailing Add:* 1687 N 18th St Laramie WY 82070

HINDS, JAMES WADSWORTH, ANATOMY. *Current Pos:* ACCT, LOISELLE & BEATHAM, CPA'S. *Personal Data:* b Waterville, Maine, May 20, 41; m 67; c 1. *Educ:* Williams Col, AB, 63; Harvard Univ, PhD(anat), 68. *Prof Exp:* From instr to asst prof anat, Sch Med, Boston Univ, 67-75, assoc prof, 75- *Concurrent Pos:* USPHS res grants, Sch Med, Boston Univ, 69-74, 74-80 & 80-85. *Mem:* AAAS; Am Asn Anat; Soc Neurosci. *Res:* Neuroembryology; neurocytology; neuroanatomy; aging. *Mailing Add:* Loiselle & Beatham CPA's PO Box 62 Bangor ME 04402-0062

HINDS, MARVIN HAROLD, PHYSIOLOGY, BIOMEDICAL ENGINEERING. *Current Pos:* RETIRED. *Personal Data:* b Brookville, Ind, Oct 25, 28; m 52; c 2. *Educ:* Marion Col, BS, 51; Valparaiso Tech Inst, BS, 57; Tex A&M Univ, PhD(vet physiol), 71. *Prof Exp:* TV engr, M D Anderson Hosp, Univ Tex, 57-59; electronics supvr, Dept Physiol, Baylor Col Med, 59-67; asst prof physiol, Dept Vet Physiol & Pharmacol, Tex A&M Univ, 69-73; asst prof, Ind Wesleyan Univ, 73-80, prof, Biol Dept & coordr, 80-95. *Mem:* Med Electronics & Data Soc; Am Sci Affil. *Res:* New instrumentation for cardiac defibrillation; use of skeletal muscle for cardiac assist. *Mailing Add:* Dept Biol Ind Wesleyan Univ 4201 S Washington St Marion IN 46953-4999

HINDS, NANCY WEBB, PHYSICAL CHEMISTRY. *Current Pos:* ASST PROF CHEM, UNIV TENN, MARTIN, 80- *Personal Data:* b Milan, Tenn, Jan 14, 47; m 75; c 1. *Educ:* Univ Tenn, AB, 69; Memphis State Univ, PhD(phys chem), 73. *Prof Exp:* From res asst to res assoc phys biochem, Ctr Health Sci, Univ Tenn, 73-75; asst prof chem, Christian Brothers Col, 75-80. *Mem:* Am Chem Soc; Sigma Xi. *Res:* Physical parameters of drug interactions. *Mailing Add:* Chem Dept Univ Tenn Martin TN 38238-0001

HINDS, THOMAS EDWARD, PLANT PATHOLOGY. *Current Pos:* RETIRED. *Personal Data:* b Albuquerque, NMex, Nov 30, 22; m 56, Carmelita Benander; c Carl, Kevin & Keith. *Educ:* Colo State Univ, BS, 58, MS, 68. *Prof Exp:* Plant pathologist, Rocky Mountain Forest & Range Exp Sta, 59-70, res plant pathologist tree dis, 70-84. *Mem:* Am Phytopath Soc; Mycol Soc Am; AAAS. *Res:* Diseases of forest trees in general; aspen diseases in particular; decays and stains in forest trees. *Mailing Add:* 1212 Emigh St Ft Collins CO 80524

HINE, FREDERICK ROY, PSYCHIATRY. *Current Pos:* from asst prof to assoc prof, 59-71, PROF PSYCHIAT, MED CTR, DUKE UNIV, 71- *Personal Data:* b Cincinnati, Ohio, Nov 16, 25; m 48; c 1. *Educ:* Yale Univ, BS, 46, MD, 49. *Prof Exp:* Intern, Charity Hosp La, New Orleans, 49-50; resident fel psychiat, Sch Med, Tulane Univ, 50-53; psychiatrist, dir training & res & clin dir, Southeast La Hosp, 53-59. *Concurrent Pos:* Instr psychiat, Sch Med, Tulane Univ, 52-59; attend psychiat, Durham Vet Admin Hosp, 59-74, consult psychiat, 74- *Mem:* Am Psychiat Asn; Asn Dir Med Student Educ Psychiat. *Res:* Medical education. *Mailing Add:* Med Ctr Duke Univ Durham NC 27710

HINE, JACK, chemistry; deceased, see previous edition for last biography

HINE, JOHN MAYNARD, ORGANIC POLYMER CHEMISTRY. *Current Pos:* RETIRED. *Personal Data:* b Tacoma, Wash, Aug 1, 20; m 44; c 2. *Educ:* Col Puget Sound, BS, 44. *Prof Exp:* Asst chem, Univ Ore, 43-44; resin chemist, Borden Inc, 46-53, lab mgr, 53-54, West Coast develop mgr, 54-63, develop mgr, Thermosetting Prod Dept, Western Opers, 63-70, Borden Chem Co Div, 70-80, dir res & develop, Resins & Chem Div, 80-87. *Mem:* Am Inst Chemists. *Res:* Synthetic resins; plastics. *Mailing Add:* 26226 131st Pl SE Kent WA 98031

HINE, MAYNARD KIPLINGER, DENTISTRY, DENTAL HISTORY. *Current Pos:* chancellor, 69-73, exec assoc, Ind Univ Found, 73-78, EMER CHANCELLOR, IND UNIV-PURDUE UNIV, INDIANAPOLIS, 78- *Personal Data:* b Waterloo, Ind, Aug 25, 07; m 32, Harriet A Foulke; c Maynard K Jr, Judith V (Hyde) & William C. *Educ:* Univ Ill, DDS, 30, MS, 32. *Hon Degrees:* DSc, Case Western Res Univ, 67, Univ Ill, 69, Boston Univ, 69, Ohio State Univ, 70, Marian Col, 73, Temple Univ, 73, Ind Univ, 79. *Honors & Awards:* Presidential Award, Fedn Dentaire Int, 87; Hayden Harris Award, Am Acad Hist Dent, 83. *Prof Exp:* From instr to assoc prof oral path & periodontia, Col Dent, Univ Ill, 36-44; prof oral histopath & periodontia & head dept, Sch Dent, Ind Univ, Indianapolis, 44-78, dean, 45-69. *Concurrent Pos:* Rockefeller fel, Univ Rochester, 34-35, Carnegie fel, 35-36; pres, Am Asn Dent Sch, 53; mem, US Adv Panel Med Sci, 54; mem bd regents, Nat Libr Med, 59-63; mem, Nat Adv Dent Res Coun, 48-50 & 64-68 & Dept Defense Dent Adv Comt, 65-68; ed, Jour, Am Acad Periodont, 50-70; pres, Bd Cent Ind Coun on Aging, 80-83; pres, Am Asn; dent ed, Indianapolis Dist Dent Soc, Ind State Dent Asn, 58. *Mem:* AAAS; Am Dent Asn (pres elect, 64, pres, 65); Am Acad Periodont (pres, 64); Am Acad Hist Dent (pres, 81); Fedn Dent Int (pres, 75); Am Asn Dent Schs (pres, 53); Am Asn Endodontists (pres, 47); hon fel Royal Col Surgeons, Ireland; hon fel Royal Col Surgeons, Can. *Res:* Oral pathology; periodontia; dental hygiene; dental history. *Mailing Add:* 5354 W 62nd St Indianapolis IN 46268

HINE, RICHARD BATES, PLANT PATHOLOGY. *Current Pos:* PROF PLANT PATH & PLANT PATHOLOGIST, UNIV ARIZ, 67- *Personal Data:* b Los Angeles, Calif, June 2, 29; m 51; c 4. *Educ:* Univ Calif, Los Angeles, BA, 52; Univ Calif, Davis, PhD(plant path), 58. *Prof Exp:* Asst, Univ Calif, 56-58; tech rep, E I du Pont de Nemours & Co, 59-61; assoc prof, Univ Hawaii, 61-67, chmn dept, 63-67. *Concurrent Pos:* Staff mem, Calif Packing Corp, Philippines, 65-67. *Mem:* Am Phytopath Soc; Mycol Soc Am. *Res:* Soil fungi; fungus diseases of plants; agricultural chemicals. *Mailing Add:* 5933 N Via Del Chiquiri Tucson AZ 85718

HINE, RUTH LOUISE, WILDLIFE CONSERVATION, EARTH STEWARDSHIP. *Current Pos:* NATURALIST, BETHEL HORIZONS NATURE CTR, 86- *Personal Data:* b Columbus, Ohio, Aug 19, 23. *Educ:* Conn Col, BA, 44; Univ Wis, MA, 47, PhD, 52. *Honors & Awards:* Am Motors Conserv Award, 63; Commendation Award, Am Soil Conserv Soc, 64; Steven Mather Award, Nat Park & Conserv Assoc, 84. *Prof Exp:* Asst biol, Wesleyan Univ, 44-46; asst zool, Univ Wis, 46-48, asst wildlife mgt, 48-49; conserv aid, Dept Natural Resources, 49-52, biologist, 52-57, ed res publ, Natural Resources, Ecol & Environ, 57-74, natural resource specialist, 74-86. *Concurrent Pos:* Mem conf biol eds, Nat Conservancy; consult naturalist Lutheran Outdoor Ministries of Wis & Upper Mich, 84-85. *Mem:* Fel Am Soil Conserv Soc; Nature Conservancy; Green Cross Wilderness Soc. *Res:* Conservation of natural resources, especially game, fish, natural areas and endangered species; surveys and investigations on nongame, threatened and endangered species. *Mailing Add:* 6209 Mineral Point Rd No 516 Madison WI 53705-4535

HINEGARDNER, RALPH, DEVELOPMENTAL BIOLOGY. *Current Pos:* assoc prof natural sci, 68-72, PROF BIOL, CROWN COL, UNIV CALIF, SANTA CRUZ, 72- *Personal Data:* b New York, NY, Feb 18, 31; m 56; c 1. *Educ:* Denison Univ, BA, 53; Univ Southern Calif, MS, 57; Univ Hawaii, PhD(zool), 61. *Prof Exp:* USPHS res fel, Univ Hawaii, 60-63; from asst prof to assoc prof zool, Columbia Univ, 63-68. *Mem:* Fel AAAS; Soc Gen Physiol; Soc Develop Biol; Sigma Xi. *Res:* Theoretical biology; invertebrate development; nucleic acid synthesis and evolution. *Mailing Add:* Dept Biol Univ Calif Santa Cruz CA 95060

HINERMAN, DORIN LEE, PATHOLOGY. *Current Pos:* resident, Hosp, 43-45, from instr to prof, Med Sch, 45-84, med sch counsr, 63-75, EMER PROF PATH, UNIV MICH, ANN ARBOR, 84- *Personal Data:* b Huntington, WVa, Apr 19, 14; m 44; c 2. *Educ:* Marshall Col, AB, 37; Univ Mich, MD, 42; Am Bd Path, dipl, 48. *Prof Exp:* Intern, Milwaukee Hosp, 42-43. *Concurrent Pos:* Consult, Vet Admin Hosp, Ann Arbor, 54- & Mich Tumor Registry, 54-61; chmn bd trustees, Mich Cancer Found, 81-84; chmn, Mich Cancer Registry Comt; chmn spec admis comt, Univ Mich, Ann Arbor, mem exec comt, Fac Gov Body & mem intercol athletics control bd. *Mem:* Fel Am Soc Clin Path; AMA; Am Asn Path & Bact; Int Acad Path. *Res:* Endocrine pathology; oncology; medical education. *Mailing Add:* 1240 Chelsea Manchester Rd Univ Mich Chelsea MI 48118

HINES, ANSON HEMINGWAY, ZOOLOGY, MARINE BIOLOGY. *Current Pos:* RES ECOLOGIST & ASST DIR, SMITHSONIAN INST, 79- *Personal Data:* b Honolulu, Hawaii, Jan 4, 47. *Educ:* Pomona Col, BA, 69; Univ Calif, Berkeley, PhD(zool), 76. *Prof Exp:* Res fel zool, Univ Calif, Santa Cruz, 75-78; sr marine biologist, Tera Corp, 78-79. *Concurrent Pos:* Adj prof, Dept Zool, Univ Md, College Park. *Mem:* Am Soc Zoologists; Sigma Xi; Ecol Soc Am. *Res:* Marine invertebrate zoology; population and community ecology. *Mailing Add:* PO Box 28 Edgewater MD 21037

HINES, ANTHONY LORING, MASS TRANSFER, SYNTHETIC FUELS. *Current Pos:* RETIRED. *Personal Data:* b Sept 19, 41; m 63; c 7. *Educ:* Univ Okla, BS, 67; Okla State Univ, MS, 69; Univ Tex, Austin, PhD(mech eng), 73. *Prof Exp:* Chem process & plant engr, Gulf Oil Co, 67-69; sr assoc chem engr, IBM, 69-73; instr mech eng, Univ Tex, Austin, 72-73; asst prof chem eng, Ga Tech, 73-75; from asst to assoc prof, Colo Sch Mines, 75-80; dept head & prof, Chem Eng, Univ Wyo, 80-83; assoc dean & prof chem eng, Okla State Univ, 83-87; dean & prof, Col Eng, Univ Mo, Columbia, 87-93. *Concurrent Pos:* Consult, Laramie Energy Res Ctr, Dept Energy, 76-83, Western Oil Sands, Ltd, 77-81, Solar Energy Res Inst, 79-81; proj dir synthetic fuel studies, US Dept Energy, 78; proj dir adsorption studies, Solar Energy Res Inst, 80-81; vis prof, Assoc Western Univs, US Dept Energy, 82; prin investr weapon studies, Dept Air Force, 83- *Mem:* Am Inst Chem Engrs; Sigma Xi; AAAS; Am Soc Eng Educ; Nat Soc Prof Engrs; Int Adsorption Soc. *Res:* Oil shale and tar sands; adsorption of gases and liquids on solids; mass transfer and diffusion; indoor air quality. *Mailing Add:* Honda of Am 24000 Honda Pkwy Maryville OH 43040-9251

HINES, HAROLD C, DAIRY SCIENCE, IMMUNOGENETICS. *Current Pos:* Asst prof, 65-70, ASSOC PROF DAIRY SCI, OHIO STATE UNIV, 70- *Personal Data:* b Ashville, Ohio, Dec 12, 37; m 63; c 3. *Educ:* Ohio State Univ, BS, 59, MS, 61, PhD(dairy sci), 65. *Mem:* AAAS; Am Soc Animal Sci; Int Soc Animal Blood Group Res; Am Dairy Sci Asn; Sigma Xi. *Res:* Cattle blood antigens; serum and milk genetic polymorphisms. *Mailing Add:* Animal Scis Dept Ohio State Univ 2027 Coffey Rd Columbus OH 43210-1094

HINES, JAMES R, surgery, for more information see previous edition

HINES, LEONARD RUSSELL, BIOCHEMISTRY, PHARMACOLOGY. *Current Pos:* RETIRED. *Personal Data:* b Mechanicsville, Iowa, Feb 8, 13; m 41; c 3. *Educ:* Cornell Col, BS, 34; Univ Iowa, PhD(biochem), 43. *Prof Exp:* Res chemist, Wilson & Co, Ill, 34-37; asst biochem, Univ Chicago, 37-40; asst, Univ Iowa, 40-42; head dept biochem, E R Squibb & Sons, 43-52; chief chem pharmacol, Lederle Labs Div, Am Cyanamid Co, 52-58; clin investr, Hoffmann-La Roche, Inc, 58-59, assoc dir biol res, 59-62, dir biol res, 62-78, asst vpres, 73-78. *Mem:* Fel AAAS; Am Fedn Clin Res; Am Col Clin Pharmacol; Am Col Neuropsychopharmacol; NY Acad Sci. *Res:* Drug metabolism; toxicology; chemotherapy; clinical investigation. *Mailing Add:* 17233 Cuvee Ct Poway CA 92064-1214

HINES, MARGARET H, ANATOMY. *Current Pos:* asst instr anat, 62-63, instr, 63-74, asst prof, 75-81, ASSOC PROF, OHIO STATE UNIV, 81- *Personal Data:* b Cincinnati, Ohio, Sept 29, 23; m 49; c 2. *Educ:* Univ Cincinnati, BSc, 45; Ohio State Univ, MSc, 42, PhD(anat and student personnel admin), 74. *Prof Exp:* Phys therapist, US Army, 46-48 & Elizabeth Kenny Inst, Minneapolis, 49-50. *Concurrent Pos:* Phys therapist, Children's Hosp, Columbus, Ohio, 48-, asst dir outpatient dept, 51-; fel, Elizabeth Kenny Inst, 49-51; guest lectr, Bowling Green State Univ, 73, Ohio Dominican Col, 73 & Dept Surg, Beaumont Gen Hosp, Royal Oak, Mich, 75. *Mem:* Sigma Xi; Asn Am Women Sci; Asn Am Med Cols; Am Asn Clin Anatomists. *Res:* Control, computer simulation and clinical investigation of human and biped robot locomotion; medical college admissions process and student advising systems; clinical manifestations of vascular pain. *Mailing Add:* Anat Ohio State Univ Col Med 370 W Ninth Ave Columbus OH 43210-1238

HINES, MARK EDWARD, MARINE MICROBIOLOGY, BIOGEOCHEMISTRY. *Current Pos:* asst prof, 95-97, ASSOC PROF, UNIV ALASKA, ANCHORAGE, 97- *Personal Data:* b Pasadena, Tex, Apr 30, 50; m 69, Katherine Sheridan; c David & Sarah. *Educ:* Ohio State Univ, BS, 73; Univ Conn, MS, 78; Univ NH, PhD(microbiol), 81. *Prof Exp:* Res scientist marine biol, Univ NH, 81-84, res asst prof earth sci, 84-89, res assoc prof, 89-95. *Concurrent Pos:* Prin investr sea grant, Nat Oceanic & Atmospheric Admin, Univ NH, 81-84, NSF grant, 81-84, 85-88, 92-93 & 95-96, Nat Aeronaut & Space Admin grant, 83-88, 88-91 & 91-92, Am Chem Soc, 88-90; instr, Sch Life Long Learning, 82-85; Environ Protection Agency grant, 92-96. *Mem:* Am Soc Microbiol; Am Soc Limnol & Oceanog; Sigma Xi; Estuarine Res Fedn; AAAS; Am Geophys Union. *Res:* Microbial biogeochemistry of marine sediments with emphasis on microbial activity rates; interactions with trace metals; anaerobic nutrient regeneration; hypersaline ecology; wetlands ecology; production and emission of biogenic trace gases; application of molecular biology techniques to ecology. *Mailing Add:* Dept Biol Sci Univ Alaska Anchorage AK 99508. *Fax:* 907-786-4607; *E-Mail:* afmeh@uaa.alaska.edu

HINES, PAMELA JEAN, DEVELOPMENTAL BIOLOGY. *Current Pos:* SR ED DEVELOP NEUROBIOL & PLANT BIOL, SCIENCE MAG, AAAS, 89- *Personal Data:* b Detroit, Mich, July 19, 52. *Educ:* Oberlin Col, AB, 74; Univ Wis, MS, 77; Johns Hopkins Univ, PhD(biol), 83. *Prof Exp:* Instr develop biol, Purdue Univ, 77-79; res assoc molecular biol, Univ Wash, 84-89. *Concurrent Pos:* Ed, Asn Women Sci Mag. *Mem:* Soc Develop Biol; Am Soc Cell Biol; Am Soc Plant Physiol; Asn Women Sci. *Res:* Developmental biology; human genetics; chromosomes; plant development and molecular biology; hematopoiesis; neurobiology. *Mailing Add:* 1200 New York Ave NW Washington DC 20005

HINES, PAUL STEWARD, ORGANIC CHEMISTRY. *Current Pos:* Asst prof to assoc prof, 68-78, chmn dept, 71-80, PROF CHEM, WESTERN CONN STATE UNIV, 78- *Personal Data:* b New Brighton, Pa, Aug 31, 40; m 72, Ann M Hanahoe; c Mary Beth, Paul Cyril, Ann Marie & Daniel Joseph. *Educ:* Geneva Col, BSCh, 62; Univ Pa, PhD(org chem), 69. *Concurrent Pos:* Adj prof, New Eng Inst, Inc, 70-80. *Mem:* Am Chem Soc; Nat Asn Advisors Health Professions. *Res:* Synthesis, physical properties, and medicinal structure-function relationships of heterocyclic compounds, especially nitrogen bridgehead compounds and porphyrins. *Mailing Add:* Dept Chem Western Conn State Univ 181 White St Danbury CT 06810-6885. *E-Mail:* hinesp@wcsu.ctstateu.edu

HINES, RODERICK LUDLOW, SOLID STATE PHYSICS. *Current Pos:* from asst prof to assoc prof, 57-66, PROF PHYSICS, NORTHWESTERN UNIV, EVANSTON, 66- *Personal Data:* b Cleveland, Ohio, Nov 20, 25; m 49; c 5. *Educ:* Oberlin Col, BA, 47; Univ Mich, MS, 49, PhD(physics), 54. *Prof Exp:* Trainee, Gen Elec Co, NY, 47-48; physicist, sci lab, Ford Motor Co, Mich, 53-57. *Mem:* Am Phys Soc. *Res:* Irradiation effects; ion ranges in solids; imperfections in solids; electrostatic atomization; high resolution electron microscopy. *Mailing Add:* 2252 Orrington Ave Evanston IL 60201

HINES, WILLIAM CURTIS, ELECTRICAL ENGINEERING. *Current Pos:* Mem tech staff, 67-69, supvr Systs Studies Div II, 69-82, DEPT MGR, SANDIA NAT LABS, 82- *Personal Data:* b Greenwood, Miss, Mar 23, 40; m 61, Julie A Ingram; c Virginia E & William C III. *Educ:* Miss State Univ, BS, 62, MS, 64; Auburn Univ, PhD(elec eng), 67. *Mem:* Inst Elec & Electronics Engrs. *Res:* Optical control theory. *Mailing Add:* Dept 5400 Sandia Nat Labs Albuquerque NM 87185

HINES, WILLIAM GRANT, PHYSICAL CHEMISTRY. *Current Pos:* RETIRED. *Personal Data:* b Hamilton, Ont, June 22, 16; m 39, Maureen Havery; c Gordon, Gary (deceased) & Roderick. *Educ:* Univ Toronto, BA, 37, MA, 38, PhD, 42. *Prof Exp:* Asst corrosion, Nat Res Coun Can, 38-39, asst chem warfare, 39-40; demonstr, Univ Toronto, 40-42; inspector, Res Enterprises Ltd, 42-43, head, Approvals Lab, 43-46; sr res assoc indust chem res, BC Res Coun, 46-49; dir, Sch Indust Chem, Ryerson Inst Technol, 49-56; develop chemist surface chem, Steel Co Can, 56-58, div metallurgist chem activ, 58-64, gen supv metallurgist, Labs, 64-81. *Mem:* Fel Chem Inst Can. *Res:* Surface chemistry; electrochemistry; analytical chemistry; education. *Mailing Add:* 225 Bamburgh Circle Suite 201 Scarborough ON M1W 3X9 Can

HINES, WILLIAM W, INDUSTRIAL & SYSTEMS ENGINEERING. *Current Pos:* From instr to prof indust eng, 59-96, res asst prof comput appln res, 59-64, assoc dir, Sch Indust & Systs Eng, 68-96, EMER PROF INDUST ENG, GA INST TECHNOL, 96- *Personal Data:* b Tampa, Fla, Dec 12, 32; m 59; c 2. *Educ:* Memphis State Univ, BS, 54; Ga Inst Technol, MSIE, 58, PhD(opers res), 64. *Concurrent Pos:* Asst ed & tech notes ed, J Indust Eng, 59-67; lead engr, assoc prin engr & consult, Radiation Inc, 65-70; mem, Food & Drug Admin adv comt on med device good mfg pract, 77-80; pres, Enstat, Inc, 80- *Mem:* Opers Res Soc Am; Am Statist Asn; Inst Indust Engrs; Am Soc Eng Educ; AAAS. *Res:* Sampling methods; engineering statistics; power systems load research and management. *Mailing Add:* 1989 Tall Tree Dr NE Atlanta GA 30324. *Fax:* 404-874-2301; *E-Mail:* william.hines@isye.gatech.edu

HINESLEY, CARL PHILLIP, MECHANICAL METALLURGY, ENERGY CONSERVATION TECHNOLOGY. *Current Pos:* VPRES ENG, MARLEY ELEC HEATING, 86- *Personal Data:* b Muncie, Ind, Aug 13, 44; m 66; c 3. *Educ:* Univ Ky, BS, 67, MS, 69, PhD(mat sci), 72. *Prof Exp:* Proj mgr mech metall, Brush-Wellman, Inc, 72-75; proj mgr, Gould Labs, Gould Inc, 75-76, mgr prod develop energy conserv, Elec Heat Div, 76-77, prog mgr elec mat, 77-78; dir prod develop, Energy Conserv, Chromalox Div, Emerson Elec, 78-86. *Mem:* Inst Elec & Electronics Engrs; Am Soc Metals; Am Inst Mining, Metall & Petrol Engrs. *Res:* Reciprocal relations effecting the structure, properties and elevated temperature formability of materials. *Mailing Add:* PO Box 1298 Pinehurst NC 28370

HINGERTY, BRIAN EDWARD, BIOPHYSICS, COMPUTATIONAL BIOLOGY. *Current Pos:* Eugene P Wigner fel biol, 78-80, SCI STAFF LIFE SCI, OAK RIDGE NAT LAB, 80- *Personal Data:* b Brooklyn, NY, July 30, 48. *Educ:* Brooklyn Col, BS, 69; Princeton Univ, MA, 71, PhD(biophys), 74. *Honors & Awards:* Sigma Xi Award, 69. *Prof Exp:* NATO fel chem, Max Planck Inst Exp Med, Gottingen, WGer, 74-75; NIH fel, Med Res Coun Lab Molecular Biol, Cambridge, Eng, 75-78. *Concurrent Pos:* Consult, Biol Dept, NY Univ, 77-; instr, Physics Dept & asst prof, Math Dept, Univ Tenn, Knoxville, 81-; owner, Knox Comput Consult, 96- *Mem:* Fel Am Phys Soc; Am Crystallog Asn; Biophys Soc; Sigma Xi; Neutron Scattering Soc. *Res:* X-ray and neutron structure of biologically important compounds; semi-empirical potential energy methods; nucleic acid structure; crystallography; supercomputers; structure prediction; nuclear magnetic resonance; computational biology; parallel supercomputers. *Mailing Add:* Oak Ridge Nat Lab-LSD PO Box 2009 MS 8077 Oak Ridge TN 37831-8077. *Fax:* 423-574-1274; *E-Mail:* beh@ornl.gov

HINGORANI, NARAIN G, HIGH VOLTAGE DIRECT CURRENT TRANSMISSION. *Current Pos:* RETIRED. *Personal Data:* b Karachi, Pakistan, June 15, 31; US citizen; c 2. *Educ:* Baroda Univ, BS, 53; Univ Manchester Inst Sci & Technol, MSc, 57, PhD(elec eng), 60. *Hon Degrees:* DSc, Univ Manchester, Eng, 93. *Honors & Awards:* Uno Lamm Award, Power Eng Soc, Inst Elec & Electronics Engrs, 85, Lamme Medal, 95; ASM Inst Eng Mat Achievement Award, 87. *Prof Exp:* Res fel, Inst Sci & Technol, Univ Manchester, 57-61; lectr, Loughborough Univ, Eng, 61-63; sr lectr, Univ Salford, Eng, 63-68; consult, Bonneville Power Admin, 68-74; prog mgr, AC/DC substas, Elec Power Res Inst, 74-83, dir, Transmission Dept, 83-86, vpres, Elec Systs Div, 86-94, sr exec advan technol, 94-95. *Concurrent Pos:* Mem, Joint US-USSR Subcomt Res Design & Oper Ultrahigh Voltage Transmission, 70-76; mem, Coord Comt High Power Electronics Res & Develop, Elec Power Res Inst, 85- & co-chmn, Superconducting Coord Comt, 87-; mem bd dir, Power Eng Soc, Inst Elec & Electronics Engrs; spec reporter, CIGRE SC14, 84-86, chmn, 89- *Mem:* Nat Acad Eng; fel Inst Elec & Electronics Engrs. *Res:* Electric utility power transmission; application of amorphous steel in transformer cores; zinc oxide technology for overvoltage control; advancements in power semi-conductor technology; performance and extended application of direct current transmission; flexibile AC transmission systems (FACTS); custom power. *Mailing Add:* 26480 Weston Dr Los Altos CA 94022. *Fax:* 650-941-4309

HINISH, WILMER WAYNE, AGRONOMY. *Current Pos:* RETIRED. *Personal Data:* b Curryville, Pa, Apr 1, 25; m 46, Janet M Emigh; c Pamela K & Mark A. *Educ:* Pa State Univ, BS, 51, MS, 53, PhD(agron), 55. *Prof Exp:* Asst agron, 51-54, from instr to assoc prof, 54-68, prof coordr agron ext prog, 76-80, asst dean coop exten, 80-82, assoc dean, 82-88, prof agron, Pa State Univ, 68-, actg dean agr, 85-86. *Concurrent Pos:* Chief agriculturist, Tipton & Kalmbach, Inc, consult water & power develop authority, WPakistan, 63-65. *Mem:* Am Soc Agron; Coun Soil Testing & Plant Anal. *Res:* Relationships between chemical soil test and the potash content of timothy and red clover; amino acid content of grasses as affected by nitrogen fertilizers and time of cutting; agronomy extension; soil fertility; plant nutrition. *Mailing Add:* 1851 Park Forest Ave State Col University Park PA 16803

HINK, WALTER FREDRIC, CELL BIOLOGY, NATURAL PRODUCT INSECTICIDES. *Current Pos:* from asst prof to assoc prof, 68-76, PROF ENTOM & MICROBIOL, OHIO STATE UNIV, 77 - *Personal Data:* b Alhambra, Calif, June 29, 38; m 61; c 2. *Educ:* Ashland Col, BS, 61; Ohio State Univ, MS, 63, PhD(entom), 65. *Prof Exp:* Res entomologist, Int Minerals & Chem Corp, 66-68. *Concurrent Pos:* Res grants, NSF & Environ Protection Agency, 73, WHO, 78. *Mem:* AAAS; Tissue Cult Asn (treas, 76); Entom Soc Am; Soc Invert Path; Am Soc Microbiol. *Res:* Invertebrate cell culture; characterization of cultured cells; cell nutrition; new approaches to insect control, in vitro culture of differentiated cells and cell hybridization; insecticides from natural products; biological activity of venoms; flea control with natural products and systemics. *Mailing Add:* 4310 Shelbourne Lane Columbus OH 43220

HINKAMP, JAMES BENJAMIN, CHEMISTRY. *Current Pos:* CONSULT, 83- *Personal Data:* b Holland, Mich, Mar 18, 19; m 43; c 3. *Educ:* Hope Col, AB, 40; Ohio State Univ, PhD(org chem), 43. *Honors & Awards:* Midgley Award, 85. *Prof Exp:* Asst, Ohio State Univ, 40-42; res chemist, Ethyl Corp, 43-48, sect head, 48-52, res supvr, 52-63, dir chem tech serv, 63-65, asst dir res & develop, 65-83. *Mem:* AAAS; Am Chem Soc. *Res:* Development, testing and analysis of fuel and lubricant additives for diesel and gasoline engines. *Mailing Add:* 1444 S Bates St Birmingham MI 48009-1903

HINKAMP, PAUL EUGENE, (II), organic chemistry; deceased, see previous edition for last biography

HINKE, JOSEPH ANTHONY MICHAEL, ANATOMY, BIOPHYSICS. *Current Pos:* RETIRED. *Personal Data:* b Vancouver, BC, Nov 6, 31; m 57; c 3. *Educ:* Univ BC, MD, 57. *Prof Exp:* Asst prof, Univ BC, 60-65, assoc prof, 65-68, prof anat, 68-77; prof anat & chmn dept, Sch Med, Univ Ottawa, 77-92. *Concurrent Pos:* Am Life Ins res fel, Univ Col, Univ London, 58-60; Markle scholar, Univ BC, 60-65; mem adv, BC Heart Found, 65-69 & Can Heart Found, 66-69; mem, Scholar Selection Comt, Med Res Coun Can, 69-74, mem, Grants Comt Physiol & Pharmacol, 73-92; assoc ed, Can J Physiol & Pharmacol, 69-74. *Mem:* Can Asn Anat; Can Physiol Soc; Biophys Soc; Am Physiol Soc; Am Asn Anat. *Res:* Physico-chemical state of water and ions in muscle; electrolyte permeability, transport and contraction; ion-sensitive microelectrodes. *Mailing Add:* Dept Anat Univ Ottawa Ottawa ON K1N 6N5 Can

HINKEBEIN, JOHN ARNOLD, PHYSICAL CHEMISTRY. *Current Pos:* Res chemist, 58-67, res specialist, 67-85, SR RES SPECIALIST, MONSANTO CO, 85- *Personal Data:* b Leopold, Mo, Mar 5, 31; m 55; c 6. *Educ:* Southeast Mo State Col, BS, 54; Iowa State Univ, PhD, 58. *Mem:* Am Chem Soc. *Res:* Phosphorus compounds. *Mailing Add:* 2450 Barrett Station Rd Ballwin MO 63021

HINKEL, ROBERT DALE, FUEL SCIENCE CHEMISTRY & TECHNOLOGY. *Current Pos:* assoc prof, 63-64, chmn & prof, 64-79, EMER PROF CHEM, UNIV PITTSBURGH, 79- *Personal Data:* b York, Pa, Mar 11, 14; m 38; c R James & Dorothy H (Wayne). *Educ:* Pa State Col, BS, 36, PhD(tech fuels), 46; Lawrence Col, MS, 38. *Prof Exp:* Asst petrol ref, Pa State Col, 38-43 & fuel tech, 43-47; chief anal chem sect, off synthetic liquid fuels, Res & Develop Br, US Bur Mines, 47-53; pres, R D Hinkel & Co, 53-; mgr analysis res & develop, Koppers Co, Inc, 54-62; sr proj res engr, Arnold Eng Develop Ctr, 63. *Res:* Chemical and instrumental methods of analysis of hydrocarbons, synthetic fuels, gases, polymers, coal tar oils, catalysts, latices, dyestuffs and fine organic chemicals. *Mailing Add:* 284 Streets Run Rd Pittsburgh PA 15236-2005

HINKELMANN, KLAUS HEINRICH, STATISTICS. *Current Pos:* assoc prof, 66-72, head dept, 82-93, PROF STATIST, VA POLYTECH INST & STATE UNIV, 72- *Personal Data:* b Bad Segeberg, Ger, June 6, 32; m 66, Christa Gneist; c Christoph. *Educ:* Univ Hamburg, dipl, 58; Iowa State Univ, PhD(statist), 63. *Prof Exp:* Sci asst statist, Univ Freiburg, 64-66. *Concurrent Pos:* Ed, Biomet, 90-93. *Mem:* Biomet Soc; Inst Math Statist; fel Am Statist Asn; Sigma Xi; fel AAAS; Int Statist Inst. *Res:* Experimental design; genetic statistics; linear models. *Mailing Add:* Dept Statist Va Polytech Inst & State Univ Blacksburg VA 24061-0439. *Fax:* 540-231-3863; *E-Mail:* khstat@vt.edu

HINKES, THOMAS MICHAEL, TECHNOLOGY TRANSFER, PATENT LICENSING. *Current Pos:* PRIN, INTELLECTUAL PROPERTY ASSOC, 95-; FOUNDER, EGG INNOVATIONS, 95- *Personal Data:* b Watertown, Wis, Aug 14, 29; m 53, 84, Sandra K Fitzpatrick; c 6. *Educ:* Univ Notre Dame, BS, 51. *Prof Exp:* Applns res chemist, Victor Chem Works, Ill, 51-58; sr res chemist, Trionics Corp, 58-62; vpres & gen mgr, Chem Div, Madison Res & Develop Labs, Inc, 62-67, pres & sales mgr, Madison Res, Inc, 67-68; dir, Coating Develop Lab, Wis Alumni Res Found, 68-77, assoc licensing dir & sr licensing assoc, 77-89, dir patent licensing, 87-90, sr licensing assoc, 90-95. *Concurrent Pos:* Instr, Edgewood Col, 59-60; vpres cent region, Asn Univ Technol Mgrs, 91-; consult, expert witness, lectr-intelectual prop; prin, Bus Licensing Assocs, 90-95. *Mem:* Licensing Execs Soc; Asn Univ Technol Mgrs. *Res:* Technical management; technology valuation; patent licensing. *Mailing Add:* 4934 Raymond Rd Madison WI 53711

HINKLE, BARTON L(ESLIE), CHEMICAL ENGINEERING. *Current Pos:* CONSULT, 87- *Personal Data:* b Miami Beach, Fla, Nov 2, 25; m 49, 59; c 5. *Educ:* Purdue Univ, BSChE, 49; Inst Textile Technol, MS, 51; Ga Inst Technol, PhD(chem eng), 53. *Prof Exp:* Asst, Eng Exp Sta, Ga Inst Technol, 51-53; vpres, Human Resources, Electromagnetic Sci, Inc, 84-87. *Mem:* Am Inst Chem Engrs. *Res:* Cellulose chemistry; rheology of cellulose dispersions; heat-transfer characteristics of cellulose dispersions; fine particle technology; aggregation of aerosols, pneumatic conveying. *Mailing Add:* 5773 Hunton Wood Dr Broad Run VA 20137

HINKLE, CHARLES N(ELSON), AGRICULTURAL ENGINEERING, MICROPROCESSOR CONTROLS. *Current Pos:* assoc prof, 65-69, PROF AGR ENG, PURDUE UNIV, 69- *Personal Data:* b Lafayette, Ind, Sept 12, 30; m 51; c 4. *Educ:* Purdue Univ, BSAE, 51; Mich State Univ, MS, 53; Univ Mo, PhD(agr eng), 57. *Prof Exp:* Asst farm struct, Mich State Univ, 51-52, instr, 52-53; agr market specialist, Armco Steel Corp, 53; asst farm struct, Univ Mo, 55-56, instr, 56-57; assoc prof, SDak State Univ, 57-65. *Concurrent Pos:* Adv, Freshman Eng Dept, Purdue Univ, 68-; vis prof, NC State Univ, 79. *Mem:* Fel Am Soc Agr Engrs; Am Soc Eng Educ; Am Soc Heating, Refrig & Air-Conditioning Engrs. *Res:* Environmental control for animals, plants and their products; instruments for measuring man's environment; microprocessor control systems for agricultural equipment. *Mailing Add:* 400 N Sharon Chapel Rd West Lafayette IN 47906-4838

HINKLE, DALE ALBERT, AGRONOMY. *Current Pos:* from actg head dept to head dept, 49-77, from assoc prof to prof, 48-77, EMER PROF AGRON, UNIV ARK, Fayetteville, 77- *Personal Data:* b Perkins, Okla, Feb 2, 11; m 36; c 1. *Educ:* Okla State Univ, BS, 34, MS, 36; Univ Mass, PhD(agron), 49. *Prof Exp:* Asst prof agron, NMex State Col, 36-46. *Concurrent Pos:* Sabbatical, CIMMYT, El Batan, Mex. *Mem:* Am Soc Agron; Soil Sci Soc Am. *Res:* Soil fertility; soil management; plant nutrition. *Mailing Add:* 1648 E Shadowridge Dr Fayetteville AR 72701

HINKLE, DAVID CURRIER, ENZYMOLOGY. *Current Pos:* asst prof, 74-80, ASSOC PROF BIOL, UNIV ROCHESTER, 80- *Personal Data:* b Brattleboro, Vt, June 7, 44; m 68, Patricia Mills; c Caroline, Daniel & Thomas. *Educ:* Harvard Univ, BA, 66; Univ Calif, Berkeley, PhD(biochem), 71. *Prof Exp:* Fel biochem, Harvard Med Sch, 71-74. *Concurrent Pos:* Fel, Jane Coffin Childs Mem Fund Med Res, Harvard Med Sch, 71-73. *Mem:* Am Soc Biol Chemists. *Res:* Mechanisms and biological functions of nucleic acid enzymes with a current emphasis on proteins involved in DNA replication, recombination and repair. *Mailing Add:* Dept Biol Univ Rochester Rochester NY 14627-0001. *Fax:* 716-275-2070; *E-Mail:* hinkle@dch.biology.rochester.edu

HINKLE, GEORGE HENRY, NUCLEAR MEDICINE IMAGING, RADIOIMMUNODIAGNOSIS. *Current Pos:* CLIN ASST PROF RADIOL & PHARM, COL MED, OHIO STATE UNIV, 81-, ASSOC PROF PHARM, PRACT & ADMIN, COL PHARM. *Personal Data:* b Rensselaer, Ind, May 7, 52; m 72; c 2. *Educ:* Purdue Univ, BS, 75, MS, 77. *Prof Exp:* Grad instr nuclear pharm, Sch Pharm, Purdue Univ, 75-77, instr, 77-78; asst prof nuclear pharm, Col Pharm, Univ Okla, 78-81. *Concurrent Pos:* Dir, Nuclear Pharm Serv, Ohio State Univ Med Ctr; chmn, Sect Nuclear Pharm, Acad Pharm Pract, 85-86 & Specialty Coun Nuclear Pharm, Bd Pharmaceut Specialties, 85-91. *Mem:* Soc Nuclear Med; fel Am Pharmaceut Asn; Sigma Xi; fel Am Soc Hosp Pharmacists; fel Am Health Syst Pharmacists. *Res:* Radionuclide methodology and nuclear pharmacy practice; design, development preparation, quality assessment, clinical use and disposal of radiopharmaceuticals; development of new diagnostic and therapeutic radiopharmaceuticals; development of radiolabeled antibodies for diagnosis and therapy of cancer. *Mailing Add:* 1795 Upper Chelsea Rd Columbus OH 43212. *Fax:* 614-293-4366; *E-Mail:* hinkle-1@medctr.osu.edu

HINKLE, LAWRENCE EARL, JR, CARDIOVASCULAR EPIDEMIOLOGY, HUMAN ECOLOGY. *Current Pos:* RETIRED. *Personal Data:* b Raleigh, NC, Feb 7, 18; m 42; c 6. *Educ:* Univ NC, AB, 38; Harvard Univ, MD, 42; Am Bd Internal Med, dipl, 53. *Prof Exp:* Intern, Peter Bent Brigham Hosp, Boston, 42-43; asst resident internal med, New York Hosp, 46-48; instr, Med Col, Cornell Univ, 50-51, asst prof clin med, 51-56, assoc prof, 56-61, clin assoc prof med, 61-64, assoc prof, 64-71, prof med, 71-88, dir human ecol, 84-88. *Concurrent Pos:* Commonwealth fel med, New York Hosp, 48-50; asst physician, Out-Patient Dept, New York Hosp, 50-51; physician, 51-58, from asst attend physician to assoc attend physician, 58-71; consult, Ed Dept, Time, Inc, 54-; consult, Med Dept, Am Tel & Tel Co, 56-; mem environ sci rev comt, NIH, 64-66; mem environ sci training comt, Nat Inst Environ Health Sci, 66-70, chmn, 68-71; consult, Prog Resources & Environ, Ford Found, 68-70; chmn, Interuniv Bd Collabr, Bur Community Environ Mgt, Dept Health, Educ & Welfare, 69-70; mem bldg res adv bd, Comn on Sociotech Systs, Nat Res Coun, 75-81; mem policy bd, Multictr Invest Limitation Infarction Size, Nat Heart, Lung & Blood Inst, 78-; mem coun epidemiol, Am Heart Asn. *Mem:* Am Fedn Clin Res (secy-treas, 52-54, vpres, 55, pres, 56); Am Col Physicians; Am Psychosom Soc (pres, 56); fel Am Heart Asn; fel Am Pub Health Asn. *Res:* Relation of social and man-made environment to health; natural history of coronary heart disease and sudden death; epidemiology of cardiac dysrhythmias; human ecology. *Mailing Add:* 1198 Bridle Path Lane New Canaan CT 06840

HINKLE, PATRICIA M, ENDOCRINOLOGY. *Current Pos:* from asst prof to assoc prof, 75-87, PROF PHARMACOL, UNIV ROCHESTER MED SCH, 87- *Personal Data:* b Glen Ridge, NJ, Oct 12, 43; m 68, David Currier; c Caroline, Daniel & Thomas. *Educ:* Mt Holyoke Col, BA, 65; Univ Calif, Berkeley, PhD(biochem), 70. *Prof Exp:* Fel, Harvard Univ, 71-74. *Concurrent Pos:* Mem endocrinol study sect, 87-91; ed, Endocrinol, 90. *Mem:* Endocrine Soc; Am Soc Biochem & Molecular Biol; Am Soc Pharmacol & Exp Therapeut; Am Thyroid Asn. *Res:* Molecular mechanisms of hormone action with emphasis on the role of receptors and signal transduction pathways in the anterior pituitary. *Mailing Add:* Dept Pharmacol Univ Rochester Med Sch Rochester NY 14642-0001. *Fax:* 716-461-0397

HINKLE, PETER CURRIER, BIOCHEMISTRY. *Current Pos:* from asst prof to assoc prof, 70-82, PROF BIOCHEM, CORNELL UNIV, 82- *Personal Data:* b Keene, NH, Nov 13, 40; m 66, Maija Veinbergs; c Christopher, Paul & Benjamin. *Educ:* Harvard Univ, BS, 62; NY Univ, PhD(biochem), 67. *Prof Exp:* NIH fel, Glynn Res Labs, Bodmin, Eng, 67-68; fel biochem, 68-69. *Mem:* Am Soc Biochem & Molecular Biol. *Res:* Oxidative phosphorylation; proton transport efficiency glucose transport; structure-function of transporters. *Mailing Add:* Biotech Bldg Cornell Univ Ithaca NY 14853. *Fax:* 607-255-2428; *E-Mail:* pch5@cornell.edu

HINKLEY, EVERETT DAVID, PHYSICS, ENVIRONMENT. *Current Pos:* VPRES, BAINBRIDGE TECHNOL GROUP LTD, 93-; SR SCIENTIST & MGR, SCI & TECHNOL CORP, 93- *Personal Data:* b Augusta, Maine, Nov 19, 36; m 60, Caso; c Anne, Mark, Kristin & David. *Educ:* Wash Univ, BS, 58; Northwestern Univ, MS, 61, PhD(physics), 63. *Prof Exp:* Res physicist, Automatic Elec Labs, Inc, 58-59; asst physics, Northwestern Univ, 59-60, res asst & assoc, 60-63; physicist, Lincoln Lab, Mass Inst Technol, 63-76; vpres, Laser Anal Inc, 76-77; group leader, Calif Inst Technol, 77-80, prog mgr, 80-82, mgr, Atmospheric Sci Sect, Jet Propulsion Lab, 82-84, mgr, Sensor Tech Prog, 84-86; chief electronics scientist, Lockheed Corp, 86-87; chief scientist, Hughes Aircraft Corp, 87-89 & Global Change Prog, TRW, 89-93. *Concurrent Pos:* Sr res fel, Univ Calif, Los Angeles, 91-95; chmn, Aerospace Policy Comt, Inst Elec Electronics Engrs, 94-97. *Mem:* Sigma Xi; sr mem Inst Elec & Electronics Engrs; fel Optical Soc Am. *Res:* Semiconductor heterojunctions; band structure; quantum effects; computer memory systems and components; communications techniques; tunable lasers; laser spectroscopy; air pollution monitoring; ion implantation; planetary atmospheres; infrared techniques; applications of lasers to pollution detection; remote sensing; space technology; high technology development and commercialization; author of one book. *Mailing Add:* 3916 Via Nivel Palos Verdes CA 90274

HINKLEY, ROBERT EDWIN, JR, CELL BIOLOGY, ANESTHESIOLOGY. *Current Pos:* from asst prof to assoc prof, 77-87, PROF ANAT, UNIV MIAMI, 87-, ASSOC DEAN, 89- *Personal Data:* b Kansas City, Mo, Mar 10, 43; m 66; c 1. *Educ:* Tulane Univ, BS, 65, MS, 66; Univ Kans, PhD(comp biochem & physiol), 71. *Prof Exp:* Res assoc anesthesia, Med Sch, Northwestern Univ, Chicago, 71-72, asst prof anesthesia & anat, 72-77. *Concurrent Pos:* Grant, Med Sch, Northwestern Univ, Chicago, 72-77; prin investr, Dept Health & Human Serv grant, Univ Miami, 77-; vis worker Anesthesia, Northwick Park Hosp, Harrow, 79-90; dir & chmn Honors Prog Med Educ, Univ Miami Med Sch, 80-, assoc dean Honors Med Prog, 90- *Mem:* Am Soc Cell Biol. *Res:* Effects of general anesthetics on reproduction; toxicity, teratology; medical education. *Mailing Add:* Dept Anat Rm 124 Univ Miami Med Sch 1600 NW Tenth Ave Miami FL 33136-1015

HINKS, DAVID GEORGE, SUPERCONDUCTIVITY, MAGNETISM. *Current Pos:* from asst chemist to chemist, 68-93, SR CHEMIST, ARGONNE NAT LAB, 93- *Personal Data:* b Neenah, Wis, July 11, 39; m 76, Susan L Hoaglund; c James & Stephen. *Educ:* Ill Inst Technol, BS, 62; Ore State Univ, PhD(chem), 68. *Mem:* Am Chem Soc; Am Phys Soc. *Res:* Synthesis and characterization of superconducting materials; crystal growth. *Mailing Add:* Argonne Nat Lab Bldg 223 9700 S Cass Ave Argonne IL 60439-4804. *Fax:* 630-252-7777

HINKSON, JIMMY WILFORD, BIOCHEMISTRY. *Current Pos:* RETIRED. *Personal Data:* b Los Angeles, Calif, June 18, 31; m 54; c 6. *Educ:* Brigham Young Univ, BSc, 56, MSc, 58; Ind Univ, PhD(biol chem), 62. *Prof Exp:* NIH fel biochem, Univ Minn, 62-63; res fel, Charles F Kettering Res Labs, 63-65; asst prof, Univ Ariz, 65-68; mem staff, Xerox Med Diag Opers, 68-70; prof chem, Calif State Univ, Stanislaus, 70-93. *Concurrent Pos:* NSF res grant, 66-68. *Mem:* AAAS; Am Chem Soc. *Res:* Enzymology; kinetics of enzyme reactions. *Mailing Add:* 330 E 750 Salem UT 84653

HINKSON, THOMAS CLIFFORD, PHYSICAL CHEMISTRY. *Current Pos:* from asst prof to assoc prof, 68-75, prof & head dept, 75-83, PROF CHEM & ASST VPRES ACAD AFFAIRS, TARLETON STATE UNIV, 83- *Personal Data:* b Winston-Salem, NC, July 8, 39; m 60; c 3. *Educ:* Midwestern Univ, BS, 60; Univ Fla, MS, 62; Univ Ark, Fayetteville, PhD(phys chem), 70. *Prof Exp:* Sr nuclear engr, Ling-Temco-Vought, Inc, 62-64; instr chem, Tex A&M Univ, 64-65. *Mem:* Am Chem Soc. *Res:* Nuclear emulsions; hot atom recoil chemistry, photochemistry. *Mailing Add:* IBM Corp 1605 LBJ Freeway Dallas TX 75234

HINMAN, ALANSON, pediatrics, for more information see previous edition

HINMAN, CHANNING L, NEUROSCIENCE, NEUROIMMUNOLOGY. *Current Pos:* FEL IMMUNOL, DEPT IMMUNOL & MICROBIOL, WAYNE STATE UNIV, 79- *Personal Data:* b Portland, Ore, Sept 3, 43; m 76; c 2. *Educ:* Brigham Young Univ, BS, 72; Univ Calif, Los Angeles, PhD(neurosci), 77. *Prof Exp:* Fel auditory physiol, Brain Res Inst, Univ Calif, Los Angeles, 77-79. *Res:* Amelioration of antibody-mediated Myasthenia Gravis; autoimmune and viral mechanisms involved in multiple sclerosis; single neuron and evoked potential recording of brain activity; functional power series analysis of evoked potentials. *Mailing Add:* 2334 Chriswood Toledo OH 43617-1258

HINMAN, CHARLES WILEY, ORGANIC CHEMISTRY. *Current Pos:* res chemist, Dow Chem Co, 54-55, group leader, Agr Chem Res Dept, 57-61, dir res & develop, Pitman-Moore Div, 61-64, sci adv, Dow-Ledogo S P A, Milan, 64-68, asst dir res & develop, 68-72, DIR PHARMACEUT RES & DEVELOP, DOW CHEM CO, USA, 72- *Personal Data:* b Boone, Iowa, Feb 9, 27; m 47; c 1. *Educ:* Grinnell Col, BA, 51; Univ Ill, PhD(org chem), 54. *Prof Exp:* Asst, Rubber Res Lab, Univ Ill, 51-54. *Concurrent Pos:* Dir life scis res & develop, Diamond Shamrock Corp, 76-78, dir exploratory technol, 78-; pres, Hinman Assoc, 83-; vpres, Vega Biotechnol, Inc, 85- *Mem:* AAAS; Am Chem Soc. *Res:* Scientific adviser in matters of chemistry, drug research and technical organization. *Mailing Add:* 4211 N Camino Ferreo Tucson AZ 85715-6360

HINMAN, CHESTER ARTHUR, SOLID STATE CHEMISTRY, NUCLEAR REACTOR SAFETY. *Current Pos:* SR SCIENTIST MAT RES & DEVELOP, HANFORD ENG DEVELOP LAB, WESTINGHOUSE-HANFORD, 70- *Personal Data:* b Bremerton, Wash, Apr 22, 39; m 62; c 1. *Educ:* Univ Wash, BS, 61, MS, 63, PhD(ceramic eng), 73. *Prof Exp:* Engr mat res & develop, Gen Elec Corp, 62-65; scientist, Battelle Northwest Lab, 65-70. *Mem:* Am Ceramic Soc; Nat Inst Ceramic Eng; AAAS. *Res:* Equilibrium and kinetic processes in non-metallic, inorganic solids, liquids and vapors; vapor pressure; diffusion kinetics; fission gas release from ceramic nuclear fuels, transient ceramic nuclear fuels behavior. *Mailing Add:* 2214 Camas Ave Richland WA 99352

HINMAN, EDWARD JOHN, HEALTH CARE ADMINISTRATION, INTERNAL MEDICINE. *Current Pos:* MED DIR, TOTAL HEALTH CARE, 92- *Personal Data:* b New Orleans, La, Nov 10, 31; m 54; c 3. *Educ:* Univ Okla, BA, 51; Tulane Univ, MD, 55; Johns Hopkins Univ, MPH, 71; Am Bd Prev Med, cert, 71. *Prof Exp:* Dir, Prof & Tech Develop Div, Regional Med Progs Serv, 71-73; dir res admin, Spec Res & Develop Projs, Nat Ctr Health Serv Res, USPHS, 73-74, dep dir admin, Off Prog Oper, 74, dir, Div Hosps & Clins, 74-78; exec dir admin, Group Health Asn, Inc, 78-83; med dir, PruCare Washington, 86-89; asst vpres & med dir, Lincoln Nat Ins Co, 89-92. *Concurrent Pos:* Intern, USPHS Hosp, New Orleans, La, 55-56, chief prof serv, 66-67; residency internal med, USPHS Hosp, Baltimore, Md, 58-61, dir, 68-71; asst med, Johns Hopkins Univ, 63-66, lectr pub health admin, 68-79; instr med, Tulane Univ, 66-67; renal consult, Greater Baltimore Med Ctr, 66; pres, Kidney Found Md, 68-70, mem med adv bd, 68-71, chmn dialysis & transplantation comt, 69-71; nat secy, USPHS Clin Soc, 65-66, nat pres, 66-67; pres Baltimore Chap, 68-70; fel, Am Col Prev Med, 71, Am Pub Health Asn, Am Col Physicians & charter fel Soc Adv Med Systs, 71; mem coun, Alliance for Eng Med & Biol, 75, chmn proj adv comt, 75-77, vpres, 76-77, pres, 77-79; vpres pub health, Am Col Prev Med, 76-77; mem bd, Symp Comput Applns Med Care, 80-; assoc clin prof, Health Care Sci, George Washington Univ, 79-; exec comt, Group Health Asn Am, 79-; adj assoc prof epidermol & prev med, Univ Md, 93- *Mem:* Soc Adv Med Syst (treas, 74, pres-elect, 75-76, pres, 76-77); Am Fedn Clin Res; Am Soc Nephrology. *Mailing Add:* 2305 N Charles St Baltimore MD 21218

HINMAN, EUGENE EDWARD, STRATIGRAPHY, PALEONTOLOGY. *Current Pos:* Instr, 56-58, from asst prof to assoc prof, 60-74, PROF GEOL, CORNELL COL, 74- *Personal Data:* b Dubuque, Iowa, Jan 29, 30; m 52; c 2. *Educ:* Cornell Col, BA, 52; Wash State Univ, MS, 54; Univ Iowa, PhD(geol), 63. *Mem:* AAAS; Am Asn Petrol Geol; Soc Econ Paleont & Mineral; Sigma Xi. *Res:* Jurassic Carmel-Twin Creek facies of northern Utah; Silurian bioherms of Iowa. *Mailing Add:* 414A Second Ave S Mt Vernon IA 52314-1622

HINMAN, GEORGE WHEELER, ENERGY, TECHNOLOGY ASSESSMENT. *Current Pos:* dir, Nuclear Radiation Ctr & Environ Res Ctr, 69-79, PROF PHYSICS & DIR OFF APPL ENERGY STUDIES, WASH STATE UNIV, 69-, CHAIR, PROG ENVIRON SCI & REGIONAL PLANNING, 89- *Personal Data:* b Evanston, Ill, Nov 7, 27; m 52, Mary L Cauffield; c Norman, Lydia & Nancy. *Educ:* Carnegie Inst Technol, BS, 47, MS, 50, DSc(physics), 52. *Prof Exp:* Instr physics, Carnegie Inst Technol, 51-52, res physicist, 52-54; from asst prof to assoc prof, 54-63; chmn, Exp Physics Dept, Gen Atomic Div, Gen Dynamics Corp, 63-66, Dept Physics, 66-69. *Concurrent Pos:* Consult, US Gen Acct Off, 77-; dir, NMex Energy Res & Develop Inst, 82-83; mem, Nat Nuclear Accrediting Bd, Inst Nuclear Power Oper, 92- *Mem:* Fel Am Phys Soc; Am Nuclear Soc; Am Soc Eng Educ. *Res:* Nuclear and reactor physics; systems studies on energy resources and environmental quality; technology assessments. *Mailing Add:* 305 Troy Hall Wash State Univ Pullman WA 99164-4430. *Fax:* 509-335-7636; *E-Mail:* ghimman@wsu.edu

HINMAN, JACK WILEY, BIOCHEMISTRY, RESEARCH ADMINISTRATION. *Current Pos:* RETIRED. *Personal Data:* b Pilot Mound, Iowa, June 27, 19; m 42; c 6. *Educ:* Grinnell Col, AB, 41; Univ Vt, MS, 43; Univ Ill, PhD(biochem), 47. *Honors & Awards:* W E Upjohn Prize, 63. *Prof Exp:* Res chemist, Container Corp Am, Ill, 42; instr chem, Univ Vt, 42-43; spec asst, Univ Ill, 43-44; res chemist, Upjohn Co, 44-57, head natural prod res sect, 57-73, chmn, Calcium Metab Res Proj Team & clin res monitor exp med res, 73-77; clin res scientist, Hoffmann-LaRoche, Inc, Nutley, NJ, 78-82. *Concurrent Pos:* Consult, 82- *Mem:* Fel Am Inst Chem; Am Chem Soc; Am Soc Bone & Mineral Res; Marine Technol Soc. *Res:* Chemistry of penicillin; amino acid derivatives; extraction, purification and chemistry of antibiotics, protein hormones, hypothalamic factors, prostaglandins, antihypertensive kidney lipids and vitamin D metabolites. *Mailing Add:* 717 Chalfonte Ave Portage MI 49024-5809

HINMAN, NORMAN DEAN, BIOPROCESS DEVELOPMENT. *Current Pos:* SR BIOCHEM ENGR, SOLAR ENERGY RES INST, 87- *Personal Data:* b Greeley, Colo, June 4, 44; m 66; c 2. *Educ:* Johns Hopkins Univ, BA, 66; Univ Conn, PhD(biochem), 72; Colo Sch Mines, MS, 80. *Prof Exp:* Res assoc biophys, Med Sch, Univ Colo, 72-75; asst prof biochem, Eastern Va Med Sch, 75-77; instr, Colo Sch Mines, 79-80; sales forecast coordr, Gates Rubber Co, 80; process engr, Stearns Catalytic Corp, 80-86, sr biochem engr, 86-87. *Mem:* AAAS. *Res:* Bioprocess development and demonstration; conceptual design and economic analysis of bioprocesses; bench scale and pilotscale bioprocess research. *Mailing Add:* Solar Energy Res Inst 1617 Cole Blvd Golden CO 80401

HINMAN, PETER GREAYER, RECURSION THEORY. *Current Pos:* From asst prof to assoc prof, 66-84, PROF MATH, UNIV MICH, 84- *Personal Data:* b Chicago, IL, Dec 8, 37; US citizen; m 87, Elizabeth Young; c Mira. *Educ:* Harvard Col, AB, 59; Univ Calif Berkeley, PhD(math), 66. *Concurrent Pos:* Vis prof, Univ Oslo, 71-72, Univ Heidelberg, 76-77; res fel, Math Inst, ETH, Zurich, 83-84. *Mem:* Am Math Soc; Math Asn Am; Asn Symbolic Logic. *Res:* Recursion theory (classical and generalized); complexity theory. *Mailing Add:* Dept Math Univ Mich Ann Arbor MI 48109-1109. *E-Mail:* pgh@umich.edu

HINMAN, RICHARD LESLIE, BIO-ORGANIC CHEMISTRY, BIOTECHNOLOGY. *Current Pos:* vpres, 72-81, SR VPRES, CHEM PROD RES & DEVELOP, PFIZER INC, GROTON, CONN, 81- *Personal Data:* b Utica, NY, Mar 8, 27; m 67; c 4. *Educ:* Columbia Col, AB, 49; Univ Ill, Urbana, PhD, 52. *Prof Exp:* Merck fel, Cambridge Univ, Eng, 52-53; instr orgn chem, State Univ Iowa, 53-57; res chemist & group leader, Union Carbide Res Inst, 58-65, dir med chem, 65-67, mgr pharm technol, 67-69, prog mgr, chem sci, 69-72. *Concurrent Pos:* Mem Energy Res Adv Bd, Wash, DC, 79-82; vis comt dept chem, Mass Inst Technol, 81-, Indust Adv Bd, Dept Biochem Eng, 85-; chmn, Steering Comt, Old Lyme Parents Network, Conn, 86-87; mem, Educ Comt, Conn Acad Sci & Eng, 91- *Mem:* Am Chem Soc; Chem Soc London; Sigma Xi. *Res:* Fermentation research biotechnology, bioorganic chemistry; author of over 50 scientific papers. *Mailing Add:* Pfizer Central Res Eastern Point Rd Groton CT 06340

HINNERS, NOEL W, GEOCHEMISTRY, GEOLOGY. *Current Pos:* dir, Lunar Progs, NASA, 72-74, assoc adminr, Space Sci, 74-79, dir, Nat Air & Space Mus, 79-82, dir, Goddard Space Flight Ctr, 82-87, ASSOC DEP ADMINR, NASA, 87- *Personal Data:* b Brooklyn, NY, Dec 25, 35; m 62; c 2. *Educ:* Rutgers Univ, BSc, 58; Calif Inst Technol, MSc, 60; Princeton Univ, MA, 61, PhD(geochem, geol), 63. *Prof Exp:* Mem tech staff lunar sci, Bellcomm, Inc, Washington, DC, 63-65, supvr, 65-70, dept head, 70-72. *Mem:* Am Geophys Union; AAAS; Am Inst Aeronauts & Astronauts. *Res:* Geochemistry of ore-forming fluids; lunar geology and mission planning; physics and chemistry of meteorites. *Mailing Add:* 42 Mule Deer Trail Littleton CO 80127

HINNOV, EINAR, PHYSICS. *Current Pos:* res physicist, Proj Matterhorn, 59-63 & Plasma Physics Lab, 63-74, sr res physicist, 74-80, PRIN RES PHYSICIST, PLASMA PHYSICS LAB, PRINCETON UNIV, 80- *Personal Data:* b Estonia, Mar 17, 30; nat US; m 56; c 1. *Educ:* St Olaf Col, BA, 52; Duke Univ, PhD(physics), 56. *Prof Exp:* Res assoc physics, Univ Md, 56-58, asst res prof, 58-59. *Concurrent Pos:* Lectr, Dept Astrophys Sci, Princeton Univ, 65-74. *Mem:* Fel Am Phys Soc; Sigma Xi. *Res:* Atomic physics; plasma physics. *Mailing Add:* 1-D Hibben Apts Faculty Rd Princeton NJ 08540

HINOJOSA, RAUL, EAR PATHOLOGY. *Current Pos:* Asst prof, 62-68, res assoc, 68-88, ASSOC PROF, UNIV CHICAGO, 68- *Personal Data:* b Tampico, Tamulipas, Mex, June 18, 28; nat US; m 53, Berta Ojeda; c Berta E, Raul A, Jorge A & Maria D. *Educ:* Inst Sci & Technol, Tampico, BS, 46; Nat Autonomous Univ, Mex, MD, 54. *Concurrent Pos:* Dir, Temporal Bone Prog Ear Res, Univ Chicago, 62-; res career develop award, NIH, 62-65, res grantee, 65-, Hearing Res Study Sect grantee, 88-92; res fel biophys, Harvard Univ, 63, res assoc neuropath, 64, res fel anat, 65. *Mem:* Electron Micros Soc Am; AAAS; Asn Res Otolaryngol; Am Otol Soc; NY Acad Sci. *Res:* Temporal bone histopathology. *Mailing Add:* Univ Chicago 5841 S Maryland Ave Chicago IL 60637-1470

HINRICHS, CLARENCE H, PHYSICS. *Current Pos:* assoc prof physics & registr, 66-77, actg dean fac, 74-77, PROF PHYSICS, LINFIELD COL, 77- *Personal Data:* b Basin, Wyo, Jan 21, 35; m 55; c 3. *Educ:* Linfield Col, BA, 57; Iowa State Univ, MS, 60; Washington State Univ, PhD(physics), 66. *Prof Exp:* Res asst, Ames Lab, AEC, 57-60; res physicist, Linfield Res Inst, 60-62; instr, Wash State Univ, 62-64. *Mem:* Am Asn Physics Teachers. *Res:* Vacuum, low temperature and high pressure physics; superconductivity; field emission and surface physics; geophysics. *Mailing Add:* 726 Villard St McMinnville OR 97128-6894

HINRICHS, KARL, ELECTRONICS, COMPUTER SCIENCE. *Current Pos:* VPRES ENG, NEWPORT LABS, 77- *Personal Data:* b Port Washington, NY, Aug 11, 25; m 46; c 3. *Educ:* Swarthmore Col, BS, 45; Harvard Univ, MS, 47; Univ Calif, Berkeley, PhD(elec eng), 55. *Prof Exp:* Lectr, Univ Calif, Berkeley, 47-51, asst prof, 53-55; tech staff mem, Thompson-Ramo-Wooldridge, 55-56; sr engr, Systs Div, Beckman Instruments, Inc, 56-57, chief develop engr, 57-58, asst dir res & develop, 58-60, chief scientist, 60-64, dir res, 64-65, mgr comput opers, 65-66; dir res, Zeltex, Inc, 66-67; vpres & dir eng, Comcor/Astrodata, 67-68, Astrodata, 68-69; dir eng, Data Prod Div, Lockheed Electronics Co, 69-77. *Mem:* AAAS; Inst Elec & Electronics Engrs; Instrument Soc Am; Sigma Xi. *Res:* Invention and application of large scale integrated circuits to computer memories and central processing unit, including minicomputer systems. *Mailing Add:* 5196 Piccadilly Circle Westminster CA 92683

HINRICHS, KATRIN, OOCYTE MATURATION, EMBRYO TRANSFER. *Current Pos:* ASST PROF REPRODUCTION, TUFTS SCH VET MED, 88- *Personal Data:* b Oakland, Calif, Nov 13, 54; m 88; c 1. *Educ:* Univ Calif, Davis, BS, 76, DVM, 78; Univ Pa, PhD(comp med sci), 88. *Honors & Awards:* Hamilton-Thorn Award, 90. *Prof Exp:* Vet, pvt pract, 78-82; resident reproduction, New Bolton Ctr, Univ Pa Sch Vet Med, 82-84, lectr, 84-88. *Mem:* Am Vet Med Asn; Soc Study Reproduction; Soc Theriogenol; Am Col Theriogenologists; Int Embryo Transfer Soc; Am Asn Equine Practitioners. *Res:* Early pregnancy in the mare including hormonal requirements for maintenance of pregnancy in ovariectomized mares; oocyte retrieval, maturation, fertilization; early embryonic development in the horse. *Mailing Add:* Tufts Univ Sch Vet Med 200 Westboro Rd North Grafton MA 01536

HINRICHS, LOWELL A, MATHEMATICS. *Current Pos:* ASSOC PROF MATH, UNIV VICTORIA BC, 67- *Personal Data:* b Hillsboro, Ore, June 16, 35; m 58; c 1. *Educ:* Univ Ore, BA, 58, MA, 60, PhD(math), 62. *Prof Exp:* Asst prof math, Duke Univ, 62-67. *Res:* Symmetry geometry, polyehedra and tensigrids. *Mailing Add:* Dept Math & Statist Univ Victoria Box 3045 Victoria BC V8W 3P4 Can

HINRICHS, PAUL RUTLAND, AERONAUTICAL & ASTRONAUTICAL ENGINEERING. *Current Pos:* RETIRED. *Personal Data:* b Tulsa, Okla, July 17, 28; m 49, Betty J Robinson; c Lisa N. *Educ:* Univ Okla, BS, 60, MS, 61, PhD(elec eng), 63. *Prof Exp:* Aero engr, Gen Dynamics, Ft Worth, 63-65; prof dir, Gorland Div, E-Systs, Inc, 65-78; chief engr, Missile Systs Div, Rockwell Int, 78-88; vpres eng, BEI Electronics, 88-91. *Mem:* Inst Elec & Electronics Engrs; Am Inst Aeronaut & Astronaut. *Res:* Integrated position updating navigation systems using terrain correlation, for use in navigating long range cruise missiles. *Mailing Add:* 2317 Meandering Way Arlington TX 76011-2619

HINSCH, GERTRUDE WILMA, ZOOLOGY, EMBRYOLOGY. *Current Pos:* assoc prof, 74-80, PROF, UNIV SFLA, 80- *Personal Data:* b Chicago, Ill, Oct 20, 32; wid. *Educ:* Northern Ill Univ, BS, 53; Iowa State Univ, MS, 55, PhD, 57. *Prof Exp:* Instr zool, Mt Holyoke Col, 57-60; from asst prof to assoc prof, Mt Union Col, 60-66; res scientist, Inst Molecular Evolution, Univ Miami, 66-69, assoc prof, Inst Molecular Evolution & Dept Biol, 69-74. *Concurrent Pos:* Corp mem, Marine Biol Lab. *Mem:* AAAS; Am Soc Zool; Soc Develop Biol; Am Soc Cell Biol; Int Soc Develop Biol. *Res:* Ultrastructure of fertilization and gamete structure in coelenterates and crustaceans; hormonal control of reproduction in crustaceans. *Mailing Add:* Dept Biol Univ SFla Tampa FL 33620

HINSCH, JAMES E, CHEMICAL ENGINEERING. *Current Pos:* OPERS MGR, AKZONOBEL, 93- *Personal Data:* b Pontiac, Mich, Oct 18, 37; m 58, Beverly Corner; c 4. *Educ:* Univ Detroit, BChE, 60; Wayne State Univ, MSChE, 63. *Prof Exp:* Res scientist, sci res staff, Ford Motor Co, 60-66, sr res scientist, 66-67, sect supvr, Indust & Chem Prod Div, 67-71, sales & mkt mgr, electrocure opers, 71-72, asst mgr res & develop, 72-75, mgr, res & develop, 75-80, mfg mgr, Mt Clemens Paint Opers, 80-83 & Milan Plastics Plant, 83-85, mfg mgr, Mt Clemens Paint & Vinyl Opers, 85-86; qual mgr, Du Pont Co, 86-87, lab mgr, 87-90, supply chain mgr, 90-93. *Mem:* Am Chem Soc; Sigma Xi. *Res:* Automotive coatings development including body enamels; electrodeposition and low emission systems. *Mailing Add:* 14757 Yale Livonia MI 48154-5162. *Fax:* 248-253-2517; *E-Mail:* jhinsch@aol.com

HINSDILL, RONALD D, IMMUNOTOXICOLOGY. *Current Pos:* Prof, 66-96, chmn dept, 82-95, EMER PROF BACT, UNIV WIS-MADISON, 96- *Personal Data:* b Chicago, Ill, Dec 6, 33; m 60, Jeanette W Boehrnsen; c Kevin, Tyson & Dawn. *Educ:* Univ Ill, BS, 56, MS, 58; Univ Wis-Madison, PhD(bact), 63. *Concurrent Pos:* Dir, Environ Toxicol Ctr, 74-83; prof prev med, Univ Wis-Madison, 76-96. *Mem:* Am Soc Microbiol; Am Asn Immunol; Sigma Xi. *Res:* Investigation of the impact of environmental and agricultural chemicals on the immune system. *Mailing Add:* 3006 Park St Middleton WI 53562

HINSHAW, ADA SUE, NURSING. *Current Pos:* DEAN, SCH NURSING, UNIV MICH, 94- *Personal Data:* b Arkansas City, Kans, May 20, 39. *Educ:* Univ Kans, BS, 61; Yale Univ, MSN, 63; Univ Ariz, MA, 73, PhD(sociol), 75. *Hon Degrees:* DSc, Univ Md, 88, Med Col Ohio, 88, Marquette Univ, 90. *Honors & Awards:* Nurse Scientist Year Award, Am Nurses' Asn, 85; Helen Denne Schulte Vis Lectr, Univ Wis-Madison, 86. *Prof Exp:* Instr nursing, Univ Kans, 63-65; instr, Sch Nursing, Univ Calif, San Francisco, 66-67, asst prof, 67-71; assoc dir nursing res, Dept Nursing, Univ Med Ctr, Tucson, Ariz, 75-87; dir, Nat Inst Nursing Res, Dept Health & Human Serv, NIH, Bethesda, MD, 87-94. *Concurrent Pos:* Nurse-scientist fel, Univ Ariz, 71-75; green chair vis prof, Sch Nursing, Tex Christian Univ, 80; comnr, Comn Nursing Res, Am Nurses Asn, 80; vis prof, Sch Nursing, Univ Tex, 86, Univ Mich, Ann Arbor, 87; mem, Comt Advise Pub Health Serv Med Pract Guidelines, Inst Med, 89-90; co-chair, Int Task Force Nursing Res, Nat Ctr Nursing Res & Int Coun Nurses, Geneva, Switz, 90. *Mem:* Inst Med-Nat Acad Sci; Sigma Xi; fel Am Acad Nursing; Am Nurses Asn. *Res:* Clinical nursing and nursing administration; theory construction and testing; instrument development and testing; field designs and issues. *Mailing Add:* Univ Mich Sch Nursing 400 N Ingalls Bldg Rm 1320 Ann Arbor MI 48109-0482

HINSHAW, CHARLES THERON, JR, CLINICAL PATHOLOGY, NUCLEAR MEDICINE. *Current Pos:* clin asst prof path, 81-84, preceptor, 85-92, CLIN INSTR PATH, UNIV KANS SCH MED, 93- *Personal Data:* b Wichita, Kans, Jan 31, 32; m 88, Bobbie J Meier; c 3. *Educ:* Univ Kans, BA, 54, MD, 58. *Prof Exp:* Intern, Med Ctr, Univ Kans, 58-59, resident fel path, 61-65; assoc pathologist, Hutchinson Hosp, 65-79, dir, Biol Ctr Lab, 79-83. *Concurrent Pos:* Assoc dir, Lettner-Hinshaw Labs, 72-79; med dir, Sci Labs, 80-83, Ice Dream Int, 85-90; dir, Clin Specialties Lab, 92-93. *Mem:* Am Soc Clin Pathologists; Col Am Pathologists; AMA; AAAS; Am Acad Environ Med. *Res:* Food allergy; multiple chemical sensitivities. *Mailing Add:* 1833 N Rock Road Ct Wichita KS 67206. *Fax:* 316-685-4628

HINSHAW, DAVID B, SURGERY. *Current Pos:* From instr to asst prof surg, 54-61, dean sch med, 62-74, PROF SURG, LOMA LINDA UNIV, 61-, CHMN DEPT, 74-; DEAN, SCH MED, ORAL ROBERTS UNIV. *Personal Data:* b Whittier, Calif, Nov 24, 23; m 43; c 3. *Educ:* Loma Linda Univ, MD, 47. *Mem:* Am Surg Asn; Am Col Surgeons; Soc Univ Surg; Int Soc Surg. *Res:* Dumping syndrome; homograft rejection factor; metabolic and hemodynamic studies in surgical diseases. *Mailing Add:* Dept Radiol B623A Loma Linda Univ Loma Linda CA 92350-0001

HINSHAW, J RAYMOND, surgery; deceased, see previous edition for last biography

HINSHAW, JERALD CLYDE, ORGANIC CHEMISTRY. *Current Pos:* scientist, Res & Develop Lab, 78-84, supvr, 84-90, MGR APPL RES DEPT, RES & DEVELOP LAB, THIOKOL CORP, 90- *Personal Data:* b Weiser, Idaho, May 6, 44. *Educ:* Ore State Univ, BS, 66; Univ Utah, PhD(org chem), 70. *Prof Exp:* Sr chemist, 70-76, res assoc, res labs, Eastman Kodak Co, 76-78. *Mem:* Am Chem Soc; AAAS. *Res:* Synthesis and properties of unusual and or theoretically interesting molecules; high energy compounds; applications of chemistry to problems in geology and biology; research management. *Mailing Add:* Res & Develop Lab Thiokol Corp PO Box 707 MS 244 Brigham City UT 84302-0707

HINSHAW, LERNER BRADY, PHYSIOLOGY & PATHOPHYSIOLOGY. *Current Pos:* from assoc prof to prof physiol, 61-71, GEORGE LYNN CROSS RES PROF, UNIV OKLA, 85- *Personal Data:* b San Diego, Calif, June 9, 21; m 46; c 4. *Educ:* Univ Southern Calif, AB, 49, MS, 50, MA, 52, PhD(physiol), 55. *Prof Exp:* From instr to asst prof physiol, Med Sch, Univ Minn, 58-61; supvry res physiologist, Civil Aeromed Res Inst, 61-65. *Concurrent Pos:* Fel, Life Ins Med Res Fund, Med Sch, Univ Minn, 55-58; Lederle med fac award, 59-62; adj prof surg, med sch, Univ Okla, 66-; chmn, res & develop comt, Vet Admin Med Ctr, Oklahoma City, 71-73 & 80-82, prin proponent & co-chmn, Vet Admin coop study No 209 (nat clin trial study); med investr, Vet Admin Hosp, Oklahoma City, 73-82; res career scientist, Vet Admin Med Ctr, Oklahoma City, 83-87; mem, Okla Med Res Found, 87- *Mem:* West Soc Clin Res; Soc Critical Care Med; Soc Exp Biol & Med; Am Physiol Soc; Shock Soc (pres, 85); fel Am Col Critical Care Med; Am Soc Exp Therapeuts. *Res:* Cardiovascular physiology; shock; response of nonhuman primate in septic shock; treatment of baboon shock model to prevent morbidity and mortality. *Mailing Add:* Okla Med Res Found 825 NE 13th St Oklahoma City OK 73104-5097. *Fax:* 201-271-7893

HINSHAW, VIRGINIA SNYDER, VIROLOGY, IMMUNOLOGY. *Current Pos:* assoc prof, 85-88, PROF VIROL, SCH VET MED, UNIV WIS-MADISON, 88- *Personal Data:* b Oak Ridge, Tenn, Mar 25, 44; m 63; c 2. *Educ:* Auburn Univ, BS, 66, MS, 67, PhD(microbiol), 72. *Prof Exp:* Clin & res microbiologist bacteriol, Med Col Va, 67-68; res virologist oncogenic viruses, Univ Calif, Berkeley, 74-75; res assoc influenza, St Jude Children's Res Hosp, 75-77, asst mem, Influenza, 77-80, assoc mem, 81-85. *Mem:* Am Soc Microbiol; AAAS. *Res:* Ecology; structure and immunology of influenza viruses in humans, lower animals and birds. *Mailing Add:* Sch Vet Med 2015 Linden Dr Madison WI 53706-1100

HINSMAN, EDWARD JAMES, VETERINARY ANATOMY, COMPARATIVE NEUROLOGY. *Current Pos:* From instr to assoc prof, 59-70, PROF VET ANAT, PURDUE UNIV, 70- *Personal Data:* b Wyandotte, Mich, Aug 5, 34; m 59, Merry E Sullivan; c Matthew J, William J & Nora J. *Educ:* Mich State Univ, BS, 56, DVM, 58, MS, 60; Purdue Univ, PhD(vet anat), 63. *Mem:* Am Asn Anatomists; World Asn Vet Anatomists; Am Asn Vet Anat (pres, 82-83). *Res:* Use of electron microscope to study the nervous system. *Mailing Add:* Dept Anat Purdue Univ Sch Med Lynn Hall 2450 Lindberg Rd West Lafayette IN 47907-1242. *Fax:* 765-494-1772

HINSON, DAVID, AVIATION. *Current Pos:* CHIEF EXEC OFFICER & CHMN, INT AEROSPACE SOLUTIONS, 97- *Personal Data:* b Muskogee, Okla, Mar 2, 33. *Educ:* Univ Wash, BA, 55. *Prof Exp:* Chmn, Midway Airlines, 85-90; exec vpres, McDonnell Douglas, 91-93; adminr, Fed Aviation Admin, 93-97. *Concurrent Pos:* Dir, Midway Airlines, 78-90, Continental Bank, 89-91 & Chicago Northwestern Railroad, 90-91; trustee, Grad Sch Bus, Univ Chicago, 87-90 & Grad Sch Bus, Univ Wash, 87-90. *Mailing Add:* 114 Rail Rd PO Box 6930 Ketchum ID 83340

HINSON, DAVID CHANDLER, physics, for more information see previous edition

HINSON, JACK ALLSBROOK, TOXICOLOGY, DRUG METABOLISM. *Current Pos:* DIR, DIV TOXICOL, DIR & PROF, INTERDISCIPLINARY TOXICOL PROG, DIR & PROF, OCCUP & ENVIRON HEALTH PROG & PROF PHARMACOL, UNIV ARK MED SCI, 90- *Personal Data:* b Aug 18, 44; m 71; c 2. *Educ:* Col of Charleston, BS, 66, Univ SC, MS, 68, Vanderbilt Univ, PhD(biochem), 72. *Prof Exp:* Sr staff fel, Nat Heart, Lung & Blood Inst, 75-80; chief, Biochem Mechanisms Br, Nat Ctr Toxicol Res, 80-90. *Concurrent Pos:* Fel, NIH, 72-75; adj prof toxicol, Med Sch, Univ Ark, 80-90; vis fel, Can Res Campaign, Middlesex Hosp Med Sch, London, 82; adj assoc prof, Col Pharm, Univ Tenn, 82-90; vis prof, Div Toxicol, Univ Leiden, Neth, 86; pres, SCent Chap, Soc Toxicol, 90- *Mem:* Soc Toxicol; Am Soc Pharmacol & Exp Therapeut; Am Indust Hyg Asn; Int Soc Study Xenobiotics. *Res:* Toxicology; drug metabolism, carcinogenesis. *Mailing Add:* Div Toxicol Univ Ark Med Sci 4301 W Markham Little Rock AR 72205-7101. *Fax:* 501-686-5521

HINSON, KUELL, GENETICS, PLANT BREEDING. *Current Pos:* Geneticist, 54-73, RES AGRONOMIST, AGR RES SERV, USDA, 73- *Personal Data:* b Moss, Tenn, Jan 8, 24; m 55; c 4. *Educ:* Tenn Polytech Inst, BS, 49; Univ Wis, MS, 51, PhD(genetics, agron), 54. *Mem:* Am Soc Agron; Crop Sci Soc Am. *Res:* Soybean breeding and genetics; pyramiding pest-resistance factors into high yielding genotypes; adapting genotypes to broader bands of latitude; soybean production research. *Mailing Add:* 1303 NW 30th St Gainesville FL 32605

HINTERBUCHNER, CATHERINE NICOLAIDES, PHYSICAL MEDICINE & REHABILITATION. *Current Pos:* from asst prof to assoc prof, 64-71, DIR METROP HOSP, NY, 64-, PROF REHAB MED & CHMN DEPT, NY MED COL, 71- *Personal Data:* b Corfu, Greece, Nov 22, 26; US citizen; m 55, L P. *Educ:* Nat Univ Athens, MD, 51; Am Phys Med & Rehab, dipl, 62. *Prof Exp:* Asst instr, NY Med Col, 59-60; instr, State Univ NY Downstate Med Ctr, 60-64. *Concurrent Pos:* Fel rehab med, Jewish Chronic Dis Hosp, Brooklyn, NY, 56-57 & Metrop Hosp, 59-60; vis physician, Kings County Hosp, Brooklyn, 60-64; asst attend, Jewish Chronic Dis Hosp, 60-66; attend Vet Admin Hosp, 61-64; assoc attend, Flower & Fifth Ave, 64-71, attend, 71-78, Metrop, 64- & Bird S Coler Hosps, 64-88; attend, Westchester County Med Ctr, Valhalla, NY, 71-, Lincoln Hosp, 79-; mem, Am Bd Phys Med & Rehab & Accreditation Coun Grad Med Ed. *Mem:* AMA; fel Am Col Physicians; NY Acad Med; Am Acad Phys Med & Rehab; Am Cong Rehab Med; NY Acad Sci. *Mailing Add:* Polly Park Rd Rye NY 10580

HINTERBUCHNER, L P, NEUROLOGY. *Current Pos:* asst prof, State Univ NY Downstate Med Ctr, 59-61, from clin asst prof to clin assoc prof, 61-76, chmn neurol dept, Brooklyn Hosp Med Ctr, 71-85, EMER PROF NEUROL, STATE UNIV NY DOWNSTATE MED CTR, 76- *Personal Data:* b Slovakia, Dec 10, 22; m 55. *Educ:* Univ Bratislava, MD, 47. *Prof Exp:* From asst instr to instr neurol, State Univ NY Downstate Med Ctr, 55-57; USPHS trainee neurochem, Col Physicians & Surgeons, Columbia Univ, 57-59. *Concurrent Pos:* Dir neurol & psychiat, Kingsbrook Jewish Med Ctr, 61-66. *Mem:* NY Acad Sci; fel Am Acad Neurol; Asn Res Nerv & Ment Dis; fel Am Col Med; AMA. *Res:* Muscle physiology and its application to clinical neurology. *Mailing Add:* 10 Polly Park Rd Rye NY 10580

HINTEREGGER, HANS ERICH, PHYSICS. *Current Pos:* physicist, 51-53, SR SCIENTIST, AIR FORCE GEOPHYS LAB, 61- *Personal Data:* b Waidhofen, Austria, Sept 3, 19; nat US; m 42; c 6. *Educ:* Vienna Inst Technol, Dipl Ing, 44, Dr Tech(physics), 47. *Prof Exp:* Asst physics, Univ Gottingen, 44-46; asst prof, Vienna Inst Technol, 46-51. *Concurrent Pos:* Consult, Los Alamos Sci Labs, 60-64. *Mem:* Int Astron Union; Int Union Geod & Geophys; fel Optical Soc Am; Am Geophys Union. *Res:* Physical electronics; extreme ultraviolet radiation; ionospheric physics; solar physics; space research; aeronomy. *Mailing Add:* 140 Newtonville Ave Newton MA 02158

HINTHORNE, JAMES ROSCOE, MINERALOGY, COMPUTER SOFTWARE. *Current Pos:* PROF GEOL, CENT WASH UNIV, 80- *Personal Data:* b Los Angeles, Calif, Dec 23, 42; m 64; c 2. *Educ:* Univ Calif, BA, 65, PhD(geol), 74; Univ Mass, MS, 67. *Prof Exp:* Assoc scientist microprobe res, 69-73, scientist, 73-75, res scientist, 75-76, mgr methods & appl div, Appl Res Labs, 76-80. *Concurrent Pos:* Consult mineral & comput appln. *Mem:* Geol Soc Am; Mineral Soc Am; Microbeam Anal Soc. *Res:* Ion microprobe; electron microprobe; trace element contents of minerals; U-Pb ages in lunar minerals and very old terrestrial rocks; control of analytical instruments by minicomputer; applications software for geographic information systems. *Mailing Add:* Dept Geol Cent Wash Univ Ellensburg WA 98926-7500

HINTON, BARRY THOMAS, MALE REPRODUCTIVE CELL & MOLECULAR BIOLOGY, SPERM PHYSIOLOGY. *Current Pos:* Assoc prof gross anat & reproductive biol, 83-95, PROF, DEPT CELL BIOL, SCH MED, UNIV VA, 95- *Personal Data:* b 1950. *Educ:* Inst Animal Physiol, Cambridge, Eng, PhD(male reproductive physiol), 79. *Honors & Awards:* Young Andrologist Award, Am Soc Andrology, 89. *Mem:* Soc Study Reproduction; Am Soc Andrology. *Res:* Cell and molecular biology of testicular and epididymal function; role of epididymal epithelium in regulating the luminal microenvironment necessary for sperm development, maturation and survival. *Mailing Add:* Dept Cell Biol Sch Med Univ Va Box 439 Charlottesville VA 22908. *Fax:* 804-982-3912; *E-Mail:* bth7c@virginia.edu

HINTON, CLAUDE WILLEY, GENETICS. *Current Pos:* MATEER PROF BIOL, COL WOOSTER, 68- *Personal Data:* b Gatesville, NC, Aug 1, 28; m 52; c 2. *Educ:* Univ NC, AB, 48, MA, 50; Calif Inst Technol, PhD(biol), 54. *Prof Exp:* Res assoc, Biol Div, Oak Ridge Nat Lab, 54-55; from asst prof to prof zool, Univ Ga, 55-68. *Concurrent Pos:* Res grants, NIH, 55-; consult, Oak Ridge Nat Lab, 59-68; guest investr, Div Plant Indust, Commonwealth Sci & Indust Res Orgn, Canberra, Australia, 72-73; vis res biologist, Univ Calif, San Diego, 77-78; Univ NC, Chapel Hill, 82-83. *Mem:* AAAS; Genetics Soc Am; Am Soc Naturalists; Am Genetic Asn. *Res:* Chromosome behavior in Drosophila; hybrid dysgenesis. *Mailing Add:* 994 Birsch Creek Dr Wilmington NC 28403

HINTON, DAVID EARL, COMPARATIVE PATHOLOGY, AQUATIC TOXICOLOGY. *Current Pos:* PROF VET MED & AQUATIC TOXICOLOGIST, EXP STA, SCH VET MED, UNIV CALIF, DAVIS, 86-, CHAIR, GRAD GROUP PHARMACOL & TOXICOL, LEADER, AQUATIC TOXICOL UNIT. *Personal Data:* b Hattiesburg, Miss, Jan 4, 42; div; c David Jr, Michah, Emily & Ben. *Educ:* Miss Col, BS, 65; Univ Miss, MS, 67, PhD(anat), 69. *Prof Exp:* From instr to asst prof gross anat, Sch Med, Univ Louisville, 70-73, res assoc water resources biol, 70-73; res assoc path, Sch Med, Univ Md, Baltimore, 73-77, asst prof, 73-77; from assoc prof to prof, Dept Anat & Path, Sch Med, WVa Univ, Morgantown, 77-86. *Mem:* Soc Environ Toxicol & Chem; US & Can Acad Path; Soc Toxicol; Soc Toxicol Pathologists; Am Asn Cancer Researchers. *Res:* Electron microscopy; toxicology; comparative and environmental pathobiology; fishes; aquatic pollutants. *Mailing Add:* Dept Anat, Physiol & Cell Biol Sch Vet Med Univ Calif Davis CA 95616-8732

HINTON, DEBORAH M, NUCLEIC ACIDS BIOCHEMISTRY. *Current Pos:* fel, Cancer Biol Prog, Nat Cancer Inst, NIH, 80-82, staff fel, Sect Pharmacol, Lab Biochem Pharmacol, Nat Inst Arthritis, Diabetes & Digestive & Kidney Dis, 82-83, sr staff fel, 83-86, res chemist, Sect Nucleic Acid Biochem, Lab Biochem Pharmacol, 86-92, RES CHEMIST, SECT NUCLEIC ACID BIOCHEM, LAB MOLECULAR & CELLULAR BIOL, 92- *Personal Data:* b Greenville, SC, July 7, 53; m, J Reid Rowlett; c Maggie & Matt. *Educ:* Univ NC, Chapel Hill, BS, 74; Univ Ill, MS, 76, PhD(biochem), 80. *Prof Exp:* Res asst, Dept Biochem, Univ Ill, 75-80. *Concurrent Pos:* Fel, Am Cancer Soc, 80-82. *Mem:* Sigma Xi; AAAS; Am Soc Biol Chemists; Am Soc Microbiol. *Res:* Regulation of transcription; mechanisms of protein-DNA interaction. *Mailing Add:* Nat Inst Diabetes Digestive & Kidney Dis NIH Bldg 8 Rm 2A13 9000 Rockville Pike Bethesda MD 20892-0001

HINTON, DON BARKER, DIFFERENTIAL EQUATIONS. *Current Pos:* assoc prof, 70-74, PROF MATH, UNIV TENN, KNOXVILLE, 74- *Personal Data:* b Savannah, Tenn, Aug 11, 37; m 58, Ella J Pitts; c John. *Educ:* Univ Tenn, BSEE, 60, PhD(math), 63. *Prof Exp:* Asst prof math, Univ Tenn, 63-64; from asst prof to assoc prof, Univ Ga, 64-70. *Mem:* Am Math Soc; Soc Indust & Appl Math. *Res:* Differential equations-spectral properties of linear differential operators and inequalities. *Mailing Add:* Dept Math Univ Tenn Knoxville TN 37996. *Fax:* 423-974-6576; *E-Mail:* hinton@math.utk.edu

HINTON, FREDERICK LEE, PLASMA PHYSICS. *Current Pos:* SR TECH ADV, GEN ATOMIC, 81- *Personal Data:* b Yale, Mich, Aug 4, 39. *Educ:* Univ Mich, BSE, 62, MS, 63; Calif Inst Technol, PhD(physics), 67. *Prof Exp:* Res assoc physics, Plasma Physics Lab, Princeton Univ, 67-69; from asst prof to assoc prof physics, Univ Tex, Austin, 73-81. *Concurrent Pos:* Alfred P Sloan Found res fel, 74-76; assoc ed, Physics of Fluids, 75-77. *Mem:* Am Phys Soc. *Res:* Stability and transport properties of magnetically confined plasmas. *Mailing Add:* Gen Atomics PO Box 85608 San Diego CA 92138. *Fax:* 619-455-3586

HINTON, GEORGE GREENOUGH, PEDIATRIC NEUROLOGY. *Current Pos:* PROF PEDIAT, FAC MED, UNIV WESTERN ONT, 62-, PEDIAT NEUROLOGIST, WAR MEM CHILDREN'S HOSP, 62- *Personal Data:* b Shipley, Eng, July 31, 25; Can citizen; m 56, Patricia; c Patricia & Thomas. *Educ:* McGill Univ, BSc, 51, MD, CM, 55; Univ London, dipl child health, 60; FRCP(C). *Concurrent Pos:* Chief of staff, Parkwood Hosp. *Mem:* Can Med Asn; Can Pediat Soc; Can Neurol Soc; Can Psychiat Asn; Am Acad Cerebral Palsy; Can Asn Pediat Neurologists. *Res:* Mental retardation; epilepsy; learning disability. *Mailing Add:* Dept Pediat Univ Western Ont London ON N6C 2V5 Can

HINTON, JAMES FAULK, PHYSICAL CHEMISTRY. *Current Pos:* From asst prof to assoc prof, 67-75, PROF PHYS CHEM, UNIV ARK, FAYETTEVILLE, 75- *Personal Data:* b Bessemer, Ala, May 5, 38; m 61; c 1. *Educ:* Univ Ala, BS, 60; Univ Ga, MS, 62, PhD(chem), 64. *Concurrent Pos:* Res fels, Univ Ga, 64-65 & Univ Ark, 65-67. *Mem:* Am Chem Soc; NY Acad Sci. *Res:* Kinetics of reactions in solution kinetic salt and solution effects; photochemically induced reactions in solution; magnetic resonance applications to solution phenomena. *Mailing Add:* Dept Chem 114 Chem Bldg Univ Ark Fayetteville AR 72701-1202

HINTON, JONATHAN WAYNE, CERAMIC ENGINEERING. *Current Pos:* SR VPRES, LANXIDE CORP, 91- *Personal Data:* b Canton, Ohio, Apr 12, 44; m 66. *Educ:* Ohio State Univ, BS, 66, MS, 68, PhD(ceramic eng), 70. *Prof Exp:* Staff engr ceramic eng, Champion Spark Plug Co, 70-75, sect head, Cermaic Div, 75-91. *Concurrent Pos:* Trustee, Edward Orton Jr Ceramic Found. *Mem:* Fel Am Ceramic Soc; Nat Inst Ceramic Engrs; Fed Mats Soc. *Res:* Chemical vapor deposition; sonic compaction; bioceramics; refractory, dielectric, and high temperature ceramics; materials for energy conservation; environmental effects of ceramic components and methods; ceramics for spark plug components. *Mailing Add:* 10 Creek Crossing Newark DE 19711

HINTON, RAYMOND PRICE, TELECOMMUNICATION SYSTEMS, TELEPHONE & DATA SWITCHING. *Current Pos:* RETIRED. *Personal Data:* b Hereford, Gt Brit, Jan 18, 25; US citizen; wid; c Christopher, Michael & Alexander. *Educ:* Univ Bristol, Gt Brit, BSc, 45. *Prof Exp:* Engr, Stand Tel & Cables, 46-53; lab dir, ITT, 53-65; vpres, Comput Sci Corp, 65-67; tech dir, Ford Aerospace, 67-77; chief engr, Sperry Univac, 78-81; pres, Telecommun Res Inc, 82-85; prin engr, Gen Elec, 85-91. *Mem:* Fel Inst Elec & Electronics Engrs. *Res:* Electronic telecommunications; digital devices for data switching systems and telephone switching equipment; awarded 22 US and British patents. *Mailing Add:* 901 Carroll Rd Wynnewood PA 19096

HINTZ, HAROLD FRANKLIN, ANIMAL NUTRITION. *Current Pos:* asst prof animal sci, 67-70, assoc prof, 70-78, PROF ANIMAL NUTRIT, CORNELL UNIV, 78- *Personal Data:* b Frank, Ohio, Oct 28, 37; m 59. *Educ:* Ohio State Univ, BS, 59; Cornell Univ, MS, 61, PhD(animal nutrit), 64. *Prof Exp:* Asst prof animal husb, Univ Calif, Davis, 64-67. *Mem:* Am Soc Animal Sci. *Res:* Horse nutrition; Ca and P metabolism. *Mailing Add:* Animal Sci Cornell Univ 149 Morrison Hall Ithaca NY 14853. *Fax:* 607-255-9829

HINTZ, HOWARD WILLIAM, ZOOLOGY, ENTOMOLOGY. *Current Pos:* RETIRED. *Personal Data:* b Dubuque, Iowa, Nov 27, 21; m 52; c 3. *Educ:* Iowa State Col, BS, 47; Ohio State Univ, MS, 49, PhD, 52. *Prof Exp:* Asst, Ohio State Univ, 47-51; from asst prof to prof biol, Heidelberg Col, 51-87. *Mem:* Entom Soc Am; Sigma Xi. *Res:* Insect ecology and taxonomy. *Mailing Add:* 500 E Perry St Tiffin OH 44883

HINTZ, NORTON MARK, NUCLEAR REACTIONS. *Current Pos:* from asst prof to assoc prof, 52-61, PROF PHYSICS, UNIV MINN, MINNEAPOLIS, 61- *Personal Data:* b Milwaukee, Wis, Nov 22, 22; m 43, 90, Mary Abbe; c Matthew, Megan & Mark. *Educ:* Univ Calif, Los Angeles, BA, 43; Harvard Univ, PhD, 51. *Prof Exp:* AEC fel, Cavendish Lab, Eng, 51-52. *Concurrent Pos:* NSF sr fel, Inst Theoret Physics, Copenhagen, 59-60; Guggenheim award, Israel & Copenhagen, 64; NSF physics adv panel, Los Alamos Meson Physics Fac, 69-; NATO sr fel, Europ Orgn Nuclear Res, Geneva, 72; US-Japan Co-op Sci Fel, Kyoto Univ, 74-75; vis scientist, IPN, Onsay, 89. *Mem:* Am Phys Soc. *Res:* Nuclear reactions and spectroscopy. *Mailing Add:* Sch Physics 165 Physics Univ Minn Minneapolis MN 55455. *Fax:* 612-624-4578; *E-Mail:* fvs6259@umn.edu

HINTZ, RICHARD LEE, BIOSTATISTICS. *Current Pos:* STATISTICIAN, MONSANTO INC, ST LOUIS, MGR, STATIST; ASST PROF SYSTS ANALYSIS, ANIMAL BREEDING, OKLA STATE UNIV, 77- *Personal Data:* b Norwalk, Ohio, Mar 30, 49. *Educ:* Ohio State Univ, BS, 71; Cornell Univ, PhD(animal breeding), 77. *Mem:* Am Soc Animal Sci; Am Soc Dairy Sci; Biomet Soc; Am Statist Asn. *Res:* Manage a statistics group for the animal science division of Monsanto. *Mailing Add:* 700 Chesterfield Village Pkwy St Louis MO 63198-0001

HINTZE, LEHI FERDINAND, GEOLOGY. *Current Pos:* prof geol, 55-59, chmn dept, 60-69, prof, 60-86, EMER PROF, BRIGHAM YOUNG UNIV, 86- *Personal Data:* b Denver, Colo, Apr 14, 21; m 42, Ione Nelson; c Sharon, David, Paul & Wayne. *Educ:* Univ Utah, AB, 41; Columbia Univ, AM, 48, PhD(geol), 51. *Prof Exp:* From instr to asst prof geol, Ore State Col, 49-54; regional geologist, Utah Geol Surv, 81-96. *Concurrent Pos:* Consult, US Geol Surv, 60-86. *Mem:* Geol Soc Am; Am Asn Petrol Geol. *Res:* Environmental geology; Ordovician stratigraphy of Utah and Nevada; Ordovician trilobites; geologic maps of Oregon and Utah; geologic mapping; structure and stratigraphy of western Utah; geologic history of Utah. *Mailing Add:* 1835 N 1450 E Provo UT 84604

HINTZE, THOMAS HENRY, PHYSIOLOGY OF ATREAL ANTRURETIC FACTORS. *Current Pos:* ASST PROF PHYSIOL, NY MED COL, 82- *Educ:* NY Med Col, PhD(physiol), 79. *Mailing Add:* Dept Physiol NY Med Col 95 Grasslands Rd Valhalla NY 10595-1600

HINTZEN, PAUL MICHAEL, ASTRONOMY. *Current Pos:* AT GODDARD SPACE FLIGHT CTR, NASA. *Personal Data:* b Glenwood, Minn, Feb 17, 50. *Educ:* Univ Minn, BSc, 71; Univ Ariz, PhD(astron), 75. *Prof Exp:* Res asst astron, Univ Ariz, 74-75; fel astron, Kitt Peak Nat Observ, 75- *Res:* Observations and atmospheric analysis of white dwarfs. *Mailing Add:* Goddard Space Flight Ctr NASA Greenbelt Rd MS 681 Greenbelt MD 20771

HINZ, CARL FREDERICK, JR, INTERNAL MEDICINE, HEMATOLOGY. *Current Pos:* prof & assoc dean, 67-92, EMER PROF MED & EMER ASSOC DEAN, SCH MED, UNIV CONN, 92- *Personal Data:* b Cleveland, Ohio, Apr 9, 27; m 53, Joan Herndon; c Elizabeth, Richard, Catherine & Gretchen. *Educ:* Western Res Univ, BS, 48, MD, 51. *Prof Exp:* Res fel med, 53-57, from instr to assoc prof, Western Res Univ, 57-67. *Concurrent Pos:* Markle scholar, 59-64. *Mem:* Am Fedn Clin Res; Am Soc Clin Invest; Am Asn Immunol; Am Soc Hemat. *Res:* Immunochemistry; mechanisms of hemolysis of red cells; complement and properdin; lymphocyte mediated cytotoxicity. *Mailing Add:* 11 Highwood Dr Avon CT 06001

HINZ, PAUL NORMAN, STATISTICS. *Current Pos:* asst prof, 68-72, assoc prof statist, 72-77, PROF STATIST & FORESTRY, IOWA STATE UNIV, 78- *Personal Data:* b Tarentum, Pa, Dec 23, 35; m 61; c 3. *Educ:* Pa State Univ, BS, 57; NC State Univ, MS, 60; Univ Wis, MS, 63, PhD(statist), 67. *Prof Exp:* Wood technologist, US Forest Prod Lab, 59-62, math statistician, 63-64 & 67-68. *Mem:* Biomet Soc; Am Statist Asn. *Res:* Statistical methods. *Mailing Add:* 504 26th St Ames IA 50010

HINZE, HARRY CLIFFORD, VIROLOGY, VIRAL IMMUNOLOGY. *Current Pos:* Proj assoc virol, 58-59, asst prof, 61-72, ASSOC PROF MED MICROBIOL, SCH MED, UNIV WIS-MADISON, 72- *Personal Data:* b Middleton, Wis, July 18, 30; m 57; c 3. *Educ:* Univ Wis, BS, 53, MS, 55, PhD(med microbiol), 58. *Concurrent Pos:* USPHS trainee, Children's Hosp, Philadelphia, 59-61; prin investr, Meharry Med Sch, 65-, vis prof virol, 79-81. *Mem:* Am Soc Microbiol; Am Asn Immunol; Am Soc Virol. *Res:* Oncogenic herpes viruses; tumor virus-host cell interactions; tumor virus immunology. *Mailing Add:* Dept Med Microbiol Univ Wis Med Sch 1300 University Ave Madison WI 53706-1585

HINZE, WILLIAM JAMES, GEOPHYSICS. *Current Pos:* PROF GEOPHYS, PURDUE UNIV, 72- *Personal Data:* b Milwaukee, Wis, July 26, 30; m 56; c 2. *Educ:* Univ Wis, BS, 51, PhD(geol), 57. *Prof Exp:* Staff geophysicist, Jones & Laughlin Steel Corp, 53 & 56-58; from asst prof to prof geol, Mich State Univ, 58-72. *Mem:* Soc Explor Geophys; Am Geophys Union. *Res:* Regional geophysical studies; mining and engineering geophysics; geoscience data management. *Mailing Add:* Geosci Purdue Univ West Lafayette IN 47907-1968

HINZE, WILLIE LEE, ANALYTICAL & MEMBRANE MIMETIC CHEMISTRY, SEPARATION SCIENCE. *Current Pos:* chmn, 90-94, from asst prof to prof, 75-89, UNIV PROF CHEM, WAKE FOREST UNIV, 89- *Personal Data:* b Burton, Tex, Jan 17, 49; m 80, Wen-Wen Chu. *Educ:* Sam Houston State Univ, BS, 70, MA, 72; Tex A&M Univ, PhD(chem), 74. *Prof Exp:* Instr chem, Blinn Col, 74-75. *Concurrent Pos:* Lectr & NIH fel chem, Tex A&M Univ, 74-75. *Mem:* Am Chem Soc; Am Inst Chemists; Soc Appl Spectros; Sigma Xi; Royal Soc Chem; Assoc Off Anal Chemists. *Res:* Use of membrane mimetic agents in analytical chemistry; luminescence methods; separations; enzymology. *Mailing Add:* Dept Chem Wake Forest Univ Box 7486 Winston-Salem NC 27109-7486. *Fax:* 910-759-4656; *E-Mail:* hinze@pop.wfu.edu

HIOE, FOIK TJIONG, QUANTUM OPTICS, STATISTICAL MECHANICS & NONLINEAR DYNAMICS. *Current Pos:* assoc prof, 81-84, PROF PHYSICS, ST JOHN FISHER COL, 84- *Personal Data:* b Jakarta, Indonesia, Apr 20, 41; US citizen; m, Siew H Toh; c Wayne, Elliot & Nelson. *Educ:* Imp Col Sci & Technol, BSc (Hon) & ARCS, 63; Univ London, PhD(theoret physics), 67. *Prof Exp:* Res chemist, Univ Calif, San Diego, 67-70; res fel, Ill Inst Technol, 70-71; res assoc physics, Univ Rochester, 75-80, sr res assoc, 75-81. *Concurrent Pos:* Vis assoc prof physics, State Univ NY, Buffalo, 78-79; prin investr, US Dept Energy, 82-91. *Mem:* Am Phys Soc. *Res:* Excluded volume effect in polymers; multilevel and multiphoton effect in laser-induced atomic and molecular excitation; nonlinear dynamics in two-dimensional Hamiltonian systems; published over 80 articles. *Mailing Add:* St John Fisher Col 3690 East Ave Rochester NY 14618-3537

HIPEL, KEITH WILLIAM, STOCHASTIC MODELLING, CONFLICT ANALYSIS. *Current Pos:* from asst prof to assoc prof, 76-85, PROF, DEPT SYSTS DESIGN ENG, UNIV WATERLOO, 85- *Personal Data:* b Kitchener, Ont, Mar 15, 46; m 71; c Melita, Lloyd, Conrad & Warren. *Educ:* Univ Waterloo, BASc, 70, MASc, 72, PhD(civil eng), 75. *Honors & Awards:* W R Boggess Award, Am Water Resources Asn, 83; Outstanding Contrib Award, Inst Elec & Electronics Engrs, 95. *Prof Exp:* Teaching asst eng, Univ Waterloo, 71-75; vis prof civil eng, Fed Univ, Brazil, 75-76. *Concurrent Pos:* Vis prof, Univ Sao Paulo, Brazil, 80 & State Sci & Technol, China, 82; consult, Environ Can & Elec Utilities, 77-; Japan Soc Prom Sci res fel, Dept Appl Math & Physics, Kyoto Univ, 84; assoc ed, J Info Sci & Technol, J Conflict Processes, J Chinese Mgt Issues. *Mem:* Am Geophys Union; fel Am Water Resources Asn; fel Inst Elec & Electronics Engrs; Int Environmetrics Soc. *Res:* Conflict resolution; time series analysis; systems design engineering; decision technologies; water resources management; environmental engineering; author of numerous publications. *Mailing Add:* Dept Syst Sci Univ Waterloo Waterloo ON N2L 3G1 Can. *Fax:* 519-746-4791; *E-Mail:* kwhipel@sysoffice.watstar.uwaterloo.ca

HIPP, BILLY WAYNE, SOIL FERTILITY. *Current Pos:* RETIRED. *Personal Data:* b Blackwell, Tex, June 18, 33; m 54; c 2. *Educ:* Tex Tech Univ, BS, 55; Tex A&M Univ, MS, 63, PhD(soil chem), 66. *Prof Exp:* Field rep fertilizer, Wood Chem Co, 55-56 & 58-60; instr soils, Tex A&M Univ, Agr Res & Exten Ctr, Dallas, 60-65, prof, 65- *Mem:* Am Soc Agron; Am Hort Soc. *Res:* Soil fertility; nutrient movement in soils. *Mailing Add:* Tex A&M Univ Res & Exten Ctr 17360 Coit Rd Dallas TX 75252

HIPP, SALLY SLOAN, SEXUALLY TRANSMISSIBLE DISEASE. *Current Pos:* res scientist, Div Labs & Res, 71-87, STD CONTROL PROG, NY STATE DEPT HEALTH, 87- *Personal Data:* b Philadelphia, Pa, Apr 5, 37; c 1. *Educ:* Pa State Univ, BS, 58; Albany Med Col, PhD(biochem), 69. *Prof Exp:* Res scientist, NY State Dept Health, 62-70; sr res scientist, London Sch Hyg & Trop Med, 70-71. *Concurrent Pos:* Adj asst prof, Dept Obstet & Gynec, Albany Med Col, 81-; vis lectr, Dept Biol, Skidmore Col, 72-73; WHO fel, UK, 77. *Mem:* Int Soc Human & Animal Mycol; Am Soc Microbiol; Sigma Xi; Am Venereal Dis Asn; NY Acad Sci. *Res:* Chlamydea; mycoplasma; sexually transmissible diseases of women; identification of causes of chronic vaginitis; role of microorganisms in reproductive failure; transport systems for genital microorganisms. *Mailing Add:* 15 Pineridge Pl Delmar NY 12054

HIPPS, KERRY W, PHYSICAL CHEMISTRY OF SURFACES & FILMS, MATERIALS SCIENCE. *Current Pos:* from asst prof to prof, 78-90, PROF CHEM & MAT SCI, WASH STATE UNIV, 91- *Personal Data:* b El Paso, Tex, Mar 16, 48; c 2. *Educ:* Univ Tex, BS, 70; Wash State Univ, PhD(chem physics), 76. *Prof Exp:* Lectr phys chem, Univ Mich, 76-78. *Concurrent Pos:* Alfred P Sloan fel; energy related fel, NSF. *Mem:* Am Chem Soc; Am Phys Soc; Sigma Xi; Mat Res Soc. *Res:* Spectroscopy of solids and surfaces; chemical physics of inorganic materials; materials chemistry and physics of thin films. *Mailing Add:* Chem Dept Wash State Univ Pullman WA 99164-4630. *E-Mail:* hipps@wsu.edu

HIRAMOTO, RAYMOND NATSUO, BACTERIOLOGY, IMMUNOLOGY. *Current Pos:* PROF MICROBIOL, MED CTR, UNIV ALA, BIRMINGHAM, 66- *Personal Data:* b Honolulu, Hawaii, June 12, 30; m 52; c 5. *Educ:* Univ Mich, Ann Arbor, BA, 52, MS, 53, PhD(bact), 56. *Prof Exp:* Teaching asst, Univ Mich, Ann Arbor, 55-56; cancer res scientist biochem, Roswell Park Mem Inst, NY, 56-59, sr cancer res scientist, 59-62; from asst prof to assoc prof microbiol, Univ Tenn, Memphis, 61-66. *Concurrent Pos:* Chief immunol sect, St Jude Children's Res Hosp, Memphis, 62-66, dir blood bank, 63-66. *Mem:* Fel Am Acad Microbiol; Am Asn Immunol; Am Asn Cancer Res; Soc Exp Biol & Med; NY Acad Sci. *Res:* Site of fixation in various organs of antikidney antibodies; penetration of antibodies and globulins into viable cells; immuno-histochemical studies on human tumors and related tissues; antibody formation; Pavlovian conditioning of immune resistance. *Mailing Add:* Dept Microbiol Sch Med Univ Ala Univ Sta Birmingham AL 35294-0007

HIRANO, ASAO, NEUROPATHOLOGY. *Current Pos:* HEAD, DIV NEUROPATH, MONTEFIORE HOSP, 65-; HARRY M ZIMMERMAN PROF NEUROPATH, MONTEFIORE MED CTR, 95- *Personal Data:* b Tomioka, Japan, Nov 26, 26; m 59, Keiko; c Michio, Ikuo, Yoko & Shigeo. *Educ:* Univ Niigata, BS, 47; Univ Kyoto, MD, 52. *Honors & Awards:* Billings Silver Medal, AMA, 59; Annual Prize, Am Asn Neuropath, 61; Henry Moses Res Award, 68; Royal Col lectr, Can Asn Neuropathologists, Royal Col Physicians & Surgeons Can, 80; Jack Prichard Mem lectr, Queen's Univ, Belfast, Ireland, 81; Rajan Bharati Mem lectr, Madras Med Col, India, 84; Neuropath Meritorious Contrib Award, Am Asn Neuropathologists, 95. *Prof Exp:* Intern, Osaka US Army Hosp, Japan, 52-53 & Harlem Hosp, NY, 53-54; resident neurol, Bellevue Hosp, New York, 54-55 & Montefiore Hosp, 55-56, chief resident, 57-58; vis scientist, Nat Inst Neurol Dis & Blindness, 59-65. *Concurrent Pos:* Fel neuropath, Montefiore Hosp, 56-69; asst, Columbia Univ, 59; assoc prof, Albert Einstein Col Med, 65-71, prof, 71-; vis prof, Kansai Med Univ, Osaka, Japan, 85, Univ Western Australia, 86, Nippon Med Sch, 93. *Mem:* Am Asn Neuropath (pres, 77-78); Am Acad Neurol; Asn Res Nervous & Ment Dis; Am Neurol Asn; Japanese Neuropath Asn; hon mem Japanese Soc Neurol. *Res:* Fine structure of normal and pathological nervous tissue; pathology of motor neuron diseases. *Mailing Add:* Montefiore Med Ctr 111 E 210th St Bronx NY 10467. *Fax:* 718-653-3409

HIRANO, TOSHIO, SIGNAL TRANSDUCTION, GENE EXPRESSION. *Current Pos:* from assoc prof to prof, Inst Molecular Cell Biol, 84-93, PROF, BIOMED RES CTR, OSAKA UNIV MED SCH, 89- *Personal Data:* b Osaka, Apr 17, 47; m 74, Chiyoko; c 2. *Educ:* Osaka Univ, med degree, 72, PhD, 79. *Honors & Awards:* Erwin von Belz Prize, 86; Rheumatism Prize, Japanese Found Rheumatism, 90; Sandoz Prize, 92. *Prof Exp:* Assoc prof, Kumamoto Univ Med Sch, 80-84. *Mem:* Am Asn Immunologists. *Res:* Molecular mechanism(s) of growth and differentiation of hematopoietic lineage cells; gene expression and signal transduction mechanism(s) of interleukin 6; molecular mechanism(s) of autoimmune diseases and oncogenesis of lymphoid cells. *Mailing Add:* Dept Molecular Oncol Biomed Res Ctr Osaka Univ Med Sch 2-2 Yamada-oka Suita Osaka 565 Japan. *Fax:* 81-6-879-3889; *E-Mail:* hirano@molonc.med.osaka-u-ac.jp

HIRASAKI, GEORGE J, INTERFACIAL PHENOMONA. *Current Pos:* PROF, DEPT CHEM ENG, RICE UNIV, 93- *Personal Data:* b Beaumont, Tex, Sept 26, 39. *Educ:* Lamar State Col Technol, BS, 63; Rice Univ, PhD(chem eng), 67. *Honors & Awards:* Lester C Uren Award, Soc Petrol Engrs, 89. *Prof Exp:* Engr, Shell Develop Co, 67-70, res engr, 70-71, res assoc, 71-72, staff reservoir engr, Shell Oil Co, 72-74, staff res engr, Shell Develop Co, 74-78, sr staff res engr, 78-83, res adv, 83-93. *Concurrent Pos:* Mem, Monograph Comt, Soc Petrol Engrs, 74-75 & 82-87, Nat Petrol Comt Enhanced Oil Recovery, 92; mem, Comt Appl Res Related to Extraction Oil & Gas, Nat Res Coun, 82-84, Bd Chem Sci & Technol, 94-; moderator, World Cong Emulsions, Paris, 93-; consult enhanced oil recovery, Saga Petrol, Norway, 93-; mem, Panel Rev Oil Recovery Demonstration Prog, Nat Res Coun, Dept Energy, 94-95. *Mem:* Nat Acad Eng; Soc Petrol Engrs; Am Inst Chem Engrs; Am Chem Soc; Soc Core Analyst; Soc Indust & Appl Math; Soc Prof Well Log Analysis. *Res:* Interfacial phenomena; numerical simulation; multiphase flow in porous media; wettability; foam in porous media; surfactant flooding; author of various publications; granted 3 patents. *Mailing Add:* Dept Chem Eng Rice Univ MS362 6100 S Main St Houston TX 77251-1892

HIRASUNA, ALAN RYO, MECHANICAL ENGINEERING. *Current Pos:* VPRES, L'GARDE, INC, 71- *Personal Data:* b Fresno, Calif, Sept 27, 39; m 86; c 1. *Educ:* Univ Calif, Berkeley, BS, 62; Univ SCalif, MS, 69. *Prof Exp:* Refinery engr, Chevron, 62-64; heat transfer analyst, NAm Rockwell, 64; prog engr, Ford Aerospace, 64-71. *Concurrent Pos:* Dir, bd L'Garde Inc, 71-; dir, bd Am Assoc SML Res Cos, 84-; comt mem, Comt Elastomers, Geothermal Resources Coun, 84. *Mem:* Am Chem Soc; Am Soc Mech Engrs; Geothermal Res Coun; Soc Petrol Engrs; Am Defense Preparedness Assoc. *Res:* Develop new elastomer compounds for extremely hostile environments; developed Y267 EPDM which has become a standard in the geothermal industry for wells up to 320 centigrade; developed compounds for army tank track and strategic missile applications which must survive a nuclear encounter. *Mailing Add:* L'Garde Inc 15181 Woodland Ave Tustin CA 92780

HIRATA, FUSAO, MOLECULAR & BIOCHEMICAL PHARMACOLOGY, DEVELOPMENT PHARMACEUTICS BY BIOTECHNOLOGY. *Current Pos:* PROF PHARMACOL, FAC PHARM, WAYNE STATE UNIV, 90-, PROF TOXICOL, INS CHEM TOXICOL, 90- *Personal Data:* b Ube, Yamagulhi, Japan, Aug 28, 41; m 68; c 3. *Educ:* Tokyo Med & Dent Univ, MD, 67; Kyoto Univ, PhD(biochem), 72. *Honors & Awards:* Distinguished Young Scientist Award, Japanese Biochem Soc, 77. *Prof Exp:* Asst prof biochem, Fac Med, Kyoto Univ, 72-80; vis scientist pharmacol, NIMH, 77-84, unit chief cell biol, 84-86; assoc prof toxicol, Johns Hopkins Univ, 86-90. *Concurrent Pos:* State-of-the-Art lect, Am Asn Endocrinol, 82; adj fac, Sch Hyg & Pub Health, Johns Hopkins Univ, 90-; prof pharmacol, Sch Med, Wayne State Univ, 91- *Mem:* AAAS; Am Soc Biochem & Molecular Biol; NY Acad Sci. *Res:* Pathophysiology of hyperreactive airways with respect to dysfunction of neuroreceptors induced by inflammatory cytokine networks and mechanisms of therapeutic action of glucocorticoids. *Mailing Add:* Dept Pharmaceut Sci Wayne State Univ Shapero Hall 528 Detroit MI 48202. *Fax:* 313-577-2033

HIRATSUKA, YASUYUKI, MYCOLOGY, PLANT PATHOLOGY. *Current Pos:* RES SCIENTIST MYCOL, CAN FORESTRY SERV, CAN GOVT, 64- *Personal Data:* b Tottori, Japan, Dec 27, 33; Can citizen; m 59; c 3. *Educ:* Int Christian Univ, Tokyo, BS, 57; Hokkaido Univ, MS, 59; Purdue Univ, PhD(mycol, plant path), 62. *Honors & Awards:* Dr & Mrs D L Bailey Award, Can Phytopath Soc, 88; Distinguished Award, Soc Tech Commun, 88. *Concurrent Pos:* Nat Res Coun Can fel, 62-65; adj prof bot, Univ Man, 83-; adj prof forest & plant sci, Univ Alta, 81-; res scientist, Dir Mycological Inst, 96- *Mem:* Am Mycol Soc; Phytopath Soc Japan; Mycol Soc Japan; Int Soc Plant Taxon; Can Bot Asn; Am Phytopath Soc. *Res:* Taxonomy and biology of uredinales; taxonomy and morphology of forest disease pathogens; biochemical study of metabolites of tree disease pathogens; pine stem rusts of the world; armillaria root rot of conifers; aspen decay and stain. *Mailing Add:* Northern Forestry Ctr 5320 122nd St Edmonton AB T6H 3S5 Can

HIRAYAMA, CHIKARA, PHYSICAL CHEMISTRY, INORGANIC CHEMISTRY. *Current Pos:* CONSULT, 86- *Personal Data:* b Honolulu, Hawaii, Feb 12, 24; m 56, Kay K Imamura; c 5. *Educ:* Univ Hawaii, BS, 46, MS, 48; Univ Minn, PhD(chem), 57. *Prof Exp:* Chemist, Coca Cola Co, 48-50, Wailuku Sugar Co, 51-52 & US Fish & Wildlife Serv, 52-53; res chemist, Res Labs, Westinghouse Elec Corp, 57-73, consult scientist, 85-86. *Mem:* AAAS; Am Chem Soc. *Res:* Dielectric properties of inorganic electrical insulators; physics and chemistry of glasses; chemistry of coordination compounds, kinetics and optical properties; lasers; electroluminescence; high temperature chemistry and thermodynamics; mass spectrometry; solid electrolyte sensors; thin dielectric films. *Mailing Add:* PO Box 318 Kaunakakai HI 96748-0318

HIRD, DAVID WILLIAM, VETERINARY MEDICINE, PUBLIC HEALTH & EPIDEMIOLOGY. *Current Pos:* from asst prof to assoc prof, 80-92, PROF, UNIV CALIF, DAVIS, 92- *Personal Data:* b Newport News, Va, June 30, 42; m 73, Shelley A Carter; c Laurel & Andreco. *Educ:* Stanford Univ, AB, 64; Univ Calif-Davis, DVM, 68, MPVM, 73; Univ Minn, PhD(epidemiol), 80. *Honors & Awards:* Fulbright Res Award, Costa Rica, 87. *Prof Exp:* Res vet, Univ Chile, Santiago, 68-70; clin vet, Australia, 71-72; livestock prod specialist, Food & Agr Orgn, Venezuela, 70-71; county vet, Imp County, Calif, 73-77. *Concurrent Pos:* Hon prof, Univ Chile. *Res:* Quantitative epidemiologic approaches to livestock, health and productivity; food safety. *Mailing Add:* Dept Med & Epidemiol Univ Calif Davis CA 95616. *Fax:* 530-752-5845

HIREGOWDARA, DANANAGOUD, MEDICINE. *Current Pos:* POSTDOCTORAL FEL, SCH MED, BOSTON UNIV, 89- *Mailing Add:* Dept Biochem K234 New England Deaconess Hosp 21-27 Burlington Ave Boston MA 02115

HIREMATH, SHIVANAND T, MOLECULAR ENTOMOLOGY, BIOLOGICAL CONTROL OF FOREST PESTS. *Current Pos:* RES BIOLOGIST, USDA FOREST SERV, 88- *Personal Data:* b Bijapur, India, Jan 26, 52; m 80; c 1. *Educ:* Karnatak Univ, Dharwar, India, BS, 71, MS, 73; Poona Univ, India, PhD(biochem), 78. *Prof Exp:* Res assoc, State Univ NY, Buffalo, 78-82, Univ Ky, Lexington, 83-87; res scientist, Univ Calif, Riverside, 87-88. *Mem:* Am Soc Biochem & Molecular Biol; Am Soc Microbiologists; AAAS. *Res:* Safe and effective microbial agents for use in integrated forest pest management systems. *Mailing Add:* USDA Forestry Sci Lab 359 Main Rd Delaware OH 43015-8640

HIRES, RICHARD IVES, PHYSICAL OCEANOGRAPHY. *Current Pos:* Asst prof, 67-73, ASSOC PROF OCEAN ENG, STEVENS INST TECHNOL, 73- *Personal Data:* b Camden, NJ, Aug 19, 39; m 63; c 4. *Educ:* Rensselaer Polytech Inst, BS, 61; Johns Hopkins Univ, MA, 64, PhD(oceanog), 68. *Concurrent Pos:* Instr, NJ Marine Sci Consortium, 69-; consult, Woodward Envicon Inc, 72-74 & Enviro Sci Inc, 74- *Mem:* Soc Naval Architects & Marine Engrs; Am Geophys Union. *Res:* Wind generation of waves; interactions across the air-sea interface; diffusion of contaminants in coastal waters; estuarine circulation; wind engineering. *Mailing Add:* 14 Farragut Pl Morristown NJ 07960

HIRKO, RONALD JOHN, MAGNETIC PARTICLE ORIENTATION & POLYURETHANE RESINS, TRIBOLOGY & SURFACE CHARACTERIZATION. *Current Pos:* MGR CHEM & PHYSICS, QUANTEGY INC, 95- *Personal Data:* b Cleveland, Ohio, Mar 3, 43; m 65, Mary Catherine Linn; c Andrew Ronald, Kimberly Ann & Tamara Agnes. *Educ:* Kent State Univ, BS, 65; Utah State Univ, PhD(chem), 69. *Prof Exp:* Sect head chem, Occidental Chem Co, White Springs, 69-79, mgr qual assurance, 79-90; anal lab mgr, Ampex Media Recording Corp, 91-95. *Mem:* Am Chem Soc. *Mailing Add:* 410 Green St Auburn AL 36830-6164

HIRLEMAN, EDWIN DANIEL, JR, THERMAL SCIENCES. *Current Pos:* from asst prof to assoc prof mech eng, 81-87, PROF MECH ENG, ARIZ STATE UNIV, 88-, PROF & VCHAIR AEROSPACE, 89- *Personal Data:* b Wichita, Kans, Dec 1, 51; m 75; c 3. *Educ:* Purdue Univ, BSME, 72, ME, 74, PhD(mech eng), 77. *Prof Exp:* Res assoc laser diag, Tech Univ Denmark, 74-75; staff engr, Hughes Aircraft Co, 74-77. *Concurrent Pos:* Prin investr, various grants founded by NSF, Off Naval Res, Air Force Off Sci Res, Semiconductor Res Corp, IBM, Allied-Signal Aerospace, McDonnell-Douglas Helicopter. *Mem:* Combustion Inst; Am Soc Mech Engrs; Am Inst Aeronaut & Astronaut; Optical Soc Am. *Res:* Laser optical diagnostics for thermo-fluid science; optical sensors for manufacturing; optical characterization of surface microfeatures design theory; design methodology. *Mailing Add:* Mech Eng Dept Ariz State Univ Tempe AZ 85287

HIRNING, LANE D, MOLECULAR BIOLOGY. *Current Pos:* SR SCIENTIST, NPS PHARMACEUT INC, 89-, MIS MGR, INFO SERVS. *Personal Data:* b Twin Falls, Idaho, Oct 1, 58. *Educ:* Idaho State Univ, BS, 81; Univ Ariz, PhD(pharmacol), 85. *Prof Exp:* Postdoctoral fel, Dept Pharmacol & Phys Sci, Univ Chicago, 85-89. *Mem:* Am Soc Pharmacol & Exp Therapeut; AAAS; Soc Neurosci. *Mailing Add:* Dept Neurophysiol NPS Pharmaceut Inc 420 Chipeta Way Salt Lake City UT 84108

HIROKAWA, KATSUIKU, STRUCTURE & IMMUNOLOGICAL FUNCTION OF THE THYMUS, BIOLOGY OF AGING. *Current Pos:* chief, 81-85, DIR PATH, TOKYO METROP INST GERONT, 85- *Personal Data:* b Tokyo, Japan, Nov 5, 39; m 68; c 3. *Educ:* Tokyo Med & Dent Univ, MD, 64, DMed Sci, 69. *Prof Exp:* Sr instr path, Tokyo Med & Dent Univ, 69-76, assoc prof, 76-81. *Mem:* Am Asn Immunologists; NY Acad Sci. *Res:* Ontogenic development and aging of the thymus and T cell dependent immune functions; mechanism of the age-related alteration of the immune system; neuroendocrine control of the thymus and the immune system. *Mailing Add:* Dept Path Immunol Tokyo Med & Dent Univ 1-5-45 Yushima Bunkyo-ku Tokyo Japan. *Fax:* 813-3813-1790; *E-Mail:* hiro.pth2@med.tmd.ac.jp

HIROSE, AKIRA, PHYSICAL MATHEMATICS. *Current Pos:* res assoc, Univ Sask, 71-74, res scientist, 75-77, assoc prof, 77-79, PROF, DEPT PHYSICS, UNIV SASK, 79- *Personal Data:* b Nagano Prefecture, Japan, Aug 16, 41; m 69, Yamamoto Kimiko; c Tadashi & Kyoko. *Educ:* Yokohama Nat Univ, BS, 65, MS, 67; Univ Tenn, PhD(elec eng), 69. *Hon Degrees:* DSc, Univ Sask, 94. *Honors & Awards:* Merit Award, Inst Elect & Electronics Engrs Nuclear & Plasma Sci Soc, 93. *Prof Exp:* Consult, Oak Ridge Nat Lab, 68-69, mem res staff, Thermonuclear Div, 69-71. *Concurrent Pos:* Res fel, Japan Soc Prom Sci, 84. *Mem:* Fel Am Phys Soc; fel Inst Elec & Electronics Engrs; Can Asn Physicists. *Res:* Plasma turbulence; linear and nonlinear waves and instabilities; turbulent heating; toroidal confinement. *Mailing Add:* Dept Physics & Eng Physics Univ Sask Saskatoon SK S7N 0W0 Can. *Fax:* 306-966-6400; *E-Mail:* hirose@sask.usask.ca

HIROTA, JED, BIOLOGICAL OCEANOGRAPHY. *Current Pos:* fel, 73-74, asst prof, 74-79, ASSOC PROF OCEANOG, HAWAII INST MARINE BIOL, 79- *Personal Data:* b Honolulu, Hawaii, Mar 2, 43; m 70; c 2. *Educ:* Univ Wash, BSc, 65, MSc, 67; Scripps Inst Oceanog, PhD(biol oceanog), 73. *Honors & Awards:* Calif Acad Sci Award, Am Soc Limnol & Oceanog, 71. *Prof Exp:* Res asst biol oceanog, Scripps Inst & Dept Oceanog, Univ Wash, 65-72. *Mem:* Am Soc Limnol & Oceanog; Ecol Soc Am. *Res:* Ecology of zooplankton distribution, faunal assemblages, metabolism, secondary production, natural history, feeding behavior; biological and chemical oceanographic methodology. *Mailing Add:* 186 Kuukama St Kailua HI 96734

HIROYASU, HIROYUJI, mechanical engineering, for more information see previous edition

HIROYASU, HIROYUKI, MECHANICAL ENGINEERING. *Current Pos:* assoc prof, 66-67, PROF, DEPT MECH ENG, UNIV HIROSHIMA, 68- *Personal Data:* b Hiroshima, Japan, Jan 13, 35; m 64, Yoshiko Ikeda; c Tomoyuki & Shoko. *Educ:* Tohoku Univ, BA, 57, MS, 59, PhD(mech eng), 62. *Honors & Awards:* Soichiro Honda Medal, Am Soc Mech Engrs, 92. *Prof Exp:* Res engr, Toyota Cent Res & Develop Co Ltd, 62-64; res assoc, Dept Mech Eng, Univ Wis, 64-66. *Concurrent Pos:* Vis prof, Dept Mech Eng, Wayne State Univ, Detroit, 79-80; adv prof, Shanghai Jiao Tong Univ, China; ed, Atomization, 92. *Mem:* Fel Soc Automotive Engrs; Japan Soc Mech Engrs; Japan Soc Automotive Engrs; Japan Soc Energy & Resources; Japan Soc Aeronaut & Space Sci; Japan Soc Eng Educ; Gas Turbine Soc Japan; Visualization Soc Japan; Fuel Soc Japan; Heat Transfer Soc Japan. *Res:* Internal combution engines. *Mailing Add:* Nagatsukanishi 5-9-21 Asamiuamiku Hiroshima 73101 Japan

HIRS, CHRISTOPHE HENRI WERNER, ORGANIC CHEMISTRY. *Current Pos:* PROF & CHMN, DEPT BIOCHEM, BIOPHYS & GENETICS, SCH MED, UNIV COLO, DENVER, 78- *Personal Data:* b Bern, Switz, Apr 25, 23; nat US; m 49. *Educ:* Manchester Univ, BSc, 44; Columbia Univ, PhD(biochem), 49. *Prof Exp:* Assoc in biochem, Rockefeller Inst Med Res, 49-58; from assoc biochemist to biochemist, Brookhaven Nat Lab, 58-63, sr biochemist, 63-65, chmn dept biol, 65-69; dir, Div Biol Sci, Ind Univ, Bloomington, 69-77, prof biol, 69-78. *Concurrent Pos:* Mem Am Inst Biol Sci adv comt biochem, Off Naval Res, 60-63 & physiol chem study sect, Div Res Grants, NIH, 63-67; exec ed, Arch Biochem & Biophys, 63-72; mem adv panel molecular biol, NSF, 71-74; assoc ed, J Biol Chem, 72- *Mem:* AAAS; Am Chem Soc; Am Soc Biochem & Molecular Biol. *Res:* Protein chemistry. *Mailing Add:* Dept Biochem Biophys Genetics Univ Colo Health Sci Ctr 4200 E Ninth Ave Denver CO 80262-0001. *Fax:* 303-270-8215

HIRSCH, ALBERT EDGAR, CHEMICAL ENGINEERING. *Current Pos:* RETIRED. *Personal Data:* b Buffalo, NY, Nov 27, 24; m 48; c 1. *Educ:* Univ Mich, BS, 48, Univ Tenn, MS, 62, PhD(chem eng), 64. *Prof Exp:* Engr chem eng, E I du Pont de Nemours & Co Inc, 48-57, proc control supt, 51-61, res engr chem eng, 64-69, res engr mat sci, 69-70. *Concurrent Pos:* Consult, 90- *Mem:* Am Chem Soc. *Res:* Engineering and materials science; chemical engineering; materials science engineering. *Mailing Add:* 2410 Raven Rd Wilmington DE 19810

HIRSCH, ALLEN FREDERICK, MEDICINAL CHEMISTRY, CLINICAL & PRECLINICAL QUALITY. *Current Pos:* PRES, QUAL CONSULT, 93- *Personal Data:* b New York, NY, May 24, 35; m 57; c 3. *Educ:* Fordham Univ, BS, 57; Univ NC, MS, 62, PhD(med chem), 64. *Prof Exp:* Res assoc org chem, Sloan-Kettering Inst Cancer Res, 63-65; fel, Albert Einstein Col Med, 65-67; group leader, Ortho Pharmaceut Corp, 67-77, dir res qual assurance, 77-89; sr dir, Regulatory Affairs Admin Worldwide, R W Johnson Pharmaceut Res Inst, 89-92. *Concurrent Pos:* Course Dir, Ctr Prof Advan. *Mem:* Soc Qual; Drug Info Asn. *Res:* Organic synthesis in plasmalogens, thiosulfinates, nitrogen mustards, pseudouridine, steroids and nucleic acids; male and female antifertility agents. *Mailing Add:* 4 N Cadillac Dr Somerville NJ 08876

HIRSCH, ANN MARY, PLANT MOLECULAR BIOLOGY, PLANT DEVELOPMENT. *Current Pos:* ASSOC PROF BIOL, UNIV CALIF, LOS ANGELES, 88- *Personal Data:* b Milwaukee, Wis, June 2, 47; m 70. *Educ:* Marquette Univ, BS, 69; Univ Calif, PhD(bot), 74. *Prof Exp:* Asst prof bot, Univ Minn, 74-76; res assoc, Harvard Univ, 76-78; from asst prof to assoc prof biol, Wellesley Col, 78-88, dir greenhouses, 84-87. *Concurrent Pos:* Biol tutor, Harvard Univ, 77-80, vis scientist, 81-82; vis scientist, Stanford Univ, 83; panel mem, comt res grants, Nat Acad Sci-Nat Res Coun, 84-87 & nitrogen fixation prog, USDA, 86, NSF, 86. *Mem:* Am Asn Plant Physiologists; Am Soc Microbiol; Am Soc Cell Biol; Sigma Xi; Bot Soc Am. *Res:* Symbiotic nitrogen fixation; plant and rhizobial genes expressed during the early stages of nodule development. *Mailing Add:* Dept Biol Univ Calif 405 Hilgard Ave Los Angeles CA 90024-7009

HIRSCH, ARNOLD, CHEMISTRY. *Current Pos:* DIR, RES & DEVELOP LAB, AL LABS, INC, 82- *Educ:* Univ Ill, BS, 60, PhD(chem), 65; Miami Univ, MS, 62. *Prof Exp:* Res chemist, Julian Res Inst, 65-75; lab supvr, Diamond Shamrock Corp, Franklin Park, Ill, 75-77, gen mgr, 77-79, mgr res & develop, 79-81. *Concurrent Pos:* Instr (part-time) org chem, Murton Col, 66-73. *Mem:* Am Chem Soc; AAAS; Chem Soc London; fel Am Inst Chemists. *Res:* Synthesis of 4'-Flavonecarboxylic Acid; nucleophilic substitution of picoline and pyrazine N-oxides; studies in the steroid field involving process development and synthesis; corticoids; manufacture and synthesis of progestational compounds; sterols manufacture and synthesis; author of 16 publications. *Mailing Add:* AL Labs 400 State St Chicago Heights IL 60411

HIRSCH, ARTHUR, PACKAGING. *Current Pos:* CONSULT, 89- *Personal Data:* b Vienna, Austria, Dec 10, 21; US citizen; m 49, Ruth Jaul; c Steven N. *Educ:* City Col New York, BS, 46; Brooklyn Col, MS, 56; NY Univ, PhD, 60. *Honors & Awards:* NY Univ Founders Day Award, 60. *Prof Exp:* Chemist, Pease Labs, 46-52; chief chemist, Atlantic Gummed Paper Co, 52-54 & Swingline Indust Corp, 54-55; tech dir, Gen Gummed Prod, 55-60; dir res, Can Tech Tape, Ltd, 62-68; dir res, Standard Packaging Corp, Clifton, 68-78; tech dir, Arvey Corp, Chicago & Cedar Grove, 78-89. *Concurrent Pos:* Lectr, Wagner Lutheran Col, 56-58; Nat Res Coun Can & Defense Res Bd Can, grants, 63, 64 & 65; chmn educ comt, Nat Flexible Packaging Asn; mem comt adhesives, Am Soc Testing & Mat; adj prof, BCCC, 89- *Mem:* Am Chem Soc; Tech Asn Pulp & Paper Indust; Chem Inst Can; fel Am Inst Chem; sr mem Inst Elec & Electronics Engrs. *Res:* Polymers; adhesives; functional paper coatings; heterocyclic organic chemistry; packaging; extrusion and lamination; paper saturation. *Mailing Add:* 2000 Linwood Ave Ft Lee NJ 07024

HIRSCH, CARL ALVIN, CHEMISTRY. *Current Pos:* DIR CLIN CHEM, NEW ENG MED CTR HOSP, BOSTON, 75-; ASSOC CLIN PROF PATH, SCH MED, TUFTS UNIV, 75- *Personal Data:* b Los Angeles, Calif, Sept 21, 29. *Educ:* Calif Inst Technol, BS, 51; Wash Univ, MD, 59; Am Bd Path, cert, 75. *Prof Exp:* Chemist, Army Chem Corps Biol Labs, Md, 53-55; intern, Eastern Marine Gen Hosp, 59-60; res fel, Dept Bact, Harvard Med Sch, 60-63, instr bact, 63-64, instr med, 64-68, assoc, 68-69, asst prof, 69-72; asst clin prof lab med & clin path, Sch Med, Univ Calif, San Francisco, 72-74. *Concurrent Pos:* Res assoc med, Beth Israel Hosp, Boston, 64-72; NSF grant, 71-73; asst chief, Clin Path Serv, San Francisco Vet Admin Hosp, 72-74, actg chief, 74; pathologist, New Eng Deaconess Hosp, Boston, 74-75, New Eng Baptist Hosp, Boston, 74-75. *Mem:* AAAS; Am Soc Biochem & Molecular Biol; Col Am Pathologists; Am Asn Clin Chem; Acad Clin Lab Physicians & Scientists. *Res:* Clinical pathology. *Mailing Add:* Clin Chem Dept Tufts-New Eng Med Ctr 171 Harrison Ave Boston MA 02111-1854

HIRSCH, DONALD EARL, CHEMICAL ENGINEERING, COGENERATION. *Current Pos:* PVT CONSULT, 91- *Personal Data:* b Erie, Pa, Sept 17, 24; m 46, Mary Alice Buseck; c Robert P, Susan J (Glass), Karl F & Donald E Jr. *Educ:* Univ Pittsburgh, BS, 47, MS, 48, PhD(chem eng), 54. *Prof Exp:* Chemist, Los Alamos Sci Lab, 45-46; instr chem eng, Univ Pittsburgh, 48-50; chemist, E I du Pont de Nemours & Co, 50-57, proj mgr, 57-58, sr assoc engr, 59-62; adv engr, Am Potash & Chem Co, 63-65, mgr plant tech serv, 65-68; consult engr, Kerr McGee Co, 68-69, tech asst to pres, 69-72, chief process design engr, 72-77, dir mfg servs, 77-80, mgr process eng, 80-81; dir tech serv, IMC Fertilizer, Inc, 81-91. *Mem:* Nat Soc Prof Engrs; Sigma Xi; Am Inst Chem Engrs. *Res:* High temperature kinetics and thermodynamics; phase chemistry; process design; plant optimization; winning of metals by chlorine technology; industrial cogeneration of electrical power; automation & computerization of process control systems. *Mailing Add:* 4852 Leisurewood Lane Lakeland FL 33811-1592. *Fax:* 941-644-6859; *E-Mail:* dhirsch713@aol.com

HIRSCH, HELMUT V B, NEUROBIOLOGY. *Current Pos:* asst prof, 72-77, ASSOC PROF BIOL, STATE UNIV NY ALBANY, 77- *Personal Data:* b Chicago, Ill, Sept 22, 43; div; c 1. *Educ:* Univ Chicago, BA, 65; Stanford Univ, PhD(psychol), 70. *Prof Exp:* Fel, Johns Hopkins Univ, 70-72. *Concurrent Pos:* Alfred P Sloan Found fel, 75; adj assoc prof psychol, State Univ NY, Albany, 77- *Mem:* AAAS; Soc Neurosci; Sigma Xi; Asn Res Vision & Ophthalmol; Sigma Xi. *Res:* Role of early visual experience in the development of the mammalian visual system; neuronal mechanisms underlying the perception of form and pattern. *Mailing Add:* Dept Biol State Univ NY 1400 Washington Ave Albany NY 12222

HIRSCH, HENRY RICHARD, GERONTOLOGY. *Current Pos:* asst prof, 63-67, assoc prof, 67-76, PROF PHYSIOL & BIOPHYS, UNIV KY, 76- *Personal Data:* b New York, NY, Mar 27, 33; m 54, Genevieve Tenen; c Steven & Samuel. *Educ:* Mass Inst Technol, SB, 54, PhD(physics), 60. *Prof Exp:* Elec engr, Bell Tel Labs, 54-57; physicist, NIH, 61-63. *Concurrent Pos:* Reviewer, Zentralblatt fur Mathematik, 67-; coordr nat corresp, Fed Am Soc Exp Biol, 71-79; guest assoc biophysicist, Brookhaven Nat Lab, 71; mem pub affairs comt, Fedn Am Soc Exp Biol, 79-85, pub affairs adv comt, Am Physiol Soc, 83-, pub affairs exec comt, 91-92. *Mem:* Am Physiol Soc; Am Phys Soc; Biophys Soc; fel Geront Soc; sr mem Inst Elec & Electronics Engrs; AAAS. *Res:* Theoretical biology; physiology; aging. *Mailing Add:* Dept Physiol Univ Ky Col Med Lexington KY 40536-0084. *Fax:* 606-323-1070; *E-Mail:* hrhirsch@pop.uky.edu

HIRSCH, HORST EBERHARD, EXTRACTIVE METALLURGY, SEMICONDUCTORS. *Current Pos:* pres, 89-91, M-SM, JOHNSON MATTHEY ELECTRONICS, 92- *Personal Data:* b Woelsendorf, W Germany, July 26, 33; Can citizen; m 61; c 3. *Educ:* Univ Karlsruhe, W Germany, dipl chem, 58, Dr rer nat(chem tech), 60. *Prof Exp:* Res engr extractive metall, Cominco Electronic Mats, Inc, 62-64, group leader mineral process, 65-68, develop supvr process develop, 69-70, supt elec mat, 71-76, asst mgr, 76-79, mgr tech res, 79-81, gen mgr, Elec Mat Div, 82-84, pres, Elec Mat Div, 84-89. *Concurrent Pos:* Nat Res Coun Can fel, 61-62. *Mem:* Chem Inst Can; Am Inst Mining & Metall Engrs; Am Soc Metals; German Soc Mining Metals Eng. *Res:* Extractive metallurgy process development; new compound semiconductors; ultrapurification of metals-less common and precious metals. *Mailing Add:* 1005 E 54th Ave Spokane WA 99223

HIRSCH, IRA J, OTOLARYNGOLOGY. *Current Pos:* RES PROD OTOGLARYNGOL, WASHINGTON UNIV, ST LOUIS. *Educ:* Harvard Univ, PhD, 48. *Honors & Awards:* Gold Medal, Acoust Soc Am, 92. *Res:* Otolaryngology. *Mailing Add:* Cent Inst Deaf 818 S Euclid Ave St Louis MO 63110

HIRSCH, JACOB IRWIN, CARDIOVASCULAR DISEASE, BIOMEDICAL ENGINEERING. *Current Pos:* From instr to asst prof, 59-71, ASSOC PROF MED, SCH MED, NY UNIV, 71- *Personal Data:* b New York, NY, Aug 27, 26; m 50, Gloria L Mallin; c Robert M, Russell L & Laurel A. *Educ:* Brooklyn Col, AB, 48; NY Univ, MD, 52. *Concurrent Pos:* Consult, Biomed Eng Training Comt, Nat Inst Gen Med Sci, 62- *Mem:* AAAS; AMA; Am Heart Asn; fel NY Acad Sci; Inst Elec & Electronics Engrs; fel NY Acad Med; Sigma Xi; fel Am Col Cardiol; fel Am Col Physicians. *Res:* Volume conductor characteristics of human torso; application of computers to monitoring of patient electrocardiograms on line; biomedical engineering education; experimental myocardial infarction. *Mailing Add:* 1 Greenacre Ct Great Neck NY 11021

HIRSCH, JAY G, CHILD PSYCHIATRY. *Current Pos:* assoc prof, 71-74, PROF PSYCHIAT, ABRAHAM LINCOLN SCH MED, UNIV ILL COL MED, 74- *Personal Data:* b Cleveland, Ohio, Aug 6, 30; m 62; c 4. *Educ:* Univ Cincinnati, BS, 50, MD, 54; Am Bd Psychiat & Neurol, dipl, psychiat, 63 & child psychiat, 64. *Prof Exp:* Intern, Philadelphia Gen Hosp, Pa, 54-55; res psychiat, Univ Ill, 57-60; fel child psychiat, Inst Juv Res, 60-62, res child psychiatrist, 62-66, chief div prev psychiat, 66-71. *Concurrent Pos:* Dir prof educ, Inst Juv Res, Chicago, 73-77. *Mem:* Fel Am Acad Child Psychiat; fel Am Psychiat Asn; fel Am Orthopsychiat Asn; Soc Res Child Develop. *Mailing Add:* 912 S Wood St Chicago IL 60612

HIRSCH, JERRY, PSYCHOLOGY GENETICS, RACISM. *Current Pos:* from assoc prof to prof psychol, Univ Ill, 60-93, prof zool, 67-76, prof ecol, ethology & evolution, 76-93, EMER PROF PSYCHOL, UNIV ILL, URBANA-CHAMPAIGN, 93-, EMER PROF ECOL, ETHOLOGY & EVOLUTION, 93- *Personal Data:* b New York, NY, Sept 20, 22; m 50, Marjorie Barrie; c Wesley M. *Educ:* Univ Calif, BA, 52, PhD(psychol), 55. *Hon Degrees:* Dr, Univ Rene Descartes, Sorbonne, Paris, France, 87. *Honors & Awards:* Auxillary Res Award, Soc Sci Res Coun, 62; Robert Choate Tryon Mem lectr, Univ Calif, Berkeley, 87. *Prof Exp:* Asst prof psychol, Columbia Univ, 56-60. *Concurrent Pos:* NSF fel, 55-57; NIMH fel, Ctr Advan Study Behav Sci, 60-61; dir, NIMH pre- & postdoctoral Biopsych Res training prog, 66-78; vis res scholar, Zool Dept, Univ Edinburgh, 68; ed, Animal Behav, 68-72, J Comp Psychol, 83-88; mem, US Nat Comt, Int Union Biol Sci, 75-81, Int Ethological Conf Comt, 75-83; co-dir, NIMH pre- & postdoctoral training prog for res on Instnl Racism, Univ Ill, 77-86. *Mem:* AAAS; Animal Behav Soc (pres, 75); Am Psychol Asn; Sigma Xi. *Res:* Heredity-environment analysis of behavior, measuring individual differences in tropisms, excitatory states, conditioning, etc; behavior-genetic component analyses of species; methodological, theoretical and scholarly analyses of institutional and scientific racism. *Mailing Add:* Psychol Dept Univ Ill 603 E Daniel Champaign IL 61820. *Fax:* 217-244-5876; *E-Mail:* jhirsch@s.psych.uiuc.edu

HIRSCH, JERRY ALLAN, ORGANIC CHEMISTRY. *Current Pos:* from asst prof to assoc prof, 67-75, dean, Col Arts & Sci, 86-96, PROF CHEM, SETON HALL UNIV, 75- *Personal Data:* b Louisville, Ky, June 6, 41; m 69; c 3. *Educ:* Vanderbilt Univ, AB, 62; Stanford Univ, PhD(org chem), 66. *Prof Exp:* Res assoc chem, Wayne State Univ, 66-67. *Concurrent Pos:* Vis prof, State Univ Leiden, Neth, 74-75 & Weizmann Inst, Israel, 81-82. *Mem:* Am Chem Soc. *Res:* Stereochemistry and conformational analysis; ionene polymers; nonconjugated chromophores; heterocyclic systems related to trans-decalin; medium-ring carbocyclic systems. *Mailing Add:* Dept Chem Seton Hall Univ South Orange NJ 07079. *Fax:* 973-761-9772; *E-Mail:* hirschje@lanmail.shu.edu

HIRSCH, JOHN MICHELE, EXPERIMENTAL PHYSICS, PETROLEUM PHYSICS. *Current Pos:* Physicist, 75-77, RES PHYSICIST, SHELL DEVELOP CO, 77- *Personal Data:* b Cleveland, Ohio, Feb 1, 47; m 69. *Educ:* Mass Inst Technol, SB, 69; Harvard Univ, MA, 72, PhD(physics), 74. *Mem:* Am Inst Physics; Am Asn Physics Teachers; Soc Petrol Engrs. *Res:* Application of physical techniques to the location of petroleum in the subsurface. *Mailing Add:* 1502 Cedarbrook Dr Houston TX 77055

HIRSCH, JORGE E, PHYSICS. *Current Pos:* from asst prof to assoc prof, 83-87, PROF PHYSICS, UNIV CALIF, SAN DIEGO, 87- *Personal Data:* b Buenos Aires, Arg, Aug 5, 51; c 3. *Educ:* Univ Chicago, MSc, 77, PhD(physics), 80. *Prof Exp:* Res assoc, Univ Calif, Santa Barbara, Inst Theoret Physics, 80-82. *Concurrent Pos:* Sloan fel, Sloan Found, 84. *Mem:* Fel Am Phys Soc. *Res:* Superconductivity; magnetism; theory; mechanisms. *Mailing Add:* Dept Physics 0319 Univ Calif San Diego La Jolla CA 92093

HIRSCH, JUDITH ANN, CARDIOPULMONARY PHYSIOLOGY, PEDIATRIC PULMONARY MEDICINE. *Current Pos:* ASST RES PROF PEDIAT PULMONARY MED, STATE UNIV NY, BUFFALO, 79- *Educ:* State Univ NY, Buffalo, PhD(physiol), 79. *Mailing Add:* Dept Physiol State Univ NY 120 Sherman Hall Buffalo NY 14214

HIRSCH, JULES, MEDICINE. *Current Pos:* asst prof biochem & assoc physician, 54-60, assoc prof & physician, 60-67, PROF & SR PHYSICIAN, ROCKEFELLER UNIV, 67- *Personal Data:* b New York, NY, Apr 6, 27. *Educ:* Rutgers Univ, 43-45; Univ Tex, MD, 48. *Hon Degrees:* DSC, State Univ NY. *Honors & Awards:* Robert R Herman Award, Am Soc Clin Nutrit, McCollum Award; Jos B Goldberger Award, AMA; Jonathan E Rhoads Award, Am Soc Parenteral & Enteral Nutrit. *Prof Exp:* Intern path & med, Duke Hosp, NC, 48-50; from asst resident to resident, State Univ NY Col Med, Syracuse, 50-52. *Concurrent Pos:* Physician-in-chief, Rockefeller Univ Hosp, 92-96; adj prof med, Columbia Univ. *Mem:* Inst Med-Nat Acad Sci; Am Soc Clin Invest; Harvey Soc; Asn Am Physicians; Am Fedn Clin Res; AAAS; Am Soc Clin Nutrit; Am Inst Nutrit. *Res:* Obesity; human behavior; internal medicine; biochemistry and physiology of lipids; lipid metabolism and nutrition. *Mailing Add:* Lab Human Behav & Med Rockefeller Univ New York NY 10021

HIRSCH, LAWRENCE LEONARD, FAMILY MEDICINE, MEDICAL SOCIOECONOMICS. *Current Pos:* PROF FAMILY MED & CHMN DEPT, CHICAGO MED SCH, 75- *Personal Data:* b Chicago, Ill, Aug 20, 22. *Educ:* Univ Ill, BS, 43, MD, 50. *Prof Exp:* Pvt pract, 51-70; dir ambulatory care, Ill Masonic Med Ctr, 70-75, dir family pract residency, 71-75. *Concurrent Pos:* Vis fac, Great Lakes Naval Hosp, 75-; trustee, Cook Co Grad Med Sch, 84- *Mem:* Fel AAAS; fel Am Acad Family Physicians; fel Am Geriat Soc; AMA; Am Geront Soc; Soc Teachers Family Med. *Res:* Family physicians. *Mailing Add:* Dept Family Med Univ Health Sci Chicago Med Sch 3333 Green Bay Rd North Chicago IL 60064-3037

HIRSCH, MARTIN STANLEY, IMMUNOLOGY, VIROLOGY. *Current Pos:* from asst prof to assoc prof, 71-88, PROF, DEPT MED, HARVARD MED SCH, 88- *Personal Data:* b Cortland, NY, Apr 16, 39; m 64, Corinne Becker; c Tera & Michael. *Educ:* Hamilton Col, AB, 60; Johns Hopkins Univ, MD, 64; Am Bd Internal Med, dipl, 72; Harvard Univ, MA, 90. *Prof Exp:* Intern med, Univ Chicago Clins & Hosps, 64-65, resident, Univ Chicago Clins, 65-66; med officer virol, Nat Commun Dis Ctr, 66-68. *Concurrent Pos:* Fel immunol, Nat Inst Med Res, London, 68-69; fel infectious dis, Mass Gen Hosp, 69-71. *Mem:* Infectious Dis Soc Am; Am Asn Immunol; Am Soc Clin Investr; NIH AIDS Adv Comt; Am Found AIDS Res Sci Adv Comt; Asn Am Physicians. *Res:* Host response, both cellular and humoral, to viral infections; therapy of viral infections; AIDS. *Mailing Add:* Mass Gen Hosp Dept Med Harvard Med Sch Boston MA 02114. *Fax:* 617-726-7416

HIRSCH, MORRIS WILLIAM, TOPOLOGY OF MANIFOLDS, DYNAMICAL SYSTEMS. *Current Pos:* asst prof, Univ Calif, Berkeley, 60-65, vchmn dept, 66-67, chmn dept, 81-83, prof, 65-93, EMER PROF MATH, UNIV CALIF, BERKELEY, 93- *Personal Data:* b Chicago, Ill, June 28, 33; m 57, Charity Burns; c Jennifer & Michael. *Educ:* Univ Chicago, PhD(math), 58. *Prof Exp:* NSF fel math, Inst Adv Study, 58-60 & 83-84. *Concurrent Pos:* Vis prof, Cambridge Univ, 63-64, Geneva Univ, 68-69 & Harvard Univ, 75-76; Sloan fel, 64-66; fel, Miller Inst Basic Res, in Sci, 71-72; Zyskind prof, Brandeis Univ, 76-77. *Mem:* Am Math Soc; Soc Indust & Appl Math; Int Neural Network Soc; Soc Indust & Appl Math. *Res:* Neural computation; dynamical systems; mathematical models in applied sciences; history and philosophy of mathematics. *Mailing Add:* Dept Math Univ Calif Berkeley CA 94720-3840

HIRSCH, PETER M, MATHEMATICS, COMPUTER SCIENCE MANAGEMENT. *Current Pos:* MEM STAFF, ELEC POWER RES INST, 91- *Personal Data:* b Cortland, NY, Apr 12, 39; m 61; c 3. *Educ:* Univ Wis, BS, 61, MS, 63, PhD(math), 66. *Prof Exp:* Teaching asst math, Univ Wis, 61-65; instr, Pa State Univ, 65-66; mem staff, IBM Corp, 66-91. *Res:* Numerical analysis; holography; electric power simulation; object oriental programming. *Mailing Add:* Power Syst Eng Elec Power Res Inst 3412 Hillview Ave Palo Alto CA 94303

HIRSCH, PHILIP FRANCIS, PHARMACOLOGY. *Current Pos:* assoc prof, Univ NC, Chapel Hill, 66-70, prof pharmacol, 70-92, dir, Dent Res Ctr, 75-83, prof, Dept Dent Ecol, 88-92, EMER PROF PHARMACOL, SCH MED, UNIV NC, CHAPEL HILL, 92-, EMER PROF, DEPT DENT ECOL, SCH DENT, 92- *Personal Data:* b Stockton, Calif, June 24, 25; m 56, Eugenia Isaeff; c Steven, Lisa, Kenny & Nancy. *Educ:* Univ Calif, Berkeley, BS, 50, PhD(physiol), 54. *Prof Exp:* Asst physiol, Univ Calif, Berkeley, 53-54, lectr & jr res physiol, 54-55; instr pharmacol, Sch Dent Med, Harvard Univ, 55-57, assoc, 57-64, asst prof, 64; physiologist, Lawrence Radiation Lab, Univ Calif, Livermore, 64-66. *Concurrent Pos:* Res fel biochem, Brandeis Univ, 58-59. *Mem:* AAAS; Endocrine Soc; Am Soc Pharmacol & Exp Therapeut; Am Soc Bone & Mineral Res. *Res:* Carbohydrate and lipid metabolism of mammary gland and liver; physiological control of serum calcium; pharmacological action of parathyroid hormone, calcitonin and glucocorticoids. *Mailing Add:* Dent Res Ctr Univ NC Chapel Hill NC 27599-7455. *Fax:* 919-966-3683; *E-Mail:* pfh@med.unc.edu

HIRSCH, ROBERT GEORGE, ATOMIC & MOLECULAR PHYSICS. *Current Pos:* Res physicist appl physics, E I Du Pont de Nemours Co, Inc, 74-76, res supvr, 76-78, div prog coordr, Eng Res & Develop, 78-79, sr res supvr, Mat Res, 79-81, prin consult, Corp Res & Develop Planning, 81-84, mkt mgr adv electronics systs, 84-85, dir & site mgr, Electronics Tech Lab, 85-88, dir IBM account, 89-90, tech dir polyester film enterprise, 91-93, TECH DIR DUPONT FILM, E I DU PONT DE NEMOURS CO, INC, 91- *Personal Data:* b Baltimore, Md, Nov 25, 46; m 70; c 2. *Educ:* Univ Scranton, Pa, BS, 69; Harvard Univ, MA, 70; Univ Va, PhD(physics), 74. *Concurrent Pos:* Woodrow Wilson Found fel, 69-74; NSF trainee, Harvard Univ, 69-70; consult, Teledyne Avionics, 73-74; mem, Indust Adv Bd, NC A&T Univ, 85-88; mem, Duke Univ Bd Visitors Eng, 87-91; mem, NC State Univ Physics & Math Sci Found, 87-91. *Mem:* Am Phys Soc; Am Inst Physics; Sigma Xi; Am Inst Chem Engrs. *Res:* Atomic and molecular physics; ion-molecule reactions; atmospheric physics; mass spectroscopy; plasma chromatography; trace substance analysis; research and development strategy; microelectronic packaging; tech ceramics; high-density ceramic packaging; polyester film technology; research and development management. *Mailing Add:* 115 Chalfonte Lane Kennett Square PA 19348

HIRSCH, ROBERT L, VIRAL IMMUNOLOGY, NEUROIMMUNOLOGY. *Current Pos:* group mgr clin develop, Immunobiol Res Inst, 86-87, asst dir clin invest, 88-89, dir clin invest, 90-93, SR DIR CLIN DEVELOP, IMMUNOBIOL RES INST, 94- *Personal Data:* b Boston, Mass. *Educ:* Brandeis Univ, AB, 73; Georgetown Univ, PhD(immunobiol), 77. *Prof Exp:* Fel neurovirol, Sch Med, Johns Hopkins Univ, 77-79, asst prof, 79-82; asst prof neurol & microbiol, Sch Med, Univ Md, 82-85; mgr med info serv, Ortho Pharmaceut Corp, 85-86. *Concurrent Pos:* Instr neurol, Sch Med, Johns Hopkins Univ, 79; res assoc, Howard Hughes Med Inst, 79-82. *Mem:* Am Asn Immunologists; Am Soc Microbiol; AAAS; Sigma Xi. *Res:* Autoimmunity; AIDS; peptides-immunomodulators in HIV infection; role of complement in recovery from acute viral infections; immunobiology of multiple sclerosis; therapeutic trials in multiple sclerosis; monoclonal antibodies in organ transplantation in man. *Mailing Add:* Immunobiol Res Inst Rt 22 E PO Box 999 Annandale NJ 08801-0999

HIRSCH, ROBERT LOUIS, nuclear engineering & physics, for more information see previous edition

HIRSCH, ROBERT M, HYDROLOGY, WATER RESOURCES. *Current Pos:* Hydrologist, Water Resources Div, 80-87, staff asst to asst secy water & sci, Dept Interior, 87-88, asst chief hydrologist res & external coord, 88-93, actg dir, 93-94, CHIEF, HYDROLOGIST, US GEOL SURV, 94- *Personal Data:* b Highland, Park, Ill, June 6, 49; m, Franna Kuddell; c Benjamin & Jacob. *Educ:* Earlham Col, BA, 71; Univ Wash, MS, 74; Johns Hopkins Univ, PhD(geog & environ eng), 76. *Honors & Awards:* Water Mgt Achievement Award, Interstate Coun Water Policy, 96. *Concurrent Pos:* US Geol Surv spokesman, Nat Water-Qual Assessment Prog, 85-88. *Mem:* fel AAAS; Am Water Resources Asn. *Res:* Development and application of new methods of analysis of hydrologist systems and the presentation of those analyses in a way that is useful to public decision making. *Mailing Add:* US Dept Interior Geol Surv Reston VA 20192

HIRSCH, ROLAND FELIX, ANALYTICAL CHEMISTRY. *Current Pos:* prog mgr, US Dept Energy, 84-88 & 91-95, ACTG DIV DIR, US DEPT ENERGY, 95- *Personal Data:* b Rhinebeck, NY, Nov 30, 39; m 71; c 3. *Educ:* Oberlin Col, BA, 61; Univ Mich, MS, 63, PhD(analytical chem), 65. *Prof Exp:* From instr to assoc prof, 65-83, from asst chmn to chmn dept, 71-75, assoc dean, Arts & Sci, 81-86, prof chem, Seton Hall Univ, 83-88; prog mgr, NIH, 88-91. *Concurrent Pos:* Vis scientist, Inorg Chem Labs, Oxford Univ, 75-76; adv bd, Advan Chem, 85-88; chair, Comt Int Activ, Am Chem Soc, 90-92. *Mem:* Am Chem Soc; Am Soc Testing & Mat. *Res:* Analytical chemistry; structural molecular biology. *Mailing Add:* US Dept Energy ER-73 Germantown MD 20874-1290. *Fax:* 301-903-0567; *E-Mail:* roland.hirsch@oer.doe.gov

HIRSCH, SAMUEL ROGER, ALLERGY, IMMUNOLOGY. *Current Pos:* assoc clin prof, 73-87, CLIN PROF MED, MED COL WIS, 87-, ASSOC CLIN PROF MED, UNIV WIS, 76- *Personal Data:* b Chicago, Ill, Dec 19, 30; m 90, Sharon Brochhansen; c Rachel, Daniel, Michael & Brian. *Educ:* Univ Wis, BA, 53, MD, 56. *Prof Exp:* Res assoc, Vet Admin Ctr, Milwaukee, 64-73, chief, Allergy & Pulmonary Res Lab, 75-82. *Concurrent Pos:* Pvt pract, Allergy Assocs, Ltd, 63-80; attending physician, Milwaukee County Med Complex, 63-78; consult staff mem, Milwaukee Children's Hosp, 63-, Samaritan Hosp, Milwaukee, 65- & St Michael's Hosp, 65-80; assoc attending physician, Mt Sinai Hosp, 67-; consult, Panel on Diphenhydramine, FDA, 76-77. *Mem:* Fel Am Acad Allergy; fel Am Col Physicians; fel Am Col Allergy; Am Col Chest Physicians. *Res:* Pulmonary disease. *Mailing Add:* Allergic Dis SC 5020 W Oklahoma Ave Milwaukee WI 53219-4543. *Fax:* 414-546-3142

HIRSCH, SOLOMON, MEDICINE, PSYCHIATRY. *Current Pos:* assoc prof, 58-64, PROF PSYCHIAT, DALHOUSIE UNIV, 64-, DEP HEAD DEPT, 81- *Personal Data:* b Sydney, NS, Jan 24, 26; m 54; c 3. *Educ:* Dalhousie Univ, BSc, 45, MD, 49; Royal Col Physicians & Surgeons Can, cert, 53. *Prof Exp:* Resident psychiat, Dalhousie Univ, 49-50, asst prof, 53-54; asst resident, Johns Hopkins Univ, 50-52; Head dept psychiat, Victoria Gen Hosp, 75-85. *Concurrent Pos:* Asst psychiatrist, Victoria Gen Hosp, Can, 43-54, assoc psychiatrist, 59-; psychiatrist, NS Hosp, 53-54; consult psychiatrist, Grace Maternity Hosp, 54- *Mem:* Am Psychiat Asn; fel Am Col Psychiat; Can Psychiat Asn. *Res:* suicidology. *Mailing Add:* Dept Psychiat Victoria Gen Hosp 1278 Tower Rd Halifax NS B3H 2Y9 Can

HIRSCH, STEPHEN SIMEON, ORGANIC CHEMISTRY, POLYMER CHEMISTRY. *Current Pos:* DIR NEW BUS DEVELOP & PLANNING, GAF CHEM, 85- *Personal Data:* b New York, NY, Mar 25, 37; m 59; c 2. *Educ:* Polytech Inst Brooklyn, BS, 58; Univ Md, PhD(chem), 62. *Prof Exp:* Sr res chemist, Goodyear Tire & Rubber Co, Ohio, 62-63; res chemist, Monsanto Co, 64-66, group leader, 67-68; res group leader, Allied Chem Corp, 68-69; assoc dir, Res Dept, Ciba-Geigy Corp, 69-71, prod mgr, Resins Dept, 71-72; mgr bus develop plastics, 72-75; dir res & develop, Hooker Chem & Plastics Corp, 75-78; vpres technol & bus develop, Plastics & Chem Spec Group, Hooker Chem Co, 78-81; dir chem res, Armand Hammer Tech Ctr, 81-84, dir, Oper Anal, Occidental Petrol Corp, 84-85. *Mem:* Am Chem Soc; Am Mgt Asn; Com Develop Asn. *Res:* Plastics, fiber, composites; advanced materials; high temperature chemistry; flammability; organics; metal plating chemicals; new business development. *Mailing Add:* 202 Steeplechase Dr North Wales PA 19454-4231

HIRSCH, TEDDY JAMES, CIVIL ENGINEERING, ENGINEERING MECHANICS. *Current Pos:* res engr, 67-92, instr & res asst civil eng prof, 67-92, EMER PROF CIVIL ENG, TEX A&M UNIV, 92- *Personal Data:* b Beaumont, Tex, Aug 11, 29; m 55; c 4. *Educ:* Tex A&M Univ, BS, 52, MEng, 53, PhD(civil eng), 61. *Honors & Awards:* Paul Gray Hoffman Award, Automobile Safety Found, 68. *Prof Exp:* Struct engr, Stone & Pitts Architects & Engrs, 55-56. *Concurrent Pos:* Assoc head, Struct Eng Div, Tex Transp Inst, 64-65, head, 65-83; mem grad fac, Tex A&M Univ, 63-, head, Struct Eng Div, 66-, assoc head dept, 80-83, interim head, Dept Civil Eng, 83-85; consult engr. *Res:* Structural engineering and materials; motor vehicle impact; dynamic behavior of piling; dynamic loads; heavy truck and railroad barriers; foundations of structures; highway safety appurtenances; human tolerance to impact free fall life boats. *Mailing Add:* Dept Civil Eng & Tex Transp Inst Tex A&M Univ College Station TX 77843-3136

HIRSCH, WARREN MAURICE, MATHEMATICS. *Current Pos:* Asst, NY Univ, 47-52, instr, 48-51, lectr, grad dept, 52, vis lectr, 52-53, from asst prof to assoc prof, 53-60, PROF MATH, COURANT INST MATH SCI, NY UNIV, 57- *Personal Data:* b New York, NY, Aug 3, 23; m 60; c 2. *Educ:* NY Univ, AB, 47, MS, 48, PhD(math), 52. *Concurrent Pos:* Lectr, Columbia Univ, 52-53; consult Rand Corp, 53- *Mem:* AAAS; Am Math Soc; Math Asn Am; Am Statist Asn; Sigma Xi. *Res:* Theory of probability; mathematical statistics. *Mailing Add:* 51 Kettle Creek Rd Weston CT 06883-2208

HIRSCHBERG, ALBERT I, ORGANIC CHEMISTRY. *Current Pos:* from asst prof to assoc prof, 62-71, dept chmn, 79-85, PROF CHEM, LONG ISLAND UNIV, 71- *Personal Data:* b Brooklyn, NY, May 9, 34; m 60; c 2. *Educ:* Brooklyn Col, BS, 54, Polytech Inst New York, MS, 56, PhD(chem), 60. *Prof Exp:* NIH fel, 60-61. *Concurrent Pos:* Fac res fel, Seiler Res Lab, US Air Force Acad, 87. *Mem:* Am Chem Soc; Royal Soc Chem. *Res:* Heterocyclic synthesis; chemotherapy; reaction mechanisms; chemical education. *Mailing Add:* 3733 E Oceanside Rd Oceanside NY 11572-5939

HIRSCHBERG, CARLOS BENJAMIN, CELL BIOLOGY, GENETICS. *Current Pos:* PROF BIOCHEM & MOLECULAR BIOL, UNIV MASS MED CTR, 87- *Personal Data:* b Santiago, Chile, Feb 1, 43; m 73. *Educ:* Rutgers Univ, MS, 66; Univ Ill, Urbana, PhD(chem), 70. *Prof Exp:* Res fel biol chem, Harvard Univ, 70-72; res assoc biol, Mass Inst Technol, 72-74; from asst prof to assoc prof, Sch Med, St Louis Univ, 74-82, prof biochem, 82-87. *Concurrent Pos:* Jane Coffin Childs fel, Harvard Med Sch, 70-72 & Mass Inst Technol, 72-73; mem, Cell Biol Study Sect, NIH, 78-82, MERIT grant awardee, 91-; mem adv comt biochem & carcinogenesis, Am Cancer Soc, 84-87. *Mem:* AAAS; Am Soc Cell Biol; Am Soc Biochem & Molecular Biol. *Res:* Metabolism and function of glycoproteins and lipids in membranes and cell surfaces; biosynthesis of glycosaminolycans. *Mailing Add:* Dept Biochem & Molecular Biol Univ Mass Med Ctr 55 Lake Ave N Worcester MA 01655-0001. *E-Mail:* carlos.hirschberg@ummed.edu

HIRSCHBERG, ERICH, biochemistry, for more information see previous edition

HIRSCHBERG, JOSEPH GUSTAV, PHYSICS. *Current Pos:* chmn, Dept Physics, Univ Miami, 65-72, dir, Optical Physics Lab, 67-77, prof, 65-86, EMER PROF PHYSICS, UNIV MIAMI, 86- *Personal Data:* b Chicago, Ill, Apr 13, 21; m 47; c 4. *Educ:* Dartmouth Col, AB, 43; Univ Wis, PhD(physics), 52. *Prof Exp:* Fulbright scholar physics, Ecole Normale Superieure, Paris, 52-53; res assoc, Univ Wis, 53-58; head, Optical Sect, Plasma Physics Lab, Princeton Univ, 58-65, res physicist, 62-65. *Concurrent Pos:* Pres, Fed Eng Co, 54-59; exchange prof, Univ Paris, 64; res assoc, French Asn Atomic Energy Comn-Europ Atomic Energy Comn, Paris, 64; consult, Plasma Physics Lab, Princeton Univ, 65-68 & Langley Res Ctr, NASA, 66-67; coun, Oak Ridge Assoc Univs, 70-72; fel, Papanicolaou Cancer Res Inst, Miami; vis astron, Sacramento Peak Observ, 77; vis scientist, Princeton Univ, 81-; exchange researcher, Mus Natural Hist, Paris, France, 83, 87 & 88. *Mem:* Fel Am Phys Soc; fel Am Optical Soc; Sigma Xi; Europ Acad Sci, Arts & Humanities. *Res:* Meteorology; atomic spectra; physical optics; Fabry-Perot interferometer; plasma spectroscopy; holographic interferometry; solar physics; infrared imaging; fluoromicroscopy of living cells; optical oceanography. *Mailing Add:* Dept Physics Univ Miami Coral Gables FL 33124

HIRSCHBERG, RONA L, GENE REGULATION, NITROGEN FIXATION. *Current Pos:* asst prof biol, 75-81, ASSOC PROF BASIC LIFE SCI, UNIV MO-KANSAS CITY, 81-, ASSOC DEAN BASIC LIFE SCI, 89- *Personal Data:* b Gary, Ind, Mar 26, 43. *Educ:* Purdue Univ, BS, 65; Univ Wis-Madison, MS, 68, PhD(bacteriol), 70. *Prof Exp:* Fel molecular biol & biochem, Albert Einstein Col Med, 69-73; instr biol, Hunter Col, City Univ NY, 73-75. *Concurrent Pos:* Vis scientist, Univ Wis-Madison, 81. *Mem:* Am Soc Microbiol; Soc Gen Microbiol; AAAS; Am Soc Biochem & Molecular Biol. *Res:* Regulation of gene expression in procaryotes; molecular genetics of microbial pathogens. *Mailing Add:* Sch Basic Life Sci Univ Mo Kansas City MO 64110. *Fax:* 816-235-5158

HIRSCHFELD, RONALD COLMAN, CIVIL ENGINEERING. *Current Pos:* PRIN, GEOTECH ENGRS, INC, 70- *Personal Data:* b Amsterdam, NY, Nov 23, 30; m 64; c 2. *Educ:* Union Col, NY, BSCE, 50; Harvard Univ, SM, 57, PhD, 58. *Prof Exp:* From instr to asst prof soil mech, Harvard Univ, 58-64; assoc prof, Mass Inst Technol, 64-72. *Concurrent Pos:* Mem, US Comt Large Dams; nat dir, Asn Eng Geol, 72-73, Am Soc Civil Engrs, 72-73 & Am Consult Engrs Coun, 83-84. *Mem:* Am Soc Civil Engrs; Geol Soc Am; Int Soc Soil Mech & Found Eng; Asn Eng Geol. *Res:* Engineering geology; soil and rock mechanics. *Mailing Add:* 47 Emerson Rd Winchester MA 01890-3407

HIRSCHFELD, SUE ELLEN, GEOLOGY, PALEONTOLOGY. *Current Pos:* instr, Calif State Univ, Hayward, 71-75, assoc prof earth sci, 75-80, dept chair, 88-94, PROF GEOL SCI, CALIF STATE UNIV, HAYWARD, 80- *Personal Data:* b Ossining, NY, Jan 12, 41; div. *Educ:* Univ Fla, BS, 63, MS, 65; Univ Calif, Berkeley, PhD(paleont), 71. *Prof Exp:* Instr earth sci, St Petersburg Jr Col, 65-66. *Concurrent Pos:* Consult. *Mem:* AAAS; hon mem, Golden Key Soc; Asn Women Geoscientists (nat secy, 79-80); Geol Soc Am; Soc Econ Paleontologists & Mineralogists. *Res:* Earthquake hazards of the San Francisco Bay area. *Mailing Add:* Dept Geol Sci Calif State Univ Hayward CA 94542. *E-Mail:* shirschf@csuhayward.edu

HIRSCHFELDER, JOHN JOSEPH, MATHEMATICS. *Current Pos:* SR PRIN ENGR, HUGHES AIRCRAFT, 75- *Personal Data:* b Ft Wayne, Ind, Sept 12, 43; m 66; c 3. *Educ:* Univ Notre Dame, BS, 65, MS, 66, PhD(math), 68. *Prof Exp:* Asst prof math, Univ Wash, 68-75. *Mem:* Asn Comput Mech; Am Math Soc. *Res:* Several complex variables; complex manifolds. *Mailing Add:* 12066 Lakeside Pl NE Seattle WA 98125

HIRSCHHORN, JOEL S(TEPHEN), SCIENCE POLICY, TECHNICAL MANAGEMENT. *Current Pos:* PRES, HIRSCHHORN & ASSOCS, INC, 90- *Personal Data:* b New York, NY, Sept 8, 39; m 61, Jacqueline Rams; c 2. *Educ:* Polytech Inst Brooklyn, BMetE, 61, MS, 62; Rensselaer Polytech Inst, PhD(mat eng), 65. *Honors & Awards:* Clean Water Found Award. *Prof Exp:* Res metallurgist, adv mat res & develop lab, Pratt & Whitney Aircraft Div, United Aircraft Corp, 62-63; from asst prof to prof metall eng, Univ Wis-Madison, 65-78; sr assoc, Off Technol Assessment, US Cong, 78-90. *Concurrent Pos:* Consult, Friction Prod Co, 67-68, dir res, 68-72; consult, Stellite Div, Cabot Corp, 70-71, Advan Prod Corp, 71-73 & Que Metal Powders, 75-76; ed Remediation J Environ Cleanup Costs, Technol & Techn, 97- *Mem:* Am Soc Testing & Mat; Nat Soc Prof Engrs; Air & Waste Mgt. *Res:* Indust waste reduction; environmental technology; hazardous waste; strategic planning; environmental regulations; technology assessment; science and technology policy; risk assessment; waste site remediation; environmental justice. *Mailing Add:* 3231 Coquelin Terr Chevy Chase MD 20815

HIRSCHHORN, KURT, HUMAN GENETICS, PEDIATRICS. *Current Pos:* prof pediat & chief, Div Med Genetics, Mt Sinai Sch Med, 66-76, Arthur J & Nellie Z Cohen prof pediat, 68-76, Herbert H Lehman prof & chmn, Dept Pediat, 76-95, PROF PEDIAT, HUMAN GENETICS MED, MT SINAI SCH MED, 95- *Personal Data:* b Vienna, Austria, May 18, 26; nat US; m 52; c 3. *Educ:* NY Univ, BA, 50, MD, 54, MS, 58. *Honors & Awards:* Allan Award, Am Soc Human Genetics, 95. *Prof Exp:* Intern internal med, Bellevue Hosp, NY, 54-55, asst resident, 55-56; from instr to assoc prof med, Sch Med, NY Univ, 55-66. *Concurrent Pos:* USPHS clin trainee metab dis, 56-57; from asst vis physician to assoc vis physician, Bellevue Hosp, 56-66; from asst attend physician to assoc attend physician, NY Univ Hosp, 56-66; Berquist & Pop Coun fels, Inst Med Genetics, Uppsala, 57-58; Am Heart Asn res fel, NY Univ, 58-60, estab investr, 60-65; career scientist, New York City Health Res Coun, 65-75; attend pediat, Mt Sinai Hosp, 66-; vis prof, Galton Lab, Dept Human Genetics, Univ Col, Univ London, 71-72; mem, Coun Arteriosclerosis, Am Heart Asn; vis prof, Harvard Med Sch, 86- *Mem:* Inst Med-Nat Acad Sci; Am Soc Human Genetics (dir, 64-65 & 68-71, pres, 69); Harvey Soc (vpres, 79-80, pres, 80-81); Am Asn Immunol; Asn Am Physicians; Am Pediat Soc (coun, 81-84); fel AAAS. *Res:* Immunogenetics; human biochemical, molecular and cytogenetics. *Mailing Add:* Mt Sinai Sch Med One Gustave L Levy Pl New York NY 10029-6574. *Fax:* 212-360-1809; *E-Mail:* khirschorn@smtplink.mssm.edu

HIRSCHHORN, ROCHELLE, IMMUNOBIOLOGY, HUMAN GENETICS. *Current Pos:* Intern, Bellevue IV Med Div, NY Univ, 58-59, assoc res scientist, 65-66, from instr to assoc prof, 66-79, PROF MED, DEPT MED, SCH MED, NY UNIV, 79- HEAD, DIV MED GENETICS, 84- *Personal Data:* b New York, NY, Mar 19, 32; m 52, Kurt; c Melanie D (Vetter), Lisa E (Goldberg) & Joel N. *Educ:* Barnard Col, Columbia Univ, BA, 53; NY Univ, MD, 57. *Honors & Awards:* Jeffrey Modell Found Lifetime Achievement Award, 90. *Concurrent Pos:* Fel, Arthritis Found, 66-69; sr investr, NY Heart Asn, 69-72; res career develop award, NIH, 72-77; hon fel, Dept Human Genetics & Biomet, Univ Col, Univ London, 71-72; mem, NIH Study Sect, Allergy & Immunol Clin Res Adv Comt, Nat Found March Dimes, 77-94; vis prof, Harvard Med Sch, 85-86; fel rev comt, Arthritis Found, 86-88; mem, Inst Allergy & Infectious Dis Bd Sci Counr, NIH, 87-91. *Mem:* Inst Med-Nat Acad Sci; Am Asn Immunologists; Am Soc Human Genetics; Am Asn Physicians; fel AAAS; Harvey Soc; fel Am Col Rheumatology; Soc Inherited Metab Dis; fel Am Col Med Genetics; Am Soc Clin Invest. *Res:* Control of differentiation and activation of immunocompetent cells; inherited disorders of man and genetic polymorphism. *Mailing Add:* Dept Med Sch Med NY Univ 550 First Ave New York NY 10016. *Fax:* 212-263-7151; *E-Mail:* hirscr01@mcrcr0.med.nyu.edu

HIRSCHI, MICHAEL CARL, SOIL & WATER CONSERVATION, WATER QUALITY. *Current Pos:* asst prof, 85-91, ASSOC PROF, AGR ENG DEPT, UNIV ILL, 91- *Personal Data:* b Minneapolis, Minn, Dec 29, 55; m 78, Debra Germundsen; c 2. *Educ:* Univ Minn, BAgE, 78, MSAgE, 80, PhD(agr eng), 85. *Prof Exp:* Res specialist, Agr Eng Dept, Univ Ky, 80-85. *Concurrent Pos:* Res assoc, US Army Construct Eng Res Lab, 89-; actg asst dir, Ill Coop Ext Serv, 91, interim assoc dir, 92, coordr, Water Qual Prog, 92- *Mem:* Am Soc Agr Engrs; Sigma Xi. *Res:* Mechanisms, prediction and control of surface and ground water contamination; soil erosion and sedimentation processes and their influences on surface water quality. *Mailing Add:* 332P AESB 1304 W Pennsylvania Ave Urbana IL 61801. *E-Mail:* mch@uiuc.edu

HIRSCHMAN, ALBERT, BIOCHEMISTRY, HISTOLOGY. *Current Pos:* instr histol, 48-54, from asst prof to assoc prof anat, 54-93, EMER ASSOC PROF, STATE UNIV NY DOWNSTATE MED CTR, 93- *Personal Data:* b New York, NY, Oct 20, 21; m 43, Mildred Gottschall; c Beverly, Sally & Robert. *Educ:* City Col New York, BS, 42; Polytech Univ Brooklyn, MS, 46, PhD(biochem), 52. *Prof Exp:* Chem technician, Jewish Hosp, Brooklyn, 42-43; asst chemist, 43-47. *Concurrent Pos:* Adj prof, Ctr Biomed Educ, Touro Col, Dix Hills, NY, 82-; vis prof, Rockefeller Univ, 60-61 & Hebrew Univ, Jerusalem, Israel, 80-81. *Mem:* Am Chem Soc; Am Asn Anat; Am Crystallog Asn; NY Acad Sci; AAAS; Sigma Xi. *Res:* Physical, chemical and histochemical studies of bone and the mechanism of calcification; x-ray diffraction of mineralized tissue; biochemical studies of enzymes and proteoglycans in bone and in calcifying and non-calcifying cartilages; cell biology. *Mailing Add:* Health Sci Ctr State Univ NY Box 5 Brooklyn NY 11203-2098

HIRSCHMAN, ISIDORE ISAAC, JR, mathematics; deceased, see previous edition for last biography

HIRSCHMAN, LYNETTE, NATURAL LANGUAGE PROCESSING, LOGIC PROGRAMMING. *Current Pos:* mgr, 82-86, TECH DIR, LOGIC-BAND SYSTS, PAOLI RES CTR, UNISYS DEFENSE SYSTS, 86- *Personal Data:* b Huntington, WVa, Nov 22, 45. *Educ:* Oberlin Col, BA, 66; Univ Calif, Santa Barbara, MA, 68; Univ Pa, PhD(linguistics), 72. *Prof Exp:* Res scientist, NY Univ, 75-82. *Concurrent Pos:* Adj asst prof, Dept Comput Sci, NY Univ, 80-81; adj prof, Dept Comput Sci, Univ Pa, 87- *Mem:* Am Asn Artificial Intelligence; Asn Comput Mach; Asn Logic Prog; Asn Comput Ling. *Res:* Natural language processing and applications of logic programming to natural language; parallel processing and biomedical information processing. *Mailing Add:* Mitre Corp 202 Burlington Rd 545 Technology Sq MS K 329 Bedford MA 01730

HIRSCHMAN, SHALOM ZARACH, INFECTIOUS DISEASE, MOLECULAR BIOLOGY. *Current Pos:* assoc prof, 69-71, dir, Div Infectious Dis, Med Ctr, 69-96, PROF MED, MT SINAI SCH MED, 71-, EMER DIR, DIV INFECTIOUS DIS, 97-, ATTEND PHYSICIAN, MT SINAI HOSP, 71-; PRES & CHIEF EXEC OFFICER, ADV VIRAL RES CORP, 96- *Personal Data:* b Troy, NY, Aug 5, 36; div; c 2. *Educ:* Yeshiva Univ, BA, 57; Albert Einstein Col Med, MD, 61; FRSTM. *Prof Exp:* Intern, Mass Gen Hosp, Harvard Med Sch, Boston, 61-62, asst resident, 62-63; NIH res assoc, Nat Inst Arthritis & Metab Dis, Md, 63-66; sr investr molecular virol, Nat Cancer Inst, Md, 67-69. *Concurrent Pos:* NIH spec fel, 64; fel, Columbia-Presby Med Ctr, NY, 66-67; vchmn, Microbiol Sect, NY Acad Sci, 73-, chmn, 75; mem, Merit Rev Bd, Vet Admin, 79-82 & Microbiol Rev Bd, Am Cancer Soc, 80-85. *Mem:* AAAS; fel Am Col Physicians; NY Acad Sci; Am Soc Clin Invest; Soc Exp Biol Med; Asn Am Physicians; Biophys Soc; Infectious Dis Soc Am; Am Soc Microbiol; Royal Soc Trop Hyg Med; Am Col Pharamacol; Liver Soc; Harvey Soc. *Res:* Molecular biology of bacteria and viruses; biology of hepatitis B virus; internal medicine; replication of human immunodeficiency virus. *Mailing Add:* 5240 Blackstone Ave Riverdale NY 10471. *Fax:* 718-601-8892

HIRSCHMANN, ERWIN, MICROWAVE PHYSICS. *Current Pos:* RETIRED. *Personal Data:* b Vienna, Austria, July 17, 24; m 63; c Eric & Paula. *Educ:* Vienna Tech Univ, dipl, 49. *Prof Exp:* Prod technician, Siemens & Halske Co, Inc, Austria, 42-45, prod engr, 50-52; mem staff, Sound-Frequency Lab, Hasler Co, Inc, Switz, 54-55; mem staff develop transistor field, Siemens & Halske, Ger, 56-58; researcher semiconductors, Diamond Ord Fuze Labs, 58-62; researcher laser commun & millimeter propagation, Goddard Space Flight Ctr, NASA, 62-80, command & control-commun & data handling subsysts tv infrared observ satellite weather satellites, 81-95. *Mem:* Inst Elec & Electronics Engrs; Am Phys Soc. *Res:* Microwave and laser propagation and communication; semiconductor, solid state physics; theoretical physics. *Mailing Add:* 35 Lakeside Dr Greenbelt MD 20770

HIRSCHMANN, HANS, BIOLOGICAL CHEMISTRY. *Current Pos:* from asst prof to prof biochem, 42-78, prof chem, 68-78, EMER PROF, CASE WESTERN RES UNIV, 78- *Personal Data:* b Bavaria, Ger, July 1, 09; US citizen; m 38; c 1. *Educ:* Univ Basel, MD, 34; Columbia Univ, PhD(biochem), 38. *Honors & Awards:* Morley Award, Am Chem Soc, 84. *Prof Exp:* Res fel, Univ Pa, 38-42. *Mem:* AAAS; Am Chem Soc; Endocrine Soc; Am Soc Biochem & Molecular Biol. *Res:* Chemistry of steroids, adrenal steroids; stereochemistry. *Mailing Add:* Judson Manor Apt 825 1890 E 107th St Cleveland OH 44106-2245

HIRSCHMANN, RALPH FRANZ, ORGANIC CHEMISTRY, BIO-ORGANIC CHEMISTRY. *Current Pos:* RES PROF CHEM, UNIV PA, PHILADELPHIA, 87- *Personal Data:* b Bavaria, Ger, May 6, 22; nat US; m 51; c Ralph F & Carla H (Hummel). *Educ:* Oberlin Col, AB, 43; Univ Wis, MA, 48, PhD(org chem), 50. *Hon Degrees:* DSc, Oberlin Col, 69. *Honors & Awards:* Intrasci Res Found Award, 70; Alan E Pierce Award, 83; Romanes lectr, Univ Edinburgh, 85; Agnes Borrowman Spec lectr in Pharm, London Univ, 85; Hurd Lectr, Northwestern Univ, 85; Nichols Medal, Darmouth Lectr, 88; Chem Pioneer Award, Inst Chemists, 92; Max Bergmann Medal, 93; Grothers Award, Am Chem Soc, 94, Alfred Burger Award, 94. *Prof Exp:* Chemist process res, Res Labs, Merck Sharp & Dohme, Inc, Rahway, 50-54, sr chemist, 54-56, sect head, 57-58, res assoc fundamental res, 58-63, res assoc explor, 63-64, asst dir explor res, 64-68; dir peptide res, Merck Sharp & Dohme Res Labs, Rahway, NJ, 68-69, dir protein chem, 69-71, sr dir new lead discovery, 71-72, sr dir med chem, 72-74, exec dir, med chem, West Point, Pa, 74-76, vpres, 76-78, sr vpres basic res, 78-84, sr vpres chem, 84-87. *Concurrent Pos:* Vis prof, Univ Wis, 73; mem, NIH Med Chem A Study Sect, 79-82; distinguished lectr, Wesleyan Univ, 79; co-chmn, Gordon Res Conf, 78 & bd trustees, 81-; mem, Comt Surv Opportunities Chem Sci, Nat Res Coun, 82-; adv comt chem, NSF, 85-; med prof, Univ SC, 87-; univ prof biomed res, Med Univ SC, Charleston, 87-; consult, expert witness-patents. *Mem:* Fel AAAS; NY Acad Sci; Am Soc Biol Chemists; Am Acad Arts & Sci; Am Chem Soc. *Res:* Organic synthesis; steroids; vitamin K; first total synthesis of ribonuclease; chemistry and biology relating to human and animal health; peptides; peptidomimetics. *Mailing Add:* Dept Chem Univ Pa 231 S 34th St Philadelphia PA 19104-6323. *Fax:* 215-898-5129

HIRSCHMANN, ROBERT P, APPLIED CHEMISTRY. *Current Pos:* group leader, 70-82, asst mgr chem res, 82-88, DIR RES & DEVELOP, VULCAN MAT CORP, 88- *Personal Data:* b New York, NY, Dec 26, 34; m 57; c 4. *Educ:* City Col New York, BS, 56; Iowa State Univ, PhD(phys chem), 63; Wichita State Univ, MBA, 82. *Prof Exp:* Res chemist, Gen Chem Div, Allied Chem Corp, NJ, 56-58, spectroscopist, Ill, 58-59, sr res chemist, Morristown, 63-66, sr res scientist, Indust Chem Div, 66-70. *Mem:* Am Chem Soc. *Res:* Vibrational spectra of -X-Y-Z compounds such as alkyl isocyanates and isothiocyanates; the study of oxidative chlorination of simple aliphatic molecules. *Mailing Add:* 9919 W 12th Wichita KS 67212-4204

HIRSCHOWITZ, BASIL ISAAC, MEDICINE. *Current Pos:* assoc prof med, 59-64, physiol, 68-71, PROF MED, MED COL ALA, 64-, PHYSIOL, 71-, DIR DIV GASTROENTEROL, 59- *Personal Data:* b Bethal, SAfrica, May 29, 25; m 58. *Educ:* Univ Witwatersrand, BSc, 43, MB, ChB, 47, MD, 54; FRCP(Ed); FRCP. *Honors & Awards:* Schindler Medal, Am Soc Gastrointestinal Endoscopy, 73; Kettering Prize, Gen Motors Cancer Res Found, 87. *Prof Exp:* House officer med, Johannesburg Gen Hosp, SAfrica, 48-50; house officer, Postgrad Med Sch, London, 50; registr, Cent Middlesex Hosp, 51-53; from instr to asst prof internal med, Med Sch, Univ Mich, 53-56; asst prof, Sch Med, Temple Univ, 57-59. *Mem:* AAAS; Am Physiol Soc; Sigma Xi; NY Acad Sci; Med Res Soc Gt Britain; Am Gastroenterol Asn. *Res:* Diseases of the gastrointestinal tract; physiology of the stomach. *Mailing Add:* Div Gastroenterol Univ Ala Birmingham AL 35294-0007. *Fax:* 205-975-6381

HIRSH, ALLEN GENE, stress physiology of freezing in woody plants, for more information see previous edition

HIRSH, DWIGHT CHARLES, III, VETERINARY MICROBIOLOGY. *Current Pos:* from asst prof to assoc prof, 73-83, PROF MICROBIOL, UNIV CALIF, DAVIS, 83- *Personal Data:* b Los Angeles, Calif, Oct 5, 38; m 67, Lucy Tushak; c Dwight & Elizabeth. *Educ:* Loyola Univ, Calif, BS, 60; Univ Calif, Davis, DVM, 66; Stanford Univ, PhD(med microbiol), 71. *Prof Exp:* Fel med microbiol, Stanford Univ, 66-68; asst prof vet microbiol, Univ Mo-Columbia, 71-73. *Mem:* Am Soc Microbiol; Sigma Xi; Am Asn Immunologists. *Res:* Host-parasite relationships, especially immunological and ecological aspects; plasmid mediated resistance and virulence determinants in Pasteurella. *Mailing Add:* Microbiol Univ Calif Davis CA 95616-5200. *Fax:* 530-752-3349

HIRSH, EVA MARIA HAUPTMANN, PHARMACOLOGY, PHYSIOLOGY. *Current Pos:* ASST PROF PHARMACOL, NY MED COL, 75- *Personal Data:* b Freiburg, Ger, July 14, 28; US citizen; m 62; c 2. *Educ:* Bryn Mawr Col, AB, 50; NY Univ, PhD(physiol-pharmacol), 73. *Prof Exp:* Instr physiol & pharmacol, NY Univ Col Dent, 60-68; lectr Philadelphia Col Osteop Med, 69-72; fel pharmacol & psychiat, NY Med Col, 73-74; res assoc psychopharmacol, Med Sch Thomas Jefferson Univ, 74-75. *Mem:* NY Acad Sci; AAAS; Am Asn Electroencephalographers; Sigma Xi. *Res:* Mechanisms involved in production of experimental myocardial ischemia and necrosis by means of cardiotoxic adrenergic amines; measurement of blood flow by electrical impedance plethysmography; neuropsychopharmacology of hallucinogens. *Mailing Add:* 6 James St Norwalk CT 06850-1631

HIRSH, IRA JEAN, PSYCHOPHYSICS. *Current Pos:* from assoc prof to prof, 52-85, dean, Fac Arts & Sci, 69-73, Malinckrodt distinguished prof, 85-92, dir, Cent Inst Deaf, 92-94, SR SCIENTIST, CENT INST DEAF, WASHINGTON UNIV, 83-, EMER MALINCKRODT DISTINGUISHED PROF PSYCHOL, 92- *Personal Data:* b New York, NY, Feb 22, 22; m 43; c 4. *Educ:* NY State Col Teachers, AB, 42; Northwestern Univ, MA, 43; Harvard Univ, PhD(exp psychol), 48. *Honors & Awards:* Biennial Award, Acoust Soc Am, 56; Honors Award, Am Speech & Hearing Asn, 68; Gold Medal, Acoust Soc Am, 92. *Prof Exp:* Asst, Psycho-acoustic Lab, Harvard Univ, 46-48, res fel, 48-51; res assoc, Cent Inst Deaf, 51-60, from asst dir res to dir res, 60-83. *Concurrent Pos:* Vis prof, Sorbonne, 62-63 & Tsukuba Univ, Japan, 81-82; consult, USAF, 55-61, Vet Admin, 56-65, NIH, 63-66 & Dept Trans, 67-73; mem comt hearing & bio-acoustics, Armed Forces-Nat Acad Sci, 56-59 & 63-66, chmn, 64-65; chmn eval panel acoustics, Nat Bur Stand, 71-74. *Mem:* Nat Acad Sci; fel Acoust Soc Am (pres, 67-68); fel Am Psychol Asn; fel Am Speech & Hearing Asn; Soc Exp Psychol. *Res:* Hearing, auditory perception, communication, speech and language, communication disorders. *Mailing Add:* Cent Inst Deaf 818 S Euclid St Louis MO 63110

HIRSH, MERLE NORMAN, MATERIALS SCIENCE, ATOMIC PHYSICS. *Current Pos:* sr scientist, Lab Laser Energetics, 80-81, PRES, PLASMA RESOURCES, UNIV ROCHESTER, 81- *Personal Data:* b New York, NY, Apr 27, 31; m 54; c 4. *Educ:* Univ Pittsburgh, BS, 52; Johns Hopkins Univ, PhD(physics), 58. *Prof Exp:* Proj dir maser res, ITT Fed Labs, 58-61; tech dir space physics, G C Dewey Corp, 61-71 & Dewey Electronics Corp, 71-72; chmn, Sci-Math Div, Univ Minn, Morris, 72-78, prof physics, 72-80. *Concurrent Pos:* Mem staff, Physics Discharge Lab, Superior Sch Elec, Gif-sur-Yvette, France, 76-77. *Mem:* Am Asn Physics Teachers; Inst Elec & Electronics Engrs; Indust Appln Soc; Am Phys Soc; Am Vacuum Soc. *Res:* Plasma modification of surfaces; plasma chemistry; gaseous electronics, particularly electron and ion production processes in the upper atmosphere; laboratory investigation of ionospheric reactions. *Mailing Add:* 1600 East Ave No 810 Rochester NY 14610

HIRSHAUT, YASHAR, INTERNAL MEDICINE, ONCOLOGY. *Current Pos:* ADJ RES PROF BIOL, YESHIVA UNIV, 86- *Personal Data:* b Berlin, Ger, Feb 27, 38; US citizen; m 64; c 8. *Educ:* Yeshiva Univ, BA, 59, Albert Einstein Col Med, MD, 63; Am Bd Internal Med, dipl, 72, dipl med oncol, 75. *Prof Exp:* Intern, Montefiore Hosp, 63-64, asst resident, 64-65; clin assoc, Med Br, Nat Cancer Inst, 65-68; res assoc, Inst, Med Col, Cornell Univ, 68-72, assoc, 72-75, asst prof, 72-79, assoc prof med, Med Col, 79-86, head, Lab Immunodiag, Sloan-Kettering Inst Cancer Res, 75-86, asst mem, Inst, 81-86. *Concurrent Pos:* Fel med oncol, Dept Med, Mem Hosp, New York, 69-70; fel, Dept Med, Cornell Univ Med Sch, 69-70, instr med, 70-72; clin asst physician, Clin Immunol Serv, Mem Hosp, New York, 70-73, asst attend physician, 73-79, assoc attend physician, 79-86; adj attend, Lenox Hill Hosp, 85-; assoc attend, Beth Israel Hosp, NY, 87- *Mem:* Am Asn Immunol; Am Asn Cancer Res; Am Soc Clin Oncol; NY Acad Sci; AMA. *Res:* Tumor immunology; clinical immunology; cancer chemotherapy and immunotherapy. *Mailing Add:* 860 Fifth Ave New York NY 10021

HIRSHBURG, ROBERT IVAN, MECHANICAL ENGINEERING. *Current Pos:* RES ENGR, E I DU PONT DE NEMOURS & CO, INC, 80- *Personal Data:* b Dallas, Tex, June 19, 49; m 74; c 1. *Educ:* Auburn Univ, BME, 72, MS, 74; Ariz State Univ, PhD(mech eng), 80. *Prof Exp:* Proj engr, Sperry Flight Systs, 74-75; res asst, Ariz State Univ, 75-79. *Mem:* Am Soc Mech Engrs. *Res:* Theoretical and experimental investigations of free-surface liquid flows, particularly analysis and development of precision coating equipment. *Mailing Add:* RR 4 Hendersonville NC 28739

HIRSHFIELD, JAY LEONARD, PLASMA PHYSICS. *Current Pos:* from instr to asst prof physics, 62-63, from asst prof to assoc prof appl sci, 63-68, PROF APPL PHYSICS, YALE UNIV, 68- *Personal Data:* b Washington, DC, Oct 24, 31; m 57; c 4. *Educ:* Univ Md, BS, 52; Ohio State Univ, MS, 56; US Air Force Inst Technol, MS, 58; Mass Inst Technol, PhD(physics), 60. *Prof Exp:* Proj engr, Air Develop Ctr, Wright-Patterson AFB, Ohio, 54-57; res assoc physics, Mass Inst Technol, 60; NATO fel, Inst Plasma Physics, Jutphaas, Neth, 61-62. *Concurrent Pos:* Guggenheim fel, Lab Gas Ionization, Frascati, Italy, 68; vis prof, Racah Inst Physics, Hebrew Univ, Jerusalem, Israel, 72 & 77-78. *Mem:* Fel Am Phys Soc. *Res:* Microwave optics; microwave gas discharge and plasma physics; interactions of radiation with relativistic electron beams, including gyrotrons, free electron lasers, slow cyclotron wave amplifiers and related mechanisms; laser-produced plasmas; plasma diagnostics. *Mailing Add:* 55 Killdeer Rd Hamden CT 06517

HIRSHMAN, CAROL A, ANESTHESIOLOGY, PHARMACOLOGY. *Current Pos:* PROF ANESTHESIOL MED & ENVIRON HEALTH SCI, JOHNS HOPKINS UNIV, 86- *Personal Data:* b Montreal, Can, Aug 12, 44; m 70; c 1. *Educ:* McGill Univ, BSc, 65, MD, 69. *Prof Exp:* Asst prof anesthesiol, Univ Colo Med Ctr, 74-75; asst prof anesthesiol, Ore Health Sci Univ, 76-80, from assoc prof to prof anesthesiol & pharmacol, 80-86. *Concurrent Pos:* Prin investr, NIH, 90-95. *Mem:* Am Soc Anesthesiologists; Am Physiol Soc; Am Thoracic Soc; Asn Univ Anesthetists. *Mailing Add:* Physiol Div Rm 7006 615 N Wolfe St Baltimore MD 21205. *Fax:* 410-955-0299

HIRSHMAN, JUSTIN LEONARD, ORGANIC & ORGANOMETALLIC CHEMISTRY. *Current Pos:* DIR MKT RES, ATOCHEM N AM, INC, 90- *Personal Data:* b New York, NY, Dec 13, 30; m 59; c 2. *Educ:* City Col, City Univ New York, BS, 53; Brooklyn Col, City Univ New York, MA, 59; Fairleigh Dickinson Univ, MBA, 77. *Prof Exp:* Develop chemist, US Vitamin & Pharmaceut Corp, 55-59 & Specific Pharmaceut, Chemetron Co, 59-63; res chemist, M&T Chem, Inc, 63-68, res suprv, 68-72, res mgr, 72-74, res dir, Chem Div, 74-80, res dir chem, 80-86, dir, comm eval & develop, 86-89. *Mem:* Am Chem Soc; CDA; Licensing Exec Soc. *Res:* Product and process research and development; organic and organometallic chemicals; condensation catalysis; polymer stabilization and biocidal activity of organometallic chemicals. *Mailing Add:* 47 Landsdowne Rd East Brunswick NJ 08816

HIRSHON, JORDON BARRY, BIOLOGICAL RHYTHMS, DNA SEQUENCES. *Current Pos:* From asst prof to assoc prof, 64-76, PROF BIOL, LONG ISLAND UNIV, 76- *Personal Data:* b Brooklyn, NY, Feb 26, 39; m 60; c 2. *Educ:* City Col New York, BS, 60; Rutgers Univ, PhD(bot), 64. *Concurrent Pos:* Vis prof, Chungang Univ, Korea, 65-66; partic, NSF Summer Inst Math. *Mem:* Sigma Xi. *Res:* Circadian rhythms in Neurospora; computer analysis of DNA sequences. *Mailing Add:* Dept Biol Long Island Univ Brooklyn Ctr Brooklyn NY 11201

HIRSHON, RONALD, MATHEMATICS. *Current Pos:* from asst prof to assoc prof, 67-79, PROF MATH, POLYTECH INST NEW YORK, 80- *Personal Data:* b May 17, 39; US citizen; m 62; c 2. *Educ:* Brooklyn Col, BS, 61, MA, 63; Adelphi Univ, PhD(math), 67. *Prof Exp:* Instr math, State Univ NY Stony Brook, 65-66; asst prof, Staten Island Community Col, 66-67. *Mem:* Am Math Soc; Math Asn Am. *Res:* Group theory, particularly hopfian groups. *Mailing Add:* Polytech Univ 333 Jay St Brooklyn NY 11201

HIRST, ALBERT EDMUND, MEDICINE. *Current Pos:* RETIRED. *Personal Data:* b Riverside, Calif, June 13, 15; m 52; c 3. *Educ:* Pac Union Col, BA, 38; Loma Linda Univ, MD, 42; Am Bd Path, dipl, 47. *Prof Exp:* From instr to prof path, Sch Med, Loma Linda Univ, 43-97, chmn dept, 64-73. *Concurrent Pos:* Jr attend physician, Los Angeles Co Hosp, 46-64; consult pathologist, San Antonio Community Hosp, Upland, 50-52; dir labs, John Wesley Co Hosp, 59-60; res assoc, Harvard Univ, 61-62; vis prof, Univ Ala, Birmingham, 71-72; chief lab serv, Loma Linda Vet Admin Hosp, 77-87; assoc pathologist, San Bernardino Community Hosp, 83-84 & Loma Linda Community Hosp, 85. *Mem:* Am Soc Clin Path. *Res:* Arterial disease, especially arteriosclerosis and dissecting aneurysm. *Mailing Add:* 24681 Lawton Ave Loma Linda CA 92354

HIRST, MAURICE, CHEMICAL PHARMACOLOGY. *Current Pos:* NIH fel org chem, 65-66, from asst prof to assoc prof, 67-79, PROF PHARMACOL, UNIV WESTERN ONT, 79- *Personal Data:* b Leeds, Eng, Aug 23, 40; m 65; Sylvia Beryl; c Paul B, Jason O & Claire N. *Educ:* Univ Liverpool, BSc, 62, PhD(org chem), 65; Univ Western Ont, PhD(pharmacol), 69. *Concurrent Pos:* Sci rev mem, Comt Biomed Res, Health & Welfare, Med Res Coun Can, 75-78; mem fel comt, Ont Ment Health Found, 81-86; mem, biol, chem & toxicol comt, Health & Welfare, Can, 84-89; vis sr scientist, Addiction Res Found, Toronto, Can, 91-92. *Mem:* NY Acad Sci; Soc Toxicol Can; Can Col Neuropsychopharmacol; Pharmacol Soc Can; Res Soc Alcoholism. *Res:* Dependence producing drugs and their mechanisms of action; cardiotoxic effects of ethanol; therapeutic biosensors. *Mailing Add:* Dept Pharmacol & Toxicol Health Sci Ctr Univ Western Ont London ON N6A 5C1 Can. *Fax:* 519-661-4051; *E-Mail:* mhirst@julian.uwo.ca

HIRST, ROBERT CHARLES, PHYSICAL CHEMISTRY. *Current Pos:* sr res chemist res dept, 69-75, group leader, NMR Spectros, 75-77, SECT HEAD SPECTROS, GOODYEAR TIRE & RUBBER CO, 77- *Personal Data:* b Chillicothe, Mo, Nov 2, 32; m 61; c 2. *Educ:* Univ Calif, Berkeley, BS, 54; Univ Utah, PhD(phys chem), 63. *Prof Exp:* Fel, Div Pure Chem, Nat Res Coun Can, 63-64; res chemist, Cent Res Div Lab, Socony Mobil Oil Co, 64-68, sr res chemist, Mobil Res & Develop Corp, 68-69. *Mem:* Am Phys Soc; Am Chem Soc. *Res:* Polymer characterization and analysis by nuclear magnetic resonance spectroscopy, including high resolution, pulse and carbon-13 nuclear magnetic resonance of solids; characterization of polymers and surfaces by Fourier transform infrared spectroscopy. *Mailing Add:* 1082 Greenvale Ave Akron OH 44313-6702

HIRSTY, SYLVAIN MAX, RUBBER CHEMISTRY, POLYMER CHEMISTRY. *Current Pos:* TECH DIR, GATES ENG, 71- *Personal Data:* b Antwerp, Belg, Apr 11, 25; nat US; m 46; c 3. *Educ:* Rensselaer Polytech Inst, BS, 46, PhD(org chem), 53. *Prof Exp:* Instr, NY State Col Teachers, Albany, 52; res chemist rubber chem, E I du Pont de Nemours & Co, 53-71. *Mem:* Am Chem Soc. *Res:* Elastomers technology; rubber chemicals; fluorine and neoprene chemistry; elastomeric coatings. *Mailing Add:* 5481 White Sands Lakeworth Wilmington FL 33469

HIRT, ANDREW MICHAEL, SURFACE & INTERFACE CHEMISTRY, MATERIALS CHARACTERIZATION. *Current Pos:* PRES & SR SCIENTIST, MAT RES LABS, INC, 88- *Personal Data:* b Youngstown, Ohio, Mar 30, 55; m 83, Carol J McKenna; c James. *Educ:* Case Inst Technol, BS, 77. *Prof Exp:* Sr scientist, Struct Probe, Inc, 77-80, lab mgr, 82-88; lab scientist, Phys Electronics Div, Perkin-Elmer, 80-82; vpres res, Lasir Systs, Inc, 90-93. *Concurrent Pos:* Publicity chmn, Int Soc Hybrid Microelectronics, Garden State, 85-93, prog comt, Ann Joint Symp, 89-; course instr, Instrumental Surface Anal, Ctr Prof Advan, 89; consult electron spectros, Dept Physics, Rutgers Univ, 90- *Mem:* Am Vacuum Soc; Am Soc Metals Int; Int Soc Hybrid Microelectronics (pres, 88-89); Soc Appl Spectros; Catalysis Soc Am; Eastern Electron Spectros Soc; Microbeam Anal Soc. *Res:* Surface and interface chemistry; interaction of solid-solid and solid-gas interfaces; thermal transport mechanisms; materials characterization; experimental design; evaporation and sputtering techniques for metallization; metallographic preparation petrography and fractography; computer programming. *Mailing Add:* 290 N Bridge St Struthers OH 44471. *Fax:* 216-750-0778

HIRT, CYRIL WILLIAM, JR, THEORETICAL PHYSICS. *Current Pos:* PRES, FLOW SCI, INC, 80- *Personal Data:* b Flushing, NY, Dec 20, 36; m 68, Ginger Warren; c Heather & Amber. *Educ:* Univ Mich, BS, 58, MS, 60, PhD(plasma physics), 63. *Prof Exp:* Staff mem, Los Alamos Nat Lab, 63-80. *Concurrent Pos:* Sr scientist, Sci Appl Inc, 72-73; consult. *Res:* Fluid mechanics; numerical fluid dynamics; commercial software development. *Mailing Add:* Flow Sci Inc 1325 Trinity Dr Los Alamos NM 87544. *Fax:* 505-662-6564; *E-Mail:* cfd@flow3d.com

HIRT, THOMAS J(AMES), PHYSICAL CHEMISTRY, FUEL TECHNOLOGY. *Current Pos:* RETIRED. *Personal Data:* b Cincinnati, Ohio, Mar 24, 31; m 52, Janet H Helnen; c Diane J, Thomas J Jr & Nancy A. *Educ:* Xavier Univ, Ohio, BS, 56; Pa State Univ, PhD(fuel tech), 62. *Prof Exp:* Chemist, Carbon & Ribbon Div, Interchem Corp, 56-57; res asst fuel tech, Pa State Univ, 57-62; sr res chemist, Allison Div, Gen Motors Corp, 62-64; res scientist, HNG/Internorth Inc, 64-67, mgr, Corp Res & Develop, Northern Natural Gas Co, 67-75, vpres res, HNG/Internorth, 75-86. *Mem:* Am Chem Soc; Electrochem Soc; Indust Res Inst. *Res:* Chemical kinetics in the middle and high temperature ranges; combustion phenomena reactions of element carbon; structure of carbon; electrochemistry; energy conversion. *Mailing Add:* 1 Cypress Run Haines City FL 33844

HIRTH, HAROLD FREDERICK, ANIMAL ECOLOGY. *Current Pos:* asst prof zool, 63-68, assoc prof biol, 68-71, PROF BIOL, UNIV UTAH, 72- *Personal Data:* b Rockville, Conn, Dec 6, 32; m 62; c 2. *Educ:* Univ Conn, BA, 54, MS, 58; Univ Fla, PhD(biol), 62. *Prof Exp:* Asst prof biol, Univ Fla, 62-63. *Concurrent Pos:* NIH, Food & Agr Org & AEC res grants; Fulbright scholar. *Mem:* Ecol Soc Am; Animal Behav Soc; Sigma Xi. *Res:* Ecology and behavior of animals. *Mailing Add:* Dept Biol Univ Utah 201 S Biol Bldg Salt Lake City UT 84112-1196

HIRTH, JOHN P(RICE), PHYSICAL METALLURGY. *Current Pos:* PROF MAT ENG, WASH STATE UNIV, 88- *Personal Data:* b Cincinnati, Ohio, Dec 16, 30; m 53, Martha Davis; c Marc, Laura, Gregory & Christina. *Educ:* Ohio State Univ, BMetE & MS, 53; Carnegie Inst Technol, PhD(metall eng), 58. *Honors & Awards:* Hardy Medal, Am Inst Mining, Metall & Petrol Engrs, 61, Mehl Medal, 80, Mathewson Medal, 82; Stoughton Award, Am Soc Metals, 64; Curtis McGraw Award, Am Soc Eng Educ, 67. *Prof Exp:* Fulbright res fel, Univ Bristol, 57-58; asst prof metall eng, Carnegie Inst Technol, 58-61; Mershon assoc prof, Ohio State Univ, 61-64, prof phys metall, 64-88. *Concurrent Pos:* Consult, Crucible Steel Co. *Mem:* Nat Acad Sci; Nat Acad Eng; Am Soc Eng Educ; fel Am Soc Metals; fel Metall Soc; Am Inst Mining, Metall & Petrol Engrs. *Res:* Crystal growth; dislocation theory. *Mailing Add:* Dept Mech & Mat Eng Wash State Univ Pullman WA 99164. *Fax:* 509-335-4662

HIRTH, ROBERT STEPHEN, veterinary pathology, for more information see previous edition

HIRTZEL, CYNTHIA S, APPLIED MATHEMATICS, SYSTEMS SIMULATION. *Current Pos:* assoc prof, 86-90, PROF CHEM ENG & MAT SCI, SYRACUSE UNIV, 90-, CHAIRPERSON DEPT, 90- *Personal Data:* b Ind. *Educ:* Wash Univ, AB, 73; Northwestern Univ, MS, 77, PhD(civil & environ eng), 80. *Prof Exp:* Vis scholar environ eng, Northwestern Univ, 80-81; asst prof chem & environ eng, Rensselaer Polytech Inst, 81-86. *Concurrent Pos:* Consult, various environ, indust & other consult firms, 82- *Mem:* AAAS; Am Inst Chem Engrs; Am Soc Eng Educ; Am Phys Soc; Am Chem Soc; Soc Insust & Appl Math; Asn Women Sci. *Res:* Adsorption/ desorption phenomena; colloidal and interfacial phenomena; stochastic processes and applications to engineering systems; environmental analysis and modeling (including air pollution); computer experiments for colloidal systems; atmospheric sciences and modeling. *Mailing Add:* 2300 Schlosser Rd Harleysville PA 19438

HIRUKI, CHUJI, VIROLOGY, MYCOPLASMOLOGY. *Current Pos:* RETIRED. *Personal Data:* b Fukue, Nagasaki-Ken, Japan, June 16, 31; m 61, Yasuko Hijikata; c Tadaaki & Lisa. *Educ:* Kyushu Univ, Japan, BSC, 54, PhD(plant virol), 63. *Honors & Awards:* Nat Sci Coun lectr, Gov Repub China, 89; Award Excellence, Phytopath Soc Japan, 90; Res Award Distinguished Foreign Specialist, Gov Japan, 91; Lifetime Achievement Award, Am Phytopath Soc, 93; Outstanding Res Plant Path Award, 96; J Gordin Kaplan Award Excellence Res, 93; Award Outstanding Res, Can

Phytopath Soc. *Prof Exp:* Plant pathologist, Hatano Tobacco Exp Sta, Japan, 54-65; from asst prof to prof, Dept Plant Sci, Univ Alta, 66-91, univ prof, 91-. *Concurrent Pos:* Vis plant pathologist, Univ Calif Berkeley, 63-64; hon fel, Univ Wis-Madison, 64-66, Neth Int Ctr, 73; vis scientist, Nat Inst Agron Res, Versailles, France 72, Agr Univ, Wageningen, Neth, 73, Forestry & Forest Prod Res Inst, Japan, 91-92; vis prof several foreign univs, 73-96. *Mem:* Fel Royal Soc Can; fel Can Phytopath Soc (pres, 90-91); fel Am Phythopath Soc; NY Acad Sci; Phythopath Soc Japan; Int Soc Plant Molecular Biol; Int Orgn Mycoplasmology. *Res:* Studies of plant diseases with special emphasis on pathogen characteriaction diagnostic techniques and analysis of genome interaction between host and pathogen under controlled and natural environment conditions. *Mailing Add:* 410D Agr Forest Ctr Univ Alta Edmonton AB T6G 2P5 Can. *Fax:* 403-492-4265; *E-Mail:* chiruki@afns.ualberta.ca

HIRWE, ASHALATA SHYAMSUNDER, SYNTHETIC ORGANIC CHEMISTRY. *Current Pos:* res chemist, 74-80, SR RES CHEMIST, RES CTR, HERCULES, INC, 80- *Personal Data:* b Goa, India, Aug 20, 38; m 62; c 2. *Educ:* Wilson Col, India, BSc, 59; Univ Col, Ireland, PhD(org chem), 65. *Prof Exp:* Sr demonstr chem, Univ Col, Dublin, Ireland, 62-65; sr res chemist org chem, Fraco-India Pharmaceut, 65-68; res assoc radiochem, Dept Chem, Univ Ill, 68-69, res assoc synthetic org chem, Dept Entom, 70-74. *Concurrent Pos:* Mgr, Tech Info Div, Hercules, Inc. *Mem:* Am Chem Soc. *Res:* Synthesis of bioactive compounds; application of radioisotopes to industrial problems and surface chemistry. *Mailing Add:* Res Ctr Bldg 8100 Rm 304 500 Hercules Rd Wilmington DE 19808

HIRZY, JOHN WILLIAM, PLASTICS CHEMISTRY, RISK ASSESSMENT. *Current Pos:* SR SCIENTIST, ASSESSMENT DIV, US ENVIRON PROTECTION AGENCY, 81- *Personal Data:* b St Louis, Mo, Sept 19, 36; m 87; c 3. *Educ:* Univ Mo, BS, 58, PhD(org chem), 62. *Prof Exp:* Res specialist plasticizers, Monsanto Indust Chem Co, 62-81. *Concurrent Pos:* Instr, St Louis-St Louis Co Jr Col, 63-68, 70-71 & 75-76; asst prof, Univ Mo, St Louis, 68-70; pres, Local 2050, Nat Fedn Fed Employees; adj prof chem, Am Univ, Wash, DC, 95- *Mem:* Am Chem Soc; AAAS; Soc Risk Anal. *Res:* Reduction of nitroaromatic compounds; effect of substituents on ultraviolet spectra of aromatic compounds; chemical modification of polymers; plasticizer theory and technology, environmental effects of plasticizers; flame retardants synthesis; risk assessment; industrial chemicals; carpet toxicity; indoor air quality. *Mailing Add:* US Environ Protection Agency 401 M St SW 7402 Washington DC 20460

HISADA, MITUHIKO, NEUROSCIENCES. *Current Pos:* PROF & DEAN, SCI UNIV TOKYO, 93- *Personal Data:* b Nagoya, Japan, Oct 30, 29; m 56; c 1. *Educ:* Univ Tokyo, BSc, 52; Hokkaido Univ, DSc, 60. *Honors & Awards:* Soc prize, Zool Soc Japan, 88. *Prof Exp:* Res assoc zool, Univ Tokyo, 52-54; res assoc, Hokkaido Univ, 54-56, lectr physiol, 56-60, from assoc prof to prof, 60-93. *Concurrent Pos:* Coun, Physiol Soc Japan, 61-, Biol Soc Japan, 77- & Jap Soc Comp Physiol & Biochem, 91-; vis lectr, Univ Pa, 62-64, vis assoc prof, 71-73; lectr, Sapporo Med Col, 78-, Asahikawa Med Col, 85-; dir, Ctr Exp Plants & Animals, Hokkaido Univ, 81-91. *Mem:* Biol Soc Japan; Physiol Soc Japan; Japanese Soc Comp Physiol & Biochem; Int Soc Neuroethology (secy, 89-); Am Physiol Soc; Soc Neurosci. *Res:* Neuronal substrates of invertebrate behavior; anthropod interneurons; nonspiking integration of sensory input and motor output; neural network subserving gravitational responses of crustacea; neural circuit simulation study. *Mailing Add:* Sci Univ Tokyo Oshamambe Campus 102 Tomino Oshamambe Hokkaido 045-39 Japan. *Fax:* 81-1377-3430

HISATSUNE, ISAMU CLARENCE, PHYSICAL CHEMISTRY, BUDDHISM & SCIENCE. *Current Pos:* from asst prof to prof, 60-84, EMER PROF CHEM, PA STATE UNIV, 84- *Personal Data:* b Stockton, Calif, Jan 3, 24; m 51, Kim Yonemura. *Educ:* Univ Calif, BS, 51; Univ Wash, PhD(chem), 54. *Prof Exp:* Asst aeronaut eng, Aeronaut Res Inst, Tokyo, 44-45; civil censor, US Army, 45-47; asst chem, Univ Calif, 51 & Univ Wash, 51-52; res fel, 52-54; res fel, Univ Minn, 54-56; asst prof, Kans State Univ, 56-60. *Concurrent Pos:* Vis prof, Inst Org Chem, Univ Florence, 66 & Dept Chem, Fac Sci, Univ Tokyo, 68 & 75; adj prof sci & buddhism, Inst Buddhist Studies, Berkeley, Calif, 88- *Mem:* Am Chem Soc; Am Phys Soc. *Res:* Molecular structure; kinetics; buddhism and science. *Mailing Add:* 888 O'Farrell St Apt W-1206 San Francisco CA 94109

HISAW, FREDERICK LEE, JR, ZOOLOGY, ENDOCRINOLOGY. *Current Pos:* asst prof, 58-61, ASSOC PROF ZOOL, ORE STATE UNIV, 61- *Personal Data:* b Madison, Wis, Mar 26, 27; m 48; c 6. *Educ:* Univ Mo, BS, 50, MS, 52; Harvard Univ, PhD(zool), 55. *Prof Exp:* Res fel endocrinol, Biol Labs, Harvard Univ, 55-58. *Mem:* Am Soc Zool; Endocrine Soc; Soc Gen Physiol. *Res:* Endocrinology and the comparative physiology of reproduction. *Mailing Add:* 5925 SW Plymouth Dr Corvallis OR 97333

HISCOCK, WILLIAM ALLEN, THEORETICAL GENERAL RELATIVITY, QUANTUM FIELD THEORY. *Current Pos:* asst prof, 84-88, ASSOC PROF PHYSICS, DEPT PHYSICS, MONT STATE UNIV, 88- *Personal Data:* b Santa Monica, Calif, Oct 31, 51; m 75; c 2. *Educ:* Calif Inst Technol, Bs, 73; Univ Md, MS, 75, PhD(physics), 79. *Honors & Awards:* Wiley Res Award, 90. *Prof Exp:* Res assoc, dept physics, Yale Univ, 79-81; res assoc, dept physics, Ctr Relativity, Univ Tex, 81-82, lectr, 82-83; res assoc, dept physics, Univ Calif, Santa Barbara, 83-84. *Concurrent Pos:* Mem, Quantum Gravity Group, Nat Inst Theoret Physics, Univ Calif, Santa Barbara, 80. *Mem:* Am Phys Soc; Sigma Xi. *Res:* Quantum field theory in curved spacetimes, especially black hole evaporation; relativistic dissipative fluid mechanics; early universe cosmology; physics of neutron stars and black holes; quantum gravity. *Mailing Add:* Dept Physics Mont State Univ Bozeman MT 59717

HISCOE, HELEN BRUSH, REPRODUCTIVE BIOLOGY. *Current Pos:* RETIRED. *Personal Data:* b New London, Conn, Mar 10, 19; m 46, D Bonta; c Susan (Wisser), Elaine (Charney), Lenore (Starr) & Nancy (Clark). *Educ:* Vassar Col, AB, 39; Brown Univ, MS, 40; Univ Calif, Los Angeles, PhD(zool), 43. *Prof Exp:* Asst zool, Vassar Col, 40-41, instr, 43-46; res assoc for Dr Paul Weiss, Univ Chicago, 46-47; lectr, Mich State Univ, 59-68, from asst prof to prof, 68-86, emer prof, Dept Natural Sci, 86-97. *Mem:* AAAS; Asn Gen & Liberal Studies; Soc Col Sci Teachers. *Res:* General education in natural sciences. *Mailing Add:* 1817 Walnut Heights Dr East Lansing MI 48823

HISCOTT, RICHARD NICHOLAS, DEEP-SEA CLASTIC SEDIMENTOLOGY, BASIN ANALYSIS. *Current Pos:* PROF EARTH SCI, MEM UNIV NFLD, 77- *Personal Data:* b St Catharines, Ont, Feb 12, 51; m 80; c 1. *Educ:* Brock Univ, BSc, 74; McMaster Univ, PhD(geol), 77. *Concurrent Pos:* Res fel, Husky Oil Opers, 85-87, Japanese Sci & Technol Agency, 89; contract prof, Univ Bologna, Italy, 90. *Mem:* Soc Econ Paleontologists & Mineralogists; Am Asn Petrol Geologists; Can Soc Petrol Geologists; Int Asn Sedimentologists; Geol Assn Can. *Res:* Sedimentology of ancient deep-sea fans, slopes and shallow-marine clastics; ocean drilling program. *Mailing Add:* Dept Earth Sci Mem Univ Nfld St John's NF A1B 3X5 Can. *Fax:* 709-737-2589; *E-Mail:* rhiscott@kean.ucs.mun.ca

HISER, HOMER WENDELL, AEROSPACE ENGINEERING & REMOTE SENSING, ENVIRONMENTAL ENGINEERING. *Current Pos:* prof & dir, Radar Meteorol Lab, Rosenstiel Sch Marine & Atmospheric Sci, 55-73, PROF & DIR REMOTE SENSING LAB, COL ENG, UNIV MIAMI, 74- *Personal Data:* b Ava, Ill, Nov 21, 24; m 53, Wanda Jean Leach. *Educ:* Univ Ill, BS, 51, MS, 54; Washington Univ, St Louis, DSc(environ eng), 72. *Honors & Awards:* Cert Appreciation, Nat Weather Serv, US Dept Commerce, 71. *Prof Exp:* Res assoc & res radar meteorologist, Ill State Water Surv, Univ Ill, 50-55. *Concurrent Pos:* Consult, Battelle Columbus Labs, 74 & adv panel, NASA, 75; consult, Europ Space Agency, Spain, 86. *Mem:* Am Meteorol Soc; Am Geophys Union; sr mem Inst Elec & Electronics Engrs; sr mem Am Inst Aeronauts & Astronauts; Sigma Xi. *Res:* Applications of satellites, radar, and other remote sensing systems to meteorology, atmospheric physics, hydrology, solar energy, communications, electromagnetic propagation, and air pollution problems. *Mailing Add:* 272 Coconut Palm Rd Boca Raton FL 33432-7914

HISEY, ROBERT WARREN, ORGANIC CHEMISTRY, CHEMICAL ENGINEERING. *Current Pos:* CONSULT, 86- *Personal Data:* b Chicago, Ill, May 7, 31; c 5. *Educ:* Middlebury Col, AB, 52; Inst Paper Chem, MS, 54, PhD(chem eng), 55. *Honors & Awards:* Westbrook Steel Gold Medal, 55. *Prof Exp:* Tech serv dir, S D Warren Co, Cumberland Mills, 55-60, chief engr, 60-64; vpres, tech dir & div mgr, Brown Co, NH, 64-67; vpres-gen mgr, Bleached Prod, Continental Can Co, 67-77; exec vpres, Bleached Syst Oper, Continental Forest Indusrs, 77-86. *Mem:* Tech Asn Pulp & Paper Indust. *Res:* Filtration; pulp and paper processing. *Mailing Add:* 7227 Sparta Rd Sebring FL 33872

HISKES, JOHN ROBERT, THEORETICAL PHYSICS. *Current Pos:* Physicist, Calif Res & Develop Co, 52-54, Lawrence Livermore Lab, Univ Calif, 54-55 & Univ Calif, Berkeley, 55-60, PHYSICIST, LAWRENCE LIVERMORE LAB, UNIV CALIF, 60- *Personal Data:* b Chicago, Ill, May 30, 28; m 51, Dolores Grant; c Robin C & John G. *Educ:* Univ Calif, AB, 51, MA, 52, PhD, 60. *Concurrent Pos:* Consult, Gen Elec Co, 62-63; vis physicist, Culham Lab, Berkshire, Eng, 63-64, Ecole Polytecnic, France, 80, Japan At Eu R Inst, NAKA, Ibara Ki-Ken, 87-89; Nat Inst Fusion Sci, Nagoya, Japan, 91. *Mem:* Fel Am Phys Soc; Sigma Xi. *Res:* Atomic and molecular physics; controlled fusion; particle accelerators; liquid drop model of nuclear fission; negative ions. *Mailing Add:* Lawrence Livermore Nat Lab Livermore CA 94550. *Fax:* 510-447-6983

HISKES, RONALD, SOLID STATE PHYSICS. *Current Pos:* mem tech staff mat res, 70-77, PROF MGR, HEWLETT-PACKARD LAB, 77- *Personal Data:* b Evergreen Park, Ill, Jan 30, 41. *Educ:* Calvin Col, BS, 63; Univ Mich, BSE(chem eng) & BSE(metal eng), 63; Stanford Univ, MS, 64, PhD(mat sci), 68. *Prof Exp:* Instr mat sci, Stanford Univ, 69-70. *Concurrent Pos:* Res assoc & staff scientist crystal growth, Ctr Mat Res, Stanford Univ, 68-70; consult, Battelle Mem Inst, 68-70. *Mem:* Am Asn Crystal Growth. *Res:* Crystal growth and characterization of magnetic oxides; materials research; molecular beam epitaxy; fiber optics. *Mailing Add:* 3484 Waverley St Palo Alto CA 94306

HISKEY, CLARENCE FRANCIS, ANALYTICAL CHEMISTRY. *Current Pos:* RETIRED. *Personal Data:* b Milwaukee, Wis, June 5, 12; wid; c Iris. *Educ:* Univ Wis, BA, 35, MA, 36, PhD(inorg & phys chem), 39. *Prof Exp:* Instr chem, Univ Tenn, 39-41; instr, Columbia Univ, 41-42, res sect mgr, Manhattan Dist Proj, s a m labs, 42-43; sect chief metall lab, Univ Chicago, 43-44; assoc prof chem, Polytech Inst Brooklyn, 46-53; vpres, Transition Metals & Chems, 55-58; dir analytical res, Endo Labs Inc 58-73; researcher, E I DuPont de Nemours, 73-78. *Concurrent Pos:* Chem consult. *Mem:* AAAS; Am Chem Soc; Am Geophys Union; NY Acad Sci. *Res:* Analytical and metallurgical chemistry of niobium, tantalum, rhenium, molybdenum and manganese; spectrophotometry; isotope fractionation; instrumental techniques of analysis; pharmaceutical analysis; development of analytical methods of a pharmaceutical and inorganic chemical character. *Mailing Add:* 49 Long Hill Farm Guilford CT 06437-1868

HISKEY, J BRENT, CHEMICAL METALLURGY, HYDROMETALLURGY. *Current Pos:* dir, Ariz Mining & Mineral Resources Res Inst, 85-96, PROF EXTRACTIVE METALL, DEPT MAT SCI & ENG, UNIV ARIZ, 84-, DIR, COPPER RES CTR, 89- *Personal Data:* b Salina, Utah, Aug 18, 44; m 67; c 2. *Educ:* Univ Utah, BS, 67, MS, 71, PhD(metall), 73. *Honors & Awards:* Taggart Award, Soc Mining Engrs, Am Inst Mining, Metall & Petrol Engrs, 74; James Douglas Gold Medal, Am Inst Mech Engrs, 93. *Prof Exp:* Extractive metallurgist res, Alcoa Labs, 73-74; asst prof extractive metall, NMex Inst Mining & Technol, 74-77; res scientist, US Steel Res Labs, 77-80; mgr, Metall Res, Kennecott Copper Corp, 80-84. *Concurrent Pos:* Lectr, Carnegie Mellon Univ, 77-79; consult, E I du Pont de Nemours & Co, Inc, 84-, Phelps Dodge, 85-, Newcrest Gold Co, 85-95, Kennecott Corp, 85-96; chmn, Nat Asn Mineral Inst Dirs, 90-91; chmn, Mineral & Metall Processing Div, Soc Mining, Metall & Explor Inc, 91-92; Cyrus AMAX Metals Corp, 94- *Mem:* Nat Acad Eng; Sigma Xi; Soc Metall Engrs; Soc Mining Metall & Explor Inc. *Res:* Hydrometallurgy and mineral processing, specifically the physical chemistry of leaching, ion exchange, solvent extraction and metal recovery; kinetics of hydrometallurgical reactions with special emphasis on electrochemical processes; extraction of copper, gold and silver, and critical and strategic metals. *Mailing Add:* Dept Mat Sci & Eng Univ Ariz Tucson AZ 85721. *Fax:* 520-621-8159; *E-Mail:* jbh@bigdog.engr.arizona.edu

HISKEY, RICHARD GRANT, SYNTHETIC ORGANIC CHEMISTRY, PROTEIN CHEMISTRY. *Current Pos:* from assoc prof to prof, 58-75, chmn dept, 70-75, ALUMNI PROF CHEM, UNIV NC, CHAPEL HILL, 75- *Personal Data:* b Emporia, Kans, May 21, 29; m 53; c 5. *Educ:* Emporia State Univ, AB, 51; Kans State Col, MS, 53; Wayne State Col, PhD(chem), 55. *Honors & Awards:* Standard Oil Award, 69. *Prof Exp:* Res assoc org chem, Polytech Inst Brooklyn, 55-58. *Concurrent Pos:* Guggenheim fel, 70-71; consult, NIH, 74- *Mem:* fel AAAS; Am Chem Soc; fel Japan Soc Prom Sci; Sigma Xi. *Res:* Protein-metalion-lipid interactions; peptide synthesis; enzyme modification; model enzyme systems; role of gamma-carboxy glutamic acid in blood coagulation. *Mailing Add:* Dept Chem CB 3290 Univ NC Chapel Hill NC 27599-3290

HISLE, JOHN W, ADMINISTRATION. *Current Pos:* DIR, FED OCCUP HEALTH, HEALTH & HUMAN SERVS, 93- *Personal Data:* b Takema Park, Md, Jan 20, 42. *Educ:* Fairfield Univ, AB, 64; Fordham Univ, MA, 70; Baruck Col, MBA, 75. *Prof Exp:* Dep dir, Nat Health Serv Corps, 87-90, Community & Migrant Health Ctrs Prog, USPHS, 90-93. *Mailing Add:* Fed Occup Health 4350 East West Hwy Bethesda MD 20814. *Fax:* 301-594-4991; *E-Mail:* jhisle@foh.dhhs.gov

HISLOP, HELEN JEAN, MEDICAL PHYSIOLOGY, EXERCISE PHYSIOLOGY. *Current Pos:* chmn dept, 76-87, PROF PHYS THER, UNIV SOUTHERN CALIF, 68- *Personal Data:* b Linden, NJ, Mar 13, 29. *Educ:* Cent Col Iowa, BA, 50, cert phys ther, 51; Univ Iowa, MS, 53, PhD, 60. *Hon Degrees:* ScD, Cent Col, 79. *Honors & Awards:* Golden Pen Award, Am Phys Ther Asn, 69; John Stanley Coulter Lectr, Am Congress Rehab Med, 77; McMillan Lect, Am Phys Ther Asn, 75. *Prof Exp:* Instr phys ther, Sch Med, Univ Minn, 53-55; asst to dir prof educ, Nat Found, 55-58; res assoc physiol & pharmacol, Sch Med, Univ Pittsburgh, 60-62; ed j, Am Phys Ther Asn, 62-68. *Concurrent Pos:* Sr res consult, Inst Rehab Med, NY Med Ctr, 66-68; consult phys ther, Surg Gen, US Army, 67-69; dir phys ther, Rehab Res & Training Ctr, Univ Southern Calif, 68-74; Worthingham fel, Am Phys Ther Asn, 82; consult, S Ill Univ Sch Med, 86-, SUNY, Buffalo, 86-87. *Mem:* Fel AAAS; fel Am Col Sports Med; Am Phys Ther Asn; Am Cong Rehab Med; Sigma Xi. *Res:* Physiology of exercise; nerve-muscle physiology; adaptations to exercise; pathokinesiology; physical therapy. *Mailing Add:* 12313 Brock Ave Downey CA 90242-3503

HISSERICH, JOHN CHARLES, HEALTH ADMINISTRATION. *Current Pos:* admin dir, Comprehensive Cancer Ctr, 71-86, ASSOC VPRES, HEALTH AFFAIRS, UNIV SOUTHERN CALIF, 86- *Personal Data:* b Los Angeles, Calif, Apr 29, 39; m 73; c 4. *Educ:* Calif State Univ, Los Angeles, BA, 65; Univ Calif, Los Angeles, MPH, 66, DrPH, 70. *Prof Exp:* Adminr, Charles R Drew Med Sch, Univ Calif, Los Angeles, 70-71. *Concurrent Pos:* Assoc clin prof preventive med & pharm, Sch Med, Univ Southern Calif, 72-; WHO study fel, 75; Nat Cancer Inst Interventions Comt, NIH, 77-79. *Mem:* Am Pub Health Asn; Am Asn Cancer Educ; Inst Soc, Ethics & Life Sci; Soc Health & Human Values; AAAS; Am Soc Prev Oncol. *Res:* Cancer control; technology transfer; biomedical ethics; confidentiality of medical data. *Mailing Add:* Off Assoc VPres Health Affairs Univ Southern Calif 1540 Alcar St CHP 100 Los Angeles CA 90033

HISTAND, MICHAEL B(ENJAMIN), BIOENGINEERING, BIOMECHANICS. *Current Pos:* From asst prof to assoc prof, 69-80, PROF MECH ENG, PHYSIOL & BIOPHYS, COLO STATE UNIV, 80- *Personal Data:* b Ft Lewis, Wash, Oct 31, 42; m 67; c 2. *Educ:* Lehigh Univ, BS, 64; Stanford Univ, MS, 65, PhD(aeronaut, astron), 69. *Mem:* Am Soc Mech Engrs. *Res:* Medical ultrasound; hemodynamics; medical instrumentation. *Mailing Add:* 1630 W Vine Dr Ft Collins CO 80521

HISTED, JOHN ALLAN, PULP CHEMISTRY, PULP BLEACHING. *Current Pos:* RETIRED. *Personal Data:* b Hamilton, Ont, Feb 14, 29; m 53; c 3. *Educ:* McMaster Univ, BSc, 53. *Honors & Awards:* Douglas Jones Award, Tech Sect, Can Pulp & Paper Asn, 73, I H Weldon Medal, 83. *Prof Exp:* Res chemist, CIP Res Ltd, 53-66, group leader specialty pulps & bleaching, 66-73, res assoc, 73-75, sr res assoc, C P Forest Prod Res Ltd, 75-91. *Concurrent Pos:* Tappi fel, Tech Asn Pulp & Paper Indust, 85. *Mem:* Can Pulp & Paper Asn; sr mem Tech Asn Pulp & Paper Indust; Chem Inst Can. *Res:* Optimization and simplification of bleach sequences; development of bleachery control systems; reduction of pollution from bleacheries; development of new bleaching process. *Mailing Add:* 285 Front St L'Original ON K0B 1K0 Can

HITCHCOCK, ADAM PERCIVAL, ELECTRON AND X-RAY ABSORPTION. *Current Pos:* from asst prof to assoc prof, 79-89, PROF CHEM, MCMASTER UNIV, 89- *Personal Data:* b Hamilton, Ont, June 27, 51; m 72; c 2. *Educ:* McMaster Univ, BSc, 74; Univ British Columbia, PhD(chem), 78. *Honors & Awards:* Rutherford Medal, Royal Soc Can, 78; Noranda Award, Can Soc Chem, 89. *Prof Exp:* Fel, Univ BC, 78-79. *Concurrent Pos:* Prin investr, Ont Ctr Mat Res, 88- *Mem:* Am Chem Soc; Am Vacuum Soc; Can Soc Chem; Can Inst Physics. *Res:* Inner-shell excitations and ionization phenomena in molecules; surfaces and solids studied by electron impact and X-ray absorption. *Mailing Add:* Dept Chem McMaster Univ Hamilton ON L8S 4M1 Can. *Fax:* 905-521-2773; *E-Mail:* aph@mcmaster.ca

HITCHCOCK, CLAUDE RAYMOND, surgery; deceased, see previous edition for last biography

HITCHCOCK, DANIEL AUGUSTUS, PLASMA PHYSICS, APPLIED MATHEMATICS. *Current Pos:* ACTG DIV DIR, MATH INFO & COMPUTATIONAL SCI DIV, OFF COMPUT & TECH RES, OFF ENERGY RES, DEPT ENERGY, 91- *Personal Data:* b Cleveland, Ohio, Oct 14, 47; m 73. *Educ:* Univ Calif, Berkeley, AB, 69; Princeton Univ, MA, 71, PhD(appl math), 75. *Prof Exp:* Res assoc plasma physics, Fusion Res Ctr, Univ Tex Austin, 75-91. *Mem:* Am Phys Soc. *Res:* Stability theory for two component tokomaks, nonlinear plasma theory, especially resonance broadening techniques; singular perturbation theory for integro-differential equations. *Mailing Add:* 4507 Chestnut St Bethesda MD 20814-4740. *Fax:* 301-903-7774

HITCHCOCK, DOROTHY JEAN, biology, for more information see previous edition

HITCHCOCK, ELDON TITUS, ANALYTICAL CHEMISTRY. *Current Pos:* from asst prof to assoc prof, 57-69, chmn dept, 79-85, PROF CHEM, COLO COL, 69- *Personal Data:* b Leonard, Mich, Feb 2, 24; m 54, Monique Ariege; c Renee, Janine & Daniel. *Educ:* Western Mich Univ, BS, 46; Univ Mich, PhD, 61. *Prof Exp:* Du Pont instr chem, Univ Mich, 56-57; chmn dept, Bob Jones Univ, 48-54. *Concurrent Pos:* Vis staff mem, Los Alamos Sci Lab, 65- *Mem:* Am Chem Soc; Am Sci Affil; Sigma Xi; fel AAAS; Nat Asn Advisors Health Prof. *Res:* Nonaqueous and high frequency titrimetry; acid-base theory; electroanalytical methods; teaching techniques and curricula in undergraduate chemistry training. *Mailing Add:* Dept Chem Colo Col Colorado Springs CO 80903

HITCHCOCK, HAROLD BRADFORD, science education; deceased, see previous edition for last biography

HITCHCOCK, JOHN PAUL, ANIMAL NUTRITION. *Current Pos:* ASST PROF ANIMAL SCI, UNIV TENN, KNOXVILLE, 75- *Personal Data:* b Muscatine, Iowa, Apr 13, 48; m 75. *Educ:* Iowa State Univ, BS, 68; Pa State Univ, MS, 70; Mich State Univ, PhD(animal husb), 75. *Mem:* Am Soc Animal Sci. *Res:* Vitamin and trace mineral research; amino acid and fatty acid requirements of swine. *Mailing Add:* Dept Animal Sci Univ Tenn 1345 Circle Park Knoxville TN 37996-0001

HITCHCOCK, MARGARET, pharmacology, metabolism, for more information see previous edition

HITCHCOCK-DEGREGORI, SARAH ELLEN, BIOLOGY, BIOCHEMISTRY. *Current Pos:* PROF NEUROSCI & CELL BIOL, ROBERT WOOD JOHNSON MED SCH, UNIV MED & DENT NJ, 85- *Personal Data:* b Washington, DC, Nov 19, 43; 80, Alessandro DeGregori. *Educ:* Smith Col, AB, 65; Wesleyan Univ, MA, 67; Case Western Reserve Univ, PhD(biol), 70. *Honors & Awards:* Res Career Develop Award, NIH, 82-87. *Prof Exp:* Fel Brandeis Univ, 70-73 & MRC Lab Molecular Biol, Cambridge, Eng, 73-76; asst prof biol sci, Carnegie-Mellon Univ, 76-81, assoc prof, 80-85. *Concurrent Pos:* Fel, Muscular Dystrophy Asn, 71-73, Brit-Am Heart Asn, 73-75 & NIH, 75-76; Res Career Develop Award, NIH, 82-87. *Mem:* Am Soc Cell Biol; Biophys Soc. *Res:* Molecular biology of contractile proteins in muscle and non-muscle cells. *Mailing Add:* Dept Neurosci & Cell Biol UMDNJ Robert Wood Johnson Med Sch 675 Hoes Lane Piscataway NJ 08854-5635. *Fax:* 732-235-4029

HITCHINGS, GEORGE HERBERT, BIOCHEMISTRY. *Current Pos:* RETIRED. *Personal Data:* b Hoquiam, Wash, Apr 18, 05; m 33, 89; c 2. *Educ:* Univ Wash, BS, 27, MS, 28; Harvard Univ, PhD(biol chem), 33. *Hon Degrees:* DSc, Univ Mich, Ann Arbor, 71, Univ Strathclyde, 77, NY Med Col & Emory Univ, 81, Duke Univ & Univ NC, 82 & Mt Sinai Sch Med, 83. *Honors & Awards:* Nobel Prize in Physiol & Med, 88; Clowes Mem Lectr & Award, Am Asn Cancer Res, 68, Bruce F Cain Award, 84; Charles E Dohme Lectr & Award, Johns Hopkins, 69; Robert de Villier Sci Award, Leukemia Soc Am, 69; Walter H Hartung Mem Lectr, Univ NC, 72; Med Chem Award, Am Chem Soc, 72, Alfred Burger Award Med Chem, 84; Michael Cross Mem Lectr, Cambridge Univ, 74; Pfizer Lectr, State Univ NY, Stony Brook, 81;

Oscar B Hunter Award, Am Soc Clin Pharmacol, 84; Matthia Lectr Chemother, 84; Award Sci Achievement, Nat Cancer Soc, 78; Papanicolaou Award, 78; C Chester Stock Medal, 81; Burroughs Wellcome Distinguished Lectr, Philadelphia Col Pharm & Sci, 81, Oscar B Hunter Award, Bruce F Cain Award, 84. *Prof Exp:* Instr & tutor biochem sci, Harvard Univ, 32-36, assoc, 36-39; sr instr biochem, Western Res Univ, 39-42; biochemist, Burroughs Wellcome Co, 42-46, chief biochemist, 46-55, assoc res dir, 55-63, res dir, Chemother Div, 63-67, vpres chg res, 67-75, dir, 68-77, dir, Burroughs Wellcome Fund, 68-, emer scientist & consult, 75- *Concurrent Pos:* Res fel, Harvard Univ, 34-36; mem, Comt Growth, Nat Res Coun, 52-53; mem, Chem Panel, Cancer Chemother Nat Serv Ctr, 55-57; mem, Indust Subcomt, Cancer Chemother Nat Comt, 55-57; consult, Cancer Chemother Study Sect, USPHS, 56-60; mem, Ther Comt, Am Cancer Soc, 63-66; vis prof, Brown Univ, 68-80; mem bd trustees, Leukemia Soc, 69-73; adj prof exp med & pharmacol, Duke Univ, 70-85, pharmacol, Univ NC, Chapel Hill, 72-85; adj prof pharmacol, Univ NC, Chapel Hill, 72-; mem vis comt, Drug Res Bd, Nat Res Coun-Nat Acad Sci, 74-75, mem bd sci technol, Nat Res Coun, 75-79; mem, Drug Develop Comt, Nat Cancer Inst, 75-79. *Mem:* Nat Acad Sci; fel AAAS; foreign mem Royal Soc, London; hon fel Royal Soc Med, London; hon mem Am Asn Cancer Res; hon fel Royal Soc Chem; Sigma Xi; Am Chem Soc; Am Soc Biol Chem; Soc Exp Biol Chem. *Res:* Chemistry of condensed pyrimidine systems; purine and pyrimidine antagonists; nutrition and disease; anti-malarials; anti-bacterials; cancer chemotherapy; immunosuppressive drugs; anti-metabolites; organic chemistry of heterocycles; nucleic acids; anti-tumor, anti-malarial and anti-bacterial drugs; medical education and care. *Mailing Add:* Burroughs Wellcome Co 3030 Cornwallis Rd Research Triangle Park NC 27709

HITCHNER, STEPHEN BALLINGER, POULTRY PATHOLOGY. *Current Pos:* chmn dept, 66-76, prof, 66-81, EMER PROF AVIAN DIS, NY STATE COL VET MED, CORNELL UNIV, 81- *Personal Data:* b Daretown, NJ, Feb 4, 16; m 43, Mariana White; c Stephen (deceased), Roger, Sarabelle, Thomas & Robert. *Educ:* Rutgers Univ, BS, 39; Univ Pa, VMD, 43. *Honors & Awards:* Special Serv Award, Am Asn Avian Path, 81. *Prof Exp:* Instr avian path, Col Vet Med, Univ Ill, 46; assoc animal & poultry path, Agr Exp Sta, Va Polytech Inst, 47-49; res prof poultry path, Agr Exp Sta, Mass State Col, 49-53; res vet, Am Sci Labs, 53-58, dir res, 59-60; dir res, I&M Labs, 60-64, Amdal Co, 64-65 & infectious dis res div, Abbott Labs, 65-66. *Concurrent Pos:* Lectr, VOCA, Bolivia, 87, 89; vaccine consult, Int Execs Serv Corps, Peru, 87-88; poultry path consult, Int Exec Serv Corps, Egypt, 94. *Mem:* Am Vet Med Asn; Poultry Sci Asn; Am Asn Avian Path (pres, 60-61); NY Acad Sci; Asn Avian Vet. *Res:* Virology; poultry vaccine production. *Mailing Add:* 24110 Kinnairds Point Dr Worton MD 21678

HITCHON, BRIAN, geochemistry, for more information see previous edition

HITE, GILBERT J, MEDICINAL CHEMISTRY. *Current Pos:* PROF MED CHEM, SCH PHARM, UNIV CONN, 73-, HEAD SECT MED CHEM & PHARMACOGNOSY, 76- *Personal Data:* b Boston, Mass, Jan 24, 31; m 60; c 2. *Educ:* New Eng Col Pharm, BS, 54; Univ Wis, MS, 57, PhD(pharmaceut chem), 59. *Prof Exp:* Assoc prof pharmaceut chem & chmn dept, Col Pharm, Howard Univ, 59-61; from asst prof to prof pharmaceut chem, Col Pharm, Columbia Univ, 61-73, chmn dept chem, 67-72. *Concurrent Pos:* Vis prof, Dept Crystallog, Univ Pittsburgh, 71-73. *Mem:* Am Pharmaceut Asn; Am Chem Soc; Am Asn Col Pharm; Am Asn Pharmaceut Scientists; Am Crystallog Asn. *Res:* Mechanisms of organic reactions; structure-activity relationships; modes of drug action; stereochemical aspects of drug action. *Mailing Add:* Sch Pharm Univ Conn U-92 372 Fairfield Rd Storrs CT 06269-0001

HITE, J ROGER, CHEMICAL ENGINEERING. *Current Pos:* chem engr, Shell Develop Co, 66-69, res engr, 69-74, res engr, 75-79, mgr engr, Shell Oil Co, 80-90, DIR PROD RES, SHELL DEVELOP DIV, 90- *Personal Data:* b Houston, Tex, Aug 18, 39; m 60; c 3. *Educ:* Tulane Univ, BS, 61; Princeton Univ, MA, 63, PhD(chem eng), 65. *Prof Exp:* NATO fel, Phys Chem Inst, Munich, 65-66. *Mem:* Am Chem Soc; Am Inst Chem Engrs; Soc Petrol Engrs. *Res:* Reservoir engineering. *Mailing Add:* 3734 Ella Lee Lane Houston TX 77027

HITE, MARK, TOXICOLOGY, SAFETY ASSESSMENT. *Current Pos:* DIR, DRUG SAFETY EVAL, WYETH-AYERST RES, 85- *Personal Data:* b Cambridge, Mass, Feb 7, 35; m 60, Nancy S Gordon; c Gary & Deborah. *Educ:* Rensselaer Polytech Inst, BCE, 56; Univ Rochester, MS, 57; Univ Cincinnati, SCD(indust toxicol), 60; Am Bd Toxicol, dipl. *Prof Exp:* Sr asst scientist, USPHS, 60-63; toxicologist, Dow Chem Co, 63-64; sr res toxicologist, Merck Inst Therapeut Res, 64-70, dir toxicol, 67-70, dir toxicol & path, 70-85. *Mem:* AAAS; Environ Mutagen Soc; Sigma Xi; Soc Toxicol; Am Col Toxicol; fel Acad Toxicol Sci. *Res:* Pharmaceutical and chemical safety evaluations; mutagenic and carcinogenic effects of chemicals and drugs; genetic toxicology; safety assessment; risk analysis. *Mailing Add:* 628 North Hampton Rd Norristown PA 19403. *Fax:* 732-274-5325

HITE, S(AMUEL) C(HARLES), CHEMICAL ENGINEERING. *Current Pos:* PROF CHEM ENG & CHMN DEPT, ROSE-HULMAN INST TECHNOL, 70- *Personal Data:* b Ft Wayne, Ind, Aug 20, 22; m 53; c 1. *Educ:* Purdue Univ, BSChE, 43, PhD(chem eng), 51. *Prof Exp:* From instr to assoc prof chem eng, Purdue Univ, 43-57; prof & chmn dept, Univ Ky, 57-70. *Concurrent Pos:* Res assoc, Purdue Univ, 46-51; consult, Com Solvents Corp & Eli Lilly & Co. *Mem:* Am Chem Soc; Am Inst Chem Engrs. *Res:* Gas engineering; unit process and operations. *Mailing Add:* 5577 S Canal St Terre Haute IN 47802

HITES, RONALD ATLEE, ANALYTICAL CHEMISTRY, ENVIRONMENTAL CHEMISTRY. *Current Pos:* prof, 79-89, DISTINGUISHED PROF PUB & ENVIRON AFFAIRS & CHEM, INDIANA UNIV, 89- *Personal Data:* b Jackson, Mich, Sept 19, 42; m 64, Bonnie R Carlson; c Veronica, Karin & David. *Educ:* Oakland Univ, BA, 64; Mass Inst Technol, PhD(anal chem), 68. *Honors & Awards:* Award for Creative Advan in Environ Sci & Technol, Am Chem Soc, 91; Founders Award, Soc Environ Toxicol & Chem, 93. *Prof Exp:* Fel chem, Arg Res Serv, 68-69; res staff chem, Mass Inst Technol, 69-72, from asst prof to assoc prof chem eng, 72-79. *Concurrent Pos:* Pres, Am Soc Mass Spec, 88-90; assoc ed, Environ Sci & Technol, 90-; mem, Comt Toxicol, Nat Res Coun, 91-93. *Mem:* Am Chem Soc; Am Soc Mass Spectrometry; AAAS; Int Asn Great Lakes Res; Sigma Xi. *Res:* Organic analytical chemistry; organic environmental chemistry; mass spectrometry; atmospheric deposition. *Mailing Add:* Sch Public & Environ Affairs Indiana Univ Bloomington IN 47405. *Fax:* 812-855-1076; *E-Mail:* hitesr@indiana.edu

HITLIN, DAVID G, ELEMENTARY PARTICLE PHYSICS. *Current Pos:* assoc prof, 79-85, PROF PHYSICS, CALIF INST TECHNOL, 85- *Personal Data:* b Brooklyn, NY, Apr 15, 42; m 66, 82, Abigail Gumbiner. *Educ:* Columbia Univ, BA, 63, MA, 65, PhD(physics), 68. *Prof Exp:* Instr physics, Columbia Univ, 67-69; res assoc, Stanford Linear Accelerator Ctr, 69-72; asst prof, Stanford Univ, 72-75; asst prof, Stanford Linear Accelerator Ctr, 75-79. *Concurrent Pos:* Spokesman, Babar Collab. *Mem:* Fel Am Phys Soc. *Res:* Experimental high energy physics; with emphasis on e plus e minus annihilation; weak decays of elementary particles. *Mailing Add:* 356-48 Lauritsen Lab Calif Inst Technol Pasadena CA 91125. *Fax:* 626-795-3951

HITNER, HENRY WILLIAM, PHARMACOLOGY, PHYSIOLOGY. *Current Pos:* from asst prof to assoc prof, 77-88, PROF PHARMACOL, PHILADELPHIA COL OSTEOPATH, 88-, VCHMN, DEPT PHYSIOL & PHARMACOL, 82- *Personal Data:* b Bethlehem, Pa, Oct 9, 39; m 66; c 2. *Educ:* Moravian Col, BS, 65; Hahnemann Med Col, MS, 72, PhD(pharmacol), 74. *Prof Exp:* Biologist toxicol, Pharmachem Corp, 66; res asst toxicol, Wyeth Labs, Inc, 66-69; pharmacologist, Nat Drug Co, 69-70; instr biol, Montgomery Co Community Col, 74-77. *Mem:* Am Soc Pharmacol & Exp Therapeut; Sigma Xi; Mid Atlantic Reproduction & Teratology Asn. *Res:* Autonomic nervous system; shock; drug abuse; hallucinogens; teratology. *Mailing Add:* Philadelphia Col Osteopath 506 Madison Ave Ft Washington PA 19034

HITT, JOHN BURTON, CELL BIOLOGY. *Current Pos:* RETIRED. *Personal Data:* b Springfield, Ohio, June 15, 31; m 57, 85; c 7. *Educ:* Wittenberg Univ, BS, 57; Ohio State Univ, MS, 60, PhD(zool), 69. *Prof Exp:* Teacher gen sci, High Sch, Ohio, 60-61; from instr to assoc prof biol, Wittenberg Univ, 61-94. *Mem:* AAAS; Sigma Xi. *Res:* Studies of calcium transport in mitochondria of the earthworm calciferous gland; glucose as a depressor of menstrual cramps. *Mailing Add:* 224 Souters Lane Brunswick GA 31520

HITTELMAN, ALLEN M, DATA MANAGEMENT, MAPPING. *Current Pos:* DIR, WORLD DATA CTR-A SOLID EARTH GEOPHYS & CHIEF, SOLID EARTH GEOPHYS DIV, NAT OCEANIC & ATMOSPHERIC ADMIN, 94- *Personal Data:* b New York, NY, Dec 21, 45; div; c 2. *Educ:* Queen's Col, BS, 67; Univ Chicago, MS, 69. *Honors & Awards:* Super Accomplishment Award, US Naval Oceanog Off, 73. *Prof Exp:* Geophysicist oceanog, US Naval Oceanog Off, 67-75; sect chief geophys, Nat Geophys & Solar Terrestrial Data Ctr, 75-82; mgr, Data Mgt, Arco Explor & Technol Co, 82-86. *Concurrent Pos:* Res asst, Advan Res Proj Admin, 67-69; chmn, Marine Geophys Data Exchange Format Task Group, 77. *Mem:* Sigma Xi; Am Geophys Union; Soc Explor Geophysicists; Am Asn Petrol Geologists; Am Petrol Inst. *Res:* Geophysical database systems; potential field continuation; data access on web; CD-ROM access technologies. *Mailing Add:* Nat Geophys Data Ctr NOAA Mail Code E/GC 325 Broadway Boulder CO 80303. *Fax:* 303-497-6513; *E-Mail:* amh@ngdc.noaa.gov

HITTELMAN, WALTER NATHAN, CELL BIOLOGY, CYTOGENETICS. *Current Pos:* Fel, 72-74, res assoc, 74-75, from asst prof to assoc prof, 75-85, PROF CELL BIOL, M D ANDERSON HOSP & TUMOR INST, UNIV TEX, HOUSTON, 85- *Personal Data:* b Fontana, Calif, May 22, 44; div; c 3. *Educ:* Univ Calif, Berkeley, BS, 66, MS, 68, PhD(biophys), 72. *Mem:* Am Soc Cell Biol; Fedn Am Scientists; Am Asn Cancer Res. *Res:* Growth regulation and cytogenetics of mammalian cells with special regard to the process of malignancy in humans. *Mailing Add:* M D Anderson Cancer Ctr Univ Tex 1515 Holcombe Blvd Houston TX 77030-4095. *Fax:* 713-792-3754

HITTINGER, WILLIAM C(HARLES), PHYSICAL METALLURGY. *Current Pos:* RETIRED. *Personal Data:* b Bethlehem, Pa, Nov 10, 22; m 44, Elizabeth Herman; c Patricia (Bunche), William J, David C & Nancy (Lehrer). *Educ:* Lehigh Univ, BS, 44. *Hon Degrees:* Dr, Lehigh Univ, 74. *Honors & Awards:* Frederik Philips Medal, Inst Elec & Electronics Engrs, 86. *Prof Exp:* Mat Engr, Western Elec Co, 46-52; prod mgr, Nat Union Radio Corp, 52-54; mem tech staff semiconductor res & develop, Bell Tel Labs, 54-57, dept head, 57-60, dir, 60-62, exec dir, NJ, 62-66; pres, Bellcomm, Inc, DC, 66-68; pres, Gen Instrument Corp, 68-70; gen mgr & pres, RCA Solid State Div, RCA Corp, 70-73, exec vpres consumer elec & solid state electronics, 73-75, exec vpres, 74-86. *Concurrent Pos:* Corp dir. *Mem:* Nat Acad Eng; fel Inst Elec & Electronics Engrs; Am Inst Mining Metall & Petrol Engrs; fel Royal Soc Arts. *Res:* Germanium crystal growth; diffused silicon transistors; management of electronics research and development. *Mailing Add:* 149 Bellview Ave Summit NJ 07901. *Fax:* 908-277-1261

HITTLE, DOUGLAS CARL, ENERGY CONSERVATION, HEAT TRANSFER & THERMODYNAMICS. *Current Pos:* DIR, SOLAR ENERGY APPLNS LAB, COLO STATE UNIV, 89- *Personal Data:* b Ft Collins, Colo, Apr 16, 47; m 69; c 2. *Educ:* Univ Ill, BS, 69, MS, 75, PhD(mech eng), 81. *Prof Exp:* Mech engr, Chanute AFB, 69-73; prin investr, US Army Construct Eng Res Lab, 73-81, res team leader, 81-86; assoc prof, Purdue Univ, 86-89. *Concurrent Pos:* Consult, Architect US Capitol, 77- & Elec Power Res Inst, 87-; vis researcher, Bldg Res Estab, UK, 84. *Mem:* Fel Am Soc Heating Refrig & Air-Conditioning Engrs; Am Soc Mech Engrs; Int Solar Energy Soc; Sigma Xi; AAAS. *Res:* Building energy conservation; simulation of building energy systems; control of heating and air-conditioning systems; renewable solar energy system development; expert systems for hvac design; air flow and ventilation; heat transfer and thermodynamics; neural networks. *Mailing Add:* 2640 Centennial Dr Ft Collins CO 80526-5400. *Fax:* 970-491-8544; *E-Mail:* hittle@longs.lance.colostate.edu

HITZ, CHESTER W, pomology; deceased, see previous edition for last biography

HITZEMAN, JEAN WALTER, CELL BIOLOGY. *Current Pos:* PROF ANAT & PHYSIOL, DEPT BIOL SCI, STATE UNIV NY, BROCKPORT, 77-; AT ZOOL DEPT, WASHINGTON STATE UNIV, PULLMAN. *Personal Data:* b Chicago, Ill, Oct 29, 26. *Educ:* Barry Col, BS, 50; DePaul Univ, MS, 56; Univ Mich, PhD(zool), 62. *Prof Exp:* Teacher parochial elem schs, Fla, 45-53; teacher parochial sec schs, Mich, 53-59; from instr to prof biol, Siena Heights Col, 62-70; prof & chmn dept biol, J C Smith Univ, 70-73; dir of studies, Adrian Dominican Generalate, 73-75; prof biol & chmn div natural sci & math, Johnson State Col, Vt, 75-77. *Concurrent Pos:* NIH res grant gen med, 63-70; chmn dept biol, Siena Heights Col, 68-70. *Mem:* AAAS; Sigma Xi. *Res:* Pathways of metabolism in Leydig cells of the mouse; hormonal control of sperm differentiation. *Mailing Add:* Dept Biol Sci State Univ NY Col 350 New Campus Dr Brockport NY 14420-2915

HITZMAN, DONALD OLIVER, BACTERIOLOGY, GEOCHEMISTRY. *Current Pos:* RES DIR, GEO-MICROBIAL TECHNOL INC, 85-; VPRES RES, INJECTECH INC, 85- *Personal Data:* b Milwaukee, Wis, Dec 2, 26; m 49, Mary E Neumann; c Murray W & Daniel C. *Educ:* Carleton Col, AB, 48; Univ Ill, MS, 50, PhD(bact), 56. *Prof Exp:* Asst, Univ Ill, 48-50 & 52-54; res bacteriologist, Tex Co, 50; asst, Univ Southern Calif, 50-51; res bacteriologist, Phillips Petrol Co, 54-85. *Concurrent Pos:* Consult petrol microbiol & fermentation, 85- *Mem:* Am Chem Soc; Am Soc Microbiol; Soc Indust Microbiol; AAAS; Geochem Soc; Soc Petrol Engrs. *Res:* Bacteriological aspects of petroleum and petroleum products; microbial prospection; microbial enhanced oil recovery; geochemical prospection for oil and gas. *Mailing Add:* 1717 Church Ct Bartlesville OK 74006. *Fax:* 918-535-2564; *E-Mail:* gmtgeochem@aol.com

HIU, DAWES NYUKLEU, ORGANIC CHEMISTRY. *Current Pos:* PRES, CHAMINADE UNIV EDUC FOUND, 94- *Personal Data:* b Honolulu, Hawaii, Feb 14, 27; m 55, Leonora Lum; c Stephen, Michael, Vincent, Sharon & Brenda (Shin). *Educ:* Univ Southern Calif, BA, 50; Univ Hawaii, PhD(chem), 59. *Prof Exp:* Chemist, Res Div, Allis-Chalmers Mfg Co, Wis, 52-54; asst chem, Univ Hawaii, 54-56, from instr to asst prof, 57-60; from asst prof to prof chem, Chaminade Col, Honolulu, 60-67, acad dean, 68-76, vpres acad affairs, 78-89. *Mem:* Am Chem Soc; Sigma Xi. *Res:* Analysis and structural determination of volatiles and pigments from natural products, especially by chromatographic means; infra-red spectroscopy. *Mailing Add:* 3276 Ala Laulani Honolulu HI 96818

HIVELY, ROBERT ARLAND, ANALYTICAL CHEMISTRY, CHROMATOGRAPHY. *Current Pos:* RETIRED. *Personal Data:* b Salem, Ohio, Apr 27, 21; m 48, Miriam E Braziell; c William R & Jane A. *Educ:* Mt Union Col, BS, 43; Univ Akron, MS, 53. *Prof Exp:* Control chemist, Goodyear Tire & Rubber Co, 45-53, from res chemist to sr res chemist, 53-65, sect head chromatography, 65-74, sect head quant anal, 74-77, sect head separations & identifications, 77-80, res scientist, 80-81, res & develop Assoc, 81-87. *Mem:* Am Chem Soc. *Res:* Separations and identifications; gas and liquid partition chromatography; mass spectroscopy; ion exchange; organic qualitative analysis; ultraviolet spectrophotometry; polarography; atomic absorption spectroscopy. *Mailing Add:* 2431 27th St Cuyahoga Falls OH 44223

HIX, ELLIOTT LEE, PHARMACOLOGY. *Current Pos:* from instr to assoc prof, 53-67, chmn dept, 67-75, PROF PHARMACOL, KIRKSVILLE COL OSTEOP MED, 67- *Personal Data:* b Rock Hill, SC, July 28, 25; m 50; c 4. *Educ:* Univ Ga, BS, 49; Kans State Univ, MS, 50, PhD(mammal physiol, biochem), 53. *Prof Exp:* Asst physiol, Kans State Univ, 49-50, asst animal sci, 50-52, instr nutrit physiol, 52-53. *Mem:* Am Physiol Soc; Sigma Xi. *Res:* Renal physiology; autonomic innervation of kidney and its influence on kidney function; somato-renal and viscero-renal reflexology; trophic functions of kidney innervation; biochemical synthesis in transplanted kidney; experimental surgery. *Mailing Add:* 811 S Cottage Grove Ave Kirksville MO 63501

HIX, HOMER BENNETT, organic chemistry; deceased, see previous edition for last biography

HIXON, MARK A, MARINE ICHTHYOLOGY. *Current Pos:* asst prof, 84-89, ASSOC PROF, ORE STATE UNIV, 89- *Personal Data:* b San Diego, Calif, June 10, 51; m 88; c 1. *Educ:* Univ Calif, Santa Barbara, BA, 73, MA, 74, PhD(pop & aquatic biol), 79. *Prof Exp:* Seasonal aide, Calif Dept Fish & Game, 73-74; teaching asst, Univ Calif, Santa Barbara, 74-76, res asst, 77-79; NSF fel, Univ Calif, Irvine, 79 & Univ Hawaii, 79-80; vis prof, Univ Hawaii, 80-81; lectr, Univ Calif, Irvine, 81-84. *Concurrent Pos:* vis prof, Univ VI, 83- *Mem:* AAAS; Am Soc Zoologists; Animal Behav Soc; Ecol Soc Am; Soc Study Evolution. *Res:* Community ecology of marine reef fishes and benthos; behavioral ecology of reef fishes and hummingbirds; theories of territoriality, foraging and mechanisms maintaining local species diversity. *Mailing Add:* Dept Biol Ore State Univ 2042 Cordley Hall Corvallis OR 97331-2908

HIXON, SUMNER B, IMAGE INTERPRETATION, PETROGRAPHY. *Current Pos:* PROGRAMMER, UNISYS, 88- *Personal Data:* b La Junta, Colo, Sept 7, 30; m 61, Helen Bicknell; c Nancy, Edward & Richard. *Educ:* Univ Colo, BA, 52; Univ Tex, MA, 59; Univ Mich, PhD(chem metall), 64. *Prof Exp:* Asst, Univs Tex, Mich & Eastern Mich; asst prof geol & geol eng, Univ Miss, 64-67; engr sr, Lockheed Electronics Co, Houston, 67-81; sr geologist, geophysicist & image interpreter, Aero Serv, Houston, 81-83; consult, Monarch Int, 83-85, chief geologist, 85- *Concurrent Pos:* Jr geologist, Pa State Geol Surv, 59 & Great Lakes Res, Mich, 61; geologist, Que Dept Mines, 60 & 64 & NASA, Ala, 65; consult, Consumers Power Co, Mich, 62 & Dow Chem Co, 63; fac fel, NASA, Johnson Space Ctr, Houston, 67. *Mem:* Am Asn Petrol Geol; Am Soc Photogram. *Res:* Sedimentary petrography; computer programming applications to photometry, to earth, moon, and martian photography and to data storage and retrieval; lunar geology; remote sensing applications from space and aircraft. *Mailing Add:* 504 Misty Lane Friendswood TX 77546-4532

HIXSON, ELMER LAVERNE, ELECTROACOUSTICS. *Current Pos:* from asst prof to assoc prof elec eng, 54-70, PROF ELEC ENG, UNIV TEX, AUSTIN, 71- *Personal Data:* b Arlington, Calif, Sept 29, 24; m 45; c 5. *Educ:* Univ Tex, BS, 47, MS, 48, PhD(elec eng), 60. *Prof Exp:* Res engr, Elec Eng Res Lab, Univ Tex, 47-48; electronic scientist, Electronics Lab, US Navy, 48-54. *Mem:* Fel Acoust Soc Am; sr mem Inst Elec & Electronics Engrs; Inst Noise Control Eng; fel Am Soc Eng Educ (vpres, 78-79). *Res:* Acoustics; transducers; mechanical vibrations. *Mailing Add:* Dept Elec & Comput Eng Univ Tex Austin TX 78712

HIXSON, FLOYD MARCUS, ANIMAL BREEDING, ENVIRONMENTAL PHYSIOLOGY. *Current Pos:* RETIRED. *Personal Data:* b Holdenville, Okla, May 15, 18; m 41; c 5. *Educ:* Okla State Univ, BS, 41; Kans State Univ, MS, 48, PhD(genetics), 60. *Prof Exp:* Assoc prof poultry husb, Okla State Univ, 49-50; prof animal sci, Calif State Univ, Fresno, 51-80. *Mem:* Poultry Sci Asn. *Mailing Add:* 1712 Harvard Ave Clovis CA 93612

HIXSON, JAMES ELMER, GENETICS. *Current Pos:* asst scientist, 85-89, ASSOC SCIENTIST, SOUTHWEST FOUND, BIOMED RES, 90- *Personal Data:* b San Diego, Calif, Nov 24, 52; m 87. *Educ:* Univ Tex, Austin, BA, 78; Univ Mich, Ann Arbor, PhD(human genetics), 83. *Prof Exp:* Teaching asst human genetics, Univ Mich, 79-80; fel, Stanford Univ, Sch Med, 83-85. *Concurrent Pos:* Adj asst prof, Univ Tex, Health Sci Ctr, San Antonio, 85-90, adj assoc prof, 90-; prin investr, NIH grant, 88-93. *Mem:* Am Heart Asn; Int Soc Heart Res; Am Soc Human Genetics. *Res:* Identification of genetic factors that cause predisposition to heart disease; genetic analysis of atherosclerosis in human populations; lipid metabolism in non-human primates. *Mailing Add:* 19820 Chimney Creek Rd Helotes TX 78023

HIXSON, STEPHEN SHERWIN, ORGANIC CHEMISTRY. *Current Pos:* from asst prof to assoc prof, 70-80, PROF CHEM, UNIV MASS, 80- *Personal Data:* b Philadelphia, Pa, Sept 4, 43; m 67, 86; c 3. *Educ:* Univ Pa, BA, 65; Univ Wis, PhD(chem), 70. *Prof Exp:* Fel chem, Harvard Univ, 69-70. *Concurrent Pos:* NSF fel, 69-70. *Mem:* Am Chem Soc. *Res:* Organic photochemistry; photochemical probes of the structure of biological systems. *Mailing Add:* Dept Chem Univ Mass Amherst MA 01003-0002

HIXSON, SUSAN HARVILL, BIO-ORGANIC CHEMISTRY. *Current Pos:* PROG DIR, DIV UNDERGRAD EDUC, NSF, 92- *Personal Data:* b Orange, NJ, Sept 26, 44; c Thomas & David. *Educ:* Univ Mich, Ann Arbor, BSCh, 65; Univ Wis-Madison, PhD(biochem), 70. *Prof Exp:* Instr chem, Boston Univ, 69-70; res assoc, Univ Mass, Amherst, 70-73; from asst prof to prof chem, Mt Holyoke Col, 73-93. *Concurrent Pos:* NIH fel, 71-72; vis prof, Dept Biochem, Univ NC, Chapel Hill, 80; vis scientist, Dept Biochem & Molecular Biol, Univ Tex Health Sci Ctr, Houston; coun, Council Undergrad Res, AAAS, 82-88. *Mem:* Am Chem Soc; Sigma Xi; Asn Women Sci; Am Soc Biol Chemists; AAAS; Coun Undergrad Res. *Res:* Photoaffinity labeling of enzymes; enzyme chemistry; glycoprotein biochemistry. *Mailing Add:* NSF Div Undergrad Educ 4201 Wilson Blvd Arlington VA 22230. *Fax:* 703-306-0445; *E-Mail:* shixson@nsf.gov

HIYAMA, TETSUO, BIOCHEMISTRY. *Current Pos:* assoc prof, 79-87, PROF, SAITAMA UNIV, JAPAN, 87-, DEPT CHMN, 89- *Personal Data:* b Tokyo, Japan, Jan 28, 39; m 80, Aiko Narui; c Noriko & Junko. *Educ:* Univ Tokyo, BS, 62, MA, 64, PhD(biochem), 67. *Prof Exp:* Asst instr microbiol, Univ Tokyo, 67; NIH fel, Johnson Found, Univ Pa, 67-69; NSF fel, C F Kettering Lab, Ohio, 69-71; Carnegie Inst res fel, Carnegie Inst, Dept Plant Biol, 71-74; asst res biochemist, Univ Calif, Berkeley, 74-79; assoc prof, Nat Inst Basic Biol, Japan, 79-82; prof, Univ Tokyo, 91-93. *Mem:* AAAS; Am Soc Plant Physiologists; Am Soc Photobiol; Int Soc Plant Molecular Biol. *Res:* Photosynthesis and bioenergetics; photosynthesis; thermophilic organisms; heat shock proteins. *Mailing Add:* Dept Biochem Saitama Univ Urawa Saitama 338 Japan. *Fax:* 81-48-858-3698

HIZA, MICHAEL JOHN, JR, PHASE EQUILIBRIA, GAS SEPARATION & PURIFICATION. *Current Pos:* PRES, DELTA-MH INC, BOULDER, COLO, 87- *Personal Data:* b Pueblo, Colo, Sept 8, 31; m 53, Beverly Masters; c Michael D & Margaret M. *Educ:* Univ Colo, BS, 53, MS, 60. *Honors & Awards:* Russell B Scott Mem Award, Cryogenic Eng Conf Bd, 67. *Prof Exp:* Res chem engr properties mat, Cryogenics Div, Nat Bur Stand, 56, proj engr hydrogen & helium liquefaction, 56-59, res chem engr gas purification, 59-60, proj leader properties cryogenic fluid mixtures, 60-78, res chem engr properties fluid mixtures, 78-80, leader, unit opers & process group, Chem Eng Sci Div, 80-83, actg chief, Chem Process Metrol Div, 83, actg chief, Chem Eng Sci Div, Nat Bur Stand, 84-86. *Concurrent Pos:* Res assoc chem eng, Univ Colo, 62-68; consult hydrogen safety, Lockheed Calif Co & NAm Aviation, Inc, 63-64; mem, task group, Comt Data Sci & Technol Chem Indust, 78-86; adj prof chem eng, Univ Wyo, 77-85. *Mem:* Am Inst Chem Engrs; Am Chem Soc; AAAS; Sigma Xi. *Res:* Low temperature phase equilibria properties of fluid mixtures; physical adsorption of pure fluids and of fluid mixtures at high pressure and low temperatures; measurement and prediction of liquified natural gas densities for equity in trade. *Mailing Add:* PO Box 490 Story WY 82842

HJELLE, JOSEPH THOMAS, CELLULAR PHARMACOLOGY, MESOTHELIAL CELL BIOLOGY. *Current Pos:* asst prof, 80-86, ASSOC PROF PHARMACOL, COL MED, UNIV ILL, PEORIA, 87- *Personal Data:* b LaCrosse, Wis, Aug 26, 49; m 93, Marcia Miller; c Kate & Andrew. *Educ:* Univ Wis-LaCrosse, BS, 71; Univ Ariz, PhD(pharmacol), 76. *Prof Exp:* Fel pharmacol, Roche Inst Molecular Biol, 76-78; fel cell biol, Pharmaceutical Mfrs Asn, Found Inst Cellular & Molecular Path, 78-80. *Concurrent Pos:* Prin investr, Univ Ill, 80-; consult, 85- *Mem:* Sigma Xi; Am Soc Pharmacol & Exp Therapeut; AAAS; Int Soc Peritoneal Dialysis. *Res:* Studies of drug localization and action on subcellular organelles; mesothelial cell biology; peritoneal dialysis; polycystic kidney disease; renal toxicology; effects of endotoxin in disease and toxicology. *Mailing Add:* Univ Ill Col Med One Illinios Dr PO Box 1649 Peoria IL 61656-1649. *Fax:* 309-671-8403

HJELME, DAG ROAR, ELECTRICAL ENGINEERING. *Current Pos:* res asst, 84-88, RES ASSOC, UNIV COLO, 88- *Personal Data:* b Valldal, Norway, Mar 25, 59. *Educ:* Norweg Inst Technol, dipl eng, 82; Univ Colo, PhD(elec eng), 88. *Prof Exp:* Res asst, Norweg Inst Technol, 83-84. *Mem:* Optical Soc Am; Inst Elec & Electronics Engrs; Int Soc Optical Eng. *Res:* Semiconductor lasers; spectral and dynamic properties, stabilization, optical feedback and noise; injection locking; ultrafast lasers; noise analysis and application to optical sampling; microwave optics; application to integrated optics and microwave device characterization. *Mailing Add:* Nidaroyat Eight N 7034 Trondheim N 7030 Trondheim Norway

HJELMELAND, LEONARD M, GROWTH FACTORS, FIBROSIS. *Current Pos:* ASSOC PROF OPHTHAL, UNIV CALIF, DAVIS, 86- *Educ:* Stanford Univ, PhD(phys biochem), 79. *Mailing Add:* Dept Biol Chem Univ Calif Sch Med Davis CA 95616

HJELMFELT, ALLEN T, JR, HYDROLOGY, CIVIL ENGINEERING. *Current Pos:* PROF AGR ENG, UNIV MO, COLUMBIA, 78-; RES HYDRAUL ENGR & RES LEADER, AGR RES SERV, USDA, 78- *Personal Data:* b Holdrege, Nebr, Oct 21, 37; m 80, Marian Parks; c 4. *Educ:* Kans State Univ, BS, 59; Univ Kans, MS, 61; Northwestern Univ, PhD(fluid mech), 65. *Honors & Awards:* J C Stevens Award, Am Soc Civil Engrs, 83; Fel, Am Soc Civil Engrs, 85. *Prof Exp:* Jr civil engr, State Calif Dept Water Resources, 59; asst instr eng mech, Univ Kans, 59-62; assoc develop engr, Nuclear Div, Union Carbide Corp, 62-63; res engr, Northwestern Univ, 63-64; from asst prof to prof civil eng, Univ Mo, Columbia, 65-77. *Concurrent Pos:* Consult, Mineracao Vera Cruz, 76; vis prof, Univ Fed do Para, Belem, Brazil, 76. *Mem:* Fel Am Soc Civil Engrs; Am Geophys Union; Int Asn Hydraul Res; Am Water Resources Asn; fel Indian Asn Hydrologists. *Res:* Hydrologic processes on small watersheds. *Mailing Add:* 269 Agr Engr Bldg Univ Mo Columbia MO 65211. *E-Mail:* aeallenh@muccmail.missouri.edu

HLA, TIMOTHY TUN, ANGIOGENESIS, VASCULAR BIOLOGY. *Current Pos:* Fel, 88-91, SCIENTIST I, HOLLAND LABS, AM RED CROSS, 91- *Personal Data:* b Rangoon, Burma, June 9, 62; m 88, Jeanne Wadsworth; c Hilary M & Jonathan M. *Educ:* Western Ill Univ, BS, 82; George Washington Univ, PhD(biochem), 88. *Concurrent Pos:* Fac mem biol, Immaculata Col High Sch, 86-87; adj asst prof, Genetics Prog, George Washington Univ, 92- *Mem:* Am Soc Cell Biol; AAAS; NY Acad Scis. *Res:* Molecular mechanisms of blood vessel function, growth and differentiation. *Mailing Add:* Holland Lab Molecular Biol Am Red Cross 15601 Crabbs Branch Way Rockville MD 20855-2743. *E-Mail:* hlatim@hlsun.red-cross.org

HLASTA, DENNIS JOHN, MEDICINAL CHEMISTRY. *Current Pos:* Sr res chemist, Sterling Winthrop Res Inst, 79-83, group leader, 83-90, RES LEADER, STERLING RES GROUP, 90- *Personal Data:* b Youngstown, Ohio, July 13, 53; m 75; c 4. *Educ:* Ohio State Univ, BS, 75; Yale Univ, MS, 77, MPh, 78, PhD(org chem), 79. *Mem:* Am Chem Soc; Int Soc Heterocyclic Chem; AAAS. *Res:* Design and synthesis of organic compounds as potential therapeutic agents. *Mailing Add:* R W Johnson Pharmaceut Res Inst Raritan NJ 08869

HLAVACEK, ROBERT ALLEN, MATERIAL SCIENCE. *Current Pos:* sr res scientist, 82-95, GROUP LEADER TECH SERVS, DAVIS & GECK, DIV AM CYANAMID, 95- *Personal Data:* b Bridgeport, Conn, June 14, 49; m 72, Elaine Valko; c Robert & Kara. *Educ:* Univ Conn, BS, 71, MS, 74. *Prof Exp:* Develop engr, Uniroyal Chem, 71-79; sr proj engr, Raymark Corp, 79-82. *Mem:* AAAS. *Res:* Development of biodegradeable, implantable, surgical devices. *Mailing Add:* 42 Visconti Dr Naugatuck CT 06770

HLAVACEK, ROBERT JOHN, FOOD CHEMISTRY, QUALITY SYSTEMS-FOODS. *Current Pos:* RETIRED. *Personal Data:* b Chicago, Ill, Apr 18, 23; m 51; c 3. *Educ:* Lawrence Col, BA, 44; Northwestern Univ, PhD(org chem), 49. *Prof Exp:* Chemist, Swift & Co, Ill, 48-50, head indust oils res, 50-53, asst to dir labs, 53, spec assignment, 53-54, head finished prod qual div, 54-56, asst head fresh meats res, 56-59, head table ready meats res, 59-63; asst to tech dir, Hunt-Wesson Foods, 63-64, assoc dir res & develop, 64-73; vpres res & qual control, Best Foods Div, CPC Int, Inc, Union, NJ, 73-76; asst vpres, 76-77, vpres qual assurance, Thomas J Lipton, 77-88. *Mem:* Am Chem Soc; Am Oil Chemists Soc; fel Inst Food Technologists. *Res:* Fats and oils chemistry and processing, sensory evaluation methodology; packaging; analytical methods; quality control methodology. *Mailing Add:* 16 Oechsner Ct Berkeley Heights NJ 07922-1492

HLAVACEK, VLADIMIR, CHEMICAL ENGINEERING. *Current Pos:* PROF CHEM ENG, STATE UNIV NY, BUFFALO, 81- *Personal Data:* b Prague, Czech, Feb 28, 39; US citizen; m 92, Zdena Pundova. *Educ:* Inst Chem Technol, Prague, MS, 61, PhD, 64; Charles Univ, Prague, BS, 67. *Honors & Awards:* Wilhelm Award. *Prof Exp:* Prof & sr res scientist, chem eng, Inst Chem Technol, Prague, 67-80; prof chem eng, Cath Univ, Leuven, Belg, 80-81. *Concurrent Pos:* Ed, Chem Eng Sci, 75-81; vis prof, Cath Univ, Leuven, Belg, 74 & 80-81, Leningrad, USSR, 73 & Zurich, Switz, 77; consult, var co; C C Furmes Prof, 91. *Mem:* Am Inst Chem Engrs; Am Ceramic Soc; Soc Indust & Appl Math; Mat Res Soc. *Res:* Chemical reactor theory; flames; separation process; nonlinear boundary value problems; bifurcation theory; synthesis of ceramic materials. *Mailing Add:* 4921 Pineledge Dr W Clarence NY 14031

HLAVKA, JOSEPH JOHN, ORGANIC CHEMISTRY. *Current Pos:* RES CHEMIST, LEDERLE LABS, AM CYANAMID CO, 57- *Personal Data:* b Franklin, NJ, Feb 13, 27; m 54; c 2. *Educ:* Rutgers Univ, 50; Mass Inst Technol, PhD(org chem), 57. *Concurrent Pos:* Am Cyanamid sr ed award, Imp Col, Univ London, 62. *Mem:* Am Chem Soc. *Res:* Photochemistry; peptide synthesis; chemistry of antibiotics. *Mailing Add:* Tower Hill Rd Tuxedo Park NY 10987

HNATIUK, BOHDAN T, AERONAUTICAL ENGINEERING. *Current Pos:* PRES AEROSPACE ENG, DREXEL UNIV, 60- *Personal Data:* b Zaliszczyki, Ukraine, July 25, 15; nat US; m 44; c 3. *Educ:* State Sem, Ukraine, BSEd, 35; Danzig Tech Univ, Dipl, 43, DrIng, 45. *Prof Exp:* Sci asst aeronaut eng, Danzig Tech Univ, 42-44; res scientist & asst to Prof Schrenk & Prof Katzmayer, Vienna Tech Univ, 44-45; anal engr, Dornier Works, Ger, 45-47; teacher & dir, UNRRA, Mech Training Sch, Ger, 47-48; with Displaced Persons Serv, Tettnang Dist, French Zone, Ger, 48-49; engr, Link Belt Co, Pa, 50-51; from asst prof to assoc prof aeronaut eng, Univ Notre Dame, 51-57; prof aerospace eng, Univ WVa, 57-60. *Concurrent Pos:* Consult, Guided Missile Sect, Bendix Aviation Corp, Ind, 55-57, Pneumo Dynamics Corp, Systs Eng Div, Md, 61-63 & George C Marshall Space Flight Ctr, Ala, 67-69; lectr & consult, Allegany Ballistics Lab, Dept Navy, 59-; fel, Am Soc Eng Educ-NASA; Alexander von Humboldt scholar. *Mem:* AAAS; Am Ord Asn; AAUP; Shevchenko Sci Soc; Am Inst Aeronaut & Astronaut. *Res:* Thermodynamics, heat transfer; fluid mechanics, aerodynamics; gas dynamics; aircraft and missile propulsion; gas turbines; space flight dynamics. *Mailing Add:* 535 Prescott Rd Merion Station PA 19066

HNATOW, MIQUEL ALEXANDER, CHEMICAL ENGINEERING. *Current Pos:* VPRES & TREAS, CATALYSIS RES CORP, 73- *Personal Data:* b Arg, Feb 26, 42; US citizen; m 66; c 3. *Educ:* Univ Mass, BS, 65; NY Univ, MS, 67, PhD(chem eng), 70. *Prof Exp:* Engr, Esso Res & Eng Co, 69-70; asst prof chem eng, NY Univ, 70-73; asst prof, Polytech Inst NY, 73-75. *Mem:* Am Inst Chem Engrs; Am Chem Soc; NY Acad Sci; Catalysis Soc; Sigma Xi. *Res:* Kinetics and catalysis; use of tracers in elucidating structure and mechanisms in heterogeneous catalysis; use of complex oxides as catalysts; catalyst synthesis; hydrates, kinetics of formation and decomposition. *Mailing Add:* 45 Cedars Rd Caldwell NJ 07006

HNATOWICH, DONALD JOHN, NUCLEAR MEDICINE, RADIOPHARMACEUTICAL DEVELOPMENT. *Current Pos:* PROF NUCLEAR MED, MED SCH, UNIV MASS, WORCESTER, 79- *Personal Data:* b Winnipeg, Man, Apr 20, 40; m 68, Marcia; c Rachael & Shayna. *Educ:* Univ Man, BSc, 63, MSc, 64; Mass Inst Technol, PhD(chem), 68. *Prof Exp:* Res assoc, Europ Inst Nuclear Res, 68-69; res collabr, Brookhaven Nat Lab, 69-70; mem res staff nuclear eng, Mass Inst Technol, 71-78. *Concurrent Pos:* Nat Res Coun Can fels, Europ Inst Nuclear Res, 68-69 & Brookhaven Nat Lab, 69-70; asst chemist, Dept Radiol, Mass Gen Hosp, 71-78, Hammersmith Hosp, London, 87. *Mem:* Soc Nuclear Med; Int Asn Radiopharmacol. *Res:* Diagnostic nuclear medicine; development of new radioactive imaging agents; preparation and characterization of diagnostic and therapeutic radiopharmaceuticals; development of methods for labeling of proteins, peptides, oligonucleotides with technetium-99m, indium-111, yttrium-90. *Mailing Add:* Dept Nuclear Med Univ Mass Med Ctr Worcester MA 01655. *Fax:* 508-856-4572; *E-Mail:* dhnatowich@bangate.ummed.edu

HO, ANDREW KONG-SUN, PHARMACOLOGY, MUSCARINIC ACETYLCHOLINE RECEPTOR. *Current Pos:* PROF PHARMACOL, COL MED, UNIV ILL, PEORIA & URBANA, 75- *Personal Data:* b Apr 22, 39. *Educ:* Monash Univ, Victoria, Australia, PhD(pharmacol & cell biol), 67. *Concurrent Pos:* Prin investr grants, NIH, Am Heart Asn & Am Fedn on Aging; vis prof, Fac Med, Univ Calgary, 84-85. *Mem:* Am Soc Pharmacol & Exp Therapeut; Int Soc Biomed Res Alcoholism. *Res:* Calcium binding proteins; muscarinic acetylcholine receptors; signal transduction; role of receptor mechanisms in aging, developmental pharmacology. *Mailing Add:* Dept Pharmacol Col Med Univ Ill One Illini Dr Peoria IL 61605. *Fax:* 307-671-8403

HO, BEGONIA Y, RECEPTOR PHARMACOLOGY, DRUG DESIGN. *Current Pos:* RES FEL BIOL, CALIF INST TECHNOL, 89- *Personal Data:* b Hong Kong, July 8, 62. *Educ:* Chinese Univ Hong Kong, BS, 84; Univ Minn, Minneapolis, PhD(pharmacol), 89. *Prof Exp:* Res asst, Behav Pharmacol Lab, Univ Minn, Minneapolis, 84-85, res asst pharmacol, 85-89. *Mem:* Fel Am Soc Pharmacol & Exp Therapeut; Soc Neurosci. *Res:* Expression of neurotransmitter, hormone, drug receptors and ion channels in mammalian cells and characterization of their structure-function relationship in ligand binding and signal transduction by molecular biological, biochemical and electrophysiological approaches. *Mailing Add:* Dept Pharmacol Med Col Wis 8701 Watertown Plank Rd Milwaukee WI 53226-4801. *Fax:* 414-266-8460

HO, BENG THONG, BIOCHEMICAL PHARMACOLOGY. *Current Pos:* from asst prof to assoc prof, 68-71, PROF MENT SCI, GRAD SCH BIOMED SCI, UNIV TEX, HOUSTON, 71-, HEAD NEUROCHEM & NEUROPHARMACOL RES SECT, TEX RES INST MENT SCI, 69- *Personal Data:* b Malacca, Malaysia, Sept 3, 32; US citizen; m 62. *Educ:* Nat Taiwan Univ, BS, 55; Univ Ore, MS, 59; Univ Wash, PhD(pharmaceut chem), 62. *Prof Exp:* Res assoc med chem, Sch Pharm, State Univ NY Buffalo, 62-64, asst res prof, 64-65; asst prof biochem & psychiat, Col Med, Baylor Univ, 65-68. *Concurrent Pos:* Fel, Sch Pharm, State Univ NY Buffalo, 62-64; chief chem res sect, Tex Res Inst Ment Sci, 65-68, chief neurochem & chem res sect, 68-69. *Mem:* Fel NY Acad Sci; fel Acad Pharmaceut Sci; Am Soc Neurochem; Am Chem Soc; Sigma Xi. *Res:* Neurochemical adaptation to chronic treatment of psychotherapeutic agents; evaluation of agents capable of selectively altering the actions of a specific biogenic amine; behavioral correlates of drug actions at the subcellular level; effects of nutritional state on bioavailability of psychotherapeutic agents, and on alcohol dependency and withdrawal. *Mailing Add:* Dept Neuro Oncol Univ Tex 2615 S Glen Haven Houston TX 77025-2131

HO, BONG, ELECTRICAL ENGINEERING. *Current Pos:* RETIRED. *Personal Data:* b Hong Kong, Dec 23, 31; m 59; c 2. *Educ:* Chung Kung Univ, BS, 56; SDak State Univ, MS, 61; Univ Mich, PhD(elec eng), 67. *Prof Exp:* From asst prof to assoc prof elec eng, Mich State Univ, 67-96. *Mem:* Inst Elec & Electronics Engrs. *Res:* Microwave electronics. *Mailing Add:* Dept Elec Eng 2120 Eng Bldg Mich State Univ East Lansing MI 48824-1126

HO, CHIEN, BIOCHEMISTRY, BIOPHYSICS. *Current Pos:* head, 79-86, prof, 79-86, ALUMNI PROF, DEPT BIOL SCI, CARNEGIE MELLON UNIV, 85-; DIR, PITTSBURGH NUCLEAR MAGNETIC RESONANCE CTR BIOMED RES, 85- *Personal Data:* b Shanghai, China, Oct 23, 34; US citizen; m 63, Nancy Tseng; c Jeanette & Carolyn. *Educ:* Williams Col, BA, 57; Yale Univ, PhD(phys chem), 61. *Honors & Awards:* Merit Award, Nat Heart, Lung & Blood Inst, 86. *Prof Exp:* Res chemist, Linde Co, Union Carbide Corp, 60-61; res assoc chem, Mass Inst Technol, 61-62, res assoc biol, 62-64; asst prof biophys, Univ Pittsburg, 64-67, assoc prof molecular biol, 67-70, chmn dept biophys & microbiol, 67-69, prof molecular biol & biochem, 71-79. *Concurrent Pos:* Guggenheim fels, 70-71; mem, Biophysics & Biophys Chem B Study Sect, NIH, 74-78, Biotechnol Resources Rev Comt, 79-83; mem, Molecular Biol Adv Panel, NSF, 80-83; mem Cellular & Molecular Basis Dis Rev Comt, NIH, 87-90. *Mem:* AAAS; Am Chem Soc; Biophys Soc; Am Soc Biochem & Molecular Biol; Soc Magnetic Resonance Med; Protein Soc. *Res:* Structure-function relationships in biological systems; application of nuclear magnetic resonance to biological and biomedical problems; conformations of macromolecules in solution; normal and abnormal hemoglobins; biological membranes. *Mailing Add:* Dept Biol Sci Carnegie-Mellon Univ Pittsburgh PA 15213. *Fax:* 412-268-7083; *E-Mail:* chienho@andrew.cmu.edu

HO, CHIH-MING, AEROSPACE ENGINEERING, NUCLEAR ENGINEERING. *Current Pos:* PROF, MECH, AEROSPACE & NUCLEAR ENG DEPT, UNIV CALIF, LOS ANGELES, 91-, DIR, CTR MICRO SYSTS, 93-, BEN RICH-LOCKHEED MARTIN PROF, 97- *Personal Data:* b Aug 16, 45; m 72, Shirley; c Dean. *Educ:* Nat Taiwan Univ, BS, 67; Johns Hopkins Univ, PhD(mech & mat sci), 74. *Prof Exp:* Assoc res scientist, Dept Mech & Mat Sci, Johns Hopkins Univ, 74-75; adj asst prof & res assoc, Dept Aerospace Eng, Univ Southern Calif, 75-76, from asst prof to prof, 76-91. *Concurrent Pos:* Indust consult, Dynamics Technol Inc, 77-85, Rockwell Int Inc, 80-83, Flow Indust, 82-, Brunswick Co, 84-85, United Technols, 84, Oak Ridge Nat Lab, 85-89, Int Technol, 87-, Ronsco, 89-; mem, tech comt aerocoust, Am Inst Aeronaut & Astrounaut, 80-84, adv, Nat Cheng-Kung Univ, Taiwan, 87-89; assoc ed, Am Inst Aeronaut & Astronaut J, 85-87, Am Soc Mech Eng J Fluids Eng, 91-93; hon prof, Nanjing Univ Aeronaut & Astronaut, China. *Mem:* Nat Acad Eng; Am Soc Mech Engrs; fel Am Inst Aeronaut & Astronaut; fel Am Phys Soc. *Res:* Control of turbulent flows; applying microtransducers to aerospace science; aerodynamics; micro-eletro-mechanical systems; noise bio-fluid mechanics; granted 4 patents. *Mailing Add:* Mech Aero & Nuclear Eng Dept Univ Calif Los Angeles CA 90024

HO, CHI-TANG, FOOD SCIENCE & TECHNOLOGY. *Current Pos:* Fel, Rutgers Univ, Sch Chem, 75-76, asst res fel, 76-78, asst prof, 78-83, assoc res prof, 83-87, PROF, DEPT FOOD SCI, RUTGERS UNIV, 87- *Personal Data:* b Fuzhou, Fujian, China, Dec 26, 44; m 74; c Gregory & Joseph. *Educ:* Nat Taiwan Univ, BS, 68; Washington Univ, St Louis, MA, 71, PhD(chem), 74. *Concurrent Pos:* Ed bd mem Food Reviews Int, 87, ed bd adv, Reviews in Food Sci & Nutrit, 87; chmn Flavor subdiv, Agr Food Div, Am Chem Soc, 90. *Mem:* Fel Am Chem Soc; Am Oil & Chemists Soc; Inst Food Technologists. *Res:* Mechanisms of the formulation of flavor compounds in foods; antimutagenic and anticarcinogenic compounds from natural products; antoxidative mechanism of lipids. *Mailing Add:* 32 Jernee Dr East Brunswick NJ 08816

HO, CHONG CHEONG, POLYMER SCIENCE. *Current Pos:* RETIRED. *Personal Data:* b Singapore, July 5, 38; m 68; c 2. *Educ:* Univ Idaho, BS, 59, MS, 61; Rensselaer Polytech Inst, PhD(chem eng), 64. *Prof Exp:* NASA res asst, Rensselaer Polytech Inst, 64; res engr, Uniroyal Res Ctr, 64-66, sr res engr, Uniroyal Chem, Naugatuck, 66-71, sr group leader, Uniroyal Chem, Uniroyal Inc, Naugatuck, 71-85, sr res scientist, Uniroyal Chem, Geismar, La, 86- *Mem:* Am Chem Soc. *Res:* Relationship between molecular structure and properties of polymers; melt rheology and polymer processing; physical properties and morphology of polymer blends; rubber-reinforced plastics; physical testing. *Mailing Add:* Uniroyal Chem Co PO Box 397 Geismar LA 70734-0397

HO, CHO-YEN, THERMAL PHYSICS, RESEARCH ADMINISTRATION. *Current Pos:* SR RES, PURDUE UNIV, WEST LAFAYETTE, 74, DIR, 82- *Personal Data:* b Kweiping, China, Aug 11, 28; nat US; m 63, Nancy Yang Wang; c Chris & Chester. *Educ:* Nat Taiwan Univ, BS, 55; Univ Ky, MSME, 60; Purdue Univ, PhD(thermodyn, heat transfer), 64. *Honors & Awards:* Thermal Conductivity Award, Thermal Conductivity Conf Gov Bd, 81. *Prof Exp:* Mech engr, Sung-I Textile Co, 55-57; asst, Univ Ky, 58-60; res asst, Thermophys Properties Res Ctr, 60-64; from asst sr researcher to assoc sr researcher, Purdue Univ, West Lafayette, 64-69, head ref data tables div, 67-73, asst dir, ctr info & numerical data analysis & synthesis, 73-81, interim dir, 81-82, dir, US Dept Defense High Temperature Mat Info Analysis Ctr, 86-96, dir, DOD Ceramics Info Analysis Ctr, 90-96, dir, DOD Metals Info Analysis Ctr, 90-96; dir, DOD Metal Matrix Composited Info Analysis Ctr, 92-96. *Concurrent Pos:* Indexer, Appl Mech Rev, 67-72; reviewer & referee, Int J Heat & Mass Transfer & Am Soc Mech Eng J Heat Transfer, 68-; co-chmn, Eighth Int Thermal Conductivity Conf, 68; mem, Standing Comt on Thermophys Properties, Am Soc Mech Engrs, 68-; short course instr, NSF, 73; treas & mem, Gov Bd, Int Thermal Conductivity Conf, 73- *Mem:* Am Soc Mech Engrs; Am Phys Soc; Sigma Xi; Am Soc Metals; Inst Elec & Electronic Engrs; Mat Res Soc. *Res:* Thermophysics, thermophysical and electrical properties of materials, thermoelectric power generation and conversion, thermodynamics and heat transfer; engineering physics; mechanical engineering; author or co-author of 8 books, 54 research articles, 128 technical reports, and editor or co-editor of 30 books; principal investigator or co-principal investigator of ninety-three research contracts and grants with a total amount of research funds of twenty-six million dollars acquired from government agencies, research institutes and industrial organizations. *Mailing Add:* 606 Riley Lane West Lafayette IN 47906-2370

HO, CHUNG WEN, HIGH DENSITY INTERCONNECT & PACKAGING, MULTICHIP MODULE TECHNOLOGY. *Current Pos:* vpres process eng, 92-96, CHIEF TECH OFFICER, MICRO MODULE SYSTS INC, 96- *Personal Data:* b Yunan, China, Sept 8, 40; US citizen; m, Heidi Chu; c Charles & Frank. *Educ:* Nat Taiwan Univ, BS, 61; Univ Calif, Berkeley, MS, 63, PhD(elec eng), 66. *Prof Exp:* Asst prof, Univ Calif, Berkeley, 66-67; res staff mem, IBM TJ Watson Res Ctr, 67-75, semiconductor eng mgr, 75-84; tech dir, Trilogy Systs Inc, 84-86; group eng mgr, Digital Equip Corp, 86-92. *Mem:* Fel Inst Elec & Electronics Engrs. *Res:* Interconnect, assembly and packaging development for high performance and high density electronics devices, including computer applications, telecommunications, portable electronics. *Mailing Add:* 10500-A Ridgeview Ct Cupertino CA 95014. *Fax:* 408-864-5950; *E-Mail:* cho@mms.com

HO, CHUNG YOU (PETER), APPLIED MATHEMATICS, COMPUTER SCIENCE. *Current Pos:* assoc prof comput sci & mech eng, 67-81, PROF COMPUT SCI, UNIV MO, ROLLA, 82- *Personal Data:* b China, Sept 12, 33; US citizen; m 60; c 3. *Educ:* Univ Taiwan, BS, 56; Univ Tex, MS, 59; Rensselaer Polytech Inst, PhD, 62. *Prof Exp:* Sr engr, Bendix Corp, NY, 62-63; syst analyst, Int Bus Mach, Minn & Vt, 63-67. *Concurrent Pos:* Asst prof, St Mary's Col, Minn, 63-65. *Mem:* Inst Elec & Electronics Engrs; Am Soc Mech Engrs. *Res:* Operations research; spatial kinematics; robotics; computer integrated manufacturing. *Mailing Add:* Dept Comput Sci Univ Mo Rolla MO 65401

HO, CHUNG-WU, GEOMETRIC TOPOLOGY, DYNAMICAL SYSTEMS. *Current Pos:* From assoc prof to prof, 70-78, chmn dept, 88-94, SOUTHERN ILL UNIV, 78- *Personal Data:* b Hankow, China; m 64, Yin-hsin Hsieh; c Minnie & Ronald. *Educ:* Univ Wash, BS(physics) & BS(math), 64, MA, 65; Mass Inst Technol, PhD(math), 70. *Concurrent Pos:* Vis prof, Univ Tex, 80, Washington Univ, 84-85; hon prof, Hefei Educ Inst, Hefei, Anhui, China, 85, Hangzhou Teachers Col, 92; overseas consult, Gifted Prog, Univ Sci & Technol China, 85-; panel mem vis lect, Prog Math Asn Am, 93-97. *Mem:* Am Math Soc; Math Asn Am; NY Acad Sci; Sigma Xi. *Res:* Differential and geometric topology; differential geometry; topological dynamics. *Mailing Add:* Dept Math Southern Ill Univ Edwardsville IL 62026-1653. *Fax:* 618-692-3174; *E-Mail:* cho@siue.edu

HO, DAH-HSI, BIOCHEMICAL PHARMACOLOGY, CLINICAL PHARMACOLOGY. *Current Pos:* PHARMACOLOGIST & PROF PHARMACOL, GRAD SCH BIOMED SCI, UNIV TEX HEALTH SCI CTR, HOUSTON, 81- *Personal Data:* b Shanghai, China, June 22, 31; m 63, Beng T. *Educ:* Nat Taiwan Univ, BS, 55; Univ Ore, MS, 59, PhD(physiol), 62. *Prof Exp:* Cancer res scientist biochem, Roswell Park Mem Inst, 64-65; asst prof, Univ Tex Syst, M D Anderson Hosp & Tumor Inst, 65-72, assoc, 72-80. *Concurrent Pos:* From asst to assoc prof biochem, Grad Sch Sci, Univ Tex Health Sci Ctr, Houston, 68-81. *Mem:* Am Asn Cancer Res; Am Soc Pharmacol & Exp Therapeut; Am Soc Clin Oncol; Am Asn Microbiol. *Res:* Drug metabolism mechanism of action of anticancer drugs; clinical and biochemical pharmacology of anticancer drugs; radioimmunoassay enzymeassay, high performance liquid chromotography and gas chromatography/mass spectrometry for phase I; anticancer agents. *Mailing Add:* M D Anderson Hosp & Tumor Inst 1515 Holcombe Box 52 Houston TX 77030. *Fax:* 713-792-6759

HO, DAR-VEIG, APPLIED MATHEMATICS. *Current Pos:* Asst prof math, 62-67, ASSOC PROF MATH, GA INST TECHNOL, 67- *Personal Data:* b Peiping, China, Jan 3, 31; US citizen; m 55; c 3. *Educ:* Nat Taiwan Univ, BS, 53; Univ Tenn, MS, 55; Brown Univ, PhD(appl math), 62. *Mem:* Am Math Soc; Soc Indust & Appl Math. *Res:* Fluid dynamics; partial differential equations. *Mailing Add:* Dept Math Ga Inst Technol 225 N Ave Atlanta GA 30332

HO, DAVID DA-I, INFECTIOUS DISEASE, AIDS. *Current Pos:* co-dir, 90-94, PROF MED & MICROBIOL, CTR AIDS RES, NY UNIV, 90-; DIR, 94-; DIR, DIAMOND AIDS RES CTR, 90- *Personal Data:* b Taichung, Taiwan, Nov 3, 52. *Educ:* Calif Inst Technol, BS, 74; Harvard Univ, MD, 78. *Honors & Awards:* Ernst Jung Prize in Med, AAAS. *Prof Exp:* Resident internal med, Sch Med, Univ Calif, Los Angeles, 81; chief resident, 82; clin & res fel, Infectious Dis Unit, Mass Gen Hosp, 82-85; physician & res scientist, Dept Med, Div Infectious Dis, Cedars-Sinai Med Ctr, 86-90. *Concurrent Pos:* Res fel med, Harvard Univ, 82-85. *Mem:* Inst Med-Nat Acad Sci; Am Fedn AIDS Res; fel AAAS. *Mailing Add:* Aaron Diamond AIDS Res Ctr 455 First Ave 7th Floor New York NY 10016

HO, DAVID TUAN-HUA, PLANT BIOCHEMISTRY, DEVELOPMENTAL BIOLOGY. *Current Pos:* ASSOC PROF, DEPT BIOL, WASH UNIV, ST LOUIS, MO, 84- *Personal Data:* b Nanking, China, Oct 1, 48; c 1. *Educ:* Nat Taiwan Univ, BS, 70; Mich State Univ, PhD(biochem), 76. *Prof Exp:* Res asst plant biochem, Mich State Univ, 71-75; fel plant biochem, Wash Univ, 75-76; fel molecular biol, Mass Inst Technol, 76-78; asst prof bot, Univ Ill, 78-84. *Concurrent Pos:* Fel, Jane Coffin Child Mem Fund for Med Res, 76-78. *Mem:* Am Soc Plant Physiologists; AAAS; Am Soc Biochem & Molecular Biol; Int Asn Plant Molecular Biol. *Res:* Plant biochemistry; action of plant hormones; molecular biology; plant physiology. *Mailing Add:* Biol Campus Box 1137 Wash State Univ One Brookings Dr St Louis MO 63130-4862. *Fax:* 314-935-4432

HO, FANGHUAI H(UBERT), MECHANICAL SYSTEMS, PROJECT & PEOPLE MANAGEMENT. *Current Pos:* res engr, B F Goodrich Res Ctr, 65-69, res assoc, 69-81, res fel, 81-90, RES & DEVELOP FEL MGR, B F GOODRICH AEROSPACE, 90- *Personal Data:* b Nanking, China, Dec 25, 34; m 61; c 2. *Educ:* Nat Cheng Kung Univ, Taiwan, BS, 56; Univ Fla, PhD(eng mech), 64. *Prof Exp:* Asst prof eng sci & mech, Univ Fla, 64-65. *Concurrent Pos:* Lectr, Cleveland State Univ, 80-84. *Mem:* Am Inst Aeronaut & Astronaut. *Res:* Research of high-temperature composite materials and structures; system modeling and simulation. *Mailing Add:* B F Goodrich Res Ctr 9921 Brecksville Rd Brecksville OH 44141. *E-Mail:* ho@brk.bfg.com

HO, FLOYD FONG-LOK, ANALYTICAL CHEMISTRY, CATALYSIS. *Current Pos:* Res chemist, 69-76, SR RES CHEMIST, HERCULES, INC, 76- *Personal Data:* b China; nat US. *Educ:* Hong Kong Baptist Col, BS, 63; Stetson Univ, Fla, MS, 64; Univ NC, PhD(chem), 69. *Mem:* Am Chem Soc. *Res:* Research and development of analytical methods and technology, mainly in the fields of nuclear magnetic resonance, electron spin resonance and ESCA, and applied mostly to polymers and polymerization catalysts; catalysis research involving Zeigler-Natta type catalysis. *Mailing Add:* 8 Grenable Ct Wilmington DC 19807

HO, GRACE PING-POO, MATHEMATICS. *Current Pos:* RETIRED. *Personal Data:* b Surabaia, Indonesia. *Educ:* Ore State Univ, BA, 57; Iowa State Univ, MA, 60; Pa State Univ, PhD(math), 68. *Prof Exp:* Instr physics, Winona State Col, 60-61; from asst prof to assoc prof math, Univ Bridgeport, 67-96. *Mem:* Am Math Soc; Math Asn Am; Soc Indust & Appl Math. *Res:* Partial differential equation. *Mailing Add:* 109 Village Dr Shelton CT 06484-1732

HO, HENRY SOKORE, BIOPHYSICS, ELECTRONICS ENGINEERING. *Current Pos:* RES MICROWAVE ENGR BIOL EFFECTS, BUR RADIOL HEALTH, FOOD & DRUG ADMIN, 71- *Personal Data:* b Fukien, China, Sept 8, 42; US citizen; m 72; c 2. *Educ:* Univ Wash, BS, 65, MS, 67, PhD(elec eng), 70. *Concurrent Pos:* Res medical device electronics engr. *Mem:* Sigma Xi; Inst Elec & Electronics Engrs. *Res:* Biological effects and dosimetry of microwaves; medical devices. *Mailing Add:* Ctr Devices & Radiolog Div Phys Sci 5600 Fishers Lane/HFZ 133 Rockville MD 20857

HO, HON HING, MYCOLOGY, PHYTOPATHOLOGY. *Current Pos:* from asst prof to assoc prof, 68-79, PROF BIOL, STATE UNIV NY COL, NEW PALTZ, 79- *Personal Data:* b Hong Kong, May 3, 39; m 68, Lucinda Chui; c Cynthia & Nancy. *Educ:* Univ Hong Kong, BSc, 62, Hons, 63; Univ Western Ont, PhD(bot), 66. *Prof Exp:* Can fel, 66-67; asst prof bot & bact, Ohio Wesleyan Univ, 67-68. *Concurrent Pos:* Vis prof, Inst Microbiol, Acad Sinica, Beijing & Dept Plant Protection, Nanjing Agr Univ, China, 82-83, 92-93, Inst Bot, Acad Sinica, Taipei, 89-90, 91 & 96-97; fac exchange scholar, State Univ NY, 90-93, chmn biol, New Paltz, 92- *Mem:* Mycol Soc Am; Am Phytopath Soc. *Res:* Biology of plant-pathogenic phycomycetes; morphology and taxonomy of phytophthora. *Mailing Add:* Dept Biol State Univ NY Col New Paltz NY 12561. *Fax:* 914-257-3791; *E-Mail:* hoh@npum.newpaltz.edu

HO, HUNG-TA, APPLIED MATHEMATICS, FLUID DYNAMICS. *Current Pos:* from asst prof to assoc prof, 66-72, PROF MATH, SAN DIEGO STATE UNIV, 72- *Personal Data:* b Anking, Anhui, China, Oct 14, 21; m 61; c 2. *Educ:* Ord Eng Col, China, BSc, 45; Va Polytech Inst, MSc, 56; Brown Univ, PhD(appl math), 61. *Prof Exp:* Res engr, Chinese Ord Bur, 45-49, res assoc mech eng, Chinese Ord Res Inst, 49-54; res asst, Va Polytech Inst, 54-55; appl math & hypersonic aerodyn, Brown Univ, 55-60; res scientist, Hydronautics Inc, 60-63; asst prof aerospace, Univ Okla, 63-66. *Concurrent Pos:* Instr, Taiwan Prov Taipei First Tech Col, 49-54; consult, ARO, Inc, Arnold Air Force Sta, Tenn, 66-68. *Mem:* Am Math Soc. *Res:* Aerodynamics, hydrodynamics. *Mailing Add:* 11156 Orian Way San Diego CA 92126

HO, ING KANG, NEUROCHEMISTRY, PHARMACOLOGY. *Current Pos:* assoc prof, 75-78, PROF PHARMACOL, MED CTR, UNIV MISS, 78-, CHMN, 82- *Personal Data:* b Taiwan, China, May 7, 39; m 65; c 3. *Educ:* Nat Taiwan Univ, BS, 62; Univ Calif, San Francisco, PhD(biochem), 68. *Prof Exp:* Res assoc anesthesiol, Baylor Col Med, 68-69, instr, 69-70; res pharmacologist, Univ Calif, San Francisco, 70-71; asst res pharmacologist, 71-73, asst prof, 73-75. *Mem:* Soc Neurosci; Am Soc Pharmacol & Exp Therapeuts; Soc Toxicol. *Res:* Drug addiction; mechanism of development of tolerance to and dependence on psychoactive agents; neurotoxicity. *Mailing Add:* Dept Pharmacol/Toxology Univ Miss Med Ctr 2500 N State St Jackson MS 39216-4505. *Fax:* 601-984-1637

HO, IWAN, MYCORPHIZAE PHYSIOLOGY, ENZYMES. *Current Pos:* RES PLANT PATHOLOGIST, FORESTRY SCI LAB, US FORESTRY SERV, 70- *Personal Data:* b Souzhou, Kiangsu, China, Apr 15, 25; US citizen; m 75; c 1. *Educ:* Nat Shanghai Univ, BS, 46; La State Univ, MS, 56; Ore State Univ, PhD(forest sci), 84. *Prof Exp:* Specialist pest mgt, Taiwan Agr Sta, Taiwan, 47-51; supvr res, Taichung Sugarcane Exp Sta, 51-56; microbiologist diagnostics, Seattle-King Co Health Dept, 62-67. *Concurrent Pos:* Grant, Sigma Xi, 72; vis prof, Academia Sinica, 85; courtesy adj prof, Col Forestry, Ore State Univ. *Mem:* Sigma Xi; Mycol Soc Am; Am Soc Plant Physiologists; Int Soc Molecular Biol. *Res:* Physiological and biochemical process of mycorrhizae and their ecological significance in relationship with their hosts and site condition; genetic variations in enzyme activity and phytohormone production of various species. *Mailing Add:* 1686 SW Bullevard St Philomath OR 97370

HO, JAMES CHIEN MING, SOLID STATE PHYSICS. *Current Pos:* from assoc prof to prof physics, 71-85, prof physics & chem, 85-91, SR STAFF SCIENTIST, NAT INST AVIATION RES, WICHITA STATE UNIV, 87-, TRUSTEES, DISTINGUISHED PROF PHYSICS & CHEM, 91- *Personal Data:* b China, July 31, 37; US Citizen; m 64, Lydia S Hsu; c Claudia & Marilyn. *Educ:* Nat Taiwan Univ, BS, 59; Univ Calif, Berkeley, MS, 63, PhD(chem), 66. *Prof Exp:* Fel chem, Lawrence Radiation Lab, Univ Calif, Berkeley, 65-67; sr scientist, Battelle Mem Inst, 67-71. *Concurrent Pos:* Vis prof chem, Univ Calif, Berkeley, 77-78; vis prof physics, Nat Tsing Hua Univ, Taiwan, 91-92. *Mem:* AAAS; Am Phys Soc; Am Soc Testing & Mat; Am Chem Soc; Sigma Xi; Mat Res Soc. *Res:* Low-temperature calorimetry; superconductivity; metals and alloys. *Mailing Add:* Dept Physics Wichita State Univ Wichita KS 67260

HO, JOHN TING-SUM, EXPERIMENTAL CONDENSED MATTER PHYSICS. *Current Pos:* assoc prof, State Univ NY, Buffalo, 75-83, prof physics, 83-95, interim dean, 84-85, ASSOC DEAN NATURAL SCI & MATH, STATE UNIV NY, BUFFALO, 83-, PROF DISTINGUISHED SERV, 95- *Personal Data:* b Hong Kong, July 5, 42; US citizen; m 70, Martha C Leung. *Educ:* Univ Hong Kong, BSc Gen, 64, BSc Spec, 65; Mass Inst Technol, PhD(physics), 69. *Prof Exp:* Asst prof physics, Univ Pa, 69-74; assoc prof, Univ Houston, 74-75. *Concurrent Pos:* Vis prof physics, Haverford Col, 84; Guggenheim fel, 90-91; vis scientist, AT&T Bell Labs, 91. *Mem:* Fel Am Phys Soc; Biophys. Soc. *Res:* Critical phenomena; biophysics; light scattering; liquid crystals. *Mailing Add:* Dept Physics State Univ NY Buffalo NY 14260. *Fax:* 716-645-2534; *E-Mail:* proho@acsu.buffalo.edu

HO, JU-SHEY, ZOOLOGY, PARASITOLOGY. *Current Pos:* from asst prof to assoc prof, 70-79, PROF, CALIF STATE UNIV, LONG BEACH, 79- *Personal Data:* b Taipei, Formosa, Dec 20, 35; m 65; c 2. *Educ:* Nat Taiwan Univ, BS, 58; Boston Univ, MA, 65, PhD(zool), 69. *Prof Exp:* Lab instr zool, Nat Taiwan Univ, 60-62; NSF fel, Boston Univ, 69-70. *Mem:* AAAS; Soc Syst Biol; Crustacean Soc; World Asn Copepodologists (vpres, 93-). *Res:* Crustacean parasites of fish; copepod parasites of marine invertebrates. *Mailing Add:* Dept Biol Calif State Univ 3702 Csulb Long Beach CA 90840-0004. *Fax:* 562-985-8887; *E-Mail:* jsho@csulb.edu

HO, KANG-JEY, PATHOLOGY. *Current Pos:* from asst prof to assoc prof, 70-75, PROF PATH, MED CTR, UNIV ALA, BIRMINGHAM, 76-; CHIEF PATH RES, VET ADMIN HOSP, BIRMINGHAM, 76- *Personal Data:* b Tainan, Taiwan, China, Aug 2, 37; m 69, Le-Hong C; c Yen-Ching & Yen-Dong. *Educ:* Nat Taiwan Univ, MD, 63; Northwestern Univ, PhD(path), 68. *Prof Exp:* From instr to asst prof path, Med Sch, Northwestern Univ, 68-70. *Concurrent Pos:* Res fel, Evanston Hosp, Ill, 68-69; Schweppe Found fel, 73; dir path res, Evanston Hosp, 69-70; interim chief path serv, Vet Admin Hosp, Birmingham, 75-76 & 90-92; hon prof, Guiyang Med Col, Guiyang, China, 87. *Mem:* Am Heart Asn; Am Soc Clin Nutrit; Am Inst Nutrit; Soc Exp Biol & Med; Int Soc Chronobiol; Am Soc Invest Path. *Res:* Lipid metabolism and its relationship to atherosclerogenesis and cholelithiasis. *Mailing Add:* Dept Path Univ Ala Med Ctr Birmingham AL 35294. *Fax:* 205-933-4484

HO, KAY T, MARINE TOXICOLOGY, ENVIRONMENTAL CHEMISTRY. *Current Pos:* Environ res scientist, 92-94, ENVIRON RES SCIENTIST & TECH PROG COORDR, US ENVIRON PROTECTION AGENCY, 94- *Personal Data:* b Yonkers, NY, July 15, 57. *Educ:* Univ Calif, Davis, BS, 82; Cornell Univ, MS, 85; Univ RI, PhD(chem oceanog), 91. *Prof Exp:* Res assoc, Univ RI, 89-90. *Concurrent Pos:* Adj prof marine toxicol,

Hampton Univ, 93- *Mem:* Soc Environ Toxicol & Chem. *Res:* Develop methods for determining chemical compound(s) responsible for toxicity in marine sediments; developing novel chemical methods to separate and remove different classes of compounds from sediments as well as develop new toxicity tests compatible with these chemical methods. *Mailing Add:* 27 Tarzwell Dr Narragansett RI 02874. *Fax:* 401-782-3030; *E-Mail:* kho%narvax@epavax.rtpnc.epa.gov

HO, KEH MING, crop breeding, cytogenetics, for more information see previous edition

HO, LOUIS T, ACOUSTICS. *Current Pos:* RETIRED. *Personal Data:* b Shanghai, China, July 22, 30; m 61, Claudine Jiang; c Charlton & Denise. *Educ:* Cath Univ Am, BS, 53, MS, 61, PhD(acoust), 72. *Prof Exp:* Res assoc, Molecular Physics Lab, Univ Md, 55-61; res physicist, Gen Kinetics, Inc, 61-63; res physicist, Marine Eng Lab, 63-67, sr proj engr, Naval Ship Res & Develop Ctr, 67-87; res scientist, David Taylor Res Ctr, Annapolis, 87-89; br head, Mach Struct Acousts Br, Naval Surface Warfare Ctr, Annapolis, 89-95. *Mem:* Am Phys Soc; Acoust Soc Am. *Res:* Sound radiation and propagation; noise reduction techniques; acoustic measurements; fluid-structure interaction. *Mailing Add:* 11607 Candor Dr Mitchellville MD 20721

HO, LYDIA SU-YONG, chemistry, statistical quality control, for more information see previous edition

HO, MAT H, ANALYTICAL BIOCHEMISTRY, CLINICAL CHEMISTRY. *Current Pos:* Asst prof chem, Univ Ala, Birmingham, 71-77, from asst prof forensic sci to assocs prof, 83-87, from asst prof biomed eng to assoc prof, 87-88, ASSOC PROF CHEM, UNIV ALA, BIRMINGHAM, 87- *Personal Data:* b May 29, 51; m 81; c 2. *Educ:* Univ New Orleans, PhD(chem), 81; Univ S Ala, MD, 96. *Honors & Awards:* Outstanding Res Award, Sigma Xi. *Concurrent Pos:* Consult, Southern Res Inst, 82-85; chmn, Symposium Biol Monitioring Exposure Chem, Am Chem Soc, 84-85, Symposium Methods Forensic Chem, 85. *Mem:* Am Chem Soc; Sigma Xi; fel Nat Acad Clin Biochem. *Res:* Fundamental studies of bio-electro chemistry and development of biosensor based on electrochemical, piezoelectric and fiber optical detections; study of immobilized enzymes, antibodies, and DNA and use them as analytical reagents in clinical, environmental and forensic chemistry; investigation of flow injection analysis, biosensors, and chemical sensors. *Mailing Add:* 1744 Napier Dr Birmingham AL 35226

HO, MAY-KIN, IMMUNOLOGY. *Current Pos:* VPRES, GOLDMAN SACHS & CO, 92- *Personal Data:* b Hong Kong, Oct 16, 52. *Educ:* State Univ NY, Downstate Med Ctr, BS, 75, PhD(immunol), 80. *Prof Exp:* Supvr immunol res, E I du Pont de Nemours Co, 82-92. *Mem:* Am Asn Immunologists; Reticuloendothelial Soc; AAAS; Am Asn Women Sci; NY Acad Sci. *Mailing Add:* Goldman Sachs & Co 85 Broad St 16th Floor New York NY 10004. *Fax:* 212-902-6723

HO, MONTO, VIROLOGY, MEDICINE. *Current Pos:* asst prof med & microbiol, 59-62, PROF MICROBIOL, UNIV PITTSBURGH, 64-, CHMN DEPT INFECTIOUS DIS & MICROBIOL, GRAD SCH PUB HEALTH, 69- *Personal Data:* b Hunan, China, Mar 28, 27; m 52; c 2. *Educ:* Harvard Univ, AB, 49; Harvard Med Sch, MD, 54; Am Bd Internal Med, dipl; Am Bd Microbiol, dipl. *Prof Exp:* Intern & resident, Boston City Hosp, 54-56. *Concurrent Pos:* Res fel med & bact, Harvard Med Sch, 56-59; prof med & chief infectious dis, Med Sch, Univ Pittsburgh, 70- *Mem:* Fel Am Acad Microbiol; Am Asn Immunol; Am Soc Clin Invest; fel Am Col Physicians; Asn Am Physicians; Academia Sinica. *Res:* Interferon, cytomegalovirus, pathogenesis of infectious diseases. *Mailing Add:* Dept Infectious Dis & Microbiol Univ Pittsburgh Grad Sch Pub Health Crabtree A-427 Pittsburgh PA 15261-0001. *Fax:* 412-624-4953

HO, NANCY WANG-YANG, MOLECULAR BIOLOGY, BIOCHEMISTRY. *Current Pos:* res assoc, Dept Biol Sci, 68-69, NIH res fel, 69-71, res assoc molecular biol, 71-77, ASST RES SCIENTIST & ASST PROF, DEPT BIOL SCI, PURDUE UNIV, 77- *Personal Data:* b Tai-City, Kiangsu, China; US citizen; m 63; c 2. *Educ:* Nat Taiwan Univ, BS, 57; Temple Univ, MA, 60; Purdue Univ, PhD(molecular biol), 68. *Prof Exp:* Res asst biochem, LaRabida-Univ Chicago Inst, 62-63. *Concurrent Pos:* Co-prin investr, NIH res grants, 71- *Mem:* Am Soc Biol Chemists; Am Inst Biol Sci; Sigma Xi. *Res:* Nucleic acids; organic chemistry. *Mailing Add:* Molecular Genetics Purdue Univ 1295 Potter Ctr West Lafayette IN 47907-1295

HO, PATIENCE CHING-RU, PHYSICAL CHEMISTRY, ORGANIC CHEMISTRY. *Current Pos:* RES SCIENTIST PHYS CHEM, OAK RIDGE NAT LAB, 76- *Personal Data:* b Peiping, China; US citizen. *Educ:* Nat Taiwan Norm Univ, BS, 63; Univ Calif, MS, 66; Univ Bonn, WGer, PhD(org chem), 71. *Prof Exp:* Chemist, Hogan Faximile Corp, 66-67; res asst, Upjohn Co, 68; assoc org synthesis, Stanford Univ, 72; assoc med res, State Univ NY, Buffalo, 72-74. *Mem:* Am Chem Soc. *Res:* Solution chemistry. *Mailing Add:* Oak Ridge Nat Lab PO Box 2008 Oak Ridge TN 37831-6110

HO, PAUL SIU-CHUNG, MATERIALS SCIENCE ENGINEERING. *Current Pos:* COCKRELL FAMILY REGENTS CHAIR, UNIV TEX, AUSTIN. *Personal Data:* b Canton, China, Oct 6, 36; m 67; c 2. *Educ:* Nat Chengkung Univ, Taiwan, BS, 57; Nat Tsinghue Univ, Taiwan, MS, 59; Rensselaer Polytech, NY, PhD(physics), 65. *Prof Exp:* From asst prof to assoc prof mat sci, Cornell Univ, 67-72; res staff mem, IBM Res Ctr, 72-75, sr mgr, 85-91. *Mem:* Fel Am Phys Soc; Am Vacuum Soc; Mat Res Soc; Am Soc Metals. *Res:* Thin films and interfaces in multilayeral structures for ULSI applications; published articles in numerous journals. *Mailing Add:* Mats Lab Interconnect & Packaging Univ Tex BRC/MER Mail Code 78650 Austin TX 78712-1100

HO, PETER PECK KOH, BIOCHEMISTRY, IMMUNOLOGY. *Current Pos:* ATTY, NORRIS, CHOPLIN & SCHROEDER, 94- *Personal Data:* b Fukien, China, Sept 12, 37; US citizen; m 62; c 2. *Educ:* Chung Chi Col, Hong Kong, BS, 58; Univ Wash, PhD(biochem), 63. *Hon Degrees:* JD, Ind Univ, 84. *Prof Exp:* Res assoc biochem, Univ Calif, Berkeley, 63-64; sr biochemist virol, Eli Lilly & Co 64-69, from res scientist to sr res scientist, 69-82, res adv, Res Labs, 82-93. *Mem:* Am Chem Soc; Am Soc Biol Chemists; NY Acad Sci; Sigma Xi. *Res:* Virus-induced enzyme systems; biochemical studies on virus replication; mechanism of antibiotics; metabolic inhibitors; prostaglandin and leukotriene biosynthesis and metabolism; asthma; cellular immunology, arthritis and inflammation. *Mailing Add:* 6329 Cherbourg Dr Indianapolis IN 46220

HO, PING-PEI, PHYSICS, LASERS. *Current Pos:* PROF, DEPT ELEC ENG, CITY COL NY, 83- *Personal Data:* b Kao-Hsiung, Taiwan, May 19, 49; m 73, 88; c 3. *Educ:* Nat Tsing-Hua Univ, Taiwan, BS, 70; City Col New York, MA, 74, PhD(physics), 78; Kent State Univ, Ohio, MBA, 83. *Prof Exp:* Sr res assoc physics, City Col New York, 78-79; sr engr, NCR Corp, 79-83. *Mem:* Optical Soc Am. *Res:* Ultrafast phenomena in solid state physics; chemical reaction of biological systems; nonlinear optical research in liquids and solids; state of arts laser research and development. *Mailing Add:* Dept Elec Eng City Col NY 138 Convent Ave New York NY 10031-9198

HO, REN-JYE, ADENYLATE CYCLASE, ADIPOSE TISSUES. *Current Pos:* PROF BIOCHEM, SCH MED, UNIV MIAMI, 73- *Educ:* Vanderbilt Univ, PhD(physiol), 63. *Mailing Add:* Dept Biochem & Molecular Biol Univ Miami Sch Med PO Box 016129 Miami FL 33101-6129. *Fax:* 305-243-3955

HO, S(HUI), OPERATIONS RESEARCH. *Current Pos:* SCI ADV, US NCCS SUPPORT STAFF, 88- *Personal Data:* b Macao, Sept 16, 31; US citizen; m 59, Kean Yue; c Vincent B. *Educ:* Univ Adelaide, BE, 55; Mass Inst Technol, SM, 57, ScD(struct eng), 63. *Prof Exp:* Res asst struct dynamics & comput appln, Mass Inst Technol, 55-57 & 60-62; designer, Jackson & Moreland Inc, Engrs, Mass, 57-58, jr engr, 58-60; mem tech staff, Mitre Corp, 62-66; mem prof staff, Ctr Naval Anal, 66-83, opers res analyst, Naval Res Lab, 83-84 & US Army Concept Anal Agency 84-88. *Concurrent Pos:* Adj asst prof, Howard Univ, 67-68, adj prof, 68-69; fel opers res, Stanford Univ, 71-72. *Mem:* Opers Res Soc Am. *Res:* Command and control; nuclear weapons effects; operations research; computer applications. *Mailing Add:* 9114 Ashmeade Dr Fairfax VA 22032

HO, THOMAS INN MIN, telecommunications, information networking, for more information see previous edition

HO, THOMAS TONG-YUN, ORGANIC GEOCHEMISTRY. *Current Pos:* group leader, Continental Oil Co, 75-80, sr res assoc, 80-83, res fel, 83-84, DUPONT FEL, CONOCO, INC, 85- *Personal Data:* b Taiwan, China, July 2, 31; m 63; c 2. *Educ:* Nat Taiwan Univ, BS, 54; Univ Kans, MA, 61, PhD(paleont), 64. *Prof Exp:* Teaching asst zool, Nat Taiwan Univ, 56-58; res assoc org geochem, Univ Ariz, 64-67; sr geologist, Exxon Prod Res Co, 67-75. *Concurrent Pos:* Vis scientist, Univ Calif, Los Angeles, 67; UN Adv, 80. *Mem:* AAAS; fel Geol Soc Am; Am Geophys Union; Geochem Soc; Am Asn Petrol Geologists. *Res:* Fishery biology; paleontology; organic geochemistry; quaternary, marine and petroleum geology; computer application in geology, basin modeling. *Mailing Add:* 2409 Hummingbird Lane Ponca City OK 74604

HO, TIMOTHY WAI-CHUNG, BIOCHEMISTRY, BIOTECHNOLOGY. *Current Pos:* SCIENTIST, BIO-RAD LABS, 95- *Personal Data:* b Hong Kong, Nov 2, 49; US citizen; c 2. *Educ:* Nat Taiwan Univ, MD, 75. *Prof Exp:* Head, Dept Urol, China Med Col Hosp, Taichung, Taiwan, 80-84; postdoctoral, Univ Calif, Riverside, 86-87, res scientist, 87-92; fel, Children's Hosp Med Ctr, Cincinnati, 92; mgr res & develop, Hemosphere Inc, 92-95. *Mem:* Endocrine Soc; AMA; Urol Asn Repub China. *Res:* Biochemistry and activity of different isoforms of prolactin; manufacturing and application of artificial platelets; manufacturing and application of protein microspheres; development of diagnostic controls. *Mailing Add:* 3726 E Miraloma Ave Anaheim CA 92806. *Fax:* 714-666-1383; *E-Mail:* timothy_ho@bio-rad.com

HO, YEW KAM, ATOMIC SCATTERING, POSITRON PHYSICS. *Current Pos:* RES FEL, INST ATOMIC & MOLECULAR SCIS, ACAD SINICIA, TAIPEI, TAIWAN, REP CHINA, 93- *Personal Data:* b Macau, June 5, 46; Can citizen; m 72, Agnes Law; c Hubert. *Educ:* Sir George Williams Univ, Can, BSc, 69; Univ Western Ont, MSc, 71, PhD(appl math), 75. *Prof Exp:* Res assoc, NASA-Goddard Space Flight Ctr, 75-77; asst prof physics, Wayne State Univ, 77-80; res asst prof, La State Univ, 84-87, res assoc prof, 87-93. *Concurrent Pos:* Excellence Res Award, Nat Sci Coun, 94-95. *Mem:* Am Phys Soc. *Res:* Theoretical studies of atomic resonance phenomena; interactions between positrons and positroniums with atoms; electron-ion interaction phenomena related to astrophysics and laboratory plasmas; atomic systems in external electric and magnetic fields. *Mailing Add:* Inst Atomic & Molecular Scis Acad Sinicia PO Box 23-166 Taipei Taiwan. *Fax:* 886-2-362-0200; *E-Mail:* ykho@atom.iams.sinica.edu.tw

HO, YU-CHI, APPLIED MATHEMATICS, SYSTEMS ENGINEERING. *Current Pos:* from asst prof to assoc prof eng & appl physics, 61-69, GORDON MCKAY PROF ENG, DIV APPL SCI, HARVARD UNIV, 69-, T JEFFERSON COOLIDGE PROF APPL MATH, 88- *Personal Data:* b China, Mar 1, 34; US citizen; m 59, Sophia Hu; c 3. *Educ:* Mass Inst Technol, SB, 53, SM, 55; Harvard Univ, PhD(appl math), 61. *Honors & Awards:* Field Award, Control Eng, Inst Elec & Electronics Engrs. *Prof Exp:* Sr engr, Res Lab Div, Bendix Corp, 55-58. *Concurrent Pos:* Mem, Army Sci Adv Panel, 68-74; Guggenheim fel, 70; gen chmn, Conf Robotics & Automation, Inst Elec & Electronics Engrs, 87, pres, Coun Robotics & Automation, 88; vis Cockrell Family Chair prof eng, Univ Tex, Austin, 88-89. *Mem:* Nat Acad Eng; fel Inst Elec & Electronics Engrs. *Res:* Control and information science; manufacturing automation. *Mailing Add:* Pierce Hall G12j Div Appl Sci Harvard Univ 29 Oxford St Cambridge MA 02138. *Fax:* 617-496-6404; *E-Mail:* ho@paone.harvard.edu

HOA, SUONG VAN, STRESS ANALYSIS, ACOUSTIC EMISSION. *Current Pos:* Design Engineer, Canadian Fram Ltd, 76-77, asst prof, 77-81, PROF MECH ENG, CONCORDIA UNIV, 81- *Personal Data:* b Longan, Viet Nam, Mar 20, 48; m 83; c 3. *Educ:* Calif State Univ, San Luis Obispo, BEng, 71; Univ Toronto, MS, 73 & PhD(mech eng), 76. *Honors & Awards:* Ralph R Teetor Award, Soc Automotive Engr, 80. *Concurrent Pos:* Consult, CPF Dualan Ltd, 79-, SPAR Aerospace, 81-87, comt mem, Am Soc Mech Engr Boiler & Pressure Vessel Code, 83- *Mem:* Am Soc Mech Eng; Am Soc Mat; Am Soc for Testing & Mat; Soc Exp Mech. *Res:* Composite structures and materials; graphite, glass, keular fibers; epoxy, polyester and thermoplastic matrix materials. *Mailing Add:* 1455 de Maisonneuve W No 549 Montreal PQ H3G 1M8 Can

HOADLEY, GEORGE B(URNHAM), electrical engineering; deceased, see previous edition for last biography

HOADLEY, ROBERT BRUCE, WOOD IDENTIFICATION, WOOD SCIENCE & TECHNOLOGY. *Current Pos:* from asst prof to assoc prof, 62-78, PROF WOOD SCI & TECHNOL, UNIV MASS, AMHERST, 78- *Personal Data:* b Waterbury, Conn, July 24, 33; m 57; c 2. *Educ:* Univ Conn, BS, 55; Yale Univ, MF, 57, DFor, 62. *Prof Exp:* Lab supvr & res technician wood tech, Yale Univ, 57-62. *Mem:* Forest Prod Soc; Soc Wood Sci & Technol; Sigma Xi; Int Asn Wood Anatomists. *Res:* Wood machining; veneer cutting; fundamental properties of wood. *Mailing Add:* Holdsworth Nat Res Ctr Univ Mass Amherst MA 01002. *Fax:* 413-545-4358

HOAG, ARTHUR ALLEN, ASTRONOMY. *Current Pos:* RETIRED. *Personal Data:* b Ann Arbor, Mich, Jan 28, 21; m 49; c 2. *Educ:* Brown Univ, AB, 42; Harvard Univ, PhD(astron) 51. *Prof Exp:* Physicist, US Naval Ord Lab, 42-44; astronomer, US Naval Observ, 50-65; astronomer, Kitt Peak Nat Observ, 65-77; dir, Lowell Observ, 77-86. *Mem:* AAAS; Am Astron Soc; Int Astron Union; Fel Royal Astron Soc. *Res:* Photoelectric and photographic photometry; astronomical sites and instruments; quasi-stellar sources. *Mailing Add:* 4410 E 14th St Tucson AZ 85711

HOAG, DAVID GARRATT, SYSTEM ENGINEERING. *Current Pos:* CONSULT, 89- *Personal Data:* b Boston, Mass, Oct 11, 25; m 52, Grace E Griffith; c Rebecca, Peter, Jeffrey, Nicholas & Lucy. *Educ:* Mass Inst Technol, BS, 46, MS, 50. *Honors & Awards:* Thurlow Award, Inst Navigation, 70; Lewis W Hill Space Transp Award, Am Inst Aeronaut & Astronaut, 72. *Prof Exp:* Tech dir polaris missile guid, Mass Inst Technol, 58-61, prog mgr, Apollo guid & navigation, 61-73; dept head, adv systs, C S Draper Lab, Inc, 73-85, sr tech adv, 85-89. *Mem:* Nat Acad Eng; Int Acad Astronaut; Inst Navigation (pres, 78-79); fel Am Inst Aeronaut & Astronaut. *Res:* System engineering for aerospace vehicles specializing in guidance, navigation, control, and precision pointing with emphasis on inertial and electro-optical sensing; real time computing; trajectory analysis and accuracy. *Mailing Add:* 116 Winthrop St Medway MA 02053-2310. *E-Mail:* dghoag@sprynet.com

HOAG, ROLAND BOYDEN, JR, EXPLORATION GEOCHEMISTRY. *Current Pos:* PRES, HYDRO SOURCE & ASSOC, 91- *Personal Data:* b Boston, Mass, Sept 3, 45; m 68; c 2. *Educ:* Univ NH, BS, 67; McGill Univ, PhD(geol), 75. *Prof Exp:* Geologist stream sediment geochem, NAm Explor, 67; consult geologist, Scandia Mining & Explor Co & Labrador Mining & Explor Co, 71; res assoc, McGill Univ, 76; consult geologist, 76-77; vpres, BCI Geonetics, Inc, 77-91. *Mem:* Sigma Xi; Geol Soc Am; Soc Explor Geochemists; Soc Econ Geologists; Newcomen Soc. *Res:* Innovation techniques applying remote sensing, geophysics, geochemistry, and hydrogeology for the exploration and evaluation of municipal groundwater supplies in fractured crystalline rock. *Mailing Add:* Miles Pond Rd Center Sandwich NH 03227

HOAGBERG, RUDOLPH KARL, GEOLOGY. *Current Pos:* PRES, R K HOAGBERG ASSOCS, 82- *Personal Data:* b Ironwood, Mich, Mar 11, 30; m 53; c 5. *Educ:* Mich State Univ, BS, 52, MS, 57. *Prof Exp:* Geophysicist, Humble Oil Div, Stand Oil Co, NJ, Ill & Mont, 52-56; mining geologist, Properties & Indust Develop Dept, Northern Pac Rwy Co, Minn, 57-62; instr phys geol, Sch Earth Sci, Univ Minn, 62-63; asst to dir indust minerals & environ geol, Minn Geol Surv, 63-69; managing assoc, Lindgren Explor Co, 69-70; geologist, Minn Geol Surv, 70-76; sr geologist, E K Lehmann & Assocs, Inc, 76-82. *Mem:* AAAS; Geol Soc Am; Am Inst Prof Geologists. *Res:* Glacial geology studies re industrial minerals; environmental geology and hydrogeology of glaciated and Karst terranes. *Mailing Add:* R K Hoagberg Assoc 12 S Sixth St Suite 1047 Minneapolis MN 55402-1514

HOAGE, TERRELL RUDOLPH, CELL BIOLOGY, REPRODUCTIVE ULTRASTRUCTURE. *Current Pos:* RETIRED. *Personal Data:* b Fairfield, Iowa, Aug, 12, 34; m 57, Mary L Reneker; c Terrell L & Jay B. *Educ:* Parsons Col, BS, 57; Iowa State Univ, MS, 63, PhD(entom), 64. *Prof Exp:* Res entomologist, Bee Mgt Invests, USDA, 64-65; asst prof zool, Parsons Col, 65-68; assoc prof, Sam Houston State Univ, 68-75, Path Serv Prog, Nat Ctr Toxicol Res, 81-83, prof biol, 75-97. *Concurrent Pos:* Dir, BARC, Inc, Microeng Cellular Graphics; fel, Univ Iowa, 67; res dir, Sewage Aeration Waste Water. *Res:* Metabolic DNA in post-mitotic cells; molecular genetics; regenerative tissue toxicology; lyme disease; waste water research; microbubble aeration; restaurant grease removal; environmental control of swine waste; septic tank remediation. *Mailing Add:* Dept Biol Sam Houston State Univ Huntsville TX 77341. *Fax:* 409-294-3940; *E-Mail:* bio__trh@shsu.edu

HOAGLAND, A(LBERT) S(MILEY), ELECTRICAL ENGINEERING, MAGNETIC RECORDING & DATA STORAGE TECHNOLOGY. *Current Pos:* DIR, INST INFO STORAGE TECHNOL, SANTA CLARA UNIV, 84- *Personal Data:* b Berkeley, Calif, Sept 13, 26; m 50, Janine; c Katherine, Nicole & Richard. *Educ:* Univ Calif, BS, 47, MS, 48, PhD(elec eng), 54. *Honors & Awards:* Centennial Medal, Inst Elec & Electronics Engrs, 84, Golden Core Award, 96. *Prof Exp:* Res engr elec eng, Univ Calif, 47-52, from instr to asst prof, 52-56; mgr, Magnetic Record Technol Res Lab, IBM Corp, Calif, 56-59, mgr eng sci, 59-61, systs mgr, Adv Systs Div, 61-62, sr tech consult, World Trade Corp, 62-64; mgr eng sci, Res Ctr Yorktown Heights, 64-68, dir tech planning, 68-71, corp prog coordr, Boulder, 71-76, mgr explor magnetic recording, 76-80; tech adv pres, GPD, 80-84. *Concurrent Pos:* Consult, IBM Corp, 54-56 & State Calif, 56; dir bd, Inst Elec & Electronics Engrs, 74-76; adj prof, Harvey Mudd Col, 78- & Univ Calif, San Diego, 83-85; trustee, Charles Babbage Found, 79- *Mem:* Fel Inst Elec & Electronics Engrs; Am Fedn Info Processing Soc (vpres, 75-78, pres, 78-80); Sigma Xi. *Res:* Digital computers, especially technologies exploiting magnetic recording for storage; magnetic recording theory; memory and storage for data processing systems; magnetic disk drive technology and design. *Mailing Add:* Inst Info Storage Technol Sch Eng Santa Clara Univ Santa Clara CA 95053

HOAGLAND, ALAN D, GEOLOGY. *Current Pos:* CONSULT GEOLOGIST, 76- *Personal Data:* b Winnetka, Ill, Mar 25, 11; m 39; c 3. *Educ:* Northwestern Univ, BSc, 33, MA, 35. *Prof Exp:* Chief geologist, NJ Zinc Co, 41-70, mgr eastern explor, 70-76. *Mem:* Geol Soc Am; Soc Econ Geol. *Res:* Metal and industrial mineral exploration. *Mailing Add:* 3749 Amesbury Lane #5608 Sarasota FL 34232

HOAGLAND, GORDON WOOD, NUMERICAL ANALYSIS, PARTIAL DIFFERENTIAL EQUATIONS. *Current Pos:* chmn dept, 79-84, PROF MATH & COMPUT SCI, RICKS COL, 69- *Personal Data:* b Nampa, Idaho, Oct 22, 36; m 62; c 3. *Educ:* Brigham Young Univ, BS, 66, MS, 68. *Prof Exp:* Res consult, Ore State Univ, 68-69. *Mem:* Soc Indust & Appl Math; Am Math Soc. *Res:* Gamma ray spectroscopy; numerical forestry analysis; applied mathematics. *Mailing Add:* 206 E 2nd St Rexburg ID 83440

HOAGLAND, K ELAINE, SCIENCE POLICY, BIODIVERSITY. *Current Pos:* EXEC DIR, ASN SYSTS COLLECTIONS, 87- *Personal Data:* b Los Angeles, Calif, Dec 10, 47; m 75. *Educ:* Pomona Col, AB, 70; Harvard Univ, AM, 73, PhD(biol), 75. *Prof Exp:* Asst prof biol, 75-82, sr res scientist, ctr marine & environ studies, Lehigh Univ, 83-87. *Concurrent Pos:* Res assoc, Acad Natural Sci Philadelphia, 75- *Mem:* Ecol Soc Am; fel AAAS; Am Malacol Union; Soc Conserv Biol. *Res:* Population dynamics and population genetics of marine invertebrates; ecology of colonizing species; molluscan systematics; science policy. *Mailing Add:* Asn Systs Collections 1725 K St NW Suite 601 Washington DC 20006

HOAGLAND, LAWRENCE CLAY, MECHANICAL ENGINEERING. *Current Pos:* VPRES & DIR RES, AIRXCHANGE INC, ROCKLAND, MASS, 80- *Personal Data:* b Marion, Ohio, Nov 15, 31; m 51, Carol Carsten; c Kathryn A (Nourse), Douglas C, Janet L (Richards) & Sandra J. *Educ:* Gen Motors Inst, BMech Eng, 54; Mass Inst Technol, MS, 55, ME, 56, ScD(mech eng), 60. *Prof Exp:* Jr engr, Small Gas Turbine Dept, Gen Motors Corp, 53-54; from instr to asst prof heat transfer & thermodyn, Mass Inst Technol, 56-59; vpres eng res, Dynatech Corp, 60-68, vpres & dir res, Steam Engine Systs Corp, Newton, 68-75; dir develop, CTI-Cryogenics Div, Helix Tech Corp, 75-77; dir res & develop, Amtech Inc, Newton, Mass, 77-80. *Concurrent Pos:* Consult heat transfer, 85- *Mem:* Am Soc Mech Engrs; Soc Automotive Engrs; Am Soc Heating, Refrig & Air-Conditioning Engrs. *Res:* Development of heat engines, heat exchanger applications and heat transfer and flow processes of interest in heat exchange equipment; heat transfer and flow in non circular ducts. *Mailing Add:* Star Rte 62 Box 412A Center Harbor NH 03226. *Fax:* 781-871-3029

HOAGLAND, MAHLON BUSH, MOLECULAR BIOLOGY, RESEARCH ADMINISTRATION. *Current Pos:* pres & sci dir, 70-85, EMER PRES, WORCESTER FOUND EXP BIOL, 85- *Personal Data:* b Boston, Mass, Oct 5, 21; m 43, 61, Olley V Jones; c Judith (Hauck), Mahlon Jr & Robin (Hoy). *Educ:* Harvard Med Sch, MD, 48. *Hon Degrees:* ScD, Worcester Polytech Inst, 73; ScD, Univ Mass, 84. *Honors & Awards:* Franklin Medal, 76. *Prof Exp:* From asst to asst prof med, Huntington Lab, Mass Gen Hosp, Harvard Med Sch, 48-60, assoc prof bact & immunol, 60-67, exec secy comt res, Hosp 54-57; prof biochem & chmn dept, Dartmouth Med Sch, 67-70; founder & spokesman, Deleg Basic Biomed Res, 78-87. *Concurrent Pos:* Res fel med, Huntington Lab, Mass Gen Hosp, 48-51; fel, Am Cancer Soc, Carlsberg Lab, Copenhagen, 51-52, Biochem Res Lab, Mass Gen Hosp, 52-53; scholar cancer res, Am Cancer Soc, 53-58; mem med res coun unit molecular biol, Cavendish

Lab, Cambridge Univ, 57-58; mem biochem study sect, NIH, 61-64; mem comt etiol cancer, Am Cancer Soc, 65-68, chmn med res comt, Mass Div, 74-76; res prof, Med Sch Univ Mass, 70-85; mem bd sci counrs, Nat Heart & Lung Inst, 72-74; mem, Corp Woods Hole Oceanog Inst, 74-85, trustee, 82-87; vis prof biochem, Dartmouth Med Sch, 86-; trustee, Montshire Mus Sci, 90- & Hitchcock Found, 91. *Mem:* Nat Acad Sci; Am Acad Arts & Sci. *Res:* Carcinogenic and biological effects of beryllium; biosynthesis of co-enzyme A; biosynthesis of protein; discoverer of transfer RNA and of mechanisms of amino acid activation. *Mailing Add:* PO Box 183 Thetford VT 05074. *Fax:* 802-785-2333

HOAGLAND, ROBERT EDWARD, BIOCHEMISTRY, PLANT PHYSIOLOGY. *Current Pos:* res chemist, Metab & Radiation Res Lab, Fargo, NDak, 72, RES BIOCHEMIST HERBICIDE ACTION, SOUTHERN WEED SCI LAB, SCI & EDUC ADMIN-AGR RES, USDA, STONEVILLE, MISS, 72- *Personal Data:* b Cleveland, Ohio, Feb 3, 42. *Educ:* Youngstown State Univ, BS, 64; Univ Cincinnati, MS, 68; NDak State Univ, PhD(biochem), 70. *Prof Exp:* Res assoc chem, NDak State Univ, 67-69, res chemist herbicide metab, 70-72. *Mem:* Sigma Xi; Am Chem Soc; Am Soc Plant Physiologists; Weed Sci Soc Am; Bot Soc Am. *Res:* Plant biochemistry; physiology and enzymology; aspects of phenolic metabolism; mode and mechanisms of herbicide action. *Mailing Add:* Southern Weed Sci Lab USDA PO Box 350 Stoneville MS 38776-0350

HOAGLAND, VINCENT DEFOREST, JR, BIOCHEMISTRY. *Current Pos:* from asst prof to assoc prof, 69-78, chmn dept, 74-77, PROF CHEM, SONOMA STATE UNIV, 78- *Personal Data:* b Waltham, Mass, June 10, 40; m 70, Margo Bell. *Educ:* Wesleyan Univ, BA, 62; Fla State Univ, PhD(chem), 67. *Prof Exp:* NIH res fel biochem, Univ Wash, 67-69. *Concurrent Pos:* Chair, Health Professions Adv Comt, Sonoma State Univ, 75-; pres, Western Asn Advisors Health Professions, 93- *Mem:* Am Chem Soc; AAAS; Sigma Xi. *Res:* Enzymology; quaternary structure of enzymes; enzyme kinetics. *Mailing Add:* Dept Chem Sonoma State Univ Rohnert Park CA 94928. *Fax:* 707-664-2505; *E-Mail:* vin.hoagland@sonoma.edu

HOAGLIN, DAVID CASTER, DATA ANALYSIS, SURVEY RESEARCH. *Current Pos:* sr analyst, 77-78, SR SCIENTIST, ABT ASSOCS INC, CAMBRIDGE, MASS, 78- *Personal Data:* b Charleston, WVa, Mar 4, 44; m 68, Dianne J Mendenhall; c Christopher D. *Educ:* Duke Univ, BS, 66; Princeton Univ, PhD(statist), 71. *Prof Exp:* From instr to asst prof statist, Harvard Univ, 70-72, lectr statist, 72-77; res assoc statist, Harvard Univ, 77-94. *Concurrent Pos:* Biostatistician, Harvard Anaesthetical Ctr, Mass Gen Hosp, 83-88. *Mem:* Fel AAAS; Soc Indust & Appl Math; fel Am Statist Asn (vpres, 96-98); Inst Math Statist; Int Statist Inst. *Res:* Exploratory data analysis; survey research methods; applications of statistics to policy problems. *Mailing Add:* Abt Assoc Inc 55 Wheeler St Cambridge MA 02138. *Fax:* 617-492-5219; *E-Mail:* dave__hoaglin@abtassoc.com

HOAGSTROM, CARL WILLIAM, BIOGEOGRAPHY, MAMMALOGY. *Current Pos:* PROF, OHIO NORTHERN UNIV, ADA, 75- *Personal Data:* b Holdrege, Nebr, Aug 24, 40; m 65; c Rebecca A, Christopher W & Sherwin C. *Educ:* Kearney State Col, Nebr, BS, 66; Purdue Univ, MS, 68; Univ Ariz, PhD(zool), 78. *Prof Exp:* Instr sci, Arcadia Nebr Sch, 68-69; instr biol & chem, Grand Island Nebr Sch, 69-71. *Mem:* AAAS; Am Inst Biol Sci; Ecol Soc Am; Am Soc Mammalogists. *Res:* Monitoring population fluctuations and community organization in small mammals. *Mailing Add:* Dept Biol Sci Ohio Northern Univ 525 S Main St Ada OH 45810-1555

HOAR, RICHARD MORGAN, DEVELOPMENTAL ANATOMY, REPRODUCTIVE BIOLOGY. *Current Pos:* CONSULT DEVELOP TOXICOL, ARGUS INT INC, HORSHAM, PA, 86- *Personal Data:* b Boston, Mass, Nov 22, 27; m 49; c 1. *Educ:* Dartmouth Col, AB, 50; Univ Kans, PhD(anat), 56. *Prof Exp:* Instr anat, Col Med, Univ Cincinnati, 56-58, from asst prof to assoc prof, 58-69; head teratology, Res Div, Hoffmann-La Roche Inc, 69-77, from asst dir to assoc dir, dept toxicol & path, 77-85; Findley Res, Inc, Fall River, Mass, 85-86. *Concurrent Pos:* Consult, Nat Inst Environ Health Sci, NIH, 70-72 & 76-78 & Environ Prof Protection Agency, 80-82; adj assoc prof anat, Col Physicians & Surgeons, Columbia Univ, 73-85; lectr anat, Mt Sinai Sch Med, 76-85; adj assoc prof anat, Albany Med Col; consult, develop toxicol & reproduction. *Mem:* AAAS; Am Asn Anat; Teratology Soc (treas, 74-78, pres, 80-81); Soc Study Reproduction; Am Asn Lab Animal Sci; Sigma Xi; Am Col Toxicol (pres, 88-89). *Res:* Endocrinology of reproduction, teratology, and biochemistry of development in guinea pigs; reproduction and teratology in ferrets. *Mailing Add:* 179 Cold Spring Rd Williamstown MA 01267-2753. *Fax:* 413-458-0930

HOAR, WILLIAM STEWART, COMPARATIVE PHYSIOLOGY. *Current Pos:* prof zool & fisheries, Univ BC, 45-64, head dept, 64-71, prof, 64-79, EMER PROF ZOOL, UNIV BC, 79- *Personal Data:* b Moncton, NB, Aug 31, 13; m 41, Margaret Mackenzie; c Stewart, David, Kenzie & Melanie. *Educ:* Univ NB, BA, 34; Univ Western Ont, MA, 36; Boston Univ, PhD(med sci), 39; FRSC, 55. *Hon Degrees:* DSc, Univ NB, 65, Mem Univ, 67, St Francis Xavier Univ, 76 & Univ Western Ont, 78; LLD, Simon Fraser, 80, Toronto, 85. *Honors & Awards:* Flavelle Medal, Royal Soc Can, 65; Officer, Order of Can, 75; Fry Medal, Can Soc Zool, 74; Shinkishi Hatai Medal, Pac Sci Asn, 91. *Prof Exp:* Demonstr zool, Univ Western Ont, 34-36; asst histol & embryol, Med Sch, Boston Univ, 36-39; asst prof biol, Univ NB, 39-42, prof zool, 42-45. *Concurrent Pos:* Guggenheim fel, Oxford Univ, 58-59. *Mem:* Can Soc Zoologists; Am Soc Zoologists; Sigma Xi. *Res:* Physiology; aspects of histology, embryology behavior and physiology of salmon; fish endocrinology especially pituitary and reproductive hormones. *Mailing Add:* Dept Zool Univ BC Vancouver BC V6T 2A9 Can

HOARD, DONALD ELLSWORTH, BIOCHEMISTRY. *Current Pos:* CONTRACT, LOS ALAMOS SCI LAB, UNIV CALIF, 96- *Personal Data:* b Seattle, Wash, Apr 14, 28; m 54, Dorothy Goetz; c Emily (Johnson), Robin, Allison (deForest) & Matthew. *Educ:* Univ Wash, BS, 52; Univ Calif, PhD(biochem), 57. *Prof Exp:* Res chemist, Pabst Labs, Pabst Brewing Co, 60-63; mem staff, Los Alamos Sci Lab, Univ Calif, 63-82, biomed res group, 63-82, data anal, 82-86; Amparo Corp, Santa Fe, NM, 86-95. *Concurrent Pos:* Res fel biochem, Calif Inst Technol, 57-60. *Mem:* AAAS. *Res:* Organic and radiation chemistry of nucleotides; oligonucleotides and nucleic acids. *Mailing Add:* 11 Los Arboles Dr Los Alamos NM 87544

HOARE, JAMES PATRICK, ELECTROCHEMISTRY. *Current Pos:* CONSULT, 87- *Personal Data:* b Denver, Colo, Jan 9, 21; m 53, Therese Tressel; c Karen M, Patrick J & John P. *Educ:* Regis Col, BS, 43; Cath Univ, MS, 48, PhD(phys chem), 49. *Honors & Awards:* John Campbell Award, Gen Motors Corp, 80, 86; Silver Medal Award, Am Electroplaters Soc, 81 & 83, Gold Medal Award, 85, Sci Achievement Award, 89; Sci Achievement Award, Cath Univ Am, 84; Res Award, Electrochem Soc, 87. *Prof Exp:* Asst chem, Cath Univ, 46-49; from instr to asst prof physics & chem, Trinity Col, DC, 49-54; phys chemist, Naval Res Lab, Washington, DC, 54-57; prin res engr, Sci Lab, Ford Motor Co, 57-60; sr res chemist, Gen Motors Corp, 60-70, mem sr tech staff electrochem dept, Res Labs Div, 70-77, dept res scientist, 77-79, res fel, 79-87. *Concurrent Pos:* Bonfils scholar, 39-43; Mullen fel, 43-44; electronic technician, US Navy, 44-46; grant, Res Corp, 52-54. *Mem:* Am Chem Soc; Electrochem Soc; Int Soc Electrochem; NY Acad Sci; Am Electroplaters Soc; Catalyst Soc. *Res:* Chemical kinetics; electrochemistry; mechanisms of electrode reactions; catalysts; surface chemistry; fuel cells; electrochemical machining; mechanisms of chromium electrodeposition. *Mailing Add:* 24860 Davenport Novi MI 48374

HOARE, RICHARD DAVID, INVERTEBRATE PALEONTOLOGY. *Current Pos:* chmn dept, 67-70, 71-75 & 80-84, assoc vpres acad affairs, 84-88, PROF GEOL, BOWLING GREEN STATE UNIV, 57- *Personal Data:* b Rosiclare, Ill, May 14, 27; m 47, 71; c 4. *Educ:* Augustana Col, AB, 51; Univ Mo, MA, 53, PhD, 57. *Prof Exp:* Instr geol, Univ Mo, 53-57. *Concurrent Pos:* Geologist, Cartier Mining Co, Can, 56; asst prof, Univ Mo, 57-58; managing ed, J Paleontology, 85- *Mem:* Paleont Soc; Brit Palaeont Asn. *Res:* Upper Paleozoic invertebrate paleontology; Pennsylvanian gastropods and polyplacophora. *Mailing Add:* 1337 Clark St Bowling Green OH 43402

HOBACK, JOHN HOLLAND, physical chemistry; deceased, see previous edition for last biography

HOBART, DAVID EDWARD, SPECTROELECTROCHEMISTRY, ACTINIDE SOLUTION AND SOLID STATE CHEMISTRY. *Current Pos:* GROUP LEADER, ACTINIDE GEOCHEM GROUP, LAWRENCE BERKELEY LAB, 93- *Personal Data:* b Middletown, Ohio, Jan 5, 49; m 86; c Michelle A & Carson H. *Educ:* Rollins Col, BA, 71; Univ Tenn, Knoxville, PhD(chem), 81. *Prof Exp:* Teaching asst chem, Univ Tenn, Knoxville, 75-77, res asst, 77-81, res assoc, 81-83; adj prof, Univ NMex, Los Alamos Br, 83-93. *Concurrent Pos:* Reviewer, NSF, Inorg Chem, Chem Reviews, Lanth Act Res, Radiochim Acta. *Mem:* Am Chem Soc; Sigma Xi; Soc Electroanalysis Chem. *Res:* Less stable oxidation states of lanthanide and actinide elements via spectroelectrochemistry in complexing aqueous media; preparation and analysis of solid state actinides and actinides in near-neutral aqueous media as pertains to nuclear waste isolation and the environment. *Mailing Add:* RE/SPEC Inc 4775 Indian School Rd NE Suite 300 Albuquerque NM 87110

HOBART, EVERETT W, ANALYTICAL CHEMISTRY. *Current Pos:* asst res dir, 65-71, LAB DIR, LEDOUX & CO, 71-76 & 80- *Personal Data:* b Cincinnati, Ohio, Dec 15, 31; m 56; c 5. *Educ:* Mass Inst Technol, BS, 53. *Prof Exp:* Jr chemist, Am Cyanamid Co, Conn, 53-55, chemist, 55-56; sr chemist, Pratt & Whitney Aircraft Div, United Aircraft Corp, Conn, 56-60, supvr analytical chem, 60-65; tech dir, Spectrochem Labs, Inc, 76-80. *Mem:* Am Chem Soc; Am Soc Test & Mat. *Res:* Chemical and instrumental analysis. *Mailing Add:* 81 Kirkgate Dr Spencerport NY 14559-2179

HOBART, PETER MERRILL, MOLECULAR BIOLOGY. *Current Pos:* ADJ PROF, CONN COL, 83- *Personal Data:* b Nov 13, 46; US citizen. *Educ:* Colby Col, AB, 68; Wesleyan Univ, PhD(molecular biol), 78. *Prof Exp:* Fel molecular genetics, Univ Calif, San Francisco, 77-81. *Mem:* Am Soc Biochem & Molecular Biol; NY Acad Sci. *Res:* Molecular mechanisms of cellular regulation; contribution of primary structure of macromolecules and deriving information from primary structure and levels of expression of the macromolecules which may reveal regulating mechanisms. *Mailing Add:* Dept Molecular Biol Vical Inc 9373 Towne Center Dr Suite 100 San Diego CA 92121

HOBART, ROBERT H, MATHEMATICAL PHYSICS. *Current Pos:* RETIRED. *Personal Data:* b New York, NY, Feb 2, 32. *Educ:* Mass Inst Technol, BS, 54; Stanford Univ, MS, 55; Univ Ill, PhD, 61. *Prof Exp:* Asst prof physics, Dalhousie Univ, 61-63; sr physicist, Battelle Meem Inst, 63-70; lectr, Mid Tech Univ, Ankara, 70-71; hons tutor, St Andrews Univ, 71-72; prof & head dept, Ft Hare Univ, 73-75 & Kenyatta Univ Col, 76-78; adj prof, Western Ky Univ, 78-79; prof physics & math, Mid Ga Col, 80-82; physicist, Foreign Sci & Technol Ctr, 83-92. *Res:* Nonlinear modeling; electrodynamics; nonlinear field theory. *Mailing Add:* 500 Court Square No 702 Charlottesville VA 22902

HOBART, WILLIAM CHESTER, JR, MEMORY SYSTEMS DESIGN, PROGRAM BEHAVIOR. *Current Pos:* asst prof elec eng, 89-94, DEP HEAD, DEPT ELEC & COMPUT ENG, USAF INST TECHNOL, 94- *Personal Data:* b Valparaiso, Fla, June 26, 54; m 77, Linnea Gundersen; c Keith, Stephen & William. *Educ:* USAF Acad, BS, 76; Air Force Inst Technol, MSEE, 81; Univ Tex, Austin, PhD(elec eng), 89. *Prof Exp:* Tactical air base commun maintenance officer, 3rd Combat Commun Group, USAF, 77-79, chief, Tactical Data Link Implementaion Br, Interoperability Group, 83-86; instr elec eng, USAF Acad, 81-83. *Concurrent Pos:* Prin investr, Advan Res Projs Agency, 93-; Nat Aerospace Plane Joint Prog Off, 93-; consult technol insertion, High Performance Comput Working Group, Dept Defense, 93- *Mem:* Inst Elec & Electronics Engrs Comput Soc; Asn Comput Mach. *Res:* Modeling of memory reference behavior, design of memory systems, and parallelization of discrete event simulations, collaborating in parallelization of computational fluid dynamics codes. *Mailing Add:* USAF Acad DFCS 2354 Fairchild Dr Suite 6K41 USAF Academy CO 80840. *E-Mail:* whobart@afit.af.mil

HOBBIE, JOHN EYRES, HYDROBIOLOGY. *Current Pos:* SR SCIENTIST, MARINE BIOL LAB, 76-, CO-DIR, ECOSYSTS CTR, 85- *Personal Data:* b Buffalo, NY, June 5, 35; m 59, Olivann Rumph; c Lawrence J, Erik A & David B. *Educ:* Dartmouth Col, BA, 57; Univ Calif, Berkeley, MA, 59; Ind Univ, PhD(zool), 62. *Honors & Awards:* Hutchinson Medal, Am Soc Limnol & Oceanog, 83. *Prof Exp:* Res assoc zool, Univ Calif, Davis, 62-63; NIH fel, Inst Limnol, Uppsala, 63-65; from asst prof zool to prof, NC State Univ, 65-75. *Concurrent Pos:* NSF sr fel, Norweg Inst Water Res, Oslo, 71-72; dir, Tundra Biome Aquatic Prog, US Int Biol Prog, 71-74; Tage Erlander professorship, Sweden, 88-89; Co-chair, NSF Land Margin Ecosys Res Coord Comt, 92- *Mem:* Ecol Soc Am; Am Soc Limnol & Oceanog (pres, 84-86); Am Soc Microbiol. *Res:* Arctic and antarctic limnology; heterotrophic bacteria in aquatic ecosystems; estuarine ecology; global carbon cycle. *Mailing Add:* 52 McCallum Dr Falmouth MA 02540. *Fax:* 508-457-1548; *E-Mail:* jhobbie@lupine.mbl.edu

HOBBIE, RUSSELL KLYVER, PHYSICS, MEDICAL. *Current Pos:* Res assoc, Univ Minn, 60-62, from asst prof to assoc prof, 62-72, dir, Space Sci Ctr, 79-84, assoc dean, 84-95, PROF PHYSICS, UNIV MINN, MINNEAPOLIS, 72- *Personal Data:* b Albany, NY, Nov 3, 34; m 57, Cynthia A Borcherding; c Lynn, Eric, Sarah & Ann. *Educ:* Mass Inst Technol, BS, 56; Harvard Univ, AM, 57, PhD(physics), 60. *Mem:* Am Phys Soc; Am Asn Physics Teachers; Am Asn Physicists Med; AAAS; Inst Elec & Electronics Engrs. *Res:* Radiological physics; biophysics. *Mailing Add:* Sch Physics Univ Minn 116 Church St SE Minneapolis MN 55455. *Fax:* 612-624-4578; *E-Mail:* hobbie@umn.edu

HOBBINS, JOHN CLARK, MATERNAL-FETAL MEDICINE, DIAGNOSTIC ULTRASONOGRAPHY. *Current Pos:* Instr, 70-71, asst prof to assoc prof 74-80, PROF OBSTET & GYNEC, YALE UNIV, SCH MED, 80-, DIR OBSTET, NEW HAVEN MED CTR, 76- *Personal Data:* b New York, NY, July 13, 36. *Educ:* Hamilton Col, MS, 58; NY Med Col, MD, 63; Yale Univ, MS, 80. *Concurrent Pos:* Ed, Clin Diag Ultrasound & Ultrasound Med & Biol; examr, Maternal-Fetal Med Bds. *Mem:* Fel Am Col Obstet & Gynec; Soc Gynec Invest; Am Inst Ultrasound Med; Soc Perinatal Obstetricians (vpres). *Res:* Prenatal diagnosis of congenital anomalies by ultrasound and fetal treatment of some of these anomalies such as hydrocephalus and posterior urethral obstruction. *Mailing Add:* Univ Col Health Sci Ctr 4200 E North Ave Denver CO 80262

HOBBS, ANN SNOW, ION TRANSPORT, ENZYME KINETICS. *Current Pos:* RES ASST PROF, DEPT PHYSIOL, SCH MED, UNIV MD, 84- *Personal Data:* b Washington, DC, Nov 20, 45. *Educ:* Univ Md, BS, 68, PhD(biophysics), 73. *Prof Exp:* Res assoc, Dept Biol, Syracuse Univ, 73-75; fel, Lab Biophysics & Neurochem, NIH, 75-77, staff fel, 77-79, sr staff fel, Lab Neurochem, Neurol Commun Disorders & Strokes, 79-84. *Concurrent Pos:* Fel Grass Found, Marine Biol Lab, 74; adj asst prof, Dept Physiol, Uniformed Serv Univ Health Sci, 78- *Mem:* Biophys Soc; AAAS. *Res:* Enzyme mechanisms and regulatory processes for active ion transport across cell membranes, particularly the transport of sodium and potassium. *Mailing Add:* Cushman Darby & Cushman 1100 New York Ave NW E Tower 9th Floor Washington DC 20005-3918. *Fax:* 202-822-0944

HOBBS, ANSON PARKER, PHYSICAL CHEMISTRY. *Current Pos:* RETIRED. *Personal Data:* b Greensburg, Ind, Mar 4, 15; m; c 3. *Educ:* Univ Ind, AB, 36. *Prof Exp:* Chemist, Dow Chem Co, 37-44, group leader anal chem, 44, asst dir spec serv lab, 44-69; res chemist, Helium Res Ctr, Tex, 69-70, res chemist, Pittsburgh Energy Res Ctr. Energy Res & Develop Admin, 70-77. *Concurrent Pos:* Rep, Natural Gas Processors Asn, 55-; mem, Gas Asn. *Mem:* AAAS; fel Am Inst Chem; Am Chem Soc; Alzheimers Found (vpres). *Res:* Gas analysis; catalyst research; physical properties and other reactions of gaseous materials. *Mailing Add:* 8555 S Lewis 24C Tulsa OK 74137-1298

HOBBS, BENJAMIN F, ENVIRONMENTAL SYSTEMS ENGINEERING, ELECTRIC UTILITY SYSTEMS PLANNING. *Current Pos:* from asst prof to assoc prof, 88-93, PROF, SYSTS ENG, CASE WESTERN RES UNIV, 95- *Personal Data:* b Summit, NJ, July 31, 54; m 80, Julie R McDill; c Jeannette C & Paul M. *Educ:* SDak State Univ, BS, 76; State Univ NY, Syracuse, MS, 78; Cornell Univ, PhD(environ systs eng), 83. *Prof Exp:* Econ assoc, Brookhaven Nat Lab, 77-79; Wigner fel, Oak Ridge Nat Lab, 82-84. *Concurrent Pos:* NSF presidential young investr, 86; inst assoc, Nat Regulatory Res Inst; consult, Fed Energy Regulatory Comn. *Mem:* Am Soc Civil Engrs; Am Geophys Union; Inst Elec & Electronics Engrs; Inst Opers Res & Mgt Sci; Asn Energy Serv Prof. *Res:* Energy and environmental engineering problems using systems analysis and economics; energy conservation planning; acid rain compliance planning; multiobjective decision analysis method development. *Mailing Add:* Dept Geog & Environ Eng Johns Hopkins Univ 313 Ames Hall Baltimore MD 21218. *Fax:* 410-516-8996; *E-Mail:* bhobbs@jhu.edu

HOBBS, BILLY FRANKEL, MATHEMATICS. *Current Pos:* chmn dept, 70-80, PROF, POINT LOMA COL, 70-, CHMN, 87- *Personal Data:* b Hiltons, Va, Mar 5, 31; m 53; c 2. *Educ:* Ball State Univ, BS, 54, MA, 55; Purdue Univ, PhD, 67. *Prof Exp:* Teacher pub sch, Ind, 54-57; asst prof math, Olivet Nazarene Col, 57-66, chmn dept, 60-66; asst prof, Purdue Univ, 66-67; prof, Olivet Nazarene Col, 67-70, prof & chmn dept, Pasadena Col, 70. *Concurrent Pos:* NSF sci fac fel, 62-63, grad fel, 64-65, grad trainee, 65-66; mem, deleg math educ to China, 83, Nat Coun Teacher Math. *Mem:* Am Math Soc; Math Asn Am. *Res:* Topological and commutative algebra; general topology; use of logo in problem solving. *Mailing Add:* Math & Comput Sci Dept Point Loma Nazarene Col 3900 Lomaland Dr San Diego CA 92106-2899

HOBBS, CHARLES CLIFTON, JR, ORGANIC CHEMISTRY, FREE RADICAL OXIDATIONS OF PARAFFINS & ALKYLAROMATICS MATHEMATICAL MODELING OF OXIDATIONS. *Current Pos:* CONSULT LIQUID PHASE OXIDATION, 85- *Personal Data:* b Wewoka, Okla, Mar 23, 27; m 50, Hsiao-Hsia Tsai; c Jeffrey, Jennifer & John. *Educ:* Univ Okla, BS, 49, MS, 51, PhD(chem), 53. *Honors & Awards:* Chem Pioneer Award, Am Inst Chemists, 74. *Prof Exp:* From res chemist to sr res chemist, Celanese Corp Am, 52-58, from res assoc, Explor Res Dept to group leader, basic process res sect, Chem Div, 58-67, sr res assoc, Chem Res Dept, Celanese Chem Co, 67-85. *Mem:* Am Chem Soc; fel Am Inst Chemists. *Res:* Chromyl chloride oxidation of saturated hydrocarbons; derivatives of petroleum chemicals; organic electrochemistry; peroxygen chemicals; free radical reactions; liquid phase oxidation; mathematical modeling; vapor phase oxidation; organic syntheses. *Mailing Add:* 1437 Casa Verde Dr Corpus Christi TX 78411-3331. *E-Mail:* cch@corpus.enet.hcc.com

HOBBS, CHARLES FLOYD, ORGANIC CHEMISTRY. *Current Pos:* CONSULT, 93- *Personal Data:* b Lebo, Kans, Jan 17, 35; m 55; c 2. *Educ:* Emporia Kans State Univ, AB, 56; Univ Kans, PhD(org chem), 60. *Prof Exp:* Res asst org chem, Univ Kans, 56-60; sr res chemist, Monsanto Agr Chem Co, 60-68, res specialist, 68-73, sr res specialist org chem, Corp Res Labs, 73-79, sr res specialist, Monsanto Chem Intermediates Co, 79-83, sr res specialist, Monsanto Agr Chem Co, 83-88, group leader, 88-93. *Mem:* Am Chem Soc; fel Am Inst Chemists; Sigma Xi. *Res:* Homogeneous catalysis; organic nitrogen chemistry; organometallic chemistry; olefin metathesis; heterocyclic chemistry. *Mailing Add:* 1100 Trinket Ct St Louis MO 63131

HOBBS, CHARLES HENRY, TOXICOLOGY & VETERINARY TOXICOLOGY. *Current Pos:* toxicologist, 69-73, asst dir, 74-93, ASSOC DIR, INHALATION TOXICOL RES INST, 94-, VPRES, LOVELACE BIOMED & ENVIRON RES INST, 94-; CLIN PROF, UNIV NMEX, 86- *Personal Data:* b Longmont, Colo, Oct 4, 42; div; c Carrie A & Kathryn L. *Educ:* Colo State Univ, DVM, 66; Am Bd Vet Toxicol, dipl, 72; Am Bd Toxicol, cert, 81. *Prof Exp:* Capt, US Army Vet Corps, 66-69. *Concurrent Pos:* Toxicologist, Div Biomed & Environ Res, US Energy Res & Develop Admin, 75-76. *Mem:* Am Acad Vet & Comp Toxicol (secy-treas, 76-80); Am Vet Med Asn; Radiation Res Soc; Soc Toxicol. *Res:* Inhalation toxicology; toxicology of inhaled chemicals; late effects of radiation; long-term toxicity studies. *Mailing Add:* Inhalation Toxicol Res Inst PO Box 5890 Albuquerque NM 87185. *Fax:* 505-845-1193; *E-Mail:* chobbs@audrey.lmf.org

HOBBS, CHARLES RODERICK BRUCE, JR, GEOLOGY. *Current Pos:* RETIRED. *Personal Data:* b Englewood, NJ, Dec 24, 29; m 62, Anne Pierce. *Educ:* Va Polytech Inst, BS, 52, MS, 53, PhD(geol), 57. *Prof Exp:* Geologist, Div Mineral Resources, Va Dept Conserv & Econ Develop, 57-70, from asst state geologist & asst comnr mineral resources to dep state geologist & dep comnr mineral resources, 70-85; dep state geologist, Div Mineral Resources, Va Dept Mines, Minerals & Energy, 85-91. *Mem:* Geol Soc Am; Am Asn Petrol Geol; Sigma Xi. *Res:* Carbonate petrology. *Mailing Add:* 717 Cargil Lane Charlottesville VA 22902

HOBBS, CLIFFORD DEAN, PLANT PATHOLOGY, GENERAL AGRICULTURE. *Current Pos:* OWNER, HOBBS GARDEN CTR, 91- *Personal Data:* b Atlanta, Tex, June 9, 33; m 56, Betty J Nichols; c Donna J, David D & Joel R. *Educ:* Tex A&M Univ, BS, 55, MS, 60, PHD(plant path), 64. *Prof Exp:* Res agronomist, Crops Res Div, Agr Res Serv, USDA, 58-61, res plant pathologist, 61-65; exten plant pathologist, Tex Agr Exten Serv, 65-67; plant sci rep, Eli Lilly & Co, 67-74; consult, Agr Mgt & Consult Serv, 75-77; pres, Valley Garden Ctr, Inc, 76-85; agr missionary, Foreign Mission Bd, Southern Baptist Conv, 85-90. *Concurrent Pos:* Sales rep, Kinney Bonded Warehouse, Inc. *Res:* Manage garden center; educational seminars; consultant on ornamental crops; evaluation of mung bean varieties for use as high protein food in Liberia and other West African countries; physiology of disease resistance to wheat stem rust. *Mailing Add:* 10806 Burnwood Dr Austin TX 78758

HOBBS, CLINTON HOWARD, BOTANY. *Current Pos:* from asst prof to prof biol, 45-80, EMER PROF BIOL SCI, KENT STATE UNIV, 80- *Personal Data:* b Indianapolis, Ind, Jan 16, 15; m 44; c 4. *Educ:* Purdue Univ, BSA, 36, MS, 39, PhD(plant physiol), 42. *Prof Exp:* Asst biol, Purdue Univ, 36-42; teacher pub sch, Ind, 43; asst plant physiologist, Guayule Rubber Res Proj, USDA, Calif, 43-45. *Mem:* AAAS; Am Inst Biol Sci; Am Nature Study Soc. *Res:* Plant respiration; mineral deficiency in pine; polygonaceae of Ohio. *Mailing Add:* 952 Ravenna Rd Kent OH 44240-6155

HOBBS, DAVID E, MECHANICAL ENGINEERING, GAS TURBINE TURBOMACHINERY DESIGN, TESTING AND PRODUCT DEVELOPMENT. *Current Pos:* CONSULT, 94- *Personal Data:* b Aug 23, 41; m, Rayona; c Jeffrey & Andrew. *Educ:* Dartmouth Col, BA, 63; Case Inst Technol, BS, 64; Rensselaer Polytech Inst, MS, 67, PhD(mech eng), 83. *Honors & Awards:* Gas Turbine Award, Am Soc Mech Engrs, 88. *Prof Exp:* Staff mem, Turbine Component Design Group, Pratt & Whitney, 64-67, Turbine Anal & Technol Develop Group, 67-77, staff mem, Compressor Anal & Technol Develop Group, 77-94. *Concurrent Pos:* Mem, Gas Turbine Turbomach Comt & Axial Compressor Panel, Am Soc Mech Engrs. *Mem:* Am Soc Mech Engrs; Am Inst Aeronaut & Astronaut. *Res:* Gas turbines; turbomachinery; experimental and computational modelling of flows in turbomachinery; design system development. *Mailing Add:* 20 Bayberry Trail South Windsor CT 06074

HOBBS, DONALD CLIFFORD, BIOCHEMISTRY. *Personal Data:* b Edmonton, Alta, Apr 12, 30; m 52, Donna Thompson; c Dale, David & Diane. *Educ:* Univ Alta, BSc, 52, MSc, 55; Univ Tenn, PhD(biochem), 57. *Prof Exp:* Lectr, Univ Alta, 52-54; res biochemist, Pfizer, Inc, 57-73, mgr, 73-78, asst dir, 78-81, dir, Drug Metab Dept, 81-90. *Mem:* AAAS; Am Soc Pharmacol & Therapeut. *Res:* Intermediary metabolism; peptide chemistry; isolation and chemistry of antibiotics and other natural products; drug disposition and biotransformation; nutrition. *Mailing Add:* 7 N Ledge Rock Rd Niantic CT 06357. *E-Mail:* 103320.3310@compuserve.com

HOBBS, HERMAN HEDBERG, SOLID STATE PHYSICS, ATROPHYSICS. *Current Pos:* chmn dept, 61-68, 74-77, prof, 59-93, EMER PROF PHYSICS, GEORGE WASHINGTON UNIV, 93- *Personal Data:* b Dallas, Tex, Jun 25, 27; m 48, Joyce Pritchett. *Educ:* George Washington Univ, BS, 53, MS, 55; Univ Va, PhD(physics), 58. *Prof Exp:* Physicist, Nat Bur Stand, 53; instr physics, George Washington Univ, 54-55; instr, Univ Va, 56-58, res fel, 58-59. *Mem:* Am Phys Soc; Am Asn Physics Teachers; Sigma Xi; AAAS; Am Asn Univ Prof; Exp Aircraft Asn. *Res:* Growth and perfection of metal crystals; electrical conductivity and piezo-resistance effects in metal crystals; microwave electronics; growth of metal whiskers under conditions which resemble those on an orbiting space station sponsored by NASA. *Mailing Add:* Dept Physics George Washington Univ Washington DC 20052

HOBBS, HORTON HOLCOMBE, JR, systematic zoology; deceased, see previous edition for last biography

HOBBS, HORTON HOLCOMBE, III, LIMNOLOGY, BIOSPELEOLOGY. *Current Pos:* PROF BIOL, WITTENBERG UNIV, 76- *Personal Data:* b Gainesville, Fla, Dec 17, 44; m 67; c Heather H (Killion) & Horton H IV. *Educ:* Univ Richmond, BA, 67; Miss State Univ, MS, 69; Ind Univ, PhD(zool), 73. *Honors & Awards:* Cert of Merit, Nat Speleol Soc. *Prof Exp:* Instr biol, Christopher Newport Col, 73-75; asst prof biol, George Mason Univ, 75-76. *Concurrent Pos:* Dir Nat Speleol Soc, bd gov, Ohio Valley Region; bd mem, Cave Conserv, Va; bd trustees, Island Cave Res Ctr. *Mem:* Am Soc Limnol & Oceanog; Am Inst Biol Sci; fel Nat Speleol Soc; Sigma Xi; Cave Res Found; Crustacean Soc; fel Explorers Club. *Res:* Cave ecology; systematics, evolution and ecology of aquatic decapods and entocytherid ostracods. *Mailing Add:* Dept Biol Wittenberg Univ Springfield OH 45501. *Fax:* 937-327-6340; *E-Mail:* hhobbs@wittenberg.edu

HOBBS, JAMES ARTHUR, AGRONOMY, SOILS. *Current Pos:* asst agronomist & asst prof, Kans State Univ, 50-52, assoc agronomist & assoc prof, 52-58, agronomist & prof, 58-85, EMER PROF SOILS, EXP STA, KANS STATE UNIV, 85- *Personal Data:* b East Kildonan, Can, Dec 5, 14; nat US; m 40; c 3. *Educ:* Univ Man, BSA, 35, MSc, 40; Purdue Univ, PhD(soils), 48. *Prof Exp:* Asst, Dom Exp Farms, Ottawa, 35-41; agr rep exten serv, Dept Agr, Man, 41-48; asst prof soils, Univ Man, 48-49. *Concurrent Pos:* Head, Dept Soil Sci, Ahmadu Bello Univ, Nigeria, 64-66 & 70-74, dean agr, 65-66 & 71-72; consult, Dept Agr, Sri Lanka, 79, Min Agr, Tanzania, 79, Fac Agr, Univ Zimbabwe, 82 & INRA, Min Agr, Morocco, 87; res exten liaison officer, Min Agr, Botswana, 82-85. *Mem:* Am Soc Agron; Soil Sci Soc Am; Int Soc Soil Sci; Soil Water Conserv Soc. *Res:* Soil management, soil conservation. *Mailing Add:* 571 Jessie Ave Winnipeg MB R3L 0R1 Can

HOBBS, JOHN ROBERT, PHYSICAL CHEMISTRY, ANALYTICAL CHEMISTRY. *Current Pos:* RES CHEMIST, SAFETY & ENVIRON TECHNOL DIV, VOLPE NAT TRANSP SYST CTR, RES & SPEC PROG ADMIN, US DEPT TRANSP, 70- *Personal Data:* b Plainfield, Ind, Aug 22, 41; m 69. *Educ:* Rose Polytech Inst, BS, 63; Univ NH, PhD(phys chem), 68. *Prof Exp:* Nat Acad Sci-Nat Res Coun fels, Army Mat & Mech Res Ctr, 68-69; NSF fel chem, Cornell Univ, 69-70. *Mem:* Am Chem Soc; NY Acad Sci; Am Soc Mass Spectrometry; Am Soc Testing & Mat. *Res:* Mass spectroscopy applied to trace analysis; trace analysis of impurities in materials; high energy chemical kinetics; trace gas analysis; explosive vapor detection methods; security in transportation systems. *Mailing Add:* Volpe Nat Transp Syst Ctr Code 75 US Dept Transp Kendall Sq Cambridge MA 02142. *E-Mail:* hobbsj@volpez.dot.gov

HOBBS, LEWIS MANKIN, ASTRONOMY, ASTROPHYSICS. *Current Pos:* from asst prof to assoc prof, 66-76, dir, Yerkes Observ, 74-82, PROF ASTRON & ASTROPHYS, UNIV CHICAGO, 76- *Personal Data:* b Upper Darby, Pa, May 16, 37; m 62, JoAnn Hagele; c John, Michael & Dara. *Educ:* Cornell Univ, BEngPhys, 60; Univ Wis, MS, 62, PhD(physics), 66. *Prof Exp:* Jr astronomer, Univ Calif, Santa Cruz, 65-66. *Concurrent Pos:* Alfred P Sloan scholar, 56-60; mem, bd dirs, Asn Univs for Res Astron, Inc, Washington, DC, 74-85; mem, Astron Comt of Bd Trustees, Univs Res Asn, Inc, Washington, DC, 79-83, chmn, 79-81; mem, Space Telescope Inst Coun Asn Univs for Res Astron, Inc, 82-87; mem, bd govs, Astrophys Res Consortium, Inc, ARC, Seattle, Wash, 84-91; mem, Hubble Space Telescope Users' Comt, NASA, 90-94. *Mem:* Am Astron Soc; Am Phys Soc; Int Astron Union. *Res:* Interstellar medium; observational cosmology. *Mailing Add:* Yerkes Observ Univ Chicago Williams Bay WI 53191-0258

HOBBS, M FLOYD, PHYSICAL CHEMISTRY, ORGANIC CHEMISTRY. *Current Pos:* PRES, M FLOYD HOBBS & ASSOC INC, 83- *Personal Data:* b San Jose, Calif, Dec 19, 24; m 47; c 5. *Educ:* Univ Calif, Berkeley, BA, 48. *Prof Exp:* Analytical chemist, Marine Magnesium Div, Merck & Co, 48-51; chemist, Bioferm Div, Int Minerals & Chem Corp, 51-54, proj chemist, 54-61, head org chem, 61-65; sr res chemist, FMC Corp, 65-82. *Mem:* Am Chem Soc; fel Am Inst Chem; Am Soc Enol & Viticult. *Res:* Isolation of organic chemicals from fermentation media; ion exchange; liquid ion exchange; kinetics; phase relationships; solvent extraction; waste and waste water chemistry. *Mailing Add:* 15604 Kavin Lane Monte Sereno CA 95030-3224

HOBBS, MARCUS EDWIN, PHYSICAL CHEMISTRY. *Current Pos:* Asst, Indust Chem Lab, Duke Univ, 31-35, from instr to asst prof, 35-45, assoc prof, 45-49, prof chem, 49-79, chmn dept, 51-54, dean, Grad Sch Arts & Sci, 54-59, dean univ, 58-63, provost, 69-70, UNIV DISTINGUISHED SERV EMER PROF CHEM, DUKE UNIV, 79- *Personal Data:* b Chadbourn, NC, Aug 11, 09; m 37, Sarah F Blanchard; c Sarah H (Jackson) & Joan H (Gray). *Educ:* Duke Univ, AB, 32, MA, 34, PhD(chem), 36. *Honors & Awards:* Civilian Serv Medal, Dept Army, 59. *Concurrent Pos:* Civilian, Off Sci Res & Develop; actg chief scientist, Off Ord Res, 51-52; mem predoctoral fels bd, Nat Res Coun, NSF, 51-53, Adv Comt Spec Projs Sci Ed, 58-65; chmn, Exec Comt, Res Triangle Inst, 64-69 & 77-; mem, Adv Comt Utilization Res & Develop, USDA, 64-70. *Mem:* AAAS; Am Chem Soc; Am Inst Physics; Am Inst Chemists. *Res:* Dielectric constants and dipole moments; infrared and ultraviolet absorption spectra; colloids; chemistry of tobacco and smoke; nuclear magnetic resonance; relaxation times. *Mailing Add:* Dept Chem Box 90346 Duke Univ Durham NC 27708. *Fax:* 919-660-1605

HOBBS, PETER VICTOR, ATMOSPHERIC PHYSICS. *Current Pos:* Asst prof, 63-65, assoc prof, 65-70, PROF ATMOSPHERIC SCI, UNIV WASH, 70-, DIR CLOUD PHYSICS GROUP, 63-, ADJ PROF GEOPHYS, 74- *Personal Data:* b London, Eng, May 31, 36; US citizen; m 63; c 3. *Educ:* Univ London, BSc, 60, DIC & PhD(cloud physics), 63. *Mem:* AAAS; Am Geophys Union; Am Meteorol Soc; Royal Meteorol Soc. *Res:* Physics of clouds, rain, snow, thunderstorms and weather modification; air pollution; atmospheric chemistry; mesometeorology. *Mailing Add:* Dept Atmospheric Sci AK-40 Univ Wash Seattle WA 98195-0001

HOBBS, ROBERT WESLEY, RADIO ASTRONOMY. *Current Pos:* CONSULT, 93- *Personal Data:* b Chester, WVa, Jan 28, 38; m 62, Belinda L Delung; c David & Anne M. *Educ:* Case Inst Technol, BS, 60; Univ Mich, MS, 62, PhD(astron), 64. *Prof Exp:* Sect head, Radio Astron Br, US Naval Res Lab, 64-69; br head, Lab Astron & Solar Physics, Goddard Space Flight Ctr, NASA, 69-82; chief scientist, CTA Inc, 82-90, dir eng, 90-92, vpres, 92-93. *Concurrent Pos:* Guest lectr, Univ Md, 64. *Mem:* Am Astron Soc; Int Sci Radio Union; Int Astron Union. *Res:* Radio, ultraviolet and optical astronomy; polarization of radio sources; flux density variations in quasars; solar active regions; radio emission from comets; author of 120 technical publications. *Mailing Add:* 737 Walnut Ave North Beach MD 20714

HOBBS, STANLEY YOUNG, POLYMER PHYSICS. *Current Pos:* MEM STAFF POLYMER PHYSICS, GEN ELEC CORP RES & DEVELOP, 69-, TECH COORDR LAB ADMIN, 75-, MGR STRUCT PLASTICS PROJ, 76-, MGR POLYMER PHYSICS UNIT, 78-, STAFF SCIENTIST, 88- *Personal Data:* b Gloversville, NY, June 1, 44; m 68; c 1. *Educ:* Dartmouth Col, BA, 66; Rensselaer Polytech Inst, PhD(chem), 69. *Mem:* Am Phys Soc; Electron Micros Soc Am; Sigma Xi. *Res:* Polymer crystallization and morphology; nucleation phenomena; polymer blends. *Mailing Add:* 33 Gould Dr Scotia NY 12302

HOBBS, WILLARD EARL, RADIATION TRANSPORT, RISK ASSESSMENT OF NUCLEAR RADIATION. *Current Pos:* CHIEF SCIENTIST, RADON REDUCTION & RESEARCH, 89- *Personal Data:* m 73, Ronda Kaufman; c Christopher & Carrie. *Educ:* USDAF Acad, BS, 65; Univ Calif, Davis, MS, 68, PhD(appl sci), 75. *Prof Exp:* Nuclear res officer, Air Force Tech Appln Ctr, 68-75; AEC special fel nuclear sci, Univ Calif-Davis, 73-75; resident res assoc, Naval Res Lab, 75-77; sr scientist, Jaycor, 77-81; prog mgr, Kaman Sci Corp, 81-89. *Concurrent Pos:* Lectr, Solano Col, 69-72; organizer, Missle In-Flight Working group, 81-88; mem, Radon Task Force, S Calif, 90-93. *Mem:* Am Phys Soc; AAAS. *Res:* Numerical analysis of gas dynamics for indoor pollution; numerical analysis of electromagnetic fields induced by nuclear radiation; microwave environments induced by nuclear radiation. *Mailing Add:* 515 Foxen Dr Santa Barbara CA 93105

HOBBY, CHARLES R, MATHEMATICS. *Current Pos:* chmn dept, 73-84, prof, 84-96, EMER PROF MATH, UNIV ALA, 96- *Personal Data:* b Tyler, Tex, Sept 5, 30; m 53; c 2. *Educ:* Univ Calif, Berkeley, BA, 53; Univ Houston, MS, 57; Calif Inst Technol, PhD(math), 60. *Prof Exp:* Mathematician, Inst Defense Anal, 60-61; from asst prof to prof math, Univ Wash, 61-73. *Mem:* Am Math Soc. *Res:* Group theory; probability. *Mailing Add:* Dept Math Univ Ala Box 870350 Tuscaloosa AL 35487-0350

HOBEIKA, ANTOINE GEORGE, TRANSPORTATION ENGINEERING. *Current Pos:* from asst prof to assoc prof, 73-83, PROF TEACHING & RES, VA POLYTECH INST & STATE UNIV, 83- *Personal Data:* b Homsieh, Lebanon, Sept 28, 43; US citizen. *Educ:* Am Univ Beirut, Lebanon, BS, 67, MS, 70; Purdue Univ, PhD(civil eng), 73. *Prof Exp:* Training engr construct & design, Victoria Line, London, 66; site engr construct, Esso Gas Liquification Plant, Libya, 67; teaching asst, Am Univ Beirut, 69-70; supv engr civil works, Off Reconstruct, Beirut, 68-70; res asst, Purdue Univ, 70-73. *Concurrent Pos:* Consult, Ministry Planning, Iraq, 74-75 & RR Orgn, Saudi-Arabia, 78; prin investr, Va Div Motor Vehicles, 77-82, NASA, Langley, 78-81, Dept Energy, 79-81 & Urban Mass Transp Admin, 82-85, NSF, Va Elec & Power Co, Va Dept Emergency Serv, Va Dept Highways & Transp. *Mem:* Am Soc Civil Engrs; Inst Transp Engrs; Am Rd & Transp Builders Asn; Sigma Xi. *Res:* Transportation evacuation planning particularly in emergency management; airfield runway geometrics under future air traffic control systems; transportation and development in less developed countries; increasing productivity of mass transit systems; shipment of hazardous materials. *Mailing Add:* Dept Civil Eng Va Polytech Inst 200 Patton Hall Blacksburg VA 24061-0105

HOBERG, ERIC PAUL, SYSTEMATICS OF ANIMAL PARASITES, HISTORICAL BIOGEOGRAPHY. *Current Pos:* ZOOLOGIST & ASSOC CUR US NAT PARASITE COLLECTION, USDA, AGR RES SERV, BIOSYSTEMATIC PARASITOL LAB, 90- *Personal Data:* b San Francisco, Calif, Oct 18, 53; m 79, Margaret I Dykes. *Educ:* Univ Alaska, Fairbanks, BS, 75; Univ Sask, MS, 79; Univ Wash, Seattle, PhD(parasite syst & wildlife sci), 84. *Honors & Awards:* Henry Baldwin Ward Medal, Am Soc Parasitologists, 92. *Prof Exp:* Instr gen parasitol & wildlife parasitol, Western Col Vet Med, Univ Sask, 78; res asst parasitol, Dept Pathobiol, Univ Wash, 79-84, sr fel, 84-85; res assoc parasitol, Col Vet Med, Ore State Univ, 85-89; asst prof vet parasitol, Atlantic Vet Col, Univ Prince Edward Island, 89-90. *Concurrent Pos:* Prin investr, Arctic Inst NAm, 81 & 82, NSF, 82-84, Nat Sci & Eng Res Coun Can, 90-93; vis scientist, Labs Ornith & Parasitol, Inst Biol Probs North, Russian Acad Sci, 81 & 88; Interacad Exchange Prog, Nat Acad Scis, 88; RL & VR Rausch vis prof, Univ Sask Western Col Vet Med, 92; assoc ed systs & phylogenetics, J Parasitol, 93- *Mem:* AAAS; Am Soc Parasitologists; Am Asn Zool Nomenclature; Soc Syst Biol; Am Ornithologists Union. *Res:* Systematics, phylogenetic reconstruction and biodiversity of helminthic parasites of vertebrates; coevolution, historical biogeography and historical ecology of host-parasite systems among seabirds and marine mammals in Holarctic and antarctic seas; higher-level phylogeny of tapeworms; evolution of nematodes among ruminants. *Mailing Add:* BARC E 1180 USDA Agr Res Serv 10300 Baltimore Ave Beltsville MD 20705-2850. *Fax:* 301-504-8979; *E-Mail:* ehoberg@asrr.arsusda.gov

HOBERMAN, ALFRED ELLIOTT, EDUCATION. *Current Pos:* PROF & CHMN DEPT CHEM, PHYSICS & GEOSCI, LOCK HAVEN UNIV, 67- *Personal Data:* b Lock Haven, Pa, Aug 24, 39; m 67; c 2. *Educ:* Lock Haven Univ, BS, 62; Univ Miss, MSc, 67; Louisiana State Univ, ABD. *Prof Exp:* Teacher chem, Spec Sch Dist, Dover, Del, 62-65 & Chichester Sch Dist, 65-66. *Concurrent Pos:* Instr chem, Louisiana State Univ, 72-74; prin investr, stream acidification, Lock Haven Univ, 85- *Mem:* Am Chem Soc. *Res:* Stream acidification in central Pennsylvania; the effect of acid precipitation on limestone and free stone streams. *Mailing Add:* Lock Haven Univ Lock Haven PA 17745-2390

HOBERMAN, HENRY DON, BIOCHEMISTRY. *Current Pos:* from assoc prof to prof, 53-90, EMER PROF BIOCHEM, ALBERT EINSTEIN COL MED, 90- *Personal Data:* b Bridgeport, Conn, Apr 23, 14; m 43, 74, Hilda Carnicero; c John, David, Ruth & Michael. *Educ:* Columbia Univ, AB, 36, PhD(biochem), 43; Harvard Univ, MD, 47. *Prof Exp:* Asst trop med & tutor biochem sci, Harvard Univ, 43-44; asst prof internal med, Yale Univ, 47-48, asst prof physiol chem, 48-53; assoc attend physician, Bronx Minic Hosp Ctr, 81- *Concurrent Pos:* Markle scholar, Yale Univ, 48-53. *Mem:* Am Soc Biol Chemists; Nat Asn Appl Arts & Sci; Am Chem Soc. *Res:* Regulation of intermediary metabolism of amino acids, coupling of intracellular oxidation-reduction reactions; alcohol metabolism; post-translational modifications of human hemoglobin. *Mailing Add:* 28436 Verde Lane Bonita Springs FL 34135

HOBEROCK, LAWRENCE L, AUTOMATIC CONTROL, DRILLING MECHANICS. *Current Pos:* PROF & HEAD, SCH MECH & AEROSPACE ENG, OKLA STATE UNIV, 87- *Personal Data:* b Wichita, Kans, Oct 21, 39; m 64, Judith L Anderson; c Michael J, Barbara T & Timmothy M. *Educ:* Univ Mo, Rolla, BSME, 61; Purdue Univ, MSME, 63, PhD(mech eng), 66. *Honors & Awards:* Dedicated Serv Award, Am Soc Mech Engrs, 95. *Prof Exp:* Res coordr, US Army Ballistic Res Labs, 66-68; from asst prof to assoc prof mech eng, Univ Tex, Austin, 68-78; res assoc, Amoco Prod Co, 78-81, res supvr, 81-85; vpres res, Derrick Mfg Corp, 85-86; eng consult, 86-87. *Concurrent Pos:* Assoc ed, J Dyn Systs, Am Soc Mech Engrs, 74-77, mem, Bd Eng Educ, 97; consult, Amoco Prod Co 77-78 & 88, Shell Develop Co, 89-91 & Conoco Inc, 90; assoc ed, Drilling Eng, Soc Petrol Engrs, 87-90. *Mem:* Fel Am Soc Mech Engrs; Soc Petrol Engrs; Am Soc Eng Educ; Inst Elec & Electronics Engrs; Am Inst Aeronaut & Astronaut. *Res:* drilling mechanics; oilfield soil/liquid separation; artificial neural networks; robotics systems applications. *Mailing Add:* Dept Mech & Aerospace Eng 218 EN Okla State Univ Stillwater OK 74078-5016. *E-Mail:* lhobero@master.ceat.okstate.edu

HOBEY, WILLIAM DAVID, BIOMEMBRANE STRUCTURE, DYNAMICS. *Current Pos:* asst prof, 63-67, ASSOC PROF CHEM & BIOCHEM, WORCESTER POLYTECH INST, 67- *Personal Data:* b Lynn, Mass, Aug 8, 35; m 61; c 3. *Educ:* Tufts Univ, BS, 57; Calif Inst Technol, PhD(theoret chem), 62. *Prof Exp:* NSF res fel, Trinity Col, Cambridge Univ, 62-63. *Concurrent Pos:* Gen Elec found grant, 72-76; NSF microcomput grant, 81-83. *Mem:* Fel Am Inst Chem; Sigma Xi; Am Chem Soc. *Res:* Kinetics and mechanisms of passive cation transport in human erythrocytes; modes of action of beta adrenergic blockers and related compounds on human erythrocytes; mechanism of activation of erythrocytic acetylcholinesterase. *Mailing Add:* Dept Chem & Biochem Worcester Polytech Inst 100 Inst Rd Worcester MA 01609-2247

HOBGOOD, RICHARD TROY, JR, PHYSICAL CHEMISTRY. *Current Pos:* CONSULT, 89- *Personal Data:* b Calhoun, Ga, Jan 15, 39. *Educ:* Emory Univ, AB, 60, MS, 61, PhD(phys chem), 63. *Prof Exp:* Res chemist, ICI Americas Inc, 63-77, sr res chemist, 77-81, supvr, Corp Res Dept, 81-89. *Mem:* Am Chem Soc; Soc Appl Spectros; Sigma Xi. *Res:* Theoretical and applied spectroscopy, particularly nuclear magnetic resonance; studies of conjugated systems; unsaturated hetero atom containing hydrocarbons; carbohydrates and their dehydrated derivatives; heterocyclic ring systems. *Mailing Add:* PO Box 626 Calhoun GA 30703

HOBKIRK, RONALD, BIOCHEMISTRY, ENDOCRINOLOGY. *Current Pos:* RETIRED. *Personal Data:* b Peebles, Scotland, June 13, 30; m 54; c Carole J (Wallace), Ruth E (Boate) & Neil R. *Educ:* Univ Edinburgh, BSc, 52, PhD(biochem), 55, DSc, 73. *Prof Exp:* Asst lectr biochem, Univ Edinburgh, 52-55; asst lectr biochem & surg, Univ Glasgow, 55-57; res asst, McGill Univ, 57-58, from asst prof to prof exp med, 60-71; prof biochem, Univ Western Ont, 72- *Concurrent Pos:* Brit Empire Cancer Campaign jr fel, 55-57; Med Res Coun Can grants, 59-; Banting Res Found grants, 60-; res asst biochem, Div Metab Dis, Montreal Gen Hosp, 58-60, lab dir endocrinol, 60-66; career investr, Med Res Coun Can, 66-; prof path chem, Univ Western Ont, 71-72. *Mem:* Am Soc Biol Chemists; Endocrine Soc; Can Biochem Soc. *Res:* Biochemistry and regulation of steroid sulfotransferases, sulfohydrolases, glucuronyltransferases and B-glucuronidases; their roles in controlling steroid hormone concentrations in uterus and intrauterine tissues in pregnancy; steroid sulfate hydroxylation; 17B-OH-steroid dehydrogenase. *Mailing Add:* Dept Biochem Univ Western Ont London ON N6A 5C1 Can. *Fax:* 519-661 3175

HOBLIT, LOUIS DOUGLAS, organic chemistry; deceased, see previous edition for last biography

HOBLITT, RICHARD PATRICK, GEOLOGY, GEOPHYSICS. *Current Pos:* Geophysicist paleomagnetism, 75-77, GEOLOGIST, US GEOL SURV, 77- *Personal Data:* b Stockton, Calif, Oct 14, 44; m 67. *Educ:* Univ Wash, BS, 67; Univ Colo, MS, 70, PhD(geol), 78. *Mem:* Geol Soc Am; Am Geophys Union; Sigma Xi. *Res:* Volcanology; volcanic hazards; paleomagnetism; petrology; organic chemistry. *Mailing Add:* US Geol Surv 5400 MacArthur Blvd Vancouver WA 98661

HOBSON, ARTHUR STANLEY, THEORETICAL PHYSICS. *Current Pos:* Assoc prof, 64-74, PROF PHYSICSS UNIV ARK, FAYETTEVILLE, 74- *Personal Data:* b Philadelphia, Pa, Nov 27, 34; div; c Ziva & David. *Educ:* NTex State Univ, BMusic, 55; Kans State Univ, BSc, 60, PhD(physics), 64. *Mem:* AAAS; fel, Am Phys Soc; Am Assoc Physics Teachers; Fedn Am Sci; Union Concerned Scientists; Nat Sci Teachers Asn. *Res:* Foundations of statistical mechanics; study of the social and cultural implications of physics; physics for non-science college students. *Mailing Add:* Dept Physics Univ Ark Fayetteville AR 72701. *Fax:* 501-575-4580; *E-Mail:* ahobson@uafsysb.uark.edu

HOBSON, EDMUND SCHOFIELD, ICHTHYOLOGY. *Current Pos:* RES FISHERY BIOLOGIST, US NAT MARINE FISHERIES SERV, 62- *Personal Data:* b White Plains, NY, Apr 7, 31; m 59, Karen Gronli; c Brett, Joanna & Eric. *Educ:* Univ Hawaii, BA, 58, MA, 61; Univ Calif, Los Angeles, PhD(zool), 67. *Honors & Awards:* Publ Award, Am Inst Fishery Res Biologists, 64; Silver Medal Award, US Dept Com, 76. *Concurrent Pos:* Res assoc, Scripps Inst Oceanog, Univ Calif, San Diego, 68-76. *Mem:* Am Soc Ichthyologists & Herpetologists; Am Fisheries Soc; Am Inst Fishery Res Biologists; West Soc Naturalists. *Res:* Behavior and ecology of marine fishes. *Mailing Add:* Tiburon Lab 3150 Paradise Dr Tiburon CA 94920. *Fax:* 415-435-3675

HOBSON, GEORGE DONALD, GEOPHYSICS. *Current Pos:* RETIRED. *Personal Data:* b Hamilton, Ont, Jan 8, 23; m 48, Arletta L Russell; c Robert, Linda, Douglas & Donna. *Educ:* McMaster Univ, BA, 46; Toronto Univ, MA, 48. *Hon Degrees:* DSc, McMaster Univ, 91. *Honors & Awards:* Centennial Medal, Dept Indian & Northern Affairs Can, 91; Indust Achievement Award, Am Soc Mech Engrs; Massey Medal, Royal Can Geog Soc, 91. *Prof Exp:* Partner, Heiland Explor Can Ltd, Calgary, Alta, 48-55; geophysicist, Can Fina Oil Co, 55-56; chief geophysicist, Merrill Petrol Ltd, 56-57; geophysicist, Pac Petrol Ltd, 57-58; chief, Seismic Sect, Geol Surv Can, Ottawa, 58-69, chief, Geophys Div, 69-71; dir, Polar Shelf Proj, Ottawa, 72-88, sr adv, 88-90. *Mem:* Fel Explor Geophysicists India; fel Royal Can Geog Soc; fel Arctic Inst NAm; Soc Explor Geophysicists (vpres, 68); Can Soc Explor Geophysicists. *Res:* Petroleum. *Mailing Add:* 5428 Long Island Rd PO Box 161 Manotick ON K4M 1A3 Can

HOBSON, JOHN ALLAN, PSYCHIATRY, NEUROPHYSIOLOGY. *Current Pos:* res assoc, 64-66, from asst prof to assoc prof, 69-78, PROF PSYCHIAT, HARVARD MED SCH, 78-; PRIN PSYCHIATRIST & DIR LAB NEUROPHYSIOL, MASS MENT HEALTH CTR, 67- *Personal Data:*

b Hartford, Conn, June 3, 33; m 56; c 3. *Educ:* Wesleyan Univ, AB, 55; Harvard Med Sch, MD, 59. *Honors & Awards:* Benjamin Rush Gold Medal, Am Psychiat Asn, 78. *Prof Exp:* Intern med, Bellevue Hosp, NY, 59-60; resident psychiat, Mass Ment Health Ctr, Boston, 60-61; clin assoc exp psychiat, NIMH, 61-63; resident psychiat, Mass Ment Health Ctr, Boston, 64-66; res assoc neurophysiol, Lyon, 63-64. *Concurrent Pos:* NIMH spec fel, 63-64, grant, 67-; psychiat consult, Mass Rehab Comn, 66-; chmn Intramural Rev Panel, NIMH, 82-84; vis comt, Max Planck Inst, Munich, 85- *Mem:* Asn Psychophysiol Study Sleep; Soc Neurosci; Int Brain Res Orgn. *Res:* Physiological correlates of behavior, especially sleep, in man and animals. *Res:* Cellular and molecular basis of sleep cycle control with special reference to REM sleep and dreaming. *Mailing Add:* Harvard Med Sch 74 Fenwood Rd Boston MA 02115-6106

HOBSON, JOHN PETER, ELECTRON PHYSICS. *Current Pos:* PRES, NAT VACUUM TECHNOLOGIES, INC, 86- *Personal Data:* b India, Aug 25, 24; nat Can; m 48, Isabel Clay; c Daniel, Eric, James & Alan. *Educ:* Univ BC, BASc, 49, MASc, 50; Univ Calif, PhD(physics), 54. *Honors & Awards:* Albert Nerken Award, Am Vacuum Soc, 90. *Prof Exp:* From asst res officer to assoc res officer, Nat Res Coun Can, 54-62, sr res officer, 62-73, prin res officer, 73-81, asst dir, Elec Eng Div, 81-86. *Mem:* Hon mem fel Am Vacuum Soc; Can Asn Physicists. *Res:* Molecular beams; electron physics; physical adsorption; vacuum physics. *Mailing Add:* Nat Vacuum Technologies Inc PO Box 4160 Postal Sta E Ottawa ON K1S 5B2 Can

HOBSON, KEITH ALAN, COMMUNITY ECOLOGY, STABLE ISOTOPE APPLICATIONS TO FOOD WEB STUDIES. *Current Pos:* RES SCIENTIST, CAN WILDLIFE SERV, 92- *Personal Data:* b Harrow, Middlesex, Eng, July 10, 54; Can citizen. *Educ:* Simon Fraser Univ, BSc, 77; Univ Man, MSc, 88; Univ Sask, PhD(biol), 92. *Prof Exp:* Res technologist, Simon Fraser Univ, 78-85; Nat Sci & Eng Res Coun fel, Freshwater Inst, 92. *Mem:* Am Ornithologists Union; Arctic Inst NAm; Wilson Ornith Soc; Cooper Ornith Soc. *Res:* Investigating the use of stable isotope analysis in aviam dietary and energetics studies; influence of fragmentation and landscape-level perturbations on aviam communities. *Mailing Add:* 115 Perimeter Rd Saskatoon SK S7N 0X4 Can. *Fax:* 306-975-4087

HOBSON, MELVIN CLAY, JR, physical chemistry, for more information see previous edition

HOBSTETTER, JOHN NORMAN, MATERIALS SCIENCE. *Current Pos:* from assoc prof to prof metall, 58-69, dir lab res struct of matter, 60-76, vprovost res, 67-71, dean grad sch arts & sci, 68-69, prof metall & mat sci, 69-80, PROF MAT SCI & ENG, UNIV PA, 80-, ASSOC PROVOST ACAD PLANNING, 71- *Personal Data:* b Dayton, Ohio, Feb 19, 17. *Educ:* Mass Inst Technol, SB, 39; Harvard Univ, SD(phys metall), 46. *Prof Exp:* Instr metall, Harvard Univ, 41-46, instr eng sci, 46-47, asst prof, 47-52; mem tech staff, Bell Tel Labs, 52-58. *Mem:* AAAS; Am Phys Soc; Am Inst Mining, Metall & Petrol Engrs; Sigma Xi. *Res:* Erosion of materials under extreme conditions; phase transformations in solids; physics of solids; defect structures in metals and semiconductors; biomaterials. *Mailing Add:* Cape May Ave Sewell NJ 08080

HOBURG, JAMES FREDERICK, APPLIED ELECTROMAGNETICS, CONTINUUM ELECTROMECHANICS. *Current Pos:* from asst prof to assoc prof, 75-84, PROF ELEC & COMP ENG, CARNEGIE-MELLON UNIV, 84-, ASSOC DEPT HEAD, 85- *Personal Data:* b Pittsburgh, Pa, Dec 30, 46; m 78, Ryan; c Warren & Russell. *Educ:* Drexel Univ, BS, 69; Mass Inst Technol, SM, 71, PhD(elec eng), 75. *Prof Exp:* Instr, Mass Inst Technol, 73-75. *Concurrent Pos:* Consult, Westinghouse Elec Corp, 79-82, Midland Ross Corp, 85, Mentor Robotics, 85, US Steel Corp, 86, McGraw-Hill Book Co, 86-87, Bethlehem Steel, 87. *Mem:* Inst Elec & Electronics Engrs; Sigma Xi; Electrostatics Soc; Am Soc Eng Educ. *Res:* Electromagnetic field theory and engineering; continuum electromechanics; electrohydrodynamics; electrostatic precipitation; magnetohydro dynamics; magnetic confinement and shaping; magnetic shielding. *Mailing Add:* 1000 Oak Creek Lane Baden PA 15005-2856. *Fax:* 412-268-2860; *E-Mail:* hoburg@katahdin.ece.cmu.edu

HOCART, SIMON, CHEMISTRY. *Current Pos:* ASST PROF CHEM, TULANE UNIV, 90- *Personal Data:* b Stanford, Eng, Aug 17, 55. *Educ:* Willver Hampton Polytech, BA, 78, PhD(chem), 82. *Mem:* Am Asn Sci; Royal Chem Soc. *Res:* Chemistry. *Mailing Add:* Tulane Med Ctr 1430 Tulane Ave New Orleans LA 70112

HOCH, FREDERIC LOUIS, ENDOCRINOLOGY, BIOCHEMISTRY. *Current Pos:* From assoc prof to prof internal med, 68-86, from assoc prof to prof biochem, 70-86, EMER PROF INTERNAL MED & BIOCHEM, UNIV MICH MED SCH, 87- *Personal Data:* b Vienna, Austria, Apr 14, 20; nat US; m 61, Martha L Ludwig. *Educ:* City Col New York, BS, 39; NY Univ, MD, 43; Mass Inst Technol, MS, 52. *Prof Exp:* Intern, Michael Reese Hosp, 43-44; resident & teaching fel, Dept Path, Tufts Med Sch & Mt Auburn Hosp, 47-48; res assoc, dept biol, Mass Inst Technol, 48-51; res fel biochem, Mass Gen Hosp, 51-53; from res assoc to asst prof med, Harvard Med Sch, 53-67. *Concurrent Pos:* Second, 1st Lt, Med Corps, US Army, 41-44, capt, 44-46; fel clin physiol, McLean Hosp, 48; from jr assoc to sr assoc med, Peter Bent Brigham Hosp, 53-67; tutor med sci, Harvard Med Sch, 57-66; vis scientist, Biophys Res Div, Inst Sci & Technol, Univ Mich, 67-68; vis prof, Arrhenius Lab, Univ Stockholm, Sweden, 77-78, Lab Nuclear Med & Radiation Biol, Univ Calif, Los Angeles, 78. *Mem:* AAAS; Am Chem Soc; Am Soc Biol Chem; Brit Biochem Soc. *Res:* Mechanism of action of hormones; cellular intermediary metabolism and energy transfer mechanisms in biomembranes. *Mailing Add:* 3455 Woodland Rd Ann Arbor MI 48104-4257. *E-Mail:* fredhoch@umich.edu

HOCH, GEORGE EDWARD, BIOCHEMISTRY. *Current Pos:* assoc prof, 65-74, PROF BIOL, UNIV ROCHESTER, 74-, CHMN DEPT, 80- *Personal Data:* b Brookings, SDak, Mar 11, 31; m 53; c 4. *Educ:* SDak State Col, BS, 53; Univ Wis, MS, 56, PhD(biochem), 58. *Prof Exp:* Staff scientist, Res Inst Adv Studies, Martin Co, 58-64; mem staff, Univ Pa, 64-65. *Res:* Photosynthesis; biological nitrogen fixation. *Mailing Add:* Dept Biol Univ Rochester Rochester NY 14627

HOCH, HARVEY C, FUNGAL ULTRA-STRUCTURE, CYTOLOGY. *Current Pos:* ASSOC PROF, NY STATE AGR EXP STA, CORNELL UNIV, 86- *Educ:* Univ Wis, PhD(plant path). *Mailing Add:* Dept Plant Path Cornell Univ NY State Agr Exp Sta Geneva NY 14456-0462. *Fax:* 315-787-2389

HOCH, JAMES ALFRED, MICROBIOLOGY, BIOCHEMISTRY. *Current Pos:* fel, Scripps Clin & Res Found, 67-68, from asst to assoc, 68-72, assoc mem microbiol, 72-77, assoc mem cellular biol, 78-80, MEM & HEAD, DIV CELLULAR BIOL, SCRIPPS CLIN & RES FOUND, 80- *Personal Data:* b Brookings, SDak, Jan 22, 39; m 69; c 2. *Educ:* SDak State Univ, BSc, 61; Univ Ill, PhD(microbiol), 65. *Prof Exp:* USPHS fel, Ctr Molecular Genetics, Gif-sur-Yvette, France, 65-67. *Concurrent Pos:* Am Cancer Soc fac res assoc awardee, 69-74; mem ed bd, Bact Rev, 73-79 & J of Bact, 75-78; mem microbiol chem, NIH, 77-81, microbiol physiol & genetics, 85-88. *Mem:* AAAS; Am Soc Microbiol; Genetics Soc Am; Am Soc Biol Chemists. *Res:* Genetics and regulation of development in microorganisms. *Mailing Add:* Dept Molecular & Exp Med Res Inst Scripps Clin 10666 N Torrey Pines Rd La Jolla CA 92037-1027. *Fax:* 619-784-7966; *E-Mail:* hoch@scripps.edu

HOCH, MICHAEL, MATERIALS SCIENCE. *Current Pos:* from asst prof to assoc prof metall eng, 56-63, head dept, 68-75, PROF MAT SCI & METALL ENG, UNIV CINCINNATI, 63- *Personal Data:* b Budapest, Hungary, Feb 9, 23; nat US; m 56. *Educ:* Swiss Fed Inst Technol, DSc, 47. *Prof Exp:* Res assoc, Univ Zurich, 48-50; res assoc, Res Found, Ohio State Univ, 51-53, assoc supvr, 53-56. *Concurrent Pos:* Consult, Solid State Sci Div, Argonne Nat Lab, 58-59, NMPO, Gen Elec Co, 62- & Mound Lab, Monsanto Chem Corp, 62- *Mem:* Am Soc Metals; Am Chem Soc; Am Phys Soc; Am Ceramic Soc; Am Inst Mining, Metall & Petrol Engrs. *Res:* High temperature chemistry and metallurgy; thermophysical properties; alloys of transition metals; deviation from stoichiometry. *Mailing Add:* 5300 Hamilton Ave No 1706 Cincinnati OH 45224

HOCH, ORION L, PHYSICS, ELECTRICAL ENGINEERING. *Current Pos:* PRES, LITTON INDUSTS INC. *Personal Data:* b Canonsburg, Pa, Dec 21, 28; m 52; c 3. *Educ:* Carnegie Inst Technol, BS, 52; Univ Calif, Los Angeles, MS, 54; Stanford Univ, PhD(elec eng), 57. *Prof Exp:* Electronics engr, Res & Develop Labs, Hughes Aircraft Corp, 52-54; res engr microwave tubes, Electronics Labs, Stanford Univ, 54-57; sr engr & dept mgr, Electron Tube Div, Litton Industs, Inc, 57-63, pres & gen mgr, 63-68, vpres, Components Group, 68-70, corp sr vpres, 70-77; pres & chief exec officer, Advan Memory Systs, 77- *Mem:* Inst Elec & Electronics Engrs. *Mailing Add:* 55 Melanie Lane Atherton CA 94027

HOCH, PAUL EDWIN, organic chemistry, for more information see previous edition

HOCH, RICHMOND JOEL, AERONOMY, SPACE SCIENCE. *Current Pos:* chmn, bd dirs & chief exec officer, Sigma Res Inc, 74-87, PRES, SIGMA FINANCIAL GROUP, INC, 74- *Personal Data:* b Oak Park, Ill, Oct 5, 35; m 53; c 2. *Educ:* Harvey Mudd Col, BS, 63; Univ Wash, MS, 65, PhD(physics), 70. *Prof Exp:* Instrument designer, Davidson Optronics Inc, 58-63; res scientist nuclear reactor physics, Gen Elec Co, 63-65; res scientist, Battelle-Northwest Lab, Wash, 65-66, sr res scientist & mgr aeronomy & space sci, 66-74; pres, Benton-Franklin Ventures, Inc, 89-91. *Concurrent Pos:* Prof math & physics, Columbia Basin Col, 88-89; chmn, Pac Rim Technol Conf, 89; lectr physics, Wash State Univ, Tri Cities, 90-; trustee, Wash State Univ, 93- *Mem:* AAAS; Am Geophys Union; Sigma Xi. *Res:* Photometric and spectroscopic research on auroras; airglow; zodiacal light and astronomical objects; theoretical studies in plasma physics; hydromagnetics and atomic physics; design of automated measuring instruments. *Mailing Add:* 2921 S Auburn Pl Kennewick WA 99337

HOCH, SALLIE O'NEIL, CELLULAR BIOLOGY, BIOCHEMISTRY. *Current Pos:* PRIN SCIENTIST, AGOURON INST, 83- *Personal Data:* b Mineola, NY, Feb 15, 41; m 69, James A; c James A Jr & Patrick E. *Educ:* St Bonaventure Univ, BS, 64; Univ Ill, MS, 66, PhD(microbiol), 69. *Prof Exp:* Am Cancer Soc fel cellular biol, Scripps Clin & Res Found, 69-71, asst, 71-72, assoc, 72-83; sr scientist, Agouron Pharmaceut, Inc, 84-93. *Concurrent Pos:* Fel, Am Cancer Soc, 69-71; prin investr res grants, NIH, NSF, Lupus Found Am, 71-; res career develop award, Nat Cancer Inst, NIH, 75-80; mem rev comts, NIH, 81, 90, 93 & 95; mem, Fel Comt, Arthritis Found, 89-90. *Mem:* Am Soc Microbiol; Am Soc Biochem & Molecular Biol; Am Soc Cell Biol; Sigma Xi; Am Col Rheumatology; RNA Soc. *Res:* Structure and function of autoimmunity-associated antigens; immunodiagnostic markers; ribonucleoprotein complexes. *Mailing Add:* Agouron Inst 505 Coast Blvd S La Jolla CA 92037-4696. *Fax:* 619-456-5339

HOCHACHKA, PETER WILLIAM, COMPARATIVE BIOCHEMISTRY. *Current Pos:* from asst prof to assoc prof, 66-75, PROF BIOL & ZOOL, UNIV BC, 75- *Personal Data:* b Therien, Alta, Mar 9, 37; c 3. *Educ:* Univ Alta, BSc, 59; Dalhousie Univ, MSc, 61; Duke Univ, PhD(zool), 65. *Honors*

& Awards: Killiam Res Prizes, 87 & 88. Prof Exp: Asst prof biol, Univ Toronto, 64-65; fel biochem, Duke Univ, 65-66. Concurrent Pos: Vis investr, Inst Arctic Biol, Univ Alaska, 71, Univ Hawaii, 73, 75 & 76, Plymouth Marine Lab, 78, Nat Marine Fisheries, Honolulu, 81, 82 & 84 & Concord Field Sta, Harvard Univ, 84; vis prof, Friday Harbor Marine Lab, Univ Wash, 75, Med Sch, Harvard Univ, 76-77 & Monash Univ, 83; NSF grant, 78-79; Nat Sci & Eng Coun Can grants, 78-81, 82-85 & 85- Mem: Fel AAAS; NY Acad Sci; Am Soc Zoologists; Am Soc Biol Chemists; Soc Exp Biol; fel Royal Soc Can; Can Soc Zoologists; Sigma Xi. Res: Unique problems of metabolic control faced by animals unable to maintain classical homeostasis; examination of three levels of organization whole animal, multienzyme preparations and enzyme systems. Mailing Add: Dept Zool Univ BC 2354-6270 University Blvd Vancouver BC V6T 1Z4 Can. Fax: 604-822-2416

HOCHANADEL, CLARENCE JOSEPH, PHYSICAL CHEMISTRY, ATMOSPHERIC CHEMISTRY. Current Pos: RETIRED. Personal Data: b Gibsonburg, Ohio, Nov 25, 16; m 44; c 8. Educ: Bowling Green State Univ, AB, 40; Ind Univ, MA, 41, PhD(phys chem), 43. Prof Exp: Res chemist, Metall Lab, 43-46; sr chemist, Oak Ridge Nat Lab, 46-80. Mem: Am Chem Soc; Radiation Res Soc. Res: Radiation chemistry; photochemistry; chemical kinetics. Mailing Add: 101 Endicott Lane Oak Ridge TN 37830

HOCHBERG, IRVING, AUDIOLOGY. Current Pos: PROF AUDIOL, CITY UNIV NY BROOKLYN COL, 70-, EXEC OFFICER SPEECH & HEARING SCI, GRAD SCH, 74- Personal Data: b Brooklyn, NY, Apr 17, 34; c 2. Educ: Brooklyn Col, BA, 55; Teachers Col, Columbia, MA, 57; Pa State Univ, PhD(audiol), 62. Prof Exp: Prof audiol, NY Univ, 62-70. Concurrent Pos: Danforth Assoc, 68-71; dir, Ctr Res Speech & Hearing Sci, City Univ NY Grad Ctr, 79- Mem: Fel Am Speech-Lang-Hearing Asn; Acoust Soc Am; Am Acad Audiol. Res: Clinical audiology; psychoacoustic behavior of children and the aged; cochlear implants. Mailing Add: City Univ NY Grad Sch 33 W 42nd St New York NY 10036. Fax: 212-642-2379; E-Mail: hochberg@mailhub.gc.cuny.edu

HOCHBERG, JEROME, CHEMICAL ENGINEERING. Current Pos: res engr coated fabrics, E I du Pont de Nemours & Co, 50-63, assoc, 63-65, res supvr, 65-68, RES FEL, EXP STA, E I DU PONT DE NEMOURS & CO, 68- Personal Data: b New York, NY, Dec 21, 25; m 48; c 2. Educ: City Col New York, BChE, 48; NY Univ, MChE, 51. Prof Exp: Res chem engr, Laurel Hill Res Lab, Gen Chem Div, Allied Chem & Dye Corp, 48-50. Mem: Am Chem Soc. Res: Coated fabrics, finishes, poromeric materials; polymer manufacture; air pollution control. Mailing Add: 2413 Chatham Dr Wilmington DE 19803-2709

HOCHBERG, KENNETH J, STOCHASTIC PROCESSES, MATHEMATICAL BIOLOGY. Current Pos: assoc prof math & comput sci, 87-95, CHMN, BAR-ILAN UNIV, 93-, PROF, 95- Personal Data: b New York, NY, July 26, 50; m 71; c 4. Educ: Yeshiva Univ, BA, 71; New York Univ, MS, 73, PhD(math), 76. Prof Exp: Asst prof math, Carleton Univ, 76-78; asst prof math & statist, Case Western Res Univ, 78-82, assoc prof, 82-88. Concurrent Pos: Vis asst prof, Northwestern Univ, 78; prin investr res grants, NIH, 80-83, NSF, 84-89, Nat Soc Agency, 88-89; vis prof, Hebrew Univ, 83-84, Cornell Univ, 93 & 95; Fulbright scholar, 86-87; adj prof, Hebrew Univ, 87-96; vis scientist, Cornell Univ, 92-93. Mem: Am Math Soc; Inst Math Statist; Israel Math Union; Israel Statist Asn. Res: Mathematical areas of probability theory and stochastic processes; measure-valued diffusion processes with applications to epidemiology and population genetics. Mailing Add: Dept Math & Comput Sci Bar Ilan Univ Ramat Gan 52900 Israel. Fax: 972-3-535-3325; E-Mail: hochberg@macs.biu.ac.il

HOCHBERG, MURRAY, MATHEMATICS. Current Pos: Asst prof, 68-70, ASSOC PROF MATH, BROOKLYN COL, 70- Personal Data: b Brooklyn, NY, May 30, 43; m 67; c 2. Educ: Yeshiva Univ, BA, 64; NY Univ, MS, 66, PhD(math), 69. Mem: Am Math Soc; Math Asn Am. Res: Probability; combinatorial analysis; reliability theory and biostatistics. Mailing Add: 1182 E Tenth St Brooklyn NY 11230-4706

HOCHEL, ROBERT CHARLES, INSTRUMENTATION, SYSTEMS DEVELOPMENT. Current Pos: res chemist, 73-76, staff chemist, 76-77, res supvr, 78-80, RES STAFF CHEMIST, SAVANNAH RIVER LAB, WESTINGHOUSE INC, 80- Personal Data: b Chicago, Ill, Oct 10, 44; m 69; c 3. Educ: Univ Ill, BS, 67; Purdue Univ, PhD(nuclear chem), 73. Prof Exp: Chemist, Babcock & Wilcox Nuclear Develop Ctr, 67-68. Mem: Am Nuclear Soc. Res: Development of nuclear and radio chemical techniques; neutron activation analysis; automated or specialized counting systems. Mailing Add: 1058 Kismet Dr Aiken SC 29803

HOCHELLA, NORMAN JOSEPH, ANALYTICAL CHEMISTRY, BIOCHEMISTRY. Current Pos: RES CHEMIST, BOSTON HEART FOUND, 93- Personal Data: b Hazleton, Pa, June 28, 30; m 66; c 2. Educ: Lafayette Col, AB, 52. Prof Exp: Res chemist, Univ Pa, 52-56 & Thomas Jefferson Univ, 56-58; res assoc, Inst Cancer Res, 58-60, Fels Res Inst, Temple Univ, 60-66 & Sch Med, Univ NC, 66-70; sr res chemist, Damon Corp, 70-72; res assoc, Mass Inst Technol, 72-75; chief chemist, Precision Syst, Inc, 75-89; res chemist, Mass Inst Technol, 90-93. Concurrent Pos: Consult, Women's Med Col Pa, 58-60. Mem: Am Chem Soc; fel Am Inst Chemists; Sigma Xi; AAAS. Res: Boron chemistry; endocrine chemistry; automated chemical analysis; glucose metabolism; chemistry of bladder cancer; inborn errors of metabolism; mitogenic agents; calcium analysis; osmometry; molecular weight characterization; arteriosclerosis research. Mailing Add: 4 Milford St West Medway MA 02053

HOCHHAUS, LARRY, COGNITIVE PSYCHOLOGY, APPLIED STATISTICS & EXPERIMENTAL DESIGN. Current Pos: PROF EDUC & PSYCHOL, ALCORN STATE UNIV, 96- Personal Data: b Britt, Iowa, Mar 9, 42; div; c 2. Educ: Iowa State, BS, 67, MS, 69, PhD(psychol), 70. Prof Exp: Asst prof psychol, Cent Col, 70-71; from asst prof to prof, Okla State Univ, 71-96. Concurrent Pos: Vis assoc prof res, Okla Univ Health Sci Ctr, 80-81; assoc ed, Behav Res Methods, Instr & Comput, 82- & J Exp Psych: Human Perception & Performance, 83-, J Gen Psychol. Mem: Am Psychol Soc; Psychonomic Soc. Res: Cognitive psychology; perception, memory and language processes; selective attention. Mailing Add: Psychol Dept Okla State Univ Stillwater OK 74078-0002. E-Mail: hoch1@osuunx.ucc.okstate. edu

HOCHHEIMER, BERNARD FORD, OPTICS, SPECTROSCOPY. Current Pos: PHYSICIST, APPL PHYSICS LAB, JOHNS HOPKINS UNIV, 60-, INSTR OPHTHAL HOSP, 70- Personal Data: b Rochester, NY, May 24, 29; m 55; c 6. Educ: St Bonaventure Univ, BS, 51; Univ Rochester, MS, 53. Prof Exp: Tech assoc optics, Univ Rochester, 53-54; assoc physicist, Appl Physics Lab, Johns Hopkins Univ, 54-56; scientist, Hayes Aircraft Corp, 56-60. Mem: Optical Soc Am. Res: Gas dynamics and gas lasers; infrared spectroscopy and physics; medical instrumentation and research; applications of lasers to medicine. Mailing Add: 5390 N Church St Manchester MD 21102

HOCHMAN, BENJAMIN, GENETICS, ZOOLOGY. Current Pos: assoc prof, 63-72, PROF GENETICS, UNIV TENN, KNOXVILLE, 72- Personal Data: b New York, Apr 8, 25; m 69. Educ: Univ Calif, AB, 49, MA, 52, PhD, 56. Prof Exp: Asst zool, Univ Calif, 52-54, assoc, 54-55; res assoc genetics, City of Hope Med Ctr, 56-57; asst prof, Univ Utah, 57-63. Concurrent Pos: Res partic biol div, Oak Ridge Nat Lab, 60-61. Mem: Genetics Soc Am; Soc Study Evolution; NY Acad Sci; Am Asn Univ Prof. Res: Genetics of Drosophila; cytogenetics & developmental effects of chromosome 4. Mailing Add: 8116 W Cliff Dr Knoxville TN 37909

HOCHMAN, JACK M(ARTIN), CHEMICAL ENGINEERING. Current Pos: PRES, EXXON BIOMED SCI INC, 96. Personal Data: b Brooklyn, NY, Jan 26, 39; m 78, Jane D Finneman, c Diane (Gallo), Jennifer, Amy & Rarin. Educ: Polytech Inst Brooklyn, BChE, 59; Yale Univ, MEng, 60; Columbia Univ, DEngSc, 64. Prof Exp: Sr res engr, Atomics Int Div, NAm Aviation Inc, 64-65; sr res engr, Esso Res & Eng Co, 65-93, dept mgr, Equip Oil Processing, Exxon Res & Eng Co, 86-89, mgr planning & prog, 89-93, proj exec, Singapore, 93-96. Concurrent Pos: Adj asst prof, NY Univ, 68-69. Mem: Am Inst Chem Engrs; Am Chem Soc. Res: Petroleum refinery planning; chemical reactor engineering; conversion of coal and gas to petroleum products via liquefaction/gasification; heavy oil processing plus broad research management experience in products research; engineering technology research and process research; biomedical sciences. Mailing Add: Esso Singapore Pvt Centers OUB Centre No 1 Ruffles Pl Singapore 0104 Singapore

HOCHMAN, JEROME HENRY, CELL BIOLOGY & BIOCHEMISTRY, CELL BIOLOGY & BIOCHEMISTRY OF DRUG METABOLISM, DEVELOPMENT OF CELL POLARITY. Current Pos: SR RES BIOLOGIST, INTERX DIV, MERCK & CO, 88- Personal Data: b Camden, NJ, Sept 10, 55; m 85, Martha Purdon; c Abigail. Educ: Univ Calif Davis, BS, 77; Mich State Univ, PhD(biochem), 84. Prof Exp: Fel, Johns Hopkins Univ, 84-88. Concurrent Pos: Res fel, Damon Runyon-Walter Winchel Cancer Fund, 84. Mem: AAAS; Am Soc Cell Biol. Res: Using cell biology approaches to understand barriers to systematic absorbtion of drugs through oral routes of administration, this work focusses on developing models and studying transport properties of the intestinal epithelium and the liver. Mailing Add: 895 Carriage Way Lansdale PA 19446

HOCHMAN, MARCELO LUIS, FACIAL PLASTIC & RECONSTRUCTIVE SURGERY. Current Pos: ASSOC PROF OTOLARYNGOL & DERMAT & DIR FACIAL PLASTIC & RECONSTRUCTIVE SURG, MED UNIV SC, 91- Personal Data: b Buenos Aires, Arg, Sept 14, 59; US citizen; c Joseph & Adam. Educ: Univ Tex, Austin, BA, 81; Univ Tex, San Antonio, MD, 85; Am Bd Otolaryngol, cert, 90. Honors & Awards: John Orlando Roe Award, Am Acad Facial Plastic & Reconstructive Surg, 92, Investr Develop Award, 92. Prof Exp: Clin instr, Dept Otolaryngol, St Louis Univ, 90-91, Univ Ark Med Sci, 91. Concurrent Pos: Residency otolaryngol, Stanford Med Ctr, 90; mem, Med Devices & Drugs Comt, Am Acad Otolaryngol-Head & Neck Surg, 91-, Plastic & Reconstructive Surg Comt, 92-, Task Force New Mats, 93-; fel facial plastic & reconstructive surg, Washington Univ, 91; fel cleft lip & palate & clin instr otolaryngol-head & neck surg, Univ Ark Med Sci, 91. Mem: Am Acad Facial Plastic & Reconstructive Surg; Am Acad Otolaryngol-Head & Neck Surg; Am Soc Dermal Surg; Am Cleft Palate-Craniofacial Asn. Res: Bone repair materials including in-vitro grown bone; mechanisms of ischemia tolerance of microvascular free tissue transfers. Mailing Add: Dept Otolaryngol Med Univ SC Charleston SC 29425. Fax: 803-792-0546

HOCHMAN, PAULA S, IMMUNOGENETICS. Current Pos: Fel, 81-83, instr, 83-85, RES ASST PROF PATH, TUFTS UNIV, 85- Personal Data: b Brooklyn, NY, Feb 14, 53. Educ: State Univ NY, Buffalo, PhD(microbiol & immunol), 79. Mem: Am Asn Immunologists. Mailing Add: Dept Cell Biol Biogen 14 Cambridge Ctr Cambridge MA 02142-1481

HOCHMAN, ROBERT F(RANCIS), METALLURGY. Current Pos: from asst prof to prof & assoc dir metall, Sch Chem Eng, 59-82, PROF METALL, SCH MAT ENG, GA INST TECHNOL, 80- Personal Data: b Chicago, Ill, May 1, 28; m 60; c 2. Educ: Univ Notre Dame, BS, 50, MS, 54, PhD(metall),

59. *Honors & Awards:* Res Award, Sigma Xi, 77. *Prof Exp:* Foundry metallurgist, Dodge Mfg Corp, Ind, 50-51; metallurgist, Bendix Aviation Corp, 54-55; spec instr, Eve Div, Mich State Univ, 58-59. *Concurrent Pos:* Consult, Zimmer Mfg Co, 57-; Lockheed Ga Ford Motor Co, 64-; Howmedica Inc, 85- *Mem:* Fel Am Soc Metals; Nat Asn Corrosion Engrs; Am Soc Nondestructive Testing; Am Soc Testing & Mat. *Res:* Physical metallurgy surface modification, ion implantation and plating; basic and applied corrosion; biomedical materials. *Mailing Add:* 5425 Hoylake Ct Duluth GA 30155

HOCHMUTH, ROBERT MILO, CELL BIOMECHANICS, BIORHEOLOGY. *Current Pos:* chair dept, 86-94, PROF BIOMED ENG, DUKE UNIV, 78-, PROF MECH ENG, 86- *Personal Data:* b Berkeley, Calif, May 29, 39; m 64, Doris Ann Schwartz; c 1. *Educ:* Univ Colo, BS, 61; Ohio State Univ, MS, 62; Brown Univ, PhD(eng), 67. *Prof Exp:* From asst prof to prof chem eng, Wash Univ, 67-78. *Concurrent Pos:* NIH res career develop award, 73-78; vis prof, Dept Biophys, Univ Rochester, 85-86; assoc ed, J Biomech Eng, 87-; mem bd dirs, Biomed Eng Soc, 87-91, pres, 93-94; chmn, Bioprocess Eng Prog, Am Soc Mech Engrs, 89-91; consult, NIH & NSF; vis scientist, Los Alamos Nat Lab, 94; vis prof, Dept Bioeng, Univ Calif, San Diego. *Mem:* Am Soc Mech Engrs; Biophys Soc; Soc Rheology; Biomed Eng Soc (pres, 93-94); AAAS; NAm Soc Biorheology; Am Inst Biol Eng. *Res:* Elastic and viscous properties of cells and cell membranes; biorheology; viscous and adhesive properties of cells, cellular biomechanics. *Mailing Add:* Dept Mech Eng & Mat Sci Duke Univ Box 90300 Durham NC 27708-0300. *Fax:* 919-660-8963; *E-Mail:* hochmuth@acpub.duke.edu

HOCHSCHILD, GERHARD P, MATHEMATICS. *Current Pos:* EMER PROF MATH, UNIV CALIF, BERKELEY, 86- *Mem:* Nat Acad Sci. *Mailing Add:* Dept Math Univ Calif Berkeley CA 94720

HOCHSTADT, HARRY, MATHEMATICS. *Current Pos:* assoc prof, Polytech Inst NY, 57-59, head dept, 63-90, dean arts & sci, 74-75, PROF MATH, POLYTECH INST NY, 59- *Personal Data:* b Vienna, Austria, Sept 7, 25; nat US; m 53; c 2. *Educ:* Cooper Union, BChE, 49; NY Univ, MS, 50, PhD(math), 56. *Prof Exp:* Res engr, W L Maxson Corp, 51-57. *Mem:* Am Math Soc; Math Asn Am; Soc Indust & Appl Math; Sigma Xi. *Res:* Special functions; partial differential equations; problems of wave propagation. *Mailing Add:* 126 Joralemon St Brooklyn NY 11201-6610

HOCHSTADT, JOY, BIOCHEMISTRY, MICROBIOLOGY. *Current Pos:* vpres & sci dir, Hercon Lab, 88-90, SR VPRES BIOMED TECHNOL, PRINCETON POLYMER LABS, 88-, PRES, DIAG DEVELOP TEAM, 93- *Personal Data:* b New York, NY, May 6, 39; m 60. *Educ:* Columbia Univ, AB, 60; Stanford Univ, AM 63; Georgetown Univ, PhD(microbiol), 69. *Prof Exp:* USPHS res fel, Lab Biochem, Nat Heart & Lung Inst, 68-70, guest worker, 70-72; sr scientist molecular biol, Worcester Found Exp Biol, 72-76; vis prof, Weizmann Inst, Israel, 76; vis prof biochem & biophysics, Univ RI, 76-77; res prof microbiol, NY Med Col, 77-81; dir, Cell Genetics Res Lab & Div Clin Biochem, Catholic Med Ctr, Woodhaven, NY, 81-88. *Concurrent Pos:* Estab investigatorship, Am Heart Asn, 70-75, mem coun, Basic Sci, 71-; adj prof biochem, Cent New England Col, 74-75; mem NSF fel educ panel, Nat Res Coun, 75-; prin investr res grants, Nat Inst Gen Med Sci, 73-76, & Nat Cancer Inst, 73- & Nat Sci Found, 78-81; mem NATO fel panel, 78 & cell biol study sect, 79-; vis scholar, Columbia Univ, 84- *Mem:* Am Soc Microbiol; fel Am Inst Chemists; Am Soc Biol Chemists; fel Am Acad Microbiol; Am Soc Cell Biol. *Res:* Cell division and cell differentiation; molecular biology of regulation of differentiation in lens cells and hepatoma cells; cell genetics including gene isolation for cell division specific genes. *Mailing Add:* 300 Central Park W New York NY 10024-1513. *Fax:* 212-580-9930

HOCHSTEIN, HERBERT DONALD, MICROBIOLOGY. *Current Pos:* MICROBIOLOGIST, BUR BIOLOGICS, FOOD & DRUG ADMIN, 72- *Personal Data:* b Johnstown, Pa, Sept 12, 29; m 54; c 3. *Educ:* Univ Md, BS, 56; George Washington Univ, MS, 59; Univ NC, MPH, 68, DrPH, 70. *Prof Exp:* Med technician med microbiol, Clin Path Dept, NIH, 56-67, microbiologist, Div Biol Stands, 70-72. *Mem:* Am Pub Health Asn; Am Soc Microbiol. *Res:* Detecting endotoxin in biological products using both the rabbit pyrogen test and the Limulus amebocyte lysate test. *Mailing Add:* 11313 Orleans Way Kensington MD 20895

HOCHSTEIN, JOHN ISAAC, COMPUTATIONAL FLUID DYNAMICS, MICROGRAVITY PROCESSES. *Current Pos:* ASSOC PROF MECH ENG, UNIV MEMPHIS, 91- *Personal Data:* b Brooklyn, NY, Jan 29, 53; m 76, Deborah Colecom; c David, Ann, Marie & Daniel. *Educ:* Stevens Inst Technol, BE, 73; Pa State Univ, MS, 79; Univ Akron, PhD(eng), 84. *Prof Exp:* Design engr, Elec Boat Div, Gen Dynamics, 75-77; thermal-hydraul engr, Nuclear Power Generation Div, Babcok & Wilcox, 78-79; spec lectr mech eng, Univ Akron, 79-84; asst prof, Washington Univ, 84-88, assoc prof, 88-91. *Concurrent Pos:* Mem, Nat Tech Comt Space Processing, Am Inst Aeronaut & Astronaut, 88-91 & 96-, chmn, 96-97. *Mem:* Assoc fel Am Inst Aeronaut & Astronaut; Am Soc Mech Engrs; Am Soc Eng Educ. *Res:* Fluid flow and heat transfer in a reduced gravity environment with emphasis on modeling flows with gas/liquid interfaces. *Mailing Add:* 9312 Hawthorn Hill Dr Germantown TN 38139. *E-Mail:* j__hochstein@memphis.edu

HOCHSTEIN, LAWRENCE I, BACTERIOLOGY, MICROBIAL PHYSIOLOGY. *Current Pos:* SR SCIENTIST, AMES RES CTR, 63- *Personal Data:* b Chicago, Ill, June 16, 28; m 55, 92; c Karen & Lisa. *Educ:* Univ Southern Calif, BA, 53, MS, 55, PhD(bact, biochem), 58. *Prof Exp:* Instr biochem, Univ Southern Calif, 55-56, res assoc bact, 57-58, lectr 58, res assoc dept med microbiol, 58-59; res assoc, Elgin State Hosp, 59-60; instr microbiol, Col Med, Univ Ill, 60-61; res assoc dept genetics, Sch Med, Stanford Univ, 61-63. *Mem:* Am Soc Microbiol; Brit Soc Gen Microbiol. *Res:* Physiology of halophilic bacteria and sulfolobus; denitrification; archael atpases. *Mailing Add:* Dept Chem & Biochem Univ Calif, Santa Cruz Santa Cruz CA 95064. *Fax:* 650-604-1088

HOCHSTEIN, PAUL EUGENE, PHARMACOLOGY. *Current Pos:* prof pharmacol, 69-80, prof toxicol & biochem, 80-93, DIR INST TOXICOL & ASSOC DEAN, UNIV SOUTHERN CALIF, 80-, EMER DISTINGUISHED PROF TOXICOL & BIOCHEM, 93- *Personal Data:* b New York, NY, Feb 7, 26; m 56; c 2. *Educ:* Rutgers Univ, BS, 50; Univ Md, MS, 52, PhD(phytopath), 54. *Hon Degrees:* PhD, Univ Stockholm, 86. *Prof Exp:* Assoc biochem, Col Physicians & Surgeons, Columbia Univ, 57-62; from asst prof to assoc prof pharmacol, Duke Univ, 63-69. *Concurrent Pos:* NIH res fel, 54-57, career award, 65-69; NSF sr fel, Wenner-Gren Inst, 62-63; vis prof, Univ Stockholm, 78-79, Univ Genoa, 86. *Mem:* AAAS; Am Asn Cancer Res; Am Soc Biol Chemists; Soc Gen Physiol; Am Soc Pharmacol & Exp Therapeut; Soc Toxicol. *Res:* Toxicological mechanisms; hydrogen peroxide and organic peroxide formation and detoxification; oxygen toxicity; hemolytic mechanisms. *Mailing Add:* Inst Toxicol Univ Southern Calif 1110 Kenneth Dr Cambria CA 93428. *Fax:* 802-927-5400

HOCHSTER, MELVIN, COMMUTATIVE ALGEBRA, ALGEBRAIC GEOMETRY. *Current Pos:* prof, 77-84, R L Wilder prof, 84-93, R W & L H ROWNE PROF MATH, UNIV MICH, 93- *Personal Data:* b Brooklyn, NY, Aug 2, 43; m 87, Margie R Morris; c Michael A & Hallie M (Morris). *Educ:* Harvard Univ, BA, 64; Princeton Univ, MA, 66, PhD(math), 67. *Honors & Awards:* Frank Nelson Cole Prize, Am Math Soc, 80. *Prof Exp:* From asst prof to assoc prof math, Univ Minn, 67-73; prof, Purdue Univ, 73-77. *Concurrent Pos:* Guest prof, Math Inst Aarhn, Denmark, 73-74; fel, John Simon Guggenheim Mem Found, 82; bd gov, Inst Math & Applns, 85-87; bd trustees, Math Sci Res Inst, Berkeley, 85-87 & Scientific Adv Coun, 89-93. *Mem:* Nat Acad Sci; Math Asn Am; Am Math Soc; Am Acad Arts & Sci; Am Women Sci. *Res:* Commutative Noetherian rings including Cohen-Macaulay rings and modules; invariant theory; algebraic geometry. *Mailing Add:* Math Dept Univ Mich Ann Arbor MI 48109-1109. *Fax:* 313-763-0937; *E-Mail:* hochster@math.lsa.umich.edu

HOCHSTETLER, ALAN RAY, synthetic organic chemistry, for more information see previous edition

HOCHSTRASSER, DONALD LEE, MEDICAL ANTHROPOLOGY, COMMUNITY HEALTH. *Current Pos:* from instr to prof anthrop & community med, Col Arts & Sci & Col Med, Univ Ky, 61-80, assoc dir, Ctr Develop Change, 70-73; prof anthrop, Community Health & Pub Admin, Col Arts & Sci, Col Allied Health & Sch Pub Admin, 80-92, EMER PROF, UNIV KY, 93- *Personal Data:* b Taylorsville, Ky, June 10, 27; m 60, Marie Emlen; c Laura A (Dickinson), Elosie Q (Fishcer) & Letitia C (Fickel). *Educ:* Univ Ky, BA, 52, MA, 55; Univ Ore, PhD(anthrop), 63; Univ Calif, Berkeley, MPH, 69. *Prof Exp:* Instr anthrop, Univ Ky, 56-57; instr, Univ Ore, 58-59. *Concurrent Pos:* Nat Tuberc Asn res grant, Cent Ky, Univ Ky, 62-65, USPHS proj grant, Appalachia, 64-65, Nat Inst Child Health & Human Develop res grant, Appalachia, 71-74, US AID proj grant, 72, US Agency Action prog grant, 72-73 & Robert Wood Johnson Found res & prog eval grant, 74-77; mem, Nat Guid Comt, TB Control Prog, Nat Asn-Am Thoracic Soc, 64-67; NIMH spec res fel, Univ Calif, Berkeley, 68-69, vis scholar, Sch Pub Health, 79-80; chmn, State Family Planning Prog Rev Comt, Ky State Comprehensive Health Planning Coun, 72-74; consult regionalization effectiveness study, Southeastern Ky Regional Health Demonstration, Inc, Lexington, 73-74; res consult, Infant-Child Care Eval Prog, Hazard Hosp, Appalachian Hosps, Lexington, 74-78; primary care eval proj, Ohio Valley Regional Med Prog Spec Res Contract, 74-75; sickle cell prog eval study res grant, Ky State Bur Health Serv, 75-78; Appalachian fertil study contract res proj, Nat Inst Child Health & Human Develop, Pop Res Ctr, 80-83; Appalachian Fertil Study, Nat Inst Child Health & Develop res proj, Univ Ky Res Found, 83-85; res consult, State Family Planning Prog, Eval Study, Access to Family Planning Serv in Appalachia, Ky, State Dept Health Serv, 88-89. *Mem:* Am Pub Health Asn; fel Soc Appl Anthrop; fel Am Anthrop Asn; Am Asn Univ Prof; NY Acad Sci; Sigma Xi. *Res:* Medical anthropology, cultural and social change, community study research; health services research and program evaluation, population and fertility study, social and behavioral aspects of health behavior; health services utilization and patient compliance; rural health care. *Mailing Add:* Dept Health Serv Univ Ky 110 CAHP Bldg Chandler Med Ctr Lexington KY 40536-0003. *Fax:* 606-257-2454

HOCHSTRASSER, ROBIN, CHEMISTRY, CHEMICAL PHYSICS. *Current Pos:* from assoc prof to prof, 63-71, Blanchard prof, 71-83, DONNER PROF CHEM, UNIV PA, 83- *Personal Data:* b Edinburgh, Scotland, Jan 4, 31; US citizen; m 60; c 2. *Educ:* Heriot-Watt Univ, BSc, 52; Univ Edinburgh, PhD(pure chem), 55. *Hon Degrees:* DSc, Heriot-Watt Univ, 84. *Honors & Awards:* Sherwin-Williams Lectr, Univ Ill, 77; Phillips Lectr, Haverford Col, 78; Bourke Lectr, Faraday Soc, Royal Inst, 81; Noyes Distinguished Lectr, Oxford Univ, 82; Cyril Hinshelwood Lectr, Oxford Univ, 82; Reilly Lectr, Notre Dame Univ, 86; Spec Presidents Award, Int Soc Optical Physics, 86; Dreyfus Lectr, Univ Kans, 86; William Drape-Harkins Lectr, Univ Chicago, 90; Peter Debye Award, Am Chem Soc, 96; numerous named lectureships. *Prof Exp:* Instr, Univ BC, 57-60, asst prof, 60-63. *Concurrent Pos:* Alfred P Sloan fel, 63-67; Guggenheim fel, 71-72; vis prof, Cambridge Univ, Eng, 72, Australian Nat Univ, 73, Univ Grenoble, 74 & Calif Inst Technol, 75; Alexander von Humboldt sr fel, 78; dir, Regional Laser Lab,

78- *Mem:* Nat Acad Sci; AAAS; Am Chem Soc; Am Acad Arts & Sci; Royal Inst Chem; Am Phys Soc; Am Inst Physics; Am Asn Univ Profs; Biophys Soc; Optical Soc Am. *Res:* Molecular spectroscopy with fentosecond and other laser methods; photo properties of large molecules and solids with emphasis on primary processes; author of numerous publications. *Mailing Add:* 242 S Phillip Pl Philadelphia PA 19106

HOCHULI, URS ERWIN, ELECTRICAL ENGINEERING, PHYSICS. *Current Pos:* from asst prof to prof, 55-92, EMER PROF ELEC ENG, UNIV MD, COLLEGE PARK, 92- *Personal Data:* b Biel, Switz, Feb 9, 27; m 54, Helen Gebhard; c Christian, Stephan & Juerg. *Educ:* Univ Md, MS, 55; Cath Univ, PhD, 61. *Honors & Awards:* Cert Recognition, NASA. *Prof Exp:* Elec engr, Brown Boveri Co, Switz, 50-52; asst inst fluid dynamics, Univ Md, 52-55. *Mem:* Am Phys Soc; Inst Elec & Electronics Engrs. *Res:* Quantum electronics; laser technology. *Mailing Add:* Dept Elec Eng Univ Md College Park MD 20742

HOCHWALD, GERALD MARTIN, NEUROLOGY, IMMUNOLOGY. *Current Pos:* resident neurol, 60-64, from instr to prof neurol, 64-77, PROF PHYSIOL & BIOPHYS, MED CTR, NY UNIV, 77- *Personal Data:* b New York, NY, June 13, 32; m 59; c 1. *Educ:* Alfred Univ, BA, 53; State Univ Leiden, MD, 59. *Prof Exp:* Intern, Bronx Hosp, NY, 59-60. *Concurrent Pos:* Fel path, Med Ctr, NY Univ, 61-62; Nat Inst Neurol Dis & Stroke fel, 61-62, spec fel & res grant, 64-67, career develop award, 67-; assoc attend physician, Bellevue & Univ Hosps, 65. *Mem:* Am Acad Neurol; Am Asn Immunol; Am Physiol Soc; Brit Soc Res Hydrocephalus & Spina Bifida; Am Neurol Asn. *Res:* Origin of serum and spinal fluid proteins; blood-brain barrier for proteins; experimental hydrocephalus; autoimmune diseases. *Mailing Add:* Dept Neurol NY Univ Med Ctr 550 First Ave New York NY 10016-6451

HOCK, ARTHUR GEORGE, AGRONOMY, SOIL MORPHOLOGY. *Current Pos:* agronomist, 71-77, dir res & agron serv, 77-79, MGR SEED AGRON SERV & RES, COUNTRYMARK, INC, 79- *Personal Data:* b Hamilton, Ohio, Nov 20, 41; m 70. *Educ:* Ohio State Univ, BS, 67, MS, 71. *Prof Exp:* Soil scientist, Div Lands & Soils, Ohio Dept Natural Resources, 66-68; soils consult, Hock & Assocs, 69-71. *Mem:* Am Soc Agron; Soil Sci Soc Am; Crop Sci Soc Am; Coun Agr Sci & Technol. *Res:* Development of soybean, corn and forage varieties; soil fertility; use of sewage sludge as a fertilizer. *Mailing Add:* 3340 Pebble Beach Rd Grove City OH 43123

HOCK, DONALD CHARLES, PHYSICS. *Current Pos:* RETIRED. *Personal Data:* b North Tonawanda, NY, Apr 18, 29; m 57; c 2. *Educ:* Univ Buffalo, BA, 51; Agr & Mech Col, Tex, MS, 52; Pa State Univ, PhD(physics), 56. *Prof Exp:* Sr staff mem, Appl Physics Lab, Johns Hopkins Univ, 55-58; res physicist, Res Div, Radiation, Inc, 58-61; design engr, Orlando Div, Martin Co, 61-64; sr mem tech staff, Data Dynamics, Inc, 64-65; sr mem prof staff, Orlando Div, Martin Marietta Corp, 65-89. *Mailing Add:* 2480 Temple Dr Winter Park FL 32789

HOCKEL, GREGORY MARTIN, REGULATORY AFFAIRS, MEDICINAL DRUG DEVELOPMENT. *Current Pos:* res scientist, 80-83, sr res scientist, 83-85, SR REGULATORY AFFAIRS SCIENTIST, PFIZER CENT RES, 85- *Personal Data:* b Philadelphia, Pa, Nov 10, 50; m 76; c 2. *Educ:* Calif State Univ, Long Beach, BA, 72; Ind Univ, PhD(physiol), 77. *Prof Exp:* From instr to asst prof physiol, Sch Med, Univ Miss, 77-80. *Mem:* Am Physiol Soc; Regulatory Affairs Prof Soc; NY Acad Sci. *Res:* Role of the kidney and renal prostaglandins in the control of arterial blood pressure; renin-angiotensin-aldosterone system; design of renin inhibitors for treatment of hypertension. *Mailing Add:* British Biotech Inc 201 Defense Hwy Suite 260 Annapolis MD 21401

HOCKEN, ROBERT JOHN, PHYSICS, METROLOGY. *Current Pos:* NORVIN KENNEDY DICKERSON DISTINGUISHED PROF PRECISION ENG, UNIV NC, CHARLOTTE, 89- *Personal Data:* b Dinuba, Calif, Feb 20, 44; m 80; c 3. *Educ:* Ore State Univ, BA, 68; State Univ NY, Stony Brook, MA, 69, PhD(physics), 73. *Honors & Awards:* Silver Medal, Dept Com, 78; F W Taylor Medal, Int Inst Prod Eng Res, 79; IR-100 Award, 80; Nat Bur Stand Appl Res Award, 80; Fredrick W Taylor Res Award, Soc Mfg Engrs, 85. *Prof Exp:* Fel, Equation State Sect, Nat Bur Stand, 73-75, physicist dimensional technol, 75-76, group leader dimensional metrol, 76-80, chief, automated prod technol, 80-85, chief, Precision Eng Div, 85-89. *Concurrent Pos:* Pres, Hochen Assoc, Inc, 89- *Mem:* Am Soc Mech Eng; Int Inst Prod Eng Res; fel Soc Mfg Engrs. *Res:* Laser interferometry; three-dimensional metrology; machine tool metrology; dimensional measurement of large structures; critical phenomena; machine tool automation; robotics; computer aided design/computer aided manufacturing. *Mailing Add:* Dept Mech Eng Univ NC Charlotte NC 28223

HOCKENBERRY, TERRY OLIVER, ELECTRICAL ENGINEERING. *Current Pos:* PRES, TOH LABS, 90- *Personal Data:* b Butler, Pa, Apr 13, 38. *Educ:* Univ Cincinnati, Elec Eng, 61; Carnegie Inst Technol, MSc, 62, PhD(elec eng), 64. *Prof Exp:* Asst elec eng, Particle Accelerator Div, Argonne Nat Lab, 61; asst prof, Carnegie-Mellon Univ, 64-70; consult engr, 70-90. *Concurrent Pos:* Sci consult, Siltronics, Inc, 64-65, dir res, 66-70; expert witness, var legal firms, 66-78; dir res, Krux, Inc, 70-73; lectr, Carnegie-Mellon Univ, 70-79. *Mem:* Inst Elec & Electronic Engrs; NY Acad Sci; AAAS; Soc Mfg Engrs; Nat Fire Protection Asn; Sigma Xi. *Res:* Electrical discharge machining; basic research in spark erosion of metallic conductors; effects of electrical arcs on materials; electrical distress conditions; fire causation research. *Mailing Add:* 112 Wynnwood Dr Pittsburgh PA 15215-1548

HOCKENBURY, ROBERT WESLEY, NUCLEAR ENGINEERING. *Current Pos:* res asst, Nuclear Eng & Sci Div, 58-67, res assoc, 67-74, ASSOC PROF NUCLEAR ENG & SCI DIV, RENSSELAER POLYTECH INST, 74- *Personal Data:* b Springfield, Mass, July 31, 28; m 55; c 3. *Educ:* Union Col, BS, 52; Rensselaer Polytech Inst, MS, 59, PhD(nuclear sci), 67. *Prof Exp:* Nuclear analyst, Knolls Atomic Power Lab, Gen Elec Co, 56-58. *Concurrent Pos:* Consult reactor safety, NY risk assessment, availability; mem, Exec Coun, Soc Risk Analysis. *Mem:* Am Nuclear Soc; Am Phys Soc; Soc Risk Analysis. *Res:* Reliability; risk analysis; failure data analysis; probabilistic methods; radiation induced curing of polymers. *Mailing Add:* 8 Oak Dr Albany NY 12203

HOCKER, GEORGE BENJAMIN, SENSORS. *Current Pos:* sect head, 76-85, dept mgr, 85-87, PRIN RES FEL, HONEYWELL SENSOR & SYST DEVELOP CTR, 87- *Personal Data:* b Harrisburg, Pa, Sept 11, 42; m 72; c 2. *Educ:* Cornell Univ, BEP, 65, PhD(appl physics), 70. *Prof Exp:* Asst prof elec eng, Univ Minn, Minneapolis, 70-76. *Concurrent Pos:* Prog chmn, Inst Elect & Electronic Engrs Solid State Sensor & Actuator Works Lab, 88, gen chmn, 90. *Mem:* Inst Elec & Electronics Engrs. *Res:* Sensor technology and applications, especially silicon sensors, micromachining, and micro-structure devices. *Mailing Add:* 5730 Covington Circle Minnetonka MN 55345

HOCKING, GEORGE MACDONALD, PHARMACOGNOSY. *Current Pos:* PROF PHARMACOG, SCH PHARM, AUBURN UNIV, 51- *Personal Data:* b Newquay, Eng, Mar 21, 08; US citizen; m 33, Betty S Willis; c Joan (Anderson). *Educ:* Univ Wash, BSP, 31; Univ Fla, MSP, 32, PhD(pharmacog), 42. *Honors & Awards:* ACS Award, Am Chem Soc, 26. *Prof Exp:* Instr, Col Pharm, George Washington Univ, 33-35; chief pharmacognosist, S B Penick & Co, New York, 42-46; prof pharmacog, Col Pharm, Univ Buffalo, 46-48; prof pharmacog & pharmacol, Col Pharm, Univ NMex, 48-51. *Concurrent Pos:* Instr, Col Pharm, Ohio Northern Univ, 37-40; abstr, Biol Abstracts, Excerpta Botanica Sect A & Phytologia, 46-; mem, Comt Nat Formulary & chmn, Subcomt Pharmacog, 47-60; vis prof, Univ Miss, 47-50; consult med plants, Food & Agr Orgn, Govt Pakistan, 51; mem, Comn Study Med & Toxic Plants Brazil, 52 & Int Comn Plant Raw Mat, 65; ed, Int J Crude Drug Res, Lisse, Neth, 75. *Mem:* Am Pharmaceut Asn; Nat Asn Stand Med Vocab. *Res:* Crude plant drug materials and drug plants, including plants belonging to genera Liatris, Mentha and Iris; terminology drugs; abstracting and book reviewing. *Mailing Add:* Sch Pharm Auburn Univ Auburn AL 36849-5503

HOCKING, JOHN GILBERT, MATHEMATICS. *Current Pos:* from instr to assoc prof, 51-63, PROF MATH, MICH STATE UNIV, 63- *Personal Data:* b Caspian, Mich, Sept 26, 20; m 44; c 4. *Educ:* Univ Mich, PhD(math), 53. *Prof Exp:* Asst, Off Naval Res, Univ Mich, 48-51. *Concurrent Pos:* Fulbright guest prof, Univ Tubingen, 62-63. *Mem:* Am Math Soc; Math Asn Am. *Res:* Topology of manifolds; game theory; logic. *Mailing Add:* Math Dept Mich State Univ East Lansing MI 48824

HOCKING, MARTIN BLAKE, ORGANIC REDOX RATES & MECHANISMS, ORGANIC WATER-SOLUBLE COPOLYMER SYNTHESIS. *Current Pos:* asst prof, Univ Victoria, 71-75, chair, Environ Studies Prog, 75-76, assoc prof, 75-96, PROF CHEM, UNIV VICTORIA, 96- *Personal Data:* b London, Nov 25, 38; Can citizen; m 62, Diana Crane; c Jennifer, Philippa & Jeffrey. *Educ:* Univ Alta, BSc, 59; Univ Southampton, PhD(org chem), 63. *Prof Exp:* Res chemist, Dow Chem Can, Ltd, 63-68, group leader, 69-71. *Concurrent Pos:* Vis prof, McGill Univ, Montreal, 78-79; vis scientist, Pulp & Paper Res Inst Can, 78-79; Harold Hibbert Mem fel, 78-79; consult, MacMillan Bloedel Ltd, 85-87; res fel, Univ Col London, 87-88; distinguished visitor, Massey Univ, NZ, 91; vis prof, Univ NSW, Australia, 92. *Mem:* Fel Royal Inst Chem; fel Chem Inst Can; Royal Soc Chem; Am Chem Soc; Can Soc Chem & Biochem Technol. *Res:* Application of principles of aqueous aromatic oxidation chemistry to development of peroxide bleaching of mechanical pulps; synthesis and stereochemistry of bridged ring phosphorus heterocycles; environmental chemistry; life cycle analysis. *Mailing Add:* Dept Chem Univ Victoria PO Box 3065 Victoria BC V8W 3V6 Can. *Fax:* 250-721-7147

HOCKING, RONALD RAYMOND, MATHEMATICS, STATISTICS. *Current Pos:* PROF STATIST, TEX A&M UNIV, 80- *Personal Data:* b Ishpeming, Mich, June 4, 32; m 54; c 3. *Educ:* Mich Tech Univ, BS, 54; Univ Mich, MS, 57; Iowa State Univ, PhD(math, statist), 62. *Honors & Awards:* Snedecor Award, Iowa State Univ, 62; Wilcoxon Award, 71 & 76; Shewell Prize, 78 & 80. *Prof Exp:* Res assoc, Boeing Airplane Co, 57-58; asst prof math, Mich Tech Univ, 58-63; from assoc prof to prof statist, Tex A&M Univ, 63-71; prof mgt sci, Univ Houston, 71-76; prof statist & head dept, Miss State Univ, 76-80. *Mem:* Fel Am Statist Asn. *Res:* Linear models; regression; statistical estimation theory, especially minimum variance estimation; multivariate analysis. *Mailing Add:* 10629 Northboro St Dallas TX 75230

HOCKMAN, CHARLES HENRY, NEUROPHYSIOLOGY, NEUROPHARMACOLOGY. *Current Pos:* PROF NEUROSCI, SCH MED, MERCER UNIV, MACON, GA, 82- *Personal Data:* b Montreal, Que, Mar 15, 23; m 52; c 3. *Educ:* Queen's Univ, Ont, BA, 58; Brown Univ, ScM, 60, PhD(exp psychol, electrophysiol), 63. *Prof Exp:* Asst prof neurophysiol, Med Col Va, 62-66; assoc prof pharmacol, Fac Med, Univ Toronto, 66-72; assoc prof neurosci, Sch Basic Med Sci, Univ Ill Col Med, 72-82. *Concurrent Pos:* Consult, Hoffman-LaRoche, US, 62-66, Can, 66-71; sci officer, Dept Health & Welfare, Can, 72-73. *Mem:* Am Physiol Soc; Can Physiol Soc; Soc Neurosci; Sigma Xi; World Fedn Neurol; Int Brain Res Orgn. *Res:* Neurophysiol and neuropharmacol relationships between basal forebrain and bulbar motor functions; CNS regulation of autonomic function; effects of psychotropic drugs on cortical and subcortical regions of the brain. *Mailing Add:* Sch Med Mercer Univ 1400 Coleman Ave Macon GA 31207

HOCKMAN, DEBORAH C, RESEARCH & DEVELOPMENT. *Current Pos:* from asst dir, to sr dir, 87-92, PRES, WMI ENVIRON MONITORING LABS, INC, 92- *Personal Data:* b Sept 1, 55; m, Peter Cihak; c Justin & Katie. *Educ:* Northeastern Ill Univ, BS, 77; Loyola Univ, Chicago, PhD(anal Chem) 82. *Honors & Awards:* Poehlman Award Outstanding Achievement, Nat Soc Appl Spectros. *Prof Exp:* Spectroscopist & lab coordr, Anal Serv Lab, Northwestern Univ, 82; res scientist, Prod Develop Anal Dept, G D Searle & Co, 82-84; group leader formulations res, Med Res Div, Am Cyanamid Co, 84-87. *Concurrent Pos:* Schmitt fel. *Mem:* Am Chem Soc; Soc Appl Spectros (pres, 90-91); Asn Women Sci. *Res:* Lab robotics; chromatography; spectroscopy. *Mailing Add:* WMX Technologies Inc 2100 Clearwater Dr Geneva IL 60134-4101. *Fax:* 630-208-9064

HOCKNEY, RICHARD L, ACTIVE MOTION CONTROL, ENERGY CONVERSION & STORAGE. *Current Pos:* div leader, 86-90, vpres eng, 91-94, VPRES & CHIEF TECH OFFICER, SATCON TECHNOL, 94- *Educ:* Northeastern Univ, BS, 72, MS, 80. *Prof Exp:* Design engr, C S Draper Lab, 72-75, sr engr, 76-79, prin engr, 80-85. *Mem:* Sr mem Inst Elec & Electronics Engrs. *Res:* Electro-mechanical control systems including magnetic bearings, magnetic suspensions, vibration isolators; power electronics for actuator and motor drives; energy conversion and storage including flywheels. *Mailing Add:* SatCon Technol Corp 161 First St Cambridge MA 02142. *Fax:* 617-661-3373; *E-Mail:* hockney@satc.com

HOCKSTRA, DALE JON, MANAGEMENT SCIENCE, OPERATIONS MANAGEMENT. *Current Pos:* assoc prof mgt, Univ Evansville, 76-77, asst dean, 77-80, dean, 81-90, PROF MGT, UNIV EVANSVILLE, 90- *Personal Data:* b San Diego, Calif, Mar 29, 48; m 72, Carolyn Fitzmaurice. *Educ:* Occidental Col, BA, 69; Stanford Univ, MS, 70, PhD(opers res), 74. *Prof Exp:* Asst prof mgt sci, Wash State Univ, 72-76. *Concurrent Pos:* Assoc prof, Univ Denver, 80-81. *Mem:* Inst Opers Res & Mgt Sci; Decision Sci Inst. *Res:* Mathematical models in production/operations management. *Mailing Add:* Sch Bus Admin Univ Evansville 1800 Lincoln Ave Evansville IN 47722. *E-Mail:* dh3@evansville.edu

HOCKSWENDER, THOMAS RICHARD, POLYMER MODELING & SIMULATION, TECHNOLOGY INNOVATION & PLANNING. *Current Pos:* Sr res chemist, PPG C&R Res, 73-78, res assoc, 78-82, sr res assoc, 82-87, mgr indust res, 88-91, SCIENTIST, PPG C&R RES, 87-, MGR APPL SCI COMPUT, 91- *Personal Data:* b Pittsburgh, Pa, Feb 16, 48; m 70, Christine Bucci; c Thomas R III. *Educ:* Duquesne Univ, BS, 70; Case Western Res Univ, PhD(org chem), 73. *Concurrent Pos:* Consult scientist, PPG Corp Technol Group, 91- *Mem:* Am Chem Soc; AAAS. *Res:* Synthesis, design and production of polymers for high solids and water borne coatings; computer modeling of polymers; development of new quality and research management systems. *Mailing Add:* c/o M L Jordan PPG Industs Pittsburgh PA 15272

HOCOTT, C(LAUDE) R(ICHARD), PETROLEUM ENGINEERING. *Current Pos:* dir, Petrol Res Comt, 77-79, prof, 77-80, EMER PROF ENG, UNIV TEX, AUSTIN, 80- *Personal Data:* b Excelsior, Ark, Nov 16, 09; m 37; c 2. *Educ:* Univ Tex, BS, 33, MS, 34, PhD(chem eng), 37. *Honors & Awards:* Anthony Lucas Medal, Soc Petrol Engrs, 74. *Prof Exp:* Tutor chem, Univ Tex, 33-34, instr chem eng, 34-35, chem, 35-37; res engr, Humble Oil & Refining Co, Stand Oil Co, NJ, 37-42, asst head prod res, 42-54, div head, 54-58, res mgr, 58-64, vpres, Esso Prod Res Co, 64-71, exec vpres, 71-77. *Mem:* Nat Acad Eng; Am Asn Petrol Geol; Am Inst Mining, Metall & Petrol Engrs; Am Inst Chem Engrs; Soc Petrol Engrs. *Res:* Occurrence and recovery of petroleum; cooling tower for suspensions; geochemical prospecting; well logging; decomposition of methane in electrical discharge. *Mailing Add:* Col Eng CPE 5182 Univ Tex Austin TX 78712

HOCUTT, CHARLES H, aquatic ecology, ichthyology, for more information see previous edition

HODDER, ROBERT WILLIAM, GEOLOGY. *Current Pos:* from asst prof to assoc prof, 70-75, prof geol, 75-93, CHMN, DEPT GEOL, UNIV WESTERN ONT, 83-, EMER PROF, 93- *Personal Data:* b Ottawa, Ont, Apr 10, 32; m 65; c 2. *Educ:* Queen's Univ, Ont, BA, 55; Univ Calif, Berkeley, PhD(geol), 59. *Prof Exp:* Geologist, Am Metal Climax Inc, 59-64; geologist & vpres, Callahan Mining Corp, 64-70. *Concurrent Pos:* Consult, Callahan Mining Corp, 70- *Mem:* Am Inst Prof Geologists; Am Inst Mining, Metall & Petrol Engrs; Soc Econ Geologists; Geol Asn Can. *Res:* Metallogenetic relationships of mineral deposits and their economic significance; physical volcanolgy and its role in metal concentration. *Mailing Add:* Dept Earth Sci Univ Western Ont London ON N6A 5B9 Can

HODEL, MARGARET JONES, COMBINATORIAL ANALYSIS, NUMBER THEORY. *Current Pos:* instr, 74-93, LECTR MATH, DUKE UNIV, 93- *Personal Data:* b Lewistown, Pa, July 6, 41; m 70, Richard E; c Richard G & Katherine (Kennedy). *Educ:* Vassar Col, AB, 63; Duke Univ, PhD(math), 72. *Prof Exp:* Math teacher, Am Community Sch, Athens, Greece, 63-65 & St Stephens Sch, Rome, Italy, 65-68. *Mem:* Am Math Soc. *Res:* Enumeration of sequences of nonnegative integers, of weighted sequences, of weighted rectangular arrays; Dedekind sums. *Mailing Add:* Dept Math Duke Univ Box 90320 Durham NC 27708-0320

HODEL, RICHARD EARL, MATHEMATICS. *Current Pos:* Asst prof, 65-70, ASSOC PROF MATH, DUKE UNIV, 70- *Personal Data:* b Winston-Salem, NC, Sept 24, 37; m 70, Margaret Jones; c Richard G Jones & Katherine (Kennedy). *Educ:* Davidson Col, BS, 59; Duke Univ, PhD(math), 62. *Mem:* Am Math Soc; Math Asn Am; Symbolic Logic Asn. *Res:* Set-theoretic topology. *Mailing Add:* Dept Math Duke Univ Durham NC 27708-0320

HODES, LOUIS, APPLICATIONS IN CHEMISTRY, STRUCTURE ACTIVITY RELATIONSHIPS. *Current Pos:* RETIRED. *Personal Data:* b New York, NY, June 19, 34; m 67. *Educ:* Polytech Inst Brooklyn, BEE, 56, MS, 58; Mass Inst Technol, PhD(math), 62. *Prof Exp:* Staff mem math, IBM Res Ctr, 61-65; vis mem, Courant Inst Math Sci, NY Univ, 65-66; res mathematician, Div Comp Res & Technol, NIH, 66-74, res mathematician, Div Cancer Treatment, nat Cancer Inst, 74-94. *Concurrent Pos:* Vis mathematician, Appl Logic Group, Hebrew Univ, Jerusalem, 64. *Mem:* Am Chem Soc; Soc Indust & Appl Math; Inst Elec & Electronics Engrs Comput Soc. *Res:* Theory of pattern recognition on a discrete space; biomedical applications of computers, radiation treatment planning; information theory applied to chemical structure searching; quantitative structure-activity relationships in biochemistry. *Mailing Add:* 10201 Grosvenor Pl Rockville MD 20852

HODES, MARION EDWARD, MEDICAL GENETICS, MOLECULAR GENETICS. *Current Pos:* from asst prof to assoc prof, Sch Med, Ind Univ, Indianapolis, 55-66, prof med & biochem, 66-72, prof med genetics, 72-92, PROF MED, SCH MED, IND UNIV, INDIANAPOLIS, 72-, PROF MED & MOLECULAR GENETICS, 92-, PROF PATH, 92- *Personal Data:* b New York, NY, Aug 6, 25; m 49, Halina Markowicz; c Marquis Z, Zachary I, Jonathan E & Abigail J. *Educ:* Univ Buffalo, MD, 47; Columbia Univ, PhD(biochem), 55; Am Bd Clin Chem, dipl, 52, Am Bd Med Genetics, dipl, 82, 93. *Prof Exp:* Asst med, Columbia Univ, 55-56, assoc, 56. *Concurrent Pos:* Consult, Regional Genetics Counseling Clin, South Bend, Ind, 80-96 & Evansville Ind, 83-86 & Med Genetics Clin, Richmond, Ind, 81-82; chmn, Int Sci Coun, Israel Cancer Res Fund, 88-95. *Mem:* Am Soc Biochem & Molecular Biol; Am Chem Soc; Am Asn Clin Chem; Am Asn Cancer Res; Am Soc Human Genetics; Soc Neurosci. *Res:* Genetic diseases (molecular and clinical); recombinant DNA; preservation of DNA; molecular genetics of Pelizaeus; Merzbacher disease. *Mailing Add:* Dept Med & Molecular Genetics Ind Univ Med Ctr Indianapolis IN 46202-5251. *Fax:* 317-274-1069; *E-Mail:* mhodes@medgen.iupui.edu

HODES, PHILIP J, radiology; deceased, see previous edition for last biography

HODES, WILLIAM, ORGANIC CHEMISTRY, POLYMER CHEMISTRY. *Current Pos:* mgr chem develop lab, 69-80, dir chem develop & gen mgr, chem oper, 80-87, GEN MGR COM CHEM, POLAROID CORP, 87- *Personal Data:* b Newark, NJ, May 25, 25; m 55; c 4. *Educ:* NY Univ, AB, 48; Ind Univ, MA, 50, PhD(chem), 52. *Prof Exp:* Asst proj chemist, Standard Oil Co, Ind, 52-56; res chemist, Am Cyanamid Co, 56-60; mgr chem dept, Res Div, Am-Standard Corp, 60-69. *Mem:* AAAS; Am Chem Soc. *Res:* Synthetic chemicals-process research and development; polymerization processes; polyelectrolyte properties and applications; membrane separations; steric control of organic reactions; catalysis; manufacture of fine organics and chemical specialties; marketing. *Mailing Add:* 21 Oxford St Winchester MA 01890-3536

HODGDON, F(RANK) E(LLIS), MECHANICAL ENGINEERING. *Current Pos:* RETIRED. *Personal Data:* b Malden, Mass, Aug 21, 15; m 47; c 4. *Educ:* Ga Sch Technol, BS, 37. *Prof Exp:* Engr, Gen Elec Co, Ind, 37-38 & Hydril Co, Pa, 38-39; res engr labs, Am Gas Asn, 39-42, asst chief res engr, 46-49, chief engr, 49-52, from asst to dir to dir, 52-71, asst managing dir, 62-71, vpres & dir labs, 71-77, sr vpres consumer affairs & safety, 77-80. *Mem:* Int Gas Union; Am Soc Testing & Mat; Newcomen Soc; Nat Soc Prof Engrs. *Res:* Gas appliances and accessories. *Mailing Add:* 1152 Verdon Dr Atlanta GA 30338

HODGDON, HARRY EDWARD, SCIENTIFIC SOCIETY ADMINISTRATION. *Current Pos:* field dir, 77-82, EXEC DIR, WILDLIFE SOC, 82- *Personal Data:* b Brattleboro, Vt, Sept 4, 46; m 67, 93, Mary S Van Horn; c Christopher Ross, Scott Gerald & Ryan David. *Educ:* Univ Maine, Orono, BS, 68; Univ Mass, Amherst, MS, 71, PhD(wildlife biol), 78. *Prof Exp:* Mgr, Conserv Activ Dept, Nat Rifle Asn, 75-76, dir, Hunting & Conserv Div, 76-77. *Concurrent Pos:* Mem, Nat Nongame Bird Steering Comt, Forest Serv, USDA, 76-80 & Rangeland Policy Comt, Off Secy, 78-80; mem, Exec Comt, Renewable Natural Resources Found, 81-92 & 96-; ed, The Wildlifer, Wildlife Soc, 82-; mem, Conserv Adv Coun, Sen Roger W Jepson, Chmn, US Sen Subcomt Soil, Conserv, Forestry & Environ, 83-84; mem, Fish & Wildlife Adv C mt, Conserv Found, 83-84; mem, Info & Commun Study Team, President's Comn Americans Outdoors, 85-86; mem, Nat Threatened & Endangered Species Task Force, USDA, 88-89, US Implementation Bd, NAm Waterfowl Mgt Plan, 88-, Nat Adv Comt for Eval of the Conserv Title of the Food Security Act of 1985, Soil & Water Conserv Soc, 88-92; Proactive Strategies Fish Wildlife Mgt Task Force, 90-94. *Mem:* Sigma Xi; AAAS; Am Inst Biol Sci; Wildlife Soc; Soc Am Foresters; Soc Range Mgt. *Res:* Integration of wildlife research findings into the political decisionmaking process; improvement of the status of wildlife professionals; enhancement of wildlife education programs; furbearer management; behavior, ecology and population dynamics of beaver. *Mailing Add:* Wildlife Soc Suite 200 5410 Grosvenor Lane Bethesda MD 20814

HODGDON, RUSSELL BATES, PHYSICAL ORGANIC CHEMISTRY. *Current Pos:* RETIRED. *Personal Data:* b Medford, Mass, Nov 9, 24; m 58, Doris Senfleben; c Paul, Gail & Ellen (Dreher). *Educ:* Mass Inst Technol, BS, 51; Columbia Univ, MS, 54, PhD(phys org chem), 57. *Prof Exp:* Res chemist, Monsanto Chem Co, 59-60; sr scientist, Gen Elec Co, Mass, 60-69; mgr membrane res & develop, Ionics Inc, 69-89, consult, 89-94. *Mem:* Am Chem Soc. *Res:* Polyelectrolyte chemistry; ion exchange membranes synthesis, rheological behavior and solution thermodynamics; pressure driven membrane science; hyperfiltration, nanofiltration and ultrafiltration; membrane synthesis; awarded over 25 patents. *Mailing Add:* 71 Captain Bearse Lane Harwich MA 02645

HODGE, BARTOW, INFORMATION SCIENCE. *Current Pos:* PROF INFO SYSTS, SCH BUS, VA COMMONWEALTH UNIV, 82- *Personal Data:* b Winnfield, La, Jan 11, 20; m 46; c 3. *Educ:* La State Univ, BS, 47, MS, 48, PhD, 54. *Prof Exp:* Asst physics, La State Univ, 47-51; physicist, Esso Labs, Esso Standard Oil Co, 51-55; appl scientist, IBM Corp, Tex, 55-56, appl sci mgr, La, 57-58, mgr petrol industs, NY, 58-60, mgr control systs, Ill, 60, mgr advan systs, 61-64, prog adminr process industs, White Plains, 64-68, sr prog adminr sensor based syst, 68-73; dis lectr info syst, Col Bus Admin, Univ SC, 73-82. *Concurrent Pos:* Consult, Cert Syst Prof, 86. *Mem:* Am Phys Soc; Data Processing Mgt Asn; Asn Syst Mgr; Acad Mgt; Asn Comput Mach. *Res:* Information theory and sciences; application to management information and organization; health care administration. *Mailing Add:* Va Commonwealth Univ Bus Sch 11220 Tumley Lane Midlothian VA 23113

HODGE, DANIEL B, ELECTRICAL ENGINEERING. *Current Pos:* CHMN, DEPT ELEC ENG, VA POLYTECH INST & STATE UNIV. *Personal Data:* b Warsaw, Ind, Nov 29, 38; m 64; c 1. *Educ:* Purdue Univ, BSEE, 60, MSEE, 61, PhD(elec eng), 65. *Prof Exp:* Vis asst prof elec eng, Univ Ill, 64-65; Royal Norweg Coun Sci & Indust res fel, 65-66; asst prof, Ohio State Univ, 66-80, prod elec eng, 80- *Mem:* Inst Elec & Electronics Engrs. *Res:* Electromagnetic theory; wave propagation and scattering. *Mailing Add:* 3969 Newhall Rd Columbus OH 43220

HODGE, DAVID CHARLES, HUMAN FACTORS ENGINEERING, ROBOTICS. *Current Pos:* Res psychologist, 62-85, eng psychologist, Human Eng Lab, 85-92, CHIEF, INT PROGS BR, ARMY RES LAB, US ARMY, 92- *Personal Data:* b Ft Worth, Tex, July 5, 31; m 57. *Educ:* Univ Rochester, PhD(exp psychol), 63. *Concurrent Pos:* Chmn, Operator Robot Interaction, NATO RS6-18, 89- *Mem:* Sigma Xi; Asn Unmanned Vehicle Systs. *Res:* assessment of science and technology worldwide; initiation and management of international S and T cooperation. *Mailing Add:* 3103 Woolsey Dr Churchville MD 21028-1328. *Fax:* 410-278-5820; *E-Mail:* darch@brl.mil

HODGE, DENNIS, GEOPHYSICS, PETROLOGY. *Current Pos:* From asst prof to assoc prof, 66-81, chmn dept, 73-75, PROF GEOL SCI, STATE UNIV NY BUFFALO, 81- *Personal Data:* b Chicago, Ill, Jun 17, 39; m 62; c 2. *Educ:* Beloit Col, BS, 61; Univ Wyo, MS, 63, PhD(geol, geophys), 66. *Mem:* Am Geophys Union; Soc Expl Geophysicists. *Res:* Field geophysical studies of New England; heat flow studies of New York; earth molds of flexine. *Mailing Add:* Dept Geol State Univ NY PO Box 600001 Buffalo NY 14260-0001

HODGE, DONALD RAY, INFORMATION ENGINEERING, INTEROPERABILITY. *Current Pos:* PRES & SR CONSULT, DR HODGE & ASSOCS, 96- *Personal Data:* b Springfield, Mo, Aug 22, 39; m 79, Elizabeth A Brown; c Kristin M & Carrie L. *Educ:* Drury Col, BS, 61; Univ Wis-Madison, MS, 63, PhD(physics), 68. *Prof Exp:* Analyst opers res, Ctr Naval Analysis, 68-71; opers res analyst, US Army Commun, Electronics Comput Appln Agency, 71-73; sr scientist, BDM Corp, 73-77; sr staff, TRW Defense Systs Group, TRW Corp, 77-88; sr analyst, Jaycor, 88-89; exec staff, Comput Sci Corp, 89-96. *Concurrent Pos:* Staff mem, Nat Acad Sci, 71- *Mem:* Am Phys Soc; Opers Res Soc Am; Inst Elec & Electronics Engrs Comput Soc. *Res:* Information systems architecture; systems engineering; command and control systems; standards and protocols; information interfaces; communications compatibility and interoperability; system development methodologies; measures of effectiveness; simulation and modeling. *Mailing Add:* 2907 Farm Rd Alexandria VA 22302-2411

HODGE, FREDERICK ALLEN, RADIOBIOLOGY, ENVIRONMENTAL SCIENCE. *Current Pos:* SR ENVIRON SCIENTIST, ENERGETICS, INC, 92- *Personal Data:* b Durango, Colo, Jan 10, 39; m 63, 85, Linda M Smith; c Heather, Holly, Heath & Jason M. *Educ:* Colo State Univ, BS, 64, MS, 65; Ore State Univ, PhD(radiation biol), 71. *Prof Exp:* Microbiologist, Naval Radiol Defense Lab, 65-68 & Naval Biomed Res Lab, Calif, 71-73; head bact div & head med physics dept, Naval Med Res Unit 2, Taipei, Taiwan, 73-76; radiobiologist, Spec Effects Biomed Res Detachment, Naval Med Res Inst, 76-77; radiobiologist & actg chief, Bioeffects Analysis Br, Off Radiation Progs, US Environ Protection Agency, 77-91. *Concurrent Pos:* Med Serv Corps, US Navy, 65-76; capt, USPHS, 77-91. *Mem:* Radiation Res Soc; AAAS; Sigma Xi; NY Acad Sci; Asn Mil Surgeons US. *Res:* Effects of ionizing and non-ionizing radiation on cells; role of lysosomes in cellular responses to various physical, chemical and biological agents; mechanisms of division delay in synchronized cells; radiation protection of man and his environment; radiation risk assessment. *Mailing Add:* 1206 Governor Bridge Rd Davidsonville MD 21035. *Fax:* 301-621-8997

HODGE, IAN MOIR, PHYSICAL CHEMISTRY, POLYMER PHYSICS. *Current Pos:* MEM STAFF, EASTMAN KODAK RES LABS, ROCHESTER, NY, 85- *Personal Data:* b Auckland, NZ, Jan 28, 46; m, Kathalee Grant. *Educ:* Univ Auckland, BSc, 67, MSc, 68; Purdue Univ, PhD(phys chem), 74. *Prof Exp:* Res chemist, B F Goodrich Co, 78-85. *Concurrent Pos:* Fel, Univ Aberdeen, UK, 74-75; McGill Univ, Montreal, 75-76 & Purdue Univ, 77-78. *Mem:* Am Chem Soc; Am Physical Soc. *Res:* Conductivity and dielectric relaxation; glass transition; physical aging. *Mailing Add:* 55 Seville Dr Rochester NY 14617. *Fax:* 716-477-5970

HODGE, JAMES DWIGHT, POLYMER CHEMISTRY, FLAME RESISTANT FIBERS & CLOTHING. *Current Pos:* RETIRED. *Personal Data:* b Mechanicsburg, Ohio, July 14, 33; m 55, Louise Frady; c Sharon, Marcia & James A. *Educ:* Bob Jones Univ, BS, 56; Univ Mich, MS, 59; Pa State Univ, PhD(org chem), 63. *Prof Exp:* Chemist, Plastics & Resins Div, Shell Chem Co, Houston, Tex, 59-61; res chemist, Dacron Res Lab, Textiles Fibers Dept, E I Du Pont de Nemours & Co, Inc, Kinston, NC, 63-66, sr res chemist, 66-81, res assoc, 81-86, sr res assoc, Advan Fiber Systs, Richmond, Va, 86-93. *Concurrent Pos:* Consult flame resistant clothing. *Mem:* Am Chem Soc; Am Asn Textile Chemist & Colorists. *Res:* Organic reaction mechanisms; carbonium ions; epoxy compounds; polyesters; aramid polymerization, flame resistant polymers; string of arhmio fabrics. *Mailing Add:* 2101 Oakengate Lane Midlothian VA 23113-4047

HODGE, JAMES EDGAR, MATHEMATICS. *Current Pos:* assoc prof, 71-77, PROF MATH, ANGELO STATE UNIV, 77- *Personal Data:* b Corsicana, Tex, Apr 19, 29; m 48; c 2. *Educ:* NTex State Univ, BS, 50, MS, 57; Univ Ga, PhD(math), 65. *Prof Exp:* Teacher pub sch, Tex, 50-52, prin high sch, 54-56; instr math, NTex State Univ, 57-60, asst prof, 65-71. *Mem:* Am Math Soc; Math Asn Am. *Res:* Mathematical topology. *Mailing Add:* 413 Millstone Dr PO Box AG Beckley WV 25801

HODGE, JOHN EDWARD, CARBOHYDRATE CHEMISTRY. *Current Pos:* ADJ PROF CHEM, BRADLEY UNIV, PEORIA, ILL, 84- *Personal Data:* b Oct 12, 14; US citizen; m 48; c 4. *Educ:* Univ Kans, AB, 36, MA, 40. *Honors & Awards:* Super Serv Award, USDA, 53. *Prof Exp:* Prin chemist gasoline oils, State Kans Dept Inspections & Regist, Topeka, 37-39; teacher chem, State Indust Dept, Western Univ, Kansas City, Kans, 39-41; org chemist carbohydrates, Northern Regional Res Lab, Sci & Educ Admin, Agr Res, USDA, Peoria, Ill, 41-73, supvry res chemist, 73-81. *Concurrent Pos:* Mem comt food stability, Adv Bd Mil Personnel Supplies, Nat Res Coun, Nat Acad Sci, 77-, supvr grant res prog; consult chemist carbohydrates, 81- *Mem:* Emer mem Am Chem Soc; emer mem Am Asn Cereal Chemists. *Res:* Organic, food and cereal chemistry; sweeteners; gums. *Mailing Add:* 1107 W Groveland Ave Peoria IL 61604-3131

HODGE, PAUL WILLIAM, ASTRONOMY. *Current Pos:* assoc prof, Univ Wash, 65-69, assoc dean, Grad Sch, 70-72, assoc dean arts & sci, 78-79, chmn, Astron Dept, 87-90, PROF ASTRON, UNIV WASH, 69- *Personal Data:* b Seattle, Wash, Nov 8, 34; m 62; c 3. *Educ:* Yale Univ, BS, 56; Harvard Univ, PhD(astron), 60. *Honors & Awards:* Bok Astron Prize; Beckwith Astron Prize. *Prof Exp:* Lectr astron, Harvard Univ, 60-61; asst prof, Univ Calif, Berkeley, 61-65. *Concurrent Pos:* Physicist, Astrophys Observ, Smithsonian Inst, 56-65; NSF fel, 60-61; fel, Mt Wilson & Palomar Observs & Calif Inst Technol, 60-61; ed, Astron J, 84- *Mem:* Am Astron Soc (vpres, 90-93); Int Astron Union; Meteoritical Soc; AAAS. *Res:* Structure of galaxies; evolution of galaxies; meteorite craters. *Mailing Add:* Dept Astron Box 351580 Univ Wash Seattle WA 98195

HODGE, PHILIP G(IBSON), JR, PLASTICITY, COMPUTATIONS. *Current Pos:* EMER PROF MECH, UNIV MINN, MINNEAPOLIS, 91-; VIS EMER PROF, STANFORD UNIV, 93- *Personal Data:* b New Haven, Conn, Nov 9, 20; m 43, Thea Drell; c Susan E, Philip T & Elizabeth M. *Educ:* Antioch Col, AB, 43; Brown Univ, PhD(appl math), 49. *Honors & Awards:* Worcester Reed Warner Medal, Am Soc Mech Engrs, 75, Medal, 87; Theodore von Karman Medal, Am Soc Civil Engrs, 85; Distinguished Serv Award, Am Acad Mech, 85. *Prof Exp:* Res assoc appl math, Brown Univ, 47-49; asst prof math, Univ Calif, Los Angeles, 49-53; from assoc prof to prof appl mech, Polytech Inst Brooklyn, 53-57; prof mech, Ill Inst Technol, 57-71; prof mech, Univ Minn, Minneapolis, 71-91. *Concurrent Pos:* Consult, NAm Aviation, Inc, 51-52, AiResearch Mfg Co, 52-53 & IIT Res Inst, 57-71; NSF sr fel, 63-64; tech ed, J Appl Mech, 71-76; secy, US Nat Comn Theo & Appl Mech, 82-; asst treas, Int Union Theo & Appl Mech, 84-92. *Mem:* Nat Acad Eng; hon mem Am Soc Mech Engrs. *Res:* Theory of plasticity; plastic analysis of structures; numerical analysis. *Mailing Add:* 350 Sharon Park Dr No C-21 Menlo Park CA 94025. *E-Mail:* hodge@am-sun2.stanford.edu

HODGE, RICHARD PAUL, nucleic acid chemistry, applied research & process development, for more information see previous edition

HODGE, SANDRA S, COMMUNITY FORESTRY, AGROFORESTRY. *Current Pos:* exten assoc, 96-97, RES ASST PROF AGROFORESTRY, UNIV MO, COLUMBIA, 97- *Personal Data:* b Biloxi, Miss, Jan 30, 50; m 79, Robert H; c 1. *Educ:* Univ RI, BA, 73; Mich State Univ, MSc, 89, PhD(forestry), 93. *Prof Exp:* Adj asst prof forestry, Va Inst Technol, 93-95. *Concurrent Pos:* Natural resources consult, 91-94; lectr, Sch Archit, Univ Va, 93. *Mem:* Soc Am Foresters; Rural Sociol Soc; Int Soc Trop Foresters; Asn Temperate Agroforestry. *Res:* Social dimensions of forestry-affects of forest policy on communities; adoption of forestry practices by communities; reasons for participation/nonparticipation in forestry/agroforestry on private lands. *Mailing Add:* Sch Natural Resources I-30 Agr Bldg Univ Mo Columbia MO 65211. *Fax:* 573-882-1977; *E-Mail:* sandra_hodge@muccmail.missouri.edu

HODGE, STEVEN MCNIVEN, GLACIOLOGY. *Current Pos:* GEOPHYSICIST, WATER RESOURCES DIV, US GEOL SURV, 72- *Personal Data:* b London, Eng, Oct 15, 42; US citizen; div; c 2. *Educ:* Univ BC, BSc, 64; Univ Wash, PhD(geophys), 72. *Concurrent Pos:* Mem, Comt Snow & Ice, Am Geophys Union, 74-77; mem, Glaciol Comt, Polar Res Bd, US Nat Acad Sci, 76-79. *Mem:* Int Glaciol Soc; Am Geophys Union. *Res:* Radar sounding of ice sheets and glaciers; satellite remote sensing of glaciers and ice sheets; the interaction between glaciers and climate. *Mailing Add:* US Geol Surv Ice & Climate Proj Univ Puget Sound Tacoma WA 98416

HODGEN, GARY DEAN, ENDOCRINOLOGY. *Current Pos:* Staff fel endocrinol, NIH, 69-71, sr staff fel, 71-73, chief, Sect Endocrinol, Reproduction Res Br, 73-76, CHIEF, PREGNANCY RES BR, NAT INST CHILD HEALTH & HUMAN DEVELOP, 77- *Personal Data:* b Frankfort, Ind, May 10, 43; m 64; c 2. *Educ:* Purdue Univ, BS, 65, MS, 66; Ohio State Univ, PhD(endocrinol), 69. *Honors & Awards:* Ayerst Lectr, Am Fertility Soc, 82; Gregory Pincus Mem Lectr, Laurentian Hormone Conf, 82. *Concurrent Pos:* Res award, Soc Study Reproduction, 81. *Mem:* Endocrine Soc; Soc Study Reproduction; Soc Gynec Invest; Am Fertil Soc. *Res:* Primate reproductive physiology, including intrauterine fetal development and ovarian and testicular function during puberty and adulthood. *Mailing Add:* 105 44th St Virginia Beach VA 23451

HODGES, BILLY GENE, MATHEMATICS. *Current Pos:* assoc prof, 65-74, chmn dept, 74-77, PROF MATH, WINTHROP COL, 74- *Personal Data:* b Wayne, Okla, Nov 2, 29; m 60; c 3. *Educ:* Univ Okla, BA, 52, MA, 58, PhD(differential geom), 64. *Prof Exp:* Spec instr math, Univ Okla, 58-62; asst prof, Winthrop Col, 62-64; assoc prof, Ill State Univ, 64-65. *Mem:* Am Math Soc; Math Asn Am. *Res:* Riemannian geometry. *Mailing Add:* 781 Bridgewood Dr Rock Hill SC 29732

HODGES, CARL NORRIS, CONTROLLED ENVIRONMENTS, FOOD PRODUCTION. *Current Pos:* CHIEF EXEC OFFICER, PLANETARY DESIGN CORP, 85- *Personal Data:* b New Braunfels, Tex, Mar 19, 37; m 60, 87; c 4. *Educ:* Univ Ariz, BS, 59. *Prof Exp:* Res assoc, Univ Ariz, 61-63, supvr, Solar Energy Res Lab, 63-67, dir, Environ Res Lab, 67- *Concurrent Pos:* Mem, Comt Arid Lands, AAAS, 67-75 & Desertification Adv Comt, 76-78; mem bd trustees, Oceanic Found, Waimanalo, Hawaii, 72-82, Western Behav Sci Inst, La Jolla, Calif, 85-; pres, Desert Develop Found, Puerto Penasco, Mex, 75-; mem, Comt Aquacult, Nat Acad Sci, Washington, DC, 77, Panel Aquacult Eng & Simulation, 84-85, Adv Comt Technol Innovation & Comt Climate & Weather Fluctuations & Agr Prod; mem, Technol Assessment Adv Coun, Off Technol Assessment, US Cong, Washington, DC, 79-87, Adv Panel Technol Transfer to Middle East, 83 & Adv Panel Energy, Technol & Environ Develop Countries, 90; mem, Tarrytown One Hundred, NY, 83-85 & PRONATURA (Mex Asn Conserv Nature) Hermosillo, Mex, 84-; mem adv bd, Ariz Cancer Ctr, Tucson, 87-; mem bd dirs, Nat Asn Homebuilders Res Ctr, Washington, DC, 88-89 & Univ Phoenix, 90-; mem adv coun, Kino Learning Ctr, Tucson, Ariz, 89-; chmn, Ariz Solar Energy Comm, Phoenix, Ariz; first Pierson vis fel, Pierson Col, Yale Univ, 90. *Mem:* Fel World Acad Art & Sci; fel AAAS; Int Solar Energy Soc/Am Solar Energy Soc; World Maricult Soc. *Res:* Controlled environments and growing systems, future food production including greenhouses, aquatic animals and halophytes; development of totally closed ecological "biospheres" for the study of environmental problems on earth and ultimately use in space colonies; integrating biology into urban environments; seawater technology for irrigation of coastal desert areas and its effect on global warming. *Mailing Add:* 4230 E Whittier St Tucson AZ 85711

HODGES, CARROLL ANN, PLANETARY GEOLOGY, GEOMORPHOLOGY. *Current Pos:* asst chief geologist, Western Region, 84-88, GEOLOGIST, US GEOL SURV, 70- *Personal Data:* b Pomona, Calif, June 30, 36. *Educ:* Univ Tex, Austin, BA, 58; Univ Wis, MS, 60; Stanford Univ, PhD(geol), 66. *Prof Exp:* Geologist, Shell Oil Co, 60-62; ranger/ naturalist, Grand Canyon Nat Park, 63; asst prof geol, Colo State Univ, 65-66; geologist, Utah Construct & Mining Co, 66-69; asst prof geol, San Jose State Univ, 69-70. *Concurrent Pos:* Lectr, San Francisco State Univ, 78; Am Geophys Union Cong Sci fel, Washington, DC, 80-81; NSF is prof, Stanford Univ, 92, consult prof, 93-94. *Mem:* Fel Geol Soc Am; AAAS; fel Am Geophys Union; Mineral Econs & Mgt Soc. *Res:* Analysis and interpretation of lunar and Martian landforms of volcanic and impact origin; mineral resource assessment; mineral resources and world affairs; the changing role of minerals in the international economy of the 90s. *Mailing Add:* US Geol Surv MS 984 345 Middlefield Rd Menlo Park CA 94025. *Fax:* 650-329-5110; *E-Mail:* hodges@mojave.wr.usgs.gov

HODGES, CHARLES THOMAS, CHEMISTRY. *Current Pos:* develop biochemist, 78-84, RES SUPVR, E I DU PONT DE NEMOURS & CO, INC, 84- *Personal Data:* b Birmingham, Ala, Apr 28, 51; m 75; c 2. *Educ:* Univ South, BA, 73; Univ NC, Chapel Hill, PhD(biochem), 78. *Mem:* Am Asn Clin Chemists. *Res:* Chemical modification of proteins; development of clinical chemistry assays; immunoassay techniques. *Mailing Add:* 28 Pierson Dr Hockessin DE 19707

HODGES, CLINTON FREDERICK, PLANT PHYSIOLOGY. *Current Pos:* Assoc prof agron & hort, 67-76, PROF HORT, AGRON & PLANT PATH, IOWA STATE UNIV, 76- *Personal Data:* b Danville, Ill, Apr 20, 39; m 60; c 3. *Educ:* Univ Ill, Urbana, BS, 62, MS, 64, PhD(plant path), 67. *Mem:* Am Phytopath Soc; Am Soc Plant Physiologists. *Res:* Physiology of host-pathogen interactions. *Mailing Add:* Horticulture Iowa State Univ Ames IA 50011-2010

HODGES, DAVID A(LBERT), ELECTRICAL ENGINEERING. *Current Pos:* from assoc prof to prof, 70-97, dean, Col Eng, 90-96, DANIEL TELLEP DISTINGUISHED PROF ELEC ENG & COMPUT SCI, UNIV CALIF, BERKELEY, 97- *Personal Data:* b Hackensack, NJ, Aug 25, 37; m 65; c 2. *Educ:* Cornell Univ, BEE, 60; Univ Calif, Berkeley, MS, 61, PhD(elec eng), 66. *Honors & Awards:* Educ Medal, Inst Elec & Electronics Engrs, 97. *Prof Exp:* Mem tech staff, Functional Integration Group, Bell Tel Labs, Inc, 66-68, tech supvr, 68-69, head, Systs Elements Res Dept, 69-70. *Concurrent Pos:* Indust consult, 70- *Mem:* Nat Acad Eng; Inst Elec & Electronics Engrs. *Res:* Semiconductor; integrated circuits; computer integrated manufacturing. *Mailing Add:* Elec Eng & Comput Sci Dept Univ Calif 516 Corey Hall Berkeley CA 94720-1770. *Fax:* 510-643-5052; *E-Mail:* hodges@eecs.berkeley.edu

HODGES, DEAN T, JR, QUANTUM ELECTRONICS. *Current Pos:* SR VPRES, NEWPORT CORP, 84- *Personal Data:* b Bremerton, Wash, Mar 28, 44; m 76. *Educ:* Calif State Univ, Humboldt, BS, 66; Cornell Univ, PhD(appl physics), 71. *Prof Exp:* Mgr, Lasers & Optics Dept, Electronics Res Lab, Aerospace Corp, 71-80, eng mgr, Laser Prod, Spectra Physics, 80-84. *Concurrent Pos:* Adj prof, Univ Calif, Los Angeles, 76-77. *Mem:* Optical Soc Am; fel Inst Elec & Electronics Engrs. *Res:* Quantum electronic processes of rare-gas and metal-vapor ion lasers, discharge molecular lasers, and optically pumped infrared and far infrared molecular lasers; development of near millimeter wave detectors and radiometers. *Mailing Add:* Laser Power Corp 12777 High Bluff Dr San Diego CA 92130

HODGES, DEWEY HARPER, STRUCTURAL DYNAMICS AEROELASTICITY, STRUCTURAL MECHANICS & DYNAMICS. *Current Pos:* PROF AEROSPACE ENG, GA INST TECHNOL, ATLANTA, 86- *Personal Data:* b Clarksville, Tenn, May 18, 48; m 71, Margaret Elin Jones; c Timothy, Jonathan, David, Philip & Benjamin. *Educ:* Univ Tenn, BS, 69; Stanford Univ, MS, 70, PhD(aeronaut & astronaut eng), 73. *Prof Exp:* Res scientist, US Army Aeroflight Dynamics Directorate, Ames Res Ctr, Moffett Field, Calif, 70-80, sr res scientist & theoret group leader, 80-86. *Concurrent Pos:* Instr, NC Bible Col, San Jose, 74-86; lectr, Stanford Univ, 80-86; guest res scientist, DLR Inst Structural Mech, Braunschweig, Ger, 84. *Mem:* Fel Am Inst Aeronaut & Astronaut; Am Acad Mech; Am Helicopter Soc; Sigma Xi. *Res:* Helicopter dynamics; aeroelasticity; computational methods in structural dynamics; computational mechanics of thin structural elements; structural mechanics; optimal control, including space and time element methods; published over 160 articles; co-patentee on 2 US patents. *Mailing Add:* Sch Aerospace Eng Ga Inst Technol Atlanta GA 30332-0150. *E-Mail:* dewey.hodges@ae.gatech.edu

HODGES, DONALD GLENN, NATURAL RESOURCE-ENVIRONMENTAL POLICY & ECONOMICS, POLICY ANALYSIS. *Current Pos:* ASST PROF FOREST MGT & POLICY, DEPT FORESTRY, MISS STATE UNIV, 91- *Personal Data:* b Chattanooga, Tenn, July 21, 59; m 80, Cynthia Green; c Andrew, Alison & Deidre. *Educ:* Univ Tenn, Knoxville, BS, 82; Univ Ga, MS, 85, PhD(forest econ & policy), 88. *Prof Exp:* Res assoc, USDA Forest Serv, Southern Forest Exp Sta, 88-89; asst prof natural resource mgt & policy, Univ NH Dept Natural Resources, 89-91. *Mem:* Soc Am Foresters. *Res:* Socioeconomic aspects of environmental and natural resource policies, with emphasis on assessing the impact of federal and state policies on natural resource management. *Mailing Add:* 210 Seville Pl Starkville MS 39759. *Fax:* 601-325-8726; *E-Mail:* dgh2@msstate.edu

HODGES, FLOYD NORMAN, ENVIRONMENTAL GEOCHEMISTRY, GEOHYDROLOGY. *Current Pos:* SR SCIENTIST, WESTINGHOUSE, 89- *Personal Data:* b San Antonio, Tex, Sept 16, 39; m 66; c 2. *Educ:* Univ Tex, Austin, BS, 69, PhD(geol), 75. *Prof Exp:* Fel Geophys Lab, Carnegie Inst, Washington, 72-74; fel, State Univ NY, Stony Brook, 74-76; asst prof geol, Furman Univ, 76-79; staff scientist geochem, Rockwell Int, 79-81; sr scientist geochem, Battelle Northwest Lab, 81-88. *Concurrent Pos:* Lectr chem, Joint Ctr Grad Studies, Washington State Univ, Richland, Wash, 80- *Mem:* Geol Soc Am; Mineral Soc Am; Am Geophys Union; Geochem Soc; AAAS. *Res:* Application of geochemistry to problems of hazardous waste disposal and remediation; igneous and metamorphic petrogenesis and the role of these processes in the evolution of planetary crusts. *Mailing Add:* 8130 W Falls Pl Kennewick WA 99336

HODGES, GLENN R(OSS), INFECTIOUS DISEASES, INTERNAL MEDICINE. *Current Pos:* from asst prof to assoc prof, 74-84, assoc dean vet affairs, 87-96, PROF MED, COL MED, UNIV KANS, 84- *Personal Data:* b Cleveland, Ohio, Aug 28, 41; m 64, Carolyn Read; c Diane, Cheryl, Kristine & Janice. *Educ:* Muskingum Col, BA, 63; Univ Chicago, MD, 67; Ohio State Univ, MS, 72. *Prof Exp:* Clin instr med, Col Med, Ohio State Univ, 70-72. *Concurrent Pos:* Head, Sect Infectious dis, Naval Hosp, Great Lakes, Ill, 72-74; chief, Sect, Infectious Dis, Vet Admin Med Ctr Kansas City, Mo, 74-90, Leavenworth, Mo, 96- *Mem:* Am Col Physicians; Am Col Physician Execs; Infectious Dis Soc Am; Am Soc Microbiol. *Res:* Antimicrobial therapy; nosocomial infections; infection control and hospital epidemiology. *Mailing Add:* Med Serv Dwight D Eisenhower VA Med Ctr 4101 S Fourth St Trafficway Leavenworth KS 66048. *Fax:* 913-758-4225; *E-Mail:* hodges.glenn@leavenworth.va.gov

HODGES, HARDY M, COSMOLOGY. *Current Pos:* SMITHSONIAN FEL, HARVARD-SMITHSONIAN CTR ASTROPHYS, 90- *Personal Data:* b Tampa, Fla, Nov 26, 63. *Educ:* Fla State Univ, BS, 83; Univ Chicago, PhD(physics), 88. *Prof Exp:* Res assoc, Santa Cruz Inst Particle Physics, Univ Calif, 88-90. *Res:* Particle physics and astrophysics interface; cosmology; inflation; topological defects; phase transitions; origin of large-scale structure; stochastic processes in cosmology. *Mailing Add:* 72 Garden St Hoboken NJ 07030. *Fax:* 617-495-7093

HODGES, HARRY FRANKLIN, PLANT PHYSIOLOGY. *Current Pos:* PROF AGRON, MISS STATE UNIV, 75- *Personal Data:* b Bedford, Ind, Nov 17, 33; m 55; c 3. *Educ:* Purdue Univ, BS, 56, MS, 58, PhD(plant physiol), 64. *Prof Exp:* Instr res agron, Purdue Univ, 56-65, from asst prof to assoc prof plant physiol, 65-75. *Concurrent Pos:* Res asst, Pa State Univ, 64-65. *Mem:* Am Soc Agron; Crop Sci Soc Am; Am Soc Plant Plysiologists; Sigma Xi. *Res:* Regulation of physiological development. *Mailing Add:* Agron Miss State Univ PO Box 9655 Starkville MS 39762-9555

HODGES, JOHN DEAVOURS, PLANT PHYSIOLOGY, SILVICULTURE. *Current Pos:* SILVICULTURIST, MISS STATE UNIV, 75- *Personal Data:* b Laurel, Miss, Apr 12, 37; m 58; c 2. *Educ:* Miss State Univ, BS, 59; Univ Wash, MS, 62, PhD(tree physiol), 65. *Prof Exp:* Res forester, Southern Forest Exp Sta, USDA, 59-61, res plant physiologist, 65-75. *Mem:* Soc Am Foresters; Am Soc Plant Physiol. *Res:* Silviculture of southern hardwoods; plant water relations; plant chemistry; environmental physiology; physiology of disease and insect resistance in plants; ecology. *Mailing Add:* Dept Forestry Miss State Univ Box 9681 Mississippi State MS 39762-9637

HODGES, JOHN HENDRICKS, MEDICINE. *Current Pos:* Asst demonstr, Jefferson Med Col, 44-53, asst prof, 53-63, prof clin med, 63, prof, 64-79, bd trustees, Children's Rehab Hosp, 78-89, Magee Rehab Hosp, 87-93, LUDWIG A KIND EMER PROF MED, JEFFERSON MED COL, 79- *Personal Data:* b Harpers Ferry, WVa, Aug 1, 14; m 40; Elizabeth M Wallace; c John H Jr. *Educ:* Cath Univ, BS, 35; Jefferson Med Col, MD, 39; Am Bd Internal Med, dipl, 48, recert, 77. *Concurrent Pos:* Fel med, Jefferson Med Col, 42-44; Mary Markle fel trop med, Walter Reed Hosp & Cent Am, 43; consult hemat, Lankenau Hosp, 64-88; assoc, Cardeza Found, 69-79; mem bd dir, Mercy Cath Med Ctr, 71-81; mem bd trustees, Thomas Jefferson Univ, 78- *Mem:* Fel Am Col Physicians; Am Soc Hemat; Am Soc Trop Med & Hyg; Am Heart Asn; Int Soc Hemat; AMA; Sigma Xi. *Res:* Original clinical and laboratory studies on the origin of viral dysentery; studies on sickle cell disease, bone marrow and coagulation. *Mailing Add:* 436 Sabine Ave Wynnewood PA 19096-1402

HODGES, JOHN HERBERT, MATHEMATICS. *Current Pos:* from asst prof to assoc prof, 60-66, PROF MATH, UNIV COLO, BOULDER, 66- *Personal Data:* b Pittsburgh, Pa, Sept 30, 28; m 55; c 3. *Educ:* Westminster Col, Pa, BS, 51; Duke Univ, MA, 53, PhD, 55. *Prof Exp:* Instr math, Duke Univ, 54-55; asst prof, Univ Buffalo, 55-58; res mathematician, Cornell Aeronaut Lab, Inc, 58-60. *Concurrent Pos:* NSF res grants, 56-58 & 61-71 & sci fel, 64-65. *Mem:* Am Math Soc; Math Asn Am. *Res:* Number-theoretic properties of matrices over a finite field; matrix equations; distribution of matrices with given properties; weighted partitions; exponential sums. *Mailing Add:* Univ Colo Campus Box 395 Boulder CO 80309-0001

HODGES, JOSEPH LAWSON, JR, THEORETICAL STATISTICS. *Current Pos:* RETIRED. *Personal Data:* b Shreveport, La, Apr 10, 22; m 47; c 5. *Educ:* Univ Calif, BA, 42, PhD(math), 48. *Prof Exp:* From instr to assoc prof math, Univ Calif, Berkeley, 48-57, prof statist, 57-90. *Concurrent Pos:* Asst prof, Univ Chicago, 51-52; Guggenheim fel, 56-57. *Mailing Add:* Dept Statist Univ Calif 2120 Oxford St Berkeley CA 94720

HODGES, LANCE THOMAS, SEDIMENTARY PETROLOGY, PALEOECOLOGY. *Current Pos:* SR RES ASSOC, PHYSIOL & PHARMACOL, LOMA LINDA UNIV, 87- *Personal Data:* b Windsor, Ont, May 20, 34; US citizen; m 86, Debbie Munroe. *Educ:* Andrews Univ, BA, 57; Univ Waterloo, MSc, 63; Loma Linda Univ, PhD(geol), 77. *Prof Exp:* Instr phys sci, Andrews Univ, 65-66; engr elec eng, Calif Inst Technol, 67-68; instr eng, Grantham Eng Sch, 69-71; asst prof geol, NMex Highlands Univ, 77; staff geologist, CER Corp, 78-79; res geologist, C K Geoenergy Corp, 79-86. *Mem:* Am Asn Petrol Geologists; Geol Soc Am; Int Asn Sedimentologists; Int Asn Study Fossil Cnidaria; Soc Econ Paleontologists & Mineralogists. *Res:* Fossil reef paleoecology and sedimentology; carbonate petrology and petrography; bioherm structure; structure, stratigraphy and natural gas of the Green River Basin; drug metabolism in animals. *Mailing Add:* 23078 Peacock Ct Grand Terrace CA 92313

HODGES, LAURENT, SOLAR ENERGY, GENERAL PHYSICS. *Current Pos:* Assoc, 66-68, from asst prof to assoc prof, 68-78, PROF PHYSICS, IOWA STATE UNIV, 78- *Personal Data:* b Houston, Tex, Jan 16, 40; m 66; c 2. *Educ:* Harvard Univ, AB, 60, AM, 61, PhD(physics), 66. *Concurrent Pos:* From asst physicist to sr physicist, Ames Lab, US Dept Energy, 66-81; energy specialist, Iowa Energy Exten Serv, 81- *Mem:* AAAS; Am Phys Soc; Am Solar Soc; Am Asn Phys Teachers; Am Math Soc. *Res:* Energy conservation and passive solar energy; environmental pollution. *Mailing Add:* Dept Physics Iowa State Univ 12 Physics Hall Ames IA 50011-3660

HODGES, LAWRENCE H, AGRICULTURAL ENGINEERING. *Current Pos:* CONSULT AGR & MECH ENG. *Mem:* Nat Acad Eng. *Mailing Add:* 601 Lake Ave PO Box 307 Racine WI 53401-0307

HODGES, LINDA CAROL, BIOCHEMISTRY. *Current Pos:* ASST PROF CHEM, KENNESAW COL, 80- *Personal Data:* b Covington, Ky, Jan 24, 51. *Educ:* Centre Col, Ky, BS, 72; Univ Ky, PhD(biochem), 79. *Prof Exp:* Instr chem, Georgetown Col, 77, Berea Col, 78-79; vis prof, Centre Col, 79-80. *Concurrent Pos:* Res scientist, Ga Inst Technol, 81- *Mem:* Sigma Xi; Am Chem Soc. *Res:* Glycoprotein structure and function; carbohydrate structures and sites of glycosidic linkage in protease-inhibitor; structural studies on a polysaccharides from Cannabis that lower inner ocular pressure. *Mailing Add:* 2886 Cherokee St Kennesaw GA 30144-2800

HODGES, NEAL HOWARD, II, INTELLIGENT SYSTEMS. *Current Pos:* DATA PROCESSING SPECIALIST, SDAK SCH MINES & TECHNOL, 77- *Personal Data:* b Tacoma, Wash, Oct 22, 48; m 78; c 2. *Educ:* Black Hills State Univ, BS, 74. *Concurrent Pos:* Adj assoc prof, SDak Sch Mines & Technol, 80-91. *Mem:* Am Asn Artificial Intel. *Res:* Mobile semi-autonomous robots for exploration and military applications. *Mailing Add:* 2327 S Valley Dr Rapid City SD 57701-5997. *E-Mail:* nhodges@silver.sdsmt.edu

HODGES, RALPH RICHARD, JR, PLANETARY ATMOSPHERES. *Current Pos:* res scientist, 65-67, asst prof atmospheric & space sci, 67-72, RES SCIENTIST, UNIV TEX, DALLAS, 72- *Personal Data:* b St Louis, Mo, Aug 18, 33; m 57; c 4. *Educ:* Univ Ill, BS, 55, MS, 57, PhD(elec eng), 64. *Prof Exp:* Res asst, Antenna Lab, Univ Ill, 55-56, res assoc, 56-58, proj engr, Collins Radio Co, 58-60, head, Appl Sci Dept, 64-65. *Mem:* Am Geophys Union; Inst Elec & Electronics Engrs; Sigma Xi. *Res:* Planetary atmospheres and ionospheres; electromagnetic theory. *Mailing Add:* 7620 Tophill Lane Dallas TX 75248

HODGES, ROBERT EDGAR, INTERNAL MEDICINE. *Current Pos:* RETIRED. *Personal Data:* b Marshalltown, Iowa, July 30, 22; m 46; c 4. *Educ:* Univ Iowa, BA, 44, MD, 49; Am Bd Internal Med, dipl, 54; Am Bd Nutrit, cert. *Prof Exp:* Intern, Mem Hosp, Pa, 47-48; resident internal med, Univ Iowa, 49-52, instr, 52-53, assoc, 53-54, from asst prof to prof 54-71, dir metab ward, Hosp, 52-54 & 56-71; prof, Sch Med, Univ Calif, Davis, 71-80; at Dept Biochem & Internal Med, Med Ctr, Univ Nebr. *Concurrent Pos:* Fel coun arteriosclerosis & coun epidemiol, Am Heart Asn. *Mem:* AMA; Am Heart Asn; fel Am Col Physicians; Am Fedn Clin Res; Am Soc Clin Nutrit (pres, 66). *Res:* Nutrition; physiology; diet in atherosclerosis; experimental human deficiencies of pantothenic acid, ascorbic acid and vitamin A. *Mailing Add:* RR1 Box 147 Oxford IA 52322-9752

HODGES, ROBERT STANLEY, PROTEIN CHEMISTRY, PEPTIDE VACCINES. *Current Pos:* from asst prof to assoc prof, 74-84, PROF BIOCHEM, UNIV ALTA, 84-; PRES, ALTA PEPTIDE INST, 85-; PRES & CHIEF EXEC OFFICER, SYNTHETIC PEPTIDES INC, 86- *Personal Data:* b Saskatoon, Sask, Dec 30, 43; m 62, Phyllis; c 2. *Educ:* Univ Sask, BSc, 65; Univ Alta, PhD(biochem), 71. *Prof Exp:* Defense sci serv officer, Dept Nat Defense, Defense Res Bd, Defense Res Estab, Suffield, 65-67; Med Res Coun Can fel, Rockefeller Univ, 71-73, res assoc, 73-74. *Mem:* Can Biochem Soc; Biophys Soc; Am Soc Biol Chemists; NY Acad Sci; Am Chem Soc; fel Royal Soc Can; Protein Soc; Am Peptide Soc; Sigma Xi. *Res:* Structure and function of muscle protein systems involved in contraction and relaxation (tropomyosin, troponin I, troponin T, troponin C and calmodulin); chemical modification and sequence determination; chemical synthesis of peptides and proteins; synthesis and use of heterobifunctional crosslinking reagents; immunogenicity-antigenicity of proteins; synthetic vaccines; de novo design of proteins; high-performance liquid chromatography, methodology development. *Mailing Add:* Dept Biochem Univ Alta Edmonton AB T6G 2H7 Can. *Fax:* 403-492-0095

HODGES, RONALD WILLIAM, SYSTEMATIC ENTOMOLOGY. *Current Pos:* res entomologist, 62-76, chief, syst entom lab, 76-80, RES ENTOMOLOGIST, SCI & EDUC ADMIN, AGR RES, USDA, 80- *Personal Data:* b Lansing, Mich, Aug 7, 34; m 67, Elaine R Snyder; c Steven E & Lawrence B. *Educ:* Mich State Univ, BSc, 56, MSc, 57; Cornell Univ, PhD(entom), 61. *Honors & Awards:* Thomas Say Award, Entom Soc Am. *Prof Exp:* Res asst, Mich State Univ, 56-57; NSF jr fel, 61-62. *Concurrent Pos:* Ed-in-chief, Moths Am NMex. *Mem:* Soc Syst Biol; Lepidop Soc (pres, 75-76); Entom Soc Can; Entom Soc Am. *Res:* Taxonomy of Lepidoptera, particularly Gelechioidea. *Mailing Add:* Syst Entom Lab USDA US Nat Mus NHB 168 Washington DC 20560

HODGES, SIDNEY EDWARD, PHYSICS. *Current Pos:* RETIRED. *Personal Data:* b Booneville, Miss, Feb 11, 24; m 47, Linda Susan Neal; c Philippe, Annette, Sean, Chadwick & Angela. *Educ:* Southern Methodist Univ, BS, 49; Agr & Mech Col, Univ Tex, PhD(physics), 58. *Prof Exp:* Instr physics, ETex State Col, 50-54, asst prof, 56-58; prof & head dept, Stephen F Austin State Col, 58-65 & Howard Payne Col, 65-67; prof physics, Southeast Mo State Univ, 67-88. *Concurrent Pos:* Founder non-profit sci mus, Denton, Tex, 92- *Mem:* Am Asn Physics Teachers; Sigma Xi. *Res:* Molecular spectroscopy; acoustics; laboratory standard for absolute intensities; optics. *Mailing Add:* 1821 Emery St Denton TX 76201. *E-Mail:* ishooo2@unt.edu

HODGES, THOMAS KENT, PLANT PHYSIOLOGY. *Current Pos:* assoc prof, 68-74, head dept bot & plant path, 77-82, PROF PLANT PHYSIOL, PURDUE UNIV, 71- *Personal Data:* b Bedford, Ind, Oct 18, 36; c 3. *Educ:* Purdue Univ, BS, 58; Univ Calif, Davis, MS, 60, PhD(plant physiol), 62. *Honors & Awards:* Charles Albert Shull Award, Am Soc Plant Physiol, 75. *Prof Exp:* Res assoc plant physiol, Univ Ill, 62-63, from asst prof to assoc prof, 63-68. *Mem:* Am Soc Plant Physiol. *Res:* Plant biochemistry; membrane transport; plant regeneration. *Mailing Add:* Dept Bot Purdue Univ West Lafayette IN 47907-1968

HODGETTS, ROSS BIRNIE, DEVELOPMENTAL GENETICS. *Current Pos:* asst prof, 70-75, ASSOC PROF GENETICS, UNIV ALTA, 75- *Personal Data:* b Ont, May 27, 41; m 64. *Educ:* Queen's Univ, Ont, BSc, 63; Yale Univ, MS, 65, PhD(biophys), 67. *Prof Exp:* Jane Coffin Childs fel, 67-69. *Mem:* Genetics Soc Can. *Res:* Gene-enzyme studies on dope decarboxylase in Drosophila. *Mailing Add:* Biol Scis Univ Alta Edmonton AB T6G 2E9 Can

HODGIN, EZRA CLAY, IMMUNOLOGY, VETERINARY PATHOLOGY. *Current Pos:* MEM STAFF, DEPT PATH, MICH STATE UNIV, 79- *Personal Data:* b Greensboro, NC, Apr 1, 47; m 74; c 1. *Educ:* NC State Univ, BS, 68; Okla State Univ, DVM, 72; Wash State Univ, PhD(path), 76. *Prof Exp:* Asst prof immunopath, NC State Univ, 76-79. *Mem:* Asn Am Vet Med Cols. *Res:* Modulation of immune responses; lymphocyte function; mechanisms of host defense and disease; eosinophil function. *Mailing Add:* 1710 May St Baton Rouge LA 70808

HODGINS, DANIEL STEPHEN, BIOCHEMISTRY. *Current Pos:* assoc, 84-90, PARTNER, ARNOLD, WHITE & DURKEE, 91- *Personal Data:* b Scranton, Pa, June 21, 39; m 65; c 3. *Educ:* Elizabethtown Col, BS, 61; Univ Del, PhD(chem), 66; Okla City Univ, JD, 81. *Prof Exp:* NIH fel, Brandeis Univ, 65-67; from asst prof to assoc prof biochem & molecular biol, Med Sch, Univ Okla, 67-81; assoc, Dunlap & Codding Patent Attorneys, 81-84. *Mem:* Am Soc Biol Chemists; Am Chem Soc; Soc Exp Biol Med; AAAS; Am Bar Asn. *Res:* Enzyme mechanism; cancer therapy; cyclic adenosine monophosphate and hypertension; cardiac hypertrophy. *Mailing Add:* Arnold White & Durkee One American Pl Suite 1900 600 Congress Ave Austin TX 78701. *Fax:* 512-474-7577

HODGINS, GEORGE RAYMOND, PHOTOGRAPHIC CHEMISTRY. *Current Pos:* RETIRED. *Personal Data:* b East Rockaway, NY, May 24, 26; m 52; c 3. *Educ:* Hofstra Col, BA, 50; Adelphi Col, MS, 56. *Prof Exp:* Dir res, Litho Chem & Supply Co, 50-59; group leader basic res, Technifax Corp, 59-64, res supvr, 64-70; mgr contract develop, James River Graphics Inc, 70-73, res mgr, 73-89. *Mem:* Am Chem Soc; Soc Photog Scientists & Engr; Tech Asn Pulp & Paper Indust; Nat Microfilm Asn; Tech Asn Graphic Arts. *Res:* Light sensitive materials used in the reproduction of printed materials; diazotypes; lithography; photography; photopolymerization; organic synthesis; electrophotographic imaging materials and processes; non-silver photoimaging materials and processes; photopolymers. *Mailing Add:* 666 Amherst Rd Granby MA 01033-9784

HODGKIN, ALAN LLOYD, BIOPHYSICS. *Current Pos:* RETIRED. *Personal Data:* b Feb 5, 14; m 44, Marion de Kay Rous; c 4. *Educ:* Cambridge Univ, fel, 36, MA, ScD; Univ Aberdeen, LLD. *Hon Degrees:* Several from foreign univs. *Honors & Awards:* Nobel Prize in Med or Physiol, 63; Royal Medal, Royal Soc, 58, Copley Medal, 65. *Prof Exp:* Sci officer radar, Air Ministry Aircraft Prod, 39-45; from lectr to asst dir res, Cambridge Univ, 45-52, John Humphrey Plummer prof biophysics, 70-81; Foulerton res prof, Royal Soc, 52-69; Chancellor, Univ Leicester, 71-84; master, Trinity Col, 78-84. *Concurrent Pos:* mem, Med Res Coun, 59-63. *Mem:* Nat Acad Sci; fel Royal Soc (pres, 70-75); hon fel Indian Nat Sci Acad; Physiol Soc (secy, 60-67); hon foreign mem Am Acad Arts & Sci; foreign mem Royal Danish Acad Sci; foreign mem Royal Swedish Acad Sci; foreign mem Am Philos Soc; foreign mem USSR Acad Sci; Marine Biol Asn UK (pres, 66-76); hon mem Royal Irish Acad. *Res:* Conduction of the nervous impulse; nature of nervous conduction, muscle and vision; devised system of mathematical equations describing nerve impulse; giant nerve fibers of squid, proving that electricity was direct causal agent of impulse propagation. *Mailing Add:* 18 Panton St Cambridge CB2 1HP England

HODGKIN, BRIAN CHARLES, BIOENGINEERING & BIOMEDICAL ENGINEERING. *Current Pos:* res assoc med res, Biomed Res Inst, 76-82, coordr elec eng, 82-85, DEAN, SCH APPL SCI, UNIV SOUTHERN MAINE, 85- *Personal Data:* b Lewiston, Maine, May 1, 41; m 69; c 2. *Educ:* Univ Maine, BSc, 63 & 64; Johns Hopkins Univ, PhD(biomed eng), 69. *Prof Exp:* Instr surg, Sch Med, Johns Hopkins Univ, 69-72; res assoc electrocardiology, Maine Med Ctr, 72-75. *Concurrent Pos:* Res assoc, Maine Med Ctr, 76- *Mem:* Inst Elec & Electronics Engrs. *Mailing Add:* Sch Appl Sci John Mitchel Ctr Univ Southern Maine 37 College Ave Gorham ME 04038

HODGKINS, EARL JOSEPH, forest ecology; deceased, see previous edition for last biography

HODGMAN, JOAN ELIZABETH, MEDICINE, NEONATOLOGY. *Current Pos:* from instr to assoc prof, 51-69, PROF PEDIAT, SCH MED, UNIV SOUTHERN CALIF, 69-; MEM ATTEND STAFF, LOS ANGELES CO-UNIV SOUTHERN CALIF MED CTR, 50- *Personal Data:* b Portland, Ore, Sept 7, 23; wid; c Ann V (Schwartz) & Susan L (DiPietro). *Educ:* Stanford Univ, BA, 43; Univ Calif, MD, 46; Am Pediat Bd, dipl, 56; Am Bd Neonatal-Prenatal Med, cert, 75. *Prof Exp:* Intern pediat, Univ Calif Hosp, 46-47; resident, Los Angeles Co Hosp, 48-50. *Concurrent Pos:* Resident, Harbor Gen Hosp, Torrance, 48; mem attend staff, Rancho Los Amigos, 53-; consult nursery, Booth Mem Hosp, 50-63. *Mem:* AMA; Am Pediat Soc; Am Acad Pediat. *Res:* Problems of the newborn, especially the premature infant. *Mailing Add:* Womens Hosp L919 1240 Mission Rd Los Angeles CA 90033-1078. *Fax:* 213-226-3440

HODGSON, DEREK JOHN, STRUCTURAL CHEMISTRY, INORGANIC CHEMISTRY. *Current Pos:* prof & head chem, 87-90, VPRES RES, UNIV WYO, 90-, PRES, UNIV WYO TECH TRANSFER FOUND, INC, 91- *Personal Data:* b Watford, Eng, July 1, 42; m 78; c 1. *Educ:* Harvard Univ, AB, 65; Northwestern Univ, Ill, MS, 68, PhD(chem), 69. *Honors & Awards:* Tanner Award, 85. *Prof Exp:* From asst prof to prof chem, Univ NC, Chapel, 69-87. *Concurrent Pos:* Acad vis, Oxford Univ, 80; vis prof, Univ Copenhagen, 80 & Univ Aukland, 87; dir, Western Res Inst, 91- *Mem:* Am Chem Soc; Am Crystallog Asn; Coun Chem Res. *Res:* Structures of magnetically condensed materials; redox-active dimers and oligomers; aza analogs of nucleic acid constituents; calcium binding in biological systems. *Mailing Add:* Off Provost PO Box BQ Mississippi State MS 39762

HODGSON, EDWARD SHILLING, COMPARATIVE PHYSIOLOGY. *Current Pos:* prof biol, 69-89, chmn dept, 69-76, EMER PROF BIOL, TUFTS UNIV, 90- *Personal Data:* b Wilmington, Del, Oct 28, 26; m 49; c 2. *Educ:* Allegheny Col, BS, 47; Johns Hopkins Univ, PhD(biol), 51. *Prof Exp:* Jr instr, Johns Hopkins Univ, 47-51; from instr to prof zool, Barnard Col, Columbia Univ, 51-69. *Concurrent Pos:* USPHS fel, 54-55; Fulbright res fel, Australia, 59-60; hon fel, Australian Nat Univ. *Mem:* AAAS; Am Soc Zool; Am Physiol Soc; NY Acad Sci. *Res:* Sensory physiology; invertebrate physiology; neurophysiology; neurosecretion; animal behavior. *Mailing Add:* Dept Biol Tufts Univ Medford MA 02155

HODGSON, ERNEST, BIOCHEMICAL & COMPARATIVE TOXICOLOGY, RISK ANALYSIS. *Current Pos:* from asst prof to prof, NC State Univ, 61-77, William Neal Reynolds prof toxicol, 77, chmn toxicol prog, 83-89, HEAD, DEPT TOXICOL, NC STATE UNIV, 89- *Personal Data:* b Hetton-le-Hole, Eng, July 26, 32; US citizen; m 57, Mary K Devlin; c Mary E, Audrey C (Myers), Patricia E & Ernest. *Educ:* Univ Durham, BSc, 54; Ore State Univ, PhD, 59. *Honors & Awards:* Educ Award, Soc Toxicol, 84; Burdick & Jackson Award, Am Chem Soc, 89; Merit Award, Soc Toxicol, 94. *Prof Exp:* Demonstr zool, Kings Col, Univ Durham, 54-55; fel entom, Univ Wis, 59-61. *Concurrent Pos:* Ed, J Biochem Toxicol, Reviews Biochem Toxicol, Environ Toxicol; pres, Toxicol Commun, Inc. *Mem:* AAAS; Am Soc Pharmacol & Exp Therapeut; Soc Toxicol; Am Chem Soc; Int Soc Study Xenobiotics. *Res:* Enzymatic aspects of toxicology; comparative toxicology; pesticide toxicology; risk analysis. *Mailing Add:* Dept Toxicol Box 7633 NC State Univ Raleigh NC 27695-7633. *Fax:* 919-515-7169; *E-Mail:* ernest_hodglow@ncsu.edu

HODGSON, GORDON WESLEY, PHYSICAL CHEMISTRY. *Current Pos:* RETIRED. *Personal Data:* b Alta, May 25, 24; m 53; c 5. *Educ:* Univ Alta, BSc, 46, MSc, 47; McGill Univ, PhD(phys chem), 49. *Prof Exp:* Chief chemist, Oil Sands Proj, 49; res chemist, Res Coun Alta, 49-58, head petrol res, 58-67; Nat Acad Sci res assoc, NASA Ames Res Ctr, 67-68; NASA res assoc, Sch Med, Stanford Univ, 68-69; fac prof, 69-72, Kananaskis Ctr, Univ Calgary, 69-72, prof environ sci, 72-73, prof & dir, fac eng, 82-85. *Concurrent Pos:* Vis prof, Tohoku, Japan, 62. *Mem:* Am Chem Soc; Geochem Soc; Am Geophys Union; Am Astron Soc; Chem Inst Can. *Res:* Organic geochemistry; solids pipelining; exobiology; cosmochemistry; chemical oceanography; environmental science; environmental management; technology transfer. *Mailing Add:* 18 Varbay Pl NW 18 Varbay Pl NW Calgary AB T3A 0C8 Can

HODGSON, J(EFFREY) WILLIAM, MECHANICAL ENGINEERING. *Current Pos:* from asst prof to assoc prof, 67-76, PROF MECH ENG, UNIV TENN, KNOXVILLE, 76- *Personal Data:* b Stockport, Eng, Nov 15, 40; US citizen; m 63; c 2. *Educ:* Ga Inst Technol, BME, 63, MSME, 65, PhD(mech eng), 67. *Prof Exp:* Asst mech eng, Ga Inst Technol, 63-67. *Mem:* Am Soc Mech Engrs; Soc Automotive Engrs. *Res:* Heat transfer; fluid mechanics; thermodynamics; automotive safety; dynamic sealing. *Mailing Add:* 7677 Williams Ferry Rd Lenoir City TN 37771

HODGSON, JAMES B, JR, information science, for more information see previous edition

HODGSON, JAMES RUSSELL, ZOOLOGY. *Current Pos:* Asst prof, 70-76, ASSOC PROF BIOL, ST NORBERT COL, 76- *Personal Data:* b Sept 1, 42; US citizen; m 67; c 2. *Educ:* Univ Wis, BS, 65; Western Mich Univ, MA, 69; Mont State Univ, PhD(zool), 70. *Concurrent Pos:* Environ consult, 77-; vis prof zool & hon fel, Univ Wis-Madison, 80-81. *Mem:* AAAS; Am Soc Mammalogists. *Res:* Habitat preference and niche utilization of small mammals; prey-predator interactions in aquatic ecosystems. *Mailing Add:* Div Natural Sci St Norbert Col 100 Grant Ave De Pere WI 54115-2099

HODGSON, JOHN HUMPHREY, SEISMOLOGY. *Current Pos:* RETIRED. *Personal Data:* b Toronto, Ont, Sept 24, 13; m 40; c 3. *Educ:* Univ Toronto, BA, 40, MA, 46, PhD(geophys), 51. *Prof Exp:* Field engr, Schlumberger Well Surv Corp, 40-44; asst prof geophys, Univ Toronto, 45-49; seismologist, Dom Observ, Dept Mines & Tech Survs, 49-51, chief, Seismol Div, 52-65, dir earth physics br, Dept Energy, Mines & Resources, 65-73; proj mgr, UNESCO-UN Develop Prog Seismol Prog for Southeast Asia, 73-79. *Concurrent Pos:* Consult, Seismol Orgn, 79- *Mem:* Seismol Soc Am; Asn Seismol & Physics Earth's Interior (pres, 63-67); fel Royal Soc Can; Geol Soc London. *Res:* Structure of the earth's crust; mechanics of earthquakes. *Mailing Add:* 60 McLeod, Apt 707 Ottawa ON K2P 2G1 Can

HODGSON, JONATHAN PETER EDWARD, GEOMETRIC TOPOLOGY, MATHEMATICAL BIOLOGY. *Current Pos:* assoc prof, 74-80, PROF MATH, ADELPHI UNIV, 80-, CHMN, DEPT MATH & CORP SCI, 81- *Personal Data:* b Sheffield, Eng, Sept 3, 42; m 67. *Educ:* Cambridge Univ, BA, 63, MA & PhD(math), 67. *Prof Exp:* Instr math, Univ Pa, 66-68; Sci Res Coun fel, Univ Warwick, 68-69; asst prof, Univ BC, 69-70 & Univ Pa, 71-74. *Mem:* Am Math Soc; NY Acad Sci. *Res:* Automorphisms of manifolds, structure of manifolds and poincare spaces; diffusion in ecological systems. *Mailing Add:* 533 Riverview Rd Swarthmore PA 19081-1021

HODGSON, KEITH OWEN, BIOINORGANIC CHEMISTRY, STRUCTURAL CHEMISTRY. *Current Pos:* asst prof, 73-78, ASSOC PROF CHEM, STANFORD UNIV, 79- *Personal Data:* b Sept 28, 47; US citizen; m 69. *Educ:* Univ Va, BS, 69; Univ Calif, Berkeley, PhD(chem), 72. *Prof Exp:* Fel chem, Swiss Fed Inst Technol, 72-73. *Mem:* Am Chem Soc; Am Crystallog Soc; AAAS. *Res:* Synthetic and structural organometallic chemistry; application of x-ray absorption spectroscopy for investigation of molecular structure; anomalous scattering in protein crystallography and use of synchrotron radiation in such studies. *Mailing Add:* Chem Dept Stanford Univ Stanford CA 94305

HODGSON, LYNN MORRISON, MARINE ECOLOGY, MARINE PHYCOLOGY. *Current Pos:* ASSOC PROF BIOL, UNIV HAWAII, WEST OAHU, 92- *Personal Data:* b Atlanta, Ga, July 30, 48. *Educ:* Col William & Mary, BS, 70; Univ Wash, MS, 72; Stanford Univ, PhD(biol sci), 79. *Prof Exp:* Asst res scientist aquatic ecol, Ctr Aquatic Weeds, Univ Fla, 79-81; asst prof biol & bot, Univ Ark, 81-82; res assoc aquacult, Div Appl Biol, Harbor Br Inst, 82-85; from asst prof to assoc prof biol, Northern State Univ, 85-92, chair, Dept Math & Natural Sci, 88-92. *Concurrent Pos:* Nominating comt chair, Phycological Soc Am, 87-89. *Mem:* Int Phycological Soc; Phycological Soc Am; Sigma Xi; Pac Sci Asn; Western Soc Naturalists. *Res:* Quantitative marine assessment of algal, invertebrate and fish populations of West Maui. *Mailing Add:* Univ Hawaii 96-043 Ala Ike Pearl City HI 96782. *Fax:* 808-456-5208

HODGSON, PAUL EDMUND, SURGERY. *Current Pos:* asst dean curric, Col Med, Univ Nebr Med Ctr, Omaha, 69-72, chmn dept, 72-84, prof, 62-88, EMER PROF SURG, COL MED, UNIV NEBR MED CTR, 88- *Personal Data:* b Wilwaukee, Wis, Dec 14, 21; m 45, Barbara Osborne; c Ann B & Paul C. *Educ:* Beloit Col, BS, 43; Univ Mich, MD, 45; Am Bd Surg, dipl, 53. *Prof Exp:* Resident, Univ Mich Hosp, Ann Arbor, 48-52, from instr to assoc prof surg, Med Sch, 52-62. *Concurrent Pos:* Chief surg serv, Ann Arbor Vet Admin Hosp, 56-60. *Mem:* Am Col Surg; Soc Univ Surg; Am Surg Asn; Soc Surg Alimentary Tract; Cent Surg Asn; Western Surg Asn; Am Asn Surg & Trauma. *Res:* Blood coagulation; metabolism; vascular disease. *Mailing Add:* 600 S 42nd St Omaha NE 68198-3280

HODGSON, RICHARD HOLMES, BOTANY. *Current Pos:* RETIRED. *Personal Data:* b Orange, NJ, Aug 30, 29; m 51; c 1. *Educ:* Duke Univ, BS, 51, MA, 54; Ohio State Univ, PhD(bot), 59. *Prof Exp:* Plant physiologist, Denver Fed Ctr, USDA, 59-64, res plant physiologist, Metab & Radiation Res Lab, Fargo, NDak, 64-78, res leader, Weed Physiol & Growth Regulator Res Lab, Sci & Educ Admin, Frederick, Md, 78- *Mem:* AAAS; Weed Sci Soc Am; Am Soc Plant Physiol; Scand Soc Plant Physiol; Am Soc Hort Sci. *Res:* Pesticide and growth regulator metabolism; organic translocation in plants; radiobiology; general plant physiology; weed science; air pollution; environmental physiology. *Mailing Add:* 3132 Odl National Pike Middletown MD 21769

HODGSON, RICHARD JOHN WESLEY, THEORETICAL PHYSICS, INVERSE PROBLEMS. *Current Pos:* from asst prof to assoc prof, 69-92, dept chmn, 91-97, PROF THEORET PHYSICS, UNIV OTTAWA, 92- *Personal Data:* b Edmonton, Alta, Dec 10, 41; m 66, Lynne Day; c Anthony & Erica. *Educ:* Univ Alta, BSc, 63; Univ Sydney, PhD(physics), 68. *Prof Exp:* Fel theoret physics, Univ Alta, 67-69. *Mem:* Can Asn Physicists; Am Asn Physics Teachers; Am Phys Soc. *Res:* Inverse problems, quantum mechanics; Bayesian inference. *Mailing Add:* Dept Physics 150 Louis Pasteus Univ Ottawa Ottawa ON K1N 6N5 Can. *Fax:* 613-562-5190; *E-Mail:* hodgson@physics.uottawa.ca

HODGSON, ROBERT ARNOLD, ENVIRONMENTAL POLLUTION BY HYDROCARBONS. *Current Pos:* CONSULT OIL & GAS EXPLOR, RAH GEOL CONSULT SERV, 83- *Personal Data:* b Orange, NJ, Sept 22, 24; m 48, Lorna E Biberthaler; c Cynthia E. *Educ:* Antioch Col, BA, 50; Brigham Young Univ, MS, 51; Yale Univ, MS, 57, PhD(struct geol), 58. *Prof Exp:* Sr scientist, Gulf Res & Develop Corp, 58-83. *Concurrent Pos:* Geologist, Ohio Oil Co, 51-54. *Mem:* Fel Geol Soc Am; fel AAAS; fel Am Cong Surveying & Mapping; Sigma Xi; fel Explorers Club. *Res:* Natural rock fracturing and lineaments and their implications with respect to global structure and modes of origin. *Mailing Add:* 403 Liberty St PO Box 531 Jamestown PA 16134

HODGSON, RODNEY, PHYSICS, MICROMECHANICS. *Current Pos:* CONSULT, 92- *Personal Data:* b Salmon Arm, BC, Jan 6, 39; m 62; c 3. *Educ:* Univ BC, BSc, 60, PhD(physics), 64. *Prof Exp:* Scientist, Max Planck Inst, Plasma Physics, 64-67; asst prof mech eng, Colo State Univ, 67-68; mem res staff, Res Div, IBM Corp, 68-92. *Concurrent Pos:* Nat Res Coun Can fel, 64; vis fel, Imperial Col, 74. *Mem:* Fel Am Phys Soc; fel Am Optical Soc. *Res:* Plasma instabilities; non-equilibrium ionization in plasmas; ion engines; atomic and electronic collision phenomena; vacuum ultraviolet lasers; four wave parametric generation; laser and rapid annealing of semiconductors; laser welding; high power transmission of laser light through fibers; holography; materials research; micromechanics registered patent agent. *Mailing Add:* IBM T J Watson Res Ctr PO Box 218 Yorktown Heights NY 10598. *Fax:* 914-945-3715; *E-Mail:* hodgson@watson.ibm.com

HODGSON, THOM JOEL, OPERATIONS RESEARCH, INDUSTRIAL ENGINEERING. *Current Pos:* prof & head dept, 83-90, PROF INDUST ENG DEPT, NC STATE UNIV, 90- *Personal Data:* b Hillsdale, Mich, Mar 6, 38; m 65; c 2. *Educ:* Univ Mich, Ann Arbor, BSE, 61, MBA, 65, PhD(indust eng), 70. *Prof Exp:* Opers res analyst, Ford Motor Co, 66-67; from asst prof to prof indust & systs eng, Univ Fla, 70-78. *Concurrent Pos:* Consult, Ford Motor Co, 68-71. *Mem:* Opers Res Soc Am; Inst Mgt Sci; Am Inst Indust Engrs. *Res:* Analytic models of production-inventory and manufacturing systems. *Mailing Add:* Dept Indust Eng NC State Univ Raleigh NC 27695-7906

HODGSON, THOMAS A, HEALTH ECONOMICS. *Current Pos:* Dir, Div Health & Utilization Anal, 82-95, CHIEF ECONOMIST, OFF ANALYSIS EPIDEMIOL & HEALTH PROMOTIONS, 95- *Personal Data:* b Scranton, Pa, Nov 7, 40. *Educ:* Swarthmore, BA, 62; Cornell, MA, 66, PhD(econs), 69. *Mem:* Am Econ Asn; Am Pub Health Asn. *Mailing Add:* 6525 Belcrest Rd Hyattsville MD 20782. *Fax:* 301-436-8459; *E-Mail:* tah2@cdc.gov

HODGSON, VOIGT R, biomechanics; deceased, see previous edition for last biography

HODNETT, ERNEST MATELLE, MEDICINAL CHEMISTRY. *Current Pos:* from asst prof to prof, 45-79, EMER PROF CHEM, OKLA STATE UNIV, 79- *Personal Data:* b Hartford, Ala, Feb 6, 14; m 39, Mary E Gunn; c Mary K (Doro). *Educ:* Univ Fla, BS, 36, MS, 39; Purdue Univ, PhD(org chem), 45. *Prof Exp:* Asst chem, Univ Fla, 36-39; state food chemist, Fla, 40-43. *Concurrent Pos:* Assoc chemist, Argonne Nat Lab, 52-53; res partic, Oak Ridge Nat Lab, 54; sr scientist, NIH, 62-63; scientist dir, USPHS Res Corps. *Mem:* Am Chem Soc; Sigma Xi. *Res:* Chemotherapy of cancer; synthesis and study of drugs used for treatment of cancer. *Mailing Add:* Dept Chem Okla State Univ Stillwater OK 74078

HODSON, CHARLES ANDREW, NEUROENDOCRINOLOGY, REPRODUCTIVE PHYSIOLOGY. *Current Pos:* from asst prof to assoc prof, 84-91, PROF OBSTET & GYNEC, ECAROLINA UNIV, 91- *Personal Data:* b Mason City, Iowa, Aug 9, 47; m 84; c 1. *Educ:* Iowa State Univ, BS, 69, MS, 71, PhD(zool), 75. *Prof Exp:* Res assoc physiol, Mich State Univ, 75-78. *Mem:* Endocrine Soc; Am Physiol Soc; Soc Study Reproduction; Sigma Xi; AAAS; Am Soc Zoologists. *Res:* Neuroendocrinology of the female reproductive process; neural regulation of gonadotropin and prolactin and mammary tumor growth. *Mailing Add:* Dept Obstet & Gynec ECarolina Univ Sch Med Greenville NC 27834

HODSON, HAROLD H, JR, ANIMAL NUTRITION. *Current Pos:* assoc prof, 71-75, CHMN DEPT, SOUTHERN ILL UNIV, CARBONDALE, 73-, PROF ANIMAL INDUSTS, 75- *Personal Data:* b Grand Forks, NDak, Mar 20, 39; m 59; c 3. *Educ:* Iowa State Univ, BS, 61, PhD(animal nutrit), 65. *Prof Exp:* Instr animal sci, Iowa State Univ, 63-65; instr night sch, Alamogordo Commun Col, 65-68; asst prof, Iowa State Univ, 68-71. *Mem:* Am Soc Animal Sci; Sigma Xi. *Res:* Nutritional requirements and general production problems of swine. *Mailing Add:* RR 4 Box 173 Ames IA 50014-9804

HODSON, JEAN TURNBAUGH, RESTORATIVE DENTISTRY. *Current Pos:* RETIRED. *Personal Data:* b Anthony, Kans, July 10, 20. *Educ:* Univ Wash, BA, 52, MS, 58. *Prof Exp:* From instr to assoc prof oral anat & dent ceramics, Univ Wash, 52-69, prof oper dent, 69-70, prof restorative dent, 70-87. *Mem:* Am Asn Dent Schs; assoc Am Dent Asn; Int Asn Dent Res; hon mem Am Acad Gold Foil Opers; Sigma Xi. *Res:* Human tooth morphology teaching methods; microstructure, strength and physical properties of dental porcelains; dental amalgam and pure gold dental restorative materials; dental anatomy and occlusion. *Mailing Add:* 3624 Meridian Ave N Seattle WA 91803

HODSON, PHILLIP HARVEY, INDUSTRIAL MICROBIOLOGY. *Current Pos:* RETIRED. *Personal Data:* b Springville, Utah, July 25, 31; m 55, Maxine Reinhardt; c Phillip Max, Marian, Elaine & Cheryl. *Educ:* Brigham Young Univ, BS, 53, MS, 57; Univ Tex, PhD(bact), 62. *Prof Exp:* Res biochemist, Cent Res Dept, Monsanto Co, 62-69, group leader, Inorg Res & Develop Div, 69-72; team leader & res scientist, Eli Lilly & Co, 72-94. *Mem:* Am Soc Microbiol; Sigma Xi; Am Chem Soc. *Res:* Bacterial endospores; production of dipicolinic acid by fungi; Bacillus exo-enzymes amylase, protease; citric acid; cellulase, microbial detection of chemical carcinogen; large scale production of antibiotics monensin, tylosin, penicillin, vancomycin and hygromycin; use of genetically engineered microorganisms to commercially produce human insulin (Humulin R). *Mailing Add:* 8928 Dandy Creek Dr Indianapolis IN 46234

HODSON, ROBERT CLEAVES, GENE STRUCTURE & REGULATION. *Current Pos:* asst prof biol sci, 69-75, ASSOC PROF, SCH LIFE & HEALTH SCI, UNIV DEL, 75- *Personal Data:* b St Paul, Minn, Apr 21, 37; m 64; c 2. *Educ:* Univ Minn, BA, 59; Cornell Univ, MS, 63, PhD(plant physiol), 66. *Prof Exp:* NIH fel, 65-67; NIH traineeship biol, Brandeis Univ, 67-69. *Concurrent Pos:* Prin investr, Crop Res Grants Off, USDA, 81-83. *Mem:* AAAS; Am Soc Plant Physiol; Int Soc Plant Molecular Biol; Am Soc Microbiol; Sigma Xi. *Res:* Nitrogen metabolism in algae; regulation of genes for nitrogen assimilation in chlamydomonas; regulation of gametogenesis in chlamydomonas; plant cell transformation; plant gene cloning. *Mailing Add:* Dept Biol Univ Del Newark DE 19716

HODSON, WILLIAM MYRON, geographic analysis, computer modeling, for more information see previous edition

HOEBEL, BARTLEY GORE, NEURAL BASIS OF EATING & REINFORCEMENT OF BEHAVIOR. *Current Pos:* MEM FAC PSYCHOL DEPT, PRINCETON UNIV, 62-, PROF, 70- *Personal Data:* b New York, NY, May 29, 35; m 62, Cynthia A Eney; c Valerie, Carolyn & Brett. *Educ:* Harvard Univ, AB, 57; Univ Pa, PhD, 62. *Hon Degrees:* PhD, Cath Univ, Louvain, France, 91. *Concurrent Pos:* Pres, Div 6, Am Psychol Asn, 95. *Mem:* Fel AAAS; fel Am Psychol Soc; fel Am Psychol Asn; Soc Neurosci; Soc Study Ingestive Behav (pres, 96); NAm Soc Study Obesity; fel Int Behav Neurosci Soc. *Res:* Psychology; neuroscience; ingestive behavior; investigation of the neural basis of appetite and reward as they relate to eating disorders and drug addiction through brain stimulation, drug injection and microdialysis in rats. *Mailing Add:* 207 Hartley Ave Princeton NJ 08540-5615. *Fax:* 609-258-1113; *E-Mail:* hoebel@princeton.edu

HOEFELMEYER, ALBERT BERNARD, COSMETIC CHEMISTRY. *Current Pos:* PRES & OWNER, EAGLE BEAUTY LABS INC, 75- *Personal Data:* b San Antonio, Tex, Mar 27, 28; div; c 2. *Educ:* St Mary's Univ, BS, 49; Univ Tex, MA, 50; Tex A&M Univ, PhD, 54. *Prof Exp:* Res chemist, Petrochem Res Lab, Celanese Corp Am, 53-55; asst prof chem, Tex Col Arts

& Indust, 55-57; sr nuclear engr, Radiation Effects Group, Nuclear Aerospace Res Facility, Gen Dynamics Corp, 57-63, sr res scientist, Solid State Physics Group, Appl Sci Lab, Tex, 63-71, sr res scientist, Mat Group, Appl Res Lab, 71; chem consult, 71-74; sr testing engr, Bell Helicopter Co, 74-81. *Concurrent Pos:* Adj prof, Tex Christian Univ, 59- *Mem:* Am Chem Soc; Radiation Res Soc; Soc Cosmetic Chemists; Sigma Xi. *Mailing Add:* 7355 Greenacres Dr Ft Worth TX 76112-3533

HOEFER, JACOB A, ANIMAL HUSBANDRY. *Current Pos:* prof, Mich State Univ, 50-66, actg chmn, Dept Animal Husb, 66-68 & Dept Food Sci & Human Nutrit, 70-71, actg dean, Col Agr & Natural Resources, 75-77, ASSOC DIR, AGR EXP STA, MICH STATE UNIV, 67-, ASST DEAN, COL AGR & NATURAL RESOURCES & COL NATURAL SCI, 78- *Personal Data:* b Lafayette, Ind, Nov 21, 15; m 42; c 5. *Educ:* Purdue Univ, BSA, 37, MSA, 40, PhD(animal nutrit), 46. *Prof Exp:* From asst to instr animal husb, Purdue Univ, 37-43; asst prof, Okla Agr & Mech Col, 44-46; from asst prof to assoc prof, Purdue Univ, 46-50. *Mem:* Am Inst Nutrit. *Res:* Animal nutrition; swine, cattle and sheep. *Mailing Add:* 1337 Albert Ave East Lansing MI 48823

HOEFER, RAYMOND H, EXPERT SYSTEMS, PLANT PHYSIOLOGY. *Current Pos:* head, plant sci chem res, 89-90, mgr tech serv & develop, 90-92, MGR TECHNOL TRANSFER, DOWELANCO, 93- *Personal Data:* b Sutherland, Nebr, Mar 30, 52; m 79, Gachia Kiburz; c Anna & Caitlin. *Educ:* Hastings Col, BS, 74; Univ Nebr, MS, 77, PhD(agron), 81. *Prof Exp:* Plant sci rep, Eli Lilly & Co, 81-85, regional res rep, 85, regulatory mgr, 85-86, proj mgr, 86-87, head, agr anal chem, 87- 89. *Mem:* Weed Sci Soc Am; Am Chem Soc. *Res:* Crop protection chemic; pesticide registration. *Mailing Add:* 9330 Zionsville Rd 308 c/2 Indianapolis IN 46268-1054

HOEFER, WOLFGANG JOHANNES REINHARD, ELECTRICAL ENGINEERING, ELECTROMAGNETICS & MICROWAVES. *Current Pos:* PROF ELEC & COMPUT ENG, UNIV VICTORIA, 92- *Personal Data:* b Urmitz Rhein, Ger, Feb 6, 41; m 70; c 2. *Educ:* Aachen Tech Univ, Dipl Ing, 65; Univ Grenoble, Dr Ing, 68. *Prof Exp:* Asst elec eng, Univ Grenoble, 68-69; from asst prof to prof, Univ Ottawa, 69-92, chmn dept, 78-81. *Concurrent Pos:* Nat Res Coun Can fel, 70-81; consult, Dept Commun, Govt Can, 74-85, AEG-Telfunken, 76 & Can Int Develop Agency, 78; vis prof, Univ Grenoble, 77, Univ Rome II, 90 U Univ Nice, 91; managing ed, Int J Numerical Modelling, 88-; res chair, replacement factor eng, Nat Sci Eng Res Coun/Mgt Prog Rev, 92- *Mem:* Fel Inst Elec & Electronics Engrs. *Res:* Microwave and millimeter-wave integrated circuits; planar microwave structures; microwave and millimeter-wave communication systems; numerical techniques; numerical modelling of electromagnetic fields. *Mailing Add:* Dept Elec & Comput Eng Univ Victoria Victoria BC V8W 3P6 Can. *Fax:* 250-721-6230, 721-6052; *E-Mail:* whoefer@ece.uvic.ca

HOEFERT, LYNN LUCRETIA, BOTANY. *Current Pos:* BOTANIST, AGR RES SERV, USDA, 66- *Personal Data:* b Billings, Mont, July 7, 35. *Educ:* Mont State Univ, BS, 58, MS, 61; Univ Calif, Davis, PhD(bot), 65. *Prof Exp:* Lab technician, Univ Calif, Davis, 64-65; res botanist, Univ Calif, Santa Barbara, 65-66. *Mem:* Bot Soc Am; Electron Microscopy Soc Am; Am Soc Sugar Beet Technol; Am Inst Biol Sci; Am Phytopathol Soc; Sigma Xi. *Res:* Pathological plant anatomy and cytology. *Mailing Add:* 405 Lena Ave Gilroy CA 95020

HOEFLE, MILTON LOUIS, ORGANIC CHEMISTRY. *Current Pos:* RETIRED. *Personal Data:* b Manhattan, Kans, Feb 19, 22; m 45; c 5. *Educ:* Univ Ill, BS, 43; Univ Minn, MS, 44, PhD(org chem), 49. *Prof Exp:* Res chemist, Gen Aniline & Film Corp, 49-53; sr res chemist, Parke, Davis & Co, 53-70, sect dir chem, 70-77, sect dir chem, Pharmaceut Res Div, Warner-Lambert/Parke-Davis, 77- *Mem:* Am Chem Soc; AAAS. *Res:* Pharmaceutical chemistry; development of cardiovascular agents. *Mailing Add:* 1020 Belmont Ann Arbor MI 48104-2818

HOEFT, LOTHAR OTTO, APPLIED PHYSICS, ELECTROMAGNETISM. *Current Pos:* SR PRIN ELECTRO MAGNETIC EFFECTS, BDM INT, INC, ALBUQUERQUE, NMEX, 79- *Personal Data:* b Antigo, Wis, Sept 17, 31; m 58; c 3. *Educ:* Univ Wis, BS, 53, MS, 54; Pa State Univ, PhD(physics, biophys), 61. *Prof Exp:* Asst chief phys acoust, Aero Med Lab, Wright Air Develop Ctr, Wright-Patterson AFB, Ohio, 54-58 & Neurophysiol Br, Aerospace Med Res Lab, 61-65; group leader, Simulation Group, Air Force Weapons Lab, Kirtland AFB NMex, 66-69, dep chief, Technol Div, 69-71, sci & tech coordr, 76-79; physicist, Europ Off Aerospace Res & Develop, London Eng, 71-75, spec asst for spec studies, Anal Div, 75-76. *Mem:* AAAS; Int Solar Energy Soc; Inst Elec & Electronics Engrs; Soc Aerospace Engrs. *Res:* Electromagnetic compolibility; pulse power technology; alternative energy technology. *Mailing Add:* 9013 Haines Ave NE Albuquerque NM 87112

HOEFT, ROBERT GENE, SOIL SCIENCE, AGRONOMY. *Current Pos:* from asst prof to assoc prof, 73-81, PROF AGRON, SOIL FERTILITY EXTEN, UNIV ILL, 81- *Personal Data:* b David City, Nebr, May 21, 44; m 90, Nancy Bussen; c 2. *Educ:* Univ Nebr, Lincoln, BSc, 65, MSc, 67; Univ Wis-Madison, PhD(soils), 72. *Honors & Awards:* Ciba-Geigy Award, Am Soc Agron, 78; Funk Award, Univ Ill, 89. *Prof Exp:* Fel, Univ Wis-Madison, 71-72; asst prof soil & plant sci, SDak State Univ, 72-73. *Mem:* Fel Am Soc Agron; fel Soil Sci Soc Am; Coun Agr Sci & Technol; Sigma Xi. *Res:* Soil fertility, macro and micro-nutrients; municipal and industrial waste disposal; air and water pollution; nitrification inhibitors. *Mailing Add:* Agron/N305 Turner-MC-046 Univ Ill Urbana IL 61801. *E-Mail:* rhoeft@uiuc.edu

HOEG, DONALD FRANCIS, PHYSICAL ORGANIC CHEMISTRY. *Current Pos:* CONSULT, DFH ASSOCS, 88- *Personal Data:* b Brooklyn, NY, Aug 2, 31; m 52, Patricia C Fogarty; c Thomas E, Robert F, Donald J, Mary B & Susan C. *Educ:* St John's Univ, NY, BS, 53; Ill Inst Technol, PhD(chem), 57. *Prof Exp:* Sr res chemist, Polymer Res Dept, Res Div, W R Grace & Co, 56-61; from group leader addition polymers to mgr polymer chem, Borg-Warner Corp, 61-66, assoc dir, 66-75, dir, res ctr, 75-88. *Concurrent Pos:* Adj prof, Ill Inst Technol Bus Sch, 87. *Mem:* AAAS; Am Chem Soc; Am Mgt Asn; Sigma Xi. *Res:* Organic and polymer chemistry; reaction kinetics and mechanisms; isotope effects; organometallic chemistry; stereospecific polymerizations; chemical reactions of macromolecules. *Mailing Add:* 313 S Elmhurst Ave Mt Prospect IL 60056-3128. *Fax:* 847-259-1230

HOEG, JEFFREY MICHAEL, MOLECULAR BIOLOGY. *Current Pos:* med staff fel, 83-87, SR INVESTR, MOLECULAR DIS BR, NIH, 87- *Personal Data:* b Gary, Ind; m 73; c 2. *Educ:* Ind Univ, AB, 74, MD, 77. *Prof Exp:* Intern, Barnes Hosp, St Louis, 77-78, resident, 78-79, chief resident, 79-80; res assoc, Wash Univ Vet Admin Hosp, 80-83. *Concurrent Pos:* Head, Sect Cellular Biol, NIH. *Mem:* Am Fedn Clin Res; Am Col Physicians; AAAS; Am Col Nutrit; Am Col Cardiol. *Res:* Apolipoproteins recognized by specific membrane-associated receptors within the human liver; regulation of hepatic apolipoprotein output; posttranslational modifications of apolipoproteins A-I and B including glycosylation, phosphorylation, and fatty acid acylation. *Mailing Add:* Cell Biol Sect Bldg 10 Rm 7N115 Bethesda MD 20892-1666. *Fax:* 301-402-0190

HOEGERMAN, STANTON FRED, CYTOGENETICS, RADIOBIOLOGY. *Current Pos:* asst prof, 76-80, ASSOC PROF BIOL, COL WILLIAM & MARY, 80- *Personal Data:* b Brooklyn, NY, May 13, 44; m 92, Carol Winkelman; c 2. *Educ:* Cornell Univ, BS, 65; NC State Univ, MS, 68, PhD(genetics), 72; Am Bd Med Genetics, dipl Clin Cytogenetics. *Prof Exp:* Instr biol, Lincoln Univ, Pa, 70-72; asst biologist, Radiol & Environ Res Div, Argonne Nat Lab, 72-76. *Concurrent Pos:* Adj assoc prof, Dept Pediat, Eastern Va Med Sch. *Mem:* AAAS; Genetics Soc Am; Bot Soc Am; Am Soc Human Genetics. *Res:* Cytogenetics of fragile sites in humans; general human cytogenetics. *Mailing Add:* Biol Dept Col William & Mary Williamsburg VA 23185. *Fax:* 757-221-6483

HOEGGER, ERHARD FRITZ, CHEMICAL CONSULTING, GENERAL CHEMISTRY. *Current Pos:* INDEPENDENT CONSULT, 85- *Personal Data:* b Baden, Switz, July 3, 24; nat US; m 56; c 1. *Educ:* Basel Univ, PhD(chem), 52. *Prof Exp:* Asst lectr, Univ Basel, 50-54; res fel, Univ Colo, 54-55; res assoc, L Givaudan & Co SA, Switz, 56; sr res & staff chemist, Film & Plastic Prods & Resins Depts, E I du Pont de Nemours & Co, Inc, 56-88. *Concurrent Pos:* Mem gov bd, Fedn Anal Chemists & Spectros Socs, 86- *Mem:* Am Chem Soc; Sigma Xi; Fedn Anal Chemists & Spectros Socs. *Res:* Polymer synthesis, characterization and new applications; films and foams; liquid and gas chromatography; gel permeation chromatography. *Mailing Add:* 1513 Harvey Rd Wilmington DE 19810

HOEHN, A(LFRED) J(OSEPH), ELECTRICAL ENGINEERING, MATHEMATICS. *Current Pos:* PROPRIETOR, ETA ENGRS, 85- *Personal Data:* b Ft Dodge, Iowa, Mar 31, 19; m 72, Iona Provance; c Cheryl. *Educ:* Iowa State Univ, BS, 41; Univ Minn, MS, 48; Univ Ariz, PhD(elec eng), 60. *Prof Exp:* Jr engr, Commonwealth Edison Co, Ill, 41-42; instr rotating elec mach, Naval Training Sch, Iowa State Col, 42-43; elec engr, Stromberg Carlson Co, 43-46; instr elec eng & radio, Univ Minn, 46-47; elec engr & supvr elec eng res, Armour Res Found, 47-52, asst mgr, 52-55, mgr southwestern labs, 55-57; instr radio & electromagnetic theory, Univ Ariz, 57-60; mgr theoret analysis, Bell Aerosysts Co, Ariz, 60-61, res dir, 61-62; consult, pvt pract, 62-64; vpres & res dir, Electro Tech Analysis Corp, 64-69, pres & res dir, 69-71; consult elec eng, 71-85. *Concurrent Pos:* Consult, Fed Aviation Admin, 64-65, 74-75; ed, Inst Elec & Electronics Engrs Region Six Conf Record, 66; ad hoc visitor, Accreditation Examr Engrs Coun Prof Develop, 72-76. *Mem:* Inst Elec & Electronics Engrs; Sigma Xi. *Res:* Nonlinear phenomena in electrical engineering; electromagnetic engineering; antenna design and measurement techniques; accurate timekeeping methods; electromagnetic interference and compatibility. *Mailing Add:* 3325 N Forgeus Ave Tucson AZ 85716-1165

HOEHN, G(USTAVE) L(EO), ELECTRICAL ENGINEERING. *Current Pos:* PVT CONSULT, 85- *Personal Data:* b Dallas, Tex, June 27, 25; m 50; c 2. *Educ:* Southern Methodist Univ, BS, 47; Stanford Univ, MS, 49, PhD(elec eng), 58. *Prof Exp:* Prod engr, geophys instruments, Geotronic Labs, 47-50; vpres, Radian Instrument Co, 50-52; res technologist, Field Res Labs, Magnolia Petrol Co, Socony Mobil Oil Co, Inc, 52-54, sr res technologist, 54-59, res assoc, Mobil Res & Develop Corp, 59-85. *Mem:* Sigma Xi; Inst Elec & Electronics Engrs; AAAS. *Res:* Geophysical electromagnetics, geophysical instrumentation; data processing. *Mailing Add:* 3512 S Franklin St Dallas TX 75233

HOEHN, HARVEY HERBERT, organic polymer chemistry; deceased, see previous edition for last biography

HOEHN, MARVIN MARTIN, MICROBIOLOGY. *Current Pos:* RETIRED. *Personal Data:* b Fall Creek, Wis, May 4, 20; m 44, Helen Hedegaard; c William, Elizabeth & Theodore. *Educ:* Wis State Col, BS, 42; Univ Wis, MS, 49. *Prof Exp:* Sr microbiologist, Eli Lily & Co, 49-68, res scientist, 68-74, res assoc, 74-84. *Mem:* Am Soc Microbiol; Soc Indust Microbiol; US Fedn Cult Collections. *Res:* Isolation and study of actinophages; fermentation and development of new antibiotics. *Mailing Add:* 4975 E 79th St Indianapolis IN 46250

HOEHN-SARIC, RUDOLF, PSYCHIATRY. *Current Pos:* from instr to assoc prof, 60-93, PROF PSYCHIAT, SCH MED, JOHNS HOPKINS UNIV, 93- *Personal Data:* b Graz, Austria, Feb 5, 29; US citizen; m 60; c 3. *Educ:* Graz Univ, MD, 54; McGill Univ, dipl psychiat, 59. *Prof Exp:* Fel med, Johns Hopkins Univ, 58-59. *Concurrent Pos:* Res assoc, Springfield State Hosp, Md, 60-61. *Mem:* Am Psychiat Asn; AAAS; Am Psychopath Asn. *Res:* Psychopharmacology and psychophysiology and imaging of anxiety disorders. *Mailing Add:* 115 Meyer Bldg Johns Hopkins Hosp Baltimore MD 21287-7144. *Fax:* 410-955-0946; *E-Mail:* rhoehn@welchlink.welch.jhu.edu

HOEK, JOANNES (JAN) BERNARDUS, CELL SIGNALING, MEMBRANE BIOCHEMISTRY. *Current Pos:* Assoc prof, 86-88, PROF PATH & CELL BIOL, THOMAS JEFFERSON UNIV, 88- *Personal Data:* b Haarlem, Neth, Jan 25, 42; m 66, Marja C Smit; c Maarten, Joost & Jasper J. *Educ:* Univ Amsterdam, Neth, PhD(biochem), 72. *Prof Exp:* Lectr, biochem, Univ Nairobi, Kenya, 74-77; asst prof, Univ Pa, 77-81; assoc prof path, Hahnemann Univ, Pa, 81-86. *Mem:* AAAS; Am Soc Biochem & Molecular Biol; Biophys Soc; Res Soc Alcoholism; Int Soc Biomed Res Alcoholism. *Res:* Intracellular signalling; control of intracellular calcium homeostasis; mechanisms of adaptation to ethanol; hormonal control of metabolism in liver cells; alcoholism. *Mailing Add:* Dept Path Anat & Cell Biol Thomas Jefferson Univ Philadelphia PA 19107. *Fax:* 215-923-2218

HOEKENGA, MARK T, INTERNAL MEDICINE, RESEARCH ADMINISTRATION. *Current Pos:* assoc dir clin res, Merrell-Nat Labs, Div Richardson-Merrell Inc, 61-63, dir med & sci coord, 63-70, vpres res, 70-80, VPRES, MERRELL DOW PHARMACEUT INC, 80- *Personal Data:* b Ripon, Calif, Apr 6, 20; m 44; c 5. *Educ:* Stanford Univ, AB, 41, MD, 43. *Honors & Awards:* Commendation, Minister Health & Soc Assistance, Honduras, 61. *Prof Exp:* Intern, Gorgas Hosp, CZ, Stanford Univ, 44, sr res med, 48-49; USPHS sr res fel, Johns Hopkins Hosp, 47-48; physician & chief res sect, United Fruit Co, Honduras, 49-56, med supt, Chiriqui Land Co, Panama, 56-61. *Concurrent Pos:* Physician, Kuwait Oil Co Ltd, 49; vpres, Col Med Chiriqui, 57-60; vis prof, Sch Med, Univ Miami, 60-72; asst prof, Sch Med, Univ Cincinnati, 61-; clinician, Out-Patient Dept, Cincinnati Gen Hosp; attend physician, Daniel Drake Mem Hosp, Cincinnati, 61-, pres med staff, 73-, med dir, 76-78; Rockefeller Found consult, Valle, Colombia, 63; vchmn sect clin & path malaria, Int Cong Trop Med & Malaria, Rio de Janeiro, Brazil, 63; clin prof, Sch Med, Univ Ky, 64- *Mem:* Fel Am Col Physicians; Am Soc Trop Med & Hyg (secy-treas, 75-80, pres elect, 80-81 & pres, 81-82); Am Soc Clin Pharmacol & Therapeut; Am Acad Clin Toxicol; NY Acad Sci. *Res:* Chemotherapy of tropical diseases; tropical public health; pharmaceutical scientific administration. *Mailing Add:* 925 Congress Ave Cincinnati OH 45246

HOEKMAN, THEODORE BERNARD, PHARMACOLOGY, BIOPHYSICS. *Current Pos:* ASSOC PROF BIOPHYS, MEM UNIV NFLD, 77- *Personal Data:* b Lethbridge, Alta, Nov 1, 39; div; c 5. *Educ:* Hope Col, AB, 62; Univ Ill, Urbana, PhD(biophys), 68. *Prof Exp:* Res assoc pharmacol, Vanderbilt Univ Sch Med, 68-70, instr, 70-71; from instr to asst prof, Sch Med, Georgetown Univ, 71-77. *Concurrent Pos:* Prin investr, NIH res grant, 74-77, Med Res Coun res grant, 78-82 & Muscular Dystrophy Asn Can res grant, 80-82. *Mem:* Am Soc Pharmacol & Exp Therapeut; Soc Neurosci. *Res:* Physiology and pharmacology of neuromuscular junction; muscle; neurotrophic regulation of muscle in relation to muscular dystrophy; expert testimony in drug and alcohol cases; developed computer assisted medical education software for microcomputers; medical and informatics research and development. *Mailing Add:* Fac Med Mem Univ Nfld St John's NF A1B 3V6 Can. *Fax:* 709-737-7010; *E-Mail:* thoekman@morgan.ucs.mun.ca

HOEKSEMA, HERMAN, JR, ORGANIC CHEMISTRY. *Current Pos:* RES ASSOC, UPJOHN CO, 51- *Personal Data:* b Grand Rapids, Mich, Mar 21, 20; m 43; c 4. *Educ:* Calvin Col, AB, 42; Univ Nebr, MS, 44, PhD(org chem), 48. *Prof Exp:* Res chemist, Standard Oil Co Ind, 48-51. *Mem:* Am Chem Soc. *Res:* Chemistry of antibiotics. *Mailing Add:* 6898 Blue Star Hwy Coloma MI 49038-9316

HOEKSEMA, WALTER DAVID, MICROBIOLOGY, BIOCHEMISTRY. *Current Pos:* asst prof, 71-80, ASSOC PROF BIOL, FERRIS STATE COL, 80- *Personal Data:* b Holland, Mich, Apr 22, 42; m 66; c 1. *Educ:* Calvin Col, BS, 64; Western Mich Univ, MA, 66; Mich State Univ, PhD(microbiol), 71. *Prof Exp:* Teaching asst biol, Western Mich Univ, 64-66. *Mem:* Am Soc Microbiol. *Res:* Physiology, genetics and biochemistry of the synthesis of amino acids and proteins in the bacteria; control mechanisms in catabolic and anabolic pathways. *Mailing Add:* Dept Biol Ferris State Univ 901 S State St Big Rapids MI 49307-2251

HOEKSTRA, JOHN JUNIOR, PHYSICAL CHEMISTRY. *Current Pos:* assoc prof, 72-77, PROF CHEM, UNIV DUBUQUE, 77-, ACTG ACAD DEAN, 80- *Personal Data:* b Grand Rapids, Mich, Jan 18, 29; m 57; c 3. *Educ:* Calvin Col, BS, 51; Wayne State Univ, PhD(phys chem), 58. *Prof Exp:* Asst, Wayne State Univ, 51-52, res assoc, 52-54; chemist, Dow Chem Co, 57-63, res chemist, 64-69; assoc prof chem, Cent Col, Iowa, 69-72. *Mem:* Am Chem Soc; Electrochem Soc. *Res:* Electrochemistry; batteries; electro-deposition; single crystal studies; short contact time hydrocarbon cracking studies. *Mailing Add:* 405 Moore Heights Dubuque IA 52003

HOEKSTRA, KARL EGMOND, MINERALOGY, GLASS TECHNOLOGY. *Current Pos:* PRES & GEN MGR, RANSOM & RANDOLPH, 91- *Personal Data:* b Battle Creek, Mich, Oct 9, 35; m 57; c 3. *Educ:* Miami Univ, BA, 58, MS, 65; Ohio State Univ, PhD(mineral), 69. *Prof Exp:* Res engr, Ferro Corp; mgr mat eval lab, Precision Furnace Div, Harrop Ceramic Serv Co, 64-67, dir lab div, 67-70; consult, Tradet, Inc, 70-71; sr res scientist, Corning Glass Works, 72- *Concurrent Pos:* Res fel, Corning Glass Works, 71-72. *Mem:* Mineral Soc Am; Am Ceramic Soc. *Res:* Diffusion and crystallization in the glassy phase, glass-glass and glass-plastic composites. *Mailing Add:* 407 W Front St Perrysburg OH 43551

HOEKSTRA, WILLIAM GEORGE, NUTRITIONAL BIOCHEMISTRY. *Current Pos:* From instr to assoc prof, 54-64, PROF BIOCHEM, UNIV WIS-MADISON, 64-, PROF NUTRIT SCI, 69- *Personal Data:* b Golden, Colo, Aug 14, 28; m 55; c 3. *Educ:* Colo State Univ, BS, 50; Univ Wis, MS, 52, PhD(biochem), 54. *Honors & Awards:* Gustav Bohstedt Award, Am Soc Animal Sci, 67; Borden Award, Am Inst Nutrit, 75. *Concurrent Pos:* Merck sr fel, Nat Inst Res Dairying, Reading, Eng, 57-58; mem, Nutrit Study Sect, NIH, 70-74; NIH fel, Rowett Res Inst, Aberdeen, Scotland, 75-76. *Mem:* Am Inst Nutrit (pres, 80); Am Soc Animal Sci; Am Chem Soc; Soc Exp Biol & Med; Am Soc Biol Chemists; Sigma Xi. *Res:* General animal metabolism and nutrition; mineral nutrition of animals; biochemical function and metabolism of trace elements. *Mailing Add:* 5529 Greenleaf Dr Madison WI 53713

HOEL, DAVID GERHARD, PUBLIC HEALTH & EPIDEMIOLOGY. *Current Pos:* chief, Environ Biomet Br, 73-81, math statistician, 70-73, DIR, BIOMET & RISK ASSESSMENT PROG, NAT INST ENVIRON HEALTH SCI, NIH, 81-, ACTG DIR, 90- *Personal Data:* b Los Angeles, Calif, Nov 18, 39; m 61; c 3. *Educ:* Univ Calif, Berkeley, AB, 61; Univ NC, Chapel Hill, PhD(statist), 66. *Prof Exp:* Fel, Stanford Univ, 66-67; sr mathematician, Westinghouse Res Labs, 67-68; res statistician, Oak Ridge Nat Labs, 68-70. *Concurrent Pos:* Assoc dir, Radiation Effects Res Found, Hiroshima, 84-86. *Mem:* Inst Med-Nat Acad Sci; Am Statist Asn; Royal Statist Soc; Biomet Soc; Int Statist Inst; Soc Risk Anal. *Res:* Statistical inference particularly sequential procedures; statistical and mathematical applications in biology and medicine; epidemiology; radiation health effects. *Mailing Add:* 365 Battery St Charleston SC 29401

HOEL, LESTER A, CIVIL ENGINEERING. *Current Pos:* chmn & Hamilton prof civil eng, 74-89, FAC RES SCIENTIST, VA TRANSP RES COUN, UNIV VA, CHARLOTTESVILLE, 75-, HAMILTON PROF CIVIL ENG, 91- *Personal Data:* b Feb 26, 35. *Educ:* City Col New York, BCE, 57; Polytech Inst New York, MCE, 60; Univ Calif, Berkeley, DEng, 63. *Honors & Awards:* Walter L Huber Civil Eng Res Prize, Am Soc Civil Engrs, Frank M Masters Transp Eng Award; Pyke Johnson Award, Transp Res Bd, W N Cary Jr Distinguished Serv Award; Stanley W Gustafson Leadership Award, Hwy Users Fedn. *Prof Exp:* Lectr civil eng, City Col, New York, 58-60; asst prof eng, San Diego State Col, Calif, 62-64; Fulbright res scholar & vis prof transp, Norweg Tech Univ, Trondheim & Inst Transp Econ, Oslo, Norway, 64-65; prin engr, Wilbur Smith & Assocs, 65-66; from assoc prof to prof civil eng, Carnegie-Mellon Univ, Pittsburgh, Pa, 66-74, assoc dir, Transp Res Inst, 66-74. *Concurrent Pos:* Consult var firms; mem, Transp Res Coun, Am Soc Civil Engrs, chmn, Transp Educ Comt, Hwy Safety Comt & Nat Conf Educ; chmn, Comt Transp Prof Needs, Nat Res Coun & Truck Weight Study Comt; dir, Transp Exec Inst, Am Asn State Hwy & Transp Officials; vis prof civil eng, Univ Calif, Irvine & Inst Hwy & RR Eng, Norway, 90-91. *Mem:* Nat Acad Eng; fel Am Soc Civil Engrs; Inst Transp Engrs; Transp Res Bd; Am Soc Eng Educ; Transp Res Forum; Am Road & Transp Builders Asn; Sigma Xi; Am Soc Eng Educ. *Res:* Author of various publications; highway and urban transportation system. *Mailing Add:* Dept Civil Eng Thornton Hall Univ Va Charlottesville VA 22903

HOEL, PAUL GERHARD, MATHEMATICS. *Current Pos:* from instr to assoc prof, 39-48, PROF MATH, UNIV CALIF, LOS ANGELES, 48- *Personal Data:* b Iola, Wis, Mar 23, 05; m 32; c 3. *Educ:* Luther Col, BA, 26; Univ Minn, MA, 29, PhD(math), 33. *Prof Exp:* Instr math, Rose Polytech Inst, 31-35, asst prof, 35-36; Am-Scandinavian Found fel, 36-37; instr math, Ore State Col, 37-39. *Concurrent Pos:* Fulbright fel, Norway, 53-54. *Mem:* Am Math Soc; Math Asn Am; Am Statist Asn; fel Inst Math Statist. *Res:* Mathematical statistics; theory of computational errors; theoretical statistics; approximation theory. *Mailing Add:* Dept Math Univ Calif Los Angeles CA 90095-1555

HOELSCHER, DOUGLAS RICHARD, MECHANICAL ENGINEERING. *Current Pos:* SR VPRES, TENNANT CO, 73- *Personal Data:* b St Paul, Minn, Aug 1, 38; m 60, Barbara J Thorson; c Steven, Donna (Olson) & Scott. *Educ:* Univ Minn, BSME, 61. *Honors & Awards:* Outstanding Achievement Award, Nat Soc Prof Engrs, 90. *Prof Exp:* Process engr, Modine Mfg Co, 61-63; mfg engr, Trance Co, 63-68; mgr & mfg engr, Chrysler Corp, 68-73. *Concurrent Pos:* Bush leadership fel, Bush Found, 76; adj prof, St Thomas Univ, 88- *Mem:* Nat Soc Prof Engrs. *Mailing Add:* Tennant Co 701 Lilac Dr N Minneapolis MN 55422-4611

HOELZEL, CHARLES BERNARD, TECHNICAL MANAGEMENT. *Current Pos:* LECTR GEN SCI, ELIZABETH CITY STATE UNIV, 89- *Personal Data:* b St Paul, Minn, Nov 21, 32; m 56; c 2. *Educ:* Hamline Univ, BS, 54; Vanderbilt Univ, PhD(chem), 60. *Prof Exp:* Chemist, Tenn Prod & Chem Corp, 56; sr res chemist, Hercules Powder Co, 59-65; res & develop engr, Fiber Industs, Inc, 65-67, res chemist, Halocarbon Prod Corp, 67-70; res scientist, Philip Morris Inc, 70-78, assoc sr scientist, 78-84; lectr chem, Univ NC, Wilmington, 84-89. *Mem:* Am Chem Soc; Sigma Xi. *Res:* Organosulfur compounds; disulfides and sulfinate esters; nitrogen heterocyclics; propellant binder systems; tobacco properties; liquid adhesive rheology. *Mailing Add:* 109 Small Dr Elizabeth City NC 27909-9490

HOELZEMAN, RONALD G, ELECTRICAL & COMPUTER ENGINEERING. *Current Pos:* asst prof, 70-77, dir continuing eng educ, 77-80, ASSOC PROF ELEC ENG & ASSOC CHMN DEPT, UNIV PITTSBURGH, 80- *Personal Data:* b Pittsburgh, Pa, Oct 6, 40; m, Bonnie Hall; c Barbara. *Educ:* Univ Pittsburgh, BSEE, 64, MSEE, 67, PhD(elec eng), 70. *Honors & Awards:* Undergrad Teaching Award, Inst Elect & Electronics Engrs, 93. *Prof Exp:* Engr, Westinghouse Elec Co, 64-67; instr elec eng, Univ Pittsburgh, 67-69; instr, Am Univ Beirut, 69-70. *Concurrent Pos:* Assoc ed, Inst Elect & Electronics Engrs Comput Soc. *Mem:* Fel Inst Elec & Electronics Engrs; Am Soc Eng Educ; Inst Elec & Electronics Engrs Comput Soc (pres, 95). *Res:* Optimization; computer design; mathematical programming; computer graphics. *Mailing Add:* Dept Elec Eng 348 BEH Pittsburgh PA 15261. *Fax:* 412-624-8003

HOELZER, GUY ANDREW, CONSERVATION GENETICS. *Current Pos:* ASST PROF BIOL, UNIV NEV, RENO, 91- *Personal Data:* Adam M. *Educ:* Williams Col, AB(biol) & AB(psychol), 78; San Jose State Univ, MS, 82; Univ Ariz, PhD(ecol & evolutionary biol), 89. *Prof Exp:* Res scientist, Dept Anthrop, Columbia Univ, 89-91. *Mem:* AAAS; Animal Behav Soc; Int Soc Study Behav Ecol; Molecular Biol & Evolution Soc; Soc Study Org Evolution. *Res:* Evolution of social behavior in vertebrates; use techniques from molecular genetics to examine the phylogenetic and filial relationships of organisms with the aim of elucidating the patterns and processes of social evolution. *Mailing Add:* 1400 Webster Way Reno NV 89509. *E-Mail:* hoelzer@vnr.edu

HOENER, BETTY-ANN, BIOPHARMACEUTICS. *Current Pos:* PROF BIOPHARM SCI & PHARMACEUT CHEM, SCH PHARM, UNIV CALIF, SAN FRANCISCO, 95-, ASSOC DEAN STUD AFFAIRS, 92- *Personal Data:* b Dayton, Ohio, Nov 25, 46. *Educ:* Univ Cincinnati, BS, 70; Ohio State Univ, PhD(pharmaceut chem), 74. *Concurrent Pos:* Secy, Pharmaceut Sci Sect, AAAS, 85-; mem-at-large, exec comt, Acad Pharmaceut Res Sci, 93-, Pres, 96-97. *Mem:* AAAS; Am Asn Cols Pharm; fel Am Pharmaceut Asn; Am Asn Pharmaceut Scientists; Int Soc Study Xenobiotics. *Res:* Disposition of 5-nitrofurans in isolated perfused rat liver, kidney and lung. *Mailing Add:* Dept Biopharmaceut Sci Univ Calif San Francisco CA 94143. *Fax:* 415-476-0688; *E-Mail:* hoener@itsa.ucsf.edu

HOENIG, ALAN, FRACTURE MECHANICS, COMPUTER TYPESETTING. *Current Pos:* From asst prof to assoc prof, 79-90, PROF MATH, JOHN JAY COL, CITY UNIV NY, 91- *Personal Data:* b Brooklyn, NY, June 18, 49; m 80; c 2. *Educ:* Yale Univ, BA, 71; Harvard Univ, MA, 72, PhD(appl math), 77. *Mem:* NY Acad Sci; Math Asn Am; Am Math Soc; Am Acad Mech. *Res:* Mathematical analysis of fracture and crack analysis; effects of cracking on large-scale physical properties of a specimen. *Mailing Add:* 17 Bay Ave Huntington NY 11743-1205

HOENIG, CLARENCE L, ceramic engineering, for more information see previous edition

HOENIG, STUART ALFRED, ELECTRICAL ENGINEERING, AIR POLLUTION. *Current Pos:* from assoc prof to prof eng, 59-87, EMER PROF ELEC ENG, UNIV ARIZ, 71- *Personal Data:* b Bridgeport, Conn, May 2, 28; m 52; c 2. *Educ:* Univ Mich, BS, 51; Univ Md, MS, 54; Univ Calif, Berkeley, PhD(eng sci), 61. *Prof Exp:* Physicist, US Naval Ord Lab, Md, 51-52; asst, Inst Fluid Dynamics & Appl Math, Univ Md, 52-54; asst engr, Sperry Gyroscope Co, NY, 54-55; assoc engr, Armour Res Inst, 55-57; asst, Low Pressure Lab, Univ Calif, Berkeley, 57-79. *Concurrent Pos:* Mem, Nat Acad Sci Comts, 77- *Mem:* AAAS; Inst Elec & Electronics Engrs; Electrostatic Soc Am. *Res:* New technology for control of fugitive dust pollution; sulfur dioxide and diesel engine exhaust particulates; new medical devices for operating room and burn unit use; apparatus for detection of under ground rock failure. *Mailing Add:* Dept Elec & Comput Eng Univ Ariz Tucson AZ 85721

HOEPFINGER, LYNN MORRIS, QUALITY ASSURANCE, FOOD CHEMISTRY. *Current Pos:* MGR QUAL ASSURANCE, HENKEL CORP, 84- *Personal Data:* b Neligh, Nebr, Aug 7, 41; m 65; c 2. *Educ:* Hastings Col, AB, 63; Purdue Univ, PhD(biochem), 68. *Prof Exp:* Asst prof chem, Hope Col, 67-71, assoc prof, 71-74; mgr, Mead Johnson & Co, 74-84. *Mem:* Am Soc Qual Control; Am Chem Soc. *Res:* Enzyme isolation and inhibition studies; biochemistry of ascorbic acid. *Mailing Add:* Henkel Corp PO Box 191 Kankakee IL 60901

HOEPPNER, CONRAD HENRY, ELECTRO-OPTICS, RADAR ENGINEERING. *Current Pos:* CONSULT, HOEPPNER ASSOC, 80- *Personal Data:* b Spooner, Wis, March 12, 28; m 52; c 2. *Educ:* Univ Wis, BS, 49, MS, 50; Mass Inst Technol, EE, 57. *Prof Exp:* Dept mgr, Raytheon Corp, 60-65; chief scientist, Harris Corp, 65-70; pres, Indust Electronetics Corp, 70-80. *Concurrent Pos:* Mem, US Govt Res & Develop Bd Comt Guided Missiles, Dept Defense, 50-53; deleg, Int Space Conf, London, Paris, Vienna & Tokyo; deleg, UN Int Space Conf, Vienna. *Mem:* Fel Inst Radio Engrs; fel Inst Elec & Electronics Engrs; fel Am Inst Aeronaut & Astronaut; Instrument Soc Am; Soc Exp Stress Anal; Soc Mfg Engrs; Soc Automotive Engrs; Sigma Xi. *Res:* High field electron emission; radar target characterization; high performance radio telemetry; author of numerous publications. *Mailing Add:* 320 12th Terr Indialantic FL 32903

HOEPPNER, DAVID WILLIAM, FATIGUE DESIGN, FRACTURE MECHANICS. *Current Pos:* chmn, 85-92, PROF MECH ENG, UNIV UTAH, 92-, DIR, QUAL & INTEGRITY DESIGN CTR. *Personal Data:* b Waukesha, Wis, Dec 17, 35; m 59; c 3. *Educ:* Marquette Univ, BME, 58; Univ Wis-Madison, MS, 60, PhD(metall & eng mech), 63. *Prof Exp:* Asst prof mat eng, Calif State Univ, 63; asst prof mat & mech eng, Univ Wis, Milwaukee, 63-64; res metallurgist struct mat eng, Battelle Mem Inst, 64-69; group engr fatigue & fracture mech, Lockheed Calif Co, 69-74; prof mech & aerospace eng, Univ Mo, Columbia, 74-78; Cockburn prof eng design, Univ Toronto, 78-85. *Concurrent Pos:* Prin investr, USN USAF, 70-78 & Elec Power Res Inst, 75-78; consult, Metal Properties Coun, 78-82, Detroit Diesel Allison, 79-81, Woodward Assoc, US Bur Mines, 78-, Rolls Royce Aero Engine Div, 80-, Lockheed Corp, Boeing Corp, McDonnell-Douglas Corp, Garrett Turbine, Pratt & Whitney & NIH, 85- *Mem:* Am Soc Mech Engrs; Am Soc Testing & Mat; Soc Automotive Engrs; Am Soc Metals; Am Soc Eng Educ; Am Inst Aeronaut & Astronaut; Nat Soc Prof Engrs. *Res:* Reliability and quality of engineered structures; fatigue, fracture; environmentally assisted crack propagation; corrosion fatigue; fretting fatigue; influence of structure on fatigue; physics of fatigue; design methods. *Mailing Add:* PO Box 581197 Salt Lake City UT 84158-1197. *Fax:* 801-585-5889; *E-Mail:* hoeppner@me.utah.edu

HOEPRICH, PAUL DANIEL, INTERNAL MEDICINE, INFECTIOUS DISEASES. *Current Pos:* prof med, 67-91, prof path, 68-86, EMER PROF, SCH MED, UNIV CALIF, DAVIS, 91- *Personal Data:* b Alliance, Ohio, Jan 3, 24; m 48, Muriel L Blackwell; c Martha S (Kennedy), Paul D Jr, T Eric & Kurt L. *Educ:* Harvard Med Sch, MD, 47; Am Bd Internal Med, dipl; Am Bd Med Microbiol, dipl. *Honors & Awards:* Mod Med Monographs Award, 58; Alice Sneed West lectr, Univ Tex Med Sch, 73; Paul A Rhoads lectr, Northwestern Univ, 75. *Prof Exp:* Med house officer, Peter Bent Brigham Hosp, 47-48; res fel bact & immunol, Harvard Med Sch, 49-51; asst resident internal med, New Haven Hosp, 53-54; resident infectious dis, Western Res Univ Hosp, 54-55; instr med, Sch Med & instr epidemiol, Sch Hyg & Pub Health, Johns Hopkins Univ, 56-57; asst prof med & asst res prof path, Col Med, Univ Utah, 57-62, assoc prof med & assoc res prof path, 62-67. *Concurrent Pos:* Asst physician, Outpatient Dept, Johns Hopkins Hosp, 55-57; consult, Vet Admin Hosp, 56-67; prof dir, Clin Microbial Lab & assoc physician, Salt Lake Co Gen Hosp, 65-67; consult med specialist, David Grant USAF Med Ctr, Travis AFB, 68-91; consult, Letterman Gen Hosp, San Francisco, 70-76; vis prof med, St Joseph Hosp & Univ Tex Med Sch, Houston, 73; lectr, Found Microbiol, 74-75; vis prof, Med Sch, Northwestern Univ, Chicago, 75; Fogerty Sr Int fel, 76; distinguished fac award, Med Ctr, Univ Calif, Davis, 86; H Wm Harris vis prof med, Am Bur Med Advan China, 89. *Mem:* Am Acad Microbiol; Fel Am Col Physicians; Am Fedn Clin Res; Am Soc Clin Invest; Am Soc Exp Path; Am Soc Microbiol; Am Thoracic Soc; Fel Infectious Dis Soc Am; AAAS; Am Asn Path Bacteriol; Am Asn Univ Prof; Asn Am Physicians; Sigma Xi. *Res:* Clinical investigation in infectious diseases; laboratory investigation of methods of microbiology; mechanisms of action of antimicrobial agents; antifungal chemotherapy. *Mailing Add:* 1305 Grayson Rd Wilmington DE 19803-4119. *Fax:* 302-764-5838

HOERCHER, HENRY E(RHARDT), THERMODYNAMICS. *Current Pos:* sr scientist, 55-64, CHIEF, ENERGY TRANSFER SECT, SYSTS DIV, AVCO CORP, 64- *Personal Data:* b New York, NY, Oct 19, 30; m 57; c 2. *Educ:* Polytech Inst Brooklyn, BME, 52. *Prof Exp:* Asst, Mech Eng Lab, Polytech Inst Brooklyn, 51-52; res scientist, Rocketdyne Div, NAm Aviation, Inc, 53-55. *Mem:* Am Inst Aeronaut & Astronaut; Am Soc Mech Engrs; Sigma Xi. *Res:* Heat transfer and thermodynamics of reentry vehicles and nozzles; laboratory simulation devices for reentry vehicles and rocket nozzles; space propulsion. *Mailing Add:* One Candlewood Rd Lynnfield MA 01940

HOERGER, FRED DONALD, ENVIRONMENTAL SCIENCE POLICY, REGULATORY AFFAIRS. *Current Pos:* CONSULT SCI & PUB POLICY, 91- *Personal Data:* b Wadsworth, Ohio, Jan 3, 29; m 51, Helen Goodin; c Bruce E, Carl R, Thomas J, David L & Steven F. *Educ:* Heidelberg Col, BS, 51; Purdue Univ, MS, 53; PhD(chem), 54. *Prof Exp:* Chemist, Strosackers Lab, Dow Chem Co, 54-57, asst lab dir, Ethylene Res Lab, 57-62, lab dir, 62-68, prod registr mgr, 68-74, opers mgr, Health-Environ Res, 74-77, dir regulatory & legis issues, Health-Environ Sci, 77-84, regulatory & policy consult, 84-91. *Concurrent Pos:* Mem, Comt Environ Improv, Am Chem Soc, 89-; consult, Resources Future, 92-93. *Mem:* AAAS; Am Chem Soc; fel Soc Risk Anal. *Res:* Agricultural chemicals; toxicology of biologically active compounds; safety and environmental fate of chemicals and pesticides; regulatory policy in occupational health, toxic substances and environmental affairs; science policy; risk assessment, risk communication. *Mailing Add:* 2813 Schade West Dr Midland MI 48640. *E-Mail:* fhoerger@aol.com

HOERING, THOMAS CARL, GEOCHEMISTRY, PHYSICAL CHEMISTRY. *Current Pos:* STAFF MEM, CARNEGIE INST WASH, 59- *Personal Data:* b Alton, Ill, May 4, 25; m 50; c 2. *Educ:* Wash Univ, BA, 48, MA, 50, PhD(chem), 52. *Honors & Awards:* Treibs Medal, Geochemical Soc. *Prof Exp:* From asst prof to assoc prof chem, Univ Ark, 52-58. *Mem:* Am Chem Soc; AAAS; Geochem Soc; Am Soc Limnol & Oceanog. *Res:* Geochemistry of stable isotopes; geochemistry of organic substances. *Mailing Add:* 3124 Quesada St NW Washington DC 20015-1305

HOERL, BRYAN G, microbiology, pathology; deceased, see previous edition for last biography

HOERLEIN, ALVIN BERNARD, animal pathology, for more information see previous edition

HOERMAN, KIRK CONKLIN, biochemistry, for more information see previous edition

HOERNER, GEORGE M, JR, DESIGN, INSTRUMENTATION. *Current Pos:* from asst prof to prof, Lafayette Col, 58-91, exec officer, 77-81, dept head, 81-91, EMER PROF CHEM ENG, LAFAYETTE COL, 91- *Personal Data:* b Hershey, Pa, Feb 12, 29; m 57, Margaret Dewart; c Eric & Nancy. *Educ:* Lafayette Col, BS, 51; Univ Rochester, MEd, 58; Lehigh Univ, PhD(chem eng), 63. *Honors & Awards:* Jones Lectr Award, Lafayette Col, 64. *Prof Exp:* Shift supvr, E I du Pont de Nemours & Co, Inc, 51-54 & 56-57. *Concurrent Pos:* Res assoc, Lewis Res Ctr, NASA, summers 64 & 65; resident process engr, Sun Oil Co, 66-67; eng consult, J T Baker Chem Co, 68-83. *Mem:* Fel Am Inst Chem Engrs; Am Soc Eng Educ. *Res:* Dynamics of packed-tower gas absorption; chemical process instrumentation; chemical process design and economics. *Mailing Add:* 2763 Queen St Easton PA 18042

HOERR, FREDERIC JOHN, AVIAN PATHOLOGY. *Current Pos:* VET PATHOLOGIST, ALA DEPT AGR & INDUSTS & C S ROBERTS VET DIAG LAB, 87- *Personal Data:* b Peoria, Ill, May 2, 52; m 75; c 2. *Educ:* Purdue Univ, DVM, 76, MS, 77, PhD(vet path), 81. *Concurrent Pos:* Assoc prof, Dept Pathobiol, Col Vet Med, Auburn Univ, 80- *Mem:* Am Vet Med Asn; Am Asn Avian Pathologists; World Vet Poultry Asn; Am Col Vet Path. *Res:* Respiratory diseases of poultry; cryptosporidiosis; trichothecene mycotoxicoses; aflatoxicosis; applied research in veterinary pathology and toxicology. *Mailing Add:* C S Roberts Vet Diag Lab PO Box 2209 Auburn AL 36831-2209

HOERTZ, CHARLES DAVID, JR, CHEMICAL ENGINEERING. *Current Pos:* sales engr, Ashland Oil Co, 54-55, chem engr, 55-60, group leader res & develop, 60-66, admin asst, 66-67, mgr res & develop, 67-80, PRES, ASHLAND SYNTHETIC FUELS, 80- *Personal Data:* b Louisville, Ky, Aug 5, 26; m 45; c 4. *Educ:* Univ Louisville, BChE, 48. *Prof Exp:* Refining engr, Aetna Oil Co, Ky, 48-54. *Mem:* Am Chem Soc; Am Inst Chem Engrs. *Res:* Process research and development in all phases of petroleum refining and petrochemical manufacturing. *Mailing Add:* 420 Bellefonte Princes Rd Ashland KY 41101

HOESCHELE, GUENTHER KURT, ORGANIC POLYMER CHEMISTRY. *Current Pos:* RETIRED. *Personal Data:* b Stuttgart, Ger, Mar 25, 25; nat US; m 55; c 2. *Educ:* Stuttgart Tech Inst, dipl, 49, Dr rer nat, 52. *Prof Exp:* Asst, Stuttgart Tech Inst, 51-53; res assoc, Polytech Inst Brooklyn, 53-54; res chemist, E I du Pont de Nemours & Co, Inc, 54-79, res fel, 79-83, sr res fel, 84-90. *Concurrent Pos:* Consult, Conolux Inc, 90- *Mem:* Am Chem Soc; Ger Chem Soc. *Res:* Organic preparative chemistry; polymer chemistry; thermoplastic elastomers; polyester elastomer. *Mailing Add:* 2007 Dogwood Lane Wilmington DE 19810-3606

HOESE, HINTON DICKSON, MARINE BIOLOGY. *Current Pos:* from asst prof to assoc prof, 67-76, PROF BIOL, UNIV SOUTHWESTERN LA, 76- *Personal Data:* b San Antonio, Tex, June 26, 35; m 58; c 3. *Educ:* Agr & Mech Col, Tex, BS, 56, MS, 59; Univ Tex, PhD(zool), 65. *Prof Exp:* Marine biologist, Marine Div, Tex Game & Fish Comn, 57-59; asst marine scientist, Va Fisheries Lab, Eastern Shore Sta, 59-62; res assoc, Marine Inst, Univ Ga, 65-66; asst prof marine biol, Univ Ala, 66-67. *Concurrent Pos:* Interim Dir, La Univ Marine Consortium, 79-80. *Mem:* Am Soc Ichthyol & Herpet; Nat Shellfisheries Asn; Am Fisheries Soc; Sigma Xi. *Res:* Distribution, ecology and taxonomy of marine fishes; ecology of marine invertebrates. *Mailing Add:* 213 Des Jardin St Univ Southwestern La Box 42451 Lafayette LA 70507-2611

HOEVE, CORNELIS ABRAHAM JACOB, PHYSICAL CHEMISTRY. *Current Pos:* RETIRED. *Personal Data:* b Landsmeer, Neth, Aug 31, 24; m 53; c 1. *Educ:* Univ Amsterdam, cand, 47, MS, 50; Univ Pretoria, DSc, 55. *Prof Exp:* Res chemist, Toegepast Natuurwetenschappelijk Onderzoek, Neth, 50-52 & coun sci & indust res, SAfrica, 52-55; fel, Nat Res Coun Can, 55-56; res assoc, Cornell Univ, 56-57; sr fel, Mellon Inst, 57-64; mem staff, Nat Bur Stand, 64-69, sect chief, 69; prof chem, Tex A&M Univ, 69-92. *Mem:* Am Chem Soc; Sigma Xi. *Res:* Polymer chemistry. *Mailing Add:* 4799 Ganymede Ct Naples FL 34105

HOEY, DANNY LEE, CHEMISTRY. *Current Pos:* PROD LINE LIAISON, HEWLETT PACKARD CO, 89- *Personal Data:* b New York, NY, Oct 13, 57. *Educ:* Queens Col, BS, 78; Univ Mass, MS, 84, PhD(chem), 88. *Prof Exp:* Salesman, 79-89. *Mem:* Am Acad Forensic Sci; Am Asn Clin Chem; Am Chem Soc; Am Inst Chemists. *Mailing Add:* Hewlett Packard Co Calif Analytic Div 1601 California Ave Palo Alto CA 94304

HOF, LISELOTTE BERTHA, MYELINATION, BRAIN DEVELOPMENT. *Current Pos:* instr, 72-73, asst prof, 73-78, ASSOC PROF BIOCHEM, ALBANY MED COL, 78- *Personal Data:* b Cologne, Ger, Jan 1, 37; m 72, Peter Weber. *Educ:* Univ Cologne, BS, 59, MS, 63, PhD(physiol chem), 65. *Prof Exp:* Res asst glycolipid metab, Ment Health Res Inst, Univ Mich, 67-68; NIH fel, Dept Pediat, Univ Chicago, 68-70; res asst, Univ Bochum, 70-72. *Concurrent Pos:* Assoc prof, Sch Pub Health, State Univ NY, Albany, 88- *Mem:* Soc Complex Carbohydrates; Asn Women in Sci; Am Chem Soc; Am Soc Biol Chemists; Am Soc Neurochem. *Res:* Glycolipids in brain development; membrane glycoconjugates; glycolipids metabolism; membranes. *Mailing Add:* Dept Biochem Albany Med Col 47 New Scotland Ave Albany NY 12208. *Fax:* 518-262-5689

HOFELDT, FRED DAN, INTERNAL MEDICINE, ENDOCRINOLOGY-METABOLISM. *Current Pos:* actg chief med, 89-92, CHIEF ENDOCRINOL, DENVER GEN HOSP, COLO, 84- *Personal Data:* b Rock Springs, Wyo, Sept 11, 36; m 77, Laurel Hendricks; c Fred D III, Scott M, LeAnn & Stacey. *Educ:* Col Idaho, BS, 59; Univ Wash, MD, 63. *Honors & Awards:* Legion of Merit, 84. *Prof Exp:* Chief endocrinol, Fitzsimons Army Med Ctr, 71-84, dir fel prog endocrinol, 78-84. *Concurrent Pos:* Prof med, Univ Colo Health Sci Ctr, Denver, 84-; assoc dir med, Denver Gen Hosp, 89- *Mem:* Fel Am Col Physicians; Am Diabetes Asn; Endocrine Soc; Am Inst Nutrit; Am Soc Clin Nutrit; Am Soc Bone & Mineral Resources. *Res:* Diabetes mellitus; hypoglycemia; thyroid cancer; metabolic bone disease and dyslipidemia. *Mailing Add:* 6680 E Mansfield Ave Denver CO 80237

HOFER, GREGORY GEORGE, SOLID STATE PHYSICS. *Current Pos:* SUPVR ENG, RAYTHEON ENGRS EBASCO, 78- *Personal Data:* b Flushing, NY, Apr 29, 52. *Educ:* Queens Col, BA, 74; Univ Chicago, MS, 76; Univ Wis, MS, 78. *Mem:* Am Phys Soc; Am Nuclear Soc. *Mailing Add:* 61-52 Little Neck Pkwy Little Neck NY 11362

HOFER, KENNETH EMIL, COMPOSITES FATIGUE & FRACTURE, UNDERGROUND STRUCTURES. *Current Pos:* VPRES MFG, TEST SYSTS TECHNOL, 83-; VPRES MAT, L J BROUTMAN & ASSOC, LTD, 82- *Personal Data:* b Chicago, Ill, Sept 26, 34; m 75; c 6. *Educ:* Ill Inst Technol, BS, 56, MS, 60. *Prof Exp:* Mgr mat sci, IIT Res Inst, 65-77, sr eng, 77-82. *Concurrent Pos:* Mem, Am Soc Testing Mat Subcomts; expert, fatigue & fracture composites, NASA. *Mem:* Soc Exp Mech Inc; Soc Advan Mat & Process Eng; Soc Mfg Eng; Am Soc Metals Int; Am Water Works Asn; Soc Plastics Indust. *Res:* Fatigue and fracture of composite materials and reinforced plastics; materials and structural, stress analysis and failure analysis; developed several testing methods and fixtures which have been adopted by the National Association for Testing. *Mailing Add:* 10601 Orchard Lane Chicago Ridge IL 60415

HOFER, KURT GABRIEL, CELL BIOLOGY, RADIATION BIOLOGY. *Current Pos:* asst prof, 71-75, assoc prof & USPHS res grant, 75-79, PROF BIOL SCI, FLA STATE UNIV, 79- *Personal Data:* b Feldkirchen, Austria, Mar 2, 39; m 65, Maria Geyer; c Andrea M & Mourlisek. *Educ:* Teacher Training Col, Austria, MEd, 59; Univ Vienna, PhD(biol), 65. *Prof Exp:* Asst radiobiol, Univ Vienna, 65-66; res assoc cancer biol, Sch Med, Tufts Univ, 66-70; asst prof radiobiol & Bremer Found Fund res grant, Ohio State Univ, 70-71. *Concurrent Pos:* Mem res comt, Fla Div, Am Cancer Soc, 72-88. *Mem:* AAAS; Radiation Res Soc; Am Asn Cancer Res; Sigma Xi. *Res:* Biological effects of radiation and antimetabolites; mechanism of radiation action damage from radioisotope decay; radiation repair; diurnal and annual rhythms of radiosensitivity; growth kinetics of normal and neoplastic cell populations. *Mailing Add:* Biol Sci Fla State Univ 600 W College Ave Tallahassee FL 32306-1096. *Fax:* 850-561-1406

HOFER, LAWRENCE JOHN EDWARD, PHYSICAL CHEMISTRY. *Current Pos:* CONSULT, MINE SAFETY & HEALTH ADMIN, US DEPT LABOR, 92- *Personal Data:* b Salt Lake City, Utah, June 26, 15; m 41, Marguerite I Tears; c Richard L. *Educ:* Univ Utah, BA, 37, MA, 39; Univ Rochester, PhD(phys chem), 41. *Prof Exp:* Sherman Clark fel, Univ Rochester, 38-40; res assoc propellants, Nat Defense Res Comt, Carnegie Inst Technol, 41-43; actg chief, Phys Chem Res & Develop Br, Off Synthetic Liquid Fuels, US Bur Mines, 43-50, chief, Phys Chem Sect, Synthetic Fuels Res Br, 50-55 & Phys & Catalytic Chem Sect, Coal-to-Oil Res Br, 55-61; supvry phys chemist adsorption, Pittsburgh Coal Res Ctr, 61-65; sr fel, Mellon Inst, 65-71, head, Adsorption Fel, 67-71; mem staff anal toxicol in mining res, US Bur Mines, 71-76; chief, Mat Toxicol Br, Pittsburgh Tech Support Ctr, 76-78, Chief Toxic Mat Div, 78-86, sr scientist, Pittsburgh Health Technol Ctr, 86-92. *Mem:* Fel Am Inst Chem; Catalysis Soc; Am Chem Soc; Air pollution Control Asn; fel AAAS. *Res:* Catalysis; Fischer-Tropsch synthesis; auto exhaust oxidation; carbides of iron, cobalt and nickel; photochemistry; fluorescence of cyanine dyes; activated carbon structure; adsorption; toxicology; mine atmospheres; structure chemistry of coal; flames and explosions. *Mailing Add:* 236 Hays Rd Upper St Clair Br Pittsburgh PA 15241

HOFERT, JOHN FREDERICK, ENDOCRINOLOGY. *Current Pos:* asst prof, 66-71, ASSOC PROF BIOCHEM & MOLECULAR BIOL, UNIV NEBR MED CTR, OMAHA, 71- *Personal Data:* b Oak Park, Ill, Oct 13, 35; m 62, Priscilla Bomberger; c Daniel W & Andrew J. *Educ:* NCent Col, Ill, BA, 57; Mich State Univ, MS, 59; Univ Wis, PhD(oncol), 63. *Prof Exp:* Res asst biochem, Mich State Univ, 57-59; res asst oncol, Univ Wis, 59-63; res fel biochem, Albert Einstein Col Med, 63-64, instr, 64-66. *Concurrent Pos:* Vis scholar, Dept Internal Med, Sch Med, Emory Univ, Atlanta, Ga, 86. *Mem:* AAAS; Am Soc Biochem & Molecular Biol; Endocrine Soc. *Res:* Metabolic control mechanisms; metabolic alterations in diabetes mellitus; metabolic effects of glucocorticoids. *Mailing Add:* Dept Biochem & Molecular Biol Univ Nebr Med Ctr 600 S 42nd St Omaha NE 68198-4525. *Fax:* 402-559-6650; *E-Mail:* jhofert@unmc.edu

HOFF, BERT JOHN, PLANT BREEDING, RICE GENETICS. *Current Pos:* ASSOC PROF AGRON, LA STATE UNIV, BATON ROUGE, 67- *Personal Data:* b Windthorst, Tex, Nov 26, 34; m 71, 86; c 2. *Educ:* Tex A&M Univ, BS, 57, MS, 63; Univ Ariz, PhD(agron), 67. *Mem:* Am Soc Agron; Crop Sci Soc Am. *Res:* Cytology and reproductive behavior of Cynodon dactylon; reproductive behavior of Zizania aquatica in Louisiana; male sterility in Oryza sativa; inheritance of disease resistance in rice; inheritance of aroma in rice. *Mailing Add:* 1242 Aster St Baton Rouge LA 70802

HOFF, CHARLES JAY, IMMUNOGENETICS. *Current Pos:* assoc prof, Dept Med Genetics, 76-86, prof, 86-88, PROF PEDIAT, COL MED, UNIV SALA, 90- *Personal Data:* b Newark, NY, Oct 28, 37; m 77, Marcia J Lasswell. *Educ:* Pa State Univ, BS, 61, MA, 67, PhD(phys anthrop), 72; Univ Oxford, dipl human biol, 68. *Prof Exp:* Comput programmer, IBM, 62-64; teaching & res asst, Dept Anthrop, Pa State Univ, 64-67, instr, 68-69, dir, Peruvian Field Sch, 69; asst prof & phys anthrop, Univ Ore, 70-76. *Concurrent Pos:* Partic growth & develop, Advan Study Inst, NATO, 79; prin investr res grants, NIH, 79-81, 86-88; adj prof, Dept Path, Univ SAla, 88-90; staff scientist, Battelle PNL, 88-90; vis prof, Dept Pharmacol & Toxicol, Wash State Univ, 89-91; clin assoc prof, Dept Epidemiol, Univ Wash, 89-91. *Mem:* Am Soc Human Genetics; Soc Study Human Biol; fel Human Biol Coun; Soc Epidemiol Res; Am Asn Phys Anthropologists; fel Am Col Epidemiol; Am Soc Reprod Immunol. *Res:* Human population genetics; physical growth and development; risk factors associated with pregnancy outcome; immunogenetics; Acquired Immune Deficiency Syndrome. *Mailing Add:* Dept Pediat POD 40130 Univ SAla Mobile AL 36640-0130. *Fax:* 334-405-5120; *E-Mail:* choff@jaguar1.usouthal.edu

HOFF, DALE RICHARD, MEDICINAL CHEMISTRY. *Current Pos:* RETIRED. *Personal Data:* b Galesburg, Ill, Nov 16, 27; m 59; c 5. *Educ:* Univ Ill, BS, 52; Mass Inst Technol, PhD(org chem), 56. *Prof Exp:* From sr chemist to asst dir, Merck Sharp & Dohme Res Labs, Rahway, 56-68, assoc dir to dir, 68-78, sr investr, 78-88. *Mem:* Am Chem Soc; The Chem Soc; AAAS. *Res:* Antiparasitic chemotherapy; computer applications to chemistry. *Mailing Add:* 2 Kings Ridge Rd Basking Ridge NJ 07920-1098

HOFF, DARREL BARTON, ASTRONOMY, SCIENCE EDUCATION. *Current Pos:* ADJ PROF PHYSICS & SCI EDUC, LUTHER COL, 93- *Personal Data:* b Victory, Wis, Dec 17, 32; m 54, Ardith Gardner; c Andrea & Adrian. *Educ:* Luther Col, Iowa, BA, 55; Univ Northern Iowa, MA, 63; Univ Iowa, PhD(sci educ & astron), 70. *Prof Exp:* Teacher chem & physics, Westby High Sch, 58-61; instr phys sci & astron, Univ Northern Iowa, 64-67, prof astron & sci educ, 70-87; proj dir, Ctr Astrophys, Harvard Univ, 87-93. *Concurrent Pos:* Consult, Am Astron Soc. *Mem:* Am Astron Soc; Am Asn Physics Teachers; Sigma Xi; Nat Sci Teachers Asn; Int Astron Union; fel Royal Astron Soc. *Res:* Astronomy education; UBV photometry-variable stars. *Mailing Add:* Phys Dept Luther Col Decorah IA 52101. *Fax:* 319-387-1080; *E-Mail:* noffdarr@Luther.edu

HOFF, GLORIA THELMA (ALBUERNE), HIGH ENERGY PHYSICS. *Current Pos:* from instr to asst prof, 64-68, ASSOC PROF PHYSICS, UNIV ILL, CHICAGO CIRCLE, 68- *Personal Data:* b Cienfuegos, Cuba, May 10, 30; m 59; c 3. *Educ:* Univ Havana, DCFM(physics, math), 54; Univ Chicago, MS, 57, PhD(physics), 65. *Prof Exp:* Asst prof physics, Sec Educ Inst, Cienfuegos, Cuba, 51-54, Sec Educ Inst, Vibora, Cuba, 55-56 & Univ Villanueva, Cuba, 57-58; asst, Univ Chicago, 58-63. *Concurrent Pos:* Referee, Phys Rev & Phys Rev Letters, 65- & Am J Physics, 75-; Res Bd grant, Univ Ill, Chicago Circle, 75-76. *Mem:* NY Acad Sci; AAAS; Am Phys Soc. *Res:* Phenomenology of pion photoproduction with polarized photons; analysis of lambda-kaon production data; interpretation of pion-nucleon differential cross section and polarization data; strongly correlated resonances model. *Mailing Add:* Dept Physics M/C 273 Univ Ill 845 W Taylor St Rm 2236 Chicago IL 60607

HOFF, HENRY FREDERICK, PATHOLOGY, BIOPHYSICS. *Current Pos:* HEAD ATHEROSCLEROSIS SECT, DEPT CARDIOVASC RES, CLEVELAND CLIN FOUND, 80-, DIR, PROG PROJ ATHEROSCLEROSIS, 83- *Personal Data:* b Vienna, Austria, Mar 22, 38; US Citizen; m 67; c 1. *Educ:* Dartmouth Col, BA, 59; Univ Calif, Berkeley, PhD(biophys), 65. *Prof Exp:* Teaching asst physiol, Univ Calif, Berkeley, 61-63; Alameda Co Heart Asn fel histol, Univ Vienna, 65-66; res assoc neuropath, Max-Planck Inst Psychiat, 66-70; asst prof neurol, Baylor Col Med, 70-74, assoc prof, 74-78, assoc prof exp med, 78-80. *Concurrent Pos:* Fel arteriosclerosis coun, Am Heart Asn; Am Heart Asn advan res fel atherosclerosis, Max-Planck Inst Psychiat, Munich, 68-70; proj in cardiovasc & stroke ctr grants, Baylor Col Med, 70-80; estab investr award, Am Heart Asn, 76-81 & mem, Prog Rev Comt, 80-81; ad hoc mem, Metabolism Study Sect, NIH, 84; mem, Parent Review Comt, Arteriosclerosis Spec Ctr Res Prog, Nat Heart, Lung & Blood Inst, 85-86; ed, Artery, 77-84. *Mem:* Am Asn Exp Path; Am Heart Asn; Am Soc Cell Biol; NY Acad Sci. *Res:* Vascular pathology, injury and repair; cerebral atherosclerosis; lipoproteins and atherosclerosis in experimental animals and humans using quantitative immunochemical, enzyme and immuno-histochemical and electron microscope techniques; interaction of lipoproteins extracted from human arteries with macrophages and arterial cells in culture-mechanism of foam cell formation; cell biology. *Mailing Add:* Cleveland Clin Found Dept Atherosclerosis 9500 Euclid Ave Cleveland OH 44195-0001. *Fax:* 216-444-9404

HOFF, JAMES GAVEN, ecology, ichthyology, for more information see previous edition

HOFF, JOHN C, MICROBIOLOGY. *Current Pos:* CONSULT, ENVIRON MICROBIOL, 89- *Personal Data:* b Billings, Mont, Mar 9, 28; m 57, L Jean Martin; c Karen, Susan & Patricia. *Educ:* Mont State Col, BS, 50; Utah State Univ, MS, 56; Wash State Univ, PhD(bact), 62. *Prof Exp:* Bacteriologist, Mont State Bd Health, 50, 52-54, virologist, 56-58; res microbiologist, Northwestern Water Supply Res Lab, Environ Protection Agency, 62-70, dir, 70-73, res microbiologist, Risk Reduction Eng Lab, 73-89. *Mem:* Am Soc Microbiol; Sigma Xi; Am Water Works Asn. *Res:* Sanitary and environmental bacteriology and virology; bacteriophage typing; bacteriological and virological methods for examination of water; microbiological aspects of water disinfection. *Mailing Add:* 6962 Gammwell Dr Cincinnati OH 45230. *Fax:* 513-232-6585

HOFF, JULIAN THEODORE, NEUROLOGY. *Current Pos:* PROF NEUROL, UNIV MICH, ANN ARBOR, 81-, HEAD SECT NEUROSURG, 81-, PROF NEUROSURG, 81- *Personal Data:* b Boise, Idaho, Sept 22, 36; m 62, Diane Shanks; c Paul, Allison & Julia. *Educ:* Stanford Univ, Calif, BA, 58; Cornell Univ, MD, 62; Am Bd Neurol Surg, dipl. *Prof Exp:* Intern, New York Hosp, 62-63, resident surg, 63-64, resident neurosurg, 66-70; from asst prof to prof neurosurg, Univ Calif, San Francisco, 74-81. *Concurrent Pos:* Macy fac scholar, London, 79; Javits neurosci investr award, NIH, 85- *Mem:* Fel Am Col Surgeons; Am Asn Neurol Surgeons (vpres, 91-93, pres, 93-); Am Surg Asn; Cong Neurol Surgeons (vpres, 82-83); Am Acad Neurosurgeons (treas, 89-92, secy, 92-). *Res:* Neurology; neurosurgery. *Mailing Add:* Univ Mich Hosp Neurosurg Taubman Bldg Rm 2128B Boc 0338 1500 E Med Ctr Dr Ann Arbor MI 48109

HOFF, KENNETH MICHAEL, NEUROCHEMISTRY, COMPARATIVE ANATOMY. *Current Pos:* RETIRED. *Personal Data:* b Dickinson, NDak, July 6, 34. *Educ:* Carroll Col, Mont, AB, 61; Wash State Univ, PhD(zool), 66. *Prof Exp:* From asst prof to prof biol, Cleveland State Univ, 66-94. *Res:* Maturation and control of indoleamine metabolism during mouse brain development; interaction of various drugs with indoleamines during mouse brain development. *Mailing Add:* 6165 Paisley Dr North Olmsted OH 44070

HOFF, MARCIAN EDWARD, JR, ELECTRICAL ENGINEERING. *Current Pos:* VPRES & CHIEF TECH OFFICER, TEKLICON INC, 90- *Personal Data:* b Rochester, NY, Oct 28, 37; m 62, 77; c 1. *Educ:* Rensselaer Polytech Inst, BEE, 58; Stanford Univ, MS, 59, PhD(elec eng), 62. *Honors & Awards:* Stuart Ballantine Medal, Franklin Inst, 79; Cledo Brunetti Award & Centennial Medal, Inst Elec & Electronics Engrs, 84. *Prof Exp:* Res assoc elec eng, Stanford Univ, 62-68; mgr applns res, Intel Corp, 68-83; vpres technol, Atari, Inc, 83-84. *Concurrent Pos:* Consult, 84- *Mem:* Fel Inst Elec & Electronics Engrs. *Res:* Electronic and adaptive computers; telecommunications. *Mailing Add:* 12226 Colina Dr Los Altos Hills CA 94024-5212

HOFF, N(ICHOLAS) J(OHN), AERONAUTICAL ENGINEERING, MECHANICS. *Current Pos:* prof & head dept, 57-71, EMER PROF AERONAUT & ASTRONAUT, STANFORD UNIV, 71- *Personal Data:* b Magyarovar, Hungary, Jan 3, 06; nat US; m 40, 72; c 1. *Educ:* Fed Polytech Inst, Zurich, Switz, Dipl Ing, 28; Stanford Univ, PhD(eng mech), 42. *Hon Degrees:* DSc Eng, Technion, Haifa, Israel, 81. *Honors & Awards:* Wilbur Wright Mem Lectr, Royal Aero Soc, London, 53; William M Murray Lectr, Soc Exp Stress Anal, 58; Theodore von Karman Mem Lectr, Israel Soc Aeronaut Sci, Tel Aviv, 66; von Karman Lectr, Am Inst Aeronaut & Astronaut, 66, G Edward Pendray Award & Struct Dynamics & Mat Award, 71; Worcester Reed Warner Medal, Am Soc Mech Engrs, 67, Medal, 74, Centennial Medal, 80; Theodore von Karman Medal, Am Soc Civil Engrs, 72; Lester D Gardner Lectr, Mass Inst Technol, 73; Monie A Ferst Award, Sigma Xi, 82; I B Laskowitz Award, NY Acad Sci, 83; Daniel Guggenheim Medal, 83. *Prof Exp:* Instr gliding & soaring, Hungarian Soaring Soc, 28; struct designer, Aeroplane Div, Manfred Weiss Aeroplane & Motor Works, Ltd, Budapest, Hungary, 29-39; res asst mech eng, Stanford Univ, 39-40; from instr to prof aeronaut eng & appl mech, Polytech Inst Brooklyn, 40-57, chmn dept, 41-57. *Concurrent Pos:* Mem, Subcomt Aircraft Struct, Nat Adv Comt Aeronaut, 48-57, Struct Design Comt, 58; mem, Subcomt Aircraft Structures, Nat Adv Comt Aeronaut, 48-57, Struct Design Comt, 58; mem, Gen Assembly Int Union for Theoret & Appl Mech, 49-; mem, US Nat Comt Theoret & Appl Mech, 49-, chmn, 57-60; mem, Ship Struct Design Comt, Nat Res Coun, 53-63, chmn, 60-63; mem, Res Adv Comt Aircraft Struct, NASA, 59-67 & Res & Technol Adv Coun, 67-70; vis prof, Univ Tokyo, 63, Univ Paris, 64, Univ NSW, Sydney, 66, Monash Univ, 71, Ga Inst Technol, 73, Cranfield Inst Technol, 73-74, Fed Polytech Inst, Zurich, 74 & Rensselaer Polytech Inst, 76-81; invited lectr, 4th Int Conf Composite Mats, Tokyo, Japan, 82 & Hungarian Acad Sci, 83. *Mem:* Nat Acad Eng; Am Acad Arts & Sci; hon fel Am Inst Aeronaut & Astronaut; hon mem Aeronaut Soc India; hon mem & fel Am Soc Mech Engrs; hon mem Hungarian Acad ci; hon mem, Japanese Rocket Soc; hon mem Nat Acad Air & Space, France; assoc mem Acad Sci, Paris, France; hon mem Hungarian Acad Sci; Inst DeFrance. *Res:* Applied mechanics; structural analysis and airplane analysis; shell theory; static and dynamic stability; high temperature effects on structures; applied mechanics. *Mailing Add:* 782 Esplanada Way Stanford CA 94305

HOFF, RAYMOND E, OLEFIN POLYMERIZATION CATALYSIS, ZIEGLER-NATTA CATALYSTS. *Current Pos:* CONSULT, 93- *Personal Data:* b Norfolk Va, Mar 24, 34; m 62, Susan Dentler; c Jonathan & David. *Educ:* Beloit Col, BS, 56; Univ Utah, PhD(org chem), 64. *Prof Exp:* Technician, Westinghouse Res Lab, 56-60; res chemist, B F Goodrich Res Ctr, 64-66, Chemplex Co, 66-85; sr res scientist, Norchem, Inc, 85-86; assoc scientist, USI Chem Co, 86-88; res scientist, Quantum Chem Corp, 88-93. *Mem:* Am Chem Soc; Sigma Xi. *Res:* Catalysis of olefin polymerization with supported Ziegler-Natta and chromium catalysts. *Mailing Add:* 244 S Oak St Palatine IL 60067

HOFF, RICHARD WILLIAM, NUCLEAR CHEMISTRY. *Current Pos:* Asst, Lawrence Livermore Lab, Univ Calif, 50-53, group leader, 59-69, assoc leader, Nuclear Chem Div, 69-79, RES CHEMIST, LAWRENCE LIVERMORE LAB, UNIV CALIF, 53- *Personal Data:* b Duluth, Minn, Jan 25, 30; m 53; c 2. *Educ:* Univ Minn, AB, 50; Univ Calif, PhD(chem), 54. *Mem:* Am Chem Soc; Am Phys Soc. *Res:* Radiochemical and nuclear properties of actinide elements; neutron capture gamma-ray spectroscopy. *Mailing Add:* L-231 Lawrence Livermore Nat Lab UCL PO Box 808 Livermore CA 94550

HOFF, VICTOR JOHN, CYTOGENETICS. *Current Pos:* assoc prof, 66-71, PROF BIOL, STEPHEN F AUSTIN STATE UNIV, 71- *Personal Data:* b Cincinnati, Ohio, Oct 18, 29; m 62. *Educ:* Univ Ky, BS, 53, MS, 58; Univ Ind, PhD(bot), 61. *Prof Exp:* Asst prof bot, Univ Ark, 61-66. *Mem:* Bot Soc Am; Am Genetic Asn; Am Inst Biol Sci. *Res:* Cytogenetics of Onagraceae. *Mailing Add:* Dept Biol Box 13003 Stephen F Austin State Univ Nacogdoches TX 75962

HOFF, WILFORD J, JR, ORGANIC CHEMISTRY. *Current Pos:* From instr to assoc prof, US Mil Acad, 58-67, dept head, 67-77, prof chem & head dept chem, 77-, EMER PROF, US MIL ACAD, 88- *Personal Data:* b Walterboro, SC, Oct 3, 28; m 3. *Educ:* The Citadel, BS, 50; Princeton Univ, MA, 55, PhD(chem), 62. *Mem:* Am Chem Soc; AAAS; Sigma Xi. *Res:* Chemical education. *Mailing Add:* Rte 3 Box 736 Manning NY 29102

HOFFBAUER, MARK ARLES, NEUTRAL BEAM PROCESSING OF SEMICONDUCTOR MATERIALS, NONLINEAR OPTICAL PROBES OF SURFACES & INTERFACES. *Current Pos:* TECH STAFF MEM, LOS ALAMOS NAT LAB, 85- *Personal Data:* b Jan 30, 54; m 75, Barbara Evans; c Christopher & Timothy. *Educ:* Abilene Christian Univ, BS, 76; Univ Minn, PhD(chem phys), 82. *Prof Exp:* Nat Res Coun fel, Naval Res Lab, 82-85; res fel, Nat Inst Stand & Technol, 85. *Mem:* Am Phys Soc; Am Chem Soc; Am Vacuum Soc. *Res:* Nonlinear optical diagnostic techniques are developed and used to study surfaces and interfaces including structure, chemical and physical properties, and ultrafast dynamics; hyperthermal neutral beams are used to make novel electronic materials through growth and removal processes. *Mailing Add:* Los Alamos Nat Lab CST-1 MS-J565 Los Alamos NM 87545. *Fax:* 505-665-4613

HOFFBECK, LOREN JOHN, AGRONOMY. *Current Pos:* res coordr, Pioneer Hi-Bred Int, Inc, 77-86, res dir, 86-90, CORN BREEDER, RES DEPT, PIONEER HI-BRED INT, INC, 66-, RES FEL, 90- *Personal Data:* b Ortonville, Minn, Aug 26, 32; m 60, Helen M Shea; c Joan K (Dubnicka), Mark D, Joseph P, Amy M (Reynolds) & Susan R (Takacs). *Educ:* SDak State Univ, BS, 54; Univ Wis, MS, 59, PhD(agron), 62. *Prof Exp:* Res agronomist, USDA, 61-66. *Mem:* Am Soc Agron; Crop Sci Soc. *Res:* Crop breeding; development of improved corn inbreds and hybrids. *Mailing Add:* Pioneer Hi-Bred Int Inc 1000 W Jefferson Tipton IN 46072

HOFFEE, PATRICIA ANNE, BIOCHEMISTRY, MICROBIOLOGY. *Current Pos:* from asst prof to assoc prof, 67-78, PROF MICROBIOL, SCH MED UNIV PITTSBURGH, 78- *Personal Data:* b Columbiana, Ohio, Oct 1, 37. *Educ:* Univ Pittsburgh, BS, 59, MS, 61, PhD(microbiol), 63. *Prof Exp:* NIH fel, Albert Einstein Col Med, 63-65, from instr to asst prof molecular biol, 65-67. *Concurrent Pos:* Career develop award, Albert Einstein Col Med, 65-67. *Mem:* AAAS; Am Soc Biol Chem & Molecular Biol; Am Soc Microbiol. *Res:* Genetic regulation; enzyme structure and function; immuno deficiency diseases-adenosine deaminase, purine nucleaside phosphorylase; purine and pyrimidine nucleotide metabolism. *Mailing Add:* Dept Molec Genet Biochem Univ Pittsburgh Sch Med Pittsburgh PA 15261-0001

HOFFELD, J TERRELL, IMMUNOLOGY, DENTAL RESEARCH. *Current Pos:* DENT OFFICER, COMN CORPS, DEPT HEALTH & HUMAN SERV, USPHS, 78-, CHIEF, SCI REV BR, AGENCY HEALTH CARE POLICY & RES, 91- *Personal Data:* b Oct 18, 46; m 73, Edwina Howe; c Erica H & Bradley J. *Educ:* Univ Cincinnati, BS, 68; Ohio State Univ, DDS, 72; Univ Rochester, PhD(microbiol & immunol), 77. *Prof Exp:* Investr, Lab Microbiol & Immunol, Nat Inst Dent Res, NIH, 77-81, sr investr, Clin Invests & Patient Care Br, 81-85, exec secy, Oral Biol & Med Study Sect, Div Res Grant, 85-91. *Concurrent Pos:* Adj res fac, Dept Microbiol, Baltimore Col Dent Surg, Univ Md, 82-; vis lectr, Dept Periodont, Naval Dent Sch, 83-; co-founder, NIH Oxygen Radicals Forum, 81, chmn, 81-87; mem, Int Asn Dent Res, Wash Acad Sci liaison, 85-, fel, 91-; secy-treas, Microbiol & Immunol Res Group, Int Asn Dent Res, 86- *Mem:* Int Asn Dent Res (secy-treas, 86-87, vpres, 87-88, pres, 88); Am Asn Immunologists; Am Soc Microbiol; Am Soc Bone & Mineral Res; fel Acad Dent Int; fel Am Col Dentists; fel Int Col Dentists. *Res:* Dental research and oral biology. *Mailing Add:* NIH 6701 Rockledge Dr Rm 4116 Rockville MD 20892-7816. *Fax:* 301-594-0154; *E-Mail:* t5h@cu.nih.gov

HOFFELDER, ANN MCINTOSH, CHEMICAL EDUCATION. *Current Pos:* RETIRED. *Personal Data:* b Creedmoor, NC, Feb 3, 35; m 59; c 2. *Educ:* Univ NC, Greensboro, BA, 57; Univ NC, Chapel Hill, MAT, 63; Univ Md, College Park, PhD(chem educ), 73. *Prof Exp:* Teacher & counr gen sci, Eng & soc studies, Pac Beach Jr High, San Diego, Calif, 57-61; teacher chem, biol & gen sci, Chapel Hill High Sch, NC, 61-62; from instr to assoc prof, Cumberland Col, Ky, 63-78, prof gen & org chem & dept head, 78-95; prof, Europe Div, Univ Md, Col Park, 96. *Concurrent Pos:* Mem bd dir, Ky Asn Progress Sci, 72-; mem coun, Ky State Sci Adv Coun, 73- *Mem:* Am Chem Soc; Nat Sci Teachers Asn. *Res:* Curriculum development in chemical education. *Mailing Add:* 54 Charles St Williamsburg KY 40769-9318

HOFFER, ABRAHAM, EARTH SCIENCES, GEOPHYSICS. *Current Pos:* CONSULT, 88- *Personal Data:* b Budapest, Hungary; US citizen. *Educ:* Univ Toronto, BASc, 56, MASc, 57; Univ Chicago, PhD(geophys sci), 59. *Prof Exp:* Res assoc solid state physics, Pa State Univ, 60-62; asst prof, Loyola Univ, 62-64 & Sir George Williams Univ, 65-66; assoc prof, Marquette Univ, 66-68; assoc ed & staff writer, Encycl Britannica, 68-71; teacher phys sci, Chicago City Col, 72-88. *Mem:* AAAS; Am Geophys Union; Am Phys Soc; Nat Soc Prof Engr. *Res:* Causes of intra-terrestrial unrest; origin of geomagnetic field; solar-planetary relationships. *Mailing Add:* 992 S Park Terr Chicago IL 60605-2018. *Fax:* 312-663-5276; *E-Mail:* hoffabra@aol.com

HOFFER, ALAN R, MATHEMATICS. *Current Pos:* assoc prof, 71-76, PROF MATH, UNIV ORE, 76- *Personal Data:* b Chicago, Ill. *Educ:* Univ Calif, BA, 58; Univ Notre Dame, MS, 63; Univ Mich, PhD(math), 69. *Prof Exp:* Teacher high schs, Calif, 58-67; asst prof math, Univ Mont, 69-71. *Concurrent Pos:* Chmn, Comn Educ Teachers Math, Nat Coun Teachers Math, 74-76; dir, Math Resource Proj, NSF, 74-78. *Mem:* Math Asn Am. *Res:* Mathematics education; group theory and geometry; combinatorics; mathematics combinatorics. *Mailing Add:* Educ Dept Univ Calif 245 Berkeley Irvine CA 92717

HOFFER, J(OAQUIN) A(NDRES), NEUROPHYSIOLOGY, SENSORIMOTOR SYSTEMS. *Current Pos:* PROF & DIR, SCH KINESIOLOGY, SIMON FRASER UNIV, 91- *Personal Data:* b Montevideo, Uruguay, Aug 4, 46; c 1. *Educ:* Harvey Mudd Col, BS, 70; Johns Hopkins Univ, PhD(biophysics), 75. *Prof Exp:* Fel nerve & muscle physiol, Dept Physiol, Univ Alberta, 75-78; staff fel integrative neurophysiol, Lab Neural Control, Nat Inst Neurol & Commun Dis & Stroke, Bethesda, Md, 78-80, sr staff fel, 80-82; from asst prof to prof, Dept Clin Neurosci, Univ Calgary, 82-91. *Concurrent Pos:* Vis prof, Nat Res Inst Physiol Cent Nerv Syst, Milano Italy, 82; med scholar, Alta Heritage Found Med Res, 82-87 & 87-92. *Mem:* Soc Neurosci; Behav & Brain Sci Asn; Inst Elec & Electronics Engrs; Emba Mink Breeders Asn. *Res:* Central control and reflex regulation of movements; activity of single sensory and motor nerve cells in freely moving animals; design of implantable electrodes for the control of prosthetic limbs. *Mailing Add:* Simon Fraser Univ Sch Kinesiol 8888 University Dr Burnaby BC V5A 1S6 Can

HOFFER, JERRY M, GEOLOGY. *Current Pos:* assoc prof, 68-72, PROF GEOL, UNIV TEX, EL PASO, 72- *Personal Data:* b Marshalltown, Iowa, Aug 10, 34; m 57; c 2. *Educ:* Univ Iowa, BA, 56, MS, 58; Wash State Univ, PhD(geol), 65. *Prof Exp:* Instr high sch, 58-59; teaching asst geol, Wash State Univ, 60-64; asst prof, Western Ill Univ, 65 & Tex Western Col, 65-68. *Mem:* AAAS; Geol Soc Am; Can Mineral Soc; Mineral Soc Am; Sigma Xi. *Res:* Vulcanism; x-ray mineralogy. *Mailing Add:* Dept Geosci Univ Tex 500 W Uni Ave El Paso TX 79968-8900

HOFFER, PAUL B, RADIOLOGY, NUCLEAR MEDICINE. *Current Pos:* PROF RADIOL & DIR SECT NUCLEAR MED, YALE UNIV, 77- *Personal Data:* b New York, NY, Apr 9, 39; m 64; c 5. *Educ:* Univ Chicago, MD, 63; Am Bd Radiol, dipl, 70, cert nuclear imaging, 74; Am Bd Nuclear Med, dipl, 72; Yale, MA, 77. *Prof Exp:* Intern med, Mary Hitchcock Mem Hosp, 63-64; resident radiol, Univ Chicago, 66-69, from instr to assoc prof, 69-74, dir, Sect Nuclear Med, Pritzker Sch Med, 70-74; prof radiol & dir, Sect Nuclear Med, Med Ctr, Univ Calif, San Francisco, 74-77. *Concurrent Pos:* James Picker Found res scholar, Pritzker Sch Med, Univ Chicago, 69-72; proj leader, Argonne Cancer Res Hosp, 69-74. *Mem:* AAAS; Soc Nuclear Med (vpres, 80-81); Am Col Radiol; Asn Univ Radiol; Am Col Nuclear Physicians. *Res:* Nuclear medicine. *Mailing Add:* 33 Cedar St TE-2 New Haven CT 06510-3289

HOFFER, ROGER M(ILTON), REMOTE SENSING, PHOTO INTERPRETATION. *Current Pos:* PROF FORESTRY & DIR REMOTE SENSING & GIS PROG, COLO STATE UNIV, 88- *Personal Data:* b Rogers City, Mich, Dec 5, 37; m 58, Constance A Steinbach; c Philip C, Douglas P & Steven E. *Educ:* Mich State Univ, BS, 59; Colo State Univ, MS, 60, PhD(watershed mgt), 62. *Honors & Awards:* Pecora Award, NASA & US Geol Surv, 76; Alan Gordon Mem Award, 78; NASA Group Achievement Award, 79, 90; Birdseye Award, Am Soc Photogram & Remote Sensing, 90. *Prof Exp:* Watershed specialist, US Forest Serv, 62; res assoc remote sensing, Purdue Univ, assoc prof, 68-75, prof forestry, 75-88, leader, Ecosyts Res Prog, Lab Appln Remote Sensing, 66-88. *Concurrent Pos:* NASA grant, 66-72; consult, AID, 71 & 76-77, US Geol Surv & US Army C Engr, 73, UN, 75 & NASA, 78 & 80; prin investr, Landsat, 72-76 & Skylab, 73-75; assoc ed, Photogram Eng & Remote Sensing, 74-75; prin investr, Spaceborne Imaging RADAR-B, 82-90. *Mem:* Soc Am Foresters; Am Soc Photogram (vpres, 87-89, pres, 89-90); Sigma Xi. *Res:* Interpretation of remote sensor imagery and color infrared photography; spectral characteristics of vegetation, soil, and water; development and evaluation of computer-aided analysis techniques for mapping earth surface features using satellite data; author of over 250 scientific publications. *Mailing Add:* Dept Forest Sci Colo State Univ Ft Collins CO 80523. *E-Mail:* roger@cnr.colostate.edu

HOFFER, THOMAS EDWARD, PHYSICAL METEOROLOGY. *Current Pos:* assoc res prof, 64-71, res prof atmospheric physics & prof physics, 71-92, EMER RES PROF, UNIV NEV, RENO, 92- *Personal Data:* b Salt Lake City, Utah, Aug 1, 27; m 76; c 2. *Educ:* Univ Utah, BS, 50, MS, 52; Univ Chicago, PhD(meteorol), 61. *Prof Exp:* Lectr meteorol, Univ NMex, 51-52 & Univ Utah, 52-56; res assoc, Univ Chicago, 56-61; sr res scientist, Lockheed-Calif Co, 61-64. *Mem:* Sigma Xi; Am Meteorol Soc; AAAS; NY Acad Sci; Air Pollution Control Asn. *Res:* Study of aerosols in pollution and nucleation; air pollution monitoring and research; aircraft sampling and analysis of particulates gases and wind field; visibility research and laser tranmissometer development. *Mailing Add:* 5570 Scarsdale Circle Reno NV 89502

HOFFERTH, BURT FREDERICK, RESEARCH ADMINISTRATION. *Current Pos:* RETIRED. *Personal Data:* b Kouts, Ind, Nov 6, 22; m 43, Madalyn Heiniger; c Sandra, Susan, Burt, Sally & Stephanie. *Educ:* Purdue Univ, BSCHE, 43, Iowa State Univ, PhD(chem), 50. *Prof Exp:* Chem engr fatty acids & derivatives, Armour & Co, 43-45; instr org chem, Iowa State Univ, 46-50; mgr, Armstrong World Indust, Inc, 61-68, gen mgr, 68-80, sr res assoc, 81-86. *Mem:* Am Chem Soc. *Res:* Fatty chemicals; organometallic chemistry; protective coatings; polymer processing. *Mailing Add:* 125 White Oak Dr Lancaster PA 17601

HOFFLEIT, ELLEN DORRIT, ASTRONOMY. *Current Pos:* res assoc, 56-69, SR RES ASTRONR, OBSERV, YALE UNIV, 69- *Personal Data:* b Florence, Ala, Mar 12, 07. *Educ:* Radcliffe Col, AB, 28, MA, 32, PhD(astron), 38. *Hon Degrees:* DSc, Smith Col, 84. *Honors & Awards:* George van Biesbroeck Award, 88; Annenberg Award, 93. *Prof Exp:* Asst, Observ, Harvard Univ, 29-38, res assoc, 38-43; mathematician, Ballistic Res Lab, Aberdeen Proving Ground, MD, 43-48; astronr, Observ, Harvard Univ, 48-56; dir, Maria Mitchell Observ, Mass, 57-78. *Concurrent Pos:* Lectr, Wellesley Col, 55-56; tech expert, Ballistic Res Lab, Aberdeen Proving Ground, 48-61; astronr adjoint, Astron Observ, Pasteur Inst, Strasbourg, France, 76. *Mem:* AAAS; Meteoretical Soc; Am Asn Variable Observers (vpres, 58-60, pres, 61-63); Int Astron Union; Am Astron Soc; Am Geophys Union. *Res:* Variable stars; stellar spectra; proper motions; meteors; galactic structure; bright stars; updating star catalogues; 19th-20th century topics in the history of astronomy. *Mailing Add:* Dept Astron Yale Univ Box 208101 New Haven CT 06520-8101

HOFFMAN, ALAN BRUCE, PHYSICAL INORGANIC CHEMISTRY. *Current Pos:* assoc prof, 71-90, PROF CHEM, LEWIS & CLARK COMMUNITY COL, 90- *Personal Data:* b Canton, Ill, Sept 22, 41; m 64; c 4. *Educ:* Univ Ill, BS, 63; Stanford Univ, PhD(inorg chem), 67. *Prof Exp:* NIH res fel crystallog, Cornell Univ, 67-69; sr res chemist phys chem, Monsanto Co, St Louis, 69-71. *Concurrent Pos:* Lectr, Southern Ill Univ, Edwardsville, Ill, 70- *Mem:* Sigma Xi; Am Chem Soc. *Res:* Kinetics and mechanism of reactions of complex ions; structures and reaction mechanisms of complex ions involved in oxygen-carrying and similar phenomena. *Mailing Add:* Dept Chem Lewis & Clark Community Col 5800 Godfrey Rd Godfrey IL 62035-2426

HOFFMAN, ALAN JEROME, MATHEMATICS. *Current Pos:* RES STAFF MEM, IBM RES CTR, 61-, FEL, 78- *Personal Data:* b New York, NY, May 30, 24; m 47, 90; c 2. *Educ:* Columbia Univ, AB, 47, PhD, 50. *Hon Degrees:* DSc, Technion, 86. *Honors & Awards:* Von Neumann Prize, Opers Res Soc & Inst Mgt Sci, 92. *Prof Exp:* Lectr & instr math, Columbia Univ, 46-50; mem, Inst Adv Study, 50-51; mathematician, Nat Bur Stand, 51-56; sci liaison officer, Off Naval Res, London, 56-57; consult, Gen Elec Co, 57-61. *Concurrent Pos:* Adj prof, City Univ New York, 65-76, Yale Univ, 76-80 & Stanford, Univ, 80-90; vis prof, Rutgers Univ, 90-; prof, Ga Tech Univ, 91-93. *Mem:* Nat Acad Sci; Math Asn Am; fel Am Acad Arts & Sci; fel NY Acad Sci; Am Math Soc; Soc Indust & Appl Math. *Res:* Combinatorial mathematics; graph theory; experimental designs; linear inequalities and programming; estimation of eigen values. *Mailing Add:* IBM Res Ctr PO Box 218 Yorktown Heights NY 10598

HOFFMAN, ALBERT CHARLES, GENETICS, BIOLOGY. *Current Pos:* From asst prof to assoc prof, Millersville Univ, 70-77, prof biol genetics, 77-81, actg dean, 81-82, DEAN, SCH SCI & MATH, MILLERSVILLE UNIV, 82- *Personal Data:* b Northumberland, Pa, July 8, 38; m 66; c 2. *Educ:* Bloomsburg State Col, BSEd, 64; NC State Univ, MS, 68, PhD(genetics), 70. *Mem:* Coun Cols Arts & Sci. *Res:* Use of insects as assay organisms to determine mutagenic effectiveness of chemical agents; repair of induced genetic damage in insect oocytes. *Mailing Add:* Dean Sci Millersville Univ Millersville PA 17551

HOFFMAN, ALEXANDER A J, THEORETICAL PHYSICS, SOLAR ENERGY. *Current Pos:* INDEPENDENT PRACT, 81- *Personal Data:* b Suffern, NY, Dec 3, 31; m 56; c 3. *Educ:* Univ Tex, Austin, BA, 55, MA, 57, PhD(physics), 62. *Prof Exp:* Teaching asst math, Univ Tex, Austin, 56-58, spec instr, 58-60, res physicist, Defense Res Labs, 60-62; from asst prof to prof math & physics, 62-81, Tex Christian Univ, dir comput sci prog, 73-81. *Mem:* Geoscience Electronics Soc (pres, 78); AAAS; Asn Comput Mach; Inst Elec & Electronics Engrs; Sigma Xi. *Res:* Insulation and climatology; solar energy; computer based mathematical models. *Mailing Add:* 4201 Hildring Dr E Ft Worth TX 76109

HOFFMAN, ALLAN JORDAN, PHARMACEUTICAL CHEMISTRY, BIOCHEMISTRY. *Current Pos:* RADIATION PHYSICIST I, DEPT ENVIRON PROTECTION, NJ STATE, 84- *Personal Data:* b Hicksville, NY, June 27, 25; m 52; c 2. *Educ:* Columbia Univ, BS, 49; Rutgers Univ, PhD(pharmaceut chem), 69. *Prof Exp:* Supvr anal chem, Carter-Wallace Inc, 54-59; anal res supvr, White Labs, Inc, Div Schering Corp, 59-66; sr scientist, Am Cyanamid Co, 66-70; head bioanal res, Hoechst-Roussel Pharmaceut Inc, Div Am Hoechst Corp, 70-81. *Mem:* AAAS; Am Chem Soc; Acad Pharmaceut Sci. *Res:* Analysis of drugs in biological matrices; pharmaceutical analysis; drug-sensitized photodynamic oxidation; analytical instrumentation; analysis and stability studies of drug formulations; thorium, uranium, radium studies on drinking water. *Mailing Add:* 223 S Fourth Ave Highland Park NJ 08904-2628

HOFFMAN, ALLAN RICHARD, SOLID STATE PHYSICS. *Current Pos:* EXEC DIR, COMT SCI, ENG & PUB POLICY, NAT ACAD SCI, 82- *Personal Data:* b New York, NY, May 31, 37; m 59; c 2. *Educ:* Cornell Univ, BEP, 59; Univ Ill, Urbana, MS, 61; Brown Univ, PhD(physics), 67. *Prof Exp:* Res physicist, Tex Instruments, Inc, 61-63; res assoc physics, Brown Univ, 66-68; asst prof, Univ Mass, Amherst, 68-75; staff scientist, US Senate Comt on Com, Sci & Transp, 75-78; dir, Advan Engery Systs Policy Div, US Dept Energy, 78-79; asst dir, Indust Prog, Energy Prod Ctr/Mellon Inst, 79-81. *Concurrent Pos:* Cong fel, Am Phys Soc, 74-75. *Mem:* AAAS; Fedn Am Sci; Am Phys Soc. *Res:* Low temperature thermometry; radiation detection; transport properties of metals; ultrasonic studies in metals; solar energy; energy conservation. *Mailing Add:* 1621 Apricot Ct Reston VA 22090

HOFFMAN, ALLAN SACHS, BIOENGINEERING, BIOMATERIALS. *Current Pos:* asst dir, Ctr Bioeng, 72-83, PROF CHEM ENG & BIOENG, UNIV WASH, 70- *Personal Data:* b Chicago, Ill, Oct 27, 32; m 62; c David & Lisa. *Educ:* Mass Inst Technol, SB, 53, SM, 55, ScD, 57. *Honors & Awards:* Clemson Award, 84; Biomat Sci Prize, Japanese Soc Biomat, 90. *Prof Exp:* Asst dir, Oak Ridge Eng Pract Sch, Mass Inst Technol, 54-55; instr chem eng, 55-56, asst prof, 58-60; res staff mem, Calif Res Corp, 60-63; assoc dir res, Amicon Corp, 63-65; assoc prof chem eng, Mass Inst Technol, 65-70. *Concurrent Pos:* Kimberly-Clark fel, 56-57; Fulbright fel, 57-58 & Battelle fel, 70-72. *Mem:* Am Chem Soc; Am Inst Chem Engrs; Am Soc Artificial Internal Organs; Soc Biomat (pres, 83-84); Int Soc Artificial Organs; Controlled Release Soc. *Res:* Materials science of surfaces, polymers and biomaterials; applied radiation and plasma chemistry; immobilized biomolecules. *Mailing Add:* Ctr Bioeng Univ Wash Box 352255 Seattle WA 98195

HOFFMAN, ALLEN HERBERT, BIOMECHANICS. *Current Pos:* From asst prof to assoc prof, 70-83, PROF MECH ENG, WORCESTER POLYTECH INST, 83- *Personal Data:* b Salem, Mass, Mar 23, 42; m 68, Carol A Snyder; c Kimberly C & Rebecca A. *Educ:* Worcester Polytech Inst, BS, 63, MS, 67; Univ Colo, PhD(mech eng), 70. *Honors & Awards:* Elizabeth W Lanir Award, Am Acad Orthop Surgeons, 88. *Concurrent Pos:* Assoc prof, Univ Mass Med Sch, 78- *Mem:* Am Soc Mech Engrs; Am Soc Eng Educ; Sigma Xi; Rehab Eng Soc NAm. *Res:* Constitutive equations to describe soft biological tissue; rehabilitation engineering. *Mailing Add:* Mech Eng Dept Worcester Polytech Inst 100 Inst Rd Worcester MA 01609-2280. *Fax:* 508-831-5680; *E-Mail:* ahoffman@wpi.wpi.edu

HOFFMAN, ARLENE FAUN, VASCULAR EVALUATION. *Current Pos:* assoc prof, Basic Sci Dept, Calif Col Podiatric Med, 67-69, dir basic sci, 68-75, assoc dean, Curric Affairs, 72-75, from asst prof to assoc prof, Dept Podiatric Med, 78-85, PROF BASIC SCI, CALIF COL PODIATRIC MED, 69-, PROF PODIATRIC MED, 85-, PVT PRACT, 78- *Personal Data:* b New York, NY, Nov 23, 41. *Educ:* Queens Col, BS, 62; State Univ NY Downstate Med Ctr, PhD(physiol), 67; Calif Col Podiatric Med, DPM, 76. *Prof Exp:* Bact technician, Maimonides Hosp, 61; high sch teacher biol, New York City Bd Educ, 62; teaching asst physiol, State Univ NY Downstate Med Ctr, 63-66; USPHS fel immunophysiol, Depts Med & Physiol, Sch Med, Stanford Univ, 66-67. *Concurrent Pos:* Instr biol & physiol, City Univ New York, 64-66; mem, Nat Bd Podiatry Examrs, 69-; spec ed basic sci in med, J Am Podiatry Asn, 72-; eval consult, Mt Zion Hosp, 74-75; mem rev comt spec proj grants, Bur Health Manpower, 75-77; resident surg, Jewish Mem Hosp, NY, 76-77; mem rev comt, Nat Heart & Lung Inst instnl res fel grant appln, 76-77; mem, Dept Health, Educ & Welfare, Women's Action Prog Task Force Comt; mem rev comt biomed res develop grants, NIH, 77-78; assoc, Med Ctr Podiatry Group, Augusta, Ga, 77-78; pvt pract, 78; gen ed, J Am Podiatric Med Asn, 80-; chief, Vascular Clin, 84-; chair, Exam Comt, Primary Podiatric Med Sect, Am Bd Podiatric Orthop & Primary Podiatric Med, 92-93; trustee, Am Bd Podiatric Orthop & Primary Podiatric Med, 93-, Am Soc Podiatric Med, Am Soc Podiatric Dermat. *Mem:* Am Podiatric Med Asn; Asn Women in Sci; Am Asn Women Podiatrists (pres, 82-84); Nat Acad Pract; fel Am Soc Podiatric Med; fel Am Soc Podiatric Dermat; fel Am Soc Ambulatory Surg; fel Nat Acad Pract. *Res:* Podiatric medicine; medical curriculum development, implementation and evaluation with special emphasis upon developing curricula compatible with health delivery systems; evaluation of blood flow in the lower extremities; utilization of physiological principles in the treatment of podiatric problems. *Mailing Add:* 2100 Webster St Stuite 202 San Francisco CA 94115

HOFFMAN, BRIAN MARK, BIOINORGANIC CHEMISTRY. *Current Pos:* from asst prof to assoc prof chem, 67-74, prof chem & biochem, 74-80, PROF CHEM, BIOCHEM, MOLECULAR & CELL BIOL, NORTHWESTERN UNIV, 80- *Personal Data:* b Chicago, Ill, Aug 7, 41; m 80. *Educ:* Univ Chicago, BS, 62; Calif Inst Technol, PhD(chem), 66. *Honors & Awards:* FMC lectr, Princeton Univ, 88. *Prof Exp:* Air Force Off Spec Res, Nat Acad Sci-Nat Res Coun res fel biol, Mass Inst Technol, 66-67. *Concurrent Pos:* Alfred P Sloan Found fel, 71-73; career develop award, NIH, 71-73; F Leon Watkins vis prof, Wichita State Univ, 81; US/USSR acad seminar on catalysis, 85; metals in biol, Gordon Res Conf, 87. *Mem:* Fel AAAS; Am Chem Soc; Am Soc Biol Chemists; Biophys Soc. *Res:* Electron paramagnetic resonance and electron-nuclear double resonance of metalloenzymes; long-range electron transfer within protein complexes; magnetism and metallic conductivity in molecular crystals. *Mailing Add:* 733 Milburn Evanston IL 60201-2408

HOFFMAN, CHARLES JOHN, PHYSICAL INORGANIC CHEMISTRY. *Current Pos:* RETIRED. *Personal Data:* b Cleveland, Ohio, July 9, 18; m 55; c 1. *Educ:* Case Inst Technol, BSc, 42, MS, 48; Univ Ill, PhD(chem), 51. *Prof Exp:* Res org chem, Diamond Alkali Co, 42-43; asst chem, Case Inst Technol, 47; phys chemist, Univ Ill, 48-50; cryogenist & mem staff, Los Alamos Nat Lab, 51-53; phys chemist, Merrill Co Div, Arthur D Little, Inc, 53-55; chemist, Lawrence Radiation Lab, Calif, 55-58; staff scientist, Lockheed Missiles & Space Co, 58-78; consult, 78. *Res:* Inorganic-physical rocket propulsion chemistry. *Mailing Add:* 1665 Edmonton Ave Sunnyvale CA 94087

HOFFMAN, CLARK SAMUEL, JR, ENVIRONMENTAL SCIENCES, ANALYTICAL CHEMISTRY. *Current Pos:* Res chemist, E I Du Pont de Nemours & Co, Inc, 66-73, res supvr, 73-75, environ mgr, 75-77, mfg mgr, 78-81, EMPLOYEE REINS MGR, E I DU PONT DE NEMOURS & CO, INC, 81- *Personal Data:* b Hershey, Pa, Nov 26, 38; div; c 2. *Educ:* Lebanon Valley Col, BS, 60; Mont State Univ, MS, 64, PhD(chem), 67. *Mem:* Am Chem Soc. *Res:* Vehicle emission research; air pollution; polycyclic aromatic hydrocarbons; halocarbon and fluorocarbon analyses; water conservation; pilot plant in-line instrumentation; gas, liquid, thin-layer and paper chromatography; moisture and aerosol propellant analyses. *Mailing Add:* 810 Painters Crossing Chadds Ford PA 19317

HOFFMAN, CYRUS MILLER, PARTICLE PHYSICS. *Current Pos:* staff mem, 74-84, assoc group leader, 84-93, PROG MGR, LOS ALAMOS NAT LAB, 93- *Personal Data:* b New York, NY, Feb 20, 42; m 63, Jane Granich; c 4. *Educ:* Brown Univ, ScB, 62; Harvard Univ, MA, 64, PhD(physics), 69. *Prof Exp:* Res asst physics, Princeton Univ, 69, from instr to asst prof, 69-74. *Mem:* Fel Am Phys Soc; Am Astron Soc; Sigma Xi. *Res:* Quantum electrodynamics, including muon inelastic scattering and properties of vector mesons; weak interactions including CP violation, hyperon beta decay and rare pion and muon decays; high energy gamma ray astronomy. *Mailing Add:* 660 Totavi St Los Alamos NM 87544-2644. *Fax:* 505-665-1712; *E-Mail:* cy@lanl.gov

HOFFMAN, DALE A, LIMNOLOGY. *Current Pos:* WATER QUAL SPECIALIST, BUR LAND MGT, 73- *Personal Data:* b Denver, Colo, Feb 25, 30; m 58; c 1. *Educ:* Colo State Univ, BS, 52, MS, 56, PhD(limnol), 62. *Prof Exp:* Aquatic biologist, US Fed Water Pollution Control Admin, 61-65; res scientist, US Bur Reclamation, 65-73. *Concurrent Pos:* Affiliate fac mem, Grad Sch, Colo State Univ, 70- *Mem:* Ecol Soc Am; Am Soc Limnol & Oceanog; Am Fisheries Soc; Sigma Xi. *Res:* Water quality and changes; regimen in reservoir; bottom fauna reactions to water quality changes. *Mailing Add:* 11514 Silver Fox Lane Conifer CO 80433

HOFFMAN, DANIEL LEWIS, MARINE INVERTEBRATE ZOOLOGY. *Current Pos:* asst prof, 70-77, ASSOC PROF BIOL, BUCKNELL UNIV, 77- *Personal Data:* b La Salle, Ill, June 23, 38; m 80; c 3. *Educ:* Univ Calif, Berkeley, BA, 61, MA, 63; Univ Wash, PhD(zool), 68. *Prof Exp:* NIH fel zool, Northwestern Univ, 68-69; instr biol sci, 69-70. *Concurrent Pos:* Vis scholar, Scripps Inst Oceanog, 83-84. *Mem:* Am Soc Zoologists; Crustacean Soc. *Res:* Life history strategies of benthic marine invertebrates; predatory-prey interactions among benthic invertebrates; settlement, recruitment and growth of pedunculate barnacles. *Mailing Add:* Dept Biol Bucknell Univ Lewisburg PA 17837-2005

HOFFMAN, DARLEANE CHRISTIAN, NUCLEAR CHEMISTRY, RADIOCHEMISTRY. *Current Pos:* prof chem, 84-91, emer prof, 91-93, PROF GRAD SCH, UNIV CALIF, BERKELEY, 93-, FAC SR SCIENTIST & GROUP LEADER, HEAVY ELEMENT NUCLEAR RADIOCHEM, NUCLEAR SCI DIV, LAWRENCE BERKELEY LAB, 84- *Personal Data:* b Terril, Iowa, Nov 8, 26; m 51, Marvin; c Maureane & Daryl. *Educ:* Iowa State Col, BS, 48, PhD(phys chem), 51. *Honors & Awards:* John Dustin Clark Award, Am Chem Soc, 76, Award for Nuclear Chem, 83, Garvan Medal, 90; Nat Medal of Sci, 97. *Prof Exp:* Asst, Ames Lab, AEC, 47-51; chemist, Oak Ridge Nat Lab, 51-52; chemist, Los Alamos Nat lab, 52-71, assoc group leader, 71-78, div leader, Chem-Nuclear Chem Div, 79-81, leader, Isotope Nuclear Chem Div, 81-84; dir, Seaborg Inst Transactinium Sci, Lawrence Livermore Nat Lab, 91-96. *Concurrent Pos:* Sr NSF fel, Oslo, Norway, 64-65; pres, NMex Inst Chemists, 76-78; Guggenheim fel mechanisms nuclear fission, Lawrence Berkeley Lab, Univ Calif, 78-79; chmn, Subcomt Nuclear & Radiochem, 82-84; dirs fel, Los Alamos Nat Lab, 90; ACS Div Nuclear Chem Tech Chmn, 78-79, Comt Sci, 86-88, exec comt, 87-90; Int Union Pur & Appl Chem, 83-87, secy, 85-87, chmn, 87-91, assoc mem, 91-93; NAS-NRC Bd Radioactive Waste Mgt, 94- *Mem:* Fel Am Inst Chem; Am Chem Soc; fel Am Phys Soc; fel AAAS. *Res:* Low energy and spontaneous fission; radionuclide migration in the environment; nuclear waste management; production mechanisms for heavy element isotopes; chemical and nuclear properties of heaviest elements. *Mailing Add:* Nuclear Sci Div 70A-3307 Lawrence Berkeley Nat Lab Berkeley CA 94720. *Fax:* 510-486-6707; *E-Mail:* hoffman@lbl.gov

HOFFMAN, DAVID ALLEN, GEOMETRY, COMPUTATION. *Current Pos:* from asst prof to prof math, 74-94, HEAD, SCI GRAPHICS PROJ MSRI, UNIV MASS, AMHERST, 94- *Personal Data:* b Far Rockaway, NY, July 21, 44; m 74, Joan Sarnat; c Michael & Jascha. *Educ:* Univ Rochester, AB, 66; Stanford Univ, MS, 69, PhD(math), 72. *Honors & Awards:* Chauvenet Prize, Math Asn Am, 90. *Prof Exp:* Lectr math, Univ Durham, 72; asst prof, Univ Mich, 72-73; prof, Univ Paris VII, 89; vis prof, Stanford, 95. *Concurrent Pos:* Co-prin investr, NSF Res Grants Geometry & Anal, 73-78 & 80-85, prin investr, 85-; vis prof, Stanford Univ, 78, Inst Pure & Appl Math, Rio de Janeiro, 81, Univ Paris VII, 89 & Ecole Technique, 90; Danforth fel; prin investr, US Dept Energy, 86- *Mem:* Am Math Soc; Math Asn Am; Inst Elec & Electronics Engrs; Asn Comput Mach. *Res:* Geometry of immersed submanifolds, including problems concerning minimal surfaces, variational inequalities, isoperimetric inequalities in Riemannian geometry; computational methods in mathematical research; computer graphics; microstructure of compound polymers. *Mailing Add:* MSRI 1000 Centennial Dr Berkeley CA 94720. *E-Mail:* david@msri.org

HOFFMAN, DAVID J, DEVELOPMENTAL PHYSIOLOGY, BIOCHEMISTRY. *Current Pos:* SR STAFF PHYSIOLOGIST, ENVIRON PHYSIOL & TOXICOL, PATUXENT RES CTR, US DEPT INTERIOR, 76- *Personal Data:* b New London, Conn, Sept 22, 44; m 66, Suzanne E O'Clair; c Michael D & James S. *Educ:* McGill Univ, BS, 66; Univ Md, PhD(develop biol), 71. *Honors & Awards:* Achievement Award, US Dept Interior, 90, 96. *Prof Exp:* Instr biol, Univ Nebr, Lincoln, 66-67; instr embryol & genetics, Univ Md, College Park, 67-70; NIH fel biochem, Oak Ridge Nat Lab, Tenn, 71-73; mem fac biol, Boston Col, 73-74; sr staff physiologist, Toxicol Div, Health Effects Lab, Environ Protection Agency, Cincinnati, Ohio, 74-76. *Concurrent Pos:* Adj prof, Univ Md. *Mem:* AAAS; Soc Environ Toxicol & Chem; Teratology Soc; Toxicol Soc; Soc Exp Biol & Med; Wildlife Soc. *Res:* Developmental physiology, teratology and environmental health, nucleic acid regulation, oxidant stress, avian and wildlife toxicology; glutathione metabolism, environmental contaminants, selenium, mercury, lead, polycyclic aromatic hydrocarbons and polychlorinated biphenyls. *Mailing Add:* Patuxent Res Ctr US Dept Interior Laurel MD 20708. *Fax:* 301-497-5675

HOFFMAN, DENNIS MARK, POLYMER CRYSTALLIZATION, POLYMER CHARACTERIZATION. *Current Pos:* RES SCIENTIST, LAWRENCE LIVERMORE NAT LAB, 79- *Personal Data:* b Huntingdon, Pa, July 22, 47; m 81; c Michael & Andrew. *Educ:* Juniata Col, Huntingdon, Pa, BS, 69; Univ Mass, Amherst, PhD(polymer sci), 79. *Mem:* Am Chem Soc; Am Phys Soc; AAAS; Soc Plastics Engrs. *Res:* Polymer blends, morphology, crystallization, solution properties, cure kinetics; thermal analysis, mechanical and rheological properties, electron and optical microscopy and molecular weight measurements; polymer explosives, polyolefins, epoxy prepregs and foams. *Mailing Add:* Lawrence Livermore Nat Lab L-282 Livermore CA 94550. *E-Mail:* hoffman2@llnl.gov

HOFFMAN, DONALD BERTRAND, OTHER MEDICAL & HEALTH SCIENCES. *Current Pos:* ASST PROF FORENSIC MED, MED CTR, NY UNIV, 77- *Personal Data:* b New York, NY, May 3, 39. *Educ:* NY Univ, BA, 59; Columbia Univ, MA, 60, PhD(chem), 67; Am Bd Forensic Toxicol, dipl, 88. *Prof Exp:* Res assoc biochem, Jewish Chronic Dis Hosp, NY, 67-68; NIMH training fel psychopharmacol, Dept Psychiat, Med Ctr, NY Univ, 68-69; sr chemist toxicol, Dept Toxicol, Off Chief Med Examr, NY, 69-87, res scientist, Dept Toxicol, 87-96. *Concurrent Pos:* Sr res scientist forensic med, Med Ctr, NY Univ, 73-76; expert testimony in court; guest lectr med, legal, law enforcement & forensic groups; adj asst prof, Dept Forensic Sci, John Jay Col Criminal Justice, 76-84; consult forensic toxicol. *Mem:* Am Acad Forensic Sci; NY Acad Sci; Int Asn Forensic Toxicol; Soc Med Jurisp; Sigma Xi. *Res:* Methodology of forensic chemistry; new techniques for isolation of drugs from tissues and biological fluids; mass urine screening procedures for detection of drugs of abuse; forensic toxicology. *Mailing Add:* 1939 Grand Concourse No 2F NY NY 10453

HOFFMAN, DONALD D, MACHINE & HUMAN VISION. *Current Pos:* from asst prof to assoc prof, 83-90, PROF COGNITIVE SCI, UNIV CALIF, IRVINE, 90- *Personal Data:* b San Antonio, Tex, 1955; m 86, Geralyn M Souza; c Melissa L. *Educ:* Univ Calif, Los Angeles, BA, 78; Mass Inst Technol, PhD(comput psychol), 83. *Honors & Awards:* Distinguished Scientific Award, Am Psychol Asn, 89. *Prof Exp:* Mem tech staff, Hughes Aircraft Co, 78-83; res scientist, Lab Artificial Intel, Mass Inst Technol, 83. *Concurrent Pos:* Troland res award, Nat Acad Sci, 94; vis prof, Zentrum fur interdisziplinare Forschung, Bielefeld, Ger, 95-96. *Res:* How we construct what we see, for instance, how human vision constructs the three-dimensional structure of the world from two-dimensional images, and how it recognizes objects. *Mailing Add:* Dept Cognitive Sci Univ Calif Irvine CA 92717. *Fax:* 714-725-2307; *E-Mail:* dhoffman@orion.oac.uci.edu

HOFFMAN, DONALD OLIVER, INDUSTRIAL CHEMISTRY. *Current Pos:* RETIRED. *Personal Data:* b Mt Pleasant, Iowa, June 14, 16; m 44, Gertrude Cheney; c 3. *Educ:* Northwestern Univ, BS, 37; Univ Minn, MS, 41; Ohio State Univ, PhD(org chem), 48. *Prof Exp:* Chemist, Columbia Chem Div, Pittsburgh Plate Glass Co, Ohio, 37-39; asst chem, Univ Minn, 41-43; res assoc, Nat Defense Res Comt Proj, Columbia Univ, 43-44; res assoc, Ohio State Univ, 44-46, asst instr org chem, 47-48, asst prof, 48-49; from biochemist to head dept biochem, US Naval Med Res Unit No 3, Egypt, 49-53; sr res chemist, Am Optical Corp, 54-65, mgr mat res, 66-68, chief surface res, 69-76. *Res:* Chromatography of sugars and related compounds; molluscicides for control of snail intermediate hosts of bilharziasis; infrared absorbing plastics; mechanism of glass polishing; surface chemistry. *Mailing Add:* 7 Ridgeview Rd Sturbridge MA 01566-1145. *E-Mail:* dhoffman@hey.net

HOFFMAN, DONALD RICHARD, IMMUNOLOGY. *Current Pos:* assoc prof path & lab med, 77-82, PROF PATH, SCH MED, ECAROLINA UNIV, 82- *Personal Data:* b Boston, Mass, Aug 25, 43; m 71, Valeria Mossey; c Anthony, Maria & Avram. *Educ:* Harvard Col, AB, 65; Calif Inst Technol, PhD(chem), 70. *Prof Exp:* Cancer res scientist immunol, Roswell Park Mem Inst, NY State Health Dept, 70-71; asst prof pediat, Sch Med, Univ Southern Calif, 71-75; assoc prof path, Sch Med, Creighton Univ, 75-77. *Concurrent Pos:* Consult, Allermed Labs Inc, 73-80, Pharmacia Labs Inc, 74-86, Allergenic Prod Adv, US Food & Drug Admin, 90- *Mem:* Am Asn Immunologists; Am Acad Allergy & Immunol; Sigma Xi; NY Acad Sci; Clin Immunol Soc. *Res:* Human immunoglobulin E antibodies and allergy; allergens; antibody sites and structure; immunopathology; autoimmune diseases; immune response in children; insect venoms. *Mailing Add:* Dept Path ECarolina Univ Sch Med Greenville NC 27858-4354. *Fax:* 919-816-3336; *E-Mail:* mdhoffman@eastnet.edu.ecu.edu

HOFFMAN, DOROTHEA HEYL, ORGANIC CHEMISTRY. *Current Pos:* RETIRED. *Personal Data:* b Easton, Pa, May 30, 19; m 46; c 2. *Educ:* Bryn Mawr Col, BA, 39, MA, 40, PhD(org chem), 42. *Honors & Awards:* James Bryant Conant Award, High Sch Chem Teaching, Am Chem Soc, 76. *Prof Exp:* Demonstr chem, Bryn Mawr Col, 39-40; res chemist, Merck & Co, 42-52; teacher, Westfield High Sch, 65-84. *Concurrent Pos:* Chem consult, 63-65; sci writing, 52- *Mem:* AAAS; Am Chem Soc. *Res:* Substituted malonic esters and barbituric acids; biotin; vitamin B6 group; codecarboxylase; vitamin B12. *Mailing Add:* Four Cowperthwaite Sq Westfield NJ 07090-4048

HOFFMAN, DOUGLAS WEIR, AGRICULTURE, EARTH SCIENCE. *Current Pos:* ADJ PROF, PLANNING & RESOURCE MGT, UNIV WATERLOO, 85-; ADJ PROF, YORK UNIV, 85- *Personal Data:* b Toronto, Ont, Feb 16, 20; m 44, Frances Noxon; c Barbara, Michael, James & Susan. *Educ:* Univ Toronto, BSA, 46, MSA, 49; Univ Waterloo, PhD(planning), 73. *Prof Exp:* Soils specialist taxon, Ont Dept Agr, 46-48; pedologist soil taxon, Can Agr Soil Res Inst, 48-62; from assoc prof to prof soil surv & land use, Univ Guelph, 62-78, dir resource develop, 73-78; dir planning & resource mgt, Sch

Urban Planning, Univ Waterloo, 78-84, prof planning & resource mgt, 85-88. *Concurrent Pos:* Mem, Can Soil Survey Comt, 55-73, Grand River Conserv Authority, 70-74, Peatlands Study Comt Nat Forest Lands, 71-75 & Land Use Comt, Soil Conserv Soc Am, 74-76; dir, Ecoplans Ltd, 76-; pres, Asn Urban & Regional Planning Progs Can Univs, 82-85; adj prof, York Univ & Univ Guelph, 85- *Mem:* Agr Inst Can; Geol Asn Can; fel Can Soil Sci Soc; Int Soil Sci Soc; Can Asn Geol; Can Asn Geog; Sigma Xi; Can Inst Planners. *Res:* Soil classification, genesis and morphology and their relationship to land evaluation and rural planning. *Mailing Add:* 45 Winston Cres Guelph ON N1E 2K1 Can

HOFFMAN, DOYT K, JR, ELECTRO-CHEMISTRY. *Current Pos:* Res chemist, Lithium Corp Am, 67-79, chemist-group leader, 67-80, proj dir, 80-87, SR DEVELOP ENG, LITHIUM CORP AM, 88- *Personal Data:* b Gas; m 66; c 2. *Educ:* Wake Forest Univ, BS, 67. *Mem:* Am Chem Soc; Sigma Xi. *Res:* Improvement of extractive metallurgical plant processes connected with efficient and economical recovery of lithium values from spodumene ore; production of battery quality lithium metal, alloys and salts; development of new and improved battery separators. *Mailing Add:* 104 Windsong Ct Gastonia NC 28056-8816

HOFFMAN, EDWARD JACK, COAL & ENERGY CONVERSION, PETROLEUM PRODUCTION & RESERVOIR ENGINEERING. *Current Pos:* RETIRED. *Personal Data:* b Marion, Kans, June 10, 25; m 53; c 3. *Educ:* Okla State Univ, BS, 44; Univ Mich, MS, 50. *Prof Exp:* Refinery control, petrol refining, Continental Oil Co, 46-48; petrol prod res, Carter Oil Co, 48-49; process engr oil & gas equip, Black, Sivalls & Bryson, 51-52; instr chem eng, Okla State Univ, 52-54; asst prof, Univ Colo, 54-57; assoc prof, Univ Tulsa, 57-62; res engr, Heat Transfer Res Inc, 63-65; assoc prof & res engr coal conversion, Univ Wyo, 65-72; consult, King-Wilkinson, Inc, 77-84 & Gas Res Inst, 78-85. *Concurrent Pos:* Prin investr, FMC Corp, 56-57; vis prof, Cities Serv Co, 57, Phillips Petrol Co, 60-61 & Humble Oil Co, 62; consult fuels & energy, 72- *Res:* Coal and energy conversion; thermodynamic behavior of non-ideal systems; net energy analysis; distillation; energy concepts; heat transfer; coal gasifiers; petroleum production; synthetic fuels; process development; hazardous wastes. *Mailing Add:* PO Box 1352 Laramie WY 82070

HOFFMAN, ERIC ALFRED, CARDIAC MECHANICS, PULMONARY VENTILATION-PERFUSION & IMAGING. *Current Pos:* assoc prof, 92-96, CHIEF, DIV PHYSIOL IMAGING, DEPT RADIOL, UNIV IOWA, 92-, PROF RADIOL & BIOMED ENG, 96- *Personal Data:* b Rochester, Minn, May 9, 51; m 87, Deanna Johnson. *Educ:* Antioch Col, Ohio, BA, 74; Univ Minn, PhD(physiol), 81. *Prof Exp:* Res asst cardiopulmonary physiol, Cardiovasc Pulmonary Res Lab, Univ Colo, Denver, 74-75 & physiol, dept physiol & biophys, Colo State Univ, Ft Collins, 75; fel, Mayo Clin, 75-81, res fel, 81-82, sr res fel, 83-84, instr, 82-84, assoc consult & asst prof physiol, Biodynamics Res Unit, 84-87; from asst prof to assoc prof radiol sci & physiol, Univ Pa, 87-92, chief, Sect Cardiothoracic Imaging Res, Dept Radiol, 88-92. *Concurrent Pos:* John G Searle-Mayo scholar, 83-86; new investr, Heart, Lung & Blood Inst, NIH, 83-86; mem exec comt, Coun Cadiopulmonary Dis, Am Heart Asn, 87-, Coun Cardiac Radiol, 90-, estab investr, 87-91; study sect mem, NIH, 90-94. *Mem:* Am Physiol Soc; Sigma Xi; Am Heart Asn; Am Thoracic Soc; Radiologic Soc NAm; Biomed Eng Soc; NAm Soc Cardiac Imaging. *Res:* New imaging techniques associated with synchronous volumetric x-ray computed tomography and magnetic resonance; the intrathoracic determinants of cardiac and pulmonary geometry to function relationships; telemedicine applications. *Mailing Add:* Dept Radiol Univ Iowa Col Med 200 Hawkins Dr Iowa City IA 52242. *Fax:* 319-356-1503; *E-Mail:* eric@everest.radiology.uiowa.edu

HOFFMAN, EUGENE JAMES, cell biology, for more information see previous edition

HOFFMAN, EVERETT JOHN, PHYSICAL CHEMISTRY. *Current Pos:* RETIRED. *Personal Data:* b Spring Valley, Minn, Dec 31, 08; m 42, Caroline Prizer; c Laura A. *Educ:* Univ Minn, BChE, 31, PhD(phys chem), 35. *Prof Exp:* Asst chem, Univ Minn, 34-35; res chemist, Armour & Co, Ill, 35-46, chief librn, Chem Res & Develop Dept, 46-50; ed, Nuclear Sci Abstracts, Div Tech Info Exten, US Atomic Energy Comn & Environ Res & Develop Admin, 50-56, sci ed, 56-58, asst to chief, Cataloging Br, 58-61, sr sci asst staff officer to chief, Catalog Opers Sect, 61-66, chief, Chem Sect, Sci & Technol Br, 66-74, asst to chief, Sci & Technol Br, 74-77. *Mem:* Am Chem Soc. *Mailing Add:* 103 Nixon Rd Oak Ridge TN 37830-5224

HOFFMAN, FREDERICK, EXPERT SYSTEMS, COMBINATORICS & FINITE GROUPS. *Current Pos:* from asst prof to assoc prof, 68-77, PROF MATH, FLA ATLANTIC UNIV, 77- *Personal Data:* b Cleveland, Ohio, Nov 10, 37; m 68; c 4. *Educ:* Georgetown Univ, BS, 58; Univ Va, PhD(math), 63. *Prof Exp:* From instr asst prof math, Univ Ill, Urbana, 62-66; mathematician, Commun Res Div, Inst Defense Analysis, 66-67; asst prof math, Drexel Inst Technol, 67-68. *Concurrent Pos:* Vis assoc prof combinatorics & optimization, Univ Waterloo, 75; fac visitor, IBM, 82-83; mem bd dirs, Teletimer Int, 87- *Mem:* Am Asn Artificial Intel; Am Math Soc; Math Asn Am; Soc Indust & Appl Math; Inst Elec & Electronics Engrs; Asn Comput Mach; Inst Elec & Electronics Engrs Comput Soc; Sigma Xi; NY Acad Sci; fel Inst Combinatorics & Appln. *Res:* Development of expert systems for configuration and experimental design; interplay of combinatorics and algebra, especially finite groups and vector spaces. *Mailing Add:* Fla Atlantic Univ 500 NW 20th St Boca Raton FL 33431-6498

HOFFMAN, G(RAHAM) W(ALTER), ELECTRICAL ENGINEERING. *Current Pos:* assoc prof, 59-65, PROF ELEC ENG, UNIV TENN, KNOXVILLE, 65- *Personal Data:* b Detroit, Mich, Jan 10, 28; wid; c 4. *Educ:* Lafayette Col, BS, 50; Harvard Univ, SM, 51, PhD(elec eng), 55. *Prof Exp:* Scientist, Bettis Atomic Power Div, Westinghouse Elec Corp, 55-59. *Concurrent Pos:* Consult, Oak Ridge Nat Lab, 60-; vis prof, Univ Nottingham, 70-71. *Mem:* Am Phys Soc; Am Nuclear Soc; Am Soc Eng Educ; Inst Elec & Electronics Engrs. *Res:* Physical electronics; conduction in gases; nuclear reactor physics; electron optics; plasma. *Mailing Add:* Ferris Hall-2100 Univ Tenn Knoxville TN 37996

HOFFMAN, GEORGE R, PLANT ECOLOGY. *Current Pos:* from asst prof to assoc prof, 64-70, PROF BIOL, UNIV SDAK, 70-, CHMN DEPT BIOL, 78- *Personal Data:* b Hastings, Nebr, Feb 5, 35; m 60; c 2. *Educ:* Hastings Col, BA, 57; Wash State Univ, PhD(bot), 62. *Prof Exp:* Instr bot, Univ Denver, 62-64. *Concurrent Pos:* Res grant, 65-67; vis scientist, Oak Ridge Nat Lab, 67-68; res assoc, Ctr Study Natural Systs, Mo Bot Gardens, 68-69; res grants, Nat Air Pollution Control Admin, 68-71, US Dept Interior 71-73, US Forest Serv, 72-74, 76-81 & 81-, US Army C Engr, 73-82, NSF, 74-76 & 76-79 & Nat Park Serv, 78-80, 84-85 & 88- *Mem:* Soc Range Mgt; Torrey Bot Club; Ecol Soc Am; Am Bryol & Lichenological Soc; Brit Ecol Soc. *Res:* Autecologic investigations of bryophytes; ecology of epiphytic bryophytes and lichens and influence of air pollution on them; studies on revegetation of reservoir shorelines; habitat type studies in Rocky Mountains and grasslands of the Great Plains. *Mailing Add:* Dept Biol Univ Northern Iowa Cedar Falls IA 50614-0001

HOFFMAN, GERALD M, OPERATIONS RESEARCH. *Current Pos:* PRES, GERALD HOFFMAN CO, 85- *Personal Data:* b Chicago, Ill, Oct 31, 26; m 60, May Weber; c 2. *Educ:* Purdue Univ, BS, 46, MS, 49; Northwestern Univ, PhD, 78. *Prof Exp:* Res physicist, Motorola, Inc, 49-51; pres, Panoramic Builders, Inc, 51-65; mgr opers res, Standard Oil Co Ind, 68-79; exec vpres & gen mgr, Amoco Comput Serv, 79-84. *Concurrent Pos:* Pres, Gerald Hoffman Co, 84-95; pres, Sr Strategy Group, LLC, 95- *Mem:* Inst Mgt Sci (pres); Soc Mgt Info Systs (pres, secy); Opers Res Soc Am; fel AAAS; Sigma Xi. *Res:* Practical applications of operations research methodology; management of information systems. *Mailing Add:* 212 E Ontario St Chicago IL 60611

HOFFMAN, GLENN JERRALD, SALINITY MANAGEMENT IN AGRICULTURE, IRRIGATION & DRAINAGE MANAGEMENT. *Current Pos:* DEPT HEAD & PROF, UNIV NEBR, 89- *Personal Data:* b Delaware, Ohio, Oct 16, 39; m 70, Maria L Hunter; c Sheryl, Karen & Kimberly. *Educ:* Ohio State Univ, BAE & MS, 63; NC State Univ, PhD(agr eng), 67. *Prof Exp:* Res engr, Salinity Lab, Agr Res Serv, USDA, 66-83; lab dir, Water Mgt Res Lab, Agr Res Serv, USDA, 83-89. *Concurrent Pos:* Adj prof, Univ Calif, Riverside, 72-; ed, Soils & Water Div, Transactions, Am Soc Agr Engrs, 72-77; vis prof, Soils & Water Inst, Bet Dagan, Israel, 77- *Mem:* Am Soc Agr Engrs; Am Soc Agron; Int Soil Sci Soc; Soil Sci Soc Am; Am Soc Eng Educ. *Res:* International authority on the management and reclamation of salt-affected soils; influence of environmental factors on crop salt tolerance and plant growth; instrumentation for measuring plant response to salt and water stress. *Mailing Add:* 8110 Dundee Dr Lincoln NE 68510. *Fax:* 402-472-6338

HOFFMAN, GLENN LYLE, PARASITOLOGY. *Current Pos:* RETIRED. *Personal Data:* b Aurora, Iowa, Dec 28, 18; m 48; c 4. *Educ:* Univ Iowa, BA, 42, PhD(zool, parasitol), 50. *Honors & Awards:* Distinguished Serv Award, Wildlife Dis Asn, 74; Distinguished Serv Award, Fish Health Sect, Am Fish Soc, 82, Fish Culture Sect, 85. *Prof Exp:* Asst prof parasitol & bact, Med Sch, Univ NDak, 50-58; parasitologist, Eastern Fish Dis Lab, US Fish & Wildlife Serv, 58-74, res fish parasitologist, Fish Farming Exp Sta, 74-85. *Concurrent Pos:* Assoc ed, J Wildlife Dis, 70-71; adj prof, Memphis State Univ, 75-85; asst ed, Int J Fish Dis, 78-; bd rev, J Protozool, 80-82. *Mem:* Am Soc Parasitol; Am Fisheries Soc; Am Micros Soc; Soc Protozool; Wildlife Dis Asn; Sigma Xi; hon mem, Czechoslovakian Fishermens Guild, Ceske Budejovice; Europ Asn Fish Path; Am Fish Soc (pres, 84). *Res:* Parasites and diseases of freshwater fish, especially strigeoid trematodes; Myxosporida; ciliates. *Mailing Add:* Rte 3 Box 36 Kearneysville WV 25430

HOFFMAN, H(ERBERT) W(ILLIAM), CHEMICAL ENGINEERING. *Current Pos:* PROG MGR, PAI CORP, 88- *Personal Data:* b Baltimore, Md, Jan 20, 23; m 47, Myra L Jacobs; c Kari, Randy, Laury & Larry. *Educ:* Johns Hopkins Univ, BE, 43, DrEng, 51. *Prof Exp:* Res engr distillation, Res & Develop Div, Socony-Vacuum Oil Co, 43-44; res assoc gaseous separations, SAM Labs, Columbia Univ, 44; engr thermal separations, Fercleve Corp, 44-45; res assoc explosives, Los Alamos Sci Labs, Univ Calif, 45-46; res assoc heat transfer, Johns Hopkins Univ, 47-50; head, Dept Heat Transfer & Fluid Dynamics, Oak Ridge Nat Lab, 50-88. *Concurrent Pos:* Lectr, Univ Tenn, 64-88. *Mem:* AAAS; Am Nuclear Soc; Am Inst Chem Engrs; Sigma Xi. *Res:* Molten salts, liquid metals, as gases and energy system coolants; water nuclear reactor safety thermal hydraulics; desalination; geothermal and ocean thermal energy conversion; space power systems; nuclear waste management. *Mailing Add:* 116 Canterbury Rd Oak Ridge TN 37830

HOFFMAN, HAROLD A, GENETICS. *Current Pos:* GENETICIST, NAT CANCER INST, 63- *Personal Data:* b Grand Rapids, Mich, Mar 21, 30; m 55; c 2. *Educ:* Univ Calif, BS, 57, MA, 60, PhD(genetics), 62. *Prof Exp:* Geneticist, Div Res Serv, NIH, 61-63. *Concurrent Pos:* Lectr, George Washington Univ, 62, Am Univ, 66 & Univ Calif, Berkeley, 69; assoc ed, J Nat Cancer Inst, 74- *Mem:* AAAS; Am Genetic Asn; Am Soc Human Genetics. *Res:* Biochemical genetics; genetic control of protein poly-morphism and regulatory mechanisms. *Mailing Add:* 11519 College View Dr Silver Spring MD 20902

HOFFMAN, HEINER, ORAL MICROBIOLOGY. *Current Pos:* from instr to prof, 54-84, EMER PROF MICROBIOL, COL DENT, NY UNIV, 84- *Personal Data:* b Cleveland, Ohio, Mar 20, 19; m 55, Claire Perlstein. *Educ:* Case Western Reserve Univ, BS, 41; Univ Louisville, DMD, 45; Ohio State Univ, MSc, 49, PhD(microbiol), 50. *Prof Exp:* Grad asst microbiol, Ohio State Univ, 48-49, res assoc, Res Found, 50-51; instr, Col Med, Univ Nebr, 51-53. *Concurrent Pos:* NIH fel, Ohio State Univ, 49-50; NIH res grants bact, NY Univ, 57-68; adj prof, York Col, NY, 74-75; vis lectr, St Lukes Hosp Roosevelt Med Ctr, 82-85; NY Col Osteop, 85-86. *Mem:* Am Soc Microbiol. *Res:* Cytology and cytochemistry of bacteria; morphogenesis of bacterial aggregations; microbial ecology of human body, especially oral cavity; infection control in dental practice; biology of fusobacteria. *Mailing Add:* 10-44 Totten St Whitestone NY 11357-2849

HOFFMAN, HENRY HARLAND, ANATOMY. *Current Pos:* RETIRED. *Personal Data:* b Hughesville, Mo, Oct 30, 22; m 55; c 3. *Educ:* Mo Valley Col, BS, 50; St Louis Univ, MS, 54, PhD(anat), 56. *Prof Exp:* Instr anat, St Louis Univ, 56-57; from instr to prof anat, Univ Ala, Birmingham, 57-88, dir med admin, Med Ctr, 70-88. *Mem:* AAAS; Sigma Xi; Acad Educ Develop; Am Asn Anat. *Res:* Neuroanatomy; comparative neuroanatomy; autonomic nervous system. *Mailing Add:* 1244 Lincoya Dr Birmingham AL 35216

HOFFMAN, HENRY TICE, JR, ANALYTICAL CHEMISTRY. *Current Pos:* RETIRED. *Personal Data:* b Lake City, Colo, Sept 14, 25; m 56, Carol Weigle; c Thomas H, Julie C & Heidi H. *Educ:* Western State Col Colo, AB, 46; Univ Iowa, PhD(phys chem), 50. *Prof Exp:* Asst, Univ Iowa, 46-49; from chemist to sr res chemist, Res Div, Am Can Co, 50-64, res assoc, 64-83; anal chemist, Environ & Health Sci Lab, Mobil Oil Corp, 83-86; res scientist, Dept Environ Protection, State NJ, 86-96. *Mem:* Am Chem Soc; Am Soc Mass Spectrometry; Sigma Xi. *Res:* Molecular spectroscopy; gas chromatography; mass spectrometry. *Mailing Add:* 22 Vanderveer Dr Lawrenceville NJ 08648-3151. *E-Mail:* hhoff67271@aol.com

HOFFMAN, HERBERT I(RVING), mechanical engineering; deceased, see previous edition for last biography

HOFFMAN, HOWARD EDGAR, DRUG DEVELOPMENT, RESEARCH ADMINISTRATION. *Current Pos:* RETIRED. *Personal Data:* b New York, NY, Nov 10, 26; m 51, Beverly Provisor; c 3. *Educ:* Univ Calif, Los Angeles, BA, 49, MA, 51; Stanford Univ, PhD(chem), 56. *Prof Exp:* Asst chem, Univ Calif, Los Angeles, 49-53; asst biochem, Stanford Univ, 53-55; res assoc, Stine-Haskell Pharmaceut Lab, Newark, Del, 55-86, admin supvr, 86-87, asst dir infectious dis clin invests, E I du Pont de Nemours & Co, Barley Mill Plaza, Wilmington, Del, 87-88. *Concurrent Pos:* Asst, Palo Alto Med Res Fedn, 54-55; instr pharmacol, Acad Life-Long Learning, Div Continuing Educ, Univ Del, 89-; sci consult, 89- *Res:* Metabolism and pharmacokinetics of drug candidates, both preclinical and clinical; clinical development of new drugs. *Mailing Add:* 222 Pennington Dr Wilmington DE 19810

HOFFMAN, HOWARD TORRENS, ELECTRONICS ENGINEERING, SCIENCE ADMINISTRATION & GENERAL MANAGEMENT. *Current Pos:* PRES & CHIEF EXEC OFFICER, HOFFMAN ASSOCS, SAN DIEGO, 69-; CHIEF EXEC OFFICER & CHIEF FINANCIAL OFFICER, HOFFMAN GROUP, SAN DIEGO, 87- *Personal Data:* b East St Louis, Ill, Dec 30, 23; m 47, Ruth Koch; c Howard, Jean & Glenn. *Educ:* Iowa State Univ, BSEE, 50; Thomas Univ, MSEE, 72, PhD(mgt sci), 77. *Prof Exp:* Head, Eng Sect, Joy Mfg Co, St Louis, 50-55; missile systs engr, McDonnell Aircraft Corp, St Louis, 55-57; exec engr, IT&T Labs, Ft Wayne, Ind, 57-59; mgr missile systs, Litton Industs, College Park, Md, 59-60; prog mgr, chief mgr & div mgr, Teledyne Ryan Co, San Diego, 60-69. *Concurrent Pos:* Chmn bd, exec dir, asset mgr, mgt consult, H&R Assocs, San Diego, 70- *Mem:* Am Inst Aeronaut & Astronaut; Inst Elec & Electronics Engrs; AAAS; Nat Soc Prof Engrs; Am Mgt Asn; Nat Mgt Asn. *Res:* Military, space and computer areas; patentee in field. *Mailing Add:* 5545 Stresemann St San Diego CA 92122

HOFFMAN, JACOB MATTHEW, JR, MEDICINAL CHEMISTRY, SYNTHETIC ORGANIC CHEMISTRY. *Current Pos:* sr res chemist, 73-79, res fel, 79-90, SR RES FEL, MERCK RES LAB, 91- *Personal Data:* b Pittsburgh, Pa, Dec 10, 44. *Educ:* Carnegie Inst Technol, BSc, 66; Univ Rochester, PhD(org chem), 71. *Prof Exp:* Res assoc, Columbia Univ, 70-72; res chemist, Univ Calif, Los Angeles, 72-73. *Mem:* Am Chem Soc; AAAS. *Res:* Synthetic methods; drug design and development. *Mailing Add:* Merck Res Labs WP26A-4044 Sumneytown Pike PO Box 4 West Point PA 19486

HOFFMAN, JACQUELINE LOUISE, GENETICS MICROBIOLOGY, BACTERIOLOGY. *Current Pos:* LECTR & LAB COURSE COORDR, GENETICS & MICROBIOL, DEPT BIOL, WASH UNIV, 84-, SCI OUTREACH COORDR, 90- *Personal Data:* b Los Angeles, Calif, 1952; m 82; c 2. *Educ:* Univ Calif, Davis, BS, 73; Harvard Univ, AM, 74, PhD(biol), 79. *Mem:* Am Soc Cell Biol; Soc Develop Biol; Sigma Xi. *Mailing Add:* 1456 Wellington View Lane Chesterfield MO 63005

HOFFMAN, JAMES IRVIE, GEOLOGY. *Current Pos:* PROVOST & SR VPRES ACAD AFFAIRS, EASTERN WASH UNIV, 93- *Personal Data:* b Trenton, NJ, Dec 23, 41; c 1. *Educ:* Allegheny Col, BS, 63; Mich State Univ, MS, 65, PhD(geol), 69. *Prof Exp:* Explor field geologist, Anaconda Am Brass, Ltd, Can, 67; instr geol, Mich State Univ, 68-69; from asst prof to prof geol, Univ Wis-Oshkosh, 69-93, chmn dept, 75-78, assoc dean, 79-84, dean letters & sci, 84-93. *Concurrent Pos:* Consult geologist, Earth Studies Inc, 72- *Mem:* Geochem Soc; Int Asn Geochem & Cosmochem; AAAS; Nat Asn Geol Teachers; Sigma Xi; Am Water Resources Asn. *Res:* Geochemical mass balance of transition metals with sediments and associated waters, with special attention to base metals in organic rich sediments. *Mailing Add:* Sr Vpres Acad Affairs, Provost, MS 132 Eastern Wash Univ 526 Fifth St Cheney WA 99004-2431

HOFFMAN, JAMES TRACY, electronics, systems engineering; deceased, see previous edition for last biography

HOFFMAN, JEFFREY ALAN, X-RAY ASTRONOMY. *Current Pos:* NASA SPACE SHUTTLE ASTRONAUT/MISSION SPECIALIST, JOHNSON SPACE CTR, 78- *Personal Data:* b New York, NY, Nov 2, 44. *Educ:* Amherst Col, BA, 66; Harvard Univ, PhD(astron), 71. *Prof Exp:* Nat Acad Sci fel astron, Smithsonian Astrophys Observ, 71-72; Harvard-Sheldon Int Fel, Univ Leicester, 72-73; NATO fel, 73-74; EXOSAT proj scientist, Physics Dept, X-ray Astronomy Group, 74-75; head-A4 proj scientist, Mass Inst Technol, 75-78. *Mem:* Am Astron Soc; Int Astron Union; Sigma Xi. *Res:* X-ray; gamma ray; space-based observations; high energy astrophysics; x-ray astronomy; high-energy astrophysics. *Mailing Add:* 6527 Rutgers Houston TX 77005

HOFFMAN, JERRY C, HAZARDOUS MATERIAL MANAGEMENT, HAZARDOUS WASTE MANAGEMENT. *Current Pos:* Proj engr, 72-73, dept head, 78-88, PROJ MGR, BURNS & MCDONNELL ENG CO, 88- *Personal Data:* b Madisonville, Ky, Apr 15, 43; m 66, Ann Curren; c Mark A, Laura L, Christopher C & Allison N. *Educ:* Western Ky Univ, BS, 72. *Concurrent Pos:* Chmn, Energy & Environ Comt, Kansas City Chamber of Com, 88-91; Air Toxic Subcomt, Mid Am Regional Coun, 89- *Mem:* Am Soc Civil Engrs; Am Soc Testing & Mat; Nat Soc Prof Engrs; Environ Audit Roundtable. *Res:* Hazardous material management; investigation of hazardous waste disposal sites; environmental regulation compliance. *Mailing Add:* Burns & McDonnell PO Box 419173 Kansas City MO 64141-6173

HOFFMAN, JOE DOUGLAS, FLUID DYNAMICS, PROPULSION. *Current Pos:* From asst prof to assoc prof, 63-73, PROF MECH ENG, PURDUE UNIV, 73- *Personal Data:* b Memphis, Tenn, Aug 9, 34; m 56; c 3. *Educ:* Tex A&M Univ, BS, 58, MS, 59; Purdue Univ, PhD(mech eng), 63. *Concurrent Pos:* Design engr, Aerojet-Gen Corp, 61-63; vis prof, Univ Colo, 74. *Mem:* Am Inst Aeronaut & Astronaut; Am Soc Eng Educ; Combustion Inst; Am Soc Mech Engrs. *Res:* Gas dynamics; computational fluid dynamics. *Mailing Add:* Dept Mech Eng Purdue Univ West Lafayette IN 47907-1968

HOFFMAN, JOHN D, CRYSTALLOGRAPHY. *Current Pos:* RES PROF, DEPT MAT SCI & ENG, JOHNS HOPKINS UNIV, 90- *Personal Data:* b Washington, DC, Nov 26, 22. *Educ:* Franklin & Marshall Col, BS, 42; Princeton Univ, MS, 48, PhD, 49. *Honors & Awards:* High Polymer Physics Prize, Am Phys Soc, 71; Presidents Meritorious Excellence Award, 80. *Prof Exp:* Dir, Inst Mat Res, Nat Bur Stand, 67-78, dir, 78-82; prof & chmn nuclear eng, Univ Md, 82-85; dir & chief exec, Mich Molecular Inst, 85-90. *Concurrent Pos:* Distinguished res fel, Mich Molecular Inst, 90. *Mem:* Nat Acad Eng; fel Am Phys Soc; Sigma Xi; NY Acad Sci; hon mem Am Dent Asn. *Mailing Add:* 6121 Maiden Lane Bethesda MD 20817. *Fax:* 301-320-9569

HOFFMAN, JOHN HAROLD, ATMOSPHERIC PHYSICS, MASS SPECTROMETRY. *Current Pos:* assoc prof physics, Southwest Ctr Advan Studies, 66-69, assoc prof, 69-78, PROF PHYSICS & HEAD DEPT, UNIV TEX, DALLAS, 78-, ASSOC DEAN, SCH NATURAL SCI & MATH, 89- *Personal Data:* b Winona, Minn, Sept 7, 29; m 59, Judith Poncelet; c Rita, Gregory, Julie & Peggy. *Educ:* St Mary's Col, Minn, BS, 51; Univ Minn, MS, 54, PhD(physics), 58. *Honors & Awards:* Group Achievement Award, NASA. *Prof Exp:* Asst physics, Univ Minn, res assoc, 58-59; physicist, US Naval Res Lab, Washington, DC, 59-66. *Mem:* Am Asn Physics Teachers; Sigma Xi. *Res:* Mass spectrometric studies of cosmogenic helium in iron meteorites; gas and ionic composition of the upper atmosphere; lunar and planetary atmospheric composition; stratospheric ion composition; cometary coma studies. *Mailing Add:* Dept Physics Univ Tex Dallas PO Box 830688 Richardson TX 75083-0688. *Fax:* 972-690-2848; *E-Mail:* jhoffman@utdallas.edu

HOFFMAN, JOHN RALEIGH, PHYSICS ENGINEERING. *Current Pos:* CONSULT, 92- *Personal Data:* b Evansville, Ind, July 7, 26; m 50, Phyllis Reindel; c J Russell & Gary P. *Educ:* Univ Richmond, BS, 49; Univ Fla, MS, 51, PhD(physics), 54. *Prof Exp:* Asst, Univ Fla, 49-53, asst physics, 53-54; mem staff, Sandia Corp, 54-57; proj scientist, Kaman Nuclear, 57-68, from vpres to sr vpres, 74-90, exec vpres, Kaman Sci Corp, 90-92. *Concurrent Pos:* Emer bd dirs, Red Spot Paint & Varnish Co, 93- *Mem:* Am Phys Soc; Inst Elec & Electronics Engrs; Sigma Xi. *Res:* Nuclear engineering; nuclear physics; atomic physics. *Mailing Add:* 5020 Lyda Lane Colorado Springs CO 80904

HOFFMAN, JOHN RUSSELL, ELECTROMAGNETIC COMPATIBILITY & INTERFERENCE, SATELLITE COMMUNICATIONS & TRACKING. *Current Pos:* SR ENGR, ALLIED SIGNAL TECH SERV CORP, 93- *Personal Data:* b Gainsville, Fla, Oct 16, 53. *Educ:* Colo Sch Mines, BS, 75; Rice Univ, MA, 78, PhD(solid state physics), 83. *Prof Exp:* Res scientist, Conoco, Inc, 81-86; res physicist, Mission Res Corp, 86-91. *Mem:* Am Phys Soc; Inst Elec & Electronics Engrs; Sigma Xi. *Mailing Add:* 425 Mesa Vista Ct Colorado Springs CO 80904

HOFFMAN, JOSEPH ELLSWORTH, JR, ELECTRICAL ENGINEERING, PHYSICS. *Current Pos:* asst chief engr, US Vet Admin Med Ctr, Newington, Conn, 71-75, chief eng, Providence, RI, 75-84, electronics eng prog mgr, Vet Admin Cent Off, Washington, DC, 84-86, proj mgr, 86-88, ASST CHIEF ENG, VET ADMIN MED CTR, BOSTON, MASS, 88- *Personal Data:* b Somerville, NJ, July 9, 35. *Educ:* Rensselaer Polytech Inst, BEE, 57; Univ Pa, MSEE, 59; Northeastern Univ, PhD(spectros instrumentation), 68; Univ Conn, MBA, 75. *Prof Exp:* Elec engr, RCA, 57-59; electronics officer & engr, USAF, 59-63; asst res engr, Utah State Univ, 63-66; electronics engr, USAF, 66-70, Canberra Industs, 70-71 & Hoffman Elec, 71. *Concurrent Pos:* Consult instrumentation, 71-; adj asst prof, Univ Hartford, 72-74; vis lectr, Providence Col & Bryant Col, 75-84, Capitol Col & Prince George Community Col, 85-88. *Mem:* Inst Elec & Electronics Engrs; Nat Soc Prof Engrs; Am Mgt Asn; Inst Indust Engrs. *Res:* Improving instrumentation and techniques of Fourier spectroscopy; lasers and their applications. *Mailing Add:* 304 N London Ave West Warwick RI 02893

HOFFMAN, JOSEPH FREDERICK, PHYSIOLOGY. *Current Pos:* prof, 65-74, chmn dept, 73-79, EUGENE HIGGINS PROF CELLULAR & MOLECULAR PHYSIOL, SCH MED, YALE UNIV, 74- *Personal Data:* b Oklahoma City, Okla, Mar 7, 25; m 74, Elena Citkowitz. *Educ:* Univ Okla, BS, 47, MS, 48; Princeton Univ, MA, 51, PhD, 52. *Hon Degrees:* MA, Yale Univ, 65. *Prof Exp:* Lab asst, Univ Okla, 47; asst instr biol, Princeton Univ, 49-51, asst, 52-53, res assoc, 53-54, lectr, 54-56; USPHS spec res fel, 56-57; from physiologist to head sect membrane physiol, Nat Heart Inst, 57-65. *Concurrent Pos:* Lectr, George Washington Univ, 58-65; mem fac, NIH Grad Sch, 59-65; mem, Woods Hole Marine Biol Lab. *Mem:* Nat Acad Sci; Soc Gen Physiol (pres, 75-76); Biophys Soc (pres, 85-86); fel AAAS; Am Physiol Soc; Sigma Xi; fel Am Acad Arts & Sci; hon mem Argentine Soc Physiol Sci. *Res:* Membrane transport processes in red blood cells. *Mailing Add:* Dept Cellular & Molecular Physiol Yale Univ Sch Med New Haven CT 06510. *Fax:* 203-785-4951

HOFFMAN, JULIEN IVOR ELLIS, PEDIATRIC CARDIOLOGY. *Current Pos:* assoc prof, pediat, 66-70, prof physiol, 81-88, PROF PEDIAT, UNIV CALIF, SAN FRANCISCO, 70-, MEM CARDIOVASC RES INST, 66- *Personal Data:* b Salisbury, SRhodesia, July 26, 25; US citizen; m 86, Kathleen W Lawless; c Anna & Daniel. *Educ:* Univ Witwatersrand, BSc, 44, Hons, 45, MB & BCh, 49, MD, 70; Am Bd Pediat, dipl pediat cardiol, 68 & dipl pediat intensive care, 87; FRCP, 73. *Honors & Awards:* George Brown Mem lectr, Am Heart Asn, 77; Lilly lectr, Royal Col Physicians, London, 81; George Alexander Gibson lectr, Royal Col Physicians, Edinburgh, 78; Isaac Starr lectr, Cardiac Systs Dynamics Soc, 82; Janet Baldwin Mem lectr, 84; John Keith lectr, Can Cardiovasc Soc, 85; First Nadas lectr, Am Heart Asn, 87; Bayer Award, 89; First Donald C Fyler lectr, Boston Children's Hosp, 90. *Prof Exp:* Vol res asst med, Postgrad Med Sch, London, Eng, 56-57; fel pediat, Children's Hosp, Boston, 57-59; sr fel cardiol, Cardiovasc Res Inst, San Francisco, 59-60; asst prof med & pediat, Albert Einstein Col Med, 61-66. *Concurrent Pos:* Estab investr, Am Heart Asn, 63-68; asst physician & pediatrician, Bronx Munic Hosp Ctr, 65-66; sub-bd Pediat Intensive Care, 85-87; distinguished physiol lectr, Am Col Chest Physicians, 85; fac lectr, Univ Calif, San Francisco, 92; hon pres, World Cong Pediat Cardiol & Cardiac Surg, Paris, 93. *Mem:* Am Heart Asn; Soc Pediat Res; Am Pediat Soc; Am Physiol Soc. *Res:* Pathophysiology and natural history of congenital heart disease; pathophysiology of regional coronary blood flow; indicator dilution studies; natural history of ventricular septal defects in infancy. *Mailing Add:* Box 0544 Univ Calif San Francisco CA 94143-0544. *E-Mail:* julien_hoffman@pedcardgateway.ucsf.edu

HOFFMAN, JULIUS, PSYCHIATRY, NEUROLOGY. *Current Pos:* RETIRED. *Personal Data:* b New York, NY, Feb 4, 21; m 43; c 3. *Educ:* NY Univ, BA, 41, MD, 44; Ohio State Univ, MA, 58, MMSc, 62; Southern Ill Univ, MS, 72; Am Bd Psychiat & Neurol, dipl neurol, 50, dipl psychiat, 53, dipl child neurol, 68; Am Bd Pediat, dipl, 64. *Honors & Awards:* Hughlings-Jackson Found Nuerol Res Award, 62. *Prof Exp:* Intern, Kings Co Hosp, NY, 44-45, resident neurol, 45-46 & 48-49; Resident psychiat, Winter Vet Admin Hosp, Kans, 49-51; sr psychiat physician, Fairfield State Hosp, Conn, 51; assoc prof psychiat, Grad Sch, Ohio State Univ, 51-53, social admin, 53-63; assoc prof neurol & pediat, Georgetown Univ, 63-65; prof pediat neurol, Sch Med, Howard Univ, 65-91. *Concurrent Pos:* Nat Inst Neurol Dis & Blindness award pediat neurol, 61-62; staff psychiatrist, Columbus Receiving Hosp, 51-63; consult, Children's Hosp, Columbus, Ohio, St Anthony, Grant & Mt Carmel Hosps, Columbus State Sch & Vet Admin, 53-56, Old Age Survivors Ins, 58-63, Columbus Receiving Hosp Children, 59-63, USAF, 59-63, Freedman's Hosp, DC & Howard Univ Hosp, 66-, Suburban Hosp, Md, 67-68; resident, Children's Hosp, Columbus, Ohio, 61-62; mem staff, Georgetown Univ, DC Gen, Children's Convalescent & Children's Hosps, Washington, DC, 63-65, Sibley Mem Hosp, 64-70, Wash Hosp Ctr, 71-; consult to Presidential Spec Asst on Ment Retardation, 63; consult, Div Res Facilities & Resources, NIH, 64-, Neurol & Sensory Dis Prog, USPHS, 65- & Civil Serv Comn, 71-; prof-in-residence, Lynchburg Training Sch & Hosp, Va, 66 & 67; spec lectr, George Washington Univ, 69-, Found Advan Educ Sci, NIH, 71-74. *Mem:* AMA; fel Am Psychiat Asn; fel Am Asn Ment Deficiency; fel Am Acad Neurol; fel Am Acad Pediat. *Res:* Pediatric neurology; basic and clinical neurological sciences; neurophysiology; psychotherapy. *Mailing Add:* 7805 Green Twig Rd Bethesda MD 20817-6917

HOFFMAN, JULIUS R, ENTOMOLOGY, ACAROLOGY. *Current Pos:* From asst res prof to assoc res prof entom, Mich State Univ, 49-63, assoc prof natural sci & entom, 63-69, asst to dean undergrad coun, 65-69, prof entom & asst dean, 69-86, EMER PROF ENTOM & EMER ASST DEAN, COL NATURAL SCI, MICH STATE UNIV, 86- *Personal Data:* b Toledo, Ohio, Aug 1, 19; m 43, Alice Jeffers; c Joel J, Peter T, Janet E & Elaine E. *Educ:* Ohio State Univ, BA, 40; Cornell Univ, MS, 47, PhD(entom), 49. *Mem:* AAAS; Entom Soc Am; Sigma Xi; Acarological Soc Am. *Res:* Virus and disease transmission by insects; greenhouse and ornamental pests control; leaf-hoppers and mites. *Mailing Add:* 246 Clarendon Rd East Lansing MI 48823

HOFFMAN, KARLA LEIGH, OPERATIONS RESEARCH, COMBINATORIAL OPTIMIZATION. *Current Pos:* assoc prof, 85-89, PROF OPERS RES, GEORGE MASON UNIV, 90-, ACTING CHMN OPERS RES & ENG DEPT, 96- *Personal Data:* b Paterson, NJ, Feb 14, 48; m 71, Allan; c Matthew Douglas. *Educ:* Rutgers Univ, BA, 69; George Washington Univ, MBA, 71, DSc, 75. *Honors & Awards:* Silver Medal, US Dept Com, 84; Appl Res Award, Nat Bur Stand, 84. *Prof Exp:* Oper res analyst, Internal Revenue Serv, 71-73; res fel, NSF & Nat Acad Sci, 75-76; mathematician, Nat Bur Stand, 76-85. *Concurrent Pos:* Consult var govt agencies, 76-86, airline indust & telecommun corp, 86-; distinguished prof eng, George Mason Univ, 89, pres-elect, Inst Opers Res & Mgt Scis. *Mem:* Opers Res Soc Am; Math Prog Soc; Soc Indust & Appl Math. *Res:* Testing of large-scale mathematical models; combinatorial optimization; nonconvex optimization. *Mailing Add:* 6921 Clifton Rd Clifton VA 22024. *Fax:* 703-993-1521; *E-Mail:* khoffman@gmu.edu

HOFFMAN, KENNETH A, GEOLOGY. *Current Pos:* lectr, 74, from asst prof to assoc prof, 74-83, PROF, PHYSICS DEPT, CALIF POLYTECH STATE UNIV, 83- *Personal Data:* b Feb 17, 45. *Educ:* Univ Calif, Berkeley, BA, 66, MA, 69, PhD(geophys), 73. *Prof Exp:* Res fel geol & geophys, Univ Minn, 72-73. *Concurrent Pos:* Vis assoc prof, Univ Minn, 77-78; res geophysicist, Univ Calif, Santa Barbara, 78; vis fel, Res Sch Earth Sci, Australian Nat Univ, 80-81 & Victoria Univ, NZ, 81; assoc physician, Inst Physic Globe Paris, 88-89; ed, J Geophys Res Solid Earth & Planets, 86-90; chair, Paleomagnetism Working Group, Int Asn Geomagnetism & Aeronomy, 89-93, Div Internal Fields, 95- *Mem:* Fel Am Geophys Union. *Res:* Geomagnetic reversal; paleomagnetic methodology; lunar magnetism; mineral physics. *Mailing Add:* Physics Dept Calif Polytech State Univ San Luis Obispo CA 93407. *Fax:* 805-756-2435

HOFFMAN, KENNETH CHARLES, MECHANICAL ENGINEERING, SYSTEM SCIENCE. *Current Pos:* PRIN ENGR, MITRETEK CORP. *Personal Data:* b Long Island City, NY, Nov 29, 33; m 55, Ann Hynes; c Kenneth M, Theresa A & Charles M. *Educ:* NY Univ, BME, 54; Adelphi Univ, MS, 68; Polytech Inst Brooklyn, PhD(systs eng), 72. *Prof Exp:* Sci staff engr, Brookhaven Nat Lab, 56-79, head, Nat Ctr Anal Energy Systs, 76-79, chmn, Dept Energy & Environ, 77-79; sr vpres, Mathtech, Inc, 79-83, pres, 84; vpres, Martin Marietta Data Systs, 84-90; dir, Oracle Complex Systs Corp, 90-92. *Concurrent Pos:* Consult, Systs Europ, Inc, 76-; mem, Commerce Tech Adv Bd, Panel Proj Independence, 76-77, Comt Renewable Resources for Indust Mats, Nat Acad Sci, 76-77, Comt Adv Energy Storage Systs, 77- & Res Coord Panel, Gas Res Inst, 77-79. *Mem:* Am Soc Mech Engrs; AAAS. *Res:* Business applications of information technology; development of engineering, materials, and advanced energy conversion systems; development of analytical models of the energy and materials system with applications to industry and national policy. *Mailing Add:* 2007 Swans Neck Way Reston VA 22091. *Fax:* 703-610-2053; *E-Mail:* khoffman@mitretek.org

HOFFMAN, KENNETH MYRON, MATHEMATICS. *Current Pos:* Instr math, Mass Inst Technol, 56-57, C L E Moore instr, 57-59, from asst prof to assoc prof, 59-64, chmn comn educ, 69-71, head dept, 71-80, PROF MATH, MASS INST TECHNOL, 64- *Personal Data:* b Long Beach, Calif, Nov 30, 30; div; c 3. *Educ:* Occidental Col, AB, 52; Univ Calif, Los Angeles, MA, 54, PhD(math), 56. *Concurrent Pos:* Fel, Sloan Found, 64-66; co-chmn, Mass Inst Technol/Wellesley Exchange Prog, 74-79; exec dir, Nat Res Coun Comn Resources Math Sci, 81-83; dir fed rel, Joint Policy Bd Math, 84-; chmn adv comt, NSF Sci & Eng Educ Directorate, 84-85; exec dir, Math Sci Educ Bd, 89-91; assoc exec officer, Nat Res Coun, 91- *Mem:* Am Math Soc; Math Asn Am; Soc Indust & Appl Math; AAAS; Oper Res Soc Am; Nat Coun Teachers Math. *Res:* Functional analysis. *Mailing Add:* 7401 Westlake Terr Suite 102 Bethesda MD 20817

HOFFMAN, KENNETH WAYNE, APPLICATION OF ANALYTICAL INSTRUMENTATION TECHNIQUES, POLYMER ANALYSIS & PROBLEM RESOLUTION. *Current Pos:* RES CHEMIST & LAB MGR, RHONE POULENC, NASHVILLE, 90- *Personal Data:* b Irvington, NJ, June 9, 55; m 76; c 1. *Educ:* Tenn Technol Univ, BS, 80. *Prof Exp:* Forensic chemist, Ga Bur Invest, 80-82, forensic chemist prin, 82-84; plating chemist, Siegel Robert Inc, 84-85, res chemist, 85-86, chief res & develop, 86-90. *Mem:* Am Chem Soc; Soc Appl Spectros. *Res:* Provide analytical instrumentation expertise for support of any research projects or troubleshooting activities of current and future production processes. *Mailing Add:* 303 Highland Dr Old Hickory TN 37138-1621

HOFFMAN, LANCE J, AUTOMATED RISK ANALYSIS, COMPUTER SECURITY. *Current Pos:* PROF COMPUT SCI & DIR, INST COMPUT & TELECOMMUN SYST POLICY, GEORGE WASHINGTON UNIV, 77- *Personal Data:* b Pittsburgh, Pa, Dec 8, 42; div; c 1. *Educ:* Carnegie Inst Technol, BS, 64; Stanford Univ, MS, 67, PhD(comput sci), 70. *Prof Exp:* Asst prof comput sci, Univ Calif, Berkeley, 70-77. *Concurrent Pos:* Pres, Info Policy, Inc, 81-84, Hoffman Bus Asn, Inc, 85-; distinguished lectr, Inst Elec & Electronics Engrs; vis lectr, Asn Comput Mach. *Mem:* Asn Comput Mach; AAAS; Inst Elec & Electronics Engrs. *Res:* Computer security, risk analysis; social impact analysis for computer systems; automated risk analysis; computer viruses; encryption policy. *Mailing Add:* Dept Elec Eng & Comput Sci George Washington Univ Washington DC 20052

HOFFMAN, LARRY RONALD, PHYCOLOGY. *Current Pos:* from asst prof to assoc prof, 62-75, PROF BOT, UNIV ILL, URBANA, 75- *Personal Data:* b Sigourney, Iowa, May 12, 36; m 59; c 3. *Educ:* Iowa State Univ, BS, 58; Univ Tex, PhD(bot), 61. *Honors & Awards:* The Darbaker Prize, Bot Soc Am, 75. *Prof Exp:* NSF res fel, Prof Manton's Lab, Univ Leeds, 61-62. *Concurrent Pos:* Vis prof, Witts Univ, Johannesburg, SAfrica, 83. *Mem:* Bot Soc Am; Phycol Soc Am (vpres, 75 & 80, pres, 81); Int Phycol Soc; Brit Phycol Soc; Am Micros Soc (secy, 88-92). *Res:* Morphology; fine structure; eukaryotic algal viruses; sexuality of algae, especially Sphaeropleales, Oedogoniales and other oogamous members of the Chlorophyta. *Mailing Add:* 202 W Grand St Joseph IL 61873

HOFFMAN, LINDA M, NEUROCHEMISTRY, CANCER RESEARCH. *Current Pos:* from asst prof to assoc prof, 77-81, PROF CHEM, BARUCH COL, 82-, CHAIR, DEPT NATURAL SCI, 95- *Personal Data:* b New York, NY, Dec 18, 39; m 58; c 1. *Educ:* Queens Col, BS, 59; NY Univ, MS, 67, PhD(org chem), 70. *Honors & Awards:* Moore Award, Am Soc Neuropathologists, 80, 84. *Prof Exp:* Fel biochem, Sloan Kettering Inst Cancer Res, 72-73; res assoc neurochem, Kingsbrook Jewish Med Ctr, 73-77. *Concurrent Pos:* Res assoc, Kingsbrook Jewish Med Ctr, 78-94. *Mem:* Am Chem Soc; AAAS; Sigma Xi; NY Acad Sci. *Res:* Relationship of glycosphingolipids to surface properties and disease in cultured cells derived from Tay-Sachs diseased brains; glycosphingolipids in neurological tumors and cell cultures derived from these tumors; porphyrins as tumor-localizing agents. *Mailing Add:* Baruch Col Box 502 17 Lexington Ave New York NY 10010

HOFFMAN, LOREN HAROLD, HISTOLOGY, REPRODUCTIVE BIOLOGY. *Current Pos:* From instr to asst prof anat, 69-84, PROF CELL BIOL, SCH MED, VANDERBILT UNIV, 84- *Personal Data:* b Los Angeles, Calif, Dec 18, 41; m 63; c 2. *Educ:* Jamestown Col, BA, 63; Cornell Univ, PhD(zool), 68. *Concurrent Pos:* USPHS res fel, Sch Med, Vanderbilt Univ, 68-70. *Mem:* Am Asn Anat; Soc Study Reproduction; Sigma Xi; Am Soc Cell Biol. *Res:* Female reproductive biology; uterus, ovo-implatation and placentation. *Mailing Add:* Dept Cell Biol Vanderbilt Univ Sch Med Nashville TN 37232-2175

HOFFMAN, MARK PETER, BEEF & SWINE PRODUCTION. *Current Pos:* From asst prof to assoc prof, 69-80, PROF ANIMAL SCI, IOWA STATE UNIV, 80- *Personal Data:* b West Reading, Pa, Feb 4, 41; m 69, Lorraine Johnson; c Kourtney K & Royelle M. *Educ:* Delaware Valley Col, BS, 63; Iowa State Univ, MS, 67, PhD(animal breeding), 69. *Honors & Awards:* Animal Mgt Award, Am Soc Animal Sci, 89. *Mem:* AAAS; Am Dairy Sci Asn; Am Soc Animal Sci; Am Inst Biol Sci; Coun Agr Sci & Technol; Am Regist Prof Animal Sci. *Res:* Bovine production; effects of genotype and environment on productivity. *Mailing Add:* 119 Kildee Hall Iowa State Univ Ames IA 50011. *Fax:* 515-294-0018; *E-Mail:* phoffman@iastate.edu

HOFFMAN, MARVIN MORRISON, PHYSICS. *Current Pos:* CONSULT, AMPARO CORP, 80- *Personal Data:* b Kans, Jan 16, 25; m 51, Darleane Christian; c Maureane R & Daryl C. *Educ:* Greenville Col, AB, 47; Iowa State Col, PhD(physics), 52; Univ NMex, MBA, 79. *Prof Exp:* Asst, Ames Lab, AEC, 48-52; physicist, Los Alamos Nat Lab, 52-80. *Mem:* Am Phys Soc; Am Asn Physics Teachers; Inst Elec & Electronics Engrs. *Res:* Photonuclear reactions; fission; nuclear structure. *Mailing Add:* 2277 Manzanita Dr Oakland CA 94611

HOFFMAN, MAUREANE RICHARDSON, HEMATOLOGY, IMMUNOLOGY. *Current Pos:* resident path, Duke Univ, 82-85, Duke-Cabarrus path fel, 84, asst prof, 85-87, ASST PROF, DEPT PATH, DUKE UNIV, 91-; DIR HEMAT, LAB SERV, DURHAM DEPT VET AFFAIRS MED CTR, 92- *Personal Data:* b Los Alamos, NMex, Apr 21, 57; m 81, Stephen G Richardson. *Educ:* NMex Stat Univ, BS, 76; Univ Iowa, MD & PhD, 82; Am Bd Path, cert anat & clin path, 85. *Prof Exp:* Tech staff, Environ Sci Div, Oak Ridge Nat Lab, 76; asst prof, Dept Path & assoc dir, Transfusion Serv, Univ NC, 87-91. *Concurrent Pos:* Prin investr, United Way NC, 85-86, Am Cancer Soc, 85-86, USPHS, 88-89, Univ NC, 89-90 & NIH, 91-; mem, Transfusion Comt, Univ NC-NC Mem Hosp, 87-91; mem, Ctr Thrombosis & Hemostasis, Univ NC, 88-, adj asst prof, Dept Med, 93-; staff physician, Lab Serv, Durham Dept Vet Affairs Med Ctr, 91-92; young investr merit travel award, Int Soc Thrombosis & Hemostasis, 91, mem, Sci Subcomt Platelet Physiol, Sci & Stand Comt, 94-; Prin investr, Travel Award, Coun Thrombosis, Am Heart Asn, 92; prog specialist path, US Dept Vet Affairs, Health Servs & Res Admin, 92-94. *Mem:* Am Asn Blood Banks; Am Asn Pathologists; An Fedn Clin Res; Am Soc Clin Pathologists; Am soc Hemat; NY Acad Sci; Soc Free Radical Res; Soc Leukocyte Biol. *Res:* Pathology. *Mailing Add:* Vet Admin Med Ctr Durham NC 27705. *Fax:* 919-286-6818; *E-Mail:* maureane@med.unc.edu

HOFFMAN, MICHAEL G, CONSTRUCTION & OVERSEAS PROJECT MANAGEMENT, ELECTRICAL ENGINEERING. *Current Pos:* SCHEDULER & ESTIMATOR SUBSTA CONSTRUCT, BONNEVILLE POWER ADMIN, 92-, PROJ MGR CONTRACT LABOR. *Personal Data:* b Sunnyside, Wash, Oct 2, 52; m 83, Suzanne C Pickgrobe. *Educ:* Univ Portland, BSEE, 78. *Honors & Awards:* Centennial Medal, Inst Elec & Electronics Engrs, 83. *Prof Exp:* Distrib engr, Pac Power & Light, 78-79; proj engr, Saudi Consol Elec Co, 79-81, 83-84; scheduler, Alusuisse Serv, 81-82; elec engr, Pac Eng, 84-86; syst engr, Comput Tools, Inc, 87-89; scheduler, Wright Schuchart Harbor, 89-90, Hoffman Construct, 91-92. *Concurrent Pos:* Founder, Saudi Arabian Inst Elec & Electronics Engrs Sect, 80-81, sect chmn, 81, chmn, Prof Activ Comt, Portland, Ore Sect, 83-85; ed, Comput Tools Mag, 87-89; mem bd dirs, NW China Coun, 87- & Delaunay Ment Health Ctr, 88-94. *Mem:* Inst Elec & Electronics Engrs. *Res:* Integration of off the shelf software and hardware for PC based project management systems running on local area networks with telecommunications links for overseas projects. *Mailing Add:* 7466 N Fiske St Portland OR 97203

HOFFMAN, MICHAEL JOHN, OPERATOR THEORY, COMPLEX ANALYSIS. *Current Pos:* from asst prof to assoc prof, 81-93, PROF MATH, CALIF STATE UNIV, LOS ANGELES, 93- *Personal Data:* b Lake Forest, Ill, Jan 12, 48; m 76, Susan Chandler. *Educ:* Mass Inst Technol, BS, 70, MA, 73; Univ Calif, Berkeley, PhD(math), 79. *Prof Exp:* Bateman res instr math, Calif Inst Technol, 79-81. *Concurrent Pos:* Chair, Dept Math & Comput Sci, Calif State Univ, Los Angeles, 96- *Mem:* Am Math Soc; fel Sigma Xi. *Res:* Function theory, disks, annuli and related operation theory in Hilbert and Banach spaces; textbooks in analysis and complex analysis. *Mailing Add:* Dept Math & Comput Sci Calif State Univ 5151 Rancho Castilla Los Angeles CA 90032-4221. *E-Mail:* mhoffma@calstate.edu

HOFFMAN, MICHAEL K, PHYSICAL ORGANIC CHEMISTRY, MASS SPECTROMETRY. *Current Pos:* chemist, 79-85, staff officer, 85-89, BR CHIEF, FOOD SAFETY & INSPECTION SERV, USDA, 89- *Personal Data:* b Philadelphia, Pa, Sept 7, 41; div; c 2. *Educ:* Univ Pa, BS, 63; Bryn Mawr Col, PhD(phys org chem), 68. *Prof Exp:* Res assoc, Univ Pa, 67-68 & Univ NC, 68-71; asst prof chem, Kans State Univ, 71-75; asst prof, Dept Biochem, Sch Med, Washington, Univ, 75-79. *Concurrent Pos:* Sr fel sci, NATO, 73; Cong fel, 88. *Mem:* Am Soc Mass Spectrometry. *Res:* Application of mass spectrometry to environmental problems; food safety, risk assessment. *Mailing Add:* 613 Elgin Lane Bethesda MD 20817

HOFFMAN, MORTON Z, PHYSICAL INORGANIC CHEMISTRY. *Current Pos:* from asst prof to assoc prof, 61-71, PROF PHYS CHEM, BOSTON UNIV, 71- *Personal Data:* b New York, NY, Apr 22, 35; m 65, Sandra Weintraub; c Linda & Julie. *Educ:* Hunter Col, AB, 55; Univ Mich, MS, 57, PhD(photochem), 60. *Prof Exp:* Res assoc phys chem, Univ Sheffield, 60-61. *Concurrent Pos:* Rackham fel, 60-61; Nat Acad Sci-Nat Res Coun sr res assoc, 69-70; vis scientist, US Army Natick Labs, 69-70. *Mem:* Fel AAAS; Am Chem Soc, Am Asn Univ Professors; Sigma Xi; Int-Am Photochem Soc; Radiation Res Soc. *Res:* Photo and radiation chemistry of transition metal coordination complexes; photochemical conversion and storage of solar energy. *Mailing Add:* Chem Boston Univ 590 Commonwealth Ave Boston MA 02215

HOFFMAN, MYRON A(RNOLD), ENGINEERING, ADVANCED ENERGY CONVERSION. *Current Pos:* PROF MECH ENG, UNIV CALIF, DAVIS, 68- *Personal Data:* b Chicago, Ill, Nov 15, 30; m 63, Sharna; c 2. *Educ:* Mass Inst Technol, SB & SM, 52, ScD(aeronaut eng), 55. *Prof Exp:* Assoc prof aeronaut & astronaut, Mass Inst Technol, 55-56, 59-68. *Mem:* Am Nuclear Soc; Am Soc Mech Engrs. *Res:* Electric power generation; heat transfer; fusion energy conversion. *Mailing Add:* Dept Mech Eng Univ Calif Davis CA 95616

HOFFMAN, NELSON MILES, III, RADIATIVE TRANSFER, HYDRODYNAMICS. *Current Pos:* Staff mem, 75-80, asst group leader to assoc group leader, Diag Physics Group, 80-85, STAFF MEM, INERTIAL FUSION & PLASMA THEORY GROUP, APPL THEORET PHYSICS DIV, LOS ALAMOS NAT LAB, 85- *Personal Data:* b Manhattan, Kans, Oct 4, 48; c 2. *Educ:* Rice Univ, BA, 70; Univ Wis, PhD(astron), 74. *Mem:* Am Phys Soc. *Res:* Inertial fusion target physics. *Mailing Add:* M/S F645 Los Alamos Nat Lab PO Box 1663 Los Alamos NM 87545

HOFFMAN, NORMAN EDWIN, SEPARATION SCIENCE. *Current Pos:* from instr to prof, 56-94, chmn dept, 72-81, EMER PROF CHEM, MARQUETTE UNIV, 94- *Personal Data:* b Chicago, Ill, Oct 26, 28; m 53, Margaret Cunningham. *Educ:* Loyola Univ, BS, 50; Northwestern Univ, PhD(chem), 54. *Prof Exp:* Res chemist, Stand Oil Co, 53-56. *Concurrent Pos:* Vis prof, Univ Wis-Madison, 85. *Mem:* AAAS; Am Chem Soc; Sigma Xi. *Res:* Development of gas and liquid chromatographic methods; chromatographic theory; chromatographic techniques for determination of therapeutic drugs in biological fluids, usually urine and blood or plasma; ion exchange chromatography. *Mailing Add:* Chem Dept Marquette Univ Milwaukee WI 53233. *Fax:* 414-288-3300

HOFFMAN, PAUL FELIX, ORIGIN AND EVOLUTION OF CONTINENTAL LITHOSPHERE, PROTEROZOIC OROGENIC BELTS & SEDIMENTARY BASINS. *Current Pos:* STURGIS HOOPER PROF GEOL, HARVARD UNIV, 94- *Personal Data:* b Toronto, Ont, Mar 21, 41; m 76, Erica J Westbrook; c Guys. *Educ:* McMaster Univ, BSc, 64; Johns Hopkins Univ, MS, 65, PhD(geol), 70. *Honors & Awards:* Sproule Award, Soc Econ Paleontologists & Mineralogists, 73; Matson Award, Am Asn Petrol Geologists, 75; Past Presidents Medal, Geol Asn Can, 76 & Logan Medal, 92; Douglas Medal, Can Soc Petrol Geologists, 92. *Prof Exp:* Lectr geol, Franklin & Marshall Col, Lancaster, Pa, 68-69; res sci, Dept Energy, Mines & Resources, Geol Surv Can, 69-92; prof earth sci, Sch Earth & Ocean Sci, Univ Victoria, 92-94. *Concurrent Pos:* Lectr geol, Univ Calif, Santa Barbara, 71-72; Fairchild scholar, Calif Inst Technol, 74-75; vis prof, Univ Tex, Dallas, 78; distinguished lectr, Am Asn Petrol Geologists, 78-79; vis prof earth sci, Univ Tex, Dallas, 78, Carleton Univ, Ottawa, 89-92, Lamont-Doherty Earth Observ, Columbia Univ, 90. *Mem:* Fel Royal Soc Can; Geol Asn Can; Geol Soc Am; foreign hon mem AAAS; Geol Asn Can. *Res:* The tectonic assembly and interactions of continents in proterozoic time and their role in the evolution of other earth systems (mantle, hydrosphere, biosphere, atmosphere). *Mailing Add:* Dept Earth Sci Harvard Univ 1350 Massachusetts Cambridge MA 02138-3800. *Fax:* 617-495-8839

HOFFMAN, PAUL NED, NEURO-OPHTHALMOLOGY. *Current Pos:* Fel neuropath, Johns Hopkins Univ, 76-77, resident ophthal, 77-80, fel ophthal, 80-81, asst prof neurol, 81-87, ASSOC PROF OPHTHAL, JOHNS HOPKINS UNIV, 87- *Personal Data:* b Cornwall, NY, Sept 16, 47; m 83, Carolyn Van Schoik. *Educ:* Cornell Univ, BS, 69; Case Western Res Univ, PhD(neurobiol), 74, MD, 76. *Mem:* Soc Neurosci; Am Soc Cell Biol; Am Soc Neurochem; Am Acad Ophthal. *Res:* The role of the neuronal cytoskeleton in axonal growth and the response of neurons to axonal injury; the control of neuronal gene expression; central nervous system regeneration. *Mailing Add:* Dept Ophthal & Neurol Johns Hopkins Univ Med Sch 600 N Wolfe St Meyer S 167 Baltimore MD 21205. *Fax:* 410-614-1008; *E-Mail:* phoffman@welchlink.welch.jhu.edu

HOFFMAN, PAUL ROGER, CHEMICAL ENGINEERING. *Current Pos:* PRES, TEXTRON SPECIALTY MAT, 78- *Personal Data:* b New York, NY, May 10, 34; m, Lynn Thompson; c Lane, Spencer & Britton. *Educ:* Yale Univ, BE, 55, MS, 58, PhD(chem eng), 59. *Prof Exp:* Mkt res analyst, Union Carbide Chem Co, 59; sect chief mat sci, Res & Adv Develop Div, Avco Corp, 62-63, mgr res projs staff, 63-64, mgr applns dept, 64-65, dir mat technol, 65-69, vpres res & eng, Avco Space Systs Div, 69-70, vpres mat & chem processes, Avco Systs Div, 70-77, vpres & gen mgr, Avco Specialty Mat Div, 77-78. *Mem:* Am Inst Aeronaut & Astronaut; Am Inst Chem. *Res:* Materials research, development and production; chemical market research. *Mailing Add:* Textron Specialty Mat Div 2 Industrial Ave Lowell MA 01851

HOFFMAN, RICHARD BRUCE, PHYSICS. *Current Pos:* asst prof, 68-72, VPRES & LECTR PHYSICS, FRANKLIN & MARSHALL COL, 72- *Personal Data:* b Manheim, Pa, Nov 29, 36; m 57; c 3. *Educ:* Lehigh Univ, BS, 62, MS, 63, PhD(physics), 67. *Prof Exp:* Instr physics, Temple Univ, 66-67, res assoc, 67-68. *Mem:* Am Phys Soc; Am Asn Physics Teachers; NY Acad Sci; Am Asn Univ Professors. *Res:* Double crystal spectrometry; celestial mechanics; general relativity. *Mailing Add:* Franklin & Marshall Col PO Box 3003 Lancaster PA 17604

HOFFMAN, RICHARD LAIRD, RHEOLOGY & COLLOID CHEMISTRY, MICROENCAPSULATION. *Current Pos:* SR RES SCIENTIST, UNIV NH, 94- *Personal Data:* b Cincinnati, Ohio, Apr 30, 39; m 63, Judith Reynolds; c Richard W & Kathryn (Reynolds). *Educ:* Ohio State Univ, BChE, 62, MS, 62; Princeton Univ, MA & PhD(chem eng), 68. *Prof Exp:* Res specialist, Monsanto Co, 68-78, sci fel, 78-86, sr fel, 86-94. *Mem:* Soc Rheol. *Res:* Fluid mechanics; flow behavior of concentrated suspensions of solids in liquid, especially dilatant flow; characterization of flow near interfaces; polymer rheology; particle size measurement; microencapsulation for controlled release. *Mailing Add:* 14 Meadowview Rd Wilbraham MA 01095

HOFFMAN, RICHARD LAWRENCE, systematic zoology, for more information see previous edition

HOFFMAN, RICHARD OTTO, INDUSTRIAL ENGINEERING, MANUFACTURING ENGINEERING. *Current Pos:* asst prof indust eng, 70-76, assoc prof, 76-81, PROF INDUST & MGT ENG, UNIV NEBR, LINCOLN, 81- *Personal Data:* b Chicago, Ill, Aug 4, 39; m 61, Patricia R Mark; c Keith & Kenneth. *Educ:* Iowa State Univ, BS, 63, MS, 66; Va Polytech Inst & State Univ, PhD(indust eng), 71. *Prof Exp:* Res asst indust eng, Iowa State Univ, 62-63, grad asst, 63-64, instr, 64-66; indust engr, Hosp Systs Res Group, Univ Mich, Ann Arbor, 66-67; indust engr, Community Systs Found, 67-68; instr indust eng, Va Polytech Inst & State Univ, 68-70. *Mem:* Am Inst Indust Engrs; Am Soc Eng Educ; Cert Network Engrs Prof Asn. *Res:* Facility design; computer-aided manufacturing; quality control systems; packaging engineering; computer networking. *Mailing Add:* Dept Indust Eng Univ Nebr Lincoln NE 68588-0518. *Fax:* 402-472-2410; *E-Mail:* rhoffman@unlinfo.unl.edu

HOFFMAN, RICHARD WAGNER, SOLID STATE PHYSICS. *Current Pos:* Res assoc, Case Western Reserve Univ, 49-52, from instr to prof, 52-81, AMBROSE SUASEY PROF PHYSICS, CASE WESTERN RES UNIV, 81- *Personal Data:* b Cleveland, Ohio, Apr 9, 27; m 50; c 3. *Educ:* Case Inst, BS, 47, MS, 49, PhD(physics), 52. *Concurrent Pos:* Mem tech staff, Bell Labs, 55-56, dep to George Kelley Reader, Oxford, 62-63. *Mem:* Am Phys Soc; Am Vacuum Soc (pres, 77). *Res:* Structure-property relations in thin film and solid surfaces, especially magnetic and mechanical properties; surface analysis, including specialized techniques of optical, electron and x-ray spectroscopy. *Mailing Add:* 34660 Sherwood Dr Solon OH 44139

HOFFMAN, ROBERT, DENTISTRY, ORTHODONTICS. *Current Pos:* DIR RES, MODULATION OPTICS INC, 76- *Personal Data:* b Brooklyn, NY, Nov 27, 28; m 52; c 3. *Educ:* Colgate Univ, BA, 50; NY Univ, DDS, 55. *Honors & Awards:* Albert Joachim Int Award, 67. *Prof Exp:* Staff scientist, Waldemar Med Res Found, 63-67, dir dent mat res, 67-76, dir micros, 74-76. *Concurrent Pos:* Adj prof, Adelphi Univ, Garden City, NY, 76-; consult. *Mem:* Soc Photo-Optical Instrumentation Engr; Am Dent Asn; Am Asn Orthod; Int Asn Dent Res; Int Dent Fedn. *Res:* Ultrasonic bonding of metal to hard tissue; ultrasonic casting; invention and development of the modulation contrast microscope for imaging phase gradient objects; differential interference microscopy; advanced optical techniques for hard tissues study; electro-optic methods for detecting and measuring motion; microstructures of dental enamel; invention of "HMOS" precision measuring device. *Mailing Add:* Modulation Optics Inc 100 Forest Dr Greenvale NY 11548

HOFFMAN, ROBERT A, SPACE PHYSICS. *Current Pos:* Mem staff aerospace technol, Lab Planetary Atmospheres, 61-80, MEM STAFF, LAB EXTRATERRESTRIAL PHYSICS, GODDARD SPACE FLIGHT CTR, NASA, 80- *Personal Data:* b Winona, Minn, Jan 30, 34; m 59, Barbara A Plunkett; c Cynthia & David. *Educ:* St Mary's Col, Minn, BS, 56; Univ Minn, MS, 61, PhD(physics), 62. *Honors & Awards:* Medal Except Sci Achievement, NASA. *Concurrent Pos:* Nat Acad Sci-NASA res fel, 61-63; lectr, Cath Univ Am, 65-68. *Mem:* Am Geophys Union. *Res:* Magnetospheric physics; auroral physics and high latitude ionospheric phenomena; magnetosphere-ionosphere coupling. *Mailing Add:* Code 696 Goddard Space Flight Ctr Greenbelt MD 20771. *E-Mail:* hoffman@eldyn2.gsfc.nasa.gov

HOFFMAN, ROBERT A, AGRICULTURAL ADMINISTRATION. *Current Pos:* RETIRED. *Personal Data:* b Portland, Ore, June 30, 19; m 43; c 2. *Educ:* Ore State Univ, BS, 47; Okla State Univ, MS, 65, PhD, 68; Am Registry Prof Entomologists, dipl. *Prof Exp:* Fishery biologist, State Game Comn, Ore, 47; res asst, Entom Res Div, Agr Res Serv, USDA, 47-49, jr entomologist, 50-56, entomologist & substa leader, Miss, 56-60, res entomologist, Tex, 60-68, agr adminr, Plant Indust Sta, Agr Res Serv, MD, 68-72, invest leader & res entomologist, Vet Toxicol & Entom Res Lab, 72-73, agr adminr, Okla-Tex Area, 73-82. *Concurrent Pos:* Mem NSF seminar, NC State Univ, 65. *Mem:* Entom Soc Am; Am Mosquito Control Asn; Sigma Xi. *Res:* Medical and veterinary entomology, especially biology and control of the blood feeding insects. *Mailing Add:* Rte 3 Box L-312 Franklin TX 77856

HOFFMAN, ROBERT FRANK, CHEMICAL ENGINEERING, PHYSICAL CHEMISTRY. *Current Pos:* tech dir, 84-88, DIR ENVIRON & HUMAN RELATIONS, ICI POLYURETHANES, 88- *Personal Data:* b Riverside, NJ, Apr 2, 35; m 60, Betty Cogswell; c Crystal & Garry. *Educ:* Drexel Univ, BS, 57; Princeton Univ, MSE, 58; Univ Pa, PhD(chem eng), 67. *Prof Exp:* Process engr chem eng, Thiokol Corp, Trenton, NJ, 58-62, pilot plant supvr, 62-67, mgr process develop, 67-74, res & develop dir, 74-77, dir tech opers chem eng & admin, 77-79; tech dir, Rubicon Chem Inc, Wilmington, 79-84. *Concurrent Pos:* Adj asst prof, Drexel Univ, 68-74. *Mem:* Am Inst Chem Engrs; Sigma Xi. *Res:* Health and environmental research on the effects of isocyanates. *Mailing Add:* 25 Horse Shoe Curve Medford NJ 08055

HOFFMAN, ROBERT M, CANCER BIOLOGY, HAIR FOLLICLE BIOLOGY. *Current Pos:* PROF CANCER BIOL, UNIV CALIF, SAN DIEGO, 79-; PRES, ANTICANCER INC, 84- *Personal Data:* b Greenwich, Conn, June 19, 44. *Educ:* Univ Buffalo, BA, 65; Harvard Univ, PhD(biol), 71. *Prof Exp:* Instr, Harvard Med Sch, Mass Gen Hosp, 75-79. *Mem:* Am Asn Cancer Res; Am Soc Clin Oncol; Tissue Cult Asn; Am Soc Cell Biol; Japanese Cancer Asn; Soc Investigative Dermat. *Res:* Cancer biology; biochemistry and molecular genetics of cancer; development of preclinical models of human cancer, in vitro and in vivo; cancer drug development; hair growth and pigmentation. *Mailing Add:* AntiCancer Inc 7917 Ostrow St San Diego CA 92111. *Fax:* 619-268-4175; *E-Mail:* antica@1x.netcom.com

HOFFMAN, ROBERT VERNON, ORGANIC CHEMISTRY. *Current Pos:* mem fac, 74-80, ASSOC PROF CHEM, NMEX STATE UNIV, 80- *Personal Data:* b Canton, Ohio, Nov 11, 44; m 69. *Educ:* Case Western Res Univ, BS, 66, PhD(chem), 70. *Prof Exp:* Res assoc org chem, Ohio State Univ, 69-74. *Mem:* Am Chem Soc; Sigma Xi. *Res:* Electrophilic aromatic substitution; peroxide decompositions and oxidation; intermolecular and intramolecular carbenic reactions. *Mailing Add:* 605 College Pl Las Cruces NM 88005-3328

HOFFMAN, ROGER ALAN, NEUROENDOCRINOLOGY, REPRODUCTIVE BIOLOGY. *Current Pos:* assoc prof, 65-70, PROF BIOL, COLGATE UNIV, 70- *Personal Data:* b Willimantic, Conn, Feb 23, 24; m 46; c 3. *Educ:* Univ Conn, BS, 50; Purdue Univ, MS, 52, PhD(physiol, endocrinol), 56. *Prof Exp:* Asst wildlife mgt, Purdue Univ, 50-52, asst zool, 53-54, wildlife biologist, Maine Dept Inland Fish & Game, 52-53; biologist, physiol & endocrinol, Army Chem Ctr, 56-65. *Concurrent Pos:* Res grant, NSF, Purdue Univ, 59; vis lectr, Loyola Col, Md, 59-; NIMH fel, Univ Rochester, 69-70; Pop Coun fel, Univ Del Valle, Colombia, 71-72; dir reg biol, NSF, 75-76; vis scientist, Bur Drug Biol, Food & Drug Admin, Washington, DC, 78-79. *Mem:* AAAS; Am Soc Zoologists; Am Physiol Soc; Am Soc Mammal; Soc Study Reproduction. *Res:* Male reproduction in seasonal breeders; thyroid-gonad relationships; psychopharmacology and temperature regulation; hormonal aspects of temperature regulation; hibernation; comparative endocrinology; pineal gland-endocrine system relationships. *Mailing Add:* Dept Biol Colgate Univ Box 231 Hamilton NY 13346-1338

HOFFMAN, ROGER ALLEN, ORGANIC CHEMISTRY. *Current Pos:* RETIRED. *Personal Data:* b LaCrosse, Wis, Sept 6, 15; m 39, Marguerite Sylvester; c Peter J & Diane (Amsel). *Educ:* Univ Wis, BS, 39; Univ Mich, MS, 40, PhD(org chem), 42. *Prof Exp:* Res chemist, Merck, Sharp & Dohme, 42-50, mgr develop res group, Cherokee Plant, 50-55, mgr, Rahway Process Develop Group, 55-58, prod mgr, India, 58-63, managing dir, Pakistan Ltd, 63-67, admin mgr, Int Div, Southeast Asia, 67-68 & Europe, 69-74, sr dir subsidiary serv Europe, 74-79, exec dir tech opers, 80-85. *Mem:* Am Chem Soc. *Res:* Developmental research on pharmaceuticals; dissociation of pentaarylethanes. *Mailing Add:* 20 Dogwood Dr Madison NJ 07940-2609

HOFFMAN, ROSS N, ASSIMILATION OF REMOTELY SENSED DATA. *Current Pos:* sr staff scientist, 83-88, PRIN SCIENTIST, ATMOSPHERIC & ENVIRON RES, INC, 89- *Personal Data:* b Brooklyn, NY, Mar 5, 49; wid; c Max & David. *Educ:* Brown Univ, ScB, 71; Boston Univ, MA, 75; Mass Inst Technol, PhD(meteorol), 80. *Prof Exp:* Nat Res

Coun, resident res assoc, Goddard Space Flight Ctr, NASA, 80-82. *Mem:* Am Meteorol Soc; Am Geophys Union; Soc Indust & Appl Math. *Res:* Improve use of satellite data for numerical weather prediction; microwave data, both passive radiometer and active scatterometer data; developed variational techniques to assimilate data; techniques to use satellite data together with pattern recognition to detect phase errors in forecasts. *Mailing Add:* Atmospheric & Environ Res Inc 840 Memorial Dr Cambridge MA 02139. *Fax:* 617-661-6479; *E-Mail:* rhoffman@aer.com

HOFFMAN, RUTH I, MATHEMATICS, EDUCATION IN COMPUTERS & MATHEMATICS. *Current Pos:* lectr, 55-63, assoc prof, 63-70, PROF MATH, UNIV DENVER, 70- *Personal Data:* b Denver, Colo, Mar 23, 25. *Educ:* Univ Colo, BA, 46, MA, 47; Univ Denver, EdD(math educ), 53. *Prof Exp:* Teacher math, Denver Pub Schs, 47-53, dean admin, 53-58, prin, 58-63. *Concurrent Pos:* Lectr, Regis Col, Colo, 55-58 & Univ Colo, 55-63; consult, Addison Wesley Pub Co, 63- & Sci Res Assocs, 72-; author and math systems dir, Educ Develop Lab, McGraw Hill, 73- *Mem:* Math Asn Am; Am Math Soc; AAAS; NY Acad Sci. *Res:* Mathematics education; geometry; topology. *Mailing Add:* Seaview Terr Castle Townbere County Cork Ireland

HOFFMAN, T(ERRENCE) W(ILLIAM), chemical engineering, for more information see previous edition

HOFFMAN, THEODORE P, ORGANIC CHEMISTRY. *Current Pos:* RETIRED. *Personal Data:* b Jersey City, NJ, Mar 9, 29; m 81, Marian E Finnie. *Educ:* Rutgers Univ, BSc, 50, MSc, 52, PhD(org chem), 55. *Prof Exp:* Develop chemist, Am Cyanamid Co, 55-57; res chemist, Esso Res & Eng Co, 57-61; res scientist, Am Stand Co, 61-65; ed chem, Acad Press, Inc, 65-66; ed, Wiley-Intersci, John Wiley & Sons, 66-84, sr ed, 85-94. *Mem:* Am Chem Soc; NY Acad Sci. *Res:* Organic, inorganic, physical chemistry; biochemistry; macromolecular chemistry. *Mailing Add:* 220 E 67th St New York NY 10021

HOFFMAN, THOMAS, CELL BIOLOGY. *Current Pos:* sr investr, Div Biochem & Biophys, Ctr Drugs & Biologics, 83-84, CHIEF, LAB CELL BIOL, DIV HEMAT, CTR BIOLOGICS EVAL & RES, US FOOD & DRUG ADMIN, NIH, 84- *Personal Data:* b Jan 31, 47. *Educ:* City Col New York, BS, 67; Univ Pittsburgh, MD, 71. *Prof Exp:* Pediat internship & residency, Johns Hopkins Hosp, 71-74; pediat immunol fel, Mem Sloan Kettering Cancer Ctr & immunol res fel, Rockefeller Univ, 74-79; sr investr, Lab Immunodiag & Biol Response Modifiers Prog, Frederick Cancer Res Ctr, Nat Cancer Inst, 79-83. *Concurrent Pos:* Med officer, USPHS Comn Corp, comd, 79-88, capt, 88-, comn corps liason rep CBER, 87-89, res officer group, 90- *Mem:* Am Asn Immunologists; Am Acad Pediat. *Res:* Cell biology; immunology; pediatrics. *Mailing Add:* Lab Cell Biol DMA HFM-558 FDA CBER 1401 Rockville Pike Rockville MD 20852-1488

HOFFMAN, THOMAS R(IPTON), VERY-LARGE-SCALE INTEGRATION DESIGN. *Current Pos:* RETIRED. *Personal Data:* b White Plains, NY, Oct 18, 23; m 45; c Thomas G, Elisabeth S, Debora R & William A. *Educ:* Union Col, NY, BS, 44, MS, 50. *Honors & Awards:* Centennial Medal, Inst Elec & Electronics Engrs. *Prof Exp:* From instr to asst prof elec eng, Union Univ, NY, 46-50; mem tech staff, Bell Tel Labs, 50-54; from assoc prof to prof elec eng, Union Col, NY, 54-79; consult engr, Gen Elec Co, Fla, 79-84, mgr microelectronic, 84-89. *Concurrent Pos:* Consult, Gen Elec Co, 54-79 & Bell Tel Labs, 70-79; Fulbright lectr, Alexandria, 60-61, Taiwan, 67-68; vis prof, Univ Canterbury, Christchurch, NZ, 74. *Mem:* Sr mem Inst Elec & Electronics Engrs; Sigma Xi. *Res:* Digital computers; logic design and programming; digital circuits; semiconductor devices and circuits; microprocessors--applications; electrical engineering. *Mailing Add:* 1115 Jacaranda Ave Daytona Beach FL 32118

HOFFMAN, WARREN E, ORGANIC CHEMISTRY. *Current Pos:* RETIRED. *Personal Data:* b Buffalo, NY, Apr 5, 23; m 48; c 3. *Educ:* Union Col, NY, BS, 51; Univ Buffalo, PhD, 55. *Prof Exp:* Res & develop chemist, Nat Analine Div, Allied Chem & Dye Corp, 54-60; from asst prof to prof chem, Ind Inst Technol, 60-83, chmn dept, 65-76, acad dean, 75-76. *Concurrent Pos:* Qual control engr, Western Elec Corp, 51-52; exp control chemist, E I du Pont de Nemours & Co, 53; consult, Protective Coatings Inc, Tokheim Corp & ITT. *Mem:* AAAS; Am Chem Soc; Am Inst Chem; Am Inst Chem Eng; Soc Appl Spectros; Sigma Xi. *Res:* Nitrogen organic compounds including isocyanates and polymers; oxamidines and cyanogen; physical organic and polymer chemistry; education and medicinal chemistry. *Mailing Add:* 1505 Ridgecrest Lane Longwood FL 32750

HOFFMAN, WAYNE LARRY, ENVIRONMENTAL SCIENCE, EARTH SCIENCE. *Current Pos:* PROF GEOG & HEAD DEPT GEOG & GEOL, WESTERN KY UNIV, 70- *Personal Data:* b Oshkosh, Wis, Aug 12, 37; m 63; c 2. *Educ:* Univ Wis-Oshkosh, BS, 62; Ohio State Univ, MA, 65; Univ Fla, PhD(geog), 70. *Prof Exp:* Instr geog, Univ Wis-Oshkosh, 66-67 & 69-70. *Mem:* Asn Am Geographers; Am Planning Asn; Am Geog Soc. *Res:* Land use and socio-economic areas of geography. *Mailing Add:* Dept Geog & Geol Western Ky Univ 1 Big Red Way St Bowling Green KY 42101-3576

HOFFMAN, WILLIAM ANDREW, JR, ANALYTICAL CHEMISTRY. *Current Pos:* from asst prof to assoc prof, 60-67, chmn dept, 64-67 & 68-69, dean admis, 73-77, PROF CHEM, DENISON UNIV, 67- *Personal Data:* b Hughesville, Mo, July 19, 28; m 51; c 5. *Educ:* Mo Valley Col, BS, 50; Purdue Univ, MS, 52, PhD(chem), 55. *Prof Exp:* Instr Wabash Col, 54-55; asst prof chem, Wesleyan Univ, 55-60. *Mem:* AAAS; Am Chem Soc. *Res:* Solution and atmospheric chemistry. *Mailing Add:* Chem Dept Denison Univ PO Box M Granville OH 43023-0613. *Fax:* 740-587-6417; *E-Mail:* HOFFMAN@CC:DENISON.EDU

HOFFMAN, WILLIAM CHARLES, PHYSICAL MATHEMATICS, MATHEMATICAL STATISTICS. *Current Pos:* prof 69-85, EMER PROF MATH, OAKLAND UNIV, 85- *Personal Data:* b Portland, Ore, Aug 11, 19; m 50, 75; c 3. *Educ:* Univ Calif, Berkeley, BA, 43; Univ Calif, Los Angeles, MA, 47, PhD(math), 53. *Honors & Awards:* Wilson Award, 85. *Prof Exp:* Head anal staff, USN Electronics Lab, 47-49; asst probability proj, Off Naval Res, 49-50; res physicist, Hughes Aircraft Co, 51-52; head anal staff, USN Electronics Lab, 52-55; consult, US Naval Air Missile Test Ctr, 55; mathematician & consult, Rand Corp, 55-59; res mathematician, Hughes Aircraft Co, 59; sr lectr physics, Univ Queensland, 60-61; res mathematician, Boeing Sci Res Labs, 61-65; prof math, Ore State Univ, 66-69. *Concurrent Pos:* Vis prof math, NMex State Univ, 85-86; fel, math psychol, Melbourne Univ, 75-76. *Mem:* Am Math Soc; Psychomet Soc; Am Educ Res Asn; Soc Indust & Appl Math; Am Statist Asn. *Res:* Lie group theory of neuropsychology; geometric psychology; electromagnetic wave propagation; statistical methods. *Mailing Add:* 2591 W Camino Llano Tucson AZ 85742-9074

HOFFMAN, WILLIAM E, anesthesiology, brain function; deceased, see previous edition for last biography

HOFFMAN, WILLIAM F, animal science, dairy science; deceased, see previous edition for last biography

HOFFMAN, WILLIAM HUBERT, PEDIATRIC ENDOCRINOLOGY. *Current Pos:* CHIEF PEDIAT ENDOCRINOL, MED COL GA, 84-, PROF PEDIAT. *Personal Data:* b Toledo, Ohio; m 65; c 3. *Educ:* Marquette Univ, BA, 61, MD, 65. *Prof Exp:* Chief, Childs Hosp Mich, 73-83; med res officer, NIH, 83-84. *Mem:* Am Diabetes Asn; Am Thyroid Asn; Am Col Nutrit; Am Soc Human Genetics; Endocrinol Soc; Pediat Endocrinol Soc. *Mailing Add:* Dept Pediat Med Col Ga Augusta GA 30912-3785. *Fax:* 706-721-7311

HOFFMAN-GOETZ, LAURIE, NUTRITIONAL IMMUNOLOGY, THERMOREGULATION. *Current Pos:* Asst prof, 80-86, ASSOC PROF HEALTH STUDIES, UNIV WATERLOO, 86- *Educ:* Univ Mich, PhD(biol anthrop & physiol), 79. *Mailing Add:* Dept Health Studies Univ Waterloo University Ave Waterloo ON N2L 3G1 Can

HOFFMANN, CONRAD EDMUND, MICROBIOLOGY & DRUG METABOLISM. *Current Pos:* res microbiologist animal med, Stine Lab, E I du Pont de Nemours & Co, 52-58, res supvr, Therapeut Chem Sect, 58-61, mgr, Microbiol Sect, 61-77, MGR MICROBIOL & DRUG METAB, PHARMACEUT DIV, STINE LAB, E I DU PONT DE NEMOURS & CO, INC, 77-, COORDR, PHARMACEUT DIV TASK FORCE, 80-, MGR, LIFE SCI CONSTRUCT, 80- *Personal Data:* b Lawrence, Kans, Apr 15, 20; m 42; c 3. *Educ:* Cornell Univ, BS, 42, MS, 43; Western Reserve Univ, PhD(microbiol), 52. *Prof Exp:* Res assoc, Owens-Ill Glass Co, 45-46; res scientist nutrit & physiol, Lederle Labs, 46-49; asst, Western Reserve Univ, 49-52. *Mem:* Am Soc Microbiol; NY Acad Sci. *Res:* Microbiology; metabolism. *Mailing Add:* 701 Crothers Rd Rising Sun MD 21911-2306

HOFFMANN, DIETRICH, BIOCHEMISTRY, ORGANIC CHEMISTRY. *Current Pos:* Res assoc, 57-60, assoc, 60-66, assoc mem, 66-70, ASSOC SCIENTIST, SLOAN-KETTERING INST CANCER RES, 70-; CHIEF, DIV ENVIRON CARCINOGENESIS, AM HEALTH FOUND, VALHALLA, NY, 70- *Personal Data:* b Danzig, Ger, Dec 10, 24; m 60; c Peter & Ralph. *Educ:* Univ Kiel, BS, 52, MS, 55; Max Planck Inst, PhD(biochem), 57. *Concurrent Pos:* Asst prof, Sloan-Kettering Div, Med Col, Cornell Univ, 61-69; assoc dir, chem & biochem, Am Health Found, Valhalla, NY, 80- *Mem:* Am Chem Soc; NY Acad Sci; Am Asn Cancer Res; fel Am Inst Chem; Soc Toxicol; Am Soc Prev Oncol; Phytochem Soc. *Res:* Experimental and environmental carcinogenesis; environmental analysis; tobacco sciences. *Mailing Add:* Am Health Found 1 Dana Rd Valhalla NY 10595-1599. *Fax:* 914-592-6317

HOFFMANN, EDWARD MARKER, IMMUNOLOGY. *Current Pos:* from asst prof to prof, 68-80, PROF MICROBIOL, CELL SCI, IMMUNOL & MED MICROBIOL, INST FOOD & AGR SCI, UNIV FLA, 80-, CHMN, DEPT MICROBIOL & CELL SCI, 89- *Personal Data:* b Mar 1, 34; US citizen; m 57; c 2. *Educ:* Fla State Univ, BS, 56; Univ Miami, MS, 62, PhD(microbiol), 67. *Prof Exp:* Lab asst bact, Fla State Bd Health, 56; res asst immunol, Univ Fla, 59; res scientist immunochem, Sch Med, Univ Miami, 66-74. *Concurrent Pos:* USPHS trainee, 59-60. *Mem:* Am Soc Microbiol; Am Asn Immunologists. *Res:* Isolation of an anticomplementary substance from human erythrocytes; complement deficiencies in lymphoproliferative diseases; phylogenetic aspects of complement system; role of complement in virus elimination; resistance to brucellosis. *Mailing Add:* Dept Microbiol & Cell Sci Univ Fla Bldg 981 Box 110700 Gainesville FL 32611-0700. *Fax:* 904-392-5922

HOFFMANN, GEOFFREY WILLIAM, IMMUNE SYSTEM NETWORK THEORY, NEURAL NETWORK THEORY. *Current Pos:* ASSOC PROF PHYSICS & MICROBIOL, UNIV BC, VANCOUVER, CAN, 79- *Personal Data:* b Hamilton, Victoria, Australia, Oct 20, 44; m 71; c 2. *Educ:* Univ Melbourne, BSc, 67, MSc, 68; Max Planck Inst, PhD(biophys chem), 72. *Prof Exp:* Postdoctoral phys chem, IBM Res Labs, San Jose, Calif, 72-73; scientist theoret biol, Max Planck Inst Biophys Chem, Gottingen, Ger, 73-74; mem theoret immunol, Basel Inst Immunol, Switz, 74-79. *Concurrent Pos:* Collabr theoret biol group, Los Alamos Nat Lab, 85-86. *Mem:* Can Soc Immunologists; Can Asn Physicists. *Res:* Theoretical biology; stochastic theory of origin of life; symmetric network theory of regulation of immune system; neural network theory. *Mailing Add:* Dept Physics Univ BC Vancouver BC V6T 2L2 Can. *Fax:* 604-222-6645

HOFFMANN, GEORGE ROBERT, MICROBIAL GENETICS, GENETIC TOXICOLOGY. *Current Pos:* from asst prof to assoc prof, 81-89, CHMN BIOL, HOLY CROSS COL, WORCESTER, MASS, 85-, PROF BIOL, 89- *Personal Data:* b Jersey City, NJ, June 6, 46; m 69, Linda Wagner; c Lisa. *Educ:* Rutgers Univ, AB, 67; Univ Tenn, Knoxville, MS, 69, PhD(bot), 72. *Prof Exp:* Instr biol, Roane State Community Col, Harriman, Tenn, 72-73; fel genetics, Nat Inst Environ Health Sci, Res Triangle Park, NC, 73-74; asst prof biol, Meredith Col, Raleigh, NC, 74-77; geneticist, Nat Inst Environ Health Sci, 77-78; sr staff off toxicol, Nat Acad Sci, Wash, DC, 79-81. *Concurrent Pos:* Mem, Nat Res Coun Panel Irritant Chem, 82-84; consult, L'Oreal Res Lab, Aulnay-sous-Bois, France, 81-94, US Environ Protection Agency, Wash, DC, 82-88 & Biol Panel Carcinogenicity of BHA, Fedn Am Socs Exp Biol, 92-94; assoc ed genetic toxicol, J Am Col Toxicol, 82-, ed-in-chief, Environ Molecular Mutagenesis, 83-88; vis scientist, Nat Ctr Sci Res, Strasbourg, France, 88-89 & 95-96. *Mem:* Genetics Soc Am; Environ Mutagen Soc (pres, 90-91); Bot Soc Am; Am Col Toxicol; Sigma Xi. *Res:* Bacterial and fungal genetics; mutagenesis; genetic toxicology testing. *Mailing Add:* Dept Biol Holy Cross Col Worcester MA 01610

HOFFMANN, JOAN CAROL, ENDOCRINOLOGY, REPRODUCTIVE BIOLOGY. *Current Pos:* ASSOC DEAN, OFF STUDENT AFFAIRS, UNIV MASS MED SCH, 83- *Personal Data:* b Cedarburg, Wis, Feb 20, 34. *Educ:* Univ Wis-Madison, BS, 59; Univ Ill, Chicago, PhD(physiol), 65. *Prof Exp:* Asst prof nursing & physiol, Sch Med & Dent, Univ Rochester, 65-70; from assoc prof to prof anat & reproductive biol, Sch Med, Univ Hawaii, 70-83. *Concurrent Pos:* Nat Inst Child Health & Human Develop res grant, 66-75. *Mem:* Sigma Xi; Am Physiol Soc; Endocrine Soc; Soc Study Reproduction; Am Asn Anat. *Res:* Factors controlling the timing of ovulation; effects of the environment, particularly light, on reproduction in mammals; control mechanisms of neuro-endocrine function. *Mailing Add:* 30 Homestead Rd Sedona AZ 86336-3236

HOFFMANN, JON ARNOLD, FLUID DYNAMICS. *Current Pos:* PROF AERONAUT ENG, CALIF POLYTECH STATE UNIV, 68- *Personal Data:* b Waukesha, Wis, Jan, 13, 42; m 73, Carol R Frye. *Educ:* Univ Wis, BS, 64, MS, 66. *Prof Exp:* Res engr, Trane Co, 66-68. *Concurrent Pos:* Res engr, Stanford Univ, 70; res fel, NASA Ames Res Ctr, 74-75, consult, 75-77, prin investr, 81-89; consult, Orvis Co, 95- *Mem:* Am Soc Mech Engrs. *Res:* Author of numerous publications. *Mailing Add:* Dept Aeronaut Eng Calif Polytech State Univ San Luis Obispo CA 93407. *Fax:* 805-756-2376

HOFFMANN, JOSEPH JOHN, RENEWABLE RESOURCES, PHYTOCHEMISTRY. *Current Pos:* teaching asst, Univ Ariz, 72-75, res assoc, 75-79, from asst prof to assoc prof, 80-92, DIR, BIORESOURCES RES FACIL, UNIV ARIZ, 81-, PROF MED CHEM, 92-, CHAIR, ARID LANDS RESOURCE SCI PHD PROG, 94- *Personal Data:* b Waukesha, Wis, Apr 26, 50; c 1. *Educ:* St Norbert Col, BS, 71; Univ Ariz, PhD(med chem), 75. *Prof Exp:* Teaching asst chem, St Norbert Col, 69-71. *Concurrent Pos:* Fel, Lloyd Found Pharm Educ, 72; vis lectr, Univs Venice & Florence, Italy, 78. *Mem:* Am Chem Soc; Soc Econ Bot; Phytochem Soc NAm; Am Soc Pytochem. *Res:* Renewable resources, especially chemicals and fuels from arid lands plants; isolation and identification of medicinal agents and agrochemical from plants and microorganisms, biotransformations. *Mailing Add:* Univ Ariz 250 E Valencia Rd Tucson AZ 85706-6800. *Fax:* 520-741-1468

HOFFMANN, LOUIS GERHARD, IMMUNOLOGY. *Current Pos:* from asst prof to assoc prof, 64-73, PROF MICROBIOL, COL MED, UNIV IOWA, 73- *Personal Data:* b Bloemendaal, Neth, July 12, 32; US citizen; m 55; c 2. *Educ:* Wesleyan Univ, BA, 53; Johns Hopkins Univ, ScM, 58, ScD(microbiol), 60. *Prof Exp:* NSF fel, Univ Calif, Berkeley, 60-62; from instr to asst prof microbiol, Sch Med, Johns Hopkins Univ, 62-64. *Concurrent Pos:* USPHS fel, 62-63, res grant, 64-67; NSF res grants, 67-73; Iowa Heart Asn res grant, 69-72; Damon Runyon-Walter Winchell Cancer Fund res grant, 71-73; Roche Res Found fel, 75; res grants, Iowa Heart Asn, 77-78 & NIH, 80-83. *Mem:* AAAS; Soc Exp Biol & Med; NY Acad Sci; Am Asn Immunol. *Res:* Chemical basis of antibody activity as manifested in cytotoxic effects in conjunction with complement. *Mailing Add:* Dept Microbiol Univ Iowa Col Med Iowa City IA 52242-0001. *Fax:* 319-335-9006

HOFFMANN, MICHAEL K, MICROBIOLOGY. *Current Pos:* PROF, NY MED COL, VALHALLA, 89- *Personal Data:* b Breslau, Ger, Mar 6, 39; wid. *Educ:* Univ Heidelberg, Physikum, 63; Univ Tubingen, MD, 66. *Prof Exp:* Postdoctoral sci teaching asst, Max-Planck Inst fur Virusforschung, Ger, 66-70; postdoctoral fel, Univ Calif, San Diego, 70-71; res assoc, Sloan-Kettering Inst Cancer Res, NY, 71-72, assoc, 73-78, assoc mem, 78-89; assoc prof, Cornell Univ Med Col, 73-89. *Mailing Add:* Dept Microbiol & Immunol NY Med Col Valhalla NY 10595. *Fax:* 914-993-4176

HOFFMANN, MICHAEL ROBERT, APPLIED CHEMICAL & MICROBIAL CATALYSIS, ENVIRONMENTAL, CLOUD & FOG CHEMISTRY. *Current Pos:* from assoc prof to prof environ eng, 80-90, prof environ chem, 90-95, JAMES IRVINE PROF, CALIF INST TECHNOL, 96- *Personal Data:* b Fond du Lac, Wis, Nov 13, 46; m; c 2. *Educ:* Northwestern Univ, BA, 68; Brown Univ, PhD(chem), 73. *Honors & Awards:* E Gordon Young Award, 95. *Prof Exp:* From asst prof to assoc prof civil eng, Univ Minn, 75-80. *Concurrent Pos:* USPHS res fel, Calif Inst Technol, 73-75; ed, Environ Div, Am Chem Soc, 78-84 & assoc ed, J Geophys Res, 84-86; chmn, Gordon Res Conf, 88; Alexander von Humboldt Prize, 91. *Mem:* AAAS; Am Chem Soc; Am Geophys Union; Asn Environ Eng Prof; Soc Limnol & Oceanog. *Res:* Air and water pollution; atmospheric and aquatic chemistry; photocatalysis, microbial and chemical catalysis; chemistry and physics of clouds and fogs; reaction kinetics; sonochemistry; pulsed plasma. *Mailing Add:* Environ Eng Sci Calif Inst Technol Pasadena CA 91125

HOFFMANN, PHILIP CRAIG, PHARMACOLOGY. *Current Pos:* from instr to assoc prof, 63-80, PROF PHARMACOL, SCH MED, UNIV CHICAGO, 80- *Personal Data:* b Evanston, Ill, June 18, 36. *Educ:* Univ Chicago, BS, 57, PhD(pharmacol), 62. *Honors & Awards:* Quantrell Prize, 71. *Prof Exp:* NSF fel, Pharmacol Inst, Univ Marburg, 62-63; guest res assoc, Royal Vet Col Sweden, 63. *Concurrent Pos:* Prin investr, USPHS res grant, 64- *Mem:* AAAS; Am Soc Pharmacol & Exp Therapeut; Soc Neurosci. *Res:* Neurochemical control of metabolism; neurochemical aspects of development. *Mailing Add:* Pharmacol & Physiol Sci Univ Chicago 947 E 58th St Chicago IL 60637-1431. *Fax:* 773-702-3774

HOFFMANN, RICHARD JOHN, POPULATION BIOLOGY, MARINE BIOLOGY. *Current Pos:* assoc prof, 80-87, PROF ZOOL & GENETICS, IOWA STATE UNIV, 87-, ASSOC DEAN, COL LIB ARTS & SCI, 93- *Personal Data:* b Ames, Iowa, Nov 8, 46; m 69; c 2. *Educ:* Col William & Mary, BS, 69; Stanford Univ, MA, 71, PhD(biol sci), 74. *Prof Exp:* Scholar biol oceanog, Woods Hole Oceanog Inst, 74-75; asst prof biol sci, Univ Pittsburgh, 75-79. *Concurrent Pos:* Woodrow Wilson fel, 69; instr invert zool, Marine Biol Lab, 77; prin investr, NSF, 78-79, 82-86, 89-90, 90-94 & NIH, 79-82. *Mem:* Fel AAAS; Soc Study Evolution; Soc Molecular Biol & Evolution; Sigma Xi. *Res:* Function of genetic variation at the enzyme level in natural populations; ecological genetics; microevolution; biology of coelenterates; population structure of asexual organisms; mt DNA genetics. *Mailing Add:* Col Lib Arts & Sci Iowa State Univ Ames IA 50011-1301. *E-Mail:* rjhoffman@iastate.edu

HOFFMANN, ROALD, THEORETICAL CHEMISTRY. *Current Pos:* from assoc prof to prof chem, 68-74, John A Newman Prof Phys Sci, 74-96, FRANK M T RHODES PROF HUMANE LETT, CORNELL UNIV, 96- *Personal Data:* b Zloczow, Poland, July 18, 37; US citizen; m 60, Eva Borjesson; c Hillel J & Ingrid H. *Educ:* Columbia Univ, BA, 58; Harvard Univ, MA, 60, PhD(chem physics), 62. *Hon Degrees:* Twenty-three from US & foreign univs, 78-93. *Honors & Awards:* Nobel Prize in Chem, 81; Pure Chem Award, Am Chem Soc, 69, Harrison Howe Award, 70, Arthur C Cope Award, 73, Pauling Award, 74, Inorg Chem Award, 82 & Priestly Medal, 90; Int Acad Quantum Molecular Sci Award, 71; Nichols Medal, 81; Inorg Chem Award, 82; Nat Medal Sci, 83; Semenov Gold Medal, Acad Sci USSR, 91. *Prof Exp:* Jr fel, Soc Fels, Harvard Univ, 62-65. *Mem:* Nat Acad Sci; AAAS; Int Acad Quantum Molecular Sci; Am Phys Soc; foreign mem Royal Swed Acad Sci; foreign mem Royal Soc; foreign fel Indian Nat Sci Acad; Am Philos Soc; foreign mem Finnish Acad Sci. *Res:* Molecular orbital calculations of electronic structure of ground and excited states of molecules; theoretical studies of transition states and intermediates in organic and inorganic reactions. *Mailing Add:* Dept Chem Cornell Univ Ithaca NY 14853

HOFFMANN, ROBERT SHAW, SYSTEMATICS, ECOLOGY. *Current Pos:* asst secy sci, Smithsonian Inst, Washington, DC, 88-92, asst secy res, 92-94, act provost, 94-96, act dir, Nat Air Space Mus, 95-96, SEN SCIENTIST, SMITHSONIAN INST, WASHINGTON, DC, 96- *Personal Data:* b Evanston, Ill, Mar 2, 29; m 51, Sally A Monson; c Karl, John, David & Brenna. *Educ:* Utah State Univ, BS, 50; Univ Calif, Berkeley, MA, 54, PhD(zool), 55. *Hon Degrees:* DSc, Utah State Univ, 88. *Prof Exp:* From instr to prof zool, Univ Mont, 55-68; Summerfield distinguished prof systs & ecol, Univ Kans, Lawrence, 68-86, chmn, Dept Systs & Ecol, Mus Natural Hist, 69-72, chmn div biol sci, 75-76, assoc dean & actg dean, Col Liberal Arts & Sci, 78-82; dir, Nat Mus Natural Hist, 86-88. *Concurrent Pos:* Nat Acad Sci exchange fel, USSR, 63-64; mem & chmn, US Nat Comt Int Union Quaternary Res, 78-82; mem, Nat Acad Sci & US-USSR joint Comt Sci Policy. *Mem:* Brit Mammal Soc; Ecol Soc Am; hon mem Am Soc Mammal (pres, 78-80); Soc Study Evolution; Soc Syst Zoologists (pres, 88-89); hon mem All-Union Theriol Soc USSR; fel AAAS; foreign mem Russ Acad Natural Sci. *Res:* Systematics, evolution and biogeography of birds and mammals; population and community ecology; evolution of biotic communities, pleistocene-recent. *Mailing Add:* Div Mammal Nat Mus Nat Hist MRC108 Smithsonian Inst Washington DC 20560. *Fax:* 202-786-2979

HOFFMANN, THOMAS RUSSELL, TECHNICAL MANAGEMENT, INDUSTRIAL & MANUFACTURING ENGINEERING. *Current Pos:* assoc prof, 63-65, PROF OPERS MGT, UNIV MINN, 65- *Personal Data:* b Milwaukee, Wis, Sept 10, 33; m 57, Lorna Graenzel; c Timothy J. *Educ:* Univ Wis, BS, 55, MS, 56, PhD(indust eng), 59. *Prof Exp:* Engr, Allis-Chalmers Mfg Co, 56-59; asst prof prod mgt, Univ Wis, 59-63. *Concurrent Pos:* Chmn, Mgt Sci Dept, Univ Minn, 69-78, dir, W Bank Comput Serv, 71-87. *Mem:* Am Prod & Inventory Control Soc; Inst Mgt Sci; Asn Comput Mach. *Res:* Computing technology in the field of operations management; assembly line balancing, shop floor scheduling and linear programming; author or co-author of five books and 50 articles. *Mailing Add:* 4501 Sedum Lane Edina MN 55435. *Fax:* 612-626-1316; *E-Mail:* THOFFMANN@CSOM.UNM.EDU

HOFFMANN, WILLIAM FREDERICK, INFRARED ASTRONOMY, ASTRONOMICAL INSTRUMENTATION. *Current Pos:* PROF ASTRON, STEWARD OBSERV, UNIV ARIZ, 73- *Personal Data:* b Manchester, NH, Feb 26, 33; m 65; c Andrea & Christopher. *Educ:* Bowdoin Col, AB, 54; Princeton Univ, PhD(physics), 62. *Honors & Awards:* Except Sci Achievement Medal, NASA, 72. *Prof Exp:* Instr physics, Princeton Univ, 58-61; resident res assoc, NASA Goddard Inst Space Studies, 62; instr, Yale Univ, 62-65; physicist, NASA Goddard Inst Space Studies, 65-73. *Concurrent Pos:* Adj assoc prof astron, Columbia Univ, 69-73; NSF fel, 54; Danforth fel, 54-58. *Mem:* Fel AAAS; Am Phys Soc; Am Astron Soc; AAAS; Sigma Xi. *Res:* Infrared astronomy; astronomical telescope construction. *Mailing Add:* Steward Observ Univ Ariz Tucson AZ 85721

HOFFMANN-PINTHER, PETER HUGO, NUCLEAR STRUCTURE CALCULATION. *Current Pos:* FAC, DEPT NATURAL SCI, UNIV HOUSTON. *Personal Data:* b Chicago, Ill, Feb 14, 35; m 62. *Educ:* St Mary's Univ, BS, 58, Ind Univ, MS, 64; Ohio Univ, PhD(physics), 73. *Prof Exp:* Res Scientist US Tank Automotive Command, 60-61; instr physics, Ohio State Univ, 71-73, vis fel, 74-77; instr physics, Ohio State Univ, 71-73, vis fel, 74-77. *Mem:* Am Phys Soc; Sigma Xi. *Res:* Theory fructuation nuclear cross-section and nuclear structure calculation; science in pre-Columbian America. *Mailing Add:* Dept Natural Sci Univ Houston Downtown 1 Main St Houston TX 77002

HOFFMASTER, DONALD EDEBURN, botany, conservation, for more information see previous edition

HOFFMEISTER, DONALD FREDERICK, ZOOLOGY. *Current Pos:* from asst prof to prof, 46-84, EMER PROF ZOOL, UNIV ILL, URBANA, 84- *Personal Data:* b San Bernardino, Calif, Mar 21, 16; m 38; c 2. *Educ:* Univ Calif, AB, 38, MA, 40, PhD(zool), 44. *Honors & Awards:* Hartley H T Jackson Award, 86. *Prof Exp:* Tech asst, Mus Vert Zool, Univ Calif, 40-41, asst, 41-42, asst zool, Univ, 42-44, assoc, 44; asst prof zool & asst cur mus natural hist, Univ Kans, 44-46. *Concurrent Pos:* Curatorial asst, Mus Vert Zool, Univ Calif, 43-44; mem natural hist field expeds, Kans, 45, Ill, Ariz & Calif; cur mus, Univ Mus Nat Hist, Univ Ill, Urbana, 46-64, dir, 64-84; res assoc, Mus NAriz, 69- *Mem:* Hon mem Am Soc Mammalogists (secy, 47-52, pres, 64-66); Soc Syst Zool; Asn Sci Mus Dirs; Am Asn Mus. *Res:* Mammalogy, especially phylogeny; taxonomy and speciation in rodents, particularly cricetine rodents, both fossil and recent; southwestern American mammals. *Mailing Add:* 20 Fields E Champaign IL 61821

HOFFSOMMER, JOHN C, ORGANIC CHEMISTRY. *Current Pos:* RES ASSOC CHEMIST, US NAVAL ORDNANCE LAB, 59- *Personal Data:* b Montgomery, Ala, Jan 23, 32; m 56; c 2. *Educ:* Univ Pa, AB, 54; Univ Md, MS, 60; George Washington Univ, PhD(chem), 64. *Mem:* Am Chem Soc. *Res:* Explosives chemistry research; synthesis; kinetics. *Mailing Add:* 12805 Lacy Dr Silver Spring MD 20904-2917

HOFFSTEIN, VICTOR, RESPIRATORY MEDICINE, RESPIRATORY PHYSIOLOGY. *Current Pos:* STAFF RESPIROLOGIST MED, ST MICHAELS HOSP, UNIV TORONTO, 80-, ASSOC PROF MED, 87- *Personal Data:* b Soviet Union, Dec 7, 42; nat US. *Educ:* Polytech Inst Brooklyn, 65, MS, 67, PhD(physics), 73; Univ Miami, MD, 73, Royal Col Physicians & Surgeons Can, 82. *Prof Exp:* Researcher physics, RCA Labs, Princeton, 65-67, Nat Sci Res Ctr, France, 70-73. *Mem:* Am Thoracic Soc; Can Thoracic Soc. *Res:* Upper airways, asthma, obstructive sleep breathing. *Mailing Add:* Dept Med St Michaels Hosp 30 Bond St Toronto ON M5B 1W8 Can

HOFMAN, EMIL THOMAS, INORGANIC CHEMISTRY. *Current Pos:* From instr to assoc prof, 53-68, asst dean, Col Sci, 65-71, PROF CHEM, UNIV NOTRE DAME, 68-, DEAN FRESHMAN YEAR STUDIES, 71- *Personal Data:* b Paterson, NJ, June 24, 21; m 57; c 3. *Educ:* Univ Miami, AB, 49; Univ Notre Dame, MS, 53, PhD(chem), 62. *Mem:* AAAS; Am Chem Soc; Nat Sci Teachers Asn; Sigma Xi. *Res:* Metal chelates; teacher training. *Mailing Add:* Dept Chem & Biochem Univ Notre Dame Notre Dame IN 46556

HOFMAN, WENDELL FEY, PHYSIOLOGY. *Current Pos:* asst prof, 70-77, ASSOC PROF PHYSIOL, MED COL GA, 77- *Personal Data:* b Grand Rapids, Mich, Oct 28, 42; m 63; c 3. *Educ:* Western Mich Univ, BS, 64, MA, 66; Mich State Univ, PhD(physiol), 70. *Prof Exp:* Teaching asst biol, Western Mich Univ, 64-66; teaching asst physiol, Mich State Univ, 66-69, spec res assoc, Endocrine Res Unit, 69-70. *Concurrent Pos:* Prin investr, NIH, 87-92, mem study sects, 89-90; mem, Ga Lung Asn Res Grants Panel, 89-, Ga Heart Asn Res Comt, 89- *Mem:* Sigma Xi; Am Lung Asn; Am Physiol Soc; Am Heart Asn. *Res:* Pulmonary edema and vasoreactivity dogs to serotorin and prostaglandins. *Mailing Add:* Dept Physiol & Endocrinol Med Col Ga Augusta GA 30912-0001

HOFMANN, ALAN FREDERICK, GASTROENTEROLOGY, HEPATOLOGY. *Current Pos:* dir, Res & Training Prog, Div Gastroenterol, 80-96, PROF MED, UNIV CALIF, SAN DIEGO, 77- *Personal Data:* b Baltimore, Md, May 17, 31; m 57, Helga K Aicher; c Anthea K (Phillips) & Cecilia R (McKenzie). *Educ:* Johns Hopkins Univ, AB, 51, MD, 55; Univ Lund, PhD, 65. *Hon Degrees:* MD, Univ Bologna, Italy, 88. *Honors & Awards:* Snell Mem lectr, Palo Alto, Calif, 73; Beaumont Mem lectr, USAF, 73; Sir Arthur Hurst Mem lectr, Brit Soc Gastroenterol, 74; Schorstein Mem lectr, London Hosp, 74; Solomon Meyers lectr, Sch Med, Wayne State Univ, 75; Eppinger Prize, Falk Found, WGer, 76; Humboldt Found Sr Scientist Award, Ger, 76 & 91; H M Pollard lectr, Univ Mich, 77; Christian Johann Berger lectr, Aalborg Hosp, Denmark, 77; William Beaumont Prize, Am Gastroenterol Asn, 78; R D McKenna lectr, Can Soc Gastroenterol, 79; Samuel D Kushlan lectr, Yale Univ, 83; Leon Schiff lectr, Univ Cincinnati, 84; Tanner lectr, St Georges Med Sch, UK, 87; Lepow lectr, Univ Conn, 88; Zyma lectr, Univ Bern, Switz, 91; Atkinson lectr, Northwestern Univ Med Ctr, 92; Walter B Cannon lectr, Soc Gastroenterol Radiol, 88; Bengt Ihre lectr, Swed Med Asn, 88; Charles Flood lectr, Columbia-Presby Med Ctr, 90; Friedenwald Medal, Am Gastroenterol Asn, 94; Thannhauser Medal, Ger Soc Digestive & Metabolic Dis, 96; Klatskin lectr, Yale Univ, 97. *Prof Exp:* Intern & res, Dept Med, Columbia-Presby Med Ctr, 55-57; clin assoc internal med, Nat Heart Inst, 57-59; res assoc, Rockefeller Univ, 62-64, asst prof med & biochem & assoc physician, 64-67; assoc prof physiol & med, Mayo Med Sch, Univ Minn, 67-70, prof med & physiol, 70-77, assoc dir, Gastroenterol Unit, Mayo Clin & Mayo Found, 66-77. *Concurrent Pos:* Nat Found fel, Univ Lund, 59-61, NIH fel, 61-62; vis prof, var univs & clins US, Scotland & Australia, 69-85; mem, Gen Med A Study Sect, NIH, 71-75; distinguished prof lectr, Univ Cincinnati, 76; attend physician, San Diego Med Ctr, Univ Calif, 77-; Fogarty Int sr fel, NIH, 86; vis prof, Royal Soc Med, UK, 87. *Mem:* Am Asn Study Liver Dis; Am Gastroenterol Asn; Am Physiol Soc; Am Soc Clin Invest; Asn Am Physicians; hon mem Ger Soc Gastroenterol; Int Asn Study Liver; hon mem Brit Soc Gastroenterol; fel AAAS; Am Fedn Clin Res; corresp mem Royal Flemish Acad Med. *Res:* Bile acid and lipid metabolism; cholelithiasis; biliary pathobiology, pathochemistry and physiology; diagnosis and treatment of digestive and hepatobiliary disease; enterohepatic circulation of endo and xenobiotics. *Mailing Add:* Dept Med 0813 Univ Calif San Diego La Jolla CA 92093-0813. *Fax:* 619-543-2770; *E-Mail:* ahofmann@ucsd.edu

HOFMANN, ALBERT JOSEF, PHYSICS, NATURAL SCIENCE. *Personal Data:* b Uznach, Switz, Feb 27, 33; m 60, Elisabeth I Bloechlinger; c Bettina, Sabine & Regula. *Educ:* Swiss Fed Inst Tech, dipl, 57, Dr(natural sci), 64. *Honors & Awards:* Robert R Wilson Prize, Am Physics Soc, 96. *Prof Exp:* Sci co-worker, Swiss Fed Inst, Tech Inst Nuclear Physics, 64-66; res fel Cambridge Electron Accelerator, Harvard Univ & Mass Inst Technol, 66-72; sr physicist, Europ Orgn Nuclear Res, Geneva, 73-83, sr physicist, superprotron sychrotron-large elctron pos ring di, 83-87; prof appl res, Synchrontron Radiation Lab, Stanford Linear Accelerator Ctr, Stanford Univ, 83-86. *Mem:* Fel Am Physics Soc. *Mailing Add:* Cern SL-div European Orgn Nuclear Res Geneva CH 1211 Switzerland

HOFMANN, BO, AIDS PATHOGENESIS, LYMPHOCYTE ACTIVATION. *Current Pos:* res fel, 88-90, ASST RESEARCHER IMMUNOL, DEPT MICROBIOL-IMMUNOL, SCH MED, UNIV CALIF, LOS ANGELES, 90- *Personal Data:* b Copenhagen, Denmark, Sept 14, 53. *Educ:* Copenhagen Univ, MD, 81, DSc(immunol), 91. *Prof Exp:* Resident med & surg, Copenhagen Univ Hosp, 81-83, resident clin immunol, 83-86, res fel immunol, 86-88. *Concurrent Pos:* Teaching asst anat, Copenhagen Univ, 79-81 & 84-85. *Mem:* Am Asn Immunologists; Int AIDS Soc. *Res:* Early events in lymphocyte activation; AIDS pathology; HIV's effect on the immune system; HIV epidemiology. *Mailing Add:* Hostrups Have 13 5th Frederiksberg DK-1954 Denmark

HOFMANN, CHARLES BARTHOLOMEW, ELECTRICAL ENGINEERING. *Current Pos:* prin engr, 69-71, dir eng proj, 71-75, vpres eng, 75-, PRES, AMECOM DIV, LITTON SYSTS, INC. *Personal Data:* b New York, NY, Sept 5, 39; m 65; c 2. *Educ:* Lehigh Univ, BSEE, 61; Columbia Univ, MBA, 63. *Prof Exp:* Engr electronic warfare, Airborne Instruments Lab, 63-66; sr engr, Maxson Electronics, 66-69. *Mem:* Inst Elec & Electronics Engrs; Armed Forces Commun & Electronics Asn; Soc Photooptical Instrumentation Engrs; Asn Old Crows. *Res:* Electronic warfare; electronic support measures equipment; air traffic control voice switching system, high frequency communications, and Loran navigation. *Mailing Add:* 13517 Middlevale Lane Silver Spring MD 20906

HOFMANN, CORRIS MABELLE, PHARMACEUTICAL CHEMISTRY. *Current Pos:* RETIRED. *Personal Data:* b Plainville, Mass, Sept 18, 15. *Educ:* Univ Ill, BS, 37; Bryn Mawr Col, PhD(org chem), 41. *Prof Exp:* Demonstr chem, Bryn Mawr Col, 37-39; res chemist, Calco Chem Div, Am Cyanamid Co, 41-55, res chemist, Lederle Labs, 55-85. *Mem:* AAAS; Am Chem Soc; Am Inst Chem. *Res:* Synthesis of unsaturated esters; molecular rearrangements; azo dyestuffs; pharmaceuticals. *Mailing Add:* 4840 Thunderbird Dr Apt 283 Boulder CO 80303

HOFMANN, DAVID JOHN, ATMOSPHERIC PHYSICS, CHEMISTRY. *Current Pos:* CHIEF SCIENTIST, NAT OCEANIC & ATMOSPHERIC ADMIN/CMDL, 90- *Personal Data:* b Albany, Minn, Jan 3, 37; m 59; c Gretchen, Jennifer & Karl. *Educ:* Univ Minn, BS, 61, MS, 63, PhD(physics), 66. *Honors & Awards:* Alexander von Humboldt Sr Scientist Award, 82. *Prof Exp:* Res assoc cosmic ray physics, Univ Minn, 65-66; from asst prof to prof physics, Univ Wyo, 66-91. *Concurrent Pos:* Res grants, NSF, 67-90, Off Naval Res, 70-85, NASA, 76-88 & Environ Protection Agency, 71-72. *Mem:* Am Geophys Union; Sigma Xi. *Res:* Stratospheric constituents; stratospheric aerosol measurements. *Mailing Add:* R/E/CG NOAA/ERL 325 Broadway St Boulder CO 80303-3328. *Fax:* 303-497-6975

HOFMANN, FREDERICK GUSTAVE, ENDOCRINOLOGY. *Current Pos:* from assoc to assoc prof, 53-68, PROF PHARMACOL, COL PHYSICIANS & SURGEONS, COLUMBIA UNIV, 68-, ASSOC DEAN, 70- *Personal Data:* b Detroit, Mich, May 25, 23; m 56; c 2. *Educ:* Univ Mich, AB, 43; Harvard Univ, PhD(physiol), 52. *Prof Exp:* Nat Res Coun fel med & res fel endocrinol, Harvard Univ, 52-53. *Concurrent Pos:* Markle scholar, 55-60; ed-in-chief, Endocrinol, Endocrine Soc, 63-67. *Mem:* Endocrine Soc; Am Soc Pharmacol & Exp Therapeut; Harvey Soc. *Res:* Adrenocortical insufficiency; pituitary-adrenal interrelationships; biogenesis of steroid hormones; drug abuse. *Mailing Add:* 923 Van Houten B-1 Clifton NJ 07013-2720

HOFMANN, GUNTER AUGUST GEORGE, PLASMA PHYSICS. *Current Pos:* sr staff physicist, 67-80, MGR PROD DEVELOP, HUGHES RES LABS, 80-, CHAIR & CHIEF SCI OFFICER, 97- *Personal Data:* b Munich, Ger, Sept 9, 35. *Educ:* Munich Tech Univ, dipl ing, 59, Dr rer nat(plasma physics), 62. *Prof Exp:* Res scientist, Max Planck Inst Plasma Physics, 62-67. *Mem:* Am Phys Soc; Europ Phys Soc; Ger Phys Soc. *Res:* Thermonuclear fusion; fast discharges; plasma diagnostics; crossed field devices; direct current interrupters; ionizing radiation; radiation transport. *Mailing Add:* 3750 Riviera Dr San Diego CA 92109

HOFMANN, HANS J, PALEONTOLOGY. *Current Pos:* PROF PALEONT, GEOL DEPT, UNIV MONTREAL. *Honors & Awards:* Willet G Miller Medal, Royal Soc Can, 95. *Mailing Add:* Dept Geol Univ Montreal CP6128 Succursale Centre-ville Montreal PQ H3C 3J7 Can

HOFMANN, KARL HEINRICH, MATHEMATICS. *Current Pos:* PROF MATH, TECHNISCHE HOCHSCHULE DARMSTADT, GER, 82- *Personal Data:* b Heilbribbm Ger, Oct 3, 32; m 63, Isolde Rosler; c Claudia & Georg. *Educ:* Unit Tübingen, Dr rer nat, 58. *Honors & Awards:* E Harris Harbison Award, Danforth Found, 70. *Prof Exp:* Asst math, Univ Tubingen, 58-59, res assoc math statist, 59-60, docent math, 61-63; res assoc math, Tulane Univ, 60-61, assoc prof, 63-65, prof, 65-, W R Irby prof, 79- *Concurrent Pos:* Fel, Alfred P Sloan Found, 67-68; vis prof, Univ Paris, 73-74 & Tech Univ, Darmstadt, 80-81; adj prof, Tulane Univ. *Mem:* Am Math Soc; Australian Math Soc; Ger Math Soc; Math Soc France; Sigma Xi; AAAS. *Res:* Topological algebraic structures; functional analysis; topological and lie groups, semigroups. *Mailing Add:* Tech Sch Darmstadt Schlossgartenstr 7 64289 Darmstadt Germany. *Fax:* 49-6151-164011

HOFMANN, KLAUS HEINRICH, biochemistry; deceased, see previous edition for last biography

HOFMANN, LENAT, GRAZING SEASONALITY. *Current Pos:* RES AGRONOMIST RANGE MGT, AGR RES SERV, USDA, 74- *Personal Data:* b Cedarburg, Wis, May 25, 34; m 59; c 3. *Educ:* Univ Wis-River Falls, BS, 62; NDak State Univ, MS, 68, PhD(agron), 69. *Prof Exp:* Soil scientist, US Army CEngr, Ill, 62-65; asst prof forage crops, Univ Md, College Park, 69-74. *Mem:* Am Soc Agron; Soil Water Conserv Soc; Soc Range Mgt. *Res:* Develop use of cool-season grass species for season-long grazing in the Northern Great Plains; range and pasture management systems. *Mailing Add:* 317 Saturn Dr Mandan ND 58554

HOFMANN, LORENZ M, PHARMACOLOGY, PHYSIOLOGY. *Current Pos:* ASSOC DIR CLIN DEVELOP, DEPT MED, ADRIA LABS. *Personal Data:* b Chicago, Ill, Jan 10, 37; m 68. *Educ:* Univ Ill, BS, 59, MS, 61, PhD(pharmacol), 64. *Prof Exp:* Sr investr renal pharmacol, Div Biol Res, G D Searle & Co, 64-77; assoc dir clin pharmacol res, Ross Labs, 77- *Concurrent Pos:* Assoc dir clin sci, Parke-Davis. *Mem:* AAAS; Am Pharmaceut Asn; Am Soc Pharmacol & Exp Therapeut; Am Soc Clin Pharmacol & Therapeut. *Res:* Renal and cardiovascular pharmacology; application of statistics in design of experiments; clinical research in antibiotics, analgesics, dermatologicals, antihypertensives, cardiotonics and devices. *Mailing Add:* 4449 N Opal Norridge IL 60656

HOFMANN, PAUL BERNARD, PUBLIC HEALTH. *Current Pos:* SR VPRES HEALTH INDUST PRACT, AON CONSULT, 97- *Personal Data:* b Portland, Ore, July 6, 41; m 69, Lois Bernstein; c Julie & Jason. *Educ:* Univ Calif, Berkeley, BS, 63, MPH, 65, DPH, 94. *Honors & Awards:* Robert S Hudgens Mem Award, Am Col Hosp Adminr, 76. *Prof Exp:* Res assoc hosp admin, Lab Comput Sci, Mass Gen Hosp, 66-68, asst dir, 68-69; from asst adminr to assoc adminr, San Antonio Community Hosp, 69-72; dep dir, Stanford Univ Hosp, 72-74, dir, 74-77; exec dir, Emory Univ Hosp, Atlanta, 78-87; exec vpres & chief opers officer, Alta Bates Corp, Emeryville, Calif, 87-91, consult, 91-92; consult, Strategic Healthcare Pract, Alexander & Alexander, 92-94, sr consult, 94-97. *Concurrent Pos:* Instr comput appl, Harvard Univ, 68-69; lectr hosp admin, Univ Calif, Los Angeles, 70-72, Sch Med, Stanford Univ, 72-77; assoc prof, Emory Univ Sch Med, Atlanta, 78-87; sr fel, Stanford Univ Hosp, 93-94; distinguished vis scholar, Ctr Biomed Ethics, Stanford Univ, 93-97. *Mem:* Fel Am Col Hosp Adminr; Am Hosp Asn; Soc Critical Care Med. *Res:* Contributed over 100 articles to professional journals on ethical issues in healthcare. *Mailing Add:* Aon Consult 333 Bush St Suite 600 San Francisco CA 94104-2828

HOFMANN, PETER L(UDWIG), TECHNICAL MANAGEMENT, SYSTEMS ANALYSIS. *Current Pos:* RETIRED. *Personal Data:* b Vienna, Austria, Jan 25, 25; nat US; m 50, Garda Steiner; c Mark E & Monica L. *Educ:* Cooper Union, BEE, 50; Union Col, NY, MS, 54; Rensselaer Polytech Inst, DEngSci, 60. *Prof Exp:* Test engr, Gen Elec Co, 50-51; nuclear engr & mgr nuclear design & anal, Knolls Atomic Power Lab, 51-61; tech consult, Hanford Lab, mgr eng physics, mgr fast flux test facil reactor physics, mgr reactor & plant technol, mgr systs anal, 61-74; assoc dir planning & anal, Battelle Corp Staff, 74-79, var mgt positions, Battelle Proj Mgt Div, 74-94. *Concurrent Pos:* Adj assoc prof, Rensselaer Polytech Inst, 60-61; assoc prof & prog chmn, Joint Ctr Grad Study, Univ Wash, 62-74; consult. *Mem:* Am Nuclear Soc; sr mem Inst Nuclear Mat Mgt; Sigma Xi. *Res:* Analysis and engineering of power reactors; nuclear strategies, fuel cycles and waste management including nuclear waste transport; environmental aspects of reactor siting; energy policy. *Mailing Add:* 11301 NE Seventh St Apt X-4 Vancouver WA 98684

HOFMANN, THEO, BIOCHEMISTRY, MOLECULAR BIOLOGY. *Current Pos:* assoc prof biochem, 64-66, prof, 66-89, EMER PROF BIOCHEM & CHEM, UNIV TORONTO, 89- *Personal Data:* b Zurich, Switz, Feb 2, 24; Can citizen; m 53, Doris T Forbes; c Martin I, Tony D & Peter A. *Educ:* Swiss Fedn Inst Technol, dipl Ing Chem, 47, DrScTech(pharmaceut chem), 50. *Prof Exp:* Agr Res Coun grant biochem, Aberdeen Univ, 50-52; from asst sci officer to sr sci officer, Hannah Dairy Res Inst, Ayr, Scotland, 52-56; lectr biochem, Univ Sheffield, 56-64. *Concurrent Pos:* Vis assoc prof, Univ Wash, 62-63; mem group comt, Med Res Coun Can, 70-74; vis scientist, Div Animal Genetics, Commonwealth Sci & Indust Res Orgn, Sydney, Australia, 72; vis prof, Dept Chem, Univ Calif, Santa Cruz, 81; vis scientist, Univ Lund, Sweden, 84, 87. *Mem:* Am Soc Biol Chem; Can Biochem Soc; Brit Biochem Soc. *Res:* Structure and function of proteolytic enzymes and calcium-binding proteins. *Mailing Add:* Dept Biochem Univ Toronto Fac Med Toronto ON M5S 1A8 Can. *Fax:* 416-978-8548; *E-Mail:* theo@hera.med.utoronto.ca

HOFMASTER, RICHARD NAMON, ENTOMOLOGY. *Current Pos:* RETIRED. *Personal Data:* b Fostoria, Ohio, Apr 12, 15; m 46. *Educ:* Ohio State Univ, BSc, 37, MSc, 40, PhD(entom), 48. *Honors & Awards:* L O Howard Award, ENT, 74. *Prof Exp:* Field aide, Sugar Beet Leafhopper Lab, Bur Entom & Plant Quarantine, USDA, Idaho, 38-41; asst entom, Ohio State Univ, 46-47; entomologist, Va Truck Exp Sta, 47-81. *Mem:* AAAS; Entom Soc Am; Sigma Xi. *Res:* Nuclear polyhedrosis virus studies on cabbage looper, its effectiveness and environmental relationships; ecology of the sugar beet leafhopper; precise insecticidal tests; biology and control of the potato tubermoth and the corn earworm; mites with special emphasis on joint insecticide-herbicide treatments; potato, tomato and fall cucurbit insects; general vegetable insects and control. *Mailing Add:* Box 327 Belle Haven VA 23306

HOFREITER, BERNARD T, ORGANIC CHEMISTRY, PAPER TECHNOLOGY. *Current Pos:* CONSULT, INT EXEC SERV CORPS, KOREA, SRI LANKA & US, 83- *Personal Data:* b Peoria, Ill, July 22, 24; m 47, Mary A Snyder; c Philip J, Ann K, William D & Janet L. *Educ:* Bradley Univ, BS, 48, MS, 50; NC State Univ, PhD, 73. *Prof Exp:* Chemist, Corn Prod Ref Co, 50; chemist, Northern Regional Res Ctr, USDA, 51-60, res leader, 60-80; mem staff, Peoria Sch Med, Univ Ill, 80-83. *Concurrent Pos:* Fac chem, Bradley Univ, 85- *Mem:* Am Chem Soc; Tech Asn Pulp & Paper Indust. *Res:* Industrial utilization of cereal derived products; physical and chemical modification of starch and related carbohydrate material to produce papermaking adjuncts. *Mailing Add:* 2516 N Woodbine Terr Peoria IL 61604

HOFRICHTER, CHARLES HENRY, CHEMISTRY. *Current Pos:* RETIRED. *Personal Data:* b Cleveland, Ohio, Sept 3, 14; m 38; c 4. *Educ:* Hiram Col, BA, 37; Univ Buffalo, PhD(org chem), 40. *Prof Exp:* Off Sci Res & Develop, Northwestern Univ, 40-41; res chemist, Durez Plastics, 41-43; res chemist, E I du Pont de Nemours & Co, 43-51; chief film res sect, Olin Industs, Inc, 51-54, mgr pesticides res & develop dept, 54-58, tech adv to vpres res, 58-62, tech dir appln res chem div, 62-69, tech dir urethanes, 69-75, dir urethane chem safety, Olin Corp, 75-78. *Concurrent Pos:* Mem safety group, Int Isocyanates Inst, 72-; chmn pub affairs tech info comt, SPI Coordinating Comt on Consumer Safety, 73-78; consult urethane & fire technol, 78- *Mem:* Fel AAAS, Am Chem Soc; fel Am Inst Chem; NY Acad Sci; Soc Fire Protection Engrs; Sigma Xi. *Res:* Silicon orthoesters; cellophane coatings; mylar and polyethylene film; agricultural chemicals; urethane; automotive fluids; biocides; plastics combustibility; fire sciences. *Mailing Add:* Six Stone Pasture Lane Killingworth CT 06419

HOFRICHTER, HARRY JAMES, PHYSICAL CHEMISTRY, BIOPHYSICS. *Current Pos:* staff fel phys chem, 72-75, sr staff fel, 75-77, RES CHEMIST PHYS CHEM, LAB CHEM PHYSICS, NIH, 77- *Personal Data:* b Buffalo, NY, Aug 21, 43; m 65; c 2. *Educ:* Dartmouth Col, BA, 65; Univ Ore, PhD(phys chem), 71. *Prof Exp:* Fel phys chem, Univ Ore, 71-72. *Res:* Polymer physical chemistry; linear and circular dichroism of biological molecules; optical spectroscopy; microspectrophotometry; protein assembly reactions; sickle cell hemoglobin; kinetics of nucleated reactions. *Mailing Add:* Bldg 5 Rm 108 NIH Bethesda MD 20892

HOFSLUND, PERSHING BENARD, ZOOLOGY. *Current Pos:* from instr to prof, 49-82, EMER PROF ZOOL, UNIV MINN, DULUTH, 82- *Personal Data:* b Jeffers, Minn, Apr 13, 18; m 40, H Elaine Warner; c 2. *Educ:* Mankato State Teachers Col, Minn, BS, 40; Univ Mich, MS, 47, PhD(zool), 54. *Honors & Awards:* Thomas Sadler Roberts Award. *Prof Exp:* Pub sch teacher, Minn, 40-45. *Mem:* Wilson Ornith Soc (secy, 63-71, pres, 71-73); Am Ornithologists Union; Am Birding Asn. *Res:* Ornithology, behavior and migrations of hawks and wood warblers. *Mailing Add:* 4726 Jay St Duluth MN 55804

HOFSTADTER, DOUGLAS RICHARD, COMPUTER SCIENCE. *Current Pos:* from asst prof to assoc prof comput sci, Ind Univ, 77-84, adj prof psychol, philos, hist, philos sci & comp lit & dir, Ctr Res Concepts & Cognition, PROF COGNITIVE SCI & COMPUT SCI, IND UNIV, BLOOMINGTON, 88- *Personal Data:* b New York, NY, Feb 15, 45; m 85, Carol A Brush; c Daniel F & Monica M. *Educ:* Stanford Univ, BS, 65; Univ Ore, MS, 72, PhD(physics), 75. *Prof Exp:* Walgreen prof cognitive sci, Univ Mich, Ann Arbor, 84-88. *Concurrent Pos:* Guggenheim fel, 80-81. *Mem:* Cognitive Sci Soc; Am Asn Artificial Intel; Am Lit Translr Asn. *Res:* Computer science; cognitive science. *Mailing Add:* 510 N Fess St Bloomington IN 47408-3822

HOFSTETTER, EDWARD, ELECTRICAL ENGINEERING, MATHEMATICS. *Current Pos:* Asst prof elec eng, 59-63, STAFF MEM, LINCOLN LAB, MASS INST TECHNOL, 63- *Personal Data:* b New York, NY, Nov 17, 32; m 55, Nancy Bennett; c Christine & Karen. *Educ:* Mass Inst Technol, SB & SM, 55, ScD(elec eng), 59. *Concurrent Pos:* Consult, Tex Instruments Inc, Tex, 60-61 & Raytheon Co, Mass, 61-63. *Mem:* Inst Elec & Electronics Engrs; Sigma Xi. *Res:* Digital signal processing; probability theory and its application to signal detection and parameter estimation; speech recognition; speech bandwidth compression. *Mailing Add:* 98 Wolf Rock Rd Carlisle MA 01741-1118

HOFSTETTER, HENRY W, VISUAL PHYSIOLOGY, EDUCATIONAL ADMINISTRATION. *Current Pos:* dir, Div Optom, 52-70, prof, 52-74, Rudy prof, 74-79, EMER PROF OPTOM, IND UNIV, 80- *Personal Data:* b Windsor, Ohio, Sept 10, 14; wid; c Ann K (Delaney) & Susan C (Mohme). *Educ:* Ohio State Univ, BSc, 39, MSc, 40, PhD(physiol optics), 42. *Hon Degrees:* DOS, Los Angeles Col Optom, 54 & Mass Col Optom, 68; ScD, Pa Col Optom, 69, Univ Waterloo, 77, State Univ NY, 91. *Honors & Awards:* Int Optical League Medal, 68; Apollo Award, Am Optom Asn, 73; Orion Award, Armed Forces Optom Soc, 74; Prentice Award, Am Acad Optom, 76. *Prof Exp:* From instr to assoc prof optom, Ohio State Univ, 42-49; dean, Los Angeles Col Optom, 49-52. *Concurrent Pos:* Mem, Adv Res Coun, Am Optom Found, 49-70, Nat Adv Coun Educ for Health Professions & Armed Forces-Nat Res Coun Comt Vision; chmn, Tech Adv Comt Light & Vision, Illum Eng Res Inst, 77-81; vis prof optom, Univ Waterloo, Can, 80; actg dean optom, Int Am Univ, PR, 81; mem adv comt, Lighting Res Inst, 88-94. *Mem:* AAAS; Optical Soc Am; Am Optom Asn (pres, 68-69); Am Acad Optom; Asn Schs & Cols Optom (pres, 53). *Res:* Ocular accommodation and convergence; ocular findings in twins; validity of clinical optometric tests; physiology of concomitant squint; environmental optics; optometric and visual science history. *Mailing Add:* 1050 Sassafras Circle Bloomington IN 47408

HOFSTETTER, KENNETH JOHN, RADIOANALYTICAL CHEMISTRY, RADIOACTIVE WASTE PROCESSING. *Current Pos:* SR RES SCIENTIST, WESTINGHOUSE SAVANNAH RIVER CO, 89- *Personal Data:* b Moline, Ill, Aug 18, 40; m 65; c 2. *Educ:* Augustana Col, AB, 62; Purdue Univ, PhD(chem), 67. *Prof Exp:* Post-doctoral fel nuclear chem, Tex A&M Univ, 67-69; asst prof chem, Univ Ky, 69-74; radiochem suprv, Allied Gen Nuclear Servs, 74-80; radiochem eng suprv, Gen Pub Utilities-TMI-2, 80-87; res staff chemist, E I Du Pont, Savannah River Lab, 87-89. *Concurrent Pos:* Consult, Int Atomic Energy Agency, 85-87; lectr, Am Chem Soc Speakers Tour, 70-74. *Mem:* Am Chem Soc; Am Nuclear Soc; AAAS. *Res:* Nuclear decay scheme spectroscopy and the study of nuclear reaction mechanisms; development of charged particle induced x-ray fluorescence and other radioanalytical methods; developed real-time monitors for special nuclear materials; developed liquid radiowaste processing techniques; monitoring of radioactive material at environmental levels. *Mailing Add:* Westhouse Savannah River Co Savannah River Lab Bldg 735-A Aiken SC 29808

HOFSTETTER, RONALD HAROLD, ECOLOGY, ENVIRONMENTAL SCIENCE. *Current Pos:* Asst prof, 68-74, ASSOC PROF BIOL, UNIV MIAMI, 74- *Personal Data:* b Kitchener, Ont, Jan 25, 39; m 62; c 3. *Educ:* McMaster Univ, BSc, 62, MSc, 64; Univ Minn, Minneapolis, PhD(bot), 69. *Mem:* Soc Wetland Scientists; Exotic Pest Plant Coun. *Res:* Ecology of wetlands and forests; plant ecology of subtropical ecosystems, particularly the role of fire. *Mailing Add:* Dept Biol Univ Miami PO Box 248106 Coral Gables FL 33124-9118. *E-Mail:* rhofstet@umiami.ir.miami.edu

HOFSTRA, GERALD GERRIT, PLANT PHYSIOLOGY, PLANT ECOLOGY. *Current Pos:* RETIRED. *Personal Data:* b Heeg, Neth, Dec 11, 38; Can citizen; m 62; c 3. *Educ:* Univ Toronto, BSA, 63, MSA, 64; Simon Fraser Univ, PhD(plant physiol), 67. *Prof Exp:* Nat Res Coun Can overseas fel, 67-68; from asst prof to assoc prof environ biol, Univ Guelph, 68-81, prof, 81- *Mem:* Can Sci & Christian Affil; Can Soc Plant Physiol. *Res:* Environmental physiology; assessment of economic losses from air pollution; low temperature stress and drought stress in crops and conifer seedlings; stress alleviation. *Mailing Add:* Dept Environ Biol Univ Guelph Guelph ON N1G 2W1 Can

HOFT, RICHARD GIBSON, ELECTRICAL ENGINEERING. *Current Pos:* RETIRED. *Personal Data:* b Wall Lake, Iowa, Dec 4, 26; m 46; c 4. *Educ:* Iowa State Univ, BS, 48, PhD(elec eng), 65; Rensselaer Polytech Inst, MEE, 54. *Prof Exp:* Develop engr, Gen Eng Lab, Gen Elec Co, 49-56, mgr elec control, 56-60, mgr converter circuits, Adv Tech Labs, 60-63; assoc prof, Univ Mo-Columbia, 65-68, prof elec eng, 68-93. *Mem:* Fel Inst Elec & Electronics Engrs; Sigma Xi; Nat Soc Prof Engrs; Am Soc Elec Engrs. *Res:* Applied research and development on power electronics, automatic control, and electrical machines. *Mailing Add:* Dept Elec Eng Univ Mo 139 EBW Columbia MO 65211

HOGABOAM, GEORGE JOSEPH, PLANT BREEDING. *Current Pos:* RETIRED. *Personal Data:* b Lewiston, Idaho, Nov 13, 19; m 43, Rachel Ott; c Nancy, Georgianne & Thomas. *Educ:* Univ Idaho, BS, 47; Mich State Univ, MS, 48, PhD(plant breeding), 56. *Prof Exp:* Mkt specialist, Fed Pea & Bean Inspector, Idaho, 46-47; asst farm crops, Mich State Col, 47-48; res agronomist & res leader, USDA & Mich State Univ, 48-84. *Mem:* Am Soc Sugar Beet Technol; Am Soc Agron; Crop Sci Soc Am. *Res:* Breeding improved varieties of sugar beets with special emphasis on resistance to black root, leaf spot diseases and rhizoctonia. *Mailing Add:* 1778 Dogwood Dr Holt MI 48842-1529

HOGAN, ALOYSIUS JOSEPH, JR, NUCLEAR ENGINEERING, PHYSICAL CHEMISTRY. *Current Pos:* RETIRED. *Personal Data:* b Albany, NY, Sept 18, 28; m 52, Rosemary Golden; c 5. *Educ:* Col Holy Cross, BS, 50; Rensselaer Polytech Inst, MS, 52. *Prof Exp:* Jr engr, Philadelphia Elec Co, 54-55; proj engr, Atomic Power Develop Assoc, Inc, 55, asst to tech dir, 55-57, asst Fermi coordr, 57-61, field engr, 61-62, proj engr, 62-63; sr engr, Philadelphia Elec Co, 63-75, group leader, 75-76, staff engr, 76-90. *Concurrent Pos:* Mem Adv Comt Radioactive Mat, Hazardous Transp Bd, Commonwealth Pa, 66-73; mem Task Force Reactor Safety Res, Elec Res Coun, 69-73, Atomic Indust Forum, 66-71 & Elec Power Res Inst, 74-80; mem Environ Res Guide Comt, Md Acad Sci, Power Plant Siting Prog, Md Dept Natural Resources, 73-82, vchmn, 77-82; mem, Am Nuclear Soc Stand Comt Environ Stand, 72-84. *Mem:* Am Chem Soc; Am Nuclear Soc; fel Am Inst Chem. *Res:* Research in sodium chemistry and nuclear chemistry using tracer techniques research, design and development of sodium-cooled fast breeder and high temperature gas cooled power reactors; design of boiling and pressurized water reactors; environmental studies in meteorology and radiation monitoring. *Mailing Add:* 1221 Concord Ave Drexel Hill PA 19026

HOGAN, BRIGID L M, MOLECULAR BIOLOGY. *Current Pos:* PROF, DEPT CELL BIOL, VANDERBILT MED SCH, 88-, HORTENSE B INGRAM CHAIR MOLECULAR ONCOL, 90-, INVESTR, HOWARD HUGHES MED INST, 93- *Personal Data:* b UK, Aug 28, 43. *Educ:* Univ Cambridge, BA, 64, PhD, 68. *Honors & Awards:* Jenkinson Mem Lectr, Univ Oxford, 95; Margaret Pittman Lectr, NIH, 96. *Prof Exp:* NATO res fel, Dr Paul Gross Lab, Dept Biol, Mass Inst Technol, 68-70; lectr biochem, Univ Sussex, UK, 70-74; sci staff, Imp Cancer Res Fund, Mill Hill Lab, 74-84; head, Lab Molecular Embryol, Nat Inst Med Res, Mill Hill, London, 85-88. *Concurrent Pos:* European ed, Cell, 73-78; comt mem, Brit Soc Cell Biol, 82-86, Brit Soc Develop Biol, 84-88; vchair, Basement Membrane Gordon Conf, 94, chair, 96; co-chair sci, Human Embryo Res Panel, NIH, 94. *Mem:* Inst Med-Nat Acad Sci; European Molecular Biol Orgn. *Res:* Published 7 articles and granted 3 patents. *Mailing Add:* Dept Cell Biol Vanderbilt Univ Med Sch 1161 21st Ave S Rm U-2219 Nashville TN 37232-2175

HOGAN, CHRISTOPHER JAMES, PLANT CELL BIOLOGY. *Current Pos:* ASST PROF, DEPT MED, UNIV COLO, DENVER, 93- *Personal Data:* b Tehran, Iran, Jan 25, 57; m 82; c 2. *Educ:* Colo State Univ, BS, 80, PhD(bot & cell biol), 86. *Prof Exp:* NSF fel cell biol mitosis, Dept Molecular & Cell Biol, Univ Calif, Berkeley, 87-93. *Mem:* Am Soc Cell Biol. *Res:* Higher plant cytoskeleton as it relates to division polarity and plant development; mitosis and meiosis, specifically the mechanism of the polypeptides involved in, and the controlling mechanisms that regulate anaphase B (spindle elongation). *Mailing Add:* Dept Med Univ Colo 4200 E Ninth Ave Campus Box B171 Denver CO 80262-0001. *Fax:* 303-270-3573

HOGAN, CLARENCE LESTER, APPLIED PHYSICS. *Current Pos:* RETIRED. *Personal Data:* b Great Falls, Mont, Feb 8, 20; m 46; c 1. *Educ:* Mont State Univ, BS, 42; Lehigh Univ, MS, 47, PhD(physics), 50; Harvard Univ, MA, 54. *Hon Degrees:* DEng, Mont State Univ, 68 & Lehigh Univ, 71; DSc, Worcester Polytech Inst, 69. *Prof Exp:* Res engr, Anaconda Copper Mining Co, 42-43; instr physics, Lehigh Univ, 47-50; mem tech staff, Bell Tel Labs, 50-53, sub dept head, 53; assoc prof appl physics, Harvard Univ, 54-56, Gordon McKay prof, 56-58; vpres & gen mgr, Motorola Inc, 58-68; pres & chief exec off, Fairchild Camera & Instrument Corp, 68-74, vchmn bd, 75-79, consult to pres & dir, 80-85. *Concurrent Pos:* Mem, Comt Undersea Warfare, Torpedo Study Group, Nat Acad Sci, 63-64; res coun comt adv, Nat Bur Stand for Radio Stand Lab, 65-67; vis comt, Lehigh Univ, 65-; C Lester Hogan chmn elec eng & comput sci, Univ Calif, Berkeley, 97. *Mem:* Nat Acad Eng; fel Inst Elec & Electronics Engrs; Am Phys Soc; hon fel Inst Elec & Electronics Engrs Gt Brit. *Res:* Thermal conductivity of metals; application of ferrites and semiconductors to microwave transmission systems; inventor of the microwave gyrator, circulator, and isolator. *Mailing Add:* 36 Barry Lane Atherton CA 94027

HOGAN, DANIEL JAMES, CONTACT DERMATITIS, WORK RELATED SKIN DISEASES. *Current Pos:* CHIEF DERMAT, BAY PINES VET ADMIN, 93-; PROF MED PEDIAT & PUB HEALTH, UNIV SFLA, 93- *Personal Data:* b Baie Comeau, Que, Feb 15, 53; US & Can citizen; m 75, Lorea A LeSelleur; c Gregory & Matthew. *Educ:* Dalhousie Univ, MD, 76. *Honors & Awards:* Barney Usher Award Dermat Research, 85. *Prof Exp:* From asst prof to assoc prof, Univ Sask, 82-89; assoc prof, Univ Miami, 90-93. *Concurrent Pos:* Exchange fel, Am Acad Dermat, 85; mem, Comt Contact Dermatitis, Am Acad Dermat, 86-90, Comt Occup Dermat, 91-; vis assoc prof, Univ Calif, San Francisco, 88; Schering travelling fel, Can Soc Clin Invest, 88; asst chief dermat, Miami Vet Admin Med Clin, 92-93. *Mem:* Am Contact Dermatitis Soc (vpres, 92); Am Acad Dermat. *Res:* Work related skin disorders, contact dermatitis, skin cancer and medical advertising; clinical trails of experimental medications to treat skin disorders. *Mailing Add:* Univ SFla Dermat 17 Davis Blvd 402 Tampa FL 33606. *Fax:* 813-398-9554

HOGAN, EDWARD L, NEUROLOGY & NEUROCHEMISTRY, GLYCONEUROPATHOLOGY. *Current Pos:* PROF NEUROL & BIOCHEM & CHMN DEPT NEUROL, MED UNIV SC, 73- *Personal Data:* b Arlington, Mass, July 26, 32; m 61; c 5. *Educ:* Tufts Univ, BS, 53, MD, 57. *Prof Exp:* Res fel neurol, Harvard Med Sch, 63-64; res fel biochem, Sch Med, Tufts Univ, 64-66; from asst prof to assoc prof neurol & from asst prof to assoc prof biochem, Sch Med, Univ NC, Chapel Hill, 66-73. *Concurrent Pos:* Nat Inst Neurol Commun Dis & Stroke res grants, 66-71 & 74-; several NIH & Vet Admin Comt appointments & chairs. *Mem:* Asn Univ Prof Neurol; Am Soc Biol Chemists; Soc Neurosci; Am Acad Neurol; Asn Res Nerv & Ment Dis. *Res:* Pathological biochemistry of developmental disorders of the brain, particularly the process of myelination and genetic disorders of myelination. *Mailing Add:* Dept Neurol Med Sch SC 171 Ashley Ave Charleston SC 29425

HOGAN, GARY D, PLANT MINERAL NUTRITION. *Current Pos:* RES SCIENTIST, CAN FORESTRY SERV, 77- *Personal Data:* b Hayes, Eng, Nov 11, 49; Can citizen; m 71; c 2. *Educ:* Univ NB, BSc, 71; Laurentian Univ, MSc, 75; Univ Guelph, PhD(plant physiol), 78. *Mem:* Can Soc Plant Physiol. *Res:* The effects of environmental chemical factors on physiological function of native trees through measurement of growth, carbon utilization and nutrient relations. *Mailing Add:* Great Lakes Forestry Ctr Forestry Can Ont Region Sault St Marie ON P6A 5M7 Can

HOGAN, GUY T, MATHEMATICS. *Current Pos:* ASSOC PROF MATH, UNIV MASS, BOSTON, 73- *Personal Data:* b La Boca, CZ, May 21, 33; US citizen; m 61; c 3. *Educ:* Talladega Col, BA, 57; Univ Chicago, MS, 59; Ohio State Univ, PhD(math), 69; Suffolk Univ Law Sch, JD, 85. *Prof Exp:* Instr natural sci & math, Talladega Col, 59-61; asst prof math, Cent State Univ, Ohio, 61-66; assoc prof, State Univ NY Col Oneonta, 69-73. *Mem:* AAAS; Am Math Soc. *Res:* Structure of finite p-groups; existence and construction of social welfare functions. *Mailing Add:* Norfolk State Univ Norfolk VA 23504

HOGAN, JAMES C, CELL BIOLOGY. *Current Pos:* CHIEF, CLIN CHEM & HEMAT, CONN DEPT HEALTH, 87- *Personal Data:* b Milledgeville, Ga, Jan 3, 39; m 59, Izola Stinson; c Pamela (Renita), Gregory K & Jeffrey D. *Educ:* Albany State Col, BS, 61; Atlanta Univ, MS, 68; Brown Univ, PhD(cell biol), 72. *Prof Exp:* Dir, Minority Student Affairs, 83-87, ASSOC PROF ALLIED HEALTH, UNIV CONN HEALTH SCI CTR, 80- *Concurrent Pos:* Josiah Macy fel, 78-80; Ford Found fel, 80-81; vis fac fel, Yale Univ, 84-85; mem, Bd Educ, North Haven, Conn, 94- *Mem:* Am Soc Cell Biol; AAAS; NY Acad Sci; Sigma Xi. *Res:* Basic and applied research on lead concentration and its impact per its existence in human blood, hair and nails. *Mailing Add:* 10 Clinton St Hartford CT 06106-1624. *Fax:* 860-566-7813

HOGAN, JAMES J(OSEPH), ELECTRICAL ENGINEERING. *Current Pos:* eng specialist, Loral Defense Systs, 64-69; head electro-optical sensors, 69-76, eng prin fl head advan guid technol, 76-80, mgr, Weapon Syst Eng, 80-82, prog dir, Missile FSD prog, 82-85, DIR SYSTS ENGR, LORAL DEFENSE SYSTS, AKRON, 85- *Personal Data:* b Cleveland, Ohio, Oct 31, 37; m 65; c 4. *Educ:* Univ Dayton, BEE, 59; Univ Ill, MS, 61, PhD(elec eng), 64. *Prof Exp:* Instr elec eng, Univ Ill, 62-64. *Mem:* Fel Inst Elec & Electronics Engrs. *Res:* Electrically sprayed liquid particles; high resolution radar sensors; area correlation, map-matching and image processing for guidance and tracking systems; missile navigation and control; digital image processor simulation and development; underwater acoustics, transducers and signal processing; antisubmarine warfare system development, smart weapons. *Mailing Add:* Loral Defense Systems Akron 1210 Massillion Rd Akron OH 44315

HOGAN, JAMES JOSEPH, NUCLEAR CHEMISTRY. *Current Pos:* from asst prof to assoc prof, 68-80, PROF CHEM, MCGILL UNIV, 81- *Personal Data:* b New Haven, Conn, May 30, 41; Can citizen; div; c Betsy, Stephanie & Catherine. *Educ:* Rensselaer Polytech, BS, 62; Univ Chicago, MSc, 66, PhD(chem), 68. *Prof Exp:* Res assoc chem, Univ Chicago, 68. *Concurrent Pos:* Vis scientist, Lawrence Berkeley Lab, Berkeley, Calif, 78-79 & UK Atomic Energy, Harwell, 83-90. *Mem:* AAAS; Am Chem Soc; Am Phys Soc; Sigma Xi; Chem Inst Can. *Res:* High energy nuclear fission; nuclear reactions; heavy ion induced reactions; fissionability of heavy nuclides. *Mailing Add:* Dept Chem McGill Univ 801 Sherbrooke St W Montreal PQ H3A 2K6 Can. *Fax:* 514-398-3797; *E-Mail:* hogan@omc.lan.mcgill.ca

HOGAN, JOHN PAUL, POLYMER CHEMISTRY, CATALYSIS. *Current Pos:* RETIRED. *Personal Data:* b Lowes, Ky, Aug 7, 19; m 43, Glenda Moultrie; c Fay (Sweney), Kenneth & Susan (Lair). *Educ:* Murray State Col, BS, 42. *Hon Degrees:* DSc, Murray State Univ, 71. *Honors & Awards:* Nat Award, Am Chem Soc, 69; Pioneer Chemist Award, Am Inst Chemists, 72, Soc Plastics Eng, 81; Perkin Medal, Soc Chem Indust, 87. *Prof Exp:* Teacher pub sch, Ky, 42-44; instr physics, Okla State Univ, 43-44; res chemist, Phillips Petrol Co, 44-54, group leader to sr group leader, 54-61, sect mgr catalysis, 61-77, sr res assoc, 77-85. *Concurrent Pos:* Consult, 85- *Mem:* Am Chem Soc; Am Inst Chemists. *Res:* Isomerization; alkylation; Fischer-Tropsch synthesis; polymer chemistry; catalysis. *Mailing Add:* 1049 SE Greystone Ave Bartlesville OK 74006-5010

HOGAN, JOHN THOMAS, PLASMA PHYSICS, NUCLEAR FUSION. *Current Pos:* RES SCIENTIST & GROUP LEADER NUCLEAR FUSION, OAK RIDGE NAT LAB, 70- *Personal Data:* b East St Louis, Ill, Aug 18, 41; m 67; c 2. *Educ:* St Louis Univ, BS, 62; Northwestern Univ, PhD(mech eng), 67. *Prof Exp:* Vis prof mech, State Univ NY, Stony Brook, 67-68; res assoc magneto-fluid dynamics, Courant Inst NY Univ, 68-70. *Mem:* AAAS; Fel Am Phys Soc. *Res:* Controlled nuclear fusion by magnetic confinement. *Mailing Add:* 103 Pomona Rd Oak Ridge TN 37830

HOGAN, JOHN WESLEY, MATHEMATICS. *Current Pos:* assoc prof, 69-72, chmn dept, 72-77, PROF MATH, MARSHALL UNIV, 72- *Personal Data:* b Monterville, WVa, Jan 20, 36; m 78; c 4. *Educ:* Berea Col, BA, 57; Univ Wis, Madison, MS, 59; Va Polytech Inst, PhD(math), 69. *Prof Exp:* Instr math, Berea Col, 59-60, WVa Univ, 62-67, Va Polytech Inst, 67-69. *Mem:* Math Asn Am; Am Math Soc. *Res:* Algebraic and topological theory of semigroups. *Mailing Add:* 342 Teays Lane Hurricane WV 25526

HOGAN, JOSEPH C(HARLES), ELECTRICAL ENGINEERING. *Current Pos:* dean eng, 67-81, prof elec eng, 67-87, EMER DEAN ENG, UNIV NOTRE DAME, 81-, EMER PROF ELEC ENG, 87- *Personal Data:* b St Louis, Mo, May 26, 22; m 44, Mary E Carreri; c Mary (Hill), Susan (Pastenack), Thomas C, Stephen J, Michael C, Martha (Massey), William G & Daniel C. *Educ:* Wash Univ, BS, 43; Univ Mo, MS, 49; Univ Wis, PhD(elec eng), 53. *Honors & Awards:* Centennial Medallion, Inst Elec & Electronics Engrs, 81 & Am Inst Eng Educ, 93. *Prof Exp:* Elec engr, Knapp-Monarch Co, 45-46 & McQuay-Norris Co, 46-47; instr elec eng, Univ NDak, 47; from instr to prof, Univ Mo, 47-67, dean eng, 61-67. *Concurrent Pos:* Instr, Univ Wis, 52-53; engr, Commonwealth Assoc, Inc, 53-54; consult, Syst Analyzer Corp, 54, Henry Elec Co, 57, Cent Elec Power Corp, 59, Aerojet-Gen Corp, 61-65, North Cent Asn, 67-81 & St Louis Univ, 68-69; bd dirs, Weldun Int, 72-87, TII Corp, 73-, Am Asn Eng Socs, 82-84, Am Biogenetics, Inc, 83- *Mem:* Fel Am Soc Eng Educ (pres-elect, 81-82, pres, 82-83); fel Inst Elec & Electronics Engrs; Nat Soc Prof Engrs; Am Asn Eng Socs Inc; Sigma Xi. *Res:* Analysis of unsymmetrical induction machines by means of derived equivalent circuits; shaded pole induction machines; analysis of power systems, electrical machinery; control systems. *Mailing Add:* 12 Sandhill Crane Hilton Head Island SC 29928

HOGAN, LE MOYNE, HORTICULTURE. *Current Pos:* RETIRED. *Personal Data:* b Choudrant, La, Apr 24, 26; m 47; c 4. *Educ:* La State Univ, BS, 53, MS, 57; Univ Md, PhD(hort), 62. *Prof Exp:* Nursery supt, La State Forestry Comn, 53-54; res assoc hort, La State Univ, 54-56; gen mgr, Fred's Greenhouses & Nursery, 56-58; asst hort, Univ Md, 58-59, instr, 59-62; asst horticulturist, Univ Ariz, 62-63, assoc prof & assoc horticulturist, 63-66, prof hort & bot, US Agency Int Develop, Brazil, 66-70, prof hort & chief of party, Univ Ariz, 70-72, horticulturist, 72-81, prof hort, 72-86, dept head, 81-84; dep proj dir, Western Sudan Agr Res Proj, 84-85; dep head, Sultan Qaboos Univ Oman, 86-87, dean, Col Agr, 87-91. *Mem:* Am Soc Hort Sci. *Res:* Nutrition of landscape and floricultural plants; domestication of jojoba (Simmondsia chinensis). *Mailing Add:* 2802 Belcara Dr Ruston LA 71270

HOGAN, MICHAEL EDWARD, BIOPHYSICS. *Current Pos:* ASSOC PROF BIOTECHNOL, BAYLOR COL MED, 88- *Personal Data:* b Phoenix, Ariz, Dec 7, 51; m 78. *Educ:* Dartmouth Col, BA, 73; Yale Univ, PhD(biochem), 78. *Prof Exp:* Asst prof phys biochem, Dept Biochem Sci, Princeton Univ, 80-88. *Res:* Structural studies of chromatin and its complexes with toxins; studies of the mechanism by which hydrocarbons induce tumors; physical studies of molecular flexibility; structural origins of eucharyotic gene control. *Mailing Add:* 30 Leeward Cove Dr Spring TX 77381

HOGAN, PHILIP, ORGANIC CHEMISTRY. *Current Pos:* from assoc prof to prof, 63-97, chmn dept, 64-76, EMER PROF CHEM, LEWIS UNIV, 97- *Personal Data:* b Chicago, Ill, Oct 22, 25; m 69; c 2. *Educ:* St Mary's Col, Minn, BS, 48; Univ Mo, MS, 53; Loyola Univ, PhD(org chem), 59. *Prof Exp:* Asst prof chem, St Mary's Col, 59-61, chmn, 61-63. *Concurrent Pos:* Res grant, NSF, Kans State Univ, 64; fac fel, Pa State Univ, 67-68, vis prof, 68. *Mem:* Am Chem Soc; NY Acad Sci; The Chem Soc. *Res:* Organic reaction mechanics; physical organic chemistry. *Mailing Add:* 2007 E Bishop St Peoria IL 61614

HOGAN, WILLIAM, physics, for more information see previous edition

HOGAN, WILLIAM JOHN, APPLIED PHYSICS. *Current Pos:* sr scientist, Lawrence Livermore Nat Lab, 66-73, assoc div leader, Spec Proj Div, 73-77, prog leader, Liquefied Gaseous Fuels Safety Prog, 78-83, leader, 83-86, DEP PROG LEADER, INERTIAL CONFINEMENT FUSION, LAWRENCE LIVERMORE NAT LAB, 86- *Personal Data:* b Omaha, Nebr, Oct 8, 40; m 62; c 3. *Educ:* Calif Inst Technol, BS, 62; Princeton Univ, MA, 64, PhD(physics), 66. *Prof Exp:* Res & teaching assoc physics, Princeton Univ, 62-66. *Concurrent Pos:* Mem adv bd, USAF Sci, 72-78 & Gas Res Inst, 80-83. *Mem:* AAAS; Am Nuclear Soc; Am Phys Soc. *Res:* Theoretical work on the physics of nuclear explosions; interaction of radiation and matter at large temperatures and densities; non-equilibrium processes; system studies and operations research on nuclear weapons systems, heavy gas dispersion, combustion and detonation phenomena; inertial confinement fusion physics; fusion reactor design; fusion program management. *Mailing Add:* 2369 Woodthrush Way Pleasanton CA 94566

HOGARTH, JACKE EDWIN, APPLIED MATHEMATICS, COSMOLOGY. *Current Pos:* RETIRED. *Personal Data:* b Huntsville, Ont, Sept 22, 23; m 44; c 3. *Educ:* Univ Toronto, BASc, 49, MA, 50; Univ London, PhD(theoret physics), 53. *Prof Exp:* Defence Res Sci Officer, Defence Res Bd, Dept Nat Defence, Can, 50-59; assoc dean, Sch Grad Studies & Res, Queens Univ, Ont, 70-76, Abitibi prof eng math, 59-86. *Concurrent Pos:* Math consult, Ont Dept Educ, 66-68. *Res:* Relativity and cosmology; algebraic coding theory. *Mailing Add:* 522 King W St Kingston ON K7L 2X8 Can

HOGBEN, CHARLES ADRIAN MICHAEL, PHYSIOLOGY. *Current Pos:* head dept, 61-73, PROF PHYSIOL, COL MED, UNIV IOWA, 61- *Personal Data:* b Eng, Nov 12, 21; nat US; m 48; c 2. *Educ:* Univ Wis, BS, 41, MD, 43; Univ Minn, PhD(med), 50. *Prof Exp:* Med officer, Sect Kidney & Electrolyte Metab, Nat Heart Inst, Md, 51-57; prof physiol & exec off dept, George Washington Univ, 57-61. *Concurrent Pos:* Fel med sci, Nat Res Coun, Copenhagen, 50-51; mem res career award comt, NIH, 58-62, med study res training prog, 61-63, physiol study sect, 63-67; mem steering comt, Gastroenterol Res Group, 60-64; trustee, Mt Desert Island Biol Lab, 60-66, mem exec comt, 64-66; mem comt to eval appln for NSF postdoctoral fels, Nat Acad Sci-Nat Res Coun, 61-63 & sr postdoctoral fels, 65, mem comt on NIH training, 72-75. *Mem:* Am Physiol Soc; Am Soc Pharmacol & Exp Therapeut; Biophys Soc; Am Gastroenterol Asn. *Res:* Mechanisms of gastric hydrochloric acid secretion; gastrointestinal physiology; membrane transport; kidney and electrolyte physiology. *Mailing Add:* Box 243 RFD 1 Ellsworth ME 04605-9722. *Fax:* 207-667-9716

HOGBEN, DAVID, STATISTICS, SOFTWARE SYSTEMS. *Current Pos:* CONSULT, 81- *Personal Data:* b Cape Town, SAfrica, Feb 28, 29; US citizen; div. *Educ:* Univ Minn, BA, 51; Rutgers Univ, MS, 58, PhD(statist), 63. *Honors & Awards:* Silver Med, Dept Com. *Prof Exp:* Actuarial asst, NAm Life & Casualty Co, 52-53; qual control analyst, Ford Motor Co, 53-55; qual control develop engr, Western Elec Co, Inc, 55-59; asst statist, Rutgers Univ, 59-61, from instr to asst prof, 61-65; mathematician, Nat Bur Standards, 65-81. *Concurrent Pos:* Consult, US Naval Res Supply & Develop Facil, NJ, 65; lectr, Univ Md, 66-67. *Mem:* Fel Am Statist Asn. *Res:* Statistical research in the computing physical sciences. *Mailing Add:* 101 Odendhal Ave Gaithersburg MD 20877

HOGBEN, LESLIE, ABSTRACT ALGEBRA. *Current Pos:* Instr, 78-80, ASSOC PROF MATH, IOWA STATE UNIV, 80- *Personal Data:* b Washington, DC, Feb 10, 52; m 78. *Educ:* Swarthmore Col, BA, 74; Yale Univ, PhD(math), 78. *Mem:* Am Math Soc. *Res:* Non-associative algebras, especially Jordan algebras; radical classes. *Mailing Add:* Dept Math Iowa State Univ Ames IA 50011

HOGE, HAROLD JAMES, THERMAL SCIENCES, FLUID MECHANICS. *Current Pos:* VIS RES ASSOC, TUFTS UNIV, 74- *Personal Data:* b Springville, Iowa, Mar 15, 07; m 34; c 1. *Educ:* Univ Iowa, AB, 32; Yale Univ, PhD(physics), 35. *Prof Exp:* Asst physics, Yale Univ, 32-35; res physicist, Nat Bur Standards, 35-50 & Leeds & Northrup Co, 50-55; head, Thermodyn Lab, US Army Natick Labs, 55-74. *Mem:* Am Phys Soc. *Res:* Thermodynamics; thermal properties; temperature measurement. *Mailing Add:* Dept Mech Eng Tufts Univ Medford MA 02155

HOGE, HARRY PORTER, SEDIMENTARY PETROLOGY. *Current Pos:* PROF GEOL, LEE COL, HUNTSVILLE, TEX, 86- *Personal Data:* b Coshocton, Ohio, Jan 12, 36; m 59; c 2. *Educ:* Ohio Univ, BSc, 61, MSc, 63; Univ NMex, PhD(geol), 71. *Prof Exp:* Explor geologist, Texaco, Inc, 63-66; instr geol, Morehead State Univ, 66-69; asst field geol, Univ NMex, 69-71; from asst prof to prof geol, Eastern Ky Univ, 71-79, chmn geol, 78-79; prof & chmn geol, Stephen F Austin State Univ, 79-85. *Concurrent Pos:* Field geologist, Ky Geol Surv-US Geol Surv, 67-69 & 71-78; secy-treas, Keystone Geol Consults Inc, 75-78; vis prof geol, San Diego State Univ, 86-88. *Mem:* Soc Econ Paleontologists & Mineralogists; Am Asn Petrol Geologists; Sigma Xi. *Res:* Sedimentology and stratigraphy of Cenozoic deposits in alluvial and paralic environments; petrology and stratigraphy of Upper Paleozoic deposits in Eastern and Southeastern United States. *Mailing Add:* 13880 Keyworth Dr Houston TX 77014

HOGENBOOM, DAVID L, HIGH PRESSURE PHYSICS, PLANETARY SCIENCE. *Current Pos:* from asst prof to assoc prof, 65-81, PROF PHYSICS, LAFAYETTE COL, 81- *Personal Data:* b Pikeville, Ky, Nov 29, 36; m 60; c 2. *Educ:* Col Wooster, BA, 57; Pa State Univ, MS, 61, PhD(physics), 63. *Prof Exp:* Nat Acad Sci-Nat Res Coun res assoc & physicist, Nat Bur Stand, 63-65. *Mem:* Am Phys Soc; Am Asn Physics Teachers; Sigma Xi; AAAS. *Res:* Phase transitions at elevated pressures; density and phase diagrams of solutions to 4000 bars and 130K that are important constituents of the icy moons of the outer planets. *Mailing Add:* 165 Parker Ave Easton PA 18042. *E-Mail:* hogenbod@lafayette.edu

HOGEN-ESCH, THIEO ELTJO, POLYMER SYNTHESIS, IONIC POLYMERIZATIONS. *Current Pos:* PROF, DEPT CHEM & LOKER HYDROCARBON INST, UNIV SOUTHERN CALIF, LOS ANGELES, 88- *Personal Data:* b Terneuzen, Neth, Feb 22, 36; m 66; c 3. *Educ:* State Univ Leiden, BSc, 58, MCSc, 61, PhD(phys org chem), 67. *Prof Exp:* Adv technologist, Shell Chem Co, ny, 67-68; res assoc polymer chem, State Univ NY Col Forestry, Syracuse, 68-69, asst prof, 69-70; from asst prof to prof polymer chem, Univ Fla, 70-88. *Concurrent Pos:* Vis prof, Univ Louvain, Belg, 77, Univ Pierre Et Marie Curie, Paris, 77, Johannes Gutenberg Univ, Mainz, Ger, 82 & Univ Bordeaux, 91; fel, Japan Soc Prom Sci, 87. *Mem:* Sigma Xi; Am Chem Soc; fel Japanese Soc Prom Sci. *Res:* Mechanisms of anionic vinyl polymerization; synthesis of self-assembling water-soluble polymers; synthesis of macrocyclic and star polymers; synthesis of self-assembling block copolymers; cationic polymerization of cyclic ethers; synthesis of stereoregular vinyl polymers. *Mailing Add:* Dept Chem & Loker Hydrocarbon Inst Univ Southern Calif Los Angeles CA 90089-1661

HOGENKAMP, HENRICUS PETRUS C, BIOCHEMISTRY. *Current Pos:* head dept, 76-92, PROF, DEPT BIOCHEM, UNIV MINN, MINNEAPOLIS, 76- *Personal Data:* b Doesburg, Neth, Dec 20, 25; US citizen; m 53, Aaltje E Ter Haar; c Harry P, Derk J & Margaret A. *Educ:* Univ BC, BSA, 57, MSc, 58; Univ Calif, Berkeley, PhD(biochem), 61. *Prof Exp:* Jr res biochemist, Univ Calif, 61-62; assoc scientist, Fisheries Res Bd Can, 62-63; from asst prof to prof chem, Univ Iowa, 63-76. *Concurrent Pos:* Vis prof, John Curtin Sch Med Res, Australian Nat Univ, 66-67, Pilipps Univ, Marburg, Ger, 86-87; guest scientist, Los Alamos Sci Labs, 74-75; John Simon Guggenheim Mem Found fel, 74-75; mem ed bd, J Biol Chem, 75-80; Alexander von Humboldt-Stiftung Sr Scientist Award, 86-87. *Mem:* Am Soc Biol Chem; Am Chem Soc. *Res:* Chemistry and biochemistry of cobamide coenzymes; ribonucleotide reduction and thymidylate synthesis. *Mailing Add:* Dept Biochem Univ Minn Minneapolis MN 55455

HOGG, ALAN MITCHELL, MASS SPECTROMETRY. *Current Pos:* Nat Res Coun Can fel chem, Univ Alta, 64-65, res assoc mass spectrometry, 65-69, prof officer, 69-76, fac serv officer mass spectrometry, 76-80, FAC SERV OFFICER CHEM, UNIV ALTA, 80- *Personal Data:* b Edinburgh, Scotland, Aug 8, 36; m 63; c 3. *Educ:* Univ Edinburgh, BSc, 58; Univ Alta, PhD(chem), 64. *Mem:* Am Soc Mass Spectrometry; Chem Inst Can. *Res:* Analytical mass spectrometry. *Mailing Add:* Dept Chem Univ Alta Edmonton AB T6G 2G2 Can

HOGG, DAVID CLARENCE, RADIO PHYSICS, ATMOSPHERIC SCIENCES. *Current Pos:* sci assoc, Colo Inst Res Environ Sci, 86-89, LECTR, UNIV COLO, 89- *Personal Data:* b Sask, Can, Sept 5, 21; m 47, Jean E MacMillan; c David Randal & Rebecca Jean. *Educ:* Univ Western Ont, BSc, 49; McGill Univ, MSc, 50, PhD, 53. *Honors & Awards:* Silver Medal Award, US Dept Com; Distinguished Achievement Award, Inst Elec & Electronics Engrs, 83. *Prof Exp:* Mem tech staff, radio res, Bell Labs, 53-66, head, Antenna & Propagation Dept, 66-77; chief radio meteorol, Wave Propagation Lab, Environ Res Lab, Nat Oceanic & Atmospheric Admin, 77-86. *Concurrent Pos:* Distinguished lectr, Antenna & Prop Soc, Inst Elec & Electronics Engrs. *Mem:* Nat Acad Eng; fel Inst Elec & Electronics Engrs; Antenna & Prop Soc; Geosci & Remote Sensing Soc. *Res:* Radio propagation; microwave diffraction; electronics, research and design of remote sensors. *Mailing Add:* 4978 Carter Ct Boulder CO 80301-3804

HOGG, DAVID EDWARD, ASTRONOMY. *Current Pos:* Asst astronr, Nat Radio Astron Observ, 61-64, assoc astronr, 64-69, asst dir, 70-74, SCIENTIST, NAT RADIO ASTRON OBSERV, 69-, ASSOC DIR, 74- *Personal Data:* b Newmarket, Ont, Jan 18, 36; m 59; c 2. *Educ:* Queen's Univ, Ont, BA, 57, MSc, 59; Univ Toronto, PhD(radio astron), 62. *Mem:* Am Astron Soc; Royal Astron Soc Can; Can Asn Physicists; Int Astron Union. *Res:* Radio emission from supernova remnants; the origin of cosmic rays; structure of radio sources by means of radio interferometry. *Mailing Add:* 270 Ipswich Pl Charlottesville VA 22901

HOGG, GARY LYNN, INDUSTRIAL ENGINEERING, OPERATIONS RESEARCH. *Current Pos:* assoc prof, Tex A&M Univ, 76-81, assoc dept head, 90-91, dept head, 91-93, PROF INDUST ENG, TEX A&M UNIV, 82-, ASSOC DEAN, 93- *Personal Data:* b Olney, Ill, July 3, 46; m 66, Judith M Harris; c Gary Jr & Emily. *Educ:* Tex A&M Univ, BS, 68; Univ Tex, Austin, MS, 70, PhD(mech eng), 71. *Prof Exp:* Teaching asst, Univ Tex, 69-71; asst prof, Univ Ill, 71-76. *Concurrent Pos:* Dir simulation res, Nat Clearinghouse Criminal Justice Planning, 72-76; eng consult, Pres Lodestane II Inc; dir, Opers Res Div, Inst Indust Engrs; asst dir, Tex Eng Exp Sta. *Mem:* Inst Indust Engrs (vpres, 90-93). *Res:* Mathematical programming; simulation languages and techniques; power generation systems; production control systems and manufacturing. *Mailing Add:* 3302 Normand Dr College Station TX 77845. *Fax:* 409-845-8986; *E-Mail:* g_hog6@tamu.edu

HOGG, HELEN (BATTLES) SAWYER, astronomy; deceased, see previous edition for last biography

HOGG, JAMES CAMERON, PATHOLOGY, PHYSIOLOGY. *Current Pos:* PROF PATH & PHYSIOL, UNIV BC, 77- *Educ:* McGill Univ, Montreal, PhD(exp med), 69. *Mailing Add:* Dir Pulmonary Res St Paul's Hosp 1081 Burrard St Vancouver BC V6Z 1Y6 Can

HOGG, JAMES FELTER, ANALYTICAL CHEMISTRY. *Current Pos:* assoc prof, Queen's Col, 64-67, chmn dept, 68-72, prof chem, 67-89, prof biochem, 80-89, EMER PROF BIOCHEM, QUEENS COL, 89- *Personal Data:* b Denison, Tex, Dec 11, 18; m 45; c 2. *Educ:* Rice Inst, BA, 41; Univ Tex, MA, 42, PhD(biol org chem), 48. *Prof Exp:* Instr chem, Univ Tex, 41-44 & 46-47; res chemist & biochemist, Chas Pfizer & Co, NY, 44-46; from instr to asst prof biol chem, Univ Mich, 47-64. *Concurrent Pos:* Exec officer biochem, City Univ New York, 66-70; chmn educ comt, Div Biol Chem, Am Chem Soc, 73-76. *Mem:* Am Chem Soc; Am Soc Biochem & Molecular Biol; Biochem Soc Eng. *Res:* Adsorption methods; biochemistry of microorganisms, especially Protozoa; hexose transport; enzyme cytology; metabolism in peroxisomes and autophagic vacuoles; gluconeogenesis. *Mailing Add:* 168 Elm Ave Queens Col Univ NY Glen Cove NY 11542-3211

HOGG, JOHN LESLIE, BIO-ORGANIC CHEMISTRY. *Current Pos:* asst prof, 75-81, ASSOC PROF CHEM, TEX A&M UNIV, 81- *Personal Data:* b Mangum, Okla, Aug 18, 48; m 69. *Educ:* Southwestern State Col, BS, 70; Univ Kans, PhD(chem), 74. *Prof Exp:* Res assoc chem, Dept Biochem, Brandeis Univ, 74-75. *Mem:* Am Chem Soc. *Res:* Bioorganic and physical organic chemistry; mechanism of enzyme action; isotope effects; solution catalysis. *Mailing Add:* Dept Chem Tex A&M Univ College Station TX 77843-3255

HOGG, RICHARD, MINERAL PROCESSING, FINE PARTICLE TECHNOLOGY. *Current Pos:* from asst prof to assoc prof, 69-79, PROF MINERAL PROCESSING, PA STATE UNIV, 79- *Personal Data:* b Redcar, Eng, Jan 6, 38; m. *Educ:* Univ Leeds, BSc, 63; Univ Calif, Berkeley, MS, 65, PhD(mineral technol), 70. *Honors & Awards:* Gaudin Award, Soc Mining Engrs-Am Inst Mining, Metall & Petrol Engrs, 94. *Prof Exp:* Asst specialist mineral technol, Univ Calif, Berkeley, 66-69. *Concurrent Pos:* Mem comt, Comminution & Energy Consumption, Nat Acad Sci, 78-80. *Mem:* Am Inst Mining, Metall & Petrol Engrs; Fine Particle Soc; Sigma Xi; Am Filtration & Separations Soc. *Res:* Fundamental basis of mineral processing operations; colloid and surface chemistry; mixing, segregation and flow of particulate solid materials; fine grinding processes. *Mailing Add:* 1232 S Garner St State College PA 16801-6326

HOGG, ROBERT VINCENT, JR, STATISTICS. *Current Pos:* From instr to assoc prof, 47-62, chmn dept, 65-83, PROF MATH, UNIV IOWA, 62-, PROF STATIST, 83- *Personal Data:* b Hannibal, Mo, Nov 8, 24; m 56; c 4. *Educ:* Univ Ill, AB, 47; Univ Iowa, MS, 48, PhD(math), 50. *Concurrent Pos:* NIH grants, 67-69 & 75-78, NSF grants, 69-74. *Mem:* Math Asn Am; fel Inst Math Statist; fel Am Statist Asn (pres, 88); Sigma Xi; Int Statist Inst. *Res:* Mathematical statistics. *Mailing Add:* Statist & Actuarial Sci Univ Iowa Iowa City IA 52242

HOGG, ROBERT W, MICROBIOLOGY, GENETICS. *Current Pos:* asst prof, 69-73, assoc prof microbiol, Sch Med, 73-, PROF, DEPT MOLECULAR BIOL & MICROBIOL, CASE WESTERN RESERVE UNIV. *Personal Data:* b New York, NY, June 30, 38; m 60; c 2. *Educ:* Univ BC, BSA, 60, MSA, 62; Univ Ill, Urbana, PhD(dairy biochem), 67. *Prof Exp:* Scholar, Univ Calif, Santa Barbara, 67-68. *Concurrent Pos:* USPHS res grant, 69, 72, 78, 84, res career develop award, 70, NSF, 90. *Mem:* Am Soc Biol Chem; Am Soc Microbiol; Protein Soc. *Res:* Genetic and molecular studies on the process of active transport of small molecules into microbial cells. *Mailing Add:* Dept Molecular Biol & Microbiol Case Western Reserve Univ Cleveland OH 44106-4960

HOGGAN, DANIEL HUNTER, CIVIL ENGINEERING, HYDROLOGY & HYDRAULIC ENGINEERING. *Current Pos:* assoc prof civil eng, 68-75, asst dir, Utah Water Res Lab, 71-76, PROF CIVIL & ENVIRON ENG, UTAH STATE UNIV, 75- *Personal Data:* b Lorenzo, Idaho, Sept 25, 29; c Sharlene, Stuart A, Terri L & Todd D. *Educ:* Utah State Univ, BS, 52, PhD(civil eng), 69; Stanford Univ, MS, 53. *Prof Exp:* Asst civil engr, Fluor Corp Ltd, 53-54; detailer & designer, US Steel Corp, 56-60; asst proj engr, US AEC, 60-61; struct engr, Ralph M Parsons Co, 61-63, proj engr, 63-65; staff specialist water resources planning, US Water Resources Coun, 67-68. *Concurrent Pos:* Consult, Pac Northwest River Basins Comn, 69, US Water Resources Coun, 70-71, Sergant, Hauskins & Beckwith, 88, Indo-Am Eng Co, 89, EG&G Idaho, Inc, 90-91; Off Water Resources Res grant, 71-73; advan technol specialist, US Energy Res & Develop Admin, 76-77; hydraul engr, Hydrol Eng Ctr, US Army CEngr, 84-86, Sacramento Dist, 89-90; consult, EG&G Co. 92 & 93, Lockheed Idaho Tech Co, 94; US Army Eng, SAC Dist, 95, Los Angeles Dist, 96. *Mem:* Am Soc Civil Engrs; Am Water Resources Asn. *Res:* Urban drainage and flood control; computer simulation models of hydrologic and hydraulic systems; real time data systems. *Mailing Add:* 955 Foothill Dr Providence UT 84332. *Fax:* 435-797-3663; *E-Mail:* danh@cc.usu.edu

HOGGAN, MALCOLM DAVID, MICROBIOLOGY. *Current Pos:* RETIRED. *Personal Data:* b Salt Lake City, Utah, Feb 28, 30; m 50; c 2. *Educ:* Univ Utah, BS, 52, MS, 53; Johns Hopkins Univ, ScD(microbiol), 59. *Prof Exp:* Asst chief, Bact Br, Sixth Army Area Med Lab, Ft Baker, Calif, 53-56; virologist, Histobact Sect, Armed Forces Inst Path, 59-63; virologist, Lab Viral Dis, Nat Inst Allergy & Infectious Dis, 63-92. *Mem:* Am Soc Microbiol; Am Asn Immunol; Electron Micros Soc Am. *Res:* Tumor virology and immunology; electron microscopy; parvoviruses. *Mailing Add:* 13709 Nells Ct Silver Spring MD 20904

HOGGAN, ROGER D, GEOLOGY. *Current Pos:* INSTR GEOL, RICKS COL, 71- *Personal Data:* b Ogden, Utah, Jan 3, 40; m 65, Karen White; c Nannette & Mark. *Educ:* Weber State Col, BS, 66; Brigham Young Univ, MS, 69, PhD(paleont), 71. *Concurrent Pos:* Mem staff, US Geol Surv, 74-81, geol dept chmn, 81-86, chmn, Nat Sci Div, 86- *Mem:* Nat Asn Geol Teachers; Paleont Soc; Sigma Xi. *Res:* Geologic mapping in eastern Idaho; paleoecologic and stratigraphic investigations of paleozoic rock units in eastern Idaho. *Mailing Add:* Geol Dept Ricks Col Rexburg ID 83440

HOGGARD, PATRICK EARLE, PHYSICAL INORGANIC CHEMISTRY. *Current Pos:* PROF CHEM, SANTA CLARA UNIV, 93- *Personal Data:* b Los Angeles, Calif, July 5, 44; m 67, Eugenie Stanton; c 2. *Educ:* Univ Calif, Berkeley, BS, 65; Wash State Univ, PhD(chem), 70. *Prof Exp:* Fel chem, Inst Phys Chem, Frankfurt, Ger, 70-73 & Univ BC, 73-75; asst prof chem, Polytech Inst NY, 75-81; from asst prof to prof chem, NDak State Univ, 81-93. *Mem:* Am Chem Soc. *Res:* Sharp line electronic spectroscopy and metal-ligand geometry of transition metal complexes; solvent-initiated photochemistry of metal complexes. *Mailing Add:* 2503 Rose Crest Terr San Jose CA 95126-2156. *Fax:* 701-237-8831; *E-Mail:* hoggard@vm1.nodak.edu

HOGLE, DONALD HUGH, PHYSICAL CHEMISTRY, DIRECT PROCESS NON WOVENS. *Current Pos:* CONSULT, NONWOVEN POLYMER PROCESS, 89- *Personal Data:* b Ticonderoga, NY, Dec 11, 24; m 45, Marilyn Daniels; c Richard, Gary & Janice. *Educ:* St Lawrence Univ, BS, 49, MS, 50; Iowa State Univ, PhD(phys org chem), 54. *Prof Exp:* Control chemist, Int Paper Co, 46; lab asst, Eastman Kodak Co, 46-47; res engr, Res Lab, Westinghouse Elec Corp, 54-61; supvr elec prod div, 3M Co, 61-68, supvr, 70-74, mgr, Bldg Serv & Cleaning Prod Div, 75-81, staff scientist, Non Wovens Technol Ctr, 82-86, staff scientist, Life Sci Sector Lab 3M Co, 86-89. *Mem:* Am Chem Soc. *Res:* Relationship of chemical structure to dielectric properties of liquids, polymers and inorganic insulators; dielectrics; semiconductors; synthetic fibers; non wovens. *Mailing Add:* 21509 Lofton Ave N Scandia MN 55073-9414

HOGMIRE, HENRY WILLIAM, JR, TREE FRUIT INSECTS, SPRAY APPLICATION. *Current Pos:* From asst prof to assoc prof, 79-90, EXTEN SPECIALIST, WVA UNIV, 79-, PROF ENTOM, 90- *Personal Data:* b South Haven, Mich, Nov 6, 52; m 82, Pamela Custer; c Renee N & Michelle D. *Educ:* Olivet Col, BA, 74; Mich State Univ, MS, 76, PhD(entom), 79. *Mem:* Entom Soc Am. *Res:* Biology, monitoring and management of arthropod pests of apples and peaches; integrated pest management programs are developed and evaluated on tree fruits; spray application technology and methodology are studied to improve efficiency and environmental compatibility of pesticide use. *Mailing Add:* PO Box 609 Kearneysville WV 25430-0609. *Fax:* 304-876-6034; *E-Mail:* hhogmire@wvu.edu

HOGNESS, DAVID SWENSON, MOLECULAR GENETICS. *Current Pos:* from asst prof to assoc prof, 59-66, chmn, 86-89, PROF, DEPT BIOCHEM, STANFORD UNIV, CALIF, 66-, PROF DEVELOP BIOL & BIOCHEM, 89- *Personal Data:* b Oakland, Calif, Nov 17, 25; m 48; c 2. *Educ:* Calif Inst Technol, BS, 49, PhD(biol & chem), 52. *Hon Degrees:* Univ Crete, Greece & Univ Basel, Switz, 86. *Honors & Awards:* Newcomb Cleveland Prize, AAAS, 66 & 88; Genetics Soc Am Medal, 84; Sonneborn lectr, Ind Univ, 85. *Prof Exp:* Nat Res Coun Lilly fel, Inst Pasteur, Paris, France, 52-54; Nat Found fel, NY Univ, 54-55; from instr to asst prof microbiol, Sch Med, Wash Univ, St Louis, Mo, 55-59. *Concurrent Pos:* Guggenheim Found fel, 68-69; co-chmn, Gordon Conf, Nucleic Acids, 70, Develop Biol, 81; mem, Nat Cancer Adv Bd, 77-78; Harvey Soc lectr, 79; mem, Alan T Waterman Award Comt, NSF, 82; Rudy J & Daphne Donohue Munzer prof, 91. *Mem:* Nat Acad Sci; Am Acad Arts & Sci. *Res:* Genetic organization and regulation of eukaryotic chromosomes. *Mailing Add:* Dept Develop Biochem Sch Med Stanford Univ Stanford CA 94305-5427

HOGNESS, JOHN RUSTEN, ACADEMIC ADMINISTRATION. *Current Pos:* EMER PROF, UNIV WASH, 79- *Personal Data:* b Oakland, Calif, June 27, 22. *Educ:* Univ Chicago, BS, 43, MD, 46; Am Bd Internal Med, dipl, 54. *Hon Degrees:* DSc, Med Col Ohio, 72 & Haverford Col, 73; LLD, George Washington Univ, 73; DLitt, Thomas Jefferson Univ, 80. *Honors & Awards:* Cartwright Medal, Columbia Univ, 78. *Prof Exp:* From asst prof to prof med, Univ Wash, 58-69, exec vpres, 69-70, dir, Health Sci Ctr, 70-71; pres, Inst Med-Nat Acad Sci, 71-74; pres, Univ Wash, 74-79; pres acad admin, Asn Acad Health Sci, 79-80. *Concurrent Pos:* From asst dean to dean, Sch Med, Univ Wash, 59-69; mem, Nat Adv Coun Regional Med Progs, USPHS, 66-70; trustee, China Med Bd, NY, 67-; mem, Task Force Medicaid & Related Progs, HEW, 69-70, adv comt to dir, NIH & adv comt to adminr, Health Sci & Ment Health Admin, 70-71; mem, Nat Cancer Adv Bd, Nat Cancer Inst, 72-76; chmn, Med Injury Compensation Study Comt, Inst Med, Nat Acad Sci, 76-78; mem, Selection Comt, Rockefeller Pub Serv Award, 76-81 & Tyle Ecol Award, 76-79; mem, Nat Sci Bd, 76-82; mem, Coun Biol Sci & Pritzker Sch Med, Univ Chicago, 77-89; mem, Nat Coun Health Care Technol, 79-; provost, Hahnemann Univ, 92-93. *Mem:* Inst Med-Nat Acad Sci; fel Am Acad Arts & Sci; Am Soc Internal Med; Archeol Inst Am; Asn Am Physicians; Am Col Physicians. *Res:* Endocrinology. *Mailing Add:* 514 Lost River Rd Mazana WA 98833

HOGUE, CAROL JANE ROWLAND, EPIDEMIOLOGY, BIOSTATISTICS. *Current Pos:* chief, Pregnancy Epidemiol Br, 82-88, DIR, DIV REPRODUCTIVE HEALTH CTRS DIS CONTROL, ATLANTA, 88- *Personal Data:* b Springfield, Mo, Dec 11, 45; m 66; c 1. *Educ:* William Jewell Col, AB, 66; Univ NC, MPH, 71, PhD(epidemiol), 73. *Honors & Awards:* First Ann Award Excellence, Statist & Epidemiol Sect, NC Pub Health Asn, 73. *Prof Exp:* Res assoc epidemiol, Univ NC, 73-74, asst prof biostatist, 74-77; from asst prof to assoc prof biomet, Univ Ark Med Sci, 77-82. *Concurrent Pos:* Prin investr grant, Ford & Rockefeller Found, 72-73; consult, Int Fertil Res Prog, 73-78, Div Biomet, Nat Ctr Toxicol Res, 78-80 & Bur Med Devices, FDA, 78-81; pos coordr, Sch Pub Health & Area Health Educ Ctrs, 75-76; res assoc, Health Serv Res Ctr, Univ NC, 76-77; res fel, Carolina Pop Ctr, 76-77; prin investr grant, Nat Inst Child Health & Human Develop, 80-82; scholar in residence, Ctrs Dis Control, 81. *Mem:* Int Epidemiol Asn; Soc Epidemiol Res (pres, 87-88); Pop Asn Am; Am Pub Health Asn; Sigma Xi. *Res:* Long-term complications of induced abortion; methodology of epidemiologic studies; epidemiology of reproduction. *Mailing Add:* Rollins Sch Pub Health 1518 Clifton Rd NE Atlanta GA 30322

HOGUE, DOUGLAS EMERSON, ANIMAL NUTRITION. *Current Pos:* From asst prof to assoc prof, 57-73, PROF ANIMAL SCI, CORNELL UNIV, 73- *Personal Data:* b Holdrege, Nebr, Aug 8, 31; m 55, Deborah Vicars; c James & Allison. *Educ:* Univ Calif, BS, 53; Cornell Univ, MS, 55, PhD(animal nutrit), 57. *Mem:* Am Soc Animal Sci; Brit Soc Animal Prod. *Res:* Animal science and nutrition. *Mailing Add:* Animal Sci Morrison Hall Cornell Univ Ithaca NY 14853-4801. *Fax:* 607-255-9829

HOGUET, ROBERT GERARD, POLYMER CHEMISTRY. *Current Pos:* RES CHEMIST, VERONA DIV, MOBAY CORP, 78- *Personal Data:* b Darby, Pa, Apr 2, 48; m 70; c 2. *Educ:* Dayton Univ, BS, 70; Syracuse Univ, PhD(chem), 76. *Prof Exp:* Res chemist, GAF Corp, 75-78. *Mem:* Am Chem Soc; Sigma Xi. *Res:* Dispersion of powders in liquids. *Mailing Add:* 200 Duncannon Rd Bel Air MD 21014

HOH, GEORGE LOK KWONG, ORGANIC CHEMISTRY, POLYMER CHEMISTRY. *Current Pos:* res chemist, Electrochem Dept, 62-71, sr res chemist, 72-81, RES ASSOC, PLASTIC PROD & RESINS DEPT, E I DU PONT DE NEMOURS & CO INC, 81- *Personal Data:* b Canton, China, Feb 22, 35; US citizen; m 62; c 2. *Educ:* Pomona Col, BA, 56; Univ Kans, PhD(org chem), 61. *Prof Exp:* Res asst ferrocene chem, Univ Kans, 58-60; res assoc, Brandeis Univ, 60-61. *Mem:* AAAS; Am Chem Soc; Sigma Xi. *Res:* Ferrocene chemistry; amine oxidation and olefin epoxidation with hydrogen peroxide; ethylene-vinyl acetate, polyamide, and polyester thermoplastics; hot melt adhesives; polymer research and development. *Mailing Add:* 1404 Fresno Rd Wilmington DE 19803-5122

HOHAM, RONALD WILLIAM, PHYCOLOGY, SNOW. *Current Pos:* From asst prof to assoc prof, 71-83, PROF BIOL, COLGATE UNIV, 83- *Personal Data:* b Omaha, Nebr, July 10, 42; c 2. *Educ:* Munic Univ Omaha, BA, 64; Mich State Univ, MS, 66; Univ Wash, PhD(bot), 71. *Concurrent Pos:* Res assoc, Northern Ariz Univ, 78; assoc ed, Physologia, 78-83; chair, Colgate Univ Res Coun, 80-84; vis prof bot, Biol Sta, Univ Mont, 80, 82, 84 & 86. *Mem:* Phycol Soc Am; Int Phycol Soc; Sigma Xi; Inst Arctic & Alpine

Res. *Res:* Snow algae, emphasizing physiological ecology; mating strategies and life histories, speciation and evolution distribution; culture collections; reviewer and contributor of photographic material of textbooks in biology, botany and phycology. *Mailing Add:* Dept Biol Colgate Univ 315 Olin Hall Hamilton NY 13346. *Fax:* 315-824-7997; *E-Mail:* rhoham@center.colgate.edu

HOHENBERG, CHARLES MORRIS, PHYSICS. *Current Pos:* from asst prof to assoc prof, 70-78, PROF PHYSICS, WASH UNIV, 78- *Personal Data:* b Selma, Ala, May 19, 40; div; c 2. *Educ:* Princeton Univ, BA, 62; Univ Calif, Berkeley, PhD(physics), 68. *Prof Exp:* Res physicist, Univ Calif, Berkeley, 68-69. *Mem:* Fel Meteoritical Soc. *Res:* Space physics; rare gas mass spectroscopy. *Mailing Add:* 11518 Cedar Walk Dr St Louis MO 63146. *Fax:* 314-935-4083; *E-Mail:* cmh@krypton.wustl.edu

HOHENBERG, PIERRE CLAUDE, THEORETICAL & CONDENSED MATTER PHYSICS. *Current Pos:* DEP PROVOST SCI & TECHNOL, YALE UNIV, 95- *Personal Data:* b Neuilly-sur-Seine, France, Oct 3, 34; US citizen; m 65, Barbara Blanchard; c Laura. *Educ:* Harvard Univ, AB, 56, PhD(physics), 62. *Honors & Awards:* Fritz London Prize Low Temperature Physics, 90. *Prof Exp:* Nat Acad Sci exchange fel physics, Inst Phys Probs, Moscow, USSR, 62-63; NATO fel, Ecole Normale Superieure, Paris, 63-64; mem tech staff, Bell Labs, 64-95. *Concurrent Pos:* Vis prof, Tech Univ Munich, 71-72, prof, 74-77; Lorentz prof, Univ Leiden, 91. *Mem:* Nat Acad Sci; fel Am Acad Arts & Sci; fel NY Acad Sci; fel AAAS; fel Am Phys Soc. *Res:* Theory of superfluids and superconductors; electronic theory of solids; magnetism, critical phenomena and phase transitions; nonlinear and nonequilibrium phenomena; statistical mechanics; instabilities in fluids. *Mailing Add:* Dept Physics PO Box 208120 Yale Univ New Haven CT 06520-8120. *Fax:* 203-432-7107; *E-Mail:* pierre.hohenberg@yale.edu

HOHENBOKEN, WILLIAM DANIEL, ANIMAL BREEDING, ANIMAL SCIENCE. *Current Pos:* PROF ANIMAL BREEDING & GENETICS, VA POLYTECH INST & STATE UNIV, 87- *Personal Data:* b Davenport, Iowa, Nov 13, 41; div; c 1. *Educ:* Okla State Univ, BS, 63; Colo State Univ, MS, 69, PhD(animal breeding & genetics), 70. *Prof Exp:* USDA Agr Res Serv fel, Univ Wis-Madison, 70-71; from asst prof to prof animal breeding & genetics, Ore State Univ, 71-87. *Concurrent Pos:* NZ Nat Res Adv Coun fel, Ruakura Animal Res Ctr, Hamilton, NZ, 85-86. *Mem:* Am Soc Animal Sci. *Res:* Quantitative animal genetics; livestock production. *Mailing Add:* 1609 Greenwood Dr Blacksburg VA 24060

HOHENEMSER, CHRISTOPH, TECHNOLOGY ASSESSMENT, SOLID PHYSICS & SCIENCE POLICY. *Current Pos:* assoc prof, 71-77, PROF PHYSICS, CLARK UNIV, 77- *Personal Data:* b Berlin, Ger, May 29, 37; US citizen; m 60, Anne Holland; c Lisa & Julia. *Educ:* Swarthmore Col, BA, 58; Wash Univ, St Louis, PhD(physics), 63. *Prof Exp:* Res assoc physics, Wash Univ, St Louis, 63-64; from instr to asst prof physics, Brandeis Univ, 64-71. *Concurrent Pos:* Vis scientist, Natuurkundig Laboratorium, Univ Groningen, Neth, 73-74 & 78-79, Physics Dept, Univ Konstanz, Ger, 86, Energy & Resources Group, Univ Calif, Berkeley, 90-91. *Mem:* AAAS; Am Phys Soc; Soc Risk Analysis; Fedn Am Scientists. *Res:* Use of nuclear physics techniques in solid state physics, such as Mossbauer effect; positron annihilation in solids; perturbed angular correlations; x-ray spectroscopy; technological hazard management; regulation of hazardous technology; risk analysis. *Mailing Add:* Dept Physics Clark Univ 950 Main St Worcester MA 01610. *Fax:* 508-793-8861; *E-Mail:* chohenemser@clark.edu

HOHENEMSER, KURT HEINRICH, MECHANICS. *Current Pos:* vis prof, 57-65, prof, 65-76, EMER PROF AEROSPACE ENG, WASH UNIV, 76- *Personal Data:* b Berlin, Ger, Jan 3, 06; nat US; m 33; c 2. *Educ:* Darmstadt Tech Univ, dipl, 27, DrIng, 29. *Honors & Awards:* Bell Award, 57; Alexander Klemin Award, 64. *Prof Exp:* Privatdocent appl mech, Univ Gottingen, 32-34; consult helicopter develop, Anton Flettner Aircraft Corp, 35-45; chief aeromech eng, McDonnell Aircraft Corp, 47-65. *Mem:* Fel Am Helicopter Soc; assoc fel Am Inst Aeronaut & Astronaut. *Res:* Helicopters; structural dynamics; aeromechanics; applied mechanics. *Mailing Add:* 2421 Remington Lane St Louis MO 63144

HOHIMER, A ROGER, PERINATAL PHYSIOLOGY. *Current Pos:* ASST PROF PHYSIOL, DEPT OBSTET & GYNEC, ORE HEALTH SCI UNIV, 81- *Educ:* Univ Wash, Seattle, PhD(physiol & biophys), 77. *Res:* Fetal-cerebral blood flow and metabolism. *Mailing Add:* Dept Obstet & Gynec Ore Health Sci Univ 3181 SW Sam Jackson Park Rd Portland OR 97201-3098

HOHL, JAKOB HANS, SOLID STATE ELECTRONICS, RELIABILITY ENGINEERING. *Current Pos:* RETIRED. *Personal Data:* b Heiden, Switz, Feb 18, 30; m 55; c 3. *Educ:* Tech Winterthur, Switz, dipl, 53; Univ Vt, MS, 70; Univ Ariz, MS, 72, PhD(elec eng), 76. *Prof Exp:* Engr tel switch circuits, Stand Tel & Radio, Int Tel & Tel Corp, 53-56; res staff mem electronics, IBM Corp, Switz, 56-66; mem staff & adv engr solid state circuits, IBM Corp, Vt, 66-78; adv engr large scale integrated circuits, IBM Corp, Tucson, Ariz, 78-85; res engr, Univ Ariz, 85-88, vis prof, 88-93. *Concurrent Pos:* Adj assoc prof, Univ Vt, 77-78 & adj prof, Univ Ariz, 81-88. *Mem:* Sr mem Inst Elec & Electronics Engrs; Int Soc Hybrid Microelectronics. *Res:* Evaluation and modeling of integrated solid state electronic devices; development, simulation and analysis of very large-scale integrated memory logics circuits; techniques for reliability and functional evaluation of such circuits; modeling of radiation effect in very large-scale integrated circuits. *Mailing Add:* 10249 E Placita Cresten Feliz Tucson AZ 85749

HOHMAN, WILLIAM H, INORGANIC CHEMISTRY. *Current Pos:* From asst prof to assoc 65-80, PROF INORG CHEM, MARIETTA COL, 80- *Personal Data:* b Canton, Ohio, May 1, 39; m 70; c 2. *Educ:* Mt Union Col, BS, 61; Univ Ohio, PhD(chem), 66. *Mem:* Am Chem Soc. *Res:* Preparation and identification of coordination compounds; transition metals. *Mailing Add:* Dept Chem Marietta Col Marietta OH 45750-3031

HOHMANN, PHILIP GEORGE, BIOCHEMISTRY. *Current Pos:* sr scientist, Roswell Park Mem Inst, 75-78, asst res prof, Dept Exp Biol, 78-81, assoc cancer res scientist, 78-92, CANCER RES SCIENTIST IV, ROSWELL PARK MEM INST, 92- *Personal Data:* b Harvey, Ill, Jan 25, 42; m 71; c 1. *Educ:* Univ Ill, Urbana, BS, 64; Univ Calif, Berkeley, PhD(biochem), 69. *Prof Exp:* Damon Runyon Mem fel, Univ Calif, Berkeley, 69-70; Am Cancer Soc fel, Nat Inst Med Res, Eng, 70-71; res assoc biochem, Col Med, Univ Iowa, 71-72; NIH fel, Dept Pharmacol, Med Sch, Univ Colo, Denver, 72-74; staff mem, Cellular & Molecular Radiobiol Group, Los Alamos Sci Lab, Los Alamos, NMex, 74-75. *Mem:* AAAS; Am Soc Cell Biol; Am Soc Biol Chemists. *Res:* Molecular diagnostics of T-cell diseases. *Mailing Add:* Dept Neurol Roswell Park Cancer Inst Buffalo NY 14263. *E-Mail:* hohmann@sc3103.med.buffalo.edu

HOHN, ARNO R, PEDIATRICS, CARDIOLOGY. *Current Pos:* HEAD, DIV PEDIAT CARDIOL, CHILDRENS HOSP, 84-; PROF PEDIAT, UNIV SOUTHERN CALIF, 84- *Personal Data:* b Paterson, NJ, Aug 4, 31; m 61; c 2. *Educ:* Rutgers Univ, New Brunswick, BS, 52; NY Med Col, MD, 56. *Prof Exp:* Fels, Buffalo Children's Hosp, NY, 58-59 & 62-63; from instr to asst prof, State Univ NY, Buffalo, 63-67; from assoc prof to prof pediat, Med Univ SC, 67-83, dir, Div Pediat Cardiol, 67-83. *Concurrent Pos:* Dir cardiac clins, Buffalo Children's Hosp, NY, 63-67, actg dir sect cardiol, 66-67, dir resident training, 67; consult & chmn comt hosp care, Am Acad Pediat, 69-81; actg chmn, Dept Pediat, Med Univ SC, 81-83. *Mem:* Fel Am Acad Pediat; fel Am Col Cardiol; fel Am Col Chest Physicians. *Res:* Improvement of heart catheterization techniques in children; hypertension and exercise testing; cardiac function in noncardiac diseases in infants and children. *Mailing Add:* Childrens Hosp Heart Ctr 4650 Sunset Blvd Los Angeles CA 90027-6016

HOHN, EMIL OTTO, ENDOCRINOLOGY. *Current Pos:* RETIRED. *Personal Data:* b Basel, Switz, Mar 14, 19; m 44; c 2. *Educ:* Univ London, MB & BS, 43, MSc, 46, PhD(physiol), 51. *Prof Exp:* From demonstr to asst lectr physiol, Guy's Hosp, Med Sch, Univ London, 44-47; from asst prof to prof physiol, Univ Alta, 47-83. *Mem:* Arctic Inst NAm; Can Physiol Soc; Brit Physiol Soc; Brit Soc Endocrinol; Am Ornithologists Union. *Res:* Ornithology; endocrinology of mammals and birds. *Mailing Add:* 11511 78th Ave Edmonton AB T6G 0N4 Can

HOHN, MATTHEW HENRY, ECONOMIC BOTANY, LIMNOLOGY. *Current Pos:* RETIRED. *Personal Data:* b New Stanton, Pa, Nov 9, 20; m 47; c 4. *Educ:* Pa State Teachers Col, Ind, BS, 43; Cornell Univ, MS, 49, PhD(econ bot), 51. *Prof Exp:* Asst bot, Cornell Univ, 48-50, instr, 50-59; assoc prof biol, Bloomsburg State Col, 59-61; assoc prof, Beaver Island, Cent Mich Univ, 61-67, prof biol & dir biol sta, 67-83. *Mem:* Am Soc Limnol & Oceanog; Phycol Soc Am; Am Micros Soc; Int Phycol Soc. *Res:* Diatom taxonomy and population structure with reference to stream pollution. *Mailing Add:* 1600 W Columbia Terr Peoria IL 61606-1003

HOHNADEL, DAVID CHARLES, CLINICAL CHEMISTRY, BIOCHEMISTRY. *Current Pos:* DIR CLIN CHEM, DEPT LAB MED, CHRIST HOSP, 78- *Personal Data:* b Englewood, NJ, Dec 12, 41; m 62; c 2. *Educ:* Antioch Col, BS, 63; Case Western Reserve Univ, PhD(biochem), 70. *Honors & Awards:* B J Katchman Award, 87. *Prof Exp:* IBM fel, Dept Lab Med, Univ Conn, 69-71; clin chemist, Bristol Hosp, 71-73; dir clin chem, Dept Lab Med, Univ Conn, 73-78. *Concurrent Pos:* Consult, Int Bus Mach Co, NY, 69-73; US Vet Admin Hosp, Newington, Conn, 70-73 & New Brit Gen Hosp, Conn, 71-73. *Mem:* Sigma Xi; Am Asn Clin Chemists; AAAS; Asn Clin Scientists; Am Chem Soc; Nat Acad Clin Biochem. *Mailing Add:* Genesee Hosp 224 Alexander St Rochester NY 14607-4055

HOHNKE, DIETER KARL, MATERIALS SCIENCE. *Current Pos:* Sr res scientist, 68-73, PRIN RES SCI ASSOC, DEPT PHYSICS, FORD MOTOR CO, 73- *Personal Data:* b Ger, Dec 22, 36. *Educ:* Univ Hamburg, BS, 60; Univ Pa, MS, 65, PhD(mat sci), 68. *Mem:* Am Phys Soc; Electrochem Soc. *Res:* Electrical transport processes and defects in ionic solids and semiconductors; interaction of gases with solid surface (solid state chemical sensors). *Mailing Add:* 1201 Harbrooke Ann Arbor MI 48103

HOHNSTEDT, LEO FRANK, BORON COMPOUNDS. *Current Pos:* from assoc prof to prof chem, 63-83, chmn dept, 66-77, EMER PROF, ST LOUIS UNIV, 92- *Personal Data:* b Alton, Ill, June 12, 24; m 60, Margaret Gorman. *Educ:* St Louis Univ, BS, 49; Univ Chicago, PhD(chem), 55. *Prof Exp:* From instr to asst prof chem, St Louis Univ, 54-60; assoc prof chem, Polytech Inst Brooklyn, 60-61; mem weapon systs anal div, Inst Defense Anal, 61-63. *Mem:* Sigma Xi; Fel Am Inst Chemists. *Res:* Boron-nitrogen and boron-sulfur compounds. *Mailing Add:* 4811 Kaskaskia Trail Godfrey IL 62035

HOINESS, DAVID ELDON, ORGANIC CHEMISTRY, TECHNICAL MANAGEMENT. *Current Pos:* CONSULT, 93- *Personal Data:* b Decorah, Iowa, Aug 14, 35; wid; c Valerie. *Educ:* St Olaf Col, BA, 57; Purdue Univ, MS, 61; Baylor Univ, PhD(org chem), 64. *Prof Exp:* Fel & res assoc, Southern Regional Res Lab, USDA, New Orleans, 64-66; res assoc, Textile Fibers

Dept, E I du Pont De Nemours & Co, Inc, 66-93. *Concurrent Pos:* Adj prof chem, Univ Mo, Rolla, 95- *Mem:* AAAS; Am Chem Soc; Soc Advan Mat & Process Eng; Soc Automotive Engrs. *Res:* Electrical insulation materials; organic polymer chemistry; paper and fiber chemistry; friction materials; materials engineering; non-structural composites; vebris analysis; environmental science; air particulates. *Mailing Add:* 1421 Commercial Dr Rolla MO 65401. *Fax:* 573-368-4730; *E-Mail:* hoiness@umr.edu

HOISIE, ADOLFY, COMPUTATIONAL LINEAR ALGEBRA, PARALLEL COMPUTING & ALGORITHMS. *Current Pos:* sci software analyst, 88-91, mgr, 91-93, PROJ LEADER PARALLEL ALGORITHMS & PERFORMANCE, CORNELL THEORY CTR, CORNELL UNIV, 93- *Personal Data:* b Botosani, Romania, May 15, 57; US citizen; m 83, Silvia Brad; c Daniel & Michael. *Educ:* Bucharest Univ, Romania, BS, 80, MS, 81. *Honors & Awards:* Gordon Bell Award Computational Sci, Inst Elec & Electronics Engrs. *Prof Exp:* Res assoc, Nuclear Power Reactors Inst, Romania, 81-88. *Concurrent Pos:* Consult, New York City Bd Educ, 88. *Mem:* Soc Indust & Appl Math. *Res:* Parallel algorithms for shared and distributed computing; performance evaluation of parallel architectures; modal techniques for three dimensional nuclear reactor dynamics. *Mailing Add:* Cornell Univ 623 E&TC Bldg Ithaca NY 14853. *Fax:* 607-254-8888; *E-Mail:* hoisie@tc.cornell.edu

HOISINGTON, DAVID A, molecular genetics, genetic engineering, for more information see previous edition

HOISINGTON, DAVID B(OYSEN), ELECTRONICS SYSTEMS DESIGN & SYSTEMS SCIENCE. *Current Pos:* PARTNER, E W ENTERPRISES, FRIDAY HARBOR, WASH, 80- *Personal Data:* b Philadelphia, Pa, Feb 11, 20; m 40, Elizabeth Stockwell; c Charles M, Helen (Campbell) & Nancy (Bly). *Educ:* Mass Inst Technol, SB, 40; Univ Pa, MS, 41. *Honors & Awards:* Straton Prize, Mass Inst Technol, 40. *Prof Exp:* Develop engr, Hazeltine Electronics Corp, NY, 41-46; proj engr in charge develop radar equip, Sperry Gyroscope Co, 46-47; from asst prof to prof elec eng, Naval Postgrad Sch, 57-80, chmn, Electronic Warfare Acad Group, 76-80. *Concurrent Pos:* Instr night sch, City Col New York, 45-46; consult engr, Carmel Valley, Calif, 51-80. *Mem:* Inst Elec & Electronics Engrs; Sigma Xi; Asn Old Crows; Armed Forces Commun & Electronics Asn. *Res:* Design of radar equipment; antijamming radar receiver; detector for antijamming receiver; electronic warfare; electronic countermeasures; direction finding systems. *Mailing Add:* 5661 Davison Head Dr Friday Harbor WA 98250-9728

HOITINK, HARRY A J, PLANT PATHOLOGY, BACTERIOLOGY. *Current Pos:* Assoc prof, 67-74, PROF PLANT PATH, OHIO AGR RES & DEVELOP CTR, 74- *Personal Data:* b Neth, July 28, 38; m 64; c 2. *Educ:* Univ Wis, PhD(plant path), 67. *Mem:* Am Phytopath Soc; AAAS. *Res:* Soil microbiology; ornamental pathology. *Mailing Add:* 946 Linden Dr Wooster OH 44691

HOJNACKI, JEROME LOUIS, BIOCHEMISTRY, ATHEROSCLEROSIS. *Current Pos:* PROF BIOL SCI, UNIV MASS, LOWELL, 78-, DEAN GRAD SCH, 87-; RES FEL, DEPT PATH, MASS GEN HOSP, 92- *Personal Data:* b Stamford, Conn, Mar 9, 47; m 78. *Educ:* Southern Conn State Univ, BS, 69; Univ Bridgeport, MS, 71; Univ NH, PhD(lipid biochem), 75; Clark Univ, MHA, 82. *Honors & Awards:* Stamford Med Asn Award, 65. *Prof Exp:* Instr biol & physiol, Stamford Pub Sch, Stamford, Conn, 69-71. *Concurrent Pos:* Res asst, Univ NH, 71-75; Am Heart Asn res fel, Harvard Univ Sch Pub Health, 75-76 & NIH res fel, 76-77; res consult, Beth Israel Hosp, Harvard Med Sch, 77-; res grant-in-aid, Am Heart Asn, 78-86, Coun Tobaccco Res, USA Inc, US Brewer's Asn & Distilled Spirits Coun US Inc & Nat Inst Alcohol Abuse & Alcoholism, Alcoholic Beverage Med Res Found, Johns Hopkins Univ; fel, Coun Arteriosclerosis. *Mem:* Soc Exp Biol & Med; Am Heart Asn; AAAS; Sigma Xi; NY Acad Sci; Am Inst Nutrit; Am Fedn Clin Res; fel Coun Arteriosclerosis; fel Am Col Nutrit. *Res:* Lipid chemistry; lipoprotein metabolism; pathology. *Mailing Add:* Grad Sch Falmouth Hall Univ Mass Lowell 1 University Ave Lowell MA 01854. *Fax:* 978-934-3010

HOJVAT, CARLOS F, ACCELERATOR PHYSICS. *Current Pos:* head, Antiproton Prod Group, 80-85, asst head res facil, 85-90, SCIENTIST II, FERMI NAT ACCELERATOR LAB, 77- *Personal Data:* b Buenos Aires, Arg, May 5, 39; Can citizen; m 67; c 1. *Educ:* Inst Balseiro, Arg, Lic physics, 62; Univ BC, PhD(physics), 67. *Prof Exp:* Fel, Univ BC, 68-69; res assoc, Queen Mary Col, 70-74 & McGill Univ, 74-77. *Concurrent Pos:* Dir off, Fermi Nat Accelerator Lab, 90- *Mem:* Can Asn Physics; Am Phys Soc; AAAS. *Res:* Elementary particle physics; accelerator physics. *Mailing Add:* Fermi Nat Accelerator Lab MS 105 PO Box 500 Batavia IL 60510

HOKAMA, TAKEO, ORGANIC CHEMISTRY. *Current Pos:* res chemist, 65-71, group leader polymer synthesis, 71-78, GROUP LEADER AGR CHEM SYNTHESIS, VELSICOL CHEM CORP, 78- *Personal Data:* b Hilo, Hawaii, June 20, 31. *Educ:* Univ Hawaii, BA, 53; Purdue Univ, MS, 56, PhD(chem), 58. *Prof Exp:* Res chemist, Koppers Chem Co, 58-65. *Mem:* Am Chem Soc. *Res:* Organic synthesis in nitroparaffins, phenols and hydrocarbons. *Mailing Add:* 707 Continental Circle Apt 625 Mountain View CA 94040

HOKAMA, YOSHITSUGI, IMMUNOLOGY, PATHOLOGY. *Current Pos:* assoc prof, 66-68, PROF PATH, MED SCH, UNIV HAWAII, 68- *Personal Data:* b Kohala, Hawaii, Oct 25, 26; m 51; c 2. *Educ:* Univ Calif, Los Angeles, BA, 51, MA, 53, PhD(microbiol), 57. *Prof Exp:* Asst, Univ Calif, Los Angeles, 52-53, from microbiologist to asst res microbiologist, 53-66. *Concurrent Pos:* Consult, Courtland Labs, 62-66 & Accupath Lab, 74-94; assoc prof microbiol, Calif State Univ, Los Angeles, 63-66. *Mem:* Sigma Xi; Am Asn Immunologists; Am Soc Microbiol; NY Acad Sci; Am Asn Pathologists; Int Soc Toxinology; Am Asn Cancer Res. *Res:* Medical bacteriology; mycology; physiology and biochemistry of acute phase proteins; C-reactive protein; influenza sialidases; catalase biochemistry and physiology; prostaglandins and drugs in immune response; peroxisome-functions; ciguatoxin (fish toxin) assay; marine toxicology. *Mailing Add:* Dept Path Med Sch Univ Hawaii Honolulu HI 96822

HOKANSON, GERARD CLIFFORD, MEDICINAL CHEMISTRY. *Current Pos:* sr scientist, Parke-Davis Pharmaceut, 81-83, res assoc to sr res assoc, 83-90, SECT DIR, PARKE-DAVIS PHARMACEUT, 90- *Personal Data:* b Elgin, Ill, Dec 19, 49; m 76. *Educ:* DePauw Univ, BA, 71; Purdue Univ, PhD(med chem), 75. *Prof Exp:* asst prof pharmacog 75-79, assoc prof pharmaceut chem, Col Pharm & Allied Health Professions, Wayne State Univ, 79-81. *Concurrent Pos:* Res Div, Warner-Lambert Co & Parke-Davis Pharmaceut. *Mem:* Am Chem Soc; Am Asn Pharmaceut Scientists. *Res:* Analytical methods development; stability of drug substances in pharmaceutical dosage forms. *Mailing Add:* One Hunter Dr Long Valley NJ 07853-8808

HOKANSON, KENNETH ERIC FABIAN, FISH BIOLOGY. *Current Pos:* Chief, Monticello Field Sta, 73-78, RES AQUATIC BIOLOGIST, NAT WATER QUAL LAB, 78-; ENVIRON RES LAB-DULUTH, ENVIRON PROTECTION AGENCY, 68- *Personal Data:* b Minneapolis, Minn, Nov 10, 41; m 70; c 2. *Educ:* Univ Minn, St Paul, BS, 63, PhD(fishery biol), 68. *Concurrent Pos:* Adj assoc prof, Univ Minn, Duluth, 71- *Mem:* Am Fisheries Soc; Am Inst Fishery Res; Sigma Xi. *Res:* Thermal requirements of fishes; population dynamics; water quality effects; toxicology; bioassay methods; aquatic entomology; biometrics; experimental design. *Mailing Add:* 401 Pinewood Lane Duluth MN 55804

HOKE, DONALD I, CHEMICAL CONTROL LAWS, POLYMER CHEMISTRY. *Current Pos:* Res chemist, Lubrizol Corp, 57-60, group leader develop lubricant additives, 60-62, staff asst to vpres res & develop, 63-64, supvr chem prod res dept, 64-71, supvr lubricant additive res, 71-73, dept head additive res, 73-81, dir, Corp Prod Safety & Compliance, 81-95, RES MGR, LUBRIZOL CORP, 96- *Personal Data:* b Elgin, Ill, Dec 19, 30; m 60, Joan Gooch; c David & Kevin. *Educ:* Ill Inst Technol, BS, 53; Purdue Univ, MS, 56, PhD(org chem), 58. *Honors & Awards:* Outstanding Contrib Chem, Am Chem Soc, 88. *Mem:* Am Chem Soc. *Res:* Lubricant additives; chemical process development; synthesis of monomers and polymers. *Mailing Add:* 15440 Dale Rd Chagrin Falls OH 44022

HOKE, JOHN HENRY, METALLURGY. *Current Pos:* from asst prof to prof, 60-85, EMER PROF METALL, PA STATE UNIV, 85- *Personal Data:* b Greencastle, Pa, July 24, 22; m 44; c 5. *Educ:* Pa State Univ, BS, 46, MS, 48; Johns Hopkins Univ, DEng(mech eng), 55. *Prof Exp:* Res asst, Armco Steel Corp, 47-50; instr, Johns Hopkins Univ, 50-54; res metallurgist, Babcock & Wilcox Co, 54-57; res supvr stainless steel, Crucible Steel Co Am, 57-60. *Mem:* Am Soc Metals; Am Inst Mining, Metall & Petrol Engrs; Nat Asn Corrosion Eng; Am Soc Testing & Mat; Am Soc Eng Educ. *Res:* Stainless steels and high temperature materials; mechanical properties, especially brittle fracture and creep. *Mailing Add:* 142 October Dr State College PA 16801

HOKE, JOHN HUMPHREYS, PETROLEUM GEOLOGY, GEOPHYSICAL INTERPRETATION. *Current Pos:* RETIRED. *Personal Data:* b Toledo, Ohio, Aug 5, 26; m 51, 81, Anne M Brabben; c David, Karl & Jennifer. *Educ:* Duke Univ, BS, 46; Univ Mich, MS, 51. *Prof Exp:* Res geo chemist, Plaskon Div, Libbey-Owens-Ford Glass Co, 47-49; geologist & geophysicist, Stand Oil Co Calif, 51-54; seismog geologist, Arabian Am Oil Co, Saudi Arabia, 54-56, sr geophysicist, NY & Tex, 56-59, sr geologist, Hq Staff, Saudi Arabia, 59-64, sr staff geophysicist, Explor Dept, 64-66, chief geophysicist, Explor Dept, 66-80, mgr, Geophys Dept, 80-86. *Mem:* Fel Geol Soc Am; Soc Explor Geophys; Seismol Soc Am; Am Asn Petrol Geol; Am Geophys Union; AAAS. *Res:* Geophysical interpretation; organic geochemistry. *Mailing Add:* PO Porto Cervo Costa Smeralda Sardinia 07020 Italy

HO-KIM, QUANG, THEORETICAL PHYSICS, QUANTUM FIELD THEORIES. *Current Pos:* from asst prof to assoc prof, 66-75, PROF PHYSICS, LAVAL UNIV, 75- *Personal Data:* b Saigon, Vietnam; m; c 2. *Educ:* Syracuse Univ, BS, 61; Mass Inst Technol, MS, 63, PhD(physics), 65. *Prof Exp:* Res asst physics, Mass Inst Technol, 63-65; Nat Res Coun Can fel & res assoc, McGill Univ, 65-66; vis prof, Univ Paris, 73-74, Univ Ind, 74, Univ Tours, 93. *Mem:* Am Phys Soc; Can Asn Physicists. *Res:* Particles and field theory. *Mailing Add:* Dept Physics Laval Univ Quebec PQ G1K 7P4 Can. *Fax:* 418-656-2040; *E-Mail:* qhokim@phy.ulaval.ca

HOKIN, LOWELL EDWARD, PHARMACOLOGY. *Current Pos:* from asst prof to prof physiol chem, 57-68, chmn Dept Pharmacol, 68-93, PROF PHARMACOL, UNIV WIS-MADISON, 93- *Personal Data:* b Chicago, Ill, Sept 20, 24; m 78, Barbara Gallagher; c Linda, Catherine (deceased), Samuel & Ian. *Educ:* Univ Louisville, MD, 48; Univ Sheffield, PhD, 52. *Honors &*

Awards: Hilldale Award, 93. *Prof Exp:* From lectr to asst prof pharmacol, McGill Univ, 53-57. *Mem:* Am Soc Biochem & Molecular Biol; Brit Biochem Soc; Am Chem Soc; Am Soc Pharmacol & Exp Therapeut; NY Acad Sci; AAAS. *Res:* Discovered the phosphoinositide signalling system; proposed the phosphoinositide-phosphatidic acid cycle; studied the action of antibipolar drugs in the brain. *Mailing Add:* 383 Med Sci Bldg Univ Wis Madison WI 53706. *Fax:* 608-262-1257; *E-Mail:* hokin@macc.wisc.edu

HOKIN-NEAVERSON, MABEL, PSYCHOPHARMACOLOGY. *Current Pos:* PROF PSYCHOPHARMACOL, UNIV WIS, 57- *Educ:* Univ Sheffield, Eng, PhD(biochem), 52. *Mailing Add:* Dept Psychiat Univ Wis Madison WI 53706

HOLADAY, BONNIE, CHRONICALLY ILL CHILDREN & FAMILY, INFECTIOUS DISEASE IN CHILD DAY CARE. *Current Pos:* CONSULT, 95- *Personal Data:* b St Joseph, Mich, May 27, 47. *Educ:* Ariz State Univ, BS, 69; Univ Calif, Los Angeles, MN, 73; Univ Calif, San Francisco, DNS, 79. *Prof Exp:* Staff & charge nurse, Naval Hosp, San Diego, 69-71; instr pediat nursing, Univ Utah, 73-75; asst prof pediat nursing, Univ Calif, Los Angeles, 80-83, assoc prof, San Francisco, 83-90; prof & chair pediat nursing, Sch Nursing, Vanderbilt Univ, 90-95. *Concurrent Pos:* Clin Nurse specialist pediat, Univ Utah Med Ctr, 73-75, Univ Calif Med Ctr, Los Angeles, 80-83; clin nurse researcher, Oakland Children's Hosp, 88-90; Fulbright scholar, 92; co-chair, Res Child Care Group, Nat Asn Pediat Nurse Practrs, 93- *Mem:* Fel Am Acad Nursing; Soc Pediat Nurses (secy, 90-92); Am Nurses Asn; Nat Asn Pediat Nurse Practrs; Asn Care Childrens Health; Soc Res Child Develop. *Res:* Impact of chronic illness on child development. *Mailing Add:* 11404 W Douglas Ave Wichita KS 67212. *Fax:* 615-343-7711; *E-Mail:* bonnie.holaday@mcmail.vanderbilt.edu

HOLADAY, DUNCAN ASA, ANESTHESIOLOGY. *Current Pos:* PROF ANESTHESIOL, SCH MED, VANDERBILT UNIV, 80- *Personal Data:* b Denver, Colo, July 22, 16; m 41; c 5. *Educ:* Univ Chicago, BS, 40, MD, 43; Am Bd Anesthesiol, dipl. *Prof Exp:* Intern, St Luke's Hosp, New York, 43-44; resident anesthesiol, 44-45, Sharp & Dohme fel pharmacol & exp therapeut, Sch Med, Johns Hopkins Univ, 47-50; from asst prof to assoc prof, Col Physicians & Surgeons, Columbia Univ, 50-59; prof surg & anesthesiol, Sch Med, Univ Chicago, 59-68; prof anesthesiol, Sch Med, Univ Miami, 68-80. *Concurrent Pos:* Asst attend anesthetist, Presby Hosp, NY, 50-59. *Mem:* Am Physiol Soc; Am Soc Pharmacol & Exp Therapeut; Am Soc Anesthesiol; Asn Univ Anesthetists; fel NY Acad Sci; Sigma Xi. *Res:* Physiology of respiration and acid-base balance; pharmacology of curariform drugs and other anesthetic agents; respiratory therapy; management of acute respiratory failure; biotransformation of volatile halogenated hydrocarbons; medical instrumentation. *Mailing Add:* 4166 Dingman Dr Sanibel FL 33957-5107

HOLADAY, JOHN W, NEUROPHARMACOLOGY, PSYCHOSOMATIC MEDICINE. *Current Pos:* PRES & CHIEF EXEC OFFICER, ENTREMED, INC, 92- *Personal Data:* b New York, NY, June 9, 45; div. *Educ:* Univ Ala, Tuscaloosa, BA, 66, MS, 69; Univ Calif, San Francisco, PhD(pharmacol), 77. *Honors & Awards:* Dean Calvert Award, Am Soc Pharmacol & Exp Therapeut, 77; US Army Res & Develop Award & Bronze Medallion, 80 & 84; US Army Serv Conf Award & Bronze Medallion Outstanding Sci Achievement, 80. *Prof Exp:* Chief, Neuropharmacol Br, Walter Reed Army Inst Res, 81-89; sr vpres res & develop, Medicis Pharmaceut Corp, 89-92. *Concurrent Pos:* Prof pharmacol & psychiat, Uniformed Serv Univ Health Sci. *Mem:* Am Soc Pharmacol & Exp Therapeut; Am Col Neuropsychopharmacol; Shock Soc (treas, 83-); Soc Critical Care Med; Soc Neurosci; Sigma Xi. *Res:* Pathophysiological mechanisms and therapeutics in circulatory shock and central nervous system injury; biochemical basis of antidepressants; mechanisms of seizures and anticonvulsant pharmacology; immune correlates of endocrine function; stress and immunity relationships to neuroendocrine status; pain and antonomic regulation; peptide physiology; opiate receptor coupling through allostene mechanisms. *Mailing Add:* Entremed Inc 9610 Medical Ctr Dr Suite 200 Rockville MD 20850-3336. *Fax:* 301-217-9594

HOLADAY, WILLIAM J, medicine, surgical pathology, for more information see previous edition

HOLBEIN, BRUCE EDWARD, BIOINORGANIC CHEMISTRY, HYDROMETALLURGY. *Current Pos:* PRES & DIR RES, TALLON METAL TECHNOL INC, 87- *Personal Data:* b Arnprior, Ont, May 12, 50; m 71, Sharon Marie Griffin; c Marc & Paul. *Educ:* Univ Guelph, BSc, 73, PhD(microbial biochem), 77. *Prof Exp:* Scientist, Nat Defence Can, 77-79; assoc prof microbiol, McGill Univ, 79-84; pres, DeVoe-Holbein Can Inc, 84-87. *Concurrent Pos:* Prin investr, Ont Ministry Environ & Energy, 95. *Res:* Role of metals in biological systems including infectious disease and cancer; technology for sequestration and recovery of environmentally significant heavy metals. *Mailing Add:* 44 Shadybrook Crescent Guelph ON N1G 3G5 Can. *Fax:* 514-335-8279, 519-766-9760; *E-Mail:* tmtbeh@ibm.net

HOLBERT, DONALD, APPLIED STATISTICS. *Current Pos:* ASST PROF STATIST, OKLA STATE UNIV, 74- *Personal Data:* b NSW, Australia, Aug 27, 41; m 73. *Educ:* Univ Ore, BS, 67; Wash State Univ, MA, 69; Okla State Univ, PhD(statist), 73. *Prof Exp:* Teacher math, Australian Sec Schs, 61-65; asst prof statist, Med Univ SC, 73-74. *Mem:* Sigma Xi; Am Statist Asn; Biomet Soc. *Res:* Methods in applied statistics. *Mailing Add:* Sch Allied Health ECU Greenville NC 27858

HOLBERT, GENE W(ARWICK), CHEMISTRY. *Current Pos:* Res chemist, Merrell-Nat Labs, 79-81, SR RES CHEMIST, MARION MERRELL DOW RES INST, 81- *Personal Data:* b Honesdale, Pa, Aug 8, 48; m 72, Teresa G Malloy; c Tim & Beth. *Educ:* Pa State Univ, BS, 70; Cornell Univ, MS, 77, PhD(chem), 79. *Mem:* Am Chem Soc. *Res:* Design and synthesis of potentially useful therapeutic agents, especially suicide enzyme inhibitors; natural products synthesis and synthetic methods. *Mailing Add:* 1961 Stockton Dr Loveland OH 45140

HOLBROOK, ANTHONY, MICRO DEVICES. *Current Pos:* Staff, 73-86, pres & chief oper officer, 86-90, VCHMN & CHIEF TECH OFFICER, ADVAN MICRO DEVICES INC, 90- *Mailing Add:* Advan Micro Devices Inc 915 DeGuigne St Box 3453 Sunnyvale CA 94088

HOLBROOK, DAVID JAMES, JR, BIOCHEMISTRY, TOXICOLOGY. *Current Pos:* Res assoc, 59-60, from instr to asst prof, 60-71, ASSOC PROF BIOCHEM, SCH MED, UNIV NC, CHAPEL HILL, 71-, DIR GRAD STUDIES TOXICOL, 79- *Personal Data:* b Norfolk, Va, Apr 16, 33; m 65; c 1. *Educ:* Col William & Mary, BS, 55; Univ NC, PhD(biochem), 59. *Mem:* Am Soc Biol Chem; Am Soc Pharmacol & Exp Therapeut; Soc Toxicol. *Res:* Metabolism and chemistry of nucleic acids; biochemical pharmacology and toxicology. *Mailing Add:* Dept Biochem Sch Med Univ NC CB 7260 Chapel Hill NC 27599-7260. *Fax:* 919-966-6357; *E-Mail:* david_holbrook@unc.edu

HOLBROOK, FREDERICK R, INSECT ECOLOGY, ECOLOGY OF ARBOVIRUS VECTORS. *Current Pos:* RETIRED. *Personal Data:* b Warwick, Mass, Nov 15, 35; m 89, Joyce M Pulvermacher; c Randall F & Glenn L. *Educ:* Univ NH, BS, 61; Univ Mass, Amherst, MS, 64, PhD(entom, Simuliidae), 67. *Honors & Awards:* Cert of Merit, USDA, 89. *Prof Exp:* Entomologist, USDA, Agr Res Serv, USDA Hawaii, 67-68, res entomologist, Fla, 68-71, res entomologist, Maine, 71-73, res leader, Maine, 73-78, supvry res entomologist, Arthropod-Borne Animal Dis Res Lab, Colo, 78-85, res entomologist, Laramie, Wyo, 85-96. *Concurrent Pos:* Adj prof, Univ Wyo & Colo State Univ; consult, Off Technol Assessment, 77-80. *Mem:* Entom Soc Am; Am Mosquito Control Asn; Soc Invert Path; Soc Vector Ecol; NAm Benthological Soc. *Res:* Ecology of gypsy moth and Simuliidae; ecology and control of alfalfa weevil; Mediterranean, Oriental, Caribbean and melon flies; aphids on potatoes; development of mycological insect control; biology and control of insect vectors of animal virus disease. *Mailing Add:* USDA-Agr Res Serv PO Box 3965-Univ Sta Laramie WY 82071-3965. *Fax:* 307-766-3500

HOLBROOK, GABRIEL PETER, PHOTOSYNTHESIS, CARBON METABOLISM. *Current Pos:* ASST PROF, DEPT BIOL SCI, NORTHERN ILL UNIV, 87- *Personal Data:* b Ilfracombe, Eng, Nov 20, 57; m 88; c 1. *Educ:* Univ York, Eng, BS, 79, PhD(plant biochem), 86. *Prof Exp:* Res assoc, Biochem Dept, Univ Nebr, 83-85; postdoctoral assoc, Bot Dept, Univ Fla, 85-87. *Mem:* Am Soc Plant Physiol. *Res:* Photosynthesis; carbon metabolism; biochemistry and enzymology of photosynthetic reactions; enzyme regulation; mechanisms for reducing photorespiration in higher plants and algae. *Mailing Add:* Dept Biol Sci Northern Ill Univ 1425 W Lincoln Hwy De Kalb IL 60115-2825

HOLBROOK, KAREN ANN, BIOLOGICAL STRUCTURE. *Current Pos:* from instr to assoc prof, 71-79, VCHMN DEPT BIOL STRUCT, SCH MED, UNIV WASH, 81-, PROF, 84-, ASSOC DEAN SCI AFFAIRS, 85- *Personal Data:* b Des Moines, Iowa, Nov 6, 42; m 73; c 1. *Educ:* Univ Wis, BS, 63, MS, 66; Univ Wash, PhD(biol struct), 72. *Prof Exp:* Instr biol, Ripon Col, 66-69. *Concurrent Pos:* NIH trainee, Univ Wash, 69-72, NIH trainee & sr fel dermat, 76-78, mem, Study Sect, Gen Med, NIH, 80-; adj assoc prof med dermat, Sch Med, Univ Wash, 79-; Nat Inst Arthritis & Metab Dis, Nat Inst Arthritis, Diabetes & Digestive Kidney Dis Spec Study Sect, 85-88; adj prof, Med Dermat, 84- *Mem:* Am Asn Anatomists; Soc Invest Dermat; AAAS; Sigma Xi; Am Soc Cell Biol; Soc Pediat Dermat. *Res:* Fine structural & biochemical analysis of human skin including development of the human epidermis and dermis in vivo prenatal diagnosis of inherited skin diseases, and structural abnormalities of the dermis in individuals with inherited disorders of connective tissue metabolism and of epidermis in inherited disorders of keratinization. *Mailing Add:* Dept Anat & Cell Biol Univ Fla 223 Grinter Hall Gainesville FL 32611

HOLBROOK, NIKKI J, MOLECULAR GENETICS. *Current Pos:* CHIEF UNIT GENE EXPRESSION & AGING, LAB MOLECULAR GENETICS, NAT INST AGING, 83- *Mailing Add:* Molecular Genetics Lab Nat Inst Aging Geront Res Ctr 4940 Eastern Ave Baltimore MD 21224-2735. *Fax:* 410-558-8335

HOLBROW, CHARLES H, EXPERIMENTAL NUCLEAR PHYSICS. *Current Pos:* assoc prof, Colgate Univ, 67-75, assoc dir, Comput Ctr, 68-69, sr assoc, 70-72, chmn, Dept Physics & Astron, 70-71, 77-80 & 82-84, prof physics, 75-86, dir, Div Natural Sci & Math, 85-88, CHARLES A DANA PROF PHYSICS, COLGATE UNIV, 86- *Personal Data:* b Melrose, Mass, Sept 23, 35; m 56, Mary Ross; c 5. *Educ:* Univ Wis, BA, 55; Columbia Univ, MA, 57; Univ Wis, MS, 60, PhD(physics), 63. *Prof Exp:* Asst prof physics, Haverford Col, 62-65; res investr, Univ Pa, 65-67. *Concurrent Pos:* Am Coun Educ acad admin intern, Stanford Univ, 72-73; vis assoc, Calif Inst Technol, 75-76; vis physicist, Brookhaven Nat Lab, 80-81; vis prof, Spectros Lab, Mass Inst Technol, 82 & 88-89; guest scientist, dept physics, State Univ NY, Stony Brook, 83-93; vis scientist, GSJ-Darmstadt, Ger, 94-95; guest scholar, Dept History Sci, Harvard Univ, 95. *Mem:* Am Phys Soc; Am Asn Physics Teachers; Am Asn Univ Professors. *Res:* Charged-particle nuclear spectroscopy with magnetic spectrograph; laser-based atomic spectroscopy relevant to nuclear properties; history of nuclear physics. *Mailing Add:* Dept Physics & Astron Colgate Univ Hamilton NY 13346-1398. *Fax:* 315-824-7187; *E-Mail:* cwolbrow@center.colgate.edu

HOLCENBERG, JOHN STANLEY, CLINICAL PHARMACOLOGY, ONCOLOGY. *Current Pos:* DIR, CLIN AFFAIRS, IMMUNEX CORP, SEATTLE, WASH, 91- *Personal Data:* b San Francisco, Calif, Oct 9, 35; m 58; c 2. *Educ:* Harvard Univ, AB, 56; Univ Wash, MD, 61. *Prof Exp:* Intern & resident ward med, Barnes Hosp, St Louis, 61-63; surgeon, Clin Endocrine Br, Nat Inst Arthritis & Metab Dis, 63-65; Am Cancer Soc res fel, Lab Biochem, Nat Heart Inst, 65-67; from asst prof to assoc prof med & pharmacol, Sch Med, Univ Wash, 67-76; prof pharmacol, med & pediat, Med Col Wis & dir pharmacol, Midwest Childhood Cancer Ctr, Milwaukee, 76-82; prof pediat & biochem, Dept Pediat, Univ Southern Calif Children's Hosp, 82-90. *Concurrent Pos:* Pharmaceut Mfrs Asn Found career develop award, 67-70; Leukemia Soc scholar, 70; NIH career develop award, 71-76; Burroughs Wellcome clin pharmacol scholar, 78-83. *Mem:* AAAS; Am Soc Biol Chemists; Am Soc Pharmacol & Exp Therapeut; Am Soc Clin Pharmacol & Therapeut; Am Asn Cancer Res; Am Soc Clin Invest. *Mailing Add:* Hematol/Oncol Children's Hosp Los Angeles PO Box 54700 Los Angeles CA 90054-0700

HOLCK, GARY LEROY, ANIMAL NUTRITION. *Current Pos:* ANIMAL NUTRITIONIST, HOLCO AGRI-PROD, INC, 72- *Personal Data:* b Paullina, Iowa, Dec 30, 38; m 60; c 3. *Educ:* Iowa State Univ, BS, 60; Univ Vt, MS, 62; Univ Mo, PhD(animal nutrit), 66. *Prof Exp:* Swine res specialist, Cent Soya Co, Inc, 65-72. *Mem:* Am Soc Animal Sci. *Res:* Calcium and phosphorus nutrition of growing dairy calves; the relationship between lysine and tryptophan and their effect upon growth; nitrogen retention and plasma levels of these amino acids in swine. *Mailing Add:* 1406 St Lukes Dr Spencer IA 51301

HOLCOMB, CHARLES EDWARD, DRYING, HEAT TRANSFER. *Current Pos:* RETIRED. *Personal Data:* b Colorado Springs, Colo, July 17, 24; m 46, Margaret S Turnbull; c Brett & Karen. *Educ:* Univ Colo, BS, 49; Univ Wis, MS, 51, PhD(chem eng), 53. *Prof Exp:* Instr chem eng, Univ Wis, 49-53. *Concurrent Pos:* Res engr, E I du Pont de Nemours & Co, 53-58, staff engr, 58-60, res assoc, 60-74, res fel, 74-85. *Mem:* Am Inst Chem Engrs. *Res:* Process development for plastic films; photographic films from emulsion making to coating; drying of photographic films. *Mailing Add:* 3210 Laurel Park Hwy Hendersonville NC 28739

HOLCOMB, DAVID NELSON, PHYSICAL CHEMISTRY. *Current Pos:* group leader, 66-80, mgr res & develop, 80-87, TECHNOL MGR, BASIC FOOD SCI LAB, KRAFT, INC, 87- *Personal Data:* b Sioux City, Iowa, Sept 12, 36; m 65; c 4. *Educ:* Univ Nebr, BS, 58; Univ Ill, PhD(chem), 62; Roosevelt Univ, MBA, 77. *Prof Exp:* NSF fel chem, Univ Calif, Berkeley, 62-64; res chemist, Agr Res Serv, USDA, 64-66. *Concurrent Pos:* Ed, Food Microstruct. *Mem:* AAAS; Am Chem Soc; Electron Micros Soc Am; Am Oil Chemists Soc; Sigma Xi. *Res:* physical chemistry; thermodynamics, rheology and microscopy of foods and food components; research management; analytical data quality control. *Mailing Add:* 903 Elder Rd Homewood IL 60430-2061

HOLCOMB, DONALD FRANK, PHYSICS EDUCATION. *Current Pos:* From instr to assoc prof physics, 54-62, chmn dept, 69-74 & 82-86, dir lab atomic & solid state physics, 64-68, PROF PHYSICS, CORNELL UNIV, 62- *Personal Data:* b Chesterton, Ind, Nov 8, 25; m 50, Barbara Page; c Douglas P, Jane (Bryant) & Nancy (Miller). *Educ:* DePauw Univ, AB, 49; Univ Ill, MS, 50, PhD(physics), 54. *Honors & Awards:* Oersted Medal, Am Asn Physics Teachers, 96. *Concurrent Pos:* Guggenheim fel, 68-69; Sci Res Coun sr vis fel, 78. *Mem:* Fel Am Phys Soc; Am Asn Physics Teachers (pres, 87); fel AAAS. *Res:* Spin resonance phenomena; physics solids; studies of electron localization phenomena in disordered systems such as heavily-doped, compensated semiconductors; strong engagement in modernizing undergraduate physics curricula. *Mailing Add:* Dept Physics Clark Hall Cornell Univ Ithaca NY 14853. *Fax:* 607-255-6428; *E-Mail:* dfh1@cornell.edu

HOLCOMB, GEORGE RUHLE, physical anthropology, research administration; deceased, see previous edition for last biography

HOLCOMB, GORDON ERNEST, DISEASES OF ORNAMENTAL PLANTS & TURFGRASSES, ETIOLOGY & DISEASE MANAGEMENT. *Current Pos:* From asst prof to assoc prof, 65-70, PROF PLANT PATH, LA STATE UNIV, BATON ROUGE, 78- *Personal Data:* b Monroe, Wis, July 6, 32; m 64, Alice H Duff; c Janette L & Amy F. *Educ:* Univ Wis, Platteville, BS, 59; Univ Wis, Madison, PhD(plant path), 66. *Honors & Awards:* Dave Feathers Award, Am Camellia Soc, 82-83 & 85. *Mem:* AAAS; Am Phytopath Soc; Am Inst Biol Sci; Sigma Xi. *Res:* Diseases of ornamental plants and turfgrasses; disease etiology and management; mycology; cultivar screening for disease resistance. *Mailing Add:* Dept Plant Path & Crop Phys La State Univ Baton Rouge LA 70803-1720. *Fax:* 504-388-1415

HOLCOMB, HERMAN PERRY, ANALYTICAL CHEMISTRY, RADIOCHEMISTRY. *Current Pos:* INDEPENDENT CONSULT, 96- *Personal Data:* b Jonesville, NC, Dec 30, 34; m 90, Evalyn Wood; c Robert & Martha. *Educ:* Duke Univ, BS, 56; Univ Va, MS, 58, PhD(anal chem), 60. *Prof Exp:* Res chemist, Separations Chem Div, E I du Pont de Nemours & Co, Inc, Westinghouse Savannah River Co, 60-75, staff chemist, Environ Effects Div, Savannah River Lab, 75-80, process staff chemist, Separations Technol Dept, Savannah River Plant, 80-84, fel scientist, Separations Technol Dept, 84-92, fel scientist, Environ Restoration Dept, Savannah River Site, 92-96. *Concurrent Pos:* Asst res prof, Med Col Ga, 65-68. *Mem:* Am Chem Soc; Sigma Xi. *Res:* Separation and purification of actinide elements; radioactive waste studies; environmental restoration; groundwater remediation; characterization of waste sites and solid waste. *Mailing Add:* 1891 Green Forest Dr North Augusta SC 29841-2157. *E-Mail:* pholcomb@home.ifx.net

HOLCOMB, IRA JAMES, ANALYTICAL CHEMISTRY. *Current Pos:* control chemist, 64-78, SR RES ASSOC, PARKE DAVIS & CO, DIV WARNER LAMBERT CO, 78-, MGR, QUALITY CONTROL TESTING. *Personal Data:* b Flint, Mich, June 10, 34; m 60, Jean Potts; c Elizabeth, Ira J & Matthew J. *Educ:* Wayne State Univ, BS, 59, MS, 61, PhD(anal chem), 64, MBA, 80. *Prof Exp:* Instr chem, Detroit Inst Technol, 60-62; res fel, Wayne State Univ, 62-64. *Mem:* Am Chem Soc; Coblentz Soc; fel Asn Anal Chemists; Fed Anal Chem & Spectros Soc. *Res:* Thin layer and paper chromatography; ultraviolet and infrared spectrophotometry; non-aqueous titrations; functional group analysis; liquid chromatography; chemical microscopy; quality control. *Mailing Add:* 3603 28 M Rd Washington MI 48094-9584

HOLCOMB, ROBERT M(ARION), CIVIL ENGINEERING. *Current Pos:* RETIRED. *Personal Data:* b Sapulpa, Okla, Mar 7, 16; m 38; c 3. *Educ:* Univ Ariz, BS, 36; Iowa State Col, MS, 41, PhD(struct eng), 56. *Prof Exp:* Jr engr, Ariz Hwy Dept, Phoenix, 36-37 & US Bur Reclamation, 37-38; instr civil eng, Univ Ariz, 38-40; instr gen eng, Iowa State Col, 40-41; civil engr & designer, Donald R Warren, Los Angeles, 41-43 & Barrett & Hilp, San Francisco, 43; designer, Radiation Lab, Calif, 43-47; prof struct eng, Tex A&M Univ, 47-79. *Concurrent Pos:* Consult engr, 47-; dean, Seato Grad Sch Eng, Bangkok, 61-63. *Mem:* Am Soc Civil Engrs; Am Soc Eng Educ; Am Concrete Inst. *Res:* Structural engineering; comparative economy of various structural types. *Mailing Add:* 1100 Ashburn Ave College Station TX 77840

HOLCOMB, ROBIN TERRY, VOLCANOLOGY, MARINE GEOLOGY. *Current Pos:* AFFIL PROF, UNIV WASH, 88- *Personal Data:* b Sterling, Ill, Mar 11, 43; m 65, Annette Shuck; c Chris & Maui. *Educ:* Cornell Col, BA, 65; Univ Ariz, MS, 75; Stanford Univ, PhD(geol), 81. *Prof Exp:* Res geologist, Hawaiian Volcano Observ, US Geol Surv, 71-75, Cascades Volcano Observ, 80-86, res geologist, Gloria Sidescan Sonar Surv, 87-97. *Mem:* Am Geophys Union; Geol Soc Am; AAAS; Marine Technol Soc; Am Soc Photogram & Remote Sensing. *Res:* Volcanic geomorphology, including studies of active volcanic eruption processes; morphologic interpretation of subaerial and submarine lava flows; long-range forecasting of volcanic eruptions; regional reconnaissance of seafloor using side-scan sonar; growth and collapse of large oceanic shield volcanoes. *Mailing Add:* Sch Oceanog US Geol Surv Univ Wash Seattle WA 98195-7940. *E-Mail:* rholcomb@u.washington.edu

HOLCOMBE, CRESSIE EARL, JR, HIGH TEMPERATURE INTERACTIONS & REACTIONS, MICROWAVE PROCESSING AT ULTRA HIGH TEMPERATURES. *Current Pos:* advan staff, Martin Marietta Energy Systs, Inc, 84-88, sr develop staff, 88-90, advan sr develop staff, 90-92, CORP FEL, MARTIN MARIETTA ENERGY SYSTS, 92- *Personal Data:* b Anderson, SC, Dec 18, 45; m 66, Catherine J Brockman; c Justin K & Eric B. *Educ:* Clemson Univ, BS, 66, MS, 67. *Honors & Awards:* Weapons Complex Award Excellence, US Dept Energy, 86 & 89; IR 100 Award for Innovation, Res & Develop Mag, 87; Indust Applns Award Excellence, Titanium Develop Asn, 90. *Prof Exp:* From assoc develop engr to advan staff, Union Carbide Nuclear Div, 67-84. *Concurrent Pos:* Dir & pres, Zyp Coatings, Inc, 82-, Orpac, Inc, 89- *Mem:* Fel Am Ceramic Soc; Nat Inst Ceramic Engrs; Sigma Xi. *Res:* High temperature material science; foundry speciality crucibles, coatings and casting processes; microwave sintering and processing refractories; diamond syntheses; published over 50 articles and granted 45 US patents. *Mailing Add:* 440 Sugarwood Dr Knoxville TN 37922. *E-Mail:* cvh@ornl.gov

HOLCOMBE, JAMES ANDREW, ANALYTICAL CHEMISTRY. *Current Pos:* PROF CHEM, UNIV TEX, AUSTIN, 74- *Personal Data:* b Denver, Colo, Nov 12, 48; m 69; c 2. *Educ:* Colo Col, BA, 70; Univ Mich, MS, 72, PhD(chem), 74. *Concurrent Pos:* Ed-in-chief, Appl Spectros. *Mem:* Am Chem Soc; Soc Appl Spectros. *Res:* Graphite furnace atomic absorption spectrometry; trace and ultratrace metal analysis; surface studies using sims; computer simulation and interfacing analytical instrumentation to computers; software development. *Mailing Add:* Dept Chem Univ Tex Austin TX 78712-1104. *Fax:* 512-471-0985; *E-Mail:* holcombe@uts.ce.utexas.edu

HOLCOMBE, TROY LEON, OCEAN MAPPING, SCIENTIFIC DATA MANAGEMENT & ADMINISTRATION. *Current Pos:* sr scientist, 84-96, ACTG CHIEF, MARINE GEOL & GEOPHYS DIV, NAT GEOPHYS DATA CTR, NAT OCEANIC & ATMOSPHERIC ADMIN, BOULDER, COLO, 96- *Personal Data:* b Roxton, Tex, Mar 8, 40; m 71, Janis O'Neal; c Leigh, Virginia & Terry. *Educ:* Hardin-Simmons Univ, BA, 61; Univ Mo, AM, 64; Columbia Univ, PhD(geol), 72. *Prof Exp:* Res oceanogr, US Naval Oceanog Off, Chesapeake Beach, Md, 68-75; head, Geol Br, Naval Ocean Res & Develop Activ, NSTL, Miss, 75-84. *Concurrent Pos:* Vis assoc prof oceanog, Dept Oceanog, Tex A&M Univ, College Station, 80-81; assoc prof, Ctr Wetland Resources, La State Univ, Baton Rouge, 82-83; prog mgr & prin investr, NGDC Prog Paleoclimatol, Nat Oceanic & Atmospheric Admin, 87-91; US sci coordr, Int Bathymetric Chart Caribbean Sea & Gulf Mex proj, Intergovt Oceanog Comn, UNESCO, 87-; reviewer, Caribbean & Gulf Mex, Gen Bathymetric Chart Oceans, 89- *Mem:* Geol Soc Am; Am Asn Petrol Geologists. *Res:* Origin and evolution of seafloor fabric and the accumulation of ocean sediments in space and time-supported by ocean mapping and studies of acoustic stratigraphy; areas of concentration, Caribbean Sea, Gulf of Mexico and Laurentian Great Lakes. *Mailing Add:* Nat Geophys Data Ctr Nat Oceanic & Atmospheric Admin 325 Broadway Boulder CO 80303. *Fax:* 303-497-6513; *E-Mail:* tholcombe@ngdc.noaa.gov

HOLCSLAW, TERRY LEE, PHARMACOLOGY. *Current Pos:* ASST PROF PHARMACOL, UNIV NEBR, 74- *Personal Data:* b Hammond, Ind, July 1, 46; m 67; c 1. *Educ:* Univ Ariz, BS, 68; Purdue Univ, MS, 72, PhD(pharmacol), 74. *Mem:* AAAS; Am Asn Cols Pharm. *Res:* Overall regulation of drug metabolizing enzyme activity as well as environmental and pharmacological agent which modifies drug metabolism; biochemical mechanisms in the development and maintenance of essential hypertension. *Mailing Add:* 1250 S Collegeville Rd Smith Kline French Labs Smith Kline & French Labs Collegeville PA 19426

HOLDAWAY, MICHAEL JON, METAMORPHIC PETROLOGY, MINERALOGY. *Current Pos:* From asst prof to assoc prof, 62-74, chmn, 77-82 & 86-91, PROF GEOL, SOUTHERN METHODIST UNIV, 74- *Personal Data:* b Canberra, Australia, Jan 1, 36; US citizen; m 58, 92, Angeline Koolstra; c Mark, Scott & Ian. *Educ:* Yale Univ, BS, 58; Univ Calif, Berkeley, PhD(geol), 62. *Concurrent Pos:* Res grants, NSF, 63-65, 72-75, 76-79, 81-83, 83-85, 86-90, 91-93 & 93-95 & NASA, 66-67; ed, Am Mineralogist, 80-84. *Mem:* Mineral Soc Am (pres, 91-92); Sigma Xi. *Res:* Stability relations of epidote, aluminum silicates, cordierite, almandine, staurolite; pelitic metamorphic rocks in Maine and New Mexico; crystal chemistry of staurolite, cordierite, muscovite, biotite. *Mailing Add:* Dept Geol Sci Southern Methodist Univ Dallas TX 75275. *Fax:* 214-768-2701

HOLDEMAN, JONAS TILLMAN, JR, PHYSICS, COMPUTATIONAL FLUID MECHANICS & COMPUTATIONAL ELECTROMAGNETICS. *Current Pos:* PROP & PRIN INVESTR, OBELISK RES, 96- *Personal Data:* b Baton Rouge, La, Feb 9, 37; m 64, Judith Ann Serban; c Jonas III, Steven J & Jeffrey D. *Educ:* La State Univ, BS, 58, MS, 60; Case Western Reserve Univ, PhD(physics), 66. *Prof Exp:* Mem staff physics, Los Alamos Sci Lab, 66-68; res assoc, Mich State Univ, 69-71, asst prof, 71-72; asst prof, Univ Southwestern La, 72-74; res & develop group leader, Oak Ridge Nat Lab, 74-96. *Mem:* Am Phys Soc; Sigma Xi; AAAS; Am Inst Aeronaut & Astronaut; Am Comput Electromagnetics Soc. *Res:* Numerical analysis; mathematical physics; computational fluid mechanics and computational electromagnetics. *Mailing Add:* 1056 Lovell Rd Knoxville TN 37932

HOLDEMAN, LOUIS BRIAN, CRYOGENICS, MICROELECTRONICS. *Current Pos:* AT COMSAT LABS, CLARKSBURG, MD. *Personal Data:* b Baton Rouge, La, Aug 9, 38; m 59; c 2. *Educ:* La State Univ, BS, 62; Stanford Univ, MS, 65, PhD(physics), 73. *Honors & Awards:* Bronze Medal, Dept Comn, 81. *Prof Exp:* Planetarium lectr & instr astron, La State Univ, 62; res assoc space sci, George C Marshall Space Flight Ctr, NASA, 73-75; physicist, Elec Div, 75-78 & Nat Bur Stand, 75-83. *Concurrent Pos:* Res assoc, Nat Acad Sci/Nat Res Coun, 73-75. *Mem:* Am Phys Soc; Sigma Xi; Inst Elec & Electronics Engrs; Am Vacuum Soc. *Res:* Microelectronics fabrication technology for GaAs field; effect transistors; monolithic microwave intigrated circuits. *Mailing Add:* 9 Diller Ct Boyds MD 20841-9015

HOLDEN, ALISTAIR DAVID CRAIG, ELECTRICAL ENGINEERING, COMPUTER SCIENCE. *Current Pos:* from asst prof to prof elec eng & computer sci, 64-89, PROF COMPUTE SCI & ENG & ELEC ENG, UNIV WASH, 89- *Personal Data:* b Lochgilphead, Argyll, Scotland, Nov 8, 28; US citizen; m 59; c 2. *Educ:* Glasgow Univ, BSc, 55; Yale Univ, MEng, 58; Univ Wash, PhD(elec eng), 64. *Prof Exp:* Grad apprentice, Brit Broadcasting Corp, London, 55-57; res engr, Boeing Co, 58-60. *Concurrent Pos:* Gen chmn, 1st Int Joint Conf Artificial Intel, 69; sect ed, artificial intel, Int J Cybernetics & Gen Systs, 72-; consult, expert systs & artificial intel. *Mem:* Asn Comput Mach; Inst Elec & Electronics Engrs. *Res:* Artificial intelligence, the attempt to use digital computers to augment human intelligence, to simulate human intelligent activities and to shed light on the learning, problem-solving abilities and development of concepts in children; man and machine communication involving natural language, speech and vision. *Mailing Add:* Dept Elec Eng FT-10 Univ Wash Seattle WA 98195

HOLDEN, FRANK C(HARLES), PHYSICAL METALLURGY. *Current Pos:* RETIRED. *Personal Data:* b Bangor, Maine, Nov 28, 21; m 59, Donna Abel; c Jane R. *Educ:* Univ Maine, BS, 43; Harvard Univ, MS, 47, MES, 49. *Prof Exp:* Jr engr, Explosives Div, Los Alamos Labs, 44-46; instr mech eng, Univ Maine, 49-51; prin res metallurgist, 51-56, from asst div chief to div chief, 56-67, assoc mgr, 67-70, mgr process & phys metall, 70-73, mgr, Metall Dept, 73-78, mgr metall sci, 78-81, mgr phys metall, 81-83, mgr ceramics & glass, 83-85, mgr corrosion & electrochem, Battelle Mem Inst, 85-86. *Mem:* Am Soc Metals; Am Inst Mining, Metall & Petrol Engrs. *Res:* Titanium alloys; mechanical metallurgy. *Mailing Add:* 1763 Merriweather Dr Columbus OH 43221

HOLDEN, FREDERICK THOMPSON, PETROLEUM GEOLOGY. *Current Pos:* RETIRED. *Personal Data:* b New York, NY, June 23, 15. *Educ:* Denison Univ, AB, 37; Univ Chicago, PhD(geol), 41. *Hon Degrees:* DSc, Denison Univ, 80. *Prof Exp:* Field geologist, US Geol Surv, Kans, 38-39; subsurface geologist, Carter Oil Co, La, 41-46, dist geologist, Miss, 46-52, staff geologist, Okla, 52-53, asst to div geologist, southern US, 53-56, sr geologist, 56-60, sr geologist, Humble Oil & Ref Co, 60-67, sr prof geologist, 67-71, explor geologist, 71-73; sr explor geologist, Exxon Corp, CO, USA, 73-75, geol scientist, 75-78, sr geol scientist, 78-85. *Mem:* Fel Geol Soc Am; Am Asn Petrol Geol; Am Inst Prof Geologists. *Res:* Mississippian stratigraphy of Ohio; stratigraphy and structure of eastern Gulf Coast and western Mid-Continent; stratigraphy and geologic history of Mid-Continent. *Mailing Add:* 118 Bridgewater Circle Midland TX 79707-6112

HOLDEN, HAROLD WILLIAM, POLYMER SCIENCE, EXPLOSIVES & PROPELLANTS. *Current Pos:* PRES & PRIN SCIENTIST, CARAIGEEN INC, 94- *Personal Data:* b Toronto, Ont, Sept 29, 29; m 54, Barbara Black; c David (deceased), Paul, Kathleen, Ian, Barbara & Madeleine. *Educ:* Univ Toronto, BA, 51, PhD(phys chem), 55. *Prof Exp:* UK Nat Coal Bd res fel, Univ Birmingham, 55, univ res fel, 56-58; Nat Res Coun Can res fel photochem, Nat Res Coun Div Pure Chem, Ottawa, 58-60; res chemist, Cent Res Lab, Can Industs Ltd, 60-71, group leader pioneering, 71-73, group mgr pioneering res, Explosives Res Lab, 73-75, group mgr prod res & develop, 75-79, group mgr, explosives physics, Explosives Res Lab, 79-84, tech mgr, New Ventures, Explosives Div, C-I-L Inc, 84-94; at Explosives Tech Ctr, ICI Explosive Can, 90-92, McMasterville Tech Ctr, 92-94. *Concurrent Pos:* Consult Energeric Mat Chem. *Mem:* Chem Inst Can. *Res:* High explosives and blasting agents; polymer physics and physical chemistry; physical properties of polymers and composites; emulsions and gels; chemical kinetics; explosives formulation, sensitization and hazards; energetic propellant constituents. *Mailing Add:* Caraigeen Inc 75 Pl Courcelles Mont St-Hilaire PQ J3H 2S6 Can

HOLDEN, HOWARD T, IMMUNOLOGY. *Current Pos:* STAFF, WARNER LAMBERT, ANN ARBOR, 88- *Educ:* Univ Miami, Fla, PhD(microbiol), 73. *Prof Exp:* Sr investr, Nat Cancer Inst, 75-88. *Res:* Drug regulatory affairs. *Mailing Add:* Ligand Pharmaceut Inc 9393 Towne Ctr Dr Suite 100 San Diego CA 92121-3016

HOLDEN, JAMES EDWARD, MEDICAL PHYSICS. *Current Pos:* asst prof radiol, 74-79, assoc prof med phys & radiol, 79-80, PROF MED PHYS & RADIOL, UNIV WIS-MADISON, 80- *Personal Data:* b Yonkers, NY, Oct 19, 44; m 68; c 2. *Educ:* Providence Col, RI, BS, 66; Univ Pa, PhD(physics), 71. *Prof Exp:* Res assoc nuclear physics, Nuclear Physics Lab, Univ Pittsburgh, 71-74. *Concurrent Pos:* James Picker Found scholar, 76-80. *Mem:* Soc Nuclear Med; Soc Cerebral Blood Flow & Metab. *Res:* Linear systems analysis of medical imaging processes and of tracer kinetics for investigation of cerebral and cardiac physiology; radioactive tracer dynamics and compartmental analysis; computer assisted transverse-axial reconstruction algorithms. *Mailing Add:* 219 Lathrop St Madison WI 53705

HOLDEN, JAMES RICHARD, PHYSICAL CHEMISTRY, X-RAY CRYSTALLOGRAPHY. *Current Pos:* RETIRED. *Personal Data:* b Omaha, Nebr, Aug 1, 28; m 58, Rachel Blachly; c Carol (Zimmer) & Barbara (Newman). *Educ:* Univ Nebr, BSc, 50, MSc, 51; Univ Iowa, PhD(phys chem), 55. *Prof Exp:* Res chemist, US Naval Surface Warfare Ctr, 55-88. *Mem:* Am Crystallog Asn. *Res:* Study of the physical properties of explosives and their relation to chemical constitution; determination of crystal structure of organic compounds by x-ray crystallography; prediction of crystal structure from molecular structure. *Mailing Add:* HC 31 Box 1347 Phippsburg ME 04562

HOLDEN, JOHN B, JR, ANALYTICAL CHEMISTRY. *Current Pos:* from asst prof to assoc prof chem, 68-74, prof chem & dir Environ Studies Inst, 74-86, PROF CHEM, MANKATO STATE UNIV, 86- *Personal Data:* b Washington, DC, May 26, 35; m 64; c 3. *Educ:* Cath Univ Am, BChE, 57; Princeton Univ, MA, 59, PhD(chem), 61. *Prof Exp:* Sr res chemist, Printing Prod Div, Minn Mining & Mfg Co, 61-68. *Mem:* Am Chem Soc. *Res:* Iron III chemistry; experimentation for instructional chemistry; water chemistry. *Mailing Add:* MSU No 40 Mankato State Col Mankato MN 56001

HOLDEN, JOSEPH THADDEUS, MICROBIOLOGY. *Current Pos:* actg dir, 87-93, ASSOC DEAN, CITY OF HOPE GRAD PROGS, BECKMAN RES INST, 95- *Personal Data:* b Brooklyn, NY, Jan 18, 25; m 48; c 4. *Educ:* Polytech Inst Brooklyn, BS, 44; Univ Wis, MS, 48, PhD(biochem), 51. *Prof Exp:* Asst biochem, Univ Wis, 47-51; USPHS res fel biochem & genetics, Calif Inst Technol, 51-53; biochemist, Exp Sta, Chem Dept, E I du Pont de Nemours & Co, 53-54; res scientist, assoc div chmn & head, Cell Physiol Sect, Neurosci Div, City of Hope Res Inst, 54-80, asst dir res, 80-87. *Concurrent Pos:* Nat Inst Neurol Dis & Stroke spec trainee, Col France, Paris, 74. *Mem:* Am Soc Microbiol; Am Soc Biochemists; Am Soc Cell Biol; Am Soc Neurochem; Soc Neurosci. *Res:* Microbial amino acid and vitamin nutrition and metabolism; genetic factors in nutrition and metabolism; active transport of cell nutrients; biosynthesis of bacterial cell wall; structure and function of cell membranes. *Mailing Add:* City Hope Beckmann Res Inst Duarte CA 91010

HOLDEN, KENNETH GEORGE, MEDICINAL CHEMISTRY. *Current Pos:* DIR RES, HOLDEN LABS, 88- *Personal Data:* b Summit, NJ, Dec 19, 34; m 60, Kathryn D Tracy; c 1. *Educ:* Brown Univ, BS, 57; Univ Calif, Berkeley, PhD(chem), 61. *Prof Exp:* Sr med chemist, Smith Kline & French Labs, 61-67, asst dir chem, 67-72, sr investr, Res & Develop Div, 72-79, assoc sci dir, 79-80, dep dir med chem, 80-84, dir chemotherapeut res, 84-88. *Mem:* AAAS; Am Chem Soc. *Res:* Natural products chemistry; synthesis and structure determination of alkaloids, microorganism metabolites, steroids, prostaglandins, glycoproteins, B-lactam antibiotics and enzyme inhibitors; anticancer agents; serotonergic agents. *Mailing Add:* RD 5 Box 336 Horseshoe Trail Malvern PA 19355-9501

HOLDEN, NORMAN EDWARD, NUCLEAR PHYSICS. *Current Pos:* physicist nuclear physics, 74-90, RES COORDR, BROOKHAVEN NAT LAB, 90- *Personal Data:* b New York, NY, Feb 1, 36; m 62, Gail Rafferty; c Sean, Kristen, Maurisa, Gregory, Megan, Victoria, Keith, Kathleen & Kevin. *Educ:* Fordham Univ, BS, 57; Cath Univ Am, MS, 59, PhD(physics), 64. *Prof Exp:* Officer nuclear physics, Air Force Tech Appln Ctr, 62-65; physicist, G E Knolls Atomic Power Lab, 65-74. *Concurrent Pos:* Mem Int

Comn Atomic Weights, 71-87, secy, 75-79, pres, 79-83; mem Subcomt Assessment Isotopic Compos, Int Union Pure & Appl Chem, 73-83, Comt Inorg Chem, 79-85, Subcomt, Isotopic Abundance Measurements, 83-, Natural Isotopic Fractionation, 87-; US adv nuclear struct & decay data, Int Atomic Energy Agency, 76-78; mem Int Comt Radionuclide Metrol, 77- & Int Comt Radiochem & Nuclear Tech, 83- *Mem:* Am Phys Soc; Am Nuclear Soc; NY Acad Sci; AAAS. *Res:* Atomic weights; isotopic abundances of elements; neutron cross sections; radioactivity and nuclear data; reactor physics; radiation analysis. *Mailing Add:* High Flux Beam Reactor Brookhaven Nat Lab Upton NY 11973

HOLDEN, PALMER JOSEPH, ANIMAL NUTRITION, ANIMAL HUSBANDRY. *Current Pos:* EXTEN SPECIALIST SWINE NUTRIT, IOWA STATE UNIV, 72- *Personal Data:* b Apr 10, 43; US citizen; m 74, V Sheryl Gift; c Daniel. *Educ:* NDak State Univ, BS, 63; Iowa State Univ, MS, 67, PhD(animal nutrit), 70. *Prof Exp:* Exten adv agr, US Army, Vietnam, 70-71. *Concurrent Pos:* Swine consult, Monterey Farms, Philippines, 73-86, Univ Costa Rica, 78, 81 & 89, Poland, Bulgaria & Ger Dem Repub, 86, Honduras, 87, Sardenia & Malaysia, 89, Sweden, Denmark & Holland, 89, Malaysia & Thailand, 93. *Mem:* Am Soc Animal Sci. *Res:* Swine nutrition research of practical problems related directly to production. *Mailing Add:* Dept Animal Sci Iowa State Univ Ames IA 50011-2010. *Fax:* 515-294-3795; *E-Mail:* pholden@iastate.edu

HOLDEN, THOMAS MORE, METALLIC MAGNETISM, APPLIED PHYSICS. *Current Pos:* SR RES OFFICER, NAT RES COUN CAN, 96- *Personal Data:* b Ilkley, Yorkshire, Eng; Can citizen. *Educ:* Univ Leeds, Eng, BSc, 61, PhD(physics), 65. *Prof Exp:* Indust fel, Atomic Energy Res Estab, Harwell, UK, 64-66; Nat Res Coun fel, Chalk River Nuclear Labs, Atomic Energy can Ltd, Ont, 66-67, asst res officer, 67-75, assoc res officer, 75-84, sr res officer, 84-95. *Mem:* Can Asn Physicists. *Res:* Application of thermal neutrons to the study of the structure and dynamics of magnetic materials, particularly rare-earth and actinide compounds; engineering applications of thermal neutron diffraction methods. *Mailing Add:* Neutron Prog Mat Res Steacle Inst Molecular Sci Nat Res Coun Can Chalk River ON K0J 1J0 Can. *Fax:* 613-584-4040; *E-Mail:* holdent@aecl.ca

HOLDEN, WILLIAM DOUGLAS, surgery; deceased, see previous edition for last biography

HOLDEN, WILLIAM R(OBERT), ENGINEERING PHYSICS. *Current Pos:* From asst prof to assoc prof, 55-77, PROF PETROL ENG, LA STATE UNIV, BATON ROUGE, 77- *Personal Data:* b Ft Worth, Tex, Dec 20, 28; m 57; c 1. *Educ:* Univ Okla, BS, 53, MS, 55. *Mem:* Am Inst Mining, Metall & Petrol Engrs; Soc Petrol Engrs. *Res:* Turbulent flow properties of non-Newtonian fluids. *Mailing Add:* 2066 Columbine St Baton Rouge LA 70808

HOLDER, CHARLES BURT, JR, CHEMISTRY. *Current Pos:* RETIRED. *Personal Data:* b Berea, Ky, Aug 29, 14; m 53, Thelma MacPherson; c 5. *Educ:* Transylvania Col, AB, 36; Ga Inst Technol, MS, 38; Univ Tex, PhD(org chem), 41. *Prof Exp:* Chemist, Texaco, Inc, 41-65, res chemist petrol prod res, 65-80. *Mem:* Am Chem Soc; Sigma Xi. *Res:* Polymers; synthesis of hydantoin derivatives; petroleum derivatives; organic chemistry. *Mailing Add:* 33 Edge Hill Dr Wappingers Falls NY 12590-3631

HOLDER, DAVID GORDON, PLANT BREEDING. *Current Pos:* GENETICIST, US SUGAR CORP, 73- *Personal Data:* b Louisville, Miss, Oct 18, 43; m 67, Sandra Eaves; c Amy. *Educ:* Miss State Univ, BS, 65, MS, 67; Purdue Univ, PhD(plant genetics), 71. *Prof Exp:* Rockefeller Found res grant entom, Miss State Univ, 71-73. *Mem:* Am Soc Agron; Crop Sci Soc Am; Int Soc Sugarcane Technologists; Am Soc Sugarcane Technologists. *Res:* Sugarcane genetics and breeding, sugarcane pathology. *Mailing Add:* 1035 Palmetto St Clewiston FL 33440

HOLDER, GERALD D, NATURAL GAS RECOVERY, THERMODYNAMICS. *Current Pos:* from asst prof to assoc prof, 79-86, PROF CHEM ENG, UNIV PITTSBURGH, 86-, CHMN, 87-, DEAN ENG, 96- *Personal Data:* b Los Angeles, Calif, July 29, 50; m 68, Diane Bicknell; c Nancy, Elizabeth & Jonathan. *Educ:* Kalamazoo Col, BA, 72; Univ Mich, BSE, 73, MSE, 74, PhD(chem eng), 76. *Prof Exp:* Asst prof, Columbia Univ, 76-79. *Concurrent Pos:* Consult, Exxon Res & Eng, 77, Gulf Sci & Technol, 80-81, Norks-Nyddo, 87, Petrobas, 87. *Mem:* Am Chem Soc; Am Inst Chem Engrs; Soc Petrol Engrs. *Res:* Thermodynamics of natural gas hydrates and their potential as an alternative energy source; molecular dynamics; extraction and reaction of substances using supercritical fluids. *Mailing Add:* 240 Benedum Hall Univ Pittsburgh Pittsburgh PA 15261. *Fax:* 412-624-9639; *E-Mail:* Holder@engrng.pitt.edu

HOLDER, HAROLD DOUGLAS, PUBLIC HEALTH. *Current Pos:* LECTR, HEALTH EDUC PROG SCH PUB HEALTH, UNIV CALIF, BERKELEY, 87-, DIR PREV RES CTR, PAC INST RES & EVAL, BERKELEY, 87- *Personal Data:* b Raleigh, NC, Aug 9, 39; m 80; c 3. *Educ:* Samford Univ, AB, 61; Syracuse Univ, MA, 62, PhD(commun sci), 65. *Prof Exp:* Dir, Community Res Ctr & asst prof, Dept Journalism & Oral Commun, Baylor Univ, 65-67; assoc prof & mem grad fac, Dept Sociol, NC State Univ, 67-75; site mgr, Human Ecol Inst, Wellesley, 73-75; sr scientist, 77-87, dir, 80-87; mgr develop, City of Portsmouth, Va, 75-76. *Concurrent Pos:* Bd dirs, Cent Tex Res Coun, 65-67; lectr, Sch Pub Health, Univ NC, Chapel Hill, 67-68; Dept Psychiat, 67-68; res scientist, Div Res & dir systs analysis & prog eval, NC Dept Ment Health, 67-69; sr analyst, Caseway, Inc, Brockton, Mass, 77-78; vis prof, Newhouse Community Ctr, 66, Univ NC, Chapel Hill, 79-80; chmn, Off Sci Affairs Nat Inst Alcohol Abuse & Alcoholism, 86-87; consult, Nat Inst Alcohol Abuse & Alcoholism, Tex Educ Agency, Cent Tex Regional Educ Ctr, James Connally Tech Inst, Tech Educ Res Ctr, Univ NC, Chapel Hill, NC Dept Health, Child Advocacy Ctr, Nat Inst Ment Health, Serv Integration Tech Inst & Boston Learning Inst NC. *Mem:* Am Pub Health Asn; Am Sociol Asn; Am Asn Pub Opinion Res; Nat Asn Pub Health Policy (secy/treas, 85-86); Soc Gen Systs Res; Res Soc Alcoholism. *Res:* Contributed various chapters to books and articles to journals. *Mailing Add:* Prev Res Ctr Pac Inst Res & Eval 2150 Shattuck Ave Suite 900 Berkeley CA 94704-1306

HOLDER, IAN ALAN, MICROBIOLOGY. *Current Pos:* DIR, DEPT MICROBIOL, SHRINERS BURNS INST, CINCINNATI, 67- *Personal Data:* b Brooklyn, NY, July 23, 34. *Educ:* Brooklyn Col, BS, 58, MA, 63; Univ Kans, PhD(microbiol), 67. *Honors & Awards:* Am Burn Asn Award, 85; Tanner Vandeput Prize, 86; Martin Ramelot Prize Sci Res, 91. *Prof Exp:* Res asst microbiol, Brooklyn Col, 58-59; res & develop biologist, Res & Develop Lab, Schieffelin & Co, 59-61; res assoc, Bellevue Hosp, 61-63; from asst prof to prof exp surg, Col Med, Univ Cincinnati, 67-79, from asst prof to prof microbiol, 70-80, actg dir, Div Microbiol, Med Ctr, 73-75. *Concurrent Pos:* Vis prof, Kitasato Inst, Tokyo, Japan, 84, Dept Surg & Pediat, Univ Tex Health & Sci Ctr, Houston, 85 & Dept Biol, Youngstown State Univ, Youngstown, Ohio, 88. *Mem:* Am Soc Microbiol; Am Burn Asn; Sigma Xi; fel Am Acad Microbiol; Int Soc Burn Injuries; Japan Pseudomonas aeruginosa Soc. *Res:* Host parasite interactions, virulence factors, mechanisms of pathogenesis and clinical aspects of Pseudomonas aeruginosa and Candida albicans infections. *Mailing Add:* Shriners Burns Inst 3229 Burnet Ave Cincinnati OH 45229-3095. *Fax:* 513-872-6999; *E-Mail:* iaholder@juno.com

HOLDER, LEONARD IRVIN, MATHEMATICS. *Current Pos:* chmn dept, 64-75, 80-, PROF MATH, GETTYSBURG COL, 64-, DEAN, 75- *Personal Data:* b Ft Worth, Tex, Nov 30, 23; m 49; c 2. *Educ:* Agr & Mech Col Tex, BS, 47, MS, 51; Purdue Univ, PhD(math), 55. *Prof Exp:* Asst prof math, Arlington State Col, 47-49; instr, Agr & Mech Col Tex, 51-52; engr-designer, Boeing Co, Kans, 52; asst math, Purdue Univ, 52-55; assoc prof, San Jose State Col, 55-64. *Mem:* Am Math Soc; Math Asn Am. *Res:* Infinite series, particularly summability of series as applied to Fourier series. *Mailing Add:* Dept Math Gettysburg Col Gettysburg PA 17325-1486

HOLDER, THOMAS M, pediatric surgery, for more information see previous edition

HOLDERBAUM, DANIEL, VASCULAR & CONNECTIVE TISSUE. *Current Pos:* ASST STAFF, CLEVELAND CLIN FOUND, 82- *Educ:* Cleveland State Univ, PhD(regulatory biol), 80. *Mailing Add:* Div Rheumatol Case Western Res Univ Cleveland OH 44106

HOLDHUSEN, JAMES S(TAFFORD), AERONAUTICAL ENGINEERING. *Current Pos:* RETIRED. *Personal Data:* b Houghton, SDak, Apr 2, 25; m 55; c 3. *Educ:* Univ Minn, BCE, 45, MS, 47, PhD(fluid mech), 52. *Honors & Awards:* J C Stevens Award, Am Soc Civil Engrs, 51. *Prof Exp:* Instr civil eng, Univ Minn, 49-52; chief res engr, Fluidyne Eng Corp, 52-57, vpres res & planning, 57-71, exec vpres, 71-90. *Mem:* Am Inst Aeronaut & Astronaut; Am Soc Mech Engrs. *Res:* Propulsion aerodynamics; wind tunnel development; aerodynamics. *Mailing Add:* 4520 Sunset Ridge Golden Valley MN 55427

HOLDITCH, STEPHEN ALLEN, PETROLEUM ENGINEERING. *Current Pos:* PROF, TEX A&M UNIV, 76-; PRES, S A HOLDITCH & ASSOCS, COLLEGE STATION, 77- *Personal Data:* b Corsicana, Tex, Oct 20, 46; m 71, Ann Friddle; c Katie J (Rowe) & Abbie Diane. *Educ:* Tex A&M Univ, BS, 69, MS, 70, PhD(petrol eng), 76. *Honors & Awards:* Lester C Uren Award, Soc Petrol Engrs, 95. *Prof Exp:* Engr, Pan Am Petro Corp, Tyler, Tex, 68-69; prod engr, Shell Oil Co, Vicksburg, Wilcox, Tex, 70-74; consult engr pvt pract, College Station, Tex, 74-76. *Concurrent Pos:* Shell distinguished chair petrol eng, Tex A&M Univ, 83-87. *Mem:* Nat Acad Eng; Soc Petrol Engrs; Am Asn Petrol Geologists; Soc Prof Well Log Analysts; Soc Petrol Eval Engrs; Sigma Xi. *Res:* Contributed numerous articles to professional journals. *Mailing Add:* 8600 Rosewood College Station TX 77845

HOLDREDGE, RUSSELL M, MECHANICAL ENGINEERING. *Current Pos:* from asst prof to assoc prof, 59-70, head dept, 70-76, PROF MECH ENG, COL ENG, UTAH STATE UNIV, 70-; ASSOC DEAN, 76- *Personal Data:* b Paonia, Colo, July 22, 33; m 55; c 4. *Educ:* Univ Colo, BS(mech eng) & BS(bus admin), 56, MS, 59; Purdue Univ, PhD(mech eng), 65. *Prof Exp:* Systs engr, Sandia Corp, 56-57; instr mech eng, Univ Colo, 57-59. *Concurrent Pos:* NSF fac fel, Purdue Univ, 65-66. *Mem:* Am Soc Mech Engrs; Am Soc Eng Educ. *Res:* Cryogenic heat transfer, primarily transient cooling and pool boiling; reactor heat transfer, primarily transient cooling and conduction in nonhomogeneous materials. *Mailing Add:* 1436 N 1640 E Logan UT 84321

HOLDREN, JOHN PAUL, ENERGY CONVERSION, ENVIRONMENTAL PHYSICS. *Current Pos:* PROF, DIV SCI TECH & PUB POLICY PROG CTR SCI & INT AFFAIRS, KENNEDY SCH GOVT, HARVARD UNIV, 96- *Personal Data:* b Sewickley, Pa, Mar 1, 44; m 66, Cheryl Edgar; c John C & Jill V. *Educ:* Mass Inst Technol, BS, 65, MS, 66; Stanford Univ, PhD(aeronaut, astronaut & elec eng), 70. *Hon Degrees:* ScD, Univ Puget Sound, 75. *Honors & Awards:* Gustavsen lectr, Univ Chicago, 78;

MacArthur Found Prize fel, 81-86; Volvo Environ Prize, 93. *Prof Exp:* Physicist, Magnetic Fusion Energy, Lawrence Livermore Nat Lab, Univ Calif, 70-73; from asst prof to prof energy & resources, Univ Calif, Berkeley, 73-96. *Concurrent Pos:* Mem, Int Environ Prog Comt, Nat Acad Sci-Nat Acad Eng, 70-75, mem, Comt Nuclear & Alt Energy Systs & Comt Rev Lit Nuclear Risks, 75-79; lectr, Univ Calif, Berkeley, 71-72; sr res fel, Pop Prog, Calif Inst Technol, 72-73; consult, Magnetic Fusion Energy Div, Lawrence Livermore Lab, 73-, Energy & Environ Div, Lawrence Berkeley Lab, 74- & Int Inst Appl Systs Anal, 75-; sr investr, Rocky Mountain Biol Lab, 76-88; mem, Energy Res Adv Bd, US Dept Energy, 78-79; vis fel, Resource Systs Inst & Environ & Policy Inst, East West Ctr, Honolulu, 79 & 80; vchair, Comt Int Security Studies, Am Acad Arts & Sci, 83-; chmn, Fedn Am Scientists, 84-86; chmn, Sr Comt Environ Safety & Econ Aspects Magnetic Fusion Energy, US Dept Energy, 85-89; Kistiakowsky vis scholar, AAAS, 86-87; vis prof, Univ Rome, 87; guest res, Max-Plank Soc, WGer, 87-88; vis scholar, Ctr Int Studies, Mass Inst Technol, 88; mem, Comt Int Security & Arms Control, Nat Acad Sci, 92-, chmn, 93-; vis scholar, Woods Hole Res Ctr, 92, 93- *Mem:* Nat Acad Sci; fel Am Phys Soc; Fedn Am Scientists; Am Nuclear Soc; Sigma Xi; fel Am Acad Arts & Sci; fel AAAS. *Res:* Environmental aspects of coal, fusion and fission; national and international problems in energy and environment, nuclear weapons and arms control; plasma physics, energy technology and policy. *Mailing Add:* Kennedy Sch Govt Harvard Univ 79 JFK St Cambridge MA 02138. *Fax:* 617-495-8963; *E-Mail:* john_holdren@harvard.edu

HOLDSWORTH, ROBERT POWELL, ENTOMOLOGY. *Current Pos:* RETIRED. *Personal Data:* b Stoughton, Mass, Jan 12, 15; m 40, Jeannette Houghton; c Ann J, Robert H & Nancy. *Educ:* Univ Mass, BS, 37; Harvard Univ, MA, 38, PhD(zool), 41. *Prof Exp:* Agt entom, USDA, 46-47; salesman, E I du Pont de Nemours & Co, 47-56, prod mgr, 56-58; exten entomologist, Ohio State Univ, 58-65, resident teacher entom & researcher, 65-81. *Mem:* Entom Soc Am. *Res:* Integrated pest management of apple arthropods. *Mailing Add:* 2739 Westmont Blvd Columbus OH 43221-3334

HOLE, FRANCIS DOAN, SOIL ZOOLOGY, SOIL LANDSCAPE DYNAMICS. *Current Pos:* asst prof soil sci, 46-51, assoc prof, 52-57, prof, 58-83, EMER PROF SOIL SCI & GEOG, UNIV WIS-MADISON, 83- *Personal Data:* b Muncie, Ind, Aug 25, 13; m 41; c 2. *Educ:* Earlham Col, AB, 33; Haverford Col, MA, 34; Univ Wis-Madison, PhD(geol soil sci), 43. *Prof Exp:* Instr Ger, Friends Cent Country Day Sch, 34-35; instr French, Ger, music, & physiography, Westtown Friends Boarding Sch, 35-38; instr geol & soil sci, Earlham Col, 40-41 & 43-44. *Concurrent Pos:* Ed, Soil Surv Horizons, 60-63; vis prof, Dept Soils, Water & Eng, Univ Ariz, 81. *Mem:* Soil Sci Soc Am; Geol Soc Am; Asn Am Geographers; Sigma Xi; Soc Social Responsibility in Sci. *Res:* Influence of animals on soils; factors affecting the incorporation of organic matter into soil; numerical classification of soils; soil landscape analysis. *Mailing Add:* 2201 Center Ave Madison WI 53704-5624

HOLECHEK, JERRY LEE, RANGE NUTRITION, RANGELAND. *Current Pos:* PROF RANGE SCI, DEPT ANIMAL & RANGE SCI, NMEX STATE UNIV, 79- *Personal Data:* b Lebanon, Ore, Mar 6, 48. *Educ:* Mont State Univ, MS, 76; Ore State Univ, BS, 71, PhD(animal sci), 80. *Mem:* Soc Range Mgt; Am Soc Animal Sci; Soil Conserv Soc Am; Wildlife Soc. *Res:* Nutrition of free ranging animals; reclamation of deteriorated ranges; range/wildlife interactions; techniques for studying food habits and nutrition of wild and domestic ruminant animals; range economics, rangeland public policy. *Mailing Add:* Dept Animal & Range Sci NMex State Univ Las Cruces NM 88003

HOLEMAN, DENNIS LEIGH, MAN-MACHINE INTELLIGENCE. *Current Pos:* PRIN ENGR, SRI INT, 78- *Personal Data:* b Portland, Ore, May 10, 46; m 81, Jeanette M Sill. *Educ:* Harvey Mudd Col, BSE, 68; Univ Calif, Berkeley, MEME, 70. *Prof Exp:* Sr engr, Oceanic Div, Westinghouse Elec Corp, 68-75; co-founder & coordr eng, IMSAI Mfg Corp, 75-78. *Concurrent Pos:* Prin, Heuristica: A Systs Consultancy, 72-75. *Mem:* Am Asn Artificial Intel; Inst Elec & Electronics Engrs; Am Inst Aeronaut & Astronaut; AAAS. *Res:* Development of systems integrating human and machine intelligence capabilities in a synergistic fashion for defense, aerospace and other complex system control functions. *Mailing Add:* SRI Int MS BN390 333 Ravenswood Ave Menlo Park CA 94025. *Fax:* 650-859-4175; *E-Mail:* dennis_holeman@qm.sri.com

HOLESKI, PAUL MICHAEL, INSECT ECOLOGY, TAXONOMY. *Current Pos:* ASSOC PROF BIOL, RIO GRANDE COL, 80- *Personal Data:* b Akron, Ohio, July 7, 43. *Educ:* Wilmington Col, AB, 66; Univ Akron, MS, 69; Bowling Green State Univ, PhD(biol), 76. *Prof Exp:* Teacher biol, Wayne Trace Local Sch, 68-72; fel, Bowling Green State Univ, 75-76, asst prof biol, Firelands Br, 76-77; asst prof biol, Agr Tech Inst, Ohio State Univ, 79-80. *Concurrent Pos:* Vpres elect, Zool Sect, Ohio Acad Sci. *Mem:* Sigma Xi; Entom Soc Am; Coleopterists Soc. *Res:* Adaptions and changes in the composition of shore-inhabiting insect communities in response to environmental change; taxonomy of Coleoptera which inhabit the shore. *Mailing Add:* Math & Sci Univ Rio Grande Rio Grande OH 45674-9999

HOLFELD, WINFRIED THOMAS, ORGANIC CHEMISTRY. *Current Pos:* sr res chemist, Tech Div, 56-69, tech specialist, Mkt Div, 69-78, DEVELOP ASSOC, TECH DIV, E I DU PONT DE NEMOURS & CO, INC, 78- *Personal Data:* b Essen, Ger, June 1, 26; nat US; m 53; c 3. *Educ:* Fordham Univ, BS, 47, MS, 49; Rutgers Univ, PhD(chem), 57. *Prof Exp:* Asst supvr, Biochem Lab, St Vincent's Hosp, NY, 49-51; biochemist, Carter Prod Inc, NJ, 51-54; asst instr, Rutgers Univ, 54-55. *Mem:* Am Asn Textile Chemists & Colorists. *Res:* Natural products; textiles. *Mailing Add:* 700 Thornby Rd Wilmington DE 19803

HOLFORD, RICHARD L, APPLIED MATHEMATICS. *Current Pos:* MEM TECH STAFF, BELL LABS, 68- *Personal Data:* b London, Eng, Apr 1, 37; m 94, Susan Faber; c 2. *Educ:* Cambridge Univ, BA, 58, PhD(math), 64. *Prof Exp:* Res fel math, Manchester Univ, 63-64; lectr, Stanford Univ, 64-65; res scientist, NY Univ, 65-66; sr scientist, TRG, Inc Div, Control Data Corp, 66-68. *Mem:* Assoc mem Acoust Soc Am. *Res:* Water waves; rough surface scattering; asymptotic methods in acoustics. *Mailing Add:* Lucent Technol Bell Labs 15F-310 Whippany NJ 07981. *E-Mail:* rholford@lucent.com

HOLFORD, RICHARD MOORE, HEALTH PHYSICS, NUCLEAR INSTRUMENTATION. *Current Pos:* COMPUT PROGRAMMER (SMALL SYSTS), HAMILTON DIGITAL DESIGNS, 89- *Personal Data:* b Cheltenham, UK, June 25, 38; m 61, Anne M E French; c Stephen F, Philip E & Mark R. *Educ:* Cambridge Univ, BA, 61, PhD, 66. *Prof Exp:* Res asst radiotherapeut, Cambridge Univ, 61-62; from asst res officer to res officer, Atomic Energy Can Ltd, 66-89. *Res:* Design of firmware for out-door graphical displays; design of health physics instruments. *Mailing Add:* Hamilton Digital Designs 3342 Main Way Dr Burlington ON L7M 1A7 Can. *Fax:* 905-332-1518

HOLFORD, THEODORE RICHARD, BIOSTATISTICS. *Current Pos:* Mem res biomet, 72-73, from asst prof to assoc prof pub health, 74-89, PROF PUB HEALTH, MED SCH, YALE UNIV, 89- *Personal Data:* b Columbus, Ohio, May 19, 47; m 69, Maryellen Hutchinson; c Matthew & Lesley. *Educ:* Andrews Univ, BA, 69; Yale Univ, MPhil, 72, PhD(biomet), 73. *Honors & Awards:* Wakeman Award, 89. *Concurrent Pos:* Eleanor Roosevelt int fel, Am Union Int Contre Cancer, Univ Oxford; Epidemiol & Dis Control Study Sect, NIH, 86-89; assoc ed, Biomet, 84-88, Am J Epidemiol, 89-92. *Mem:* Am Statist Soc; Soc Epidemiol Res; Biomet Soc. *Res:* Formulation of mathematical models to describe and explain the underlying mechanics of fundamental processes and the development and application of statistical methods in the field of health. *Mailing Add:* Dept Epidemiol & Pub Health Yale Univ Sch Med PO Box 3333 New Haven CT 06510. *E-Mail:* theodore.holford@yale.edu

HOLGUIN, ALFONSO HUDSON, EPIDEMIOLOGY. *Current Pos:* vis prof, 74-78, PROF EPIDEMIOL, SCH PUB HEALTH, UNIV TEX, HOUSTON, 78-, ASST DEAN, SAN ANTONIO, MASTER PHYS EDUC & HEALTH PROG. *Personal Data:* b El Paso, Tex, Apr 3, 31; m 54, Irby H Spring; c Laura, Mark, Theresa, Carol, Paul & Stephen. *Educ:* Univ Tex, El Paso, BA, 51, Galveston, MD, 57; Harvard Univ, MPH, 64. *Prof Exp:* Med officer, USPHS, Seattle, 57-58; med officer virus res, Lab Br, Ctr Dis Control, USPHS, 58-62, asst to chief, 62-64, chief, Tuberc Prog, 64-68, dir, Bur Training, 70-74. *Concurrent Pos:* Prin investr, Epidemiol Res Univ, 79-; consult, Southwest Res Inst, 79- & Nat Inst Heart, Lung & Blood, 80- *Mem:* Am Pub Health Asn. *Res:* Epidemiology of infectious diseases, especially tuberculosis and nosocomial infections; epidemiology of environments and occupationally related health problems. *Mailing Add:* 12819 Queens Forest St San Antonio TX 78230

HOLICK, MICHAEL FRANCIS, ENDOCRINOLOGY, NUTRITIONAL BIOCHEMISTRY. *Current Pos:* Clin fel, 76-78, asst prof, 78-81, ASSOC PROF MED, HARVARD MED SCH, 81-; ASSOC PROF NUTRIT BIOCHEM, MASS INST TECHNOL, 81- *Personal Data:* b Mar 15, 46; c 1. *Educ:* Seton Hall Univ, BS, 68; Univ Wis, MS, 70, PhD, 71, MD, 76. *Honors & Awards:* Wilson S Stone Mem Award, M D Anderson Hosp, 72; Fuller Albright Young Investr Award, 80. *Concurrent Pos:* Clin asst med, Mass Gen Hosp, 78-81, assoc prof, 81-; lectr, Mass Inst Technol, 79-81. *Mem:* Am Soc Bone & Mineral Res; Am Soc Clin Invest; Endocrine Soc; Am Soc Photobiol; Am Col Physicians. *Res:* Photobiology of vitamin D; chemical synthesis of vitamin D analogs; role of caffeine on fetal bone growth and development; metabolism of vitamin D in health and disease. *Mailing Add:* Boston Univ Sch Med 80 E Concord St M-1013 Boston MA 02118-2394

HOLICK, SALLY ANN, VITAMIN D CHEMISTRY. *Current Pos:* CONSULT, VITAMIN D, 88- *Personal Data:* b Harrisburg, Pa, Dec 11, 48; m 72; c 1. *Educ:* Bloomsburg Col, Pa, BA, 70; Univ Wis, PhD(biochem), 74. *Prof Exp:* Fel biochem, Univ Wis, 74-75; instr chem, Boston Univ, 75-77; res fel med, Harvard Med Sch & Mass Gen Hosp, 77-81; instr med, Harvard Med Sch, 77-82; res scientist nutrit, Mass Inst Technol, 82-85 & Tufts Univ, 85-88. *Mem:* Am Chem Soc; Am Soc Biol Chemists; Sigma Xi. *Res:* Metabolism of vitamin D; structure function relationships; photobiology. *Mailing Add:* 31 Bishop Lane Sudbury MA 01776-1701

HOLIFIELD, CHARLES LESLIE, ANALYTICAL CHEMISTRY, INORGANIC CHEMISTRY. *Current Pos:* RES CHEMIST ANALYTICAL, CHEM DIV, PPG INDUSTS, INC, 65-, RES ASSOC, ANALYTICAL INSTRUMENTAL ANALYSIS. *Personal Data:* b Minneapolis, Minn, May 16, 40; m 65; c 2. *Educ:* Univ Tex, BS, 62; Univ Minn, MS, 65. *Mem:* Am Chem Soc; Electron Micros Soc Am. *Res:* X-ray fluorescence and diffraction; atomic absorption spectroscopy; emission spectroscopy; thermal analysis; scanning electron microscopy; transmission electron microscopy. *Mailing Add:* PPG Indust Chem Div 440 College Park Dr Monroeville PA 15146-1536

HOLKEBOER, PAUL EDWARD, ANALYTICAL CHEMISTRY. *Current Pos:* RETIRED. *Personal Data:* b Holland, Mich, Jan 16, 28; m 51; c 4. *Educ:* Hope Col, AB, 51; Purdue Univ, MS, 53, PhD(chem), 56. *Prof Exp:* From asst prof to prof chem, Western Mich Univ, 55-58, Coordr Grad Sci Educ Prog, 66-88, Coordr Acad Adv, 80-88. *Mem:* Am Chem Soc. *Res:* Inorganic chemistry; coordination compounds and their application to analytical chemistry; science education. *Mailing Add:* 2381 W Lakewood Blvd Holland MI 49424

HOLL, FREDERICK BRIAN, PLANT GENETICS, SUSTAINABLE AGRICULTURE. *Current Pos:* ASSOC PROF, DEPT PLANT SCI, UNIV BC, 78- *Personal Data:* b Winnipeg, Man, 1944. *Educ:* Univ Man, BSA, 66, MSc, 68; Univ Cambridge, Eng, PhD(genetics), 71. *Prof Exp:* Res officer plant genetics, Prairie Regional Lab, Nat Res Coun, 72-78. *Concurrent Pos:* Sr consult, Lamorna Enterprises Ltd. *Mem:* Genetics Soc Can; Genetical Soc Brit. *Res:* Inheritance of dinitrogen fixation in legumes; use of rhizosphere microorganisms in sustainable agriculture and forestry. *Mailing Add:* Dept Plant Sci Univ BC 2329 Westmall Vancouver BC V6T 1W5 Can

HOLL, J(OHN) WILLIAM, MECHANICAL & AERONAUTICAL ENGINEERING. *Current Pos:* from assoc prof to prof, 63-91, EMER PROF AEROSPACE ENG, PA STATE UNIV, 91- *Personal Data:* b Danville, Ill, Feb 20, 28; m 50, Antoinette Fillhouer; c Jessica, Vanessa, Melissa, Cassandra, Alyssa, Nathan & Zachary. *Educ:* Univ Ill, BS, 49, MS, 51; Pa State Univ, PhD(mech eng), 58. *Honors & Awards:* R T Knapp Award, Am Soc Mech Engrs, 70 & 90, Melville Medal, 70. *Prof Exp:* Asst mech eng, Univ Ill, 49-51; res assoc ord res lab, Pa State Univ, 51-55; res engr subsonic wind tunnel, Chem Warfare Lab, Chem Ctr, US Army, Md, 55-56; res assoc Appl Res Lab, Pa State Univ, 56-58, asst prof, 58-59; assoc prof mech eng, Univ Nebr, 59-63. *Mem:* Assoc fel Aeronaut & Astronaut; fel Am Soc Mech Engrs; Sigma Xi. *Res:* Fluid mechanics; two phase flow; cavitation. *Mailing Add:* 1108 Mayberry Lane State College PA 16801

HOLL, MANFRED MATTHIAS, MARINE WEATHER ANALYSIS & PREDICTION. *Current Pos:* CONSULT, 90- *Personal Data:* b Cologne, Ger, Nov 12, 28; nat US; m 52; c 2. *Educ:* McGill Univ, BSc, 50; Univ Toronto, MA, 51; Univ Calif, Los Angeles, PhD(meteorol), 57. *Prof Exp:* Meteorologist, Meteorol Serv Can, 50-52; instr meteorol & jr res meteorologist, Univ Calif, Los Angeles, 52-57; proj scientist & sect chief geophys res directorate, Air Force Cambridge Res Ctr, 57-58; head weather dynamics prog, Stanford Res Inst, 58-61; pres & dir res, Meteorol Int, Inc, 61-84; sr scientist, Nat Ocean Serv, Nat Oceanic & Atmospheric Admin, US Dept Com, 84-90. *Mem:* Am Meteorol Soc. *Res:* Numerical models of atmosphere and ocean structures for analysis and forecasting of significant variabilities; environmental-data evaluation; processing and objective assembly; inherent-scale techniques; mathematical-physical, statistical and probabalistic approaches to weather studies; related exploitation of computers. *Mailing Add:* 25526 Carmel Knolls Dr Carmel CA 93923

HOLLAAR, LEE ALLEN, INFORMATION RETRIEVAL, SYSTEMS ENGINEERING. *Current Pos:* assoc prof comput sci, 80-86, PROF COMPUT SCI & ELEC ENG, UNIV UTAH, 86-, DIR CAMPUS NETWORKING, 86-; PRES, CONTEXTURE, INC, 83- *Personal Data:* b Litchfield, Minn, Mar 9, 47; m 68; c 1. *Educ:* Ill Inst Technol, BS, 69; Univ Ill, Urbana-Champaign, MS, 74, PhD(comput sci), 75. *Prof Exp:* Eng mgr, Datalogics, Inc, 69-74; asst prof comput sci, Univ Ill, 75-80. *Concurrent Pos:* Distinguished visitor, Inst Elec & Electronics Engrs Comput Soc, 85-86. *Mem:* Sr mem Inst Elec & Electronics Engrs; Asn Comput Mach. *Res:* Hardware and software system for the retrieval and handling of text; development of special purpose backend processors; high-speed text search engine implemented in custom very-large-scale integration; design and implementation of a distributed software architecture for text handling; very-large-scale integration design tools and databases. *Mailing Add:* 3190 Merrill Eng Bldg Salt Lake City UT 84112

HOLLAND, ANDREW BRIAN, SOLID STATE PHYSICS, PHOTOGRAPHIC CHEMISTRY. *Current Pos:* SCIENTIST, POLAROID CORP, 75- *Personal Data:* b Nashville, Tenn, Feb 24, 40; m 63; c 2. *Educ:* Vanderbilt Univ, AB, 61; Univ Wis, MS, 64, PhD(physics), 69. *Prof Exp:* Res physicist, Photo Prod Dept, Exp Sta, E I du Pont de Nemours & Co, 69-75. *Mem:* Am Phys Soc; Soc Photog Scientists & Engrs. *Res:* Fermi surfaces of solids; electroluminesence; solid state electronics; electrooptics; photographic science; particle sizing; sensitometry. *Mailing Add:* 7 Autumn Lane Wayland MA 01778

HOLLAND, BURT S, SIMULTANEOUS STATISTICAL INFERENCE, LINEAR STATISTICAL MODELS. *Current Pos:* from asst prof to assoc prof, 70-91, dept chair, 91-96, PROF, DEPT STATIST, TEMPLE UNIV, 91- *Personal Data:* b Brooklyn, NY, Dec 4, 45; m 75, Robin Margaret; c Irene V, Andrew P & Benjamin K. *Educ:* Binghamton Univ, BA, 66; NC State Univ, MES, 68, PhD(statist), 70. *Mem:* Am Statist Asn; Inst Math Statist; Biometric Soc. *Res:* Multiple comparisons especially computing intensive techniques; methods for alternative measures of error control and methods for multi-group comparisons. *Mailing Add:* Dept Statistics 006-00 Temple Univ Philadelphia PA 19122. *Fax:* 215-204-1501; *E-Mail:* v5730e@vm.temple.edu

HOLLAND, CHARLES D(ONALD), SEPARATION PROCESSES, CHEMICALS & CANCER. *Current Pos:* from asst prof to prof, 52-87, head dept, 64-87, EMER PROF CHEM ENG, TEX A&M UNIV, 87-; PRES, TEX INST ADVAN CHEM TECHNOL, 88- *Personal Data:* b Iredell Co, NC, Oct 9, 21; m 45, Eleanore Williams; c Nancy L, Charlotte C & Thomas P. *Educ:* NC State Col, BS, 43; Agr & Mech Col, Tex, MS, 49, PhD(chem eng), 53. *Prof Exp:* Engr, Burlington Mills Corp, 47-48. *Mem:* Fel Am Inst Chem Engrs; Am Chem Soc; Am Soc Eng Educ; AAAS; Sigma Xi; fel Am Inst Chemists. *Res:* Design of distillation columns; catalysis and kinetics; reactor design; published 150 technical papers and seven books. *Mailing Add:* Tex Inst Advan Chem Technol MS 3125 Tex A&M Univ College Station TX 77843

HOLLAND, CHARLES JORDAN, APPLIED MATHEMATICS, COMPUTER SCIENCE. *Current Pos:* DIR, MATH & INFO SCI, AIR FORCE OFF SCI RES, 88- *Personal Data:* b Dublin, Ga, Mar 28, 48; m 86; c 2. *Educ:* Ga Inst Technol, BS, 68, MS, 69; Brown Univ, PhD(appl math), 72. *Prof Exp:* From asst prof to assoc prof math, Purdue Univ, 72-81; sci officer math, 81-84, liaison scientist, London, 84-85; head, Computer Sci Div, Off Naval Res, 85-88. *Concurrent Pos:* Vis mem, Courant Inst Math Sci, 76-78; mem staff, Off Technol Assessment, US Cong, 79-81. *Mem:* Soc Indust & Appl Math; sr mem Inst Elec & Electronics Engrs. *Res:* Deterministic and stochastic optimal control, filtering; probabilistic methods in applied mathematics; nonlinear diffusion equations; stochastic control theory. *Mailing Add:* Air Force Off Sci Res/NM 110 Duncan Ave Suite B115 Bolling AFB DC 20332-0001

HOLLAND, CHRISTIE ANNA, VIROLOGY, RECOMBINATE DNA. *Current Pos:* DIR CTR VIROL, IMMUNOL & INFECTIOUS DIS RES PROF PEDIAT, GEORGE WASHINGTON UNIV MED CTR. *Personal Data:* b 1950; m 89; c Joshua. *Educ:* Univ Tenn, PhD(biomed sci), 77. *Prof Exp:* from assist to assoc prof, Univ Mass, 85-91. *Mem:* AAAS; Am Soc Cell Biol; Am Soc Virol. *Res:* Pathogenesis of murine leukemia viruses and HIV-1 infection of children and adolescents. *Mailing Add:* Ctr Virol Immunol/Infectious Dis Res Children's Nat Med Ctr 111 Michigan Ave NW Washington DC 20010

HOLLAND, DEWEY G, POLYMER SYNTHESIS, POLYMER APPLICATIONS. *Current Pos:* PRES, RD&E CONSULT. *Personal Data:* b New York, NY, Apr 15, 37; m 59; c 4. *Educ:* Fordham Univ, BS, 58; Lehigh Univ, PhD(chem), 62. *Prof Exp:* Res chemist, Mil Res & Develop, Polymer Br, Air Force Mat Lab, 62-65; sect head corp res & develop, Air Prod & Chem, Inc, 65-71, dir indust res & develop, 71-78; vpres technol, Eschem, Inc, 78-85 & Reichhold Chem, Inc, 85. *Mem:* Am Chem Soc; Am Asn Consult Chemists & Chem Engrs. *Res:* Monomer and polymer synthesis; polymerization; electrochemistry adhesives; coatings and adhesives; product formulation and applications; surface chemistry; process development; reaction catalysts; foamed plastics. *Mailing Add:* 7046 Sauk Trail Beach Cedar Grove WI 53013

HOLLAND, EUGENE PAUL, structural engineering, for more information see previous edition

HOLLAND, F D, JR, PALEONTOLOGY. *Current Pos:* from asst prof to prof, 54-89, EMER PROF GEOL, UNIV NDAK, 89- *Personal Data:* b Leavenworth, Kans, Mar 6, 24; m 45, Margine McVey; c Frank D III & Erik L. *Educ:* Univ Kans, BS, 48; Univ Mo, AM, 50; Univ Cincinnati, PhD(geol), 58. *Prof Exp:* Asst to cur geol mus, Univ Kans, 47-48; asst, Univ Cincinnati, 50-51, cur mus, 51-54. *Concurrent Pos:* Dir coun educ geol sci & AGI dir educ & manpower, Am Geol Inst, 70-72. *Mem:* Paleont Res Inst; Am Asn Petrol Geol; Paleont Soc; Palaeont Asn; Geol Soc Am. *Res:* Paleozoic invertebrates; Devonian and Mississippian stratigraphy and paleontology; stratigraphy and paleontology of North Dakota; earth science education. *Mailing Add:* Dept Geol & Geol Eng Univ NDak PO Box 8358 Grand Forks ND 58202-8358. *E-Mail:* budholland@aol.com

HOLLAND, GERALD FAGAN, MEDICINAL CHEMISTRY. *Current Pos:* sr res investr, 74-87, SR PROJ ANALYST, PFIZER CENT RES, 87- *Personal Data:* b Boston, Mass, Aug 16, 31; m 62; c 4. *Educ:* Boston Col, BS, 52; Mass Inst Technol, PhD(chem), 56. *Prof Exp:* Sr asst scientist, NIH, 56-58; chemist, Med Res Labs, Pfizer Inc, 58-74. *Mem:* Am Chem Soc. *Res:* Atherosclerosis and lipid metabolism; metabolic diseases; diabetes; organic chemistry; amino acids and proteins; heterocyclic compounds. *Mailing Add:* 22 Coult Lane Old Lyme CT 06371

HOLLAND, GRAHAM REX, ANATOMY, DENTISTRY. *Current Pos:* assoc prof, Div Endodontics, 83-85, prof & chmn, 85-90, CHAIR & PROF, DEPT RESTORATIVE DENT, UNIV ALTA, 90-, ASSOC DEAN, GRAD STUDIES & RES, 91- *Personal Data:* b Rainford, Eng, Dec 3, 46; m 69, Margaret Ashcroft; c Sara, Tom & Amy. *Educ:* Univ Bristol, BSc, 68, BDS, 71, PhD(anat), 73. *Honors & Awards:* Murray L Barr Jr Scientist Award, 80. *Prof Exp:* Res asst, Med Res Coun Gt Brit, 72-75; asst prof endodontics, Univ Iowa, 75-77; from asst prof to assoc prof anat, Univ Man, 77-81; assoc prof, Dept Endodontics, Col Dent, Univ Iowa, 81-83. *Concurrent Pos:* McCalla prof, 89-90. *Mem:* Brit Asn Clin Anatomists; Int Asn Dent Res; Anat Soc Gt Brit & Ireland. *Res:* Structural basis of pain; neural damage and recovery. *Mailing Add:* Sch Dent Univ Mich 1011 N University Ann Arbor MI 48104-1078

HOLLAND, HANS J, INORGANIC CHEMISTRY. *Current Pos:* RES ASSOC, CORNING GLASS WORKS, 63- *Personal Data:* b Mannheim, Ger, July 1, 29; US citizen; m 54; c 5. *Educ:* Houghton Col, BS, 50; Columbia Univ, MA, 52; Univ Utah, PhD(chem), 63. *Prof Exp:* Phys scientist, Dugway Proving Ground, Utah, 51-52; res chemist, Continental Oil Co, 54-59. *Mem:* Am Chem Soc; Am Crystallog Asn; Mineral Soc Am. *Res:* Carbon dating; coprecipitation of cations with calcium carbonate; structure of alkali earth hexammoniates; glass devitrification products and their structure and mechanism of formation; x-ray diffraction instrumentation and automation; x-ray crystallography. *Mailing Add:* Corning Inc SP Corning NY 14831-0001

HOLLAND, HEINRICH DIETER, GEOCHEMISTRY. *Current Pos:* PROF GEOCHEM, HARVARD UNIV, 72- *Personal Data:* b Mannheim, Ger, May 27, 27; US citizen; m 53; c 4. *Educ:* Princeton Univ, BA, 46; Columbia Univ, MS, 48, PhD(geol), 52; Harvard Univ, MA, 72. *Prof Exp:* Asst, Columbia Univ, 47-50; from instr to prof geochem, Princeton Univ, 50-72, dir summer studies, 62-66. *Concurrent Pos:* Instr, Shelton Col, 48-50; NSF fel, Oxford Univ, 56-57; Fulbright lectr, Univ Durham, 63-64; vis prof, Univ Hawaii, 68-69 & 81, Pa State Univ, 85-86; Guggenheim fel, 75-76; dir, Ctr Earth & Planetary Physics, Harvard Univ, 78-; sr scientist award, Alexander von Humboldt Found, 80-81. *Mem:* Nat Acad Sci; fel Geol Soc Am; Geochem Soc (vpres, 69-70, pres, 70-71); fel Am Geophys Union; fel Am Acad Arts & Sci; Soc Econ Geologists; Am Mineral Soc; AAAS; fel Geol Soc Am. *Res:* Chemistry of ore forming fluids; chemical evolution of the atmosphere and ocean; planetary geology; author of numerous publications. *Mailing Add:* 306 Hoffman Labs Harvard Univ 20 Oxford St Cambridge MA 02138. *Fax:* 617-495-8839; *E-Mail:* solomon@ets

HOLLAND, HERBERT LESLIE, ORGANIC CHEMISTRY. *Current Pos:* from asst prof to assoc prof, 76-85, PROF CHEM, BROCK UNIV, 85- *Personal Data:* b Bolton, Eng, Aug 2, 47; m 73; c 2. *Educ:* Univ Cambridge, BA, 68, MA, 71; Univ Warwick, MSc, 69; Queen's Univ Belfast, PhD(chem), 72. *Prof Exp:* Univ demonstr chem, Queen's Univ Belfast, 69-72; fel, McMaster Univ, 72-74, teaching fel, 74-76. *Concurrent Pos:* Res grants, Nat Res Coun Can, 76-, Imp Oil, 78-79, Ont Ministry Environ, 79 & 80 & Petrol Res Fund, Am Chem Soc, 82. *Mem:* Royal Soc Chem; Can Inst Chem. *Res:* Bioorganic chemistry; mechanistic chemistry of biological oxidation processes; natural products chemistry. *Mailing Add:* Dept Chem Brock Univ Merrittville Hwy St Catharines ON L2S 3A1 Can

HOLLAND, ISRAEL IRVING, FOREST ECONOMICS. *Current Pos:* RETIRED. *Personal Data:* b Houston, Tex, Nov 25, 15; m 42; c 3. *Educ:* Univ Calif, BS, 40, MS, 41, PhD, 55. *Prof Exp:* Field asst range mgt res, Rocky Mountain Forest & Range Exp Sta, US Forest Serv, 41, logging time studies, Calif, 41, chief, War Mapping Proj Party, 42, forester, 46-49, forest economist, Div Forest Econ Res, Washington, DC, 52-57; asst prof forestry, Iowa State Univ, 57-59; from assoc prof to prof forest econ, Univ Ill, Urbana, 59-80, from assoc dept head to dept head, 71-81. *Mem:* Soc Am Foresters. *Mailing Add:* 1004 E Harding Dr No 103 Urbana IL 61801

HOLLAND, JACK CALVIN, BIOCHEMISTRY, CLINICAL CHEMISTRY. *Current Pos:* RETIRED. *Personal Data:* b Alameda, Calif, Mar 11, 25; m 49; c 3. *Educ:* Mich Col Mining & Technol, BS, 48, MS, 49; Mich Technol Univ, PhD(chem), 68. *Prof Exp:* Res engr chem eng, Copper Range Mining Co, Houghton, Mich, 49-50; clin biochemist, St Luke's Hosp, Duluth, Minn, 50-54; instr chem, Univ Minn, 50-54; dir med lab, Duluth Clin, Minn, 54-63; prof med tech, Mich Technol Univ, 65-90. *Concurrent Pos:* Res assoc, Am Cancer Soc, Mich Technol Univ, 63-65; consult, Allied Health Planning Asn, 73-76 & Mich Dept Pub Health-Continuing Educ, 76- *Mem:* Am Chem Soc; Sigma Xi; Am Asn Clin Chem. *Res:* Hepatic cancer; fluorescent analysis of cervical smears; adrenalin levels in football players; femur fat in deer bone marrow; hyperthermia; medicinal value of the Finnish sauna; hibernation phenomenon; comparative biochemistry; effects of nutritional variation in deer herds of Michigan; high density lipoprotein cholesterol variations in Michigan populations. *Mailing Add:* 1624 Jasberg St Hancock MI 49930

HOLLAND, JAMES FREDERICK, ONCOLOGY. *Current Pos:* prof neoplastic dis & chmn dept & prof med, 73-93, dir, Cancer Ctr, Univ & Hosp, 73-93, DISTINGUISHED PROF NEOPLASTIC DIS, MT SINAI SCH MED, 93- *Personal Data:* b Morristown, NJ, May 16, 25; m 56; c 6. *Educ:* Princeton Univ, AB, 44; Columbia Univ, MD, 47. *Honors & Awards:* Albert Lasker Award Cancer Chemother, 72; Nat Annual Award, Am Cancer Soc, 81; David A Karnofsky Mem Lectr, 82; Katherine Berkan Judd Award, Mem Sloan-Kettering Cancer Ctr, 84; Return of the Child Award, Leukemia Soc Am, 86; Cancer Res Award, Milken Family Med Found, 86; Distinguished Sci Award, Am Soc Clin Oncol, 93. *Prof Exp:* House staff, Presby Hosp, NY, 47-49; resident med, Francis Delafield Hosp, 51-52; asst, Columbia Univ, 52-53; sr asst surgeon, Nat Cancer Inst, 53-54; from assoc chief to chief med, Roswell Park Mem Inst, 54-73, from assoc res prof to res prof med, State Univ NY, Buffalo, 62-73, dir, Cancer Clin Res Ctr, 63-73. *Concurrent Pos:* Consult, Cancer World Health Orgn; mem, Bd Sci Counselors, Div Cancer Prev & Control, Nat Cancer Inst. *Mem:* Am Soc Clin Invest; Am Asn Cancer Res (pres, 70); Am Fedn Clin Res; Am Soc Hemat; Am Soc Clin Oncol (pres, 76); Sigma Xi; Asn Am Physicians. *Res:* Internal medicine; neoplastic diseases; chemotherapy, immunotherapy and molecular biology of cancer; breast cancer; acute leukemia; medical oncology and therapeutics; possible viral etiology human breast cancer. *Mailing Add:* Mt Sinai Sch Med 5th Ave & 100th St New York NY 10029

HOLLAND, JAMES PHILIP, ENDOCRINOLOGY. *Current Pos:* assoc prof, Ind Univ, 67-74, prof zool & assoc dean, Grad Sch, 74-77, interim dean, 77-78, PROF BIOL, IND UNIV, BLOOMINGTON, 78- *Personal Data:* b Bowling Green, Ky, Dec 31, 34; m 67. *Educ:* Ky State Col, BS, 56; Ind Univ, MS, 58, PhD(endocrinol), 61. *Prof Exp:* Fel endocrinol, Sch Med, Univ Wis, 61-62; asst prof zool, Howard Univ, 62-67. *Concurrent Pos:* Prin investr, NIH res grants & NSF res grants; mem, NSF Grad Fel Eval Panel, 83- *Mem:* AAAS; Am Soc Zool; Endocrine Soc; Soc Study Reproduction. *Res:* Reproduction physiology; interrelationships of the thyroid gland and the ovary. *Mailing Add:* Dept Biol Ind Univ Bloomington IN 47405-6800

HOLLAND, JAMES READ, physical metallurgy, for more information see previous edition

HOLLAND, JIMMIE C, PSYCHIATRY. *Current Pos:* CHAIR, DEPT PSYCHIAT & BEHAV SCI, PSYCHIAT SERV & ATTEND PSYCHIATRIST, MEM SLOAN-KETTERING CANCER CTR, NEW YORK, 77-, MEM, 84-, WAYNE E CHAPMAN CHAIR PSYCHIAT ONCOL, 89-; PROF, DEPT PSYCHIAT, CORNELL UNIV MED SCH & ATTEND PSYCHIATRIST, NY HOSP, 77-, VCHMN, DEPT PSYCHIAT, CORNELL UNIV MED SCH, 94- *Personal Data:* b Neveda, Tex, Apr 9, 28; m, James F; c Steven, Mary, Sally, Peter, David & Diane. *Educ:* Baylor Univ, BA, 48, MD, 52; Am Bd Psychiat & Neurol, dipl, 66. *Hon Degrees:* DSc, Iona Col, New Rochelle, NY, 95. *Honors & Awards:* Barrett Mem Lectr, Baylor Univ Cancer Ctr, Dallas, 83, Susan Koman Mem Lectr, 84; Irene Owens Mem Lectr, Brown Univ Col Med, Providence, RI, 87; Paul C Weinberg Mem Lectr, 21st Ann Meeting, Am Soc Psychosomatic Obstet & Gynec, Charleston, 93; Edward Weiss Lectr, 51st Ann Meeting, Am Psychosomatic Soc, 93; Mary Swartz Rose Mem Lectr, Greater NY Dietetic Asn, NY, 94; Medal Hon Clin Res, Am Cancer Soc, 94; Thomas P Hackett Mem Award, Acad Psychosomatic Med, 94. *Prof Exp:* Rotating intern, St Louis City Hosp, 52-53; asst resident psychiat, Malcolm Bliss Health Ctr, St Louis, 53-54; resident, Mass Gen Hosp, Boston, 55-56 & Edward J Meyer Mem Hosp, Buffalo, 56; clin instr, Dept Psychiat, State Univ NY, Buffalo, 56-62, clin assoc, 62-66, from asst prof to assoc prof, 66-72; assoc prof, attend psychiatrist, asst dir & consult/liaison, Dept Psychiat Albert Einstein Col Med & Montefiore Hosp, Bronk, NY, 73-77. *Concurrent Pos:* Psychiat res fel, Washington Univ Sch Med, USPHS, St Louis, Mo, 53-54; teaching fel, Harvard Univ, Boston, 55-56; attend psychiatrist, E J Meyer Mem Hosp, Erie Co Med Ctr, Buffalo, 58-72, chief, Liaison-Consult Serv, 65-68, clin dir, Dept Psychiat, 68-70, dir, 70-72; consult, NIMH Joint Schizophrenia Res Study, Psychiat Res Inst, Moscow, 72-73; chmn, Psycho-Oncol Comt, Cancer & Leukemia Group B, Clin Trials Group, Nat Cancer Inst, 76-; mem, Serv & Rehab Comt, NYC Div, Am Cancer Soc, 76-78, Psychosocial Educ & Res Comt, 79 & Coun Res & Clin Awards, 83-86; prin investr, Cancer & Leukemia Group B, Psychosocial & Qual Life Res, Nat Cancer Inst, 77-, Psychosocial & Pain Res Cancer Training Grant, 84, Psychosocial Res AIDS, NIMH, 89-94 & Study Childhood Cancer Survivors & Family Intervention, 91-96; examr, Am Bd Psychiat & Neurol, 80-; mem, Comt Study Health Consequences Stress Bereavement, Inst Med-Nat Acad Sci, 83-84; lectr, Tata Mem Hosp, Bombay, India, 89; chmn, Comt Consult-Laison, Am Psychiat Asn. *Mem:* Sr mem Inst Med-Nat Acad Sci; Int Psycho-Oncol Soc; fel Am Psychiat Asn; Am Psychosomatic Soc; fel Acad Psychosomatic Med; Am Soc Clin Oncol; NY Acad Med; Am Cancer Soc; Am Soc Psychiat Oncol/AIDS (pres, 88-); fel Am Col Psychiatrists. *Res:* Published 142 articles. *Mailing Add:* Mem Sloan-Kettering Cancer Ctr 1275 York Ave New York NY 10021

HOLLAND, JOHN HENRY, APPLIED MATHEMATICS, COMPUTER SCIENCE. *Current Pos:* res assoc, Univ Mich, Ann Arbor, 56-59, assoc res mathematician & lectr psychol, 59-61, from asst prof to assoc prof commun sci, 61-67, actg dir, Logic of Comput Group, 65-66, prof, 67-80, actg chmn, Dept Comput & Commun Sci, 71-72 & 74, assoc dir, Logic of Comput Group, 71-86, prof comput & commun sci, 80-86, PROF COMPUT SCI & ENG, UNIV MICH, ANN ARBOR, 86-, PROF PSYCHOL, 88- *Personal Data:* b Ft Wayne, Ind, Feb 2, 29; m 56, Maurita L Peterson; c 3. *Educ:* Mass Inst Technol, BS, 50; Univ Mich, MA, 54, PhD(commun sci), 59. *Honors & Awards:* Levy Medal, Franklin Inst; Russel Lectr, Univ Mich; MacArthur Fel, John D & Catherine T MacArthur Found, 92. *Prof Exp:* Assoc engr, Int Bus Mach Corp, 50-52, consult, 52-56. *Concurrent Pos:* Res assoc, Carnegie Inst, Washington, DC, 61-64; consult, Univ Mich, 64-, actg dir, 77-78; fel, Franklin Inst, 71; mem, Steering Comt, Sci Adv Bd, Santa Fe Inst, 87-, dir, Adaptive Comput, 89-, dir, Santa Fe Inst Res Prog, Univ Mich, 90- *Mem:* AAAS; Asn Comput Mach; Am Math Soc; Sigma Xi; Am Asn Artificial Intel; AAAS. *Res:* Logical and mathematical theory of computers and automata; theories and models of cognition; adaptive systems. *Mailing Add:* 3800 W Huron River Dr Ann Arbor MI 48103

HOLLAND, JOHN JOSEPH, MICROBIOLOGY. *Current Pos:* PROF BIOL, UNIV CALIF, SAN DIEGO, 68- *Personal Data:* b Pittsburgh, Pa, Nov 16, 29; m 60; c 2. *Educ:* Loyola Univ, La, BS, 53; Univ Calif, Los Angeles, PhD(microbiol), 57. *Honors & Awards:* Eli Lilly Award Microbiol, 63. *Prof Exp:* From instr to asst prof bact, Univ Minn, 57-60; from asst prof to assoc prof microbiol, Univ Wash, 60-64; prof, Univ Calif, Irvine, 64-68. *Mem:* AAAS; Soc Exp Biol & Med; Am Soc Microbiol. *Res:* Virology; cell biology. *Mailing Add:* Dept Biol Univ Calif San Diego 9500 Gilman Dr La Jolla CA 92093-0322

HOLLAND, JOSHUA ZALMAN, METEOROLOGY. *Current Pos:* RETIRED. *Personal Data:* b Chicago, Ill, June 23, 21; m 84; c 3. *Educ:* Univ Chicago, BS, 41; Univ Wash, PhD(atmospheric sci), 68. *Honors & Awards:* Silver Medal, Dept Com, 56, Gold Medal, 74. *Prof Exp:* Instr meteorol, Univ Chicago, 42 & NY Univ, 42-43; weather officer, US Army Air Forces, 43-46; meteorologist in charge, Oak Ridge Off, US Weather Bur, Tenn, 48-53; meteorologist, Washington, DC, 53-55; exec secy, Adv Comt Reactor Safeguards, US AEC, 56-57, meteorologist, Environ Sci Br, Div Biol & Med, 57-59, chief fallout studies br, 59-69; dir, Barbados Oceanog & Meteorol Anal Proj, Nat Oceanog & Atmospheric Admin, US Dept Com, 69-71, dir, Ctr Exp Design & Data Anal, 71-78, dir, Environ Data & Info Serv, Ctr Environ Assessment Servs, 78-79; adj prof meteorol, Univ Md, 79-83, res assoc, 83-89. *Concurrent Pos:* Consult, Comt Meteorol Aspects Effects Atomic Radiation, Nat Acad Sci, 56-60, mem, Interdept Comt Community Air Pollution, 57-59, mem, Interdept Comt Atmospheric Sci, 59-62, mem, Subcomt Mesometeorol, 61-62, mem, Ad Hoc Comt Int Progs Atmospheric Sci & chmn, Subcomt Atmospheric Chem, 62-63, mem, Adv Comt Civil Defense, 67-70, mem, Data Mgt Panel, US Comt Global Atmospheric Res Prog, 70-, mem, Adv Panel, Atlantic Trop Exp, Nat Acad Sci, 78-; chief scientist, Barbados Oceanog & Meteorol Exp, Sea-Air Interaction Prog, 69; mem, Adv Comt Oceanic Meteorol Res, World Meteorol Orgn, 70-77; mem pub comn, Am Meteorol Soc, 80-88; mem, Comt Geophys Data, Nat Res Coun, 84-87.

Mem: Am Geophys Union; fel Am Meteorol Soc. *Res:* Atmospheric transport, dispersion and deposition of contaminants; atmospheric turbulence; micrometeorology; stack plume rise; air-sea exchange processes; environmental experiment design and data analysis. *Mailing Add:* 2448 39th St NW Washington DC 20007

HOLLAND, LENE J, REGULATION OF GENE EXPRESSION. *Current Pos:* asst prof, 90-94, ASSOC PROF, DEPT PHYSIOL, UNIV MO SCH MED, 94- *Personal Data:* b July 5, 49. *Educ:* Univ Calif, Berkeley, BA, 72; Univ Calif, San Francisco, PhD(biochem), 79. *Prof Exp:* Fel, Brandeis Univ, 79-85; asst prof, Univ Iowa, 85-90. *Concurrent Pos:* Fel, Damon Runyon-Walter Winchell Cancer Fund, 79-81, Am Heart Asn, 81-82, Am Cancer Soc, 82-84, Charles A King Trust, 84-85; NIH res career develop award, 93- *Mem:* Endocrine Soc; Am Soc Biochem & Molecular Biol; Am Soc Microbiol; AAAS; Women in Endocrinol. *Res:* Regulation of gene expression, steroid hormone action, transcription factors. *Mailing Add:* Dept Physiol Univ Mo Sch Med Columbia MO 65212. *Fax:* 573-884-4276; *E-Mail:* physljh@muccmail.missouri.edu

HOLLAND, LEWIS, ANIMAL BREEDING, GENETICS. *Current Pos:* RETIRED. *Personal Data:* b Somerton, Ariz, July 3, 25; m 48; c 6. *Educ:* NMex State Univ, BS, 49; Colo State Univ, MS, 51; Iowa State Univ, PhD(animal breeding, genetics), 57. *Prof Exp:* Instr animal husb, Colo State Univ, 49-50; asst prof, Kans State Univ, 51-54 & 56-58; assoc prof, NMex State Univ, 59-69, prof animal sci, 69-81, assoc dean, Col Agr & Home Econ, 71-81, admin adv, NMex State Univ-Paraguay Aid, 76-81. *Concurrent Pos:* Asst, Iowa State Univ, 55. *Mem:* Am Soc Animal Sci; Am Genetics Asn. *Res:* Animal breeding and genetics of sheep and cattle. *Mailing Add:* 1992 Crescent Dr Las Cruces NM 88005

HOLLAND, LOUIS EDWARD, II, VIROLOGY. *Current Pos:* sr virologist, Life Sci Dept, 88-96, SCI ADV, IIT RES INST, 96- *Personal Data:* b Kansas City, Mo, Nov 15, 48; m 77, Mary Lambert; c Michael & Jeffrey. *Educ:* Baker Univ, BS, 70; Univ Calif, Irvine, PhD(molecular biol), 79. *Prof Exp:* Res fel virol, Univ Mich, 79-84; sr molecular biologist, Dept Biochem, Southern Res Inst, 84-88. *Mem:* Am Soc Microbiol; Am Soc Virol; AAAS; Sigma Xi; Int Soc Antiviral Res. *Res:* Mechanism of action for antiviral chemotherapeutic agents; pathogenesis of human immunodeficiency virus; discovery of new antiviral agents; molecular diagnostics for infectious agents. *Mailing Add:* Life Sci Dept IIT Res Inst 10 W 35th St Chicago IL 60616-3799. *Fax:* 312-567-4466; *E-Mail:* lholland@hq.iitri.com

HOLLAND, LYMAN LYLE, CHEMICAL & ENVIRONMENTAL ENGINEERING. *Current Pos:* SR RES ENGR, DACRON STAPLE RES & DEVELOP CTR, KINSTON, E I DUPONT DE NEMOURS & CO, INC, 69- *Personal Data:* b Portsmouth, Va, Apr 20, 40; m 68; c 2. *Educ:* Univ Va, BChE, 63; Clemson Univ, MSChE, 65, PhD(chem eng, environ systs eng), 68. *Mem:* Am Inst Chem Engrs. *Res:* Modeling photobiological processes using chemical engineering photochemical kinetics; effect of mixing on kinetic growth rates of Chlorella pyrenoidosa in parallel plate flow reactor; process development; waste recovery, recycle and utilization; polymer melt rheology. *Mailing Add:* 1805 Sauret Ave Kingston NC 28504

HOLLAND, MARJORIE MIRIAM, PLANT ECOLOGY, ENVIRONMENTAL SCIENCE. *Current Pos:* DIR, FIELD STA, UNIV MISS, OXFORD, 95- *Personal Data:* b Boston, Mass, Aug 18, 47; m, Raymond W Prach; c Hannah R. *Educ:* Conn Col, BA, 69; Smith Col, MA, 74; Univ Mass, PhD(bot), 77. *Prof Exp:* Teacher biol, Mountain Sch, Vershire, Vt, 69-70 & Dover-Sherborn Regional High Sch, Mass, 70-72; teaching fel, Smith Col, 72-76; vis lectr, Amherst Col, 76-77, vis asst prof, 77-78; exec dir environ sci, Water Supply Citizen's Adv Comt, Springfield, Mass, 78-80; from asst prof to assoc prof, Col New Rochelle, 80-89; Environ Monitoring & Assessment Prog, US Environ Protection Agency, 93-95. *Concurrent Pos:* Res assoc, Dept Biol Sci, Smith Col, 77-; ed, Lawrence Erdang Publ, 78-; consult, US Army CEngr, 79-80; consult, Secretariat of Unesco's MAB (Man & the Biosphere Prog), Paris, 86-88; dir, Ecol Soc Am, 87-93. *Mem:* AAAS; Ecol Soc Am; Sigma Xi; Am Inst Biol Sci; Soc Wetland Scientists; Int Limnol Soc. *Res:* Plant systematics; wetlands ecology; riverine ecology; phytosociology; brackish tidal wetlands; water resource management; public policy development; integration and assessment. *Mailing Add:* 21 County Rd-202 Oxford MS 38655. *Fax:* 601-232-5144; *E-Mail:* mholland@olemiss.edu

HOLLAND, MARK ALEXANDER, PLANT-BACTERIA INTERACTIONS, BIOLOGY-BIOTECHNOLOGY EDUCATION. *Current Pos:* ASST PROF BIOL, SALISBURY STATE UNIV, 93- *Personal Data:* b Paterson, NJ, May 7, 53; m 79, Catherine Goodloe. *Educ:* Muhlenberg Col, BS, 75; Wake Forest Univ, MA, 79; Rutgers Univ, PhD(hort), 85. *Prof Exp:* Fel, Dept Biochem, Univ Mo, 86-90, res asst prof, 90-93. *Mem:* AAAS; Am Soc Plant Physiol. *Res:* Plant genetics and molecular biology; studying relationship between plants and nonpathogenic phylloplane bacteria, especially as it applies to plant metabolism; interest in applying research to plant improvement. *Mailing Add:* Dept Biol Salisbury State Univ Salisbury MD 21801. *E-Mail:* maholland@sae.ssu.umd.edu

HOLLAND, MARY JEAN CAREY, PAIN MANAGEMENT, PHARMACOKINETICS. *Current Pos:* from asst prof to assoc prof, 82-90, PROF BIOL, BARUCH COL, CITY UNIV NY, 91- *Personal Data:* b Dearborn, Mich, Feb 14, 42; m 68, Cecil Jr. *Educ:* Vassar Col, AB, 63; NY Univ, MS, 69, PhD(biol), 71. *Prof Exp:* Res asst biophys, Parke-Davis & Co, 64-65; assoc microbiologist, Merck & Co, 65-67; instr biol, Lehman Col, City Univ New York, 70-71; NIH fel, 72-74, instr exp med, 75-79, asst prof med, Med Ctr, NY Univ, 79-82. *Concurrent Pos:* Fels, Fulbright, 63-64, Nat Found, March of Dimes, 74-75 & Arthritis Found, 76-79; adj fac mem biochem, Grad Prog, Sarah Lawrence Col, 77-79; young investr grant, NY Arthritis Found, 78-79; vis asst prof microbiol, NY Col Osteop Med, 79-82; res collabr, Chem Dept, Brookhaven Nat Lab, 81-93; res asst prof psychiat, NY Univ Med Ctr, 82- *Mem:* Am Soc Microbiol; Am Soc Cell Biol; Soc Neurosci; Soc Math Biol; NY Acad Sci. *Res:* Mathematical models for receptor-mediated processes; pharmocokinetics and tissue distribution of opiates; opiate receptor binding kinetics; analgesia. *Mailing Add:* Dept Nat Sci Baruch Col 17 Lexington Ave New York NY 10010. *Fax:* 212-387-1229; *E-Mail:* mjhbb@cunyvm.cuny.edu

HOLLAND, MONTE W, PHYSICS. *Current Pos:* RETIRED. *Personal Data:* b De Kalb, NY, June 12, 38; m 66. *Educ:* Union Col, NY, BS, 59; Northwestern Univ, PhD(physics), 63. *Prof Exp:* Lectr physics, State Univ NY, Buffalo, 63-64, asst prof, 64-69, asst chmn dept, 67-69; assoc prof, Slippery Rock State Col, 69-73, chmn dept, 69-73, prof physics, 72- *Mem:* Am Phys Soc; Am Asn Physics Teachers. *Res:* Particle physics; properties of hyperfragments; equipment of science instruction; uses of computers for instruction; basic physics textbook preparation. *Mailing Add:* PO Box 222 Slippery Rock PA 16057

HOLLAND, NANCY H, pediatrics, nephrology, for more information see previous edition

HOLLAND, NEAL STEWART, HORTICULTURE. *Current Pos:* RETIRED. *Personal Data:* b Bracken, Sask, Oct 26, 29; US citizen. *Educ:* NDak State Univ, BS, 51, MS, 60. *Honors & Awards:* Silver Medal, All-Am Selections Award, 66; R L Wodarz Award, 77. *Prof Exp:* Teacher pub schs, Minn, 51-52; asst, NDak State Univ, 54-60, from asst prof to prof, 60-69, actg head, 81-83, emer prof hort, 83-86. *Mem:* Am Pomol Soc; Int Lilac Soc. *Res:* Fruit culture and breeding; tomatoes, squash, and ornamentals breeding programs and genetic studies. *Mailing Add:* 17010 29th St SE Harwood ND 58042

HOLLAND, NICHOLAS DREW, INVERTEBRATE & VERTEBRATE ZOOLOGY & EVOLUTION. *Current Pos:* from asst prof to assoc prof, 66-78, PROF MARINE BIOL & REGIONAL ED, MARINE ECOL PROGRESS SERIES, SCRIPPS INST OCEANOG, 78- *Personal Data:* b Washington, DC, Apr 24, 38; m 61, Linda Zimmerman; c 3. *Educ:* Carleton Col, AB, 60; Stanford Univ, PhD(biol), 64. *Prof Exp:* NSF fel zool, Naples Zool Sta, Italy, 64-66. *Res:* Invertebrate zoology (echinoderms and cephalochordates); vertebrate zoology (agnathans); comparative molecular evolution; phylogenetic origin of the vertebrates from the invertebrates. *Mailing Add:* Marine Biol Res Div 0202 Scripps Inst Oceanog Univ Calif San Diego La Jolla CA 92093

HOLLAND, PAUL VINCENT, INTERNAL MEDICINE. *Current Pos:* asst chief, 68-74, CHIEF BLOOD BANK, NIH, 74- *Personal Data:* b Toronto, Ont, Oct 29, 37; US citizen; m 62; c 4. *Educ:* Univ Calif, Riverside, BA, 58; Univ Calif, Los Angeles, MD, 62; Am Bd Internal Med, dipl, 69; Am Bd Path, dipl, 73, cert blood banking. *Prof Exp:* Intern med, Univ Calif, Los Angeles, 62-63; staff physician blood bank, NIH, 63-66; asst res med, San Francisco Med Ctr, Univ Calif, 66-68. *Concurrent Pos:* Clin instr med, Med Sch, George Washington Univ, 69-74, clin asst prof, 74-75, clin assoc prof, 75-; clin assoc prof path, Sch Med, Georgetown Univ, 74- *Mem:* Am Fedn Clin Res; Am Soc Hemat; NY Acad Sci; Am Asn Blood Banks. *Res:* Hepatitis, especially re Australia antigen and antibody; immunohematology; blood transfusion; component therapy. *Mailing Add:* Sacramento Med Fed Blood Ctr 1625 Stockton Blvd Sacramento CA 95816-7089

HOLLAND, PAUL WILLIAM, STATISTICS, BIOSTATISTICS. *Current Pos:* DIR STATIST RES, EDUC TESTING SERV, 75- *Personal Data:* b Tulsa, Okla, Apr 25, 40; m 61; c 2. *Educ:* Univ Mich, BA, 62; Stanford Univ, MS, 64, PhD(statist), 66. *Prof Exp:* Asst prof statist, Mich State Univ, 66; from asst prof to assoc prof statist, Harvard Univ, 66-72; sr res assoc, Nat Bur Econ Res, 72-75. *Concurrent Pos:* Fac Res Grant, Social Sci Res Coun, 70-71; lectr statist, Harvard Univ, 72-75; mem, Panel Productivity Statist, Nat Res Coun, 77-78. *Mem:* Fel Inst Math Statist; Biomet Soc; Am Sociol Asn; fel AAAS; Psychomet Soc (pres, 89-90). *Res:* Application of statistics and mathematical models to sociology, education and the behavioral sciences; problems of inference in studies of human populations. *Mailing Add:* GE Spacenet Eng Dept 1750 Old Meadow Rd McLean VA 22102

HOLLAND, RAY W(ALTER), MECHANICAL ENGINEERING & AEROSPACE ENGINEERING. *Current Pos:* RETIRED. *Personal Data:* b Afton, Tenn, Feb 11, 24; m 46, Mary B Balding; c Ray W Jr & Connie L. *Educ:* Duke Univ, BS, 47; Univ Tenn, MS, 52. *Prof Exp:* From instr to asst prof mech eng design, Duke Univ, 47-55; assoc prof mech & aerospace eng, Univ Tenn, Knoxville, 55-69, emer prof, 69-89. *Concurrent Pos:* Indust consult, 52-89. *Mem:* Am Soc Mech Engrs; Soc Mfg Engrs; Am Soc Eng Educ; Sigma Xi; Soc Exp Mech. *Res:* Experimental stress analysis; machine design. *Mailing Add:* 2004 McClain Rd Knoxville TN 37912-4617

HOLLAND, REDUS FOY, MOLECULAR SPECTROSCOPY. *Current Pos:* RES PHYSICIST, LOS ALAMOS NAT LAB, UNIV CALIF, 61- *Personal Data:* b Frederick, Okla, Jan 8, 30; m 56; c Brennan, Gavin & Kiernan. *Educ:* Panhandle State Col, BS, 51; Univ Okla, PhD(physics), 61. *Mem:* Laser Inst Am; Optical Soc Am. *Res:* Emission spectra of atmospheric gases; probability of excitation by collisions with electrons and ions; long-lived states of diatomic ions; vibrational spectroscopy of polyatomic molecules; cryogenic solution spectroscopy; chemical kinetics. *Mailing Add:* 2774 Walnut St Los Alamos NM 87544

HOLLAND, ROBERT CAMPBELL, NEUROSCIENCES. *Current Pos:* prof & chmn, Dept Anat, 77-90, EMER PROF ANAT, MOREHOUSE SCH MED, 90- *Personal Data:* b Bushnell, Ill, Aug 16, 23; m 89; c 1. *Educ:* Univ Wis, BS, 48, MS, 49, PhD(anat, zool), 55. *Prof Exp:* Instr histol & path, Dent Sch, Northwestern Univ, 49-51; res asst anat, Univ Wis, 51-54; from instr to asst prof neuroanat, Univ NDak, 54-60; assoc prof anat, Sch Med, Univ Ark, 60-66; vis prof & actg chmn dept, Mahidol Univ, Thailand, 66-75; fel anat, Med Sch, Univ Calif, Los Angeles, 76-77. *Concurrent Pos:* Nat Found Infantile Paralysis fel, Univ Calif, Los Angeles, 57-58; mem field staff, Rockefeller Found, 66-77; vis prof anat, Med Sch, Univ Calif, Los Angeles, 76. *Mem:* AAAS; Am Asn Anatomists; Am Acad Neurol; Soc Exp Biol & Med; Soc Neurosci; Sigma Xi. *Res:* Neuroendocrinology; neuroanatomy; neurophysiology. *Mailing Add:* 2704 Hampton Trail Woodstock GA 30188

HOLLAND, ROBERT EMMETT, EXPERIMENTAL NUCLEAR PHYSICS. *Current Pos:* assoc physicist, Argonne Nat Lab, 50-68, sr physicist, 68-82, assoc ed, Appl Physics Lett, 83-89, ASSOC ED, J APPL PHYSICS, ARGONNE NAT LABS, ARGONNE, ILL, 83- *Personal Data:* b Chicago, Ill, May 21, 20; m 49; c 3. *Educ:* Univ Iowa, BA, 42, MS, 44, PhD(physics), 50. *Prof Exp:* From res assoc to instr physics, Univ Iowa, 44-48. *Concurrent Pos:* Fulbright res grant, Univ Helsinki, 61-62. *Mem:* Am Phys Soc. *Res:* Nuclear physics; bombardment by fast particles; lifetimes of nuclear states. *Mailing Add:* 5406 Florence Ave Downers Grove IL 60515

HOLLAND, ROBERT FRANCIS, FOOD SCIENCE. *Current Pos:* prof dairy indust, 45-72, head depts dairy indust & food sci, 55-72, EMER PROF DAIRY INDUST, CORNELL UNIV, 73- *Personal Data:* b Holley, NY, Sept 21, 08; m 30; c 4. *Educ:* Cornell Univ, BS, 36, MS, 38, PhD(dairy indust), 40. *Prof Exp:* Instr dairy chem, Cornell Univ, 35-39; prof, NY Agr Exp Sta, Geneva, 39-41; dir chem res, Coop G L F Soil Bldg Serv, Inc, Ithaca, 41-45. *Mem:* Am Dairy Sci Asn; Inst Food Technologists. *Res:* Milk pasteurization; sanitary chemistry; dairy products marketing. *Mailing Add:* 114 Seneca Rd Trumansburg NY 14886

HOLLAND, RUSSELL SEDGWICK, PHOTOGRAPHIC SCIENCE. *Current Pos:* RETIRED. *Personal Data:* b Westerly, RI, May 4, 29; m 57; c 2. *Educ:* Brown Univ, BSc, 51; Princeton Univ, PhD(chem), 55. *Prof Exp:* Res chemist, Med Prod Dept, E I du Pont de Nemours & Co Inc, 54-66, tech specialist, 66-77, sr tech specialist, 77-78, tech assoc, 78-90. *Mem:* Am Chem Soc; Soc Photog Sci & Eng. *Res:* Photographic chemistry; image evaluation; photographic film testing. *Mailing Add:* 20 E Parkway Elkton MD 21921

HOLLAND, SAMUEL S, JR, VALUATION THEORY, HERMITIAN FORMS. *Current Pos:* assoc prof, 67-71, PROF MATH, UNIV MASS, AMHERST, 71- *Personal Data:* b Lawrence, Mass, June 29, 28; m 58; c 4. *Educ:* Mass Inst Technol, BS, 50; Univ Chicago, MS, 52; Harvard Univ, PhD(math), 61. *Prof Exp:* Staff scientist math physics, Tech Opers, Inc, 55-57; Nat Acad Sci-Nat Res Coun res assoc, 60-61; from asst prof to assoc prof math, Boston Col, 61-67. *Concurrent Pos:* Consult, Tech Opers, Inc, 61-67; NSF res grant, 63- *Mem:* Am Math Soc. *Res:* Study of division rings with involution, their orderings, valuations, and the infinite dimensional hermitian forms they may support. *Mailing Add:* Dept Math & Statist Univ Mass Box 34515 Amherst MA 01003-4515. *E-Mail:* holland@math.umass.edu

HOLLAND, STEVEN WILLIAM, ARTIFICIAL INTELLIGENCE, COMPUTER INTEGRATED MANUFACTURING. *Current Pos:* Assoc sr res scientist, Gen Motors Res Labs, 75-77, staff res scientist, 77-79, sr staff res scientist, 79-82, asst dept head, 83-87, sect mgr, 87-91, DIR & MGR ROBOTICS, GEN MOTORS NAO MFG CTR, 91- *Personal Data:* b Detroit, Mich, Dec 4, 51; m 75, Connie Anderson; c Jessica & Kathryn. *Educ:* Gen Motors Inst, BA, 76; Stanford Univ, MS, 76. *Honors & Awards:* Arch T Colwell Award, Soc Automotive Engrs, 80. *Concurrent Pos:* Adj fac, Wayne State Univ, 77-81. *Mem:* Sr mem Inst Elec & Electronics Engrs; Am Asn Artificial Intel; Sigma Xi; Soc Mech Engrs; Robotics Indust Asn. *Res:* Application of computer science and artificial intelligence to the problems and processes of a large manufacturing corporation; robotics; agile manufacturing; US patents. *Mailing Add:* 1670 Sumac Dr Rochester Hills MI 48309-2227. *E-Mail:* holland@gmr.com

HOLLAND, WILBUR CHARLES, ORDERED ALGEBRAIC STRUCTURES. *Current Pos:* chmn, Dept Math & Statist, 81-83, PROF MATH, BOWLING GREEN STATE UNIV, 72- *Personal Data:* b Parkersburg, WVa, Feb 24, 35; m 55, Claudia Brown; c Eric, Paul, Claudia, Rebecca & David. *Educ:* Tulane Univ, BS, 57, MS, 59, PhD(math), 61. *Prof Exp:* NATO fel, Univ Tubingen, 61-62; instr math, Univ Chicago, 62-64; from asst prof to prof math, Univ Wis-Madison, 64-72. *Concurrent Pos:* Vis prof, Simon Fraser Univ, 83-84. *Mem:* Am Math Soc; Math Asn Am. *Res:* Lattice-ordered permutation groups. *Mailing Add:* Dept Math Bowling Green Univ Bowling Green OH 43403-0001. *E-Mail:* chollan@andy.bgso.edu

HOLLAND, WILLIAM FREDERICK, INDUSTRIAL & POLYMER CHEMISTRY. *Current Pos:* RETIRED. *Personal Data:* b Jersey City, NJ, Sept 30, 14; m 39; c 1. *Educ:* City Col New York, BS, 42; Polytech Inst Brooklyn, MS, 48. *Prof Exp:* Asst dir labs, Standard Varnish Works, NY, 43-50; tech dir org coatings, Benjamin Franklin Paint & Varnish Co, Pa, 50-53; vpres, Hanline Bros Inc, Baltimore, 53-67; res supvr chem div, PPG Industs, Inc, 67-71; chief chemist, Akron Paint & Varnish Co, 71-82. *Concurrent Pos:* Coatings Consult. *Mem:* Emer mem Am Chem Soc; Fedn Soc Coatings Technol. *Res:* Protective and decorative organic coatings and allied specialties; high polymer chemistry. *Mailing Add:* 1194 Highview Dr Wadsworth OH 44281-9224

HOLLAND, WILLIAM JOHN, ANALYTICAL CHEMISTRY. *Current Pos:* RETIRED. *Personal Data:* b Belleville, Ont, Jan 6, 20; m 45; c 2. *Educ:* Queen's Univ, Ont, BSc, 45; Wayne State Univ, MSc, 53, PhD(chem), 56. *Prof Exp:* Chief chemist, R P Scherer Co, 46-59; fel org chem, Wayne State Univ, 59-60; from asst prof to assoc prof anal chem, Univ Windsor, 60-70, prof, 70-86. *Mem:* Chem Inst Can. *Res:* Synthesis of organic chelating agents and application to trace metal analysis and transition metal separations by solvent extraction. *Mailing Add:* 2293 Gladstone Ave Windsor ON N8W 2N8 Can

HOLLAND, WILLIAM ROBERT, PHYSICAL OCEANOGRAPHY. *Current Pos:* RES OCEANOGR, NAT CTR ATMOSPHERIC RES, 74- *Personal Data:* b Van Nuys, Calif, July 31, 38; m 57; c 3. *Educ:* Univ Calif, Los Angeles, AB, 60; Mass Inst Technol, MS, 61; Univ Calif, San Diego, PhD(oceanog), 66. *Prof Exp:* Fel oceanog, Cambridge Univ, 66-67; res oceanographer, Nat Oceanic & Atmospheric Admin, 67-74. *Mem:* AAAS; Am Geophys Union; Am Meterol Soc. *Res:* Numerical models of ocean circulation. *Mailing Add:* 1525 Wildwood Ln Boulder CO 80303

HOLLAND-BEETON, RUTH ELIZABETH, HYDROBIOLOGY, ECOLOGY. *Current Pos:* PRIMARY RES INVESTR, DEPT ATMOSPHERIC & OCEANIC STUDIES, UNIV MICH, 76- *Personal Data:* b Weatherly, Pa, Apr 17, 36; m 66, Alfred M; c Jonathan E & Daniel P. *Educ:* St Olaf Col, BA, 58; Univ Mich, MS, 62. *Prof Exp:* Fishery res biologist, US Bur Com Fisheries, 63-66; res specialist, Ctr Great Lakes Studies, Univ Wis-Milwaukee, 66-76. *Concurrent Pos:* Consult, Atty Gen Off, Wis, 72-73; prin investr, Environ Protection Agency, 77-78, Sea Grant Prog, Wis, 70-76 & Sea Grant Col, Mich, 79-86 & 92-94; res assoc, Dept Oceanog, Ore State Univ, 82-83. *Mem:* AAAS; Int Asn Theoret & Appl Limnol; Fresh Biol Asn Gt Brit; Int Asn Great Lakes Res; Int Soc Diatom Res. *Res:* Ecology, growth rates, population fluxes and distribution of planktonic diatoms, especially of the Great Lakes region; planktonic diatoms, water transparency and water chemistry before and after the zebra mussel. *Mailing Add:* 2761 Oakcleft Ct Ann Arbor MI 48103-2247

HOLLANDER, GERHARD LUDWIG, SYSTEM ARCHITECTURE, COMPUTER SYSTEMS. *Current Pos:* PRES & TECH DIR, HOLLANDER ASSOCS, 61- *Personal Data:* b Berlin, Ger, Feb 27, 22; nat US; m 57, Marianne Scheupp; c Susan, Jeffrey & Carolyn. *Educ:* Ill Inst Technol, BS, 47; Wash Univ, St Louis, MS, 48; Mass Inst Technol, EE, 53. *Honors & Awards:* Centennial Medal, Inst Elec & Electronics Engrs, 84- *Prof Exp:* Radio buyer, Spiegel, Inc, 40-42; res engr, McDonnell Aircraft Co, 47; asst prof eng, St Louis Univ, 48-49; sr engr, Servo Lab, Raytheon Mfg Co, 49-51; res asst, Servomechanisms Lab, Mass Inst Technol, 52-54; sect head, data processing syst, Clevite Res Ctr, 54-57; sect mgr comput systs, Philco Corp, 57-60; mgr gen purpose comput dept, Hughes Aircraft Co, 60-61. *Concurrent Pos:* Consult, indust & govt, 53-; mem, Nat Joint Comput Comt, 59-61; mem, Control Adv Comt, Am Automatic Control Coun, 60-62; dir, Am Fedn Info Processing Socs, 62-65; gen chmn, Joint Nat Conf Major Systs, 71; dir & chmn bd, Inst Elec & Electronics Engrs Winter Conv on Mil Systs, 75-79; gen chmn & chmn bd dir, Inst Elec & Electronics Engrs Conf Expert Systems, Westex, 85-91; vpres & pres, Inst Elec & Electronics Engrs Computer Soc, 62-65, chmn, Los Angeles coun, Region 6 S, 71-73. *Mem:* Fel Inst Elec & Electronics Engrs; Sigma Xi; fel Nat Contract Mgt Asn. *Res:* Computer system design and application; general methodology for decision making and for optimal structuring of large systems; system architecture and acquisition strategies for major systems. *Mailing Add:* Hollander Assocs PO Box 2276 Fullerton CA 92837-0276. *E-Mail:* g.hollander@ieee.org

HOLLANDER, JACK M, ENERGY, RESOURCES. *Current Pos:* dir, Energy & Environ Div, Lawrence Berkeley Lab, 73-76, prof, 79-89, EMER PROF ENERGY & RESOURCES, UNIV CALIF, BERKELEY, 89- *Personal Data:* b Youngstown, Ohio, Apr 13, 27; m 85, Sharon Mann; c Judy, Jeffrey & Allan. *Educ:* Ohio State Univ, BS, 48; Univ Calif, Berkeley, PhD(chem), 51. *Prof Exp:* Vpres, Ohio State Univ, 83-89. *Concurrent Pos:* Sr staff scientist, Lawrence Berkeley Lab, 53-; Guggenheim fel, 58-59 & 65-66; mem, Subcomt Nuclear Struct, Nat Acad Sci-Nat Res Coun, 60-70; ed, Ann Rev Energy, 76-; mem & founding chair bd, Beijer Int Inst Energy & Human Ecol, Stockholm, 76-; exec dir, Comt Nuclear & Alternative Energy Systs, Nat Acad Sci, 76-77. *Mem:* AAAS; Am Phys Soc; Am Chem Soc; Royal Swed Acad Sci; World Acad Arts & Sci. *Res:* Nuclear spectroscopy and models; compilations of nuclear data; energy policy; energy conservation research. *Mailing Add:* 168 Southampton Ave Berkeley CA 94707

HOLLANDER, JOSEPH LEE, RHEUMATOLOGY. *Current Pos:* instr med, Univ Pa, 46-48, assoc, 48-51, assoc prof clin med, 53-58, assoc prof med, 58-62, chief arthritis sect, Univ Hosp, 46-72, prof, 62-78, EMER PROF MED, UNIV PA, SCH MED, 78- *Personal Data:* b St Louis, Mo, Mar 8, 10; m 36, 74; c 2. *Educ:* Cornell Univ, AB, 32; Univ Pa, MD, 35. *Honors & Awards:* Harding Medal, Arthritis Found, 82; Master, Am Rheumatism Asn,

87. *Prof Exp:* Asst physician, Pa Hosp, Philadelphia, 37-46. *Concurrent Pos:* Asst demonstr, Jefferson Med Col, 40-46; consult to Surgeon Gen, US Dept Army, 48-50, Valley Forge Gen Hosp, 50-52 & Childrens' Hosp, 51-; hon prof med, Univ Guadalajara, Mex & Univ Peruana Cayetano Heredia, Lima, Peru; mem, Comt of Honor, 15th Int Cong Rheumatology, Paris, 81. *Mem:* AMA; Am Rheumatism Asn; Asn Am Physicians; master Am Col Physicians. *Res:* Arthritis; clinical and basic research on joint physiology and action of cortisone-like hormones on joint tissues; effects of climate on arthritis; immunopathogenesis of rheumatoid arthritis. *Mailing Add:* 3400 Spruce Havertown PA 19083

HOLLANDER, JOSHUA, NEUROLOGY, BIOCHEMISTRY. *Current Pos:* asst prof, 69-77, ASSOC PROF NEUROL, SCH MED & DENT, UNIV ROCHESTER, 69-, SR ASSOC NEUROLOGIST, STRONG MEM HOSP, 77- *Personal Data:* b New York, NY, Dec 28, 36; m 60; c 3. *Educ:* Columbia Univ, BA, 56, MD, 60. *Prof Exp:* Intern med, Univ Hosp, Vanderbilt Univ, 60-61, asst resident, 61-62; resident neurol, Mass Gen Hosp, 62-63, actg resident, 64-65; clin & res assoc biochem, Geront Res Ctr, Nat Inst Child Health & Human Develop, 65-67; asst res biochemist, Ment Health Res Inst, Univ Mich, Ann Arbor, 67-69. *Concurrent Pos:* Clin fel neuropath, Mass Gen Hosp, 63-64; Nat Inst Neurol Dis & Blindness spec fel, 67-69; chief neurol serv, Rochester Gen Hosp, 69- *Mem:* AAAS; Am Acad Neurol; Geront Soc. *Res:* Biochemistry of aging nervous system; brain phospholipid metabolism-physiologic aspects. *Mailing Add:* 1425 Portland Ave Rochester NY 14621-3001

HOLLANDER, LEONORE, CLINICAL BIOCHEMISTRY, SUPERVISION & ACCURACY CONTROL. *Current Pos:* RETIRED. *Personal Data:* b Ferguson, Mo, May 27, 06; div; c Gerda Winifred, Cichon Eckehart & Ullrike Nan (Solomon). *Educ:* Bryn Mawr Col, AB, 28; Univ Ill, MS, 29, PhD(physiol chem), 32. *Honors & Awards:* Meritorious Serv Award, Am Inst Chem. *Prof Exp:* Asst biochem, Cancer Res Inst, 31-33; grad scholar, Ger Polytech Inst, Prague, 33-35, Kaiser Hilhelm Inst, Heidelberg, 35-37; asst prof chem, Cedar Crest Col, Allentown, Pa, 47-49; res asst biochem, Inst Cancer Res, Fox Chase, Pa, 50-53; clin biochemist, St Luke's Hosp, Bethlehem, Pa, 53-62, Philadelphia Gen Hosp, 62-63. *Mem:* Fel Am Inst Chemists; fel AAAS; Am Inst Chem; Am Chem Soc; Am Asn Clin Chemists. *Res:* Salivary and pancreatic amylase, isolation and study of crystalline dextrine; elucidating bacterial polysaccharide complex from serratia marcescens, involving systemizing use of the anthrone reaction in identifying, distinguishing and quantifying sugars. *Mailing Add:* 684 Benicia Dr Apt 35 Santa Rosa CA 95409-3060

HOLLANDER, MAX LEO, CHEMISTRY. *Current Pos:* RETIRED. *Personal Data:* b Cologne, Ger, Dec 3, 23; nat US; m 48; c 3. *Educ:* Rutgers Univ, BS, 44, PhD(chem), 47. *Prof Exp:* Instr chem, Rutgers Univ, 47; res chemist, Am Smelting & Refining Co, 47-66, sect leader, 66-70, supt chem res, 70-76, supt chem res, Asarco, Inc, 76-84. *Res:* Non-ferrous chemistry; electrochemistry; extractive metallurgy; water pollution control. *Mailing Add:* 740 Hart Dr Bridgewater NJ 08807

HOLLANDER, MILTON B(ERNARD), mechanical engineering, for more information see previous edition

HOLLANDER, MYLES, MATHEMATICAL STATISTICS, APPLIED STATISTICS. *Current Pos:* From asst prof to prof, 65-96, chmn dept, 78-81, DISTINGUISHED RES PROF STATIST, FLA STATE UNIV, 96- *Personal Data:* b Brooklyn, NY, Mar 21, 41; m 63; c 2. *Educ:* Carnegie Inst Technol, BS, 61; Stanford Univ, MS, 62, PhD(statist), 65. *Concurrent Pos:* Vis prof biostatist, Stanford Univ, 72-73 & 81-82, Univ Wash, 89-90. *Mem:* AAAS; fel Am Statist Asn; Int Statist Inst; fel Inst Math Statist; Sigma Xi. *Res:* Nonparametric statistics; biostatistics; medical consulting. *Mailing Add:* Dept Statist Fla State Univ Tallahassee FL 32306

HOLLANDER, PHILIP B, PHARMACOLOGY, BIOPHYSICS & COMPUTER SCIENCES. *Current Pos:* RETIRED. *Personal Data:* b Chicago, Ill, May 4, 24; div; c Marc Joel, Carol Ruth, Daniel Charles, Rachel Blyth & Sara Elizabeth. *Educ:* Univ Calif, Los Angeles, BS, 48, Univ Southern Calif, MSc, 55, PhD(pharmacol), 60. *Prof Exp:* USPHS fel, 60-61; sr engr, Radio Corp Am, NJ, 61-64; asst prof pharmacol, Woman's Med Col Pa, 62-64; assoc prof, Col Med, Ohio State Univ, 64-69, dep chmn, 77-83, prof pharmacol & biophys, 69-92. *Concurrent Pos:* Mem fac, Jefferson Med Sch, 63-64; NIH develop award fel, 64-74. *Mem:* AAAS; Am Soc Pharmacol & Exp Therapeut; NY Acad Sci; Biomed Eng Soc; Am Heart Asn; Sigma Xi; Inst Elec & Electronics Engrs. *Res:* Electropharmacological principles of pharmacological activities as related to cardiac activity; information processing by biological systems; man-machine interrelationships for closed loop design analysis; substance abuse. *Mailing Add:* PO Box 8463 Columbus OH 43210-0463. *Fax:* 614-294-4499; *E-Mail:* hollander.2@osu.edu

HOLLANDER, VINCENT PAUL, INTERNAL MEDICINE. *Current Pos:* PROF INTERNAL MED & RES PROF BIOCHEM, MT SINAI SCH MED, 69-, RES PROF SURG & NEOPLASTIC DIS, 80- *Personal Data:* b New York, NY, June 18, 17; m 52; c 4. *Educ:* Univ Chicago, BS, 41, MS & PhD(biochem), 44; Northwestern Univ, MD, 47; Am Bd Internal Med, dipl, 54. *Prof Exp:* Asst resident med, Montefiore Hosp, 49-50; res fel, Sloan-Kettering Inst Cancer Res, 50-52; assoc prof internal med, Sch Med, Univ Va, 52-60, Am Cancer Soc prof internal med, 60-63; dir Res Inst Skeletomuscular Dis, Hosp Joint & Med Ctr, 63-80. *Concurrent Pos:* Clin asst, Mem Hosp Cancer & Allied Dis, 51-52; asst prof biochem, Sch Med, Univ Va, 52-63, physician & chief tumor clin, Univ Hosp, 52-58, coordr cancer prog, Univ, 52-63; mem endocrine study sect, Div Res Grants, NIH, 64-, mem cancer res training comt, Nat Cancer Inst, 69-; prof med & biochem, Am Cancer Soc, 77; attend physician Internal Med, Mt Sinai Hosp, 64-, attend physician Neoplastic dis, 82- *Mem:* AAAS; Am Soc Cancer Res; Endocrine Soc; Am Soc Biol Chem; Am Fedn Clin Res; Am Chem Soc. *Res:* Endocrinology; malignant disease; steroid chemistry. *Mailing Add:* 2 Beekman Pl New York NY 10022

HOLLANDER, WALTER, JR, INTERNAL MEDICINE, NEPHROLOGY. *Current Pos:* RETIRED. *Personal Data:* b Baltimore, Md, Aug 12, 22; m 55, Jennie L Laughon; c 2. *Educ:* Haverford Col, BS, 44; Harvard Univ, MD, 50; Am Bd Internal Med, dipl, 60. *Prof Exp:* Intern & asst resident med, Presby Hosp, New York, 50-53; sr resident, Boston Vet Admin Hosp, 53-54; from instr to emer prof med, Sch Med, Univ NC, Chapel Hill, 56-88, dir, Gen Clin Res Unit, 60-66, asst to dean, 66-72. *Concurrent Pos:* USPHS fel, Sch Med, Univ NC, Chapel Hill, 54-56 & 72-73; Am Heart Asn res grant, 58-61; Markle scholar, 58-63; USPHS res grant, 61-66; asst, Sch Med, Boston Univ, 53-54 & Harvard Med Serv, Boston City Hosp, 53-54. *Mem:* AAAS; emer mem Am Fedn Clin Res; emer mem Am Soc Clin Invest; Am Asn Univ Professors; Sigma Xi. *Res:* Renal and body fluid normal and abnormal function and structure. *Mailing Add:* 531 Dogwood Dr Chapel Hill NC 27516-2807

HOLLANDER, WILLIAM, INTERNAL MEDICINE. *Current Pos:* Asst med, Boston Univ, 51-55, instr, 55-57, assoc, 57-59, from asst prof to assoc prof, 59-69, from asst mem to assoc mem, Hosp, 57-65, vis physician, 57-65, PROF MED, SCH MED, BOSTON UNIV, 69-, DIR HYPERTENSION & ATHEROSCLEROSIS RES UNIT, UNIV HOSP, 65- *Personal Data:* b Brooklyn, NY, May 21, 25; m 54; c 3. *Educ:* NY Univ, BA, 45; Long Island Col Med, MD, 49. *Mem:* AAAS; Am Heart Asn; Am Fedn Clin Res. *Res:* Metabolic and pharmacological studies in arterial hypertension and atherosclerosis. *Mailing Add:* Boston Univ Sch Med 15 Stoughton St Rm E438 Boston MA 02118-2313

HOLLANDSWORTH, CLINTON E, NUCLEAR PHYSICS, ELECTRO MAGNETISM. *Current Pos:* RES PHYSICIST, US ARMY RES LAB, 92- *Personal Data:* b Pulaski, Va, Dec 7, 30. *Educ:* Va Polytech Inst, BS, 58, MS, 61; Duke Univ, PhD(nuclear physics), 63. *Prof Exp:* Asst nuclear physics, Duke Univ, 59-63, res assoc, 63-65; res physicist, US Army Nuclear Defense Lab, 65-71 & US Army Ballistic Res Lab, 71-92. *Mem:* Am Phys Soc; Inst Elec & Electronics Engrs; Sigma Xi. *Res:* Experimental physics; fast neutron physics including elastic and inelastic scattering of neutrons; accelerator technology; physics of charged particle beams; pulsed power electromagnetics; electromagnetism. *Mailing Add:* 830 Chesney Lane Bel Air MD 21014. *Fax:* 410-278-9699; *E-Mail:* holland@arl.army.mil

HOLLDOBLER, BERTHOLD KARL, BEHAVIORAL ECOLOGY, SOCIOBIOLOGY. *Current Pos:* PROF ZOOL, UNIV WURZBURG, GER, 89- *Personal Data:* b Erling-Andechs, Ger, June 25, 36; m 80, Friederike Probst; c Jakob, Stefan & Sebastian. *Educ:* Univ Wurzburg, Dr rer nat, 65; Univ Frankfurt, Dr habil, 69. *Hon Degrees:* Am, Harvard Univ. *Honors & Awards:* Leibniz Prize, 89; Karl Ritter von Frisch Medal & Sci Prize, Ger Zool Soc, 96; Korber Prize for Europ Sci, 96. *Prof Exp:* Asst prof zool, Univ Frankfurt, 66-69, privatdozent on leave, 69-71, prof zool, 71-72; prof biol, Harvard Univ, 73-90, Alexander Agassiz prof zool, 82-90. *Concurrent Pos:* Res assoc zool, Harvard Univ, 69-71; co-ed, Psyche, 73- & Behav Ecol & Sociobiol, 76-; John Simon Guggenheim fel, 80; Psychobiol Panel, NSF, 84-87; Alexander von Humboldt Sr Scientist Award, 86-87; adj prof, Univ Ariz, 89- *Mem:* Am Acad Arts & Sci; Leopoldina Ger Acad Sci; fel AAAS; Animal Behav Soc; Int Union Study Social Insects; Ger Zool Soc; Cambridge Entom Soc; Ecol Soc Am; Soc Study Evolution; Soc Am Naturalists; Int Soc Chem Ecol; Bavarian Acad Sci. *Res:* Behavioral ecology and sociobiology of insects; animal communication; chemical ecology. *Mailing Add:* 26 Oxford St Cambridge MA 02138-2902

HOLLE, MIGUEL, HORTICULTURE, PLANT BREEDING. *Current Pos:* CONSULT, 92- *Personal Data:* b Berlin, Ger, Jan 13, 37; Peru citizen; m 66, Amparo Fernandez; c Kurt M, Juan A & Karin E. *Educ:* Colo State Univ, BS, 58; Iowa State Univ, MS, 60, PhD(hort), 65. *Prof Exp:* From asst prof to prof hort, Univ Nac Agraria La Molina, Lima, Peru, 61-76; horticulturist, Res & Training Ctr, Turrialba, Costa Rica, 76-82; regional officer, Int Bd Plant Genetic Resources, Cali, Colombia, 82-88; Plant Genetic Resources Prog, Lima, Peru, 88-89; dir, Andean Crop & Animal Res Proj, Nat Agr Inst Res, Peru, 89-92. *Concurrent Pos:* Guggenheim Found fel, 74-75; specialist, Int Potato Ctr, Lima, Peru. *Mem:* Am Soc Hort Sci; Latin Am Asn Agr Sci; Int Soc Hort Sci; Nat Acad Sci & Technol Peru. *Res:* Vegetable crops, especially germ plasm and field management studies within the cropping systems context. *Mailing Add:* Callez No 183 Urb El Rancho-Miraflores Lima 18 Peru. *E-Mail:* mholle@cipa.pe

HOLLE, PAUL AUGUST, BIOLOGY. *Current Pos:* prof & chmn dept, 57-89, EMER PROF BIOL, WORCESTER STATE COL, 89- *Personal Data:* b Decatur, Ind, July 5, 23; m 54; c 2. *Educ:* Valparaiso Univ, AB, 47; Univ Notre Dame, MS, 49, PhD(zool), 56. *Prof Exp:* Asst prof zool, Univ NH, 50-57. *Concurrent Pos:* Mem staff, Marine Biol Lab, Woods Hole, 50-51, Bermuda Marine Biol Labs, 51 & Mus Comp Zool, Harvard Univ, 53-55. *Mem:* AAAS; Soc Syst Zool; Nat Asn Biol Teachers; Am Malacol Union. *Res:* Malacology; marine invertebrates; science education; amphibian osteology. *Mailing Add:* 35 Julio Dr Apt 215 Shrewsbury MA 01545

HOLLEBEEK, ROBERT JOHN, DATA INTENSIVE COMPUTING, WIDE AREA METACOMPUTING. *Current Pos:* assoc prof, 86-89, PROF PHYSICS, UNIV PA, 89-; DIR, NAT SCALABLE CLUSTER PROJ, 94- *Personal Data:* m 69, Ardith Razenberg; c David, Timothy & Mark. *Educ:* Calvin Col, AB & BS, 70; Univ Calif, Berkeley, PhD(physics), 74. *Hon Degrees:* MA, Univ Pa, 87. *Prof Exp:* Postdoctoral fel, Columbia Univ, 74-79; asst prof, Stanford Univ, 79-85. *Concurrent Pos:* Mem, Stanford Sci Policy Comt, 91-96; grad chair physics, Univ Pa, 95-, prin investr, 96- *Res:* Applications in science, medicine and business where the solution requires large scale data intensive computing tools; building large scale systems including wide area meta-computers for these applications. *Mailing Add:* Dept Phys & Astron Univ Pa 209 S 33rd St Philadelphia PA 19104-6396. *Fax:* 215-898-8512; *E-Mail:* hollebeek@nscp.upenn.edu

HOLLEIN, HELEN CONWAY FARIS, EDUCATIONAL ADMINISTRATION. *Current Pos:* from asst prof to assoc prof, 82-92, DEPT CHAIR, MANHATTAN COL, RIVERDALE, NY, 89-, PROF CHEM ENG, 92- *Personal Data:* b Ft Bragg, NC, Mar 21, 43; m 66, Leo B Jr; c Mary E, Kathleen R & Michael C. *Educ:* Univ SC, BS, 65; NJ Inst Technol, MS, 79, DEng, 82. *Honors & Awards:* Ralph R Teetor Award, Soc Automotive Engrs, 84. *Prof Exp:* Process engr, chem div, Exxon Res & Eng Co, 65-67; teacher chem & physics, Livingston High Sch, NJ, 67-69; substitute teacher math, Singapore Am High Sch, 70-71; teaching asst, Dept Chem Eng & Chem, NJ Inst Technol, 77-78, adj instr, 78-81. *Mem:* Am Inst Chem Engrs; Am Chem Soc; Am Soc Eng Educ; Sigma Xi. *Res:* Adsorption and ion exchange; biotechnology; ultrafiltration. *Mailing Add:* Dept Chem Eng Manhattan Col Riverdale NY 10471. *Fax:* 718-920-7819

HOLLEMAN, KENDRICK ALFRED, POULTRY SCIENCE. *Current Pos:* RETIRED. *Personal Data:* b Normangee, Tex, Dec 11, 34; m 56; c 2. *Educ:* Tex A&M Col, BS, 58; Univ Nebr, Lincoln, MS, 62; Univ Mo, Columbis, PhD(poultry sci), 71. *Honors & Awards:* Egg Sci Award, Am Egg Bd, 73. *Prof Exp:* Asst exten poultryman, Coop Exten Serv, Univ Nebr, Lincoln, 58-59; asst mgr turkey processing & mkt, Nebr Turkey Growers Coop Asn, 59-64; mgr small animal nutrit res, Small Animal Labs, Ralston Purina Co, Mo, 64-66; instr physiol res, Univ Mo-Columbia, 66-70; prof poultry sci & proj leader, Poultry Sci Exten, Clemson Univ, 70-80; prog leader poultry sci, Exten Serv, USDA, 81 95. *Mem:* Poultry Sci Asn; World's Poultry Sci Asn; Sigma Xi. *Res:* Physiology of reproduction in avian species; environmental studies on domestic poultry; nutrition of domestic poultry; egg science and technology; PCB research. *Mailing Add:* Dept Animal Sci Ore State Univ 112 Withcombe Hall Corvallis OR 97331-6702

HOLLEMAN, WILLIAM H, BIOCHEMISTRY. *Current Pos:* Res biochemist, Abbott Labs, 66-70, group leader, 70-77, sect head, antithrombosis, 77-80, head, Dept Virol & Biochem, 80-84, proj leader, cardiovasc res, 84-90, HEAD, TECHNOL ASSESESSMENT, ABBOTT LABS, 90- *Personal Data:* b Jamestown, Mich, Aug 18, 40; m 63, Mary B Roters; c William K & Thomas E. *Educ:* Hope Col, AB, 62; Mich State Univ, PhD(biochem), 66. *Concurrent Pos:* Lectr, Med Sch, Loyola Univ Chicago, 70-80, Harvard Med Sch, Boston, 83-84. *Mem:* Am Soc Biol Chem; AAAS. *Res:* Biochemistry of macromolecules, ultracentrifugation; isolation and characterization of enzymes which have therapeutic importance; drug development for cardiovascular diseases; science administration; pharmaceutical drug discovery. *Mailing Add:* Dept 473 Abbott Labs Abbott Park IL 60064-3500. *Fax:* 847-938-5290

HOLLENBACH, DAVID JOHN, INFRARED ASTRONOMY, STAR FORMATION & INTERSTELLAR MEDIUM STUDIES. *Current Pos:* Nat Res Coun Assoc, 79-80, RES SCIENTIST, NASA AMES RES CTR, 80- *Personal Data:* b Kirksville, Mo, Oct 10, 42; m 71, Jane E Rosenthal; c Anna E. *Educ:* Hope Col, BA, 64; Cornell Univ, PhD(theoret physics), 69. *Prof Exp:* Fel, Harvard Univ, 68-70; vis asst prof, Colo Col, 71-73; asst prof, Univ Colo, Colorado Springs, 73-75; fel, Univ Calif, Berkeley, 75-79. *Concurrent Pos:* Prin investr, Ctr Star Formation Studies, 85- *Mem:* Am Astron Soc; Int Astron Union. *Res:* Theoretical research on the interstellar medium, star formation and the galactic center; interstellar processes in galaxies and infrared astronomy. *Mailing Add:* 6434 Regent St Oakland CA 94618

HOLLENBACH, EDWIN, MECHANICAL & ELECTRICAL ENGINEERING. *Current Pos:* RETIRED. *Personal Data:* b West Leesport, Pa, Nov 2, 18; m 44; c 1. *Educ:* Wyomissing Polytech, BSME, 39. *Prof Exp:* Designer, Birdsboro Steel, Steel Foundry & Mach Co, 39-41; eclipse-pioneer div, Bendix Corp, 41-45; instr math, Wyomissing Polytech, 45-46; design engr, Rheem Mfg Co, 46-49; proj engr, Air Prod, Inc, 49-50; sr engr, Scott Paper Co, 50-52; mgr serv, Burroughs Corp, 52-55; mgr serv sr res engr, Univac Corp, 55-56; vpres eng, Briggs Assocs, Inc, 56-59; exec vpres, Chem Serv, Inc, 60-69, pres, 69-80; vpres, Drexel Dynamics Corp, 59-80. *Mem:* Int Mat Mgt Soc; Am Chem Soc. *Res:* Design and development of automation and computer equipment; input-output automatic controls; general material handling equipment. *Mailing Add:* 30 Lyman Ave Woodbury NJ 08096-2837

HOLLENBAUGH, KENNETH MALCOLM, ENVIRONMENTAL GEOLOGY. *Current Pos:* from asst prof to assoc prof geol, 68-73, chmn dept, 71-77, PROF GEOL, BOISE STATE UNIV, 73-, DEAN GRAD COL, 75-, DIR, UNIV RES CTR, 81-, ASSOC EXEC VPRES, 81- *Personal Data:* b Fostoria, Ohio, Sept 8, 34; m 61; c 3. *Educ:* Bowling Green State Univ, BS, 57; Univ Idaho, MS, 59, PhD(geol), 68. *Prof Exp:* Teaching asst phys geol & paleont, Univ Idaho, 57-58, mine geologist, Idaho Bur Mines & Geol, 58-59; mine engr, Kaiser Cement & Gypsum Corp, 60-63, mine supt, 63-65; geologist, Kaiser Steel Corp, 65-68. *Concurrent Pos:* Pres, Kash Enterprises; vpres, Idaho Quartzite. *Mem:* Am Inst Mining, Metall & Petrol Engrs; Sigma Xi. *Res:* Research and consulting in environmental geology, geothermal geology and mineral economics. *Mailing Add:* Grad Col Boise State Univ 1910 University Dr Math Geosci Bldg Rm 140 Boise ID 83725-1110

HOLLENBECK, CLARIE BEALL, EXPERIMENTAL BIOLOGY. *Current Pos:* res scholar, 82-85, RES SCIENTIST, DEPT MED, STANFORD UNIV SCH MED, 85-, RES SCIENTIST, GERIAT EDUC & CLIN CTR, VET ADMIN MED CTR, PALO ALTO, CALIF, 85- *Personal Data:* b San Francisco, Calif, Apr 18, 47; m; c 4. *Educ:* Calif State Univ, BA, 71; Ore State Univ, PhD(nutrit biochem), 82. *Prof Exp:* Res asst, Univ Ore Health Sci Ctr, Portland, 79-81, Ore State Univ, Corvallis, 80-81, teaching asst, Dept Foods & Nutrit, 81-82, res asst, Nutrit Res Inst, 81-82. *Concurrent Pos:* Nat res serv award, Nat Heart, Lung & Blood Inst, NIH, 83-85; mem, Prog Comt, Coun Nutrit Sci & Metab, Am Diabetes Asn, 84-88, chair, Educ Comt, 85-87, chair, Prof Educ Comt, 86-87, chair, Educ & Prog Comt, Coun Nutrit Sci & Metab, 86-88, vchair, Prof Educ Comt, 87-88, mem, 87-90, mem, Comt on Sci & Med Progs, 87-89, chair, Prof Educ Subcomt, 87-, vchair, Coun Nutrit Sci & Metab, 88-90, co-chmn, Task Force on Nutrit & Pregnancy, 88-91, chmn, Coun Nutrit Sci & Metab, 90-, mem, Med-Sci Comt, 90-; coordr diabetes res, Dept Med, Stanford Univ Sch Med, 85-86, assoc dir & res coordr, Gen Clin Res Ctr, 86-90, vis scholar, Dept Med, 86-87. *Mem:* Am Diabetes Asn; Am Fedn Clin Res; Am Heart Asn; Am Inst Nutrit; Am Soc Clin Nutrit; Sigma Xi. *Res:* Diabetes. *Mailing Add:* 940 Green Ave San Bruno CA 94066

HOLLENBECK, ROBERT GARY, PHARMACEUTICS, PHYSICAL PHARMACY. *Current Pos:* Asst prof, 77-83, assoc dean, 90-96, ASSOC PROF PHARMACEUT, SCH PHARM, UNIV MD, 83- *Personal Data:* b Oneida, NY, Oct 8, 49; m 80, Olesia Melnit Schenko; c 2. *Educ:* Albany Col Pharm, BS, 72; Purdue Univ, PhD(indust & phys pharm), 77. *Mem:* Am Asn Pharmaceut Scientists; Am Pharmaceut Asn; Am Asn Col Pharm. *Res:* Application of physical-chemical principles to the design, development and evaluation of drug delivery systems. *Mailing Add:* Univ Md Sch Pharm 20 N Pine St Baltimore MD 21201-1180. *Fax:* 410-706-4012; *E-Mail:* hollenbe@pharmacy.ab.umd.edu

HOLLENBERG, CHARLES H, MEDICINE. *Current Pos:* chmn dept, Univ Toronto, 70-81, Charles H Best prof med res, 81-83, vprovost, 83-89, PROF MED, UNIV TORONTO, 70-, DIR, BANTING & BEST DIABETES CTR, 81- *Personal Data:* b Winnipeg, Man, Sept 15, 30; m 56; c 1. *Educ:* Univ Man, BSc, 50, BSc & MD, 55; FRCP(C), 59; FACP(US), 73. *Hon Degrees:* DSc, Univ Man, 83, McGill Univ, 85. *Prof Exp:* Asst med, Tufts Univ, 58-60; Markle scholar, 60; from lectr to prof, McGill Univ, 60-70. *Concurrent Pos:* Physician-in-chief, Toronto Gen Hosp, 70-81, sr physician, 81- *Mem:* Fel Am Col Physicians; Endocrine Soc; Am Physiol Soc; Asn Am Physicians; Am Soc Clin Invest; Sigma Xi. *Res:* Endocrinology and lipid metabolism. *Mailing Add:* CCRW3-836 Ont Cancer Treatment & Res 620 University Ave Suite 1500 Toronto ON M5G 2L7 Can. *Fax:* 416-971-6888

HOLLENBERG, DAVID HENRY, CELLULOSE CHEMISTRY, HEMICELLULOSE CHEMISTRY. *Current Pos:* RES FEL, KIMBERLY-CLARK CORP, 91- *Personal Data:* b Philadelphia, Pa, Feb 3, 46; m 67; c 3. *Educ:* Wittenberg Univ, BS, 67; Univ Maine, PhD(chem), 72. *Prof Exp:* Fel, Sloan-Kettering Inst, 72-73, Am Cancer Soc, 73-74; sr develop chemist wood chem, St Regis Paper Co, 77-79, sr staff chemist, 79-82; mem staff, W R Grace & Co, 82-84; sr res assoc, James River Corp, 84-86, res fel, 86-91. *Mem:* Am Chem Soc; AAAS; Tech Asn Pulp & Paper Indust; Sigma Xi; NY Acad Sci. *Res:* Mechanisms of pulping and bleaching of wood fibers and natural products including tall oil, turpentine, polysaccharides and other natural polymers; chemical modification of cellulosic fibers; mechanisms of fiber-fiber bonding; papermaking chemistry surface and colloid science. *Mailing Add:* Kimberly-Clark Corp PO Box 999 Neenah WI 54957-0999

HOLLENBERG, J LELAND, PHYSICAL CHEMISTRY. *Current Pos:* PROF CHEM, UNIV REDLANDS, 63- *Personal Data:* b La Verne, Calif, Sept 17, 26; m 51; c 5. *Educ:* Univ Redlands, BA, 49, BS, 52; Univ Calif, Berkeley, MS, 52; Univ Southern Calif, PhD(chem), 62. *Prof Exp:* High sch instr chem & physics, 49-50 & 52-54; instr chem, Fullerton City Col, 54-59; staff consult, Chem Study, 61-63. *Concurrent Pos:* NSF fac fel, Univ Calif, Riverside, 71-72. *Mem:* Am Chem Soc. *Res:* Absolute infrared intensities of ions and molecules, especially in condensed phases; hydration numbers of small, biologically important molecules. *Mailing Add:* 31350 Alta Vista Dr Redlands CA 92373

HOLLENBERG, JOEL WARREN, TURBOMACHINERY, ALTERNATE ENERGY. *Current Pos:* from asst prof to assoc prof, 77-82, PROF MECH ENG, COOPER UNION, 82- *Personal Data:* b New York, NY, Oct 20, 38; m 60, 74, C J Puotinen; c David & Rachel. *Educ:* Cooper Union, BME, 60; Stevens Inst Technol, MS, 62, PhD(mech eng), 78. *Prof Exp:* Res asst, Stevens Inst Technol, 60-61, res engr, Davidson Lab, 61-65; eng sect mgr, Diehl Div, Singer Co, 65-67; mem tech staff, Ingersoll Band Res, Inc, 67-71, prog mgr govt contracts, 71-73; instr, Stevens Inst Technol, 73-77. *Concurrent Pos:* Consult & expert witness for indust, 74-; prof in charge mech eng labs, Cooper Union, 81- *Mem:* Am Soc Mech Engrs; Am Soc Heating, Refrig & Air Conditioning Engrs; Am Soc Eng Educ; Sigma Xi. *Res:* Regenerative turbomachinery; transverse fans; unusual low speed aerodynamic problems; computer aided experimentation and alternative energy systems. *Mailing Add:* Cooper Union Cooper Square New York NY 10003

HOLLENBERG, MARTIN JAMES, ANATOMY. *Current Pos:* DEAN, FAC MED, UNIV BC, 85- *Personal Data:* b Winnipeg, Man, June 30, 34; m 59; c 2. *Educ:* Univ Man, BSc & MD, 58; Wayne State Univ, MSc, 64, PhD(anat), 65. *Prof Exp:* From asst prof to assoc prof anat, Univ Western Ont, 65-71; prof anat, Univ BC, 71-75; prof morphol sci & head div, Fac Med, Univ Calgary, 75-78; dean med & prof anat, Univ Western Ont, 78-85. *Mem:* Am Asn Anat; Can Asn Anat. *Res:* Structure of vertebrate eye. *Mailing Add:* Fac Med Univ BC 2194 Health Sci Mall Vancouver BC V6T 1Z3 Can

HOLLENBERG, MILTON, MEDICINE, CARDIOVASCULAR PHYSIOLOGY. *Current Pos:* assoc prof, 68-78, PROF, MED CTR, UNIV CALIF, SAN FRANCISCO, 78- *Personal Data:* b New York, NY, July 29, 30; m 64; c 1. *Educ:* Brooklyn Col, AB, 51; Cornell Univ, MD, 55. *Prof Exp:* Intern, Bellevue Hosp, New York, 55-56; resident, Med Ctr, Univ Calif, San Francisco, 58-61; fel physiol, Harvard Med Sch, 61-63; from instr to asst prof, Med Col, Cornell Univ, 63-68. *Concurrent Pos:* Health Res Coun NY career scientist, 63-68; chief cardiol, San Francisco Vet Admin Hosp, 68-77. *Mem:* AAAS; Am Fedn Clin Res; Am Heart Asn; Vet Admin Cardiovasc Asn (pres, 84-85, vpres, 83-84, secy-treas, 82-83). *Res:* Exercise testing; uses of computers in science; cardiovascular pharmacology. *Mailing Add:* Vet Admin Hosp 111C-3 Univ Calif San Francisco 4150 Clement St San Francisco CA 94121

HOLLENBERG, MORLEY DONALD, ENDOCRINOLOGY. *Current Pos:* PROF & HEAD PHARMACOL DEPT, FAC MED, UNIV CALGARY, 79- *Personal Data:* b Winnipeg, Man, July 2, 42; m 65; c 2. *Educ:* Univ Man, Can, BSc, 63, MSc, 64; Oxford Univ, PhD(pharmacol), 67; Johns Hopkins Med Sch, MD, 72. *Prof Exp:* Fel pharmacol, Oxford Univ, 67-68; intern internal med, Johns Hopkins Hosp, 71-72, fel pharmacol, Johns Hopkins Med Sch, 72-73, asst prof pharmacol, 73-79, asst prof med, 74-79. *Concurrent Pos:* Investr med & pharmacol, Howard Hughes Med Inst, 74-79. *Mem:* Am Soc Pharmacol & Exp Therapeut; Am Soc Clin Invest; Can Soc Clin Invest. *Res:* Studies of the receptors and mechanisms of action of growth factors like insulin, somatomedins and epidermal growth factor-urogastrone. *Mailing Add:* Dept Pharmacol Univ Calgary Fac Med Calgary AB T2N 1N4 Can

HOLLENBERG, NORMAN KENNETH, INTERNAL MEDICINE, NEPHROLOGY & HYPERTENSION. *Current Pos:* res fel, Harvard Med Sch, 65-67, res assoc, 67-68, from asst prof to assoc prof radiol, 68-76, PROF & DIR PHYSIOL RES, HARVARD MED SCH, 76-; DIR PHYSIOL RES, DEPT RADIOL, PETER BENT BRIGHAM HOSP, 68- *Personal Data:* b Winnipeg, Man, Sept 10, 36; US citizen. *Educ:* Univ Man, BS, & MD, 60, PhD, 65; Royal Col Physicians, Cert, 61. *Hon Degrees:* MA, Harvard Univ, 76. *Honors & Awards:* Prowse Prize & Medal for Clin Res, 65; Neil John McLean Award for Res in Basic Sci, 66; Gold Medal & Prize, Royal Col Physicians, 69. *Prof Exp:* Jr intern, Winnipeg Gen Hosp, 60-61, resident, Dept Med, 63-65; intern, Dept Pharmacol, Karolinska Inst, Sweden, 61-63. *Concurrent Pos:* Can Heart Found res fel & assoc med, Dept Clin Investr, Deer Lodge Hosp, Winnipeg, 62-64; advanced Am Heart Found fel, Dept Med, Peter Bent Brigham Hosp, 65-67, jr assoc med, 67-68, sr assoc radiol & med, 71-76, sr assoc med, Cardiorenal Div, Dept Med, 71-; chmn, Subcomt Radionuclides in Nephrology, Int Soc Nephrology, 74-78; consult, Children's Hosp Med Ctr, Dana-Farber Cancer Inst, Parker Hill Med Ctr, New Eng Deaconess Hosp & Vet Admin Hosp, Boston, 76-; co-prin investr, NIH Radiol Ctr, 76-88; tutor, Cabot House, Harvard Col, 90- *Mem:* Am Soc Nephrology; Int Soc Nephrology; Am Heart Asn; Am Soc Clin Invest; Am Soc Pharmacol & Exp Therapeut; Int Soc Hypertension. *Res:* Pathogenesis and treatment of hypertension, including the renin system, sodium homeostasis, the kidney and genetics; collateral arterial growth and reactivity; author of several publications. *Mailing Add:* Brighan & Womens Hosp 75 Francis St Boston MA 02115-6195. *Fax:* 617-732-4144

HOLLENBERG, PAUL FREDERICK, DRUG & XENOBIOTIC METABOLISM, ENZYMOLOGY. *Current Pos:* MAURICE SERVERS COL PROF & CHAIR PHARMACOL, UNIV MICH, 94- *Personal Data:* b Philadelphia, Pa, Sept 18, 42; m 67, Emily Vanootighem; c David & Kathryn. *Educ:* Wittenberg Univ, BS, 64; Univ Mich, MS, 66, PhD(biochem), 69. *Prof Exp:* Postdoctoral fel, Univ Mich, 69, Univ Ill, 69-72; asst prof biochem, Med Sch, Northwestern Univ, Chicago, 72-81, assoc prof path & pharmacol, 81-84, prof path & molecular biol, 84-87; prof & chair pharmacol, Wayne State Univ, 87-94. *Concurrent Pos:* Schweppe Found Res Fel; mem, Chem Path Study Sect, NIH, 87-91; assoc ed, Chem Res in Toxicol, 88- *Mem:* Am Chem Soc; Am Asn Cancer Res; Am Soc Pharmacol & Exp Therapeut(secy/treas, 97-); Soc Toxicol; Am Soc Biochem & Molecular Biol. *Res:* Enzyme mechanisms; role of enzyme structure in catalytic function; structure and properties of heme proteins; biological oxidations and peroxidations; mechanisms of carcinogensis and toxicity. *Mailing Add:* Pharmacol 2301 MSRB Frl Univ Mich Med Ctr 1150 W Medical Center Dr Ann Arbor MI 41809-0632. *Fax:* 313-763-4450; *E-Mail:* phollen@umich.edu

HOLLENDER, MARC HALE, psychiatry, psychoanalysis, for more information see previous edition

HOLLENHORST, ROBERT WILLIAM, SR, MEDICINE, NEURO-OPHTHALMOLOGY. *Current Pos:* from instr to prof, 49-79, consult, Mayo Clin, 49-79, EMER PROF OPHTHAL, MAYO GRAD SCH MED, 79- *Personal Data:* b St Cloud, Minn, Aug 12, 13; m 39, Alice Nolan; c Robert W Jr, Michael J, Mary H (Lazarus), John T, F Mark, James N, Kathleen H (Tassen), Thomas M & Stephen E. *Educ:* Univ Minn, BS, 38, MB, 40, MD, 41, MS, 48; Am Bd Ophthal, dipl. *Honors & Awards:* Howe Medal, Am Ophthal Soc. *Prof Exp:* Intern, Abbott Hosp, Minneapolis, 40; intern, Ancker Hosp, St Paul, 40-41; Mayo Found fel, Univ Minn, 46-48. *Concurrent Pos:* State consult ophthal, Minn State Dept Pub Welfare, 63-91. *Mem:* Am Ophthal Soc; Am Acad Ophthal; Sigma Xi; AMA. *Res:* Neuro-ophthalmology with particular emphasis on intracranial vascular disease. *Mailing Add:* Charter House 1617 Rochester MN 55901

HOLLENSEN, RAYMOND HANS, BRYOLOGY. *Current Pos:* from asst prof to prof natural sci, Mich State Univ, 65-89, asst chairperson, 75-84, actg asst dir, Undergrad Univ Div, 87-90, PROF BOT & PLANT PATH, MICH STATE UNIV, 77-, ASSOC DIR, UNDERGRAD UNIV DIV, 90- *Personal Data:* b Madison Co, Nebr, Nov 5, 31; m 55; c 3. *Educ:* Capital Univ, BA, 53; Univ Mich, MS, 58; Univ Cincinnati, PhD(bot), 62. *Prof Exp:* Asst bot, Univ Mich, 56-58 & Univ Cincinnati, 58-61; instr biol, Keuka Col, 61-63, actg chmn dept, 62-63, asst prof, 63-65. *Concurrent Pos:* Curator, Cryptogamic Herbarium, Mich State Univ, 90- *Mem:* Am Bryol & Lichenological Soc. *Res:* Developmental morphology; tissue differentiation; systematics of the Hepaticae. *Mailing Add:* Botany Mich State Univ 166 Plant Biol East Lansing MI 48824-1312

HOLLER, ALBERT COCHRAN, CHEMISTRY. *Current Pos:* RETIRED. *Personal Data:* b Erie, Pa, Mar 17, 21; m 46; c 5. *Educ:* Univ Minn, BChem, 47. *Honors & Awards:* Thomas F Andrews Prize, 47. *Prof Exp:* Chief chemist, US Metal Prod Co, Pa, 41-44; res fel chem, Off Naval Res Proj, Univ Minn, 47-49; chief anal chemist, Twin City Testing & Eng Lab, 49-52, dir chem div, 52-58, vpres chem div, 58-85. *Mem:* AAAS; Am Chem Soc; Am Inst Chemists; Sigma Xi; Nat Asn Corrosion Engrs; Royal Soc Chem London; Am Indust Hyg Assoc. *Res:* Visible and ultraviolet absorption spectrophotometry; chromatography; analytical methods for nitric acid esters; metallurgy of copper base alloys and their analysis; corrosion of metals; ferrous metals analysis; mineralogy; sampling of metals, alloys, vegetable oils and petroleum. *Mailing Add:* 3205 Wendhurst Ave NE Minneapolis MN 55418-1727

HOLLER, FLOYD JAMES, ANALYTICAL CHEMISTRY. *Current Pos:* from asst prof to assoc prof, 77-95, PROF CHEM, UNIV KY, 95- *Personal Data:* b Muncie, Ind, Aug 6, 46; m 67, Vicki P; c Brian J, Brad A & Scott A. *Educ:* Ball State Univ, BS, 68, MS, 73; Mich State Univ, PhD(chem), 77. *Prof Exp:* Teacher chem & physics, Western Wayne Schs, 68-73; grad asst, Mich State Univ, 73-77. *Mem:* Am Chem Soc. *Res:* Reaction rate methods; analytical instrumentation; mini and micro computer applications; science education. *Mailing Add:* Dept Chem Univ Ky Lexington KY 40506. *Fax:* 606-323-1069; *E-Mail:* holler@pop.uky.edu

HOLLER, JACOB WILLIAM, medicine, for more information see previous edition

HOLLER, JAMES STEWART, TOXICOLOGY, INDUSTRIAL & PUBLIC HEALTH. *Current Pos:* CHIEF, EMERGENCY RESPONSE & SCI ASSESSMENT BR, DIV TOXICOL, AGENCY TOXIC SUBSTANCES & DIS REGISTRY, 93- *Educ:* St Andrews Presby Col, BA, 69; Ariz State Univ, PhD(org chem), 78. *Prof Exp:* Chem staff specialist, US Army, 70-72; res chemist, Mass Spectrometry Lab, Anal Div, Hercules Inc, 76-78; chief, Mass Spectros Lab, Toxicol Br, Div Environ Health Lab Sci, Ctr Dis Control, 78-88, asst to br chief, 88-92, supvry res chemist, Spec Activities Br, 92-93. *Mem:* Am Chem Soc. *Res:* Public health assessment of dioxins exposure from soil; volatile organic compounds. *Mailing Add:* Div Toxicol Agency Toxic Substances & Dis Registry 1600 Clifton Rd NE MSE-29 Atlanta GA 30333

HOLLER, NICHOLAS ROBERT, WILDLIFE MANAGEMENT, MAMMALOGY. *Current Pos:* Staff specialist wildlife res, US Fish & Wildlife Serv, 70-73, supvr wildlife biologist animal damage, Patuxent Wildlife Res Ctr, 73-75, sr proj biologist, CFBC study, Fla Game & Fresh Water Fish Comn, 75-85, SUPV WILDLIFE BIOLOGIST ANIMAL DAMAGE, DENVER WILDLIFE RES CTR, US FISH & WILDLIFE SERV, 85-, LEADER, ALA COOP FISH & WILDLIFE RES UNIT, 85- *Personal Data:* b Plymouth, Ind, May 14, 39; m 67; c 2. *Educ:* Univ Mo, AB, 61, AM, 63, PhD(zool), 73. *Concurrent Pos:* Assoc ed, J Wildlife Mgt, 80-81; ed, Wildlife Soc Bull, 90-91. *Mem:* Wildlife Soc; Am Soc Mammalogists; Soc Conserv Biol. *Res:* Wildlife damage control; mammalian ecology; social behavior; endangered species. *Mailing Add:* 209 S Cedarbrook Dr Auburn AL 36830

HOLLERAN, EUGENE MARTIN, PHYSICAL CHEMISTRY. *Current Pos:* from asst prof to prof, St John's Univ, 50-89, chmn dept, 61-65 & 70-73, dir sci, 65-67, EMER PROF CHEM, GRAD SCH, ST JOHN'S UNIV, NY, 89- *Personal Data:* b Pa, June 25, 22; m 47; c 8. *Educ:* Univ Scranton, BS, 43; Cath Univ Am, PhD(chem), 49. *Prof Exp:* Instr chem, Regis Col, 48-50. *Mem:* AAAS; Am Chem Soc; Sigma Xi. *Res:* Kinetic theory of gases; correlation of fluid properties; equations of state. *Mailing Add:* 57 S Corona Ave Valley Stream NY 11580

HOLLEY, CHARLES H, POWER GENERATION & TECHNICAL MANAGEMENT. *Current Pos:* RETIRED. *Personal Data:* b Pittsburgh, Pa, Apr 15, 19; c 4. *Educ:* Duke Univ, BSEE, 41. *Honors & Awards:* Tesla Award & Centennial Award, Inst Elec & Electronics Engrs. *Prof Exp:* Mem staff, Gen Elec Co, 41-74, mgr TB-Generator Eng, 62-74, gen mgr, Elec Utility Syst Eng Dept, Energy Syst/Technol Div, 74-80, mgr turbine technol assessment oper, Turbine Bus Group, 80-83. *Concurrent Pos:* Consult, elec eng, power generation systs & tech mgt, 83- *Mem:* Nat Acad Eng; fel Inst Elec & Electronics Engrs. *Mailing Add:* 5603 Pipers Waite Sarasota FL 34235

HOLLEY, DANIEL CHARLES, BIOLOGICAL SCIENCE. *Current Pos:* staff mem, 78-86, PROF, DEPT BIOL SCI, SAN JOSE STATE UNIV, 86- *Personal Data:* b San Jose, Calif, Aug 1, 49. *Educ:* Cabrillo Col, AS, 69; Univ Calif, Davis, BS, 71, MS, 73, PhD(physiol), 76. *Prof Exp:* Staff res assoc I, Dept Surg, Sch Med, Univ Calif, Davis, 69-73, teaching asst, Dept Animal Physiol, 73-74, res & teaching asst, Dept Animal Sci, 71-76; instr physiol, Dept Physiol, La State Univ Med Sch, 76-78. *Concurrent Pos:* Consult, NIH; grants, San Jose State Univ, 80-82, NASA, 81-82, 82-86 & 82-85, NIH, 83-87; mem, People to People Aerospace Deleg, Peoples Repub China, 87. *Mem:* Sigma Xi; Fedn Am Soc Exp Biol; AAAS; Aerospace Med Asn; Am Asn Univ

Prof; Am Inst Biol Sci. *Res:* Chronobiology, particularly physiological circadian rhythms; role of light as it relates to the circadian system; control of carbohydrate metabolism (endocrine aspects especially insulin); environmental physiology; space biology; numerous technical publications. *Mailing Add:* Dept Biol Sci San Jose State Univ San Jose CA 95912-0100

HOLLEY, EDWARD R, CIVIL ENGINEERING. *Current Pos:* MEM FAC, UNIV TEX, AUSTIN, 79-, STANLEY P FINCH CENTENNIAL PROF ENG. *Educ:* Ga Inst Technol, BSCE, MSCE, 60; Mass Inst Technol, ScD, 65. *Concurrent Pos:* Staff mem, Bur Reclamation, Denver, Delft Hydraul Lab, Neth & Univ Queensland, Australia; hydrologist, Geol Surv, 74- *Mem:* Am Geol Union; Int Asn Hydraul Res. *Res:* Environmental fluid mechanics; transport of pollutants in surface and groundwaters; outfalls and difussers; thermal discharges; deepwell disposal. *Mailing Add:* 8902 Rockcrest Dr Austin TX 78759

HOLLEY, FRIEDA KOSTER, MATHEMATICS. *Current Pos:* from asst prof to assoc prof, 75-83, PROF MATH, METROP STATE COL, DENVER, 83-, DIR PROG EVAL, 88- *Personal Data:* b Albuquerque, NMex, Mar 12, 44; m 67, Richard. *Educ:* Colo Col, BA, 65; Univ NMex, MA, 67, PhD(math), 70. *Prof Exp:* Lectr math, Ithaca Col, 68-69; asst prof, Col Notre Dame, 69-71; lectr asst prof level, Douglass Col, Rutgers Univ, 71-74. *Mem:* Math Asn Am; Am Math Soc; Asn Women Math; AAAS; Sigma Xi. *Res:* Topology, lattices. *Mailing Add:* 830 Columbia Pl Boulder CO 80303-3210. *Fax:* 303-556-4558; *E-Mail:* Holley@zeno.mscd.colorado.edu

HOLLEY, HOWARD LAMAR, medicine; deceased, see previous edition for last biography

HOLLEY, RICHARD ANDREW, MATHEMATICS. *Current Pos:* PROF MATH, UNIV COLO, BOULDER, 74- *Personal Data:* b Champaign, Ill, Sept 15, 43; m 67. *Educ:* Univ NMex, BS, 65, MA, 66; Cornell Univ, PhD(math), 69. *Prof Exp:* Instr math, Cornell Univ, 69; Miller Inst fel, Univ Calif, Berkeley, 69-71; asst prof, Princeton Univ, 71-74. *Concurrent Pos:* Sloan Found fel, 75- *Mem:* Am Math Soc. *Res:* Infinite particle systems; random fields. *Mailing Add:* Dept Math Univ Colo Box 395 Boulder CO 80309-0395

HOLLEY, RICHARD HOWARD, CHEMICAL ENGINEERING, POLYMER SCIENCE. *Current Pos:* res engr, Textiles, Deering Milliken Res Corp, Deering Milliken, Inc, Spartanburg, 74-77, dept head, 77-80, PLANT & BUS TECH MGR, DEERING MILLIKEN CO, 80- *Personal Data:* b Washington, DC, Nov 24, 43; m 66; c 3. *Educ:* NC State Univ, BS, 65, PhD(chem eng), 69. *Prof Exp:* Ciba fel & res assoc, Swiss Fed Inst Technol, 69-70. *Mem:* Am Chem Soc; Am Inst Chem Engrs. *Res:* Polymer membrane technology and science; textile coating and dyeing technology. *Mailing Add:* 729 Camellia Dr La Grange GA 30240-1646

HOLLIBAUGH, WILLIAM CALVERT, petroleum products & lubricants; deceased, see previous edition for last biography

HOLLIDAY, CHARLES WALTER, EPITHELIAL TRANSPORT, INVERTEBRATE OSMOREGULATION. *Current Pos:* from asst prof to assoc prof, 82-95, PROF BIOL, LAFAYETTE COL, 95- *Personal Data:* b Alexandria, Va, Sept 19, 46; m 71, Patricia A Roseman. *Educ:* Marietta Col, BS, 68; Univ Ore, PhD(biol), 78. *Honors & Awards:* Jones Fac lectr, Lafayette Col, 87-88. *Prof Exp:* Marine sci technician, USCG, 69-73; assoc res scientist, Mt Desert Island Biol Lab, Salisbury Cove, Maine, 78-81; asst prof-in-residence, biol sci group, Univ Conn, 81-82. *Mem:* Soc Integrated Comp Biol; Sigma Xi; Crustacean Soc; Western Soc Naturalists. *Res:* Osmoregulatory ion transport in crustacean and other invertebrate groups; organic anion and cation excretion in crustacean kidney; salt and water balance; physiological ecology of cicada-killer wasps. *Mailing Add:* Dept Biol Lafayette Col Easton PA 18042-1778

HOLLIDAY, DALE VANCE, UNDERWATER ACOUSTICS, ACOUSTICAL OCEANOGRAPHY. *Current Pos:* Engr/scientist, Tracor Inc, 62-66, sr scientist, 67-72, dir, San Diego Lab, 72-84, dir ocean sci, 82-84, DIR RES, ANAL & APPL RES DIV, TRACOR APPL SCI, 84- *Personal Data:* b Ennis, Tex, May 29, 40; m 62, Mary E Freeman; c Kathryn A (Bento), Karen E (Lindquist) & Mary C (Carroll). *Educ:* Univ Tex, Austin, BS, 62, MA, 65; Univ Calif, San Diego, PhD(appl physics), 72. *Concurrent Pos:* Mem US deleg, Int Coun Explor Sea, 87- *Mem:* Fel Acoust Soc Am; Am Soc Limnol & Oceanog; Oceanog Soc. *Res:* Acoustical oceanography, including reverberation, ambient noise, propagation and signal processing; development of instrumentation to measure, study and monitor the marine ecosystem, including the assessment of oceanic plankton, nekton and marine mammals. *Mailing Add:* Tracor Inc 4669 Murphy Canyon Rd No 102 San Diego CA 92123. *Fax:* 619-268-9775; *E-Mail:* holliday@galileo.tracor.com

HOLLIDAY, DENNIS, FLUID DYNAMICS. *Current Pos:* RESEARCHER REMOTE OCEAN IMAGING PROG, LOGICON RDA, 71- *Educ:* Stanford Univ, BS, 57; Princeton Univ, PhD(theoret physics), 61. *Prof Exp:* Mem, Physics Dept, Rand Corp, 63-71. *Concurrent Pos:* NATO fel, Univ Lund, Sweden, 60-61. *Mem:* Sigma Xi. *Res:* Radar scattering theory; ocean remote sensing phenomenology, including the generation and detectability of wakes and the interaction of nonlinear water waves with internal waves; author of numerous publications. *Mailing Add:* Logicon RDA 6053 W Century Blvd Los Angeles CA 90045

HOLLIDAY, GEORGE HAYES, GENERAL ENVIRONMENTAL SCIENCES. *Current Pos:* ENVIRON ENGR, HOLLIDAY ENVIRON ENG SERV INC, 86- *Personal Data:* b Toledo, Ohio, Oct 26, 22; m 44, Doris Stelling; c Kathy, Karen & William. *Educ:* Univ Calif, BSME, 48; Univ Southern Calif, MSCE, 62, EME, 65; Univ Houston, PhD(civil eng), 70. *Prof Exp:* Mech engr drilling, Shell Oil Co, 48-52, sr mech engr prod, 53-57, asst chief engr prod, 57-65, environ engr, 71-85; res engr offshore, Shell Develop Co, 66-70. *Concurrent Pos:* Distinguished lectr, Soc Petrol Engrs, 80-81; comt man, Safety & Environ Comt, Soc Petrol Engrs, 88- & Govt Affairs Comt, Am Acad Environ Engrs, 89- *Mem:* Fel Am Soc Mech Engrs; Am Petrol Inst; Soc Petrol Engrs. *Res:* Offshore civil engineering research on fatigue of leg connections and fracture mechanics of leg connections; coauthor of one publication and author of one publication. *Mailing Add:* PO Box 2508 Bellaire TX 77402. *Fax:* 713-668-5184; *E-Mail:* ghh@sccsi.com

HOLLIDAY, MALCOLM A, PEDIATRICS. *Current Pos:* clin prof, 63-66, PROF PEDIAT & DIR, CHILDREN'S RENAL CTR, UNIV CALIF, SAN FRANCISCO, 66- *Personal Data:* b Staunton, Va, Jan 12, 24; m 46; c 5. *Educ:* Univ Va, BA, 43, MD, 46. *Prof Exp:* Intern pediat, Children's Hosp, Boston, 46-47; asst resident, Vanderbilt Univ Hosp, Nashville, Tenn, 47-48; resident, Children's Hosp, Boston, 48-49; res fel, Harvard Med Sch, 49-50; res fel, Med Sch, Yale Univ, 50-51; asst prof, Sch Med, Ind Univ, 51-56; from asst prof to assoc prof, Sch Med, Univ Pittsburgh, 56-63. *Concurrent Pos:* Physician-in-chief, Children's Hosp Med Ctr, Oakland, Calif, 63-66. *Mem:* Am Pediat Soc; Soc Pediat Res (vpres, 68); Am Acad Pediat; Am Soc Pediat Nephrology (pres, 74-75); Perinatal Res Soc. *Res:* Pediatric renal-electrolyte problem; nutrition in chronic renal disease; calorie balance and protein turnover; growth and kidney function; renal failure in children; problems in body fluids and osmolality. *Mailing Add:* Dept Pediat A-276 Univ Calif Children's Renal Ctr 12701 Sir Francis Drake Inverness CA 94937-0648. *Fax:* 415-669-1719

HOLLIDAY, VANCE TERRELL, SOIL-GEOMORPHOLOGY, GEOARCHEOLOGY. *Current Pos:* PROF GEOG, UNIV WIS MADISON, 86- *Personal Data:* b San Antonio, Tex, Sept 23, 50; m 86, Diane Young; c Cora M H. *Educ:* Univ Tex, Austin, BA, 72; Tex Tech Univ, MS, 77; Univ Colo, Boulder, PhD(geol), 82. *Prof Exp:* Asst prof geog & anthrop, Tex A&M Univ, 84-86. *Concurrent Pos:* Prin investr, NSF, 88-96; vis prof, Alaska Quaternary Ctr, Univ Alaska, Fairbanks, 94; mem, US Nat Comt, Int Union Quaternary Res, 97. *Mem:* Am Quaternary Asn (pres, 96-98); fel Geol Soc Am; Asn Am Geographers; AAAS; Sigma Xi; Soc Am Archeol. *Res:* Quaternary paleoenvironments, soil-geomorphology, soils and geomorphology in archeology and the peopling of the New World; quaternary landscape evolution, paleoenvironments and Paleoindian geoarcheology of the Great Plains. *Mailing Add:* Dept Geog Univ Wis 550 N Park St Madison WI 53706-1491

HOLLIEN, HARRY FRANCIS, PHONETIC SCIENCE, PSYCHOACOUSTICS. *Current Pos:* assoc prof commun sci, Univ Fla, 62-68, from assoc dir to dir, commun sci lab, 62-75, prof speech, 68-75, prof ling, 76, assoc dir ling, 89-91, DIR INST ADVAN STUDY COMMUN PROCESSES, UNIV FLA, 75-, PROF CRIMINAL JUSTICE, 79- *Personal Data:* b Brockton, Mass, July 16, 26; m 69, Patricia Ann Milanowksi; c Karen, Kevin, Keith, Brian, Stephanie & Christine. *Educ:* Boston Univ, BS, 49, MEd, 51; Univ Iowa, MA, 53, PhD(exp phonetics), 55. *Honors & Awards:* Manuel Garcia Int Award, Int Asn Logopedics & Phoniatrics, 71; Gould Int Res Prize, 78; Gutzmann Res Medal, Union Europ Phoniatrists & Int Asn Logopedics & Phoniatrics, 80; Kay Elemetrics Prize Res Phonetics, Int Soc Phonetic Sci, 87, Svend Smith Prize, 91; John R Hunt Award, Am Acad Forensic Sci, 88. *Prof Exp:* Dir, Speech & Hearing Prog, Baylor Univ, 55-58; asst prof logopedics, Univ Wichita, 58-62. *Concurrent Pos:* Guest prof, Paul Quinn Col, 56-58; fel, Northwestern Univ, 58; prin investr grants, NIH, 60-81, Univ Fla, 62-90, Off Naval Res, 65-74, Am Speech & Hearing Asn, 71, US Dept Com, 77-78, Voice Found, 78-80, Sea Grant, 79-83, Dreyfus Found, 80-, US Justice Dept, 89, Army Res Off, 81-84 & USN, 85-; co-dir grants, Rehab Serv Admin, 63-68 & 70-72, NIH, 64- & NSF, 74-77; mem, Commun Sci Study Sect, Div Res Grants, NIH, 63-67; pres, Hollien Assocs, 66-; res consult, Vet Admin Hosp, San Francisco, 67-93; mem, Nerv & Sensory Systs Res Eval Comt, Vet Admin, 69-74; vis scientist, Speech Transmission Lab, Royal Inst Technol, Sweden, 70; mem bd dirs, Div Sponsored Res, Univ Fla, 71-73 & 79-81; vis prof, Wroclaw Tech Univ, Poland, 74; chmn bd dirs, Wild Animal, 86-90; sr Fulbright prof, Univ Trier, Ger, 87. *Mem:* Fel AAAS; fel Acoust Soc Am; fel Int Soc Phonetic Sci (secy gen, 75-89, exec vpres, 83-89, pres, 89-); fel Am Speech & Hearing Asn; Marine Technol Soc; Am Asn Phonetic Sci (pres, 73-75); fel Am Acad Forensic Sci; Am Asn Underwater Sci; Japan Soc Phonetic Sci; Int Asn Forensic Phonetics; Sigma Xi. *Res:* Diver communication; voice science; laryngeal function; psychoacoustics; underwater communication; forensic communication; author of 221 major books, articles and 161 minor publications; granted 1 patent. *Mailing Add:* Inst Advan Study Commun Processes 50 Dauer Hall Univ Fla Gainesville FL 32611-2005. *Fax:* 904-392-6170; *E-Mail:* hollien@ufcc.ufl.edu

HOLLIMAN, DAN CLARK, VERTEBRATE ZOOLOGY. *Current Pos:* From asst prof to assoc prof, 62-71, PROF BIOL, BIRMINGHAM-SOUTHERN COL, 71- *Personal Data:* b Birmingham, Ala, Aug 25, 32; m 58; c 1. *Educ:* Univ Ala, BS, 57, MS, 59, PhD(zool), 63. *Res:* Taxonomy of mammals of the southeastern United States; ornithology in Alabama. *Mailing Add:* Dept Biol Birmingham-Southern Col Birmingham AL 35204

HOLLIMAN, RHODES BURNS, PARASITOLOGY. *Current Pos:* assoc prof, 62-71, PROF ZOOL, VA POLYTECH INST & STATE UNIV, 71- *Personal Data:* b Birmingham, Ala, Feb 28, 28; m 50; c 2. *Educ:* Howard Col, BS, 50; Univ Miami, MS, 53; Fla State Univ, PhD(zool), 60. *Prof Exp:* Asst invert anat, Univ Miami, 51-53; res assoc microbiol, Med Col Ala, 55-56; asst gen biol, Fla State Univ, 56-57, asst schistosomiasis, 57-59; asst prof zool, Jacksonville Univ, 60-61; instr gen biol, Fla State Univ, 61-62. *Concurrent Pos:* Fel trop med, La State Univ Med Sch, 73. *Mem:* Am Soc Parasitol; Am Soc Trop Med & Hyg; Paleopath Soc. *Res:* Infectious and parasitic diseases in tropical Americas; epidemiology of trichinosis; medical protozoology and medical helminthology. *Mailing Add:* 101 Howell St Dublin VA 24084-2210

HOLLING, CRAWFORD STANLEY, ZOOLOGY. *Current Pos:* PROF ZOOL & EMER SCHOLAR ECOL SCI, UNIV FLA, 88- *Personal Data:* b Theresa, NY, Dec 6, 30; Can citizen; m 53, 78. *Educ:* Univ Toronto, BA, 52, MA, 54; Univ BC, PhD, 57. *Prof Exp:* Agr res officer predation, Forest Biol Div, Res Br, Can Dept Agr, 52-67; dir, Inst Resource Ecol, Inst Fisheries, Univ BC, 69-73, prof zool, 67-88. *Concurrent Pos:* Dir, Inst Appl Systs Anal, Laxenburg, Austria, 81-84; mem bd, Int Statist Ecol Prog. *Mem:* Ecol Soc Am; Entom Soc Can; Can Soc Zool; fel Royal Soc Can; Brit Ecol Soc; Japanese Ecol Soc; fel AAAS. *Res:* Systems ecology; population dynamics; policy analysis. *Mailing Add:* Zool Dept 223 Bartram Hall Univ Fla Gainesville FL 32611-2009. *Fax:* 904-392-3704, 375-2362

HOLLING, HERBERT EDWARD, medicine, for more information see previous edition

HOLLINGDALE, MICHAEL RICHARD, vaccine development, epidemiology, for more information see previous edition

HOLLINGER, F(REDERICK) BLAINE, HEPATOLOGY, AIDS. *Current Pos:* NIH spec fel, 68-70, from asst prof to assoc prof, 70-78, PROF VIROL & EPIDEMIOL, BAYLOR COL MED, 78-, PROF MED, 81- *Personal Data:* b Hays, Kans, June 22, 35; m 78; c 4. *Educ:* Univ Kans, BA, 57, MD, 62. *Prof Exp:* Asst chief, Arbovirus Infection Unit, Ctr Dis Control, USPHS, Ga, 67-68. *Concurrent Pos:* Adv & consult prog projs, grants & contracts related to hepatitis & AIDS res, Nat Heart & Lung Inst, Nat Inst Allergy & Infectious Dis & Bur Biologics, Food & Drug Admin, 72-; consult ed, J Immunol, Gastro, Hepatology, New Eng J Med, Ann Internal Med, Intervirol & JAMA, 72-; consult, Expert Group Viral Hepatitis, Nat Libr Med, NIH, 78-84; Am Asn Blood Banks Transfusion Transmitted Dis Comt, 85-; comn, Health Task Force AIDS, State of Tex, 86-; assoc ed, J Inf Dis, 87-88; assoc ed, Hepatitis Knowledge-Base Proj, Mass Med Soc, 87-90; chmn, Int Symp Viral Hepatitis & Liver Dis, 87-90. *Mem:* Am Gastroenterol Asn; fel Infectious Dis Soc; Am Asn Study Liver Dis; Int Asn Study Liver Dis. *Res:* Characterization of hepatitis agents; develop of sensitive assays for hepatitis; prophylaxis of hepatitis; vaccine development; immunopathogenesis of viral hepatitis; epidemiol of hepatitis; AIDS research, virology quality assurance programs, isolation of agent, immunodiagnosis, immunopathogenesis and virology endpoints of therapy. *Mailing Add:* 6550 Fannin St No 1101 Houston TX 77030

HOLLINGER, HENRY BOUGHTON, PHYSICAL CHEMISTRY. *Current Pos:* asst prof, 61-64, assoc prof, 64-80, PROF PHYS CHEM, RENSSELAER POLYTECH INST, 80- *Personal Data:* b Jacksonville, Fla, Feb 20, 33; m; c 3. *Educ:* Lebanon Valley Col, BS, 55; Univ Wis, PhD, 60. *Prof Exp:* Mem staff, Lebanon Valley Col, 59-61. *Mem:* Am Chem Soc; Am Phys Soc; Sigma Xi. *Res:* Kinetic theory of dense gases; nonequilibrium mechanics. *Mailing Add:* Dept Chem Rensselaer Polytech Inst 110 Eighth St Troy NY 12180-3522

HOLLINGER, JAMES PIPPERT, REMOTE SENSING, PHYSICS. *Current Pos:* RETIRED. *Personal Data:* b Elyria, Ohio, Oct 1, 33; m 60; c 2. *Educ:* NMex Inst Mining & Technol, BS, 56; Univ Va, MS, 58, PhD(physics), 61. *Prof Exp:* Asst prof physics, George Washington Univ, 61-62; res physicist, US Naval Res Lab, 63-93. *Mem:* Int Sci Radio Union. *Res:* Polarization of the radio wavelength radiation from discrete cosmic sources; remote microwave sensing of the earth's surface; millimeter wave passive imaging systems. *Mailing Add:* 795 Skinner Turn Rd Owings MD 20736

HOLLINGER, MANNFRED ALAN, PHARMACOLOGY. *Current Pos:* from asst prof to assoc prof, 69-86, PROF PHARMACOL, SCH MED, UNIV CALIF, DAVIS, 86- *Personal Data:* b Chicago, Ill, June 28, 39; m 61; c 2. *Educ:* NPark Col, BS, 61; Loyola Univ Chicago, MS, 65, PhD(pharmacol), 67. *Prof Exp:* Res pharmacologist, B Baxter Labs, 61-63; instr pharmacol, Med Sch, Stanford Univ, 67-69. *Concurrent Pos:* Fogarty Sr Int Fel, NIH, Burroughs-Wellcome Int Fel. *Mem:* Am Soc Pharmacol & Exp Therapeut; Soc Toxicol. *Res:* Reproductive biology; biochemistry of spermatogenesis; factors influencing gamete formation; drug-receptor interaction; pharmacology of fibrosis and pulmonary pharmacology and toxicology. *Mailing Add:* Dept Med Pharmacol & Toxicol Sch Med MSI Univ Calif Davis CA 95616-5224. *Fax:* 530-752-7710

HOLLINGER, THOMAS GARBER, REPRODUCTIVE BIOLOGY, DEVELOPMENTAL BIOLOGY. *Current Pos:* asst prof, 78-81, ASSOC PROF ANAT, COL MED, UNIV FLA, 81- *Personal Data:* b Chicago, Ill, Oct 23, 42; m 65, Sandra Hill; c Amanda, Randall & Amy. *Educ:* Northwestern Univ, BS, 66; Northern Ill Univ, MS, 69; Purdue Univ, PhD(zool), 74. *Prof Exp:* Investr biol, Oak Ridge Nat Labs, 74-76. *Mem:* Am Asn Anat; Soc Develop Biol; Am Soc Cell Biol; Am Ageing Asn; AAAS. *Res:* Yolk proteins in teleost fish oocytes; biological basis of meiosis and the initiation of cell division. *Mailing Add:* Dept Anat & Cell Biol Box 100235 JHMHSC Univ Fla Col Med Gainesville FL 32610-0235. *Fax:* 904-392-3305

HOLLINGSWORTH, CHARLES ALVIN, PHYSICAL CHEMISTRY. *Current Pos:* from instr to prof, 48-82, EMER PROF CHEM, UNIV PITTSBURGH, 82- *Personal Data:* b Earl, Colo, June 22, 17; m 44; c 3. *Educ:* Western State Col Colo, BA, 41; Univ Iowa, PhD(phys chem), 46. *Prof Exp:* Res chemist, E I du Pont de Nemours & Co, 46-48. *Mem:* Am Chem Soc. *Res:* Mathematical theoretical; rate processes; colloids; thermodynamics. *Mailing Add:* Dept Chem Univ Pittsburgh Pittsburgh PA 15260

HOLLINGSWORTH, CHARLES GLENN, EPIDEMIOLOGY, BIOSTATISTICS. *Current Pos:* CLIN APPLNS PROG DIABETES, NAT INST ARTHRITIS, METAB & DIGESTIVE DIS, NIH, 79- *Personal Data:* b Erie, Pa, Aug 7, 46; m 70; c 2. *Educ:* Univ Pittsburgh, BS, 69, MSH, 70; Univ Mich, DrPH, 74. *Prof Exp:* Res asst asbestosis, Grad Sch Pub Health, Univ Pittsburgh, 70-71, biostatistician clin trials, Abbott Labs, 70-72; epidemiologist, Heart Dis & Clin Trial, Sch Med, Univ Minn, 74-76; asst prof epidemiol, Sch Pub Health, Univ Mass, 76-78. *Concurrent Pos:* Biomed res grant prostatic cancer, Sch Pub Health, Univ Mass, 78-79. *Mem:* Soc Epidemiol Res; Soc Clin Trials; Am Col Epidemiol. *Res:* Major chronic diseases; epidemiology of heart disease diabetes; clinical trials in heart disease diabetes and new pharmaceuticals. *Mailing Add:* 535 Chestertown St Gaithersburg MD 20878

HOLLINGSWORTH, CORNELIA ANN, MEAT SCIENCE, PROTEIN CHEMISTRY. *Current Pos:* MGR PROD DEVELOP, BIL MAR FOODS-SARA LEE CORP, 88- *Personal Data:* b Carrollton, Ga, Mar 6, 57. *Educ:* Auburn Univ, BS, 79; Univ Nebr-Lincoln, MS, 81, PhD(animal sci), 84. *Prof Exp:* Res scientist, Armour Food Co-Con Agra, 84-88. *Concurrent Pos:* Res & teaching asst, Univ Nebr-Lincoln, 79-84; chmn, Meat Indust Res Conf, 90-91; qual facilitator, Bil Mar Foods, 90-; mem, Nutrit Labeling Adv Comt, Am Meat Inst, USDA, 91-93. *Mem:* Inst Food Technologists; Am Meat Sci Asn. *Res:* Development of new products for a major meat processing company through application of chemistry, microbiology, sensory and textural evaluation. *Mailing Add:* 64 Highpoint Dr Berwyn PA 19312

HOLLINGSWORTH, DAVID S, CHEMICAL ENGINEERING. *Current Pos:* RETIRED. *Educ:* Lehigh Univ, BS, 48. *Honors & Awards:* Nat Medal of Technol, 91. *Prof Exp:* Chem engr, Res Ctr, Hercules Inc, Wilmington, Del, 48-49, Kalamazoo, Mich, 49-53, tech rep sales, New Orleans, La & Wilmington, Del, 53-61, asst sales mgr paper chem, 61-63, sales mgr specialty chem, 63-65, mgr specialty paper chem, 65-67, dir sales paper chem, Pine & Paper Chem Dept, 67-72, dir mkt, 72, asst gen mgr, 72-74, gen mgr, New Enterprise Dept, 74-75, gen mgr, Food & Fragrance Develop Dept, 75-78, dir organics, Worldwide Bus Ctr, 78-79, vpres planning, 79-82, group vpres water-soluble polymers, 82-83, group vpres polypropylene, 83, div vpres mkt, 83-84, pres, Specialty Chem Co, 84-86, mem bd dirs, Hercules Inc, 82-90, vchmn, 86-90, chief exec officer, 87-90. *Concurrent Pos:* Mem bd dirs, Orbital Sci Corp II, Oryx Energy Co, Econ Strategy Inst & Chem Mfrs Asn; mem adv bd, Beckman Ctr History Chem; mem, Vis Comt Chem Eng, Lehigh Univ. *Mem:* Am Inst Chem Engrs; distinguished mem Am Soc Metals Int. *Res:* Marketing of specialty chemicals. *Mailing Add:* 21700 Atlantic Blvd Dulles VA 20166-6801

HOLLINGSWORTH, JACK W, MATHEMATICS. *Current Pos:* dir, Sch Comput Sci & Technol, Rochester Inst Technol,80-82, prof comput sci, 79-86, prof 86-96, EMER PROF MATH, ROCHESTER INST TECHNOL, 96- *Personal Data:* b South Haven, Kans, Mar 3, 24; m 50, Nancy Harris; c Joel, Priscilla & Seth (deceased). *Educ:* Univ Kans, BS, 48, AB, 49; Univ Wis, MS, 51, PhD(math), 54. *Prof Exp:* Asst, Univ Kans, 48-49 & Univ Wis, 49-54; mathematician, Gen Elec Co, 54-57; assoc prof math, Rensselaer Polytech Inst, 57-61, supvr comput lab, 57-70, chmn interdisciplinary comt comput sci, 68-73, prof math, 61-79. *Mem:* Am Math Soc; Soc Indust & Appl Math; Math Asn Am; Asn Comput Mach. *Res:* Numerical analysis; computing. *Mailing Add:* 55 Crestview Dr Pittsford NY 14534

HOLLINGSWORTH, JAMES W, internal medicine, for more information see previous edition

HOLLINGSWORTH, JOHN GRESSETT, MATHEMATICS. *Current Pos:* asst prof to assoc prof, 67-81, PROF MATH, UNIV GA, 81- *Personal Data:* b Decatur, Miss, July 15, 38; m 60; c 2. *Educ:* Miss State Univ, BA, 59, MS, 61; Rice Univ, PhD(math), 67. *Prof Exp:* Assoc mathematician, Texaco Inc, 61-64; instr math, Rice Univ, 66-67. *Mem:* Am Math Soc. *Res:* Geometric topology; topology of manifolds. *Mailing Add:* Dept Math Univ Ga Athens GA 30602-7403

HOLLINGSWORTH, JOSEPH PETTUS, INSECT TRAP DESIGN & OPERATION. *Current Pos:* RETIRED. *Personal Data:* b Mertens, Tex, Aug 20, 22; m 63, Peggy L Wilsford; c Philip J. *Educ:* Tex A&M Univ, BS, 43, MS, 61. *Prof Exp:* Res asst, Tex A&M Univ, 46-48; proj leader, Agr Res Serv, USDA, 48-78. *Concurrent Pos:* Owner/operator, TV Sales & Serv Bus, 79-83; consult, Entom Consult Group, 84-88. *Mem:* Am Soc Agr Engrs; Entom Soc Am. *Res:* Measuring effects of near-ultraviolet and visible electromagnetic stimuli on phototactic responses of insects; developing equipment for using proven attractants in traps for survey and control applications. *Mailing Add:* 2204 Sharon Dr Bryan TX 77802-2438

HOLLINGSWORTH, RALPH GEORGE, USER INTERFACE DESIGN, SOFTWARE ENGINEERING. *Current Pos:* ASSOC PROF COMPUT SCI & CHMN DEPT, MUSKINGUM COL, 81- *Personal Data:* b Wheeling, WVa, Mar 4, 47; m 66; c 2. *Educ:* Univ Cincinnati, BSChE, 70; Univ Mich, MS, 71, PhD(bioeng), 74. *Prof Exp:* NSF Fel, Univ Mich, 74-75; asst prof physiol, Med Univ SC, 75-78; sr systs analyst, NCR, 78-81. *Concurrent Pos:* Consult analyst, SDRC, 84. *Mem:* Inst Elec & Electronics Engrs; Sigma Xi; Math Asn Am; Asn Comput Mach. *Res:* The application of expert system technology to the design of user interfaces, including the use of sound, color, N-dimensionality and cognitive style matching; applications neural networks. *Mailing Add:* Crows Nest 76147 Peoli Rd Port Washington OH 43837

HOLLINGWORTH, ROBERT MICHAEL, TOXICOLOGY, PESTICIDE CHEMISTRY & FOOD SAFETY. *Current Pos:* DIR, PESTICIDE RES CTR & PROF ENTOM & ZOOL, MICH STATE UNIV, 87-, DIR, NAT FOOD SAFETY & TOXICOL CTR, 94- *Personal Data:* b Yorkshire, Eng, Oct 4, 39; m 61; c 2. *Educ:* Univ Reading, BSc, 62; Univ Calif, Riverside, PhD(insect toxicol), 66. *Prof Exp:* From asst prof to prof insect toxicol, Purdue Univ, West Lafayette, 66-87. *Concurrent Pos:* Vis prof, Stauffer Chem Co, 74-75; mem, Toxicol Study Sect, NIH, 76-80; Environ Protection Agency sci adv panel, Fifra, 82-84; chmn, Div Pesticide Chem, Am Chem Soc, 84. *Mem:* AAAS; fel Am Chem Soc; Soc Toxicol; Soc Risk Anal; Am Coun Sci Health. *Res:* Metabolism and mode of action of insecticides and related chemicals; selective toxicity, neurotoxicology, comparative neuropharmacology; pesticide resistance. *Mailing Add:* 124 E Sherwood Rd Williamston MI 48895

HOLLINS, ROBERT EDWARD, ENZYME KINETICS, INSTRUMENTAL TECHNIQUES. *Current Pos:* ASSOC PROF CHEM, CHICAGO STATE UNIV, 77- *Personal Data:* b Chicago, Ill, Oct 19, 40. *Educ:* Roosevelt Univ, BS, 64; Northwestern Univ, PhD(phys chem), 70. *Prof Exp:* Sr res chemist, Sherwin-Williams Co, 69-72; asst prof chem, Roosevelt Univ, 72-77. *Mem:* Am Chem Soc; Am Asn Black Prof; Nat Orgn Black Chemists. *Res:* Observing the effects of lead and trace metals on the biochemical parameters in rats, specifically how they affect the metalloenzymes; instrumental analytical techniques as applied to the superoxide dismutase and the cytochrome oxioase enzymes. *Mailing Add:* Dept Chem Chicago State Univ 95th St at King Dr Chicago IL 60628-1598

HOLLINSHEAD, ARIEL CAHILL, PHARMACOLOGY, VIROLOGY. *Current Pos:* Res fel pharmacol, Med Sch, George Washington Univ, 57-58 & 59, asst prof pharmacol, 59-61, from asst prof to assoc prof med, 61-73, dir, Lab Virus & Cancer Res, 64-89, EMER PROF MED, MED SCH, GEORGE WASHINGTON UNIV, 74- *Personal Data:* b Allentown, Pa, Aug 24, 29; m 58, Montgomery Hyun; c William & Christopher. *Educ:* Ohio Univ, AB, 51; George Washington Univ, MA, 55, PhD(pharmacol), 57. *Hon Degrees:* DSc, Ohio Univ, 77. *Honors & Awards:* Star of Europe Medal, 80; Distinguished Scientist Award, Soc Exp Biol & Med, 85, Emer distinguished Scientist Award, 96. *Concurrent Pos:* Res fel virol & assoc prof, Col Med, Baylor Univ, 58-59; hon consult, Beijing Thoracic Tumor Res Inst, 92- *Mem:* Soc Exp Biol & Med; Am Soc Clin Oncol; Am Asn Cancer Res; Int Agency Res Cancer; NY Acad Sci; Int Lung Cancer Asn; AAAS; Am Med Writers Asn. *Res:* Chemotherapy of animal virus diseases and cancer; nucleoprotein chemistry of viruses; cancer immunogenetics; oncology; cancer immunochemotherapy and immunoprophylaxis; environmental carcinogens; first isolation, purification and identification of animal and human tumor-associated antigens; human-human hybridoma research, and development of epitopes for study and use in human cancers; development of new forms of combination immunochemotheraph for HIV/AIDS. *Mailing Add:* Pres HT Virus & Cancer Res Inc 3637 Van Ness St NW Washington DC 20008

HOLLINSHEAD, MAY B, ANATOMY, EMBRYOLOGY. *Current Pos:* RETIRED. *Personal Data:* b New York, NY, Nov 28, 13; m 42, Merrill Taylor; c Richard C. *Educ:* Hunter Col, AB, 36; Columbia Univ, PhD, 51. *Prof Exp:* Asst anat, Col Physicians & Surgeons, Columbia Univ, 49-51; instr, Col Med, NY Univ, 51-56; from asst prof to prof anat, Col Med & Dent NJ, Newark, 56-89. *Mem:* Am Asn Anat; AAAS; Sigma Xi. *Res:* Embryology; histochemistry of skeletal muscle; development of teeth and periodontal tissues in osteopetrotic mouse; effect of ascorbic acid on burns, frostbite and barbiturates; effect of aqueous humor on blood coaqulation. *Mailing Add:* 2 Winthrop Pl Leonia NJ 07605

HOLLIS, BRUCE WARREN, METHODS DEVELOPMENT, CHROMATOGRAPHY METHODOLOGY. *Current Pos:* assoc prof pediat 86-94, assoc prof biochem & molecular biol, 89-94, PROF PEDIAT & PROF BIOCHEM & MOLECULAR BIOL, MED UNIV SC, 94- *Personal Data:* b Elyria, Ohio, May 29, 51; m 80, Betsy Eberle; c Ian, Sam, Sarah & Stephen. *Educ:* Ohio State Univ, BSc, 73, MSc, 76; Univ Guelph, PhD(exp nutrit), 79. *Honors & Awards:* Mead Johnson Award, Am Inst Nutrit, 91; Mitchell Rubin Res Award, Med Univ SC, 91. *Prof Exp:* Teaching fel med, Case Western Res Univ, 79-82, asst prof nutrit, 82-86. *Concurrent Pos:* Nat Res Serv Award, NIH, 80-82, Res Career Develop Award, 82-; acad consult, INSTAR Corp, 82- & Teltech Resource Network, 85- *Mem:* Endocrine Soc; Am Soc Bone & Mineral Res; Am Inst Nutrit; NY Acad Sci; Sigma Xi. *Res:* Nutrient requirements of premature infants; development of new hormone analysis. *Mailing Add:* Dept Pediat Med Univ SC 171 Ashley Ave Charleston SC 29425. *Fax:* 803-792-9223; *E-Mail:* hollisb@musc.edu

HOLLIS, CECIL GEORGE, MYCOLOGY. *Current Pos:* RETIRED. *Personal Data:* b Eden, Ala, Nov 6, 24; c 3. *Educ:* Univ Ala, PhD(bot), 54. *Prof Exp:* Asst biol, Univ Ala, 50-51; asst prof, Furman Univ, 51-52; jr res assoc plant physiol, Univ Ala, 52-53; prof biol, Ark Col, 54-57; microbiologist, Buckman Labs, Inc, Tenn, 57-70; prof biol, Memphis State Univ, 70-83; vpres res & develop, Buckman Labs, 83-97. *Mem:* Mycol Soc Am; Am Soc Microbiol; Sigma Xi; Soc Indust Microbiol (pres, 88-89). *Res:* Taxonomy and physiology of fungi; industrial microbiology; biocides. *Mailing Add:* 1767 Poplar Estates Pkwy Germantown TN 38138

HOLLIS, DANIEL LESTER, JR, NUCLEAR ENGINEERING. *Current Pos:* RETIRED. *Personal Data:* b Mexico City, Mex, Mar 7, 24; US citizen; m 56; c 2. *Educ:* US Naval Acad, BS, 46; Univ Ala, MS, 58, MA, 59; Tex A&M Univ, PhD(nuclear eng), 67. *Prof Exp:* Instr, Univ Ala, Tuscaloosa, 59-61, asst prof, 61-62, from asst prof to prof elec & nuclear eng, 65-89. *Mem:* Am Nuclear Soc; Am Soc Eng Educ; Sigma Xi; Inst Elec & Electronics Engrs. *Res:* Plasma-thermonuclear engineering; hydromagnetic models of magnetically confined plasmas; bremsstrahlung and space shielding; neutron activation and prompt gamma analyses. *Mailing Add:* 10852 Mallard Lake Lane Cottondale AL 35453-6762

HOLLIS, GILBERT RAY, ANIMAL NUTRITION, SWINE. *Current Pos:* PROF & EXTEN SWINE SPECIALIST, UNIV ILL, URBANA, 77- *Personal Data:* b Poplar Bluff, Mo, Nov 26, 39; m 61; c 3. *Educ:* Univ Ark, BSA, 61, MS, 63; Purdue Univ, PhD(animal nutrit), 66. *Prof Exp:* Asst animal nutritionist, Univ Fla, 66-70; area swine specialist, Tex Agr Exten Serv, 70-77. *Mem:* Am Soc Animal Sci. *Res:* Swine nutrition and management. *Mailing Add:* 1623 Broadmoor Dr Champaign IL 61821-5931

HOLLIS, J(OHN) SEARCY, electrical engineering; deceased, see previous edition for last biography

HOLLIS, JAN MICHAEL, RADIO ASTRONOMY, COMPUTER SCIENCE. *Current Pos:* astronr, 79-82, head sci opers br, 82-88, ASST CHIEF, SPACE DATA & COMPUT DIV, NASA GODDARD SPACE FLIGHT CTR, 88- *Personal Data:* b Martinsburg, WVa, June 5, 41; m, Joan Ellen Grunow; c David & Morgan. *Educ:* Duke Univ, AB, 63; Univ Va, MA, 72, PhD(astron), 76. *Honors & Awards:* Except Sci Achievement Medal, NASA, 90. *Prof Exp:* Comput systs analyst astron, Nat Radio Astron Observ, 73-79. *Mem:* Am Astron Soc; Int Astron Union; Royal Astron Soc. *Res:* Radio astronomy as it pertains to the physical conditions and chemical composition of the interstellar medium, comets and stars. *Mailing Add:* Code 930 NASA Goddard Space Flight Ctr Greenbelt MD 20771. *Fax:* 301-286-1777; *E-Mail:* jan.m.hollis@gsfc.nasa.gov

HOLLIS, MARK DEXTER, ENGINEERING, ENVIRONMENTAL SCIENCES. *Current Pos:* CONSULT, ENVIRON ENG, 81- *Personal Data:* b Buena Vista, Ga, Sept 24, 08; m 27; c 2. *Educ:* Univ Ga, BSCE, 31, CE, 37. *Hon Degrees:* DSc, Univ Fla, 56. *Honors & Awards:* Arthur Bedell Award & Charles A Emerson Medal, Water Pollution Control Fedn, 64; Distinguished Serv Medal, USPHS. *Prof Exp:* Officer, USPHS, 31-47, asst surgeon gen, 47-61; dir environ health, UN World Health, Geneva, Switz, 61-73; vchmn, Fla State Environ Regulation Comn, 74-81. *Concurrent Pos:* Mem, Interstate Comn, Potomac River Basin, 50-61; chmn, Bd Nat Sanit Found, 52-60; mem, Interstate Compact Comn, Ohio River Basin, 54-58. *Mem:* Nat Acad Eng; Am Acad Environ Engrs; Am Soc Civil Engrs; Water Pollution Control Fedn (pres, 59-60). *Res:* Tropical diseases, especially malaria and typhus; pollution control, particularly air, water and land. *Mailing Add:* Carpenters Home Estates 1001 Carpenters Way No 1-520 Lakeland FL 33809

HOLLIS, THEODORE M, PHYSIOLOGY. *Current Pos:* DEAN, SCH GRAD STUDIES, ST GEORGES UNIV, GRENADA. *Personal Data:* b Palo Alto, Calif, Dec 22, 39; m 63; c 3. *Educ:* San Jose State Col, BA, 63; Ohio State Univ, MS, 67, PhD(physiol), 69. *Prof Exp:* Instr biol, Ohio Northern Univ, 66-69; from asst prof to assoc prof biol, Pa State Univ, 69-84, prof physiol, 84-94, emer prof, 94- *Mem:* AAAS; Am Physiol Soc; Soc Exp Biol; Am Diabetic Asn; Asn Res in Vision & Ophthal. *Res:* Arterial metabolic changes associated with experimental atherogenesis, hypertension and diabetes; hemodynamics; vascular histamine. *Mailing Add:* St Georges Univ Ctr St Georges Grenada

HOLLIS, WALTER JESSE, internal medicine, cardiology, for more information see previous edition

HOLLIS, WALTER WINSLOW, OPTICAL ENGINEERING. *Current Pos:* Sci Adv, Combat Develop Exp Command, 68-73, Oper Test & Eval Agency, 73-80, DEP UNDER SECY OPERS RES, DEPT DEFENSE, US ARMY, 80- *Personal Data:* b Braintree, Mass, Nov 13, 26; wid; c Nancy A, Jeffrey L, David M & Susan J. *Educ:* Northeastern Univ, BA, 49; George Washington Univ, MS, 73. *Honors & Awards:* Presidential Distinguished Exec Award, Allen R Matthews Award, Int Test & Eval Asn, 92. *Prof Exp:* Optical designer & engr fire control syst eng, Frankford Arsenal, 51-65, chief, Combat Vehicle & Gen Instruments Fire Control Lab, 65-68. *Mailing Add:* Dep Under Secy of Army Ops Res Rm 2E660 The Pentagon Washington DC 20310

HOLLIS, WILLIAM FREDERICK, EXPERT SYSTEMS, COMPUTER BASED INFORMATION STORAGE & RETRIEVAL. *Current Pos:* sr info specialist, 84, actg head, 85, HEAD INFO CTR POLYMER SCI, GENCORP RES, 86- *Personal Data:* b Cleveland, Ohio, May 25, 54; m 77, Jo Anne Kohlenberg; c George & Dawn. *Educ:* Bowling Green State Univ, BS, 76; Kent State Univ, MLS, 79, EDS(instrnl technol), 92. *Prof Exp:* Info specialist polymer sci, B F Goodrich Res & Develop Ctr, 79-82; instr libr & info sci, Col Wooster, 82-84. *Concurrent Pos:* Instr, Stark Tech Col, 83-84. *Mem:* Am Chem Soc; Am Inst Physics; Am Soc Info Sci; Asn Educ Commun & Technol. *Res:* Information science, especially as it relates to the handling of science/technical information. *Mailing Add:* GenCorp Technol Ctr 2990 Gilchrist Rd Akron OH 44305

HOLLISTER, ALAN SCUDDER, CLINICAL PHARMACOLOGY, HYPERTENSION. *Current Pos:* ASSOC PROF MED, UNIV COLO, 90- *Personal Data:* b Baltimore, Md, Feb 28, 47; m 70; c 2. *Educ:* Swarthmore Col, BA, 70; Univ NC, PhD(pharmacol), 76, MD, 77. *Prof Exp:* Intern & resident internal med, Univ Fla, 77-80; fel clin pharmacol, Vanderbilt Univ, 80-83, asst prof med, 83-90. *Concurrent Pos:* Clin assoc physician, Clin Res Ctr, Vanderbilt Univ, 83-85. *Mem:* Am Fedn Clin Res; Am Soc Pharmacol & Exp Therapeut; Am Heart Asn; Am Col Physicians; AAAS; Soc Neurosci. *Res:* Clinical pharmacology and pharmacological interactions in the control of blood pressure; adrenergic receptor mechanisms; atrial natriuretic factor; evaluation and treatment of hypertension and hypotension; autonomic pharmacology. *Mailing Add:* Div Clin Pharmacol Univ Colo Health Sci Ctr Denver CO 80262. *Fax:* 303-315-4334

HOLLISTER, CHARLES DAVIS, MARINE GEOLOGY, OCEANOGRAPHY. *Current Pos:* assoc scientist, 67-79, scientist & dean grad studies, 79-, VPRES, WOODS HOLE OCEANOG INST. *Personal Data:* b Santa Barbara, Calif, Mar 18, 36. *Educ:* Ore State Univ, BS, 60; Columbia Univ, PhD(geol), 66. *Honors & Awards:* John Oliver La Gorce Medal, Nat Geog Soc. *Prof Exp:* Teaching asst geol, Ore State Univ, 60-61; oceanogr, US Dept Interior, 61; res asst submarine geol, Columbia Univ, 61-67. *Mem:* Fel AAAS; fel Geol Soc Am; Am Asn Petrol Geol; Sigma Xi. *Res:* Ocean bottom currents and their effects on the deep sea floor; sediment dynamics of the deep sea; sub-seabed disposal of radioactive waste; graduate education in oceanography. *Mailing Add:* Woods Hole Oceanog Inst MS 40 Woods Hole MA 02543-1522

HOLLISTER, FLOYD HILL, ELECTRICAL ENGINEERING. *Current Pos:* DIR, SCI TECH DIV, SOFTWARE ENG INST, CARNEGIE-MELLON UNIV, PITTSBURGH, 91- *Personal Data:* b Cortland, NY, Apr 28, 37; m 89, Lilliana Pejovich; c James K, William H & Robert E. *Educ:* Columbia Coll, AB, 58; Naval Postgrad Sch, PhD(elec eng), 65. *Prof Exp:* Control syst engr, Naval Ocean Syst Ctr, San Diego, 65-69; spec asst to commanding officer, Naval Shore Electronics Eng, Activ-Pac, Honolulu, 69-71; staff asst info & commun, Directorate Defense Res & Eng, Washington, 71-73; dir, Info Systs Div, Naval Electronics Systs Command, Washington, 73-75; prog mgr info systs, Defense Advan Res Proj Agency, Va, 75-78; vpres corp res, develop & eng & dir, Comput Sci Ctr, Tex Instruments, Dallas, 78-91. *Concurrent Pos:* Mem eng sch adv bd, Univ Ill, Urbana, 87-92, Univ Tex, 87-91. *Mem:* Soc Mfg Engrs. *Res:* Electrical engineering. *Mailing Add:* Carnegie-Mellon Univ Fed Aviation Admin 800 Independence Ave SW Washington DC 20591. *E-Mail:* fhh@sei.cmu.edu

HOLLISTER, LEO E, PHARMACOLOGY. *Current Pos:* MED DIR, HARRIS COUNTY PSYCH CTR. *Personal Data:* b Cincinnati, Ohio, Dec 3, 20; div; c Stephen, David, Cynmiv & Matthew. *Educ:* Univ Cincinnati, BS, 40, MD, 43; Am Bd Internal Med, dipl, 51 & 74. *Honors & Awards:* Menninger Award, Am Col Physicians; Hunter Award, Am Soc Clin Pharmacologists; Eddy Award, Col Prob Drug Dependence; Hoch Award, Am Col Neruropsychopharmacol. *Prof Exp:* Chief med serv, 53-60, assoc chief staff, 60-70, sr med investr, Vet Admin Hosp, 70-78 & 82-86. *Concurrent Pos:* Prof med, psychiat & pharmacol, Sch Med, Stanford Univ, 70-86; prof psychiat & pharmacol, Univ Tex Med Sch, Houston, 87-91. *Mem:* Am Col Physicians; Am Soc Pharmacol & Exp Therapeut; Am Soc Clin Pharmacol & Therapeut (past pres); Int Col Neuropsychopharmacol (past pres); Am Col Neuropsychopharmacol (past pres). *Res:* Clinical psychopharmacology; drugs of abuse; adverse drug reactions. *Mailing Add:* Harris County Psych Ctr PO Box 20249 Houston TX 77225-0249. *Fax:* 713-741-7832

HOLLISTER, LINCOLN STEFFENS, GEOLOGY, STRUCTURAL. *Current Pos:* from asst prof to assoc prof, 69-76, PROF GEOL, PRINCETON UNIV, 76- *Personal Data:* b Rochester, Minn, Oct 16, 38; m 60, Sarah Walford; c John & William. *Educ:* Harvard Univ, AB, 61; Calif Inst Technol, PhD(geol & geochem), 66. *Honors & Awards:* Group Achievement Award, NASA, 73; Past Presidents' Medal, Mineral Asn Can, 90. *Prof Exp:* Asst prof geol, Univ Calif, Los Angeles, 66-69. *Concurrent Pos:* Mem, Lunar Sample Rev Bd, 71-73; NATO fel, Ctr Res Petrol & Geochem, France, 72-73; vis geologist, Geol Surv Can, Vancouver, 81; assoc ed, Geol Soc Am, 82-88; gastdozent, ETH, Switz, 87-88; assoc ed, Can Mineralogist, 90-94. *Mem:* Mineral Asn Can; Am Geophys Union; Mineral Soc Am; Geol Soc Am. *Res:* Petrogenetic interpretations of compositional zoning in minerals from metamorphic and igneous rocks; tectonics of the coast Orogen, BC; fluid inclusion studies; geology of the kingdom of Bhutan. *Mailing Add:* Dept Geosci Princeton Univ Princeton NJ 08544. *Fax:* 609-258-1274

HOLLISTER, VICTOR F, MINING ENGINEERING. *Current Pos:* CONSULT, 80- *Personal Data:* b Chicago, Ill, Mar 25, 25; Can citizen; c 4. *Educ:* Univ Calif, Berkeley, BS, 48, MS,49. *Prof Exp:* Geologist, Am Smell & Refining Co, 49-62; mgr, Duval Corp, 62-80. *Mem:* Soc Econ Geologists; Geol Asn Can; Assoc Inst Mining Engrs; Can Inst Mining Metall. *Res:* Author of twenty publications. *Mailing Add:* 8069 Philbert St Mission BC V2V 3W9 Can

HOLLISTER, WALTER M(ARK), ASTRONAUTICAL ENGINEERING. *Current Pos:* teaching asst, 60-61, from instr to assoc prof, 62-82, PROF AERONAUT & ASTRONAUT, MASS INST TECHNOL, 82- *Personal Data:* b St Johnsbury, Vt, Nov 22, 30; m 61; c 3. *Educ:* Middlebury Col, BA, 53; Mass Inst Technol, BS, 53, SM, 59, ScD(instrumentation), 63. *Prof Exp:* Eng asst, Sperry Gyroscope Co, 52, field serv engr, 53-54. *Res:* Technology in gyroscopic instrument theory; inertial guidance; instrumentation; air traffic control. *Mailing Add:* Dept Aeronaut Mass Inst Technol 77 Massachusetts Ave Cambridge MA 02139-4307

HOLLOCHER, THOMAS CLYDE, JR, REDOX BIOCHEMISTRY. *Current Pos:* from asst prof to assoc prof, 61-81, PROF BIOCHEM, BRANDEIS UNIV, 81- *Personal Data:* b Norristown, Pa, June 6, 31; m 53, Pamela; c 3. *Educ:* Worcester Polytech Inst, BS, 53; Univ Rochester, PhD(biochem), 58. *Prof Exp:* Res assoc bot, Wash Univ, 58. *Concurrent Pos:* Vis scientist, Karolinska Inst, Sweden, 68; vis prof, Univ Iceland, 75; Fulbright-Hays res fel, Waite Agr Inst, Adelaide, Australia, 80-81, Biotechnol Inst, Reykjavik, Ireland, 90; traveling lectr, Peoples Repub China, 84; chmn environ studies prog, Brandeis Univ, 72-74. *Mem:* Am Soc Biol Chem; Am Soc Microbiol. *Res:* Mechanisms of action of oxidation reduction enzymes; denitrification; nitrification; inorganic chemistry of N-oxides. *Mailing Add:* Dept Biochem Brandeis Univ Waltham MA 02254-9110

HOLLOMAN, JOHN L S, JR, MEDICINE, HEALTH ADMINISTRATION. *Current Pos:* MED DIR, RYAN HEALTH CTR, 81- *Personal Data:* b Washington, DC, Nov 22, 19; c 5. *Educ:* Va Union Univ, BS, 40; Univ Mich, MD, 43. *Hon Degrees:* DSc, Va Union Univ, 83. *Prof Exp:* Dir, Riverton Lab, 47-74; pres, New York City Health & Hosp Corp, 74-77; regional med officer, US Food & Drug Admin, 80-86. *Concurrent Pos:* Pvt med pract, NY, 47-; dir, Diag Lab, 69-74; chmn bd, Health Manpower Develop Corp, 69-79; dir, Health Ins Plan, 71-73, vpres, 73-74; prof staff, Ways & Means Health Subcomt, US Cong, 78-80; chmn, Clin Dirs Task Force on AIDS, Nat Asn Community Health Ctr, 87- *Mem:* Inst Med-Nat Acad Sci; AMA; Nat Med Asn (pres, 66-67); Am Pub Health Asn. *Res:* Clinical, pharmaceutical, social and administrative medicine. *Mailing Add:* 27-40 Ericsson St East Elmhurst NY 11369

HOLLOSZY, JOHN O, PHYSIOLOGY. *Current Pos:* from asst prof to assoc prof, 65-74, prof prev med & pub health & dir div appl physiol, 74-84, PROF MED & DIR SECT APPL PHYSIOL, SCH MED, WASHINGTON UNIV, 84-, DIR, DIV GERIAT GERONT, 94- *Personal Data:* b Vienna, Austria, Jan 2, 33; US citizen; m 57. *Educ:* Ore State Univ, 50-53; Wash Univ, MD, 57. *Prof Exp:* Intern med, Wash Univ Med Ctr, 57-58, from asst resident to chief resident, 58-61. *Concurrent Pos:* Nat Inst Arthritis & Metab Dis spec res fel biochem, Sch Med, Washington Univ, 63-65; USPHS res grant, 65-94, res career develop award, 69-73. *Mem:* Am Inst Nutrit; Am Fedn Clin Res; Am Soc Clin Invest; Am Heart Asn; Am Physiol Soc; Am Soc Biol Chem; Geront Soc Am; Am Diabetes Asn. *Res:* Effects of exercise on sugar transport into muscle; serum lipids; cardiovascular function; enzymes involved in energy metabolism in muscle; body composition and food intake; aging health maintenance. *Mailing Add:* Dept Med Campus Box 8113 Washington Univ 4566 Scott Ave St Louis MO 63110. *Fax:* 314-362-7657

HOLLOWAY, CAROLINE T, LIPIDS, ENZYMES & PROTEINS. *Current Pos:* grants assoc, 84-85, head biol str sect, 85-90, DIR, OFF SCI POLICY, NAT CTR RES RESOURCES, NIH, 90- *Personal Data:* b New York, NY, July 29, 37; m; c 2. *Educ:* City Col NY, BS, 59; Duke Univ, PhD(biochem), 64. *Prof Exp:* Postdoctoral fel, NIMH, Duke Univ, 67; res asst prof, Med Ctr, Univ Va, 76-83; vis res scientist, E I Du Pont de Nemours & Co, Inc, 83-84. *Mem:* Am Soc Biochem & Molecular Biol; AAAS. *Res:* Develop planning, evaluation, legislation and science policy for intramural and extramural components of National Center Research Resources. *Mailing Add:* Off Sci Policy Nat Ctr Res Resources NIH Bldg 12A-4045 6209 Hollins Dr Bethesda MD 20817-0001. *Fax:* 301-402-1775

HOLLOWAY, CLARKE L, HISTOLOGY, GERONTOLOGY. *Current Pos:* RETIRED. *Personal Data:* b Atmore, Ala, May 2, 26; m 48; c 3. *Educ:* Auburn Univ, DVM, 49, MS, 62; Iowa State Univ, PhD(anat), 69. *Prof Exp:* Pvt pract, 49-60; from instr to assoc prof anat, Auburn Univ, 60-67; assoc prof, Univ Ga, 67-68; prof anat & head dept, Sch Vet Med, Auburn Univ, 68-88. *Concurrent Pos:* Nat Inst Neurol Dis & Blindness spec fel, 64-68. *Mem:* Am Vet Med Asn; Am Asn Vet Anat. *Res:* Anatomy and histology of olfactory mechanism of the dog; changes with age in eye of domestic animals. *Mailing Add:* Dept Anat & Histol Auburn Univ Sch Vet Med Auburn AL 36830

HOLLOWAY, CLIVE EDWARD, EDUCATION ADMINISTRATION, GENERAL ENVIRONMENTAL SCIENCES. *Current Pos:* From asst prof to assoc prof, 68-93, PROF CHEM, YORK UNIV, 93- *Personal Data:* b Bristol, Eng, Jan 28, 38; Can citizen. *Educ:* Bristol Col Advan Technol, ARIC, 60; Univ Western Ont, MSc, 62, PhD(chem), 66. *Concurrent Pos:* Counr, Chem Inst Can, Toronto, 86-88; pres, Asn Chem Prof Ont, 87-89; dir, Natural Sci, York Univ, 89-; mem, Biol & Chem Defence Rev Comt, Defence Res Bd, Ottawa, Can, 90-93, chmn, 93-; expert witness, Corp & Consumer Affairs Can, 90- *Mem:* Chem Inst Can. *Res:* Coordination complexes and organometallic compounds with emphasis on the transition elements and x-ray, electron and neutron diffraction stucture correlations. *Mailing Add:* Dept Chem York Univ 4700 Keele St North York ON M3J 1P3 Can. *Fax:* 416-736-5700; *E-Mail:* fs300554@sol.yorku.ca

HOLLOWAY, FRANK A, BEHAVIORAL PHARMACOLOGY, BEHAVIORAL MEDICINE. *Current Pos:* Instr & asst prof med & biol psychol, 66-74, instr & assoc prof, 74-77, PROF BIOL PSYCHOL, DEPT PSYCHIAT & BEHAV SCI, HEALTH SCI CTR, UNIV OKLA, 77-, DIR BIOL, PSYCHOL PhD PROG, 78- *Personal Data:* b Houston, Tex, Jan 1, 40; m 67, Joan Buchanan; c Karen J, Benjamin S & Jason L. *Educ:* Univ Houston, BS, 61, MA, 64, PhD(exp psychol), 66. *Mem:* Am Psychol Asn; Psychol Soc; Soc Neurosci; AAAS; Am Psychological Soc. *Res:* Psychopharmacology of learning and motivation; state-dependent learning; behavioral pharmacology of ethanol and drugs of abuse; biological rhythms & behavior; behavioral neuroscience. *Mailing Add:* 10516 Admiral Dr Oklahoma City OK 73162-6804. *Fax:* 405-271-2356

HOLLOWAY, G ALLEN, JR, WOUND HEALING, VASCULAR MEDICINE. *Current Pos:* med staff pres, 91, DIR MED, VASCULAR LAB, MARICOPA MED CTR, 88-, DIR MED RES, 92-, PRES, MARICOPA MED CTR RES FOUND, 92- *Personal Data:* b New York, NY, Oct 14, 38; m 87, Eileen J; c Mara R & Brett C. *Educ:* Yale Univ, BA, 60; Harvard Univ, MD, 64. *Prof Exp:* Chief med, US Army Hosp, Camp Zama, Japan, 70-72; from asst prof to assoc prof bioeng, Ctr Bioeng, Univ Wash, Seattle, 75-88. *Concurrent Pos:* Consult & lectr, mult orgn; renal fel, Pub Health Serv, 78-79, career develop award, 80-85; adj prof chem, biol & mat eng, Ariz State Univ. *Mem:* Biomed Eng Soc; Vascular Technol Soc. *Res:* Vascular disease of both the macrovascular and microvascular systems as well as clinical aspects of wound healing. *Mailing Add:* Dept Surg Maricopa Med Ctr 2601 E Roosevelt Phoenix AZ 85008

HOLLOWAY, HARRY, AEROSPACE MEDICINE. *Current Pos:* RETIRED. *Educ:* Univ Okla, dipl, 58. *Prof Exp:* Chmn, Dept Psychiat & actg dean, Uniformed Servs Univ Health Sci, 90-92, dep dean, Sch Med, 92- *Concurrent Pos:* Dir neuropsychiat, Walter Reed Army Inst; consult, WHO. *Res:* Impact of extreme environments on human adaption. *Mailing Add:* Biol Dept Univ NDak PO Box 9019 Grand Forks ND 58202

HOLLOWAY, HARRY CHARLES, NEUROPSYCHIATRY. *Current Pos:* PROF, DEPT PSYCHIAT, UNIFORM SERV UNIV HEALTH SCI, 77-, CHMN, 79- *Personal Data:* b Yukon, Okla, May 4, 33; m 55; c 3. *Educ:* Univ Okla, MD, 58; Am Bd Psychiat & Neurol, dipl, 66. *Prof Exp:* Chief Neurol & Psychiat Sect, 121st Evacuation Hosp, Korea, 62-63; res psychiatrist, Div Neuropsychiat, Walter Reed Army Inst Res, 63-65; chief Neuropsychiat Dept, USA Component, SEATO Med Res Lab, Thailand, 65-69; dep dir, Walter Reed Army Inst Res, 69-70, dir, Div Neuropsychiat, 70-77. *Concurrent Pos:* Consult, Eighth US Army, 62-63; fac mem, Washington Sch Psychiat, 74-; consult, Community Ment Health Training Prog, 74-, mem, Res Study Sect & Res Adv Comt, Ill Dept Ment Health & Develop Disabilities, 75-; fac mem, Life Sci Comt, NASA, 75-; fac mem, Georgetown Univ, Sch Med, 76-79; mem, Leukemia Core Comt, Cancer & Leukemia Group B, 81-82. *Mem:* Fel Am Psychiat Asn; AAAS; Soc Neurosci; Acad Soc & Polit Sci. *Res:* Psychiatric epidemiology and psychopharmacology with emphasis on the impact of social and environmental factors upon the occurrence of psychiatric disease psychophysiology of cancer chemotherapy and drug abuse. *Mailing Add:* 4301 Jones Bridge Rd Bethesda MD 20814-4799

HOLLOWAY, HARRY LEE, JR, PARASITOLOGY. *Current Pos:* chmn dept, 71-74, PROF BIOL, UNIV NDAK, 71- *Personal Data:* b York Co, Va, May 22, 26; m 48; c 4. *Educ:* Randolph-Macon Col, BS, 48; Univ Richmond, MA, 51; Univ Va, PhD, 56. *Prof Exp:* Asst, Univ Richmond, 50-51 & Univ Va, 51-53; from asst prof to prof biol, Roanoke Col, 53-69; prof biol & dean fac, Western Md Col, 69-71. *Concurrent Pos:* Chmn dept biol, Roanoke Col, 59-69; US Antarctic Res Prog grants, 64-69, McMurdo Facil Antarctica, 64-65. *Mem:* Fel AAAS; Am Soc Parasitol; Am Micros Soc; Am Inst Biol Sci; Sigma Xi. *Res:* Morphology and taxonomy, development and life cycles, macroecology and zoogeography of animal parasites. *Mailing Add:* Biol Dept Univ NDak PO Box 8238 Grand Forks ND 58202

HOLLOWAY, JAMES ASHLEY, NEUROPHYSIOLOGY. *Current Pos:* asst prof, Howard Univ, 71-73, assoc prof neurophysiol, 73-80, assoc prof physiol & biophys, 80-90, PROF & CHMN, DEPT PHYSIOL & BIOPHYS, COL MED, HOWARD UNIV, 90- *Personal Data:* b Stanton, Tenn, Feb 7, 36. *Educ:* San Jose State Univ, BA, 65; Univ Calif, PhD(physiol), 71. *Prof Exp:* Indust engr, Campbell Soup Co, 65-67, anal chemist, 67-68. *Concurrent Pos:* Comnr Parks & Recreation, State Calif, 70-71; consult, Am Cancer Soc, 70-71, Field Educ Publ, 72-73 & Nat Insts Gen Med Sci, 73-; fel, Johns Hopkins Univ, 71-72; NSF res grant, 72 & 73; Porter lectr, Meharry Med Col, 72- & Tuskegee Inst, 73-; NIH training grant, 74-78. *Mem:* AAAS; Am Physiol Soc; Soc Neurosci; Int Asn Study Pain. *Res:* Response characteristics of spinal cord dorsal horn cells to natural and electrical stimulation. *Mailing Add:* Dept Physiol & Biophys Howard Univ Col Med Washington DC 20059-0001

HOLLOWAY, JOAN PARISE, PUBLIC HEALTH SERVICES. *Current Pos:* DIR, DIV PROGS SPEC POP BUR PRIMARY HEALTH CARE, HEALTH RESOURCES & SERVS ADMIN, BETHESDA, MD, 88- *Personal Data:* b New York, NY, Aug 25, 41; c 1. *Educ:* Hunter Col, AB, 62. *Prof Exp:* Instr, New York Bd Educ, 62-64; statist supvr, Med Records Dept, Univ Ky, 64-67; dep dir, Med Records Dept, US Pub Health Hosp, Baltimore, Md, 68-70; asst dir, Pub Health Serv Prog Health Record Admin, Baltimore, Md, 70-72; health record consult, Regional Med Prog Servs, Rockville, Md, 72-73; health consult/proj officer, Nat Ctr Health Servs Res, Rockville, Md, 73-75; asst dir prog mgt, Div Hosp & Clinics, Bur Med Servs, Hyattsville, Md, 75-78; mgr, Med Info Proj, US Privacy Protection Study Comn, Washington, DC, 76-77; dir, US Pub Health Serv Clin, Portland, Me, 78-80, Off Ambulatory Care, Hyattsville, Md, 81-82; dir, Off Ambulatory CAr, Hyattsville, Md, 81-82; dir, Clin Servs staff, Bureau Health Care Delivery & Assistance, 83-87, dep dir, Div Primary CAre Servs, 87-88. *Concurrent Pos:* Consult, Baltimore City Hosp, 70-71, Dept Continuing Educ, Md Reg Med Prog, 71-74, W Baltimore Comprehensive Health Care Ctr, 71-72, Emergency Med Servs Comt, Regional Plannng Coun, CHP, Baltimore Region, 72, Nat Ctr Health Servs Res, 79-80, House Rep, Gov Info & Individual Rights Subcomt, Comt Gov Opers, 77; mem, Health Rec Task Force Coop Health Serv Proj, N Baltimore Community Health Orgn, 72; chmn, Coun Educ, Am Med Rec Asn, 80. *Res:* Health status of special and underserved populations through the development, implementation and evaluation of community-based service delivery systems. *Mailing Add:* Div Progs Spec Pop 4350 EW Hwy Rm 9-10A2 9th flr EW Tower Bldg Bethesda MD 20814

HOLLOWAY, JOHN LEITH, JR, DYNAMIC METEOROLOGY. *Current Pos:* RETIRED. *Personal Data:* b Hickory, NC, Dec 18, 27. *Educ:* Mass Inst Technol, BS, 52, MS, 53. *Honors & Awards:* Silver Medal, US Dept Com, 63. *Prof Exp:* Res meteorologist, Univ Pa, 53-55 & Off Meteorol Res, US Weather Bur, 55-57; meteorologist, Geophys Fluid Dynamics Lab, Nat Oceanic & Atmospheric Admin, 57-83 & 89-90. *Mem:* Am Meteorol Soc; Am Soc Photobiol; Int Dark-Sky Asn. *Res:* Simulation of climate by numerical solution of meteorological equations on computers; smoothing, filtering and spectral analysis of meteorological time series; analysis of solar ultraviolet radiation measurements at surface of earth. *Mailing Add:* 10500 Rockville Pike No M10 Rockville MD 20852-3331

HOLLOWAY, JOHN REQUA, PETROLOGY, GEOCHEMISTRY. *Current Pos:* From asst prof to assoc prof, 69-79, PROF CHEM & GEOL, ARIZ STATE UNIV, 80- *Personal Data:* b Portland, Ore, Aug 2, 40; div; c 2. *Educ:* Univ Ore, BS, 63; Pa State Univ, PhD(geochem), 70. *Concurrent Pos:* Vis scientist, Geophys Lab, 75-76; vis prof, Stanford Univ, 79, Calif Inst Technol, 87, Bristol, Eng; vis fel, Royal Soc, 90. *Mem:* Geol Soc Am; Mineral Soc Am; fel Am Geophys Union; Geochem Soc. *Res:* Experimental measurement and theoretical calculation of the stability of hydrous silicate phases. *Mailing Add:* Dept Chem Ariz State Univ Tempe AZ 85287-0001

HOLLOWAY, JOHN THOMAS, EXPERIMENTAL PHYSICS. *Current Pos:* RETIRED. *Personal Data:* b Cape Girardeau, Mo, June 19, 22; m 65, Kay Vickers; c Linda & Kim. *Educ:* Millikin Univ, AB, 43; Iowa State Univ, PhD(physics), 57. *Prof Exp:* Mem nuclear physics br, Off Naval Res, 46-53, actg br head, 51-52; asst, Iowa State Univ, 53-57; chief phys sci div, Off Dir Defense Res & Eng, 58-59, dept dir, Off Sci, 59-61; chief, Univ Progs & dept dir, Off Grants & Res Contracts, NASA, 61-65, actg dir, 65-67, with space applns div, 67-68; dir, Nat Hwy Safety Res Ctr, Nat Hwy Safety Bur, US Dept Transp, 68-69; vpres res, Ins Inst for Hwy Safety, 69-72; assoc dir opers, Interdisciplinary Commun Prog, Smithsonian Inst, 72-77; consult hwy safety, biomed electronics & energy conserv, 77-78; sr staff officer, Radioactive Waste Mgt Bd, Nat Acad Sci-Nat Res Coun, 78-85. *Concurrent Pos:* Consult, radioactive waste mgt & hwy safety, 85- *Mem:* Am Phys Soc; Sigma Xi. *Res:* Research administration and management; experimental nuclear physics; space science and engineering; highway safety; international population policy; radioactive waste management. *Mailing Add:* 2220 Cathedral Ave NW Washington DC 20008. *E-Mail:* jholloway@worldnet.att.net

HOLLOWAY, LELAND EDGAR, EXPERIMENTAL HIGH ENERGY PHYSICS. *Current Pos:* from asst prof to assoc prof, 67-74, PROF PHYSICS, UNIV ILL, URBANA, 74- *Personal Data:* b Kansas City, Mo, Aug 19, 36; m 65; c 1. *Educ:* Mass Inst Technol, BS, 58; Univ Pa, PhD(physics), 62. *Prof Exp:* NSF fel, 62-63; res physicist, Lawrence Radiation Lab, 63-66 & Inst Nuclear Physics, Orsay, France, 66-67. *Mem:* Fel Am Phys Soc. *Mailing Add:* Dept Physics Univ Ill 1110 W Green St Urbana IL 61801

HOLLOWAY, PAUL FAYETTE, AEROSPACE. *Current Pos:* RETIRED. *Personal Data:* b Hampton, Va, June 7, 38; m 56, Barbara J Menetech; c Paul M (deceased) & Eric S. *Educ:* Va Polytech Inst & State Univ, BS, 60. *Hon Degrees:* DSc, Old Dominion Univ, 94. *Prof Exp:* Aerospace res engr, Langley Res Ctr, NASA, 60-69, head, Systs Anal Sect, Aerophys Div, 69-71, head, Opers Anal Br, Space Systs Div, 71-72, chief, 72-75, dir space, Off Aeronaut & Space Technol, 75-85, dep dir, 85-91, dir 91-97. *Concurrent Pos:* mem space shuttle task group, Langley Res Ctr, 69-97; co-dir, Joint NASA/Dept of Defense Nat Space Transp Archit Study Task Team, 85 & 86. *Mem:* Fel Am Inst Aeronaut & Astronaut; fel Am Astron Soc; Int Acad Astronaut. *Mailing Add:* 16 N Westover Dr Hampton VA 23662-1424

HOLLOWAY, PAUL HOWARD, MATERIAL SCIENCE, SURFACE SCIENCE. *Current Pos:* assoc prof, 78-81, PROF MAT SCI & ENG, UNIV FLA, 81- *Personal Data:* b Marion, Ind, Oct 31, 43; m 64, Bette Zubrod; c Michael, Brian & Kimberly. *Educ:* Fla State Univ, BS, 65, MS, 66; Rensselaer Polytech Inst, PhD(mat eng), 72. *Honors & Awards:* E W Muller Award. *Prof Exp:* Phys metallurgist, Knolls Atomic Power Lab, Gen Elec Co, 66-69; staff mem mat eng, Sandia Labs, 72-78. *Mem:* Fel Am Vacuum Soc; Am Soc Testing & Mat; Am Soc Metals; Am Inst Mining, Metall & Petrol Engrs; Mat Res Soc. *Res:* Surface science; kinetics and thermodynamics of gas/solid interactions; metallurgical reactions in thin films; defect enhanced solid state atomic transport; electronic materials; compound semiconductors. *Mailing Add:* 3520 NW 143d St Gainesville FL 32606. *Fax:* 904-392-4911; *E-Mail:* pholl@mse.ufl.edu

HOLLOWAY, PETER WILLIAM, MEMBRANE PROTEIN STRUCTURE. *Current Pos:* PROF BIOCHEM, SCH MED, UNIV VA, 69- *Personal Data:* b Manchester, UK, June 30, 38. *Educ:* Univ Manchester, PhD(chem), 62. *Mem:* Am Biol Chemist; Biophys Soc. *Res:* Interaction of cytochrome b5 with membranes; fatty acid desaturation. *Mailing Add:* Dept Biochem Sch Med Univ Va Jordan Hall Box 440 Charlottesville VA 22908-0001

HOLLOWAY, RALPH L, JR, PHYSICAL ANTHROPOLOGY, NEUROSCIENCES. *Current Pos:* From asst prof to assoc prof, 64-69, chmn, 79-81, PROF ANTHROP, COLUMBIA UNIV, 73- *Personal Data:* b Philadelphia, Pa, Feb 6, 35; div; c Marguerite, Eric & Benjamin. *Educ:* Univ NMex, BS, 59; Univ Calif, Berkeley, PhD(anthrop), 64. *Concurrent Pos:* NIMH res fel, 64; NSF res grant, 69-; vis prof, New Sch Social Res, 72-85; Guggenheim Found fel, 74-75; L S B Leakey Found Grant, 85. *Mem:* Fel AAAS; Am Anthrop Asn; Am Asn Phys Anthrop; fel NY Acad Sci; Soc Neurosci. *Res:* Evolution of human brain and behavior; comparative primate neuroanatomy; primate aggression and social evolution; fossil man; dendritic branching in cortex; fossil brain endocasts; cerebral asymmetrics; sexual dimorphism of the brain. *Mailing Add:* Dept Anthrop Columbia Univ New York NY 10027. *Fax:* 212-854-7347

HOLLOWAY, RICHARD GEORGE, PALYNOLOGY, QUATERNARY PERIOD. *Current Pos:* CONSULT, 95- *Personal Data:* b Norristown, Pa, Apr 19, 51. *Educ:* Eastern NMex Univ, BA, 73; Tex A&M Univ, MS, 78, PhD(bot), 81. *Prof Exp:* Archaeol technician I, US Forest Serv, Sitka, Alaska, 79; palynologist, Res Found, State Univ NY, Binghamton, 81; res scientist, Anthrop Res Lab, Tex A&M Univ, 81-87; vis asst prof anthrop, Eastern NMex Univ, 87-89; res assoc, Biol Dept, Univ NMex, 89-95. *Concurrent Pos:* Fel, Anthrop Prog, Tex A&M Univ, 81-87. *Mem:* AAAS; Am Asn Stratig Palynologists; Am Quaternary Asn; Electron Micros Soc Am; Int Asn Wood Anatomists; Int Asn Aerobiol; Am Bot Soc. *Res:* Quaternary palynology and quaternary plant ecology; palynological statistics; fossil pollen morphology and taxonomy; arctic and subarctic paleoecology; archaeological palynology; coprolite analysis; macro-botanical analysis of archaeological materials; prehistoric diets and nutrition; southeastern US paleoecology. *Mailing Add:* 5000 N Country Club Lane Flagstaff AZ 86004

HOLLOWELL, JOSEPH GURNEY, JR, PEDIATRIC ENDOCRINOLOGY, GENETICS. *Current Pos:* CHIEF, DEVELOP DISABILITIES BR, CTRS DIS CONTROL & PREV, ATLANTA, GA, 85- *Personal Data:* b Charleston, SC, Nov 19, 32; m 55, Emily Allen; c Joseph G III, Kyra (Morris), Susan H (Ledsetter), Barbara H (Wagner), H Edith & Janet L. *Educ:* Med Univ SC, MD, 56; Univ Calif, Berkeley, MPH, 77. *Prof Exp:* Intern, Hosp, Med Col SC, 56-57, resident pediat, 57-59; res fel pediat endocrinol & genetics, State Univ NY Upstate Ctr, 61-63; from instr to assoc prof pediat, Med Col Ga, 63-70; assoc prof pediat, Univ Kans Med Ctr, 70-72, assoc prof pediat & prev med, 72-90, mem grad fac anthrop, 74-90. *Concurrent Pos:* Pediat consult & dir, Birth Defects Ctr, Gracewood State Sch & Hosp; US HEW grants, 64-67; dir, Div Health, Kans Dept Health & Environ, 79-85. *Mem:* Am Soc Human Genetics; Soc Teachers Family Med; Ambulatory Pediat Asn; Sigma Xi; NY Acad Sci; Am Acad Pediat; Soc Develop Pediat. *Res:* Catecholamine metabolism; endocrinology, regulation of sodium transport; developmental aspects of transporting membranes; medical education; health care delivery; developmental aspects of mental retardation and disability; health concepts; public health and spidemiology of developmental disabilities. *Mailing Add:* 7116 Pennsylvania Ave Kansas City MO 64114

HOLLSTEIN, ULRICH, ORGANIC CHEMISTRY. *Current Pos:* assoc prof org chem, 67-74, PROF CHEM, UNIV NMEX, 74- *Personal Data:* b Berlin, Ger, July 7, 27; nat US; m 57; c 3. *Educ:* Univ Amsterdam, BS, 48, MS, 53, PhD(chem), 56. *Prof Exp:* Nat Res Coun Can fel natural prod chem, 56-57; res chemist org radiochem, Inst Nuclear Res, Neth, 58-59; fel natural prod chem, Univ Calif, Berkeley, 60-63; from asst prof to assoc prof org chem, Eastern NMex Univ, 63-67. *Concurrent Pos:* Fulbright fel, Univ Tubingen, WGer, 73-74. *Mem:* Am Chem Soc; Royal Neth Chem Soc. *Res:* Natural products; alkaloids; ca-antagonists antibiotics; microbial metabolites; biosynthesis; interaction with polydeoxyribonucleotides; optical rotatory dispersion and circular dichroism; carbon-13 nuclear magnetic resonance; mass spectrometry. *Mailing Add:* Dept Chem Univ NMex Albuquerque NM 87131-0002

HOLLUB, RAYMOND M(ATHEW), AERONAUTICAL ENGINEERING. *Current Pos:* RETIRED. *Personal Data:* b Passaic, NJ, Mar 9, 28; m 52; c 2. *Educ:* Univ Ala, BS, 55, MS, 58. *Honors & Awards:* Frank Oppenheimer Award, Am Soc Eng Educ, 78. *Prof Exp:* Assoc res engr, Lockheed Aircraft Corp, Ga, 55-56; instr eng mech, Univ Ala, 56-58, from asst prof to assoc prof aeronaut eng, 58-90, dir res comt proj, 59, dir NASA res contracts, 61-65, dir continuing eng educ, 72-90, dir off campus masters degree prog, 75-90, spec asst continuing ed, 80-90. *Concurrent Pos:* Consult, Lockheed Aircraft Corp, 58-61, Southern Serv Corp & Astro Space Labs, Ala; assoc dir, Am Soc Eng Educ-NASA fac fel prog, Marshall Space Flight Ctr & Univ Ala, 66, co-dir, 67; NSF-W Alton Jones fel, Ga Inst Technol, 67-70; dir contract consultation training, Occup Safety & Health Admin, US Dept Labor, 78- *Mem:* Am Soc Eng Educ; Am Inst Aeronaut & Astronaut; Nat Univ Exten Asn. *Res:* Mechanical properties of materials; structural analysis; heat transfer. *Mailing Add:* 3601 Blackberry Ln Northport AL 35476

HOLLWEG, JOSEPH VINCENT, SPACE PHYSICS, SOLAR PHYSICS. *Current Pos:* dir, Space Sci Ctr, 82-83, PROF, DEPT PHYSICS, UNIV NH, 80- *Personal Data:* b New York, NY, Mar 20, 44; m 76, Leslie F Losch; c 2. *Educ:* Mass Inst Technol, BS & MS, 65, PhD(plasma physics), 68. *Prof Exp:* Res fel space physics, Ctr Space Res, Mass Inst Technol, 67-68; vis scientist, Max Planck Inst Physics & Astrophys, 68-70; res assoc, Calif Inst Technol, 70-72; mem sci staff solar physics, Nat Ctr Atmospheric Res, 72-80. *Concurrent Pos:* Vis scientist, Max Planck Inst Aeronomy, 75-76; assoc ed, J Geophys Res, 82-85, 93-96. *Mem:* Am Geophys Union; Am Astron Soc; Int Astron Union. *Res:* Physical processes of the solar and interplanetary plasma, with emphasis on mechanisms of energy and momentum balance. *Mailing Add:* Dept Physics Univ NH Durham NH 03824. *Fax:* 603-862-1915; *E-Mail:* joe.hollweg@unh.edu

HOLLY, FRANK JOSEPH, OPTOMETRY, DENTISTRY. *Current Pos:* DIR-OWNER, DAKRYON PHARMACEUT, 90- *Personal Data:* b Budapest, Hungary, Dec 3, 34; US citizen; m 69; c 4. *Educ:* Cornell Univ, PhD(phys chem), 62. *Prof Exp:* Staff Scientist dent res, Procter & Gamble, 62-65; prof chem, Univ El Salvador, 65-66; staff scientist biomat, Thermo Electron Corp, 66-68; sr scientist cornea & retina, Eye Res Inst Retina Found, 68-78; prof ophthal & biochem, Health Sci Ctr, Tex Tech Univ, 78-90. *Concurrent Pos:* Pres, Dry Eye Inst, 83- *Mem:* Am Chem Soc; Int Soc Contact Lens Res; Asn Res Vision & Ophthal; Int Soc Colloid & Interface Scientists; Int Soc Dakryology (pres, 84-90); hon fel Am Acad Optom; assoc fel Am Acad Ophthal. *Res:* Interface science, rheology, kinetics (physical chemistry) applied to biological systems, prosthesis, and pharmaceuticals; dental decay, biocompatibility of materials, lacrimal physiology, cell interaction, and bioadhesion; ocular surface disease. *Mailing Add:* 3106 29th St Lubbock TX 79410

HOLLYDAY, MARGARET ANNE, DEVELOPMENTAL NEUROBIOLOGY. *Current Pos:* PROF BIOL, BRYN MAWR COL, 87- *Personal Data:* b Elizabeth, NJ, June 23, 47; c Jediah P & Rachel E. *Educ:* Swarthmore Col, BA, 69; Duke Univ, PhD(physiol), 74. *Prof Exp:* Res assoc, Washington Univ, 74-76; asst prof pharmacol & physiol sci, Univ Chicago, 76-83, assoc prof, 83-87. *Res:* Development of the vertebrate nervous system including pattern formation, gene expression, histogenesis, cell migration and patterns of connections; experimental embryological techniques and various forms of morphological tools to study development. *Mailing Add:* 213 Pheasant Run Dr Paoli PA 19301-2049

HOLLYFIELD, JOE G, DEVELOPMENTAL BIOLOGY. *Current Pos:* assoc prof, 77-80, PROF OPHTHAL, BAYLOR COL MED, 80- *Personal Data:* b El Dorado, Ark, Aug 6, 38. *Educ:* Hendrix Col, BA, 60; La State Univ, MS, 63; Univ Tex, Austin, PhD(zool), 66. *Honors & Awards:* Marjorie W Margohn Prize, Retina Res Found. *Prof Exp:* Asst prof bot & zool, Univ Tex, Austin, 66-67; asst prof ophthal res, Col Physicians & Surgeons, Columbia Univ, 69-75, assoc prof anat, 75-77. *Concurrent Pos:* Fel, Hubrecht Lab, Utrecht, Neth, 67-69; Olga K Weiss Scholars Award, Res Prevent Blindness Inc. *Mem:* Fel AAAS; Am Soc Zoologists; Asn Res Vision & Ophthal; Soc Develop Biol. *Res:* Development and cell biology of the retina and pigment epithelium. *Mailing Add:* Dept Ophthal Cleveland Clin Found 9500 Euclid Ave Cleveland OH 44195-0001. *Fax:* 216-445-3670

HOLLYWOOD, JOHN M(ATTHEW), ELECTRONICS. *Current Pos:* CONSULT, 79- *Personal Data:* b Red Bank, NJ, Feb 4, 10; wid. *Educ:* Mass Inst Technol, BS, 31, MS, 32. *Prof Exp:* Chief engr, Electron Res Labs, NY, 32-35; circuitry develop engr, Ken-Rad Tube & Lamp Corp, 35-36; electronics res engr, Columbia Broadcasting Syst, Inc, 36-42; consult, Am-Brit Lab, Harvard Univ-Radio Res Lab, Eng, 42-45, Naval Res Lab, 45-46 & Airborne Instruments Lab, 46-49; sr engr in charge adv res & develop, Columbia Broadcasting Syst, Inc, 49-54, coordr res, 54-58, sci aide to pres, 58-71; consult, Goldmark Commun Corp, 72-79. *Mem:* Audio Eng Soc; fel Inst Elec & Electronics Engrs. *Res:* Circuit and information theory; monochrome; color television; audio; acoustics applications; stereo; radar; radio countermeasures; radar systems and displays; transistor applications. *Mailing Add:* 33 Peters Pl Red Bank NJ 07701

HOLM, DALE M, BIOPHYSICS, NUCLEAR PHYSICS. *Current Pos:* RETIRED. *Personal Data:* b Portland, Ore, Jan 23, 24; m 49; c 3. *Educ:* Lewis & Clark Col, BS, 49; Ore State Univ, MS, 52, PhD(physics), 55. *Prof Exp:* Res asst, Los Alamos Nat Lab, 52-55, staff mem, 55-73, group leader agr biosci & liaison between Los Alamos Nat Lab & USDA, 73-81, group leader, Biophys Instrumentation, 81-82a, intel analyst, 82-87. *Concurrent Pos:* Consult, 87- *Mem:* AAAS. *Res:* Reactor design, construction, and diagnosis; gamma scanning of reactor fuel elements; activation analysis. *Mailing Add:* 264 Andanada St Los Alamos NM 87544

HOLM, DANIEL K, STRUCTURAL GEOLOGY. *Current Pos:* Asst prof, 92-97, ASSOC PROF GEOL, KENT STATE UNIV, 97- *Personal Data:* b Korea, Mar 2, 62. *Educ:* Univ Rochester, BS, 84; Univ Minn, MS, 86; Harvard Univ, PhD(geol), 92. *Honors & Awards:* NSF Career Award, 95. *Mem:* Geol Soc Am. *Mailing Add:* Dept Geol Kent State Univ Kent OH 44242. *Fax:* 330-672-7949; *E-Mail:* dholm@kent.edu

HOLM, DAVID GARTH, HORTICULTURE, POTATO BREEDING. *Current Pos:* from asst prof to assoc prof, 78-96, PROF HORT, COLO STATE UNIV, 96-, SUPT, 83- *Personal Data:* b Shelley, Idaho, Aug 17, 50; m 74, Vonda L Jones; c Cameron & Ansley. *Educ:* Univ Idaho, BS, 72, MS, 74; Univ Minn, PhD(hort), 77. *Prof Exp:* jr scientist, 77-78. *Concurrent Pos:* Mem, Western Regional Coord Comt Potato Variety Develop, 83, Potato Asn

Am, 83-, dir, Potato Asn Am, 85-88. *Mem:* Sigma Xi; Potato Asn Am; Am Soc Hort Sci; Europ Asn Potato Res. *Res:* Genotype-environment interactions of food crops; physiological and morphological characters associated with high yielding food crops; potato breeding for improved yield and quality. *Mailing Add:* San Luis Valley Res Ctr 0249 E Rd 9 N Center CO 81125

HOLM, DAVID GEORGE, GENETICS. *Current Pos:* from asst prof to assoc prof, 69-83, chmn biol prog, 85-88, PROF, DEPT ZOOL, UNIV BC, 83-, ASSOC DEAN FAC SCI, 90- *Personal Data:* b Rossland, BC, Apr 21, 35; m 57; c 2. *Educ:* Univ BC, BSc, 64; Univ Conn, PhD(genetics), 69. *Prof Exp:* Assayer, COMINCO, 55-61. *Concurrent Pos:* Consult, biol course, Open Learning Inst, 80; mem, Acad Coun, OLI, 90- *Mem:* Genetics Soc Am; Can Genetics Soc; Environ Mutagen Soc. *Res:* Meiotic behavior of chromosomes in Drosophila melanogaster; genetic properties of heterochromatin; radiation and chemical mutagenesis; genetic imprinting in D melanogaster. *Mailing Add:* Dept Zool Univ BC 6270 University Blvd Vancouver BC V6T 1Z4 Can. *Fax:* 604-822-5558; *E-Mail:* dave_holm@mtsa.ubc.ca

HOLM, HARVEY WILLIAM, MICROBIOLOGY, BIOCHEMISTRY. *Current Pos:* res microbiologist, Environ Res Lab, 70-80, CHIEF, ENVIRON SYSTS BR, US ENVIRON PROTECTION AGENCY, 80- *Personal Data:* b Williston, NDak, Mar 3, 41; m 78; c 3. *Educ:* Minot State Col, BS, 63; Univ NDak, MS, 65, PhD(microbiol), 69. *Prof Exp:* Res assoc microbiol, Univ Ga, 68-70. *Mem:* Am Soc Microbiol; Am Inst Biol Sci; Am Soc Limnol & Oceanog. *Res:* Fate of pollutants in aquatic ecosystems; impact of pollutants on aquatic ecosystem structure and function. *Mailing Add:* Environ Res Div US Environ Protection Agency 960 College Station Rd Athens GA 30577

HOLM, LEROY GEORGE, COMPILATION, BIOLOGY & DISTRIBUTION OF MAJOR WORLD WEED SPECIES. *Current Pos:* COMPILATION OF WORLD WEED INVENTORY, 72- *Personal Data:* b Wyeville, Wis, Oct 2, 17; m 45; c 3. *Educ:* Wis State Univ, La Crosse, BS, 39; Univ Wis, PhD, 49. *Honors & Awards:* Distinguished Serv Award, Int Weed Sci Soc. *Prof Exp:* From asst prof to prof hort, Univ Wis-Madison, 49-71; sr fel, East-West Ctr, Univ Hawaii, 71-72. *Concurrent Pos:* Nat Acad Sci exchange prof, USSR, 63; mem staff, Div Plant Protection, UN Food & Agr Orgn, Rome, 65-66; consult weed sci, 60 countries, 72-; sr res scholar, East-West Ctr, Hawaii, 71-72. *Mem:* Hon fel Weed Sci Soc Am; Europ Weed Res Soc; Int Weed Sci Soc; Asian-Pac Weed Sci Soc. *Res:* Distribution and biology of world weeds; survey of world weed vegetation. *Mailing Add:* 714 Miami Pass Madison WI 53711

HOLM, MYRON JAMES, ORGANIC CHEMISTRY. *Current Pos:* RETIRED. *Personal Data:* b York, Nebr, May 31, 30; m 54; c 3. *Educ:* Univ Nebr, AB, 52, MS, 56, PhD(chem), 58. *Prof Exp:* Res assoc chem, Ohio State Univ, 58-59; res chemist, Monsanto Co, 59-63, res specialist, 63-80, sr res specialist, 80-90. *Res:* Paper chemicals; photochemistry; antineoplastics; plant growth regulators; fungicides. *Mailing Add:* 9734 Mansfield Dr St Louis MO 63132-3319

HOLM, REIMER, surface & interface analysis, catalysis corrosion & adhesion, for more information see previous edition

HOLM, RICHARD H, INORGANIC CHEMISTRY. *Current Pos:* PROF CHEM, HARVARD UNIV, 80- *Personal Data:* b Sept 24, 33; m 58; c 4. *Educ:* Univ Mass, BS, 55; Mass Inst Technol, PhD(inorg chem), 59. *Hon Degrees:* DSc, Univ Mass, 79, Univ Chicago, 93. *Honors & Awards:* Bailar Medal, 73; Inorg Chem Award, Am Chem Soc, 76, Distinguished Serv Inorg Chem Award, 90, Alfred Bader Award, 92; Harrison Howe Award, 77; Centenary Medal, Royal Chem Soc, 80; Dwyer Medal, Australia Chem Soc, 88; Linus Pauling Medal, 92; Award Chem Sci, Nat Acad Sci, 93; Theodore Wm Richards Medal, 94. *Prof Exp:* Prof chem, Mass Inst Technol, 67-75 & Stanford Univ, 75-80. *Concurrent Pos:* Sloan fel, 64-67. *Mem:* Nat Acad Sci; Am Chem Soc; Royal Soc Chem; Am Acad Arts & Sci. *Res:* Inorganic and bioinorganic chemistry. *Mailing Add:* Dept Chem Rm M-306 Harvard Univ Cambridge MA 02138

HOLM, ROBERT E, AGRICULTURE. *Current Pos:* DIR, AGROCHEM SCI DEPT, AGROCHEM DIV, RHONE-POULENC INC, 81- *Personal Data:* b Lafayette, Ind, Feb 18, 40; m 64; c 2. *Educ:* Purdue Univ, BS, 62, MS, 64, PhD(plant physiol & biochem), 69. *Honors & Awards:* Wilson Popenoe Award, Am Soc Hort Sci, 78. *Prof Exp:* Sr res biochemist, Diamond Shamrock Corp, 69-75, res assoc, 75-76, sr res assoc, 76-78; head biol testing, Mobil Chem Co, 78-80, mgr crop chem res & develop, 80-81. *Concurrent Pos:* Chmn, Plant Growth Regulator Working Group, 76-77; asst ed, J Plant Physiol, 80-82. *Mem:* Plant Growth Regulator Soc Am (pres, 76-77); Weed Sci Soc Am; Coun Agr Sci & Technol; Am Soc Plant Physiologists. *Res:* Mode-of-action of plant hormones, regulators and herbicides; biological evaluation of herbicides and plant growth regulants; uptake, translocation and metabolism of agricultural chemicals. *Mailing Add:* Rhone-Poulenc Agr Co PO Box 12014 TW Alexander Dr Research Triangle Park NC 27709

HOLM, VANJA ADELE, PEDIATRICS. *Current Pos:* resident pediat, Univ Wash Sch Med, 56 & 62-64, fel develop pediat, 64-65, instr pediat, 65-69, asst prof, 69-81, ASSOC PROF PEDIAT, UNIV WASH SCH MED, 81- *Personal Data:* b Kiruna, Sweden, Oct 5, 28; m 52, Carl; c Ingrid Adele & Erik Carl. *Educ:* Karolinska Inst, Med Kand, 50, MD, 55. *Honors & Awards:* Am Med Writers Award, 79; Aesculapius Award, 79. *Prof Exp:* Intern Swedish Hosp, Seattle, 55-56. *Concurrent Pos:* Attend pediatrician, Children's Orthop Hosp, Univ Hosp; med dir, Boyer Children's Clin Presch. *Mem:* Fel Am Acad Pediat; Soc Develop Pediat; Soc Behav Pediat; fel Am Acad Cerebral Palsy & Develop Med; fel Am Asn Ment Retardation. *Res:* Contributed over 60 articles to professional journals. *Mailing Add:* 4309 34th Ave W Seattle WA 98199-1393

HOLMAN, B LEONARD, NUCLEAR MEDICINE, RADIOLOGY. *Current Pos:* from instr to prof, 70-88, PHILIP H COOK PROF RADIOL, HARVARD MED SCH, 88-, dir Clin Nuclear Med Serv, 80-88, CHMN DEPT RADIOL, BRIGHAM & WOMEN'S HOSP, 88- *Personal Data:* b Sheboygan, Wis, June 26, 41; m 71; c Amy Lynn & Allison Stacy. *Educ:* Univ Wis, BS, 63; Wash Univ, MD, 66; Am Bd Radiol, cert diag radiol, 72, cert nuclear radiol, 79; Am Bd Nuclear Med, cert, 72. *Hon Degrees:* AM, Harvard Univ, 88, DSc, Pannon Univ Agr Scis, 96. *Honors & Awards:* Taplin Lectr Award, Soc Nuclear Med, 85; Blumgart Pioneer Award, Soc Nuclear Med, 86. *Prof Exp:* Intern, Mt Zion Hosp Med Ctr, San Francisco, 66-67; resident & fel, Edward Mallinckrodt Inst Radiol, Wash Univ Med Sch, 67-70. *Concurrent Pos:* Mem, Radiopharmaceut Panel, US Pharmacopeia, 70-86; radiologist nuclear med, Children's Hosp Med Ctr, 70-; consult, W Roxbury Vet Admin Hosp, 74-; chief clin nuclear med, Peter Bent Bringham Hosp, 75-80; radiologist nuclear med, Dana Farber Cancer Inst, 76-; assoc ed, Cardiovasc Radiol, 77-90; fel, Coun Cardiovasc Radiol & Coun Circulation; mem, Nuclear Cardiol Rev Panel, Intersoc Comn Heart Dis Resources, 79-81 & Adv Comt Med Uses Isotopes, US Nuclear Regulatory Comn, 79-; ed, Diag Imaging Sect, Med Instrumentation, 80-85. *Mem:* Am Heart Asn; fel Am Col Radiol. *Res:* Neuronuclear medicine; functional brain imaging, using spect evaluation of Alzheimer's disease, brain tumor, cocaine abuse, Lyme disease, CFS; neuroreceptor imaging (SPECT). *Mailing Add:* Brigham & Women's Hosp/Chmn Dept Radiol 75 Francis St Boston MA 02115. *Fax:* 617-732-6336; *E-Mail:* holman@ulna.bwh.harvard.edu

HOLMAN, GERALD HALL, PEDIATRICS, ENDOCRINOLOGY & CLINICAL GENETICS. *Current Pos:* MED DIR & MED DIR ADOLESCENT SUBSTANCE ABUSE, ST ANTHONY'S HOSPICE, AMARILLO, 85-, EXEC DIR, 87-; ASSOC CHIEF STAFF, VA MED CTR, 89-; VPRES, MED EDUC CROWN TEX HOSPICE, AMARILLO, 96- *Personal Data:* b Winnipeg, Man, June 7, 29; m 53; c 4. *Educ:* Univ Man, BSc & MD, 53; FRCPS(C), 59, FAAP, 58. *Honors & Awards:* Schwentker Res Award, Johns Hopkins Hosp, 56. *Prof Exp:* Res fel physiol & med res, Univ Man, 50-52; rotating intern, Winnipeg Gen Hosp, 52-53; asst resident pediat, Winnipeg Children's Hosp, 53-54; from jr to sr asst resident, Harriet Lane Home, 54-56; NSF fel pediat endocrinol, Johns Hopkins Hosp, 56-58; asst prof pediat, Univ Hosp, Univ Sask, 58-61; assoc prof, Sch Med, Univ Kans, 61-64; prof & chmn dept, Med Col Ga, 64-69; chief dept pediat & head div, Univ Calgary, 69-73; prof pediat, Eastern Va Med Sch, 73-79, head dept, 73-75, dean & vpres acad affairs, 75-79; assoc dean & asst to pres, Tex Tech Health Sci Ctr, Amarillo, 79-84. *Concurrent Pos:* John & Mary Markle scholar acad med, 58-63; NIH res grants, 59-; consult, Proj Headstart, 65- *Res:* Developmental adrenal metabolism and growth disorders in newborns, infants and children; fragile X-syndrome; clinical genetics. *Mailing Add:* 2802 Travis Amarillo TX 79109-3524

HOLMAN, GORDON DEAN, THEORETICAL PLASMA ASTROPHYSICS, SOLAR-STELLAR ASTROPHYSICS. *Current Pos:* res assoc, Nat Acad Sci & Nat Res Coun, 83-85, ASTROPHYSICIST, NASA, GODDARD SPACE FLIGHT CTR, GREENBELT, MD, 85- *Personal Data:* b Ft Lauderdale, Fla, July 15, 49; wid; c Trisha M & Lisa C. *Educ:* Fla State Univ, BS, 71; Univ NC, Chapel Hill, MS, 73, PhD(astrophys), 77. *Prof Exp:* Teaching asst, Dept Physics & Astron, Univ NC, Chapel Hill, 71-77; lectr astron, Astron Prog, Univ Md, College Park, 77-83, fel, Ctr Theoret Physics, 77-79, res assoc, Astron Prog, 79-83. *Concurrent Pos:* Prin investr & co-prin investr, var NASA grants, 78- *Mem:* Am Astron Soc; Am Geophys Union; Int Astron Union. *Res:* Physical processes involved in solar and stellar flares and solar-stellar coronal heating; comet ion tail-solar wind interaction; radio and x-ray emission from clusters of galaxies; propagation of cosmic ray electrons. *Mailing Add:* Lab Astron & Solar Physics Goddard Space Flight Ctr NASA Code 682 Greenbelt MD 20771. *Fax:* 301-286-1617; *E-Mail:* holman@stars.gsfc.nasa.gov

HOLMAN, HALSTED REID, INTERNAL MEDICINE, IMMUNOLOGY. *Current Pos:* chmn dept, 60-71, PROF MED, SCH MED, STANFORD UNIV, 60-, CO- CHIEF, DIV FAMILY & COMMUNITY MED, 87- *Personal Data:* b Cleveland, Ohio, Jan 17, 25; m 49, 84, Diana Dutton; c Michael, Andrea, Alison & Geoffrey. *Educ:* Yale Univ, MD, 49. *Honors & Awards:* Walter Bauer Mem Award, Arthritis Found, 64; Hewlett Award, 85. *Prof Exp:* Intern med, Montefiore Hosp, Bronx, NY, 52-53, resident, 53-55; asst physician immunol, Rockefeller Univ, 55-58, asst prof, 58-60. *Concurrent Pos:* Nat Res Coun fel, Carlsberg Labs, Copenhagen, Denmark, 49-50; dir, R W Johnson Clin Scholar Prog, Stanford Univ, 69-; dir, Stanford Multipurpose Arthritis Ctr, 77- *Mem:* Am Soc Clin Invest (pres, 70-71); Asn Am Physicians; Asn Prof Med (treas, 67-70); AAAS. *Res:* Rheumatic disease; health services research. *Mailing Add:* Family-Community Med Sch Med Stanford Univ Stanford CA 94305-9991

HOLMAN, J ALAN, VERTEBRATE PALEONTOLOGY, HERPETOLOGY. *Current Pos:* assoc prof, 66-69, PROF GEOL & ZOOL, MICH STATE UNIV, 69-, CUR VERT PALEONT, 67- *Personal Data:* b Indianapolis, Ind, Sept 24, 31. *Educ:* Franklin Col, AB, 53; Univ Fla, MS, 57, PhD(biol), 61. *Prof Exp:* Asst prof biol, Howard Col, 60-61; assoc prof vert zool, Ill State Univ, 61-67. *Mem:* Soc Study Amphibious Reptiles; Soc Vert Paleont; Herpet League. *Res:* Paleontology of Cenozoic amphibians and reptiles. *Mailing Add:* 540 Linden St East Lansing MI 48823

HOLMAN, JACK PHILIP, MECHANICAL ENGINEERING. *Current Pos:* assoc prof, 60-66, chmn, dept civil & mech eng, 73-78, PROF MECH ENG, SOUTHERN METHODIST UNIV, 66-, DIR, THERMAL & FLUID CTR, 67- *Personal Data:* b Dallas, Tex, July 11, 34; m 64. *Educ:* Southern Methodist Univ, BS, 55, MS, 56; Okla State Univ, PhD(mech eng), 58. *Honors & Awards:* Convair Award, 55-58; George Westinghouse Award, Am Soc Eng Educ, 72; James Harry Potter Gold Medal, 86; Worcester Reed Warner Gold Medal, Am Soc Mech Engrs, 87. *Prof Exp:* Asst mech eng, Southern Methodist Univ, 55-56 & Okla State Univ, 56-58; task scientist fluid dynamics, USAF Aeronaut Res Lab, Wright-Patterson AFB, Ohio, 58-60. *Concurrent Pos:* Consult ed, McGraw-Hill Book Co, 66 - *Mem:* Fel Am Soc Mech Engrs; Am Soc Eng Educ. *Res:* Heat transfer; thermodynamics; fluid dynamics; fluidized and vortex heat transfer; programmed learning methods; audio tutorial instruction techniques; air pollution technology. *Mailing Add:* 11407 Crestbrook Dr Dallas TX 75230

HOLMAN, JOHN ERVIN, JR, VETERINARY PATHOLOGY. *Current Pos:* RETIRED. *Personal Data:* b St Louis, Mo, Nov 26, 33; m 54; c 3. *Educ:* Univ Mo, BS, 56, DVM, 56; Ohio State Univ, PhD(vet path), 65. *Prof Exp:* Vet, Nat Heart Inst, 56-62; vet pathologist, Vet Path Div, Armed Forces Inst Path, 65-67; scientist adminr, Animal Resources Br, Div Res Resources, NIH, 67-71, chief, Lab Animal Med & Vivarial Sci Sect, 71-73, dir, Lab Animal Sci Prog, Animal Resources Br, 73-87. *Mem:* Am Vet Med Asn; Am Col Vet Path. *Res:* Comparative pathology; laboratory animal medicine. *Mailing Add:* 11807 Enid Dr Potomac MD 20854

HOLMAN, KERMIT LAYTON, PROCESS ENGINEERING-PUMP & PAPER, PROCESS CONTROL & ANALYSIS. *Current Pos:* SR PROCESS ENG SPECIALIST, WEYERHAEUSER CO,81- *Personal Data:* b Morris, Minn, Nov 16, 35; m 59, Audrey Mae Redwing; c Erik, Jennifer(Zichel) & Peter. *Educ:* Univ NDak, BS, 57; Univ Idaho, MS, 61; Iowa State Univ, PhD(chem eng), 64. *Prof Exp:* Process engr, 3M Co, 57-60; sr chem engr, Dow Chem Co, 64-65; prof & dept head, Dept Chem Eng, NMex State Univ, 65-76; prof & chmn, Dept Chem Eng, Univ Idaho, 76-81. *Concurrent Pos:* Vis staff mem, Los Alamos Nat Lab, 66-81; chair, Forest Products Div, Am Inst Chem Engrs, 95-97. *Mem:* Am Inst Chem Engrs. *Res:* Process analysis and control in chemical recovery systems and pulping/bleaching systems in pulp/paper manufacture; project engineering and safety analysis in pulp/paper. *Mailing Add:* 31619 37th Ave SW Federal Way WA 98023-4008. *Fax:* 253-924-6324; *E-Mail:* holmank@wdni.com

HOLMAN, RALPH THEODORE, LIPIDS, POLYUNSATURATED ACIDS. *Current Pos:* assoc prof physiol chem, 51-56, exec dir, 75-85, PROF BIOCHEM, HORMEL INST, UNIV MINN, 56-, EMER PROF BIOCHEM, MED SCH; ADJ PROF BIOCHEM, MAYO MED SCH, 77- *Personal Data:* b Minneapolis, Minn, Mar 4, 18; m 43, Karla Calais; c Nils T. *Educ:* Univ Minn, BS, 39, PhD(physiol chem), 44; Rutgers Univ, MS, 41. *Honors & Awards:* Borden Award, Am Inst Nutrit, 66; Bailey Award, Am Oil Chem Soc, 72 & Lipid Chem Award, 78; Fachini Prize, Italian Oil Chem Soc, 74. *Prof Exp:* Instr physiol chem, Med Sch, Univ Minn, 44-46; Nat Res Coun fel, Med Nobel Inst, Stockholm, 46-47; Am Scand Found fel, Inst Biochem, Univ Uppsala, 47; assoc prof biochem & nutrit, Tex A&M Univ, 48-51. *Concurrent Pos:* Consult nutrit study sect, NIH, 59-62; NIH spec fel, Univ Gothenburg, 62; mem, Hormel Found, 79-86; organizer & pres, First Int Cong Essential Fatty Acids and Prostaglandins, 80; bd dir, Minn affil, Am Heart Asn, 90-92. *Mem:* Nat Acad Sci; Am Chem Soc; fel Am Inst Nutrit; Am Oil Chem Soc (vpres, 73-74, pres, 74-75); Am Soc Biol Chemists. *Res:* Essential fatty acids; polyunsaturated fatty acids in disease; metabolism of unsaturated fatty acids; metabolism of hydrogenated fats, quantitative requirements for essential fatty acids; mass spectrometry of lipids; lipoxidase; quantitative chemical taxonomy. *Mailing Add:* Hormel Inst Univ Minn Austin MN 55912. *E-Mail:* rtholman@maroon.tc.umn.edu

HOLMAN, RICHARD BRUCE, BEHAVIORAL NEUROCHEMISTRY. *Current Pos:* DIR BUS DEVELOP, CELEBRUS LTD, 97- *Personal Data:* b Washington, DC, Oct 26, 43; m 87; c 2. *Educ:* Colgate Univ, BA, 65; Purdue Univ, MSc, 67, PhD(psychol), 70. *Prof Exp:* Postdoctoral fel pharmacol, Inst Animal Physiol, Babraham, Cambridge, UK, 70-72; sr res assoc psychiat, Stanford Med Ctr, Stanford Univ, 72-79; lectr & reader, Physiol & Biochem, Univ Reading, UK, 79-88; prin scientist pharmacol, Reckitt & Colman Psychopharmacol Unit, Dept Pharmacol, Univ Bristol, UK, 88-96, sr res fel, 88-96. *Mem:* Am Soc Pharmacol & Exp Therapeut; Soc Neurosci; Int Brain Res Orgn; Int Soc Biomed Res Alcoholism. *Res:* Neurochemical basis of central nervous system disorders; monitoring changes in cerebral neurochemistry, in vivo microdialysis; behavioral modeling to investigate neurochemical regulation of behavior; HPLC techniques for monitoring changes in endogenous neurotransmitters. *Mailing Add:* Celebrus Ltd Forwood Park Bukharst Rd Ascot SL5 7PN England

HOLMBERG, CHARLES ARTHUR, VETERINARY PATHOLOGY. *Current Pos:* AT DEPT VET MED, UNIV CALIF, DAVIS. *Personal Data:* b Sayre, Okla, Nov 21, 44; m 64; c 3. *Educ:* Okla State Univ, BS, 67, DVM, 71; Univ Calif, PhD(comp path), 75. *Prof Exp:* Assoc prof path, Tex A&M Univ, 71- *Concurrent Pos:* Adj prof path, Univ Calif, Davis, 75-79. *Mem:* Am Col Vet Pathologists. *Mailing Add:* Univ Calif Davis VMTRC 18830 Rd 112 Tulare CA 93274

HOLME, THOMAS T(IMINGS), INDUSTRIAL ENGINEERING. *Current Pos:* exec dir, 53-81, EMER DIR, SIGMA XI, 81-; EMER PROF INDUST ENG, YALE UNIV, 73- *Personal Data:* b Frankford, Pa, Mar 12, 13; m 36; c 3. *Educ:* Lehigh Univ, BS, 35, MS, 40, IE, 48; Yale Univ, MA, 50. *Hon Degrees:* DEng, Lehigh Univ, 70. *Prof Exp:* Indust engr, E I du Pont de Nemours & Co, Del & Conn, 35-37; asst prof mech eng, Lehigh Univ, 37-41, assoc prof indust eng, 46-49, prof & head dept & dir curriculum, 49-50; chmn dept indust admin, Yale Univ, 54-63, prof, 50-73. *Concurrent Pos:* Fel, Trumbull Col, Yale Univ, dir Yale Coop Asn & Henry G Thompson Co; spec consult, Springfield Ord Dist, Ord Corps, US Army, 52-53, 56-57; consult, Hughes Aircraft Co, 58, 61 & 62, Southern New Eng Tel Co, 61, Hamilton Standard-United Aircraft, 63 & United Illum Co, 64; AAAS rep, exec comt, Sigma Xi. *Mem:* Fel AAAS; Am Soc Eng Educ; Sigma Xi; Am Inst Indust Engrs. *Res:* Engineering economy; industrial relations; education; operations research. *Mailing Add:* 773 Marlin Dr St Helena Island SC 29920

HOLMEN, REYNOLD EMANUEL, POLYMER CHEMISTRY, ORGANIC CHEMISTRY. *Current Pos:* VPRES, RES & DEVELOP, KEMSERCH, 85- *Personal Data:* b Essex, Iowa, Oct 23, 16; m 42, 93, Johnnie Gause; c Karen, John & Robert. *Educ:* Augustana Col, Ill, AB, 36; Univ Mich, MS, 37, PhD(org chem), 49. *Prof Exp:* Res chemist, E I du Pont de Nemours & Co, Mich, 37-43 & Philadelphia, 43-46; res chemist, Cent Res Dept, 3M Co, 48-54, group supvr, 54-55, head, Tech Info Sect, 55-57, head, Inorg Sect, 57-62, head, Org Scouting Group, 59-62, mgr gen res, Reflective Prod Div, 62-70, mgr gen res & vacuum coating, Spec Enterprises Dept, 70-73, mgr res & develop, Spec Enterprises Dept, 73-81, mgr, Life Sci Sector Develop Lab, 81-82. *Concurrent Pos:* Consult, 82- *Mem:* AAAS; emer mem Am Chem Soc. *Res:* Synthetic resins; chemical specialties; elastomers; catalysis; vinyl monomers; boron compounds; coordination compounds; chemical binding; vacuum coating; electroluminescence; glass microbubbles; retroflection. *Mailing Add:* 2225 Lilac Lane White Bear Lake MN 55110

HOLMER, DONALD A, ORGANIC CHEMISTRY. *Current Pos:* res specialist, 68-81, SR SPECIALIST, MONSANTO TEXTILES CO, 81- *Personal Data:* b Lead, SDak, Mar 29, 34; m 63; c 2. *Educ:* SDak Sch Mines & Technol, BS, 56; Okla State Univ, PhD(org chem), 61. *Prof Exp:* Res chemist, Ethyl Corp, 61-68. *Mem:* Am Chem Soc. *Res:* Synthesis and characterization of high polymers; textile fibers. *Mailing Add:* 164 Mirabelle Circle Pensacola FL 32514

HOLMER, RALPH CARROL, EXPLORATION GEOPHYSICS. *Current Pos:* PROF GEOPHYS, COLO SCH MINES, 72- *Personal Data:* b Chicago, Ill, Nov 24, 16; m 39; c 3. *Educ:* Colo Sch Mines, Geol Engr, 38, DSc(geophys), 54. *Prof Exp:* Geophysicist petrol explor, Mott-Smith Corp, 39-42; physicist, US Naval Bur Ord, 42-43; geophysicist petrol explor, Calif Co, 43-46; instr geophys, Colo Sch Mines, 46-50; geophysicist petrol explor, Exp Surv, Inc, 50-51; instr geophys, Colo Sch Mines, 51-52; chief geophysicist mineral explor, Kennecott Copper Corp, Colo, 52-64, dir, Explor Serv, Utah, 64-72. *Mem:* Soc Explor Geophys; Am Inst Mining, Metall & Petrol Engr. *Res:* Application of geophysical and geochemical methods to mineral exploration and to regional and local structural geological problems; geologic research for application in mineral exploration; application of computers to exploration problems. *Mailing Add:* 1943 Foothills Rd Golden CO 80401

HOLMES, CALVIN VIRGIL, MATHEMATICS. *Current Pos:* from asst prof to assoc prof, 56-64, PROF MATH, SAN DIEGO STATE UNIV, 64- *Personal Data:* b Newhebron, Miss, Oct 21, 24; m 56, Alvene I Hull; c Michael L & Julie A. *Educ:* Univ Miss, BA, 47, MA, 48; Univ Ill, MS, 52; Univ Kans, PhD, 55. *Prof Exp:* From instr to asst prof math, Murray State Col, 48-51; mathematician, Northrop Aircraft, Inc, 55-56. *Mem:* Am Math Soc; Math Asn Am. *Res:* Group theory. *Mailing Add:* Dept Math San Diego State Univ San Diego CA 92182

HOLMES, CHARLES ROBERT, GEOPHYSICS. *Current Pos:* RETIRED. *Personal Data:* b Kemmerer, Wyo, Oct 11, 18; m 46; c 3. *Educ:* St Louis Univ, BS, 48, MS, 50; Pa State Univ, PhD, 58. *Prof Exp:* Geophysicist & instr physics & geophys, NMex Inst Mining & Technol, 49-52, res geophysicist, 54-56; asst, Pa State Univ, 52-54; res geophysicist, Atomic Energy Comn, 56-57 & Birdwell, Inc, Pa, 57-59; from assoc prof to prof geophys, NMex Inst Mining & Technol, 59-89, sr geophysicist, 59-89. *Mem:* Fel AAAS; Am Geophys Union; Sigma Xi. *Res:* Atmospheric physics; thunderstorm acoustics; thunderstorm electrification; solid earth geophysics; electrical properties; tritium tracing and isotope exchange. *Mailing Add:* 1006 Lopezville Rd Socorro NM 87801

HOLMES, CLAYTON ERNEST, POULTRY SCIENCE. *Current Pos:* from assoc prof to prof, 49-70, EMER PROF POULTRY HUSB, VA POLYTECH INST & STATE UNIV, 70- *Personal Data:* b Sechlerville, Wis, July 20, 04; m 31, Alyce V Hahn; c Rolf F & Clayton J. *Educ:* Univ Wis, BS, 27, MS, 31, PhD(poultry genetics), 38. *Prof Exp:* Asst poultry husb, Pa State Col, 27-28; from instr to asst prof, Univ Wis, 28-41; assoc prof, Ore State Col, 41-46; mgr owner poultry breeding farm, 46-49. *Concurrent Pos:* Owner, Polled Hereford Breeding Farm, 51- *Mem:* Am Genetic Asn; Poultry Sci Asn. *Res:* Nutrition of poultry; control of intestinal parasites of poultry; genetics of poultry. *Mailing Add:* 2409 Bishop Rd NE Blacksburg VA 24060

HOLMES, CLIFFORD NEWTON, GEOLOGY. *Current Pos:* sr geologist, Phillips Petrol Co, 52, asst dir explor sect, 53, dir strategic minerals, 54-58, asst mgr mining & milling dept, 58-63, mgr minerals div, 63-71, VPRES & DIR, WESTERN HEMISPHERE & PHOSPHATE MINES, INC, PHILLIPS PETROL CO, 71-, ENERGY ADV, 72-, MGR MINERALS, PHILLIPS CHEM CO, 75- *Personal Data:* b Escanaba, Mich, Jan 1, 22; m 45; c 7. *Educ:* Univ Mich, BS, 43; Yale Univ, MS, 47; Univ Utah, PhD, 60. *Prof Exp:* Jr geologist, US Geol Surv, Kans & Calif, 43-45, asst geologist, Utah & La, 45-46, assoc geologist, Colo Plateau, 48-50. *Concurrent Pos:* Mem, Gov Energy Adv Coun, 75- *Mem:* Fel Geol Soc Am; Am Asn Petrol Geologists; Am Inst Mining, Metall & Petrol Eng; Am Petrol Inst; Soc Econ Geologists. *Res:* Mineral deposits. *Mailing Add:* 1431 Valley Rd Bartlesville OK 74003

HOLMES, CURTIS FRANK, ELECTROCHEMISTRY. *Current Pos:* VPRES TECHNOL, WILSON GREATBATCH LTD, 76- *Personal Data:* b Baton Rouge, La, Feb 14, 43; m 70; c 1. *Educ:* La State Univ, BS, 65; Ind Univ, PhD(chem physics), 69. *Prof Exp:* Fel & instr chem, La State Univ, 71-72; prin chemist, Calspan Advan Technol, 73-76. *Concurrent Pos:* Adj instr, State Univ NY, Buffalo, 83- *Mem:* Electrochem Soc; Am Chem Soc; Asn Advan Med Instrumentation; Nat Elec Mfrs Asn; fel Am Inst Med Biol Eng. *Res:* High energy density, high reliability lithium batteries for implantable devices and other speciality applications. *Mailing Add:* Wilson Greatbatch Ltd 10000 Wehrle Dr Clarence NY 14031

HOLMES, D BRAINERD, ELECTRICAL ENGINEERING. *Current Pos:* PRES, HOLMES ASSOC INC, 86- *Personal Data:* b New York, NY, May 24, 21. *Educ:* Cornell Univ, BSEE, 43. *Hon Degrees:* DSc, Univ NMex; DEng, Worcester Polytech. *Honors & Awards:* Paul T Johns Award, Arnold Air Soc. *Prof Exp:* Design engr, Western Elec Co, 45-53; mem staff, RCA Corp, 53-61, gen mgr, Major Defense Systs Div, 61; dir manned space flight, NASA, 61-63; sr vpres, Raytheon Co, 63-69, exec vpres, 69-75, dir, 63-86, pres, 75-86. *Concurrent Pos:* Mem tech staff, Bell Tel Labs, 45-53; proj mgr, Navy Talos Land Based Missile Syst Develop, 54-57, Air Force Atlas Launch Control & Checkout Equip Develop, 57 & Air Force Ballistic Missile Early Warning Syst, 58-61. *Mem:* Nat Acad Eng; fel Inst Elec & Electronics Eng; fel Am Inst Aeronaut & Astronaut; Aerospace Indust Asn; Nat Aeronaut Asn. *Mailing Add:* 166 Edmunds Rd Wellesley Hills MA 02181

HOLMES, DALE ARTHUR, ELECTRICAL ENGINEERING, OPTICS. *Current Pos:* CHIEF SCIENTIST OPTICS, LASER PROGS, ROCKETDYNE DIV, BOEING NAM, 74- *Personal Data:* b Biwabik, Minn, Dec 31, 37; m 62; c 2. *Educ:* Purdue Univ, BS, 60; Carnegie Inst Technol, MS, 61, PhD(elec eng), 65; Univ Rochester, MS, 69. *Honors & Awards:* Air Force Res & Develop Award, 71. *Prof Exp:* Asst prof elec eng, Carnegie Inst Technol, 65-66; chief optical integration group, Laser Div, Air Force Weapons Lab, Kirtland AFB, NMex, 66-74. *Mem:* Optical Soc Am; Inst Elec & Electronics Engrs. *Res:* Optical systems; high energy lasers. *Mailing Add:* 32850 Canyon Quail Trail Agua Dulce CA 91350

HOLMES, DAVID G, FOOD SCIENCE, BIOCHEMISTRY. *Current Pos:* PRES, NAT FOOD LAB INC, 85- *Personal Data:* b Lethbridge, Can, Mar 29, 43; m 67; c 5. *Educ:* Univ Alta, BS, 68; Brigham Young Univ, MS, 70; Utah State Univ, PhD(food sci), 73. *Prof Exp:* Teaching asst physiol, Brigham Young Univ, 68-70; biochemist & proj leader, Beatrice Foods Res, Chicago, 73-75; group leader res & develop, Foremost Foods, 75-77, mgr prod & process develop, Foremost-Mckesson Res, 77-82, dir res & develop, 82-85. *Mem:* Am Dairy Sci Asn; Inst Food Technologists. *Res:* Sell contract research in sensory evaluation, analytical testing, new product and process development for the food industry. *Mailing Add:* 18017 22nd St East Court Apt 22 Sumner WA 98390

HOLMES, DAVID SALWAY, BIOSENSORS, BIOREMEDIATION & BIOLOGICAL METAL RECOVERY. *Current Pos:* PROF BIOL, CLARKSON UNIV, 90- *Personal Data:* b Eastbourne, Eng, July 6, 46; m 69, Patricia J Lewis-Crosby; c Elizabeth, Timothy & Molly. *Educ:* Trinity Col, Ireland, BS, 69; Calif Inst Technol, PhD(molecular biol), 73. *Prof Exp:* Res fel, Calif Inst Technol, 73-75; asst prof, Duke Univ, 75-80; staff scientist, Gen Elec, 81-87; res prof, Rensellear Polytech Inst, 87-90. *Concurrent Pos:* Prin investr, NSF, Off Naval Res & NIH, 77-; vis scholar, UN, 85-90; vis prof, Am Soc Microbiol, 88, Univ Chile, 93- *Mem:* Am Soc Microbiol; NY Acad Sci; AAAS; Int Biotechnol Union. *Res:* Develop genetically engineered microorganisms for biotechnological applications including waste remediation, metal recovery and for biosensing. *Mailing Add:* May Rd PO Box 100 Potsdam NY 13676

HOLMES, DAVID W, PHARMACOLOGY. *Current Pos:* PRES & CHIEF EXEC OFFICER, ALLIED HEALTHCARE, 93- *Personal Data:* m 94, Marjorie E Coulson; c 4. *Educ:* Ball State Univ, BS, 64, MS, 67; Syracuse Univ, PhD(audiol), 72. *Prof Exp:* Assoc prof, Univ NC, 76-84, Tex Womans Univ, 84-88 & Univ NTex, 88-93. *Mem:* Fel Am Acad Audiol; Am Speech & Hearing Asn; Asn Clin Pharmacol. *Res:* Pharmaceutical new drug investigations. *Mailing Add:* 8215 Westchester Suite 150 Dallas TX 75225

HOLMES, DAVID WILLIS, ORGANIC CHEMISTRY. *Current Pos:* RETIRED. *Personal Data:* b Fremont, Ohio, Nov 24, 14; m 40; c 3. *Educ:* Amherst Col, AB, 37; Univ Mich, MS, 38, PhD(org chem), 40. *Prof Exp:* Rackham fel, Univ Mich, 40-41; res chemist, E I du Pont de Nemours & Co, Inc, 41-42, supvr, Chambers Works, 42-49, tech supt, Louisville Works, 49-50, asst works mgr, 51-52, prod mgr, Org Chem Dept, 52-56, dir mfg, Elastomer Chem Dept, 57-66, dir sales, 66-77. *Concurrent Pos:* consult, 80- *Mem:* Am Chem Soc. *Res:* Synthetic hormone synthesis; synthetic rubber polymers and latices; synthesis of compounds related to female sex hormones. *Mailing Add:* 4619 Weldin Rd Wilmington DE 19803-4825

HOLMES, DONALD EUGENE, MEDICAL PHYSICS, MAGNETIC RESONANCE. *Current Pos:* PROF PHYSICS, CALIF STATE UNIV, FRESNO, 76- *Personal Data:* b Wellington, Tex, Feb 17, 34; m 55; c 2. *Educ:* Univ Okla, BS, 58; Calif State Col San Diego, MS, 60; Univ Calif, Los Angeles, PhD(biophys & nuclear med), 66. *Prof Exp:* Res biophysicist, Gen Atomics, 59 & Northrop Aircraft-Norair Nuclear Sci, 60-61; chemist, Lab Nuclear Med, Univ Calif, Los Angeles, 61-66; Nat Acad Sci-James Picker Found fel, Lab Radiation Chem, Univ Newcastle-upon-Tyne, Eng, 66-67; Nat Acad Sci-James Picker Found fel, Dept Biophys, Univ Hawaii, 67-68, res biophysicist, 68-69; res biophysicist, Lawrence Berkeley Lab, Univ Calif, 69-71. *Concurrent Pos:* Assoc prof physics, Calif State Univ, Fresno, 71-76, sabbatical leave med physics, Univ Calif, Los Angeles, 77-78. *Mem:* Health Physics Soc; Biophys Soc; Am Asn Ultrasound Med; Radiation Res Soc; Am Asn Physicists Med. *Res:* Biophysics of membranes; radiation biophysics of nucleic acids; proteins and nucleoproteins; radiation chemistry of aqueous systems; radiation physics of solids; magnetic resonance spectroscopy; physical chemistry of biochemical systems; radioisotope technology; medical physics. *Mailing Add:* 2345 E San Ramon MS 37 Calif State Univ Fresno CA 93740-8030

HOLMES, DOUGLAS BURNHAM, RHEOLOGY, HEAT TRANSFER. *Current Pos:* PRIN/CONSULT, MINERGY ASSOCS, 90- *Personal Data:* b Indianapolis, Ind, June 16, 38; m 67, Elske Weijmarshausen; c 2. *Educ:* Rice Univ, BA, 60, MS, 62; T H Delft, Neth, DEng(appl physics), 67. *Prof Exp:* Res asst & lectr fluid mech, Tech Physics Lab, T H Delft, Neth, 63-68; res & develop engr, Res Labs, Polaroid Corp, 68-72; mgr camera opers, Polaroid, Europa, BV, 72-74; sr prin engr, Appl Tech Div, Polaroid Corp, 74-77, sr tech mgr, Battery Div, 77-84, sr mgr prod planning, 84-88; chief oper officer, Ecol Eng Assocs, 89. *Mem:* Am Solar Energy Soc; Brit Soc Rheology; Water Pollution Control Fedn; Koninkl Inst Eng; Sigma Xi. *Res:* Laminar, non-Newtonian fluid flow; heat transfer to such flows; heat transfer and fluid flow in solar heated dwellings. *Mailing Add:* Minergy House 4 John Wilson Lane Lexington MA 02173-6033. *E-Mail:* dbholmes@aol.com

HOLMES, E(DWARD) BRUCE, COMPARATIVE ANATOMY. *Current Pos:* assoc prof, 65-72, PROF BIOL, WESTERN ILL UNIV, 72- *Personal Data:* b Iola, Kans, Sept 29, 27; m 47, Lucille Anderson. *Educ:* Kans State Col Pittsburg, BS, 48; Univ Ill, MS, 50; Univ Kans, PhD(zool), 62. *Prof Exp:* Instr biol, Ark Polytech Col, 50-53 & Tex Col Arts & Indust, 53-56; asst prof, Westminster Col, 60-62 & St Olaf Col, 62-65. *Res:* Comparative vertebrate anatomy; avian myology; reptilian neuroanatomy; vertebrate heart. *Mailing Add:* 11 Woodland Lane Macomb IL 61445

HOLMES, EDWARD WARREN, BIOCHEMICAL GENETICS. *Current Pos:* resident med, Duke Univ, 70-74, fel metab & genetic dis, 71-73, chief resident med, 73-74, asst prof med to assoc prof, 74-81, PROF MED, DUKE UNIV MED CTR, 81-, ASST PROF BIOCHEM, 75- *Personal Data:* b Winona, Miss, Jan 25, 41; m 67. *Educ:* Washington & Lee Univ, BS, 63; Univ Pa, MD, 67. *Prof Exp:* Intern med, Hosp Univ Pa, 67-68; res assoc nephrology, USPHS, 68-70. *Mem:* Am Soc Human Genetics; Am Fedn Clin Res; Am Soc Nephrology; Am Rheumatism Asn; AAAS. *Res:* Studies on the control of purine biosynthesis de novo; regulation of human PP-ribose-P amidotransferase and prime metabolism in muscle function. *Mailing Add:* 7-131 Maysbelle School Rd Mt Olive NC 28365

HOLMES, FRANCIS W(ILLIAM), PLANT PATHOLOGY, SHADE TREE PATHOLOGY. *Current Pos:* CONSULT, 91- *Personal Data:* b Yonkers, NY, May 21, 29; m 53, Helen Bequaert; c Peter, Sarah & Joseph. *Educ:* Oberlin Col, AB, 50; Cornell Univ, PhD(plant path), 54. *Honors & Awards:* Nat Arbor Day Fedn Award, 79; Environ Merit Award, US Environ Protection Agency, 80; Merit Award, Int Soc Arboricult, 93. *Prof Exp:* Asst plant path, Cornell Univ, 50-54; from asst prof to prof, Shade Tree Labs, Univ Mass, Amherst, 54-91, dir, 73-88, Mass urban forestry coordr, 79-85. *Concurrent Pos:* NSF sr fel, Neth, 62-63 & Fulbright scholar, 62-63 & 70-71; Chair, Int Soc Arboricult Res Grants Comt, 80-92; Am Phil Soc grant, Neth, 84-85; sr res fel, Neth Agr Univ, 84-85; fel, Int Agr Ctr, Wageningen, Neth, 84-85. *Mem:* Emer mem Am Phythopath Soc; corresp mem Royal Dutch Bot Soc; emer mem Can Phythopath soc; hon mem Int Soc Arboriculture; Sigma Xi. *Res:* Dutch elm disease; urban street- and shade-tree disease diagnosis; inheritance and mechanisms of pathogenicity and disease resistance; salt injuries to trees; phytopathological translations; shade tree pathology; biological control of tree diseases; urban forestry; author of three books. *Mailing Add:* 24 Berkshire Terr Amherst MA 01002-1302

HOLMES, GEORGE EDWARD, MOLECULAR BIOLOGY. *Current Pos:* ASSOC PROF MICROBIOL, COL MED, HOWARD UNIV, 74- *Personal Data:* b Chicago, Ill, May 8, 37; m 67. *Educ:* Wiley Col, BS, 60; Chicago State Univ, MS, 67; Univ Ariz, Med Ctr, PhD(molecular biol, biochem), 73. *Prof Exp:* Med technologist area hosps, Chicago, 61-67; teaching asst molecular genetics, Univ Calif, Davis, 67-68; res assoc hemoglobinopathies, Rockefeller Univ, 73-74. *Concurrent Pos:* Teacher high sch, Chicago Bd Educ, 64-67. *Mem:* Soc Protozoologists; Am Soc Microbiol; Am Soc Clin Pathologists; Am Soc Biol Chemists; Fedn Am Scientists; Am Soc Virologists. *Res:* Molecular basis of aging; apurinic/apyrimidinic lesions and DNA repair mechanisms; alterations of essential components of protein-synthesizing machinery by virus-specified proteins; intragenic complementation; protein-protein interaction. *Mailing Add:* Dept Microbiol Howard Univ Col Med Washington DC 20059-0001. *Fax:* 202-806-4508

HOLMES, HELEN BEQUAERT, BIOETHICS, MEDICAL TECHNOLOGY ASSESSMENT. *Current Pos:* proj dir, 93-96, COORDR, CTR GENETICS, ETHICS & WOMEN, FERRE INST, UTICA, NY, 92- *Personal Data:* b Boston, Mass, Sept 6, 29; m 53, Francis W; c Peter, Virginia & Joseph. *Educ:* Oberlin Col, BA, 51; Cornell Univ, MS, 53; Univ Mass, PhD(zool), 70. *Prof Exp:* Tech asst parasitol, Col Vet Med, Cornell Univ, 53-54; teacher biol & chmn dept sci, Northampton Sch Girls, 65-67; teacher, Int Sch Beverweerd, Neth, 70-71; asst prof, Springfield Tech Community Col, 71-73; vis asst prof, Div Sci & Math, Eisenhower Col, 75-76; asst prof, Russell Sage Col, 76-78; vis lectr, Dept Biol, Tufts Univ, 78-80; scholar assoc, Womens Res Inst, Hartford Col Women, 86-87; scholar assoc, Off Womens Res, 90-91; assoc fel, Inst Advan Studies Humanities, Univ Mass, Amherst, 88-90. *Concurrent Pos:* Teaching asst, Dept Zool, Univ Mass, 67-70; Adelia

Field Johnston fel, Oberlin Col, 68-69; vis investr, Dept Biol, Amherst Col, 73-75; NSF & NEH grants, 78-80 & 82-83; reviewer, NSF-Ethics & Values Sci & Technol grant, 80 & 83; res assoc, Fedn Orgn Prof Women, 79-82; vis scholar, bioethics, Spelman Col, 82-83; vis scientist, Sci & Soc, Univ Groningen, Neth, 84-85; Fulbright scholar, Univ Waikato, NZ, 86; contractor, US Cong Technol Assessment, 87; guest ed, Hypatia Issue Feminist Ethics & Med, 89, ed, Issues Reproductive Technol I, 90-91; mem, Sci & Technol Task Force, Nat Women's Studies Asn; co-founder & co-coordr, Network on Feminist Approaches to Bioethics, 92-; NIH grants, 95-96. *Mem:* Sigma Xi; Inst Soc Ethics Life Sci; Am Philos Asn. *Res:* Population genetics of parasitic hymenoptera; technology assessment and ethical issues in reproductive medicine especially the new reproductive technlgies; women and science; ethical and social issues in genetics. *Mailing Add:* 24 Berkshire Terr Amherst MA 01002-1302. *E-Mail:* fholmes@pltpath.umass.edu

HOLMES, HOWARD FRANK, AQUEOUS CHEMISTRY. *Current Pos:* CHEMIST, OAK RIDGE NAT LAB, 58- *Personal Data:* b Toledo, Ohio, May 21, 31; m 61; c 2. *Educ:* Tenn Tech Univ, BS, 50; Univ Tenn, PhD(chem), 58. *Prof Exp:* Tech asst, Oak Ridge Nat Lab, 55; asst, Univ Tenn, 55-58. *Mem:* Sigma Xi; Am Chem Soc. *Res:* Surface chemistry; calorimetry; electrochemistry; electrokinetics; thermodynamics, solutions. *Mailing Add:* 5209 Yosemite Trail Knoxville TN 37909-1844

HOLMES, IVAN GREGORY, ANALYTICAL CHEMISTRY, HISTORY OF SCIENCE. *Current Pos:* assoc acad dean, Col Arts & Sci, 74-77, dean col, 77-80, PROF CHEM, LOMA LINDA UNIV, 72- *Personal Data:* b Castana, Iowa, Mar 26, 35; m 56; c 2. *Educ:* Ariz State Univ, BS, 57, MS, 61; Ore State Univ, PhD(chem), 68- *Prof Exp:* From instr to assoc prof chem, Andrews Univ, 60-72, assoc prof hist of sci, 70-72, dir freshman educ, 71-72. *Concurrent Pos:* consult, X-Ray & Nuclear Radiation Physics & Chem, Med & Gen Res Appln. *Mem:* AAAS; Am Chem Soc; Sigma Xi. *Res:* Analytical applications of metal chelates with emphasis on ultraviolet spectroscopy; x-ray fluorescence analysis of copper; unique instructional techniques using motion picture film; x-ray diffraction analysis of volcanic minerals. *Mailing Add:* Chem Dept La Sierra Univ Riverside CA 92515

HOLMES, JAMES FREDERICK, OPTICAL PROPAGATION THROUGH TURBULENCE, OPTICAL REMOTE SENSING. *Current Pos:* assoc prof, 74-78, chmn dept physics & elec eng, 74-88, PROF APPL PHYSICS & ELEC ENG, ORE GRAD CTR, 78-, CHMN, DEPT ELECT ENG, 94- *Personal Data:* b Billings, Mont, Sept 10, 37; m 59, Avon Ferne Opland; c 3. *Educ:* Univ Wash, BSEE, 59, PhD(electromagnetic waves), 68; Univ Md, MSEE, 63. *Prof Exp:* Engr, US Atomic Energy Comm, 57-63; res engr, Boeing Co, 63-66; res assoc electromagnetic waves, Univ Wash, 66-68; asst prof elec eng, Ore State Univ, 69-74. *Mem:* Inst Elec & Electronics Engrs; fel Optical Soc Am. *Res:* Experimental and analytical work on laser beam and speckle propagation through the atmosphere and its application to optical remote sensing. *Mailing Add:* Dept Elec Eng PO Box 91000 Portland OR 97291-1000. *Fax:* 503-690-1121; *E-Mail:* jfred@eeap.ogi.edu

HOLMES, JERRY DELL, ORGANIC CHEMISTRY, CHEMICAL & POLYMER RESEARCH & DEVELOPMENT. *Current Pos:* RETIRED. *Personal Data:* b Mt Vernon, Tex, Nov 30, 35; m 57, Margaret L King; c Lisa, Melinda, Jerry Jr & James. *Educ:* ETex State Col, BS, 56; Univ Tex, PhD(org chem), 64. *Prof Exp:* Jr chemist, Am Oil Co, Tex, 56-60; chemist to sr chemist res & develop, Tenn Eastman Co, 63-73, group leader org chem res, 73-74, div head, Res Div, 74-77, div dir, Develop Div, Tex Eastman Co, 77-80, asst to works mgr, 80-81, staff asst, Develop, Eastman Chem Div, 81-82, dir, Res & Develop, Tex Eastman, 82-84; dir, develop, Eastman Chem Co, 84-88, assoc dir, res, 88-89, vpres, 90-95, vpres, res & develop, 95-96. *Mem:* Am Chem Soc; Sigma Xi. *Res:* Product and process development and improvement in organic chemicals and polymers; management experience for a major chemical company research and development organization; extensive expertise in using TQM to increase productivity of research and development. *Mailing Add:* 1908 Fleetwood Dr Kingsport TN 37660-5729. *Fax:* 423-245-0235; *E-Mail:* jdholmes@preferred.com

HOLMES, JOHN CARL, HELMINTH COMMUNITY ECOLOGY. *Current Pos:* From asst prof to assoc prof, 59-71, PROF ZOOL, UNIV ALTA, 71- *Personal Data:* b St Paul, Minn, Aug 30, 32; m 57; c 2. *Educ:* Univ Minn, BA, 54; Rice Univ, MA, 57, PhD(biol), 59. *Honors & Awards:* H B Ward Medal, Am Soc Parasitol, 72; R A Wardle lectr, Can Soc Zoologists, 86. *Mem:* Ecol Soc Am; Am Soc Parasitologists (vpres, 80, pres, 91); Arctic Inst NAm; Wildlife Dis Asn; Can Soc Zool; Am Soc Naturalists. *Res:* Ecology of parasitic helminths, especially factors associated with the development and maintenance of communities of helminths. *Mailing Add:* Biol Sci Univ Alta Edmonton AB T6G 2E9 Can. *Fax:* 403-492-9234; *E-Mail:* jholmes@vm.ucs.ualberta.ca

HOLMES, JOHN LEONARD, PHYSICAL CHEMISTRY OF GAS PHASE IONS, ANALYTICAL MASS SPECTROMETRY. *Current Pos:* from asst prof to assoc prof, 62-73, PROF CHEM, UNIV OTTAWA, 73- *Personal Data:* b London, Eng, Nov 29, 31; Can citizen; m 58; c Susan & Jonathan. *Educ:* Univ London, BSc, 54, PhD(chem), 57; DSc, 83. *Honors & Awards:* Barringer Res Award, Can Spectros Soc, 80, Herzberg Award, 90; Medal, Chem Inst Can, 89. *Prof Exp:* Nat Res Coun Can fel, Ottawa, 58-60; Imp Chem Indust fel, Univ Edinburgh, 60-61, lectr chem, 61-62. *Concurrent Pos:* NAm Ed, Org Mass Spectrometry, 77-93; Overbeek vis prof, Univ Utrecht, 79; distinguished vis scientist, Univ Adelaide, 84; vis res fel, Australian Nat Univ, Canberra, 84, 93; mem, NSERC Chem Comt, 90-93. *Mem:* Fel Can Inst Chemists; Royal Soc Chem; Am Soc Mass Spectrometry; fel Royal Soc Can; Brit Mass Spectrometry Soc. *Res:* Kinetics of gas phase reactions; mechanisms and energetics of positive ion fragmentation; ion structures in the gas phase; ion beam chemistry and physics. *Mailing Add:* Dept Chem Univ Ottawa Ottawa ON K1N 6N5 Can. *Fax:* 613-562-5170; *E-Mail:* jholmes@oreo.chem.uottawa.ca

HOLMES, JOHN RICHARD, ATOMIC SPECTROSCOPY. *Current Pos:* chmn, Dept Physics & Astron, 63-72, PROF PHYSICS, UNIV HAWAII, HONOLULU, 63- *Personal Data:* b Chula Vista, Calif, Sept 24, 17; m 51; c 3. *Educ:* Univ Calif, AB, 38, AM, 41, PhD(physics), 42. *Prof Exp:* Asst physics, Univ Calif, 38-41, res physicist, Manhattan Proj, Radiation Lab, 42-45; from asst prof to prof & head dept, 45-63. *Concurrent Pos:* Fulbright lectr, Univ Madrid, 62-63; UNESCO Consult, Univ Buenos Aires, Arg, 70. *Mem:* AAAS; fel Am Phys Soc; fel Optical Soc Am; Sigma Xi. *Res:* Spectroscopy; optics of thin films; atomic transition probabilities. *Mailing Add:* Dept Physics & Astron Univ Hawaii Honolulu HI 96822

HOLMES, JOHN THOMAS, RADIOACTIVE WASTE DISPOSAL. *Current Pos:* mem tech staff, 76-85, MGR, SANDIA NAT LABS, ALBUQUERQUE, NMEX, 85- *Personal Data:* b Oak Park, Ill, Aug 10, 36; m 63; c 2. *Educ:* Univ Wis-Madison, BS, 58: Univ Calif, Berkeley, MS, 60. *Honors & Awards:* IR-100 Award, 74 & 92. *Prof Exp:* Chem engr, Argonne Nat Lab, 60-76. *Res:* Solar power-tower, component development and testing, systems analysis and system operation; nuclear reactor fuel cycle process development; reactor coolant purity; radioactive waste disposal. *Mailing Add:* Sandia Nat Labs Orgn 6348 PO Box 5800 M/S 1341 Albuquerque NM 87185-1341. *Fax:* 505-848-0881

HOLMES, JOSEPH CHARLES, chemistry; deceased, see previous edition for last biography

HOLMES, KATHRYN VOELKER, VIROLOGY, CELL BIOLOGY. *Current Pos:* assoc prof, 76-83, PROF PATH, UNIFORMED SERV UNIV HEALTH SCI, 83- *Personal Data:* b Philadelphia, Pa, Sept 14, 40; m 62; c 2. *Educ:* Radcliffe Col, AB, 62; Rockefeller Univ, PhD(virol), 68. *Prof Exp:* USPHS fel, Harvard Univ, 68-70; asst prof microbiol, Schs Med & Dent, Georgetown Univ, 70-72; asst prof microbiol, Southwestern Med Sch, Univ Tex Health Sci Ctr, Dallas, 72-76. *Concurrent Pos:* Consult, Molecular Anat Prog, NIH-Oak Ridge Nat Lab-Union Carbide Inc, 70-72. *Mem:* AAAS; Am Soc Microbiol; Sigma Xi; Electron Micros Soc Am; Am Soc Virol. *Res:* Virus-cell interactions, especially of moderate and cell fusing viruses; ultrastructure of virions and virus infected cells; pathogenesis of virus diseases; virus receptors. *Mailing Add:* Univ Colo Health Sci Ctr 4200 E Ninth Ave CB-B175 Denver CO 80262-0001

HOLMES, KENNETH ROBERT, TISSUE BLOOD FLOW, BIOHEAT TRANSFER. *Current Pos:* PRES, PERFTEC INC, URBANA, ILL, 86- *Personal Data:* b Lansing, Mich, Dec 14, 37; m 63; c 4. *Educ:* Mich State Univ, BS, 59, MS, 66, PhD(physiol), 72. *Prof Exp:* Assoc engr, Martin-Marietta Corp, Baltimore, 59-62; elec engr, Mich Dept State Hwys, 62-66; instr anat, Mich State Univ, 71-72; asst prof physiol, Southern Ill Univ, Edwardsville, 72-75; asst prof, 75-83, assoc prof anat, Physiol & Bioeng & asst head dept, Univ Ill, Urbana-Champaign, 83- *Mem:* Am Physiol Soc; Sigma Xi; Am Asn Vet Anatomists. *Res:* Development of a new thermal method of measuring local tissue blood flow; effects of toxins on tissue blood flow; biophysical properties of tissues; bioheat transfer. *Mailing Add:* Dept Vet Biosci Univ Ill 3639 Vet Basic Sci 2001 S Lincoln Urbana IL 61802. *Fax:* 217-333-4628; *E-Mail:* krholmes@uiuc.edu

HOLMES, KING KENNARD, MEDICINE. *Current Pos:* Resident, Univ Wash, 67-68, chief resident, 68-69, from instr to assoc prof med, 69-78, vchmn, Dept Med, 84-89, PROF MED, UNIV WASH, 78-, DIR, CTR SEXUALLY TRANSMITTED DIS, 89-, HEAD INFECTIOUS DIS, HARBORVIEW MED CTR, 95- *Personal Data:* b St Paul, Minn, Sept 1, 37; c 3. *Educ:* Harvard Col, AB, 59; Cornell Univ, MD, 63; Univ Hawaii, PhD(microbiol), 67; Am Bd Internal Med, dipl, 71, dipl infectious dis, 74; FRCP(E), 90. *Honors & Awards:* Squibb Award, Infectious Dis Soc Am, 78; Thomas Parran Award, Am Venereal Dis Asn, 83. *Concurrent Pos:* Epidemiologist, Div Prev Med, USN, Pearl Harbor, 65-67; head, Div Pulmonary Dis, USPHS Hosp, Seattle, 69-70, asst chief, Dept Med, 69-83, head, Div Infectious Dis, 70-83; dir, Sexually Transmitted Dis Clin, Harborview Med Ctr, Univ Wash, 72-79, adj prof microbiol & immunol, 78-, adj prof edpidemiol, 80-, chief med, 84-89; mem numerous adv comts, Nat Inst Allergy & Infectious Dis, NIH, USPHS, WHO & Nat Acad Sci, 74-; prin investr, NIH, Nat Cancer Inst, Nat Inst Allergy & Infectious Dis, Nat Inst Child Health & Human Develop, Centers Dis Control, 83- *Mem:* Inst Med-Nat Acad Sci; Asn Am Physicians; fel Am Col Physicians; Am Epidemiol Soc; Am Fedn Clin Res; AMA. *Res:* Sexually transmitted diseases and AIDS; etiology and natural history of cervical neoplasia; surveillance of gonorrhea. *Mailing Add:* Harborview Med Ctr Univ Wash 1001 Broadway Suite 215 Seattle WA 98122. *Fax:* 206-720-5003; *E-Mail:* worthy@u.washington.edu

HOLMES, L(AWRENCE) B(RUCE), astronautical & mechanical engineering, for more information see previous edition

HOLMES, MARK HAYDEN, MODELING & ANALYSIS OF SENSORY SYSTEMS & TISSUE. *Current Pos:* From asst prof to assoc prof, 78-89, PROF MATH, RENSSELAER POLYTECH INST, 89-, CHAIR MATH SCI, 94- *Personal Data:* b Onawa, Iowa, Nov 7, 50; m 88, Colette O'Connell;

c Matthew H & Marianna. *Educ:* Colo State Univ, BS, 73; Univ Calif, Los Angeles, PhD(appl math), 78. *Honors & Awards:* Y C Fung Young Investr Award, Am Soc Mech Engrs, 87. *Concurrent Pos:* Guggenheim Found fel, 86; vis prof, Imp Col, 86-87, Columbia Univ, 87 & Univ NSW, 94; ed, J Appl Math, Soc Indust & Appl Math 95-; prin investr, Proj Links, 97- *Mem:* Soc Indust & Appl Math; Am Soc Mech Eng. *Res:* Development and analysis of mathematical models of physiological systems; mechanoreception, how we sense and recognize mechanical signals like sound and touch and mechanics of hydrated tissues like skin and cartilage. *Mailing Add:* Dept Math Sci Rensselaer Polytech Inst 110 Eighth St Troy NY 12180. *E-Mail:* holmes@rpi.edu

HOLMES, MARK LAWRENCE, GEOLOGY. *Current Pos:* GEOLOGIST, US GEOL SURV, 75- *Personal Data:* b Tulsa, Okla, Sept 18, 38; m 74; c 2. *Educ:* Princeton Univ, BSE, 60; Univ Wash, MS, 67, PhD(oceanog), 75. *Prof Exp:* Sr oceanographer, Univ Wash, 67-75. *Concurrent Pos:* Res assoc, Univ Wash, 75-81, affil asst prof, 81-82, affil assoc prof, 82- *Mem:* Geol Soc Am; Am Geophys Union; Soc Explor Geophysicist. *Res:* Structure and evolution of continental shelves on the west coast of North America, with particular emphasis on evaluating hydrocarbon potential and identifying geologic hazards to economic development. *Mailing Add:* US Geol Surv Univ Wash Sch Oceanog Box 357940 Seattle WA 98195-7940

HOLMES, NEAL JAY, SCIENCE EDUCATION. *Current Pos:* prof sci educ, Cent Mo State Univ, 67-72, from assoc prof to prof chem, 72-87, head Dept Chem, 76-81, PROF SCI EDUC, CENT MO STATE UNIV, 87- *Personal Data:* b Mercer, Mo, Aug 2, 31; m 91, Carol Rollins; c 4. *Educ:* Northeast Mo State Col, BS, 57; Wash Univ, MA, 62; Okla State Univ, EdD(sci educ), 67. *Prof Exp:* Pub sch teacher, 57-61; sci consult, Parkway Schs, 62-67. *Concurrent Pos:* Consult, McGraw-Hill Publ Co, Mo, 63-66; panelist, Coop Col Sch Sci Proj Eval Comt, NSF, 68; mem, Teachers Indust & Environ Comt, 85- *Mem:* Nat Sci Teachers Asn. *Res:* Observational systems; systems to reliably determine the behavior of students, elementary and secondary, in science learning environments. *Mailing Add:* RR 4 Warrensburg MO 64093

HOLMES, OWEN GORDON, CHEMISTRY. *Current Pos:* from assoc prof to prof, 65-87, dean arts & sci, 66-71, ACAD VPRES, UNIV LETHBRIDGE, 72-, EMER PROF CHEM, 87- *Personal Data:* b Swift Current, Sask, Apr 1, 29; m 55; c 3. *Educ:* Univ Sask, BA, 48, MA, 50; Univ Calif, PhD(chem), 55. *Prof Exp:* Asst chem, Univ Calif, 51-52, res assoc, 54; asst prof, Regina Col, 55-61; assoc prof, Univ Sask, 61-65. *Mem:* Fel Chem Inst Can. *Res:* Inorganic chemistry; spectroscopy of material in condensed states; fused salt solutions. *Mailing Add:* 2708 S Parkside Dr Lethbridge AB T1K 0C5 Can

HOLMES, PAUL THAYER, STATISTICS. *Current Pos:* assoc prof, 69-77, PROF MATH SCI, CLEMSON UNIV, 77- *Personal Data:* b Sept 25, 35; US citizen; m 56; c 2. *Educ:* Wash State Univ, BA, 57, MA, 59; Stanford Univ, PhD(statist), 66. *Prof Exp:* Asst prof statist, Purdue Univ, 63-67; assoc prof, Rutgers Univ, 67-69. *Mem:* Am Statist Asn; Inst Math Statist. *Res:* Probability theory; Markov chains; mathematical statistics. *Mailing Add:* Dept Math Sci Clemson Univ Rm O Martin Hall Clemson SC 29634-1907

HOLMES, PHILIP JOHN, NONLINEAR MECHANICS, DYNAMICAL SYSTEMS. *Current Pos:* from asst prof to assoc prof theoret & appl mech, Cornell Univ, 77-84, dir, Ctr Appl Math, 81-86, PROF THEORET & APPL MECH & MATH, CORNELL UNIV, 84-, CHARLES N MELLOWES PROF ENG & MATH, 92- *Personal Data:* b Lincolnshire, UK, May 24, 45; m 70; c 4. *Educ:* Oxford Univ, UK, BA, 67; Southampton Univ, UK, PhD(eng), 74. *Prof Exp:* Res asst eng, Southampton Univ, 70-74, res fel, 74-77. *Concurrent Pos:* Prin investr, NSF, Air Force Off Sci Res & Off Naval Res grants, 78-; ed, Soc Indust & Appl Math J Appl Math, 84-89, Arch Rational Mech & Anal, 86-, J Nonlinear Sci, 89-; Aisenstadt chair, Ctr Math Res, Univ Montreal, 85-86; Fairchild scholar, Calif Inst Technol, 88-89; Guggenheim fel, 93-94. *Mem:* Am Math Soc; Soc Indust & Appl Math; Soc Natural Philos; Int Soc Interaction Math & Mech. *Res:* Mathematical theory of dynamical systems, with applications to the nonlinear dynamics of fluid and solid systems; nonlinear oscillations; Hamiltonian mechanics. *Mailing Add:* Appl Comput & Math Dept Princeton Univ Fine Hall Washington Rd Princeton NJ 08544-1000

HOLMES, RANDALL KENT, INTERNAL MEDICINE, MICROBIOLOGY. *Current Pos:* assoc dean acad affairs, 84-93, actg chmn, Dept Biochem, 93, PROF MICROBIOL & INTERNAL MED & CHMN DEPT MICROBIOL & IMMUNOL, UNIFORMED SERV UNIV HEALTH SCI, 76-, CHMN, DEPT BIOCHEM, 96- *Personal Data:* b Muskegon, Mich, Nov 7, 40; m 62, Kathryn Voelker; c Rebecca & Elisabeth. *Educ:* Harvard Col, AB, 62; NY Univ, MD & PhD(microbiol), 68. *Prof Exp:* Intern med, Beth Israel Hosp, Boston, 68-69, resident, 69-70; res assoc, Lab Biochem & Metab, Nat Inst Arthritis & Metab Dis, 70-72; from instr to assoc prof internal med, Univ Tex Health Sci Ctr, Dallas, 72-76. *Concurrent Pos:* NIH fel infectious dis, Univ Tex Health Sci Ctr, 72-73; mem, Vaccines Adv Comt, Nat Ctr Drugs & Biologics, 83-87, consult, 87-93; mem, Microbiol Test Comt, Nat Bd Med Examrs, 84-86, chmn, 87-93; mem, Bact Dis Rev Panel, Am Inst Biol Sci-Army Med Res & Develop Command, 85-, US Cholera Panel, NIH, 87-92 & Nat Bd Med Examrs, Comprehensive Part I Comt, 90-92; Bact & Mycol Study Sect, NIH, 92- *Mem:* Am Soc Microbiol; Am Acad Microbiol; Am Soc Clin Invest; Infectious Dis Soc Am; Am Col Physicians. *Res:* Pathogenesis of bacterial infectious diseases. *Mailing Add:* UCHSC-SOM Microbiol Dept 4200 E Ninth Ave B175 Denver CO 80262

HOLMES, RICHARD, biochemistry, for more information see previous edition

HOLMES, RICHARD BROOKS, MATHEMATICAL PHYSICS, OPTICS. *Current Pos:* SR STAFF SCIENTIST, LOCKHEED MARTIN PALO ALTO ADVAN TECHNOL CTR, 95-; PRES, NUTTRONICS, INC, 95- *Personal Data:* b Milwaukee, Wis, Jan 7, 59. *Educ:* Calif Inst Technol, BS, 81; Stanford Univ, MS, 83. *Prof Exp:* Sr syst analyst, Comptek Res, Inc, 82-83; staff scientist, Western Res Corp, 83-85; from staff scientist to prin res scientist, Avco Res Lab, 85-88; prin res scientist, North East Res Assocs, 88-90; sr mem tech staff, Rockwell Int Corp, 90-95. *Concurrent Pos:* Consult, 90- *Mem:* AAAS; Am Phys Soc; Optical Soc Am; Soc Photog Instrumentation Engrs. *Res:* Propagation of light in homogeneous and nonlinear media and related practical applications. *Mailing Add:* 101 First St Apt S331 Los Altos CA 94022

HOLMES, RICHARD BRUCE, mathematical analysis, systems analysis, for more information see previous edition

HOLMES, RICHARD TURNER, ANIMAL ECOLOGY & BEHAVIOR, AVIAN ECOLOGY. *Current Pos:* from asst prof to assoc prof, 67-75, chmn dept, 83-91, PROF BIOL, DARTMOUTH COL, 76-, HARRIS PROF ENVIRON BIOL, 92- *Personal Data:* b Monterey Park, Calif, Aug 7, 36; m 62; c 2. *Educ:* Humboldt State Univ, BS, 59; Univ Calif, Berkeley, PhD(zool), 64. *Honors & Awards:* Howell Award, Cooper Ornith Soc, 64, H R Painter Award, 67, 85; Brewster Medal, Am Ornithologists Union, 93. *Prof Exp:* Lectr biol, Univ Calif, Santa Barbara, 64-65; asst prof, Tufts Univ, 65-67. *Concurrent Pos:* Res grants, Arctic Inst NAm, 66 & NSF, 67- *Mem:* Animal Behav Soc; Ecol Soc Am; fel Am Ornith Union; Cooper Ornith Soc; fel AAAS; Soc Conserv Biol; Brit Ecol Soc. *Res:* Population and community ecology; structure and functioning of animal communities in forest ecosystems; behavioral and population ecology of migrant birds in breeding and wintering areas. *Mailing Add:* Dept Biol Dartmouth Col Hanover NH 03755

HOLMES, ROBERT RICHARD, INORGANIC CHEMISTRY, STRUCTURAL CHEMISTRY. *Current Pos:* PROF CHEM, UNIV MASS, AMHERST, 66- *Personal Data:* b Chicago, Ill, Aug 25, 28; m 56, Joan M Hickey; c Mary A, Kathryn & Robert. *Educ:* Ill Inst Technol, BS, 50; Purdue Univ, PhD(chem), 53. *Prof Exp:* From instr to assoc prof inorg chem, Carnegie Inst Technol, 53-62; mem tech staff, Bell Tel Labs, Inc, NJ, 62-66. *Concurrent Pos:* Ed-in-chief, Phosphorus, Sulfur & Silicon & Related Elements; vis prof, Nat Inst Arthritis, Metab & Digestive Dis, NIH, Bethesda, MD, 73, Univ Braunschweig, Ger, 73, Louis Pasteur Univ, Strasbourg, France, 80, Univ Calif, San Diego, 87, 91 & 94 & Univ Sci & Technol, Lanquedoc, Montpellier, France, 92; expert witness organotin chem; fac fel, Univ Mass, Amherst, 87. *Mem:* Am Chem Soc. *Res:* Synthesis, nuclear magnetic resonance, single crystal x-ray and spectroscopic studies of main group compounds, particularly organo phosphorus, silicon, and tin compounds; stereochemistry and mechanisms of nucleophilic substitution reactions at phosphorus and silicon; formation of new classes of organotin cluster compounds; the development of an active site model for cyclic AMP action; abinitio studies of the comparative reactivity at pentacoordinate phosphorus and silicon centers; 200 publications and two invited ACS monographs. *Mailing Add:* Dept Chem Univ Mass Amherst MA 01003. *Fax:* 413-545-4490; *E-Mail:* rrh@chemistry.umass.edu

HOLMES, ROBERT W, BIOLOGICAL OCEANOGRAPHY, ECOLOGY. *Current Pos:* assoc prof biol, 67-74, PROF BIOL SCI, UNIV CALIF, SANTA BARBARA, 74-, DIR, MARINE SCI INST, 69- *Personal Data:* b Dover, NH, Sept 9, 25; m 49; c 3. *Educ:* Haverford Col, BS, 49; Univ Calif, MS, 61; Univ Oslo, PhD, 61. *Prof Exp:* From jr res biologist to assoc res biologist, Scripps Inst Oceanog, Univ Calif, San Diego, 52-67. *Mem:* Am Soc Limnol & Oceanog; AAAS; Phycol Soc Am; Sigma Xi. *Res:* Diatom taxonomy, morphology and ecology; primary productivity of oceans. *Mailing Add:* 3749 Brenner Dr Santa Barbara CA 93105

HOLMES, ROGER ARNOLD, ELECTRICAL ENGINEERING. *Current Pos:* DEAN ACAD AFFAIRS, GEN MOTORS INST, 78- *Personal Data:* b Peekskill, NY, Aug 31, 31; m 55; c 3. *Educ:* USCG Acad, BSc, 53; Mass Inst Technol, SM, 58; Purdue Univ, PhD(elec eng), 62. *Prof Exp:* Asst elec eng, Mass Inst Technol, 56-58; from instr to assoc prof, Purdue Univ, 58-70; dean, Col Eng, Univ SC, 70-77. *Concurrent Pos:* Jr scientist, Midwest Appl Sci Corp, 59-64; scientist, Adv Res Corp, Ga, 61-64; teaching consult, Western Elec Co, 62-63; dir res, Radiation Dynamics, Inc, NY, 63-64; consult, Nat Aeronaut & Space Admin, 73- *Mem:* Inst Elec & Electronics Engrs. *Res:* Remote sensing of earth resources; electronics. *Mailing Add:* 5590 Old Pond Dr Dublin OH 43017

HOLMES, WILLIAM FARRAR, BIOLOGICAL STRUCTURE, COMPUTER SCIENCE. *Current Pos:* SR RES SCIENTIST, UNIV ARIZ, 87- *Personal Data:* b St Louis, Mo, June 6, 32; m 79; c 2. *Educ:* Princeton Univ, AB, 53; Univ Pa, PhD(biophys), 60. *Prof Exp:* Res fel biophys, Johnson Found, Univ Pa, 60-64; res assoc comput sci, Wash Univ, 65-68, asst prof, 68-74, assoc prof biochem, 74-87. *Mem:* Biophys Soc; Asn Comput Mach; Am Soc Mass Spectrometry. *Res:* Computer controlled mass spectrometry; computer analysis of biochemical self assembly. *Mailing Add:* 2335 E Seneca Tucson AZ 85719

HOLMES, WILLIAM NEIL, ENDOCRINOLOGY. *Current Pos:* assoc prof, 64-67, PROF PHYSIOL, UNIV CALIF, SANTA BARBARA, 67- *Personal Data:* b New Mills, Eng, June 2, 27; m 55; c 4. *Educ:* Univ Liverpool, Eng, BSc, 52, MSc, 54, PhD(zool), 57. *Hon Degrees:* DSc, Univ Liverpool, 68. *Prof Exp:* From asst prof to assoc prof zool, Univ BC, 57-64. *Concurrent Pos:*

Guggenheim Found fel, 61-62; external examr undergrad degrees in zool, Univ Hong Kong, 76-79 & 85-88; vis prof, dept zool, Univ Hong Kong, 73 & 82-83; dir, exp animal res, Univ Calif, Santa Barbara, 68-82. *Mem:* Endocrine Soc; Am Physiol Soc; Am Soc Zool; Brit Soc Endocrinol; Brit Soc Exp Biol. *Res:* Endocrinology of salt and water balance in lower vertebrates; interactions between hormonal regulators and petroleum pollutants; ultrastructual characteristics of steroidogenic cells of the adrenal gland in relation to their embryological development and specific functional properties. *Mailing Add:* Dept Biol Sci Univ Calif Santa Barbara CA 93106

HOLMES, ZOE ANN, FOOD QUALITY. *Current Pos:* from asst prof to assoc prof, 74-86, PROF FOODS, ORE STAT UNIV, 87- *Personal Data:* b Pittsburg, Kans, Feb 28, 42. *Educ:* Kans State Univ, Manhattan, BS, 64, MS, 65; Univ Tenn, Knoxville, PhD(food sci), 72. *Prof Exp:* Instr foods, Ore State Univ, 65-68 & Univ Tenn, Knoxville, 70; asst prof foods, Univ Tex, Austin, 72-74. *Concurrent Pos:* Reviewer, Instrnl Sci Equip Prog, NSF, 78-81; sr consult, Nutrit Res & Develop Ctr, Borgor, Indonesia, 82. *Mem:* Inst Food Technologists; Am Asn Cereal Chemists; Am Chem Soc; Asn Develop Comput-Based Instrnl Systs; Am Meat Sci Asn; Am Home Econ Asn. *Res:* Food science. *Mailing Add:* Sch Home Economics Ore State Univ Corvallis OR 97331

HOLMGREN, ARTHUR HERMAN, plant taxonomy, ecology; deceased, see previous edition for last biography

HOLMGREN, HARRY D, NUCLEAR PHYSICS. *Current Pos:* from assoc prof to prof nuclear physics, 61-74, PROF PHYSICS, UNIV MD, COLLEGE PARK, 74- *Personal Data:* b Minneapolis, Minn, Apr 21, 28; m 49; c 4. *Educ:* Univ Minn, BS, 49, MA, 50, PhD, 54. *Prof Exp:* Physicist, US Naval Res Lab, 54-61. *Mem:* Am Phys Soc. *Res:* The study of the mechanisms of nuclear interactions and the structure of nuclei; cyclotrons. *Mailing Add:* Dept Physics & Astron Univ Md College Park MD 20742

HOLMGREN, NOEL HERMAN, PLANT TAXONOMY. *Current Pos:* res assoc, 68-69, assoc cur, 69-74, CUR, NY BOT GARDEN, 74- *Personal Data:* b Salt Lake City, Utah, Nov 18, 37; m 69. *Educ:* Utah State Univ, BS, 62; Columbia Univ, PhD(taxon), 68. *Prof Exp:* Asst prof bot, Ore State Univ, 67-68. *Concurrent Pos:* Adj asst prof, Lehman Col, 74-; assoc ed, Brittonia, 75-77, ed, 77- *Mem:* AAAS; Am Soc Plant Taxon; Int Soc Plant Taxon; Bot Soc Am. *Res:* Floristic and biosystematic research; floristics of western United States; Penstemon and Castilleja; Scrophulariaceae of North and South America. *Mailing Add:* 401 Park Ridge Ln White Plains NY 10603

HOLMGREN, PATRICIA KERN, PLANT TAXONOMY. *Current Pos:* Herbarium specialist, NY Bot Garden, 68-69, assoc cur, 69-71, herbarium adminr, 71-73, herbarium supvr & adminr, Phanerogamic Herbarium, 73-75, head cur, 75-81, actg vpres bot sci, 88-91, ASST VPRES SCI & DIR HERBARIUM, NY BOT GARDEN, 81- *Personal Data:* b Athens, Ind, Jan 21, 40; m 69. *Educ:* Ind Univ, BS, 62; Univ Wash, NY Bot Garden, MS, 64, PhD(bot), 68. *Honors & Awards:* Merit Award, Bot Soc Am, 91. *Concurrent Pos:* Assoc ed, Brittonia, 75-91, managing ed, 84-91, ed, News & Notes, Taxon, 83-88; copy ed, Intermountain Flora, 74-; bd dirs, Am Inst Biol Sci, 81-85, Asn Systs Collections, 89-91, Int Asn Plant Taxon, 91-99. *Mem:* Am Soc Plant Taxon (treas, 85-88, pres-elect, 89, pres, 90); Int Asn Plant Taxon; Bot Soc Am (secy, 75-79, vpres, 80, pres, 81); Am Inst Biol Sci; Asn Systs Collections (secy, 92-94). *Res:* Floristics of western United States. *Mailing Add:* New York Bot Garden Bronx NY 10458-5126

HOLMGREN, PAUL, CELL BIOLOGY, ELECTRON MICROSCOPY. *Current Pos:* asst prof, 69-76, ASSOC PROF BIOL, NORTHERN ARIZ UNIV, 76- *Personal Data:* b Gary, Ind, Sept 25, 37; m 58; c 2. *Educ:* Ind Univ, BS, 60; Southern Methodist Univ, MA, 65; NTex State Univ, PhD(biol), 69. *Prof Exp:* High sch teacher, Ind, 60-65; asst prof biol, Pasadena Col, 65-66; teaching fel, NTex State Univ, 66-69. *Mem:* Am Soc Cell Biol. *Mailing Add:* Dept Biol Northern Ariz Univ Box 5640 Flagstaff AZ 86011-0001

HOLM-HANSEN, OSMUND, PLANT PHYSIOLOGY. *Current Pos:* RES BIOLOGIST, SCRIPPS INST OCEANOG, UNIV CALIF, SAN DIEGO, 62- *Personal Data:* b Sandefjord, Norway, Sept 9, 28; nat US; m 63; c 1. *Educ:* Harvard Univ, BA, 50; Univ Wis, PhD(plant physiol), 54. *Prof Exp:* Fulbright res award, Univ Oslo, 54-55; res biochemist, Radiation Lab, Univ Calif, 55-58; asst prof bot, Univ Wis, 58-62. *Res:* Intermediary metabolism of algae, especially photosynthesis, nitrogen-metabolism and microelement nutrition; biological and biochemical oceanography; nucleotide analyses. *Mailing Add:* 2336 Calle Chiquita La Jolla CA 92037

HOLM-KENNEDY, JAMES WILLIAM, PHYSICS, ELECTRICAL ENGINEERING. *Current Pos:* mem fac, 77-80, PROF ELEC ENG, SCH ENG, UNIV HAWAII, 80- *Personal Data:* b Los Angeles, Calif, Jan 2, 39. *Educ:* Univ Calif, Riverside, AB, 60; Univ Minn, MS, 63, PhD(elec eng), 69. *Prof Exp:* Sta & dist mgr, Riverside Press-Enterprise Co, 55-59; lab asst & reader, Univ Calif, Riverside, 59-60; teaching asst physics, Univ Minn, 60-63; lectr elec eng, Univ Calif, Santa Barbara, 69; asst prof elec sci & eng, Univ Calif, Los Angeles, 69-77. *Concurrent Pos:* Physicist, US Naval Ord Lab, 58-61. *Mem:* Am Inst Physics. *Res:* High field transport in semiconductors; semiconductor devices and device physics; solid state physics. *Mailing Add:* Dept Elec Eng-Hol 445 Univ Hawaii 2540 Dole St Honolulu HI 96822

HOLMLUND, CHESTER ERIC, BIOCHEMISTRY. *Current Pos:* from assoc prof to prof biochem, 67-74, PROF CHEM, UNIV MD, COLLEGE PARK, 74- *Personal Data:* b Worcester, Mass, Dec 14, 21; m 49; c 2. *Educ:* Worcester Polytech Inst, BS, 43, MS, 51; Univ Wis, PhD(biochem), 54. *Prof Exp:* Res chemist, E I du Pont de Nemours & Co, 46-47; adhesives chemist, US Envelope Co, 48-51; asst, Univ Wis, 51-54; res biochemist, Lederle Labs, Am Cyanamid Corp, 54-57, group leader, NY, 57-67. *Mem:* AAAS; Am Soc Microbiol; Am Soc Biol Chem; Am Oil Chemists Soc; Sigma Xi. *Res:* Biochemistry of microorganisms; mode of action of drugs on microorganisms and cell cultures; sterol metabolism in yeast and cell cultures; metabolic control mechanisms. *Mailing Add:* 4 Junco Lane Brevard NC 28712-9767

HOLMQUEST, DONALD LEE, NUCLEAR MEDICINE. *Current Pos:* PARTNER, HOLMQUEST & ASSOCS, HOUSTON, 91- *Personal Data:* b Dallas, Tex, Apr 7, 39; m 72, Ann N James. *Educ:* Southern Methodist Univ, BS, 62; Baylor Univ, MD, 67, PhD(physiol), 68, Univ Houston, JD, 80. *Prof Exp:* Electronic engr, Tex Instruments, Inc, Dallas, 62; intern, Methodist Hosp, Houston, 67-68; res assoc, Mass Inst Technol, 68-70; ast prof radiol & physiol, Baylor Col Med, 70-73; dir nuclear med, Eisenhower Med Ctr, Calif, 73-74; assoc dean med & assoc prof Tex A&M Univ, 74-76; dir nuclear med, Navasota Med Ctr, 76-84, Med Arts Hosp, 77-85; partner, Wood Lucksinger & Epstein, Houston, 80-91. *Concurrent Pos:* Scientist & astronaut, NASA, 67-73. *Mem:* Soc Nuclear Med; Am Col Nuclear Physicians; Sigma Xi. *Res:* Nuclear medicine; radiology; physiology; astronautics. *Mailing Add:* 1617 Ash Valley Rd Nashville TN 37215-4021

HOLMQUIST, BARTON, BIOLOGICAL CHEMISTRY, PEPTIDE CHEMISTRY. *Current Pos:* Res assoc, 68-86, ASSOC PROF, DEPT BIOCHEM & MOLECULAR PHARM, HARVARD MED SCH, 86- *Personal Data:* b Los Angeles, Calif, Mar 12, 43; div; c Brett & Kara. *Educ:* Univ Calif, Santa Barbara, BA, 65, PhD(chem), 68. *Concurrent Pos:* Vpres res & develop, BioNebraska. *Mem:* Am Chem Soc; AAAS. *Res:* Biophysical and mechanistic studies of enzymes and enzyme catalysis; magnetic circular dichroism of metalloproteins; peptide synthesis and production; amidation. *Mailing Add:* BioNebraska 3820 NW 46th St Lincoln NE 68524. *Fax:* 402-470-2100

HOLMQUIST, NELSON D, PATHOLOGY, CYTOPATHOLOGY. *Current Pos:* from asst prof to prof, 59-89, EMER PROF PATH, SCH MED, LA STATE UNIV MED CTR, NEW ORLEANS, 89- *Personal Data:* b Waterbury, Conn, Sept 27, 24; m 75, Marion Lowe; c 5. *Educ:* Princeton Univ, AB, 47; Columbia Univ, MD, 51. *Prof Exp:* Intern surg, NY Hosp, 51-52, asst resident, 53-55; instr path, Med Col, Cornell Univ, 55-59. *Concurrent Pos:* Nat Cancer Inst trainee diag cytol, Med Col, Cornell Univ, 52-53; asst attend pathologist, NY Hosp, 58-59; vis pathologist, Charity Hosp La, New Orleans, 59-70, sr vis pathologist, 70-89; consult, Vet Admin Hosp, New Orleans, 67-94. *Mem:* Am Soc Cytol; Am Soc Clin Path; Sigma Xi. *Res:* Diagnostic cytology; cancer research. *Mailing Add:* 12380 River Ridge Dr Folsom LA 70437. *Fax:* 504-796-3653; *E-Mail:* nHolmquist@Juno.com

HOLMQUIST, WALTER RICHARD, BIOCHEMISTRY, MOLECULAR EVOLUTION. *Current Pos:* asst res chemist, Univ Calif, 70-74, assoc res chemist, 74-80, sr res fel, 80-82, RES CHEMIST, SPACE SCI LAB, UNIV CALIF, BERKELEY, 80- *Personal Data:* b Kansas City, Mo, Dec 23, 34; wid; c Laurie M & Jon A. *Educ:* Washington & Lee Univ, BS, 57; Calif Inst Technol, BS, 61, PhD(chem), 66. *Prof Exp:* Lectr org chem & biochem, Univ Ife, Nigeria, 66-68; res fel biol, Harvard Univ, 68-70. *Concurrent Pos:* Prin investr, Nat Heart & Lung Inst grant, Univ Calif, Berkeley, 71-73; NSF grant, 77-81 & 83-87; math educr, WContra Costa Unified Sch Dist. *Mem:* AAAS; Am Chem Soc; Am Soc Biochem & Molecular Biol; Sigma Xi; NY Acad Sci; Soc Study Evolution; Am Inst Chemists. *Res:* Chemistry of heme- and electron transfer proteins; human hemoglobin, cytochrome c1; structure of thermostable bacterial spores; molecular evolution of proteins and nucleic acids; paleogenetics, methanobacteria. *Mailing Add:* 760 Mesa Way Richmond CA 94805-1743. *Fax:* 510-232-9205; *E-Mail:* kmnjo8a@prodigg.com

HOLMSEN, THEODORE WAAGE, APPLIED PHYSIOLOGY. *Current Pos:* RETIRED. *Personal Data:* b Teaneck, NJ, Mar 1, 30; m 53; c 4. *Educ:* Rutgers Univ, BS & MS, 58; Univ Fla, PhD(plant physiol), 61. *Prof Exp:* Plant physiologist, Dow Chem Co, 61-63; fel, Lab Chem Biodyn, Univ Calif, Berkeley, 63-65; group leader herbicide res, Agr Res Ctr, Dow Chem Co, 65-67, res plant physiologist, 68-69, assoc scientist, 69-78, sr assoc scientist, 79-84, res scientist, 84-88. *Mem:* AAAS; Am Soc Agron; Crop Sci Soc; Plant Growth Regulator Soc Am. *Res:* Applied and basic phyto-pharmacology. *Mailing Add:* 20 Mt Scott Ct Clayton CA 94517

HOLMSTEDT, JAN OLLE VALTER, dental research, for more information see previous edition

HOLMSTROM, FRANK ROSS, ELECTRICAL ENGINEERING. *Current Pos:* from asst prof to assoc prof, 70-81, chair elec eng, 81-84, PROF, UNIV MASS LOWELL, 81- *Personal Data:* b Port Angeles, Wash, Dec 28, 36; m 61, Lynda Lytle; c 2. *Educ:* Univ Wash, Seattle, BS, 58; Stanford Univ, MS, 60, PhD(elec eng), 65. *Prof Exp:* Res asst elec eng, Stanford Univ, 58-63; elec engr, NASA Electronics Res Ctr, 64-70. *Concurrent Pos:* Elec engr, Transp Syst Ctr, Dept Transp, 70. *Mem:* AAAS; Inst Elec & Electronics Engrs. *Res:* Electronic aspects of rapid transit safety; semiconductor electronics. *Mailing Add:* Dept Elec Eng Univ Mass Lowell One University Ave Lowell MA 01854. *Fax:* 978-934-3027; *E-Mail:* holmstrof@woods.uml.edu

HOLMSTROM, FRED EDWARD, ASTRONOMY. *Current Pos:* prof & chmn dept, 63-82, PROF PHYSICS, SAN JOSE STATE COL, 82- *Personal Data:* b Salt Lake City, Utah, Mar 31, 27; m 51, Ruth Walton; c 5. *Educ:* Univ Utah, BA, 55, PhD(physics), 59. *Prof Exp:* Res physicist, IBM Corp, 58-61; res specialist, Rocketdyne Div, NAm Aviation, Inc, Calif, 61-63. *Concurrent Pos:* Asst prof, San Jose State Col, 59-61 & San Fernando State Col, 61-63; indust consult, 64-; Esso Found grant, 68-69; NASA Consortium grant, 78-85. *Mem:* Am Phys Soc; Am Asn Physics Teachers. *Res:* Solid state, electron, ion, and MOS physics. *Mailing Add:* Dept Physics San Jose State Univ One Washington Sq San Jose CA 95192-0106

HOLOB, GARY M, CHEMICAL ENGINEERING, MATERIAL SCIENCE. *Current Pos:* RES & DEVELOP ENGR SYNTHETIC RUBBERS, E I DU PONT DE NEMOURS & CO, INC, 73- *Personal Data:* b Buffalo, NY, Feb 4, 47; m 70; c 1. *Educ:* State Univ NY Buffalo, BS, 69, MS, 70, PhD(chem eng), 75. *Mem:* Am Inst Chem Engrs. *Res:* Synthesis and refining of organic compounds; polymerization of synthetic rubbers; extrusion of non Newtonian materials; electrical conductivity of polymers. *Mailing Add:* 702 Westcliff Rd Wilmington DE 19803

HOLOIEN, MARTIN O, GENERAL COMPUTER SCIENCES, APPLIED MATHEMATICS. *Current Pos:* LECTR COMPUT SCI, UNIV CALIF, SANTA BARBARA, 84- *Personal Data:* b Wolf Point, Mont, Nov 13, 28; m 48; c 4. *Educ:* Moorhead State Univ, BS, 51; NDak State Univ, MS, 59; Univ Minn, PhD(math educ), 70. *Prof Exp:* Sci instr math & sci, Hillcrest Lutheran Acad, 51-58; math instr col math, NDak State Univ, 58-60, asst prof math, 61-68; sci comput programmer, Boeing Co, 60-61; from asst prof to prof comput sci, Moorhead State Univ, 68-84. *Concurrent Pos:* Chmn, Minn Statewide Comt Educ Comput, 75-76; mem, Taxon Comt, Develop Comput Sci Taxon, US Off Educ, 76; mem, Spec Interest Group, Comp Sci Educ, Am Comput Mach & Spec Interest Group, Comput & Soc. *Mem:* Asn Comput Mach. *Res:* Author of four computer science textbooks. *Mailing Add:* 3810 Pueblo Ave Santa Barbara CA 93110

HOLONYAK, N(ICK), JR, SEMICONDUCTOR MATERIAL & DEVICES, APPLIED SOLID STATE PHYSICS. *Current Pos:* PROF ELEC ENG, UNIV ILL, URBANA, 63-, MEM, CTR ADVAN STUDY, 77-, JOHN BARDEEN PROF ELEC & COMPUT ENG & PHYSICS, 93- *Personal Data:* b Zeigler, Ill, Nov 3, 28; m 55, Katherine Verger. *Educ:* Univ Ill, BS, 50, MS, 51, PhD(elec eng), 54. *Hon Degrees:* DSc, Northwestern Univ, 92, DEng, Notre Dame, 94. *Honors & Awards:* Cordiner Award, Gen Elec Co, 62; Morris Liebmann Prize, Inst Elec & Electronics Engrs, 73, Jack A Morton Award, 81, Edison Medal, 89; John Scott Medal, 75; Welker Award, 76; Solid State Sci & Technol Award, Electrochem Soc, 83; Monie A Ferst Award, Sigma Xi, 88; US Nat Medal Sci, 90; Charles H Townes Award, Optical Soc Am, 92; Nat Acad Sci Award Indust Appl Sci, 93; Am Soc Elec Engrs Centennial Medal, 93; Am Electronics Asn 50th Anniversary Award; Japan Prize, 95; John Bardeen Award, Metal Minerals Mat Soc, 95. *Prof Exp:* Mem tech staff, Transistor Develop Dept, Bell Tel Labs, NJ, 54-55; physicist & mgr, Advan Semiconductor Lab, Semiconductor Prod Dept, Gen Elec Co, 57-63. *Concurrent Pos:* Army instr, Univ Md, Yokohama, Japan, 56. *Mem:* Nat Acad Sci; Nat Acad Eng; Electrochem Soc; fel Am Phys Soc; Math Asn Am; fel Inst Elec & Electronics Engrs; AAAS; Elec Chem Soc; fel AAAS; fel Optical Soc Am; fel Int Eng Consortium. *Res:* Solid state electronic devices; transistors; diodes; switches; negative resistance devices; semiconductor technology; semiconductor controlled rectifiers; semiconductor devices; III-V compounds; semiconductor lasers and light emitters; semiconductor materials; light emitting diodes; lasers; quantum well devices. *Mailing Add:* Dept Elec & Comput Eng Univ Ill 1406 W Green St Urbana IL 61801. *Fax:* 217-244-6375

HOLOUBEK, VIKTOR, BIOCHEMISTRY, MOLECULAR BIOLOGY. *Current Pos:* from asst prof to assoc prof, 68-77, PROF BIOCHEM, UNIV TEX MED BR GALVESTON, 77- *Personal Data:* b Brno, Czech, Apr 19, 28; US citizen; m 64; c 2. *Educ:* Charles Univ, Prague, PhD(physiol, biochem), 52. *Prof Exp:* Res fel chem, Fac Med, Charles Univ, Prague, 52-53; res fel, Cancer Res Inst, Bratislava, Czech, 53-54, assoc res biochemist, 54-60; res biochemist, Cancer Res Inst, Vienna, 60-61; asst res biochemist, Virus Lab, Univ Calif, Berkeley, 61-63; asst res biochemist, Cancer Res Inst, Med Ctr, Univ Calif, San Francisco, 63-68. *Concurrent Pos:* Vis prof, Australia, 80-82. *Mem:* Am Soc Biol Chem; Am Soc Cell Biol; Am Asn Cancer Res; Sigma Xi. *Res:* Chemistry of histones and acidic nuclear proteins; regulation of gene expression, interaction of hormones, carcinogens and viruses with the cellular genome. *Mailing Add:* Dept Human Biol Chem & Genetics Univ Tex Med Br Galveston TX 77550

HOLOWATY, MICHAEL O, INORGANIC CHEMISTRY. *Current Pos:* RETIRED. *Personal Data:* b Stanislav, Ukraine, Nov 21, 22; nat US; m 45; c 4. *Educ:* Breslau Univ, PhD(chem), 44. *Honors & Awards:* J E Johnson Award, Am Inst Mining, Metall & Petrol Eng, 56; J Metals Award, 57; Interprof Coop Award, Am Soc Tool & Mfg Eng, Soc Mfg Eng, 67; Joseph Becker Award, 81. *Prof Exp:* Asst, Breslau Univ, 43-44; res assoc, Univ Heidelberg, 45-48; res engr, Cleveland Cliffs Iron Co, Mich, 49-51; metallurgist, Inland Steel Co, 51-54, chief raw mat res, 54-57, chief res engr raw mat, 57-59, raw mat & reduction, 59-62, assoc mgr, Res Dept, 62-74, dir raw mat & mineral res, 74-76, sr adv, Res Dept, 76-91. *Concurrent Pos:* Mem, US Del Steel Indust Execs to USSR, 58. *Mem:* Am Inst Mining, Metall & Petrol Eng. *Res:* Raw materials; beneficiation and agglomeration of iron ores; coal; preparation and coal chemistry; cooking processes; reduction of ferrous metals; heavy inorganic chemistry. *Mailing Add:* 12405 Clark St Crown Point IN 46307

HOLOWENKO, A(LFRED) R(ICHARD), MECHANICAL ENGINEERING. *Current Pos:* RETIRED. *Personal Data:* b Boston, Mass, Dec 10, 16; m 49, Virginia Irwin; c Richard I & Robbin D. *Educ:* Harvard Univ, AB & MS, 38, 39. *Prof Exp:* Mech engr, Westinghouse Elec Corp, Pa, 39-42; asst prof mech eng, Pittsburgh, 42-44; instr, Rice Inst, 44-46; from asst prof to emer prof mech eng, Purdue Univ, 46-82. *Mem:* Am Soc Mech Engrs; Am Soc Eng Educ. *Res:* Dynamics of machinery; machine design. *Mailing Add:* 300 Chippewa West Lafayette IN 47906

HOLOWINSKY, ANDREW WOLODYMYR, BIOCHEMISTRY, SCIENCE EDUCATION. *Current Pos:* ASSOC PROF BIOL, BROWN UNIV, 68- *Personal Data:* b Ukraine, Oct 25, 36; US citizen; m 59; c 1. *Educ:* La Salle Col, BA, 56; Univ Pa, PhD(bot), 61. *Prof Exp:* USPHS fel biol, Harvard Univ, 61-63, from instr to asst prof, 63-68. *Concurrent Pos:* Vis sr res assoc, Brandeis Univ, 67-68, vis assoc prof photobiology, 76. *Mem:* Am Soc Plant Physiol; Sigma Xi; AAAS. *Res:* Plant growth and development; chloroplast development and light physiology. *Mailing Add:* Box G-J 264 Providence RI 02912

HOLOWKA, DAVID ALLAN, MOLECULAR IMMUNOLOGY, CELL SURFACE RECEPTORS. *Current Pos:* res assoc, 80-86, SR RES ASSOC, DEPT CHEM, CORNELL UNIV, 86- *Personal Data:* b Rochester, NY, Aug 21, 48; m 79; c 3. *Educ:* St John Fisher Col, BS, 70; Tufts Univ, PhD(biochem), 75. *Prof Exp:* NIH fel biophys chem, dept chem, Cornell Univ, 75-77; Arthritis Found fel molecular immunol, Arthritis & Rheumatism Br, Nat Inst Arthritis, Metab & Digestive Dis, NIH, 77-80. *Concurrent Pos:* Reg ed, Molecular Immunol, 90- *Mem:* Am Asn Immunologists. *Res:* Biophysical and biochemical studies on the structure and function of cell surface receptors in the immune response, including spectroscopic studies on the receptor for immunoglobulin E. *Mailing Add:* Dept Chem Cornell Univ Baker Lab Ithaca NY 14853. *Fax:* 607-255-4137

HOLPER, JACOB CHARLES, CANCER, IMMUNOLOGY. *Current Pos:* RETIRED. *Personal Data:* b Bosworth, Mo, May 20, 24; m 46, Patricia Johnson; c Ann (Staton) & David. *Educ:* Univ Kans, AB, 49, MA, 51; Univ Mich, PhD(virol), 54. *Prof Exp:* Head, Infectious Dis Sect, Res Div, Abbott Labs, 54-64, dir, Infectious Dis & Parasitol Div Ill, 64-69, dir res & develop, Abbott Sci Prod Div, 69-72; dir, Cancer Res Br, Organon Teknika, 72-75, gen mgr, Biomed Res Div, 75-80, dir sci affairs, Bionetics Lab Prod, 80-89. *Concurrent Pos:* Mem, Virus Cancer Prog Sci Rev Comt B, Nat Cancer Inst, 74-78. *Mem:* Am Soc Microbiol; fel Am Acad Microbiol; Am Asn Immunol; Soc Exp Biol & Med. *Res:* Infectious diseases; antibiotics; chemotherapy of viruses; viral induced cancer; virus vaccines; biologic products research and development; immunodiagnostics. *Mailing Add:* 12 Windsor Dr Charleston SC 29407-3410

HOLROYD, LOUIS VINCENT, PHYSICS. *Current Pos:* From asst prof to assoc prof, Univ Mo, Columbia, 50-61, chmn dept, 56-74, prof physics, 61-87, campus safety coordr, 77-87, EMER PROF PHYSICS, UNIV MO, COLUMBIA, 87- *Personal Data:* b Vancouver, BC, Jan 22, 25; m 50; c 4. *Educ:* Univ BC, BA, 45, MA, 47; Univ Notre Dame, PhD(physics), 50. *Concurrent Pos:* Chmn, Hazardous Waste Task Force, Mo. *Mem:* Am Phys Soc; Am Asn Physics Teachers. *Res:* Electron spin resonance of ions and defects in crystals; improvement of high school teaching; enviromental science. *Mailing Add:* 2235 Bluff Blvd Columbia MO 65201-6101

HOLROYD, RICHARD ALLAN, RADIATION CHEMISTRY. *Current Pos:* chemist, 69-89, SR CHEMIST, BROOKHAVEN NAT LAB, 89- *Personal Data:* b Jamestown, NY, Dec 31, 30; m 57, Dwana Thomas; c 2. *Educ:* Col Wooster, BA, 52; Univ Rochester, PhD(phys chem), 56. *Prof Exp:* Asst prof eng, Univ Calif, Los Angeles-AID Prog Indonesia, 57-59; fel radiation chem, Mellon Inst, 59-64; res specialist, Atomics Int Div, NAm Rockwell Corp, Calif, 64-69. *Concurrent Pos:* US sr scientist award, Humboldt Found, WGer, 75-76; assoc ed, Radiation Res Soc, 75-78. *Mem:* Radiation Res Soc; Am Chem Soc. *Res:* Photoionization and photodetachment processes in non-polar fluids; photolysis of aliphatic hydrocarbons; pulse radiolysis; electron mobility in fluids; reactions and energies of electrons in fluids; electron reactions in non-polar liquids; pressure effects. *Mailing Add:* Brookhaven Nat Lab 555 Upton NY 11973

HOLROYDE, CHRISTOPHER PETER, oncology, for more information see previous edition

HOLSAPPLE, CLYDE W, DECISION SUPPORT SYSTEMS & KNOWLEDGE MANAGEMENT, ORGANIZATIONAL COMPUTING & ELECTRONIC COMMERCE TECHNOLOGY. *Current Pos:* PROF DECISION SCI & INFO SYSTS, UNIV KY, 88-, ROSENTHAL ENDOWED CHAIR MGT INFO SYSTS, 88-, COORDR, DECISION SCI & INFO SYSTS AREA, 94- *Personal Data:* b Raleigh, NC, Nov 1, 50; m 90, Carol Eades; c Christina & Claire. *Educ:* Purdue Univ, BS, 72, MS, 75, PhD(mgt sci info systs), 77. *Prof Exp:* Vis asst prof mgt, Purdue Univ, 77-78, vis assoc prof mgt & comput sci, 81-82, from assoc prof to prof mgt, 83-89. *Concurrent Pos:* Asst & assoc prof bus admin, Univ Ill, 78-83; co-dir, NATO Advan Study Inst, 85 & 91; area ed, J Comput, Opers Res Soc Am, 88-92, Decision Support Systs, 92-; adj prof mgt sci & info systs, Univ Tex, 89-; assoc ed, J Orgn Comput & Electronic Com, 90-, Mgt Sci, 91-; chmn, Dept Decision Sci & Info Systs, Univ Ky, 93-94. *Mem:* Asn Mgt Info Systs; Decision Sci Inst; Int Soc Decision Support Systs; Inst Elec & Electronics Engrs Comput Soc; Inst Opers Res & Mgt Sci. *Res:* Artificially intelligent systems; tools and methods for creating systems that support decision making; computer based means for conduct of commerce and business. *Mailing Add:* Gatton Bus & Econ Bldg Univ Ky Lexington KY 40506-0034. *Fax:* 606-257-8031; *E-Mail:* cwhols@ukcc.uky.edu

HOLSCLAW, DOUGLAS S, JR, PEDIATRICS, PULMONARY DISEASES. *Current Pos:* from asst prof to assoc prof, 70-78, PROF PEDIAT, HAHNEMAN UNIV, 78- *Personal Data:* b Tucson, Ariz, Nov 25, 34; m 77, Anne Topham; c Douglas III & Alison. *Educ:* Univ Ariz, BA, 56; Columbia Univ, MD, 60; Inst Child Health, London, DCH, 64. *Prof Exp:* Intern med, Univ Chicago Clins, 60-61; resident, Children's Hosp, Cincinnati, 61-63; registr, Hosp Sick Children, 63-64; fel, Children's Hosp, Boston, 66-68; instr pediat, Harvard Med Sch, 68-70. *Concurrent Pos:* Dir, Pediat Pulmonary & Cystic Fibrosis Ctrs, 70-; mem, Med Adv Coun, Cystic Fibrosis Found, 73-77; gov appointee, Adv Health Bd & Secy Health, 80-90; Pulmonary Acad Award, Nat Heart & Lung Inst, 74-77; interim chmn, Dept Pediat, Hahnemann Univ, 88-90. *Mem:* Am Pediat Soc; Am Thoracic Soc; Am Acad Pediat. *Res:* Acute and chronic pediatric pulmonary disorders with particular attention to children and adults with cystic fibrosis. *Mailing Add:* Dept Pediat Hahnemann Univ 230 N Broad St Philadelphia PA 19102. *Fax:* 215-762-1601

HOLSEN, JAMES N(OBLE), THERMODYNAMICS & MATERIAL PROPERTIES. *Current Pos:* CONSULT ENGR, 92- *Personal Data:* b Palo Alto, Calif, June 20, 24; m 50, 77, Margot Meyer; c James III & David. *Educ:* Princeton Univ, BS, 48; Washington Univ, DSc, 54. *Prof Exp:* Chem engr, Olin Mathieson Chem Corp, 54-55; from asst prof to prof chem eng, Washington Univ, 55-73; prof chem eng, Univ Mo, Rolla, 73-76; sr tech prog mgr, McDonnell Douglas Corp, 77-92. *Concurrent Pos:* Vis prof mech eng, Kabul Univ, Afghanistan, 63-64 & 69-73, chem eng, Nat Tech Inst, Saigon, Vietnam, 73-74. *Mem:* Am Chem Soc; assoc fel Am Inst Aeronaut & Astronaut; Am Inst Chem Engrs; Am Soc Eng Educ; AAAS; Sigma Xi. *Res:* Mass transfer and chemical kinetics; shock tube studies in high temperature chemical kinetics; gas dynamics and re-entry thermodynamics; materials processing in space; satellite components and structural materials; chemical engineering. *Mailing Add:* 419 E Argonne Dr Kirkwood MO 63122. *Fax:* 314-822-0410

HOLSEN, THOMAS MICHAEL, ENVIRONMENTAL CHEMISTRY, DRY DEPOSITION. *Current Pos:* ASST PROF ENVIRON ENG, ILL INST TECHNOL, 88- *Personal Data:* b Milwaukee, Wis, Oct 16, 59; m 82; c 2. *Educ:* Univ Calif, Berkeley, BS, 83, MS, 85, PhD(civil & environ eng), 88. *Prof Exp:* Environ scientist, Kennedy-Jenks Engrs, 83-84. *Mem:* Am Chem Soc; Asn Environ Eng Professors; Int Asn Water Pollution. *Res:* Environmental chemistry; fate and transport of organic chemicals in the environment; air toxics; dry deposition; sorption of organic chemicals on natural surfaces. *Mailing Add:* IIT Ctr Environ Eng Chicago IL 60616

HOLSER, WILLIAM THOMAS, MINERALOGY. *Current Pos:* prof, 70-86, EMER PROF GEOL, UNIV ORE, 86- *Personal Data:* b Bakersfield, Calif, July 4, 20; m 54, Mary A Harris; c Thomas D, Alec S & Margaret (Anolfo). *Educ:* Calif Inst Technol, BS, 42, MSc, 46; Columbia Univ, PhD(ore deposits), 50. *Prof Exp:* Asst geol, Calif Inst Technol, 45-46; lectr, Columbia Univ, 46-48; asst prof, Cornell Univ, 48-54; geologist, US Geol Surv, 48-54; prin geochemist, Battelle Mem Inst, 54-55; res geochemist, Inst Geophys, Univ Calif, Los Angeles, 55-58; sr res assoc mineral, Chevron Oil Field Res Co, 58-70. *Concurrent Pos:* Mem comt int tables, Int Union Crystallog, 63-65, 71-76; ed, Am Mineral, 66-72; Fulbright fel, 76; Alexander von Humboldt US sr scientist award, 76; Caswell Silver Res Prof, Univ NMex, 83; counr, Geochem Soc, 86-88; vis scientist, Cornell Univ, 89- *Mem:* Geol Soc Am; Am Geophys Union; hon life fel Mineral Soc Am; Geochem Soc; Soc Econ Geologists. *Res:* Mineralogy and geochemistry of bromine, sulfur, carbon, strontium and rare earths; geology of evaporites; stable isotope geochemistry and chemical history of the oceans and sediments; mass extinction events. *Mailing Add:* 2620 Cresta De Ruta St Eugene OR 97403

HOLSHOUSER, DON F, PHYSICAL ELECTRONICS. *Current Pos:* res assoc microwave tubes, Dept Elec Eng, Univ Ill, Urbana, 46-51, asst prof, 51-58, assoc prof & prof dir, 58-65, prof microwave & optical electronics, 65-82, EMER PROF, DEPT ELEC ENG, UNIV ILL, URBANA, 82- *Personal Data:* b Dwight, Kans, Mar 23, 20; m 43; c 3. *Educ:* Kans State Col, BS, 42; Univ Ill, MS, 50, PhD(elec eng), 59. *Prof Exp:* Develop engr cathode ray tubes, Radio Corp of Am, Pa, 42-46. *Concurrent Pos:* Air Force Off Sci Res grants, 58-72; vis prof, Athens Tech, 64-65. *Mem:* Fel AAAS. *Res:* Modulation and demodulation of light at microwave frequencies; solar energy. *Mailing Add:* Off Two Lights Rd Cape Elizabeth ME 04107

HOLSHOUSER, W(ILLIAM) L(UTHER), METALLURGY. *Current Pos:* RETIRED. *Personal Data:* b Blowing Rock, NC, Oct 23, 11; m 35, Louise Von Canon; c William, Elizabeth & Linda. *Educ:* Davidson Col, BS, 33. *Prof Exp:* Phys sci aide, Nat Bur Standards, 39-41, jr metallurgist to assoc metallurgist, 41-47, metallurgist, 47-57, aeronaut struct mat res engr, 57-59, phys metallurgist, 59-62; staff metallurgist, Civil Aeronaut Bd, 62-67; staff metallurgist, Nat Transp Safety Bd, 67-73, chief, Lab Serv staff, 71-73. *Concurrent Pos:* Conferee World Metall Cong, Chicago, 57; consult aircraft metall, 73-81. *Mem:* Am Soc Metals; Am Soc Testing & Mat. *Res:* Fatigue of metals; quality of aircraft welding; service failures and corrosion of metals; effects of prior fatigue stressing on the impact resistance of chromium molybdenum aircraft steel; evaluation of fatigue damage of steel by supplementary tension impact tests; investigation of aircraft accidents. *Mailing Add:* RR 1 Banner Elk NC 28604

HOLSINGER, JOHN ROBERT, BIOSPELEOLOGY, INVERTEBRATE SYSTEMATICS. *Current Pos:* from asst prof to assoc prof, 68-78, PROF BIOL, OLD DOMINION UNIV, 78- *Personal Data:* b Harrisonburg, Va, Apr 6, 34; m 85, Linda J Bogen. *Educ:* Va Polytech Inst, BS, 55; James Madison Univ, MS, 63; Univ Ky, PhD(biol), 66. *Honors & Awards:* Award for Lifetime Contribs to Sci off Speleol, Nat Speleol Soc, 95. *Prof Exp:* Instr, Fairfax Co Sec Sch Syst, 58-63; asst zool, Univ Ky, 63-66; asst prof biol & zool, ETenn State Univ, 66-68. *Concurrent Pos:* Vis assoc cur, Dept Invert Zool, Smithsonian Inst, 72-73 & res assoc, 90-; eminent scholar, Old Dominion Univ, 90-; res assoc, Va Mus Natural Hist, 93- *Mem:* AAAS; hon life mem Nat Speleol Soc; Soc Syst Biol; Crustacean Soc; Sigma Xi; Willi Hennig Soc. *Res:* Systematics, ecology and zoogeography of freshwater amphipod crustaceans of North America, especially subterranean forms; zoogeography of cavernicolous invertebrates of the Appalachians; groundwater ecology. *Mailing Add:* Dept Biol Old Dominion Univ Norfolk VA 23529-0266. *Fax:* 757-683-5283; *E-Mail:* jrh100f@viper.mgb.odu.edu

HOLSINGER, KENT EUGENE, THEORETICAL POPULATION GENETICS, PLANT POPULATION GENETICS. *Current Pos:* ASST PROF ECOL & EVOLUTIONARY BIOL, UNIV CONN, 86- *Personal Data:* b Oregon City, Ore, Oct 15, 56. *Educ:* Col Idaho, BS, 78; Stanford Univ, PhD(biol sci), 82. *Prof Exp:* Res fel, Miller Inst Basic Res Sci, Univ Calif, Berkeley, 82-84; res assoc, Dept Biol Sci, Stanford Univ, 84-86. *Concurrent Pos:* Assoc, dept genetics, Agr Exp Sta, Univ Calif, Davis, 85, adj lectr, 85. *Mem:* Soc Study Evolution; Am Soc Naturalists; Genetics Soc Am; Bot Soc Am; Am Soc Plant Taxonomists; Int Asn Plant Taxonomists. *Res:* Plant evolutionary biology, including systematics; theoretical population genetics, especially the evolution and consequences of self-fertilization in plants; comparative and experimental studies on genetic and phenotypic variation in natural populations of plants; philosophy of biology, especially theories of systematics and theories of explanation in the fields of organismal and evolutionary biology. *Mailing Add:* Univ Conn U-43 75 N Eagleville Rd Storrs CT 06268

HOLSINGER, VIRGINIA HARRIS, FOOD SCIENCES & TECHNOLOGY. *Current Pos:* Res chemist, 58-80, SUPVR RES CHEMIST, US DEPT AGR, 80- *Personal Data:* b Washington, DC. *Educ:* Col William & Mary, BS, 58; Ohio State Univ, PhD(food sci & nutrit), 80. *Honors & Awards:* Col Rohland A Isker Award, 84; Indust Achievement Award (Team), Inst Food Technologists, 87. *Mem:* Am Chem Soc; Am Dairy Sci Asn; Inst Food Technologists; Int Dairy Fedn. *Res:* Plan, supervise and execute research directed toward maintenance of quality and safety of processed dairy products and other foods. *Mailing Add:* Agr Res Serv US Dept Agr 600 E Mermaid Lane Philadelphia PA 19118

HOLSON, RALPH ROBERT, NEUROBIOLOGY OF NEOCORTEX, DEVELOPMENTAL PSYCHOBIOLOGY. *Current Pos:* Staff fel, 84-86, res psychologist, 86-88, ACTG CHIEF, PERINATAL & POSTNATAL EVAL BR, DIV REPRODUCTIVE & DEVELOP TOXICOL, NAT CTR TOXICOL RES, 88- *Personal Data:* b Nashville, Tenn, July 26, 41; m 66; c 2. *Educ:* Univ Calif, Berkeley, BA, 66; Univ Wash, PhD(psychol), 84. *Mem:* Behav Teratology Soc; Soc Neurosci; Int Soc Develop Psychobiol; AAAS. *Res:* Effect of perinatal drug exposure on the developing dopamine system; effect of isolation rearing on brain and behavior; development and function of the pre-frontal cortex. *Mailing Add:* Perinatal Assessment Br Nat Ctr Toxicol Res Nat Ctr Toxicol Res Dr Jefferson AR 72079

HOLST, EDWARD HARLAND, ORGANIC CHEMISTRY. *Current Pos:* CONSULT, 89- *Personal Data:* b Beaumont, Tex, Jan 25, 30; m 49; c 5. *Educ:* NTex State Col, BA, 51, MS, 53; Pa State Univ, PhD(org chem), 55. *Prof Exp:* Asst, Pa State Univ, 54; res chemist, Texaco, Inc, 55-61, sr proj chemist, 61-67, asst supvr chem res, 67-74, supvr res, 74-87. *Mem:* AAAS; Am Chem Soc. *Res:* Polymers; metal organic condensation and olefin metal alkyl catalysts; organic synthesis; fuel and lubricant additives process development; feasibility studies of commercial foreign joint ventures. *Mailing Add:* 2909 Lawrence Nederland TX 77627

HOLST, GERALD CARL, ELECTRO-OPTICAL SYSTEM ANALYSIS, THERMAL IMAGING. *Current Pos:* PRES, E O TECHNOL, WINTER PARK, FLA, 93- *Personal Data:* b Brooklyn, NY, Oct 29, 42. *Educ:* Brooklyn Polytech Inst, BSEE, 63; Univ Conn, MS, 65, PhD(mat sci), 68; George Washington Univ, MEngAd, 81. *Prof Exp:* Physicist, Am Optical Corp, 66-68; physicist, Frankford Arsenal, US Army, Philadelphia, 68-77, physicist, Chem Systs Lab, Aberdeen Proving Ground, Md, 77-84; sr tech staff mem, Martin Marietta, Orlando, Fla, 84-93. *Concurrent Pos:* Chmn, NATO Proj Group 16, 81-84; lectr, Martin Marietta Cont Educ Prog, 87-93, SPIE Conf, 90-; adj prof, Univ Cent Fla, 88-; chmn, Conf Infrared Imaging Systs, Soc Photo-Optical Instrumentation Engrs, 90- *Mem:* Optical Soc Am; Soc Photo-Optical Instrumentation Engrs. *Res:* Fully conversant with infrared electro-optical system theory, design and modeling; proficient in lab and field testing; authored four books and over 60 publications. *Mailing Add:* 2932 Cove Trail Winter Park FL 32789-1159. *Fax:* 407-629-5370

HOLST, TIMOTHY BAILEY, STRUCTURAL GEOLOGY, TECTONICS. *Current Pos:* ASST PROF GEOL, UNIV MINN, DULUTH, 79- *Personal Data:* b Minneapolis, Minn, Mar 24,.51; m 74. *Educ:* Univ Minn, BA, 73, PhD(geol), 77. *Prof Exp:* asst prof geol, Hope Col, 77-79. *Mem:* Geol Soc Am; Sigma Xi. *Res:* Methods of strain determination in rocks; regional joint patterns; joint formation; theory and modeling of fold development in rock; mechanism of overthrust faulting. *Mailing Add:* Col Sci & Engr Univ Minn-Duluth 10 University Dr Duluth MN 55812

HOLST, WILLIAM FREDERICK, computer sciences; deceased, see previous edition for last biography

HOLSTE, JAMES CLIFTON, THERMOPHYSICAL PROPERTIES MEASUREMENTS, GAS FLOW METER DEVELOPMENT. *Current Pos:* from asst prof to assoc prof, 75-85, assoc dir, Off Grad Studies, 93-95, PROF CHEM ENG, TEX A&M UNIV, 85- *Personal Data:* m 69, Cathleen A Haring; c Rachel S & Jill C. *Educ:* Concordia Teachers Col, BS, 66; Iowa State Univ, PhD(solid state physics), 73. *Prof Exp:* Res assoc, Nat Res Coun, Nat Bur Stand, 73-75. *Concurrent Pos:* Mem, Nat Prog Comt Thermodynamics, Am Inst Chem Engrs, 85-90, Comt Thermophys Properties, Heat Transfer Div, Am Soc Mech Engrs, 88-; asst dean eng, Tex A&M Univ. *Mem:* Am Inst Chem Engrs; Am Phys Soc; Am Chem Soc; Instrument Soc Am; AAAS; Sigma Xi. *Res:* Experimental measurements of thermodynamic properties of natural gas mixtures and of alternative refrigerants; development of new experimental methods for thermodynamic properties; development of natural gas flow meters and meter provers. *Mailing Add:* 3025 Hummingbird Circle Bryan TX 77807. *Fax:* 409-845-6446; *E-Mail:* jch6931@rigel.tamu.edu

HOLSTEIN, ARTHUR G, BIOCHEMISTRY. *Current Pos:* RETIRED. *Personal Data:* b Mason City, Iowa, Oct 13, 11; m 37; c 2. *Educ:* Univ Ill, BS, 33. *Honors & Awards:* Melville Wolfrom Award, Carbohydrate Div, Am Chem Soc. *Prof Exp:* Chief control chemist, Keokuk Electro Metals, 33-34 & anal & develop, Armour By-Prod, 34-37; tech sales adv, Gen Dye Stuffs Corp, 37-38; res chemist, Visking Corp, 38-42; ord officer, US Army, 42-46; chem eng & prod, Chicago Copper & Chem Co, 46-47; mgr, Chem Div, Pfanstiehl Chem Co, 47-54, pres, Pfanstiehl Labs Inc, 54-75. *Concurrent Pos:* Mem sub-comt carbohydrates & comt specifications & criteria for biochem compounds & chmn subcomt carbohydrates, Nat Acad Sci-Nat Res Coun. *Mem:* Am Chem Soc; Am Inst Chemists. *Res:* Cellulose viscose; carbohydrates. *Mailing Add:* PO Box 439 Waukegan IL 60079-0439

HOLSTEIN, BARRY RALPH, THEORETICAL PHYSICS. *Current Pos:* from asst prof to assoc prof, 71-79, PROF PHYSICS, UNIV MASS, 79- *Personal Data:* b Youngstown, Ohio, Nov 19, 43; m 66, Carolyn Morrow; c Jeremy B & Jesse M. *Educ:* Carnegie Inst Technol, BS, 65, MS, 67; Carnegie-Mellon Univ, PhD(physics), 69. *Prof Exp:* Vis fel, Princeton Univ, 69-71. *Concurrent Pos:* Vis fel, Princeton Univ, 75-76; prog officer theoret physics, NSF, 77-79; vis prof, Princeton Univ, 85. *Mem:* Fel Am Phys Soc; Am Asn Physics Teachers. *Res:* Theoretical physics, especially weak interaction theory; study of nonleptonic weak processes and of weak decays of nuclei; chiral symmetry. *Mailing Add:* Dept Physics & Astron Univ Mass Amherst MA 01003. *E-Mail:* holstein@phast.umass.edu

HOLSTEIN, THOMAS JAMES, DEVELOPMENTAL GENETICS. *Current Pos:* TEACHER BIOL, ROGER WILLIAMS COL, 69- *Personal Data:* b Lansdowne, Pa, May 8, 43; m 65; c 2. *Educ:* Providence Col, BS, 65; Brown Univ, MS, 67, PhD(biol), 69. *Concurrent Pos:* Vis investr, Brown Univ, 78- *Mem:* AAAS; Int Pigment Cell Soc. *Res:* Developmental genetics of the multiple forms of tyrosinase from mammalian melanocytes; chemically induced hypo and hypermelanosis. *Mailing Add:* Dept Math & Sci Roger Williams Univ One Old Ferry Rd Bristol RI 02809-2921

HOLSTEN, JOHN ROBERT, ORGANIC CHEMISTRY, TEXTILE CHEMISTRY. *Current Pos:* RES CHEMIST, SPRINGS INDUSTS INC, 87- *Personal Data:* b Tulsa, Okla, Feb 27, 31; m 51; c 3. *Educ:* Vanderbilt Univ, BA, 52, MA, 55, PhD(chem), 57. *Prof Exp:* Sr res chemist, Chemstrand Res Ctr, Inc, NC, 56-71; res specialist, M Lowenstein Corp, 71-75; dir chem res, 75-78, dir reg affairs, 78-83, chemist, 83-87. *Mem:* Am Chem Soc; Am Asn Textile Chemists & Colorists; Am Oil Chemists Soc. *Res:* Condensation-type polymerizations; high temperature stable polymer systems; organic intermediates; acetylene chemistry; solvent effects; fabric flammability and flame retardants; textile chemical environmental and health problems; electroforming technology; textile printing technology. *Mailing Add:* 115 Normandy Ave Spartanburg SC 29301-1308

HOLSTIUS, ELVIN ALBERT, PHARMACY. *Current Pos:* DIR PHARMACEUT RES & DEVELOP, BURROUGHS WELLCOME CO, RESEARCH TRIANGLE PARK, 68- *Personal Data:* b Woonsocket, RI, Feb 9, 21; m 42; c 2. *Educ:* RI Col Pharm, BS, 43; Purdue Univ, MS, 49, PhD(pharm chem), 50. *Prof Exp:* Pharm res chemist, Burroughs & Wellcome, NY, 45-47; sr chemist, Merck & Co, Inc, NJ, 50-53; assoc prof pharm, Univ Kansas City, 53-56, dir pharmaceut res, 54-56; dir pharm develop labs, Res Div, Geigy Chem Corp, 56-67; tech dir, Endo Labs, Inc, 67-68. *Mem:* NY Acad Sci; Acad Pharmaceut Sci; Am Chem Soc; Am Pharmaceut Asn. *Res:* Physical characteristics which affect drugs and tableting. *Mailing Add:* 4A Dogwood Ct Orange City FL 32763-6105

HOLSTON, JAMES L, PUBLIC HEALTH. *Current Pos:* RETIRED. *Personal Data:* b Montgomery, Ala, Feb 9, 42; m 64; c 2. *Educ:* Huntingdon Col, BA, 64; Univ NC, MS, 70, PhD, 72. *Prof Exp:* Microbiologist, Clin Lab Admin, Ala Dept Pub Admin, 64-69, asst dir labs, 73-78, dir labs, 78-87; doctrite, Pub Health, 87-92. *Mem:* Sigma Xi; Am Pub Health Asn. *Res:* Development of a neuraminidase hemagglutination assay for Hong Kong influenza; development and evaluation of an isolation and transport system for gonorrhoeae. *Mailing Add:* 631 County Downs Rd Montgomery AL 36109

HOLSZTYNSKI, WLODZIMIERZ, MATHEMATICS, COMPUTER ARCHITECTURE. *Current Pos:* CONSULT, 85- *Personal Data:* b Nizny Tagil, USSR, Mar 3, 42; US citizen; m 62; c 4. *Educ:* Univ Warsaw, MS, 62, PhD(math), 65. *Prof Exp:* Mem staff math, Inst Advan Studies, 73-74; lectr, Univ Southern Ill, 74-75; from assoc prof to prof math, Univ Western Ont, 75-79; mem, Sr Prof Staff, Martin Marietta Aerospace, 81-85. *Concurrent Pos:* Fel, Lomonosoff Univ, 67-68; res grants, NSF, 69-74; grant, Univ Westen Ont, 75-76; Nat Res Coun Can grants, 76-77 & 77-80; res mathematician to sr res mathematician, Environ Res Inst Mich, 77-81; vis prof, Bowling Green State Univ, 78 & 84; consult, 85- *Res:* Mathematics, especially topology and algebra; statistical mechanics; computer architecture, especially parallel processors, image processing, data compression; patents parallel processing-image processing including patents for Geometric Arithmetic Parallel Processor. *Mailing Add:* 4175 Chester Dr Apt 11 Ypsilanti MI 48197

HOLT, ALAN CRAIG, space utilization & payload integration, advanced space systems concepts, for more information see previous edition

HOLT, BEN DANCE, DEVELOPMENT OF ANALYTICAL METHODS FOR RESEARCH IN GEOCHEMISTRY. *Current Pos:* from jr chemist to assoc chemist, 44-72, CHEMIST, ARGONNE NAT LAB, 72- *Personal Data:* b Tenn, June 3, 19; m 43, Louise Goode; c Benja, Mary Lou, Jane & Tom. *Educ:* Univ Tenn, BS, 41; Univ Chicago, SM, 51; Ill Inst Technol, PhD, 69. *Honors & Awards:* Mat Sci Award, US Dept Energy, 83. *Prof Exp:* Jr chemist, Tenn Valley Auth, 41-43. *Mem:* Am Chem Soc; Sigma Xi. *Res:* Gases in metals and oxides by high temperature; mass spectrometric techniques; extraction of gases from ground water and other earth materials for stable isotope ratio measurements. *Mailing Add:* Argonne Nat Lab Bldg 205 9700 S Cass Ave Argonne IL 60439

HOLT, CHARLENE POLAND, PEDIATRICS, ONCOLOGY. *Current Pos:* mem staff adolescent med & chief pediat oncol, Madigan Army Med Ctr, Tacoma Wash, 78-81, MEM, PEDIAT STAFF & CLIN ONCOL, GORGAS ARMY MED DEPT ACTIV, US ARMY MED CORP, REPUB PANAMA, 81- *Personal Data:* b Memphis, Tenn, Mar 2, 38; m 75; c 2. *Educ:* Fla Southern Col, BS, 59; Univ Miami, MD, 63; Am Bd Pediat, dipl. *Prof Exp:* Intern med pediat, Baptist Hosp, Memphis, 64, resident, 65; res fel pediat oncol, St Jude Children's Res Hosp, 66-68; asst prof pediat, Univ Tenn, 68-69; asst prof pediat, Med Ctr, Univ Colo, Denver, 69-75, assoc prof, 75-77; dir pediat oncol, Children's Hosp, 69-77. *Concurrent Pos:* Pediatrician chemother phase I-II liaison comt, Nat Cancer Inst; exec dir, Colo Regional Cancer Ctr, Inc, 74-75; pediat oncologist, Mountain States Tumor Inst, Idaho; dir, Intermountain Youth Cancer Ctr, Boise, Idaho; pvt practice, Weiser Idaho; assoc prof, Univ Wash, 78-81. *Mem:* Am Med Women's Asn; Am Asn Cancer Res; Am Soc Clin Oncol; Int Soc Lymphology; Int Soc Pediat Oncol. *Res:* Evaluation of new treatment modalities and chemotherapeutic agents in pediatric neoplasia. *Mailing Add:* Madigan Army Med Ctr Tacoma WA 98431

HOLT, CHARLES A(SBURY), ELECTRICAL ENGINEERING. *Current Pos:* RETIRED. *Personal Data:* b Staunton, Va, Feb 22, 21; m 47; c 4. *Educ:* US Mil Acad, BS, 43; Univ Ill, MS, 47, PhD(elec eng), 49. *Prof Exp:* Asst prof elec eng, US Mil Acad, 51-54; prof elec eng, Va Polytech Inst & State Univ, 54-85. *Mem:* Am Soc Eng Educ. *Res:* Electromagnetic waves; semiconductors; electric and magnetic phenomena in materials. *Mailing Add:* 1815 Winston Rd Charlottesville VA 22903

HOLT, CHARLES LEE ROY, JR, GEOLOGY, STRATIGRAPHY & SEDIMENTATION. *Current Pos:* CONSULT, 80- *Personal Data:* b Evanston, Ill, June 10, 24; m 82, Patricia Wood; c Charles L. *Educ:* Univ Tex, BS, 48, MA, 50. *Honors & Awards:* Distinguished Serv Award, Dept Interior, 80. *Prof Exp:* Geologist, Tex Bd Water Engrs, 48-49; geologist, US Geol Surv, Ga, 50-59, dist geologist, 59-66, dist chief, Wis, 66-75, prog & planning officer, Southeastern Region, Water Resource Div, 75-80. *Concurrent Pos:* Mem US nat comt, Int Asn Hydrologists; consult groundwater, Amman Jordan, 80-84, Muscat, Oman, 84 & San Antonio, Tex, 85-88; consult, Water Resources Mgt, Corpus Christi, 89- *Mem:* Fel Geol Soc Am; Am Water Resources Asn; Am Geophys Union; Hydroenological Asn (pres); Hydrologists Am (pres). *Res:* Ground water geology; water resources; limestone hydrology. *Mailing Add:* PO Box 164 Port Aransas TX 78373

HOLT, CHARLES STEELE, LIMNOLOGY, AQUATIC BIOLOGY. *Current Pos:* From asst prof to assoc prof, 65-76, PROF BIOL, BEMIDJI STATE UNIV, 76- *Personal Data:* b Chicago, Ill, June 18, 37; m 63; c 2. *Educ:* Beloit Col, BS, 59; Univ Wis-Madison, MS, 62; Univ Minn, PhD(fisheries sci), 65. *Concurrent Pos:* Consult, US Army CEngr, 73-74; vis scientist, Sci Mus Minn, St Paul, 76-77. *Mem:* Am Fisheries Soc; Am Soc Limnol & Oceanog. *Res:* Eutrophication of aquatic ecosystems; biotelemetry studies of walleye. *Mailing Add:* 8734 Cranberry Ct NE Bemidji MN 56601

HOLT, DAVID LOWELL, PROCESS FLOWSHEET DEVELOPMENT. *Current Pos:* ENGR & ACCT, HARTFORD STEAM BOILER INSPECTION & INSURANCE CO, 97- *Personal Data:* b Greensville, SC, Apr 16, 61. *Educ:* Clemson Univ, BS, 83, MS, 85. *Prof Exp:* Process engr, E I du Pont de Nemours & Co, 84-89; tech mgr, Westinghouse Savannah River Site, 89-92; vpres, Martin Color, Fla, 92-95; proj eng, Lockwood Greene Eng, 95-96. *Mem:* Am Inst Chem Engrs. *Res:* Spent nuclear fuel processing. *Mailing Add:* 3435 N Main Walnut Creek CA 94596

HOLT, DONALD ALEXANDER, AG SYSTEMS. *Current Pos:* instr agron, 56, dir, Ill Agr Exp Sta & assoc dean, Col Agr, 82-96, SR ASSOC DEAN, COL AGR, CONSUMER & ENVIRON SCI, UNIV ILL, 96- *Personal Data:* b Joliet, Ill, Jan 29, 32; m 53; c 4. *Educ:* Univ Ill, Urbana, BS, 54, MS, 56; Purdue Univ, PhD(agron), 67. *Prof Exp:* self-employed farmer, 56-63; from instr to assoc prof, Purdue Univ, 64-77, prof agron, 77-87. *Concurrent Pos:*

Consult, Environ Protection Agency, 81 & res admin, Coun Agr, Repub China, 91. *Mem:* Fel Am Soc Agron (pres, 87-89); fel Crop Sci Soc Am; fel AAAS; Sigma Xi; Agr Res Inst (pres, 90-92). *Res:* Physiological response of plants to environmental changes; diurnal variation in plant constituency; hay management; large area yield prediction models; computer simulation of plant growth; research administration. *Mailing Add:* Univ Ill Agr Expt Sta 109 Mumford Hall 1301 W Gregory Dr Urbana IL 61801-3608

HOLT, EDWARD C(HESTER), JR, STRUCTURAL ENGINEERING. *Current Pos:* from asst prof to assoc prof, 56-84, PROF CIVIL ENG, RICE UNIV, 84- *Personal Data:* b Philadelphia, Pa, Dec 23, 23; m 57; c 3. *Educ:* Mass Inst Technol, BS, 45, MS, 47; Pa State Univ, PhD(civil eng), 56. *Prof Exp:* Instr civil eng, Pa State Univ, 49-56. *Mem:* Am Soc Civil Engrs; Am Soc Eng Educ. *Res:* Structural engineering. *Mailing Add:* 4053 Nenana Dr Houston TX 77025-5419

HOLT, ELIZABETH MANNERS, FLUORESCENT COMPLEXES OF COPPER I, CALCIUM-ALLERGEN INTERACTIONS. *Current Pos:* adj asst prof & assoc researcher, 80-81, from asst prof to assoc prof, 81-87, PROF CHEM, OLKA STATE UNIV, 87- *Personal Data:* b NJ, Aug 2, 39; m 63, Smith L Jr; c Alexandra & Smith L III. *Educ:* Smith Col, BA, 61; Brown Univ, PhD(chem), 66. *Prof Exp:* Res assoc, Polytech Laereanstalt, Copenhagen, 65-66; adj assoc prof, Polytech Inst Brooklyn, 66-67, inst res fel physics, 67-68, instr chem, 68-69; fel, Univ Wyo, 69-74, temp asst prof, 75-78; res assoc, Dept Biochem, Univ Ga, 78-80. *Concurrent Pos:* Fulbright res fel, 88 & 92, 94-97. *Mem:* Am Chem Soc; Am Crystallog Asn. *Mailing Add:* Dept Chem Okla State Univ Stillwater OK 74078. *E-Mail:* chememh@succ

HOLT, ETHAN CLEDDY, PLANT BREEDING, AGRONOMY. *Current Pos:* From asst prof to assoc prof grass breeding, 48-57, PROF FORAGE CROPS, TEX A&M UNIV, 57- *Personal Data:* b Brilliant, Ala, Feb 6, 21; m 44; c 2. *Educ:* Auburn Univ, BS, 43 Purdue Univ, MS, 48, PhD(plant breeding), 50. *Honors & Awards:* Tex A&M Univ Distinguished Achievement Award Res, 70. *Mem:* Fel Am Soc Agron; Crop Sci Soc Am. *Res:* Grass breeding, including variety development, methodology, genetics, heritability and cytogenetics, especially warm-season grasses; forage physiology; pasture management. *Mailing Add:* 1110 Ashburn Ave College Station TX 77840

HOLT, FREDERICK SHEPPARD, MICROWAVE PHYSICS, MICROWAVE OPTICS. *Current Pos:* RETIRED. *Personal Data:* b Washington, DC, July 12, 20; m 49, Emily K Wright; c Caroline (Larson), Craig S & Alison C. *Educ:* Kenyon Col, AB, 41; Mass Inst Technol, PhD(appl math), 50. *Prof Exp:* Res assoc theory group, Radiation Lab, Mass Inst Technol, 42-43, instr math, 47-50; radar officer, Combat Submarine, 44-45; mathematician, Microwave Physics Lab, Rome Air Develop Command, Air Force Cambridge Res Labs, 59-75, physicist, Electromagnetic Sci Div, 76-80; prof math, Tufts Univ, 70-85. *Concurrent Pos:* From asst prof to assoc prof, Tufts Univ, 55-69. *Mem:* Sigma Xi. *Res:* Design and analysis of antennas; microwave optics devices; 11 Air Force patent awards. *Mailing Add:* 46 Emerson Rd Winchester MA 01890

HOLT, HARVEY ALLEN, URBAN FORESTRY, INDUSTRIAL WEED SCIENCE. *Current Pos:* assoc prof, 75-83, PROF FORESTRY, PURDUE UNIV, 83- *Personal Data:* b San Jose, Calif, Oct 15, 43; m 64; c 2. *Educ:* Okla State Univ, BS, 65; Ore State Univ, MS, 67, PhD(forest ecol), 70. *Prof Exp:* Res asst forestry, Ore State Univ, 65-70; asst prof, Univ Ark, Fayetteville, 70-75. *Mem:* Soc Am Foresters; Weed Sci Soc Am; Coun Agr Sci & Technol; Int Soc Arboricult; Am Railway Eng Asn; Arboricult Res & Educ Acad. *Res:* Effects of types and levels of vegetation on the desired species; rights-of-way and industrial vegetation management; use of tree growth regulators. *Mailing Add:* Dept Forestry & Natural Res Purdue Univ West Lafayette IN 47907-1159. *Fax:* 765-494-0409; *E-Mail:* holt@mace.cc.purdue.edu

HOLT, HELEN KEIL, ATOMIC PHYSICS, LASERS. *Current Pos:* CONSULT, 86- *Personal Data:* b West Palm Beach, Mar 23, 37; m 58, Lawrence G; c Daphne J & Leslie E. *Educ:* Barnard Col, BA, 58; Yale Univ, MS, 60, PhD(physics), 65. *Prof Exp:* Physicist, Ctr Absolute Phys Quantities, Nat Bur Stand, 65-86. *Mem:* Fel Am Phys Soc; Sigma Xi. *Res:* Electron-atom scattering, theory of gas lasers, correlated cascade spontaneous emission; stark quenching in hydrogen and helium, resonance trapping; laser intracavity absorption, saturated flourescence in a laser field; publications in journals. *Mailing Add:* 6740 Melody Lane Bethesda MD 20817

HOLT, IMY VINCENT, BOTANY. *Current Pos:* from assoc prof to prof, 60-84, EMER PROF BIOL, WESTERN MICH UNIV, 84- *Personal Data:* b Billings, Okla, Apr 3, 19; m 46, Waldeen Duree; c Garland (DeWayne). *Educ:* NMex Col, BS, 50; Iowa State Col, MS, 52, PhD, 53. *Prof Exp:* From asst prof to assoc prof bot, Okla State Univ, 53-60. *Mem:* Am Soc Agron; Sigma Xi. *Res:* Plant morphology; floral initiation. *Mailing Add:* 1200 Ficklin Circle Corsicana TX 75110

HOLT, JAMES ALLEN, BIOCHEMISTRY. *Current Pos:* prog officer, Western & Cent Eur, 90-96, PROG OFFICER, JAPAN & CHINA, FOGARTY INT CTR, NIH, 96- *Personal Data:* b Antlers, Okla, May 24, 34; m 61, Phyllis M Phelps; c Gregory N & Brett R. *Educ:* Okla Baptist Univ, AB, 56; Univ Ill, PhD(biochem), 61. *Prof Exp:* Res assoc biochem, Rockefeller Univ, 61-62; from asst prof to assoc prof chem, Okla Baptist Univ, 62-68; sr lectr & chmn dept, Fac Basic Sci, Njala Univ Col, Univ Sierra Leone, 66-67; asst prof chem, Williams Col, 68-71; prof chem, Univ Agr Malaysia, Peace Corps, 71-73; sci curric specialist, Maret Sch, 73-74; spec asst, Off Int Progs, 74-76, Prog Mgr, US-East Asia Coop Sci Prog, 76-81, Dep Dir, Div Int Prog, NSF, 81-84; dean, Warren Wilson Col, 84-88; provost, Servant Leadership Sch, 89-90. *Concurrent Pos:* Consult, Jersey Prod Res Co, 62. *Mem:* Sigma Xi. *Res:* Physical and chemical characterization of enzymes; mechanisms of enzyme catalysis; science education, policy and administration; management of international scientific activities; curriculum design and professional development in higher education. *Mailing Add:* Fogarty Int Ctr NIH 9000 Rockville Pike Bldg 31 Rm B2C11 Bethesda MD 20892-2220. *Fax:* 301-480-3414; *E-Mail:* ah50r@nih.gov

HOLT, JAMES FRANKLIN, SOLAR PHOTOVOLTAICS, MAGNETOHYDRODYNAMICS. *Current Pos:* RETIRED. *Personal Data:* b Murray City, Ohio, June 14, 24; m 51. *Educ:* Ohio State Univ, BSc, 49, MSc, 51, PhD(physics), 62. *Prof Exp:* Electronics engr, Farnsworth Electronics Co, 51-56; res assoc plasma physics, Ohio State Univ, 58-62, assoc res supvr, 62-66; physicist, USAF Aero Propulsion Lab, Wright-Patterson AFB, 66-85; physicist, IAP Res, Inc, 85-90. *Concurrent Pos:* Vis lectr, Ohio Acad Sci, 64-68. *Mem:* Am Phys Soc; Sigma Xi. *Res:* Magnetohydrodynamic power generation experiments and theory; gas lasers; electromagnetic heating and confinement of plasmas; thermonuclear fusion; television electronics; infrared radiation detection; solar V5 cells and solar power; EM accelerators. *Mailing Add:* 3795 Osborn Rd Medway OH 45341

HOLT, JOHN FLOYD, radiology; deceased, see previous edition for last biography

HOLT, JOHN GILBERT, MICROBIOLOGY. *Current Pos:* RETIRED. *Personal Data:* b Buffalo, NY, Dec 16, 29; m 55; c 3. *Educ:* Cornell Univ, BS, 52; Syracuse Univ, MS, 54; Purdue Univ, PhD(microbiol), 60. *Honors & Awards:* J Roger Porter Award, US Fed Cult Collections, 85. *Prof Exp:* Instr microbiol, Purdue Univ, 60; res assoc, Iowa State Univ, 60-62, USPHS fel, 62, from asst prof to prof microbiol, 63-90; prof microbiol, Mich State Univ, 90-96. *Mem:* Am Soc Microbiol; Can Soc Microbiol; Sigma Xi. *Res:* Classification and nomenclature of the bacteria; ecology of soil bacteria. *Mailing Add:* 1686 N College Rd Mason MI 48854

HOLT, JOSEPH PAYNTER, SR, physiology; deceased, see previous edition for last biography

HOLT, MATTHEW LESLIE, ELECTROCHEMISTRY. *Current Pos:* RETIRED. *Personal Data:* b Ellsworth, Iowa, June 19, 04; m 52. *Educ:* St Olaf Col, BA, 26; Univ Wis, MS, 28, PhD(inorg chem), 30. *Prof Exp:* from instr to prof, Univ Wis-Madison, 30-73, emer prof chem, 73- *Concurrent Pos:* Instr, US Army Univ, France, 45-46; vis sr chemist, Argonne Nat Lab, 50. *Mem:* Am Chem Soc; Electrochemical Soc. *Res:* Inorganic chemistry; electrodeposition of tungsten alloys and less common metals and alloys. *Mailing Add:* 6209 Mineral Pt Rd Madison WI 53705

HOLT, MAURICE, APPLIED MATHEMATICS. *Current Pos:* vis prof, 60-63, prof, 63-88, EMER PROF AERONAUT SCI, UNIV CALIF, BERKELEY, 88- *Personal Data:* b Wildboarclough, Eng, May 16, 18; US citizen; m 42; c 5. *Educ:* Univ Manchester, BSc, 40, MSc, 44, PhD, 48. *Prof Exp:* Asst lectr appl math, Univ Liverpool, 48-49; lectr, Univ Sheffield, 49-51; prin sci off, Ministry of Supply, 52-55; vis lectr math, Harvard Univ, 55-56; assoc prof appl math, Brown Univ, 56-60. *Concurrent Pos:* Consult, US Aerospace Co & US Res Labs. *Mem:* Fel Am Phys Soc; fel Am Inst Aeronaut & Astronaut. *Res:* Fluid dynamics; non-linear theory of compressible flow; hypersonic aerodynamics; shock wave phenomena; flutter and vibrations; numerical treatment of partial differential equations of hyperbolic and mixed type. *Mailing Add:* Div Mech Eng Univ Calif Berkeley CA 94720

HOLT, PERRY CECIL, INVERTEBRATE ZOOLOGY, SYSTEMATICS. *Current Pos:* from asst prof to prof zool, 56-78, dir, Ctr Systs Collections, 72-76, EMER PROF ZOOL, VA POLYTECH INST & STATE UNIV, 78- *Personal Data:* b Overton Co, Tenn, June 26, 12; m 42. *Educ:* Tenn Polytech Univ, BS, 42; Univ Va, MA, 48, PhD(biol), 51. *Prof Exp:* Instr biol, Univ Richmond, 48-50; from asst prof to assoc prof, ETenn State Col, 50-56. *Concurrent Pos:* Found Advan Educ fel, Univ Chicago, 55-56; vis res assoc, Smithsonian Inst, 67-68. *Mem:* Fel AAAS; Asn Southeastern Biologists (pres); Am Soc Zoologists; Am Micros Soc. *Res:* Morphology, taxonomy and zoogeography of the Branchiobdellida. *Mailing Add:* 1308 Crestview Dr Blacksburg VA 24060

HOLT, PETER STEPHEN, IMMUNOLOGY. *Current Pos:* res assoc, Vet Toxicol & Entom Res Lab, 85-87, RES IMMUNOL, SOUTHEAST POULTRY RES LAB, AGR RES SERV, USDA, 87- *Personal Data:* b Aberdeen, Md, Feb 19, 51; m 75, Julia Reagan. *Educ:* Southern Ill Univ, BA, 73; Cath Univ Am, MS, 78; Univ Mo, PhD(microbiol), 85. *Honors & Awards:* Glenn Smoeyenbos New Investr Award, Am Asn Avian Pathologists. *Prof Exp:* Sci asst microbiol, Walter Reed Army Inst Res, 75-78; chief bact, Letterman Army Med Ctr, 78-81. *Mem:* Am Asn Immunologists; Am Soc Microbiol; Am Asn Vet Immunologists; Am Asn Avian Pathologists; Sigma Xi. *Res:* Stress effects on immunity in chickens; role of various components of chicken immune response in protecting against Salmonella enteritidis infection; development of intestinal mucosal immunity in the chicken. *Mailing Add:* 934 College Station Rd Athens GA 30605

HOLT, RICHARD A(RNOLD), LASER SPECTROSCOPY, ATOMIC LIFETIMES. *Current Pos:* res scientist, 74-76, from asst prof to assoc prof, 76-89, PROF PHYSICS, UNIV WESTERN ONT, 89- *Personal Data:* b New York, NY, Sept 4, 42; m 78, Renee Silberman; c Benjamin, Daniel & Nina. *Educ:* Harvard Univ, AB, 64, AM, 66, PhD(physics), 73. *Prof Exp:* Fel physics, Brown Univ, 73-74. *Concurrent Pos:* Assoc researcher, Spectrometry Lab, Univ Lyon, France, 82-83; vis scientist, Oxford Univ, 83, Lawrence Berkeley Lab & Lawrence Livermore Nat Lab, Calif, 89-90. *Mem:* Am Phys Soc; Sigma Xi; Can Asn Physicists. *Res:* Laser and radiofrequency spectroscopy of atomic and molecular fast ion beams; measurement of fine and hyperfine structure; quantum electrodynamic effects; measurement of excited atomic state lifetimes. *Mailing Add:* Dept Physics & Astron Univ Western Ont London ON N6A 3K7 Can. *E-Mail:* r.a.holt@uwo.ca

HOLT, RICHARD E(DWIN), metallurgy, for more information see previous edition

HOLT, RICHARD THOMAS, PHYSICAL METALLURGY. *Current Pos:* SR RES OFFICER, NAT RES COUN CAN, 73- *Personal Data:* b Derby, Eng, Dec 2, 38; Can citizen; m 69; c 2. *Educ:* Univ Sheffield, BMet, 60; Univ BC, PhD(metall), 68. *Prof Exp:* Fel mech eng, Univ Man, 68-70, asst prof civil eng, 70-72. *Concurrent Pos:* Secy, Subcomt Aerospace Mat & Processes, Int Stand Orgn; Can Coun lectr, Am Soc Metals, 95-96. *Mem:* Am Soc Metals; Asn Prof Engrs. *Res:* Metal and ceramic matrix composites reinforced with ceramic fibers; aluminum alloys for aerospace applications; hot isostatic pressing of metal and ceramic matrix composites. *Mailing Add:* Inst Aerospace Res Nat Res Coun Can Ottawa ON K1A 0R6 Can. *Fax:* 613-990-7444; *E-Mail:* richard.holt@nrc.ca

HOLT, ROBERT LOUIS, organic chemistry, analytical chemistry; deceased, see previous edition for last biography

HOLT, ROY JAMES, NUCLEAR PHYSICS. *Current Pos:* PROF, UNIV ILL, URBANA-CHAMPAIGN, 94- *Personal Data:* b Borger, Tex, Jan 22, 47; m 66, Nancy Cox; c Luanne, Shelley & Stephen. *Educ:* Southern Methodist Univ, BS, 69; Yale Univ, MPhil, 71, PhD(physics), 72. *Prof Exp:* Res staff physicist, Yale Univ, 72-74; asst scientist, Argonne Nat Lab, 74-77, physicist, 77-88, sr physicist, 88-94. *Concurrent Pos:* Mem bd dirs, Continuous Electron Beam Accelerator Facil, 83-84, 89-92, chmn, 90; chmn, Gordon Res Conf Photonuclear Reactions, 90. *Mem:* Fel Am Phys Soc; AAAS. *Res:* Photonuclear reactions and electron scattering studies of nuclei; polarization phenomena; medium energy physics. *Mailing Add:* Physics Div Argonne Nat Lab Argonne IL 60439. *E-Mail:* r.holt@uine.eud

HOLT, RUSH D(EW), JR, SOLAR PHYSICS, ENERGY POLICY. *Current Pos:* ASST DIR, PLASMA PHYSICS LAB, PRINCETON UNIV, 89- *Personal Data:* b Weston, WVa, Oct 15, 48; m 85, Margaret Lancefield; c 3. *Educ:* Carleton Col, BA, 70; NY Univ, MA, PhD(physics), 81. *Prof Exp:* Acoust physicist, New York City Environ Protection Admin, 73; asst prof phys, Swarthmore Col, 80-88; sci res specialist, US Dept State, 88-89. *Concurrent Pos:* Consult, solar energy & environ planning, 75-; Cong scientist fel, Am Phys Soc, 82-83. *Mem:* Am Phys Soc; Sigma Xi; Am Astron Soc; AAAS. *Res:* Energy balance of the solar chromosphere; world energy production and consumption. *Mailing Add:* Princeton Plasma Phtsics Lab PO Box 451 Princeton NJ 08543. *Fax:* 609-243-2749; *E-Mail:* rholt@ppl.gov

HOLT, SMITH LEWIS, JR, INORGANIC CHEMISTRY. *Current Pos:* PROF CHEM & DEAN ARTS & SCI, OKLA STATE UNIV, 80-86 & 88- *Personal Data:* b Ponca City, Okla, Dec 8, 38; m 63; c 2. *Educ:* Northwestern Univ, BSc, 61; Brown Univ, PhD(inorg chem), 65. *Prof Exp:* Res fel, Brown Univ, 65; NATO res fel, Univ Copenhagen, 65-66; asst prof inorg chem, Polytech Inst Brooklyn, 66-69; assoc prof chem, Univ Wyo, 69-73, prof, 73-78; prof chem & head dept, Univ Ga, 78-80; Okla secy educ, 86-87. *Concurrent Pos:* Fulbright grant & prof assoc, Univ Bordeaux, 74-75. *Mem:* Am Chem Soc; AAAS; Sigma Xi. *Res:* Structural inorganic chemistry; x-ray crystallography; inorganic synthesis; spectroscopy of transition metal ions; solid state chemistry. *Mailing Add:* Arts & Sci Col Okla State Univ Stillwater OK 74078

HOLT, STEPHEN S, HIGH ENERGY ASTROPHYSICS, X-RAY ASTRONOMY. *Current Pos:* chief, High Energy Astrophys Progs, NASA, Washington, DC, 80-81, dir, Lab High Energy Astrophys, 83-90, ASTROPHYSICIST, GODDARD SPACE FLIGHT CTR, NASA, 66-, DIR, SPACE SCI, 90- *Personal Data:* b New York, NY, May 17, 40; m 61, Carol Weissman; c Peter, Eric & Laura. *Educ:* New York Univ, BS, 61, PhD(physics), 66. *Honors & Awards:* Except Sci Achievement Medal, NASA, 77 & 80, Outstanding Leadership Medal, 91; John C Lindsay Mem Award, 93. *Prof Exp:* Instr physics, NY Univ, 64-67. *Concurrent Pos:* Lectr physics & astron, Univ Md, 67-88; adj prof astron, 88-; chmn, High Energy Astrophys Div, Am Astron Soc, 83, ed, Exp Astron (Sci J), 89-; vice chair, astrophysics Subdiv, Comt Space Res, Int Coun Sci Unions, 94- *Mem:* AAAS; fel Am Phys Soc; Am Geophys Union; Am Astron Soc; Int Astron Union; Sigma Xi. *Res:* Balloon, rocket and satellite-borne studies in cosmic ray physics and x-ray astronomy; space-borne scientific investigations, including the Einstein Observatory (the first X-ray astronomy telescope). *Mailing Add:* Code 600 Goddard Space Flight Ctr NASA Greenbelt MD 20771. *E-Mail:* steve.holt@gsfc.nasa.gov

HOLT, THOMAS MANNING, NEUROCHEMISTRY. *Current Pos:* PROF, MANNING PROFESSIONAL CTR, 84- *Personal Data:* b Detroit, Mich, July 19, 43; m 63; c 2. *Educ:* ECarolina Univ, BS, 66, MS, 68; La State Univ, PhD(anat), 74. *Prof Exp:* Instr biol, ECarolina Univ, 68-69; from instr to asst prof anat, Col Med, Univ SFla, 74-78; asst prof anat, Col Med, Med Univ SC, 78-84. *Mem:* Am Asn Anatomists. *Res:* Plasticity of central nervous system catecholaminergic neurons. *Mailing Add:* 1005 Mar Walt Dr Ft Walton Beach FL 32547

HOLT, VERNON EMERSON, HEAT TRANSFER, ENVIRONMENTAL CONTROL. *Current Pos:* adj assoc prof, 90-95, EMER PROF ENG, HAMPTON UNIV, 95- *Personal Data:* b Miller, SDak, May 13, 30; m 56; c David, Brian, Alan & Diane. *Educ:* SDak Sch Mines & Technol, BS, 51; NC State Univ, MS, 58; Purdue Univ, PhD, 61. *Prof Exp:* Mem lab staff, Gen Elec Co, Wash, 51-54; instr eng, NC State Univ, 56-58; mem tech staff, Bell Tel Labs, NJ, 60-65; asst prof eng mech, NC State Univ, 65-66, assoc prof & asst dean grad sch, 66-68; mem tech staff, Bell Labs, 68-90, supvr environ studies 72-86, design qual assurance, 86-90. *Concurrent Pos:* Consult, Comput Lab, Gen Elec Co, 65- & Hayes Int Co, Ala, 65- *Mem:* Am Phys Soc; Sigma Xi. *Res:* Effect of environment on materials properties; phonon transport; superconductive devices; thermal radiation and emissivities; control of temperature, humidity and pollutants and effects on materials, devices and equipment; design and development quality assurance; reliability and failure mode effects analyses. *Mailing Add:* 45 Franklin Rd Mendham NJ 07945

HOLT, WILLIAM HENRY, SOLID STATE PHYSICS. *Current Pos:* PHYSICIST, NAVAL SURFACE WARFARE CTR, 69- *Personal Data:* b San Antonio, Tex, Aug 5, 39; m 63; c 2. *Educ:* St Mary's Univ, Tex, BS, 60; Univ Tex, MA, 62, PhD(physics), 67. *Prof Exp:* Fel & lectr physics, Univ Man, 66-69. *Mem:* Am Phys Soc; Can Asn Physicists; Sigma Xi; Mat Res Soc. *Res:* Shock waves in solids; positron annihilation. *Mailing Add:* 906 Carol Lane Fredericksburg VA 22405-1618

HOLT, WILLIAM ROBERT, mathematical statistics, medical statistics, for more information see previous edition

HOLTAN, HEGGIE NORDAHL, AGRICULTURAL ENGINEERING, HYDROLOGY. *Current Pos:* CONSULT, 81- *Personal Data:* b Stoughton, Wis, Apr 10, 09; m 38; c 3. *Educ:* Wis State Univ, La Crosse, BA, 33. *Prof Exp:* Lab aide off res, Soil Conserv Serv, USDA, Wis, 34-37, sci aide, DC, 37-39, eng aide, Edwardsville, Ill, 40-43, hydraul engr, Elmwood, Ill, 43-47 & Va, 47-54, hydraul engr, Cent Tech Unit, DC, 54-56, hydraul engr watershed hydrol, Agr Res Serv, 56-58, invests leader, 58-60, asst br chief, Northeast Br, 60-61, dir, Hydrograph Lab, 61-75; lectr agr eng, Univ Md, 75-81. *Concurrent Pos:* Team mem preparation hydrol guide, Soil Conserv Serv, USDA, 54-56, mem, Subcomt Hydrol, Interagency Comt Water Resources, 57-, chmn, Comt Preparation Field Manual Res Agr Hydrol, Agr Res Serv, 59-62, mem work group, Subcomt Rep & Exp Basins & Subcomt Floods & Their Comput, UNESCO-Int Hydrol Decade, 67-69; mem staff, Agr Res Sta, Univ Md, 75-80. *Mem:* Soil Conserv Soc Am. *Res:* Watershed hydrology including precipitation and evaporation, soils treatment and vegetation, hydrogeology and hydrodynamics as to their effect on water quality and the hydrologic performance of agricultural watersheds; computer model for watershed hydrology including sediment and chemical transports. *Mailing Add:* 1734 27th Ave Vero Beach FL 32960

HOLTBY, KENNETH F, AERODYNAMICS. *Current Pos:* RETIRED. *Personal Data:* b Escanaba, Mich, May 18, 22; c 5. *Educ:* Calif Inst Technol, BS, 47; Mass Inst Technol, MS, 61. *Honors & Awards:* Design Award, Am Inst Aeronaut & Astronaut. *Prof Exp:* Vpres 747 prog, Boeing Aircraft Co, 72-78, vpres new progs, 78-81, sr vpres, 81-87. *Mem:* Nat Acad Eng; fel Royal Aeronaut Soc; hon fel Am Inst Aeronaut & Astronaut. *Mailing Add:* 4907 Croatian Way Anacortes WA 98221

HOLTE, JAMES EDWARD, ELECTRICAL ENGINEERING. *Current Pos:* From instr to asst prof, 55-63, dir continuing educ eng & sci, 64-69, ASSOC PROF ELEC ENG, UNIV MINN, MINNEAPOLIS, 63- *Personal Data:* b Grand Forks, NDak, Apr 9, 31; m 55; c 3. *Educ:* Univ Minn, BS, 53, MS, 56, PhD(elec eng), 60. *Mem:* Inst Elec & Electronics Engrs; Am Soc Eng Educ; Sigma Xi. *Res:* Electron gun design; computer-assisted problem solving; distributed system analysis and synthesis; network theory; continuing engineering education. *Mailing Add:* Dept Elec Eng Univ Minn CSci/EE Bldg 200 Union St SE Minneapolis MN 55455-0154

HOLTE, KARL E, PLANT TAXONOMY, PLANT ECOLOGY. *Current Pos:* From asst prof to assoc prof, 65-83, PROF BOT, IDAHO STATE UNIV, 83- *Personal Data:* b Graettinger, Iowa, Apr 25, 31; div; c 3. *Educ:* Augustana Col, SDak, BA, 54; Northern Iowa Univ, MA, 61; Univ Iowa, PhD(bot), 66. *Concurrent Pos:* Curator, Ray J Davis Herbarium; consult, govt agencies. *Mem:* Am Soc Plant Taxon; Bot Soc Am; Ecol Soc Am; Int Asn Plant Taxon. *Res:* Floristic studies in Idaho; threatened and endangered plants in Idaho and southeastern Oregon. *Mailing Add:* Dept Biol Sci Idaho State Univ 921 S Eighth Ave Pocatello ID 83209-0001

HOLTEN, DAROLD DUANE, BIOCHEMISTRY, ENZYMOLOGY. *Current Pos:* RETIRED. *Personal Data:* b Devils Lake, NDak, Sept 26, 35; m 62. *Educ:* NDak State Univ, BS, 58, MS, 60; Univ NDak, PhD(biochem), 65. *Prof Exp:* Am Cancer Soc fel biochem, Oak Ridge Nat Lab, Tenn, 65-67; res scientist, Armour Pharmaceut Co, Ill, 67-68; from asst prof to prof biochem, Univ Calif, Riverside, 68-94. *Mem:* Am Inst Nutrit; Am Soc Biol Chemists; AAAS. *Res:* Mechanisms by which diet regulates the synthesis of lipogenic enzymes and apolipoproteins. *Mailing Add:* Dept Biochem Univ Calif 2615 Piedmont Dr Riverside CA 92506

HOLTEN, VIRGINIA ZEWE, biochemistry, for more information see previous edition

HOLTER, JAMES BURGESS, DAIRY SCIENCE. *Current Pos:* Assoc prof, 63-78, PROF ANIMAL SCI, UNIV NH, 78- *Personal Data:* b New Bethlehem, Pa, Sept 7, 34; m 59; c 2. *Educ:* Pa State Univ, BS, 56, PhD(dairy sci), 63; Univ Md, MS, 59. *Concurrent Pos:* Consult, Dairy Nutrit, Venezuela & Can. *Mem:* Am Soc Animal Sci; Am Dairy Sci Asn; Am Inst Nutrit. *Res:* Efficiency of utilization of forages by dairy cattle; energy metabolism; computer dairy ration balancing; optimum supplementation in dairy rations. *Mailing Add:* Dept Animal Sci Univ NH Durham NH 03824-4724

HOLTER, MARVIN ROSENKRANTZ, physics, mathematics; deceased, see previous edition for last biography

HOLTKAMP, DORSEY EMIL, MEDICAL SCIENCE, ENDOCRINOLOGY. *Current Pos:* INDEPENDENT CONSULT, 87- *Personal Data:* b New Knoxville, Ohio, May 28, 19; m 42, 57, 84; c 7. *Educ:* Univ Colo, AB, 45, MS, 49, PhD(biochem), 51. *Prof Exp:* Asst chem & biol, Univ Colo, 45-46, biochem, Sch Med, 47-51; sr res scientist biochem sect, Smith, Kline & French Labs, 51-57, group leader, 57-58; head dept endocrinol, Merrell-Nat Labs Div, Richardson-Merrell, Inc, 58-70, group dir, Endocrine Clin Res, 70-81, group dir, Med Res Dept, Merrell Dow Pharmaceut Inc, Dow Chem Co, 81-87. *Mem:* Am Chem Soc; Endocrine Soc; Am Soc Pharmacol & Exp Therapeut; Am Soc Clin Pharmacol & Therapeut; Am Fertil Soc; AAAS. *Res:* Homoiothermia control; manganese and thiamin nutrition; tumor, adjacent tissue metabolism; reticulo-endothelial system stimulation; endocrinodynamics; antihistaminic, anti-inflammatory, cholesterol-lowering, thyroidal, estrogenic, fertility-sterility drugs; reproduction; teratology; basic and clinical drug research and development. *Mailing Add:* 130 S Liberty-Keuter Rd Lebanon OH 45036-9333

HOLTKAMP, FREDDY HENRY, ORGANIC CHEMISTRY. *Current Pos:* asst prof, Mars Hill Col, 68-74, Piedmont Univ Ctr fel, 70-74, assoc prof, 74-77, PROF CHEM, MARS HILL COL, 77-, CHMN DEPT, 74- *Personal Data:* b Needville, Tex, Jan 19, 34; m 57; c 3. *Educ:* Tex Lutheran Col, BS, 57; Tex A&M Univ, MS, 64, PhD(chem), 69. *Prof Exp:* Chemist, Dow Chem Co, 59-61. *Mem:* AAAS; Am Chem Soc. *Res:* Organic synthesis of phosphonic acid analogs of naturally occurring heterocyclic amino acids and sulfur containing amino acids. *Mailing Add:* Box 838 Mt Vernon GA 30445-0838

HOLTMAN, MARK STEVEN, CHEMICAL APPLICATIONS OF COMPUTERS. *Current Pos:* CORP QUAL MGR, AM ANALYTICAL LABS, INC, 93- *Personal Data:* b Dayton, Ohio, Apr 3, 49; m 80, Patricia R Blum; c Robert. *Educ:* Univ Dayton, BS, 71; Wright State Univ, MS, 73; Ohio State Univ, PhD(inorg chem), 79. *Prof Exp:* Sr res chemist, PPG Indust, Inc, 79-84; proj engr, BP Am, 85-92. *Mem:* Am Chem Soc; Am Soc Qual Control. *Res:* Interfacing laboratory instrumentation/reactors to computers for data acquisition and process control; laboratory information management systems, software for chemical applications; laboratory quality control/quality assurance. *Mailing Add:* 970 Brookpoint Dr Macedonia OH 44056-1606. *Fax:* 216-535-7246

HOLTMANN, WILFRIED, ANIMAL BREEDING. *Current Pos:* MEM STAFF, SEMEN MKT, CTR D'INSEMINATION ARTIFICIELLE DU QUEBEC, CIAQ INC, 76- *Personal Data:* b Winnipeg, Man, June 18, 39; m 62; c 4. *Educ:* Univ Man, BSA, 61; Univ Guelph, MSA, 62; Univ Wis, PhD(dairy sci), 66. *Prof Exp:* Res scientist, Can Dept Agr, 66-67; asst prof animal sci, Laval Univ, 67-70, assoc prof, 70-76. *Mem:* Am Soc Animal Sci; Can Soc Animal Sci. *Res:* Animal production, especially animal breeding; crossbreeding in swine and beef cattle; selection and improvement in dairy cattle. *Mailing Add:* CIAQ Box 518 St-Hyacinthe PQ J2S 7B8 Can

HOLTMYER, MARLIN DEAN, PETROLEUM & POLYMER CHEMISTRY. *Current Pos:* Sr res chemist, Halliburton Serv, 66-70, group leader, 70-73, asst mgr, 73-78, RES ASSOC CHEM RES & DEVELOP, HALLIBURTON SERV, 78- *Personal Data:* b Red Oak, Iowa, Feb 1, 37; m 60; c 2. *Educ:* Northwestern Mo State Col, BS, 62; Okla State Univ, PhD(phys chem), 67. *Mem:* Am Chem Soc. *Res:* Solution properties of polymers in both aqueous and nonaqueous media; chemistry of natural and synthetic polymers (solution properties), surfactants, emulsions, and their application in the petroleum well service industry. *Mailing Add:* 1219 N 12th Duncan OK 73533-3711

HOLTON, ADOLPHUS, GEOLOGY. *Current Pos:* stud financial aid dir, New Eng Col, 63-69, dir placement, 69-70, dir phys plant develop, 71-72, prof eng & geol, 48-78, res engr phys plant develop, 72-78, EMER PROF ENG, NEW ENG COL, 87- *Personal Data:* b Norwood, Mass, June 1, 12; m 32, M Elizabeth Leroy; c David, Peter & Philip. *Educ:* Northeastern Univ, BS, 36. *Prof Exp:* Inspector qual control, B F Sturtevant Co, Mass, 34-37; engr design & drafting, Tobe Deutschmann Corp, 38-40; real estate operator, 40-42; engr qual control, Bendix Aviation Corp, 42-43; design engr, Raytheon Mfg Co, 43-46; instr math, drawing & blueprint reading, Feener Tech Inst, 46-48. *Concurrent Pos:* Engr, Eng Design Serv, Mass, 46-48; consult, 48-, consult engr, 78- *Mem:* Am Soc Mech Engrs. *Res:* Geology of New Hampshire, southern Rockies and gulf area of Mississippi. *Mailing Add:* 227 Pleasant St Concord NH 03301

HOLTON, GERALD, PHYSICS, HISTORY OF SCIENCE. *Current Pos:* mem staff, Off Sci Res & Develop, Harvard Univ, 43-46, instr physics, 47-49, from asst prof to prof, 49-75, MALLINCKRODT PROF PHYSICS & PROF HIST SCI, HARVARD UNIV, 75- *Personal Data:* b Berlin, Ger, May 23, 22; nat US; m 47, Nina Rossfort; c Thomas & Stephan. *Educ:* Wesleyan Univ, BA, 41, MA, 42; Harvard Univ, MA, 46, PhD(physics), 48. *Hon Degrees:* DSc, Grinnell Col, 67, Kenyon Col, 77, Bates Col, 79, Trinity Col, 81; LLD, Duke Univ, 81; LHD, Wesleyan Univ, 81. *Honors & Awards:* George Sarton Mem lectr, AAAS, 62; R A Millikan Medal, Am Asn Physics Teachers, 67, Oersted Medal, 80; Herbert Spence lectr, Oxford Univ, 79; Jefferson lectr, 81; Presidential Citation Serv to Educ, 84; J D Bernal Prize, Soc Social Studies Sci, 89; Sarton Medal, Hist Sci Soc, 89; Gemant Award, Am Inst Physics, 89; Joseph Priestley Medal, Dickinson Col, 94; Rothschild lectr, Harvard Univ, 97. *Prof Exp:* Instr, Brown Univ, 42-43. *Concurrent Pos:* Founding Ed, Daedalus, 57-61; vis mem, Inst Advan Study, 64 & 67; trustee, Boston Mus Sci, 65-67, Sci Serv, 72-78, Wesleyan Univ, 75-89, Nat Humanities Ctr, 89-93; mem bd dirs, AAAS, 67-71; mem, Comt Scholarly Commun with People's Repub China, Nat Acad Sci, 69-72, Nat Comt Hist & Philos Sci, 82-89; mem gov bd, Am Inst Physics, 69-74; mem, Adv Comt Ethical & Human Impact of Sci, NSF, 73-78, Adv Comt Sci & Eng Educ, 85-93; mem, US Nat Comn, UNESCO, 75-80, US Nat Comn Excellence in Educ, 81-83; fel, Ctr Advan Study Behav Sci, Stanford Univ, 75-76; vis prof, Mass Inst Technol, 76-; Guggenheim fel, 80-81; mem, Coun Scholars, Libr Cong, 80-85 & 88-; mem adv bd, Radcliffe Inst Women, 82-85; coun, Am Acad Arts & Sci, 91-95. *Mem:* Am Philos Soc; Fel Am Phys Soc; Hist Sci Soc (pres, 83-84); fel Am Acad Arts & Sci; Int Acad Hist Sci (vpres, 81-89). *Res:* High pressure phenomena; molecular physics; history and philosophy of physical science; science education. *Mailing Add:* 358 Jefferson Physics Lab Harvard Univ Cambridge MA 02138

HOLTON, JAMES R, DYNAMIC METEOROLOGY. *Current Pos:* from asst prof to assoc prof, 65-73, PROF ATMOSPHERIC SCI, UNIV WASH, 73- *Personal Data:* b Spokane, Wash, Apr 16, 38; m 62; c 2. *Educ:* Harvard Univ, BA, 60; Mass Inst Technol, PhD(meteorol), 64. *Honors & Awards:* Meisinger Award, Am Meteorol Soc, 73, Second Half Century Award, 82. *Prof Exp:* NSF fel, Univ Stockholm, 64-65. *Concurrent Pos:* Co-chief ed, J Atmospheric Sci, 78-83. *Mem:* Nat Acad Sci; fel Am Geophys Union; Am Meterol Soc. *Res:* Stratospheric dynamics and tropical dynamics. *Mailing Add:* Dept Atmospheric Sci Box 351640 Univ Wash Seattle WA 98195. *E-Mail:* holton@atmos.washington.edu

HOLTON, RAYMOND WILLIAM, PLANT PHYSIOLOGY. *Current Pos:* from asst prof to assoc prof, Univ Tenn, 63-65, actg head dept, 64-65, head dept, 65-84, co-chairperson biol consortium, 84-86, actg chairperson, 92-93, PROF BOT, UNIV TENN, KNOXVILLE, 65- *Personal Data:* b Riverside, Calif, Apr 30, 29; div; c Betsey, Nancy, William & Thomas. *Educ:* Pomona Col, BA, 51; Univ Mich, MS, 54, PhD(bot), 58. *Prof Exp:* Chemist, US Naval Ord Test Sta, Calif, 51-52; instr bot, Flint Col, Univ Mich, 57-59, asst prof, 59-61; res scientist zool, Univ Tex, 61-62, USPHS trainee, 62-63. *Concurrent Pos:* Sr Fulbright fel, Univ Durham, UK, 72-73; vis prof, Univ Groningen, Neth, 87. *Mem:* AAAS; Am Soc Plant Physiol; Bot Soc Am; Brit Phycol Soc; Phycol Soc Am. *Res:* Biochemistry and physiology of algae and fungi. *Mailing Add:* Bot Univ Tenn 437 Hesler Knoxville TN 37996

HOLTON, ROBERT LAWRENCE, MARINE BIOLOGY, POLLUTION BIOLOGY. *Current Pos:* res assoc, 71-77, ASST PROF OCEANOG, SCH OCEANOG, ORE STATE UNIV, 77- *Personal Data:* b Billings, Mont, Nov 1, 28; m 53; c 3. *Educ:* Univ Mont, BA, 50, ME, 58; Ore State Univ, MS, 62, PhD(biol oceanog), 68; Univ Minn, MS, 65. *Prof Exp:* Teacher high sch, Idaho, 50-51, Mont, 51-59, Wash, 59-60 & Ore, 61-64; assoc prof sci educ, Eastern Ore Col, 67-69; marine biologist, US AEC, 69-71. *Concurrent Pos:* Res assoc, Ore Regional Primate Res Ctr, 62-63; consult, Nuclear Regulatory Comn, US Energy Res & Develop Admin, 73- *Mem:* Am Soc Limnol & Oceanog; Sigma Xi; Pac Estuarine Res Soc; Estuarine Res Fedn. *Res:* Effect of various pollutants on individuals, populations and communities of marine organisms; effects of pollutants at low sub-lethal levels on reproduction, behavior and productivity. *Mailing Add:* 8624 SW Miller Ct Portland OR 97224

HOLTON, WILLIAM COFFEEN, SOLID STATE PHYSICS. *Current Pos:* DIR MICROSTRUCT SCI, SEMICONDUCTOR RES CORP & VPRES RES OPERS, 84- *Personal Data:* b Washington, DC, July 24, 30; m 54; c 3. *Educ:* Univ NC, BS, 52; Univ Ill, MS, 58, PhD(physics), 60. *Prof Exp:* Asst physics, Univ Ill, 56-60; mem tech staff, Texas Instruments Inc, 60-65, mgr, Quantum Electronics Br, Physics Res Lab, 65-74, dir Advan Components Lab, 74-78, dir res develop eng, semiconductor group, 78-84. *Mem:* Fel Inst Elec & Electronics Engrs; fel Am Phys Soc. *Res:* Electron paramagnetic resonance; luminescence and defects or imperfections in crystalline solids; quantum electronics; lasers; microwave devices; integrated circuits (LSI and VLSI); infrared physics; displays. *Mailing Add:* Semiconductor Res Corp 601 Brookview Dr Chapel Hill NC 27514. *Fax:* 919-541-9450

HOLTSLANDER, WILLIAM JOHN, PHYSICAL CHEMISTRY, CHEMICAL ENGINEERING. *Current Pos:* RETIRED. *Personal Data:* b Moose Jaw, Sask, July 25, 37; m 60; c 3. *Educ:* Univ Sask, BE & MSc, 60; Univ Alta, PhD(radiation chem), 67. *Prof Exp:* Res chemist, Chemcell Ltd, 60-61; teaching asst chem, Univ Alta, 61-66; prof chem eng, Atomic Energy Can, Ltd, 67-97. *Concurrent Pos:* Mgr, Int Prog Nat Fusion Prog, Atomic Energy Can, Ltd; mem, Int Atomic Energy Agency Tech Comt Tritium Technol; prog chmn, Third Trop Meeting Tritium Technol, Toronto, 88. *Mem:* Fel Chem Inst Can; Can Soc Chem Eng. *Res:* Immobilization, storage and disposal of tritium containing wastes from nuclear power reactors; chemistry of aqueous sulfur containing systems; recovery of tritium from nuclear reactors; technology of handling concentrated tritium in fission and fusion systems; deuterium exchange reaction; recovery of tritium from nuclear reactors; technology of handling concentrated tritium. *Mailing Add:* 256 Thomas St Box 930 Deep River ON K0J 1P0 Can

HOLTUM, ALFRED G(ERARD), ELECTRICAL ENGINEERING, MATHEMATICS. *Current Pos:* CONSULT, 84- *Personal Data:* b Freeport, Ill, Aug 26, 18; m 41, Betty L Larson; c Sally (Ryan), Edwin A, Ellen (Bierbaum), Susan (O'Connell), Faith (Harwood) & Paul A. *Educ:* NY Univ, BA, 49; Rutgers Univ, MS, 52; Ill Inst Technol, PhD(elec eng), 72. *Prof Exp:* Electronic engr, Sig Corps Eng Labs, NJ, 45-54; chief, Radio Commun Div, Sig Commun Dept, Army Electronic Proving Ground, Ariz, 54-57; chief engr, Andrew Corp, Calif, 57-61, dir antenna design, Orland Park, Ill, 61-66, dir new prod develop, 66-68, sr scientist, 68-70; mem tech staff, Justice Assocs, Bridgeview, Ill, 70-72; prin engr, Harris Corp, 72-75; consult, US Govt, 75-78; asst prof, Univ NC, Charlotte, 78-84. *Concurrent Pos:* Adj prof, Fla Inst Technol, 72-74; consult electromagnetics, waveguides & antennas. *Mem:* Inst Elec & Electronics Engrs; Sigma Xi. *Res:* Antennas; electromagetic theory; research, development, design of advanced antenna technology, including multiple frequency and dual polarization techniques, high efficiency and front to back ratios for microwave radio relay links, and leaky coaxial cable for communications with trains in tunnels. *Mailing Add:* 300 Lakeview Ridge E Roswell GA 30076. *E-Mail:* dragh@prodigy.com

HOLTZ, ALIZA, BIOMEDICAL COMMUNICATIONS & CONSULTING, MEDICAL WRITING. *Current Pos:* PRES, HOLTZ COMMUN, INC, 85- *Personal Data:* b New York, NY, Jan 10, 52. *Educ:* Brandeis Univ, BA, 73; Boston Univ, PhD(biochem), 80. *Prof Exp:* Fel, NY State Psychiat Inst, 80-82; mgr educ proj, med, 83-84. *Concurrent Pos:* Med writer, Revlon Health Care Group, 82-; adj fac, Col New Rochelle, 84-85; consult, Ketchum Pub Rels, 87- *Mem:* AAAS; Sigma Xi; Am Med Writers Asn. *Res:* Antibiotics; gastro-intestinal; metabolism; endocrinology; reproduction; respiratory; cancer; psychiatry; central nervous system; veterinary; cardiovascular; diabetes; recombinant DNA products; author of various publications. *Mailing Add:* 275 Ft Washington Ave Apt 5C New York NY 10032-1231

HOLTZ, CARL FREDERICK, PHOTOGRAPHIC & CLINICAL CHEMISTRY. *Current Pos:* Sr res chemist org synthesis, Eastman Kodak Co Res Labs, 65-68, res assoc photog develop work, 68-74, lab head, 74-76, asst dir, Color Photog Div, 76-78, ASST DIR, BIOSCI DIV, EASTMAN KODAK CO RES LABS, 78- *Personal Data:* b Baltimore, Md, Sept 7, 40; m 61. *Educ:* Rensselaer Polytech Inst, BS, 61, PhD(org chem), 66. *Mem:* Am Chem Soc; Am Asn Clin Chem. *Res:* Administration of research and development work in the biosciences and clinical chemistry. *Mailing Add:* 13 Woodcliff Terr Fairport NY 14450

HOLTZ, DAVID, ADMINISTRATION. *Current Pos:* PRES, GLATT-HOLTZ INC, 78- *Personal Data:* b Los Angeles, Calif, Nov 11, 42; m 73, Diane Glatt; c 3. *Educ:* Calif Inst Technol, BS, 64; Univ Calif, Berkeley, PhD(org chem), 68; Univ Calif, Los Angeles, MBA, 83. *Prof Exp:* Instr chem, Calif Inst Technol, 68-71; staff officer, Environ Studies Bd, Nat Acad Sci, 71-74; asst dir, Holcomb Res Inst, Butler Univ, 75-77. *Concurrent Pos:* Adv, Comt Econ Develop, 71-74; mem, Eval Panel Air Qual, Nat Bur Stand, 71-74; cert pub acct, 85-; vpres finance, GNP Develop Corp, 85-86; pres, Medivest Corp, 86-87; mem bd dirs, Caltech Alumni Asn, 89-92. *Mem:* Am Chem Soc; Am Inst Cert Pub Acct. *Res:* Entrepreneurship with companies based on new technologies. *Mailing Add:* 18203 Sheffield Lane Northridge CA 91326. *Fax:* 818-366-9708; *E-Mail:* holtzdavid@aol.com

HOLTZ, WESLEY G, earthwork field & laboratory testing of soils; deceased, see previous edition for last biography

HOLTZAPPLE, MARK THOMAS, BIOMASS CONVERSION TECHNOLOGY. *Current Pos:* ASSOC PROF CHEM ENG, TEX A&M UNIV, 91- *Personal Data:* b Enid, Okla, Nov 16, 56; m 92, Carol Kamps. *Educ:* Cornell Univ, BS, 78; Univ Pa, PhD(chem eng), 81. *Honors & Awards:* Presidential Green Chem Challenge Award. *Prof Exp:* Capt & res engr, Natick Res, Develop & Eval Ctr, US Army, 82-85. *Mem:* Am Inst Chem Engrs; Am Soc Mech Engrs; Sigma Xi; Am Soc Eng Educ; Am Chem Soc. *Res:* Energy production and conservation; biological process to convert waste biomass to useful fuels and chemicals; author of papers and have patents related to efficient air conditioning systems. *Mailing Add:* 1805 Southwood Dr College Station TX 77840. *E-Mail:* mth4500@chennov1.tamu.edu

HOLTZBERG, FREDERIC, SYNTHETIC, INORGANIC & ORGANOMETALLIC CHEMISTRY. *Current Pos:* Staff mem, Watson Sci Comput Lab, IBM Corp, 52-60, res staff mem, T J Watson Res Ctr, 60-74, mgr Mat Sci Dept, 74-81, res staff mem, T J Watson Res Ctr, 81- 93, EMER RES, IBM CORP, 93- *Personal Data:* b New York, NY, Apr 12, 22; m 50; c 1. *Educ:* Brooklyn Col, BS, 47; Polytech Inst Brooklyn, PhD, 52. *Hon Degrees:* Dr, Mod Sci Univ, Grenoble. *Honors & Awards:* Int Prize New Mat, Am Phys Soc, 91. *Concurrent Pos:* Tech asst to spec asst to President for sci & technol, 59-60; consult, Off Sci & Technol, 60-61; adj prof, Univ Grenoble, 75-76. *Mem:* Am Chem Soc; fel Am Phys Soc; Am Crystallog Asn; fel Am Inst Chemists; Sigma Xi. *Res:* X-ray diffraction structure analysis; low temperature diffraction studies; crystal chemistry; phase equilibria in inorganic oxide systems; ferroelectric materials; physics and chemistry of rare earth semiconducting, ferromagnetic, magnetic intermediate valence and superconducting materials; high temperature superconductivity. *Mailing Add:* 14 Cradle Rock Rd E Pound Ridge NY 10576

HOLTZCLAW, HENRY FULLER, JR, INORGANIC CHEMISTRY. *Current Pos:* from instr to prof chem, Univ Nebr, 47-67, found regents prof, 67-88, dean grad studies, 76-85, FOUND REGENTS EMER PROF CHEM, UNIV NEBR, LINCOLN, 88- *Personal Data:* b Stillwater, Okla, July 30, 21; m 49; c 2. *Educ:* Univ Kans, AB, 42; Univ Ill, MS, 46, PhD(inorg chem), 47. *Prof Exp:* Asst instr chem, Univ Kans, 42-43, instr math, 43; asst chem, Univ Ill, 43-44; shift foreman, Clinton Eng Works & Tenn Eastman Corp, Oak Ridge, 44-45; asst chem, Univ Ill, 45-46. *Concurrent Pos:* Ed-in-chief, Inorg Synthesis, Vol VIII. *Mem:* AAAS; Am Chem Soc; Sigma Xi. *Res:* Inorganic coordination compounds; polarography; metal chelates; inorganic polymers. *Mailing Add:* 7140 S Hampton Rd Lincoln NE 68506-1625

HOLTZER, ALFRED MELVIN, BIOPHYSICAL CHEMISTRY. *Current Pos:* from asst prof to assoc prof, 57-65, PROF CHEM, WASHINGTON UNIV, 65- *Personal Data:* b Brooklyn, NY, Feb 22, 29; m 54, 69, Marilyn Emerson; c Rachel & Dan. *Educ:* Washington Univ, AB, 50; Harvard Univ, PhD(chem), 54. *Prof Exp:* Instr chem, Yale Univ, 54-57. *Mem:* Am Chem Soc; Am Soc Biochem & Molecular Biol; Biophys Soc; Protein Soc. *Res:* Physical chemistry of macromolecules; protein folding; alpha-helical proteins. *Mailing Add:* Dept Chem Washington Univ Box 1134 St Louis MO 63130

HOLTZER, HOWARD, EMBRYOLOGY. *Current Pos:* From assoc to assoc prof, 54-63, PROF ANAT, SCH MED, UNIV PA, 63-, DIR PROG CELL DIFFERENTIATION, 73- *Personal Data:* b New York, NY, Mar 8, 23; m 53; c 1. *Educ:* Univ Chicago, PhD(zool), 52. *Concurrent Pos:* USPHS fel, Col Physicians & Surgeons, Columbia Univ, 52-54; Fulbright & Guggenheim fels, Carlsberg Labs, Denmark & Sweden, 58-59; vis prof, Inst Molecular Biol, Cambridge, Eng, 70-71; consult, Nat Inst Child Health & Human Develop. *Mem:* Am Soc Zool; Am Asn Anat. *Res:* Differentiation of embryonic nervous system; influence of embryonic spinal cord on differentiation of cartilage and muscle; regeneration; tissue culture. *Mailing Add:* Dept Anat Univ Pa Sch Med Philadelphia PA 19104-6058

HOLTZER, MARILYN EMERSON, MACROMOLECULAR PHYSICAL CHEMISTRY, PROTEIN PHYSICAL CHEMISTRY. *Current Pos:* instr chem, 73-80, res assoc, 80-90, RES ASST PROF, WASHINGTON UNIV, 90- *Personal Data:* b Belleville, Ill, July 22, 38; m 69, Alfred; c E Rachel & Dan. *Educ:* Washington Univ, AB, 60, AM, 63, PhD(chem), 66. *Prof Exp:* Res assoc, Washington Univ, 66-67; asst prof chem, Webster Col, 67-69; instr physics, John Burroughs Sch, 69-70; vis asst prof chem, Univ Mo, 71-72. *Concurrent Pos:* Vis prof chem, Chiba Univ, Japan, 92. *Mem:* Biophys Soc. *Res:* Stability of alpha-helical; two-chain coiled-coils; strength and specificity of interactions between alpha-helical chains in tropomyosin, tropomyosin segments, and paramyosin; protein folding kinetics in two-chain coiled coil molecules; unfolding in two-chain coiled coils. *Mailing Add:* Dept Chem Washington Univ St Louis MO 63130. *Fax:* 314-935-4481; *E-Mail:* emerson@wuchem.wush.edu

HOLTZMAN, DAVID ALLEN, CHEMICAL SENSES, DEVELOPMENTAL NEUROBIOLOGY. *Current Pos:* ASST PROF NEUROSCI & ANIMAL BEHAV, OBERLIN COL, 92- *Personal Data:* b Perth Amboy, NJ, Mar 4, 62. *Educ:* Cornell Univ, BS, 84; State Univ NY, Brooklyn, PhD(neural & behav sci), 89. *Prof Exp:* Fel, Rockefeller Univ, 90-92. *Concurrent Pos:* Lectr anat & physiol, Nassau Co Community Col, 91; guest ed, Brain, Behav & Evolution, 93; prin investr, NIH First Award-Oberlin Col, 93- *Mem:* Soc Neurosci; Asn Chemoreception Sci; Fac Undergrad Neuro Sci; Int Brain Res Orgn. *Res:* Focus on neurogenesis in the olfactory and vomeronasal systems of reptiles and on spatial learning and memory in reptiles. *Mailing Add:* Sperry Neurosci Bldg Oberlin Col 130 W Lorain St Oberlin OH 44071-1082. *Fax:* 440-775-8960; *E-Mail:* fholtzman@ocvaxa.cc.oberlin.edu

HOLTZMAN, GOLDE IVAN, STATISTICS, STATISTICAL CONSULTING. *Current Pos:* asst prof, Va Polytech Inst & State Univ, 80-86, dir, Grad Prog, 87-92, actg dept head, 89-90, ASSOC PROF STATIST, VA POLYTECH INST & STATE UNIV, 86-, DIR, STATIST CONSULT CTR, 92- *Personal Data:* b Pittsburgh, Pa, Feb 10, 46; m 72, Rona Herman; c Duna & Banney. *Educ:* Univ Calif, Los Angeles, AB, 72; Univ Ariz, MA, 75; NC State Univ, PhD(biomath), 80. *Concurrent Pos:* Chair, Comt Prof Ethics, Am Statist Asn. *Mem:* Am Statist Soc; Biomet Soc; AAAS; Sigma Xi. *Res:* Statistical computing; environmental trend analysis; statistical consulting and ethics; water quality assessment. *Mailing Add:* Dept Statist Va Polytech Inst & State Univ PO Box 0439 Blacksburg VA 24063-0001. *Fax:* 540-231-3863

HOLTZMAN, JORDAN L, PHARMACOLOGY. *Current Pos:* CHIEF CLIN PHARMACOL SECT, VET ADMIN HOSP, 71-; PROF PHARMACOL & MED, MED SCH, UNIV IINN, MINNEAPOLIS, 71- *Personal Data:* b Chicago, Ill, July 12, 33; m 58; c 3. *Educ:* Univ Chicago, BA, 52, MS, 55, MD, 59, PhD(pharmacol), 64. *Prof Exp:* Pharmacologist, Lab Parasite Chemother, Nat Inst Allergy & Infectious Dis, 64-65; pharmacologist, Lab Chem Pharmacol, Nat Heart Inst, 65-67; sr scientist, Lab Pharmacol, Nat Cancer Inst, 67-71. *Concurrent Pos:* Vis lectr, Sch Med, George Washington Univ, 65. *Mem:* Am Soc Pharmacol & Exp Therapeut; Am Soc Biol Chemists; Am Soc Clin Pharmacol Therapeut; Soc Toxicol. *Res:* Investigations into the metabolic transformation of therapeutic and environmental agents; role of mechanism of toxicity of toxic metabolites. *Mailing Add:* Vet Admin Med Ctr One Veterans Dr Minneapolis MN 55417-2213

HOLTZMAN, JULIAN CHARLES, ELECTRICAL ENGINEERING, REMOTE SENSING. *Current Pos:* asst prof, 69-76, assoc prof, 76-80, PROF ELEC ENG & ACTG CHMN DEPT, CTR RES IN ENG SCI, UNIV KANS, 80- *Personal Data:* b Staten Island, NY, Aug 14, 35; m 58. *Educ:* Polytech Inst Brooklyn, BS, 58; Univ Calif, Los Angeles, MS, 62; Cornell Univ, PhD(elec eng), 67. *Prof Exp:* Mem tech staff, Hughes Aircraft Co, 58-62; asst prof elec eng, San Jose State Col, 65-68. *Concurrent Pos:* Res scientist, Lockheed Missiles & Space Co, 66-67; consult, Appl Technol Inc, 67- *Mem:* Inst Elec & Electronics Engrs. *Res:* Communications theory; systems theory; radar systems; antennas; remote sensing. *Mailing Add:* Dept Elec & Comput Eng Univ Kans Cecase 2291 Irving Hill Dr Lawrence KS 66045

HOLTZMAN, NEIL ANTON, PEDIATRICS, MEDICAL GENETICS. *Current Pos:* From intern to sr asst resident, Harriet Lane Home, Johns Hopkins Hosp, 59-62, USPHS fel biophys, Sch Med, Johns Hopkins Univ, 62-64, from asst prof to assoc prof, 64-84, PROF PEDIAT, SCH MED, JOHNS HOPKINS UNIV, 84-, PEDIATRICIAN, JOHNS HOPKINS HOSP, 64- *Personal Data:* b Brooklyn, NY, Apr 8, 34; m 55, Barbara Starfield; c Robert, Jon, Steven & Deborah. *Educ:* Swarthmore Col, BA, 55; NY Univ, MD, 59; Univ Calif, Berkeley, MPH, 84; Am Bd Pediat, dipl, 65. *Concurrent Pos:* Fel pediat, Harriet Lane Home, Johns Hopkins Hosp, 59-64; USPHS res career develop award, 69-73; Joseph P Kennedy Jr Mem Found res scholar ment retardation, 72-74; dir genetics unit, John Hopkins Univ, 72-74; mem, comt study inborn errors metab, Nat Res Coun-Nat Acad Sci, 72-76; resident fel, Nat Acad Sci, 74-75; mem, comn hereditary dis, State of Md, 74-83; mem, comt genetics, Am Acad Pediat, 78- & chmn comn, 83-87; coordr, Hereditary Dis Serv, Dept Health & Ment Hyg, State Md, 78-83; dir, Robert Wood Johnson Gen Pediat Acad Develop Prog, Johns Hopkins Univ, 79-83; dept epidemiol, Sch Hyg, Johns Hopkins Univ, 81, dept health policy & mgt, 88; fel epidemiol, Milbank Mem Fund, 83-84; sr analyst, US Cong Off Technol Assessment, 86-87; mem, comt assessing genetic risks, Inst Med, 91-93; vchair, Md Coun Hereditary & Congenital Dis, 93- *Mem:* AAAS; fel Am Acad Pediat; Am Soc Human Genetics (secy, 83-88); Am Pediat Soc; Soc Pediat Res. *Res:* Genetic screening and services; medical technology; diffusion of biotechnology. *Mailing Add:* Johns Hopkins Med Insts 550 N Broadway Suite 301 Baltimore MD 21205

HOLTZMAN, RICHARD BEVES, RADIOCHEMISTRY, HEALTH PHYSICS. *Current Pos:* GROUP LEADER, INTERNAL DOSIMETRY, ARGONNE NAT LAB, 92- *Personal Data:* b Chicago, Ill, Sept 24, 27; m 53, Mariln Wasserman; c Faye (Brislawn), Alan & Jill (Larson). *Educ:* Univ Chicago, PhB, 45, BS, 46, MS, 50, PhD(chem), 53. *Prof Exp:* Res assoc geochem, Columbia Univ, 53-54; res physicist, Armour Res Found, Ill Inst Technol, 54 & 56-59; assoc chemist, Radiol Physics Div, Argonne Nat Lab, 59-74, chemist, Radiol & Environ Res Div, 74-84; radiation specialist, US Nuclear Regulatory Comn, 84-90. *Concurrent Pos:* Mem, Nat Coun Radiation Protection & Measurements. *Mem:* Am Chem Soc; fel Health Physics Soc; Sigma Xi; AAAS. *Res:* Natural radioactivity in the environment; metabolism of radioactive and stable trace elements; reaction kinetics of radioactive tracers in biological and physical systems; dosimetry. *Mailing Add:* 6108 Carpenter St Downers Grove IL 60516-1809. *Fax:* 630-252-5657; *E-Mail:* holtzmanrb@anl.gov

HOLTZMAN, SAMUEL, INTELLIGENT DECISION SYSTEMS, DECISION ANALYSIS. *Current Pos:* res asst, 80-83, instr, 83-84, CONSULT ASST PROF ENG & ECON SYSTS, STANFORD UNIV, 85-, STRATEGIC DECISIONS GROUP, 89- *Personal Data:* b Mexico City, Mex, Feb 9, 55; m 85; c 2. *Educ:* Mass Inst Technol, SB, 77, SM & EE, 80; Stanford Univ, MS & PhD(eng-econ systs), 85. *Prof Exp:* Res asst comput sci, Mass Inst Technol, 77-80. *Concurrent Pos:* assoc, Strategic Decisions Group, 81-86, sr assoc, 86-89, prin, 89- *Mem:* Sigma Xi; Inst Elec & Electronics Engrs; Am Asn Artificial Intel; AAAS; Inst Mgt Sci; Asn Comput Math; Comput Scientists for Social Responsibility. *Res:* Decision analysis artificial intelligence; intelligent decision systems; medical decision making, medical ethics. *Mailing Add:* 2440 Sand Hill Rd Menlo Park CA 94025-6900

HOLTZMAN, SEYMOUR, ENVIRONMENTAL HEALTH & SCIENCES. *Current Pos:* CONSULT, ENVIRON RISK ANALYSIS, 97- *Personal Data:* b Brooklyn, NY, June 22, 34; m 61, Victoria E Cueva; c David A & Ruth E. *Educ:* City Col New York, BS, 55; City Univ New York, MA, 65, PhD(biol), 73. *Prof Exp:* Res asst histol, Cols Dent & Med, NY Univ, 58-59; res asst, Downstate Med Ctr, State Univ NY, 59-60; biologist endocrinol, Squibb Inst Med Res, 60-63; res assoc physiol, Inst Phys Med & Rehab, Med Ctr, NY Univ, 63-67; vis asst prof biol, Col VI, 73-74; NIH fel, Brookhaven Nat Lab, 74-75, res assoc radiobiol, 74-76, asst scientist, 76-78, assoc scientist carcinogenesis, Med Dept, 78-80; scientist, Off Res & Develop, US Environ Protection Agency, 80-82 & Brookhaven Nat Lab, 82-84; asst prof physiol, NY Col Oseopath Med, 85-87; res assoc, Biol Dept, Brooklyn Col, 88-90; scientist, Dept Appl Sci, Brookhaven Nat Lab, 90-97. *Concurrent Pos:* Adj asst prof biol, Brooklyn Col, 73-74; adj asst prof, Queensborough Community Col, 74-76, adj assoc prof, 84- *Mem:* Fel AAAS; Soc Risk Anal; Sigma Xi. *Res:* Superfund and probabilistic analyses of risks to human health and biota, from chemical and radioactive agents. *Mailing Add:* PO Box 902 Medford NY 11763-0902. *Fax:* 516-344-7867; *E-Mail:* holtzman@mail.bnl.gov

HOLTZMAN, WAYNE HAROLD, PSYCHOLOGY, MENTAL HEALTH. *Current Pos:* From asst prof to assoc prof, 49-59, dean, Col Educ, 64-70, PROF PSYCHOL, UNIV TEX, AUSTIN, 59-, HOGG PROF PSYCHOL & EDUC, 64- *Personal Data:* b Chicago, Ill, Jan 16, 23; m 47, Joan King; c Wayne H, James K, Scott E & Karl H. *Educ:* Northwestern Univ, BS, 44, MS, 47; Stanford Univ, PhD, 50. *Hon Degrees:* LHD, Southwestern Univ, 80. *Honors & Awards:* Klopper Prize, Soc Personality Assessment, 88; Centennial Citation, Am Psychol Asn, 92; Award Distinguished Contrib Int Psychol, Am Psychol Asn, 96. *Concurrent Pos:* Assoc dir, Hogg Found Ment Health, Univ Tex, Austin, 55-64, pres, 70-93, spec coun, 93-; mem behav sci study sect, USPHS, 57-59, ment health study sect, 60; dir, Soc Sci Res Coun, 57-63, Ctr Invest Soc, Mex, 60-70; fac res fel Soc Sci Res Coun, 63-65, Ctr Advan Study Behav Sci, 62-63; consult, USAF; mem basic res comt, Nat Res Coun, 68-71; mem comput sci & eng bd, Nat Acad Sci, 71-73; bd dirs, Found Fund Res Psychiat, 73-77; dir, Conf SW Found, 76-84, pres, 78-79; trustee, Menninger Found, 80-; mem acad info systems adv coun, IBM, 82-85. *Mem:* Fel Am Psychol Asn; AAAS; Am Statist Asn; InterAm Soc Psychol (pres, 66-67); Am Educ Res Asn; Int Union Psychol Sci (pres, 84-88); Sigma Xi. *Res:* Psychology; cross-cultural studies of personality development and psychiatric assessment; impact of human services on mental health. *Mailing Add:* 3300 Foothill Dr Austin TX 78731-5823. *Fax:* 512-471-9608; *E-Mail:* wayne.holtzman@mail.utexas.edu

HOLTZMANN, OLIVER VINCENT, PLANT PATHOLOGY. *Current Pos:* asst plant pathologist, Univ Hawaii, 56-66, from assoc prof to prof, 66-86, chmn dept, 70-83 & 85-86, EMER PROF PLANT PATH, UNIV HAWAII, 86- *Personal Data:* b Highmore, SDak, June 26, 22; m 57; c 5. *Educ:* Colo State Univ, BS, 50, MS, 52; Wash State Univ, PhD(plant path), 55. *Prof Exp:* Res asst plant path, Wash State Univ, 52-55; res asst prof, NC State Col, 55-56. *Concurrent Pos:* Adv, Hawaii Turfgrass Asn; adv, Dept Agr, Plant Quarantine. *Mem:* Am Phytopath Soc; Soc Nematol. *Res:* Phytonematol; diseases of turf grass; teaching of tropical plant pathology. *Mailing Add:* 1235 Manu Mele St Kailua HI 96734

HOLUB, BRUCE JOHN, NUTRITIONAL BIOCHEMISTRY. *Current Pos:* from asst prof to assoc prof, 73-83, PROF NUTRIT, UNIV GUELPH, 83- *Personal Data:* b Sudbury, Ont, Nov 3, 44; m 72; c 2. *Educ:* Univ Guelph, BSA, 67; Univ Toronto, MSc, 69, PhD(biochem, nutrit), 71. *Honors & Awards:* Borden Award Nutrit. *Prof Exp:* Res chemist, Imperial Oil Ltd, 67. *Concurrent Pos:* Med Res Coun Can fel biol chem, Univ Mich, 71-73. *Mem:* Am Oil Chemists Soc; Am Inst Nutrit; Can Biochem Soc; Nutrit Soc Can. *Res:* Metabolism of essential fatty acids; biological function of inositol; nutritional regulation of lipid metabolism. *Mailing Add:* Dept Nutrit Sci Univ Guelph Guelph ON N1G 2W1 Can

HOLUB, DONALD ARTHUR, internal medicine; deceased, see previous edition for last biography

HOLUB, FRED F, ORGANIC CHEMISTRY, POLYMER CHEMISTRY. *Current Pos:* CONSULT, 86- *Personal Data:* b Cleveland, Ohio, June 20, 21; m 49, Maxine Maxwell; c Karen. *Educ:* Western Reserve Univ, BA; Duke Univ, PhD. *Honors & Awards:* Meritorious Serv Award, NY Sect, Am Chem Soc. *Prof Exp:* Res scientist, Res & Develop Ctr, Gen Elec Co, 56-86. *Concurrent Pos:* Consult mat sci & technol. *Mem:* Am Chem Soc; Sigma Xi; AAAS. *Res:* Fluorination of organic compounds; synthesis and high temperature polymers; aromatic polyesters and nitrogen polymers; synthetic elastomers; chemical modification of polymers; composite structures; radiation chemistry; polymer blends; polyimide-siloxanes copolymers; polymer auto headlamps; electrical polymer switches; flame resistant blends and insulation; very large screen television system. *Mailing Add:* 726 St Thomas Cove Niceville FL 32578

HOLUB, JAMES ROBERT, MATHEMATICS. *Current Pos:* From asst prof to assoc prof, 69-78, PROF MATH, VA POLYTECH INST & STATE UNIV, 78- *Personal Data:* b New Prague, Minn, Dec 5, 42; m 67; c 2. *Educ:* Col St Thomas, BA, 64; La State Univ, MS, 66, PhD(math), 69. *Mem:* Am Math Soc. *Res:* Functional analysis; operator, tensor product and basis theory. *Mailing Add:* 220 Craig Dr Blacksburg VA 24060

HOLUBEC, ZENOWIE MICHAEL, PETROLEUM CHEMISTRY, TRIBOLOGY. *Current Pos:* Res chemist, Lubrizol Corp, 60-63 & 68-70, proj leader, 70-71, res supvr, 71-72, proj mgr, 72-78, dir phys & anal chem, 78-86, SR PROJ COORDR, LUBRIZOL CORP, 86- *Personal Data:* b Ukraine, Nov 21, 37; US citizen; m 63; c 3. *Educ:* Case Western Reserve Univ, BA, 60; John Carroll Univ, MS, 64; Univ Ill, PhD(org chem), 68. *Mem:* Am Chem Soc; Am Soc Testing & Mat; Soc Automotive Engrs. *Res:* Tribology; synthesis; use and mode of action of additives for industrial, tractor transmission, gear, engine lubricants and railroad diesel lubricants; physical properties of lubricants; analysis of new and old lubricants. *Mailing Add:* 6908 Anthony Lane Cleveland OH 44130-4655

HOLUBKA, JOSEPH WALTER, ORGANIC CHEMISTRY, POLYMER CHEMISTRY. *Current Pos:* SR STAFF SCIENTIST POLYMER CHEM, FORD MOTOR CO, 77- *Personal Data:* b Detroit, Mich, Jan 10, 50. *Educ:* Univ Detroit, BS, 72; Wayne State Univ, PhD(chem), 77. *Mem:* Am Chem Soc. *Res:* Physical chemistry of polymer films, polymer synthesis and modification; surface analysis of polymer films. *Mailing Add:* 17902 Myron Livonia MI 48152-1997

HOLUJ, FRANK, SOLID STATE PHYSICS. *Current Pos:* from asst prof to prof, 61-94, EMER PROF PHYSICS, UNIV WINDSOR, 94- *Personal Data:* b Poland, Oct 28, 27; Can citizen. *Educ:* Univ London, BSc, 54; McMaster Univ, MSc, 56, PhD(physics), 58. *Prof Exp:* Fel physics, McMaster Univ, 58-59; res officer gas masers, Appl Physics Div, Nat Res Coun Can, 59-61. *Mem:* Can Asn Physicists; Am Phys Soc. *Res:* Nuclear and electron spin (magnetic) resonance in solids; optical study of solids using lasers; gamma-gamma correlation study in solids. *Mailing Add:* Dept Physics Univ Windsor Windsor ON N9B 3S4 Can

HOLUM, JOHN ROBERT, ORGANIC CHEMISTRY. *Current Pos:* RETIRED. *Personal Data:* b Tracy, Minn, Aug 31, 28; m 50, Mary Mattili; c Elizabeth, Ann & Kathryn. *Educ:* St Olaf Col, BA, 50; Univ Minn, Minneapolis, PhD(org chem), 54. *Honors & Awards:* Minn Sect Col Chem Teaching Award, Am Chem Soc, 73. *Prof Exp:* Chemist, Eastman Kodak Co, NY, 54; instr org chem, Augsburg Col, 57-58 & Pac Lutheran Col, 58-59; from assoc prof to prof org chem, Augsburg Col, 59-93. *Concurrent Pos:* NSF grants, 59-60, 61-62 & 64-65; NSF sci fac fel, Calif, Inst Technol; consult, John Wiley & Sons, Inc, NY, 63-; consult, Control Data Corp, Minn, 66-67 & Plastics Inc, 67-69; sabbatical leave, Harvard Univ, 69-70, Univ Minn, 78-79. *Mem:* AAAS; Am Chem Soc; Sigma Xi. *Res:* The keto group as a neighboring group in chloroketones. *Mailing Add:* 750 S Miss River Blvd No 322 St Paul MN 55116

HOLVECK, DAVID P, PHARMACOLOGY. *Current Pos:* staff mem, Centocor Inc, 83-86, exec vpres NAm, 86-87, exec vpres vitro diag prod, 87-88, EXEC VPRES & PRES DIAG DIV, CENTOCOR INC, 88- *Prof Exp:* Staff mem, Corning Glass Works, 64-79; mgr digital x-ray, Gen Elec Corp, 79-83. *Mailing Add:* Centocor Inc 200 Great Valley Pkwy Malvern PA 19355-1307

HOLVERSON, EDWIN LEROY, SOLID STATE PHYSICS. *Current Pos:* from asst prof to assoc prof, 71-73, PROF PHYSICS, MIDWESTERN UNIV, 73- *Personal Data:* b Cottage Grove, Ore, Feb 1, 34; m 60; c 1. *Educ:* Humboldt State Col, AB, 58; Ariz State Univ, MS, 62, PhD(physics), 65. *Prof Exp:* Instr, Humboldt State Col, 57-58, AV technician, 58-59; asst physics, Ariz State Univ, 59-64, res fac assoc, 64-65; asst prof, Mont Col Mineral Sci & Technol, 65-67 & Midwestern Univ, 67-69; vis assoc prof, Am Univ Cairo, 69-70. *Mem:* Am Phys Soc; Sigma Xi. *Res:* Pollution control utilizing electrokinetic techniques. *Mailing Add:* 4022 Kingsbury Dr Wichita Falls TX 76309

HOLWAY, JAMES GARY, HUMAN ECOLOGY. *Current Pos:* from asst prof to assoc prof, 63-68, PROF BIOL, STATE UNIV NY COL ONEONTA, 68- *Personal Data:* b Lake Placid, NY, Sept 28, 31; m 53; c 3. *Educ:* State Univ NY Col Ed, Albany, AB, 59; Colo State Univ, MS, 61, PhD(bot sci), 62. *Prof Exp:* Prof biol, Yampa Valley Col, 62-63. *Res:* Life history of angiosperm alpine plants in Colorado; ecological study of forest-climate relationships in Adirondacks, NY; man-environment relationships. *Mailing Add:* Dept Biol State Univ NY Col PO Box 4015 Oneonta NY 13820-4015

HOLWAY, LOWELL HOYT, JR, PHYSICS, APPLIED MATHEMATICS. *Current Pos:* Assoc res staff mem, Res Div, Raytheon Co, 55-58, sr engr, Govt Equip Div, 58-63, sr res scientist, 63-65, PRIN RES SCIENTIST, RES DIV, RAYTHEON CO, LEXINGTON, 65- *Personal Data:* b St Louis, Mo, Oct 7, 31; m 55; c 1. *Educ:* Dartmouth Col, AB, 53; Harvard Univ, AM, 55, PhD(appl math), 64. *Mem:* Am Phys Soc; Inst Elec & Electronics Engrs; Am Nuclear Soc. *Res:* Kinetic theory of gases; shock waves; plasma physics; carrier transport in semiconductors; neutron diffusion; laser self-focusing; microwave breakdown, ionospheric and magnetospheric propagation; heat transfer; electron traps and deep levels in semiconductors; Impatt diodes. *Mailing Add:* 4 Everett St Natick MA 01760

HOLWERDA, JAMES G, GEOLOGY. *Current Pos:* proj geologist, Ralph M Parsons Co, Iraq, 53-55, proj mgr, 55-57, proj mgr, Ethiopia, 58-64, VPRES, PARSONS CORP, 64-, VPRES, RALPH M PARSONS CO PTY LTD, 71- *Personal Data:* b Los Angeles, Calif, Dec 9, 25; m 55; c 2. *Educ:* Univ Southern Calif, BA, 48, MA, 51, PhD(geol), 58. *Prof Exp:* Proj geologist, Ralph M Parsons Co, Taiwan, 50-51; geologist, Johnston Int, Calif, 51-53. *Mem:* AAAS; Geol Soc Am; Asn Eng Geol; Am Asn Petrol Geol; Am Geophys Union; Sigma Xi. *Res:* Ground water and engineering geology; mineral exploration; project management; negotiations. *Mailing Add:* 1217 W Paseo Del Mar San Pedro CA 90731-6060

HOLWERDA, ROBERT ALAN, INORGANIC CHEMISTRY. *Current Pos:* From asst prof to assoc prof, 74-85, assoc dean, 85-87, PROF, COL ARTS & SCI, TEX TECH UNIV, 86- *Personal Data:* b Detroit, Mich, Sept 13, 47; m 71; c 3. *Educ:* Stanford Univ, BS, 69; Calif Inst Technol, PhD(chem), 74. *Mem:* Am Chem Soc; Sigma Xi. *Res:* Reactivity and electronic structure of oxo-bridged polynuclear transition metal complexes; chemistry of metal stabilized organic free radical ligands; Kinetic stability of the copper (II) mercaptide sulphur bond; thermodynamic and kinetic aspects of palladium (II) carbon bond formation. *Mailing Add:* 6905 Flint Ave Lubbock TX 79413-6218

HOLY, NORMAN LEE, ORGANIC CHEMISTRY, POLYACRYLICS. *Current Pos:* RES FEL, ROHM & HAAS, 84- *Personal Data:* b Sturgis, Mich, June 3, 41; m 67; c 2. *Educ:* Western Mich Univ, BA, 63; Purdue Univ, PhD(chem), 68. *Prof Exp:* Prof chem, Western Ky Univ, 67-84. *Mem:* Am Chem Soc. *Res:* Making novel polyacrylates; degradable surfactants; degradable plastics. *Mailing Add:* PO Box 107 Penns Park PA 18943-0107

HOLYOKE, CALEB WILLIAM, JR, AGRICHEMICALS. *Current Pos:* RES ASSOC, E I DU PONT DE NEMOURS & CO, INC, 73- *Personal Data:* b York, Pa, Sept 22, 43; m 66; c 2. *Educ:* Washington Univ, BS, 67; Vanderbilt Univ, PhD(chem), 73. *Prof Exp:* Chemist, Petrolite Corp, 66-68. *Concurrent Pos:* Adj prof, Dept Entom & Appl Ecol, Univ Del, 81- *Mem:* Am Chem Soc; Sigma Xi; Soc Neurosci. *Res:* Combinatorial chemistry; insecticide design and synthesis; structure-activity relationships. *Mailing Add:* 120 Country Club Dr Newark DE 19711. *Fax:* 302-366-5738; *E-Mail:* holyoke@al@esvax@umc.com

HOLYOKE, EDWARD AUGUSTUS, ANATOMY, EMBRYOLOGY. *Current Pos:* From instr to assoc prof, Univ Nebr, 32-46, chmn dept, 60-73, prof anat, 46-83, EMER PROF, COL MED, UNIV NEBR, OMAHA, 83- *Personal Data:* b Madrid, Nebr, Mar 10, 08; m 40, 81, Frances Brockmeier; c Edward A Jr & Thomas T. *Educ:* Univ Nebr, BSc, 30, MA, 32, MD, 34, PhD(anat), 38. *Mem:* AAAS; Am Asn Anatomists; Sigma Xi; Anatomical Soc Gt Brit & Ireland. *Res:* Experimental embryology; gross anatomy; hematology. *Mailing Add:* Col Med Univ Nebr Omaha NE 68105

HOLYOKE, THOMAS CAMPBELL, ALGEBRA. *Current Pos:* RETIRED. *Personal Data:* b Milwaukee, Wis, June 9, 22; m 47; c 3. *Educ:* Harvard Univ, AB, 43; Ohio State Univ, MA, 47, PhD(math), 50. *Prof Exp:* Instr math, Ohio State Univ, 49-50; instr, Northwestern Univ, 50-53, asst prof, 53-55; asst prof, Miami Univ, 55-58; assoc prof, Antioch Col, 58-63, prof math, 63-84, assoc acad dean, 77-80. *Concurrent Pos:* Vis mem, Dept Math, Air Develop Ctr, Wright-Patterson AFB, 56CF; dir, NSF Inst Teachers Math, Miami Univ, 57; NSF fel, Univ Calif, 57-58; chmn, Dept Math, Antioch Col, 61-64, dir, Sci Inst, 69-72; Fulbright-Hays lectr, Mindanao State Univ, 64-65, vis prof, 67-69; Fulbright-Hays lectr, prof math & head dept, Chancellor Col, Univ Malawi, 75-77; vis prof, Col Wooster, Ohio, 80-81; Chancellor Col, Univ Malawi, 75-77; Fulbright lect grant, Univ Botswana, 87-88. *Res:* Permutation groups; abstract algebra; elementary number theory; multiply transitive permutation groups. *Mailing Add:* 608 S High St Yellow Springs OH 45387

HOLZAPFEL, CHRISTINA MARIE, BIOGEOGRAPHY, QUANTITATIVE GENETICS. *Current Pos:* RES ASSOC BIOGEOG, UNIV ORE, 71- *Personal Data:* b Baltimore, Md, Jan 24, 42; m 70, William E Bradshaw; c Pilar A Bradshaw. *Educ:* Goucher Col, BA, 64; Univ Mich, Ann Arbor, MS, 68, PhD(zool), 70. *Prof Exp:* NSF res asst biogeog plants, Canary Islands, Spain, 65-66; NSF res trainee biogeog insects, Univ Mich, Ann Arbor, 66-70, lectr exp biol, 70; res fel biogeog plants, Harvard Univ, 70-71. *Concurrent Pos:* Res assoc, Tall Timbers Res Sta, Tallahassee, Fla, 77-78; res fel, Imp Col, Silwood Park, Eng, 86; fel, Woods Hole Oceanog Inst, 63. *Mem:* Sigma Xi; Soc Study Evolution; Ecol Soc Am. *Res:* Population biology, life history patterns and genetic differentiation of container-breeding mosquitoes. *Mailing Add:* Dept Biol 1210 Univ Ore Eugene OR 97403-1210. *Fax:* 541-346-2364; *E-Mail:* holz@darkwing.uoregon.edu

HOLZBACH, R THOMAS, HUMAN GALLSTONE PATHOGENESIS, CLINICAL GASTROENTEROLOGY & HEPATOLOGY. *Current Pos:* HEAD, GASTROINTESTINAL RES UNIT, DEPT GASTROENTEROL, CLEVELAND CLIN FOUND, OHIO, 73- *Personal Data:* b Salem, Ohio, Aug 19, 29; m 56, Lorraine Cozza; c Ellen, Mark & James. *Educ:* Georgetown Univ, BS, 51; Case Western Res Univ, MD, 55; Nat Bd Med Examiners, dipl, 56; Am Bd Internal Med, cert, 62, Med Subspecialty Gastroenterol, 64. *Prof Exp:* Internship & asst resident med, Univ Ill, Res & Educ Hosps, Chicago, 55-57; sr resident internal med, Cleveland Metrop Gen Hosp, Ohio, 59-60; fel gastroenterol, Case Western Res Univ, Cleveland, Ohio, 60-61; pvt pract gastroenterol, Cleveland, Ohio, 63-67; head, Gastrointestinal Res Unit & assoc physician, Div Med, St Luke's Hosp, Cleveland, Ohio, 67-73; dir, Div Gastroenterol, 70-73. *Concurrent Pos:* Instr med, Sch Med, Case Western Res Univ, Cleveland, Ohio, 61-64, clin instr, 64-71; asst physician, Univ Hosps, Cleveland, Ohio, 61-63; asst chief, Sect Gastroenterol, Vet Admin Med Ctr, Cleveland, Ohio, 61-63; sci dir, Res Projs Area, Cleveland Clin Found, 74-82; vis prof & lectr, numerous univs & hosps, foreign & US, 74-94; Alexander von Humboldt traveling fel, Univ Heidelberg, Ger, 78, Univ Munich, 82. *Mem:* Am Gastroenterol Asn; Am Asn Study Liver Dis; fel Am Col Physicians; Am Physiol Asn; Am Soc Biochem & Molecular Biol; AAAS; Sigma Xi; Am Soc Biol Chemists; Int Asn Study Liver Asn; Am Fedn Clin Res. *Res:* Discovered: glycoproteins secreted by liver are present in human bile; glycoproteins have opposing effects; an inhibitor form delays the growth of cholesterol crystals, an essential prelude to gallstone formation; promoter forms, of which there may be several, accelerate crystals formation and growth; characterizing these unique glycoproteins. *Mailing Add:* Gastrointestinal Res Unit Dept Gastroenterol Cleveland Clin Found 9500 Euclid Ave Cleveland OH 44195. *Fax:* 216-444-9366

HOLZBECHER, JIRI, PHYSICAL CHEMISTRY. *Current Pos:* res assoc, Trace Anal Res Ctr, 76-79, PRIN SLOWPOKE OPERATOR ANALYTICAL CHEM, SLOWPOKE FACIL, DALHOUSIE UNIV, 79- *Personal Data:* b Prague, Czech, Nov 14, 43; Can citizen; m 68. *Educ:* Univ Chem Technol, Prague, MSc, 67; Dalhousie Univ, PhD(anal chem), 73. *Prof Exp:* Fel anal chem, Dalhousie Univ, 73-74; sr technologist clin chem, Grace Maternity Hosp, Halifax, 75-76. *Mem:* Chem Inst Can. *Res:* Neutron activation analysis; infrared spectrometry; fluorimetry analysis. *Mailing Add:* Slowpoke Facil Life Sci Bldg Dalhousie Univ Halifax NS B3H 4J1 Can

HOLZBERLEIN, THOMAS M, atomic physics, solar materials; deceased, see previous edition for last biography

HOLZER, ALFRED, NUCLEAR PHYSICS. *Current Pos:* RETIRED. *Personal Data:* b Vienna, Austria, Jan 23, 25; US citizen; m 50; c 2. *Educ:* Univ Mich, BS(physics) & BS(math), 50, MS, 51; Case Inst, PhD(physics), 60. *Prof Exp:* Chief spectroscopist, J H Herron Co, Ohio, 51-54; physicist, K Div, Univ Calif, 59-62, group leader, 62-66, from dep div leader to div leader, Plowshare Div, Lawrence Livermore Lab, 66-74, asst assoc dir, Energy & Resource Prog, 74-86. *Mem:* Am Phys Soc. *Res:* Shock waves in solids; explosion phenomena; energy & resources. *Mailing Add:* PO Box 7247 Carmel CA 93921

HOLZER, GUNTHER ULRICH, GEOCHEMISTRY. *Current Pos:* ASSOC PROF, SCH BIOL & CTR BIOTECHNOL GA INST TECHNOL, 86- *Personal Data:* b Lahr, Ger, May 22, 42; m 81. *Educ:* Acad Chem & Physics, Isny, Ger, BS, 68; Univ Houston, Tex, PhD(org chem), 73. *Prof Exp:* Chem engr synthetic rubber, Farbenfabriken Bayer, Ger, 68-69; res asst peptide chem, Inst Org Chem, Univ Tubingen, Ger, 74; res assoc & vis asst prof chem & biochem, Dept Biophys Sci, Univ Houston, Tex, 75-80; from asst prof to assoc prof chem & geochem, Colo Sch Mines, 80-86. *Concurrent Pos:* Consult, Solar Energy Res Inst, 81- *Mem:* Sigma Xi. *Res:* Lipids in archaebacteria; role of microorganisms in petroleum formation; organic analysis of ancient and recent sediments by gas chromatography mass spectrometry; development of supercritical fluid chromatography. *Mailing Add:* Sch Biol Ga Inst Technol 225 N Ave NW Atlanta GA 30332-0001

HOLZER, ROBERT EDWARD, SPACE PHYSICS, PLASMA PHYSICS. *Current Pos:* head dept planetary & space sci, Univ Calif, 67-69, dean div phys sci, 73-74, prof, 47-74, EMER PROF GEOPHYS, UNIV CALIF, LOS ANGELES, 74- *Personal Data:* b Portland, Ore, Nov 21, 06; m 31; c 3. *Educ:* Reed Inst, AB, 26, Univ Calif, Berkeley, MA, 28; PhD (physics), 30. *Hon Degrees:* DSc, Univ NMex, 89. *Prof Exp:* Instr physics, Univ Calif, 30-31; Nat Res Coun fel, Univ Chicago, 31-33; asst prof, Fenn Col, 33-34; instr, Univ Calif, 34-35; from instr to prof, Univ NMex, 35-46; prof & head dept, Pomona Col, 46-47. *Concurrent Pos:* Assoc dir war res proj, Univ NMex, 41-46; mem sci adv bd, USAF, 56-62; asst sci dir, Off Naval Res, London, 59-60. *Mem:* AAAS; fel Am Phys Soc; fel Am Geophys Union; Am Asn Physics Teachers. *Res:* Atmospheric electricity; electrical structure of thunderstorms; propagation of low audiofrequency atmospherics; experimental space physics; magnetospheric physics; auroral phenomena. *Mailing Add:* 10517 Wynton Dr Los Angeles CA 90024

HOLZER, THOMAS EDWARD, SOLAR TERRESTRIAL PHYSICS, SPACE PLASMA PHYSICS. *Current Pos:* scientist, 73-78, dir, 90-95, SR SCIENTIST, HIGH ALTITUDE OBSERV, NAT CTR ATMOSPHERIC RES, 78-; PROF ADJOINT, DEPT ASTROPHYS, PLANETARY & ATMOSPHERIC SCI, UNIV COLO, 81- *Personal Data:* b Albuquerque, NMex, June 24, 44; m 68. *Educ:* Pomona Col, BA, 65; Univ Calif, San Diego, PhD(appl physics), 70. *Honors & Awards:* James B Macelwane Award, Am Geophys Union, 78. *Prof Exp:* NATO fel space physics, Imp Col, Univ London, 70-71; Nat Res Coun res assoc, Aeronomy Lab, Nat Oceanic & Atmospheric Admin, Boulder, Colo, 71-73. *Concurrent Pos:* Lectr, Dept Astrophys, Planetary & Atmospheric Sci, Univ Colo, 72-81; mem, Heliospheric Hydromagnetics Subpanel, Space Plasma Physics Panel, Nat Acad Sci, 76-77, Comt Solar & Space Physics, 77-80, Advocacy Comt Study Physics of the Sun, 80-83, Ad Hoc Comt Role of Theory in Space Sci, 80-82, Study Major Directions Space Sci, Solar & Space Physics Task Group, Space Sci Bd, 84-86, Solar Panel, Astron & Astrophys Surv Comt, 89-90; mem, Solar Terrestrial Theory Panel, NASA, 78-79, Solar Cycle & Dynamics Mission Working Group, 78-79, Space Sci Steering Comt, Solar Terrestrial Theory Prog, Ad Hoc Adv Subcomt, 79-80, Solar Physics Working Group, Astron Surv Comt, 79-80, Solar Physics Mgt Opers Working Group, 79-80, Ad Hoc Comt, Prog Nex Solar Maximum, 84-86, Cosmic & Heliospheric Mgt Opers Working Group, Space Physics Div, 87-, Heliospheric Physics Working Group, 87-, Solar Probe Sci Working Team 88-; head, Coronal-Interplanetary Physics Sect, High Altitude Observ; mem steering comt, Off Interdisciplinary Earth Studies, Univ Corp Atmospheric Res, 86-88, Solar-Interplanetary Variability Study, Sci Comt Solar Terrestrial Physics, 87-, Solar-Terrestrial Energy Prog, Sci Comt Solar-Terrestrial Physics, 87-90; chmn, Heliospheric SR&T Rev Panel, Space Physics Div, NASA, 89, Solar Theory & Modelling SR&T Rev Panel, 90, Theory Working Group, 90-; chmn, Organizing Comt Workshop on Solar-Terrestrial Impacts on Global Change, 89-; mem, rev comt solar prog, NASA Goddard Space Flight Ctr, 90, rev comt, Inst Space & Terrestrial Sci, Ontario, Can, 90, theory panel, NASA Space Physics Study, 90, cosmic & heliospheric panel, 90; co-organizer, Interstellar Probe Workshop, 90; vis comt, Bartol Res Inst, Univ Del, 90- *Mem:* Fel Am Geophys Union; Am Astron Soc; Int Astron Union; Int Union Radio Sci; Norweg Acad Sci & Lett. *Res:* Physics of the sun; heliosphere; terrestrial magnetosphere,ionosphere and upper atmosphere. *Mailing Add:* High Altitude Observ Nat Cter Atmospheric Res PO Box 3000 Boulder CO 80307. *Fax:* 303-497-1589; *E-Mail:* holzer@hao.ucar.edu

HOLZER, THOMAS LEQUEAR, GEOLOGY. *Current Pos:* geologist, US Geol Surv, 75-82 & 84-88, dep asst dir res, 82-84, br chief, 88-92, GEOLOGIST, US GEOL SURV, 92-; CONSULT PROF, STANFORD UNIV, 94- *Personal Data:* b Lafayette, Ind, June 26, 44; m 68, Mary Burbach; c 2. *Educ:* Princeton Univ, BSE, 65; Stanford Univ, MS, 66, PhD(geol), 70. *Honors & Awards:* Distinguished Serv Award, Hydrogeol Div, Geol Soc Am. *Prof Exp:* Asst prof geol, Univ Conn, 70-75. *Mem:* Geol Soc Am; Asn Ground Water Scientists & Engrs; Am Geophys Union; Sigma Xi; AAAS. *Res:* Rheology of fine grained sediments; land subsidence; ground water hydrology; earthquake liquefaction. *Mailing Add:* PO Box 851 Palo Alto CA 94302

HOLZER, TIMOTHY J, retrovirology & host defense, macrophage-t cell biology, for more information see previous edition

HOLZHEY, CHARLES STEVEN, SCIENCE ADMINISTRATION. *Current Pos:* Soil scientist, Soil Conserv Serv, USDA, Mont, 58-68, res soil scientist, Soil Surv Lab, Plant Indust Sta, 68-72, head, Soil Surv Invest Unit, 72-75 & Nat Soil Surv Lab, 75-88, ASST DIR, SOIL SURV DIV, SOIL CONSERV SERV, USDA, 88- *Personal Data:* b Malta, Mont, Apr 29, 36; m 66; c 2. *Educ:* Univ Idaho, BS, 58, MS, 64; Univ Calif, Riverside, PhD(soil sci), 68. *Mem:* Am Soc Agron; Soil Sci Soc Am; Soils Conserv Soc Am; Nat Asn Conserv Dist; Sigma Xi. *Res:* Soil formation and classification; soil survey applications to land use and environmental concerns. *Mailing Add:* 430 Haverford Dr Lincoln NE 68510

HOLZINGER, JOSEPH ROSE, MATHEMATICS. *Current Pos:* RETIRED. *Personal Data:* b Annville, Pa, Sept 30, 14; m 39; c 3. *Educ:* Franklin & Marshall Col, BS, 35; Cornell Univ, MS, 48. *Prof Exp:* Teacher pub sch, Pa, 36-42; instr math, Wyomissing Polytech Inst, 45-46; prof math & astron, Franklin & Marshall Col, 48-80. *Concurrent Pos:* Dir Grundy Observ, Franklin & Marshall Col; NSF sci fac fel, 59-60. *Mem:* AAAS; Am Astron Soc; Math Asn Am. *Res:* Astronomy. *Mailing Add:* 2001 Harrisburg Pike Apt 21 Lancaster PA 17601

HOLZINGER, THOMAS WALTER, FOOD SCIENCE, MICROBIOLOGY. *Current Pos:* res assoc, Milk & Ice Cream Div, Borden Inc, 61-63, coordr res & qual control, 63-65, dir res, Dairy & Serv Div, NY, 66-68, dir qual assurance, Ohio, 68-73, assoc dir corp qual assurance, 73 & 76, dir qual assurance & compliance, 76-85, corp tech dir, 85-92, CORP DIR QUAL ASSURANCE, DAIRY & FOODS INT, BORDEN INC, 92- *Personal Data:* b Nurnberg, Ger, Feb 23, 30; US citizen. *Educ:* Univ Vt, BS, 53; Iowa State Univ, MS, 54. *Prof Exp:* Res asst biochem, Univ Vt, 54-55; asst mgr, NJ Dairy Labs, 55-61. *Concurrent Pos:* Mem, Interstate Milk Shippers Conf, 66- & Milk Indust Found Tech Comt, 67-; dir, Am Cultured Dairy Prod Inst; chmn, Nat Dairy Bd, Sci Adv Comt; dir, Int Dairy Fedn, Am Dairy Sci Asn; tech comt mem, Nat Food Processors Asn; chair, Dairy Tech Div, Inst Food Technologists. *Mem:* Am Dairy Sci Asn; Inst Food Technologists; NY Acad Sci; fel Am Inst Chemists; Am Soc Microbiol; Nat Food Processors Asn; Int Dairy Fedn. *Res:* Food technology; food chemistry; microbiology; food safety. *Mailing Add:* 3440 Olentangy River Rd Columbus OH 43202

HOLZMAN, GEORGE, ORGANIC CHEMISTRY. *Current Pos:* TRUSTEE & DIR, SOUTHWEST WASH HOSPS, 85-; DIR, HEALTH & WELFARE PLANNING COUN, 87- *Personal Data:* b Los Angeles, Calif, Jan 25, 20; m 44; c 3. *Educ:* Calif Inst Technol, BS, 42, PhD(org chem), 48. *Prof Exp:* Asst, Calif Inst Technol, 42-46; A D Little fel, Mass Inst Technol, 47-49; chemist, Shell Develop Co Div, Shell Oil Co, Calif, 49-53, res supvr, 53-62, spec technologist, 62-64, mgr, Aromatics Dept, 64, supt Woodriver Refining, 64-67, chief technologist, 67-68, mgr mfg technol, 68-70, refinery mgr, 70-71, gen mgr refining, 71-77, gen mgr logistics, 77-80. *Concurrent Pos:* Dir fuels & petrochem, Am Inst Chem Engrs, 70-71; chmn coord subcomt factors affecting petrol refining capacity, Nat Petrol Coun, 72-73. *Mem:* AAAS; Am Chem Soc; Am Inst Chem Engrs; The Chem Soc. *Res:* Petroleum process chemistry and processing. *Mailing Add:* PO Box 1909 Vancouver WA 98668-1909

HOLZMAN, GEORGE ROBERT, PHYSICS, ELECTRICAL ENGINEERING. *Current Pos:* RETIRED. *Personal Data:* b Long Island, NY, Dec 31, 19; m 44; c 2. *Educ:* Rensselaer Polytech Inst, BEE, 42, PhD(physics), 51. *Prof Exp:* Radio engr radar, Naval Res Lab, 42; jr instr physics, Johns Hopkins Univ, 46; sr physicist, Behr-Manning Corp, 50-52; fel, Mellon Inst, 52-58; physicist, Int Bus Mach Corp, 58-59, mathematician programmer, 59-61, mgr phys sci, 61-63, mgr adv tech, 63-65, mgr new mkts develop, 65-69, planning mgr, Electromagnetic Compatibility Power Systs, 69-72, gas panel coordr, 72-76, electromagnetic compatibility mgr, ion implant, diffusion, IBM Corp, 76-84. *Mem:* Am Phys Soc. *Res:* Nuclear and electron spin resonance; electrical charging of small particles; study of surfaces, films and interfaces; ferroelectrics; laser communications; computer systems. *Mailing Add:* 166 Echo Dr Vernon CT 06066

HOLZMAN, GERALD BRUCE, MEDICINE. *Current Pos:* DIR EDUC, AM COL OBSTET & GYNEC. *Personal Data:* b Los Angeles, Calif, Apr 22, 33; m 57, Barbara Hexter; c Ruth (Clemans), Michael & Gregory. *Educ:* Stanford Univ, BA, 54, MD, 57. *Prof Exp:* Intern, Los Angeles County Gen Hosp, 57-58; resident gynec & obstet, Johns Hopkins Hosp, Johns Hopkins Univ, 59, chief resident, 64-65, instr, Sch Med, 66-67; asst prof, Univ Calif, Sch Med, Los Angeles, 69-72; from assoc prof to prof, Dept Obstet, Gynec & Reproductive Biol, Mich State UNiv, Col Human Med, 72-83, prof, Off Med Educ Res & Develop, 77-83, assoc chmn, 78-83; prof & vchmn, Dept Obstet & Gynec, Med Col Ga, 83- *Concurrent Pos:* Fel, Am Cancer Soc, 61-64, Joshi Macy Found, 65-66, Johns Hopkins Hosp, 66-67 & Off Med Educ Res & Develop, Mich State Univ, 72-73; private prac obstet & gynec, Baltimore, 65-68, Shelton Clin, Los Angeles, Calif, 68-69; assoc prof, Off Med Educ Res & Develop, Col Human Med, Mich State Univ, 73-77, actg asst dean for Lansing, 78; examr, Am Bd Obstet Gynec. *Mem:* Nat Bd Med Examiners; Am Col Obstetricians & Gynecologists; Asn Professors Gynec & Obstet. *Res:* Modeling medical decision making. *Mailing Add:* Am Col Obstet & Gynec Box 96920 Washington DC 20090-6920. *Fax:* 202-863-4994

HOLZMAN, PHILIP S, PSYCHOLOGY. *Current Pos:* Esther & Sidney R Rabb Prof, 77-92, EMER PROF PSYCHOL, HARVARD UNIV, 92- *Personal Data:* b New York, NY, May 2, 22; m 46, Hannah; c Natalie Kay, Carl David & Paul Benjamin. *Educ:* City Col New York, BA, 43; Univ Kans, PhD, 52. *Hon Degrees:* AM, Harvard Univ, 77. *Honors & Awards:* Stanley Dean Award, Am Col Psychiatrists; Lieber Prize, Nat Alliance Res Schizophrenia & Depression; Salmon Lectr & Medal NY Acad Med; Joseph Zubin Award, Soc Res Psychopath. *Prof Exp:* Psychologist & dir, Res Training, Menninger Found, 50-68; prof psychiat & behav sci, Univ Chicago, 68-77. *Concurrent Pos:* Dir, Lab Psychol, McLean Hosp, Belmont, Mass. *Mem:* Inst Med-Nat Acad Sci; Am Acad Arts & Sci; fel Am Psychol Asn; fel Am Col Neuropsychopharmacol; fel Am Psychol Soc; fel AAAS. *Res:* Cognitive, psychophysiological and genetic aspects of mental disorders. *Mailing Add:* Harvard Univ 33 Kirkland St Cambridge MA 02138. *Fax:* 617-855-2778; *E-Mail:* psh@wjh.harvard.edu

HOLZMAN, ROBERT STEPHEN, IMMUNOLOGY, INFECTIOUS DISEASES. *Current Pos:* From intern to resident, Med Ctr, NY Univ, 65-70, fel immunol & infectious dis, 70-73, asst prof med & asst epidemiologist, Bellevue Hosp, 73-79, HOSP EPIDEMIOLOGIST, BELLEVUE HOSP, 79-; ASSOC PROF MED, NY UNIV. *Personal Data:* b New York, NY, Apr 13, 40; m 63; c 2. *Educ:* Rutgers Univ, BA, 61; Johns Hopkins Univ, MD, 65. *Mem:* Am Fedn Clin Res; fel Am Col Physicians; fel Infectious Dis Soc Am. *Res:* Hospital acquired infections; delayed-type hypersensitivity; transfer factor; acquired immune deficiency syndrome. *Mailing Add:* Dept Med NY Univ Med Ctr 550 First Ave New York NY 10016

HOLZMANN, ERNEST G(UNTHER), EXPERT SYSTEMS, OPERATIONS RESEARCH. *Current Pos:* SR ENG SPECIALIST, LORAL AEROSYS CORP, 88- *Personal Data:* b Ger, Nov 20, 21; US citizen; m 52; c 6. *Educ:* Univ London, BSc, 47; Mass Inst Technol, MSEE, 51; Stanford Univ, MS, 66, PhD(elec eng), 69. *Honors & Awards:* Region Award New Tech Concepts, Inst Elec & Electronics Engrs, 77 & 79. *Prof Exp:* Engr process control, Shell Develop Co, 51-56; reactor safeguards, Atomic Power Equip Dept, Gen Elec Co, San Jose, 56-60, sr systs engr, Electronics Lab, Syracuse, 60-64; res assoc mat sci, Stanford Univ, 67-69; systs anal engr, Corp Res & Develop, Gen Elec Co, Schenectady, 69-83; mem tech staff, Anal Sci Corp, 83-85; mem tech staff, Sci Int Applns Corp, 85-88. *Concurrent Pos:* Adj prof, Dept Elec Eng, Union Col, 69-74 & Rensselaer Polytech Inst, 72-74. *Mem:* Inst Elec & Electronics Engrs. *Res:* Systems and operations analysis; expert systems; computer simulation for planning and design. *Mailing Add:* 2333 Barbour Rd Falls Church VA 22043

HOLZMANN, GERARD J, VALIDATION OF COMPUTER PROTOCOLS, DIGITAL IMAGE MANIPULATION. *Current Pos:* DISTINGUISHED MEM TECH STAFF COMPUT SCI, BELL LABS, MURRAY HILL, 83- *Personal Data:* b Amsterdam, Neth, Nov 12, 51. *Educ:* Delft Univ, BSc, 73, MSc, 76, PhD(tech sci), 79. *Honors & Awards:* Bahler Award, Royal Dutch Inst Engrs, 81. *Prof Exp:* Fulbright fel oper systs, Univ Southern Calif, 78-80, AT&T Bell Labs, Murray Hill, 80-81; asst prof data commun, Delft Univ, 81-83. *Concurrent Pos:* Vis lectr, Comput Sci Dept, Princeton Univ, NJ, 90-91, Elec Eng Dept, Columbia Univ, NY, 91-92. *Res:* Validation methods for distributed systems; history of telecommunications; model checking techniques. *Mailing Add:* Bell Labs Rm 2C-521 600 Mountain Ave Murray Hill NJ 07974-2070. *E-Mail:* gerard@research.bell-labs.com

HOLZMANN, RICHARD THOMAS, INORGANIC CHEMISTRY, PHYSICAL CHEMISTRY. *Current Pos:* MGR & DIR, CHRISTOPHER GROUP, LAGUNA HILLS, CALIF, 79- *Personal Data:* b New York, NY, Mar 24, 27; m 47; c 5. *Educ:* St John's Univ, NY, BS, 51; Univ Del, MS, 55; Pa State Univ, PhD(inorg chem), 62; Georgetown Univ, LLB, 64. *Prof Exp:* Res chemist, Claymont Develop Lab, Gen Chem, 51-54 & Lawrence Radiation Lab, Univ Calif, 57-58; res supvr, Reaction Motors Div, Thiokol Chem Corp, 58-61; prog mgr, Advan Res Proj Agency, Washington, DC, 61-64, actg dir chem, 64; asst mgr chem & struct prod div, Von Karman Ctr, Aerojet-Gen Corp, 64-65, mgr chem prod div, 65-68; dir res, Quaker Chem Corp, 68-74; pres, Dynachem Corp, Santa Fe Springs, Calif, 74-79. *Concurrent Pos:* Mem, Interagency Chem Rocket Propulsion Group, 62-64; consult, Advan Res Proj Agency, 64- *Mem:* Am Chem Soc; assoc fel Am Inst Aeronaut & Astronaut; Am Ord Asn; fel Am Inst Chemists; Am Inst Chem Engrs. *Res:* Hydride, fluorine and interhalogen chemistry; uranium recovery; phosphoric acid; microanalytical chemical surveillance; propellants and explosives; glass technology; composite structure; chemical specialties; lubricants; hydraulics; cryogenics; textile and paper making auxiliaries; pollution chemistry and control. *Mailing Add:* Christopher Group Attn Matthew Holzmann 3617 W Macarthur Blvd Suite 507 Santa Ana CA 92704-6847

HOLZRICHTER, JOHN FREDERICK, LASERS, OPTICS. *Current Pos:* solid state laser design leader, Lawrence Livermore Nat Lab, 73-74, dep group leader laser & plasma group, 74-75, assoc prog leader solid state lasers, 75-80, assoc prog leader, Fusion Lasers Prog, 80-81, leader Inertial Confinement Fusion, 81-84, leader adv solid state lasers, 84-87, DIR INST RES DEVELOP, LAWRENCE LIVERMORE NAT LAB, 87- *Personal Data:* b Chicago, Ill, June 8, 41; c 2. *Educ:* Univ Wis, BS, 64; Stanford Univ, ME, 66, PhD(physics), 71. *Prof Exp:* Physicist, Res & Develop, Naval Res Lab, 71-73. *Concurrent Pos:* Consult, ILC Technol, 69-70; Fulbright fel, Sloan Found & Hertz Found. *Mem:* Am Phys Soc; Sigma Xi; Optical Soc Am; AAAS. *Res:* Design and construction of high power lasers for fusion research; scientific management for research, development and construction of large scientific projects. *Mailing Add:* Lawrence Livermore Nat Lab Llnl L003 PO Box 808 Livermore CA 94551-0808

HOLZWARTH, GEORGE MICHAEL, BIOPHYSICS, BIOPHYSICAL CHEMISTRY. *Current Pos:* lectr, physics, 84-87, assoc prof, 88-89, PROF, WAKE FOREST UNIV, WINSTON-SALEM, NC, 89- *Personal Data:* b Dusseldorf, Ger, May 7, 37; US citizen; m 70; c 2. *Educ:* Wesleyan Univ, BA, 59; Harvard Univ, PhD(biophys), 64. *Prof Exp:* Res assoc, Fla State Univ, 64-66; asst prof biophys & chem, Univ Chicago, 67-74; mem staff, Corp Res Lab, Exxon Res & Eng Co, 74-83. *Mem:* Biophys Soc; Am Chem Soc; Am Phys Soc; Electrophoresis Soc. *Res:* Physical chemistry of water-soluble polymers; biophysical chemistry, especially solution conformation of polysaccharides, nucleic acids, and proteins; molecular spectroscopy, especially optical activity; polymer physics. *Mailing Add:* Dept Physics Wake Forest Univ PO Box 7507 Winston Salem NC 27109

HOLZWARTH, JAMES C, METALLURGICAL ENGINEERING, CORROSION. *Current Pos:* RETIRED. *Personal Data:* b Ft Wayne, Ind, June 20, 24; m 45; c 3. *Educ:* Purdue Univ, BS, 46, MS, 48. *Prof Exp:* Instr metall eng, Purdue Univ, 47-48; res metallurgist, Gen Motors Res Labs, 48-55, supvr, Metall Eng Dept, 55-60, asst head dept, 60-69, head dept, 69-73, tech dir, 73-87. *Mem:* Am Soc Metals; Am Soc Testing & Mat; Am Foundrymen's Soc; Soc Automotive Engrs; Sigma Xi. *Res:* Environmental simulation in corrosion of automobile bodies and components; corrosion product characterization; development of alloys for wear, fatigue and corrosion resistance; new technology in scrap metal reclamation and recycling. *Mailing Add:* PO Box 1317 Breckenridge CO 80424-1317

HOLZWORTH, JEAN, VETERINARY MEDICINE, FELINE SPECIALTY. *Current Pos:* RETIRED. *Personal Data:* b Port Chester, NY, Mar 26, 15. *Educ:* Bryn Mawr Col, AB, 36, MA, 37, PhD(Latin), 40; State Univ NY Vet Col, Cornell Univ, DVM, 50. *Prof Exp:* Instr Latin, Mt Holyoke Col, 40-41, Bryn Mawr Col, 41-44 & Latin & Greek, Brearley Sch, NY, 45-46; intern, Angell Mem Animal Hosp, 50-51, resident, 51-52, clin staff vet med, 52-86. *Concurrent Pos:* Grants, USPHS, 56-57 & 64-66 & Am Philos Soc, 57. *Mem:* Am Vet Med Asn; Am Col Vet Int Med. *Res:* Diseases of cats. *Mailing Add:* PO Box 2305 New Preston CT 06777

HOLZWORTH, ROBERT H, II, SPACE SCIENCE, MAGNETOSPHERIC PHYSICS. *Current Pos:* asst prof, 82-88, ASSOC PROF GEOPHYS & PHYSICS, UNIV WASH, SEATTLE, 88- *Personal Data:* b Winston-Salem, NC, June 20, 50; m 70; Phyllis C Poch; c Eric C, Leah C & Ross H. *Educ:* Univ Colo, BA, 72; Univ Calif, Berkeley, MA, 74, PhD(physics), 77. *Prof Exp:* Res asst physics, Univ Calif, Berkeley, 74-77, asst res physicist space physics, Space Sci Lab, 78; mem tech staff space physics, Space Sci Lab, Aerospace Corp, 78-82. *Concurrent Pos:* Prin Investr, NASA & NSF, 79- *Mem:* Am Geophys Union. *Res:* Ionospheric physics and atmospheric physics; particles and fields above tropopause; experimental work in electric fields. *Mailing Add:* 713 16th Ave Seattle WA 98112. *Fax:* 206-685-3815; *E-Mail:* bobholz@geophys.washington.edu

HOM, BEN LIN, HEMATOLOGY, BLOOD TRANSFUSION. *Current Pos:* PATHOLOGIST, MERCY HOSP MED CTR, DES MOINES, IOWA, 88- *Personal Data:* b New York, NY, Feb 5, 36; m 83. *Educ:* Colby Col, BA, 57; NY Univ, MD, 61; Am Bd Path, cert anal & clin path, 69, cert hemat, 83 & cert blood banking, 84; Royal Col Pathologists, Australia, cert anat path-hemat, 85. *Prof Exp:* Intern med, Queen's Hosp, 61-62, resident path, 62-63; resident path, Univ Calif, Los Angeles, 63-64, New Eng Deaconess Hosp, Boston, 64-65 & Va Hosp, San Francisco, 68; res fel hemat, Bispeguerg Hosp, Copenhagen, 65-67; pathologist, Kaiser Hosp, Honolulu, 69-70; pathologist, Queen's Med Ctr, Honolulu, 70-84, fel hemat, 71-72; sr lectr, Chinese Univ, Hong Kong, 84-87; pathologist, Wagga Wagga Base Hosp, Australia, 87 & St John's Hosp, Springfield, Ill, 88. *Concurrent Pos:* Consult hematologist, Prince of Wales Hosp, 84- *Mem:* Col Am Pathologists; Am Soc Clin Pathologists; Am Soc Hematologists; Int Soc Blood Transfusion; Am Asn Blood Banks. *Res:* Biology of lung cancer; physiology of plasma cells; immune thrombocytopenia; biology of blood coagulation. *Mailing Add:* Dept Path Mercy Hosp Med Ctr Des Moines IA 50314

HOM, FOO SONG, PHYSICAL PHARMACY. *Current Pos:* SR RES SCIENTIST, R P SCHERER CORP, 68- *Personal Data:* b Kwangtung, China, Sept 17, 29; US citizen; m 63; c 2. *Educ:* Philadelphia Col Pharm, BS, 54; Temple Univ, MS, 56; Univ Wis, PhD(pharm), 62. *Prof Exp:* Res asst chem, C P Hall Chem Co, 58-59; res assoc pharm develop, Parke, Davis & Co, 61-66; res scientist, Warner-Lambert Res Inst, 66-68. *Mem:* Am Pharmaceut Asn; Am Chem Soc; Acad Pharmaceut Sci. *Res:* Product developments; analytical developments, including spectrophotometry, gas chromatography, thin layer chromatography, titrimetry, and electrochemistry; dosage form design effect on bioavailability; gelatin properties; behavior of gelatin to oxygen permeation and light transmission and other physical parameters. *Mailing Add:* 3102 Blue Heron St Safety Harbor FL 34695

HOMAIDAN, FADIA RAFIC, INFLAMMATION, CELL-CELL COMMUNICATION. *Current Pos:* ASSOC PROF, AM UNIV BEIRUT, 97- *Personal Data:* b Kfarnabragh, Lebanon, June 25, 56; m 85, Marwan El-Sabban; c Maya & Rami. *Educ:* Lebanese Univ, BSc, 78; Am Univ Beirut, MSc, 81; Univ Birmingham, UK, PhD(clin chem), 85. *Prof Exp:* Postdoctoral fel, Cornell Univ, 85-88, res assoc, 88-89, res assoc II, 89-92; dir, GI Labs, Winthrop Univ Hosp, 92-97. *Concurrent Pos:* Vis prof, Am Univ Beirut, 90-91; prin investr, Winthrop Univ Hosp, 92-97; asst prof, Stony Brook Col Med, 92-97. *Mem:* AAAS; Am Genetic Asn; Soc Gen Physiologists. *Res:* Cytokines such as IL-1, and cell-cell interaction in the regulation of inflammation. *Mailing Add:* Am Univ Beirut Physiol 850 Third Ave 18th Floor New York NY 10022. *E-Mail:* fh01@aub.edu.lb

HOMAN, CLARKE GILBERT, SOLID STATE PHYSICS, PHYSICAL METALLURGY. *Current Pos:* RETIRED. *Personal Data:* b Providence, RI, July 16, 31; m 54; c 4. *Educ:* Univ RI, BS, 58; Rensselaer Polytech Inst, MS, 65. *Honors & Awards:* Paul Siple Medal, USA, 79; Res & Develop Achievement Award, US Army, 81 & 85. *Prof Exp:* Teaching asst physics, Rensselaer Polytech Inst, 58-60; solid state physicist, US Army, 60-64, proj leader solid state physics, 64-70, sr proj leader, 70-73, group leader solid state physics, 73-85, chief mat eng, Benet Weapons Lab, Watervliet Arsenal, 85-87. *Concurrent Pos:* Adj prof, NY State Univ Albany, 76- *Mem:* Am Phys Soc; Asn Int Res Pressions & Temperature (corresp secy). *Res:* Solid state properties of materials at high pressure and cryogenic temperatures such as superconductivity, phase transitions, magnetic and electronic properties; diffusion and lattice defects; ion beam modification of materials. *Mailing Add:* 2084 Maple Ave Ballston Lake NY 12019

HOMAN, ELTON RICHARD, TOXICOLOGY. *Current Pos:* SR TOXICOLOGIST & MGR TOXICOL, HERCULES, INC, 87- *Personal Data:* b Glen Ridge, NJ, Oct 19, 32; m 54, Esther Boettler; c Janice, Benjamin & Connie. *Educ:* Rutgers Univ, BSc, 54; Cornell Univ, PhD(econ entom), 62. *Prof Exp:* Fel, Kettering Lab, Med Ctr, Univ Cincinnati, 62-63, sr res assoc toxicol, 63-64; pharmacologist, Div Air Pollution, Taft Sanit Eng Ctr, USPHS, 64-65; pharmacologist, Lab Toxicol, Nat Cancer Inst, 65-74; pharmacologist, Off Toxic Substances, Environ Protection Agency, 74-75; fel chem hyg, Carnegie-Mellon Inst Res, 75-77; mgr, Union Carbide Corp, 77-79, assoc dir, Bushy Run Res Ctr, 80-85, assoc corp dir, Appl Toxicol, 85-87. *Mem:* AAAS; Soc Toxicol; NY Acad Sci; Sigma Xi; Am Chem Soc. *Res:* Toxicology of antineoplastic chemotherapeutic agents; regulatory toxicology; toxicology of household and industrial chemicals; risk assessment; mathematical modelling. *Mailing Add:* 107 Pennbrook Dr Lincoln University PA 19352. *Fax:* 302-594-7255

HOMAN, RUTH ELIZABETH, ANALYTICAL CHEMISTRY, BIOCHEMISTRY. *Current Pos:* res chemist analytical chem, 69-79, SECT HEAD ANALYTICAL CHEM, MERRELL NAT LABS, MERRELL DOW PHARMACEUT, INC, 79- *Personal Data:* b Cincinnati, Ohio, Sept 24, 44. *Educ:* Edgecliff Col, BA, 66; Xavier Univ, MEd, 72, MS, 75; St Thomas Inst, PhD(chem, biochem), 78. *Prof Exp:* Res chemist analytical, Lab Serv Sect, Air Qual & Emissions Data Proj, Nat Ctr Air Pollution Control, USPHS, 66-68; teacher sec physics, Williamsburg Sch Dist, 68-69. *Mem:* Am Chem Soc; NAm Thermal Analysis Soc; Soc Appl Spectros. *Res:* Characterization of organic compounds using differential scanning calorimetry, optical microscopy, infrared spectroscopy; organic elemental analysis. *Mailing Add:* 2110 E Galbraith Rd Cincinnati OH 45237-1625

HOMANN, FREDERICK ANTHONY, MATHEMATICS. *Current Pos:* RETIRED. *Personal Data:* b Philadelphia, Pa, July 3, 29. *Educ:* St Louis Univ, AB, 53, PhL, 54, MS, 56; Univ Pa, PhD(math), 59; Woodstock Col, Md, STL, 63. *Prof Exp:* Instr math, Loyola Col, Md, 58-59 & 64-65; from asst prof to assoc prof, 65-70; assoc prof, St Joseph's Univ, Pa, 70- *Concurrent Pos:* Chmn, Dept Math, Loyola Col, Md, 66-70, trustee, 70-77; rector, Jesuit Fac, St Joseph's Col, 71-74, actg chmn, Dept Philos, 72-74. *Mem:* Soc Archit Historians. *Res:* Study of improper integrals arising in H Rademacher's analytic additive number theory; generalizations of algebraic and differential inequalities; history of Renaissance mathematics; history of calculus. *Mailing Add:* Dept Math St Joseph's Univ Philadelphia PA 19131

HOMANN, H ROBERT, BIOCHEMISTRY. *Current Pos:* from asst prof to assoc prof chem, 64-78, assoc acad dean, 69-73, NERE SUNDET PROF CHEM, CONCORDIA COL, MOORHEAD, MINN, 78-, ASSOC DEAN COL, 73- *Personal Data:* b Hinsdale, Ill, Dec 11, 37; m 62. *Educ:* Beloit Col, BS, 59; Wash State Univ, PhD(biochem), 64. *Prof Exp:* Res fel, Wash State Univ, 64. *Mem:* Am Chem Soc; Am Soc Microbiol. *Res:* Metabolism of facultative autotrophic bacteria. *Mailing Add:* VP Academic Affairs Concordia Col Moorhead MN 56560

HOMANN, PETER H, PLANT PHYSIOLOGY, BIOCHEMISTRY. *Current Pos:* Res assoc, 62-66, from asst prof to assoc prof biol sci, 66-78, PROF PLANT PHYSIOL, INST MOLECULAR BIOPHYS, FLA STATE UNIV, 78- *Personal Data:* b Wittenberge, Ger, Apr 3, 33; m 64; c 2. *Educ:* Karlsruhe Tech Univ, Dipl chem, 59, Dr rer nat(chem, biochem), 62. *Mem:* AAAS; Am Soc Plant Physiol; Am Soc Photobiol. *Res:* Photosynthesis; photobiology; plant biochemistry; organization of the protein complex of photosynthetic water oxidation, and its interaction with inorganic cofactors. *Mailing Add:* Biol Sci Fla State Univ 600 W College Ave Tallahassee FL 32306-1096

HOMBERG, OTTO ALBERT, ORGANIC CHEMISTRY. *Current Pos:* CONSULT, 83- *Personal Data:* b New York, NY, Jan 10, 31; m 55, Jane Grissinger; c Carol A & Martha S. *Educ:* Polytech Inst Brooklyn, BS, 52; Univ Md, MS, 60; Univ Cincinnati, PhD(chem), 65. *Prof Exp:* Res chemist, Gen Chem Div, Allied Chem Corp, 52-53; res chemist, US Indust Chem Div, Nat Distillers & Chem Corp, 57-59; sr chemist, Carlisle Chem Works, Inc, 59-64; res chemist, Cent Res Labs, GAF Corp, 65-67; res engr, Homer Res Labs, Bethlehem Steel Corp, 67-74, supvr chem, 74-77, res engr cokemaking, 77-83. *Res:* Synthetic organic chemistry; organosulfur compounds; coal tar aromatics; heterocyclics; organometallics; process development; organophosphorus compounds; vapor phase oxidation; bio-oxidation; plastic additives; gas processing; environmental control. *Mailing Add:* Indian Purchase 5954 Green Point Rd East New Market MD 21631-9767

HOMBERGER, DOMINIQUE GABRIELLE, FUNCTIONAL ANATOMY. *Current Pos:* from asst prof to assoc prof, 79-91, PROF COMP ANAT, LA STATE UNIV, 91- *Personal Data:* b Zurich, Switz, Apr 10, 48; m 85. *Educ:* Univ Zurich, Switz, MS, 72, PhD(zool), 76. *Honors & Awards:* Erwin-Strasemann Prize, German Ornithologists' Soc, 88. *Prof Exp:* Asst, Zool Mus, Univ Zurich, Switz, 72-76; res assoc, Dept Biol Sci, Columbia Univ, 77-79. *Concurrent Pos:* Teacher, Sch Blind Adults, Zurich, 72-75; fel, NSF, Switz, 77-78; vis scientist, Am Mus Natural Hist, 77-79; res assoc, Mus Natural Sci, La State Univ, Baton Rouge, 79-; prin invest, sect syst biol, NSF, 84-87; hon mem, CSIRO-Wildlife & Ecol, Canberra, Australia, 87-88. *Mem:* Am Soc Zoologists; Am Asn Anatomists; Am Ornithologists Union; Brit Ornithologists Union; Ger Ornithologists Union. *Res:* Comparative, functional and ecological morphology of the avian feeding apparatus; feeding and drinking behavior of birds; biomechanical analysis of complex anatomical systems; systematics, phylogeny and biogeography of birds; theoretical foundations and methods of phylogenetic reconstruction and functional morphology. *Mailing Add:* Dept Zool & Physiol La State Univ Baton Rouge LA 70803-1725. *Fax:* 504-388-1763; *E-Mail:* zodhomb@lsuvm.sncc.lsu.edu

HOMBURGER, FREDDY, MEDICINE, PATHOLOGY. *Current Pos:* RES PROF PATH, SCH MED, BOSTON UNIV, 74- *Personal Data:* b St Gall, Switz, Feb 8, 16; nat US; m 39, Regina T. *Educ:* Univ Geneva, MD, 41; Am Bd Toxicol, dipl, 82. *Honors & Awards:* Julius A Stratton Prize, Friends of Switz, 91. *Prof Exp:* Res fel path, Sch Med, Yale Univ, 41-42; intern, New Haven Hosp, Conn, 42-43; intern med, Boston City Hosp, 43-44; res fel, Thorndike Mem Lab, Harvard Med Sch, 44-45; Teagle res fel, Sloan-Kettering Inst Cancer Res, New York, 45-46, chief dept clin invest, 46-48; res prof med, Med Sch, Tufts Univ, 48-57; pres & dir, Bio-Res Inst, Inc & Bio-Res Consults, Inc, 57-84. *Concurrent Pos:* Instr, Med Col, Cornell Univ, 46-48; dir cancer res & control unit, New Eng Med Ctr, 48-57; sci assoc, Jackson Lab, Maine, 52-59; visitor dept Ger lang & cultures, Harvard Univ, 65-71, 74-80 & Consul of Switz, Boston, 64-86; spec consult cancer control br, Nat Cancer Inst; consult adv comn serum albumins, Comn Plasma Fractionation & Related Processes; mem, Nat Adv Coun, Nat Hypertension Asn, Inc. *Mem:* Endocrine Soc; Soc Exp Biol & Med; Am Asn Pathologists; Am Soc Pharmacol & Exp Therapeut; Toxicol Soc; Sci Acad Toxicol. *Res:* Protein metabolism; clinical investigation; experimental pathology of tumors; environmental carcinogenesis; toxicology; experimental pathology of Syrian hamster; cardiomyopathy. *Mailing Add:* 675 Massachusetts Ave Cambridge MA 02139-3309. *Fax:* 617-441-5591

HOMBURGER, HENRY A, PATHOLOGY, CLINICAL IMMUNOLOGY. *Current Pos:* intern path, Mayo Grad Sch Med, 72-73, resident, 74-76, from asst prof to assoc prof, 77-87, PROF LAB MED, MAYO MED SCH & GRAD SCH MED, 87-, HEAD, SECT IMMUNOPATH, DIV PATH, DEPT LAB MED & PATH, 90-; DIR, SPECIFIC ANTIBODY LAB & CELLULAR CYTOTOXICITY LAB, SECT IMMUNOPATH, MAYO CLIN, 81- *Personal Data:* b Detroit, Mich, July 20, 40. *Educ:* Univ Mich, BS, 68, MD, 72; Am Bd Path, cert anat & clin path, 76. *Prof Exp:* Resident path, Univ Calif, San Francisco, 73-74. *Concurrent Pos:* Consult lab med, Sect Clin Chem & Regional Lab Serv, Mayo Clin, 76-81 & Sect Immunopath, 81-; resource consult, Dept Health & Human Serv, Food & Drug Admin, 91-; mem, var adv comts, Col Am Pathologists, Am Soc Clin Pathologists & Nat Comt Clin Lab Standards. *Mem:* Am Asn Immunologists; Sigma Xi; Col Am Pathologists; Am Soc Clin Pathologists; AAAS; Acad Clin Lab Physicians & Scientists; Am Fedn Clin Res; Am Acad Allergy & Immunol; AMA; Soc Anal Cytol. *Res:* Immunopathology. *Mailing Add:* Mayo Med Sch Dept Lab Med & Pathol Mayo Clin 920 Hilton Bldg Rochester MN 55905-0001

HOMEIER, EDWIN H, JR, PHYSICAL INORGANIC CHEMISTRY. *Current Pos:* res chemist, UOP Inc, 67-80, res specialist, 80-83, assoc res scientist, 83-85, assoc anal scientist, 85-89, sr anal specialist, 89-92, SR RES SPECIALIST, UOP INC, 92- *Personal Data:* b Louisville, Ky, Dec 6, 37; m 59, Arlene M Leege; c Michael D, Steven P & Daniel S. *Educ:* Concordia Teachers Col, Ill, BS, 59; Univ Wis, Madison, PhD(inorg chem), 68. *Prof Exp:* Instr, High Sch, Chicago, 59-62; teaching asst chem, Univ Wis, 62-64. *Concurrent Pos:* From asst prof to assoc prof chem, Concordia Teachers Col, Ill, 67-74; consult, Phys Sci for Nonsci Students Testing Prog, Rensselaer Polytech Inst, 69-70. *Mem:* Catalyst Soc NAm; Am Chem Soc; AAAS; Int Precious Metal Inst. *Res:* Characterization of catalysts, feed and products for petroleum refinery and petrochemical applications; characterization of catalysts for pollution abatement processes; characterization of engineered materials; reduced states of the early transition metals. *Mailing Add:* 2 Atrium Way Elmhurst IL 60126. *Fax:* 847-391-3337

HOMER, GEORGE MOHN, MEDICAL SCIENCE, TOXICOLOGY. *Current Pos:* DIR CHEM, DR R G THOMAS & ASSOC, ELYRIA MEM HOSP, OHIO, 80- *Personal Data:* b Cleveland, Ohio, Mar 28, 24; m 51; c 2. *Educ:* Ohio State Univ, BA, 48, PhD(physiol chem), 58; Univ Colo, MS, 51; Nat Registry Clin Chem, cert, 69; Am Bd Clin Chem, dipl, 71. *Prof Exp:* Asst pharmacol, Wyeth Inst Med Res, 51-52; asst biochem & biophys, Dept Med, Ohio State Univ, 52-58; res chemist, Miami Valley Hosp, Akron, 58-63, asst dir res, Dept Res, 63-65; biochemist, Dept Path, Akron City Hosp, 65-80; instr chem & mem grad fac, Youngstown State Univ, 73-80; asst prof path, Northeastern Ohio Univs Col Med, 70-80. *Concurrent Pos:* Mem adj sci staff, med & dent Staff, Akron City Hosp, 74-80; health prof affil staff, Elyria Mem Hosp, 81-; inspector, forensic urine drug testing, Am Asn Clin Chem/CAP, 87- *Mem:* Nat Acad Clin Biochemists; Am Asn Clin Chemists; Sigma Xi. *Res:* Clinical chemistry techniques; TDM and toxicology pharmacokinetics. *Mailing Add:* 32111 Lake Rd Avon Lake OH 44012-1807

HOMER, LOUIS DAVID, BIOMETRICS, PHYSIOLOGY. *Current Pos:* MED OFFICER, NAVAL MED RES INST, NAT NAVAL MED CTR, 71- *Personal Data:* b Washington, DC, Mar 21, 35; m 61; c 3. *Educ:* Columbia Univ, BA, 55; Med Col Va, PhD(physiol), 62, MD, 63. *Prof Exp:* Assoc biomet, Emory Univ, 63-64, asst prof, 63-69; assoc prof, Brown Univ, 69-71. *Mem:* Am Physiol Soc; Biometrics Soc; Math Asn Am; Soc Math Biol. *Res:* Mathematical models of capillary solute exchange. *Mailing Add:* Dept Res Legacy Emanuel Hosp 2801 N Gatenbein Ave Portland OR 97227. *Fax:* 503-413-4942

HOMER, PAUL BRUCE, PHYSICS, ENGINEERING. *Current Pos:* Physicist weapons res & develop, Naval Ord Test Sta, Naval Weapons Ctr, 62-68, br head, 68-74, dir head weapons res & develop, 74-82, dept head electronic warfare, 82-87, dept head aircraft weapons integration, 87-88, DEPT HEAD ATTACK WEAPONS, NAVAL WEAPONS CTR, 88- *Personal Data:* b Hempstead County, Ark, Feb 28, 39. *Educ:* NMex Inst Mining & Technol, BS, 62; Univ Calif, Los Angeles, MS, 68; Mass Inst Technol, SM, 88. *Concurrent Pos:* Task leader, TTCP Panel W-6, Generic Weapons Systs Effectiveness, 75-78; chmn, Joint Munitions Effectiveness manuals, Air-to-Surface Steering Comt, 75-79; Sloan fel, Mass Inst Technol, 87-88; panel mem, Adv Group Aerospace Res & Develop, NATO, 88- *Mem:*

Res Soc Am; Sigma Xi. *Res:* Weapons systems research and development; warhead optimization; target vulnerability; fire control design analysis; combat assessment; military operations analysis; electronic warfare. *Mailing Add:* 248 N Jacks Ranch Rd Ridgecrest CA 93555

HOMER, ROGER HARRY, MATHEMATICS. *Current Pos:* From asst prof to prof, 59-88, EMER PROF MATH, IOWA STATE UNIV, 88- *Personal Data:* b Long Beach, Calif, Dec 3, 24; m 52, Annette Dingmau; c Margaret, Mark, Melinda, Mary & Molly. *Educ:* Univ Southern Calif, AB, 51; Univ Calif, Berkeley, PhD(math), 59. *Mem:* Am Math Soc. *Res:* Mathematical analysis; applied functional analysis. *Mailing Add:* 2212 Knapp St Ames IA 50014-7312

HOMER, STEVEN ELLIOTT, COMPLEXITY THEORY. *Current Pos:* from asst prof to assoc prof, 81-93, PROF COMPUT SCI, BOSTON UNIV, 93- *Personal Data:* b Chicago, Ill, Mar 27, 52; m 78, Michelle Buron; c 3. *Educ:* Univ Calif Berkeley, BA, 73; Mass Inst Technol, PhD(math), 78. *Prof Exp:* Asst prof math, DePaul Univ, 78-81. *Concurrent Pos:* Vis scholar, Mass Inst Technol, 79-80 & 84-88; Fulbright prof comput sci, Heidelburg Univ, 88-89. *Mem:* Sigmi Xi; Asn Symbolic Logic; Asn Comput Math. *Res:* Theory of computation; study combinatorial problems, trying to determine whether they are computable and if so, how difficult they are to solve. *Mailing Add:* Comput Sci Dept Boston Univ Boston MA 02215. *Fax:* 617-353-6457; *E-Mail:* homer@cs.bu.edu

HOMEYER, AUGUST HENRY, CHEMISTRY. *Current Pos:* RETIRED. *Personal Data:* b Chicago, Ill, Apr 21, 08; m 34; c 2. *Educ:* Wash Univ, BS, ChE, 30; Pa State Col, MS, 31, PhD(org chem), 33. *Prof Exp:* Chemist, Mallinckrodt Chem Works, 33-49, assoc dir res, 49-56, dir mkt res med chem, 52-60, dir foreign develop, 60-62, gen mgr, Int Div, 62-69, vpres, 69-73, consult, Mallinckrodt Inc, 73-83. *Concurrent Pos:* Mem, Comt Opium Scientists, UN, Geneva, 58. *Mem:* AAAS; Am Chem Soc; Am Inst Chemists. *Res:* Organic synthesis; alkaloids of opium; medicinal chemicals; compounds containing a neopentyl system; syntheses employing dialkyl carbonates. *Mailing Add:* 9033 Green Ridge Dr St Louis MO 63117

HOMMERSAND, MAX HOYT, BOTANY. *Current Pos:* from instr to assoc prof, 59-71, PROF BOT, UNIV NC, CHAPEL HILL, 71- *Personal Data:* b San Diego, Calif, July 10, 30. *Educ:* Univ Calif, BA, 54, PhD(bot), 58. *Prof Exp:* NSF res fel plant physiol, Harvard Univ, 57-59. *Mem:* AAAS; Int Phycol Soc; Bot Soc Am; Phycol Soc Am. *Res:* Algal morphology, physiology and systematics. *Mailing Add:* Dept Biol Univ NC Chapel Hill NC 27599-3280

HOMMES, FRITS A, BIOCHEMISTRY, DEVELOPMENTAL BIOCHEMISTRY. *Current Pos:* PROF, DEPT PATH, NY MED COL, VAHALLA, 96- *Personal Data:* b Bellingwolde, Neth, May 28, 34; m 58, Greet Renes; c Peter & Anne. *Educ:* Univ Groningen, MSc, 58; Univ Nymegen, PhD(biochem), 60; Am Bd Med Genetics, dipl, 87. *Prof Exp:* Res assoc chem, Univ Groningen, Neth, 56-58, res assoc biochem, Univ Nymegen, 60-61 & Univ Pa, 61-63; instr, Dept Biochem, Univ Nymegen, 65-66, head lab, Dept Pediat, Univ Groningen, 66-72, assoc prof, 72-79; prof, Dept Cell & Molecular Biol, Med Col Ga, Augusta, 79-93; prof, Dept Pediats, NY Univ Med Ctr, New York, 93-96. *Concurrent Pos:* Fulbright fel, 61-63; lectr, Am Soc Biol Chemists, 65; consult, Dutch Health Coun, 74-79; chmn, Bioenergetics Study Sect, Neth, 74-76; lectr, Third Genetics Sem, Tokyo, 81. *Mem:* Europ Soc Pediat Res; Am Soc Human Genetics; Soc Study Inherited Metab Dis; AAAS; Am Soc Biol Chemists; Soc Inherited Metab Dis; Soc Pediat Res; Am Col Med Genetics. *Res:* Molecular defects of in-born errors of metabolism; mechanism of brain dysfunction in amino acidemias; cerebral sulfate metabolism. *Mailing Add:* Dept Path NY Med Col Nalhalla NY 10595. *Fax:* 914-285-4500

HOMSHER, EARL EDWIN, II, PHYSIOLOGY. *Current Pos:* USPHS fel physiol, 69-70, asst prof to assoc prof 70-81, PROF PHYSIOL, UNIV CALIF, LOS ANGELES, 81-, ASSOC MEM, BRAIN RES INST, 70- *Personal Data:* b Painesville, Ohio, Feb 19, 42; m 65; c 1. *Educ:* Marietta Col, BS, 64; Univ Pittsburgh, PhD(physiol), 69. *Concurrent Pos:* Assoc mem USPHS proj, Univ Calif, Los Angeles, 72-82. *Mem:* Am Physiol Soc; Biophys Soc. *Res:* Chemical and thermal energetics of excitation-contraction coupling and chemomechanical transduction in skeletal and cardiac muscle. *Mailing Add:* Dept Physiol Univ Calif Los Angeles Med Sch, Ctr Health Scis Los Angeles CA 90024. *Fax:* 310-206-5661

HOMSHER, PAUL JOHN, REPRODUCTIVE BIOLOGY, ACAROLOGY. *Current Pos:* from asst prof to assoc prof biol, Old Dominion Univ, 62-77, dir, Biomed Sci Prog, 79-82, assoc dean, Col Sci, 85-91, interim dean, 91-93, PROF BIOL, OLD DOMINION UNIV, 77-, ASSOC DEAN, 93- *Personal Data:* b Philadelphia, Pa, May 17, 31; m 59, Judith Wharton; c Michael P, Christine E & Mary J. *Educ:* Pa State Univ, BS, 53, MS, 59, PhD(genetics), 67. *Prof Exp:* Instr bot, Forestry Sch, Pa State Univ, 59. *Concurrent Pos:* Asst prof dept biol & Old Dominion Univ Educ Found study grant, Ga Southern Col, 69-70; assoc prof & geneticist, Am Soc Eng Educ/NASA summer fel, 68, US Food & Drug Admin proj on miniature swine breeding, 79-86; sr res assoc & ext consult, US Naval Med Res, Cairo, Egypt, 79-82. *Mem:* Entom Soc Am; Am Genetic Asn; Acarology Soc Am; Sigma Xi. *Res:* Systematics and reproductive biology of ticks; ultrastructure of pheromone glands; analysis of pheromone biosynthesis; nucleic acid biochemistry of tick cells; viral host cell interactions in tick borne viruses. *Mailing Add:* Biol Col Sci Old Dominion Univ Hampton Blvd Norfolk VA 23529-0163. *Fax:* 757-683-3034; *E-Mail:* homsher@cs.du.edu

HOMSY, CHARLES ALBERT, BIOMEDICAL ENGINEERING. *Current Pos:* coordr prosthetic mat & develop, 66-67, DIR PROSTHESIS RES LAB, METHODIST HOSP, HOUSTON, TEX, 66- *Personal Data:* b Boston, Mass, June 21, 32; m 56; c 3. *Educ:* Mass Inst Technol, SB, 53, ScD(chem eng), 59. *Prof Exp:* Asst chem eng, Mass Inst Technol, 53-54, asst dir sch chem eng pract, 54-55, asst chem eng, 55-59; res engr, E I du Pont de Nemours & Co, 59-61, tech rep, 61-64, mkt rep, 64-66. *Concurrent Pos:* Fulbright scholar eng, Univ Sheffield, 57-58; res asst prof, Baylor Col Med, 69-77 & res assoc prof, 77-; pres, Vitek Inc. *Mem:* Orthop Res Soc; Soc Biomat; Am Inst Chem Eng; Am Chem Soc; Nat Asn Corrosion Eng; Am Soc Testing & Biomat; assoc & fel Am Acad Orthop Surgeons. *Res:* Industrial management; combustion similitude; process design for high polymer synthesis; prosthetic implant materials. *Mailing Add:* 11526 Raintree Circle Houston TX 77024-7304

HON, DAVID NYOK-SAI, WOOD CHEMISTRY & PULP & PAPER CHEMISTRY, ADHESIVES & COATINGS. *Current Pos:* assoc prof, 84-85, DIR RES, CLEMSON UNIV 84-, PROF RES & TEACHING, 85- *Personal Data:* b Kluang Johor, Malaysia, June 19, 47; US citizen; m 72, Michelle Sudo; c Gordon & Hong-Yi. *Educ:* Tokyo Univ Agr & Technol, BS, 72; Gunma Univ, MS, 74; Va Polytech Inst, PhD(wood chem) 77. *Honors & Awards:* Japanese Govt Res Award Foreign Specialists, 82; Nat Coun Res Award, Repub China, 96. *Prof Exp:* From asst prof to assoc prof res & teaching, Va Polytech Inst & State Univ, 77-84. *Concurrent Pos:* Consult, Buckyle Cellulose, 77-78, Squibb, 83-84, Johnson Wax, 85-87, Carib-Med, 86-, Resource Chem & Off Technol Assessment (Congress), 88-89; ed, Am Chem Soc, 82 & Mercer Dekker, 90, 94 & 97. *Mem:* Am Chem Soc; Tech Asn Pulp & Paper Indust; Forest Prods Res Soc; Soc Plastics Engrs. *Res:* Wood chemical modification and utilization; chemical modification of wood and polymer; weathering of wood; photochemistry of polymers; preservation of papers and woods with historic values. *Mailing Add:* Clemson Univ 127 Lehotsky Hall Clemson SC 29634-1003. *E-Mail:* dhon@clemson.edu

HON, EDWARD HARRY GEE, OBSTETRICS & GYNECOLOGY. *Current Pos:* RETIRED. *Personal Data:* b Canton, China, Jan 12, 17; m 48; c 3. *Educ:* Union Col, Nebr, BS, 50; Col Med Evangelists, MD, 50. *Prof Exp:* From instr to asst prof obstet & gynec, Sch Med, Yale Univ, 55-60; prof, Col Med Evangelists, 60-64; from assoc prof to prof, Sch Med, Yale Univ, 64-69; prof obstet & gynec, Sch Med, Univ Southern Calif, 69-83. *Concurrent Pos:* Markle scholar, 55-60. *Mem:* Sigma Xi. *Res:* Evaluation of fetal responses to the stresses of labor and delivery; use of biophysical techniques for the study of uterine contractility. *Mailing Add:* 11 Bradbury Hills Rd Duarte CA 91010-1106

HONAKER, CARL BOGGESS, INORGANIC CHEMISTRY. *Current Pos:* RETIRED. *Personal Data:* b Oakvale, WVa, Sept 10, 26; m 90, Bonnie Waechter; c Susan M. *Educ:* Concord Col, BS, 48; Univ Tenn, MS, 50, PhD(inorg chem), 57. *Hon Degrees:* DSc, Tenn Wesleyan Col, 78. *Prof Exp:* Asst chem, Univ Tenn, 48-50; pub sch teacher, SC, 50-51; prof chem & physics & chmn, Dept Phys Sci, Tenn Wesleyan Col, 51-77; staff chemist, Res Dept, Rockwell Hanford Opers, Richland, 77-83; prin chemist, Bioorg Chem Dept, Midwest Res Inst, Kansas City, Mo, 83-85; res analyst, Boeing Tenn, Inc, Oak Ridge, Tenn, 85-91. *Concurrent Pos:* Univ fel anal chem, Univ Ariz, 60-61. *Mem:* Am Chem Soc; Sigma Xi; Royal Soc Chem. *Res:* Complex compounds; solvent extraction; emission spectroscopy; chromatography; low energy beta emitters. *Mailing Add:* 5940 Tennyson Dr Knoxville TN 37909-1071

HONDA, BARRY MARVIN, MOLECULAR BIOLOGY. *Current Pos:* asst prof, 81-87, ASSOC PROF BIOL, SIMON FRASER UNIV, VANCOUVER, BC, 87- *Personal Data:* b Hamilton, Ont, July 5, 50. *Educ:* McMaster Univ, BSc, 71; Univ BC, PhD(biochem), 75. *Prof Exp:* Fel molecular biol, MRC Lab, Cambridge, UK, 75-79; res assoc, Med Sch, Wash Univ, St Louis, 79-81. *Mem:* Can Biochem Soc. *Res:* Molecular studies of the structure, organization, packaging and expression of genes in higher organisms, aimed at understanding gene regulation during differentiation and development. *Mailing Add:* IMB & B Simon Fraser Univ Burnaby BC V5A 1S6 Can

HONDA, KAZUO, GASTROENTEROLOGY, CARDIOVASCULAR PHARMACOLOGY. *Current Pos:* SR PHARMACOLOGIST, YAMANOUCHI PHARMACEUT CO LTD, 79- *Educ:* Univ Tokyo, PhD(pharmacol), 85. *Prof Exp:* Pharmacologist, Mitsubishi Chem Indust, 74-79. *Concurrent Pos:* Postdoctoral, Stanford Univ, 88-89. *Res:* Cardiovascular, renal, gastrointestinal and receptor pharmacology. *Mailing Add:* Dept Pharmacol Cent Res Labs Yamanouchi Pharmaceut 1-8 Azusawa Itabashi-Ku 21 Miyukigaoka Tsukuba-shi Ibaraki 305 Japan. *Fax:* 81-298-52-5391

HONDA, SHIGERU IRWIN, CELL PHYSIOLOGY. *Current Pos:* assoc prof, 67-71, PROF BIOL, WRIGHT STATE UNIV, 71- *Personal Data:* b Seattle, Wash, Nov 16, 27. *Educ:* Calif Inst Technol, BS, 50; Univ Wis, MS, 52, PhD(bot), 54. *Honors & Awards:* Dipl Merit, NZ Sci Cong, 66. *Prof Exp:* Asst bot, Univ Wis, 50-53; res off, Commonwealth Sci & Indust Res Orgn, Div Food Preserv & Transport, Sydney, 54-56; chemist, US Plant, Soil & Nutrit Lab, USDA, 56-61; asst prof bot, Cornell Univ, 60-61; assoc res plant biochemist, Dept Bot & Plant Biochem, Univ Calif, Los Angeles, 62-67. *Concurrent Pos:* Fulbright grantee, Australia, 53-54; spec res fel, Div Gen Med Sci, USPHS, 61-62, res career develop award, 62-66; vis prof, Kasetsart Univ, Bangkok, 68 & Univ Chiengmai, 70; vis res plant physiologist, Univ Calif, Los Angeles, 71; NASA-Am Soc Eng Educ fel, Johnson Space Ctr, Houston, 73 & 74; vis plant physiologist, Commonwealth Sci & Indust Res Orgn, Div Hort Res, Adelaite, 85-86 & 88. *Res:* Chloroplast replication and senescence. *Mailing Add:* Dept Biol Sci Wright State Univ 3640 Colonel Glenn Hwy Dayton OH 45435-0001

HONDEGHEM, LUC M, PHARMACOLOGY. *Current Pos:* PROF MED & PHARMACOL & STAHLMAN CHMN, CARDIOVASC RES PROG, VANDERBILT UNIV, 85- *Personal Data:* b Jabbeke, Belg, Sept 22, 44; c 3. *Educ:* Univ Louvain, Belg, MD, 70, MS, 71; Univ Calif, San Francisco, PhD(pharmacol), 73. *Prof Exp:* From asst prof to assoc prof pharmacol, Univ Calif, San Francisco, 73-85. *Concurrent Pos:* Ed, Biophys J, 78. *Mem:* Am Heart Asn; Sigma Xi; Med Electronics & Data Soc; Am Soc Pharmacol & Exp Therapeut. *Res:* Ultrastructural and electrophysiological aspects of impulse transmission in cardiac tissue; mechanisms of cardiac arrhythmias; effects of antiarrhythmic drugs on normal and abnormal impulse transmission in the heart. *Mailing Add:* Sch Med Vanderbilt Univ Nashville TN 37203

HONE, DANIEL W, THEORETICAL CONDENSED MATTER PHYSICS. *Current Pos:* vis lectr, Univ Calif, Santa Barbara, 67-68, assoc prof 68-74, assoc dean, 91-92, actg dean , 92-94, PROF PHYSICS, UNIV CALIF, SANTA BARBARA, 74-, DEP DIR, INST THEORET PHYSICS, 87-88 & 94- *Personal Data:* b San Francisco, Calif, Jan 7, 37; m 58, Donna Orbach; c Jennifer, Laurie & Cheryl. *Educ:* Univ Calif, Berkeley, AB, 58; Univ Ill, MS, 60, PhD(physics), 62. *Prof Exp:* Nat Acad Sci-Nat Res Coun fel, 62-63; asst prof physics, Univ Pa, 63-67. *Concurrent Pos:* Exchange prof, Univ Paris, Orsay, 73; sr vis lectr, Nat Res Coun, Oxford Univ, 74; res fel, Japan Soc Prom Sci, Inst Solid State Physics, Tokyo Univ, 82; chmn, Physics Dept, Inst Theoret Physics, Univ Calif, 82-86, vchmn, 86-87, assoc dean, Col Lett & Sci, 91-92, actg dean, Div Math Life & Phys Sci, 92-94. *Mem:* Fel Am Phys Soc. *Res:* Theory of many body problems; magnetism; magnetic resonance theory; polymers; nonlinear behavior of mesoscopic quantum systems. *Mailing Add:* Inst Theoret Physics Univ Calif Santa Barbara CA 93106. *Fax:* 805-893-2431; *E-Mail:* hone@itp.ucsb.edu

HONE, JENNIFER, insulin receptor mutations causing clinical syndromes of insulin resistance, for more information see previous edition

HONEA, FRANKLIN IVAN, CHEMICAL & MECHANICAL ENGINEERING. *Current Pos:* PROJ MGR COMBUSTION & GAS CLEANUP, ILL CLEAN COAL INST, 90- *Personal Data:* b Hope, Ark, Aug 9, 31; m 59, Marvine Lakedon; c Mary, Rose, John, Paul, Jane, Luci, Joan, Luke, Rita & Love. *Educ:* Univ Calif, Berkeley, BS, 55; Univ Southern Calif, MS, 62; Univ Denver, PhD(chem eng), 69. *Prof Exp:* Thermodynamicist, Aviation Div, NAm Rockwell Corp, Calif, 55-58; heat transfer engr, Northrop Corp, 58-61; res specialist, Space Div, NAm Rockwell Corp, 61-66; sr staff engr, Martin Marietta Corp, 66-68; adj prof chem eng, Univ Denver, 69; dept engr develop, Pantex Atomic Energy Comn Plant, Mason & Hanger-Silas Mason Co, Inc, 70-74; sr environ engr, Midwest Res Inst, Kansas City, 74-76; chem engr & proj mgr, Grand Forks Proj Off, US Dept Energy, NDak, 76-87; consult energy & environ, 88-90. *Concurrent Pos:* Staff, Southern Ill Univ Carbondale, 90- *Mem:* Am Soc Testing & Mat; Am Inst Chem Engrs; Am Soc Mech Engrs; Sigma Xi. *Res:* Nationwide fossil energy project performance evaluations; technical and economic evaluation studies of energy-related processes; research project management for coal combustion; environmental control systems. *Mailing Add:* 3109 Edgewood Park Marion IL 62959-5511

HONECK, HENRY CHARLES, REACTOR PHYSICS, APPLIED MATHEMATICS. *Current Pos:* PRES, COMPUT APPL TECHNOL INC, 80- *Personal Data:* b Batavia, NY, Oct 4, 30; m 52; c 2. *Educ:* Rensselaer Polytech Inst, BS, 52; Mass Inst Technol, ScD(nuclear eng), 59. *Honors & Awards:* E O Lawrence Award, AEC, 74. *Prof Exp:* Test engr reactor physics, Pratt & Whitney Aircraft, 52-56; scientist, Brookhaven Nat Lab, 59-65 & AEC, 65-67; res mgr, Comput Appln Div, Savannah River Lab, E I du Pont de Nemours & Co, 67-73, res fel, comput sci div, 73-80. *Concurrent Pos:* Consult, Gen Atomic Div, Gen Dynamics Corp, 61-65. *Mem:* Fel Am Nuclear Soc. *Res:* Neutron transport theory; neutron thermalization; reactor theory computer codes; data management; modular systems; computer science. *Mailing Add:* 621 Colleton Ave SE Aiken SC 29801-4607

HONES, EDWARD W, MECHANICAL ENGINEERING, PLASMA PHYSICS. *Current Pos:* RETIRED. *Educ:* Duke Univ, BS, 43, MA, 49, PhD(physics), 51. *Prof Exp:* Staff scientist, Los Alamos Nat Lab, 65-87. *Mailing Add:* 129 Monte Rey Dr Los Alamos NM 87544

HONES, MICHAEL J, PARTICLE PHYSICS. *Current Pos:* ASST PROF PHYSICS, VILLANOVA UNIV, 69- *Personal Data:* b Rahway, NJ, Apr 18, 42; m 64. *Educ:* Holy Cross Col, BS, 64; Univ Notre Dame, PhD(physics), 69. *Mem:* Am Phys Soc. *Res:* Experimental high energy physics; meson and baryon spectroscopy. *Mailing Add:* Dept Physics Villanova Univ Villanova PA 19085-1672

HONEY, RICHARD CHURCHILL, ELECTROOPTICS. *Current Pos:* sr res engr, Microwave Group, Electromagnetics Lab, Stanford Res Inst, 52-60, tech prog coordr, Electromagnetic Tech Lab, 60-64, mgr, 64-70, staff scientist, 70-84, sr staff scientist, Electromagnetic Sci Lab, 85-89, SR PRIN SCIENTIST, APPL ELECTROMAGNETICS & OPTICS LAB, SRI INT, 89- *Personal Data:* b Portland, Ore, Mar 9, 24; div; c Leslie, Steven, Laura & Janine. *Educ:* Calif Inst Technol, BS, 45; Stanford Univ, PhD(elec eng), 53. *Prof Exp:* Asst, Electronics Res Labs, Stanford Univ, 48-52. *Concurrent Pos:* Chmn working group lasers, Adv Group Electron Devices, Dir Defense Res & Eng, 69-75; mem, Army Sci Bd, 78-84. *Mem:* Fel Inst Elec & Electronics Engrs; Am Phys Soc; fel Optical Soc Am. *Res:* Lasers; microwave theory; antennae and measurements; medical applications of lasers; ocean optics. *Mailing Add:* SRI Int 333 Ravenswood Ave Menlo Park CA 94025. *Fax:* 650-859-6259

HONEYCUTT, JAY F, AERONAUTICAL ENGINEERING. *Current Pos:* engr, NASA, 66-81, tech asst to assoc admin space transp syst, 81, mgr, 82-86, spec asst to assoc adminr space flight, 86-87, dep mgr, Space Shuttle Prog Off, Johnson Space Ctr, 87-89, dir shuttle mgt & opers, Kennedy Space Ctr, 89-95, CTR DIR, KENNEDY SPACE CTR, NASA, 95- *Personal Data:* b Jena, La, May 7, 37; m; c Barry, Jeff, Delise & Daniel. *Educ:* Univ Southwestern La, BS. *Prof Exp:* Engr, Redstone Arsenal, Huntsville, Ala, 60-66. *Mailing Add:* NASA Kennedy Space Center FL 32899

HONEYCUTT, RODNEY LEE, MOLECULAR EVOLUTIONARY BIOLOGY, SYSTEMATIC BIOLOGY & MAMMALIAN EVOLUTION. *Current Pos:* PROF GENETICS & WILDLIFE FISHERIES, TEX A&M UNIV, 89- *Personal Data:* b Houston, Tex, Aug 5, 48; m 74, Dierdre A Hale; c Heather A & Morgan L. *Educ:* Univ Tex, BA, 70; Tex A&M Univ, MS, 78, PhD(biol), 81. *Prof Exp:* Environ consult, Stearns-Roger, Inc, 75-77; res asst, Tex Tech Univ, 77-81; res fel, Australian Nat Univ, 81-83; fel, Univ Mich, 83-84; assoc prof biol, Harvard Univ, 84-89. *Concurrent Pos:* Prog officer biol, NSF, 92-93, prin investr. *Mem:* Am Soc Mammalogists; Soc Molecular Biol & Evolution; Soc Study Evolution; Soc Systematic Biol. *Res:* Molecular evolution and mammalian genetics; published over 60 papers. *Mailing Add:* Wildlife & Fisheries Sci Tex A&M Univ College Station TX 77843-0100

HONEYCUTT, THOMAS LYNN, OPERATIONS RESEARCH, COMPUTER SCIENCE. *Current Pos:* asst prof, NC State Univ, 70-80, assoc head dept, 76-, ADJ ASSOC PROF, NC STATE UNIV, 80-, ASSOC PROF COMPUT SCI. *Personal Data:* b Louisville, Ky, Aug 28, 42; m 63; c 1. *Educ:* NC State Univ, BS, 65, MS, 67, PhD(eng), 69. *Prof Exp:* Sr analyst opers res, US Plywood-Champion Papers, 69-70. *Concurrent Pos:* Assoc consult, Mgt Decisions Develop Corp, 69- *Mem:* Opers Res Soc Am; Am Soc Agr Engrs. *Res:* Industrial plant location analysis. *Mailing Add:* 4550 Mill Village Rd Raleigh NC 27612

HONEYMAN, MERTON SEYMOUR, GENETICS. *Current Pos:* CONSULT, CONN DEPT PUB HEALTH & ADDICTION SERV. *Personal Data:* b Hartford, Conn, Sept 27, 25; m 52, Harriet Chatzek; c Elisa, Michael & Jason. *Educ:* Univ Conn, BA, 50, MS, 51; Ohio State Univ, PhD(zool), 54. *Prof Exp:* Fel genetics, Yale Univ, 54-57; geneticist, Nat Cancer Inst, 57-59; geneticist, Chronic Dis Control Sect, Conn State Dept Health, 59-66, dir, Div Res, Off Ment Retardation, 66-74, dir, Div Health Statist, 74-84, res scientist, 84-89. *Concurrent Pos:* Instr eve col, Teachers Col, Conn, 54-55; adj asst prof, Hillyer Col, 55-56 & Univ Hartford, 60-72; lectr, Dept Epidemiol & Pub Health, Sch Med, Yale Univ, 60-69; mem, Expert Adv Comt Method of Twin Studies, WHO, Geneva, 65; consult, Swed Twin Registry, Karolinska Inst, 67 & Rheumatic Fever Clin, Hadassah Med Sch, Hebrew Univ, Israel, 67; lectr, Manchester Community Col, 71-73 & Tunxis Community Col, 73-75; consult, Dept Med, Hartford Hosp. *Mem:* Am Soc Human Genetics; Am Cancer Soc; Am Pub Health Asn; Am Heart Asn. *Res:* Human genetics; twin research; genetics of chronic disease; demography; genetic counseling; public health statistics. *Mailing Add:* 17109 Waterbend Dr No 124 Jupiter FL 33477

HONEYWELL, WALLACE I(RVING), CHEMICAL ENGINEERING & PHYSICS. *Current Pos:* asst prof chem eng, 65-67, assoc dean, Cullen Col Eng, 76-80, ASSOC PROF CHEM ENG, UNIV HOUSTON, 67-, DIR, ACAD ADV CTR, 80- *Personal Data:* b North Platte, Nebr, Feb 6, 36; m 59; c 4. *Educ:* Stanford Univ, BS, 59; Calif Inst Technol, PhD(chem eng), 64. *Prof Exp:* NSF fel physics, State Univ Leiden, 64-65. *Mem:* Am Chem Soc; Am Inst Chem Engrs; Am Soc Eng Educ. *Res:* Magnetic field effects on transport properties of gases; non-equilibrium thermodynamics; high gradient magnetic separation processes; magnetothermal convection in gases. *Mailing Add:* 3720 Parkwood Dr Houston TX 77021

HONG, ALLAN JIXIAN, ARTIFICIAL INTELLIGENCE APPLICATION IN DECISION MAKING & INTERNATIONAL BUSINESS MANAGEMENT. *Current Pos:* Sr scientist, 90-92, CHEM PORTFOLIO MGR, HOFFMANN-LA ROCHE, 92- *Personal Data:* b Shanghai, China, May 27, 54. *Educ:* Univ Del, BS, 83; Yale Univ, MS, 85, PhD(eng & appl sci), 88. *Concurrent Pos:* Adj asst prof, Stevens Inst Technol, 91. *Mem:* Am Inst Chem Engrs; Am Chem Soc; Sigma Xi. *Res:* Project management, strategic planning and decision making logistics combined with computer technology in artificial intelligence applications; international business management. *Mailing Add:* Brookdale Gardens Glen Ridge NJ 07028

HONG, BOR-SHYUE, OPHTHALMOLOGY. *Current Pos:* ADJ ASSOC PROF OPHTHAL, TEX TECH UNIV HEALTH SCI CTR, 82- *Educ:* Colo State Univ, PhD(neurotoxins), 70. *Res:* structure and function of collagen cornea; calcium dependent neutral protease in eye lenses; catherization of vitamin A binding in tears. *Mailing Add:* Optic Prog Alcon Labs Inc 6201 S Freeway Ft Worth TX 76134-2099

HONG, CHIA-SWEE, ENVIRONMENTAL SCIENCES, ORGANIC CHEMISTRY. *Current Pos:* instr, 93-97, ASST PROF, STATE UNIV NY, 97-; RES SCIENTIST, WADSWORTH CTR, NY STATE DEPT HEALTH, 84- *Personal Data:* m 78, Sai-Pei Ting; c Grace Ting & Gary Ting. *Educ:* Fu-Jen Univ, Taiwan, BS, 75; City Univ NY, Brooklyn, MS, 78, PhD(anal chem), 80. *Prof Exp:* Proj asst, Wadsworth Ctr, NY State Dept Health, 80-84. *Concurrent Pos:* Prin investr, NY Sea grant, 90 & Nat Inst Environ Health Sci, 95- *Mem:* Am Chem Soc; Soc Environ Toxicol & Chem; Hazardous Mat Control Resources Inst; Am Water Works Asn; Marine Environ Res Inst; Overseas Chinese Environ Engr & Scientist Asn. *Res:* Development of remediation technology. *Mailing Add:* Wadsworth Ctr PO Box 509 Albany NY 12201-0509. *Fax:* 518-473-7689; *E-Mail:* hongc@wadsworth.org

HONG, CHUNG IL, MEDICINAL CHEMISTRY. *Current Pos:* NSF grants & res scientist med chem, Gen Clin Res Ctr, Roswell Park Cancer Inst, 69-73, cancer res scientist, 73-74, sr res scientist, 74-80, CANCER RES SCIENTIST IV, DEPT NEUROSURG, ROSWELL PARK CANCER INST, 80- *Personal Data:* b Koo-Sung, Korea, Dec 22, 38; m 64, Jung J Ahn; c 3. *Educ:* Seoul Nat Univ, BS, 61; Univ NC, Chapel Hill, MS, 67, PhD(med chem), 68. *Prof Exp:* Instr biochem, Sch Pharm, Univ NC, 69. *Concurrent Pos:* Asst res prof, Dept Chem, Roswell Park Grad Div, State Univ NY, Buffalo, 82- *Mem:* Am Chem Soc; Am Pharmaceut Asn; Am Asn Cancer Res; NY Acad Sci; Korean Scientists & Engrs Asn Am. *Res:* Synthesis and biochemical studies of nucleic acid components and 3', 5'- cyclic nucleotides; kinetics of entry, distribution, and metabolism of antitumor agents in experimental animals; development of antitumor and antiviral agents by conjugation with natural carrier molecules; prodrugs of antitumor and antiviral nucleosides conjugating with ether and thioether phospholipids; micellar formulation of the nucleoside conjugates; platinum complexes of corticosteroids; combination chemotherapy. *Mailing Add:* Roswell Park Cancer Inst Elm & Carlton St Buffalo NY 14263-0001. *Fax:* 716-845-3545; *E-Mail:* hongci@ubvms.cc.buffalo.edu

HONG, DANIEL C, THEORETICAL PHYSICS. *Current Pos:* asst prof, 88-94, ASSOC PROF PHYSICS, LEHIGH UNIV, 94- *Personal Data:* b Seoul, Korea; m 81, Susy S Lee; c Susan, Annie, Daniel & Julianna. *Educ:* Seoul Nat Univ, BS, 79, MS, 81; Boston Univ, PhD(physics), 85. *Prof Exp:* Lectr physics, Korean Mil Acad, 81; postdoctoral fel, Inst Theoret Physics, Univ Calif, Santa Barbara, 85-87; vis res scholar, Emory Univ, 87-88. *Concurrent Pos:* Emerson fel, Emory Univ, 95. *Mem:* Am Phys Soc; Mat Res Soc; Asn Korean Physicists Am (secy, 95-96); Korean Scientists & Engrs Asn (vpres, 94-95, pres, 95-96). *Res:* Theoretical studies of equilibrium and nonequilibrium statistical mechanics of complex systems with particular emphasis on nonlinear dynamics, interfacial instability and pattern formation, phase transitions and critical phenomena; author of numerous articles and publications in the field. *Mailing Add:* Dept Physics Lewis Lab Lehigh Univ Bethlehem PA 18015. *Fax:* 610-758-5730, 867-1973; *E-Mail:* dh09@lehigh.edu

HONG, DONALD DAVID, methods development, for more information see previous edition

HONG, JAU-SHYONG, NEUROPHARMACOLOGY. *Current Pos:* PROF NEUROPHARMACOL, DUKE UNIV, 80-; HEAD, NEUROPHARMACOL SECT, LAB BEHAV & NEUROL TOXICOL, NAT INST ENVIRON HEALTH SCI, 80- *Personal Data:* b Nov 8, 43; m; c 2. *Educ:* Univ Kans, PhD(pharmacol), 73. *Concurrent Pos:* Acting chief, Lab Molecular & Integrative Neuroscience, Nat Inst Environ Health Sci, NIH. *Mem:* Am Soc Pharmacol & Exp Therapeut; Neurosci Soc. *Res:* Neuropeptides; neurotransmitters. *Mailing Add:* Lab Molecular Integrative Neurosci Nat Inst Environ Health Sci NIH PO Box 12233 Research Triangle Park NC 27709-2233

HONG, JEN SHIANG, GENETICS. *Current Pos:* SR SCIENTIST, BOSTON BIOMED RES INST, 81- *Personal Data:* b Mar 3, 39; m; c 2. *Educ:* Univ Calif, Berkeley, PhD(biochem), 69. *Mem:* AAAS; Am Soc Biochem & Molecular Biol; Am Soc Microbiol. *Res:* Molecular genetics of membrane transport; gene regulation. *Mailing Add:* Dept Cell Physiol Boston Biomed Res Inst 20 Staniford St Boston MA 02114-2500

HONG, KEELUNG, MEMBRANE FUSION, ENDOCYTOSIS. *Current Pos:* asst res biochemist, 79-91, ASSOC RES BIOCHEMIST, UNIV CALIF, SAN FRANCISCO, 91- *Personal Data:* b Taiwan, Apr 8, 43; US citizen. *Educ:* Taiwan Cheng Kung Univ, BS, 65; Univ Tex, MS, 70; Univ Calif, Berkeley, PhD(chem), 75. *Prof Exp:* Postdoctoral res, Univ Calif, San Francisco, 75-76 & Univ Calif, Berkeley, 76-77; postdoctoral res, Stanford Univ, 77-78, assoc res, 78-79. *Concurrent Pos:* Consult, Biotech Co. *Mem:* AAAS; Am Chem Soc; Biophys Soc; Am Soc Cell Biol; NY Acad Sci; fel Am Inst Chemists. *Res:* Biomembrane structure and function; mechanism of membrane fusion; protein-lipid interactions; liposome as drug carrier; liposome-cell interactions; critique of social science research. *Mailing Add:* Univ Calif Box 0450 San Francisco CA 94143-0450

HONG, KI C(HOONG), CHEMICAL & PETROLEUM ENGINEERING, THERMAL ENHANCED OIL RECOVERY & STEAMFLOODING. *Current Pos:* SR ADV, PETROL ENG-ENHANCED OIL RECOVERY, CHEVRON USA PROD CO, BAKERSFIELD, 92- *Personal Data:* b Seoul, Korea, May 1, 36; m 63, Koon J Pang; c Caroline, Marjorie, Sandra & Deborah. *Educ:* Iowa State Univ, BSc, 59, MSc, 61, PhD(chem eng), 62. *Prof Exp:* Sr eng assoc, Chevron Oil Field Res Co, La Habra, 62-92. *Concurrent Pos:* Lectr environ eng, Univ Calif, Irvine, 74-76; lectr mech eng, Calif State Univ, Fullerton, 83-86; lectr steamflood reservoir mgt, Res Inst Petrol Explor & Develop, Beijing, China, 93. *Mem:* Am Chem Soc; Am Inst Chem Engrs; Am Inst Mining, Metall & Petrol Engrs. *Res:* High analysis fertilizers; mathematical simulation; optimization; flow through porous media; thermal recovery of petroleum; well completion methods; multiphase flow in pipes; reservoir engineering and analysis; laboratory, numercal, and field studies of steamflood process. *Mailing Add:* 7 Glenhaven Lane Irvine CA 92620

HONG, KUOCHIH, PHYSICAL CHEMISTRY, HYDRIDE TECHNOLOGY. *Current Pos:* PRES, HONG ENTERPRISES CO, 80- *Personal Data:* b Ping-Tong, Taiwan. *Educ:* Nat Taiwan Normal Univ, BS, 65; Nat Tsing Hua Univ, MS, 69; Univ Chicago, PhD(chem), 75. *Prof Exp:* Teacher sci, Taipei Girls' Mid Sch, 65-66; instr chem, Tamkung Col, 69-70; res assoc, Univ Chicago, 75-77; asst chemist, Brookhaven Nat Lab, 77-80. *Concurrent Pos:* Prof, Dept Mat Eng, Tsing Hua Univ, Taiwan. *Mem:* Am Chem Soc; Int Hydrogen Energy Asn. *Res:* Hydride batteries, hydride heat pump, fuel cells. *Mailing Add:* 1790 Rolling Woods Dr Troy MI 48098

HONG, MINGHWIE, MATERIALS SCIENCE & ENGINEERING. *Current Pos:* mem tech staff, Mat Res Lab, 81-88, MEM TECH STAFF, SEMICONDUCTOR RES LAB, AT&T BELL LABS, MURRAY HILL, NJ, 88- *Educ:* Nat Taiwan Univ, BS, 73; Univ Calif, Berkeley, MS, 78, PhD(mat sci & eng), 80. *Prof Exp:* Staff scientist II, Mat & Molecular Res Div, Lawrence Berkeley Lab, Univ Calif, 80-81. *Concurrent Pos:* Mem, Electronic Device Mat Comt, Metall Soc, 85-90, Magnetic Mat Comt, 89-, Electronic & Photonic Device Mat Comt, 90- *Mem:* Am Phys Soc; Metall Soc; Inst Elec & Electronics Engrs; Mat Res Soc. *Mailing Add:* AT&T Bell Labs Rm 1T-204 600 Mountain Ave Murray Hill NJ 07974

HONG, PILL WHOON, SURGERY. *Current Pos:* RETIRED. *Personal Data:* b Ichon, Korea, Oct 10, 21; m 56; c 3. *Educ:* Yonsei Univ, Korea, MB, 42, DMSc(physiol), 60. *Honors & Awards:* Acad Awards, Korean Med Asn, 62. *Prof Exp:* From asst prof to prof surg, Col Med, Yonsei Univ, Korea, 56-67; from assoc prof to prof surg, Sch Med, Univ Hawaii, 67-80; prof, Yonsei Univ, 80-87, vpres, 84-86. *Concurrent Pos:* China Med Bd NY, Inc, travel fel, 60-66; Brit Nat Coun fel, 66. *Mem:* Fel Am Col Surg; fel Am Col Chest Physicians; Korean Surg Soc (pres, 66). *Res:* Thoracic surgery. *Mailing Add:* 2766 A Manoa Rd Honolulu HI 96822

HONG, RICHARD, PEDIATRICS, IMMUNOLOGY. *Current Pos:* assoc dean clin affairs, 71-74, PROF PEDIAT & MICROBIOL, MED CTR, UNIV WIS-MADISON, 69- *Personal Data:* b Danville, Ill, Jan 10, 29; m 52; c 4. *Educ:* Univ Ill, Urbana-Champaign, BS, 49; Univ Ill, Chicago, MD, 53. *Prof Exp:* Sr res assoc immunol, Univ Cincinnati, 60-65; from asst prof to prof pediat & immunol, Univ Minn, Minneapolis, 65-69. *Concurrent Pos:* USPHS fel, 60-62, res career develop award, 63-69; mem, Transplant Registry, 68-69. *Mem:* Am Soc Clin Invest; Am Asn Immunol; Soc Pediat Res; Am Pediat Soc. *Res:* Immunoglobulin structure and function; immunochemistry of hypogammaglobulinemia; treatment of immunological deficiency states; physiology of immunity. *Mailing Add:* Dept Pediat Univ Vt Genetic Lab 32 N Prospect Ave Burlington VT 05401-0508

HONG, SE JUNE, COMPUTER & ELECTRICAL ENGINEERING. *Current Pos:* Staff engr, IBM Corp, 69-72, adv engr, 73-76, sr engr, 77-78, sr mgr, 82-94, RES MEM STAFF, IBM CORP, 78- *Personal Data:* b Seoul, Korea, May 15, 44; m 68, Karen McCully; c 1. *Educ:* Seoul Nat Univ, BSc, 65; Univ Ill, Urbana, MS, 67, PhD(elec eng), 69. *Honors & Awards:* Outstanding Young Elect Engr, Inst Elec & Electronics Engrs, 75. *Concurrent Pos:* Vis assoc prof, Univ Ill, 74-75; vis prof, Korean Advan Inst Sci & Technol, 80. *Mem:* Fel Inst Elec & Electronics Engrs; Asn Comput Mach; Sigma Xi; Korean Scientists & Engrs in Am; Am Asn Artificial Intel. *Res:* Coding theory; fault tolerant computing; array logic; switching theory and minimization; test pattern generation; design automation; expert systems; data mining; artificial intelligence. *Mailing Add:* 1374 White Hill Rd Yorktown Heights NY 10598

HONG, SONG, ADVANCED OXIDATION & ELECTROCHEMICAL-FENTION REACTION TO TREAT ORGANIC POLLANTS. *Current Pos:* POSTDOCTORAL RES ASSOC, CORNELL UNIV, 94- *Educ:* Jilin Agr Univ, BS, 83; Beijing Agr Univ, MS, 86; Univ Ga, PhD(pesticidal chem), 96. *Concurrent Pos:* Analytical chemist, Cert Anal Lab, 96. *Mem:* Am Chem Soc. *Res:* Pesticide degration using electrochemical advanced oxidation methods; herbicide degradation on golf course; pesticide formulation. *Mailing Add:* Dept Textiles & Apparel MVR Hall Cornell Univ Ithaca NY 14853

HONG, SUK KI, PHYSIOLOGY. *Current Pos:* asst prof, 62, assoc prof 65, PROF PHYSIOL, STATE UNIV NY BUFFALO, 75- *Personal Data:* b Kyonggi Do, Korea, Oct 16, 28; m 59, Kay; c Robert & Peggy. *Educ:* Yonsei Univ, MD, 49; Univ Rochester, PhD(physiol), 56. *Hon Degrees:* DSc, Kyungpook Nat Grad Sch, Daegu, Korea, 83. *Honors & Awards:* Samil Cult Found Award, 63; Stover Link Award, Undersea Med Soc, 84; Stockton Kimball Award, SUNY at Buffalo, 87. *Prof Exp:* From instr to asst prof physiol, Univ Buffalo, 56-59; asst prof physiol, Yonsei Univ Korea, 59-62, assoc prof, 63-65, prof & chmn dept, 66-68; prof physiol, Univ Hawaii, 68-75, chmn dept, 71-75. *Concurrent Pos:* Consult, Off Surg Gen, Repub Korea Air Force, 60-68 & Korea Amateur Sports Asn, 62-68; deleg, Int Cong Physiol Sci, 68; consult, Tripler Army Med Ctr, Honolulu, 72-75; mem US-Japan coop prog natural resources, 72- *Mem:* Am Physiol Soc; Am Soc Nephrology; Undersea Med Soc; Int Soc Nephrology; Soc Exp Biol & Med. *Res:* Renal and membrane physiology; diving physiology; adaptation of man to cold environment. *Mailing Add:* Dept Physiol State Univ NY Buffalo NY 14214. *Fax:* 716-829-2344

HONG, WAUN KI, ONCOLOGY. *Current Pos:* internist & prof med, M D Anderson Cancer Ctr, Univ Tex, Houston, 84-88, chief, Sect Thoracic Med Oncol, 87-88, dep head, Div Med, 92-93, CHMN, DEPT THORACIC HEAD & NECK MED ONCOL, M D ANDERSON CANCER CTR, UNIV TEX, HOUSTON, 93- *Personal Data:* b Kyung gi Do, SKorea, Aug 13, 42; US citizen; m 69, Mi H Yoo; c Edward & Burton J. *Educ:* Yon-Sei Univ, MD, 67; Am Bd Internal Med, dipl, 76 & 79. *Honors & Awards:* Richard & Hinda Rosenthal Found Award, Am Asn Cancer Res, 93; Distinguished Serv Award, Am Cancer Soc, 93; KBS Korean Overseas Compatriots Award Sci, 94; Ho-Am Prize Med, Sam-Sung Found, 94. *Prof*

Exp: Teaching assoc, Sch Med, Boston Univ, 71-73, from asst prof to assoc prof med, 75-84; clin instr med, Cornell Univ, 73-75. *Concurrent Pos:* Rotating intern, Bronz Lebanon Hosp, New York, 70-71; jr med resident, Boston Vet Affairs Med Ctr, 71-72, sr med resident, 72-73, chief med oncol, 75-84, prog dir hemat oncol training prog, 82-84; lectr med, Tufts Univ, 75-84; attend physician med, Boston City Hosp, 78-84; clin assoc prof pharm, Northeastern Univ, Boston, 80-84; adj prof med, Baylor Col Med, 91-; vis prof, Tex Tech Univ, Sch Med, 92, Tufts Univ, Sch Med, Dana Farber Cancer Ctr & Johns Hopkins Oncol Ctr, 93. *Mem:* AMA; AAAS; Am Radium Soc; Am Fedn Clin Res; Am Asn Physicians; Am Asn Cancer Res; Am Soc Clin Oncol; Nat Cancer Inst; Soc Head & Neck Surgeons. *Res:* Innovative, translational research approaches to investigate the use of retinoids, either singly or in combination with other agents, for the chemoprevention of human aerodigestive epithelial tumors. *Mailing Add:* M D Anderson Cancer Ctr Dept Thoracic Head Neck Med Oncol Houston TX 77030. *Fax:* 713-796-8655

HONG, WEN-HAI, PHYSICAL PHARMACY. *Current Pos:* SR RES ASSOC, WARNER LAMBERT & PARKE DAVIS & CO, 69- *Personal Data:* b Tainan, Taiwan, Apr 11, 34; m 61; c 3. *Educ:* Nat Taiwan Univ, BS, 57; Univ Wis, MS, 66, PhD(pharm), 69. *Prof Exp:* Teaching asst pharm, Nat Taiwan Univ, 59-64, instr, 64-65. *Mem:* Am Chem Soc. *Res:* Development of selective methods for analysis of investigational new dosage forms intended for use in humans. *Mailing Add:* 10 Sylvan Dr Pine Brook NJ 07058

HONG, WON-PYO, TELECOMMUNICATION NETWORKS & SERVICES. *Current Pos:* PROJ LEADER, BELLCORE, 88- *Personal Data:* b Seoul, Korea, Feb 8, 60; m 90, Yoo-Kyung Hong-Lim. *Educ:* Seoul Nat Univ, BS, 83; Univ Mich, MS, 84, PhD(elec eng), 88. *Honors & Awards:* Int Res Coop Trust Award, Japan Key Tech Ctr, 91. *Mem:* Inst Elec & Electronics Engrs. *Res:* Advanced semiconductor devices and systems to support broadband communication networks and wireless communication systems. *Mailing Add:* Bellcore 331 Newman Springs Rd Rm 3X-367 Red Bank NJ 07701. *Fax:* 732-758-4372; *E-Mail:* wphong@cc.bellcore.com

HONIG, ARNOLD, SEMICONDUCTORS, LOW TEMPERATURE PHYSICS. *Current Pos:* from asst prof to assoc prof physics, 56-62, PROF PHYSICS, SYRACUSE UNIV, 62- *Personal Data:* b New York, NY, Feb 28, 28; m 47, 79, Dolly Roth; c 3. *Educ:* Cornell Univ, BA, 48; Columbia Univ, MA, 50, PhD(physics), 53. *Honors & Awards:* Glover Mem Award, Dickinson Col, 66. *Prof Exp:* Asst microwave spectros, Columbia Univ, 51-53; res physicist, Solid State Physics, Univ Calif, 53-54; res fel molecular physics, Ecole Normale Superieure, Paris, 54-56. *Concurrent Pos:* Vis prof, Hebrew Univ, 62, Comn Atomic Energy, Saclay, France, 65. *Mem:* Am Phys Soc; Fedn Am Scientists. *Res:* Spin-polarized nuclear fusion fuels; nuclear and electronic magnetic resonance in semiconductors and quantum solids at very low temperatures; luminescence and transport in semiconductors under conditions of high electron and hole spin-polarizations; bio-luminescence. *Mailing Add:* Dept Physics Syracuse Univ Syracuse NY 13244. *Fax:* 315-443-9103; *E-Mail:* honig@suhep.phy.sgr.edu

HONIG, BARRY, COMPUTATIONAL BIOLOGY. *Current Pos:* lectr biol sci, 70-73, PROF BIOCHEM & BIOPHYS, COLUMBIA UNIV, 81- *Personal Data:* b New York, NY, Nov 30, 41; m 68, Marjorie Hanson; c Michael & Adam. *Educ:* Polytech Inst, NY, BSc, 63; Johns Hopkins Univ, MA, 64; Weizmann Inst Sci, Israel, PhD(chem physics), 68. *Honors & Awards:* Merit Award, NIH, 95. *Prof Exp:* NIH postdoctoral fel chem, Harvard Univ, 68-70; sr lectr phys chem, Hebrew Univ, 73-77, assoc prof, 77-79; assoc prof biophys, Univ Ill, 79-81. *Concurrent Pos:* Mem, NIH Study Sect, 89-93; ed, J Molecular Biol; NSF Blue Ribbon Panel High Performance Comput, 93. *Mem:* AAAS; Am Chem Soc; Biophys Soc (pres); Am Soc Biochem & Molecular Biol. *Res:* Theoretical and computational studies of biological macromolecules. *Mailing Add:* Dept Biochem & Molecular Biophys 630 W 168th St BB221 New York NY 10032-3702. *Fax:* 212-305-6926

HONIG, CARL ROBERT, TOXICOLOGY. *Current Pos:* asst, Univ Rochester, 54-57, from instr to assoc prof, 57-67, actg chmn dept, 68-69, PROF PHYSIOL, SCH MED & DENT, UNIV ROCHESTER, 67- *Personal Data:* b New York, NY, July 15, 25; m 47; c 2. *Educ:* Univ Rochester, BS, 45; Long Island Col Med, MD, 49; Am Bd Internal Med, dipl, 58. *Honors & Awards:* Merit Award USPHS. *Prof Exp:* Instr, Col Med, Univ Cincinnati, 52-53. *Mem:* Am Physiol Soc; Microcirculatory Soc; Int Soc Oxygen Transp to Tissue. *Res:* Circulation-metabolism coupling; oxygen transport; myoglobin microspectroscopy in vivo. *Mailing Add:* Dept Physiol Univ Rochester Med Sch 601 Elmwood Ave Rochester NY 14642-0001

HONIG, DAVID HERMAN, FOOD CHEMISTRY. *Current Pos:* RETIRED. *Personal Data:* b Turtleford, Sask, Sept 9, 28; US citizen; m 67, Judith Bell; c Elizabeth, Sarah & Daniel. *Educ:* Bethany Col, BSc, 62; Kans State Univ, MSc, 65. *Prof Exp:* Res chemist, Northern Regional Res Ctr, Sci & Educ Admin-Fed Res, USDA, 65-93. *Mem:* Am Chem Soc; Am Asn Cereal Chemists. *Res:* Sources, causes and modification of flavor in soybeans and soybean products; chemical nature of soybeans and physiological effects of components; interactions of the components; characterization of cornstarch-polyacrylonitrile copolymers. *Mailing Add:* 2305 N University St Peoria IL 61604-3222

HONIG, GEORGE RAYMOND, PEDIATRIC HEMATOLOGY, ONCOLOGY. *Current Pos:* PROF PEDIAT & HEAD DEPT, COL MED, UNIV ILL, 84- *Personal Data:* b May 5, 36. *Educ:* Univ Ill, MD, 61; George Washington Univ, PhD(biochem), 66. *Mem:* Am Soc Biochem & Molecular Biol; Am Soc Hemat; Am Soc Cancer Res. *Res:* Thalassemia; sickle cell anemia. *Mailing Add:* Dept Pediat Univ Ill Col Med 840 S Wood St Chicago IL 60612. *Fax:* 312-413-1526

HONIG, JOHN GERHART, OPERATIONS RESEARCH, MANAGEMENT. *Current Pos:* PRIN SCIENTIST, MGT ANALYSIS INC, 88-; CONSULT, 88-; SR CONSULT, INST DEFENSE ANALYSIS, 89- *Personal Data:* b Vienna, Austria, Oct 30, 23; nat US; m 80, Elaine Souliere; c Gary, Judy & David. *Educ:* Drew Univ, AB, 47; Univ Mich, MS, 48; Georgetown Univ, PhD(phys chem), 56. *Honors & Awards:* David Rist Prize, Mil Opers Res Soc, 71. *Prof Exp:* Phys chemist, Nat Inst Cleaning & Dyeing, 48-50; phys chemist, Naval Res Lab, Washington, DC, 50-56; opers analyst, Opers Eval Group, Mass Inst Technol, 56-59; assoc proj leader, Weapons Syst Eval Group, Inst Defense Analyst, 59-62; chief naval warfare tech, Honeywell Inc, 62-65; opers res officer, US Arms Control & Disarmament Agency, 65-66; sci adv, Dir Studies, Off Chief of Staff Army, 66-68, chief weapons requirements & analyst, 68-74, asst dir systs rev, Off Res, Develop & Acquisitions, 74-78, chief of aircraft, missiles & electronics, Comptroller Army, 78-84; sr consult, Analysis Serv Inc, 84-86, prin physicist, 86-88. *Concurrent Pos:* Mem, Gov Sci Adv Coun, Md, 70-; sect chmn, Opers Res Soc Am, 74. *Mem:* Fel AAAS; Am Chem Soc; Mil Opers Res Soc (pres, 69-70); Inst Mgt Sci; Nat Coun Asns Policy Sci (pres, 77); fel World Acad Arts & Sci; Opers Res Soc Am. *Res:* Military operations research; military and industrial long-range planning; research and development management; systems analysis; large molecular systems in nonaqueous media; non-Newtonian flow in nonaqueous media; decision science, research and development management. *Mailing Add:* 7701 Glenmore Spring Way Bethesda MD 20817. *Fax:* 703-845-2211; *E-Mail:* jhonig@ida.org

HONIG, JURGEN MICHAEL, METAL-INSULATOR PHASE TRANSITIONS, SINGLE CRYSTAL GROWTH. *Current Pos:* from asst prof to assoc prof, 53-59, PROF CHEM, PURDUE UNIV, 67- *Personal Data:* b Gottingen Ger, Sept 29, 24; US citizen; m 47, Gertrude C Dahlbam; c Valerie A (Gramman) & Robert E. *Educ:* Amherst Col, BS, 46; Univ Minn, PhD(chem physics), 52. *Prof Exp:* Group leader, Mass Inst Technol, Lincoln Lab, 53-59. *Concurrent Pos:* Dir, Mat Res Lab, Purdue Univ, 69-82; consult, Hooker Chem Co, 76-79, Ill Inst Technol, 78-80; ed, J Solid State Chem, 82- *Mem:* Hon mem Mat Res Soc Indian; fel NY Acad Sci; Am Chem Soc; Am Phys Soc; Am Ceramic Soc. *Res:* Studies of metal-insulator transitions; superconductivity; growth of single crystals; development of theories pertaining to electron correlation effects; measurement of thermodynamic and electron transport properties of solids. *Mailing Add:* Dept Chem Purdue Univ West Lafayette IN 47907-1399. *Fax:* 765-494-0239; *E-Mail:* jmb@chem.purdue.edu

HONIG, LAWRENCE STERLING, DEVELOPMENTAL NEUROBIOLOGY, NEURODEGENERATIVE DISEASES. *Current Pos:* ASST PROF NEUROL, SOUTHWESTERN MED CTR, UNIV TEX, 94- *Personal Data:* b Calif, Oct 26, 53; m 93, Genia B Billote; c Maija & Edouardo. *Educ:* Cornell Univ, AB, 73; Univ Calif, Berkeley, PhD(molecular biol), 78; Univ Miami, MD, 86. *Prof Exp:* Anna Fuller Fund fel, Middlesex Hosp Med Sch, Eng, 78-79; mem sci staff develop biol, Nat Inst Med Res, Eng, 80; res asst prof basic sci, Univ Southern Calif, 81-83; clin instr neurol, Sch Med, Stanford Univ, 90-92, clin asst prof neurol, 92-94. *Concurrent Pos:* Dana fel neurosci, Stanford Univ, 90-94, Walter Berry fel neurobiol, 91-94; coordr, Alzheimers Neurosci res, Southwestern Med Ctr, Univ Tex, 94-; asst ed, Neurol, 97- *Mem:* Am Acad Neurol; AAAS; Sigma Xi; Soc Neurosci. *Res:* Mechanisms of neural development, especially synapse formation between neurons; mechanisms of neurological disease, especially neurodegenerative disorders, such as Alzheimers disease. *Mailing Add:* 5323 Harry Hines Blvd MC 9036 Dallas TX 75235-9036. *Fax:* 214-648-7992; *E-Mail:* lhonig@mednet.swmed.edu

HONIG, MILTON LESLIE, ORGANIC CHEMISTRY. *Current Pos:* VPRES RES & DEVELOP, STAND LUBRICANTS INC, 77- *Personal Data:* b New York, NY, Apr 10, 44;. *Educ:* City Col New York, BS, 65; Polytech Inst Brooklyn, PhD(chem), 70. *Prof Exp:* Res chemist, Stauffer Chem Co, 70-77 & Fordham Univ Law Sch, 80. *Concurrent Pos:* Adj lectr, Hunter Col, 72-73 & Barnard Col, 81-82. *Mem:* Am Chem Soc; Chem Soc; Am Soc Lubrication Engrs. *Res:* Synthetic lubricant development; organophosphorus chemistry; flame retardant chemistry. *Mailing Add:* 3240 Henry Hudson Pkwy Bronx NY 10463-3212

HONIG, RICHARD EDWARD, MASS SPECTROMETRY. *Current Pos:* RETIRED. *Personal Data:* b Gottingen, Ger, June 4, 17; nat US; m 43; c 2. *Educ:* Robert Col, Istanbul, BS, 38; Mass Inst Technol, MS, 39, PhD(molecular physics), 44. *Prof Exp:* Asst physics, Mass Inst Technol, 39-40 & 41-44, res assoc, 44-46; sr physicist, Res Labs, Socony-Vacuum Oil Co, Inc, 46-50; tech staff mem, RCA Labs, 50-68, head mat characterization, 68-82, staff scientist, 82-87. *Concurrent Pos:* Instr, Bluffton Col, 40-41; res fel, Univ Brussels, 55-56; adj res prof, Rensselaer Polytech Inst. *Mem:* Fel Am Phys Soc; Am Soc Mass Spectrometry (pres, 70-72); Am Vacuum Soc. *Res:* Ion physics; mass spectrometry; solid state. *Mailing Add:* 3300 Darby Rd Pine No 7305 Haverford PA 19041

HONIGBERG, BRONISLAW MARK, immunology, microbiology; deceased, see previous edition for last biography

HONIGBERG, IRWIN LEON, MEDICINAL CHEMISTRY. *Current Pos:* from asst prof to assoc prof, 64-79, PROF MED, SCH PHARM, UNIV GA, 79- *Personal Data:* b Brooklyn, NY, Jan 31, 30; m 58; c 4. *Educ:* Univ Conn, BS, 51; Univ NC, PhD(pharmaceut chem), 57. *Prof Exp:* Assoc prof pharmaceut chem, New Eng Col Pharm, 56-57; assoc chemist, Midwest Res Inst, 57-64. *Mem:* AAAS; Am Chem Soc; Am Asn Pharmaceut Sci. *Res:* Pharmacy; liquid chromatography in pharmaceutical analysis; analysis of drugs in biological fluids; organic medicinals; mechanisms of antiallergy action. *Mailing Add:* 180 Ravenwood Ct Athens GA 30605

HONKALA, FRED SAUL, geology; deceased, see previous edition for last biography

HONKANEN, PENTTI A, COMPUTER SCIENCE, ELECTRICAL ENGINEERING. *Current Pos:* assoc prof, 73-, PROF INFO SYSTS, GA STATE UNIV, ATLANTA. *Personal Data:* b Brooklyn, NY, Nov 25, 32; m 54; c 5. *Educ:* Univ Colo, BS(elec eng) & BS(appl math), 59; Syracuse Univ, MEE, 62; Pa State Univ, PhD(elec eng), 67. *Prof Exp:* Staff engr, IBM Corp, 59-64; res assoc, Ord Res Lab, Pa State Univ, 64-68, asst prof comput sci, 68-73, chmn grad affairs, 71-73. *Mem:* Sigma Xi; Inst Elec & Electronics Engrs; Asn Comput Mach. *Res:* Database systems and data structures; computer simulation; analysis and simulations of nonlinear electrical networks on a digital computer; graph theory; numerical solution on nonlinear differential equations; systems simulation on a digital computer. *Mailing Add:* 2442 Cravey Dr Atlanta GA 30345

HONMA, SHIGEMI, HORTICULTURE. *Current Pos:* from asst prof to assoc prof, 56-66, prof, 66-86, EMER PROF HORT, MICH STATE UNIV, 86- *Personal Data:* b Haina, Hawaii, Feb 14, 20; m 45, Isao Okajima; c Alan K & Valerie E (Kennedy). *Educ:* Cornell Univ, BA, 49; Univ Minn, PhD, 53. *Prof Exp:* Asst horticulturist, Univ Nebr, 53-55. *Mem:* Fel Am Soc Hort Sci. *Res:* Plant geneticist and plant breeder. *Mailing Add:* Dept Hort Mich State Univ East Lansing MI 48824

HONNELL, MARTIAL A(LFRED), ELECTROMAGNETIC COMPATIBILITY. *Current Pos:* prof, 58-81, EMER PROF ELEC ENG & ADJ PROF, AUBURN UNIV, 81- *Personal Data:* b Lyons, France, Oct 23, 10; nat US; m 38, Ann Cullum; c Martial S & Angeline H. *Educ:* Ga Inst Technol, BS, 34, MS, 40, EE, 45. *Honors & Awards:* M A Ferst Sigma Xi Res Award, Ga Tech, 51. *Prof Exp:* Radio engr, WGST, Atlanta, 30-35, 38-44 & Pan Am Airways, Inc, Fla, 36-37; from instr to prof elec eng, Ga Inst Technol, 37-53, instr, Civilian Pilot Training Prog, 40-43, supvr pre-radar sch, 42-43 & ultrahigh frequency course, Eng Sci & Mgt War Training, 42-44, fac res assoc, 44-53; vpres & chief engr, Measurements Corp Div, McGraw-Edison Co, NJ, 53-58. *Concurrent Pos:* Consult, Redstone Arsenal Proj, NASA & Auburn Res Found, 58-81; vchmn, Comt Electronic & High-Frequency Instruments, Inst Elec & Electronics Engrs, 63-65, chmn, Subcomt Signal Generators, 64; distinguised grad fac lectr, Auburn Univ, 76-77. *Mem:* Am Soc Eng Educ; fel Inst Elec & Electronics Engrs. *Res:* Instrumentation; electronics; antennas; lightning. *Mailing Add:* Dept Elec Eng Auburn Univ Auburn AL 36849. *Fax:* 334-844-1809; *E-Mail:* mhonnell@eng.auburn.edu

HONNELL, PIERRE M(ARCEL), ELECTRICAL ENGINEERING. *Current Pos:* from assoc prof to prof, 46-76, EMER PROF ELEC ENG, WASHINGTON UNIV, 76- *Personal Data:* b Paris, France, Jan 28, 08; US citizen; m 37; c 2. *Educ:* Agr & Mech Col Tex, BSc, 30, EE, 38; Mass Inst Technol, MSc, 39; Calif Inst Technol, MSc, 40; St Louis Univ, PhD(geophys), 50. *Honors & Awards:* Marconi Premium, Brit Inst Radio Engrs, 56. *Prof Exp:* Radio operator stas WCAR & WOAI, Tex, 23-24; radio officer, US Merchant Marine, Tex Co & Gulf Refining Co, 26-28; mem tech staff, Bell Tel Labs, 30-33; geophysicist, Tex Co, 34-38; asst prof elec eng, Southern Methodist Univ, 40-41 & Univ Ill, 46. *Concurrent Pos:* Consult, McDonnell Aircraft Corp, Carter Carburetor Co & Martin Co, Colo. *Mem:* Fel AAAS; fel Inst Elec & Electronics Engrs; Am Soc Eng Educ; Am Asn Physics Teachers; Int Asn Analogue Comput; fel Inst Radio Engrs. *Res:* Stability theory, electronic and mechanic networks; seismological instruments; matric computors over reals and integers; didactic applications of matric computors. *Mailing Add:* Dept Elec Eng Washington Univ St Louis MO 63130

HONNOLD, VINCENT RICHARD, SOLID STATE PHYSICS. *Current Pos:* RETIRED. *Personal Data:* b Los Angeles, Calif, Feb 10, 24; m 48; c 5. *Educ:* Calif Inst Technol, BS, 48; Notre Dame Univ, PhD(physics), 54. *Prof Exp:* Physicist, Solid State Physics Br, US Naval Ord Test Sta, 54-57, head, 57-59; mem tech staff, Hughes Aircraft Co, 59-63, head basic mechanisms sect, Radiation Effects Res Dept, Fullerton Res & Develop, 63-69, mem staff, Vulnerability & Hardness Lab, TRW Systs, 70-77; mem staff, B-1 Div, Rockwell Int, 77-78; sr staff physicist, Hughes Aircraft Co, 78-86. *Concurrent Pos:* Instr, Univ Calif, Los Angeles, 55-56. *Mem:* Am Phys Soc; Sigma Xi. *Res:* High energy radiation effects; photoconductive and conduction processes in semiconductors and insulators; magnetic resonance. *Mailing Add:* 656 17th St Manhattan Beach CA 90266

HONRUBIA, VICENTE, OTOLARYNGOLOGY, NEUROPHYSIOLOGY. *Current Pos:* assoc prof, 68-70, PROF OTOLARYNGOL & DIR RES, DIV HEAD & NECK SURG, UNIV CALIF, LOS ANGELES, 70- *Personal Data:* b Valencia, Spain, July 13, 34; m 62; c 2. *Educ:* Univ Valencia, MD, 57, dipl pub health, 58, DMSc, 59. *Hon Degrees:* Dr, Univ Valencia, Spain, 82. *Honors & Awards:* Ugo Foscolo Medallion, Univ Pavia, Italy, 85. *Prof Exp:* Intern otolaryngol, Univ Valencia, 55-58; Marques de Urquijo Found fel, Univ Madrid, 58-60; NIH fel, Univ Chicago, 60-62 & Rockefeller Inst, 62-63; res assoc & guest investr neurophysiol, Rockefeller Univ, 63-64; asst prof physiol & otolaryngol, Vanderbilt Univ, 65-66, assoc prof otolaryngol & audiol & dir otolaryngol res, 66-68. *Concurrent Pos:* Dir res, Hope for Hearing Found, 76- *Mem:* Fel Acoust Soc Am; Am Physiol Soc; Collegium Oto-Rhino-Laryngologicum Amicitiae Sacrum; Asn Res Otolaryngol (pres, 77-78); Am Neurotology Soc; Soc Neurosci. *Res:* Physiopathology of the auditory and vestibular systems. *Mailing Add:* Div Head & Neck Surg Univ Calif Sch Med Los Angeles CA 90095-1624

HONSAKER, JOHN LEONARD, ATMOSPHERIC PHYSICS, COMPUTER GRAPHICS. *Current Pos:* RETIRED. *Personal Data:* b Pasadena, Calif, May 4, 34; m 56. *Educ:* Calif Inst Technol, BS, 55, PhD(physics), 65. *Prof Exp:* Physicist & staff mem, Los Alamos Sci Lab, 57-58; instr physics, Univ Chicago, 64-67; mem fac, Inst Earth & Planetary Physics, Univ Alta, 67-90. *Mem:* AAAS; Can Cartog Asn. *Res:* Nuclear structure and reaction mechanisms; controlled thermonuclear reactions; climatic change; computer cartography; micrometeorology; erosion analysis; multidimensional scaling and geometry. *Mailing Add:* 20450 Township Rd 510 Sherwood Park AB T8G 1E5 Can

HONSBERG, WOLFGANG, ORGANIC CHEMISTRY, POLYMER CHEMISTRY. *Current Pos:* SR TECH ASSOC, E I DU PONT DE NEMOURS & CO, 63- *Personal Data:* b Ludwigshafen, Ger, Aug 17, 29; m 58; c 2. *Educ:* Karlsruhe Tech Univ, dipl chem, 55, Dr rer nat, 58. *Prof Exp:* Res assoc radiation chem, Univ Chicago, 58-59, res assoc peroxides, Fla State Univ, 59-61, res assoc peptides, 62-63. *Mem:* Am Chem Soc Rubber Div. *Res:* Organic polyvalent iodine compounds; radiation chemistry; peroxides; peptides; heterocycles; polymerization; emulsions; curing of elastomers; polymer blends. *Mailing Add:* 2401 S Lori Lane Wilmington DE 19810

HONSINGER, VERNON BERTRAM, ELECTRICAL ENGINEERING. *Current Pos:* ELEC MACH CONSULT, 82- *Educ:* Univ Mich, BS. *Prof Exp:* From engr to mgr develop eng, Allis Chalmers, Norwood, Ohio, 45-73; consult develop eng, Advan Technol Ctr & mgr, Elec Systs Prog, Allis Chalmers, Milwaukee, Wis, 73-76; elec engr, Corp Res & Develop, Gen Elec, 76-82. *Concurrent Pos:* Elec engr, USN; lectr, Rensselaer Polytech Inst, 80. *Mem:* Fel Inst Elec & Electronics Engrs. *Res:* Electrical machinery; computer programming; permanent magnet machines; reluctance machines; induction machines; actuators; author of over 25 technical publication; 50 internal and contractual technical reports. *Mailing Add:* 6 Woodstead Rd Ballston Lake NY 12019

HONSTEAD, WILLIAM HENRY, CHEMICAL ENGINEERING. *Current Pos:* RETIRED. *Personal Data:* b Waterville, Kans, May 21, 16; m 40; c 3. *Educ:* Kans State Col, BS, 39, MS, 46; Iowa State Univ, PhD, 56. *Prof Exp:* Plant control chemist, Nat Aniline Div, Allied Chem & Dye Corp, NY, 39-43; from instr to prof chem eng, Kans State Univ, 43-83, head dept, 60-68, tech field rep, 68-70, dir, Kans Indust Exten Serv, 70-81, exec vpres, Res Found, 72-83. *Mem:* Am Chem Soc; Am Soc Eng Educ; Nat Soc Prof Engrs; Am Inst Chem Engrs. *Res:* Dehydration of vegetable materials, including grasses; industrial utilization of sorghum grains; heat transfer; fertilizer technology. *Mailing Add:* 2130 Meadowlark Rd Manhattan KS 66502-4557

HONTZEAS, S, nuclear chemistry, for more information see previous edition

HOO, CHEONG SENG, MATHEMATICS. *Current Pos:* from asst prof to assoc prof, 65-74, PROF MATH, UNIV ALTA, 74- *Personal Data:* b Malacca, Malaysia, Sept 15, 38; Can citizen; m 88, Wah S Tan. *Educ:* Univ Auckland, BSc, 60, MSc, 61; Syracuse Univ, PhD(math), 64. *Prof Exp:* Instr math, Univ Ill, Urbana, 64-65. *Concurrent Pos:* Nat Res Coun Can res grant, 66-91. *Mem:* Am Math Soc; Math Asn Am; Can Math Cong; Southeast Asia Math Soc. *Res:* Algebraic topology; category theory and theory of topological semigroups; homotopy theory and the theory of H-spaces; lattice theory; topological semigroups, MV, BCI, and BCK algebras. *Mailing Add:* Dept Math Sci Univ Alta Edmonton AB T6G 2G1 Can. *Fax:* 403-492-6826

HOO, JOE JIE, MEDICAL GENETICS, PEDIATRICS. *Current Pos:* PROF PEDIAT, STATE UNIV NY, SYRACUSE, 93- *Personal Data:* b Malang, Indonesia, July 7, 44; Can citizen; m 73, Lanlan Koo. *Educ:* Philipps Univ Marburg, WGer, MD, 72; FAAP(pediat) Am Acad Pediat, cert; Am Bd Med Genetics, 82. *Prof Exp:* Sr res assoc, Inst Human Genetics, Univ Hamburg, WGer, 79-81, med geneticist, 81-82; asst prof pediat, Univ Calgary, 82-85; assoc prof pediat, Univ Ill, Chicago, 85-93. *Mem:* Am Acad Pediat; Am Soc Human Genetics; Am Col Med Genetics. *Res:* Human karyotype-phenotype correlation; the origin and behavior of ring chromosome; usage of molecular genetic techniques in clinical cytogenetics; gene mapping; dysmorphology. *Mailing Add:* Dept Pediat State Univ NY Health Sci Ctr 750 E Adams St Syracuse NY 13210. *Fax:* 315-464-7564

HOOBER, J KENNETH, CHLOROPLAST MEMBRANE ASSEMBLY, CHLOROPHYLL SYNTHESIS. *Current Pos:* PROF & CHAIR BOT, ARIZ STATE UNIV, 91- *Personal Data:* b Lancaster, Pa, Sept 5, 38; m 60, Doris Zook; c Rebecca & Maria. *Educ:* Goshen Col, BA, 60; Univ Mich, PhD(biochem), 65. *Prof Exp:* USPHS fel cell biol, Rockefeller Univ, 66-68; asst prof biochem, Rutgers Med Sch, Col Med & Dent NJ, 68-71; assoc prof, Med Sch, Temple Univ, 71-77, prof biochem, 77-91. *Mem:* AAAS; Am Soc Plant Physiologists; Am Soc Biochem & Molecular Biol; Am Soc Photobiol; Am Soc Cell Biol; Am Soc Photobiol; Sigma Xi. *Res:* Assembly of chlorophyll-protein complexes and synthesis of the individual components; regulation of gene expression examined at the transcriptional and post-translational levels. *Mailing Add:* Ariz State Univ Box 871601 Tempe AZ 85287-1601. *Fax:* 602-965-6899; *E-Mail:* icjkh@asuvm.inre.asu.edu

HOOBLER, RAYMOND TAYLOR, ALGEBRAIC GEOMETRY. *Current Pos:* assoc prof, 75-77, PROF MATH CITY COL NY & GRAD CTR, CITY UNIV NEW YORK, 77- *Personal Data:* b Boston, Mass, Aug 14, 1941; m 90, Frances Kuehn; c Jason V & Aurora J. *Educ:* Oberlin Col, AB, 62; Univ Calif, Berkeley, MA, 64, PhD(math), 66. *Prof Exp:* Ritt instr math, Columbia Univ, 66-69; asst prof math, Grad Ctr, City Univ New York, 69-71, Rice Univ, 71-75. *Concurrent Pos:* Vis prof math, Tata Inst Fundamental Res, Bombay, 90-91; US-Indo res fel, Fulbright Found, 90-91. *Mem:* Am Math Soc. *Mailing Add:* 789 West End Ave No 4D New York NY 10025. *E-Mail:* rthcc@cunyvm.cuny.edu

HOOD, CLAUDE IAN, PATHOLOGY. *Current Pos:* from instr to prof, 56-91, EMER PROF PATH, COL MED, UNIV FLA, 91- *Personal Data:* b Purley, Eng, Jan 25, 25; nat US; m 52, Helen Hlobil; c Colin P & Sarah J. *Educ:* Univ Liverpool, MB, ChB, 48. *Prof Exp:* Casualty officer, Liverpool Stanley Hosp, 48-49; house physician, Kettering Gen Hosp, 49; resident med officer, St Andrews Hosp, 49-50; instr path, Cornell Univ, 50-56. *Concurrent Pos:* From asst resident to resident, NY Hosp, 50-56; asst med examr, Alachua County, Fla, 59-75; consult, Vet Admin Hosp, Gainesville, Fla, 74-78, chief lab serv, 78-88. *Mem:* Int Acad Path. *Res:* Medical teaching. *Mailing Add:* 4025 SW 18th St Gainesville FL 32608

HOOD, DONALD C, VISUAL SCIENCE. *Current Pos:* From asst prof to assoc prof psychol, Columbia Univ, 69-78, chmn dept, 75-78, vpres arts & sci, 82-87, PROF PSYCHOL, COLUMBIA UNIV, 78-, JAMES F BENDER PROF, 90- *Personal Data:* b North Merrick, NY, June 2, 42; m 78, Nancy E Epstein. *Educ:* State Univ NY, BA, 65; Brown Univ, MSc, 68, PhD(psychol), 70. *Concurrent Pos:* Mem, Comt Vision, Nat Acad Sci-Nat Res Coun, 87-91; trustee, Smith Col, 89- & Harry Guggenheim Found, 96- *Mem:* Asn Res Vision & Ophthal; Optical Soc Am; Am Asn Univ Professors; AAAS; Psychonomic Soc. *Res:* Behavioral and physiological structures of vision; academic administration. *Mailing Add:* 450 Riverside Dr New York NY 10027

HOOD, DONALD WILBUR, OCEANOGRAPHY. *Current Pos:* from assoc prof to prof, 54-65, prof marine sci & dir inst, 65-76, EMER PROF MARINE SCI, UNIV ALASKA, FAIRBANKS, 78-; OCEANOG CONSULT, 77- *Personal Data:* b New Castle, Pa, July 12, 18; m 45, Betty Jackson; c Beckie J (Davis), Barbara J & Susan M. *Educ:* Pa State Col, BS, 40; Okla Agr & Mech Col, MS, 42; Agr & Mech Col Tex, PhD(biochem, nutrit), 50. *Prof Exp:* Chem engr, E I Du Pont de Nemours & Co, Inc, 42-43; res chemist, Manhattan Proj, Univ Chicago, 44; chemist, Hanford Eng Works, 44-46; instr chem, Tex A&M Univ, 46-47, asst prof chem oceanog, 50-54. *Concurrent Pos:* NSF sr fel, 63-64; mem study sect environ sci & eng, NIH, 65-68 Int Comt Port & Coastal Eng under Arctic Conditions, 71, 73 & 75 & adv panel int decade ocean explor, NSF, 72-76; chmn, Gordon Conf Chem Oceanog, 72 & Alaska Comn Oceanog Advan Sci & Technol; consult, US Plywood/Champion Paper Co, Alyeska Pipeline Serv Co & US CEngr; vis prof, Seoul Nat Univ, 77-78. *Mem:* Am Chem Soc; Am Soc Limnol & Oceanog. *Res:* Chemical oceanography; organic chemistry of seawater; chemistry of carbon dioxide system; waste disposal and marine pollution. *Mailing Add:* PO Box 57 Friday Harbor WA 98250-0057

HOOD, EDWARD E, JR, NUCLEAR ENGINEERING. *Current Pos:* RETIRED. *Personal Data:* b Jonesville, NC, Sept 15, 30. *Educ:* NC State Col, BS, 52, MS, 53. *Prof Exp:* Engr, Gen Elec Co, 57-62, mgr supersonic trans eng proj, 62-67, vpres group exec, 72-73, vpres group exec power generation group, 73-77, vpres gen mgr, Com Eng Div, 68-93, vchmn, 79-93. *Concurrent Pos:* Mem, USAF, 52-56; mem bd, Nat Elec Mfrs Asn, Nat Action Coun Minorities Eng; chmn, bd gov, Aerospace Industs Asn, bd trustees, Rensselaer Polytech Inst, Steering Comt, Defense Indust Initiative Bus Ethics & Conduct & Adv Comt, Nat Security Telecommun. *Mem:* Nat Acad Eng; fel Am Inst Aeronaut & Astronaut; Aerospace Indust Asn. *Mailing Add:* 11674 Lake House Ct West Palm Beach FL 33408

HOOD, HORACE EDWARD, CHEMICAL PROCESS HAZARDS, RUNAWAY REACTIONS. *Current Pos:* PRES, H E HOOD INC, 91- *Personal Data:* b Sparta, Ill, Sept 16, 23; m 49, Gertrude Trygestad; c James, Chris, Robert & John. *Educ:* Univ Ill, BS, 44; Univ Minn, PhD(org chem), 50. *Prof Exp:* Res chemist, Res Ctr, Hercules Powder Co, 50-63, res supvr, 64-66; chem res supvr, Mo Chem Works, Hercules Inc, 67, tech supt, 67-70, res scientist, 71-77, res proj leader, Hercofina, 78-79, res assoc, 80-91. *Concurrent Pos:* Lectr reactive chem, Am Inst Chem Engrs, 91-95. *Mem:* Emer mem Am Chem Soc. *Res:* Process development; hydrocarbon oxidation; peroxides; production technology; chemical process hazards. *Mailing Add:* 1980 Superfine Lane Unit No 304 Wilmington DE 19802-4913. *E-Mail:* hehood@aol.com

HOOD, J MYRON, MATHEMATICS, BIOMATHEMATICS. *Current Pos:* PROF MATH, CALIF POLYTECH STATE UNIV, 77- *Personal Data:* b Billings, Mont, 41. *Educ:* Grinnell Col, BA, 63; Northwestern Univ, MS, 65; Wash Univ, PhD, 70. *Mem:* Math Asn Am; Acad Arts & Sci Am; Soc Conserv Biol Resource Modeling Asn. *Res:* Mathematics and biomathematics. *Mailing Add:* Math Dept Calif Polytech State Univ San Luis Obispo CA 93407

HOOD, JAMES WARREN, GEOLOGY. *Current Pos:* RETIRED. *Personal Data:* b Houston, Tex, Nov, 18, 25; m 46; c 3. *Educ:* Univ Tex-Austin, BS, 48. *Prof Exp:* Ground water hydrologist, Water Resources Div, US Geol Surv, 48-84. *Concurrent Pos:* Consult & tech editing, 84-88. *Mem:* Geol Soc Am; Am Geophys Union. *Res:* Analysis of ground water systems; assisted in preparation of technical reports for publication, results given in 40 plus publications. *Mailing Add:* 1209 Princeton Ave Salt Lake City UT 84105

HOOD, JERRY A, electrical engineering, for more information see previous edition

HOOD, JOHN MACK, JR, PHYSICS. *Current Pos:* LECTR NATURAL SCI, SAN DIEGO STATE UNIV, 75- *Personal Data:* b Alamosa, Colo, June 11, 25; m 46; c 3. *Educ:* Univ Colo, BA, 49, MA, 51; Univ Reading, PhD, 69; Univ London, DIC, 67. *Prof Exp:* Instr physics, Univ Colo, 49-51; res engr, NAm Aviation Co, 51-53; assoc engr, Univ Calif, 53-55; supvry physicist, USN Electronics Lab, 55-75. *Concurrent Pos:* Consult, Galileo Electrooptics, 80- *Mem:* Optical Soc Am; Soc Photo-Optical Instrumentation Engrs; Sigma Xi. *Res:* Geophysics; optical instrument design; laser technology and systems; visual systems engineering; theory of coherent imaging systems; history of science. *Mailing Add:* 3802 Point Loma Ave San Diego CA 92106-2028

HOOD, JOSEPH, SOILS. *Current Pos:* From asst prof to assoc prof, 49-59, PROF AGRON & SOILS, AUBURN UNIV, 59- *Personal Data:* b Commerce, Ga, Apr 14, 24; m 46; c 1. *Educ:* Univ Ga, BSA, 47; Purdue Univ, MS, 49; Cornell Univ, PhD(soils), 54. *Mem:* Fel Am Soc Agron; Soil Sci Soc Am; Sigma Xi. *Res:* Ion interactions in soils and plants; potassium status of soils; fertilizer placement; soil classification and land use. *Mailing Add:* Dept Agron & Soils Auburn Univ Auburn AL 36830

HOOD, LAMARTINE FRAIN, FOOD CHEMISTRY. *Current Pos:* DEAN, COL AGR, PA STATE UNIV, 86- *Personal Data:* b Johnstown, Pa, Feb 25, 37; m 60; c 3. *Educ:* Pa State Univ, BS, 59, PhD(food sci), 68; Univ Minn, MS, 63. *Honors & Awards:* William F Geddis Mem Lectr, NW sect, Am Asn Cereal Chemists, 85. *Prof Exp:* From asst to prof, Food Sci & Dir Agr Exp Sta, Cornell Univ, 68-86. *Mem:* Am Asn Cereal Chemists; Inst Food Technologists. *Res:* Starch chemistry; comparative electron microscopic and chemical studies of the interactions among food ingredients during processing and storage; effect of processing on the nutritional quality of foods. *Mailing Add:* Pa State Univ 201 Ag Admin Bldg University Park PA 16802-2600

HOOD, LEROY E, IMMUNOGENETICS, GENETICS. *Current Pos:* from asst prof to prof, Univ Wash, 70-77, Bowles prof biol, 77-92, chmn biol, 80-89, GATES PROF & CHAIR MOLECULAR BIOTECHNOL, UNIV WASH, 92-; DIR, NSF CTR MOLECULAR BIOTECHNOL, 89- *Personal Data:* b Missoula, Mont, Oct 10, 38; m 63, Valerie Logan; c Eran & Margie. *Educ:* Calif Inst Technol, BS, 60, PhD(biochem), 68; Johns Hopkins Univ, MD, 64. *Hon Degrees:* DSc, Mont State Univ, 86, Mt Sinai Sch Med, City Univ New York, 87, Univ BC, Vancouver, Can, 88, Univ Southern Calif, 89, Wesleyan Univ, 92; DHL, Johns Hopkins Univ. *Honors & Awards:* Lasker Award; Dickson Prize. *Prof Exp:* USPHS fel, Calif Inst Technol, 64-67; sr investr immunol, Nat Cancer Inst, 67-70. *Concurrent Pos:* Dreyfus teacher-scholar, 74. *Mem:* Nat Acad Sci; AAAS; Am Asn Immunologists. *Res:* Genetics & evolution of multigene systems; genetics & evolution of immune recognition antibodies, T-cell receptors, MHC molecules; protein evolution; recombinant DNA; biotechnology; genomics large scale DNA sequencing. *Mailing Add:* Dept Molecular Biotechnol Univ Wash Box 357730 Seattle WA 98195-7730. *Fax:* 206-685-7301; *E-Mail:* tawney@u.washington.edu

HOOD, LON(NIE) LAMAR, STRATOSPHERIC PHYSICS, PHYSICS OF EARLY SOLAR SYSTEMS. *Current Pos:* from res assoc to sr res assoc, 79-83, from asst res scientist to assoc res scientist, 83-95, SR RES SCIENTIST, LUNAR & PLANETARY LAB, UNIV ARIZ, 95- *Personal Data:* b Marshall, Tex, June 13, 49; m 74; c Teresa, Christina & James. *Educ:* Northeast La Univ, BS, 71, MS, 73; Univ Calif, Los Angeles, PhD(geophys), 79. *Prof Exp:* Teaching asst, Dept Physics, Northeastern LA Univ, 71-73; res asst, Inst Geophys & Planetary Physics, Univ Calif, Los Angeles, 75-79. *Concurrent Pos:* Prin investr res grants, NASA, 81-, NSF, 90- & Dept Energy, 93- *Mem:* Am Geophys Union; AAAS; Int Asn Geomagnetism & Aeronomy; Europ Geophys Soc; Am Meteorol Soc; Int Asn Meteorol & Atmospheric Sci. *Res:* Physics and chemistry of the stratosphere; lunar geophysics with emphasis on paleomagnetism; anthropogenic trends in ozone; effects of solar ultraviolet variability on the stratosphere. *Mailing Add:* Lunar & Planetary Lab Univ Ariz Tucson AZ 85721-0092. *E-Mail:* lon@lpl.arizona.edu

HOOD, RICHARD FRED, physics; deceased, see previous edition for last biography

HOOD, ROBERT L, INORGANIC CHEMISTRY. *Current Pos:* MGR LAB SERV, COUNTRY PRIDE FOODS, 76- *Personal Data:* b Shreveport, La, Dec 7, 29; m 56; c 3. *Educ:* Centenary Col, BS, 50; Univ Tex, Austin, PhD(chem), 69. *Prof Exp:* Eng clerk, Gas Measurement Dept, Tex Eastern Transmission Corp, 50-54; dir, Gas Lab, Centenary Col, 54-76, asst prof, 68-72, lectr chem, 72-76. *Mem:* AAAS; Am Chem Soc. *Res:* Reactions of the coordinated ethylenediamine ligand in his (ethylenediamine)-palladium (II) iodide. *Mailing Add:* 1922 Ridgewood El Dorado AR 71730

HOOD, ROBIN JAMES, PHYSICAL CHEMISTRY, ANALYTICAL CHEMISTRY. *Current Pos:* DIR, CENT INSTRUMENTATION FACIL, WAYNE STATE UNIV, 81- *Personal Data:* b Detroit, Mich, Apr 1, 42; m 65; c 2. *Educ:* Mich State Univ, BS, 66; Wayne State Univ, PhD(chem), 73. *Prof Exp:* Asst prof chem, Univ Nebr, 73-75; asst prof chem, Marygrove Col, 75-81. *Mem:* AAAS; Am Chem Soc; Am Phys Soc. *Res:* Solid state spectroscopy; microcomputers in undergraduate teaching laboratory. *Mailing Add:* 75 Chem Wayne State Univ Detroit MI 48202

HOOD, RODNEY TABER, HISTORY OF MATHEMATICS. *Current Pos:* from assoc prof to prof, 60-86, chmn dept, 62-72, 75-78, EMER PROF MATH, FRANKLIN COL, 87. *Personal Data:* b Kenmore, NY, Sept 29, 24; m 49; c 3. *Educ:* Oberlin Col, AB, 46; Univ Wis, MA, 47, PhD, 50; Colgate-Rochester Divinity Sch, BD, 53; Univ Chicago, MA, 65. *Honors &*

Awards: Cert Meritorious Serv, Math Asn Am, 89. *Prof Exp:* Instr math, Beloit Col, 49-50; asst Greek, Colgate-Rochester Divinity Sch, 52-53; asst math, Univ Chicago, 54-56; asst prof, Ohio Univ,56-60. *Mem:* Math Asn Am; Am Math Soc; Sigma Xi. *Res:* Differential equations; geometry; history of mathematics; number theory. *Mailing Add:* 1015 Ina Circle Franklin IN 46131-9194

HOOD, RONALD DAVID, TERATOLOGY, DEVELOPMENTAL TOXICOLOGY. *Current Pos:* From asst prof to assoc prof, 68-78, PROF BIOL, UNIV ALA, 78- *Personal Data:* b El Paso, Tex, July 5, 41; m 72, Barbara K Owen; c Rebecca. *Educ:* Tex Tech Univ, BS, 63, MS, 65; Purdue Univ, PhD(physiol), 69. *Concurrent Pos:* Consult, 78-; consult environ med, US Vet Admin, 83-84; spec consult, Sci Adv Bd, US Environ Protection Agency, 83-93; adj prof pub health, Univ Ala, Birmingham, 88- *Mem:* Soc Study Reproduction; Teratol Soc; Am Asn Lab Animal Sci; Soc Toxicol. *Res:* Experimental teratology and developmental toxicology: arsenic teratogenicity, including metabolism and distribution; mycotoxin teratogenicity; in vitro teratogenicity testing; contract research in teratology; teratogenic mechanisms; teratogenicity screening systems; maternally-mediated effects. *Mailing Add:* Dept Biol Sci Univ Ala Box 870344 Tuscaloosa AL 35487-0344. *Fax:* 205-348-1786

HOOD, SAMUEL LOWRY, BIOLOGY GENERAL, RADIATION BIOLOGY. *Current Pos:* prof, 69-83, EMER PROF BIOL, CALIF UNIV PA, 83- *Personal Data:* b Cambridge, Ohio, July 28, 18; m 50; c 1. *Educ:* Col Wooster, AB, 40; Cornell Univ, PhD(biochem), 49. *Prof Exp:* Biochemist soil fertil, Ohio Agr Exp Sta, 41; biochemist cereal chem, Fed Soft Wheat Lab, 42-43, USDA Nutrit Lab, Cornell Univ, 43-44 & 46-48; biochemist agr radiotracer chem, Agr Res Prog, AEC, Oak Ridge, 48-53; biochemist & radiation biologist, Charles F Kettering Found, 53-63; sr scientist, Nuclear Sci & Eng Corp, 63-68; res assoc, Univ Pittsburgh, 68-69. *Mem:* AAAS; Am Chem Soc; Radiation Res Soc; Am Inst Biol Sci; NY Acad Sci; Sigma Xi. *Res:* Mineral metabolism; radioisotope tracers; agricultural chemistry; cell culture; radiation biology, exobiology. *Mailing Add:* 301 Milstead Way Greenville SC 29615

HOOD, WILLIAM BOYD, JR, INTERNAL MEDICINE, CARDIOLOGY. *Current Pos:* PROF, DEPT MED, CARDIOL UNIT, UNIV ROCHESTER MED CTR, 82- *Personal Data:* b Sylacauga, Ala, Mar 25, 32; m 72, Katherine Todd; c Jefferson B. *Educ:* Davidson Col, BS, 54; Harvard Med Sch, MD, 58; Am Bd Internal Med, dipl, 67. *Prof Exp:* House officer med, Peter Bent Brigham Hosp, 58-59, jr resident to sr resident, 59-60 & 62-63; res assoc, Sch Pub Health, Harvard Univ, 65-67, assoc, Sch Med, 67-69, from asst prof to assoc prof, Harvard Med Sch, 69-71; from assoc prof to prof med, Sch Med, Boston Univ, 71-82. *Concurrent Pos:* NSF fels, Cardiol Lab, St Thomas' Hosp, London, Eng, 60-61 & Cardiol Lab, Peter Bent Brigham Hosp, Boston, 61-62; Mass Heart Asn, Am Heart Asn & NIH grants, 71- *Mem:* AAAS; Am Soc Clin Invest; Am Fedn Clin Res; Am Col Cardiol; Am Physiol Soc; Asn Am Physicians. *Res:* Investigation of normal and abnormal cardiovascular hemodynamics in man and animals; coronary artery disease and coronary ischemia; congestive heart failure. *Mailing Add:* Dept Med Cardiol Unit Univ Rochester Med Ctr Box 679 Rochester NY 14642. *Fax:* 716-473-1573

HOOD, WILLIAM CALVIN, PETROLEUM GEOLOGY, GEOCHEMISTRY. *Current Pos:* RETIRED. *Personal Data:* b Kansas City, Mo, June 7, 37; m 69, Sandra D Peterson; c 3. *Educ:* Univ Mo, BA, 59; Univ Mont, PhD(geol), 64. *Prof Exp:* Lectr geol, Southern Ill Univ, 62-63; asst prof, NC State Univ, 63-65 & Univ SFla, 65-68; from assoc prof to prof, Southern Ill Univ, Carbondale, 68-81; area geologist, Amoco Prod Co, 81-87, proj geologist, 87-91, mgr strategic staffing, 91-93, explor renewal team, 93-95. *Mem:* Clay Minerals Soc; Am Inst Prof Geologists; Am Asn Petrol Geologists. *Res:* Mineralogy and geochemistry of surface and near surface geologic processes; origin and migration of hydrocarbons. *Mailing Add:* 515 Dove Ct Grand Junction CO 81503

HOOFNAGLE, JAY H, DIGESTIVE DISEASES. *Current Pos:* clin dir, 86-88, SR INVESTR, LIVER DIS SECT, DIGESTIVE DIS BR, NAT INST DIABETES & DIGESTIVE & KIDNEY DIS, NIH, 78-, DIR, DIV DIGESTIVE DIS & NUTRIT, 88- *Personal Data:* b Washington, DC, July 31, 43; m; c 3. *Educ:* Univ Va, BA, 65; Yale Med Sch, MD, 77; Am Bd Internal Med, cert, 76; Am Bd Gastroenterol, cert, 79. *Prof Exp:* Intern, Internal Med, Univ Va Hosp, 70-71, resident, 71-72; staff assoc Hepatitis Br, Div Blood & Blood Prod, Bur Biologics, Food & Drug Admin, 72-74, actg dir, 74-76; asst chief res med, Vet Admin Hosp, Washington, DC, 75-76, res gastroenterol-hepatology, 76-78. *Concurrent Pos:* Mem, Clin Res Subpanel, Nat Inst Diabetes & Digestive & Kidney Dis, NIH, 80-, med bd, Clin Ctr 86-88; chmn, Credentials Comt, Clin Ctr, NIH, 87-88, Digestive Dis, Interagency Coord Comt, 88- *Mem:* Am Asn Study Liver Dis (pres elect, 90-); Am Soc Clin Invest; AAAS; Int Soc Interferon Res; Am Gastroenterol Asn; Am Soc Parenteral & Enteral Nutrit. *Res:* Viral hepatitis, types A, B, C and D; epidemiology and serology of viral hepatitis; immunology of acute and chronic viral hepatitis; therapy of viral hepatitis; autoimmune liver disease including autoimmune chronic active hepatitis primary biliary cirrhosis and sclerosing cholangitis. *Mailing Add:* NIH Bldg D10 Rm 4D52 Bethesda MD 20816-1423

HOOGENBOOM, GERRIT, CROP SIMULATION, AGROMETEOROLOGY. *Current Pos:* asst prof, Dept Agr Eng, 89-95, ASSOC PROF, DEPT BIOL & AGR ENG, UNIV GA, 95- *Personal Data:* b Monster, Neth, Dec 19, 55; m 84, Carol J Wilkerson. *Educ:* Agr Univ, Wageningen, Neth, BSc, 78, MSc, 81; Auburn Univ, PhD(agron & soils), 85. *Honors & Awards:* Step Award, Am Soc Agron, 84. *Prof Exp:* Res asst, Auburn Univ, 81-85; assoc, Univ Fla, 85-89. *Concurrent Pos:* Vis res scientist, Scottish Hort Res Orgn, Dundee, 78-79, Agr Res Orgn, Israel, 79; consult, Winrock Int, 91; lectr, Res Inst Soil Sci & Agr Chem, Budapest, Hungary, 91 & 92, Univ Hawaii, 92 & Int Fertilizer Develop Ctr, 93. *Mem:* Am Soc Agr Engrs; Am Soc Agron; Crop Sci Soc Am; Soil Sci Soc Am; Am Geophys Union; Soc Comput Simulation. *Res:* Effects of environment on crop growth, development and production using computer simulation; develop an automated environmental monitoring network for the state of Georgia. *Mailing Add:* Dept Biol & Agr Eng Univ Ga Griffin GA 30223-1797. *E-Mail:* gerrit@bae.uga.edu

HOOGHEEM, THOMAS JOHN, ENVIRONMENTAL ENGINEERING, CIVIL ENGINEERING. *Current Pos:* environ specialist water, 76-82, sr environ specialist, 82-84, ENVIRON MGR, MONSANTO AGR PROD CO, MONSANTO CO, 85- *Personal Data:* b Fulton, Ill, Dec 18, 51; m 74. *Educ:* Univ Ill, BS, 73, MS, 74. *Prof Exp:* Engr civil eng, Moline, Ill, 66-72; res asst water pollution, Univ Ill, 73-74; environ engr, Tenn Valley Authority, 74-76. *Mem:* Water Pollution Control Fedn; Am Inst Chem Engrs; Soc Environ Toxicol & Chem. *Res:* Water pollution control, especially desalination, removal of toxic organics and sampling of priority pollutants; chemical surveillance and monitoring systems; air pollution and control of hydrocarbons from tire manufcture and styrene-butadiene manufacture; dioxin and hazardous waste sampling; health and environmental aspects of herbicides. *Mailing Add:* 651 Charbray Dr Ballwin MO 63011

HOOK, DEREK JOHN, MICROBIAL BIOCHEMISTRY. *Current Pos:* ASSOC DIR, NPS PHARMACEUT, 97-, DIR DRUG DISCOVERY. *Personal Data:* b London, UK, Aug 2, 47. *Educ:* Hull Univ, UK, BSc, 68; Dalhousie Univ, NS, PhD(biol), 72. *Prof Exp:* Fel biosynthesis, Purdue Univ, 72-74; biochemist pharmaceut, Raylo Chem, Bristol Myers Indust Div, 74-77, biochemist, 78-83, res inst, 83-96. *Mem:* Am Chem Soc; Soc Microbiol; AAAS; Am Soc Biochem & Molecular Biol. *Res:* Natural product isolation and fermentations of microorganisms in connection with the development of new drugs and antibiotics; biosynthesis of pharmacologically important compounds; high throughput screening automation, robotics drug discovery. *Mailing Add:* NPS Pharmaceut 420 Chipeta Way Salt Lake City UT 84108. *E-Mail:* dhook@npsp.com

HOOK, DONALD D, FORESTRY, TREE PHYSIOLOGY. *Current Pos:* prof & dir, Belle W Baruch Forest Sci Inst, 73-81, PROF, DEPT FORESTRY, CLEMSON UNIV, 81-, PROF & DIR, FOREST WETLANDS RES PROG, SOUTHEASTERN FOREST EXP STA, CLEMSON UNIV & USDA. *Personal Data:* b Cleveland, Okla, June 21, 33; m 56; c 3. *Educ:* Utah State Univ, BS, 61, MS, 62; Univ Ga, PhD(tree physiol), 68. *Prof Exp:* Res forester, Intermountain Forest & Exp Sta, 62; res asst physiol, Univ Minn, 62-63; asst silviculturist, Southeastern Forest Exp Sta, 63-64; from assoc silviculturist to silviculturist, Forest Serv, USDA, 65-68, from plant physiologist to prin plant physiologist, 68-70; assoc prof silvicult & physiol, Univ Ky, 70-73. *Concurrent Pos:* Mem, Southeastern Forest Exp Sta Ecol Res Comt, 64-68 & Southern Forest Environ Res Coun, 64-70; sabattical leave, Pac Northwest Res Sta, 84-85; chair, Appalachian Soc Am Foresters, 92. *Mem:* Soc Am Foresters; Soc Wetland Scientists. *Res:* Factors affecting the relative flood tolerance of tree species; aeration systems in trees; vegetative propagation of tree species; physiology and ecology of wetland species and ecosystems. *Mailing Add:* Dept Forestry Clemson Univ Clemson SC 29632-0001. *Fax:* 803-724-4152

HOOK, EDWARD WATSON, JR, INTERNAL MEDICINE, INFECTIOUS DISEASES. *Current Pos:* chmn, Dept Med & physician-in-chief, Hosp, 69-90, dir humanities Med, 90-96, HENRY B MULHOLLAND PROF MED, DEPT HUMANITIES IN MED, SCH MED, UNIV VA, 69- *Personal Data:* b Sumter, SC, Aug 10, 24; m 49, Jessie Thurecht; c Robert R, Jane (Brosig), Susan (Norton) & Edward W III. *Educ:* Wofford Col, BS, 43; Emory Univ, MD, 49; Am Bd Internal Med, dipl, 58. *Hon Degrees:* Med Col Pa, DMSc, 86. *Honors & Awards:* Helen & Payne Whitney Distinguished Lectr, North Shore Univ, 77; Paul S Rhoads Lectr, 77; Shaia Lectr, Med Col Va, 77; Robert H Moser Lectr, Am Col Physicians, 85; George Pedigo Lectr, Univ Louisville, 88; Marion D Hargrove Sr lectr, La State Univ, 90. *Prof Exp:* Intern med, Univ Hosps, Univ Minn, Minneapolis, 49-50; from jr asst resident to resident, Grady Mem Hosp, Atlanta, Ga, 50-55; instr, Sch Med, Emory Univ, 54-56; from instr to asst prof, Johns Hopkins Univ, 56-59; from assoc prof to prof, Cornell Univ, 59-69. *Concurrent Pos:* Attend physician, NY Hosp, 59-69; mem, Allergy & Immunol Study Sect, Nat Inst Allergy & Infectious Dis, 66-70, numerous comts, Am Bd Internal Med & Am Col Physicians, 72-90, Bd Int Health, Nat Acad Sci, 84-87 & US deleg, US-Japan Coop Med Sci Prog, 84-; ed, Antimicrobial Agents & Chemother, 72-80, Am J Med, 74-79 & Current Opinion Infectious Dis, 88-90; Mary W Barr vis prof med, NY Hosp, Cornell Med Ctr, 76, Aaron Feder vis prof, Med Col, 88; M Glenn Koenig vis prof, Vanderbilt Univ, 76; vis prof, Tufts-New Eng Med Ctr, 78, Sch Med, Univ Louisville, 88 & La State Univ, 90; hon prof, Univ Bahia, Brazil. *Mem:* Inst Med-Nat Acad Sci; fel Infectious Dis Soc Am (pres, 75-76); Am Soc Clin Invest; Asn Am Physicians; Am Clin & Climat Asn; fel Am Col Physicians (pres elect, 84-85, pres, 85-86); hon fel Royal Australian Col Physicians; Asn Professors Med (pres, 81-82); fel AAAS; Am Asn Immunologists; NY Acad Sci. *Res:* Infectious diseases with emphasis on pathogenesis; salmonella infections; activity of antibiotics; interactions between the humanities and medicine. *Mailing Add:* Dept Med Univ Va Sch Med PO Box 359 Charlottesville VA 22908. *Fax:* 804-924-5986; *E-Mail:* ewh@virginia.edu

HOOK, ERNEST, EPIDEMIOLOGY, TERATOLOGY. *Current Pos:* PROF PEDIAT, UNIV CALIF, 88- *Personal Data:* b New York, NY. *Educ:* Oberlin Col, BA, 56; Univ Calif, Berkeley, MA, 58; NU Univ, MD, 62. *Prof Exp:* From intern to resident pediat, Univ Minn, 62-65; fel, Univ Wash, 65-68; from asst prof to prof, Albany Med Col, 68-78, prof pediat, 78-88; chief human ecol sect, State Dept Health, NY, 69-74, chief epidemiol & human ecol, Birth Defects Inst, 74-81, chief genetics sect, Bur Child Health, 81-88, res physician, 81-88. *Mem:* Am Soc Human Genetics; Soc Epidemiol Res; Soc Pediat Res; Teratology Soc; Environ Mutagen Soc; Am Statist Asn. *Res:* Epidemiology of birth defects; human population cytogenetics; human mutagenesis; teratology; pediatrics and medical genetics. *Mailing Add:* Warren Hall MCH Sch Pub Health Warren Hall Berkeley CA 94720-0001

HOOK, GARY EDWARD RAUMATI, PULMONARY BIOCHEMISTRY. *Current Pos:* vis assoc, Nat Inst Environ Health Sci, 70-74, sr staff fel, 74-79, sect head biochem path, 79-93, CHIEF ENVIRON HEALTH REOSPECTIVE, 93- *Personal Data:* b Wellington, NZ, Jan 31, 42; US citizen; m 65; c 4. *Educ:* Victoria Univ, Wellington, NZ, BSc, 63, MSc, 64, PhD(biochem), 68, DSc, 86. *Honors & Awards:* Award of Merit, NIH, 87. *Prof Exp:* Jr lectr biochem, Victoria Univ, Wellington, NZ, 67-68; lectr, Univ Wales, Gt Brit, 68-70. *Concurrent Pos:* Co-ed, Environ Health Perspectives, 73-; asst prof, Dept Med, Duke Univ, 76-; assoc prof curric toxicol, Univ NC, 80-85, prof 85- *Mem:* Biochem Soc Gt Brit. *Res:* Regulation of pulmonary epithelial secretions; research aimed at elucidating mechanisms through which alveolar type II cells are activated and the subcellular events that lead to increased synthesis and hypersecretion of surfactant phosphospholids by those activated cells. *Mailing Add:* Nat Inst Environ Health Sci (WC-01) PO Box 12233 Research Triangle Park NC 27709

HOOK, JAMES EDWARD, AGRONOMY, ENVIRONMENTAL SCIENCE. *Current Pos:* from asst prof to assoc prof, 78-95, PROF AGRON, UNIV GA, 95- *Personal Data:* b Washington, DC, Apr 24, 47; m 68; c 5. *Educ:* Pa State Univ, BS, 69, MS, 71, PhD(agron), 75. *Prof Exp:* Res asst agron, Pa State Univ, 71-75; res assoc, Mich State Univ, 75-78. *Concurrent Pos:* Assoc ed, J Prod Agr & Soil Sci Soc Am J. *Mem:* Fel Am Soc Agron; Soil Sci Soc Am; Coun Agr Sci & Technol; AAAS. *Res:* Soil-water-plant relations; irrigation management; waste water, sludge and solid waste treatment on land; regional water resources; pesticide impact assessments. *Mailing Add:* Dept Crop & Soil Sci Coastal Plain Exp Sta PO Box 748 Tifton GA 31793-0748. *Fax:* 912-386-7293; *E-Mail:* jimhook@tifton.cpes.peachnet.edu

HOOK, JERRY B, TOXICOLOGY, DRUG DEVELOPMENT. *Current Pos:* PRES & CHIEF EXEC OFFICER, SPARTA PHARMACEUT, INC, 96- *Personal Data:* b Elk City, Okla, Sept 7, 37; m 85, Jacqueline H Smith; c Bruce G & Marilyn (McKenna). *Educ:* Wash State Univ, BS & BPharm, 60; Univ Iowa, MS, 64, PhD(pharm), 66. *Hon Degrees:* DSc, John Jay Col Criminal Justice, New York. *Prof Exp:* Asst, Wash State Univ, 57-60; from asst prof to prof pharmacol, Mich State Univ, 66-85, prof toxicol, 78-83, dir, Ctr Environ Toxicol, 80-83; vpres, Preclin Res & Develop, Smith Kline & French Labs, 83-87, vpres, Worldwide, 87-88, actg vpres res, 88-89, vpres, Res & Develop, 89-90, sr vpres & dir, Res & Develop, Smithkline Beecham Pharmaceut, 90-93; pres & chief exec officer, Lexin Pharmaceut Corp, 93-96. *Concurrent Pos:* Adj prof, Univ Mich, 77 & Philadelphia Col Pharm & Sci, 83-86; vis scientist, Imp Chem Industs, Alderley Park, Eng, 79-80; Burroughs-Wellcome vis prof, Univ NDak, 81; mem adv comt, Nat Toxicol Prog, 82-86, Deer rev panel experts, 82-86, chmn, 84-86, adv bd, Toxicol Res & Training Ctr, John Jay Col Criminal Justice, New York, 86-91; adj prof pharmacol & toxicol, Mich State Univ, 83-; vis sci, Fedn Am Soc Exp Biol, Univ PR Med Sch, 84, Herbert H Lehman Col of City Univ, Bronx, NY, 85, John Jay Col Criminal Justice, New York, 87, Calif State Univ, Long Beach, 88, Pembroke State Univ, NC, 89; adj prof pharmacol, Temple Univ, 86-93. *Mem:* Am Soc Pharmacol & Exp Therapeut; Soc Toxicol (vpres elect, 85-86, vpres, 86-87, pres, 87-88). *Res:* Renal toxicology with emphasis on biomedical mechanisms of cellular damage; role of kidney in metabolic activation; nephrotoxicity in senescence; perinatal toxicology; developmental nephrology; developmental pharmacology. *Mailing Add:* Sparta Pharmaceut Inc Pa Bus Campus Rock Plaza III 111 Rock Rd Horsham PA 19044-2310

HOOK, JOHN W, GEOLOGY, APPLIED, ECONOMIC & ENGINEERING. *Current Pos:* RETIRED. *Personal Data:* b Capon Bridge, WVa, June 11, 22; m 49; c 4. *Educ:* Univ Tenn, AB, 47. *Prof Exp:* Geologist, Am Zinc Co, 47-54 & Reynolds Metals Co, 54-74; consult, John W Hook & Assoc, 74-86. *Concurrent Pos:* Prin investr, Minerals availability Syst, Bauxite Pac NW State Ore & US Bur Mines, 74-76; geothermal consult, NW Natural Gas Co, 76-80 & Eugene Water & elect Bd, 78-81; mem, Geothermal Resources Coun; gen partner, Sea-Tac Geothermal Co, 79-; pres, Blue Lake Geothermal Co, 87. *Mem:* Fel Geol Soc Am; Soc Econ Geologists. *Res:* Geological structure and hydrothermal systems; development of the theory of solution breccias in the East Tennesse Zinc District which led to the discovery of Young Mine. *Mailing Add:* 7315 Battle Creek Rd SE Salem OR 97301

HOOK, MAGNUS AO, CONNECTIVE TISSUE. *Current Pos:* DIR, CTR MATRIX BIOL, 92- *Personal Data:* b St Malm, Sweden, Sept 10, 46. *Educ:* Univ Uppsala, Sweden, PhD(med chem), 74. *Prof Exp:* Assoc prof biochem, Univ Ala, Birmingham, 80-92. *Mem:* Am Soc Cell Biol; Am Soc Biol Chemists. *Mailing Add:* Ctr Matrix Biol Tex A&M Univ IBT 2121 W Holcombe Blvd Houston TX 77030-3303. *Fax:* 713-677-7576

HOOK, ROLLIN EARL, METALLURGICAL ENGINEERING. *Current Pos:* res engr, Armco Steel Corp, 67-68, sr res metallurgist, 68-70, res assoc, 70-75, sr staff metallurgist, 75-81, PRIN RES METALLURGIST, ARMCO INC, 81- *Personal Data:* b Highland, Ind, Nov 26, 34; m 56, Lois Cotter; c Paul & Cheryl. *Educ:* Purdue Univ, BS, 56; Ohio State Univ, MS, 59, PhD(metall eng), 66. *Prof Exp:* Metallurgist, Dow Chem Co, 56-57 & Aerospace Res Labs, Wright-Patterson AFB, 57-67. *Concurrent Pos:* Vis prof, Ohio State Univ, 81, var comts, Am Soc Metals Int. *Mem:* Fel Am Soc Metals Int. *Res:* Deep drawing sheet steels; alloy development; plastic deformation and fracture; yielding phenomena; strain aging behavior; iron and nickel aluminides; formability; crystallographic textures; strip casting. *Mailing Add:* Res Technol Armco Inc 705 Curtis St Middletown OH 45044-3999. *Fax:* 937-425-2587

HOOK, WILLIAM ARTHUR, MICROBIOLOGY, IMMUNOLOGY. *Current Pos:* CONSULT, 92- *Personal Data:* b Washington, DC, Apr 24, 30; m 56; c Carol S & Walter B. *Educ:* Univ Md, BS, 53, MS, 56, PhD(microbiol), 65. *Prof Exp:* Lab asst bact, Livestock Sanit Serv Lab, Md, 51-53, lab technician, 53-54; asst, Univ Md, 54-56; microbiologist serol, Walter Reed Army Inst Res, 56-66; microbiologist, Nat Cancer Inst, 66-68; res microbiologist, Lab Immunol, Nat Inst Dent Res, 68-92. *Mem:* Emer mem Am Asn Immunol; emer mem Am Soc Microbiol; fel Am Acad Microbiol. *Res:* Substances in natural resistance to infection; immunological mediators of inflammation; histamine release from basophils and mast cells. *Mailing Add:* 4008 Jeffrey St Wheaton MD 20906-4227. *Fax:* 301-496-2443; *E-Mail:* cwa@cu.nih.gov

HOOKE, ROBERT, MATHEMATICS, STATISTICS. *Current Pos:* RETIRED. *Personal Data:* b Chattanooga, Tenn, Apr 8, 18; m 41, Annis Hines; c William Hines & John A. *Educ:* Univ NC, BA, 38, MA, 39; Princeton Univ, AM, 40, PhD(math), 42. *Prof Exp:* Instr math, NC State Univ, 41-43, asst prof, 43-46; assoc prof, Univ of the South, 46-51; mem staff, Opers Eval Group, US Navy, Mass Inst Technol, 51-52; res assoc, Princeton Univ, 52-55; res mathematician, Westinghouse Elec Corp, 54-56, mgr statist sect, 56-63, mgr, Math Dept, 63-79. *Concurrent Pos:* Consult, 79-83. *Mem:* Fel AAAS; fel Am Statist Asn. *Res:* Applied statistics; design of experiments; sampling from finite populations. *Mailing Add:* 592 Central Dr Southern Pines NC 28387

HOOKE, ROGER LEBARON, GEOLOGY. *Current Pos:* From asst prof to assoc prof 65-79, PROF GEOL, UNIV MINN, MINNEAPOLIS, 79- *Personal Data:* b Glenridge, NJ, Jan 3, 39; m 61, Ann Peck; c Bruce G & Lyn P. *Educ:* Harvard Univ, BA, 61; Calif Inst Technol, PhD(geol), 65. *Honors & Awards:* Wiley Award, Brit Geomorphological Res Group, 93. *Concurrent Pos:* Guest researcher, Univ Uppsala, Sweden, 72-73 & Univ Stockholm, Sweden, 80-81; assoc dir res, Tarfala Field Sta, Sweden, 81- *Mem:* Fel Geol Soc Am; Glaciol Soc. *Res:* Processes on alluvial fans in arid regions; geomorphic evolution of the tongue of the ocean, Bahamas, using deep submersible Alvin; glaciological studies, Barnes Ice Cap, Baffin Island, Canada; distribution of shear stress and sediment in meandering rivers; glaciological studies on subpolar glaciers, Tarfala Field Station, Sweden. *Mailing Add:* 1917 Pleasant St St Paul MN 55113. *Fax:* 612-625-3819

HOOKE, WILLIAM HINES, ATMOSPHERIC PHYSICS. *Current Pos:* Physicist, Inst Telecommun Sci, 67-70 & Wave Propagation Lab, 70-73, supvry physicist, Wave Propagation Lab, 73-83, DIR, ENVIRON SCI GROUP, NAT OCEANIC & ATMOSPHERIC ADMIN, US DEPT COM, 84- *Personal Data:* b Raleigh, NC, Apr 23, 43; m 76; c 2. *Educ:* Swarthmore Col, BA, 64; Univ Chicago, SM, 66, PhD(geophys sci), 67. *Concurrent Pos:* Lectr astro-geophys, Univ Colo, Boulder, 69-74; fel, Coop Inst Res Environ Sci, 71-78; adjoint assoc prof astro-geophys, Univ Colo, Boulder, 74- *Mem:* Am Geophys Union; Int Sci Radio Union; fel Am Meteorol Soc. *Res:* Gravity-wave propagation and dynamics in the atmosphere; meso-scale and boundary-layer dynamics; upper atmosphere and ionospheric physics; remote sensing of the atmosphere. *Mailing Add:* 7813 Lee Ave Alexandria VA 22308

HOOKER, MARK L, soil fertility, irrigation water management; deceased, see previous edition for last biography

HOOKER, THOMAS M, JR, BIOPHYSICAL CHEMISTRY. *Current Pos:* from asst prof to assoc prof, 69-81, PROF CHEM, UNIV CALIF, SANTA BARBARA, 81- *Personal Data:* b Arlington, Ky, May 9, 36; m 58; c 3. *Educ:* Univ Ky, AB, 58, BS, 61; Univ Mo-Kansas City, MS, 66; Duke Univ, PhD(biochem), 67. *Prof Exp:* NIH res assoc chem, Univ Ore, 66-69. *Mem:* Am Chem Soc; Soc Appl Spectros. *Res:* Theoretical and experimental aspects of optical activity; molecular conformation in solution; conformation and biological activity of biopolymers; thermodynamics of molecular interactions of biological significance; biochemical applications of digital computers; Raman spectroscopy. *Mailing Add:* Dept Chem Univ Calif Santa Barbara CA 93106

HOOKER, WILLIAM JAMES, plant pathology; deceased, see previous edition for last biography

HOOKER, WILLIAM MEAD, MICROSCOPIC ANATOMY. *Current Pos:* asst prof, 69-77, ASSOC PROF ANAT & ASSOC DEAN, SCH MED, LOMA LINDA UNIV, 77- *Personal Data:* b Takoma Park, Md, Sept 9, 42; m 64; c 3. *Educ:* Columbia Union Col, BA, 64; Loma Linda Univ, PhD(anat), 69. *Concurrent Pos:* Fel, Univ Iowa, 70-71. *Mem:* Am Asn Anatomists; Electron Micros Soc Am; Sigma Xi. *Res:* Quantitative ultrastructural descriptions of endocrine and other cell systems. *Mailing Add:* Dept Anat Loma Linda Univ Sch Med 25027 Mound St Loma Linda CA 92350-0001

HOOKS, RONALD FRED, POMOLOGY, PLANT SCIENCE. *Current Pos:* from asst prof to assoc prof, 69-75, PROF HORT, NMEX STATE UNIV, 75- *Personal Data:* b San Antonio, Tex, Dec 2, 41; m 71; c 3. *Educ:* Tex A&M Univ, BS, 64, MS, 66; Mich State Univ, PhD(pomol), 69. *Prof Exp:* Grad asst hort, Tex A&M Univ, 64-66. *Mem:* Am Soc Hort Sci; Sigma Xi. *Res:* Fruit production; growth regulators; cultural practices; nutrition; chile pepper cultural practices; fertilizer and growth regulators. *Mailing Add:* 8516 Princess Jeanne NE Albuquerque NM 87112

HOOKS, WILLIAM GARY, STRATIGRAPHY. *Current Pos:* from asst prof to assoc prof, Univ Ala, 54-66, head dept geol & geog, 69-77, actg head, 81-82, PROF GEOL, UNIV ALA, TUSCALOOSA, 77-. *Personal Data:* b Asheville, NC, Oct 4, 27; m 51; c 4. *Educ:* Univ NC, SB, 50, MS, 53, PhD, 61. *Prof Exp:* Asst geol, Univ NC, 50-54. *Concurrent Pos:* Consult, 55- *Mem:* Am Asn Petrol Geologists. *Res:* Geomorphology; environmental geology; sedimentation-stratigraphy. *Mailing Add:* Dept Geol Univ Ala PO Box 870338 Tuscaloosa AL 35487

HOOL, JAMES N, INDUSTRIAL ENGINEERING, FOREST MANAGEMENT. *Current Pos:* Asst prof, 65-68, assoc prof, 68-79, PROF INDUST ENG, AUBURN UNIV, 79- *Personal Data:* b Streator, Ill, May 28, 38; m 66. *Educ:* Purdue Univ, BS, 60, MS, 62, PhD(forest mgt), 65. *Mem:* Am Statist Asn; Am Inst Indust Engrs. *Res:* Experimental statistics; operations research; systems analysis; normal approximation of linear combinations. *Mailing Add:* Dept Indust Eng Auburn Univ Auburn AL 36849-3501. *Fax:* 334-844-1381

HOON, WILLIAM LEROY, HEALTH SERVICES MANAGEMENT. *Current Pos:* DIR, DENT SERVS, WESTERN CTR, 84- *Personal Data:* b Camp Lockett, Calif, Nov 27, 45; m 73. *Educ:* Duquesne Univ, Med, 72, MLS, 88; Univ Pittsburgh, DMD, 80, MPH, 81. *Prof Exp:* Dentist, 81-86. *Concurrent Pos:* Dent officer, US Army Res, 81- *Mem:* Fel Acad Dent Int; master Acad Gen Dent. *Mailing Add:* 456 Coolidge Ave Pittsburgh PA 15228 1222. *Fax:* 412-873-3401

HOOP, BERNARD, JR, PHYSICS IN MEDICINE & THE LIFE SCIENCES. *Current Pos:* assoc physicist, 73-87, PHYSICIST, MASS GEN HOSP, 87-; ASSOC PROF MED PHYSICS, HARVARD MED SCH, 87- *Personal Data:* b San Francisco, Calif, Feb 17, 39; m 65, Nancy Hulbert; c Heidi A & Katrina (Clark). *Educ:* Stanford Univ, BS, 60; Univ Wis-Madison, MS, 62, PhD(physics), 66. *Honors & Awards:* Fulbright Lectr Award, India, 93. *Prof Exp:* Res asst nuclear physics, Univ Wis-Madison, 62-65; res assoc, Physics Inst, Univ Basel, 65-67; asst appl physics, Mass Gen Hosp, 67-70, asst appl physicist, 70-73. *Mem:* Am Phys Soc; Am Physiol Soc. *Res:* Central nervous system control of respiration; non-linear phenomena in living systems; physics of the circulation. *Mailing Add:* 266 Main St Wakefield MA 01880. *Fax:* 617-726-6878; *E-Mail:* bhoop@helix.mgh.harvard.edu

HOOPER, ALAN BACON, MICROBIAL BIOCHEMISTRY. *Current Pos:* assoc prof, 68-75, PROF GENETICS & CELL BIOL, UNIV MINN, ST PAUL, 75- *Personal Data:* b Berkeley, Calif, Nov 30, 37; c Nadja M (Leonhard-Hooper). *Educ:* Oberlin Col, BA, 59; Johns Hopkins Univ, PhD(biol), 64. *Prof Exp:* Asst prof zool, Univ Minn, Minneapolis, 64-68. *Mem:* Am Soc Microbiol; Am Soc Chem & Molecular Biol; Am Soc Cell Biol. *Res:* Biochemistry of nitrification in microorganisms. *Mailing Add:* Dept Genetics & Cell Biol Univ Minn 250 Biosci St Paul MN 55108-1011. *Fax:* 612-625-5754; *E-Mail:* hooper@molbio.cbs.umn.edu

HOOPER, ANNE CAROLINE DODGE, FORENSIC PATHOLOGY. *Current Pos:* asst prof path, 77-78, ASSOC PROF PATH, WVA SCH OSTEOP MED, 78- *Personal Data:* b Groton, Mass, July 16, 26; m 52, W Dale; c Betsy, Joan & Caroline. *Educ:* Wash Univ, AB, 47, MD, 52, Am Bd Path, cert, path anat, 58, forensic path, 60, clin path, 61. *Honors & Awards:* Borden Award, 52. *Prof Exp:* Jackson-Johnson res fel pharmacol, Wash Univ, 49-50; intern, Virginia Mason Hosp, Seattle, 52-53; resident internal med, St Francis Hosp, Hartford, Conn, 53-54; resident path, New Britain Gen Hosp, Conn, 54-57 & Presby Hosp, Philadelphia, 57-58; forensic pathologist, Med Examr Off, Philadelphia, 58-60; consult radioisotopes, Vet Admin Hosp, Coatesville, Pa, 63, dir lab, 66; dir lab, Kerbs Hosp, St Albans, Vt, 66-71 & Williamson Appalachian Regional Hosp, Williamson, WVa, 71-74; pathologist, Beckley Appalachian Regional Hosp, 74-75, dir lab, 75-76. *Concurrent Pos:* Dir lab, St Albans Hosp, Vt, 66-69; consult radioisotopes, Coatesville Hosp, Pa, 63. *Mem:* Fel Am Soc Clin Pathologists; fel Am Acad Forensic Sci; Int Acad Path; Sigma Xi; Col Am Pathologists; AMA. *Mailing Add:* WVa Sch Osteop Med 400 N Lee St Lewisburg WV 24901. *Fax:* 304-645-4859

HOOPER, BILLY ERNEST, VETERINARY MEDICINE, EDUCATION ADMINISTRATION. *Current Pos:* RETIRED. *Personal Data:* b Pawnee City, Nebr, June 22, 31; m 54; c 2. *Educ:* Univ Mo, BS & DVM, 61; Purdue Univ, MS, 63, PhD(vet path), 65. *Prof Exp:* From asst prof to assoc prof vet path, Purdue Univ, 65-68; mem, Fac Dept Path, Sch Vet Med, Univ Mo, Columbia, 68, assoc prof, 68-71, chmn dept, 69-71; prof vet path, Col Vet Med, Univ Ga, 71-73; prof, Sch Vet Med & assoc dean acad affairs, Purdue Univ, West Lafayette, 73-86; exec dir, Asn Am Vet Med Col, 86-92; assoc dean student affairs, Okla State Univ, 92-97. *Mem:* Am Vet Med Asn; Am Col Vet Path. *Res:* Gastrointestinal pathology; virus induced enteric disease of swine. *Mailing Add:* 5224 W Eighth Ave Stillwater OK 74074

HOOPER, CATHERINE EVELYN, HIGH ELECTRON MOBILITY TRANSFER TECHNOLOGY, GALLIUM ARSENIDE TECHNOLOGY. *Current Pos:* SR DEVELOP ENGR, HUGHES RES LABS, 84- *Personal Data:* b Brooklyn, NY, Nov 10, 39; m 74; c 2. *Prof Exp:* Inspector, Amelco Semiconductor, 66-68; technician, Fairchild Res & Develop, 68-73; sr technician, Varian Cent Res, 73-84. *Concurrent Pos:* Lectr, Grad Women Sci, Nat Speakers Bur, 90. *Mem:* Sigma Xi; Int Soc Optical Engrs; Am Vacuum Soc; Mat Res Soc. *Res:* Gallium arsenide field effect transistor; high electron mobility transistors for satellite and space applications. *Mailing Add:* 1741 Royal St George Dr Thousand Oaks CA 91362

HOOPER, CHARLES FREDERICK, JR, THEORETICAL ATOMIC & PLASMA PHYSICS. *Current Pos:* From asst prof to assoc prof, 63-76, PROF PHYSICS, UNIV FLA, 76-, dept chmn, 80-86. *Personal Data:* b Cambridge, Mass, June 3, 32; m 71; c 2. *Educ:* Dartmouth Col, AB, 54; Johns Hopkins Univ, PhD(physics), 63. *Mem:* Fel Am Phys Soc. *Res:* Spectral line broadening in plasmas; electric microfield distributions; statistical physics; dense plasma physics. *Mailing Add:* Dept Physics Univ Fla 231 Williamson Hall Gainesville FL 32611. *E-Mail:* chooper@phys.ufl.edu

HOOPER, DONALD LLOYD, NUCLEAR MAGNETIC RESONANCE. *Current Pos:* asst prof, 66-73, ASSOC PROF CHEM, DALHOUSIE UNIV, 73-; MGR, NUCLEAR MAGNETIC RESONANCE, ATLANTIC REGION MAGNETIC RES CTR, 82- *Personal Data:* b St Stephen, NB, Can, Nov 18, 38; m 61, Shirley Smillie; c Lorraine. *Educ:* Univ NB, BSc, 60, MSc, 61, PhD(nuclear magnetic resonance), 64. *Prof Exp:* NRC postdoctoral chem, Univ E Anglia, 64-66. *Mem:* fel Chem Inst Can; Royal Soc Chem; Am Chem Soc. *Res:* Application of spectroscopic methods, primarily high field nuclear magnetic resonance to solution of problems in structure and dynamics of compounds. *Mailing Add:* Dept Chem Dalhousie Univ Halifax NS B3H 3J5 Can. *Fax:* 902-494-1310

HOOPER, EDWIN BICKFORD, JR, MAGNETIC FUSION ENERGY, MIRROR & TOKAMAC CONFINEMENT & HEATING. *Current Pos:* PHYSICIST FUSION RES & ASST DEP ASSOC DIR, LAWRENCE LIVERMORE NAT LAB, 70- *Personal Data:* b Bremerton, Wash, June 18, 37; m 63, Virginia; c Edwin, Sarah & William. *Educ:* Mass Inst Technol, SB, 59, PhD(physics), 65. *Prof Exp:* Asst prof appl sci, Yale Univ, 66-70. *Concurrent Pos:* Mem bd dirs, Div Plasma Physics, Am Phys Soc, 90-91. *Mem:* Fel Am Phys Soc; AAAS; Am Inst Aeronaut & Astronaut. *Res:* Experimental and supporting theoretical research on magnetic fusion energy, with special attention to plasma physics and atomic physics issues; mirror machines and high energy neutral beams based on negative ions; Tokamak heating by electron cyclotron resonance; spherowak physics. *Mailing Add:* L-637 Lawrence Livermore Nat Lab PO Box 808 Livermore CA 94551

HOOPER, F(RANK) C(LEMENTS), HEAT TRANSFER, HEAT ENGINEERING. *Current Pos:* Demonstr mech eng, Univ Toronto, 46-47, lectr, 47-55, from asst prof to assoc prof, 55-65, prof mech eng, 65-89, chmn, Div Eng Sci, 77-82, chmn, Div Eng Sci, 88-89, EMER PROF ENG, UNIV TORONTO, 89- *Personal Data:* b Toronto, Ont, Apr 10, 24; m 52, Gay Jones; c Della E (Burns) & Jeffrey T. *Educ:* Univ Toronto, BASc, 46; Univ London, DIC, 53. *Honors & Awards:* Eng Medal, Asn Prof Engrs Ont, 76; Can Cong Appl Mech Medal, 77; Silver Jubilee Medal, 77; E K Campbell Award, Am Soc Heating Refrig & Air Conditioning Engrs, 80; Stachiewic Heat Transfer Medal, 86. *Concurrent Pos:* Exchange lectr, Univ London, 52-53; mem, Engines Comt, Nat Res Coun Can, 52-54, Heat Transfer Comt, 59-72, chmn, Assoc Comt Heat Transfer, 66-72; consult, ERDA & Dept Energy, 74- & Sci Coun, 76-78, pres Hooper & Angus Assoc, 77-87; pres, Int Assembly Heat Transfer Conf, 78-82 & pres, Royal Can Inst, 81-82, pres, Can Soc Mech Eng, 87-88; pres, Int Assembly Heat Transfer Conf, 78-82, Royal Can Inst, 81-82 & Can Soc Mech Eng, 87-88; consult eng univ lectr, 90-; pres, Thermal Conversion Ltd, 95- *Mem:* Am Soc Mech Engrs; fel Eng Inst Can; fel Can Soc Mech Engrs (pres, 87-88); Solar Energy Soc Can; fel Can Acad Eng. *Res:* Conduction and radiation heat transfer; thermal storage; heat pumps; diffuse solar radiation; boiling and flashing of liquids - low temperature engines. *Mailing Add:* Dept Mech & Indust Eng Univ Toronto Toronto ON M5S 3G8 Can. *Fax:* 416-978-7753

HOOPER, FRANK FINCHER, ZOOLOGY. *Current Pos:* RETIRED. *Personal Data:* b Phoenix, Ariz, Jan 17, 18; m 43. *Educ:* Univ Calif, BA, 39; Univ Minn, PhD(zool), 48. *Prof Exp:* Asst zool, Univ Minn, 40-42; instr, Univ Mich, 48-52, biologist, Inst Fisheries Res, 58-62; aquatic ecologist, Div Biol & Med, US AEC, 62-63; biologist-in-charge, Inst Fisheries Res, Univ Mich, Ann Arbor, 65-66, prof fisheries & zool, 66-91. *Mem:* Ecol Soc Am; Am Micros Soc (treas, 52-55); Am Fisheries Soc; Am Soc Zool; Am Soc Limnol & Oceanog (pres elect, 65, pres, 66). *Res:* Limnochemistry; aquatic food chains. *Mailing Add:* 4155 Clark Rd Ann Arbor MI 48105

HOOPER, GEORGE BATES, BIOLOGY. *Current Pos:* RETIRED. *Personal Data:* b Philadelphia, Pa, Nov 23, 24; m 53; c 4. *Educ:* Seton Hall Col, BS, 49; Princeton Univ, PhD(biol), 56. *Prof Exp:* Asst biol, Princeton Univ, 55-56, instr, 56-57; asst prof, Bard Col, 57-60; from asst prof to assoc prof biol, Marist Col, NY, 60-67, chmn dept, 60-68, chmn, Div Sci, 68-75 & 78-90, prof biol, 68-90. *Concurrent Pos:* Vis lectr, Princeton Univ, 64-65. *Mem:* AAAS; Am Soc Zoologists; Soc Study Evolution; Am Soc Naturalists. *Res:* Drosophila ecology, physiology and evolution. *Mailing Add:* 36 Circle Dr Hyde Park NY 12538

HOOPER, HENRY OLCOTT, SOLID STATE PHYSICS. *Current Pos:* ASSOC PROVOST & DEAN GRAD COL, NORTHERN ARIZ UNIV, 81- *Personal Data:* b Washington, DC, Mar 9, 35; m 96, M Jeanne Riley; c Deborah (MacDonald), Michael, Andrew, Katherine (Kittridge) & Bruce H. *Educ:* Univ Maine, ScB, 56; Brown Univ, ScM, 59, PhD(physics), 61. *Prof Exp:* Asst prof physics, Brown Univ, 61-64; from asst prof to prof, Wayne State Univ, 64-73; prof physics & chmn dept, Univ Maine, Orono, 73-80, dean grad sch, 77-80, act vpres acad affairs, 79-80. *Mem:* AAAS; Am Phys Soc; Am Asn Physics Teachers. *Res:* Nuclear magnetic resonance; nuclear quadrupole resonance; amorphous magnetic materials. *Mailing Add:* 1300 University Heights Dr S Flagstaff AZ 86001. *Fax:* 520-523-1075; *E-Mail:* henry.hooper@nau.edu

HOOPER, IRVIN P(LATT), mechanical engineering; deceased, see previous edition for last biography

HOOPER, IRVING R, MEDICINAL CHEMISTRY. *Current Pos:* CONSULT, 77- *Personal Data:* b South Lyon, Mich, June 16, 21; m 44; c 3. *Educ:* Mich State Normal Col, AB, 41; Univ Ill, PhD(biochem), 44. *Prof Exp:* Sr chemist, Parke, Davis & Co, Detroit, 44-45; Res Found fel, Ohio State Univ, 45-46; proj leader, Bristol Labs Div, Bristol-Myers Co, 46-49, dir biochem res, 49-65, dir chem res, 65-72, assoc dir res, 72-77; res assoc, Marine Lab, Duke Univ, 78-87. *Concurrent Pos:* Lectr, State Univ NY Upstate Med Ctr, 68-77. *Mem:* Am Chem Soc. *Res:* Isolation of natural products; structure determination; antibiotics; carbohydrate chemistry; immobilized enzymes; marine pheromones; anti-fouling surfaces. *Mailing Add:* 775 Hwy 101 Beaufort NC 28516-9713

HOOPER, JAMES R(IPLEY), SCIENCE EDUCATION. *Current Pos:* RETIRED. *Personal Data:* b Boston, Mass, Mar 30, 15; m 40, Helen Lang; c Ethel H (Farny), Katharine A, Anne H (Webb), James R III & Rosamond (Hamersley). *Educ:* Harvard Univ, AB, 37, MS, 39, PhD(physics), 57. *Prof Exp:* Asst physics, Williams Col, 40-41; instr, Union Col, 41-42; instr & res assoc, Harvard Univ, 42-50; from instr to assoc prof elec eng, Case Western Res Univ, 50-75, dir spec progs, 58-60, assoc dean instr, 60-64, dean undergrad studies, 64-69, dean spec undergrad studies, 69-75. *Mem:* Am Phys Soc. *Res:* Innovation in undergraduate eductional programs. *Mailing Add:* 4 Jerusalem Lane Cohasset MA 02025

HOOPER, JOHN WILLIAM, PHYSICAL ELECTRONICS, ACADEMIC ADMINISTRATION. *Current Pos:* RETIRED. *Personal Data:* b Clarendon, Ark, June 9, 31; m 57; c 2. *Educ:* Kans State Univ, BS(elec eng) & BS(bus admin), 54; Ga Inst Technol, MS, 55, PhD(elec eng), 61. *Prof Exp:* Instr math, Martin Br, Univ Tenn, 54; asst elec eng, Ga Inst Technol, 54-55; engr, Gen Elec Co, 55; res assoc, Army Ballistic Missile Agency, 55-57; asst elec eng, Ga Inst Technol, 57-58, from instr to prof, 58-71, regents' prof, 71-72; assoc vchancellor, Bd Regents Univ Syst Ga, 72-76, vchancellor, 76-79; regents prof & dir, Microelectronics Res Ctr, Ga Inst Technol, 79-86, actg vpres acad affairs, 86-87. *Concurrent Pos:* Consult, Ga Power Co, 57-65 & Oak Ridge Nat Lab, 65-79. *Mem:* Fel Am Phys Soc; Inst Elec & Electronics Engrs; Sigma Xi. *Res:* Atomic collisions; atomic cross section measurements; ion molecule reactions in gases at low and high pressures; charged and neutral beam detectors; solid state theory; ultra-high vacuum technology. *Mailing Add:* 350 Camp Dobbs Rd Jasper GA 30143

HOOPER, NIGEL, BIOCHEMISTRY. *Current Pos:* RES INSTR, DIV MOLECULAR BIOL & BIOCHEM, SCH BASIC LIFE SCI, UNIV MO, 90- *Personal Data:* b Bristol, Eng, June 18, 61. *Educ:* Univ Salford, UK, BSc, 83; Univ Surrey, UK, MSc, 84; Univ Aston, UK, PhD(biochem), 87. *Prof Exp:* Researcher, Dept Biomed & Environ Health Sci, Sch Pub Health, Univ Calif, 87-89. *Mem:* AAAS; Protein Soc; Am Soc Biochem & Molecular Biol. *Res:* Biomedical; molecular biology. *Mailing Add:* Dept Biochem Univ Leeds Leeds LS2 9JT England

HOOPER, RICHARD PAUL, WATER QUALITY, WATERSHED HYDROCHEMICAL MODELING. *Current Pos:* RES HYDROLOGIST, US GEOL SURV, 87- *Personal Data:* b Huntingdon, Pa, May 14, 57; m 87, Susanne Borges. *Educ:* Harvard Univ, BA, 79; Cornell Univ, MS, 84, PhD(civil eng), 86. *Prof Exp:* Fel, NATO, 86. *Concurrent Pos:* Assoc ed, Water Resources Res, 91-96. *Mem:* Am Geophys Union; Am Soc Civil Engrs. *Res:* Multivariate techniques for the interpretation of ambient water quality; determination of hydrological flowpaths through the terrestrial environment to determine fate and transport of non-point source pollutants. *Mailing Add:* 3039 Amwiler Rd Suite 130 Atlanta GA 30341. *Fax:* 770-903-9199; *E-Mail:* rphooper@usgs.gov

HOOPER, ROBERT JOHN, INORGANIC CHEMISTRY, MOLECULAR SPECTROSCOPY. *Current Pos:* PROF CHEM, SOUTHEASTERN MASS UNIV, 67- *Personal Data:* b Wyoming, Pa, June 10, 31; m 60; c 1. *Educ:* King's Col, Pa, BS, 53; Univ Notre Dame, MS, 59, PhD(inorg chem), 62. *Prof Exp:* Res assoc, Radiation Lab, Univ Notre Dame, 62-64; asst prof chem, Marist Col, 64-67. *Mem:* Am Chem Soc; Soc Appl Spectros. *Res:* Spectroscopic studies of the structure and bonding in transition metal complexes. *Mailing Add:* 12 Costa St North Dartmouth MA 02747

HOOPER, WILLIAM JOHN, JR, PHYSICS, ASTRONOMY. *Current Pos:* assoc prof physics, 67-72, chmn dept phys sci, 67-74, PROF PHYSICS,CLINCH VALLEY CO,L 72-, CHMN NATURAL SCI DEPT, 86- *Personal Data:* b Buffalo, NY, July 15, 35; m 59; c 2. *Educ:* Rensselaer Polytech Inst, BS, 57, MS, 59; Boston Univ, EdD, 67. *Prof Exp:* Asst prof physics, Clinch Valley Col, 59-63; instr, Simmons Col, 63-64; assoc prof, Boston State Col, 64-67. *Mem:* US Metric Asn; Am Asn Physics Teachers. *Res:* Physics and physical science education. *Mailing Add:* Laurel Hills Wise VA 24293

HOOPES, JOHN A, FLUID MECHANICS, HYDRAULIC ENGINEERING. *Current Pos:* From asst prof to assoc prof, 68-72, PROF CIVIL ENG, UNIV WIS-MADISON, 72- *Personal Data:* b Berkeley, Calif, Mar 29, 36; m 59; c 3. *Educ:* Univ Calif, Berkeley, BS, 58, MS, 60; Mass Inst Technol, PhD(civil eng), 65. *Honors & Awards:* Walter L Huber Civil Eng Res Prize, 72 & Karl Emil Hilgard Prize, 72, Am Soc Civil Engrs. *Mem:* Am Soc Civil Engrs; Am Geophys Union. *Res:* Transport and mixing of substances discharged into river, lake and groundwater flows; sediment erosion and transport; hydrology; wind and thermally driven circulations in impoundments. *Mailing Add:* 3124 Harvey St Madison WI 53705

HOOPES, JOHN W(ALKER), JR, CHEMICAL ENGINEERING. *Current Pos:* RETIRED. *Personal Data:* b Wilmington, Del, May 30, 22; m 49, Marjorie S Twombly; c Kathryn P & Pamela S. *Educ:* Bowdoin Col, BS, 43; Mass Inst Technol, BChE, 44; Columbia Univ, MS, 46, PhD(chem eng), 51. *Prof Exp:* Res engr, Sam Lab, Columbia Univ, 44, instr chem eng, 47-49, from assoc prof to asst prof, 50-55; sr chem engr, Atlas Chem Industs, Inc, 55-57; mgr, Process Eng Sect, Chem Eng Dept, ICI Americas Inc, 57-58, from asst dir to dir chem eng, 58-81. *Concurrent Pos:* Co-ed, Advances Chem Eng, 56-81; vis prof, Widener Univ, 83-86, prof, 86-92, adj prof, 92-97. *Mem:* Am Chem Soc; Am Inst Chem Engrs; Sigma Xi; Am Soc Eng Educ. *Mailing Add:* PO Box 3992 Greenville Wilmington DE 19807

HOOPES, KEITH HALE, VETERINARY MEDICINE. *Current Pos:* from asst prof to assoc prof animal sci, 57-69, PROF ANIMAL SCI, BRIGHAM YOUNG UNIV, 69- *Personal Data:* b Fairview, Wyo, July 23, 30; m 53; c 6. *Educ:* Wash State Univ, DVM, 56; Utah State Univ, BS, 57. *Prof Exp:* Asst vet microbiol, Wash State Univ, 53-56; pvt pract, 56-57. *Concurrent Pos:* Res asst vet sci, Univ Nebr, 63-64. *Mem:* Am Vet Med Asn; Am Asn Sheep & Goat Practrs; Am Asn Bovine Practrs. *Res:* Pathology; physiology. *Mailing Add:* 3356 Cherokee Lane Provo UT 84604

HOOPES, LAURA LIVINGSTON MAYS, MOLECULAR BIOLOGY, GERONTOLOGY. *Current Pos:* VPRES, DEAN COL & PROF BIOL, POMONA COL, 93- *Personal Data:* b Richmond, Va, Dec 1, 42; m 81, Michael; c Lyle M & Heather. *Educ:* Goucher Col, AB, 64; Yale Univ, PhD(biol), 68. *Hon Degrees:* LHD, Goucher Col, 95. *Prof Exp:* Fel microbiol, Scripps Clin & Res Found, 68-69; res assoc, Med Sch, Univ Colo, 69-73; from asst prof to prof biol, Occidental Col, 73-93, chair, 78-80 & 81-82. *Concurrent Pos:* NSF fel, Yale Univ, 64-68; NIH fel, Scripps Clinic & Res Found, 68-69 & Med Sch, Univ Colo, 69-70; NIH res grant, Occidental Col, 74-80; mem Nat Bd, Am Aging Asn, 75-84; guest scientist, Nat Inst Aging, 80-81; res corp grants, 81-82 & 84-85; consult genetics & biochem, Addison-Wesley/Benjamin Cummings, 82, Merck undergrad res prog, 87; counr, Coun Undergrad Res, 85-, exec secy, 87-90; NSF panelist, Col Sci Improv Prog, 86; vis assoc, Caltech Div Biol, 86-87 & 87-88; mem, Western Assoc Sch & Col accreditation team, 87-; co-auth & coordr, Pew Western Cluster grant, 87-90, mem, Am Fedn Aging Res grants, 86-93. *Mem:* Am Aging Asn (pres, 76-78); fel Geront Soc Am; Coun Undergrad Res (pres, 90-91); Genetics Soc Am; Am Soc Microbiol (secy-treas, 94-96); fel AAAS. *Res:* Molecular basis of changes during rodent aging; changes in DNA methylation during development and aging; changes in DNA repair in development and aging. *Mailing Add:* VPres & Dean Col Pomona Col 550 N College Ave Claremont CA 91711. *Fax:* 909-621-8836

HOOPINGARNER, ROGER A, ENTOMOLOGY. *Current Pos:* from asst prof to assoc prof, 59-72, PROF ENTOM, MICH STATE UNIV, 72- *Personal Data:* b Mich, May 27, 33; m 56; c 3. *Educ:* Mich State Univ, BS, 55; Univ Wis, MS, 57, PhD(entom), 59. *Prof Exp:* Fel entom, Univ Wis, 59. *Mem:* AAAS; Int Bee Res Asn; Int Union Study Social Insects; Entom Soc Am. *Res:* Insect behavior; apiculture. *Mailing Add:* 2712 Fontaine Trail Holt MI 48842-9724

HOOPS, RICHARD ALLEN, SPEECH PATHOLOGY, AUDIOLOGY. *Current Pos:* RETIRED. *Personal Data:* b Ft Wayne, Ind, Mar 3, 33; m 57, Helen Johnson; c Keriann, Mark, Drake & Kent. *Educ:* Oberlin Col, BA, 54; Univ Ill, MS, 56, PhD(audiol, speech path), 61. *Prof Exp:* Out-patient clinician speech path & audiol, Ball State Univ, 56-63; dir, Audiol Unit, Univ Wis, 63-64; dir, Speech, Lang & Hearing Clin, Ball State Univ, 64-76, chmn, Dept Speech Path & Audiol, 76-89 & 92-94, prof speech path & audiol, 79-95. *Mem:* Am Speech & Hearing Asn. *Mailing Add:* 405 S Umbarger Rd Muncie IN 47304

HOOPS, STEPHEN C, ORGANIC CHEMISTRY. *Current Pos:* ASST PROF CHEM, PA STATE UNIV, 68- *Personal Data:* b Denver, Colo, Nov 15, 40; m 64; c 2. *Educ:* Grinnell Col, BA, 62; Univ Kans, PhD(chem), 68. *Prof Exp:* Res chemist, Union Carbide Corp, NJ, 66-68. *Mem:* Am Chem Soc. *Res:* Reaction mechanisms; structure-reactivity correlations. *Mailing Add:* 524 Woodland Ave Oakmont PA 15139-1226

HOORY, SHLOMO, MEDICAL PHYSICS. *Current Pos:* HEALTH PHYSICS & RADIATION SAFETY OFFICER NUCLEAR MED PHYSICS, LONG ISLAND JEWISH HILL-SIDE MED CTR, 74- *Personal Data:* b Baghdad, Iraq, June 1, 35; Israeli citizen; m 67; c 2. *Educ:* Hebrew Univ, Jerusalem, MSc, 63, PhD(physics), 70. *Honors & Awards:* Nuclear

Med & Radiopharmacol Prize, Tel-Aviv Univ, 82; Res Award, Dept Physics, Hebrew Univ, Jerasulem, 70. *Prof Exp:* Med physicist nuclear med, Med Ctr, Hadassah Univ & Tel-Hashamer, Jerusalem, 61-63; solar physicist-in-chg, Observ, Tel-Aviv Univ, Israel, 70-74. *Mem:* Soc Nuclear Med; Am Asn Physicists Med; AAAS; Health Physics Soc. *Res:* Multilayer imaging reconstructions in the field of nuclear medicine; computerized radioisotope inventory and patient studies with radiopharmaceuticals; computerized approach of quality assurance in nuclear medicine; internal dosimetry evaluations using computerized models; new approach in evaluating bone mineral content using gamma camera. *Mailing Add:* 345 S End Ave Apt 4K New York NY 10280

HOOTMAN, HARRY EDWARD, NUCLEAR ENGINEERING, ENVIRONMENTAL ENGINEERING. *Current Pos:* ADV ENGR, STRATEGIC PLANNING & ANALYSIS DEPT, WESTINGHOUSE SAVANNAH RIVER CO, 92- *Personal Data:* b Oak Park, Ill, June 5, 33; m 63, Linda P Smith; c David, Holly & John. *Educ:* Mich Col Mining & Technol, BS, 59, MS, 61. *Prof Exp:* Res assoc chem eng, Argonne Nat Lab, 60-62; reactor engr hydraul, Savannah River Plant, E I du Pont de Nemours & Co, Inc, 62-65, sr engr fuel design, Reactor Eng Div, Savannah River Lab, 65-68, staff physicist reactor physics, Theoret Physics Div, 68-74, res staff engr nuclear waste mgt, Environ Effects Div, 74-80, res staff engr, Isotope Separations Div, 80-85, res assoc, Nuclear Eng Div, 85-88. *Concurrent Pos:* Instr, Dept Math & Eng, Univ SC, Aiken. *Mem:* Am Nuclear Soc; Nat Soc Prof Engrs; Am Phys Soc; Sigma Xi; Am Acad Environ Engrs. *Res:* Design and development of isotope production separation processing and disposal; incineration of nuclear wastes, shielding and criticality problems with nuclear wastes; production reactor design. *Mailing Add:* 820 Brandy Rd Aiken SC 29801-7281

HOOTS, FELIX R, CELESTIAL MECHANICS, MATHEMATICS. *Current Pos:* SPACE OPER GROUP DIR, GEN RES CORP, 86- *Personal Data:* b Nashville, Tenn, Sept 29, 47; m 72, 81; c 2. *Educ:* Tenn Technol Univ, BS, 69, MS, 71; Auburn Univ, PhD(math), 76. *Prof Exp:* Mathematician celestial mech, Air Force Space Commad, 74-86. *Mem:* Am Inst Aeronaut & Astronaut. *Res:* General perturbations math models for satellite orbit prediction under the influence of Earth and third body gravitation as well as atmospheric drag; rotational motion of satellites; satellite relative motion. *Mailing Add:* 19530 Broken Fenceway Monument CO 80132

HOOVER, CAROL GRISWOLD, COMPUTATIONAL STRUCTURAL MECHANICS, STATISTICAL MECHANICS & NONLINEAR DYNAMICS. *Current Pos:* COMPUT SCIENTIST/PHYSICIST, LAWRENCE LIVERMORE NAT LAB, 72- *Personal Data:* b Ft Madison, Iowa, June 4, 45; m 88. *Educ:* Auburn Univ, BS, 67; Univ Calif, Davis, MS, 73, PhD(appl sci), 78. *Prof Exp:* Mathematician, Air Force Flight Test Ctr, 68-72. *Mem:* Am Phys Soc. *Res:* Modeling of indentation and plastic flow with molecular dynamics, smooth particle applied mechanics and continuum mechanics; hybrid particle-continuum models for massively parallel computers; research in nonequilibrium statistical mechanics. *Mailing Add:* PO Box 808 L-122 Livermore CA 94550. *Fax:* 510-422-4095; *E-Mail:* hoover1@llnl.gov

HOOVER, CHARLES WILSON, JR, MANUFACTURING ENGINEERING, ELECTRICAL ENGINEERING. *Current Pos:* PROF & DIR MFG ENG PROG, POLYTECH UNIV, 88- *Personal Data:* b Akron, Ohio, Oct 7, 25; m 53; c 3. *Educ:* Yale Univ, BE, 46, MS, 51, PhD(physics), 54; Mass Inst Technol, BS, 47. *Prof Exp:* Mem tech staff, Bell Tell Labs Inc, 54-55, supvr memory syst develop, 55-58, supvr mil res dept, 58-60, head mil electronics res dept, 60-64, dir mil electronics res lab, 64-69, exec dir mil res div, 69-70 & commun systs res div, 70-71, exec dir systs assembly technol div, 71-82, exec dir interconnections & power technol div, 82-88. *Concurrent Pos:* Chmn, Comt Tech Educ, AT&T Res & Develop Community; pres & trustee, Summit Civic Found; adv, NAE Comt Career Long Educ Engrs; co-chmn, Comt Eng Design Theory & Methodology; mem, Mfg Studies Bd, Nat Res Coun, 90- *Mem:* Am Phys Soc; fel Inst Elec & Electronics Engrs; Am Soc Mech Engrs. *Res:* Optics; techniques for assembly and interconnection of large electronic systems; electronic power systems; computer aided design; production flows in manufacturing; manufacturing systems engineering. *Mailing Add:* 87 Tanglewood Dr Polytech Univ 6 Metrotech Ctr Brooklyn NY 11201

HOOVER, DALLAS GENE, BIOTECHNOLOGY, FOOD MICROBIOLOGY. *Current Pos:* asst prof, 84-90, ASSOC PROF FOOD MICROBIOL & BIOTECHNOL, UNIV DEL, 90- *Personal Data:* b York, Pa, Apr 20, 51; m 77; c 1. *Educ:* Elizabethtown Col, BS, 73; Univ Del, MS, 77; Univ Minn, PhD(food sci & biochem), 81. *Prof Exp:* Res assoc toxicol, Univ Minn, 80-81; asst prof food microbiol, Drexel Univ, 81-82; res assoc toxicol, Cornell Univ, 82-84. *Mem:* Am Soc Microbiol; Inst Food Technologists; Int Asn Milk, Food & Environ Sanitarians. *Res:* Physiology and genetics of bacteria in the genus Pediococcus. *Mailing Add:* 312 Stamford Dr Newark DE 19711. *Fax:* 302-453-9055

HOOVER, DONALD BARRY, AUTONOMIC, CARDIOVASCULAR. *Current Pos:* from asst prof to assoc prof, 78-90, PROF PHARMACOL, JAMES H QUILLEN COL MED, ETENN STATE UNIV, 90- *Personal Data:* b Sunbury, Pa, July 20, 50; m 71, Joyce A Mettler; c Bryan & Jeffrey. *Educ:* Grove City Col, BS, 72; WVa Univ, PhD(pharmacol), 76. *Prof Exp:* Res asst, Dept Pharmacol, Med Ctr, WVa Univ, 72-76; res assoc pharmacol, Lab Clin Sci, NIMH, 76-78. *Concurrent Pos:* Nat Inst Gen Med Sci fel, 76-78. *Mem:* Am Soc Pharmacol & Exp Therapeut; Soc Neurosci. *Res:* Functions and pharmacology of cholinergic neurons; role of neuropeptides in regulation of the heart and coronary circulation. *Mailing Add:* Dept Pharmacol Col Med ETenn State Univ PO Box 70577 Johnson City TN 37614-0577

HOOVER, DONALD BRUNTON, GEOPHYSICS, ELECTRICAL ENGINEERING. *Current Pos:* geophysicist, Br Crustal Studies, 60-67, GEOPHYSICIST, BR REGIONAL GEOPHYS, US GEOL SURV, 67- *Personal Data:* b Cleveland, Ohio, June 17, 30; m 77, Lucille E Tippins. *Educ:* Case Inst Technol, BS, 52; Univ Mich, MSE, 53; Colo Sch Mines, DSc(geophys), 66. *Prof Exp:* Res engr, Gulf Res & Develop Co, 56-58. *Concurrent Pos:* Adv, Dept Nat Prod Mineral, Rio di Janeiro, 69-72; US rep, Geophys PanAm Inst Geog & Hist, 88-90. *Mem:* AAAS; Inst Elec & Electronics Engrs; Soc Explor Geophys; Mineral Soc Am; Soc Brasileria Geog. *Res:* Geophysical instrumentation applied to solid earth problems, particularly seismic and electrical methods; ore deposit model; electrogeochemical methods. *Mailing Add:* 14142 W 59th Ave Arvada CO 80004. *Fax:* 303-236-1425

HOOVER, FRED WAYNE, ORGANIC CHEMISTRY, ISOCYANIC ACID CHEMISTRY. *Current Pos:* RETIRED. *Personal Data:* b North Manchester, Ind, Sept 26, 14; m 46, Winnie Guy; c Judith (Boyle), Gayle (Baseboar), Jill & Mark. *Educ:* Manchester Col, AB, 36; Purdue Univ, MS, 38, PhD(chem), 41. *Prof Exp:* Asst chem, Purdue Univ, 36-39; res chemist, Org Chem Dept, E I du Pont de Nemours & Co, Inc, 40-68, res assoc, 68-78. *Mem:* Royal Soc Chem; Am Chem Soc. *Res:* Finishes, plastics and organic syntheses; membrane technology; catalysis; photochemistry. *Mailing Add:* 206 W Pemtrey Dr Wilmington DE 19803

HOOVER, GARY MCCLELLAN, PHYSICS. *Current Pos:* Engr, Atomic Energy Div, 61-63, res physicist, 68-78, SUPVR SEISMIC MEASUREMENTS RES, RES & DEVELOP, PHILLIPS PETROL CO, 78- *Personal Data:* b Falls City, Nebr, Dec 10, 39; m 62; c 3. *Educ:* Univ Nebr, Lincoln, BS, 61; Kans State Univ, MS, 65, PhD(physics), 68. *Concurrent Pos:* Res assoc, Dept Physics, Kans State Univ, 68. *Mem:* Optical Soc Am; Soc Explor Geophys; Sigma Xi. *Res:* Molecular physics; infrared spectroscopy; elastic and electromagnetic wave propagation; computer data processing. *Mailing Add:* 2919 Ridge Ct Bartlesville OK 74006-4615

HOOVER, JOHN RUSSEL EUGENE, MEDICINAL CHEMISTRY. *Current Pos:* RETIRED. *Personal Data:* b New Enterprise, Pa, Jan 3, 25; m 45; c 3. *Educ:* Juniata Col, BS, 47; Univ Pa, MS, 49, PhD(org chem), 53. *Prof Exp:* Asst instr org chem, Univ Pa, 47-51, res assoc, 53-56; sr scientist natural prod, Wyeth Inst Appl Biochem, Am Home Prod Corp, 51-53; sr med chemist, Smith Kline & French Labs, Philadelphia, 56-59, group leader, 59-61, med chem sect head, 61-67, assoc dir chem, 67-86. *Mem:* AAAS; Am Chem Soc; NY Acad Sci; Sigma Xi. *Res:* Medicinal chemistry related to microbial, viral and cancer chemotherapy; heterocycles; cage compounds; antibiotics; semisynthetic penicillins and cephalospores. *Mailing Add:* 624 Crescent Ave Glenside PA 19038

HOOVER, JOHN W(ESLEY), AEROSPACE ENGINEERING. *Current Pos:* RETIRED. *Personal Data:* b Demopolis, Ala, Feb 24, 16; m 39; c 2. *Educ:* Ala Polytech Inst, BS, 36; Ga Inst Technol, MS, 53. *Prof Exp:* Instr physics & english, Marion Inst, 36-37; engr hwy design, Ala State Hwy Dept, 37-41; dir academics, Southern Aviation Sch, 41-44; asst proj engr, Taylorcraft Aviation Corp, 44-45; design group engr, Globe Aircraft Corp, 45-46; assoc prof aeronaut eng, Univ Ala, 46-51; from assoc prof to prof, Univ Fla, 51-85, interim head, 56-59, asst chmn dept, 72, emer prof aerospace eng, 85-86. *Concurrent Pos:* Consult, Umbaugh Aircraft, 58-60, United Fruit Co, 59-61, US Naval Air Sta, JAX, 69 & Piper Aircraft Corp, 76-78; assoc & actg dir, Fla State Technol Appln Ctr, NASA, 77-80. *Mem:* Assoc fel Am Inst Aeronaut & Astronaut; Am Soc Eng Educ; Nat Soc Prof Engrs. *Res:* Aircraft design; structures; aerodynamic loads on ground structures. *Mailing Add:* 2107 NW Fourth Pl Gainesville FL 32603

HOOVER, LORETTA WHITE, DIETETICS, COMPUTER SCIENCES. *Current Pos:* from instr to assoc prof, 72-83, PROF FOOD SYSTS MGT, UNIV MO, COLUMBIA, 83- *Personal Data:* b Stamford, Tex. *Educ:* NTex State Univ, BS, 62; Tex Tech Univ, MS, 69; Univ Mo, Columbia, PhD(food systs mgt), 73, MBA, 79. *Prof Exp:* Teacher home econ, Ozona Pub Schs, Tex, 62-67; vis instr food & nutrit, Tex Tech Univ, 69. *Concurrent Pos:* Mem ed bd, J Am Dietetic Asn, 74-77, 83-89. *Mem:* Am Dietetic Asn; Decision Sci Inst; Sigma Xi; Foodserv Systs Mgt Educ Coun. *Res:* Computer-assisted food management systems including inventory control, production control, food cost accounting, statistical forecasting, nutrient analyses, diet patterning, patient information systems, labor cost accounting, menu management, decision support systems and financial simulation models. *Mailing Add:* 601 Thilly Ave Columbia MO 65203-3462. *E-Mail:* hnffsmlh@mizzou1.missouri.edu

HOOVER, M FREDERICK, ORGANIC POLYMER CHEMISTRY, PAPER CHEMISTRY. *Current Pos:* DIR TECH OPERS, VENTRON CORP, 74- *Personal Data:* b Pittsburgh, Pa, Apr 11, 38; m 59; c 3. *Educ:* Carnegie-Mellon Univ, BS, 60. *Prof Exp:* Chemist, Calgon Corp, 60-61, group leader org res, 61-67, mgr polymer res, 67-70, asst dir res, 70-74. *Mem:* Tech Asn Pulp & Paper Indust; Am Chem Soc; Soc Plastics Engrs; Asn Res Dirs. *Res:* Water soluble polymers, structure, synthesis, production and applications; water treatment chemicals; corrosion inhibitors, biocides, dispersants; specialty chemicals for paper, oil and detergent industries; ion exchange resins; polyelectrolytes; metal hydrides; antimicrobials; catalysts. *Mailing Add:* 86 Rowley Bridge Rd Topsfield MA 01983

HOOVER, MARK DOUGLAS, AEROSOL SCIENCE, HEALTH PHYSICS & INDUSTRIAL HYGIENE. *Current Pos:* AEROSOL SCIENTIST, INHALATION TOXICOL RES INST, LOVELACE BIOMED & ENVIRON RES INST, 77- *Personal Data:* b Faribault, Minn, Aug 9, 48; m 70, Martha Price; c Alison & Ryan. *Educ:* Carnegie-Mellon Univ, BS, 70; Univ NMex, MS, 75, PhD(nuclear eng), 80. *Prof Exp:* Guest researcher, Inhalation Toxicol Res Inst, 75-77; vis scientist, Inst Aerobiol, Grafschaft, WGer, 77. *Concurrent Pos:* Mem, Biomed & Environ Effects Subpanel, Interagency Nuclear Safety Rev Panel, 88-; chmn, Environ Monitoring Working Group, Beryllium Monitoring Subcomt, Dept Energy-Dept Defense Beryllium Coordinating Comt, 90-; clin assoc prof, Col Pharm, Univ NMex, 91-; mem, US Deleg, Int Electrotech Comn; mem, Am Nat Stand Inst Comt. *Mem:* Am Nuclear Soc; Am Asn Aerosol Res; Health Physics Soc; Am Acad Health Physics; Am Acad Indust Hygiene. *Res:* Aerosol science and technology; inhalation toxicity associated with inhaled particles; sampling and characterization of aerosol sources; design and operation of aerosol instrumentation; measurement; exposure systems; health physics; industrial hygiene. *Mailing Add:* Lovelace Respiratory Res Inst PO Box 5890 Albuquerque NM 87185-5890. *Fax:* 505-845-1180; *E-Mail:* mdhoover@lucy.tli.org

HOOVER, PETER REDFIELD, RESOURCES FOR PALEONTOLOGIC RESEARCH. *Current Pos:* Asst dir, 77-78, DIR, ED & CUR, PALEONT RES INST, 78- *Personal Data:* b Ann Arbor, Mich, Apr 29, 39; m 69; c 1. *Educ:* Univ Pittsburgh, BS, 64; Ind Univ, MA, 66; Case-Western Reserve Univ, PhD(geol), 76. *Concurrent Pos:* Fel, Smithsonian Inst, 74 & Nat Res Coun, 75. *Mem:* Paleont Asn UK; Int Paleont Asn. *Res:* Permian and Triassic brachiopods; paleontology, paleoecology and functional morphology. *Mailing Add:* 5785 Rumsey Rd Trumansburg NY 14886

HOOVER, RICHARD BRICE, X-RAY OPTICS, SOLAR PHYSICS. *Current Pos:* physicist optics, Appl Res Div, Astrionics Lab, 66-70, space scientist x-ray optics & solar physics, Solar Physics Br, Space Sci Lab, 70-76, space scientist x-ray astron, High Energy Astrophys Br, Space Sci Lab 76-80, ASTROPHYSICIST X-RAY TELESCOPES & SOLAR X-RAY ASTRON, SOLAR PHYSICS BR, SPACE-TERRESTRIAL PHYSICS DIV, SPACE SCI LAB, MARSHALL SPACE FLIGHT CTR, 80- *Personal Data:* b Sikeston, Mo, Jan 3, 43; m 70, Miriam Jackson. *Educ:* Henderson State Univ, BS, 64. *Prof Exp:* Instr physics, Univ Ark, 65-66. *Concurrent Pos:* NSF grant math, Duke Univ, 64-65; consult gamma ray imaging systs, SCI Systs, Inc, Huntsville, Ala, 69-70; consult diatom community anal water pollution monitor, Environ Sci Lab, Teledyne Brown Eng, 70-71; dir, Environ Sci Lab, UNIDEV Inc, Huntsville, 70-72; Soc Photo-Optical Instrumentation Engrs; consult diatom taxon, Henri Van Heurck Mus, Royal Soc Zool, Antwerp, Belg, 75-80; pres & chmn bd, Micromega Inc, 83-; prin scientist, UHRXS Space Sta & MSSTA Rocket Exp. *Mem:* Fel Soc Photo-Optical Instrumentation Engrs. *Res:* X-ray optics, especially development of glancing incidence and multilayer x-ray telescope and microscope systems; solar physics, especially rapid changes in x-ray flare features; high energy astrophysics; micropaleontology, especially study of morphology and taxonomy of fossil & marine diatoms of the genera Entogonia and Actinoptychus; multiplate gamma ray collimator and multiplate focussing gamma ray collimator; develops advanced x-ray imaging systems; authored over 150 articles and 14 patents on x-ray telescopes and microscopes; international authority on x-ray optics and diatoms; produced diatom display for Smithsonian Museum of Natural History. *Mailing Add:* Marshall Space Flight Ctr Mail Code ES 52 Marshall Space Flight Ctr AL 35812. *Fax:* 205-544-5956; *E-Mail:* hoover@ssl.msfc.nasa.gov

HOOVER, RICHARD LEE, CELL-CELL INTERACTIONS, ENDOTHELIAL CELL BIOLOGY. *Current Pos:* assoc prof, 85-89, PROF, DEPT PATH, VANDERBILT UNIV, 89- *Personal Data:* b Beaver, Ohio, Dec 22, 44; m 85; c 2. *Educ:* Ohio State Univ, BA, 66; Univ Ky, MS, 69; Mich State Univ, PhD(zool), 72. *Prof Exp:* Instr parasitol, Mich State Univ, 72-73; fel, Univ Glasgow, 73-75; fel, Harvard Med Sch, 75-78, from asst prof to assoc prof, 78-85. *Concurrent Pos:* Vis prof physiol, Univ Vienna, 93. *Mem:* Am Soc Cell Biol; Am Soc Invest Path; AAAS; NY Acad Sci; Tissue Cult Asn. *Res:* Interactions between leukocytes and the endothelial cells that line blood vessels, this research is relevent to basic research in that it is applicable to cell-cell interactions and to medical research and the study of the acute inflammatory response and atherogenesis. *Mailing Add:* Dept Path Vanderbilt Univ Nashville TN 37232-2561. *Fax:* 613-343-7023

HOOVER, THOMAS BURDETT, ENVIRONMENTAL CHEMISTRY, ELECTROANALYTICAL CHEMISTRY. *Current Pos:* RETIRED. *Personal Data:* b Wellsville, Pa, Jan 17, 20; m 45; c 2. *Educ:* Pa State Univ, BS, 42, MS, 46, PhD(chem), 60; Am Inst Chemists, cert, 84. *Prof Exp:* Instr, Pa State Univ, 42-44; chemist, Union Carbide Nuclear Co Div, Union Carbide Corp, 48-52; sr chemist, Appl Sci Labs, Inc, 53-60; chemist, Nat Bur Standards, 60-70; res chemist, Environ Protection Agency, 70-85. *Mem:* AAAS; Am Inst Chem; Am Chem Soc. *Res:* Multielement analysis of water; electrochemical analysis. *Mailing Add:* Rte 1 Box 752 Winterville GA 30693-9641

HOOVER, THOMAS EARL, ENERGY TECHNOLOGY. *Personal Data:* b Temple, Tex, May 3, 41. *Educ:* Univ Tex, BA, 62; Tex A&M Univ, PhD(marine chem), 66. *Prof Exp:* Sr res scientist, United Aircraft Res Labs, Conn, 67-70; dir energy technol, Advan Technol, Parsons, Brinckerhoff, Quade & Douglas, 70-90. *Concurrent Pos:* Environ consult; mem, Geothermal Resources Coun. *Mem:* AAAS; Am Geophys Union; Am Chem Soc; Am Soc Oceanog; Am Nuclear Soc. *Res:* Evaluation of new applications for advanced technology; gas exchange and heat exchange across liquid surface; use of computer modeling to evaluate river pollution; computer modeling of subway environment; long-term management of nuclear waste; ocean thermal energy conversion; geothermal energy direct-use application. *Mailing Add:* 93 Bedford St New York NY 10014

HOOVER, WILLIAM G(EORGE), electrical engineering; deceased, see previous edition for last biography

HOOVER, WILLIAM GRAHAM, CHEMICAL PHYSICS. *Current Pos:* PHYSICIST, LAWRENCE LIVERMORE LAB, UNIV CALIF, 62- *Personal Data:* b Boston, Mass, Apr 18, 36; div; c 2. *Educ:* Oberlin Col, AB, 58; Univ Mich, MS, 60, PhD(chem), 61. *Prof Exp:* Alfred P Sloan Found fel, Duke Univ, 61-62; instr, 66-73, PROF APPL SCI, UNIV CALIF, DAVIS, 74- *Concurrent Pos:* Fulbright-Hays fel, Australian Nat Univ, 77-78; vis prof, Univ Australia, Univ Rome & Univ Vienna, 85, Keio Univ, Japan, 90-91. *Mem:* Fel Am Phys Soc. *Res:* Statistical mechanics; equilibrium and nonequilibrium molecular dynamics; solid phase cell models; irreversibility and time's arrow; phase diagrams; fracture; plasticity; transport and hydrodynamics. *Mailing Add:* Lawrence Livermore Nat Lab PO Box 808 L-794 Livermore CA 94550

HOOVER, WILLIAM JAY, FOOD SCIENCE. *Current Pos:* RETIRED. *Personal Data:* b Champaign, Ill, Mar 26, 28; m 50, Ellen Kesler; c Michael, Jane & Laura. *Educ:* Univ Ill, BS, 50, MS, 54, PhD(food technol), 63. *Prof Exp:* Food technologist, Qm Food & Container Inst, 51-52; asst, Univ Ill, 52-53; asst to dir, Refrig Res Found, 53-56; mgr tech serv, Corn Indust Res Found, Inc, 56-62, admin vpres, 62-66; dir, Food & Feed Grain Inst & head, Dept Grain Sci & Indust, Kans State Univ, 66-76; pres, Am Inst Baking, Manhattan, Kans, 76- *Mem:* Am Asn Cereal Chemists; Inst Food Technologists. *Res:* Research and development on grains, pulses and oilseeds and their products. *Mailing Add:* Am Inst Baking 1213 Bakers Way Manhattan KS 66502

HOPCROFT, JOHN E(DWARD), COMPUTER SCIENCES THEORY. *Current Pos:* assoc prof, Cornell Univ, 67-71, chmn, Dept Comput Sci, 87-92, assoc dean col affairs, Col Eng, 92-93, PROF COMPUT SCI, CORNELL UNIV, 72-, DEAN, COL ENG, 94- *Personal Data:* b Seattle, Wash, Oct 7, 39; m 64; c 3. *Educ:* Seattle Univ, BS, 61; Stanford Univ, MS, 62, PhD(elec eng), 64. *Hon Degrees:* DHH, Seattle Univ, 90. *Honors & Awards:* A M Turing Award, Asn Comput Mach, 86. *Prof Exp:* NSF fel, 61-64; asst prof theory comput, Princeton Univ, 64-67. *Concurrent Pos:* Consult, 66-; vis assoc prof, Stanford Univ, 70-71; vchmn, Switching & Automata Theory Comt, Comput Group, Inst Elec & Electronics Engrs, 70-72; ed, J Comput, Soc Indust & Appl Math, 72-87; mem, Comput Sci & Technol Bd, Nat Res Coun, 80-82; assoc ed, J Comput & Systs Sci, 80-; Joseph C Ford prof comput sci, 85-; mem, Comput Sci & Technol Bd, Nat Acad Sci/Nat Res Coun, 88-91; ed, Int J Computational Geom & Appln, 90-; mem, Comn Phys Sci, Math & Appln, Nat Res Coun, 95-98; mem var bds. *Mem:* Nat Acad Eng; fel Inst Elec & Electronics Engrs; Soc Indust & Appl Math; fel Asn Comput Mach; fel Am Acad Arts & Sci; fel AAAS; NY Acad Sci. *Res:* Theoretical computer science; author or co-author of numerous books and publications. *Mailing Add:* Joseph Silbert Dean Eng Cornell Univ 242 Carpenter Hall Ithaca NY 14853. *Fax:* 607-255-9606

HOPE, BRIAN BRADSHAW, CONCRETE MATERIALS, CORROSION OF STEEL IN CONCRETE. *Current Pos:* assoc prof, 67-76, PROF CIVIL ENG, QUEEN'S UNIV, ONT, 76- *Personal Data:* b Preston, Eng, Apr 21, 36; Can citizen; m 64, Anita Heron; c John & James. *Educ:* Victoria Univ Manchester, BSc, 57; Queen's Univ, Ont, MSc, 59, PhD(civil eng), 62. *Honors & Awards:* Duggan Medal, Eng Inst Can, 60. *Prof Exp:* Struct specialist, H G Acres & Co Ltd, 61-65; asst prof civil eng, Univ Calgary, 65-67. *Mem:* Fel Am Concrete Inst; Nat Asn Corrosion Engrs. *Res:* Corrosion inhibitors in concrete; cathodic protection of concrete structures; corrosion of reinforcing steel; chloride extraction from concrete. *Mailing Add:* Dept Civil Eng Queen's Univ Kingston ON K7L 3N6 Can. *Fax:* 613-545-2128

HOPE, ELIZABETH GREELEY, SEISMOLOGY. *Current Pos:* tech rep, 79-80, field supvr, 80-81, area mgr, 81-83, VPRES, PHILIP R BERGER & ASSOCS, 83- *Personal Data:* b Arlington, Mass, Jan 1, 43; m 85; c 5. *Educ:* Emmanuel Col, BS, 64. *Prof Exp:* Software analyst, Blue Cross-Blue Shield, 65. *Concurrent Pos:* Dir, Soc Explosives Engrs, 80-; ed, Leadline, Soc Explosives Engrs, 82-; mem, Div Pub Safety, Blasting Rev Bd, Commonwealth Mass, 85- *Mem:* Soc Explosives Engrs. *Res:* Theory of seismic vibrations; selective attenuation of wave components; correlation studies. *Mailing Add:* 7 Apple Ridge Maynard MA 01754

HOPE, GEORGE MARION, VISION, NEUROSCIENCE. *Current Pos:* ASSOC RES SCIENTIST, DEPT OPHTHAL, COL MED, UNIV FLA, 80-, DIR, LOW VISION SERV, EYE CTR, 80- & CTR LOW VISION, 81- *Personal Data:* b Waycross, Ga, Jan 24, 38; m 56; c 1. *Educ:* Mercer Univ, AB, 65; Univ Fla, MA, 67, PhD(physiol psychol), 71. *Prof Exp:* Res asst vision, dept psychol, Univ Fla, 66-67 & dept ophthal, Wash Univ, 70-72; from instr to asst prof ophthal, Univ Louisville, 72-79, co-dir, Low Vision Clin, 73-79. *Concurrent Pos:* dir, Placement Serv, Asn Res Vision & Ophthal, 72-84; investr, numerous res contracts & grants, 74-; consult, Defense Div, Brunswick Corp, Deland, Fla, 80-81; mem low vision consults comt, Div Blind Serv, State Fla, 84- *Mem:* AAAS; Asn Res Vision & Ophthal; Sigma Xi. *Res:* Neuroanatomy; neurophysiology; function of the normal and abnormal vertebrate visual system. *Mailing Add:* Univ Fla Col Med Dept Ophthal PO Box J100284 Gainesville FL 32610

HOPE, HAKON, X-RAY CRYSTALLOGRAPHY. *Current Pos:* from asst prof to assoc prof, 65-73, PROF CHEM, UNIV CALIF, DAVIS, 73- *Personal Data:* b Forde, Norway, Dec 15, 30; m 57; c 3. *Educ:* Univ Oslo, Cand Mag, 54, Cand Real(chem), 58. *Prof Exp:* Res fel chem, Univ Oslo, 58-60; lectr,

61-65. *Concurrent Pos:* Asst res chemist, Univ Calif, Los Angeles, 61-63; Fulbright travel grant, 61-63; NSF grants, 66-; US-Israel. *Mem:* Am Crystallog Asn; Norweg Chem Soc. *Res:* Determination of crystal structures; diffraction methods; biological macromolecules; low temperature methods; co-ed, Acta Cyst, 84. *Mailing Add:* Dept Chem Univ Calif Davis CA 95616-5224

HOPE, HUGH JOHNSON, LOW TEMPERATURE TOLERANCE, WINTER SURVIVAL. *Current Pos:* RETIRED. *Personal Data:* b Ottawa, Ont, Sept 12, 38; m 74; c 2. *Educ:* Carleton Univ, BSc, 60, MSc, 63; Dalhousie Univ, PhD(plant biochem), 68. *Prof Exp:* Fel, Univ Calif, Riverside, 68-70; res scientist, Can Dept Agr, 70- *Mem:* Phytochem Soc NAm; Am Soc Cryobiol; Can Soc Plant Physiologists; Am Soc Plant Physiologists; Am Soc Agron. *Res:* Cold tolerance improvement during germination; early growth in Zea mays and soy beans; protein metabolism during acquisition of cold and ice-encasement tolerance in cereals and forages; forage quality improvement in timothy; alfalfa by selection for reduced protein losses. *Mailing Add:* ECORC KW Neatby Bldg Agr & Agri-Food Can Ottawa ON K1A 0C6 Can

HOPE, LAWRENCE LATIMER, ELECTROLUMINESCENCE, ELECTRON DEVICES. *Current Pos:* Physicist, Gen Tel & Electronics Labs Inc, Waltham, Mass, 66-76, prog mgr, GTE Prods Corp, 76-93, PROG MGR, OSRAM SYLVANIA INC, 93- *Personal Data:* b New York, NY, Dec 28, 39; m 85, Elizabeth Greeley; c Timothy. *Educ:* Queens Col, BS, 61; Stevens Inst Technol, MS, 63, PhD(physics), 66; Mass Inst Technol, SM, 76. *Concurrent Pos:* Lectr, Hofstra Univ, 68-72. *Mem:* AAAS; Am Phys Soc; Sigma Xi; Inst Elec & Electronics Engrs; Soc Info Display. *Res:* Thin film electroluminescence; optical systems; lighting technology. *Mailing Add:* 7 Apple Ridge Rd Maynard MA 01754. *Fax:* 978-740-3528; *E-Mail:* hope@salem.sylvania.com

HOPE, RONALD RICHMOND, CARDIOLOGY. *Current Pos:* assoc prof, 78-80, CLIN ASSOC PROF MED, COL MED, UNIV OKLA, 80- *Personal Data:* b Melbourne, Australia, Aug 12, 43; m 66; c 5. *Educ:* Univ Melbourne, MB & BS, 66; FRACP, 75; Am Bd Internal Med, dipl. *Prof Exp:* Jr resident med officer, Prince Henry's Hosp, Melbourne, 67-68; sr resident med officer, 68-69, registr gen med, 69-70; registr respiratory intensive care med & gen med, Dunedin Pub Hosp, NZ & asst lectr med, Otago Univ, 70-71, fel cardiol & lectr, Otago Univ, 71-72; house officer, Royal Children's Hosp, Melbourne, 72; fel pediat cardiol, Hosp Sick Children, Toronto, Ont, 72-73; fel adult cardiol, Mt Sinai Med Ctr, Miami Beach, Fla, 73-74; specialist adult & pediat cardiol, Waikato Hosp, Hamilton, NZ, 74-75; asst prof med, Sch Med, Univ Miami, 77-78. *Mem:* Am Physiol Soc; Am Geriat Soc; Cardiac Soc Australasia. *Res:* Electrophysiology of ventricular arrhythmias in the context of myocardial infarction. *Mailing Add:* 608 NW Ninth St Oklahoma City OK 73102

HOPE, WILLIAM DUANE, NEMATOLOGY, SYSTEMATIC ZOOLOGY. *Current Pos:* Assoc cur, 64-72, chmn dept, 76-81, CUR DEPT INVERT ZOOL, MUS NATURAL HIST, SMITHSONIAN INST, 72- *Personal Data:* b Ft Collins, Colo, June 7, 35; div; c Pam (Herbert), Karen (Torabi) & Linda (Greene). *Educ:* Colo State Univ, BS, 57, MS, 60; Univ Calif, PhD(nematol), 65. *Concurrent Pos:* Res Award, Smithsonian Inst, 66-67 & 78-79; fel parasitol, Univ Toronto, 67-68; chmn, Int Asn Meiobenthologists & ed Newsletter, 68-69; assoc ed, J Nematol, 70-75. *Mem:* Am Micros Soc; Int Asn Meiobenthologists; Soc Nematologists; Soc Syst Zool; Sigma Xi; Am Asn Zool Nomenclature (pres, 90-91). *Res:* Comparative and functional morphology, ultrastructure and systematics of marine nematodes. *Mailing Add:* Invert Zool Smithsonian Inst Nat Mus Natural Hist Washington DC 20560. *Fax:* 202-357-3043; *E-Mail:* mnhiv005@sivm

HOPEN, HERBERT, HORTICULTURE. *Current Pos:* head veg crops div, 71-72, asst prof, 65-78, PROF HORT, UNIV ILL, URBANA, 78- *Personal Data:* b Madison, Wis, Jan 7, 34; m 59; c 1. *Educ:* Univ Wis, BS, 56, MS, 59; Mich State Univ, PhD(hort), 62. *Honors & Awards:* Campbell Award, Am Phytopath Soc, 80. *Prof Exp:* Asst prof agr, Univ Minn, 62-64. *Concurrent Pos:* Vis assoc prof, Univ Ariz, 72-73; vis fel, Agr Univ Norway, 77. *Mem:* Weed Sci Soc Am; Am Soc Hort Sci; Int Soc Hort Sci. *Res:* Chemical and biological weed control. *Mailing Add:* Dept Hort 385 Hort Univ Wis 1575 Linden Dr Madison WI 53706-1514

HOPENFIELD, JORAM, MECHANICAL ENGINEERING, TECHNICAL MANAGEMENT. *Current Pos:* PRES, NOVERFLO & SENSOR MFR. *Personal Data:* b Warsaw, Poland, Jan 6, 34; US citizen; m 63; c 3. *Educ:* Univ Calif, Los Angeles, BS, 60, MS, 62, PhD(mech eng), 68. *Honors & Awards:* Blackall Award, Am Soc Mech Engrs, 67. *Prof Exp:* Mem tech staff mech eng, Atomics Int Div, NAm Rockwell Corp, 62-71; reactor engr, Div Reactor Develop & Technol, US AEC, 71-77; res engr, Magnetohydrodyn Div, Dept Energy, 77-82; nuclear engr, Nuclear Regulatory Comn, 82- *Concurrent Pos:* Lectr, Automotive Diesels, Montgomery Col, Md. *Res:* Heat transfer; mass transfer; electrochemical machining; patented method for the on-line detection of pipe thinning due to corrosion and advanced fiberoptic sensors for oil leaks and chemical warfare agents monitoring; embedded corrosion sensors. *Mailing Add:* 1724 Yale Pl Rockville MD 20850

HOPF, HARRIET DUDEY WILLIAMS, ANESTHESIOLOGY, WOUND HEALING RESEARCH. *Current Pos:* res fel surg, Univ Calif, 87-88, resident anesthesia, 89-91, res fel anesthesiol, 91-92, ASST PROF ANESTHESIA, UNIV CALIF, SAN FRANCISCO, 92- *Personal Data:* b Madison, Wis, May 28, 60; m 88, Leo. *Educ:* Yale Univ, BA, 82; Dartmouth Col, MD, 86. *Prof Exp:* Resident surg, Univ Minn Hosp & Clin, 86-87. *Concurrent Pos:* Co-prin investr, Univ Calif, San Francisco, NIHGM Prog Proj Grant, 90- *Mem:* Am Bd Anesthesiol; Wound Healing Soc; Am Soc Anesthesiologists; Int Soc Oxygen Transp Tissue; AAAS; Soc Critical Care Med. *Res:* Tissue oxygen measurement; predictive value of wound tissue oxygen measurements for wound healing and the efficiency of interventions to increase wound oxygen tension; basic mechanisms, including the requirements of leukocytes for oxygen, glucose and other factors for optimal bacterial killing; effect of anemia on wound healing; relationship between gut hypoxia and bacterial translocation during shock. *Mailing Add:* Univ Calif Dept Anesthesiol 513 Parnassus San Francisco CA 94143-0522

HOPFENBERG, HAROLD BRUCE, CHEMICAL ENGINEERING, POLYMER SCIENCE. *Current Pos:* From asst to prof chem eng, NC State Univ, 67-80, head chem eng dept, 80-87, assoc dean, Col Eng, 87-90, exec asst to chancellor, 90-92, vchancellor instnl advan, 91-92, CAMILLE DREYFUS PROF, NC STATE UNIV, 80-, DIR, KENAN INST ENG, TECHNOL & SCI, 92- *Personal Data:* b New York, NY, Aug 28, 38; m 78, Patsy Graham; c 4. *Educ:* Mass Inst Technol, SB, 60, SM, 61, PhD(chem eng), 65. *Honors & Awards:* Alcoa Found Eng Awards, 78 & 80; R J Reynolds Industs Award, 85; Res Achievement Award, Plastics Inst Am, 89. *Concurrent Pos:* Grants, NSF & Army Res Off; consult, B Alza Corp, 74-, Am Can Co, 76-, Hoechst-Celanese, 81-, Hercules Inc, 83-, Duracell Inc, 84-, Grace Sierra Chem, 85-, Biosys, 86-; sr vis fel, Sci Res Coun, UK & vis fel, Clare Hall, Univ Cambridge, 77; res grants, Owens Ill, Inc, Alza Corp, E I du Pont Plastics Inst Am, Alcoa Corp & Hoechst-Celanese; vis prof, Univ Bologna, 82 & 84; vis prof, Appalachian State Univ, 85, Univ Naples, 89, Cambridge Univ; vis-fel, Trinity Col, 97- *Mem:* Am Inst Chem Engrs; Am Chem Soc; Sigma Xi. *Res:* Transport of small molecules in polymeric materials; controlled release; barrier plastics; migration and relaxation in glassy polymers; complex-biased separation processes; membrane separations. *Mailing Add:* Kenan Inst Eng Technol & Sci NC State Univ Box 7006 Raleigh NC 27695-7006. *Fax:* 919-515-5831; *E-Mail:* hal_hopfenberg@ncsu.edu

HOPFER, ROY L, MEDICAL MYCOLOGY, MEDICAL MICROBIOLOGY. *Current Pos:* ASSOC DIR CLIN MICROBIOL, UNIV NC HOSPS, 87- *Personal Data:* b Guthrie, Okla, Mar 20, 44; m 74; c 3. *Educ:* Okla State Univ, BS, 67, PhD(microbiol), 72. *Prof Exp:* Fel med mycol, Skin & Cancer Hosp, Temple Univ, 72-74; asst microbiologist, Univ Tex M D Anderson Hosp & Tumor Inst, 74-81, asst prof, 76-81, assoc microbiologist, assoc prof lab med microbiol & chief sect microbiol, 81-87; assoc prof, Univ Tex Grad Sch Biomed Sci, 82-87, Univ Tex Med Sch, Houston, 82-87. *Mem:* Am Soc Microbiol; Am Bd Med Microbiol; Med Mycol Soc Am; Sigma Xi. *Res:* Host-parasite relationships of fungi; infections in the immunosuppressed patient; diagnosis of systemic candidiasis in the cancer patient. *Mailing Add:* 1007 Monterey Valley Dr 101 Manning Dr Rm 1035 Chapel Hill NC 27516

HOPFER, SAMUEL, PHYSICS. *Current Pos:* VPRES & DIR RES & DEVELOP, GEN MICROWAVE CORP, 63- *Personal Data:* b Rexingen, Ger, Nov 21, 14; nat US; m 42, Hannah Pollak; c 4. *Educ:* WVa Univ, BA, 44; Cornell Univ, MA, 46; Polytech Inst Brooklyn, PhD(physics), 54. *Prof Exp:* Mgr microwave res, PRD Electronics Co, 46-63. *Concurrent Pos:* Adj prof, Polytech Inst Brooklyn, 56-65. *Mem:* Fel Inst Elec & Electronics Engrs. *Res:* Microwave broadband transmission systems, multimode coupling structures; instrumentation microwave power, radiation and impedance measurement; broadband solid-state switching, attenuation, modulation components; microstrip hybrids and microwave integrated circuit technology. *Mailing Add:* 17 Casuto Jerusalem Israel

HOPFER, ULRICH, CELL BIOLOGY. *Current Pos:* from asst prof to assoc prof anat, 74-83, prof develop genetics & anat, 83-88, PROF PHYSIOL & BIOPHYS, CASE WESTERN RESERVE UNIV, 86- *Personal Data:* b Burg, Ger, Apr 7, 39; m 63; c 2. *Educ:* Univ Gottingen, MD, 66; Johns Hopkins Univ, PhD(biochem), 70. *Honors & Awards:* Hoffmann-LaRoche Prize, Am Phys Soc, 83. *Prof Exp:* Fel biochem, Mass Gen Hosp, Harvard Med Sch, 70-71, res assoc, 71; dozent, Swiss Fed Inst Technol, 72-74. *Concurrent Pos:* Vis scientist, Max Planck Inst Biophys, Frankfurt, Fed Repub Ger, 80-81. *Mem:* AAAS; Am Soc Biol Chemists; Biophys Soc Am; Am Physiol Soc; Brit Biochem Soc; Soc Gen Physiol. *Res:* Structure and function of biomembranes; solute transport across plasma membranes; epithelial transport. *Mailing Add:* Dept Physiol & Biophys Sch Med Case Western Reserve Univ Sch Med 2119 Abington Rd Cleveland OH 44106-4970. *Fax:* 216-368-3952; *E-Mail:* uxu@vo.cwku.edu

HOPFIELD, JOHN JOSEPH, BIOPHYSICS, COMPUTATIONAL NEUROSCIENCE. *Current Pos:* PROF MOLECULAR BIOL, PRINCETON UNIV, 97- *Personal Data:* b Chicago, Ill, July 15, 33; m, Mary Waltham. *Educ:* Swarthmore Col, BA, 54; Cornell Univ, PhD(physics), 58. *Hon Degrees:* DSc, Swarthmore Col, 92. *Honors & Awards:* Oliver E Buckley Prize, Am Phys Soc, 69; Biophys Prize, 85; MacArthur fel, 83-88; Michelson-Morley Award, 88; Dudley Wright Prize, 89. *Prof Exp:* Mem tech staff, AT&T Bell Tel Labs, NJ, 58-60 & 73-90; vis res physicist, Ecole Normale Superieure, Paris, 60-61; from asst prof to assoc prof physics, Univ Calif, Berkeley, 61-64; prof, Princeton Univ, 64-80; prof chem & biol, Calif Inst Technol, 80-96. *Concurrent Pos:* trustee, Battelle Mem Inst, 83- *Mem:* Nat Acad Sci; Am Acad Arts & Sci; Am Phys Soc; Am Philos Soc. *Res:* Computational neurobiology; artificial neural networks in engineering; the physics of biological molecules and processes. *Mailing Add:* Dept Molecular Biol Princeton Univ Princeton NJ 08544

HOPFINGER, J ANTHONY, CALCIUM NUTRITION, FRUIT QUALITY. *Current Pos:* SPECIALIST POMOLOGY EXTEN RES, AGR EXP STA, RUTGERS COOP EXTEN RUTGERS UNIV, NJ, 84- *Personal Data:* b Salem Ore, Sept 13, 51. *Educ:* Univ Calif, BS, 73, MS, 75; Wash State Univ, PhD(hort), 78. *Prof Exp:* Asst prof hort, Univ Mo, Columbia, 78-82, systs oper officer, analyst & programmer, Univ Mo Hosp & Clins, 82-84. *Concurrent Pos:* Consult, Laura Exports USA, Inc, 87-, Blank, Rome, Cominsky & McCauley, Esqs, Philadelphia, 85-, Chubb Ins Co NAm, 86-; chmn, Nat Pcach Coun, 88-89. *Mem:* Am Soc Hort Sci; Am Pomol Soc; Sigma Xi. *Res:* Whole plant nutrition (especially calcium) and its effect on post harvest fruit quality of apples and peaches; peach skin discoloration (inking); development of maturity standards for New Jersey peach industry; physiological disorders of apples and peaches. *Mailing Add:* 2613 Ravens Crest Dr Plainsboro NJ 08536

HOPKE, PHILIP KARL, RADON & RADON PROGENY BEHAVIOR, RECEPTOR MODELING. *Current Pos:* ROBERT A PLANE PROF CHEM, CLARKSON UNIV, POTSDAM, 89- *Personal Data:* b Sherman, Tex, Mar 22, 44; m 68, Eleanor Lois Fritz; c Jane C & Frederick K. *Educ:* Trinity Col, Hartford, BS, 65; Princeton Univ, MA, 67, PhD(chem), 69. *Prof Exp:* Res assoc nuclear chem, Mass Inst Technol, 69-70; asst prof chem, State Univ Col, Fredonia, NY, 70-74; from asst prof to prof environ chem, Univ Ill, Urbana-Champaign, 75-89. *Concurrent Pos:* Vis asst prof chem, Univ Ill, Urbana-Champaign, 74-75; vis prof, Vrije Univ Brussels, Belg, 84-85; chmn, Sci Rev Panel Air Chem & Physics, US Environ Protection Agency, 87-; mem, Comt Advan Assessing Human Exposure Airborne Pollutants, Nat Acad Sci, Nat Res Coun, 89-90, Comt Dosimetric Extrapolations Beir IV Risk Estimates Gen Pub, 89-91, Comt Assess Nat Inst Standards & Technol Lab Chem Sci & Technol, 91 & Task Force Air Toxics, Am Chem Soc, 89-; dir, Am Asn Aerosol Res, 89-94; chair, Tech Comt EM2, Air & Waste Mgt Asn, 90-92; mem, Comt Risk Assessment Hazardous Air Pollutants, Nat Acad Sci/Nat Res Coun, 91-94, Comt Biol Effects Ionizing Radiation VI, 94-97; prin investr award air qual res, Ont Ministry Environ, 91; ed-in-chief, Aerosol Sci Technol, 93- *Mem:* Sigma Xi; Am Asn Aerosol Res; Am Chem Soc; Am Phys Soc; Air & Waste Mgt Asn; Health Physics Soc; AAAS; Air Pollution Control Asn; Ger Soc Aerosol Res. *Res:* Atmospheric of radon and its progeny; measurement of environmental radioactivity; sampling, physical, and chemical characterization of airborne particles; multivariate statistical and pattern recognition analysis of environmental data sets; source-receptor relationships for airborne pollutants; homogeneous and ion-induced nucleation. *Mailing Add:* Dept Chem Clarkson Univ Potsdam NY 13699-5810. *Fax:* 315-268-6610; *E-Mail:* hopkepk@draco.clarkson.edu

HOPKIN, A(RTHUR) M(CMURRIN), ELECTRICAL ENGINEERING. *Current Pos:* assoc prof, 54-60, PROF ELEC ENG & COMPUT SCI, UNIV CALIF, BERKELEY, 60- *Personal Data:* b Burley, Idaho, Feb 25, 19; m 44; c 5. *Educ:* Ga Inst Technol, BS, 42; Northwestern Univ, MS, 47, PhD(elec eng), 50. *Prof Exp:* From instr to asst prof elec eng, Northwestern Univ, 46-54. *Mem:* Inst Elec & Electronics Engrs. *Res:* Rotating electrical machines; control systems and components. *Mailing Add:* Univ Calif 2200 University Ave Berkeley CA 94720

HOPKINS, ALLEN JOHN, POLYMER CHEMISTRY. *Current Pos:* res chemist, Hoechst Fiber Industs, Hoechst Celanese Corp, 77-83, group leader process assistance, 83-87, tech supt, 87-91, MKT MGR RECYCLE SERVS, HOECHST CELANESE CORP, 91. *Personal Data:* b Liverpool, Eng, Feb 8, 42; m 65, Kathleen Parker; c Jana L & Sean L. *Educ:* Liverpool Col Technol, BSc, 64; Univ Manchester Inst Sci & Technol, PhD(polymer chem), 68; Furman Univ, MBA, 76. *Prof Exp:* Res asst radiochem, UK Atomic Energy Authority, 64-65 & Unilever Corp, 65-66; res chemist fiber chem, Phillips Petrol Co, 68-70, res chemist fiber technol, Phillips Fibers Corp, 70-77. *Mem:* Am Asn Textile Chemists & Colorists. *Res:* Polymer adsorption studies; synthetic fiber technology particularly with respect to texturing of partially drawn polyester yarn; recycle technologies for polyester. *Mailing Add:* 119 Continental Dr Greenville SC 29615

HOPKINS, AMOS LAWRENCE, PHYSIOLOGY. *Current Pos:* From instr to asst prof, 55-66, ASSOC PROF ANAT, SCH MED, CASE WESTERN RESERVE UNIV, 66- *Personal Data:* b Boston, Mass, Jan 27, 26; m 49, 70; c 3. *Educ:* Harvard Univ, BA, 48; Wash Univ, PhD(zool), 55. *Mem:* NY Acad Sci; Soc Magnetic Resonance Med. *Res:* Membrane oxygenator; dielectric behavior of bound water; nuclear magnetic resonance of living muscle; nuclear magnetic resonance of human cerebrospinal fluid in vivo; oxygen-17 as a proton MRI contrast agent in cerebral blood flow studies. *Mailing Add:* Dept Anat Case Western Res Sch Med 2119 Abington Rd Cleveland OH 44106-2333

HOPKINS, BETTY JO HENDERSON, radiation biology, experimental embryology, for more information see previous edition

HOPKINS, CARL DOUGLAS, ANIMAL BEHAVIOR. *Current Pos:* AT NEUROL-BEHAV DEPT, CORNELL UNIV, ITHACA, NY. *Personal Data:* b Rochester, NY, Apr 8, 44; m 70; c 2. *Educ:* Bowdoin Col, AB, 66; Rockefeller Univ, PhD(behav sci), 72. *Prof Exp:* Fel neurosci, Univ Calif, San Diego, 72-73; asst prof ecol & behav biol, Univ Minn, Minneapolis, 73-78, assoc prof, 78- *Mem:* Sigma Xi; Animal Behav Soc; Am Physiol Soc; Am Soc Ichthyologists & Herpetologists. *Res:* Evolution of animal communication; electric communication among fish; sensory filtering and species recognition. *Mailing Add:* Neurobiol-Behav Cornell Univ Ithaca NY 14853

HOPKINS, CHARLES B(EVERLEY), JR, CHEMICAL ENGINEERING. *Current Pos:* RETIRED. *Personal Data:* b Birmingham, Ala, Aug 15, 22; m 48, Virginia Pope; c 4. *Educ:* Ala Polytech Inst, BS, 43; Univ Wyo, MS, 54. *Prof Exp:* Anal chemist, Cities Serv Refining Corp, La, 43-46; pyrometrist, Tenn Coal, Iron & RR Co, Ala, 47-49; from chemist to chem engr, petrol & oil shale exp sta, US Bur Mines, Wyo, 49-56; res engr, Cities Serv Res & Develop, La, 56-60; chem engr, Chem Res & Develop Ctr, FMC Corp, 60-74, environ engr, 74-85. *Mem:* AAAS; Am Chem Soc; Sigma Xi. *Res:* Petroleum refining; catalytic processing; properties of porous solids; synthetic fuels; coal carbonization; reactivity of carbons; active carbon; water treating. *Mailing Add:* 11 Rosetree Lane Lawrenceville NJ 08648-3232

HOPKINS, CLARENCE YARDLEY, ORGANIC CHEMISTRY, PHYTOCHEMISTRY. *Current Pos:* RETIRED. *Personal Data:* b Kinmount, Ont, June 20, 03; wid, Kathleen Kerr; c Edward. *Educ:* Queen's Univ, Ont, BA, 24, MA, 26; NY Univ, PhD(org chem), 29. *Prof Exp:* Demonstr chem eng, Univ Toronto, 29-30; from asst res chemist to sr res chemist, Nat Res Coun Can, 30-68. *Concurrent Pos:* Lectr, Carleton Univ, 45-49; writer, 65-90; consult, 68-70. *Mem:* Am Oil Chem Soc; fel Chem Inst Can. *Res:* Protective coatings; oils and fats; novel fatty acids of seed oils; other natural products; discovery and identification of 11 new fatty acids. *Mailing Add:* 180 Carleton St Ottawa ON K1M 0G7 Can

HOPKINS, COLIN RUSSELL, CELL BIOLOGY. *Current Pos:* PROF CELL BIOL, UNIV COL LONDON, 90-, DIR BIOL/MED, MRC LAB MOLECULAR CELL BIOL, 90- *Personal Data:* b Wales, June 4, 39; m 64; c 2. *Educ:* Univ Wales, BSc, 61, PhD(biol), 64. *Prof Exp:* Lectr cell biol, Med Sch, Liverpool Univ, 64-70, prof, 70-85; prof cell biol, Imp Col London, 86-90. *Concurrent Pos:* Vis prof, Rockefeller Univ, 69-71. *Mem:* Am Soc Cell Biol; Brit Soc Cell Biol. *Res:* Cell biology; drug delivery; uptake and intracellular processing of cell surface receptors. *Mailing Add:* Lab Molecular Cell Biol Univ Col London Gower St London WC1E 6BT England

HOPKINS, DANIEL T, NUTRITIONAL BIOCHEMISTRY. *Current Pos:* TECH DIR SPECIALTY BUS GROUP, PURINA MILLS, INC, 87- *Personal Data:* b Peterborough, NH, Oct 3, 32; m 93, Madeline Whitten; c 3. *Educ:* Cornell Univ, BS, 56, MNS, 58, PhD(animal nutrit), 63. *Prof Exp:* From res asst to res assoc, Cornell Univ, 57-63; asst mgr broiler & roaster res, Ralston Purina Co, 63-65, coordr, Nutrit Labs, 65-66, mgr, Nutrit Biochem Lab, 66-73, dir, nutrit biochem lab, 73-83; vpres, Agr Nutrit Consult, Inc, 83-87. *Mem:* AAAS; Am Poultry Sci Asn; Am Inst Nutrit; Inst Food Technol; Sigma Xi; Am Dairy Sci Asn; Am Soc Animal Sci. *Res:* Lipid transport and metabolism; energy metabolism; protein quality of foods and feedstuffs; nutrition of laboratory and exotic animals. *Mailing Add:* Purma Mills Inc PO Box 66812 St Louis MO 63166. *Fax:* 573-678-4859

HOPKINS, DAVID ALAN, LIMBIC SYSTEM, AUTONOMIC NERVOUS SYSTEM. *Current Pos:* assoc prof, 77-85, PROF NEUROANAT, DALHOUSIE UNIV, 85-, HEAD DEPT, 91- *Personal Data:* b Victoria, BC, Aug 31, 42; m 76; c 3. *Educ:* Univ Alberta, BSc, 64; McMaster Univ, MA, 67, PhD(psychol), 70. *Honors & Awards:* Murray L Barr Jr Scientist Award, Can Asn Anatomists, 83. *Prof Exp:* Fel neuroanat, Erasmus Univ, Rotterdam, 70-72, asst prof, 72-77. *Concurrent Pos:* Fel, Int Brain Res Orgn, 69. *Mem:* Neurosci Soc; Am Asn Anatomists; Can Asn Anatomists; Europ Neurosci Asn. *Res:* Functional and anatomical organization of motor systems; limbic and basal ganglia connections with the brain stem; organization of the autonomic nervous system. *Mailing Add:* Dept Anat Dalhousie Univ Sir Charles Tupper Med Bldg Halifax NS B3H 4H7 Can. *Fax:* 902-494-1212

HOPKINS, DAVID MOODY, QUATERNARY GEOLOGY. *Current Pos:* distinguished prof quaternary sci, 84-94, dir, Alaska Quaternary Ctr, 84-90, EMER PROF & DIR QUATERNARY SCI, UNIV ALASKA, FAIRBANKS, 94- *Personal Data:* b Nashua, NH, Dec 26, 21; m 49, 57, 70, Rachel C Chouinard; c Dana (Weiss), Chindi (Peavey), Alexander, Vincent Stanley, Christopher Stanley & Gregory Stanley. *Educ:* Univ NH, BS, 42; Harvard Univ, MS, 48, PhD(geol), 55. *Honors & Awards:* Kirk Bryan Award, Geol Soc Am, 68, Archaeol Geol Award, 90; Roal Fryxell Award, Soc Am Archeol, 88; Franklin Burr Award, Nat Geog Soc, 93. *Prof Exp:* Jr geologist, US Geol Surv, 42-44, asst geologist, 46, assoc geologist, 47-48, geologist, 48-84. *Concurrent Pos:* Mem, Int Geog Cong Comn Evolution of Slopes & Comn Periglacial Morphol, 59-63; vis prof, Stanford Univ, 61; mem, Alaska Glacial Map comn, US Geol Surv, 56-63, Quaternary Shorelines comn, Int Quaternary Asn, 65-, geol names comn, US Geol Surv, 66-82, Early Man Res comn, Nat Geog Soc, 75-80, vis comt, Univ Wash Quaternary Res Ctr, 81-82, adv bd, Univ Maine Ctr Early Man Studies, 85-, US Nat Comn Int Permafrost Asn, 86-90, sci adv comt, div polar progs, USNSF, 86-88; panelist, Tundra Biome, Int Biol Prog, 68,; co-convenor, Burg-Wartenstein Conf Paleoecol of Beringia, 79; Nat Acad Sci exchange fel, USSR, 69. *Mem:* Fel AAAS; fel Geol Soc Am; fel Arctic Inst NAm; Int Quaternary Asn (pres, 75-76); Soc Am Archaeol; Sigma Xi; Am Quaternary Asn (pres, 75-76). *Res:* Oceanography, geology, tectonics and paleogeography of Bering and Chukchi Seas and Bering land bridge; Cenozoic stratigraphy of Alaska; worldwide Pleistocene correlations; geomorphology of arctic and subarctic regions; geology of placers; paleoecology of Beringia; offshore permafrost; Cenozoic stratigraphy of Alaska. *Mailing Add:* Univ Alaska Alaska Quaternary Ctr Fairbanks AK 99775-1200. *Fax:* 907-474-5163; *E-Mail:* ffomh@alaska.edu

HOPKINS, DON CARLOS, PHYSICS. *Current Pos:* RETIRED. *Personal Data:* b Charleston, Ill, Feb 18, 36; m 59; c 2. *Educ:* Eastern Ill Univ, BS, 57; Univ Ill, MS, 59, PhD(physics), 62. *Prof Exp:* From asst prof to assoc prof physics, Univ Mo, Rolla, 62-68; head dept, SDak Sch Mines & Technol, 68-88, prof physics, 68-93. *Mem:* AAAS; Am Phys Soc; Am Asn Physics

Teachers; Sigma Xi. *Res:* Thermodynamic properties of superconductors; magnetic alloy systems at low temperatures; use of computers in undergraduate education. *Mailing Add:* 2590 Wheeler St N Roseville MN 55113-2815

HOPKINS, DONALD LEE, PLANT PATHOLOGY. *Current Pos:* asst plant pathologist, 69-74, assoc plant pathologist, 74-79, PLANT PATHOLOGIST, UNIV FLA, 79- *Personal Data:* b Sacramento, Ky, Mar 13, 43; m 67; c 3. *Educ:* Western Ky Univ, BS, 65; Univ Ky, PhD(plant path), 68. *Prof Exp:* USDA res assoc, 68-69. *Mem:* AAAS; Sigma Xi; Am Phytopath Soc; Am Soc Microbiol. *Res:* Physiology of plant diseases and plant disease resistance; chemical control of fungus diseases; plant bacterial and virus diseases; Pierce's disease of grape; biological control of plant diseases. *Mailing Add:* CFREC Leesburg 5336 University Ave Leesburg FL 34748

HOPKINS, DONALD R, TROPICAL PUBLIC HEALTH. *Current Pos:* sr consult, 87-97, DIR HEALTH PROG, CARTER CTR, 97- *Personal Data:* b Miami, Fla, Sept 25, 41; m 67, Ernestine Mathis. *Educ:* Morehouse Col, BS, 62; Univ Chicago Sch Med, MD, 66; Harvard Univ, MPH, 70. *Hon Degrees:* DSc, Morehouse Col, 88. *Honors & Awards:* One Millionth Dollar Award, Nat Med Fel Inc, 62; Joseph Mountin Lect Award, 81; Distinguished Serv Med, USPHS, 86; Cert Commendation, Pres William Clinton, 93; MacArthur Fel, John D & Catherine T MacArthur Found, 95. *Prof Exp:* Researcher, Dept Microbiol, Univ Chicago, 63-66; intern, San Francisco Gen Hosp, 66-67; med epidemiologist & dir, Sierra Leone Smallpox & Measles Prog, 67-69; resident pediat, Univ Chicago Hosp & Clin, 70-72; med officer, Off Prog Planning & Eval, Off Ctr Dir, Ctr Dis Control, 72-74; asst prof trop pub health, Harvard Sch Pub Health, 74-77; asst dir opers, Ctr Dis Control, 77-80, Int Health, 80-84, dep dir, 84-87. *Concurrent Pos:* LSU fel trop med & parasitol, Gorgas Mem Lab, Panama City, 65; consult epidemiologist, Training Course Ethiopian Smallpox Eradication Prog, Peace Corps, WHO, 71, Yaws Prog, PAHO & WHO, Dominica, 72, Smallpox Prog, W Bengal, India, 73 & Anti-Yaws Campaign, Colombia, 75; dep chief, Environ Health Serv Div, Bur State Serv, Ctr Dis Control, 74; consult WHO hq staff, Expanded Immunization Prog, Geneva, 75; mem, US Del World Health Assembly, 77-86, Global Adv Group, Expanded Prog Immunization, WHO, 78-80, Steering Comt, Sci Working Group Epidemiol, Spec Prog Res & Training Trop Dis, 80-83, Tech Adv Group, Diarrhcal Dis Control, 83-84, Vaccines & Rel Biol Prod Adv Comt, Nat Cancer Drugs & Biol, Food & Drug Admin, 81-85; chmn, Interagency Working Group, Int Health Res Develop & Demo & spec adv, Int Health Res & African Regional Health Strategy, 78; vis lectr, Harvard Sch Pub Health, 78-, Emory Univ Sch Med, Dept Community Health, Master Pub Health Prog, 84-, Stony Brook State Univ, 82-; dep adminr, Agency Toxic Substance & Dis Registry, 84-87; actg dir, Ctr Dis Control, 85; mem, Overseers Comt Vis Sch Pub Health, Harvard Univ, 86-92, Gov Bd, Nat Coun Int Health, 87-92, Bd Dirs, Int Serv Asn Health & Adv Bd & Health Pub, 86-92, adv bd, Edna McConnell Clark Found & WHO Collab Ctr, Int Ctr Health Sci, Meharry Med Col, 87-90; mem, Chicago Bd Health, 89- *Mem:* Inst Med-Nat Acad Sci; Royal Acad Sci; Am Soc Trop Med & Hyg. *Res:* Author of over 75 publications in medicine; disease eradication; history of medicine. *Mailing Add:* Global 2000 Carter Ctr Atlanta GA 30307

HOPKINS, ESTHER ARVILLA HARRISON, PHYSICAL CHEMISTRY. *Current Pos:* DEPT GEN COUN, DEPT ENVIRON PROTECTION, BOSTON, MASS. *Personal Data:* b Stamford, Conn, Sept 18, 26; m 53, 59; c 2. *Educ:* Boston Univ, AB, 47; Howard Univ, MS, 49; Yale Univ, PhD(phys chem), 67; Suffolk Univ, JD, 77. *Prof Exp:* Instr chem, Va State Col, 49-52; res asst biophys, New Eng Inst Med Res, 55-59; res chemist, Am Cyanamid Co, 59-61; scientist, Polaroid Corp, 66-72, patent atty, 73-79, sr proj admin, 79-86, technol liaison mgr, 86-90. *Concurrent Pos:* Adv comt minority prog, Sci Educ Directorate, NSF. *Mem:* Am Chem Soc; AAAS. *Res:* Biophysical chemistry; metal catalysis of enzyme reactions; emulsion research and coating technology; fiber optics. *Mailing Add:* 1550 Worcester Rd Unit 524 W Framingham MA 01702

HOPKINS, FREDERICK SHERMAN, JR, FORESTRY, ECONOMICS & POLICY. *Current Pos:* prof, 59-89, EMER PROF FORESTRY, IOWA STATE UNIV, 89- *Personal Data:* b Springfield, Mass, June 12, 22; m 46; c 4. *Educ:* Univ Mich, BSF, 46, BBA & MF, 47; State Univ NY, PhD(forest econ), 59. *Prof Exp:* Asst forester, Exp Sta & asst prof forestry, Univ Vt, 50-54; instr forest econ, State Univ NY Col Forestry, Syracuse Univ, 57-59. *Mem:* Soc Am Foresters. *Res:* Forestry economics. *Mailing Add:* 715 Ridgewood Ave Ames IA 50010

HOPKINS, GEORGE C, POLYMER CHEMISTRY. *Current Pos:* Technician chem, Hooker Chem Corp, 58-60, chemist, 60-68, proj coordr PVC & related polymers, 68-72, sect mgr, 72-75, ASSOC DIR RES & DEVELOP, HOOKER CHEM CORP, 75- *Personal Data:* b Buffalo, NY, June 29, 35; m 54; c 3. *Educ:* State Univ NY Buffalo, BA, 61, PhD(org chem), 67. *Mem:* Am Chem Soc; Soc Plastics Engrs. *Res:* Polymer and plastics synthesis, evaluation and process development. *Mailing Add:* 1730 Pinon Circle St Cloud FL 34769-1644

HOPKINS, GEORGE H, JR, ELECTRICAL ENGINEERING, GEOPHYSICS. *Current Pos:* ASSOC PROF ELEC ENG, TEX A&I UNIV, 88- *Personal Data:* b San Saba, Tex, Jan 1, 33; m 93, Galina K Lesnitchaya; c Heather J & Tamara L. *Educ:* Univ Tex, BS, 56, MS, 57, PhD, 66. *Prof Exp:* Instr elec eng, Univ Tex, 57-61, res engr, Elec Eng Res Lab, 61-65; chief engr, Geosci, Inc, Mass, 65-66, sr vpres, 66-68; pres, Geotronics Corp, 68-85. *Concurrent Pos:* Consult, Geosci, Inc, Mass, 64-65. *Mem:* Inst Elec & Electronics Engrs; Am Geophys Union; Soc Explor Geophys. *Res:* Electrical geoscience; magnetotellurics; instrumentation. *Mailing Add:* Dept Elec Eng Comput Sci Tex A&I Univ Campus Box 192 Kingsville TX 78363

HOPKINS, GEORGE WILLIAM, II, OPTICAL ENGINEERING. *Current Pos:* develop engr, Hewlett-Packard Co, 77-80, 84-86 & 89-90, mem tech staff, 80-84, prod mgr, 86-89, mem tech staff, 90-92, PRIN PROJ ENGR, HEWLETT-PACKARD CO, 92- *Personal Data:* b Sewanee, Tenn, Mar 30, 47; m 70, Karen Melby; c Dawn D. *Educ:* Univ of the South, BA, 68; Univ Mass, MS, 70; Univ Ariz, PhD(optical sci), 76. *Prof Exp:* Res assoc, Univ Ariz, 76-77. *Mem:* Optical Soc Am; Soc Photo-Optical Instrumentation Engrs. *Res:* Instrumentation using optical techniques; granted two United States patents. *Mailing Add:* Hewlett-Packard Co 3500 Deercreek Rd Palo Alto CA 94304-1392. *Fax:* 650-857-2862; *E-Mail:* hopkins@hpl.hp.com

HOPKINS, GORDON BRUCE, PATHOLOGY, NUCLEAR MEDICINE. *Current Pos:* LAB DIR, SHARP REESE-STEALY LAB, 92- *Personal Data:* b Seattle, Wash; m 67. *Educ:* Gonzaga Univ, BA, 62; Med Col Wis, MD, 66. *Prof Exp:* Intern path, Univ Wash, 66-67, resident, 67-70; resident path & nuclear med, Univ Ore, 70-71; asst clin prof, Univ Calif, Med Sch, San Diego, 72-93; dir, Div Nuclear Med, Dept Path, Scripps Mem Hosp, 73-92. *Mem:* Col Am Path; Am Soc Clin Path; Am Col Nuclear Physicians; Soc Nuclear Med. *Res:* Clinical evaluation of diagnostic radiopharmaceuticals. *Mailing Add:* Dept Path Scipps Mem Hosp Dept La Jolla CA 92037

HOPKINS, HARRY P, JR, PHYSICAL CHEMISTRY. *Current Pos:* from asst prof to assoc prof chem, 67-74, PROF CHEM, GA STATE UNIV, 74- *Personal Data:* b Norfolk, Va, July 10, 39; m; c 1. *Educ:* Univ Va, BA, 61; Carnegie Inst Technol, PhD(phys chem), 65. *Prof Exp:* AEC fel, Univ Pittsburgh, 65; Welch res fel, Rice Univ, 65-67. *Mem:* Am Chem Soc. *Res:* Calorimetry; solution chemistry; infrared and magnetic resonance spectroscopy. *Mailing Add:* 5066 Shadow Glen Ct Atlanta GA 30338

HOPKINS, HOMER THAWLEY, PLANT PHYSIOLOGY, INTERNATIONAL AGRICULTURAL DEVELOPMENT. *Current Pos:* VOL COORDR INTL PROG, UNIV MD, INST APPL AGR, 84- *Personal Data:* b Frederica, Del, July 27, 13; m 40; c 1. *Educ:* Univ Del, BS, 35, Cornell Univ, MS, 39; Univ Md, PhD(plant physiol), 51. *Prof Exp:* Asst chemist, State Bd Agr, Del, 35-37; anal chemist, Forest Soils Lab, Cornell Univ, 37-38; soil conservationist, Soil Conserv Serv, USDA, 39-42, asst chemist, Bur Plant Indust, Agr Res Admin, 46-47, assoc soil scientist, 47-53, plant physiologist, AEC Proj, Agr Res Serv, 53-56, supvr chemist human nutrit, Agr Res Serv; chemist-in-charge invests membrane transport, Nutrit Div, US Food & Drug Admin, 61-69; biol sci adminr, Radiation Biol Lab, Smithsonian Inst, 69-70; staff officer, Food & Nutrit Bd, Nat Acad Sci-Nat Res Coun, Washington, DC, 70-71; consult tech & sci info, life & earth sci, 71-73; prog mgr environ sci & geochem, Hittman Assocs, Inc, 73-81; consult tech & sci info, life & health sci, 81-84. *Concurrent Pos:* Asst adj prof, Univ Md Inst Appl Agr, 85- *Mem:* Fel AAAS; Am Soc Plant Physiol; Am Chem Soc; Am Inst Biol Sci; NY Acad Sci; Sigma Xi; Asn Int Agr & Exten Educ; Am Asn Adult & Continuing Educ. *Res:* Ion transport across living membranes; nutrient composition of national food supplies; phytotoxicity and persistence of chlorinated hydrocarbon insecticides in soils; soil biology; plant materials for the rehabilitation of lands disturbed by construction, mining and related activities; assessment of potential ecological and health effects of synthetic fuel technologies. *Mailing Add:* 4500 Elmwood Rd Beltsville MD 20705-2618

HOPKINS, HORACE H, JR, PHYSICAL CHEMISTRY, INDUSTRIAL ENGINEERING. *Current Pos:* staff engr, Res & Develop Dept, Atlantic Richfield-Hanford Co, 69-76, mgr, Strategic Planning Dept, 74-75, staff engr res & develop, Rockwell Hanford Opers, 76-86, STAFF ENGR, WESTINGHOUSE HANFORD OPERS, ATLANTIC RICHFIELD-HANFORD CO, 86- *Personal Data:* b Orange, NJ, Dec 24, 22; m 57; c 2. *Educ:* Oberlin Col, BS, 43; Univ Calif, PhD(chem), 49. *Prof Exp:* Chemist, Metall Lab, Univ Chicago, 43-46; chemist, Gen Elec Co, 49-65; mgr, Puchem Lab, Isochem Co, 66-69. *Mem:* Am Nuclear Soc; Am Chem Soc. *Res:* Radiochemistry; nuclear materials processing; inorganic chemistry; manufacturing engineering. *Mailing Add:* 25301 103rd Ave E Graham WA 98338-8971

HOPKINS, JOHN CHAPMAN, NUCLEAR PHYSICS. *Current Pos:* RETIRED. *Personal Data:* b Palo Alto, Calif, June 30, 33; m 54, Adele Herrigel; c Anna & Barbara. *Educ:* Univ Wash, BSc, 55, PhD(physics), 60. *Prof Exp:* Physics staff, Los Alamos Nat Lab, 60-72, asst div leader, Field Test Div, 72-74, div leader, 74-82, dep assoc dir, 82-84, assoc dir, 84-92. *Concurrent Pos:* Vis scientist, Nuclear Res Div, Atomic Weapons Res Estab, Eng, 63-64; vis scholar, Univ Calif, San Diego, 92-93. *Mem:* Fel Am Phys Soc. *Res:* Beta decay; beta polarization; fission; neutron scattering; nuclear weapons policy. *Mailing Add:* 1251 41st St Los Alamos NM 87544. *E-Mail:* johnchopki@aol.com

HOPKINS, JOHN RAYMOND, GEOPHYSICS. *Current Pos:* at CONOCO INC, KATY, TEX. *Personal Data:* b Greenup, Ill, Nov 19, 44; m 66; c 2. *Educ:* Eastern Ill Univ, BS, 66; Iowa State Univ, PhD(physics), 72. *Prof Exp:* Res assoc physics, Okla State Univ, 72-74; res scientist, Continental Oil Co, 74-77, sr res scientist, 77-78, sr staff geophysicist, 78-80, assoc div explor mgr, enver, 74- *Mem:* Sigma Xi; Soc Explor Geophysicists. *Res:* Shear and compressional wave propagation and reflection properties and their applications in geophysics; Gulf Coast and Rocky Mountains hydrocarbon exploration. *Mailing Add:* 907 Caswell Ct Katy TX 77450-2814

HOPKINS, JOHNS WILSON, MOLECULAR BIOLOGY. *Current Pos:* assoc prof, 66-69, chmn dept, 66-75, PROF BIOL, WASH UNIV, 69- *Personal Data:* b Darlington, Md, Apr 1, 33; m 55; c 1. *Educ:* Haverford Col, BS, 55; Rockefeller Inst, PhD(biol), 60. *Prof Exp:* From instr to asst prof biol, Harvard Univ, 60-66. *Res:* Science education. *Mailing Add:* Dept Biol Campus Box 1137 Wash Univ 1 Brookings Dr St Louis MO 63130-4862

HOPKINS, LAURIE BOYLE, IMPROVEMENT OF MATHEMATICAL PEDOGOGY. *Current Pos:* Asst prof math, 84-89, ASSOC PROF MATH, COLUMBIA COL, 89- *Personal Data:* b Columbia, SC, Apr 12, 51; m, Christie; c Earle, Alice & Tommy. *Educ:* Univ SC, BS, 76, PhD(math), 81. *Concurrent Pos:* Chmn math dept, Columbia Col, 92- *Mem:* Math Asn Am; Am Asn Math; Nat Coun Teachers Math. *Res:* Techniques which motivate and encourage women to study and learn mathematics; techniques for enabling mathematics teachers to improve their instruction; alternative formats for instruction of traditional courses. *Mailing Add:* 1301 Columbia Col Columbia SC 29206

HOPKINS, LEON LORRAINE, nutrition, for more information see previous edition

HOPKINS, M E, GEOLOGY. *Current Pos:* RETIRED. *Personal Data:* b Grove, Okla, Feb 4, 28; m 57; c 1. *Educ:* Univ Ark, BS, 50, MS, 51; Univ Ill, PhD(geol), 57. *Prof Exp:* Asst, Univ Ark, 50-51; asst, Coal Div, State Geol Surv, Ill, 51-53, asst geologist, 53-55; asst prof geol, Univ Tulsa, 55-63; assoc geologist, Ill Geol Surv, 63-68, actg head sect, 68-69, geologist & head coal sect, 69-75; consult coal geol, H Williamson, Inc, 75-81; dir geol, Peabody Coal Co, 81-83, dir geol, Peabody Develop Co, 83-93. *Mem:* Geol Soc Am; Soc Econ Paleont & Mineral; Am Inst Mining, Metall & Petrol Engrs. *Res:* Coal mining geology; stratigraphy; sedimentation; field geology; subsurface geology; sedimentary petrology. *Mailing Add:* 35 Club Grounds North Dr Florissant MO 63033

HOPKINS, MANSELL HERBERT, JR, ELECTRICAL ENGINEERING. *Current Pos:* asst prof, 55-58, ASSOC PROF ELEC ENG, VA POLYTECH INST & STATE UNIV, 58- *Personal Data:* b Warrenton, Va, Oct 2, 27; m 52; c 3. *Educ:* Va Polytech Inst, BSEE, 53, MSEE, 58; Iowa State Univ, PhD(elec eng), 64. *Prof Exp:* Qual control engr, Lamp Div, Gen Elec Co, 53-55. *Concurrent Pos:* NSF Res fel, Iowa State Univ, 60-61. *Mem:* Am Soc Eng Educ; Inst Elec & Electronics Engrs. *Res:* Power systems; instrumentation and protection; controls. *Mailing Add:* Dept Elec Eng Va Polytech Inst & State Univ Blacksburg VA 24061

HOPKINS, NIGEL JOHN, OPERATIONS RESEARCH. *Current Pos:* PRES, H C CAMIRRAL LTD, 85-; PRES ORBITA CONSULTS, LTD, 90- *Personal Data:* b Indian Head, Sask, July 2, 22; m 45, 84, Sally Carling; c John. *Educ:* McGill Univ, BSc, 48, MSc, 49, PhD(nuclear physics), 52. *Prof Exp:* Res physicist, Atomic Energy Can Ltd, 52-53; staff mem, Nat Defense Hq, 53-68, dir maritime oper res, 68-70, dir land opers res, Can Forces Hq, 70-74, sr planning officer, 74-77, dir sci & tech intel, Nat Defense HQ, 77-85. *Mem:* Can Oper Res Soc (pres, 72-73). *Res:* Operational research; systems analysis; planning of research and development; scientific intelligence. *Mailing Add:* 304-200 Rideau Terr Ottawa ON K1M 0Z3 Can. *E-Mail:* nhopkins@sympatico.ca

HOPKINS, PAUL BRINK, CHEMISTRY. *Current Pos:* asst prof, 82-88, ASSOC PROF CHEM, DEPT CHEM, UNIV WASH, 88- *Personal Data:* b Indianapolis, Ind, June 13, 56. *Educ:* Purdue Univ, BS, 77; Harvard Univ, PhD(chem), 82. *Honors & Awards:* ICI Awardee, 88. *Concurrent Pos:* Searle scholar, 84-87; Sloan fel, 88-90. *Mem:* Am Chem Soc; AAAS. *Res:* Organic and bio-organic chemistry. *Mailing Add:* Dept Chem Box 351700 Seattle WA 98195-1700

HOPKINS, PAUL DONALD, INORGANIC CHEMISTRY. *Current Pos:* Asst proj chemist, Amoco Oil Co, 63-65, proj chemist, 65-67, rr proj chemist, 67-74, res chemist, 74-81, sr res chemist, 81-89, RES ASSOC, AMOCO OIL CO, 89- *Personal Data:* b Woodbury, NJ, Apr 1, 35; m 63; c 3. *Educ:* Haverford Col, BS, 57; Univ Pittsburgh, PhD(inorg chem), 63. *Mem:* Am Chem Soc; Chem Soc; Catalysis Soc; Clay Minerals Soc. *Res:* Transition metal, coordination and surface chemistry; catalytic conversions of petroleum; oxidation of liquid hydrocarbons; synthesis of heterogeneous catalysts and zeolites. *Mailing Add:* 1402 S Seventh St St Charles IL 60174-3809

HOPKINS, RICHARD A, ENGINEERING GEOPHYSICS. *Current Pos:* CONSULT, 88- *Personal Data:* b New Rochelle, NY, Apr 4, 43; m 70, Martha E; c Matthew L & Nathan T. *Educ:* Murray State Univ, BA, 70; Univ Tenn, MS, 76. *Prof Exp:* Mem staff eng geophys, Tenn Valley Authority, 72-88. *Concurrent Pos:* Asst instr, Univ Tenn, 78. *Mem:* Soc Explor Geophysicists; Am Geophys Union; Asn Eng Geologists; Nat Water Well Asn; Am Soc Testing & Mat. *Res:* Borehole and surface techniques as applied to geotechnical, geohydrological and environmental investigations. *Mailing Add:* Marrich Inc PO Box 9179 Knoxville TN 37940-0179

HOPKINS, RICHARD H(ENRY), MATERIALS SCIENCE, METALLURGY. *Current Pos:* Sr engr res labs, Westinghouse Elec Corp, 67-73, fel engr, Westinghouse Res & Develop Ctr, 73-77, prog mgr, 77-80, mgr crystal sci, 80-87, mgr, Silicon WEB Technol Develop, 84-87, mgr electro-optical mat, 88-90, mgr electronic & photonic mat, Westinghouse Res & Develop Ctr, 90-91, mgr, Silicon Carbide Electronics, Westinghouse Sci & Technol Ctr, 91-95, MGR MICROELECTRONICS, NORTHROP GRUMMAN SCI & TECHNOL CTR, WESTINGHOUSE ELEC CORP, 96- *Personal Data:* b Hartford, Conn, Dec 23, 40; m 68, Donna J; c Brian. *Educ:* Lehigh Univ, BS, 63, MS, 65, PhD(metall), 67. *Concurrent Pos:* Bd dirs, Am Inst Mat Engrs, 82-; invited lectr, Int Conf Crystal Growth, 84; pres, Pittsburgh Chapter-Crystal Grower; chmn, Am Asn Crystal Growth (East), 92-97. *Mem:* AAAS; Am Soc Metals Int; Am Inst Mining, Metall & Petrol Engrs; Am Asn Crystal Growth; Mat Res Soc. *Res:* Solidification and crystal perfection of metallic alloys; development of high melting inorganic materials for optical devices; growth and evaluation of synthetic crystals; crystal growth and perfection of metals, alloys, inorganic compounds and semiconductors; studies of composites, optical devices, and solar cells; ribbon crystal growth of silicon; development of acoustical crystals; studies of epitaxial ferrite films; silicon carbide crystal growth and development of silicon carbide microwave and high temperature electronics. *Mailing Add:* Northrop Grumman Sci & Technol Ctr 1350 Bueluh Rd Pittsburgh PA 15235. *Fax:* 412-256-1331

HOPKINS, ROBERT CHARLES, DNA STRUCTURE, DNA FUNCTION. *Current Pos:* assoc prof & dir sci, 76-81, interim dean, Sch Natural & Appl Sci, 94-95, PROF CHEM & BIOPHYS, UNIV HOUSTON, CLEAR LAKE, 81- *Personal Data:* b Pasadena, Calif, July 23, 37; m 65, Star Martin; c Karen M & Rand C. *Educ:* Univ Calif, Los Angeles, BS, 59; Harvard Univ, MA, 62, PhD(phys chem), 65. *Prof Exp:* Staff physicist, Shell Develop Co, 65-76. *Concurrent Pos:* Vis prof, Molecular Biol Inst, Univ Calif, Los Angeles, 82, dept chem, Univ Mich, 86. *Mem:* Am Phys Soc; Biophys Soc. *Res:* Theoretical studies of implications for a new family of double-helical DNA models including four-stranded structures; physical and biological investigations seeking evidence for such DNA forms. *Mailing Add:* Univ Houston-Clear Lake 2700 Bay Area Blvd Houston TX 77058

HOPKINS, ROBERT WEST, VASCULAR SURGERY. *Current Pos:* PROF MED SCI, BROWN UNIV, 70- *Personal Data:* b Springfield, Mass, May 26, 24; m 60, Ann Demetreou; c Mary A & Elizabeth C. *Educ:* Harvard Med Sch, MD, 47. *Prof Exp:* Instr surg, Sch Med, Univ Pa, 55-58; from sr instr to assoc prof, Case Western Res Univ, 58-70. *Concurrent Pos:* Asst surgeon, Pa Hosp, Philadelphia, 55-58; lower fel, Case Western Res Univ, 58-59; asst vis surgeon, Cleveland Metrop Gen Hosp, 55-65, assoc surgeon, 65-70; assoc surgeon-in-chief, Miriam Hosp, Providence, RI, 70-80, surgeon-in-chief, 80-86, sr surgeon, 86- *Mem:* Am Surg Asn; Soc Vascular Surg; Am Asn Surg Trauma; Sigma Xi. *Res:* Surgical physiology; physiologic and biochemical changes in circulatory shock in animals and in man. *Mailing Add:* 164 Summit Ave Providence RI 02906-2800

HOPKINS, RONALD MURRAY, TOXICOLOGY, PHARMACY. *Current Pos:* VPRES RES & DEVELOP, ALLIANCE PHARMACEUT CORP, 90- *Personal Data:* b Baltimore, Md, Jan 4, 42; m 87, 62; c Carol McNail. *Educ:* Univ Md, BS, 63, MS, 67, PhD(pharmacol), 70. *Prof Exp:* Pharmacologist, Huntingdon Res Ctr, Inc, 65-69; instr pharmacol, Univ Md Sch Dent, 69-70; from res pharmacologist to sr res pharmacologist, Mallinckrodt, Inc, 70-76, asst pharm dir & toxicol, 76-80, from assoc dir to dir res, 80-84, dir res & develop, Opers Div, 84-88, bus dir, Nuclear Med Prod, 88-89, vpres tech planning, 89-90. *Mem:* Am Soc Pharmacol & Exp Therapeut; Am Inst Ultrasound Medsci; Magnetic Resonance Imaging Soc. *Res:* All phases of toxicological evaluation primarily involving diagnostic radiographic media and radiopharmaceuticals; cardiovascular and pulmonary pharmacology; industrial pharmaceutical formulation, primarily parenterals; medical device. *Mailing Add:* Alliance Pharmaceut Corp 3040 Science Park Rd San Diego CA 92121-1102

HOPKINS, THEODORE LOUIS, ENTOMOLOGY. *Current Pos:* from instr to assoc prof, 58-70, PROF ENTOM, KANS STATE UNIV, 70- *Personal Data:* b San Diego, Calif, June 12, 29; m 51, 71, Arlene McGregor; c David A, Gail J, Linda A, Annaliese (Briggs), Albert E Goedde & Terezie S (Stanberry). *Educ:* Ore State Univ, BS, 51, MS, 56; Kans State Univ, PhD(entom), 60. *Prof Exp:* Entomologist, USDA, 53-57. *Mem:* Entom Soc Am; Sigma Xi; Orthop Soc. *Res:* Biochemistry and physiology of insect cuticle formation and structure; chemistry of insect/plant interactions. *Mailing Add:* 5501 Turkeyfoot Lane Manhattan KS 66503. *Fax:* 785-532-6232; *E-Mail:* thopkins@oz.oznet.ksu.edu

HOPKINS, THOMAS FRANKLIN, REPRODUCTIVE ENDOCRINOLOGY. *Current Pos:* RETIRED. *Personal Data:* b Culpepper, Va, Dec 16, 24; c Thea Louise, Thomas M, Charles M, Arthur G & Michael. *Educ:* Calvin Coolidge Col, BS, 55; Mich State Univ, MS, 61; Boston Univ, PhD(physiol), 70. *Prof Exp:* Res asst, Worcester Found Exp Biol, 48-59, staff scientist, 61-70; assoc prof physiol, Univ Conn, 70-75; prof biol & head, Dept Natural Sci, Univ Md, Eastern Shore, 75-94. *Mem:* AAAS; Am Soc Zool; Am Physiol Soc; Soc Study Reprod. *Res:* Toxic effects of heavy metals; physiology of aging. *Mailing Add:* 1602 Camden Ave Salisbury MD 21801

HOPKINS, THOMAS LEE, OCEANIC FOOD WEBS, OCEANIC & NEARSHORE ENVIRONMENTS. *Current Pos:* PROF BIOL OCEANOG, DEPT MARINE SCI, UNIV SFLA, 67- *Personal Data:* b Harve De Grace, Md, Sept 25, 30; m 59, Gerrie Ethridge; c Eric & Elaine. *Educ:* Univ Del, BA, 55, MA, 57; Fla State Univ, PhD(zool), 64. *Prof Exp:* Fel, Univ Southern Calif, 64-67. *Mem:* Am Soc Limnol & Oceanog; Crustation Soc. *Res:* Oceanic food webs in the Antarctic and low latitudes; investigate role of zooplankton both as consumers and as food in marine ecosystems. *Mailing Add:* Dept Marine Sci Univ SFla 140 Seventh Ave S St Petersburg FL 33701-5016. *Fax:* 813-893-9189; *E-Mail:* t.hopkins.usf@omnet.nasa.gov

HOPKINS, THOMAS R (TIM), ENZYMOLOGY, PROTEIN CHEMISTRY. *Current Pos:* PRES & CEO, BIOSPEC PROD INC, 81- *Personal Data:* b Urbana, Ill, Oct 12, 38; m 90, Sharon Ginn; c Bryan, James, Steve, Chris & Tara. *Educ:* Univ Calif, Berkeley, BA, 61; Univ Utah, MS, 65, PhD(molecular biol), 67. *Honors & Awards:* IR 100 Award. *Prof Exp:* USPHS fel phys chem, Univ Minn, Minneapolis, 67-69; sr lectr biochem, Med Sch,

Univ Otago, NZ, 69-76; mgr biochem processes, Biotech Div, Phillips Petrol Co, 76-88. *Concurrent Pos:* Consult, Biochem Instrumentation; tech mgr, S&T Promotions, Inc. *Mem:* Am Soc Photobiol; Am Soc Biol Chemists; Biophys Soc. *Res:* Protein biophysics and chemistry; excited and ground state energy transfer in biomolecules; biochemical instrumentation; industrial applications of enzymes and proteins. *Mailing Add:* Biospec Prod Inc PO Box 722 Bartlesville OK 74005-0722. Fax: 918-336-3363

HOPKINS, WILLIAM GEORGE, PLANT PHYSIOLOGY. *Current Pos:* from asst prof to prof, 69-89, EMER PROF BIOL, UNIV WESTERN ONT, 95- *Personal Data:* b Woodbury, NJ, Aug 15, 37; m 59; c 2. *Educ:* Wesleyan Univ, AB, 59; Ind Univ, PhD(bot), 64. *Prof Exp:* Res assoc plant physiol, Brookhaven Nat Lab, 63-65; asst prof biol, Bryn Mawr Col, 65-69. *Mem:* Am Soc Plant Physiol; Can Soc Plant Physiol; Scand Soc Plant Physiol. *Res:* Growth and development of higher plants; organization and development of photosynthetic membranes; bioenergetics. *Mailing Add:* Dept Plant Sci Univ Western Ont London ON N6A 5B7 Can

HOPKINS, WILLIAM STEPHEN, PALYNOLOGY, GEOLOGY. *Personal Data:* b Palo Alto, Calif, July 29, 31; m 64; c 2. *Educ:* Univ Wash, BSc, 54; Univ BC, MSc, 62; PhD(palynology, geol), 66. *Prof Exp:* Geologist, Humble Oil & Refining Co, 58-60; res scientist, Pan Am Petrol Res Ctr, Okla, 66-68; res scientist, Inst Sedimentary & Petrol Geol, Geol Surv Can, 68-84. *Concurrent Pos:* Consult & adv polynology & geol, San Juan Islands, Wash, 84-; founder & pres, Waldron Geol Consult, Inc. *Mem:* AAAS; fel Geol Soc Am; Am Asn Stratig Palynologists. *Res:* Palynology, paleoecology and past floral distributions in Tertiary and Cretaceous sedimentary rocks from British Columbia and Washington State. *Mailing Add:* PO Box 610 Eastsound WA 98245

HOPLA, CLUFF EARL, MEDICAL ENTOMOLOGY. *Current Pos:* asst prof entom, 51-59, from assoc prof to prof zool, 59-69, GEORGE LYNN CROSS RES PROF ZOOL, UNIV OKLA, 69-, CHMN DEPT, 62-, CUR ENTOM, STOVALL MUS, 59- *Personal Data:* b Mapleton, Utah, Dec 28, 17; m 41; c 3. *Educ:* Brigham Young Univ, BS, 41, MS, 47; Univ Kans, PhD(entom, bact), 50. *Prof Exp:* Res assoc, Univ Kans, 50-51. *Mem:* Am Soc Parasitol; Am Soc Trop Med & Hyg; Entom Soc Am; Soc Syst Zool. *Res:* Zoonoses; bionomics and taxonomy of Acarina, Culicidae and Siphonaptera. *Mailing Add:* Dept Zool Univ Okla 730 Van Vleet Oval Norman OK 73019

HOPP, WILLIAM BEECHER, ZOOLOGY. *Current Pos:* RETIRED. *Personal Data:* b Terre Haute, Ind, Sept 4, 17; m 49; c 1. *Educ:* Ind State Teachers Col, BS, 39; Purdue Univ, MS, 41, PhD(zool), 53. *Prof Exp:* Instr biol, Purdue Univ, 46-47; asst prof zool, Eastern Ky State Col, 47-55; from asst prof to assoc prof zool, Ind State Univ, 55-61, chmn div sci, 61-69, prof zool, 61- *Mem:* AAAS; Am Soc Parasitol; Am Soc Ichthyol & Herpet; Sigma Xi. *Res:* Parasitology; herpetology. *Mailing Add:* 335 S Brown Ave Terre Haute IN 47813

HOPPE, DAVID MATTHEW, VERTEBRATE BIOLOGY, EVOLUTIONARY ECOLOGY. *Current Pos:* PROF BIOL, UNIV MINN, MORRIS, 75- *Personal Data:* b West Concord, Minn, Aug 22, 42; div. *Educ:* Univ Minn, BA, 64, MS, 68; Colo State Univ, PhD(zool), 75. *Prof Exp:* Asst scientist genetics, Univ Minn, 64-66; asst prof biol, Mayville State Col, 68-72; instr zool, Colo State Univ, 73-74. *Concurrent Pos:* Consult ecol, Houston Eng, Inc, 75- *Mem:* Sigma Xi; Soc Study Amphibians & Reptiles; Herpet League; Nat Wildlife Fedn. *Res:* Genetics and ecology of amphibian adaptations, particularly color polymorphism and various developmental phenomena; xenopus albinism; amphibian declines. *Mailing Add:* Dept Math & Sci Univ Minn Morris MN 56267-2134

HOPPE, JOHN CAMERON, APPLIED PHYSICS. *Current Pos:* electronics engr appl physics, 65-83, sect head, Photo-Optical Inst, 83-93, TM.LDRY APPL OPTICS, LANGLEY RES CTR, NASA, 93- *Personal Data:* b San Diego, Calif, Aug 18, 43; m 89, Patricia A Colosi; c 3. *Educ:* Col William & Mary, BS, 64, MS, 67; Va Polytech Inst & State Univ, PhD(physics), 77. *Prof Exp:* Engr appl physics, Va Assoc Res Ctr, 64-65. *Concurrent Pos:* Adj prof, St Leo Col, 80- 89. *Mem:* Am Phys Soc; Optical Soc Am; Inst Elec & Electronics Engrs; Soc Indust & Appl Math; Am Soc Photogram & Remote Sensing; Am Inst Aeronaut & Astronaut. *Res:* Applied optics; laser applications; scattering of electromagnetic radiation; applications of laser light scattering methods to measure properties of gas flows; applications of video close-range photogrammetry; flow visualization technology. *Mailing Add:* Langley Res Ctr NASA Mail Stop 236 Hampton VA 23681. Fax: 757-864-7607

HOPPE, PETER CHRISTIAN, REPRODUCTIVE BIOLOGY. *Current Pos:* Fel, 68-70, assoc staff scientist to staff scientist, 70-81, SR STAFF SCIENTIST, JACKSON LAB, 81- *Personal Data:* b Long Beach, Calif, Feb 16, 42; m 63; c 3. *Educ:* Calif State Polytech Univ, BS, 64; Kans State Univ, MS, 66, PhD(reprod physiol), 68. *Mem:* Soc Study Reprod. *Res:* Mammalian reproductive physiology; fertilization; parthenogenesis; differentiation; transgenic mice. *Mailing Add:* Jackson Lab Bar Harbor ME 04609

HOPPENJANS, DONALD WILLIAM, PHYSICAL INORGANIC CHEMISTRY. *Current Pos:* res chemist, 69-73, tech supvr, 73, tech mgr, 74-78, prod mgr, 78-83, SR RES SUPVR, E I DU PONT DE NEMOURS & CO, INC, 83-; BIOMAT PROG CONSULT. *Personal Data:* b Covington, Ky, June 21, 41; m; c 4. *Educ:* Bellarmine Col, AB, 63; Cath Univ Am, PhD(phys inorg chem), 67. *Prof Exp:* Fel, Univ Iowa, 67-69. *Mem:* Am Chem Soc. *Res:* Kinetics and mechanisms of the reactions of coordination compounds; fused salts; paint technology; TiO_2 product development; biomaterials. *Mailing Add:* 315 Hampton Rd Wilmington DE 19803

HOPPENSTEADT, FRANK CHARLES, MATHEMATICS. *Current Pos:* asst prof math, 65-68, DEAN, COL NATURAL SCI, MICH STATE UNIV, EAST LANSING, 86- *Personal Data:* b Oak Park, Ill, Apr 29, 38; m 86, Leslie Thomas; c Charles, Matthew & Sarah. *Educ:* Butler Univ, BA, 60; Univ Wis, MS, 62, PhD, 65. *Prof Exp:* From assoc prof to prof, NY Univ, 68-79; prof, Univ Utah, Salt Lake City, 77-86, chmn, Dept Math, 82-85. *Mem:* Am Math Soc; Soc Indust & Appl Math; Sigma Xi. *Res:* Mathematics. *Mailing Add:* Box 7606 Ariz State Univ Tempe AZ 85287

HOPPER, ANITA KLEIN, GENETICS, MOLECULAR BIOLOGY. *Current Pos:* assoc prof, 79-87, PROF BIOCHEM, HERSHEY MED CTR, PA, 87- *Personal Data:* b Chicago, Ill, Sept 24, 45; m 71, James; c Julie. *Educ:* Univ Ill, Chicago, BS, 67; Univ Ill, Urbana, PhD(biol), 72. *Prof Exp:* Fel genetics & molecular biol, Univ Wash, 72-75; from asst prof to assoc prof genetics & molecular biol, Med Sch, Univ Mass, 75-79. *Concurrent Pos:* Mem NSF panel genetic biol, 81-85, NIH genetics study sect, 85-89; ed, Molecular Cell Biol, 89-; mem, Sci Adv Comt, Am Cancer Soc, 94- *Mem:* Am Soc Microbiol; Am Soc Biol Chemists; AAAS; fel Am Acad Microbiol. *Res:* Molecular mechanisms of import of proteins into mitochondria and nuclei; synthesis and maturation of transfer RNA in yeast; cell biology. *Mailing Add:* Dept Biochem & Molecular Biol Milton S Hershey Med Ctr Hershey PA 17033. Fax: 717-531-7072

HOPPER, ARTHUR FREDERICK, RADIATION BIOLOGY. *Current Pos:* from asst prof to prof, 49-80, EMER PROF ZOOL, RUTGERS UNIV, NEW BRUNSWICK, 80- *Personal Data:* b Plainfield, NJ, Sept 7, 17; m 40, 86, Patricia Vennett; c Arthur F, Geoffrey V, Christopher J & Gregory L. *Educ:* Princeton Univ, AB, 38; Yale Univ, MS, 42; Northwestern Univ, PhD(zool), 48. *Prof Exp:* Instr zool, Northwestern Univ, 48; asst prof, Wayne Univ, 48-49. *Concurrent Pos:* Mem sci staff, Detroit Inst Cancer Res, 48-49; res collabr, Brookhaven Nat Lab, 63-80; vis prof, Univ Liege, 67-68; vis investr, Jackson Lab, 71 & 73. *Mem:* AAAS; Soc Develop Biol; Radiation Res Soc; Sigma Xi; Soc Integrated & Comp Biol. *Res:* Embryology and regeneration in fish and amphibians; cell population kinetics in the intestinal mucosa; radiation biology. *Mailing Add:* 231 Cocoanut Row Palm Beach FL 33480-4132

HOPPER, JACK R, CHEMICAL ENGINEERING, CATALYSIS. *Current Pos:* from asst prof to assoc prof, 69-75, PROF CHEM ENG, LAMAR UNIV, 75-, HEAD DEPT, 74- *Personal Data:* b Highlands, Tex, May 12, 37; m 58; c 2. *Educ:* Tex A&M Univ, BS, 59; Univ Del, MChE, 64; La State Univ, Baton Rouge, PhD(catalysis), 69. *Honors & Awards:* Dow Chem Co Award, Am Soc Eng Educ, 71. *Prof Exp:* Jr res engr, Humble Oil & Ref Co, 59-60, asst res engr, 60-61; res engr, Esso Res & Eng Co, 64-67; res assoc catalysis, La State Univ, Baton Rouge, 67-69. *Mem:* Fel Am Inst Chem Engrs; Am Chem Soc; Catalysis Soc; Am Soc Eng Educ. *Res:* Reaction engineering; catalysis, hazardous waste treatment and minimization; pollution prevention; environmental engineering. *Mailing Add:* 3590 Crestwood Dr Beaumont TX 77706-3731

HOPPER, JAMES ERNEST, CELL BIOLOGY, DEVELOPMENTAL BIOLOGY. *Current Pos:* ASSOC PROF, DEPT BIOL CHEM, MILTON S HERSHEY MED CTR, PA STATE UNIV. *Personal Data:* b Madison, Wis, July 16, 42; m 71. *Educ:* Univ Wis-Madison, BS, 64, MS, 67; PhD(genetics), 70. *Prof Exp:* Comt Instnl Coop traveling scholar & res assoc plant physiol, Univ Ill, Urbana, 69-71; NIH res fel biochem, Univ Wash, 71-75; mem staff, Med Ctr, Univ Mass, Worcester, 75- *Res:* Molecular basis of regulatory mechanisms underlying metabolic differentiation and developmental transitions. *Mailing Add:* Dept Biol Chem Pa State Univ Col Med PO Box 850 Hershey PA 17033-0850

HOPPER, JOHN HENRY, NUTRITION. *Current Pos:* RETIRED. *Personal Data:* b Briggsville, Ark, Mar 17, 25; m 51, Betty Johnston; c John B & Shirlee J. *Educ:* Univ Ark, BSA, 49, MS, 51; Univ Ill, PhD(nutrit), 55. *Prof Exp:* Asst nutrit, Univ Ark, 50-51; instr animal nutrit, Ark Agr & Mech Col, 51-52; asst nutrit, Univ Ill, 52-55; asst prof, Univ Nebr, 55-56; head animal nutrit res sect, Armour & Co, 56-60, dir nutrit, 60-69, dir res, 69-70, vpres & dir food res, 70-76, sr vpres sci affairs, Kellog Co, 76-79. *Res:* Vitamin, amino acid and protein metabolism; trace minerals, food composition; food metabolism; development of new foods. *Mailing Add:* PO Box 97 Hampton AR 71744

HOPPER, KENNETH DAVID, ULTRASOUND & MAGNETIC RESOURCE IMAGING, COMPUTED TOMOGRAPHY. *Current Pos:* PROF RADIOL, PA STATE UNIV, 89-, CHIEF BODY IMAGING & RADIOL RES. *Personal Data:* b Ada, Okla, Aug 18, 48; m 72, Margaret Guiney; c David, Katie & Tom. *Educ:* US Mil Acad, BS, 72; Med Sch, Univ Okla, MD, 79. *Honors & Awards:* Sir Henry Welcome Medal, Welcome & Co, 88; Cert Merit, Radiol Soc NAm, 90; Silver Medal, Am Roentgen Ray Soc, 91. *Prof Exp:* Chief computed tomography imaging, Fitzsimons Army Med Ctr, 85-87, chief diag, 87-88, chief dept & residency prog dir, 88-89. *Concurrent Pos:* Chief res, Pa State Univ, 89-, chief magnetic resource imaging, 89-91, chief computed tomography, 90-, chief body imaging, 91-; clin asst prof radiol, Univ Colo, 87-89, Uniformed Univ Health Studies, 87-90; prin investr, Meadox Surgimed, 91-92, Berlin Nickinson, 92, Amedic, 93, Shiley, 93-95, Mendl, 93-95. *Mem:* Soc Magnetic Resonance; Am Heart Asn; Radiol Soc NAm; Am Roentgen Ray Soc; Asn Univ Radiologists; Am Col Radiol. *Res:* Percutaneous biopsy techniques, informed consent, 3-dimensional imaging, computed tomography and radiology peer review. *Mailing Add:* 1620 Nottingham Dr Hummelstown PA 17036-8712. Fax: 717-531-5596

HOPPER, MAX D, DATA PROCESSING. *Current Pos:* Sr vpres info systs, CONSULT, AMR CORP, DALLAS. *Honors & Awards:* Distinguished Info Sci Award, Data Processing Mgt Asn, 95. *Mailing Add:* AMR Corp PO Box 619616 Dallas TX 75261-9616

HOPPER, MICHAEL JAMES, SPECTROSCOPY, ANALYTICAL CHEMISTRY. *Current Pos:* DEVELOP MGR RES & DEVELOP, FILM DIV, HOECHST-CELANESE CORP, 79- *Personal Data:* b Los Angeles, Calif, Sept 23, 40; m 68; c 2. *Educ:* Univ Calif, Riverside, BA, 62; Univ Minn, PhD(phys chem), 67. *Prof Exp:* Teaching asst inorg chem, Univ Calif, Riverside, 60-62; gen teaching asst gen chem, Univ Minn, 62-64, phys chem, 64-66; mem staff, Celanese Res Co, NJ, 67-71, supvr, Analytical & Phys Testing Dept, Celanar Res & Develop Div, 71-75, res & develop group leader appln & prod develop, Celanese Plastics Mat Co, 76-78, res & develop mgr film develop, 78-79. *Mem:* Am Chem Soc; Soc Appl Spectros; Coblentz Soc; Sigma Xi. *Res:* Ultraviolet spectroscopy; infrared spectroscopy of polymers; attenuated total reflectance spectroscopy of surfaces; thermal analysis; atomic absorption spectroscopy; gas chromatography; biaxially oriented polyester film technology; magnetic tape product development; dyed UV stabilized film development; process development; polarizing film technology. *Mailing Add:* Hoechst Celanese PO Box 1400 Greer SC 29652-1400

HOPPER, NORMAN WAYNE, CROP PHYSIOLOGY, SEED PHYSIOLOGY. *Current Pos:* ASSOC PROF AGRON, TEX TECH UNIV, 76- *Personal Data:* b Ralls, Tex, Sept 1, 43; m 66; c 3. *Educ:* Tex Tech Univ, BS, 65, MS, 67; Iowa State Univ, PhD(agron), 70. *Prof Exp:* Asst prof agron, Ohio State Univ, 70-76. *Mem:* Am Soc Agron; Crop Sci Soc Am. *Res:* Factors affecting seed quality; measurement of seed quality; seedling vigor studies. *Mailing Add:* Plant & Soil Sci Tex Tech Univ Lubbock TX 79409-0001

HOPPER, PAUL FREDERICK, ORGANIC CHEMISTRY, TOXICOLOGY. *Current Pos:* CONSULT, 88-; ADJ PROF FOOD SCI, CORNELL UNIV, 88- *Personal Data:* b Troy, NY, Oct 26, 24; m 50; c 4. *Educ:* Holy Cross Col, BS, 44; Univ Notre Dame, PhD(chem), 51. *Prof Exp:* Res chemist, Stamford Res Labs, Am Cyanamid Co, 49-52, group leader develop res, 52-53, tech rep, Govt Res Liaison, Washington, DC, 53-56, mgr consumer prod develop, Farm & Home Div, NY, 56-57, dir food indust develop, Agr Div, 57-60; prod mgr, Ethicon, Inc, NJ, 60-61; mgr prod develop, Devro Div, Johnson & Johnson, 61-63, vpres prod mgt, 64-70, vpres corp planning, 70-71; dir environ health sci, Gen Foods Corp, Tarrytown, 71-72, dir nutrit & health sci, 72-74, corp dir strategic tech planning, 74-78, corp dir sci affairs, White Plains, 78-88. *Concurrent Pos:* Pres, Flavor Mfr; adj prof, Cornell Univ. *Mem:* Am Chem Soc; fel Inst Food Technologists; fel Am Inst Chemists; AAAS; Coun Agr Sci & Technol. *Res:* Barbituates; methylene-dioxy compounds; cyanamide derivatives; cyanoethylation; s-triazines; organic nitrogen chemistry; synthetic organic chemistry; food science and technology; protein chemistry; food microbiology; food additives safety; nutrition; toxicology; biomedicine; research planning; food law. *Mailing Add:* 84 Londonderry Dr Greenwich CT 06830-3536

HOPPER, ROBERT WILLIAM, GLASS SCIENCE. *Current Pos:* MAT SCIENTIST, CHEM & MAT SCI DEPT, LAWRENCE LIVERMORE LAB, UNIV CALIF, 76- *Personal Data:* b New York, NY. *Educ:* Univ Wash, BS, 63; Harvard Univ, SM, 67; Mass Inst Technol, PhD(mat sci), 71. *Prof Exp:* Staff scientist metall, Manlabs, Inc, 65-67; mat engr, Microwave & Power Tube Div, Raytheon Co, 67-68; vpres res, Am Res & Instrument Corp, 71-72; asst prof polymers, Mass Inst Technol, 72-76. *Mem:* Am Ceramic Soc; Am Soc Metals; Soc Rheology; Am Phys Soc; AAAS. *Res:* Glasses, particularly inorganic, low molecular weight organic, polymeric and metallic; rheology of complex materials and its relationship to induced structural changes; interfaces; phase changes; mathematical modelling; low-density foams. *Mailing Add:* Lawrence Livermore Nat Labs PO Box 808 Livermore CA 94550

HOPPER, SAMUEL HERSEY, BACTERIOLOGY, PUBLIC HEALTH. *Current Pos:* RETIRED. *Personal Data:* b Boston, Mass, July 4, 11; m 37; c 2. *Educ:* Mass Inst Technol, BS, 33, MS, 34, PhD(bact), 37. *Prof Exp:* Res assoc, Mass Inst Technol, 37-39; asst prof bact & chem, Ga Inst Technol, 39-42; assoc prof chem, bact & sanit, Sch Pub Health, Univ NC, 42-44; mem staff sanit prog, War Shipping Admin, USPHS, Washington, DC, 44-45; from assoc prof to prof pub health, Sch Med, Ind Univ, Indianapolis, 45-81, chmn dept, 50-81. *Concurrent Pos:* Vis prof, Butler Univ; consult, Ind State Bd Health; consult & dir scientist res corp, USPHS. *Mem:* AAAS; Am Soc Microbiol; fel Am Pub Health Asn; Sigma Xi; fel AAAS; Inst Food Tech; NY Acad Med. *Res:* Biochemistry of bacteria; bacteriology and pharmacology of wetting agents; flotation process for detection of toxins or bacteria; food microbiology. *Mailing Add:* 5064 Boardwalk Pl Indianapolis IN 46220-5382

HOPPER, STEVEN PHILLIP, ORGANOMETALLIC CHEMISTRY. *Current Pos:* MGR MKT, C P HALL, CHICAGO, 90- *Personal Data:* b Tucson, Ariz, June 14, 45; div; c 2. *Educ:* Wabash Col, BA, 67; Mass Inst Technol, PhD(inorg chem), 72. *Prof Exp:* Asst prof org chem, Wabash Col, 72-73; asst prof inorg chem, Vassar Col, 73-80; proj scientist, Union Carbide Corp, Tarrytown, NY, 80-84, res chemist, 84-86, mgr, Nat Tech Sales, 86-88, prog mgr, 88-90. *Mem:* Am Chem Soc. *Res:* Preparative organometallic chemistry of the main group elements, particularly silicon and boron groups; organosilicon polymers. *Mailing Add:* 532 Turner Ave Glen Ellyn IL 60137

HOPPES, DALE DUBOIS, NUCLEAR PHYSICS. *Current Pos:* RETIRED. *Personal Data:* b Liberty, Ind, Sept 13, 28; m 50; c 4. *Educ:* Purdue Univ, BS, 50; Cath Univ Am, MS, 56, PhD(nuclear physics), 61. *Prof Exp:* Leader, Radioactivity Group, Nat Inst Stand & Technol, 50-92. *Mem:* Am Phys Soc. *Res:* Radioactivity standardization. *Mailing Add:* 5671 Crabapple Dr Frederick MD 21703. *E-Mail:* ddhoppes@erols.com

HOPPIN, RICHARD ARTHUR, GEOLOGY. *Current Pos:* from asst prof to assoc prof, 52-61, chmn dept, 74-83, PROF STRUCT, UNIV IOWA, 61- *Personal Data:* b St Paul, Minn, May 15, 21; m 47; c 4. *Educ:* Univ Minn, AB, 42, AM, 47; Calif Inst Technol, PhD(geol), 51. *Prof Exp:* Asst mineral, Univ Minn, 46-47; asst optical mineral & petrol, Calif Inst Technol, 47-49. *Concurrent Pos:* Jr geologist, US Geol Surv, 47-48. *Mem:* AAAS; Nat Asn Geol Teachers; Geol Soc Am; Am Geophys Union; Am Asn Petrol Geologists; Am Asn Photogram Remote Sensing. *Res:* Structural geology; geotectonics; remote sensing. *Mailing Add:* Dept Geol Univ Iowa Iowa City IA 52242

HOPPING, RICHARD LEE, OPTOMETRY. *Current Pos:* PRES, SOUTHERN CALIF COL OPTOM, 73- *Personal Data:* b Dayton, Ohio, July 26, 28; m 51, Patricia L Vance; c Ronald L, Debra L (Davis) & Jerrold A. *Educ:* Southern Col Optom, BS & OD, 52. *Hon Degrees:* DOS, Southern Col Optom, 72; DSc, State Univ NY, 95. *Honors & Awards:* Dr Raymond Myers Award, Am Optom Student Asn, 90; Eminent Serv Award, Am Acad Optometry, 91; Distinguished Serv Award, Am Optomet Asn, 93; Dir Choice Award, Optical Lab Asn, 95; Leo Award Excellence Global Eye Care, Nat Eye Res Found, 95. *Prof Exp:* Optometrist, pvt pract, 52-73. *Concurrent Pos:* Chmn, Nat Acad Optom, 83-89; pres, Asn Schs & Cols Optom, 83-85; vchmn, 13th Dist Med Qual Rev Comt, State Calif Bd Med Qual Assurance, 85-92; chmn, Nat Educ Summit Conf, Am Optom Asn/Asn Schs & Cols Optom, 91, chmn, summit Optom Educ, 92. *Res:* Numerous articles written on vision care. *Mailing Add:* Southern Calif Col Optom 2575 Yorba Linda Blvd Fullerton CA 92831

HOPPONEN, JERRY DALE, ELECTROMAGNETIC PROPAGATION. *Current Pos:* STAFF ENGR, LOCKHEED MARTIN TELECOMMUN, 77- *Personal Data:* b Fargo, NDak, Mar 26, 46; m 83; c 2. *Educ:* NDak State Univ, BS; Univ Ariz, MS; Univ Colo, PhD(math). *Prof Exp:* Mathematician, Inst Telecommun Sci, 72-77. *Mem:* Math Asn Am. *Res:* Simulation of electromagnetic wave propagation through the terrestrial atmosphere, with emphasis on efficient numerical methods, absorption by molecular oxygen and water vapor and basic ionospheric phenomena; matrix theory over special algebraic structures. *Mailing Add:* Lockheed Martin Telecommun 1272 Borregas Ave Bldg 551 Sunnyvale CA 94089

HOPPS, HOWARD CARL, GEOGRAPHIC PATHOLOGY. *Current Pos:* curators prof path, 70-82, EMER PROF, UNIV MO, COLUMBIA, 82-; ADJ PROF PATH, MED COL, OHIO, 82- *Personal Data:* b Schenectady, NY, Aug 14, 14; m 37, 68, Hilda P; c Christopher R, David C & Susan (Nathiel). *Educ:* Univ Okla, BS, 35, MD, 37; Univ Chicago, PhD(path), 70. *Honors & Awards:* Howard Taylor Ricketts Prize, 42; Distinguished Serv Award, Soc Environ Geochem & Health, 83. *Prof Exp:* Intern, Evanston Hosp, Ill, 37-39; asst path, Univ Chicago, 40-41, from instr to asst prof, 41-44; prof & chmn dept, Univ Okla, 44-56; prof path & chmn dept & pathologist-in-chief, Univ Hosp, Univ Tex Med Br, 57-63; vis prof anat, Northwestern Univ, 64; chief div geog path, Armed Forces Inst Path, 64-70. *Concurrent Pos:* Chmn subcomt motion pictures, Intersoc Comt Res Potential Path, Inc, 54-55 & 60-64; mem, Path Study Sect, NIH, 54-59, Adv Comt Staph Infection & Influenza, 58, Gen Res Training Grants Comt, 58 & Res Career Award Comt, 59-64; Fulbright vis prof, Univ Otago, NZ, 55; mem path test comt, Nat Bd Med Exam, 56-60; mem adv comt personnel for res, Am Cancer Soc, 58-61, vchmn, 60-61, mem adv comt res pathogenesis of cancer, 61-65, chmn, 63-65; mem res adv coun, 67-73, chmn, 71-73; mem adv comt regulatory biol, NSF, 60-61; ed sect educ & res, Bull Col Am Path, 60-64 & Int Path, 64-70; NIH res training fel, Northwestern Univ, 64; registr, Am Registry Geog Path, 64-70; clin prof, Univ Md, 65-70; vis prof, Temple Univ, 67-70; consult geog path, NASA, 69-70 & WHO, 71; mem subcomt geochem environ related to health & dis, Nat Acad Sci, 69-75, co-chmn, 70-75; chmn, Nat Acad Sci Panel Aging & Geochem Environ, 75-; consult, Int Atomic Energy Agency, 77 & Water Resources Div, US Geol Surv, 79-82; vpres, Mo Acad Sci, 75-76, pres, 76-77; pres, Med Col Ohio Sigma Xi Club, 88-89 & 90-91. *Mem:* Am Asn Immunol; Am Soc Clin Path; Am Soc Tropical Med & Hyg; Int Acad Path; Soc Environ Geochem & Health (secy-treas, 71-78, pres elect, 78-79, pres, 79-80); Am Asn Path. *Res:* Geographic pathology; medical ecology; infectious diseases; parasitic diseases; trace elements; epidemiology; inflammation; immunity and allergy; reticuloendothelial system; cardiovascular and renal disease; forensic pathology; medical education; graduate education in environmental sciences. *Mailing Add:* Med Col Ohio 5939 Swan Creek Dr Toledo OH 43614-1038

HOPSON, CLIFFORD ANDRAE, GEOLOGY, IGNEOUS PETROLOGY. *Current Pos:* assoc prof, Univ Calif, Santa Barbara, 64-66, chmn dept, 66-69, prof geol, 66-92, EMER PROF GEOL, UNIV CALIF, SANTA BARBARA, 93- *Personal Data:* b Portland, Ore, Feb 2, 28; m 55, Mary Arrowood; c Forrest, Erin & Eric. *Educ:* Stanford Univ, BS, 51; Johns Hopkins Univ, PhD(geol), 55. *Prof Exp:* Guest investr geophys lab, Carnegie Inst, 53-55; from asst prof to assoc prof geol, Johns Hopkins Univ, 55-64; geologist, US Geol Surv, 52-93. *Concurrent Pos:* Mem, Earth Sci Adv Panel, NSF, 72-75, chmn, 74-75; vchmn, Cordilleran Sect, Geol Soc Am, 74-75, chmn, 75-76; US Plate Tectonics Deleg to China & Tibet, 79; assoc ed, Geol Soc Am Bull, 82-87. *Mem:* AAAS; fel Geol Soc Am; Geochem Soc; Am Geophys Union. *Res:* Igneous and metamorphic petrology; volcanology; tectonics; ophiolites; geology of Cascade Mountains, Central Appalachian Piedmont, California Coast Ranges, Oman, NW China and Inner Mongolia; diving scientist AMAR-78 project. *Mailing Add:* Dept Geol Sci Univ Calif Santa Barbara CA 93106. *Fax:* 805-893-2314; *E-Mail:* hopson@magic.geol.ucsb.edu

HOPSON, JAMES A, VERTEBRATE PALEONTOLOGY. *Current Pos:* from asst prof to assoc prof anat, 67-86, PROF ORGANISMAL BIOL & ANAT, UNIV CHICAGO, 86- *Personal Data:* b New Haven, Conn, Aug 27, 35; m 61, Susan Dickerson; c Andrew & Peter. *Educ:* Yale Univ, BS, 57; Univ Chicago, PhD(paleozool), 65. *Prof Exp:* Res asst vert paleont, Peabody Mus Natural Hist, Yale Univ, 63-65, res assoc geol, 65-67. *Concurrent Pos:* NSF res grants, 65-; res assoc, Dept Geol, Field Mus Natural History, 71-; mem, Comt Evolutionary Biol, Univ Chicago, 80-; Nat Geog Soc res grants, 85-86 & 87-88. *Mem:* Soc Vert Paleont (pres, 84); Soc Integrative & Comp Biol; Paleont Soc; Soc Syst Biols; Sigma Xi. *Res:* Functional anatomy and evolution of mammal-like reptiles; origin of mammals and evolution of Mesozoic mammals; vertebrate faunas of the Permian and Triassic. *Mailing Add:* Dept Organismal Biol & Anat Univ Chicago 1027 E 57th St Chicago IL 60637-1508

HOPSON, JOHN WILBUR, JR, PHYSICS. *Current Pos:* Res staff mem physics, 68-76, leader shock wave physics group, 76-78, ALT DIV LEADER DYNAMIC TESTING, LOS ALAMOS SCI LAB, 78- *Personal Data:* b San Antonio, Tex, Feb 3, 40; div; c 2. *Educ:* Southwest Tex State Univ, BS, 60; Univ Tex, Austin, PhD(physics), 68. *Mem:* Am Phys Soc. *Res:* Shock waves in condensed materials; solid state physics; dynamic mechanical properties of solids. *Mailing Add:* 1940 Camino Mora Los Alamos NM 87544

HOPSON, KEVIN MATTHEW, REGULATORY AFFAIRS. *Current Pos:* int investr, 92-94, CHEMIST, OFF REGULATORY AFFAIRS, US FOOD & DRUG ADMIN, 90- *Personal Data:* b Roanoke, Va, May 11, 59. *Educ:* Va Polytech Inst & State Univ, BS(microbiol) & BS(biochem), 83. *Prof Exp:* Area foreman, Hercules Inc, 83-84, chem engr, 84-87, chemist, 87-89. *Mem:* Am Chem Soc; Am Inst Chem Engrs; Nat Soc Black Engrs; Nat Orgn Black Chemists & Chem Engrs; Am Asn Pharmaceut Scientists. *Res:* Food additive analysis, antioxidants research, natural product additive research in adulteration of fruit juices, abbreviated new drug application/new drug application forensic technology and in-vitro drug bioequivalency studies for government. *Mailing Add:* 2098 Gaither Rd Rockville MD 20850

HOPTON, FREDERICK JAMES, environmental chemistry, environmental engineering, for more information see previous edition

HOPWOOD, LARRY EUGENE, RADIATION BIOLOGY, CELL BIOLOGY. *Current Pos:* THERAPY CONSULT, 90- *Personal Data:* b Frederick, Md, Dec 11, 45; m 83; c 2. *Educ:* Johns Hopkins Univ, BA, 67; Wash Univ, St Louis, PhD(molecular biol), 71. *Prof Exp:* Res instr radiol, Wash Univ Sch Med, 71-72; res assoc radiation & biol, Colo State Univ, 72-74, asst prof, 75-77; co-chmn biophysics grad prog, Med Col Wis, 80-84, assoc prof radiol, 77-90, assoc prof pharmacol, 78-90, assoc prof radiation oncol, 82-90. *Concurrent Pos:* Res Career Develop Award, Nat Cancer Inst, 77-82; prin investr, Nat Cancer Inst grant, 78-82, 84-90; grant, Am Cancer Soc, 79-82. *Mem:* Radiation Res Soc; AAAS; Am Soc Therapeut Radiologists; Am Soc Clin Oncologists; Am Asn Cancer Res. *Res:* Cell killing and mutation by combined hyperthermia and x-rays; membrane fluidity changes in mammalian cells; radiation response of human tumor cells; metal bound antineoplastic agents as radiosensitizers; molecular biology; resistance of tumors to drugs. *Mailing Add:* 2436 N 88th St Milwaukee WI 53226

HORA, MANINDER SINGH, PROTEIN STABILIZATION & FORMULATION, SUSTAINED DELIVERY OF PROTEINS. *Current Pos:* DIR FORMULATION DEVELOP, CHIRON CORP, 91- *Personal Data:* b Jabalpur, India, Apr 13, 53; US citizen; m 80, Jasbir Gambhir; c Sandeep & Harmeet. *Educ:* Univ Jabalpur, India, BS, 72; Indian Inst Technol, MS 75, PhD(biomed eng), 80. *Prof Exp:* Fulbright scholar, Univ Wash, Seattle, 79-81; fel, Marquette Univ, 81-83; scientist, SK&F Labs, 83-85; group leader, Ayerst Labs, 85-86; scientist, Cetus Corp, 86-90, sr scientist, 90-91. *Mem:* Am Asn Pharmaceut Scientists; Am Chem Soc; Controlled Release Soc. *Res:* Develop strategies for stabilization of therapeutic agents, especially proteins for administration to humans; develop controlled delivery formulations for proteins; characterization of proteins. *Mailing Add:* 20 Gait Ct San Ramon CA 94583

HORABIN, JAMILA IDDI, GERMLINE SEX DETERMINATION PROCESS. *Current Pos:* ASST PROF, UNIV ALA, BIRMINGHAM, 93- *Personal Data:* b Mombasa, Kenya, Oct 30, 58; m 81, Ivan. *Educ:* Duke Univ, BA, 81, PhD(biochem & genetics), 87. *Concurrent Pos:* Fel, Damon Runyon-Walter Winchell Cancer Fund, 88. *Res:* Understanding Drosophila sex determination in the soma and germline; maintenance of the female determined state in the soma involving splicing regulation, while the germline sex determination process implicates a signalling mechanism from the soma to the germline. *Mailing Add:* Dept Biochem Univ Ala 845 19th St S Rm 834 Birmingham AL 35294. *Fax:* 205-934-0758; *E-Mail:* jhorabin@bmg.bhs.uab.edu

HORACKOVA, MAGDA, CELLULAR CARDIOLOGY. *Current Pos:* Assoc prof, 78-83, PROF PHYSIOL & BIOPHYS, DALHOUSIE UNIV, 68- *Personal Data:* b Braque, Czechoslovakia, Nov 5, 40. *Educ:* Acad Sci, PhD(physiol), 68. *Mailing Add:* Dept Physiol & Biophys Dalhousie Univ Halifax NS B3H 4H7 Can

HORAI, KI-ITI, geophysics, lunar science, for more information see previous edition

HORAK, DONALD L, FISHERIES. *Current Pos:* FISH RES CHIEF, COLO DIV WILDLIFE, 62- *Personal Data:* b Wahoo, Nebr, July 13, 37; m 59; c 3. *Educ:* Colo A&M Col, BS, 60; Colo State Univ, MS, 62, PhD(fish sci), 70. *Mem:* Am Fisheries Soc; Wildlife Soc; Sigma Xi. *Res:* Rainbow trout, especially development of practical dry diets, culture techniques and disease control; forage species introductions; heavy metal studies; lake aeration. *Mailing Add:* 745 S Summit View Dr Ft Collins CO 80524

HORAK, JAMES ALBERT, MATERIALS SCIENCE, NUCLEAR REACTOR TECHNOLOGY. *Current Pos:* SR DEVELOP ENGR, LOCKHEED MARTIN ENERGY SYST K-25 TECHNOL SUPPORT ORGN. *Personal Data:* b Plainfield, NJ, Oct 28, 31; m 54, Diane J Herman; c Ralph J, Kendell J & Gregory E. *Educ:* Univ Ill, Urbana, BS, 58; Northwestern Univ, MS, 63, PhD(mat sci), 66. *Prof Exp:* Asst metallurgist, Argonne Nat Lab, 58-68; staff scientist, Reactor Tech Div, Los Alamos Sci Lab, 68-69; assoc prof nuclear eng, Univ NMex, 69-74, prof, 74; sr res scientist, Oak Ridge Nat Lab, 74-93. *Concurrent Pos:* Consult, 68-70; staff mem, Reactor Studies Div, Sandia Labs, 69-71, staff scientist, 71-74; guest scientist, Los Alamos Sci Lab, 72-74; USA-USSR exchange team on fusion energy, US Dept Energy, 74-; US rep, working group on fast reactors, specialists meeting on mech properties of struct mat, Int Atomic Energy Agency, 83-; vchmn, Mat Sci & Technol Div, Am Nuclear Soc, 77-78, chmn, 78-79. *Mem:* Am Soc Testing & Mat; fel Am Nuclear Soc (secy-treas, 76-77). *Res:* Irradiation effects in metals, alloys and nuclear fuels; development of the materials to harness fission and fusion energy; development of improved fuels and structural materials for nuclear power reactors; development of refractory alloys for space nuclear power. *Mailing Add:* 304 Calloway Circle Lenoir City TN 37771. *E-Mail:* horakja@ornl.gov

HORAK, MARTIN GEORGE, APPLIED MATHEMATICS. *Current Pos:* from asst prof to assoc prof, 67-73, PROF MATH, TOWSON STATE UNIV, 73-, CHMN, DEPT MATH, 73-76, 84- *Personal Data:* b Baltimore, Md, Dec 28, 36; m 64; c 3. *Educ:* Loyola Col, Md, BS, 58; Univ Notre Dame, MS, 60; Univ Md, College Park, PhD(math), 70. *Prof Exp:* Assoc mathematician, Appl Physics Lab, Johns Hopkins Univ, 60-62; asst prof math, Loyola Col, Md, 62-67. *Mem:* Math Asn Am. *Res:* Bochner p integrable solution of nonlinear hyperbolic partial differential equations; periodic solutions of hyperbolic partial differential equations in the large. *Mailing Add:* Dept Math Towson State Univ Baltimore MD 21204

HORAK, VACLAV, ELECTROCHEMISTRY, SURFACE CHEMISTRY. *Current Pos:* prof, 68-93, EMER PROF CHEM, GEORGETOWN UNIV, 93- *Personal Data:* b Prague, Czech, Dec 9, 22; US citizen; m 49, Zdenka Zahutova; c 1. *Educ:* Charles Univ, Czech, RNDr, 48, CSc, 61. *Prof Exp:* Assoc prof chem, Charles Univ, Prague, Czech, 48-68. *Concurrent Pos:* Vis scientist, NIH/Nat Health Inst Lab Chem Pharmacol, 65-66 & 68 & Inst Phys Chem Acad Sci, Prague, Czech, 89-90; vis prof, Univ Indust, Italy, 77, Univ Utah, 79 & 80 & Univ Belo Horizonte, Brazil, 78, Univ Ariz, 84, Inst Phys Chem Acad Sci, Prague, Czech, 89-90 & Charles Univ, 92-95; vpres, Found Biosocial Behav & Human Health, 78-82. *Mem:* Am Chem Soc; Czech Soc Art & Sci; Electrochem Soc. *Res:* Chemistry of organic sulfur compounds, guinones, pharmaceuticals; organic synthesis; electrosynthesis; electrochemistry; polymer reactive and chemical modification and analysis; bioorganic chemistry of melanin; electron transfer; drug distribution. *Mailing Add:* Dept Chem Georgetown Univ 37th & O Sts NW Washington DC 20057-0002. *E-Mail:* vhorak@guvax.georgetown.edu

HORAKOVA, ZDENKA, PHARMACOLOGY, PHARMACY. *Current Pos:* toxicologist, Food Safety & Inspection Serv, 78-87, TOXICOLOGIST, FOREST SERV, USDA, 87- *Personal Data:* b Jindrichuv Hradec, Czech, Apr 6, 25; US citizen; m 49; c 1. *Educ:* Charles Univ, Prague, Magister Pharm, 49, RNDr, 52; Czechoslovakian Acad Sci, Prague, PhD(pharmacol), 61. *Prof Exp:* Teaching asst pharmacol, Med Fac Charles Univ, Prague, 49-50; res pharmacologist, Res Inst Pharm & Biochem, Prague, 50-68, exp therapeut br, Nat Heart, Lung & Blood Inst, NIH, Bethesda, 69-74, sect molecular pharmacol, Pulmonary Br, 74-77 & lab cellular metab, 77-78. *Concurrent Pos:* Head pharmacol dept, Res Inst Pharm & Biochem, Prague, 58-68; vis guest, Lab Chem Pharmacol, Nat Heart Inst, 65-66. *Mem:* Am Soc Pharmacol & Exp Therapeut; Soc Exp Biol & Med; Inflammation Res Asn; Soc Toxicol; Asn Govt Toxicologists. *Res:* Inflammation, specifically mediators, cell involvement, role of the H receptors and the effect of drugs in inflammatory processes; the role of histamine in immediate hypertensivity reactions in the stomach and the lungs; toxicology, particularly the screening of new drugs; toxicological evaluation of potentially toxic chemical residues such as drugs and pesticides in meat and poultry and environment, risk assessment evaluation; toxicology. *Mailing Add:* 5508 Oakmont Ave Bethesda MD 20817-3528. *Fax:* 202-453-8272

HORAN, FRANCIS E, PHYSICAL ORGANIC CHEMISTRY. *Current Pos:* res mgr agr prod, 59-66, assoc dir res, 66-69, DIR, ARCHER DANIELS MIDLAND CO, 69- *Personal Data:* b Atchison, Kans, Mar 1, 14; m 46; c 4. *Educ:* St Benedict's Col, Kans, AB, 35; Columbia Univ, MA, 36, PhD(chem), 45. *Prof Exp:* Prof chem, St Francis Xavier, Can, 36-39; res assoc, Midwest Res Inst, 45-48; asst prof phys chem, Univ Ariz, 48; fel phys biochem, Med Col, Cornell Univ, 48-49; assoc prof chem, St Martin's Col, 49-52; res chemist, Huron Milling Co, 52-56; res chemist, Hercules Powder Co, 56-59. *Mem:* Am Chem Soc; Am Asn Cereal Chem. *Res:* Physico-chemical aspects of starch chemistry; industrial starch chemistry and utilization of grain sorghums; electrical conductivity of blood; streaming potentials of blood; ultrasonic investigations on high polymers; vegetable proteins; food and industrial grades; fermentation; research management. *Mailing Add:* 50 Malaga Way Hot Springs Village AR 71909-2620

HORAN, MICHAEL, CARDIOVASCULAR DISEASES. *Current Pos:* spec asst to dir, Div Heart & Vascular Dis, Nat Heart, Lung & Blood Inst, 81-82, chief, Hypertension & Kidney Dis Br, 82-89, assoc dir cardiol, 89-93, DIR, DIV HEART & VASCULAR DIS, NAT HEART, LUNG & BLOOD INST, 93- *Personal Data:* b Rochester, Minn, June 27, 45. *Educ:* Manhattan Col, BA, 67; Georgetown Univ, MD, 71; Johns Hopkins Univ, ScM, 78. *Prof Exp:* Attend physician, Baltimore USPHS Hosp, 77-81, asst chief ambulatory care, 77-81, dir, 81; instr med, Johns Hopkins Univ, 77-81, dir, Johns Hopkins Hosp Hypertension Mgt Clin, 78-81, asst prof med, 81-93. *Concurrent Pos:* Active staff, Johns Hopkins Hosp, 77-93; sci adv, Nat High Blood Pressure Educ Prog, 82-; NIH coordr, US-USSR Sci Exchange Agreement in Hypertension, 82-; chmn, Nat Heart, Lung & Blood Inst Task Force Control of Blood Pressure in Children, 83-86, Res Activ Related to Blacks & other Minorities, 84-88; mem, Coun High Blood Pressure Res Educ Comt, Am Heart Asn, 89-, Nat Kidney & Urologic Dis Adv Bd, 89-, Nat Comn on Sleep Dis, 90-; sci adv, Nat Heart Attack Alert Prog, 91- *Mem:* Am Col Physicians; Am Pub Health Asn; Am Fedn Clin Res; Am Heart Asn. *Res:* Purification of thrombin and its amino acid sequence; primary care; hypertension; ischemic heart disease; ventricular ectopy; vascular biology and diseases. *Mailing Add:* Nat Heart Lung & Blood Inst Two Rockledge Centre Suite 9044 6701 Rockledge Dr MSC 7940 Bethesda MD 20892-7940

HORAN, PAUL KARL, PATHOLOGY, CELL BIOLOGY. *Current Pos:* PARTNER, QED TECHNOLOGIES, 93- *Personal Data:* b Schenectady, NY, Sept 25, 42; div; c Colleen, Paul K II, Andrew & Kelly. *Educ:* State Univ NY, Albany, BS, 65; Pa State Univ, MS, 67, PhD(biophys), 70. *Prof Exp:* Emer lab technician, Albany Med Col Hosp, 63-65; guest researcher med physics, Donner Lab, Lawrence Radiation Lab, Berkeley, 68-69; exten lectr phys sci, Pa State Univ, 70; res fel cell biol, Donald S Walker Lab, Sloan-Kettering Inst Cancer Res, 71-72; staff mem, Los Alamos Sci Lab, 72-74; from asst prof to assoc prof path, Med Sch, Univ Rochester, 74-82; assoc dir immunol, Smith Kline & Fr, 82-88; chmn bd, Pres Pharmaceut Div, chief sci officer & founder, Zynaxis Cell Sci, Inc, 88-93. *Concurrent Pos:* NIH fel, Pa State Univ, 70-71; Nat Acad Sci nat sci travel award to IV Int Cong Radiation Biol, Evian, France, 70; lectr, Proj Newgate, Pa State Penitentiary, 70; dir, Zynaxis, Inc, 88-93. *Mem:* AAAS; Soc Anal Cytol; fel Am Acad Microbiol; Am Asn Exp Path; Nat Physics Hon Soc. *Res:* Cell surface antigens on tumor cells using monoclonal antibodies; development of new methodologies in flow cytometry. *Mailing Add:* QED Technologies 20 Valley Stream Pkwy Suite 265 Malvern PA 19355-1457. *Fax:* 610-695-2517; *E-Mail:* pkhoran@aol.com

HORBATSCH, MARKO M, SCATTERING THEORY, FIELD THEORY. *Current Pos:* from asst prof to assoc prof, 88-96, PROF PHYSICS, DEPT PHYSICS, YORK UNIV, 96- *Personal Data:* b Goettingen, Repub Fed Ger, Mar 3, 54; m 82, Roma Chumak-H; c Michael & Olena. *Educ:* JWV Goethe Universitat, Frankfurt, Vordipln, 74, Dipl, 76, Dr phil nat(physics), 81. *Prof Exp:* Postdoctoral fel, Dept Physics, York Univ, 82-84; res assoc, Inst Physic Theory, JWV Goethe Universitat, 84-85; res fel, Dept Physics, Nat Sci & Eng Res Coun Can, 85-88. *Res:* Theoretical description of scattering processes in atomic physics involving many particles by semiclassical time dependent field theory; quantum mechanical few body problem; atoms in intense laser fields. *Mailing Add:* Dept Physics York Univ 4700 Keele St Toronto ON M3J 1P3 Can. *Fax:* 416-736-5516

HORBETT, THOMAS ALAN, BIOCHEMISTRY. *Current Pos:* Res assoc bioeng, 71-75, from res asst prof to res prof, 75-88, PROF BIOENG & CHEM ENG, UNIV WASH, 88- *Personal Data:* b Buffalo, NY, Aug 27, 43; m 81, Pamela Tuffield. *Educ:* State Univ NY, BSc, 65; Univ Wash, PhD(biochem), 70. *Honors & Awards:* Clemson Award for Basic Res, Soc Biomat, 89. *Concurrent Pos:* Fel, Univ Wash, 70-71 & 71-72; prin investr grants, 76-91; distinguished lectr, Controlled Drug Delivery, Col Pharm, Rutgers Univ, 89. *Mem:* AAAS; Soc Biomat; Am Chem Soc; Controlled Release Soc. *Res:* Protein-protein interactions; protein modification; interfacial proteins; cell adhesion; biomaterials; insulin delivery devices. *Mailing Add:* Dept Chem Eng Univ Wash Box 351750 Seattle WA 98195-1750. *Fax:* 206-543-3778; *E-Mail:* horbett@chemevax.cheme.washington.edu

HORCH, KENNETH WILLIAM, NEUROPHYSIOLOGY, SENSORY PHYSIOLOGY. *Current Pos:* fel physiol, Sch Med, Univ Utah, 71-74, res instr, 73-75, from asst prof to assoc prof, 75-93, assoc prof bioeng, 86-92, PROF BIOENG, UNIV UTAH, 92-, PROF PHYSIOL, 93- *Personal Data:* b Cleveland, Ohio, 1942; m 87, Mary L Stewart; c 2. *Educ:* Lehigh Univ, BS, 65; Yale Univ, MPhil, 68, PhD(biol), 71. *Prof Exp:* Instr biol, Purdue Univ, 70-71. *Concurrent Pos:* Prin investr, NIH, NSF, 74-; vis prof, Univ Sci & Med, Grenoble, France, 86; dir neurol testing, Topical Testing Inc, 86-93; agent, Ztech L C, 95- *Mem:* Biomed Eng Soc; NY Acad Sci; Soc Neurosci; Sigma Xi; Inst Elec & Electronics Engrs. *Res:* Somatosensory physiology; nerve regeneration and repair; neuroprosthetics. *Mailing Add:* Dept Bioeng Univ Utah 2480 MEB Salt Lake City UT 84112. *Fax:* 801-585-5361; *E-Mail:* k.horch@m.cc.utah.edu

HORD, CHARLES W, PHYSICS, ATMOSPHERIC PHYSICS. *Current Pos:* res physicist, Lab Atmospheric & Space Physics, Univ Colo, 66-74, adj assoc prof, 74-76, adj prof, 76-80, PROF ASTRO-GEOPHYS, UNIV COLO, BOULDER, 80- *Personal Data:* b Casper, Wyo, Feb 16, 37; m 59; c 2. *Educ:* Univ Colo, BA, 59, PhD(physics), 64. *Prof Exp:* Scientist, Rocky Flats Div, Dow Chem Co, 59-60; asst prof physics, Southern Colo State Col, 64-66. *Concurrent Pos:* Planetary exploration missions; Mariner 6 and 7, 1969; Mariner 9, 1971; prin investr, Galileo Ultraviolet spectrometer exp, 77-; Voyager, 1978 and Pioneer Venus, 1978. *Mem:* Am Inst Physics. *Res:* Planetary exploration. *Mailing Add:* 980 Hartford Dr Boulder CO 80303

HORD, WILLIAM EUGENE, ELECTRICAL ENGINEERING. *Current Pos:* chmn dept, 74-80, ASSOC PROF ENG, SOUTHERN ILL UNIV, EDWARDSVILLE, 74-; VPRES, MICROWAVE APPLNS GROUP, SANTA MARIA, CALIF. *Personal Data:* b Leola, SDak. *Educ:* Mo Sch Mines, BSc, 59; Univ Mo-Rolla, MSc, 63, PhD(elec eng), 66. *Prof Exp:* Assoc engr microwave, Sperry Gyroscope Co, 59-60; instr eng, Univ Mo-Rolla, 60-66; group engr microwave, Emerson Elec Co, 66-69. *Concurrent Pos:* Consult, Emerson Elec Co, 69-, Monsanto Res Corp, 72. *Mem:* Sr mem Inst Elec & Electronics Engrs; Sigma Xi. *Res:* Propagation in ferrite-loaded waveguides; application of ferrite devices to phased array antennas. *Mailing Add:* Microwave Applns Group 3030 Industrial Pkwy Santa Maria CA 93455

HORDON, ROBERT M, HYDROLOGY, PHYSICAL GEOGRAPHY. *Current Pos:* From instr to asst prof, 67-76, ASSOC PROF GEOG, RUTGERS UNIV, 76- *Personal Data:* b New York, NY, July 10, 36; m 59, Sheila Feldman; c Laurence & Bruce. *Educ:* Brooklyn Col, BA, 59; Columbia Univ, MA, 65, PhD(geog), 70. *Mem:* Am Geophys Union; AAAS; Am Inst Hydrol; Am Water Resources Asn; Asn Am Geogr; Am Geog Soc. *Res:* Surface and ground water hydrology; ground water yield; wetlands; water quality; water demand; yield of consolidated rock areas. *Mailing Add:* Dept Geog Rutgers Univ New Brunswick NJ 08903-5080. *Fax:* 732-445-0006

HORECKER, BERNARD LEONARD, BIOCHEMISTRY. *Current Pos:* RETIRED. *Personal Data:* b Chicago, Ill, Oct 31, 14; m 36; c 3. *Educ:* Univ Chicago, SB, 36, PhD(chem), 39. *Honors & Awards:* Award Biol Chem, Wash Acad Sci, 54; Phillips Lectr, Haverford Col, 65; Reilly Lectr, Notre Dame Univ, 69; Merck Award, Am Soc Biol Chemists, 81; Neuberg Medal, Virchow-Pirquet Med Soc, 81. *Prof Exp:* Res assoc enzymes, Univ Chicago, 39-40; jr examr phys sci, US Civil Serv Comn, 40-41; biochemist, NIH, 41-53, chief, Biochem & Metab Lab, Nat Inst Arthritis & Metab Dis, 53-59; prof microbiol & chmn dept, Col Med, NY Univ-Bellevue Med Ctr, 59-63; prof molecular biol & chmn dept, Albert Einstein Col Med, 63-71, assoc dean sci affairs, 71-72; mem, Roche Inst Molecular Biol, 72-84; head, Lab Molecular Enzym, 77-84; prof, Med Col, Cornell Univ, 84-89, emer prof biochem, 89-, dean, Grad Sch Med Sci, 84- *Concurrent Pos:* Vis prof, Univ Calif, Berkeley, 54, Univ Ill, 57, Univ Parana, Brazil, 60 & 63, Cornell Univ, Ithaca, NY, 65, Univ Rotterdam, 70, Indian Inst Sci, Bangalore, 71 & Albert Einstein Col Med, 72-84; consult, Lederle Labs, 59-72; Fulbright scholar, 64; Career Develop Award Study Sect, NIH, 66-70; mem, Comt Personnel, Am Cancer Soc, 69-73, Sci Adv Comt Biochem & Chem Carcinogenesis, 74-78 & Coun Res & Clin Invest Awards, 84-88; mem, Biol Div Adv Comt, Oak Ridge Nat Lab, 76-80; adj mem, Roche Inst Molecular Biol, 84-89; assoc dean, Res & Sponsored Progs, Med Col, Cornell Univ, 84- *Mem:* Nat Acad Sci; fel Am Acad Arts & Sci; Am Soc Biol Chemists (pres, 68-69); fel AAAS; Harvey Soc (vpres, 69-70, pres, 70-71); hon mem Brazil Acad Sci; Am Chem Soc; hon mem Swiss Biochem Soc; hon mem Japan Biochem Soc; hon mem Indian Sci Acad. *Res:* Isolation and characterization of respiratory enzymes; spectrophotometry of hemoglobin and derivatives; enzymology; carbohydrate metabolism; enzyme structure; mechanism of action regulation; thymic peptides. *Mailing Add:* 340 E 64th St New York NY 10021

HORECZY, JOSEPH THOMAS, ORGANIC CHEMISTRY. *Current Pos:* res chemist, Humble Oil & Refining Co, 41-48, sr res chemist, 48-54, sect head, 54-60, res assoc, 60-64, sr res assoc, 64-65, sr res assoc, Esso Res & Eng Co, 65-66, assoc sci adv, 66-67, sci adv, 67-75, chief scientist, plastic properties, 75-78, CONSULT, PLASTIC TECHNOL DIV, EXXON, CHEM CO, 78- *Personal Data:* b Falls City, Tex, Nov 2, 13; m 42; c 1. *Educ:* Southwest Tex State Teachers Col, BS, 34; Univ Tex, Austin, MA, 39, PhD(org chem), 41. *Prof Exp:* Teacher, Pub Schs, Tex, 34-41. *Concurrent Pos:* Staff Consult, S & B Engrs, Inc, Houston, TX. *Mem:* AAAS; Am Chem Soc; Am Inst Chem Eng; Soc Plastic Engr. *Res:* Synthetic organic chemicals from petroleum; aviation gasoline; motor gasoline; analytical chemistry; synthesis of new polymers; fibers from polymers; dyeability of fibers; flame retardancy of plastics and fibers; solids handling. *Mailing Add:* 105 Edgewood St Baytown TX 77520

HOREL, JAMES ALAN, COGNITIVE NEUROSCIENCE. *Current Pos:* assoc prof, 69-74, PROF ANAT, STATE UNIV NY UPSTATE MED CTR, 74- *Personal Data:* b Eureka, Calif, Sept 11, 31; m 52; c 3. *Educ:* Humboldt State Col, AB, 58; Ohio State Univ, MA, 60, PhD(physiol psychol), 63. *Prof Exp:* Fel anat, Univ Fla, 62-63, Nat Inst Neurol Dis & Blindness fel, 63-64; from asst prof to assoc prof anat, Univ Fla, 64-69. *Mem:* AAAS; Am Asn Anatomists; fel Am Psychol Asn; Soc Neurosci; fel Am Psychol Soc. *Res:* Neuroanatomy of behavior; neuroanatomy of learning and memory processes. *Mailing Add:* Dept Anat State Univ NY SUNY Health Sci Ctr Syracuse NY 13210. *Fax:* 315-464-8835

HORELICK, BRINDELL, GENERAL MATHEMATICS. *Current Pos:* RETIRED. *Personal Data:* b New York, NY, Sept 5, 32; m 65, Kathleen. *Educ:* Mass Inst Technol, BS, 52; Univ Chicago, MS, 53; Wesleyan Univ, PhD(math), 67. *Prof Exp:* Instr math, Villanova Univ, 59-60; from instr to asst prof, Lafayette Col, 60-67; assoc prof, State Univ NY Col Cortland, 67-68; asst prof math, Univ Md, 68-87. *Mem:* Math Asn Am. *Res:* Topological dynamics. *Mailing Add:* 59 Glenwood Ave Catonsville MD 21228

HOREN, DANIEL J, nuclear physics, for more information see previous edition

HORENSTEIN, SIMON, NEUROLOGY. *Current Pos:* ASSOC, VET ADMIN HOSP, 70-, CHIEF NEUROL, 72- *Personal Data:* b Providence, RI, Sept 8, 24; m 48; c 3. *Educ:* Univ Ill, BS, 46, MD, 48. *Prof Exp:* Assoc neurol, Sch Med, Harvard Univ, 60-62; from asst prof to assoc prof, Case Western Reserve Univ, 62-70; PROF NEUROL & CHIEF DEPT, UNIV & CHIEF NEUROL, HOSPS, ST LOUIS UNIV, 70-, CHMN DEPT, 72- *Concurrent Pos:* Nat Heart Inst fel, Boston City Hosp, 53-54; vis physician, Boston City Hosp, 54-62; neurologist, Mass Ment Health Ctr, 60-62; consult, Vet Admin Hosp, Cleveland, Ohio, 62-70, chief neurol, Highland View Hosp, 62-70; chmn stroke comt, Bistate Regional Med Prog, 71-; spec consult to dir, NIH, Neurol Sci Res Training Comt A, 71- *Mem:* Am Neurol Asn; fel Am Col Physicians; fel Am Acad Neurol (2nd vpres, 65-67); Asn Res Nerv & Ment Dis. *Res:* Behavioral consequences of visual field defects. *Mailing Add:* 3655 Vista Ave St Louis MO 63110-2594

HORGAN, CORNELIUS OLIVER, APPLIED MECHANICS, APPLIED MATHEMATICS. *Current Pos:* PROF APPL MATH, UNIV VA, 88-, WILLS JOHNSON PROF APPL MATH & MECH, 94- *Personal Data:* b Cork, Ireland, May 16, 44; US citizen; m 71, Myra; c Olivia & David. *Educ:* Nat Univ Ireland, BS, 64, MS, 65; Calif Inst Technol, PhD(appl mech), 70. *Hon Degrees:* DSc, Nat Univ Ireland, 83. *Prof Exp:* Lectr eng mech, Univ Mich, 70-72; sr res assoc appl math, Univ E Anglia, 72-74; assoc prof appl mech, Univ Houston, 74-78; from assoc prof to prof appl mech, Mich State Univ, 78-88. *Concurrent Pos:* Vis prof appl math, Northwestern Univ, 77-78 & Cornell Univ, 82; vis assoc appl mech, Calif Inst Technol, 79 & 81, vis prof, 84-85; mem bd dirs, Soc Eng Sci, 93-; vis prof, Univ di Pisa, Italy, 96. *Mem:* Fel Am Soc Mech Engrs; Soc Indust & Appl Math; Am Math Soc; fel Am Acad Mech; Soc Eng Sci; Soc Natural Philos. *Res:* Continuum mechanics; partial differential equations arising in the physical sciences; linear and nonlinear elasticity; author of over 120 publications in field. *Mailing Add:* Inst Appl Math Olsson Hall Univ Va Charlottesville VA 22903-1226

HORGAN, JAMES D(ONALD), ELECTRICAL ENGINEERING. *Current Pos:* RETIRED. *Personal Data:* b Grand Rapids, Mich, May 21, 22; m 45; c 2. *Educ:* Marquette Univ, BEE, 47, MS, 51; Univ Wis, PhD, 57. *Prof Exp:* Mem staff, Radiation Labs, Mass Inst Technol, 43-45; from instr to assoc prof, 47-56, chmn dept elec eng, 56-61, prof elec eng, Marquette Univ, 57-87, clin prof eng med, Med Col Wis, 68-87. *Concurrent Pos:* Consult, Square D Co, Wis, 54-59, A C Spark Plug Div, Gen Motors Corp, 59- & Vet Admin Hosp, Wood, Wis, 63- *Mem:* Am Soc Eng Educ; Inst Elec & Electronics Engrs. *Res:* Biomedical engineering, particularly computer simulation of biological systems including human respiratory and circulatory systems. *Mailing Add:* 1530 N Longwood Ave Elm Grove WI 53122

HORGAN, STEPHEN WILLIAM, MEDICINAL CHEMISTRY. *Current Pos:* Res asst med chem, Merrell Nat Labs, 66-70, org res chemist, 70-74, proj leader, Chem Develop Dept, Richardson-Merrell, Inc, 74-79, sect head, Chem Develop Dept, Merrell Nat Labs, 79-81, res assoc, Merrell Dow Pharmaceut, 81-90, res scientist, Marion Merrell Dow, 90-93, sr res scientist, 93-95, SR RES SCIENTIST, HOECHST MARION ROUSSEL, 95- *Personal Data:* b Springfield, Mass, Aug 23, 42; m 64, Peggy J Shepherd; c Karin & Kelly. *Educ:* Xavier Univ, Ohio, BS, 64, MS, 66; Univ Cincinnati, PhD(org chem), 71. *Mem:* Am Chem Soc; Sigma Xi. *Res:* Synthetic medicinal agents; product process development including pilot plant scale-up. *Mailing Add:* Hoechst Marion Roussel 2110 Galbraith Rd Cincinnati OH 45215. *Fax:* 513-948-4676

HORGEN, PAUL ARTHUR, cell biology, molecular biology, for more information see previous edition

HORGER, EDGAR OLIN, III, OBSTETRICS. *Current Pos:* from asst prof to prof obstet & gynec, Med Univ Sc, 69-90, dir maternal & fetal med, 73-90, prof radiol, 78-90, PROF OBSTET & GYNEC, MED UNIV SC, 90-, CHMN OBSTET & GYNEC, 93- *Personal Data:* b Eutawville, SC, May 30, 37; m 60, Polly Collins; c Edgar O IV, David C & Patricia H (McDaniel). *Educ:* Furman Univ, BS, 59; Med Col SC, MD, 62, Am Bd Obstet & Gynec, cert, 70, cert maternal & fetal med, 74. *Prof Exp:* Intern med, Hosp, Med Col SC, 62-63, resident, obstet & gynec, 63-67; fel fetal physiol, Univ Pittsburgh, 67-68, asst prof obstet & gynec, 68-69. *Concurrent Pos:* Bd examrs, Am Bd Obstet & Gynec, 75-79 & 81-85; State Bd Med Examiners, SC, 85-87. *Mem:* AMA; Am Col Obstet & Gynec; Am Gynec & Obstet Soc; Soc Perinatal Obstetricians. *Res:* Assessment of fetal physiology and pathophysiology; detection of fetal abnormalities; management of maternal and fetal problems caused by complications of pregnancy; author or coauthor of over 100 publications. *Mailing Add:* Dept Obstetrics & Gynec Univ SC Sch Med Columbia SC 29203

HORGER, LEWIS MILTON, PHYSIOLOGY, PHARMACEUTICAL REGULATORY AFFAIRS. *Current Pos:* RETIRED. *Personal Data:* b Dearborn, Mich, June 22, 27; m 52; c 3. *Educ:* Univ Detroit, BS, 51; Purdue Univ, MS, 53, PhD(physiol), 56. *Prof Exp:* Res physiologist, Sherman Labs, Mich, 56-57; sr lit scientist, Smith Kline & French Labs, 57-60, group leader biochem, 60-66, assoc dir regulatory affairs, 69-71, dir res & develop, 71-80, vpres, Regulatory Affairs, US Pharmaceut Prod, 80-83; corp vpres, Regulatory Affairs, Alcon Labs, 83-88; consult, Pharmaceut Regulatory Affairs, 89-97. *Mem:* AAAS; emer mem Endocrine Soc; Drug Info Asn. *Res:* Pharmaceutical research and development; federal drug regulations; data processing; new drugs and medical devices. *Mailing Add:* 422 Pebble Creek Ct Venice FL 34292

HORHOTA, STEPHEN THOMAS, PHARMACY. *Current Pos:* sr scientist res & develop, 80-85, SR PRIN SCIENTIST, BOEHRINGER INGELHEIM PHARMACEUT, 85- *Personal Data:* b Buffalo, NY, June 9, 50; m 73; c 3. *Educ:* Clarkson Col Technol, BS, 72; State Univ NY, Buffalo, PhD(pharmaceut), 78. *Prof Exp:* Pharmacist res & develop, Ayerst Labs, 72-74, group leader, 77. *Concurrent Pos:* Vis prof, Sch Pharm, State Univ NY Buffalo, 82-; adj prof, Sch Pharm, Univ RI, 84- *Mem:* Am Asn Pharmaceut Scientists. *Res:* Multivariate relations between properties of materials and methods of manufacture on features and attributes of pharmaceutical dosage forms. *Mailing Add:* 13 Prospect Dr Brookfield CT 06804

HORIE, YASUYUKI, PHYSICS. *Current Pos:* assoc prof, 78-80, PROF CIVIL ENG & ASSOC MEM MAT SCI & ENG, NC STATE UNIV, 80- *Personal Data:* b Tokyo, Japan, July 6, 37; m 64; c 1. *Educ:* Int Christian Univ, Tokyo, BA, 61; Yale Univ, MS, 63; Wash State Univ, PhD(physics), 66. *Prof Exp:* Vis lectr math, Univ Strathclyde, 66-67; lectr, Manchester Col Sci & Technol, Eng, 67-68; assoc prof eng sci mech, Stanford Res Inst, 69-76, sr physicist, 77. *Concurrent Pos:* Mem staff, US Army Res Off, 79-81, Sandia Nat Lab, 85, 86, US Army Mat Technol Lab, 87, US ARO, 87-88. *Mem:* Am Phys Soc; Mat Res Soc. *Res:* Physics of shock waves; nonlinear continuum physics; shock compression chemistry in materials synthesis. *Mailing Add:* Dept Civil Engr NC State Univ PO Box 7908 Raleigh NC 27695-7908

HORING, SHELDON, ELECTRICAL ENGINEERING. *Current Pos:* pres, CBIS Federal, 90, PRES, CBIS, 91- *Personal Data:* b Brooklyn, NY, June 1, 36; m 61; c 2. *Educ:* City Col New York, BEE, 57; NY Univ, MEE, 59; Polytech Inst Brooklyn, PhD(elec eng), 61. *Prof Exp:* Instr elec eng, Polytech Inst Brooklyn, 60-61, asst prof, 61-62; mem tech staff, 57-60 & 62-72, head dept, 70-79, dir, 79-81, exec dir, Bell Tel Labs, 81-89. *Concurrent Pos:* Adj asst prof, Newark Col Eng, 62-63, adj assoc prof, 63-64; vis prof, Stevens Inst Technol, 64-68, assoc prof, 68-74. *Mem:* Inst Elec & Electronics Engrs. *Res:* Optimal control theory, particularly application and extension of the theory to terminal control problems which arise in guidance theory; teletraffic and congestion theory. *Mailing Add:* 65 Cornell Dr Livingston NJ 07039

HORITA, AKIRA, PHARMACOLOGY. *Current Pos:* From instr to assoc prof, 56-66, PROF PHARMACOL, MED SCH, UNIV WASH, 66-, PROF PSYCHIAT, 80- *Personal Data:* b Seattle, Wash, June 10, 28; m 54; c 2. *Educ:* Univ Wash, AB, 50, MS, 51, PhD(pharmacol), 54. *Mem:* AAAS; Am Soc Pharmacol & Exp Therapeut; Sigma Xi. *Res:* Chemical pharmacology; biochemistry and pharmacology of the central nervous system and the autonomic nervous system. *Mailing Add:* Dept Pharmacol SJ-30 Univ Wash Sch Med Seattle WA 98195-0001. *Fax:* 206-543-9520

HORITA, ROBERT EIJI, SPACE PHYSICS, GEOPHYSICS. *Current Pos:* from asst prof to assoc prof, 70-80, PROF PHYSICS, UNIV VICTORIA, 80- *Personal Data:* b Vancouver, BC, Mar 15, 37; m 70; c 5. *Educ:* Univ BC, BASc, 60, MASc, 62, PhD, 68. *Prof Exp:* Sci officer, Naval Res Estab, 62-66; res scientist, Commun Res Ctr, 68-69; Nat Res Coun Can Overseas Fel, Kyoto Univ, 69-70. *Concurrent Pos:* Guest worker, Space Environ Lab, Nat Oceanic & Atmospheric Admin, 76-77; Exchange Prog Scientist, Nat Ctr Sci Res, France, 77. *Mem:* Can Asn Physicists; Am Geophys Union; Soc Terrestrial Magnetism & Elec Japan; Acoustic Soc Am; Inst Elec & Electronics Engrs. *Res:* Aeronomy; upper atmosphere physics; solar-terrestrial relationships; geomagnetic micropulsations. *Mailing Add:* Dept Physics Univ Victoria Box 3055 Elliott Bldg Rm 115 Victoria BC V8W 3P6 Can

HORIUCHI, KENSUKE, MOLECULAR BIOLOGY. *Current Pos:* res assoc genetics, Rockefeller Univ, 69-73, asst prof, 73-78, assoc prof, 78-89, ADJ PROF GENETICS, ROCKEFELLER UNIV, 89-; PROF, NAT INST GENETICS, JAPAN, 89- *Personal Data:* b Tokyo, Japan, Sept 21, 33; m 62; c 3. *Educ:* Univ Tokyo, BSc, 57, MSc, 59, PhD(biol), 62. *Prof Exp:* Fel microbiol, Yale Univ, 63-64; res assoc genetics, Rockefeller Inst, 64-66; asst biophys, Univ Tokyo, 66-69. *Mem:* Am Soc Microbiol. *Res:* Genetic and biochemical studies on small bacteriophages; restriction and modification enzymes. *Mailing Add:* 500 E 63rd St New York NY 10021

HORLICK, GARY, ANALYTICAL CHEMISTRY. *Current Pos:* PROF CHEM, UNIV ALTA, 69- *Personal Data:* b Regina, Can, Apr 15, 44. *Educ:* Univ Alta, BSc Hons, 65; Univ Ill, PhD(chem), 70. *Honors & Awards:* Barringer Award, Spectros Soc Can, 77. *Res:* Analytical spectroscopy. *Mailing Add:* Dept Chem Univ Alta Edmonton AB T6G 2G2 Can. *Fax:* 403-492-8231

HORLICK, LOUIS, MEDICINE. *Current Pos:* lectr med & biochem, Univ Sask, 53-55, asst prof med & co-dir, Cardiopulmonary Lab, 55-57, assoc prof med, 57-62, head dept, 68-74, PROF MED, UNIV SASK, 62-, DIR, DEPT ELECTROCARDIOGRAPHY, 55- *Personal Data:* b Montreal, Que, Dec 2, 21; m 54; c 4. *Educ:* McGill Univ, BSc, 44, MD & CM, 45, MSc, 52; FRCPS(C). *Prof Exp:* Demonstr med, McGill Univ, 50-53. *Concurrent Pos:* Mem Coun Arteriosclerosis & Clin Cardiol, Am Heart Asn; mem Can Coun Hosp Accreditation. *Mem:* Am Col Physicians; Am Col Cardiol; Can Cardiovasc Soc; Can Med Asn; Can Soc Clin Invest; Can Soc Internal Med; Can Soc Arteriosclerosis. *Res:* Arteriosclerosis; clinical investigation; lipid metabolism; cardiac rehabilitation. *Mailing Add:* Dept Med Univ Hosp Saskatoon SK S7N 0X0 Can

HORMATS, ELLIS IRVING, ELECTRON MICROSCOPY, APPLIED CHEMISTRY. *Current Pos:* RETIRED. *Personal Data:* b Albany, NY, Dec 10, 19; m 61; c 4. *Educ:* Rensselaer Polytech Inst, BChE, 41, Univ Cincinnati, MS, 43; Cornell Univ, PhD(chem), 50. *Prof Exp:* Asst, Univ Cincinnati, 41-42; jr engr prod, Chem Warfare Serv, Edgewood Arsenal, 42-43, asst engr develop, Pineblauff Arsenal, 43-44; assoc scientist, Los Alamos Sci Lab, 45-46; chemist, Aerojet Gen Corp, 50-57; prin scientist, Basic Sci Lab, Stromberg-Carlson Co, 57-60; sr res staff mem, Gen Dynamics Electronics Div, 60-69; prin engr, Stromberg Carlson Co, 69-85. *Mem:* Am Chem Soc; fel Am Inst Chem; Sigma Xi. *Res:* Chemical kinetics; solid state chemistry and crystal growth; photochemistry; thin film techniques; electron microscopy; analytical chemistry; microelectronics. *Mailing Add:* 639 Lake Shores Dr Maitland FL 32751

HORN, ALFRED, LATTICE THEORY. *Current Pos:* from instr to prof, 47-88, EMER PROF MATH, UNIV CALIF, LOS ANGELES, 88- *Personal Data:* b New York, NY, Feb 17, 18; m 45, Carole Christiansen; c Julian & Karen. *Educ:* City Col New York, BS, 38; NY Univ, MA, 41; Univ Calif, PhD(math), 46. *Prof Exp:* Asst math, Univ Calif, Berkeley, 41-42 & 45-46, instr, 46-47, mathematician, Radiation Lab, 42-45. *Concurrent Pos:* Mem, Inst Advan Study, 52-53. *Res:* Lattice theory; universal algebra. *Mailing Add:* Dept Math Univ Calif Los Angeles CA 90024-1555

HORN, ALLEN FREDERICK, JR, FOREST MANAGEMENT. *Current Pos:* RETIRED. *Personal Data:* b Milwaukee, Wis, Apr 25, 29; m 54; c 3. *Educ:* Mich State Univ, BS, 50, MS, 51; State Univ NY, PhD(forest mgt), 57; Syracuse Univ, LLB, 67. *Prof Exp:* Instr forestry, Mich State Univ, 51-53; asst prof & asst forester exp sta, Miss State Univ, 53-55; from asst prof to assoc prof, Col Environ Sci & Forestry, State Univ NY, Syracuse Univ, 57-69, prof forest mgt, 69- *Concurrent Pos:* Consult, Wood Industs, Pa, 57 & Area Redevelop Admin, 63-64; forester, USDA Coop Stat Res Serv, 75-76. *Mem:* Soc Am Foresters. *Res:* Legal problems relating to the administration of natural resources; environmental law; business and financial aspects of forest management. *Mailing Add:* 2255 Plantation Dr Beaufort SC 29902-5255

HORN, CHARLES NORMAN, SYSTEMATICS OF AQUATIC PLANTS, ECOLOGY OF AQUATIC PLANTS. *Current Pos:* asst prof, 86-89, ASSOC PROF BIOL, NEWBERRY COL, 89-, CAUGHMAN ENDOWED CHAIR SCI, 89- *Personal Data:* b Washington, DC, Nov 22, 56. *Educ:* George Mason Univ, BS, 78; Ohio State Univ, MS, 80; Univ Ala, PhD(biol), 85. *Prof Exp:* Instr biol, Shelton State Univ, 85-86. *Mem:* Ecol Soc Am; Bot Soc Am; Am Soc Plant Taxonomists; Nat Asn Biol Teachers; Am Inst Biol Sci. *Res:* Systematics, taxonomy, and ecology of a group of aquatic plants of the family pontederiaceae. *Mailing Add:* Dept Biol & Chem Newberry Col 2100 College Newberry SC 29108-2126. *Fax:* 803-321-5232

HORN, CHRISTIAN FRIEDRICH, GENERAL CHEMISTRY, POLYMER CHEMISTRY. *Current Pos:* mem bd dirs, 85-91, PRES, GRACE VENTURES CORP, 83-, MANAGING PARTNER, HORN VENTURE PARTNERS & HORN VENTURE PARTNERS II, 83-, SR VPRES, W R GRACE & CO, 91-; CORP SR VPRES & HEAD INT DEVELOP, CHEMED CORP, 81- *Personal Data:* b Dresden, Ger, Dec 23, 27; US citizen; m 54; c 1. *Educ:* Dresden Tech Univ, dipl chem, 51; Aachen Tech Univ, Dr rer nat(polymer chem), 58. *Prof Exp:* Res chemist synthetic fibers, Ger Acad Sci, 52-53; res chemist, Farbenwerke Hoechst, 53-54; res chemist, Union Carbide Chem Co, 54-57, group leader synthetic fibers, 58-61, res & develop mgr urethane polymers, 61-63, asst licensing mgr, 63-65; pres, Polymer Technol Inc, 65-71; managing dir & mem exec bd, Zimmer AG, 71-73; pres, Chrislon Corp, 73-74; vpres off opers, W R Grace & Co, 74-76, vpres, Corp Off Res & Tech Serv, 76-78, corp vpres & bd dirs, 78-81. *Concurrent Pos:* Res chemist, Europ Res Assocs, Belg, 57-58; consult, 65-71; mem bd, ASI Controls, Caelus, Inc, Home Town Buffet, Inc, Interlink Electronics, Inc, Nature's Elements Int, Roasters Corp & Timothy's Coffees of the World. *Mem:* Am Chem Soc. *Res:* Chemical process engineering in synthetic fibers; plastics; fiber technology; synthesis of monomers; chemical processes; international development; granted 47 US patents. *Mailing Add:* HOR Ventures Ptrs 20300 Stevens Creek Blvd No 330 Cupertino CA 95014

HORN, DAG, NUCLEAR PHYSICS, HEAVY ION REACTIONS. *Current Pos:* RES OFFICER, CHALK RIVER LABS, ATOMIC ENERGY CAN, LTD, 81- *Personal Data:* b Oslo, Norway, June 4, 50; m 76, Maria Kemp; c Marianna & Katherine. *Educ:* Mass Inst Technol, SB, 72, PhD(nuclear physics), 76. *Prof Exp:* Res asst nuclear physics, Mass Inst Technol, 72-76; fel, Atomic Energy Can Ltd, Chalk River Nuclear Lab, 76-78; asst nuclear physicist, Brookhaven Nat Labs, 78-80; res fel, Australian Nat Univ, 80-81. *Concurrent Pos:* Nat Sci Found Can fel, 76-78; vis scientist, Lab Phys Corpuslaire, Caen, France, 89-90. *Mem:* Am Phys Soc; Can Asn Physicists; Sigma Xi. *Res:* Experimental nuclear physics with heavy ions; nuclear reaction studies and spectroscopy: production and decay of highly excited nuclear systems. *Mailing Add:* Nuclear Physics Sta 49 Nuclear Lab Chalk River ON K0J 1J0 Can. *E-Mail:* horn@crl.aecl.ca

HORN, DAVID JACOBS, ECOLOGY, ENTOMOLOGY. *Current Pos:* assoc prof, 72-78, PROF ENTOM, OHIO STATE UNIV, 78- *Personal Data:* b Philadelphia, Pa, Feb 12, 43; m 66; c 2. *Educ:* Harvard Univ, BA, 65; Cornell Univ MS, 67, PhD(entom), 69. *Prof Exp:* Asst prof biol, Calif State Col, Hayward, 69-72. *Mem:* AAAS; Am Inst Biol Sci; Ecol Soc Am; Entom Soc Am; Entom Soc Can. *Res:* Biological control of insects; predator-prey interrelationships; population and community ecology; human influences on insect ecology. *Mailing Add:* Dept Entom Ohio State Univ 1735 Neil Ave Columbus OH 43210

HORN, DAVID NICHOLAS, multipoint multimedia communications systems & network services, distributed & parallel computing architectures & systems; deceased, see previous edition for last biography

HORN, DIANE, SCIENCE COMMUNICATIONS, SUSTAINABILITY & THE ENVIRONMENT. *Current Pos:* PRIN, ENVIRON CONSULT SERV, SEATTLE, WASH, 92- *Personal Data:* b Iowa City, Iowa. *Educ:* Stanford Univ, BA, 65; Purdue Univ, PhD(biol sci), 71. *Prof Exp:* Res fel cell biol & genetics, Harvard Med Sch, 71-75; asst prof biol sci, Univ Southern Calif, 75-83; sr scientist, Oncogen, Seattle, Wash, 83-90; sr res investr, Bristol-Myers Squibb Pharmaceut Res Inst, Seattle, Wash, 90-92. *Concurrent Pos:* NIH fel, 71-73; res fel genetics, Clin Genetics Div, Children's Hosp Med Ctr, Boston, 71-75; fel, Workshops Huntington's Dis, 73-74. *Res:* Control of gene expression in mammalian cells in tissue culture, particularly the regulation of growth and differentiated functions; biology of oncostatin M, monoclonal antibodies for cancer diagnosis and therapy; cover sustainability and environmental issues for media. *Mailing Add:* 202 W Olympic Pl Suite 104 Seattle WA 98119. *E-Mail:* dhorncs@ad.com

HORN, EDWARD GUSTAV, ECOLOGY, ENVIRONMENTAL SCIENCE. *Current Pos:* ENVIRON SCIENTIST VI, NY STATE DEPT HEALTH, 87- *Personal Data:* b Tucson, Ariz, Dec 18, 42; m 76; c 2. *Educ:* Duke Univ, BS, 64; Princeton Univ, PhD(biol), 69. *Prof Exp:* From asst prof to assoc prof biol, Russell Sage Col, 69-77, chmn dept, 71-76; res scientist III, NY State Dept Environ Conserv, 77-79, chief, Bur Environ Protection, 79-87. *Mem:* AAAS; Ecol Soc Am. *Res:* Role of food competition in community structure of cellular slime molds; ecology of aquatic macrophytes; fate of toxic substances in the environment; environmental remediation. *Mailing Add:* 2 University Pl Albany NY 12203

HORN, EUGENE HAROLD, ENDOCRINOLOGY, ANATOMY. *Current Pos:* instr histol, neuroanat & gross anat, 53-60, assoc prof anat, 60-68, asst dean, 62-66, assoc dean, 66-79, PROF ANAT, ALBANY MED COL, 68-, INTERIM CHMN, 87- *Personal Data:* b Lancaster, Pa, Sept 27, 26; m 52; c 2. *Educ:* Franklin & Marshall Col, BS, 49; Rutgers Univ, PhD(endocrinol), 53. *Prof Exp:* Asst, Bur Biol Res, Rutgers Univ, 50-53. *Mem:* AAAS; Asn Am Med Cols; NY Acad Sci; Sigma Xi; Am Asn Anatomist; Asn Anat Chmn. *Res:* Reproductive maturation; nutrition; thyroid physiology, relaxin. *Mailing Add:* 33 N Helderberg Pkwy Slingerlands NY 12159

HORN, HARRY MOORE, CIVIL ENGINEERING. *Current Pos:* RETIRED. *Personal Data:* b Brooklyn, NY, Jan 28, 31. *Educ:* Polytech Inst Brooklyn, BCE, 53; Columbia Univ, MS, 56; Univ Ill, PhD(civil eng), 61. *Honors & Awards:* C A Hogentogler Award, Am Soc Testing & Mat, 74. *Prof Exp:* Struct engr, Howard, Needles, Tammen & Bergendoff, NY, 53-55; soils engr, Tippetts, Abbett, McCarthy, Stratton, 56-57 & Haley & Aldrich, Mass, 60-62; asst prof civil eng, Mass Inst Technol, 62-65; assoc prof, Univ Ill, 65-67; prin, Woodward Clyde Consults, 67- *Mem:* Am Soc Civil Engrs. *Res:* Frictional properties of minerals; performance of building foundations; foundation instrumentation. *Mailing Add:* Woodward-Clyde Consult 201 Willow Brook Blvd Wayne NJ 07470

HORN, HENRY STAINKEN, POPULATION ECOLOGY, ANIMAL BEHAVIOR. *Current Pos:* From asst prof to assoc prof, 66-78, PROF BIOL, PRINCETON UNIV, 78- *Personal Data:* b Philadelphia, Pa, Nov 12, 41; m 63. *Educ:* Harvard Univ, BA, 62; Univ Wash, PhD(ecol), 66. *Mem:* AAAS; Ecol Soc Am; Animal Behav Soc; Lepidopterists Soc. *Res:* Spatial patterns of plants and animals; behavioral ecology of vertebrates and butterflies. *Mailing Add:* Dept Biol Princeton Univ Thomas Lewis Lab Princeton NJ 08544-1099

HORN, J(OHN) W(ILLIAM), TRANSPORTATION, CIVIL ENGINEERING. *Current Pos:* RETIRED. *Personal Data:* b Martinsburg, WVa, Aug 6, 29; m 51; c 4. *Educ:* WVa Univ, BS, 52; Mass Inst Technol, MS, 56. *Prof Exp:* Asst transp, Mass Inst Technol, 54-56; from asst prof to assoc prof, NC State Univ, 56-69, tech dir hwy res, 58-74, admin coordr joint hwy res prog, 64-65, prof civil eng, 69-89. *Concurrent Pos:* Res engr, Bruce Campbell & Assocs, Mass, 54-56; consult engr, 56-81; chmn bd, Kimley-Horn & Assocs, Prof Engrs, 66-84; prin & sr consult, Kimley-Horn & Assoc, Engrs, 84-88. *Mem:* Am Soc Civil Engrs; Inst Traffic Engrs; Am Pub Works Asn; Am Consult Engrs Coun; Sigma Xi. *Res:* Transportation planning, design and operations. *Mailing Add:* 3612 Anclote Pl Raleigh NC 27607

HORN, JOANNE MARIE, generation of biodegradative pollution abatement systems, engineering of genetic regulatory systems & proteins, for more information see previous edition

HORN, KENNETH PORTER, FLUID MECHANICS, SYSTEMS ENGINEERING. *Current Pos:* dept head, 88-90, PROG DIR, RAND CORP, 75- *Personal Data:* b Ft Worth, Tex, Dec 10, 37; m 79, Ann Harper. *Educ:* Rice Univ, BA, 60, MS, 62; Stanford Univ, PhD(aeronaut & astronaut), 66. *Prof Exp:* Aerospace engr, NASA Manned Spacecraft Ctr, 62; mem tech staff, Plasma Res Lab & Satellite Systs Div, Aerospace Corp, 66-75. *Mem:* Am Phys Soc; Am Inst Aeronaut & Astronaut. *Res:* High-temperature gas dynamics, including radiation-coupled flow and nonequilibrium processes; systems engineering, particularly space and missile systems. *Mailing Add:* Rand Corp 1700 Main St Santa Monica CA 90406. *Fax:* 310-827-4059; *E-Mail:* kenneth_horn@rand.org

HORN, LEIF, BIOPHYSICS. *Current Pos:* assoc prof, 67-68, PROF PHYSIOL, COL MED & DENT NJ, 68- *Personal Data:* b Tromso, Norway, Mar 15, 25; m 49, 79; c 3. *Educ:* Univ Oslo, Cand Phil, 47, PhD(physiol & biochem), 56. *Honors & Awards:* Angiol Res Found-Purdue Frederick Co Achievement Award, 64-65. *Prof Exp:* Asst physiol, Univ Oslo, 49-50, asst,

Inst Nutrit Res, 50-53; res assoc surg, Med Col Va, 57, from instr to asst prof biophys, 57-59; asst prof path, Sch Med, NY Univ, 59-62, asst prof exp surg, 62-64; assoc prof physiol, NY Med Col, 64-67. *Concurrent Pos:* Res chemist, Aeromed Inst, Norway, 50; spec fel with Prof Benjamin W Zweifach, Nat Heart Inst, 59-61. *Mem:* Microcirc Soc; Fedn Am Soc Exp Biol; Am Physiol Soc; Am Heart Asn. *Res:* Electrophysiology of vascular smooth muscle; vascular physiology and biophysics. *Mailing Add:* Dept Physiol UMDNJ NJ Med Sch 185 S Orange Ave Newark NJ 07103-2714

HORN, LYLE WILLIAM, BIOPHYSICS, CELL MEMBRANE TRANSPORT. *Current Pos:* ASSOC PROF PHYSIOL & BIOPHYS, TEMPLE UNIV, 81- *Personal Data:* b St Paul, Minn, July 22, 43; m 70. *Educ:* Univ Colo, BS, 66; Johns Hopkins Univ, PhD(biomed eng), 73. *Prof Exp:* Res assoc mech, Johns Hopkins Univ, 73-74; asst prof physiol, Sch Med, Univ Md, 74-81. *Mem:* Biophys Soc; Soc Gen Physiol; AAAS. *Res:* Kinetics of cell membrane transport of amino acids; sodium-coupling; giant axon membranes; surfactants; muscle membranes. *Mailing Add:* Dept Physiol Temple Univ Sch Med 3223 N Broad St Philadelphia PA 19140-5211

HORN, MARK WILLIAM, PLASMA PROCESSING OF INTEGRATED CIRCUIT MATERIALS, PLASMA DEPOSITION OF POLYMERS & INORGANIC MATERIALS. *Current Pos:* STAFF MEM, MASS INST TECHNOL LINCOLN LAB, 88- *Personal Data:* m 85, Mary L (Snyder); c Christian, Chelsey & Kyle. *Educ:* Pa State Univ, BS, 82, MS, 85, PhD(eng sci & mech), 89. *Prof Exp:* Instr eng sci, Pa State Univ, 87-88. *Res:* Developing plasma etching processes for metals, semiconductors and polymers, plasma-deposited photorfesist for all-dry lithography, silylation processes for sub-0.25 micrometer lithography, and chemical-mechanical polishing (CMP) for integrated circuits. *Mailing Add:* Mass Inst Technol Lincoln Lab 244 Wood St Lexington MA 02173-6499. *Fax:* 781-981-4983; *E-Mail:* hom@submicron.ll.mit.edu

HORN, MICHAEL HASTINGS, ICHTHYOLOGY, MARINE BIOLOGY. *Current Pos:* from asst prof to assoc prof zool, 70-77, PROF BIOL, CALIF STATE UNIV, FULLERTON, 77- *Personal Data:* b Tahlequah, Okla, Nov 14, 42. *Educ:* Northeastern State Col, BS, 63; Univ Okla, MS, 65; Harvard Univ, PhD(biol), 69. *Prof Exp:* Fel biol oceanog, Woods Hole Oceanog Inst, 68-69; NATO fel sci, Brit Mus, London, 70. *Concurrent Pos:* Ed, Ichthyol Book Rev, 85-92; vis res scientist, Dunstaff Nage Mar Res Lab, Oban, Scotland, 86. *Mem:* AAAS; Am Soc Ichthyol & Herpet; Am Fish Soc; Sigma Xi; Ecol Soc Am; Soc Conserv Biol. *Res:* Fish-plant interactions in coastal seas and tropical rainforests; physiological ecology of rocky shore fishes; feeding ecology and digestive physiology of fishes; feeding ecology and digestive physiology of fish-eating seabirds. *Mailing Add:* Dept Biol Calif State Univ Fullerton CA 92834. *Fax:* 714-773-3426; *E-Mail:* mhorn@fullerton.edu

HORN, MYRON K, PETROLEUM GEOLOGY. *Current Pos:* head dept geol res, Res Lab, 65-70, DIR RES, E&P RES LAB, CITIES SERV CO, 70- *Personal Data:* b Miami, Fla, Jan 28, 30; m 55; c 3. *Educ:* Univ Colo, BA, 52; Univ Houston, MS, 58; Rice Univ, PhD(geol), 64. *Prof Exp:* Sr res geologist, Pure Oil Co Res Ctr, 60-64. *Concurrent Pos:* Assoc ed, Am Asn Petrol Geologists, 75-78, ed, 79-; sci adv, Ocean Margin Drilling Proj, 81- *Mem:* AAAS; Sigma Xi; Soc Petrol Engrs; Am Petrol Inst; Am Asn Petrol Geologists. *Res:* Computer systems for well log interpretation; computer-derived retrieval systems; computer-derived geochemical balances; simulated neutron activation spectra; habitat of oil and gas on continental margins; production geology; remote sensing applications; composition of formation waters; global geology. *Mailing Add:* 5919 S Gary Pl Tulsa OK 74105

HORN, ROGER ALAN, MATRIX ANALYSIS. *Current Pos:* RES PROF MATH, UNIV UTAH, 92- *Personal Data:* b Macon, Ga, Jan 19, 42; m 65, Susan Dadakis; c 3. *Educ:* Cornell Univ, BA, 63; Stanford Univ, MS, 64, PhD(math), 67. *Prof Exp:* Asst prof math, Univ Santa Clara, 67-68; from asst prof to prof math sci, Johns Hopkins Univ, 68-92, chmn dept, 72-79; assoc prof, Univ Md, Baltimore Co, 71-72. *Concurrent Pos:* Alfred P Sloan Found res fel, 75-79. *Mem:* Am Math Soc; Soc Indust & Appl Math; Math Asn Am. *Res:* Analysis, complex variables; matrix analysis; probability. *Mailing Add:* Math Dept Univ Utah Salt Lake City UT 84112

HORN, SUSAN DADAKIS, HEALTH SERVICES RESEARCH, MEDICAL STATISTICS. *Current Pos:* SR SCIENTIST, INST CLIN OUTCOMES RES, 96- *Personal Data:* b Cleveland, Ohio, Aug 30, 43; m 65, Roger; c 3. *Educ:* Cornell Univ, AB, 64; Stanford Univ, MS, 66, PhD(statist), 68. *Prof Exp:* Asst prof biostatist, Johns Hopkins Univ, 68-74, asst prof statist, 68-72, assoc prof math sci, 72-77, asst prof health care orgn, 73-77, assoc prof health policy & mgt, 77-86, prof health policy & mgt, 86-92; sr scientist, Intermountain Health Care, 92-95. *Concurrent Pos:* Statistician consult, var US hosps, 74- *Mem:* Asn Health Serv Res; fel Am Statist Asn; Biomet Soc; Am Pub Health Asn. *Res:* Statistical methods; measuring patient's severity of illness for management, quality and prospective reimbursement; applications of statistics in public health; clinical practice improvement research. *Mailing Add:* Inst Clin Outcomes Res 2681 Parleys Way Suite 201 Salt Lake City UT 84109. *Fax:* 801-582-0626

HORN, WILLIAM EVERETT, PHYSICS. *Current Pos:* RETIRED. *Personal Data:* b Zanesville, Ohio, Aug 27, 28; m 54, 78. *Educ:* Ohio State Univ, BSc, 50, MSc, 51; Johns Hopkins Univ, cert bus mgt, 60. *Prof Exp:* Res asst optical physics, Res Found, Ohio State Univ, 50-52; res engr, Res Labs, Westinghouse Elec Co, 52-54; sr engr, Aerospace Div, Md, 56-59, proj engr, 59-61, supvr physicist, 61-65, dir, Westinghouse Cambridge Lab, 65-69, mgr res & develop Progs, Syst Develop Div, 69-97. *Mem:* Am Phys Soc; Optical Soc Am; sr mem Inst Elec & Electronics Engrs; assoc fel Am Inst Aeronaut & Astronaut; Am Defense Preparedness Ord Asn; Sigma Xi. *Res:* Electromagnetic areas of laser techniques; infrared reconnaissance and aerospace applications; molecular electronics; microwaves; systems applications involving radar and optical guidance, control, stabilization and computation areas. *Mailing Add:* 2 Thorndyke Garth Phoenix MD 21131

HORNA, OTAKAR ANTHONY, COMMUNICATION ENGINEERING, MATHEMATICAL LOGIC. *Current Pos:* RETIRED. *Personal Data:* b Prague, Czech, Jan 8, 22; US citizen; m 57; c 1. *Educ:* Czech Inst Technol, MSEE, 48; Inst Radiotechnol & Electronics, Prague, PhD(electronics), 62; Charles Univ, Prague, dipl math logic, 63. *Honors & Awards:* Gold Medal, World Exhib, Brussels, 58 & Brno Int Fair & Exhib, Czech, 67; Res Award, COMSAT Labs, 76. *Prof Exp:* Res asst measurement technol, Inst Theoret & Exp Mech, 48-55; res engr med electronics, Inst Med Electronics, Prague, 55; sr staff scientist comput, Inst Math Mach, Prague, 55-68; sr engr mil electronics, Multronics Corp, Rockville, Md, 68-69; sr staff scientist communs, Comsat Labs, Clarksburg, Md, 69-84; sr engr, IBM, 84-92. *Concurrent Pos:* Consult, Automotive Res Inst, Prague, 52-66; sci secy, Govt Adv Coun Comput, Prague, 63-65; consult, Turbine Test Dept, SKODA Works, Czech, 64-68; actg vchmn, Sci Coun, Res Inst Math Mach, Prague, 66-68; co-chmn, Govt Adv Bd Electronics Indust Planning, Prague, 67. *Mem:* Sr mem Inst Elec & Electronics Engrs; Czech Soc Arts & Sci Am. *Res:* Satellite communication; real-time signal processing; self-adaptive systems and filters; mathematical logic. *Mailing Add:* IBM 9211 Corporate Blvd Rockville MD 20850

HORNACK, FREDERICK MATHEW, PHYSICAL CHEMISTRY. *Current Pos:* PROF CHEM, UNIV NC, WILMINGTON, 64- *Personal Data:* b Philadelphia, Pa, June 10, 29; m 53; c 3. *Educ:* Lowell Technol Inst, BS, 50; Fla State Univ, PhD(chem), 55. *Honors & Awards:* Olney Prize, 50. *Prof Exp:* Asst, Fla State Univ, 50-55; res assoc chem, Univ Ark, 55-56; chemist, Robert A Taft Eng Ctr, USPHS, 56-58; asst prof chem, Univ Tampa, 58-60; asst prof, Va Polytech Inst, 60-64. *Mem:* Am Chem Soc. *Res:* Education in chemistry; solubility of gases. *Mailing Add:* 114 Green Forest Dr Wilmington NC 28409

HORNAK, THOMAS, ELECTRONICS. *Current Pos:* mem tech staff solid state circuits & optoelectronics, 68-73, Dept Mgr Solid State Circuits, Optoelectronics & Commun Technol, 73-92, PRIN LAB SCIENTIST, HEWLETT PACKARD LABS, 92- *Personal Data:* b Bratislava, Czech, Oct 14, 24; US citizen; m 58; c 1. *Educ:* Slovak Tech Univ, Bratislava, Czech, BSEE, 46, MSEE, 47; Czech Tech Univ, Prague, PhD(electronic eng), 66. *Prof Exp:* Sect mgr electronics, Tesla Radio Res Lab, Prague, 47-61; head adv, Comput Res Inst, Prague, 62-68. *Concurrent Pos:* Vis prof, Tech Univ, Prague & Brno, Czech, 52-56. *Mem:* Fel Inst Elec & Electronics Engrs. *Res:* Advanced solid state circuits and optoelectronics and their applications to instrumentation, communication, computation and signal processing. *Mailing Add:* Hewlett Packard Co Bldg 26U4 PO Box 10350 Palo Alto CA 94303

HORNBACK, JOSEPH MICHAEL, ORGANIC CHEMISTRY. *Current Pos:* asst prof, 70-75, assoc dean, 88-95, ASSOC PROF CHEM, UNIV DENVER, 75- *Personal Data:* b Middletown, Ohio, Sept 16, 43; m 85, Melani Poundstone; c Joseph, Patrick & Jordan. *Educ:* Univ Notre Dame, BS, 65; Ohio State Univ, PhD(chem), 68. *Prof Exp:* Res assoc chem, Univ Wis, 68-70. *Mem:* Am Chem Soc. *Res:* Photochemical reactions of organic compounds; synthesis of organic compounds. *Mailing Add:* Dept Chem Univ Denver Denver CO 80208. *Fax:* 303-871-2254; *E-Mail:* jhornbac@du.edu

HORNBAKER, EDWIN DALE, SPECIALTY POLYMERS, CERAMICS. *Current Pos:* RETIRED. *Personal Data:* b Louisburg, Kans, June 19, 29; m 57, Judy; c Vanessa & Dorinda. *Educ:* Univ Kans, BS, 51; Univ Va, MS, 53, PhD(chem), 55. *Prof Exp:* Sr res chemist, J T Baker Chem Co, 55-57; res chemist, Ethyl Corp, 57-62, from res assoc to sr res assoc, 62-64, supvr, 64-81, asst dir, 81-89, mat res dir, 89-90, sr res adv, 90-91. *Mem:* Am Chem Soc. *Res:* Development of specialty polymers; high softening thermoplastics; specialty elastomers; water soluble polymers; ceramic precursor polymers; ceramics. *Mailing Add:* 10968 Worthington Ave Baton Rouge LA 70815-5341

HORNBEIN, THOMAS F, ANESTHESIOLOGY, PHYSIOLOGY. *Personal Data:* b St Louis, Mo, Nov 6, 30; m 51; c 5. *Educ:* Univ Colo, BA, 52; Wash Univ, MD, 56; Am Bd Anesthesiol, dipl. *Honors & Awards:* Hubbard Medal; George Norlin Award, Univ Colo, Denver, 70. *Prof Exp:* Instr anesthesiol, Sch Med, Wash Univ, 60-61, from asst prof to prof anesthesiol, physiol & biophys, 63-78, vchmn, Dept Anesthesiol, 72-74, prof & chmn, 78-93. *Concurrent Pos:* USPHS res fel, 59-61, res grant, 64-67, career develop award, 65-75; chmn, Soc Acad Anesthesia, 78-93. *Mem:* Am Physiol Soc; Am Soc Anesthesiol; Asn Univ Anesthetists (pres, 75-76); Inst Med; Soc Acad Anesthesia Chmn; fel AAAS. *Res:* Respiratory physiology; chemical regulation of ventilation; quantification of neural discharge from peripheral chemoreceptors in response to hypoxia, hypercapnia and acidosis; role of acidosis or carbon dioxide; ion regulation across blood-brain barrier; high altitude physiology and pathophysiology; cerebral hypoxiz. *Mailing Add:* Dept Anesthesiol Box 356540 Univ Wash Sch Med Seattle WA 98195. *Fax:* 206-543-2958

HORNBERGER, CARL STANLEY, JR, ORGANIC CHEMISTRY. *Current Pos:* CONSULT, 82- *Personal Data:* b Chicago, Ill, June 27, 23; m 50; c 3. *Educ:* NCent Col, Ill, AB, 47; Univ Ill, PhD(chem), 51; Am Bd Indust Hyg, cert. *Prof Exp:* Res fel, Univ Ill, 51-53; res chemist agr chem, E I Du Pont de Nemours & Co, Inc, 53-58, biochemist pharmaceut res, Stine Lab, 58-64, biochemist drug metab, 64-67, toxicologist, Haskell Lab, 67-74, chief dermalocular toxicol, 70-74, plant indust hygenist, 74-76, consult indust hyg, 76-80, sr info specialist, Haskell Lab, 80-82. *Concurrent Pos:* Consult, indust hyg; adj prof toxicol, math modelling & on-line retrieval info (modem), Del State Col, Dover. *Mem:* Am Chem Soc; Am Indust Hyg Asn. *Res:* Biomolecular reduction of hindered keytones; lipoic acid, isolation, characterization and synthesis; agricultural chemicals; pharmaceuticals; drug metabolism; managerial methods for identification and assessment of chemical health hazards; setting standards for work place contaminants. *Mailing Add:* 11 N Cliffe Dr Wilmington DE 19809

HORNBERGER, GEORGE MILTON, HYDROLOGY. *Current Pos:* From asst prof to prof, Univ Va, 70-90, chmn dept, 79-83, distinguished prof, 90-93, ERNEST H ERN PROF ENVIRON SCI, UNIV VA, 93- *Personal Data:* b Ashland, Pa, June 22, 42; m 65, Joan Azckey; c Rachel J (Kessinger) & George Z. *Educ:* Drexel Univ, BSCE, 65, MSCE, 67; Stanford Univ, PhD(hydrol), 70. *Honors & Awards:* Robert Horton Award, Hydrol Sect, Am Geophys Union, 93; John Wesley Powell Award, US Geol Surv, 95. *Concurrent Pos:* Vis fel, Centre Resource & Environ Studies, Australian Nat Univ, Canberra, 77-78; hon vis prof, Univ Lancaster, Eng, 84-85; NAm ed, Hydrol Processes, 85-93; mem, Bd Radioactive Waste Mgt, Nat Acad Sci, 86-91; vis prof, Stanford Univ, 90-91; vis scientist, US Geol Surv, 90-91; ed, Water Resources Res, 93-96; mem, Comn Geosci, Environ & Resources, 94-, chmn, 96- *Mem:* Nat Acad Eng; Am Geol Inst; Sigma Xi; Geol Soc Am; fel Am Women Sci; fel Am Geophys Union. *Res:* Modelling of environmental systems with uncertainty; hydrogeochemical response of small cathments; transport of microbes in groundwater. *Mailing Add:* Dept Environ Sci Clark Hall Univ Va Charlottesville VA 22903. *E-Mail:* gmh3k@virginia.edu

HORNBLASS, ALBERT, ORBITAL ONCOLOGY, LACRIMOLOGY. *Current Pos:* DIR OPHTHAL PLASTIC SURG, MANHATTAN EYE, EAR & THROAT HOSP, 79-; CLIN PROF OPHTHAL, NY STATE UNIV HEALTH SCI CTR, 88- *Personal Data:* b New York, NY, July 5, 39; m 73, Bernice M Brooks; c David, Moshe & Elana. *Educ:* Yeshiva Univ, BA & BRE, 60; Univ Cincinnati, MD, 64. *Honors & Awards:* Honor Award, Am Acad Ophthal, 82, Sr Award, 93; Reeh Award, Am Soc Ophthal & Plastic Surg, 86; Jack Crawford Award, Univ Toronto, 92; Ruedeman lectr, Am Soc Ocularists, 92. *Concurrent Pos:* Vis prof, Univ Philippines, Univ Toronto, Sinai Hosp, Ohio State Univ, Hebrew Univ Jerusalem, Mt Sinai Hosp, New York & Korea Univ. *Mem:* Am Soc Ophthal & Plastic Surg (pres, 93); Am Israeli Ophthal Soc; Am Acad Ophthal; Am Soc Ocularists; fel Am Col Surgeons; fel Ophthal Laser Surg Soc. *Res:* Ophthalmic plastic and orbital surgery; eyelid and orbital oncology; congenital eyelid defects; orbital trauma; thyroid ophthalmology. *Mailing Add:* Ophthal Dept 130 E 67th St New York NY 10021

HORNBOGEN, ERHARD, SHAPE MEMORY ALLOYS, LIGHT STRUCTURAL MATERIALS. *Current Pos:* PROF MAT SCI, RUHR UNIV, 68- *Personal Data:* b Feb 2, 30; m 64, Dorothy Bitterhof; c Martin. *Educ:* Tech Univ, Clausthal, dipl phys metab, 54, Dr Ing, 56; Tech Univ, Stuttgart, Dr Habil, 64. *Hon Degrees:* Dr, Univ Miskolz, Hungary, 96. *Honors & Awards:* Grossman Award, Am Soc Mat, 62 & 63; Masing Prize, Ger Soc Mat, 65, Heyn Award, 91; R E Mehl Award, Am Inst Mining & Metal Engrs, 79; Reaumur Medal, Fr Soc Metall, 84; R Mitsche Award, Austrian Metall Soc, 90; Sorby Award, Int Metallog Soc, 95. *Prof Exp:* Res engr, US Steel Corp, Pittsburgh, 58-62; scientist, Max-Planck-Inst, Stuttgart, 63-65; prof, Univ Gottingen, 65-68. *Mem:* Fel Am Soc Mat; Ger Phys Soc; Ger Soc Math. *Res:* Light metals; natural polymers; smart materials; recycling of materials. *Mailing Add:* Ruhr Univ 44780 Bochum Germany. *Fax:* 49-234-7094-235

HORNBROOK, K ROGER, PHARMACOLOGY. *Current Pos:* assoc prof, 72-77, PROF PHARMACOL, UNIV OKLA HEALTH SCI CTR, OKLAHOMA CITY, 77-, PROF & CHAIR PHARMACOL & TOXICOL, 94- *Personal Data:* b New Martinsville, WVa, Oct 23, 36; m 58, Lois J Schupbach; c Jane. *Educ:* WVa Univ, BS, 58; Univ Mich, PhD(pharmacol), 63. *Prof Exp:* Res assoc pharmacol, Univ Mich, 63; asst prof, Emory Univ, 65-72. *Concurrent Pos:* Fel, Washington Univ, 63-65; Nat Inst Arthritis & Metab Dis spec fel, 67-70. *Mem:* Am Soc Pharmacol & Exp Therapeut; Soc Exp Biol & Med. *Res:* Biochemical pharmacology; regulation of carbohydrate metabolism; mechanisms of hepatotoxicity. *Mailing Add:* Dept Pharmacol & Toxicol Univ Okla Health Sci Ctr Oklahoma City OK 73190. *E-Mail:* roger_hornbrook@uokhsc.edu

HORNBUCKLE, FRANKLIN L, ENGINEERING. *Current Pos:* VPRES, DEFENSE SYST, INC, 91- *Personal Data:* b Birmingham, Ala, Jan 19, 41. *Educ:* Tenn State Univ, BSEE, 62; Rutgers Univ, MSEE, 71. *Prof Exp:* Engr, RCA Space Div, 62-72; mgr spacecraft elec, Fairchild Space Co, 72-75, dir, Elec Eng Dept, 75-81, Dir, Eng Dept, 81-86, vpres, 86-88, vpres spacecraft eng, 88-91. *Mem:* Inst Elec & Electronics Engrs; Am Inst Aeronaut & Astronaut; Asn Naval Aviation; Armed Forces Commun & Electronics Asn. *Res:* Advanced satellite power systems concepts; high density solid state memory applications. *Mailing Add:* Fairfield Space Co 20301 Century Blvd Germantown MD 20874

HORNBUCKLE, PHYLLIS ANN, PSYCHOPHYSIOLOGY. *Current Pos:* RETIRED. *Personal Data:* b Mooresville, NC, Nov 18, 38. *Educ:* Pfeiffer Col, BA, 59; Col William & Mary, MA, 66; Emory Univ, PhD(psychophysiol), 69. *Prof Exp:* Asst prof psychol, Med Col Va, Va Commonwealth Univ, 68-92, asst prof med, 75-92. *Mem:* Sigma Xi. *Res:* Therapeutic and non-therapeutic chemical effects on behavior. *Mailing Add:* RR 1 Mathews VA 23109

HORNE, ALEXANDER JOHN, AQUATIC BIOLOGY. *Current Pos:* assoc prof aquatic ecol, Dept Eng, 71-80, PROF SANITARY, ENVIRON, COASTAL & HYDRAULIC ENG, DEPT CIVIL ENG, UNIV CALIF, BERKELEY, 80-, ASSOC BIOLOGIST, SANIT ENG RES LAB, 71- *Personal Data:* b Doncaster, Eng. *Educ:* Univ Bristol, BSc, 64; Univ Dundee, Scotland, PhD(limnol & oceanog), 69. *Prof Exp:* Res asst nitrogen fixation, Dept Bot, Westfield Col, Univ London, 64-68; res fel nitrogen fixation, Dept Biol Sci, Univ Dundee, Scotland, 69-70; res fel limnol, Dept Ecol, Univ Calif, Davis, 70-71. *Concurrent Pos:* Consult, Lake County Flood Control & Water Conserv Dist, 70- & Calif Dept Water Resources, 73- *Mem:* Am Soc Limnol & Oceanog; Brit Phycol Soc; Int Soc Limnol. *Res:* Aquatic ecology; environmental engineering; nitrogen-fixation; eutrophication, lakes, reservoirs, estuaries, rivers and coastal waters; pollution control; lake and estuarine management; oil pollution; geothermal pollution; sewage pollution. *Mailing Add:* Dept Civil Eng Univ Calif 760 Davis Hall Berkeley CA 94720-0001

HORNE, FRANCIS R, COMPARATIVE PHYSIOLOGY. *Current Pos:* from asst prof to assoc prof biol, 67-77, PROF BIOL, SOUTHWEST TEX STATE UNIV, 77- *Personal Data:* b San Antonio, Tex, Dec 22, 39; c 3. *Educ:* Tex Tech Col, BS, 62; Univ Wyo, MS, 64, PhD(physiol), 66. *Prof Exp:* NIH res fel, Inst Marine Sci, 66-67. *Mem:* Am Soc Zool. *Res:* Comparative physiology and biochemistry of nitrogen excretion; respiratory pigments and ion regulation. *Mailing Add:* Dept Biol Southwest Tex State Univ San Marcos TX 78666-4602

HORNE, FREDERICK HERBERT, PHYSICAL CHEMISTRY, THEORETICAL CHEMISTRY. *Current Pos:* PROF CHEM & DEAN, COL SCI, ORE STATE UNIV, 86- *Personal Data:* b Kans City, Mo, Mar 11, 34; m 59, Clara A Johnson; c Frederick J, James H & Nancy C. *Educ:* Harvard Univ, AB, 56; Univ Kans, PhD(phys chem), 62. *Prof Exp:* NSF fel, Stanford Univ, 62-63, instr chem, 63-64; from asst prof to assoc prof, Mich State Univ, 64-73, assoc chmn dept, 75-82, prof chem, 73-86, assoc dean, Col Natural Sci, 82-86. *Concurrent Pos:* Vis scientist, Lawrence Livermore Lab, 71 & Odense Univ, Denmark, 79; vis prof chem, Arya Mehr Univ Technol, Iran, 75; Bd Sci & Technol Int Develop, Nat Res Coun, 88- *Mem:* Am Chem Soc; Mat Res Soc; AAAS. *Res:* Chemical and nonequilibrium thermodynamics; nonequilibrium statistical mechanics; thermal diffusion; membrane transport; ion transport in liquids and solids; applied mathematics and statistics. *Mailing Add:* Kidder Hall 128 Ore State Univ Corvallis OR 97331-4608. *Fax:* 541-737-1009; *E-Mail:* hornef@ccmail.orst.edu

HORNE, G(ERALD) T(ERENCE), METALLURGY. *Current Pos:* VPRES, INDUST TESTING LAB SERV CO, 69- *Personal Data:* b New York, NY, June 24, 24; m 46; c 5. *Educ:* Mont Sch Mines, BSc, 48; Carnegie Inst Technol, MS, 51, PhD(metall), 52; Univ Pittsburgh, MBA, 72. *Honors & Awards:* Andrew Carnegie Lectr, 78. *Prof Exp:* Mem staff, Metals Res Lab, Carnegie Inst Technol, 52-64, from asst prof to assoc prof, Dept Metall Eng, 52-64; staff engr, Glass Res Ctr, PPG Indust, Inc, 64-65; asst mgr, 65-69. *Mem:* Am Soc Metals; Am Soc Testing & Mat; Am Inst Mining, Metall & Petrol Engrs; Am Soc Eng Educ; NY Acad Sci; Sigma Xi; Am Soc Mech Engr; AAAS. *Res:* Deformation of metals; fracture; fatigue of metals; diffusion in solids; mechanical metallurgy. *Mailing Add:* 302 Fox Chapel Rd Apt 212 Pittsburgh PA 15238

HORNE, GREGORY STUART, STRATIGRAPHY, MARINE GEOLOGY. *Current Pos:* assoc prof earth sci, 67-80, PROF EARTH & ENVIRON SCI, WESLEYAN UNIV, 80; PRES, ESSEX MARINE LAB, 75- *Personal Data:* b Minneapolis, Minn, June 11, 35; m 57; c 2. *Educ:* Dartmouth Col, AB 57; Columbia Univ, PhD(geol), 68. *Prof Exp:* Geologist, Tidewater Oil Co, 57-64; geologist, Pan Am Petrol Corp, 65. *Mem:* Geol Soc Am; Am Asn Petrol Geologists; Soc Econ Paleont & Mineral. *Res:* Petroleum geology; stratigraphy and structural geology of orogenic belts; sedimentology of chaotic deposits; paleoecology of Lower Paleozoic carbonate sequences; coastal processes and nearshore geological oceanography. *Mailing Add:* Soc Sci Middlesex Community Tech Col 100 Training Hill Rd Middletown CT 06457-4825

HORNE, RALPH ALBERT, ENVIRONMENTAL CHEMISTRY. *Current Pos:* CONSULT, 87- *Personal Data:* b Haverhill, Mass, Mar 10, 29. *Educ:* Mass Inst Technol, BS, 50; Univ Vt, MS, 52; Boston Univ, MA, 53; Columbia Univ, PhD(phys chem), 55; Suffolk Univ Law Sch, JD, 79. *Prof Exp:* Asst, Columbia Univ, 53; res assoc chem, Brookhaven Nat Lab, 53-55; res assoc, Nuclear Sci Lab, Mass Inst Technol, 55-57; mem sr tech staff, Radio Corp Am, 57-59; sr scientist, Joseph Kaye & Co, Inc, 59-60 & Arthur D Little, Inc, Mass, 60-68; assoc scientist, Woods Hole Oceanog Inst, 69-71; prin scientist, JBF Sci Corp, 71-72; mem sci staff, Arthur D Little, Inc, 72-78; sr scientist, GCA Tech Div, 78-80, & Energy & Environ Eng Inc, 81-87. *Res:* Electron exchange reactions; structure of aqueous solutions; transport processes in aqueous solutions; chemical oceanography; high pressure; environmental law; history and philosophy of science; environmental chemistry; energy and resources. *Mailing Add:* 9 Wellington St Boston MA 02118

HORNE, ROBERT D, VETERINARY SURGERY. *Personal Data:* b Eufaula, Ala, June 17, 35; m 57; c 1. *Educ:* Auburn Univ, DVM, 59, MSc, 61; Am Col Vet Surg, dipl, 70. *Honors & Awards:* Am Animal Hosp Asn Merit Award in Orthop, 73. *Prof Exp:* From instr to assoc prof, Auburn Univ, 59-70, alumni assoc prof, 70, alumni prof small animal surg & med, Sch Vet Med, 70-95. *Concurrent Pos:* Orthop Res Soc grant, 63-64; Scott Rickey Grant, Orthopedic Res, 79-81; fac grant, Orthopedic Res, 78- *Mem:* Am Vet Med Asn; Am Asn Vet Clinicians; Animal Hosp Asn. *Res:* Thoracic, cardiovascular and orthopedic surgery. *Mailing Add:* 295 Chewacla Dr Auburn AL 36830

HORNE, ROLAND NICHOLAS, GEOTHERMAL RESERVOIR ENGINEERING. *Current Pos:* from asst prof to assoc prof, 80-91, PROF PETROL ENG, STANFORD UNIV, 91-, CHMN, 95- *Personal Data:* b London, Eng, Nov 27, 52; US citizen; m 78; c 1. *Educ:* Univ Auckland, NZ, BE, 72, PhD(appl mech), 75, DSc, 86. *Prof Exp:* Res fel, Univ Auckland, 74-76; actg asst prof chem eng, Stanford Univ, 76-77, actg asst prof petrol eng, 77-78; lectr appl mech, Univ Auckland, 78-79. *Concurrent Pos:* Prin investr, Stanford Geothermal Prog, 81- *Mem:* Sigma Xi; Am Inst Mining, Metall & Petrol Engrs; Am Soc Mech Engrs; Soc Petrol Engrs. *Res:* Geothermal reservoir engineering; heat and mass transfer in porous media; pressure transient analysis of oil, gas and geothermal wells; hydrodynamic stability; reservoir simulation; optimisation of reservoir performance. *Mailing Add:* Dept Petrol Eng Stanford Univ Stanford CA 94305-2220

HORNE, SAMUEL EMMETT, JR, POLYMER CHEMISTRY, ORGANIC CHEMISTRY. *Current Pos:* RETIRED. *Personal Data:* b Jacksonville, Fla, July 26, 24; m 49, Sue Ross; c Vicki, Peggy, Melanie & Sam III. *Educ:* Emory Univ, AB, 47, MA, 48, PhD(chem), 50. *Hon Degrees:* DSc, Emory Univ, 82. *Honors & Awards:* Pioneer Award, Am Inst Chemists, 74; Midgley Medal, Am Chem Soc, 78, & Goodyear Medal Rubber Div, 80. *Prof Exp:* Tech man, B F Goodrich Co, 50-54, sr tech man, 54-59, res assoc, 59-68, sr res assoc, res ctr, 68-82; sci adv, Rubber Tech Ctr, Polysar, Inc, Stow, Ohio, 82-84; prin scientist, 84-87. *Concurrent Pos:* Chmn, Gordon Conf Hydrocarbon Chem, 69; asst counr, Rubber Div, Am Chem Soc, 88-; polymer consult. *Mem:* Am Chem Soc; NY Acad Sci; fel Am Inst Chemists; Sigma Xi; Tire Soc; AAAS. *Res:* Terpene research; natural products; polymerization, diene and vinyl; hydrocarbon reactions; stereospecific polymerization; organometallics; catalysis. *Mailing Add:* 10205 Echo Hill Dr Brecksville OH 44141

HORNEMANN, ULFERT, GENETICS, MOLECULAR BIOLOGY. *Current Pos:* PROF PHARMACEUT BIOCHEM, SCH PHARM, UNIV WIS-MADISON, 81- *Personal Data:* b Dresden, Ger, Apr 22, 39; m 70, Kathleen M Hornemann; c 4. *Educ:* Hannover Tech Univ, BS, 61; Munich Tech Univ, MS, 64, PhD(org chem), 66. *Prof Exp:* From instr to prof med chem, Purdue Univ, 67-81. *Concurrent Pos:* Vis scientist, Dept Genetics, John Inmes Inst, Norwich, Eng, 76-77, Dept Biotechnol, Inst Pasteur, Paris, France, 90-91. *Mem:* Ger Chem Soc; Am Chem Soc; Am Soc Microbiol; Chem Soc; Am Soc Biol Chem. *Res:* Biosynthesis and chemistry of antibiotics; isolation and studies on regulation of enzymes of antibiotic biosynthesis; mode of action of antibiotics; biochemical genetics of antibiotic production; genetic engineering; DNA amplification in streptomycetes; evolution of translation. *Mailing Add:* Sch Pharm Univ Wis 425 N Charter St Madison WI 53706-1515. *Fax:* 608-262-3397

HORNER, ALAN ALFRED, BIOCHEMISTRY, PHYSIOLOGY. *Current Pos:* from asst prof to assoc prof, Banting & Best Dept Med Res, 63-70, assoc prof, 70-80, PROF PHYSIOL, UNIV TORONTO, 80- *Personal Data:* b York, Eng, Feb 23, 34; m 58; c 3. *Educ:* Univ Liverpool, BSc, 55, PhD(biochem), 58. *Prof Exp:* Biochemist, Blood Prods Lab, Lister Inst Prev Med, Eng, 58-59; sr biochemist, Res & Develop Labs, Can Packers Ltd, 59-63. *Mem:* Can Biochem Soc; Can Physiol Soc. *Res:* Biochemistry and physiology of heparin. *Mailing Add:* Dept Physiol Univ Toronto One Kings College Circle Toronto ON M5S 1A8 Can

HORNER, B ELIZABETH, ZOOLOGY. *Current Pos:* Asst zool, Smith Col, 40-41, instr, 41-44 & 46-48, from asst prof to prof, 48-70, MYRA M SAMPSON PROF BIOL SCI, SMITH COL, 70- *Personal Data:* b Merchantville, NJ, Apr 29, 16. *Educ:* Rutgers Univ, BS, 38; Smith Col, MA, 40; Univ Mich, PhD(zool), 48. *Concurrent Pos:* Am Asn Univ Women fel, Univ Sydney, 54-55. *Mem:* AAAS; Ecol Soc Am; Am Soc Mammal; Soc Study Evolution; Animal Behav Soc. *Res:* Postnatal skeletal development of carnivores and rodents; animal ecology; behavior and systematics of rodents and marsupials. *Mailing Add:* Dept Biol Sci Smith Col Northampton MA 01063-0001

HORNER, CHESTER ELLSWORTH, PLANT PATHOLOGY. *Current Pos:* RETIRED. *Personal Data:* b McMinnville, Ore, Mar 2, 25; m 53; c 3. *Educ:* Walla Walla Col, BA, 50; Ore State Col, PhD(plant path), 54. *Prof Exp:* From asst prof to assoc prof, Ore State Univ, 54-64, prof bot & plant path, 65-80, leader hops & mint invests, USDA, 68-72, res leader hops, mint & field crops, Agr Res Serv, 72-80. *Mem:* Am Phytopath Soc; Am Inst Biol Sci; Am Soc Agron; Crop Sci Soc Am. *Res:* Fungus diseases of plants; soil microbiology; breeding for disease resistance. *Mailing Add:* 1760 NW Menlo Dr Corvallis OR 97330

HORNER, DONALD RAY, MATHEMATICAL ANALYSIS. *Current Pos:* assoc prof, 66-69, PROF MATH, EASTERN WASH UNIV, 69-, CHMN, DEPT MATH & COMPUT SCI, 76- *Personal Data:* b Beatrice, Nebr, Aug 8, 35; m 54; c 2. *Educ:* Univ Tex, Arlington, BS, 61; NTex State Univ, MS, 62; NMex State Univ, PhD(math), 67. *Prof Exp:* Instr electronics, Philco Corp, 58-59; instr math, Univ Tex, El Paso, 62-66. *Concurrent Pos:* Res mathematician, Schellenger Res Labs, 63-65; res assoc, Phys Sci Labs, 65-66; mathematician, Air Force Grant, 66. *Mem:* Math Asn Am; Am Math Soc. *Res:* Measure theory; locally convex spaces; general topology. *Mailing Add:* Dept Comput Sci Eastern Wash Univ MS-86 Cheney WA 99004

HORNER, EARL STEWART, PLANT BREEDING. *Current Pos:* From asst prof to assoc prof, 50-64, PROF AGRON, UNIV FLA, 64- *Personal Data:* b Allison, Colo, Aug 22, 18; m 48; c 3. *Educ:* State Col Wash, BS, 40; Mich State Col, MS, 42; Cornell Univ, PhD(plant breeding), 50. *Mem:* AAAS; Genetics Soc Am; fel Am Soc Agron; Sigma Xi. *Res:* Methods of corn breeding; genetics of heterosis in corn; alfalfa breeding. *Mailing Add:* 1941 NW 23rd Terr Gainesville FL 32605

HORNER, GEORGE JOHN, CARDIOPULMONARY MEDICINE, CLINICAL CARDIOPULMONARY PHYSIOLOGY. *Current Pos:* RETIRED. *Personal Data:* b Sept 15, 23; US citizen; m 52, Lili R Berman; c Daniel J & Michael D. *Educ:* Univ Sydney, MB & BS, 60. *Prof Exp:* Australian Heart Found res fel med & surg, Univ Sydney, 62-64; fel chest dis, Sch Med, Yale Univ, 64-65, Am Heart Asn res fel, 65-66; from instr to asst prof med, Yale Univ, 66-68, dir, Cardiopulmonary Lab, 67-68; assoc prof med, Jefferson Med Col, 68-81; head, Respiratory Res Dept, Lankenau Hosp, 68-81, chief, Pulmonary Serv Lab, 72-81, consult med, 81-90. *Concurrent Pos:* Clin prof med, Jefferson Med Col, 81-90, emer prof & emer consult med, 90- *Mem:* Am Fedn Clin Res; Am Thoracic Soc; AMA; fel Am Col Chest Physicians. *Res:* Experimental acute cor pulmonale in pulmonary embolism, incompatible blood transfusion and endotoxin shock; aging and pulmonary function; pulmonary gas exchange in patients with heart and/or lung disease. *Mailing Add:* 717 Old Eagle School Rd Wayne PA 19087-2009. *Fax:* 610-687-1492; *E-Mail:* georgehorner@prodigy.com

HORNER, HARRY THEODORE, BOTANY, CELL & DEVELOPMENTAL BIOLOGY & MICROCOPY. *Current Pos:* NIH fel, 62-66, from asst prof to assoc prof, 66-73, PROF BOT, IOWA STATE UNIV, 73- *Personal Data:* b Chicago, Ill, Jan 28, 36; m 61, Cecilia A Midthun; c Kevin S, Amy L & Allison L. *Educ:* Northwestern Univ, BA, 59, MS, 61, PhD(biol), 64. *Prof Exp:* Asst biol, Northwestern Univ, 60-62. *Concurrent Pos:* Sigma Xi & Sci Res Soc Am grants, 62 & 65; grant, Coop State Res Serv, USDA, 71-73 & 82-84; NSF grant, 74; mem, Iowa Soybean Prom Bd, 81-85; res grant, Monsanto, 82-86 & Iowa State Univ, 88-89. *Mem:* Bot Soc Am (pres elect); Am Inst Biol Sci; Sigma Xi; Am Soc Plant Physiol; Micros Soc Am. *Res:* Sporogenesis; cytoplasmic and nuclear sterility; plant secretion and calcification; bacterial leaf nodulation. *Mailing Add:* Dept Bot Iowa State Univ Ames IA 50011-1020. *Fax:* 515-294-1337; *E-Mail:* hth@iastate.edu

HORNER, JAMES M, MATHEMATICS. *Current Pos:* DIR ACAD AFFAIRS, AIR FORCE INST TECHNOL, 90- *Personal Data:* b Phillipsburg, Mo, Feb 26, 35; m 57, Evelyn J Thiene; c 2. *Educ:* Univ Ala, BS, 61, MA, 62, PhD(math), 64. *Prof Exp:* Assoc sr res mathematician, Gen Motors Res Labs, 64-65; from asst prof to prof math, Univ Ala, Huntsville, 65-75, chmn dept, 66-68 & 70-72, dean fac, 73-77; vpres, provost & prof math, Ill State Univ, 75-79; pres, Cent Mo State Univ, 79-85, prof math, 79-90. *Res:* Functions of a complex variable, differential equations and special functions. *Mailing Add:* Air Force Inst Technol 2950 P St Wright Patterson AFB OH 45433-7765. *Fax:* 937-476-7600; *E-Mail:* jhorner@afit.af.mil

HORNER, JAMES WILLIAM, JR, chemical information; deceased, see previous edition for last biography

HORNER, JOHN ROBERT, PALEONTOLOGY. *Current Pos:* CUR PALEONT, MUS ROCKIES, MONT STATE UNIV, 82-; ADJ PROF, DEPT GEOL, 82- *Personal Data:* b Shelby, Mont, June 15, 46; m 86, Joann K Raffelson; c Jason J. *Hon Degrees:* DSc, Univ Mont, 86. *Prof Exp:* Res scientist, Am Mus Natural Hist, NY, 80-82. *Concurrent Pos:* MacArthur fel, 86. *Res:* Paleontology. *Mailing Add:* Mont State Univ Mus Rockies Bozeman MT 59717

HORNER, NORMAN V, ARACHNOLOGY, ENTOMOLOGY. *Current Pos:* Instr, Midwestern State Univ, 67-69, asst prof, 71-74, assoc prof, 75-80, PROF BIOL, MIDWESTERN STATE UNIV, 81- *Personal Data:* b Brownwood, Tex, June 1, 42; m 63; c 2. *Educ:* NTex State Univ, BS, 65, MS, 67; Okla State Univ, PhD(entom), 71. *Mem:* Entom Soc Am; Am Arachnological Soc; Brit Arachnological Soc; Sigma Xi. *Res:* Life histories and taxonomy of local spider fauna. *Mailing Add:* Dept Biol Midwestern State Univ 3410 Taft Wichita Falls TX 76308

HORNER, SALLY MELVIN, INORGANIC CHEMISTRY. *Current Pos:* vchancellor admin & finance, 84-90, vchancellor planning & fiscal affairs, 90-93, EXEC VPRES, COASTAL CAROLINA UNIV, 93- *Personal Data:* b Fayetteville, NC, Nov 17, 35; div; c Stephanie (Toney) & John W. *Educ:* Univ NC, BS, 57, PhD(inorg chem), 61. *Prof Exp:* Res assoc chem, Univ NC, Chapel Hill, 61-62, instr, 62-63, res assoc, 63-67; from instr to asst prof, Meredith Col, 65-72, chmn dept, 72-77, assoc prof chem & chmn dept, 72-78, prof, 78; univ provost & dean, Col Arts & Sci, Univ Charleston, WVa, 78-81, actg dean, Col Health Sci, 80-81, vpres admin serv, 81-84, actg pres, 84. *Concurrent Pos:* Consult, Res Triangle Inst, 66; sr vis res assoc chem, Duke Univ, 72; dir, Inst Res, Meredith Col, 75-78, dir financial aid, 78; consult, Univ NC Gen Admin, 77 & WVa Bd Regents, 83-86; chmn, Statewide Comt Planning, SC Comn Higher Educ, 93-; chmn, Finance Study Comt, 94-; comnr, Comn Cols Southern Asn Col & Schs, 95- *Mem:* AAAS; Am Chem Soc; Sigma Xi. *Res:* Coordination compounds of transition metals; spectra of transition metal ions; molecular orbital theory; institutional planning, integration of budgeting and planning. *Mailing Add:* 608 D 35th Ave N Myrtle Beach SC 29578-2856. *E-Mail:* horner@coastal.edu

HORNER, THEODORE WRIGHT, STATISTICS, GENETICS. *Current Pos:* STATIST CONSULT, 70- *Personal Data:* b Clarksburg, WVa, Feb 29, 24; m 50, Barbara Ward; c Ward P & Theodore W Jr. *Educ:* NC State Col, BS, 49, MS, 51, PhD, 53. *Prof Exp:* Asst statistician, NC State Col, 51-53; asst prof statist, Iowa State Col, 53-57; sr opers res analyst, Gen Mills, Inc, 57-59; prin statistician, Booz-Allen Appl Res, Inc, 59-70. *Concurrent Pos:* Statist consult, 70- *Mem:* Am Statist Asn; Biomet Soc; Inst Math Statist. *Res:* Mathematical theory of epistasis; operations research; industrial statistics; biometry; social statistics. *Mailing Add:* 659 Western Blvd Ext Suite 438 Cary NC 27511-4219

HORNER, WILLIAM HARRY, BIOCHEMISTRY. *Current Pos:* assoc prof, 59-60, chmn dept, 60-81, PROF BIOCHEM, SCHS MED & DENT, GEORGETOWN UNIV, 60- *Personal Data:* b Kenmore, NY, Sept 30, 23; m 62; c 4. *Educ:* Western Res Univ, MD, 47; Cornell Univ, PhD(biochem), 52. *Prof Exp:* From asst prof to assoc prof biochem, Med Col, State Univ NY Downstate Med Ctr, 52-59. *Concurrent Pos:* Prin investr res grants, 59-85. *Mem:* AAAS; Harvey Soc; Am Soc Biol Chemists; Sigma Xi. *Res:* Metabolism, amino acids and derivatives; metabolism of guanidine compounds; muscle disease. *Mailing Add:* 7 Moonshell Dr 1500C Ocean Pines Berlin MD 21811-9139

HORNG, ARBEIT JWUHSIUNG, WASTEPAPER RECYCLING & DEINKING, PULPING & PAPERMAKING. *Current Pos:* ADV & DIR TECHNOL, PT INDAH KIAT PULP & PAPER CO, 97- *Personal Data:* m, Su-Chin Lin; c Stella F & Anne I. *Educ:* Nat Cheng Kung Univ, BSc, 65; Univ Calif, PhC, 70, PhD(org chem), 72. *Prof Exp:* Chief chemist, Chinese Petrol Corp, 66-68; postdoctoral fel, Univ Calif, 72-73; sr res chemist, MacMillan Bloedel Res, 74-82, sect head chem fiber, MacMillan Bloedel Ltd Res & Develop Ctr, 82-90, sec fiber, 90-95, packaging res, 95-97. *Concurrent Pos:* Postdoctoral lectr, Brock Univ, 72-73; postdoctoral fel, Nat Res Coun Can, 74-; conf chmn & prog chmn, Can Pulp & Paper Asn, 95 & 97. *Mem:* Am Chem Soc; Sigma Xi; Tech Asn Pulp & Paper Indust; Can Pulp & Paper Asn. *Res:* Explore novel methods to enhance quality of recycled fiber for higher value paper and board products while improve the economical and environmental impacts on the society; new deinking processes for water based ink printed papers and hard to deink grades; reduce water/energy consumption and pollution. *Mailing Add:* Wisma Indah Kiat Gedung B Km8 JL Raya Serpong Tangerang Jawa Indonesia. *Fax:* 6221-538-0020/1474

HORNG, WAYNE J, idiotype, genetics, for more information see previous edition

HORNICEK, FRANCIS JOHN, ORTHOPAEDICS & CELL MEMBRANE BIOPHYSICS, CYTOKINE INTERACTION & FUROCOUMARINS MECHANISM OF ACTION. *Current Pos:* res fel, Univ Miami, 83-85, res asst prof, 85-87, res assoc, 91-96, ASSOC PROF, SCH MED, UNIV MIAMI, 96- *Personal Data:* m 84. *Educ:* Washington & Jefferson Col, BA, 79; Georgetown Univ, MS, 82, PhD(biophys), 83; Univ Pittsburgh, MD, 91. *Prof Exp:* Res assoc, Wash Hosp Ctr, 81-83. *Concurrent Pos:* Guest scientist, NIH, 82-83; res fel, Allegheny Singer Res Lab, 89-91; sr biochemist, US Environ Protection Agency, Washington, DC, 89; orthoped surg resident, Univ Miami, Sch Med, 91-96; orthoped oncol fel, Harvard Univ, 96-97. *Mem:* Soc Leukocyte Biol; AAAS; Am Soc Cell Biol; Sigma Xi; AMA. *Res:* Characterization of the cytokine and 8-methoxypsoralen interactions with cell membranes (photo biochemistry- photobiophysics of cell membranes); evaluation of chemical modifications of cell membranes in cellular proliterative responses (cellular biophysics). *Mailing Add:* 1 Longfellow Pl No 517 Boston MA 02114. *Fax:* 305-548-4622

HORNICK, RICHARD B, INTERNAL MEDICINE, INFECTIOUS DISEASES. *Current Pos:* VPRES MED EDUC ORLANDO REG MED CTR, 87- *Personal Data:* b Johnstown, Pa, Jan 27, 29; m 54, Susan; c Douglas, Thomas, Martha A & Adele B. *Educ:* Johns Hopkins Univ, AB, 51, MD, 55. *Honors & Awards:* Smadel Award, Infectious Dis Soc Am, 83; Bruce Award, Am Col Physicians, 86. *Prof Exp:* From instr to prof med, Univ Md, Sch Med, Baltimore, 71-79, dir, Div Infectious Dis, 63-79; chmn dept med, Univ Rochester, Sch Med, 79-85, assoc dean, Affil Hosps, 85-87. *Concurrent Pos:* Mem epidemiol staff, USPH Lab, Mont, 60; consult, USPHS Hosp, 63-; mem comn epidemiol surv, US Armed Forces Epidemiol Bd, 65-86. *Mem:* Am Soc Microbiol; Infectious Dis Soc Am, (treas, 78-82, pres, 85-86); Am Fedn Clin Res; Am Soc Clin Invest; Am Col Physicians. *Res:* Value of immunoprophylactic agents in preventing infectious diseases in man; associated host defense mechanisms. *Mailing Add:* Orlando RegionalHealth Care Syst 1414 Kuhl Ave Orlando FL 32806-2093

HORNIG, DONALD FREDERICK, MOLECULAR SPECTROSCOPY, SHOCK WAVES. *Current Pos:* hon res assoc appl physics, Harvard Univ, 76-77, Alfred North Whitehead Prof chem, 81-86, prof chem, Sch Pub Health, 77-90, dir interdisciplinary progs in health, 77-90, chmn, Dept Environ Health & Toxicol, 88-90, EMER PROF CHEM, HARVARD UNIV, 90- *Personal Data:* b Milwaukee, Wis, Mar 17, 20; m 43, Lilli Schwenk; c Joanna, Christopher, Ellen & Leslie. *Educ:* Harvard Univ, BS, 40, PhD(phys chem), 43. *Hon Degrees:* LLD, Temple Univ, 64, Notre Dame, 65, Boston Col, 66 & Dartmouth Col, 74; DHL, Yeshiva Univ, 65; ScD, Rensselaer Polytech Inst, 65, Univ Md, 65, Ripon Col, 66, Widener Col, 67, Univ Wis, 67, Univ Puget Sound, 68, Syracuse Univ, 68, Princeton Univ, 69, Seoul Nat Univ, Korea, 73, Univ Pa, 75 & Lycoming Col, 80; DEng, Worcester Polytech Inst, 67. *Honors & Awards:* Eng Centennial Award, Widener Col, 67; Charles Lathrop Parsons Award, Am Chem Soc, 67; First Mellon Inst Award, Carnegie-Mellon Univ, 68; Moranjang Medal, Korean Govt, 68. *Prof Exp:* Res assoc, Woods Hole Oceanog Lab, 43-44; scientist & group leader, AEC, Los Alamos Sci Lab, Univ Calif, 44-46; from asst prof to prof chem, Brown Univ, 46-57, dir, Metcalf Res Lab, 49-57, from assoc dean to actg dean grad sch, 52-54; Donner prof sci, Princeton Univ, 57-64, chmn, Dept Chem, 58-64; spec asst sci & technol to President, Washington, DC, 64-69; vpres & dir, Eastman Kodak Co, NY, 69-70; pres, Brown Univ, 70-76. *Concurrent Pos:* Pres, Radiation Instruments Co, 46-48; Guggenheim & Fulbright fel, St John's Col, Oxford, 54-55; mem adv panel chem, NSF, 57-60 & Physics Adv Comt, Off Sci Res, USAF, 59-61; mem space sci bd, Nat Acad Sci, 58-64; mem bd dirs, W A Benjamin, Inc, 60-64; mem, President's Sci Adv Comt, 60-69, chmn, 64-69, consult-at-large, 69-72; vis prof, Calif Inst Technol, 62, mem, US deleg to negotiate space coop with USSR, 62-63; chmn, Fed Coun Sci & Technol, 64-69; dir off sci & technol, Exec Off President, 64-69; mem bd overseers, Harvard Univ, 64-70; prof, Univ Rochester, 69-70; dir, Overseas Develop Coun, 69-77; mem bd dirs, Upjohn Co, 71-92 & Westinghouse Elec Corp, 72-90; mem, Adv Comt Health Sci & Tech Enterprise, Off Technol Assessment, 76-78, chmn, Adv Comt Effect Regulation Innovation, 79; chmn, Comt Instnl Arrangements Space Telescope Sci Inst, Nat Acad Sci, 76, mem, Comt Satellite Power Syst, 79, Comt Post-Doctorals & Doctoral Res Staff, 79, vchmn, Bd Toxicol & Environ Health Hazards, 84-86; mem, Am Assembly Workshop, Improving Am Innovation, 83; mem, Twentieth Century Fund Task Force, Improving Am Innovation, 83; mem, Security Telecomm Policy Planning, 84-86, chmn, Bd Environ Studies & Toxicol, 86-88, Nat Acad Sci, 87-90, Comn Life Sci, Report Rev Com, 95-; dir & treas, Overseas Develop Network, Inc, 85-92; pres, Cambridge Water Bd, 86-94; chmn, Bd Environ Studies & Toxicol, 86-88, Comn Life Sci, 87-; mem, comt to consider long term changes that may affect the habitability of the earth, NASA, 82; bd dirs, Chem Indust Inst Toxicol. *Mem:* Nat Acad Sci; Am Chem Soc; fel Am Phys Soc; Am Acad Arts & Sci; Romanian Acad; Am Philos Soc. *Res:* Molecular spectroscopy; spectra of crystals; shock and detonation waves; fast reactions; theoretical chemistry. *Mailing Add:* 16 Longfellow Park Cambridge MA 02138-4831. *Fax:* 617-432-4710; *E-Mail:* dhornig@hsph.harvard.edu

HORNIG, HOWARD CHESTER, PHYSICAL CHEMISTRY, EXPLOSIVES. *Current Pos:* Res chemist, Lawrence Livermore Nat Lab, Univ Calif, 52-74, proj mgr, 74-76, group leader, 76-79, PROJ LEADER, LAWRENCE LIVERMORE NAT LAB, UNIV CALIF, 79- *Personal Data:* b Fond du Lac, Wis, July 14, 24; m 56; c 3. *Educ:* Univ Chicago, BS, 48, MS, 49, PhD(chem), 52. *Mem:* AAAS; Combustion Inst; Sigma Xi. *Res:* Energetic chemical systems, explosives, detonation, hydrodynamics, blasting and pyrotechnics; coal recovery; boron hydrides; high speed photography; radiochemical tracer techniques; kinetics of ionic reactions in solution; quality assurance. *Mailing Add:* 4763 E Wing Rd Castro Valley CA 94546

HORNIG, JAMES FREDERICK, PHYSICAL CHEMISTRY, ENVIRONMENTAL CHEMISTRY. *Current Pos:* assoc prof, 62-66, dean grad sch, chmn sci div & assoc dean fac, 64-65, PROF CHEM, DARTMOUTH COL, 66-, ALBERT BRADLEY PROF SCI, 75-, DARTMOUTH PROF CHEM & ENVIRON STUDIES, 92- *Personal Data:* b Milwaukee, Wis, Feb 22, 29; m 52; c David, Douglas & Linda. *Educ:* Harvard Univ, AB, 50; Univ Wis, MS, 52, PhD(chem), 54. *Prof Exp:* NSF fel, Univ Marburg, 54-55; res chemist, E I du Pont de Nemours & Co, 56-58; asst prof chem, Univ Calif, Riverside, 58-62. *Concurrent Pos:* NSF fel, Marburg, Ger, 69. *Mem:* Am Chem Soc; Am Phys Soc; Sigma Xi. *Res:* Energy transfer in organic crystals; environmental chemistry. *Mailing Add:* Dept Chem Dartmouth Col Hanover NH 03755. *Fax:* 603-646-1682; *E-Mail:* j.hornig@dartmouth.edu

HORNING, MARJORIE G, PHARMACOLOGY. *Current Pos:* RETIRED. *Personal Data:* b Detroit, Mich, Aug 23, 17; m 42. *Educ:* Goucher Col, AB, 38; Univ Mich, MS, 40, PhD(biol chem), 43. *Hon Degrees:* DSc, Goucher Col, 77. *Honors & Awards:* Warner-Lambert Award, Am Asn Clin Chemists, 76; Garvan Medal, Am Chem Soc, 77. *Prof Exp:* Res assoc pediat, Univ Mich Hosp, 44-45; res chemist, Univ Pa, 45-50; biochemist, Nat Heart Inst, 51-61; assoc prof, Baylor Col Med, 61-69, prof biochem, Inst Lipid Res, 69-85. *Mem:* AAAS; Am Soc Pharmacol & Exp Therapeut; Am Chem Soc; NY Acad Sci. *Res:* Analytical biochemistry; drug metabolism; gas chromatography and mass spectrometry; toxicology. *Mailing Add:* 11610 Starwood Dr Houston TX 77024-5113

HORNOF, VLADIMIR, ENHANCED OIL RECOVERY, OIL SANDS RESEARCH. *Current Pos:* PROF CHEM ENG, UNIV OTTAWA, 76- CHMN, DEPT, 84-87 & 96- *Personal Data:* m 69, Alexandra Hamplova; c Monica & Christina. *Educ:* Univ Chem Technol, Czech, chem engr, 63; Simon Fraser Univ, PhD(phys chem), 71. *Prof Exp:* Res asst, Univ Chem Technol, 64-67; postdoctoral fel, Laval Univ, 71-73; res prof, Univ Que, Trois-Rivieres, 74-76. *Concurrent Pos:* Vis scientist, NMex Petrol Recovery Res Ctr, 82-83; consult, Revenue Can, 85-86, Syncrude Can Ltd, 89-90 & Ontario Col Grad Studies, 95. *Mem:* Fel Can Soc Chem Eng; sr mem Can Pulp & Paper Asn; Soc Petrol Engrs; Sigma Xi; Int Union Pure & Appl Chem. *Res:* Enhanced oil recovery; interfacial phenomena in liquid-liquid systems; oil-water displacements in porous media; oil sands: recovery of bitumen and treatment of sludges. *Mailing Add:* Univ Ottawa PO Box 450 Sta A Ottawa ON K1N 6N5 Can. *Fax:* 613-562-5172; *E-Mail:* hornof@eng.uottawa.ca

HORNOR, SALLY GRAHAM, MICROBIAL ECOLOGY, AQUATIC ECOLOGY. *Current Pos:* ASST PROF BIOL, ANNE ARUNDEL COMMUNITY COL, 86- *Personal Data:* b Boston, Mass, June 10, 49; m 83; c 2. *Educ:* Goucher Col, BA, 71; Univ Conn, MS, 74, PhD(ecol), 77. *Prof Exp:* Res assoc microbiol ecol, State Univ NY, Syracuse, 77-79; asst prof microbiol, Va Polytech Inst & State Univ, 79-85. *Mem:* AAAS; Am Soc Limnol & Oceanog; Am Soc Microbiol; Sigma Xi. *Res:* Energetics and comparative microbial decomposition processes in aquatic and terrestrial ecosystems; biochemical ecology of aquatic sediments and submerged soils. *Mailing Add:* 787 Mago Vista Rd Arnold MD 21012-1103

HORNSBY, ARTHUR GRADY, SOIL PHYSICS, SOIL CHEMISTRY. *Current Pos:* STAFF MEM, SOIL SCI DEPT, UNIV FLA, GAINESVILLE. *Personal Data:* b Marks, Miss, Feb 5, 40; m 66. *Educ:* Univ Ark, BS, 62, MS, 64; Okla State Univ, PhD(soil sci), 72. *Prof Exp:* Lab technician, Dept Water Sci & Eng, Univ Calif, Davis, 67-69; soil scientist, Robert S Kerr environ res lab, Environ Protection Agency, 71- *Concurrent Pos:* Adj prof, Soil Sci Dept, Univ Fla, 81-, mem, Innovative Res Proj, 81-82. *Mem:* Am Soc Agron; Am Geophys Union; Soil Sci Soc Am; Sigma Xi. *Res:* Movement of water, salts and organics in soil systems; simulation techniques for water resource management; salinity control in irrigation return flows. *Mailing Add:* Hwy 24 Archer FL 32618

HORNSEY, EDWARD EUGENE, ENGINEERING MECHANICS. *Current Pos:* from instr to asst prof, 63-75, ASSOC PROF ENG MECH, UNIV MO, ROLLA, 75-, ASSOC PROF BASIC ENG, 88- *Personal Data:* b Potosi, Mo, May 31, 37; m 59, Joyce Albert; c Philip & Neil. *Educ:* Univ Mo, Rolla, BS, 59, MS, 61, PhD(mining eng), 67. *Prof Exp:* Instr eng mech, Univ Mo, Rolla, 60-62; mining methods res engr, Appl Physics Res Lab, US Bur Mines, Md, 62-63. *Concurrent Pos:* Pvt consult. *Mem:* Am Soc Eng Educ. *Res:* Solid mechanics; mechanics of materials, dynamics, vibrations and stability; rock mechanics. *Mailing Add:* Dept Basic Eng Univ Mo Rolla MO 65409. *Fax:* 573-341-4979, 573-341-4082; *E-Mail:* eeh@umr.edu

HORNSTEIN, IRWIN, NUTRITIONAL BIOCHEMISTRY. *Current Pos:* mgr, Proj Sustain, 82-90, CONSULT, 90- *Personal Data:* b New York, NY, Jan 4, 17; m 42, Lydia Rolf; c Robert & Charles. *Educ:* City Col New York, BChE, 37; Univ Md, MS, 51; Georgetown Univ, PhD, 60. *Prof Exp:* Chemist alloys, US Naval Gun Factory, 40-45; org chemist, Nat Bur Stand, 45-46; res chemist, Glenn L Martin Co, 46-48; res chemist, Agr Res Serv, USDA, 48-67; chief food qual & use, Lab Human Nutrit, Res Div, 67-69; mem staff, Aid US State Dept, 69-73, dep dir, Off Nutrit, 73-80. *Concurrent Pos:* Adj prof, Flavor Chem, Univ Md, 68-70; chmn, Div Agr & Food Chem, Am Chem Soc, 70, Flavor Subdiv; chmn, Gordon Conf Psychophysiol Odor & Flavor, 71; co-ed, Food Rev Int, 84-; instr, USDA Grad Sch. *Mem:* Fel AAAS; Am Chem Soc; Inst Food Technol; Sigma Xi. *Res:* Analytical methods; insecticides; flavors; lipids; meats; nutrition; technology transfer. *Mailing Add:* 5920 Bryn Mawr Rd College Park MD 20740

HORNSTEIN, JOHN STANLEY, REMOTE SENSING, ATMOSPHERIC RADIATION. *Current Pos:* RES PHYSICIST, NAVAL RES LAB, 83- *Personal Data:* b New York, NY, Nov 18, 41; m 77, Juline Larsen. *Educ:* Mass Inst Technol, BS, 63; Cornell Univ, PhD(physics), 75. *Prof Exp:* Staff scientist, Comput Sci Corp, 74-83. *Concurrent Pos:* Proj scientist, Polar Ozone & Aerosol Measurement Orbiting Ozone & Aerosol Monitor; pres, Nat Capital Sect, Optical Asn Am. *Mem:* Am Phys Soc; Am Optical Soc; Inst Elec & Electronics Engrs; Am Math Soc; Am Geophys Union. *Res:* Atmospheric remote sensing, polar stratospheric clouds, infrared sensors (especially focal plane arrays); infrared, visible, ultraviolet and microwave radiation in the atmosphere; detection and estimation (classical); atmospheric remote sensing; quantum detection and estimation theory. *Mailing Add:* Naval Res Lab Code 7227 Washington DC 20375-5351. *Fax:* 202-767-0005; *E-Mail:* hornstei@poamb.nrl.navy.mil

HORNTVEDT, EARL W, DESALINATION EQUIPMENT, PRODUCT & MARKET RESEARCH FLOW CONTROL. *Current Pos:* MGR NEW PROD DEVELOP, HAMILTON INDUSTS, 89- *Personal Data:* b Detroit, Mich, Aug 21, 48; m 81; c 2. *Educ:* Western Mich Univ, BS, 78; Cardinal Stritch Col, MBA, 88. *Prof Exp:* Dir new prod develop, Aqua-Catem, Inc, 81-88; dir eng, Northland Stainless, 88-89. *Mem:* Am Soc Heating Refrig & Air Conditioning Engrs; Am Soc Testing & Mat. *Mailing Add:* 215 Cleveland Ave Manitowoc WI 54220

HORNUNG, DAVID EUGENE, PHYSIOLOGY. *Current Pos:* teaching fel, State Univ NY Upstate Med Ctr, 73-75, from asst prof to assoc prof physiol, 75-83, res assoc prof, 80-85, chmn dept biol, 86-89, dir int educ, 89-93, RES PROF PHYSIOL, STATE UNIV NY UPSTATE MED CTR, 85-; CHARLES A DANA PROF BIOL, ST LAWRENCE UNIV, 83- *Personal Data:* b Latrobe, Pa, Apr 30, 45, Susan E Ward. *Educ:* Geneva Col, BS, 67; Kent State Univ, MS, 69; State Univ NY Upstate Med Ctr, PhD(physiol), 75. *Prof Exp:* Teaching asst gen biol, Kent State Univ, 67-69; instr physiol, St Lawrence Univ, 69-73. *Mem:* AAAS; Am Physiol Soc; Am Chemoreception Sci; Europ Chemoreception Res Orgn; NY Acad Sci. *Res:* Mechanism and function of the olfactory and taste systems in health and disease. *Mailing Add:* Dept Biol St Lawrence Univ Canton NY 13617. *E-Mail:* hornung@stlawu.edu

HORNUNG, ERWIN WILLIAM, PHYSICAL CHEMISTRY, CRYOGENICS. *Current Pos:* RETIRED. *Personal Data:* b Chicago, Ill, Mar 3, 19. *Educ:* Univ Chicago, MS, 49; Univ Calif, PhD(chem), 54. *Prof Exp:* From asst res chemist to assoc res chemist, Univ Calif, Berkeley, 54-83. *Mem:* Sigma Xi. *Res:* Low temperature physical chemistry; magnetic properties of matter. *Mailing Add:* 975 Alvarado Berkeley CA 94705

HORNUNG, HANS G, AERONAUTIC ENGINEERING. *Current Pos:* DIR GRAD AERONAUT LAB & C L KELLY JOHNSON PROF AERONAUT, CALIF INST TECHNOL, 87- *Personal Data:* b Jufta, Palestine, Dec 26, 34. *Educ:* Univ Melbourne, Australia, BS, 60, MS, 62; London Univ, PhD(aeronaut), 65. *Honors & Awards:* Joint Award, Int Coun Aeronaut Sci, Ger, 91. *Prof Exp:* Res & teaching, Australia, 67-80; dir, Inst Exp Fluid Mech DLR, Ger, 80-87. *Mem:* Foreign assoc Nat Acad Eng; foreign mem Royal Swed Acad Eng Sci. *Mailing Add:* Grad Aeronaut Lab Calif Inst Technol 1201 E California Blvd Pasadena CA 91125

HORNYAK, WILLIAM FRANK, nuclear physics, for more information see previous edition

HORODYSKI, ROBERT JOSEPH, stratigraphy, paleontology; deceased, see previous edition for last biography

HOROVITZ, ZOLA PHILLIP, PHARMACOLOGY. *Current Pos:* res pharmacologist, Squibb Inst Med Res, 59-67, dir, Dept Pharmacol, 67-72, assoc dir res, 72-78, vpres drug develop, 79-85, vpres planning, 85-89, VPRES LICENSING, BRISTOL-MYERS SQUIBB, 90- *Personal Data:* b Pittsburgh, Pa, Oct 12, 34; m 58; c 2. *Educ:* Univ Pittsburgh, BS, 55, MS, 58, PhD(pharmacol), 60. *Honors & Awards:* A E Bennett Award, 65. *Prof Exp:* Vis investr, Neuropsychiat Res Labs, Vet Admin, Pa, 58-59. *Concurrent Pos:* Vis prof, Sch Med, Rutgers Univ, 67-; fel, Am Found Pharmaceut Educ; mem adv coun, Rutgers Sch Pharm, 77- *Mem:* Fel AAAS; Am Pharmaceut Asn; Am Soc Pharmacol & Exp Therapeut; NY Acad Sci; assoc Brit Pharmacol Soc; Sigma Xi. *Res:* Neuropharmacology; neurophysiology; neurochemistry; behavioral and psychopharmacology; cardiovascular work. *Mailing Add:* 30 Philip Dr Princeton NJ 08540-5410

HOROWICZ, PAUL, physiology, biophysics; deceased, see previous edition for last biography

HOROWITZ, ALAN STANLEY, PALEONTOLOGY, GEOLOGY. *Current Pos:* CUR PALEONT & PROF GEOL, IND UNIV, BLOOMINGTON, 64- *Personal Data:* b Ashland, Ky, June 12, 30; wid. *Educ:* Washington & Lee Univ, AB, 52; Ohio State Univ, MS, 54; Ind Univ, PhD, 57. *Prof Exp:* Res geologist, Marathon Oil Co, 56-64. *Concurrent Pos:* Guest prof, Aarhus Univ, Denmark, 71-72. *Mem:* Geol Soc Am; Paleont Soc; Soc Econ Paleontologists & Mineralogists. *Res:* Invertebrate paleontology; lower carboniferous bryozoans and echinoderms. *Mailing Add:* Dept Geol Sci Ind Univ 1005 E Tenth St Bloomington IN 47405. *Fax:* 812-855-7899; *E-Mail:* horowitz@vcs.indiana.edu

HOROWITZ, ARIE, MUSCLE CONTRACTILE & REGULATORY PROTEINS, CONFICAL MICROSCOPY & IMAGING. *Current Pos:* RES FEL, DEPT MED, HARVARD MED SCH, 94- *Personal Data:* b Bucharest, Romania, Sept 13, 54. *Educ:* Israel Inst Technol, BA, 80, MSc, 84, DSc, 88. *Prof Exp:* Res fel, Dept Bioeng, Univ Wash, 88-90; res assoc, Rosenstiel Res Ctr, Brandeis Univ, 90-93. *Concurrent Pos:* Res assoc, Boston Biomed Res Inst, 94- *Mem:* Biophys Soc; Am Soc Cell Biol. *Res:* Cell biology. *Mailing Add:* Cardiol-Beth Israel Hosp Harvard Med Sch 330 Brookline Ave Boston MA 02215. *Fax:* 617-667-4833

HOROWITZ, BARRY MARTIN, SYSTEMS RESEARCH. *Current Pos:* CHMN & CHIEF EXEC OFFICER, CONCEPT FIVE TECHNOLOGIES, INC, 96- *Personal Data:* b Brooklyn, NY, Apr 20, 43; m 65, Sheryl R Lang; c Hillary & Charles. *Educ:* City Col New York, BSEE, 65; NY Univ, MSEE, 67, PhD(elec eng), 69. *Honors & Awards:* Gold Medal Eng, Armed Forces Commun & Electronics Asn, 90. *Prof Exp:* Asst proj engr, Bendix Corp, 65-66, sr proj engr, 67-69; tech staff, Mitre Corp, McLean, Va, 69-71, group leader, 71-74, dept head, 74-79, dir spec studies, Bedford, Mass, 79-80, tech dir, 80-84, vpres strategic progs, 84-85, vpres progs, 85-86, sr vpres & gen mgr, 86, group vpres & gen mgr, 86-87, exec vpres, dir & chief opers officer, 87-90, pres & chief exec officer, 90-95, pres & chief exec officer, Mitretek Systs, Inc, 95-96. *Concurrent Pos:* Proj engr, Gen Precision, 66-67; consult, USAF, 82-, Defense Bd, Pentagon, 88- *Mem:* Nat Acad Eng; Am Inst Aeronaut & Astronaut; Armed Forces Commun & Electronics Asn (pres, 87-88); Ctr Sci & Int Affairs; Inst Elec & Electronics Engrs. *Res:* Electronics; communications; aeronautics; information systems technology. *Mailing Add:* Concept Five Technologies Inc 7525 Colshire Dr McLean VA 22102-7400. *Fax:* 703-610-2001; *E-Mail:* bah@concept5.com

HOROWITZ, CARL, POLYMER & TEXTILE CHEMISTRY, ELECTROCHEMISTRY. *Current Pos:* PRES, POLYMER RES CORP, 63- *Personal Data:* b Lvov, Poland, Aug 10, 23; m 46, Irene Mandel; c Alice & Terry. *Educ:* Columbia Univ, BS, 50; Polytech Inst Brooklyn, MA & PhD, 63. *Honors & Awards:* John C Vaaler Awards, Chem Processing Mag, 64 & 72. *Prof Exp:* Vpres, Yardney Chem Corp, 51-63. *Mem:* Am Chem Soc; Am Inst Chem Engr. *Res:* Chemical grafting; fabric nonflammability; semipermeable membranes; silver zinc storage batteries; pollution protection; corrosion and abrasion protection. *Mailing Add:* 2719 Whitman Dr Brooklyn NY 11234. *Fax:* 718-241-3930

HOROWITZ, ELLIS, COMPUTER SCIENCE. *Current Pos:* PROF COMPUT SCI, UNIV SOUTHERN CALIF, 73- *Personal Data:* b New York, NY, Feb 11, 44; m 68; c 3. *Educ:* Brooklyn Col, BS, 64; Univ Wis, MS, 67, PhD(comput sci), 70. *Concurrent Pos:* Ed, Trans Math Software, 76-80, Comt ACM, 78-82. *Mem:* Soc Indust & Appl Math; Sigma Xi; Asn Comput Mach; Inst Elec & Electronics Engs. *Mailing Add:* Comput Sci Dept Univ Southern Calif Los Angeles CA 90089

HOROWITZ, EMANUEL, MATERIALS SCIENCE & ENGINEERING, BIOMATERIALS. *Current Pos:* CONSULT, MAT SCI & ENG, BIOMAT, SURG & DENT IMPLANTS, 88- *Personal Data:* b New York, NY, Mar 29, 23; m 50, Diane Silverman; c Amy, Andrew, Alice & Alan. *Educ:* City Col New York, BS, 48; George Washington Univ, MS, 56, PhD, 63. *Honors & Awards:* Meritorious Awards, Nat Bur Stand, 61 & 65-68, Rosa Award, 72, Gold Medal, 75. *Prof Exp:* Chemist, Smithsonian Inst, 49-51; supvry chemist, Nat Bur Stand, 51-61; vis scientist, Univ Ill, 61-62; phys polymer chemist, Nat Bur Stand, 62-64, Dept Com sci & technol fel, 64-65, chief polymer characterization sect, 65-67, dep chief polymers div, 67-69, dep dir inst mat res, 69-76, dep dir resources & opers, Nat Meas Lab, 76-80; dir, Ctr Mat Res, Johns Hopkins Univ, 80-85, prof mat sci & eng, 80-88. *Concurrent Pos:* Chmn task group TC-38 (textiles), Int Orgn Standardization, 57-65, chmn task group polymer stand ref mat ISO/TC-61 (plastics), 65-80, mem, ISO/TC 150 (surg implants), ISO/TC 194 (biocompatibility), 90-; leader, US Sci Team,

Yugoslavia, 70, 72; chmn, Interagency Comn on Mat, 73-75; trustee, Inst Standards Res; prof, Johns Hopkins Univ, 88- *Mem:* Am Chem Soc; hon mem Am Soc Testing & Mat; NY Acad Sci; Cosmos Club; Fedn Mat Socs (pres, 83). *Res:* Synthesis and characterization of organic and coordination polymers; relation between structure and physical and chemical properties of materials; development of new or improved methods of chemical analysis and characterization of materials; properties and performance of surgical implant materials; biomaterials-polymers, metals and alloys, ceramics, composites, biosynthethics, biocompatibility. *Mailing Add:* 14100 N Gate Dr Silver Spring MD 20906. *Fax:* 410-516-5293

HOROWITZ, ESTHER, SPEECH PATHOLOGY, PSYCHOLOGY. *Current Pos:* RETIRED. *Personal Data:* b New York, NY, Dec 17, 20. *Educ:* Brooklyn Col, BA, 40; Univ Wis, MA, 49; Columbia Univ, PhD(psychol), 59. *Prof Exp:* Speech clinician, Queen's Col, 44-46; teacher, NY Schs, 46-50; assoc prof speech path, Hofstra Univ, 50-72, dir speech clin, 53-67, prof, 72-81. *Concurrent Pos:* Res grant speech path, Hofstra Univ, 61. *Mem:* Am Speech & Hearing Asn; Speech Asn Am. *Res:* Stuttering; aphasia. *Mailing Add:* 147-07 Charter Rd Apt 14A Jamaica NY 11435

HOROWITZ, GARY T, GENERAL RELATIVITY, QUANTUM GRAVITY. *Current Pos:* PROF, DEPT PHYSICS, UNIV CALIF, SANTA BARBARA, 83- *Personal Data:* b Washington, DC, Apr 14, 55; m 80, Corinne Gillet; c Diane & Caroline. *Educ:* Princeton Univ, BA, 76; Univ Chicago, PhD(physics), 79. *Honors & Awards:* Xanthopoulos Award, 93. *Prof Exp:* Fel, Univ Calif, Santa Barbara, 79-80; NATO fel, Oxford Univ, 80-81; mem, Inst Advan Study, 81-83. *Mem:* Sigma Xi. *Res:* Aspects of Einstein's theory of general relativity, approaches to quantum gravity, especially string theory, interested in nonperturbative formulations of the theory. *Mailing Add:* Dept Physics Univ Calif Santa Barbara CA 93106. *E-Mail:* gary@physics.ucsb.edu

HOROWITZ, HUGH H(ARRIS), ELECTROCHEMISTRY, ORGANIC CHEMISTRY. *Current Pos:* RETIRED. *Personal Data:* b New York, NY, Sept 8, 28; m 53, Enid Garmise; c Amy A, Alan M & Lawrence S. *Educ:* City Col New York, BS, 49; Columbia Univ, AM, 51, PhD(org chem), 53. *Prof Exp:* Chemist, Prod Res Div, Exxon Res & Eng Co, 52-55, proj leader lube oil additives, 55-61, proj leader & res assoc fuel cells, 61-66, proj leader & sr res assoc org electrochem, 66-71, proj leader & sr res assoc, Alsthom-Exxon Joint Fuel Cell Venture, 71-76, group leader, Corp Res Lab, 77-80, sr res assoc, Eng Mat Technol Div, 80-86, sr res assoc, Prods Res Div, 86-93. *Mem:* Am Chem Soc; Electrochem Soc. *Res:* Copolymerization; viscometry and rheology; hydrodynamic lubrication; automotive cold cranking; thermogravimetry; lubricant additives; catalysis; electrochemical oxidation of organics; fuel cells; electroanalytical chemistry; batteries; corrosion; antioxidants. *Mailing Add:* 1350 Summit Lane Mountainside NJ 07092

HOROWITZ, ISAAC, FEEDBACK CONTROL SYSTEMS. *Current Pos:* prof, 85-91, EMER PROF, DEPT ELEC ENG, UNIV CALIF, DAVIS, 91-; CONSULT SANDIA NAT LABS, LIVERMORE, CALIF. *Personal Data:* b Safed, Israel, Dec 15, 20; nat US; m 45, 84, Gloria August; c Chaya, Ruth, David, Dafna, Matanya & Benyakir. *Educ:* Univ Man, BSc, 44; Mass Inst Technol, SB, 48; Polytech Inst Brooklyn, MEE, 53, DEE, 56. *Honors & Awards:* Ann Award, Nat Electronics Conf, 56; Oldenburger Award, Am Soc Mech Engrs, 92. *Prof Exp:* Asst prof elec eng, Polytech Inst Brooklyn, 56-58; sr scientist guid & controls div, Hughes Aircraft Corp, Calif, 58-66; prof elec eng, City Univ New York, 66-67 & Univ Colo, Boulder, 67-85; Cohen prof appl math, Weizmann Inst Sci, Israel, 69-85, emer prof appl math, 85-91. *Concurrent Pos:* Guest lectr, Delft Technol Univ, 62 & Haifa Technion, 62; lectr, Calif Inst Technol, 64-; distinguished vis prof, Air Force Inst Technol, 83-92; vis prof, Mech Eng Dept, Univ Witwatersrand, Johannesburg, 94. *Mem:* Fel Inst Elec & Electronics Engrs. *Res:* Feedback theory; active network synthesis; adaptive systems. *Mailing Add:* 4470 Grinnell Ave Boulder CO 80303. *Fax:* 303-492-2758; *E-Mail:* horowitz@schof.colorado.edu

HOROWITZ, JACK, BIOCHEMISTRY. *Current Pos:* from asst prof to prof biochem, Iowa State Univ, 61-95, chmn, Dept Biochem & Biophys, 71-74, coordr molecular, cellular & develop biol prog, 77-80, UNIV PROF, IOWA STATE UNIV, 95- *Personal Data:* b Vienna, Austria, Nov 25, 31; nat US; m 61, Carole Sager; c 2. *Educ:* City Col New York, BS, 52; Ind Univ, PhD(biochem), 57. *Prof Exp:* Asst chem, Ind Univ, 54-57; fel biochem, NSF, Columbia Univ, 57-59, res biochemist, 59-60, res assoc biochem, Col Physicians & Surgeons, 60-61. *Concurrent Pos:* Vis scientist, Rockefeller Univ, 68, Mass Inst Technol, 90-91; vis prof, Yale Univ, 74-75; travel awards, Am Soc Biochem & Molecular Biol, 67, 73 & 82; prog dir biochem & biophys, NSF, 93-94. *Mem:* AAAS; Am Soc Biochem & Molecular Biol; RNA Soc. *Res:* Nucleic acids; protein biosynthesis; nucleoproteins; transfer RNA. *Mailing Add:* Dept Biochem & Biophys Iowa State Univ Ames IA 50011

HOROWITZ, JILL ANN, gene expression, rna expression, for more information see previous edition

HOROWITZ, JOHN M, HIBERNATION, HIPPOCAMPAL NETWORKS. *Current Pos:* from asst prof to assoc prof, 69-78, PROF PHYSIOL, UNIV CALIF, DAVIS, 78- *Personal Data:* b San Francisco, Calif, Sept 16, 34; m 70. *Educ:* Univ Calif, Berkeley, BS, 59, MS, 61, PhD(biophys), 68. *Prof Exp:* Res engr biophys, Univ Calif, Berkeley, 61-63. *Mem:* Soc Neurosci; Am Physiol Soc. *Res:* Neural control of temperature regulation and neural mechanisms associated with hibernation; hippocampal neural networks; coupling of signals from nerve cells to other cell types. *Mailing Add:* Dept Neurobiol Physiol & Behavior Univ Calif-Davis Davis CA 95616

HOROWITZ, JOSEPH, APPLICATIONS OF PROBABILITY & STATISTICS IN MEDICAL & ASTRONOMICAL IMAGE ANALYSIS, EQUATIONS OF MATHEMATICAL PHYSICS. *Current Pos:* PROF, DEPT MATH & STATIST, UNIV MASS, 69- *Personal Data:* b Washington DC, Apr 2, 41; m 69, Paula Boer; c Gaia, Brett D, Jason H. *Educ:* Mass Inst Technol, BS, 62; Univ Mich, MS, 63, PhD(math), 67. *Prof Exp:* Asst prof, Univ Toledo, 67-69. *Concurrent Pos:* Grantee, NSF, 72-90; vis, Stanford Univ, 74, Univ Strasbourg, 76, ETH Zurich, 79, Technion Haifa, 83, Indian Statist Inst, 88 & 92; dir, Statist Consult Ctr, Univ Mass, 84-87; Indo-Am fel, Coun Int Exchange Scholars, 88, Fulbright fel, 92. *Mem:* Inst Math Statist; Bernoulli Soc; Am Statist Asn. *Res:* Applications of probability and statistics image analysis; decision analysis for medical, policy and other decisions; theory and applications of stoclastic processes. *Mailing Add:* Dept Math & Statist Univ Mass Amherst MA 01003. *E-Mail:* joeh@math.umass.edu

HOROWITZ, LARRY LOWELL, ESTIMATION THEORY, ADAPTIVE ANTENNAS. *Current Pos:* staff mem, 75-83, asst group leader, 83-90, SR STAFF, LINCOLN LAB, MASS INST TECHNOL, 90- *Personal Data:* b Flushing, NY, Apr 17, 49; m 78, Allene H Edelman; c 2. *Educ:* Mass Inst Technol, SB, 72, SM, 72, PhD(elec eng), 74. *Prof Exp:* Engr, Appl Physics Lab, Johns Hopkins Univ, 74-75. *Mem:* Inst Elec & Electronics Engrs; Sigma Xi. *Res:* Estimation theory and signal processing; practical superresolution techniques; adaptive antenna processing. *Mailing Add:* 11 Turning Mill Rd Lexington MA 02173-1313

HOROWITZ, MARDI J, PSYCHIATRY, PSYCHOANALYSIS. *Current Pos:* from instr to assoc prof, 69-74, PROF PSYCHIAT, UNIV CALIF, SCH MED, SAN FRANCISCO, 74- *Personal Data:* b Los Angeles, Calif. *Educ:* Univ Calif, Los Angeles, BA, 55, MD, 58. *Honors & Awards:* Found Fund Prize; Royer Award; Strecker Award. *Prof Exp:* Intern, Univ Ore, 59; resident psychiat, Langley Porter Neuropsychiat Inst, 62. *Concurrent Pos:* NIMH res career award, Mt Zion Med Ctr, 64-72; dir, Prog Conscious & Unconscious Processes, John D & Catherine T MacArthur Found. *Mem:* Am Psychoanal Asn; Am Psychiat Asn; Am Psychosom Soc; Psychother Res Soc. *Res:* Visual imagery; abnormal thought; stress; character and character change. *Mailing Add:* Langley Porter Psych Inst 401 Parnassus Ave San Francisco CA 94143-0001

HOROWITZ, MARILYN STEPHENS, MEDICINE, SCIENCE POLICY. *Current Pos:* res fel plasma proteins, NY Blood Ctr, 68-73, fel, 73-77, assoc dir qual assurance, Blood Derivatives Prog, 77-80, dir planning, educ & regulatory affairs, 80-82, dir clin studies & regulatory affairs, 82-90, DIR, OFF PATENTS & LICENSES, NY BLOOD CTR, 86-, DIR CLIN AFFAIRS, MELVILLE BIOLOGICS DIV, 90- *Personal Data:* b New York, NY, Sept 2, 40; m 71, Bernard Horowitz; c Cara A, Gregory & Stephen. *Educ:* Marymount Col, BS, 62; Georgetown Univ, MS, 65; Cornell Univ, PhD(biochem), 73. *Prof Exp:* From instr to asst prof chem, Marymount Manhattan Col, 64-69. *Concurrent Pos:* Lectr chem, Marymount Manhattan Col, 71-74; consult, NJ regulatory affairs, CellTech, Ltd, 83 & clin studies & regulatory affairs, Exovir, Inc, 84-85. *Mem:* Am Chem Soc; AAAS; NY Acad Sci; Int Soc Thrombosis & Hemostasis; Asn Univ Technol Mgrs. *Res:* Immunochemistry; blood coagulation chemistry; new blood-derived products. *Mailing Add:* 156 Taymil Rd New Rochelle NY 10804

HOROWITZ, MARK CHARLES, IMMUNOBIOLOGY. *Current Pos:* Fel immunol, 77-78, res assoc, Dept Path, 78-80, RES ASSOC, DEPT ORTHOP, HOWARD HUGHES MED INST, YALE UNIV, 81- *Personal Data:* b New York, NY, Aug 5, 50. *Educ:* Syracuse Univ, BS, 72; State Univ NY Upstate Med Ctr, PhD(immunol), 78. *Mem:* Sigma Xi. *Res:* Immunoregulation mediated by different subsets of T and B cells; immunoregulatory defects in autoimmunity; control mechanisms of the immune response. *Mailing Add:* Dept Surg & Orthop Yale Univ Sch Med PO Box 208071 New Haven CT 06520-8071

HOROWITZ, MARTIN I, BIOCHEMISTRY. *Current Pos:* assoc prof, 61-69, PROF BIOCHEM, NY MED COL, 69- *Personal Data:* b May 17, 29; m 53; c 2. *Educ:* Brooklyn Col, MA, 52; Rutgers Univ, PhD(microbial chem), 57. *Prof Exp:* Asst nutrit chem, Sch Pub Health, Columbia Univ, 51-52; biochemist, Mt Sinai Hosp, 57-61. *Mem:* AAAS; Am Oil Chem Soc; Am Soc Biol Chemists; Am Chem Soc. *Res:* Biochemistry of mucins; digestive enzymes; glycolipids; nutrition; immunochemistry-blood group substances. *Mailing Add:* Dept Biochem NY Med Col Valhalla NY 10595

HOROWITZ, MYER GEORGE, BIOCHEMISTRY. *Current Pos:* RETIRED. *Personal Data:* b Boston, Mass, July 23, 24; m 50, Evelyn G Jacobs; c Irviugh, Golda C & Louise J. *Educ:* Harvard Univ, BA, 45; Univ Ore, MA, 49, PhD(biochem), 52. *Prof Exp:* Asst biochemist, Univ Ore, 49-51; Nat Found Infantile Paralysis fel, Northwestern Univ, 52-54; USPHS fel, 54-55; clin chemist, Clin Lab, Jewish Hosp, Cincinnati, 55-89. *Mem:* AAAS; Am Chem Soc; Am Asn Clin Chem; Sigma Xi. *Res:* Mechanism of lactose biosynthesis; glycolytic processes in mammary tissue homogenates; interaction of dyes with proteins. *Mailing Add:* 1239 Avon Dr Cincinnati OH 45229

HOROWITZ, NORMAN HAROLD, GENETICS, BIOCHEMISTRY. *Current Pos:* res fel biochem, Calif Inst Technol, 40-42, from assoc prof to prof biol, 47-82, mgr, Biosci Sect, Jet Propulsion Lab, 65-70, chmn div, 77-80, EMER PROF BIOL, CALIF INST TECHNOL, 82- *Personal Data:* b Pittsburgh, Pa, Mar 19, 15; wid; c Joel & Elizabeth. *Educ:* Univ Pittsburgh, BS, 36; Calif Inst Technol, PhD(biol), 39. *Honors & Awards:* Pub Serv Medal, NASA, 77. *Prof Exp:* Fel, Nat Res Coun, Univ & Hopkins Marine Sta,

Stanford Univ, 39-40; res assoc biol, Stanford Univ, 42-46. *Concurrent Pos:* Fulbright & Guggenheim fel, Genetics Lab, Univ Paris, 54-55; mem, Space Sci Bd, Nat Acad Sci, 71-75. *Mem:* Nat Acad Sci; AAAS; Am Acad Arts & Sci; Am Soc Biol Chemists; Genetics Soc Am. *Res:* Biochemical genetics of Neurospora; enzymes; molecular evolution; exploration of Mars. *Mailing Add:* Div Biol Calif Inst Technol Pasadena CA 91125

HOROWITZ, PAUL MARTIN, BIOCHEMISTRY, PHYSICAL CHEMISTRY. *Current Pos:* assoc prof, 77-84, PROF DEPT BIOCHEM, UNIV TEX HEALTH SCI CTR, 84- *Personal Data:* b Jersey City, NJ, Oct 5, 39; m 65; c 3. *Educ:* NY Univ, BA, 62; Univ Chicago, PhD(biochem), 68. *Prof Exp:* AEC res fel spectros, Inst Molecular Biophys, Fla State Univ, 68-70; asst prof phys biochem, Dartmouth Col, 70-77. *Concurrent Pos:* Cottrell grant, 71; Petrol Res Fund grant, 71-74; adj asst prof, Dartmouth Med Sch, 73-; Erna & Jakob Michael vis prof, Weizman Inst Sci, Israel. *Mem:* AAAS. *Res:* Structure function relationships in biological macromolecules; enzymes and nucleic acids. *Mailing Add:* Dept Biochem Univ Tex Health Sci Ctr San Antonio TX 78284-7760

HOROWITZ, RICHARD E, PATHOLOGY, COMPUTER SCIENCES. *Current Pos:* from asst prof to assoc prof, 63-72, CLIN PROF PATH, SCH MED, UNIV SOUTHERN CALIF, 72-; CLIN PROF PATH, SCH MED, UNIV CALIF, LOS ANGELES, 83- *Personal Data:* b Vienna, Austria, May 17, 31; US citizen; div; c 1. *Educ:* Univ Calif, Los Angeles, AB, 53; Univ Calif, San Francisco, MD, 57; Am Bd Path, cert path anat & clin path, 63. *Prof Exp:* Intern, Los Angeles Co Hosp, 58; supvr, Dept Germfree Res, Walter Reed Army Inst Res, 58-60; fel path, Mt Sinai Hosp, NY, 60-63; instr path, Col Physicians & Surgeons, Columbia Univ, 61-63. *Concurrent Pos:* Pathologist, Los Angeles Co Gen Hosp, 63-66, asst dir labs, 66-68; consult pathologist, Vet Admin Hosp, Los Angeles, 64-, sr attend physician, Los Angeles Co, Univ Southern Calif Med Ctr, 68-; assoc pathologist, St Joseph Med Ctr, 68-71, dir labs, 71-90, sr pathologist, 90-; mem, Comt Life Sci & Pub Policy, Nat Res Coun-Nat Acad Sci, 68-75; chmn, Verdugo Div, Am Heart Asn, 72-74; mem, Comt Computerized Lab Systs, Col Am Pathologists, 77-85, Calif Deleg to House of Delegates, 84-, bd dirs, vpres, 93-; mem comt Comput in Health Sci, Inst Elec & Electronics Engrs; mem bd dirs, Los Angeles Soc Pathologists, 82-87, pres, 86-; mem bd trustees, St Joseph Med Ctr Found, 82-, adv bd, 91-, chmn bd trustees, 91-; mem, Path Sci Adv Panel, Calif Med Asn, 85-89, chmn, 87-88; mem, Finance Comt, Am Soc Clin Pathologists, 85-88, vchair Res, Develop & Strategic Planning Comt, 86-90, bd dirs, 88-, treas, 88- *Mem:* Col Am Path; Am Soc Clin Path (treas, 88-); AMA. *Res:* Pathologic anatomy; laboratory computer and information sciences; laboratory management. *Mailing Add:* 14590 Peervale Pl Sherman Oaks CA 91403. *Fax:* 818-843-0627

HOROWITZ, SAMUEL BORIS, CELL PHYSIOLOGY, ZOOLOGY. *Current Pos:* chmn, Dept Biol, 75-78, res scientist, 72-81, LAB CHIEF, MICH CANCER FOUND, 72-, CHMN, DEPT PHYSIOL & BIOPHYS, 81- *Personal Data:* b Perth Amboy, NJ, Aug 26, 27; m 55, 73; c 1. *Educ:* Hunter Col, AB, 51; Univ Chicago, PhD(zool), 56. *Prof Exp:* Res assoc, Col Med, Univ Ill, 56-57; sr res fel basic res, Eastern Pa Psychiat Inst, 57-62; vis investr, Int Physiol & Med Biophys, Uppsala Univ, 62-63; assoc mem & co-head lab cellular biophys, Albert Einstein Med Ctr, 63-69, head, 69-72. *Concurrent Pos:* Vis investr, Physiol Lab, Cambridge Univ, 71-72; adj prof, Dept Biol, Wayne State Univ, 72-89; mem, Biophys & Biophysical Chem Study Sect, NIH, 78-79. *Mem:* Am Asn Cancer Res; AAAS; Am Soc Cell Biol; Biophys Soc; Soc Study Develop & Growth. *Res:* Intracellular transport; hormonal action at cellular level; solute transport; physics and chemistry of transport and solubility in proteinaceous systems; growth control. *Mailing Add:* Mich Cancer Found 110 E Warren Ave Detroit MI 48201-1379

HOROWITZ, SIDNEY LESTER, ORTHODONTICS. *Current Pos:* res asst dent, 51-54, from res assoc to asst clin prof, 54-69, PROF DENT & DIR DIV OROFACIAL DEVELOP, SCH DENT & ORAL SURG, COLUMBIA UNIV, 69- *Personal Data:* b Jersey City, NJ, June 26, 21; m 50; c 4. *Educ:* Columbia Univ, BS, 42, cert, 49; NY Univ, DDS, 45. *Prof Exp:* Asst vis dentist, Children's Hosp, Philadelphia, 49-51. *Concurrent Pos:* Assoc attend orthodontist, Manhattan Eye, Ear & Throat Hosp, New York, 58-; consult, Roosevelt Hosp, 69- *Mem:* AAAS; Int Asn Dent Res; Sigma Xi. *Res:* Genetic variations in skull and dentition; orthodontic management in reconstructive plastic surgery of the face. *Mailing Add:* Sch Dent & Oral Surg Columbia Univ New York NY 10032

HOROWITZ, STANLEY H, ELECTRICAL POWER SYSTEMS, ELECTRICAL ENGINEERING. *Current Pos:* CONSULT, ELEC POWER SYSTS. *Mem:* Nat Acad Eng. *Res:* Electric power systems reliability and integrity through advanced protective relaying concept. *Mailing Add:* 3143 Griggsview Ct Columbus OH 43221

HOROWITZ, SYLVIA TEICH, BIO-ORGANIC CHEMISTRY. *Current Pos:* vis lectr biochem, 69-88, EMER CALIF STATE UNIV, LOS ANGELES, 88- *Personal Data:* b Brooklyn, NY; wid; c 3. *Educ:* Brooklyn Col, BA, 43; Columbia Univ, PhD(org chem), 49. *Prof Exp:* Res assoc org chem, Amherst Col, 49-50; res assoc steroid chem, Col Physicians & Surgeons, Columbia Univ, 50-53; res assoc biochem, Sch Med, Univ Mich, 53-55. *Mem:* Am Chem Soc; Am Women Sci; Sigma Xi; AAAS. *Res:* Metabolism of steroid hormones; synthesis of steroid conjugates; synthesis of analogues of penicillin. *Mailing Add:* 800 Fairfield Circle Calif State Univ Pasadena CA 91106-3900

HORRES, ALAN DIXON, PHYSIOLOGY. *Current Pos:* from asst prof to assoc prof physiol, 65-71, asst prof exp med, 65-67, PROF PHYSIOL, MED UNIV SC, 71- *Personal Data:* b Charleston, SC, Jan 12, 29; m 49; c 3. *Educ:* Col Charleston, BS, 48; Syracuse Univ, MS, 50; Med Col SC, PhD(physiol), 55. *Prof Exp:* Asst prof biol, The Citadel, 55-56; instr physiol, Med Col SC, 56-58; from instr to asst prof physiol, Emory Univ, 58-63, instr surg, 60-63, assoc surg, 65-65, dir pulmonary function lab, 60-65. *Concurrent Pos:* Dir pulmonary function lab, Vet Admin Hosp, 65-67. *Mem:* Am Physiol Soc. *Res:* Respiratory control; cardiovascular physiology; neurophysiology. *Mailing Add:* Dept Physiol Med Univ SC 171 Ashely Ave Charleston SC 29425-0001

HORRES, CHARLES RUSSELL, JR, PHYSIOLOGY, BIOMEDICAL ENGINEERING. *Current Pos:* PRES, CYBERRX INC, 91- *Personal Data:* b Charleston, SC, Aug 6, 45; m 67. *Educ:* Ga Inst Technol, BS, 68; Duke Univ, PhD(physiol & pharmacol), 75. *Prof Exp:* Res engr membrane develop, Chemstrand Res Ctr, Monsanto, 68-69; spec asst sanitary engr air pollution control, Nat Air Pollution Control Admin, 69-71; prin investr biochem & pharmacol, Becton-Dickenson Res Ctr, 75-77 & prin investr mat res, 77-78, dept mgr appl physiol, 78-83; vpres res & develop, Pancretec, Inc, 83-86; pres res & develop, Ivac, Inc, 86-90. *Concurrent Pos:* Adj res assoc physiol, Duke Univ, 76-78, adj asst prof, 78-82, adj assoc prof, 82-; lectr physiol, Univ NC, Chapel Hill, 78-80, adj asst prof, 80-83; vpres res & develop, Pancretec Inc, 83-86. *Mem:* Biophys Soc; Am Soc Artificial Internal Organs; Cardiac Muscle Soc; Soc Gen Physiologists. *Res:* Membrane transport phenomena; cardiac cellular physiology. *Mailing Add:* 13071 Via Grimaldi Del Mar CA 92014

HORRIDGE, PATRICIA EMILY, TEXTILE CHEMISTRY. *Current Pos:* chairperson textile & clothing, 76-85, chairperson merchandising, environ design & consumer econ, 85-90, PROF, TEX TECH UNIV, 90- *Personal Data:* b Marshall, Tex, Jan 17, 37; c 1. *Educ:* Univ Tex, Austin, BS, 58; Univ Houston, MS, 65; Tex Woman's Univ, PhD(textile sci), 69. *Prof Exp:* Asst prof textile & clothing, Baylor Univ, 66-68; res asst, Tex Woman's Univ, 68; asst prof, Fla State Univ, 69-71; assoc prof, Univ Southwestern La, 72; chairperson, Univ Ky, 73-76. *Concurrent Pos:* Numerous grants, Univs & Indust, 76-91. *Mem:* Int Fed Home Econ; fel Asn Col Prof Textiles & Clothing; Am Home Econ Asn. *Res:* Energy, especially determination of the effectiveness of window treatments as fuel savers; flammability of Cordelan/cotton blend fabrics. *Mailing Add:* 3812 53rd St Lubbock TX 79413

HORRIGAN, FRANK ANTHONY, THEORETICAL PHYSICS. *Current Pos:* tech mkt mgr, Equip Div, 80-87, prog mgr, AOSP, 81-85, TECH DIR ADVAN TECHNOL, EQUIP DEVELOP LABS, RAYTHEON, 85- *Personal Data:* b Butte, Mont, Apr 19, 33; m 58, 75; c 4. *Educ:* Fordham Univ, BS, 54; Harvard Univ, AM, 55, PhD(physics), 61. *Prof Exp:* Sr res scientist, 61-65, prin res scientist, Res Div, Raytheon Co, 65-74, mgr, Electrooptics Lab, 70-74; div mgr, Sci Appln, Inc, 74-80. *Concurrent Pos:* NATO fel, Saclay Nuclear Res Ctr, France, 62-63. *Mem:* Am Phys Soc. *Res:* Quantum mechanical many body theory; statistical mechanics; atomic and electron processes; plasma and laser physics; applied mathematics; fault tolerant computers; electro optic systems. *Mailing Add:* 283 Davis Rd Bedford MA 01730

HORRIGAN, JACK ALLEN, MODELING & SIMULATION, ALGORITHM DEVELOPMENT & TEST DESIGN. *Current Pos:* ASSOC, B&J WESTERN, 86- *Personal Data:* b Des Moines, Iowa, Aug 30, 30; m 63, Patricia Ann Austin; c Marianne M, Aileen E & William G. *Educ:* Iowa State Col Agr & Mech Arts, BS, 55; Neotarian Fel & Col Philos, PhD(philos & econ), 69. *Prof Exp:* Field engr, TechRep Div, Philco Corp, Philadelphia, 58-60; mathematician, Vitro Labs, Vitro Corp, Silver Spring, Md, 60-61; sr mathematician, Data Systs Div, Litton Indust, Van Nuys, Calif, 62-66; asst dept mgr, Western Div, Wolf Res & Develop, Encino, Calif, 66-67; design engr, Pac Div, AAI, Van Nuys, Calif, 67-68; consult, Volt Info Systs, Tucson, 68-69; Westinghouse Elec Co, 76-77, Lear Siegler Inc, 79, Struct Dynamics, 80; staff engr, Hughes Aircraft Co, 69-70; laborer, Clarett McCoy Inc, 70-71; chief opers res, Psychol Dept, Univ Denver, 72-76; contract programmer & analyst, Am Home Video Corp, 81-82, Gen Elec Co, 82-83, E I du Pont de Nemours & Co Inc, 83-84. *Concurrent Pos:* Mem bd, Clarett McCoy Inc, 72-87; writer, Colo QRP Club, 97. *Res:* Monosodium glutamate syndrome. *Mailing Add:* PO Box 200626 Denver CO 80220-0626. *Fax:* 303-333-2261

HORRIGAN, PHILIP ARCHIBALD, INORGANIC CHEMISTRY. *Current Pos:* from asst prof to assoc prof chem, 62-67, chmn dept, 67-80, PROF CHEM, SOUTHERN CONN STATE COL, 68- *Personal Data:* b Brighton, Mass, Oct 8, 28; m 55; c 2. *Educ:* Mass Inst Technol, BS, 48; Boston Col, MS, 50; Univ Ill, PhD(chem), 53. *Prof Exp:* Res chemist, Lever Bros Co, 50-51; mem staff tech sales, Rohm and Haas Co, 55-56; pres detergent mfg, Jet Prods, Inc, 57-62. *Mem:* Am Chem Soc. *Res:* Manufacturing and marketing of chemical specialties. *Mailing Add:* Dept Chem Southern Conn State Univ 501 Crescent St New Haven CT 06515-1330

HORRIGAN, ROBERT V(INCENT), CHEMICAL & NUCLEAR ENGINEERING. *Current Pos:* RETIRED. *Personal Data:* b Brookline, Mass, June 8, 24; m 50; c 3. *Educ:* Mass Inst Technol, BS, 44, MS, 47; Yale Univ, PhD(chem eng), 51. *Prof Exp:* Assoc engr, Brookhaven Nat Lab, 50-52; res investr, Titanium Alloy Mfg Div, Nat Lead Co, 52-57, chief develop div, 57-61; pres & tech dir, Transelco, Inc, 61-76, div mgr, Transelco Div, Ferro Corp, 76-79. *Concurrent Pos:* Consult, US AEC, 52-55. *Mem:* Am Chem Soc; Am Inst Chem Engrs; Am Ceramic Soc. *Res:* Industrial applications of titanium and zirconium products; concentration, disposal and utilization of radioactive wastes. *Mailing Add:* 6941 Country Lake Circle Sarasota FL 34243

HORROBIN, DAVID FREDERICK, endocrinology, cardiovascular physiology, for more information see previous edition

HORROCKS, LLOYD ALLEN, NEUROCHEMISTRY, BIOCHEMICAL NEUROPATHOLOGY. *Current Pos:* from asst prof to prof physiol chem, 68-90, prof med biochem, 90-91, EMER PROF, COL MED, OHIO STATE UNIV, 92-; PRES & CHIEF EXEC OFFICER, BRAINCHEMTECH CORP, 90- *Personal Data:* b Cincinnati, Ohio, July 13, 32; m 56, Marjorie Werstler; c Richard & Rebecca. *Educ:* Ohio Wesleyan Univ, BA, 53; Ohio State Univ, MSc, 55, PhD(physiol chem), 60. *Prof Exp:* Res assoc neurochem, Cleveland Psychiat Inst, 60-68. *Concurrent Pos:* NIH fel, Univ Birmingham, 64-65; Josiah Macy Jr Found fac scholar, Ctr Neurochem, Nat Sci Res Ctr, Louis Pasteur Univ, Strasbourg, France, 74-75; mem rev B comt, Neurol Disorders Prog Proj, NIH, 81-85; vis prof, Nat Res Coun Italy, NATO, 86; chmn & chief exec officer, Jarrow-Lloyd Pharmaceut, Inc, 90-93. *Mem:* Soc Neurosci; Am Soc Biochem Molecular Biol; Am Soc Neurochem; Int Soc Neurochem; Brit Biochem Soc; Neurotrauma Soc; AAAS; Am Asn Clin Chem; Am Asn Univ Professors; Am Oil Chemists Soc; corresp mem Royal Acad Sci, Spain, 93; Int Soc Develop Neurosci. *Res:* Brain lipid metabolism; brain function, membrane composition and structure; methods of lipid analysis; chromatography; experimental neuropathology; neurological diseases; fatty acid metabolism. *Mailing Add:* Ohio State Univ Dept Med Biochem 465 Hamilton Hall 1645 Neil Ave Columbus OH 43210-1218. *Fax:* 614-292-5482

HORROCKS, ROBERT H, ORGANIC CHEMISTRY. *Current Pos:* asst prof, Univ Bridgeport, 65-72, assoc prof chem, 72-81, chmn, Dept Chem, 81-86, PROF CHEM, UNIV BRIDGEPORT, 81- *Personal Data:* b North Attleboro, Mass, Dec 23, 28; m 52; c 5. *Educ:* Univ RI, BS, 51, MS, 61, PhD(chem), 64; Am Int Col, MBA, 57. *Prof Exp:* Plant chem engr, Plastics Div, Monsanto Co, 51 & 53-55, res chem engr, 55-61; asst, Univ RI, 61-63, res asst, 63-64; res assoc, Iowa State Univ, 64-65. *Concurrent Pos:* Res asst, Univ RI, 59-61; NSF grant, Boston Univ, 66-67; consult, Geigy Chem Co, 67. *Mem:* Am Chem Soc; Sigma Xi. *Res:* Free radical reactions, particularly hydrogen bromide additions to olefins and perester decompositions; both thermosetting and thermoplastic polymers; radical ions such as semidiones; mechanisms of phenazine formation. *Mailing Add:* 140 Salem Rd Stratford CT 06497

HORROCKS, RODNEY DWAIN, AGRONOMY. *Current Pos:* chmn dept, 81-89, PROF DEPT AGRON & HORT, BRIGHAM YOUNG UNIV, 78- *Personal Data:* b Maeser, Utah, Oct 4, 38; m 60; c Rodney Dwain Jr, Sharilyn, Janene, Richard Lloyd & Russell David. *Educ:* Brigham Young Univ, BS, 62; Pa State Univ, MS, 64, PhD(agron), 67. *Prof Exp:* From asst prof to prof agron, Univ Mo, Columbia, 71-78. *Concurrent Pos:* Vis prof, Dept Soils, Water & Eng, Univ Ariz, 75-76 & Dept Agron & Range Sci, Univ Calif, Davis, 89-90; USAID consult, Sierra Leone & Liberia, 76; assoc ed, Agron J, 83-87, tech ed, 87-93. *Mem:* Am Soc Agron; Crop Sci Soc Am; Sigma Xi; Am Inst Biol Sci. *Res:* Ecological modeling; forage crop production, management, physiology and ecology. *Mailing Add:* Dept Agron & Hort 273 Widtsoe Bldg Provo UT 84602

HORROCKS, WILLIAM DEWITT, JR, INORGANIC CHEMISTRY, BIOINORGANIC CHEMISTRY. *Current Pos:* assoc prof, 69-72, PROF CHEM, PA STATE UNIV, 72- *Personal Data:* b Orange, NJ, Dec 7, 34; m 63, E Joan Allan; c Allan. *Educ:* Wesleyan Univ, BA, 56; Mass Inst Technol, PhD(inorg chem), 60. *Prof Exp:* From instr to asst prof chem, Princeton Univ, 60-69. *Concurrent Pos:* Vis lectr biol chem, Harvard Med Sch & Guggenheim fel, 74-75, vis prof, Mass Inst Technol, 88. *Mem:* Fel AAAS; Am Chem Soc; Am Soc Biochem & Molecular Biol; Biophys Soc. *Res:* Physical and inorganic chemistry, spectra and structure of transition metal compounds; physical inorganic and bioinorganic chemistry; transition metal and lanthanide coordination chemistry; paramagnetic nuclear magnetic resonance; laser luminescence spectroscopy. *Mailing Add:* Dept Chem Pa State Univ University Park PA 16802. *E-Mail:* wdh2@psuvm.psu.edu

HORSBURGH, ROBERT LAURIE, ENTOMOLOGICAL EXTENSION. *Current Pos:* LAB SUPT & ENTOMOLOGIST, VA POLYTECH INST & STATE UNIV WINCHESTER FRUIT RES LAB, 81-, PROF ENTOM, 81- *Personal Data:* b Coronach, Sask, June 23, 31; m 55; c 3. *Educ:* McGill Univ, BSc, 56; Pa State Univ, MS, 69, PhD(entom), 70. *Prof Exp:* Tree fruit entomologist, NS Dept Agr, 56-66 & 70-74; res assoc, Pa State Univ, 66-70; tree fruit entomologist, Va Polytech Inst & State Univ, 74-81. *Mem:* Etomologic Soc Am; Can Entom Soc. *Res:* Pest management of fruit pests with emphasis on biology of spiders, mirids, and anthocorids; efficacy of experimental pesticides on major pests and beneficial species on apple and peach. *Mailing Add:* 109 Mulberry Circle Stephens City VA 22655

HORSCH, ROBERT BRUCE, PLANT TRANSFORMATION, AGRICULTURAL BIOTECHNOLOGY. *Current Pos:* sr res biologist, res specialist & res group leader, Monsanto Agr Co, 81-85, sr res group leader, Corp Res Lab, 85-87, mgr, 87-91, DIR, CROP TRANSFORMATION, MONSANTO AGR CO, 91- *Personal Data:* b Pittsburgh, Pa, Sept 28, 52; m 72, Linda L Lanshaw; c Elisa, Laura & Michael. *Educ:* Univ Calif, Riverside, BSc, 74, PhD(genetics), 79. *Honors & Awards:* Monsanto's Thomas & Hochwalt Award. *Prof Exp:* Fel, Univ Sask, 79-81. *Concurrent Pos:* Organizer for plant molecular biol course, Cold Spring, Harbor Labs, 85-88; adj prof biol, Washington Univ. *Mem:* Am Soc Plant Physiol. *Res:* Crop improvement via biotechnology; gene-transfer techniques for genetic engineering of plants. *Mailing Add:* 12768 Whispering Hills Lane St Louis MO 63146. *Fax:* 314-537-6567; *E-Mail:* rbhors@ccmail.monsanto.com

HORSEMAN, NELSON DOUGLAS, ENDOCRINOLOGY. *Current Pos:* assoc prof, 89-91, dir grad studies, 90-96, PROF PHYSIOL, UNIV CINCINNATI, 91- *Personal Data:* b Dayton, Ohio, Sept 30, 51; m 75; c 2. *Educ:* Eastern Ky Univ, BS, 73, MS, 75; La State Univ, PhD(physiol), 78. *Prof Exp:* Res assoc, La State Univ, 75-78; appointee, Argonne Nat Lab, 78-80; from asst prof to assoc prof physiol, Marquette Univ, 80-89. *Concurrent Pos:* Dir, Biol & Biomed Res Inst, Marquette Univ, 87-89. *Mem:* Endocrine Soc; Am Soc Biochem & Molecular Biol; AAAS. *Res:* Molecular biology of prolactin actions; transcription factor identification, receptor signal transduction and gene structure; function of annexin, lipocortin genes and proteins. *Mailing Add:* Dept Molecular & Cell Physiol Univ Cincinnati ML 576 Cincinnati OH 45267-0576. *Fax:* 513-558-5738; *E-Mail:* nelson.horseman@uc.edu

HORSFALL, JAMES GORDON, plant pathology; deceased, see previous edition for last biography

HORSFALL, WILLIAM ROBERT, ENTOMOLOGY. *Current Pos:* from asst prof to prof, 47-76, EMER PROF ENTOM, UNIV ILL, URBANA, 76- *Personal Data:* b Mountain Grove, Mo, Jan 11, 08; m 30, Annie L Ellis. *Educ:* Univ Ark, BS, 28; Kans State Col, MS, 29; Cornell Univ, PhD(entom), 33. *Honors & Awards:* Award of Merit, Zool Soc Finland, 64; Harold Gray Award, Am Mosquito Control Asn, 70; Hoogstraal Medal, Am Soc Trop Dis, 91. *Prof Exp:* Asst, Kans State Col, 28-29; asst, Cornell Univ, 30-33; prof biol, Agr & Mech Col, Monticello, 33-36; instr entom, Univ Ark, 36-37; asst prof entom & zool, Exp Sta, SDak State Col, 37-38; from asst prof to assoc prof entom, Univ Ark, 38-47. *Concurrent Pos:* Asst entomologist, Exp Sta, Univ Ark, 38-45; malariologist, US Army, 43-44; lion mem, Am Mosquito Control Asn, 86. *Mem:* Fel AAAS; fel Entom Soc Am; hon mem Am Mosquito Control Asn. *Res:* Bionomics of mosquitoes and ticks; medical entomology. *Mailing Add:* 101 W Windsor St Urbana IL 61801

HORSLEY, JOHN ANTHONY, SURFACE CHEMISTRY, LASER CHEMISTRY. *Current Pos:* SR RES FEL, CATALYTICA, INC, 86- *Personal Data:* b Scarborough, Eng, Mar 10, 43; m 69; c 2. *Educ:* Oxford Univ, BA, 64, DPhil, 68. *Prof Exp:* NATO fel, Ctr Appl Wave Mech, Paris, 67-68; res scientist, French Nat Sci Res Ctr, 68-75; res chemist, Exxon Res & Eng Co, 75-77, staff chemist, 77-80, sr staff chemist, 80-81, head, Surface Chem Group, 81-86. *Mem:* Am Chem Soc. *Res:* Quantum chemistry; surface chemistry; electronic structure of catalysts; metal clusters; x-ray near edge spectroscopy; laser chemistry; laser isotope separation. *Mailing Add:* 689 Torrington Dr Sunnyvale CA 94087-2446

HORSLEY, JOHN SHELTON, III, SURGERY. *Current Pos:* PROF SURG, DIV SURG ONCOL, MED COL VA, 76- *Personal Data:* b Richmond, Va, Oct 3, 27; m 55; c 3. *Educ:* Univ Va, BA, 50, MD, 53; Am Bd Surg, cert, 60. *Honors & Awards:* Horsley Mem Award Merit, Am Cancer Soc, 73. *Prof Exp:* From intern to asst resident surg, Peter Bent Brigham Hosp, Boston, 53-58, chief resident, 59; clin instr surg, Med Col Va, 59-65; from asst prof to assoc prof, Med Col Va, Univ Va, 65-72, Am Cancer Soc prof clin oncol, 72-76, dir, McIntire Tumor Clin, 65-76, dir, Div Cancer Studies, 75-80, prof surg, 72-76, assoc dir, Cancer Ctr & dir, Joint Cancer Clin, 76-78. *Concurrent Pos:* Nat Cancer Inst trainee, Col Physicians & Surgeons, Columbia Univ, Mem Ctr, New York, 55-56; Arthur Cabot teaching fel, Harvard Med Sch, 59; attend surgeon, St Elizabeth's Hosp & Sheltering Arms Hosp, Richmond, 59-65; surg consult, McGuire Vet Admin Hosp, Richmond, 59-65; mem courtesy staff, Richmond Mem Hosp, 59-65; clin cancer coordr, Univ Va, 65-, clin dir, Div Cancer Studies, 70-73; co-ed, Cancer Trends, 67-; consult, Salem Vet Admin Hosp, 68-76; asst chief surg serv, McGuire Vet Hosp, 78-80, chief, surg oncol, 80- *Mem:* Am Col Surg; Asn Acad Surg; James Ewing Soc; Int Soc Surg; Soc Surg Oncol; Am Surg Asn. *Res:* Cancer. *Mailing Add:* Med Col Va Box 980011 Richmond VA 23298-0011

HORSMA, DAVID AUGUST, ELECTRONIC PACKING, ELECTRICAL PROPERTIES OF MATERIALS. *Current Pos:* group leader, Raychem Corp, 72-78, tech dir, 78-82 & 84-89, tech mkt mgr, 82-84, sr scientist, 89-92, DEVELOP MGR, RAYCHEM CORP, 92- *Personal Data:* b Hubbell, Mich, Sept 3, 40; m 66, Geri Booker; c Jennifer & Amy. *Educ:* Mich Tech Univ, BS, 62; Univ Calif, Davis, PhD(chem), 66. *Prof Exp:* Res assoc chem, Univ Calif, Los Angeles, 66-67; asst prof, Calif Polytech State Univ, 66-68; group leader plastics appln, Rohm & Haas Co, 68-71; sr engr mat develop, Crown Zellerbach Corp, 71-72. *Mem:* Am Chem Soc; Inst Elec & Electronics Engrs. *Res:* Physical and electrical properties of polymers and the applications of these materials to products; granted 22 US patents. *Mailing Add:* 1141 Parkinson Ave Palo Alto CA 94301. *Fax:* 650-361-2261; *E-Mail:* dhorsma@raychem.com

HORST, G ROY, ZOOLOGY, HISTOLOGY. *Current Pos:* prof biol & chmn dept, State Univ NY Col Potsdam, 75-80. *Personal Data:* b Lancaster, Pa, July 13, 33; m 58; c 2. *Educ:* Wagner Col, BS, 59; Cornell Univ, PhD(zool), 67. *Prof Exp:* From instr to asst prof anat, Univ Ariz, 67-71; asst prof, Univ Vt, 71-75, USPHS grant, 72-75. *Concurrent Pos:* USPHS grant, Univ Ariz, 68-71; chmn, Ann NAm Symp Bat Res, 70-; mem exec comt, Desert Bighorn Sheep Coun, 71-72. *Mem:* AAAS; Am Asn Anatomists; Am Soc Mammalogists; Am Soc Zoologists; Sigma Xi. *Res:* Renal physiology and morphology in desert mammals; mammalian development osmoregulation and thermoregulation. *Mailing Add:* RR 2 Box 246 Potsdam NY 13676-9626

HORST, JOHN ALBERT, CONTROL OF AUTONOMOUS SEMI-AUTONOMOUS VEHICLES, MATHEMATICAL MODELING. *Current Pos:* ELECTRONICS ENGR, ROBOT SYSTS DIV, NAT INST STAND & TECHNOL, 89- *Personal Data:* b Cinton, Iowa, Feb 24, 53; m 83; c Justin, Palmer, Stephen & Gilbert. *Educ:* Univ Md, Col Park, BA, 76, BS, 85, MS, 89. *Prof Exp:* Electronics engr, Dept Defense, 85-89. *Mem:* Inst Elec & Electronics Engrs. *Res:* Autonomous vehicle control in unknown and unstructured environments; development and implementation of methods for intelligent control system design; computer simulation of phenomena in sensor-interactive mobile robotics; vision based hearing through motion. *Mailing Add:* Bldg 220 Rm B-124 Nat Inst Stand & Technol Gaithersburg MD 20899. *Fax:* 301-990-9688; *E-Mail:* horst@cme.nist.gov

HORST, RALPH KENNETH, PLANT PHYSIOLOGY, MICROBIOLOGY. *Current Pos:* from asst prof to assoc prof, 68-80, PROF PLANT PATH, CORNELL UNIV, 80- *Personal Data:* b Massillon, Ohio, June 22, 35; m 60, 69; c 4. *Educ:* Ohio Univ, BS, 57; Ohio State Univ, MS, 59, PhD(plant path), 61. *Prof Exp:* Supvr virus indexing, Yoder Bros, Inc, 62-63, dir, Lab Plant Path, 63-68. *Concurrent Pos:* Pres & secy, H&I Agritech, Inc. *Mem:* Am Phytopath Soc; AAAS; Tissue Cult Asn; Int Soc Hort Sci; Int Soc Hort Path; Soc Am Florists. *Res:* Virus indexing of mums, carnations, roses and meristem culture; characterization and investigations on viroid, virus and virusl; epidemiology of Fusaria ornamentals; biocompatible chemicals for control of plant diseases. *Mailing Add:* Dept Plant Path Cornell Univ Ithaca NY 14853-5098. *Fax:* 607-266-0193; *E-Mail:* rkh@cornell.edu

HORST, RALPH L, JR, CHEMICAL ENGINEERING, CORROSION. *Current Pos:* Sales develop engr, Aluminum Co Am, 48-60, head petrol & chem sect, Sales Develop Div, 60-64, prod develop engr, 64-65, res engr, Alcoa Res Labs, 65-66, sr res engr, Alcoa Tech Ctr, 66-78, staff engr, 78-81, tech supvr, 81-84, ENG ASSOC, ALCOA LABS, 84- *Personal Data:* b New Orleans, La, July 14, 25; m 54; c 3. *Educ:* Columbia Univ, BS, 47, MS, 48. *Mem:* Sigma Xi; Nat Asn Corrosion Engrs. *Res:* Corrosion science; electrochemistry and metallurgy of corrosion processes; materials evaluation; aluminum alloy corrosion mechanisms; cathodic protection engineering. *Mailing Add:* 1568 Linden Ave Lancaster PA 17601

HORST, RONALD LEE, PHYSIOLOGY, BIOCHEMISTRY. *Current Pos:* MEM STAFF, NAT ANIMAL DIS CTR, SCI & EDUC ADMIN, USDA, 78- *Personal Data:* b Waynesboro, Pa, Aug 16, 49; m 73; c 1. *Educ:* WVa Univ, BS, 71; Univ Wis, MS, 72, PhD(dairy sci, biochem), 76. *Prof Exp:* Fel biochem, Univ Wis, 76-77. *Mem:* Am Dairy Sci Asn; Am Soc Bone & Mineral Res; Am Inst Nutrit. *Res:* Vitamin D and calcium metabolism in the bovine. *Mailing Add:* Nat Animal Dis Ctr USDA ARS 2300 Dayton Ave PO Box 70 Ames IA 50010-0070

HORSTMAN, ARDEN WILLIAM, GEOLOGY. *Current Pos:* RETIRED. *Personal Data:* b Manitowoc, Wis, Aug 23, 30; m 66, 78; c 2. *Educ:* Lawrence Univ, BS, 52; Univ Cincinnati, MS, 54; Univ Colo, PhD(geol), 66. *Prof Exp:* Geologist, Shell Oil Co, 54-56, Mene Grande Oil Co, Venezuela, Gulf Oil Corp, 57-59 & Belco Petrol Corp, 60; vis lectr geol, Univ Mont, 65 & Lawrence Univ, 66; from asst prof to assoc prof geol, Western Carolina Univ, 66-93. *Mem:* Fel AAAS; Am Asn Petrol Geologists; Sigma Xi. *Res:* Stratigraphy and sedimentation. *Mailing Add:* Rte 67 PO Box 36P Cullowhee NC 28723

HORSTMAN, DONALD H, PULMONARY PHYSIOLOGY. *Current Pos:* RES PHYSIOLOGIST, US ENVIRON PROTECTION AGENCY, UNIV NC, 63- *Personal Data:* b St Louis, Mo, Jan 4, 39. *Educ:* Pa State Univ, PhD(physiol), 67. *Mailing Add:* Glaxo Wellcome 5 Moore Dr Res Triangle Park NC 27709

HORSTMANN, DOROTHY MILLICENT, VIROLOGY, INFECTIOUS DISEASES. *Current Pos:* from instr to assoc prof prev med, Yale Univ, 45-61, assoc prof pediat, 56-61, prof epidemiol & pediat, 61-69, J R Paul prof epidemiol & prof pediat, 69-82, EMER J R PAUL EPIDEMIOL, EMER PROF PEDIAT & SR RES SCIENTIST, EPIDEMIOL, SCH MED, YALE UNIV, 82- *Personal Data:* b Spokane, Wash, July 2, 11. *Educ:* Univ Calif, AB, 36, MD, 40; Am Bd Internal Med, dipl, 47. *Hon Degrees:* DSc, Smith Col, 61; MA, Yale Univ, 61; DrMedSc, Woman's Med Col Pa, 63. *Honors & Awards:* James D Bruce Award, Am Col Physicians, 75; Maxwell Finland Award, Infectious Dis Soc Am; Thorvald Madsen Award, State Serum Inst, Copenhagen. *Prof Exp:* Instr prev med, Yale Univ, 43-44; instr med, Med Sch, Univ Calif, 44-45. *Concurrent Pos:* Commonwealth Fund fel, Sch Med, Yale Univ, 42-43; NIH fel, Nat Inst Med Res, London, 47-48; distinguished alumni fac vis prof, Med Sch, Univ Calif, San Francisco, 79. *Mem:* Nat Acad Sci; Am Soc Clin Invest; Am Epidemiol Soc; Infectious Dis Soc Am (pres, 74-75); Asn Am Physicians; Pan-Am Med Asn; Am Pediat Soc; fel Am Acad Pediat; Europ Asn Virus Dis; master Am Col Physicians; hon mem Royal Soc Med. *Res:* Infectious disease; clinical virology; clinical epidemiology; poliomyelitis, pathogenesis, immunization and prevention. *Mailing Add:* Dept Epidemiol & Pub Health Sch Med Yale Univ 208034 60 College St New Haven CT 06520-8034. *Fax:* 203-785-7296

HORT, EUGENE VICTOR, ORGANIC CHEMISTRY. *Current Pos:* CONSULT, 86- *Personal Data:* b New York, NY, May 25, 21; m 43; c 3. *Educ:* City Col New York, BS, 42; Polytech Inst Brooklyn, MS, 48, PhD(chem), 50. *Prof Exp:* Res chemist, Nopco Chem Co, 50-51; dir res, Marco Chem Co, 51-53; sr chemist, Air Reduction Res Labs, 53-55; asst mgr acetylene chem & polymer sect, Gen Aniline & Film Corp, 55-62, tech assoc, 62-63, mgr cent res lab, 63-68, sr tech assoc, GAF Corp, 68-72, mgr acetylene chem res & devel, cent res lab, 72-81, sr scientist, 81-86. *Mem:* Am Chem Soc; Catalysis Soc. *Res:* Research management; synthetic organic chemistry; polymerization; catalysis. *Mailing Add:* 300 Winston Dr Cliffside Park NJ 07010

HORTICK, HARVEY J, GENETICS, AGRICULTURAL CHEMISTRY. *Current Pos:* DIR, FRUIT, VEG & TROP CROPS, AGR RES, NESTLE ENTERPRISES, INC, 78- *Personal Data:* b Leyden Twp, May 28, 35; m 59; c 2. *Educ:* Univ Ill, BS, 57, MS, 59, PhD(hort & plant physiol), 62. *Prof Exp:* Plant physiologist veg crops res, Libby, McNeill & Libby, Inc, 62-65, asst dir, 65-67, assoc dir, 67-69 dir agr res, 69-78. *Concurrent Pos:* Rep, Agr Res Inst, 74- *Res:* Effect of environment on plant growth and development; management and technical implementation for fruit, vegetable and tropical crops (pesticides, nutrient fertility, plant genetics, agricultural engineering and cultural programs). *Mailing Add:* 12526 Lt Nichols Rd Fairfax VA 22033-2431

HORTMANN, ALFRED GUENTHER, ORGANIC CHEMISTRY. *Current Pos:* from asst prof to assoc prof, 69-76, PROF ORG CHEM, WASH UNIV, 76- *Personal Data:* b New York, NY, Mar 1, 37; m 89, Charlotte Teeklin. *Educ:* Mass Inst Technol, SB, 58; Harvard Univ, PhD(chem), 64. *Prof Exp:* NIH fel org chem, Harvard Univ, 64. *Mem:* Am Chem Soc; AAAS. *Res:* Synthesis and structure determination in natural product area; photochemistry; synthesis of heterocyclic systems; C102 as an oxidant in organic synthesis. *Mailing Add:* Dept Chem Campus Box 1134 Wash Univ 1 Brookings Dr St Louis MO 63130-4899

HORTON, AARON WESLEY, GEOGRAPHIC CANCER EPIDEMIOLOGY. *Current Pos:* prof biochem & environ med, Med Sch, Ore Health Sci Univ, 62-76, actg head div environ med, 69-72, prof pub health, prev med & biochem, 76-89, head Sect Chem Biol & Oncol, 76-89, EMER PROF, PUB HEALTH & PREV MED, ORE HEALTH SCI UNIV, 89- *Personal Data:* b Detroit, Mich, June 13, 19; m 41, Virginia Cole; c 5. *Educ:* Yale Univ, BS, 40, MS, 47, PhD(phys/org chem), 48. *Prof Exp:* Sr res chemist, Socony-Vacuum Labs, 41-46; res engr, Res & Develop Dept, Franklin Inst, 48; from asst prof to prof indust health, Kettering Lab, Univ Cincinnati, 49-63. *Concurrent Pos:* Consult, indust and govt toxicol probs, 50-89; vis prof, Kettering Lab, Univ Cincinnati, 63-65 & Nat Inst Health & Med Res, Debrousse Hosp, Lyon, France, 72. *Mem:* Am Chem Soc; Sigma Xi. *Res:* Carcinogens, cocarcinogens and inhibitors in petroleum; physical models of biological membranes and their interactions with cocarcinogens and steroids; membrane-mediated control of latent cancer; etiologic factors in the geographical distribution of breast, lung and oesophageal cancer. *Mailing Add:* Dept Pub Health Med Sch Ore Health Sci Univ Portland OR 97201

HORTON, BILLY D, plant physiology, horticulture, for more information see previous edition

HORTON, BILLY MITCHUSSON, CONTROL SYSTEMS, INNOVATIONS. *Current Pos:* RETIRED. *Personal Data:* b Bartlett, Tex, Dec 27, 18; m 41, Hattie Grace Schultz; c Phillip & Stephen. *Educ:* Univ Tex, BA, 41; Univ Md, MS, 49. *Honors & Awards:* Arnold O Beckman Award, Inst Soc Am, 60; John Scott Award, 66. *Prof Exp:* Instr, Chanute Field, US Army, 41-42; Radar Officer, Signal Corp, 42-46; physicist, Naval Res Lab, 46-51; proj physicist, Nat Bur Stand, 51-53; lab chief & tech dir, Harry Diamond Labs, 61-74; prof mech & aero eng, Case Western Res Univ, 75-89. *Concurrent Pos:* Lectr, Univ Md, 54-58; consult, Chamberlain Mfg Corp, 75-79. *Mem:* Nat Acad Eng; fel Inst Elec & Electronics Engrs. *Res:* Amplification processes: fluid, mechanical, parametric; frictional processes; correlation in signal processing; noise modulation in detection and ranging systems; high intensity radiation detectors; high pressure physics; noise generated in sliding electrical contacts. *Mailing Add:* 14250 Larchmere Blvd Shaker Heights OH 44120

HORTON, CARL FREDERICK, PLANT PATHOLOGY, MOLECULAR BIOLOGY. *Current Pos:* PRES, INST MARINE & AGR RES INC, 93- *Personal Data:* m 76, Danette McYoung; c Eric & Jennifer. *Educ:* Univ NC, Wilmington, BS, 85; NC State Univ, PhD(biochem), 94. *Mem:* Am Chem Soc; Am Soc Plant Physiologists; AAAS. *Res:* Exploratory research in plant signal mechanisms; oversee the creation and description of environmentally associated plant and microorganism cultures in a semi-closed system. *Mailing Add:* 7474-110 Creedmore Rd Raleigh NC 27613. *Fax:* 919-821-1137

HORTON, CHARLES ABELL, ANALYTICAL CHEMISTRY. *Current Pos:* RETIRED. *Personal Data:* b Buffalo, NY, Mar 31, 18; m 47, E Carmen (Hart); c Nancy H (Burch) & John C. *Educ:* Cornell Univ, AB, 41; Univ Mich, MS, 46, PhD, 50. *Prof Exp:* Chemist, Mead Johnson Co, Trojan Powder Co & Bell Aircraft Corp, 41-44; res assoc, Manhattan Proj, Univ Rochester, 44-45 & Univ Mich, 46-49; res assoc nuclear div, Union Carbide Corp, 49-71; consult, 71-76. *Concurrent Pos:* Sr officer, Int Atomic Agency, Vienna, 66-68. *Mem:* Fel AAAS; fel Am Inst Chemists; Am Chem Soc; Sigma Xi. *Res:* Analytical chemistry, instrumental, metals and fluorides; analysis of biochemicals; uranium compounds; chemical documentation. *Mailing Add:* 384 East Dr Oak Ridge TN 37830

HORTON, CLAUDE WENDELL, JR, THEORETICAL PHYSICS. *Current Pos:* PROF PHYSICS, UNIV TEX, AUSTIN, 69- *Personal Data:* b Houston, Tex, Feb 3, 42; m 63; c 1. *Educ:* Univ Tex, Austin, BS, 63; Univ Calif, San Diego, MS, 65, PhD(physics), 67. *Concurrent Pos:* Fel Inst Advan Study, Princeton, 67-69; consult, Lawrence Livermore Lab, 73-, Sloan fel, 75; res scientist, Inst Fusion Studies, Univ Tex. *Mem:* Fel Am Phys Soc; Am Geophys Union. *Res:* Stability theory of plasmas. *Mailing Add:* R L Moore Bldg 11-320 Univ Tex Austin TX 78712

HORTON, CLAUDE WENDELL, SR, UNDERWATER ACOUSTICS. *Current Pos:* asst prof, Univ Tex, 46-50, chmn dept, 57-63, prof physics, 50-76, prof geol, 65-76, res physicist, Defense Res Lab, 45-, EMER PROF, UNIV TEX, AUSTIN, 76- *Personal Data:* b Cherryvale, Kans, Sept 23, 15; m 38; c 2. *Educ:* Rice Inst Technol, BA, 35, MA, 36; Univ Tex, PhD(physics), 48. *Honors & Awards:* Pioneers Underwater Acoust Medal, Acoust Soc Am, 80. *Prof Exp:* Asst seismologist, Shell Oil Co, 36-37, party chief, 38-43; asst math, Princeton Univ, 37-38; res assoc, Underwater Sound Lab, Harvard Univ, 43-45. *Concurrent Pos:* Consult, 45-; mem corp, Woods Hole Oceanog Inst. *Mem:* Fel Am Phys Soc; Soc Explor Geophys; fel Acoust Soc Am; Am Geophys Union. *Res:* Interpretation of geophysical data; electromagnetic radiation problems; theory of underwater sound problems; propagation of sound in the ocean. *Mailing Add:* 6501 Mesa Dr Austin TX 78731

HORTON, CLIFFORD E(DWARD), PHYSICS, ELECTRICAL ENGINEERING. *Current Pos:* RETIRED. *Personal Data:* b Worcester, Mass, Oct 19, 22; m 45; c 2. *Educ:* Purdue Univ, BS, 43. *Prof Exp:* Engr power tube develop, Victor Div, Radio Corp Am, 43-46; circuit develop, Gen Elec Co, 46-49, receiving tubes, 49-59, actg mgr circuit develop unit, 59-60, consult engr, 60-63; res scientist weapons effect, Kaman Sci Corp, 63-87. *Concurrent Pos:* Vis lectr, Ky Wesleyan Col, 48-49; instr eng graphics, Univ Colo, 74- *Res:* Physics of nuclear weapons effects; electronic receiving tubes. *Mailing Add:* 310 W Woodmen Rd Colorado Springs CO 80919

HORTON, DEREK, ORGANIC CHEMISTRY. *Current Pos:* res assoc, 59-60, assoc res supvr, 60-62, from asst prof to prof, 62-93, EMER PROF CHEM, OHIO STATE UNIV, 93-; ISABELL PROF CARBOHYDRATE CHEM, AM UNIV, 93- *Personal Data:* b Brit, Aug 31, 32; m 57; c 4. *Educ:* Univ Birmingham, BSc, 54, PhD(chem), 57, DSc, 72. *Honors & Awards:* C S Hudson Award, Am Chem Soc, 72, Morley Medal, 91; Humboldt Sr Scientist Award, 88; Haworth Medal, Royal Soc Chem, 90. *Prof Exp:* Head sci dept, Sebright Sch, Eng, 57-59. *Concurrent Pos:* Vis prof, Univ Paris, 70 & Univ Grenoble, 71, 72 & 75; chmn, Gordon Res Conf Carbohydrates, 71; mem Med Chem Study Sect, NIH; regional ed, Carbohydrate Res. *Mem:* Argentine Acad Sci; Am Chem Soc; fel Royal Soc Chem; fel Am Inst Chemists. *Res:* Carbohydrate chemistry, carbohydrate antibiotics; synthesis, reactions, stereochemistry; mechanistic and biochemical aspects; bacterial antigens. *Mailing Add:* Chem Dept Am Univ 4400 Massachusetts Ave NW Washington DC 20016-8014. *E-Mail:* carbchm@american.edu

HORTON, EDWARD S, MEDICINE, ENDOCRINOLOGY & METABOLISM. *Current Pos:* VPRES & MED DIR, JOSLIN DIABETES CTR & PROF MED, HARVARD MED SCH. *Personal Data:* b Sept 21, 32; m 55, Elizabeth Duffett; c Jane T, Edward S Jr & Thomas G. *Educ:* Dartmouth Col, AB; Harvard Med Sch, MD. *Honors & Awards:* Herman Award, Am Soc Clin Nutrit; Banting Award, Am Diabetes Asn. *Prof Exp:* Prof med & chmn, E L Amidon, Col Med, Univ Vt, 89- *Mem:* Am Diabetes Asn; Am Psychol Soc; Endocrine Soc; Am Soc Clin Nutrit. *Res:* Regulation of glucose transplant in skeletal muscle; insulin resistance; obesity; diabetes; regulation of energy metabolism. *Mailing Add:* Joslin Diabetes Ctr One Joslin Pl Boston MA 02215

HORTON, GLYN MICHAEL JOHN, animal nutrition; deceased, see previous edition for last biography

HORTON, HORACE ROBERT, BIOCHEMISTRY. *Current Pos:* from asst prof to prof, NC State Univ, 64-95, alumni distinguished prof, 79-95, William Neal Reynolds prof, 81-95, WILLIAM NEAL REYNOLDS EMER PROF, NC STATE UNIV, 96- *Personal Data:* b St Louis, Mo, Aug 26, 35; m 59, Roberta A Geehan; c Robert R, Michael E, Richard A & Rebecca A. *Educ:* Mo Sch Mines, BS, 56; Univ Mo, MS, 58, PhD(biochem), 62. *Prof Exp:* Asst instr biochem, Univ Mo, 58-59; Nat Acad Sci-Nat Res Coun fel, Brookhaven Nat Lab, 61-62, res assoc, 62-64. *Concurrent Pos:* Mem, Danforth Assoc, Carolinas Assoc, 68-; guest prof biochem, Univ Lund, 74. *Mem:* Am Soc Biochem & Molecular Biol; AAAS. *Res:* Mechanisms of enzyme action; enzyme structure as related to catalytic activity; immobilized enzyme systems; formation of disulfide bonds in proteins and peptides. *Mailing Add:* Dept Biochem NC State Univ Box 7622 Raleigh NC 27695-7622. *Fax:* 919-515-2047; *E-Mail:* hrhorton@aol.com

HORTON, HOWARD FRANKLIN, FISH BIOLOGY. *Current Pos:* from instr to assoc prof, 58-69, marine adv prof leader, 80-87, PROF FISHERIES, ORE STATE UNIV, 69- *Personal Data:* b Glendale, Calif, Sept 6, 26; m 54; c 4. *Educ:* Calif State Polytech Col, BS, 53; Ore State Univ, MS, 55, PhD(fisheries), 63. *Honors & Awards:* Outstanding Publ Res Award, Western Agr Econ Asn; Prof Excellence Publ Res Award, Am Agr Econ Asn; Award Excellence, Soc Tech Publ. *Prof Exp:* Fishery biologist, Calif Dept Fish & Game, 53 & Ore State Game Comn, 58. *Concurrent Pos:* Dir, Pond Dynamics/Aquaculture CRSP, 87- *Mem:* Am Fisheries Soc; Wildlife Soc; Am Inst Fishery Res Biol; Nat Shellfisheries Asn; Wildlife Soc. *Res:* Population dynamics; reproductive biology and ecology of fishes and invertebrates. *Mailing Add:* Dept Fisheries & Wildlife Ore State Univ Corvallis OR 97331

HORTON, JAMES HEATHMAN, TAXONOMY, BOTANY. *Current Pos:* RETIRED. *Personal Data:* b Winston-Salem, NC, Jan 9, 31; m 54; c 5. *Educ:* Univ NC, AB, 52, MA, 58, PhD(bot), 61. *Prof Exp:* Instr bot, Univ NC, 60-61; assoc prof biol, Western Carolina Univ, 61-70, head dept, 67-74, prof biol, 70-89. *Res:* Floristic research in Rowan County, North Carolina; taxonomy of Polygonella; floristics and descriptive ecology, Great Smoky Mountains. *Mailing Add:* 30 Old Longbranch Rd Cullowhee NC 28723

HORTON, JAMES WRIGHT, JR, STRUCTURAL GEOLOGY, PETROLOGY. *Current Pos:* res assoc, 78-80, asst br chief, 84-85, RES GEOLOGIST, US GEOL SURV, 80- *Personal Data:* b Anderson, SC, June 14, 50; m 73, Beverly Rose; c James F & Sarah R. *Educ:* Furman Univ, BA, 72; Univ NC, Chapel Hill, MS, 74, PhD(geol), 77. *Honors & Awards:* Spec Achievement Award, US Geol Surv, 86. *Prof Exp:* Asst prof geol, Univ Southern Maine, 77-79. *Concurrent Pos:* Adj asst prof, Univ NC, Chapel Hill, 78-79; Penrose Conf Comt, Geol Soc Am, 83-85; Sci Adv Comt, US Geol Surv, Geol Div, 88-90; assoc ed, Geol Soc Am Bull, 88-90, 91-93. *Mem:* Fel Geol Soc Am; Am Geophys Union; AAAS. *Res:* Structural, metamorphic and igneous geology of the Appalachian Piedmont and Blue Ridge; regional tectonics; fault zones. *Mailing Add:* 926A Nat Ctr US Geol Surv Reston VA 20192. *E-Mail:* whorton@usgs.gov

HORTON, JOHN, ONCOLOGY. *Current Pos:* resident, Albany Med Ctr Hosp, 60-62, Nat Cancer Inst res fel, 62-63, from instr to assoc prof, 64-74, PROF MED, ALBANY MED COL, 74- *Personal Data:* b Sheffield, Eng, June 25, 34; US citizen; c 3. *Educ:* Univ Sheffield, MB & ChB, 57. *Prof Exp:* Intern med, Albany Hosp, NY, 57-58; sr house officer, Royal Hosp, Sheffield, Eng, 58-59. *Concurrent Pos:* Consult, NY State, 65-; dir, Natalie Warren Bryant Cancer Ctr, 75-77; ECOG grant; Cancer Educ grant. *Mem:* Am Asn Cancer Educ (pres, 81); Am Asn Cancer Res; Am Soc Clin Oncol; fel Am Col Physicians; fel Am Col Gastroenterol. *Res:* Clinical treatment trials, principally in relationship to cancer chemotherapy; cancer education; cancer prevention. *Mailing Add:* Div Med Oncol Albany Med Col 47 New Scotland Ave Albany NY 12208-3412

HORTON, JOHN EDWARD, IMMUNOLOGY, PERIODONTOLOGY. *Current Pos:* PROF & CHMN, DEPT PERIODONT, COL DENT, OHIO STATE UNIV, 81- *Personal Data:* b Brockton, Mass, Dec 30, 30; m 51; c 5. *Educ:* Providence Col, BS, 52; Tufts Univ, DMD, 57; Baylor Univ, MSD, 65; George Washington Univ, MA, 78. *Prof Exp:* Vis scientist cellular immunol, Lab Microbiol & Immunol, Nat Inst Dent Res, 70-73; chief dept immunol, Inst Dent Res, Walter Reed Army Med Ctr, 73-77; assoc prof, Harvard Sch Dent Med, 80-, chmn dept periodont, 77-81. *Concurrent Pos:* Asst prof lectr oral biol, Grad Sch Arts & Sci, George Washington Univ, 72-74, assoc prof lectr, 74-76, prof lectr, Sch Hyg & Pub Health, Johns Hopkins Univ, 75-80; consult, Vet Admin Hosp, West Roxbury, 78- *Mem:* AAAS; Int Asn Dent Res; Am Acad Periodont; Am Acad Oral Med; Am Acad Oral Path. *Res:* Investigations in cell-mediated immunological mechanisms as related to the pathogenesis of periodontal disease; specifically, actions of macrophages, lymphocytes and lymphokines in the host response to inflammation and bone resorption. *Mailing Add:* Ohio State Univ Col Dent Dept Periodont 305 W 12th Ave Columbus OH 43210. *Fax:* 614-292-4612; *E-Mail:* horton.1@osu.edu

HORTON, JOSEPH ARNO, JR, ORDERED INTERMETALIC ALLOYS. *Current Pos:* RES STAFF MEM, OAK RIDGE NAT LAB, MARTIN MARIETTA ENERGY SYSTS, 79- *Personal Data:* b Johnson City, Tenn, Feb 21, 51; m 78, Linda Schiestle; c Derek, Leanna & Scott. *Educ:* Tenn Technol Univ, BS, 73; Univ Va, MS, 75, PhD(mat sci), 79. *Prof Exp:* Res asst, Res Labs Eng Sci, Univ Va, 73-79. *Mem:* Am Soc Metals; Metall Soc; Electron Micros Soc Am; Sigma Xi; Assoc Inst Mech Engrs; Mat Res Soc. *Res:* Transmission electron microscopy and microstructural studies of ordered intermetallic alloys; mechanical properties of permanent magnets. *Mailing Add:* Metals & Ceramics Div Bldg 4500S-MS6115 Oak Ridge Nat Lab PO Box 2008 Oak Ridge TN 37831-6115. *Fax:* 423-574-7659; *E-Mail:* htn@ornl.gov

HORTON, JOSEPH WILLIAM, ORGANIC CHEMISTRY, ENVIRONMENTAL CHEMISTRY. *Current Pos:* from instr to asst prof, 52-55, assoc prof, 58-71, PROF CHEM, UNIV WIS-SUPERIOR, 71- *Personal Data:* b Corpus Christi, Tex, Nov 9, 29; m 51; c 3. *Educ:* Univ Portland, BS, 50, MS, 52; Mich State Univ, PhD(chem), 60. *Prof Exp:* Res assoc chem, Reed Col, 52. *Concurrent Pos:* Fel, Kans State Univ, 66. *Mem:* Am Chem Soc; Sigma Xi. *Res:* Nitrogen heterocyclics, especially in tetrazoles; tetrazole analogs of amino acids; pharmaceuticals; amino acids in peptides; organic mechanisms; trace metals in fuels, hydrosphere and biosphere; environmental quality of lakes and streams. *Mailing Add:* 2422 Hughitt Ave Superior WI 54880

HORTON, JURETA, TRAUMA & SHOCK. *Current Pos:* Asst prof, 86-90, RES INSTR SURG, UNIV TEX HEALTH SCI CTR, 80-, ASSOC PROF, 90- *Personal Data:* b Ennis, Tex, Feb 11, 41. *Educ:* Univ Tex, PhD(cardiophysiol), 81. *Mailing Add:* Dept Gen Surgery Univ Tex Southwestern Med Ctr 5323 Harry Hines Blvd Dallas TX 75235-9031. *Fax:* 214-648-8420

HORTON, KENNETH EDWIN, PHYSICAL & NUCLEAR METALLURGY. *Current Pos:* INT SPECIALIST, US DEPT ENERGY, 78- *Personal Data:* b Buffalo, NY, Aug 14, 32; m 58; c 2. *Educ:* Rensselaer Polytech Inst, BMetE, 54; Univ Wis, MS, 55. *Prof Exp:* Res engr, Atomics Int Div, NAm Aviation, Inc, 55-57; res lab analyst, Douglas Aircraft Co,

57-60; sr metallurgist, Adv Tech Labs Div, Am-Standard Corp, 60-65; metallurgist, US Atomic Energy Comn, 65-78. *Concurrent Pos:* Asst prof, Long Beach State Col, 59-60. *Mem:* Am Soc Metals; Am Inst Mining Metall & Petrol Engrs. *Res:* Nuclear fuel elements; thermal stress fatigue; alloy development; liquid metals compatibilities; high temperature measurements. *Mailing Add:* US Dept Energy Energy Technol 1000 Independence SW Washington DC 20585

HORTON, LINDA LOUISE SCHIESTLE, EFFECTS OF RADIATION ON MATERIALS, ELECTRON MICROSCOPY. *Current Pos:* res staff mem defect mechanisms group, Metals & Ceramic Div, Oak Ridge Nat Lab, 81-86, tech asst to assoc dir phys sci, 86-88, tech asst to dir, 88-89, group leader surfaces & interfaces group, 90-91, group leader micros & microanalytical sci group, Metals & Ceramic Div, 91-93, MGR, BASIC ENERGY SCI PROG, OAK RIDGE NAT LAB, 90- *Personal Data:* b Mercer, Pa, July 13, 55; m 78, Joseph A Jr; c Derek, Leanna & Scott. *Educ:* Grove City Col, BS, 76; Univ Va, MS, 78, PhD(mat sci), 81. *Honors & Awards:* Award Distinguished Achievement Sci, Am Asn Women Sci, 87; Outstanding Young Mem Award, Am Soc Mat, 90. *Concurrent Pos:* Prin investr, Basic Energy Sci Res & Develop Tasks, 81-86 & 89-92, vchmn, Basic Energy & Sci Adv Comt, 96. *Mem:* Fel Am Soc Mat Int; Micros Soc Am; Mat Res Soc; Am Ceramics Soc. *Res:* Manages basic science programs in theoretical studies, materials characterization, radiation effects, inter-metallics and ceramic composites; applications of electron microscopy to radiation effects, diamond thin films and ion implantation. *Mailing Add:* Oak Ridge Nat Lab Bldg 4500S MS6132 PO Box 2008 Oak Ridge TN 37831-6132. *Fax:* 423-574-7659; *E-Mail:* horton11@ornl.gov

HORTON, M DUANE, CHEMICAL ENGINEERING. *Current Pos:* EXEC VPRES, MEGADIAMOND INDUST, 81- *Personal Data:* b Salt Lake City, Utah, Nov 21, 35; m 60; c 2. *Educ:* Univ Utah, BS, 57, PhD(chem eng), 61. *Prof Exp:* Chem engr, US Naval Ord Test Sta, 60-63; from asst prof to prof chem eng, Brigham Young Univ, 63-81. *Concurrent Pos:* Air Force Off Sci & Res grant, 65-74; consult, Hercules Powder Co, 65-75; co-founder, Megadiamond Corp; chmn bd, DBT Co. *Mem:* Am Inst Chem Engrs; Combustion Inst. *Res:* High pressure synthesis; combustion of pulverized coal. *Mailing Add:* 2900 Iroquois Dr Provo UT 84604

HORTON, MAURICE LEE, PLANT SCIENCE, SOIL PHYSICS. *Current Pos:* USCA CSRS NAT RES, 90- *Personal Data:* b Norman, Ind, May 23, 31; m 55; c 1. *Educ:* Purdue Univ, BS, 53, MS, 59; Iowa State Univ, PhD(soil physics), 62. *Prof Exp:* Res assoc agron, Iowa State Univ, 61-62; asst prof soil physics, Southern Ill Univ, 62-64; assoc prof soil physics, SDak State Univ, 64-74, prof soil & water resources, 74-78, prof & head plant sci dept, 78-90. *Mem:* Soil Conserv Soc Am; Am Soc Agron; Soil Sci Soc Am. *Res:* Effects of compaction on soil properties; movement of air, heat, and water through soils; soil-plant-climate relationships; soil and water resources. *Mailing Add:* USCA CSRS Nat Res Rm 807 Aerospace Washington DC 20250-2210

HORTON, OTIS HOWARD, DAIRY HUSBANDRY. *Current Pos:* RETIRED. *Personal Data:* b Des Moines, NMex, Nov 28, 17; m 46; c 2. *Educ:* NMex State Univ, BS, 41; Univ Mo, MA, 47; Univ Ill, PhD(nutrit prod), 54. *Prof Exp:* Asst dairying, Univ Mo, 46-47; asst prof dairy sci, Univ Ark, 47-50; asst prof, Univ Ill, 50-51 & 53-54; from asst prof to prof, Univ Ark, 54-70; prof dairy sci, ETex State Univ, 70-85. *Res:* Pasture quality; roughage utilization by young animals; baby calf nutrition and digestibility by ruminants. *Mailing Add:* 1200 Northwood Dr Commerce TX 75428

HORTON, PHILIP BISH, SOLID STATE PHYSICS. *Current Pos:* From asst prof to prof, 51-89, EMER PROF PHYSICS, PHILLIPS UNIV, 89- *Personal Data:* b Newark, Ohio, May 10, 26; m 58; c 2. *Educ:* Denison Univ, BS, 49; Univ Ark, MS, 54; La State Univ, PhD(physics), 64. *Mem:* Am Asn Physics Teachers. *Res:* Galvanomagnetic and thermomagnetic transport phenomena in soilds; theoretical magnetotransport. *Mailing Add:* 117 Sammie Dr Hot Springs National Park AR 71913

HORTON, RALPH M, METALLURGY. *Current Pos:* MGR METALL, DIAMOND TECHNOL CTR, HUGHES-CHRISTENSEN INC, 82- *Personal Data:* b Salt Lake City, Utah, Oct 4, 34; m 61; c 6. *Educ:* Univ Utah, BS, 57, PhD(metall), 61. *Prof Exp:* From asst prof to assoc prof, Metall Dept, Wash State Univ, 61-75; supvr, Mat Lab, Idaho Nat Eng Lab, 75-81. *Concurrent Pos:* Vis prof, Hanford Ed Develop Labs, 63, 64 & 73; res trainee high pressure physics & chem, Brigham Young Univ, 71. *Mem:* Am Soc Metals; Am Powder Metall Inst; Soc Petrol Engrs. *Res:* Oxidation and corrosion; materials for coal gasification equipment; industrial diamond utilization. *Mailing Add:* 5184 Spring Clover Dr Murray UT 84123. *Fax:* 801-488-4452

HORTON, RICHARD, MEDICINE, PHYSIOLOGY. *Current Pos:* assoc prof, 69-73, PROF MED & CHIEF SECT ENDOCRINOL, SCH MED, UNIV SOUTHERN CALIF, 73- *Personal Data:* b New York, NY, May 3, 32; c 2. *Educ:* Univ Wash, BA, 54, MD, 58. *Prof Exp:* Intern med, Swed Hosp, Seattle, 58-59; resident, Vet Admin Hosp & Univ Calif, Los Angeles, 59-61; fel, Med Ctr, Univ Calif, San Francisco, 61-63, NIH spec res fel, Worcester Found Exp Biol, 63-65; asst prof med, Med Sch, Univ Calif, Los Angeles, 65-67; assoc prof med & physiol, Univ Ala, 67-68. *Concurrent Pos:* NIH career develop award, 65-67; Am Cancer Soc grant, 65-70; NIH grant, 65-; prof & div head, Univ Ala, 74-; ed, Jour Clin Endocrine, 78-93. *Mem:* AAAS; Am Fedn Clin Res; Endocrine Soc; NY Acad Sci; Am Soc Clin Invest; Am Asn Physicians. *Res:* Aldosterone pathophysiology and the study of sex hormone metabolism in man; androgen physiology; prostaglandens, renin and the kidney. *Mailing Add:* Dept Med & Endocrinol Univ Southern Calif Med Ctr 1200 N State St Los Angeles CA 90033-4525. *Fax:* 213-226-2652

HORTON, RICHARD E, ELECTRICAL ENGINEERING. *Current Pos:* Instr electronics technol, 63-67, asst prof electronics technol & elec eng, 67-68, asst prof, 68-80, ASSOC PROF ELEC ENG, IOWA STATE UNIV, 80- *Personal Data:* b Marshalltown, Iowa, Feb 5, 40; m 62; c 1. *Educ:* Iowa State Univ, BS, 62, MS, 63, PhD(elec eng), 67. *Mem:* Inst Elec & Electronics Engrs. *Res:* Estimation theory in random processes; simulation of random processes; data communications. *Mailing Add:* Dept Elec Eng Iowa State Univ Coover Hall Ames IA 50011

HORTON, RICHARD GREENFIELD, physiology; deceased, see previous edition for last biography

HORTON, ROBERT, JR, SOIL PHYSICS. *Current Pos:* ASST PROF SOIL PHYSICS, IOWA STATE UNIV, 81- *Personal Data:* b Ger, July 9, 54; US citizen; m 75; c 2. *Educ:* Tex A&M Univ, BS, 75, MS, 77; NMex State Univ, PhD(soil physics), 81. *Prof Exp:* Trainee soil scientist, Soil Conserv Serv, 75; asst instr soil, Tex A&M Univ, 76, asst instr res, 76-77; asst instr res, NMex State Univ, 77-81. *Mem:* Soil Sci Soc Am; Am Soc Agron. *Res:* Heat and/or mass transport in soil; irrigation; drainage; pollution; waste disposal; nutrient uptake; soil temperature; tillage. *Mailing Add:* 3618 Oakland St Ames IA 50010

HORTON, ROBERT A, JR, SEDIMENTARY PETROLOGY, GROUNDWATER GEOCHEMISTRY. *Current Pos:* PROF, DEPT PHYSICS & GEOL, CALIF STATE UNIV, BAKERSFIELD, 84-, CHAIR, 92- *Personal Data:* b Hackensack, NJ, Aug 18, 51. *Educ:* State Univ NY, BS, 73; Univ Tenn, MS, 77, Colo Sch Mines, PhD(geol), 84. *Prof Exp:* Geologist, Getty Minerals Co, 76-77; sr geologist, Bendix Field Eng Corp, 77-79; geochemist, Anaconda Minerals Corp, 82-83. *Concurrent Pos:* Secy, San Joaquin Geol Soc, 86-88, vpres, 88-89, pres-elect, 89-90, vpres, 90-91; deleg, Am Asn Petrol Geologists, 91-; vpres, Pac Sect, Soc Sedimentary Geol, 94-95. *Mem:* Geol Soc Am; Am Asn Petrol Geologists; Soc Sedimentary Geologists; Nat Asn Geosci Teachers. *Res:* Investigation of diagenetic processes in arkosic and volcanolithic sandstones and development of porosity in these rocks; investigation of dolomitization in modern and ancient limestones; investigation of groundwater geochemical evolution. *Mailing Add:* Dept Physics & Geol Calif State Univ Bakersfield CA 93311

HORTON, ROBERT CARLTON, MINERAL ECONOMICS & POLICY. *Current Pos:* dir, Ctr Strategic Mat Res & Policy Study, 87-90, assoc dean, 88-90, EMER ASSOC DEAN, MACKAY SCH MINES, UNIV NEV, RENO, 90- *Personal Data:* b Tonopah, Nev, July 25, 26; m 50, Beverly J Burhans; c 3. *Educ:* Univ Nev, BSc, 49. *Hon Degrees:* DSc, Univ Nev, 86. *Prof Exp:* Field asst geol, US Geol Surv, 49-50; geol consult, 51-53; mining engr econ geol, Nev Bur Mines, Univ Nev, Reno, 56-65, assoc dir, 65-66; pres, Nev Geoserv Inc, 66-76; regional geologist, Bendix Field Eng Corp, 76-77, dir, Geol Div, 77-81; dir, US Bur Mines, Dept Interior, 81-87. *Concurrent Pos:* Mem, Nev Pollution Control Hearing Bd, 66-68 & Gov Adv Mining Bd, Nev, 66-73. *Mem:* Am Inst Mining, Metall & Petrol Engrs; Soc Econ Geologists; Mining & Metall Soc Am. *Res:* Mineral deposits of Nevada; development and utilization of geothermal resources; mineral economics and policy. *Mailing Add:* 654 W Riverview Circle Reno NV 89509

HORTON, ROBERT LOUIS, PHYSICAL CHEMISTRY, ENHANCED OIL RECOVERY. *Current Pos:* SR RES ASSOC, TEXACO, 90- *Personal Data:* b Shreveport, La, Apr 28, 44; m 66; c 2. *Educ:* Rice Univ, BA, 66; Univ Calif, Berkeley, PhD(phys chem), 71. *Prof Exp:* Asst prof chem & physics, La State Univ, Alexandria, 71-75; res chemist, Phillips Petrol Co, 75-79, sr res chemist, Res & Develop Dept, 79-82; group leader II, BP Am, 82-85; enhanced oil recovery supvr, OXY USA, 85-90. *Concurrent Pos:* Fel chem, Rice Univ, 73-75. *Mem:* Sigma Xi; Soc Petrol Engrs; Can Inst Mining; Gas Processors Asn; Soc Mining Engrs. *Res:* Enhanced oil recovery; alternative fuels; uranium extraction and refining; aqueous ionic/polyelectrolytic equilibria; reactions of non-aqueous polyelectrolytes; thermophysical properties of mixtures; phase equilibria; kinetics; gaseous ionic equilibria; ion-molecule reactions. *Mailing Add:* 301 Doug Dr Lafayette LA 70508-6305. *Fax:* 713-954-6911

HORTON, ROBERT LOUIS, ORGANIC CHEMISTRY. *Current Pos:* RETIRED. *Personal Data:* b Miami, Fla, Sept 2, 20; m 41; c 1. *Educ:* Cornell Univ, BA, 47, PhD(chem), 51. *Prof Exp:* Asst analytical chem, Cornell Univ, 47-50; res chemist, Pharmaceut Res Dept, Am Cyanamid Co, 50-54, chief chemist, Pharmaceut Prod Dept, 54-56, group leader, Res & Develop Dept, 56-67, proj leader elastomers prod, 67-83. *Mem:* Am Chem Soc. *Res:* Antimetabolites; anticoagulants; tranquilizers; organic process research and development; antioxidents; ultraviolet adsorbers; synthetic polymers. *Mailing Add:* PO Box 132 Bound Brook NJ 08805-0132

HORTON, ROGER FRANCIS, PLANT GROWTH REGULATORS, AQUATIC AND AMPHIBIOUS PLANTS. *Current Pos:* Fel, 67-69, asst prof, 69-74, ASSOC PROF PLANT PHYSIOL, UNIV GUELPH, 74- *Personal Data:* b Chislehurst, Eng, June 22, 43; Can citizen; m 66, Josephine Phillips; c Simon, James & Matthew. *Educ:* Univ Col Wales, BSc(Hons), 64; Oxford Univ, DPhil, 67. *Concurrent Pos:* Vis scientist, Univ Cambridge, UK, 76. *Mem:* Can Soc Plant Physiologists (secy, 80-81); Am Soc Plant Physiologists. *Res:* Role of plant growth regulations in the growth of aquatic and amphibious plants; roles of abscitic acid, ethylene and j asmorabes in plant growth and development. *Mailing Add:* Dept Bot Univ Guelph Guelph ON N1G 2W1 Can

HORTON, THOMAS EDWARD, JR, FLUID MECHANICS, APPLIED MECHANICS. *Current Pos:* assoc prof & res engr, 66-71, PROF & RES ENGR MECH ENG, UNIV MISS, 71- *Personal Data:* b Houston, Tex, Jan 12, 35; m 63; c 2. *Educ:* Univ Tex, BS, 57, PhD(eng mech), 64; Stanford Univ, MS, 58. *Prof Exp:* Jr mech engr, Shell Develop Co, 58-59; teaching asst eng mech, Univ Tex, 60-62; sr res engr, Jet Propulsion Lab, Calif Inst Technol, 62-66. *Concurrent Pos:* Consult, Jet Propulsion Lab, Calif Inst Technol, 66-75, numerous govt & indust orgns, 68-; dir laser sci, US Army High Energy Laser Lab, 75-76; ed, Am Inst Aeronaut & Astronaut Progress Series, 81; chmn, Am Inst Aeronaut & Astronaut Thermophysic Tech Comt, 82-84; mem, Am Soc Mech Engrs Heat Transfer Div Tech Comt, 72-87. *Mem:* Am Soc Mech Engrs; Am Inst Aeronaut & Astronaut; Am Phys Soc; Sigma Xi (pres, 75). *Res:* Unsteady flow and acoustics, non-equilibrium phenomena, radiative transfer, and thermochemistry of high temperature gases. *Mailing Add:* 209 St Andrews Circle Oxford MS 38655-2518

HORTON, THOMAS ROSCOE, MATHEMATICS-NUMBER THEORY, MANAGEMENT. *Current Pos:* UNIV ADV, STETSON UNIV, 91- *Personal Data:* b Ft Pierce, Fla, Nov 17, 26; m 47; c Susan, Jean & Marilyn. *Educ:* Stetson Univ, BS, 49; Univ Fla, MS, 50, PhD(math), 54. *Hon Degrees:* LLD, Pace Univ, 76; DLitt, Univ Charleston, 80; DHum, Stetson Univ, 82. *Honors & Awards:* Distinguished Serv Award, Int Coun Innovation in Higher Educ. *Prof Exp:* Asst headmaster, Bolles Sch, Fla, 50-52; instr, Univ Fla, 53-54; appl sci res, IBM Corp, 54-55, mgr, Space Comput Ctr, 56, mgr spec systs mkt, 57-59, systs mgr intermediates systs, 59, mgr systs develop, Fed Systs Div, 59-64, vpres, Systs Develop Div, 64-67, dir, Univ Rels, 68-82; pres, Am Mgt Asn, 82-91. *Concurrent Pos:* Sr vpres, Nat Coun Philanthropy, 73-80; mem vis comt ling & philos, Mass Inst Technol, 71-82; trustee, Pace Univ, 75-, Am Grad Sch Int Mgt, 82-; chmn, Asn Gov Bds Univs & Cols, 82-83; dir, Mastery Educ Corp, 82-; dir, Am Precision Indust, 89-94; Stanhome Corp, 91-; chair, Kids Voting USA, 93- *Mem:* AAAS; Am Math Soc; Math Asn Am; Inst Elec & Electronics Engrs; fel Acad Mgt; fel Int Acad Mgt. *Res:* Number theory, especially quadratic forms; high-speed computational techniques; computer systems design; technical management; education administration; author. *Mailing Add:* 825 Pine Tree Ct DeLand FL 32724

HORTON, WALTER JAMES, synthetic organic chemistry; deceased, see previous edition for last biography

HORTON, WILLIAM A, PEDIATRICS. *Current Pos:* DIR RES, SHRINERS HOSP, PORTLAND, 94- *Prof Exp:* Prof med & pediat, Health Sci Ctr, Univ Tex, 89-94. *Mailing Add:* Shriners Hosp 3101 SW Sam Jackson Pkwy Portland OR 97201

HORVAT, ROBERT EMIL, ENVIRONMENTAL EDUCATION, ENERGY EDUCATION. *Current Pos:* from asst prof to assoc prof, 73-89, CHMN, DEPT EARTH SCI & EDUC, STATE UNIV NY COL BUFFALO, 78-81 & 86-, PROF, 89- *Personal Data:* b Chicago, Ill, Nov 4, 40. *Educ:* Valparaiso Univ, BS, 62; Univ Kans, MS, 69; Univ Wis, Madison, PhD(sci & environ educ), 74. *Prof Exp:* Instr chem, State Univ NY, Oneonta, 66-69; res asst, Univ Wis, Madison, 70-73. *Concurrent Pos:* Panel reviewer, NSF, 77-78; consult individualized sci instruct syst, 74-78 & proj for energy-enriched curriculum, 80-81; proj assoc, NY Sci, Technol Soc Educ Proj, 82-; coop sci educator, Chem Educ Prog Pub Understanding, 90- *Mem:* Asn Educ Teachers Sci; Nat Asn Sci Technol & Soc; Nat Sci Teachers Asn; AAAS. *Res:* Science, technology & society cirriculum development/dissemination; energy and environmental science curriculum development, kindergarten through 12th grade. *Mailing Add:* Dept Earth Sci & Sci Educ Buffalo State Col 1300 Elmwood Ave Buffalo NY 14222-1095

HORVATH, CSABA GYULA, BIOTECHNOLOGY, SEPARATION SCIENCE. *Current Pos:* res assoc, Yale Univ, 64-70, lectr, 67-72, assoc prof, 70-75, from assoc prof to prof eng & appl sci, 72-81, prof chem eng, 81-93, chmn, 87-93, LLEWELLIN WEST JR, PROF CHEM ENG, YALE UNIV, 93- *Personal Data:* b Szolnok, Hungary, Jan 25, 30; US citizen; m 63; c Donatella & Katalin. *Educ:* Budapest Tech Univ, Dipl chem eng, 52; Univ Frankfurt, DrPhil, 63. *Hon Degrees:* MA, Yale Univ, 79; Dr, Budapest Tech Univ, 86. *Honors & Awards:* S Dal Nogare Award, 78; M Tswett Award, 80 & Medal, 82; Humboldt US Sr Scientist Award, 82; Chromatography Award, Am Chem Soc, 83; Merit Award, NIH, 93; AP Martin Gold Medal, Chromatographic Soc. *Prof Exp:* Asst prof chem technol, Budapest Tech Univ, 52-56; res fel, Mass Gen Hosp & Harvard Univ, 63-64. *Mem:* Am Chem Soc; Inst Food Technol; fel Am Inst Chem Engr; Deutsch Gesellschaft fuer Chemisches Apparatewesen; Hungarian Acad Sci; Hungarian Chem Soc; fel, Am Inst Med Biomed Eng. *Res:* Biochemical separations; high performance liquid chromatography; electrophoresis biotechnology, enzyme engineering; separation science; biochemical engineering; biomedical engineering, capillary electrochromatography, ultrapurification of biopolymers. *Mailing Add:* 41 Temple Ct New Haven CT 06511. *Fax:* 203-432-4360; *E-Mail:* csaba.horvath@yale.edu

HORVATH, DONALD JAMES, ANIMAL NUTRITION. *Current Pos:* RETIRED. *Personal Data:* b Newark, NJ, Sept 8, 29; m 53; c 4. *Educ:* Rutgers Univ, BS, 51, MS, 54; Cornell Univ, PhD, 57. *Prof Exp:* From asst prof to assoc prof, WVa Univ, 57-69, prof animal nutrit & physiol, 69- *Concurrent Pos:* Co-chmn subcomt, Geochem Environ Rel Health & Dis, Nat Acad Sci. *Mem:* Am Soc Animal Sci; Soc Environ Geochem & Health. *Res:* Swine nutrition; hypomagnesemic tetany of ruminants; minor element nutrition; environmental geochemistry and health. *Mailing Add:* Div Animal Sci WVa Univ Box 6108 Morgantown WV 26506-6108

HORVATH, FRED ERNEST, NEUROPHYSIOLOGY. *Current Pos:* from asst prof to assoc prof, 66-81, PROF PHYSIOL, NY MED COL, 81- *Personal Data:* b Pittsburgh, Pa, Nov 26, 24; m 87. *Educ:* US Naval Acad, BS, 47; Univ Mich, PhD(physiol, psychol), 61. *Prof Exp:* Res asst psychol, Ment Health Res Inst, Univ Mich, 56-60; NIH fel neurophysiol, Univ Calif, Los Angeles, 60-61, res asst neurophysiol, 61-64; NIH spec fel, Paris, 64-66. *Mem:* AAAS; Am Physiol Soc; Soc Neurosci. *Res:* Caudate-thalamic-cortical spindles; termination of convulsant seizure activity; regulation of vasopressin release. *Mailing Add:* Dept Physiol NY Med Col 95 Grasslands Rd Valhalla NY 10595-1600

HORVATH, JOHN MICHAEL, MATHEMATICAL ANALYSIS. *Current Pos:* from asst prof to assoc prof, 57-63, PROF MATH, UNIV MD, COLLEGE PARK, 63- *Personal Data:* b Budapest, Hungary, July 30, 24; US citizen; m 53, Teresa Low; c Ann. *Educ:* Univ Budapest, PhD(math physics), 47. *Prof Exp:* Attache res math, Nat Ctr Sci Res, Paris, France, 48-51; prof math, Univ of the Andes, 51-57. *Concurrent Pos:* Vis prof, Univ Nancy, 63-64 & Univ Paris, 72-73. *Mem:* Am Math Soc; Math Asn Am; corresp mem Span Acad Sci. *Res:* Functional analysis, especially topological vector spaces, Schwartz distributions and their applications. *Mailing Add:* Dept Math Univ Md College Park MD 20742. *E-Mail:* john_m_horvath@umail.umd.edu

HORVATH, KALMAN, QUALITY ASSURANCE MANAGEMENT, MICROBIOLOGY. *Current Pos:* qual assurance microbiol mgr, Cutter Biol, 76-92, QUAL ASSURANCE AUDITS & STAND MGR, BIOTECHNOL/PHARMACEUT DIV, MILES INC, 92- *Personal Data:* b Gyor, Hungary, Feb 13, 40; US citizen; m 64; c 2. *Educ:* Univ Calif, Los Angeles, BA, 63, MA, 65; Rice Univ, PhD(biol), 69. *Prof Exp:* Asst prof biol, Tex A&M Univ, 68-73; sr pharmacologist, Am McGaw Labs, 74-75; biol lab mgr, Cutter Labs, Inc, 75-76. *Mem:* Sigma Xi; Parenteral Drug Asn. *Res:* Resistance of microorganisms to industrial sterilization; environmental microbiology; environmental control for sterile drug manufacture; sterility, pyrogenicity, toxicity studies on MAb genetic engineered products; development of test methods in microbiology, biochemistry, immunology, chemistry. *Mailing Add:* 1166 Moccasin Ct Clayton CA 94517. *Fax:* 510-420-5143

HORVATH, RALPH S(TEVE), ELECTRONICS ENGINEERING, MICROCOMPUTER APPLICATIONS. *Current Pos:* from instr to asst prof, 62-72, ASSOC PROF ELEC ENG, MICH TECHNOL UNIV, 73- *Personal Data:* b Scranton, Pa, Feb 9, 36; m 82; c 1. *Educ:* Mich Technol Univ, BS, 60; NY Univ, MS, 62; Worcester Polytech Inst, PhD(elec eng), 68. *Honors & Awards:* Ralph R Teetor Award, Soc Automotive Engrs, 81. *Prof Exp:* Mem tech staff, Bell Tel Labs, 60-62. *Concurrent Pos:* Pacemaker consult, Medico Italia, Padua, Italy, 77-78; continuing educ consult, Gen Motors Inst, 78-; mem conf comt, Inst Life, Paris, 72-; lectr, Univ Md-Europe, 84-85; vis prof, Darling Downs Inst Advan Educ, Toowoomba, Queensland, Australia, 88; vis assoc prof, Univ Auckland, 92-93. *Mem:* Inst Elec & Electronics Engrs; Int Inst Arson Investigators; Sigma Xi; Int Asn Mini & Micro Comput. *Res:* Electronic circuits; computer applications in real time; neurophysiology; heart pacemaker design; continuing education (in-plant training) in microprocessor applications in industrial control. *Mailing Add:* Dept Elec Eng Mich Technol Univ Houghton MI 49931

HORVATH, STEVEN MICHAEL, PHYSIOLOGY & TOXICOLOGY, BIOMEDICAL ENGINEERING. *Current Pos:* prof physiol & biomed eng & dir, Inst Environ Stress, 61-86, PROF PHYSIOL & BIOMED ENG & DIR, NEUROSCI RES INST, UNIV CALIF, SANTA BARBARA, 86- *Personal Data:* b Cleveland, Ohio, Sept 15, 11; m 40; c 3. *Educ:* Miami Univ, BS, 34, MS, 35; Ohio State Univ, MS, 39; Harvard Univ, PhD(physiol),42. *Prof Exp:* Asst physiol & zool, Miami Univ, 31-35; asst physiol, Col Med, Ohio State Univ, 35-37; instr physiol & zool, Miami Univ, 37-39; asst physiol, Fatigue Lab, Harvard Univ, 39-42; dir res & asst prof phys med, Grad Sch Med, Univ Pa, 46-48, assoc prof, 48-49; from assoc prof to prof physiol, Col Med, Univ Iowa, 49-51, actg dir, Inst Geront, 51-58; head dept physiol, Div Res, Lankenau Hosp, 58-61. *Concurrent Pos:* Asst, Woods Hole Marine Biol Lab, 36; res dir, Metrop State Hosp, Mass, 39-42; tutor, Harvard Univ, 40-42; assoc prof, Sch Med, Univ Pa, 58-61; consult, Off Surgeon, US Army, EPA & var industs. *Mem:* AAAS; Am Col Cardiol; Am Heart Asn; Am Physiol Soc; Am Pub Health Asn. *Res:* Environmental, stress, cardiovascular and respiratory physiology; gerontology; endocrinology; exercise biochemistry. *Mailing Add:* Environ Stress Lab 5210 Austin Rd Santa Barbara CA 93111. *Fax:* 805-682-3332

HORVATH, THOMAS B, PSYCHIATRY. *Current Pos:* Chief staff, Vet Admin Med Ctr, Dept Vet Affairs, 89, clin dir psychiat, Bronx Vet Admin Med Ctr, chief psychiat, dir, Mental Health & Behav Sci Serv, 94-95, CHIEF STRATEGIC HEALTH CARE GROUP, DEPT VET AFFAIRS, 95- *Personal Data:* b Hungary; nat US; m, Csilla; c Andrea & Kristine. *Educ:* Univ Melbourne, Australia, MD, 65; Am Bd Psychiat & Neurol, dipl, 78. *Concurrent Pos:* Assoc vpres clin affairs & prof psychiat, State Univ NY, 89-, assoc dean, 92-94; chief staff, NPort Vet Admin Med Ctr, 92-94. *Mem:* Fel Royal Australian Col Physicians. *Res:* Psychobiological study substance abuse; clinical assessment in neuropsychiatry; spirituality in medicine; resource allocation; quality management in health care; impact health care reform on mental health services; author of numerous articles. *Mailing Add:* Dept Vet Affairs Ment Health Strategic Health Group 810 Vermont Ave NW Washington DC 20420. *Fax:* 202-273-9069

HORVATH, WILLIAM JOHN, BIOPHYSICS. *Current Pos:* prof health systs, 74-88, RES SCIENTIST, MENT HEALTH RES INST, UNIV MICH, ANN ARBOR, 58-, EMER PROF HEALTH SYSTS, 88- *Personal Data:* b New York, NY, Sept 13, 17; m 63, Rebecca S Badger; c Susan G & John S.

Educ: City Col New York, BS, 36; NY Univ, MS, 38, PhD(physics), 40. *Honors & Awards:* Naval Ord Develop Award, 45; Presidential Cert of Merit, 47; Kimball Medal, Opers Res Soc, 77. *Prof Exp:* Instr physics, NY Univ, 39; instr, Polytech Inst Brooklyn, 40; physicist, Bur Ord, US Dept Navy, 40-43, consult, Nat Defense Res Comt & Off Sci Res & Develop, USN, 43-45, analyst, Div Indust Co-op, Mass Inst Technol, 46-48, dept dir, Opers Eval Group, US Navy, 48-49, mem rev bd, Weapons Systs Eval Group, Joint Chiefs of Staff, 49-52, consult, 52-55; sect head dept med & biol physics, Airborne Instrument Lab, NY, 55-58. *Concurrent Pos:* Mem health serv res study sect, NIH, 62-66, mem health care systs study sect, 68-70. *Mem:* Am Phys Soc; Opers Res Soc Am (vpres, 55); fel AAAS; fel Am Pub Health Asn; Royal Soc Health; Sigma Xi. *Res:* Nuclear physics; slow neutron absorption; electricity and magnetism; degaussing; cryogenics; properties of liquid helium; medical physics; mathematical models of behavior; health care research. *Mailing Add:* Ment Health Res Inst Univ Mich Ann Arbor MI 48109

HORVE, LESLIE A, RHEOLOGY OF ELASTOMERS, OIL SEAL FUNCTION & DESIGN. *Current Pos:* appln engr, 67-69, mgr res & develop, 69-71, mgr prod eng, 72-75, vpres technol, OE Div, 75-83, vpres opers, Replacement Div, 83-85, vpres corp technol & qual assurance, 85-86, vpres technol, OE Group, Corp Staff, 86-90, SR VPRES, INT OPERS, CR INDUSTS, 90- *Personal Data:* b Decatur, Ill, Dec 5, 38; m 60; c 4. *Educ:* Univ Ill, Urbana, BS, 60, MS, 64; Midwest Col Eng, Prof Degree Mech Eng, 71; Keller Grad Sch Mgt, MBA, 79. *Hon Degrees:* Dr Eng, Midwest Col Eng, 73. *Honors & Awards:* Walter D Hobson Award, Am Soc Lubrication Engrs, 71. *Prof Exp:* Anal engr, Pratt & Whitney Aircraft, United Technologies, 64-67. *Concurrent Pos:* Instr, Midwest Col Eng, 69- & Judson Col, 70-75; chmn, Seals Tech Comt, Rubber Mfrs Asn, 82-83 & Soc Automotive Engrs, 82- *Mem:* Soc Automotive Engrs; Rubber Mfrs Asn; Am Soc Lubrication Eng; Am Chem Soc. *Res:* Function of elastomeric sealing devices; rheology of elastomers. *Mailing Add:* 515 Rue Chamonix Barrington IL 60010

HORVITZ, DANIEL GOODMAN, STATISTICS, SOCIAL SURVEYS. *Current Pos:* RETIRED. *Personal Data:* b New Bedford, Mass, Mar 4, 21; m 45, Shirley Gordon; c Gary, Paul & Barbara. *Educ:* Mass State Col, BS, 43; Iowa State Col, PhD(statist), 53. *Prof Exp:* Assoc scientist, Manhattan Proj, Univ Calif, 46; asst statist, Iowa State Col, 46-49, instr, 49-51; asst prof biostatist, Grad Sch Pub Health, Univ Pittsburgh, 51-53; assoc prof statist, NC State Col, 53-56; vpres, A J Wood Res Corp, 56-60; vis prof statist, Univ Rangoon-Univ Chicago Proj, 60-62; group leader, Res Triangle Inst, 62-66, dep dir, Statist Res Div, 66-71, dir, Ctr Pop Res & Serv, 71-72; prof biostatist, Sch Pub Health, Univ NC, Chapel Hill, 73-74; vpres statist sci, Res Triangle Inst, 74-83, exec vpres, 83-88, distinguished inst scientist, 89-91. *Concurrent Pos:* Lectr, Villanova Univ, 58-60; adj prof statist, NC State Univ, 62-72; vis prof statist health sci, Univ NC, 63-64; consult, Nat Ctr Health Statist, 67-69 & 73; mem, Nat Defense Exec Res, 67-70; assoc ed, J Am Statist Asn, 69-71; mem adv comt to Bur Census, Am Statist Asn, 69-72 & 80-85; consult, Ctr Pop Res, NIH, 72-74; adj prof biostatist, Univ NC, 74-91; chmn, Panel Statist Family Assistance & Related Progs, Comt Nat Statist, Nat Res Coun, 80-82, Panel Qual Control Family Assistance Progs, 86-87, Panel on Nat Health Care Surv, 90-91; mem bd, Int Comp Studies in Educ, Nat Acad Sci, 90-93. *Mem:* Fel AAAS; fel Am Statist Asn (vpres, 85-87); Int Asn Surv Statist; Int Statist Inst; Nat Inst Statist Sci (treas, 91-). *Res:* Demographic simulation models; sample survey methods; measurement error research; social program evaluation; demographic measurement designs; health care expenditure surveys; randomized responses. *Mailing Add:* 3115 Eton Rd Raleigh NC 27608. *E-Mail:* dgh@rcc.rti.org

HORVITZ, HOWARD ROBERT, DEVELOPMENTAL GENETICS, BEHAVIORAL GENETICS. *Current Pos:* From asst prof to assoc prof, 78-86, PROF BIOL, MASS INST TECHNOL, 86-, INVESTR, HOWARD HUGHES MED INST, 88- *Personal Data:* b Chicago, Ill, May 8, 47; m 93, Martha Constantine Paton; c Alexandra. *Educ:* Mass Inst Technol, SB(math) & SB(econ), 68; Harvard Univ, MA, 72, PhD(biol), 74. *Honors & Awards:* Spencer Award in Neurobiol, Columbia Univ, 86; Warren Triennial Prize, Mass Gen Hosp, 86; US Steel Found Award in Molecular Biol, Nat Acad Sci, 88; VD Mattia Award, Roche Inst Molecular Biol, 93; Hans Sigrist Award, Univ Bern, 94; Charles A Dana Award Pioneering Achievements in Health, 95; Ciba-Drew Award Biomed Sci, 96. *Concurrent Pos:* Res fel, Muscular Dystrophy Asn, 74-77; NIH res career develop award, 81-86; assoc prof biol, Whitehead Inst Career Develop, 82-85; adv, Dept Biochem & Molecular Biol, Harvard Univ, 85-90 & Cold Spring Harbor Lab, 84-; mem, Sci Adv Bd, Hereditary Dis Found, 87- & Comt on Scholarly Commun with China, People's Rep of China, US Nat Acad Sci, 87-; neurobiologist, Mass Gen Hosp, 89-, geneticist, 89-; lectr, Harvey Soc, 89; mem sci rev comt, Amyotrophic Lateral Sclerosis Asn, 90- *Mem:* Nat Acad Sci; Soc Develop Biol; Soc Nematologists; Soc Neurosci; Am Soc Cell Biol; Am Soc Microbiol; Am Asn Cancer Res; fel AAAS; Genetics Soc Am (vpres, 94, pres, 95); fel Am Acad Arts & Scis; Am Soc Microbiol. *Res:* Developmental and behavioral genetics of the nematode caenorhabditis elegans, with particular emphasis on the cellular and genetic mechanisms utilized to control cell lineage and cell fate; author of numerous publications. *Mailing Add:* Mass Inst Technol 77 Mass Ave Rm 68-425 Cambridge MA 02139

HORWATH, EWALD, PSYCHIATRIC EPIDEMIOLOGY. *Current Pos:* Asst clin prof, 85-92, ASSOC CLIN PROF PSYCHIAT, COLUMBIA UNIV, 92- *Personal Data:* b Koflach, Austria, Apr 12, 53; US citizen; m 96, Glaucia K Santos; c Juliana & Elena. *Educ:* Univ Chicago, BA, 75; Univ Chicago Pritzker Sch Med, MD, 79; Columbia Univ Sch Pub Health, MSc, 88. *Concurrent Pos:* Dir intensive care unit, NY State Psychiat Inst, 85-, pres med staff orgn, 91- *Mem:* Am Psychiat Asn; Asn Clin Psychosocial Res; Asn Res Nerv Ment Dis. *Res:* Public health issues in psychiatry; epidemiology of mood and anxiety disorders and the epidemiology of human immunodeficiency virus in the seriously mentally ill. *Mailing Add:* 722 W 168th St New York NY 10032

HORWEDEL, CHARLES RICHARD, physical metallurgy, for more information see previous edition

HORWITT, MAX KENNETH, NUTRITION, BIOCHEMISTRY. *Current Pos:* EMER PROF BIOCHEM & INTERNAL MED, DIV GERIATRIC MED, SCH MED, ST LOUIS UNIV, 77-; CONSULT NUTRIT SCI, 77- *Personal Data:* b New York, NY, Mar 21, 08; m 33, 74, Mildred W; c Ruth (Singer), Mary (Goldman), Judy (Kraner), Charles W & Sharon (Soltman). *Educ:* Dartmouth Col, BA, 30; Yale Univ, PhD(physiol chem), 35; Am Bd Clin Chem, dipl; Am Bd Nutrit, dipl. *Honors & Awards:* Osborne & Mendel Award, Am Inst Nutrit, 61. *Prof Exp:* Asst physiol chem, Sch Med, Yale Univ, 32-35, lead res fel, 35-37; assoc biochem, Univ Ill Col Med, 40-43, from asst prof to prof, 43-68. *Concurrent Pos:* Dir biochem res lab, Elgin State Hosp, 37-59, dir, L B Mendel Res Lab, 60-67; mem, Comts Food & Nutrit Bd, Nat Res Coun, 42-85, consult, 66-; mem study sect metab & nutrit, NIH, 55-58, mem study sect psychopharmacol, 59-63; mem WHO expert group vitamin requirements, Food & Agr Orgn, 65-67; consult human nutrit, USDA, 66-67; dir div res serv, Ill Dept Ment Health, 66-67; vis prof nutrit, Univ Hawaii, 66; consult med, Rush Med Sch, 66-84; field dir, Anemia & Malnutrit Res Ctr, Chiangmai Med Sch, Thailand, 68-69; mem, Comt Dietary Allowances, Nat Res Coun, 80-85; chmn, 81-83, mem, Inst Review Bd, St Louis Univ, 83-89. *Mem:* Fel AAAS; fel Am Soc Biol Chemists; fel Am Inst Nutrit; Am Soc Clin Nutrit; Soc Exp Biol & Med; fel Am Inst Chemists; fel Geront Soc. *Res:* Evaluation of nutritional requirements in collaboration with the National Research Council; use of vitamin E as an antioxidant supplement to minimize oxidation of tissue lipids. *Mailing Add:* Div Geriat Med Dept Internal Med St Louis Univ Sch Med St Louis MO 63104. *Fax:* 314-997-4508

HORWITZ, ALAN FREDRICK, CELL BIOLOGY, DEVELOPMENTAL BIOLOGY. *Current Pos:* dir, Cellular & Molecular Biol Training Prog, 87-93, head, Dept Cell & Struct Biol, 87-95, PROF CELL BIOL, UNIV ILL, URBANA-CHAMPAIGN, 87- *Personal Data:* b Minneapolis, Minn, Oct 26, 44; m 72, Carole Rosen; c Jeremy J & Rachel T. *Educ:* Univ Wis-Madison, BA, 66; Stanford Univ PhD(biophys), 69. *Hon Degrees:* MA, Univ Pa, 78. *Honors & Awards:* Merit Award, Nat Inst Gen Med Sci; W D Stroud Estab Investr, Am Heart Asn. *Prof Exp:* NIH fel, Univ Calif, Berkeley, 70-73; res assoc cell biol, Bio Ctr, Univ Basel, 73-74; from asst prof to prof biochem, Univ Pa Med Sch, 74-87. *Concurrent Pos:* Mem, Pub Policy Comt, Am Soc Cell Biol, 87-; ed, J Cell Biol, 88- & J Cell Sci, 90-; assoc ed, Develop Biol, 89-95. *Mem:* Am Soc Cell Biol; Soc Develop Biol; Am Soc Biol Chemists; AAAS. *Res:* Cell adhesion molecules; membrane cytoskeletal linkages; muscle and neuronal development; cell migration. *Mailing Add:* Dept Cell & Struct Biol Univ Ill Urbana IL 61801. *Fax:* 217-244-1698; *E-Mail:* afh@uiuc.edu

HORWITZ, BARBARA ANN, ANIMAL PHYSIOLOGY, CELL PHYSIOLOGY. *Current Pos:* USPHS res fel, Univ Calif, Davis, 67-68, asst res physiologist, 68-72, asst prof, 72-75, assoc prof & assoc physiologist, 75-78, PROF PHYSIOL & PHYSIOLOGIST, AGR EXP STA, UNIV CALIF, DAVIS, 78-, CHAIR, 91- *Personal Data:* b Chicago, Ill, Sept 26, 40; m 70, John M. *Educ:* Univ Fla, BS, 61, MS, 62; Emory Univ, PhD(physiol), 66. *Honors & Awards:* Merit Award, NIH, 92. *Prof Exp:* Asst biol, Univ Fla, 59-61; res physiologist, Emory Univ, 66; USPHS res fel physiol, Sch Med, Univ Calif, Los Angeles, 66-67. *Concurrent Pos:* Consult, Physiol Dept, Sch Med, Univ Calif, Los Angeles, 66-67, NSF, 80-83; consult, NSF, 80-83. *Mem:* Am Physiol Soc; NY Acad Sci; Am Inst Nutrit; fel AAAS; Sigma Xi; Soc Exp Biol & Med; NAm Asn Study of Obesity. *Res:* Cellular physiology; bioenergetics; hormonal and neural control of cellular metabolism; thermogenesis; obesity. *Mailing Add:* Sect Neurobiol Physiol & Behav Div Biol Sci Univ Calif Davis CA 95616-8519. *Fax:* 530-752-5582; *E-Mail:* bahorwitz@ucdavis.edu

HORWITZ, DAVID A, MICROBIOLOGY. *Current Pos:* PROF MED & MICROBIOL & CHIEF, DIV RHEUMATOLOGY & IMMUNOL, SCH MED, UNIV SOUTERN CALIF, LOS ANGELES, 80- *Educ:* Univ Mich, BA, 58; Univ Chicago, MD, 62. *Prof Exp:* Intern resident, Michael Reese Hosp, Chicago, 66; instr internal med, Southwestern Med Sch, Univ Tex, 68-69, rheumatol fel, 69; from asst prof to prof med, Sch Med, Univ Va, Charlottesville, 69-80. *Concurrent Pos:* Vis prof, Clin Res Ctr, Harrow, Eng, 76-77; vis investr, Imp Cancer Res Fund, London, 88-89. *Res:* Research in human blood lymphocytes with iC3b (type 3) complement receptors; characterization of immunologic function in homosexual males with persistent generalized lymphadenopathy and AIDS; abnormalities in patients with active systemic lupus erythematosus, human CD8 lymphocytes stimulated in the absence of CD-4 cells enhance immunoglobulin G production by antibody-secreting B cells. *Mailing Add:* Div Rheumatol & Immunol Univ Southern Calif 2011 Zonal No 711 Los Angeles CA 90033-1034. *Fax:* 213-342-2874

HORWITZ, DAVID LARRY, ENDOCRINOLOGY, METABOLISM. *Current Pos:* vpres regulatory affairs, 91-94, EXEC VPRES, SCICLONE PHARMACEUT INC, 94- *Personal Data:* b Chicago, Ill, July 13, 42; m 65; c 2. *Educ:* Harvard Univ, BA, 63; Univ Chicago, MD, 67, PhD(physiol), 68; Lake Forest Grad Sch Mgt, MBA, 91. *Honors & Awards:* Res & Develop Award, Am Diabetes Asn, 74, 75. *Prof Exp:* Med officer, USN, 69-71; res fel endocrinol, Univ Chicago, 72-74, instr, 74-75, asst prof med endocrinol, 75-79; assoc prof med endocrinol, Univ Ill, 79-90, clin prof med, 90-91. *Concurrent Pos:* Med dir, Baxter Healthcare Corp, 82-91; vpres, Med Prof Affairs, 91-92. *Mem:* Fel Am Col Physicians; Am Fedn Clin Res; Am Diabetes Asn; AAAS; Endocrine Soc. *Res:* Factors affecting the regulation of insulin secretion; clinical pharmacology of insulin; dietary treatment of diabetes mellitus; carbohydrate metabolism; exercise physiology; pharmaceutical development. *Mailing Add:* SciClone Pharmaceut 901 Mariners Island Blvd Suite 315 San Mateo CA 94404. *Fax:* 650-358-3469; *E-Mail:* davidh@sciclone.com

HORWITZ, EARL PHILIP, SEPARATIONS CHEMISTRY. *Current Pos:* chemist, 59-80, SR CHEMIST, ARGONNE NAT LAB, 80- *Personal Data:* b Cincinnati, Ohio, June 3, 30; m 55; c 2. *Educ:* Univ Cincinnati, BS, 53; Univ Ill, MS, 55, PhD(chem), 57. *Honors & Awards:* IR-100 Award, 87; Distinguished Assoc Award, US Dept Energy, 90; RD-100 Award, 91 & 94; Glenn T Seaborg Actinide Separations Award, 92. *Prof Exp:* Res chemist, Dow Chem Co, 57-59. *Mem:* AAAS; Am Chem Soc; Sigma Xi. *Res:* Chemistry of the less familiar elements; chelate chemistry; liquid-liquid extraction; liquid chromatography; actinide chemistry; high speed-high efficiency liquid chromatography; nuclear fuel reprocessing; nuclear waste processing; radioanalytical chemistry; separation of kerogen and bitumen from oil shale; separation of maceral constituents of coal; hydrometallurgy. *Mailing Add:* Argonne Nat Lab 9700 S Cass Ave Argonne IL 60439

HORWITZ, EDWIN M, HEMATOLOGOY, ONCOLOGY. *Current Pos:* MED SCIENTIST, TRAINING PROG, DEPT PEDIAT, SCH MED, WASHINGTON UNIV, 88- *Personal Data:* b Indianapolis, Ind, June 29, 59. *Educ:* Ind Univ, AB, 81, PhD, 85, MD, 88. *Prof Exp:* Assoc instr biol chem, Ind Univ, 81, res assoc, Dept Chem, 82-85, postdoctoral res assoc, Med Sci Prog, 85-86; intern, 88-89, pediat resident, St Louis Childrens Hosp, 89- *Concurrent Pos:* Assoc instr human anat, Ind Univ, 82 & physiol chem, 83, vis asst prof biochem, Med Sci Prog, 87. *Mem:* Am Acad Pediat; AMA; Am Soc Cell Biol. *Res:* Author of 16 technical publications. *Mailing Add:* 1254 Vinton Ave Memphis TN 38103-0939

HORWITZ, JEROME PHILIP, ORGANIC CHEMISTRY, ONCOLOGY. *Current Pos:* prof chem, div oncol, Sch Med, 71-90, PROF DEPT INTERNAL MED, SCH MED, WAYNE STATE UNIV, 90- *Personal Data:* b Detroit, Mich, Jan 16, 19; m 51; c Carol K & Suzanne G. *Educ:* Univ Detroit, BS, 42, MS, 44; Univ Mich, PhD(chem), 48. *Hon Degrees:* Dr, Univ Detroit, 87. *Honors & Awards:* William L Simpson Award, Wayne State Univ, 87. *Prof Exp:* US Army fel, Northwestern Univ, Evanston, 48-50; Parke Davis fel, Univ Mich, Ann Arbor, 50-51; asst prof chem, Ill Inst Technol, 51-55; res assoc org chem, Detroit Inst Cancer Res, 56-64. *Concurrent Pos:* dir, Div Chem, 65-69, sci dir, 70-73, dir, Div Basic Sci, Mich Cancer Found, 73- *Mem:* Am Chem Soc; Am Asn Cancer Res. *Res:* Nucleic acid metabolism and new cancer chemotherapeutic agents. *Mailing Add:* PO Box 02188 Detroit MI 48202-0188. *E-Mail:* horwitz@sgih.voc.wayne.edu

HORWITZ, JOSEPH, BIOPHYSICS. *Current Pos:* Fel, Lab Nuclear Med & Radiation Biol, Univ Calif, 70-71, asst prof, 71-76, assoc prof, 76-80, PROF BIOPHYS, JULES STEIN EYE INST, SCH MED, UNIV CALIF, LOS ANGELES, 80- *Personal Data:* b Petach-Tikva, Israel, Jan 10, 36; US citizen; m 64; c 2. *Educ:* Univ Calif, Los Angeles, BS, 65, PhD(biophysics), 70. *Mem:* Am Chem Soc; Biophys Soc; Am Soc Photobiol; Sigma Xi. *Res:* Proteins, structure and function; vision on the molecular level. *Mailing Add:* J Stein Eye Inst Univ Calif Los Angeles Sch Med Los Angeles CA 90024-7008

HORWITZ, KATHRYN BLOCH, MOLECULAR & CELL BIOLOGY, ENDORINOLOGY. *Current Pos:* from asst prof to assoc prof, 79-89, PROF MED, UNIV COLO MED CTR, 89- *Personal Data:* b Sosua, Dominican Repub; US citizen; c 2. *Educ:* NY Univ, MS, 66; Southwestern Med Sch, Dallas, PhD(med physiol), 75. *Honors & Awards:* Wilson S Stone Award, M D Anderson Inst, 76. *Prof Exp:* Fel, Univ Tex Health Sci Ctr, San Antonio, 78-79. *Concurrent Pos:* Res career develop award, Nat Cancer Inst, 81-86. *Mem:* Am Fedn Clin Res; Endocrine Soc; Soc Cell Biol; Am Soc Cancer Res. *Res:* Steroid hormone action; estrogen, progesterone receptors; breast cancer; endocrinology. *Mailing Add:* Dept Med Univ Colo Sch Med 4200 E Ninth Ave Box B-151 Denver CO 80262-0001. *Fax:* 303-270-5082

HORWITZ, LAWRENCE D, CARDIOLOGY. *Current Pos:* head, Div Cardiol, 79-89, PROF MED, HEALTH SCI CTR, UNIV COLO, 79- *Personal Data:* b Nov 29, 39; m; c 2. *Educ:* Univ Rochester, BA, 61; Yale Univ, MD, 64; Am Bd Internal Med, dipl internal med & cardiovasc dis, 73. *Prof Exp:* Intern med, Bellevue Hosp, 64-65, asst resident, 65-66; med res officer, USAF Sch Aerospace Med, Brooks AFB, 66-68; Nat Heart Inst spec fel, Peter Bent Brigham Hosp & Harvard Med Sch, 68-70; asst prof med, Southwestern Med Sch, Univ Tex, Dallas, 70-73; from assoc prof to prof, Health Sci Ctr, Univ Tex, San Antonio, 73-79. *Concurrent Pos:* Attend physician, Parkland Mem Hosp, Dallas, 70-73, Bexar County Hosp, San Antonio, 73-79 & Univ Hosp, Denver, 79-; staff physician, Vet Admin Hosp, San Antonio, 73-79 & Vet Admin Med Ctr, Denver, 79-83; mem, Cardiovasc Study Comt, Vet Admin, 79-82, chmn, 82; mem, Clin & Circulation Coun, Am Heart Asn. *Mem:* Am Fedn Clin Res; Am Heart Asn; Am Physiol Soc; fel Am Col Cardiol; Am Soc Clin Invest; Am Asn Physicians. *Res:* Author of numerous technical publications. *Mailing Add:* Health Sci Ctr Dept Med Univ Colo 4200 E Ninth Ave Denver CO 80262-0001

HORWITZ, LAWRENCE PAUL, THEORETICAL PHYSICS. *Current Pos:* PROF PHYSICS, TEL AVIV UNIV, 72-, PROF PHYSICS, BAR ILAN UNIV, 91- *Personal Data:* b New York, NY, Oct 14, 30; m 51, Ruth Abeles; c Benjamin, Dorothy & Deborah. *Educ:* NY Univ, BS, 52; Harvard Univ, PhD(physics), 57. *Prof Exp:* Staff consult commun & electronics, Pickard & Burns, Inc, 54-55; physicist, Res Lab, IBM Corp, 57-64; vis res assoc, Inst Theoret Physics, Univ Geneva, 64-66; from assoc prof to prof physics, Univ Denver, 66-71. *Concurrent Pos:* Vis assoc prof, Tel Aviv Univ, 67-68; vis prof, Inst Theoret Physics, Univ Geneva, 71-72, Syracuse Univ, 80, Eidgenossische Technische Hochschule, Zurich, Switz, 81, Inst Hautes Etudes Sci, Buros/Yvette, 90 & Inst Advan Study, Princeton, 96. *Mem:* Am Phys Soc; Israeli Phys Soc; Swiss Phys Soc; Europ Phys Soc; NY Acad Sci; Int Asn Quantum Struct. *Res:* Functional analysis and algebraic methods in quantum mechanics and particle physics; relativistic quantum theory; algebraic approach to non-Abelian gauge fields using modules over Clifford algebras; Steuckelberg-Feynman approach to relativistic quantum theory; unstable systems; relativistic statistical mechanics. *Mailing Add:* Sch Physics & Astron Tel Aviv Univ Ramat Aviv 69978 Israel. *E-Mail:* larry@post.tav.ac.il

HORWITZ, MARCUS AARON, INFECTIOUS DISEASES, IMMUNOLOGY. *Current Pos:* chief, Div Infectious Dis, 85-92, PROF MED, MICROBIOL & IMMUNOL, UNIV CALIF, LOS ANGELES, 85- *Personal Data:* b Elmira, NY, May 3, 46; m 81; c 2. *Educ:* Cornell Univ, BA, 68; Columbia Univ, MD, 72. *Honors & Awards:* Alexander D Langmuir Award, Ctr Dis Control, 76; Squibb Award, Infectious Dis Soc Am, 91; James C Feeley Award, 91 & 93. *Prof Exp:* Internship med, Bronx Munic Hosp, 73, residency, 73-74; epidemic intel serv officer, Ctr Dis Control, 74-76; fel infectious dis, Albert Einstein Col Med, Affil Hosps, 76-77; NIH fel res, Rockefeller Univ, 77-80, asst prof res, 80-85. *Mem:* Am Fedn Clin Res; Am Soc Microbiol; Infectious Dis Soc Am; Am Soc Clin Invest. *Res:* Interaction between infectious agents and leukocytes; macrophage activation; intracellular parasitism; immunobiology of Legionnella pneumophila, Mycobacterium leprae and Mycobacterium tuberculosis. *Mailing Add:* Div Infectious Dis Dept Med Univ Calif Sch Med Ctr Health Sci Rm 37-121 Los Angeles CA 90024

HORWITZ, MARSHALL SYDNEY, MICROBIOLOGY, PEDIATRICS. *Current Pos:* asst prof cell biol, Albert Einstein Col Med, 69-70, asst prof pediat, 69-73, asst prof microbiol & immunol, 70-73, assoc prof, 73-78, PROF PEDIAT, MICROBIOL & IMMUNOL, ALBERT EINSTEIN COL MED, 78-, DIR, DIV PEDIAT INFECTIOUS DIS, 81- *Personal Data:* b Boston, Mass, Mar 26, 37; m 60; c 2. *Educ:* Harvard Univ, BA, 58; Tufts Univ, MD, 62. *Prof Exp:* From intern to resident pediat, New Eng Med Ctr, Boston, Mass, 62-65; instr, Med Sch, Emory Univ, 65-67. *Concurrent Pos:* Virologist, Ctr Dis Control, US Dept Health, Educ & Welfare, 65-67; Am Cancer Soc fel, Albert Einstein Col Med, 67-69; career scientist, Health Res Coun, New York, 69-72; Nat Cancer Inst grant, 69-; NIH res career develop award, 72-77; Irma T Hirscl Career Develop Award, 76-81; mem study sect exp virol, NIH, 78-82, chmn, 85-87; mem, FDA adv comt on vaccines. *Mem:* Am Soc Microbiol; Harvey Soc; Soc Pediat Res; Am Soc Virol. *Res:* Virus replication; DNA synthesis; antiviral chemotherapy. *Mailing Add:* Albert Einstein Col Med 1300 Morris Park Ave Bronx NY 10461-1924

HORWITZ, NAHMIN, PHYSICS. *Current Pos:* from asst prof to assoc prof, 59-65, PROF PHYSICS, SYRACUSE UNIV, 65- *Personal Data:* b Duluth, Minn, Oct 28, 27; m 49, Leah Gressel; c David, Susan, Ann & Amy. *Educ:* Western Res Univ, BS, 49; Univ Minn, MS, 51, PhD(physics), 54. *Prof Exp:* Physicist, Lawrence Radiation Lab, Univ Calif, 54-59. *Concurrent Pos:* Physicist, Rutherford High Energy Lab, Eng, 65-66; sci assoc, Europ Orgn Nuclear Res, Geneva, Switz, 75-76; Fulbright scholar & Lady Davis fel, Technion, Haifa, Israel, 82-83; Fulbright scholar, Univ Valencia, Spain, 93. *Mem:* Fel Am Phys Soc; Am Asn Physics Teachers. *Res:* Elementary particle physics. *Mailing Add:* Dept Physics Syracuse Univ Syracuse NY 13244

HORWITZ, ORVILLE, MEDICINE. *Current Pos:* From asst instr to instr pharmacol, Univ Pa, 40-52, from asst instr to instr med, 45-49, assoc, 49-53, from asst prof to assoc prof, 53-70, prof med, 70-80, PROF MED & PHARM, SCH MED, UNIV PA, 80-, SR WARD CHIEF, HOSP, 53- *Personal Data:* b Strafford, Pa, Nov 20, 09; m 34, Nataline Dulles; c 3. *Educ:* Harvard Univ, SB, 32; Johns Hopkins Univ, MD, 38. *Concurrent Pos:* Consult, US Vet Admin & US Dept Navy; trustee, Jackson Lab, 51-; chmn coun circulation & fel coun arteriosclerosis, Am Heart Asn, 65-67. *Mem:* Am Physiol Soc; AMA; Am Heart Asn; Am Clin & Climat Asn; fel Am Col Physicians; Sigma Xi. *Res:* Cardiovascular diseases; physiology; pathology and treatment. *Mailing Add:* 2 Private Way Wayne PA 19087

HORWITZ, PAUL, SCIENCE EDUCATION. *Current Pos:* DIV SCIENTIST, BOLT BERANEK & NEWMAN, INC, 79- *Personal Data:* b New York, NY, Dec 4, 38; m 64; c 3. *Educ:* Harvard Univ, BA, 60; Columbia Univ, MA, 63; NY Univ, PhD(physics), 67. *Concurrent Pos:* Chmn, Forum Physics & Soc, 78-79. *Mem:* Am Phys Soc; Am Asn Physics Teachers. *Res:* Use of computers for teaching science and mathematics, particularly chaos theory, visual modeling, special relativity and quantum mechanics. *Mailing Add:* 32 Riverside Ave Concord MA 01742. *E-Mail:* phorwitz@bbn.com

HORWITZ, RALPH IRVING, INTERNAL MEDICINE, CLINICAL EPIDEMIOLOGY. *Current Pos:* Asst prof med, 78-95, asst dir, 78-95, EMER DIR, ROBERT WOOD JOHNSON CLIN SCHOLAR PROG, 95-, HAROLD H HINES JR PROF MED & EPIDEMIOL & CHAIR, DEPT INTERNAL MED, YALE UNIV SCH MED. *Personal Data:* b Philadelphia, Pa, June 25, 47; m 70, Sarah McCue; c Rebecca Margaret (Taylor). *Educ:* Albright Col, BA, 69; Pa State Univ, MD, 73. *Prof Exp:* Chief, Sec Gen Med, 82-94, vchmn, Internal Med, 93. *Concurrent Pos:* Robert Wood Johnson clin scholar prog, 75-77, co-dir, 78-95, emer dir, 95-; chmn internal med, Beeson Med Serv, 94- , chief. *Mem:* Inst Med-Nat Acad Sci; Soc Epidemiol Res; Am Col Physicians; Am Fedn Clin Res. *Res:* Quantification of prognosis and therapy in clinical care; clinical epidemiology; evaluation of diagnostic tests; methodology of case-control research. *Mailing Add:* Yale Univ Sch Med 333 Cedar St 1072 LMP New Haven CT 06520-8056

HORWITZ, SUSAN BAND, MOLECULAR PHARMACOLOGY, BIOCHEMISTRY. *Current Pos:* from instr to asst prof pharmacol, 68-75, assoc prof, 75-80, PROF PHARMACOL & CELL BIOL, ALBERT EINSTEIN COL MED, 80-, CO-CHMN, DEPT MOLECULAR PHARMACOL, 85- *Personal Data:* b Cambridge, Mass; m 60; c 2. *Educ:*

Bryn Mawr Col, BA, 58; Brandeis Univ, PhD(biochem), 63. *Prof Exp:* Fel pharmacol, Med Sch, Tufts Univ, 63-65; fel, Med Sch, Emory Univ, 65-67. *Mem:* Am Cancer Soc; Am Soc Pharmacol & Exp Therapeut; Am Chem Soc; Am Soc Microbiol; Am Soc Cell Biol. *Res:* Mechanism of action of chemotherapeutic agents which affect macromolecular synthesis in mammalian cells and their viruses; interaction of antitumor and antiviral drugs with nucleic acids. *Mailing Add:* Dept Molecular Pharmacol Albert Einstein Col Med 1300 Morris Park Ave Rm 248F Bronx NY 10461-1975. *Fax:* 718-430-8922

HORWITZ, WILLIAM, FOOD CHEMISTRY. *Current Pos:* from chemist to chief chemist, Food & Drug Admin, Minn, 39-51, food & drug officer, 51-52, chief food res br, 52-63, asst to asst comnr sci resources, 63-67, asst dir ,Bur Sci, 67-70, dep dir, Off Sci, 70-81, SCI ADV, CTR FOOD SAFETY & APPL NUTRIT, FOOD & DRUG ADMIN, 81- *Personal Data:* b Gilbert, Minn, Feb 4, 18; m 40, Selma Gilberstadt; c 3. *Educ:* Univ Chicago, BS, 37; Univ Minn, MS, 38, PhD(phys chem), 47. *Honors & Awards:* Harvey W Wiley Award, Asn Off Analytical Chemists, 75. *Prof Exp:* Asst chem, Univ Minn, 38-39. *Concurrent Pos:* Instr, USDA Grad Sch, 51-61; sect ed foods, Chem Abstr, 55-; ed, Off Methods Analysis, 55, 60, 65, 70, 75 & 80; US mem, adv & deleg, Food & Agr Orgn/WHO Codex Alimentarius Comts, 58- *Mem:* AAAS; Am Chem Soc; Asn Off Analytical Chemists (secy, 52-79); Inst Food Technologists. *Res:* Methods of analysis for foods; research administration; reliability of chemical analysis. *Mailing Add:* 14800 Pennfield Circle Silver Spring MD 20906. *Fax:* 202-401-7740

HORZ, FRIEDRICH, GEOLOGY, PETROGRAPHY. *Current Pos:* SPACE TECHNOLOGIST, MANNED SPACECRAFT CTR, NASA, 71- *Personal Data:* b Blaubeuren, Ger, Mar 23, 40; m 74, Eleni Panagiotopolous; c Christina & Marianna. *Educ:* Univ Tubingen, BS, 62, PhD(petrog), 65. *Honors & Awards:* Commendation, Geol Soc Am, 74; Barringer Award, Meteorological Soc, 96. *Prof Exp:* Nat Res Coun resident assoc, Ames Res Ctr, NASA, Calif, 66-68; res fel, Calif Inst Technol, 68-69; vis scientist, Lunar Sci Inst, Houston, Tex, 69-70. *Concurrent Pos:* Mission sci trainer for Apollo 16 astronauts, NASA, 71-; vis scientist, Max Planck Inst Neurol Res, Heidelberg, Ger, 81-92; proj scientist, Cosmic Dust Collection facil, 85-92; co-investr, Stardust Mission, 95- *Mem:* Fel Meteoritical Soc; Am Geophys Union; Ger Mineral Soc. *Res:* Impact cratering mechanics and experimental shock studies of geological materials; micrometeoroid impact and other small scale processes on the lunar surface; capture and analysis of cosmic dust and space debris in low earth orbit. *Mailing Add:* 907 Layfair Pl Friendswood TX 77546

HORZEMPA, LEWIS MICHAEL, ENVIRONMENTAL CHEMISTRY, GEOCHEMISTRY. *Current Pos:* CHEMIST, EVASCO, BOSTON, MASS, 95- *Personal Data:* b Beverly, Mass, Sept 5, 49. *Educ:* Rensselaer Polytech Inst, BS, 71; Univ Mass, MS, 73; Univ Md, PhD(geochem), 77. *Prof Exp:* Asst prof earth sci, Western Conn State Col, 77-78; res assoc environ chem, Manhattan Col, 78-80; sr environ chemist, Envirosphere Co, NY, 80-95. *Mem:* Geochem Soc; Soil Sci Soc Am; Sigma Xi; Am Chem Soc. *Res:* Evaluation of the mobility and fate of chemicals in the environment; environmental chemical assessments and studies relating to hazardous waste disposal, site contamination, treatment technologies, combustion emissions, energy development and associated environmental health risks. *Mailing Add:* 4 Marions Way Georgetown MA 01833

HORZEPA, JOHN PHILIP, PROCESS ENGINEERING, INTERNATIONAL PROJECT MANAGER. *Current Pos:* DIR ENG, NOBEL MET INDUST, 90- *Personal Data:* b Bayonne, NJ, May 22, 43; m 85; c 3. *Educ:* NJ Inst Technol, BS, 65, MS, 70. *Prof Exp:* Jr res engr, Engelhard Minerals & Chem Corp, 65-68, from res engr to sr res engr, 68-75, group leader, 75-78, mgr process develop catalyst & chem, Minerals & Chem Div, 78-82, mgr, Div Process Eng, 83-85, proj mgr corp eng, 85-90. *Mem:* Am Inst Chem Engrs. *Res:* Catalysts, sorbents, and pigments, especially kaolin; precious metals. *Mailing Add:* 7430 E Chaparral Rd Scottsdale AZ 85250

HOSAIN, FAZLE, NUCLEAR MEDICINE. *Current Pos:* assoc prof nuclear med, 75-78, DIR RADIOPHYSICS, DEPT NUCLEAR MED, UNIV CONN HEALTH CTR, 75-, PROF NUCLEAR MED, 78- *Personal Data:* b Murshidabad, India, Apr 1, 32; US citizen. *Educ:* Univ Calcutta, India, BSc Hons, 51, MSc, 53, AINP, 55, DPhil, 59. *Prof Exp:* Lectr physics, Chary Chandra Col, 55-56; Govt India nat res fel sci, Saha Inst Nuclear Physics, 59-61; Fulbright scholar & res fel hemat, Sch Med, Univ Wash, Seattle, 61-64; reader & in-chg, Dept Nuclear Med, Med Col, Banaras Hindu Univ, 64-66; fel radiol, Div Nuclear Med, Sch Med, Johns Hopkins Univ, 67-69, asst prof, Sch Hyg & Med, Div Nuclear Med & Radiation Health, 69-74, assoc prof environ health, Sch Hyg & Pub Health & asst prof radiol & radiation sci, Sch Med, 74-75. *Concurrent Pos:* Vis staff mem, Brookhaven Nat Lab, Mem Sloan-Kettering Cancer Ctr, NY & Naval Res Lab, Washington, DC. *Mem:* Soc Nuclear Med; Am Chem Soc; Am Physiol Soc. *Res:* Nuclear medicine; radiophysics and radiopharmacy; biomedical investigations with radionuclide tracers; author of more than 170 technical publications. *Mailing Add:* Dept Nuclear Med Univ Conn Health Ctr Farmington CT 06030-0001

HOSAIN, MAHBUB UL, STRUCTURAL ENGINEERING. *Current Pos:* from asst prof to assoc prof, 69-75, PROF STRUCT ENG, UNIV SASK, 79- *Personal Data:* b Calcutta, W Bengal, India, Feb 4, 38; Can citizen; m 67; c 3. *Educ:* Univ Dacca, BSc, 60; Univ Man, Winnipeg, MSc, 63; Tech Univ of NS, Halifax, PhD (structure eng), 71. *Prof Exp:* Asst engr bldgs, Coun Sci & Indust Res, 60-61; engr class I struct design, Assoc Consult Engrs Ltd, 64-65; design engr bldgs & bridges, J Philip Vaughan & Assocs, Halifax, 67-68. *Concurrent Pos:* Commonwealth scholar, Univ Man, 61-63; postdoctoral fel, Univ Alta, Edmonton, 68-69; vis prof, Univ Ottawa, 78-79; pres, Sask Eng Soc, 81-82; comt, Can Standards Asn, 87- *Mem:* Assoc Am Soc Civil Engrs; fel Can Soc Civil Engrs; Eng Inst Can; Am Soc Engr Educ; Can Standards Asn. *Res:* Experimental investigation of steel and composite structures particularly stub-girders; computer aided design & analysis; finite element analysis and boundary element method; computer aided instruction. *Mailing Add:* Dept Civil Eng Univ Sask Saskatoon SK S7N 5A9 Can

HOSANSKY, NORMAN LEON, ORGANIC CHEMISTRY. *Current Pos:* asst ed, 63-68, asst dept head org editing, 68-71, ORG CHEM MGR, CHEM ABSTR SERV, 71- *Personal Data:* b NY, Feb 12, 24; m 49, 61; c 2. *Educ:* Queens Col, NY, BS, 47; Columbia Univ, AM, 48; Rutgers Univ, PhD(chem), 53. *Prof Exp:* Prof asst antibiotics, E R Squibb & Sons, 48-50; res chemist natural prod, S B Penick & Co, 53-62. *Mem:* Am Chem Soc. *Res:* Chemical documentation; antibiotics; steroids; alkaloids and other natural products; isolation and structural identification. *Mailing Add:* 181 S Chesterfield Rd Columbus OH 43209-1912

HOSE, RICHARD K, PETROLEUM GEOLOGY. *Current Pos:* CONSULT, 86- *Personal Data:* b Newark, NJ, March 23, 20. *Educ:* Univ Ala, BS, 43. *Prof Exp:* Geologist, US Geol Surv, 44-80; sr geol assoc & adv, Atlantic Richfield Co, 80-85. *Mem:* Fel Geol Soc Am; Am Asn Petrol Geologists; Sigma Xi; AAAS. *Res:* Geologic mapping, basin range province in Nevada and Utah; structural and stratigraphic studies in Wyoming. *Mailing Add:* 10335 Stonydale Dr Cupertino CA 95014-1073

HOSEA, JOEL CARLTON, PLASMA PHYSICS. *Current Pos:* res fel, 68-69, MEM RES STAFF PLASMA PHYSICS, PRINCETON UNIV, 69- *Personal Data:* b Atlanta, Ga, Dec 12, 38; m 61; c 3. *Educ:* Auburn Univ, BS, 61; Stanford Univ, MS, 62, PhD(plasma physics), 66. *Prof Exp:* Res asst plasma physics, Stanford Univ, 61-66; NSF fel, Saclay Nuclear Res Ctr, France, 66-68. *Mem:* Am Phys Soc. *Res:* Interaction of electromagnetic energy with plasmas and solids; study of basic phenomena in all types of plasmas, especially in fusion oriented plasmas. *Mailing Add:* Plasma Physics Lab B329 Princeton Univ Princeton NJ 08543. *Fax:* 609-243-3248; *E-Mail:* Jhosea@pppl.gov

HOSEIN, ESAU ABBAS, BIOCHEMISTRY. *Current Pos:* RETIRED. *Personal Data:* b Trinidad, WI, Dec 4, 22. *Educ:* McGill Univ, BSc, 47, MSc, 50, PhD(biochem), 52. *Prof Exp:* Lectr biochem, McGill Univ, 52-58, from asst prof to prof, 58-93. *Mem:* Can Physiol Soc. *Res:* Epilepsy; myasthenia gravis; muscular dystrophy; neurohumoral transmitters in brain and muscle; neuropharmacology; molecular basis of action of narcotic drugs. *Mailing Add:* 654 Lanseolune Ave Westmount PQ H3Y 2V8 Can

HOSENEY, RUSSELL CARL, CEREAL CHEMISTRY. *Current Pos:* res assoc cereal chem, 67-71, assoc prof grain sci, 71-75, PROF GRAIN SCI, KANS STATE UNIV, 75- *Personal Data:* b Coffeyville, Kans, Dec 3, 34; m 56; c 3. *Educ:* Kans State Univ, BS, 57, MS, 60, PhD(cereal chem), 68. *Prof Exp:* Res chemist, Crops Res Div, Agr Res Serv, USDA, 56-70. *Mem:* Am Chem Soc; Am Asn Cereal Chemists; Inst Food Technologists. *Res:* Wheat and flour quality, including the role of proteins, carbohydrates and lipids. *Mailing Add:* Flour/Feed Mill Dept Kans State Univ Manhattan KS 66504

HOSEY, M MARLENE, PROTEIN PHOSPHORYLATION, MUSCARINIC RECEPTORS. *Current Pos:* ASSOC PROF BIOCHEM, CHICAGO MED SCH, 78- *Educ:* Univ Ill, PhD(pharmacol), 74. *Res:* Signal transduction in muscle. *Mailing Add:* Dept Molecular Pharm & Biochem Northwestern Univ Med Sch 303 E Chicago Ave 5215 Chicago IL 60611-3008. *Fax:* 312-503-3692

HOSFORD, ROBERT MORGAN, JR, PLANT PATHOLOGY. *Current Pos:* from asst prof to assoc prof, 67-75, PROF PLANT PATH, NDAK STATE UNIV, 75- *Personal Data:* b Bremerton, Wash, Aug 18, 33; m 67. *Educ:* Ore State Univ, BS, 56, MS, 59; Univ Ariz, PhD(plant path), 65. *Prof Exp:* Grad asst, Univ Ariz, 61-65; asst plant pathologist, Potato Invests Field Lab, Univ Fla, 65-67. *Concurrent Pos:* Mem wheat comt, Nat Plant Dis Detection & Info Prog, 73- *Mem:* Am Phytopath Soc; Soc Nematol. *Res:* Identification, epidemiology, biology, control, physiology, genetics, cytogenetics of disease-causing organisms; root, foliage and seed diseases; field and horticultural crops; foliar diseases of wheat excluding rusts; biological control of leafy spurge; teaching & trouble shooting (nematology, diseases of horticultural crops). *Mailing Add:* Dept Plant Path ND State Univ Fargo ND 58102

HOSFORD, WILLIAM FULLER, JR, METALLURGY & PHYSICAL METALLURGICAL ENGINEERING. *Current Pos:* assoc prof, 63-68, PROF METALL ENG, UNIV MICH, 68- *Personal Data:* b Orange, NJ, Mar 17, 28; m 54, Margaret Waldeck; c Jean F, John S, Kenneth R & Thaddeus J. *Educ:* Lehigh Univ, BS, 50; Yale Univ, ME, 51; Mass Inst Technol, ScD(metall), 59. *Prof Exp:* Asst prof metall, Mass Inst Technol, 59-63. *Mem:* Am Inst Mining, Metall & Petrol Engrs; fel Am Soc Metals Int. *Res:* Mechanical metallurgy; sheet metal forming. *Mailing Add:* Dept Mat Sci & Eng Univ Mich 3062 Dow Bldg 2300 Hayward St Ann Arbor MI 48109-2136. *Fax:* 313-763-4788; *E-Mail:* whosford@engin.umich.edu

HOSHAW, ROBERT WILLIAM, phycology; deceased, see previous edition for last biography

HOSHIKO, MICHAEL S, BIOFEEDBACK, RADIO COMMUNICATION. *Current Pos:* CONSULT. *Personal Data:* b Surrey, BC; US citizen; m 55, Rose Dege; c Cecily, Sumi & Lance. *Educ:* Heidelburg Col, BA, 48; Bowling Green State Univ, MA, 49; Purdue Univ, PhD(speech & hearing sci), 57. *Prof Exp:* Instr psychol, Univ Kans, 49-50; intern, Peoria State Hosp, 50 & Ill Inst Technol, 51; sch psychologist, Prep Sch, Montreal, 51-52; res psychologist, Univ Toronto Med Sch, 52-55; prof commun dis, Southern Ill Univ, 57-92, coordr, Speech & Hearing Clin Ctr, 86-91. *Concurrent Pos:* Prin investr, NIH, 61-66, State Ill Ment Health, 62-64 & Am Cancer Soc, 63-65; Am Speech-Lang-Hearing Asn int travel award, 62; res fel, Johns Hopkins Med Sch, 66-67; voiceprint consult, Southern Ill Univ, 75-; vis prof behav med, Med Sch, MacMaster Univ, 81; site visitor, Am Speech-Lang-Hearing Asn, 84-, mem, Multicult Bd, 91-93. *Mem:* Fel Am Speech-Lang-Hearing Asn; Am Psychol Asn. *Res:* Electromyographic research respiratory muscles during speech; radio telemetry of physiological activity during speaking situations; radiophonic research communication without acoustic speech signals; skin potential as an indicator of hearing response; voiceprint research. *Mailing Add:* Dept Commun Dis & Sci Southern Ill Univ Carbondale IL 62901

HOSHIKO, TOMUO, PHYSIOLOGY, MEMBRANE BIOPHYSICS & SCIENTIFIC MISCONDUCT. *Current Pos:* from sr instr to assoc prof, 57-69, PROF PHYSIOL, SCH MED, CASE WESTERN RES UNIV, 69- *Personal Data:* b BC, Can, Oct 5, 27; nat US; m 62; c 3. *Educ:* Kent State Univ, BS, 49; Univ Minn, PhD(physiol), 53. *Prof Exp:* Asst physiol, Univ Minn, 49-53; instr, Univ Utah, 53-55; res fel zoophysiol, Am Heart Asn, Copenhagen Univ, 55-56. *Concurrent Pos:* Vis asst prof, Tokyo Med & Dent Univ, 64-65; vis prof, Dept Biol, Ill Inst Technol, 71-72; guest prof, Lab Physiol, Kath Univ, Leuven, Belgium, 80-81; mem prof adv comt, Ctr Biomed Ethics, Case Western Res Univ, 85- *Mem:* AAAS; Biophys Soc; Am Physiol Soc; Am Asn Univ Prof; Soc Gen Physiologists (secy, 73-75, pres, 81); Coun Sci Soc Pres; fel Am Sci Affil. *Res:* Ion transport through membranes; renal physiology; active transport. *Mailing Add:* Dept Physiol & Biophys Case Western Res Univ Sch Med Cleveland OH 44106-4970. *Fax:* 216-368-5586

HOSICK, HOWARD LAWRENCE, GROWTH FACTORS, CANCER. *Current Pos:* from asst prof to assoc prof cell biol & cancer, Wash State Univ, 73-83, chmn, 83-87, Dept Genetics & Cell Biol, 87-91, PROF ZOOL & CELL BIOL, DEPT ZOOL, WASH STATE UNIV, 83- *Personal Data:* b Champaign, Ill, Nov 1, 43; m 68, Cynthia Jacobson; c Steven, Anna & Rachel. *Educ:* Univ Colo, Boulder, BA, 65; Univ Calif, Berkeley, PhD(zool), 70. *Honors & Awards:* Fac Develop Award, Shell Co Found, 84. *Prof Exp:* Fel molecular genetics, Karolinska Inst, Sweden, 70-72; asst res biochemist, Cancer Res Lab, Univ Calif, Berkeley, 72-73. *Concurrent Pos:* Fel, Danon Runyon Mem Fund & Am Cancer Soc, 70-73; courtesy prof, Genetics Prog, Wash State Univ, 74-83, Pharmacol & Toxicol Prog, 84-; vis scientist, Univ Reading, Eng, 79 & Aichi Cancer Res Inst, Nagoya, Japan, 86; res comt, Am Heart Asn, 83-; mem bd gov, Int Asn Breast Cancer Res, 93-; foreign fel, Cambridge Univ, 94. *Mem:* Am Soc Cell Biol; Int Asn Breast Cancer Res; Am Asn Cancer Res; Tissue Cult Asn. *Res:* Cell biology of growth regulation during normal development and tumorigenesis, particularly in the mammary gland; molecular basis of cell interaction in mammary gland and blood vessel wall; use and improvement of cell culture methods. *Mailing Add:* Dept Zool Wash State Univ Pullman WA 99164-4236. *Fax:* 509-335-1907

HOSKEN, WILLIAM H, COMPUTER SCIENCE. *Current Pos:* proj mgr, 77-80, MGR INFO SYSTS, UNIV CHICAGO, 80- *Personal Data:* b Zion, Ill, June 26, 37; c 3. *Educ:* Antioch Col, AB, 60; Ohio State Univ, MA, 62; Purdue Univ, PhD(comput sci), 68. *Prof Exp:* Asst prof math & comput sci, Purdue Univ, 68; asst prof comput sci, Univ Nebr, 68-69 & Pa State Univ, 69-76; assoc prof, Univ NMex, 76-77. *Mem:* Asn Comput Mach. *Res:* Logic; automata theory; formal systems; data processing systems. *Mailing Add:* 3022 Enoch Ave Zion IL 60099

HOSKER, RAYFORD PETER, JR, AIR POLLUTION METEOROLOGY, MICROMETEOROLOGY. *Current Pos:* phys scientist, 71-90, DIR, ATMOSPHERIC TURBULENCE & DIFFUSION DIV, ENVIRON RES LABS, NAT OCEANIC & ATMOSPHERIC ADMIN, US DEPT COM, 90- *Personal Data:* b Lynn, Mass, June 17, 43; m 66, Marilyn A Kane; c Richard P & Elizabeth A. *Educ:* Boston Col, BS, 65; Univ Minn, MS, 67; Northwestern Univ, PhD(mech eng), 71. *Prof Exp:* Res fel, von Karman Inst Fluid Dynamics, NATO, Belgium, 70-71. *Concurrent Pos:* Consult, Adv Comt Reactor Safeguards, US Nuclear Regulatory Comn, 82-89, Nat Coun Radiation Protection & Measurement, 84-89; field dir, US Dept Energy Atmospheric Studies Complex Terrain Prog, 85-90. *Mem:* AAAS; Am Meteorol Soc; Air Pollution Control Asn; Am Soc Testing & Mat. *Res:* Transport and dispersion in complex terrain, including design and direction of large field experiments; theoretical and experimental studies of flow and dispersion near buildings; theory and monitoring of dry deposition of acidifying pollutants. *Mailing Add:* 108 Norton Rd Oak Ridge TN 37830. *Fax:* 423-576-1327

HOSKIN, FRANCIS CLIFFORD GEORGE, NEUROSCIENCES, TOXICOLOGY. *Current Pos:* res prof, 69-96, EMER PROF BIOL, ILL INST TECHNOL, 96- *Personal Data:* b Hanna, Alta, Oct 19, 22; nat US; m 45, 92, Elizabeth M Farnham; c Laura A. *Educ:* Queen's Univ, Ont, BA, 50, MA, 51; Univ Sask, PhD(org chem), 53. *Prof Exp:* Asst, Queen's Univ, Ont, 49-51 & Univ Sask, 51-53; biochemist, Defence Res Bd, Suffield Exp Sta, Can, 53-57; res assoc & asst prof neurol, Col Physicians & Surgeons, Columbia Univ, 57-69. *Concurrent Pos:* Res collabr, Brookhaven Nat Lab, 59-60; NIH spec fel, Leicester Univ, Eng, 67-68; mem, Marine Biol Lab Corps; vis prof biochem, Med Col, Rush Univ, 72-; mem, Chem Systs Labs Adv Panel, 81. *Mem:* AAAS; Am Soc Biol Chemists; Am Soc Neurochem. *Res:* Chemistry and biochemistry of phosphorus and sulfur compounds; biochemical basis of nerve function; neurochemistry; intermediary metabolism; quinones. *Mailing Add:* Marine Biol Lab Woods Hole MA 02543

HOSKIN, GEORGE PERRY, SEAFOOD SAFETY PHYSIOLOGY. *Current Pos:* assoc dir, 80-96, DIR, DIV SCI APPL TECHNOL, FOOD & DRUG ADMIN, 96- *Personal Data:* b Seattle, Wash, Oct 4, 41; m 67, Somsong Pitarachart; c Mark Jaran & Sumalee. *Educ:* Univ Wash, BS, 63; Univ Hawaii, MS, 68; Lehigh Univ, PhD(biol), 72. *Prof Exp:* Instr biol, Lafayette Col, 71-72, asst prof, 72-80. *Concurrent Pos:* Consult, Brandt Water Testing Lab, 75-79. *Mem:* Sigma Xi; AAAS. *Res:* Molluscan physiology and pathobiology; invertebrate lipid metabolism; symbiosis among invertebrates, especially histo-pathological and biochemical alterations of host organisms in host-parasite relationships. *Mailing Add:* 9706 Lawndale Dr Silver Spring MD 20901. *Fax:* 202-418-3196; *E-Mail:* gph@fdacf.ssw.dhhs.gov

HOSKINS, BETH, AGING, PHARMACOLOGY & TOXICOLOGY. *Current Pos:* ASSOC PROF PHARMACOL & TOXICOL, MED SCH, UNIV MISS, 72- *Educ:* Univ Miss, PhD(pharmacol), 70. *Mailing Add:* Dept Pharmacol & Toxicol Univ Miss Med Ctr 2500 N State St Jackson MS 39216-4505. *Fax:* 601-984-1637

HOSKINS, BETTY B, DEVELOPMENTAL EDITING & WRITING, FEMINIST BIOETHICS. *Current Pos:* ASSOC PROF BIOL, MASS COL ART, 90- *Personal Data:* b Baltimore, Md, June 29, 36; c Betty K & Kent E (deceased). *Educ:* Goucher Col, BA, 56; Amherst Col, MA, 58; Tex Woman's Univ, PhD(molecular biol), 73. *Prof Exp:* Assoc prof life sci, Worcester Polytech Inst, 73-79; develop ed, High Sch Biol, Ginn & Co & asst prof sci, El Centro Community Col, Dallas County Dist, 79-82; sect mgr, Third Party Pubs, Prime Comput, 82-90. *Concurrent Pos:* Freelance ed & proj mgr & publ consult, 79-; vis prof embryol, Assumption Col, 79, anat & physiol, Quinsigamond Community Col, 80. *Mem:* AAAS; Sigma Xi; Nat Asn Biol Teachers. *Mailing Add:* 5 Paradox Dr Worcester MA 01602

HOSKINS, CAROL N, NURSING RESEARCH, FAMILY THERAPY. *Current Pos:* from asst prof to assoc prof, 77-87, PROF NURSING, NY UNIV, 87. *Educ:* Cornell Univ, BSN, 55; NY Univ, MA, 73, PhD(nursing res & family ther), 78. *Prof Exp:* Pub health nurse, NY, 55-58. *Concurrent Pos:* postdoctoral nurse fel, Nat Res Serv Award, Pub Health Serv, 80-82; nat res grantee, Sigma Theta Tau, 79; dir, Prog Res & Theory Develop Nursing, NY Univ, 85-90; prin investr, Walter Lanauer Found, 90-94; sr highlight award, US Educ Found Greece, Univ Athens, 95; Joan M Stout res scholar, Lienhard Sch Nursing, Pace Univ, 96-97. *Mem:* Fel Am Acad Nursing. *Mailing Add:* Div Nursing NY Univ 429 Shimkin Hall Washington Sq New York NY 11357. *Fax:* 212-995-3143; *E-Mail:* hoskins@is.nyu.edu

HOSKINS, CORTEZ WILLIAM, PETROLEUM GEOLOGY, PALEOECOLOGY. *Current Pos:* RETIRED. *Personal Data:* b Long Beach, Calif, May 17, 30; m 54; c 3. *Educ:* Pomona Col, BA, 53; Claremont Col, MA, 54; Stanford Univ, PhD(geol), 57. *Prof Exp:* Res geologist paleont, Jersey Prod Res Co, 57-64; res geologist paleont prod res, Richfield Oil Corp, 65-66; res assoc, Unocal Sci & Technol Div, Union Oil Co Calif Res Ctr, 66-73, suprv geol & geochem, 73-74, mgr explor res, 74-90, mgr geol res & staff consult, explor res, 90-92. *Mem:* Am Asn Petrol Geologists; Sigma Xi. *Res:* Sedimentology; stratigraphy; paleontology. *Mailing Add:* 11872 Simon Ranch Rd Santa Ana CA 92705

HOSKINS, DALE DOUGLAS, BIOCHEMISTRY, REPRODUCTIVE PHYSIOLOGY. *Current Pos:* from asst scientist to assoc scientist, Res Ctr, 61-69, from asst prof to assoc prof, 63-76, scientist, Res Ctr, 69-76, PROF BIOCHEM, UNIV ORE, 76-, SR SCIENTIST, ORE REGIONAL PRIMATE RES CTR, 76- *Personal Data:* b Exeter, Calif, Feb 12, 28; m 53; c 2. *Educ:* Ore State Univ, BS, 53, MS, 55; Univ Colo, PhD(biochem), 60. *Prof Exp:* Res asst biochem, Arctic Health Res Ctr, 55-57; instr dept pediat, Sch Med, Univ Wash, 60-61. *Concurrent Pos:* USPHS fel, 60-61 & spec res fel, Johns Hopkins Univ, 67-68; mem reproductive biol study sect, Div Res Grants, Nat Inst Child Health & Human Develop, 76-80; Fogarty int scholar, 81. *Mem:* Am Chem Soc; Am Soc Biol Chemists; Soc Study Reproduction. *Res:* Cellular respiration; mechanism of enzyme action; flavoproteins in electron transport; biochemistry of the male reproductive tract; enzymology of sperm maturation. *Mailing Add:* 4145 SW Washouga Ave Portland OR 97201

HOSKINS, DONALD MARTIN, GEOLOGY. *Current Pos:* Geologist, 56-68, asst state geologist, Dept Environ Resources, 68-86, STATE GEOLOGIST, BUR TOPOG & GEOL SURV, PA GEOL SURV, 86- *Personal Data:* b Lyons Fall, NY, May 22, 30; m 53; c 3. *Educ:* Union Col, NY, BS, 52; Univ Rochester, MS, 54; Bryn Mawr Col, PhD(geol), 60; Univ Pa, MGA, 74. *Honors & Awards:* Ralph Digman Award, 90. *Mem:* Geol Soc Am; Paleont Soc. *Res:* Stratigraphy and structure of the Appalachian Mountain section of the Valley and Ridge province of Pennsylvania; paleontology of Silurian ostracodes; history of science. *Mailing Add:* 5403 Rodgers Ave Harrisburg PA 17112

HOSKINS, EARL R, JR, MINING ENGINEERING, GEOPHYS. *Current Pos:* Brockett prof geophys, geol & geog & prof mining eng, 77-88, head, Dept Geophysics, 83-88, dept dean, 88-96, EMER PROF GEOPHYS, COL GEOSCI, TEX A&M UNIV, 96. *Personal Data:* b Chicago, Ill, May 2, 34; m 61; c 2. *Educ:* SDak Sch Mines & Technol, BS, 56, MS, 64; Australian Nat Univ, PhD(geophysics), 68. *Prof Exp:* From instr to prof mining eng, SDak Sch Mines & Technol, 56-77, head, Dept Mining Eng, 73-77. *Concurrent Pos:* Mem panel on earthquake modification, Nat Acad Sci, 69-75, mem, Comt Mech Rope & Cable, 72-75, US Nat Comt Rock Mech, 72-76 & 81- & Panel Tectonophys, 76-78; geophysicist, US Geol Surv, 69-75; vpres & mem bd dirs, Re, Spec Inc, 70-, chmn bd dirs, 94-; exec dir, DOSECC Inc, 91-96. *Mem:*

Asn Eng Geologists; Am Inst Mining, Metall & Petrol Engrs; Geol Soc Am; Am Geophys Union; Soc Exp Stress Anal; Am Soc Photogram & Remote Sensing. *Res:* Rock mechanics; engineering geology; remote sensing; scientific drilling; mined land reclamation; mineral economics. *Mailing Add:* Dept Geophys Tex A&M Univ College Station TX 77843. *Fax:* 409-846-6658; *E-Mail:* ehoskins@aol.com

HOSKINS, FREDERICK HALL, FOOD SCIENCE, NUTRITION. *Current Pos:* chair dept, 84-86, PROF FOOD SCI & HUMAN NUTRIT, WASH STATE UNIV, PULLMAN, 84- *Personal Data:* b Cincinnati, Ohio, May 17, 36; m 57, Mildred A Ball; c Michael & Darrell. *Educ:* Univ Ariz, BS, 58, MS, 59; La State Univ, PhD(nutrit), 63. *Prof Exp:* Assoc animal sci & univ fel, La State Univ, Baton Rouge, 63-64, instr animal nutrit, 64-65, asst prof food sci & technol, 65-71, from assoc prof to prof food sci, 71-84. *Concurrent Pos:* Consult, Ethyl Corp, 65-66 & Int Food Technol Inc, 67-78; mem, Nutrit Res Coun; vis prof human nutrit, Univ Uppsala, Sweden, 78; mem bd dir, Nat Nutrit Consortium. *Mem:* Soc Animal Sci; Inst Food Technologists; Am Inst Nutrit; Soc Nutrit Educ; Asn Off Anal Chem. *Res:* Nutritional composition of meat; world food problems; nutrition as related to food processing; protein and amino acid relationships to rice and other cereal grains; nutritional interrelationships; food toxicology; therapeutic nutrition. *Mailing Add:* Dept Food Sci & Human Nutrit Wash State Univ Pullman WA 99164-0001. *Fax:* 509-335-4815

HOSKINS, HARTLEY, GEOPHYSICS, SCIENCE COMMUNICATION. *Current Pos:* asst scientist, 68-72, RES ASSOC GEOL & GEOPHYS, WOODS HOLE OCEANOG INST, 72- *Personal Data:* b Rochester, NY, Feb 15, 38; m 75, Rosemary E Kelley; c Andrew M. *Educ:* Mass Inst Technol, BS, 59; Univ Chicago, MS, 61, PhD(geophys), 65. *Prof Exp:* Fel geophys sci, Univ Chicago, 65-66; lectr, Univ Ghana, 66-68. *Concurrent Pos:* Coordr, Ocean Indust Prog, 77-90 & Off Comm Affairs, 91- *Mem:* Am Geophys Union; Soc Explor Geophys; Sigma Xi. *Res:* Oceanic rocks and sediments and their distribution; telecommunications; intellectual property; oceanography. *Mailing Add:* Dept Geol & Geophys Woods Hole Oceanog Woods Hole MA 02543. *Fax:* 508-457-2189; *E-Mail:* hhoskins@whoi.edu

HOSKINS, JOHN RICHARD, MINING ENGINEERING. *Current Pos:* RETIRED. *Personal Data:* b Brewster, Wash, June 9, 19; m 46; c 3. *Educ:* Univ Idaho, BS, 47; Univ Utah, PhD(mining eng), 62. *Prof Exp:* Proj engr, US Gypsum Co, 47-48, dept supt, 48-49; mining engr, Am Smelting & Refining Co, 49-50, shift boss, 50-51, foreman, 51-52; from instr to assoc prof mining eng, Col Mines, Univ Alaska, 52-59; dept asst, Univ Utah, 59-62; mining methods res engr, US Bur Mines, 62-67; prof mining eng, Univ Idaho, 67-90, head dept, 69-90; Spokane Res Ctr, 90-95. *Concurrent Pos:* Consult, Prof Engrs Exam Mining Engrs, Alaska, 58-59 & US Bur Mines. *Mem:* Am Inst Mining, Metall & Petrol Engrs. *Res:* Applied research in explosives and rock mechanics problems dealing primarily with rock strength properties. *Mailing Add:* 702 E Brentwood Dr Spokane WA 99208

HOSKINS, LEO CLARON, PHYSICAL CHEMISTRY. *Current Pos:* From asst prof to assoc prof, 65-75, PROF CHEM, UNIV ALASKA, 75- *Personal Data:* b Logan, Utah, July 27, 40; m 60; c 3. *Educ:* Utah State Univ, BS, 62; Mass Inst Technol, PhD(phys chem), 65. *Mem:* Am Phys Soc; Sigma Xi. *Res:* Theory of resonanance raman spectroscopy of carotenoids; laser Raman studies in oceanography. *Mailing Add:* 3291 Bluebird Ave Fairbanks AK 99709

HOSKINS, SAM WHITWORTH, JR, PERIODONTOLOGY. *Current Pos:* RETIRED. *Personal Data:* b Poplarville, Miss, Mar 29, 21; m 47; c 2. *Educ:* Atlanta-Southern Dent Col, DDS, 44; Northwestern Univ, Chicago, MSD(periodont), 50; Am Bd Periodont, dipl. *Prof Exp:* Dent officer, US Vet Admin, 46-48 & USAF, 50-70; prof periodont & coordr curric, Univ Tex Sci Ctr, San Antonio, 70-83. *Mem:* Am Dent Asn; Am Acad Periodont; fel Am Col Dent. *Res:* Periodontal therapy; mouth hygiene methods and practices including motivational factors. *Mailing Add:* 6243 Babcock Rd San Antonio TX 78240

HOSLER, CHARLES FREDERICK, JR, BIOCHEMISTRY. *Current Pos:* Asst prof, 66-68, Bd Regents fac res grant, 66-78, admin dir nuclear radiation ctr, 68-70, assoc prof, 68-77, PROF CHEM, UNIV WIS-LA CROSSE, 77- *Personal Data:* b Flint, Mich, Sept 26, 39; m 62; c 2. *Educ:* Univ Mich, BS, 61; Univ Ill, MS, 63, PhD(biochem), 67. *Mem:* Am Col Sports Med; Am Chem Soc. *Res:* Biochemistry related to exercise; physical fitness assessment; human performance; serum lipoprotein analysis. *Mailing Add:* Chem Dept Univ Wis 1725 State St La Crosse WI 54601-3742

HOSLER, CHARLES LUTHER, JR, METEOROLOGY. *Current Pos:* From instr to prof meteorol, Pa State Univ, 48-92, head dept, 60-65, dean, Col Mineral Industs, 65-66, Col Earth & Mineral Sci, 66-85, actg exec vpres & provost, 90-92, EMER PROF, SR VPRES & PROVOST, PA STATE UNIV, 92- *Personal Data:* b Honey Brook, Pa, June 3, 24; m 47, 71; c 4. *Educ:* Pa State Univ, BS, 47, MS, 48 & PhD(meteorol), 51. *Concurrent Pos:* Hydrographer, Pa Dept Forests & Waters, 49-59; consult numerous pvt corps & fed agencies, 51-; mem, Nat Adv Comt Oceans & Atmosphere, 72-75; mem, Comt Atmospheric Sci, Nat Acad Sci, 75-78; mem, Nat Sci Bd, 85; vpres, Res & Dean Grad Sch, 85-91. *Mem:* Nat Acad Eng; fel Am Meteorol Soc (pres, 76-77); Am Geophys Union. *Res:* Cloud physics; weather modification. *Mailing Add:* Pa State Univ Walker Bldg Rm 617 University Park PA 16802. *Fax:* 814-865-3363

HOSLER, E(ARL) RAMON, CHEMICAL ENGINEERING. *Current Pos:* assoc prof, 79-85, PROF, UNIV CENT FLA, 85- *Personal Data:* b Columbus, Ohio, Dec 24, 35; m 57, Judith Lorenz; c Dianne, Dennis, Donald, Richard & Robert. *Educ:* Univ Dayton, BChE, 57; Univ Ill, MS, 59, PhD(chem eng), 61. *Prof Exp:* Engr thermal & hydraul res, Bettis Atomic Power Lab, Westinghouse Elec Corp, 61-63, sr engr, 63-73, eng mgr, 73-76, tech consult, 76-79. *Concurrent Pos:* Consult, Elec Power Res Inst; chmn, Heat Transfer & Energy Conversion Divs, Am Inst Chem Engrs, 81 & Fla Sect, Am Soc Mech Engrs, 90. *Mem:* Fel Am Inst Chem Engrs; Am Soc Mech Engrs; Am Soc Eng Educ. *Res:* Heat transfer and fluid mechanics, using high speed photography to discern basic mechanisms. *Mailing Add:* Univ Cent Fla PO Box 162450 Orlando FL 32816-2450

HOSLER, JOHN FREDERICK, ORGANIC CHEMISTRY. *Current Pos:* MGR DECORATIVE PROD RES & DEVELOP, FORMICA CORP, 68- *Personal Data:* b Berwick, Pa, Apr 13, 20; m 44; c 3. *Educ:* Pa State Col, BS, 42, MS, 48, PhD(chem), 51. *Prof Exp:* Chemist, Gen Chem Defense Corp, 42-43; res chemist, Calco Chem Div, Am Cyanamid Co, 51-54, group leader, 54-57, mgt pigment res, 57-58, asst to dir chem res, 58-59, mgr intermediate & explosives res, Org Chem Div, 59-61, mgr intermediates res & develop, NJ, 61-68. *Mem:* Am Chem Soc. *Res:* Organic intermediates and plastic additives; high pressure laminates and plastics. *Mailing Add:* 1094 Little Shag Lake Rd Gwinn MI 49841-9214

HOSLER, PETER, PETROLEUM CHEMISTRY. *Current Pos:* RETIRED. *Personal Data:* b Cleveland, Ohio, Mar 12, 27; m 48; c 5. *Educ:* Case Inst Technol, BS, 49; Univ Wis, MS, 51, PhD(biochem), 53. *Prof Exp:* Biochemist, Antibiotics Dept, Eli Lilly & Co, 53-61; res engr process develop, Sun Oil Co, 61-91. *Concurrent Pos:* Secy, Div Microbial Chem, Am Chem Soc, 65-67. *Mem:* Am Chem Soc. *Res:* Development of industrial fermentation processes at pilot plant scale; applied studies of microbiol metabolism as related to environmental factors; petrochemicals; lubricants and industrial oils. *Mailing Add:* 620 Morris Lane Wallingford PA 19086-6935

HOSLEY, ROBERT JAMES, MICROBIOLOGY. *Current Pos:* RETIRED. *Personal Data:* b Lima, NY, Apr 9, 23. *Educ:* Univ Rochester, AB, 49; Univ Mich, MS, 51 PhD(bact), 55. *Prof Exp:* Bacteriologist, Eli Lilly & Co, 55-58, head dept poliomyelitis vaccine develop, 58-59, head dept tissue cult develop, 60-62, mgr biol develop, 62-64, staff asst, Biol-Pharmacol Res Div, 65-71, admin asst, Res Grants Admin, 71-79. *Mem:* Sigma Xi. *Res:* Biologics. *Mailing Add:* 2120 Fairway Dr Bozeman MT 59715. *E-Mail:* tario@mcn.net

HOSMANE, NARAYAN SADASHIV, CARBORANES & METALLACARBORANES. *Current Pos:* from asst prof to assoc prof, 82-89, PROF INORG CHEM, SOUTHERN METHODIST UNIV, 89- *Personal Data:* b Gokarn, Karnataka, India, June 30, 48; nat US; m 76, Sumathy Rao; c Suneil & Nina. *Educ:* Karnatak Univ, Dharwar, India, BSc, 68, MSc, 70; Edinburgh Univ, Scotland, PhD(inorg chem), 74. *Honors & Awards:* Outstanding Res Award, Sigma Xi, 87. *Prof Exp:* Res asst organometallic chem, Queen's Univ Belfast, 74-75; res scientist pollution control, Lambeg Indust Res Asn, 75-76; res assoc inorg chem, Auburn Univ, 76-77 & Univ Va, 78-79; asst prof, Va Polytech Inst & State Univ, 79-82. *Concurrent Pos:* Vis prof, Ohio State Univ, 85-86; consult, Nat Cancer Inst, NIH, 90, Veritech, 90- *Mem:* Fel Royal Soc Chem; Am Chem Soc; fel Am Inst Chemists; Sigma Xi. *Res:* Synthetic and structural investigations of cluster compounds, especially those of boron, carbon and transition metals in concert with a number of other elements including group 4 hetero atoms; organosilicon chemistry. *Mailing Add:* Dept Chem Southern Methodist Univ Dallas TX 75275. *Fax:* 214-768-4089; *E-Mail:* nhosmane@sun.cis.smu.edu

HOSMANE, RAMACHANDRA SADASHIV, HETEROCYCLIC CHEMISTRY, NUCLEOSIDES & NUCLEOTIDES. *Current Pos:* from asst prof to assoc prof, 82-93, PROF CHEM, UNIV MD, BALTIMORE CO, 94- *Personal Data:* b Gokarn, India, Dec 12, 44; US citizen; m 75, T S Raji; c Mala. *Educ:* Karnatak Univ, Dharwar, India, BSc, 66, MSc, 68; Univ SFla, MS, 76, PhD (chem), 78. *Prof Exp:* Res assoc chem, Univ Ill, Urbana, 79-82. *Concurrent Pos:* NIH new investr res award, 84; mem sci rev study sect, Md Affil, Am Heart Asn, 88-91; ad hoc mem, Sci Rev Study Sect, Bioorg & Nat Prod Chem, NIH, 95 & 96. *Mem:* Sigma Xi; Am Chem Soc; affil mem Int Union Pure & Appl Chem; Int Soc Heterocyclic Chem; AAAS. *Res:* Developing new and novel reagents for organic/biorganic synthesis; synthesis of medicinally significant analogues of natural products, heterocycles, and nucleosides; synthesis of polycyclic heterocycles and study of concepts of heteroaromaticity, stability, and reactivity; rearrangements in organic synthesis; cross-linking reagents for proteins and nucleic acids; author of more than 60 publications in international journals; reagents for bioorganic synthesis; blood substitutes. *Mailing Add:* Dept Chem & Biochem Univ Md, Baltimore Co 1000 Hilltop Circle Baltimore MD 21250. *Fax:* 410-455-1148; *E-Mail:* hosmane@umbc7.umbc.edu

HOSNER, JOHN FRANK, FORESTRY. *Current Pos:* asst dean, Col Agr & Life Sci, 73-80, PROF FORESTRY, VA POLYTECH INST & STATE UNIV, 61-, DIR SCH FORESTRY & WILDLIFE RESOURCES, 69-, ASSOC DEAN, COL AGR & LIFE SCI, 80- *Personal Data:* b Gillespie, Ill, Feb 25, 25; m 51; c 2. *Educ:* Mich State Univ, BS, 48; Duke Univ, MF, 50; State Univ NY, PhD, 57. *Prof Exp:* Dist forester, State of Ill, 48-50; from instr to assoc prof forestry, Southern Ill Univ, 50-61. *Concurrent Pos:* Vis prof, Col Forestry, State Univ NY, 58-59. *Mem:* Fel AAAS; fel Soc Am Foresters; Ecol Soc Am; Am Inst Biol Sci; Soil Conserv Soc Am; Sigma Xi. *Res:* Ecology and silviculture of piedmont and mountain forests. *Mailing Add:* 1505 Lincoln Lane SW Blacksburg VA 24060

HOSNI, MOHAMMAD HOSEIN, FLUID MECHANICS, HEAT TRANSFER. *Current Pos:* asst prof, 90-94, DIR, INST ENVIRON RES, KANS STATE UNIV, 93-, ASSOC PROF, DEPT MECH ENG, 94- *Personal Data:* b Yazd, June 25, 55; m 83, Fakhry; c Mehrdad & Mina. *Educ:* Southern Univ, BS, 81; La State Univ, MS, 84; Miss State Univ, PhD(mech eng), 89. *Prof Exp:* Res assoc, Miss State Univ, 89-90. *Concurrent Pos:* Consult engr, Coast Machinery, 84-86; asst prof, Southern Univ, 84-86; prin investr, Am Soc Heating, Refrig & Air Conditioning Engrs, 92-94. *Mem:* Am Soc Mech Engrs; Am Inst Aeronaut & Astronaut; Am Soc Heating Refrig & Air Conditioning Engrs; Am Soc Eng Educ. *Res:* Fluid mechanics; heat transfer; experimental techniques; uncertainty analysis and design of experiments. *Mailing Add:* Dept Mech Eng Kans State Univ Manhattan KS 66506-5106. *Fax:* 785-532-6642; *E-Mail:* hosni@ksu.edu

HOSNI, YASSER ALI, COMPUTER-AIDED MANUFACTURING, APPLIED OPERATIONS RESEARCH. *Current Pos:* PROF INDUST ENG, UNIV CENT FLA, 77- *Personal Data:* b Cairo, Egypt, July 30, 41; m 76, Djehane; c Nadine & Nerine. *Educ:* Cairo Univ, BSc, 63, MSc, 67; Univ Ark, PhD(eng), 77. *Prof Exp:* Engr, Semaf Co, 53-64; chief eng, Prod Dept, Nasr Boiler & Mfg Co, 64-70; software specialist software design, NCR Co, 70-73; asst indust eng, Univ Ark, 73-77. *Concurrent Pos:* Consult, Morton Co, Fla Plumbing & Wakenhut, 76-81; prin investr, Dept Educ, 77-79, Fla Energy Off, 77-80 & Naval Training Equip Ctr, 78-82, NASA, 90-96. *Mem:* Inst Indust Engrs; Inst Elec & Electronics Engrs; Am Soc Eng Educ; Soc Mfg Engrs; Am Soc Qual Control; Int Ref Orgn Forensic Med & Sci. *Res:* Software design and development; productivity and quality in manufacturing; applied operations research; simulation; developing of industrial packages for decision making operations; energy conservation techniques; rapid prototyping and reverse engineering. *Mailing Add:* Indust Eng & Mgt Systs Univ Cent Fla PO Box 25000 Orlando FL 32816-0001. *Fax:* 407-823-3413; *E-Mail:* hosni@iems.engr.ucf.edu

HOSODA, JUNKO, BIOCHEMISTRY, MOLECULAR BIOLOGY. *Current Pos:* assoc res biochemist, Space Sci Lab, 67-76, STAFF SCIENTIST, LAWRENCE BERKELEY LAB, UNIV CALIF, BERKELEY, 77- *Personal Data:* b Apr 10, 32. *Educ:* Univ Tokyo, PhD(biochem), 60. *Prof Exp:* Res asst, Inst Appl Microbiol, Univ Tokyo, 60-63; res assoc, Mass Inst Technol, 63-66. *Concurrent Pos:* Vis scholar, Biozentrum Univ Basel, 73-76. *Mem:* Am Soc Biochem & Molecular Biol; Am Soc Microbiol; AAAS; Protein Soc. *Res:* DNA replication, repair and recombination; protein interactions; protein analysis of human mammary epithelial cell culture; protein chemistry. *Mailing Add:* CMB Dept Bldg 934 Rm 8 Lawrence Berkeley Lab Univ Calif Berkeley CA 94720-0001. *Fax:* 510-486-5735

HOSOKAWA, KEIICHI, MOLECULAR CELL BIOLOGY, MOLECULAR VIROLOGY. *Current Pos:* PROF & CHMN, DEPT BIOCHEM, KAWASAKI MED SCH, 76- *Personal Data:* b Minoh, Japan, Sept 19, 29; m 62; c Mika, Krista A & Ken. *Educ:* Osaka Univ, MD, 55, PhD(physiol chem), 61. *Honors & Awards:* Sci Achievement Award, Sanyo Broadcasting Found Sci & Cult, 88. *Prof Exp:* Res fel biochem, Osaka Univ Dent Sch, 60-66; asst prof biochem, Univ Calif, Berkeley, 63-65, prof, 66-71; sr scientist, Worcester Found Exp Biol, 71-76. *Concurrent Pos:* Res fel radiation med, Radiation Ctr Osaka Prefecture, 61-62; Miller res fel bact, Univ Calif, Berkeley, 63-65; proj assoc, Univ Wis, 65; Med Res Coun res fel biochem, Ont Cancer Inst, 65-66; vis scientist, City Hope Res Inst, 80; lectr, Dept Virol, Okayama Univ Med Sch, 80-82, Dept Biochem, 80- & Inst Cancer Res, 91-; vis sr scientist, Southern Ill Univ, 83; adj prof, Dept Nutrit Biochem & Chem Biopolymers, Kawasaki Col Allied Health Prof, 83-86; guest prof, Inst Genetics, Univ Cologne, 84-93; vis prof, Okayama Univ Med Sch, 93-94. *Mem:* Am Soc Biochem & Molecular Biol; Am Soc Microbiol; Am Chem Soc; NY Acad Sci; Protein Soc. *Res:* Functionally active ribosome reconstituted from inactive subparticles and proteins and from RNAs and proteins; in vitro assembled adenovirus chromatin as a highly efficient probe for transfection; regulation of gene expression in adenovirus infected HeLa all host response against virus; structure and function of ribosome; enzymatic mechanism and evolution of oxygenase in soil bacteria. *Mailing Add:* 2-2-7 Minowa Taito-Ku Tokyo 110 Japan. *Fax:* 81-86-272-8077

HOSS, DONALD EARL, PHYSIOLOGICAL ECOLOGY. *Current Pos:* fishery biologist, prog leader physiol ecol, 72-87, CHIEF, RESOURCE ECOL DIV, NAT MARINE FISHERIES SERV, BEAUFORT LAB, 87- *Personal Data:* b Mexico, Mo, Dec 17, 36; m 60, Carolyn Reasch; c Timothy & Patrick. *Educ:* Univ Mo-Columbia, BS, 58; NC State Univ, MS, 65, PhD(zool), 71. *Prof Exp:* Fishery biologist radiobiol, Bur Com Fisheries Radiobiol Lab, 58-69. *Concurrent Pos:* Lab rep, Secy Interior Oil-Spill Comt, 70-71; adj fac mem, NC State Univ, 74-; vis investr, Dunstaffnage Marine Res Lab, Scottish Marine Biol Asn, Oban, 76-77. *Mem:* Am Fisheries Soc; Estuarine Res Fedn; Sigma Xi. *Res:* Effects of natural and man-induced changes on the survival and growth of fish; larval fish development and physiology; karval fish recruitment processes. *Mailing Add:* 118 Straits Haven Rd Beaufort NC 28516. *E-Mail:* cdhoss@hatteras.bea.nmfs.gov

HOSS, WAYNE PAUL, NEUROSCIENCE. *Current Pos:* PROF MED CHEM, UNIV TOLEDO, 85-, CO-DIR, CTR DRUG DESIGN & DEVELOP & ASSOC VPRES, RES & DEVELOP, 89- *Personal Data:* b Paso Robles, Calif, Dec 11, 43; m 67, Dorothy Hart. *Educ:* Univ Idaho, BS, 66; Univ Nebr, PhD(chem), 71. *Prof Exp:* NSF teaching fel, Ctr Brain Res, Univ Rochester, 70-72, NIH fel, 72-75, from asst prof to assoc prof, Ctr Brain Res, 80-85. *Concurrent Pos:* Vis assoc prof biochem, Nagoya City Univ, Japan, 77; NIMH res career develop award, 76-81; dir, Undergrad Neurosci Prog, Univ Rochester, 80-84. *Mem:* Am Soc Pharmacol & Exp Ther; Am Asn Cols Pharm; NY Acad Sci; Soc Neurosci; Am Chem Soc. *Res:* Biochemistry and pharmacology of cns receptors, including opioid, cholinergic and histaminergic; drugs of abuse; G-proteins; aging and dementia; development of new therapeutics. *Mailing Add:* Univ Toledo Col Univ Off Res 2801 W Bancroft St Toledo OH 43606-3390. *Fax:* 419-530-7893; *E-Mail:* whoss@uofto2.utoledo.edu

HOSSAIN, SHAFI UL, chemistry, for more information see previous edition

HOSSAINI, ALI A, CLINICAL PATHOLOGY. *Current Pos:* from asst prof to assoc prof clin path, 63-76, PROF PATH, MED COL VA, 67-, DIR BLOOD BANK, 63-, DIR SCH BLOOD BANKING, 65- *Personal Data:* b Basra, Iraq, Sept 24, 28; nat US; m 61; c 4. *Educ:* Am Univ Beirut, BA, 53; Tex Christian Univ, MS, 57; Ohio State Univ, PhD(path), 60. *Prof Exp:* Dir health educ, Am Point IV Prog, Iran, 53-55; asst instr clin path, Ohio State Univ, 59-60; dir, Ports Hosp, Basra, Iraq, 60-62; dir biochem, Med Ctr, Univ WVa, 62-63. *Concurrent Pos:* Am Cancer Soc grant, 64-; consult, Vet Admin Hosp, 65- *Mem:* AAAS; Am Soc Clin Path; Am Thoracic. *Res:* Serologic differentiation between leukemic and normal leukocytes; diagnosis of leukemias serologically; attempts at finding antagonists destroying leukemic leukocytes; relationship between leukoagglutinins and febrile transfusion reactions. *Mailing Add:* Path Box 662 Va Commonwealth Univ Sch Med Richmond VA 23298-1900

HOSSLER, FRED E, HISTOLOGY, CELL BIOLOGY. *Current Pos:* assoc prof, 80-89, PROF HISTOL & ELECTRON MICROS, ETENN STATE UNIV, 89- *Personal Data:* b Hamburg, Pa, May 7, 41; m 74; c 3. *Educ:* Muhlenberg Col, BS, 63; Pa State Univ, MS, 65; Univ Colo, PhD(path), 71. *Prof Exp:* Postdoctoral cell biol, Yale Univ, 71-74; from asst prof to assoc prof anat, histol & cell biol, La State Univ, 74-80. *Concurrent Pos:* Asst dean, Sch Grad Studies, ETenn State Univ, 87-89, actg dean & assoc vpres, 89-90. *Mem:* Am Asn Anatomists; Am Soc Cell Biol; Electron Micros Soc Am. *Res:* Sodium, potassium-astatine-pase-rich epithelia and their changes with changing osmotic conditions; microvascular of heart, lung, ion-transporting tissues as viewed with corrosion casting and scanning electron microscopy. *Mailing Add:* Dept Anat Col Med ETenn State Univ PO Box 70582 Johnson City TN 37614-0582. *Fax:* 423-461-7040

HOSSNER, KIM L, ENDOCRINE REGULATION OF ANIMAL GROWTH. *Current Pos:* asst prof, 85-91, ASSOC PROF, DEPT ANIMAL SCI, COLO STATE UNIV, 91- *Personal Data:* b Idaho Falls, Idaho, Jan 3, 49; m 71, Linda Timmons; c Nathan & Matt. *Educ:* Univ Idaho, BS, 71; Univ Tenn, PhD(zool), 76. *Prof Exp:* Fel, Case Western Res Univ, 76-80; instr & res assoc endocrinol, Univ Idaho, 80-85. *Concurrent Pos:* Prin investr insulin-like growth factor receptors, Colo State Univ, 86-89, prof animal growth regulation, 85- *Mem:* AAAS; Am Soc Animal Sci; Endocrine Soc. *Res:* Hormonal regulation of animal growth, with a primary focus on insulin-like growth factors and growth hormone in sheep and cattle; gene expression, receptors and binding proteins. *Mailing Add:* Dept Animal Sci Colo State Univ Ft Collins CO 80523

HOSSNER, LLOYD RICHARD, SOIL CHEMISTRY, SOIL FERTILITY. *Current Pos:* from asst prof to assoc prof, 68-77, PROF SOIL CHEM, TEX A&M UNIV, 77- *Personal Data:* b Ashton, Idaho, July 24, 36; m 58, Yvonne Rees; c Gregory, Layne & Eric. *Educ:* Utah State Univ, BS, 58, MS, 61; Mich State Univ, PhD(soil chem), 65. *Honors & Awards:* Super Achievement Award Res, Soil & Crop Sci, 89; Super Serv Res Award, USDA, 93; Soil Sci Appl Res Award, Soil Sci Soc Am, 96. *Prof Exp:* Res asst soil chem, Utah State Univ, 59-61; instr, Mont State Univ, 61-62; res asst, Mich State Univ, 62-65; res soil chemist, Int Minerals & Chem Corp, 65-68. *Concurrent Pos:* Ed, Soil Sci Soc Am J; assoc ed, Nutrit Cycling in Agroecosyst. *Mem:* AAAS; fel Am Soc Agron; fel Soil Sci Soc Am; Sigma Xi; Int Soil Sci Soc. *Res:* Applied soil chemistry; soil-fertilizer reaction products; waste management; surface mine reclamation; author of over 100 publications. *Mailing Add:* Dept Soil & Crop Sci Tex A&M Univ College Station TX 77843. *Fax:* 409-845-0456; *E-Mail:* l_hossner@tamu.edu

HOSTER, DONALD PAUL, INORGANIC CHEMISTRY. *Current Pos:* from asst prof to assoc prof, 70-90, coordr physics & phys sci, 86-90, PROF CHEM, BALTIMORE CITY COMMUNITY COL, 90- *Personal Data:* b Seneca Falls, NY, Aug 30, 41; m 82, Joanne E Price. *Educ:* Union Col, NY, BS, 63; Univ Del, MS, 65, PhD(phys org chem), 68. *Honors & Awards:* NSF Equip Grant, 77. *Prof Exp:* Asst prof chem, St Joseph Col, Md, 67-70. *Concurrent Pos:* Lectr, Mt St Mary's Col, Md, 69-70; res partic, NSF, 68; summer res prog fac, US Army, 90; Md collab sci-math teacher prep, NSF, 93- *Mem:* Am Chem Soc; Nat Sci Teachers Asn. *Res:* Gas phase reactions and pyrolysis of organic chlorides and acetates; deuterium exchange reactions; individualizing instruction; audio-visual aids; biochemistry for dental hygiene curriculum; computer applications in chemical education; chemistry for nonscientists; FTIR in chemical analysis; constructivist approach to teaching science (chemistry); chemical science for the elementary grades. *Mailing Add:* 625 Parkwyrth Ave Baltimore MD 21218-1956

HOSTETLER, JEPTHA RAY, PREVENTIVE MEDICINE, DRUG & ALCOHOL ABUSE MEDICINE. *Current Pos:* from asst prof to assoc prof anat, 70-81, assoc prof prev med, 81-95, ASSOC PROF PSYCHIAT, OHIO STATE UNIV. *Personal Data:* b Orrville, Ohio, June 23, 39; m 62, A Joyce Metzler; c Jodi, Jill & Julie. *Educ:* Goshen Col, BA, 62; Ohio State Univ, PhD(anat), 69. *Prof Exp:* NIH fel, Col Med, Tufts Univ, 68-70; instr anat, Univ Ky, 68-70. *Mem:* Asn Med Educ & Res Substance Abuse. *Res:* Medical student teaching/training in alcohol & other drug abuse medicine. *Mailing Add:* 193 E Frambes Columbus OH 43201-1409. *Fax:* 614-293-3937

HOSTETLER, KARL YODER, MEDICINE, BIOCHEMISTRY. *Current Pos:* from asst prof to assoc prof, 73-84, PROF MED, UNIV CALIF, SAN DIEGO, 84-,; PHYSICIAN, VET ADMIN MED CTR, SAN DIEGO, CALIF, 73- *Personal Data:* b Goshen, Ind, Nov 17, 39; m 71, Margaretha Steur; c Saskia E, Kirsten C & Carl M. *Educ:* De Pauw Univ, BA, 61; Western Res Univ, MD, 65. *Concurrent Pos:* Fel, John Simon Guggenheim Found, 80-81 & Japan Soc Prom Sci, 86; founder & vpres res & develop, Vical Inc, San Diego, 87-92, consult, 92-; bd dirs, Triangle Pharmaceut Inc, 95- *Mem:* Am Soc Biochem & Molecular Biol; Am Soc Clin Invest; Int Soc Antiviral Res; Endocrine Soc; Western Asn Phys; Am Soc Microbiol. *Res:* Clinical endocrinology and metabolism; chemistry and biochemistry of phospholipids; mechanisms of drug-induced lipidosis; design, synthesis and evaluation of lipid prodrugs of antiviral and anticancer agents. *Mailing Add:* 14024 Rue St Raphael Del Mar CA 92014-3043. *Fax:* 619-534-6133; *E-Mail:* khostetl@ ucsd.edu

HOSTETLER, ROBERT PAUL, MATHEMATICS EDUCATION. *Current Pos:* instr, Behrend Col, Pa State Univ, 64-67, asst prof, 70-79, assoc prof math, 79-96, EMER ASSOC PROF MATH, BEHREND COL, PA STATE UNIV, 96- *Personal Data:* b Holsopple, Pa, Apr 8, 37; m 60, Eloise Beyeler; c Lori, Eric, Chad, Greg & Pamela. *Educ:* Eastern Mennonite Col, BS, 59; Pa State Univ, MA, 65, PhD(math educ), 70. *Prof Exp:* High sch teacher, Pa, 59-62. *Mem:* Math Asn Am; Nat Coun Teachers Math. *Res:* Effective sequencing of mathematical content; mathematics as skill, art and process; textbook author in elementary, intermediate & college algebra; precalculus; calculus. *Mailing Add:* Dept Math Behrend Col Pa State Univ Erie PA 16563

HOSTETLER, ROY IVAN, VETERINARY MEDICINE. *Current Pos:* RETIRED. *Personal Data:* b Asotin, Wash, Sept 9, 16; m 41; c 3. *Educ:* Wash State Univ, BS & DVM, 39. *Prof Exp:* Jr vet, USDA, 39-42; pvt pract, Wash, 46-58; supvr animal indust div, Wash State Dept Agr, 58-60; exten vet, Coop Exten Serv, Wash State Univ, 60-78. *Concurrent Pos:* Mem, Nat Mastitis Coun. *Mem:* Am Vet Med Asn; US Animal Health Asn. *Res:* Mastitis control; nitrate toxicity; selenium toxicity and industry contamination; internal parasites. *Mailing Add:* 2365 Valleyview Ct Clarkston WA 99403

HOSTETTER, DONALD LEE, insect pathology, for more information see previous edition

HOSTETTLER, JOHN DAVISON, PHYSICAL CHEMISTRY. *Current Pos:* PROF CHEM, SAN JOSE STATE UNIV, 95- *Personal Data:* b Rockford, Ill, June 22, 41; m 65; c 2. *Educ:* Monmouth Col, BA, 62; Univ Wis-Madison, PhD(phys chem), 70. *Prof Exp:* Asst prof, chem, Univ Colo, Colo Colo Springs, 70-77, assoc prof, 77-95. *Mem:* AAAS; Am Chem Soc. *Res:* Fluorescence applied to polymers C-13 nuclear magnetic resonance; chemical education. *Mailing Add:* Dept Chem San Jose State Univ One Washington Sq San Jose CA 95192-0101

HOTCHIN, JOHN ELTON, VIROLOGY. *Current Pos:* RETIRED. *Personal Data:* b Sutton-On-Sea, Eng, Apr 7, 21; m 52; c 1. *Educ:* Univ London, MD & BS, 44, PhD, 52; FRCPath, 72. *Prof Exp:* House surgeon & physician, Kings Col Hosp, London, 43-44; mem res staff, Nat Insts Med Res, London, 48-55; asst prof bact & immunol, Univ BC, 55-57; asst dir, div labs & res, NY State Dept Health, Albany, 57-87. *Concurrent Pos:* Rockefeller travelling fel, Johns Hopkins Univ & Kerckhoff Lab, Calif Inst Technol, 52-54; res assoc, Western Div, Connaught Med Res Labs, 55-57; prof, Med Sch, Albany Hosp, 57-; ed, Infection & Immunity. *Mem:* Am Soc Microbiol; Am Asn Immunol; Infectious Dis Soc Am. *Res:* Pathogenesis of persistent and slow virus infections; virus induced behavioral disorders. *Mailing Add:* 18 Paxwood Rd Delmar NY 12054

HOTCHKISS, DONALD K, APPLIED STATISTICS. *Current Pos:* RETIRED. *Personal Data:* b Eldora, Iowa, Dec 23, 28; m 52, Dorothy Ives; c Thomas, William & Elizabeth. *Educ:* Iowa State Univ, BS, 50, PhD(animal nutrit), 60. *Prof Exp:* Co exten dir, Iowa State Univ, 54-56, asst dairy nutrit, 56-59; res statistician, Design & Analytical Exp, Ralston Purina Co, 59-61; prof & consult statist, Iowa Stat Univ, 61-90. *Concurrent Pos:* Vis prof, Nat Sch Agr, Mex, 67-68; vis lectr, Univ Costa Rica, 83. *Mem:* Biomet Soc; Am Statist Asn. *Res:* Nutrition of dairy cows; design of experiments in area of biological sciences. *Mailing Add:* Statist Lab Iowa State Univ Ames IA 50011

HOTCHKISS, JULANE, REPRODUCTIVE PHYSIOLOGY. *Current Pos:* RES PROF PHYSIOL, MED SCH, UNIV TEX, 82- *Personal Data:* b 1934; c 2. *Educ:* Harvard Univ, PhD(physiol), 62. *Prof Exp:* From instr to res prof, Dept Physiol, Univ Pittsburgh Sch Med, 62-85. *Concurrent Pos:* Sect mem, Women Caucus, Endocrine Soc, 83-86, pres, 88-90. *Mem:* Endocrine Soc; Am Physiol Soc; Int Soc Neuroendocrinol. *Res:* Reproductive endocrinology. *Mailing Add:* Dept Integrative Biol Med Sch Univ Tex PO Box 20708 Houston TX 77225. *Fax:* 713-500-7444; *E-Mail:* hotchkis@girch1.med.uth. tmc.edu

HOTCHKISS, ROLLIN DOUGLAS, BIOCHEMISTRY. *Current Pos:* asst chem, Rockefeller Inst, 38-42, assoc path & microbiol, 42-50, assoc mem, 50-55, prof physiol, 55-82, EMER PROF PHYSIOL, ROCKEFELLER UNIV, 82- *Personal Data:* b South Britain, Conn, Sept 8, 11; m 33, 67, Magda Gabor; c Paul & Cynthia. *Educ:* Yale Univ, BS, 32, PhD(org chem), 35. *Hon Degrees:* ScD, Yale Univ, 62 & Univ Paris-South, 80, State Univ NY, Albany 86, Rockefeller Univ, 88. *Honors & Awards:* Commercial Solvents Co Award, Am Soc Bact, 53; Dyer lectr, NIH, 61; Griffith lectr, Soc Gen Microbiol, 74. *Prof Exp:* Asst elem chem, Yale Univ, 32-34; fel chem, Rockefeller Inst, 35-36, asst, 36-37; Rockefeller Found fel, Carlsberg Lab, Copenhagen, 37-38. *Concurrent Pos:* Vis prof, Mass Inst Technol, 58, Univ Calif, Berkeley, 68 & Corpus Christi Col, Univ Cambridge, 70; mem sci adv bds, Roswell Park Mem Inst, Univ Buffalo, 58-65, Inst Cancer Res, 60-74, & Nat Inst Allergy & Infectious Dis, 61-64; mem adv bd, Biol Div, Oak Ridge Nat Lab, 62-70 & Nat Cancer Inst, 64-68; scholar, Fogarty Ctr, NIH, 71-72, UNESCO vis scholar, Biol Res Ctr, Szeged, 72-78; vis prof, Biol Sci Div, Univ Utah, 72 & 73, Univ Paris, Orsay, 75 & 79, Raine vis prof, Univ Perth, 80; res prof biol, State Univ NY, Albany, 82-85, adj prof, 85- *Mem:* Nat Acad Sci; fel Am Acad Naturalists (vpres, 65); Harvey Soc (pres, 58-59); fel Am Acad Arts & Sci; Genetics Soc Am (pres, 72); fel AAAS; Hungarian Acad Sci; Royal Danish Acad Sci; Am Soc Cell Biol. *Res:* Bacterial metabolism; mode of action of anti-bacterial agents; bacterial genetics; fusion bacterial protoplasts; immunochemistry; protein chemistry; carbohydrates; nucleic acids; exonucleases; bacterial diploidy. *Mailing Add:* 2-4 Rolling Hills Condominium Lenox MA 01240

HOTCHKISS, SHARON K, BIOLOGY. *Current Pos:* DIR, POTSDAM MATH & READING CTR, 91- *Personal Data:* b Eau Claire, Wis, Dec 1, 42; m 82, David Kaup; c Galen. *Educ:* Univ Wis-Eau Claire, BS, 67; Univ Ky, PhD(microbiol), 73. *Prof Exp:* Instr cell biol, Med Sch, Univ Ky, 73-74; asst prof biol, Univ Wis-River Falls, 75-78; lectr, Northwestern Univ, 78-79; asst prof, Clarkson Col, 79-85. *Res:* Genetics and developmental events associated with the circadian rhythm of eclosion in Drosophila; cell division cycle. *Mailing Add:* 133 Leroy St Potsdam NY 13676. *Fax:* 315-265-3039

HOTCHKISS, WILLIAM ROUSE, GROUNDWATER MODELING, SNOW HYDROLOGY. *Current Pos:* Hydrologist, Water Resources Div, US Geol Surv, 65-78, proj leader, Northern Great Plains Regional Aquifer Syst Assessment, 78-82, supv hydrologist & chief, Nat Training Ctr, 82-89, CENT REGION STAFF, US GEOL SURV, 89- *Personal Data:* b Schenectady, NY, June 12, 37; m 65; c 6. *Educ:* Dartmouth Col, 55-59, Mont State Col, BS, 62, MS, 65; Colo State Univ, PhD(civil eng), 88. *Honors & Awards:* Montgomery M Atwater Award, Nat Avalanche Found, 89. *Mem:* Am Inst Hydrol; Am Geophys Union; fel Geol Soc Am; Int Glaciological Soc; Am Asn Avalanche Prof. *Res:* Glacial ablation studies in Montana & California; ground water studies in the San Joaquin & Sacramento Valleys of California; snow hydrology & the study of snow avalanches; author of 50 publications & reports. *Mailing Add:* Geol Surv WRD Cent Region Staff MS 406 Box 25046 Lakewood CO 80225-0046

HOTH, DANIEL F, MEDICAL RESEARCH. *Current Pos:* RESEARCHER, CELL GENSYS, 92- *Personal Data:* b Washington, DC, Apr 3, 46; m. *Educ:* Franklin & Marshall Col, AB, 68; Georgetown Univ, MD, 72; Am Bd Internal Med, dipl, 76, dipl oncol, 77. *Prof Exp:* Intern med, Med Sch, Georgetown Univ, 72-73, jr & sr resident internal med, Georgetown Univ Med Hosp, 73-75, fel med oncol, 77-75, from instr to asst prof med, 77-80; head Drug Eval & Reporting Sect, Nat Cancer Inst, 80-81, chief Investigational Drug Br, Cancer Ther Eval Prog, Div Cancer Treatment, 81-87, actg assoc dir, 82-83; actg dir, Div Aids, Nat Inst Allergy & Infectious Dis, 87-88, dir, 88-92. *Concurrent Pos:* Jr fac clin fel, Am Cancer Soc, 78-80. *Mem:* Am Soc Clin Oncol; Am Col Physicians; Am Soc Clin Pharmacol & Therapeut; Soc Clin Trials; Infectious Dis Soc Am. *Res:* Internal medicine; AIDS. *Mailing Add:* 9517 Accord Dr Potomac MD 20854

HOTTA, SHOICHI STEVEN, BIOCHEMISTRY, MEDICINE. *Current Pos:* MED OFFICER, PUB HEALTH SERV, 89- *Personal Data:* b Stockton, Calif, Jan 8, 29; m 54, Mary M Furukawa; c Gregory T & Stephanie H. *Educ:* Univ Calif, Berkeley, BA, 50, PhD(biochem), 53; Johns Hopkins Univ, MD, 58. *Prof Exp:* Jr asst physiologist biochem, Univ Calif, Berkeley, 53-54; asst prof, Med Col, Cornell Univ, 61-73; from assoc prof to prof biochem, Eastern Va Med Sch, 73-85; med officer, Food & Drug Admin, 85-89. *Mem:* AAAS; Am Chem Soc; Soc Exp Biol & Med; NY Acad Sci; Am Soc Biol Chemists; Am Soc Clin Nutrit. *Res:* Cholesterol metabolism in diabetic and normal animals; pathways of glucose and glutamate metabolism in brain; roles of hexosemonophosphate shunt and glutathione in cells; biochemical basis for effects of compounds in brain; regulation of cholesterol metabolism. *Mailing Add:* 7001 Roundtree Rd Falls Church VA 22042-3912

HOTTA, YASUO, CELL BIOLOGY, GENETICS. *Current Pos:* assoc res biologist, 65-73, RES BIOLOGIST, UNIV CALIF, SAN DIEGO, 73- *Personal Data:* b Nagoya, Japan, Jan 12, 32; m 59; c 2. *Educ:* Nagoya Univ, BSc, 54, MSc, 56, DSc(biol), 59. *Prof Exp:* Nat Res Coun Can res fel, 59-60; res assoc bot, Univ Ill, 60-65. *Concurrent Pos:* Consult, Hirokawa Publ Co, Tokyo, Japan, 70- & Eisai Pharmaceut Co, Tokyo, 74-80; Oriental Nutrit Res Corp, San Diego, 83- *Mem:* Am Soc Cell Biol; Soc Develop Biol; Japan Soc Genetics. *Res:* Mechanisms and control of homologous chromosome pairing and crossing-over in meiosis; recombination, repair mechanisms and modification of DNA molecules in eukaryotic cells; analysis and control of chromosome pairing and chiasmata formation in meiosis. *Mailing Add:* Sch Biosci NARA Inst Sci & Tech Takayama-cho Ikoma-shi 630-01 Japan. *Fax:* 81-052-781-4763

HOTTEL, HOYT C(LARKE), CHEMICAL ENGINEERING, COMBUSTION. *Current Pos:* Asst, Mass Inst Technol, 24-25, res assoc, 27-28, from asst prof to prof, 28-66, dir, Fuel Res Lab, 34-69, Carbon P Dubbs prof, 66-69, EMER PROF, MASS INST TECHNOL, 69- *Personal Data:* b Salem, Ind, Jan 15, 03; m 29, Nellie L Rich; c Lois H (Wood), Hoyt C Jr, Barbara H (Willis) & Elizabeth H (Barrett). *Educ:* Univ Ind, AB, 22; Mass Inst Technol, MS, 24. *Honors & Awards:* King's Medal, Eng, 47; William H Walker Award, Am Inst Chem Eng, 47; Edgerton Medal, Combustion Inst, 60; Melchett Medal, Brit Inst Fuel, 60; Max Jakob Award, Am Soc Mech

Engrs & Am Inst Chem Eng, 66; Farrington Daniels Award, Int Solar Energy Soc, 75; Royal Soc Esso Energy Award, 75; Founders Award, Nat Acad Eng, 80; Hottel lectr, Mass Inst Technol, 85; Biennial Hottel Plenary Lectr, Combustion Inst, 85. *Concurrent Pos:* Tech aide & sect chief, Fire Warfare Sect, Nat Defense Res Comt, 42-45; mem, Gas Turbine Subcomt, Nat Adv Comt Aerospace, 42-46, ad hoc comt, status jet propulsion, Whitman Comt, US Dept Defense, 43, Panel Coal Gasification Technol, Nat Acad Eng-Nat Res Coun, 71-73, rev comt, Task Force Energy, Nat Acad Eng, 74, Adv Group Arid Zone Probs Brazil, Nat Acad Sci, 74-75, ad hoc Panel Advan Power Cycles, Nat Res Coun, 75-78, Eval Panel Energy Conserv Prog, US Bur Stand, 76-80, Comt Chem Coal Utilization, Nat Res Coun, 76-80, Comt Assessment Indust Energy Conserv Prog, Dept Energy, 80-82, Panel Fire Res, Assessment Nat Bur Stand, Prog, 85-91; chmn, Thermal Panel, Armed Forces Spec Weapons Proj, US Dept Defense, 46-56; chmn, Am Flame Res Comt, 53-74, hon chmn, 74-; chmn, Comt Fire Res, Nat Acad Sci-Nat Res Coun, 56-67, mem adv panel, Bldg Res Div, US Bur Stand, 65-69, Ctr Fire Res, 85-91. *Mem:* Nat Acad Sci; Nat Acad Eng; Am Chem Soc; Combustion Inst (vpres, 53-64); Am Acad Arts & Sci. *Res:* Radiant heat transmission; optical methods of temperature measurement; flame propagation; combustion mechanisms; combustion in ramjets and turbines; radiative transfer; solar energy utilization; new energy technology. *Mailing Add:* 27 Cambridge St Winchester MA 01890. *Fax:* 617-258-5042

HOTTON, NICHOLAS, III, VERTEBRATE PALEONTOLOGY. *Current Pos:* assoc cur to cur, Div Vert Paleont, 59-68, res cur, 68-93, EMER RES PALEONTOLOGIST, DEPT PALEOBIOL, NAT MUS NAT HIST, SMITHSONIAN INST, 93- *Personal Data:* b Sault Ste Marie, Mich, Jan 28, 21; wid; c Albert T, Nicholas IV & Carol L. *Educ:* Univ Chicago, BS, 47, PhD(paleozool), 50. *Prof Exp:* Asst instr zool, Univ Ill, 50-51; instr anat, Univ Kans Sch Med, 51-54, asst prof, 54-59. *Mem:* Soc Vert Paleont; Sigma Xi; AAAS. *Res:* Paleontology of lower tetrapods; cranial morphology; functional anatomy. *Mailing Add:* 101 Sheridan Ave Takoma Park MD 20912-5741

HOTZ, HENRY PALMER, INSTRUMENTAL ANALYSIS. *Current Pos:* CONSULT, 91- *Personal Data:* b Fayetteville, Ark, Oct 17, 25; m 52, Marie Brase; c Henry B, Mary (Hogen) & Martha (Vitaterna). *Educ:* Univ Ark, BS, 48; Wash Univ, PhD(physics), 53. *Prof Exp:* Asst prof physics, Auburn Univ, 53-58 & Okla State Univ, 58-64; assoc prof, Marietta Col, 64-66; scientist-in-residence, US Naval Radiol Defense Lab, 66-67; assoc prof physics, Univ Mo, Rolla, 67-71; physicist, Qanta Metrix Corp, 71-74; sr scientist, Nuclear Equip Corp, 74-79, Wemco Div, Envirotech Corp, 79-82, Dohrmann Div, Xertex Corp, 82-86 & Dohrmann Div, Rosemount Anal Corp, 86-91. *Concurrent Pos:* Consult, Air Force Missile Develop Ctr, Holloman AFB, 58-61 & US Naval Radiol Defense Lab, 64-65. *Mem:* AAAS; Am Phys Soc; Am Asn Physics Teachers; Comput Soc; Asn Comput Mach. *Res:* Design chemical analytical instruments. *Mailing Add:* 290 Stilt Ct Foster City CA 94404. *Fax:* 650-342-8595

HOTZ, PRESTON ENSLOW, GEOLOGY. *Current Pos:* RETIRED. *Personal Data:* b Sonoma, Calif, Mar 24, 13; m 40; c 3. *Educ:* Univ Calif, Berkeley, AB, 37, MA, 40; Princeton Univ, PhD, 49. *Prof Exp:* Recorder & mem field party, US Geol Surv, Ore, 38-41, geol field asst & jr geologist, Ore, 41, from jr geologist to geologist, Calif, NJ & Pa, 42-49, Washington, DC, 50 & Nev, 51-57, area supvr, Mineral Deposits Br, 58-59, geologist, 60-77. *Mem:* Fel Geol Soc Am. *Res:* Petrology of Triassic diabases of Pennsylvania; magnetite deposits of the Dillsburg district, Pennsylvania, and of New Jersey; structure and stratigraphy of northern Nevada; gold and nickel deposits of northern California and southwest Oregon; geology of northern Klamath Mountains, California. *Mailing Add:* 209 Blackburn Ave Menlo Park CA 94025

HOU, CHING-TSANG, BIOCATALYSIS, BIOTRANSFORMATION. *Current Pos:* LEAD SCIENTIST, NAT CTR AGR UTILIZATION RES, USDA, PEORIA, ILL, 88- *Personal Data:* b Taiwan, June 26, 35; US citizen; m 61, Manhua Chen; c Susan, Janey & Nancy. *Educ:* Nat Taiwan Univ, BS, 58; Univ Tokyo, MS, 64, PhD(biochem), 67. *Prof Exp:* Chemist, Taiwan Sugar Coop, 60-62; res assoc biochem, Sch Pharm, Univ Wis-Madison, 68-69; microbiologist, Northern Regional Res Lab, USDA, 69-71; res biochemist, Exxon Res Ctr, Linden, NJ, 71-74, sr res biochemist, 74-77, staff biochemist, 77-79, sr staff biochemist, 79-82, prin investr, Annandale, NJ, 82-86; dir natural prod, Squibb Inst Med Res, 86-88. *Concurrent Pos:* Consult, Exxon Res Ctr, Annandale, NJ, 90-92; assoc ed, J Am Oil Chemists Soc, 92-; vchair, Biotechnol Div, Am Oil Chemists Soc, 95- *Mem:* Am Chem Soc; fel Am Soc Microbiol; Am Oil Chemists Soc; fel Soc Indust Microbiol; Chinese-Am Microbiol Soc (pres, 95-96). *Res:* Oil and fatty acids bioconversion; biocatalysis; antimicrobial agents; natural products; petrochemicals; hydrocarbon oxidation enzymes; mono and dioxygenases; mycotoxins; peptide antibiotic lactonases; steryl glucoside biosynthesis; vitamin A biosynthesis; alcohol production. *Mailing Add:* USDA Agr Res Serv Nat Ctr Agr Utilization Res 1815 N University St Peoria IL 61604. *Fax:* 309-681-6686

HOU, DAQING, POWER SYSTEM PROTECTION RELAYING, DIGITAL SIGNAL PROCESSING. *Current Pos:* develop engr, 90-92, ROTATING MACHINERY ENG MGR, SCHWEITZER ENG LABS, 97- *Personal Data:* b Fushun, China, Oct 1, 59; m 84, Jian Chen; c Andy E & Brilliana X. *Educ:* Northeast Univ, China, BS, 82, MS, 84; Wash State Univ, PhD(elec & comput eng), 92. *Prof Exp:* Asst prof, Northeast Univ, China, 84-85. *Mem:* Inst Elec & Electronics Engrs. *Res:* Research and design protection algorithms to be used in microprocessor relays which protect power system transmission and distribution lines, power transformers buses, motors and generator; simulate power systems and protection logic; design signal processing algorithms and study general linear systems. *Mailing Add:* 2350 NE Hopkins Ct Pullman WA 99163. *Fax:* 509-334-4935; *E-Mail:* daqing_hou@selinc.com

HOU, GENE JEAN-WIN, ENGINEERING DESIGN OPTIMIZATION, COMPUTATIONAL MECHANICS. *Current Pos:* Asst prof, 83-90, ASSOC PROF MECH ENG, OLD DOMINION UNIV, 89- *Personal Data:* b Yunlin, Taiwan, Feb 2, 52; US citizen; m 80; c 3. *Educ:* Nat Cheng Kung Univ, Taiwan, BS, 74; Nat Taiwan Univ, MS, 76; Univ Iowa, PhD(mech eng), 83. *Honors & Awards:* Ralph R Teeter Educ Award, Eng Soc Advancing Mobility Land Sea Air & Space, 88. *Concurrent Pos:* Prin investr, NSF, NASA & local indust, 83-91; NSF presidential young investr, 87; liaison officer, Comt Design Theory & Methodology, Am Soc Mech Engrs, 88-89. *Mem:* Am Soc Mech Engrs; Am Inst Aeronaut & Astronaut; Eng Soc Advancing Mobility Land Sea Air & Space. *Res:* Analysis tools supporting the engineering design machines; structural reanalysis techniques and design sensitivity analysis and optimization methodologies for multidisciplinary applications. *Mailing Add:* Dept Mech Eng KDH Rm 137C Old Dominion Univ Norfolk VA 23529

HOU, KENNETH C, RESEARCH & DEVELOPMENT ADMINISTRATION. *Current Pos:* res engr, Cuno Div, AMF, 72-79, dir res, 79-85, VPRES RES & DEVELOP, CUNO INC, 85- *Personal Data:* b Kiangsui, China, Apr 22, 29; m 66, Catherine Feng; c 2. *Educ:* Taiwan Univ, BS, 52; Univ Idaho, MS, 57; Univ Tex, PhD(phys chem), 62. *Prof Exp:* Res chemist, Celanese Res Co, 66-72. *Mem:* Am Chem Soc; Sigma Xi. *Res:* Bioseparation and purification in large scale bioprocessing engineering; affinity chromatography; membrane filtration. *Mailing Add:* CUNO Inc 400 Research Pkwy Meriden CT 06450

HOU, ROGER HSIANG-DAH, algebra, for more information see previous edition

HOUBOLT, JOHN C(ORNELIUS), CIVIL, AERONAUTICAL & ASTRONAUTICAL ENGINEERING. *Current Pos:* RETIRED. *Personal Data:* b Altoona, Iowa, Apr 10, 19; m 49, Mary Morris; c Mary C, Joanna & Julie. *Educ:* Univ Ill, BS, 40, MS, 42; Swiss Fed Inst Technol, PhD(tech sci), 58. *Hon Degrees:* Dr, Swiss Fed Inst Technol, 75, Clarkston Univ. *Honors & Awards:* Except Sci Achievement Award, NASA, 64; Structures, Structural Dynamics & Mat Award, Am Inst Aeronaut & Astronaut, 68, Dryden Res Lectr, 71 & 72. *Prof Exp:* Bridge engr, Ill Cent RR, 40; asst, Univ Ill, 40-42; aeronaut res engr, Langley Res Ctr, NASA, 42-48, exchange scientist, Eng, 49, asst chief, Dynamic Loads Div, 49-62, chief, Theoret Mech Div, 62-63; exec vpres & sr consult, Aeronaut Res Assocs, Princeton, 63-67, sr vpres & sr consult, 67-69; dir, Doweave, Inc, 69-73; chief scientist, Langley Res Ctr, NASA, 73-85. *Concurrent Pos:* Jr city engr, Waukegan, Ill, 41; instr, Univ Va, 43-; mem div adv group, Air Force Sci Adv Bd; consult, Air Force, Navy, Army & var com firms; assoc ed, Am Inst Aeronaut & Astronaut J Spacecraft & Rockets. *Mem:* Nat Acad Eng; hon fel Am Inst Aeronaut & Astronaut. *Res:* Aeroelastic and structural problems of earthbound and space flight vehicles; author of over 200 technical publications. *Mailing Add:* 51 Winster Fax Williamsburg VA 23185. *Fax:* 757-229-5434

HOUCHENS, DAVID PAUL, IMMUNOLOGY, CHEMOTHERAPY. *Current Pos:* DIR, LAB & CLIN SCI, NEOPROBE CORP, 90- *Personal Data:* b Louisville, Ky, Jan 26, 37; m 63; c 3. *Educ:* Stetson Univ, BS, 59; George Washington Univ, MS, 64, PhD(microbiol), 71. *Prof Exp:* Bacteriologist, Ft Detrick, Md, 60-62; supv technician immunol, Microbiol Assoc, Bethesda, 62-68; jr prof, Bionetics Res Labs, Kensington, 68-71; sr staff fel immunochemother, Nat Cancer Inst, 71-76; res immunologist, Battelle Mem Inst, 76-79, assoc sect mgr, 79-84, proj mgr, Columbus Div, 84-90. *Concurrent Pos:* Fel microbiol, George Washington Univ, 68-71; instr, Montgomery Col, 71-73; adj assoc prof, Ohio State Univ, 85- *Mem:* Am Asn Cancer Res; Am Soc Microbiol; Am Asn Immunologists; Drug Info Asn. *Res:* Immunotherapy and combine modality therapy of animal and human tumors; immunologic effects of chemotherapy; radioimmunologates for radioimmunodetection and radioimmunotherapy. *Mailing Add:* Neoprobe Corp 425 Metro Pl N Suite 300 Dublin OH 43017. *Fax:* 614-786-7188

HOUCK, DAVID R, biochemistry, natural products chemistry, for more information see previous edition

HOUCK, FRANK SCANLAND, INTERNATIONAL NUCLEAR SAFEGUARDS. *Current Pos:* oper res officer, 63-72, phys sci officer, 72-81, SR SCIENTIST INT SAFEGUARDS, US ARMS CONTROL & DISARMAMENT AGENCY, 81- *Personal Data:* b Philadelphia, Pa, Aug 27, 30; m 55; c 3. *Educ:* Dickinson Col, BS, 52; Columbia Univ, MS, 57, PhD(chem), 59. *Honors & Awards:* Meritorious Honor Awards, US Arms Control & Disarmament Agency, 67 & 80. *Prof Exp:* Opers analyst, Opers Eval Group, US Navy, 57-61 & Ctr for Naval Anal, Franklin Inst, 61-63. *Concurrent Pos:* Guest researcher, Mass Inst Technol, 60-62; standing adv group safeguards implementation, Int Atomic Energy Asn, 80- *Res:* Operations research in naval and nuclear warfare; research and testing of inspection and verification for arms control; nuclear materials safeguards. *Mailing Add:* 320 21st St NW US AC & D Agency Washington DC 20451

HOUCK, JAMES RICHARD, ASTROPHYSICS. *Current Pos:* Res assoc astron, 67-69, from asst prof to assoc prof, 69-79, PROF ASTRON, CORNELL UNIV, 79- *Personal Data:* b Mobile, Ala, Oct 5, 40; m 64, Elaine Vezzani; c Robert & Christopher. *Educ:* Carnegie Inst Technol, BS, 62; Cornell Univ, PhD(physics), 67. *Concurrent Pos:* Mem, Infrared Panel, Nat Acad Sci, 69-71, 75 & Infrared Satellite Team, NASA, 75-; Sloan res fel, 71-75; mem, Bahcall Comt. *Mem:* Int Astron Union; Am Astron Soc; AAAS. *Res:* Infrared studies of H II regions and ultraluminous galaxies. *Mailing Add:* Dept Astron Cornell Univ Ithaca NY 14853. *Fax:* 607-255-5875; *E-Mail:* houck@astrosun.tn.cornell.edu

HOUCK, JOHN CANDEE, IMMUNOBIOLOGY, CELL BIOLOGY. *Current Pos:* PRES, BIOPROD, INC, 81- *Personal Data:* b New York, NY, Feb 19, 31; m 53; c 6. *Educ:* Columbia Univ, BA, 53; Univ Western Ont, MSc, 55, PhD(path chem), 56. *Honors & Awards:* A Cressy Mem Award, NY Acad Sci, 62; Am Dermat Asn Award, 65. *Prof Exp:* Dir, Surg Res Lab, Sch Med, Georgetown Univ, 58-60; dir biochem res lab, Children's Hosp, 59-76, sci dir res found, 69-76; dir, Virginia Mason Res Ctr, 76-81. *Concurrent Pos:* Sr res fel surg res lab, Sch Med, Georgetown Univ, 57-58, from asst prof to prof lectr dept biochem, 58-76, asst prof dept pediat & biochem, 67-69, prof pediat, 69-71, prof child health & develop, 71-76. *Mem:* AAAS; Am Soc Biol Chemists; Soc Exp Biol & Med; Am Rheumatism Asn; Am Soc Exp Path. *Res:* Biochemistry of inflammation; biochemical control of cell growth; chalones. *Mailing Add:* 3219 NE 68th St Seattle WA 98115-7335

HOUCK, LAURIE GERALD, PLANT PATHOLOGY, HORTICULTURE. *Current Pos:* RES PLANT PATHOLOGIST, HORT CROPS RES STA, USDA, 78- *Personal Data:* b Tucson, Ariz, Aug 13, 28; m 58, Margaret Evers; c Lorna & Marlys. *Educ:* Univ Ariz, BS, 52, MS, 54; Ore State Univ, PhD(plant path), 62. *Prof Exp:* Plant physiologist, Agr Res Serv, USDA, 54-55; asst horticulturist, Univ Ariz, 55-57; res asst plant path, Ore State Univ, 57-61; res plant pathologist, Mkt Qual Res, Riverside, 62-78. *Concurrent Pos:* Instr, Calif State Polytech Univ, 63, lectr, 64 & 66. *Mem:* Am Phytopath Soc; Am Soc Hort Sci; Coun Agr Sci & Technol; Food Distrib Res Soc; Sigma Xi. *Res:* Post-harvest storing; chemical and nonchemical disease control; shipping, both domestic and export; marketing problems of citrus, avocados, dates and other subtropical fruits; herbicides for weed control; effect of maleic hydrazide upon respiration of roots; root rots and vascular diseases of strawberries and other small fruits of the Pacific Northwest; fumigation, heat treatment and cold treatment of citrus. *Mailing Add:* Hort Crops Res Sta Agr Res Serv USDA 2021 S Peach Ave Fresno CA 93727. *Fax:* 209-453-3088

HOUCK, MARK HEDRICH, ENVIRONMENTAL ENGINEERING, WATER RESOURCES ENGINEERING. *Current Pos:* PROF, GEORGE MASON UNIV, 92-, INTERIM DIR CIVIL, ENVIRON, INFRASTRUCTURE ENG, 96- *Personal Data:* b Baltimore, Md, May 14, 51; m 72; c 3. *Educ:* Johns Hopkins Univ, BES, 72, PhD(eng), 76. *Honors & Awards:* Huber Res Prize, Am Soc Civil Engrs, 88. *Prof Exp:* Res asst prof civil eng, Univ Wash, 75-77; from asst prof to prof civil eng, Purdue Univ, 77-91. *Concurrent Pos:* Assoc ed, Water Resources Res, 81-85; pres, Omtek Eng Inc, 84-; chmn, Water Resources Systs Comt, Am Soc Civil Engrs, 84; chmn, Expert Systs & Water Resources Comt, Am Soc Civil Engrs, 86-, Applns Emerging Technol Comt, 87-; vpres, Water Resources Mgt Inc, 88-89; Dr, Johns Hopkins Univ, 89-90. *Mem:* Am Geophys Union; Am Soc Civil Engrs; Forensic Med & Sci; Sigma Xi; Int Reference Orgn. *Res:* Engineering systems analysis with a focus on civil, water resources and environmental engineering, management, planning and design; operations research; civil engineering. *Mailing Add:* Civil, Environ & Infrastructure Eng MS 4A6 George Mason Univ Fairfax VA 22030-4444

HOUDE, EDWARD DONALD, FISHERIES, BIOLOGICAL OCEANOGRAPHY. *Current Pos:* PROF, CHESAPEAKE BIOL LAB, UNIV MD, 80- *Personal Data:* b Attleboro, Mass, Sept 4, 41; m 83; c 1. *Educ:* Univ Mass, BA, 63; Cornell Univ, MS, 65, PhD(fishery sci), 68. *Prof Exp:* Res biologist fishery sci, US Bur Com Fisheries, Fla, 68-70; res scientist, Div Biol & Living Resources, 70-71, from asst prof to prof fishery sci, Rosentiel Sch Marine & Atmospheric Sci, Univ Miami, 71-80. *Concurrent Pos:* Prog dir, Biol Oceanog, NSF, 83-85. *Mem:* Am Fisheries Soc; Am Soc Limnol & Oceanog; AAAS; Oceanog Soc; Estuarine Res Fed. *Res:* Ecology of fish eggs and larvae; assessment of pelagic resources abundance; factors affecting distribution and abundance; feeding and energetics of fish larvae; experimental rearing of larval fishes in the laboratory; predator-prey relationships; fishery management. *Mailing Add:* Univ Md PO Box 38 Solomons MD 20688. *Fax:* 410-326-7318; *E-Mail:* ehoude@cbl.cees.edu

HOUDE, RAYMOND WILFRED, CLINICAL PHARMACOLOGY, ANALGESIOLOGY. *Current Pos:* PROF MED, MED COL, CORNELL UNIV, 82-; MEM SLOAN-KETTERING INST CANCER RES, 84-, SR ATTEND PHYSICIAN, DEPT MED & NEUROL PAIN, 86- *Personal Data:* b Claremont, NH, May 11, 16; c Susan (Walter) & Peter. *Educ:* NY Univ, AB, 40, MD, 43. *Honors & Awards:* John J Bonica Mem Lectureship Award, Eastern Pain Asn, 81; Nathan B Eddy Mem Award, Col Probs Drug Dependence, 84; Oscan B Hunter Award, Am Soc Clin Pharmacol & Therapeut, 85; Bristol-Myer Squibb Award, Am Pain Soc, 92. *Prof Exp:* Intern, Bellevue Hosp, 44; asst resident med, Mem Hosp, 47-48; from instr to assoc prof, Med col, Cornell Univ, 50-82. *Concurrent Pos:* Vis fel, Univ Mich, 48-49; res fel clin invest, Mem Sloan-Kettering Cancer Ctr, 48-50, asst attend physician, 55-65, attend physician, 65-; Nat Res Coun fel, Nat Cancer Inst, 49-51; mem res unit, USPHS Hosp, Ky, 49-50; assoc mem, Sloan-Kettering Inst Cancer Res, 60-63, mem 83-; prof pharmacol, Grad Sch Med Sci, Cornell Univ, 84-86. *Mem:* AAAS; Am Soc Clin Pharmacol & Therapeut; Am Soc Pharmacol & Exp Therapeut; NY Acad Sci; Am Pain Soc. *Res:* Clinical investigation of analgesic agents; psychophysiology of pain. *Mailing Add:* Mem Sloan-Kettering Cancer Ctr 1275 York Ave New York NY 10021-6007

HOUDE, ROBERT A, COMMUNICATIONS SCIENCE. *Current Pos:* RETIRED. *Personal Data:* b Fall River, Mass, Apr 12, 31; m 57; c 2. *Educ:* Northeastern Univ, BS, 54; Univ Rochester, MS, 65; Univ Mich, PhD(commun sci), 67. *Prof Exp:* Res staff mem, Gen Dynamics/Electronics, 56-68, mgr res dept, 68-70; pres & dir res, Ctr Commun Res Inc, 70-90. *Mem:* Acoust Soc Am; Sigma Xi; Am Speech & Hearing Asn; NY Acad Sci. *Res:* Speech acoustics. *Mailing Add:* 75 High Power Rd Rochester NY 14623

HOUDE-WALTER, SUSAN N, OPTOELECTRONIC DESIGN, OPTICAL GLASS. *Current Pos:* asst prof, 87-93, ASSOC PROF, INST OPTICS, UNIV ROCHESTER, 93-; CO-FOUNDER, LASERMAX INC, 89- *Personal Data:* b New York, NY, Aug 20, 54. *Educ:* Sarah Lawrence Col, NY, BA, 76; Univ Rochester, MS, 83, PhD(optics), 87. *Prof Exp:* Bkstore mgr, Mus Holography, NY, 78-79; holographer, Cambridge Sterographics, 79. *Concurrent Pos:* Bd dirs, Optical Soc Am, 94-96. *Mem:* Fel Optical Soc Am. *Res:* New optical materials; design of long-chain integrated-optics and optoelectronic systems. *Mailing Add:* Inst Optics Univ Rochester Rochester NY 14627. *Fax:* 716-271-1027; *E-Mail:* shw@optics.rochester.edu

HOUGAS, ROBERT WAYNE, plant breeding, genetics, for more information see previous edition

HOUGEN, FRITHJOF W, PLANT CHEMISTRY. *Current Pos:* RETIRED. *Personal Data:* b Oslo, Norway, Dec 22, 20. *Educ:* Norway Inst Technol, Chem Engr, 48; Univ Cape Town, PhD(org chem), 55. *Prof Exp:* Sci asst, Nat Chem Res Lab, Coun Sci & Indust Res SAfrica, 48-49, asst res officer, 50-53, res officer, 54-55; fel, Prairie Regional Lab, Nat Res Coun Can, 56-58; res chemist, Univ Man, 58-67, assoc prof, 67-77, prof plant sci, 77-86. *Mem:* Chem Inst Can; Am Oil Chem Soc; Am Chem Soc; Sigma Xi. *Res:* Chemical composition of fats and lipids; development of chemical analytical methods for use in plant breeding research. *Mailing Add:* 69 Linacre Rd Winnipeg MB R3T 3G7 Can

HOUGEN, JOEL O(LIVER), CHEMICAL ENGINEERING. *Current Pos:* vis prof chem, 67, prof, 67-80, EMER PROF CHEM, UNIV TEX, AUSTIN, 80- *Personal Data:* b Tacoma, Wash, Feb 26, 14; m 38; c 4. *Educ:* Univ Wis, BS, 36; Univ Minn, MS, 46, PhD(chem eng), 48. *Honors & Awards:* Instrument Technol Award, Instrument Soc Am, 70. *Prof Exp:* Res chem engr, Pan Am Ref Corp, Tex, 37-41; instr chem eng, Univ Minn, 41-44; process engr, Union Oil Co, Calif, 44-46; instr chem eng, Univ Ill, 46-48; from assoc prof to prof, Rensselaer Polytech Inst, 48-56; systs engr, Monsanto Chem Co, 56-66 & Monsanto Co, 66-67; independent consult process control & optimization, 67. *Concurrent Pos:* Consult, Gen Elec Co, 49-56, Boeing Airplane Co, 54 & Amoco Chem Co, 76; mem sci adv bd, Environ Protection Agency, 76-78. *Mem:* Am Soc Eng Educ; Am Inst Chem Engrs; Instrument Soc Am. *Res:* Process dynamics and control. *Mailing Add:* 1206 Falcon Ledge Dr Austin TX 78746

HOUGEN, JON T, MOLECULAR SPECTROSCOPY. *Current Pos:* physicist, Nat Inst Stand & Technol, 67-69, chief, Molecular Spectros Sect, 69-73, res scientist, 74-85, SR FEL, NAT INST STAND & TECHNOL, 85- *Personal Data:* b Sheboygan, Wis, Oct 23, 36. *Educ:* Univ Wis, BSc, 56; Harvard Univ, AM, 58, PhD(phys chem), 60. *Honors & Awards:* Coblentz Award, 68; Silver Medal, Nat Bur Stand, 74, Gold Medal, 80; Plyler Prize, 84; Lippincott Award, 84. *Prof Exp:* Fel, Nat Res Coun Can, 60-62, assoc res officer, 62-66. *Mem:* Am Phys Soc; Optical Soc Am; Coblentz Soc. *Res:* Quantum mechanical and group theoretical problems in high-resolution molecular spectroscopy. *Mailing Add:* Molecular Physics Div Nat Inst Stand & Technol Gaithersburg MD 20899. *Fax:* 301-975-3038; *E-Mail:* hougen@tiber.nist.gov

HOUGH, AUBREY JOHNSTON, JR, ORTHOPEDIC & METABOLIC DISEASES. *Current Pos:* prof & vchmn, Dept Path, 80-81, prof, 81-95, CHMN, DEPT PATH, UNIV ARK MED SCI, LITTLE ROCK, 81-, DISTINGUISHED PROF, 95- *Personal Data:* b Little Rock, Ark, July 20, 44; m 68, Linda Ann Yaeger; c Charles Prentiss & Robert Page. *Educ:* Hendrix Col, BA, 66; Vanderbilt Univ, MD, 70; Am Bd Path, dipl. *Honors & Awards:* Dirs Commendation, Vet Admin, 80; Brown Mem Lectr, Asn Clin Scientists, 86. *Prof Exp:* Resident, Dept Path, Vanderbilt Univ, 70-72, chief resident, 74-75, asst prof, 75-78, asst prof, Dept Orthop, 77-78, assoc prof, Depts Path & Orthop, 78-80. *Concurrent Pos:* Clin assoc, Nat Inst Arthritis & Metab Dis, 72-74; surgeon, USPHS, 72-74; basic sci grantee, Nat Inst Gen Med Studies, 78, Altheimer Found, 84, Nat Inst Arthritis, 88; pres, Ark Acad Path, 82-86; chief staff, Univ Ark Hosp, Little Rock, 86-88; coun dept chmn, Univ Ark Col Med, 87-88; assoc ed, Human Path, 88-; mem path test comt, Nat Bd Med Examrs, 89-92, chmn, 93-95, comp II comt, 92-95, mem, 96-; mem, Residency Rev Comt Path, Accreditation Coun Med Educ, 90-96; chmn, Shideler Chem Educ Endowmnt. *Mem:* Fel Col Am Pathologists; AMA; Int Acad Path; Am Soc Clin Pathologists; Am Asn Path; Asn Clin Scientists; Arthur Purdy Stout Soc; Asn Path Chmn; Orthop Res Soc; Hist Med Assocs; Am Asn Univ Profs. *Res:* Contributed numerous articles on orthopedic diseases to professional journals, chapters to books. *Mailing Add:* Univ Ark Med Sci 4301 W Markham Slot 517 Little Rock AR 72205. *Fax:* 501-296-1184; *E-Mail:* ahough@pathology.uams.edu

HOUGH, HUGH WALTER, SOIL SCIENCE. *Current Pos:* asst prof, 56-66, ASSOC PROF SOILS, UNIV WYO, 66- *Personal Data:* b Hebron, Ind, Feb 10, 22; m 47; c 3. *Educ:* Purdue Univ, BSA, 47, MS, 50; Mich State Univ, PhD(soil sci), 54. *Prof Exp:* Asst soils, Purdue Univ, 47-49; instr, Mich State Univ, 49-55. *Mem:* Soil Sci Soc Am; Am Soc Agron. *Res:* Soil structure; crops response to fertilizers; soil testing; effects of soil amendments. *Mailing Add:* 1703 Ord St Laramie WY 82070

HOUGH, JANE LINSCOTT, lipid biochemistry, for more information see previous edition

HOUGH, LINDSAY B, NEUROPHARMACOLOGY, NEUROSCIENCES. *Current Pos:* assoc prof, 84-86, PROF PHARMACOL, ALBANY MED COL, 86- *Personal Data:* b Paris, Ky, Oct 16, 50; m 79, Claudia; c Andrew & Matthew. *Educ:* Univ Ky, Lexington, BS, 73; Univ Mich, Ann Arbor, PhD(pharmacol), 78. *Prof Exp:* Fel pharmacol, Mt Sinai Med Sch, NY, 78-79, from asst prof to assoc prof, 80-84. *Concurrent Pos:* Prin investr, Nat Inst Drug Abuse, 82- *Mem:* Am Soc Pharmacol; Soc Neurosci; Am Pain Soc. *Res:* Exploration of the neurochemistry and neuropharmacology of histamine in the central nervous system; investigation of the antinociceptive properties of histamine. *Mailing Add:* Dept Pharmacol & Toxicol Albany Med Col Albany NY 12208-3479

HOUGH, PAUL VAN CAMPEN, STRUCTURAL BIOLOGY, ATOMIC FORCE MICROSCOPY. *Current Pos:* from physicist to sr physicist, 61-74, SR BIOPHYSICIST, BROOKHAVEN NAT LAB, 74- *Personal Data:* b Ellwood City, Pa, May 21, 25; m 76, Iris A Mastrangelo; c David & Judith. *Educ:* Swarthmore Col, BA, 45; Cornell Univ, PhD(physics), 50. *Prof Exp:* Jr scientist, Los Alamos Sci Lab, 45; from instr to assoc prof physics, Univ Mich, 50-60. *Concurrent Pos:* Guggenheim fel, 59-60 & 73-74. *Mem:* Biophys Soc; fel Am Phys Soc; Micros Soc Am. *Res:* Initiation of transcription and replication in eukaryotes; DNA-binding proteins by electron microscopy, land atomic force microscopy. *Mailing Add:* Dept Biol Brookhaven Nat Lab Upton NY 11973. *Fax:* 516-344-3407; *E-Mail:* hough@bnl.gov

HOUGH, RALPH L, MATERIALS SCIENCE. *Current Pos:* PRES, HOUGH LAB, RUSSELLS POINT, 66- *Personal Data:* b Springfield, Ohio, Jan 13, 30; m 53, Lois G Hallam; c Harold J, Patricia M & Pamela M. *Educ:* Wittenberg Univ, BA, 54. *Prof Exp:* Engr, Equip Lab, Wright-Patterson AFB, 55-59, engr, Air Force Mat Lab, 59-63, res team leader reinforcements formation, 63-66. *Concurrent Pos:* Consult, Space Gen Corp, Los Angeles, 66-67, Dow-Corning Corp, Midland & Univ Cincinnati, 67, Res Found, Ohio State Univ, 67-70 & Res Inst, Univ Dayton, 69; consult engr, Specialties Develop Corp, Hilliard, Ohio, 78- *Mem:* Sigma Xi; AAAS; Am Chem Soc; fel Am Inst Chem; Soc Aerospace Mat & Process Engrs. *Res:* Developing diffusion barriers for boron and silicon carbide filaments; development of large diameter carbonbased fibers; new coatings to enhance the strength of boron and other fibers currently being used as reinforcements; design, develop and install special halon fire suppression system for Air Force Avionics Lab Anachoic Chamber; design and developing microprosser controlled test stands for industrial materials industries; designing integrated computer systems for office or terminal use. *Mailing Add:* Hough Lab Box 81 Russells Point OH 43348-0081

HOUGH, RICHARD ANTON, LIMNOLOGY. *Current Pos:* asst prof, 73-80, assoc prof, 80-90, PROF BIOL, WAYNE STATE UNIV, 90-, ASSOC CHAIR, 90- *Personal Data:* b Houston, Tex, Sept 4, 42; m 69, Evelyn DePrince; c Jack & Robert. *Educ:* Univ Ill, BS, 64; Univ Mich, MS, 66; Mich State Univ, PhD(bot), 73. *Prof Exp:* Oceanogr marine biol, US Naval Oceanogr Off, 66-69. *Mem:* Am Soc Limnol & Oceanogr; Ecol Soc Am; Int Soc Aquatic Vascular Plant Biologists; Int Soc Theoret & Appl Limnol; Sigma Xi. *Res:* Physiological ecology and productivity of aquatic macrophytes and algae. *Mailing Add:* Dept Biol Sci Wayne State Univ Detroit MI 48202. *Fax:* 313-577-6891; *E-Mail:* rhough@lifesci.wayne.edu

HOUGH, RICHARD R(ALSTON), electrical engineering; deceased, see previous edition for last biography

HOUGH, WALTER ANDREW, RESEARCH ADMINISTRATION, FORESTRY. *Current Pos:* RETIRED. *Personal Data:* b Philadelphia, Pa, May 3, 32; m 61, Frances E Baker; c Winnie V. *Educ:* Pa State Univ, BS, 55; Duke Univ, MF, 60, DF, 63. *Prof Exp:* Forester, US Forest Serv, 55-56, res forester, Southern Forest Fire Lab, 58-61; res assoc, Duke Univ, 63; res forester, Southern Forest Fire Lab, US Forest Serv, 63-67, proj leader fuel physics, 67-73, team leader mechanism of smoke generation, 73-75, staff specialist fire sci, Div Forest Fire & Atmospheric Sci Res, Washington, DC, 75-78, asst dir planning & appln, Southeastern Forest Exp Sta, Asheville, NC, 78-81, asst dir res progs, Southern Forest Exp Sta, 81-94. *Mem:* Soc Am Foresters; Am Soc Plant Physiologists; Sigma Xi. *Res:* Use of prescribed fire in the forest; effect of forest fire on living vegetation; heat content and rate of energy release for forest fuels; influence of forest fuels on production and quality of forest fire smoke. *Mailing Add:* US Forest Serv Southern Stn 701 Loyola Ave New Orleans LA 70113

HOUGH-GOLDSTEIN, JUDITH ANNE, ENTOMOLOGY. *Current Pos:* asst prof, 81-88, ASSOC PROF ENTOM, UNIV DEL, 88- *Personal Data:* b Ann Arbor, Mich, Aug 27, 50; m 83; c 2. *Educ:* Harvard Univ, BA, 72; Cornell Univ, MS, 77, PhD(entom), 81. *Mem:* Entom Soc Am; AAAS. *Res:* Insect/plant interactions; insect pest management. *Mailing Add:* Dept Entom & Applied Ecol Univ Del Newark DE 19717-1303

HOUGHTON, ALAN N, MEDICAL ONCOLOGY, TUMOR IMMUNOLOGY. *Current Pos:* ASSOC MEM MED & IMMUNOL, MEM SLOAN-KETTERING CANCER CTR, 88-, CHIEF CLIN IMMUNOL SERV, 89-; ASSOC PROF MED & IMMUNOL, CORNELL UNIV MED COL, 88- *Personal Data:* b Boston, Mass, Apr 12, 47; m 75; c 2. *Educ:* Stanford Univ, BA, 70; Univ Conn, MD, 74. *Honors & Awards:* Boyer Award, Mem Sloan-Kettering Cancer Ctr, 85. *Concurrent Pos:* Assoc/adv ed, Hybridoma, 86-, J Exp Med, 88- & Cancer Immunol Immunother, 90-; mem bd sci adv, Sterling Res Group, Eastman-Kodak, 87-; mem sci adv bd, Am Cancer Soc, 89-; mem exp ther study sect, Nat Cancer Inst, NIH, 90-; mem bd dirs, Soc Biol Ther, 90- *Mem:* Am Soc Clin Invest; Soc Biol Ther; Am Asn Cancer Res; Am Soc Clin Oncol; Am Asn Immunologists. *Res:* Experimental cancer therapy with special emphasis on biologic treatments, including cytokines, monoclonal antibodies and cancer vaccines; pathogenesis and treatment of human melanoma; pigment cell biology; human tumor antigens. *Mailing Add:* Dept Med & Immunol Mem Sloan-Kettering Cancer Ctr 1275 York Ave New York NY 10021-6094. *Fax:* 212-717-3036

HOUGHTON, ANTHONY, PHYSICS, EDUCATION. *Current Pos:* asst prof physics, 63-67, assoc prof, 67-71, PROF, BROWN UNIV, 71-, CHMN, DEPT PHYSICS, 92- *Personal Data:* b Heanor, Eng, Oct 4, 35; m 61, Patricia Sanchez-Cerani. *Educ:* Univ Birmingham, Eng, BSc, 56, PhD, 59. *Prof Exp:* Res physicist, McMaster Univ, Hamilton, Ont, 60-63. *Concurrent Pos:* Postdoctoral fel, Carnegie Inst Technol, 59-60, Univ Calif, San Diego, 59-60; vis prof, Oxford Univ, Eng, 70, Univ Paris Orsay, 70, UK Army Educ Corps, Harwell, 71, Univ Southern Calif, 75-76, Univ Sussex, Eng, 77, Univ Heidelberg, Ger, 77 & 78, Dalhousie Univ, Halifax, NS, 79, Imp Col, London, 82-83, Univ Calif, San Diego, 89-90; consult, Los Alamos Nat Labs, 88- *Mem:* Fel Am Physics Soc. *Res:* Contributed numerous articles to professional journals. *Mailing Add:* 173 Matthewson Rd Barrington RI 02806-4426

HOUGHTON, CHARLES JOSEPH, TOPOLOGY. *Current Pos:* asst prof, 64-69, ASSOC PROF MATH, STATE UNIV NY BINGHAMTON, 69- *Personal Data:* b Castle Gate, Utah, June 26, 32; m 61; c 3. *Educ:* Univ Utah, BA, 58; Ohio State Univ, MA, 61, PhD(math), 64. *Prof Exp:* Ballistics computer, Sign Missile Support Agency, White Sands Missile Range, NMex, 58-59. *Mem:* Math Asn Am. *Mailing Add:* Dept Math State Univ NY Binghamton Binghamton NY 13902-6000

HOUGHTON, DAVID DREW, METEOROLOGY. *Current Pos:* from asst prof to assoc prof, Univ Wis-Madison, 68-72, assoc chmn grad affairs, 70-72, chmn dept, 76-79, 91-94, PROF ATMOSPHERIC & OCEANIC SCI, UNIV WIS-MADISON, 72-, ASSOC CHMN, UNDERGRAD AFFAIRS, 94- *Personal Data:* b Philadelphia, Pa, Apr 26, 38; m 63, Barbara Coan; c Eric, Karen & Steven. *Educ:* Pa State Univ, BS, 59; Wash Univ, MS, 61, PhD(atmospheric sci), 63. *Prof Exp:* Res scientist dynamic meteorol, Nat Ctr Atmospheric Res, 63-68. *Concurrent Pos:* Prin investr & co-prin investr, NSF Grants; exchange scientist, Inst Atmospheric Physics, Moscow, USSR, 66; vis scientist, Courant Inst Math Sci, New York, 66; invited lectr, Nanjing Univ, People's Repub China, 80; vis sr scientist, Nat Meteorol Ctr, Washington, DC, 88 & Inst Atmospheric Physics, Beijing & Nanjing Univ, Nanjing, Peoples Repub China, 89. *Mem:* Fel AAAS; fel Am Meteorol Soc. *Res:* General circulation; large-scale atmospheric dynamics; subsynoptic scale motions; initialization for numerical models; flow over mountains; gravity waves; short range prediction; large scale annual cycle dynamics; satellite meteorology climate dynamics. *Mailing Add:* Dept Atmospheric & Oceanic Sci Univ Wis 1225 W Dayton St Madison WI 53706-1612. *Fax:* 608-262-0166; *E-Mail:* ddhought@facstaff.wisc.edu

HOUGHTON, JAMES RICHARD, MECHANICAL ENGINEERING, APPLIED MECHANICS. *Current Pos:* PROF MECH ENG, TENN TECHNOL UNIV, 77- *Personal Data:* b Morgantown, WVa, Aug 31, 36; m 61, Maaret Koivula; c June (Kingsbury) & Paul Eugene. *Educ:* George Washington Univ, BME, 58; Univ Md, MSME, 65; Vanderbilt Univ, PhD(mech eng), 76. *Prof Exp:* Designer & supvr construct, Friends Africa Mission, 58-60; proj leader mech eng, Nat Bur Stand, 61-66; lectr mech eng, Univ Sierra Leone, 66-68 & Univ Nairobi, Kenya, 68-72; asst prof, Tenn State Univ, 72-77. *Concurrent Pos:* Mem acoust emission working group; prod liabilities consult. *Mem:* Am Soc Mech Engrs; Soc Exp Mech. *Res:* Shock, vibrations, nondestructive testing and acoustic emission; signature analysis by mathematical model development for a system transfer function; computer aided machine design; modal analysis. *Mailing Add:* 1070 McGregor Lane Cookeville TN 38501. *Fax:* 615-372-6340; *E-Mail:* jrh6911@tntech.edu

HOUGHTON, JAMES RICHARDSON, GLASS WORKS. *Current Pos:* RETIRED. *Personal Data:* b Corning, NY, Apr 6, 36; m 62, May Tuckerman Kinnicutt; c James DeKay & Nina Bayard. *Educ:* Harvard Univ, AB, 58, MBA, 62. *Prof Exp:* Staff, Goldman, Sachs & Co, 59-61; staff, Corning Glass Works, 62-64, mgr, Zurich, Switz, 64-68, vpres & gen mgr, Consumer Prod Div, 68-71, vchmn bd, dir & chmn exec comt, 71-83, chmn bd & chief exec officer, 83-96. *Mailing Add:* Corning Inc 80 E Market St Suite 201 Corning NY 14830

HOUGHTON, JANET ANNE, PHARMACOLOGY. *Current Pos:* Fel, Dept Biochem & Clin Pharmacol, St Jude Children's Res Hosp, 77-80, res assoc, 80-82, asst mem, 82-85, ASSOC MEM, DEPT BIOCHEM & CLIN PHARMACOL, ST JUDE CHILDREN'S RES HOSP, MEMPHIS, 85- *Personal Data:* b Grantham, Eng, May 21, 52. *Educ:* Univ Bradford, Eng, BPh Hons, 73; Univ London, PhD(biophys), 77. *Mem:* Am Asn Cancer Res; Pharmaceut Soc Gt Brit. *Res:* Tumor models; human tumor xenografts; experimental chemotherapy; selectivity of drug action in vivo, drug resistance; 5-fluoropyrimidines; Vinca alkaloids; colon carcinoma and rhabdomyosarcoma as specific human diseases; tumor heterogeneity; folate metabolism; heterogeneity of thymidylate synthase; author of more than 120 technical publications. *Mailing Add:* Dept Biochem & Clin Pharmacol St Jude Children's Res Hosp 332 N Lauderdale Memphis TN 38105-2729

HOUGHTON, JOHN M, BIOTECHNOLOGY DEVELOPMENT & ASSESSMENT, NEW PRODUCT COMMERCIALIZATION. *Current Pos:* DIR, STEWART TECHNOL MGT, 91- *Personal Data:* b Knobnoster, Mo, July 18, 41; m 66; c 1. *Educ:* Southern Ill Univ, BS, 67; Univ Ill, MS, 70, PhD(agron), 73. *Prof Exp:* Sales rep, Ciba-Geigy Corp, 67-68; prod develop assoc & res group leader, Monsanto Agr Co, 73-78, mgr prod develop, Latin Am & US, 78-84, dir new prod, 84-88, dir new technol, 88-90; pres, J M Houghton & Assocs, 90-91. *Concurrent Pos:* Partic, Comt Strategies Mgt Pesticides Resistant Pest Populations, 86. *Mem:* AAAS; Weed Sci Soc Am. *Mailing Add:* One Duddin Ct Ballwin MO 63021

HOUGHTON, KENNETH SINCLAIR, SR, INDOLE ALKALOIDS, TECHNICAL MANAGEMENT. *Current Pos:* tech dir, Lightfoot Co, Philip Morris USA, 70-72, gen mgr, 72-74, mgr, Process Control & Qual Assurance, Park 500, 74-76 & Tech Serv, 76-77, gen mgr, Park 500, 77-80 & Richmond Processing Plants, 80-83, dir res & develop, Europe, Mid East, Africa, Philip Morris Int, 83-86, VPRES RES & DEVELOP, PHILIP MORRIS USA, 86- *Personal Data:* b Hackensack, NJ, Aug 31, 40; m 63; c 4. *Educ:* St Peters Col, BS, 62; Seton Hall Univ, MS, 69, PhD(org chem), 72. *Prof Exp:* Chief chemist, Continental Chem Co, 66-68, plant mgr, 68-69; grad asst, Seton Hall Univ, 69-70. *Mem:* Am Chem Soc; Indust Res Inst; Sigma Xi. *Res:* Organic chemistry of natural products and flavors; extract and recombine processes; industrial waste water treatment; high-speed manufacturing techniques; tobacco chemistry and processing techniques; cigarette design, construction and product evaluation. *Mailing Add:* Philip Morris USA PO Box 26583 Richmond VA 23261-6583

HOUGHTON, ROB, SIMULATION & MODELING, NAVIGATION. *Current Pos:* VPRES, ILLGEN SIMULATION TECHNOLOGIES INC, 96- *Personal Data:* m 84, Barbara Suzan Douds; c Elizabeth Anne & Grant Landon. *Educ:* Fla State Univ, BS, 72; Auburn Univ, MS, 78, PhD(physics), 82. *Prof Exp:* Mem tech staff, Mission Res Corp, 82-86; dir, Gen Res Corp, 86-89; consult, 89-96. *Mem:* Am Phys Soc; Inst Elec & Electronics Engrs. *Res:* Design and implementation of next generation navigation systems including WAAS and GPS III; state-of-the-art simulation and modeling tools. *Mailing Add:* 4801 Shamrock Dr Fair Oaks CA 95628. *Fax:* 805-692-2334; *E-Mail:* epi@ix.netcom.com

HOUGHTON, ROBERT W, PHYSICAL OCEANOGRAPHY. *Current Pos:* res scientist, 77-78, RES ASSOC, DEPT OCEANOG, LAMONT-DOHERTY GEOL OBSERV, COLUMBIA UNIV, 78- *Personal Data:* b Philadelphia, Pa, Sept 4, 41; m 64; c 1. *Educ:* Oberlin Col, Ohio, AB, 63; Univ Minn, PhD(physics), 68. *Prof Exp:* Res assoc physics, City Col, New York, 68-71; lectr, physics, statist & thermo, Univ Ghana, Legon, Accra, 71-75; science teacher, Friends Acad, NY, 75-76; res assoc, Dept Oceanog, Dalhousie Univ, 76-77. *Mem:* Am Phys Soc; Am Meteorol Soc; AAAS; Am Geophys Union. *Res:* Experimental physical oceanographic research on the thermal structure of the equatorial Atlantic Ocean; structure and exchange processes at the Middle Atlantic Bight coastal front. *Mailing Add:* 87 Piermont Pl Piermont NY 10968

HOUGIE, CECIL, PATHOLOGY. *Current Pos:* prof, 68-89, EMER PROF PATH, UNIV CALIF, SAN DIEGO, 89- *Personal Data:* b Eng, Oct 29, 22; m 50; c 2. *Educ:* Univ Manchester, MB, BS, 46. *Prof Exp:* Registr path, West London Hosp, 50-52, sr registr, 54-55; instr, Sch Med, Univ NC, 55-56; asst prof, Sch Med, Univ Va, 56-60; assoc prof, Sch Med, Univ Wash, 60-68. *Concurrent Pos:* Mason res fel, Med Sch, WLondon Hosp, 52-54; established investr, Am Head Asn, 60-65. *Mem:* Soc Exp Biol & Med. *Res:* Coagulation of blood and fibrinolytic enzymes. *Mailing Add:* 7982 Roseland Dr La Jolla CA 92037. *Fax:* 619-459-1988; *E-Mail:* bbh@cts.com

HOUGLAND, ARTHUR ELDON, MICROBIOLOGY, VIROLOGY. *Current Pos:* asst prof, 73-78, ASSOC PROF MICROBIOL, E TENN STATE UNIV, 79-, SPECIAL ASST TO DEAN, SCH PUB & ALLIED HEALTH, 90- *Personal Data:* b Omaha, Nebr, Jan 5, 35; m 61; c 3. *Educ:* State Univ Iowa, BA, 58; Brigham Young Univ, MS, 61; Univ SDak, PhD(microbiol), 75. *Prof Exp:* Chief microbiol, Med Field Serv Sch, 62-64; res, Ft Detrick, 64-69. *Concurrent Pos:* Am Cancer Soc fel, 69-71; Fraternal Order Eagles grant, 71-73; res consult, Oak Ridge Assoc Univ, 78- *Mem:* Am Soc Microbiol; Am Mil Surgeons; Sigma Xi; Tissue Cult Asn. *Res:* Lipids of biological membranes; sulphydryl groups of cells and bacteria; cancer. *Mailing Add:* E Tenn State Univ PO Box 70673 Johnson City TN 37614

HOUH, CHORNG SHI, MATHEMATICS. *Current Pos:* assoc prof, 67-75, PROF MATH, WAYNE STATE UNIV, 75- *Personal Data:* b Canton, China, Mar 23, 26; m 66, Fu M Chang; c Henry & Emily. *Educ:* Nat Taiwan Univ, BSc, 49; Tokyo Metrop Univ, PhD(math), 62. *Prof Exp:* Asst math, Nat Taiwan Univ, 49-56; from instr to asst prof, Univ Fla, 62-64; asst prof, Univ Man, 64-67. *Mem:* Am Math Soc; Math Soc Japan. *Res:* Connection theory of a Riemannian manifold; differential geometry on complex and almost complex spaces; differential geometry on submanifolds. *Mailing Add:* Dept Math 1150 FAB Wayne State Univ 5950 Cass Ave Detroit MI 48202. *E-Mail:* houh@math.Wayne.edu

HOUK, ALBERT EDWARD HENNESSEE, CHEMISTRY, BIOPHYSICS. *Current Pos:* CONSULT, 81- *Personal Data:* b Glen Alpine, NC, May 20, 14; m 41, Vivian; c William, Lawrence & James. *Educ:* Univ Minn, BS, 36, MS, 38; Columbia Univ, PhD(chem), 44. *Prof Exp:* Asst agr biochem, Univ Minn, 36-38; instr chem & agr chem, Purdue Univ, 38-39; from assoc to asst prof physiol chem, Chicago Med Sch, 44-45; admin asst & proj chief, Stand Brands, Inc, NY, 45-46; head, Nutrit Res Dept, H J Heinz Co, 46-48; capt to LTC, Med Serv Corp, US Army, 49-69; asst dir lab serv, St Mary's Hosp, 55-56; chief chemist, Providence Hosp, 56; chemist, Food & Drug Admin, Rockville, 56-81. *Concurrent Pos:* Fel, Yale Univ, 43-44. *Mem:* Sigma Xi; emer mem Am Chem Soc. *Res:* Drug manufacture and controls; sanitary engineering and preventive medicine; nutrition; pesticides and food additives. *Mailing Add:* 3661 Jennings Chapel Rd PO Box 250 Woodbine MD 21797-7505

HOUK, CLIFFORD C, INORGANIC CHEMISTRY. *Current Pos:* asst prof, 66-71, assoc prof, 71-80, PROF CHEM, OHIO UNIV, 80-, DIR GEN CHEM, 66- *Personal Data:* b Dayton, Ohio, July 7, 33; m 54; c 3. *Educ:* Ohio Univ, BSEd, 55, MEd, 56; Mont State Univ, PhD(chem), 66. *Prof Exp:* Teacher, High Sch, Ohio, 56-62; asst chem, Mont State Univ, 62-63. *Mem:* AAAS; Am Chem Soc; Sigma Xi. *Res:* Synthesis of transition metal complexes; magnetic properties of transition metal compounds; chemical education. *Mailing Add:* C2H Enterprises Inc 12 Northwood Dr Athens OH 45701-1341

HOUK, JAMES CHARLES, CENTRAL NERVOUS SYSTEM NEUROPHYSIOLOGY. *Current Pos:* NATHAN SMITH DAVIS PROF PHYSIOL & CHMN DEPT, SCH MED, NORTHWESTERN UNIV, 78-, PROF BIOMED ENG, 79- *Personal Data:* b Northville, Mich, June 3, 39; m 63; c 3. *Educ:* Mich Technol Univ, BS, 61; Mass Inst Technol, SM, 63; Harvard Univ, PhD(physiol), 66. *Honors & Awards:* Javits Neurosci Investr Award, Nat Inst Neurol & Commun Disorders & Stroke, NIH. *Prof Exp:* Postdoctoral fel, Fac Med, Toulouse, France, 66-67; from instr to asst prof physiol, Harvard Med Sch, 67-73; assoc prof physiol, Sch Med, Johns Hopkins Univ, 73-78. *Concurrent Pos:* Lectr, Dept Elec Eng, Mass Inst Technol, 71-73; adj assoc prof, Dept Physiol, Univ NC, 75. *Mem:* AAAS; Am Physiol Soc; Soc Neurosci; Sigma Xi; Inst Elec & Electronics Engrs; Europ Neurosci Asn; Int Neural Networks Soc. *Res:* Neural mechanisms controlling movement; cerebellar mechanisms for sensorimotor learning. *Mailing Add:* Ward Bldg 5-319 Physiol Northwestern Univ 303 E Chicago Ave Chicago IL 60611

HOUK, KENDALL N, THEORETICAL ORGANIC CHEMISTRY. *Current Pos:* PROF CHEM, UNIV CALIF, LOS ANGELES, 86- *Personal Data:* b Nashville, Tenn, Feb 27, 43; m 66, 90; c 1. *Educ:* Harvard Univ, AB, 64, MS, 66, PhD(chem), 68. *Honors & Awards:* Von Humboldt Sr Res Scientist Award, 82; James Flack Norris Award, Am Chem Soc, 91. *Prof Exp:* From asst prof to assoc prof chem, La State Univ, 68-80; prof chem, Univ Pittsburgh, 80-85. *Concurrent Pos:* Vis prof, Princeton Univ, 75. *Mem:* Chem Soc; NAm Photochem Soc; Asn Quantum Biol. *Res:* Theoretical organic chemistry; photochemistry; cycloaddition reactions; asymmetric reagents; transition state modeling. *Mailing Add:* Dept Chem & Biochem Univ California Los Angeles CA 90095-1569. *Fax:* 310-206-1843; *E-Mail:* houk@chem.ucla.edu

HOUK, LARRY WAYNE, INORGANIC CHEMISTRY. *Current Pos:* From asst prof to assoc prof, 68-78, PROF DEPT CHEM, UNIV MEMPHIS, 78- *Personal Data:* b Glasgow, Ky, Aug 25, 41; m 62; c 3. *Educ:* Mid Tenn State Col, BS, 63; Univ Ga, PhD(inorg chem), 68. *Mem:* Am Chem Soc. *Res:* Low valence organophosphorus transition metal complexes. *Mailing Add:* Dept Chem Univ Memphis Memphis TN 38152-6060

HOUK, NANCY (MIA), ASTRONOMY. *Current Pos:* res assoc astron, 71-74, from asst res scientist to assoc res scientist, 75-83, RES SCIENTIST ASTRON, UNIV MICH, ANN ARBOR, 84- *Personal Data:* b Potsdam, NY, July 18, 40. *Educ:* Univ Mich, BS, 62; Case Western Reserve Univ, MS, 64, PhD(astron), 67. *Prof Exp:* Res assoc astron, Warner & Swasey Observ, Case Western Reserve Univ, 67-69; Netherlands Orgn Advan Pure Res grant & vis res assoc, Kapteyn Astron Lab, 70. *Mem:* Am Astron Soc; Int Astron Union; AAAS. *Res:* Spectral classification; M-type variable stars; stellar spectroscopy; galactic structure. *Mailing Add:* 826 Granger Ave Ann Arbor MI 48104

HOUK, RICHARD DUNCAN, BOTANY, TAXONOMY. *Current Pos:* RETIRED. *Personal Data:* b Hobart, Okla, June 13, 33; m 55; c 2. *Educ:* Southwest Mo State Col, BS, 59; Fla State Univ, PhD(bot), 66. *Prof Exp:* Instr biol, Southwest Mo State Col, 59-60; from asst prof to assoc prof, Winthrop Col, 64-73, asst vpres acad affairs, 74-75, vprovost, 75-80, prof biol, 75- *Mem:* Int Asn Plant Taxon; Nat Sci Teachers Asn; Am Soc Plant Taxonomists; Nat Asn Biol Teachers; Bot Soc Am. *Res:* Biology of Helianthus Schweinitzii; methodology of biology teaching; conservation education. *Mailing Add:* 629 University Dr Rock Hill SC 29730

HOUK, ROBERT SAMUEL, CHEMICAL INSTRUMENTATION. *Current Pos:* from asst prof to assoc prof, 81-90, PROF ANALYTICAL CHEM, IOWA STATE UNIV, 91-; SR CHEMIST, AMES LAB, US DEPT ENERGY, 91- *Personal Data:* b New Castle, Pa, Nov 23, 52; m 81; c 2. *Educ:* Slippery Rock State Col, BS, 74; Iowa State Univ, PhD(analytical chem), 80. *Honors & Awards:* Lester W Strock Medal, Soc Appl Spectros, 85; Award in Chem Instrumentation, Am Chem Soc, 93. *Prof Exp:* Grad res asst, Ames Lab, US Dept Energy, 75-80, asst chemist, 80-81. *Concurrent Pos:* Prin investr, Plasma Mass Spectrometry Proj, Ames Lab, US Dept Energy, 80- *Mem:* Am Chem Soc; Soc Appl Spectros; Am Soc Mass Spectrometry; Sigma Xi; AAAS. *Res:* Ionization principles and methods for mass spectrometry; applications and diagnostics of inductively coupled plasmas; trace elemental isotopic and organic analysis; mass spectrometry; high vacuum technology. *Mailing Add:* Dept Chem Iowa State Univ Ames IA 50011-0061

HOUK, THOMAS WILLIAM, BIOPHYSICS. *Current Pos:* from asst prof to assoc prof, 74-82, PROF PHYSICS, MIAMI UNIV, OXFORD OHIO, 82-, CHMN DEPT, 85- *Personal Data:* b Johnson City, Tenn, June 4, 44; m 73; c 3. *Educ:* NC State Univ, Raleigh, BS, 66; Univ Md, College Park, PhD(physics), 71. *Prof Exp:* USPHS fel, Univ Calif Med Ctr, Cardiovasc Res Inst, Med Sch, Univ Calif, San Francisco, 71-73; Robert A Welch fel, Dept Biomath, M D Anderson Hosp & Tumor Inst, Houston, 73-74. *Mem:* Biophys Soc; Am Phys Soc; Am Asn Physics Teachers; Sigma Xi; AAAS; Am Asn

Higher Educ. *Res:* Statistical physics; applications of the theory of stochastic processes in biology, medicine, and chemistry; diffusion coupled reaction theory; experimental biophysics; physical properties of macromolecules employing fluorescence spectroscopy, especially vertebrate striated muscle; effects of electromagnetic fields on biological systems and macromolecules. *Mailing Add:* Dept Physics Miami Univ Oxford OH 45056-1637. *Fax:* 513-523-3841

HOULE, FRANCES ANNE, SURFACE CHEMISTRY, KINETIC MODELLING. *Current Pos:* MEM RES STAFF, RES DIV, IBM, 81- *Personal Data:* b Pasadena, Calif, Oct 22, 52; m 78, William Minsberg; c William, Monique & Martin. *Educ:* Univ Calif, Irvine, BA, 74, Calif Inst Technol, PhD(chem), 79. *Prof Exp:* Fel, Lawrence Berkeley Lab, Univ Calif, 79-80. *Concurrent Pos:* assoc ed, J Vacuum Sci & Technol, 89-93; scholar trustee, Am Vacuum Soc, 90-92, officer, Electronics Mat & Processing Div, 93-96. *Mem:* Am Chem Soc; fel Am Phys Soc; Am Vacuum Soc; Mat Res Soc. *Res:* Stochastic simulations of reaction kinetics; materials processing chemistry; photoinduced processes at surfaces and in thin films. *Mailing Add:* IBM Almaden Res Ctr 650 Harry Rd K18/D1 San Jose CA 95120-6099. *E-Mail:* houle@almaden.ibm.com

HOULE, JOSEPH E, MATHEMATICS, ACADEMIC ADMINISTRATION. *Current Pos:* chmn dept, Pace Univ, NY, 63-70, dean, Dyson Col Arts & Sci, 71-90, vprovost, 87-90, dir ctr appl ethics, 83-93, PROF MATH, PACE UNIV, NY & WESTCHESTER CAMPUS, 63- *Personal Data:* b Hartford, Conn, Oct 11, 30; m 54, Constance Deschamps; c Marie, Joseph, Celia, Elizabeth, Amy & Bernice. *Educ:* Cath Univ Am, AB, 52, MA, 54, PhD(math), 59. *Prof Exp:* Asst math, Cath Univ Am, 52-53; from instr to assoc prof, Georgetown Univ, 53-62; assoc prof, Seton Hall Univ, 62-63. *Mem:* Math Asn Am. *Mailing Add:* 227 Garfield Pl South Orange NJ 07079-2108

HOULIHAN, JOHN FRANK, PHOTOELECTROCHEMICAL MATERIALS. *Current Pos:* from instr to assoc prof physics, 67-82, PROF PHYSICS, PA STATE UNIV, 82- *Personal Data:* b Springfield, Ill, Sept 9, 42; m 65; c 2. *Educ:* Ind Cent Univ, BA, 64; DePauw Univ, MA, 66; Pa State Univ, PhD(physics), 73. *Prof Exp:* Engr solid state, device group, Avco Electronic, 66-67. *Mem:* Am Phys Soc; Electrochem Soc; Am Asn Physics Teachers. *Res:* Materials preparation and characterization for use in photoelectrochemical device applications. *Mailing Add:* Dept Physics Pa State Univ Shenango Valley Campus Sharon PA 16146

HOULIHAN, RODNEY T, PHYSIOLOGY, ENDOCRINOLOGY. *Current Pos:* RETIRED. *Personal Data:* b Los Angeles, Calif, Dec 12, 26; m 48; c 4. *Educ:* Univ Redlands, BS, 57; Univ NMex, MSc, 58; Univ Calif, Davis, PhD(zool), 60. *Prof Exp:* Asst zool, Univ Calif, Davis, 58-60; instr biol, St Mary's Col, Calif, 60-61; from asst prof to assoc prof zool, Pa State Univ, 61-69; prof osteop med, Mich State Univ, 69-73; prof physiol, dean acad admin & dir res, Okla Col Osteop Med & Surg, 73-81, vpres res & develop, 81-88. *Mem:* AAAS; Am Physiol Soc; Aerospace Med Soc; NY Acad Sci. *Res:* Adrenal gland function during chronic and acute stress; interrelations of steroids and catecholamine metabolism, hyperbaric medicine and oxygen toxicity, water and electrolyte metabolism. *Mailing Add:* Rte 2 PO Box 2560 Mounds OK 74047

HOULIHAN, WILLIAM JOSEPH, ORGANIC CHEMISTRY, MEDICINAL CHEMISTRY. *Current Pos:* EMER RES SCIENTIST, C A DANA RES INST, DREW UNIV, 93-, PROF CHEM, 95- *Personal Data:* b South Amboy, NJ, July 24, 30; m 59, Piroska Bizony; c Anna, Michael & Peter. *Educ:* Seton Hall Univ, BS, 51; Rutgers Univ, PhD(org chem), 55. *Prof Exp:* Asst prof chem, St John's Univ, NY, 55-56; group leader, Universal Oil Prod Chem Co, 56-58; asst prof chem, Seton Hall Univ, 58-60; group leader, Universal Oil Prod Chem Co, 60-62; sect head, Sandoz Res Inst, Hanover, NJ, 62-73, sect dir chem develop & res, 73-84, dir med, Chem Dept, 84-93. *Concurrent Pos:* Lectr, Rutgers Univ, 61-62; co-chmn, Residential Sch Med Chem, Drew Univ, 87- *Mem:* Am Chem Soc. *Res:* Heterocyclic synthesis; synthesis of medicinal agents; organolithium reagents. *Mailing Add:* C A Dana Res Inst Sci Bldg Drew Univ Madison NJ 07940. *Fax:* 973-408-3504; *E-Mail:* whouliha@drew.edu

HOUN, FLORENCE, PUBLIC EPIDEMIOLOGY, MEDICINE. *Current Pos:* Clin fel, Oncol Ctr, 93-94, INSTR ONCOL, JOHNS HOPKINS SCH MED, 94-; DIR, DIV MAMMOGRAPHY QUAL & RADIATION PROGS, CTR DEVICES RADIOL HEALTH, FOOD & DRUG ADMIN, 93- *Educ:* Harvard Univ, MA, 80; Albert Einstein Col Med, MD, 84; Johns Hopkins Univ, MPH, 92; Am Bd Internal Med, cert, 87. *Honors & Awards:* Janet M Glasgow Mem Achievement Citation, Am Med Women's Asn, 84. *Prof Exp:* Intern & resident, Presby Hosp-Columbia Univ, 84-87; physician & med ctr liaison, Matilda Koval Med Ctr, Baltimore Med Syst Inc, 87-91; cancer prev & control fel, Div Cancer Control & Prev, Prev Oncol Br, Nat Cancer Inst, 91-93. *Concurrent Pos:* Int health fel, Albert Einstein Col Med, Philippines, 83. *Mem:* Am Col Physicians; Am Soc Prev Oncol; Asian Health Forum; Nat Asian Women's Health Orgn. *Res:* Contributed numerous articles to professional publications. *Mailing Add:* Food & Drug Admin 5600 Fishers Lane HFZ-240 Rockville MD 20857

HOUNSFIELD, G NEWBOLD, X-RAY TECHNOLOGY. *Current Pos:* Staff, EMI Ltd, 51-72, head, Med Systs Sect, 72-76, sr res scientist, 77-87, CONSULT, CENT RES LABS, EMI LTD, 87- *Personal Data:* b Aug 28, 19. *Educ:* City & Guild, Col, London, educ; Faraday House Elec Eng Col, London, dipl, 76. *Hon Degrees:* MD, Univ Basel, 75; DSc, City Univ, 76 & Univ London, 76; DTech, Univ Loughborough, 76; DHC, Cambridge Univ, 92. *Honors & Awards:* Nobel Prize in Med, 79; Churchill Gold Medal, 76; Gairdner Found Award, 76; Medal, Inst Physics, 76; MacRobert Award, 72; Wilhelm-Exner Medal, Austrian Indust Asn, 74; Ziedses des Plantes Medal, Physikalishe Medizinishe Gesellschaft, 74; Prince Philip Medal Award, 75; Lasker Award, Lasker Found, 75; Duddell Bronze Medal Inst Physics, 76; Golden Plate Award Am Acad Achievement, 76; Reginald Mitchell Gold Medal, Stoke-on-Trent Asn Engrs, 76; Decorated Comdr, Order Brit Empire, 76, Knight, 81. *Mem:* Fel Royal Soc. *Res:* Led design team for first all transistor computer to be built in Great Britain; invented EMI-scanner computerized transverse axial tomography system for x-ray exam; developed new x-ray technique (EMI scanner system). *Mailing Add:* 15 Crane Park Rd Whitton Twickenham Middlesex England

HOUNSHELL, DAVID A, HISTORY OF TECHNOLOGY, INNOVATION STUDIES. *Current Pos:* HENRY R LUCE PROF TECHNOL & SOCIAL CHANGE, CARNEGIE MELLON UNIV, 91- *Personal Data:* b Denver, Colo, Oct 18, 50; m 73, Nancy Burr Eddy; c Jennie B, Bernard B & Eric T. *Educ:* Southern Methodist Univ, BSEE, 72; Univ Del, MA, 75, PhD(hist), 78. *Honors & Awards:* Browder J Thompson Prize, Inst Elec & Electronics Engrs, 78; Dexter Prize, Soc Hist Technol, 87. *Prof Exp:* Asst prof hist, Harvey Mudd Col, 77-79; from asst prof to prof hist, Univ Del, 79-91. *Concurrent Pos:* Cur technol, Hagley Mus & Libr, 79-86, sr scholar, 86-87; Marvin Bower fel, Harvard Bus Sch, 87-88, Ctr Advan Study, Univ Del, 91-92. *Mem:* AAAS; Inst Elec & Electronics Engrs; Soc Hist Technol; Orgn Am Historians; Am Hist Asn; Hist Sci Soc. *Res:* History of science, technology, and business in the United States, 1776-1990; history of innovation in the public and private sectors; cold war studies. *Mailing Add:* Dept Hist Carnegie Mellon Univ 5000 Forbes Ave Pittsburgh PA 15213-3890. *Fax:* 412-268-1019; *E-Mail:* hounshel@andrew.cmu.edu

HOUNSHELL, WILLIAM DOUGLAS, ORGANIC CHEMISTRY. *Current Pos:* MEM STAFF, MOLECULAR DESIGN LTD, 80- *Personal Data:* b Atlanta, Ga, Aug 8, 51; m 73. *Educ:* Calif Inst Technol, BS, 73; Princeton Univ, PhD(chem), 77. *Prof Exp:* Instr, Princeton Univ, 77-78; asst prof chem, Wake Forest Univ, 78-80. *Mem:* Am Chem Soc; Sigma Xi. *Res:* Stereochemical analysis; computational chemistry; strained compounds; chemical information. *Mailing Add:* MDL Info Systs Inc 14600 Catalina St San Leandro CA 94577

HOUNSLOW, ARTHUR WILLIAM, HYDROGEOCHEMISTRY, TRACE ELEMENTS. *Current Pos:* PROF GEOL, OKLA STATE UNIV, STILLWATER, 82- *Personal Data:* b Reservoir, Australia, July 17, 33; m 70; c 3. *Educ:* Univ Melbourne, BSc, 60; Carleton Univ, MSc, 65, PhD(geol), 68. *Prof Exp:* Anal technician, Queen's Univ, Ont, 61-62; asst prof geol, Idaho State Univ, 69-74; sr proj mineralogist, Colo Sch Mines Res Inst, 74-81; geochemist, US Environ Protection Agency, Ada, Okla, 81-82. *Mem:* Nat Ground Water Asn; Nat Waterwell Asn; Geol Soc Am. *Res:* Prediction of rock/water interactions; materials analysis; determination of sources of pollutant as well as their rate of absorption retardation and degradation; hydrogeochemistry; pollutant attenuation in ground water systems; brine contamination and hydrocarbon/solvents spills. *Mailing Add:* Geol Dept Rm 105 NRC Okla State Univ Stillwater OK 74078-0002. *E-Mail:* awh@okway.okstate.edu

HOUPIS, CONSTANTINE H, CONTROL THEORY, FLIGHT CONTROL APPLICATIONS. *Current Pos:* instr to prof elec engr, 52-96, EMER PROF ELEC ENGR, AIR FORCE INST TECHNOL, 96-, SR RES ASSOC, FLIGHT DYNAMICS DIRECTORATE, WRIGHT LAB, 80- *Personal Data:* b Lowell, Mass, June 16, 22; m 60, Mary Stephens; c Harry & Angella. *Educ:* Univ Ill, BS, 47, MS, 48; Univ Wyo, PhD(control theory), 71. *Prof Exp:* Elec engr, Babcock & Willcox Corp, 49-51; instr elec engr, Wayne State Univ, 49-51; prin elec engr, Batelle Inst, 51-52. *Mem:* Fel Inst Elec & Electronics Engrs; Am Soc Eng Educ. *Res:* Design of robust multivariable control systems containing structured parametric uncertainty, specific emphasis on aerospace flight control system. *Mailing Add:* Dept Elec Eng Air Force Inst Technol Bldg 640 2950 P St Wright-Patterson AFB OH 45433-7765

HOUPIS, JAMES LOUIS JOSEPH, AIR POLLUTION EFFECTS & CLIMATE CHANGE EFFECTS ON FOREST SPECIES. *Current Pos:* ASSOC PROF BIOL SCIS, SOUTHERN ILL UNIV, 97-, ASST DIR, ENVIRON STUDIES PROG, 97- *Personal Data:* b Binghamton, NY, Oct 11, 56; m 80, Valerie Wood; c Elias, Aaron, Joseph & Jacob. *Educ:* Univ Calif, Berkeley, BA, 78, PhD(forest sci), 89; San Diego State Univ, MS, 84. *Prof Exp:* Res asst, Univ Calif, Berkeley, 80-86; tree ecophysiologist, Lawrence Livermore Nat Lab, 86-97, prog mgr, Biotechnol Educ Prog, 93-97. *Concurrent Pos:* Teaching assoc silvicult, Univ Calif, Berkeley, 84, scientist, 86; prin investr, US Environ Protection Agency, US Forest Serv, 87-91, 88-89 & 88-91; adj prof, Calif State Univ, Chico, 91-; fel, Southern Ill Univ, 97. *Mem:* Am Soc Plant Physiologists; Am Soc Agron. *Res:* Comparison of physiological, morphological, biochemical and growth response of mature trees and seedlings to air pollution and climate change; author and co-author of over 50 publications. *Mailing Add:* Dept Biol Scis Southern Ill Univ PO Box 1099 Edwardsville IL 62026. *Fax:* 618-692-3174; *E-Mail:* jhoupis@sive.edu

HOUPT, KATHERINE ALBRO, VETERINARY PHYSIOLOGY, ANIMAL BEHAVIOR. *Current Pos:* res assoc, 73-75, asst prof, 75-80, PROF PHYSIOL, CORNELL UNIV, 80- *Personal Data:* b Buffalo, NY, Jan 11, 39; m 62; c 2. *Educ:* Pa State Univ, BS, 60; Univ Pa, VMD, 63, PhD(biol), 72. *Prof Exp:* Instr physiol, Univ Pa, 63-64. *Concurrent Pos:* NIH fel, 63-64, spec fel, 73-75; vis scientist, Agr Res Coun, Inst Animal Physiol, Babraham, Cambridge, Eng, 78-79. *Mem:* Sigma Xi; Am Physiol Soc; Am Vet Med Asn; Animal Behav Soc; Am Soc Animal Sci. *Res:* Comparative control of ingestive behavior in swine, horses and laboratory rodents; dominance hierarchies in horses. *Mailing Add:* Dept Physiol NYS Col Vet Med Cornell Univ Ithaca NY 14853-6401

HOUPT, THOMAS RICHARD, ANIMAL PHYSIOLOGY. *Current Pos:* PROF VET PHYSIOL, NY STATE COL VET MED, CORNELL UNIV, 71- *Personal Data:* b Roslyn, Pa, Oct 9, 25; m 62, Katherine Albro; c Thomas A & Charles E. *Educ:* Univ Pa, VMD, 50, PhD(physiol), 58; Univ Ill, MS, 53. *Prof Exp:* Instr vet physiol & pharmacol, Col Vet Med, Univ Ill, 50-53; from instr to prof physiol, Sch Vet Med, Univ Pa, 53-71. *Concurrent Pos:* Res assoc, Duke Univ, 53-54; res career develop award, NIH, 62-67; vis scientist, Agr Res Coun, Inst Animal Physiol, Babraham & vis scholar Corpus Christi Col, Cambridge Univ, Eng, 78-79 & 86-87. *Mem:* AAAS; Am Physiol Soc; Am Soc Vet Physiologists & Pharmacologists; Soc Neurosci; Soc Study Ingestive Behav. *Res:* Comparative physiology of birds and mammals; environmental physiology; gastro-intestinal adaptations related to adverse nutritional conditions; nitrogen metabolism; controls of food and water intake. *Mailing Add:* Dept Physiol Vet Col Cornell Univ Ithaca NY 14853. *Fax:* 607-253-3846; *E-Mail:* trh1@cornell.edu

HOURIGAN, WILLIAM R, SOIL CHEMISTRY. *Current Pos:* prof soil chem, 60-74, PROF AGR, WESTERN KY UNIV, 74-, ASSOC DEAN UNDERGRAD INSTR, 60-, DEAN COL APPL ARTS & HEALTH, 69- *Personal Data:* b Lebanon, Ky, May 11, 29; c 1. *Educ:* Univ Ky, BS, 52, MS, 56; Ohio State Univ, PhD(soil chem), 60. *Prof Exp:* Asst county agent, Univ Ky, 52-53 & 56-57. *Res:* Effect of aluminum in soils. *Mailing Add:* Pub Health Western Ky Univ 1 Big Red Way St Bowling Green KY 42101-3576

HOURSTON, ALAN STEWART, FISHERIES. *Current Pos:* CONSULT FISHERIES BIOL, 81- *Personal Data:* b Toronto, Ont, July 9, 26; m 55, Barbara R Foster; c Kim L, Ian M, Wendy R, Roy A & Peter. *Educ:* Univ Toronto, BA, 47, MA, 49; Univ Calif, PhD(oceanog), 56. *Prof Exp:* Demonstr zool, Univ Toronto, 48-49; from asst scientist to res scientist, Fisheries Res Bd Can, 49-72, sci asst to dir, 59-62, asst dir, 62-63; prog coordr, Int Fisheries Br, Dept Fisheries & Oceans, 73, head herring prog, Pac Biol Sta, Resource Serv Br, 73-80. *Res:* Population dynamics and ecology of Pacific and Atlantic herring and Pacific salmon; theoretical population studies; scientific editing. *Mailing Add:* 2948 Hammond Bay Rd Nanaimo BC V9T 1E2 Can

HOUSE, ARTHUR STEPHEN, SPEECH COMMUNICATION. *Current Pos:* ADJ STAFF MEM, COMMUN RES DIV, INST DEFENSE ANALYSIS, 71- *Personal Data:* b New York, NY, May 1, 21; m 43; c 2. *Educ:* City Col New York, BS, 42; Univ Denver, MA, 48; Univ Ill, PhD(speech), 51. *Prof Exp:* Instr speech sci, Univ Ill, 51-52; res assoc audition, Control Systs Lab, 52-53; staff mem speech commun, Acoustics Lab, Mass Inst Technol, 53-57; assoc prof audiol & speech path, Syracuse Univ, 57-59; staff mem, Res Lab Electronics, Mass Inst Technol, 59-64; prof audiol & speech sci, Purdue Univ, West Lafayette, 64-71. *Concurrent Pos:* Mem comt hearing, bioacoustics & biomech, Nat Acad Sci-Nat Res Coun, 65-66. *Mem:* Fel AAAS; fel NY Acad Sci; fel Am Speech & Hearing Asn; fel Acoustical Soc Am. *Res:* Experimental study of processes used to decode acoustic speech signals into sequences of discrete linguistic symbols, and to encode sequences of discrete linguistic symbols into acoustic signals. *Mailing Add:* 11 Thorngate Ct Princeton NJ 08540-7807

HOUSE, EDWARD HOLCOMBE, PHYSICAL CHEMISTRY. *Current Pos:* chmn dept, 67-70, PROF CHEM, MERCER COUNTY COL, 70- *Personal Data:* b Trenton, NJ, Sept 10, 29. *Educ:* Princeton Univ, AB, 50; Dartmouth Col, AM, 52; Univ Rochester, PhD(chem), 60. *Prof Exp:* Instr chem, Hobart & William Smith Cols, 55-59; asst prof, Univ NDak, 59-62; prof math & phys sci & chmn dept, Trenton Jr Col, NJ, 62-67. *Mem:* AAAS; Am Chem Soc; Sigma Xi. *Res:* Reaction kinetics and catalysis; molecular spectroscopy; history and philosophy of science. *Mailing Add:* Dept Chem Box B Mercer County Col Trenton NJ 08690

HOUSE, EDWIN W, ANIMAL PHYSIOLOGY, PATHOLOGY. *Current Pos:* asst prof biol, 66-70, assoc prof, 70-75, PROF BIOL, IDAHO STATE UNIV, 75- *Personal Data:* b Corning, NY, Oct 20, 39; m 64, Janet Gryth; c Naomi & Matthew. *Educ:* Western Mont Col, BS, 60; Univ Mont, MS, 62; Univ NDak, PhD(physiol), 65. *Prof Exp:* Asst prof zool, Univ Mont, 65-66. *Concurrent Pos:* Dept chair, 81-86, Hosp Ethics Comt mem, 85-; chair, Idaho Higher Educ Res Coun; pres bd dirs, Environ Sci & Res Found. *Mem:* AAAS; Sigma Xi; Am Physiol Soc. *Res:* Newborn mammalian physiology; atherosclerosis; cardiovascular development and control; comparative mammalian physiology; cardiovascular control systems; comparative temperature regulation in mammals and reptiles; comparative anatomy and physiology of renal function in mammals; bioethics. *Mailing Add:* Res Idaho State Univ Campus Box 8130 Pocatello ID 83209-0001. *Fax:* 208-236-4529; *E-Mail:* housedwi@fs.isu.edu

HOUSE, GARY LAWRENCE, CHEMICAL ENGINEERING, SOLID STATE PHYSICS. *Current Pos:* Res chemist, 77-91, LAB HEAD, EASTMAN KODAK CO, 91- *Personal Data:* b St Marys, Pa, Dec 12, 47; m 70; c 3. *Educ:* Grove City Col, BS, 73; Univ Ill, MS, 75, PhD(chem eng), 77. *Mem:* Am Inst Chem Engrs; Soc Imaging Sci & Technol. *Res:* Luminescence properties of inorganic semiconductors; photographic properties of silver halide imaging systems. *Mailing Add:* 1037 Oak Ridge Dr Victor NY 14564

HOUSE, HERBERT OTIS, ORGANIC CHEMISTRY. *Current Pos:* RETIRED. *Personal Data:* b Willoughby, Ohio, Dec 5, 29; m 80; c 2. *Educ:* Miami Univ, BS, 50; Univ Ill, PhD(org chem), 53. *Honors & Awards:* Award for Creative Work in Synthetic Org Chem, Am Chem Soc, 75 & Award Chem Health & Safety, 83. *Prof Exp:* From instr to prof org chem, Mass Inst Technol, 53-71; prof chem, Ga Inst Technol, 71-90. *Concurrent Pos:* Consult, Union Carbide Chem Co; mem, Adv Bd, Org Reactions, Inc, 71-79 & Org Syntheses, 74-79; chmn comt on handling hazardous substances in labs, Nat Res Coun, 79-81. *Mem:* Am Chem Soc; The Chem Soc; Swiss Chem Soc. *Res:* Organic synthetic methods; chemistry of carbanions; stereochemistry of organic reactions; reactions involving electron transfer. *Mailing Add:* 20 Lambets Way Alpharetta GA 30202-3903

HOUSE, HOWARD LESLIE, INSECT PHYSIOLOGY, INSECT NUTRITION. *Current Pos:* RETIRED. *Personal Data:* b Brantford, Ont, Jan 20, 18; m 45, Fern A McMullen; c Linda, David & John. *Educ:* Ont Agr Col, BSA, 43; Cornell Univ, PhD(entom), 48. *Prof Exp:* Agr scientist, Res Br, Can Dept Agr, 52-71, res officer, 71-79. *Mem:* Entom Soc Am; fel Entom Soc Can; Sigma Xi. *Res:* Insect nutrition and dietetics; food preference; biological control. *Mailing Add:* RR 1 Corbyville ON K0K 1V0 Can

HOUSE, JAMES EVAN, JR, SOLID STATE INORGANIC CHEMISTRY & CHEMISTRY INDUCED BY ULTRASOUND, CHEMICAL DYNAMICS. *Current Pos:* from asst prof to assoc prof, Ill State Univ, 66-70, asst dean fac, 70-72, assoc dean univ, 72-74, PROF CHEM, ILL STATE UNIV, 74- *Personal Data:* b Benton, Ill, July 7, 36; m 93, Kathleen Kemper; c 4. *Educ:* Southern Ill Univ, BS, 58, MA, 61; Univ Ill, Urbana, PhD(inorg chem), 70. *Prof Exp:* Instr chem, Southern Ill Univ, 60-61; fac asst phys sci, Univ Ill, Urbana, 62-63; asst prof chem, Western Ky Univ, 63-64; res chemist, A E Staley Co, 64-66. *Concurrent Pos:* Vis Prof Chem & Adv Studies, Univ Ill, Urbana, 91. *Mem:* Am Chem Soc; Sigma Xi. *Res:* Thermal properties and mechanisms of reactions of coordination compounds; kinetics of solid state reactions; chemical computations and data analysis; chemical dynamics. *Mailing Add:* Dept Chem Ill State Univ Normal IL 61790-4160

HOUSE, JAMES STEPHEN, PSYCHOSOCIAL FACTORS IN HEALTH. *Current Pos:* assoc prof sociol & assoc res scientist, Surv Res Ctr & Epidemiol, Univ Mich, 78-83, assoc chair sociol, 81-84, chair sociol, 86-90, PROF SOCIOL & RES SCIENTIST, SURV RES CTR & EPIDEMIOL, UNIV MICH, 83-, DIR, SURV RES CTR, 91- *Personal Data:* b Philadelphia, Pa, Jan 27, 44; m 67, Wendy Fisher; c Jeffrey T & Erin H. *Educ:* Haverford Col, BA, 65; Univ Mich, PhD(social psychol), 72. *Prof Exp:* From instr to prof sociol, Duke Univ, 70-78. *Concurrent Pos:* From adj asst prof to adj assoc prof epidemiol, Univ NC, 75-78; assoc ed, J Health & Social Behav, Am Sociol Asn, 80-82, prin investr, Nat Inst on Aging Proj grant, 85-, chair, Social Psychol Sect, 87-88; Guggenheim fel, 86-87. *Mem:* Am Sociol Asn; fel AAAS; Soc Epidemiol Res; Soc Psychol Study Social Issue; fel Soc Behav Med. *Res:* Socioeconomic studies of health relation of social stress and social support to health, and the structural determinants of social stress and social support; health in middle and late life occupational stress and health; productive activity; stress. *Mailing Add:* Inst Social Res Univ Mich PO Box 1248 Ann Arbor MI 48106

HOUSE, JOE ESTES, CHEMISTRY. *Current Pos:* CONSULT, 87- *Personal Data:* b Newton County, Mo, Sept 28, 23; m 54, Marydella L Millsap; c Jordan E & Laura G. *Educ:* SW Mo State Univ, BS, 47; Univ Okla, MS, 50; Washington Univ, St Louis, MBA, 51. *Honors & Awards:* Gaudine Award, Am Inst Mining & Metall, 81, Douglas Award, 88; Wadsworth Award, Soc Mining Metall & Explor, 96. *Prof Exp:* Vpres, Henkel Corp, 56-86. *Mem:* Nat Acad Eng; distinguished mem Soc Mining & Metall Eng. *Res:* Solution chemistry of metallic ions using organic complexing reagents for separation and purification of aqueous solutions in heterogeneous mixtures. *Mailing Add:* 3735 Larchwood Dr Minnetonka MN 55345-1234. *Fax:* 612-404-1933; *E-Mail:* joehouse@inspect.usa

HOUSE, JOHN W, OTOLOGY. *Current Pos:* PRES, HOUSE EAR INST, LOS ANGELES, 87- *Personal Data:* b Los Angeles, Calif, July 12, 41; m 67, Patricia Roberts; c Hans, Chris & Kurt. *Educ:* Univ Southern Calif, Los Angeles, BS, 64, MD, 67. *Honors & Awards:* Hocks Mem Award, Am Tinnitus Asn, 88. *Prof Exp:* Resident, Glendale Adventist Hosp, 71-72, Los Angeles Co Med Ctr, 72-74. *Concurrent Pos:* Fel, Otologic Med Group, Los Angeles, 74; pvt pract, 75- *Mem:* Fel Am Acad Otolaryngol; Am Neurotology Soc; AMA; Am Soc Mil Otolaryngologists; Pan Am Asn Otorhinolaryngol Broncho Esophagology. *Res:* Otolaryngology. *Mailing Add:* House Ear Div 2100 W Third St 1st Floor Los Angeles CA 90057

HOUSE, KATHLEEN ANN, SONOCHEMISTRY, THERMAL ANALYSIS. *Current Pos:* AT DEPT CHEM, ILL WESLEYAN UNIV, 94- *Personal Data:* b Peoria, Ill, July 6, 66; m 93, James. *Educ:* Ill State Univ, BS, 87, MS, 89. *Prof Exp:* Grad teaching asst gen chem, Ill State Univ, 88-89; chemist, Bloomington-Normal Sanit Dist, 88-89; grad teaching asst, instrumental analysis, Univ Ill, Urbana-Champaign, 90-91, grad res asst, 91-94. *Mem:* Am Chem Soc. *Res:* Sonoluminescence from inorganic systems; chemical and physical effects of ultrasound; phase transitions in inorganic solids; rates and mechanisms of solid state reactions. *Mailing Add:* Dept Chem Box 2900 Ill Wesleyan Univ Bloomington IL 61702-2900

HOUSE, LELAND RICHMOND, OTOLARYNGOLOGY. *Current Pos:* RETIRED. *Personal Data:* b Richmond, Va, July 16, 08; div; c 4. *Educ:* Pac Union Col, BS, 32; Loma Linda Univ, MD, 34; Univ Pa, MSc, 45. *Prof Exp:* From instr to prof otolaryngol & head dept, Sch Med, Loma Linda Univ,

38-45 & 47-66; clin prof otolaryngol, Med Sch, Univ Southern Calif & chmn dept otolaryngol, Rancho Los Amigos Hosp, 66-95. *Concurrent Pos:* Mem attend staff, White Mem Hosp, 38-90, Calif Lutheran Hosp, 38-80, Glendale Adventist Med Ctr, 44-84 & Los Angeles County-Univ Southern Calif Med Ctr, 52-90; consult, St Francis Hosp, 44-70 & Cedars-Sinai Hosp, 56-90. *Mem:* Am Laryngol, Rhinol & Otol Soc; AMA; Am Acad Otolaryngol & Head & Neck Surg; Am Rhinologic Soc. *Res:* Problems of deafness and surgery on the ears for its correction; rhinological surgery for correction of nasal deformities and nasal disfunctions. *Mailing Add:* 620 S Glassell St Apt 319 Orange CA 92866-3043

HOUSE, ROBERT W(ILLIAM), SCIENCE POLICY, SYSTEMS ENGINEERING. *Current Pos:* prof technol & pub policy & dir, Vanderbilt Univ, 75-82, from assoc dean to dean acad sch, 81-84, dir mgt technol prog, 82-90, Orrin Henry Ingram Distinguished prof, 84-90, EMER ORRIN HENRY INGRAM DISTINGUISHED PROF & EMER PROF ELEC ENG, VANDERBILT UNIV, 90- *Personal Data:* b Wellsville, Ohio, May 31, 27; m 48, Pauline M Krebs; c Tamara L (Joba), Deborah J (Cohen), Linda K (Knebel), Pamela M (Hughes) & Karen A (Byerly). *Educ:* Ohio Univ, BS, 49, MS, 52; Pa State Univ, PhD(elec eng), 59; Harvard Bus Sch, PMD, 66. *Honors & Awards:* Centennial Medal & Commendation, Inst Elec & Electronics Engrs. *Prof Exp:* Mathematician, US Naval Proving Grounds, 50-51; electronic scientist, Wright-Patterson AFB, 51-54; sr mathematician, HRB-Singer, 54; from instr to asst prof elec eng, Pa State Univ, 54-59; consult, Systs Eng Div, Battelle-Columbus, 59-65, dir comput sci res, 65-66, assoc mgr, Systs & Electronics Dept, 66-70, mgr, Social & Systs Sci Dept, 70-74; pres exec, President's Exec Interchange Prog/AID, 74-75. *Concurrent Pos:* Adj prof, Ohio State Univ, 65-70; consult, Secy Sci & Technol, State of Sao Paulo, 75-78, Nat Ctr Productivity, 78, Brazilian Nat Alcohol Fuels Prog, 78-82 & US Biomass Energy Prog, 84-85. *Mem:* Fel Inst Elec & Electronics Engrs; Eng Mgt Soc; Syst, Man & Cybernetics Soc. *Res:* Management of technology; systems analysis and synthesis; technological innovation process; technology and public policy; systems engineering; project management. *Mailing Add:* Mgt Technol Prog Vanderbilt Univ Box 6188 Sta B Nashville TN 37235. *Fax:* 615-322-7996

HOUSE, VERL LEE, genetics; deceased, see previous edition for last biography

HOUSE, WILLIAM BURTNER, BIOCHEMISTRY, NUTRITION. *Current Pos:* RETIRED. *Personal Data:* b Kansas City, Mo, Aug 24, 18; m 42, Lora E Wiley; c Roger, Alan, James, William, Virginia & Mary. *Educ:* Univ Mo, BS, 42, AM, 49, PhD, 58. *Prof Exp:* Chemist, Hercules Powder Co, Del, 42-43, res chemist smokeless powder, 43-45, supvr & res chemist, 45-46; asst, Univ Mo, 46-52; nutritionist, Nat Alfalfa Dehydrating & Milling Co, 52-54; from assoc chemist to prin scientist, Midwest Res Inst, 54-60; dir res, Plan Foods, Inc, 60-61; dir biol, Sci Div, Midwest Res Inst, 63-77, prin adv, 81-82. *Concurrent Pos:* Tech dir, US Contract Mgt, Consumer Protection Dept, Saudi Arabia, 78-80. *Mem:* AAAS; Am Chem Soc; Sigma Xi. *Res:* Nutrition; inhalation toxicity; ecological assessment. *Mailing Add:* 5745 Grand Kansas City MO 64113

HOUSECROFT, CATHERINE ELIZABETH, cluster chemistry, metallaborane chemistry, for more information see previous edition

HOUSEHOLDER, ALSTON SCOTT, MATHEMATICS. *Current Pos:* CONSULT, CALIF INST TECHNOL, 74- *Personal Data:* b Rockford, Ill, May 5, 04; m 26; c 2. *Educ:* Northwestern Univ, BS, 25; Cornell Univ, MA, 27; Univ Chicago, PhD(math), 37. *Hon Degrees:* Dr, Munich Tech Inst, 65. *Honors & Awards:* Harry Goode Mem Award, 69. *Prof Exp:* Instr math, Northwestern Univ, 26-28; tutor, Miss Harris Schs, Chicago, 29-30; from instr to asst prof, Washburn Col, 30-37; Rockefeller Found fel, Univ Chicago, 37-39, from res assoc to asst prof math biophys, 39-44; sr res psychophysiologist, Nat Defense Res Comt, Brown Univ, 44-45; math consult, Naval Res Lab, Washington, DC, 45-46; sr mathematician, Oak Ridge Nat Lab, 46-69; prof math, Univ Tenn, Knoxville, 64-74. *Concurrent Pos:* Instr, Northern Ill Col Optom, 40; mem div math, Nat Res Coun, 55-58 & 70-72. *Mem:* Fel AAAS; fel Am Acad Arts & Sci; Soc Indust & Appl Math (vpres, 62-63, pres, 63-64); Asn Comput Mach (vpres, 52-54, pres, 54-56); Math Asn Am (vpres, 60); Sigma Xi. *Res:* Numerical analysis; programming for high speed digital computation. *Mailing Add:* 6235 Tapia Dr Malibu CA 90265-3110

HOUSEHOLDER, JAMES EARL, MATHEMATICS. *Current Pos:* RETIRED. *Personal Data:* b West Newton, Pa, Dec 26, 16; m 38, Carolyn Magers; c 2. *Educ:* Univ Ariz, BS, 52, MS, 53; Univ Colo, PhD(math), 59. *Prof Exp:* From asst prof to assoc prof, Humboldt State Univ, 59-69, prof math, 69-87. *Mem:* Am Math Soc; Math Asn Am. *Res:* Theory of numbers. *Mailing Add:* PO Box 4386 Arcata CA 95518

HOUSEKNECHT, DAVID WAYNE, SEDIMENTARY GEOLOGY. *Current Pos:* STAFF MEM, US GEOL SURV, 92- *Personal Data:* b Muncy, Pa, Mar 18, 51; m 73; c 2. *Educ:* Pa State Univ, BS, 73, PhD(geol), 78; Southern Ill Univ, MS, 75. *Prof Exp:* Asst prof geol, Univ Mo, Columbia, 78-92. *Concurrent Pos:* Res geologist, US Bur Mines, 75- *Mem:* Soc Econ Paleontologists & Mineralogists; Int Asn Sedimentologists. *Res:* Sandstone petrogenesis; reconstruction of ancient depositional environments; statistical applications in sedimentary geology; coal geology. *Mailing Add:* US Geol Surv 12201 Sunrise Valley Dr MS 915 Reston VA 20192

HOUSEMAN, BARTON L, PHYSICAL CHEMISTRY. *Current Pos:* Asst prof, 61-67, assoc prof, 67-73, PROF CHEM, GOUCHER COL, 73- *Personal Data:* b Silver Spring, Md, Nov 12, 33; m 55, Doris Vande Ree; c Mark E & Jeanne E (Maguire). *Educ:* Calvin Col, AB, 55; Wayne State Univ, PhD(phys chem), 61. *Concurrent Pos:* Danforth assoc, Danford Found, 64-81; consult, Nuclear Defense Lab, Edgewood Arsenal, 64-65; vis staff mem, Los Alamos Sci Lab, 66-82; res assoc, Univ Calif, Berkeley, 69-70; consult, Inorg Mat Res Div, Lawrence Radiation Lab, 69-70. *Res:* Chemical education; solution thermodynamics; ion mobility spectrometry. *Mailing Add:* Dept Chem Goucher Col Baltimore MD 21204. *E-Mail:* houseman@goucher.edu

HOUSEPIAN, EDGAR M, NEUROSURGERY, NEUROONCOLOGY. *Current Pos:* From instr to prof neurol surg, 59-96, EMER PROF CLIN NEUROL SURG, COL PHYSICIANS & SURGEONS, COLUMBIA UNIV, 97-, SPEC ADV INT AFFIL VPRES/DEAN, 97- *Personal Data:* b New York, NY, Mar 18, 28; m 54, Marion G Lyon; c David, Stephen & Jean. *Educ:* Columbia Univ, BA, 49, MD, 53; Am Bd Neurol Surg, 61. *Honors & Awards:* Fulbright Traveling Fel, 68. *Concurrent Pos:* Parkinson's Dis Found res fel, 59-61; asst neurol surgeon, Columbia-Presby Med Ctr, 59-61, asst attend neurol surgeon, 61-64, assoc attend neurol surgeon, 64-; asst attend neurol surgeon, NY State Psychiat Inst, 61-; consult, Englewood Hosp, NJ, 64- & Greenwich Hosp, Conn, 65- *Mem:* Fel Am Col Surgeons; Am Asn Neurol Surgeons; Soc Neurosci; Int Soc Res Stereoencephalomy; Am Acad Neurosci; Res Soc Neurol Surg. *Res:* Basic and applied electrophysiology; clinical research in brain tumor chemotherapy; transphenoidal microsurgery; telemedicine. *Mailing Add:* Dept Neurol Surg Columbia Univ 710 W 168th St New York NY 10032. *Fax:* 212-305-3250; *E-Mail:* housepiemh4@columbia.edu

HOUSER, DONALD RUSSELL, MECHANICAL ENGINEERING. *Current Pos:* from asst prof to assoc prof, PROF, OHIO STATE UNIV, COLUMBUS, 68- *Personal Data:* b River Falls, Wis, Sept 2, 41; m 67, Colleen M Collins; c Kelle, Kerri & Joshua. *Educ:* Univ Wis, BS, 64, MS, 65, PhD, 69. *Prof Exp:* Instr, Univ Wis-Madison, 67-68. *Concurrent Pos:* Dir, Gear Dynamics & Gear Noise Res Lab, 79-; vpres, Gear Res Inst, Evanston, Ill, 90-; dir, Ctr Automobile Res, 94- *Mem:* Fel Am Soc Mech Engrs; Am Gear Mfr Asn; Soc Automotive Engrs; Am Helicopter Soc. *Res:* Development of technology for measuring gear transmission error under load; extend gear transmition error analysis methods and incorporate them in gear train dynamic models. *Mailing Add:* Ohio State Univ 206 W 18th Ave Columbus OH 43210-1107. *Fax:* 614-292-3163; *E-Mail:* houser.4@osu.edu

HOUSER, HAROLD BYRON, EPIDEMIOLOGY. *Current Pos:* from asst prof to assoc prof prev med, Case Western Res Univ, 58-74, actg dir, Dept Biomet, 69-75, dir, 75-85, prof epidemiol, 74-92, assoc prof med, 58-92, dir, Dept Epidemiol Biostat, 85-92, EMER PROF, CASE WESTERN RES UNIV, 92- *Personal Data:* b North Liberty, Ind, Nov 22, 21; m 44, Clara Jane Goin; c Cristene, Edgar, John, Susan & James. *Educ:* Ind Univ, AB, 42, MD, 44. *Honors & Awards:* Group Lasker Award. *Prof Exp:* Resident internal med, Crile Vet Admin Hosp, Ohio, 47-49; res fel, Dept Prev Med, Western Reserve Univ, 49-52; from instr to asst prof med, Col Med, State Univ NY Upstate Med Ctr, 53-58. *Concurrent Pos:* Arthritis & Rheumatism Found res fel, Col Med, State Univ NY Upstate Med Ctr, 53; dir lab, Housing & Illness, Armed Forces Epidemiol Bd, Sampson AFB, NY, 54-58; consult prev med, Surg Gen, US Army; dir, Dept Epidemiol Biostat, Case Western Res Univ, 85-92. *Mem:* Infectious Dis Soc Am; Am Epidemiol Soc (pres, 91). *Res:* Long term illness; streptococcal diseases; rheumatic fever; nutrition epidemiology; AIDS epidemiology. *Mailing Add:* 10409 E Windflower Ct Sun Lakes AZ 85248. *E-Mail:* halhous@aol.com

HOUSER, JOHN J, PHOTOCHEMISTRY, CARBOCATIONS. *Current Pos:* PROF CHEM, UNIV NMEX. *Personal Data:* b Abington, Pa, Feb 24, 39; m 68. *Educ:* Villanova Univ, BS, 60; Pa State Univ, PhD(chem), 64. *Prof Exp:* Prof chem, Univ Akron, 65-94. *Concurrent Pos:* Vis prof, Case Western Res Univ, 85. *Mem:* Am Chem Soc; Royal Soc Chem; Sigma Xi. *Res:* Photo dehalogenation; carbocation rearrangements; theoretical chemistry; computational chemistry. *Mailing Add:* Dept Chem Univ NMex Albuquerque NM 87131

HOUSER, THOMAS J, SUPERCRITICAL WATER REACTIONS, GAS PHASE KINETICS. *Current Pos:* from asst prof to assoc prof phys chem, 64-76, PROF CHEM, WESTERN MICH UNIV, 76- *Personal Data:* b Chicago, Ill, Feb 9, 30; m 53, Carol A Adair; c Kenneth R, Judith E, Brian D & Janet A. *Educ:* Ill Inst Technol, BS, 52, Univ Mich, MS, 54, PhD(phys chem), 57. *Prof Exp:* Chemist, Stand Oil Co, Ind, 57-58, asst proj chemist, 58-59; sr res engr, Rocketdyne Div, NAm Aviation, Inc, 59-62, prin scientist, 62-64. *Mem:* Am Chem Soc. *Res:* Gas phase kinetics and mechanisms using flow systems; coal liquefaction mechanisms; supercritical fluid chemistry. *Mailing Add:* 3635 Berrington Dr Kalamazoo MI 49006-5401. *Fax:* 616-387-2909

HOUSEWRIGHT, RILEY DEE, TECHNICAL MANAGEMENT, SCIENCE ADMINISTRATION. *Current Pos:* RETIRED. *Personal Data:* b Wylie, Tex, Oct 17, 13; m 39, 69, Antomis Skevakis; c Kim B (Housewright). *Educ:* NTex State Univ, BS, 34; Univ Tex, MA, 38; Univ Chicago, PhD(bact), 44; Am Bd Med Microbiol, dipl, 61. *Honors & Awards:* Barnett L Cohen Award in Microbiol, 67. *Prof Exp:* Pub sch teacher, Tex, 34-36; instr biol & supvr sci teacher training, SW Tex State Col, 37-41; med consult, Fed Security Agency, 43-44; res & chief med microbiol div, Ft Detrick Md, 44-56, sci dir, 56-70; vpres & sci dir, Microbiol Assocs, Inc, Bethesda, Md, 70-75; prin staff officer, Nat Res Coun-Nat Acad Sci, Washington, DC, 75-81; exec dir, Am Soc Microbiol, Washington, DC,

81-84. *Concurrent Pos:* Am Mgt Asn fel, 57-58; mem, Fed Exec Prog, Brookings Inst, 60 & 69; Nat Acad Sci & US rep to Int Asn Microbiol Socs, Moscow, 66; consult, Nat Acad Sci, 67-68 & 71; mem panel regulatory biol & consult, NSF, 67-71; mem, Aspen Exec Prog, 68; Found Microbiol lectr, 68; mem, Gov Sci Adv Bd, Md, 68; consult, NIH, 68-70 & 81, Off Educ, Dept Health, Educ & Welfare, 73 & 75, NASA, 75, Leonard Wood Mem Found, 75-81 & US State Dept, 80-81; consult, US Ctr Dis Control, 76; US State Dept, 80-81; consult, Nat Can Inst, 86-93. *Mem:* Fel AAAS; fel NY Acad Sci; fel Am Acad Microbiol; hon mem Am Soc Microbiol (pres, 66); Soc Exp Biol & Med; Cosmos Club; Brit Soc Gen Microbiol. *Res:* Research and development management; chemotherapy; amino acid metabolism; nutrition and enzymology of pathogenic bacteria; bacterial toxins and antitoxins; holder of one US patent. *Mailing Add:* 147 Fairview Ave Frederick MD 21701

HOUSHOLDER, GLENN ETTA (THOLEN), MEDICAL SCIENCES. *Current Pos:* from asst prof to assoc prof, 70-81, PROF PHARMACOL, DENT BR, HEALTH SCI CTR, UNIV TEX, HOUSTON, 81- *Personal Data:* b Granbury, Tex, Dec 29, 25; m 48, Dwight E. *Educ:* Univ Houston, BS, 47; Univ Tex, Houston, PhD(pharmacol), 70. *Mem:* AAAS; Am Chem Soc; Soc Exp Biol & Med; NY Acad Sci; Am Asn Dent Schs. *Res:* Biological effects of dental materials; inflammation; hemostasis; inflammation mediators. *Mailing Add:* Univ Tex Health Sci Dent Br 6515 John Freeman Ave Houston TX 77225. *Fax:* 713-500-4500; *E-Mail:* ghoushol@mail.db.uth.tmc.edu

HOUSKA, CHARLES ROBERT, PHYSICS. *Current Pos:* from assoc prof to prof metall, 63-69, prof metals & ceramic eng & head dept, 69-71, PROF MAT ENG, VA POLYTECH INST & STATE UNIV, 71- *Personal Data:* b Cleveland, Ohio, May 16, 27; m 53; c 3. *Educ:* Mass Inst Technol, SB, 51, SM, 54, ScD(metall), 57. *Prof Exp:* Mem res staff, Metall Dept, Mass Inst Technol, 57-59 & Union Carbide Res Inst, 59-63. *Mem:* Am Crystallog Asn; Am Inst Mining, Metall & Petrol Engrs; Sigma Xi. *Res:* Solid state diffusion and transformation kinetics; x-ray diffraction. *Mailing Add:* 2301 Spring Hollow Lane Blacksburg VA 24060

HOUSLEY, ROBERT MELVIN, PLANETOLOGY, SURFACE SCIENCE. *Current Pos:* STAFF MEM, ROCKWELL INT SCI CTR, 65- *Personal Data:* b Roseburg, Ore, June 24, 34; m 63, Mitzi Imamoto; c Helen T & Robert D. *Educ:* Reed Col, BA, 56; Univ Wash, PhD(physics), 64. *Prof Exp:* Res instr solid state physics, Univ Wash, 64; fel, State Univ Groningen, 64-65. *Concurrent Pos:* Prin investr contract for lunar sample & meteorite studies, NASA; vis prof, Dept Physics, Calif Inst Technol, 84-86. *Mem:* AAAS; Am Phys Soc; Am Geophys Union; Microbeam Analytical Soc; Meteoritical Soc; Am Ceramic Soc. *Res:* Lattice dynamics and spin interactions in solids via the Mossbauer effect; origin and evolution of the solar system; solar wind and micrometeorite interactions with the lunar surface; structure and origin of meteorites; high temperature materials. *Mailing Add:* Rockwell Int Sci Ctr 1049 Camino Dos Rios Thousand Oaks CA 91360. *Fax:* 626-683-9060; *E-Mail:* bob@styx.caltech.edu

HOUSLEY, THOMAS LEE, PLANT PHYSIOLOGY, CROP PHYSIOLOGIST. *Current Pos:* from asst prof to assoc prof, 75-90, PROF AGRON, PURDUE UNIV, 90- *Personal Data:* b Akron, Ohio, Feb 22, 42; m 66, Margaret McGrath; c Andrew & Dale. *Educ:* Taylor Univ, BS, 64; Univ Conn, MA, 69; Univ Ga, PhD(bot), 74. *Prof Exp:* Teacher life sci, Rocky Hill Jr High Sch, 64-66 & 68 & biol, Edwin O Smith High Sch, 66-68; fel agron, Univ Wis, 74-75. *Mem:* Am Soc Plant Physiologists; Crop Sci Soc Am; Am Inst Biol Sci. *Res:* Long distance translocation; the interrelationship between sources of transported compounds and sinks, in crops; environmental factors that influence dry matter accumulation in corn, small grains and soybeans. *Mailing Add:* Dept Agron Purdue Univ West Lafayette IN 47907-1968. *Fax:* 765-496-1368; *E-Mail:* thousley@dept.agry.purdue.edu

HOUSMAN, DAVID E, GENETICS, NEUROLOGY, BIOPHYSICS. *Current Pos:* fel, Jane Coffin Childs Found, Mass Inst Technol, 71-73, asst prof biol, 75-78, assoc prof, 78-85, PROF, MASS INST TECHNOL, 85-; ASSOC, NEUROL & GENETICS, MASS GENERAL HOSP, 79- *Personal Data:* b July 30, 46. *Educ:* Brandeis Univ, BA, 66, MA, 71; Mass Inst Technol, PhD(molecular biol), 73. *Prof Exp:* Staff mem, Div Biol Res, Ont Cancer Inst, 73-75; asst prof, Dept Med Biophys, Univ Toronto, 73-75. *Concurrent Pos:* mem adv bd, Mammalian Genetics Study Sect, NIH, 80-84, Hereditary Dis Found, 80-, Nat Neurofibromatosis Found, 82-, Tourette's Syndrome Asn, 83-, Eleanor Roosevelt Inst Cancer Res, 91-, Muscular Dystrophy Asn, 92-, Nat Ctr Human Genome Res, 92- *Mem:* Nat Acad Sci; Inst Med-Nat Acad Sci; fel Am Acad Microbiol; fel AAAS. *Mailing Add:* Ctr Cancer Res Mass Inst Technol, 77 Mass Ave Cambridge MA 02139

HOUSMANS, PHILIPPE ROBERT H P, ANESTHESIOLOGY. *Current Pos:* asst prof, 85-92, ASSOC PROF, ANESTHESIOL & PHARMACOL, 92-, SPEC CLIN FEL, ANESTHESIOL, MAYO FOUND 92- *Personal Data:* b Oostende, Belg, Aug 27, 53. *Educ:* Univ Antwerp, Belg, BS, 74, MD, 78, PhD(physiol), 84. *Prof Exp:* Investr physiol, Nat Res Found, 83-84. *Concurrent Pos:* Consult, Dept Anesthesiol, Univ Antwerp, Belg, 83-84. *Mem:* Biophys Soc; NY Acad Sci; Int Anesthesia Res Soc; Am Soc Anesthesiologists. *Res:* Physiology and pharmacology of cardiac muscle. *Mailing Add:* Dept Anesthesiol OLV Hosp Moorselbaan 164 Aalst B-9300 Belgium

HOUSMYER, CARL LEONIDAS, analytical chemistry, for more information see previous edition

HOUSNER, GEORGE W(ILLIAM), EARTHQUAKE ENGINEERING. *Current Pos:* from asst prof to prof civil eng & appl mech, 45-74, C F Braun prof, 74-81, EMER C F BRAUN PROF ENG, CALIF INST TECHNOL, 81- *Personal Data:* b Saginaw, Mich, Dec 9, 10. *Educ:* Univ Mich, BS, 33; Calif Inst Technol, MS, 34, PhD(civil eng), 41. *Hon Degrees:* PhD, Univ Mich, 92. *Honors & Awards:* Vincent Bendix Res Award, Am Soc Eng Educ, 67; Von Karman Medal, Am Soc Civil Engrs, 74, Newmark Medal, 81; Seismol Soc Medal, 81; Nat Medal Sci, 88; Earthquake Eng Res Inst Medal, 89. *Prof Exp:* Struct engr, Los Angeles, 34-39; group leader, Eng Seismol Res, Calif Inst Technol, 39-41; engr, US Eng Corps, 41-42; chief opers anal, USAF, Europe & Africa, 43-45. *Concurrent Pos:* Consult seismic eng, TransArabian Pipe Line, Lisbon, Portugal Supension Bridge, Calif Water Proj, San Francisco Bay Area Rapid Transit Syst, Taiwan High Speed Railway, Exxon Hondo Drilling Platform & Los Angeles Metro-Rail Proj; mem or chmn numerous comts & councils, earthquake res & eng; lectr, Univ Nev, Reno, 84, Univ Ill, 84, Rensselaer Polytech Inst, 88, Carnegie-Mellon Univ, 90, Univ Ill, 93, Hong Kong Univ Sci & Technol, 93; hon prof, Inst Eng Mech, 93. *Mem:* Nat Acad Eng; Nat Acad Eng; hon mem Int Asn Earthquake Eng (pres, 69-73); Seismol Soc Am (pres, 77-78); hon mem Earthquake Eng Res Inst (pres, 55-60); Indian Nat Sci Acad; fel AAAS; Am Soc Civil Engrs; Am Geophys Union; Japan Acad. *Res:* Earthquake engineering; structural dynamics; author or co-author of over 15 books and 174 technical papers. *Mailing Add:* 211 Thomas Lab Calif Inst Technol Pasadena CA 91125. *Fax:* 626-568-2719

HOUSTIS, ELIAS N, APPLIED MATHEMATICS, COMPUTER SCIENCE. *Current Pos:* asst prof appl math, 78-79, ASSOC PROF COMPUT SCI, UNIV SC, 79- *Personal Data:* b Portaria, Greece, Sept 12, 45. *Educ:* Univ Athens, BS, 69; Purdue Univ, PhD(math), 74. *Prof Exp:* Asst prof comput sci, Purdue Univ, 75-78. *Mem:* Am Comput Mach; Int Asn Math & Comput Simulation; Soc Indust & Appl Math. *Res:* Numerical analysis; mathematical software; modelling and performance evaluation of computer systems. *Mailing Add:* 600 N Ridgewood Dr West Lafayette IN 47906-2367

HOUSTON, ARTHUR HILLIER, ENVIRONMENTAL PHYSIOLOGY. *Current Pos:* chmn, Dept Biol Sci, Brock Univ, 71-75, prof, 71-96, actg dean, Div Math & Sci, 77-78 & 81-82, dean, 84-89, EMER PROF BIOL SCI, DIV MATH & SCI, BROCK UNIV, 96- *Personal Data:* b Quebec City, Que, May 7, 31; m 55, Ida M Graber; c 2. *Educ:* McMaster Univ, BSc, 54; Univ BC, MA, 56, PhD(comp physiol), 58. *Prof Exp:* Asst prof zool, Dalhousie Univ, 58-60; from asst prof to assoc prof, Univ Man, 60-64; assoc prof, Univ Wis-Milwaukee, 64-65; from assoc prof to prof biol & asst chmn dept, Marquette Univ, 65-71; adj assoc prof physiol, Med Sch, 68-71, mem biomed eng group, 68-71. *Concurrent Pos:* Mem panel lab instr, Comn Undergrad Educ Biol Sci, 68; appraisals comt, Ont Coun Grad Studies, 74-77 & 82-84; adj prof zool, Univ Toronto, 82-87 & Univ Guelph, 82-96; consult, Maclaren Planseunt Inc, 82-85; sr univ adminr course, Univ Western Ont, 84; mem, Res Develop Comt, NSERC, 84-87. *Mem:* Am Soc Zool; Soc Exp Biol & Med; Can Soc Zool; AAAS. *Res:* Respiratory and metabolic adaptations of fishes to natural and induced environmental variation; water electrolyte and acid-base regulation; erythropoiesis and leucopoiesis in fishes. *Mailing Add:* Brock Univ St Catharines ON L2S 3A1 Can. *Fax:* 905-688-1855

HOUSTON, BLAND BRYAN, JR, SOLID STATE PHYSICS. *Current Pos:* SOLID STATE PHYSICIST, WHITE OAK LAB, NAVAL SURFACE WEAPONS CTR, 55- *Personal Data:* b Vero Beach, Fla, Sept 19, 26; m 51; c 2. *Educ:* Vanderbilt Univ, BA, 49, MS, 50; Univ Ill, PhD(physics), 55. *Mem:* Am Phys Soc. *Res:* Lead and tin chalcogenide semiconductors; study of high and low-field transport properties related to the use of these materials in devices, infrared and thermoelectric in particular. *Mailing Add:* 10711 Blossom Lane Silver Spring MD 20903

HOUSTON, CHARLES SNEAD, INTERNAL MEDICINE. *Current Pos:* prof community med & chmn dept, 66-77, prof 77-80, EMER PROF EPIDEMIOL & ENVIRON HEALTH & MED, COL MED, UNIV VT, 80- *Personal Data:* b New York, NY, Aug 24, 13; m 41; c 3. *Educ:* Harvard Univ, AB, 35; Columbia Univ, MD, 39. *Prof Exp:* Intern med, Presby Hosp, New York, 39-41; internist & cardiologist, Exeter Clin, 47-56; med dir, Aspen Inst, 56-58, internist & cardiologist, Aspen Clin, 58-62; dir prog, Peace Corps, India, 62-65; spec asst to dir in chg vol dr progs, Washington, DC, 65-66. *Concurrent Pos:* Consult, Vet Admin Hosp, Manchester, NH, 49-56; res assoc, Cleveland Clin, Ohio, 59; consult, Vet Admin Hosp, Denver, Colo, 59-62; mem adv bd, Water Pollution Control Admin, 66-69. *Mem:* Am Col Physicians; Am Col Cardiol. *Res:* High altitude physiology; cardiovascular physiology; mechanical replacement of damaged heart; environmental health; pollution abatement. *Mailing Add:* 77 Ledge Rd Burlington VT 05401-4140

HOUSTON, CLARENCE STUART, RADIOLOGY. *Current Pos:* RETIRED. *Personal Data:* b Williston, NDak, Sept 26, 27; Can citizen; m 51, Mary I Belcher; c Stan, Margaret (Sigrithur), David V & Donald S. *Educ:* Univ Man, MD, 51; FRCPC, 64. *Hon Degrees:* DLitt, Univ Sask, 87. *Honors & Awards:* Roland Michener Conserv Award, Can Wildlife Fedn, 86; Douglas H Pimlott Award; Doris Huestis Speirs Award, Can Soc Ornithologists, 89; Can 125 Medal, 93; Officer Order Can, 93; John B Neilson Award, 93. *Prof Exp:* Lectr, Univ Sask, 64-65, from asst prof to assoc prof, 65-69, asst dir, Dept Diag Radiol, Univ Hosp, 68-82, prof diag radiol, 69-95, head, Dept Med Imaging, 82-87. *Concurrent Pos:* Ed, J Can Asn Radiologists, 76-81. *Mem:* Radiol Soc NAm; fel Am Ornith Union; Can Asn Radiol. *Res:* Pediatric radiology; congenital dislocation of hip; fetal dwarfism; raptor and colonial bird banding; history of science; history of medicine; history of natural history. *Mailing Add:* 863 University Dr Saskatoon SK S7N 0J8 Can. *E-Mail:* houstons@duke.usask.ca

HOUSTON, DAVID ROYCE, FOREST PATHOLOGY. *Current Pos:* PLANT PATHOLOGIST, CTR BIOL CONTROL, NORTHEASTERN FOREST EXP STA, US FOREST SERV, 61- *Personal Data:* b Worcester, Mass, Sept 18, 32; m 54; c 3. *Educ:* Univ Mass, BS, 54; Yale Univ, MF, 55; Univ Wis, PhD(plant path), 61. *Prof Exp:* From instr to asst prof plant path, Univ Wis, 58-61. *Concurrent Pos:* Exchange scientist, Forestry Comn, Alice Holt Res Lab, Eng, 75-76; lectr, Sch Forestry & Environ Studies, Yale Univ, 84- *Mem:* Soc Am Foresters; Am Phytopath Soc. *Res:* Forest tree diseases; ecological aspects of dieback and decline diseases, with special attention to oak decline, beech bark disease and sapstreak disease of sugar maple. *Mailing Add:* 404 Opening Hill Rd Madison CT 06443. *Fax:* 203-230-4305

HOUSTON, FORREST GISH, BIOCHEMISTRY. *Current Pos:* ASSOC PROF BIOCHEM, UNIV TEX MED BR, GALVESTON, 53- *Personal Data:* b Devol, Okla, July 18, 16; m 42; c 3. *Educ:* Tex Tech Col, BS, 38; Univ Tex, MA, 42; Ohio State Univ, PhD(biochem), 47. *Prof Exp:* Instr biochem, Univ Tex, 42-46; asst chemist, Ky Agr Exp Sta, 47-53. *Mem:* AAAS; Am Chem Soc; Soc Exp Biol & Med. *Res:* Iron metabolism; metalloproteins; analytical methods in biochemistry. *Mailing Add:* 6713 E Bayou Dr Hitchcock TX 77563-3531

HOUSTON, JACK E, surface physics, for more information see previous edition

HOUSTON, JAMES GREY, ORGANIC CHEMISTRY, PHOTOCHEMISTRY. *Current Pos:* head dept, 66-68, dean grad studies, 71-75, PROF CHEM, SUL ROSS STATE UNIV, 68- *Personal Data:* b Farris, Okla, June 13, 38. *Educ:* Okla State Univ, BS, 60; Ga Inst Technol, PhD(chem), 65. *Prof Exp:* Res chemist, Esso Res & Eng Corp, 65-66. *Concurrent Pos:* Consult, Dow Chem Co, 67-69; vpres, Agrihol Corp, 80- *Mem:* Am Chem Soc; Sigma Xi. *Res:* Natural products; creosote bush and cedar oil; feasibility of feeding creosote bush to cattle; fermentation of carbohydrates. *Mailing Add:* Dept Chem Sul Ross State Univ Box 6080 Alpine TX 79832. *Fax:* 915-837-8692; *E-Mail:* jhouston@sul-ross-1.sulross.edu

HOUSTON, JAMES ROBERT, ENGINEERING MECHANICS, PHYSICS. *Current Pos:* Res physicist weapons effects, US Army Corps Engrs, 70-72, res physicist hydraul, 72-79, res hydraul engr, 79-86, CHIEF, COASTAL ENG RES CTR, WATERWAYS EXP STA, US ARMY CORPS ENGRS, 86- *Personal Data:* b Berkeley, Calif, Mar 31, 47; m 76. *Educ:* Univ Calif, Berkeley, BA, 69; Univ Chicago, MS, 70; Univ Fla, MS, 74, PhD(eng mech), 78. *Concurrent Pos:* Mem steering comt & chmn subcomt Tsunamis, Interagency Comt Seismic Safety Construct, Off President, 78- *Mem:* Am Soc Civil Engrs. *Res:* Numerical modeling of water waves; the phenomena modeled include tsuanmis, waves generated by seismic events, harbor seiching and interaction of waves, structures and sediment. *Mailing Add:* 112 Woodstock Dr Vicksburg MS 39180

HOUSTON, JOHNNY LEE, MATHEMATICS. *Current Pos:* ASSOC PROF & CHMN DEPT MATH, ATLANTA UNIV, 75-; SR RES PROF, DEPT MATH & COMPUT SCI, ELIZABETH CITY STATE UNIV, 88- *Personal Data:* b Sandersville, Ga, Nov 19, 41; m 69. *Educ:* Morehouse Col, BA, 64; Atlanta Univ, MS, 66; Purdue Univ, PhD(math), 74. *Prof Exp:* Instr math, E E Smith High Sch, 64-65 & Stillman Col, 67-69; dir black cult ctr, Purdue Univ, 72-73; assoc prof, Savannah State Col, 74-75. *Concurrent Pos:* Merrill grant, Atlanta Univ-Univ Strasbourg, 66-67; Spencer Found res grant, Atlanta Univ, 76-77; lectr statist, Atlanta Univ, 76-; lectr math, Math Asn Am-BAM prog, 77-; reviewer math, Zentralblatt Math, 77- *Mem:* Nat Asn Math; Am Math Soc; Math Asn Am; Nat Coun Teachers Math; AAAS. *Res:* Algebra, particularly group theory, matrices and generalized inverses; categorical algebra; graph theory, combinatorics and applications. *Mailing Add:* Dept Math & Comput Sci Elizabeth City Univ Elizabeth City NC 27909

HOUSTON, L L, BIOTECHNOLOGY, DRUG DELIVERY. *Current Pos:* VPRES RES & DEVELOP, PRIZIN PHARMACEUT, INC, 93-; CONSULT, 97- *Personal Data:* b Wichita, Kans, June 3, 40; m 62; Teri DeHou; c Leslie A & Scott E. *Educ:* Kans State Univ, BS, 62; Univ Wash, PhD(biochem), 67. *Prof Exp:* Fel, Univ Calif, Berkeley, 67-69; from asst prof to prof biochem, Univ Kans, 69-84; sr scientist, Cetus Corp, 84-91; dir res targeted drug ther, Chiron Corp, 91-93. *Concurrent Pos:* Res career develop award, Nat Cancer Inst, NIH, 75-80; guest prof, Swiss Nat Sci Found, Univ Basel, 75-76; consult, Study Sect, Nat Cancer Inst, 74- *Mem:* Am Soc Biochem & Molecular Biol; Protein Soc; AAAS. *Res:* Creation and investigation of target and drug reagents for the treatment of cancer and other diseases that involve unwanted cellular proliferation. *Mailing Add:* 11035 Roselle St San Diego CA 92121

HOUSTON, MARSHALL LEE, EMBRYOLOGY, TERATOLOGY. *Current Pos:* asst prof anat, 70-73, ASSOC PROF ANAT & OBSTET & GYNEC, TEX HEALTH SCI CTR SAN ANTONIO, 73- *Personal Data:* b Poplar Bluff, Mo, Jan 27, 38; m 62; c 2. *Educ:* William Jewell Col, BA, 60; Kans State Univ, MS, 64, PhD(anat), 67. *Prof Exp:* Res assoc embryol, Southwest Found Res & Educ, Tex, 66-69; asst prof anat, Med Col Va, 69-70. *Mem:* Perinatal Res Soc; Am Asn Anatomists. *Res:* Comparative embryology and placentology of primates; anatomical and behavioral teratology of the brain; development of the hypothalamo-pituitary-adrenal axis. *Mailing Add:* Dept Anat Univ Tex Med Sch 7703 Floyd Curl Dr San Antonio TX 78284-6200

HOUSTON, PAUL LYON, CHEMICAL PHYSICS. *Current Pos:* from asst prof to assoc prof, 75-85, PROF CHEM, CORNELL UNIV, 85- *Personal Data:* b Hartford, Conn, Jan 27, 47. *Educ:* Yale Univ, BS, 69; Mass Inst Technol, PhD(chem), 73. *Prof Exp:* Fel chem, Univ Calif, Berkeley, 73-75. *Concurrent Pos:* Vis scientist, Max Planck Inst for Quantum Optus; Camille & Henry Dreyfus Teacher Scholar Award, 80; Guggenheim fel, 87. *Mem:* Am Phys Soc; AAAS; Am Chem Soc. *Res:* Reaction kinetics of molecules in selected vibrational and electronic states; laser-induced chemical reactions, photodissociation and vibrational energy transfer; gas-surface interactions. *Mailing Add:* Dept Chem Baker Lab Cornell Univ Ithaca NY 14853. *Fax:* 607-255-8549; *E-Mail:* plh2@cornell.edu

HOUSTON, ROBERT EDGAR, JR, PHYSICS. *Current Pos:* RETIRED. *Personal Data:* b Detroit, Mich, Feb 17, 24; m 46; c 3. *Educ:* Mich State Col, BS, 49, MS, 51; Pa State Univ, PhD, 57. *Prof Exp:* Instr physics, Mo Sch Mines, 51-53; from asst prof to assoc prof, Univ NH, 57-66, actg chmn dept, 65-66, chmn dept, 66-69, 72-73, prof, 66-, chmn dept, 76- *Mem:* Am Phys Soc; Am Asn Physics Teachers; Am Geophys Union. *Res:* Ionospheric physics; tracking of earth satellites; electron distributions through rocket borne instrumentation. *Mailing Add:* Dept Physics Univ NH Durham NH 03824

HOUSTON, ROBERT S, ECONOMIC GEOLOGY, PETROLOGY. *Current Pos:* from instr to assoc prof, 53-70, PROF GEOL & HEAD DEPT GEOL & GEOPHYSICS, UNIV WYO, 70- *Personal Data:* b Monroe, NC, May 11, 23; m 52; c 1. *Educ:* NC State Univ, BE, 48, MS, 50; Columbia Univ, PhD(econ geol), 54. *Prof Exp:* Geophysicist, Atlantic Refining Co, 48-49. *Concurrent Pos:* US Geol Surv grants, 55-57 & 67-82; Geol Surv Wyo grant, 57-66; NSF grant, 67-82; NASA grant, 71-75; Dept Energy grants, 75-81; Consult, Los Alamos, 76-80; provost & vpres acad affairs, Univ Wyo, 86-88. *Mem:* Fel Geol Soc Am; Am Asn Petrol Geol; Soc Econ Geol; Soc Econ Paleont & Mineral; Am Geophys Union; Sigma Xi. *Res:* Study of layered mafic complexes; fossil marine and non-marine placers of the Rocky Mountain region; Precambrian geology of Wyoming province of Rocky Mountain region; uranium geology, remote sensing and Antarctic geology. *Mailing Add:* 1410 Sublette St Laramie WY 82070

HOUSTON, ROY SEAMANDS, MALACOLOGY, MARINE ECOLOGY. *Current Pos:* asst prof,74-80, ASSOC PROF MARINE BIOL, LOYOLA MARYMOUNT UNIV, 80- *Personal Data:* b Lubbock, Tex, Dec 28, 42; m 61; c 4. *Educ:* Univ Ariz, BS, 68, PhD(zool), 74; Univ of the Pac, MS, 70. *Mem:* Malacol Soc London; Sigma Xi. *Res:* Functional morphology of reproductive and alimentary systems of marine molluscs. *Mailing Add:* Dept Biol Loyola Marymount Univ 7101 W 80th St Los Angeles CA 90045-2659

HOUSTON, SAMUEL ROBERT, APPLIED STATISTICS. *Current Pos:* from asst prof to assoc prof, 68-74, PROF MATH & APPL STATIST, UNIV NORTHERN COLO, 74-, CHMN DEPT, 75-78, 81-82, 89- *Personal Data:* b Los Angeles, Calif, May 20, 35; m 63; c 3. *Educ:* Univ Calif, Los Angeles, BA, 57; Calif State Univ, Los Angeles, MA, 61; Univ Ore, MA, 64; Colo State Col, PhD(appl statist), 67. *Prof Exp:* Instr math, Los Angeles City Sch Dist, 57-65; res fel, Bur Res, Colo State Col, 65-66; prog assoc, Grants Div, Charles F Kettering Found, 66-67, res specialist, Res & Develop Div, 67-68. *Concurrent Pos:* Scholar biostatist & psychol, Univ Calif, Los Angeles, 67-68; consult, CFK, Ltd, Colo, 68-73; pres, Multiple Linear Regression Spec Interest Group, Am Educ Res Asn; Nat Cancer Inst fel biomet, Sch Med, Yale Univ, 73-74; vis prof, Univ Wyo, 82-83; lectr & consult, Zagazig Univ, Egypt, 83; exec ed, J Exp Educ, 75-78; reviewer, Computing Reviews, 82-86; reviewer, Mult Linear Regression Viewpoints, 84-; vis prof, Univ Ga, 85-86. *Mem:* Am Educ Res Asn; Am Statist Asn; Sigma Xi. *Res:* Judgment analysis; policy capturing models; multidimensional policy models; evaluation models; management styles and stress; personality profile systems. *Mailing Add:* 3711 W 230th Apt 136 Torrance CA 90505

HOUSTON, VERN LYNN, REHABILITATION ENGINEERING. *Current Pos:* INSTR REHAB MED, MED CTR, NY UNIV, 86- *Personal Data:* b Denver Colo, July 4, 47; m 70; c 3. *Educ:* Univ Colo, BSAE, 69; Univ Calif, MSE, 72; Columbia Univ, MPh, 80, PhD(elec eng), 87. *Prof Exp:* Staff engr, Vet Admin Res Ctr, 74-77; mem tech staff, AT&T Bell Labs, 81-86. *Mem:* NY Acad Med; Inst Elec & Electronics Engrs; Am Soc Mech Engrs; Soc Indust & Appl Math; Biomed Eng Soc; Int Soc Prosthetics & orthotics. *Res:* Research and development in prosthetics and orthotics computer-aided manufacturing; soft tissue viscoelastic finite element modeling and analysis; biomedical signal modeling and procssing with application in rehabilitation engineering. *Mailing Add:* 14 Erwin Park Montclair NJ 07042-3033

HOUSTON, WILLIAM BERNARD, JR, GEOMETRY. *Current Pos:* from asst prof to assoc prof, 62-70, prof, 70-92, EMER PROF MATH, ANTIOCH COL, 92- *Personal Data:* b Macon, Ga, July 3, 29; m 55, Hazel Bachelor Tulecke; c Alice & Judy. *Educ:* Ga Inst Technol, BEE, 52; Mass Inst Technol, PhD(math), 57. *Prof Exp:* Asst prof math, Morehouse Col, 57-59 & Carleton Col, 59-62. *Concurrent Pos:* Vis assoc prof, Univ Col Cape Coast, Ghana, 66-67. *Res:* Connexions; functional analysis; calculus of variations; differential geometry. *Mailing Add:* Dept Math Antioch Univ Yellow Springs OH 45387

HOUSTON, WILLIE WALTER, JR, CELL BIOLOGY, HISTOLOGY. *Current Pos:* PROF BIOL & CHMN, CENT STATE UNIV, 80- *Personal Data:* b Cedartown, Ga, Sept 14, 51. *Educ:* Morehouse Col, BS, 74; Atlanta Univ, MS, 76, PhD(biol), 81. *Prof Exp:* Lectr biol, Spelman Col, 79; instr, Ky State Univ, 79-80. *Concurrent Pos:* Instr cell biol, Wright State Univ, 81.

Mem: Nat Inst Sci; AAAS. *Res:* Changes in inferred proteins synthetic activity and its association with hyaluronic acid changes in chick brains development from 4 day-old embryos to 8 day-old embryos. *Mailing Add:* Dept Biol Cent State Univ Wilberforce OH 45384-9999

HOUTMAN, THOMAS, JR, organic chemistry, for more information see previous edition

HOUTS, GARNETTE EDWIN, VIROLOGY. *Current Pos:* FOUNDER & PRES, MOLECULAR GENETIC RESOURCES, INC, 83- *Personal Data:* b Chattanooga, Tenn, July 26, 36; m 65; c 3. *Educ:* Univ Tenn, Knoxville, BA, 58, MS, 64; Univ Tenn, Memphis, PhD(virol), 71. *Prof Exp:* Technician bact, Tenn State Health Dept, 58-59; technician biochem, Oak Ridge Nat Lab, 59-60, 62-64 & 65; res assoc, Med Ctr, Univ Ky, 65-68; res assoc oncornaviruses, St Joseph's Hosp, 71-73; assoc virologist oncornaviruses, Life Sci Res Lab, 73-83. *Res:* Physical, chemical and functional characterizations of reverse transcriptase enzyme from avian myeloblastosis virus; isolation of other proteins from AMV for use in screening drugs for AIDS treatment. *Mailing Add:* 6201 Johns Rd Suite 8 Tampa FL 33634

HOUTS, LARRY LEE, DEVELOPMENTAL BIOLOGY, ANATOMY. *Current Pos:* FAMILY PRACT, 89- *Personal Data:* b Three Rivers, Mich, Oct 1, 42; m 73, Karen A Priddle; c 2. *Educ:* Rockford Col, AB, 64; Fla State Univ, MS, 66; State Univ NY, Albany, PhD(biol), 77, WVa Sch Osteop Med, DO, 86. *Prof Exp:* Instr biol, Winthrop Col, 66-69; res biologist, Vet Admin Hosp, 74-76; asst prof biol, Bethany Col, 76-81 & Wheeling Col, 81-82; intern, Garden City Hosp, 86-87. *Concurrent Pos:* Consult allied health, East Cent Col Consortium, 77-81. *Mem:* Soc Develop Biol; Sigma Xi; Tissue Cult Asn; AAAS. *Res:* Aging of inductive tissue and control of anteroposterior polarity in the limb bud of the chick embryo; effects of various wavelengths of light on the estrous cycle of Mus musculus; zoology. *Mailing Add:* 131 Wake Robin Trail Lewisburg WV 24901

HOUTS, PETER STEVENS, SOCIAL PSYCHOLOGY, IMPACT OF ILLNESS ON PATIENTS & FAMILIES. *Current Pos:* from asst prof to assoc prof, 67-71, PROF SOC PSYCHOL, PA STATE UNIV, 95- *Personal Data:* b Great Neck, NY, March 17, 33; m 60, Mary Davidoff; c Thomas & David. *Educ:* Antioch Col, BA, 55; Univ Mich, PhD(soc psychol), 63. *Prof Exp:* Asst prof psychol, Goucher Col, 63-65; postdoctoral fel social psychol, psychiat dept, Stanford Med Sch, 65-67. *Mem:* Am Psychol Asn; Am Asn Univ Prof; Am Asn Soc Ctr Edu. *Res:* Psychological, social, and economic impact of cancer on patients and their families; need for support services among cancer patients; use of cancer screening among persons at risk for cancer; long term psychological, social and economic impacts of the Three Mile Island crisis. *Mailing Add:* Dept Behav Sci Col Med Pa State Univ PO Box 850 Hershey PA 17033. *E-Mail:* psh2@psu.edu

HOUTS, RONALD C(ARL), DIGITAL SIGNAL PROCESSING, STATISTICAL COMMUNICATIONS. *Current Pos:* DIR, UF/UWF JOINT PROG ELEC ENG, UNIV FLA, 91-92 & 93- *Personal Data:* b Chicago, Ill, Sept 22, 37; m 60; c 2. *Educ:* Univ Fla, BSE, 59, MSE, 60, PhD(elec eng), 63. *Prof Exp:* From asst prof to prof elec eng, Univ Ala, 66-91. *Concurrent Pos:* Researcher, Astrionics Labs, Telemetry Systs Br, Marshall Space Flight Ctr, Ala, 66-74; vis res prof, US Army Missile Res & Develop Command, 74-75, vis prof, US Mil Acad, West Point, 83-84; recipient grant, Electronics Div, US Army Res Off, 76-78; consult, US Army Missile Command, 79-82 & 87, Universal Data Systs, 83-86. *Mem:* Sr mem Inst Elec & Electronics Engrs; Sigma Xi. *Res:* Statistical communications; data transmission; digital filtering; signal and system theory, especially digital signal processing techniques as applied to communications and radar; author of two textbooks and over 60 publications. *Mailing Add:* UT/UWF Dept Elec Eng 11000 University Pkwy Pensacola FL 32514

HOUZE, RICHARD NEAL, CHEMICAL ENGINEERING. *Current Pos:* from asst prof to assoc prof, 69-82, PROF CHEM ENG, PURDUE UNIV, 82- *Personal Data:* b Atlanta, Ga, Oct 2, 38; m 60; c 2. *Educ:* Ga Inst Technol, BChE, 60; Univ Houston, MS, 66, PhD(chem eng), 68. *Prof Exp:* Res engr, Esso Res & Eng Co, 60-63; NSF fel, Delft Technol Univ, 68-69. *Mem:* Am Inst Chem Engrs. *Res:* Transport processes at gas-liquid interfaces; turbulent flow of fluids; transport processes in physiological systems and respiratory processes. *Mailing Add:* 3342 Division Rd West Lafayette IN 47906

HOVANEC, B(ERNARD) MICHAEL, INDUCTIVITY COUPLED PLASMA MASS SPECTROMETRY, PARTICLE BEAM & LIQUID CHROMATOGRAPH MASS SPECTROMETRY. *Current Pos:* SR STAFF CHEMIST, W COAST ANALYTICAL SERV, 86- *Personal Data:* b Riverside, Calif, May 26, 52; m 79; c 3. *Educ:* Univ Calif, Riverside, BA, 75. *Prof Exp:* Chemist, Indust Polymers, 76-77, Lever Bros, 77-78; sr chemist, W Coast Tech, 78-80; sr analytical chemist, Rockwell Int, 80-86. *Mem:* Am Chem Soc; Am Soc Mass Spectrometry; Am Welding Soc. *Res:* Application of sample introduction methodologies to permit the determination of trace level metals in various pure solutions or compounds; development of appropriate automated sampling systems for hazardous chemicals; application of same for trace organics via particle beam interfaces into organic mass specs with on-line HPLC separation. *Mailing Add:* W Coast Analytical Serv 9840 Alburtis Ave Santa Fe Springs CA 90670-5086

HOVANESIAN, JOSEPH DER, ENGINEERING MECHANICS, MECHANICAL ENGINEERING. *Current Pos:* PROF ENG & CHMN, MECH ENG DEPT, OAKLAND UNIV, 70- *Personal Data:* b Detroit, Mich, Aug 14, 30; m 60; c 2. *Educ:* Mich State Univ, BS, 53, MA, 54, PhD, 58. *Honors & Awards:* Fel, Soc Exp Mech Analysts; Shield of Strathelyde. *Prof Exp:* Res asst eng, Mich State Univ, 54-58; asst prof, Pa State Univ, 58-60; assoc prof eng mech, Wayne State Univ, 60-70. *Mem:* Optical Soc Am; fel Soc Exp Mech Anal; Am Soc Mech Engrs. *Res:* Coherent optics and holography; photelasticity; theory of elasticity; experimental stress analysis; noise & vibration control; non-destructive testing. *Mailing Add:* 34550 Freedom Rd Farmington MI 48335

HOVANESSIAN, SHAHEN ALEXANDER, ELECTRONICS ENGINEERING, APPLIED MATHEMATICS. *Current Pos:* LECTR ENG, UNIV CALIF, LOS ANGELES, 61-; SR SCIENTIST, HUGHES AIRCRAFT CO, 63-; CONSULT ENGR, AEROSPACE CORP, 63- *Personal Data:* b Teheran, Iran, Sept 6, 31; nat US; m 60; c 2. *Educ:* Univ Calif, Los Angeles, BS, 54, MS, 55, PhD(appl math, eng), 58. *Prof Exp:* Instr eng, Univ Calif, Los Angeles, 54-58; res engr, Stand Oil Co Calif, 58-61. *Mem:* Am Soc Mech Engrs; Inst Elec & Electronics Engrs. *Res:* Radar detection and missile trajectory problems; signal processing and information theory studies; formulation of mathematical models and subsequent digital computer simulation; numerical solution of fluid flow and heat transfer problems; mathematical programming methods in economic studies; author of over 35 publications on radars and computers. *Mailing Add:* Aerospace Corp PO Box 92957 Los Angeles CA 90009

HOVDE, CHRISTIAN ARNESON, ANATOMY, NEURO-ANATOMY. *Current Pos:* RETIRED. *Personal Data:* b Decorah, Iowa, Dec 25, 22; m 48, Rachel Hinman. *Educ:* St John's Col, AB, 48; Bucknell Univ, MA, 50; Columbia Univ, PhD(anat), 53. *Hon Degrees:* DD, Seabury-Western Theol Sem, 68. *Prof Exp:* Jr instr, Johns Hopkins Univ, 48-49; lab asst, Bucknell Univ, 49-50; asst neurol, Columbia Univ, 50-52, asst anat, 51-52, from instr to asst prof, 52-56; from asst prof to assoc prof, Seton Hall Col Med & Dent, 56-63; dir, Bishop Anderson Found, 63-88; prof & chmn, Dept Relig & Health, Col Sci, Rush Univ, 76-88, emer prof, 88- *Mem:* Assoc Asn Res Nerv & Ment Dis; Am Asn Anatomists; NY Acad Sci; Am Neurol Asn. *Res:* Physiology and disorders of the nervous system. *Mailing Add:* 2245 Club Hause Dr Lillian AL 36549

HOVE, JOHN EDWARD, physics, materials science, for more information see previous edition

HOVEL, HAROLD JOHN, SOLID STATE PHYSICS, MATERIALS SCIENCE. *Current Pos:* MEM RES STAFF, SOLID STATE DEVICE RES, IBM CORP, 68- *Personal Data:* b Middletown, Ohio, July 6, 42; m 65; c 2. *Educ:* Carnegie-Mellon Univ, BS, 64, MS, 65, PhD(elec eng), 68. *Mem:* Electrochem Soc; Am Phys Soc; Am Inst Physics; Inst Elec & Electronics Engrs. *Res:* Liquid phase epitaxy; solid state lasers; heterojunctions and heterojunction devices; vapor epitaxy; bistable switching and memory device; optical properties of thin films; investigations of trapping effects in solids. *Mailing Add:* Diane Ct Katonah NY 10536

HOVELAND, CARL SOREN, AGRONOMY. *Current Pos:* prof, 81-85, TERRELL DISTINGUISHED PROF AGRON, UNIV GA, 86- *Personal Data:* b Sand Creek, Wis, Oct 25, 27; m 51, 88, Pat King. *Educ:* Univ Wis, BS, 50, MS, 52; Univ Fla, PhD(agron), 59. *Honors & Awards:* Goddard lectr, Univ Tenn, 81; King Found lectr, Univ Ark, 83; Silver Medallion Award, Am Forage & Grassland Coun, 86; Thornton lectr, Texas Tech Univ, 92. *Prof Exp:* Asst, Univ Wis, 50-52; asst agronomist, Exp Sta, Agr & Mech Col, Tex, 52-55; asst agron, Exp Sta, Univ Fla, 55-58, asst bot, 58-59; assoc agronomist, Auburn Univ, 59-68, prof agron, 68-81. *Concurrent Pos:* Staff scientist, Grassland Div, Dept Sci & Indust Res, NZ, 70 & 79; lectr, Univ Zagreb, Yugoslavia, 78 & Univ Rio Grande do Sul, Brazil, 79; consult, SAfrica Dept Agr, 79 & Partners Am, Ecuador, 83; vis prof, Univ Guelph, Ontario, Can, 84; pres, Am Forage & Grassland Coun, 83; lectr, Georgian Acad Sci, Rep Ga, 92, 93 & 94. *Mem:* Fel Am Soc Agron; fel Crop Sci Soc Am; fel AAAS. *Res:* Pasture management and utilization; crop ecology; forage plant physiology; pasture ecology; grazing management. *Mailing Add:* Crop & Soil Sci Dept Univ Ga Athens GA 30602

HOVERMALE, JOHN BRUCE, meteorology; deceased, see previous edition for last biography

HOVERSLAND, ARTHUR STANLEY, REPRODUCTIVE PHYSIOLOGY, COMPARATIVE PHYSIOLOGY. *Current Pos:* EXEC SECY, HUMAN EMBRYOLOGY & DEVELOP STUDY SECT, NIH, 78- *Personal Data:* b Hallock, Minn, Apr 20, 22; m 46; c 4. *Educ:* Mont State Univ, BS, 51, MS, 58; Ore State Univ, PhD, 70. *Prof Exp:* From instr to assoc prof animal sci, Mont State Univ, 51-67; res assoc, Med Sch, Univ Ore, 68-70; assoc prof, Calif State Univ, Fresno, 71-73, prof animal sci & chmn dept, 73-78. *Concurrent Pos:* Vis scientist, Univ of Calif, Davis, 77. *Mem:* Am Soc Animal Sci; Soc Study Fertil; Soc Study Reproduction; Am Physiol Soc; NY Acad Sci. *Res:* Comparative animal reproductive physiology, hemodynamic adjustments during pregnancy, fetal-maternal relationships; growth and maturation, respiratory and biochemical properties of mammalian blood; perinatal physiology and embryology; animal science. *Mailing Add:* Harmony Rd Middleton MD 21769

HOVERSLAND, ROGER CARL, EMBRYO IMPLANTATION, SEX DEPENDENT TYPE II DIABETES. *Current Pos:* ASSOC PROF, DEPT ANAT, SCH MED, IND UNIV, 88- *Personal Data:* b Bozeman, Mont, June 10, 51; m 71; c 2. *Educ:* Calif State Univ, Fresno, BA, 74; Univ Ore, PhD(anat), 80. *Prof Exp:* NIH postdoctoral res, Dept Obstet & Gynec, Univ Kans, 80-82; asst prof, Dept Anat, Chicago Med Sch, 82-88. *Concurrent Pos:* Postdoctoral fel, individual nat res award, Nat Inst Child Health & Human Develop, 80-82; prin investr, NIH new investr award, Nat Inst Child Health & Human Develop, 82-87, Am Diabetes Found Feasibility grant, 86-88 & NIH Res Grant, 91- *Mem:* Sigma Xi; Soc Study Reproduction; Am Asn Anatomists. *Res:* Endocrine and maternal/fetal interactions of the immune regulatory responses in mice during embryo implanatation and pregnancy; hormone influences in genetic obesity and subsequent sex dependent diabetes in hypertensive rats. *Mailing Add:* Dept Anat Sch Med Ind Univ 2101 Colliseum Blvd E Ft Wayne IN 46805. *Fax:* 219-481-6408; *E-Mail:* hoversla@smtplink.iffw.indiana.edu

HOVERSON, SIGMUND JOHN, PHYSICS. *Current Pos:* Technician, 72-75, SCIENTIST LASER RES & COMPUT MODELING, MATH SCI, NORTHWEST INC, 75-; COMPUTER SYST ANALYSIS, KING COUNTY. *Personal Data:* b Seattle, Wash, Oct 18, 41; m 65; c 3. *Educ:* Calif Inst Technol, BS, 63; Univ Wash, MS, 67; Tex A&M Univ, PhD(physics), 74. *Mem:* Am Phys Soc. *Res:* Alternate energy source research especially those involving high power laser applications; computer modeling of physical systems. *Mailing Add:* 9642 NE 121st Ln Kirkland WA 98034

HOVEY, HARRY HENRY, JR, ENVIRONMENTAL ENGINEERING, AIR POLLUTION. *Current Pos:* PRIN CONSULT ENG, TRC ENVIRON CONSULTS INC, 88- *Personal Data:* b Pittsfield, Mass, Aug 28, 30; m 57; c 2. *Educ:* Rensselaer Polytech Inst, BCE, 52; Univ Minn, MPH, 60. *Honors & Awards:* S Smith Griswald Award, Air Pollution Control Asn, 82. *Prof Exp:* Hydraul engr, Fish & Wildlife Br, US Dept Interior, 56-57; sanit engr, Robert Wheeler Consult, 57-58; sr sanit engr, NY State Dept Environ Conserv, 58-65, assoc engr, 65-67, assoc dir, 67-76, dir, Div Air Resources, 76-88. *Concurrent Pos:* Mem, Clean Air Sci Adv Comt, US Environ Protection Agency, 78-82; mem, Int Air Qual Adv Bd & Int Joint Comt, 80-88. *Mem:* Air Pollution Control Asn (vpres, 77-79); Am Acad Environ Engrs; Nat Soc Prof Engrs. *Res:* Development of atmospheric pollution control regulations and ambient air quality standards; development of air pollution survey techniques. *Mailing Add:* 15 Sylvan Lane Troy NY 12180

HOVIN, ARNE WILLIAM, GENETICS, PLANT BREEDING. *Current Pos:* assoc dir, Mont Agr Exp Sta, 81-87, EMER PROF, MONT STATE UNIV, BOZEMAN, 87- *Personal Data:* b Norway, Dec 30, 22; nat US; m 53, Carol H Frink; c Randi (Rigg) & Leif E. *Educ:* Norwegian Col Agr, BS, 49; Univ Calif, Los Angeles, PhD(plant genetics), 57. *Honors & Awards:* Merit Award, Am Forage & Grassland Coun. *Prof Exp:* Asst, Norwegian Col Agr, 49-52 & Univ Calif, Los Angeles, 53-57; res geneticist, Regional Pasture Res Lab, Agr Res Serv, USDA, 58-65, res leader grass & turf invests, 65-69; prof agron & plant genetics, Univ Minn, St Paul, 69-81. *Mem:* Am Soc Agron; Crop Sci Soc Am. *Res:* Grass breeding; quantitative and qualitative genetics. *Mailing Add:* 7734 Springhill Comm Rd Belgrade MT 58714-8421

HOVINGH, JACK, NUCLEAR ENGINEERING. *Current Pos:* NUCLEAR ENGR, UNIV CALIF, LAWRENCE LIVERMORE NAT LAB, 58- *Personal Data:* b Grand Rapids, Mich, May 5, 35; c Mary, Mark (deceased) & James (deceased). *Educ:* Univ Mich, Ann Arbor, BSE(mech eng) & BSE(math), 58; Univ Calif, Berkeley, MS, 73. *Mem:* Am Nuclear Soc. *Res:* Design and analysis of both magnetically and inertially confined fusion reactors for energy applications. *Mailing Add:* 4250 Muirwood Dr Pleasanton CA 94588-4376

HOVIS, LOUIS SAMUEL, CHEMISTRY, PHYSICS. *Current Pos:* asst prof chem & math, 68-71, assoc prof chem & physics & chmn dept physics, 71-72, PROF NATURAL SCI & PHYSICS, CAMPBELL COL, NC, 72- *Personal Data:* b Gastonia, NC, May 2, 26; m 49; c 2. *Educ:* NC State Col, BChE, 48, MS, 49; Univ Tenn, PhD(chem eng), 55. *Prof Exp:* Chem engr, Polychems Dept, E I du Pont de Nemours & Co, 49-52, res engr, Indust & Biochems Dept, 55-62; sr res engr, Chemstrand Res Ctr Inc, Monsanto Co, 62-68. *Mem:* AAAS; Am Inst Chem Engr; Am Chem Soc; Am Soc Qual Control; Am Asn Physics Teachers. *Res:* Heat and mass transfer in heterogeneous systems; statistics and computer applications in education; experimental design; reaction kinetics; experimental education. *Mailing Add:* 233 Marilyn Circle Cary NC 27513

HOVMAND, SVEND, PARTICLE TECHNOLOGY & FLUIDIZATION OF PARTICLES, PORCELAIN TILE. *Current Pos:* PRES, CROSSVILLE CERAMICS, TENN, 89- *Personal Data:* b Nakskov, Denmark, Jan 3, 39; m 66, Beverly Cocolella; c Peter & Lars. *Educ:* Denmark Tech Univ, MSci, 61; Cambridge Univ, Eng, PhD(chem eng), 68. *Prof Exp:* Postdoctoral fluidization, Cambridge Univ, Eng, 68-69; res engr, Haldor Topsoe, Denmark, 69-70; dir res, Niro Atomizer, Denmark, 71-77, vpres, Columbia, Md, 77-89. *Concurrent Pos:* Course dir, Indust Drying Technol, Ctr Prof Develop, NJ, 80-90; pres, Bowen Eng, NJ, 81-89 & Niro Ceramic, Inc, Md, 82-89. *Mem:* Am Ceramic Soc. *Res:* Industrial development of equipment for spray drying; fluid bed technology including chemical reactions; drying processes and particle agglomeration. *Mailing Add:* 3711 Spring Meadow Dr Ellicott City MD 21042. *Fax:* 615-456-3993

HOVNANIAN, H(RAIR) PHILIP, BIOMEDICAL ENGINEERING, PHYSICS. *Current Pos:* CONSULT & CORP DIR MED DEVICE RES & DEVELOP, SONOKINETICS CO & VITAL SIGNS, BEI MED SYST, INC, 89- *Personal Data:* b Aleppo, Syria, Dec 17, 20; US citizen; m 48, Siran Norian; c John P, Joan A & Rosemary J. *Educ:* Am Univ Beirut, AB, 42; Mass State Col Boston, MA, 50; State Univ NY, PE, 64; Univ Beverly Hills, PhD, 79; Chartered Physicist, UK, 84. *Prof Exp:* Instr physics, Am Univ Beirut, 42-47; teaching fel, Brown Univ, 47-49; sr engr, Western Elec Co, 51-52; asst chief engr electro-mech, Calidyne Co, 52-53; asst dir res, Boston Electronics Div, Norden-Ketay Corp, 53-56; dir physics, Neutronics Res Co, 56-58; dir med sci dept, Res & Advan Develop Div, Avco Corp, 58-66; consult & proj mgr biosci progs, NASA Hq, 66-67; dir biomed eng & biophys, Kollsman Instrument Corp, 67-69; vpres & corp dir biomed eng, Cavitron Corp, Cooper Labs, Inc, 69-85. *Concurrent Pos:* Prin investr, Nat Health Inst res grants, 59-63, co-prin investr, 63-66; vis lectr, Northeastern Univ, 62-68; res assoc surg res, Lahey Clin Found, 62-; exec secy biosci working group, NASA Hq, 66-67; guest lectr, Mass Inst Technol-Harvard Med Sch Study Group Biomed Eng, 68; mem Nat Acad Eng workshop on interaction between indust & biomed eng, 70; mem obstet & gynec devices panel, Food & Drug Admin; consult, BEI Medical Syst, 89-; corp dir, Vital Signs Inc. *Mem:* AAAS; Optical Soc Am; Inst Elec & Electronics Engrs; Sigma Xi; NY Acad Sci; fel Inst Physics London; fel Am Acad Dent Electrosurg; fel Am Soc Laser Med & Surg; Biomed Eng Soc; Int Microscopy Asn. *Res:* Fiber optic endoscopy; ultraviolet and fluorescence microscopy and microspectrophotometry; low frequency ultrasound surgery of tissue; diagnostic and therapeutic respiratory instrumentation; exobiology measurements; carbon dioxide, YAG and argon lasers in medicine and surgery; medical-dental instrumentation; intra-oral TV & fluoroscopy inventor; fifty-five journal publications and USA patents mainly on medical/surgical devices and instrumentation. *Mailing Add:* 3902 Manhattan Col Pkwy Suite 1B Bronx NY 10471. *Fax:* 718-601-3825

HOVORKA, JOHN, PHYSICS, SYSTEMS DESIGN & SYSTEMS SCIENCE. *Current Pos:* chmn, Div Sci & Math, 69-81, prof, 69-94, EMER PROF PHYSICS, CURRY COL, 95- *Personal Data:* b New York, NY, Oct 17, 21; m 50; c 2. *Educ:* Queens Col, NY, BS, 42; Univ Ill, MS, 43; Mass Inst Technol, ScD, 61. *Prof Exp:* Physicist, Mass Inst Technol, 44-46, Instrumentation Lab, 50-63 & Gulf Res & Develop Co, 46-48; instr physics, Univ Buffalo, 48-50; prof & head dept, Hobart & William Smith Cols, 63-67; lectr aeronaut & astronaut, Mass Inst Technol, 67-88. *Concurrent Pos:* Consult, Inst Defense Anal, 62, Dept Army, 62, lunar astronauts, Manned Spaceflight Ctr, NASA, 62-63, Off Secy Defense, 63 & Exp Astron Lab, Mass Inst Technol, 64-72; sr res assoc aeronaut & astronaut, Mass Inst Technol, 69-72; fac fel, US Dept Transp, 79-81. *Mem:* NY Acad Sci; Am Phys Soc; Sigma Xi. *Res:* Fire control; servomechanisms; infrared spectroscopy; inertial navigation; general relativity, experimental. *Mailing Add:* 38 Lantern Lane Cohasset MA 02025

HOWALD, JEREMIAH MARK, ORGANIC CHEMISTRY. *Current Pos:* tech dir, Glaskyd Dept, 65-73, CONSULT, PERRYSBURG LABS, AM CYANAMID CO, 73- *Personal Data:* b Pittsburgh, Pa, Nov 19, 27; m 53; c 5. *Educ:* Oberlin Col, AB, 49; Cornell Univ, PhD(chem), 53. *Prof Exp:* Asst org chem, Cornell Univ, 49-52; chemist, Shell Chem Corp, 52-57; tech rep, Glaskyd, Inc, 57-65. *Mem:* Am Chem Soc. *Res:* Organic fluorine compounds; petrochemicals; plastics. *Mailing Add:* 13906 Roachton Rd Perrysburg OH 43551-1162

HOWALD, REED ANDERSON, THERMODYNAMICS & MATERIAL PROPERTIES. *Current Pos:* from asst prof to prof, 63-93, ADJ PROF CHEM, MONT STATE UNIV, 93- *Personal Data:* b Pittsburgh, Pa, Nov 23, 30; m 61, Elaine Sheperd; c 3. *Educ:* Oberlin Col, BA, 52; Univ Wis, PhD(phys chem), 55. *Prof Exp:* Instr chem, Univ Calif, Los Angeles, 55-56 & Harvard Univ, 56-59; asst prof, Oberlin Col, 59-60 & St John's Univ, NY, 60-63. *Mem:* Am Chem Soc. *Res:* Chemical kinetics; radiochemistry; geochemistry; phase equilibria; activity coefficient. *Mailing Add:* Dept Chem Mont State Univ Bozeman MT 59717. *Fax:* 406-994-5407; *E-Mail:* uchrh@earth.oscs.montana.edu

HOWARD, AUGHTUM SMITH, mathematics; deceased, see previous edition for last biography

HOWARD, BARBARA V, BIOCHEMISTRY, CELL CULTURE. *Current Pos:* PRES MEDLANTIC RES FOUND, 91- *Personal Data:* b East Orange, NJ, June 26, 41; m 62; c 3. *Educ:* Bryn Mawr Col, BA, 63; Univ Pa, PhD(microbiol), 68. *Prof Exp:* Instr microbiol, Sch Med, Univ NC, Chapel Hill, 68-69; asst prof biochem, Sch Med, George Washington Univ, 69-72 & Sch Dent Med, Univ Pa, 72-75; asst prof biochem & physiol, Med Col Pa, 75-76; res biochemist, NIH, 76-80, assoc chief, Phoenix Clin Res Sect, Nat Inst Arthritis, Diabetes & Digestive & Kidney Dis, 80-88. *Mem:* Am Soc Biol Chemists; AAAS; Tissue Cult Asn; fel Am Heart Asn. *Res:* Lipoproteins in plasma and in cultured cells. *Mailing Add:* Medlantic Res Inst Hyman 242 108 Irving St NW Washington DC 20010-2933

HOWARD, BERNARD EUFINGER, APPLIED MATHEMATICS, COMPUTER SCIENCE. *Current Pos:* dir, Sci Comput Ctr, Univ Miami, 61-64, prof, 60-91, EMER PROF MATH & COMPUT SCI, 91-; ASSOC FAC, GRAD SCH INT STUDIES, UNIV MIAMI, 96- *Personal Data:* b Ludlow, Vt, Sept 22, 20; m 42. *Educ:* Mass Inst Technol, SB, 44; Univ Ill, MS, 47, PhD(math), 51. *Prof Exp:* Mem staff, Radiation Lab, Mass Inst Technol, 42-45; asst math, Univ Ill, 45-49; sr mathematician, Inst Air Weapons Res, Univ Chicago, 51, asst to dir, 52-56, assoc dir, Inst Syst Res, 56-60, assoc dir, Appl Sci Labs, 58-60. *Concurrent Pos:* Exec secy, Air Force Adv Bd Simulation, 51-54; consult, Syst Res Labs, Inc, Dayton, Ohio, 63-67, actg dir,

Math Sci Div, 65; consult, Electronics Assocs, Inc, Princeton, NJ, 64, Variety Children's Res Found, Miami, 64-66, Fla Power & Light Co, 68 & Shaw & Assocs, 64-75; vis fel, Dartmouth Col, 76; Am Soc Eng Educ & Off Naval Res fel, Naval Underwater Systs Ctr, New London, Conn, 80 & 81; co-investr, Positron Emission Tomography Ctr & Dept Neurol, Mt Sinai Med Ctr, 81-84; chmn, bd dirs, Sociobernetics Inc, 93- *Mem:* Am Math Soc; Soc Indust & Appl Math; Asn Comput Mach; Am Phys Soc; Inst Elec & Electronics Engrs; Sigma Xi. *Res:* System analysis; simulation; plasma dynamics; electromagnetic wave propagation; guided missiles; weapon system evaluation; numerical analysis and computation; optimum curvature and torsion principles in highway routing; sociocybernetics; underwater sound propagation; position-emission tomography; artificial intelligence. *Mailing Add:* Dept Math & Comput Sci Univ Miami PO Box 249085 Coral Gables FL 33124-9085

HOWARD, BRUCE DAVID, BIOCHEMISTRY, MOLECULAR BIOLOGY. *Current Pos:* asst prof biol chem, 66-75, assoc prof, 75-81, PROF BIOL CHEM, MED SCH, UNIV CALIF, LOS ANGELES, 81- *Personal Data:* b Minneapolis, Minn, Oct 19, 37; m 64; c 1. *Educ:* Univ Minn, BA, 59, MD, 62. *Prof Exp:* Res assoc biol, Mass Inst Technol, 62; Nat Cancer Inst fel, Purdue Univ, 62-64; fel biochem, Albert Einstein Col Med, 64-66. *Mem:* AAAS; Int Soc Neurochem; Soc Neurosci; Am Soc Biol Chemists. *Res:* Neurobiology; neurochemistry. *Mailing Add:* Dept Biol Chem Univ Calif Med Sch Los Angeles CA 90024. *Fax:* 310-206-5272

HOWARD, CARLETON JAMES, PHYSICAL CHEMISTRY, ATMOSPHERIC CHEMISTRY. *Current Pos:* RES CHEMIST, AERONOMY LAB, NAT OCEANIC & ATMOSPHERIC ADMIN, 71- *Personal Data:* b Anacortes, Wash, July 20, 44; m 82, Veronica M Bierbaum; c Benjamin J & Daniel J. *Educ:* Linfield Col, BA, 66; Univ Pittsburgh, PhD(chem), 71. *Concurrent Pos:* NSF grad traineeship, Univ Pittsburgh, 66. *Mem:* Am Chem Soc; Am Phys Soc; Combustion Inst; Am Geophys Union. *Res:* Gas kinetics of atoms, radicals, and ions with small molecules. *Mailing Add:* Aeronomy Lab Nat Oceanic & Atmospheric Admin R/E/AL2 325 Broadway Boulder CO 80303

HOWARD, CHARLES, ANALYTICAL CHEMISTRY, INORGANIC CHEMISTRY. *Current Pos:* RETIRED. *Personal Data:* b Evanston, Ill, Apr 2, 19; m 45; c 3. *Educ:* Univ Wis, BS, 40, PhD(chem), 43. *Prof Exp:* Chemist, Oscar Mayer & Co, Wis, 41-46, actg chief chemist, 46-50; dir prof control, Arbogast & Bastian, Inc, Pa, 51-54; asst supt, Valleydale Packers, Inc, Va, 55-60; supt, Roegelein Provision Co, Tex, 60-61; from instr to prof chem, San Antonio Col, 61-73, chmn dept, 67-73; prof chem, Univ Tex, San Antonio, 73-86. *Concurrent Pos:* Adj prof, St Mary's Univ, San Antonio. *Mem:* Am Chem Soc; Sigma Xi; Inst Food Technologists; Water Quality Asn. *Res:* Reduction of alumina; determination of structure of complex ions by radiotracer study; analytical chemistry of phosphorus compounds; ion selective electrodes education drinking water analysis. *Mailing Add:* 518 Northridge Dr San Antonio TX 78209

HOWARD, CHARLES FRANK, JR, BIOCHEMISTRY. *Current Pos:* ASSOC DEAN, COL HEALTH & HUMAN SERV, WESTERN MICH UNIV, 90-, PROF, SCH COMMUNITY HEALTH SERV, 90- *Personal Data:* b Colon, Panama, Dec 30, 32; US citizen; m 53, 75; c 4. *Educ:* Univ Northern Colo, BA, 54, MA, 58; Univ Wis-Madison, MS, 61, PhD(biochem), 63. *Prof Exp:* Fel biochem, Brandeis Univ, 63-65; from asst scientist to assoc scientist, Ore Regional Primate Res Ctr, 65-74, scientist, Metab Dis Res Sect, 74-90, div head, 83-87. *Concurrent Pos:* Asst prof, 65-75, res prof biochem, Dept Biochem, Sch Med, Ore Health Sci Univ, Portland, 84-90; assoc prof physiol chem, Col Optom, Pac Univ, 73-79; affil scientist, Yerkes Regional Primate Res Ctr, Emory Univ, Atlanta, Ga, 79-88; collaborating scientist, Caribbean Primate Res Ctr, Univ PR, 88- *Mem:* Nat Coun Univ Res Admin; Am Soc Biochemists & Molecular Biologists; Am Diabetes Asn; Am Soc Primatol; Am Soc Allied Health Prof. *Res:* Academic research administration; diabetes; islet amyloid. *Mailing Add:* Col Health & Human Serv Western Mich Univ Kalamazoo MI 49008. *Fax:* 616-387-2683; *E-Mail:* chuck.howard@wmich.edu

HOWARD, CLARENCE EDWARD, MINERALOGY, CRYSTALLOGRAPHY. *Current Pos:* RETIRED. *Personal Data:* b Roseboro, NC, May 31, 29; m 55, 81, Anne Barker; c Wendy H, Pam G & Brad S. *Educ:* Duke Univ, BS, 53; NC State Univ, MS, 55; La State Univ, PhD(geol), 63. *Prof Exp:* Teaching asst geol, NC State Univ, 53-55; mining engr, Tungsten Mining Corp, 55-57; teaching asst geol, La State Univ, 59-63; from asst prof to prof geol, Campbell Univ, NC, 63-76, chmn dept, 64-76; pres, Carolina Earth Resources Co, 76-81 & 83-84; dir, Div Soil & Water Conserv, NC Dept Natural Resources & Commun Develop, 81-82; vis prof geol, NC State Univ, 82-83; mgr, Earth & Mineral Sci Dept, Ctr Environ Measurements & Qual Assurance, Res Triangle Inst, 84-95. *Concurrent Pos:* Pres, Carolina Earth Resources Co, 77-; dir, Div Soil & Water Conserv, NC Dept Nat Resources & Commun Develop. *Mem:* Fel Geol Soc Am; Soc Mining Eng; Asn Eng Geologists; Asn Prof Geol Scientists; Sigma Xi; Am Inst Prof Geologists. *Res:* Optical mineralogy; petrographic and statistical studies of sediments and sedimentary rocks. *Mailing Add:* PO Box 1386 Lillington NC 27546

HOWARD, DAVID K, MOLECULAR BIOLOGY. *Current Pos:* mgr, 83-88, DIR, PITMAN-MOORE INC, 88- *Personal Data:* b Glasgow, Scotland, Oct 15, 49; m 85; c 2. *Educ:* Univ Glasgow, Scotland, BSc Hons, 71, PhD(biochem), 74. *Prof Exp:* Postdoctoral virol & oncol, Stanford Univ Sch Med, 74-75; sr res scientist, Meloy Labs, 76-80, prin res scientist, 80-81; scientist, IMC Corp, 81-83. *Concurrent Pos:* Prin investr, Nat Cancer Inst, NIH. *Mem:* Sigma Xi; Am Soc Microbiol; Soc Gen Microbiol. *Res:* Developing new products for animal health industry; molecular biology; endocrinology. *Mailing Add:* 2559 Forest Ct Lake Villa IL 60046

HOWARD, DEAN DENTON, TRACKING RADAR & COUNTER MEASURES DEVELOPMENT. *Current Pos:* STAFF SCIENTIST ELECTRONICS, LOCUS INC, 84- *Personal Data:* b Chatham, NJ, Jan 2, 27; m 50, Eileen I Russow; c Barry L & Greg W. *Educ:* Purdue Univ, BS, 49; Univ Md, MS, 52. *Honors & Awards:* Meritorious Civilian Serv Award, 80. *Prof Exp:* Sect head microwaves, Naval Res Lab, 49-84. *Concurrent Pos:* Lectr, George Washington Univ, 84- *Mem:* Fel Inst Elec & Electronics Engrs; Res Soc Am. *Res:* Monopulse tracking radar; system development, measurement and analysis of target caused errors and other sources of error; counter measures; development of error reduction techniques; computer modelling of monopulse radar. *Mailing Add:* Kaman Corp 2560 Huntington Ave Alexandria VA 22303

HOWARD, DEXTER HERBERT, MEDICAL MYCOLOGY. *Current Pos:* Asst bact, Univ Calif, Los Angeles, 51-54, res microbiologist infectious diseases, Sch Med, 54-55, from instr to asst prof, 57-63, assoc prof microbiol & immunol, 63-71, prof, 71-94 EMER PROF MICROBIOL & IMMUNOL, SCH MED, UNIV CALIF, LOS ANGELES, 94- *Personal Data:* b Santa Monica, Calif, Apr 17, 27; m 51; c 2. *Educ:* Univ Calif, Los Angeles, BA, 51, MA, 53, PhD(microbiol). 54. *Concurrent Pos:* Consult, Univ Calif Hosp, Los Angeles; consult ed, Sabouraudia, 69-; ed, Infection & Immunity, 86-96. *Mem:* Am Soc Microbiol; Am Acad Microbiol; Mycol Soc Am; Int Soc Human & Animal Mycol; AAAS; NY Acad Sci. *Res:* Medical mycology, especially factors involved in the host-fungus relationship; dimorphism of fungi; genetics of zoopathogenic fungi; diagnostic mycology. *Mailing Add:* Microbiol & Immunol Univ Calif Los Angeles Sch Med 10833 Le Conte Ave Los Angeles CA 90095-1747

HOWARD, DONALD GRANT, SOLID STATE PHYSICS. *Current Pos:* asst prof, 65-69, assoc prof, 69-77, PROF PHYSICS, PORTLAND STATE UNIV, 77- *Personal Data:* b Richmond, Calif, Nov 28, 37; m 60; c 2. *Educ:* Univ Calif, Berkeley, AB, 59, PhD(physics), 64. *Prof Exp:* Res asst prof physics, Univ Wash, 63-65. *Mem:* Am Phys Soc; Sigma Xi. *Res:* Atoms and molecules adsorbed on surfaces; Mossbauer effect studies; phase transitions; lattice dynamics; micrometallurgy. *Mailing Add:* 356 SE 44th Ave Portland OR 97215-1007

HOWARD, DONALD ROBERT, EDUCATION ADMINISTRATION, VETERINARY MEDICINE. *Current Pos:* RETIRED. *Personal Data:* b Orange, NJ, Apr 9, 40; m 64; c 2. *Educ:* Mich State Univ, BS, 63, DVM, 65; Tex A&M Univ, MS, 69; Univ Mo, PhD(neuroanat), 72. *Prof Exp:* Assoc prof surg, Tex A&M Univ, 66-72; res assoc anat, Univ Mo, 69-72; prof surg, Col Vet Med, Mich State Univ, 72-79, asst dean surg, 77-79; assoc dean surg, Col Vet Med, NC State Univ, 80-94. *Concurrent Pos:* Fel admin, Univ Mich-Am Coun Educ Prog, 75-76; regent, Am Col Vet Surgeons, 75-80, chmn bd, 83-85. *Mem:* Am Vet Med Asn; Am Col Vet Surgeons; Am Asn Vet Clinicians. *Res:* Retinal geniculate projections in the dog; mapped the retinal projections to the lateral geniculate nucleus in the canine; developed cortical evoked potentials as normal study; surgical correcting procedure for cleft palate and esophageal rent repairs. *Mailing Add:* Box 796 Beulah MI 49617

HOWARD, EDGAR, JR, ORGANOPHOSPHORUS CHEMISTRY. *Current Pos:* from instr to prof chem, Temple Univ, 47-86, chmn dept, 63-68, sr prof, 86-89, EMER PROF CHEM, TEMPLE UNIV, 89- *Personal Data:* b Westerly, RI, Aug 14, 22; m 53; c 3. *Educ:* Brown Univ, ScB, 43; Univ Ill, PhD(org chem), 46. *Prof Exp:* Pittsburgh Plate Glass Co fel, Harvard Univ, 46-47. *Mem:* Am Chem Soc; Sigma Xi. *Res:* Mechanism of organic reactions; synthesis and reactions of organophosphorus compounds. *Mailing Add:* 2323 Old Arch Rd Norristown PA 19401-2013

HOWARD, EDWARD GEORGE, JR, COMPOSITE STRUCTURES, FLUORO ORGANIC CHEMISTRY. *Current Pos:* RETIRED. *Personal Data:* b Atco, NJ, Feb 17, 21; m 51, Elizabeth Proctor; c Patricia S, Anne K & Joan M. *Educ:* Temple Univ, BA, 43, MA, 45; Indiana Univ, PhD(org chem), 48. *Honors & Awards:* du Pont La oisier Award. *Concurrent Pos:* du Pont Fel Scientist, Central Res & Develop Dept, E I du Pont De Nemours & Co, Inc, 48- *Mem:* Am Chem Soc. *Res:* Free radical chemistry; flouro-organic chemistry; organic chemistry; catalysis; polymer chemistry; inorganic chemistry; numerous publications and patents. *Mailing Add:* 844 Old Public Rd Hockessin DE 19707-9630

HOWARD, EUGENE FRANK, CELL BIOLOGY. *Current Pos:* asst prof, 71-76, ASSOC PROF CELL & MOLECULAR BIOL, MED COL GA, 76- *Personal Data:* b Milwaukee, Wis, Aug 11, 38; m 61; c 2. *Educ:* Univ Wis, BS, 60, MS, 62, PhD(molecular biol), 67. *Prof Exp:* Asst bot, Univ Wis, 60-62, asst zool, 62-67, res assoc, 67-68; asst in biol, M D Anderson Hosp, Houston, 69-71; asst prof, Grad Sch Biomed Sci, Univ Tex, Houston, 69-71. *Concurrent Pos:* Fel pharmacol, Col Med, Baylor Univ, 68-69. *Mem:* Am Soc Cell Biol; Am Asn Cancer Res; Tissue Cult Asn. *Res:* Cell proliferation; cancer biology; small nuclear RNA molecules. *Mailing Add:* Dept Biochem & Molecular Biol Med Col Ga Augusta GA 30912-2100. *Fax:* 706-721-6608

HOWARD, FORREST WILLIAM, TROPICAL HORTICULTURAL ENTOMOLOGY. *Current Pos:* asst prof, 76-81, ASSOC PROF ENTOM, FT LAUDERDALE RES & EDUC CTR, UNIV FLA, 81- *Personal Data:* b Denver, Colo, Feb 8, 36; m 66, Gloria Cleves; c Andrea & Martha. *Educ:* NY State Col Forestry, BS, 61; La State Univ, MS, 71, PhD(entom), 75. *Prof Exp:* Jr forester surv, Fla Forest Serv, 58-59; forester mgt, Olinkraft, Brazil, 61-62 & US Forest Serv, 62-63; biologist wetland ecol, Fla Div Health, 65-70. *Mem:* Int Palm Soc. *Res:* Insects and diseases of palms and other tropical horticultural plants; bionomics of scale insects. *Mailing Add:* Ft Lauderdale Res & Educ Ctr Univ Fla 3205 College Ave Ft Lauderdale FL 33314. *Fax:* 954-475-4125; *E-Mail:* fwh@icon.ifas.ufl.edu

HOWARD, FRANK LESLIE, plant pathology, mycology; deceased, see previous edition for last biography

HOWARD, FREDRIC TIMOTHY, SPECIAL FUNCTIONS, COMBINATORICS. *Current Pos:* From asst prof to assoc prof, 66-78, PROF MATH, WAKE FOREST UNIV, 78- *Personal Data:* b Ft Worth, Tex, May 17, 39; m 65. *Educ:* Vanderbilt Univ, BA, 61, MA, 63; Duke Univ, PhD(math), 66. *Mem:* Am Math Soc; Math Asn Am; Fibonacci Soc. *Res:* Number theory. *Mailing Add:* 1873 Faculty Dr Winston-Salem NC 27106-5239

HOWARD, G(EORGE) MICHAEL, CHEMICAL ENGINEERING. *Current Pos:* from instr to assoc prof chem eng, Univ Conn, 61-78, actg head dept, 69-70 & 76, assoc dean res, 79-82, assoc dean Sch Eng, 74-88, PROF CHEM ENG, UNIV CONN, 78- *Personal Data:* b Washington, DC, July 4, 35; m 59, Jane Deans; c 3. *Educ:* Univ Rochester, BS, 57; Yale Univ, MEng, 59; Univ Conn, PhD(chem eng), 67. *Prof Exp:* Develop engr, res & develop, Humphrey-Wilkinson, Inc, 59-61. *Concurrent Pos:* Grant, Foxboro Corp, Chas Pfizer & Co, Olin Corp, 68-69. *Mem:* Am Inst Chem Engrs; Am Chem Soc; Am Soc Eng Educ. *Res:* Unsteady state behavior of processes; process safety & health; engineering education. *Mailing Add:* Dept Chem Eng U-222 191 Auditorium Univ Conn Storrs CT 06269-3222. *Fax:* 860-486-2959

HOWARD, GILBERT THOREAU, OPERATIONS RESEARCH, OPTIMIZATION. *Current Pos:* Prof oper res, Naval Postgrad Sch, 67-84, dir res admin, 84-91, assoc dean res, 91-93, DIR INSTNL RES, NAVAL POSTGRAD SCH, 93-, DIR ACAD PLANNING, 95- *Personal Data:* b Torrington, Wyo, Sept 21, 41; m 63; c 2. *Educ:* Northwestern Univ, BS, 63; Johns Hopkins Univ, PhD(opers res), 67. *Mem:* Opers Res Soc Am; Inst Mgt Sci; Nat Coun Res Admin; Asn Instnl Res. *Res:* Mathematical programming. *Mailing Add:* Naval Post Grad Sch Code 0011 Monterey CA 93948

HOWARD, GLENN WILLARD, JR, MOLECULAR BIOLOGY. *Current Pos:* MGR BIOL CONTROLS, PALL CORP, 76-, ASSOC DIR, SCIENTIFIC & LABORATORY SERVICES DEPT, 82- *Personal Data:* b Columbus, Ohio, Feb 16, 39; m 70; c 2. *Educ:* Rice Univ, BA, 62; Purdue Univ, MS, 69, PhD(molecular biol), 70. *Prof Exp:* Asst prof biol, Adelphi Univ, 70-73; dir res, Environ 200 Ltd, 73-74, tech prod mgr, 74-76. *Concurrent Pos:* Mem, Planning Bd City of Glen Cove, NY, 86-, Bd Dir, Glen Cove Chamber Com, 87- *Mem:* Am Soc Microbiol; Am Soc Testing & Mat. *Res:* Microbiology in regard to development of microbially and endotoxin retentive filters. *Mailing Add:* 11 Eastland Dr Glen Cove NY 11542

HOWARD, GUY ALLEN, ENDOCRINOLOGY. *Current Pos:* RES PROF, DEPT MED & CHIEF, MINERAL METAB RES, DIV ENDOCRINOL, SCH MED, UNIV MIAMI, 89-, RES PROF, DEPT BIOCHEM & MOLECULAR BIOL, 90- *Personal Data:* US citizen. *Educ:* Univ Wash, Seattle, BA, 65; Cent Wash Univ, MS, 67; Univ Ore, PhD(biochem), 70. *Prof Exp:* Postdoctoral fel, Dept Chem, Univ Ore, 70-71 & Dept Biol Chem, Sch Med, Univ Calif, Davis, 71-73; res assoc, Friedrich Miescher Inst, Basel, Switz, 73-76; from res asst prof to res assoc prof, Dept Med, Sch Med, Univ Wash, Seattle, 76-89, res assoc prof, Dept Oral Biol, Sch Dent & mem grad fac, 82-89, res prof, Dept Med, 89. *Concurrent Pos:* Res chemist, Vet Admin Med Ctr, Tacoma, Wash, 76-82, assoc res career scientist, 82-89; mem, Int Conf Calcium Regulating Hormones, Japan, 83 & France, 86, Prog Comt, Am Soc Bone & Mineral Res, 84, 88 & 90; sect head bone metab, Biochem Dept, Ayerst Labs Res, Inc, Princeton, 84-85; session chmn, Second Int Conf Basic & Clin Factors Influencing Bone Growth, 85; vis prof, Dept Orthop, Univ Zurich, Switz, 88; res career scientist, Vet Admin Med Ctr, Miami, 90- *Mem:* Am Fedn Clin Res; Soc Exp Biol & Med; Am Soc Bone & Mineral Res; Am Soc Biochem & Molecular Biol; Endocrine Soc; NY Acad Sci. *Res:* Author of more than 150 technical publications. *Mailing Add:* Res Serv 151 Vet Admin Med Ctr Miami FL 33125. *Fax:* 305-324-3365

HOWARD, H(ENRY) TAYLOR, ELECTRICAL ENGINEERING. *Current Pos:* Res asst, Radio Propagation Lab, Stanford Univ, 55-56, res assoc, Radio Sci Lab, 59-67, sr res assoc, 67-76, Ctr Radar Astron, 71-76, res prof elec eng, 76-82, EMER PROF, STANFORD UNIV, 82-; CHIEF TECHNOL OFFICER & VCHMN, CHAPARRAL COMMUN, 80- *Personal Data:* b Peoria, Ill, Apr 5, 32; m 55; c 3. *Educ:* Purdue Univ, EE, 51; Stanford Univ, BSEE, 55. *Honors & Awards:* Medal for Except Sci Acheivement, NASA. *Concurrent Pos:* Leader, Celestial Mech & Radiosci Team, Mariner Venus-Mercury 73, NASA, prin investr, Apollo Bistatic Radar Exp, team leader, Radio Propagation Team, Galileo Mission to Jupiter. *Mem:* Nat Acad Eng; Am Astron Soc; Am Geophys Union; Int Union Radio Sci; fel Inst Elec & Electronics Engrs; AAAS. *Res:* Radar astronomy; solar terrestrial relationships, interplanetary gas density and magnetic fields. *Mailing Add:* Chaparral Commun 2450 N First St San Jose CA 95131

HOWARD, HAROLD HENRY, BOTANY, LIMNOLOGY. *Current Pos:* RETIRED. *Personal Data:* b New Britain, Conn, May 2, 28; m 53; c 2. *Educ:* Cornell Univ, BS, 53, MS, 56, PhD(limnol), 63. *Prof Exp:* Instr bot, Mont State Univ, 58-59; investr tundra lake biol, Arctic Res Lab, 59-60; instr bot, Mont State Univ, 60-61, instr biol, 61-63; from asst prof to assoc prof biol, Skidmore Col, 63-83. *Mem:* AAAS; Ecol Soc Am; Torrey Bot Club. *Res:* Floristic botany; studies of Cayuga Lake, New York, arctic tundra lakes and Adirondack mountain lakes; Adirondack vascular flora. *Mailing Add:* Rte 2 Box 202 Greenwich NY 12834

HOWARD, HENRY COBOURN, MATHEMATICS, ORDINARY DIFFERENTIAL EQUATIONS. *Current Pos:* assoc prof, 67-72, PROF MATH, UNIV KY, 72- *Personal Data:* b Akron, Ohio, Sept 20, 28; m 64; c 2. *Educ:* Col Wooster, BA, 50; Carnegie Inst Technol, MS, 55, PhD(math), 58. *Prof Exp:* Instr math, Carnegie Inst Technol, 57-58 & Univ Wis- Madison, 58-60; asst prof, Univ Wis-Milwaukee, 60-63; vis asst res prof, Fluid Dynamics Inst, Univ Md, 63-65; assoc prof, Univ Wis-Milwaukee, 65-67. *Concurrent Pos:* Vis prof math, Univ BC, 73-74. *Mem:* Am Math Soc; Math Asn Am. *Res:* Classical analysis; ordinary and partial differential equations. *Mailing Add:* Dept Math Univ Ky 5005 Limestone St Lexington KY 40506-0027

HOWARD, HILDEGARDE, ORNITHOLOGY. *Current Pos:* RETIRED. *Personal Data:* b Washington, DC, Apr 3, 01; m 30. *Educ:* Univ Calif, BA, 24, MA, 26, PhD(zool), 28. *Honors & Awards:* Brewster Mem Award, Am Ornith Union, 53. *Prof Exp:* Asst zool, Los Angeles, 24-25; res asst, Los Angeles County Mus, 24-25; teaching fel paleont & geol, Univ Calif, Berkeley, 25-27; res asst, Los Angeles County Mus, 28; avian paleontologist, Nat Hist Mus Los Angeles County, 29-38, cur avian paleont, 39-50, chief cur, Div Sci, 51-61, res assoc vert paleont, 61-73, emer chief cur, 74-90. *Concurrent Pos:* Guggenheim Found res fel, 62-63. *Mem:* Fel AAAS; hon mem Soc Vert Paleont; fel Geol Soc Am; hon mem Cooper Ornith Soc; fel Am Ornith Union. *Res:* Fossil birds, especially from southern California sites, Rancho La Brea Pleistocene and marine Pliocene and Miocene; cave deposits of western states; Pliocene and Pleistocene of Mexico. *Mailing Add:* 2045 Apt Q Via Mariposa E Laguna Hills CA 92653

HOWARD, IAN PORTEOUS, HUMAN VISION, VESTIBULAR SYSTEM. *Current Pos:* assoc prof, 66-68, chmn, 68-70, PROF PSYCHOL, YORK UNIV, 68- , DISTINGUISHED RES PROF, 88-, DIR, LAB STUDY HUMAN PERFORMANCE SPACE, INST SPACE & TERRESTRIAL SCI, 88-, DIR, CTR VISION RES, 92- *Personal Data:* b Rochdale, Eng, July 20, 27; Brit & Can citizen; m 56, Antonie Eber; c Ruth, Neil & Martin. *Educ:* Univ Manchester, BSc, 52; Durham Univ, PhD(psychol), 66. *Prof Exp:* Res asst psychol, Univ Durham, 52-54, lectr, 54-65; assoc prof, NY Univ, 65-66. *Mem:* Asn Res Vision & Ophthal. *Res:* Sensory-motor mechanisms responsible for human spatially coordinated behavior; visual and vestibular systems, eye movements and their interactions; stereoscopic vision; psychophysical and objective recording procedures. *Mailing Add:* Human Performance Space Lab 103 Farquharson Bldg York Univ North York ON M3J 1P3 Can. *Fax:* 416-736-5857; *E-Mail:* 1howard@hpl.ists.ca

HOWARD, IRIS ANNE, SOLID STATE PHYSICS. *Current Pos:* at DEPT PHYSICS, UNIV TEX, ARLINGTON. *Personal Data:* b Knoxville, Tenn, Sept 20, 53. *Educ:* Mass Inst Technol, SB, 75, PhD(physics), 81. *Prof Exp:* Res assoc, Webster Res Ctr, Xerox Corp, 81-; dept physics & astron, Univ NMex. *Mem:* Am Phys Soc; Asn Women Sci. *Res:* Transport properties of quasi-one-dimensional materials; soliton effects in quasi-one-dimensional crystals. *Mailing Add:* Dept Physics Univ Tex PO Box 19059 Arlington TX 76019

HOWARD, IRMGARD MATILDA KEELER, CLINICAL CHEMISTRY, PROTEIN CHEMISTRY. *Current Pos:* From asst prof to assoc prof, 70-93, PROF CHEM, HOUGHTON COL, 93- *Personal Data:* b Philadelphia, Pa, Jan 21, 41; m 69, David A; c Deborah, William, Eleanor E & Stephen J. *Educ:* Duke Univ, AB, 62, PhD(biochem), 70. *Concurrent Pos:* Res assoc biochem, Duke Univ, 80-81; nat tour speaker, Am Chem Soc, 90- *Mem:* Am Chem Soc. *Res:* Pytohemagglutinin lectin chemistry; molecular genetics; nutrition; consumer chemistry. *Mailing Add:* Houghton Col Houghton NY 14744-0128

HOWARD, JACK BENNY, CHEMICAL ENGINEERING. *Current Pos:* Ford Found res fel, 65-67, from asst prof to assoc prof, 65-75, PROF CHEM ENG, MASS INST TECHNOL, 75- *Personal Data:* b Monroe Co, Ky, Oct 16, 37; m 69, Carolyn Butler; c Courtenay & Jonathan. *Educ:* Univ Ky, BS, 60, MS, 61; Pa State Univ, PhD(fuel tech), 65. *Honors & Awards:* Richard H Wilhelm Lectr, Princeton Univ, 77; Henry H Storch Award, Am Chem Soc, 83; Silver Medal, Combustion Inst, 84; Oblad lectr, Univ Utah, 89; Bernard Lewis Gold Medal, Combustion Inst, 92. *Concurrent Pos:* Dir, Ctr Airborne Org, Mass Inst Technol. *Mem:* AAAS; Am Chem Soc; Am Inst Chem Engrs; Combustion Inst. *Res:* Combustion and pyrolysis of solid fuels; heterogeneous reaction kinetics; carbon formation in flames; energy technology; combustion generated pollution; coal gasification. *Mailing Add:* Dept Chem Eng Mass Inst Technol Cambridge MA 02139

HOWARD, JAMES ANTHONY, PHYSICAL CHEMISTRY, ORGANIC CHEMISTRY. *Current Pos:* RETIRED. *Personal Data:* b Liverpool, Eng, Feb 9, 37; Can citizen; m 61; c 3. *Educ:* Univ Birmingham, BSc, 58, PhD(chem), 61. *Prof Exp:* Sr res officer chem, Nat Res Coun Can, Ottawa, 63-95. *Concurrent Pos:* Guest worker, Steacie Inst Molecular Sci. *Mem:* Chem Inst Can. *Res:* Kinetics and mechanistic studies of free-radical reactions in solution; metal vapor chemistry. *Mailing Add:* 38 Wick Crescent Gloucester ON K1J 7H3 Can. *E-Mail:* jah@ned1.sims.nrc.ca

HOWARD, JAMES BRYANT, BIOCHEMISTRY. *Current Pos:* Asst prof biochem, 71-77, assoc prof, 77-82, PROF BIOCHEM MED, UNIV MINN, MINNEAPOLIS, 82- *Personal Data:* b Indianapolis, Ind, Apr 25, 42; m 64; c 1. *Educ:* De Pauw Univ, BA, 64; Univ Calif, Los Angeles, PhD(biochem), 68. *Concurrent Pos:* Fel, Univ Calif, Berkeley, 69-71; vis prof, Dept Chem, Harvard Univ, 80-81. *Mem:* AAAS; Am Soc Biol Chemists; Am Chem Soc; Sigma Xi. *Res:* Protein chemistry; structure-function studies; sequencing methodology; enzymology; proteins of nitrogenase system, flavoproteins, and non-heme iron proteins; protein chemistry of blood protease inhibitors; protein chemistry of complement fixation. *Mailing Add:* Dept Biochem Univ Minn 4-225 Millard Hall 435 Delaware St SE Minneapolis MN 55455

HOWARD, JAMES LAWRENCE, BEHAVIORAL PHARMACOLOGY, DRUG DEVELOPMENT. *Current Pos:* STAFF MEM, HOWARD ASSOC, 95- *Personal Data:* b Glen Ellyn, Ill, Nov 30, 41; m 63, Judith Bennett; c David L & Erin K. *Educ:* Univ NC, BA, 63; Tulane Univ, MS, 66, PhD(psychol), 68. *Prof Exp:* Asst prof psychol, Psychiat Dept, Univ NC, 68-74; sr res scientist, Pharmacol Div, Burroughs Wellcome Co, 74-95. *Concurrent Pos:* Sci consult, NC Alcohol Res Authority, 75-; adj prof, Psychol Dept, NC State Univ, 78-; coun rep, Am Psychol Asn, 85-87. *Mem:* Fel Am Psychol Asn; fel Am Psychol Soc; Soc Stimulus Properties of Drugs (pres, 83-84); Soc Neurosci; Am Soc Pharmacol & Exp Therapeut; Behav Pharmacol Soc. *Res:* Behavioral pharmacology; drugs to treat psychiatric disorders, especially anxiety; animal models of human disorders and the effect of drugs on these models. *Mailing Add:* 8240 Morrow Mill Rd Chapel Hill NC 27516. *Fax:* 919-315-8890

HOWARD, JEFFREY LYNN, SEDIMENTATION & STRATIGRAPHY, HEAVY METAL CONTAMINATION OF SOILS. *Current Pos:* Asst prof, 87-93, ASSOC PROF, WAYNE STATE UNIV 93- *Personal Data:* b Concord, NC Sept 20, 54. *Educ:* Va Polytech Inst & State Univ, BS, 76, MS, 79; Univ Calif, Santa Barbara, PhD(geol), 87. *Mem:* Soc Luminescence Micros. *Res:* Provenance of conglomerates, Los Angeles Basin, California; tectonics of Cenozoic of Southwestern US; heavy metal contamination of urban soils. *Mailing Add:* Wayne State Univ 201 Oldmain Detroit MI 48202. *Fax:* 313-577-0517

HOWARD, JOHN, ORGANIC CHEMISTRY, INORGANIC CHEMISTRY. *Current Pos:* res scientist gen chem, 77-80, SR RES CHEMIST, BC RES, 80-; IND TECH ADV, NAT RES COUN, CAN, 93- *Personal Data:* b Clitheroe, UK, Aug 26, 33; Can citizen; m 58, Cynthia; c Samanth & Sarah. *Educ:* Leeds Univ, BSc, 54, PhD(org chem), 58. *Prof Exp:* Tech officer plastics technol, Imp Chem Indust, 57-59; fel carbohydrate res, Univ Ottawa, 59-61 & penicillin res, Univ Alta, 61-62; res chemist, R&L Molecular Res, 63-65, ITT Rayonier, 65-69, Columbia Cellulose, 69-73, Econotech Serv, 73-75, Multifibre Process Ltd, 75-77 & BC Res Corp, 77-93. *Mem:* Chem Inst Can; Can Pulp & Paper Asn. *Res:* Wood, pulp and cellulose chemistry; process development and optimization. *Mailing Add:* Pace Technol Inc 3650 Wesbrook Mall Vancouver BC V6S 2L2 Can. *Fax:* 604-224-0540

HOWARD, JOHN CHARLES, ORGANIC CHEMISTRY, BIOCHEMISTRY. *Current Pos:* asst prof, 61-66, ASSOC PROF BIOCHEM, MED COL GA, 66- *Personal Data:* b Franklin, NY, Apr 19, 24; m 49; c 2. *Educ:* Hobart Col, BS, 44; Cornell Univ, PhD(org chem), 51. *Prof Exp:* Sr res chemist, Stauffer Chem Co, 53-55; sr res chemist, Eaton Labs Div, Norwich Pharmacal Co, 55-57, unit leader & asst sect chief, 57-60. *Concurrent Pos:* USPHS grants, 61-63 & 64-67; NSF grants, 65 & 68. *Mem:* Am Chem Soc; The Chem Soc; Sigma Xi. *Res:* Heterocyclic compounds; bioorganic and physical organic chemistry. *Mailing Add:* 3008 Stratford Dr Augusta GA 30909-3530

HOWARD, JOHN MALONE, SURGERY. *Current Pos:* SURGEON, MERCY HOSP TOLEDO. *Personal Data:* b Autaugaville, Ala, Aug 25, 19; m 43; c 6. *Educ:* Birmingham Southern Col, BS, 41; Univ Pa, MD, 44; Am Bd Surg, dipl; Am Bd Thoracic Surg, dipl. *Honors & Awards:* Legion of Merit, Dept Defense. *Prof Exp:* Intern & resident surg, Hosp Univ Pa, 44-50, Am Cancer Soc fel, 49-50; asst prof surg, Col Med, Baylor Univ, 50-58; prof surg, Univ & surgeon, Hosp, Hahnemann Med Col, 58-74; prof surg, Med Col Ohio, 74-90. *Concurrent Pos:* Attend surgeon, Jefferson Davis, Methodist & Vet Admin Hosps, 50-58; consult, US Vet Admin, 55- & USPHS, 68-; surgeon-in-chief, Crozer-Chester Med Ctr, 71-73; hon fel, Royal Col Surgeons Edinburgh & Col Surgeons Brazil, 93. *Mem:* Am Col Surgeons; Soc Univ Surg; AMA; Am Surg Asn; Pan-Pac Surg Asn; Int Asn Pancreatology. *Res:* Physiology and surgery in the fields of the pancreas with emphasis on pancreatic cancer. *Mailing Add:* PO Box 10008 Toledo OH 43699-0008

HOWARD, JOHN NELSON, PHYSICS, INFRARED. *Current Pos:* RETIRED. *Personal Data:* b Philadelphia, Pa, Feb 27, 21; m 50, Irene Rogers; c Martha, Katherine, Van & John J. *Educ:* Univ Fla, BS, 43; Ohio State Univ, MS, 49, PhD(physics), 54. *Honors & Awards:* Distinguished Serv Award, Optical Soc Am, 87. *Prof Exp:* Asst chemist, Dept Soils, Univ Fla, 43-44; assoc physicist, Spectros Lab, Nat Adv Comt Aeronaut, 44-46; res assoc physics, Ohio State Univ, 48-54; head infrared tech br, 54-60, chief optical physics lab, 60-64, chief scientist, Air Force Geophys Lab, 64-82. *Concurrent Pos:* Ed, Appl Optics, 60-87, Physics News, 83-89; gov bd, Am Inst Physics, 89-92. *Mem:* Fel Am Phys Soc; History Sci Soc; fel Optical Soc Am (vpres, 89, pres-elect, 90, pres, 91); Int Comn Optics (vpres & treas, 81-87). *Res:* Infrared physics; atmospheric optics; life and research of Lord Rayleigh. *Mailing Add:* 25 Woodcliff Rd Newton Highlands MA 02161

HOWARD, JOHN WILLIAM, ANALYTICAL CHEMISTRY. *Current Pos:* RETIRED. *Personal Data:* b Dayton, Md, Sept 1, 25; m 52; c 4. *Educ:* Cath Univ Am, BS, 49; George Washington Univ, MS, 51; Georgetown Univ, PhD(chem), 55. *Prof Exp:* Chemist, Hazleton Labs, Inc, Va, 51-57 & Nat Cotton Coun Am, Washington, DC, 57-60; Food & Drug Admin, Washington, DC, 60-70; chief org & additives chem br, Bur Food, Food & Drug Admin, Washington, DC, 70-74; dir div chem & physics, 74-85. *Mem:* AAAS; Am Chem Soc. *Res:* Procedures for determining polycyclic aromatic hydrocarbons in petroleum products, smoked foods, and other food products; N-nitrosamines in foods; administration and research in development of analytical methods for determination of food additives, industrial chemicals, heavy metals, natural toxins, and others in foods and products of food additive significance. *Mailing Add:* HRC 32 Box 59C Middlebrook VA 24459

HOWARD, JOSEPH H, AGRICULTURAL RESEARCH. *Current Pos:* RETIRED. *Personal Data:* b Olustee, Okla, Jan 15, 31. *Educ:* Univ Okla, BS, 52, MS, 57. *Honors & Awards:* Melvil Dewey Medal, Am Libr Asn, 85. *Prof Exp:* Vocal music instr, Kiowa Pub Sch, Kans, 54-56; music librn, Univ Colo, 57-58, circulation librn, 58-59, assoc dir pub serv, 59-63; Peace Corp vol, Univ Malaya Libr & Malayan Teachers Col, 63-65; chief, Catalog Dept, Wash Univ Librs, St Louis, Mo, 65-67; asst chief, Descriptive Cataloging Div, Libr Cong, 67-68, chief, 68-72, chief, Ser Rec Div, 72-75, asst dir cataloging, Processing Dept, 75-76, asst librn, Processing Servs, 76-83; dir, Nat Agr Libr, USDA, 83-93. *Concurrent Pos:* Mem Joint Coun Food & Agr Sci, 83-, Am Libr Asn Historically Black Col & Univ Task Force, 87-, Nat Adv Comt, Libr Cong, 88-89; bd mem, Forest Press, 86-88; mem, Bd Regents, Nat Libr Med, gen admin bd, USDA grad sch, 88- *Mem:* Am Libr Asn; Spec Libr Asn; Nat Info Stand Orgn; Int Asn Agr Librn & Documentalists (pres, 90-). *Mailing Add:* Nat Agr Libr USDA c/o Mary Silva 10301 Baltimore Blvd Rm 200 Beltsville MD 20705

HOWARD, JOSEPH H(ERMAN) G(REGG), FLUID MECHANICS, TURBOMACHINERY. *Current Pos:* RETIRED. *Personal Data:* b Grafton, Ont, Nov 13, 33; m 60; c 1. *Educ:* Queen's Univ, Ont, BSc, 56; Univ Birmingham, MSc, 58, PhD(turbomach), 60. *Prof Exp:* Analytical engr, United Aircraft Can Ltd, 60-64; assoc prof mech eng, Univ Waterloo, 64-71, prof, 71- *Concurrent Pos:* Lectr, Loyola Col, Montreal, 63-64; consult, Dominion Eng, 67-76, Creare, 73-83 & Concepts, 84-; vis res assoc, Creare, Hanover, NH, 73-74; vis res engr, Sundstrand Corp, 80-81; vis res assoc, Concepts ETI, Norwich, Vt, 85-86. *Mem:* Am Soc Mech Engrs; Eng Inst Can. *Res:* Flow in passages of axial and centrifugal compressors and pumps; internal aerodynamics of ducts; computer-aided design methods for compressors and pumps. *Mailing Add:* Dept Mech Eng Univ Waterloo Waterloo ON N2L 3G1 Can

HOWARD, KEITH ARTHUR, GEOLOGY. *Current Pos:* Astrogeol br, US Geol Surv, 66-75, 96, chief, nat active-faults map, 74-79, dep chief off environ geol, 75-77, chief techonics needles, 77-95, chief crustal exp, 84-92, GEOLOGIST, WESTERN GEOL MAPPING TEAM, US GEOL SURV, 66- *Personal Data:* b Price, Utah, Sept 12, 39; m 95, Linda S Thompson Cox, c Crystal A. *Educ:* Univ Calif, Berkeley, BS, 61, MS, 62; Yale Univ, PhD(geol), 66. *Concurrent Pos:* Fulbright scholar, 88. *Mem:* Geol Soc Am; Am Geophys Union; Sigma Xi. *Res:* Structural geology; deformation and metamorphism in the western United States; planetology; volcanology; tectonics; volcanic structure and morphology. *Mailing Add:* US Geol Surv Menlo Park CA 94025

HOWARD, LORN LAMBIER, MICROELECTRONIC SYSTEMS FOR NEURAL NETWORK ANALYSIS. *Current Pos:* dir, biomed eng, 64-72 & 72-88, PROF ELEC ENG, SOUTHERN METHODIST UNIV, 59- *Personal Data:* b Poplar Bluff, Mo, Nov 28, 17; m 41; c 3. *Educ:* Univ Ill, BSc, 47, MSc, 48; Mich State Univ, PhD(elec eng), 59. *Prof Exp:* Lab asst elec eng, Univ Ill, 43-44, res asst, physics, 46-47, res asst elec eng, 47-55; instr elec eng, Mich State Univ, 55-59. *Concurrent Pos:* Consult & founder, Ill Res Group, 53-58; sci consult, Wadley Res Inst, Tex, 61-; sr res staff mem, Gen Dynamics/ Electronics, NY, 63; clin prof biophys, Univ Tex Health Sci Ctr, Dallas, 64-; sr assoc engr, Collins Radio Co, Tex, 67; consult, numerous elec accident invests, 67-, Graham Magnetics, Inc, Tex, 68 & Armoloy, Inc, 70-71; consult biomed eng, Emarand, SA, Neuchatel, Switz, 71-77; sci exchange, Soviet Acad Sci, 90. *Mem:* Inst Elec & Electronics Engrs; Electron Micros Soc Am; Am Vacuum Soc; Sigma Xi. *Res:* Thin conducting films; microstructural analysis; simulation of biological systems; measurement of micropotentials in biological systems, especially neuronal networks. *Mailing Add:* Dept Elec Eng Southern Methodist Univ Dallas TX 75275-0001

HOWARD, LOUIS NORBERG, APPLIED MATHEMATICS, FLUID DYNAMICS. *Current Pos:* prof math, 81-97, EMER PROF MATH, FLA STATE UNIV, 97-; EMER PROF MATH, MASS INST TECHNOL. *Personal Data:* b Chicago, Ill, Mar 12, 29; m 51; c 2. *Educ:* Swarthmore Col, AB, 50; Princeton Univ, MA, 52, PhD(math physics), 53. *Prof Exp:* Higgins lectr math, Princeton Univ, 54-55; from asst prof to prof math, Mass Inst Technol, 55-84. *Concurrent Pos:* Found fel, Guggenheim, 61. *Mem:* Nat Acad Sci; Am Phys Soc; Am Math Soc; Math Asn Am; Soc Indust & Appl Math; Soc Math Biol. *Res:* Fluid dynamics; chemical oscillations and waves; rotating stratified flow. *Mailing Add:* Dept Math Fla State Univ Tallahassee FL 32306

HOWARD, PAUL EDWARD, SET THEORY, AXIOM OF CHOICE. *Current Pos:* From asst prof to assoc prof, 70-83, PROF MATH, EASTERN MICH UNIV, 83- *Personal Data:* b St Louis, Mo, Aug 31, 43; m 65; c 2. *Educ:* Univ Mo, BA, 65; Univ Mich, PhD(math), 70. *Mem:* Am Math Soc; Asn Symbolic Logic. *Res:* Zermelo-Fraenkel set theory; relationships between weakenings of the axiom of choice. *Mailing Add:* Dept Math Eastern Mich Univ Ypsilanti MI 48197

HOWARD, PHILIP HALL, ENVIRONMENTAL FATE OF ORGANIC CHEMICALS. *Current Pos:* Res assoc environ res, 70-72, SR ENVIRON CHEMIST, ENVIRON SCI CTR, SYRACUSE RES CORP, 72- *Personal Data:* b Worcester, Mass, Oct 7, 43; m 67, 82; c 4. *Educ:* Norwich Univ, BS, 65; Syracuse Univ, PhD(org chem), 70. *Mem:* Am Chem Soc; AAAS; Soc Environ Toxicol & Chem; Am Soc Microbiol. *Res:* Persistance of organic chemicals; biodegradation; environmental pollutants; commercial chemistry. *Mailing Add:* Syracuse Res Corp Merrill Lane Syracuse NY 13210. *Fax:* 315-426-3429; *E-Mail:* howardp@syrres.com

HOWARD, RICHARD ALDEN, BOTANY. *Current Pos:* Asst, Harvard Univ, 38-39, jr fel, Soc Fels, 42 & 46-47, asst prof biol, 48-53, Arnold prof bot & dir, Arnold Arboretum, 54-78, prof dendrol, 54-87, EMER PROF DENDROL & BOT, HARVARD UNIV, 88-; EMER VPRES BOT SCI, NY BOT GARDEN, 91- *Personal Data:* b Stamford, Conn, July 1, 17; m 44, Elizabeth Solie; c Jean E, Barbara J, Bruce R & Philip G. *Educ:* Miami Univ, AB, 38; Harvard Univ, AM, 40, PhD(biol), 42. *Hon Degrees:* DSc, Framingham State Col, 77. *Prof Exp:* Asst cur, NY Bot Garden, 47-48; prof bot & chmn dept, Univ Conn, 53-54; vpres, NY Bot Garden, 88-90. *Concurrent Pos:* Chmn, Plant Records Ctr, 68-70; mem bot expeds, Caribbean Islands, Cent Am & Mex; Guggenheim fel, 78-79. *Mem:* Int Asn Bot Gardens (pres, 59-64); Bot Soc Am; Am Soc Plant Taxon (treas, 49-54); Am Acad Arts & Sci; Asn Trop Biol. *Res:* Floristic studies of the Caribbean Islands; monographic studies of the Icacinaceae, Magnoliaceae, Malvaceae, Coccoloba, and tropical American flowering plants; history of botanical gardens; flora of the lesser antilles. *Mailing Add:* Arnold Arboretum 22 Divinity Ave Cambridge MA 02138. *Fax:* 617-495-9484

HOWARD, RICHARD JAMES, MYCOLOGY, CELL BIOLOGY. *Current Pos:* res biologist, E I Du Pont De Nemours & Co, Inc, 81-84, sect res biologist, 84-85, sr res biologist, 85-94, RES ASSOC, E I DU PONT DE NEMOURS & CO, INC, 94- *Personal Data:* b Appleton, Wis, May 29, 52; m 79, Marybeth Weinberg; c 2. *Educ:* Univ Wis-Madison, BS, 74; Cornell Univ, MS, 77, PhD(plant path), 80. *Honors & Awards:* Alexopoulos Prize, 90. *Prof Exp:* NIH trainee, Sch Med, Wash Univ, 79-80, NSF fel, 80. *Concurrent Pos:* Mem chmn, Mycol Soc Am, 89-91; assoc ed, J Mycologia, 94- *Mem:* Mycol Soc Am, (treas, 96-). *Res:* Cell biology of growth and morphogenesis in fungi. *Mailing Add:* Cent Res & Develop DuPont Exp Sta Wilmington DE 19880-0402. *Fax:* 302-695-4296; *E-Mail:* howardrj@esvax.dnet.dupont.com

HOWARD, RICHARD JOHN, physics; deceased, see previous edition for last biography

HOWARD, ROBERT ADRIAN, PHYSICS. *Current Pos:* from asst prof to assoc prof physics, Univ Okla, 47-54, chmn dept phys & sch eng phys, 52-55, dir nuclear reactor lab, 58-60, chmn dept physics & astron, 64-66, prof physics, 55-76, EMER PROF PHYSICS, UNIV OKLA, 76- *Personal Data:* b Los Angeles, Calif, Feb 23, 13; m 39, 71, Phyllis I Miller; c Eileen, Brian, Donald S, Kathleen, Janet L (Miller) & Susan (Mummery). *Educ:* Calif Inst Technol, BS, 34, MS, 35; Wash Univ, PhD(physics), 38. *Prof Exp:* Asst, Wash Univ, 35-38; res physicist, Carter Oil Co, Okla, 38-42; staff mem, Radiation Lab, Mass Inst Technol, 43-45; asst, Calif Inst Technol, 34-35, res physicist, Hydrodyn Lab, 46-47. *Concurrent Pos:* Consult, Boeing Airplane Co, 52 & Oak Ridge Nat Lab, 54; mem tech staff, Thompson-Ramo-Wooldridge Corp, 55-57, consult, Space Technol Labs, 58-62; dir, Cent Inst Physics, Concepcion Univ, 62-64; vis res scientist, Inst High Energy Physics, Univ Heidelberg, 69-70. *Mem:* Am Phys Soc. *Res:* Geophysics; migration and accumulation of petroleum; design of microwave power and frequency measuring devices; x-rays; hydrodynamics; nuclear physics; high energy particle physics. *Mailing Add:* 711 W Timberdell Rd Norman OK 73072-6324. *E-Mail:* rahoward@ou.edu

HOWARD, ROBERT BRUCE, medicine, for more information see previous edition

HOWARD, ROBERT E, SOLID STATE PHYSICS. *Current Pos:* supvr, Nat Security Div, 93-95, CONSULT, OFF MGT & BUDGET, 95- *Personal Data:* b New York, NY, Feb 19, 33. *Educ:* Columbia Univ, BA, 53; Oxford Univ, DPhil, 57. *Prof Exp:* Instr, Nat Indust Col Armed Forces, 93. *Mem:* Am Physics Soc. *Mailing Add:* 3212 Garfield St NW Washington DC 20008

HOWARD, ROBERT ERNEST, PHYSICAL CHEMISTRY, SCIENCE EDUCATION. *Current Pos:* assoc prof, 81-95, chmn, Chem Dept, 86-96, PROF, UNIV TULSA, 95- *Personal Data:* b Tulsa, Okla, Oct 29, 47; m 69, Marilyn Thomso; c 2. *Educ:* Cornell Col, BA, 69; Ind Univ, PhD(chem physics), 75. *Prof Exp:* Res assoc, IBM Res Labs, 75-76; fel chem physics, Univ Calif, Berkeley, 76-77; asst prof chem, Univ Tex, Permian Basin, 77-81. *Concurrent Pos:* grantee, NSF, 76-77 & 89-, Robert A Welch Found, 78-81, Res Corp, 88-90. *Mem:* Am Chem Soc; Am Phys Soc; Sigma Xi. *Res:* Theoretical chemical physics; ab initio molecular structure calculations; construction of potential energy surfaces; quasi-classical trajectory molecular dynamics; science education. *Mailing Add:* Chem Dept Univ Tulsa 600 S College Tulsa OK 74107. *Fax:* 918-631-3404; *E-Mail:* reh_chem@centum.utulsa.edu

HOWARD, ROBERT EUGENE, MEDICAL INFORMATION SYSTEMS, PATHOLOGY. *Current Pos:* ASSOC PROF PATH, SCH MED, UNIV NMEX, 72-; CONSULT, MED COMPUT MGT & COMPUT INFO SYSTS, 81- *Personal Data:* b St Louis, Mo, Mar 27, 37; m 66; c 2. *Educ:* Wash Univ, AB, 59, MD, 65, PhD(pharmacol), 68. *Prof Exp:* From intern to resident path, Barnes Hosp, Wash Univ, 65-67, asst, Sch Med, 65-67; instr, Med Ctr, Univ Colo, 67-68; from asst prof to assoc prof, Univ Tex Med Sch San Antonio, 68-72, dep chmn dept, 70-71; chief clin chem, Path Serv, Bernalillo County Med Ctr, 72-79; chief clin chem, Path Serv, Univ NMex Hosp, 79-80. *Concurrent Pos:* USPHS trainee exp path, 66-67; Nat Inst Gen Med Sci res & Univ Colo Med Ctr fluid res grants, 67-68; co-dir biochem path labs, Bexar County Hosp Dist, Tex, 68-72, assoc chief path serv, 70-71; res subcontractor, Southwest Res Inst-Brooks Sch Aerospace Med, 70-71. *Mem:* Am Soc Clin Pathologists; Sigma Xi. *Res:* Computer-assisted interpretation of clinical data; clinical pathology and chemistry; computer-assisted medical decision making; endocrinology; laboratory management; computer utilization in pathology. *Mailing Add:* 2400 Mission Ave Eugene OR 97402

HOWARD, ROBERT FRANKLIN, ASTRONOMY. *Current Pos:* dir, 84-88, ASTRONOMER, NAT SOLAR OBSERV, 88- *Personal Data:* b Delaware, Ohio, Dec 30, 32; m 58, Margaret T Farnon; c Thomas C, Alan R & Moira C. *Educ:* Ohio Wesleyan Univ, BA, 54; Princeton Univ, PhD(astron), 57. *Prof Exp:* Carnegie fel, Mt Wilson & Palomar Observs, 57-59; asst prof astron, Univ Mass, 59-61; mem staff, Mt Wilson & Las Campanas Observ, 61-84, assist dir, 81-84. *Concurrent Pos:* Ed, J Solar Physics, 87- *Mem:* Am Astron Soc; Int Astron Union. *Res:* Magnetic field of the sun; sunspots; solar rotation and velocity fields. *Mailing Add:* PO Box 26732 Tucson AZ 85726

HOWARD, ROBERT T(URNER), MATERIALS SCIENCE, ENGINEERING. *Current Pos:* RETIRED. *Personal Data:* b Frederick, Okla, Sept 24, 20; m 47; c 5. *Educ:* Mass Inst Technol, SB, 42, ScD(metall), 47. *Prof Exp:* Asst tool steels res, Mass Inst Technol, 43-46; mem staff, Los Alamos Sci Lab, Calif, 47-48; metallurgist & dir metall qual control lab, Black, Sivalls & Bryson, Inc, 48-52; sr staff engr & asst to dir eng, Bendix Aviation Corp, 52-56; assoc prof eng & chmn dept, Univ Kansas City, 56-60; prof, Univ Wichita, 60-65; vis prof metall & mat eng, Univ Kans, 65-66, prof, 66-68; adv metallurgist, IBM Corp, 68-74, sr engr, Gen Technol Div, 86-90. *Concurrent Pos:* Consult metallurgist, James W Weldon Lab, 52-60; NSF grant mat sci, Univ Wichita, 61-63; consult, IBM Corp, 65-68. *Mem:* Am Soc Eng Educ; Am Soc Metals; Am Welding Soc; Int Soc Hybrid Microelectronics; Inst Elec & Electronics Engrs; Mfg Technol Soc. *Res:* Diffusion in single and polycrystalline cobalt below 1000 degrees C; metallurgy of soldering; development and manufacture of hybrid microcircuits, reliability of solder joints in semiconductor packages; laser trimming of resistors; adhesive bonding; microcircuit welding; hybrid microelectronics; corrosion of microelectronic circuits, curing kinetics of encapsulants for semiconductor devices. *Mailing Add:* 2 Forest Rd Essex Junction VT 05452-3817

HOWARD, ROGER, THEORETICAL PHYSICS. *Current Pos:* From instr to asst prof, 59-69, ASSOC PROF PHYSICS, UNIV BC, 69- *Personal Data:* b Bristol, Eng, Sept 11, 35; Can citizen. *Educ:* Univ Nottingham, BSc, 56, PhD(theoret physics), 60. *Mem:* Can Asn Physicists; Am Asn Physics Teachers. *Res:* Lattice dynamics, thermal properties and structure of solidified inert gases. *Mailing Add:* Dept Physics Univ BC 2075 Wesbrook Pl Vancouver BC V6T 1W5 Can

HOWARD, RONALD A(RTHUR), ENGINEERING. *Current Pos:* PROF ENG-ECON SYSTS, STANFORD UNIV, 65- *Personal Data:* b New York, NY, Aug 27, 34; m 55; c 4. *Educ:* Mass Inst Technol, SB(elec eng) & SB(econ), 55, SMEE, 56, EE, 57, ScD(elec eng), 58. *Prof Exp:* From asst prof to assoc prof elec eng & indust mgt, Mass Inst Technol, 58-65. *Concurrent Pos:* Consult, Gen Elec Co, Stanford Res Inst & Xerox Corp. *Mem:* Soc Indust & Appl Math; Opers Res Soc Am; Inst Elec & Electronics Engrs; Inst Mgt Sci; Brit Opers Res Soc; Sigma Xi. *Res:* Decision analysis and probabilistic systems; operations research; systems engineering; economic systems. *Mailing Add:* Dept Eng Econ Terman Eng Ctr Stanford CA 94301

HOWARD, RONALD M, BACTERIOLOGY, IMMUNOLOGY. *Current Pos:* RETIRED. *Personal Data:* b Minneapolis, Minn, Aug 20, 20; m 43, Delle Doty; c 1. *Educ:* Macalester Col, BA, 42; Univ Minn, MS, 50. *Prof Exp:* USAF, 43-66, chief res & develop br, Fitzsimons Army Hosp, 52-54, asst chief biophys br, Aeromed Lab, Wright Air Develop Ctr, Ohio, 54, asst prof chem, USAF Acad, 54-59, chief opers div & dir life sci, Hqs, Air Res & Develop Command, 59-60, dir life sci div, Off Aerospace Res, 60-64, dir res prog, Washington, DC, 65-66; staff scientist, Human Res & Biotechnol Div, NASA Hq, 66-68; dir, Inst Biol Sci, SDak State Univ, 68-82. *Mem:* AAAS; Am Soc Microbiol; Sigma Xi. *Res:* Bacteriology and immunology of tuberculosis; manned space flight; science education in elementary grades. *Mailing Add:* 1808 Derdall Dr Brookings SD 57006

HOWARD, RUFUS OLIVER, MEDICINE, OPHTHALMOLOGY. *Current Pos:* res fel ophthal, 62-65, from asst prof to assoc prof, 66-76, CLIN PROF OPHTHAL, MED SCH, YALE UNIV, 76- *Personal Data:* b Knoxville, Tenn, June 30, 29; m 55, Martha G Lang; c Margaret M, James C, Amy R, Thomas A, Mary F, Martha A & Emily L. *Educ:* Col William & Mary, BS, 49; Mass Inst Technol, SB, 49, PhD(phys properties of polymers), 53; Med Col Va, MD, 61. *Prof Exp:* Res chemist, E I du Pont de Nemours & Co, Inc, 54-57. *Mem:* Am Ophthal Soc. *Res:* Metabolism of ocular tissues; ophthalmic genetics. *Mailing Add:* Grove Hill Clin PC One Lake St New Britain CT 06052. *Fax:* 860-826-4436

HOWARD, RUSSELL ALFRED, SOLAR PHYSICS. *Current Pos:* Nat Acad Sci-Nat Res Coun resident res assoc, 69-71, res physicist, 71-73, ASTROPHYSICIST, NAVAL RES LAB, 73- *Personal Data:* b Baltimore, Md, Aug 17, 41; m 66, Rosalie Nasuta; c Geoffrey & Matthew. *Educ:* Univ Md, BS, 64, PhD(chem physics), 69. *Mem:* Am Geophys Union; Am Astron Soc. *Res:* Structure and dynamics of solar corona; solar-terrestrial relationships; solar wind; atomic and molecular spectroscopy; upper atmospheric research. *Mailing Add:* 9936 Woodgrouse Ct Burke VA 22015. *E-Mail:* howard@nsd0.nrl.navy.mil

HOWARD, RUSSELL JOHN, molecular parasitology, biochemistry, for more information see previous edition

HOWARD, SETHANNE, TIDAL INTERACTIONS, SCIENCE TEACHING. *Current Pos:* CONSULT, NASA, 90-, US RES ASN DEP DIR, GODDARD SPACE FLIGHT CTR, GVSP, 93- *Personal Data:* b Coronado, Calif, Feb 2, 44. *Educ:* Univ Calif, Davis, BS, 65; Rensselaer

Polytech Inst, MS, 73; Ga State Univ, PhD, 89. *Prof Exp:* Astron asst, Lick Observ, 65-67; assoc res astron, Kitt Peak Nat Observ, 72-80; comput programmer analyst, Fleet Numerical Oceanog Ctr, Monterey, Calif, 80-84; adj fac, Ga State Univ, Atlanta, 84-89; fel, Los Alamos Nat Lab, 89-90. *Mem:* Am Astron Soc; AAAS; Math Asn Am; Astron Soc Pac. *Res:* Science and computer education; astrophysics; n-body simulations of tidally; interacting galaxies in three dimensions. *Mailing Add:* 8910 Good Harvest Ct Jessup MD 20794. *E-Mail:* sethanne.howard@hq.nasa.gov

HOWARD, STEPHEN ARTHUR, pharmaceutics, for more information see previous edition

HOWARD, SUSAN CAROL PEARCY, GLYCOPROTEIN STRUCTURE-FUNCTION RELATIONSHIPS, ENZYMOLOGY. *Current Pos:* RES SCIENTIST, G D SEARLE, 94- *Personal Data:* b Enid, Okla, Jan 7, 54; m, Jeffrey L; c Heather & Brandon. *Educ:* Okla State Univ, BS, 75; PhD(biochem), 80. *Prof Exp:* Fel, Johns Hopkins Univ Sch Med, 80-81; sr res biochem, Corp Res Lab, Monsanto Co, 86-90, res specialist, 90-93. *Mem:* Am Soc Cell Biol; Sigma Xi. *Res:* Development of antivirals targetting a critical protease; enzyme purification and development of highly specific protease inhibitors; twenty-two publications, two patents and nine technical reports; purification and characterization of adhesion molecules involved in inflammation; development of peptide-based inhibitors. *Mailing Add:* Monsanto Co 700 Chesterfield Village Pkwy St Louis MO 63198. *Fax:* 314-694-4575

HOWARD, THOMAS E(DWARD), MINING ENGINEERING, GEOLOGY. *Current Pos:* RETIRED. *Personal Data:* b Longmont, Colo, Feb 25, 19; m 41, Betty Johnson; c Michael S. *Educ:* Colo Sch Mines, EM, 41. *Honors & Awards:* D C Jacking Award, Soc Mining Engrs, 75. *Prof Exp:* Asst engr, Anaconda Copper Co, 41-44; mining engr, St Louis Smelting & Ref Div, Nat Lead Co, 46-48; asst engr, Union Pac RR, 48-49; construct engr, US Army Corps Engrs, 49-51; mining engr, Spokane Field Off, US Bur Mines, 51-54, asst chief mining res & mineral develop, 54-59, br chief ceramic & fertilizer mat, 59-60, dir mining res, 60-70; dir res, Joy Mfg Co, 70-74, dir tech develop, Hard Rock Mining Div, 74-81; consult, 81-82. *Res:* Applied scientific and engineering research, principally in earth sciences as related to earth excavation technology. *Mailing Add:* 4730 Nelson St Wheat Ridge CO 80033

HOWARD, THOMAS HYLAND, VIROLOGY. *Current Pos:* PVT VET CONSULT, 91- *Personal Data:* b Princeton, Ind, May 16, 45; m 76; c 1. *Educ:* Purdue Univ, DVM, 69; Colo State Univ, PhD(physiol), 82. *Prof Exp:* From asst vet to vet, Am Breeders Serv, 75-91. *Mem:* Am Vet Med Asn; Am Asn Bovine Practr; Soc Theriogenology. *Res:* Virus diseases of cattle, particularly those affecting reproduction or transmitted via the reproductive process; artificial insemination of cattle. *Mailing Add:* N2194 Meilke Rd Poynette WI 53955

HOWARD, VOLNEY WARD, JR, WILDLIFE RESEARCH. *Current Pos:* PROF WILDLIFE SCI, NMEX STATE UNIV, 69- *Personal Data:* b Catarina, Tex, Apr 9, 41; m 67; c 2. *Educ:* Tex A&M Univ, BS, 64; NMex State Univ, MS, 66; Univ Idaho, PhD(wildlife sci), 69. *Mem:* Wildlife Soc; Soc Range Mgt; Sigma Xi. *Res:* Big game; research with muledeer, whitetailed deer, pronghorned antelope, desert bighorn sheep, coyotes, Iranian and Siberian ibex and Persian gazelle, bobcats, elk (wapiti), feral horses. *Mailing Add:* Dept Fishery & Wildlife Sci NMex State Univ Las Cruces NM 88003. *Fax:* 505-646-1281

HOWARD, W TERRY, ANIMAL NUTRITION, DAIRY MANAGEMENT. *Current Pos:* from asst prof to prof, 71-96, EMER PROF DAIRY SCI, UNIV WIS-MADISON, 96- *Personal Data:* b Pueblo, Colo, Apr 14, 36; m 60, Karen Boning; c Steven, Matthew & Rachel. *Educ:* Univ Nebr, BS, 58, MS, 64; Purdue Univ, PhD(dairy mgt), 67. *Honors & Awards:* Delaval Exten Award, Am Dairy Sci Asn. *Prof Exp:* Instr dairy sci, Univ Nebr, 59-64. *Concurrent Pos:* Nutritionist, Prof Prod & Serv, Inc, Pisirie du Sec, Wis. *Mem:* Am Dairy Sci Asn. *Res:* Total mixed rations and computer ration formulation for dairy cattle and forage quality evaluation and use. *Mailing Add:* Dept Dairy Sci 266 An Sci Bldg Univ Wis Madison WI 53706. *Fax:* 608-643-8798; *E-Mail:* howard@calshp.cals.wisc.edu

HOWARD, WALTER B(URKE), CHEMICAL ENGINEERING. *Current Pos:* RETIRED. *Personal Data:* b Corpus Christi, Tex, Jan 22, 16; m 42; c 2. *Educ:* Univ Tex, BA, 37, BS, 38, MS, 40, PhD(chem eng), 43. *Prof Exp:* From asst to sr chem engr, Bur Indust Chem, Tex, 39-52; from sr chem engr to scientist res dept, Plastics Div, Monsanto Co, 52-64, process safety mgr cent eng dept, 65-81. *Mem:* Am Chem Soc; Am Inst Chem Engrs; Combustion Inst. *Res:* Process hazard prevention; chemical technology; explosion phenomena as related to safety protection of plant equipment; acetylene manufacture from hydrocarbons; high temperature technology and fundamentals as applied to chemicals production; resonating electric circuits for large power supply; electric discharges in gases; engineering analysis. *Mailing Add:* 1415 Bopp Rd Des Peres MO 63131-4135

HOWARD, WALTER EGNER, ECOLOGY, ANIMAL CONTROL. *Current Pos:* instr zool & jr zoologist, San Joaquin Exp Range, Col Agr, Univ Calif, 47-49, lectr & asst zool, 49-54, from assoc specialist to specialist, 54-60, assoc vert ecologist, 60-64, prof wildlife biol & vert ecologist, Dept Animal Physiol, 64-73, prof, 74-87, EMER PROF, DEPT WILDLIFE & FISH BIOL, AGR EXP STA, UNIV CALIF, DAVIS, 87- *Personal Data:* b Woodland, Calif, Apr 9, 17; m 40, Elizabeth A Kendall; c Thomas K, Kathryn S & J Casey. *Educ:* Univ Calif, AB, 39; Univ Mich, MS, 41, PhD(vert ecol), 47. *Prof Exp:* Asst lab vert biol, Univ Mich, 40-42. *Concurrent Pos:* Fulbright res fel, NZ & Australia, 57; grant-in-aid, Animal Ecol Div, NZ Dept Sci Indust Res & Travel Grant, NZ Forest Serv, 62-63; UN consult, Food & Agr Orgn, Mex, 69, Arg, 69 & 72, SKorea, 74 & 77, Peninsular Malaysia, 75; WHO consult, Lebanon, 69, Qatar, 69 & 71, Bahrain, 71, Egypt, 74 & Barbados, 79 & 80; consult & lectr, Nat Sci Coun, Taiwan, 80, 81 & 85, Chinese Acad Med, China & Mil Acad Med, Inst Zool Acad, Sinica, 81, 84, 85 & 88, Kuwait, 82, 83 & 85, Qatar, 84 & 85, India, 82, Finland, 82, Norway, 82, Denmark, 82, Peru, 83, Japan, 84 & Commonwealth N Marianas, 85, Brazil, 87, Italy, 87, NZ, 88, Eng, Scotland, 89, 93, NZ, 95, Kenya, 96. *Mem:* Am Soc Mammal; Wildlife Soc; Ecol Soc Am; Animal Behav Soc; Brit Ecol Soc; Soc Range Mgt. *Res:* Population dynamics and control; rodents, coyotes and other wild vertebrates, ecology and behavior; defending society's right to use animals responsibly; lecturing and writing; animal welfare. *Mailing Add:* Dept Wildlife, Fish & Conserv Biol Univ Calif Davis CA 95616. *Fax:* 530-752-4154

HOWARD, WEBSTER EUGENE, semiconductor devices, for more information see previous edition

HOWARD, WILLIAM EAGER, III, ASTRONOMY, TECHNICAL MANAGEMENT. *Current Pos:* DIR, ASTRON & SPACE PHYSICS PROG, UNIV SPACE RES ASN, 95- *Personal Data:* b Washington, DC, Aug 25, 32; m 57, Miriam Sitler; c William IV & Jennifer. *Educ:* Rensselaer Polytech Inst, BS, 54; Harvard Univ, AM, 56, PhD(astron), 58. *Prof Exp:* Astronr, Harvard Radio Astron Sta, Tex, 58; from instr to assoc prof astron, Univ Mich, 59-64, res assoc radio astron, 59-61; assoc scientist, Nat Radio Astron Observ, Charlottesville, Va, 64-67, asst to dir, 64-74, scientist, 67-77, asst dir, Green Bank Opers, 74-77; dir div Astron Sci, NSF, 77-82; staff mem, Fed Govt, 82-84; tech dir, Naval Space Command, 85-91; dir space & strategic technol, US Army Secretariat, 91-93, dir advan concepts & space, 93-95. *Concurrent Pos:* Mem comn 40 radio astron, Int Astron Union, 61-; mem comn J, Int Sci Radio Union, 69-; chmn, Subcomt Radio Astron & Comt Radio Frequencies, Nat Acad Sci, 71-76; mem, US Study Group 2, Int Radio Consult Comt, 71-79, mem, US deleg, Geneva, 72-78. *Mem:* AAAS; Am Astron Soc (treas, 75-77); Sigma Xi; US Naval Inst; Int Astron Union; Astron Soc Pac. *Res:* Galactic and extra-galactic studies; optical and radio astronomy in the continuum and in the 21-centimeter line of neutral hydrogen; science administration. *Mailing Add:* 1653 Quail Hollow Ct McLean VA 22101-3234. *Fax:* 202-479-2613; *E-Mail:* whoward@usra.edu

HOWARD, WILLIAM GATES, JR, ELECTRICAL ENGINEERING, ELECTRONICS. *Current Pos:* INDEPENDENT CONSULT, 90- *Personal Data:* b Boston, Mass, Nov 6, 41; m 83, Kathleen. *Educ:* Cornell Univ, BEE, 64, MSc, 65; Univ Calif, PhD(elec eng), 67. *Prof Exp:* Asst prof elec eng, Univ Calif, Berkeley, 67-70; mgr, Advan Linear Integrated Circuits Develop, Motorola, 70-74, group opers mgr, Linear Integrated Circuits, 74-76, vpres & dir strategic opers, 76-79, vpres & dir technol, Planning Semiconductor Sect, 79-83, sr vpres & dir corp res develop, 83-90. *Concurrent Pos:* Mem, Defense Sci Bd. *Mem:* Nat Acad Eng; fel Inst Elec & Electronics Engrs; AAAS. *Res:* Electronic function realization in integrated circuit form. *Mailing Add:* 10642 E San Salvador Scottsdale AZ 85258

HOWARD, WILLIAM JACK, ENGINEERING. *Current Pos:* CONSULT, 82- *Personal Data:* b Kimball, Nebr, Aug 25, 22; m 46; c 2. *Educ:* NMex State Univ, BS, 46. *Hon Degrees:* Dr, NMex State Univ, 82. *Honors & Awards:* Distinguished Pub Serv Medal, US Dept Defense. *Prof Exp:* Asst to secy defense atomic energy, Dept Defense, Sandia Nat Labs, 63-66, vpres, 66-73, exec vpres, 73-82. *Concurrent Pos:* Deleg, Strategic Arms Limitation Talks, 76. *Mem:* Nat Acad Eng. *Res:* Design and development of nuclear ordnance. *Mailing Add:* 920 McDuffie Circle NE Albuquerque NM 87110

HOWARD, WILLIAM WEAVER, FIXED PROSTHODONTICS, OCCLUSION. *Current Pos:* prof & chmn fixed prosthodontics, 73-94, EMER PROF DENT, SCH DENT, ORE HEALTH SCI UNIV, 94- *Personal Data:* b Ontario, Ore, Apr 25, 22; m 60, Emma J Pearson; c John P, Jane (Martin), Alexandra M (Woodworth) & David M. *Educ:* Ore State Univ, BS, 47; Univ Ore, DMD, 50. *Honors & Awards:* Geis Ed Award, Geis Found, 82, 89, 90 & 92; Golden Pen Award, Int Col Dentists, 81 & 92, Golden Scroll Award, 82, Golden Pencil Award, 86; Horace Hayden Award, Conn State Dent Asn, 89; Barish Award, Acad Gen Dent, 93. *Prof Exp:* Pvt pract dent, 50-73. *Concurrent Pos:* Ed, Gen Dent, Acad Gen Dent, 74- *Mem:* Am Dent Asn; Am Acad Restorative Dent; Acad Gen Dent; fel Am Col Dentists; Am Asn Dent Ed; Int Col Dentists. *Res:* Clinical dentistry; oral myofunction. *Mailing Add:* 460 NW Greenleaf Rd Portland OR 97229. *Fax:* 503-494-4332

HOWARD, WILMONT FREDERICK, JR, TECHNICAL SERVICE, PROCESS DEVELOPMENT. *Current Pos:* SR SCIENTIST, COVALENT ASSOC, INC, 93- *Personal Data:* b Brattleboro, Vt, Oct 27, 46; m 73, Mary F Jukes; c Sara F & Zachary N. *Educ:* Univ Vt, BS, 69; St Michaels Col, MS, 72; Univ Va, MS, 74; Univ RI, PhD(inorg chem), 80. *Prof Exp:* Asst dir, Ctr Catalytic Sci & Technol, Univ Del, 80-84; res mgr, EMCA, subsid Rohm & Haas, 84-87; proj leader, Cermalloy Div, Heraeus Inc, 87-89; mgr chem res, Cyprus Foote Mineral Co, 90-93. *Mem:* Am Chem Soc; Electrochem Soc. *Res:* Production methods development of inorganic lithium chemicals; intercalation materials for rechargeable batteries. *Mailing Add:* Covalent Assoc Inc 10 State St Woburn MA 01801. *Fax:* 781-938-1364; *E-Mail:* howard@usa1.com

HOWARD-LOCK, HELEN ELAINE, MOLECULAR SPECTROSCOPY. *Current Pos:* asst prof eng physics, 70-78, PROF SCIENTIST, INST FOR MAT RES, MCMASTER UNIV, 81-, ASSOC PROF PATH, 87- *Personal Data:* b Hamilton, Ont, Jan 5, 38; m 60, Colin J; c Nicola E (Simmons) & Philippa E. *Educ:* McMaster Univ, BSc, 59, PhD(chem physics), 68. *Honors & Awards:* R Samuel McLaughlin Career Scientist Geront. *Prof Exp:* Nat Res Coun Can fel light scattering, Univ Toronto, 68-70. *Concurrent Pos:* Nat coordr remote sensing oil spills, Environ Can, 73-74; trustee, Halton Pub Sch, 73-81; vpres res, Castle Cement Co Ltd, Burlington, Ont, 77-82; treas, Howard Concrete & Mat Ltd, Burlington, Ont, 80-82; pres, Howard-Lock Assocs, Inc, 88. *Mem:* Fel Chem Inst Can; Can Asn Physicists. *Res:* Molecular spectra and structures; properties of cement and other potential building materials; platinum anti-tumor agents; gold, D-penicillamine and non-steroidal anti-inflammatory anti-arthritic agents; structures of materials; medical research; chiral pharmacology. *Mailing Add:* Dept Chem McMaster Univ Hamilton ON L8S 4M1 Can. *Fax:* 905-522-2509

HOWARD-PEEBLES, PATRICIA NELL, HUMAN GENETICS, CLINICAL CYTOGENETICS. *Current Pos:* CLIN CYTOGENETICIST & DIR, POSTNATAL LAB, GENETICS & IVF INST, FAIRFAX, VA, 87-; PROF, DEPT HUMAN GENETICS, MED COL VA, RICHMOND, 87- *Personal Data:* b Lawton, Okla, Nov 24, 41; m 75, Thomas M. *Educ:* Univ Cent Okla, BSEd, 63; Univ Tex, Austin, PhD(genetics), 69; Am Bd Med Genetics, dipl, 82. *Prof Exp:* Biochem technician, Biol Div, Oak Ridge Nat Lab, 64-66; instr res pediat, Univ Okla Health Sci Ctr, 71-72, cytotechnol, 71-72; from asst prof to assoc prof microbiol, Inst Genetics, Univ Southern Miss, & dir, Cytogenetics Lab, 73-80; assoc prof, Dept Pub Health & mem staff, Lab Med Genetics, Univ Ala, Birmingham, 80-81; assoc prof & dir, Cytogenetics Lab, Dept Path, Univ Tex Health Sci Ctr, Dallas, 81-85, prof & dir, 85-87. *Concurrent Pos:* Am Cancer Soc fel human genetics, Med Sch, Univ Mich, 69-70 & human genetics & develop, Col Physicians & Surgeons, Columbia Univ, 70-71; genetic consult, Ellisville State Sch, Miss, 73-80; attend staff, Dept Path, Parkland Mem Hosp, Dallas Co Hosp Dist, 81-87; referee cytogeneticist, CAP Cytogenetics Survey, 88-92; mem, Int Standing Comt Human Cytogenetic Nomenclature, 91- *Mem:* Sigma Xi; Am Soc Human Genetics; Genetics Soc Am; AAAS; fel Am Col Med Genetics. *Res:* Human cytogenetics, especially delineation of chromosomal disorders and mental retardation; X-linked mental retardation with and without fragile X, chromosomal fragile sites. *Mailing Add:* Genetics & IVF Inst 3020 Javier Rd Fairfax VA 22031-4627. *Fax:* 703-698-3988

HOWARDS, STUART S, PHYSIOLOGY, UROLOGY. *Current Pos:* PROF PHYSIOL, UNIV VA, 71- *Personal Data:* b Milwaukee, Wis, Mar 29, 37; m 66, Cartez Randolph; c Penelope (Page) & Hugh. *Educ:* Yale Univ, BA, 59; Columbia Univ, MD, 63. *Honors & Awards:* Gold Cystocope Award, Am Urol Asn; Scott Award, Am Urol Asn, 90. *Prof Exp:* Staff assoc renal physiol, NIH, 65-68; resident virol, Peter Bent Brigham Hosp, Boston, 68-71. *Concurrent Pos:* Nat Inst Childhood Develop fel, 76-81; assoc ed, J Investigative Urol, 77-85, ed, 85-; co-ed, Year Book Urology, 79-86; chmn exam comt, AVA/ABU, 87-92; mem, Am Bd Urol, 87-93, pres, 93, exec secy, 97; bd dirs, Am Soc Reproduction Med, 93-96, treas, 96- *Mem:* Soc Genitourinary Surgeons; Am Col Surgeons; Soc Study Reproduction; Am Soc Andrology; Am Soc Nephrology; Clin Soc Genitourinary Surgeons (secy/treas, 92-97). *Res:* Reproductive biology; physiology of testis and epididymis. *Mailing Add:* Univ Va Box 422 Charlottesville VA 22908-0422. *Fax:* 804-982-3652; *E-Mail:* sch4e@virginia.edu

HOWARTH, BIRKETT, JR, REPRODUCTIVE PHYSIOLOGY. *Current Pos:* from asst prof to assoc prof, 68-86, PROF POULTRY SCI, UNIV GA, 86- *Personal Data:* b Sellersville, Pa, Dec 1, 36; m 61, Sandra Shaw; c Scott, Mark, Buck & John. *Educ:* Del Valley Col, BS, 58; SDak State Univ, MS, 60; NC State Univ, PhD(reproductive physiol), 65. *Prof Exp:* Staff fel reproductive physiol, Intramural Res Prog, Develop Biol Br, Nat Inst Child Health & Human Develop, 65-68. *Mem:* Soc Study Reprod; Am Poultry Sci Asn; World's Poultry Sci Asn. *Res:* Embryo transfer and in vitro culture techniques to investigate early development of mammalian embryos; effects of environment on mammalian spermatozoa and embryos; avian sperm physiology and sperm-egg interaction. *Mailing Add:* Dept Poultry Sci L-P Univ Ga Athens GA 30602. *Fax:* 706-542-1827; *E-Mail:* bhowarth@uga.cc.uga.edu

HOWARTH, FRANCIS GARD, BIOSPELEOLOGY, CONSERVATION BIOLOGY. *Current Pos:* assoc entom, 70-74, ENTOMOLOGIST, B P BISHOP MUS, HONOLULU, 74- *Personal Data:* b Worcester, Mass, Oct 23, 40; m 65, Cadwallader; c Francis, Dianella & Vanessa. *Educ:* Univ Mass, Amherst, BS, 62; Cornell Univ, MS, 66; Univ Hawaii, Honolulu, PhD(entom), 74. *Prof Exp:* Vol agr exten, Int Vol Serv, Laos, 66-68; NIH trainee, B P Bishop Mus, 68-69; teaching asst entom, Univ Hawaii, Honolulu, 69-70. *Concurrent Pos:* Assoc ed, Int J Entom, 74-85; life sci ed, Nat Speleol Soc Bull, 75-85; prin investr, NSF grants, 76-77, 79-83 & 86-89; grad affil fac, dept entom, Univ Hawaii, 78-; chmn, Cave Species Specialist Group, Species Survival Comm, Int Union Conserv Nature & Natural Resources, 79-90; mem, Sci Adv Comt, Cave Res Found, 83-; ecologist & co-dir, Explorer's Club Chillagoe Caves Exped, 85; mem bd, Am Cave Conserv Asn, 84- *Mem:* Fel Nat Speleol Soc; Cave Res Found; Int Union Conserv Nature & Natural Resources; Am Cave Conserv Asn; Entom Soc Am; Explorer's Club; AAAS. *Res:* Ecology and evolution of cave animals; tropical island ecology; biogeography; conservation; impact of alien species; biosystematics of aythropods, especially biting midges, Diptera, Ceratopogonidae. *Mailing Add:* BP Bishop Mus PO Box 19000 Honolulu HI 96817-0916. *E-Mail:* fhowarth@bishop.bishop.hawaii.org

HOWARTH, ROBERT W, BIOGEOCHEMISTRY, ECOSYSTEM BIOLOGY. *Current Pos:* assoc prof ecol, 85-90, dir, Ecosysts Res Ctr, 87-88, PROF ECOL, CORNELL UNIV, 91- *Personal Data:* b Boston, Mass, Feb 11, 52; m 87. *Educ:* Amherst Col, BA, 74; Mass Inst Technol & Woods Hole Oceanog Inst, PhD(oceanog), 79. *Prof Exp:* Fel, Marine Biol Lab, 79-80, asst scientist, 80-84, assoc scientist, 84-85. *Concurrent Pos:* Adj prof, Univ RI, 82-; ed-in-chief, Biogeochem, 83-; consult, Nat Acad Sci Comt on Petrol in Marine Environ, 81. Comt on Health & Ecol, 83; vis scientist, Inst Ecosyst Studies; NY Bot Garden, 85; mem, US Nat Comt SCOPE, 88-90; mem, Comt on the Coastal Oceans, Nat Acad Sci, 89, Alternatives for Wastewater Disposal in Coastal Areas, 90; consult, state of Alaska on Exxon Valdez oil spill. *Mem:* Am Soc Limnol & Oceanog; Ecol Soc Am; Estuarine Res Fedn; AAAS; Sigma Xi. *Res:* Sulfur and molybdenum biogeochemistry; interactions of element cycles in aquatic ecosystems; environmental management and the effects of pollution on aquatic ecosystems and commercial fisheries; wetland ecosystems; microbial production and activity. *Mailing Add:* Ecol Cornell Univ E145 Corson Bldg Ithaca NY 14853-0001

HOWATSON, JOHN, X-RAY CRYSTALLOGRAPHY, SOLID STATE CHEMISTRY. *Current Pos:* from asst prof to assoc prof, 56-66, PROF CHEM, UNIV WYO, 66- *Personal Data:* b Calgary, Alta, June 6, 20; nat US; m 45; c 2. *Educ:* Univ Wash, BSc, 43; Univ Wis, PhD(chem), 50. *Prof Exp:* Jr chemist, Corning Glass Works, 43-44; asst, SAM Labs, Columbia Univ, 44-45; jr physicist, Tenn-Eastman Co, 45-46; asst chem, Univ Wis, 46-47 & Wis Alumni Res Found, 47-49; res asst, Corning Glass Works, 49-55; instr chem, Colo Sch Mines, 55-56. *Mem:* Am Chem Soc; Sigma Xi. *Res:* Structure of small molecules; chemical reactions of oil shale minerals during thermal and hydrothermal processing; aqueous chemistry of aluminum. *Mailing Add:* 64 Riverbend Dr Brownsville TX 78520-9522

HOWATT, WILLIAM FREDERICK, PEDIATRICS, PHYSIOLOGY. *Current Pos:* From instr to assoc prof, 59-75, PROF PEDIAT, UNIV MICH, ANN ARBOR, 75- *Personal Data:* b Brewer, Maine, Aug 22, 29; m 61; c 4. *Educ:* Univ Maine, BS, 51; Boston Univ, MD, 55. *Concurrent Pos:* NIH fel, 63-64. *Mem:* Soc Pediat Res. *Res:* Pulmonary function in children; respiratory control of the neonate; pulmonary function changes in infants with congenital heart diesase undergoing surgical repair. *Mailing Add:* Dept Pediat D/209-0718 Univ Mich Ann Arbor MI 48109

HOWD, FRANK HAWVER, ECONOMIC GEOLOGY, ENVIRONMENTAL GEOLOGY. *Current Pos:* RETIRED. *Personal Data:* b Delmar, NY, Dec 2, 24; m 51, Barbara M Campbell; c Peter, Thomas & Christopher. *Educ:* Univ Rochester, AB, 51, MS, 53; Wash State Univ, PhD(geol), 56. *Prof Exp:* Asst geol, Univ Rochester, 52-53; geologist, Div Mines & Geol, State Wash, 53; asst, Wash State Univ, 53-56; geologist, Bear Creek Mining Co, 56-59; from asst prof to assoc prof, Univ Maine, Orono, 59-90. *Concurrent Pos:* Consult, Kennecott Copper Corp, 60-70, US Soil Conserv Serv, 74-75 & US Geol Surv, 79-83. *Mem:* Fel Geol Soc Am; Geochem Soc; Soc Econ Geologists. *Res:* Relationship of trace element dispersion and hydrothermal alteration to metallic mineral deposits; experimental replacement of rocks by sulfide minerals; geochemistry of stream sediments. *Mailing Add:* 14 Spencer St Orono ME 04473

HOWD, ROBERT A, TOXICOLOGY, REGULATORY AFFAIRS & RISK ASSESSMENT. *Current Pos:* toxicologist regulation, Toxic Substances Control Prog, 88-91, TOXICOLOGIST REGULATION, OFF ENVIRON HEALTH HAZARD ASSESSMENT, CALIF ENVIRON PROTECTION AGENCY, 91- *Personal Data:* b McMinnville, Ore, Nov 19, 44; m 66, Sherry Rock; c Jennifer. *Educ:* Linfield Col, BA, 66; Univ Wash, PhD(pharmacol), 73. *Prof Exp:* Biochem pharmacologist res, SRI Int, 75-88. *Concurrent Pos:* Fel, Lab Neuroendocrine Regulation, Mass Inst Technol, 73-75. *Mem:* Soc Toxicol; Am Soc Pharmacol & Exp Therapeut; Soc Risk Analysts; AAAS. *Res:* Neurotoxicology; drug abuse; drug metabolism; risk assessment for solvents and pesticides; evaluation of dermal absorption of chemicals; exposure assessment. *Mailing Add:* 2151 Berkeley Way Annex 11 PETS Berkeley CA 94704. *E-Mail:* berkeley.bhowd@hw1.cahwnet.gov

HOWDEN, DAVID GORDON, METALLURGY, WELDING & FABRICATION. *Current Pos:* ASSOC PROF WELDING ENG, OHIO STATE UNIV, 77- *Personal Data:* b Scarborough, Eng, Aug 22, 37; m 62; c 1. *Educ:* Univ Eng, BSc, 59, PhD(metall), 62. *Honors & Awards:* Oxygen of Brazil Prize, Asn Brazil de Metais, 75; James F Lincoln Award, Am Welding Soc, 82. *Prof Exp:* Asst prof & researcher metall, Cent Tech Aeronaut, Sao Jose dos Campos, Brazil, 63-65; sr scientist welding metall, Dept Energy Mines & Resources, Can, 65-67; assoc mgr welding & fabric, Battelle Columbus Labs, 67-77. *Concurrent Pos:* US Deleg, Int Inst Welding, 77-81. *Mem:* Am Welding Soc; Am Soc Metals; Welding Res Coun. *Res:* Welding metallurgy; gas metal reactions in arc welding; health and safety in welding; welding process development; component failure analysis. *Mailing Add:* 3285 Wilson Rd Sunbury OH 43074

HOWDEN, HENRY FULLER, ENTOMOLOGY. *Current Pos:* RETIRED. *Personal Data:* b Baltimore, Md, Aug 19, 25; m 49; c 3. *Educ:* Univ Md, BS, 46, MS, 49; NC State Univ, PhD(entom), 53. *Honors & Awards:* Cert Merit, Nat Mus Can, 88. *Prof Exp:* Asst prof entom, Univ Tenn, 53-57; res scientist, Entom Res Inst, Can Dept Agr, Ont, 57-68; prof syst zool, Carleton Univ, 68-94. *Concurrent Pos:* Res partic, Oak Ridge Inst Nuclear Studies, 55; consult, US AEC, 56-58; Alexander Agassiz vis lectr, Mus Comp Zool, Harvard Univ, 67; dir, Entomol Res Group, Carleton Univ, 75- *Mem:* Entom Soc Am; Asn Trop Biol; Soc Syst Zool; fel Entom Soc Can. *Res:* Taxonomy and biology of North American and world Scarabaeidae. *Mailing Add:* Dept Biol 1125 Cornel By Ottawa ON K1S 5B6 Can

HOWE, CALDERON, MICROBIOLOGY. *Current Pos:* RETIRED. *Personal Data:* b Washington, DC, Mar 8, 16; m 44; c 4. *Educ:* Yale Univ, AB, 38; Harvard Univ, MD, 42. *Prof Exp:* Chief res physician, Peter Bent Brigham Hosp, Boston, 47-48; assoc microbiol, Columbia Univ, 52-55, from asst prof to prof, Col Physicians & Surgeons, 55-71; asst physician, Presby Hosp, 52-57, asst attend physician, 57-64, assoc microbiologist, 64-71, attend microbiologist, 71; prof microbiol & chmn dept, Med Ctr, La State Univ, New Orleans, 72-82. *Concurrent Pos:* Assoc ed, J Virol, 74-, ed bd, Proc Soc Exp Biol & Med, 75. *Mem:* Am Soc Clin Invest; Am Soc Microbiol; Am Soc Cell Biol; Soc Exp Biol & Med; Am Asn Immunologists (secy-treas, 58-61). *Res:* Infectious diseases; immunology and immunochemistry; blood groups; virology; virus-erythrocyte, virus-cell interactions; immunochemical and immunoelectron microscopic investigations of membranes. *Mailing Add:* 90 Annandale Rd Newport RI 02840-6925

HOWE, CHARLES W, ENVIRONMENTAL & NATURAL RESOURCE ECONOMICS. *Current Pos:* chmn, Dept Econ, 72-76, PROF ECON, UNIV COLO, 70-, DIR, ENVIRON & BEHAVIOR PROG, INST BEHAV SCI, 86- *Personal Data:* b Dayton, Ohio, Mar 28, 31; m 52, JoAnne Blanke; c John, Karen, Marilyn & Kathy. *Educ:* Rice Univ, BA, 52; Stanford Univ, MA, 55, PhD(econ), 59. *Honors & Awards:* Icko Iben Award, Am Water Resources Asn, 94. *Prof Exp:* Instr econ, Stanford Univ, 56-57; asst prof & assoc prof econ, Purdue Univ, 58-64; Rockefeller Found field staff & vis prof econ, Univ Col Nairobi, Kenya, 64-65; dir, Water Resources Prog, Resources Future Inc, 65-70. *Concurrent Pos:* Co-ed, Water Resource Res, Am Geophys Union, 67-75; consult, Nat Water Planning Proj Eval, Govt Mex & World Bank, 71 & 73, UN Develop Prog & Govt Kenya, 71-72, Orgn Econ Coop & Develop, Paris, 77-81, Middle Rio Grande Water Conserv Dist, Albuquerque, NMex, 88 & 92, Attorney Gen Tex, Tex vs NMex, 89-90; Water Prog fel, Int Inst Appl Systs Analysts, Lexembura, Austria, 76; Hill vis prof, Dept Agr & Appl Econ, Univ Minn, 77-78; mem, Climate Bd, Nat Res Coun-Nat Acad Sci, 77-81, chmn, Panel Climate Impact Res, 80-81, mem, Subcomt Econ & Policy, Water Sci Texhnol Bd, 86-90, Comt Int Soil & Water Res & Develop, 90-91; Rockefeller Found field staff & vis prof econ, Gadjah Mada Univ, Indonesia, 81-83; consult, Gambia River Basin Comn, Dakar, Senegal, 85-87, Senegal River Basin Comn, 86-87; Fulbright scholar, Wageningen Agr Univ, Neth, 91; mem, Nat Panel Eval 54 State Water Resources Res Inst Prog, US Geol Surv, 93-94. *Mem:* Fel Am Geophys Union; Am Econ Asn; Am Agr Econ Asn; Asn Environ & Resource Economists (pres, 88-90); Europ Asn Environ & Resource Economists; Am Water Resources Asn. *Res:* Water institution reform; operational meaning of sustainability; contributed numerous publications to professional journals. *Mailing Add:* Univ Colo Campus Box 468 Boulder CO 80309. *Fax:* 303-492-1231; *E-Mail:* charles.howe@colorado.edu

HOWE, CHIN CHEN, MOLECULAR BIOLOGY, DEVELOPMENTAL BIOLOGY. *Current Pos:* Fel virol, 73-76, STAFF DEVELOP BIOL, WISTAR INST ANAT & BIOL, 76- *Personal Data:* b Taipei, Taiwan, June 22, 33; US citizen; m 60; c 2. *Educ:* Univ Taiwan, BS, 56; Univ Pa, MS, 60, PhD(molecular biol), 72. *Concurrent Pos:* NIH fel, 75-76. *Mem:* Soc Develop Biol. *Res:* Gene expression during development and differentiation in mouse system; biochemical aspects of gene action and regulation during development. *Mailing Add:* Wistar Inst Anat & Biol 36th at Spruce Philadelphia PA 19104

HOWE, DAVID ALLAN, HIGH RESOLUTION SPECTROSCOPY. *Current Pos:* PHYSICIST ATOMIC BEAM SPECTROS, DEPT COM, NAT INST STAND & TECHNOL, 69- *Personal Data:* b Clark AFB, Philippines, Apr 6, 49; div; c 2. *Educ:* Univ Colo, BA, 70. *Honors & Awards:* Gold Medal, Dept Com. *Mem:* Am Inst Physics. *Res:* Development of very high frequency-stability using atomic and molecular spectroscopy techniques such as cesium beam and hydrogen maser devices; amplifier design; estimation of time and frequency variance. *Mailing Add:* Dept Com Nat Inst Stand & Technol Boulder CO 80303

HOWE, DENNIS GEORGE, OPTICS, OPTICAL DAM STORAGE. *Current Pos:* RES PROF, OPTICAL SCI CTR, UNIV ARIZ, 92- *Personal Data:* b Reading, Pa, Apr 8, 43; m 69, Carol Grzymkoxskf. *Educ:* Cornell Univ, AB, 65; Univ Rochester, MS, 68, PhD(optics), 76. *Prof Exp:* Photog systs analyst & sr engr, Res & Eng Dept, Kodak Apparatus Div, Eastman Kodak Co Res Labs, 65-73, proj engr video imaging systs, Consumers Prod Dept, 73-75, sr physicist, 75-78, res assoc optical, Laser & Video Systs, 78-87, sr res assoc, Eastman Kodak Co, 87-92. *Mem:* Optical Soc Am; Soc Info Display. *Res:* High density optical data storage and retrieval systems; electro-optical coherent and non-coherent light scanners for high resolution graphic arts, facsimile and video storage and display; quasi-phase-matched wavegrids second harmonic generation. *Mailing Add:* 6141 N Paseo Valdeas Tucson AZ 85750

HOWE, EUGENE EVERETT, PHARMACEUTICAL CHEMISTRY. *Current Pos:* RETIRED. *Personal Data:* b Keats, Kans, June 6, 12; m 38, 96, Alice Lupenski; c Jean & Daniel. *Educ:* Kans State Col, BS, 36, MS, 37; Univ Ill, PhD(biochem), 40. *Prof Exp:* Asst chem, Kans State Col, 37; asst, Univ Ill, 38-40; res chemist, Merck & Co, Inc, 41-47, head process develop natural prod, 48-56, dir nutrit, Inst Therapeut Res, 57-67, dir exp biol, Calgon Consumers Products Res Lab, 67-74; chem res consult, 75-80. *Mem:* AAAS; Am Chem Soc; Am Soc Biol Chemists; Am Inst Nutrit; NY Acad Sci. *Res:* Supplementation of cereals; bile acid and cholesterol metabolism; dental therapeutics. *Mailing Add:* 538 Elizabeth Ave Somerset NJ 08873-9764

HOWE, GEOFFREY RICHARD, cancer epidemiology & biostatistics, for more information see previous edition

HOWE, GEORGE FRANKLIN, PLANT PHYSIOLOGY. *Current Pos:* prof, 68-96, chmn, Div Natural Sci, 68-91, EMER PROF BIOL, THE MASTER'S COL, 97- *Personal Data:* b Buffalo, NY, Nov 15, 31; m 55; c 4. *Educ:* Wheaton Col, Ill, BS, 53; Ohio State Univ, MS, 56, PhD(plant physiol), 59. *Prof Exp:* Asst gen bot, Ohio State Univ, 55, asst plant physiol, 55-57; instr biol & bot, Westmont Col, 59-60, from asst prof to assoc prof biol, 60-68. *Concurrent Pos:* Partic, NSF Acad Yr Inst Radiation Biol, Cornell Univ, 65-66; ed, Creation Res Soc Quart, 69-74; dir, Grand Canyon Exp Sta, Creation Res Soc, 83-89, managing ed, 93- *Mem:* Creation Res Soc (pres, 77-82). *Res:* Relationship of the degree of stomatal opening to the time course of photosynthetic induction periods and photosynthetic rhythms; creation model of origins; plant physiology; botanical courses; radiation biology; post-fire regrowth of chaparral shrubs; pollination biology; micropaleontology; plant taxonomy. *Mailing Add:* Div Natural Sci The Master's Col Santa Clarita CA 91322

HOWE, GEORGE R, REPRODUCTIVE PHYSIOLOGY. *Current Pos:* asst prof physiol & biophys, 68-73, ASSOC PROF ANIMAL SCI, UNIV MASS, AMHERST, 73- *Personal Data:* b Brattleboro, Vt, Apr 14, 33; m 55; c 4. *Educ:* Univ Vt, BS; Pa State Univ, MS, 59; Univ Mass, PhD(physiol), 61. *Prof Exp:* Asst prof physiol & biophys, Col Med, Univ Vt, 61-68. *Concurrent Pos:* Grants, Pop Coun, 63 & 67, NIH, 63-65 & 69-76, Whitehall Found, 69-72, US Naval Res, 67-72 & Pop Coun, 72-74. *Mem:* Am Fertil Soc. *Res:* Equine reproduction; anabolic steroids and reproduction. *Mailing Add:* Animal Sci Univ Mass Amherst Paige Amherst MA 01003-0002

HOWE, HENRY BRANCH, JR, MICROBIAL GENETICS. *Current Pos:* from asst prof to assoc prof, Univ Ga, 59-70, prof, 70-90, assoc dean, Grad Sch, 81-90, EMER PROF MICROBIOL, UNIV GA, 90-, EMER ASSOC DEAN, GRAD SCH, 90- *Personal Data:* b Atlanta, Ga, Aug 5, 24; m 51, Margaret A Haden; c Stephen, Barbara (McArthur) & Alan. *Educ:* Emory Univ, AB, 48, MA, 50; Univ Wis, PhD(genetics), 55. *Honors & Awards:* Res Prize, Asn Southeastern Biologists, 67 & 71. *Prof Exp:* Asst prof biol, Union Col, Ky, 54-57 & Wake Forest Univ, 57-59. *Concurrent Pos:* NSF sci fac fel, Yale Univ, 59. *Mem:* Genetics Soc Am; Am Soc Microbiol; Mycol Soc Am; Am Ornith Union; Sigma Xi. *Res:* Genetics of neurospora. *Mailing Add:* 130 Bishop Dr Athens GA 30606

HOWE, HENRY FRANKLIN, ECOLOGY. *Current Pos:* PROF BIOL, UNIV ILL, CHICAGO, 88- *Personal Data:* b Gardner, Mass, Dec 24, 46. *Educ:* Earlham Col, AB, 68; Univ Mich, AM, PhD(zool), 77. *Prof Exp:* Wildlife biologist, US Army, 69-71; instr biol, Phillips Acad, 71-72; asst prof zool, Univ Iowa, 78-82, assoc prof biol, 82-88. *Concurrent Pos:* Fel Smithsonian Trop Res Inst, 77-78. *Mem:* Soc Study Evolution; Brit Ecol Soc; Ecol Soc Am; Am Soc Naturalists; Asn Trop Biol; AAAS. *Res:* Evolutionary ecology; sex ratio, sexual selection, sexual dimorphism, and reproductive biology of birds; frugivory and the ecology of tropical seed-dispersal systems; reproductive ecology of plants; desert ecology; prairie ecology. *Mailing Add:* Biol Sci Univ Ill 845 W Taylor St Chicago IL 60607-7060

HOWE, HERBERT JAMES, STRATIGRAPHY. *Current Pos:* assoc prof geosci, 67-88, EMER PROF, PURDUE UNIV, 88- *Personal Data:* b Baton Rouge, La, Jan 31, 31; m 56; c 2. *Educ:* La State Univ, BS, 52; Columbia Univ, MA, 53, PhD(geol), 59. *Prof Exp:* Explor geologist, Humble Oil & Refining Co, 53-56; from asst prof to assoc prof geol, La State Univ, New Orleans, 58-67. *Mem:* Paleont Soc; Am Asn Petrol Geologists. *Res:* Stratigraphy; invertebrate paleontology. *Mailing Add:* 2611 SE Blairmont Dr Vancouver WA 98683

HOWE, JOHN A, VERTEBRATE PALEONTOLOGY. *Current Pos:* from instr to asst prof, 65-70, ASSOC PROF GEOL, BOWLING GREEN STATE UNIV, 70- *Personal Data:* b Uniopolis, Ohio, May 22, 27; m 53; c 1. *Educ:* Bowling Green State Univ, BS, 53; Univ Nebr, MS, 56, PhD(geol), 61. *Prof Exp:* Instr & cur, Univ Educ Serv, Univ Nebr State Mus, 58-65. *Concurrent Pos:* Bowling Green State Univ res grant, 66- *Mem:* Paleont Soc; Am Quaternary Asn; Soc Vert Paleont; Sigma Xi. *Res:* Pleistocene vertebrates. *Mailing Add:* Dept Geol Bowling Green State Univ 1001 E Wooster St Bowling Green OH 43403-0001

HOWE, JOHN P(ERRY), NUCLEAR ENGINEERING, MATERIAL SCIENCE ENGINEERING. *Current Pos:* RETIRED. *Personal Data:* b Groton, NY, June 24, 10; m 41; c 4. *Educ:* Hobart Col, BS, 33; Brown Univ, PhD(phys chem), 36. *Prof Exp:* Instr chem, Ohio State Univ, 36-38; asst prof, Brown Univ, 38-42; res assoc, Metall Lab, Univ Chicago, 42-44, assoc dir, 45; mgr metall, Knolls Atomic Power Lab, Gen Elec Co, 45-52, mgr res energy conversion & storage, Gen Elec Res Lab, 52-53; sect chief reactor mat, Atomics Int, 53-57, dir res dept, 57-61; Ford prof eng, Cornell Univ, 61-67, dir dept eng physics & mat sci, 62-65 & dept eng physics, 65; res staff mem, Sci & Technol Div, Inst Defense Anal, 67-68; asst lab dir, Gen Atomic Co, 68-69, assoc lab dir, 69-71, tech dir mat advan energy systs, 71-75. *Concurrent Pos:* Mem comt sr reviewers, Div Classification, AEC, 52-67, mem adv comt reactor safeguards, 61-63, mem bd atomic safety & licensing, 65-68; adv AEC deleg & vchmn session radiation effects, Geneva Conf Peaceful Uses Atomic Energy, Switz, 55, deleg, 58; mem rev comt fundamental res in mat, Nat Acad Sci-Dept Defense, 57-58; consult, Inst Defense Anal, 67-68 & Off Tech Assessment, US Congress, 75; mem sci adv group, Air Force Off Aerospace Res, 63-71; adj prof nuclear eng, Univ Calif, San Diego, 73-82. *Mem:* Fel AAAS; Am Chem Soc; fel Am Phys Soc; fel Am Nuclear Soc; fel Am Soc Metals; Sigma Xi. *Res:* Nuclear science and engineering; nuclear materials irradiation effects; energy policy. *Mailing Add:* 5725 Waverly Ave La Jolla CA 92037

HOWE, JULIETTE COUPAIN, NUTRITION. *Current Pos:* Res biologist, Agr Res Serv, Protein Nutrit Lab, 77-79, res nutritionist, Sci & Educ Admin, High Nutrit, 79-80, RES CHEMIST, AGR RES SERV, BELTSVILLE HUMAN NUTRIT RES CTR, ENERGY & PROTEIN NUTRIT LAB, 81- *Personal Data:* b Woonsocket, RI, Aug 16, 44; m 79; c 2. *Educ:* Univ RI, BS, 65; Univ Md, MS, 78, PhD(nutrit sci), 87. *Mem:* Am Inst Nutrit; Am Chem Soc. *Res:* Effects of varying nutrient intake on energy metabolism in normal and hyperinsulinemic individuals; physiological bases of variation among individuals in resting energy expenditure; role of hormones in energy metabolism. *Mailing Add:* USDA ARS BHNRC EPNL Bldg 308 Rm 201 BARC East Beltsville MD 20705. *Fax:* 301-504-9098

HOWE, KENNETH JESSE, PLANT PHYSIOLOGY. *Current Pos:* RETIRED. *Personal Data:* b Rochester, NY, Nov 13, 23; m 50, Pauline Patterson; c Spencer, Holly, Wendy & Rhonda. *Educ:* Univ Rochester, BA, 50, MS, 51; Cornell Univ, PhD(plant physiol), 56. *Prof Exp:* Asst gen bot & cytol, Univ Rochester, 48-51; asst gen bot, Cornell Univ, 52-54, instr, 54-56; asst prof plant physiol & gen bot, Univ Fla, 56-57; from asst prof to prof gen bot & plant physiol, Bridgewater State Col, 57-88, chmn, Dept Biol Sci, 65-78, dean & head, Div Sci & Math, 78-81, inst coordr, Col Accreditation, dir coop progs & coordr aviation sci prog, 82-87. *Mem:* Am Soc Plant Physiol; Bot Soc Am; Sigma Xi. *Res:* Structure and function of plants, especially as affected by environment and growth regulators; production of essential oils in plants. *Mailing Add:* 47 Vernon St Bridgewater MA 02324

HOWE, KING LAU, PHYSICAL ORGANIC CHEMISTRY, POLYMER CHEMISTRY. *Current Pos:* From res chemist to sr res chemist, E I du Pont de Nemours & Co, Inc, 57-68, supvr, 68, sr res chemist, 69-70, res assoc, 70-83, SR RES ASSOC, E I DU PONT DE NEMOURS & CO, INC, 83- *Personal Data:* b Shanghai, China, Sept 4, 28; US citizen; m 60; c 2. *Educ:* Dartmouth Col, AB, 52; Univ Wis, PhD(chem), 57. *Mem:* Am Chem Soc. *Res:* Solvolysis reaction mechanism; stereochemistry of radical addition reaction; mechanism of base promoted dehydro-halogenation reaction; vinyl polymers; process and product development; ethylene copolymers and polymer blends; polyester engineering resins. *Mailing Add:* 414 Brentwood Dr Carrcroft Crest Wilmington DE 19803-4308

HOWE, MARSHALL ATHERTON, ORNITHOLOGY. *Current Pos:* Zoologist, US Fish & Wildlife Serv, 72-75, chief, Ornith, Bird Sect, Nat Fish & Wildlife Lab, 75-78, res zoologist, sect migratory nongame birds, 78-81, sect leader, 82-85, team leader, Br Migratory Bird Res, Patuxent Wildlife Res Ctr, 85-90, ASST CHIEF, OFF MIGRATORY BIRD MGT, US FISH & WILDLIFE SERV, 90- *Personal Data:* b Mt Kisco, NY, Dec 2, 44; m 87. *Educ:* Alfred Univ, BA, 66; Univ Minn, PhD(zool), 72. *Concurrent Pos:* Gen secy, Wader Study Group; treas, Pan-Am sect, Int Coun Bird Preserv. *Mem:* Am Ornith Union; Cooper Ornith Soc; Int Coun Bird Preserv; Int Asn Fish & Wildlife Agencies. *Res:* Behavior and ecology of birds, particularly social behavior, social organization and habitat utilization in shorebirds. *Mailing Add:* 12004 Amblewood Dr Laurel MD 20708

HOWE, MARTHA MORGAN, MOLECULAR GENETICS, VIROLOGY. *Current Pos:* VAN VLEET PROF VIROL, COL MED, UNIV TENN, MEMPHIS, 86- *Personal Data:* b New York, NY, Sept 29, 45; m 94, Terrance C Cooper. *Educ:* Bryn Mawr Col, AB, 66; Mass Inst Technol, PhD(microbiol), 72. *Honors & Awards:* Award, Eli Lilly & Co, 85, Am Acad Microbiol, 91. *Prof Exp:* Europ Molecular Biol Orgn fel, Cent Nuclear Acad, Nat Res Coun Italy, 72; fel molecular biol, Cold Spring Harbor Lab, Cold Spring Harbor, NY, 72-74; fel Am Cancer Soc, 74; from asst prof to prof, Univ Wis-Madison, 75-84, Vilas prof bact, Col Agr & Life Sci, 84-86. *Concurrent Pos:* NIH res career develop award, 78-83; assoc ed, Virol, 83-92; mem, rev panel, NSF, Howard Hughes Med Inst & Am Cancer Soc; counr, Am Soc Microbiol, 89-91; dir, Genetics Soc Am, 89-91. *Mem:* Am Soc Microbiol; Am Soc Biochem & Molecular Biol; Genetics Soc Am. *Res:* Analyses of the molecular mechanisms of genetic recombination and gene regulation, the study of these processes using bacteriophage Mu. *Mailing Add:* Dept Microbiol & Immunol 858 Madison Ave Memphis TN 38163. *Fax:* 901-448-8462; *E-Mail:* mhowe@utmem1.utmem.edu

HOWE, NORMAN ELTON, JR, PHYSICAL ORGANIC CHEMISTRY. *Current Pos:* plant supt vitamins, 77-85, prod mgr, 85-93, PLANT MGR VITAMIN PLANT, BASF CORP, 93- *Personal Data:* b San Antonio, Tex, Jan 16, 46; m 75; c Eleanor & Clarissa. *Educ:* Univ Calif, Berkeley, BA, 68; Univ Calif, Los Angeles, PhD(org chem), 73. *Prof Exp:* Fel bio-org chem, Univ Chicago, 73-75, res chemist, 75-77. *Mem:* Am Chem Soc. *Res:* High molecular weight block polymers. *Mailing Add:* 1529 Boxford Trenton MI 48183-1808. *Fax:* 313-246-6449

HOWE, RICHARD HILDRETH, DURABILITY OF AGGREGATES & CONCRETE, PAVEMENT SKID RESISTANCE. *Current Pos:* RETIRED. *Personal Data:* b Providence, RI, Dec 25, 27; m 61; c 1. *Educ:* Mass Inst Technol, SB, 51. *Prof Exp:* Petrol geologist, Calif Co, 53-54; grad student, Pa State Univ, 54-60, instr, Geol Dept, 60-61; asst dist soils engr, Pa Dept Trans, 61-66, soils res engr, 66-69, concrete & aggregate testing engr, 69-87, staff soils engr, 87-91. *Mem:* Fel Geol Soc Am; Am Soc Testing & Mat; Int Asn Eng Geologists; Am Inst Prof Geologists; Asn Eng Geologists; Am Concrete Inst. *Res:* Factors affecting the level & seasonal variability of pavement skid resistance, especially those related to the properties of aggregates; development of procedures for evaluating the durability of aggregates & concrete. *Mailing Add:* 2911 Chestnut St Camp Hill PA 17011

HOWE, RICHARD SAMUEL, WATER RESOURCE POLICY PLANNING MANAGEMENT, RECRUITING & RETENTING YOUNG WOMEN & MEN TO CAREERS IN ENGINEERING. *Current Pos:* PROF, ENG & ENVIRON SCI, UNIV TEX, SAN ANTONIO, 76- *Personal Data:* b Centralia, Ill, Aug 30, 36; m 68; c 2. *Educ:* Univ Ky, BS, 59; Mass Inst Technol, SM, 61; Univ Wis-Madison, MS, 68, MS, 69, PhD(resource mgt), 71. *Prof Exp:* Sanit engr, USPHS, 61-63; instr eng, Southern Ill Univ, 63-67; dir planning & res, City Chicago Dept Environ Control, 70-72; assoc prof environ sci, Ind Univ, 72-76. *Concurrent Pos:* Prin, Design San Antonio, 88-; chmn bd, Hemisphere Inst Pub Serv, 89-; co-prin investr, Tex Water Develop Bd Proj, Univ Tex, San Antonio, 90-; prin investr, Comprehensive Regional Ctr Minorities, 90-; dir, Univ Tex, San Antonio, Alliance for Educ, 90-; dipl, Am Acad Environ Engrs. *Mem:* Am Acad Environ Engrs; Am Soc Civil Engrs; Nat Soc Prof Engrs; Am Inst Cert Planners; Am Soc Pub Admin; Water Pollution Control Fedn. *Res:* Decision support systems for resource management-water and solid waste; resource diplomacy; management of technology and technology transfer. *Mailing Add:* 3214 Woodcrest Dr San Antonio TX 78209-3138

HOWE, ROBERT C, REMOTE SENSING, MICROPALEONTOLOGY. *Current Pos:* from asst prof to assoc prof, 68-77, PROF GEOL, IND STATE UNIV, TERRE HAUTE, 77- *Personal Data:* b Baton Rouge, La, June 13, 39; m 88. *Educ:* La State Univ, BS, 61; Univ Wis, MS, 62, PhD(geol), 65. *Prof Exp:* Jr geologist, Humble Oil & Refining Co, 61; geologist, Atlantic Refining Co, 65; instr geol, Beloit Col, 67-68. *Mem:* AAAS; Am Asn Petrol Geol; Geol Soc Am; Sigma Xi; Am Soc Photogram & Remote Sensing. *Res:* Remote sensing, utilization of landsat, TIMS and other types of remote sensing data for geologic applications; nannofossils; ostracodes. *Mailing Add:* Dept Geog & Geol Ind State Univ Terre Haute IN 47809-0001

HOWE, ROBERT GEORGE, ENTOMOLOGY. *Current Pos:* RETIRED. *Personal Data:* b Sault Ste Marie, Ont, Apr 27, 26; m 52, Barbara Louise Griffin; c Robert Gary, William Quentin & David Owen. *Educ:* Ont Agr Col, BSA, 51; Cornell Univ, PhD(entom), 55. *Prof Exp:* Asst forest entom, Can Dept Agr, 48-49, asst med entom, 50; asst veg insects, NY Exp Sta, Geneva, 51-55; field specialist agr chem develop, Dow Chem Co, 55-67, mgr bioprod res & develop, Dow Chem Europe, Switz, 67-70, tech prod specialist, 70-78, prod develop mgr, 78-89. *Mem:* Entom Soc Am. *Res:* Insecticides; space, grain and soil fumigants; urban entomology row crops. *Mailing Add:* 714 Hollybrook Dr Midland MI 48642

HOWE, ROBERT JOHNSTON, BEHAVIORAL BIOLOGY, VERTEBRATE BIOLOGY. *Current Pos:* asst prof, 75-81, ASST PROF BIOL, SUFFOLK UNIV, 81- *Personal Data:* b Providence, RI, May 2, 36. *Educ:* Univ RI, BS, 67, MS, 71; Northern Ariz Univ, PhD(animal behav, zool), 77. *Concurrent Pos:* Instr biol, Northeastern Univ, 76-77. *Mem:* Animal Behav Soc; Am Soc Mammalogists. *Res:* Social behavior of small mammals with an emphasis on scent marking and olfactory communication as it relates to reproduction. *Mailing Add:* 253 Bellman Ave Warwick RI 02889-2834

HOWE, ROBERT KENNETH, PESTICIDE METABOLISM & ENVIRONMENTAL FATE. *Current Pos:* RETIRED. *Personal Data:* b Kewanee, Ill, June 27, 39; m 64, Ann Keith; c Stephanie. *Educ:* Univ Ill, BS, 61; Univ Calif, Los Angeles, PhD(org chem), 65. *Prof Exp:* Monsanto sr fel, New Prod Div, Ag Group, Monsanto Co, 65-93; pres, Howe Xenbiotic Technol, 93. *Mem:* Am Chem Soc; Int Soc Study Xenobiotics. *Res:* Metabolism studies of pesticides. *Mailing Add:* 9276 Maler Rd San Diego CA 92129-3814. *Fax:* 619-538-0531

HOWE, ROBERT T(HEODORE), civil engineering, for more information see previous edition

HOWE, ROGER, LIE THEORY, INVARIANT THEORY. *Current Pos:* PROF MATH, YALE UNIV, 74- *Personal Data:* b Chicago, Ill, May 23, 45; m 67; c 2. *Educ:* Harvard Univ, BA, 66; Univ Calif, Berkeley, PhD(math), 69. *Honors & Awards:* Lester R Ford Award, Math Asn Am. *Prof Exp:* Asst prof math, State Univ NY Stony Brook, 69-74. *Concurrent Pos:* Mem, Inst Advan Study, 71-72; vis prof, Inst Theoret Math Res, Bonn, Ger, 73-74, Oxford Univ, Eng, 78, Tel Aviv Univ, Israel, 80, Univ Calif, San Diego, 81 & Rutgers Univ, 89-90; Guggenheim fel, 84-85; assoc ed, 85-87, ed, Res Announcements, Bull of AMS, 88-90; fel, Inst Advan Studies, Hebrew Univ, Jerusalem, 88. *Mem:* Nat Acad Sci; Math Asn Am; Am Math Soc. *Res:* Harmonic analysis and group representation theory, particularly of algebraic groups, and with emphasis on the theory of automorphic forms. *Mailing Add:* Dept Math Yale Univ Box 208283 Yale Sta New Haven CT 06520-8283. *Fax:* 203-432-7316; *E-Mail:* howe@math.yale.edu

HOWE, VIRGIL K, FOREST PATHOLOGY. *Current Pos:* DEAN, COL HEALTH & LIFE SCI, FT HAYS STATE UNIV, 88- *Personal Data:* b King City, Mo, Apr 22, 31; m 56, Virginia M Birbeck; c Christine & Daniel. *Educ:* Northwest Mo State Col, BS, 56; Univ NMex, MS, 61; Iowa State Univ, PhD(forest path), 64. *Prof Exp:* High sch instr, Mo, 56-57; asst prof biol, Northwestern State Col, La, 64-68; from asst prof to prof biol, Western Ill Univ, 68-88, chmn dept, 78-80, assoc provost, 80-82 & 83-86, actg provost, 82-83 & 86-88. *Concurrent Pos:* Res assoc, Morton Arboretum, 70-82. *Mem:* Am Phytopath Soc; Mycol Soc Am; Int Soc Arboricult; Sigma Xi. *Res:* Forest mycology; mycorrhizae of forest and shade trees; urban tree problems. *Mailing Add:* Off Dean Col Health & Life Sci Ft Hays State Univ Hays KS 67601. *Fax:* 785-628-4290; *E-Mail:* devh@fhsuvm.fhso.edu

HOWE, WALLACE BRADY, geology; deceased, see previous edition for last biography

HOWE, WILLIAM EDWARD, MAMMALIAN CELL CULTURE, IMMUNOFLUORESCENCE. *Current Pos:* CELL BIOLOGIST, ALCON LABS, 76- *Personal Data:* b Jakarta, Indonesia, June 16, 48. *Educ:* Univ Ariz, PhD(molecular biol), 76. *Mailing Add:* Code R2-41 Alcon Labs 6201 S Freeway Ft Worth TX 76134

HOWE, WILLIAM JEFFREY, ORGANIC CHEMISTRY, COMPUTER SCIENCES. *Current Pos:* res scientist, 74-80, SR RES SCIENTIST, UPJOHN CO, 80- *Personal Data:* b Ottawa, Ont, July 15, 46; m 69; c 1. *Educ:* Carleton Univ, BSc, 68; Harvard Univ, PhD(chem), 72. *Prof Exp:* Fel org chem, Harvard Univ, 72-74. *Mem:* Am Chem Soc. *Res:* Computer handling of chemical structure information; computer graphics; drug design research. *Mailing Add:* Upjohn Co Unit 7247-267-110K Kalamazoo MI 49001-0199

HOWELL, ALVIN H(AROLD), ELECTRICAL ENGINEERING, ELECTRONICS. *Current Pos:* asst prof elec eng, Tufts Univ, 40-41, assoc prof, 41-43, chmn dept, 41-70, prof & dir res, Balloon Instrumentation Lab, 43-78, EMER PROF ELEC ENG & EMER DIR RES, TUFTS UNIV, 78- *Personal Data:* b Sedgwick, Kans, Feb 5, 08; m 34; c 4. *Educ:* Univ Kans, BS, 29; Mich Col Mining & Technol, MS, 34; Mass Inst Technol, ScD, 38. *Prof Exp:* Test engr, Gen Elec Co, 29-31; instr elec eng, Mich Col Mining & Technol, 31-34; res asst, Mass Inst Technol, 37-39, res assoc, 39-40. *Concurrent Pos:* Prof, Radar Sch, Mass Inst Technol, 42-43; dir, Doble Eng Co, 60-, vpres, 61-63, chmn exec comt, 69-, chmn bd dirs, 79-; mem & chmn panel sci use of balloons, Nat Ctr Atmospheric Res, Univ Corp Atmospheric Res, 61-63; mem, Nat Res Coun. *Mem:* Am Soc Eng Educ; Am Phys Soc; Inst Elec & Electronics Engrs; Am Asn Univ Professors. *Res:* Instrumentation in the upper air research program for the Air Forces; microwave measurements; gas discharges; dieelectrics; electro-mechanical instrumentation; instrumentation for large plastic balloon systems; development of balloon-borne telescope for tracking planets and stars. *Mailing Add:* Dept Elec Eng Tufts Univ Boston MA 02155

HOWELL, BARBARA FENNEMA, PHYSICAL CHEMISTRY & POLYMER SCIENCE, EPOXIES & COATINGS. *Current Pos:* RETIRED. *Personal Data:* b Chicago, Ill, Dec 18, 24; m 46; c Susan B, Gary M & Howard O. *Educ:* Univ Minn, BA, 46; Kansas State Univ, MS, 49; Univ Mo, Columbia, PhD(phys chem), 64. *Prof Exp:* Instr chem, Kans State Univ, 46-49 & Univ Tex, Arlington, 57-61; asst prof, Kans State Teachers Col, 64-69; res assoc, Space Sci Res Ctr, Univ Mo, Rolla, 69-71; res chemist, Inorg Glass Sect, Nat Inst Stand & Technol, 71-72, Org Analysis Res Div, 72-81, res chemist polymer sci & stand, 81-87; mat engr, Polymer Composites & Resins Br & Paints & Processes Br, Carderock Div, Naval Surface Warfare Ctr, Annapolis Detachment, 87-96. *Mem:* AAAS; Sigma Xi; Am Chem Soc. *Res:* Isotope exchange reactions; polymer morphol; electron microscopy; conducting polymers; radiation curing of resins. *Mailing Add:* 6694 Flamingo Rd Melbourne Village FL 32904

HOWELL, BARBARA JANE, PHYSIOLOGY. *Current Pos:* from instr to assoc prof, 59-75, PROF PHYSIOL, STATE UNIV NY BUFFALO, 75- *Personal Data:* b Waynesfield, Ohio, May 19, 27. *Educ:* Kent State Univ, BS, 50; Univ Ill, MS, 54, PhD(physiol), 57. *Prof Exp:* Asst prof physiol, Mont State Univ, 57-58. *Mem:* Am Physiol Soc; Am Soc Zool. *Res:* Respiratory research; comparative physiology. *Mailing Add:* Dept Physiol State Univ NY Sch Med & Dent Buffalo NY 14214

HOWELL, BARTON JOHN, OPTICS. *Current Pos:* RETIRED. *Personal Data:* b Salt Lake City, Utah, June 5, 17; wid; c Barton Jr, Michael, Louise, Frances, Thomas & Holly. *Educ:* Univ Utah, AB, 40, PhD(physics), 54; Univ Mich, MS, 44. *Honors & Awards:* Second Prize, Int Photog in Sci Exhib, AAAS, 48. *Prof Exp:* Dir, USAF Photog Sch, Utah, 43; asst contract, Off Sci Res & Develop, 45-46; instr AV educ & chg photog dept, Ind Univ, 46; instr physics, Univ Utah, 46-51; secy-treas, Universal Microfilming Corp, 51-55, res physicist, Explosives Res Dept, 55-56; prin engr, Sperry Utah Eng Lab, 56-57, eng sect head, 57-61; eng dept head, Sperry Gyroscope Co, 61-65; sect supvr, Sperry Support Facility, NASA, 65-71; optical physicist, Goddard Space Flight Ctr, NASA, 71-84, sect head optical design, 84-86. *Concurrent Pos:* Chmn patents panel, Appl Optics, 78- *Mem:* Optical Soc Am; Soc Photog Scientists & Engrs. *Res:* Infrared systems; optical analog computers; microfilming techniques; optical design; laser holography. *Mailing Add:* 287 Sixth Ave Salt Lake City UT 84103. *E-Mail:* bhowell@slkc.uswest.net

HOWELL, BENJAMIN F, JR, SEISMOLOGY. *Current Pos:* head, Dept Geophys & Geochem, Pa State Univ, 49-63, asst dean, Grad Sch, 68-70, assoc dean, 70-82, prof, 49-85, EMER PROF GEOPHYS, PA STATE UNIV, UNIVERSITY PARK, 85- *Personal Data:* b Princeton, NJ, June 12, 17; wid, Constance M Benson; c Barbara C (Raphael), Catherine A (deceased), Bonnie A (Garside) & James B. *Educ:* Princeton Univ, AB, 39; Calif Inst Technol, MSc, 42, PhD(geophys), 49. *Prof Exp:* Res engr, Div War Res, Univ Calif, 42-44 & United Geophys Co, 45-49. *Concurrent Pos:* Chief seismologist consult, Vibratech Eng Co, Hazleton, Pa, 52-69; mem exec comt, Div Earth Sci, Nat Res Coun, 65-67. *Mem:* Geol Soc Am; Soc Explor Geophys; Seismol Soc Am (vpres, 60-63, pres, 63-64); Am Geophys Union (secy, 56-64). *Res:* Seismology; tectonics; geophysical surveying. *Mailing Add:* Pa State Univ 406 Deike Bldg University Park PA 16802

HOWELL, BOB A, REACTION MECHANISM, POLYMER DEGRADATION & STABILIZATION. *Current Pos:* from asst prof to assoc prof, 76-88, PROF ORG/POLYMER CHEM, CENT MICH UNIV, 88- *Personal Data:* b Jefferson, NC, Jan 14, 42; m 65; c 1. *Educ:* Berea Col, BA, 64; Ohio Univ, PhD(org chem), 71. *Prof Exp:* Assoc fel, Ohio Univ, 69-70, instr org chem, 70-71; assoc fel, Iowa State Univ, 71-74; asst prof, Univ Louisville, 74-76. *Concurrent Pos:* Res chemist, Tenn Corp, 63, E I Du Pont de Nemours & Co, 64; indust fel, Dow Chem Co, 85, consult, 85-, vis scientist, 89. *Mem:* Am Chem Soc; Royal Soc Chem; AAAS; Sigma Xi. *Res:* Organic and polymer chemistry; carbocation rearrangements; acid-catalyzed aldehyde and oxirane rearrangements; polymer-supported organoplatinum antitumor agents; polymer degradation; polymer synthesis and characterization; chromium carbonyl compounds; hydrogenolysis. *Mailing Add:* Dept Chem Cent Mich Univ Mt Pleasant MI 48858

HOWELL, CHARLES FREDERICK, MEDICINAL CHEMISTRY. *Current Pos:* res chemist, 59-68, SR RES CHEMIST, LEDERLE LABS DIV, AM CYANAMID CO, 68- *Personal Data:* b Beardstown, Ill, July 14, 32; m 54; c 2. *Educ:* Univ Ill, BS, 54; Mass Inst Technol, PhD(org chem), 58. *Prof Exp:* Fulbright fel, Australian Nat Univ, Canberra, 58-59. *Mem:* Am Chem Soc; NY Acad Sci. *Res:* Nitrogenous heterocycles; psychotropic agents; peptides; metabolism of drugs; renin inhibitors. *Mailing Add:* 28 Drake Lane Upper Saddle River NJ 07458-1699

HOWELL, CHARLES MAITLAND, DERMATOLOGY, ALLERGY. *Current Pos:* PVT PRACT, 83- *Personal Data:* b Thomasville, NC, Apr 14, 14; m 49; c 2. *Educ:* Wake Forest Univ, BS, 35; Univ Pa, MD, 37; Am Bd Dermat, dipl, 54. *Prof Exp:* Intern med, Charity Hosp, New Orleans, 37-38; resident, Burlington County Hosp, NJ, 38-39; physician, Lawrenceville Sch, 39-42; asst resident path, NC Baptist Hosp, Winston-Salem, 47-48; asst resident & resident dermat, Presby Hosp, NY, 48-50; resident allergy, Roosevelt Hosp, NY, 50-51; prof dermat & allergy & assoc path, Bowman Gray Sch Med, Wake Forest Univ, 51-83. *Mem:* Fel Am Acad Dermat; fel Am Acad Allergy; fel NY Acad Sci; Int Soc Trop Dermat. *Res:* Improved methods for identification and treatment for cutaneous allergies; topical and intralesional use of corticosteroids; topical and systematic control of acne. *Mailing Add:* 340 Pershing Ave Winston Salem NC 27103-2513

HOWELL, DANIEL BUNCE, INORGANIC CHEMISTRY. *Current Pos:* asst prof, 65-67, assoc prof phys chem, 67-79, PROF CHEM, NEBR WESLEYAN UNIV, 79-, CHAIR, CHEM DEPT, 94- *Personal Data:* b Mitchell, SDak, Aug 23, 37; m 62, Mary Davis; c Sarah & Catherine. *Educ:* Yankton Col, BA, 59; Univ Nebr, MS, 62, PhD(phys chem), 65. *Prof Exp:* Great Lakes Col Asn teaching intern chem, Col Wooster, 64-65. *Mem:* AAAS; Am Chem Soc; Sigma Xi. *Res:* Molecular spectra and molecular structure; inorganic coordination chemistry; nuclear magnetic resonance spectroscopy. *Mailing Add:* Dept Chem Nebr Wesleyan Univ 50th St Paul Lincoln NE 68504. *E-Mail:* dbh@nebrwesleyan.edu

HOWELL, DAVID MCBRIER, VIROLOGY. *Current Pos:* assoc viral oncol, Spec Animal Leukemia Ecol Segment, NIH, 71-72, staff scientist viral oncol, Off Prog Resources & Logistics, 72-77, spec asst to assoc dir viral oncol, 77-78, asst to dir div cancer cause & prev, 78-83, SPEC ASST TO DIR, DIV CANCER ETIOLOGY, NAT CANCER INST, NIH, 84- *Personal Data:* b Erie, Pa, July 30, 33. *Educ:* Princeton Univ, AB, 55; Pa State Univ, MS, 63, PhD(microbiol), 66. *Prof Exp:* Res virologist, Virus & Rickettsia Div, US Army Biol Labs, Ft Detrick, 66-71. *Mem:* Am Soc Microbiol; AAAS; Tissue Cult Asn; Sigma Xi. *Res:* Viral oncology; arthropod-borne viruses. *Mailing Add:* 1001 Carroll Pkwy Apt 205 Frederick MD 21701-4047

HOWELL, DAVID MOORE, ORGANIC CHEMISTRY, INORGANIC CHEMISTRY. *Current Pos:* from instr to assoc prof, 51-90, EMER PROF CHEM, NORTHEASTERN UNIV, 90- *Personal Data:* b San Diego, Calif, July 7, 25; m 49, Valeska Haydon; c Stephen B & Elisabeth K (Chapman). *Educ:* Univ Calif, BS, 45; Univ Mich, MS, 47; PhD(chem), 52. *Prof Exp:* Asst, Univ Calif, 44-45; instr chem, Univ Pa, 49-51. *Concurrent Pos:* Res dir, Cherquist Consult Labs, 90- *Mem:* Am Chem Soc; The Royal Chem Soc; Sigma Xi. *Res:* Schmidt reaction; metal chelates; organic hydroxylamine derivatives; polymethine derivatives; nickel triolates. *Mailing Add:* 110 Blake St Needham MA 02192-2205. *E-Mail:* rhhwyel@aol.com

HOWELL, DAVID SANDERS, RHEUMATOLOGY, CARTILAGE. *Current Pos:* asst prof, 55-69, PROF MED, SCH MED, UNIV MIAMI, 69-; MED INVEST, VET ADMIN MED CTR, 69- *Personal Data:* b Montclair, NJ, Oct 4, 23; m 48, Margaret Blue; c Linda, David & Walter. *Educ:* Bowdoin Col, AB, 44; Harvard Med Sch, MD, 47; Am Bd Internal Med, dipl, 58. *Honors & Awards:* Pemberton lectr, 73; AF-Help & Hope Award, 93. *Prof Exp:* Intern, RI Hosp, 47-48, intern med res, 48-50; resident path, Hosp Univ Pa, 50-51; asst investr, Res Div, Nat Heart Inst, 51-54; vis fel med, Columbia Univ, 54-55. *Concurrent Pos:* Markle Found scholar, 57-62; vis investr, Nobel Inst, Sweden, 61-62; consult, Coral Gables Vet Admin Hosp; merit award, NIH, 90- *Mem:* Am Physiol Soc; fel Am Col Physicians; Am Soc Clin Invest; Asn Am Physicians; Am Soc Cell Biol; Am Rheumatology Asn. *Res:* Electrolyte physiology; cartilage and other connective tissues; rheumatic diseases. *Mailing Add:* Univ Miami Sch Med Box 016960 D26 Miami FL 33101-6960. *Fax:* 305-324-9212

HOWELL, DORIS AHLEE, PEDIATRICS, HEMATOLOGY. *Current Pos:* chmn, Dept Community Med, 75-81, prof, 74-92, EMER PROF PEDIAT, UNIV CALIF, SAN DIEGO, 92- *Personal Data:* b Brooklyn, NY, Dec 2, 23. *Educ:* Park Col, BA, 44; McGill Univ, MD, CM, 49. *Honors & Awards:* Menninger Lectr, Am Psychol Asn; Job Lewis Smith Award, Am Acad Pediat. *Prof Exp:* From intern to jr asst resident, Children's Mem Hosp, Montreal, 49-51; sr asst resident pediat, Duke Univ Hosp, 51-52; fel med, Children's Med Ctr, Harvard Med Sch, 52-53, res fel, 52-54, asst hematologist, 53-55, asst physician, 54-55, instr pediat, 54-55; from asst prof to assoc prof, Duke Univ, Sch Med, 55-63; prof & chmn dept, Med Col Pa, 63-73; dep dir instnl develop, Asn Am Med Cols, 73-74. *Concurrent Pos:* Pediat hematologist, Duke Univ, Med Ctr, 55-63; consult hemat, USN; vis prof pediat, Med Col Pa, 73-74; mem, Bd Maternal, Child & Family Health, Nat Acad Sci. *Mem:* Am Acad Pediat; Soc Pediat Res; Am Soc Hemat; Am Pediat Soc. *Res:* Hematological disorders of children; palliative care and hospice care research. *Mailing Add:* Dept Pediat 0802 Univ Calif San Diego La Jolla CA 92093. *Fax:* 619-298-5649

HOWELL, EDWARD TILLSON, organic chemistry, for more information see previous edition

HOWELL, ELIZABETH E, ENZYME KINETICS & MECHANISM, SITE-DIRECTED MUTAGENESIS. *Current Pos:* ASST PROF BIOCHEM, UNIV TENN, KNOXVILLE, 88- *Personal Data:* b Jersey City, NJ, Mar 16, 51. *Educ:* Muhlenburg Col, BS, 73; Lehigh Univ, MS, 80, PhD(chem), 82. *Prof Exp:* Postdoctoral, Agouron Inst, La Jolla, Calif, 82-85, res scientist, 85-88. *Concurrent Pos:* Prin investr, NIH, 85- *Mem:* Am Chem Soc; AAAS; Protein Soc; Fedn Am Socs Exp Biol. *Res:* Structure-function studies of E coli dihydrofolate reductase and R plasmid encoded R67 dihydrofolate reductase; site-directed mutagenesis and second site reversion techniques applied to study catalysis. *Mailing Add:* Dept Biochem Univ Tenn Knoxville TN 37996-0840

HOWELL, EMBRY MARTIN, PUBLIC HEALTH & EPIDEMIOLOGY. *Current Pos:* RES MGR SYSTEMETRICS, MCGRAW HILL INC, 80- *Personal Data:* b Bethesda, Md, Nov 18, 45; m 65; c 2. *Educ:* Barnard Col, AB, 68; Univ NC, MSPH, 72. *Prof Exp:* Health planner, Health Systs Agency, NVa, 73-74; statistician, Nat Cap Med Found, 75-79. *Mem:* Am Pub Health Asn; Asn Social Sci & Health; Am Eval Asn. *Res:* Health care financing and access to medical care, particularly for low income persons. *Mailing Add:* 2923 Macomb St NW Washington DC 20008

HOWELL, EVELYN ANNE, PLANT ECOLOGY, RESTORATION. *Current Pos:* Asst prof, 75-81, ASSOC PROF, UNIV WIS-MADISON, 82-, CHAIR, DEPT LANDSCAPE ARCHIT, 88- *Personal Data:* b Milwaukee, Wis, Feb 28, 47. *Educ:* Carleton Col, BA, 69; Univ Wis, MS, 73, PhD(bot), 75. *Concurrent Pos:* Chair, Ctr Restoration Ecol Restoration & Mgt Notes; contrib ed, Univ Wis-Madison; mem, Comt to Rev Glen Canyon Environ Studies, Water Sci & Technol Bd, Nat Res Coun. *Mem:* Ecol Soc Am; AAAS; Am Inst Biol Sci. *Res:* Plant community analysis for purposes of preservation, management, and landscape design; impact analysis with emphasis on plant communities; restoration of natural plant communities, especially prairies and woodland. *Mailing Add:* Dept Landscape Archit 25 Agr Hall Univ Wis-Madison 1450 Linden Dr Madison WI 53706-1522

HOWELL, EVERETTE IRL, PHYSICS. *Current Pos:* RETIRED. *Personal Data:* b Shelby, Miss, Jan 4, 14; m 43; c 3. *Educ:* Miss Col, BA, 36; Vanderbilt Univ, MS, 37; Univ NC, PhD(physics), 40. *Prof Exp:* From assoc prof to prof phys sci, Belhaven Col, 40-48; prof physics & head dept, Miss State Univ, 48-79. *Mem:* Am Phys Soc; Am Asn Physics Teachers. *Res:* Electron scattering; production of secondary electrons by electrons of energy between .7 and 2.6 million electron volts. *Mailing Add:* PO Box 5384 Mississippi State MS 39762

HOWELL, FRANCIS CLARK, BIOLOGICAL ANTHROPOLOGY. *Current Pos:* prof, 70-91, EMER PROF ANTHROP, UNIV CALIF, BERKELEY, 91- *Personal Data:* b Kansas City, Mo, Nov 27, 25; m 55, Betty A Tomsen; c 2. *Educ:* Univ Chicago, PhB, 49, MA, 51, PhD(anthrop), 53. *Hon Degrees:* DSc, Univ Chicago, 92. *Prof Exp:* Instr anat, Sch Med, Wash Univ, 53-55; from asst prof to prof anthrop, Univ Chicago, 55-70. *Mem:* Nat Acad Sci; AAAS; Am Anthrop Asn; Am Asn Phys Anthrop; Soc Vert Paleont; Am Philos Soc; Am Acad Arts & Sci; Fr Acad Sci. *Res:* Human evolution; paleoanthropology. *Mailing Add:* Dept Anthrop Univ Calif Berkeley CA 94720. *Fax:* 510-643-8231

HOWELL, FRANCIS V, ORAL PATHOLOGY. *Current Pos:* PROF ORAL MED, GRAD SCH, LOMA LINDA UNIV, 63- *Personal Data:* b Salt Lake City, Utah, Jan 12, 23; m 51; c 4. *Educ:* Stanford Univ, AB, 48; Univ Pac, DDS, 50; Univ Ore, MS, 56. *Prof Exp:* From asst prof to assoc prof oral path & head dept, Univ Ore, 52-56; assoc clin prof path, Sch Med, Univ Southern Calif, 56-69. *Concurrent Pos:* Pvt pract, Calif, 56-; consult, US Navy Hosps, San Diego, 57-, Camp Pendleton, 60-72, Vet Admin Hosp, Long Beach, 61-74 & Vet Admin Hosp, San Diego, 74-; dir, Am Bd Oral Path, 69-; vis prof, Technol Univ Mex, 70-; coordr continuing educ, Sch Dent, Univ Baja Calif; chmn dept oral med, Scripps Clin & Res Found. *Mem:* AAAS; Am Dent Asn; Am Soc Clin Path; Am Acad Oral Path (pres, 68-69); fel Am Col Dent. *Res:* Diseases of the mouth, especially the tongue; fungus diseases; clinical pathological features of oral cancer. *Mailing Add:* PO Box 1839 La Jolla CA 92038-1839

HOWELL, GOLDEN LEON, PLANT PHYSIOLOGY. *Current Pos:* assoc prof, 61-69, PROF BIOL, MEMPHIS STATE UNIV, 69- *Personal Data:* b Hamilton, Ala, July 10, 28. *Educ:* Univ Ala, BS, 50, MS, 54, PhD(bot), 59. *Prof Exp:* Asst prof biol, High Point Col, 58-61. *Mem:* AAAS; Am Soc Plant Physiol. *Res:* Cellular processes investigation by methods utilizing chromatography and radio-isotopes. *Mailing Add:* Biol Dept Univ Memphis 3706 Alumni St Memphis TN 38152-0001

HOWELL, GORDON STANLEY, JR, HORTICULTURE, PLANT PHYSIOLOGY. *Current Pos:* Asst prof to assoc prof, 69-80, PROF HORT, MICH STATE UNIV, 80- *Personal Data:* b Mobile, Ala, Mar 7, 41; m 64; c 3. *Educ:* Miss State Univ, BS, 63, MS, 65; Univ Minn, St Paul, PhD(hort), 69. *Mem:* Am Soc Hort Sci; Am Soc Enologists; Sigma Xi. *Res:* Cold hardiness in woody plants; pomology; viticulture; enology. *Mailing Add:* Dept Hort Mich State Univ 288 Plant Sci Bldg East Lansing MI 48824-1325

HOWELL, GREGORY A, CIVIL ENGINEERING, CONSTRUCTION MANAGEMENT. *Current Pos:* PRES, TIMELAPSE, INC, 75-; PRES, HOWELL ASSOCS, 81- *Personal Data:* b Springfield, Mo, Feb 3, 43. *Educ:* Stanford Univ, BS, 66, MS, 71. *Prof Exp:* Proj engr, Arcosanti Proj, 70-71 & Kingston Quarries, 72-75. *Concurrent Pos:* Consult, Harrison Fraker, 73-75. *Mem:* Am Soc Civil Engrs; Am Inst Indust Engrs; Inst Transp Engrs. *Res:* Productivity improvement and measurement, management of the improvement process. *Mailing Add:* Dept Civil Eng Univ NMex Main Campus Albuquerque NM 87131-0002

HOWELL, JAMES ARNOLD, ANALYTICAL CHEMISTRY. *Current Pos:* from asst prof to assoc prof, 64-78, PROF ANALYTICAL CHEM, WESTERN MICH UNIV, 78- *Personal Data:* b Murphysboro, Ill, Apr 19, 32; m 52, Theresa Res; c Patrick. *Educ:* Southern Ill Univ, BA, 59; Univ Ill, MS, 61; Wayne State Univ, PhD(analytical chem), 64. *Concurrent Pos:* Sci adv, US Food & Drug Admin, 76- *Mem:* Am Chem Soc; Asn Analytical Chemists Inc. *Res:* Ultraviolet and visible absorption spectroscopy; flame photometry and atomic absorption spectroscopy; chemical instrumentation; chemical separations. *Mailing Add:* 912 Weaver St Kalamazoo MI 49007-5539. *Fax:* 616-387-2909; *E-Mail:* james.howell@w.mich.edu

HOWELL, JAMES LEVERT, MATHEMATICS. *Current Pos:* from asst to prof, 55-85, EMER PROF MATH, UNIV ALA, TUSCALOOSA, 85- *Personal Data:* b Gordo, Ala, June 16, 17; m 66. *Educ:* Univ Ala, AB, 42; Yale Univ, MA, 48, PhD(math), 54. *Prof Exp:* Asst math, Lehigh Univ, 42-43; instr, Muhlenberg Col, 43-44 & Univ Ga, 45-46; asst instr, Yale Univ, 46-52; instr, Univ Del, 52-55. *Concurrent Pos:* Instr, New Haven YMCA Jr Col, 50-52; consult & lectr, Vis Scientist Prog, Ala Acad Sci, 62-69. *Mem:* Math Asn Am. *Res:* Mathematical analysis; differential equations; complex variables. *Mailing Add:* 3411 Arcadia Dr Tuscaloosa AL 35404-4371

HOWELL, JAMES MACGREGOR, QUANTUM CHEMISTRY. *Current Pos:* asst prof, 73-77, ASSOC PROF CHEM, BROOKLYN COL, 78- *Personal Data:* b Quincy, Mass, Apr 10, 42; m 67; c 2. *Educ:* Harvard Univ, AB, 64; Cornell Univ, MS, 70, PhD(chem), 71. *Mem:* Am Chem Soc. *Res:* Quantum chemical investigation of the structure and reactions of organic and inorganic molecules. *Mailing Add:* Dept Chem City Univ NY Brooklyn Col 2901 Bedford Ave Brooklyn NY 11210-2813

HOWELL, JAMES MILTON, PHYSICAL CHEMISTRY, SOLID STATE PHYSICS. *Current Pos:* RES CHEMIST, E I DU PONT DE NEMOURS, 78- *Personal Data:* b Durham, NC, Nov 8, 44. *Educ:* Univ Miss, BS, 66; Univ NC, PhD(chem), 73. *Prof Exp:* Res assoc solid state physics, Univ NC, Chapel Hill, 72-77. *Mem:* Am Chem Soc. *Res:* Electrical effects in thin films, organic and metallic; electrical characteristics of polymeric fibers and films; surface chemistry and physics. *Mailing Add:* 108 S Baywood Lane Greenville NC 27834-6945

HOWELL, JANICE A, ELECTRICAL ENGINEERING, OPTICS. *Current Pos:* Staff, Patent & Trademark Off, US Dept Com, 77-84, primary examr, 84-88, sr examr, 88, supvr patent examr, 88-90, mem, Com Sci & Technol Fel Prog, 90-91, DEP DIR, PATENT EXAM GROUP, PATENT & TRADEMARK OFF, US DEPT COM, 92- *Personal Data:* b Jessica & Adam. *Honors & Awards:* Bronze Medal, US Dept Com, 88, Silver Medal, 96. *Concurrent Pos:* Sr Policy Analyst, Com Sci & Technol Fel Prog, US Dept Com, 90-91. *Mailing Add:* US Dept Com Patent Office Crystal Plaza Two 2011 Jefferson Davis Hwy Arlington VA 22202

HOWELL, JERRY FONCE, JR, ECOLOGY, ICHTHYOLOGY. *Current Pos:* prof & adminr environ studies, 72-80, prof & chmn, dept biol & environ sci, 80-86, PROF & ADMIN ENVIRON STUDIES, MOREHEAD STATE UNIV, 86- *Personal Data:* b McDowell, Ky, Oct 18, 41; m 63. *Educ:* NC State Univ, BS, 63 & 64; Eastern Ky Univ, MS, 68; Univ Tenn, Knoxville, PhD(zool), 71. *Prof Exp:* Forester, US Forest Serv, Dept Agr, 64-66. *Concurrent Pos:* HEW grant, 72-73 & 73-74; consult, SMiss Elec Power Asn, 76-78 & Gateway Area Develop Dist, 76-77; Area Health Educ Syst grant, 78, 79 & 80; NSF grant, 78-80; US Army Corps Engrs grants, 79 & 80; mem Southeastern Fisheries Coun. *Mem:* Sigma Xi; Wildlife Soc; Am Fisheries Soc. *Res:* Environmental education; ichthyology; land use; ecology; forestry; wildlife; environmental impact. *Mailing Add:* Biol Dept Morehead State Univ 150 University Blvd Morehead KY 40351-1684

HOWELL, JO ANN SHAW, COMPUTER SCIENCES, COMPUTER SECURITY. *Current Pos:* STAFF MEM, LOS ALAMOS NAT LAB, UNIV CALIF, 73- *Personal Data:* b Bonham, Tex, Sept 28, 45; m, Sarah Elizabeth & Adam Tillman; c 2. *Educ:* Univ Tex, Austin, BA, 67, MA, 69, PhD(comput sci), 71. *Prof Exp:* Res scientist, Ctr Numerical Analysis & asst prof comput sci, Univ Tex, Austin, 71-72; J Willard Gibbs Instr, Yale Univ, 72-73. *Concurrent Pos:* Secy, Spec Interest Group Symbolic & Algebraic Manipulation; mem, Bd Dirs, Special Interest Group Numerical Math, 73-74. *Mem:* Inst Elec & Electronics Engrs; Asn Comput Mach; Inst Nuclear Mat Mgt. *Res:* Control systems; computer security. *Mailing Add:* Group NIS-7 Mail Stop E541 Los Alamos Nat Lab Los Alamos NM 87545. *E-Mail:* howell@ang.gov

HOWELL, JOHN ANTHONY, BIOCHEMICAL ENGINEERING. *Current Pos:* dir, Membrane Appln Ctr, 85-96, head, Sch Chem Eng, 87-93, PROF BIOCHEM ENG, UNIV BATH, ENG, 85- *Personal Data:* b Hyde, Eng, Apr 26, 39; m 65, Patricia Thomasson; c Jason & Justin. *Educ:* Univ Cambridge, MA, 64; Univ Minn, Minneapolis, PhD(chem eng), 66. *Prof Exp:* Jr chem engr, Petrocarbon Develop Ltd, 61-63; res asst chem eng, Univ Minn, 63-66; asst prof, Fed Univ Rio de Janeiro, 66-67; from asst prof to assoc prof, State Univ NY, Buffalo, 67-75; reader biochem eng, Univ Col Swansea, Wales, 75-85. *Concurrent Pos:* Sr vis fel, Univ Col Swansea, Wales, 73-74; vis prof, Univ Waterloo, Can, 81-82; dir, Bio-Isolates Ltd, 84-87; vis dir res, Nat Ctr Sci Res, France, 95. *Mem:* Brit Inst Chem Engrs; Royal Soc Arts; Europ Soc Membrane Sci & Technol. *Res:* Waste water treatment by biological and physical means; membrane separations; chromatographic separations; computer control of fermenters and downstream processing; continuous electrophoresis. *Mailing Add:* Sch Chem Eng Univ Bath Bath BA2 7AY England. *E-Mail:* j.a.howell@bath.ac.uk

HOWELL, JOHN EMORY, CATALYSIS, INORGANIC CHEMISTRY. *Current Pos:* asst prof, 70-74, assoc prof, 74-78, PROF CHEM, UNIV SOUTHERN MISS, 78- *Personal Data:* b Charles City, Iowa, Mar 14, 38; m 58; c 3. *Educ:* Marion Col, BS, 59; Ariz State Univ, MNS, 64; Univ Iowa, PhD(chem), 70. *Prof Exp:* Instr chem, Miltonvale Wesleyan Col, 59-66. *Mem:* Am Chem Soc; Sigma Xi. *Res:* Transition and rare earth metal catalyzed stereospecific polymerization of dienes is being studied to determine the role of the metal and the cocatalyst. *Mailing Add:* Chem Southern Sta Box 5043 Univ Southern Miss Hattiesburg MS 39406

HOWELL, JOHN H(ANCOCK), CHEMICAL ENGINEERING. *Current Pos:* RETIRED. *Personal Data:* b New York, NY, Feb 23, 13; m 38; c 3. *Educ:* Mass Inst Technol, SB, 35, SM, 36. *Prof Exp:* Proj engr, Carbide & Carbon Chem Corp, 36-46, sr design engr, 47-56, proj leader, 57-60, asst dir, 60-63, assoc dir, 63-78. *Concurrent Pos:* Spec consult, USN, 44. *Mem:* Am Inst Chem Engrs. *Res:* High pressure hydrogenation of organic materials. *Mailing Add:* 2105 Weberwood Dr Charleston WV 25303

HOWELL, JOHN N, PHYSIOLOGY. *Current Pos:* ASSOC PROF ZOOL & BIOMED SCI, OHIO UNIV, 77- *Personal Data:* b Franklin, NH, Jan 20, 40; m 61, Suzanne Horiszny; c Steven G & Eric N. *Educ:* Kalamazoo Col, BA, 61; Univ Calif, Los Angeles, PhD(pharmacol), 68. *Honors & Awards:* Gutensohn & Denslow Award, Am Osteopath Asn, 96. *Prof Exp:* Asst prof biol sci, Calif State Polytech Col, 67-68; fel physiol, Univ Calif, Los Angeles, 68-70; from instr to asst prof physiol, Univ Pittsburgh, 70-77. *Concurrent Pos:* Danforth Found Fel, 61-65; vis prof, Berne Univ, Switz, 84-85; vis fel, John B Pierce Lab, New Haven, Conn, 94; neural control of skeletal muscle. *Mem:* Am Physiol Soc; Soc Neurosci; Am Col Sports Med. *Res:* Cellular aspects of muscle physiology, especially excitation-contraction coupling; EMG and muscle pathophysiology. *Mailing Add:* Col Osteop Med Ohio Univ Athens OH 45701. *E-Mail:* jhowell1@ohiou.edu

HOWELL, JOHN REID, HEAT TRANSFER, ENERGY. *Current Pos:* vis prof, Univ Tex, Austin, 78-79, prof mech eng, 79-83, E C H Bantel prof, 83-90, chmn mech eng, 87-90, dir, Ctr Energy Studies, 88-90, BAKER-HUGHES PROF, UNIV TEX, AUSTIN, 90-, ASSOC DEAN RES, 96- *Personal Data:* b Columbus, Ohio, June 13, 36; m 79, Susan Conway; c Reid, Keli & David. *Educ:* Case Inst Technol, BSChE, 58, MSChE, 60, PhD(eng), 62. *Honors & Awards:* Ralph Coats Roe Award, Am Soc Eng Educ, 87; Thermophysics Award, Am Inst Aeronaut & Astronaut, 90; Heat Transfer Mem Award, Am Soc Mech Engrs, 91. *Prof Exp:* Aerospace technologist heat transfer, NASA Lewis Res Ctr, 61-68; from assoc prof to prof mech eng, Univ Houston, 68-78. *Concurrent Pos:* Assoc dir res, Univ Houston, 73-75; prog mgr heating & cooling, Solar Energy Lab, Univ Houston, 74-75; dir Energy Inst, 75-78; vis scholar, Japan Soc Prom of Sci, various Japanese Univs, 85. *Mem:* Fel Am Soc Mech Engrs; fel Am Inst Aeronaut & Astronaut. *Res:* Thermal radiation heat transfer; inverse thermal design. *Mailing Add:* Dept Mech Eng Univ Tex Austin TX 78712. *Fax:* 512-471-1045; *E-Mail:* jhowell@mail.utexas.edu

HOWELL, LARRY JAMES, STRUCTURAL DYNAMICS. *Current Pos:* assoc sr res engr, Gen Motors, 72-75, staff res engr, 75-77, asst dept head eng mech, 77-82, DEPT HEAD ENG MECH, GEN MOTORS RES LABS, 82- *Personal Data:* b West Frankfort, Ill, July 1, 43; m 65; c 2. *Educ:* Univ Ill, Urbana, BS, 66, MS, 68, PhD(aeronaut eng), 71. *Prof Exp:* Instr, Univ Ill, Urbana, 67-70; sr dynamics engr structural dynamics, Gen Dynamics, Convair, 70-72. *Concurrent Pos:* Lectr, Oakland Univ, 81- *Mem:* Am Inst Aeronaut & Astronaut; Soc Automotive Engrs; Am Soc Mech Engrs. *Res:* Structural analysis; structural dynamics (noise and vibration). *Mailing Add:* 1026 Pinehurst Ave Royal Oak MI 48073-3314

HOWELL, LARRY L, MECHANICAL ENGINEERING. *Current Pos:* ASST PROF, BRIGHAM YOUNG UNIV, 94- *Educ:* Brigham Young Univ, BS, 87; Purdue Univ, MSME, 91, PhD(mech eng), 93. *Prof Exp:* Struct design engr, Gen Dynamics, Ft Worth, Tex, 88-89; res/teaching asst, Purdue Univ, 89-93, vis asst prof, 94. *Concurrent Pos:* Proj engr, Eng Methods Inc, 91-92 & 93; consult, Eng Methods, Inc, 91-93, AMP Inc, 93, Ashok Midha, Ray Cipra & Gordon Pennock, 93, Nelson Lee, 94, Spindyne Inc, 95, Beechcraft, 95, Victor Jay Liechty, Jr, 96 & Skyhook Technologies, 96; grantee, NSF, 95-97, career award, 96- *Mem:* Assoc Am Soc Mech Engrs; assoc Am Soc Eng Educ. *Res:* Compliant mechanism design and analysis; microelectromechanical systems; mechanical design; nonlinear solid mechanics; finite element analysis. *Mailing Add:* Mech Eng Dept Brigham Young Univ Provo UT 84602-4138

HOWELL, LEONARD RUDOLPH, JR, TOPOLOGY. *Current Pos:* RETIRED. *Personal Data:* b Valdosta, Ga, May 19, 25; m 44, Myrtis Avera; c Leonard R III, David A, Paul M & Elizabeth Nordan. *Educ:* Mercer Univ, AB, 48; Emory Univ, MS, 51; Fla State Univ, PhD(math), 65. *Prof Exp:* Instr math & chem, Emory Jr Col, 48-53; mathematician, Air Forces Europe, USAF, 57-58, asst prof math, Air Force Acad, 58-62, mathematician, Air Force Hq, 65-69, from asst prof to assoc prof math, Air Force Inst Technol, 69-72; assoc prof math, Valdosta State Col, 72-81. *Res:* Point set topology. *Mailing Add:* 3105 Huntington Ridge Circle Valdosta GA 31602

HOWELL, MARY GERTRUDE, PHARMACEUTICAL CHEMISTRY. *Current Pos:* res lit scientist, 59-67, head lit serv, 67-70, dir tech info serv sect, 71-76, HEAD, TECH INFO SERV DEPT, CYANAMID MED RES DIV, LEDERLE LABS, AM CYANAMID CO, 77- *Personal Data:* b Wenona, Ill, May 25, 32; m 54; c 2. *Educ:* Univ Ill, BS, 54; Mass Inst Technol, PhD(org chem), 59. *Prof Exp:* Chemist, E I du Pont de Nemours & Co, 54; res chemist, Div Plant Indust, Commonwealth Sci & Indust Res Orgn, Canberra, Australia, 59. *Concurrent Pos:* Mem, Nat Res Coun Comt Chem Info, Nat Acad Sci, 72-74 & Toxicol Info Prog Comt, 87- *Mem:* Am Chem Soc; Am Soc Info Sci. *Res:* Technical information and research; drug development. *Mailing Add:* 28 Drake Lane Upper Saddle River NJ 07458-1699

HOWELL, NORMAN GARY, ANALYTICAL CHEMISTRY, PHYSICAL CHEMISTRY. *Current Pos:* Res chemist & group leader, 76-81, RES CHEMIST & SECT HEAD, CORP TECH DIV, PROCTER & GAMBLE, 81- *Personal Data:* b Ithaca, NY, June 8, 49; m 71; c 1. *Educ:* State Univ NY, Cortland, BS, 71; Cornell Univ, MS, 74, PhD(analytical chem), 76. *Mem:* Soc Appl Spectros; Sigma Xi. *Res:* Atomic spectroscopy for chemical analysis; X-ray fluorescence; molecular spectroscopy; digital image processing; analytical microscopy; their application to personal care products. *Mailing Add:* Procter & Gamble Co PO Box 398707 Cincinnati OH 45239-8707

HOWELL, PAUL RAYMOND, TRANSMISSION ELECTRON MICROSCOPY, CRYSTALLOGRAPHY. *Current Pos:* ASSOC PROF, PA STATE UNIV, 81- *Personal Data:* b Coleford, Gloucestershire, Sept 9, 46; m 71; c 1. *Educ:* Univ Cambridge, BA, 69, MA, 73, PhD(metall), 73. *Prof Exp:* Res fel, Univ Cambridge, 72-81. *Mailing Add:* Dept Mat Sci Pa State Univ Main Campus 206-A Steidle University Park PA 16802-5005

HOWELL, PETER ADAM, PHYSICAL INORGANIC CHEMISTRY. *Current Pos:* RETIRED. *Personal Data:* b Des Moines, Iowa, Sept 11, 28; m 52; c 3. *Educ:* Calif Inst Technol, BS, 50; Univ Minn, PhD(chem), 55. *Prof Exp:* Asst, Univ Minn, 50-55; res chemist, Tonawanda Lab, Linde Co Div, Union Carbide Corp, 55-61; res chemist, 3M Co, 61-69, res specialist, 69-83, sr res specialist, 83-92. *Concurrent Pos:* Adj assoc prof chem, Macalester Col, 68-69; ed, Minn chemist, 94- *Mem:* Am Crystallog Asn; Am Ceramic Soc. *Res:* Crystal structures and chemistry of zeolite minerals; structures of boron compounds; clay mineralogy; x-ray structure determination; synthesis and properties of zeolites; polymer structure versus properties; chemical reactions in grinding processes; glass composition versus properties; particle properties and behavior. *Mailing Add:* 1896 Yorkshire Ave St Paul MN 55116. *Fax:* 612-696-6432

HOWELL, RALPH RODNEY, PEDIATRICS, GENETICS. *Current Pos:* DAVID R PARK PROF PEDIAT, UNIV TEX, HOUSTON, 72-; PEDIATRICIANS, UNIV CHILDREN'S HOSP HERMANN, HOUSTON, 72- *Personal Data:* b Concord, NC, June 10, 31; m 60; c 3. *Educ:* Davidson Col, BS, 53; Duke Univ, MD, 57. *Prof Exp:* Intern pediat, Duke Univ, Sch Med, 57-58, asst resident, 59-60; clin assoc metab dis, Nat Inst Arthritis & Metab Dis, 60-62, investr molecular biol, 62-64; assoc prof pediat, Johns Hopkins Univ, Sch Med, 64-72. *Concurrent Pos:* Res fel pediat & med, Duke Univ, Med Ctr, 58-59; Joseph P Kennedy, Jr sr res scholar, 64-72; pediatrician, Johns Hopkins Hosp, 64-72. *Mem:* Soc Pediat Res; Am Fedn Clin Res; Am Rheumatism Asn; Am Soc Human Genetics; Am Pediat Soc; Soc Inherited Metab Dis. *Res:* Inherited biochemical defects; cloning; isolation of human genes; genetic diagnosis and treatment. *Mailing Add:* Univ Miami D820 PO Box 016820 Miami FL 33101

HOWELL, ROBERT RICHARD, SPECKLE INTERFEROMETRY, PLANETARY SCIENCES. *Current Pos:* ASST PROF, PHYSICS & ASTRON DEPT, UNIV WYO, 86- *Personal Data:* b Chincoteague, Va, June 26, 52. *Educ:* Univ Mich, BSc, 74; Univ Ariz, PhD(planetary sci), 80. *Prof Exp:* Res asst, Lunar & Planetary Lab, Univ Ariz, 74-78, Steward Observ, 78-80; asst astron, Inst Astron, Univ Hawaii, 80-86. *Mem:* Am Astron Sci; Astron Soc Pac; Am Geophys Union. *Res:* Infrared speckle interferometry; infrared observations of young and evolved stars; volcanism on Jupiter's satellite Io. *Mailing Add:* 1710 Arnold St Laramie WY 82070

HOWELL, ROBERT WAYNE, plant physiology, agronomy; deceased, see previous edition for last biography

HOWELL, RONALD HUNTER, MECHANICAL ENGINEERING, ENERGY ANALYSIS. *Current Pos:* FAC MEM, DEPT MECH ENG, UNIV S FLA, 92- *Personal Data:* b Chicago, Ill, Oct 19, 35; m 56; c 3. *Educ:* Univ Ill, BS, 58, MS, 59, PhD, 67. *Honors & Awards:* Teetor Award, Soc Automotive Engrs, 78. *Prof Exp:* Instr mech eng, Univ Ill, 59-63, res assoc, 63-66; from asst prof to assoc prof, Univ Mo, Rolla, 66-73, prof mech eng, 73-92. *Concurrent Pos:* Consult, Union Elec Co, Am Soc Heating, Refrig & Air-Conditioning Engrs, 73-78 & Hussmann Refrig, 78- *Mem:* Am Soc Mech Engrs; Am Soc Heating, Refrig & Air Conditioning Engrs; Soc Automotive

Engrs; Sigma Xi; Am Soc Eng Educ. *Res:* Measurement of drag forces in separated flows; dynamics and thermodynamics of fluid flow; turbulent wakes; emptying and filling processes; air curtain design; energy analysis and conversion; system simulation. *Mailing Add:* Dept Mech Eng Univ SFla Tampa FL 33620-5350

HOWELL, RUSSELL W, COMPUTER SCIENCE. *Current Pos:* PROF, DEPT MATH & COMPUT SCI, WESTMONT COL, 78- *Educ:* Wheaton Col, BS, 69; Univ Edinburgh, Scotland, MSc, 86; Ohio State Univ, PhD(math0, 74. *Mem:* Am Math Soc; Math Asn Am. *Res:* Computer science. *Mailing Add:* Math & Comp Sci Dept Westmont Col Santa Barbara CA 93108

HOWELL, STEPHEN HERBERT, PLANT MOLECULAR BIOLOGY. *Current Pos:* BOYCE SCHULZE DOWNEY SCIENTIST & PROG DIR IN MOLECULAR BIOL, BOYCE THOMPSON INST, 88- *Personal Data:* b Davenport, Iowa, May 30, 41; m 64. *Educ:* Grinnell Col, BA, 63; Johns Hopkins Univ, PhD(biol), 67. *Prof Exp:* USPHS fel biol, 67-69, res biologist, 69-70, actg asst prof biol, 70-71, from asst prof to prof biol, 71-88,. *Concurrent Pos:* Simon Guggenheim Fel, 76. *Mem:* AAAS. *Res:* Plant viruses; molecular aspects of plant development. *Mailing Add:* Dept Plant Biol Cornell Univ 237 Plant Sci Bldg Ithaca NY 14853-0001

HOWELL, TERRY ALLEN, IRRIGATION, EVAPOTRANSPIRATION. *Current Pos:* agr engr, Fresno, Calif, 79-83, AGR ENGR, USDA, AGR RES SERV, BUSHLAND, TEX, 83- *Personal Data:* b Dallas, Sept 7, 47; m 69, Mary S Parkerson; c Terry A Jr, Lisa K (Dreibrodt) & Michael S. *Educ:* Tex A&M Univ, BS, 69, MS, 70, PhD, 74. *Prof Exp:* From res asst to res assoc, Tex A&M Univ, College Station, 69-74; asst prof, NMex State Univ, Las Cruces, 75 & Tex A&M Univ, 76-79. *Concurrent Pos:* Chmn, Soil & Water Div, Am Soc Agr Eng, 87-88; chmn, Irrigation Water Requirements Comt, Am Soc Civil Engrs, 90-93, ed, Soil & Water Div, 93- *Mem:* Fel Am Soc Agr Engrs; Am Soc Civil Engrs; Am Soc Agron; Soil Sci Soc Am. *Res:* Irrigation systems; irrigation management; evapotranspiration and irrigation systems to conserve water and enhance water use efficiency. *Mailing Add:* USDA Agr Res Serv PO Drawer 10 Bushland TX 79012

HOWELL, THOMAS HOWARD, DENTISTRY, PERIODONTAL DISEASE. *Current Pos:* Fel periodont, 73-76, assoc dean student affairs, 78-93, DIR UNDERGRAD PERIODONT DENT, HARVARD SCH DENT MED, 76-, ASSOC DEAN DENT EDUC, 93- *Personal Data:* b Atlanta, Ga, Oct 7, 45. *Educ:* Ga State Univ, BS, 67, MS, 69; Emory Univ, DDS, 73. *Concurrent Pos:* Pvt pract, Mass & Ga. *Mem:* Am Acad Periodont; Am Asn Dent Schs. *Res:* Periodontal disease; antimetabolites and their effect on bone loss; growth factors to enhance peridontal regeneration. *Mailing Add:* Harvard Sch Dent Med 188 Longwood Ave Boston MA 02115

HOWELL, THOMAS RAYMOND, VERTEBRATE ZOOLOGY. *Current Pos:* RETIRED. *Personal Data:* b New Orleans, La, June 17, 24; m 81, Eleanor Stendahl; c Thomas R Jr, Yvonne H & Heidi F. *Educ:* La State Univ, BS, 46; Univ Calif, MA, 49, PhD(zool), 51. *Honors & Awards:* Elliot Coues Award, Am Ornith Union, 85. *Prof Exp:* From asst prof to prof zool, Univ Calif, Los Angeles, 51-86. *Mem:* AAAS; Cooper Ornith Soc; Wilson Ornith Soc; Am Ornith Union (pres, 82-84); Brit Ornith Union. *Res:* Ornithology; systematics, distribution, evolution, behavior and ecology. *Mailing Add:* PO Box 677 Gualala CA 95445

HOWELL, WALLACE EGBERT, METEOROLOGY. *Current Pos:* asst to chief, 71-84, SCI CONSULT, DIV ATMOSPHERIC RESOURCES MGT, BUR RECLAMATION, 84- *Personal Data:* b Central Valley, NY, Sept 14, 14; m 42; c 5. *Educ:* Harvard Univ, AB, 36; Mass Inst Technol, ScD, 48. *Honors & Awards:* Am Meteorol Soc Award, 68. *Prof Exp:* Chief meteorologist, Mid-Continent Airlines, Kans, 37-39; assoc meteorologist, Yankee Network Weather Serv, Mass, 39-40; asst regional forecaster, US Weather Bur, 40-41; field dir, Harvard-Mt Washington Icing Res Proj, Harvard Univ, 46-47; res fel meteorol, Blue Hill Observ, 47-51; pres, W E Howell Assocs, Inc, 51-67; vpres, E Bollay Assocs, Inc, 67-71. *Concurrent Pos:* Actg dir, Mt Washington Observ, 48-53, pres, 58-67, trustee, 65-; consult meteorologist, 59-; adj prof, Northeastern Univ, 66-71. *Mem:* Fel Am Meteorol Soc; Am Geophys Union. *Res:* Cloud classification; physics of clouds; energy-environmental interactions; weather modification; weather-environment impacts. *Mailing Add:* 12983 Caminito Del Pasaje Del Mar CA 92014-3760

HOWELLS, THOMAS ALFRED, paper chemistry; deceased, see previous edition for last biography

HOWELLS, WILLIAM WHITE, PHYSICAL ANTHROPOLOGY. *Current Pos:* prof, 54-74, cur somatol, Peabody Mus, 55-74, EMER PROF ANTHROP, HARVARD UNIV, 74-, EMER CUR SOMATOL, PEABODY MUS, 74- *Personal Data:* b New York, Nov 27, 08; m 29, Muriel Seabury; c 2. *Educ:* Harvard Univ, BS, 30, PhD(anthrop), 34. *Hon Degrees:* DSc, Beloit Col, 75 & Univ Witwatersrand, 85. *Honors & Awards:* Viking Fund Medal, Wenner-Gren Found, 55; Broca Prix du Centenaire, Paris Soc Anthrop, 80. *Prof Exp:* Res assoc phys anthrop, Am Mus Natural Hist, 32-43; from asst prof to prof anthrop, Univ Wis, 39-54. *Concurrent Pos:* Lectr, Hunter Col, 37-39; ed, J Am Asn Phys Anthrop, 49-54. *Mem:* Nat Acad Sci; fel AAAS; fel Am Anthrop Asn (pres, 51); Am Asn Phys Anthrop; fel Am Acad Arts & Sci; fel Soc Antiquaries London; hon foreign assoc Royal Soc SAfrica. *Res:* Human paleontology; morphological population variation in man. *Mailing Add:* 11 Lawrence Lane Kittery Point ME 03905. *Fax:* 207-439-1380

HOWER, ARTHUR AARON, JR, ENTOMOLOGY. *Current Pos:* asst prof, 66-75, assoc prof entom, 75-80, PROF ENTOM, PA STATE UNIV, UNIVERSITY PARK, 80- *Personal Data:* b Royalton, Pa, Oct 21, 37; m 62; c 2. *Educ:* Shippensburg State Col, BS, 59; Bucknell Univ, MS, 63; Pa State Univ, PhD(zool, entom), 67. *Prof Exp:* Teacher, Cent Dauphin Joint Sch Syst, 59-61. *Mem:* Entom Soc Am; Entom Soc Can; Int Orgn Biol Control. *Res:* Ecology, biology and control of forage insects; radiation and parasites as a control mechanism for alfalfa weevil Hypera postica; impact of insecticides on parasite populations. *Mailing Add:* Dept Entom Pa State Univ 501 Agr Sci University Park PA 16802-3508

HOWER, CHARLES OLIVER, NUCLEAR CHEMISTRY, PHYSICAL CHEMISTRY. *Current Pos:* PROF CHEM, SOUTHWESTERN ORE COMMUNITY COL, 71-, PROF PHYS SCI, 80- *Personal Data:* b Emmett, Idaho, May 13, 35; m 60; c 2. *Educ:* Whitman Col, BA, 56; Univ Wash, PhD(chem), 62. *Prof Exp:* Res assoc chem, Princeton Univ, 62-64; res assoc physics, Inst Nuclear Physics Res, 64-66; asst prof chem, Univ Idaho, 66-71. *Mem:* AAAS. *Res:* Nuclear reaction cross sections; activation analysis; hot atom chemistry of halogen and nitrogen atoms. *Mailing Add:* 1090 Ocean Ct Coos Bay OR 97420

HOWER, GLEN L, ELECTRICAL ENGINEERING. *Current Pos:* from instr to assoc prof, 57-73, PROF ELEC ENG, WASH STATE UNIV, 73- *Personal Data:* b Wenatchee, Wash, Feb 8, 34; m 56; c 3. *Educ:* Wash State Univ, BS, 56, MS, 61; Stanford Univ, PhD(elec eng), 63. *Prof Exp:* Mem staff, Gen Elec Co, 56-57. *Mem:* Am Geophys Union; Am Soc Eng Educ; Inst Elec & Electronics Engrs. *Res:* Radio wave propagation; electromagnetics. *Mailing Add:* Sch Elec Eng & Comput Sci Wash State Univ Pullman WA 99164

HOWER, MEADE M, physics, for more information see previous edition

HOWERTON, ROBERT JAMES, NUCLEAR PHYSICS, NUCLEAR ENGINEERING. *Current Pos:* lab consult, 91-92, LAB ASSOC, LAWRENCE LIVERMORE NAT LAB, 92- *Personal Data:* b Hammond, Ind, Sept 27, 23; m 46. *Educ:* Northwestern Univ, BS, 46, MS, 47. *Prof Exp:* Asst prof math, Regis Col, 48-54; nuclear engr, Phillips Petrol Co, 56-57; asst div leader, Theoret Physics Div, 80-84, group leader phys data group, Lawrence Livermore Nat Lab, Univ Calif, 57-86, asst div leader, Comput Physics Div, 84-86; consult, Phys Data Systs, 86-91. *Concurrent Pos:* Consult, Am Inst Physics, 61-70 & Cent Intel Agency, 59-63. *Mem:* Fel Am Nuclear Soc. *Res:* Development of theoretical and empirical methods for providing nuclear and atomic data required for design of energy producing devices and shielding of radiation from such devices. *Mailing Add:* Lawrence Livermore Lab L298 Univ Calif Box 808 Livermore CA 94550. *E-Mail:* howerton1@llnl.gov

HOWERY, DARRYL GILMER, PHYSICAL CHEMISTRY. *Current Pos:* from asst prof to assoc prof, 65-75, PROF CHEM, BROOKLYN COL, 75- *Personal Data:* b Christiansburg, Va, June 19, 36; m 66; c 1. *Educ:* Roanoke Col, BS, 58; Univ NC, PhD(phys chem), 63. *Prof Exp:* Chemist, Univ Calif, Berkeley, 63-65. *Concurrent Pos:* Vis chemist & lectr, Kyoto Univ, 71-72, 79-80. *Mem:* Am Chem Soc. *Res:* Chemometrics, especially factor analysis. *Mailing Add:* Dept Chem Brooklyn Col Brooklyn NY 11210-2889

HOWES, CECIL EDGAR, GENETICS, PHYSIOLOGY. *Current Pos:* RETIRED. *Personal Data:* b Patten, Maine, Sept 23, 18; m 44; c 3. *Educ:* Univ Maine, BS, 41; Cornell Univ, MS, 48, PhD(genetics physiol), 54. *Prof Exp:* Instr & asst poultry husb, Univ Maine, 46, from asst prof & asst poultry husbandman to prof & poultry husbandman, 48-58; head, Dept Poultry Sci, Va Polytech Inst & State Univ, 58-78, prof, 58-86, col liaison officer, 78-86. *Mem:* Poultry Sci Asn. *Res:* Avian genetics; genetic resistance to diseases; genetic and physiological correlations. *Mailing Add:* 714 Gracelyn Ct Blacksburg VA 24060

HOWES, JOHN FRANCIS, PHARMACOLOGY, MEDICINAL CHEMISTRY. *Current Pos:* VPRES DEVELOP, XENON VISION, INC. *Personal Data:* b London, Eng, Jan 4, 43; m 69; c 2. *Educ:* Univ London, BPharm, 64, PhD(pharmacol), 67. *Prof Exp:* Res assoc pharmacol, Sch Med, Univ NC, 67-69; sr scientist, Arthur D Little Inc, 69-70; dir, SISA Inc, 70-80, vpres pharmacol, 80-; dir, New Drug Develop, Key Pharmaceut Inc. *Concurrent Pos:* Asst prof, Sch Pharm & Allied Health Sci, Northeastern Univ, 74- *Mem:* Am Soc Pharmacol & Exp Therapeut; Am Soc Clin Pharmacol Therapeut. *Res:* Pharmacology of centrally active drugs with reference to analgesics. *Mailing Add:* HGP Inc Pharmos Corp One Progress Blvd PO Box 362 Innovation Dr Alachua FL 32615-9537. *Fax:* 904-462-5401

HOWES, ROBERT INGERSOLL, JR, ANATOMY, DENTAL RESEARCH. *Current Pos:* Asst prof, 71-78, ASSOC PROF ANAT, HEALTH SCI CTR, UNIV OKLA, 78- *Personal Data:* b Santa Fe, NMex, Aug 3, 41; m 66, Ruth Hege; c Rachel & Prudence. *Educ:* Amherst Col, AB, 63; Columbia Univ, DDS, 67, PhD(anat), 71. *Concurrent Pos:* Nat Inst Dent Res grant, 73- *Mem:* Am Asn Anatomists; Int Asn Dent Res; Soc Vert Paleont; AAAS; Sigma Xi. *Res:* Hard tissue research with interest in comparative odontology using experimental approaches to study tooth attachment, tooth development, and jaw regeneration in lower vertebrates. *Mailing Add:* 1012 Brookside Norman OK 73069

HOWES, RUTH HEGE, PHYSICS OF THE ARMS RACE, PHYSICS EDUCATION. *Current Pos:* PROF PHYSICS, BALL STATE UNIV, 76-, GEORGE & FRANCES BALL DISTINGUISHED PROF, 91- *Personal Data:* b Montpelier, Vt, Oct 18, 44; m 66, Robert I; c Rachel T & Prudence N. *Educ:* Mt Holyoke Col, BA, 65; Columbia Univ, MA, 67, PhD(physics), 71. *Prof Exp:* Vis asst prof physics, Univ Okla, 71-72; adj instr, Okla City Univ, 72-76. *Concurrent Pos:* Foster fel, US Arms Control & Disarmament Agency, 84-85; cong fel, AAAS, 93-94; prof officer, NSF, 94-95. *Mem:* Fel Am Phys Soc; Sigma Xi; AAAS. *Res:* Applications in physics that have impact on the society; status of energy technology in United States; physics education. *Mailing Add:* Dept Phys & Astron Ball State Univ Muncie IN 47306. *Fax:* 765-285-5674; *E-Mail:* 00rhhowes@bsuuc.bsu.edu

HOWES, TREVOR DENIS, METALLURGY. *Current Pos:* PROF METALL, UNIV CONN, 88-, DIR, CTR GRINDING RES & DEVELOP, 88-, DIR, ADVAN TECHNOL CTR PRECISION MFG, 90- *Educ:* Univ Col, Cardiff, Wales, BSME, 60; Univ Bristol, Eng, PhD(mech eng); 63. *Prof Exp:* Tech officer, Imp Chem Industs Ltd, Severside, UK, 63-65; from proj eng to mgr eng, Strachan & Henshaw Ltd-Dickinson Robinson Group, UK, 65-71; res fel, Univ Bristol, 71-85, managing dir, Inst Grinding Technol, 85-88, dir mfg group, 85-88. *Mem:* Fel Royal Soc Arts; Am Soc Mech Engrs; Japan Soc Precision Eng; Am Soc Precision Eng; Soc Mfg Engrs; Abrasive Eng Soc. *Res:* Metallurgical engineering. *Mailing Add:* 339 Storrs Rd Mansfield Center CT 06250

HOWGATE, DAVID W, LASER PHYSICS, PROJECT MANAGEMENT. *Current Pos:* PRES, LASER TOOLS INC, HUNTSVILLE, ALA, 88- *Personal Data:* b Swedesboro, NJ, Oct 11, 32; m 64; c 3. *Educ:* Marshall Univ, BS, 54; WVa Univ, MS, 55; Univ Ala, PhD(physics), 67. *Honors & Awards:* Paul A Siple Mem Award, 78. *Prof Exp:* Physicist, Army Missile Command, Redstone Arsenal, 59-63, res physicist, 63-75, tech mgr, 75-84, consult, 84-88. *Mem:* AAAS; Am Phys Soc; NY Acad Sci; Sigma Xi. *Res:* Mathematical physics; chemical lasers; computational physics; electron spin resonance and infrared diagnostics; gas and solid state lasers; nonlinear optics. *Mailing Add:* 7800 Smoke Rise Rd SE Huntsville AL 35802

HOWICK, LESTER CARL, ANALYTICAL CHEMISTRY. *Current Pos:* From asst prof to assoc prof, 57-67, PROF CHEM, UNIV ARK, 67- *Personal Data:* b Manchester, Iowa, Nov 2, 28; m 53. *Educ:* Cornell Col, BA, 53; Univ Iowa, MS, 55, PhD(analytical chem); 57. *Mem:* Am Chem Soc; Sigma Xi. *Res:* Homogeneous precipitation; complex ions and the mechanism of their reactions. *Mailing Add:* Dept Chem Univ Ark Fayetteville AR 72701

HOWIE, DONALD LAVERN, INTERNAL MEDICINE, RESEARCH ADMINISTRATION. *Current Pos:* RETIRED. *Personal Data:* b Monticello, Iowa, June 3, 24; m 47, Lucile Srange; c Patricia, Stephen, Elizabeth & Douglas. *Educ:* Univ Iowa, MD, 48; Am Bd Internal Med, dipl, 56; Harvard Univ, AMP, 65. *Prof Exp:* Intern med, Denver Gen Hosp, Med Corps, US Army, 48-49, regimental surgeon, Seventh Inf Div, Hokkaido, Japan, 49-50, commanding off, Hq Med Detachment, First Calvary Div, Korea, 50-51, off-in-chg hepatitis annex, 31st Sta Hosp, Kyoto & Tokyo, 51, res med, Brooke Gen Hosp, Ft Sam Houston, 52-54, student mil med & allied sci, Walter Reed Army Inst Res, Walter Reed Army Med Ctr, 54-55, fel hemat, 57-58, chief med & prof serv, Ft Riley, Kans, 55-56, sr med specialist, Queen Alexandria Mil Hosp, London, 58-59, commanding off, 46th Surg Hosp, Landstuhl, Ger & consult hemat, Surgeon, US Army, Europe, 59-60, dept dir div med & asst chief dept hemat, Walter Reed Army Inst Res, 60-62, chief med res br, US Army Med Res & Develop Command, Off of the Surgeon Gen, 62-63, chief plans, progs & funds div, 63-65, dep comdr, 65-67, chief life & sci div, Army Res Off Chief Res & Develop, Dept Army, 67-72, internist, Army Phys Disability Agency, 72-93. *Concurrent Pos:* Mem, NIH Study Sect Hemat, 61-65; student defense mgt, USN Postgrad Sch, 65; mem army res coun, Dept Army, 67-71. *Mem:* AMA; fel Royal Soc Med; fel Am Col Physicians; Asn Mil Surg US. *Res:* Research in laboratory and clinical hematology and oncology; bone marrow transplantation; research management. *Mailing Add:* 1051 Carnation Dr Rockville MD 20850-1001

HOWKINS, STUART D, ACOUSTICS. *Current Pos:* SR SCIENTIST, DATA PROD CORP, 79- *Personal Data:* b London, Eng, Jan 24, 38; m 64, Nan L Rivers; c Heidi & Julie. *Educ:* Univ London, BSc, 59, MSc, 60, PhD(physics), 62. *Prof Exp:* Res assoc acoust, Univ Vt, 63-64; assoc physicist, IIT Res Inst, Ill, 64-69; mem res staff, Schlumberger-Doll Res Ctr, 69-75; mgr, Appln Lab, Krautkramer-Branson Inc, 76-79. *Concurrent Pos:* Eve instr, Ill Inst Technol, 65-69. *Res:* High-amplitude sound propagation in liquids including experimental studies of attenuation of shock waves; cavitation phenomena including nonlinear bubble oscillations and cavitation erosion; ultrasonic nondestructive testing and transducer development; physics of impulse ink jet devices. *Mailing Add:* 29 Farrar Lane Ridgefield CT 06877. *Fax:* 203-830-4736

HOWLAND, FRANK L, ENGINEERING, APPLIED MATHEMATICS. *Current Pos:* PRES, FRANK L HOWLAND INC, 89- *Personal Data:* b Long Branch, NJ, July 19, 26; m 50, Irene Lamb; c Jonathan, Rebecca & Elizabeth. *Educ:* Rutgers Univ, BS, 50; Univ Ill, MS, 52, PhD(struct eng), 55. *Prof Exp:* Res assoc struct res, Univ Ill, 52-55; mem tech staff eng mech, Bell Tel Labs, 55-59, supvr, 59-65, head, Dept Appl Mech, 65-78, head, Dept Fiber & Hybrid Lab, 76-89, head, Technol Dept, 78-89. *Mem:* AAAS; Inst Elec & Electronics Engrs; Int Soc Hybrid Microelectronics. *Res:* Mechanical engineering; electronic device assembly process and package design development; materials; fatigue; joining technology development; heat transfer; fracture mechanics. *Mailing Add:* 3076 Lindberg Ave Allentown PA 18103-5510

HOWLAND, HOWARD CHASE, SENSORY PHYSIOLOGY, PHYSIOLOGICAL OPTICS. *Current Pos:* from asst prof to assoc prof, 68-85, PROF NEUROBIOL & BEHAV, CORNELL UNIV, 85- *Personal Data:* b Lafayette, Ind, May 26, 33; m 65; c 3. *Educ:* Univ Chicago, BA, 52; Tufts Univ, MS, 58; Cornell Univ, PhD, 68. *Prof Exp:* Instr biosci, State Univ NY, Stony Brook, 60-66, asst prof, 66-67. *Concurrent Pos:* Res inst guest, Max Planck Inst Physiol Behav, 60, 62-63 & 63-66, Wissenschaftliche asst, 72-73; vis researcher, Physiol Lab, Downing Site, Cambridge, 76-77; sr res fel, Inst Ophthal, Univ London, 76-77; vis scientist, Regional Primate Ctr, Univ Wash, 80. *Mem:* Am Physiol Soc; Soc Neurosci; Optical Soc Am; Asn Res Vision & Ophthal; AAAS. *Res:* Vertebrate vision, especially the development of focusing ability in infant humans and other vertebrates. *Mailing Add:* Dept Neurobiol & Behav Cornell Univ Ithaca NY 14853

HOWLAND, JAMES LUCIEN, mathematical analysis; deceased, see previous edition for last biography

HOWLAND, JAMES SECORD, MATHEMATICS. *Current Pos:* From asst prof to assoc prof, 66-75, PROF MATH, UNIV VA, 75- *Personal Data:* b Jacksonville, Fla, Dec 27, 37; m 63; c 2. *Educ:* Univ Fla, BS, 59; Calif Inst Technol, MS, 62; Univ Calif, Berkeley, PhD, 66. *Concurrent Pos:* Assoc ed, J Math Physics, 80-82, J Math Analysis Appl, 87- *Res:* Functional analysis and mathematical physics. *Mailing Add:* 284 Turkey Ridge Rd Charlottesville VA 22903-3199

HOWLAND, JOHN LAFOLLETTE, BIOCHEMISTRY. *Current Pos:* from asst prof to assoc prof, 63-71, PROF BIOL, BOWDOIN COL, 71-, JOSIAH LITTLE PROF NATURAL SCI, 75- *Personal Data:* b Quincy, Mass, Dec 14, 35; m 61, Cynthia Birge; c Ethan & Hannah. *Educ:* Bowdoin Col, AB, 57; Harvard Univ, PhD(biol), 61. *Prof Exp:* USPHS fel biochem, Univ Amsterdam, 61-63. *Concurrent Pos:* NSF res grant, 63-; USPHS res career develop award. *Mem:* Am Chem Soc; Am Soc Biol Chemists; Biophys Soc. *Res:* Oxidative phosphorylation; membrane transport and evolution of bioenergetic mechanisms. *Mailing Add:* Dept Biol Bowdoin Col Brunswick ME 04011. *Fax:* 207-725-3405; *E-Mail:* Jhowland@polar.bowdoin.edu

HOWLAND, JOSEPH E(MERY), PLANT PHYSIOLOGY. *Current Pos:* prof hort, 78-85, prof advert & mkt, 80-90, EMER PROF, UNIV NEV, RENO, 90- *Personal Data:* b Providence, RI, Apr 2, 18; m 43, 69; c Joy & Hornby. *Educ:* RI State Col, BS, 40; Mich State Univ, MS, 42; Cornell Univ, PhD(hort), 45. *Honors & Awards:* Bradford Williams Medal, Am Soc Landscape Architects, 81. *Prof Exp:* Asst, Mich State Col, 40-42, Cornell Univ, 42-45; assoc ed, Better Homes & Gardens, 45-48; garden ed, House Beautiful, 48-54, asst to publ, 53-54, dir spec projs, 55-56; asst to pres, O M Scott & Sons, 56-68; prof hort, Univ Nev, 69-73; vpres, George J Ball Inc, 73-78; pres, Pan Am Seed Co, 73-75 & Burgess Seed & Plant Co, 75-76; dir, Peto Seed, Peters-Wheeler Seed, Denholm Seed, 73-76, Carefree Garden Prods, 76-77; dir, Am Seed Inst, 80-83. *Concurrent Pos:* Headmaster, Du Page Hort Sch, 74-78; China Daily Sem, Beijing, 83; vis prof, Victoria Agr Col, Melbourne, Australia, 85-; Winrock & Rockefeller Found Seed Proj, Thailand, 85-92. *Mem:* Am Soc Hort Sci; Am Soc Agron; Am Hort Soc; Am Mgt Asn; Garden Writers Asn Am; fel Sci Writers. *Res:* Ornamental phytopathology; plant nutrition; commercial greenhouse; lawns and commercial turf; horticultural marketing; psychographic marketing research. *Mailing Add:* 350 W Riverview Circle Reno NV 89509

HOWLAND, LOUIS PHILIP, SOLID STATE PHYSICS, THEORETICAL PHYSICS. *Current Pos:* from assoc prof to prof, Whitman Col, 65-85, chmn dept, 69-71, 74-76, 80-81, 82-85 & 91-93, Paul Garrett fel, 71-74, fac chmn, 76-78, BENJAMIN BROWN PROF PHYSICS, WHITMAN COL, 85- *Personal Data:* b Somerville, NJ, Dec 19, 29; m 56; c 5. *Educ:* Cornell Univ, BEngPhys, 52; Mass Inst Technol, PhD(physics), 57. *Prof Exp:* Mem staff physics res, Lincoln Lab, Mass Inst Technol, 56-58; from instr to asst prof physics, Dartmouth Col, 58-65. *Concurrent Pos:* Vis assoc prof, Univ Calif, Berkeley, 71-72; vis prof, Univ Wash, 79-80. *Mem:* Am Phys Soc; Am Asn Physics Teachers; Sigma Xi. *Mailing Add:* 903 Woodlawn St Walla Walla WA 99362

HOWLAND, RICHARD DAVID, PHARMACOLOGY. *Current Pos:* asst prof, 72-82, ASSOC PROF PHARMACOL, UNIV MED & DENT NJ, 82- *Personal Data:* b New York, NY, Oct 19, 42; m 65; c 7. *Educ:* Drew Univ, BA, 64; Univ Calif, San Francisco, PhD(pharmacol), 70. *Prof Exp:* USPHS fel, Univ Calif, San Francisco, 70; fel, Roche Inst Molecular Biol, Nutley, NJ, 70-72. *Concurrent Pos:* Assoc grad fac, Newark Col Arts & Sci, Rutgers Univ, 74- *Mem:* AAAS; Soc Neurosci; NY Acad Sci; Am Soc Pharmacol & Exp Therapeut. *Res:* Biochemical mechanisms of acrylamide neurotoxicity; neuron-specific enolase and its role in acrylamide neurotoxicity; neurotoxicology. *Mailing Add:* Dept Pharmacol Univ Med & Dent NJ Med Sch 185 S Orange Ave Newark NJ 07103-2714

HOWLAND, WILLARD J, RADIOLOGY. *Current Pos:* CONSULT, 87- *Personal Data:* b Neosho, Mo, Aug 28, 27; m 45, Kathleen V Jones; c Wyckliffe J, Candice H, Charles S, Thomas P & Heather K. *Educ:* Univ Kans, BS, 48, MD, 50; Univ Minn, MS, 58. *Hon Degrees:* DSc, Northeastern Ohio Univ, 90. *Honors & Awards:* Silver Medal, DSRS, 82; Scroll of Appreciation, Radiol Soc NAm, 84. *Prof Exp:* Intern, US Naval Hosp, Newport, RI, 50-51; gen pract med, Kans, 51-55; fel radiol, Mayo Clin, 55-58; assoc radiologist, Columbia Hosp, Milwaukee, Wis, 58-59; radiologist, Ohio Valley Gen Hosp, Wheeling, WVa, 59-67; prof radiol & dir diag radiol sect, Univ Tenn, 67-68; dir & chmn dept radiol, Aultman Hosp, 68-87; chmn coun radiol, Northeastern Ohio Univs Col Med, 74-87, dir integrated diag radiol, 76-87.

Concurrent Pos: NSF res grants radiol, 62-63 & 67-68; consult, Radiol Outreach Found, Doctors Hosp, Massillon, OH & Peoples Hosp, Mansfield, Ohio. Mem: Fel Am Col Radiol; Roentgen Ray Soc; Radiol Soc NAm; AMA. Res: Diagnostic radiology; arteriography; radiobiology; radiology education. Mailing Add: 1405 Harbor Dr NW Canton OH 44708

HOWLAND, WILLIAM STAPLETON, MEDICINE, ANESTHESIOLOGY. Current Pos: ASSOC PROF EXP SURG, SLOAN-KETTERING INST, 54-, MEM STAFF, 76-, CHMN, DEPT CRITICAL CARE, 78-; PROF ANESTHESIOL IN SURG, CORNELL UNIV, 68- Personal Data: b Savannah, Ga, July 21, 19; c 2. Educ: Univ Notre Dame, BS, 41; Columbia Univ, MD, 44; Am Bd Anesthesiol, dipl, 53. Prof Exp: Asst prof anesthesiol, Col Physicians & Surgeons, Columbia Univ, 53; assoc prof surg, Sloan-Kettering Div, Cornell Univ, Med Col, 54-55, assoc prof anesthesiol in surg, 55-68. Concurrent Pos: Attend anesthesiologist & chmn, Dept Anesthesiol, Mem Hosp, New York, 53-, dep chief med off, Dept Anesthesiol, 67-78, dep gen dir, 74-, vpres clin affairs, 77- Mem: Am Soc Anesthesiol. Res: Problems of hemorrhage and shock; post-operative care. Mailing Add: RR 3 Box 50A Brattleboro VT 05301-8506

HOWLETT, ALLYN C, PHARMACOLOGY, PHYSIOLOGY. Current Pos: from asst prof to prof, Dept Pharmacol, 79-90, PROF, DEPT PHARMACOL & PHYSIOL SCI, MED SCH, ST LOUIS UNIV, 90- Personal Data: b Rowan Co, NC, June 21, 50; c 1. Educ: Pa State Univ, BS, 71; Rutgers Univ, PhD(pharmacol & toxicol), 76. Prof Exp: Postdoctoral fel, Dept Pharmacol, Sch Med, Univ Va, 76-79. Concurrent Pos: NIH nat res serv award, 76-78; Pharmaceut Mfrs Asn Found res starter award, 80 & fac develop award basic pharmacol, 81-83; mem, Neurol Sci Study Sect, NIH, 84-85 & Biochem Study Sect, Nat Inst Drug Abuse, 90-91; Nat Inst Neurol & Communicative Dis & Stroke res career develop award, 85-89; prin investr, Nat Inst Drug Abuse, 89-92 & 90-93, NIH, 91-96. Mem: Am Soc Pharmacol & Exp Therapeut; Soc Neurosci. Res: Author of numerous technical publications. Mailing Add: Dept Pharmacol Med Sch St Louis Univ 1402 S Grand Blvd St Louis MO 63104-1080. Fax: 314-577-8554

HOWLETT, SUSAN ELLEN, CARDIOVASCULAR PHARMACOLOGY, CARDIAC PATHOPHYSIOLOGY. Current Pos: ASST PROF PHARMACOL, DALHOUSIE UNIV, 89- Personal Data: b Montreal, Que, Sept 2, 57; m 84; c 2. Educ: Concordia Univ, BSc, 79; Mem Univ, MSc, 82, PhD(physiol), 85. Prof Exp: Fel pharmacol, Univ Alta, 85-89. Mem: Soc Neurosci. Res: Role of calcium in the development of heart disease, especially in aging; techniques including voltage clamp of single cells and receptor binding studies to study calcium handling in the heart. Mailing Add: Dept Pharmacol Sir Charles Tupper Med Bldg Dalhousie Univ Halifax NS B3H 4H7 Can. Fax: 902-494-1388

HOWLEY, PETER MAXWELL, PATHOLOGY. Current Pos: CHMN, DEPT PATH, HARVARD UNIV, 93- Personal Data: b New Brunswick, NJ, Oct 9, 46; m 69; c 3. Educ: Princeton Univ, AB, 68; Rutgers Univ, MMS, 70; Harvard Univ, MD, 72. Honors & Awards: Warner Lambert-Parke Davis Award, Am Asn Pathologists, 83; Wallace Rowe Award, Nat Inst Allergy & Infectious Dis, 86; Meritorious Serv Award, USPHS, 89. Prof Exp: Resident path, Mass Gen Hosp, 72-73; res assoc virol, Nat Inst Allergy & Infectious Dis, NIH, 73-75; resident, Nat Cancer Inst, 75-77, sr investr, 77-79, sect chief path, 79-84, chief, Lab Tumor Viro. Bio. 84-93. Concurrent Pos: Ed, J Virol, 89- Mem: Nat Acad Sci; Inst Med-Nat Acad Sci; Am Asn Pathologists; Am Soc Clin Invest; Am Soc Microbiol; Am Soc Virol. Res: Molecular virology and oncology with a particular interest in the molecular biology and genetic organization of the papilloma viruses; development of eukaryotic vectors for studying gene regulation; gene expression. Mailing Add: Dept Path Harvard Univ 200 Longwood Ave Cambridge MA 02115-5701. Fax: 617-432-2882

HOWSE, HAROLD DARROW, CELL BIOLOGY. Current Pos: RETIRED. Personal Data: b Poplarville, Miss, Nov 8, 28; m 60; c 2. Educ: Univ Southern Miss, BS, 59, MS, 60; Tulane Univ, PhD(anat), 67. Prof Exp: Instr zool, Miss Col, 60; instr biol, Univ Southern Miss, 60-63; head sect micros, Gulf Coast Res Lab, 67-71, dir, 71-89. Concurrent Pos: Mem, Miss Marine Resources Coun, 71-; prof zool, Miss State Univ & prof biol, Univ Miss, 72-; prof biol, Univ Southern Miss, 73-; chmn adv comt, Miss Coastal Zone Mgt & Coastal Energy Impact Prog, 81. Mem: Am Asn Anatomists; AAAS; Am Micros Soc; Am Soc Cell Biol; Am Soc Zoologists; Electron Micros Soc Am; NY Acad Sci; Sigma Xi; Oceanog Soc. Res: Comparative histology, histochemistry and ultrastructure of the heart of marine invertebrates and vertebrates; histopathology of certain marine fishes and invertebrates. Mailing Add: 4713 Hilma St Moss Point MS 39563

HOWSMON, JOHN ARTHUR, CHEMISTRY, RESEARCH ADMINISTRATION. Current Pos: RETIRED. Personal Data: b Dayton, Ohio, July 4, 19; m 53, Maria Economides; c John D & George C. Educ: Berea Col, AB, 41; Univ Ill, PhD, 44. Prof Exp: Res chemist, Am Viscose Corp, 44-57, mgr basic res, 57-59, mgr polyolefin dept, 59-62; assoc dir res & develop, Avisun Corp, Pa, 62-68, admin dir res & eng, 68-70; admin res & develop mgr, Amoco Chem Corp, 70-84. Res: Rayon fibers; relation of structure to properties of fibers; polyolefin plastics. Mailing Add: 4604 Flagship Dr No 303 Ft Myers FL 33919

HOWTON, DAVID RONALD, BIOCHEMISTRY, RADIATION CHEMISTRY. Current Pos: PROF ALLIED MED SCI, JOHN A BURNS SCH MED, UNIV HAWAII, MANOA, 78- Personal Data: b Tacoma, Wash, July 8, 20; m 73, Georgia Zakonyi. Educ: Calif Inst Technol, BS, 42, PhD(org chem), 46. Prof Exp: Asst res biochemist, Atomic Energy Proj, Sch Med, 48-56, assoc res biochemist, 56-64, res biochemist, Lab Nuclear Med & Radiation Biol & prof physiol chem, Sch Med, Univ Calif, Los Angeles, 64-76; prof chem & chmn dept, Cols Med & Med Sci, King Faisal Univ, Dammam, Saudi Arabia, 76-78. Concurrent Pos: Res corp fel, Calif Inst Technol, 46-48; from clin instr to assoc prof physiol chem, Sch Med, Univ Calif, Los Angeles, 52-64, assoc prof biophys & nuclear med, 61-64, prof, 64-70. Mem: Am Chem Soc. Res: Radiation chemistry of lipids. Mailing Add: 2467 AAPI Pl Pearl City HI 96782-1002. Fax: 808-956-9547

HOY, CASEY WILLIAM, QUANTITATIVE BEHAVIORAL ECOLOGY. Current Pos: asst prof systs analysis insect pest mgt, 87-93, ASSOC PROF ENTOM, OHIO STATE UNIV, 93- Personal Data: b Berea, Ohio, Jan 11, 54; m 82, Karen A Skubik; c Briana & Sean. Educ: Cornell Univ, BS, 81, PhD(entom), 88. Prof Exp: Pest mgt control consult, 81-83; grad res asst insect biol, Cornell Univ, 83-87. Mem: Entom Soc Am; Sigma Xi; Soc Invertebrate Path; Potato Asn Am. Res: Application of systems analysis to problems in vegetable pest management; spatial dynamics of insect pests at various scales. Mailing Add: Dept Entom Ohio State Univ OARDC 1680 Madison Ave Wooster OH 44691

HOY, GILBERT RICHARD, GAMMA-RAY OPTICS. Current Pos: prof & chmn, 80-89, PROF & EMINENT SCHOLAR, OLD DOMINION UNIV, 90- Personal Data: b Cleveland, Ohio, June 17, 32; m 52, 81; c 4. Educ: Davis & Elkins Col, BS, 54; Cornell Univ, MS, 58; Carnegie Inst Technol, PhD(physics), 63. Prof Exp: Scientist, Solid State Res Dept, Xerox Corp, 62-63; instr physics, Carnegie Inst Technol, 63-65; from asst prof to prof physics, 65-80, actg chair, Boston Univ, 79-80. Concurrent Pos: Hon res assoc, Harvard Univ, 72; scientist, Centre Nuclear Studies, Grenoble, France, 76-77; consult, NIH, 78-81 & Inst Defense Analysis, 85-90; collabr, Los Alamos Nat Lab, 87- Mem: Am Phys Soc. Res: Gamma-ray optics; application of Mossbauer spectroscopy to the study of solid state physics. Mailing Add: Physics Dept Old Dominion Univ Norfolk VA 23529

HOY, JAMES BENJAMIN, ECOLOGY. Current Pos: res entomologist, Dept Entom, 94-96, ASSOC RES SCIENTIST, DEPT PSYCHOL, UNIV FLA, 96- Personal Data: b Wauseon, Ohio, Apr 13, 35; m 61, Marjorie A Wolf; c 1. Educ: Ohio Wesleyan Univ, BS, 57; Univ Mich, MS, 59; Univ Kans, PhD(entom), 66. Prof Exp: Res parasitologist, Univ Calif, Berkeley, 63-65; res entomologist, Agr Res Serv, USDA, 66-73; asst prof biol, State Univ NY Purchase & Mt Vernon, 74-76; mem res staff, Dept Entom Sci, Univ Calif, Berkeley, 76-86; entomologist, Forest Serv, USDA, Berkeley, 87-91. Concurrent Pos: Field rep, Coun on Econ Priorities, 73-75. Mem: Animal Behav Soc; Entom Soc Am. Res: Animal behavior; medical and veterinary entomology; aquatic ecology; soil ecology. Mailing Add: 4320 SW 83rd Way Gainesville FL 32608-4131. E-Mail: jimhoy@biotech.ufl.org

HOY, MARJORIE ANN, INSECT ECOLOGY, GENETICS. Current Pos: from asst prof to assoc prof, 76-82, prof, 82-92, EMER PROF ENTOM SCI, UNIV CALIF, BERKELEY, 92-; EMINENT SCHOLAR, FISCHER DAVIES & ECKES PROF BIOL CONTROL, DEPT ENTOM & NEMATOL, UNIV FLA, GAINESVILLE, 92- Personal Data: b Kansas City, Kans; m 61, James B; c Benjamin. Educ: Univ Kans, AB, 63; Univ Calif, MS, 66, PhD(entom), 72. Honors & Awards: Bussart Mem Award, Entom Soc Am, 86; Founders Award, Entom Soc Am, 92; Outstanding Sr Researcher, Sigma Xi, 96. Prof Exp: Res geneticist, Univ Calif, Berkeley, 64-66; lectr biol, Fresno State Col, 67-68; lab technician, Div Biol Control, Univ Calif, Berkeley, 68-70; lectr, Calif State Univ, Fresno, 73; res entomologist, Conn Agr Exp Sta, 73-75; res entomologist, Northeast Forest Exp Sta, US Forest Serv, USDA, 75-76. Concurrent Pos: Counc mem, Am Inst Biol Sci, 96- Mem: Sigma Xi; fel Entom Soc Am; Int Orgn Biol Control; Acarology Soc Am; fel AAAS; Am Inst Biol Serv. Res: Genetics and biological control of insect and mite pests; genetic selection of a pesticide-resistant predators and parasites for integrated pest management programs; risk assessment for releases of transgenic arthropod natural enemies developing transgenic arthropods. Mailing Add: Dept Entom & Nematol Inst Food & Agr Sci Univ Fla Gainesville FL 32611-0620. Fax: 904-392-0190; E-Mail: mahoy@gnv.ifas.ufl.edu

HOY, ROBERT C, SOLID STATE PHYSICS, CRYSTALLOGRAPHY. Current Pos: PRES, GULF FOOD PROD CO, INC, 73- Personal Data: b New Orleans, La, Dec 2, 33; m 67, Rose K Jung. Educ: Tulane Univ, BS, 54, MS, 60, PhD(physics), 65. Prof Exp: Res asst, Tulane Univ, 60-62, res assoc, 65-66; res assoc, Columbia Univ, 66; sr res engr, Space Div, Chrysler Corp, 66-67; asst prof physics, La State Univ, New Orleans, 67-73. Concurrent Pos: Spec lectr, Univ New Orleans, 75- Mem: AAAS; Am Phys Soc. Res: Electron diffraction; surface physics; x-ray crystallography. Mailing Add: 1005 Andrews Ave Metairie LA 70005-1701

HOY, RONALD RAYMOND, BIOLOGY. Current Pos: asst prof, 73-77, ASSOC PROF BIOL, CORNELL UNIV, 77- Personal Data: b Walla Walla, Wash, Jan 12, 39. Educ: Wash State Univ, BS, 62; Stanford Univ, PhD(biol), 68. Prof Exp: Asst prof biol, State Univ NY, Stony Brook, 71-73. Concurrent Pos: NIH fel, 68-70 & 78. Mem: Sigma Xi; Am Soc Zoologists; AAAS; Soc Neurosci. Res: Physiological and behavioral studies of insect audition; neuroethology; regeneration in the nervous system; developmental neurobiology. Mailing Add: Cornell Univ W 214 Mudd Hall Ithaca NY 14850

HOYE, ROBERT EARL, HEALTH CARE MANAGEMENT, URBAN POLICY. Current Pos: asst vpres, Univ Louisville, 74-81, prof urban policy & coordr Grad Prog Health Systs, 81-95, prof educ, 92-95, EMER PROF, UNIV LOUISVILLE, 95- Personal Data: b Warwick, RI, Jan 12, 31; m 55,

Patricia Bushwell; c Robert E Jr, Joanne D, Peter M & Kathleen B. *Educ:* Providence Col, BA, 53; St John's Univ, NY, MS, 55; Univ Wis-Madison, PhD, 73. *Honors & Awards:* Statesman Healthcare Admin Award, Royal Soc Health. *Prof Exp:* Instr, St John's Univ, 53-55; dir guid pub schs, Middleboro, Mass, 55-56, Rutland, Vt, 56-57; dean, Champlain Col, Vt, 57-58; supt, Frontier Regional Sch Dist, Deerfield, Mass, 58-60; New Eng dir, Sci Res Assocs, subsid IBM, Chicago, 60-65; nat dir, Learning Systs Div, Xerox Corp, NY, 65-66; dir, Instrnl Media Lab, Univ Wis-Milwaukee, 66-73. *Concurrent Pos:* Consult mgt, Louisville, 66-; ed, Educ J, 68-73. *Mem:* Fel AMA; Royal Soc Health. *Res:* Healthcare management. *Mailing Add:* 2238 Wynewood Circle Louisville KY 40222

HOYE, THOMAS ROBERT, ORGANIC CHEMISTRY. *Current Pos:* From asst prof to assoc prof, 76-88, PROF CHEM, UNIV MINN, 88- *Personal Data:* b New Castle, Pa, June 19, 50; m 73; c 3. *Educ:* Bucknell Univ, BS & MS, 72; Harvard Univ, PhD(chem), 76. *Concurrent Pos:* Adv comt mem, Res Corp Grants, 83-88; fel, Alfred P Sloan Found, 85-89. *Mem:* Am Chem Soc. *Res:* Synthetic organic chemistry; development and application of synthetic methodology to natural products total synthesis; synthetic applications of Fischer carbene complexes; stereochemistry; symmetry; NMR analysis; natural product structure determination. *Mailing Add:* Dept Chem 422 Smith Hall Univ Minn 207 Pleasant St SE Minneapolis MN 55455

HOYER, BILL HENRIKSEN, MICROBIOLOGY. *Current Pos:* STAFF MEM, DEPT TERRESTRIAL MAGNETISM, CARNEGIE INST WASHINGTON, 68- *Personal Data:* b Seattle, Wash, Dec 4, 21; m 48; c 2. *Educ:* Univ Wash, BS, 43, MS, 45; Univ Minn, PhD(microbiol), 48. *Prof Exp:* Instr, Univ Minn, 46-48; bacteriologist, NIH, Md, 48-50, Rocky Mt Lab, 50-64, sci dir lab biol viruses, 64-68. *Concurrent Pos:* Lectr, Mont State Univ, 52-64; mem, Human Develop & Aging Res & Training Comn, Nat Inst Child Health & Human Develop, 70-; sci dir, USPHS, 48-68. *Mem:* AAAS; Am Soc Microbiol; Sigma Xi. *Res:* Physiology of microorganisms and mammalian cells; chromatography and purification of viruses and viral components; DNA-DNA and DNA-RNA relationships of viruses, bacteria and animals; primate relationships; evolution. *Mailing Add:* 5901 Lone Oak Dr Bethesda MD 20814

HOYER, LEON WILLIAM, BLOOD COAGULATION RESEARCH, HEMATOLOGY. *Current Pos:* from assoc prof to prof, 70-85, CLIN PROF MED, SCH MED, UNIV CONN, 85-; DIR, HOLLAND LAB, AM RED CROSS BLOOD SERV, 85- *Personal Data:* b Minneapolis, Minn, Mar 6, 36; m 60, Diane Lawrence; c Helen K, Sharon A & Erik W. *Educ:* Harvard Col, AB, 58; Univ Minn, MD, 62; Am Bd Internal Med, dipl, 70. *Honors & Awards:* Murray Theilin Res Award, Nat Hemophilia Asn, 81; Hemophilia Res Award, French Hemophilia Asn, 83. *Prof Exp:* Asst prof med, Univ Rochester, Sch Med & Dent, 68-70. *Concurrent Pos:* Prin investr, NIH grants res factor VIII, 74-; mem, Hemat Study Sect, NIH, 76-80 & 87-91; vis scientist, Karolinska Inst, Stockholm, Sweden, 78-79; chair, Med & Sci Adv Comn, Nat Hemophilia Found, 82-85; chmn, Van Willebrand factor subcomt, 87-90, Int Comt Haemostasis & Thrombosis, 89-93; dir, Spec Ctr Res Transfusion Med, 91-96; prof med & genetics, Sch Med George Washington Univ, 88- *Mem:* Am Soc Hemat; Am Soc Clin Invest; Am Heart Asn Coun Thrombosis; Am Asn Immunologists; Int Soc Hematol. *Res:* Structure and function of coagulation on factor VIII; molecular basis of hemophilia A; immunochemical properties of human antibodies that inactivate factor VIII. *Mailing Add:* Holland Lab 15601 Crabbs Branch Way Rockville MD 20855. *Fax:* 301-738-0553; *E-Mail:* hoyer@usa.redcross.org

HOYER-ELLEFSEN, SIGURD, ELECTRICAL ENGINEERING. *Current Pos:* PRES & CHIEF EXEC OFFICER, LINTON ROOF TRUSS INC, 86- *Personal Data:* b Olso, Norway, July 24, 32; US citizen; div; c 5. *Educ:* Mass Inst Technol, BSME, 56, MSME, 57, ScD, 62. *Prof Exp:* Sr engr, Potter Instrument Co, Inc, 57-69, vpres res & develop, 70-76; vpres res & develop, Smith-Corona, SCM Corp, 76-83; sr vpres, Servo Corp Am, 83-84; consult, 84-86. *Concurrent Pos:* Chief scientist & asst prog dir, Fairchild Industs, Inc, 64-70. *Mem:* Inst Elec & Electronics Engrs. *Mailing Add:* 540 Kay Terr Boca Raton FL 33432

HOYLE, FRED, ASTRONOMY. *Current Pos:* HON PROF PHYSICS & ASTRON, MANCHESTER UNIV, 73-; HON RES PROF, CARDIFF UNIV, 75- *Personal Data:* b Gilstead, Eng, June 24, 15; m 39, Barbara Clark; c 2. *Educ:* Emmanuel Col, MA; St John's Col, MA; Cambridge Univ, MA. *Honors & Awards:* Mayhew Prize, 36; Smith's Prize, 38; Goldsmith Exhibitioner, 38, Sr Exhibitioner, Royal Comn 1851, 38; Kalinga Prize, 68; Gold Medal, Royal Astron Soc, 68; Bruce Medal, Astron Soc Pacific, 70, Dorothea Klumpke Roberts Award, 77; Royal Medal, Royal Soc, 74; Balzan Prize, 94; Karl Schwarzchild Medal, Ger Astron Soc, 92; Crafoord Prize, Royal Swed Acad Sci, 97. *Prof Exp:* Univ lectr math, Cambridge Univ, 45-58, Plumian prof astron & exp philos, 58-72, dir, Inst Theoret Astron, 66-72. *Concurrent Pos:* Staff mem, Mt Wilson & Palomar Observ, 56-62; vis prof astrophys, Calif Inst Technol, 58-, Cornell Univ, 73-79; prof astron, Royal Inst, 69-72. *Mem:* Foreign assoc Nat Acad Sci; hon mem Am Acad Arts & Sci; foreign mem Am Philos Soc. *Res:* Author of numerous books on astronomy. *Mailing Add:* Royal Six Carlton House Terr London SWIY 5AG England

HOYT, CHARLES D, JR, INDUSTRIAL ENGINEERING. *Current Pos:* assoc prof, 62-69, PROF INDUST ENG, ARIZ STATE UNIV, 69- *Personal Data:* b Indianapolis, Ind, Mar 17, 12; m 37; c 2. *Educ:* Purdue Univ, BSChE, 35, MSIE, 60, PhD(indust eng), 62. *Prof Exp:* With Am Brass Co, Wis, 35-36; off mgr, Hoyt Mach Co, Ind, 36-37; off mgr, Charles D Hoyt Co, 37-45, pres & treas, 46-59; teaching asst indust eng, Purdue Univ, 60-62. *Mem:* Am Inst Indust Engrs; Am Soc Eng Educ; Nat Soc Prof Engrs; Inst Mgt Sci. *Res:* Industrial productivity; manufacturing organization and management; rank-frequency statistics and its applications to organization, wage and salary administration, industrial marketing and manufacturing production; variable budget control of manufacturing operations. *Mailing Add:* 1311 W Baseline Rd Tempe AZ 85283

HOYT, DONALD FRANK, PHYSIOLOGICAL ECOLOGY, ANIMAL ENERGETICS. *Current Pos:* from assoc prof to asst prof, 80-88, PROF BIOL, CALIF STATE POLYTECH UNIV, 88- *Personal Data:* b San Francisco, Calif, May 22, 45; m 69, Gwendolyn Denes; c Benjamin, Andrew & Elizabeth. *Educ:* Pomona Col, Calif, BA, 67; Univ Calif, Los Angeles, PhD(biol), 77. *Prof Exp:* Res assoc, Dept Physiol, State Univ NY, 77-78; res fel, Mus Comparative Zool, Harvard Univ, 78-79, preceptor, Dept Biol, 79-80. *Mem:* Am Physiol Soc. *Res:* Physiological ecology of terrestrial vertebrates, in particular comparative aspects of energetics of locomotion in mammals and the relation between metabolic rate and growth in avian embryos; comparative aspects of energetics of locomotion in mammals; comparative physiology of detraining; the relation between metabolic rate and growth in avian embryos. *Mailing Add:* Dept Biol Sci Calif State Polytech Univ Pomona CA 91768. *Fax:* 909-869-4078; *E-Mail:* dhoyt@csupomona.edu

HOYT, EARLE B, JR, ORGANIC CHEMISTRY. *Current Pos:* asst prof, 67-74, ASSOC PROF CHEM, NORTHERN ARIZ UNIV, 67- *Personal Data:* b New York, NY, July 14, 37; m 59; c 1. *Educ:* Middlebury Col, BA, 59; Alliance Francaise, dipl, 60; Tufts Univ, PhD(chem), 66. *Prof Exp:* Instr chem, Northwestern Univ, 65-66; NIH fel, Cornell Univ, 66-67. *Mem:* AAAS; Am Chem Soc; Sigma Xi. *Res:* Organic synthesis, especially highly strained compounds and natural products. *Mailing Add:* 7500 Old Walnut Canyon Rd Flagstaff AZ 86004-1442

HOYT, HARRY CHARLES, PHYSICS, SYSTEMS ANALYSIS. *Current Pos:* RETIRED. *Personal Data:* b Grinnell, Iowa, June 20, 24; m 59, Martha; c Andrea & Brian. *Educ:* Univ Colo, BS, 46; Calif Inst Technol, PhD(physics), 52. *Prof Exp:* Instr physics, Univ Colo, 47-48; res fel, Calif Inst Technol, 52-53; staff mem, Los Alamos Nat Lab, Univ Calif, 53-59, alt group leader, 59-68, asst div leader, Weapons Div, 68-70, assoc div leader, 70-71, alt div leader, Theoret Design Div, 71-72, asst dir, Weapon Planning, 72-76, asst dir, Weapon Planning & Coord, 76-79, asst dir policy, 79, assoc dir energy prog, 79-81, asst dir special prog, 81-86. *Concurrent Pos:* Consult, 75-76, 86- *Mem:* AAAS; Am Phys Soc; Opers Res Soc Am; Sigma Xi. *Res:* Nuclear spectroscopy; hydrodynamics; electricity and magnetism; numerical analysis. *Mailing Add:* 650 Barranca Rd Los Alamos NM 87544

HOYT, JACK W(ALLACE), FLUID MECHANICS. *Current Pos:* prof, 81-92, EMER PROF MECH ENG, SAN DIEGO STATE UNIV, 92- *Personal Data:* b Chicago, Ill, Oct 19, 22; m 45, Helen Erickson; c John A, Katheryn M (Everett), Annette M (Butler) & Denise M (Kreusi). *Educ:* Ill Inst Technol, BS, 44; Univ Calif, Los Angeles, MS, 52, PhD(eng), 62. *Prof Exp:* Aero-engr, Nat Adv Comt Aeronaut, 44-48; mech engr, Naval Ocean Systs Ctr, 48-79; prof mech eng, Rutgers Univ, 79-81. *Concurrent Pos:* Am Soc Mech Engrs Freeman scholar, 71; Benjamin Meaker vis prof, Univ Bristol, Eng, 87. *Mem:* Fel Am Soc Mech Engrs; Soc Naval Architects & Marine Engrs; NY Acad Sci. *Res:* Fluid mechanics; drag-reducing polymer solutions; ocean engineering. *Mailing Add:* 4694 Lisann St San Diego CA 92117. *Fax:* 619-594-6005

HOYT, ROBERT DAN, ICHTHYOLOGY. *Current Pos:* asst prof, 69-74, assoc prof, 74-78, PROF BIOL, WESTERN KY UNIV, 78- *Personal Data:* b Conway, Ark, Sept 24, 41; m 62, Theresa Lachowsky; c Roberta, Louis, Michael, Stuart & Matthew. *Educ:* Univ Cent Ark, BS, 63; Univ Ark, MS, 65; Univ Louisville, PhD(biol), 69. *Prof Exp:* Res asst fisheries, Univ Ark, 63-65; interpretive naturalist, Bernheim Forest Nature Mus, 65-66. *Concurrent Pos:* Actg dir, Univ Hons Prog, Western Ky Univ, 83-84, assoc dean, Ogden Sci Col, 85-86. *Mem:* Am Soc Ichthyol & Herpet. *Res:* Larval fish ecology; early anatomical development of fish. *Mailing Add:* Dept Biol Western Ky Univ 1 Big Red Way St Bowling Green KY 42101-3576. *Fax:* 502-745-6471

HOYT, ROSALIE CHASE, PHYSICS. *Current Pos:* from instr to assoc prof, 41-69, Marion Reilly prof, 69-82, EMER MARION REILLY PROF PHYSICS, BRYN MAWR COL, 82- *Personal Data:* b New York, NY, May 20, 14. *Educ:* Columbia Univ, BA, 40; Bryn Mawr Col, MA, 41, PhD(physics), 45. *Prof Exp:* Instr physics, Univ Rochester, 45-48. *Mem:* Am Phys Soc. *Res:* Bioelectrics; bioelectric instrumentation; nerve models; counters and detectors for nuclear research. *Mailing Add:* Parker Head Rd Phippsburg ME 04562

HOYT, STANLEY CHARLES, ACAROLOGY, ADMINISTRATION. *Current Pos:* RETIRED. *Personal Data:* b Oakland, Calif, Oct 4, 29; m 55; c 3. *Educ:* Univ Calif, BS, 51, PhD, 58. *Honors & Awards:* Ciba-Geigy Award, Entom Soc Am, 73; C W Woodworth Award, Pac Br, Entom Soc Am, 89. *Prof Exp:* Asst entomologist, Wash State Univ, 57-63, assoc entomologist, 63-69, entomologist, Tree Fruit Res Ctr, 69-94, supt, 83-91. *Concurrent Pos:* Fulbright grant, 70-71; FAO consult, China, 87. *Mem:* Entom Soc Am; Acarological Soc Am. *Res:* Biology, ecology and control of insects affecting apples; host plant-pest interactions. *Mailing Add:* 351 N E No 12 East Wenatchee WA 98802

HOYT, WILLIAM F, NEUROLOGY, OPHTHALMOLOGY. *Current Pos:* From asst prof to assoc prof, 58-70, PROF NEURO-OPHTHAL, UNIV CALIF, SCH MED, SAN FRANCISCO, 70- *Personal Data:* b Berkeley, Calif, June 17, 26; m 56; c 2. *Educ:* Univ Calif, San Francisco, AB, 47, MD, 50; Am Bd Ophthal, dipl, 58. *Concurrent Pos:* Fulbright fel, Univ Vienna, Sch Med, 56-57; Heed fel, Johns Hopkins Hosp, 57-58; asst ed, Arch Ophthal, 62-65, assoc ed, 65- *Mem:* Soc Neurol Surg; Barany Soc. *Res:* Clinical teaching and laboratory investigation of problems related to anatomy, physiology and pathology of visual and oculomotor systems. *Mailing Add:* Dept Ophthal & Neurosurg Univ Calif San Francisco CA 94143-0350

HOYT, WILLIAM LIND, MATHEMATICS. *Current Pos:* ASSOC PROF MATH, RUTGERS UNIV, 67- *Personal Data:* b Nephi, Utah, Sept 8, 28; m 57; c 1. *Educ:* Univ Utah, BA, 50, MS, 51; Univ Chicago, PhD(math), 58. *Prof Exp:* Instr math, Northwestern Univ, 56-57; instr, Hopkins, 58-59; asst prof, Brandeis Univ, 59; mem fac, Univ Ind, Bloomington, 59-67. *Mem:* Am Math Soc. *Res:* Algebraic geometry; algebraic number theory. *Mailing Add:* 153 N Eighth Ave Highland Park NJ 08904-2921

HOYTE, ROBERT MIKELL, ORGANIC CHEMISTRY, BIOCHEMISTRY. *Current Pos:* from asst prof to prof, 72-90, DISTINGUISHED TEACHING PROF CHEM, COL OLD WESTBURY, STATE UNIV NY, 90- *Personal Data:* b New York, NY, Nov 8, 43; m 87, Cheryl Browne; c Imara-Safi. *Educ:* Long Island Univ, BS, 64; Rutgers Univ, New Brunswick, MS, 67, PhD(chem), 68. *Prof Exp:* Asst chemist, Brookhaven Nat Lab, 68-71; asst prof chem, Medgar Evers Col, 71-72. *Concurrent Pos:* Vis fel, Dept Obstet & Gynec, Yale Univ Sch Med, 80-81; res affil, Dept Obsted & Gynec, Sch Med, Yale Univ, 82- *Mem:* AAAS; Am Chem Soc; Sigma Xi. *Res:* Synthetic organic chemistry; steroid biochemistry; synthesis of radiopharmaceuticals. *Mailing Add:* Col Old Westbury State Univ NY Old Westbury NY 11568-0210

HOYUMPA, ANASTACIO MANINGO, INTERNAL MEDICINE, GASTROENTEROLOGY. *Current Pos:* PROF MED, UNIV TEX HEALTH SCI CTR, SAN ANTONIO, 82- *Personal Data:* b Baybay, Leyte, Philippines, July 4, 37; m 63; c Rebecca, Dan, Amelia & Benjamin. *Educ:* Univ Santo Tomas, MD, 61. *Prof Exp:* Instr, Univ Cincinnati, 67-68, asst prof med, 68-72, actg assoc dir, 72; GE sect chief, Vet Admin Hosp, 72; from asst prof to assoc prof med A, Vanderbilt Univ, 72-82; chief gastroenterol, Audie Murphy Mem Vet Admin Hosp, San Antonio, Tex, 82-87. *Concurrent Pos:* Fel, Univ Cincinnati, 65-67; consult, Longview State Hosp, 71-72; res & educ assoc, Vet Admin Hosp, 73-75, clin investr, 76-78, investr alcoholism, 79-81. *Mem:* Am Soc Gastrointestinal Endoscopy; Am Asn Liver Dis; Am Gastroenterol Asn; Res Soc Alcoholism; Cent Soc Clin Res; Int Asn Study Liver. *Res:* Thiamine intestinal transport and mechanism of alcohol inhibition; effect of liver disease and alcohol on drug metabolism; fetal alcohol syndrome. *Mailing Add:* Dept Med Health Sci Ctr Univ Tex 7703 Floyd Curl Dr San Antonio TX 78284. *Fax:* 210-567-1976

HOZUMI, NOBUMICHI, IMMUNOLOGY. *Current Pos:* asst prof molecular biol, Dept Med Biophys, 79-84, assoc prof immunol, Dept Immunol, 84-88, PROF IMMUNOL, UNIV TORONTO, 88- *Personal Data:* b Kitakata-City, Japan, Feb 25, 43. *Educ:* Keio Univ, Japan, MD, 68, PhD(molecular biol), 72. *Honors & Awards:* David Pressman Mem Award, 83; Boehringer Mannheim Can Prize, Can Biochem Soc, 84. *Prof Exp:* Lectr molecular biol, Dept Molecular Biol, Keio Univ, Japan, 72-75; mem immunol, Basel Inst Immunol, 75-78. *Concurrent Pos:* Reviewer, Nat Cancer Inst Can, 86-87. *Mem:* Am Asn Immunol; Can Soc Immunologists. *Res:* Molecular mechanisms involved in B cell differentiation and immunological self-nonself recognition. *Mailing Add:* Immunol & Med Genetics Dept Mt Sinai Hosp 600 University Ave Toronto ON M5G 1X5 Can. *Fax:* 416-586-8588

HRABA, JOHN BURNETT, ELECTRICAL ENGINEERING. *Current Pos:* Prof elec eng, Univ NH, 49-73, assoc dean col technol, 49-68, dean instnl res & planning, 68-, systs dir planning & anal, 73-, EMER PROF ELEC & COMPUT ENG, UNIV NH. *Personal Data:* b New York, NY, Nov 21, 21; m 46; c 2. *Educ:* Univ NH, BS, 48; Yale Univ, MEng, 49; Univ Ill, PhD(elec eng), 55. *Concurrent Pos:* Instr, Univ Ill, 55; asst prog dir eng sci, NSF, 59-60. *Mem:* Assoc Inst Elec & Electronics Engrs. *Res:* System electromagnetics. *Mailing Add:* Dept Elec & Comput Eng Univ NH Kingsbury Hall Durham NH 03824

HRAZDINA, GEZA, BIOCHEMISTRY, BIOTECHNOLGY. *Current Pos:* From res assoc to assoc prof, 66-81, PROF BIOCHEM, NY STATE AGR EXP STA, CORNELL UNIV, 81- *Personal Data:* b Letenye, Hungary, Mar 16, 39; m 93, Minou Hemmat; c Geza K. *Educ:* Swiss Fed Inst Technol, Dipl, 63, DSc, 66. *Concurrent Pos:* Lectr fel, Alexander von Humboldt Stiftung, Ger, 74-75, 81; vis prof, Tech Univ, Budapest, 79 & Univ Cologne, Ger, 81; exchange fel, Nat Acad Sci, 81; prog dir cell biol, NSF, 93-94. *Mem:* Phytochem Soc NAm (pres, 82-83); Phytochem Soc Europe; Am Soc Plant Physiol; Int Soc Plant Molecular Biol. *Res:* Biochemistry and genetic control of plant aromatic metabolism; chemistry and biochemistry of plant natural products; cellular and subcellular localization in plant metabolism. *Mailing Add:* NY State Agr Exp Sta Cornell Univ Geneva NY 14456. *Fax:* 315-787-2284; *E-Mail:* gh10@cornell.edu

HRBEK, GEORGE W(ILLIAM), electrical engineering; deceased, see previous edition for last biography

HRDINA, PAVEL DUSAN, PSYCHIATRY, PHARMOCOLOGY. *Current Pos:* from assoc prof to prof, 69-95, DIR BAS SCI, INST MENT HEALTH RES, UNIV OTTAWA, 94-, EMER PROF PHARMACOL & PSYCHIAT, FAC MED, 95- *Personal Data:* b Uzhorod, Czech, Oct 3, 29; m 54; c 1. *Educ:* Komensky Univ, MD, 55; Czech Acad Sci, PhD(pharmacol), 64. *Honors & Awards:* Medal, Can Col Neuropsyolopharmacol, 94; John Dewan Prize, Outstanding Res Mental Health, 95. *Prof Exp:* Instr path, Med Sch, Komensky Univ, 53-54, asst prof med chem, 55-57, asst & assoc prof pharmacol, 58-68. *Concurrent Pos:* Foreign res fel, Mario Negri Pharmacol Res Inst, Milan, 65-66; res fel, Med Col Va, 66-67; Med Res Coun Can vis scientist, Univ Ottawa, 68-69; vis prof, Synthelabo Lers, Paris, 79, & Dept Pharmacol, Melbourne Univ, 87; ed, J Psychiat & Neurosci. *Mem:* Pharmacol Soc Can; Can Col Neuropsychopharmacol (vpres, 84-88, pres, 88-90); Int Soc Neurochem; Col Int Neuropscholpharmacol. *Res:* Pharmacology of antidepressant drugs; neuroscience; sertonergic system in depression and suicidal behavior. *Mailing Add:* Dept Pharmacol Univ Ottawa 451 Smyth Rd Rm 3141 Ottawa ON K1H 8M5 Can. *E-Mail:* phrdina@uottawa.ca

HRDY, SARAH BLAFFER, PRIMATE BEHAVIOR, HUMAN ECOLOGY. *Current Pos:* ASSOC, PEABODY MUS, 79-; PROF, UNIV CALIF, DAVIS, 84- *Personal Data:* b Dallas, Tex, July 11, 46; m 72, Daniel B; c 3. *Educ:* Radcliffe Col, BA, 69; Harvard Univ, PhD(behav biol), 75. *Honors & Awards:* Geneva Sayre Lectr, Russell Sage Col, 85; Spencer Lectr, Univ Oxford, 95- *Prof Exp:* Instr anthrop, Univ Mass, 73; lectr biol anthrop, Harvard Univ, 75-76, fel biol, 77-78. *Concurrent Pos:* Consult ed, Am J Primatol, Primates, Cult Anthrop; vis assoc prof anthrop, Rice Univ, 81-82; assoc ed, Human Evolution, 85-88, Human Nature, 89, Evolutionary Anthrop, 91; Guggenheim fel, 87-88. *Mem:* Nat Acad Sci; fel Animal Behav Soc; fel Am Acad Arts & Sci; Am Soc Naturalists; Am Soc Primatologists; Am Anthrop Soc; Int Primatological Soc. *Res:* Evolution of primate social behavior. *Mailing Add:* Dept Anthrop Univ Calif Davis CA 95616

HREN, JOHN J(OSEPH), MATERIALS SCIENCE, SOLID STATE PHYSICS. *Current Pos:* PROF & HEAD MAT SCI & ENG, NC STATE UNIV, 85- *Personal Data:* b Milwaukee, Wis, Dec 3, 33; m 57; c Karl, Philip, Christine, Jonathan & Stephen. *Educ:* Univ Wis, BS, 57; Univ Ill, MS, 60; Stanford Univ, PhD(mat sci), 62. *Prof Exp:* Patent exam, Metall Div, US Patent Off, 57-58; res physicist, Lawrence Radiation Lab, 61-62; NSF fels, Max Planck Inst, Stuttgart, Ger, 62-63 & Univ Cambridge, 63-64; from asst prof to assoc prof metall, Univ Fla, 64-72, prof mat sci & eng, 72-85; dir Major Ana Instrumental Ctr, 82-85. *Concurrent Pos:* Vpres, Mat Consult, Inc; vis scientist, Div Tribophysics, Csiro, Melbourne, Australia, 70-71; consult, Bendix Corp, Mo, 71- & Sandia Labs, NM, 76-, Oak Ridge Nat Lab; vis prof mat sci, Vanderbilt Univ, 75-76; pres, Metamics Inc, Fla, 76-82; chmn, Mat Sci Prog, Nat Tech Univ; external adv & chmn, Nat Ctr Electron Micros; consult, Oak Ridge Nat Lab; chair, Mat Sci Prog, Nat Tech Univ, 89- *Mem:* AAAS; Am Inst Physics; Am Inst Mining, Metall & Petrol Engrs; Am Soc Metals; Electron Micros Soc Am; Sigma Xi. *Res:* Field-ion microscopy; atom probe; atomic order; defects in crystals; radiation damage; analytical electron microscopy; vacuum microelectronics; field emission. *Mailing Add:* Dept Mat Sci & Eng NC State Univ Box 7907 Raleigh NC 27695-7907. *E-Mail:* jhren@mte.ncsu.edu

HRESHCHYSHYN, MYROSLAW M, OBSTETRICS & GYNECOLOGY. *Current Pos:* from asst prof to assoc prof, 62-70, PROF OBSTET & GYNEC, STATE UNIV NY, BUFFALO, 70-; ASSOC CHIEF CANCER RES GYNECOLOGIST, ROSWELL PARK MEM INST, 71-; STAFF, CHILDREN'S HOSP, BUFFALO, NY. *Personal Data:* b Kovel, Ukraine, Aug 30, 27; US citizen; m 58; c 4. *Educ:* Univ Frankfurt, MD, 51. *Prof Exp:* Intern, St Joseph's Hosp, Yonkers, NY, 52-53; from asst resident to resident obstet & gynec, Cumberland Hosp, Brooklyn, 53-56; sr cancer res surgeon, Dept Gynec, Roswell Park Mem Inst, 58-65, assoc cancer res gynecologist, 65-71. *Concurrent Pos:* Clin fel gynec cancer, Kings County Hosp, 56-57; fel chemother, Roswell Park Mem Inst, 57-59; chmn, Gynec Oncol Group, 71. *Mem:* AMA; Am Col Obstet & Gynec; Soc Gynec Oncol. *Res:* Gynecologic cancer; cancer chemotherapy; gonadotropins; endometriosis; osteoporosis. *Mailing Add:* 219 Bryant St Buffalo NY 14222-2206

HRIBAR, JOHN ANTHONY, CIVIL ENGINEERING. *Current Pos:* VPRES, GAI CONSULTS, INC, 58- *Personal Data:* b Pittsburgh, Pa, Jan 10, 34; m 67, Kathleen Tarker; c Suzanne, John, Laura & Amy. *Educ:* Carnegie Inst Technol, BS, 56, MS, 57, PhD(civil eng), 61. *Honors & Awards:* Collingwood Prize, Am Soc Civil Engrs, 66. *Prof Exp:* From asst prof to assoc prof civil eng, Carnegie-Mellon Univ, 60-70, sr lectr, 70-72. *Mem:* Am Soc Civil Engrs; Am Soc Eng Educ; Am Concrete Inst; Am Soc Testing & Mat. *Res:* Soil mechanics and foundation engineering; numerical and finite element analysis of plates, shells and solids; experimental and theoretical stress analysis. *Mailing Add:* 610 Driftwood Dr Pittsburgh PA 15238-2516. *Fax:* 412-856-4970

HRIBAR, LAWRENCE JOSEPH, COMPARATIVE MORPHOLOGY, MEDICAL ENTOMOLOGY. *Current Pos:* RES CONSULT, IRMCO, 96- *Personal Data:* b Rochester, Pa, Nov 22, 60. *Educ:* Pa State Univ, BS, 82; Univ Tenn, MS, 84; Auburn Univ, PhD(entom), 89. *Honors & Awards:* Comstock Award; GAST Award. *Prof Exp:* Grad res asst, Univ Tenn, 82-84; grad res asst, Auburn Univ, 85-89, lab technician, 89-90; res assoc, La State Univ, 90-91, Univ Fla, 91-96. *Concurrent Pos:* Adj fac, Indian River Community Col, 94- *Mem:* Entom Soc Am; NAm Benthological Soc; Am Mosquito Control Asn; Soc Vector Ecol; Am Archaeol Soc. *Res:* Comparative and functional morphology of flies of medical and veterinary importance. *Mailing Add:* PO Box 670 Vero Beach FL 32961

HRILJAC, JOSEPH A, CHEMICAL CRYSTALLOGRAPHY, POWDER DIFFRACTION. *Current Pos:* CHEMIST, BROOKHAVEN NAT LAB, 89- *Personal Data:* b Hazel Crest, Ill, Nov 29, 60. *Educ:* Univ Ill, Urbana, BS, 82; Northwestern Univ, PhD(chem), 87. *Prof Exp:* Fel, Chem Crystallog Lab, Oxford Univ, 86-89. *Mem:* Mat Res Soc; AAAS; Am Chem Soc. *Res:* Synthesis and structural characterization of inorganic solids, particularly molecular sieves and metal oxides; powder diffraction using synchrotron X-rays and neutrons. *Mailing Add:* Sch Chem Univ Birmingham Edgbaston Birmingham B15 2TT England. Fax: 516-282-3137; E-Mail: hriljac@bnl.gov

HRISKEVICH, MICHAEL EDWARD, GEOLOGY. *Current Pos:* PRES, BANAQU EXPLOR LTD, 83- *Personal Data:* b Timmins, Ont, Mar 7, 26; m 47; c 4. *Educ:* Queen's Univ (Ont), BSc, 47, MSc, 49; Princeton Univ, PhD(geol), 52. *Prof Exp:* Instr geol, Princeton Univ, 49-52; geologist subsurface, Stanolind Oil & Gas Co, 52-54, Triad Oil Co, 54-57 & Can Fina Oil, Ltd, 57-61; dist geologist, Atlantic Ref Co, 61-63; chief geologist, Banff Oil Co, 63-65, explor mgr, 65-70; explor mgr, Aquitaine Co, Can, 70-76, vpres, 76-80, sr vpres explor spec proj, 80-81; sr vpres, Canterra Energy Ltd, 81-83. *Concurrent Pos:* Bursary, Nat Res Coun Can. *Mem:* Am Asn Petrol Geol; Geol Soc Am; Can Soc Petrol Geologists. *Res:* Geology and petrology of basic rocks; subsurface stratigraphy. *Mailing Add:* 4103 14 A St SW Calgary AB T2T 3Y3 Can

HRIVNAK, BRUCE JOHN, EVOLVED STARS, BINARY STARS. *Current Pos:* asst prof, 84-89, ASSOC PROF, PHYSICS DEPT, VALPARAISO UNIV, 89- *Personal Data:* b Johnstown, Pa, July 10, 49; m 73, Lucy Lawyer; c 3. *Educ:* Univ Pa, BA, 71, PhD(astron), 80. *Prof Exp:* Fel & instr, Dept Physics, Univ Calgary, 80-84. *Concurrent Pos:* Vis res officer, Dom Astrophys Observ, 84; prin investr, NASA, 87-, NSF, 89- *Mem:* Am Astron Soc; Sigma Xi; Int Astron Union; Am Sci Affil. *Res:* Observation of evolved stars; observation and analysis binary stars. *Mailing Add:* Dept Physics Valparaiso Univ Valparaiso IN 46383. Fax: 219-464-5483; E-Mail: bhrivnak@exodus.valpo.edu

HRKEL, EDWARD JAMES, FUEL TECHNOLOGY, PETROLEUM ENGINEERING. *Current Pos:* PROF SPECIALIST, GETTY OIL CO, 70- *Personal Data:* b Des Moines, Iowa, July 3, 42; m 69; c 1. *Educ:* Purdue Univ, BS, ME, 64; Mass Inst Technol, SM, 65, PhD(mech eng), 69. *Prof Exp:* Engr, Shell Develop Co, 69-70. *Mem:* Sigma Xi; Soc Petrol Engrs. *Res:* Numerical models for the prediction of performance in oil and gas reservoirs; fluid flow in porous media. *Mailing Add:* 1922 Hillgreen Dr Katy TX 77494-1803

HRONES, JOHN ANTHONY, MECHANICAL ENGINEERING. *Current Pos:* vpres acad affairs, 57-64, provost, 64-77, EMER PROVOST, CASE WESTERN RESERVE UNIV, 77- *Personal Data:* b Boston, Mass, Sept 28, 12; m 38; c 4. *Educ:* Mass Inst Technol, SB, 34, SM, 36, ScD, 42. *Prof Exp:* Jr engr, Chase Brass & Cooper Co, Conn, 34; asst instr appl mech, Mass Inst Technol, 34-36, instr mech eng, 36-37; asst to factory mgr, Coldwell Lawnmower Co, NY, 37-39; from instr to prof mech eng, Mass Inst Technol, 39-57. *Concurrent Pos:* Consult mech eng, 40-; head mach design div, Mass Inst Technol, 46-57, dir dynamic analysis & control lab, 50-57; mem bd trustees, Inst Defense Anal, 58-85; hon trustee, Cleveland Mus Natural Hist; pres, AIT Found, Inc, 68-91; trustee, Asian Inst Technol, Bangkok. *Mem:* Nat Acad Eng; Am Soc Mech Engrs; Am Soc Eng Educ; Am Acad Arts & Sci; Sigma Xi. *Res:* Automatic control; design and development of machinery. *Mailing Add:* 9397 Midnight Pass Rd Apt 306 Sarasota FL 34242

HROVAT, DAVORIN, CONTROL SYSTEMS, MODELING & SIMULATION. *Current Pos:* sr res engr, 81-85, prin res engr assoc control systs, 85-89, PRIN STAFF ENG, SCI RES LAB, FORD MOTOR CO, 89- *Personal Data:* b Zagreb, Croatia, Jan 2, 49; m 74; c 2. *Educ:* Univ Zagreb, Dipl Ing mech eng, 72; Univ Calif, Davis, MS, 76, PhD(mech eng), 79. *Prof Exp:* Asst prof mech eng, Wayne State Univ, 78-81. *Mem:* Sigma Xi; Am Soc Mech Engrs; sr mem Inst Elec & Electronics Engrs. *Res:* Modeling, analysis, and control of dynamic systems; vehicle dynamics and control; optimal mechanical structures; bond-graph modeling techniques; automotive power train modeling and control. *Mailing Add:* Ford Motor Co Sci Res Lab PO Box 2053 Dearborn MI 48121

HRUBAN, ZDENEK, PATHOLOGY. *Current Pos:* USPHS res fel path, 57-60, Am Cancer Soc res fel, 60-63, from asst prof to prof, 63-91, EMER PROF PATH, UNIV CHICAGO, 91- *Personal Data:* b Czech, June 15, 21; nat US; m 55, Jarmila Stanek; c Paul Y, Ralph H & Diana M (Quinn). *Educ:* Univ Rostock, Ger, Cand Med, 44; Charles Univ, Prague, MUC, 48; Univ Chicago, MD, 56, PhD, 63. *Concurrent Pos:* Lederle award, 64-67; res career develop award, 67-72; pres, Coun Higher Educ, Am Asn Study Liver Dis, 84-; bd dir, Czechoslovak Soc Arts & Sci Am, 74-; mem fac discussants, Charles Louis Davis, DVM Found, 76. *Mem:* Sigma Xi; Electron Micros Soc Am. *Res:* Ultrastructural pathology; microbodies; peroxisomes; autophagy. *Mailing Add:* Dept Path MC 3084 Univ Chicago 5841 S Maryland Ave Chicago IL 60637-1470

HRUBANT, HENRY EVERETT, ANIMAL GENETICS. *Current Pos:* RETIRED. *Personal Data:* b Aurora, Ill, Apr 5, 29; m 52, Mary Jean Malloy; c Susan Leigh, Nancy Lynn & Mark Alan. *Educ:* Univ Ill, BS, 50; Ohio State Univ, MS, 53, PhD(genetics), 57. *Prof Exp:* Res asst, Allied Chem & Dye Corp, 50-51; from asst prof to prof biol, Calif State Univ, Long Beach, 57-88. *Mem:* AAAS; Am Genetic Asn; Genetics Soc Am; Genetics Soc Can; Geront Soc. *Res:* Physiological genetics of metabolic disorders in mammals; genetic control of aging; mammalian cytogenetics. *Mailing Add:* PO Box 570 Talent OR 97540

HRUBESH, LAWRENCE W(AYNE), MICROPOROUS MATERIALS, CHEMICAL INSTRUMENTATION. *Current Pos:* Electronic engr, Lawrence Livermore Nat Lab, Univ Calif, 67-70, physicist, 70-74, dep div leader chem, 74-79, PROJ LEADER, LAWRENCE LIVERMORE NAT LAB, UNIV CALIF, 79- *Personal Data:* b Eau Claire, Wis, Dec 6, 40; m 62, Mary Overby; c 2. *Educ:* Wis State Univ-Eau Claire, BS, 65; Univ Wyo, MS, 67, PhD(physics), 70. *Honors & Awards:* IR 100 Award Aerogels, 90. *Concurrent Pos:* Instr, Univ Calif, Berkeley, 68. *Mem:* Am Inst Physics; Optical Soc Am; Am Chem Soc. *Res:* Molecular spectroscopy, specifically in rotational & vibrational spectra, and in analytical instrumentation, including development of new systems and digital control automation; laser spectroscopy for analytical measurements; material science and corrosion; low density inorganic materials; aerogels. *Mailing Add:* Lawrence Livermore Nat Lab L-322 PO Box 808 Livermore CA 94550

HRUBY, VICTOR J, BIO-ORGANIC CHEMISTRY, BIOPHYSICS. *Current Pos:* from asst prof to assoc prof, 68-77, PROF CHEM, UNIV ARIZ, 77-, PROF BIOCHEM, 78-; PROF, ARIZ RES LABS, 81-, REGENTS PROF, 89- *Personal Data:* b Valley City, NDak, Dec 24, 38; m 66, Patricia A McGovern; c Timothy J, Stephen M & Patrick A. *Educ:* Univ NDak, BS, 60, MS, 62; Cornell Univ, PhD(org chem), 65. *Hon Degrees:* Dr, Free Univ Brussels, 89. *Honors & Awards:* Javits Neurosci Award, 87; Pierce Award, 93. *Prof Exp:* Teaching asst inorg & anal chem, Univ NDak, 60-61; teaching asst org chem, Cornell Univ, 62-63, instr biochem, Med Col, 65-67, res assoc bio-org chem, 67-68. *Concurrent Pos:* Consult, Dow Chem Co, 73-92 & NIH, 78-; Fulbright-Hays rector's lectr, Belg; mem, Physiol Chem Study Sect, NIH, 80-84, Biorg & Nat Prods Chem Study Sect, 85-89; Guggenheim fel, 84; ed, Int J Peptide & Protein Res, 88- *Mem:* Fel AAAS; Am Chem Soc; fel Am Inst Chemists; Biophys Soc; Am Peptide Soc (pres, 90-91); fel NY Acad Sci; Am Soc Biol Chemists; Protein Soc. *Res:* Synthesis, structure and properties of polypeptides, unusual amino acids and proteins; hormone and neurotransmitter chemistry; nuclear magnetic resonance as a structural tool for polypeptides; brain chemistry; use of stable isotopes in bio-organic and biophysical studies; brain chemistry; conformation-biological activity relationships; computer assisted molecular design. *Mailing Add:* Dept Chem Univ Ariz Tucson AZ 85721. Fax: 520-621-8407; E-Mail: hraby@mail.arizona.edu

HRUSCHKA, HOWARD WILBUR, HORTICULTURE, PLANT PHYSIOLOGY. *Current Pos:* COOPERATOR, PLANT INDUST STA, USDA, BELTSVILLE, MD, 80- *Personal Data:* b Brooklyn, NY, Sept 17, 15; m 40, Eudora E Hendrickson; c William R, Peter D & Violet A. *Educ:* Cornell Univ, BSA, 37. *Honors & Awards:* Species of Miocene fossil porpoise named in honor, Rhabdosteus Hruschkai. *Prof Exp:* Soil conservationist, Steuben Co, NY, Agr Res Serv, USDA, 38-44, plant physiologist, NY Mkt Lab, 46-54, Maine Potato Handling Res Ctr, Aroostook Farm, 54-57 & Qual, Maintenance & Improv Sect, Plant Indust Sta, 57-65, plant physiologist, 65-72, plant physiologist, Hort Crops Res Lab, Mkt Res Inst, 72-78; docent, Naturalist Ctr, Smithsonian Inst, Washington, DC, 78-80. *Concurrent Pos:* Civilian, Pub Serv, 44-46. *Mem:* Am Soc Hort Sci; fel AAAS. *Res:* Published 150 scientific papers as sole, senior or coauthor; invented device for producing three dimensional bar graphs; post harvest plant physiology paleobiological collection; nature study education; anthropology; handling transportation and storage of fresh fruits and vegetables. *Mailing Add:* 9710 Wichita Ave College Park MD 20740

HRUSHESKY, WILLIAM JOHN MICHAEL, MEDICAL CHRONOBIOLOGY OF CANCER. *Current Pos:* PROF MED, ALBANY MED COL, STATE UNIV NY, 89-, PROF BIOMED SCI, SCH PUB HEALTH, 94-; SR ATTEND ONCOLOGIST, STRATTON VET AFFAIRS MED CTR; PROF CHEM ENG, RENSSELAER POLYTECH INST, 89- *Personal Data:* b Poughkeepsie, NY, Nov 9, 47; m 70, 85, Patricia A Wood; c Cassandra Marie Nicole. *Educ:* Syracuse Univ, AB, 69; State Univ NY, Buffalo, MD, 73; Am Bd Internal Med & Med Oncol, cert. *Prof Exp:* Intern med, Baltimore City Hosps, Johns Hopkins Univ, 73-74; assoc, Nat Cancer Inst, NIH, 74-76; resident med, Lab Med & Path, Univ Minn, 76-78, res specialist oncol, 78-79, from asst prof to assoc prof oncol, 79-89. *Concurrent Pos:* Fel, Dept Internal Med, Johns Hopkins Univ, 73-74; instr, Dept Internal Med, George Washington Univ, 74-76 & oncol sect, VA Admin, Washington, 75-76; staff mem, Georgetown Univ Hosp, 74-76; ed, Pract Appln Chronobiol to Cancer; prin investr grants, Nat Cancer Inst, 82-, Medtronic Corp, 85- & Nat Heart, Lung & Blood Inst, 86; consult, Food & Drug Admin, Inst Med, Nat Acad Sci Cong Off Technol Assessment & Pres's Cancer Panel. *Mem:* Int Soc Chronobiol; fel Am Col Physicians; Am Soc Clin Oncol; Am Asn Cancer Res; NY Acad Sci; Am Fedn Clin Res. *Res:* Founder of medical chronotherapeutics; study of several important biological rhythms and especially of how these rhythms interact; drug delivery systems and particularly their temporal control and solid tumor oncology; invention, development and reduction to practice of a quick non-invasive urinary test to predict kidney transplant rejection; characterization of the sole useful murien kidney cancer model; completion of the first and pivotal trial of implantable programmable drug delivery technology for cancer therapy; improving the understanding of the biological consequences of physical changes induced in proteins when they contact biomedical device surfaces; a method and diagnostic device for non-invasively and precisely measuring aerobic cardiopulmonary performance. *Mailing Add:* Sr Attend Oncologist 111-C Stratton Vet Admin Med Ctr Albany NY 12208. Fax: 518-472-7019

HRUSKA, ANTONIN, SPACE PHYSICS, PLASMA PHYSICS. *Current Pos:* RETIRED. *Personal Data:* b Prague, Czech, Apr 16, 34; Can citizen. *Educ:* Charles Univ, Prague, dipl physics, 57; Czech Acad Sci, PhD(astrophys), 60. *Prof Exp:* Res scientist astrophys & geophys, Czech Acad Sci, Prague, 57-67; vis scientist space physics, Univ BC, 67-69, Univ Alta, 69-70 & Nat Ctr Atmospheric Res, 70-71; res officer space physics, Nat

Res Coun Can, 71-90. *Mem:* Am Geophys Union; Europ Geophys Soc. *Res:* Structure of the magnetosphere and magnetotail; applications of plasma physics in the magnetosphere; instabilities in collisionless plasmas. *Mailing Add:* 400 Plumtree Circle Ottawa ON K1K 2N3 Can

HRUSKA, SAMUEL JOSEPH, MATERIALS SCIENCE, METALLURGICAL ENGINEERING. *Current Pos:* from asst prof to prof mat sci & metall eng, 64-87, EMER PROF MAT ENG, PURDUE UNIV, 87- *Personal Data:* b Detroit, Mich, Dec 13, 36; m 59; c 1. *Educ:* Purdue Univ, BS, 59; Carnegie Inst Technol, MS, 62, PhD(metall eng), 63. *Prof Exp:* NSF fel physics, Bristol Univ, 63-64. *Mem:* Metall Soc; Am Soc Eng Educ; Am Soc Metals. *Res:* Kinetics of phase transformations; formation of thin films; surface and interfacial phenomena; carburizing; brazing; cermets. *Mailing Add:* 839 Liverpool Ct Lafayette IN 47905

HRUTFIORD, BJORN F, CHEMISTRY. *Current Pos:* Res instr chem eng, 59-65, asst prof wood chem, 65-73, assoc prof, 65-77, PROF WOOD CHEM & CHMN DIV PHYS SCI, COL FORESTRY, UNIV WASH, 77- *Personal Data:* b Blaine, Wash, Jan 31, 32; m 60; c 2. *Educ:* Wash State Univ, BS, 54; Univ NC, PhD(org chem), 59. *Mem:* Royal Soc Chem. *Res:* Lignin and extractives chemistry. *Mailing Add:* Col Forest Resources Univ Wash AR 10 Seattle WA 98105

HRUZA, ZDENEK, physiology, gerontology, for more information see previous edition

HRYCAK, PETER, HEAT TRANSFER, FLUID MECHANICS. *Current Pos:* prof, 75-93, EMER PROF MECH ENG, NJ INST TECHNOL, 93- *Personal Data:* b Przemysl, Poland, July 8, 23; US citizen; m 49, Rea M Limberg; c Maria (deceased), Michael P, Orest W & Alexandra M. *Educ:* Univ Minn, BS, 54, MS, 55, PhD(mech eng), 60. *Prof Exp:* Teaching asst mech eng, Univ Minn, 54-55, instr, 55-60; mem tech staff, Bell Tel Labs, 60-65; sr proj engr, Curtiss-Wright Corp, 65; from assoc prof to prof mech eng, Newark Col Eng, 65-75. *Concurrent Pos:* NASA res grant heat transfer from impinging jets, 67-68; NSF res grant, 82-85. *Mem:* Am Inst Aeronaut & Astronaut; Am Soc Mech Engrs; Nat Acad Eng Sci UK; UK Engrs Soc Am (pres, 66-67); Am Geophys Union; sr mem Inst Environ Sci; Sigma Xi. *Res:* Heat transfer with a change of phase; heat transfer from impinging jets; effects of space environment on satellites; boundary layer theory applied to impinging jets; mechanics of transition from laminar to turbulent flow; problems related to thermal and chemical pollution; carbon dioxide balance of the atmosphere; principal designer of the telstar satellite thermal system. *Mailing Add:* 19 Roselle Ave Cranford NJ 07016. *Fax:* 973-642-4282

HRYNIUK, WILLIAM, HEMATOLOGY, ONCOLOGY. *Current Pos:* dir, Cancer Ctr, 91-96, PROF MED, UNIV CALIF MED CTR, 91- *Personal Data:* b Central Patricia, Ont, Apr 29, 39; m 59, 82, Lynn; c 2. *Educ:* Univ Man, MD, 61; FRCPS(C), 79. *Prof Exp:* Resident med, Wash Univ, 64-65; asst prof, Univ Man, 69-77, assoc prof med, 77-79; prof med, McMaster Univ, Hamilton, Ont, 79-91. *Concurrent Pos:* Clin fel hemat, Wash Univ, 65-66; Leukemia Soc Am fel clin pharmacol, Yale Univ, 66-68; investr, Nat Cancer Inst Can, 69-; attend physician & consult hematologist, Winnipeg Gen Hosp, 69-79; dir, Ont Cancer Treatment & Res Found & Hamilton Regional Ctr, Hamilton, Ont, 79- *Mem:* Can Soc Clin Invest; Can Hemat Soc; Am Soc Clin Oncol; Am Asn Cancer Res; Nat Cancer Inst. *Res:* Mechanisms of action of antifolates; chemotherapy of viral infections in man; fibrinolytic therapy; dose intensity in chemotherapy. *Mailing Add:* Univ Calif San Diego Cancer Ctr 9500 Gilman Dr No 0987 La Jolla CA 92093-0987. *Fax:* 619-657-8699

HSI, BARTHOLOMEW P, BIOMETRICS. *Current Pos:* assoc prof, 70-75, PROF BIOMET, UNIV TEX SCH PUB HEALTH, HOUSTON, 75- *Personal Data:* b Shanghai, China, Dec 10, 25; m 64; c 2. *Educ:* Univ Minn, MA, 62, PhD(biostatist), 64. *Prof Exp:* Asst prof biomet, Case Western Reserve Univ, 64-70. *Concurrent Pos:* Consult, Vet Admin Coop Study Prog, 74- *Mem:* Am Pub Health Asn; Am Soc Clin Pharmacol & Therapeut; Am Statist Asn; Biomet Soc. *Res:* Laboratory quality control; applied and theoretical statistics. *Mailing Add:* 6012 Burgoyne Houston TX 77057

HSI, DAVID CHING HENG, PLANT PATHOLOGY, GENETICS. *Current Pos:* Prof, 68-92, EMER PROF, NMEX STATE UNIV, 92- *Personal Data:* b Shanghai, China, May 17, 28; nat US; m 52, Kathy Chiang; c Andrew & Steven. *Educ:* St John's Univ, BS, 48; Univ Ga, MS, 49; Univ Minn, PhD, 51. *Honors & Awards:* Distinguished Scientist, NMex Acad Sci. *Concurrent Pos:* Oilseed consult, WPakistan, US Dept State, 70; vis scientist, NSF, Taiwan, Repub China, 79 & Arg, 80; res fel, Dept Agr & Fisheries, Repub SAfrica, 81; vis scientist, Min Agr, Animal Husbandry & Fisheries, People's Repub China, 85; adj prof, Univ NMex, 86-94; mem external eval panel, Peanut Collab Res Support Prog, Univ Ga & USAID, 93- *Mem:* Am Peanut Res & Educ Soc (pres, 81-82); Sigma Xi; NMex Acad Sci (pres, 83, 84); AAAS; Nat Asn Acad Sci (pres, 93-94); Am Phytopath Soc. *Res:* Peanut and sweet potato disease and improvement. *Mailing Add:* 1611 Ridgecrest Dr SE Albuquerque NM 87108

HSI, RICHARD S P, SYNTHESIS OF ISOTOPICALLY LABELED COMPOUNDS. *Current Pos:* from res assoc to sr res scientist, 59-86, SR SCIENTIST, UPJOHN CO, 87- *Personal Data:* b Shanghai, China, Sept 18, 33; US citizen; m 58, Nancy Shang; c Jeffrey D, Eric D, Richard A & Linda C. *Educ:* Pomona Col, BA, 55; Mass Inst Technol, PhD(org chem), 58. *Prof Exp:* Res fel org chem, Mass Inst Technol, 58-59. *Mem:* Am Chem Soc; Sigma Xi. *Res:* Organic synthesis; radioisotope labelling; drug metabolism; reaction mechanism; medicinal chemistry. *Mailing Add:* Upjohn Co 7256-126-250 300 Henrietta St Kalamazoo MI 49001-0199. *Fax:* 616-833-8767; *E-Mail:* richard.sp.hsi@am.pnu.com

HSIA, HENRY TAO-SZE, FLUID MECHANICS, ENERGY SOURCES. *Current Pos:* PRES, TECON SERV, 83- *Personal Data:* b Peking, China, June 16, 23; US citizen; m 47; c 3. *Educ:* Chiao Tung Univ, BS, 44; Harvard Univ, MS, 48; Stanford Univ, Engr, 63, PhD(astronaut, aeronaut), 66. *Prof Exp:* Tech specialist, Nat Resources Comn, Repub of China, 45-47; design engr, Consol Edison Co NY, 48-50; sr design engr, Ebasco Serv Inc, 50-56; mech engr, atomic power equip dept, Gen Elec Co, 56-57, prog mgr, 76-83; res scientist, Lockheed Missile & Space Co, 57-62; sr staff scientist, United Technol Ctr, United Aircraft Corp, 62-73; sr staff engr, MB Assocs, 74-75. *Concurrent Pos:* Guest lectr, Stanford Univ, 67; consult, MB Assocs, 75-76, Bechtel Power Corp, 82-84 & Sci & Technol, Jiangsu Prov, China, 85- *Mem:* Am Inst Aeronaut & Astronaut; Chinese Inst Engrs; Chinese Cult Asn (dir & exec secy, 66-); Am Nuclear Soc. *Res:* Propulsion; thermodynamics; heat transfer; nuclear reactor plant design; alternate energy source; rocket propulsion. *Mailing Add:* 15 Anson Rd Hillsborough CA 94310

HSIA, JACK JINN-GOE, THERMAL PHYSICS, SPECTROPHOTOMETRY. *Current Pos:* physicist, 69-78 & 92-95, group leader spectrophotom, 78-92, CHIEF ACAD AFFAIRS, NAT INST STANDS & TECHNOL, 95- *Personal Data:* b Anhwei, China, Oct 1, 37; US citizen; m 67, Heidi Mei; c Albert & Amie. *Educ:* Nat Taiwan Univ, BS, 59; Purdue Univ, MS, 64, PhD(thermal physics), 68. *Honors & Awards:* Bronze Medal, US Dept Com, 88. *Prof Exp:* Res asst thermal physics, Thermal Phys Properties Res Ctr, Purdue Univ, 68-69. *Concurrent Pos:* Internal pres Int Comn Illum, 95-99. *Mem:* Optical Soc Am; Am Soc Mech Engrs; Am Soc Testing & Mat; Int Comn Illum; Inter-Soc Color Coun. *Res:* Experimental instrumentation and analytical method on reflection, scattering, transmission, retroreflection, densitometry, spectral fluorimetry and infrared methods. *Mailing Add:* Nat Inst Stand & Technol Rm A505 Bldg 101 Gaithersburg MD 20899. *Fax:* 301-975-3530; *E-Mail:* hsia@onyx.nist.gov

HSIA, JOHN S, NUMBER THEORY, ABSTRACT ALGEBRA. *Current Pos:* From asst prof to assoc prof math, 66-76, PROF MATH, OHIO STATE UNIV, 76- *Personal Data:* b Shanghai, China, Dec 16, 38; US citizen; m 68; c 2. *Educ:* Brown Univ, ScB & AB, 62; Mass Inst Technol, PhD(math), 66. *Concurrent Pos:* Prin investr, NSF, 67-; vis asst prof math, Mass Inst Technol, 67; Alexander von Humboldt fel, WGer, 68-69; vis assoc prof math, Univ Calif, Santa Barbara, 75; hon res assoc, Harvard Univ, 78; distinguished lectr, Univ Southern Calif, 79, vis prof, 87; mem, Math Scis Res Inst, Berkeley, Calif, 86; ed, J Number Theory. *Mem:* Am Math Soc; Sigma Xi. *Res:* Arithmetic theory of integral quadratic forms over global fields; modular forms; combinatorial designs and coding theory. *Mailing Add:* Dept Math Ohio State Univ 231 W 18th Ave Columbus OH 43210-1101

HSIA, STEPHEN MARK, BIOCHEMICAL TOXICOLOGY, CHEMICAL CARCINOGENESIS. *Current Pos:* DIR TOXICOL, MITRETEK SYSTS, 96- *Personal Data:* b Shanghai, China, Sept 5, 46; m 71; c 2. *Educ:* Cheng Kung Univ, Taiwan, BS, 68; Univ Calif, San Diego, PhD(org chem), 74. *Honors & Awards:* Young Environ Health Scientist Award, Nat Inst Environ Health Sci, 78. *Prof Exp:* Res asst org chem, Univ Calif, San Diego, 69-74; from asst prof to prof toxicol, Dept Entom-Environ Toxicol Ctr, Univ Wis-Madison, 78-87; toxicologist, lead scientist, prin scientist, Hazardous Substances Eval Group, Mitre Corp, 87-96. *Concurrent Pos:* Prin investr, Am Cancer Soc grant, 76-77 & Nat Inst Environ Health Sci, 78-84; co-prin investr, Nat Cancer Inst grant, 77-80 & Nat Inst Environ Health Sci, 78-84; trainer, Nat Inst Environ Health Sci, 80-87; consult, Nat Sci Coun, Repub China, 80-82. *Mem:* AAAS; Soc Toxicol; Am Col Toxicol; Soc Environ Toxicol Chem. *Res:* Chemical carcinogenesis; mammalian toxicology of halogenated pesticides; insect growth regulators; risk assessment of synthetic chemicals; in vitro toxicity testing systems; hazardous substances evaluation. *Mailing Add:* 8313 Tuckermane Lane Potomac MD 20854

HSIA, SUNG LAN, BIOCHEMISTRY. *Current Pos:* assoc prof, 63-67, PROF DERMAT & BIOCHEM, SCH MED, UNIV MIAMI, 67- *Personal Data:* b China, Feb 6, 20; m 55; c 4. *Educ:* Cath Univ, Peiping, BS, 44; St Louis Univ, PhD(biochem), 52. *Prof Exp:* Fel biochem, St Louis Univ, 52-58, from sr instr to asst prof biochem, 58-63. *Concurrent Pos:* NIH career develop award, 65-70. *Mem:* AAAS; Am Chem Soc; Am Soc Biol Chem; Soc Invest Dermat; Am Oil Chem Soc. *Res:* Chemistry and metabolism of sterols, bile acids and steroid hormones; biochemistry of the skin; atherosclerosis, serum cholesterol binding reserve. *Mailing Add:* Dept Dermat R-117 Univ Miami Sch Med PO Box 016960 Miami FL 33101

HSIA, YUKUN, SOLID STATE ELECTRONICS, MICROELECTRONICS. *Current Pos:* CONSULT PARTNER, YHL CONSULTANTS, 80- *Personal Data:* b Kunming, China, Feb 21, 41; US citizen; m 65, Helen Lee; c Eric & Curtis. *Educ:* Univ Calif, Berkeley, BS, 61; Univ Calif, Los Angeles, MS, 64, PhD(solid state electronics), 69. *Prof Exp:* Design leader circuits, Electronics Div, NCR, 61-67; mem, Tech Staff Infrared Mat, NAm Aviation, 67-68; prin investr nonvolatile memories, Guidance & Control Div, Litton Industs, 69-74; br chief advan microelectronics, McDonnell Douglas Corp, 74-82; dir eng mgr microprocessors, Fairchild-Schlumberger corp, 82-87; dir microelectronics & infrared technol, Northrop Corp, 87-95. *Concurrent Pos:* Mem stand comt, Inst Elec & Electronics Engrs, 78-88, prog chair, Comput Elements Workshop, 84; lectr, Univ Southern Calif, Los Angeles, 79-82, Santa Clara Univ, 82-87; vis scholar, Acad Sinica, 84. *Mem:* Sr mem Inst Elec & Electronics Engrs. *Res:* Granted 11 US patents; author of 39 technical papers on computer and microelectronic devices and systems, infrared sensors, multispectral imagers and systems in biomedical technology. *Mailing Add:* 1821 Park Skyline Rd Santa Ana CA 92705. *E-Mail:* yhsia@aol.com

HSIA, YU-PING, PHYSICAL CHEMISTRY. *Current Pos:* from asst prof to assoc prof, 68-76, PROF CHEM, CALIF STATE POLYTECH UNIV, 76- *Personal Data:* b Tungtai, Kiangsu, China, May 16, 36; m 61; c 2. *Educ:* Tunghai Univ, BS, 59; Univ Calif, Santa Barbara, MA, 63; Ill Inst Technol, PhD(phys chem), 67. *Prof Exp:* Asst prof chem, Univ Bridgeport, 67-68. *Concurrent Pos:* Vis assoc prof, Res Inst Chem, Tsing Hua Univ, Taiwan, 69-70; vis assoc, Calif Inst Technol, 71. *Mem:* Am Chem Soc; Chinese Chem Soc. *Res:* Molecular orbital calculations in inorganic compounds; coal chemistry; environmental chemistry. *Mailing Add:* Col Sci & Eng Nat Dong Hwa Univ Hua-lien Taiwan

HSIANG, THOMAS Y, SOLID STATE ELECTRONICS, SUPERCONDUCTIVITY. *Current Pos:* asst prof, 81-94, PROF ELEC ENG, UNIV ROCHESTER, 94- *Personal Data:* b Taiwan, China, Aug 4, 48; m; c 2. *Educ:* Nat Taiwan Univ, BS, 70; Univ Calif, Berkeley, MA, 73, PhD(physics), 77. *Prof Exp:* Res assoc physics, Ames Lab, US Dept Energy, 77-79; asst prof, Ill Inst Technol, 79-81. *Mem:* Am Phys Soc; Inst Elec & Electronics Engrs. *Mailing Add:* Dept Elec Eng Univ Rochester Rochester NY 14627-0001

HSIAO, BENJAMIN S, STRUCTURE-PROPERTY-PROCESSING RELATIONS IN POLYMERS, POLYMER CRYSTALLIZATION & MORPHOLOGY. *Current Pos:* res engr, 88-90, sr engr fibers res & develop, SR SCIENTIST CHEM RES & DEVELOP, DU PONT CO, 90- *Personal Data:* b Taipei, Taiwan, Aug 12, 58; US citizen; m 87, Caroline M Stamato. *Educ:* Nat Taiwan Univ, BS, 80; Univ Conn, MS, 85, PhD(polymer sci), 87. *Prof Exp:* Fel, Dept Polymer Sci & Eng, Univ Mass, 87-88. *Mem:* Am Chem Soc; Am Phys Soc; Soc Rheology; Soc Plastics Engrs; Mat Res Soc. *Res:* Polymer physics; structure-property-processing relations in polymers and advanced polymer composites; scattering techniques for polymers. *Mailing Add:* Exp Sta/Fibers E I Du Pont Co PO Box 80302 Wilmington DE 19880. *Fax:* 302-695-1717; *E-Mail:* hsiaobs@esvax.dnet.dupont.com

HSIAO, C C, ENGINEERING MECHANICS, PHYSICS. *Current Pos:* assoc prof aeronaut & eng mech, 55-66, PROF AEROSPACE ENG & MECH, UNIV MINN, MINNEAPOLIS, 66- *Personal Data:* b Peking, China, Oct 23, 19; m 53, C Y Yiran; c Karen, Caroline, Nina & Albert. *Educ:* Yenching & Tsinghua Univs, BS, 41; Mass Inst Technol, SM, 44, PhD(physics, appl mech), 48. *Prof Exp:* From asst prof to assoc prof eng mech, Pa State Col, 47-53; prin res physicist, Jones & Laughlin Steel Corp, 53-55; teaching asst, Mass Inst Technol; instr, Harvard Univ. *Concurrent Pos:* Vis prof, Cambridge Univ, 68-69; pres, cc Consult & Friendship Univ Found. *Mem:* Am Phys Soc. *Res:* Physics and mechanics of solids; fracture and strength of polymers; viscoelasticity; fracture mechanics; biomechanics; computer simulation of polymeric structures and molecules; polymer crazing. *Mailing Add:* 3131 Shoreline Lane Arden Hills MN 55112-3759. *Fax:* 612-484-5555; *E-Mail:* hsiao008@maroon.tc.umn.edu

HSIAO, GEORGE CHIA-CHU, APPLIED MATHEMATICS, CIVIL ENGINEERING. *Current Pos:* from asst prof to assoc prof, 69-77, PROF MATH, UNIV DEL, 77- *Personal Data:* b Shanghai, China, Sept 9, 34; US citizen; m 63, Juliet C Yeh; c Barbara & Jeffrey. *Educ:* Nat Taiwan Univ, BS, 58; Carnegie Inst Technol, MS, 62; Carnegie-Mellon Univ, PhD(math), 69. *Prof Exp:* Instr math, Carnegie-Mellon Univ, 67-69. *Concurrent Pos:* Guest prof math, T H Darmstadt, 75-76, Free Univ, Berlin, 79-80, 86; Alexander von Humboldt fel, Fed Repub Ger, 75-76, 83; vis prof, Univ Concepcion, Chile, 85. *Mem:* Sigma Xi; Soc Indust & Appl Math; Am Math Soc. *Res:* Partial differential equations; integral equations and applied mathematics. *Mailing Add:* Dept Math Sci Univ Del Newark DE 19716. *Fax:* 302-831-4511; *E-Mail:* hsiao@math.udel.edu

HSIAO, HENRY SHIH-CHAN, BIOMEDICAL ENGINEERING, ENTOMOLOGY. *Current Pos:* Asst prof, 72-77, ASSOC PROF SURG & BIOMED ENG, UNIV NC, 77- *Personal Data:* b Chungking, China, Oct 12, 43; US citizen; c 3. *Educ:* Mass Inst Technol, BS, 65, EE, 67; Univ Calif, Berkeley, PhD(elec eng), 72. *Concurrent Pos:* Asst prof neurobiol, Univ NC, 73-; NSF grant, 75-; consult, Environ Protection Agency & Northrup Serv, Inc, 77- *Mem:* Entom Soc Am; Biomed Eng Soc. *Res:* Biomedical instrumentation; insect behavior. *Mailing Add:* 1915 White Plains Rd Chapel Hill NC 27514

HSIAO, MU-YUE, COMPUTER SCIENCE. *Current Pos:* adv engr, IBM Corp, 67-69, sr engr, 69-79, sr tech staff & mgr, 79-84, FEL, IBM CORP, 84- *Personal Data:* b Changsha, Hunan, China, July 17, 33; nat US; m 62; c 3. *Educ:* Nat Taiwan Univ, BS, 56; Univ Ill, MS, 60; Univ Fla, PhD(elec eng), 67. *Prof Exp:* Jr engr, Int Bus Mach Co, 60-61, assoc engr, 61-63, sr assoc engr, 63-65; res assoc elec eng, Univ Fla, 65-67. *Mem:* Fel Inst Elec & Electronics Engrs; NY Acad Sci. *Res:* Error detecting and correcting codes; switching theory and logic design; computer hardware error checking; fault detection and testing; computer maintainability. *Mailing Add:* IBM Mail Station P126 522 S Rd Poughkeepsie NY 12601

HSIAO, THEODORE CHING-TEH, PLANT PHYSIOLOGY, ECOPHYSIOLOGY. *Current Pos:* from asst prof & asst plant physiologist to assoc prof & assoc physiologist, 65-74, PROF WATER SCI & PLANT PHYSIOLOGIST, EXP STA, UNIV CALIF, DAVIS, 74- *Personal Data:* b Peiping, China, Nov 28, 31; m 57; c 2. *Educ:* Cornell Univ, BS, 55; Univ Conn, MSc, 60; Univ Ill, PhD(crop physiol, biochem), 64. *Prof Exp:* Jr chemist, Arrow Lacquer Corp, 55-56; analytical chemist, S B Penick & Co, 58; res asst soil chem, Univ Conn, 58-60; asst res plant physiologist, Univ Calif, Los Angeles, 63-65. *Concurrent Pos:* Vis scientist, Int Rice Res Inst, Philippines, 78-79. *Mem:* Am Soc Plant Physiol; Am Soc Agron; Crop Sci Soc Am. *Res:* Plant-water relations and stress physiology; interaction of plants with hydroenvironment and the underlying physiological and physical processes; metabolism of nucleic acids in plants; biological regulation; water-plant relations. *Mailing Add:* Hydrology Univ Calif Davis CA 95616-5200

HSIAO, TING HUAN, INSECT PHYSIOLOGY. *Current Pos:* from asst prof to assoc prof, 67-79, PROF ENTOM, UTAH STATE UNIV, 79- *Personal Data:* b Hangchow, China, Feb 6, 36; m 61. *Educ:* Taiwan Prov Col Agr, BSc, 57; Univ Minn, St Paul, MSc, 61; Univ Ill, Urbana, PhD(insect physiol), 66. *Prof Exp:* Res assoc insect physiol, Dept Entom, Univ Ill, Urbana, 66-67. *Concurrent Pos:* Vis prof, Entom Lab, State Agr Univ, Wageningen, Neth, 74-75, 77, 78, 81 & 87. *Mem:* AAAS; Ecol Soc Am; Am Inst Biol Scientist; Entom Soc Am; Sigma Xi. *Res:* Physiological and ecological adaptations of insects, especially the chemical relationships in host finding and food selection of phytophagous insects; biotypes of insect pests; physiology, feeding behavior and ecological genetics. *Mailing Add:* Dept Biol Utah State Univ Logan UT 83422-0001

HSIAO, WILLIAM C, ECONOMY, MATHEMATICS. *Current Pos:* mem fac, Harvard Bus Sch, 74-77, assoc prof, 75-84, PROF, HARVARD UNIV, CAMBRIDGE, 85- *Personal Data:* b Beijing, China, Jan 17, 36; c Roderick & Douglas. *Educ:* Ohio Wesleyan Univ, BA, 59; Harvard Univ, MPA, 72, MA, 74, PhD, 82. *Prof Exp:* Finance dir, Conn Gen Life Ins, 59-68; dep chief actuary, US Social Security Admin, Washington, 68-71. *Concurrent Pos:* Consult, numerous state govts, orgns & schs, 74-; bd dir, Soc Actuaries, 91- *Mem:* Fel Actuarial Sci; Soc Actuaries; Nat Acad Social Ins. *Res:* Actuarial science. *Mailing Add:* 21 Washington Ave Cambridge MA 02140

HSIE, ABRAHAM WUHSIUNG, GENETICS, TOXICOLOGY. *Current Pos:* PROF & ASSOC DIR, DIV ENVIRON TOXICOL, DEPT PREVENTIVE MED & COMMUNITY HEALTH, UNIV TEX MED BR, GALVESTON TEX, 86- *Personal Data:* b Hsinwu, Taiwan, Mar 3, 40; m 62, Mayphoon Hsu; c Marvin S & Dora Y. *Educ:* Nat Taiwan Univ, Taipei, BS, 62; Ind Univ, Bloomington, MA, 65, PhD(microbiol), 68. *Prof Exp:* Res assoc, Nat Jewish Hosp, Denver, 68-69; NIH fel & instr biophys & genetics, Med Ctr, Univ Colo, 69-71, asst prof, 71-72; group leader somatic cell genetics, 72-77, group leader, Mammalian Cell Genetic Toxicol, 77-84, Biol Div, Oak Ridge Nat Lab, 77-86; lectr, Univ Tenn-Oak Ridge Grad Sch, Biomed Sch, 72-76, prof, 76-86. *Concurrent Pos:* Prof, Departs Human Biol Chem & Genetics, & Radiation Therapy; sr scientist, Sealy Ctr Molecular Sci, Univ Tex Med Br; fel, Japan Soc Prom Sci, 77; distinguished vis scientist, US Environ Protection Agency, 85-88. *Mem:* Am Soc Biol Chemists; Am Asn Cancer Res; Am Soc Cell Biol; Environ Mutagen Soc; Genetics Soc Am; Sigma Xi; Soc Risk Analysis; Am Soc Microbiol; 05475727xxxobiol; Soc Toxicol; Radiation Res Soc. *Res:* Studies of quantitative and molecular bases of gene mutations induced by physical and chemical agents either singly or in combination. *Mailing Add:* Prev Med Pub Health Univ Tex Med Sch 301 University Blvd Galveston TX 77550-2708

HSIEH, CHUNG KUO, THERMODYNAMICS, HEAT TRANSFER. *Current Pos:* from asst prof to assoc prof, 69-79, PROF MECH ENG, UNIV FLA, 79- *Personal Data:* b Shanghai, China, May 29, 32; US citizen; m 64, Shumin Lee; c Samuel & Stephen. *Educ:* Chinese Naval Col Technol, Taiwan, BSME, 54; Purdue Univ, MSME, 64, PhD(mech eng), 68. *Prof Exp:* From asst engr to engr, Chinese Naval Shipyards, Taiwan, 54-62; res asst thermophys properties res ctr, Purdue Univ, 62-66, res instr, 66-68; asst prof mech eng, SDak Sch Mines & Technol, 68-69. *Concurrent Pos:* Consult, Argonne Nat Lab, 76-79; vis prof, Tientsin Univ, China, 80. *Mem:* Am Soc Mech Engrs; Am Inst Aeronaut & Astronaut. *Res:* Heat transfer, thermophysical properties; solar energy; energy conversion and conservation; engineering optics; infrared scanning; nondestructive testing; computer system modeling; thermodynamics; atmospheric science. *Mailing Add:* Dept Mech Eng 237 Univ Fla Gainesville FL 32611-6300. *Fax:* 352-392-1071

HSIEH, DENNIS P H, ENVIRONMENTAL TOXICOLOGY, APPLIED MICROBIOLOGY. *Current Pos:* lectr & asst biochem engr, 69-73, asst prof environ toxicol, 73-76, assoc prof, 76-80, PROF ENVIRON TOXICOL, UNIV CALIF, DAVIS, 80- *Personal Data:* b Nantow, Taiwan, Feb 8, 37; m 60; c 3. *Educ:* Nat Taiwan Univ, BA, 59; Mass Inst Technol, MS, 67, DSc, 69; Am Bd Toxicol, cert, 79. *Prof Exp:* Food technologist, Wei-Chuan Foods Inc, Taiwan, 61-64. *Concurrent Pos:* Consult, NIH, WHO, Stauffer Chem Co & City San Diego. *Mem:* Am Chem Soc; Am Soc Microbiol; Chinese Agr Chem Soc; Soc Toxicol. *Res:* Control of fungal toxigenicity and comparative toxicology of carcinogenic mycotoxins. *Mailing Add:* 726 Lake Terrace Circle Davis CA 95616-5224

HSIEH, DIN-YU, APPLIED MATHEMATICS, FLUID MECHANICS. *Current Pos:* assoc prof, 68-78, head & prof math 90-96, PROF APPL MATH, BROWN UNIV, 78-; PROF MATH, HONG KONG UNIV SCI & TECHNOL, 96- *Personal Data:* b Nanking, China, Mar 25, 33; m 58; c 2. *Educ:* Nat Taiwan Univ, BS, 54; Brown Univ, MSc, 57; Calif Inst Technol, PhD(eng sci), 60. *Prof Exp:* Res fel appl mech, Calif Inst Technol, 60-63, asst prof eng sci, 63-68. *Mem:* Soc Indust & Appl Math; Am Phys Soc. *Res:* Two phase flows; hydrodynamical stabilities; asymptotic method on nonlinear problems; chaos. *Mailing Add:* Hong Kong Univ Sci Technol Clear Water Bay Kowloon Hong Kong People's Republic of China. *Fax:* 852-2358-1643

HSIEH, HENRY LIEN, POLYMER CHEMISTRY. *Current Pos:* explor res chemist, Phillips Petrol Co, 57-59, group leader, 59-63, sect mgr, 63-79, sr res assoc, 79-83, sr scientist, 83-91, Phillips fel, 91-92, EMER FEL, PHILLIPS PETROL CO, 92- *Personal Data:* b Shanghai, China, Jan 17, 30; nat US; m 55, Sin Wai Pai; c 3. *Educ:* Univ Akron, BS, 54; Princeton Univ, MA, 56, PhD(chem), 57. *Honors & Awards:* Distinguished Corp Inventor, Am Soc Patent Holders, 93. *Prof Exp:* Asst, Princeton Univ, 54-56. *Concurrent Pos:* Tech liaison, China; vis prof chem, Univ Akron, Ohio, 93. *Mem:* AAAS; Am Chem Soc; NY Acad Sci; Am Inst Chemists; Sigma Xi; Soc Plastics Engrs. *Res:* Solution and stereospecific polymerizations; organo-metallic chemistry; rubber chemistry and technology; reaction mechanisms; polyolefino polymerization catalysts and processes; Ziegler-Natta catalysis; anionic polymerizations. *Mailing Add:* 700 Fearrington Post Pittsboro NC 27312-8564

HSIEH, HSUNG-CHENG, ELECTRICAL ENGINEERING, PLASMA PHYSICS. *Current Pos:* assoc prof, 68-70, PROF ELEC ENG, IOWA STATE UNIV, 70- *Personal Data:* b Taichung, Taiwan, Feb 24, 29; US citizen; m 60; c 1. *Educ:* Dartmouth Col, AB, 54; Calif Inst Technol, MS, 55; Stanford Univ, EE, 57; Univ Calif, Berkeley, PhD(appl math), 60. *Prof Exp:* Res engr, Huggins Labs, Inc, Calif, 57; asst prof elec eng, Univ Wichita, 59-61; assoc prof, Univ Iowa, 61-64; vis assoc prof & scientist, Inst Sci & Technol, Univ Mich, Ann Arbor, 64-66, res engr & lectr, Electron Physics Lab, 66-68. *Mem:* Am Geophys Union. *Res:* Electromagnetic field theory and its application; microwave electronic devices; electromagnetic wave interaction with plasmas; solid-state plasma phenomena. *Mailing Add:* Dept Elec Eng & Comput Iowa State Univ 201 Coover Ames IA 50011-2011

HSIEH, HUI-KUANG, STATISTICS. *Current Pos:* ASSOC PROF STATIST, UNIV MASS, 76- *Personal Data:* b Taiwan, Repub China, Feb 3, 44; m 72; c 2. *Educ:* Fu-jen Univ, BS, 67; Nat Taiwan Univ, MA, 70; Columbia Univ, MS, 72; Univ Wis, PhD(statist), 76. *Prof Exp:* Statistician, Am Home Prod Corp, 71-73. *Concurrent Pos:* Vis expert, Inst Statist, Acad Sci, 82-83. *Mem:* Inst Math Statist; Am Statist Asn; Am Soc Qual Control. *Res:* Statistical inference; nonparametric statistics; multivariate analysis. *Mailing Add:* 36 Long Meadow Dr Amherst MA 01002

HSIEH, JUI SHENG, MECHANICAL ENGINEERING. *Current Pos:* RETIRED. *Personal Data:* b Chungking, China, Mar 5, 21; m 61; c 3. *Educ:* Wuhan Univ, China, BS, 43; Univ Ky, MS, 50; Ohio State Univ, PhD(mech eng), 55. *Prof Exp:* From asst prof to assoc prof mech eng, Univ Bridgeport, 55-60; assoc prof, NJ Inst Technol, 60-65, PROF MECH ENG, 65- *Mem:* Am Soc Mech Engrs; Am Soc Eng Educ; Am Solar Energy Soc. *Res:* Thermodynamics; solar energy. *Mailing Add:* 4 O'Conner Dr Apt O Belle Mead NJ 08502

HSIEH, KE CHIANG, COSMIC RAY PHYSICS. *Current Pos:* asst prof, 71-76, ASSOC PROF PHYSICS, UNIV ARIZ, 76- *Personal Data:* b Chungking, China, June 14, 40; m 68; c 2. *Educ:* Wabash Col, BA, 63; Univ Chicago, PhD(physics), 69. *Prof Exp:* Res assoc cosmic ray physics, Enrico Fermi Inst, Univ Chicago, 69-71. *Mem:* AAAS; Am Phys Soc; Sigma Xi; Am Geophys Union. *Res:* Cosmic rays, energetic particles from the sun; space science; astrophysics. *Mailing Add:* Dept Physics Univ Ariz Tucson AZ 85721-0001

HSIEH, MONICA C, NUTRITION, ENZYMOLOGY. *Current Pos:* CONSULT DIAG METAB DIS & NEWBORN SCREENING, 93- *Educ:* Wash State Univ, PhD(nutrit), 75. *Prof Exp:* Res instr pediat res, Children's Hosp Res Found Cincinnati, 75-91; mgr, Metab Nutrit Lab, Oakland Children's Hosp, Oakland, Calif, 91-93. *Mem:* Am Inst Nutrit; Asn Clin Scientists. *Res:* Proteolytic defects of cystic fibrosis. *Mailing Add:* 4664 Lakeridge Dr Mason OH 45040-8947

HSIEH, PAUL YAO TONG, SURFACE CHEMISTRY, CHEMICAL ENGINEERING. *Current Pos:* RETIRED. *Personal Data:* b Taichung, Taiwan, China, Oct 4, 27; US citizen; m 52, Amy Chang; c Cara, Erna, Theodore & Michael. *Educ:* Nat Taiwan Univ, BS, 50; Kans State Univ, MS, 57; Rensselaer Polytech Inst, PhD(chem eng), 59. *Prof Exp:* Asst, Nat Taiwan Univ, 50-54, instr, 54-56; sr res chemist, Nat Cash Register Co, Ohio, 59-65; res staff, Westvaco, 65-68; staff scientist, Olivetti Corp Am, 68-72; sect head, Hughes Aircraft Co, 73-75, dept mgr, 76-78, sr staff engr, 78-83, sr proj engr, 83-88, scientist & engr, 88-89; mem tech staff, Rockwell Int, 89-91. *Mem:* Am Chem Soc. *Res:* Colloid and surface chemistry; liquid crystals; display devices; microelectronics; infrared detector systems. *Mailing Add:* 3862 Banyan St Irvine CA 92606-2600

HSIEH, PHILIP KWOK-YOUNG, ENZYME PURIFICATION, ENZYME KINETICS. *Current Pos:* SCIENTIST, AMGEN, 89- *Educ:* Univ Colo, PhD(biol), 78. *Prof Exp:* Sr scientist chem eng, Biopure Inc, 84-89. *Mailing Add:* 1675 Aldercreek Pl Thousand Oaks CA 91362

HSIEH, PO-FANG (PHILIP), MATHEMATICS. *Current Pos:* PROF MATH, WESTERN MICH UNIV, 73- *Personal Data:* b Tainan, Formosa, July 10, 34; m 61, Emmy Su; c Paul S & Timothy I. *Educ:* Nat Taiwan Univ, BSc, 57; Univ Minn, MSc, 61, PhD(math), 64. *Honors & Awards:* Resl Award, US Naval Res Lab, 72. *Prof Exp:* From asst prof to assoc prof math, Western Mich Univ, 64-73; res mathematician, US Naval Res Lab, 70-71. *Concurrent Pos:* NSF res grant, 67-71. *Mem:* Am Math Soc; Math Asn Am; Soc Indust & Appl Math. *Res:* Asymptotic solutions and turning point problem of ordinary differential equations. *Mailing Add:* Dept Math & Statist Western Mich Univ Kalamazoo MI 49008

HSIEH, RICHARD KUOCHI, PUBLIC HEALTH ADMINISTRATION, OPERATIONS RESEARCH. *Current Pos:* admin health sci, extramural res prog, NCI, 81-86, DIR INT PROG, NLM, NIH, 86- *Personal Data:* b China, June 7, 32; US citizen; m 60; c 2. *Educ:* Johns Hopkins Univ, BES, 57, MS, 61, MPH, 62, DrPH, 66. *Prof Exp:* Indust engr, Johns Hopkins Hosp, 59-64; res assoc oper, Johns Hopkins Univ, 64-66; chief health serv res, USPHS Hosp, Baltimore, 66-80. *Concurrent Pos:* Sr consult, Social Security Admin, 65-66; consult, Pan Am Health Orgn, 70-71; mem task force, Nat Acad Eng, 70-72. *Mem:* Fel Am Med Informatics Asn; Oper Res Soc Am; fel Am Pub Health Asn. *Res:* Testing technological and innovative concepts in the delivery of medical care; analysis and evaluation of organizational and operational management problems in the hospitals and clinics. *Mailing Add:* 601 Stacy Ct Baltimore MD 21286

HSIEH, TAO-SHIH, DNA ENZYMOLOGY, GENE REGULATION. *Current Pos:* from asst prof to assoc prof, 80-93, PROF, DEPT BIOCHEM, DUKE UNIV MED CTR, 93- *Personal Data:* b Fu-chow, China, Mar 17, 48; US citizen; m, Ai-ly Yang; c Frances, Emily & Sonia. *Educ:* Nat Taiwan Univ, BA, 70; Univ Calif, Berkeley, PhD(biophys chem), 76. *Honors & Awards:* Jr Fac Res Award, Am Cancer Soc, 83; Basil O'Connor Award, March of Dimes, 83. *Prof Exp:* Postdoctoral fel, Stanford Univ Med Ctr, 76-80. *Mem:* Am Soc Biochem & Molecular Biol; AAAS; Soc Chinese Bioscientists Am. *Res:* Chromosome structure and function; emphasis on the function, structure and mechanism of DNA toposomerases. *Mailing Add:* Dept Biochem Duke Univ Med Ctr Box 3711 Durham NC 27710-0001. *Fax:* 919-684-8885; *E-Mail:* hsieeh@biochem.duke.edu

HSIEH, YOU-LO, POLYMER & FIBER CHEMISTRY SCIENCES. *Current Pos:* From asst prof to assoc prof, 81-93, PROF TEXTILES, UNIV CALIF, DAVIS, 93- *Personal Data:* b Taipei, Taiwan, Repub China, Feb 16, 53; m 80, A Bruce Playle; c Arlo & Alma. *Educ:* Fu-Jen Univ, Taipei, Repub China, BS, 75; Auburn Univ, MS, 77; Univ Md, College Park, PhD(polymer chem), 81. *Mem:* Am Chem Soc; Am Asn Textile Chemists & Colorists; Sigma Xi; Fiber Soc. *Res:* Fiber and polymer science; surface properties (hydrophilicity, hydrophobicity, reactivity, ionic nature, chemistry and morphology); bulk properties (hygroscopicity, mechanical properties, morphology, additives); fluid-substrate interaction and biomaterials. *Mailing Add:* Div Textiles Univ Calif Davis CA 95616-8722. *Fax:* 530-752-7584

HSIEH, YU-NIAN, SOLID STATE PHYSICS. *Current Pos:* staff engr, 77-80, ADV ENGR ENGR, IBM CORP, 81- *Personal Data:* b Chungking City, China, Nov 30, 42; m 70; c 3. *Educ:* Nat Taiwan Univ, BS, 64; Univ Notre Dame, MS, 67; Univ Calif, Berkeley, PhD(physics), 73. *Prof Exp:* Res assoc chem physics, Univ Ill, 73-75; asst prof physics, Hunter Col, City Univ New York, 75-78. *Mem:* Am Phys Soc; AAAS; Sigma Xi; Inst Elec & Electronics Engrs. *Res:* Chemical physics; nuclear double resonance; semiconductor physics and devices; very large scale integration electronics. *Mailing Add:* 1083 Foxhurst Way San Jose CA 95120

HSIUNG, ANDREW K, ENVIRONMENTAL ENGINEERING, CIVIL ENGINEERING. *Current Pos:* RETIRED. *Personal Data:* b Feng-yang, China, Jan 4, 20; US citizen; m 57; c 4. *Educ:* Chiao-Tung Univ, BS, 43; Johns Hopkins Univ, MS, 60; Iowa State Univ, PhD(environ eng), 67. *Honors & Awards:* Rudolph Hering Medal, Am Soc Civil Engrs, 70. *Prof Exp:* From jr to sr engr civil eng, var govt agencies, Repub China, 43-64; res asst environ eng, Iowa State Univ, 64-67; res engr, 67-72, sr res engr environ eng, Neptune Microfloc Inc, 72-84. *Mem:* Am Waterworks Asn. *Res:* Water and wastewater treatment processes with special interest in liquid-solids separation. *Mailing Add:* 2226 Songbird Ct SE Salem OR 97306

HSIUNG, CHUAN CHIH, MATHEMATICS. *Current Pos:* from asst prof to prof, 52-84, EMER PROF MATH, LEHIGH UNIV, 84- *Personal Data:* b Kiangsi, China, Feb 15, 16; nat US; m 42; c 1. *Educ:* Nat Univ Chekiang, BS, 36; Mich State Univ, PhD(math), 48. *Prof Exp:* Asst math, Mich State Univ, 46-48; instr, Univ Wis, 48-50; lectr, Northwestern Univ, 50; res fel, Harvard Univ, 51-52. *Concurrent Pos:* Vis assoc prof, Math Res Ctr, US Army, Univ Wis, 59-60; vis specialist, Univ Calif, Berkeley, 62; founder & managing ed, J Differential Geom, 67-; ed, Bulletin Inst Math, Academia Sinica, Taiwan, 75-; ed adv math & ed, Series in Pure Math, Singapore, 81- *Mem:* Am Math Soc; Math Asn Am. *Res:* Differential geometry. *Mailing Add:* Dept Math Lehigh Univ Bethlehem PA 18015

HSIUNG, GUEH DJEN, VIROLOGY. *Current Pos:* lectr microbiol, 67-69, assoc prof, 69-74, PROF LAB MED, SCH MED, YALE UNIV, 74- *Personal Data:* b Hupeh, China, Sept 16, 18. *Educ:* Ginling Col, BS, 42; Mich State Col, MS, 48, PhD(bact), 51. *Hon Degrees:* DSc, Mich State Univ, 89. *Honors & Awards:* Becton-Dickson Award in Clin Microbiol, 83. *Prof Exp:* Res asst microbiol, Sch Med, Yale Univ, 53-54, instr microbiol & prev med, 54-57, res assoc, 57-62, asst prof epidemiol & pub health, 62-65; assoc prof med, Sch Med, NY Univ, 65-67. *Concurrent Pos:* Dir, Virol Ref Lab, Vet Admin Med Ctr, West Haven, Conn, 84-89. *Mem:* Am Soc Microbiol; Soc Exp Biol & Med; Tissue Cult Asn; Am Asn Immunol; fel Infectious Dis Soc. *Res:* Animal viruses; simian viruses; human viruses: characterization, pathogenesis, and epidemiology of virus infection; diagnostic virology; herpes virus latency; animal model for cytomegalovirus infection; evaluation of antiviral agents. *Mailing Add:* Dept Lab Med Yale Univ Sch Med Vet Admin Med Ctr 30 W Haycock Point Rd Branford CT 06405

HSIUNG, HANSEN M, STEROIDS, GROWTH HORMONE-RELEASING HORMONE. *Current Pos:* sr scientist, 80-84, res scientist, 85-92, SR RES SCIENTIST, ELI LILLY, 93- *Personal Data:* b Wu-han, China, May 12, 47; US citizen; m, Ling-Ann Wei; c Amy & Wayne. *Educ:* Univ Ill, PhD(org chem), 75. *Mem:* Am Soc Biochem & Molecular Biol; Endocrine Soc; AAAS. *Res:* Growth hormone-releasing hormone receptor and other G-protein coupled receptor; steroid hormone receptor. *Mailing Add:* Llly Corp Ctr Indianapolis IN 46285-0001

HSU, ANDREW C T, chemical engineering, materials science, for more information see previous edition

HSU, C(HIH) C(HI), ELECTRICAL ENGINEERING. *Current Pos:* RETIRED. *Personal Data:* b Shanghai, China, June 30, 23; m 55; c 3. *Educ:* Chiao Tung Univ, BSEE, 45; Univ Mich, MSE, 49; Ohio State Univ, PhD(elec eng), 51. *Prof Exp:* Jr engr, Tsingtao Power Co, 46; asst, Univ Mich, 49 & Ohio State Univ, 50-51; asst prof elec eng, Mich Col Mining & Technol, 52; proj engr, Bendix Radio Div, Bendix Aviation Corp, 53-57; from asst prof to assoc prof elec eng, Univ Wash, 58-71, prof, 71- *Mem:* Inst Elec & Electronics Engrs. *Res:* Servomechanisms; sampled-data and digital control systems; optimal control; pattern recognition; systems optimization. *Mailing Add:* 6545 48th Ave Seattle WA 98115

HSU, CHARLES FU-JEN, NATURAL PRODUCTS CHEMISTRY. *Current Pos:* RETIRED. *Personal Data:* b Kiangsu, China, May 9, 20; US citizen; m 47, Irene Weillsu; c Phyllis, Andrew, Kenneth & Rosa. *Educ:* Nat Chung Cheng Univ, BS, 46; DePaul Univ, MS, 62; Univ Ill, PhD, 65. *Prof Exp:* Asst chem engr, Northeastern Cement Corp, China, 46-48; dir cellulose purification, Lin-Tow Co, 48-50; head teaching, Ga-Yi Indust Sch, 50-52; instr teaching & res, Taiwan Agr Col, 52-55; assoc prof, Taiwan Chung Hsin Univ, 55-59; res assoc cancer res, Ivy Cancer Res Fedn, Chicago, 61-64; res chemist, G D Searle & Co, 64-71, res chemist, Searle Labs, 71-85. *Concurrent Pos:* Adv, Taichung Technol Lab, Taiwan, 52-55 & Cent Mil Surv Sch, 55-56. *Mem:* Am Chem Soc; NY Acad Sci; Soc Indust Microbiol. *Res:* Microbial transformation of prostaglandins and steroids for search of diuretic and antiulcerogenic agents; pre-control sex of human embryo before foetal formation. *Mailing Add:* 4953 Elm St Skokie IL 60077

HSU, CHEN C, CATALYSIS, SURFACE SCIENCE. *Current Pos:* actg br chief, 90, res chemist, 82-94, PHYS SCIENTIST, US ARMY EDGEWOOD RES, DEVELOP & ENG CTR, 94- *Personal Data:* b Changhwa, Taiwan, June 29, 40; US citizen; m 66, Lai; c Samuel & Sandra. *Educ:* Nat Taiwan Normal Univ, BS, 63; Brigham Young Univ, MS, 69; Univ Utah, PhD(phys chem), 72. *Prof Exp:* Res assoc phys chem, Univ Chicago, 72-74; comput syst analyst, Electronic Div, Bell & Howell, 74-75; chemist, Argonne Nat Lab, 75-82. *Concurrent Pos:* Mem, Gas Filter Comt, US Army Chem Res, Develop & Eng Ctr, 83-85, chmn, Res Directorate Safety Comt, 89; adv, Nat Res Coun, 84-; tech consult, USAF, 87-89, USN, 93. *Mem:* Am Chem Soc; Catalysis NAm; Sigma Xi. *Res:* Catalytic reaction kinetics and mechanisms; deactivation mechanisms of catalysts; surface active metals distribution and their oxidation states of oxidation catalysts; electrochemical means for toxic chemical sensing; surface chemical analysis. *Mailing Add:* 2409 Chatau Ct Fallston MD 21047. *E-Mail:* cchsu@cbdcom.apgea.army.mil

HSU, CHEN-HSING, INTERNAL MEDICINE, NEPHROLOGY. *Current Pos:* From instr to asst prof, 72-78, ASSOC PROF MED, UNIV MICH, 78-, PROF INT MED, 92- *Personal Data:* b Taiwan, China, Apr 6, 37; US citizen; m 66; c 1. *Educ:* Nat Taiwan Univ, MD, 65. *Mem:* Am Soc Nephrology; Int Soc Nephrology; Am Fedn Clin Res. *Res:* Vitamin D metabolism in hypertension and renal failure. *Mailing Add:* 3914 Taubman Med Ctr Univ Mich Ann Arbor MI 48109-0364

HSU, CHIEH-SU, ENGINEERING EDUCATION & RESEARCH. *Current Pos:* PROF MECH ENG, UNIV CALIF, BERKELEY, 58- *Personal Data:* b Soochow, Kiangsu, China, May 27, 22; m 53, Helen Y Tse; c Raymond H & Katherine H. *Educ:* Nat Inst Technol, China, BS, 45; Stanford Univ, MS, 48, PhD(eng mech), 50. *Honors & Awards:* Alexander von Humboldt Sr Scientist Award, 86. *Prof Exp:* Engr, Shanghai Naval Dockyard, 46-47; res asst, Stanford Univ, 48-51; proj engr, IBM Corp, 51-55; assoc prof eng mech, Univ Toledo, 55-58. *Concurrent Pos:* Guggenheim fel, 64-65; chmn, Div Appl Mech, Univ Calif, 69-70; Miller res prof, Univ Calif, Berkeley, 73-74; tech ed-in-chief, J Appl Mech, Am Soc Mech Engrs, 76-82; mem, US Nat Comt Theoret & Appl Mech, Nat Acad Sci, 85-89, sci adv bd, Humboldt Found, WGer, 85- *Mem:* Nat Acad Eng; Sigma Xi; Acoust Soc Am; Am Soc Mech Engrs. *Res:* Elastic stability; nonlinear oscilations and systems analysis with emphasis on global analysis of nonlinear systems; elasticity; development of the cell to cell mapping methodology. *Mailing Add:* Dept Mech Eng Univ Calif Berkeley CA 94720

HSU, CHIN SHUNG, SYSTEMS & CONTROL, NONLINEAR SYSTEMS. *Current Pos:* Vis asst prof systs & control, 78-79, ASST PROF SYSTS & CONTROL, WASH STATE UNIV, 80- *Personal Data:* b Cha-Yi, Taiwan, Aug 10, 48; m 76; c 1. *Educ:* Nat Chiao-Tung Univ, BSEE, 70; Utah State Univ, MSEE, 74; Ore State Univ, PhD(elec eng), 79. *Concurrent Pos:* Vis asst prof systs & control, Cleveland State Univ, 78-80; asst engr, Univ Fla, 79; res asst, Ore State Univ, 73-78. *Mem:* Inst Elec & Electronics Engrs; Sigma Xi. *Res:* Analysis and control of large-scale systems; control and biomedical applications of bilinear systems; digital control systems. *Mailing Add:* Dept Elec Eng Wash State Univ Pullman WA 99164-0001

HSU, CHIN-FEI, WEATHER MODIFICATION, STATISTICS. *Current Pos:* ASSOC PROF SCI, 77-, PRIN INVESTR, ILL STATE WATER SURV, 81- *Personal Data:* b Taipei, Taiwan, Oct 29, 47; m 74; c 2. *Educ:* Nat Taiwan Univ, BS, 72; Univ NC Chapel Hill, MS, 75, PhD(statist), 77. *Prof Exp:* Res asst, statist, Univ NC, Chapel Hill, 72-77. *Concurrent Pos:* Consult, Colo State Univ, 79-80. *Mem:* Am Statist Asn; Inst Math Statist; Am Meteorol Soc; Sigma Xi. *Res:* Statistical-physical techniques to evaluate weather modification operations. *Mailing Add:* 26 Parkway Pl Holmdel NJ 07733

HSU, CLEMENT C S, CLINICAL INFECTIOUS DISEASES, HUMAN LYMPHOCYTE. *Current Pos:* med dir, 90-92, CHIEF INFECTIOUS DIS, TZU-CHI GEN HOSP, 92-; PROF, TZU-CHI JR NURSING COL, 93- *Personal Data:* b Taiwan, China, Oct 9, 37; US citizen; m 65, Yui-Li Wu; c Felix & Benedict. *Educ:* Nat Taiwan Univ, MD, 63. *Honors & Awards:* Ann Med Res Award, Leukemia Res Found, Inc, 74, 75, 77. *Prof Exp:* Intern med, Jersey City Med Ctr, 65-66; jr resident, Montefiore Hosp, NY, 66-67; sr resident, Boston City Hosp, 67-68; clin res fel, Div Liver & Nutrit, NJ Col Med & Dent, 68-69; res assoc path, Inst Cancer Res, Columbia Presby Med Ctr, NY, 69-70; clin res fel med genetics, Dept Pediat, Mt Sinai Sch Med, NY, 70-72; assoc med, Northwestern Univ, 72-74, from asst prof to assoc prof med, Infectious Dis Sect, Sch Med, 74-90. *Concurrent Pos:* Vis attend physician, Northwestern Mem Hosp, Chicago, 77-90; chief, Infectious Dis Sect, Columbus Hosp, Chicago, 77-90; comt mem, AIDS Prev Comt & Nosocomial Infection Control Comt, Dept Health, Repub China, 93- *Mem:* Am Asn Immunologists; Am Asn Cancer Res; fel Infectious Dis Soc Am; fel Am Col Physicians; AMA. *Res:* Cellular immunology and infectious diseases, specifically human lymphocyte activation in vitro, identification of lymphocyte surface molecules and geriatric clinical infectious diseases including epidemiology of methicillin-resistant staphylococcus aureus and treatment of condiduria. *Mailing Add:* Lo-Tung Po-Ai Hosp 83 Nan-Chang St Lo-Tung Taiwan. *Fax:* 3-586-1825

HSU, DAVID KUEI-YU, ULTRASONICS & COMPOSITES. *Current Pos:* SR SCIENTIST & ADJ PROF AERIAL ENG & ENG MECH, AMES LAB & CTR FOR NONDESTRUCTIVE EVAL, IOWA STATE UNIV, 84- *Personal Data:* b Shantung, China, Nov 30, 41; m 71. *Educ:* Nat Taiwan Univ, BS, 65; Wayne State Univ, PhD(physics), 71. *Prof Exp:* From instr to assoc prof physics, Colo State Univ, 71-84. *Concurrent Pos:* Translr for Chinese physics & Chinese physics lasers. *Mem:* Am Phys Soc; Acoust Soc Am; Sigma Xi. *Res:* Electromagnetic generation of ultrasonic waves in metals; nuclear acoustic resonance in metals, properties of metal hydrides and nondestructive evaluation; advanced composite materials. *Mailing Add:* 133 Appl Sci Complex II NDE Iowa State Univ 1915 Scholl Rd Ames IA 50011. *Fax:* 515-294-6368; *E-Mail:* dhsu@cnde.iastate.edu

HSU, DAVID SHIAO-YO, CHEMICAL REACTION DYNAMICS, GAS-SURFACE REACTIONS. *Current Pos:* Nat Res Coun/Naval Res Lab res assoc, 75-77, res chemist, 77-91, PRIN INVESTR, NAVAL RES LAB, 88-, SECT HEAD, 91- *Personal Data:* b Chunking, China, Nov 23, 44; m 70; c 1. *Educ:* Univ Calif, Berkeley, BS, 67; Harvard Univ, MA, 69, PhD(chem physics), 74. *Prof Exp:* Sr res assoc, Brookhaven Nat Lab, 74-75. *Mem:* Am Chem Soc; fel Am Inst Chemists; Sigma Xi. *Res:* Molecular beam reaction dynamics; chemical kinetics; energy transfer; laser-induced gas phase and surface chemistry; high temperature combustion chemistry; gas-surface reaction dynamics; thin film nucleation; nanofabrication; authored 54 publications and granted 2 patents. *Mailing Add:* 8718 Parry Lane Alexandria VA 22308

HSU, DONALD K, GLOBAL DATABASE MANAGEMENT & CLIENT SERVER TECHNOLOGY, INTERNET & INTRANET DESIGN. *Current Pos:* dir, Div Bus Admin, 90-96, ASSOC PROF COMPUT INFO SYSTS, DOMINICAN COL, 88- *Personal Data:* b Shanghai, China, Apr 17, 47; US citizen; m, Salome Hsiao; c Douglas S. *Educ:* Nat Cheng Kung Univ, BS, 69; Fordham Univ, PhD(chem physics), 75. *Honors & Awards:* Res Award, Nat Aeronaut & Space Admin, 75. *Prof Exp:* Res asst, Univ Tex, 73-74; res assoc, Princeton Univ, 75; Columbia Univ, 76; vpres, TCK Industs, NY, 77-80; asst prof physics & comput sci, St Peter's Col, NJ, 78-83; coordr comput sci, Felician Col, NJ, 83-88; tech instr, Dun & Bradstreet, NJ, 88. *Concurrent Pos:* Chmn, NY Sect Environ Comt, Am Chem Soc, 77-84; Cause award, NSF, 79-80; grant, NSF, 82 & Dept Higher Educ, State NJ, 83-88; mkt consult, Otsubo Int, 84-93, Inabata Am Corp, 91-93. *Mem:* Am Asn Univ Profs; Asn Comput Mach; Inst Elec & Electronics Engrs; NY Acad Sci. *Res:* Data communication, artificial intelligence, software development, advanced C and C++ language, laser optics and fluorescence, electron beam, lifetime studies, international trade, marketing and sales, management issues and reengineering; internet, intranet design, client server technology and global finance. *Mailing Add:* 470 Western Hwy Orangeburg NY 10962

HSU, EDWARD CHING-SHENG, PHYSICAL CHEMISTRY. *Current Pos:* SR STAFF CHEMIST, EXXON RES & ENG CO, 74- *Personal Data:* b Taiwan, May 9, 42; m 72; c 2. *Educ:* Cheng Kung Univ, Taiwan, BS, 64; Univ Chicago, PhD(phys chem), 70. *Prof Exp:* Fel appl physics, Yale Univ, 70-71; res assoc phys chem, Univ Chicago, 71-73; fel polymer sci, Univ Akron, 73-74. *Mem:* Am Chem Soc. *Res:* Electrical properties of liquid and solid hydrocarbons and their derivatives. *Mailing Add:* Exxon Res & Eng Co PO Box 101 Florham Park NJ 07932

HSU, FRANK HSIAO-HUA, SOLID STATE PHYSICS. *Current Pos:* from asst prof to assoc prof, 69-81, PROF PHYSICS, GA STATE UNIV, 81- *Personal Data:* b Hankow, China, Dec 26, 35; m 65; c 1. *Educ:* Nat Taiwan Univ, BS, 59; Columbia Univ, MS, 64, PhD(physics), 67. *Prof Exp:* Res scientist physics, Columbia Univ, 67-69. *Concurrent Pos:* Res Corp grant, 70;

adv, Int Ctr Theoret Physics; consult, Int Adv Panel. *Mem:* Nat Acad Sci; Am Asn Physics Teachers; Am Phys Soc; Nat Sci Found. *Res:* Nuclear spectroscopy; positron annihilation in solids; radiation damage in solids. *Mailing Add:* Dept Physics Ga State Univ Univ Plaza Atlanta GA 30303

HSU, H(WEI) P(IAO), ELECTRICAL ENGINEERING. *Current Pos:* PROF ELEC ENG, FAIRLEIGH DICKINSON UNIV, 86-, CHMN. *Personal Data:* b Miaoli, Taiwan, Jan 14, 30; m 53. *Educ:* Taiwan Univ, BSc, 52; Case Inst Technol, MSc, 59, PhD(elec eng), 61. *Prof Exp:* Asst prof, Univ Windsor, 61-63; assoc prof elec eng, Wayne State Univ, 63-72; dept res engr, Gen Motors Corp Res Labs, 72-83; prof & dept head elec eng, Univ Evansville, 83-86. *Concurrent Pos:* Consult, Gen Motors Corp Res Labs, 63-72. *Mem:* Inst Elec & Electronics Engrs. *Res:* Communication; electromagnetic compatability; signal analysis. *Mailing Add:* Dept Elec Eng Fairleigh Dickson Univ Teaneck NJ 07666

HSU, HOWARD HUAI TA, BIOCHEMISTRY, ENDOCRINOLOGY. *Current Pos:* asst prof path, 77-81, ASSOC PROF PATH & ONCOL, UNIV KANS MED CTR, 81- *Personal Data:* b Taipei, Taiwan, Nov 13, 38; m 65; c 2. *Educ:* Tunghai Univ, BS, 62; Univ NDak, MS, 66, PhD(biochem), 70. *Prof Exp:* Res fel, Cancer Res Inst, New Eng Deaconess Hosp, Boston, Mass, 69-71; res assoc biochem, Rockefeller Univ, 71-75; res assoc, State Univ NY, Downstate Med Ctr, 75-77. *Concurrent Pos:* USPHS fel, 70-71. *Mem:* Harvey Soc; Sigma Xi; Am Soc Molecular Biol & Biochem. *Res:* Roles of thyroid hormones in cellular metabolism and calcification; mechanism of calcification of bone and cartilage; the biochemical relationship between cancerous and embryonic cells. *Mailing Add:* Dept Path Univ Kans Med Ctr 39th & Rainbow Kansas City KS 66160-7410. *Fax:* 913-588-7073

HSU, HSIEN-WEN, CHEMICAL ENGINEERING. *Current Pos:* RETIRED. *Personal Data:* b Chia-Yi, Formosa, Apr 7, 28; m 61; c 2. *Educ:* Nat Taiwan Univ, BS, 51; Kans State Univ, MS, 55; Univ Wis, PhD(chem eng), 59. *Prof Exp:* Fel thermodyn, Sch Mech Eng, Purdue Univ, 59-61, asst prof fluid mech & heat transfer, 61-64; assoc prof chem & metall eng, Univ Tenn, Knoxville, 64-71, prof chem & metall eng, 71-95. *Concurrent Pos:* Consult, Northrop Space Labs, Ala, 65-67 & molecular anat prog, Chem Tech Div, Oak Ridge Nat Lab, 67-72 & 77-. *Mem:* Am Inst Chem Engrs; Am Chem Soc; Japanese Soc Chem Engrs. *Res:* Viral coefficients and transport properties; heat and mass transfer; cavitation problems; optimization theory and applications; biophysical separation; zonal centrifugation; chromatography; fluidization. *Mailing Add:* Dept Chem Eng Univ Tenn Knoxville TN 37996-2200

HSU, HSIUNG, APPLIED PHYSICS. *Current Pos:* assoc prof, 62-66, assoc supvr, Antenna Lab, 62-66, PROF ELEC ENG, OHIO STATE UNIV, 66- *Personal Data:* b Nantung, China, Jan 24, 20; m 55, Priscilla; c Peter, Elaine & Doreen. *Educ:* Nat Wu-han Univ, China, BS, 41; Harvard Univ, MS, 46, PhD(appl physics), 50. *Prof Exp:* Engr, Int Broadcasting Sta, 41-45; res assoc, Harvard Univ, 50; sr physicist, Gen Elec Co, 50-62. *Mem:* Am Phys Soc; Inst Elec & Electronics Engrs; Am Asn Physics Teachers; Sigma Xi; Optical Soc Am. *Res:* Microwave physics; quantum electronics; electron tubes; nonlinear optics; electronic circuits; solid state devices. *Mailing Add:* Dept Elec Eng Ohio State Univ Columbus OH 43210. *Fax:* 614-292-7596; *E-Mail:* hsu@ee.eng.ohio-state.edu

HSU, HSIU-SHENG, MEDICAL BACTERIOLOGY & IMMUNOLOGY, EXPERIMENTAL PATHOLOGY. *Current Pos:* from instr to assoc prof, 64-95, PROF MICROBIOL, MED COL VA, 95- *Personal Data:* b Guangzhou, China, Oct 26, 31; nat US; m 58, Barbara Chew; c 4. *Educ:* McGill Univ, BSc, 55; Univ Pa, MS, 56, PhD(med microbiol), 59. *Prof Exp:* Fel med microbiol, Univ Pa, 59-62; fel, Med Sch, Johns Hopkins Univ, 63-64. *Concurrent Pos:* Res grants, Am Thoracic Soc, 65-68 & Nat Inst Allergy & Infectious Dis, 65-73, 84-90 & 94-98; vis fel, Sir William Dunn Sch Path, Univ Oxford, 73. *Mem:* Reticuloendothelial Soc; Am Soc Microbiol; NY Acad Sci. *Res:* Host-parasite relationship, experimental pathology and immunology in bacterial infectious diseases; role of leucocytes in host defense against bacterial infections; mouse typhoid as an experimental model. *Mailing Add:* Dept Microbiol & Immunol Va Commonwealth Univ Richmond VA 23298-0678. *Fax:* 804-828-9946

HSU, JANG-YU, CONTROLLED FUSION, SCIENTIFIC COMPUTING & COMPUTER SOFTWARE. *Current Pos:* PRES, PHYSIONIX CORP, 90- *Personal Data:* b Kaohsiung, Taiwan, Jan 20, 49; m, Yen-Hwa Liang; c Ingrid & Jessica. *Educ:* Nat Tsing Hua Univ, BS, 70; Univ Iowa, MS, 74; Princeton Univ, PhD(plasma physics), 77. *Prof Exp:* Sr scientist, Gen Atomics, 77-89. *Mem:* Am Phys Soc. *Res:* Stochastic heating, tokamak equilibrium profile and electron cyclotron resonance heating. *Mailing Add:* Physionix Corp 6440 Lusk Blvd D-206 San Diego CA 92121. *Fax:* 619-457-1581; *E-Mail:* 72172.3352@compuserve.com

HSU, JAY C, SYSTEMS ENGINEERING. *Current Pos:* Mem tech staff, 61-67, SUPVR, BELL TEL LABS, 67- *Personal Data:* b Shanghai, China, July 18, 34; US citizen; m 61; c 3. *Educ:* Cornell Univ, BEE, 57, MEE, 58, PhD(elec eng), 61. *Mem:* Inst Elec & Electronics Engrs. *Res:* Feedback control theory, especially missile guidance and control; system engineering of operations support computer systems for the telecommunications network. *Mailing Add:* Lucent Technol 600 Mountain Ave Murray Hill NJ 07974-0636

HSU, JENG MEIN, BIOCHEMISTRY, NUTRITION. *Current Pos:* PROF CHEM, UNIV SFLA, 75-; MEM STAFF, BIOCHEM RES PROJS, VET ADMIN CTR, BAY PINES, 75- *Personal Data:* b China, Nov 27, 20; nat US; m 54; c 4. *Educ:* Nat Cent Univ, China, BS & DVM, 43; Wash State Univ, MS, 49, PhD(nutrit, biochem), 53. *Prof Exp:* Teacher, Agr Sch, China, 42-44; fel, Szechwan Exp Sta, Chengtu, China, 44-46; chief nutritionist, Nat Exp Sta, Shanghai, 46-47; asst poultry nutritionist, Wash State Univ, 50-53; res assoc biochem, Johns Hopkins Univ, 53-57; dir biochem res lab, St Joseph's Hosp, Elmira, NY, 57-58; assoc prof biochem, Johns Hopkins Univ, 58-74. *Concurrent Pos:* Fel, Nat Shanghai Demonstration Farm, 46-47; chief biochem res lab, Vet Admin Hosp, Baltimore, Md, 58-75; vis prof biochem & biophys sci, Johns Hopkins Univ, 75-76. *Mem:* AAAS; Am Chem Soc; Am Inst Nutrit; Soc Exp Biol & Med. *Res:* Zinc, vitamin B12, vitamin C and trace elements. *Mailing Add:* 1986 Georgia Circle S Clearwater FL 34620-1729

HSU, JOHN Y, COMPUTER SCIENCE. *Current Pos:* PROF COMPUT SCI, CALIF POLYTECH STATE UNIV, SAN LUIS OBISPO, 70- *Personal Data:* b Nanking, China, Mar 17, 38; US citizen; m 65, Sheryl Ku; c Mary & David. *Educ:* Nat Taiwan Univ, BS, 59; Univ Calif, Berkeley, MS, 64, PhD(comput sci), 69. *Prof Exp:* Proj engr various indust orgn, 64-67; comput architect, Varian Data Mach, 70. *Concurrent Pos:* Consult comput sci, Fed Elec Corp, Int Tel & Tel Corp, 71-, Illiac IV Proj, 73-, Control Data Corp, 81 & IBM Corp, 87-88. *Mem:* Inst Elec & Electronics Engrs; Asn Comput Mach. *Res:* Computer architecture, hardware and software. *Mailing Add:* 365 Mira Sol San Luis Obispo CA 93401

HSU, JULIE MAN-CHING, pediatric pulmonology, for more information see previous edition

HSU, KATHARINE HAN KUANG, PEDIATRICS. *Current Pos:* from asst prof to prof pediat, 53-79, dir, Pediat Chest Serv, 68-79, EMER PROF PEDIAT, BAYLOR COL MED, 79- *Personal Data:* b Foochow, China, Feb 12, 14; m 41, Tien Lu; c Dahlia. *Educ:* Yenching Univ, China, BS, 35; Peking Union Med Col, MD, 39. *Prof Exp:* From instr to asst prof pediat, Nat Chung Cheng Med Col, China, 42-47; researcher chemother tuberc, Henry Phipps Inst, Univ Pa, 49-50; sr physician, Children's Hosp, Mont Alto State Sanatorium, South Mountain, Pa, 50-53. *Concurrent Pos:* Pediatrician-in-chg, Children's Tuberc Clin, Jefferson Davis Hosp, 53-68; dir tuberc control, Dept Pub Health, Houston, 65-68; consult, Tex Children's Hosp. *Mem:* Am Thoracic Soc; Am Col Chest Physicians. *Res:* Pediatric tuberculosis and respiratory diseases; pulmonary disease; chemotherapy, epidemiology and immunology of tuberculosis in children. *Mailing Add:* Pediat Baylor Col Med 1 Baylor Plaza Houston TX 77030-3411

HSU, KENNETH HSUEHCHIA, FOOD ENGINEERING. *Current Pos:* supvr eng, 87-91, PRIN ENGR, NABISCO BRANDS INC, 91- *Personal Data:* b Taiwan, Aug 21, 50. *Educ:* Kans State Univ, BS, 72, MS, 74, PhD(cereal sci), 78. *Prof Exp:* Chemist I prod develop, Durkee Food Co, SCM Corp, 78-79, sr chemist, 79-80; asst prof, Dept Food Technol, Iowa State Univ, 80-85, assoc prof, 85-87. *Mem:* Am Asn Cereal Chemists; Am Inst Chem Engrs; Inst Food Technologists. *Res:* Determination of physical, chemical and functional properties of food systems, particularly as related to cereals and oilseeds; modeling of food processes and kinetics of food reactions. *Mailing Add:* Nabisco Brands Inc 200 DeForest Ave East Hanover NJ 07936

HSU, KENNETH JINGHWA, GEOLOGY. *Current Pos:* VIS PROF, COLO SCH MINES, 97- *Personal Data:* b Nanking, China, July 1, 29; m 67, Christine Eugster; c Elisabeth, Martin, Andrew & Peter. *Educ:* Nat Cent Univ, BS, 48; Ohio State Univ, MA, 50; Univ Calif, Los Angeles, PhD(geol), 54. *Hon Degrees:* DSc, Nanjing Univ, 87. *Honors & Awards:* Wollaston Medal, Geol Soc London, 84; Twenhofel Medal, Soc Econ Paleontologists & Mineralogists, 84. *Prof Exp:* Asst geol, Ohio State Univ, 48-49; asst geophys, Inst Geophys, Univ Calif, Los Angeles, 50-51, asst geol, 51-54; geologist, Shell Develop Co, 54-56, proj head, 57-62, res assoc, 63; assoc prof geol, Harpur Col, 63-64; assoc prof, Univ Calif, Riverside, 64-67; prof, Swiss Fed Inst Technol, 67-94, chmn Geol Inst, 78-82. *Concurrent Pos:* Co-chief scientist, Mediter & Atlantic Cruises, Deep-Sea Drilling Proj; chmn, Mediter Panel, Atlantic Working Group, Joint Oceanog Inst Deep Earth Sampling; ed-in-chief, Sedimentol; assoc ed, J Sedimentary Petrol, Marine Geophys Res & Geophys Surv; Guggenheim Found fel, 72; chmn, Int Comn Marine Geol & Comt Global Change, Int Union Geol Sci; vis prof, Scripps Inst Oceanog, 72, Calif Inst Technol, 91, Nat Taiwan Univ, 94-95, Hebrew Univ Jerusalem, 95; fel, Berlin Inst Advan Studies, 96. *Mem:* Nat Acad Sci; hon mem Soc Econ Paleontologists & Mineralogists; Swiss Geol Soc; Int Asn Sedimentol (pres, 78-82); hon fel Geol Soc Am; Acad Sinica. *Res:* Structural geology; sedimentation; petrology. *Mailing Add:* Geol Inst Swiss Fed Inst Technol Sonneggstr 5 Zurich Switzerland. *Fax:* 303-384-2026; *E-Mail:* khsu@mines.edu

HSU, KONRAD CHANG, IMMUNOBIOLOGY. *Current Pos:* from asst to assoc prof, 54-69, PROF MICROBIOL, COL PHYSICIANS & SURGEONS, COLUMBIA UNIV, 69- *Personal Data:* b China, Aug 28, 01; nat US; m 84, Kit Y Ng; c 7. *Educ:* St John's Univ, China, BS, 21; Columbia Univ, MA, 23, PhD(chem), 24. *Prof Exp:* Prof chem & dean col sci, Great China Univ, 24-26; with govt serv, China, 26-28; chemist & gen mgr, Chan Hwa & Co, 29-46; vpres, Sino Hawaiian Corp, 46-49; adv govt sugar orgn, Thailand, 50-51; consult sugar factories, Thailand, 51-54. *Concurrent Pos:* Res consult microbiol, FDR Vet Hosp, Montrose, NY, 68-70. *Mem:* Am Asn Immunol; Am Asn Path; Soc Exp Biol & Med; Harvey Soc. *Res:* Diseases resulting from immune reactions utilizing fluorescein, ferritin and enzyme labeled antibodies and antigens; immunologic studies of tumor virus antigens using such labeled antibodies. *Mailing Add:* 41-40 Union St Apt 12-R Flushing NY 11355-2508

HSU, KUO-HOM LEE, VIROLOGY. *Current Pos:* sr microbiologist, 88-89, res scientist, 89-93, PRIN SCIENTIST, WYETH-AYERST RES, 93- *Personal Data:* m 72, Jemin Charles; c Jerry & Jennifer. *Educ:* Nat Taiwan Normal Univ, BS, 72; Clemson Univ, MS, 75; Univ Ala, Birmingham, PhD(immunol), 79. *Prof Exp:* Fel, Northwestern Univ, 79-81; from instr to asst prof, Univ SFla, 81-84; res asst prof, Hahnemann Univ, 84-88. *Mem:* Am Asn Immunol; AAAS; NY Acad Sci. *Res:* Development of live attenuated respiratory syncytial virus vaccine, including viral mutagenesis, temperature sensitive mutant isolation, pre-clinical evaluation of the vaccine; development of assays for clinical evaluation of the vaccine. *Mailing Add:* Wyeth-Ayerst Res 145-R2 PO Box 8299 Philadelphia PA 19101-8299. *Fax:* 215-989-4588

HSU, KWAN, BIOPHYSICS. *Current Pos:* assoc prof, 64-74, prof biophys, 74-77, prof physics, 77-80, EMER PROF PHYSICS, PORTLAND STATE UNIV, 80- *Personal Data:* b Kwang-Si, China, Mar 11, 13; US citizen. *Educ:* Shanghai Univ, BS, 36; Univ Minn, MS, 50; Univ Calif, Berkeley, PhD(biophys), 60. *Prof Exp:* Instr physics, Shanghai Univ, 37-47; Am Asn Univ Women int study grant, 47-48; asst physics, Univ Minn, 48-50; asst, Univ Iowa, 50- 52, Col Med, 52-53; assoc biophys, Univ Calif, Berkeley, 54-59; physicist, Vet Admin Hosp, Indianapolis, Ind, 60-61, asst chief biophys, 61-62; res assoc physics, Biophys Lab, Stanford Univ, 64. *Concurrent Pos:* Asst prof, Sch Med, Univ Ind, 60-62. *Mem:* Biophys Soc; Radiation Res Soc; Soc Nuclear Med; Am Asn Physics Teachers; NY Acad Sci. *Res:* Cellular and radiation biophysics; health physics. *Mailing Add:* Dept Physics Portland State Univ PO Box 751 Portland OR 97207

HSU, LAURA LING, EVOLUTION, MICROBIOLOGY. *Current Pos:* instr & coordr, Dept Biol, 80-84, ASST DEAN & DIR PROG, SCH CONTINUING STUDIES, RICE UNIV, 84- *Personal Data:* b Kwei-Chow, China, Aug 22, 39; m 63; c 2. *Educ:* Acadia Univ, NS, Can, 61; Cornell Univ, MS, 64; Univ Miami, Coral Gables, PhD(biol), 74. *Prof Exp:* Supvr & instr microbiol, Mycol & Parasitol Labs, Evanston Hosp Asn, Evanston, Ill, 63-66; instr sci, Sch Nursing, St Francis Hosp, Evanston, 66-68; instr parasitol, Sch Med Technol, Med Col, Northwestern Univ, Chicago, 67-68; res asst, Inst Molecular & Cellular Evolution, Univ Miami, Coral Gables, Fla, 69-71, res asst prof, 74- *Concurrent Pos:* Vis assoc prof, Nat Taiwan Univ, 78-79; vis fel plant path, Cornell Univ, Ithaca, NY, 82. *Mem:* Sigma Xi; Int Soc Study Origin Life; Am Soc Clin Pathologists; Am Soc Microbiologists; Asn Women Sci. *Res:* The origins and evolution of life on Earth; the development of metabolic systems and energy conversion in synthetic cell models; issues in continuing education. *Mailing Add:* 5034 Glenmeadow Houston TX 77096. *E-Mail:* llhsu@rice.edu

HSU, LIANG-CHI, MINERALOGY, PETROLOGY. *Current Pos:* asst prof geol & asst mineralogist, 69-72, assoc prof geol & assoc mineralogist, 72-78, PROF GEOL & MINERALOGIST, MACKAY SCH MINES, UNIV NEV, RENO, 78- *Personal Data:* b Formosa, Sept 1, 31; nat US; m 60; c 4. *Educ:* Univ Taiwan, BS, 56, MS, 61; Univ Calif, Los Angeles, PhD(geol), 66. *Prof Exp:* Instr geol, Univ Taiwan, 61-63; res assoc mineral & geochem, Pa State Univ, 66-68. *Concurrent Pos:* Res consult, Northrop Space Lab, Calif, 66; UN sr scientist, China, 82, 87 & 91; tech peer rev, Nuclear Waste Isolation Prog, 80; fel, Ministry Economic Affairs, Li Found. *Mem:* Am Geophys Union; fel Geol Soc Am; fel Mineral Soc Am; Geochem Soc; Soc Econ Geologists; Asn Explor Geochem; Sigma Xi. *Res:* Hydrothermal investigations of minerals or mineral assemblages related to genesis of ores and rocks; determinative mineralogy with instrumental techniques in geochemical studies of ores and minerals. *Mailing Add:* Dept Geol Scis Univ Nev Ninth & N Va Reno NV 89557. *Fax:* 702-784-1709; *E-Mail:* lihsu@nbmg.unr.edu

HSU, LINDA, ANATOMY, DEVELOPMENTAL BIOLOGY. *Current Pos:* ASST PROF BIOL, SETON HALL UNIV, 85- *Personal Data:* b Kunming, China, May 5, 44. *Educ:* Pomona Col, BA, 66; Univ Mich, MS, 68, PhD(anat), 71. *Prof Exp:* Fel anat, Yale Univ, 71-72; from instr to asst prof, NY Med Col, 72-75; fel, Rutgers Med Sch, 76-77; asst prof anat, NJ Sch Osteop Med, 77-85. *Concurrent Pos:* Res grant, Am Cancer Soc, 73-74; NIH grant, 78-81; Nat Oceanog Asn grant, 81-83. *Mem:* Tissue Cult Soc; Am Asn Anat; Neurosci Soc. *Res:* Nerve and muscle regeneration; amphibian limb regeneration; neurotrophic effects. *Mailing Add:* Dept Biol Seton Hall Univ S Orange Ave South Orange NJ 07079-2697

HSU, MING-TA, microbiology, for more information see previous edition

HSU, MING-TA SUNG, ORGANIC CHEMISTRY. *Current Pos:* RES CHEMIST, H C CHEM RES, 82- *Personal Data:* b Hopei, China, Aug 3, 37; m 72, Thomas; c Baldwin. *Educ:* Nat Taiwan Univ, BS, 60; NMex Highlands Univ, MA, 63; Iowa State Univ, PhD(org chem), 67. *Prof Exp:* Fel chem, Synvar Res Inst, 67-68; spectroscopist, Stanford Univ, 68-69; res chemist, Appl Space Prods Inc, 69-70; res assoc, Ames Res Ctr, NASA, 70-72; res chemist, San Jose State Univ, 72-82. *Concurrent Pos:* NASA contract, 72- *Mem:* Am Chem Soc; Soc Advan Mat & Process Eng. *Res:* Organic photochemistry; molecular complexes of psychoactive compounds; spectroscopy; characterization and thermal-oxidative degradation of polymers; polymer synthesis; organometallic polymers and high temperature materials. *Mailing Add:* 1934 Cape Hilda Pl San Jose CA 95133

HSU, NAI-CHAO, MATHEMATICS, ABSTRACT ALGEBRA. *Current Pos:* assoc prof, 66-72, PROF MATH, EASTERN ILL UNIV, 72- *Personal Data:* b Formosa; c Stephen, Susan & Saunders. *Educ:* Washington Univ, PhD(math), 60. *Prof Exp:* Assoc mathematician, Int Bus Mach Corp, 60-63; asst prof math, State Univ NY Buffalo, 63-66. *Mem:* Am Math Soc. *Res:* Homological algebra. *Mailing Add:* 1030 Colony Lane Charleston IL 61920

HSU, NELSON NAE-CHING, POLYMER SCIENCE, TECHNICAL MANAGEMENT. *Current Pos:* PRIN RES SCIENTIST, RECYCLE TECHNOL GROUP, CYTEC INDUSTS, INC, 91- *Personal Data:* b Shanghai, China, May 20, 34; US citizen; m 57, Rosaline King; c Vivian, Diane, Lydia & Nelson D. *Educ:* Mass Inst Technol, SB, 57; Univ Akron, MS, 60, PhD(polymer sci), 66; Univ Conn, MBA, 70. *Prof Exp:* Res chemist, B F Goodrich Res Ctr, 57-65; group leader, Aerospace Prod Dept, Am Cyanamid Co, 65-80, group leader, Eng Mat Dept, 80-82, mgr, Tech Serv Lab, Process Chem Dept, 86-91. *Concurrent Pos:* Res chemist, Inst Polymer Sci, Univ Akron, 63-65. *Mem:* Coated & Processed Paper Asn; Tech Asn Pulp & Paper Indust. *Res:* Physics and chemistry of polymers; polymerization processes; structural adhesives; commercial development of chemicals and polymers; latices; surfactants; paper chemicals, specialty monomers, radiation curing; paper recycling and drinking process water clarification; sludge dewatering, stickies removal. *Mailing Add:* 158 Thornwood Rd Stamford CT 06903. *Fax:* 203-321-2984; *E-Mail:* nelson_hsu@st.cytec.com

HSU, POCHANG, VERY LARGE SCALE INTEGRATION INTERCONNECTS, INTERCONNECT & ELECTRONIC PACKAGING. *Current Pos:* SR DESIGN ENGR, INTEL CORP, 93- *Personal Data:* b Taipez, Taiwan, Sept 4, 61; m 92; c 2. *Educ:* Nat Cheng-Kung Univ, Taiwan, BS, 84; Univ Ariz, PhD(elec & comput eng), 93. *Concurrent Pos:* Sr component engr, Advan Packaging Develop Div, LSI Logic Corp, Calif, 93-95; instr, Design Technol Div, Intel Corp, 95-96; adj prof microprocessor based systs, San Jose State Univ, 96. *Mem:* Inst Elec & Electronics Engrs. *Res:* Methodologies to characterize and enhance the electrical performance of high-speed interconnects and interconnect packages. *Mailing Add:* 271 Meyz Ct Milpitas CA 95035. *Fax:* 408-765-5775; *E-Mail:* phsu@tdzcad.intel.com

HSU, ROBERT YING, BIOCHEMISTRY. *Current Pos:* from asst prof to prof, 68-93, EMER PROF BIOCHEM, STATE UNIV NY HEALTH SCI CTR, 93- *Personal Data:* b China, Oct 10, 26; US citizen; m 62; c 2. *Educ:* Nanking Univ, BS, 50; Iowa State Univ, MS, 52; Cornell Univ, MS, 55; Univ Wis, PhD(biochem), 61. *Prof Exp:* Res scientist, Armour Pharmaceut Co, 61-63; fel biochem, Univ Wis, 63-66; asst prof, Rutgers Univ, 66-68. *Concurrent Pos:* Vis assoc prof, Nat Taiwan Univ, 62; travel award, Int Cong Biochem, Japan, 67; Brit Royal Soc vis scholar, Oxford Univ, 82. *Mem:* Am Soc Biol Chem & Molecular Biol; Am Chem Soc. *Res:* Enzymology of fatty acid biosynthesis; mechanism of enzyme action; purification and characterization of metabolically significant enzymes. *Mailing Add:* 3225 Hidden Creek Ave Thousand Oaks CA 91360

HSU, SHAW LING, POLYMER PHYSICS, VIBRATIONAL SPECTROSCOPY. *Current Pos:* from asst prof to assoc prof, 78-87, DIR, NSF MAT RES LAB, UNIV MASS, 85-, PROF POLYMER SCI & ENG, 87- *Personal Data:* b Shanghai, China, July 14, 48; m 70; c 2. *Educ:* Rutgers Univ, BA, 70; Univ Mich, PhD(physics), 75. *Prof Exp:* Res assoc physics, Macromolecular Res Ctr, Univ Mich, 75-76; res chemist, chem physics, Allied Chem Corp, 76-78. *Mem:* Am Phys Soc; Am Chem Soc; Optical Soc Am. *Res:* Conformational analysis of synthetic and biological polymers by infrared and Raman spectroscopy; use of the longitudinal acoustic mode to study polymer morphology; structural analysis of polyacetlylene-dopant systems; vibrational studies of phase transitions in polymeric systems; deformation studies of polymers by time resolved fourier transform infrared spectroscopy; characterization of polymer microstructure and phase transformation mechanisms. *Mailing Add:* Dept Polymer Sci & Eng Univ Mass Amherst MA 01003

HSU, SHENG TENG, SOLID STATE ELECTRONICS. *Current Pos:* mem staff, 72-85, FEL, RCA LABS, 85- *Personal Data:* b Taiwan, Oct 15, 34; m 64; c 2. *Educ:* Nat Taiwan Univ, BS, 58; Chiao Tung Univ, MS, 60; Univ Minn, PhD(elec eng), 66. *Prof Exp:* Mem staff solid state devices, Fairchild Semiconductor, 66-70; asst prof elec eng, Univ Man, 70-72. *Mem:* Inst Elec & Electronics Engrs. *Res:* Solid state devices; IC technologies. *Mailing Add:* 94 Presidents Lane Quincy MA 02169

HSU, SHIH-ANG, METEOROLOGY. *Current Pos:* from asst prof to assoc prof, 69-77, PROF COASTAL STUDIES INST & DEPT OCEANOG & COASTAL SCI, LA STATE UNIV, BATON ROUGE, 77- *Personal Data:* b Hanchou, China, Sept 15, 36; nat US; m 63, Hwei Chou; c Helen, Julie & Jerry. *Educ:* Nat Taiwan Univ, BS, 61; Univ Tex, Austin, MS, 67, PhD(meteorol), 69. *Prof Exp:* Meteorologist-in-chg, Yunlin Tidal Land Develop & Demonstration, Taiwan Sugar Corp, 61-63; meteorol officer, Ministry of Commun, Taipei, Taiwan, 63-65; res asst atmospheric sci group, Univ Tex, Austin, 65-67, res sci assoc, 67-69. *Concurrent Pos:* Meteorol consult (cert), govt & indust, 79- *Mem:* Am Meteorol Soc; Am Geophys Union. *Res:* Coastal and marine meteorology; air-sea interaction. *Mailing Add:* Coastal Studies Inst La State Univ Baton Rouge LA 70803. *Fax:* 504-388-2520; *E-Mail:* sahsu@antares.esl.lsu.edu

HSU, SHU YING LI, PARASITOLOGY, IMMUNOLOGY. *Current Pos:* from asst prof to assoc prof, 57-73, PROF PREV MED, STATE UNIV IOWA, 73- *Personal Data:* b Peking, China, Aug 16, 20; m 54. *Educ:* Nat Peking Norm Univ, BS, 38; Univ Iowa, PhD, 57. *Honors & Awards:* SC Res Award, Taiwan, 53. *Prof Exp:* Asst prof parasitol & head dept, Nat Shenyang Med Col, 47-48; instr, Mich State Univ, 52-53; res assoc, Sch Pub Health, Harvard Univ, 53-54. *Mem:* AAAS; Am Soc Parasitol; Am Soc Trop Med & Hyg; Am Asn Immunol; Soc Exp Biol & Med. *Res:* Parasitology and immunology, especially schistosomiasis. *Mailing Add:* Dept Prev Med 1-310-A MEB State Univ Iowa Iowa City IA 52242

HSU, STEPHEN M, TRIBOLOGY, ADVANCED CERAMICS. *Current Pos:* div chief, ceramics, 85-92, SR SCIENTIST, NAT INST STAND & TECHNOL, 92- *Personal Data:* b Shanghai, China, Nov 20, 43; m 68, Stella P Lee; c 2. *Educ:* Va Polytech Inst & State Univ, BS, 68; Pa State Univ, MS, 72, PhD(chem eng), 76. *Honors & Awards:* Bronze Medal, Dept Com, 84, Silver Medal, 90; Capt Alfred E Hunt Mem Medal, 80; Al Sonntag Award, 91. *Prof Exp:* Res engr, Amco Res Ctr, 74-78; res sci, Nat Bur Stands, 78-79. *Concurrent Pos:* Prog mgr, recycled oil progs, Nat Bur Stands, 78-83; bd dir, Soc Tribologist & Lub Engrs, 88-; adj prof, Pa State Univ, 83-; mem, Ceramics Subcomt, Comt Mat, 86-; chmn, Gov Steering Comt, Comput Tribology Info Syst, 86-91, IEA Int Round Robin ceramics powders, Gordon Res Conf tribology & US chmn, VAMAS Int study wear mat; bd dir, Soc Tribologist & Lub Engrs, 88-; mem, Nat Steering Comt, superconductivity for power transmission, 88-90; chmn, Am Soc Testing & Mat; vis prof chem eng, Pa State, 91-92; Esbach vis fel, Northwestern Univ, 92; adj prof mat sci, Univ Md, 94- *Mem:* Soc Tribologist & Lubrication Engrs; Am Soc Mech Engrs; Am Soc Testing & Mat; Soc Automotive Engrs; Am Ceramics Soc; NY Acad Sci; Am Inst Chem Engrs. *Res:* Tribology: lubrication mechanisms and models, microstructural and environmental effects on wear of metals, ceramics, coatings; ceramics tribology: ceramic powders characterization; tribochemistry: interface chemical reactions and kinetics. *Mailing Add:* Nat Inst Stand & Technol Gaithersburg MD 20899. *Fax:* 301-990-8729; *E-Mail:* hsu@micf.nist.gov

HSU, STEVE LIEH-CHUNG, POLYMER CHEMISTRY. *Current Pos:* SR RES CHEMIST, OLIN MICROELECTRONIC MATS, 96- *Personal Data:* b Taipei, Taiwan, Sept 20, 54. *Educ:* Chung-Yuan Univ, Taiwan, BS, 78; Tsing-hua Univ, Taiwan, MS, 82; Univ Akron, PhD(polymer sci), 91. *Prof Exp:* Asst researcher, Telecommun Res Labs, Taiwan, 82-83; res assoc, Indust Mat Res Lab, ITRI, Taiwan, 83-85; res scientist, Maxdem Inc, 90-95; sr chemist, TA Mfg Co, Esterline Co, 95-96. *Mem:* Am Chem Soc. *Res:* Synthesis, characterization and processing of high temperature polymers (polyimides, polyquinolines and polyphenylene); development of photosensitive polymer systems; epoxy formulation and composites; silicone rubber formulation and processing. *Mailing Add:* 2 Ferncrest Dr East Providence RI 02915. *Fax:* 401-438-8352; *E-Mail:* sshsu@corp.olin.com

HSU, SU-MING, PATHOLOGY, MOLECULAR BIOLOGY. *Current Pos:* PROF PATH, UNIV ARK, LITTLE ROCK, 90- *Personal Data:* b In-Lin, Tawain, Jan 28, 49; US citizen; m 77; c 1. *Educ:* Nat Taiwan Univ, MD, 74. *Honors & Awards:* Young Man of Year, Taiwan Govt, 76. *Prof Exp:* Staff fel path, Nat Cancer Inst, 81-84; asst prof path, Univ Tex, Houston, 84-89. *Mem:* Am Soc Path. *Res:* The nature of Hodgkin's disease and lymphomas; development of new tests to facilitate the diagnosis of Hodgkin's disease. *Mailing Add:* Nat Taiwan Univ Col Med 1 Jen-ai Rd Taipei Taiwan

HSU, SUSAN HU, IMMUNOGENETICS. *Current Pos:* SCI DIR & DIR HISTOCOMPATIBILITY LAB, AM RED CROSS PA-JERSEY REGION, 87- *Personal Data:* b Jan 19, 43; US citizen; m 68; c 2. *Educ:* Nat Taiwan Univ, BS, 65; Univ Ill, MS, 68, PhD(genetics), 70. *Prof Exp:* Trainee immunogenetics, Div Med Genetics, Johns Hopkins Univ, 70-74, from asst prof to assoc prof med, 74-86. *Mem:* Am Soc Human Genetics. *Res:* Genetic marker research; lymphocytes culture research. *Mailing Add:* Dept Res Histocompatibility Lab Am Red Cross Pa-Jersey Region Spring Gardens Philadelphia PA 19123. *Fax:* 215-451-2538

HSU, TSONG-HAN, ORGANIC POLYMER CHEMISTRY. *Current Pos:* SR RESIN CHEMIST PAINT & COATINGS, HILLYARD CHEM CO, 82- *Personal Data:* b Chekiang, China, Oct 10, 22; US citizen; m 50; c 1. *Educ:* Amoy Univ, BS, 47; Auburn Univ, MS, 64, PhD(org chem), 68. *Prof Exp:* Sr technologist wood chem, Taiwan Forest Res Inst, 48-61; res chemist, Lawrence Ottinger Res Ctr, Champion Bldg Prod, 68-72; sr chemist org systs, RSA Corp, 72-76; polymer expert adhesive coatings, UN Indust Develop Orgn, 76-79; sr res chemist bldg prod, Jim Walter Corp, 80-82. *Mem:* Am Chem Soc; Int Union Pure & Appl Chem. *Res:* Chemistry of thermosetting polymers such as phenolic, amino and epoxy resins and their uses for coatings, adhesives and molding compounds; high solids epoxy coatings technology; water-borne alkyl coatings development. *Mailing Add:* 1548 81st Ave N St Petersburg FL 33702

HSU, WALTER HAW, ENDOCRINE PHARMACOLOGY, VETERINARY PHARMACOLOGY. *Current Pos:* from asst prof to assoc prof, 77-86, PROF VET PHARMACOL & PHYSIOL, IOWA STATE UNIV, 86- *Personal Data:* b Fu-Jian, China, July 10, 46; m 71; c 2. *Educ:* Nat Taiwan Univ, BS, 69; Univ NC, PhD(pharmacol), 75. *Honors & Awards:* Ralston Purina Small Animal Res Award, 87. *Prof Exp:* Res assoc pharmacol, Purdue Univ, 75-77. *Mem:* Am Vet Med Asn; Am Soc Pharmacol Exp Ther; Soc Study Reproduction. *Res:* Adrenergic pharmacology; clinical pharmacology of veterinary drugs. *Mailing Add:* Dept Vet Physiol & Pharmacol Iowa State Univ Ames IA 50011-1250. *Fax:* 545-294-2315; *E-Mail:* whsu@ciastate.edu

HSU, WEN-TAH, BIOCHEMISTRY, MICROBIOLOGY. *Current Pos:* Asst prof biochem, 66-81, ASSOC PROF BIOCHEM, BEN MAY LAB, UNIV CHICAGO, 81-, RES ASSOC BIOCHEM, FRANKLIN MCLEAN MEM RES INST, 62- *Personal Data:* b Hwa-Lien, Formosa, Dec 29, 30; m 62; c 2. *Educ:* Nat Taiwan Univ, BS, 54; Mich State Univ, MS, 58; Univ Ill, PhD(microbiol), 63. *Mem:* Soc Am Biologists. *Res:* Molecular mechanism of action of polycyclic aromatic hydrocarbons. *Mailing Add:* 1471 E Park Pl Chicago IL 60637

HSU, WILLIAM YANG-HSING, POLYMER PHYSICS, SOLID STATE PHYSICS. *Current Pos:* res staff mem physics, 77-80, group leader, 80-81, res supvr, Cent Res & Develop Dept, Exp Sta, Wilmington, Del, 92, DIR, CIRCLEVILLE RES LAB, E I DU PONT DE NEMOURS & CO, INC, OHIO, 93- *Personal Data:* b Chungking, China, Apr 8, 48; m 75; c 1. *Educ:* Chinese Univ Hong Kong, BSc, 70; Univ Calif, Berkeley, PhD(physics), 75. *Prof Exp:* Res assoc physics, Univ Ill, Urbana, 75-77. *Mem:* Am Phys Soc. *Res:* Properties of ionic and covalent polymers; percolation theory; properties of ionic conductors, metals and impurities in semiconductors; galvanomagnetic properties. *Mailing Add:* 2410 Cambridge Blvd Columbus OH 43221-4022

HSU, YU KAO, mathematics, aeronautics, for more information see previous edition

HSU, YU-SHENG, MATHEMATICS, STATISTICS. *Current Pos:* AT CALIF POLYTECH STATE UNIV. *Personal Data:* b China, Oct 12, 45. *Educ:* Nat Tsing Hua Univ, BS, 68; Univ Wis, MS, 71; Purdue Univ, PhD(statist), 75. *Prof Exp:* Lectr math, Southern Ill Univ, 75-77; asst prof, Wright State Univ, 77-78; asst prof math, Eastern Mont Col, 78-79; asst prof of math, Ga State Univ, 79-84, prof 84-95. *Mem:* Inst Math Statist; Am Statist Asn. *Res:* Distribution theory of some multivariate test statistics; robustness studies of some multivariate tests; geostatistics. *Mailing Add:* Calif Polytech State Univ San Luis Obispo CA 93407

HSUAN, HULBERT C S, PLASMA PHYSICS, ELECTRICAL ENGINEERING. *Current Pos:* FROM RES PHYSICIST TO PRIN RES PHYSICIST, PLASMA PHYSICS LAB, PRINCETON UNIV, 73- *Personal Data:* b Jiangsu, China, Nov 28, 39; m 63, Catherine Wang; c Abraham B & Bryan B. *Educ:* Nat Taiwan Univ, BS, 60; Univ Ill, MS, 63; Princeton Univ, PhD(plasma physics), 67. *Prof Exp:* Electronic engr, Makong Navy Yard, Taiwan, 60-61; from asst prof to prof elec eng, Univ Iowa, 66-75. *Concurrent Pos:* Chinese scientists fel from HSU Found, 57-60; Ford Found fel, Plasma Physics, 63-64, NSF grants, 65-75; exec comt mem, PSAC-IEEE-NPS, 78-80. *Mem:* Fel Am Phys Soc; Inst Elec & Electronics Engrs. *Res:* Controlled thermonuclear fusion research; microwave and millimetrewave techniques and applications; electromagnetic theory; power electronics; plasma dynamics and applications. *Mailing Add:* 66 Wittmer Ct Princeton Univ Princeton NJ 08540. *Fax:* 609-243-2418

HSUEH, ANDIE M, NUTRITION & FOOD SCIENCE. *Current Pos:* from asst prof to assoc prof, 79-89, PROF, DEPT NUTRIT & FOOD SCI, TEX WOMAN'S UNIV, 89- *Personal Data:* b July 22, 40; div; c 1. *Educ:* Tunghai Univ, Taiwan, BS, 59; Tex Woman's Univ, MS, 63; Johns Hopkins Univ, ScD(nutrit biochem), 70. *Prof Exp:* Res assoc, Dept Biochem, Sch Hyg & Pub Health, Johns Hopkins Univ, 70-72, res asst prof, 72-79. *Concurrent Pos:* Wellcome vis prof, 81; NIH res grant, 89-92. *Mem:* Am Inst Nutrit; Sigma Xi. *Res:* Author of numerous technical publications. *Mailing Add:* Nutrit & Food Sci Tex Woman's Univ PO Box 425888 Denton TX 76204-5888. *Fax:* 940-898-2684; *E-Mail:* f__hsueh@twu.edu

HSUEH, YA, PHYSICAL OCEANOGRAPHY. *Current Pos:* from asst prof to assoc prof, 67-80, chmn dept, 82-85, PROF OCEANOG, FLA STATE UNIV, 80-, CHMN DEPT, 88- *Personal Data:* b Kiangsu, China, Mar 19, 36; m 64; c 2. *Educ:* Nat Taiwan Univ, BSc, 58; Johns Hopkins Univ, PhD(mech), 65. *Prof Exp:* Res assoc airsea interaction, Univ Wash, 65-67. *Concurrent Pos:* Prin investr, Inst Naval Oceanog, 87-90; prog dir phys oceanog, NSF, 80-81; prin investr, Off Naval Res, 89- *Mem:* Am Geophys Union; Am Meteorol Soc. *Res:* Dynamic oceanography; coastal upwelling; boundary currents of oceans; theoretical models of the circulation on the continental shelf; meanders of ocean currents in a rotating tank. *Mailing Add:* Dept Oceanog Fla State Univ 600 W College Ave Tallahassee FL 32306-1096

HSUI, ALBERT TONG-KWAN, GEOPHYSICS, MECHANICS. *Current Pos:* PROF, DEPT GEOL, UNIV ILL, 80- *Personal Data:* b Canton, China, 45; c 2. *Educ:* Univ Lowell, BS, 68; Cornell Univ, ME, 69, PhD(geol sci), 72. *Prof Exp:* Res assoc micrometeorol, Ames Res Ctr, NASA, 72-73; mem tech staff eng, Bell Labs, 73-75; res assoc geophys, Mass Inst Technol, 75-79. *Concurrent Pos:* Lectr, State Seismol Bur, China, 81. *Mem:* Am Geophys Union; Sigma Xi; NY Acad Sci; AAAS; Soc Explor Geophys. *Res:* Geodynamics; basin evolution studies; borehole geophysics. *Mailing Add:* Dept Geol Univ Ill 1301 W Green St Urbana IL 61801-2919. *Fax:* 217-244-4996; *E-Mail:* hsui@uikc.edu

HTOO, MAUNG SHWE, PHYSICAL CHEMISTRY. *Current Pos:* PRES, TECH COMMUN INT, INC, 92- *Personal Data:* b Yenangyaung, Burma, Aug 17, 27; US citizen; m 53, Anne Shraybman; c Susan, Nancy, Rhonda & Naomi. *Educ:* Univ Maine, BS, 52, MS, 54; Rensselaer Polytech Inst, PhD(phys chem), 61. *Prof Exp:* Sr res chem engr, Res Div, Int Paper Co, NY, 54-61; staff chemist supplies div, Int Bus Mach Corp, NY, 61-62, develop chemist, 62-65, adv chemist components div, Poughkeepsie, 65-67, proj mgr photosensitive processes, 67-69, mgr chem technol mfg res lab, 70-74, mgr prod technol mat res lab, 75-81, mgr tech assurance lab, 82-92. *Concurrent Pos:* Mem fac dept chem eve div, Dutchess Community Col, 67-84; sr tech staff mem, IBM, 85-92; adj prof, Rensselaer Polytech Inst, 92- *Mem:* NY Acad Sci; Soc Plastics Engrs; Am Chem Soc; fel Am Inst Chemists. *Res:* Photosensitive materials and processes; organic semiconductors; thin films; organic coatings. *Mailing Add:* 10 Rabbit Trail Rd Poughkeepsie NY 12603. *Fax:* 914-471-5462

HU, ALFRED SOY LAN, BIOCHEMISTRY. *Current Pos:* from asst prof to prof, 61-93, EMER PROF BIOCHEM, UNIV KY, 93- *Personal Data:* b Honolulu, Hawaii, Apr 1, 28; m 59; c 6. *Educ:* Univ Hawaii, BS, 50; Univ Ore, PhD(biol), 57. *Prof Exp:* Res assoc biochem, Univ Ore, 56-58; USPHS fel, Univ Wis, 58-59, Univ Res Found, 59-60; asst prof biochem, NMex Highlands Univ, 60-61. *Mem:* Am Soc Biol Chem. *Res:* Enzymology; cellular regulation; genetics. *Mailing Add:* 655 Tateswood Dr Lexington KY 40502

HU, BAMBI, STATISTICAL MECHANICS, NONLINEAR DYNAMICS. *Current Pos:* from asst prof to assoc prof, 78-87, PROF PHYSICS, UNIV HOUSTON, 87- *Personal Data:* b Chongqing, Sichuan Prov, June 4, 45; US citizen; m, Betty Lok; c Chu-Mei, Chu-Ching & Chu-Ying. *Educ:* Univ Calif, Berkeley, BA, 67; Cornell Univ, MS, 70, PhD(physics), 74. *Prof Exp:* Res assoc physics, Cornell Univ, 73-74, Centre d'Etudes Nucleaires de Saclay, 74-75, Ecole Polytechnique, France, 75-77 & Brown Univ, 77-78. *Concurrent Pos:* Vis assoc prof, Univ Calif, Santa Cruz, 82-83; collabr, Los Alamos Nat Lab, 83-; ed, Int J Modern Physics Letters B, 87-; adj prof, Beijing Normal Univ, Shandong Univ, Shandong Normal Univ, 88-; mem, Acad Adv Comt, Inst Physics, Academia Sinica, Taipei, 91-; div coordr, Overseas Chinese Physics Asn, 91-93. *Res:* Theoretical physics; nonlinear dynamics and chaos; phase transitions and critical phenomena; quantum field theory and particle physics. *Mailing Add:* 5003 Loch Lomond Dr Houston TX 77096. *Fax:* 713-743-3589; *E-Mail:* hu@uh.edu

HU, BEI-LOK BERNARD, GENERAL RELATIVITY, COSMOLOGY. *Current Pos:* from asst prof to assoc prof, 80-88, PROF PHYSICS, UNIV MD, 88- *Personal Data:* b Chungking, China, Oct 4, 47; m 72; c 2. *Educ:* Univ Calif, Berkeley, BA, 67; Princeton Univ, MA, 69, PhD(physics), 72. *Prof Exp:* Res assoc physics, Princeton Univ, 72-73 & Stanford Univ, 73-74; mem natural sci, Inst Advan Study, Princeton, 73 & 87; res assoc physics, Univ Md, 74-75; res mathematician, Univ Calif, Berkeley, 75-76; res astrophysicist, Inst Space Studies, NY, 76-77; res physicist, Univ Calif, Santa Barbara, 77-79; hon res fel physics, Harvard Univ, 79-80; vis prof, Cornell Univ, 89-90; Dyson vis prof, Inst Advan Study, Princeton, 94. *Concurrent Pos:* Coun, Chinese Soc & Gravitation Physics; bd, assoc mem Inst Advan Study, Princeton. *Mem:* Am Phys Soc; NY Acad Sci; Int Soc Gen Relativity & Gravitation; Chinese Soc Gravitation Physics & Relativistic Astrophys. *Res:* General relativity and cosmology; quantum field theory in curved spacetime; quantum theories of the early universe; quantum statistical; field theory quantum gravity. *Mailing Add:* Dept Physics Univ Md College Park MD 20742. *Fax:* 301-314-9525; *E-Mail:* hu@umdhep.umd.edu

HU, CHENMING, INTEGRATED CIRCUIT TECHNOLOGY, SEMICONDUCTOR DEVICES. *Current Pos:* dir indust liaison prog, 92-96, PROF ELEC ENG & COMPUT SCI, UNIV CALIF, BERKELEY, 76- *Personal Data:* b Beijing, China, July 12, 47; US citizen. *Educ:* Nat Taiwan Univ, BS, 68; Univ Calif, Berkeley, MS, 70, PhD(elec eng), 73. *Honors & Awards:* Jack A Morton Award, Inst Elec & Electronics Engrs, 97. *Prof Exp:* Asst prof elec eng, Mass Inst Technol, 73-76. *Concurrent Pos:* Consult electronics indust, 75-; mgr nonvolatile memory develop, Nat Semiconductor, 80-81; assoc ed, Inst Elec & Electronics Engrs, Trans Electron Devices, 86-88; hon prof, Beijing Univ, China, Tsin-hwa Univ, China. *Mem:* Nat Acad Eng; fel Inst Elec & Electronics Engrs. *Res:* Advanced integrated circuit technologies; integrated circuit reliability physics; non-volatile memory; semiconductor devices; microelectronic device physics, reliability and technology; author of 4 books and over 350 research papers; granted 8 patents. *Mailing Add:* Dept Elec Eng & Comput Sci Univ Calif Berkeley CA 94720. *Fax:* 510-643-5052; *E-Mail:* hu@eecs.berkeley.edu

HU, CHIA-REN, SUPERCONDUCTIVITY-SUPERFLUIDITY, LIGHT-SCATTERING. *Current Pos:* assoc prof, 77-85, PROF PHYSICS, TEX A&M UNIV, 85- *Personal Data:* b Anhwei, China, May 25, 39; m 67. *Educ:* Nat Taiwan Univ, BS, 62; Univ Md, College Park, PhD(physics), 68. *Prof Exp:* Res assoc physics, Univ Ill, 68-69; asst prof physics, Univ Southern Calif, 69-76. *Concurrent Pos:* Vis prof physics, Univ Southern Calif, 85-86. *Mem:* Am Phys Soc. *Res:* Quantum mechanical many body problem; theory of superconductivity magnetism and superfluid helium; theory of electromagnetic scattering. *Mailing Add:* Dept Physics Tex A&M Univ College Station TX 77843-4242

HU, CHING-YEH, HUMAN GENETICS, PLANT PHYSIOLOGY. *Current Pos:* asst prof genetics & bot, assoc prof, 73-78, PROF GENETICS & BOT, WILLIAM PATERSON COL, NJ, 79- *Personal Data:* b Chiang-su, China, Dec 15, 37; US citizen; m 65; c 2. *Educ:* Taichung Agr Col, BS, 60; WVa Univ, MS, 66, PhD(genetics), 68. *Prof Exp:* Asst prof genetics, Washington & Lee Univ, 68-69; vis res prof plain tissue cult, Academia Sinica, China, 78-79. *Mem:* Am Soc Plant Physiologists; Holly Soc Am; Int Asn Plant Tissue Cult; Am Soybean Asn. *Res:* In vitro culture of glycine max, flex, taxus; crop genetic engineering. *Mailing Add:* Dept Biol Sci William Paterson Col 300 Pompton Rd Wayne NJ 07470-2103

HU, CHI-YU, NUCLEAR PHYSICS, ATOMIC PHYSICS. *Current Pos:* from asst prof to assoc prof, 63-72, PROF PHYSICS, CALIF STATE UNIV, LONG BEACH, 72- *Personal Data:* b Szechwan, China, Feb 12, 33; c Marcia, Mark, Albert & Ham C. *Educ:* Nat Taiwan Univ, BS, 55; Mass Inst Technol, PhD(physics), 62. *Prof Exp:* Res assoc physics, St John's Univ, NY, 62-63. *Concurrent Pos:* NSF res grant, 69-70, DOE 86-88; vis prof, NSF, 88-90, res grant, 90- *Mem:* Am Phys Soc. *Res:* Collective properties of nuclei; pairing correlation and Hartree Fock approximation; nuclear three body problem; nuclear three and four body bound states; muon catalyzed fusion; few body problems. *Mailing Add:* Dept Physics Calif State Univ Long Beach CA 90840

HU, FUNAN, DERMATOLOGY, DERMATOPATHOLOGY. *Current Pos:* RETIRED. *Personal Data:* b Shanghai, China, Sept 13, 19; US citizen; m 44, L A Hsu. *Educ:* Nat Med Col Shanghai, MD, 42; Am Bd Dermatol, dipl, 58, cert, 75; Am Bd Pathol, cert, 75. *Prof Exp:* Resident, Med Br, Univ Tex, 47-48, univ fel, 50-53; assoc dermat, Henry Ford Hosp, Detroit, Mich, 53-65; prof dermat, Ore Health Sci Univ, 65-89. *Concurrent Pos:* From scientist to sr scientist, Ore Regional Primate Ctr, Ore Health Sci Univ, 65-86. *Mem:* Am Soc Dermatopath; Am Acad Dermat; Soc Investigative Dermat; Am Asn Cancer Res; Am Soc Cell Biol; Tissue Cult Asn. *Res:* Cutaneous biology; cytology; pigment cell biology; melanogenesis; pigmentary disorders. *Mailing Add:* Spring Ridge No D315 32200 SW French Prairie Rd Wilsonville OR 97070

HU, HAORAN, INTERNAL COMBUSTION ENGINES, COMBUSTION, EMISSION & VALVE ACTUATION SYSTEMS. *Current Pos:* sr proj engr, 91-92, prod develop mgr, 92-95, SR MGR ADVAN ENG, JACOBS VEHICLE SYSTS, 95- *Personal Data:* b Hubei, China, Nov 15, 56; c 2. *Educ:* Mass Inst Technol, ScD(mech eng), 87; Ohio State Univ, MBA, 89. *Prof Exp:* Postdoctoral assoc, Mass Inst Technol, 86-87; vis asst prof, Ohio State Univ, 87-90. *Mem:* Soc Automotive Engrs. *Res:* Internal combustion engines, variable valve actuation, combustion, emission, electrical control systems; electromagnetic solenoid, simulation, diesel engine retarders. *Mailing Add:* 22 E Dudley Town Rd Bloomfield CT 06002. *Fax:* 860-769-7828; *E-Mail:* hhu96@tiac.net

HU, JIA, MECHANICAL ENGINEERING, FLUID DYNAMICS. *Current Pos:* PROD DEVELOP SPECIALIST, MINN MINING & MFG INC, 96- *Personal Data:* m 84, Li Song; c Susan S. *Educ:* Chinese Acad Sci, MS, 84; Univ Minn, MS, 90, PhD(mech eng), 94. *Prof Exp:* Teaching/res asst, Univ Minn, 86-92; mech engr, Sims Deltec, 92-95; sr mech engr, Sarofi Diag, 95-96. *Mem:* Am Soc Mech Engrs; Soc Imaging Sci & Technol. *Res:* Computational and experimental fluid dynamics and heat transfer; solved various problems in energy, manufacturing and medical devices; leadership in research and development and design of medical and diagnostic devices and large format color printers. *Mailing Add:* 524 17th Ave NW New Brighton MN 55112

HU, JIMMY M, RELIABILITY ENGINEERING, COMPUTER AIDED ENGINEERING. *Current Pos:* sr engr, 92-95, TECH SPECIALIST, FORD MOTOR CO, 95- *Personal Data:* m 85, Susan; c Shirley & Diane. *Educ:* Jiao-Tong Univ, BS, 82, MS, 85; Univ Md, PhD(struct eng), 89. *Prof Exp:* Lectr eng mech, Jiao-Tong Univ, 85-86; res scientist, Univ Md, 89-92. *Concurrent Pos:* Assoc ed, Trans Reliability, Inst Elec & Electronics Engrs, 93-97; mem, Reliability & Environ Factor Comt, Soc Automotive Engrs, 94-97. *Mem:* Soc Automotive Engrs; Inst Environ Sci; Am Soc Mech Engrs; Inst Elec & Electronics Engrs. *Res:* Reliability of electronics packaging; accelerated testing methods development; computer aided engineering analysis for automotive products; granted several US and international patents; published more than 50 technical articles. *Mailing Add:* 6764 Fox Hills Rd Canton MI 48187. *Fax:* 313-323-8149; *E-Mail:* jhu2@mailhost.elo.ford.com

HU, JING-SHAN, DNA-PROTEIN INTERACTIONS, GENE REGULATION. *Current Pos:* RES FEL, DEPT GENETICS, HARVARD MED SCH, 89- *Personal Data:* b Xinyang, Henan, Peoples Repub China, Oct 20, 63; m 87. *Educ:* Beijing Univ, BS, 83; Univ Tex, PhD(cell & molecular biol), 89. *Concurrent Pos:* Fel, Leukemia Res Found, 90-91. *Mem:* Am Soc Cell Biol. *Res:* Regulation of tissue-specific gene expression by Helix-Loop Helix proteins. *Mailing Add:* Human Gerome Sci 9410 Key West Ave Rockville MD 02114

HU, JOHN NAN-HAI, CHEMICAL ENGINEERING. *Current Pos:* RETIRED. *Personal Data:* b Kaifeng, China, Aug 14, 36; m 64; c 2. *Educ:* Taiwan Univ, BS, 58; Univ Notre Dame, PhD(diffusion), 65. *Prof Exp:* Chem engr, Res Labs, Ethyl Corp, 64- *Res:* Diffusion; refinery technology; economic evaluation; new product development, innovation/creativity. *Mailing Add:* 8129 Oakbrook Dr Baton Rouge LA 70810

HU, L(ING) W(EN), ENGINEERING MECHANICS. *Current Pos:* assoc prof, 49-62, prof eng mech, 62-84, EMER PROF, PA STATE UNIV, 84- *Personal Data:* b Nanking, China, Jan 28, 22; m 53, Ling Gut; c Shih In Da-Shih. *Educ:* Nat Cent Univ, China, BS, 43; Univ Wash, MS, 49; Pa State Univ, PhD(eng mech), 52. *Prof Exp:* Designer, Nat Cent Mach Works, China, 43-45; instr mech eng, Nat Cent Univ, 45-47. *Mem:* Soc Exp Stress Anal; Am Acad Mech. *Res:* Mechanical properties of metals; plasticity; experimental stress analysis; triaxial stress experiments and high pressure testing. *Mailing Add:* 728 Westerly Pkwy State College PA 16801

HU, MING-KUEI, ELECTRICAL ENGINEERING. *Current Pos:* res asst prof, 51-56, sr res engr, 56-60, assoc prof, 60-63, PROF ELEC ENG, SYRACUSE UNIV, 63- *Personal Data:* b Anhwei, China, May 25, 18; m 46; c 1. *Educ:* Nat Cent Univ, China, BS, 41; Ore State Col, PhD(elec eng), 51. *Prof Exp:* Instr elec eng, Nat Cent Univ, China, 44-47. *Mem:* Am Phys Soc; sr mem Inst Elec & Electronics Engrs; Asn Comput Mach. *Res:* Electromagnetic theory; antenna and wave propagation; high voltage; discharge phenomena; electronic computers; switching theory; artificial intelligence; theory of automata. *Mailing Add:* Col Eng Syracuse Univ ECE University Place Syracuse NY 13210

HU, SHIU-LOK, aids vaccine research, cancer immunotherapy, for more information see previous edition

HU, STEVE SENG-CHIU, SYSTEMS RESEARCH. *Current Pos:* DIR, UNIV AM UNITED RES INST, 73-; DIR, CENTURY RES INC, 73- *Personal Data:* b Yangchou City, China; US citizen; m, Lily Li-wan Liu; c April (Swando), Yendo & Victor Weedo. *Educ:* Chiao-Tung Univ, China, BS, 39; Rensselaer Polytech Inst, MS, 40; Mass Inst Technol, ScD(aero-space), 42. *Prof Exp:* Managing tech dir, China Aircraft/China Motor Prog, Douglas Aircraft Corp, 43-48 & Kelly Eng Corp, 49-54; systs engr & meteorol specialist, RCA Corp, 55-58; consult gas dynamics, Aerojet Gen Corp, 58-60; res scientist, Jet Propulsion Labs, Calif Inst Technol, 60-61; tech dir, Northrop Corp & Northrop Huntsville, Space Lab, 61-72 73-92. *Concurrent Pos:* Vis fel, Calif Inst Technol, 43-44; consult, Nuclear Reactor Prog, Tsin-Hwa Univ, Taiwan, 54-58; vis prof & lectr, Univ Southern Calif, 58-62 & 68-73; prof aerospace, Univ Ala, Huntsville, 63-68; prof mech eng, Auburn Univ, 63-66; vis prof, Chun-Shan Inst Technol, Taiwan, 68-69 & Calif State Univ, 68-72; ed, Proceedings Missiles & Aerospace Vehicle Sci, Am Astronaut Soc, 63-71; pres, Univ Am Found, 77-; hon chmn, Shanghai Indust Asn, 91- *Mem:* Am Astronaut Soc (vpres, 63-71); Am Inst Aeronaut & Astronaut; Nat Asn Tech Schs. *Res:* Applied mathematics, applied physics, and electro-mechanical engineering in the fields of propulsion, gas dynamics, navigation and guidance, environmental science and computer science. *Mailing Add:* 6491 Saddle Dr Long Beach CA 90815

HU, SUNG CHIAO, DIGITAL SYSTEMS DESIGN, COMPUTER CONTROL. *Current Pos:* PROF, SAN FRANCISCO STATE UNIV, 80- *Personal Data:* b Chekiang, China, Nov 4, 42; m 67; c 3. *Educ:* Calif State Polytech Col, San Luis Obispo, BSEE, 65; Ore State Univ, MSEE, 67, PhD(elec eng), 70. *Prof Exp:* From asst prof to assoc prof elec eng, Cleveland State Univ, 70-80. *Concurrent Pos:* Consult, numerous co. *Mem:* Inst Elec & Electronics Engrs; Instrument Soc Am; Am Soc Eng Educ. *Res:* Microcomputers; digital systems; logic design; switching theory; electric distribution automation; biomedical systems. *Mailing Add:* San Francisco State Univ Eng 1600 Holloway Ave San Francisco CA 94132

HU, TE CHIANG, COMBINATORIAL ALGORITHMS, OPERATIONS RESEARCH. *Current Pos:* CHMN, COMPUT SCI DIV, UNIV CALIF, SAN DIEGO, 74- *Personal Data:* b Peking, China, Nov 28, 30; US citizen; m 60; c 3. *Educ:* Nat Taiwan Univ, BS, 53; Univ Ill, Urbana, MS, 56; Brown Univ, PhD(appl math), 60. *Prof Exp:* Res mathematician, IBM Res Ctr, 60-66; from assoc prof to prof math & comput sci, Univ Wis-Madison, 66-74. *Concurrent Pos:* Vis assoc prof, Univ Calif, Berkeley, 64-65; consult, Rand Corp, 64 & Off Emergency Preparedness, Exec Off President, 68-72; John von Neuman prof, Univ Bonn, Ger, 94-95. *Mem:* Soc Indust & Appl Math; Oper Res Soc Am; Inst Elec & Electronics Engrs; Asn Comput Mach. *Res:* Applied mathematics applied to computer science; mathematical programming; discrete optimization; combinatorial algorithms; very large scale intergration design. *Mailing Add:* Comput Sci Dept Univ Calif San Diego La Jolla CA 92093

HU, WEI-SHOU, BIOREACTOR DESIGN, ANIMAL CELL TECHNOLOGY. *Current Pos:* From asst prof to assoc prof, 83-94, PROF CHEM ENG, UNIV MN, 94- *Personal Data:* b Taiwan, Nov 5, 51; US citizen; m 76; c 2. *Educ:* Nat Taiwan Univ, BS, 74; Mass Inst Technol, SM, 81, PhD(biochem eng), 83. *Concurrent Pos:* NSF presidential young investr, 85; vis fel, Int Ctr Biotechnol, Fac Eng, Osaka Univ, Japan, 89, vis prof, 91; co-chmn, 2nd Eng Found Conf Cell Cult Eng, Santa Barbara, Calif, 89; mem, grant selection panel, Nat Sci & Eng Res Coun Can, 90-91, deleg, US/Japan Joint Biotechnol Conf, Hawaii, 91. *Mem:* Am Chem Soc; Am Inst Chem Engrs; Am Soc Microbiologists. *Res:* Biochemical engineering with emphasis on reactor design and reaction kinetics of animal, plant and microbiological cell processes; artificial liver. *Mailing Add:* Dept Chem Eng & Mat Sci Univ Minn 421 Washington Ave SE Minneapolis MN 55455

HU, WILLIAM H(SUN), physical metallurgy, materials science; deceased, see previous edition for last biography

HU, XIN-HUA, INTERACTION BETWEEN ELECTROMAGNETIC RADIATION & MATTERS, APPLICATION OF LASERS IN MEDICINE. *Current Pos:* ASST PROF, DEPT PHYSICS, EAST CAROLINA UNIV, 95- *Personal Data:* b Tianjin, China, Dec 18, 57; m; c Ben Yifeng & Bailey Yimeng. *Educ:* Nankai Univ, China, BA, 82, MS, 85; Ind Univ, Bloomington, MS, 86; Univ Calif, Irvine, PhD(physics), 91. *Prof Exp:* Res scientist, Intelligent Surg Lasers Inc, 92-93. *Mem:* Am Asn Physicist Med; Sigma Xi. *Res:* Interaction between short laser pulses and biological tissue and cells; coherent imaging of rough surfaces and random medium. *Mailing Add:* Dept Physics ECarolina Univ Greenville NC 27858. *Fax:* 919-328-6314; *E-Mail:* hux@mail.ecu.edu

HU, YAPING, POPULATION GENETICS OF MARINE MOLLUSKS. *Current Pos:* RESEARCHER, LA STATE UNIV, 93- *Personal Data:* b Fujian, China, Oct 22, 52; m 78, Suzhen Guo; c Ling H & Yancy H. *Educ:* Shanghai Fisheries Col, China, BS, 75; SChina Sea Inst Oceanology, Acad Sinica, 82; Rutgers, State Univ NJJD PhD(evolutionary ecol), 92. *Prof Exp:* Res assoc, SChina Sea Inst Acad Sinica, 82-86; res asst, Rutgers Univ, 86-91, assoc, 92-93. *Mem:* AAAS; Am Malacol Union; Nat Shellfish Res Asn; World Aquacult Soc; Chinese Soc Malacol. *Res:* Population genetics of oysters. *Mailing Add:* 245 S Sixth Ave Highland Park NJ 08904

HU, ZHIYU, MICROMECHANICAL ENGINEERING, MICROCONTILEVER SENSORS. *Current Pos:* RES ASST, LIFE SCI DIV, OAK RIDGE NAT LAB, 95-; TEACHING ASST, DEPT PHYSICS, UNIV TENN, KNOXVILLE, 96- *Personal Data:* b Kunming, China, June 30, 65; m 92, Hongzhi Li; c Lydia. *Educ:* Yunnan Univ, China, BS, 86; Fisk Univ, MA, 95. *Prof Exp:* Asst engr, Kunming Inst Technol, China, 86-90; vis scientist, Dept Molecular Physiol & Biol Physics, Univ Va, 90-93; res asst, Fisk Ctr, Photonic Mat & Devices, NASA, 93-95. *Concurrent Pos:* Lectr physics & Eng, Hexi Middle Sch, 88-89; consult, Consol-Tech, 96- *Mem:* Am Physics Soc; Mat Res Soc; Asn Comput Mach. *Res:* Micromechanical engineering, microcontilever sensors, atomic force microcopy and scanning tunneling microscopy; photonic materials and devices; crystal characterization and growth; diamond film, electron microscopy and laser video disk; characterization of semiconductors and composite semiconductors; surface treatment modification of semiconductors. *Mailing Add:* Oak Ridge Nat Lab PO Box 2008 Oak Ridge TN 37831-2008. *Fax:* 423-574-6210; *E-Mail:* zhu@utk.edu

HUA, DUY HUU, ORGANIC CHEMISTRY. *Current Pos:* ASST PROF ORG CHEM, KANS STATE UNIV, 82- *Personal Data:* b Saigon, Vietnam, June 30, 52; Taiwan citizen; m 76; c 2. *Educ:* Kyoto Univ, Japan, BS, 76; Southern Ill Univ, PhD(chem), 80. *Prof Exp:* Asst chem, Harvard Univ, 80-82. *Mem:* Am Chem Soc. *Res:* Asymmetric synthesis and stereocontrolled total synthesis of natural products. *Mailing Add:* Dept Chem Kans State Univ Willard Hall Manhattan KS 66506

HUA, PING, MEDICAL IMAGING, IMAGING PROCESSING. *Current Pos:* prin res scientist, 90-93, SR PRIN RES SCIENTIST, SIEMENS AG, 93- *Personal Data:* b Nanchang, China, July 18, 63; m 91, Linda L Lin; c Margaret. *Educ:* Shanghai Jiao Tong Univ, Shanghai, China, BS, 82; Univ Wis-Madison, MS, 84, PhD(elec eng), 90. *Prof Exp:* Instr elec eng, Shanghai Jiao Tong Univ, 82-83. *Concurrent Pos:* Mem image compression comt, Am Col Radiol & Nat Elec Mfr Asn. *Mem:* Inst Elec & Electronics Engrs; Int Soc Optical Eng. *Res:* Medical image processing; computer vision applications in medical imaging, especially in digital angiography; three dimensional reconstruction and visualization; computer-based medical instrumentation. *Mailing Add:* Siemens Gammasonics Inc Res Dept 2501 N Barrington Rd Hoffman Estates IL 60195. *Fax:* 847-304-7713; *E-Mail:* hua@sgi.siemens.com

HUA, SUSAN ZONGLU, magnetic thin films, for more information see previous edition

HUANG, ALICE SHIH-HOU, MICROBIOLOGY, VIROLOGY. *Current Pos:* DEAN SCI, NY UNIV, 91- *Personal Data:* b Kiangsi, China, Mar 22, 39; US citizen; m 68; c 1. *Educ:* Johns Hopkins Univ, BA, 61, MA, 63, PhD(microbiol), 66. *Hon Degrees:* MA, Harvard Univ, 80; DSc, Wheaton Col, 82, Mt Holyoke Col, 87, Med Col Pa, 91. *Honors & Awards:* Eli Lilly Award in Microbiol & Immunol, 77; Sixth Hattie Alexander Mem lectr, Columbia Univ, NY, 81; Sophie Jones lectr, Univ Mich, Ann Arbor, 86; Orton K Stark lectr, Miami Univ, Ohio, 88. *Prof Exp:* Asst prof zool, Taiwan, 66; from asst prof to assoc prof, 71-79, prof microbiol & molecular genetics, Harvard Med Sch, 79-91. *Concurrent Pos:* USPHS fel biochem virol, Salk Inst Biol Studies, 67 & Mass Inst Technol, 68-69; mem virol study sect, NIH, 73-77; dir, Lab Infectious Dis, Children's Hosp Med Ctr, Boston, 79-89. *Mem:* AAAS; Am Soc Biochem & Molecular Biol; Am Soc Microbiol (pres, 88-89); fel Infectious Dis Soc Am; Am Soc Virol; Am Acad Microbiol; Acad Sinica (Taiwan); Sigma Xi; NY Acad Sci; Soc Chinese Bioscientists Am. *Res:* Replication of RNA animal viruses; author of numerous publications. *Mailing Add:* NY Univ 6 Washington Sq N New York NY 10003-6635

HUANG, ANTHONY HWOON CHUNG, PLANT CELL BIOLOGY, MOLECULAR BIOLOGY. *Current Pos:* PROF BOT, UNIV CALIF, RIVERSIDE, 88- *Personal Data:* b China, Oct 10, 45; m 72; c 1. *Educ:* Nat Taiwan Univ, BS; Univ Calif, Santa Cruz, PhD(biol), 73. *Prof Exp:* From asst prof to prof, Univ SC, 73-88, Carolina res prof, 87-88. *Mem:* Am Soc Plant Physiologists. *Res:* Plant cell and molecular biology; metabolic compartmentation; seed maturation and germination; seed oil genetic engineering; flower and pollen lipids. *Mailing Add:* Dept Bot & Plant Sci Univ Calif Riverside CA 92521. *Fax:* 909-787-4437; *E-Mail:* ahuang@ucracl.ucr.edu

HUANG, BARNEY K(UO-YEN), BIOLOGICAL & AGRICULTURAL ENGINEERING. *Current Pos:* From asst prof to prof biol & agr eng, 63-93, EMER PROF BIOL & AGR ENG, NC STATE UNIV, 93-; PRES, INT INNOVATION TECHNOL, INC, 91- *Personal Data:* b Taiwan, China, Jan 27, 31; US citizen; m 64, Lindy Wang; c Lucas, Rosa & Ulric. *Educ:* Nat Taiwan Univ, BS, 54; Univ Ill, MS, 60; Purdue Univ, PhD(agr eng), 63. *Honors & Awards:* Distinguished Leadership Award, ABI, 88. *Prof Exp:* Instr & asst agr eng, Nat Taiwan Univ, 54-58; asst, Univ Ill, 58-60 & Purdue Univ, 60-62. *Concurrent Pos:* NSF lectr human eng, NC State Univ; prin investr, NSF, Energy Res & Develop Asn, US Dept Agr, Dept Energy, HEW, Pub Health Serv, R J Reynolds Co, Am Can Co, NC Energy Inst & Dept Transp grants; vis prof, Tehran Univ, 75, Japan Adv Sci, 79, Nat Taiwan Univ, 79-80, Korea Tobacco Res Inst, 80 & Jilin Univ Technol, 87; consult, Coun Agr, 74-75, Taiwan Tabacco Bur, 76, Res Triangle Inst, 76-77, Union Carbide Corp, 77-79, UN, 80-81, Valmont Indust, 83-84, NC Agr & Technol State Univ, 88, Precision Measurment Corp, 90-93, World Bank, 91, Jilin Univ Technol, 92, Henan Agr Univ, 92, Shijiazhuang Agr Mach Plant, 92, Harbin Farm Mach Plant, 92, Taylor Mfg, Inc, Inc, 94-, Independent Systs, Inc, 95-, Aquatic Bionhancement Systs, 96-; hon prof, Shenyang Agr Univ, 87. *Mem:* Am Soc Agr Engrs; Am Soc Eng Educ; Nat Geog Soc; AAAS; Sigma Xi. *Res:* Solar energy utilization in agriculture; biological servo-systems and human engineering; computer simulation and data acquisition; computer aided design and analysis of biological and physical systems; mechanics of vibrations, sounds and locomotion; agricultural power and machinery design;

author & co-author of over 100 technical and research articles and books; granted 30 national and international patents; systems design and systems; environmental engineering. *Mailing Add:* 3332 Manor Ridge Dr Raleigh NC 27603. *Fax:* 919-772-8446; *E-Mail:* ulric@bellsouth.net

HUANG, BING SHAUN, HYPERTENSION. *Current Pos:* RES SCIENTIST, UNIV OTTAWA HEART INST, 90- *Personal Data:* b Kobe, Japan, Sept 13, 45; Can citizen; m 90, Angela Q He; c Joanna. *Educ:* Tonji Med Univ, China, MD, 70; Univ Mich, PhD(physiol), 84. *Prof Exp:* Sr lectr surg, Wuhan Med Col, 73-79; assoc prof physiol, Jinan Univ, Sch Med, China, 85-86; res assoc, Univ Mich Med Sch, 86-87, Marshall Univ Sch Med, 87-89. *Concurrent Pos:* Vis surgeon, Chinese Acad Med Scis, 78-80, Univ Mich Med Sch, 79-81; prin investr, China, 85-87. *Mem:* Am Physiol Soc; Can Hypertension Soc. *Res:* Physiology. *Mailing Add:* Heart Inst 1053 Carling Ave Ottowa ON K1Y 4E9 Can

HUANG, C C, POWDER SCIENCE & TECHNOLOGY, POWDER PROCESSING. *Current Pos:* Powder technol specialist, 89-90, RES & DEVELOP MGR, MICRON POWDER SYSTS, 90- *Personal Data:* b Taiwan, Dec, 1953. *Educ:* Tunghai Univ, BS, 77; Ill Inst Technol, MS, 82; WVa Univ, PhD(chem eng), 86. *Prof Exp:* Res assoc, WVa Univ, 87-89. *Mem:* Sigma Xi; Am Chem Soc; Am Soc Testing & Mat. *Res:* Field of powder technology and science, specializing in powder processing, powder characterization, powder granulation and fluidization. *Mailing Add:* Hosokawa Micron Powder systs 10 Chatham Rd Summit NJ 07901

HUANG, C YUAN, DIGITAL SIGNAL PROCESSING. *Current Pos:* SR STAFF SCIENTIST PHYSICS, LOCKHEED RES LAB, 87- *Personal Data:* b Tainan, Taiwan, Mar 14, 35; US citizen; m 61; c 3. *Educ:* Nat Taiwan Univ, BS, 57; Harvard Univ, MS, 60, PhD(appl physics), 64. *Honors & Awards:* Alan Berman Award, 85. *Prof Exp:* Asst prof elec eng, Wash Univ, 65-66; assoc prof physics, Case Western Reserve Univ, 66-75; staff mem physics, Los Alamos Nat Lab, 75-87. *Concurrent Pos:* Adj prof, Dept Physics, Univ Houston, 87- *Mem:* Fel Am Phys Soc. *Res:* Superconductivity; magnetism; optics. *Mailing Add:* Ctr Condensed Matter Sci Nat Taiwan Univ Taipei Taiwan

HUANG, CHARLES T L, ORGANIC CHEMISTRY, BIOCHEMISTRY. *Current Pos:* SR RES CHEMIST, MERICHEM CO, 82- *Personal Data:* b Fukien, China, Oct 12, 38; m 70; c 1. *Educ:* Nat Chung Hsing Univ, BSc, 60; La State Univ, PhD(chem), 70. *Prof Exp:* Res assoc biochem eng, La State Univ, 70-71; res assoc pediat, Baylor Col Med, 72-73; from instr to asst prof pediat, 73-82. *Mem:* AAAS; Am Chem Soc; Inst Food Technologists; Am Asn Univ Prof; fel Am Inst Chemists. *Res:* Lipid metabolism; diarrheal disease; lipid chemistry; organic synthesis process development. *Mailing Add:* Merichem Co Res Ctr 1503 Cent Houston TX 77012

HUANG, CHARLES Y, ENZYME KINETICS & MECHANISMS, CALCIUM REGULATION. *Current Pos:* RES CHEMIST, LAB BIOCHEM, NAT HEART LUNG & BLOOD INST, NIH, 76- *Personal Data:* b Nanking, China; US citizen. *Educ:* Iowa State Univ, Ames, PhD(biochem), 68. *Prof Exp:* Pub Health Serv fel, Med Sch, Wash Univ, 68-70; staff fel, NIMH, NIH, 70-73; group leader, Dow Chem Co, 73-75; chemist I, Abbott Labs, 75-76. *Concurrent Pos:* Consult, Enzyme Kinetics Nomenclature, Int Union Biochem, 78-80, comt mem, Kinetics & Mechanisms Enzymes & Metab Interest Group, 83-; mem, Prog Comt, Am Soc Biochem & Molecular Biol, 81; guest lectr, Dept Chem, Georgetown Univ, 82; contract prof, Dept Cellular Biol, Univ Camerino, Italy, 83, 84 & 88; vis prof, Dept Biochem, Nanjing Univ, China, 85 & Inst Med Sci, Henan Med Univ, Zhengzhov, China, 85. *Mem:* Am Soc Biochem & Molecular Biol; Am Chem Soc; AAAS. *Res:* Enzyme regulatory mechanisms and kinetic behaviors, particularly enzyme systems involving calcium/calmodulin and phosphorylation/dephosphorylation; development of methods and theories applicable to enzyme research. *Mailing Add:* Bldg 3 Rm 218 NIH Bethesda MD 20892-0340. *Fax:* 301-496-0599

HUANG, CHAU-TING, PHYSIOLOGY, PHARMACOLOGY. *Current Pos:* RES SCIENTIST, NORWICH EATON PHARMACEUT INC, 78- *Personal Data:* b Mar 28, 39; c 2. *Educ:* Univ Alta, Can, PhD(biochem toxicol), 70. *Mem:* Am Physiol Soc. *Res:* Cardiac; hypertension. *Mailing Add:* Cardiac Dept Proctor & Gamble Pharmaceut PO Box 191 Norwich NY 13815-0191

HUANG, CHE C, RADIOCHEMISTRY. *Current Pos:* sr scientist, Warner-Lambert/Parke-Davis, 80-83, res assoc, 84-88, sr mgr, 88-93, ASSOC RES FEL, WARNER-LAMBERT/PARKE DAVIS, 93- *Personal Data:* US citizen; m. *Educ:* Tunghai Univ, BS, 69; State Univ NY, Binghamton, MA, 73; Univ Mich, PhD(med chem), 77. *Prof Exp:* Res fel nuclear med, Argonne Nat Lab, 77-80. *Concurrent Pos:* Chmn bd publ, Int Isotope Soc. *Mem:* Am Chem Soc; Int Isotope Soc. *Res:* Synthesis and design of radiolabeled drugs for metabolism and medical imaging; central nervous system drugs and steroid chemistry; development of new techniques for tritiation and radiohalogenation. *Mailing Add:* Warner-Lambert/Parke-Davis 2800 Plymouth Ann Arbor MI 48105

HUANG, CHENG-CHER, PHYSICS. *Current Pos:* from asst prof to assoc prof, 77-87, PROF PHYSICS, UNIV MINN, 87- *Personal Data:* b Taipei, Taiwan, May 25, 47; m 72; c 2. *Educ:* Nat Taiwan Univ, BS, 69; Univ Pa, PhD(physics), 75. *Prof Exp:* Res asst physics, Univ Pa, 72-75; res assoc, Univ Ill, 75-77. *Concurrent Pos:* Vis scientist, AT&T Bell Labs, 80, 81 & 85; consult, 3M Tech Res Lab, 83-85, vis prof, 84; vis prof, Chalmers Univ Technol, Sweden, 84 & Nat Su-Yet-Sen Univ Taiwan, 92. *Mem:* Am Physics Soc; Int Liquid Crystal Soc; fel Am Phys Soc. *Res:* Fundamental investigations of phase transitions in liquid crystals, in particular the thermal and optical properties of substrate-free two-dimensional systems. *Mailing Add:* Dept Physics Univ Minn Minneapolis MN 55455. *Fax:* 612-624-4578; *E-Mail:* huang001@maroon.tc.umn.edu

HUANG, CHENG-CHUN, OTOLARYNGOLOGY. *Current Pos:* from asst prof to assoc prof, 77-89, PROF OTOLARYNGOL, COLUMBIA UNIV, 89- *Personal Data:* b Taipei, Taiwan, Feb 2, 38; m 67; c 2. *Educ:* Taiwan Univ, BS, 63; Vanderbilt Univ, MS, 66; Univ Iowa, Iowa City, PhD(biochem), 70. *Honors & Awards:* First Prize Award, Am Acad Ophthal & Otolaryngol, 78. *Prof Exp:* Res assoc biochem, Univ Iowa, 70-71, assoc res scientist otolaryngol, 73-76, res scientist, 76-77; res assoc pharmacol, Yale Univ, 71-73. *Concurrent Pos:* Mem, Fac Coun, Col Physicians & Surgeons, Columbia Univ, 82- *Mem:* Am Soc Biol Chemists; Asn Res Otolaryngol; AAAS; Centurions Deafness Res Asn; Chinese Agr Chem Soc. *Res:* Pathogenesis of bone destruction in chronic middle ear cyst (called cholesteatoma) and in inner ear (called otosclerosis). *Mailing Add:* Dept Otolaryngol 17-450 Columbia Univ 630 W 168th St New York NY 10032-3702. *Fax:* 212-305-2249

HUANG, CHESTER CHEN-CHIU, BIOLOGY, CYTOGENETICS. *Current Pos:* RETIRED. *Personal Data:* b Kiangsu, China, Jan 16, 27; m 61; c 3. *Educ:* Sun Yat-Sen Univ, BS, 49; SDak State Univ, MS, 61; State Univ NY Buffalo, PhD, 66. *Prof Exp:* Teacher agron, Prov Chi-yi Sr Agr Sch, Taiwan, 49-54 & Prov Col Agr, 55-58; res asst, SDak State Univ, 59-61; cancer res scientist, Roswell Park Mem Inst, 61-66, sr cancer res scientist, 66-76, cancer res scientist V, 77-96. *Concurrent Pos:* Asst prof, State Univ NY, Buffalo, 68-74, assoc prof, 74- *Mem:* Am Soc Mammalian chromosome cytology; effects of viruses, carcinogens, radiation and other chemicals to chromosomes in vivo and vitro. *Mailing Add:* 47 Melrose Rd Williamsville NY 14221

HUANG, CHI-LUNG DOMINIC, ENGINEERING MATHEMATICS, SYSTEM MODELING. *Current Pos:* from asst prof to assoc prof, 64-74, PROF TEACHING & RES, KANS STATE UNIV, 74. *Personal Data:* b Fujian, China, Oct 10, 30; US citizen; m 60; c 4. *Educ:* Nat Taiwan Univ, BS, 55; Univ Ill, MS, 60; Yale Univ, DEngSc, 64. *Prof Exp:* Engr design, Taiwan Power Co, 55-59, Amman & Whitney, 60-61; res asst res, Univ Ill, 59-60 & Yale Univ, 61-64. *Concurrent Pos:* Vis prof, Chico-Tung Univ, China, 79; hon prof, Hua-Chico Univ, China, 86- *Mem:* Am Inst Aeronaut & Astronaut; Soc Eng Sci; Am Acad Mech; Am Soc Mech Engrs. *Res:* Continuum mechanics; mass and heat transfer; fluid mechanics; structural dynamics and machine design; engineering mathematics. *Mailing Add:* Dept Mech Eng Durland Kans State Univ Manhattan KS 66506. *Fax:* 785-532-7057; *E-Mail:* huang@ksume.me.ksu.edu

HUANG, CHIN PAO, AQUATIC CHEMISTRY. *Current Pos:* from asst prof to assoc prof, 74-80, PROF CIVIL ENG, 80-, PROF MARINE CHEM, UNIV DEL, 87-, DISTINGUISHED PROF ENVIRON ENG, 91- *Personal Data:* b Taiwan, China, Oct 4, 41; US citizen; m 71; c 2. *Educ:* Nat Taiwan Univ, BS, 65; Harvard Univ, MS, 67, PhD(environ eng), 71. *Prof Exp:* Asst prof civil eng, Wayne State Univ, 71-74. *Mem:* Am Chem Soc; Am Soc Civil Engrs; Water Pollution Control Fedn; Int Asn Colloid & Surface Scientists; Am Soc Limnol & Oceanog; Asn Environ Eng Profs. *Res:* Applied colloid and surface chemistry; industrial waste management; physical-chemical processes for water and wastewater treatment; chemistry and biology of natural waters. *Mailing Add:* Dept Civil & Environ Eng Univ Del Newark DE 19716

HUANG, CHING-HSIEN, BIOCHEMISTRY. *Current Pos:* vis asst prof, 67-68, from asst prof to assoc prof, 68-77, PROF BIOCHEM, SCH MED, UNIV VA, 77- *Personal Data:* b Tientsin, China, Oct 24, 35. *Educ:* Tunghai Univ, BS, 59; Johns Hopkins Univ, PhD(biochem), 65. *Prof Exp:* Fel phys chem, Max Planck Inst Phys Chem, Ger, 65-67. *Concurrent Pos:* Helen Hay Whitney Found res fels phys chem, 66-67 & biochem, 67-69. *Mem:* Am Soc Biol Chem; Biophys Soc. *Res:* Membrane biophysics and biochemistry; biophysical chemistry of phospholipids; molecular structure and mechanism of protein kinase. *Mailing Add:* Dept Biochem Sch Med Univ Va Box 440 Charlottesville VA 22908-0001. *Fax:* 804-924-5069

HUANG, CHING-RONG, CHEMICAL & BIOMEDICAL ENGINEERING. *Current Pos:* PROF, NJ INST TECHNOL, 78-, ASST CHMN GRAD STUDIES, DEPT CHEM ENG, 81- *Personal Data:* b Hong Kong, Jan 19, 32; m 59; c 3. *Educ:* Nat Taiwan Univ, BS, 54; Mass Inst Technol, SM, 58; Univ Mich, MS, 65, PhD(chem eng), 66. *Prof Exp:* Res engr, Am Polyplastics Lab, Mass, 58-62; asst prof chem eng, Newark Col Eng, 66-68, assoc prof, 68-78. *Concurrent Pos:* Hon prof biomed eng, Sichuan Med Univ, Peoples Repub China, 85. *Mem:* Am Inst Chem Engrs; Soc Rheology; Int Soc Biorheology. *Res:* Heterogeneous catalysis; applied mathematics; rheology. *Mailing Add:* Dept Chem Eng & Chem 323 Martin Luther King Jr Blvd Newark NJ 07102

HUANG, DAO PEI, POLYMERASE CHAIN REACTION, OLIGONUCLEOTIDE SYNTHESIS & HYBRIDIZATION. *Current Pos:* SR SCIENTIST, ROCHE MOLECULAR SYSTS, 92- *Personal Data:* b Jan 9, 43; m, Ming Q Zhang; c Ao L Huang. *Educ:* Fu Dan Univ, Shanghai, China, BS, 65; Shanghai Inst Biochem, PhD, 78. *Honors & Awards:* Frist Award, Health Dept Shanghai, 77, Chinese Acad Sci, 78. *Prof Exp:* Res asst, Shanghai Inst Biochem, Chinese Acad Sci, 65-80, assoc prof, 85-86; fel, Dept Clin Biochem, Banting Inst, 81-82, Dept Biochem, Univ Vt, 82-85; sr scientist, Cambridge

Biotech Corp, 86-92. *Concurrent Pos:* Vis sr scientist, Dept Pharmacol, Yale Univ, 85 & Dept Biochem, Univ Vt, 86; sr scientist, Cambridge Biotech Corp, 86-92. *Mem:* Soc Chinese Bioscientists Am; Am Soc Mat. *Res:* Designation and synthesis oligonucleotides to detect polymerase chain reactions products for diagnosis of clinical samples. *Mailing Add:* 7 Bev Ave Piscataway NJ 08854. *Fax:* 908-253-7665

HUANG, DENIS K, CHEMICAL ENGINEERING, POLYMER CHEMISTRY. *Current Pos:* RETIRED. *Personal Data:* b China, May 14, 25; US citizen; m 57, Betty J; c Lloyd K. *Educ:* St John's Univ, China, BS, 44; Univ Calif, BS, 50; Univ Maine, MS, 51; Polytech Inst Brooklyn, DChE, 58. *Prof Exp:* Res engr, Single Serv Div, Int Paper Co, 58-62; sr chemist, Simoniz Div, Morton Int, Inc, 62-65; sr res engr, Laurel Res Lab, Westvaco Corp, 65-78; res consult, Fed Paper Bd, 78-90; assoc consult, Tech Consults Int, 90-93. *Concurrent Pos:* UN expert, India, 70; expert, Orgn Am States, Argentina, 72; UN Develop Prog assignment, China, 83. *Mem:* Tech Asn Pulp & Paper Indust; Sigma Xi. *Res:* Emulsion and suspension polymerization; polymer application; pulp and paper technology; petroleum technology; paper coating; coal slurries; forest products. *Mailing Add:* 426 SW Fairway Landing Port St Lucie FL 34986. *Fax:* 706-738-9825

HUANG, DI-HUI (DAVID), COMPLEMENTARY METAL-OXIDE SEMICONDUCTOR TRANSISTOR DEVICE RELIABILITY, SEMICONDUCTOR DEVICE PHYSICS. *Current Pos:* SR ENGR & PROG MGR, CIRRUS LOGIC, INC, 94- *Personal Data:* b Beijing, China, Mar 12, 61; m, Joanne Jin. *Educ:* Xian Jiaotong Univ, BS, 82, MS, 84; Univ Md, PhD (microelectronics), 89. *Prof Exp:* res engr & prin investr, Advan Res & Appln Corp, 90-94. *Concurrent Pos:* Prin investr, Advan Res & Appln Corp, 90- *Mem:* Electronic Devices Soc. *Res:* Semiconductor device reliability study in complementary metal-oxide semiconductor transmitter technology; characterization of radiation hardness and oxide integrity of buried oxide; hot-carrier effect in advanced complementary metal-oxide semiconductor transistor devices. *Mailing Add:* Cirrus Logic Inc 3100 Warren Ave MS 220/B3 Fremont CA 94538. *Fax:* 408-732-1996; *E-Mail:* dhuang@cirrus.com

HUANG, ENG-SHANG (CLARK), VIROLOGY, CANCER RESEARCH. *Current Pos:* Res fel virol, Dept Microbiol & Immunol, Univ NC, Chapel Hill, 71-73, vis asst prof, Dept Microbiol & Immunol & Dept Med, 73-74, from asst prof to assoc prof, Dept Med, 74-85, PROF VIROL & CANCER RES, DEPT MED, CANCER RES CTR, UNIV NC, CHAPEL HILL, 86- *Personal Data:* b Chia-Yi, Taiwan, Mar 17, 40; US citizen; m 65, Shu M Huong; c David & Benjamin. *Educ:* Nat Taiwan Univ, BS, 62, MS, 64; Univ NC, Chapel Hill, PhD(microbiol & immunol), 71. *Honors & Awards:* Outstanding Achievement Award in Res, Soc Pub Health, 92. *Concurrent Pos:* Res Career Develop Award, Nat Inst Allergy & Infectious Dis, NIH, 78-83; mem virol study sect, res & grant div, NIH, 79-83; head virol prog, Cancer Res Ctr, Univ NC, Chapel Hill, 79-91; consult, Wu-han Inst Virol, Acad Sci, 86-; vis prof, IBMS, Academia Sinica, Taipei, 88; mem, AIDS, Res Rev Comt, Nat Inst Allergy & Infectious Dis, NIH, 88-90. *Mem:* Am Soc Microbiol; AAAS; NY Acad Sci; Am Asn Cancer Res. *Res:* Molecular biology and pathobiology of human cytomegalovirus; rule of cytomegalovirus infection in sexually transmitted diseases; search for anti-herpes virus compound; the oncogenicity of cytomegalovirus; viral epidemiology; recombinant DNA research. *Mailing Add:* CB No 7295 Lineberger Cancer Res 237H Univ NC Chapel Hill NC 27599-7295. *Fax:* 919-966-4303; *E-Mail:* eshuang@med.unc.edu

HUANG, EUGENE YUCHING, CIVIL ENGINEERING. *Current Pos:* prof, 63-84, EMER PROF TRANSP ENG, MICH TECHNOL UNIV, 84- *Personal Data:* b Changsha, China, Nov 28, 17; nat US; m 55, Helen Woo; c Martha, Pearl, William, Mary, Priscilla & Stephen. *Educ:* Univ Utah, BS, 50; Univ Mich, ScD(civil eng), 54. *Prof Exp:* From asst prof to assoc prof civil eng, Univ Ill, 54-63. *Concurrent Pos:* Mem, Transp Res Bd; fac res award, Mich Technol Univ, 67. *Mem:* AAAS; fel Am Soc Civil Engrs; Am Soc Eng Educ; Am Rwy Eng Asn; Am Soc Testing & Mat; Inst Ops Res Mgt Sci. *Res:* Highway and transportation engineering; pavement analysis and design. *Mailing Add:* 400 Garnet St Houghton MI 49931-1420

HUANG, FAN-HSIUNG FRANK, EXPERIMENTAL SOLID STATE PHYSICS. *Current Pos:* PRIN SCIENTIST, FLUOR DANIEL NW, INC, 96- *Personal Data:* b Pingtung, Taiwan, May 13, 40; m 69; c 3. *Educ:* Nat Taiwan Normal Univ, BS, 65; Rensselaer Polytech Inst, PhD(physics), 73. *Prof Exp:* Res assoc mat sci, Cornell Univ, NY, 73-77; prin scientist mech properties, Westinghouse Hanford Co, 77-96. *Mem:* Am Soc Testing & Mat; Am Nuclear Soc. *Res:* Surface diffusion and morphological instability of ceramics; the mechanical behavior of metals and alloys at elevated temperatures; fracture toughness of irradiated materials. *Mailing Add:* Fluor Daniel NW, Inc PO Box 1050 Richland WA 99352. *Fax:* 509-376-8277; *E-Mail:* f_h_frank_huang@rl.gov

HUANG, FENG HOU, FORESTRY, HORTICULTURE. *Current Pos:* PROF PLANT BIOTECHNOL, UNIV ARK, 79- *Personal Data:* b Taiwan, Sept 23, 30; US citizen; m 55, Sue Y Chyu; c Linda W & Tracy W. *Educ:* Nat C H Univ, BS, 54; Colo State Univ, MS, 67; WVa Univ, PhD(biochem genetics), 72. *Prof Exp:* Res assoc, WVa Univ, 72-74; res chemist, Beckman Inst, 75-78. *Mem:* Tissue Cult Asn; Int Plant Tissue Cult Asn; Sigma Xi. *Res:* Agriculture-forest-biotechnology of higher plants. *Mailing Add:* 316 Plant Sci Univ Ark Fayetteville AR 72701. *Fax:* 501-575-8619

HUANG, FRANCIS F, ENGINEERING THERMODYNAMICS. *Current Pos:* from asst prof to prof, 58-91, chmn dept, 73-81, EMER PROF MECH ENG, SAN JOSE STATE UNIV, 91- *Personal Data:* b Hong Kong, Aug 27, 22; US citizen; m 54, Fung Y Fung; c Raymond & Stanley. *Educ:* San Jose State Col, BS, 51; Stanford Univ, MS, 52; Columbia Univ, ME, 64. *Hon Degrees:* DSc, World Univ, 90. *Prof Exp:* Engr & job coordr, M W Kellogg Co, NY, 52-58. *Concurrent Pos:* Hon prof, Taiyuan Univ Technol, Peoples Repub China, 81- *Mem:* AAAS; Am Soc Mech Engrs; Am Soc Eng Educ; Am Inst Aeronaut & Astronaut; NY Acad Sci; Int Asn Sci & Tech Develop. *Res:* Engineering thermodynamics; intermolecular forces of gases through use of free expansion coefficients; energy systems design; second law analysis of energy processes. *Mailing Add:* Dept Mech & Aerospace Eng San Jose State Univ San Jose CA 95192-0087. *Fax:* 408-924-3995

HUANG, H(SING) T(SUNG), MICROBIOLOGY. *Current Pos:* RETIRED. *Personal Data:* b Malaysia, Sept 9, 21; m 49; c 2. *Educ:* Hong Kong Univ, BSc, 41; Oxford Univ, Eng, Dr Phil, 47. *Prof Exp:* Res fel chem, Univ Rochester, 47-48, Calif Inst Technol, 48-51; res biochemist, Rohm & Haas Co, 51-55; res supvr biochem, Chas Pfizer Inc, 55-64; dir biol sci, Inst Minerals & Chem Corp, 67-73; dir, Tech Serv, Wallerstein Div, Baxter Labs, 73-75; prog dir, Alternative Biol Resources, NSF, 75-90. *Concurrent Pos:* Dep dir, Needham Res Inst, Cambridge, Eng, 90- *Mem:* Am Chem Soc; Am Soc Biochem & Molecular Biol; Soc Invert Pathol; Hist Sci Soc. *Res:* Organic synthesis and metabolism of amino acids, peptides and related compounds; fermentation and enzyme technology; microbial control of insect pests. *Mailing Add:* 309 Yoakum Pkwy Apt 403 Alexandria VA 22304-3921

HUANG, HENRY HUNG-CHANG, PLANT PATHOLOGY, MYCOLOGY. *Current Pos:* RES SCIENTIST, AGR CAN LETHBRIDGE RES STA, 81-, LEADER FIELD CROPS PROG, 87-, CHMN ELECTRON MICROSCOPE & IMAGE ANALYZER COMT, 93- *Personal Data:* b Taiwan, May 22, 39; Can citizen; m 67, She S Dao; c Timothy Y & Sarah L. *Educ:* Chung-Hsing Univ, BSc, 63; Univ Toronto, MSc, 69, PhD(plant path), 72. *Honors & Awards:* Japanese Govt Res Award for Foreign Specialist, Sci & Technol Agency Japan, 87. *Prof Exp:* Teaching asst, Chung Hsing Univ, 64-67; res scientist plant path, Agr Can Morden Res Sta, 74-81. *Concurrent Pos:* Agr Can fel, Saskatoon Res Sta, 72-74; res grant, CSP Foods Ltd, 75-77; new crop develop fund, CSP Foods Ltd & Agr Can, 77-78, Canola Coun Can, 84; adj prof, Univ Man, 80-90, Huazhong Agr Univ, China, 91-94; assoc ed, Plant Path Bull, Phytopath Soc Repub China. *Mem:* Am Phytopath Soc; Can Phytopath Soc; Plant Protection Soc Republic China; Phytopath Soc Repub China; Can Forum Biol Control. *Res:* Soilborne diseases such as sclerotinia diseases of sunflower, canola, safflower, field pea and field bean, and verticillium wilt of alfalfa; biological control of soilborne diseases; disease resistance and fungal cytology. *Mailing Add:* 3 Tudor Ct Lethbridge AB T1K 5C9 Can. *Fax:* 403-382-3156

HUANG, HSIEN-LU, SUBSYSTEM RELIABILITY MODELING, EQUIPMENT WEAROUT ANALYSIS. *Current Pos:* MEM TECH STAFF, V/RELIABILITY, UNITED SPACE ALLIANCE, 96- *Personal Data:* m 46, Hui-Lien Peng; c Su (Chang), Kung, Chin (Lin), Hsin (Lu), Sung Ping (Lin) & Peter Sung-An. *Educ:* Nat Hunan Univ, BS, 44; Va Polytech Inst & State Univ, MS, 68, PhD(elec eng), 69. *Honors & Awards:* Group Achievement Award, Lyndon B Johnson Space Ctr, 83. *Prof Exp:* Aircraft maintenance officer, Chinese Air Force, 46-59, tech translr, 60-64; adj assoc prof eng math & elec mach, Taipei Inst Technol, 60-66; asst prof elec eng, WVa Univ, 70-74; design engr, Barbor Coleman Co, 75-76; control design engr, Bridgeport Mach Control, 77-79; sr elec engr reliability, 79-80, engr, 81-83, specialist reliability, Ford Aerospace & Commun Corp, 84-85; lead engr V/reliability, Rockwell Space Opers Co, 86-96. *Mem:* Inst Elec & Electronics Engrs; assoc fel Am Inst Aeronaut & Astronaut. *Res:* Circuits design; electronic control; applied math-numerical analysis; instrumentation sensors; microprocessor-based control systems; reliability maintenance analysis of ground equipment; equipment wearout analysis using Weibul model; critical systems reliability modeling using Markov state transition analysis; published 24 reports and 30 technical papers. *Mailing Add:* 470 Buoy Webster TX 77598

HUANG, HUEY WEN, BIOPHYSICS, STATISTICAL PHYSICS. *Current Pos:* from asst prof to assoc prof, 73-82, PROF PHYSICS, RICE UNIV, 82- *Personal Data:* b Tokyo, Japan, Feb 22, 40; m 89, Yu-Ru Yeh; c Emily & Patrick. *Educ:* Nat Taiwan Univ, BS, 62; Cornell Univ, PhD(theoret physics), 67. *Prof Exp:* Res assoc theoret physics, Columbia Univ, 67-69; lectr & res assoc biophys, Yale Univ, 69-71; asst prof physics, Southern Ill Univ, 71-73. *Concurrent Pos:* Vis prof biophys, Yale Univ, 87-88. *Mem:* Fel Am Phys Soc; AAAS; Biophys Soc. *Res:* Developing structural methods for studying peptide-membrane interactions; oriented circular dichroism and membrane in-plane scattering and their applications to antimicrobiol peptides; biophysics. *Mailing Add:* Dept Physics Rice Univ 6100 Main St Houston TX 77005. *Fax:* 713-527-9033; *E-Mail:* huang@ion.rice.edu

HUANG, JACK SHIH TA, APPLIED PHYSICS. *Current Pos:* SECT HEAD, EXXON RES CO, 91- *Personal Data:* b Nanchang, China, Aug 31, 33; US citizen; m 63; c 2. *Educ:* Univ Pa, BS, 55; Harvard Univ, MS, 58, PhD(appl physics), 63. *Prof Exp:* Mem tech staff, Bell Tel Labs, Inc, 63-67; asst prof elec eng, Univ Minn, 67-69; staff scientist, Solid State Electronics Ctr, Honey Inc, 69-75, mgr advan technol, 75-81, mgr advan technol planning, 81- *Mem:* Inst Elec & Electronics Engrs; Electrochem Soc. *Res:* Semiconductor devices and integrated circuits. *Mailing Add:* Exxon Res Co Clinton Township Rte 22E Annadale NJ 08801

HUANG, JACOB WEN-KUANG, OPTICAL PHYSICS, SOLID STATE PHYSICS. *Current Pos:* From asst prof to assoc prof, 67-78, vchmn dept, 73-78, PROF PHYSICS, TOWSON STATE UNIV, 78- *Personal Data:* b Kuangehow, China, Nov 7, 35; m 67; c 2. *Educ:* Nat Taiwan Univ, BS, 58; Johns Hopkins Univ, PhD(physics), 68. *Mem:* Am Phys Soc; Am Asn Physics Teachers; Sigma Xi; Am Sci Res Soc; Optical Soc Am. *Res:* Optics; spectroscopy; luminescence; lasers; holography; atomic physics; excited state absorption spectrum of ions in crystals and liquids; optical modulation spectroscopy of solids; physics education; holography; optical information processing. *Mailing Add:* Dept Physics Towson State Univ 8000 York Rd Baltimore MD 21204-2010

HUANG, JAMIN, PESTICIDAL CHEMISTRY. *Current Pos:* proj scientist, 87-91, sr res scientist, 91-93, GROUP LEADER, RHONE-POULENC AG CO, 93-, PROJ LEADER, 96- *Personal Data:* b Taipei, Taiwan, Aug 1, 51; m 79, Gloria W Wong; c Diana W & Bernice K. *Educ:* Nat Chung-Hsing Univ, BA, 73; Cornell Univ, MS, 78, PhD(org chem), 80. *Prof Exp:* Teaching asst org chem, Cornell Univ, 76-77, res asst, 77-80; sr chemist, Union Carbide Agr Prod Co, 80-83, proj scientist, 83-86. *Mem:* Am Chem Soc. *Res:* Natural product isolation; natural product total synthesis; exploration and syntheses of novel pesticides; development of novel pesticides for commercialization; interdisciplinary project management. *Mailing Add:* Rhone-Poulenc Ag Co PO Box 12014 Research Triangle Park NC 27709. *Fax:* 919-549-0054

HUANG, JAN-CHAN, ENGINEERING. *Current Pos:* PROF, PLASTICS ENG DEPT, UNIV MASS, LOWELL, 84- *Personal Data:* b Taichung, Taiwan, Oct 17, 53; US citizen; c Charles. *Educ:* Taiwan Univ, BS, 75; Univ Wis, PhD(chem eng), 80. *Prof Exp:* Res assoc, Kent State Univ, 80-82; res engr, Gen Elec Co, 82-84. *Mem:* Am Chem Soc; Soc Plastics Engrs. *Res:* Physical properties of plastics; reactive processing of plastics; electric properties of plastics. *Mailing Add:* Plastics Eng Dept Univ Mass Lowell MA 01854-2881. *Fax:* 978-458-4141

HUANG, JENG-SHENG, PHYSIOLOGY OF PARASITISM, BIOCHEMISTRY OF HOST PLANT-PARASITE INTERACTIONS. *Current Pos:* from asst prof to assoc prof, 75-86, PROF PLANT PATH, NC STATE UNIV, 86- *Personal Data:* b Taiwan, Repub China, May 11, 40; m 67, Pi-Yu Lin; c Jennifer & Robert. *Educ:* Nat Chung-Hsing Univ, Taiwan, BS, 62; Univ Mo-Columbia, MS, 69, PhD(plant path), 72. *Prof Exp:* Teaching asst plant path, Chung-Hsing Univ, Taiwan, 63-67; res asst plant path, Univ Mo-Columbia, 67-72, res microbiologist, 72-75. *Concurrent Pos:* Vis res fel, Liaoning Acad Agr Sci, China, 88-; vis prof, Shenyang Agr Univ, China, 88- *Mem:* Am Phytopath Soc; Am Soc Plant Physiologists. *Res:* Biochemistry and physiology of host plant-parasite interactions with special emphasis on plant disease resistance mechanisms. *Mailing Add:* Plant Path NC State Univ Box 7616 Raleigh NC 27695-0001. *Fax:* 919-515-7716; *E-Mail:* jengsheng_huang@ncsu.edu

HUANG, JENNMING STEPHEN, BATCH PROCESS AUTOMATION, COMPUTER INTEGRATED MANUFACTURING. *Current Pos:* res engr mixing & heat transfer, Int Flavors & Fragrances, Inc, 76-77, sr res engr separation technol, 78-79, proj engr batch process control, 79-81, mgr corp eng technol, mfg automation, 81-82, dir corp eng technol, comput integrated mfg, 83-92, VPRES US, INT FLAVORS & FRAGRANCES, INC, 93- *Personal Data:* b Changhua, Taiwan, July 30, 47; m 68, Yuhua Shy; c Raymond & Rayleen. *Educ:* Nat Taiwan Univ, Taipei, BS, 69; Syracuse Univ, NY, MS, 72, PhD(chem eng), 75. *Honors & Awards:* Int Distinguished Leadership, Am Biog Inst, 90. *Prof Exp:* Fel, Syracuse Univ, 75-76. *Concurrent Pos:* Bd dir, IFF, Hangzhou Co, 94-; adj prof, Hangzhou Univ, Hangzhou, People's Repub China, 95- *Mem:* Am Inst Chem Engrs. *Res:* Architecture and software of automation system for complex batch process manufacturing to capitalize advanced computer technology; assess the impact of automation systems on process performance, manpower issues and overall efficiency of production. *Mailing Add:* 3 Magnolia Dr Marlboro NJ 07746. *Fax:* 732-888-3565

HUANG, JOHN S, CHEMICAL PHYSICS, COMPLEX FLUIDS. *Current Pos:* res physicist, 76-81, res assoc, 81-88 & 89-93, sr staff physicist, 88-89, SECT HEAD COMPLEX FLUIDS, EXXON RES & ENG CO, 93- *Personal Data:* b Chung-King, China, Feb 22, 40; m 67. *Educ:* Nat Taiwan Univ, BS, 62; Cornell Univ, MS, 66, PhD(physics), 69. *Honors & Awards:* Max Planck Res Prize. *Prof Exp:* Asst prof physics, Rutgers Univ, New Brunswick, 69-76. *Concurrent Pos:* Adj prof, Rutgers Univ, 81-85. *Mem:* Fel Am Phys Soc; NY Acad Sci; Am Chem Soc. *Res:* Critical phenomena in binary fluid mixtures; critical interface; dynamic light scattering; nucleation phenomena; microemulsions and colloid science; complex fluids. *Mailing Add:* Exxon Res & Eng Co Clinton Township Rte 22 E Annandale NJ 08801. *E-Mail:* jshuang@erenj.com

HUANG, JOSEPH CHI KAN, OCEANOGRAPHY, METEOROLOGY. *Current Pos:* SR SCIENTIST & PROJ MGR, NAT OCEANIC & ATMOSPHERIC ADMIN, 81- *Personal Data:* b Hang Chow, China, May 21, 38; m 67, Nancy Wang; c Pearl, Jade & Cara. *Educ:* Chiao Tung Univ, BS, 58; Univ Mich, MS, 65, PhD(oceanog), 69. *Prof Exp:* Oceanogr, Scripps Inst Oceanog, Univ Calif, San Diego, 69-75; phys oceanogr & numerical modeler, Great Lakes Environ Res Lab, Nat Oceanic & Atmospheric Admin & assoc prof, Univ Mich, 75-81. *Mem:* AAAS; Am Geophys Union; Am Meteorol Soc; Sigma Xi. *Res:* Large-scale air-sea interaction and numerical modeling of ocean and lake; topographic wave and ecosystem study; climate study. *Mailing Add:* 9813 Korman Ct Potomac MD 20854

HUANG, JU-CHANG, SANITARY & ENVIRONMENTAL ENGINEERING, CIVIL ENGINEERING. *Current Pos:* PROF CIVIL ENG, HONG KONG UNIV SCI & TECHNOL, 93- *Personal Data:* b Kaohsiung, Taiwan, Jan 3, 41; m 65, 85, Jolynn Chen; c Alina, Nancy & Jacqueline. *Educ:* Nat Taiwan Univ, BS, 63; Univ Tex, Austin, MS, 66, PhD(civil eng), 67. *Honors & Awards:* Walker L Huber Civil Eng Res Prize, Am Soc Civil Engrs, 79. *Prof Exp:* From asst prof to assoc prof civil eng, Univ Mo, Rolla, 67-70, prof & dir, Environ Res Ctr, 75-92. *Concurrent Pos:* Prin investr, US Dept Interior grants, US Environ Protection Agency grants, NSF grants, Mo DNR grants, indust res grants, Hong Kong RGC grants & Hong Kong Indust Dept res grants, 68-97; consult, US & Foreign Govt Agencies, WHO, indusits & munic, 72- *Mem:* Water Environ Fedn; Am Soc Civil Engrs; Am Acad Environ Engrs; Asn Environ Eng Prof; Hong Kong Inst Engrs; Int Water Qual Asn. *Res:* Water and wastewater treatment; water quality management; sludge handlings and disposals; hazardous waste management and disposal; low-cost, energy saving waste treatment technologies. *Mailing Add:* Dept Civil Eng Hong Kong Univ Sci & Technol Clearwater Bay Kowloon Hong Kong People's Republic of China. *Fax:* 852-2358-1534; *E-Mail:* cehoward@ust.hk.ust.hk

HUANG, JUNG SAN, CANCER, PROTEINS. *Current Pos:* ASSOC PROF BIOCHEM, ST LOUIS UNIV, 84- *Educ:* Nat Taiwan Univ, Taipei, PhD(biochem), 72. *Mailing Add:* St Louis Univ Med Sch St Louis MO 63104

HUANG, JUNG-CHANG, COMPUTER SCIENCE, ELECTRICAL ENGINEERING. *Current Pos:* from asst to assoc prof, 69-80, PROF COMPUT SCI, UNIV HOUSTON, 80-, CHMN, DEPT COMPUT SCI, 92- *Personal Data:* b Taiwan, Apr 7, 35; m 67; c 3. *Educ:* Taipei Inst Technol, Taiwan, Dipl, 56; Kans State Univ, MS, 62; Univ Pa, PhD(elec eng), 69. *Prof Exp:* Engr telecommun, Chinese Govt Radio Admin, 58-60; electronics, Western Elec Co, 62-66. *Concurrent Pos:* NSF res grant, 77-82. *Mem:* Inst Elec & Electronics Engrs; Asn Comput Mach. *Res:* Programming methodology; software engineering; real-time systems. *Mailing Add:* Dept Comput Sci Univ Houston Houston TX 77204. *Fax:* 713-743-3335; *E-Mail:* jhuang@cs.uh.edu

HUANG, JUSTIN C, THEORETICAL PHYSICS. *Current Pos:* asst prof, 62-69, ASSOC PROF PHYSICS, UNIV MO, COLUMBIA, 69- *Personal Data:* b Honolulu, Hawaii, Oct 10, 35; m 65, Helga Shen; c Linus & Daphne. *Educ:* Univ Wash, Seattle, BS, 57; Mich State Univ, MS, 59, PhD(physics), 61. *Prof Exp:* Fulbright fel, Univ Tokyo, 61-62. *Mem:* Am Phys Soc; Sigma Xi. *Res:* Quantum mechanics; scattering theory; theory of elementary particles and fields. *Mailing Add:* Dept Physics Univ Mo Columbia MO 65211. *Fax:* 573-882-4195; *E-Mail:* physjch@mizzou1

HUANG, KEE-CHANG, PHARMACOLOGY, PHYSIOLOGY. *Current Pos:* res assoc, 53-56, from asst prof to assoc prof, 56-63, prof pharmacol, 63-88, EMER PROF PHARMACOL & TOXICOL, SCH MED, UNIV LOUISVILLE, 88- *Personal Data:* b Canton, China, July 22, 17; nat US; m 47, Shou-shan; c Kou Chu, Anna K & Karen T. *Educ:* Dr Sun Yat-sen Univ, China, MD, 40; Columbia Univ, PhD, 53. *Honors & Awards:* Fulbright Professorship Award, 78 & 86. *Prof Exp:* Res fel pharmacol, NIH, China, 40-46; instr, Nat Col Shanghai, China, 46-47; fel, Columbia Univ, 49-53. *Mem:* AAAS; Am Physiol Soc; Am Soc Pharmacol & Exp Therapeut; Soc Exp Biol & Med; Am Soc Nephrology. *Res:* Renal and intestinal transport of electrolytes, sugars and amino acids. *Mailing Add:* Health Sci Ctr Univ Louisville Sch Med Louisville KY 40292. *Fax:* 502-852-7868; *E-Mail:* kchuan01@ulkyvm.louisville.edu

HUANG, KEH-NING, THEORETICAL PHYSICS. *Current Pos:* PROF, NAT TAIWAN UNIV, 84-; RES FEL, INST ATOMIC & MOLECULAR SCI, ACADEMIA SINICA, TAIWAN, 84- *Personal Data:* b Nanking, China, Dec 6, 47; nat US; m 69, Yueh-Miaw Yu; c Wei-Hwa & Wei-Chung. *Educ:* Nat Cheng-Kung Univ, Taiwan, BS, 68; Yale Univ, PhD(physics), 74. *Honors & Awards:* Distinguished Res Award, Nat Sci Coun, Repub China; Serv Award, Phys Soc, Repub China. *Prof Exp:* Fel physics, Univ Ore, 74-76; res assoc physics, Univ Nebr, 76-78; asst prof physics, Univ Notre Dame, 78-81; physicist, Argonne Nat Lab, 81-84. *Concurrent Pos:* Manuscript referee, Nuclear Physics, 76-, Phys Rev, 78- & J Optical Soc Am, 81-; co-prin investr, NSF grant, 79-81, prin investr, Res Corp grant, 80-82; assoc ed-in-chief, Chinese J Physics, 86-88, ed-in-chief, 88-89; exec dir, Chinese Phys Soc, 86-87. *Mem:* Am Phys Soc; Sigma Xi; Chinese Phys Soc (pres, 87-88). *Res:* Relativistic many-body theory; kinematics in scattering theory; structure and properties of exotic atoms; fusion related atomic spectroscopic data; interactions of atoms and ions with radiation. *Mailing Add:* Inst Atomic & Molecular Sci Acad Sinica PO Box 23-166 Taipei 106 Taiwan. *Fax:* 886-2-362-0200; *E-Mail:* knhuang@mcrrpa.iams.sinica.edu.tw

HUANG, KERSON, THEORETICAL PHYSICS. *Current Pos:* from asst prof to assoc prof, 57-66, PROF PHYSICS, MASS INST TECHNOL, 66- *Personal Data:* b Nan Ning, China, Mar 15, 28; nat US; m 56. *Educ:* Mass Inst Technol, BS, 50, PhD, 53. *Prof Exp:* Instr physics, Mass Inst Technol, 53-55; mem staff math, Inst Advan Study, 55-57. *Concurrent Pos:* Sloan fel, 61-64; Guggenheim fel, 65-66. *Mem:* Am Phys Soc; Am Acad Arts & Sci. *Res:* Statistical mechanics; theory of elementary particles. *Mailing Add:* Dept Physics Mass Inst Technol 77 Massachusetts Ave Cambridge MA 02139

HUANG, KUN-YEN, VIROLOGY, MEDICINE. *Current Pos:* DEAN, COL MED, NAT CHENG KUNG UNIV, TAIWAN, REPUB CHINA. *Personal Data:* b Taiwan, Dec 11, 33; m 61, Amy Hsieh; c Susan, Amelia & Nellie. *Educ:* Taiwan Univ, MD, 59; George Washington Univ, PhD(microbiol), 67.

Prof Exp: Resident surg, Taiwan Univ Hosp, 61-62; teaching asst microbiol, Sch Med, George Washington Univ, 63-64; med officer, US Naval Med Res Inst, 64-67, Nat Acad Sci res assoc, 67-68; from asst prof to prof microbiol, Sch Med, George Washington Univ, 68- *Concurrent Pos:* Res fel virol, US Naval Med Res Unit II, 62-63. *Mem:* AAAS; NY Acad Sci; Am Soc Microbiol; Infectious Dis Soc Am; Int Soc Interferon Res. *Res:* Metabolic studies of Rickettsia quintana; interferon and macrophages; interferon and protozoan parasites; effects of abnormal gaseous environments on the resistance to infection. *Mailing Add:* Dean Col Med Nat Cheng Kung Univ One Ta-Hsueh Rd Tianan Taiwan. *Fax:* 886-6-2353660

HUANG, KUO-PING, BIOCHEMISTRY. *Current Pos:* sr staff fel, 73-77, RES CHEMIST, NAT INST CHILD HEALTH & HUMAN DEVELOP, NIH, 77- *Personal Data:* b Taichung, Taiwan, Jan 3, 42; US citizen; m 70; c 2. *Educ:* Nat Taiwan Univ, BS, 64; Univ Calif, Davis, PhD(biochem), 70. *Prof Exp:* Vis assoc, Nat Inst Arthritis, Metab & Digestive Dis, NIH, 72-73. *Mem:* Am Soc Biol Chemists. *Res:* Regulation of glycogen metabolism in mammalian tissues and cells grown in culture. *Mailing Add:* Nat Inst Child Health & Human Develop NIH Bldg 49 Rm 6A36 Bethesda MD 20892-4510. *Fax:* 301-496-7434

HUANG, LAURA CHI, BIOCHEMISTRY. *Current Pos:* asst prof pharmacol, 69-74, ASSOC PROF PHARMACOL, UNIV VA, 74- *Personal Data:* b Nanking, China, Nov 17, 37; c 2. *Educ:* Nat Taiwan Univ, BS, 60; Univ Calif, Davis, PhD(comp biochem), 65. *Prof Exp:* Vis fel, NIH, 65-67; res chemist, Univ Calif, Los Angeles, 67-69. *Concurrent Pos:* Res career develop award, 78-82. *Mem:* Am Soc Biol Chemists; Chinese Soc Biochemists. *Res:* Biological control mechanisms. *Mailing Add:* Dept Pharmacol Univ Va 300 La Rd Charlottesville VA 22908-0001. *Fax:* 804-924-1992

HUANG, LEAF, BIOPHYSICS, BIOCHEMISTRY & CELL BIOLOGY. *Current Pos:* from asst prof to assoc prof, 76-85, PROF BIOCHEM, UNIV TENN, KNOXVILLE, 85-; PROF PHARMACOL, UNIV PITTSBURGH, 91- *Personal Data:* b Hunan, China, Sept 23, 46; m 72; c Benjamin & Jennifer. *Educ:* Nat Taiwan Univ, BS, 68; Mich State Univ, PhD(biophysics), 74. *Prof Exp:* Fel biophysics, Carnegie Inst Washington 74-76. *Concurrent Pos:* Prin investr, NIH grants; res career develop award, NIH, 81-86; distinguished speaker, Nat Sci Comn, China; distinguished lectr, Chinese Pharmaceut Soc, China, 96- *Mem:* Biophys Soc; Am Asn Cell Biologists; Am Soc Bio Chemists; Soc Chinese Bioscientists Am; Controlled Release Soc. *Res:* Structure and function of biological membranes; membrane fusion; membrane receptors; liposome-cell interactions; liposomes in immunology; liposome technology. *Mailing Add:* Dept Pharmacol Univ Pittsburgh W1351 Biomed Sci Tower Pittsburgh PA 16561. *E-Mail:* leaf@prophet.pharm.pitt.edu

HUANG, LEO W, HIGH TEMPERATURE CHEMISTRY, PHYSICAL ORGANIC CHEMISTRY. *Current Pos:* ASST PROF CHEM, CITY COL CHICAGO, 74- *Personal Data:* b Taiwan, China, Apr 10, 42; US citizen; m 68; c 1. *Educ:* Nat Chung-Hsing Univ, BS, 64; Kans State Univ, MS, 68; Ill Inst Technol, PhD(phys chem), 73. *Prof Exp:* Res assoc, Univ Wis, Milwaukee, 73-74. *Mem:* Am Chem Soc. *Res:* Gas-surface interaction at high temperatures. *Mailing Add:* 445 Brookside Dr Wilmette IL 60091-3048

HUANG, LIANG HSIUNG, TAXONOMY, FERMENTATION. *Current Pos:* sr res investr, 75-91, PRIN RES INVESTR, CTR RES, PFIZER INC, 91- *Personal Data:* b I-Lan, Taiwan, July 16, 39; US citizen; m 70, Jane; c Grace & Amy. *Educ:* Nat Taiwan Univ, Taipei, BS, 62; Univ Wis-Madison, MS, 66, PhD(bot), 71. *Prof Exp:* Res asst, Inst Enzyme Res, Univ Wis-Madison, 65-66; res fel, Ohio State Univ, Columbus, 72-73; res assoc, Univ Ga, Athens, 73-75. *Concurrent Pos:* Ed, Newslett US Fedn Cult Collections, 87- *Mem:* Am Soc Microbiol; Mycol Soc Am; Soc Indust Microbiol; US Fedn Cult Collections (pres, 90-91). *Res:* Taxonomy of actinomycetes and soil fungi; strain development in antibiotic research; morphology of ascomycetes; isolation of microorganisms; culture collection. *Mailing Add:* Cent Res Pfizer Inc Eastern Point Rd Groton CT 06340. *Fax:* 860-441-8851; *E-Mail:* liang__h__huang@groton.pfizer.com

HUANG, MING-HUI, NONLINEAR DYNAMICS-CHAOS, MICROCOMPUTER BASED LABORATORY SYSTEM DESIGN. *Current Pos:* from asst prof to assoc prof physics, 83-94, chmn dept, 90-93, ASSOC PROF COMPUT & INFO SCI, IONA COL, 94- *Personal Data:* m 76, Christina Chow; c Connie & Sylvia. *Educ:* Tunghai Univ, BS, 73; Ohio Univ, PhD(physics), 81; Iona Col, MS, 87. *Prof Exp:* Instr elect, Hocking Tech Col, 80-81; asst prof sci, Shawnee State Col, 81-83. *Concurrent Pos:* vis scientist, Ohio Univ, 92-93. *Mem:* Am Phys Soc; Am Asn Physics Teachers. *Res:* Theoretical solid state physics; microcomputer interfacing design and laboratory automation systems; chaos research. *Mailing Add:* 930 Webster Ave New Rochelle NY 10804. *Fax:* 914-633-2240; *E-Mail:* mxh1%iona.bitnet@cunyvm.cuny.edu

HUANG, MOU-TUAN, CANCER PREVENTION, CHEMOTHERAPY. *Current Pos:* ASSOC PROF, DEPT BIOCHEM & PHARMACOL & DIR BIOCHEM RES LAB, RUTGERS UNIV, 87- *Educ:* Univ NC, PhD(biochem), 69. *Prof Exp:* Sr scientist, Hoffmann-La Roche Inc, 77-87. *Res:* Drug metabolism. *Mailing Add:* Dept Chem Biol Lab Cancer Res Rutgers Univ Col Pharm Piscataway NJ 08855-0789

HUANG, NAI-CHIEN, SOLID MECHANICS. *Current Pos:* assoc prof, 69-83, PROF AEROSPACE & MECH ENG, UNIV NOTRE DAME, 83- *Personal Data:* b Nantong, China, July 8, 32; US citizen; m 63, Geraldine S Wang; c Sheila & Nathan. *Educ:* Nat Taiwan Univ, BS, 53; Brown Univ, MS, 58; Harvard Univ, PhD(appl mech), 63. *Prof Exp:* Res assoc eng mech, Stanford Univ, 63-65; asst prof appl mech, Univ Calif, San Diego, 65-69. *Concurrent Pos:* Vis assoc prof, Univ Wis-Madison, 74-75 & Mass Inst Technol, 79; consult, Amoco Prod Co, 78-86. *Mem:* Am Soc Mech Engrs; Am Inst Aeronaut & Astronaut; Soc Rheology; Sigma Xi; Am Fiber Soc; Am Soc Rheology; Am Soc Comput Mech. *Res:* Viscoelasticity; stability; optimal design; textile mechanics; fracture mechanics; solid mechanics; structural mechanics; deformation and flow fields in an oil reservoir associated with hydraulic fracturing process; fracture of composite materials. *Mailing Add:* PO Box 309 Notre Dame IN 46556-0309. *Fax:* 219-631-8341; *E-Mail:* nai-chien.huang.1@nd.edu

HUANG, P M, SOIL CHEMISTRY & MINERALOGY, ENVIRONMENTAL CHEMISTRY. *Current Pos:* From asst prof to assoc prof, 65-78, PROF SOIL SCI, UNIV SASK, 78- *Personal Data:* b Putze, Taiwan, Sept 2, 34; Can citizen; m 64, Yun Y Lin; c Daniel C & Crystal L. *Educ:* Nat Chung Hsing Univ, BSA, 57; Univ Manitoba, MSc, 62; Univ Wis-Madison, PhD (soil sci), 66. *Concurrent Pos:* Nat vis prof, Nat Chung Hsing Univ, 75-76, head dept soil sci & dir soil res inst, 75-76; assoc ed, Soil Sci Soc Am J, 87-92 & ed, J Chinese Agr Chem Soc, 75-76; prin investr, Agr Can, 67-79 & Am Potash Inst, 67-69, Nat Sci Eng Res Coun Can, 78-, Found Agron Res, 82-83, Sask Agr Res Found, 77-82; mem, Rev Panel, US Dept Energy, 86-87 & Potash & Phosphate Inst Can, 84-; vis prof, Environ Resources Res Inst, Pa State Univ, 96; spec res chair, Dept Agr Chem, Nat Taiwan Univ, Taipei, Taiwan, 96. *Mem:* Fel Am Soc Agron; fel Soil Sci Soc Am; fel Can Soc Soil Sci; Clay Minerals Soc; Can Asn Water Pollution & Res; Chinese Agr Chem Soc; Int Union Pure & Appl Chem; Am Chem Soc; NY Acad Sci. *Res:* Solution and surface chemistry and mineralogy of soils and sediments; pedogenesis, dynamics and fate of nutrients and toxic pollutants in terrestrial and aquatic environments; food chain contamination and human health. *Mailing Add:* Dept Soil Sci Univ Sask 51 Campus Dr Saskatoon SK S7N 5A8 Can. *Fax:* 306-966-6881

HUANG, PIEN-CHIEN, BIOCHEMISTRY, GENETICS. *Current Pos:* from asst prof to assoc prof, 65-76, PROF BIOCHEM, JOHNS HOPKINS UNIV, 76- *Personal Data:* b Shanghai, China, July 13, 31; US citizen; m 65, Ru-Chih Chow; c Suber S & Suzanne S. *Educ:* Nat Taiwan Univ, BS, 53; Va Polytech Inst & State Univ, MS, 56; Ohio State Univ, PhD(genetics & biochem), 60. *Honors & Awards:* NIH Res Career Develop Award. *Prof Exp:* NIH res fel biochem genetics & chem biol, Calif Inst Technol, 60-65. *Concurrent Pos:* Abstractor, Chem Abstr Serv, 59-69; NIH res career develop award, 66-71; Am Cancer Soc & NSF fel, Fedn Europ Biochem Soc Sch Nucleic Acid Sequencing, 68; Med Res Coun vis scholar, Lab Molecular Biol, Post-Grad Med Sch, Univ Cambridge, 72; partic, NIH Cell Cult Workshop, Los Alamos, 73; NSC chair prof, Academia Sinica, Taipei, 87-88; Fogarty Sr Int fel, 87-88. *Mem:* Genetics Soc Am; Biophys Soc Am; Am Soc Biol Chem; Am Soc Cell Biol; Sigma Xi; Academia Sinica. *Res:* Genetic chemistry; gene regulation. *Mailing Add:* Nat Sci Found 4201 Wilson Blvd Arlington VA 22230. *Fax:* 410-955-2926

HUANG, ROBERT Y M, POLYMER CHEMISTRY, CHEMICAL ENGINEERING. *Current Pos:* from asst prof to assoc prof, 65-96, PROF CHEM ENG, UNIV WATERLOO, 96- *Personal Data:* b Keelung, Taiwon, China, Dec 23, 30; Can citizen; m 59, Ritsuko; c Steven, Douglas & Peter M. *Educ:* Nat Taiwan Univ, BS, 53; Univ Toronto, MASc, 58, PhD(chem eng), 63. *Prof Exp:* Chem engr, Taiwan Fertilizer Co, Ltd, 53-56; res chemist, Int Cellulose Res Ltd & Can Int Paper Co, 62-65. *Mem:* Am Chem Soc; Chem Inst Can; NAm Membrane Soc. *Res:* Polymer science and engineering, especially properties of permselective polymer membranes applied cellulose chemistry; pervaporation membrane separation processes; synthesis and transport properties of thin film composite membranes for various separation processes. *Mailing Add:* Dept Chem Eng Univ Waterloo Waterloo ON N2L 3G1 Can. *Fax:* 519-746-4979; *E-Mail:* ryhvong@chemical.watstdr.uwaterloo.ca

HUANG, RU-CHIH CHOW, MOLECULAR BIOLOGY. *Current Pos:* from asst prof to assoc prof, 65-75, PROF BIOL, JOHNS HOPKINS UNIV, 75- *Personal Data:* b Nanking, China, Apr 2, 32; m 56; c 2. *Educ:* Nat Taiwan Univ, BS, 53; Va Polytech Inst, MS, 56; Ohio State Univ, PhD, 60. *Prof Exp:* Asst plant physiol, Va Polytech Inst, 54-56; asst plant physiol, Ohio State Univ, 56-57, asst biochem, 57-58; abstracter biol, Chem Abstr Serv, 58-60; res fel, Calif Inst Technol, 60-65. *Mem:* Am Soc Biol Chemists; Biophys Soc; Chinese Acad Sci. *Res:* Biochemistry and enzymology of chromosomal nucleoproteins; gene action; differentiation and development. *Mailing Add:* Dept Biol Johns Hopkins Univ Baltimore MD 21218. *Fax:* 410-516-5213

HUANG, SAMUEL J, ORGANIC CHEMISTRY, POLYMER CHEMISTRY. *Current Pos:* from asst prof to assoc prof, 67-78, PROF CHEM, UNIV CONN, 78- *Personal Data:* b Canton, China, Mar 14, 37; m 68; c 1. *Educ:* Nat Taiwan Univ, BS, 58; Polytech Inst Brooklyn, PhD(chem), 64. *Prof Exp:* Res fel, Univ Ill, 63-64. *Mem:* Am Chem Soc; The Chem Soc; Chinese Chem Soc. *Mailing Add:* IMS O-136 Univ Conn Mansfield CT 06268

HUANG, SHAO-NAN, LIVER PATHOLOGY, VIRAL HEPITITIS. *Current Pos:* HEAD PATH, SUNNYBROOK MED CTR, 84- *Educ:* Nat Taiwan Univ, Tai Pei, MD, 54. *Mailing Add:* Dept Path Sunnybrook Health Sci Ctr 2075 Bayview Ave Don Mills ON M4N 3M5 Can

HUANG, SHAW-GUANG, NUCLEAR MAGNETIC RESONANCE. *Current Pos:* DIR, MAGNETIC RESONANCE FACIL, HARVARD UNIV, 82- *Personal Data:* b Taiwan, Aug 22, 49; US citizen; m 75; c 3. *Educ:* Nat Taiwan Univ, BS, 71; Mich State Univ, PhD(phys chem), 77. *Prof Exp:* Res assoc, Univ Ill, Urbana, 77-78; head electronic shop, dept chem, Cornell Univ, 78, dir nuclear magnetic resonance facil, 78-82. *Mem:* Am Chem Soc. *Res:* Molecular motions in molecules by nuclear magnetic resonance and other spectroscopic techniques; reaction kinetics; new nuclear magnetic resonance instrumental methodologies through both software and hardware designs. *Mailing Add:* Dept Chem Magnetic Resonance Lab Harvard Univ 12 Oxford St Cambridge MA 02138. *Fax:* 617-495-3939

HUANG, SHU-JEN WU, COAGULANTS, SURFACE ACTIVE AGENTS. *Current Pos:* sr chemist, 81-83, group leader, 84-87, TECH DIR, NALCO CHEM CO, 88- *Personal Data:* b Tainan, Taiwan, July 24, 45; US citizen; m 68; c 2. *Educ:* Cheng Kung Univ, Taiwan, BS, 67; Univ Rochester, MS, 69. *Prof Exp:* Chief chemist, Universal Div, Lonza, Inc, 70-74; chemist, Hodag Chem, 74-75; assoc proj leader, Consumer Prod Div, A E Staley, 75; group leader, Org Chem Div, Richardson Co, 75-81. *Mem:* Am Oil Chemists Soc; Am Water Works Asn; Soc Cosmetic Chemists; Soc Mfg Engrs. *Res:* Water clarification area; new coagulants development and testing; paint detackification; spray booth maintenance; waste treatment. *Mailing Add:* Nalco Chem Co One Nalco Ctr Naperville IL 60563-1198

HUANG, SHYI YI, MONOCLONAL ANTIBODY PRODUCTION, NEUTRALIZATION VENOM ACTIVITY. *Current Pos:* RETIRED. *Personal Data:* b Tainan, Taiwan, June 12, 33; US citizen; m 33, Mei Tau; c K Fon, Song X, Sophia & Margaret. *Educ:* Univ Tex, Austin, MS, 67; Baylor Univ, PhD(micobiol), 77. *Prof Exp:* Asst prof biol, Tex A&I Univ, 78-79; res scientist, Tex A&M Univ, Kingsville, 80-83, prin investr immunol, 83-94. *Concurrent Pos:* Co-investr, NIH, 83-; prin investr, NSF, 86-89. *Res:* Production of monoclonal antibody to neutralize venom activities; mechanisms of venom neutralization by naturally occurring anti-venom factors. *Mailing Add:* 1004 S 18th St Kingsville TX 78363

HUANG, SUEI-RONG, CHEMISTRY. *Current Pos:* From asst prof to assoc prof chem, 64-75, PROF CHEM, LONG ISLAND UNIV, 75- *Personal Data:* b Tainan, Taiwan, Jan 1, 32; m 65, Lily P T Chen; c Eric, Fritz, Jeffrey & Nina. *Educ:* Taiwan Univ, BS, 55; NMex Highlands Univ, MS, 60; Stevens Inst Technol, PhD(chem), 64. *Mem:* Am Chem Soc. *Res:* Radiation chemistry of inorganic salts; theoretical study of biological membrane structures; diffusion process of ions through biological membranes; analysis and elucidation of chemical components and their structures in ginseng; quantum mechanical calculations. *Mailing Add:* Dept Chem Long Island Univ Brooklyn NY 11201

HUANG, SUNG-CHENG, TOMOGRAPHIC IMAGE RECONSTRUCTION. *Current Pos:* from asst prof to prof, Dept Radiol Sci, 86-93, PROF NUCLEAR MED & BIOPHYSICS, DEPT MOLECULAR & MED PHARMACOL, SCH MED, UNIV CALIF, LOS ANGELES, 93- *Personal Data:* b Canton, China, Oct 26, 44; US citizen; m 71, Caroline; c Michael & Dennis. *Educ:* Nat Taiwan Univ, BS, 66; Wash Univ, MS, 69, DSc, 73. *Honors & Awards:* George Von Heresy Prize, World Congress of Nuclear Med & Biol, 82. *Prof Exp:* Res assoc biomed comput, Biomed Comput Lab, Wash Univ, 74; proj engr, Picker Corp, 74-77. *Concurrent Pos:* Prin investr, Lab Biomed & Environ Sci, Univ Calif Los Angeles, 77-; mem adv comt, Simulation Resource Facil, Univ Wash, 88; dep chief ed, Jour Cerebral Blood Flow & Metabolism, 93- *Mem:* Soc Nuclear Med; Inst Elec & Electronics Engrs; AAAS. *Res:* Mathematical modeling of radionuclei tracer kinetics in positron emission tomography for quantitative assessment of blood perfusion; substrate utilization and receptor density in local brain-myocardial regions; tomographic image reconstruction in nuclear medicine and radiology; digital signal and image processing. *Mailing Add:* Div Nuclear Med & Biophys Dept Molecular & Med Pharmacol Univ Calif Sch Med Los Angeles CA 90095

HUANG, SYLVIA LEE, BIOPHYSICS, BIOCHEMISTRY & MOLECULAR BIOLOGY. *Current Pos:* from res asst prof to res assoc prof, 69-71, ASSOC PROF BIOCHEM, SCH MED, NY UNIV, 71- *Personal Data:* b Shanghai, China, July 14, 30; US citizen; m 57; c 3. *Educ:* Nat Taiwan Univ, BS, 52; Univ Idaho, MS, 56; Univ Pittsburgh, PhD(biophys), 61. *Prof Exp:* Res asst biophys, Univ Pittsburgh, 58-61; res assoc, Sloan-Kettering Inst, 62-66. *Concurrent Pos:* Instr, Sch Med, Cornell Univ, 64-66; prin investr, 72- *Mem:* Biophys Soc; Am Soc Biol Chemists; Harvey Soc. *Res:* Physical chemistry of nucleic acids; structure and function of macromolecules; regulation of gene expression during development and differentiation; erythropoietin and the control of erythropoiesis; mechanism of protein biosynthesis; mechanism of anti-HIV action of plant proteins and polycyclic compounds. *Mailing Add:* Dept Biochem NY Univ Sch Med New York NY 10016

HUANG, T(ZU) C(HUEN), ENGINEERING MECHANICS. *Current Pos:* RETIRED. *Personal Data:* b Shanghai, China; nat US; m 50; c 2. *Educ:* Nat Chiao-Tung Univ, China, BS, 46; Univ Ill, MS, 49, PhD(eng mech), 52. *Prof Exp:* Res stress analyst, Int Harvester Co, 52-55; asst prof mech eng, Ore State Col, 55-56; assoc prof eng mech, Univ Fla, 56-62; prof eng mech, Univ Wis-Madison, 62- *Concurrent Pos:* Consult, NASA. *Mem:* Am Soc Mech Engrs; Am Soc Eng Educ; Am Soc Testing & Mat; Am Inst Aeronaut & Astronaut; Acoust Soc Am. *Res:* Vibration and dynamics; nonlinear mechanics and solid mechanics in elasticity; wave propagation; stress analysis. *Mailing Add:* Dept Eng Mech 1500 Eng Dr Univ Wis 1415 Johnson Dr Madison WI 53706-1607

HUANG, THOMAS SHI-TAO, ELECTRICAL ENGINEERING. *Current Pos:* PROF ELEC ENG, UNIV ILL, URBANA-CHAMPAIGN, 80- *Personal Data:* b Shanghai, China, June 26, 36; m 59; c 4. *Educ:* Nat Taiwan Univ, BS, 56; Mass Inst Technol, MS, 60, ScD(elec eng), 63. *Honors & Awards:* Tech Achievement Award, Inst Elec & Electronics Engrs, 87. *Prof Exp:* From instr elec eng to assoc prof, Mass Inst Technol, 63-72; prof elec eng, Purdue Univ, 72-80. *Concurrent Pos:* Ford fel, 63-65; Alexander von Humboldt sr scientist award. *Mem:* AAAS; fel Inst Elec & Electronics Engrs; fel Optical Soc Am. *Res:* Electrical communications; data processing; transmission and processing of pictorial information; design of efficient systems; picture quality evaluation. *Mailing Add:* Dept Elec Eng Univ Ill 1406 W Green St Urbana IL 61801-2918

HUANG, THOMAS TAO SHING, PHYSICAL CHEMISTRY. *Current Pos:* from asst prof to assoc prof, 71-82, CHMN DEPT, E TENN STATE UNIV, 79-, PROF PHYS CHEM, 82- *Personal Data:* b China, July 3, 39; m 65, M Janice Fernald; c Margaret & Steven. *Educ:* Taiwan Univ, BS, 61; East Tenn State Univ, MA, 64; Univ Ill, PhD(chem), 69. *Prof Exp:* Tech specialist, Great Lakes Res Co, 64; US AEC grant, Univ Ill, 68-69; asst prof phys chem, Univ Ky, 69-71. *Concurrent Pos:* Vis prof, Beijing Norm Univ, Cent China Norm Univ & Tsinghua Univ. *Mem:* Am Chem Soc; Sigma Xi. *Res:* Theoretical and experimental studies of chemical kinetics; kinetic isotope effects; oxidation of ascorbic acid in aqueous solutions. *Mailing Add:* 812 W Maple St Johnson City TN 37604-6510. *Fax:* 423-929-5835; *E-Mail:* i21huang@etsu.east-tenn-st.edu

HUANG, THOMAS TSUNG-TSE, FLUID DYNAMICS, ENGINEERING. *Current Pos:* CHIEF HYDRODYNAMIST, SR RES SCIENTIST & NAVAL ARCHIT FLUID DYNAMICS & HYDRODYN, DAVID TAYLOR MODEL BASIN, CDNSWC, DEPT NAVY, 68- *Personal Data:* b Taoyuan, Taiwan, Sept 1, 38; US citizen; m 62, Suiteh K; c Margaret W & Mitchell T. *Educ:* Nat Taiwan Univ, BS, 61; State Univ Iowa, MS, 64; Cath Univ Am, PhD(fluid dynamics & appl physics), 69. *Prof Exp:* Res asst hydraul & mech, Iowa Inst Hydraul Res, State Univ Iowa, 62-63; assoc res scientist, Hydronautics, Inc, 63-68. *Concurrent Pos:* Res prof, Johns Hopkins Univ, 88- *Mem:* Soc Naval Architects & Marine Engrs, fel Am Soc Mech Engrs, Soc Prof Engrs. *Res:* Ship hydrodynamics; boundary layers; wakes; flow transition; drag reduction; cavitation; applied research in full scale ship performance prediction techniques; propeller/hull interaction; computational fluid dynamics. *Mailing Add:* David Taylor Model Basin CDNSWC Code 5030 9500 MacArthur Blvd West Bethesda MD 20817-5700. *Fax:* 301-227-4589; *E-Mail:* huang@oasys.dt.navy.mil

HUANG, TIAO-YUAN, VERY LARGE SCALE INTEGRATION, SEMICONDUCTOR MEMORIES. *Current Pos:* DEVICE MGR, INTEGRATED DEVICE TECHNOL, INC, 91- *Personal Data:* b Kaohsiung, Taiwan, May 5, 49; US citizen; m 81; c 1. *Educ:* Nat Cheng Kung Univ, Taiwan, BS, 71, MS, 73; Univ NMex, MS, 79, PhD(elec eng), 81. *Prof Exp:* Proj leader telemetry, Chung Shan Inst Sci & Technol, 75-77; mem tech staff, Semiconductor Process & Design Ctr, Tex Instruments, 81-83; mem res staff, Integrated Circuit Lab, Xerox Palo Alto Res Ctr, 84-86 & Electronics & Imaging Lab, 87-91. *Concurrent Pos:* Comt mem, Int Electron Devices Meeting, Inst Elec & Electronics Engrs, 90-91. *Mem:* Sr mem Inst Elec & Electronics Engrs; Electrochem Soc. *Res:* Integrated circuits; very large scale integration; novel device structures; lightly-doped drain transistors; thin film transistors; active matrix displays; static memories; eprom-eeprom; submicron cmos-bicmos technologies. *Mailing Add:* Nat Nano Device Lab Nat Chiao-Tung Univ 1001 Ta-Hsueh Rd Hsinchu Taiwan

HUANG, TIM HUI-MING, CLINICAL CYTOGENETICS, MOLECULAR GENETICS. *Current Pos:* ASST PROF & LAB DIR CYTOGENETICS, DEPT PATH, ELLIS FISCHEL CANCER CTR, 91- *Personal Data:* b Tainan, Taiwan, Nov 6, 57; US citizen; m, Susan Leu; c Victor S & Emanuel D. *Educ:* Tunghai Univ, Taiwan, BS, 80; Univ Calif, Davis, PhD(genetics), 89. *Honors & Awards:* First Award, Nat Cancer Inst. *Prof Exp:* Cytogenetic technologist, City Hope Med Ctr, 84-85; researcher, Calif Primate Res Ctr, 85-89; fel clin cytogenetics, Baylor Col Med, 89-91. *Mem:* AAAS; Am Soc Human Genetics; Asn Cytogenetic Technologists; Soc Chinese Bioscientists Am; Am Soc Cancer Res. *Res:* Genetic alterations in common forms of cancer and study their association with tumor progression. *Mailing Add:* Dept Path Ellis Fischel Cancer Ctr 115 Business Loop 70 W Columbia MO 65203. *Fax:* 573-884-5206

HUANG, TSENG, STRUCTURAL DYNAMICS, MECHANICS. *Current Pos:* from assoc prof to prof mech, 61-69, PROF CIVIL ENG & ENG MECH, UNIV TEX, ARLINGTON, 69- *Personal Data:* b Kiangsu, China, Dec 9, 25; m 60, Yoemin Y Liu; c Lawrence, Austin & Minnie. *Educ:* Chiao Tung Univ, BS, 47; Univ Okla, MCE, 55; Univ Ill, PhD(struct mech), 60. *Honors & Awards:* Eugene W Jacobson Award, Am Soc Mech Engrs, 80; Achievement Award, Am Soc Mech Engrs, Offshore Mech & Arctic Eng Div, 88; Isop Award, Int Soc Offshore Mech & Polar Eng, 93. *Prof Exp:* Civil engr, Keelung Harbour Bur, 47-54; bridge designer, Okla State Hwy Dept, 55-56; from res asst to res assoc struct dynamics, Univ Ill, 57-60, asst prof, 60-61. *Concurrent Pos:* Consult, Jersey Prod Res Co, 62-64, Esso Prod Res Co, 64-65 & Maurer Engr Inc, 78-; mem, Struct Stability Res Coun; bd dir & secy, Offshore Mechs & Polar Eng, Coun Chmn, honors & awards comt; dir, Int Soc Offshore & Polar Engrs. *Mem:* Am Soc Civil Engrs; Am Soc Mech Engrs. *Res:* Structural analysis, eye mechanics; stability, vibration and design. *Mailing Add:* 1004 Whispering Oak Ct Arlington TX 76012-2803. *Fax:* 817-273-2630

HUANG, WAI MUN, MOLECULAR BIOLOGY. *Current Pos:* asst prof microbiol, 74-77, from assoc prof to prof cellular, viral & molecular biol, 77-95, PROF ONCOL SCI, UNIV UTAH, 95- *Personal Data:* b China. *Educ:* Johns Hopkins Unv, PhD(biophys chem), 67. *Prof Exp:* Fel biochem, Albert Einstein Col Med, 67-69; fel, Stanford Univ, 69-72; res assoc biol, Mass Inst Technol, 72-74. *Concurrent Pos:* NIH career develop award, 75. *Mem:* Am Soc Microbiol; Fedn Am Soc Exp Biol. *Res:* DNA replication; nucleic acid enzymology; molecular biology of nucleic acids; protein-nucleic acid interactions. *Mailing Add:* Dept Oncol Sci Med Ctr Univ Utah Salt Lake City UT 84132-0001

HUANG, WANN SHENG, ENHANCED OIL RECOVERY, STEAM FLOODING SIMULATION. *Current Pos:* Sr chem engr, res chem engr, sr res chem engr, asst supvr, supvr, RES CONSULT, E P TECHNOL DIV TEXACO INC, 88- *Personal Data:* b Szechuan, China, Oct 3, 39; m 64; c 2. *Educ:* Cheng Kung Univ, Taiwan, BS, 61; Univ SDak, MA, 63; Ill Inst Technol, PhD(chem eng), 68. *Mem:* Am Inst Chem Engrs; Am Inst Mining, Metall & Petrol Engrs. *Res:* Telomer chemistry; mass transfer to and from bubbles and drops; oil production; thermal recovery of heavy crude oils; thermal and miscible flooding simulation. *Mailing Add:* E & P Technol Div Texaco Inc PO Box 425 Bellaire TX 77401

HUANG, WEI-FENG, PHYSICS. *Current Pos:* from asst prof to assoc prof, 64-74, PROF PHYSICS, UNIV LOUISVILLE, 74- *Personal Data:* b Shanghai, China, Jan 23, 30; m 60; c 4. *Educ:* Univ Mich, BS, 58, MS, 59; Univ Va, PhD(nuclear physics), 63. *Prof Exp:* Res scientist, Univ Va, 62-64. *Mem:* Am Phys Soc. *Res:* Positron annihilation studies of electronic structures of solids; superconductivity. *Mailing Add:* Dept Physics Univ Louisville Louisville KY 40292

HUANG, WEN HSING, CLAY MINERALOGY, GEOCHEMISTRY. *Current Pos:* RETIRED. *Personal Data:* b Taiwan, China, Dec 30, 36; US citizen; m 75. *Educ:* Nat Taiwan Univ, China, BS, 60; Wash Univ, St Louis, MA, 68; Univ Mo, Columbia, PhD(geol), 69. *Prof Exp:* Teaching asst, Wash Univ, 65-66; fel, Univ Mo, 69-70; from asst prof to assoc prof chem, Univ SFla, 70-76; assoc prof, Dept Geol, Tex A&M Univ, 76-81. *Concurrent Pos:* Wheeler fel, Wash Univ, St Louis, 64-65; Am Chem Soc Petrol Res Fund fel, Wash Univ, St Louis, 65-67; A P Green fel, Univ Mo, 68-70; NASA Res grant, NASA Apollo moon sample project, Univ Mo, 71; Fac Res Coun award, Univ San Francisco, 71-72, 72-73 & 74-75; Sigma Xi Res grant, 72; NSF grant, 72-74; Sarasota County grant, 74-75; Nat Oceanic & Atmospheric Agency sea grant, 75; assoc ed, Clay Minerals Soc, 74-76, mem publ comt; fel, Geol Soc Am, 75; adj assoc prof chem, Univ SFla, 75-76; With Dept Interior, Bur Land Mgt, 75-76. *Mem:* Clay Minerals Soc; Int Asn Study Clays; Int Asn Geochem & Cosmochem; Geol Soc Am; Sigma Xi. *Res:* Aqueous sedimentary geochemistry; exploration and production geochemistry of ores (uranium); aluminum extraction process; thermodynamics and kinetics of organo-chemical weathering processes; computer application in geology; low-temperature solution geochemistry; clay mineralogy, thermodynamics and kinetics of organochemical weathering processes; radioactivation analysis and computer application in geology. *Mailing Add:* 730 Ridge Dr McLean VA 22101-1620

HUANG, Y(EN) T(I), CIVIL ENGINEERING, EARTHQUAKE ENGINEERING. *Current Pos:* RETIRED. *Personal Data:* b Taipei, Formosa, Feb 4, 27; US citizen; m 58; c 1. *Educ:* Univ Taiwan, BSc, 50; Univ Toronto, MASc, 57; Columbia Univ, PhD(eng mech), 61. *Prof Exp:* Instr, Univ Taiwan, 50-55; res asst, Columbia Univ, 57-61; res staff mem, Sperry Rand Res Ctr, Mass, 61-63; sr res engr, Atlantic Ref Co, Tex, 63-64; proj geophysicist, Geotech div, Teledyne Indust, Inc, 64-66, sr proj geophysicist, Teledyne, Inc, 66-67; sr systs engr, Collins Radio Co, 67-70; pres, Y T Huang & Assocs, Inc, 70- *Concurrent Pos:* Adj assoc prof, Univ Tex, Arlington, 77-79. *Mem:* NY Acad Sci; Seismol Soc Am; Am Soc Civil Engrs; Nat Soc Prof Engrs; Am Concrete Inst. *Res:* Structural engineering; elastic wave propagations; earthquake science; geodetic domes. *Mailing Add:* 396 Foresesta Terr West Palm Beach FL 33415

HUANG, ZHIJIAN, ANALYTICAL BIOCHEMISTRY, BIOLOGICAL QUANTITATION. *Current Pos:* AT MOLECULAR TOOL ALPHA CTR, 95- *Personal Data:* b Shaxian, Fujian, China, Oct 7, 63; m 88, Weimin You; c Peter M. *Educ:* Zhejiang Univ, China, BA, 83; Beijing Med Univ, Dr, 88. *Prof Exp:* Staff scientist I, Molecular Probes, Inc, 90-91; staff scientist II, 91-95. *Mem:* Am Soc Cell Biol; Biophys Soc; Protein Soc. *Res:* Employing fluorescence and other spectroscopic techniques to study and quantitate biological processes or assemblies such as quantities and binding; general analytical sciences. *Mailing Add:* Molecular Tool Alpha Ctr 1419 J Winter Park Circle Baltimore MD 21221. *Fax:* 541-344-6504

HUBA, FRANCIS, ORGANIC CHEMISTRY, ELECTROCHEMISTRY. *Current Pos:* PRES & OWNER, HYCONEX, INC, 91- *Personal Data:* b Peteri, Hungary, Apr 20, 20; US citizen; m 45, Julia; c Francis & Kathie. *Educ:* Sch Commerce, Budapest, Hungary, BBA, 48; Polytech Univ, Budapest, MS, 55; Case Western Reserve Univ, PhD(electrochem), 77. *Prof Exp:* Asst vaccines, Serum & Health Inst, Budapest, 34-45; pesticides, Huba Bros, Inc, Budapest, 45-49; managing engr, Femtomegcikkmuvek Works, 52-56; sr res chemist, Hungary Acad Sci Chem Res Inst, 56-57; sr res & develop engr, Diamond Shamrock Corp, Painesville, 57-80, res assoc, Res Ctr, 80-82; vis scientist, Case Western Univ, 83-85; res & develop engr, Avery Int, 85-87; consult, E-System Int, 87-91. *Concurrent Pos:* Res & develop chemist, Indust Org Res Inst, Budapest, 49-52. *Mem:* Am Chem Soc; Electrochem Soc; Soc Mfg Engrs. *Res:* Electrochemistry, including membranes, electrophoresis, plating, anodization, electrofluorination; organic chemistry, including acetylides, dyes and intermediates and fluoroorganics; biochemistry of pesticides, sanitizers, virocides, vaccines and serums; circuit boards, semiconductors; detoxifying auto exhaust; granted 12 US and 6 foreign patents. *Mailing Add:* 5521 80th St N Apt 312 St Petersburg FL 33709

HUBA, JOSEPH D, THEORETICAL PLASMA PHYSICS. *Current Pos:* RES PHYSICIST, NAVAL RES LAB, 75- *Personal Data:* b Peekskill, NY, Feb 11, 50. *Educ:* Univ Notre Dame, BS, 71; Univ Md, PhD(physics), 75, MBA, 82. *Concurrent Pos:* Ed, Sci Tutorial Exchange, Geophys Res Lab, 92. *Mem:* Am Phys Soc. *Mailing Add:* Naval Res Lab Code 6790 4555 Overlook Ave SW Washington DC 20375. *Fax:* 202-767-0631

HUBAND, FRANK L, SYSTEMS DESIGN & SYSTEMS SCIENCE. *Current Pos:* EXEC DIR, AM SOC ENG EDUC, 90- *Personal Data:* b Washington, NC, July 12, 39; m, Carol Singer. *Educ:* Cornell Univ, BS, 61, PhD(elec eng), 67; Yale Univ, JD, 75. *Prof Exp:* Asst prof elec eng & math sci, Rice Univ, 66-72; pres, Eng Systs Inc, 72-73; atty adv, Off Gen Coun, Fed Energy Admin, 75-76; asst to gen coun, NSF, 76-78, head, Technol Policy Sect, 78-85, dir, Elec Commun & Systs Eng Div, 85-87, dir, Emerging Eng Technol Div, 87-89, dir, Elec & Commun Systs, 89-90. *Concurrent Pos:* Consult, Tex Instruments, 68-75. *Mem:* Nat Soc Prof Engrs; Sigma Xi; Inst Elec & Electronics Engrs. *Res:* Improvement in the quality of education for engineers, including enhancement of the diversity of engineers to reflect the population; increasing the effectiveness of technology transfer from academic to production. *Mailing Add:* Am Soc Eng Educ 1818 N St NW Suite 600 Washington DC 20036-1207. *Fax:* 202-265-8504; *E-Mail:* f.huband@asee.org

HUBAY, CHARLES ALFRED, surgery; deceased, see previous edition for last biography

HUBBARD, ANN LOUISE, CELL BIOLOGY. *Current Pos:* assoc prof, 80-86, PROF, DEPT CELL BIOL & ANAT, JOHNS HOPKINS SCH MED, 86- *Personal Data:* b Long Beach, Calif, May 30, 43; m 65; c 1. *Educ:* Stanford Univ, AB, 65, MA, 66; Rockefeller Univ, NY, PhD(cell biol), 73. *Prof Exp:* Sec level teacher chem, Fairfax County Sch Syst, Groveton High Sch, 66-67; res assoc electrochem, Am Univ, Washington, DC, 67-68; fel, Sch Med, Yale Univ, 73-75, asst prof cell biol, Sect Cell Biol, 75- *Concurrent Pos:* Fel Leukemia Soc Am, Inc, 73-75. *Mem:* Sigma Xi; Am Soc Cell Biol; fel Leukemia Soc Am. *Res:* Nature and biogenesis of protein constituents in the cellular membranes of eukaryotes; specific emphasis on membrane glycoproteins of the plasmalemma; receptor-mediated endocytosis. *Mailing Add:* Dept Cell Biol & Anat Johns Hopkins Sch Med 725 N Wolfe St Baltimore MD 21205-2105. *Fax:* 410-955-4129

HUBBARD, ARTHUR T, ANALYTICAL CHEMISTRY, ELECTROCHEMISTRY. *Current Pos:* PROF CHEM, UNIV CINCINNATI, 86- *Personal Data:* b Alameda, Calif, Sept 17, 41; m 93, Chiu Nan Lai; c David & Lynne. *Educ:* Westmont Col, BA, 63; Calif Inst Technol, PhD(chem), 67. *Honors & Awards:* Am Chem Soc Award Colloid or Surface Chem, 89; David C Grahame Award, Electrochem Soc, 93. *Prof Exp:* Res fel chem, Calif Inst Technol, 66-67; prof chem, Univ Hawaii, 67-76; prof chem, Univ Calif, Santa Barbara, 76-86. *Mem:* Am Chem Soc; Soc Electroanal Chem; Electrochem Soc; Am Phys Soc. *Res:* Chemistry of surfaces studied by thin layer electrochemistry and electron techniques, such as low-energy electron diffraction, auger and electron energy-loss spectroscopy. *Mailing Add:* Dept Chem Mail Loc 172 Univ Cincinnati Cincinnati OH 45221-0172. *Fax:* 513-559-1288

HUBBARD, BERTIE EARL, MATHEMATICAL ANALYSIS. *Current Pos:* RETIRED. *Personal Data:* b Cameron, Ill, Aug 6, 28; m 52; c 2. *Educ:* Western Ill Univ, BS, 49; Univ Iowa, MS, 52; Univ Md, PhD(math), 60. *Prof Exp:* Asst math, Univ Iowa, 49-52; mathematician, US Naval Ord Lab, 55-61; from res asst prof to res assoc prof, Dept Math & Inst Phys Sci & Technol, Univ Md, College Park, 61-67, res prof math, 67-91. *Mem:* Soc Indust & Appl Math; Am Math Soc. *Res:* Numerical solution of ordinary and partial differential equations. *Mailing Add:* 3820 Chipping Lane Port Republic MD 20676

HUBBARD, CAROLYN PARKS, automotive exhaust control technology, automotive catalysis, for more information see previous edition

HUBBARD, COLIN D, PHYSICAL CHEMISTRY, BIOLOGICAL CHEMISTRY. *Current Pos:* from asst prof to assoc prof, 67-79, PROF CHEM, UNIV NH, 79- *Personal Data:* b Ipswich, Eng, May 9, 39. *Educ:* Univ Sheffield, BSc, 61, PhD(chem), 64. *Prof Exp:* Res assoc chem, Mass Inst Technol, 64-65 & Cornell Univ, 65-66; res assoc biochem, Univ Calif, Berkeley, 66-67. *Concurrent Pos:* Vis res fel, Univ Kent, Canterbury, 73-74, Univ Leicester, 80-81; vis prof, Univ Alta, Edmonton, 74, Univ Witten/Hendecke, 93-94; hon res fel, Univ Leicester, 87-88; sab fel, Univ Sevilla, 88. *Mem:* Am Soc Biol Chemists; Am Chem Soc; Royal Soc Chem. *Res:* Elementary steps in chemical reactions; application of rapid reaction techniques and high pressure kinetics to mechanism determination in inorganic, bioinorganic and biological systems and enzyme catalyzed processes; solvation. *Mailing Add:* Dept Chem Univ NH Durham NH 03824. *Fax:* 603-862-4278

HUBBARD, DONALD, BIOCHEMISTRY, ASTRONOMY. *Current Pos:* RETIRED. *Personal Data:* b Terra Ceia, Fla, Oct 4, 00. *Educ:* Univ Fla, BS, 23, MS, 24; Am Univ, PhD(chem), 32. *Honors & Awards:* L J Daguerre Medal, Soc French Photog, 34. *Prof Exp:* Phys chemist res, Nat Bur Standards, 25-64. *Mem:* Am Chem Soc; Optical Soc Am; AAAS. *Res:* Photographic emulsion sensitivity; hypersentization of panchromatic emulsions; Donnan membrane heterogeneous equilibria; optical glass. *Mailing Add:* 3 Fairfax Ct Apt 1 Chevy Chase MD 20815-6560

HUBBARD, EDWARD LEONARD, PARTICLE ACCELERATORS. *Current Pos:* CONSULT, EDWARD L HUBBARD CONSULT, 86- *Personal Data:* b Phoenix, Ariz, July 7, 21; m 52, Bonnie Cushman; c Paul E, Glenda K, Ruth S (Merkel) & Alison A (Moreno). *Educ:* Univ Calif, Los Angeles, AB, 43, AM, 48, PhD(physics), 51. *Prof Exp:* Asst physics, Univ Calif, Los Angeles, 43-44; physicist, Naval Ord Lab, 44-45; physicist, Lawrence Berkeley Lab, Univ Calif, 51-68 & Fermi Nat Accelerator Lab, 68-74; mgr, Gen Atomics, San Diego, 74-86. *Mem:* Am Phys Soc. *Res:* Particle accelerators and their applications. *Mailing Add:* 5527 Chelsea Ave La Jolla CA 92037. *E-Mail:* ed__hubbard@compuserve.com

HUBBARD, ERIC R, PODIATRIC MEDICINE & SURGERY. *Current Pos:* CLIN PROF PODIATRIC SURG, CALIF COL PODIATRIC MED, 72-; CLIN PROF PODIATRIC MED, UNIV SOUTHERN CALIF, LOS ANGELES CO HOSP, 77- *Personal Data:* b Palm Springs, Calif, Oct 11, 43; c Corey, Susan, Sean, Heather & Nicolle. *Educ:* Calif Col Podiatric Med, BS, 65, DPM, 68; Pepperdine Univ, MS, 77 Am Bd Pod Surg, dipl. *Hon Degrees:* DSc, Calif Col Podiatric Med, 90. *Concurrent Pos:* Consult, Ins Indust, 72-; staff, Mem Med Ctr & Pac Hosp, Long Beach; clin instr, Univ Southern Calif; secy Nat Bd Podiatric Med Examrs; mem bd trustees, Fund Podiatry Med Educ, Am Podiatric Med Asn. *Mem:* Am Podiatry Asn; fel Am Col Foot Orthopaedists; Am Podiatric Med Asn (pres, 88); fel Am Col Foot & Ankle Surgeons; Am Col Sports Med; fel Am Acad Podiatric Admin. *Res:* Silastic implants in foot surgery; phethesmograph and its relationship to vasoconstriction; the use of nizoral in onychomycosis. *Mailing Add:* 2333 Pacific Ave Long Beach CA 90806

HUBBARD, HARMON WILLIAM, PHYSICS. *Current Pos:* PHYS SCIENTIST, R&D ASSOCS, 71- *Personal Data:* b St Louis, Mo, Apr 15, 23. *Educ:* Univ Ill, BS, 47; Univ Calif, PhD(physics), 52. *Prof Exp:* Physicist, Lawrence Radiation Lab, Univ Calif, 52-55; prof physics, Am Univ, Beirut, 56; physicist, Aeronutronic Systs, Inc, 57; phys scientist, Rand Corp, 58-71. *Mem:* Am Phys Soc. *Res:* Theoretical physics and energy applications. *Mailing Add:* 12144 Travis St Los Angeles CA 90049

HUBBARD, HAROLD MEAD, RENEWABLE ENERGY TECHNOLOGY, SUSTAINABLE ENERGY SYSTEMS. *Current Pos:* RETIRED. *Personal Data:* b Beloit, Kans, Apr 16, 24; div; c Stuart W & David D. *Educ:* Univ Kans, BS, 48, PhD, 51. *Hon Degrees:* DSc, Regis Col, 84. *Prof Exp:* Instr chem, Univ Kans, Lawrence, 49-51; res chemist & lab mgr, E I du Pont de Nemours & Co Inc, Wilmington, Del, 51-69; dir phys sci, Midwest Res Inst, Kansas City, Mo, 70-75, vpres res, 76-78, sr vpres opers, 79-82, exec vpres, 83-90; pres & chief exec officer, Pac Int Ctr High Technol Res, 90-95. *Concurrent Pos:* Dir, Solar Energy Res Inst, 82-90; Matsuhaga distinguished fel energy & environ, Univ Hawaii, Manoa, 91- *Mem:* Int Solar Energy Soc; Am Chem Soc; AAAS; NY Acad Sci; Am Solar Energy Soc; Sigma Xi. *Res:* Solar energy and renewable energy technology; development of integrated energy systems. *Mailing Add:* 3245 Newland St Wheat Ridge CO 80033. *Fax:* 808-539-3892

HUBBARD, HARVEY HART, AEROACOUSTICS. *Current Pos:* DISTINGUISHED RES ASSOC, NASA, 92- *Personal Data:* b Swanton, Vt, June 17, 21; m 47, Sadie M Miller; c 4. *Educ:* Univ Vt, BS, 42. *Honors & Awards:* Silver Medal for Noise Control, Acoust Soc Am, 78; Aeroacoust Award, Am Inst Aeronaut & Astronaut, 79. *Prof Exp:* Elec engr training, Westinghouse Elec Corp, 42; head atmosphere acoust, Br Res, Nat Adv Comt Aeronaut, 45-59; head acoust, Br Res, NASA, 59-73, asst chief, Acoust & Noise Reduction Div, 73-80; sr res assoc, Col William & Mary, 81-92. *Mem:* Assoc fel Am Inst Aeronaut & Astronaut; fel Acoust Soc Am; Inst Noise Control Eng. *Res:* Understanding of aircraft noise, its generation, propagation, and control, and its effects on people and structures. *Mailing Add:* 325 Charleston Way Newport News VA 23606

HUBBARD, JERRY S, MICROBIOLOGY. *Current Pos:* assoc prof, 74-79, prof, 79-95, EMER PROF BIOL, GA INST TECHNOL, 95- *Personal Data:* b Tipton, Okla, Dec 10, 32; m 57, Shirley Chase; c Randall C & Amy E. *Educ:* Okla State Univ, BS, 58, MS, 60; Univ Tex, Austin, PhD(microbiol), 65. *Honors & Awards:* Newcomb-Cleveland prize, AAAS, 77. *Prof Exp:* Res fel, Lab Biochem, Nat Heart Inst, 65-66; res scientist, Jet Propulsion Lab, Calif Inst Technol, 66-68; group supvr microbiol, 68-73, sr biologist, Biol Div, Calif Inst Technol, 73-74. *Concurrent Pos:* Assoc mem biol team, Viking 76 Mission, 73-77, mem surface sampler team, 74-77; speakers bur, Am Inst Chem Engrs, 79-80. *Mem:* Am Soc Microbiol. *Res:* Microbial metabolism; bioconversions with immmobilized microorganisms; biodegradation, bioremediation, and dextoxification by soil microorganisms. *Mailing Add:* Dept Biol Ga Inst Technol 225 North Ave NW Atlanta GA 30332-0230. *Fax:* 404-894-0519

HUBBARD, JOHN CASTLEMAN, PATHOLOGY. *Current Pos:* asst prof, 63-69, ASSOC PROF PATH, SCH MED, STATE UNIV NY, BUFFALO, 69- *Personal Data:* b Louisville, Ky, Nov 2, 22; m 50, Helen C Winsor; c 4. *Educ:* Univ Ky, BS, 44; Univ Louisville, MD, 51. *Prof Exp:* Sr pathologist, Div Labs & Res, NY State Dept Health, 56-59; assoc cancer res pathologist, Roswell Park Mem Inst, 59-63. *Mem:* Micros Soc Am; AAAS; NY Acad Sci. *Res:* Partial hepatectomy and other factors influencing recovery from experimental cirrhosis; primary tumor ultrastructure and induction; genesis of juxta glomerular cell granules; improved microscopy of mycoplasma. *Mailing Add:* Dept Path Rm 204 Farber Hall State Univ NY Sch Med 3435 Main St Buffalo NY 14214-3001. *Fax:* 716-829-2086

HUBBARD, JOHN EDWARD, HYDROLOGY, CLIMATOLOGY. *Current Pos:* from asst prof to assoc prof, 63-75, PROF EARTH SCI, STATE UNIV NY COL, BROCKPORT, 75-, CHAIR, DEPT EARTH SCIS. *Personal Data:* b Binghamton, NY, Apr 17, 33; m 58; c 3. *Educ:* Union Col, AB, 58; Brown Univ, MAT, 62; Colo State Univ, PhD(watershed sci), 68. *Prof Exp:* Asst prof phys sci, State Univ NY Agr & Tech Inst, Cobleskill, 61-63. *Concurrent Pos:* Chair, Educ & Pub Serv Comt, Univs Coun on Water Resources. *Mem:* Am Geophys Union; Am Meteor Soc; Am Water Res Asn. *Res:* Evapotranspiration; forest-soil-water relations; water resources education; hydrology of radwaste sites. *Mailing Add:* Dept Earth Sci State Univ NY 350 New Campus Dr Brockport NY 14420-2915

HUBBARD, JOHN LEWIS, ORGANIC CHEMISTRY, ORGANOMETALLIC CHEMISTRY. *Current Pos:* from asst prof to assoc prof, 78-90, PROF CHEM, MARSHALL UNIV, 90- *Personal Data:* b Kingsport, Tenn, June 16, 47; m 78, Jeanne M Delaney; c Elizabeth & Matthew. *Educ:* Univ NC, Chapel Hill, BS, 69; Purdue Univ, PhD(org chem), 76. *Prof Exp:* Vis asst prof, Purdue Univ, 77, res assoc, 77-78. *Mem:* Am Chem Soc; Sigma Xi. *Res:* New approaches to borohydrides; hydride transfer reactions involving boron and aluminum; hydride-induced carbonylation of organoboranes; synthesis of potential nephrotoxins. *Mailing Add:* Dept Chem Marshall Univ Huntington WV 25755-2520. *E-Mail:* hubbard@marshall.edu

HUBBARD, JOHN PATRICK, CONSERVATION, ORNITHOLOGY & NATURAL HISTORY. *Current Pos:* RETIRED. *Personal Data:* b Ft Bragg, NC, Feb 13, 35; c 2. *Educ:* Western NMex Univ, BA, 61; Univ Mich, Ann Arbor, MS, 63, PhD(zool), 67. *Prof Exp:* Res cur, Smithsonian Inst, 66-68; Bailey-Law cur birds & mammals, Va Polytech Inst & State Univ, 69-71; cur New World birds, Del Mus Natural Hist, 71 74; Supvr Endangered Species Prog, NMex Dept Game & Fish, 74-94. *Concurrent Pos:* Univ NMex res assoc. *Mem:* Am Ornith Union. *Res:* Animal systematics, distribution, status ecology and paleohistory, particularly with reference to North America; biogeography; paleoecology; North American plant distribution, status ecology and systematics. *Mailing Add:* PO Box 182 Glenwood NM 88039

HUBBARD, JOHN W, CARDIOVASCULAR PHARMACOLOGY, CLINICAL PHARMACOLOGY. *Current Pos:* sr res pharmacologist, Hoechst-Roussel Pharmaceut Inc, 86-88, res assoc pharmacol, 88-89, asst dir clin pharmacol, 89-92, DIR PROJ MGT, HOECHST-ROUSSEL PHARMACEUT INC, 92- *Personal Data:* b San Jose, Calif, June 8, 56; m 80. *Educ:* Univ Santa Clara, BS, 78; Univ Tenn, PhD(physiol & physiol psychol), 83. *Prof Exp:* Teaching asst physiol psychol, Univ Tenn, 78-83; NIH fel pharmacol, Health Sci Ctr, Univ Tex, San Antonio, 83-85; sr res pharmacologist, Rorer-Revlon Health Care Corp, 85-86. *Concurrent Pos:* Reviewer, Am J Physiol, 89-; adj assoc prof, Robert Wood Johnson Med Sch, 91. *Mem:* Am Heart Asn; Sigma Xi; Soc Neurosci; Am Physiol Soc; Am Col Clin Pharmacol; Drug Info Asn. *Res:* Cardiovascular and neuropharmacology; therapeutic agents for the treatment of hypertension, congestive heart failure, coronary artery disease, Alzheimer's disease and schizophrenia; role of enzyme adenylate cyclase in the regulation of myocardial contractility; pharmacokinetics and pharmacodynamics of new drugs in man. *Mailing Add:* Hoechst-Roussel Pharmaceut Inc Somerville NJ 08876-1258

HUBBARD, KENNETH GENE, CLIMATE INFORMATION & DECISION MAKING, CLIMATE & CROP MODELS. *Current Pos:* PROF AGR METEROROL & DIR HIGH PLAINS CLIMATE CTR, UNIV NEBR, 81-, PROF ENVIRON INSTRUMENTATION, 91- *Personal Data:* m 71, Susan E Alcorn; c Carter & Benjamin. *Educ:* Chadron State Col, BS, 71, SDak Sch Mines & Technol, MS, 73; Utah State Univ, PhD(Soil sci & biometeorol), 81. *Prof Exp:* Meteorologist, Geophys Fluid Dynamics Lab, 73-74, Utah Water Res Lab, 74-77; Climatologist, Utah Dept Agr, 77-81. *Concurrent Pos:* Rapporteur, Comn Agr Meteorol, World National Orgn, 92- *Mem:* Am Meteorol Soc; Am Asn State Climatologists (pres, 85-86); Am Soc Agron; AAAS. *Res:* Development of climate data collection, storage and retrieval system; applied research relevant to monitoring and modeling the environment. *Mailing Add:* 242 L W Chase Hall PO Box 830728 Lincoln NE 68583-0728. *Fax:* 402-472-6614; *E-Mail:* agme006@unlvm.unl.edu

HUBBARD, LINCOLN BEALS, MEDICAL PHYSICS, RADIATION SAFETY. *Current Pos:* CHIEF PHYSICIST, MT SINAI HOSP MED CTR, CHICAGO, 74-75, 80-; PRES HUBBARD, BROADBENT 7 ASSOC, LTD, 93- *Personal Data:* b Hawkesbury, Ont, Sept 8, 40; m 61, Nancy A Krieger; c 2. *Educ:* Univ NH, BS, 61; Mass Inst Technol, PhD(physics), 67. *Prof Exp:* Fel biol, Argonne Nat Lab, 66-68; asst prof math & physics, Knoxville Col, 68-70; asst prof physics, Furman Univ, 70-74; partner, Fields, Griffith, Hubbard & Broadbent Inc, 75-93. *Concurrent Pos:* Consult physics div, Oak Ridge Nat Lab, 68-73; consult, Vet Admin Hosp, Hines, Ill, 74-; chief physicist, Cook Co Hosp, Chicago, 79-88; assoc prof, Rush Univ, 83- *Mem:* Am Phys Soc; Am Asn Physicists Med; Am Asn Physics Teachers; Health Physics Soc. *Res:* Radiation dosimetry and radiological physics. *Mailing Add:* 4113 W End Rd Downers Grove IL 60515-2307

HUBBARD, M(ALCOLM) M(ACGREGOR), engineering; deceased, see previous edition for last biography

HUBBARD, PAUL STANCYL, JR, MAGNETIC RESONANCE, MOLECULAR PHYSICS. *Current Pos:* From asst prof to assoc prof physics, 58-68, assoc dean grad sch, 69-72, PROF PHYSICS, UNIV NC, CHAPEL HILL, 68- *Personal Data:* b St Petersburg, Fla, July 15, 31; m 57; c 2. *Educ:* Univ Fla, BS, 53; Harvard Univ, AM, 54, PhD(physics), 58. *Concurrent Pos:* Alfred P Sloan res fel, 62-65; NSF fel, Clarendon Lab, Oxford Univ, 64-65. *Mem:* Am Phys Soc; Sigma Xi. *Res:* Theoretical and experimental research in nuclear magnetic resonance and relaxation. *Mailing Add:* Dept Physics Univ NC Chapel Hill NC 27514

HUBBARD, PHILIP G(AMALIEL), HYDRAULICS, ELECTRICAL ENGINEERING. *Current Pos:* Res engr & instrumentation sect head, Inst Hydraul Res, 46-64, from instr to assoc prof mech & hydraul, 46-59, dean acad affairs, 66-71, PROF MECH & HYDRAUL, UNIV IOWA, 59-, PROF ENERGY ENG, 77-, VPROVOST, 69- *Personal Data:* b Macon, Mo, Mar 4, 21; m 43; c 5. *Educ:* Univ Iowa, BS, 46, MS, 49, PhD, 54; St Ambrose Col, LHD, 69. *Mem:* Am Soc Eng Educ. *Res:* Instrumentation in hydraulic research. *Mailing Add:* 2423 Walden Rd Apt 229 Iowa City IA 52246

HUBBARD, RICHARD ALEXANDER, II, physical inorganic chemistry; deceased, see previous edition for last biography

HUBBARD, RICHARD FOREST, PLASMA PHYSICS, SPACE PHYSICS. *Current Pos:* RES PHYSICIST, NAVAL RES LAB, 85- *Personal Data:* b Kansas City, Mo, July 14, 48; m 73; c 2. *Educ:* Univ Kans, BA, 70; Univ Iowa, MS, 72, MA, 75, PhD(physics), 75. *Prof Exp:* Res asst physics, Univ Iowa, 70-75; Nat Res Coun res assoc, NASA Goddard Space Flight Ctr, 76-77; res assoc, Inst Phys Sci & Technol, Univ Md, 77-79; res scientist physics, Jaycor, Inc, 79-85. *Concurrent Pos:* Consult, G T Devices, 81-88. *Mem:* Am Phys Soc; Am Geophys Union; AAAS; Planetary Soc; Fusion Power Assocs. *Res:* Stability and transport of intense charged particle beams in plasmas and neutral gases; instabilities and acceleration mechanisms in space plasmas; numerical simulation of plasmas. *Mailing Add:* Code 6790 Naval Res Lab 4555 Overlook Ave SW Washington DC 20375-5000

HUBBARD, RICHARD W, LABORATORY MEDICINE, BIOCHEMICAL NUTRITION. *Current Pos:* clin chemist & asst prof biochem & med technol, 70-73, assoc prof biochem & med technol, Sch Med & chmn med technol, Sch Allied Health Professions, 73-87, ASSOC PROF PATH & NUTRIT, SCH MED & PUB HEALTH, LOMA LINDA UNIV, 87- *Personal Data:* b Battle Creek, Mich, Dec 24, 29; m 51, Constance Gloor; c Robert, Jeff & Karen. *Educ:* Pac Union Col, BA, 51; Purdue Univ, MS, 59, PhD(biochem), 61. *Prof Exp:* Analytical chemist, Willard Storage Battery Co, Calif, 51-53; clin lab technician, Los Angeles County Gen Hosp, 53-54; res asst med res, Res Inst, Cedars of Lebanon Hosp, Los Angeles, 54-55, res assoc, 55-56; asst biochem, Purdue Univ, 56-60; instr med sch, Univ Mich, 60-63; sr res chemist, Spinco Div, Beckman Instruments Inc, 63-67; biochemist, Stanford Res Inst, 67-70. *Concurrent Pos:* Prin investr, NIH res grant, 91-93. *Mem:* Am Asn Clin Chemists; Am Chem Soc; Am Soc Clin Path; Am Soc Med Technol; Am Inst Nutrit; Sigma Xi. *Res:* Amino acid metabolism; clinical chemistry; nutrition; physiological chemistry; dietary protein and insulin; serum protein metabolism and transport; chromatography of catecholamines. *Mailing Add:* Clin Lab Loma Linda Univ Med Ctr Loma Linda CA 92350-0001. *Fax:* 909-824-4832

HUBBARD, ROBERT PHILLIP, BIOMECHANICS, ENGINEERING MECHANICS. *Current Pos:* from asst prof to prof biomech, 77-94, PROF, DEPT MAT SCI & MECH, MICH STATE UNIV, 94- *Personal Data:* b Portsmouth, Va, June 8, 43; m 66; c 2. *Educ:* Duke Univ, BSME, 65; Univ Ill, Urbana, MS, 67, PhD(theoret & appl mech), 70. *Prof Exp:* Asst biomech, Hwy Safety Res Inst, Univ Mich, 69-70, fel, 70-71; sr res engr, Gen Motors Res Labs, 71-77. *Concurrent Pos:* Consult, Franklin Res Inst, 78-, Hoover Universal, 81-, Motor Wheel Corp, 84-, Johnson Control, 84- & Ferno-Wash, 88-; pres, Biomech Design Inc, 87- *Mem:* Soc Automotive Engrs; Am Soc Mech Engrs; Am Acad Mech. *Res:* Human tolerance; head injury; tissue biomechanics; anthropometrics; biomechanics in design. *Mailing Add:* 160 Kenberry Dr East Lansing MI 48823. *Fax:* 517-353-4472

HUBBARD, ROGER W, ENVIRONMENTAL MEDICINE. *Current Pos:* RES CHEMIST, HEAT RES DIV, US ARMY RES INST ENVIRON MED, NATICK DEVELOP CTR, 66- *Personal Data:* b Colchester, Vt, Feb 23, 39; m 62; c 2. *Educ:* Northeastern Univ, AB, 62; Brown Univ, PhD(biol), 66. *Mem:* AAAS; Am Physiol Soc; Am Soc Biol Chemists; NY Acad Sci; Sigma Xi. *Res:* Conducts research on the biochemical and physiological mechanisms operative in the complex alterations that occur in animal models and humans when exposed to environmental extremes of heat and work. *Mailing Add:* US Army Res Inst Environ Med Kansas St Natick MA 01760-5007

HUBBARD, RUTH, BIOLOGY, BIOLOGY OF WOMEN. *Current Pos:* Res fel biol, Harvard Univ, 50-58, res assoc, 59-74, lectr, 68-73, prof, 73-90, EMER PROF BIOL, HARVARD UNIV, 90- *Personal Data:* b Vienna, Austria, Mar 3, 24; nat US; m 58, George Wald; c Elijah W & Deborah H. *Educ:* Radcliffe Col, PhD(biol), 50. *Hon Degrees:* DSc, Macalester Col, St Paul, Minn & Univ Toronto, 91; LHD, Southern Ill Univ, Edwardsville, 91. *Honors & Awards:* Paul Karrer Medal, Swiss Chem Soc, 67; Distinguished Serv Award, Am Inst Biol Sci, 92. *Concurrent Pos:* Guggenheim fel, Carlsberg Lab, Copenhagen, 52-53; mem corp, Marine Biol Lab, Woods Hole, trustee, 73-78, emerita, 90-; vis prof, Mass Inst Technol, 72. *Mem:* AAAS; Am Soc Biol Chemists; Biophys Soc; Soc Gen Physiol; Nat Women's Studies Asn. *Res:* Chemistry of vision; synthesis of visual pigments; health education of non-professionals; women's biology and health; sociology of science; predictive genetic testing. *Mailing Add:* Biol Labs Harvard Univ Cambridge MA 02138

HUBBARD, VAN SAXTON, GASTROENTEROLOGY, CLINICAL NUTRITION & OBESITY. *Current Pos:* fel clin assoc, Pediat Metab Br, NIH, 76-78, med officer, 78-83, dir, Nutrient Metab Prog, 83-90, dir, Gastro-Intestinal Digestion Prog, 88-90, dir, Obesity, Eating Dis & Energy Regulation Prog, 83-95, dir & prof officer, US-Japan Malnutrition Panel, Med Sci Prog, 83-94, actg dir, Div Nutrit Res Coord, 93-94, DIR, CLIN NUTRIT RES UNITS PROG, DIV DIGESTIVE DIS & NUTRIT, NAT INST DIABETES & DIGESTIVE & KIDNEY DIS, NIH, 83-, CHIEF, NUTRIT SCI BR, 94-, DIR, OBESITY NUTRIT RES CTRS PROG, 95-, DIR, DIV NUTRIT RES COORD, 95- WASH UNIV, 86-; DIR, NUTRIT SCI BR, NAT INST DIABETES, DIGESTIVE & KIDNEY DIS, NIH, 83-, ACTG DIR, DIV NUTRIT RES COORD, 93-, CHAIRPERSON, NUTRIT COORD COMT, 93- *Personal Data:* b Middletown, NY, Mar 1, 45; m 74, Linda Dell Rucker; c Brian S & Kevin S. *Educ:* Union Col, BS, 67; Med Col Va, MD & PhD(biochem), 74; Am Bd Pediat, cert, 81. *Honors & Awards:* Commendation Medal, USPHS, 91, Outstanding Serv Medal, 95. *Prof Exp:* Resident pediat, Univ Minn Hosp, 74-76. *Concurrent Pos:* Expert, Bur Drugs, Food & Drug Admin, 78-84; staff physician, Nat Naval Med Ctr, Bethesda, 79-; assoc dir, Cystic Fibrosis Ctr, NIH, 79-83; asst ed, Am J Clin Nutrit, 81-86; asst res prof child health, George Washington Univ, 81-86, assoc res prof, 86-; mem, Comt Nutrit, Am Acad Pediat, 88-; prof pediat, Uniformed Servs, Univ Health Sci, 93-; dep comdr, Pub Health Serv Clearing & Staging Unit, Nat Disaster Med Syst, 93- *Mem:* Am Inst Nutrit; Am Soc Parenteral & Enteral Nutrit; NAm Soc Pediat Gastroenterol; Soc Pediat Res; Sigma Xi; Am Soc Clin Nutrit; fel Am Acad Pediat; fel Am Col Nutrit; NY Acad Sci; Am Gastroenterol Asn; Am Fedn Clin Res. *Res:* Basic science and clinical applications relating to the study of clinical nutrition and cystic fibrosis emphasizing essential fatty acid metabolism; essential fatty acid metabolism; health and policy implications associated with obesity and other eating disorders. *Mailing Add:* NIH Natcher Bldg 45 Center Dr Rm 6AN-18F Bethesda MD 20892-6600. *Fax:* 301-480-8300

HUBBARD, WILLIAM BOGEL, PLANETARY SCIENCES. *Current Pos:* assoc prof planetary sci, 72-75, dir, Lunar & Planetary Lab & head, Dept Planetary Sci, 77-81, PROF PLANETARY SCI, UNIV ARIZ, 75- *Personal Data:* b Liberty, Tex, Nov 14, 40; m 63, Jean Gilliland; c Lynne M & Laurie N. *Educ:* Rice Univ, BA, 62; Univ Calif, Berkeley, PhD(astron), 67. *Prof Exp:* Res fel astrophys, Kellogg Radiation Lab, Calif Inst Technol, 67-68; asst prof astron, Univ Tex, Austin, 68-72. *Concurrent Pos:* Consult, NASA, 71-, prin investr, 74-; mem, Div Planetary Sci Comt, 86-88. *Mem:* Am Astron Soc; fel Am Geophys Union; Int Astron Union; Sigma Xi; AAAS. *Res:* Interior structures of Jovian planets and brown dwarfs; occultation studies of planetary atmospheres and rings. *Mailing Add:* 2618 E Devon St Tucson AZ 85716. *Fax:* 520-621-4933; *E-Mail:* hubbard@lpl.arizona.edu

HUBBARD, WILLIAM MARSHALL, COMMUNICATION ENGINEERING, OPTICAL PHYSICS. *Current Pos:* RETIRED. *Personal Data:* b Houston, Tex, June 2, 35; m 55, 83; c 3. *Educ:* Ga Inst Technol, BS, 57, PhD(physics), 63; Univ Ill, MS, 58. *Prof Exp:* Instr physics, Ga Inst Technol, 60-63; mem tech staff, Bell Labs, Bell Commun Res, 63-83, dist res mgr, 83-93. *Mem:* Am Phys Soc. *Res:* Theoretical nuclear physics, specifically orbital electron capture; millimeter wave communication; optical frequency communication; high-speed electronics & multiplexers; photonic switching and interconnects. *Mailing Add:* 11 Spradley Lane Middletown NJ 07748

HUBBARD, WILLIAM NEILL, JR, MEDICINE. *Current Pos:* RETIRED. *Personal Data:* b Fairmont, NC, Oct 15, 19; m 45, 87; c 5. *Educ:* Columbia Univ, BA, 41; NY Univ, MD, 44. *Hon Degrees:* ScD, Hillsdale Col, 67, Albany Med Col, 68, Hope Col, 79, Mich Tech Univ, 83 & Univ NC, 87. *Honors & Awards:* Award, Soc Health & Human Values, 76. *Prof Exp:* From resident to chief resident, Bellevue Hosp, 44-50; from instr to asst prof med, Col Med, NY Univ, 50-59, from asst dean to assoc dean, 51-59; from assoc prof to prof internal med, Med Sch, Univ Mich, 59-70, dean, 59-70, dir med ctr, 69-70; vpres & gen mgr, Pharmaceut Div, Upjohn Co, 70-72, exec vpres, 72-74, pres, 74-84. *Concurrent Pos:* Mem panel educ consult, Comt Educ Health Admin, 73-76; consult, Nat Libr Med, 76-80; mem bd, Sci & Technol Int Develop, Nat Acad Sci, 78-80 & comt mem, Nat Res Coun, 75-80; mem, Coun Sci & Technol Develop, 78-84; mem Nat Sci bd, NSF, 74-80, consult, 80-81; mem bd overseers Morehouse Col Med Sch, 76-81; mem bd dirs, Int Fert Res Prog, 81-90, Family Health Int, 81-90; mem bd trustees, Kellogg Found, 80-94, Columbia Univ, 82-90; bd chm, Indust Technol Inst, 82-, vchmn, 86-94; chmn, Coun Health Care Technol, 86-90; chmn vis comn, Univ Mich Med Ctr, 89- *Mem:* Inst Med-Nat Acad Sci; Harvey Soc; AMA; fel Am Col Physicians; fel AAAS; Sigma Xi. *Res:* Medical education; administrative medicine. *Mailing Add:* 4630 E Gull Lake Dr Hickory Corners MI 49060

HUBBART, JAMES E, aerodynamics, for more information see previous edition

HUBBELL, DAVID HEUSTON, soil microbiology; deceased, see previous edition for last biography

HUBBELL, DOUGLAS OSBORNE, CHEMICAL ENGINEERING. *Current Pos:* PRES, PROCESS IMPROVEMENT, INC, 96- *Personal Data:* b Norfolk, Va, Jan 6, 42; m 66; c 2. *Educ:* Va Polytech Inst, BS, 64, MS, 66; Princeton Univ, PhD(chem eng), 69. *Prof Exp:* Develop engr, Hoechst Fibers Industs, 70-73, sr engr, 73-76, group leader fiber develop, 79-81, mgr chem technol, 81-87; consult, Qualpro, 87-92; dir, Mayfair Mills, 92-93; dir, K2, Inc, 93-95. *Concurrent Pos:* Fel Swiss Fed Inst Technol, 69-70. *Mem:* Fiber Soc; Am Soc Qual Control; Sigma Xi. *Res:* Process development in melt spinning and drawing; statistical experimental design; polymer processing; management consulting. *Mailing Add:* 120 Rock Bridge Rd Spartanburg SC 29302-9678

HUBBELL, HARRY HOPKINS, JR, PHYSICS, HEALTH PHYSICS. *Current Pos:* RETIRED. *Personal Data:* b Buffalo, NY, July 23, 14; wid; c 1. *Educ:* Williams Col, BA, 35; Lafayette Col, MS, 37; Princeton Univ, PhD(physics), 47; Am Bd Health Physics, cert, 60. *Prof Exp:* Asst physics, Lafayette Col, 36-37, Princeton Univ, 37-38, Williams Col, 38-40 & Wesleyan Univ, 40-41; asst physicist, Nat Bur Standards, 41-43; asst prof physics, Amherst Col, 43-44; instr, Princeton Univ, 44-45, asst, 45-46; asst prof, Williams Col, 46-47; assoc prof, Middlebury Col, 47-50; health physicist, Oak Ridge Nat Lab, 50-73. *Concurrent Pos:* Vis health physicist, Europ Orgn Nuclear Res, Geneva, 65-66; consult, Oak Ridge Nat Lab, 75-88, Atomic Bomb Casualty Comm, Natx Acad Sci, 60, 68, 86. *Mem:* AAAS; Am Phys Soc; Health Physics Soc; Am Asn Physics Teachers. *Res:* Small angle x-ray scattering; radiation dosimetry and health physics; beta ray slowing down spectra; studies of radiation doses to survivors of atomic bombings of Hiroshima and Nagasaki; dosimetry of very high energy radiations; optical and electron beam studies of fiber and liquid surfaces. *Mailing Add:* 248 Outer Dr Oak Ridge TN 37830-3850

HUBBELL, JOHN HOWARD, RADIATION PHYSICS. *Current Pos:* CONSULT, 88- *Personal Data:* b Ann Arbor, Mich, Apr 9, 25; m 55, Jean Norford; c Anne (Cooper), Shelton & Wendy (Carballo). *Educ:* Univ Mich, Ann Arbor, BSE, 49, MS, 50. *Hon Degrees:* Dr, Univ Cordoba, Argentina, 91. *Honors & Awards:* Paul C Aebersold Award, Soc Nuclear Med, 85; Radiation Indust Award, Am Nuclear Soc, 85, Prof Excellence Award, 90. *Prof Exp:* Physicist, Nat Bur Stand, 50-51, dir, X-ray & Ionizing Radiation Data Ctr, Radiation Physics Div, Ctr Radiation Res, 63-81, staff mem, Photon & Charged Particle Data Ctr, Ionizing Radiation Div, 82-88. *Concurrent Pos:* Consult, Int Comn on Radiol Units & Measurements, 65-; mem, Shielding Subcomt, Cross Sect Eval Working Group, 65-; chmn, ANS-6 Ad Hoc Comt on SI Units, Am Nuclear Soc, 74- & Gen Radiation Protection Sect, Health Physics Soc Stand Comt, 84-90; secy, X-ray Attenuation Proj, Int Union Crystallography, 78-; consult, Particle Properties Data Proj, Europ Orgn Nuclear Res/Lawrence Berkeley Lab, 81-; exec coun, Int Radiation Physics Soc, 85-91, vpres NAm, 91-94, pres, 94-; consult, WHO, Int Atomic Energy Agency, 89-, Brookhaven Nat Lab, Upton, NY, 90-; ed, Appl Radiation & Isotopes, 88-92 editor-in-chief, Radiation Physics Chem, 92-; academician, Int Higher Educ Acad Sci, Moscow, 94- *Mem:* Fel Am Nuclear Soc; fel Health Physics Soc; Radiation Res Soc; Am Phys Soc; Soc Nuclear Med; Int Radiation Physics Soc. *Res:* Photon (x-ray, gamma-ray, bremsstrahlung) attenuation coefficients, cross sections, transport; atomic photoeffect; coherent, incoherent scattering; pair, triplet production; form factors; buildup factors; applied mathematics, especially distributed source calculations; scintillation counter response; x-ray crystallography; radiation gauging; x-ray fluorescence yields. *Mailing Add:* Nat Inst Stand & Technol Rm C-312 Radiation Phys Bldg Gaithersburg MD 20899

HUBBELL, STEPHEN PHILIP, ECOLOGY. *Current Pos:* BIOLOGIST, SMITHSONIAN INST, 83- *Personal Data:* b Gainesville, Fla, Feb 17, 42; m 76; c 2. *Educ:* Carleton Col, BA, 63; Univ Calif, Berkeley, PhD(zool), 69. *Prof Exp:* From asst prof to assoc prof zool, Univ Mich, 69-74; from assoc prof to prof, Univ Iowa, 74-83. *Concurrent Pos:* Vis distinguished prof, Univ Tex, 80; Guggenheim fel, 83. *Mem:* Ecol Soc Am; Asn Trop Biol; fel AAAS. *Res:* Tropical forest ecology; plant-animal interactions; theoretical population biology. *Mailing Add:* Dept Biol Princeton Univ Princeton NJ 08544-0001

HUBBELL, WAYNE CHARLES, MAGNETISM, MATERIALS SCIENCE. *Current Pos:* mem tech staff magnetic bubbles, 73-80, SECT HEAD PLASMA CHARACTERIZATION, TEX INSTRUMENTS INC, 80- *Personal Data:* b New Orleans, La, Dec 14, 43; m 68; c 3. *Educ:* La State Univ, New Orleans, BS, 66, MS, 68; Rice Univ, PhD(mat sci), 72. *Prof Exp:* Res assoc magnetism, Rice Univ, 72-73. *Mem:* Inst Elec & Electronics Engrs; Am Phys Soc. *Res:* Computer memories and other devices utilizing mobile cylindrical magnetic domains, magnetic bubbles, for data storage. *Mailing Add:* 7380 Carson Rd Mobile AL 36695

HUBBEN, KLAUS, VETERINARY PATHOLOGY, TOXICOLOGY. *Current Pos:* RETIRED. *Personal Data:* b Magdeburg, Ger, Jan 1, 30; US citizen; m 71; c 5. *Educ:* Univ Pa, VMD, 53, MS, 58. *Prof Exp:* Instr path, Univ Pa, 56-61, asst prof, 61-67; dir, Safety Eval Dept, ICI Americas, Inc, 67-89. *Concurrent Pos:* Co-prin investr, NIH, 62-67. *Mem:* AAAS; Am Col Vet Path; Am Vet Med Asn; Am Col Vet Toxicol. *Res:* Pathology of canine heart disease; pathogenesis of bovine mastitis; pathology of avian sarcoma 13. *Mailing Add:* 110 Mercer Mill Rd Landenberg PA 19350-0341

HUBBLE, BILLY RAY, PHYSICAL CHEMISTRY, ENVIRONMENTAL SCIENCES. *Current Pos:* MGR, CHEM SCI BR & EXPLOSIVE SCI BR, CRANE DIV, NAVAL SURFACE WARFARE CTR, 82- *Personal Data:* b South Bend, Ind, Sept 29, 44; m 74, Carolyn McKee; c Paula & Kevin. *Educ:* Vincennes Univ, AS, 64; DePauw Univ, AB, 66; Kans State Univ, MS, 69, PhD(phys chem), 71. *Prof Exp:* Asst prof chem, Kans State Univ, 71 & Benedictine Col, 71-74; mem staff, Energy & Environ Systs Div, Argonne Nat Lab, 74-82. *Mem:* Am Chem Soc; Am Phys Soc; Air Pollution Control Assoc; NAm Thermal Anal Soc. *Res:* High temperature, high pressure chemistry related to liquid state; molten salts; high temperature solid-gas reaction kinetics related to air pollution control processes; gas-liquid reaction kinetics related to air pollution control processes; environmental control technology; pyrotechnics development; propellant, explosive and pyrotechnics analysis/characterization. *Mailing Add:* 104 Laura Lane Bloomfield IN 47424

HUBBS, CLARK, ICHTHYOLOGY. *Current Pos:* RETIRED. *Personal Data:* b Ann Arbor, Mich, Mar 15, 21; m 49, Catherine V Symons; c Laura (Tait), Ann F & John C. *Educ:* Univ Mich, AB, 42; Stanford Univ, PhD, 51. *Honors & Awards:* Award of Excellence, Am Fisheries Soc; W French Blair Award, Southwestern Asn Naturalists. *Prof Exp:* From instr to prof zool, Univ Tex, Austin, 49-88, chmn div biol sci, 74-76, chmn dept zool, 78-86, Clark Hubbs regents emer prof zool, 88-91. *Concurrent Pos:* Vis prof, Biol Sta. Univ Okla, 70-84; managing ed, Am Soc Ichthyologists & Herpetologists, 73-84, pres, 87; mem, Parks & Fish & Wildlife Adv Bd, US Dept Interior, 75-77. *Mem:* AAAS; Am Soc Ichthyologists & Herpetologists; Am Fisheries Soc; Ecol Soc Am; Am Soc Zool; Am Fisheries Soc; Am Soc Naturalists; Am Inst Biol Sci. *Res:* Systematics; evolution, distribution and speciation of fishes; hybridization of fresh water fishes; environmental modification of freshwater fishes. *Mailing Add:* Dept Zool Univ Tex Austin TX 78712. *Fax:* 512-471-9651; *E-Mail:* hubbs@u.texas.edu

HUBBS, ROBERT A(LLEN), ELECTRICAL ENGINEERING. *Current Pos:* Res specialist, Autonetics Div, NAm Aviation, Inc, 62-63, res supvr, 64-73, mgr radiation effects, 73-75, mgr systs eng, 75-78, chief scientist, 78-80, MGR SYSTS ANALYSIS, NAM ROCKWELL CORP, 80- *Personal Data:* b Sheridan, Wyo, Oct 22, 35; m 61; c 3. *Educ:* Stanford Univ, BS, 57, MS, 59, PhD(elec eng), 62. *Res:* Analysis of linear and nonlinear control systems; stochastic processes; optimum filter theory; error analysis of inertial guidance systems. *Mailing Add:* 2017 Driftwood Dr Fullerton CA 92831

HUBBUCH, THEODORE N(ORBERT), CHEMICAL ENGINEERING, PHYSICAL CHEMISTRY. *Current Pos:* RETIRED. *Personal Data:* b Louisville, Ky, Aug 12, 02; m 42; c 2. *Educ:* Univ Louisville, BS, 23; Harvard Univ, BS, 25, MS, 26. *Prof Exp:* Instr chem eng res, Mass Inst Technol, 26-28; chemist, Reynolds Metals Co, 28-29; sr res chemist, Girdler Corp, 29-30; engr tech sales, Am Potash & Chem Co, 31; consult engr, KenRad Radio Tube Corp, 33-38; proj leader indust anal, Tenn Valley Authority, 38-53; staff chem engr plant oper, US Army Chem Corps, 53-57; asst prof chem, Univ N Ala, 59-75, emer prof chem, 75-92. *Concurrent Pos:* Coordr, Tenn Valley Authortiy res energy proj with Univ N Ala & Northwest Ala Coun Local Govts. *Mem:* Am Chem Soc. *Res:* Foods and gas processing; glass technology; electronics; fertilizer processing and production; nerve gas inter- mediates production; missile fuels. *Mailing Add:* 1702 Ingleside Dr Florence AL 35630-2611

HUBBY, JOHN L, BIOLOGICAL SCIENCES, GENETICS. *Current Pos:* RETIRED. *Personal Data:* b Clovis, NMex, Mar 19, 32; m 52; c 3. *Educ:* Univ Tex, BS, 55, PhD(zool), 59. *Prof Exp:* NIH fel, Univ Chicago, 59-60, univ fel, 60-61, from instr to prof zool & biol, 60-88. *Mem:* AAAS; Genetics Soc Am; Soc Study Evolution; Am Soc Cell Biol; Am Soc Naturalists. *Res:* Physiological and evolutionary genetics. *Mailing Add:* 525 Camino Cabra Sante Fe NM 87501

HUBE, DOUGLAS PETER, ASTRONOMY. *Current Pos:* asst prof physics & astron, Univ Alta, 69-74, assoc prof physics, 74-82, assoc chair, 94-96 PROF PHYSICS, UNIV ALTA, 82- *Personal Data:* b St Catharines, Ont, May 19, 41; m 65, Joan O Rieck; c 2. *Educ:* Univ Toronto, BSc, 64, MA, 65, PhD(astron), 68. *Honors & Awards:* Serv Award, Royal Astron Soc Can, 82. *Prof Exp:* Lectr astron, Univ Toronto, 67-68; Nat Res Coun Can fel, Kitt Peak Nat Observ, Ariz, 68-69. *Mem:* Am Astron Soc; Royal Astron Soc Can; Can Astron Soc; Int Astron Union; Brit Interplanetary Soc. *Res:* Stellar radial velocities; close binaries; peculiar A-type stars. *Mailing Add:* Dept Physics Univ Alta Edmonton AB T6G 2J1 Can. *Fax:* 403-492-0714; *E-Mail:* dhube@phys.ualberta.ca

HUBEL, DAVID HUNTER, NEUROPHYSIOLOGY. *Current Pos:* assoc neurophysiol & neuropharmacol, 59-60, from asst prof to assoc prof neurophysiol & neuropharmacol, Harvard Med Sch, 60-65, prof neurophysiol, 65-67, George Packer Berry prof neurobiol, 68-82, JOHN FRANKLIN ENDERS UNIV PROF, DEPT NEUROBIOL, HARVARD MED SCH, 82- *Personal Data:* b Windsor, Ont, Feb 27, 26; US citizen; m 53; c 3. *Educ:* McGill Univ, BSc, 47, MD, 51. *Hon Degrees:* AM, Harvard, 62; DSc, McGill Univ, 78, Univ Man, 83, Univ Western Ont, 92, Oxford Univ, 94, Gustavus Adolphus Col, 94 & Ohio State Univ, 95. *Honors & Awards:* Nobel Prize Med & Physiol, 81; numerous named lectureships at US & foreign univs, 64-; Jules C Stein Award, 71; Lewis S Rosenstiel Award, Brandeis Univ, 72; Friedenwald Award, Asn Res Vision & Ophthal, 75; Karl Spencer Lashley Prize, Am Philos Soc, 77; Dickson Prize, Univ Pittsburgh, 79; Ledlie Prize, Harvard Univ, 80; Paul Kayser Int Award Merit Retina Res, 89; Outstanding Sci Leadership Award, Nat Asn Biomed Res, 90; Glen A Fry Medal, Col Optom, 91; Gerard Award Soc Neurosci, 93; Charles F Prentice Medal, 93; Helen Keller Prize, 95. *Prof Exp:* Rotating intern, Montreal Gen Hosp, 51-52; asst resident neurol, Montreal Neurol Inst, 52-53, fel EEG, 53-54; asst resident neurol, Johns Hopkins Hosp, 54-55; res fel neurophysiol, Walter Reed Army Inst Res, 55-58 & Wilmer Inst, Sch Med, Johns Hopkins Univ, 58-59. *Concurrent Pos:* Sr fel, Harvard Soc Fels, 71-; mem, Bd Syndics, Harvard Univ Press, 79-83; Cecil H & Ida Green vis prof, Univ BC, Vancouver, 85. *Mem:* Nat Acad Sci; Ger Leopoldina Acad Scientists, EGer; fel Am Acad Arts & Sci; Am Physiol Soc; Soc Neurosci (pres, 88-89); Asn Res Vision & Ophthal; Am Philos Soc; foreign mem Royal Soc, London; hon mem Physiol Soc UK; hon mem Am Neurol Soc; Asn Res Vision & Opthal; fel Royal Soc Med; fel AAAS; Sigma Xi; foreign mem Acad Europ. *Res:* Neurophysiology and neuroanatomy of the visual system of higher mammals. *Mailing Add:* Dept Neurobiol Harvard Med Sch 220 Longwood Ave Boston MA 02115

HUBEL, KENNETH ANDREW, MEDICINE, NEUROSCIENCES. *Current Pos:* assoc, 62-63, from asst prof to assoc prof, 63-73, PROF MED, COL MED, UNIV IOWA, 73- *Personal Data:* b New York, NY, Nov 11, 27; m 57, Janis Greer; c Wendy, Nancy & Adam. *Educ:* Univ Rochester, AB, 50; Cornell Univ, MD, 54. *Prof Exp:* Intern med, State Univ NY Upstate Med Ctr, 54-55, resident, 55-56; assoc dir clin invest, Bristol Labs, NY, 56-59; resident med, State Univ NY Upstate Med Ctr, 59-60; Nat Found res fel physiol, George Washington Univ, 60-62. *Concurrent Pos:* NIH spec res fel, Oxford Univ, 69-70; mem, Nat Inst Diabetes & Digestive Kidney Dis Study Sect, GMA-2, 84-88, chmn, 86-88. *Mem:* AAAS; Asn Am Med Cols; Am Fedn Clin Res; Am Gastroenterol Asn (secy, 78-83); Soc Exp Biol & Med; Am Physiol Soc. *Res:* Gastrointestinal absorption and secretion of drugs, electrolytes and water, particularly in the mechanisms of bicarbonate ion transport in the intestine and pancreas; autonomic control of intestinal function; neuro-endocrine control of epithelial ion transport; gastroenterology. *Mailing Add:* Dept Med Univ Hosp 200 Hankins Dr Iowa City IA 52242-0001. *Fax:* 319-353-6399

HUBER, BRIGITTE T, IMMUNOLOGY. *Current Pos:* ASSOC PROF PATH, SCH MED, TUFTS UNIV, 83- *Personal Data:* b Sins, Switz, Aug 21, 48; m 74; c 3. *Educ:* Univ London, Eng, PhD(immunol), 74. *Mem:* Am Asn Immunologists. *Res:* Cellular and molecular biology of T lymphocytes; T cell receptor structure - function relationship; T lymphocyte subsets, growth factor production and control of expression; molecular characterization of B lymphocyte differentiation antigens. *Mailing Add:* Dept Path Tufts Univ Sch Med 136 Harrison PO Box 2267 Boston MA 02111-1800. *Fax:* 617-956-0449

HUBER, CALVIN, CHEMISTRY. *Current Pos:* from asst prof to assoc prof, 61-74, PROF CHEM, UNIV WIS-MILWAUKEE, 74- *Personal Data:* b Sheboygan Falls, Wis, June 7, 32; m 54; c 3. *Educ:* Wheaton Col, BS, 54; Univ Wis, PhD(chem), 57. *Prof Exp:* From asst prof to assoc prof chem, Rockford Col, 57-61. *Mem:* Am Chem Soc. *Res:* Electroanalytical chemistry; atomic absorption spectroscopy. *Mailing Add:* Dept Chem Univ Wis Milwaukee WI 53201

HUBER, CAROL (SAUNDERSON), PROTEIN CRYSTALLOGRAPHY. *Current Pos:* fel chem, 63-65, from asst res officer to sr res officer, Inst Biol Sci, 65-93, SR RES OFFICE, BIOTECH RES INST, NAT RES COUN CAN, 93. *Personal Data:* b Winnipeg, Man, Apr 1, 37; m 66, Klaus P. *Educ:* Univ Man, BSc, 59, MSc, 60; Oxford Univ, DPhil(chem crystallog), 63. *Concurrent Pos:* Secy, Can Nat Comt Crystallog, 78-85 & 94; elected chair, Can Div Am Crystallog Asn, 93- *Mem:* Am Crystallog Asn. *Res:* X-ray crystallography; organic and protein structures; cysteine proteinases. *Mailing Add:* Bio Chem Dept Univ Ottawa Ottawa ON K1H 8M5 Can. *Fax:* 613-941-4475; *E-Mail:* cph@nrcbsa.bio.nrc.ca

HUBER, CLAYTON SHIRL, FOOD SCIENCE. *Current Pos:* chmn, Dept Food Sci & Nutrit, 76-88, DEAN COL BIOL & AGR, BRIGHAM YOUNG UNIV, 88- *Personal Data:* b Lapoint, Utah, Feb 28, 38; m 63, Beth Briggs; c Kerry, Philip, Lanae, Douglas, Leann, Brad & Kevin. *Educ:* Utah State Univ, BS, 62, MS, 64; Purdue Univ, PhD(food sci), 68. *Honors & Awards:* Snoopy Award, NASA, 70, Sci & Technol Award, 71; Cutler Award, 80; Signal Serv Award, 85. *Prof Exp:* Assoc prin res scientist, Technol Inc, 68-71; mgr, Food Sci Sect, Life Sci Div, 71-75; res scientist, Am Potato Co, 75-76. *Mem:* Fel Inst Food Technologists; Am Dairy Sci Asn; Poultry Sci Asn; Sigma Xi. *Res:* Research and development of military feeding systems; space feeding program; chemistry of muscle and muscle proteins; food chemistry and food development; nutrition and biochemistry; dehydration of food. *Mailing Add:* 4380 N 187 E Provo UT 84601

HUBER, DAVID LAWRENCE, THEORETICAL SOLID STATE PHYSICS. *Current Pos:* from instr to assoc prof, 64-69, PROF PHYSICS, UNIV WIS-MADISON, 69-, DIR, SYNCHROTRON RADIATION CTR, 85-, DIR, PHYS SCI LAB, 89- *Personal Data:* b New Brunswick, NJ, July 31, 37; m 62, Virginia Hullinger; c Laura P, Johanna J (London), Amy L (Veltri) & William H. *Educ:* Princeton Univ, AB, 59; Harvard Univ, AM, 60, PhD(physics), 64. *Prof Exp:* Res assoc physics, Harvard Univ, 64. *Concurrent Pos:* Sloan res fel, 65-67; Guggenheim fel, 72-73; Nat Asn State Univs & Land Grant Cols/CRPGE fel, 90-91. *Mem:* Fel Am Phys Soc; Sigma Xi; AAAS. *Res:* Theoretical studies of the magnetic and optical properties of solids. *Mailing Add:* Synchrotron Radiation Ctr Univ Wis 3731 Schneider Dr Stoughton WI 53589-3097. *Fax:* 608-877-2001; *E-Mail:* huber@src.wisc.edu

HUBER, DON MORGAN, PLANT PATHOLOGY, SOIL MICROBIOLOGY. *Current Pos:* assoc prof, 71-81, PROF PLANT PATH, PURDUE UNIV, 81- *Personal Data:* b Mesa, Ariz, Mar 19, 35; m 59, Paula E Towery; c Brenda, Joyce, Aaron, Louise, Lynette, Sharon, Sarah, Elese, Natalie, Kevin & Derek. *Educ:* Univ Idaho, BS, 57, MS, 59; Mich State Univ, PhD, 63. *Honors & Awards:* Pioneering Res Leadership Award, Dow Chem Co, 80; Joint Serv Achievement Medal, US Dept Defense, 87, Defense Meritorious Serv Medal, 88 & Meritorious Serv Medal, 89. *Prof Exp:* Assoc plant pathologist, Univ Idaho, 63-71. *Concurrent Pos:* Consult, 65-; grad Army Command & gen staff col, 74; med analyst, US Army Med Intel & Info Agency, 75-83-; chief exec officer, Decah Mfg, 78-; assoc dir, Armed Forces Med Intel Ctr, 83-89; trustee, Tipp Sch Corp, 93- *Mem:* Am Phytopath Soc; Soc Prof Dispute Resolution; Sigma Xi; Int Soc Plant Path; Indust Col Armed Forces. *Res:* Soilborne diseases; biochemistry of resistance; biological control; soil microflora; microbial interactions and activities in soil; nitrification; nitrification inhibitors; nutrient-disease interactions. *Mailing Add:* Dept Bot & Plant Path Purdue Univ West Lafayette IN 47907. *Fax:* 765-494-0363; *E-Mail:* huber@btny.purdue.edu

HUBER, DONALD JOHN, POSTHARVEST PHYSIOLOGY. *Current Pos:* from asst prof to assoc prof, 81-90, PROF, UNIV FLA, 90- *Personal Data:* b Hamilton, Ohio, Sept 11, 51; m 86. *Educ:* Miami Univ, BS, 73, MS, 75; Iowa State Univ, PhD(bot), 80. *Prof Exp:* Teaching asst plant physiol, Miami Univ, 73-75 & Iowa State Univ, 76-78; res asst, Iowa State Univ 78-80, assoc fel, 80. *Mem:* Am Soc Plant Physiologists; Am Soc Hort Sci; Brit Plant Growth Regulator Group. *Res:* Molecular basis of softening in horticultural crops; isolation, identification and characterization of cell wall enzymes and polysaccharides and how these change during ripening and softening. *Mailing Add:* Dept Hort Univ Fla Gainesville FL 32611-2002

HUBER, EDWARD ALLEN, ELECTRICAL ENGINEERING. *Current Pos:* MEM STAFF, SRI INT, 88- *Personal Data:* b Alton, Ill, Aug 31, 29; m 54; c 4. *Educ:* Univ Ill, Urbana, BS & MS, 56, PhD(elec eng), 60. *Prof Exp:* Res assoc, coord sci lab, Univ Ill, 57-61; develop engr, Gen Tel & Electronics Labs, 61-63; sr eng specialist, Western Div, Sylvania Electronic Systs, 63-88. *Concurrent Pos:* Lectr, Univ Santa Clara, 64-68. *Mem:* Inst Elec & Electronics Engrs. *Res:* Electronic signal analysis; software engineering. *Mailing Add:* 4243 Los Palos Ave Palo Alto CA 94306

HUBER, FLOYD MILTON, MICROBIOLOGY. *Current Pos:* SR RES SCIENTIST, ELI LILLY & CO, 65- *Personal Data:* b Hinsdale, Ill, Dec 11, 37; m 76; c 4. *Educ:* Ind State Univ, BS, 61; Univ Ill, MS, 64, PhD(plant path), 65. *Mem:* Am Soc Microbiol. *Res:* Biosynthesis and control of antibiotic production. *Mailing Add:* 3314 W County Rd 100 S Danville IN 46122

HUBER, GARY LOUIS, MEDICINE. *Current Pos:* clin prof, Dept Med, 85-86, physician in charge, Smoking Cessation Prog, 85-89, PROF MED, UNIV TEX HEALTH SCI CTR, TYLER, 85-, PROF MED, UNIV TEX, HOUSTON, 86- & DIR, NUTRIT UNIT, DEPT MED, TYLER, 89- *Personal Data:* b Spokane, Wash, Jan 30, 39; m 87, Mary Burke; c Melissa, John & Kathryn. *Educ:* Wash State Univ, BS, 61; Univ Wash, MD, 66, MS, 70. *Prof Exp:* Res trainee, Dept Biol Struct & Dept Anesthesiol, Univ Wash, Seattle, 63-64, student investr, Dept Anesthesiol, 64-66; teaching fel, Dept Med, Harvard Med Sch, 67-68, res fel, Dept Physiol, 68-70, instr med, 70-71, asst prof med, 71-80, dir, Smoking & Health Res Prog, 72-80; chief, Respiratory Dis Unit, Dept Med & dir, Student Res Prog, Beth Israel Hosp, 73-80; dir, Tobacco & Health Res Inst, Univ Ky, 80-81, prof med, Dept Med, Col Med, 80-85, prof anat, Col Med, Grad Sch, 80-82. *Concurrent Pos:* Clin fel, Div Respiratory Dis, Thorndike Mem Lab, Harvard Med Unit, 68-70; res consult path, Peter Bent Brigham Hosp, Boston, 68-71; asst dir, Dept Med Microbiol, Channing Lab & Dept Health & Hosp, Boston, physician in charge, Mycobacteria Ref Lab, 69-71 & dir, Clin Diag Lab, Div Chronic Dis, 69-71; vis physician, Pulmonary Med & Tuberculosis, Mattapan Chronic Dis Hosp & Long Island Chronic Dis Hosp, City of Boston, 69-71, diag clin, Tuberculosis Control Unit, Southend Health Unit, 70-74; dir, Respiratory Dis Clin, City of Boston, 70-73; chief, Div Respiratory Dis, Thorndike Mem Lab & Harvard Med Unit, Boston, 70-71, assoc physician, 71-74; consult, Mass Rehab Comn, Roxbury Div, 73-80, Univ Ky Med Ctr, Vet Admin Hosp, 82-85, Lincoln Trail Health Dept, Dept Human Resources, Ky, 83-85; physician-in-charge, Thoracic Clin, Beth Israel Hosp, 73-77, attending physician, Respiratory Intensive Care, 74-76, Pulmonary Function Lab, 76-77; assoc physician, Internal Med, Mount Auburn Hosp, Mass, 74-80, Dept Med, Beth Israel Hosp, 75-80; physician, Albert B Chandler Med Ctr, Univ Ky, 81-82, Div Pulmonary Dis, 81-83, Div Gen Internal Med, 82-85, Mountain Comprehensive Health Care, 83-85. *Mem:* AAAS; Am Asn Pathologists & Bacteriologists; fel Am Col Chest Physicians; Am Geriat Asn; Am Lung Asn; AMA; Am Physiol Soc; Am Thoracic Soc; NY Acad Sci. *Res:* Nutrition and nutritional research; modification of human behavior in appetitive dysfunctions; nutritional factors in the pathogenesis of cardiopulmonary diseases; general internal medicine; cardiopulmonary medicine; computer assisted literature analyses and metanalyses; interface of medicine, science and religious influences in Renaissance English literature. *Mailing Add:* Univ Tex Health Ctr PO Box 2003 Tyler TX 75710-2003. *Fax:* 903-877-2805

HUBER, HAROLD E, PHARMACEUTICAL CHEMISTRY, PHARMACEUTICAL TECHNOLOGY. *Current Pos:* RETIRED. *Personal Data:* b Wauseon, Ohio, May 11, 25; m 64, Rose M Pelosi; c 10. *Educ:* Ohio State Univ, BS, 51, MS, 59, PhD(pharm), 62. *Prof Exp:* Pharmacist, Doast Rexall Drug, Ohio, 51-52; owner, Stryker Rexall Drug, 52-58; instr pharm, Ohio State Univ, 60-62; sr pharmaceut chemist, Div Dow Chem Co, Merrell Nat Labs, Richardson-Merrell Inc, 62-74; group leader, Merrell-Dow Pharmaceut Inc, 74-90; dir pharmaceut res & develop, Duramed Pharmaceut Inc, 90-91, vpres sci & technol, 91-96,. *Res:* Pharmacology; pharmacy; physical-chemical characterizations of pharmaceutical compounds and dosage forms; management-pharmaceutical research and development; manufacturing support. *Mailing Add:* 5021 Lord Alfred Ct Cincinnati OH 45241

HUBER, IVAN, BEHAVIOR-ETHOLOGY, GENETICS. *Current Pos:* from asst prof to assoc prof, 68-84, PROF BIOL, FAIRLEIGH DICKINSON UNIV, 84- *Personal Data:* b Zagreb, Croatia, Oct 15, 31; US citizen; m 61, Vivienne Hirchinson; c Jonathan & Mirella. *Educ:* Cornell Univ, AB, 54; Univ Kans, PhD(entom), 68. *Prof Exp:* Instr biol, Muhlenberg Col, 66-68. *Concurrent Pos:* Consult entom, biomed res & neurophysiol; pres, Periplaneta Inc. *Mem:* Soc Study Evolution; Entom Soc Am; Sigma Xi; Am Genetic Asn. *Res:* Cockroaches (Blattaria); phylogeny and biology; production of behavioral and learning mutants in cockroaches as useful models in neurobiology and biomedical research; population biology of peridomestic species. *Mailing Add:* Dept Biol Fairleigh Dickinson Univ 285 Madison Ave Madison NJ 07940. *Fax:* 973-331-1383; *E-Mail:* huber@fdumad.fdu.edu

HUBER, JOEL E, ORGANIC CHEMISTRY. *Current Pos:* RES ASSOC, UPJOHN CO, 63- *Personal Data:* b Buffalo, NY, Aug 25, 36; m 60; c 3. *Educ:* Canisius Col, BS, 58; Wayne State Univ, MS, 61, PhD(org chem), 63. *Prof Exp:* Asst chem, Wayne State Univ, 58-60, res assoc, 60-63. *Mem:* Am Chem Soc; Int Union Pure & Appl Chem. *Res:* Physical organic chemistry; partial syntheses of steroids; synthesis of physiologically active compounds. *Mailing Add:* 10049 R Ave 7000 Portage Rd Mattawan MI 49071

HUBER, JOHN G, EXPERIMENTALIST CONDENSED MATTER. *Current Pos:* INDEPENDENT RES, 91- *Personal Data:* b Seattle, Wash, Jan 9, 40. *Educ:* Stanford Univ, BS, 62; Univ Ill, MS, 63; Univ Calif, San Diego, PhD(physics), 71. *Mem:* Am Phys Soc. *Mailing Add:* 501 North Blvd No 7 Richmond VA 23220

HUBER, JOHN TALMAGE, ANIMAL NUTRITION, DAIRY SCIENCE. *Current Pos:* prof, 84-96, EMER PROF ANIMAL SCI, UNIV ARIZ, 96-; ADJ PROF DAIRY NUTRIT, UTAH STATE UNIV, 97- *Personal Data:* b Phoenix, Ariz, Sept 22, 31; m 55, Larae Jenson; c Kerri, Marcie, Tammy, Jon & Joel. *Educ:* Ariz State Univ, BS, 56; Iowa State Univ, MS, 58, PhD(dairy nutrit), 60. *Honors & Awards:* Outstanding Res in Dairy Nutrit Award, Am Feed Mfrs Asn, 68; Bordon Award, 84; Appl Dairy Nutrit Award, Nutrit Professionals, 91. *Prof Exp:* Res asst dairy nutrit, Iowa State Univ, 55-60; asst prof, Va Polytech Inst, 60-67; from assoc prof to prof dairy nutrit, Mich State Univ, 67-80, prof animal sci, 80-84. *Mem:* Am Dairy Sci Asn; Am soc Animal Sci. *Res:* Digestion in the young calf; nutritional effects on milk composition; forage utilization studies in dairy cattle; mineral interactions in dairy cattle; milk residue and replacer studies; lactation studies with dst, processed grains, varying fat levels, varying protein quality, gossypol from whol cottonseed. *Mailing Add:* 2000 W Fountain Park Dr Tucson AZ 85715

HUBER, JOSEPH WILLIAM, III, ANALYTICAL ORGANIC, SOLVENT PURIFICATION. *Current Pos:* TPRI CONSULT SERV, 92- *Personal Data:* b Texas City, Tex, Aug 9, 44; m 70, Cinda Newman; c 1. *Educ:* Univ Houston, BS, 67; Univ Miss, PhD(med chem), 74. *Prof Exp:* Res assoc, Univ Miss, 74; asst prof med chem, Sch Pharm, Northeast La Univ, 74-78; mkt chemist liquid chrom, Instrument Group, Varian Assoc, 78-80; sr chemist, Burdick & Jackson Labs Inc, 80-86; tech support mgr, LDC/Milton Roy, 86-88; org lab mgr & tech dir, McGinnes Labs, 89-92. *Mem:* Sigma Xi; Am Chem Soc; Am Pharmaceut Asn. *Res:* Organophosphorus chemistry; amino phosphonic acids and peptides derived form aminophosphonic acids; reactions of organophosphorus compounds; liquid chromatography instrumentation and applications; environmental analysis. *Mailing Add:* 12092 Sugar Pine Trail West Palm Beach FL 33414. *E-Mail:* jhuber3@aol.com

HUBER, MELVIN LEFEVER, ORGANIC CHEMISTRY, INFORMATION SCIENCE. *Current Pos:* RETIRED. *Personal Data:* b Neffsville, Pa, Oct 11, 22; m 47; c 3. *Educ:* Franklin & Marshall Col, BS, 43; Univ Del, MS, 47, PhD(org chem), 50. *Prof Exp:* Res chemist, Eastern Lab, E I du Pont de Nemours & Co Inc, 50-53, group leader, 53-56, sect head, 56-61, supt lab serv, 61-63, tech asst, Cent Patent Index, 64-67, registr, Cent Chem Registry, 67-71, group supvr, Cent Report Index, 71-85. *Mem:* Am Chem Soc; Am Soc Info Sci. *Res:* Chemical structure codes; information retrieval systems; abnormal Grignard reactions; organic synthesis; process development; catalysis; rocket propellants. *Mailing Add:* 132 Colonial Ave Pitman NJ 08071

HUBER, NORMAN KING, GEOLOGY. *Current Pos:* geologist, 52-94, EMER GEOLOGIST, US GEOL SURV, 94- *Personal Data:* b Duluth, Minn, Jan 14, 26; m 51; c 2. *Educ:* Franklin & Marshall Col, BS, 50; Northwestern Univ, MS, 52, PhD(geol), 56. *Honors & Awards:* Meritorious Serv Award, US Dept Interior, 89. *Prof Exp:* Asst, Franklin & Marshall Col, 48-50 & Northwestern Univ, 50-53. *Mem:* AAAS; fel Geol Soc Am. *Res:* Geology of central Sierra Nevada, California, particularly Yosemite National Park. *Mailing Add:* US Geol Surv MS-975 345 Middlefield Rd Menlo Park CA 94025

HUBER, OREN JOHN, PHYSICS. *Current Pos:* RETIRED. *Personal Data:* b Columbus, Ohio, Oct 9, 17; m 46. *Educ:* Ohio State Univ, BSc, 39. *Prof Exp:* Res engr, Physics Dept, Battelle Mem Inst, 39-44; radiographer, Jack & Heintz Co Inc, 44-45, exp engr, 46-48; res engr, Battelle Mem Inst, 48-59, proj leader, Metall Dept, 59-60; metall engr, Livermore Labs, Sandia Corp, 60-65; asst dir metals eng inst, Am Soc Metals, 66-78. *Concurrent Pos:* Nat adv comt aeronaut, AEC, 45-46. *Res:* X-ray and electron diffraction; x-ray radiography; vacuum fusion; structural physical chemistry; physical metallurgy of non-ferrous and refractory metals. *Mailing Add:* 1500 Shellpoint Blvd Ft Myers FL 33908

HUBER, PAUL W(ILLIAM), ELECTRICAL ENGINEERING, THERMODYNAMICS. *Current Pos:* RETIRED. *Personal Data:* b Springfield, Ohio, Dec 17, 20; m 42; c 5. *Educ:* Ohio Northern Univ, BSEE, 42. *Prof Exp:* Elec engr, Nat Adv Comt Aeronaut, 42-45, physicist, 46-48, aeronaut res scientist, 49-58; aeronaut res scientist, Langley Res Ctr, NASA, 58-62, head Plasma Appln Sect & aerospace engr, 62-70, head, Flow Field Kinetics Sect, 70-72, asst head, Hypersonic Propulsion Br, 72-80. *Mem:* AAAS; Am Inst Aeronaut & Astronaut. *Res:* Gas dynamics; plasma physics; chemical kinetics; combustion and electromagnetics. *Mailing Add:* 2 Edgewood Dr Newport News VA 23606

HUBER, PAUL WILLIAM, PROTEIN-NUCLEIC ACID INTERACTIONS, NUCLEIC ACID STRUCTURE. *Current Pos:* asst prof, 85-92, ASSOC PROF BIOCHEM, UNIV NOTRE DAME, 92- *Personal Data:* b Meford, Mass, July 23, 51. *Educ:* Boston Col, BS, 73; Purdue Univ, PhD(biochem), 78. *Prof Exp:* Res assoc, Univ Chicago, 79-85. *Concurrent Pos:* Assoc chmn, Dept Chem & Biochem, Univ Notre Dame, 93-; prin investr, NIH grant GM 38200. *Mem:* AAAS; Am Soc Biochem & Molecular Biol. *Res:* Nucleic acid structure and recognition by proteins, the emphasis has been on those aspects of higher order structure that contribute to specific recognition; localization of mrna during development. *Mailing Add:* Dept Chem & Biochem Univ Notre Dame Notre Dame IN 46556. *Fax:* 219-631-6652; *E-Mail:* paul.w.huber.1@nd.edu

HUBER, RAYMOND C, PHARMACY. *Current Pos:* RETIRED. *Personal Data:* b Woodhaven, NY, Apr 14, 17; m 41, Lillian Haack; c Richard V. *Educ:* City Col New York, BS, 38. *Prof Exp:* Res asst, Endo Labs, Inc, NY, 46-50; res scientist, Squibb Inst Med Res, 50-63, sr res investr, 63-78, proj leader, 79-80, consult, Pharmaceut Res & Develop Dept, 81-84. *Mem:* Am Chem Soc; Am Pharmaceut Asn. *Res:* New products for injection. *Mailing Add:* 1372 Crim Rd Bridgewater NJ 08807

HUBER, REUBEN EUGENE, BIOCHEMISTRY. *Current Pos:* from asst prof to assoc prof, 67-79, chmn, Div Biochem, 87-89 & 90-92, PROF BIOCHEM, DIV BIOCHEM, UNIV CALGARY, 79- *Personal Data:* b Saskatchewan, Sask, Mar 24, 40; m 65, Irene Wiebe; c Dezene, Allene & Joelene. *Educ:* Univ Alta, BSc, 61, MSc, 62; Univ Calif, PhD(biochem), 66. *Prof Exp:* Fel biochem, Univ Aix-Marseille, 66-67. *Mem:* Am Soc Biochem & Molecular Biol; Am Chem Soc; Protein Soc. *Res:* Protein and amino acid chemistry; enzymology and chemistry of disaccharidases. *Mailing Add:* Dept Biol Sci Univ Calgary Calgary AB T2N 1N4 Can. *Fax:* 403-289-9311; *E-Mail:* huber@acs.ucalgary.ca

HUBER, RICHARD V, COMPUTER NETWORKS, OPERATING SYSTEMS. *Current Pos:* mem tech staff, 77-80, SUPVR, BELL LABS, 80- *Personal Data:* b 1948. *Educ:* Mass Inst Technol, BS, 70; State Univ NY Stony Brook, MS, 72, PhD(comput sci), 75. *Prof Exp:* Asst prof comput sci, Tex A&M Univ, 75-77. *Mem:* Asn Comput Mach; Inst Elec & Electronics Engrs; Internet Soc. *Res:* Computer software and computer networks. *Mailing Add:* AT&T PO Box 3030 Holmdel NJ 07733-3030. *E-Mail:* rvh@att.com

HUBER, ROBERT, BIOCHEMISTRY. *Current Pos:* PROF & DIR DEPT, MAX-PLANCK INST BIOCHEM, GER, 72- *Personal Data:* b Feb 20, 37; m 60, Christa Essig; c Ulrike, Martin, Robert & Julia. *Educ:* Tech Univ Munchen, dipl chem, 60, Dr rer nat, 63, habilitation, 68. *Hon Degrees:* Drhc, Cath Univ Louvain, 87, Univ Ljubljana, Slovenia, 89, Univ Vergata, Italy, 91. *Honors & Awards:* Nobel Prize in Chem, 88; E K Frey Medal, Gesellschaftfur Chirurgie, 72 & 89; Otto-Warburg Medal, Soc Biol, 77; Emil von Behring Medal, Univ Marburg, 82; Keilin Medal, Biochem Soc, London, 87; E K Frey, E Werle Gedachtnismedialle, 89; Kowe Award, Asn Clin Biochemists, UK, 90; Sir Hans Krebs Medal, Fedo Europ Biochem Soc, 92; Linus Pauling Medal, 93 & 94. *Concurrent Pos:* Appl prof, Technische Universitat Munchen, 76; ed, J Molecular Biol, mem Nat Acad Sci. *Mem:* Foreign assoc Nat Acad Sci; hon mem Japanese Biochem Soc; assoc fel Third World Acad Sci; hon mem Am Soc Biol Chemists; fel Am Acad Microbiol; corresp mem Croatian Acad Sci & Arts; Ger Soc Chem; Soc Biol Chem. *Res:* Structure and function of biological macromolecules; experimental and theoretical methods for the x-ray crystallography of proteins. *Mailing Add:* Max Planck Inst Biochem Am Klopferspitz 18A 82152 Martinsried Germany

HUBER, ROBERT JOHN, SOLID STATE CHEMICAL SENSORS, SILICON MICROMACHINING. *Current Pos:* dir microcircuit lab, Inst Biomed Eng, 71-76, res assoc prof surg, mat sci & eng & adj assoc prof physics, 76-78, PROF ELEC ENG, UNIV UTAH, 76- *Personal Data:* b Payson, Utah, July 10, 35; m 57, Virginia Goldberg; c Robert W, John L & Scott E. *Educ:* Univ Utah, BS, 56, PhD(physics), 61. *Prof Exp:* Physicist & dir, Microelectronics Res & Develop Lab, Gen Instrument Corp, 66-71. *Concurrent Pos:* Consult, Microelectronics Div, Gen Instrument Corp, 72-88, silicon integrated circuits, 88; consult, integrated circuit mfrs, 88- *Mem:* Inst Elec & Electronics Engrs; Sigma Xi. *Res:* Semiconductor integrated circuits; large scale integrated circuits, semiconductor device physics; solid state chemical sensors and silicon micromachining. *Mailing Add:* 1145 E Millbrook Way Bountiful UT 84010. *E-Mail:* huber@ee.utah.edu

HUBER, ROGER THOMAS, INSECT ECOLOGY, BIOMETEOROLOGY. *Current Pos:* assoc prof, 74-80, PROF ENTOM & PROG DIR, AGR & NATURAL RESOURCES ARIZ COOP EXTEN SERV, 81-, DEPT HEAD AGR, UNIV ARIZ, 88- *Personal Data:* b Duluth, Minn, Jan 25, 34; c 2. *Educ:* Univ Del, BA, 61, MS, 63; Purdue Univ, PhD(entom), 69. *Prof Exp:* Instr entom, Purdue Univ, 65-69, asst prof, 69-74. *Concurrent Pos:* NSF Int Travel Grant, 69; rep, Int Soc Biometeorol, 69-75; pest mgt consult, Quatar, Mex, Ecuador & Peru, 77-85. *Mem:* Entom Soc Am; Int Soc Biometeorol. *Res:* Insect population ecology; insect pheromone research and utilization of pheromones for insect pest management; computer simulation and real-time forecasting of insect population phenology; pest management systems. *Mailing Add:* Dept Agr Educ Univ Ariz 1600 E University Blvd Tucson AZ 85721-0001

HUBER, SAMUEL G(EORGE), AGRICULTURAL ENGINEERING. *Current Pos:* exten engr, 46-54, instr agr eng, 56-58, assoc prof, 58-68, PROF AGR ENG, OHIO STATE UNIV, 68-, AGR ENGR, COOP EXTEN SERV, 75- *Personal Data:* b Degraff, Ohio, Mar 5, 18; m 41; c 3. *Educ:* Ohio

State Univ, BS, 40, BAgrE, 41, MS, 58. *Prof Exp:* Agr engr, USDA, 41-42; res asst agr eng, Univ Ill, 42-43. *Concurrent Pos:* Consult, Ford Found, 64-65. *Mem:* Am Soc Agr Engrs; Am Soc Eng Educ. *Res:* Development of more efficient power systems for agricultural operations; management of farm machines. *Mailing Add:* 5815 Stoney Creek Ct Columbus OH 43255

HUBER, THOMAS LEE, PHYSIOLOGY, PHARMACOLOGY. *Current Pos:* RETIRED. *Personal Data:* b Brownstown, Ind, Feb 11, 35; m 62. *Educ:* Purdue Univ, BS, 57; Kans State Univ, MS, 58; Univ Ky, PhD(physiol, nutrit), 63. *Prof Exp:* Res assoc nutrit biochem, Univ Ill, 63-64, asst prof physiol & pharmacol, 64-66; from assoc prof to prof, Univ Ga, 75-97. *Concurrent Pos:* Mem, Conf Res Workers Animal Dis NAm. *Mem:* Am Soc Vet Physiol & Pharmacol; Soc Exp Biol & Med; World Asn Vet Physiol, Pharmacol & Biochem; Am Soc Animal Sci. *Res:* Digestive physiology of ruminants; lactic acid metabolism; renal physiology of ruminants. *Mailing Add:* 1280 McRee Gin Rd Watkinsville GA 30677

HUBER, THOMAS WAYNE, MEDICAL MICROBIOLOGY, PUBLIC HEALTH. *Current Pos:* MICROBIOLOGIST, LAB SERV, OLIN E TEAGUE VET CTR, TEMPLE, TEX, 81- *Personal Data:* b Eddy, Tex, Sept 2, 42; m 63, Doris Weise; c Mollie, Samuel & Laura. *Educ:* Univ Tex, Austin, BS, 64, PhD(microbiol), 68; Am Bd Med Microbiol, dipl & cert pub health & med lab microbiol, 73. *Prof Exp:* Fel, Nat Ctr Dis Control, Ga, 68-70; instr path, Med Sch, 70-72, asst prof, Health Sci Ctr, Univ Tex, San Antonio, 72-74; chief lab serv, Houston Health Dept, 74-81; adj asst prof microbiol & immunol, Baylor Col Med & adj asst prof med lab sci, Sch Allied Health Sci, Univ Tex, 77-80. *Concurrent Pos:* Assoc prof, Univ Tex Sch Pub Health, Houston, 74-81; asst prof path & microbiol & immunol, Baylor Col Med, 75-82; adj assoc prof, dept immunol, microbiol & path, Tex A&M Med Sch, 81-; Burroughs Wellcome vis prof, 90-91; adj prof, Dept Biomed Studies, Baylor Univ, 95- *Mem:* Am Soc Microbiol; Am Acad Microbiol; Sigma Xi. *Res:* Induction and properties of spheroplasts, protoplasts and L-forms of Staphylococcus aureus; automation in microbiology; diagnostic and clinical microbiology; cultivation of L-forms, laboratory diagnosis of venereal diseases; occurrence and mechanisms of antibiotic resistance. *Mailing Add:* 4809 Arrowhead Temple TX 76502

HUBER, W(ILSON) FREDERICK, ORGANIC CHEMISTRY, SYNTHETIC ORGANIC & NATURAL PRODUCTS CHEMISTRY. *Current Pos:* RETIRED. *Personal Data:* b Lebanon, Pa, May 6, 18; m 43, Helen V Miller; c Sharon A (Meier), Barbara J (Whitaker) & Thomas F. *Educ:* Lebanon Valley Col, BS, 40; Univ Cincinnati, MS, 42, PhD(org chem), 43. *Prof Exp:* Chemist, Monsanto Chem Co, 43-46; Am Chem Soc fel, Univ Mich, 46-47; chemist, Procter & Gamble Co, Ohio, 47-56; vpres res & develop, Nease Chem Co, Inc, 56-62; dir prod develop, Martin-Marietta Chem, 63-65, dir res, 65-66, vpres opers, 67-71, sr vpres opers, Sodyeco Div, 71-80, sr vpres technol, 81-82. *Mem:* Am Chem Soc. *Res:* Organic chemicals; fatty acids and their derivatives; organophosphorous compounds; dyestuffs. *Mailing Add:* 3738 Beresford Rd Charlotte NC 28211

HUBER, WAYNE CHARLES, URBAN HYDROLOGY, POLLUTANT TRANSPORT. *Current Pos:* PROF & HEAD CIVIL ENG, ORE STATE UNIV, 91- *Personal Data:* b Shelby, Mont, Aug 2, 41; m 68, Catherine Forster; c Lydia. *Educ:* Calif Inst Technol, BS, 63; Mass Inst Technol, MS, 65, PhD(civil eng), 69. *Honors & Awards:* Karl Hilgard Prize, Am Soc Civil Engrs, 73. *Prof Exp:* Res asst civil eng, Mass Inst Technol, 63-65 & 66-68; from asst prof to prof environ eng sci, Univ Fla, 68-91. *Concurrent Pos:* Consult. *Mem:* Am Soc Civil Engrs; Am Geophys Union; Int Asn Hydraul Res; Am Water Resources Asn. *Res:* Urban and engineering hydrology; stormwater management; nonpoint source water quality control; pollutant transport; mathematical modeling; application of hydrology and hydrodynamics to environmental problems. *Mailing Add:* Dept Civil, Construct & Environ Eng Ore State Univ Corvallis OR 97331-2302. *Fax:* 541-737-3052; *E-Mail:* huberw@ccmail.orst.edu

HUBER, WILLIAM GEORGE, COMPARATIVE PHARMACOLOGY. *Current Pos:* EMER PROF, VA TECH. *Personal Data:* b Hinsdale, Ill, Jan 10, 24; m 48, Joyce Flack; c 2. *Educ:* Univ Ill, BS, 50, DVM, 52, MS, 57, PhD, 60. *Prof Exp:* Guest lectr, Univ Ill, 52-57; res vet, Chas Pfizer & Co, Ind, 58-60; from asst prof to prof pharmacol, Col Vet Med, Univ Ill, Urbana, 60-73, asst dean col, 67-70; dir res, Hoffmann-La Roche Inc, 73-76; prof & assoc dean, Col Vet Med, Wash State Univ. *Concurrent Pos:* Pvt pract, Ill, 52-57; consult, Chas Pfizer & Co, 57, Food & Drug Admin, 65-73 & Hoffmann-La Roche Inc, 76-; adj prof, Univ Ill, Urbana, 73-76. *Mem:* Am Soc Vet Physiol & Pharmacol; Am Vet Med Asn; Am Soc Pharmacol & Exp Therapeut; Soc Toxicol. *Res:* Comparative pharmacology; antibiotics; clinical pharmacology; porcine gastric ulcers. *Mailing Add:* 14668 Yosemite Dr Sun City West AZ 85375-5654

HUBER, WILLIAM RICHARD, III, ELECTRICAL ENGINEERING, INTEGRATED CIRCUIT DESIGN. *Current Pos:* PRES, ELECTRONICS CONSULT ENGRS, 94- *Personal Data:* b Indiana, Pa, Dec 23, 41; m 64; c 2. *Educ:* Univ Pittsburgh, BS, 62, DSc(elec eng), 69; Ohio State Univ, MS, 63. *Prof Exp:* Mem tech staff, Bell Tel Labs, Inc, 62-70, supvr, 70-81; mgr, Gen Elec Co, 82-89; dir, Harris Corp, 89-94. *Concurrent Pos:* Patent litigation consult. *Mem:* Sr mem Inst Elec & Electronics Engrs. *Res:* Semicustom integrated circuits; semiconductor memories; linear integrated circuits; computer-aided circuit design; integrated circuit processing; noise. *Mailing Add:* Electronics Consult Engrs PO Box 362453 Melbourne FL 32936. *E-Mail:* w.huber@ieee.org

HUBER, WOLFGANG KARL, PHARMACOLOGY. *Current Pos:* clin asst psychiat, Univ Okla, 61-63, clin consult, 63-64, instr 63-71, asst prof res med, 68-76, clin asst prof, 71-80, clin asst prof med, 76-83, CLIN ASSOC PROF, PSYCHIAT & BEHAV SCI, COL MED, UNIV OKLA, 80- *Personal Data:* b Freiburg, Ger, June 10, 27; US citizen; m 58; c 1. *Educ:* Univ Frankfurt, MD, 57. *Prof Exp:* Med asst surg, Sch Med, Univ Frankfurt, 57; chief psychiat serv, Cent State Griffin Mem Hosp, Norman, Okla, 61-62, chief, Neuropsychiat Dept, 62-66, clin dir, 66-67; dir psychiat, Cent Okla Ment Health Ctr, 67-78. *Concurrent Pos:* Instr, Cent State Griffin Mem Hosp, 61-87; clin consult, Okla State Penitentiary Hosp, 65-66; med consult, Consulate Fed Repub Ger, 69-71; clin consult neuro-psychiatry, 2792nd US Air Force Hosp, Okla, 65-78; prog dir, Hosp Improv Proj, Norman, 65-67; tech assistance specialist, Off Econ Opportunity, 68-78; pvt pract, 74-85. *Mem:* AMA; fel Am Psychiat Asn; World Psychiat Asn. *Res:* Photometric determination of blood-alcohol; neuro-psycho-pharmacology in acute and chronic schizophrenia; chronic ulcerative colitis; medical ecology and cross-cultural studies; social psychiatry. *Mailing Add:* HK Biomedical Inc 1445 Lincoln Way San Francisco CA 94122

HUBERMAN, BERNARDO ABEL, NONLINEAR DYNAMICS, MULTIAGENT SYSTEMS & DISTRIBUTED COMPUTATION. *Current Pos:* mem res staff, 71-80, sr mem res staff physics, 80-84, RES FEL, XEROX PALO ALTO RES CTR, 85- *Personal Data:* b Buenos Aires, Arg, Nov 7, 43; US citizen; m 94; c 2. *Educ:* Univ Buenos Aires, Licenciado, 66; Univ Pa, PhD(physics), 70. *Honors & Awards:* Cecoia Prize, 90. *Concurrent Pos:* Lectr, Stanford Univ, 77-80 & consult prof, 80-; vis prof, Univ Paris, France, 81 & Univ Copenhagen, Denmark, 93. *Mem:* Fel Japan Soc Prom Sci; fel Am Phys Soc. *Res:* Dynamics of distributed processes computation; multiagent systems. *Mailing Add:* Xerox Palo Alto Res Ctr 3333 Coyote Hill Rd Palo Alto CA 94304. *Fax:* 650-812-4388; *E-Mail:* huberman@parc.xerox.com

HUBERMAN, ELIEZER, CARCINOGENESIS, CELL DIFFERENTIATION. *Current Pos:* prof molecular genetics & cell biol, 82-93, PROF RADIATION & CELLULAR ONCOL, UNIV CHICAGO, 84- *Personal Data:* b Lukow, Poland, Feb 8, 39; US citizen; m 67, Lily Ginzburg; c Ilan & Ron. *Educ:* Tel-Aviv Univ, MSc, 64; Weizmann Inst Sci, PhD(genetics), 69. *Prof Exp:* Fel, McArdle Lab, Univ Wis, 69-71; sr scientist & assoc prof, Dept Genetics, Weizmann Inst Sci, 71-77; sr scientist & group leader, Biol Div, Oak Ridge Nat Lab, 76-81; dir & group leader, Biol & Med Res Div, Argonne Nat Lab, 81-93. *Concurrent Pos:* Vis assoc, Nat Cancer Inst, 68, vis scientist, 71, mem, Gene-Toxicol Comt, 79-81; chmn, Gene-Toxicol Comt, Environ Protection Agency, 79-81; mem, Comt Chem Environ Mutagens, Nat Acad Sci, 79-83; assoc ed, Cancer Res, 81-; mem, Health Sci Rev Comt, Nat Inst Environ Health Sci, 83-; fel Univ Tokyo, 86. *Mem:* Am Asn Cancer Res; Radio/Res Soc. *Res:* Mode of action of chemicals that initiate or promote tumor formation; analysis of chemically induced changes in gene expression (mutagenesis and differentiation) in cultured mammalian cells. *Mailing Add:* 424 Sunset Ave La Grange IL 60525

HUBERMAN, JOEL ANTHONY, DNA REPLICATION & REPAIR, CHROMATIN STRUCTURE. *Current Pos:* RES PROF CELLULAR & MOLECULAR BIOL, ROSWELL PARK CANCER INST, 75- *Personal Data:* b Washington, DC, Feb 13, 41; m 63, Anne Elberfeld; c Julie A & Amy L. *Educ:* Harvard Univ, BA, 63; Calif Inst Technol, PhD(biochem), 68. *Honors & Awards:* Thomas B Tomasi Hope Award; S P Ray-Choudhury Mem Lectureship. *Prof Exp:* From asst prof to assoc prof biol, Mass Inst Technol, 70-75. *Concurrent Pos:* Ed, Chromosoma, 84- *Mem:* Am Soc Cell Biol; Am Soc Microbiol; fel AAAS; Genetics Soc Am; Am Soc Biochem & Molecular Biol. *Res:* Identification and characterization of eukaryotic DNA replication origins; identification and characterization of proteins involved in initiation of DNA replication; effects of DNA damage on DNA replication. *Mailing Add:* Molecular & Cellular Biol Dept Roswell Park Cancer Inst Buffalo NY 14263. *Fax:* 716-845-8126; *E-Mail:* huberman@acsu.buffalo.edu

HUBERMAN, MARSHALL NORMAN, ENGINEERING PHYSICS, ENERGY CONVERSION. *Current Pos:* RETIRED. *Personal Data:* b Brooklyn, NY, Jan 27, 32; m 67; c 2. *Educ:* Union Univ, NY, BS, 53; Univ Chicago, MS, 57, PhD(physics), 62. *Prof Exp:* Physicist, Atomics Int Div, NAm Aviation, Inc, 58; res asst nuclear physics, Enrico Fermi Inst Nuclear Studies, Univ Chicago, 59-62; sr physicist, Atomics Int Div, NAm Aviation, Inc, 62-64, res specialist energy conversion, 65-66; mem tech staff, TRW, 66-68, head, Colloid Thruster Tech Sect, 68-74, Colloid & Ion Propulsion Sect, 74-77, sr scientist, Space & Technol Group, 77-88, asst prog mgr, 88-93; chief systs engr, ETA Technol Corp, 93-95. *Mem:* AAAS; Am Phys Soc; assoc fel Am Inst Aeronaut & Astronaut. *Res:* Low energy nuclear physics; physical electronics; work function variations on cathode surfaces; photovoltaic cells for energy conversion; electrical propulsion. *Mailing Add:* 3129 Haddington Dr Los Angeles CA 90064. *Fax:* 310-536-0862

HUBERT, HELEN BETTY, HEART DISEASE, ARTHRITIC DISEASES. *Current Pos:* SR RES SCIENTIST, STANFORD UNIV SCH MED, 88- *Personal Data:* b New York, NY, Jan 22, 50; div; c Joshua D. *Educ:* Barnard Col, BA, 70; Yale Univ, MPH, 73, MA, 76, PhD(epidemiol), 78. *Prof Exp:* Assoc res, Sch Med, Yale Univ, 77-78; epidemiologist, Div Heart & Vascular Dis, Nat Heart, Lung & Blood Inst, 78-84; dir res, Gen Health Underwriting Inc, 84-87. *Concurrent Pos:* Mem coun epidemiol, Am Heart Asn; consult, Environ Health Strategies. *Mem:* Sigma Xi; Soc Epidemiol Res; fel Am Heart Asn; Am Col Epidemiol; Arthritis Health Prof Asn; Am Pub Health Asn. *Res:* Understanding the relationship of health risks and behaviors to health care costs and utilization of services in population groups; design, conduct, and analysis of studies to elucidate the etiology of coronary heart disease and other cardiovascular diseases in human populations; design, conduct and analysis of studies to elucidate the etiology and prognosis of arthritic diseases and musculo skeletal disabilities. *Mailing Add:* 1043 Oakland Ave Menlo Park CA 94025. *Fax:* 650-725-6951

HUBERT, JAY MARVIN, CHEMICAL PHYSICS. *Current Pos:* Res physicist, Chevron Res Co, 70-75, sr res physicist, 75-80, sr res assoc, Analytical Div, 80-82, mgr, Tech Info Ctr, 82-84, team leader, Molecular Identifications, 85-91, MGR, ANALYTICAL SCI, CHEVRON RES CO, 91- *Personal Data:* b Denver, Colo, Apr 11, 44; m 68, Mary Weed; c 3. *Educ:* Reed Col, BA, 66; Tex A&M Univ, MS, 68, PhD(physics), 70. *Concurrent Pos:* Comptrollers Dept, Chevron Corp, 84-85. *Mem:* AAAS; Am Phys Soc. *Res:* Low temperatures; liquids; superfluid helium; thermal analysis; physical properties of microporous catalysts; auger electron spectroscopy. *Mailing Add:* Chevron Res Co Anal Unit 100 Chevron Way Richmond CA 94802-0627. Fax: 510-242-1792; E-Mail: jmhu@chevron.com

HUBERT, JOHN FREDERICK, GEOLOGY. *Current Pos:* PROF GEOL, UNIV MASS, AMHERST, 70- *Personal Data:* b Quincy, Mass, Nov 28, 30; m 55, Mary Alice Gorman; c John F Jr, Nancy B & Amy S. *Educ:* Harvard Univ, AB, 52; Univ Colo, MS, 54; Pa State Univ, PhD(mineral, petrol), 58. *Prof Exp:* From asst prof to prof geol, Univ Mo, 58-70. *Concurrent Pos:* Pres, eastern sect, Soc Econ Paleont & Mineral, 84-85; assoc ed Sedimentary Geol; vis prof, Desert Res Inst, Las Vegas, Nev, 84 & Utah Geol & Mineral Surv, Salt Lake City, Utah, 91. *Mem:* Fel Geol Soc Am; Soc Econ Paleont & Mineral; Am Asn Petrol Geol; Int Asn Sedimentol. *Res:* Sedimentology; sedimentary petrology; application of statistics to sedimentology. *Mailing Add:* Dept Geosci Univ Mass Amherst MA 01003. Fax: 413-545-1200; E-Mail: jhubert@geo.umass.edu

HUBERT, WAYNE ARTHUR, FISH-HABITAT RELATIONS, FISHERIES ASSESSMENT. *Current Pos:* PROF & ASST LEADER, WYO COOP FISH & WILDLIFE RES UNIT, UNIV WYO, 82- *Personal Data:* b Kankakee, Ill, Aug 20, 47; m 89; c Phillip, David & Kimberly. *Educ:* Ill State Univ, BS, 69; Southern Ill Univ, MS, 72; Va Polytech Inst & State Univ, PhD(fish & wildlife), 79. *Prof Exp:* Aquatic biologist, Tenn Valley Authority, 72-79; asst prof & asst leader, Iowa Coop Fishery Res Unit, Dept Animal Ecol, Iowa State Univ, 79-82. *Mem:* Am Fisheries Soc; Ecol Soc Am; NAm Benthological Soc; NAm Lake Mgt Soc; Sigma Xi. *Res:* Fish ecology and fisheries management issues; fish-habitat relations; trout stream ecology; fisheries assessment; community dynamics. *Mailing Add:* 1063 Colina Dr Laramie WY 82070-5014

HUBERTY, CARL J, APPLIED STATISTICS, EDUCATIONAL EVALUATION. *Current Pos:* from asst prof to assoc prof, 69-79, PROF EDUC, UNIV GA, 79-, DEPT HEAD, 92- *Personal Data:* b Lena, Wis, Nov 14, 34; m 66, Sandra Van Vonderen; c Greg, Brian, Jeff & Kurt. *Educ:* Wis State Univ, BS, 56; Univ Wis, MS, 58; Univ Iowa, PhD(educ statist), 69. *Prof Exp:* Teacher math, Seymour High Sch, Wis, 56-57, Brown Deer High Sch, 58-59 & Oconto Falls High Sch, 59-61; teacher math, US Dept Army Schs, Orleans, France, 61-64; asst prof, Wis State Univ, 65-66. *Concurrent Pos:* Consult projs, Bur Educ Handicapped. *Mem:* Am Statist Asn; Am Educ Res Asn; Soc Multivariate Exp Psychol. *Res:* Applications of multivariate analysis; special education evaluation; research in applied statistical methods; comparisons of statistical methods, techniques, indices; translation of theoretical developments for application; reviews of proposed methods; mostly in multivariate methods; educational evaluation methods. *Mailing Add:* Dept Educ Psychol Aderhold Hall Univ Ga Athens GA 30602-7143. Fax: 706-542-4240; E-Mail: chuberty@uga.cc.uga.edu

HUBIN, WILBERT N, AERONAUTICAL & ASTRONAUTICAL ENGINEERING. *Current Pos:* From asst prof to assoc prof, 68-83, PROF PHYSICS, KENT STATE UNIV, 83- *Personal Data:* b Crosby, Minn, Apr 28, 38. *Educ:* Wheaton Col, Ill, BS, 60; Univ Ill, Urbana, MS, 62, PhD(physics), 69. *Mem:* Am Phys Soc; Am Inst Aeronaut & Astronaut; Sigma Xi. *Res:* Dynamics of aircraft flight; digital electronic instrumentation. *Mailing Add:* Dept Physics Kent State Univ Kent OH 44242. Fax: 330-672-2959

HUBISZ, JOHN LAWRENCE, JR, ATOMIC & MOLECULAR PHYSICS. *Current Pos:* from instr to prof, 71-, EMER PROF PHYSICS, COL MAINLAND. *Personal Data:* b Salem, Mass, June 6, 38; m 74; c 4. *Educ:* St Francis Xavier Univ, dipl eng, 58, BSc Hons, 59; Univ Tenn, MSc, 65, PhD(physics & space sci), 68; St Thomas Univ, BTh, 75. *Prof Exp:* Lectr physics, St Francis Xavier Univ, 59-68, asst prof, 68-71. *Concurrent Pos:* Lectr, Univ Tenn, 63-65 & York Univ, 66-68; Shell merit fel, Stanford Univ, 69; vis prof physics, NC State Univ, 93- *Mem:* Am Asn Physics Teachers; Am Phys Soc; Nat Coun Teachers Math; Sigma Xi. *Res:* Teaching of mathematics and physics; theoretical studies of diatomic molecules, especially those that are aeronomically and astronomically important. *Mailing Add:* 1604 S Salem St Apex NC 27502

HUBKA, WILLIAM FRANK, ENGINEERING SCIENCE. *Current Pos:* SR STAFF SCIENTIST, SPACE SYST DIV, LOCKHEED CORP, 90- *Personal Data:* b Denver, Colo, June 18, 39; m 61; c 2. *Educ:* Univ Denver, BS, 62, MS, 65, PhD(mech eng), 72. *Prof Exp:* Engr, Martin Co, Colo, 62-64; res scientist, Kaman Sci Corp, Colo, 64-65; res engr, Univ Denver, 65-67; res scientist, Kaman Sci Corp, 67-72; div mgr, Gen Res Corp, Santa Barbara, 72-77; group opers mgr, Sci Applns, Inc, 74-89. *Mem:* Am Soc Mech Engrs; Sigma Xi; NY Acad Sci. *Res:* Defense systems; energy systems; program management. *Mailing Add:* PO Box 4656 Mountain View CA 94040-0656

HUBLER, GRAHAM KELDER, JR, APPLIED PHYSICS. *Current Pos:* Nat Res Coun assoc, 72-74, res scientist physics, 74-93, HEAD, SURFACE MODIFICATION BR, NAVAL RES LAB, 93- *Personal Data:* b Suffern, NY, Feb 29, 44; m 88, Dorothy; c Sena. *Educ:* Union Col, BS, 66; Rutgers Univ, PhD(physics), 72. *Mem:* Am Phys Soc; Mat Res Soc; Sigma Xi; Bohmische Phys Soc. *Res:* Study of the changes induced in the surfaces of metals and semiconductors by the implantation of ions, with regard to such altered surface properties as corrosion, wear, and optical properties. *Mailing Add:* Code 6670 Naval Res Labs Washington DC 20375

HUBNER, KARL FRANZ, NUCLEAR MEDICINE, RADIATION BIOLOGY. *Current Pos:* DIR RADIOL RES, UNIV TENN MED CTR, KNOXVILLE, 84-, DIR NUCLEAR MED, 86- *Personal Data:* b Striegau, Ger, Jan 20, 34; US citizen; m 60; c 2. *Educ:* Univ Heidelberg, MD, 59. *Prof Exp:* Resident clin invest, Med Div, Oak Ridge Assoc Univs, Tenn, 62-64, res assoc exp immunol, 67-70, sr clin staff mem, 71-73, dir outpatient nuclear med, Med & Health Sci Div, 75-84. *Concurrent Pos:* Mem, clin staff, Med & Health Sci Div, Oak Ridge Assoc Univ, Tenn, 71-82, chief clinician, 79-82, asst chmn & dir, Clin Nuclear Med Br, 82-84; consult, Oak Ridge Hosp of Methodist Church, 77-; courtesy staff, internal med, E Tenn Baptist Hosp, Knoxvillve, 82-84; dir, Multidisciplinary Breast Ctr, Univ Tenn, Med Ctr, Knoxville, 85- *Mem:* AMA; Soc Nuclear Med; Am Occup Med Asn; Int Asn Radiopharmacol; Radiol Soc NAm; Am Roentgen Ray Soc. *Res:* Radiopharmaceuticals; emission computerized tomography; radiobiology; treatment of radiation injury; diagnosis of neoplastic diseases. *Mailing Add:* Univ Tenn Med Ctr 1924 Alcoa Hsy Knoxville TN 37920-1511

HUBRED, GALE L, ENVIRONMENTAL ENGINEERING. *Current Pos:* CHEVRON PETROL TECH CO, 90- *Personal Data:* b Alexandria, Minn, Jan 4, 39; div; c 2. *Educ:* Univ Minn, BS, 62; Univ Hawaii, MS, 70; Univ Calif, Berkeley, PhD(metall), 73. *Prof Exp:* Supt, Dow Chem Co, 62-68; sr res engr, Kennecott Copper, 73-79 & Occidental Petrol, 79; sr scientist, Chevron Res Co, 79-90. *Concurrent Pos:* Chmn ocean technol, Am Inst Chem Engrs, 75-; vpres, Marine Technol Soc, 82- *Mem:* Fel Marine Technol Soc; Am Inst Chem Engrs; Am Inst Mining, Metall & Petrol Engrs; Water Pollution Control Fed. *Res:* Hydrometallurgical processes; manganese nodules; solvent extraction. *Mailing Add:* Chevron Petrol Tech Co 1300 Beach Blvd La Habra CA 90633

HUBSCHMAN, JERRY HENRY, INVERTEBRATE ZOOLOGY. *Current Pos:* asst prof biol, Wright State Univ, 64-65, coordr, 65-67, assoc prof, 67-70, assoc provost, 74-78, PROF BIOL, WRIGHT STATE UNIV, 70- *Personal Data:* b Great Neck, NY, Feb 4, 29; m 53; c 3. *Educ:* Ohio State Univ, BS, 59, PhD(zool), 62. *Prof Exp:* Res biologist, Robert A Taft Sanit Eng Ctr, USPHS, 62-64. *Concurrent Pos:* Secy bd trustees, Wright State Univ, 75-78. *Mem:* Am Soc Parasitol; Societas Internationalis Limnologiae. *Res:* Growth and development of Crustacea; aquatic life cycles; parasitology; planktonic crustacea, aquatic benthos. *Mailing Add:* 1544 Corry St Yellow Springs OH 45387

HUCHITAL, DANIEL H, INORGANIC CHEMISTRY. *Current Pos:* from asst prof to assoc prof, 66-79, PROF CHEM, SETON HALL UNIV, 80- *Personal Data:* b Brooklyn, NY, July 19, 40; m 60, Helene Hechtman; c Jordana & Andrew. *Educ:* City Col New York, BSc, 61; Stanford Univ, PhD(chem), 65. *Prof Exp:* Res fel chem, State Univ NY Buffalo, 65-66; res assoc, Brookhaven Nat Lab, 66. *Concurrent Pos:* Vis prof, Tex A&M Univ, 72-73, Univ SCalif, 80-81, Emory Univ, 88-89. *Mem:* Am Chem Soc. *Res:* Coordination chemistry; mechanisms of electron-transfer reactions involving transition metal ion complexes; interaction of metal complexes with DNA. *Mailing Add:* Dept Chem Seton Hall Univ South Orange NJ 07079-2689

HUCHRA, JOHN P, ASTROPHYSICS. *Current Pos:* Fel, Ctr Astrophys, 76-78, astronr, 78-89, SR ASTRONR, SMITHSONIAN ASTROPHYS OBSERV, 89-; PROF ASTRON, HARVARD UNIV, 84-; ASSOC DIR, HARVARD-SMITHSONIAN CTR ASTROPHYS, 89- *Personal Data:* b Jersey City, NJ, Dec 23, 48; m 92, Rebecca Henderson; c Harry Matthew. *Educ:* Mass Inst Technol, BS, 70; Calif Inst Technol, PhD(astron), 76. *Honors & Awards:* Newcomb-Cleveland Award, AAAS, 89; Aaronson Prize, Nat Acad Sci, 91. *Concurrent Pos:* Mem, Am Astron Soc Publ Bd, 85-89, chmn, 86-88; chmn, Galaxies Comt, NASA, 86, Extragalactic Astron Comt, 86, Astron Data Base Adv Comt, 88-92; mem, Nat New Technol Telescope Site Rev Comt, 86-87; mem, Space Telescope Inst Coun, 87-95; mem, Subcomt Info Technol, Am Inst Physics, 88-90, Subcomt J, 90-92, chmn, Subcomt Transl J, 93-; chmn, Working Group Galaxy Radial Velocities, 88-; mem, Sci & Technol Res Ctr Site Rev Panel, NSF, 88, Gemini 8-meter Independent Rev Comt, 93; vis prof, Calif Tech Inst, 91, Univ Calif, Santa Cruz, 93; mem, Gemini Sci Adv Comt, 93-94; chmn, Gemini Directorship Search Comt, 93-94; mem, Watson Prize Comt, Nat Acad Sci, 93. *Mem:* Nat Acad Sci; Sigma Xi; Am Inst Physics; Int Astron Union; fel Am Phys Soc; Royal Astron Soc; fel AAAS; Am Astron Soc; fel Am Acad Arts & Sci; Am Asn Variable Star Observers. *Res:* Extragalactic observational astronomy; galaxies and cosmology; gravitational lenses; quasars; globular starclusters; large scale distribution of matter in space; study of the dynamics of groups, clusters and superclusters of galaxies including the local supercluster; author of over 240 professional publications. *Mailing Add:* Harvard-Smithsonian Ctr Astrophys 60 Garden St Cambridge MA 02138. E-Mail: huchra@cfa.harvard.edu

HUCK, MORRIS GLEN, PLANT SCIENCE, SYSTEM ANALYSIS. *Current Pos:* DEPT AGRON, UNIV ILL, URBANA, 85- *Personal Data:* b Centralia, Ill, Mar 7, 37; m 66, Claire Hammer; c Brian. *Educ:* Univ Ill, Urbana, BS, 58, MS, 60; Mich State Univ, PhD(soil sci), 67. *Prof Exp:* Res soil scientist, Agr Res Serv, USDA & Auburn Univ, 67-85. *Mem:* AAAS; Am Soc Agron; Soil Sci Soc Am; Sigma Xi. *Res:* Root metabolism; dynamic aspects of interactions between roots and shoots and between plant roots and their soil environment; computer simulation and operations analysis of plant growth processes; crop simulation and root system physiology. *Mailing Add:* US Dept Agr S-216 Turner Hall 1102 S Goodwin Ave Urbana IL 61801. Fax: 217-333-5251

HUCKA, VLADIMIR JOSEPH, MINING ENGINEERING. *Current Pos:* PROF MINING, UNIV UTAH, SALT LAKE CITY, 78- *Personal Data:* b Ostrava, Czech, Apr 22, 25; m 61; c 1. *Educ:* Tech Univ Mines, MS, 62; Ostrava, Czech, PhD(mining), 66. *Prof Exp:* Engr, Inst Planning New Mines, Ostrava, 52-56; engr coal mine, 57-62; head rock mech, Sci Res Coal Inst, 63-68; sci officer, Coal Owner's Inst, Essen, 68; prof mining eng, Laval Univ, Que, 68-78. *Concurrent Pos:* Mining consult, Gaspe Copper Mines, Noranda Group, 74-77. *Mem:* Can Inst Mining & Metall; Soc Mining Engrs. *Res:* Longwall mining; methane drainage; robotics in mining; mine haulage systems. *Mailing Add:* 2282 E 7800 St Salt Lake City UT 84121

HUCKABA, CHARLES EDWIN, TECHNICAL MANAGEMENT, BIOENGINEERING. *Current Pos:* RETIRED. *Personal Data:* b Huntingdon, Tenn, Oct 20, 22; m 46; c 2. *Educ:* Vanderbilt Univ, BE, 44; Mass Inst Technol, MS, 47; Univ Cincinnati, PhD(chem eng). 53. *Honors & Awards:* Stephen L Tyler Award, Am Inst Chem Engrs, 72. *Prof Exp:* Asst chem eng, Mass Inst Technol, 44-45, mem res staff, USN Proj, 45-47; instr, Univ Cincinnati, 47-52; assoc prof, Lamar State Col, 53-55 & Univ Fla, 55-61; mem staff, E I du Pont de Nemours & Co, 61-62; assoc prof chem eng, Univ Fla, 62-63; prof & chmn dept, Drexel Univ, 63-67; vis prof, Columbia Univ, 67-68, sr res assoc, 68-69, mem-at-large, Fac Eng & Appl Sci & prof rehab med, Col Physicians & Surgeons, 69-74; sect head eng chem & energetics, NSF, 74-76; dir eng prog develop, Cooper Union, 76-80; pres, Charles Huckaba Assocs, 80-91. *Concurrent Pos:* Consult, Bethlehem Steel Co, 52-56, Thermal Res & Eng Corp, 65-67 & Foxboro Co, 70-71; adj prof clin eng, Med Sch, George Washington Univ, 74-78. *Mem:* Hon life mem Am Soc Eng Educ; fel Am Inst Chem Engrs; fel Am Inst Chemists; Sigma Xi. *Res:* Analysis of biochemical, genetic and chemical engineering systems; social implications of technology and public policy; impact of government regulatory activities upon industrial productivity; organization and financing of high-tech entrepreneurial companies. *Mailing Add:* 317 34th Ave N Unit 407 St Petersburg FL 33704 Spain

HUCKABA, JAMES ALBERT, ALGEBRA. *Current Pos:* From asst prof to assoc prof, 67-79, PROF MATH, UNIV MO-COLUMBIA, 79- *Personal Data:* b Charleston, Ill, Feb 6, 36; m 55; c 3. *Educ:* Univ Ill, BS, 60; Univ Iowa, MA, 64, PhD(math), 67. *Concurrent Pos:* NSF grant, 69-71. *Mem:* Am Math Soc. *Res:* Commutative ring theory; ideal theory. *Mailing Add:* Dept Math Univ Mo Columbia MO 65211-0001

HUCKABAY, HOUSTON KELLER, CHEMICAL ENGINEERING. *Current Pos:* assoc prof, 64-69, asst to dean, Col Eng, 67-71, dir eng grad studies, 67-74, PROF CHEM ENG, LA TECH UNIV, 69-, HEAD CHEM ENG, 86- *Personal Data:* b Shreveport, La, July 21, 32; m 54, 76; c 5. *Educ:* La Polytech Inst, BSChE, 54; La State Univ, Baton Rouge, MSChE, 59, PhD(chem eng), 60. *Prof Exp:* Res chem engr, Crossett Co, 60-62; sr res engr, Forest Prod Div, Olin Mathieson Chem Corp, 62-63, res supvr paper converting, 63-64. *Concurrent Pos:* Consult, La Dept Revenue & Legal Firms; expert witness fires, explosions & chemically related accidents. *Mem:* Am Inst Chem Engrs; Am Chem Soc; Am Soc Eng Educ; Nat Fire Protection Asn; Nat Soc Prof Engrs. *Res:* Prediction of flame ignition characteristics; fire and chemical process safety; alternative energy sources; biotechnology; natural polymers. *Mailing Add:* 1405 Saint John Ave Ruston LA 71272

HUCKABAY, JOHN PORTER, BOTANY, BIOSYSTEMATICS. *Current Pos:* from asst prof to assoc prof bot & cytol, 66-72, head dept biol, 72-77, PROF BIOL, SOUTHEAST MO STATE COL, 72- *Personal Data:* b Paris, Tex, Sept 24, 28; m 51; c 2. *Educ:* Southeastern State Col, BSEd, 55; Okla State Univ, MS, 60, PhD, 67. *Prof Exp:* Instr bot & biol, Cameron State Col, 58-62; instr biol, Okla State Univ, 64-66. *Mem:* AAAS; Int Asn Plant Taxon. *Res:* Biosystematics of sorghum. *Mailing Add:* 1910 Sherwood Dr Cape Girardeau MO 63701

HUCKABY, DALE ALAN, PHYSICAL CHEMISTRY. *Current Pos:* From asst prof to assoc prof, 69-81, chmn, 87-89, PROF CHEM, TEX CHRISTIAN UNIV, 81- *Personal Data:* b Vicksburg, Miss, Sept 27, 44; m 70, Lucille; c David & Daniel. *Educ:* La State Univ, Baton Rouge, BS, 66; Rice Univ, PhD(phys chem), 69. *Concurrent Pos:* NSF grants, 78, 83 & 84-85, Robert A Welch grant, 71- *Mem:* Am Chem Soc; Sigma Xi. *Res:* Statistical mechanical calculations on model systems. *Mailing Add:* Dept Chem Tex Christian Univ Ft Worth TX 76129. *Fax:* 817-921-7110

HUCKABY, DAVID GEORGE, MAMMALOGY. *Current Pos:* Asst prof, 73-78, ASSOC PROF BIOL, CALIF STATE UNIV, LONG BEACH, 78- *Personal Data:* b Ponca City, Okla, Dec 8, 42; m 67; c 2. *Educ:* La State Univ, BS, 63, MS, 67; Univ Mich, PhD(zool), 73. *Mem:* Am Soc Mammalogists; Am Inst Biol Sci; Soc Systematic Biologists; Soc Study Mammalian Evolution; Sigma Xi. *Res:* Taxonomy of muroid rodents; comparative anatomy of the reproductive system of rodents. *Mailing Add:* Dept Biol Sci Calif State Univ Long Beach CA 90840-3702

HUCKE, DOROTHY MARIE, BIOSTATISTICS. *Current Pos:* RETIRED. *Personal Data:* b Brooklyn, NY, Jan 14, 27. *Educ:* St Joseph's Col Women, BA, 49; Columbia Univ, MS, 58; NY Univ, MS, 63. *Prof Exp:* Lab technician chem, Pfizer Inc, 49-50, lab supvr, Systs Planning & Tech Info, 50-52, statistician, 52-59, supvr statist servs, 60-67, mgr spec serv, 67-71, admin asst qual control mgt, 71-72, mgr systs & planning, 72-81, assoc dir, Systs Planning & Tech Info, 81-87. *Res:* Quality control management; data processing; statistics; development of techniques that will focus on quality problems, increase efficiency, reduce cost and improve quality; computer sciences, general. *Mailing Add:* 8244 63rd Ave Flushing NY 11379-1974

HUCKE, EDWARD E, METALLURGY, CARBONS. *Current Pos:* RETIRED. *Personal Data:* b Kansas City, Mo, Sept 1, 30; div; c 4. *Educ:* Mass Inst Technol, SB, 51, SM, 52, ScD(metall), 54. *Honors & Awards:* Lilliequist Award, Steel Founders Soc Am, 56; Bradley Stoughton Award, Am Soc Metals, 63. *Prof Exp:* Res dir, LFM Mfg Co, Kans, 53-55; from asst prof to emer prof metall eng, Univ Mich, Ann Arbor, 55-90. *Concurrent Pos:* Vis prof, Max Planck Inst Metal Res, Stuttgart, WGer, 78. *Mem:* Fel Am Soc Metals; fel Am Inst Chem; Electrochem Soc; Am Inst Mining, Metall & Petrol Engrs; Brit Inst Metals. *Res:* Metallurgical thermodynamics; cemented carbides; carbons. *Mailing Add:* 2726 Hidden Valley Rd La Jolla CA 92037

HUCKER, HOWARD B(ENJAMIN), DRUG METABOLISM. *Current Pos:* RETIRED. *Personal Data:* b St Louis, Mo, Mar 5, 26; m 58; c 4. *Educ:* St Louis Univ, BS, 48; Univ Mo, PhD(org chem), 53; Med Col Va, ScD(pharmacol), 57. *Prof Exp:* Anal chemist, Shell Oil Co, 48-49; asst chem, Univ Mo, 49-53; Am Tobacco Co fel, Med Col Va, 53-56; res chemist, Nat Heart Inst, 56-60; sr res fel, Merck Inst Therapeut Res, 60-70, dir human drug metab, 70-76, sr investr, 76-84, sr scientist, 84-90. *Concurrent Pos:* Consult, Am Tobacco Co, 53-56; assoc ed, Drug Metab Disposition, 78-90. *Mem:* Sigma Xi; Am Chem Soc; Am Soc Pharmacol & Exp Therapeut. *Res:* Biochemical pharmacology; enzymology; analytical methods. *Mailing Add:* 915 Jenifer Rd Horsham PA 19044-1021

HUCKINS, HAROLD AARON, CHEMICAL PROCESSING. *Current Pos:* PRES, PRINCETON ADVAN TECH INC, 85- *Personal Data:* b Cambridge, Mass, Nov 28, 24; m 52, Elizabeth L Kearns; c Richard W, Robert M, Christopher N, Patricia A & Leslie K. *Educ:* Northeastern Univ, BSChemE, 45; Lowell Inst, ASME, 46. *Honors & Awards:* Chem Eng Pract Award, Am Inst Chem Engrs, 94. *Prof Exp:* Chem process engr & asst proj mgr, Monsanto Chem Co, 45-49; sr process engr & group leader, Chem Div, Koppers Co, 49-53; mgr pilot plants & proj mgr, Sci Design Co Inc, 53-66; vpres tech opers, Oxirane Chem Co, 66-73; vpres tech assessment, Halcon SD Group, 73-85. *Concurrent Pos:* Dir, Mat Tech Inst, St Louis, 76-85, Asn Consult Chemists & Chem Engrs, New York, 90-93; dir, Mat Eng & Sci Div, Am Inst Chem Engrs, 92-93. *Mem:* Am Soc Mat; Am Chem Soc; Am Ceramic Soc; Nat Asn Corrosion Engrs; fel Am Inst Chem Engrs. *Res:* Contributed articles to professional journals; granted patents for chemical process technology. *Mailing Add:* Princeton Advan Tech Inc 4 Bertram Pl Hilton Head Island SC 29928-3936

HUDAK, MICHAEL J, PATTERN CLASSIFICATION, ARTIFICIAL NEURAL SYSTEMS. *Current Pos:* INDEPENDENT CONSULT, 91- *Personal Data:* b Johnson City, NY, Dec 4, 52. *Educ:* State Univ NY, Binghamton, BA, 75, PhD(comput sci), 86; Northwestern Univ, MS, 77. *Prof Exp:* Instr, State Univ NY, Binghamton, 81-84; consult comput res, Digital Equip Corp, 85; res scientist, Siemens Corp Res, 86-91. *Res:* Design and empirically study pattern classifiers inspired by neural systems. *Mailing Add:* 38 Oliver St Binghamton NY 13904

HUDAK, NORMAN JOHN, ORGANIC CHEMISTRY. *Current Pos:* assoc prof, 61-65, chmn dept, 72-77 & 85-88, PROF CHEM, WILLAMETTE UNIV, 65- *Personal Data:* b Lorain, Ohio, Jan 24, 33; m 63, Mary Jo Rohland; c Lisa, Ann & Carol. *Educ:* DePauw Univ, BA, 54; Cornell Univ, PhD(chem), 59. *Prof Exp:* Instr chem, Oberlin Col, 58-60; asst prof, Haverford Col, 60-61. *Concurrent Pos:* NSF sci fac fel, Ore State Univ, 71-72. *Mem:* Am Chem Soc; Royal Soc Chem. *Res:* Natural products; enzyme-catalyzed organic reactions; reduction reactions; carbocation rearrangements; organic photochemistry. *Mailing Add:* 1732 Toucan St NW Salem OR 97304-2027. *Fax:* 503-375-5425; *E-Mail:* nhudak@willanette.edu

HUDAK, PAUL RAYMOND, PARALLEL PROCESSING, FUNCTIONAL LANGUAGES PROGRAMMING. *Current Pos:* asst prof, 82-85, ASSOC PROF COMPUT SCI, YALE UNIV, 85- *Personal Data:* b Baltimore, Md, July 15, 52; m 81; c 2. *Educ:* Vanderbilt Univ, BS, 73; Mass Inst Technol, MS, 74, Univ Utah, PhD(comput sci), 82. *Honors & Awards:* Presidential Young Investr Award, NSF, 85. *Prof Exp:* Mem tech staff, Watkins Johnson Co, 74-77, head equip eng sect, 77-79; res assoc, univ res fel, Univ Utah, 79-82. *Concurrent Pos:* Collabr, Los Alamos Nat Lab, 83-; consult, Comput Technol Assocs, 83-; prin investr, NSF, DARPA & Dept Energy grants, 83- *Mem:* Asn Comput Mach; Inst Elec & Electronics Engrs. *Res:* Formal analysis, design and implementation of very high-level programming languages; functional and logic programming languages targeted for parallel computers; developing semantic analysis methodologies and tools for optimizing. *Mailing Add:* Dept Comput Sci Yale Univ PO 3 208285 51 Prospect St New Haven CT 06520-2825

HUDAK, WILLIAM JOHN, pharmacology; deceased, see previous edition for last biography

HUDDLE, BENJAMIN PAUL, JR, PHYSICAL CHEMISTRY. *Current Pos:* ASST PROF CHEM, ROANOKE COL, 68- *Personal Data:* b Ootacamund, India, May 25, 41; US citizen; m 64; c 2. *Educ:* Lenoir-Rhyne Col, BS, 63; Univ NC, Chapel Hill, PhD(phys chem), 68. *Mem:* Am Chem Soc; Am Phys Soc; Am Crystallog Asn; Sigma Xi. *Res:* Crystal structure of coordination compounds; structure and properties of phosphorous heterocycles and molecules with highly polar bonds. *Mailing Add:* Chem Dept Roanoke Col Salem VA 24153

HUDDLESTON, CHARLES MARTIN, NUCLEAR PHYSICS. *Current Pos:* CONSULT, 89- *Personal Data:* b Dallas, Tex, Sept 27, 25; m 52. *Educ:* Northwestern Univ, BS, 48, MS, 49; Ind Univ, PhD(physics), 53. *Prof Exp:* Assoc physicist, Argonne Nat Lab, 53-61; dir, Physics & Math Div, US Naval Civil Eng Lab, 61-67; phys sci adminr, Naval Radiol Defense Lab, 67-69; res physicist & head, Shielding & Dosimetry Group, Naval Ord Lab, Naval Surface Weapons Ctr, 69-74, dir, Nuclear Radiation Br, 74-75, tech coord, Navy Charged Particle Beam Technol Prog & task mgr, Prog Strategic Defense Initiative Off & Tech Agt, Prog Defense Advan Res Projs Agency, 75-86; sr physicist, Booz Allen & Hamilton Inc, 87-89. *Concurrent Pos:* Vis prof, Univ Ill, 68-69. *Mem:* Am Nuclear Soc; Sci Res Soc Am. *Res:* Radiation transport and energy deposition for neutrons, gamma rays, x-rays and electrons; nondestructive testing, underground nuclear weapons tests; radiation simulation; accelerators, changed particle beam technology. *Mailing Add:* 3 Oyster Cove Dr Apt 3E Grasonville MD 21638

HUDDLESTON, DEBBIE ELLEN, PLANETARY MAGNETOSPHERES, SOLAR WIND & SPACE WEATHER. *Current Pos:* RESEARCHER SPACE PHYSICS, INST GEOPHYSICS & PLANETARY PHYSICS, UNIV CALIF, LOS ANGELES, 94- *Personal Data:* b Farnborough, Eng, Mar 2, 65. *Educ:* Kings Col London, BS, 86; Univ Col London, PhD(space physics), 90. *Prof Exp:* Postdoctoral res asst, Mullard Space Sci Lab, Univ Col London, 90-92; Nat Acad Sci/Nat Res Coun res assoc, Jet Propulsion Lab, NASA, 92-94. *Mem:* Am Geophys Union; Nat Aeronaut Asn. *Res:* Planetary magnetospheres; solar wind interaction with comets; evolution and variability of the solar wind and space weather. *Mailing Add:* Inst Geophys & Planetary Physics Univ Calif 405 Hilgard Ave Los Angeles CA 90095-1567. *Fax:* 310-206-8042; *E-Mail:* huddle@igpp.ucla.edu

HUDDLESTON, ELLIS WRIGHT, ECONOMIC ENTOMOLOGY, PESTICIDE APPLICATION. *Current Pos:* head dept, 75-84, PROF ENTOM & PLANT PATH & WEED SCI, NMEX STATE UNIV, 75- *Personal Data:* b Knapp, Tex, Sept 10, 35; m 55, Billie I Alford; c James R & Kimberly A. *Educ:* Tex Tech Col, BS, 56; Cornell Univ, MS, 58, PhD(entom), 60. *Prof Exp:* Asst entom, Cornell Univ, 56-59; from asst prof to prof, Tex Tech Univ, 60-75. *Concurrent Pos:* Consult, USAID, Senegal, 86-88. *Mem:* Entom Soc Am; Am Soc Agr Engrs. *Res:* Insect ecology; rangeland entomology; ecological effects of insecticides; insecticide residue sampling and decomposition; pesticide application technology. *Mailing Add:* Dept Entom & Plant Path & Weed Sci NMex State Univ Las Cruces NM 88003. *Fax:* 505-646-7913

HUDDLESTON, GEORGE RICHMOND, JR, PHYSICAL CHEMISTRY, CHEMICAL ENGINEERING. *Current Pos:* RETIRED. *Personal Data:* b Sandersville, Miss, Oct 7, 21; m 42, 77, Eileen Shaveyco; c Patricia (Heege). *Educ:* Miss State Col, BS, 43; La State Univ, MS, 49, PhD(chem), 60. *Prof Exp:* Control chemist, Copolymer Rubber & Chem Corp, 43-44, pilot plant shift chemist, 46-48, develop chemist, 48-50, supvr pilot plant, 50-54, supvr res, 54-58, mgr res lab, 58-63, res mgr, 63-67, process develop dir, 67-70; sr scientist, Independence Develop Ctr, B F Goodrich Chem Co, 70-75, res & develop assoc, Brecksville Res & Develop Ctr, 75-78, sr res & develop assoc, Avon Lake Tech Ctr, B F Goodrich Co, 78-83, res & develop fel, 83-86. *Mem:* Am Chem Soc. *Res:* Polymerization and copolymerization to elastomeric polymers and latices; fundamental colloidal and surface studies in latices and catalysts; reactions of elemental sulfur and organic materials; process development; polyvinyl chloride. *Mailing Add:* 4031 Woodstock Dr Lorain OH 44053-1568

HUDDLESTON, JAMES HERBERT, SOIL MORPHOLOGY. *Current Pos:* ASSOC PROF SOIL SCI, ORE STATE UNIV, 76- *Personal Data:* b Malone, NY, Mar 18, 42; m 62; c 4. *Educ:* Cornell Univ, BSc, 63, MS, 65; Iowa State Univ, PhD(soils), 69. *Prof Exp:* From asst prof to assoc prof ecosyst anal, Univ Wis-Green Bay, 69-76. *Concurrent Pos:* Wis Alumni Res Found res grant, 70-71; res partic, Eastern Deciduous Forest Biome, Int Biol Prog, Madison, Wis; dir NSF undergrad res participation grants, 74 & 75. *Mem:* AAAS; Am Soc Agron; Soil Conserv Soc Am. *Res:* Soil genesis and classification; soil geomorphology and landscape evolution; soil survey interpretation for agricultural and non-agricultural uses. *Mailing Add:* Dept Crop Sci Ore State Univ 3017 Agr Life Sci Corvallis OR 97331-7306

HUDDLESTON, JOHN VINCENT, COMPUTER ENGINEERING. *Current Pos:* PROF ENG & APPL SCI, STATE UNIV NY, BUFFALO, 67- *Personal Data:* b Houston, Tex, Feb 1, 28; m 52, Martha Hendry; c 3. *Educ:* Columbia Univ, BS, 52, MS, 54, PhD(appl mech), 60. *Honors & Awards:* Robert Ridgway Award, Am Soc Civil Engrs, 52. *Prof Exp:* Instr civil eng, Columbia Univ, 52-56; asst prof, Yale Univ, 56-62, assoc prof, 62-63, assoc prof eng & appl sci, 63-67. *Concurrent Pos:* Vis prof, Imp Col, London, 64-65, Univ Florence, 74, Univ Technol Malaysia, 75-76, Univ Malaya & MARA Inst Technol, 84-85; Fulbright fels, 75-76 & 84-85; consult, Custom Comput Serv, Inc, East Amherst, NY & Wan Mohamed & Khoo, Kuala Lumpur, Malaysia; prin investr, NSF, 76-79; educ consult, Inti Col, Kuala Lumpur, Malaysia. *Mem:* Am Soc Civil Engrs; Am Soc Mech Engrs; Inst Elec & Electronics Engrs Comput Soc. *Res:* Dynamic stability; computer algorithms; population dynamics; mathematical modeling. *Mailing Add:* Dept Civil Eng State Univ NY 212 Ketter Hall Buffalo NY 14260-4300

HUDDLESTON, PHILIP LEE, MATHEMATICAL PHYSICS, COMPUTATIONAL PHYSICS. *Current Pos:* sr sci programmer/analyst, McDonnell Douglas Automation Co, 79-81, res scientist, McDonnell Douglas Res Labs, 81-85, scientist, 85-89, sr scientist, McDonnell Douglas Technologies Inc, 89-92, SR PRIN TECH SPECIALIST, MCDONNELL DOUGLAS AEROSPACE, 92- *Personal Data:* b 1947; US citizen; m 73, Angela J Gryting. *Educ:* Wash Univ, BS, 67; Boston Univ, MA, 69, PhD(physics), 74. *Prof Exp:* Asst prof physics & math, Edward Waters Col, 75-76; asst prof physics, Parks Col, St Louis Univ, 76-79. *Mem:* Inst Elec & Electronics Engrs; AAAS; Sigma Xi; Optical Soc Am; Soc Indust & Appl Maths. *Res:* Computational and applied physics with an emphasis on modeling of electromagnetic and optical phenomena. *Mailing Add:* 5471 Kenrick Parke Dr St Louis MO 63119-5027. *Fax:* 314-232-7774; *E-Mail:* m189552@mdc.com

HUDDLESTON, ROBERT E, NUMERICAL ANALYSIS. *Current Pos:* mgr, Computer Appl & Res, 85-87, dept head, Computer Sci Dept, 87-90, UNIV RELS, LAWRENCE LIVERMORE NAT LAB, 90- *Personal Data:* b Hugo, Okla, Mar 28, 39; m 87. *Educ:* Tex Christian Univ, BA, 60, PhD, 66; Univ Ariz, MS, 62. *Prof Exp:* Fel & res assoc math, Inst Fluid Dynamics & Appl Math, Univ Md, 66-67; asst mem, Sandia Labs, Albuquerque, 67-69, numerical analyst, Sandia Nat Labs, Livermore, 69-76, supvr sci comput, 76-85. *Concurrent Pos:* Vis lectr, Univ NMex, 67-69. *Mem:* Soc Indust & Appl Math; Spec Interest Group Numerical Math; Asn Comput Mach; Numerical Algorithms Group. *Res:* Numerical solutions of partial differential equations. *Mailing Add:* Univ Rels L-725 Lawrence Livermore Lab PO Box 808 Livermore CA 94550

HUDDLESTONE, RICHARD H, THEORETICAL PHYSICS. *Current Pos:* RETIRED. *Personal Data:* b Huntington Park, Calif, Dec 8, 26; m 52; c 4. *Educ:* Univ Calif, AB, 48, PhD(physics), 54. *Prof Exp:* Mem, Theoret Group, Radiation Lab, Univ Calif, 50-54, jr res physicist, Dept Physics, 54-55; mem, Theoret Physics Sect, Phys Res Lab, Space Tech Labs, 55-60; head, Reentry & Plasma Electromagnetics Dept, Aerospace Corp, 60-71, sr staff scientist, Lab Opers, 71-77, eng specialist, Info Processing Div, 77-; fac mem, Comput Sci Dept, Calif State Univ, Carson. *Mem:* Am Phys Soc. *Res:* Quantum mechanics; low energy nuclear physics; plasma, thermonuclear, reentry and mathematical physics; applied mathematics. *Mailing Add:* 27337 Pasco Laguna San Juan Capistrano CA 92675

HUDECKI, MICHAEL STEPHEN, MOLECULAR BIOLOGY, BIOCHEMISTRY. *Current Pos:* Lectr biol, 76-77, res assoc, 77-78, res asst prof, 79-86, RES ASSOC PROF, DEPT BIOL SCI, STATE UNIV NY, BUFFALO, 87- *Personal Data:* b Ft Bragg, NC, Nov 7, 43; m 73. *Educ:* Niagara Univ, BS, 65, MS, 67; State Univ NY, Buffalo, MA, 70, PhD(biol), 73. *Hon Degrees:* DSc, Niagara Univ, 81. *Concurrent Pos:* Muscular Dystrophy Asn fel, Syracuse Univ, 72-73 & State Univ NY, Buffalo, 74-76; NIH fel, State Univ NY, Buffalo, 77-79; Muscular Dystrophy Asn grant, 77-89, res career develop award, 80-85, grant, 80-83, NIH; consult, Off Serv Handicapped, State Univ NY, 77-, Proj Handicapped Sci, AAAS, 77- & NSF Phys Handicapped Sci Prog, 77-78; reviewer, biomed jour. *Mem:* AAAS; Soc Neurosci; NY Acad Sci; Fedn Sci & Handicapped; Am Physiol Soc. *Res:* Drug studies in muscular dystrophy. *Mailing Add:* Dept Biol Sci State Univ NY Cooke Hall Buffalo NY 14260

HUDGENS, RICHARD WATTS, PSYCHIATRY. *Current Pos:* From instr to prof clin psychiat, 63-89, from asst dean to assoc dean sch med, 64-74, PROF PSYCHIAT, WASH UNIV, 89- *Personal Data:* b Greenville, SC, Jan 10, 31; m 52, 82; c 4. *Educ:* Princeton Univ, BA, 52; Wash Univ, MD, 56. *Mem:* Am Psychiat Asn; AMA. *Res:* Affective disorders; suicide; psychiatric disorders in adolescence; transcultural psychiatry; medical education; history of psychiatry; psychiatric disorders. *Mailing Add:* 13 Algonquin Wood St Louis MO 63122-2013

HUDGIN, DONALD EDWARD, ORGANIC CHEMISTRY. *Current Pos:* res dir, Princeton Chem Res, Inc, 67, dir res & develop, 67-70, vpres, 70-80, dir res & develop, Princeton Polymer Labs, Inc, 70-89, PRES, PRINCETON POLYMER LABS, INC, 80- *Personal Data:* b Greenville, SC, Aug 11, 17; m 43; c 3. *Educ:* Clemson Col, BS, 38; Purdue Univ, MS, 40, PhD(org chem), 47. *Prof Exp:* Res chemist, Synthetic Detergents, Procter & Gamble Co, 47-52; res chemist, Mallinckrodt Chem Works, 52-55; sr chemist, Celanese Corp Am, 55-56, group leader, 56-58, sect head, 58-60; dir res & develop, Cary Chem, Inc, 60-61; assoc dir res, Diamond Alkali Co, 61-66; sr staff adv, Esso Res & Eng Co, 66-67. *Concurrent Pos:* Assoc ed, Int J Polymer Process Eng; adv coun, Polymer Processing Inst, 83-88; sr ed, Plastics Eng. *Mem:* AAAS; Am Chem Soc; fel Am Inst Chem; Soc Plastic Eng; Asn Res Dirs (pres, 73-74); Plastics Inst Am; Sigma Xi. *Res:* Vinyl and condensation polymers; thermoset resins; polymer properties; polyolefins. *Mailing Add:* 25436 Cumberland Lane Calabasas CA 91302-3156

HUDGINGS, DANIEL W, HEALTH PHYSICS. *Current Pos:* PHYSICIAN, SAGE MEM HOSP, 91- *Personal Data:* b Tampa, Fla, Sept 22, 42. *Educ:* Mass Inst Technol, BS, 63; Univ Md, MS, 68, PhD(physics), 73. *Prof Exp:* Pub health serv, Yellowstone Nat Park, 87-91. *Mem:* Am Phys Soc. *Mailing Add:* PO Box 1089 Ganado AZ 86505

HUDGINS, ARTHUR J, APPLIED PHYSICS, PHYSICIST RECRUITMENT. *Current Pos:* RETIRED. *Personal Data:* b Boise, Idaho, June 14, 20; m 55, Dorothy M Schell; c Richard & Carol. *Educ:* Univ Calif, Berkeley, AB, 42, PhD(physics), 52. *Prof Exp:* Physicist, Lawrence Radiation Lab, Univ Calif, 42-45 & Tenn Eastman Corp, 45-46; physicist, Lawrence Livermore Nat Lab, Univ Calif, Livermore, 46-83 & 89-93; consult, 83-93. *Concurrent Pos:* Consult, 83-93; mem bd dir, Valley Med Care, Pleasanton & Livermore, Calif. *Mem:* Am Phys Soc. *Mailing Add:* 2268 Marina Ave Livermore CA 94450-0912

HUDGINS, AUBREY C, JR, EXPERIMENTAL SOLID STATE PHYSICS, COMPUTER SIMULATION. *Current Pos:* oper res analyst, 79-81, SUPVR OPER RES ANALYST GM-14, DEFENSE LOGISTICS AGENCY, DEFENSE OPER RES OFF, DEFENSE SUPPLY CTR, 81- *Personal Data:* b Richmond, Va, Oct 15, 35; m 88; c 2. *Educ:* Univ Richmond, BS, 59; WVa Univ, MS, 61, PhD(physics), 64. *Prof Exp:* Instr & res assoc physics, WVa Univ, 64-65; instr advan eng math, Univ Va Exten, 66-67; res physicist, Metall Res Div, Reynolds Metals Co, 65-71; asst prof physics, Randolph Macon Col, 72-75; instr physics, Va Commonwealth Univ, 75-77, asst prof info systs, 77-79. *Concurrent Pos:* AEC grant, 64-65. *Mem:* Am Phys Soc; Am Asn Physics Teachers; Am Soc Metals. *Res:* Magnetism; heat transfer; computer simulation; ingot casting; ultrasonic nondestructive testing; experimental solid state research energy and systems analysis; operation research; data bank. *Mailing Add:* 4000 Cogbill Rd Richmond VA 23234

HUDGINS, PATRICIA MONTAGUE, PHARMACOLOGY. *Current Pos:* assoc prof, 75-80, PROF PHYSIOL, KIRKSVILLE COL OSTEOP MED, 80- *Personal Data:* b Buckhannon, WVa, Jan 31, 38; m 75; c 2. *Educ:* WVa Univ, BS, 59, MS, 60, PhD(pharmacol), 66. *Prof Exp:* From instr to assoc prof pharmacol, Med Col Va, Va Commonwealth Univ, 66-75. *Concurrent Pos:* Consult, Astra Pharmaceut Prod, Inc, 73-77. *Mem:* Am Soc Pharmacol & Exp Therapeut; Am Physiol Soc. *Res:* Biochemical pharmacology; active cation transport; ATPase. *Mailing Add:* WVa Sch Osteop Med 400 N Lee St Lewisburg WV 24901-9981

HUDGINS, ROBERT R(OSS), CHEMICAL ENGINEERING. *Current Pos:* From asst prof to assoc prof, 64-75, PROF CHEM ENG, UNIV WATERLOO, 75- *Personal Data:* b Toronto, Ont, Jan 25, 37; m 63; c 3. *Educ:* Univ Toronto, BASc, 59, MASc, 60; Princeton Univ, PhD(chem eng), 64. *Concurrent Pos:* Invited prof, Univ Sherbrooke, 71-72; Swiss Fed Inst Technol, Lausanne, 79. *Mem:* Fel Chem Inst Can; Sigma Xi. *Res:* Chemical reaction engineering; forced cycling of chemical reactors; influence of diluent gases in catalysis; sedimentation improvement in clarification; clarifiers. *Mailing Add:* Univ Waterloo Waterloo ON N2L 3G1 Can

HUDIG, DOROTHY, LYMPHOCYTE-MEDIATED KILLING, SERINE PROTEASE BIOCHEMISTRY. *Current Pos:* assoc prof, 84-90, PROF, SCH MED, UNIV NEV, 90- *Personal Data:* b Oakland, Calif, May 29, 46. *Educ:* Bryn Mawr Col, BA, 68; Univ Calif, San Diego, PhD(biol), 77. *Prof Exp:* Bank of Am-Giannini fel, Univ Calif, San Diego Cancer Ctr, 77-79, res biochemist, 79-84. *Concurrent Pos:* Prin investr, NIH, 79-, dir, Cancer Biol Training Prog, Univ Nev, Reno, 84-; prin investr, NSF, 88-; assoc ed, J Immunol. *Mem:* Am Asn Immunol; Am Asn Path; Am Asn Cancer Res. *Res:* Discovery of the protein responsible for the destruction of virally infected cells and tumor cells by killer T and natural killer lymphocytes; how cell death is controlled by lymphocyte serine-dependent proteases. *Mailing Add:* Dept Microbiol 320 Univ Nev Sch Med Reno NV 89557-0046. *Fax:* 702-784-4430; *E-Mail:* hudig@equinox.unr.edu

HUDIS, JEROME, NUCLEAR CHEMISTRY, INORGANIC CHEMISTRY. *Current Pos:* VPRES PROGRAMMATIC AFFAIRS & CONTROLLER, ASSOC UNIVS INC, 85- *Personal Data:* b New York, NY, June 5, 25; m 53; c Jan & James Andrew. *Educ:* Wash Univ, BS, 47, PhD(chem), 52. *Prof Exp:* From assoc chemist to sr chemist, Brookhaven Nat Lab, 52-77, chmn, Chem Dept, 77-81, asst dir, 81-85. *Concurrent Pos:* Chmn, Div Nuclear Chem & Technol, Am Chem Soc, 81. *Res:* Nuclear chemistry and reactions; x-ray photoelectron spectroscopy; research administration. *Mailing Add:* 6403 Recreation Lane Washington DC 20008. *E-Mail:* hudis@bnl.gov

HUDLER, GEORGE WILLIAM, PLANT PATHOLOGY, FORESTRY. *Current Pos:* ASST PROF PLANT PATH, CORNELL UNIV, 78- *Personal Data:* b Cloquet, Minn, Aug 19, 47. *Educ:* Univ Minn, BS, 70, MS, 73; Colo State Univ, PhD(plant path), 76. *Mem:* Am Phytopath Soc; Sigma Xi. *Res:* Diseases of forest and shade trees. *Mailing Add:* 334 Plant Sci Bldg Cornell Univ Ithaca NY 14853-0001

HUDLESTON, PETER JOHN, MECHANICS FOLDING, STRAIN ANALYSIS. *Current Pos:* from asst prof to assoc prof, 70-83, head, Dept Geol & Geophys, 83-93, PROF GEOL & GEOPHYS, UNIV MINN, MINNEAPOLIS, 83-, ASSOC DEAN, INST TECHNOL, 95- *Personal Data:* b Osterley, Middlesex, UK, May 31, 44; m 71, Bronwen Heade; c 2. *Educ:* Imp Col, London Univ, BSc, 65, PhD(geol), 69. *Prof Exp:* Res fel, Univ Uppsala, Sweden, 69-70. *Concurrent Pos:* Assoc ed, J Struct Geol; chmn, Struct Geol & Tech Div, Geol Soc Am, 89-90. *Mem:* Fel Geol Soc Am; Am Geophys Union; Am Asn Petrol Geologists; Geol Asn Can; Nat Asn Geol Teachers; Sigma Xi; Am Soc Eng Educ. *Res:* Analysis of deformation in rocks by field observation, numerical modeling and experiment with particular interest in the development of folds, foliation and crystallographic fabric. *Mailing Add:* Dept Geol & Geophys Univ Minn Minneapolis MN 55455. *Fax:* 612-625-3819; *E-Mail:* hudlesto@mailbox.mail.umn.edu

HUDLICKY, MILOS, ORGANIC CHEMISTRY, FLUORINE CHEMISTRY. *Current Pos:* vis prof, 68-69, from assoc prof to prof, 69-89, EMER PROF ORG CHEM, VA POLYTECH INST & STATE UNIV, 89- *Personal Data:* b Prelouc, Czech, May 12, 19; m 46, Alena Vyskocilova; c Tomas & Eva. *Educ:* Prague Tech Univ, PhD(org chem), 46. *Honors & Awards:* Votocek's Medal, Tech Univ, Prague, 92. *Prof Exp:* Asst org chem, Prague Tech Univ, 45-54, assoc prof, 54-58; res chemist, Res Inst Pharm & Biochem, Prague, 58-68. *Concurrent Pos:* Am Chem Soc & UNESCO fel, Ohio State Univ, 48. *Mem:* Am Chem Soc; The Chem Soc; Czech Chem Soc. *Res:* Chemistry of 1,3-dichloro-2-butene; chemistry of organic fluorine compounds. *Mailing Add:* Dept Chem Va Polytech Inst & State Univ Blacksburg VA 24061. *Fax:* 540-231-3255

HUDLICKY, TOMAS, SYNTHETIC ORGANIC CHEMISTRY & NATURAL PRODUCTS, BIOTRANSFORMATIONS & ENVIRONMENTAL CHEMISTRY. *Current Pos:* PROF, DEPT CHEM, VA POLYTECH STATE UNIV, 88- *Personal Data:* b Dec 26, 49; US citizen; m; c 1. *Educ:* Va Polytech Inst & State Univ, BS, 73; Rice Univ, PhD(chem), 77. *Honors & Awards:* NSF Antarctic Serv Award, 72; Res Award, Am Cyanamid, 92. *Prof Exp:* Chemist, SPOFA Pharmaceut Works, 66-68 & Bio-Va Polytech Inst Antarctic Exped, 72; fel, Univ Geneva, 77-78; asst prof, Ill Inst Technol, 78-82. *Concurrent Pos:* A P Sloan fel, 81-85, Fulbright fel, 84 & 85; NIH res career develop award, 84-89. *Mem:* Am Chem Soc; Sigma Xi. *Res:* Synthesis of natural products, including alkaloids, terpenes, marine natural products; development of new reagents for organic synthesis; carbocyclic, heterocyclic annulation methodology; cyclopentanoid terpene synthesis; industrial consultant; pharmaceutical synthesis; biocatalysis; microbial oxidation of aromatics; carbohydrate synthesis; anti-viral agents; waste conversion. *Mailing Add:* Univ Fla PO Box 117200 Gainesville FL 32611-7200

HUDLOW, MICHAEL DALE, meteorology, hydrology, for more information see previous edition

HUDNALL, PHILLIP MONTGOMERY, ORGANIC CHEMISTRY. *Current Pos:* chemist develop & control, 72-74, sr chemist intermediates dept staff, 74-77, sr chemist dyes dept staff, 77-78, sr chemist org chem div staff, 78-80, SR CHEMIST & DEVELOP COORDR, DEVELOP & CONTROL DEPT, TENN EASTMAN CO, 80- *Personal Data:* b Ward, WVa, Jan 7, 44; m 79. *Educ:* Morris Harvey Col, BS, 67; Univ NC, PhD(org chem), 72. *Prof Exp:* Lab technician, Union Carbide Chem Co, 62-67, chemist, 67. *Mem:* Am Chem Soc. *Res:* Process development. *Mailing Add:* PO Box 3031 Kingsport TN 37664-0031

HUDOCK, GEORGE ANTHONY, EVOLUTIONARY BIOLOGY. *Current Pos:* asst prof, 65-68, assoc prof zool, 68-80, ASSOC PROF BIOL, IND UNIV, BLOOMINGTON, 80- *Personal Data:* b Bridgetown Twp, Pa, Mar 28, 37; m 60, 81, Carol Bart; c Jennifer Elizabeth (Roll) & Jessica N. *Educ:* Harvard Univ, AB, 59, PhD(biol), 63. *Prof Exp:* NSF fel, Dartmouth Med Sch, 63-64, res assoc microbiol, 64-65. *Mem:* AAAS; Am Inst Biol Sci; Soc Protozool. *Res:* Evolutionary biology. *Mailing Add:* Dept Biol Ind Univ Bloomington IN 47405-6801. *Fax:* 812-855-6705; *E-Mail:* hudock@juliet.ucs.indiana.edu

HUDRLIK, ANNE MARIE, SYNTHETIC ORGANIC CHEMISTRY, ORGANOSILICON CHEMISTRY. *Current Pos:* FEL ORG CHEM, HOWARD UNIV, 77- *Personal Data:* b Akron, Ohio, Aug 30, 41; m 67, Paul F; c Janet & Carol. *Educ:* Ohio State Univ, BS, 63; Columbia Univ, MA, 64, PhD(chem), 67. *Prof Exp:* NIH fel, Stanford Univ, 68-69; fel org chem, Rutgers Univ, New Brunswick, 69-76. *Mem:* Am Chem Soc. *Res:* Organic synthesis; organosilicon chemistry. *Mailing Add:* Dept Chem Howard Univ Washington DC 20059. *E-Mail:* ahudrlik@capaccess.org

HUDRLIK, PAUL FREDERICK, SYNTHETIC ORGANIC CHEMISTRY, ORGANOSILICON CHEMISTRY. *Current Pos:* assoc prof, 77-81, PROF CHEM, HOWARD UNIV, 81- *Personal Data:* b Portland, Ore, May 10, 41; m 67, Anne M Bachmann; c Janet & Carol. *Educ:* Ore State Univ, BS, 63; Columbia Univ, MA, 64, PhD(org chem), 68. *Prof Exp:* Fel chem, Stanford Univ, 68-69; asst prof, Sch Chem, Rutgers Univ, 69-76. *Mem:* AAAS; Royal Soc Chem; Am Chem Soc. *Res:* Development of new synthetic methods in organic chemistry; organosilicon chemistry. *Mailing Add:* Dept Chem Howard Univ Washington DC 20059. *Fax:* 202-806-5442; *E-Mail:* hudrlik@scs.howard.edu

HUDSON, ALAN P, GENETICS. *Current Pos:* RES SERV, VET ADMIN MED CTR, PHILADELPHIA, 85-; ASST PROF, DEPT BIOL, MED COL PA, 88- *Personal Data:* b Batavia, NY, Dec 7, 48. *Educ:* Hamilton Col, BA, 71; City Univ NY, PhD(biol sci), 78. *Mem:* Am Soc Microbiol; Sigma Xi; Am Soc Biol Chemists; Asn Res Vision & Ophthal. *Mailing Add:* Res Serv Vet Admin Med Ctr University & Woodland Aves Philadelphia PA 19104. *Fax:* 215-823-5171

HUDSON, ALBERT BERRY, natural products chemistry; deceased, see previous edition for last biography

HUDSON, ALICE PETERSON, SURFACE CHEMISTRY. *Current Pos:* chemist, 71-73, LAB DIR, SURFACE CHEMISTS FLA, INC, 73-, PRES, 83- *Personal Data:* b Sherburn, Minn, Aug 9, 42; m 63; c 2. *Educ:* Iowa State Univ, BS, 63; Fla Atlantic Univ, MS, 77. *Prof Exp:* Chemist, Pratt & Whitney Aircraft Co, 63-64; lab technician, SE Fla Tuberc Hosp, 64-65. *Concurrent Pos:* Dir & secy-treas bd dirs, Surface Chemists Fla, Inc, 73-83; secy bd dirs, Jessop, Prindle & Woodward, Inc, 75-81, Mining Reagents Corp, 81-83; pres, Sunrise Chem, Inc, 83-88; dir & treas, Surfactant Technol Corp, 84- *Mem:* Am Chem Soc; Am Oil Chemists Soc; Tech Asn Pulp & Paper Indust. *Res:* Mechanisms of halogen disinfection; studies of micelle-iodine interactions; applied surface chemistry in the areas of detergents; textile chemicals and cosmetics. *Mailing Add:* Surface Chemists Fla Inc 328 W 11th St Riviera Beach FL 33404. *Fax:* 561-842-2712

HUDSON, ALVIN MAYNARD, SCIENCE EDUCATION. *Current Pos:* RETIRED. *Personal Data:* b Portland, Ore, June 28, 22. *Educ:* Stanford Univ, BS, 47, MS, 50, PhD(physics), 57. *Prof Exp:* From asst prof to assoc prof physics, Occidental Col, 57-87, actg chmn dept, 58-61, chmn dept, 62-67. *Concurrent Pos:* Mem staff, Sci Teaching Ctr, Mass Inst Technol, 64-65; mem area meeting adv comt, Phys Sci Study Comt, 65-69; mem advan placement exam comt physics, Col Entrance Exam Bd, Princeton, NJ, 70-, chmn, 74-78. *Mem:* AAAS; Am Asn Physics Teachers; Sigma Xi. *Res:* Relativity; science education. *Mailing Add:* 650 Crane Blvd Los Angeles CA 90065

HUDSON, ANNE LESTER, MATHEMATICS. *Current Pos:* PROF MATH, ARMSTRONG STATE COL, 71- *Personal Data:* b Inverness, Miss, Jan 30, 32; m 60; c 2. *Educ:* Hollins Col, AB, 53; Tulane Univ, MS, 58, PhD(math), 61. *Prof Exp:* NSF res fel math, 61-63; instr, Syracuse Univ, 63-71. *Mem:* Am Math Soc; Math Asn Am. *Res:* Structure of topological semigroups. *Mailing Add:* Dept Math & Comput Sci Armstrong Col Savannah GA 31419-1997

HUDSON, BILLY GERALD, BIOCHEMISTRY. *Current Pos:* assoc prof, 74-77, dean res, Col Health Sci, 80-86, PROF BIOCHEM, UNIV KANS MED CTR, 77- *Personal Data:* b Pine Bluff, Ark, Oct 16, 41; m 88, Julie K Roberts; c 3. *Educ:* Henderson State Col, BS, 62; Univ Tenn, Memphis, MS, 64; Univ Iowa, PhD(biochem), 66. *Prof Exp:* Postdoctoral fel, US Army Res Inst Environ Med, 66-68; res fel biol chem, Harvard Med Sch, 68-70; from asst prof to assoc prof biochem, Okla State Univ, 70-74. *Mem:* Am Chem Soc; Am Soc Biol Chem. *Res:* Pathogenesis of renal diseases; glycoprotein structure; structure and function of basement membranes and type IV collagen. *Mailing Add:* Dept Biochem & Molecular Biol Univ Kans Med Ctr 39 Rainbow Blvd Kansas City KS 66160. *Fax:* 913-588-7440

HUDSON, BRUCE WILLIAM, IMMUNOLOGY, INFECTIOUS DISEASES. *Current Pos:* RETIRED. *Personal Data:* b Minn, Oct 3, 28; m 51; c 4. *Educ:* Univ Calif, BA, 54, PhD(entom), 57. *Prof Exp:* Entomologist, Kaiser Found Hosps, 57-60; biochemist, Bur State Serv, Nat Commun Dis Ctr, USPHS, Calif, 60-65, biochemist, Tech Br, Chem Sect, 65-66, supvry chemist ecologic invests prog, Zoonoses Sect, 66-74, staff mem, Immunochem Br, Vector Borne Dis Div, Ctr Dis Control, 74-82. *Concurrent Pos:* Mem, Int Comt Microbiol Stand; affil prof microbiol, Wild Animal Dis Ctr, Colo State Univ. *Mem:* AAAS; Wildlife Dis Asn; NY Acad Sci; Am Chem Soc. *Res:* Plague; biology-immunology; arbovirus; seroepidemiology. *Mailing Add:* 1136 Wabash St Unit 26 Ft Collins CO 80526-3022

HUDSON, CECIL IVAN, JR, PHYSICS. *Current Pos:* CONSULT, 94- *Personal Data:* b Atmore, Ala, Oct 21, 37; m 59; c 4. *Educ:* Ga Inst Technol, BS, 58; Univ Va, PhD(physics), 62. *Prof Exp:* Physicist, Lawrence Livermore Lab, Univ Calif, 61-67, asst to assoc dir, Nuclear Design, 67-68, staff asst to assoc dir, Mil Applns, 68-69, group leader, 69-72; dep mgr, Systs Div, Sci Applns, Inc, 72-75, vpres, 75-76, corp vpres, 76-80; group vpres, Jaycor, 80-83; dir, Advan Technol & Policy Progs, Titan Corp, 83-87; vpres, Calif Res & Technol, 87-90; dir technol progs, Expersoft, 90-94. *Concurrent Pos:* Mem reentry systs adv group, USAF Space & Missiles Systs Orgn, 69-70; mem, Reentry Body Comt, USN Strategic Systs Proj Off, 69-72; chmn, Futures Planning Coun, Episcopal Diocese Calif; chmn working group technol, arms control & foreign policy, Calif Sem Int Security & Foreign Policy. *Mem:* AAAS; Int Inst Strategic Studies; Am Inst Aeronaut & Astronaut; Am Defense Preparedness Asn; Asn; Am Phys Soc. *Res:* Experimental fast neutron physics; design of nuclear explosives; systems analysis; policy analysis; hypervelocity penetrators assumption-based truth maintenance systems. *Mailing Add:* 13005 Caminito Mar Villa Del Mar CA 92014

HUDSON, CHARLES MICHAEL, MATERIALS ENGINEERING, ENGINEERING MECHANICS. *Current Pos:* Aerospace technologist fatigue res, 58-73, aerospace technologist fract mech, 73-75, ENG SUPVR PRESSURE SYSTS, NASA, 75- *Personal Data:* b Washington, DC, Mar 31, 35; m 63, Jean Carol Creasy; c Michael Eugene, Anita Celeste, Christopher Todd & Sean Kevin. *Educ:* Va Polytech Inst, BS, 58, MS, 65; NC State Univ, PhD(mat eng), 72. *Honors & Awards:* Medal for Except Eng Achievement, NASA, 84; Award of Merit, Am Soc Testing & Mat, 87. *Concurrent Pos:* Lectr fracture mechs, George Washington Univ; chmn, Comt E-24, Am Soc Testing & Mat. *Mem:* Am Soc Testing & Mat; Sigma Xi. *Res:* Recertification of existing high-pressure systems at Langley Research Center; fracture mechanics, fatigue, failure and stress analyses; and nondestructive examinations. *Mailing Add:* Mail Stop 447 NASA Langley Res Ctr Hampton VA 23681-0001. *Fax:* 757-864-7728

HUDSON, DAVID FRANK, ATOMIC PHYSICS, GASEOUS ELECTRONICS. *Current Pos:* Physicist, Naval Weapons Lab, 67-74, physicist, Naval Surface Weapons Ctr, 74-78, RES PHYSICIST, NAVAL SURFACE WARFARE CTR, 78- *Personal Data:* b Hudson, NY, Feb 23, 37; m 65; c 2. *Educ:* Union Col, BS, 59; Univ NH, MS, 68; Cath Univ Am, PhD(physics), 77. *Mem:* Am Phys Soc. *Res:* Collisions involving and between electronically excited atoms; nonlinear processes and chaos in electric discharges; spectroscopy; laser cooling. *Mailing Add:* PO Box 178 Clarksburg MD 20871

HUDSON, DONALD E(LLIS), MECHANICAL ENGINEERING, APPLIED MECHANICS. *Current Pos:* RETIRED. *Personal Data:* b Alma, Mich, Feb 25, 16; m 73, Phyllis Arnett; c William J & Andrew R. *Educ:* Calif Inst Technol, BS, 38, MS, 39, PhD(mech eng), 42. *Honors & Awards:* Nathan N Newmark Medal, Am Soc Civil Engrs, 89; George W Housner Medal, Earthquake Eng Res Inst, 91. *Prof Exp:* Geophys engr, Gen Petrol Corp, 37-41; from instr to assoc prof, Calif Inst Technol, 41-55, prof, 55-79, emer prof mech eng & appl mech, 81-87; prof & chmn civil eng, Univ Southern Calif, 81-87, Fred Champion prof eng, 82-88. *Concurrent Pos:* Ord res engr, Off Sci Res & Develop & Nat Defense Res Comt, Calif Inst Technol, 43-45. *Mem:* Nat Acad Eng; fel Am Soc Mech Engrs; Soc Exp Mech; Earthquake Eng Res Inst; Seismol Soc Am (pres, 71-72); Indian Nat Acad Engrs. *Res:* Structural dynamics; earthquake engineering; dynamic measurements. *Mailing Add:* Div Eng & Appl Sci Thomas Lab 104-44 Calif Inst Technol Pasadena CA 91125

HUDSON, DONALD EDWIN, PHYSICS TEACHING. *Current Pos:* chmn dept, 64-67, prof, 64-83, EMER PROF PHYSICS, CALIF STATE UNIV, LOS ANGELES, 83- *Personal Data:* b Butte, Mont, July 17, 21; m 44, Hazel Gruner; c Sharon, Toren & Darrel. *Educ:* Univ Minn, BPhys, 42; Cornell Univ, PhD(physics), 50. *Honors & Awards:* Sigma Xi. *Prof Exp:* Asst physics, Univ Minn, 41-43, instr, 43-44; jr scientist, Los Alamos Sci Lab, 44-46; asst, Cornell Univ, 46-49; instr, Princeton Univ, 49-51; from asst prof to assoc prof, Iowa State Univ, 51-64. *Mem:* Am Phys Soc; Am Asn Physics Teachers. *Res:* Cosmic rays; chemical physics; solid state physics; physical electronics. *Mailing Add:* 1565 Washburn Rd Pasadena CA 91105

HUDSON, DONNA LEE, COMPUTER-ASSISTED MEDICAL DECISION MAKING, MODELING OF BIOMEDICAL SYSTEMS. *Current Pos:* from asst prof to assoc prof family med, 82-92, PROF & DIR MED INFO RESOURCES, UNIV CALIF, SAN FRANCISCO, 92- *Personal Data:* m, Samuel E. *Educ:* Calif State Univ, Fresno, BS, 68, MS, 72; Univ Calif, Los Angeles, PhD(comput sci), 81. *Prof Exp:* Assoc engr, Boeing, 68-70; programmer/analyst, Alphameric Data Processing, 72-75, City Fresno, 74-75; lectr, info systs, decision sci, Calif State Univ, Fresno, 75-81; asst prof family med, Univ Calif, Davis, 81-82. *Concurrent Pos:* Assoc ed, J Comput & Appln, 94-; exec comt, Med Info Sci Grad Group, 97- *Mem:* Fel Am Inst Med & Biol Engrs; sr mem Inst Elec & Electronics Engrs; Int Soc Comput & Applns (treas, 95-); NAm Fuzzy Info Processing Soc. *Res:* Computer-assisted medical decision making; neural network modeling; medical imaging; modeling biological time series using chaos theory; medical applications using the Internet. *Mailing Add:* Univ Calif 2615 E Clinton Fresno CA 93703

HUDSON, FRANK ALDEN, ANIMAL SCIENCE. *Current Pos:* RETIRED. *Personal Data:* b Gallup, NMex, Dec 15, 23; m 60, Elizabeth Townsend; c David T & Kathleen A. *Educ:* Ariz State Univ, BS, 52; NMex State Univ, MS, 53; Ore State Univ, PhD(genetics), 57. *Prof Exp:* Exp aide, Ore State Univ, 53-55; animal husbandman, Sheep & Fur Animal Res Br, Agr Res Serv, USDA, Md, 57-60; prof animal sci, Tex Tech Univ, 60-88. *Mem:* Am Soc Animal Sci; Soc Range Mgt. *Res:* Sheep breeding, feeding and management with emphasis on intensified production. *Mailing Add:* 3824 52nd St Lubbock TX 79413

HUDSON, FRANK M, MATHEMATICS. *Current Pos:* chmn dept, 67-83, PROF MATH, UNIV CENT ARK, 83- *Personal Data:* b Clarksville, Ark, Sept 8, 35; m 57; c 2. *Educ:* Univ Cent Ark BS, 57; Univ Tex, Austin, MA, 59, PhD(math), 65. *Prof Exp:* Grad asst math, Univ Tex, Austin, 56-59; instr, Western State Col Colo, 59-61; NSF fel, Harvard Univ, 61-62; spec instr, Univ Tex, Austin, 62-64; prof math & chmn dept, McMurry Col, 64-67. *Mem:* Math Asn Am; Nat Coun Teachers Math. *Res:* Integral transforms. *Mailing Add:* Dept Math Univ Cent Ark PO Box 4912 Conway AR 72035-0001

HUDSON, FREDERICK MITCHELL, ORGANIC CHEMISTRY, EXPLOSIVES. *Current Pos:* prin staff engr, 85-90, sr tech adv, 90-94, PRIN RES SCIENTIST, ATLANTIC RES CORP, 94- *Personal Data:* b Miami, Fla, Jan 27, 34; m 61, 76, Heather Enloe; c George, Sarah, James, Susan & Charles. *Educ:* Davidson Col, BS, 55; Univ Tenn, Knoxville, PhD(org chem), 63. *Prof Exp:* Sr chemist, Amcel Propulsion Co, Celanese Corp Am, 61-65; sr chemist, Northrop Carolina Inc, Northrop Corp, 65-69, sr scientist, 69-71; sr scientist, Airtronics, Inc, 71-73, tech dir, Chemtronics Div, 73-76; dir res & develop, Plastifax, Inc, 76-80; vpres, Chemtronics, Inc, Div Halliburton Co, 80-84. *Concurrent Pos:* Consult, Hudson Assocs. *Mem:* Am Chem Soc; AAAS; Sigma Xi; Am Defense-Preparedness Asn. *Res:* Aromatic nitration and sulfonation; halogenation of aromatics and alkyl aromatics; rates of organic reactions in nonaqueous solvents; relation of structure and composition to physical and explosive properties; explosive manufacturing processes; insensitive high explosives; environmentally acceptable methods of demilitarization of arms and ammunition; development of propellants. *Mailing Add:* 32 Chaffee Creek Trail Camden AR 71701. *Fax:* 870-574-2509; *E-Mail:* fredson@cei.net

HUDSON, GEORGE ELBERT, applied physics, mathematics; deceased, see previous edition for last biography

HUDSON, HUGH T, SOLID STATE PHYSICS, SCIENCE EDUCATION. *Current Pos:* PROF PHYSICS, UNIV INCARNATE WORD, 96- *Personal Data:* b Jackson, Miss, Nov 20, 33; div; c 3. *Educ:* Miss Col, BS, 58; Univ Va, MS, 60, PhD(physics), 62. *Prof Exp:* Asst prof physics, Univ Houston, 62-67, assoc prof, 67-96. *Concurrent Pos:* Adj asst prof, Baylor Col Med, 65-80; resident coordr, Inst Int Educ, Bangladesh, 69-71. *Mem:* Am Phys Soc; Am Asn Physics Teachers; AAAS; Sigma Xi. *Res:* Growth of high quality metal single crystals; mechanical properties of single crystals; dislocations; response of skin to ultraviolet and visible light; identifying cognitive variables that influence the study of physics and developing support systems to reduce dropout in the introductory courses; computer assisted instruction. *Mailing Add:* Dept Physics Univ Incarnate Word 4301 Broadway San Antonio TX 78209. *Fax:* 713-743-3589

HUDSON, J(OHN) L, CHEMICAL ENGINEERING. *Current Pos:* chmn dept, Univ Va, 75-85, prof chem eng, 75-85, Ctr Advan Studies, 85-86, WILLIS JOHNSON PROF CHEM ENG, UNIV VA, 88- *Personal Data:* b Chicago, Ill, June 19, 37; m 63; c 3. *Educ:* Univ Ill, BS, 59; Princeton Univ, MSE, 60; Northwestern Univ, PhD(chem eng), 62. *Honors & Awards:* Wilhelm Award, Am Inst Chem Engrs; Sr von Humboldt Prize. *Prof Exp:* Fulbright fel, Univ Grenoble, 62-63; from asst prof to assoc prof chem & chem eng, Univ Ill, Urbana, 63-74; mgr, Div Air Pollution Control, Ill Environ Protection Agency, 74-75. *Concurrent Pos:* Fulbright fel, Univ Tubingen, 82-83. *Mem:* Am Inst Chem Engrs; Am Chem Soc; Air Pollution Control Asn. *Res:* Chemical reactors; dynamics of reacting systems. *Mailing Add:* Dept Chem Eng Thornton Hall Univ Va Charlottesville VA 22903-2442. *E-Mail:* hudson@virginia.edu

HUDSON, JAMES BLOOMER, medicine, for more information see previous edition

HUDSON, JAMES GARY, CLOUD PHYSICS, AEROSOL SCIENCE. *Current Pos:* From asst res prof to assoc res prof, 76-90, RES PROF, ATMOSPHERIC SCI CTR, DESERT RES INST, 90- *Personal Data:* b Mount Clemens, Mich, Aug 11, 46; m 70, Karen Sampson; c Alexander, Annemarie, Elaine & Veronica. *Educ:* Western Mich Univ, BA, 68; Univ Mich, MS, 70; Univ Nev, Reno, PhD(atmos physics), 76. *Mem:* Am Meterol Soc; Sigma Xi; Am Geophys Union. *Res:* Instrumentation, laboratory and field measurements and climatology of cloud condensation nuclei; relationship between cloud condensation nuclei and cloud and fog droplet spectra; origin of atmospheric aerosol and atmospheric visibility. *Mailing Add:* 2055 Severn Dr Reno NV 89503. *Fax:* 702-677-3157

HUDSON, JOHN B(ALCH), SURFACE PHENOMENA. *Current Pos:* res assoc, 63-65, from asst prof to assoc prof, 65-72, PROF MAT ENG, RENSSELAER POLYTECH INST, 72- *Personal Data:* b Plymouth, Mass, Dec 11, 34; m 57, Carol J Greenhill; c Robert B, David K & Jean E (Copper). *Educ:* Rensselaer Polytech Inst, BChE, 56, MS, 58, PhD(metall), 60. *Prof Exp:* Phys chemist, Silicone Prod Dept, Gen Elec Co, 56, phys chemist, Res Lab, 57-60; sr res staff mem, Gen Dynamics/Electronics, 60-63. *Concurrent Pos:* Consult, Gen Elec Co, 64-68, Eastman Kodak Co, 64-70, Melpar, Inc, 65, Langley Res Ctr, NASA, 65-70, Aerovac Corp, 68-70, Gen Elec Co, 74-78, Mech Technol Inc, 78-79, Watervliet Arsenal, 79-83 & 97, Inficon Corp, 84-90 & 97, TPL Cordis, 87-88, Norton Co, 93 & Travelers Ins, 93-94; vis prof physics, State Univ NY, Albany, 85-86. *Mem:* Am Inst Mining, Metall & Petrol Engrs; Am Vacuum Soc; Am Phys Soc; AAAS; Mat Res Soc. *Res:* Physics and chemistry of surfaces; ultrahigh vacuum instrumentation; heterogeneous catalysis; diffusion in solids; adsorption phenomena; environmental effects on materials; electronic materials processing; chemical vapor deposition. *Mailing Add:* Dept Mat Sci & Eng Rensselaer Polytech Inst Troy NY 12180. *E-Mail:* hudsoj@rpi.edu

HUDSON, LYNN DIANE, GENETICS. *Current Pos:* staff mem, NAT INST NEUROL & COMMUN DIS & STROKE, NIH, 87- *Personal Data:* b Chicago, Ill, Aug 7, 53; m 77; c 1. *Educ:* Univ Wis-Madison, BS, 73; Univ Minn, PhD(genetics & cell biol), 77. *Prof Exp:* Fel genetics, Harvard Med Sch, 77-79; res assoc, Brown Univ, 79-87. *Mem:* Am Soc Cell Biol; Women Cell Biol; Am Soc Neurochem. *Res:* Regulation of brain-specific genes. *Mailing Add:* Bldg 36 Rm 5D04 NIH Bethesda MD 20892-4160. *Fax:* 301-496-0899

HUDSON, MARY KATHERINE, SPACE PHYSICS, PLASMA PHYSICS. *Current Pos:* ASSOC PROF PHYS & ASTRON DEPT, DARMOUTH COL. *Personal Data:* b Santa Monica, Calif, Jan 6, 49; m 84; c 2. *Educ:* Univ Calif, Los Angeles, BS, 69, MS, 71, PhD(physics), 74. *Honors & Awards:* Macelwane Award, Am Geophys Union. *Prof Exp:* Res physicist, Aerospace Corp, 69-71; res physicist space physics, Univ Calif, Berkeley, 74-84. *Concurrent Pos:* Lectr, Univ Calif, Berkeley; vis asst prof physics, Mills Col; vis staff, LLNL & LANL; assoc ed, J Geophys Res. *Mem:* Fel Am Geophys Union; Am Phys Soc. *Res:* Theoretical models of ionospheric plasma phenomena; E and F region irregularities; ionosphere-magnetosphere coupling and transport phenomena; ring current-plasmaparse interaction; other planetary magnetospheres. *Mailing Add:* Phys & Astron Dept Dartmouth Col Hanover NH 03755

HUDSON, PAGE, PATHOLOGY, FORENSIC MEDICINE. *Current Pos:* prof, 86-91, EMER PROF PATH, E CAROLINA UNIV SCH MED, 91- *Personal Data:* b Richmond, Va, Feb 14, 31; m 56; c 4. *Educ:* Univ Richmond, BA, 52; Med Col Va, MD, 56. *Prof Exp:* Asst path, Johns Hopkins Univ, 56-57, instr, 57-58; intern path, Johns Hopkins Hosp, 56-57, asst pathologist, 57-58; res fel, Dept Legal Med, Harvard Med Sch, 60-61; instr path, State Univ NY Downstate Med Ctr, 61-64; asst prof, Med Col Va, 64-65, assoc prof surg path, 65-68; chief med examr, State of NC, 68-86; chmn, Div Forensic Path, Univ NC, Chapel Hill, 68-86, prof path, 71-86. *Concurrent Pos:* Consult forensic path. *Mem:* Fel Am Acad Forensic Sci; AMA; US Can Acad Path; Nat Asn Med Examr. *Res:* Anatomic, surgical and forensic pathology; forensic toxicology. *Mailing Add:* Dept Forensic Path Sch Med E Carolina Univ Greenville NC 27858. *Fax:* 919-253-5234

HUDSON, PEGGY R, PHYCOLOGY. *Current Pos:* asst prof, 74-80, ASSOC PROF BIOL, SEATTLE UNIV, 80- *Personal Data:* b Dayton, Wash, May 31, 47; m 69. *Educ:* Univ Wash, BS, 68, PhD(bot), 74. *Prof Exp:* Consult ultrastruct & phycol, Weyerhaeuser Co, 73-74. *Mem:* Phycol Soc Am; Int Phycol Soc; Am Asn Univ Prof; Am Inst Biol Sci. *Res:* Ultrastructure of algae; algal structure and function, especially of seaweeds. *Mailing Add:* Dept Biol Seattle Univ 901 12th Ave Seattle WA 98122-4460

HUDSON, RALPH P, METROLOGY, LOW TEMPERATURE PHYSICS. *Current Pos:* RETIRED. *Personal Data:* b Wellingborough, Eng, Oct 14, 24; nat US; m 47, Nancy Brisby; c Geoffrey & Wendy. *Educ:* Oxford Univ, BA, 44, MA & PhD, 49. *Honors & Awards:* J P Wetherill Medal, Franklin Inst, 62; Stratton Award, Nat Bur Standards, 64, Condon Award, 76. *Prof Exp:* Sci officer, Brit Ministry Supply, 44-46; vis lectr physics, Purdue Univ, 49-50, asst prof, 50-51; mem cryogenics sect, Nat Bur Standards, 51-54, actg chief, 54-55, chief, 55-61, chief heat div, 61-78, dep dir, Ctr Absolute Phys Quantities, 78-80; mem staff, Int Bur Weights & Measures, France, 80-89; prog dir, NSF, Washington, DC, 89-92. *Concurrent Pos:* Guggenheim fel, 60; US rep, Consult Comt Thermometry, Int Comt Weights & Measures, 62-80; ed, Metrologia, 80-89. *Mem:* Fel Franklin Inst; fel Am Phys Soc. *Res:* Temperature measurement and temperature physics; research near absolute zero: paramagnetism, liquid helium, superconductivity, nuclear orientation, thermometry and magnetic resonance. *Mailing Add:* 5500 Uptingham St Chevy Chase MD 20815

HUDSON, REGGIE LESTER, PHYSICAL CHEMISTRY, MAGNETIC RESONANCE. *Current Pos:* from asst prof to assoc prof, 78-92, PROF CHEM, ECKERD COL, 92- *Personal Data:* b Newport News, Va, July 23, 52; m 82; c 2. *Educ:* Pfeiffer Col, AB, 74; Univ Tenn, PhD(chem), 78. *Concurrent Pos:* Vis scientist, Univ Col, London, 85-86 & NASA-Goddard Space Flight Ctr, 87-88 & 91-92. *Mem:* Am Chem Soc; Sigma Xi; Royal Soc Chem. *Res:* Structure, bonding, and reactions of free radicals using electron spin resonance and optical spectroscopies; application of infrared, mass spectral, and radiation methods to problems in cometary chemistry; astrophysical chemistry. *Mailing Add:* Chem Eckerd Col PO Box 12560 St Petersburg FL 33733. *Fax:* 813-864-8382; *E-Mail:* hudson@eckerd.edu

HUDSON, RICHARD DELANO, JR, optical physics, for more information see previous edition

HUDSON, ROBERT B, CHEMICAL ENGINEERING, INORGANIC CHEMISTRY. *Current Pos:* RETIRED. *Personal Data:* b Baltimore, Md, Oct 1, 20; m 42, Jane Clements; c Anne, Carol, Robert & Patricia. *Educ:* Auburn Univ, BS, 42; St Louis Univ, MS, 59. *Prof Exp:* Tech trainee, Monsanto Chem Co, 44-47, res chem engr, 47-57, sr res chem engr, 57-60, res specialist, 60-62, res group leader, 62-64, sr res group leader, 64-70, mgr mfg technol, 70-78, sect mgr res & develop, 78-81, mgr res & develop, 81-82. *Mem:* Am Chem Soc; Am Inst Chem Engrs. *Res:* Product and process development; phosphorus chemistry; process control system analysis and synthesis. *Mailing Add:* 10 Barberry Lane Kirkwood MO 63122-5114

HUDSON, ROBERT DOUGLAS, AERONOMY, ATOMIC SPECTROSCOPY. *Current Pos:* CHMN & PROF, UNIV MD, 90- *Personal Data:* b Walton-on-Thames, Eng, Mar 11, 31; nat US; m 56; c 5. *Educ:* Univ Reading, BS, 56, PhD(ultraviolet spectros), 59. *Prof Exp:* Asst prof physics, Univ Southern Calif, 59-62; mem tech staff labs div, Aerospace Corp, 62-69; staff scientist, Sci Applns Directorate, Johnson Space Ctr, NASA, 69-74, mgr, Environ Effects Proj Off, 74-76, head, Stratospheric Chem & Physics Br, Goddard Space Flight Ctr, 76-90. *Concurrent Pos:* Consult, Space Technol Labs, 60-61 & Aerospace Corp, 61-62. *Mem:* Am Geophys Union. *Res:* Measurements of vacuum ultraviolet absorption cross-sections of gases and vapors; applying these data to geophysical and astrophysical problems and to the formulation of rocket and spacecraft payloads; photo chemistry of the earth's and planetary atmospheres. *Mailing Add:* Dept Meteorol Univ Md College Park MD 20742-0001

HUDSON, ROBERT FRANK, GEOLOGY. *Current Pos:* CONSULT, 85- *Educ:* Colby Col, BA, 54, MS, 57; Univ Iowa, PhD, 65. *Prof Exp:* Explor & exploitation geologist, Texaco Inc, Houston, 66-78; exploitation geologist, La Land & Explor Co, Houston, 78-81; explor geologist, MCO Resources, Houston, 81-82; explor geologist, Donald C Slawson, Houston, 82-83; staff geologist, Sohio Petrol Co, Houston, 83-85. *Concurrent Pos:* Explor geologist, Texaco Inc, Corpus Christi, 59-66. *Mem:* Am Asn Petrol Geologists; fel Geol Soc Am. *Res:* Prospect generation, prospect sales, evaluation of submittals and exploration research along the Texas Gulf Coast. *Mailing Add:* 6833 Hazen St Houston TX 77074

HUDSON, ROBERT MCKIM, PHYSICAL CHEMISTRY, INORGANIC CHEMISTRY. *Current Pos:* CONSULT, 91- *Personal Data:* b Morristown, NJ, Oct 1, 26; m 52, Jean Harris; c Robert & Barbara. *Educ:* Yale Univ, BS, 47, PhD(chem), 50. *Prof Exp:* Sr res consult, Surface Chem & Gas-Metal Reactions, Light Prod Div, Res Tech Ctr, US Steel Corp, Monroeville, 50-91. *Mem:* Am Chem Soc; Sigma Xi; Iron & Steel Soc, Am Inst Mining Metall & Petrol Engrs. *Res:* Diffusion of electrolytes in aqueous solutions; gas-metal reactions during annealing of steel; hydrogen behavior in steel; reaction kinetics and mechanisms; thermodynamics; corrosion of steel and coated steel products; pickling of iron and steel; pickling inhibitors. *Mailing Add:* 1618 Williamsburg Pl Pittsburgh PA 15235

HUDSON, ROBERT Y(OUNG), civil engineering; deceased, see previous edition for last biography

HUDSON, ROY DAVAGE, NEUROPHARMACOLOGY, HEALTH BUSINESS & MANAGEMENT. *Current Pos:* RETIRED. *Personal Data:* b Hamilton Co, Tenn, June 30, 30; m 56, Constance Taylor; c Hollye L (Goler) & David K. *Educ:* Livingstone Col, BS, 55; Univ Mich, MS, 57, PhD(pharmacol), 62. *Hon Degrees:* MA, Brown Univ, 68; LLD, Lehigh Univ, 74 & Princeton Univ, 75. *Honors & Awards:* Upjohn Prize, 87. *Prof Exp:* Asst prof pharmacol, Med Sch Univ Mich, 61-66; assoc prof neurosci, Brown Univ, 66-70, assoc dean grad sch, 66-69; pres, Hampton Univ, 70-76; vis prof pharmacol, Med Sch, Univ Va, 72-74; vpres planning, Parke-Davis Co, 76-79; dir, Cent Nervous Syst Res, Upjohn Co, 81-87, vpres, Pharm Res & Develop, Europe, 87-90, corp vpres, pub rels, 90-92; exec dir & chief exec officer, Kalamazoo Guidance Clin, 93; interim pres, Livingstone Col, 95-96. *Concurrent Pos:* Chmn elect, RI Comn Econ Develop, 68-69; comnr, Norfolk Area Med Ctr Authority, Va, 70-74; mem, Adv Comt to the Dir, NIH, 74-77 & Off Technol Assessment Appln Sci & Technol, 76-77. *Mem:* AAAS; NY Acad Sci; Am Soc Pharmacol & Exp Therapeut; Am Col Neuropsychopharmacol; Am Asn Higher Educ. *Res:* Investigation of mechanisms of action underlying motor pathologies; pyramidal and extrapyramidal motor dysfunctions occurring spontaneously and as a result of drug treatment; effects of centrally acting drugs on the electroencephalogram. *Mailing Add:* 7057 Oak Highlands Kalamazoo MI 49009

HUDSON, SCOTT E, COMPUTER SCIENCE. *Current Pos:* ASSOC PROF, COL COMPUT, GA INST TECHNOL. *Educ:* Univ Colo, PhD(comput sci), 86. *Prof Exp:* Asst prof comput sci, Univ Ariz. *Concurrent Pos:* Mem, Graphics, Visualization & Usability Ctr; Assoc ed, Asn Comput Mach Trans Comput Human Interaction. *Res:* User interface toolkits; high-level specification techniques for user interfaces; constraint systems in user interfaces; tools to support user interface evaluation, multimedia, collaborative work, new input modalities; interfaces to digital libraries and other large information spaces. *Mailing Add:* Graphics Visualization & Usability Ctr Col Comput Ga Inst Technol 801 Atlantic Dr Atlanta GA 30332-0280. *E-Mail:* hudson@cc.gatech.edu

HUDSON, SIGMUND NYROP, MATHEMATICS, COMPUTER SCIENCE. *Current Pos:* PROF MATH & COMPUT SCI, ARMSTRONG STATE COL, 85- *Personal Data:* b Memphis, Tenn, Sept 29, 36; m 60; c 2. *Educ:* Dartmouth Col, AB, 58; Tulane Univ, PhD(math), 63; Clarkson Univ, MS, 85. *Prof Exp:* Asst prof math, Syracuse Univ, 63-70; asst prof, Tulane Univ, 70-71; from assoc prof to prof math, Savannah State Col, 71-85. *Mem:* Am Math Soc; Math Asn Am; Asn Comput Mach; Computer Prof Social Responsibility. *Res:* Topological algebra. *Mailing Add:* 614 E 41st St Savannah GA 31401

HUDSON, WILLIAM NATHANIEL, MATHEMATICAL ANALYSIS, MATHEMATICAL STATISTICS. *Current Pos:* PROF, AUBURN UNIV, 78- *Personal Data:* b Berkeley, Calif. *Educ:* Univ Calif, Berkeley, AB, 60, MA, 63; Univ Calif, Irvine, PhD(math), 70. *Prof Exp:* Engr, Northrop Corp, 63-65; mem tech staff, Rockwell Corp, 65-70; lectr math, Univ Calif, Santa Barbara, 70-73; vis asst prof, Univ Utah, 73-75; assoc prof math, Bowling Green State Univ, 75-77. *Concurrent Pos:* Vis assoc prof, Tulane Univ, 77-78; vis prof, Univ Ariz, 80-81, Univ NC, 84. *Mem:* Inst Math Statist. *Res:* Probability theory and stochastic processes; infinitely divisible distributions and processes with independent increments. *Mailing Add:* Dept Math Auburn Univ Auburn AL 36849-3501

HUDSON, WILLIAM RONALD, CIVIL ENGINEERING. *Current Pos:* from instr to assoc prof, 63-73, asst dean col eng, 69-70, DeWitt C Greer prof, 81, PROF CIVIL ENG, UNIV TEX, AUSTIN, 73-, RES ENGR, CTR HWY RES, 63-, ASSOC DEAN ENG ADVAN PROGS, 70- *Personal Data:* b Temple, Tex, May 17, 33; m 58; c 3. *Educ:* Tex A&M Univ, BS, 54, MS, 55; Univ Tex, Austin, PhD(civil eng), 65. *Honors & Awards:* James R Croes Medal, Am Soc Civil Engrs, 68. *Prof Exp:* Civil engr, S J Buchanan & Assocs, 57-58; asst chief rigid pavement res br, Am Asn State Hwy Officials Rd Test, Nat Acad Sci, Ill, 58-61; supv designing res engr, Hwy Design Div, Tex Hwy Dept, 61-63. *Concurrent Pos:* Mem pavement condition eval comt, Hwy Res Bd, Nat Acad Sci-Nat Res Coun, 63-, strength & deformation characteristics of pavement sect comt, 64-, award comt, 65, res needs subcomt, pavement condition eval comt, 65-66, subcomt, rigid pavement design comt, 65-69, theory of pavement design comt, 65-69, chmn, 69-, mem task force comt struct design of pavement systs, 70, adv comt struct design asphalt concrete pavement systs, 70, asst proj engr & consult, Proj 1-1, Nat Coop Hwy Res Prog, 63-64, mem adv sect, 67, surface eval subcomt, pavement condition eval comt, 67 & ad hoc comt interaction soils & design div, 67-; consult, Signal Oil & Gas Co, 65-66; prin investr, Mat Res & Develop Inc, Calif, 66- & C5A test pavement prog, Waterways Exp Sta & Ohio River Div Lab, US CEngr, 68; mem adv panel, Eric H Wany USAF Civil Eng Res Facil, 69; consult, Dow Chem Co & Shell Develop Co. *Mem:* AAAS; Nat Soc Prof Engrs; Am Soc Civil Engrs; Am Concrete Inst; NY Acad Sci. *Mailing Add:* Dept Civil Eng Univ Tex ECJ 6-10 Austin TX 78712

HUDSON, WILLIAM RUCKER, SURGERY, OTOLARYNGOLOGY. *Current Pos:* from asst prof to assoc prof, 61-65, PROF OTOLARYNGOL & CHIEF DIV, MED SCH, DUKE UNIV, 65- *Personal Data:* b Charlotte, NC, May 16, 25; m 47; c 3. *Educ:* Bowman Gray Sch Med, Wake Forest Univ, MD, 51. *Prof Exp:* NIH fel, Sch Med, Johns Hopkins Univ, 60-61. *Concurrent Pos:* Consult, Vet Admin Hosp, Durham, NC, 61- *Mem:* Am Acad Ophthal & Otolaryngol; Am Laryngol, Rhinol & Otolaryngol Soc; Am Laryngol Asn; Soc Univ Otolaryngol; Am Col Surg. *Res:* Otophysiology. *Mailing Add:* Duke Univ Med Ctr PO Box 3805 Durham NC 27710-3805

HUDSPETH, ALBERT JAMES, NEUROBIOLOGY, SENSORY TRANSDUCTION. *Current Pos:* INVESTR HOWARD HUGHES MED INST, 93-; PROF & HEAD, LAB SENSORY NEUROSCI, ROCKEFELLER UNIV, NY, 95- *Personal Data:* b Houston, Tex, Nov 9, 45; m 77, Ann Maurine Packard; c James Chalmers & Ann Maurine Demaris. *Educ:* Harvard Univ, BA, 67, MA, 68, PhD(neurobiol), 73, MD, 74. *Honors & Awards:* Dr Harold Lamport Award, NY Acad Sci, 85; K C Cole Award, Biophys Soc, 91. *Prof Exp:* Asst prof biol, Calif Inst Technol, 75-78, assoc prof, 78-82, prof, 82-83; prof, Dept Physiol & Otolaryngol, Univ Calif, San Francisco, 83-89; prof & chmn, Dept Cell Biol & Neurosci, Univ Tex Southwestern Med Ctr, 89-92, Dir, Neurosci Prog, 92-93. *Concurrent Pos:* Instr neurobiol, Cold Spring Harbor Lab, 71-72 & 78-82; vis res fel, Karolinska Hosp, Sweden, 74-; res fel neurobiol, Harvard Med Sch, 75; Alfred P Sloan res fel, 76-78; instr synapses, Cold Spring Harbor Lab, 78-82; assoc ed, J Neurosci, 81-87; mem neurosci prog, Univ Calif, San Francisco, 83-89, vchair, Dept Physiol, 85-88, dir cell biol prog, 86-89 & mem biophys prog, 86-89; Javits Neurosci Investr Award, NIH, 85-91; Claude Pepper Award, NIH, 91-93; mem, Molecular Biophys Prog, Southwestern Med Ctr Univ Tex, Dallas, 92-94, prof & dir, Ctr Basic Neurosci Res, 92-95. *Mem:* Nat Acad Sci; Asn Res Otolaryngol; Soc Neurosci; AAAS; Am Soc Cell Biol; Biophys Soc. *Res:* Transduction process whereby the sensory receptors of the inner ear, hair cells, convert acoustical and accelerational stimuli into electrical signals that the brain can interpret; author of numerous publications. *Mailing Add:* HHMI Rockefeller Univ 1230 York Ave Campus Box 314 New York NY 10021. *E-Mail:* hudspaj@rockvax.rockefeller.edu

HUDSPETH, EMMETT LEROY, NUCLEAR PHYSICS. *Current Pos:* dir, Nuclear Physics Lab, 50-71, prof, 50-87, EMER PROF PHYSICS, UNIV TEX, AUSTIN, 87- *Personal Data:* b Denton, Tex, Dec 3, 16; m 44; c 4. *Educ:* Rice Inst, AB, 37, AM, 38, PhD(nuclear physics), 40. *Honors & Awards:* Emmett L Hudspeth Centennial Lectureship in Physics. *Prof Exp:* Res fel, Bartol Res Found, Franklin Inst, 40-41, asst dir, Found, 45-50; res assoc & mem staff radiation lab, Mass Inst Technol, 41-45. *Concurrent Pos:* Mem comt undersea warfare, 47-48; sci adv comt radiobiol lab, Univ Tex & USAF, 54-58; bd dirs, Tex Nuclear Corp, 56-66; bd dirs, Nuclear-Chicago Corp, 61-66; bd dirs & consult, Medical Monitor Systems, Inc, 69-78. *Mem:* AAAS; fel Am Phys Soc; Am Asn Physicists Med; Sigma Xi. *Res:* Nuclear physics with electrostatic machines; radar wave propagation; military operation and tactics; high voltage generators; energy levels of nuclei; neutron scattering; neutron therapy; vital signs measurements. *Mailing Add:* 4100 Jackson Ave Apt 279 Austin TX 78731-6004

HUEBERT, BARRY JOE, PHYSICAL CHEMISTRY, ANALYTICAL CHEMISTRY. *Current Pos:* PROF OCEANOG, OCEAN UNIV, RI, 87- *Personal Data:* b Nebraska City, Nebr, Mar 13, 45; div; c 2. *Educ:* Occidental Col, BS, 67; Northwestern Univ, MS, 68, PhD(chem), 71. *Prof Exp:* Instr chem, Northwestern Univ, 70-71; from asst prof to assoc prof chem, Colo Col, 71-86; dir athos chem prog, SRI Int, 86-87. *Concurrent Pos:* Sr fel, Nat Ctr Atmospheric Res, 77-78; mem, Atmospheric Chem & Climate Comt, IGAC Marine Aerosol & Gas Exchange, steering comt, Int Global Atmospheric Chem Prog, Comn Atmospheric Chem & Global Pollution. *Mem:* Am Chem Soc; Am Geophys Union. *Res:* Precipitation chemistry; global measurements of tropospheric particles and acidic gases; atmospheric chemistry and physics; atmospheric nitrogen chemistry; dry-deposition of acids; air/sea exchange climate change. *Mailing Add:* Dept Oceanography 1000 Pope Rd Univ Hawaii Honolulu HI 96822-2336

HUEBNER, ALBERT LOUIS, APPLIED PHYSICS, BIOPHYSICS. *Current Pos:* ASST PROF PHYSICS, CALIF STATE UNIV, 75- *Personal Data:* b New York, NY, Feb 4, 31; m 63, Mildred Elnick; c Susan, Paul & Laura. *Educ:* Brooklyn Col, AB, 55; Univ Calif, Los Angeles, MA, 62. *Prof Exp:* Teaching asst, Columbia Univ, 55-57; from physicist to sr physicist, Rocketdyne Div, NAm Rockwell Corp, 57-66, prin scientist, 66-73. *Concurrent Pos:* Lectr, West Coast Univ, 62-65, sr lectr & coordr dept physics, 65-82; dir, Sci-Media Assocs, 73- *Mem:* AAAS; Am Asn Physics Teachers; Am Inst Med Climat. *Res:* Electrified-fluid phenomena; solid state device physics; energy development and use analysis. *Mailing Add:* 20331 Mobile St Canoga Park CA 91306

HUEBNER, ERWIN, DEVELOPMENTAL BIOLOGY, REPRODUCTIVE BIOLOGY. *Current Pos:* from asst prof to assoc prof, 72-81, PROF ZOOL, UNIV MAN, 81- *Personal Data:* b July 14, 43; Can citizen; m 71. *Educ:* Univ Alta, BSc, 65; Univ Mass, Amherst, PhD(zool), 70. *Prof Exp:* Fel insect physiol, MacDonald Col, McGill Univ, 70-72. *Mem:* Can Soc Zool; Am Soc Develop Biol; Am Soc Cell Biol; Soc Exp Biol; Am Soc Zool; Can Soc Cell Biol; Sigma Xi. *Res:* The process of oogenesis, using comparative oogenesis to determine the morphological, cytochemical, bioelectrical and physiological parameters that occur and control this process. *Mailing Add:* Dept Zool Univ Man Winnipeg MB R3T 2N2 Can. *Fax:* 204-275-6532

HUEBNER, GEORGE J, environmental research; deceased, see previous edition for last biography

HUEBNER, GEORGE L(EE), JR, ELECTRICAL ENGINEERING. *Current Pos:* from assoc prof to prof, 61-88, EMER PROF METEOROL, TEX A&M UNIV, 88-; CHMN BD, ENVIRON RES INST MICH. *Personal Data:* b Bay City, Tex, May 22, 18; m 41; c 4. *Educ:* Tex A&M Univ, BS, 46, MS, 51, PhD(elec eng), 53. *Prof Exp:* Monitoring officer, Radio Intel Div, Fed Commun Comn, 42-43; res engr, Vector Mfg Co, Tex, 46-47 & Independent Explor Co, 47-50; sr res scientist, Tex A&M Res Found, 53-59; sect head electro optics, Tex Instruments, Dallas, 60-61. *Concurrent Pos:* Consult, TRW Systs, Tex Instruments, Envicon Inc, Spectro Systs, Tri-Pak, Oceanografia, Tex Tech Univ, Am Coun Educ, 71-, Mega Labs, Tex, 90- *Mem:* Am Meteorol Soc; Inst Elec & Electronics Engrs. *Res:* Electrical activity of thunderstorms, oceanographic instrumentation, remote sensing techniques, radar meteorology and analysis of weather systems with use of radar. *Mailing Add:* Dept Meteorol Tex A&M Univ College Station TX 77843. *Fax:* 409-693-6341; *E-Mail:* metradar@aol.com

HUEBNER, JAY STANLEY, BIOPHYSICS, ELECTRONICS. *Current Pos:* from asst prof to assoc prof, 72-78, PROF NAT SCI, UNIV NFLA, 78-, DIR, CTR MEMBRANE PHYSICS, 83- *Personal Data:* b Bancroft, Kans, July 10, 39; m 61; c 3. *Educ:* Kans State Univ, BSEE, 61; San Diego State Univ, MS, 65; Univ Calif, Riverside, PhD(physics), 71. *Prof Exp:* Assoc engr astronaut, Gen Dynamics Corp, 61-63; res proj supvr, Bourns Inc, 68-70; res assoc biophys, Mich State Univ, 71-72. *Concurrent Pos:* Fulbright scholar, 88. *Mem:* Nat Space Soc; Am Asn Physics Teachers; Am Soc Photobiol; Am Chem Soc. *Res:* Photoelectric effects in biological and artificial membranes and science teaching. *Mailing Add:* Ctr Membrane Phys Univ NFla Jacksonville FL 32216-6698

HUEBNER, JOHN STEPHEN, EXPERIMENTAL PETROLOGY, MINERAL PHYSICS. *Current Pos:* RES GEOLOGIST, US GEOL SURV, 67- *Personal Data:* b Bryn Mawr, Pa, Sept 9, 40; m 62, Emily Zug; c Christopher C & Jeffrey W. *Educ:* Princeton Univ, BA, 62; Johns Hopkins Univ, PhD(geol), 67. *Honors & Awards:* Mineral Soc Am Award, 78. *Concurrent Pos:* Lectr, George Washington Univ, 71; prin investr, NASA Lunar Sample Prog, 73-84; mem, Lunar & Planetary Rev Panel, 76-78; assoc ed, J Geophys Res, 77-79; counr, Am Geol Inst, 85-88. *Mem:* AAAS; fel Mineral Soc Am; Am Geophys Union; Geochem Soc (treas, 72-75); Am Geol Inst (secy-treas, 74-75); Sigma Xi. *Res:* Phase relations of rock forming minerals at elevated temperature, pressure; control of polycomponent fluids in experimental geochemistry; geochemistry of manganese; pyroxene phase relations; high temperature electrochemistry; diffusion in silicates; electrical conductivity and impedance spectroscopy. *Mailing Add:* 6102 Cromwell Dr Bethesda MD 20816-3410. *Fax:* 703-648-6789; *E-Mail:* shuebner@igp1.er.usgs.gov

HUEBNER, JUDITH DEE, FRESHWATER ECOLOGY. *Current Pos:* instr, 75-81, ASST PROF BIOL, UNIV WINNIPEG, 81- *Personal Data:* b New York, NY, Mar 4, 47; m 71. *Educ:* Queens Col, BA, 67; Univ Mass, Amherst, MS, 70, PhD(zool), 72. *Prof Exp:* Fel ecol res, Dept Zool, Univ Man, 73-74. *Concurrent Pos:* Researcher, Northwest Fisheries Ctr, Nat Oceanic & Atmospheric Admin, Woods Hole, Mass, 79-80. *Mem:* AAAS; Am Soc Zoologists; Ecol Soc Am; Can Soc Zoologists; Sigma Xi. *Res:* Ecological energetics and physiological ecology of large intertidal and fresh water molluscs; energetics, consumption and evacuation in inshore (marine) and freshwater fish; predator-prey interactions. *Mailing Add:* Univ Winnipeg 515 Portage Ave Winnipeg MB R3B 2E9 Can

HUEBNER, ROBERT JOSEPH, VIROLOGY. *Current Pos:* RETIRED. *Personal Data:* b Cheviot, Ohio, Feb 23, 14; m 75; c 9. *Educ:* St Louis Univ, MD, 42. *Hon Degrees:* LLD, Univ Cincinnati, 65; DSc, Edgecliff Col, 70, Univ Parma, 70 & Cath Univ Louvain, 73. *Honors & Awards:* Bailey K Ashford Award, Am Soc Trop Med, 49; James D Bruce Mem Award, Am Col Physicians, 64; Pasteur Medal, Pasteur Inst, 65; Nat Medal Sci, 69; Kimble Methodology Award, 70; Guido Lenghi Award, Nat Acad Lincei, Rome, 71; Founders Award Cancer Immunol, Cancer Res Inst Inc, 75. *Prof Exp:* Intern, USPHS Hosp, 42-43; med officer, NIH, 44-47, in chg res unit & Q fever lab, 47-50, chief virus & rickettsial dis, Nat Microbiol Inst, 50-56, chief lab viral dis, Nat Inst Allergy & Infectious Dis, 56-68, chief lab RNA tumor viruses, 68-76, sci coordr immunoprevention, 76-78, mem staff, Cellular & Molecular Biol Lab, Nat Cancer Inst, 78-82. *Mem:* Nat Acad Sci; fel Am Pub Health Asn; fel AMA; fel NY Acad Sci. *Res:* Cancer viruses; medical research. *Mailing Add:* 12100 Whippoorwill Lane Rockville MD 20852

HUEBNER, RUSSELL HENRY, SR, ELECTRON PHYSICS, RADIATION PHYSICS. *Current Pos:* physicist, Radiol & Environ Res Div, Argonne Nat Lab, 70-77, prog coodr biomed & environ res, 77-83, prof mgr, ERAB Sci Support, 83-86, assoc dir & off dir, Strategic Planning Group, 86-87, RES PROG MGR-ADMIN, ADVAN PHOTON SOURCE, ARGONNE NAT LAB, 87- *Personal Data:* b Indianapolis, Ind, Jan 24, 41; m 63, Elaine M Luthman; c Karl A, Bradley S, Kathryn A & Russell H Jr. *Educ:* Purdue Univ, BS, 62; Vanderbilt Univ, MS, 65; Univ Tenn, PhD(physics), 68; Univ Chicago, MBA, 83. *Prof Exp:* Health physics fel, Oak Ridge Nat Lab, 63-68; radiol physicist, Div Biol & Med, USAEC, 68-70. *Concurrent Pos:* Guest scientist, Electron & Optical Physics Sect, Optical Physics Div, Nat Bur Stand, 70; assoc ed, Radiation Res J, 78-81. *Mem:* Sigma Xi; AAAS. *Res:* Electron energy-loss spectroscopy of molecules and determination of oscillator strength distributions for use in radiation physics; atmospheric and environmental studies; synchrotron radiation; science research management. *Mailing Add:* 326 Carriage Hill Dr Naperville IL 60565. *Fax:* 630-252-4599; *E-Mail:* rhh@anlaps.aps.anl.gov

HUEBNER, WALTER F, ATOMIC PHYSICS, ASTROPHYSICS. *Current Pos:* INST SCIENTIST, SOUTHWEST RES INST, 87- *Personal Data:* b New York, NY, Feb 22, 28; m 57, Elizabeth Putnam; c Anne (Rice), Pieter R, Elisabeth (Huebner-Schurch) & Richard P. *Educ:* Polytech Inst Brooklyn, BS, 52; Yale Univ, MS, 53, PhD(physics), 58. *Prof Exp:* Staff mem atomic physics, Los Alamos Sci Lab, Univ Calif, 57-68; vis staff mem, Max Planck Inst Astrophys, Munich, 68-70; staff mem, Los Alamos Nat Lab, Univ Calif, 70-72 & 88-91, alt group leader equation state & opacities, 72-76, group leader equation state & opacities, 77-88. *Concurrent Pos:* Mem staff, Theoret Div, NASA, 59; Fulbright grant, Nat Acad Sci, 68; Max Planck Soc grants, 64, 68-70 & 80; consult, Int Astron Union, Comn 15, 70-73, Sci Appln Inc, 72-76 & Res Inst Swed Nat Defense, Stockholm, 72-80; alt group leader theoret astrophys, Los Alamos Nat Lab, Univ Calif, 80-81, dep group leader, 81-82; mem, Team Photographed Nucleus Halley's Comet, Giotto Spacecraft, 86; ed, Physics & Chem Comets; discipline scientist planetary astron, NASA, prog scientist, Near Earth Asteroid Rendezvous Mission, Stardust Mission, New Millenium Deep Space 1 Mission & Near Earth Objects Prog, vis sr scientist, Hq, 94- *Mem:* Am Phys Soc; Am Astron Soc; Ger Astron Soc; Int Astron Union; Sigma Xi. *Res:* Calculation of opacity and equation of state data at all densities and temperatures for any material in the gaseous or plasma phase; research on the physics and chemistry of comets; identified first polymer (polyoxymethylene) in space; author of one book. *Mailing Add:* SW Res Inst PO Drawer 28510 San Antonio TX 78228-0510

HUEBSCH, IAN O, geophysics, meteorology, for more information see previous edition

HUEBSCHMAN, EUGENE CARL, solid state physics; deceased, see previous edition for last biography

HUEBSCHMANN, JOHN W, chemical engineering; deceased, see previous edition for last biography

HUEG, WILLIAM FREDERICK, JR, AGRONOMY. *Current Pos:* RETIRED. *Personal Data:* b New York, NY, Jan 12, 24; m 49, 78; c 7. *Educ:* Cornell Univ, BS, 48; Mich State Univ, MS, 54, PhD(farm crops, soils, agr econ), 59. *Prof Exp:* Asst county agr agent, NY Exten Serv, 48-50; instr crops & soils, State Univ NY Agr Tech Inst, Alfred, 50-55; instr farm crops, Mich State Univ, 55-57; assoc prof & exten agronomist, Univ Minn, 57-62, asst dir agr exp sta, 62-66, dir, 66-75, prof agron, Inst Agr, Forestry & Home Econ, 62-84, dep vpres & dean, 74-84. *Concurrent Pos:* Mem, Nat Sci Bd, 76-82; mgr, Bhella Holsteins Hammond, WI, 84- *Mem:* Fel Am Soc Agron; fel Crop Sci Soc Am; AAAS. *Res:* Forage physiology, utilization and seed production. *Mailing Add:* 1170 Dodd Rd St Paul MN 55118

HUEGE, FRED ROBERT, CLAY MINERALOGY, PAPER CHEMISTRY. *Current Pos:* Proj leader, 70-75, group leader, Phys Measurements Group, 74-75, group leader indust prod res, 75-78, mgr res pigments & extenders, 78-81, DIR RES & DEVELOP PIGMENTS & EXTENDERS, M&C DIV, ENGELHARD CORP, 81- *Personal Data:* b New York, NY, Apr 3, 43; m 72; c 2. *Educ:* Thiel Col, BA, 64; Pa State Univ, PhD(chem), 75. *Mem:* Am Chem Soc; Clay Mineral Soc; Tech Asn Pulp & Paper. *Res:* Mineral based pigments for the paper, paint and other related industries; clay minerals such as kaolinite, attapulgite, talc, to develop new pigments and manufacturing processes. *Mailing Add:* Chemical Lime PO Box 121874 Fort Worth TX 76121

HUELKE, DONALD FRED, ANATOMY, MECHANISMS. *Current Pos:* From instr to assoc prof, 54-68, PROF ANAT, UNIV MICH, ANN ARBOR, 68-, RES SCIENTIST, TRANS RES INST, 75- *Personal Data:* b Chicago, Ill, Aug 20, 30; m 52; c 2. *Educ:* Univ Ill, BS, 52, MS, 54, PhD(anat), 57. *Honors & Awards:* Automotive Safety Award, Med Tribune, 66; Outstanding Achievement in Traffic Safety & Traffic Med, Inst Am Automotive Traffic Med, 78; Ralph H Isbrandt Automotive Safety Eng Award, Soc Automotive Engrs, 80; Award of Merit, Am Asn Automotive Med, 82; Distinguished Achievement Award, Mich Driver & Traffic Safety Educ Asn, 89. *Concurrent Pos:* Consult, Mich State Police Crime Lab, Ford Motor Co, Gen Motors Corp, Chrysler Corp, Human Factors Test Devices Subcomt & Soc Automotive Engrs; mem, Nat Motor Vehicle Safety Adv Coun, 72-74. *Mem:* Int Asn Dent Res; Am Asn Anat; Am Asn Automotive Med (pres, 70); Am Trauma Soc; fel Am Acad Forensic Sci; fel Soc Automotive Engrs. *Res:* Effects of trauma on the human body. *Mailing Add:* 1885 Stonebridge Dr N Ann Arbor MI 48108-8533

HUELSMAN, LAWRENCE PAUL, ELECTRICAL ENGINEERING. *Current Pos:* assoc prof, 60-63, PROF ELEC ENG, UNIV ARIZ, 63- *Personal Data:* b Chicago, Ill, Jan 22, 26; c 1. *Educ:* Case Inst Technol, BSEE, 50; Univ Calif, MSEE, 56, PhD(elec eng), 60. *Prof Exp:* Sect chief in chg training opers, Western Elec Co, Inc, 51-56; assoc elec eng, Univ Calif, Berkeley, 56-60. *Concurrent Pos:* Vis prof, Rice Univ, 64. *Mem:* Fel Inst Elec & Electronics Engrs; Sigma Xi. *Res:* Active resistor-capacitator circuit theory; linear vector space applications to network theory; computer software applications; computer-aided design; analysis of networks. *Mailing Add:* Dept Elec & Comput Eng Univ Ariz Tucson AZ 85721

HUENEMANN, RUTH L, NUTRITION IN PUBLIC HEALTH. *Current Pos:* assoc prof nutrit, 53-67, prof, 67-80, EMER PROF PUB HEALTH NUTRIT, SCH PUB HEALTH, UNIV CALIF, BERKELEY, 80- *Personal Data:* b Waukon, Iowa, Feb 5, 10. *Educ:* Univ Wis, BS, 38; Harvard Univ DSc, 53; Am Bd Nutrit, dipl. *Prof Exp:* Teacher pub schs, SDak, 28-35; staff dietitian, clins & hosps, Chicago, 39-40; nutritionist, Zoller Dent Clin, 40-43; assoc prof nutrit, Univ Tenn, 43-53. *Concurrent Pos:* Nutrit consult, Inst Nutrit, Peru, 51-52; consult, Off Int Res, US Agency Int Develop, 67 & WHO, Geneva, 74. *Mem:* Am Dietetic Asn; Am Pub Health Asn; fel Am Inst Nutrit; Am Bd Nutrit; fel Soc Nutrit Educ. *Res:* Community service; weight control; teenage nutrition and physique. *Mailing Add:* 1925 San Antonio Berkeley CA 94707-1649

HUENING, WALTER C, JR, INDUSTRIAL POWER SYSTEMS, ELECTRICAL ENGINEERING. *Current Pos:* RETIRED. *Personal Data:* b Boston, Mass, Feb 10, 23; m 44, 88, Elizabeth Young; c Peter & Susan (Locke). *Educ:* Tufts Univ, BS, 44. *Honors & Awards:* Kaufmann Award, Inst Elec & Electronics Engrs, 88, Indust Applns Soc Achievement Award, 89. *Prof Exp:* Metal rolling elec equip eng, 63-68; consult appln engr, Gen Elec Co, 68-89. *Mem:* fel Inst Elec & Electronics Engrs. *Res:* Industrial electric power systems; calculation of short circuit currents. *Mailing Add:* 1229 Godfrey Lane Niskayuna NY 12309

HUENNEKENS, FRANK MATTHEW, JR, BIOCHEMISTRY. *Current Pos:* mem & chmn, Dept Biochem, 62-84, mem, Div Biochem, 84-92, EMER MEM, SCRIPPS RES INST, 92- *Personal Data:* b Galveston, Tex, Feb 16, 23; m 44, Betty Ennis; c Karen & John. *Educ:* Univ Calif, BS, 43, PhD(chem), 48. *Honors & Awards:* Paul Lewis Award, Am Chem Soc, 60; F Gowland Hopkins Medal, Pteridine Symp, 82; C Chester Stock Award, Mem Sloan Kettering Cancer Ctr, 89. *Prof Exp:* Asst prof enzyme chem, Univ Wis, 49-51; from asst prof to prof, Univ Wash, 51-62. *Concurrent Pos:* Williams-Waterman fel, Univ Wis, 48-49; consult, NIH, 65-91, Am Cancer Soc, 59-92; adj prof, Depts Chem & Biol, Univ Calif, San Diego, 67-92; Outstanding Investr Grant, Nat Cancer Inst, 85-92; vis prof, Dept Biol Chem, Univ Calif, Davis, 92-93. *Mem:* Fel AAAS; Am Chem Soc. *Res:* Mechanisms of enzyme action and membrane transport; cancer chemotherapy. *Mailing Add:* Div Biochem NX7 Dept Molecular & Exp Med Scripps Res Inst 10666 N Torrey Pines Rd La Jolla CA 92037. *Fax:* 619-554-6223

HUENNEKENS, JOHN PATRICK, LASER SPECTROSCOPY. *Current Pos:* from asst prof to assoc prof, 84-94, PROF PHYSICS, LEHIGH UNIV, 94- *Personal Data:* b Seattle, Wash, May 21, 52; m 78, Carol; c Kelly & Margo. *Educ:* Univ Calif, Berkeley, BA, 73, BA, 74; Univ Ill, Champaign-Urbana, MS, 76; Univ Colo, Boulder, PhD(physics), 82. *Honors & Awards:* Presidential Young Investr Award, NSF, 85. *Prof Exp:* Res assoc, Joint Inst Lab Astrophys, Univ Colo, 82 & Princeton Univ, 82-84. *Mem:* Am Phys Soc. *Res:* Atomic collision physics; collisional line-broadening; collisional excitation transfer; radiation trapping in alkali vapors; molecular spectroscopy. *Mailing Add:* Dept Physics Lehigh Univ 16 Memorial Dr E Bethlehem PA 18015. *Fax:* 610-758-5730; *E-Mail:* jph7@lehigh.edu

HUERTA, MANUEL ANDRES, PLASMA PHYSICS, COMPUTATIONAL PHYSICS. *Current Pos:* from asst prof to assoc prof 72-83, chmn Dept Physics, 80-85, PROF PHYSICS, UNIV MIAMI, CORAL GABLES, FLA, 83- *Personal Data:* b Havana, Cuba, Nov 30, 43; m 67; c 2. *Educ:* Calif Inst Technol, Pasadena, BS, 65; Univ Miami, Coral Gables, MS, 67, PhD(physics), 70. *Prof Exp:* Instr physics, Univ Miami, 67-70; assoc res scientist plasma physics, Courant Inst Math Sci, NY Univ, New York, 70-72. *Concurrent Pos:* Consult magneto-fluid dynamics div, Courant Inst Math Sci, NY Univ, New York, 73-74; prog assoc, Div Int Progs, NSF, 77-78. *Mem:* Sigma Xi; Am Phys Soc. *Res:* Plasma physics; elecromagnetic launchers. *Mailing Add:* Dept Physics Univ Miami PO Box 248046 Coral Gables FL 33124

HUESSY, HANS ROSENSTOCK, PSYCHIATRY. *Current Pos:* clin instr, Univ Vt, 59-64, from asst prof to assoc prof, 64-69, actg chmn dept, 67-70, PROF PSYCHIAT, UNIV VT, 69- *Personal Data:* b Frankfurt, Ger, Aug 15, 21; US citizen; m 58; c 11. *Educ:* Dartmouth Col, BA, 42; Yale Univ, MD, 45; Univ Colo, MS, 51; Am Bd Psychiat & Neurol, dipl, cert psychiat, 52 & child psychiat, 63. *Honors & Awards:* Ment Health Sect Award, Am Pub Health Asn, 82. *Prof Exp:* Intern pediat, Johns Hopkins Univ, 45-46; resident psychiat, USPHS Hosp, Tex, 47-48; staff psychiatrist, US Med Ctr Fed Prisoners, Springfield, Mo, 48-49; res psychiat, Univ Colo, 49-51, clin instr, 51-53; dir ment health progs, Saratoga, Warren & Washington Counties, NY, 53-58. *Concurrent Pos:* Regional psychiat consult, Pub Health Serv, Colo, 51-53; dir aftercare proj, NIMH, 58-67. *Mem:* Fel Am Orthopsychiat Asn; fel Am Pub Health Asn; fel Am Psychiat Asn; fel Am Acad Child Psychiat; Am Psychopath Asn. *Res:* Community psychiatry; hyperkinetic syndrome; learning problems; epidemiology of behavior disorders. *Mailing Add:* Child Psychiat Med Alumni Bldg Univ Vt Col Med Burlington VT 05405

HUESTIS, DAVID LEE, SPECTROSCOPY, EXCITED STATE KINETICS. *Current Pos:* fel physicist, 73, physicist, 73-77, asst prog mgr, 77-80, PROG MGR, MOLECULAR PHYSICS LAB, SRI INT, 80- *Personal Data:* b St Paul, Minn, Dec 20, 46; m 68. *Educ:* Macalester Col, Minn, BA, 68; Calif Inst Technol, MS, 69, PhD(chem), 73. *Prof Exp:* Fel, appl physics, Calif Inst Technol, 72. *Concurrent Pos:* Vis lectr, Dept Chem, Stanford Univ, 78. *Mem:* Am Phys Soc; Int Photochem Soc. *Res:* Theoretical description of molecular excited states and their interactions; scattering theory; electronic structure of solids and surfaces; experimental spectroscopic and kinetics studies of electronically excited states of molecules. *Mailing Add:* Molecular Physics Lab SRI Int Menlo Park CA 94025

HUESTIS, DOUGLAS WILLIAM, TRANSFUSION MEDICINE. *Current Pos:* prof, 69-93, EMER PROF PATH, COL MED, UNIV ARIZ, 93- *Personal Data:* b London, Ont, Mar 21, 25; US citizen; m 55, Rosemary L Colford; c Lucy, Marilyn, Andrew, Karen & Peter. *Educ:* McGill Univ, MD, 48; Am Bd Anat Path, dipl, 55; Am Bd Clin Path, dipl, 60. *Honors & Awards:* John Elliot Award, Am Asn Blood Banks, 75. *Prof Exp:* Intern, Montreal Gen Hosp, 48; res fel exp cytol & biophys, Nobel Inst Cell Res, Karolinska Inst, Sweden, 49-50; sr house officer, Mayday Hosp, Croydon, Eng, 50-51; sr intern path, Montreal Gen Hosp, 51-52; demonstr path & asst prosector, Path Inst, McGill Univ, 52, demonstr path & asst surg path, 53; instr clin path, Ohio State Univ, 54-55; asst dir inst path, Western Pa Hosp, Pittsburgh, 55-60; assoc prof path, Chicago Med Sch, 60-66, prof clin path, 66-69. *Concurrent Pos:* From clin instr to clin asst prof, Univ Pittsburgh, 55-60; dir blood ctr, Mt Sinai Med Res Found & clin pathologist, Mt Sinai Hosp, Chicago, Ill, 60-69; med dir, Southern Ariz Red Cross Blood Prog, 70-77, United Blood Serv Southern Ariz, 85-87. *Mem:* Am Asn Blood Banks; Am Soc Hemat; Am Soc Clin Path; Int Soc Blood Transfusion. *Res:* Immunohematology, especially antigens and antibodies encountered in blood transfusion; clinical use of blood components; platelet and granulocyte transfusion; histocompatibility testing; therapeutic hemapheresis; medical history. *Mailing Add:* 6750 W Camino Del Cerro Tucson AZ 85745-9336. *E-Mail:* dwhuestis@pol.net

HUESTIS, LAURENCE DEAN, ORGANIC CHEMISTRY, ANALYTICAL CHEMISTRY. *Current Pos:* from asst prof to assoc prof chem, 61-73, chmn dept, 70-73, PROF CHEM, PAC LUTHERAN UNIV, 73- *Personal Data:* b Roseville, Calif, July 19, 34; m 58, Bonny Rickter; c 2. *Educ:* Univ Calif, Berkeley, BS, 56, Univ Calif, Davis, PhD(org chem), 60. *Prof Exp:* Res fel, Univ Minn, Minneapolis, 60-61. *Concurrent Pos:* Vis prof, Univ Nev, Reno, 82, Univ NMex, 89. *Mem:* Am Chem Soc; Mineral Soc Am. *Res:* Microanalytical techniques for cation analysis; formaldehyde analysis by mass spectrometry; infrared spectra techniques for identification of minerals; organic complexes of the lanthanide elements; mineralogy. *Mailing Add:* Pac Lutheran Univ 12180 S Park Ave Tacoma WA 98447-0003

HUESTIS, STEPHEN PORTER, GEOPHYSICS. *Current Pos:* asst prof, 77-83, ASSOC PROF GEOPHYS, DEPT GEOL, UNIV NMEX, 83- *Personal Data:* b Berkeley, Calif, Sep 11, 46; m 77. *Educ:* Harvey Mudd Col, BS, 68; Univ Calif, San Diego, MS, 69, PhD(earth sci), 76. *Prof Exp:* Lectr geophys, Eng-Geosci Group, Dept Mat Sci & Eng, Univ Calif, Berkeley, 76-77; asst res geophysicist, Inst Geophys & Planetary Physics, Univ Calif, San Diego, 77. *Concurrent Pos:* Instr geosci, Geophys Sect, Sandia Nat Labs, 80-86. *Mem:* Am Geophys Union; Royal Astron Soc; Sigma Xi. *Res:* Geophysical inverse theory, with emphasis on problems in the interpretation of heat flow, gravity, and magnetic data. *Mailing Add:* Dept Geol Univ NMex Main Campus One Univ Campus Albuquerque NM 87131-0001

HUETHER, CARL ALBERT, HUMAN POPULATION GENETICS. *Current Pos:* Asst prof genetics, 66-71, assoc prof biol, 71-81, PROF BIOL, UNIV CINCINNATI, 83-, PROF ENVIRON HEALTH, 91-, DIR, PROG GENETIC COUN, 91- *Personal Data:* b Cincinnati, Ohio, Aug 22, 37; m 59, Carol; c Laurie A, Linda & Carl Jr. *Educ:* Ohio State Univ, BS, 59; NC State Univ, MS, 63; Univ Calif, Davis, PhD(evolutionary genetics), 66. *Concurrent Pos:* Assoc dean hon, Col Arts & Sci, Univ Cincinnati, 74-77; Nat Serv Res fel, Div Human Genetics, Johns Hopkins Hosp, 77-78; mem adv comt, Pop Ref Bur Inc, Washington, DC, 78-87; vis scientist, CDC, Atlanta, 87, Univ BC, Univ Calif, Berkeley & Emory Univ, 89-90. *Mem:* AAAS; Am Soc Human Genetics; Soc Social Biol; Am Asn Univ Professors; Sigma Xi; Nat Soc Genetic Counselors. *Res:* Demographic genetics; epidemiology and estimation of incidence of chromosomal aberrations, specifically Down's syndrome; probability as applied to genetic counseling; human genetics education. *Mailing Add:* Dept Biol Univ Cincinnati Cincinnati OH 45221-0001. *Fax:* 513-556-5299; *E-Mail:* huether@ucbeh.san.uc.edu

HUETTNER, DAVID JOSEPH, PHYSICAL CHEMISTRY, SILICONE RELEASE COATINGS. *Current Pos:* SR RES CHEMIST, WACKER SILICONES CORP, 89- *Personal Data:* b New London, Wis, Feb 20, 38; m 61, Charlotte M Stroobauts; c 4. *Educ:* St Norbert Col, BS, 60; Wash State Univ, PhD(chem), 66. *Prof Exp:* Res assoc chem, Univ Mass, 66-68; staff chemist appl res, IBM Corp, Endicott, NY, 68-75; asst prof & res assoc chem appl res, Inst Paper Chem, 75-78; sr res specialist, Akrosil Div, Hammermill Paper Co, 78-85; mat specialist, Dow Corning Corp, 85-89. *Concurrent Pos:* NSF & PRF grants, Univ Mass, 66-68. *Mem:* Am Chem Soc; Tech Asn Pulp & Paper Indust; Adhesion Soc; Radtech Int. *Res:* Chemistry and surface properties of silicone release coatings; radiation curing of silicone release coatings. *Mailing Add:* 516 Tilton Dr Tecumseh MI 49286-1640

HUEY, RAYMOND BRUNSON, ANIMAL ECOLOGY, ANIMAL PHYSIOLOGICAL ECOLOGY. *Current Pos:* from asst prof to assoc prof, Univ Wash, 77-84, assoc chmn, Dept Zool, 88-91, actg chmn, 91-92, PROF, UNIV WASH, 84- *Personal Data:* b Bakersfield, Calif, Sept 14, 44. *Educ:* Univ Calif, Berkeley, AB, 66; Univ Tex, Austin, MA, 69; Harvard Univ, PhD(biol), 75. *Prof Exp:* Asst cur herpet, Mus Vert Zool, Univ Calif, Berkeley, 66-67; res assoc lizard ecol, Field Res, Kalahari, Univ Tex, 69-70; Richmond fel ecol, Harvard Univ, 71-74, res assoc lizard ecol, 74-75; Miller fel, Miller Inst Basic Res Sci, Univ Calif, Berkeley, 75-77. *Mem:* Ecol Soc Am; Am Soc Ichthyologists & Herpetologists; Soc Study Evolution; Soc Study Amphibians & Reptiles; Sigma Xi; AAAS; Am Soc Naturalists (pres, 93). *Res:* Evolution of thermal sensitivity in ectotherms; lizard thermoregulation and locomotion in ecological and evolutionary contexts; evolution of physiological ecology in lizards and fruitflies, and general vertebrate ecology. *Mailing Add:* Dept Zool NJ-15 Univ Wash 3900 Seventh Ave NW Seattle WA 98195-0001

HUEY, WILLIAM S, NATURAL RESOURCES MANAGEMENT. *Current Pos:* RETIRED. *Personal Data:* b Wichita Falls, Tex, Mar 26, 25; m 48, Mary Blue. *Educ:* NMex State Univ, BS, 52. *Honors & Awards:* George Allen Mem Award, Int Wild Waterfowl Asn, 62; Winchester Award, Game Conserv Int, 71; Spec Conserv Award, Nat Wildlife Fedn, 82; Oak Leaf Award, Nature Conservancy, 83. *Prof Exp:* Wildlife biologist, NMex Dept Game & Fish, 53-62, asst chief game mgt, 63, chief spec serv, 63-64, chief game mgt, 64-69, chief wildlife opers, 70, asst dir, 70-75, dir, 75-78; secy natural resources, NMex Natural Resources Dept, 78-82. *Concurrent Pos:* Mem, Nature Conserv, 72-, nat bd gov, 86-88, state bd gov, NMex chap, 92-; trustee, Whooping Crane Conser Asn. *Mem:* Am Forestry Asn; Wildlife Soc; Am Ornith Union; Whooping Crane Conserv Asn (pres, 71-75, 87-88); Int Asn Game, Fish & Conserv Comnrs. *Res:* Beaver life historian; waterfowl life historian. *Mailing Add:* PO Box 381 Tesuque NM 87574. *Fax:* 505-983-6082

HUFF, ALBERT KEITH, PLANT SCIENCE. *Current Pos:* ASST PROF PLANT SCI, UNIV ARIZ, 77- *Personal Data:* b Burlington, Wash, Apr 16, 42; m 65; c 2. *Educ:* Univ Wash, BS, 64; Colo State Univ, PhD(plant physiol), 74. *Prof Exp:* Chemist anal chem, Lab Radiation Biol, Univ Wash, 65-67; res assoc physiol, SDak State Univ, 74-77. *Mem:* Am Soc Plant Physiologists; Am Chem Soc; AAAS; Sigma Xi; Am Inst Biol Sci. *Res:* Regulation of plant growth and development; plastid transformations; flower abortion; chlorophyll metabolism; plant productivity in desert climates; postharvest physiology and redox potentials in plant development. *Mailing Add:* 2925 E Loretta Dr Tucson AZ 85716

HUFF, CHARLES WILLIAM, MATHEMATICS. *Current Pos:* chmn dept, 60-68, prof, 60-85, EMER PROF MATH, WINTHROP COL, 85- *Personal Data:* b Greenville Co, SC; June 6, 20; m 52; c 4. *Educ:* Wofford Col, BS, 46; Univ SC, MS, 49; Univ Ga, PhD(math), 54. *Prof Exp:* Instr math, Pa State Univ, 48-49; instr, Univ SC, 49-50; from asst prof to assoc prof, Auburn Univ, 54-60. *Mem:* Am Math Soc; Math Asn Am; Sigma Xi. *Res:* Linear algebra; exponential equation. *Mailing Add:* 113 Merrifield Dr Greenville SC 29615-3340

HUFF, DALE DUANE, HYDROLOGY. *Current Pos:* staff hydrologist, Oak Ridge Nat Lab, 74-84, hydrol group leader, 84-88, sect head environ eng & hydrol, 88-89, mgr tech oversight & rev environ restoration, 90, COORDR, GROUNDWATER PROG, OAK RIDGE NAT LAB, 91- *Personal Data:* b Portland, Ore, Mar 22, 39; m 62; c 2. *Educ:* Stanford Univ, BS, 61, MS, 64, PhD(hydrol), 68. *Prof Exp:* Actg asst prof nuclear hydrol, Stanford Univ, 67-68; from asst prof to assoc prof civil eng, Univ Wis-Madison, 68-74. *Concurrent Pos:* Radiochemist, Hazelton Nuclear Sci Corp; assoc, Adtech Consult, 68-73; consult, Oak Ridge Nat Lab, 72-74. *Mem:* Sigma Xi; Am Inst Hydrol. *Res:* Hydrologic simulation; land water interactions; hydrologic transport of trace materials; shallow-land disposal hydrology. *Mailing Add:* Oak Ridge Nat Lab Bldg 1509 PO Box 2008 Oak Ridge TN 37831-6400. *Fax:* 423-574-7420; *E-Mail:* ddh@ornl.gov

HUFF, DENNIS KARL, MICROBIOLOGY, IMMUNOLOGY. *Current Pos:* MEM FAC, DEPT BIOL SCI, CALIF STATE UNIV, 73- *Personal Data:* b Des Moines, Iowa, Mar 2, 40. *Educ:* Drake Univ, BA, 61, MA, 63; Mich State Univ, PhD(microbiol), 66. *Prof Exp:* Asst prof biol, Univ Tulsa, 66-70; fel microbiol, Univ Ill Med Ctr, 70-73. *Mem:* Am Soc Microbiol; Int Soc Comp & Develop Immunol; Sigma Xi. *Res:* Immunity to protozoan infections; role of RNA in immune response. *Mailing Add:* Dept Biol Sci Calif State Univ Sacramento CA 95819

HUFF, GEORGE FRANKLIN, INDUSTRIAL CHEMISTRY. *Current Pos:* RETIRED. *Personal Data:* b Pittsburgh, Pa, Nov 4, 23; m 50; c 4. *Educ:* Yale Univ, BS, 44; Carnegie Inst Technol, DSc(chem), 49. *Prof Exp:* Res chemist, US Steel Co, 49-52; res chemist, Callery Chem Co, 52-53, mgr res dept, 53-56, dir res & develop, 56-60, vpres, 60-66; dir chem dept, Gulf Res & Develop Co, 66-68; world-wide coordr chem, Gulf Oil Corp, 68-70; vpres res & develop, Gulf Oil Chem Co, 70-80; pres, Alt Energy Assocs Inc, 80-92. *Mem:* Am Inst Chemists; Soc Chem Indust; Am Chem Soc. *Res:* Thermodynamics; thermochemistry. *Mailing Add:* 155 North Dr Pittsburgh PA 15238-2309

HUFF, JAMES ELI, CHEMICAL ENGINEERING, EMERGENCY PRESSURE RELIEF. *Current Pos:* PVT CONSULT, 88- *Personal Data:* b Moscow, Idaho, Apr 7, 28; m 53, 67, 88, Patricia A Meyerhoeffer; c Joan C, Laurence F, James E II, Kimberly J & Randal M. *Educ:* Univ Idaho, BS, 50; Yale Univ, DEng, 57. *Prof Exp:* Trainee, Dow Chem Co, 55-56, chem engr, Phys Res Lab, 56-63, sr res engr, 63-68, tech expert, 68, process specialist, 68-71, sr process specialist, 71-80, assoc process consult, Mich Div Process Eng, 80-88. *Mem:* Fel Am Inst Chem Engrs; Sigma Xi. *Res:* Kinetics and reactor design; computer applications; phase equilibria; process development, analysis and control; emergency pressure relief systems. *Mailing Add:* 3628 Wood Duck Circle Stockton CA 95207

HUFF, JESSE WILLIAM, BIOCHEMISTRY. *Current Pos:* dir physiol chem, 66-71, asst dir exp path, 71-75, SR INVESTR, MERCK INST THERAPEUT RES, 75- *Personal Data:* b Westmoreland Co, Pa, Dec 8, 16; m 44; c 5. *Educ:* Univ Pittsburgh, BS, 40; Duke Univ, PhD(biochem), 45. *Prof Exp:* Asst biochem, Med Sch, Duke Univ, 40-42, instr, 45-46; res biochemist, Sharp & Dohme Res Labs, 46-49, asst dir biochem res, 49-50, dir, 50-58, biochem, Merck Inst Therapeut Res, 58, dir biochem, Merck Sharp & Dohme Res Labs, 58-66. *Concurrent Pos:* Biochemist, Off Sci Res & Develop contract, Duke Univ, 44-46. *Mem:* Am Soc Biol Chem; Am Heart Asn; NY Acad Sci. *Res:* Metabolism of nicotinic acid and of pyridoxine; isolation and identification of unknown biological compounds; nucleic acid and cholesterol metabolism; nutrition of experimental animals; lipid chemistry and metabolism; experimental atherosclerosis; human cardiovascular disease; lipoprotein metabolism. *Mailing Add:* 977 Woodmere Dr Westfield NJ 07090-4233

HUFF, KENNETH O, PETROLEUM GEOLOGY, SUBSURFACE GEOLOGY. *Current Pos:* PRES, ADVENTURES, INC, 70- *Personal Data:* b Daleville, Ind, Dec 17, 26; m 57; c 4. *Educ:* Indiana Univ, BS, 56. *Prof Exp:* Lab technician, Core Labs, Inc, 56-58, lab mgr & sales eng, 58-67, Rocky Mountain dist supv, 67-69; consult geologist, numerous energy co, 69-70. *Concurrent Pos:* Geol consult, numerous oil co, 70- *Mem:* Am Inst Prof Geologists; Am Asn Petrol Geologists; Soc Petrol Engrs. *Res:* Rotary drill rig design; tools for more efficient evaluation of subsurface rock samples for geological purposes. *Mailing Add:* 1106 Payne Ave Casper WY 82609

HUFF, NORMAN THOMAS, GLASS FORMING, GLASS COMPOSITIONS. *Current Pos:* res scientist, Owens-Ill Glass Co, 66-67, sr chemist, Owens-Ill, Inc, 67-85, sr scientist, Owens Corning Fiberglass, 85-92, RES ASSOC, OWENS CORNING FIBERGLASS, 92- *Personal Data:* b St Joseph, Mo, Jan 6, 40; m 64, Andrea Henry; c Rebecca & David. *Educ:* Mont State Univ, BS, 61; Carnegie-Mellon Univ, PhD(theoret chem), 64. *Prof Exp:* NSF fel, Indiana Univ, 64-66. *Concurrent Pos:* Vpres, Ultra Pure Chem, 78-82. *Mem:* Am Chem Soc; Am Ceramic Soc; Am Soc Testing & Mat. *Res:* Computerized data retrieval systems; molecular structure of glasses; formulation of container and specialty glasses; glass container forming processes; glass melting reactions; continuous filament fiber glass forming processes. *Mailing Add:* 1684 Bryn Mawr Dr Newark OH 43055-1545

HUFF, SHEELA J, BIOCHEMISTRY. *Current Pos:* PATIENT EXAMR, AM RED CROSS, 91- *Personal Data:* b London, Eng, July 3, 62. *Educ:* Univ Calif, Davis, BS, 84; Univ SC, PhD(chem), 90. *Mem:* AAAS; Am Soc Biochem & Molecular Biol; Sigma Xi. *Mailing Add:* Am Red Cross 3008 Viburnum Pl Olney MD 20832-2743

HUFF, THOMAS ALLEN, INTERNAL MEDICINE. *Current Pos:* from asst prof to assoc prof endocrinol & metab, 71-80, PROF MED, MED COL GA, 80- *Personal Data:* b Washington, DC, Oct 9, 35; m 59, Anne Hixon; c Laura A, Thomas A Jr, Joseph H & David K. *Educ:* Southwestern at Memphis, AB, 57; Emory Univ, MD, 61. *Prof Exp:* From intern to resident, Grady Mem Hosp, 61-63; fel endocrinol, Med Ctr, Duke Univ, 65-68, assoc med, 68-70. *Mem:* Am Diabetes Asn; Endocrine Soc; Am Fedn Clin Res. *Res:* Physiology of diabetes syndromes associated with insulin resistance; medical communications. *Mailing Add:* Dept Med Med Col Ga Augusta GA 30912

HUFF, WARREN D, GEOLOGY. *Current Pos:* From asst prof to assoc prof geol, 63-69, PROF GEOL, UNIV CINCINNATI, 69- *Personal Data:* b Omaha, Nebr, Apr 16, 37; m 70; c 1. *Educ:* Harvard Univ, AB, 59; Univ Cincinnati, PhD(geol), 63. *Concurrent Pos:* NSF fac fel, 71-72. *Mem:* Geol Soc Am; Asn Int Study Clay; Soc Econ Paleont & Mineral; Clay Minerals Soc. *Res:* Diagenesis of clay minerals and characteristics of fine-grained sediments; stratigraphy and geochemistry of Paleozoic Bentonites. *Mailing Add:* Dept Geol Univ Cincinnati 2600 Clifton Ave Cincinnati OH 45220-2872

HUFF, WILLIAM J, MICROPALEONTOLOGY, STRATIGRAPHY. *Current Pos:* RETIRED. *Personal Data:* b Summerland, Miss, Mar 3, 19; m 44, Frances Rossman; c John. *Educ:* Univ Miss, LLB, 47, JD, 68; Miss State Univ, BS, 56; Rice Univ, MA, 57, PhD(geol), 60. *Prof Exp:* Assoc prof geol, Southern Miss Univ, 60-65; consult geologist & atty-at-law, 65-66; asst prof natural sci, Mich State Univ, 66-68; assoc prof geol, Univ SAla, 68-82. *Concurrent Pos:* Atty-at-law, law, Pascagoula, Miss, 75-90. *Mem:* Am Asn Petrol Geol; Soc Econ Paleont & Mineral; Paleont Soc; NY Acad Sci; Sigma Xi; Paleontological Res Inst. *Res:* Taxonomy, paleoecology and stratigraphic distribution of Ostracoda and Foraminifera. *Mailing Add:* 5917 Montfort Rd S Mobile AL 36608

HUFF, WILLIAM NATHAN, MATHEMATICAL ANALYSIS. *Current Pos:* RETIRED. *Personal Data:* b Bryn Mawr, Pa, Dec 30, 12; m 38; c 3. *Educ:* Haverford Col, AB, 35; Univ Pa, MA, 37, PhD(math), 47. *Prof Exp:* Asst math, Univ Pa, 37-40; instr, Northwestern Univ, 40-41; instr pvt sch, Pa, 41-43; instr army specialized training prog, Univ Nebr, 43-44; instr, Univ Rochester, 44-46; from asst prof to assoc prof math, Univ Okla, 46-60, chmn dept, 55-61, prof math, 61-82. *Mem:* Am Math Soc; Math Asn Am; Sigma Xi. *Res:* Special functions; differential equations. *Mailing Add:* PO Box 6162 Norman OK 73070-6162

HUFFAKER, CARL BARTON, insect ecology, biological control; deceased, see previous edition for last biography

HUFFAKER, JAMES NEAL, PHYSICS. *Current Pos:* ASSOC PROF PHYSICS, UNIV OKLA, 67- *Personal Data:* b Atlanta, Ga, June 18, 37; m 73; c 4. *Educ:* Univ Chicago, BA, 55; Emory Univ, MS, 59; Duke Univ, PhD(physics), 63. *Prof Exp:* Res assoc physics, Duke Univ, 62-63; asst prof, Univ Ala, Tuscaloosa, 63-67. *Concurrent Pos:* Res grant, 65-68; fel, Japan Soc Prom Sci, Kobe Univ, 75-76; vis assoc prof, Dartmouth Col, 86-87. *Mem:* Am Phys Soc. *Res:* Theory of weak interactions, especially beta decay and mu capture; theory of nuclear structure; rovibrational states of diatomic molecules/quasiparticle surface states in superconductors. *Mailing Add:* Dept Physics Univ Okla 440 W Brooks Norman OK 73019

HUFFAKER, RAY C, BIOCHEMISTRY, PLANT PHYSIOLOGY. *Current Pos:* from asst agronomist to assoc agronomist, 60-70, PROF PLANT BIOCHEM, UNIV CALIF, DAVIS, 70- *Personal Data:* b Murray, Utah, Dec 6, 29; m 52; c 4. *Educ:* Brigham Young Univ, AB, 55; Univ Calif, Los Angeles, PhD(hort sci), 60. *Prof Exp:* Lab technician plant biochem, Univ Calif, Los Angeles, 56-60. *Mem:* Am Soc Plant Physiol; Am Soc Agron; Am Fedn Biol Chem; Scand Soc Plant Physiol; Sigma Xi; fel Crop Sci Soc Am. *Res:* Regulation of transport and assimilation of inorganic nitrogen by plants; biochemistry and physiology of plant senescence. *Mailing Add:* 526 Pole Dr Heber City UT 84032-9612

HUFFINE, COY L(EE), CHEMICAL ENGINEERING, MATERIALS SCIENCE. *Current Pos:* CONSULT & LECTR, 86- *Personal Data:* b Knoxville, Tenn, Apr 2, 24; m 51, Virginia Browne; c Jeremy & Lucinda. *Educ:* Univ Tenn, BS, 45, MS, 47; Columbia Univ, PhD(chem eng), 53. *Prof Exp:* Engr metall & ceramic develop, Aircraft Nuclear Propulsion Dept, Gen Elec Co, 51-59, res ceramist, Res Lab, 59-60; proj mgr mat develop & fabrication, Res & Adv Develop Div, Avco Corp, 60-68; adv engr, Systs Prod Div, IBM Corp, 68-70, mgr prod technol, 71-80, mgr component technol, 81-86. *Mem:* AAAS; Am Inst Chem Engrs; Minerals, Metals & Mat Soc; NY

Acad Sci; Nat Inst Ceramic Engrs; Sigma Xi. *Res:* Materials for nuclear reactors and for high temperature applications; powder processing technology; metal hydrides; ablative materials; composite materials; ferrites and magnetic recording components. *Mailing Add:* 2247 Fifth Ave NE Rochester MN 55906-4017

HUFFINES, WILLIAM DAVIS, MEDICINE, PATHOLOGY. *Current Pos:* from instr to assoc prof path, 57-68, assoc dean basic sci, 71-80, PROF PATH, SCH MED, UNIV NC, CHAPEL HILL, 68- *Personal Data:* b Reidsville, NC, Jan 23, 27; m 57; c 4. *Educ:* Univ NC, BS, 51, MD, 55; Am Bd Path, dipl & cert anat & clin path, 63. *Prof Exp:* Intern, Osler Med Serv, Johns Hopkins Hosp, 55-56; asst resident path, NC Mem Hosp, 56-57. *Concurrent Pos:* Resident, Med Div, Oak Ridge Inst Nuclear Studies, 57-58; chief resident, NC Mem Hosp, 58-59; Markle scholar, 60-65. *Mem:* Sigma Xi. *Res:* Structural changes in renal diseases correlated with functional changes. *Mailing Add:* Dept Path Univ NC Sch Med Berryhill Hall CB No 7525 Chapel Hill NC 27599-7525. *Fax:* 919-966-6354

HUFFINGTON, NORRIS J(ACKSON), JR, ENGINEERING MECHANICS, STRUCTURAL DYNAMICS. *Current Pos:* RETIRED. *Personal Data:* b Baltimore, Md, July 23, 21; m 52; c 4. *Educ:* Johns Hopkins Univ, BE, 49, MSE, 51, DE(eng mech), 54. *Prof Exp:* Draftsman & designer, Glenn L Martin Co, 40-46; jr instr mech eng, Johns Hopkins Univ, 49-50, instr, 53-54; staff mem, Opers Res Off, 50-53; assoc prof appl mech, Va Polytech Inst, 54-56, prof eng mech, 56-58; chief dynamics res staff, Martin Co, 59-67; chief, Struct Mech Br, US Army Ballistic Res Lab, 67-73, chief, Target Loading & Response Br, 73-80, res mech eng, 80-92, res mech engr, US Army Res Lab, 92-95. *Concurrent Pos:* Prof, Univ Del, 74-82; fel, Ballistic Res Lab; sr lectr, Johns Hopkins Univ, 83- *Mem:* Am Soc Mech Engrs; Am Acad Mech. *Res:* Structural dynamics; stiffened plate structures; dynamic properties of materials; terminal ballistics; air blast analysis. *Mailing Add:* 3101 Rolling Green Dr Churchville MD 21028

HUFFINGTON, ROY MICHAEL, INTERNATIONAL OIL & GAS EXPLORATION. *Current Pos:* pres, 56-83, CHMN BD & DIR, ROY M HUFFINGTON INC, 58-90 & 93- *Personal Data:* b Tomball, Tex, Oct 4, 17; m 45, Phyllis Gough; c Michael & Terry (Dittman). *Educ:* Southern Methodist Univ, BS, 38; Harvard Univ, MA, 41, PhD(geol), 42; Harvard Univ, AMP, 76. *Hon Degrees:* LHD, Southern Methodist Univ, 90. *Honors & Awards:* Petrol Indust Award, Am Soc Mech Engrs, 85; Gold Medallion Oil Pioneer Award, 85; Michel T Halbouty Human Needs Award, Am Asn Petrol Geologists, 91. *Prof Exp:* Instr geol, Harvard Univ, 42; from field geologist to sr geologist, Explor Geol Div, Humble Oil & Refining Co, 46-56; ambassador, US Embassy, Vienna, Austria, 90-93. *Concurrent Pos:* Dir, Independent Petrol Asn Am, 79-80 & Am Petrol Inst, 83-90 & 93-; trustee assoc, Am Asn Petrol Geologists Found, 80-90 & 93-; trustee, Geol Soc Am Found, 88-90, hon trustee, 93- *Mem:* Fel AAAS; fel Geol Soc Am; Am Asn Petrol Geologists; Am Inst Prof Geologists; Independent Petrol Asn Am. *Res:* International oil and gas exploration, production, engineering activities and gas liquefaction operations; author of articles on stratigraphic, structural and petroleum geology. *Mailing Add:* Roy M Huffington Inc 1100 Louisiana St Suite 2500 PO Box 4337 Houston TX 77210-4337. *Fax:* 713-659-2521

HUFFMAN, ALLAN MURRAY, ORGANIC CHEMISTRY. *Current Pos:* GROUP LEADER RES & DEVELOP, CROMPTON & KNOWLES CORP, NY, 80- *Personal Data:* b Kennedy, Sask, Jan 6, 36; US citizen; m 65, Laura Santilli; c David, Janet, John, Mark & Mathew. *Educ:* Univ Minn, BA, 59; Carnegie Inst Technol, MS, 63, PhD(org chem), 64. *Prof Exp:* Res chemist, E I du Pont de Nemours & Co, Del, 64-70; group leader res & develop, Am Color & Chem Corp, Inc, Charlotte, NC, 70-80. *Mem:* Am Chem Soc; Am Asn Textile Chemists & Colorists. *Res:* Development of new dyes for textiles. *Mailing Add:* PO Box 341 Reading PA 19603

HUFFMAN, CLARENCE W, PROCESSES FOR PESTICIDES, PROCESSES FOR SYNTHETIC VITAMINS. *Current Pos:* CONSULT, 75- *Personal Data:* b Withie, Wis, June 6, 13; m 41, C Virginia Salinas; c James, Lee, Dian & Joan. *Educ:* Univ Minn, PhD(org chem), 41. *Prof Exp:* Chemist, Merck & Co, 45-52, Monsanto Co, 52-57 & Int Minerals & Chem, 57-75. *Mem:* Am Chem Soc. *Res:* Processes to make pesticides. *Mailing Add:* 1141 Heatherfield Glenview IL 60025

HUFFMAN, D C, JR, PHARMACY PRACTICE & MANAGEMENT. *Current Pos:* EXEC VPRES, AM COL APOTHECARIES. *Educ:* Univ Ark, BS, 66; Univ Miss, PhD(pharm admin), 71. *Prof Exp:* Prof, Col Pharm, Univ Tenn, chmn dept, adminr & vpres pharm & mgt servs. *Concurrent Pos:* Sr vpres pharm pract & mgt servs, Nat Asn Retail Druggists. *Mem:* Am Found Pharm Educ; Am Col Apothecaries; Nat Asn Retail Druggists. *Res:* Pharmacy practice and management services; contributed articles to professional journals. *Mailing Add:* Am Col Apothecaries 205 Daingerfield Rd Alexandria VA 22314

HUFFMAN, DALE L, MEAT SCIENCE, FOOD SAFETY. *Current Pos:* from assoc prof to prof meat sci, 63-95, EMER PROF MEAT SCI & EMER DIR, FOOD TECHNOL INST, AUBURN UNIV, 95- *Personal Data:* b Churchville, Va, July 23, 31; m 56, Jo-Ann Johnson; c Shari, Randy & Emily. *Educ:* Cornell Univ, BS, 59; Univ Fla, MS, 60, PhD(meats), 62. *Honors & Awards:* Meat Processing Award, Am Meat Sci Asn, 83, Signal Serv Award, 88; Harry L Rudnick Educr Award, Nat Asn Meat Purveyors, 84; Food Technol Indust Achievement Award, Inst Food Technologists, 92; Man of Year Serv Agr Award, Progressive Farmer Mag, 92; Nat Award Agr Excellence Technol, Nat Atri-Marketing Asn, 95. *Prof Exp:* Asst meats, Univ Fla, 59-62; meat scientist, Res & Develop Ctr, Swift & Co, 62-63. *Concurrent Pos:* Indust fel, Armour & Co, 69-70; dir, Food Technol Inst, Auburn Univ, 94-95. *Mem:* Am Soc Animal Sci; Am Meat Sci Asn (pres-elect, 80-81, pres, 81-82); Inst Food Technol; Royal Soc Health; Sigma Xi. *Res:* Low-fat ground beef; restructured fresh meats; lean beef production; food safety. *Mailing Add:* 219 Deer Run Rd Auburn AL 36832-4103. *Fax:* 334-502-6171; *E-Mail:* dhuffman@auburn.campus.mci.net

HUFFMAN, DAVID A(LBERT), ELECTRICAL ENGINEERING. *Current Pos:* PROF INFO SCI, UNIV CALIF, SANTA CRUZ, 67- *Personal Data:* b Alliance, Ohio, Aug 9, 25. *Educ:* Ohio State Univ, BEE, 44, MSE, 49; Mass Inst Technol, ScD, 53. *Honors & Awards:* Levy Medal, Franklin Inst, 55; W Wallace McDowell Award, Inst Elec & Electronics Engrs, 74. *Prof Exp:* Instr elec eng & res assoc, Univ Res Found, Ohio State Univ, 46-50; from asst prof to assoc prof elec eng, Mass Inst Technol, 50-67. *Mem:* Inst Elec & Electronics Engrs; Asn Comput Mach. *Res:* Switching theory; information theory; picture analysis; signal design. *Mailing Add:* Dept Comput & Info Sci Univ Calif Santa Cruz CA 95064-1099

HUFFMAN, DAVID GEORGE, PARASITOLOGY. *Current Pos:* Asst prof, 73-78, ASSOC PROF BIOL, SOUTHWEST TEX STATE UNIV, 78- *Personal Data:* b Charleston, WVa, May 8, 41; div. *Educ:* WVa Univ, AB, 68; Marshall Univ, MS, 70; Univ NH, PhD(zool), 73. *Mem:* Sigma Xi; Am Asn Parasitologists; Am Ornithologists Soc. *Res:* Freshwater parasitology, especially natural history, systematics, morphology and ecology of fish helminths. *Mailing Add:* Dept Biol Southwest Tex State Univ San Marcos TX 78666-4602

HUFFMAN, DONALD MARION, MYCOLOGY. *Current Pos:* chmn, 63-76, PROF BIOL, DIV NATURAL SCI, CENT COL, IOWA, 63- *Personal Data:* b Pittsburg, Kans, Sept 28, 29; m 53. *Educ:* Kans State Col, Pittsburg, BS, 51; Kans State Univ, MS, 52; Iowa State Univ, PhD(plant path), 55. *Prof Exp:* Asst prof plant path & bot, Kans State Univ, 55-57; from asst prof to assoc prof biol, Cent Col, Iowa, 57-61; NIH res fel mycol, Columbia Univ, 61-63. *Concurrent Pos:* Univ Iowa vis scientist & lectr, 60-65. *Mem:* AAAS; Mycol Soc Am; Am Inst Biol Sci. *Res:* Higher fungi. *Mailing Add:* Dept Nat Sci Cent Col Pella IA 50219-1999

HUFFMAN, DONALD RAY, SOLID STATE PHYSICS, ASTROPHYSICS. *Current Pos:* from asst prof to assoc prof, 67-75, PROF PHYSICS, UNIV ARIZ, 75- *Personal Data:* b Ft Worth, Tex, June 19, 35; m 63. *Educ:* Tex A&M Univ, BS, 57; Rice Univ, MA, 59; Univ Calif, Riverside, PhD(physics), 66. *Prof Exp:* Res engr, Res Div, Humble Oil Co, 59-60; instr physics, Pepperdine Col, 60-62; NSF fel, Univ Frankfurt, 66-67. *Concurrent Pos:* Consult, Europ Space Agency, 75; vis scientist, Max Planck Inst Solid State Res, Stuttgart, WGer, 76. *Mem:* Am Phys Soc. *Res:* Low temperature physics of solids; thermal and optical studies of the antiferromagnetic phase transition; crystal field spectra; laboratory studies of likely interstellar and circumstellar dust particles. *Mailing Add:* Dept Physics Univ Ariz Tucson AZ 85721

HUFFMAN, ERNEST OTTO, PHYSICAL CHEMISTRY. *Current Pos:* CONSULT, J C BARBER & ASSOC, 76- *Personal Data:* b Hickory, NC, Aug 30, 11; m 35, Bobbie Mitchell; c 3. *Educ:* Lenoir-Rhyne Col, BS, 32; Univ NC, MS, 34. *Prof Exp:* Control chemist, Tenn Eastman Corp, 35-36; res chemist, Tenn Valley Authority, 36-64, chief, Fundamental Res Br, 64-73, asst dir chem develop, 73-74, dir chem develop, 74-76. *Mem:* Am Chem Soc. *Res:* Fixation of atmospheric nitrogen; synthesis of phosphorous-nitrogen compounds; defluorination of phosphate rock in the molten state; rate of solution of phosphates; kinetics of heterogeneous processes; research administration; fertilizer science and production. *Mailing Add:* 3995 Kernachan Dr Muscle Shoals AL 35661

HUFFMAN, FRED NORMAN, ENERGY CONVERSION, NUCLEAR ENGINEERING. *Current Pos:* THERMO ELECTRON CORP, WALTHAM, 86- *Personal Data:* b Catawba Co, NC, Sept 25, 32; m 55; c 4. *Educ:* Lenoir-Rhyne Col, BS, 54; Vanderbilt Univ, MS, 56; Johns Hopkins Univ, PhD(physics), 64. *Honors & Awards:* Fourth Hastings Lectr. *Prof Exp:* Asst proj eng, Martin Marietta Corp, Md, 57-59, sr res scientist, 64-67, sect mgr biomed eng, 67-84, mgr direct energy conversion dept vpres, res & develop ctr, 74-85. *Concurrent Pos:* Nuclear consult, Gen Instrument Corp, 62-64. *Mem:* Am Phys Soc; Inst Elec & Electronics Engrs; Am Ceramics Soc. *Res:* Energy conversion, particularly from nuclear sources; applied physics aspects of thermionic, thermoelectric and artificial heart development; vapor deposition; thermal insulation, heat pipe and high temperature technology. *Mailing Add:* 25 Colonial Rd Sudbury MA 01776

HUFFMAN, GEORGE WALLEN, BIOCHEMISTRY, ORGANIC CHEMISTRY. *Current Pos:* RETIRED. *Personal Data:* b Renville Co, NDak, Dec 7, 21; m 42; c 3. *Educ:* NDak State Univ, BS, 48, MS, 50; Univ Minn, Minneapolis, PhD(biochem), 56. *Prof Exp:* Chemist, Abbott Labs, 50-51; proj leader res, Quaker Oats Co, 56-61, group leader chem res, 61-64, cent dist sales mgr, 64-68, from com develop assoc to sr com develop assoc, Chem Div, 68-75, proj mgr bus develop, 75-77, mgr mkt develop, 77-84. *Mem:* AAAS; Am Chem Soc; Com Develop Asn. *Res:* Commercial development of organic chemicals; furan chemicals; carbohydrates and proteins. *Mailing Add:* 6502 Vermont Trail Crystal Lake IL 60012-3257

HUFFMAN, GERALD P, SPECTROSCOPY & SPECTROMETRY, SOLID STATE PHYSICS. *Current Pos:* DIR, CONSORTIUM FOSSIL FUEL LIQUEFACTION SCI & RES PROF, UNIV KY, 86- *Personal Data:* b Steubenville, Ohio, Sept 12, 38; m 61; c 3. *Educ:* West Liberty State Col, BS, 60; Univ WVa, MS, 62, PhD(physics), 65. *Prof Exp:* Scientist, US Steel Corp Res Ctr, 65-75, assoc res consult, E C Bain Lab Fundamental Res, 75-80, res consult, 80-85; pres, Macroatom, Inc, 85-86. *Mem:* Am Phys Soc; Am Chem Soc; Metall Soc; AAAS. *Res:* Coal structure; mineralogy; liquefaction; ash behavior; catalysis; XAFS spectroscopy; Mossbauer spectroscopy; electron microscopy. *Mailing Add:* CFFLS Univ Ky 533 S Limestone St Rm 111 Lexington KY 40506

HUFFMAN, JACOB BRAINARD, FORESTRY, WOOD SCIENCE TECHNOLOGY. *Current Pos:* prof, 52-87, EMER PROF FOREST PROD, SCH FOREST RESOURCES & CONSERV, UNIV FLA, 87- *Personal Data:* b Maggie, Va, July 21, 19; m 48, Dorothy F Kammerer; c Blair M & Gregory L. *Educ:* Va Polytech Inst, BS, 41; Duke Univ, MF, 47, DF(wood technol), 53. *Prof Exp:* Wood technologist, Tidewater Plywood Co, Ga, 47-49; instr, Sch Forestry, WVa Univ, 49-50. *Concurrent Pos:* Consult, 53- *Mem:* Forest Prod Soc; Soc Wood Sci & Technol; Soc Am Foresters; Am Wood Preservers' Asn; Hardwood Res Coun. *Res:* Wood properties, seasoning, gluing and preservation. *Mailing Add:* 528 NW 36th St Gainesville FL 32607-2445. *Fax:* 352-372-8234

HUFFMAN, JOHN CURTIS, X-RAY CRYSTALLOGRAPHY. *Current Pos:* Crystallographer, 74-80, SR SCIENTIST & DIR, MOLECULAR STRUCT CTR, IND UNIV, 80- *Personal Data:* b Kokomo, Ind, Dec 9, 41; m 65, Carolyn J Nash; c John N & Charles C. *Educ:* Ind Univ, BS, 64, MS, 68 & PhD(chem), 74. *Mem:* Am Crystallog Asn; Am Chem Soc; Sigma Xi; AAAS; Am Inst Physics. *Res:* Single crystal x-ray diffraction of small molecules; development of computers and techniques in crystallography; author of over 400 papers in field of structural chemistry. *Mailing Add:* Dept Chem Box 130 Bloomington IN 47401. *E-Mail:* huffman@ucs.indiana.edu

HUFFMAN, JOHN WILLIAM, JR, ORGANIC CHEMISTRY. *Current Pos:* from asst prof to assoc prof, 60-67, PROF CHEM, CLEMSON UNIV, 67- *Personal Data:* b Evanston, Ill, July 21, 32; m 54, 75, Dana Holderby; c Paul, James, George & John E. *Educ:* Northwestern Univ, BS, 54; Harvard Univ, AM, 56, PhD(chem), 57. *Prof Exp:* Asst prof chem, Ga Inst Technol, 57-60. *Concurrent Pos:* NIH career develop award, 65-70. *Mem:* Am Chem Soc; Int Cannabinoid Res Soc. *Res:* Structure and synthesis of natural products; stereochemistry of carbocyclic systems; synthesis and medicinal chemistry of traditional and non-traditional cannabinoids. *Mailing Add:* Dept Chem Clemson Univ Clemson SC 29634-1905. *Fax:* 864-656-6613; *E-Mail:* john_huffman@quickmail.clemson.edu

HUFFMAN, K(ENNETH) ROBERT, INFORMATION RETRIEVAL & CONSULTING. *Current Pos:* TEKTRIEVAL INFO CONSULT, 86- *Personal Data:* b Akron, Ohio, Nov 13, 33; m 57; c 3. *Educ:* Oberlin Col, AB, 55; Univ Rochester, PhD(org chem), 59. *Honors & Awards:* IR-100, Indust Res, Inc, 71. *Prof Exp:* Res chemist, Am Cyanamid Co, 58-65, sr res chemist, 65-86. *Mem:* Am Chem Soc. *Res:* Synthetic organic chemistry; heterocyclic chemistry; organic photochemistry; polymer synthesis; bioabsorbable polymers; water soluble polymers; polymeric surfactants. *Mailing Add:* 207 Maple Hill Dr Flat Rock NC 28731

HUFFMAN, LOUIE CLARENCE, MATHEMATICS. *Current Pos:* From instr to assoc prof math, 55-68, PROF MATH, MIDWESTERN STATE UNIV, 68-, CHMN DEPT, 69-, DIR DIV MATH SCI, 83- *Personal Data:* b Dundee, Tex, Dec 29, 26; m 54; c 3. *Educ:* Midwestern Univ, BS, 52, ME, 54; Univ Tex, Austin, MA, 62, PhD(math), 69. *Res:* Generalized discrete functions of more than one variable. *Mailing Add:* Math Sci Div Midwestern State Univ Wichita Falls TX 76308-1923

HUFFMAN, ROBERT EUGENE, PHYSICAL CHEMISTRY. *Current Pos:* Res chemist, Air Force Cambridge Res Labs, 58-67, supvry res chemist, 67-74, supvry res chemist, 75-86, chief, Ultraviolet Br, Air Force Geophys Lab, 86-89, SUPVRY PHYSICAL SCIENTIST, GEOPHYS DIRECTORATE, PHILLIPS LAB, HANSCOMB AFB, BEDFORD, MA, 89- *Personal Data:* b Breckenridge, Tex, Apr 23, 31; m 56; c 3. *Educ:* Tex A&M Univ, BS, 53; Calif Inst Technol, PhD(chem, physics), 58. *Concurrent Pos:* Dept Phys, Imp Col London, 67-68. *Mem:* Am Chem Soc; Am Phys Soc; Optical Soc Am; Am Geophys Union; Am Inst Aeronaut & Astronaut; Soc Photo-Optical Instrumentation Engrs. *Res:* Atmospheric ultraviolet radiation; vacuum ultraviolet spectroscopy; vacuum ultraviolet spectroscopy; atmospheric chemistry and physics. *Mailing Add:* PO Box 919 Sudbury MA 01776-0919

HUFFMAN, ROBERT WESLY, ORGANIC CHEMISTRY. *Current Pos:* from asst prof to prof, 67-97, EMER PROF CHEM, NORTHERN ARIZ UNIV, 97- *Personal Data:* b North Lewisburg, Ohio, June 6, 32; m 56, Constance Sue Moore; c Michael Lynn, Timothy Dustin & Charlotte Ann. *Educ:* Ohio Univ, BS, 59; Ind Univ, Bloomington, PhD(org chem), 64. *Prof Exp:* Fel, Univ Calif, Santa Barbara, 64-67. *Mem:* Am Chem Soc; Sigma Xi. *Res:* Bio-organic reaction mechanisms such as mechanisms of synthetic membrane penetration in surfactant vesicles. *Mailing Add:* Northern Ariz Univ Box 5698 Flagstaff AZ 86011. *Fax:* 520-523-8111

HUFFMAN, RONALD DEAN, NEUROPHARMACOLOGY, NEUROPHYSIOLOGY. *Current Pos:* ASSOC PROF PHARMACOL, UNIV TEX HEALTH SCI CTR SAN ANTONIO, 73- *Personal Data:* b Vandergrift, Pa, Dec 13, 37. *Educ:* Pa State Univ, BS, 59; Purdue Univ, MS, 61, PhD(pharmacol), 67. *Prof Exp:* Res assoc neurophysiol, Southwest Found Res & Educ, 66-67; instr physiol, Univ BC, 67-68; asst prof pharmacol & anat, Univ Tex Med Sch San Antonio, 68-73. *Concurrent Pos:* Morrison Trust res support grants, San Antonio, 69-72 & 76-78; USPHS grants, 70-72, 74-76, 77-81 & 82-84; NSF grant 78-80. *Mem:* Soc Neurosci; Am Soc Pharmacol Exp Ther. *Res:* Physiology and pharmacology of synaptic transmission in the basal ganglia. *Mailing Add:* Dept Pharmacol Univ Tex Med Sch 7703 Floyd Curl Dr San Antonio TX 78284-6200

HUFFMAN, TOMMIE RAY, electrical engineering, semiconductors, for more information see previous edition

HUFFORD, CHARLES DAVID, PHARMACY, PHARMACOGNOSY. *Current Pos:* asst prof, 72-75, assoc prof, 75-82, PROF PHARMACOG, SCH PHARM, UNIV MISS, 82-, CHMN, 87- *Personal Data:* b Tiffin, Ohio, Oct 16, 44; m 84, Alice M Clark; c Gary & Jennifer. *Educ:* Ohio State Univ, BSPharm, 67, PhD(natural prod chem), 72. *Concurrent Pos:* Nat Cancer Inst Fel, 74- *Mem:* Sigma Xi; Am Soc Pharmacog; fel Am Asn Pharmaceut Scientists; Am Chem Soc; Am Soc Microbiol; Am Asn Cols Pharm. *Res:* Natural products chemistry of bioactive constituents; microbial metabolism of drugs, antifungal and antibacterial drugs; natural products chemistry. *Mailing Add:* Dept Pharmacog Univ Miss University MS 38677. *Fax:* 601-232-7026

HUFFORD, GEORGE (ALLEN), MATHEMATICS, ELECTROMAGNETISM. *Current Pos:* mathematician, Environ Sci Serv Admin, 65-70, Off Telecommun, 70-78, MATHEMATICIAN, NAT TELECOMMUN & INFO ADMIN, INST TELECOMMUN SCI, 78- *Personal Data:* b San Francisco, Calif, June 1, 27; m 54, Lottie Webb; c George, Richard & Lottie. *Educ:* Calif Inst Technol, BS, 46; Univ Wash, MS, 48; Princeton Univ, PhD(math), 53. *Prof Exp:* Electronic scientist, Nat Bur Standards, 48-50; instr math, Princeton Univ, 53-55; instr, Stanford Univ, 55-58; asst prof, Univ Wash, 58-64; mathematician, Nat Bur Standards, 64-65. *Mem:* Am Math Soc; Soc Indust & Appl Math; Inst Elec & Electronics Eng; Sigma Xi. *Res:* Radiowave propagation at VHF, UHF and millimeter wave frequencies. *Mailing Add:* US Dept Commerce Nat Telecommun & Info Admin Inst Telecommun Sci 325 Broadway Boulder CO 80303

HUFFORD, TERRY LEE, AQUATIC ECOLOGY. *Current Pos:* ASSOC PROF BOT, GEORGE WASHINGTON UNIV, 72- *Personal Data:* b Toledo, Ohio, Sept 19, 35; m 55; c 3. *Educ:* Bowling Green State Univ, BS, 61, MA, 62; Ohio State Univ, PhD(bot), 72. *Prof Exp:* Instr biol, Ind Cent Col, 62-63; asst prof biol, Cent Methodist Col, 63-64; asst prof biol, Grove City Col, 66-69. *Concurrent Pos:* Pres, Ctr Environ Educ & Res, 78-; chair, Four-Yr Col Sect, Nat Asn Biol Teachers, 90-91. *Mem:* Phycological Soc Am; Nat Asn Biol Teachers; Nat Sci Teachers Asn; Bot Soc Am; Am Inst Biol Sci; Am Micros Soc. *Res:* Taxonomy, morphology and anatomy of freshwater diatoms. *Mailing Add:* 7147 Parkview Ave Falls Church VA 22042-1615

HUFHAM, JAMES BIRK, BACTERIOLOGY, GENETICS. *Current Pos:* asst prof, 69-77, ASSOC PROF LIFE SCI, UNIV MO, ROLLA, 78- *Personal Data:* b Petersburg, Va, Jan 25, 35; m 57; c 2. *Educ:* Univ Ala, BS, 57; Univ Nebr, Lincoln, MS, 59, PhD(microbiol), 68. *Prof Exp:* Res assoc microbiol, Sch Med, Wayne State Univ, 61-67; head res, Space-Defense Corp, 67-68; res microbiologist, Esso Res Lab, 68-69. *Concurrent Pos:* Consult, Space-Defense Corp, 66-67, Esso Res Lab, 69-70 & Anschutz Mining Corp, 79-81. *Mem:* Am Soc Microbiol; NY Acad Sci; Sigma Xi. *Res:* Carcinogenicity testing of chemicals using Ames Test; molecular genetics. *Mailing Add:* Dept Life Sci Univ Mo Box 249 Rolla MO 65401-2631

HUFNAGEL, LINDA ANN, DEVELOPMENTAL BIOLOGY OF CILIATED PROTISTAN CELLS, ULTRASTRUCTURAL CORRELATES OF BEHAVIOR. *Current Pos:* lectr electron micros, Univ RI, 73-75, asst prof, 75-79, assoc prof, 79-86, PROF MICROBIOL, UNIV RI, 86- *Personal Data:* b Teaneck, NJ, Nov 7, 39; m 84, Robert V Zackroff; c 2. *Educ:* Univ Vt, BA, 61, MS, 63; Univ Pa, PhD(biol), 67. *Prof Exp:* Fel biol sci, Yale Univ, 67-69; res assoc biol, Columbia Univ, 69-70; res assoc path, Sch Med, Wayne State Univ, 71-73. *Concurrent Pos:* NSF fel, Yale Univ, 67-69; NSF res grant, Univ RI, 76-78; Steps fel, Marine Biol Lab, Woods Hole, 78 & 79. *Mem:* AAAS; Am Soc Cell Biol; Soc Protozoologists; Micros Soc Am. *Res:* Morphogenesis and ciliogenesis in ciliated cells; structure and function of ciliary basal bodies; positioning of organelles in cells; membrane differentiation; cell-cell interactions in mating cilioprotists; ultrastructure of epithelial conducting systems of Hydra. *Mailing Add:* Dept Biochem Microbiol & Molecular Genetics Univ RI Kingston RI 02881. *E-Mail:* aun103@uriacc.uri.edu

HUFSCHMIDT, MAYNARD MICHAEL, water resources management, public investment theory, for more information see previous edition

HUFSTEDLER, ROBERT SLOAN, inorganic chemistry; deceased, see previous edition for last biography

HUFT, MICHAEL JOHN, SYSTEMATICS, FLORISTICS. *Current Pos:* ATTY, 92- *Personal Data:* b Highland Park, Mich, Jan 15, 49; m 72, 85; c 4. *Educ:* Univ Notre Dame, BS, 71; Univ Mich, PhD(bot), 79. *Prof Exp:* Res assoc & actg cur herbarium bot, dept bot & microbiol, Univ Okla, 80; curatorial trainee, Mo Bot Garden, 80-81, res botanist, 81-83, asst cur bot, 84-92. *Concurrent Pos:* Asst vis cur bot, dept bot, Field Mus Natural Hist, 81-92. *Mem:* Am Soc Plant Taxonomists; Soc Econ Bot; Int Asn Plant Taxon. *Res:* Systematics of the Euphorbiaceae; floristics of the neotropics, especially Mexico and Central America. *Mailing Add:* 20 Park Dr Glenview IL 60025

HUG, CARL CASIMIR, JR, PHARMACOLOGY, ANESTHESIOLOGY. *Current Pos:* assoc prof, Emory Univ, 72-80, assoc prof anesthesiol, 74-78, dep chair res, 87-95, PROF ANESTHESIOL, SCH MED, EMORY UNIV, 78-, PROF PHARMACOL, 80-, DEP CHAIR ACAD AFFAIRS ANESTHESIOL, 95- *Personal Data:* b Canton, Ohio, Dec 20, 36; m 56, Marilyn A France; c Patricia A (DeStephano), Michael S, Joan M (Daniel), Mary L (Higgins) & Lori R (Mauldin). *Educ:* Duquesne Univ, BS, 58; Univ Mich, PhD(pharmacol), 63, MD, 67; Am Bd Anesthesiol, dipl, 75; FRCA, 93; Fanzca, 94. *Prof Exp:* From instr to assoc prof pharmacol, Med & Grad Schs, Univ Mich, Ann Arbor, 63-71. *Concurrent Pos:* Spec fel anesthesiol, Emory Univ, 71-73; ed, Anesthesiol, 79-88; vis res prof, Univ Leiden, Neth, 82-83; dir, Am Bd Anesthesiol, 84-, pres, 92-93; vis, Australian & NZ Col Anaesthetists Found, 94. *Mem:* Am Soc Pharmacol & Exp Therapeut; Am Soc Clin Pharmacol & Therapeut; Am Soc Anesthesiol; Int Anesthesia Res Soc; Soc Cardiovasc Anesthesiologists; Asn Univ Anesthesiologists (pres, 84-86); hon mem Belg Soc Anesthesiol & Reanimation. *Res:* Academic medicine, particularly pharmacology and anesthesiology; relationships between the biological disposition of drugs and their actions; opioids and drugs used in anesthesia and life support during cardiac and thoracic surgery and in intensive care. *Mailing Add:* Dept Anesthesiol Emory Univ Sch Med Atlanta GA 30322-1104. *Fax:* 404-778-5194; *E-Mail:* chug@emory.org

HUG, DANIEL HARTZ, PHYSIOLOGICAL BACTERIOLOGY, PHOTOBIOLOGY. *Current Pos:* RES MICROBIOLOGIST, VET ADMIN HOSP, 58- *Personal Data:* b Davenport, Iowa, Apr 9, 27; m 50; c 6. *Educ:* Iowa State Col, BS, 49, PhD(bact physiol), 56. *Prof Exp:* NIH fel, Univ Ill, 56-58. *Concurrent Pos:* Res scientist internal med, Univ Iowa. *Mem:* Am Soc Biol Chemists; Am Soc Photobiol; Am Soc Microbiol; Am Chem Soc; Sigma Xi. *Res:* Enzymology; amino acid metabolism; histidine catabolism; photoactivation of urocanase. *Mailing Add:* Gen Med Res Lab Vet Admin Hosp Iowa City IA 52246

HUG, GEORGE, PEDIATRICS, BIOCHEMISTRY. *Current Pos:* resident, 61-63, from asst prof to assoc prof, 63-71, PROF PEDIAT, COL MED, UNIV CINCINNATI, 71- *Personal Data:* b Zurich, Switz, June 2, 31; US citizen; m 63; c 5. *Educ:* Univ Zurich, MD, 57; Am Bd Pediat, dipl, 64. *Prof Exp:* Asst pediat, Univ Children's Hosp, Bern, Switz, 57-58; intern pediat path, Children's Hosp Med Ctr, Boston, Mass, 60-61. *Concurrent Pos:* Swiss Nat Found & Eli Lilly & Co fels biochem, Sch Med, Wash Univ, 58-60; attend pediatrician, Children's Hosp. *Mem:* Am Soc Clin Invest; Soc Pediat Res; Am Pediat Soc; Int Acad Path; Electron Micros Soc. *Res:* Inborn errors of metabolism; biochemical genetics. *Mailing Add:* Childrens Hosp Res Found 333 Burnett Ave Cincinnati OH 45229-3039

HUG, GORDON L, PHYSICAL CHEMISTRY. *Current Pos:* asst prof specialist, 76-86, ASSOC PROF SPECIALIST, RADIATION LAB, UNIV NOTRE DAME, 86- *Personal Data:* b Highland, Ill, Sept 15, 42; m 64. *Educ:* Southern Ill Univ, Carbondale, BA, 64; Univ Chicago, PhD (chem physics), 70. *Prof Exp:* Res assoc, Inst Molecular Biophys, Fla State Univ, 70-73; fel, Dept Chem, Univ Houston, 74-76. *Mem:* Am Chem Soc; Sigma Xi. *Res:* Photochemistry and photophysics of organic excited states in solution; compilation and evaluation of such data. *Mailing Add:* PO Box 579 Notre Dame IN 46556

HUG, VERENA, oncology, for more information see previous edition

HUGELMAN, RODNEY D(ALE), AERONAUTICAL ENGINEERING. *Current Pos:* RETIRED. *Personal Data:* b Bismarck, NDak, Aug 16, 34; wid. *Educ:* Ore State Univ, BS, 56, MS, 59; Okla State Univ, PhD(eng), 64. *Prof Exp:* Aerodynamicist, Gen Dynamics/Convair, 58; res scientist appl math, Aerospace Res Lab, Wright-Patterson AFB, 63-68; dir aerospace & eng mech, NDak State Univ, 68-72; exec consult res & develop, General Prog Corp, 72-74; dir res & develop, Warren Knaust, 74-77; prof gen eng, Univ Ill, Urbana, 77-92. *Mem:* Am Inst Aeronaut & Astronaut; Am Soc Mech Engrs; Nat Soc Prof Engrs. *Res:* Aerodynamics and applied mathematics, particularly fluidics, boundary layer flows and aircraft design; industrial controls; automation and robotics both fluidic and microprocessor controls. *Mailing Add:* 603 S Duncan Rd Champaign IL 61821

HUGER, FRANCIS P, BIOCHEMICAL PHARMACOLOGY, NEUROSCIENCE. *Current Pos:* sr res biochemist & res group mgr, Hoechst Roussel Pharmaceut Inc, 80-96, RES SCIENTIST, HOECHST MARION ROUSSEL, 96- *Personal Data:* b Lexington, Va, Oct 25, 47; m 69. *Educ:* Va Military Inst, BS, 69; Med Col Va, PhD(pharmacol), 78; Fairleigh Dickinson Univ, MBA, 93. *Prof Exp:* Analytical chemist, Va Dept Health, 69-70, Va Consol Lab, 72-74; res assoc, Uniformed Servs Univ, 79-80. *Mem:* Soc Neurosci; Am Chem Soc. *Res:* Biochemical pharmacology and development of structure-activity relationships; regulation of synthesis and turnover of central neurotransmitters and associated receptor changes. *Mailing Add:* 238 Rick Rd Milford NJ 08848

HUGGARD, RICHARD JAMES, AGRICULTURE. *Current Pos:* RETIRED. *Personal Data:* b Norton, NB, June 18, 35; m 60, Marjorie MacRae; c Richard James & Lesley Anne. *Educ:* McGill Univ, BS, 58; Univ Ill, MS, 65. *Honors & Awards:* Erland Lee Award, Federated Women's Inst Can, 92. *Prof Exp:* beef fieldman, NS Dept Agr & Mkt, Truro, 58-65, livestock supt, 65-73, dir, Livestock Br, 73-75, dir, Exten Br, 75-86, chief dir opers, Halifax, 86-90, exec dir admin, 90, dep minister, 91-94. *Concurrent Pos:* Fel award, Agr Inst Can, 92. *Mem:* Can Soc Animal Sci; Can Soc Exten; Agr Inst Can. *Mailing Add:* NS Dept Agr & Mkt 59 Shannon Dr Truro NS B2N 3V7 Can

HUGGETT, CLAYTON (MCKENNA), FIRE SAFETY, COMBUSTION. *Current Pos:* RETIRED. *Personal Data:* b Columbia Co, Wis, Mar 12, 17; m 46, Lois C Kelly; c William, Thomas & James. *Educ:* Univ Wis, BS, 38; Univ Minn, MS, 43, PhD(phys chem), 45. *Prof Exp:* Res assoc, US Navy Proj, Univ Minn, 45-48; res chemist, Rohm & Haas Co, 48-49, resident dir res, Redstone Arsenal Res Div, 50-54, head high pressure lab, 54-59; dir res, Amcel Propulsion, Inc, 59-62; sr scientist, Atlantic Res Corp, 62-66, dir chem technol dept, 66-70; chief prog chem, Nat Bur Standards, 70-77, chief off extramural fire res, 77-80, dep dir, Ctr Fire Res, 80-85. *Mem:* Am Chem Soc; Combustion Inst. *Res:* Chemistry of propellants, explosives and incendiaries; polymer and acetylene chemistry; high pressure chemical processes; combustion hazards; spacecraft atmospheres; chemistry of combustion processes relating to fire safety. *Mailing Add:* 11355 SW 84th St Apt 416 Miami FL 33175

HUGGETT, RICHARD WILLIAM, JR, PHYSICS. *Current Pos:* from asst prof to assoc prof, 57-61, prof, 65-95, EMER PROF PHYSICS, LA STATE UNIV, BATON ROUGE, 95- *Personal Data:* b Frazee, Minn, July 2, 30; div; c Laurie, James, Heather & Ariana. *Educ:* Concordia Col, AB, 51; Ind Univ, MS, 53, PhD(physics), 57. *Prof Exp:* Asst physics, Ind Univ, 51-57. *Concurrent Pos:* Vis scientist, Max Planck Inst Extraterrestrial Physics, 69-70. *Res:* Experimental nuclear physics; cosmic ray physics. *Mailing Add:* 10728 Leigh Ellen Ave Baton Rouge LA 70810-3028

HUGGETT, ROBERT JAMES, MARINE GEOCHEMISTRY, ENVIRONMENTAL SCIENCES. *Current Pos:* asst marine scientist, Va Inst Marine Sci, 68-71, sr marine scientist & chmn dept ecol pollution, 72-79, from asst prof to assoc prof, 77-81, chmn dept chem oceanog, 79-86, asst dir, 86-91, PROF, VA INST MARINE SCI, 85-; CHMN, DEPT ENVIRON SCI, 91- *Personal Data:* b Newport News, Va, Apr 26, 42; m 63; c 2. *Educ:* Scripps Inst Oceanog, MS, 68; Col William & Mary, PhD(marine chem), 77. *Honors & Awards:* Horsley Award Fundamental Res, Va Acad Sci. *Prof Exp:* Res technician chem, Dow Chem Co, 60-63. *Concurrent Pos:* Co-chmn permanent chem task force, Shellfish Sanit Br, US Food & Drug Admin, 73-77; mem eval panel, Off Air & Water Measurements, Nat Bur Standards, 74-77; lectr, Brookings Inst; mem, Sci Adv Bd, Environ Protection Agency, 82-, Water Sci Technol Bd, Nat Acad Sci/Nat Res Coun, 91- *Mem:* Soc Environ Toxicol & Chem. *Res:* Biological availability of trace metals and organics in estuarine systems; toxic substances in aqueous systems; fate and effects of anthropogenic substances in aqueous systems. *Mailing Add:* Sch Marine Sci Col William & Mary Marine Sci Gloucester Point VA 23062. *Fax:* 804-642-7186

HUGGHINS, ERNEST JAY, ANIMAL PARASITOLOGY. *Current Pos:* from asst prof to prof entom & zool, 52-80, zoologist, Agr Exp Sta, 54-85, prof & head, dept biol, 81-85, EMER PROF BIOL, SDAK STATE UNIV, 85- *Personal Data:* b Bryan, Tex, Dec 25, 20; m 52; c 3. *Educ:* Baylor Univ, BA, 43; Tex A&M Univ, MS, 49; Univ Ill, PhD(zool), 52. *Prof Exp:* Instr microbiol, Univ Houston, 46-47; asst biol, Tex A&M Univ, 47-49; asst zool, Univ Ill, 49-51. *Concurrent Pos:* Consult, Off Naval Res, First Int Cong Parasitol, Rome, 64; Fulbright vis prof, Nat Univ Villarreal, Lima, Peru, 67; vis prof, Univ Okla Biol Sta, 60 & Black Hills Natural Sci Field Sta, 72-73; fel, Interam Prog, La State Univ, 63; partic, NATO Advan Study Inst on Animal Learning, WGer, 76; sabbatical leave, Kenya, Africa, 81. *Mem:* Fel AAAS; Am Soc Parasitol; Am Micros Soc; Am Soc Zool; Am Soc Mammal. *Res:* Wildlife parasitology; zoogeographical relationships of South American fish parasites; parasites of dairy cattle. *Mailing Add:* 1034 Sixth Ave Brookings SD 57006

HUGGINS, CHARLES BRENTON, cancer; deceased, see previous edition for last biography

HUGGINS, CLYDE GRIFFIN, BIOCHEMISTRY. *Current Pos:* chmn dept biochem, 72-73, asst dean basic med sci, 72-75, prof, 72-, ASSOC DEAN, COL MED, UNIV S ALA, 75-, EMER PROF BIOCHEM. *Personal Data:* b Watertown, Tenn, June 21, 22; m 44; c 3. *Educ:* Mid Tenn State Col, BS, 45; Univ Miss, BS, 48, MS, 50; Tulane Univ, PhD(biochem), 54. *Prof Exp:* Instr pharm, Univ Miss, 48-51; asst, Univ Tex, 51-52; asst prof physiol chem, Univ Miss, 54-55; from asst prof to assoc prof pharmacol, Med Ctr, Univ Kans, 55-61; from assoc prof to prof biochem, Sch Med, Tulane Univ, 61-72. *Concurrent Pos:* Consult, Vet Admin, 64-72 & Nat Heart & Lung Inst, 68-72; coordr basic med sci, Tulane Univ, 68-72; emer prof, Tulane Med Sch, 72- *Mem:* AAAS; Am Soc Biol Chemists; Am Soc Pharmacol & Exp Therapeut; Asn Am Med Cols; Sigma Xi. *Res:* Metabolism of three-carbon compounds; biologically active polypeptides; phosphoinositides. *Mailing Add:* Tulane Univ Sch Med 2303 Lakeshore Dr Mandeville LA 70448-5736

HUGGINS, ELISHA R, THEORETICAL PHYSICS. *Current Pos:* From asst prof to assoc prof physics, 61-74, PROF PHYSICS, DARTMOUTH COL, 74- *Personal Data:* b Dover, NH, Apr 18, 34; m 58, Anne Walp; c Cleo & Robert. *Educ:* Mass Inst Technol, BS, 55; Calif Inst Technol, PhD(physics), 62. *Honors & Awards:* Am Asn Physics Teachers Award, 65. *Concurrent Pos:* Consult, C A Rypinski Co, 58-59 & Benjamin Publ Co, 64-; vis scientist, Los Alamos Sci Lab, 66-67, consult, 67-; fel, US-Japan Coop NSF Prog, Kyoto Univ, 72. *Mem:* Am Phys Soc. *Res:* Theory of gravity; theory of superfluid helium; superfluid hydrodynamics. *Mailing Add:* Dept Physics Dartmouth Col Hanover NH 03755

HUGGINS, FRANK NORRIS, MATHEMATICS. *Current Pos:* RETIRED. *Personal Data:* b Zephyr, Tex, Oct 25, 26; m 46, Caroline Bradshaw. *Educ:* Howard Payne Col, BA, 48; NTex State Col, MS, 50; Univ Tex, PhD, 67. *Prof Exp:* Teacher pub schs, Tex, 50-54; instr math, Agr & Mech Col, Tex, 54-57, asst prof, 57-61; spec instr, Univ Tex, 61-62; asst prof, Tex A&M Univ, 62-64; spec instr, Univ Tex, Austin, 64-67; from asst prof to assoc prof math, Univ Tex, Arlington, 67-84. *Concurrent Pos:* NSF fac fel, 59-60. *Mem:* Am Math Soc; Math Asn Am. *Res:* Point set theory; theory of functions of real and complex variables; pure mathematics; properties of real functions such as slope variation, generalized Lipschitz conditions and generalized convexity; theory of integration. *Mailing Add:* 1707 Tulip Dr Arlington TX 76013-4917

HUGGINS, JAMES ANTHONY, SORICID SYSTEMATICS, HOSPITAL-UNIVERSITY ALLIANCES. *Current Pos:* PROF ANAT & PHYSIOL, MICRO, PATHOPHYSIOL, HUMAN GROSS ANAT, BAPTIST MEM HOSP, UNION UNIV, 88- *Personal Data:* b Flint, Mich, Oct 1, 53; m 73; c 1. *Educ:* Ark State Univ, BSA, 75, MS, 77; Memphis State Univ, PhD(biol), 85. *Prof Exp:* Asst prof biol, Miss Indust Col, 80-82; instr anat & physiol, Memphis State Univ, 82-83; assoc prof anat & physiol, micro, Shelby State Community Col, 83-88. *Concurrent Pos:* Chair, Div Sci, Baptist Mem Hosp, Union Univ, 88-; adj fac, Memphis State Univ, 90- *Mem:* Am Soc Mammalogists; Am Soc Syst Zoologists; Creation Res Soc; Bible Sci Asn. *Res:* Shrew systematics: morphometrics and chromosomal; hospital or health care association research with universities, joint partnerships, etc. *Mailing Add:* Div Sci BMH Campus 1050 Union University Dr Jackson TN 38305

HUGGINS, LARRY FRANCIS, AGRICULTURAL ENGINEERING. *Current Pos:* From instr to assoc prof, 62-76, prof, 76-81, HEAD AGR ENGR, PURDUE UNIV, 81- *Personal Data:* b Decatur, Ill, Nov 30, 37; m 56; c 3. *Educ:* Univ Ill, Urbana, BS, 60, MS, 62; Purdue Univ, PhD(agr eng), 66. *Concurrent Pos:* Nat dir prof develop, Am Soc Agr Engrs, 88-90. *Mem:* Am Soc Agr Engrs; Am Soc Eng Educ; Soil Conserv Soc Am; Sigma Xi; Nat Soc Prof Engrs. *Res:* Hydrology; water resources planning. *Mailing Add:* 2700 Covington St West Lafayette IN 49706-1408

HUGGINS, PATRICK JOHN, GALACTIC & STELLAR ASTROPHYSICS. *Current Pos:* from asst prof to assoc prof, 78-88, PROF PHYSICS, NY UNIV, 88- *Personal Data:* b Hertfordshire, Eng, Sept 25, 48. *Educ:* Univ Cambridge, BA, 70, MA, 74, PhD(astron), 75. *Prof Exp:* Res assoc astrophys, Queen Mary Col, Univ London, 74-76; res fel, Bell Labs, 76-78. *Concurrent Pos:* Fel, Alfred P Sloan Found, 81-85. *Mem:* Fel Royal Astron Soc; Am Astron Soc; Int Astron Union. *Res:* Radio astronomy, circumstellar matter, interstellar matter. *Mailing Add:* Dept Physics NY Univ 4 Washington Pl New York NY 10003

HUGGINS, ROBERT A(LAN), FAST IONIC CONDUCTION IN SOLIDS, SOLID STATE IONICS. *Current Pos:* CHIEF SCIENTIST, CTR SOLAR ENERGY & HYDROGEN RES, ULM, GER, 91- *Personal Data:* b Stanford, Calif, Mar 26, 29; m 51; c 3. *Educ:* Amherst Col, BA, 50; Mass Inst Technol, SM, 52, ScD(metall), 54. *Honors & Awards:* Hardy Gold Medal, Am Inst Mining, Metall & Petrol Engrs, 57; Vincent Bendix Award, Am Soc Eng Educ, 78; Alexander von Humboldt Sr Scientist Award, Ger, 78. *Prof Exp:* Instr metall, Mass Inst Technol, 53-54; from asst prof to assoc prof metall eng, Stanford Univ, 54-62, actg exec head, Dept Metall Eng, 57-58, dir, Ctr Mat Res, 61-80, prof mat sci, 62-91. *Concurrent Pos:* NSF sr fel, Univ Gottingen, 65-66; dir mat sci, Advan Res Projs Agency, US Dept Defense, Washington, DC, 68-70; Case Centennial scholar, Case Western Res Univ, 80. *Mem:* Am Soc Metals; Electrochem Soc; Am Inst Mining, Metall & Petrol Engrs; Am Phys Soc; Sigma Xi; Mat Res Soc. *Res:* Solid state ionics; imperfections in crystals; solid-state kinetics; thermodynamics; solid-state electrochemistry; author or co-author of over 300 publications; high temperature superconductivity. *Mailing Add:* Ctr Solar Energy & Hydrogen Res Helmholtzstrasse 8 89081 Ulm Germany

HUGGINS, SARA ESPE, zoology, physiology, for more information see previous edition

HUGGINS, W(ILLIAM) H(ERBERT), ELECTRICAL ENGINEERING. *Current Pos:* RETIRED. *Personal Data:* b Rupert, Idaho, Jan 11, 19. *Educ:* Ore State Col, MS, 42; Mass Inst Technol, ScD, 53. *Honors & Awards:* Thompson Award, Inst Radio Engrs, 48; Nat Electronics Conf Award, 55; Christian R & Mary F Lindback Award, 61; Western Elec Fund Award, Am Soc Eng Educ, 65; Ed Medal Award, Inst Elec & Electronics Engrs, 66. *Prof Exp:* Res assoc, Ore State Col, 41-43, instr elec eng, 43-44; res assoc, Harvard Univ, 44-46 & Mass Inst Technol, 49-54; prof, Johns Hopkins Univ, 54-75, chmn dept, 70-75, emer prof elec eng, 75-86. *Concurrent Pos:* Actg chief, Comput Lab, Air Force Cambridge Res Ctr, 46-54; ed, Circuit Theory J, Inst Elec & Electronics Engrs, 53-57; consult, Rand Corp, 54-63. *Mem:* Nat Acad Eng; fel Acoust Soc Am; fel Inst Elec & Electronics Engrs; Am Soc Eng Educ. *Res:* Circuit theory; theory of hearing; signal theory; iconic communication. *Mailing Add:* One E University Pkwy Apt 1005 Baltimore MD 21218

HUGHEL, THOMAS J(OSIAH), PHYSICAL METALLURGY. *Current Pos:* RETIRED. *Personal Data:* b Anderson, Ind, Apr 9, 19; m 40; c 1. *Educ:* Purdue Univ, BS, 42, PhD(metall), 51. *Prof Exp:* Instr metall, Purdue Univ, 46-50, asst prof metall eng, 50-56; sr res metallurgist, Gen Motors Corp, 56-63, supvry res metallurgist, 63-77, staff res engr, 77-84. *Mem:* Am Soc Metals; Am Inst Mining, Metall & Petrol Engrs; Sigma Xi. *Res:* Alloy steels, x-ray diffraction, failure analysis, forensic metallurgy, hydrogen embrittlement. *Mailing Add:* 2012 Elmhurst Ave Royal Oak MI 48073-3857

HUGHES, ABBIE ANGHARAD, DESIGN & DEVELOPMENT OF EYE, RESEARCH ADMINISTRATION. *Current Pos:* VIS FEL, OPTICAL SCI CTR, AUSTRALIAN NAT UNIV, 91- *Personal Data:* b Whiston, UK, 1940; UK & Australian citizen; m 62; c 2. *Educ:* Oxford Univ, BA Hons, 63, MA, 68; London Univ, DIC, 66; Edinburgh Univ, PhD(visual neurosci), 68, DSc, 82. *Prof Exp:* Asst lectr physiol, Edinburgh Univ Med Sch, 64-68; univ demonstr, Univ Lab Physiol, Oxford Univ, 68-72; res fel, John Curtin Sch Med Res, Australian Nat Univ, 72-74, sr res fel, 74-83; prof & dir, Nat Vision Res Inst Australia, 83-90. *Concurrent Pos:* Chmn, Royal Canberra Hosp Eye Bank Comt, 79-82; vis fel, Dept Appl Math, Australian Nat Univ, 82-90, mem, Visual Sci Ctr, 85-; hon secy, Nat Vision Res Found, Australia, 84- *Mem:* Fel Optical Soc Am; Am Acad Optom; Neurosci Soc; AAAS; Physiol Soc; Australian Physiol & Pharmacol Soc. *Res:* Comparative anatomy and physiology of ocular and visual function with attention to structure and function of optics and retina of the eye; evolution; development and engineering design. *Mailing Add:* 41 Outlook Dr Eaglemont 3084 Australia. *E-Mail:* abbies@ariel.ucs.unimelb.edu.qu

HUGHES, ARTHUR D(OUGLAS), MECHANICAL ENGINEERING. *Current Pos:* prof, 46-74, EMER PROF MECH ENG, ORE STATE UNIV, 74- *Personal Data:* b Tacoma, Wash, June 16, 09; m 32; c 3. *Educ:* State Col Wash, BS & MS, 32, ME, 53. *Prof Exp:* Instr mech eng, State Col Wash, 32-36 & Ore State Col, 38-40, asst prof, 40-43, assoc prof, 43-44; res engr, Gas Turbine Develop Div, Allis-Chalmers Mfg Co, Wis, 44-46. *Concurrent Pos:* Chief proj engr, Birchfield Boiler, Inc, Wash, 63-64; pres, BTU Chasers, Inc, 74- *Mem:* Fel Am Soc Mech Engrs; Am Soc Heating, Refrig & Air-Conditioning Engrs; Am Soc Eng Educ; Am Inst Plant Engrs; Nat Soc Prof Engrs. *Res:* Gas turbines; heatpower equipment; air conditioning; peppermint oil distillation; energy audits. *Mailing Add:* 1162 Norsam Rd Gladwyne PA 19035-1420

HUGHES, AUSTIN LELAND, MOLECULAR EVOLUTION, IMMUNOGENETICS. *Current Pos:* asst prof, 90-96, ASSOC PROF BIOL, PA STATE UNIV, 96- *Personal Data:* b Washington, DC, Sept, 49; m 80, Marianne Kitzmiller; c Austin Jr & Helen. *Educ:* Georgetown Univ, BA, 69; Univ Md, BS, 77; WVa Univ, MS, 80; Ind Univ, PhD(zool), 84. *Prof Exp:* Fel, Univ Oxford, 85-86; vis asst prof biol, Univ Iowa, 86-87; res asst prof genetics, Univ Tex, Houston, 87-90. *Mem:* Soc Molecular Biol & Evolution; Genetics Soc Am; AAAS; Soc Study Evolution; Am Ornithologist's Union. *Res:* Focuses on understanding the mechanisms maintaining genetic polymorphism at major histo compatability complex loci and the evolution of this and other molecular components of one vertebrate immune system. *Mailing Add:* Pa State Univ Dept Biol 208 Mueller Lab University Park PA 16802. *Fax:* 814-865-9131; *E-Mail:* austin@hugaus3.bio.psu.edu

HUGHES, BENJAMIN G, INORGANIC CHEMISTRY, ANALYTICAL CHEMISTRY. *Current Pos:* Asst prof, 64-69, ASSOC PROF CHEM, WESTERN ILL UNIV, 69- *Personal Data:* b Lewistown, Ill, Aug 28, 37; m 60; c 4. *Educ:* Western Ill Univ, BS, 59; Iowa State Univ, MS, 62, PhD(inorg chem), 64. *Mem:* Am Chem Soc. *Res:* Polynuclear halide compounds of niobium and tantalum. *Mailing Add:* 705 E Washington Macomb IL 61455-2433

HUGHES, BLYTH ALVIN, OCEAN WAVES, INTERNAL WAVES. *Current Pos:* RETIRED. *Personal Data:* b Victoria, BC, Mar 10, 36; m 57, 90, Faith J Keifer; c Daniel J, Nicola M & Megan L. *Educ:* Univ BC, BA, 56, MA, 60; Cambridge Univ, PhD(geophys fluid mech), 64; Vancouver Sch Theol, MA, 93, MDiv, 95. *Prof Exp:* Defense sci serv officer marine physics, Pac Naval Lab, Defense Res Bd Can, 56-89, defense sci ocean physics, Defense Res Estab Pac, 69-91. *Res:* Surface and internal waves; remote sensing in oceanography; arctic acoustics; arctic ice morphology. *Mailing Add:* 760 Walema Ave Victoria BC V8Y 3B1 Can

HUGHES, BUDDY LEE, POULTRY SCIENCE, REPRODUCTIVE PHYSIOLOGY. *Current Pos:* Asst poultry sci, 65-68, assoc exten specialist, 71, asst prof poultry exten & res, 72-73, asst prof poultry res, 74-76, assoc prof, 76-81, PROF POULTRY RES & TEACHING, CLEMSON UNIV, 81- *Personal Data:* b Gastonia, NC, Apr 20, 42; m 64; c 3. *Educ:* Clemson Univ, BS, 68; Ore State Univ, MS, 70, PhD(reprod physiol), 71. *Mem:* Poultry Sci Asn; Soc Study Reprod Physiol; Sigma Xi. *Res:* Reproductive performance of artificially inseminated, caged breeder chickens; reproductive characteristics of minor poultry groups; development of the guinea fowl for commerical meat production; housing environment and animal performance. *Mailing Add:* Dept Poultry Sci Clemson Univ 201 Sikes Hall Clemson SC 29632-0001

HUGHES, CHARLES EDWARD, SOFTWARE TOOLS, SIMULATION. *Current Pos:* PROF COMPUT SCI, UNIV CENT FLA, 80- *Personal Data:* b Boston, Mass, Oct 25, 43; m 68; c 2. *Educ:* Northeastern Univ, BA, 66; Pa State Univ, MS, 68, PhD(comput sci), 70. *Prof Exp:* Programmer, Radio Corp Am, 61-66; from instr to asst prof, Pa State Univ, 68-74; from assoc prof to prof comput sci, Univ Tenn, 74-80. *Concurrent Pos:* Nat Bur Standards fel,

71-72; NSF res grant, 76-78, 79-82; vpres & co-founder, Gentleware Corp, 80-; Navy grant, 85-86, Fla high tech res grant & Army res grant, 88-89; Consult, NASA res grant, 88. *Mem:* Asn Comput Mach; Inst Elec & Electronics Engrs. *Res:* Software engineering; programming environments; simulation and training; computability theory. *Mailing Add:* Ont Res Found 130 Slater St Suite 1100 Ottawa ON K1P 6E2 Can

HUGHES, DANIEL RICHARD, ALGEBRA, GEOMETRY. *Current Pos:* reader, Westfield Col, Univ London, 64-67, prof math, 67-84, head dept, 71-74, prof, 84-92, EMER PROF, QUEEN MARY COL, UNIV LONDON, 92- *Personal Data:* b Cincinnati, Ohio, Aug 7, 27; div; c 6. *Educ:* Univ Md, BS, 50, MA, 52; Univ Wis, PhD(math), 55. *Prof Exp:* Instr math, Univ Wis, 55; NSF fel, Ohio State Univ, 55-56, lectr, 56-57, asst prof, 57-58; res lectr, Univ Chicago, 58-60; from asst prof to assoc prof, Univ Mich, 60-64. *Concurrent Pos:* Vis prof, Queen Mary Col, Univ London, 62-63, Univ Rome, 63-64 & 70-71 & Univ Perugia, 70-71. *Mem:* London Math Soc. *Res:* Finite projective planes; combinatorial analysis; finite group theory. *Mailing Add:* Dept Math Queen Mary Col Univ London 327 Mile End Rd London E1 4NS England. *Fax:* 44-181-981-9587; *E-Mail:* d.r.hughes@qmw.ac.uk

HUGHES, DAVID EDWARD, VETERINARY MICROBIOLOGY. *Current Pos:* RETIRED. *Personal Data:* b Deansboro, NY, Nov 24, 22; m 63; c 5. *Educ:* State Univ NY Vet Col, Cornell Univ, DVM, 51; Cornell Univ, MS, 52; Am Col Vet Microbiol, dipl, 67. *Prof Exp:* Res asst vet bact, Cornell Univ, 51-57; vet med off, Bact & Mycol Res Lab, Nat Animal Dis Ctr, NCent Region, Agr Res Serv, USDA, 57-79. *Concurrent Pos:* Exec secy, Leptospirosis Res Conf, 58-63; mem, Conf Res Workers Animal Dis. *Mem:* US Animal Health Asn; Am Vet Med Asn; Sigma Xi. *Res:* Infectious diseases of cattle, brucellosis and vibriosis; leptospirosis of animals; infectious bovine keratoconjunctivitis. *Mailing Add:* 4587 Cameron School Rd Ames IA 50014

HUGHES, DAVID KNOX, MATHEMATICS. *Current Pos:* from asst prof to assoc prof, 67-77, PROF MATH, ABILENE CHRISTIAN UNIV, 77- *Personal Data:* b Lubbock, Tex, Dec 7, 40; m 62; c 1. *Educ:* Abilene Christian Col, BA, 62; Univ Okla, MA, 64, PhD(math), 67. *Prof Exp:* Instr math, Univ Okla, 66-67. *Mem:* Soc Indust & Appl Math; Am Math Soc; Math Asn Am. *Res:* Differential equations; control theory. *Mailing Add:* Dept Math Foster Sci Bldg Rm 237 AC4 Box 28012 Abilene TX 79699-8012

HUGHES, DAVID WILLIAM, ORGANIC CHEMISTRY. *Current Pos:* CAN CONSULT, US PHARMACOPEIA, 94- *Personal Data:* b Leicester, Eng, Aug 4, 33; Can citizen; m 57; c 2. *Educ:* Univ Nottingham, BSc, 54, PhD(natural prod chem), 59. *Prof Exp:* Fel, Div Appl Biol, Nat Res Coun Can, 59-61; sr sci off, Nat Chem Lab, Eng, 61-64; res scientist, Can Food & Drug Directorate, Health Protection Br Can, 64-75, bur drug res, 75-94. *Mem:* Can Inst Chem. *Res:* Structural studies of compounds isolated from natural sources, especially moulds, bacteria and higher plants, analysis of medicinal plants; chemical methods of analysis of antibiotics. *Mailing Add:* 23 Donnington Pl Nepean ON K2H 7K9 Can

HUGHES, EDWIN R, CHEMISTRY, MEDICINE. *Current Pos:* prof pediat, 73-77, dir grad studies in basic med sci, 78-91, EMER PROF PEDIAT, UNIV SALA, 91- *Personal Data:* b Solano, NMex, May 27, 28; m 48; c 7. *Educ:* Eastern NMex Univ, BS, 51, MS, 52; Univ Utah, MD, 56; Am Bd Pediat, dipl. *Prof Exp:* Asst chem, Eastern NMex Univ, 51-52; asst pediat, Univ Utah, 53-56; intern, Univ Minn Hosp, 56-57; asst resident, Univ Utah, 57-58; resident pediat & path, Med Ctr, Univ Ark, 58-59; med res assoc, Brookhaven Nat Lab, 59-61; from asst prof to prof pediat & biochem, Med Ctr, Univ Ark, Little Rock, 61-72; prof, Med Ctr, WVa Univ, 72-73. *Concurrent Pos:* Res collabr, Brookhaven Nat Lab, 61-62. *Mem:* Am Soc Exp Path; Endocrine Soc; Soc Pediat Res; Am Pediat Soc; Am Chem Soc; Sigma Xi. *Res:* Pediatrics; endocrinology; adrenal cortex. *Mailing Add:* 4736 Wicker Way Mobile AL 36609

HUGHES, EUGENE MORGAN, MATHEMATICAL ANALYSIS. *Current Pos:* PRES, WICHITA STATE UNIV, 93- *Personal Data:* b Scottsbluff, Nebr, Apr 3, 34; m 54; c 3. *Educ:* Chadron State Col, BS, 56; Kans State Univ, MS, 58; George Peabody Col, PhD(math), 68. *Prof Exp:* From instr to asst prof math & head dept, Chadron State Col, 57-62, from assoc prof to prof math, 65-70, dir res, 65-66 & Head Start Prog, 66, asst to pres, 66-68, asst dir, Upward Bound, proj mgr regional training off, Proj Head Start & dir, NSF In-Serv Insts Math & Sci, 66-70, dean admin, 68-70; asst to undergrad dean, George Peabody Col, 63-64, asst to pres, 64-65; dean, Col Arts & Sci, Northern Ariz Univ, 70-71, prof math, 70-93, provost univ arts & sci, 71-72, acad vpres, 72-79, acad pres, 79-93. *Concurrent Pos:* Vis lectr, Math Asn Am, 61-62; consult, Nebr State Dept Educ, 66-70; dir, Nebr State Cols Curric Develop Teacher Educ Proj, 67-69; co-dir, NCent Asn Cols & Sec Schs Workshop Teacher Educ, Univ Minn, 68-70, coordr asn, 68-72; chmn, State Elem & Sec Educ Act Adv Coun, Nebr, 69-70; chief, Ariz Acad NSF fel, 63-64; bd dirs, Ariz Bank, 87-, adv bd, United Bank, 82-87 & Flagstaff Chamber Com. *Mem:* Math Asn Am; Nat Educ Asn; Nat Coun Teachers Math. *Res:* Impact of selected experimental curriculum projects on commercially published elementary school mathematics textbooks; properties of groups and permutation groups; mathematics education. *Mailing Add:* Wichita State Univ 1845 Fairmount Wichita KS 67260-0001

HUGHES, EVERETT C, CHEMOTHERAPY, BIOENGINEERING. *Current Pos:* RETIRED. *Personal Data:* b Wadena, Minn, Nov 22, 04; c 5. *Educ:* Carleton Col, AB, 27; Cornell Univ, PhD(chem), 30. *Honors & Awards:* Pioneer Chemist Award, Am Inst Chemists, 71; Morley Award & Medal, Am Chem Soc, 74. *Prof Exp:* Res chemist, Stand Oil Co, Ohio, 30-43, chief, Chem & Phys Res Div, 44-54, res mgr, 54-59, mgr, Res Dept, 59-61, vpres res & develop, 61-69; res assoc, asst & assoc clin prof otolaryngol, Sch Med, Univ Southern Calif, 70-96. *Concurrent Pos:* Chmn mgt comn, Gordon Res Conf, 53-54; mem aviations fuels div, Coop Fuels Res Comt, Coord Res Coun. *Mem:* Fel AAAS; Am Chem Soc; Am Inst Chemists; emer mem Soc Study Headache. *Res:* Causes and treatment of sensorineural hearing impairment and allergies; food allergy; immunology; electrochemical bioengineering. *Mailing Add:* 1225 Charles St Pasadena CA 91103

HUGHES, FRANCIS NORMAN, PHARMACY, PHYSIOLOGY & PHARMACOLOGY. *Current Pos:* RETIRED. *Personal Data:* b Dresden, Ont, Jan 23, 08; m 35, 54, Lorna F Roberts; c Judith, Mary, Margaret, Elizabeth, Donald, David & Linda. *Educ:* Univ Toronto, PharmB, 29, MA, 44; Purdue Univ, BS, 40. *Hon Degrees:* LLD, Purdue Univ, 54, Dalhousie Univ, 73, Univ Toronto, 80; DSc, Mem Univ, 90. *Honors & Awards:* Can Centennial Medal, Govt of Can, 67. *Prof Exp:* Asst prof pharm, Ont Col Pharm, 38-42, from assoc prof to prof mat med & pharm chem, 42-49, prof & asst dean, 49-52, dean, 52-53; prof/dean fac pharm, Univ Toronto, 53-73, emer dean & emer prof, fac pharm, 73- *Concurrent Pos:* Secy, Can Conf Pharmaceut Faculties, 44-50, chmn, 51-52; ed new pharmaceut sect, Can Pharmaceut J, 45-71; pres, Can Found Adv Pharm, 56-57; mem adv bd, Proprietary & Patent Med Act, 58-73; pres, Pharm Exam Bd Can, 64-66; registr-treas, 73-81; ed, Compendium Pharmaceut & Specialties, 60-67, co-ed, 67-71, consult ed, 71-79. *Mem:* Fel AAAS; Asn Faculties Pharm Can (pres, 70); Can Soc Hosp Pharmacists; Asn Deans Pharm Can (pres, 66-69); Can Pharmaceut Asn. *Mailing Add:* 74 Batson Dr Aurora ON L4G 3P8 Can

HUGHES, GEORGE MUGGAH, HYDROGEOLOGY. *Current Pos:* MEM STAFF, ONT MINISTRY ENVIRON, 74- *Personal Data:* b Sidney, NS, Aug 14, 29; m 57; c 2. *Educ:* Univ Alta, BSc, 51, MSc, 59; Univ Ill, PhD(geol), 62. *Prof Exp:* Geologist, Pan Am Petrol Corp, 52-57 & Ill State Geol Surv, 62-74. *Mem:* Am Inst Hydrol. *Res:* Pleistocene geology and hydrogeology; groundwater pollution. *Mailing Add:* RR 4 Gananoque ON K7G 2V6 Can

HUGHES, GILBERT C, botany, mycology, for more information see previous edition

HUGHES, GORDON FRIERSON, APPLIED PHYSICS. *Current Pos:* SR DIR, RECORDING TECHNOL, UNIV SAN DIEGO, 82- *Personal Data:* b Los Angeles, Calif, Sept 9, 37; m 82, Shirley Gordon; c Laura & Eric. *Educ:* Calif Inst Technol, BS, 59, MS, 60, PhD(elec eng), 64. *Prof Exp:* Mem res staff pattern recognition statist, Autonetics; prin scientist magnetic res & develop, Palo Alto Res Ctr, Xerox Corp, 69-82. *Mem:* Sr mem Inst Elec & Electronics Engrs; Sigma Xi. *Res:* Applied magnetism, mathematical analysis and theory of magnetic recording. *Mailing Add:* 6471 Norman Lane San Diego CA 92120. *Fax:* 408-438-4190

HUGHES, HARRISON GILLIATT, PLANT GENETICS, PLANT BREEDING. *Current Pos:* PROF HORT, COLO STATE UNIV, 77- *Personal Data:* b Princeton, Ind, Aug 14, 48; m. *Educ:* Eastern Ill Univ, BS, 69; Purdue Univ, PhD(plant genetics & breeding), 74. *Prof Exp:* Instr hort, Purdue Univ, 73-74; asst prof, State Univ NY, 74-76 & Univ RI, 76-77. *Concurrent Pos:* Vis prof tissue cult, Dept Agron, Univ Ky, 75, Dept Pomol, Univ Calif, 84. *Mem:* Int Asn Plant Tissue Cult; Am Soc Hort Sci; Tissue Cult Asn; Sigma Xi; Am Genetic Asn. *Res:* Tissue culture as applied to propagation and plant genetics and breeding; cryopreservation of plant parts; applied plant biotechnology. *Mailing Add:* Dept Hort Colo State Univ Ft Collins CO 80523-0001

HUGHES, IAN FRANK, METALLURGY. *Current Pos:* RETIRED. *Personal Data:* b Douglas, Eng, Apr 14, 40; m 62, Doreen; c Robert I & Vanessa. *Educ:* London Univ, BS, 62, PhD(metall), 66. *Prof Exp:* Res scientist, Richard Thomas & Baldwins Steel Co, Eng, 58-62; res fel, Nat Phys Lab, Eng, 65-67; from res engr to sr res engr, Inland Steel Co, 67-82, from asst dir to dir, 72-84, gen mgr, 84-86, vpres, 86-, vpres tech, 87- *Res:* Metallurgy. *Mailing Add:* 1479 S Indiana Ave Apt I Chicago IL 60605

HUGHES, JAMES GILLIAM, MEDICINE, PEDIATRICS. *Current Pos:* from assoc prof to prof, 46-76, chmn dept, 60-76, EMER PROF PEDIAT, UNIV TENN, COL MED, MEMPHIS, 76- *Personal Data:* b Memphis, Tenn, Sept 11, 10; m 35; c 4. *Educ:* Southwestern at Memphis, AB, 32; Univ Tenn, Memphis, MD, 35. *Honors & Awards:* Hon Prof, San Carlos Univ Guatemala, 56 & Univ Guadalajara, 63; Abraham Jacobi Award, 75. *Prof Exp:* Rotating intern, City of Memphis Hosps, 35-37; resident, Children's Mem Hosp, Chicago, 37-38 & City of Memphis Hosps, 38-39; instr pediat, Okla State Med Asn & Commonwealth Found NY, 40-42. *Concurrent Pos:* Official examr, Am Bd Pediat, 51-; consult, Surgeon Gen, US Army, 54-, WHO, 55, 56 & 58, Rockefeller Found, 56 & AID-Alliance Progress, 62. *Mem:* Am Acad Pediat (pres, 65-66); Am Pediat Soc; Soc Pediat Res; hon mem Arg, Brazilian, Colombian, Cuban, Mex, Panamanian, Uruguayan & Venezuelan Socs Pediat. *Res:* Studies on the causes of brain damage, prenatally, perinatally and postnatally. *Mailing Add:* 848 Adams Ave Memphis TN 38103-2821

HUGHES, JAMES MITCHELL, NOSOCOMIAL INFECTIONS, DIARRHEAL DISEASE. *Current Pos:* Chief, Water Related Dis Activ, Bacterial Dis Div, Bur Epidemiol, Ctrs Dis Control, 78-81, chief, Surveillance & Prev Br, Hosp Infections Prog, 81-83, dir, Hosp Infections Prog, 83-88, dept dir, 88-92, DIR, NAT CTR INFECTIOUS DIS, CTRS DIS CONTROL & PREV, ATLANTA, 92-; STAFF PHYSICIAN, DEPT MED, DIV

INFECTIOUS DIS, EMORY UNIV, 89- *Personal Data:* b Pittsburgh, Pa, Aug 11, 45; m 71; c Andrew & Mitchell. *Educ:* Stanford Univ, BA, 66, MD. *Concurrent Pos:* Co-leader, Immunization & Infectious Dis Priority Area Work Group, Year 2000 Objectives for Nation, USPHS, 91-; asst surgeon gen, USPHS. *Mem:* Fel Am Col Physicians; fel Infectious Dis Soc Am; AAAS; Am Soc Microbiol; Am Soc Trop Med & Hyg; Royal Soc Trop Med & Hyg. *Res:* Epidemiology, surveillance, prevention and control of infectious diseases in the United States and abroad, with emphasis on nosocomial infections, diarrheal disease, antimicrobial resistance and emerging infections. *Mailing Add:* Ctrs Dis Control & Prev Bldg 1 Rm 6013 MS C12 1600 Clifton Rd Atlanta GA 30333

HUGHES, JAMES PAUL, OCCUPATIONAL MEDICINE. *Current Pos:* MEM HEARING BD, BAY AREA AIR QUAL MGT DIST, CALIF, 89- *Personal Data:* b Wilkinsburg, Pa, 1920; m 44, Adelaide Mitchell; c James M. *Educ:* Univ Pittsburgh, MD, 45; Univ Cincinnati, IMD, 52. *Prof Exp:* Intern, St Francis Hosp, Pittsburgh, 45-46; res path, Univ Hosps, Cleveland, 48-49; fel indust med, Inst Indust Health, Kettering Lab, Cincinnati, 49-52; attend staff, Occup Med Sect, Clin Div Med, Ohio State Univ Hosp, 55-57; med dir, Kaiser Aluminum & Chem Corp, 57-82. *Concurrent Pos:* Asst prof indust med, Univ Cincinnati, 52-55; assoc prof prev med, Univ Ohio, 55-57; exec vpres & dir, Kaiser Found Int, 64-74; lectr med, Tulane Univ, 65-; vpres health affairs, Kaiser Industs Corp, 72-74; assoc prof occup med, Univ Calif, San Francisco, 79-96; vis scholar, Green Col, Oxford Univ, 88; vis consult, Int Labor Office, Geneva, 89. *Mem:* Inst Med-Nat Acad Sci; fel Am Col Occup & Environ Med; fel Am Acad Occup Med (pres, 76-77); fel Am Col Physicians. *Res:* Author. *Mailing Add:* 124 Guilford Rd Piedmont CA 94611-3805

HUGHES, JAMES SINCLAIR, boolean algebra in nonlinear circuits, state machine theory & design, for more information see previous edition

HUGHES, JANICE S, FISHERIES. *Current Pos:* RETIRED. *Personal Data:* b Bastrop, La, Sept 16, 37; m 88, Nathaniel Little. *Educ:* NE La Univ, BS, 59, MS, 66. *Prof Exp:* Biol aide, La Dept Wildlife & Fisheries, 59-61, fisheries biologist I, 61-70, fisheries biologist II, 70-73, fisheries biologist III, 73-83, dist fisheries supvr, 83- *Mem:* Am Fisheries Soc (vpres, 80-82, pres, 83-84); Am Inst Fishery Res Biologists. *Res:* Lake management practices including the evaluation of stocking Florida largemouth bass in a new impoundment; techniques for producing striped bass and grass carp; the toxicity of various chemicals to several species of fish. *Mailing Add:* La Wildlife & Fisheries 368 Century Park Dr Monroe LA 71203-8732

HUGHES, JAY MELVIN, FOREST ECONOMICS, NON-MARKET VALUE ANALYSIS. *Current Pos:* ADJ PROF, DEPT AGR, ECON & BUS, NMEX STATE UNIV, 91- *Personal Data:* b Pueblo, Colo, Dec 1, 30; m 53; c 2. *Educ:* Univ Colo, BA, 52; Colo State Univ, MF, 58; Mich State Univ, PhD(forestry), 64. *Prof Exp:* Forester, USDA Forest Serv, 58-59, res forester, 59-62, res forester & proj leader, 62-66, dir, Forest Resources Prog, Coop State Res Serv, 71-72, br chief, Nat Forest Surv, 72-74, dir, Forest Resources Econ Res, 74-77; prof regional anal forest mgt, Sch Forestry, Univ Minn, 66-71; dean & prof, Col Forestry & Natural Resources, Colo State Univ, 77-91. *Concurrent Pos:* Chmn, Working Group Recreation, Int Union Forest Res Orgn, 76-79, Forest Sci Bd, Soc Am Foresters, 78-80 & Fourth World Wilderness Cong, 83-87; mem, Panel Rev Natural Resources Progs Nepal, Nat Acad Sci, 82-, Nat Joint Coun Food & Agr Sci, 82-86, Nat Coop Forest Res Adv Coun, 83-87, Adv Bd Natural Resources Law Ctr, Univ Colo, 88-89 & bd trustees, Pan-Am Sch Agr, Honduras, 91-; sr Fulbright fel, Honduras, 93; consult, Bhuton Food & Agr/UNOP, 91, vol overseas coop assistance, Bolivia, 95-96. *Mem:* Soc Am Foresters; Am Agr Econ Asn. *Res:* Research administration; forest economics and marketing; feasibility studies for new forest products industries; economic impact analysis of changes in levels and kinds of industry; economic efficiency in forest management and product processing. *Mailing Add:* No 38 Las Casitas Las Cruces NM 88005. *Fax:* 505-523-7506; *E-Mail:* jayhughespc@msn.com

HUGHES, JOHN I(NGRAM), ENGINEERING, CHEMISTRY. *Current Pos:* Chem engr process develop, Ammonia Dept, 41-46, tech supt econ studies, 46-47, tech supt high pressure process develop, 47-48, asst prod supt nylon intermediates, Polychem Dept, 48-50, tech investr, Planning Div, 50-52, res supvr plastics res, 52-55, mgr mkt res plastics, 55-58, mgr mkt develop plastics, 58-61, mgr, Develop Dept, 61-63, NEW VENTURE MGR, E I DU PONT DE NEMOURS & CO, 63- *Personal Data:* b Hudson, Wis, May 8, 19; m 43; c 2. *Educ:* Univ Minn, BChE, 41. *Mem:* Am Chem Soc; Am Inst Chem Engrs. *Mailing Add:* 1302 Copley Dr Welshire Wilmington DE 19803-4118

HUGHES, JOHN LAWRENCE, ORGANIC CHEMISTRY, MEDICINAL CHEMISTRY. *Current Pos:* ASSOC DIR, PEPTIDES UNLIMITED, 90- *Personal Data:* b Evansville, Ind, June 9, 28; m 58; c 2. *Educ:* Evansville Col, BS, 53; Univ Mich, MS, 60, PhD(pharmaceut chem), 62. *Prof Exp:* Chemist, Mead Johnson & Co, 56-58, sr scientist, 61-63; chemist, Union Carbide Chem Co, 63-65; res chemist, Armour Pharmaceut Co, 65-78; prin develop chem, Beckman Instruments, 78-85; assoc dir, Smith Kline & French Labs, 85-90. *Mem:* Am Chem Soc; AAAS. *Res:* Synthesis of organic compounds with potentially useful biological properties; development of processes for the large-scale production of synthetic peptides; development of methods for the determination of composition and sequence of peptides and proteins. *Mailing Add:* 1714 Cherrytree Lane Mountain View CA 94040-3602

HUGHES, JOHN P, VETERINARY MEDICINE. *Current Pos:* from asst prof to assoc prof, 56-67, chief ambulatory, 65-71, chmn dept reprod, 77-84, PROF CLIN SCI, UNIV CALIF, DAVIS, 67-, DIR, EQUINE RES LAB, & DIR SEROL, 81- *Personal Data:* b Fresno, Calif, Mar 21, 22; c 2. *Educ:* Kans State Col, DVM, 49; Am Col Theriogenologists, dipl. *Prof Exp:* Vet, private practice, Madera, Calif, 49-56. *Concurrent Pos:* Vet, Agr Exp Sta, Univ Calif, Davis, 56-, chief equine reprod. Vet Med Teaching Hosp, 71- *Mem:* Am Vet Med Asn; Am Asn Equine Practitioners; Soc Study Reproduction; Am Asn Vet Clinicians; Am Col Theriogenologists; Soc Theriogenology. *Res:* Utero-ovarian relationships, ovarian tumors, infertility associated with chromosomal errors; estrous cycle of the mare; study of the normal physiology of the estrous cycle of the mare. *Mailing Add:* 1539 Brown Dr Davis CA 95616-0804

HUGHES, JOHN RUSSELL, ELECTROENCEPHALOGRAPHY, NEUROPHYSIOLOGY. *Current Pos:* PROF NEUROL & DIR EEG & EPILEPSY CLIN, MED CTR, UNIV ILL, 77- *Personal Data:* b Du Bois, Pa, Dec 19, 28; m 58; c 3. *Educ:* Franklin & Marshall Col, AB, 50; Oxford Univ, BA, 52, MA, 55; Harvard Univ, PhD(neurophysiol), 54; Northwestern Univ, Chicago, MD, 75. *Hon Degrees:* DM, Oxford Univ, 76. *Honors & Awards:* Cert Appreciation, Surgeon Gen Army, 91. *Prof Exp:* Res neurophysiologist, Mass Inst Technol, 54; mem staff, Sect Cortical Integration, NIMH, 55-57; chief neurophysiol & EEG, Meyer Mem Hosp, State Univ NY, 57-63; from assoc prof to prof neurol & dir div EEG & neurophysiol, Northwestern Univ, Chicago, 64-77. *Concurrent Pos:* Asst prof, Sch Med, Univ Buffalo, 57-63; chief EEG, Mercy Hosp, 57-63; consult, Gowanda State Hosp, NY & Craig Epileptic Colony, 57-63, Vet Admin Res Hosp & Evanston Hosp Assoc, 64-77, Nat Inst Neurol Dis Blind, 76-, NIMH, 76- & Nat Cancer Inst, 76-; mem staff, Chicago Wesley Mem Hosp & Passavant Mem Hosp, 64-77, Mercy Ctr, Aurora, 64-, Copley Mem Hosp, 67-, Downey Vet Admin Hosp, 71-76, Community Hosp, Geneva & Delnor Hosp, St Charles, 72-, Univ Ill Hosp & West Side Vet Admin Hosp, 77-; full colonel, USAR, Med Corps, command surgeon, 86 USARCOM; USA rep, Int Brain Death Debate, BBC, London, 83; invited lectr, Int Conf EEG, London, 85; keynote speaker, Int Cong Neurol, Oxford, 93. *Mem:* Hon mem Brit Soc Clin Neurophysiol; Am Acad Neurol; Am EEG Soc; Am Epilepsy Soc; Am Med EEG Asn. *Res:* Electrophysiology of central nervous system. *Mailing Add:* Univ Ill Med Ctr 912 S Wood St Chicago IL 60612

HUGHES, JOHN RUSSELL, ADDICTION, BEHAVORIAL MEDICINE. *Current Pos:* PROF, PSYCHIAT, UNIV VT, 84- *Personal Data:* b Columbia, SC, June 7, 49. *Educ:* Millsaps Col, BS, 71; Univ Miss, MD, 75. *Honors & Awards:* Res Scientist Develop Award, Nat Inst Drug Abuse, 84. *Prof Exp:* Asst prof, psychiat, Univ Minn. *Res:* Human behavioral pharmacology. *Mailing Add:* Dept Psychiat Univ Vt 38 Fletcher Pl Burlington VT 05401-1419

HUGHES, KAREN WOODBURY, EVOLUTION. *Current Pos:* from asst prof to assoc prof, 73-84, head dept, 85-91, PROF BOT, UNIV TENN, KNOXVILLE, 84- *Personal Data:* b Madison, Wis, Aug 15, 40; div. *Educ:* Univ Utah, BS, 62, MS, 64, PhD(genetics), 72. *Prof Exp:* NIH fel RNA develop, Univ Utah, 72-73. *Concurrent Pos:* Assoc prog dir genetic biol, NSF, 80-81. *Mem:* AAAS; Tissue Cult Asn; Int Asn Plant Molecular Biol; Bot Soc Am. *Res:* Evolution and biological diversity, biogeography. *Mailing Add:* Dept Bot Univ Tenn Knoxville TN 37996-0001

HUGHES, KENNETH E(UGENE), BIOMEDICAL ENGINEERING, MEDICAL PRODUCT DEVELOPMENT. *Current Pos:* Technologist, 70-74, res scientist bioeng, Columbus Labs, 75-90, tech liaison, 90-92, SR TECH DIR, MED PROD DEVELOP BATTELLE MEM INST, 93- *Personal Data:* b Columbus, Ohio, May 15, 39; m 64, Marollyn J Falstick; c Keith, Craig & Matthew. *Mem:* Soc Biomat; Am Soc Testing & Mat; Am Soc Qual Control; Soc Plastics Eng. *Res:* Biomedical device and equipment development; biomaterials and implantable prostheses for orthopedics and other surgery; bioengineering applications in space research; material specifications; processing for use in implantable prosthetics; orthopedic devices for bone and tendon repair; cardiovascular materials; instrumented probes and catheters; collagen biomaterials; disposable medical devices and diagnostic instuments; endoscopic surgical instruments. *Mailing Add:* Cornerstone Solution Inc 605 Deerwood Ave Gahanna OH 43230. *Fax:* 614-424-7400

HUGHES, KENNETH JAMES, CHEMICAL ENGINEERING, PHYSICAL CHEMISTRY. *Current Pos:* RETIRED. *Personal Data:* b Glencoe, Okla, May 18, 21; m 46; c 2. *Educ:* Okla State Univ, BS, 43. *Honors & Awards:* Outstanding Engr, Okla Soc Prof Engrs, 70 & Outstanding Engr in Mgt, 78. *Prof Exp:* Chem engr pilot plant fractionation, US Bur Mines, Bartlesville, 46-48, sr combustion engr, 48-55, chem engr automobile exhaust gas res, 55-59, supt mgr res ctr, 59-74; mgt officer & dir, Div Opers, Energy Tech Ctr, US Dept Energy, Bartlesville, 74-83, dir, Div Opers, NIPER, 83-85. *Concurrent Pos:* Dir admin, Emergency Petrol & Natural Gas Admin, 60- *Mem:* Nat Soc Prof Engrs; Am Chem Soc. *Res:* Fundamental investigation of heat release from combustion of liquid hydrocarbons; research dealt with thermodynamics and physical chemistry studies; application of gas chromatographic analysis of hydrocarbon combustion products. *Mailing Add:* 305 SE Rockwood Bartlesville OK 74006

HUGHES, KENNETH RUSSELL, PSYCHOPHYSIOLOGY. *Current Pos:* From asst prof to assoc prof, 61-74, actg chmn dept, 70- 74, PROF PHYSIOL, UNIV MAN, 74-, DEAN GRAD STUDIES. *Personal Data:* b Winnipeg, Man, May 7, 33; m 63. *Educ:* Univ Man, BA, 54, MA, 56; Univ Chicago, PhD(psychol), 61. *Mem:* Am Physiol Asn; Can Physiol Soc. *Res:* Central nervous system and behavior; limbic system function and stress; environmental effects on behavior. *Mailing Add:* Dean Grad Studies Univ Man University Ctr Rm 500 Winnipeg MB R3T 2N2 Can

HUGHES, MALCOLM KENNETH, PALEOCLIMATOLOGY, DENDROCHRONOLOGY. *Current Pos:* PROF & DIR DENDROCHRONOLOGY, LAB TREE-RING RES, UNIV ARIZ, 86- *Personal Data:* b Matlock, Eng, July 24, 43; c 2. *Educ:* Univ Durham, Eng, BSc, 65, PhD(ecol), 70. *Prof Exp:* Amanuensis, Soil Biol Inst, Aarhus Univ, 68-69; res fel bot, Univ Durham, 69-71; lectr ecol, Liverpool Polytech, Eng, 71-73, sr lectr, 73-80, prin lectr, 80-82, reader, 82-86. *Concurrent Pos:* Mem, Terrestrial Life Sci Grants Comt, Natural Environ Res Coun, UK, 82-85, Combined Studies (Sci) Bd, Coun Nat Acad Awards, UK, 83-86, US Nat Comt for Int Union for Quaternary Res, 88-91 & Paleoclimat Adv Panel, Nat Oceanic & Atmospheric Admin, 89-; dir, Global Change Div, Ariz Res Labs, 89- *Mem:* Fel Royal Meteorol Soc; Am Geophys Union; Tree-Ring Soc. *Res:* Exploring climate of recent centuries using annual resolution natural records, primary tree rings, currently developing 3,000 year drought history of California using annual rings of giant sequoia. *Mailing Add:* Lab Tree-Ring Res Univ Ariz 101 W Stadium Tucson AZ 85721. *Fax:* 520-621-8229

HUGHES, MARK, ORGANIC CHEMISTRY. *Current Pos:* From instr to assoc prof chem, 58-69, chmn dept, 67-77, PROF CHEM, ST JOHN'S UNIV, MINN, 69- *Personal Data:* b Hutchinson, Minn, Aug 3, 31; m 54; c 7. *Educ:* St John's Univ, Minn, BA, 53; Iowa State Col, PhD, 58. *Concurrent Pos:* Sabbatical, 65-66. *Mem:* Am Chem Soc. *Mailing Add:* 37 Fourth Ave N Waite Park MN 56387

HUGHES, MARK R, molecular disease diagnostics, human genome research, for more information see previous edition

HUGHES, MARYANNE ROBINSON, AVIAN OSMOREGULATION. *Current Pos:* RES ASSOC ZOOL, UNIV BC, 64-, LECTR, 68- *Personal Data:* b Binghamton, NY, Dec 27, 30; m 61, Gilbert C; c Amy E, Joel D & M Olwyn. *Educ:* Harpur Col, BA, 52; Duke Univ, MA, 56, PhD(zool), 62. *Prof Exp:* Res biochemist, Eaton Labs, Norwich Pharmacal Co, 52-54; asst zool, Duke Univ, 56-59; res assoc, Univ Wash, 60-61; asst prof, Univ of the Pac, 62-63 & Comp Animal Physiol, Simon Frasier Univ, 63-64. *Concurrent Pos:* NSF grant, 63-66; Natural Sci & Eng Res Coun grant, 68-; vis res scientist, Marine Sci Res Lab, Mem Univ, 68 & Dept Zool, James Cook Univ, 71-72; vis prof, Belle W Baruch Inst Marine Biol & Coastal Res, Univ SC, 78-79. *Mem:* Am Soc Zool; Am Physiol Soc. *Res:* Renal function in the octopus; renal and extrarenal salt and water excretion, body water and ion distribution, organ weight and water content in marine birds; hormonal regulation of body water and ion distribution, organ weight and water content in marine birds. *Mailing Add:* Dept Zool Univ BC 6270 University Blvd Vancouver BC V6T 1Z4 Can. *Fax:* 604-822-2416

HUGHES, MICHAEL CHARLES, ANALYTICAL CHEMISTRY. *Current Pos:* mem tech staff, 81-88, DISTINGUISHED MEM TECH STAFF, BELL TEL LABS, ALLENTOWN, PA, 88- *Personal Data:* b Schenectady, NY, May 9, 42. *Educ:* State Univ NY, Albany, BS, 65; Syracuse Univ, PhD(analytical chem), 71. *Prof Exp:* Fel chem, Univ Mich, 74-75; asst prof analytical chem, Lehigh Univ, 75-80. *Mem:* Sigma Xi; AAAS; Am Chem Soc. *Res:* Electroanalytical chemistry; environmental trace analysis; analytical chemistry in the semiconductor industry. *Mailing Add:* 498 Rosewood Dr Northampton PA 18067

HUGHES, NORMAN, DEVELOPMENTAL GENETICS. *Current Pos:* PROF BIOL, PEPPERDINE UNIV, MALIBU, 70- *Personal Data:* b Nashville, Tenn, Mar 26, 32; m 54; c 2. *Educ:* Harding Col, BA, 54; Emory Univ, MS, 56, PhD(biol), 58. *Prof Exp:* Vis instr biol, Emory Univ, 58; prof, Lubbock Christian Col, 58-63; assoc prof, Harding Col, 63-68; prof, Christian Col S W, 68-70. *Mem:* Am Soc Zool; Sigma Xi. *Res:* Cytology and physiology of fertilization; vertebrates; developmental genetics. *Mailing Add:* Seaver Col Pepperdine Univ Malibu CA 90263. *Fax:* 310-456-4785; *E-Mail:* nhughes@pepperdine.edu

HUGHES, O RICHARD, ADVANCED MATERIALS, POLYMER PROCESSING. *Current Pos:* Res chemist, Celanese Res Co, 66-71, proj leader, Catalysis, 71-75, res assoc, 75-82, coordr univ res, 82-85, res assoc advan mat, 85-90, SR RES ASSOC ADVAN MAT, CELANESE RES CO, 90- *Personal Data:* b Washington, DC, May 14, 38; m 63, Margaret L Schormuller; c Stephen R & Eric A. *Educ:* DePaul Univ, BS, 60; Purdue Univ, MS, 64, PhD(phys chem), 66. *Honors & Awards:* Shultheiss lectr, Frankfurt, Ger, 89. *Concurrent Pos:* Pres, Chatham Twp Bd Health, 87-93. *Mem:* Am Chem Soc; NY Acad Sci; Am Ceramic Soc; Mat Res Soc. *Res:* New structural polymers; synthesis and fabrication; polymer powder processing; fabrication & applications of polymer-based performance parts; fabrication of high performance synthetic fibers. *Mailing Add:* Hoechst Celanese R L Mitchell Tech Ctr 86 Morris Ave Summit NJ 07901. *E-Mail:* orh@sumhcci.hcc.com

HUGHES, PATRICK RICHARD, PLANT INSECT INTERACTIONS. *Current Pos:* res assoc, 69-72, asst, 73-77, assoc insect physiologist, 77-85, INSECT PHYSIOLOGIST, BOYCE THOMPSON INST PLANT RES, CORNELL UNIV, 85- *Personal Data:* b San Jose, Calif, March 17, 43; m 63; c 7. *Educ:* San Jose State Col, BA, 64; Univ Calif, Davis, MS, 69, PhD(entom), 73. *Prof Exp:* Lab technician, Univ Calif, Davis, 64-66, res asst, 66-67, res entom, 67-68. *Concurrent Pos:* Teaching asst entom, Univ Calif, Davis, 70-71; guest prof, Forest Zool Inst, Univ Freiburg, WGer, 77; mem, Southern Regional Proj SY135, Develop Microbiol Pesticides, 79-; chmn, organizing comt, Am Registry Prof Entomologists, Northeastern Br, 82, NY Br, 81-82, nominating comt for sr examr, physiol & biochem specialty, 84; mem, Res Design Team to Brazil, Bean/Cowpea Collab Res Support Prog, 80; mem, USDA Competitive Res Grants Off Biol Stress Panel for Entomol, Nematol, 85; chmn nominating comt, subsect CE, Insect Path & Microbiol Control, Entom Soc Am, 86; mem, USDA competitive res grants, Off Biol Strero Panel Insect Pest Sci, 88; specialty mem, Behav, Prof Maintenance & Cert Comt, Am Registry Prof Entomologists, 88-91. *Mem:* Entom Soc Am; Am Registry Prof Entomologists; Soc Invert Path; Int Soc Chem Ecol; Am Soc Virol. *Res:* Response of insects and mites to environmentally-induced changes in host quality; quantitative relationships between insects and insect pathogens. *Mailing Add:* 220 Eastern Heights Dr Ithaca NY 14850

HUGHES, PETER C(ARLISLE), AEROSPACE SCIENCE. *Current Pos:* From asst prof to assoc prof, 66-76, PROF AEROSPACE SCI, UNIV TORONTO, 76- *Personal Data:* b St Catherines, Ont, June 5, 40. *Educ:* Univ Toronto, BASc, 62, MASc, 63, PhD(aerospace sci), 66. *Concurrent Pos:* Consult, Can Defence Res Bd, 66, Aerospace Eng & Res Consults, 66-, Commun Res Ctr, 70- & Spar Aerospace Prod Ltd, 71- *Mem:* Am Inst Aeronaut & Astronaut; Can Aeronaut & Space Inst. *Res:* Spacecraft attitude dynamics, control; trajectory dynamics and control; flexible vehicle control; optimal control. *Mailing Add:* Aerospace Studies Univ Toronto Toronto ON M5S 1A1 Can

HUGHES, RAYMOND HARGETT, PHYSICS. *Current Pos:* from asst prof to prof, 54-90, EMER PROF PHYSICS, UNIV ARK, FAYETTEVILLE, 90- *Personal Data:* b Walla Walla, Wash, June 1, 27; m 52, Olive Jane Wipson; c Diane (Huston), Marshall, Clayton & Randall. *Educ:* Whitman Col, BA, 49; Univ Wis, MS, 51, PhD, 54. *Prof Exp:* Asst, Univ Wis, 49-54. *Mem:* Fel Am Phys Soc. *Res:* Spectra induced by ion and electron impact; laser generated ions; relativistic electron beams. *Mailing Add:* Dept Physics Univ Ark Fayetteville AR 72701

HUGHES, RICHARD V(AN VOORHEES), petroleum engineering; deceased, see previous edition for last biography

HUGHES, ROBERT ALAN, ENVIRONMENTAL CHEMISTRY, LIMNOLOGY. *Current Pos:* prog supvr, Environ Assessment, Dept Sci Develop, Bechtel Corp, 71-72, group mgr environ sci, 72-74, group mgr environ monitoring, 74-76, prog mgr, 76-80, coal progs supvr, 80-81, CHEM WASTE TECHNOL MGR, BECHTEL NAT INC, 81- *Personal Data:* b Milwaukee, Wis, June 27, 38; m 63; c 3. *Educ:* Univ Wis-Milwaukee, BS, 64; Univ Wis-Madison, MS, 68, PhD(water chem), 70. *Prof Exp:* Mgr environ res, Environ Systs Dept, Westinghouse Elec Corp, 70-71. *Concurrent Pos:* Consult, Westinghouse Elec Corp, 70. *Mem:* Am Chem Soc; Am Soc Limnol & Oceanog; Am Water Works Asn; Int Asn Theoret & Appl Limnol; Int Asn Water Pollution Res; Sigma Xi. *Res:* Aquatic chemistry-biology interaction; environmental chemistry of organic nonelectrolytes; mitigation of environmental effects of large construction projects through advanced technology application; hazardous waste management and remedial action implementation. *Mailing Add:* Bechtel Nevada 2621 Losee Rd MS NLV 002 North Las Vegas NV 89030-4134

HUGHES, ROBERT CLARK, MICROSENSOR SCIENCE. *Current Pos:* Mem tech staff, 66-73, supvr physics org solids, 73-78, SUPVR MICROSENSOR DIV, SANDIA NAT LAB, 84- *Personal Data:* b Cleveland, Ohio, Nov 27, 40; m 67; c 3. *Educ:* Carleton Col, BA, 63; Stanford Univ, PhD, 66. *Mem:* Fel Am Phys Soc. *Res:* Physics of dielectrics; photoconductivity and photo detectors; solid state sensors including chemical and radiation sensors. *Mailing Add:* Sandia Nat Lab PO Box 5800 MS 1425 Albuquerque NM 87185-1425

HUGHES, ROBERT DAVID, ORGANIC CHEMISTRY. *Current Pos:* PROJ CHEMIST, STANDARD OIL CO (IND), 79- *Personal Data:* b Chicago, Ill, Aug 17, 43; m 68; c 2. *Educ:* Western Ill Univ, BS, 66; Univ Iowa, MS & PhD(org chem), 70. *Prof Exp:* Proj chemist, Am Oil Co, 70-79. *Mem:* Am Chem Soc. *Res:* Organic stereochemistry; reaction mechanisms; bicyclic compounds facilitated transport through membranes; synthetic fuels. *Mailing Add:* 518 Braemar Ave Naperville IL 60563

HUGHES, ROBERT EDWARD, PHYSICAL CHEMISTRY, RESEARCH MANAGEMENT. *Current Pos:* PRES, ASSOC UNIV INC, 80- *Personal Data:* b New York, NY, May 24, 24; m 54; c 1. *Educ:* Lehigh Univ, BS, 49; Cornell Univ, PhD(chem), 52. *Prof Exp:* Res asst, Bakelite Corp, 41-42 & 46-47; instr, Cornell Univ, 52-53; from asst prof to prof, Univ Pa, 53-64; dir, Mat Sci Ctr, Cornell Univ, 68-74, prof chem, 64-80. *Concurrent Pos:* Consult, Rohm & Haas, 56-74, Sun Oil Co, 58-64 & 77-80 & Gen Motors, 78-80; sr NSF fel, Cambridge Univ, 67-68; ed, J Solid State Chem, 69-74; mem res & develop study group, US Comn Gov Proc, 71-72; mem solid state sci comt, Nat Res Coun-Nat Acad Sci, 67-74, chmn, 71-73; asst dir nat & int affairs, NSF, 74-75, astron, atmospheric, earth & ocean sci, 75-76 & actg asst dir sci, technol & int affairs, 75-76; head US deleg, 8th Antarctic Treaty Consult Meeting, Oslo, 75; assoc, Prog Sci, Technol & Soc, Cornell Univ, 77-80; mem nat mat adv bd, Nat Res Coun-Nat Acad Sci, 78-81, mem nat adv bd, Am Univ, 83-; vis prof, Oxford Univ, 79; mem, Res Coord Coun, Gas Res Inst, 85- *Mem:* Am Chem Soc; Am Crystallog Asn; AAAS; Am Astron Soc; Am Phys Soc; Sigma Xi. *Res:* X-ray crystallography; oligopeptide and antibiotic structures; boron and boride crystal chemistry; non-stoichiometric systems; physical chemistry of macromolecules. *Mailing Add:* 1400 16th St NW Suite 730 Washington DC 20036-2217

HUGHES, ROBERT MASON, REGIONAL AQUATIC ECOLOGY, FISH ASSEMBLAGE ECOLOGY. *Current Pos:* SR SCIENTIST, DYNAMAC, 96- *Personal Data:* b Mt Pleasant, Mich, Aug 19, 45; m 69, Mary Wingo; c Gregory & Elizabeth. *Educ:* Univ Mich, AB, 67, MS, 73; Ore State Univ, PhD(fisheries & wildlife), 79. *Honors & Awards:* Sci & Technol Achievement Award, US Environ Protection Agency, 87. *Prof Exp:* Biol teacher, Dexter High Sch, 67-68; gen sci teacher, Charlotte Amalie High Sch, 68-69; conserv teacher, Huron High Sch, 69-72; natural resources teaching fel, Univ Mich, 72-74; res asst, Ore State Univ, 74-77; asst prof stream ecol & field biol, Western Mich Univ, 77-80; ecologist, US Environ Protection Agency, 80-81; vis res scientist, Univ Ill, 81-82; res scientist, Man Tech Environ Technol Inc, 82-96. *Concurrent Pos:* Bot asst, Melvern F Tessene, 67; instr aquatic entom, Ore State Univ, 76; courtesy assoc prof, Ore State Univ, 90-94; instr biol diversity, US Fish & Wildlife Serv, 93. *Mem:* Am Fisheries Soc; NAm Benthological Soc. *Res:* Sampling and analysis of fish assemblages and aquatic ecosystems; developing and evaluating indicators of aquatic ecosystem health; assess ecoregional patterns of aquatic ecosystems and propose biological criteria; modify an index of biological integrity for use in large rivers in Oregon, France, India and Poland; selection and evaluation of reference streams and lakes to determine potential biological integrity. *Mailing Add:* 2895 SE Glenn Corvallis OR 97333. *E-Mail:* hughesb@mail.cor.epa.gov

HUGHES, RUSSELL PROFIT, INORGANIC CHEMISTRY, ORGANOMETALLIC CHEMISTRY. *Current Pos:* asst prof, 76-82, assoc prof, 82-86, PROF CHEM, DARTMOUTH COL, 86- *Personal Data:* b Denbigh, Wales, Dec 23, 46. *Educ:* Univ Manchester, Inst Sci & Technol, BSc, 67; Univ Toronto, PhD(chem), 72. *Prof Exp:* Res asst chem, Bristol Univ, 73-75; res assoc, McGill Univ, 75-76. *Concurrent Pos:* Alfred P Sloan res fel, 80-84; Alexander von Humboldt fel, 83-84. *Mem:* Am Chem Soc. *Res:* Organotransition metal chemistry. *Mailing Add:* Dept Chem Dartmouth Col Hanover NH 03755-3577

HUGHES, STANLEY JOHN, MYCOLOGY. *Current Pos:* mycologist, Agr Can, 52-58, sr mycologist, 58-62, prin mycologist, 62-83, HON RES ASSOC, EASTERN CEREAL & OILSEED RES CTR, CENT EXP FARM, AGR CAN, 83- *Personal Data:* b Llanelli, Wales, Sept 17, 18; m 58, Lyndell Anne Rutherford; c Robert Conway, Glenys Anne & David Stanley. *Educ:* Univ Wales, BSc, 41, MSc, 43, DSc(mycol), 54. *Honors & Awards:* Jakob Eriksson Gold Medal, Swedish Acad Sci, 69; George Lawson Medal, Can Bot Asn, 81; Distinguished Mycologist Award, Mycol Soc Am, 85. *Prof Exp:* Asst mycologist, Commonwealth Mycol Inst, Eng, 45-52. *Concurrent Pos:* Sr res fel, Dept Sci & Indust Res, NZ, 63. *Mem:* Mycol Soc Am (pres, 75); mem Brit Mycol Soc (vpres, 87); Int Mycol Asn (vpres, 77-83); fel Royal Soc Can; Linnean Soc London. *Res:* Fungi imperfecti; classification; sooty molds. *Mailing Add:* Eastern Cereal & Oilseed Res Ctr William Saunders Bldg Cent Exp Farm Agr Can Ottawa ON K1A 0C6 Can

HUGHES, STEPHEN EDWARD, TRANSPLANTATION, PHYSIOLOGY. *Current Pos:* asst prof, Dept Surg, Albany Med Col, 94-96, dir transplant res lab, 94-96, ASSOC PROF, DEPT PHYSIOL & CELL BIOL, ALBANY MED COL, 92-, ASST PROF, DEPT EMERG MED, 96-, assoc res dir, dept emerg med, 96-97, RES DIR, DEPT EMERG MED, 97- *Personal Data:* b Newton, Mass, June 1, 53; m 84, Michelle R Lenmartz; c Kelly & Austin. *Educ:* Univ Miami, BS, 74; Univ Mass, Amherst, PhD(zool), 81. *Prof Exp:* Res & teaching asst biol, Univ Miami, 72-74; teaching assoc zool, Univ Mass, Amherst, 74-79; res assoc neurosci, Univ Mich, Ann Arbor, 80-85; asst prof speech & hearing, Wash Univ, 85-92; asst res scientist neurobiol, Cent Inst Deaf, 85-92. *Concurrent Pos:* Bd mem, St Louis Chap, Retinitis Pigmentosa Found, 88. *Mem:* AAAS; Asn Res Otolaryngol; Sigma Xi; Soc Neurosci. *Res:* Restoration of sensory function through the transplantation of sensory cells in the eye and ear; development of sensory systems. *Mailing Add:* Dept Emergency Med A-139 Albany Med Col 47 New Scotland Ave Albany NY 12208. *Fax:* 518-262-3236; *E-Mail:* shughes@ccgateway.amc.edu

HUGHES, THOMAS JOSEPH, ENGINEERING. *Current Pos:* assoc prof, 80-82, PROF MECH ENG & CHMN, DIV APPL MECH, STANFORD UNIV, 83- *Personal Data:* b Brooklyn, NY, Aug 3, 43; m 72; c 3. *Educ:* Pratt Inst, BS, 65, MS, 67; Univ Calif, Berkeley, MS, 74, PhD(eng sci), 74. *Honors & Awards:* Bernard Friedman Mem Award, 74; Walter Huber Res Prize, Am Soc Civil Engrs, 78; Computational Mech Award, Japan Soc Mech Engrs, 93; Tech Achievement Award, Nat Acad Eng, 95. *Prof Exp:* Mech design engr, Grumman Aircraft Eng Co, 65-66; res & develop engr, Gen Dynamics Corp, 67-69; asst res engr, Univ Calif, Berkeley, 74-76, lectr, Dept Civil Eng, 75-76; asst prof struct mech, Calif Inst Technol, 76-78, assoc prof, 78-80. *Concurrent Pos:* Ed, J Comput Methods Appl Mech & Eng, 90. *Mem:* Nat Acad Eng; fel Am Soc Mech Engrs; Am Soc Civil Engrs; Sigma Xi; Am Inst Aeronaut & Astronaut; fel Am Acad Mech; fel Asn Comput Mach. *Res:* Development of finite-element computer procedures for fluid, solid, soil and structural mechanics problems; author of over 300 publications. *Mailing Add:* Div Mech & Comput Durand Bldg Stanford CA 94305

HUGHES, THOMAS ROGERS, JR, PHYSICS. *Current Pos:* INSTR PHYSICS, COL ALAMEDA, 70- *Personal Data:* b Staten Island, NY, Oct 3, 31; m 67. *Educ:* Yale Univ, BS, 53; Wash Univ, PhD(physics), 62. *Mem:* Am Asn Physics Teachers; Int Solar Energy Soc; Astron Soc Pac; Am Solar Energy Soc. *Res:* Application of nuclear magnetic resonance techniques to the study of the metal ammonia system. *Mailing Add:* Dept Math Physics Chem & Biol Col Alameda 555 Atlantic Ave Alameda CA 94501-2109

HUGHES, TRAVIS HUBERT, HYDROGEOLOGY, ENVIRONMENTAL GEOLOGY. *Current Pos:* VPRES & PRIN, HYDROLOGIC CONSULT, INC, 92- *Personal Data:* b Rapid City, SDak, Feb 21, 37; m 57, Suzy Hatcher; c Tracy & Travis Jr. *Educ:* Vanderbilt Univ, BA, 59, MS, 60; Univ Colo, PhD(geol), 67. *Honors & Awards:* Waldemar Lindgren Citation Award, Soc Econ Geologists, 68; NASA Citation for Innovative Res, 78; Cert Merit, Am Inst Prof Geol, 83; Distinguished Achievement Earth Sci Award, Fedn Lapidary & Mineral Socs, 79. *Prof Exp:* Geologist, Oman Construct Co, 60-62; from instr to prof geol, Univ Ala, 66-82, chmn dept, 78-81; vpres, P E LaMoreaux & Assoc, 82-92. *Concurrent Pos:* US rep, Conf Remobilization Ore Deposits, Sardinia, 68; sr staff scientist, Univ Ala Environ Inst Waste Mgt Studies, 84-88; comt Onshore Oil & Gas Leasing, Nat Acad Sci, 89. *Mem:* Am Inst Prof Geologists (pres, 86); Geochem Soc; Geol Soc Am; Am Geol Inst; Asn Ground Water Scientists & Engrs. *Res:* Hydrogeology; geochemistry; environmental geology; assessment, evaluation, characterization, and remediation of hydrogeologic and geochemical problems at industrial and mining sites. *Mailing Add:* Hydrologic Consult Inc 143 Union Blvd Suite 525 Lakewood CO 80228. *Fax:* 303-969-8357; *E-Mail:* hcilkwd@usa.net

HUGHES, VERNON WILLARD, PHYSICS. *Current Pos:* from asst prof to prof, Yale Univ, 60-69, assoc chmn dept, 60-61, chmn, 61-66, Donner prof, 69-78, Sterling prof physics, 78-91, EMER STERLING PROF PHYSICS, YALE UNIV, 91-, SR RES SCIENTIST, 91- *Personal Data:* b Kankakee, Ill, May 28, 21; m 80, Miriam Kartch; c Emlyn & Gareth. *Educ:* Columbia Univ, AB, 41, PhD(physics), 50; Calif Inst Technol, MS, 42. *Hon Degrees:* Dr, Univ Heidelberg, 77. *Honors & Awards:* Morris Loeb Lectr Physics, Harvard Univ, 72; Davisson-Germer Prize, Am Phys Soc, 78, Tom W Bonner Prize, 90; Rumford Prize, Am Acad Arts & Sci, 85. *Prof Exp:* Res assoc radiation lab, Mass Inst Technol, 42-46; instr & lectr physics, Columbia Univ, 49-52; asst prof, Univ Pa, 52-54. *Concurrent Pos:* Assoc prof physics, Columbia Univ, 58-59, vis I I Rabi prof, 84, adj prof, 84-; trustee, Assoc Univs, Inc, 82-; mem, Naval Res Adv Comt, 68-74; counr-at-large, Am Phys Soc, 70-74; vis prof, Japan Soc Prom Soc Sci, 74; Alexander von Humboldt Sr US Scientist Award, 76; Guggenheim fel, 78-79; vis prof, Slac, Stanford Univ, 78-79, Col France, 81 & Scuola Normale Superiore, Pisa, Italy, 82; consult, Los Alamos Sci Lab, Oak Ridge Nat Lab, NSF, Nat Res Coun, Dept Energy & others. *Mem:* Nat Acad Sci; fel Am Acad Arts & Sci; fel Am Phys Soc; fel AAAS. *Res:* Radiofrequency and microwave spectroscopy of atoms and molecules; particle physics. *Mailing Add:* Yale Univ Dept Physics 4655 W Gibbs 260 Whitney Ave PO Box 208181 New Haven CT 06520-8121. *Fax:* 203-432-3804; *E-Mail:* hughes@hepmail.physics.yale.edu

HUGHES, VICTOR A, PHYSICS, ASTRONOMY. *Current Pos:* prof physics & astron, 63-68, prof physics, 68-92, EMER PROF PHYSICS, QUEEN'S UNIV, ONT, 92- *Personal Data:* b Manchester, Eng, Mar 17, 25; m 58, 70; c 4. *Educ:* Univ Manchester, BSc, 45, MSc, 49, DSc, 77. *Prof Exp:* Mem staff radar & radio astron, Royal Radar Estab, Malvern, Eng, 52-61; prin sci officer, Radio Res Sta Slough, 61-63. *Concurrent Pos:* Chmn, Comn V, Can Nat Comt, Int Sci Radio Union, 65-70. *Mem:* Can Asn Physicists; Int Astron Union; fel Royal Astron Soc; Am Astron Soc; Can Astron Soc. *Res:* Galactic astronomy; interstellar medium. *Mailing Add:* Dept Physics Astron Group Queen's Univ Kingston ON K7L 3N6 Can

HUGHES, WALTER LEE, JR, BIOCHEMISTRY, MOLECULAR & RADIATION BIOLOGY. *Current Pos:* chmn dept, 63-76, prof, 63-79, EMER PROF PHYSIOL, SCH MED, TUFTS UNIV, 79- *Personal Data:* b Trenton, NJ, Nov 19, 15; wid; c Judith E & Mary L (Berger). *Educ:* Mass Inst Technol, SB, 37, PhD(org chem), 41. *Prof Exp:* Fel protein chem, Harvard Univ, 40-42, res assoc phys chem, 42-46, assoc, 46-48, asst prof, 48-53; assoc prof, Johns Hopkins Univ, 53-55; head, Div Microbiol, Med Res Ctr, Brookhaven Nat Lab, 55-58, head, Div Biochem, 58-63. *Concurrent Pos:* Guggenheim fel, Calif Inst Technol, 51-52; res collabr, Brookhaven Nat Lab. *Mem:* Am Acad Arts & Sci; Am Soc Biol Chemists; Fedn Am Scientists. *Res:* Proteins nucleic acids; mechanisms of synthesis and catabolism and cellular localization; technics for studying metabolism; labeled nucleosides; chromium labeled proteins; selenium as biological anti-oxidant and mercury detoxicant; cancer therapy. *Mailing Add:* 54 Bellport Lane Bellport NY 11713

HUGHES, WALTER T, PEDIATRICS. *Current Pos:* PROF PEDIAT, CTR HEALTH SCI, UNIV TENN, 81-; CHMN, DIV INFECTIOUS DIS, ST JUDE CHILDREN'S RES HOSP, 81- *Personal Data:* b Cleveland, Tenn, May 16, 30; m 57, Frances J Skinner; c Carla, Greg & Christopher. *Educ:* Tenn Polytech Inst, 48-50; Univ Tenn, MD, 54. *Prof Exp:* Intern, Gen Hosp, Knoxville, Tenn, 55; resident, Col Med, Univ Tenn, 57; staff mem, Walter Reed Army Med Ctr, Res & Develop Command, Ft Detrick, Md, 57-59; from instr to prof pediat, Sch Med, Univ Louisville, 61-69; prof pediat & microbiol, Univ Tenn Med Units, Memphis, 69-77; prof pediat & dir, Div Pediat Infectious Dis, Sch Med, Johns Hopkins Univ, 77-81, staff mem, Johns Hopkins Hosp, 77-81. *Concurrent Pos:* Consult, Ireland Army Hosp, US Army, Ft Knox, Ky, 63-69; lectr pediat, Sch Med, Johns Hopkins Univ, 81-; Arthur Ashe chair, Pediat AIDS Res, 93- *Mem:* Am Soc Microbiol; Soc Pediat Res; Infectious Dis Soc Am; Am Acad Pediat; Am Pediat Soc. *Res:* Infectious diseases in the immune-compromised host. *Mailing Add:* St Jude Children's Res Hosp 332 N Lauderdale Memphis TN 38101. *Fax:* 901-521-1511

HUGHES, WALTER WILLIAM, III, PATHOLOGY, ENVIRONMENTAL TOXICOLOGY. *Current Pos:* PROF BIOL, LOMA LINDA UNIV, CALIF, 93- *Personal Data:* b Glendale, Calif, Apr 23, 51; m 72, Marilyn Klebba; c Stacey, Summer & Courtney. *Educ:* Loma Linda Univ, BA, 73, PhD(biol), 78; Pac Union Col, MA, 74. *Honors & Awards:* Edmund C Jaeger Award, 76. *Prof Exp:* Prof biol, Andrews Univ, 78-91. *Concurrent*

Pos: Res assoc, Univ Newcastle, Eng, 78-79. *Mem:* Sigma Xi. *Res:* Invertebrate skeletal growth increments and their relation to paleontology, paleoecology and geophysics. *Mailing Add:* Sch Allied Health Professions Loma Linda Univ Loma Linda CA 92350

HUGHES, WILLIAM (LEWIS), ELECTRICAL ENGINEERING. *Current Pos:* RETIRED. *Personal Data:* b Rapid City, SDak, Dec 2, 26; c 4. *Educ:* SDak Sch Mines & Technol, BS, 49; Iowa State Univ, MS, 50, PhD(elec eng), 52. *Prof Exp:* TV studio & transmitter engr, WOI-TV, Ames, Iowa, 49-52; head sch elec eng, Okla State Univ, 60-76, prof elec eng, 60-86, emer prof, 86-93, dir, Eng Energy Lab, 75-86; vpres, SDak Sch Mines & Tech, 88-93. *Concurrent Pos:* Mem, TV Allocations Study Orgn, 57-60; instigator & dir unconvention energy systs work, Okla State Univ, 62-; chmn study group XI-B, US Prep Comt, Consult Comt Int Radio, 66-73; nat chmn, Comn Elec Eng Dept Heads, 66; instigator & dir Themis invest elec characteristics severe storms, US Dept Defense, 67-72; US deleg & chmn Int Color TV Stand Group, Consult Comt Int Radio meeting, Palma, Spain, 68 & Geneva, 69-71; chmn, Nat Acad Sci Comt Energy Sources Develop Nations; tech adv, Ministry Elec, Arab Repub Egypt; consult renewable energy matters var industs, govt agencies & several foreign govt; pres & owner, INEN Corp, 72-. *Mem:* Fel Inst Elec & Electronics Engrs; AAAS; Soc Motion Picture & TV Engrs; Am Soc Eng Educ; Solar Energy Soc. *Res:* Nonlinear systems; electromagnetics; color television systems; fuel cells; energy storage systems. *Mailing Add:* 6118 Greenleaf Ct Rapid City SD 57702-8845

HUGHES, WILLIAM CARROLL, CIVIL ENGINEERING. *Current Pos:* asst prof, 68-75, ASSOC PROF CIVIL ENG, UNIV COLO, DENVER, 75-. *Personal Data:* b Albuquerque, NMex, Apr 5, 38; m 60; c 2. *Educ:* Univ NMex, BS, 60, MS, 65, PhD(civil eng), 69; Univ Utah, BS, 61. *Prof Exp:* Asst engr, Calif State Dept Water Resources, 64-66. *Concurrent Pos:* NSF initiation grant, 71-72. *Mem:* Am Soc Civil Engrs; Am Soc Eng Educ; Sigma Xi. *Res:* Hydrology and hydraulics. *Mailing Add:* 207 Iroquois Dr Boulder CO 80303-4215

HUGHES, WILLIAM E, SOLID STATE PHYSICS. *Current Pos:* PROF PHYSICS & CHMN DEPT, UNIV SOUTHERN MISS, 69-. *Personal Data:* b Centreville, Miss, Sept 12, 32; m 60; c 3. *Educ:* Univ Southern Miss, BS, 58; Univ Ala, PhD(physics), 63. *Prof Exp:* Asst prof physics, Stetson Univ, 64-69. *Res:* Electron spin resonance; nuclear resonance in solids. *Mailing Add:* Dept Physics Univ Southern Miss Box 5046 Hattiesburg MS 39406

HUGHES, WILLIAM F(RANK), MECHANICAL ENGINEERING. *Current Pos:* Assoc prof mech eng, 55-67, PROF MECH & ELEC ENG, CARNEGIE-MELLON UNIV, 67-. *Personal Data:* b Ash, NC, Oct 20, 30; m 79, Sue Evans; c Christopher & Eric. *Educ:* Carnegie Inst Technol, BS, 52, MS, 53, PhD(mech eng), 55. *Honors & Awards:* Fulbright lectr, Univ Sydney, 63. *Concurrent Pos:* NSF fel, Cambridge Univ, 57-58. *Mem:* Am Soc Mech Engrs; Am Phys Soc; Am Geophys Union; Soc Tribologists & Lubrication Engrs. *Res:* Fluid dynamics and hydrodynamic lubrication and friction; magnetohydrodynamics; electromechanical systems. *Mailing Add:* PO Box 245 Oquossoc ME 04964

HUGHES, WILLIAM TAYLOR, BIOPHYSICS. *Current Pos:* from asst prof to assoc prof, 67-75, chmn dept, 71-75, PROF PHYSICS & ASTRON, BOWDOIN COL, 75-. *Personal Data:* b Vidor, Tex, Nov 15, 36; m 65; c 1. *Educ:* Ind Univ, BS, 60, MA, 62; Northwestern Univ, PhD(astron), 67. *Prof Exp:* Astronr, Smithsonian Astrophys Observ Satellite Tracking Sta, Neth, WI, 58-59; instr astron, Univ Mo, 62-63; asst prof physics & astron, WVa State Col, 63-65. *Concurrent Pos:* Consult, Southworth Planetarium, Univ Maine, 69-71; mem, Biosatellite eval panel, NASA, 70; mem staff, NATO Advan Study Inst Biophys, 71 & Cambridge Univ, 73-74. *Mem:* Fel Royal Astron Soc. *Res:* Astronomical spectroscopy and photometry; bioenergetics; membrane properties; DNA replication. *Mailing Add:* 8 McKeen St Brunswick ME 04011

HUGHETT, PAUL WILLIAM, MEDICAL IMAGING, INVERSE PROBLEMS. *Current Pos:* RES ASSOC, MED CTR, UNIV PA, 96-. *Personal Data:* b San Rafael, Calif, May 19, 50. *Educ:* Mass Inst Technol, BS, 86, MS, 86; Univ Calif, Berkeley, PhD(elec eng), 95. *Prof Exp:* Mem tech staff, Hewlett-Packard, 73-77; syst engr, Singer-Link Flight Simulation, 77-81; owner, Hughett Res, 81-91; grad stud, Univ Calif, Berkeley, 91-96. *Concurrent Pos:* Instr, Univ Calif, Santa Cruz, 90-91. *Mem:* Prof & Tech Consults Asn (pres, 87-89); Soc Photo-Optical Instrumentation Engrs; Inst Elec & Electronics Engrs Comput Soc; Soc Motion Picture & TV Engrs; Asn Comput Mach. *Res:* Applications of image processing and computer graphics to scientific and engineering research; quantitative infrared thermography; ultrasound imaging; non-destructive testing; fringe pattern analysis; inverse problems of medical imaging, especially statistical hypothesis testing and the use of prior knowledge. *Mailing Add:* Neuropsychiat Sect 10th Floor Gates Bldg Univ Pa 3400 Spruce St Philadelphia PA 19104. *E-Mail:* hughett@bbl.psycha.upenn.edu

HUGLI, TONY EDWARD, BIOCHEMISTRY, PROTEIN CHEMISTRY. *Current Pos:* assoc mem, 72-82, MEM, SCRIPPS CLIN & RES FOUND, 82-. *Personal Data:* b Logan, Ohio, June 26, 41; m 65, Judith Furay; c Kevin & Heidi. *Educ:* Otterbein Col, BS, 63; Ind Univ, Bloomington, PhD(biochem), 68. *Honors & Awards:* Ecker lectr, Case Western Res Univ, 92. *Prof Exp:* Res assoc protein chem, Rockefeller Univ, 68-72. *Concurrent Pos:* Estab investigatorship, Am Heart Asn, 72-77, grant-in-aid, 74-77; exec ed, Anal Biochem, 85-; assoc ed, Immunopharmacol, 88-, Protein Sci, 91-. *Mem:* Am Soc Immunol; Am Soc Biol Chem; Am Soc Exp Pathol. *Res:* Structural comparison of dissolved and crystalline sperm whale metmyoglobin; active site studies of bovine pancreatic deoxyribonuclease A; method for determining tryptophan in proteins following alkaline hydrolysis; chemistry and biology of human serum complement components. *Mailing Add:* 10666 N Torrey Pines Rd La Jolla CA 92037-1092. *Fax:* 619-554-6079; *E-Mail:* hugli@scripps.edu

HUGO, NORMAN ELIOT, PLASTIC SURGERY. *Current Pos:* PROF SURG, COLUMBIA PRESBY MED CTR, CHMN, PLASTIC SURG, 82-. *Personal Data:* b Beverly, Mass, Sept 23, 33; m 59; c 5. *Educ:* Williams Col, AB, 55; Cornell Univ, MD, 59. *Hon Degrees:* DSc, Williams Col, 89. *Prof Exp:* Instr surg, Med Sch, Cornell Univ, 64-66; dir plastic surg lab, Ind Univ Med Ctr & asst prof surg, Med Sch, 66-67; assoc prof surg, Med Sch, Univ Chicago, 69-70; assoc prof surg, Northwestern Univ, 70-82. *Concurrent Pos:* J J O'Neill res fel, New York Hosp-Cornell Med Ctr, 64-65; attend surgeon plastic surg, Ind Univ Med Ctr, 66-67; asst chief plastic surg, Walter Reed Army Hosp, 67-69; attend surgeon & chief plastic surg, Michael Reese Hosp, 69-70; attend surgeon, Northwestern Mem Hosp, 70-82, Columbia-Presby Med Ctr; vchmn, Am Bd Plastic Surg, 88-89. *Mem:* Plastic Surg Res Coun; Am Asn Plastic Surg; Educ Found; Am Soc Plastic & Reconstruct Surgeons (pres, 88-89); Asn Acad Surgeons. *Res:* Wound healing, especially wound contraction and the role of the dermis in controlling myofibroblastic contraction; fetal wound healing. *Mailing Add:* 161 Ft Washington Ave Suite 502 622 W 168th St New York NY 10032-3702

HUGON, JEAN S, ELECTRON MICROSCOPY, GASTROENTEROLOGY. *Current Pos:* RETIRED. *Personal Data:* b Brussels, Belg, Feb 5, 27; m 67, Elizabeth Renaud; c Claude. *Educ:* Cath Univ Louvain, MD, 51; Sch Trop Med, Antwerp, specialist gynec, 52. *Prof Exp:* Dir hosp, Queen Elizabeth Funds Med Assistance to Natives, Kenge, Kwango, 52-58; dir maternity, Cath Univ Louvain, Leopoldville, 58-59, head, Dept Obstet & Gynec, 59-60; Europ AEC grant, 61-62; dir staff electron micros, Radiobiol Dept, Nuclear Ctr, Belg, 62-68; prof path, Med Ctr, Univ Sherbrooke, 68-83, chmn, Dept Anat-Cell Biol, 76-83; scientist, CEA, France. *Concurrent Pos:* Grants, WHO, 59-60, Int Atomic Energy Agency, 66-68, Med Res Coun Can, 68-82 & Nat Defence Bd Can, 69-73. *Mem:* Can Asn Anatomists; Am Soc Cell Biol; Am Asn Anatomists; NY Acad Sci; Fr Soc Electron Micros. *Res:* Relationships between functions of gastrointestinal tract and its morphological and cytochemical ultrastructure; membrane permeability. *Mailing Add:* Clos St Michel Chaily-Sur Armancon 21320 France

HUGUENIN, GEORGE RICHARD, ASTRONOMY, ASTROPHYSICS. *Current Pos:* FOUNDER, PRES & CHIEF EXEC OFFICER, MILLIMETRIX, LLC, 96-. *Personal Data:* b East Stroudsburg, Pa, Nov 6, 37; m 75, Ellen Moore; c Paul L. *Educ:* Mass Inst Technol, SB, 59; Harvard Univ, PhD(astron), 63. *Hon Degrees:* DSc, Univ Mass, Amherst, 94. *Honors & Awards:* Bart J Bok Award. *Prof Exp:* Asst prof astron, Harvard Univ, 63-68; from assoc prof to prof, Univ Mass, Amherst, 68-82; dir, Five Col Radio Astron Observ, 71-82; founder & pres, Millitech Corp, 82-96. *Concurrent Pos:* Mem Comn J, US Nat Comt, Int Sci Radio Union, 64. *Mem:* Int Astron Union; Am Astron Soc; Inst Elec & Electronics Engrs. *Res:* Radio astronomy investigating pulsars; the sun and other rapidly varying sources; millimeter wavelength spectroscopy of the interstellar medium; millimeter systems applications. *Mailing Add:* Millimetrix LLC 100 Venture Way Hadley MA 01035-9684. *Fax:* 413-582-9610; *E-Mail:* rhuguenin@millimetrix.com

HUGULEY, CHARLES MASON, JR, internal medicine, oncology, for more information see previous edition

HUGUNIN, ALAN GODFREY, FOOD SCIENCE, TECHNICAL MANAGEMENT. *Current Pos:* PRES, HUGUNIN & ASSOC, 95-. *Personal Data:* b Janesville, Wis, Apr 22, 45; m 67, JoAnne Merwin; c Sean & Nicole. *Educ:* Univ Wis-Madison, BS, 67, MS, 70, PhD(food sci), 75; Univ Calif, Berkeley, MBA, 81. *Prof Exp:* Biosci asst serol, Walter Reed Army Inst Res, 70-71; proj leader food sci, Foremost Foods Co, Foremost-McKesson, Inc, 75-77, group leader & tech mgr indust prof, 77-85; dir prod develop, Nat Food Processors Asn, 85-87, sr dir prod technol, 87-95. *Concurrent Pos:* Consult. *Mem:* Inst Food Technologists. *Res:* Development of dairy-based ingredients and dehydrated vegetable products for use in food systems; formulation of dairy, bakery, confection and other processed food products with nutritional, functional and/or economic advantages; by-product utilization; protein functionality; enzyme applications in food systems; liqueurs; new business analysis and development. *Mailing Add:* 5958 Via del Cielo Pleasonton CA 94566

HUGUS, BARBARA SANFORD, GENETICS, IMMUNOLOGY. *Current Pos:* SCI CONSULT. *Personal Data:* b Brockton, Mass, Oct 17, 27; m 50, 92, J Edward Hugus; c Arthur, Brian, Paul & Jane (Stabile). *Educ:* Boston Univ, BS, 49; Brown Univ, MA, 60, PhD(biol), 63. *Hon Degrees:* DS, Bates Col. *Prof Exp:* Health info specialist, Mass Dept Pub Health, 49-51; from cancer res scientist to sr cancer res scientist, Roswell Park Mem Inst, 61-63; res fel, Mass Gen Hosp & Harvard Med Sch, 63-65; fel, Harvard Med Sch, 65-66, from res assoc to prin res assoc path, 69-73; biologist, NIH, 73-75, prog dir immunol, DCRRC, Nat Cancer Inst, 75-78; dir res, Dana Farber Cancer Inst, 78-81; assoc prof path, Harvard Med Sch, 78-81; dir, Jackson Lab, 81-88. *Concurrent Pos:* USPHS fel, Mass Gen Hosp, 63-64 & grants, 67-, Am Cancer Soc res grant, 65-67; asst biologist, Mass Gen Hosp, 65-73; asst mem, Inst Health Sci, Brown Univ, 71-75; mem, Animal Resources Adv Comt, NIH, 72-76; mem, Cancer Ctrs Adv Comt, Nat Cancer Inst, 77-87; mem bd, Dana Farber Cancer Inst, 81-, Jackson Lab, 87-; mem bd trustees, Univ Maine, 81-87. *Mem:* Am Genetic Asn; Genetics Soc Am; Am Asn Immunol; Transplantation Soc; Am Asn Cancer Res. *Res:* Immunogenetics; transplantation; cancer research; human genetics. *Mailing Add:* 1090 Mission Rd Pebble Beach CA 93953. *Fax:* 408-646-9730

HUGUS, Z ZIMMERMAN, JR, INORGANIC CHEMISTRY. *Current Pos:* dept head, 67-73, PROF CHEM, NC STATE UNIV, 67- *Personal Data:* b Washington, DC, Aug 14, 23; m 47; c 4. *Educ:* Williams Col, BA, 43; Univ Calif, Berkeley, PhD(chem), 49. *Prof Exp:* Res fel, Radiation Lab, Univ Calif, Berkeley, 49-52, instr chem, 50-52; asst prof, Univ Minn, 52-57, assoc prof, 57-63, prof & chief inorg chem, 63-67. *Mem:* Am Chem Soc; fel AAAS. *Res:* Application of nuclear quadrupole resonance measurements to the elucidation of the electronic structures of transition metal compounds. *Mailing Add:* Dept Chem NC State Univ Box 8204 Raleigh NC 27695-8204

HUH, CHIH-AN, CHEMICAL OCEANOGRAPHY, RADIOCHEMISTRY. *Current Pos:* asst prof, 84-90, ASSOC PROF, ORE STATE UNIV, 90- *Personal Data:* b Taiwan, Jan 30, 52; US citizen; m 78, An-Yi Chang; c David. *Educ:* Nat Taiwan Univ, BS, 74, MS, 78; Univ Southern Calif, PhD(geol), 82. *Prof Exp:* Investr, Woods Hole Oceanog Inst, 82-84. *Mem:* Am Geophys Union. *Res:* Applications of natural and anthropogenic radionuclides to environmental and oceanographic studies. *Mailing Add:* Col Oceanic Ore State Univ Corvallis OR 97331-5503. *Fax:* 541-737-2064; *E-Mail:* chuh@oce.orst.edu

HUH, OSCAR KARL, COASTAL OCEANOGRAPHY & GEOLOGY, REMOTE SENSING OF ENVIRONENT. *Current Pos:* assoc prof oceanog & marine sci, 76-84, prof geol & geophys, 84-90, PROF OCEANOG & COASTAL SCI, COASTAL STUDIES INST, LA STATE UNIV, 91-; FOUNDER & DIR EARTH SCI LAB. *Personal Data:* b Nov 29, 35; m, Wanda P Kuhn; c Melanie R. *Educ:* Rutgers Univ, BA, 57; Pa State Univ, MS, 63, PhD(geol), 68. *Honors & Awards:* Group Achievement Award, NASA, 85. *Prof Exp:* Res asst stratig & sedimentol, Pa State Univ, 57-59, res geologist, 62-67; res oceanogr coastal & satellite oceanog, US Naval Oceanog Off, Washington, DC, 67-76. *Concurrent Pos:* Substitute & guest lectr, Pa State Univ & Univ Md; NSF fel, 64; basic res grant, Off Naval Res, US Naval Oceanog Off, Coastal Oceanog, Sea of Japan, 71-72; consult, remote sensing oil spills, Tex, Kuwait, Greek coastal waters & Gulf Mex. *Mem:* Soc Econ Paleont & Mineral; AAAS; Am Geophys Union; fel Explorers Club. *Res:* Air-sea interactions during cold air outbreaks over continental shelf waters; oceanographic and hydrologic applications of satellite radiometric imagery; coastal and continental shelf oceanography and coastal sedimentary processes; oceanography of Sea of Japan, East China Sea, Yellow Sea, Bay of Bengal and Gulf Mex; stratigraphy of petrology of Mississippian Age Carbonate Strata, Overthrust Belt, Idaho-Montana; remote sensing of environment. *Mailing Add:* Coastal Studies Inst 615 Sunset Blvd La State Univ Baton Rouge LA 70803. *Fax:* 504-388-2520; *E-Mail:* oscar@antares.esl.lsu.edu

HUHEEY, JAMES EDWARD, INORGANIC CHEMISTRY, HERPETOLOGY. *Current Pos:* from asst prof to assoc prof, 65-75, PROF CHEM, UNIV MD, COLLEGE PARK, 75- *Personal Data:* b Cincinnati, Ohio, Aug 2, 35. *Educ:* Univ Cincinnati, BS, 57; Univ Ill, MS, 59, PhD(inorg chem), 61. *Prof Exp:* Res fel chem, Univ Mich, 61; asst prof, Worcester Polytech Inst, 61-65. *Concurrent Pos:* NSF grants, 65-67, 75-76 & 78-81; vis prof chem, Univ Calif, Los Angeles, 86, vis prof zool, Southern Ill Univ, Carbondale, 87, 89-90. *Mem:* Fel AAAS; Am Chem Soc; Ecol Soc Am; Soc Study Evolution; Soc Study Amphibians & Reptiles; Herpetologists League; fel Explorers Club. *Res:* Phosphorus, nitrogen and sulfur; Lewis acid-base interactions; orbital electronegativity, electronegativity equalization, group electronegativities and polar effects; zoology; mimicry; herpetology of Southern Appalachians, especially salamanders. *Mailing Add:* 6909 Carleton Terr College Park MD 20740

HUI, CHIU SHUEN, PHYSIOLOGY, BIOPHYSICS. *Current Pos:* assoc prof, 84-91, PROF PHYSIOL & BIOPHYS, IND UNIV, 91- *Personal Data:* b Hong Kong, June 7, 42; m, Siu Lui; c Ken Y. *Educ:* Univ Hong Kong, BS, 66; Mass Inst Technol, PhD(physics), 73. *Prof Exp:* Res assoc biophys, Ctr Theoret Studies, Miami, 73-74; fel physiol, Yale Med Sch, 74-79; from asst prof to assoc prof biol sci, Purdue Univ, 79-84. *Concurrent Pos:* Fel, NIH, 77, res career develop award, 83-84 & 85-89. *Mem:* Biophys Soc; Am Heart Asn. *Res:* Biophysics and physiology of excitable membrane in nerve and muscle; excitation-contraction coupling in muscle. *Mailing Add:* Dept Physiol & Biophys Ind Univ Med Ctr Indianapolis IN 46202. *Fax:* 317-274-3318

HUI, KOON-SEA, NEUROCHEMISTRY, PSYCHIATRY. *Current Pos:* CHIEF, PEPTIDE RES LAB, NATHAN S KLINE INST, 83- *Personal Data:* b Hong Kong, Sept 21, 48; m 74, Maria P Cheung; c Jacqueline & Electra. *Educ:* Chinese Univ Hong Kong, BSc, 71; Hong Kong Univ, MPhil, 74; Univ Sask, PhD(psychiat), 76. *Prof Exp:* Demonstr biol, Chinese Univ Hong Kong, 71-72; teaching asst pharmacol, Hong Kong Univ, 72-74; lab scientist II psychiat, Dept Health, Sask, 74-76; sr res scientist, NY State Res Inst Neurochem & Drug Addiction, 76-83. *Concurrent Pos:* Res assoc prof phychiat, NY Univ Med Ctr; Nat Inst Drug Abuse, 91-94. *Mem:* Int Brain Res Orgn; Am Soc Biochem & Molecular Biol; Int Soc Neurochem; NY Acad Sci. *Res:* Biochemistry of brain; brain protein and peptide turnover; neuropeptide breakdown and its regulation; inhibitors for neuropeptide breakdown. *Mailing Add:* Nathan S Kline Inst Psychiat Res Orangeburg NY 10962. *Fax:* 914-365-6017; *E-Mail:* hui@nki.rfmh.org

HUI, SEK WEN, MEMBRANE BIOPHYSICS, ELECTRON MICROSCOPY & DIFFRACTION. *Current Pos:* from asst prof to assoc prof, 76-84, PROF BIOPHYS, STATE UNIV NY, BUFFALO, 84-; HEAD, MEMBRANE BIOPHYS LAB, ROSWELL PARK CANCER INST, 76- *Personal Data:* b Yunan, China, July 15, 35; c 2. *Educ:* Univ Western Australia, BSc, 64; Monash Univ, Melboune, PhD(physics), 68. *Prof Exp:* Lectr phys sci, Flinders Univ S Australia, 68-69; res physicist, Carnegie-Mellon Univ, 70-71, res fel biophysics, 71-72. *Concurrent Pos:* Spec fel, NIH, 72; res scientist, Roswell Park Mem Inst, 72-; prin investr 6 grants, NIH & Am Cancer Soc, 74; career develop award, NIH, 75-80; mem regional high voltage electron micros facil adv comt, NIH, 82-84, Biophys Chem Study Sect, 86-90; dir, Electron Micros Soc Am, 85-87. *Mem:* Electron Micros Soc Am; Am Phys Soc; Biophys Soc; Am Soc Cell Biol. *Res:* Effects of membrane lipids on the activities of biological membranes including transport, regeneration, fusion and electrical potential; physical chemistry of membrane lipids, molecular mechanism fusion and molecular organization in biomembranes; author of over 100 papers in professional journals and 30 chapters in scientific books. *Mailing Add:* Membrane Biophys Lab Roswell Park Cancer Inst 666 Elm St Buffalo NY 14263

HUI, SIU LUI, BIOMETRICS, BIOSTATISTICS. *Current Pos:* asst prof to assoc prof, 81-88, PROF BIOSTATIST, SCH MED, IND UNIV, 88- *Personal Data:* b Hong Kong, Oct 12, 48. *Educ:* Univ Hong Kong, BSc, 70; Yale Univ, PhD(biomet), 79. *Prof Exp:* Asst prof biostatist, Med Ctr, Univ Ill, 79-81. *Concurrent Pos:* Prin investr, NIH, 80-83, 84-86, 87, mem study sect, 86-90, concensus panel, 90. *Mem:* Am Statist Asn; Biomet Soc. *Mailing Add:* Dept Med Ind Univ Regan Strief Inst 1001 W Tenth St RG 6 RR 135 702 Barnhill Dr Indianapolis IN 46202

HUIATT, TED W, MUSCLE DEVELOPMENT, MUSCLE PROTEIN ASSEMBLY. *Current Pos:* ASSOC PROF BIOCHEM, IOWA STATE UNIV, 82- *Educ:* Iowa State Univ, PhD(biochem), 79. *Mailing Add:* Muscle Biol Group Iowa State Univ 3112 Molecular Biol Med Col Ames IA 50011-3260. *Fax:* 515-294-0453

HUIE, CARMEN WAH-KIT, ANALYTICAL SPECTROSCOPY, CAPILLARY ELECTROPHORESIS. *Current Pos:* vis asst prof, 86-88, ASST PROF CHEM, STATE UNIV NY, BINGHAMTON, 89- *Personal Data:* b Hong Kong, Aug 7, 59. *Educ:* Univ Wis-Superior, BS(chem) & BS(math), 80; Iowa State Univ, PhD(analytical chem), 86. *Prof Exp:* Teaching asst, Univ Wis-Superior, 77-80, Iowa State Univ, 80-81; res asst, Ames Lab-Dept Energy, 81-85. *Mem:* Am Chem Soc; Sigma Xi. *Res:* Development of new strategies and tactics in chemical analysis and their applications to solving significant analytical problems in biological, clinical and environmental areas; use of lasers, surfactants and chemiluminescent reactions. *Mailing Add:* Alcou Labs Inc Mail Stop R2-43 6201 S Freeway Fort Worth TX 76134

HUIE, ROBERT ELLIOTT, ATMOSPHERIC CHEMISTRY & PHYSICS, FREE RADICAL CHEMISTRY. *Current Pos:* RES CHEMIST, NAT INST STAND & TECHNOL, 67-, GROUP LEADER, 96- *Personal Data:* b Atlanta, Ga, Jan 24, 45; m 96, Gilda Borbe; c Amanda, Jessica & Robert. *Educ:* Macalester Col, BA, 66; Univ Md, Col Park, PhD(phys chem), 72. *Honors & Awards:* Bronze Medal, Dept Com. *Concurrent Pos:* Vis scientist phys chem, Cambridge Univ, 75-76. *Mem:* Am Chem Soc; Am Geophys Union. *Res:* Gas phase kinetics; solution kinetics; atmospheric chemistry; pulse radiolysis; flash photolysis; free radical chemistry. *Mailing Add:* Nat Inst Stand & Technol Gaithersburg MD 20899. *Fax:* 301-975-3672; *E-Mail:* robert.huie@nist.gov

HUIJING, FRANS, CLINICAL BIOCHEMISTRY, GENETICS. *Current Pos:* assoc prof biochem & med, 68-73, prof biochem & assoc prof med, 73-86, PROF BIOCHEM & MOLECULAR BIOL, SCH MED, UNIV MIAMI, 86- *Personal Data:* b Amsterdam, Neth, Jan 28, 36; m 63; c 2. *Educ:* Univ Amsterdam, BSc, 58, Drs, 61, DSc(biochem), 64. *Prof Exp:* Asst biochem, Univ Amsterdam, 61-64; res fel, Col Med Sci, Univ Minn, Minneapolis, 64-66; res scientist med enzymol, Univ Amsterdam, 66-68. *Res:* Detection, genetics, biochemistry and nutritional management of inborn errors of metabolism, especially glycogen-storage diseases, lysosomes storage diseases; control of metabolism; computer-based medical education. *Mailing Add:* Dept Biochem & Molecular Biol PO Box 016129 Miami FL 33101. *E-Mail:* fhuijing@mednet.med.miami.edu

HUISJEN, MARTIN ALBERT, MAGNETIC RESONANCE, MICROWAVE ENGINEERING. *Current Pos:* staff consult, 76-94, SR MGR, BALL AEROSPACE SYSTS DIV, 95- *Personal Data:* b Oak Park, Ill, May 30, 44; m 69, Janet Van Dyke; c Derek & Katrina. *Educ:* Univ Ill, BS, 65; Cornell Univ, MS, 68, PhD(exp physics), 71. *Prof Exp:* Pulsed magnetic resonance, Varian Assocs, 71-73; mem tech staff microwave eng, Hughes Aircraft Co, 73-76. *Mem:* Sigma Xi; Inst Elec & Electronics Engrs. *Res:* Radar and communications systems engineering with emphasis on antenna systems; phased array antennas; adaptive array antennas; fiber optics communications. *Mailing Add:* 2209 Juniper Ct Boulder CO 80304

HUISMAN, TITUS HENDRIK JAN, BIOCHEMISTRY. *Current Pos:* from assoc prof to prof biochem & path, 59-63, prof biochem, 63-64, REGENTS PROF CELL & MOLECULAR BIOL, MED COL GA, 64-, CHMN DEPT, 77- *Personal Data:* b Leeuwarden, Neth, Sept 1, 23; m 50; c 2. *Educ:* State Univ Groningen, MS, 46, PhD(chem), 48; State Univ Utrecht, DSc(biochem), 50. *Honors & Awards:* D D Van Slyke Award, 71. *Prof Exp:* Head biochem res lab, State Univ Groningen, 51-59. *Concurrent Pos:* Mem organizing comt colloquium, St Jans Hosp, Belg. *Mem:* Am Chem Soc; Am Soc Biol Chemists; Royal Neth Chem Soc; Europ Soc Hemat. *Res:* Inhomogeneity of hemoglobin and myoglobin types; functional differences of hemoglobin variants; genetic studies of human hemoglobin abnormalities. *Mailing Add:* Dept Biochem Med Col Ga Sch Med 1120 15th St Augusta GA 30912-2100. *Fax:* 706-721-3092

HUITEMA, BRADLEY EUGENE, ANALYSIS OF COVARIANCE, TIME-SERIES EXPERIMENTS. *Current Pos:* PROF PSYCHOL & DIR INDUST/ORGN PROG, WESTERN MICH UNIV, 68- *Personal Data:* b Hammond, Ind, July 28, 38; div; c Craig B & Laura L. *Educ:* Southern Ill Univ, BA, 61; Western Mich Univ, MA, 62; Colo State Univ, PhD(psychol), 68. *Prof Exp:* Res psychologist, US Army Enlisted Eval Ctr, 62-64; res prof, Res Div, Ore State Univ, 67-68. *Concurrent Pos:* Vis prof, Univ Veracruz, Mex, 75; res design consult, 86-88; expert witness, Nabisco, 86-89; vis scholar, Univ Calif, San Diego, 88-89. *Mem:* Am Statist Asn; AAAS; Am Psychol Asn; Asn Behav Med; Asn Behav Anal; Am Educ Res Asn. *Res:* The design and analysis of single subject and group experiments; development of new methods of time-series analysis. *Mailing Add:* Dept Psychol Western Mich Univ Kalamazoo MI 49008-5052. *Fax:* 616-387-4550

HUITINK, GERALDINE M, ANALYTICAL CHEMISTRY. *Current Pos:* Asst prof chem, 67-73, ASSOC PROF CHEM, 73-, CHMN CHEM DEPT, IND UNIV SOUTH BEND, 82- *Personal Data:* b Chicago, Ill, Oct 11, 42. *Educ:* Mundelein Col, BS, 63; Iowa State Univ, MS, 65, PhD(anal chem), 67. *Mem:* Am Chem Soc; Sigma Xi; AAAS. *Res:* Synthesis and study of metallofluorochromic indicators. *Mailing Add:* Ind Univ PO Box 7111 South Bend IN 46634

HUITRIC, ALAIN CORENTIN, PHARMACEUTICAL CHEMISTRY. *Current Pos:* from asst prof to prof, 55-80, EMER PROF MED CHEM, UNIV WASH, 80- *Personal Data:* b Laurier, Man, July 28, 11; nat US. *Educ:* Loyola Univ, Calif, BS, 50; Univ Calif, MS, 52, PhD(pharmaceut chem), 54. *Prof Exp:* Asst prof, Univ San Francisco, 54-55. *Mem:* Am Chem Soc; Am Pharmaceut Asn; The Chem Soc. *Res:* Medicinal chemistry; organic synthesis; stereochemistry; configurational and conformational analysis by nuclear magnetic resonance; drug metabolism. *Mailing Add:* Dept Med Chem Univ Wash Box 357610 Seattle WA 98195

HUIZENGA, JOHN ROBERT, NUCLEAR CHEMISTRY, NUCLEAR PHYSICS. *Current Pos:* Tracy H Harris prof, 78-91; prof chem & physics, chmn, Dept Chem, 83-88, EMER TRACY H HARRIS PROF CHEM & PHYSICS, UNIV ROCHESTER, 91 *Personal Data:* b Fulton, Ill, Apr 21, 21; m 46, Dorothy J Koeze; c Linda, Jann, Robert & Joel. *Educ:* Calvin Col, AB, 44; Univ Ill, PhD(phys chem), 49. *Honors & Awards:* Ernest O Lawrence Mem Award, AEC, 66; Award for Nuclear Appln Chem, Am Chem Soc, 75, Leroy Rundle Grummans Medal, 91. *Prof Exp:* Lab supvr, Tenn Eastman Co, 44-46; instr phys chem, Calvin Col, 46-47; assoc scientist, Argonne Nat Lab, 49-58, sr scientist, 58-67; Guggenheim fel, Univ Calif, Berkeley & Niels Bohr Inst, Tech Univ Munich, 73-74. *Concurrent Pos:* Fulbright fel, Neth, 54-55; Guggenheim fel & vis prof, Univ Paris, 64-65. *Mem:* Nat Acad Sci; fel AAAS; fel Am Phys Soc; Am Chem Soc; fel Am Acad Arts & Sci. *Res:* Heavy and light ion reactions; nuclear fission; nuclear level densities; nuclear properties of actinide elements; effect of environment on radioactive decay; muon-induced reactions in actinide elements. *Mailing Add:* 43 McMichael Dr Pinehurst NC 28374-6702

HUIZINGA, HARRY WILLIAM, COMPARATIVE PATHOLOGY, PARASITOLOGY. *Current Pos:* RETIRED. *Personal Data:* b Rahway, NJ, Sept 4, 34; m 64; c 2. *Educ:* Mich State Univ, BS, 56; Univ Md, MS, 61; Univ Conn, PhD(zool), 65. *Prof Exp:* Asst zool, Univ Md, 58-60; res technician, Patuxent Wildlife Res Ctr, US Fish & Wildlife Serv, Md, 60-62; asst & instr zool, Univ Conn, 62-63, lectr, 63-65; NIH trainee parasitol, Sch Pub Health, Univ NC, 65-67; from asst prof to prof parasitol, Ill State Univ, 67-95. *Concurrent Pos:* Fel trop parasitol, La State Univ, 67; vis assoc prof path, Bull Fel, Ont Vet Col Guelph Univ, 74-75; vis assoc prof teaching, Peoria Med Sch, 72-87. *Mem:* Am Soc Trop Med & Hyg; Am Soc Parasitol; Wildlife Dis Asn; Sigma Xi. *Res:* Experimental host-parasite relationships of wildlife parasites. *Mailing Add:* 64161 E Echo Canyon Ct Tucson AZ 85739-2017

HUKILL, PETER BIGGS, PATHOLOGY. *Current Pos:* DIR LABS, CHARLOTTE HUNGERFORD HOSP, 77- *Personal Data:* b Lucerne, Switz, Feb 3, 27; US citizen; div; c 1. *Educ:* Harvard Univ, AB, 47; Yale Univ, MD, 53. *Prof Exp:* From instr to assoc prof path, Sch Med, Yale Univ, 58-68; prof, Univ Ala, Birmingham, 68-69; prof path, Sch Med, Univ Conn & pathologist, Univ Hosps, 69-77. *Concurrent Pos:* Asst attend path, Grace-New Haven Community Hosp, 59-61, attend, 61-68; clin prof path, Univ Conn, 77-; clin assoc prof, Yale Univ, 78- *Mem:* Col Am Pathologists; Am Soc Clin Pathologists; Int Acad Path; Am Soc Dermopath. *Res:* Histochemistry of human tumors; surgical pathology; dermatopathology. *Mailing Add:* Charlotte Hungerford Hosp PO Box 988 540 Litchfield St Torrington CT 06790-0988

HULAN, HOWARD WINSTON, NUTRITION, FOOD SCIENCE. *Current Pos:* PROF BIOCHEM, HEAD FOOD SCI, MEM UNIV, ST JOHN'S, NFLD, 90- *Personal Data:* b Jeffrey's, Nfld, Oct 18, 41; m 64, Shirley M Tucker; c Renee, Shelley, Heidi & Deborah. *Educ:* McGill Univ, BSc, 65, MSc, 68; Univ Maine, PhD(nutrit), 71. *Honors & Awards:* Nutrit Res Award, Am Feed Indust, 87; Res Award, Am Broiler Coun, 88; Can Packers Medal Excellence Nutrit & Meat Sci Res, 88. *Prof Exp:* Asst nutrit, Univ Maine, 68-71; Nat Res Coun fel biochem, Carleton Univ, 71-72; nutritionist, Prod & Mkt Br, Kentville Res Sta Agr Can, 72-73, res scientist lipid metab, Res Br, Animal Res Inst, 73-77, sr scientist, Poultry Sect, 77-88, prin res scientist, sect head/prog leader poultry, 88-90. *Concurrent Pos:* Consult nutrit & health, Prod & Mkt Br, Agr Can, 72-73; adj prof, Tech Univ Nova Scotia, Halifax, 88-91; prof & head, Dept Poultry Sci, Ore State Univ, Corvallis; mem, Prov House Assembly, 93-96; minister, Dept Fisheries, Food & Agr. *Mem:* Sigma Xi; Am Inst Nutrit; Poultry Sci Asn; Can Soc Nutrit Sci; World Poultry Sci Asn; Can Soc Animal Sci; Can Inst Food Sci & Technol. *Res:* Physiological, biochemical and pathological effects of feeding high levels of long chain monoenoic fatty acids on the rat, pig, chicken and monkey, with special emphasis on the myocardium; poultry nutrition-physiology; influence of strain and nutrition on leg abnormalities of chicken broilers and roasters; effect of nutrition on sudden death syndrome heart attack in chickens; nutrition-disease interrelationships; omega-3 fatty acids in broiler chickens and egg yolk lipids. *Mailing Add:* Food Sci Dept Biochem Mem Univ Nfld St John's NF A1B 3X9 Can. *Fax:* 709-737-2422; *E-Mail:* hhulan@morgan.ucs.mum.ca

HULBERT, LEWIS E(UGENE), ENGINEERING MECHANICS. *Current Pos:* RETIRED. *Personal Data:* b Somerton, Ohio, Nov 15, 24; m 48; c 3. *Educ:* Iowa State Col, BS, 47; Case Western Res Univ, MS, 51; Ohio State Univ, PhD, 63. *Prof Exp:* Asst chief metallurgist, True Temper Sporting Goods, 42-43 & 46; math consult, Res Lab, Am Soc Heating & Ventilating Engrs, 49; actuarial consult, Wyatt Co, 50-52; sr res engr, Batelle Mem Inst, 52-67, chief, Adv Solid Mech Div, 67-77, res leader, Trans & Struct Dept, 77-89. *Concurrent Pos:* Vpres, Systs & Design; mem, Bd Res & Technol Develop. *Mem:* Fel Am Soc Mech Engrs; Sigma Xi. *Res:* Mechanics of deformable bodies; heat transfer; diffusion theory; theory of fibrous composites; biomechanics; numerical and computer solution of boundary value problems. *Mailing Add:* 2871 E Shore Ct Columbus OH 43231

HULBERT, MATTHEW H, PHYSICAL CHEMISTRY, PHARMACEUTICAL MANUFACTURING PROCESSES. *Current Pos:* sr proj engr & proj mgr, 93-94, dir pharmaceut develop, 94-96, PRE-CLIN RESOURCE CTR LEADER, MALLINCKRODT, INC, 96- *Personal Data:* b Marlinton, WVa, Aug 25, 42; m 64, Linda Wooldridge; c 2. *Educ:* Washington & Lee Univ, BS, 64; Univ Wis, MS, 67, PhD(anal chem), 69; Indiana State Univ, MBA, 92. *Prof Exp:* Asst prof chem, Lehigh Univ, 69-75; Nat Res Coun res assoc, Atlantic Oceanogr & Meteorol Labs, 74-75; from asst prof to assoc prof chem, Conn Col, 75-81; sr res scientist, Int Minerals & Chem Corp, 81-87; sr res scientist, Pittman-Moore, 87-92, mgr mfg, 92-93. *Concurrent Pos:* Consult, Pharmachem Corp, 70-74; Nat Oceanic & Atmospheric Admin, 75-79; USCG Res & Develop Ctr, 79-81; proprietor, Resource Dynamics, 70-; vis fel, Yale Univ, 77-78; adv, Naval Res Lab, 89- *Mem:* Sigma Xi; Am Chem Soc; Parenteral Drug Asn; AAAS; Clay Minerals Soc. *Res:* Pharmaceutical process chemistry; resource management; new medical product development; behavior of fine-grained sedimentary materials. *Mailing Add:* 33 Orvieto Ct Florissant MO 63031. *E-Mail:* mhhulbert@aol.com

HULBERT, SAMUEL FOSTER, BIOMEDICAL ENGINEERING, MATERIALS ENGINEERING. *Current Pos:* PRES, ROSE-HULMAN INST TECHNOL, 76- *Personal Data:* b Adams Center, NY, Apr 12, 36; m 60; c 3. *Educ:* Alfred Univ, BS, 58, PhD(ceramic sci), 64. *Hon Degrees:* LLD, Ind State Univ. *Honors & Awards:* Clemson Award, Soc Biomat; George Winter Award, Europ Soc Biomat. *Prof Exp:* Instr math & physics, Alfred Univ, 60-64; asst prof ceramic & metall eng, Clemson Univ, 64-68, assoc prof mat eng & head div interdisciplinary studies, 68-73, assoc dean eng res interdisciplinary progs, 70-73; prof surg & orthop & dean sch eng, Med Ctr, Tulane Univ, 73-76. *Mem:* Am Ceramic Soc; Am Soc Artificial Internal Organs; Biomed Eng Soc; Nat Inst Ceramic Engr. *Res:* Development and evaluation of materials and prosthetic devices and artificial organs. *Mailing Add:* Rose Hulman Inst Technol Terre Haute IN 47803

HULBERT, THOMAS EUGENE, INDUSTRIAL & MANUFACTURING ENGINEERING. *Current Pos:* assoc dir, Educ Resources, Northeastern Univ, 67-69, from asst dean to actg dean eng, 69-81, from instr to assoc prof indust eng, 63-95, assoc dean & dir eng technol, 81-95, EMER PROF INDUST ENG, NORTHEASTERN UNIV, 95- *Personal Data:* b Ft Edward, NY, Sept 1, 35; m 57, Betty Frazier; c Sally (Foster), James, Barbara (Crosby), Judith (Dupuis), David & Susan (Murphy). *Educ:* Rensselaer Polytech Inst, BMgtE, 57; Northeastern Univ, MS, 64. *Prof Exp:* Indust engr, Armstrong Corr Co, 57-60; sr indust engr, Raytheon Co, 60-63. *Concurrent Pos:* Partner, Eng Mgt Assocs, 64-88; regional vpres & mem bd trustees, Inst Indust Engrs, 71-73. *Mem:* Inst Indust Engrs; Am Soc Eng Educ. *Res:* Design and analysis of manufacturing facilities to achieve maximum productivity; design and implementation of automated flexible manufacturing systems; technical education consulting. *Mailing Add:* Dept of Mech Indust & Mfg Eng Northeastern Univ 330 Snell Eng Boston MA 02115-5096. *E-Mail:* thulbert@lynx.neu.edu

HULCE, MARTIN R, EXTENDED CONJUGATE ADDITION CHEMISTRY, NEW SYNTHETIC METHODS. *Current Pos:* ASSOC PROF CHEM, CREIGHTON UNIV, 91- *Personal Data:* b Baltimore, Md, Apr 15, 56. *Educ:* Butler Univ, BS, 78; Johns Hopkins Univ, MA, 80, PhD(org chem), 83. *Prof Exp:* Res chemist, E I Du Pont de Nemours & Co Inc, 83-85; asst prof chem, Univ Md, Baltimore Co, 85-90. *Mem:* Am Chem Soc; AAAS; Int Union Pure & Appl Chem; Sigma Xi. *Res:* Extended conjugate additions to mixed hybridization state Michael acceptors provide conjugate polyenolates which are reactive as ambident C-nucleophiles; sequential application of such conjugate addition-enolate alkylation strategy leads to highly elaborated adducts in a stereoselective manner. *Mailing Add:* Dept Chem Creighton Univ Omaha NE 68178-0104. *Fax:* 402-280-5737; *E-Mail:* mhulce@creighton.edu

HULCHER, FRANK H, BIOCHEMISTRY. *Current Pos:* RETIRED. *Personal Data:* b Hampton, Va, Mar 12, 26; m 53; c 3. *Educ:* Va Polytech Inst, BS, 50, MS, 53, PhD(biochem), 57. *Honors & Awards:* Res Award, Sigma Xi, 58. *Prof Exp:* Instr bact, Va Polytech Inst, 53-54; asst biochem, 54-57; asst microbiol & fel, Yale Univ, 57-59, res assoc, 58; from instr to assoc prof biochem, Bowman Gray Sch Med, 59-92. *Concurrent Pos:* Vis scientist, Brookhaven Nat Lab, 60; problem-based tutor & evaluator med student curric, Bowman Gray Sch Med, 87-91. *Mem:* Fel AAAS; Am Chem Soc; Am Soc Microbiol; Am Soc Biol Chem; Sigma Xi. *Res:* Enzyme chemistry; biochemistry of myelin; microbial biochemistry; regulation of cholesterol metabolism, hydroxymethylglutaryl-coenzyme A reductase and cholesterol 7-alpha hydro xylase; role of isoprenoid and cholesterol synthesis in DNA replication; microbial hydroxamates and enzyme activation; control of plasma cholesterol by cortisol and cholesterol-7d hydroxylase. *Mailing Add:* 4149 Wycliff Dr Winston-Salem NC 27106-2949

HULET, CLARENCE VELOID, ANIMAL SCIENCE. *Current Pos:* RETIRED. *Personal Data:* b Chinook, Mont, July 2, 24; m 52; c 8. *Educ:* Brigham Young Univ, BS, 52; Univ Wis, MS, 53, PhD(reproductive physiol), 55. *Prof Exp:* Asst genetics, Univ Wis, 52-55; instr agr, Idaho State Col, 55-57; animal geneticist, Sheep Exp Sta, USDA, 57-62, animal physiologist, 62-76, supvry res physiologist, 76-90. *Concurrent Pos:* Fulbright-Hays sr res scholar, Ruakura Res Sta, Hamilton, NZ, 71-72. *Mem:* Fel Am Soc Animal Sci. *Res:* Physiologic and genetics factors affecting reproduction in sheep, including semen studies; effects of nutrition on fertility; mating behavior; relationship between age at puberty and subsequent fertility; environmental and genetic factors affecting fertility in both the male and female ovine; selection for ovulation rate; effects of various hormones on reproductive phenomena; accelerated lambing. *Mailing Add:* 1905 E Powerhouse Rd Spanish Fork UT 84660

HULET, ERVIN KENNETH, ACTINIDE CHEMISTRY, EXPERIMENTAL NUCLEAR PHYSICS. *Current Pos:* RETIRED. *Personal Data:* b Baker, Ore, May 7, 26; wid; c Randall E & Carri (Gicker). *Educ:* Stanford Univ, BS, 49; Univ Calif, PhD(chem), 53. *Honors & Awards:* Wech Found Lectr, 90; Nuclear Chem Award, Am Chem Soc, 94. *Prof Exp:* Chemist nuclear chem, Lawrence Radiation Lab, Lawrence Livermore Lab, Berkeley, 49-53, chemist nuclear chem, 53-91, group leader, 66-91. *Concurrent Pos:* Fulbright res scholar, Inst Atomic Energy, Univ Oslo, 62-63; co-discoverer of element 106; chmn & chmn-elect, Div Nuclear Chem & Technol, Am Chem Soc, 86-87. *Mem:* Fel AAAS; fel Am Inst Chem; Am Phys Soc; Am Chem Soc. *Res:* Chemical and nuclear properties of the transplutonium elements; discoverer of bimodal fission. *Mailing Add:* L-231 Lawrence Livermore Lab Livermore CA 94551. *Fax:* 510-422-3160; *E-Mail:* ekhulet@llnl.gov

HULET, RANDALL GARDNER, LASER COOLING OF ATOMS. *Current Pos:* from asst prof to assoc prof, 87-96, PROF PHYSICS, RICE UNIV, 96- *Personal Data:* b Walnut Creek, Calif, Apr 27, 56; m 80, Lourdes T Hernandez; c Benjamin H & Gabriella G. *Educ:* Stanford Univ, BS, 78; Mass Inst Technol, PhD(physics), 84. *Honors & Awards:* I I Rabi Prize, Am Phys Soc. *Prof Exp:* Postdoctoral assoc, Mass Inst Technol, 84-85; Nat Res Coun fel, NBS, 85-87. *Concurrent Pos:* Alfred P Sloan Found res fel, 89; NSF presidential young investr award, 89. *Mem:* Am Phys Soc; Optical Soc Am. *Res:* Experimental atomic physics; quantum optics; laser cooling of atoms; interactions between ultra-cold atoms; laser and electro-optic-technology; Bose-Einstein condensation of ultra-cold atoms. *Mailing Add:* Dept Physics MS 61 Rice Univ Houston TX 77005. *E-Mail:* randy@atomcool.rice.edu

HULET, WILLIAM HENRY, INTERNAL MEDICINE. *Current Pos:* CONSULT, 62- *Personal Data:* b Minot, NDak, June 19, 25; m 69; c 1. *Educ:* Minot State Col, BA, 47; Univ NDak, BS, 49; Univ Pa, MD, 51; Univ Miami, PhD(marine sci), 73; Am Bd Internal Med, dipl, 62. *Honors & Awards:* C V Mosby Award, 51. *Prof Exp:* Intern, George F Geisinger Mem Hosp, Danville Pa, 51-52; asst resident, Jackson Mem Hosp, Miami, Fla, 52-53; asst resident med, George F Geisinger Mem Hosp, Danville, Pa, 53-54, chief resident, 54-55; vis fel, Col Physicians & Surgeons, Columbia Univ, 55-56; NIH trainee, 55-57; fel, Sch Med, NY Univ, 56-58, instr physiol, 58-59; asst prof med, Sch Med, Univ Miami, 59-62, asst prof physiol, 60-63, from assoc prof to prof med & physiol, 63-73; prof med, physiol & biophys & chief Marine Med Div, Marine Biomed Inst, Univ Tex, Med Br Galveston, 73-83; attend physician, Jackson Mem Hosp, Miami, 61- *Concurrent Pos:* Asst physician, Presby Hosp, 55-56; clin asst vis physician, Bellevue Hosp, 56-59; Am Heart Asn res fel, 57-58; clin investr, Vet Admin Hosp, Coral Gables, Fla, 59-62, staff physician, 62-, assoc chief staff res, 62-63; NIH res career develop award, 63-; adj prof marine sci, Rosenstiel Sch Marine & Atmospheric Sci, Univ Miami, 77-83. *Mem:* AAAS; Am Fedn Clin Res; Am Physiol Soc; Am Col Physicians. *Res:* Marine science; diving medicine; renal physiology. *Mailing Add:* 1353 Long Beach Dr Big Pine Key FL 33043-3500

HULKA, BARBARA SORENSON, EPIDEMIOLOGY. *Current Pos:* res assoc, Dept Prev Med, Univ NC, Chapel Hill, 67-68, asst prof epidemiol, Sch Pub Health, 67-71, asst prof med, Dept Family Med, 68-76, assoc prof epidemiol, Sch Pub Health, 72-76, assoc clin prof med, Dept Family Med & prof epidemiol, Sch Pub Health, Sch Med, 77-86, chairperson, Dept Epidemiol, 83-93, CLIN PROF, DEPT FAMILY MED, SCH PUB HEALTH, UNIV NC, CHAPEL HILL, 86-, KENAN PROF, 87- *Personal Data:* b Minneapolis, Minn, Mar 1, 31; m 54; c 3. *Educ:* Radcliffe Col, BA, 52; Juilliard Sch Music, MS, 54; Columbia Col Physicians & Surgeons, MD, 59; Columbia Sch Pub Health & Admin Med, MPH, 61. *Honors & Awards:* Distinguished Achievement Award, Am Soc Prev Oncol, 91; Hanes Falk Award Mem Lect, Nat Inst Environ Health Sci, 94; Abraham Lienfield Award, Am Col Epidemiol, 94; Wade Hampton Frost Lect Award, Am Pub Health Asn, 96. *Prof Exp:* Asst pub health physician, Pa State Health Dept, 61-62; res instr, Dept Obstet & Gynec, Univ Pittsburgh, 62-65, res asst prof, 66-67. *Concurrent Pos:* Reviewer, Health Manpower Prog & Res Proj, Nat Ctr Health Serv Res, 71-, Health Serv Develop grants study sect, 73-77, Comn Serv Fels Prog, 75-76, Cancer Control Prog, Nat Cancer Inst, 74- & Pop Res Prog, Nat Inst Child Health & Human Develop, 74-; fel, Health Care Resources Va, Nat Acad Sci, 74-75; consult var med insts & univs, 74-; aasoc clin prof epidemiol, community health sci, Med Ctr, Duke Univ, 76-82; mem, Comt Toxic Shock Syndrome, Inst Med-Nat Acad Sci, 81-82, Comt Passive Smoking, 85, Comn Antiprogestins, 92-93, Comt Crossroads Nuclear Test, 94; mem, Sci Rev & Eval Bd, Health Serv Res Develop Serv, Vet Admin, 83-85; mem, Breast Cancer Detection Demonstration Proj Anal & Publ Comt, Nat Cancer Inst, 85; coord subcomt, Nat Acad Sci, 85, chair comt, 85-86; consult, Ortho Pharmaceut Corp, 88; chair, Data & Safety Monitoring Bd, Phys Educ Pub Info, Nat Heart Lung & Blood Inst, NIH, 89-, Bd Sci Coun, Nat Cancer Inst, 92-; mem, Bd Sci Coun, Nat Cancer Inst, NIH, 92-; mem, Endpoint Rev Safety Monitoring & Adv Comt, NIH, 92- *Mem:* Inst Med-Nat Acad Sci; Am Pub Health Asn; Asn Teachers Prev Med; Am Col Epidemiol; Int Epidemiol Asn; Soc Epidemiol Res (pres, 75-76); Am Epidemiol Soc; Am Col Prev Med; fel Royal Soc Med. *Res:* Cancer epidemiology and health services research. *Mailing Add:* Dept Epidemiol Sch Pub Health CB 7400 McGauran Greenberg Hall Chapel Hill NC 27599-7400. *Fax:* 919-966-2089

HULKA, JAROSLAV FABIAN, OBSTETRICS & GYNECOLOGY. *Current Pos:* assoc prof obstet & gynec, Sch Med, 67-76, PROF MATERNAL & CHILD HEALTH, SCH PUB HEALTH, UNIV NC, CHAPEL HILL, 76-, PROF OBSTET & GYNEC, SCH MED, 76- *Personal Data:* b New York, NY, Sept 29, 30; c 3. *Educ:* Harvard Univ, AB, 52; Columbia Univ, MD, 56. *Prof Exp:* Intern, Roosevelt Hosp, New York, 56-57; resident obstet & gynec, Sloane Hosp for Women, 57-60; Macy jr vis fel, Columbia-Presby Med Ctr, 60-61; asst prof, Univ Pittsburgh, 61-66, assoc mem microbiol, Grad Fac, 62-66, actg chmn dept obstet & gynec, Univ, 63-64. *Mem:* Fel Am Col Obstet & Gynec; Am Fertil Soc; Am Asn Gynec Laparoscopists (pres, 80). *Res:* Antigenicity of the trophoblast; reproductive physiology; delivery of contraceptive service; sterilization techniques. *Mailing Add:* Dept Obstet Gynec Univ NC Sch Med Chapel Hill NC 27514

HULL, ALVIN C, JR, PLANT ECOLOGY. *Current Pos:* CONSULT DESERT LIVESTOCK, SKULL VALLEY CO, 73- *Personal Data:* b Whitney, Idaho, Mar 25, 09; m 36, Mayme Laird; c Nancy, Susan, James & Mary K. *Educ:* Utah State Univ, BS, 36, PhD, 59; Brigham Young Univ, MS, 40. *Honors & Awards:* Outstanding Achievement Award, Soc Range Mgt, 74. *Prof Exp:* Range exam, Intermt Forest & Range Exp Sta, US Forest Serv, USDA, 36-41, forest ecologist, 42-47, range scientist, Rocky Mt Forest & Range Exp Sta, 48-51, asst, Div Range Mgt Res, Washington, DC, 51-55, coordr range seeding res, Western US, Agr Res Serv, 55-66, coordr range sci res, Western US, Agr Res Serv, 66-73. *Concurrent Pos:* Range conserv work, Egypt & Israel, 52-53; range conserv res, Peru, 58; tour leader near eastern range technicians, 76. *Mem:* Fel Soc Range Mgt; Am Soc Agron; Sigma Xi. *Res:* Range seeding; range ecology; undesirable plant control; plant competition. *Mailing Add:* 321 N 400 E Logan UT 84321

HULL, ANDREW P, HEALTH PHYSICS. *Current Pos:* RETIRED. *Personal Data:* b New Britain, Conn, Jan 11, 20; m 42, 61; c 4. *Educ:* Cent Conn State Col, BS, 56; Vanderbilt Univ, MS, 61. *Honors & Awards:* Failla Award, 97. *Prof Exp:* Res assoc meteorol, Travelers Weather Serv, 55-56; jr health physicist, Oak Ridge Nat Lab, 57-58; supvr health physics, Indust Reactor Lab, 58-61; assoc health physicist, Brookhaven Nat Lab, 61-79, health physicist, 80- *Mem:* AAAS; Health Physics Soc; fel Am Pub Health Asn. *Res:* Detection and evaluation of low level radioactivity in the natural environment; evaluation of health risks from alternate energy sources. *Mailing Add:* Safety & Environ Protection Div Mail Stop 51 Brookhaven Nat Lab Upton NY 11973

HULL, BRUCE LANSING, VETERINARY MEDICINE, SURGERY. *Current Pos:* assoc prof clin, 76-81, prof surg, 81-92, PROF & HEAD SURG, OHIO STATE UNIV, 92- *Personal Data:* b Albany, NY, Feb 15, 41; m 65; c 2. *Educ:* Cornell Univ, DVM, 65; Iowa State Univ, MS, 71. *Prof Exp:* Pvt pract, Delmar Animal Hosp, 65-66; post vet, US Army, 66-68; instr clin, Iowa State Univ, 68-71, from asst prof to assoc prof, 71-76. *Concurrent Pos:* Chair, Bd Regents, Am Col Vet Surgeons. *Mem:* Am Asn Vet Clinicians; Am Asn Bovine Practitioners; Am Vet Med Asn; Am Col Vet Surgeons. *Res:* Surgery and ultrasound of teat and udder; Stifle surgery; caprine arthritis encephalomylitis. *Mailing Add:* 1935 Coffey Rd Columbus OH 43210

HULL, CARL MAX, organic chemistry, for more information see previous edition

HULL, CLARENCE JOSEPH, ORGANIC CHEMISTRY. *Current Pos:* RETIRED. *Personal Data:* b Ft Madison, Iowa, July 14, 19; m 49; c 2. *Educ:* Univ Iowa, BS, 41; Ind Univ, MA, 42, PhD(org chem), 44. *Prof Exp:* Res chemist, Am Cyanamid Co, Conn, 44-46; from instr to assoc prof gen org chem, Univ Detroit, 46-57; chmn sci dept, Moorhead State Col, 59-62; prof chem, Ind State Univ, Terre Haute, 62- *Concurrent Pos:* Fel, Inst Int Educ, Zurich, 47; mem, Ky Contract Team, US Opers Mission, Indonesia, 57-61. *Mem:* AAAS; Am Chem Soc; Royal Soc Chem. *Res:* Indones; synthesis of isoflavones; homologues of vitamin B1; history and literature of chemistry. *Mailing Add:* 90 Deming Lane Terre Haute IN 47803

HULL, DALE O, AGRICULTURAL ENGINEERING, FARM & AGRICULTURAL INDUSTRY ACCIDENTS. *Current Pos:* prof & exten agr engr, 45-77, emer prof agr eng exten, 77-90, EMER PROF AGR ENG, IOWA STATE UNIV, 78- *Personal Data:* b Oskaloosa, Iowa, Feb 26, 12; m 40, Helen L Bentley; c Adrian D & Karen K (Craig). *Educ:* Iowa State Univ, BS, 39, MS, 40. *Prof Exp:* Automotive engr, Stand Oil Co, Ind, 40-44, lubrication engr, 44-45; eng consult, Dale O Hull Assocs, 77-91. *Mem:* Am Soc Agr Engrs; Soc Automotive Engrs; Nat Safety Coun. *Res:* Automation of agriculture; farmstead engineering; agricultural land drainage; agricultural power and implements; farm and home safety; forensic engineering farm accidents. *Mailing Add:* Dale O Hull Assocs 2925 Ross Rd Ames IA 50014

HULL, DAVID G(EORGE), OPTIMIZATION, FLIGHT MECHANICS. *Current Pos:* from asst prof to prof, 66-84, M J THOMPSON REGENTS PROF AEROSPACE ENG, UNIV TEX, AUSTIN, 85- *Personal Data:* b Oak Park, Ill, Mar 27, 37; m 83, Vicki Poole; c Kate & Emily. *Educ:* Purdue Univ, BS, 59; Univ Wash, Seattle, MS, 62; Rice Univ, PhD, 67. *Prof Exp:* Staff assoc aerospace res, Boeing Sci Res Labs, 59-64; res assoc, Aero-Astronaut Group, Rice Univ, 64-66. *Concurrent Pos:* Assoc ed, J Optimization Theory & Applns & J Astronaut Sci; vis, Sandia Nat Labs, Aerospace Syst Develop Ctr, 87, 91 & 93. *Mem:* Am Inst Aeronaut & Astronaut; Am Astronaut Soc. *Res:* Application of flight mechanics and analytical/numerical optimal control theory to the development of optimal trajectories and guidance laws for aerospace vehicles. *Mailing Add:* Dept Aerospace Eng & Eng Mech Univ Tex Austin TX 78712

HULL, DAVID LEE, APPLIED MATHEMATICS, STATISTICS. *Current Pos:* from asst prof to assoc prof, 70-80, PROF MATH, OHIO WESLEYAN UNIV, 80- *Personal Data:* b Cleveland, Ohio, Aug 4, 39; m 63; c 2. *Educ:* Ohio State Univ, BS, 61, PhD(math), 69; Univ Wis, MS, 64. *Prof Exp:* Teacher, Cleveland Bd Educ, 61-63; actuarial trainee, Nationwide Ins Co, 64-65; analyst, Ctr Naval Anal, 69-70. *Concurrent Pos:* Consult statistician, Northeastern For Exp Sta, USDA, 70-71; consult, NSF, 73-85; assoc, Environ Anal Assocs, Inc, 73-88; independent comput consult, 78-92. *Mem:* Math Asn Am; Am Statist Asn. *Res:* Applications of mathematics and statistics to societal problems; methodology for evaluating federal programs in technology transfer; methodology for evaluating educational programs in entrepreneurship. *Mailing Add:* Dept Math & Sci Ohio Wesleyan Univ Delaware OH 43015. *E-Mail:* dlhull@cc.owu.edu

HULL, DONALD ALBERT, GEOLOGY, GEOTHERMAL ENERGY. *Current Pos:* geothermal spec, 74-77, DIR, DEPT GEOL & MINERAL INDUSTS, STATE ORE, 77- *Personal Data:* b Wallace, Idaho, July 9, 38; c 3. *Educ:* Univ Idaho, BS, 60; McGill Univ, MS, 62; Univ Nev, PhD(geol), 70. *Prof Exp:* Dist mgr, Homestake Mining Co, 70-74. *Mem:* Am Asn State Geologists; Can Inst Mining & Metall. *Res:* Geologic research; economic geology; mineral exploration; geologic hazards. *Mailing Add:* 3954 N Castle Ave Portland OR 97227

HULL, DONALD R(OBERT), chemical engineering; deceased, see previous edition for last biography

HULL, FREDERICK CHARLES, METALLURGY. *Current Pos:* RETIRED. *Personal Data:* b Alliance, Ohio, Nov 9, 15; m 93, Liz Garvin; c 1. *Educ:* Univ Mich, BS, 37; Carnegie Inst Technol, DSc(metall eng), 41. *Honors & Awards:* Charles B Dudley Medal, Am Soc Testing & Mat, 62; James F Lincoln Gold Medal, Am Welding Soc, 74. *Prof Exp:* Teaching asst, Carnegie Inst Technol, 37-39; res engr, Westinghouse Elec Corp, 41-57, adv engr, Res & Develop Ctr, 57-81. *Concurrent Pos:* Consult, 81-86. *Mem:* Fel Am Soc Metals Int; Am Inst Mining, Metall & Petrol Engrs; Am Soc Testing & Mat. *Res:* Grain size; high temperature alloys; stainless steels; hot cracking. *Mailing Add:* 8501 Bluebill Ct Raleigh NC 27615

HULL, GEORGE, JR, ENTOMOLOGY. *Current Pos:* PROF BIOL & CHMN DEPT, FISK UNIV, 66-, DIR DIV NATURAL SCI & MATH, 77- *Personal Data:* b Indianola, Miss, Sept 30, 21; m 47; c 2. *Educ:* Alcorn Agr & Mech Col, BS, 45; Tenn Agr & Indust State Univ, MS, 49; Ohio State Univ, PhD(entom), 57. *Prof Exp:* Asst instr biol, Tenn Agr & Indust State Univ, 48-49, from instr to prof, 49-64; prof biol sci & head dept, Grambling Col, 64-66. *Mem:* AAAS; Entom Soc Am. *Res:* Biology and control of insects; insect pathology. *Mailing Add:* Dept Biol Fisk Univ 1000 17th Ave N Nashville TN 37208-3045

HULL, GORDON FERRIE, JR, PHYSICS. *Current Pos:* PRES, HULL ASSOCS & EDUC CONSULTS, 65- *Personal Data:* b Hanover, NH, May 23, 12; m 37, Mona Cutler; c 5. *Educ:* Dartmouth Col, AB, 33, AM, 34; Yale Univ, PhD(physics), 37. *Prof Exp:* Mem tech staff, Bell Tel Labs, Inc, NJ, 37-44; prof physics, Dartmouth Col, 44-55; sr staff mem, Lincoln Lab, Mass Inst Technol, 55-58; sr scientist, Sylvania Elec Prod, Inc, 58-63; dir res, Baird-Atomic, Inc, 63-65. *Mem:* Fel AAAS; fel Am Phys Soc. *Res:* Spectroscopy; electronics; microwaves; solid state physics; optics; astrophysics. *Mailing Add:* 2 Jewett St Rockport MA 01966

HULL, HARRY H, PHYSICAL CHEMISTRY. *Current Pos:* RETIRED. *Personal Data:* b Beaver, Pa, Jan 30, 11; m 35; c Harry F, James, Helen & Robert. *Educ:* Purdue Univ, BS, 33; Univ Chicago, MS, 40. *Prof Exp:* Chem engr, Victor Chem Works, 34-43; res engr, R R Donnelley & Sons Co, 46-62; physicist, Graphic Arts Tech Found, 62-75; chem engr, C E Lummus Co, 75-77. *Mem:* AAAS; Soc Rheol; Am Chem Soc. *Res:* Thermodynamics of rheology; printability of paper; Design of experiments. *Mailing Add:* 1710 Del Webb Blvd Sun City Center FL 33573-5010

HULL, HERBERT MITCHELL, PLANT PHYSIOLOGY, BOTANY & FORESTRY. *Current Pos:* prof, 66-85, EMER PROF RENEWABLE NATURAL RESOURCES, UNIV ARIZ, 85- *Personal Data:* b La Jolla, Calif, Aug 19, 19; m 50, Mary Mattison; c Laurinda L & Daniel J. *Educ:* Univ Calif, BS, 46; Calif Inst Technol, PhD(plant physiol), 51. *Prof Exp:* Res fel, Calif Inst Technol, 49-52. *Concurrent Pos:* Plant physiologist, Agr Res Serv, USDA, Tucson, Ariz, 52-78. *Mem:* Fel AAAS; Am Soc Plant Physiol; Bot Soc Am; Weed Sci Soc Am; Am Inst Biol Sci; Sigma Xi. *Res:* Absorption and translocation of organic substances; effect of air pollution upon plants; leaf and cuticle ultrastructure. *Mailing Add:* 4040 W Sweetwater Dr Tucson AZ 85745-9757

HULL, HUGH BODEN, CARDIOVASCULAR DISEASE. *Current Pos:* DIR CARDIOL DEPT, ST LUKE'S HOSP, PHOENIX, 59- *Personal Data:* b Greenfield, Ohio, Nov 1, 20; m 45, Eleanor Van Fossan; c Margaret, Hugh W, John E & Maryann. *Educ:* Ohio State Univ, BA, 42, MD, 44; Am Bd Internal Med, dipl, 55. *Prof Exp:* Intern, Good Samaritan Hosp, Phoenix, Ariz, 45-46; resident med, Ohio State Univ, 47-49; resident cardiol, White Cross Hosp, Columbus, 49-50; asst instr med & fel cardiol, Col Med, Ohio State Univ, 50-53, asst prof physiol, 52-59, asst prof med, 53-59. *Concurrent Pos:* Actg chief res lab, Ohio Tuberc Hosp, Columbus, 51-52; mem heart steering comt, Ariz Regional Med Prog. *Mem:* AMA; NAm Soc Pacing & Electrophysiol; fel Am Col Chest Physicians; Int Soc Endovascular Surg. *Mailing Add:* Barrow Heart Lung Ctr St Lukes Hosp 1800 E Van Buren Phoenix AZ 85006-3742. *Fax:* 602-251-8553

HULL, JAMES CLARK, PLANT ECOLOGY. *Current Pos:* PROF BIOL, TOWSON STATE UNIV, 76- *Personal Data:* b Los Angeles, Calif, Nov 29, 45; m 71, Carol Ray; c Brian & Craig. *Educ:* Univ Calif, Santa Barbara, BA, 68, MA, 73; PhD(biol), 74. *Prof Exp:* Lectr bot, Univ Calif, Santa Barbara, 74-75; asst prof bot, Bishop's Univ, 75-76. *Concurrent Pos:* Plant ecologist, Chesapeake Bay Ctr Environ Sci, Smithsonian Inst, 80; vis scholar, Stanford Univ, 84-85. *Mem:* Ecol Soc Am; Sigma Xi; Am Inst Biol Sci. *Res:* competitive and allelopathic interactions which result in dominance, stability and perturbations within vegetation; plant physiological adaptations for tolerance of adverse environmental conditions; serpentine vegetation; plant nutrient relations. *Mailing Add:* Dept Biol Sci Towson State Univ 8000 York Rd Towson MD 21252. *Fax:* 410-830-2405; *E-Mail:* e7b2hul@toe.towson.edu

HULL, JEROME, JR, AGRICULTURE, HORTICULTURE. *Current Pos:* exten horticulturist, 64-97, PROF HORT, MICH STATE UNIV, 71- *Personal Data:* b Canfield, Ohio, Dec 15, 30; m 57, Suzanne Lotze; c 4. *Educ:* Mich State Univ, BS, 52, PhD(agr), 58; Va Polytech Inst & State Univ, MS, 53. *Honors & Awards:* Pomol Res Award, Int Dwarf Fruit Tree Asn, 91. *Prof Exp:* Exten pomologist, Purdue Univ, 59-64. *Concurrent Pos:* Ed, Hoosier Hort, 69-74, Ann Report, Mich State Hort Soc, 71-97; Stewart Green fel, 75; ext ed, Hortscience, 77-80. *Mem:* Fel Am Soc Hort Sci; Coun Agr Sci & Technol; Int Dwarf Fruit Tree Asn. *Res:* Nutrition of deciduous fruit crops; chemical weed control and physiology of fruit crops; plant growth regulation for fruit production. *Mailing Add:* Dept Hort Mich State Univ East Lansing MI 48824. *Fax:* 517-353-0890

HULL, JOHN LAURENCE, POLYMER PROCESSING ENGINEERING. *Current Pos:* VCHMN, HULL CORP, HATBORO, PA, 55- *Personal Data:* b Danville, Pa, Mar 29, 24; m 47, 76; c 3. *Educ:* Mass Inst Technol, BS, 44. *Prof Exp:* Div officer, UN, China, 46-48; area officer, Ger, 48-50; design engr, Commonwealth Aircraft, Australia, 50-52; advert mgr, Fischer & Porter Co, Hatboro, Pa, 52-55. *Concurrent Pos:* Dir, Compex Corp, Hull Corp, Thinco, Inc, Barnes Corp, Finmac Corp, PCK Elastomerics, Tree Growers Inc, Kard Corp & Hull Int, Scotland, 55-; chmn, Publ Comt & Elec & Electronics Div, Soc Plastics Engrs, 55-; lectr, Ctr Prof Advan, 75-; pres, Hulltronics, Inc, 77-82. *Mem:* Sr mem Soc Plastics Engrs; Plastics Inst Am; Plastics Pioneers Asn. *Res:* Direct encapsulation of electronic components and semiconductor devices with plastic by transfer molding. *Mailing Add:* 598 Belmont Ave Apt F203 Southampton PA 18966

HULL, JOHN R, SOLAR ENERGY, SUPERCONDUCTIVITY. *Current Pos:* physicist, 80-81, engr, 82-89, SECT MGR, ARGONNE NAT LAB, 90- *Personal Data:* b Des Moines, Iowa, Aug 15, 49; m 95, Olga Kalinina; c Aron & Michael. *Educ:* Iowa State Univ, BS, 71, PhD(physics), 79. *Honors & Awards:* Award for Distinguished Performance, Univ Chicago, 95. *Prof Exp:* Fel, Iowa State Univ, 79-80. *Concurrent Pos:* Consult, UN; assoc ed, Solar Energy; chmn, Superconductivity Tech Comt, Am Soc Mech Engrs, 92-93; bd chrm, Cryog Eng Conf, 95, Appl Superconductivity Conf, 96. *Mem:* Int Solar Energy Soc; Optical Soc Am; sr mem Inst Elec & Electronics Engrs; fel Am Soc Mech Engrs; Sigma Xi. *Res:* Solar pond physics; energy storage; electromagnetic levitation; natural convection; applications of superconductivity. *Mailing Add:* Argonne Nat Lab ET-335 Argonne IL 60439. *Fax:* 630-252-5568; *E-Mail:* john_hull@qmgate.anl.gov

HULL, JOSEPH A, ELECTRICAL ENGINEERING, ENGINEERING PHYSICS. *Current Pos:* assoc dir, 70-82, PHYSICIST, HIST TELECOMMUN SCI, NAT TELECOMMUN & INFO ADMIN, DEPT COM, 82- *Personal Data:* b Portland, Kans, Jan 21, 25; m 46; c 6. *Educ:* Univ Kans, BS, 49; Univ NMex, MS, 57. *Prof Exp:* Asst cardiovasc res, Univ Kans, 49-52; res assoc high explosives, Los Alamos Sci Lab, 52-54; staff mem, 54-56; sr scientist, Avco Corp, 59-64; dept mgr space measurements, 64-67; br chief, Electronics Res Ctr, NASA, 67-70. *Mem:* Am Inst Aeronaut & Astronaut; Sigma Xi; sr mem Inst Elec & Electronics Engrs. *Res:* Ballistic missile re-entry physics; non-nuclear vulnerability of missile and satellites; electronic and optical instrumentation; instrumentation aspects of medical research and technology; optical communications; fiber optics. *Mailing Add:* ITS NI 325 S Broadway Boulder CO 80303

HULL, JOSEPH POYER DEYO, JR, PETROLEUM GEOLOGY. *Current Pos:* CONSULT GEOLOGIST, 90- *Personal Data:* b Tulsa, Okla, Jan 21, 31; m 62, Renate Kranz; c Thomas & Karen. *Educ:* Hamilton Col, AB, 52; Columbia Univ, MA, 53, PhD(geol), 55. *Prof Exp:* Subsurface geologist petrol explor, Humble Oil & Refining Co, 55-58; staff geologist, Kerr-McGee Corp, 59-68, chief geologist, Can, 69-73, mgr Can explor, 73-75; pres, Impel Energy Corp, 75-80; pres, Page Petrol Inc, 80; vpres, Ensource, Inc, 81-84; vpres, Sabine Corp, 84-86; vpres, Wolf Energy Co, 87-90. *Mem:* Geol Soc Am; Soc Econ Paleont & Mineral; Soc Econ Geol; Am Asn Petrol Geol. *Res:* Oil and gas; regional stratigraphy; sedimentary petrology; permian of Texas and New Mexico; geology of northern Canada. *Mailing Add:* 64 S Flora Way Golden CO 80401

HULL, LARRY ALLEN, FRUIT ENTOMOLOGY, INTEGRATED PEST MANAGEMENT. *Current Pos:* Res Asst, Pa State Univ, 72-74, grad res asst, 74-77, from instr to asst prof, 77-90, PROF, PA STATE UNIV, 90- *Personal Data:* b Gettysburg, Pa, April 23, 50; m 73; c 2. *Educ:* Mt St Marys Col, BS, 72; Pa State Univ, PhD(entom), 77. *Concurrent Pos:* Prin investr, Cortium Integrated Pest Mgt through Tex A&M Univ, Environ Protection Agency, USDA, 78-82. *Mem:* Entom Soc Am. *Res:* Integrated pest-management programs for deciduous tree fruits, select natural enemies with resistance to pesticides for implementation of expanding pest management systems. *Mailing Add:* Pa State Univ Fruit Res Lab PO Box 309 Biglerville PA 17307

HULL, McALLISTER HOBART, JR, THEORETICAL PHYSICS, NUCLEAR PHYSICS. *Current Pos:* prof physics & provost, 77-85, counr to pres, 85-88, EMER PROF & PROVOST, DEPT PHYSICS & ASTRON, UNIV NMEX, 88- *Personal Data:* b Birmington, Ala, Sept 1, 23; m 46, Mary Muska; c John McAllister & Wendy Ann (McCabe). *Educ:* Yale Univ, BS, 48, PhD(physics), 51. *Prof Exp:* Res technician theoret physics, Los Alamos Sci Lab, 46; asst res, Univ Wis, 46-47; asst res, Yale Univ, 47-51, from instr to assoc prof physics, 51-66; prof physics & chmn dept, Ore State Univ, 66-69; prof physics & astron & chmn dept, State Univ NY, Buffalo, 69-77, actg dean grad sch, 71-72, dean grad prof educ, 72-77. *Mem:* Fel Am Phys Soc; Am Asn Physics Teachers. *Res:* Nucleon scattering; analysis and tabulation of charged particle wave functions; interaction of radiation with matter; pion scattering; nuclear structure; planning and management in higher education. *Mailing Add:* Dept Physics & Astron Univ NMex Albuquerque NM 87131

HULL, MAURICE WALTER, VETERINARY PHYSIOLOGY. *Current Pos:* RETIRED. *Personal Data:* b Clay Center, Kans, Mar 11, 22; m 45; c 3. *Educ:* Kans State Univ, DVM, 45, MS, 61, PhD(physiol), 64. *Prof Exp:* Vet, Linden Animal Hosp, Mo, 45; owner, Clay Ctr Animal Hosp, Kans, 45-59; assoc vet physiologist, Mont State Univ, 62-71, prof vet physiol, Vet Res Lab, 71-85. *Concurrent Pos:* Vis prof, Univ Alexandria, Egypt, 80-81. *Mem:* Am Soc Vet Physiol & Pharmacol; Am Vet Med Asn. *Res:* Ruminant physiology, especially bovine pulmonary emphysema and brisket disease; trace element nutrition. *Mailing Add:* 4424 E Delta Ave Mesa AZ 85206

HULL, MICHAEL NEILL, ELECTROCHEMISTRY. *Current Pos:* MGR, INT PAPER, 82- *Personal Data:* b Belfast, Northern Ireland, Nov 7, 42; US citizen; m 67; c 3. *Educ:* Queen's Univ, BSc, 64, PhD(electrochem), 67. *Prof Exp:* Res assoc electrochem, Duke Univ & US Army Electronics Command, 67-69; sr scientist electrochem, ESB, Inc, 69-78; sect mgr, IRDC, INCO, 78-82. *Concurrent Pos:* Lectr, Quality Improv Progs. *Mem:* Electrochem Soc; Tech Asn Pulp & Paper Indust. *Res:* Development of new battery systems and fundamental research in the electrochemistry of power systems; battery electrochemistry; pulping and bleaching. *Mailing Add:* 17 Arbor Lane Nanuet NY 10954

HULL, RICHARD JAMES, PHYSIOLOGICAL ECOLOGY, PLANT NUTRITION. *Current Pos:* assoc prof, 69-78, PROF PLANT SCI, UNIV RI, 79- *Personal Data:* b Newport, RI, Nov 29, 34; m 66, Catherine C; c Stephen F & Thomas C. *Educ:* Univ RI, BS, 57, MS, 59; Univ Calif, Davis, PhD(bot), 64. *Prof Exp:* Asst prof plant physiol, Purdue Univ, 64-69. *Concurrent Pos:* Res assoc, Univ Calif, Davis, 77; chmn, Plant Sci Dept, Univ RI, 88-97; vis scholar, Univ Calif, Davis, 91. *Mem:* Am Soc Plant Physiol; Am Soc Hort Sci; Agron Soc Am; Crop Sci Soc Am; Soil Sci Soc Am; Weed Sci Soc Am. *Res:* Physiology of perennial plants; influence of environmental factors on the translocation and metabolism of photosynthetic products; stress physiology of turf, woody ornamental plants and tidal marsh halophytes; physiology of phanerogamic parasites. *Mailing Add:* Dept Plant Sci Univ RI Kingston RI 02881-0804. *Fax:* 401-874-5826; *E-Mail:* rjhull@uriacc.uri.edu

HULL, ROBERT JOSEPH, PHYSICS. *Current Pos:* STAFF MEM LINCOLN LAB, MASS INST TECHNOL, 69- *Personal Data:* b Salem, Mass, July 6, 36; m 58; c 6. *Educ:* Mass Inst Technol, SB, 57, PhD(physics), 61. *Prof Exp:* Asst res physicist & lectr, Univ Calif, Berkeley, 63-64; physicist & lectr, 64-66; asst prof physics, State Univ NY, Buffalo, 66-69. *Mem:* Optical Soc Am; Am Phys Soc. *Res:* Optics; laser technology. *Mailing Add:* 2 Minuteman Dr Concord MA 01742

HULL, THOMAS EDWARD, computer science; deceased, see previous edition for last biography

HULL, WILLIAM L(AVALDIN), mechanical engineering; deceased, see previous edition for last biography

HULLAND, THOMAS JOHN, VETERINARY MEDICINE, PATHOLOGY. *Current Pos:* RETIRED. *Personal Data:* b Redcliff, Alta, Feb 2, 30; m 56; c 4. *Educ:* Univ Toronto, DVM, 54; Univ Edinburgh, PhD(vet path), 59; dipl, Am Col Vet Path, 63. *Prof Exp:* From asst prof to assoc prof vet path, Ont Vet Col, Univ Guelph, 54-64, head, Dept Path, 64-69, prof, 64-, assoc acad dean, 69-80. *Concurrent Pos:* Mem exam bd, Am Col Vet Path, 65-68, coun, 69-74, pres, 73; consult, Armed Forces Inst Path, 71. *Mem:* Can Vet Med Asn (pres, 71-72); Can Asn Vet Path; fel Royal Soc Med. *Res:* Veterinary pathology. *Mailing Add:* Dept Path Ont Vet Col Univ Guelph Guelph ON N1G 2W1 Can

HULLAR, THEODORE LEE, ORGANIC CHEMISTRY, BIOCHEMISTRY. *Current Pos:* chancellor, 87-94, PROF ENVIRON TOXICOL, UNIV CALIF, DAVIS, 94- *Personal Data:* b Prescott, Wis, Mar 19, 35; m 58; c 2. *Educ:* Univ Minn, BS, 57, PhD(biochem), 63. *Prof Exp:* NSF fel, State Univ NY, Buffalo, 63-64; asst prof, 64-69, assoc dean grad sch, 69-71, assoc prof med chem, 69-74; comnr environ qual, Erie Co, NY, 74-75; dep comnr environ conserv, NY Dept Environ Conserv, 75-79; assoc dir res & adj prof, Cornell Univ, 79-81, dir res & prof, Col Agr & Life Sci, 81-84, dir, Agr Exp Sta, 81-84; exec vchancellor, Univ Calif, Riverside, 84-85, chancellor, 85-87. *Mem:* AAAS; Am Chem Soc; Chem Soc. *Res:* Chemistry and biochemistry of carbohydrates, nucleotides, pyridoxal phosphate; synthetic organic chemistry; mechanism of action and selective inhibition of enzymes; environmental toxicology; environmental policy; natural resources policy and management; agricultural research policy. *Mailing Add:* Dept Environ Toxicol Univ Calif Davis CA 95616-8588. *E-Mail:* tlhullar@ucdavis.edu

HULLETT, SANDRAL, PUBLIC HEALTH. *Current Pos:* HEALTH SERVS DIR, WEST ALA HEALTH SERVS, INC, 79- *Personal Data:* b Birmingham, Ala, Sept 11, 46; m, Charles A Robertson. *Educ:* Ala A&M Univ, BS, 67; Med Col Pa, MD, 76; Univ Ala, Birmingham, MPH, 87. *Hon Degrees:* LHD, AOH Theol Seminary, 88. *Honors & Awards:* Samuel U Rodgers Achievement Award, Nat Asn Community Health Ctrs Inc, 89; Rural Practioner of the Year, Nat Rural Health Asn. *Prof Exp:* Instr, Coosa County High Sch, Cottage Grove, Ala, 67-68; res asst, Charles Pfizer-Maywood Cancer Res Div, Maywood, NJ, 68-70; res asst, Inst Cancer Res, Columbia Univ, 70-72. *Concurrent Pos:* Clin asst prof, Dept Community & Prev Med, Med Col Pa; preceptor, Sch Nursing, Emory Univ; clin assoc prof, Dept Family Med Col, Community Health Sci, Univ Ala, preceptor, Community Med Clerkship; clin asst prof, Dept Community Health & Prev Med, Morehouse Sch Med; preceptor, Univ Ala, Birmingham; clin assoc prof, Dept Family Practice, Univ S Ala; clin staff, Family Pract Ctr, Selma, Ala; grantee, Center on Aging, 79, Ford Found, 84-88, Robert Wood Johnson Found, 84-90, Dept Health & Human Servs, Bureau Health Professions, 90-96, Health Resources & Servs Admin & Dept Health & Human Servs Pub Health Servs, Div Maternal & Chil Health, 92-96, Nat Cancer Inst, 92-97, Nat Cancer Inst, Robert Wood Johnson Found & W K Kellogg Found, 94-96 & Nat Heart, Lung & Blood Inst, 94- *Mem:* Inst Med-Nat Acad Sci; Nat Rural Health Asn; Am Cancer Soc; AMA; Am Pub Health Asn; Am Acad Family Physicians; US Dept Health & Human Servs. *Res:* Published several articles. *Mailing Add:* West Ala Health Servs Inc PO Box 599 Eutaw AL 35462

HULLEY, CLAIR MONTROSE, engineering, computer science; deceased, see previous edition for last biography

HULLINGER, RONALD LORAL, VETERINARY & MICROSCOPIC ANATOMY, IMMUNOLOGY. *Current Pos:* from asst prof to assoc prof, 69-84, PROF VET ANAT, PURDUE UNIV, 85- *Personal Data:* b Des Moines, Iowa, Feb 4, 41; m 59; c 3. *Educ:* Iowa State Univ, BS, 64, DVM, 65, MS, 66, PhD(vet anat), 68. *Prof Exp:* Asst prof vet anat, Iowa State Univ, 68-69. *Concurrent Pos:* Vis prof, Cornell Univ, 74-75; Utrecht Univ, Holland, 76-77 & Univ Ill, 78-79, Free Univ Berlin, 84- *Mem:* Am Asn Vet Anat; Am Vet Med Asn; World Asn Vet Anat; Europ Asn Vet Anat; Asn Am Vet Med Educ; World Asn Vet Med Educ. *Res:* Normal microscopic and fine structural anatomy of the canine endocrine system and changes with age in that system; cell biology; development of endocrine system in mammals. *Mailing Add:* Dept Vet Anat Purdue Univ West Lafayette IN 47909-1246. *Fax:* 765-494-1772

HULM, JOHN KENNETH, SOLID STATE PHYSICS. *Current Pos:* RETIRED. *Personal Data:* b Southport, Eng, July 4, 23; US citizen; m 48; c 5. *Educ:* Cambridge Univ, BA, 43, MA, 45, PhD(physics), 49. *Honors & Awards:* Wetherill Medal, Franklin Inst, Pa, 64; Int Prize New Mats, Am Phys Soc, 79. *Prof Exp:* Res fel physics, Union Carbide & Carbon Corp, Inst Study Metals, Univ Chicago, 49-51, asst prof, Univ, 51-54; adv physicist, Westinghouse Elec Corp, 54-56, mgr, Solid State Physics Dept, 56-60, assoc dir res, 60-64, dir cryogenic res, 64-69, res dir, 69-74; sci attache, US Dept State, US Embassy, London, 74-76; mgr chem res, Westinghouse Res Labs, 76-80, dir corp res, 80-96. *Mem:* Nat Acad Sci; Nat Acad Eng; Brit Nuclear Energy Soc; fel Am Phys Soc; AAAS; Brit Inst Physics. *Res:* Cryogenics; superconductivity; semiconductors; ferroelectrics; magnetism; electrotechnology and the generation of high magnetic fields; energy technology. *Mailing Add:* 51 Newgate Rd Pittsburgh PA 15202

HULME, BERNIE LEE, NUMERICAL ANALYSIS, MATHEMATICAL MODELING. *Current Pos:* CONSULT APPL MATH, HULME MATH, 86- *Personal Data:* b Chickasha, Okla, July 1, 39; m 60, Phyllis Swarts; c Bradley D. *Educ:* Univ Okla, BS, 62, MCE, 63; Harvard Univ, MS, 65, PhD(appl-math), 69. *Prof Exp:* Staff mem appl math, Sandia Nat Labs, 69-86. *Mem:* Soc Indust & Appl Math. *Res:* Numerical analysis, in particular the numerical solution of differential equations; applications of graph theory and Boolean algebra; operations research. *Mailing Add:* 3701 General Patch NE Albuquerque NM 87111

HULME, NORMAN ARTHUR, PHARMACOLOGY. *Current Pos:* RETIRED. *Personal Data:* b Philadelphia, Pa, June 9, 24; m 50; c 3. *Educ:* Philadelphia Col Pharm, BSc, 50; Johns Hopkins Univ, MS, 53; Univ Md, PhD(pharmacol), 54. *Prof Exp:* Clin pharmacologist, Sterling Winthrop Res Inst, 54-88. *Mem:* AAAS; Am Chem Soc; Brit Biochem Soc; NY Acad Sci; Am Soc Clin Pharmacol & Therapeut. *Res:* Mechanism of action of general anesthetics. *Mailing Add:* 50 Sunset Dr Delmar NY 12054-1126

HULS, BERNARDUS (BERT) JOSEPHUS, MINERAL PROCESSING, HYDROMETALLURGY. *Current Pos:* MGR PROCESS DEVELOP, BHP MINERALS, 93- *Personal Data:* b Leidschendam, Holland, Jan 5, 53; Can citizen; m 76, Gerda J Klerks; c Eldwin & Natalie. *Educ:* Delft, Univ Technol, Holland, BSc, 76, MSc, 78, PhD(metall eng), 90. *Prof Exp:* Tech asst supt, Southern Peru Copper Corp, 85-87; supt mineral processing, Falconbridge Ltd, 87-90; mgr technol, Lakefield Res, 90-93. *Concurrent Pos:* Chmn, Column 91, Can Mineral Processors, 90, second vchmn, 91, first vchmn, 92, chmn, 93. *Mem:* Can Inst Mining & Metall; Am Inst Mining, Metall & Petrol Engrs. *Res:* Mineral processing concentrated on the application and development of column floatation and instrumentation for process control; level indication, bias, holdup, redox potential; hydrometallurgy research is focused on the extraction of nickel and copper, including bio leaching and other leach routes. *Mailing Add:* 204 Edison Way Reno NV 89509. *Fax:* 702-856-1619

HULSBOS, C(ORNIE) (LEONARD), CIVIL ENGINEERING. *Current Pos:* PROF & CHMN DEPT CIVIL ENG, UNIV NMEX, 65- *Personal Data:* b Given, Iowa, Aug 23, 20; wid; c 3. *Educ:* Iowa State Univ, BS, 41, MS, 49, PhD(struct eng), 53. *Prof Exp:* Struct draftsman, Am Bridge Co, 41-46; instr theoret & appl mech, Iowa State Univ, 46-47, from instr to prof civil eng, 47-60; res prof, Lehigh Univ, 60-65. *Concurrent Pos:* Mem concrete bridges comt, Transp Res Bd. *Mem:* Am Soc Civil Engrs; Am Soc Eng Educ; Am Concrete Inst; Nat Soc Prof Engrs. *Res:* Structural engineering. *Mailing Add:* 7608 Palo Duro NE Albuquerque NM 87110

HULSE, ARTHUR CHARLES, HERPETOLOGY, ECOLOGY. *Current Pos:* from asst prof to assoc prof, 76-83, PROF BIOL, INDIANA UNIV OF PA, 83- *Personal Data:* b Jersey City, NJ, Dec 20, 45; m 79, Karen L Owens; c Caleb. *Educ:* Bloomfield Col, BA, 67; Ariz State Univ, MA, 70, PhD(zool), 74. *Prof Exp:* Fel zool, Univ Tex, Austin, 73-75. *Concurrent Pos:* Res assoc, Carnegie Mus Natural Hist, 76- *Mem:* Soc Study Evolution; Soc Study Amphibian Reptile; Soc Syst Zoologists; Am Asn Ichthyologists & Herpetologists; Herpetologists League. *Res:* Ecological herpetology with major emphasis on demographic patterns in aquatic salamanders and reproductive ecology of snakes. *Mailing Add:* Dept Biol Indiana Univ of Pa Indiana PA 15705-0001

HULSE, CHARLES O, CERAMICS. *Current Pos:* RES SCIENTIST, UNITED TECHNOL CORP, 61- *Personal Data:* b New York, NY, May 29, 28; m; c 2. *Educ:* Rutgers Univ, BS, 51; Univ Calif, Berkeley, MS, 56, PhD(eng sci), 60. *Mem:* Am Ceramic Soc; Soc Exp Mech. *Res:* Mechanical behavior of materials; thin film sensors. *Mailing Add:* 387 Foote Rd South Glastonbury CT 06073

HULSE, RUSSELL ALAN, FUSION PLASMA PHYSICS, COMPUTER MODELING. *Current Pos:* mem tech staff, Princeton Univ, 77-80, staff res physicist II, 80-84, res physicist, Plasma Physics Lab, 84-92, PRIN RES PHYSICIST, PRINCETON UNIV, 92- *Personal Data:* b New York, NY, Nov 28, 50. *Educ:* Cooper Union, BS, 70; Univ Mass, MS, 72, PhD(physics), 75. *Hon Degrees:* DSc, Univ Mass, 94. *Honors & Awards:* Nobel Prize in Physics, 93. *Prof Exp:* Res assoc, Nat Radio Astron Observ, 75-77. *Mem:* Fel Am Phys Soc; Am Astron Soc. *Res:* Computer modeling of transport and atomic processes in tokamak controlled thermonuclear fusion plasmas; advanced computational environments; science education. *Mailing Add:* Plasma Physics Lab Princeton Univ PO Box 451 Princeton NJ 08543

HULSEY, J LEROY, FINITE ELEMENT ANALYSIS, EXPERIMENTAL STRESS ANALYSIS. *Current Pos:* ASSOC PROF CIVIL ENG, UNIV ALASKA, FAIRBANKS, 87- *Personal Data:* b Sullian, Mo, Oct 6, 41; m 64; c 1. *Educ:* Mo Sch Mines & Metall, BS, 64; Univ Mo, Rolla, MS, 66, PhD(struct), 76. *Prof Exp:* Proj engr, Daily Assocs, Inc, US Army, 66-72; res asst, Univ Mo, Rolla, 72-76; asst prof, NC State Univ, 76-80; pres, Civil Eng & Appl Res, 79-85; asst dir, Inst Transp Res, 85-87. *Concurrent Pos:* Mem, Gen Struct Comt, Transp Res Bd, 76-80 & Geotech Computer Appln & Numerical Methods Comt, Am Soc Civil Engrs, 76-79; pres, Appl Computer Serv, Inc, 79- *Mem:* Sigma Xi; Am Soc Civil Engrs; Am Concrete Inst. *Res:* Numerical methods and laboratory evaluation of bridge behavior for temperature stresses, load distribution for cable-stayed bridges, long term deflections of segmental bridges and life cycle performance of bridges. *Mailing Add:* Dept Civil Eng Univ Alaska Rm 247A Fairbanks AK 99775-5900

HULSIZER, ROBERT INSLEE, JR, ELEMENTARY PARTICLE PHYSICS. *Current Pos:* dir, Educ Res Ctr, Mass Inst Technol, 64-68, chmn fac, 77-79, prof physics & mem lab nuclear sci, 64-86, EMER PROF, MASS INST TECHNOL, 86- *Personal Data:* b East Orange, NJ, Nov 25, 19; m 41, 67, Carol Kasen; c Stephen H, Ann (Wymore), Morgan (Jenkins) & Cynthia H. *Educ:* Bates Col, BS, 40; Wesleyan Univ, MA, 42; Mass Inst Technol, PhD(physics), 48. *Prof Exp:* Asst physics, Wesleyan Univ, 40-42; mem staff, Radiation Lab, Mass Inst Technol, 42-46, res assoc physics, Lab Nuclear Sci, 46-49; from asst prof to prof, Univ Ill, 49-64. *Concurrent Pos:* Consult, Off Naval Res, 57-61, Xerox Corp, 68-72 & Phys Sci Study Comt, Educ Servs, Inc, 58-60. *Mem:* Fel Am Phys Soc; Am Asn Physics Teachers. *Res:* Acoustics of quartz bars; nature of primary cosmic radiation; use of digital computers in real-time data-handling; low temperature physics; beta decay; elementary particle reactions. *Mailing Add:* MIT Rm 24-410 Cambridge MA 02139. *E-Mail:* hulsizer@mit.edu

HULT, JOHN LUTHER, ELECTRONICS, PHYSICS ENGINEERING. *Current Pos:* CONSULT, 72- *Personal Data:* b Mulino, Ore, May 21, 16; m 43; c 2. *Educ:* Ore State Col, BS, 39; Ohio State Univ, PhD(physics), 49. *Prof Exp:* Prin investr, Rand Corp, 49-72. *Mem:* Am Phys Soc; World Future Soc. *Res:* Electronic warfare; communication satellites; remotely manned vehicles; Antarctic icebergs for fresh water and cooling. *Mailing Add:* 1368 Calle De Oro Thousand Oaks CA 91360

HULT, RICHARD LEE, BIOCHEMICAL PHARMACOLOGY, TOXICOLOGY. *Current Pos:* from asst prof to assoc prof, 76-92, PROF PHARMACOL, FERRIS STATE UNIV, 92- *Personal Data:* b Grand Rapids, Mich, July 23, 45; m 69; c 3. *Educ:* Ferris State Col, BS, 68; Ore State Univ, MS, 75, PhD(pharm & toxicol), 77. *Prof Exp:* Teaching asst, Ore State Univ, 71-76. *Mem:* Am Asn Cols Pharm. *Res:* Cancer chemotherapy; improvement of toxicity efficacy ratio; toxicity of para aminophenols. *Mailing Add:* Col Pharm Ferris State Univ 901 S State St Big Rapids MI 49307-2251

HULTGREN, FRANK ALEXANDER, PHYSICAL METALLURGY. *Current Pos:* SR RES ASSOC, SOHIO METALL CO, 84- *Personal Data:* b Lakewood, Ohio, Apr 13, 36; m 66. *Educ:* Case Inst Technol, BS, 58, PhD(metall), 62; Univ Mich, MSE, 60. *Prof Exp:* Res engr, Sci Lab, Ford Motor Co, 59-60; res asst, Case Inst Technol, 60-62, res assoc, 62; nuclear res salvage, Ger, 62-65; proj leader flat-rolled & stainless steels, Repub Steel Corp, 65-67, chief fundamental res sect, 67-73, chief phys metall & formability, 73-75, develop metallurgist, 75-76, mgr process develop, 76-84. *Concurrent Pos:* Fulbright scholar, Ger, 62-63. *Mem:* Am Soc Metals; Am Inst Mining, Metall & Petrol Engrs; Am Iron & Steel Engrs. *Res:* Deformation; recrystallizations; mechanical metallurgy; metal physics; dislocation damping; internal friction; steel melting, refining and finishing. *Mailing Add:* 427 Deerfield Dr Mars Lakeville PA 16066

HULTGREN, HERBERT NILS, MEDICINE. *Current Pos:* from instr to assoc prof, 48-69, PROF MED, SCH MED, STANFORD UNIV, 69- *Personal Data:* b Santa Rosa, Calif, Aug 29, 17; m 48; c John, Bruce & Peter. *Educ:* Stanford Univ, AB, 39, MD, 43. *Prof Exp:* Intern Prof Exp: Intern, San Francisco Hosp, 42-43; asst resident med, Stanford Hosp, 43-44, asst resident path, 46-47; fel, Thorndike Mem Lab, Harvard Med Sch, 47-48. *Concurrent Pos:* Markle Found scholar, 51-56. *Mem:* Am Soc Clin Invest; Am Fedn Clin Res; Am Col Physicians; Asn Univ Cardiologists; Western Asn Physicians. *Res:* Cardiovascular diseases; valvular and congenital heart disease; phonocardiography; high altitude physiology; coronary artery disease. *Mailing Add:* Dept Med Stanford Univ Sch Med Vet Admin Med Ctr 3801 Miranda Ave C-111 Cardiol Palo Alto CA 94304. *Fax:* 650-852-3473

HULTIN, HERBERT OSCAR, FOOD SCIENCE. *Current Pos:* from asst prof to assoc prof, 59-69, PROF FOOD SCI, UNIV MASS, AMHERST, 69- *Personal Data:* b Quincy, Mass, Jan 1, 34; m 58; c 5. *Educ:* Mass Inst Technol, SB & SM, 56, PhD(food sci), 59. *Honors & Awards:* Res Award, Inst Food Technol, 68; Earl P McFee Award, Atlantic Fisheries Technologists, 85. *Prof Exp:* Res asst food sci, Mass Inst Technol, 56-58, res assoc, 58-59. *Concurrent Pos:* NIH fel, Inst Enzyme Res, Univ Wis, 62-63; prof, Assoc Grad Fac, Univ Guelph, 91- *Mem:* AAAS; fel Inst Food Technol; fel Am Chem Soc; Atlantic Fisheries Technol Conf; Oxygen Soc Int Soc Free Radical Res; Japanese Soc Sci Fisheries. *Res:* Relationship of enzymic activity to subcellular environment; immobilized enzymes; enzymic control of postharvest metabolism; biochemistry of marine foods. *Mailing Add:* Univ Mass-Marine Box 7128 Anesville Gloucester MA 01930

HULTMAN, CARL A, SURFACE CHEMISTRY, DIFFUSION COATINGS. *Current Pos:* PROF CHEM & DIR METALLIZING INST, GANNON UNIV, 84- *Personal Data:* b Milwaukee, Wis, May 21, 43; m, Kathy Kosko; c Amy & Brady. *Educ:* Univ Wis-Madison, BS, 69; Pa State Univ, PhD(phys chem), 75. *Mem:* Am Chem Soc; Am Soc Microbiol. *Res:* Producing diffusion coatings on metals and graphite using molten salt electrochemistry. *Mailing Add:* Chem Dept Univ AQ Erie PA 16541-0001. *Fax:* 814-455-2631

HULTQUIST, DONALD ELLIOTT, BIOCHEMISTRY. *Current Pos:* from instr to assoc prof, 64-79, PROF BIOL CHEM, UNIV MICH, ANN ARBOR, 79- *Personal Data:* b Jamestown, NY, Sept 14, 34; m 61, Nancy S Stoutz; c David, Cynthia, Laura, Deryl & Kevin. *Educ:* Univ Rochester, BS, 56, PhD(biochem), 62. *Prof Exp:* NIH fel, Univ Minn, 62-63 & Univ Calif, Los Angeles, 63-64. *Concurrent Pos:* Actg dir, Cellular & Molecular Biol Grad Prog, Univ Mich, 82. *Mem:* Am Chem Soc; Am Soc Biol Chemists; Oxygen Soc. *Res:* Structure, properties and function of hemeproteins and proteases of erythroid cells; mechanism by which riboflavin and PQQ protect tissues from oxidating injury. *Mailing Add:* Dept Biol Chem Med Sci Bldg 1 Univ Mich 2185 Ayrshire Ann Arbor MI 48109-0606

HULTQUIST, MARTIN EVERETT, ORGANIC CHEMISTRY. *Current Pos:* RETIRED. *Personal Data:* b Laird, Colo, Oct 31, 10; m 34; c 2. *Educ:* Univ Colo, BS, 31, MS, 33, PhD(chem), 35. *Honors & Awards:* Co-recipient Bruce M Cain Mem Award, Am Asn Cancer Res, 87. *Prof Exp:* Asst org chem, Univ Colo, 31-35; res chemist, Calco Chem Div, Am Cyanamid Co,

35-44, chief chemist pharmaceut res, 44-46, asst dir, 46-50, res assoc, 50-54; res assoc, Arapahoe Chem Div, Syntex Corp, 54-63, assoc dir res, 63-78. *Concurrent Pos:* Chem consult, 75-79. *Mem:* Am Chem Soc; fel NY Acad Sci. *Res:* Synthesis of sulfanilamide derivatives; folic acid and derivatives; synthesis of organic medicinal products. *Mailing Add:* 1560 Cress Ct Boulder CO 80304-1503

HULTQUIST, PAUL F(REDRICK), ELECTRICAL ENGINEERING, APPLIED MATHEMATICS. *Current Pos:* from asst prof to assoc prof appl math, Univ Colo, Boulder, 55-63, exec dir, Numerical Anal Ctr, 58-60 & 62-63, prof appl math & elec eng, 65-66, prof elec eng & asst dean eng, Univ Colo, Colo Springs, 66-71, prof elec & comput eng, Univ Colo, Denver, 71-88, EMER PROF ELEC ENG & COMPUT SCI, UNIV COLO, DENVER, 88- *Personal Data:* b Holdrege, Nebr, Mar 24, 20; m 46, Juanita M Tokheim; c Fred J & Ann M. *Educ:* Univ Colo, BA, 45, PhD(physics), 54. *Prof Exp:* Instr appl math, Univ Colo, 45-48 & 52-55, instr physics, 49-50 & 51-52; instr math, Univ Tex, 49. *Concurrent Pos:* Assoc res scientist, Lockheed Missile & Space Co, Calif, 56-57; consult, Ball Bros Res Corp, Colo, 58, 59-60 & 65-, staff scientist, 60-61, sr staff scientist, 63-65; consult, Kaman Nuclear Div, Kaman Aircraft Corp, 65-70; consult, US Geol Surv, 76-82; lectr, Univ Nebr, Omaha, 90-95; consult, 88- *Mem:* Soc Indust & Appl Math; Math Asn Am; Asn Comput Mach; Inst Elec & Electronics Engrs; Soc Comput Simulation; Sigma Xi. *Res:* Numerical analysis and computers; systems engineering; aerospace systems analysis; energy systems. *Mailing Add:* 6803 N 68th Plaza No 414 Omaha NE 68152-2131

HULTQUIST, ROBERT ALLAN, MATHEMATICAL STATISTICS. *Current Pos:* assoc prof, 66-71, prof statist, 71-96, EMER PROF STATIST, PA STATE UNIV, 96- *Personal Data:* b Jamestown, NY, Nov 6, 29; m 56; c 5. *Educ:* Alfred Univ, BA, 51; Purdue Univ, MS, 53; Okla State Univ, PhD, 59. *Prof Exp:* Asst prof math, DePauw Univ, 59-60; from asst prof to assoc prof, Okla State Univ, 60-66. *Mem:* Am Statist Asn; Inst Math Statist. *Res:* Statistical methods; linear models; analysis of variance; distribution theory. *Mailing Add:* Dept Statist 416 Thomas Bldg Pa State Univ University Park PA 16802-6106

HULTS, MALCOM E, PHYSICS TEACHING. *Current Pos:* RETIRED. *Personal Data:* b Whitley Co, Ind, June 30, 26; m 50, Joyce L Johnson; c Carolyn S (Hart-Hults), Richard E & Stewart L. *Educ:* Manchester Col, BA, 49; State Univ NY, Buffalo, MA, 52, PhD(physics), 64. *Prof Exp:* Asst physics, Univ Buffalo, 49-51; teacher high sch, Ind, 51-53; from instr to assoc prof, Ball State Univ, 53-67, head dept, 65-89, prof physics, 67-89. *Concurrent Pos:* Instr, State Univ NY, Buffalo, 60-61, res assoc, 61-63; vis prof, Univ Santa Maria, Brazil, 69. *Mem:* Optical Soc Am; Am Phys Soc; Am Asn Physics Teachers; Sigma Xi. *Res:* Atomic spectroscopy; solar eclipses. *Mailing Add:* 6418 Friendship Circle Indianapolis IN 46268

HULTSCH, ROLAND ARTHUR, PHYSICS. *Current Pos:* Asst prof, 61-67, ASSOC PROF PHYSICS, UNIV MO, COLUMBIA, 67- *Personal Data:* b Columbus, Ind, June 18, 31; m. *Educ:* Wabash Col, AB, 52; Univ Del, MS, 56; Iowa State Univ, PhD(physics), 61. *Mem:* Am Phys Soc; Am Asn Physics Teachers. *Res:* Nuclear magnetic resonance. *Mailing Add:* 1848 Cliff Dr Columbia MO 65201

HULUKA, GOBENA, GLOBAL CLIMATIC CHANGES EFFECT ON PLANTS, PHOSPHOROUS CHEMISTRY IN SOILS. *Current Pos:* res assoc, 90-93, ASST RES PROF, TUSKEGEE UNIV, 90- *Personal Data:* m 85, Hirut Gifawosen; c Bniyan & Liya. *Educ:* Addis Ababa Univ, BSc, 80; Auburn Univ, MSc, 85, PhD(soil chem), 90. *Prof Exp:* Asst res officer, Inst Agr Res, Addis Ababa, Ethiopia, 80-81, head, Soil & Plant Anal Lab, 81-82; asst researcher, Auburn Univ 85-90. *Mem:* Agron Soc Am; Soil Sci Soc Am; Crop Sci Soc Am. *Res:* Effects of increasing carbon dioxide in the atmosphere on plant growth, yield, photosynthesis, water relation, nutrient partitioning with interactions of soil nutrients and water; how phosphorus sorption-desorption is affected by organic acid and residue, additions, soil microbial population and activity. *Mailing Add:* 40 Woodland Terr Auburn AL 36830

HULYALKAR, RAMCHANDRA K, POLYMER SYNTHESIS, CHARACTERIZATION & APPLICATION IN PAINT & COATINGS. *Current Pos:* SR CHEMIST, BENJAMIN MOORE & CO, 91- *Personal Data:* b Mysore State, India, Jan 2, 29; m 57, Nalin; c Atul & Anjali. *Educ:* Poona Univ, BSc, 51, MSc, 55; Queen's Univ, Ont, MSc, 61, PhD(org chem), 64. *Prof Exp:* Sr sci asst, Hidustan Antibiotics Ltd, 57-60; Nat Res Coun Can fel, 64-66; sr res chemist, Polymer Corp Ltd, Can, 66-69; prin chemist, Dart & Kraft Industs Inc, 69-78, sr res assoc, 78-80, prin res assoc, 80-82; res supvr, Textron, 82-85. *Mem:* Am Chem Soc; Oil Color Chemist Asn. *Res:* Synthesis of polymers for the coatings and sealants and their evaluation; custom design the polymer for the specific applications-structure/property relationship. *Mailing Add:* Benjamin Moore & Co 134 Lister Ave Newark NJ 07105-4524. *Fax:* 201-252-2727

HUMAR, JAGMOHAN LAL, STRUCTURAL DYNAMICS & EARTHQUAKE ENGINEERING, STRUCTURAL DESIGN & ANALYSIS. *Current Pos:* from asst prof to assoc prof, 75-83, PROF CIVIL ENG, CARLETON UNIV, OTTAWA, 83-, CHMN DEPT, 90- *Personal Data:* b Udaipur, India, Sept 15, 37; Can citizen; m 62, Yash; c Rachna, Abhinav & Atul. *Educ:* Banaras Hindu Univ, BSc, 58; Indian Inst Technol, MTech, 59; Carleton Univ, PhD(civil eng), 74. *Honors & Awards:* Gzowski Medal, Can Soc Civil Eng, 89. *Prof Exp:* Exec engr, Pub Works Dept, Govt India, 63-71, superintending engr, 71-75. *Concurrent Pos:* Spec consult, Adjeleian & Assocs, 88-89; chair, Comput Appln Div, Can Soc Civil Eng, 88-92; assoc ed, Can J Civil Eng, 96- *Mem:* Fel Can Soc Civil Eng; fel Eng Inst Can; Indian Soc Earthquake Technol. *Res:* Dynamics of structures; response of structures to seismic ground motion; analysis of soil-structure interaction and dam-reservoir-foundation interaction under dynamics loading; dynamic response of bridges; computer-aided design including application of computers in civil engineering. *Mailing Add:* Dept Civil Eng & Environ Carleton Univ 1125 Colonel By Dr Ottawa ON K1S 5B6 Can. *Fax:* 613-788-3951; *E-Mail:* jhumar@ccs.carleton.ca

HUMAYDAN, HASIB SHAHEEN, BREEDING FOR MULTIPLE DISEASE RESISTANCE IN PLANTS, TISSUE CULTURE. *Current Pos:* PRES & OWNER, AGR CONSULT INT, 92- *Personal Data:* b Ain Anoub, Lebanon, Mar 6, 45; m 80; c 2. *Educ:* Am Univ Beirut, BS, 69, MS, 71; Univ Wis-Madison, PhD(plant path & plant genetics), 74. *Prof Exp:* Plant pathologist & Plant breeder, Joseph Harris Seed Co, Inc, 74-82, dir plant path & tissue cult, 82-84; eastern mgr res & develop, Harris Moran Seed Co, 84-85, vpres res & develop, 85-92. *Mem:* Am Phytopath Soc; Am Soc Hort Sci; NY Acad Sci. *Res:* Breeding improved vegetable and flower cultivators with multiple disease resistance; traditional methods supplemented by tissue culture, electrophoresis, induced mutations, and protoplasm fusion. *Mailing Add:* 317 Red Maple Dr Danville CA 94506

HUMAYUN, MIR Z, MOLECULAR BIOLOGY MUTAGENESIS. *Current Pos:* from asst prof to assoc prof microbiol, 79-89, PROF MICROBIOL & MOLECULAR GENETICS, NJ MED SCH, UNIV MED & DENT NJ, 89- *Personal Data:* b India, Feb 11, 49. *Educ:* Loyola Campus, Andhra Univ, India, BSc, 67; Madras Univ, India, MSc, 70; Indian Inst Sci, India, PhD(biochem), 75. *Prof Exp:* Res fel molecular biol, Biol Labs, Harvard Univ, 74-76; asst res scientist molecular biol, Med Ctr, NY Univ, 77-79. *Concurrent Pos:* Res Career Develop Award, US Pub Health Serv, 84-89. *Mem:* Am Soc Biochem & Molecular Biol. *Res:* Molecular mechanisms by which damage to DNA leads to mutagenesis; mechanisms of mutagenicity, genotoxicity and carcinogenicity of Alfatoxin, vinyl chloride and diethylstilbestrol. *Mailing Add:* Dept Microbiol NJ Med Sch 185 S Orange Ave MSB F607 Newark NJ 07103-2714. *Fax:* 973-982-3644; *E-Mail:* humayun@umdnj.edu

HUMBER, LESLIE GEORGE, ORGANIC CHEMISTRY. *Current Pos:* sr res chem, Wyeth-Ayerst Res, 58-67, res fel, 67-69, head, Mem Chem Sect, 69-71, assoc dir, 72-79, dir, chem dept, 80-83, DIR DRUG DESIGN & ANCILLARY SERV, WYETH-AYERST RES, 84- *Personal Data:* b Kingston, Jamaica, Dec 19, 31; Can citizen; m 59; c 2. *Educ:* Sir George Williams Univ, BSc, 53; Univ NB, PhD(org chem), 56. *Prof Exp:* Eli Lilly fel, Univ NB, 56-57; res chemist, Shawinigan Chem Ltd, 57; Sloan fel, Univ Rochester, 57-58. *Concurrent Pos:* Lectr, Concordia Univ, 59-; titular mem, Chem Med Sect, Int Union Pure & Appl Chem, 73-81. *Mem:* Am Chem Soc; Chem Inst Can. *Res:* Structure determination and synthesis of natural products; medicinal chemistry; design of enzyme inhibitors; drugs affecting the central nervous system and lipid metabolism; heterocyclic chemistry; antiinflammatory agents; dopaminergic agents; computer-assisted drug design. *Mailing Add:* Wyeth-Ayerst Res CN 8000 Princeton NJ 08543-8000

HUMBER, RICHARD ALAN, INSECT MYCOLOGY, TAXONOMY. *Current Pos:* NIH fel, 78-79, res assoc, Boyce Thompson Inst, 79-82, RES SCIENTIST INSECT MYCOL, AGR RES SERV, CORNELL UNIV, USDA, 82-, ADJ PROF, PLANT PATH, 88- *Personal Data:* b San Francisco, Calif, May 9, 47; m 77; c 2. *Educ:* Stanford Univ, AB, 69; Univ Washington, MS, 70, PhD(bot), 75. *Honors & Awards:* Grad Res Prize, Mycol Soc Am, 75; Cert Award, Nat Comn Educ, China, 89. *Prof Exp:* Lectr bot, Univ Washington, 75-76; NIH fel, Univ Maine, 76-78. *Mem:* Mycol Soc Am; Soc Invert Path. *Res:* Basic and developmental biology; taxonomy and systematics of fungal pathogens of insects; entomophthorales (zygomycetes); curation of large collection of entomopathogenic fungal cultures. *Mailing Add:* 608 N Aurora St Ithaca NY 14850. *E-Mail:* rah3@cornell.edu

HUMBERD, JESSE DAVID, MATHEMATICS, SCIENCE EDUCATION. *Current Pos:* PROF MATH & SCI, GRACE COL, 54- *Personal Data:* b Roann, Ind, Dec 21, 21; m 42, Laura Eastep; c Lenora H (Kingery) & Margaret H (Damer). *Educ:* Bryan Univ, BS, 43; Wittenberg Col, BA, 47; Ohio State Univ, MA, 50, PhD(math ed), 64; Grace Theol Sem, MDiv, 54. *Prof Exp:* Teacher pub schs, Ohio, 46-47 & 48-51; instr math & physics, Wittenberg Col, 47-48. *Concurrent Pos:* Instr, Ohio State Univ, 58-59. *Mem:* Nat Coun Teachers Math; Nat Sci Teachers Asn. *Res:* Relations between religious and mathematical history; interrelations of sciences in general and liberal education. *Mailing Add:* 411 Kings Hwy Warsaw IN 46580

HUMBERTSON, ALBERT O, JR, ANATOMY, NEUROANATOMY. *Current Pos:* From instr to assoc prof, 62-88, EMER ASSOC PROF ANAT, OHIO STATE UNIV, 89- *Personal Data:* b Cumberland, Md, Sept 30, 33; m 56, Esther Cain; c Debra, Allison & Melinda. *Educ:* Marietta Col, BS, 56; Ohio State Univ, PhD(anat), 62. *Concurrent Pos:* Assoc prof, Univ Va, 93- *Mem:* Am Asn Anat; Soc Neurosci; Sigma Xi; Int Soc Develop Neurosci; AAAS. *Res:* Neuroanatomy; neuroembryology; neurohistochemistry. *Mailing Add:* 1440 Beacon Hill Afton VA 22920

HUMBURG, NEIL EDWARD, AGRONOMY, WEED SCIENCE. *Current Pos:* AGR RESEARCHER & CONSULT, 83- *Personal Data:* b LaCrosse, Kans, May 16, 33; m 61, Renae Bygel; c Karen L & James N. *Educ:* Colo State Univ, BS, 55, MS, 65; Univ Wis-Madison, PhD(agron), 70. *Prof Exp:* Asst prof agron, Kans State Univ, 70-75; agronomist, Humburg Ranch, Inc, 75-76; asst prof weed sci, Univ Wyo, 76-83. *Concurrent Pos:* Consult, Osman-Omar,

Inc, Agr Bank Saudi Arabia, 83, Colo pesticide use surv, 89-93; consult agronomist, Russia, 94 & 96. *Mem:* Weed Sci Soc Am; Am Soc Agron; Crop Sci Soc Am; Int Weed Sci Soc; Soil Sci Soc Am; Sigma Xi. *Res:* Weed control in agronomic crops; USDA agricultural pesticide use surveys for Colorado. *Mailing Add:* XAJA Res PO Box 1992 Sierra Vista AZ 85636-1992. *E-Mail:* rhumburg@primenet.com

HUME, ARTHUR SCOTT, PHARMACOLOGY, TOXICOLOGY. *Current Pos:* from asst prof to assoc prof, 66-86, PROF PHARMACOL, MED CTR, UNIV MISS, 86- *Personal Data:* b Columbia, Tenn, June 17, 28; m 55, Barbara; c Arthur Jr, Andrew & Ann M. *Educ:* Univ Miss, BS, 58, MS, 61, PhD(pharmacol), 64. *Prof Exp:* Instr pharm, Univ Miss, 58-61; fel pharmacol, Sch Med, Vanderbilt Univ, 64-65, instr, 65-66. *Concurrent Pos:* USPHS fel, 64-66; dir, Miss Crime Lab, 72-80. *Mem:* Am Soc Pharmacol & Exp Therapeut; Soc Toxicol; Sigma Xi. *Res:* Correlation of chemical structure; physicochemical properties and biological activities of drugs; toxicology of cyanide and carbon monoxide. *Mailing Add:* Dept Pharmacol Univ Miss Med Ctr 2500 N State St Jackson MS 39216-4505. *Fax:* 601-984-1637

HUME, DAVID JOHN, CROP PHYSIOLOGY. *Current Pos:* From asst prof to assoc prof, 66-79, PROF CROP SCI, UNIV GUELPH, 79-, CHAIR, CROP SCI, 94- *Personal Data:* b Milton, Ont, Aug 7, 40; m 64, Jean Fuller; c Janice & Brian. *Educ:* Univ Toronto, BSA, 61, MSA, 63; Iowa State Univ, PhD(crop physiol), 66. *Honors & Awards:* Outstanding Res Award, Can Soc Agron, 90. *Concurrent Pos:* Assoc prof crop sci, Univ Ghana, 72-74; chmn, Oilseeds Subcomt, East Can Expert Comt on Grain Breeding, 86-91. *Mem:* Fel Am Soc Agron; Agr Inst Can; fel Crop Sci Soc Am; Can Soc Agron (pres, 84-85); Sigma Xi. *Res:* Physiology and management of soybeans and canola, including soybean nodulation, N2 fixation and crop production practices; spring and winter canola production; canola seed constituent quality; canola variety evaluation. *Mailing Add:* Dept Crop Sci Univ Guelph Guelph ON N1G 2W1 Can. *Fax:* 519-763-8933; *E-Mail:* dhume@erop.uoguelph.ca

HUME, DAVID NEWTON, ANALYTICAL CHEMISTRY. *Current Pos:* from asst prof to prof, 47-80, EMER PROF ANALYTICAL CHEM, MASS INST TECHNOL, 80- *Personal Data:* b Vancouver, BC, Dec 22, 17; nat US; m; c 2. *Educ:* Univ Calif, Los Angeles, BA, 39, MA, 40; Univ Minn, PhD(phys chem), 43. *Honors & Awards:* Fisher Award, Am Chem Soc, 63. *Prof Exp:* Res assoc plutonium proj, Metall Lab, Univ Chicago, 43; group leader, Clinton Labs, Oak Ridge, 43-44, sect chief, 45-46; asst prof chem, Univ Kans, 46-47. *Concurrent Pos:* Guggenheim fel, 54-55; NSF sr fel, 64-65; guest investr, Woods Hole Oceanog Inst, 71. *Mem:* Am Chem Soc; Am Acad Arts & Sci. *Res:* Analytical chemistry; instrumental analysis; polarography; complex ions; environmental trace analysis; chemical oceanography; forensic science. *Mailing Add:* One Sylvan Rd Wellesley Hills MA 02181-3239

HUME, HAROLD FREDERICK, TEXTILE CHEMISTRY, GENERAL ENVIRONMENTAL SCIENCES. *Current Pos:* CONSULT, ENERGY CHEM & MGT AFFAIRS, BENCH MARK ASSOCS, 77- *Personal Data:* b Genesee Falls, NY; m 53; c 2. *Educ:* Houghton Col, BSc, 39. *Prof Exp:* Proj engr, Curtiss Airplane Co, NY, 39-45; res engr & res chemist, E I du Pont de Nemours & Co, Inc, 45-64, res assoc, 64-76. *Mem:* AAAS; Am Chem Soc; Fiber Soc. *Res:* Airplane design; food processing and preservation; textiles; physical chemistry; physics of fibers; housing development and design. *Mailing Add:* 2408 Cedar Ave Wilmington DE 19808-3202

HUME, JAMES DAVID, GEOLOGY. *Current Pos:* RETIRED. *Personal Data:* b Fresno, Calif, Dec 17, 23; m 54; c 2. *Educ:* US Mil Acad, BS, 45; Univ Mich, BSE, 49, MS, 50, PhD(geol), 57. *Prof Exp:* Asst prof geol, Purdue Univ, 55-57; from asst prof to prof geol, Tufts Univ, 57-87, chmn dept, 69-77 & 81-87. *Concurrent Pos:* Investr, Arctic Inst NAm, Off Naval Res, 59-69. *Mem:* Geol Soc Am; Soc Econ Paleont & Mineral; Am Petrol Geol; Nat Asn Geol Teachers; Int Asn Sedimentologists. *Res:* Sedimentary petrology; sedimentation; shoreline processes; archeological geology. *Mailing Add:* 15 King Richard Dr Londonderry NH 03053

HUME, JAMES NAIRN PATTERSON, THEORETICAL PHYSICS. *Current Pos:* from asst prof to assoc prof, Univ Toronto, 50-63, chmn dept 75-80, prof, 63-88, EMER PROF COMPUT SCI, UNIV TORONTO, 88- *Personal Data:* b Brooklyn, NY, Mar 17, 23; m 53; c 4. *Educ:* Univ Toronto, BA, 45, MA, 46, PhD(atomic spectra), 49. *Prof Exp:* Lab asst physics, Univ Toronto, 45-46, lectr math, 46-49; instr physics, Rutgers Univ, 49-50; from asst prof to assoc prof, Univ Toronto, 50-63, chmn dept, 75-80, prof, 63-88; master, Massey Col, 81-88. *Mem:* Asn Comput Mach; Sigma Xi; fel Royal Soc Can. *Res:* Theoretical atomic spectra; high-speed digital computation; analysis of computer systems; programming languages. *Mailing Add:* Dept Comput Sci Univ Toronto Toronto ON M5S 1A4 Can. *Fax:* 416-978-1931

HUME, JOHN CHANDLER, PREVENTIVE MEDICINE, PUBLIC HEALTH. *Current Pos:* assoc dean, Sch Hyg & Pub Health, 61-67, chmn, Dept Pub Health Admin, 61-69, prof pub health admin, 61-81, dean, Sch Hyg & Pub Health, 67-77, EMER DEAN, JOHNS HOPKINS UNIV, 77-, EMER PROF HEALTH POLICY & MGT, 81- *Personal Data:* b Brooklyn, NY, May 16, 11; m 33; c 3. *Educ:* Princeton Univ, AB, 32; Vanderbilt Univ, MD, 36; Johns Hopkins Univ, MPH, 47, DrPH, 51. *Honors & Awards:* Edward W Browning Award for Prev of Dis, Am Pub Health Asn, 77; William Freeman Snow Award for Distinguished Serv to Humanity, Am Social Health Asn, 85; Thomas A Parson Award for Long & Distinguished Contrib to Field of Veneral Dis Control, Am Venereal Dis Asn, 88. *Prof Exp:* Med intern, Vanderbilt Univ Hosp, 36-37; actg dir, Hardin County Dept Health, Tenn, 37-38; clinician & dir, Tri-County Demonstration Syphilis, Ga, 38-39; practicing physician, Ga, 39-42; dir venereal dis control, Wilmington City & New Hanover County Dept Health, NC, 42-44 & State Dept Health, WVa, 44-46; res assoc, Johns Hopkins Univ, 47-51, assoc prof, 51-55, asst dir, 48-55; chief, Health Div, US Tech Coop Mission to India, Int Coop Admin, 55-61. *Concurrent Pos:* Physician-in-chg Venereal Dis Div, Med Clin (PM), Johns Hopkins Hosp, 47-55; chief, Div Venereal Dis Control, State Dept Health, Md, 52-55, mem residency rev comn prev med, 63-73; secy-treas, Am Bd Prev Med, 63-67, chmn, 67-74; mem, Am Bd Med Specialties, 64-72; mem, Nat Adv Coun Pub Health Training, 66-70; pres, Asn Schs Pub Health, 70-71; mem bd trustees & first vpres, Pan Am Health & Educ Found, 70-83, pres, 83-84; mem bd dirs, Am Asn World Health, US Comt, WHO, 70-81, pres, 72-74, vpres, 74-81; mem nat comn venereal dis, US Dept HEW, 71-72. *Mem:* Fel Am Pub Health Asn; Int Health Soc Inc (pres, 77-78); Am Venereal Dis Asn (secy, 53-55, vpres, 64-67, pres, 69-70); Sigma Xi; Am Social Health Asn. *Res:* Public health administration; education for health professions; venereal and treponemal disease control; international health. *Mailing Add:* 717 Maiden Choice Lane No 420 Baltimore MD 21228

HUME, MERRIL WAYNE, STATISTICS. *Current Pos:* RES SPECIALIST STATIST, ROCKWELL INT, 74- *Personal Data:* b San Francisco, Calif, Apr 30, 39; m 63; c 3. *Educ:* Col William & Mary, BS, 60; Va Polytech Inst, MS, 64, PhD(statist), 66. *Honors & Awards:* Harlan J Anderson Award, Am Soc Testing Mat. *Prof Exp:* Asst prof statist, Case Western Reserve Univ, 66-70; assoc prof, Univ Mo, Rolla, 70-74. *Mem:* Am Statist Asn; fel Am Soc Testing & Mat; Inst Nuclear Mat Mgt; Nat Mgt Asn. *Res:* Rank correlation; assessment of transuranics in the environment; accountability and safeguards of nuclear material. *Mailing Add:* 7560 Johnson St Arvada CO 80005

HUME, WAYNE C, ELECTRICAL ENGINEERING. *Current Pos:* OWNER & PROD DESIGNER, VINTAGE REPRODUCTIONS, 74- *Personal Data:* b Mankato, Minn, June 17, 36; m 62; c 2. *Educ:* Univ Minn, BEE, 59, MSEE, 61. *Prof Exp:* Assoc res eng, Res Lab, Univac Div, Sperry Rand Corp, Minn, 61-65; res scientist, Shock & Struct Dyn Lab, Kaman Nuclear Div, Kaman Sci Corp, 65-74. *Concurrent Pos:* res grant, Colo Energy Res Inst, 78-79. *Mem:* Inst Elec & Electronics Engrs. *Res:* Pulse power engineering; high-speed photography; shock wave experiments; solar radiation. *Mailing Add:* Vintage Reproductions 2606 Flintridge Dr Colorado Springs CO 80918

HUMENICK, MICHAEL JOHN, II, CIVIL & SANITARY ENGINEERING. *Current Pos:* AT DEPT CIVIL ENG, UNIV WYO. *Personal Data:* b Muskegon, Mich, Sept 24, 36. *Educ:* Univ Mich, BS, 59, MS, 60; Univ Calif, Berkeley, PhD(civil eng), 70. *Prof Exp:* Asst res engr, Chevron Res Co, 60-61, assoc res engr, 61-63, trainee, Standard Oil Co Calif, 63-64, res engr, Chevron Res Co, 64-67; mgr water pollution control, Environ Qual Eng, Inc, 70; assoc prof civil eng, Univ Tex, Austin, 70- *Mem:* Am Soc Civil Engrs; Am Inst Chem Engrs. *Res:* Physical, chemical and biological treatment of water and wastewaters. *Mailing Add:* Dept Civil Eng Univ Wyo Box 3295 Laramie WY 82071-3295

HUMENIK, FRANK JAMES, AGRICULTURAL WASTE MANAGEMENT, WATER QUALITY. *Current Pos:* From asst prof to assoc prof, 69-78, ASSOC HEAD, DEPT BIOL & AGR ENG, NC STATE UNIV, 73-, PROF ENG, 78- *Personal Data:* b Brooklyn, NY, May 26, 37; m 60, Sue Chancey; c Kerry & David. *Educ:* Ohio State Univ, BSCE, 63, MS, 66, PhD(sanit eng), 69. *Honors & Awards:* Duggar Lectr, Auburn Univ, 77; Gunlogson Countryside Eng Award, Am Soc Agr Engrs, 78, Presidential Distinguished Serv Citation, 93. *Concurrent Pos:* Grants, Water Resources Res Inst, 69-71 & Environ Protection Agency, 71; consult, Environ Protection Agency Animal Waste Projs, 73-78, Nat Comn Water Qual, 75, animal waste projs, pvt eng firms, 76- & state non-point source projs, 82-; chmn, Cast Publ, Agr & Water Qual, 89-92, Agr Work Group Coastal Zone Mgt Act, 92, Ecop & Escop Work Group Water Qual & Clean Water Act, 93- *Mem:* Am Soc Agr Engrs; Sigma Xi. *Res:* Animal waste management; wastewater and waste nutrient utilization; land application of waste; water quantity and quality; total watershed management. *Mailing Add:* 4008 Pepperton Dr Raleigh NC 27606. *Fax:* 919-515-6772

HUMENIK, MICHAEL, JR, CERAMICS, METALLURGY. *Current Pos:* res engr, Ford Motor Co, Dearborn, Mich, 52-54, supvr ceramic & powder metall, 54-62, mgr ceramics & glass res, 62-69, asst dir mfg res, 69-76, DIR MFG PROCESSES LAB RES, FORD MOTOR CO, 76- *Personal Data:* b Garfield, NJ, Nov 10, 24; m 48; c 3. *Educ:* Alfred Univ, BS, 49; Mass Inst Technol, ScD, 52. *Honors & Awards:* Ferro Enamels Award, 57. *Prof Exp:* Asst, Mass Inst Technol, 49-52. *Mem:* Am Ceramic Soc; Am Soc Metals; Am Inst Mining, Metall & Petrol Engrs. *Res:* Surface energy studies in ceramic and metal systems at elevated temperatures; sintering; powder metallurgy; cermets; glass. *Mailing Add:* 17097 Cambridge Ave Allen Park MI 48101

HUMER, PHILIP WILSON, ORGANIC CHEMISTRY. *Current Pos:* sr info scientist patent liaison, 74-94, CONSULT, FMC CORP, 94- *Personal Data:* b Carlisle, Pa, Nov 8, 32; m 53, 81, Felicia F Foulkes; c Jean (Reardon), Kathleen (Ries), Richard C, Alice (Foulkes-Garcia) & Ann (Foulkes). *Educ:* Dickinson Col, Pa, BS, 54; Pa State Univ, PhD(org chem), 64. *Prof Exp:* Res chemist surfactants & adhesives, Phillips Petrol Co, 64-69; sr res chemist paper additives & adhesives, Pa Indust Chem Corp, 69-73; sr res chemist adhesives, Hercules Inc, Picco Resins, 73-74. *Concurrent Pos:* Patent agt, 78- *Mem:* Am Chem Soc; AAAS. *Res:* Reaction mechanisms; reactive intermediates, such as carbenes; stereochemistry of cycloadditions, surfactants, adhesives, paper additives, insecticides, nematicides, herbicides, fungicides, plant regulators and chemical processes. *Mailing Add:* 8 Glenwood South Gate Morrisville PA 19067-1022

HUMES, ARTHUR GROVER, parasitology, for more information see previous edition

HUMES, JOHN LEROY, ENDOCRINOLOGY, BIOCHEMISTRY. *Current Pos:* biochemist, 63-68, res biochemist, 68-73, sr res biochemist, 74-78, RES FEL, MERCK INST THERAPEUT RES, 78- *Personal Data:* b Uniontown, Pa, Feb 18, 36; m 63. *Educ:* Ohio Wesleyan Univ, BA, 58; Rutgers Univ, PhD(zool), 74. *Prof Exp:* Res asst biochem, Univ Pittsburgh, 61-63. *Concurrent Pos:* Assoc prof grad fac, Rutgers Univ, 74- *Mem:* Sigma Xi; Am Physiol Soc; NY Acad Sci; Am Asn Immunologists. *Res:* Role of intracellular and extracellular regulators of cell functions, especially the role of prostaglandins and cyclic-nucleotides in cell function. *Mailing Add:* Merck Res Labs Box 2000 Rahway NJ 07065-0900

HUMES, PAUL EDWIN, ANIMAL SCIENCE, GENETICS. *Current Pos:* From asst prof to assoc prof, 68-77, PROF ANIMAL SCI, LA STATE UNIV, BATON ROUGE, 77-, HEAD DEPT, 90- *Personal Data:* b Colville, Wash, Nov 19, 42; m 65, Tamra Fae Lickfold; c Steven Roy & Krista Leigh. *Educ:* Wash State Univ, BS, 64; Ore State Univ, PhD(genetics), 68. *Mem:* Am Soc Animal Sci; Sigma Xi; Am Registry Prof Animal Scientists. *Res:* Genetic evaluation of breeds and breed crosses of sheep, cattle and swine; genetic control of hormones associated with growth and reproduction; production efficiency and mature size relationships in beef cattle. *Mailing Add:* Dept Animal Sci La State Univ Baton Rouge LA 70803. *Fax:* 504-388-3279

HUMI, MAYER, MATHEMATICAL PHYSICS, TURBULENCE. *Current Pos:* from asst prof to prof, 71-87, SINCLAIR PROF MATH, WORCESTER POLYTECH INST, 88- *Personal Data:* b Bagdad, Iraq, Sept 29, 44; m 80, Carmella Zemach; c Michelle & Joshua. *Educ:* Hebrew Univ Jerusalem, BSc, 63, MSc, 64; Weizmann Inst Sci, PhD(math physics), 69. *Prof Exp:* Fel, Univ Toronto, 69-70, asst prof math, 70-71. *Concurrent Pos:* Asst prof, Clark Univ, 75-76; assoc prof, Ga Inst Technol, 78-79; IPA fel, Natick RDLE Army Lab, Mass, 89-93; resident univ prof, Philips Lab, Hanscam AFB, Mass, 93- *Mem:* Am Math Soc; Soc Indust & Appl Math; Int Asn Math Physics. *Res:* Lie groups theory and its applications to differential equations; relativity and cosmology; theoretical physics; turbulence; author of 2 books and 40 papers. *Mailing Add:* Dept Math Worcester Polytech Inst Worcester MA 01609

HUMIEC, FRANK S, JR, INORGANIC CHEMISTRY. *Current Pos:* CHEMIST, AT&T BELL LAB, 86- *Personal Data:* b Niagara Falls, NY, June 11, 33; div; c 2. *Educ:* Niagara Univ, BS, 58; Fairleigh Dickinson Univ, MS, 68. *Prof Exp:* Anal technician, Union Carbide Corp, 51-53 & Hooker Electrochem Corp, 53-58; chemist, Mellon Inst, 58-63 & Witco Chem Soc, Inc, 63-68; res chemist, Hoffmann-La Roche Inc, 68-86. *Mem:* Am Electroplaters & Surface Finishers Soc. *Res:* Phosphorus chemistry; organic synthesis; instrumental analysis; inorganic polymers and complexes; amino acids; medicinal chemistry; isolation of natural products; electroplating. *Mailing Add:* 614 Essex Pl Fair Lawn NJ 07410

HUMKE, PAUL DANIEL, ANALYSIS & FUNCTIONAL ANALYSIS, TOPOLOGY. *Current Pos:* assoc prof, 80-85, PROF DEPT MATH, ST OLAF COL, 85- *Personal Data:* b Milwaukee, Wis, Feb 16, 45; m 67, Bonnie Ericson; c Kristi, Eric & Peter. *Educ:* Univ Wis, Milwaukee, PhD(math), 72. *Prof Exp:* From asst prof to assoc prof, Dept Math, Western Ill Univ, 72-80. *Concurrent Pos:* Vis assoc prof, Univ Calif, Santa Barbara, 83; vis res scientist, Fulbright/Hungarian Ministry Educ, 87; vis prof, Univ Wis, Milwaukee, 88 & NC State Univ, 92; NAm dir, Budapest Semesters Math, 89- *Mem:* Am Math Soc; Math Asn Am. *Res:* The exceptional behavior of real functions, fractals, set porosity, derivates and derivatives; dynamical systems. *Mailing Add:* Dept Math St Olaf Col 1520 St Olaf Ave Northfield MN 55057-1574. *E-Mail:* humke@stolaf.edu

HUMKE, RAMON L, UTILITIES. *Current Pos:* PRES & CHIEF OPERATING OFFICER, INDIANAPOLIS POWER & LIGHT CO, 90-; VCHMN, IPALCO ENTERPRISES INC, 91- *Personal Data:* b Quincy, Ill, Nov 19, 32; m 55, Carolyn Jacobs; c Steven K. *Educ:* Univ Indianapolis, LLD, 88. *Prof Exp:* Mgt, Ill Bell Tel Co, 51-73; dir forecasting & productivity, AT&T, 74-75; vpres personnel, Ill Bell Tel Co, 78-82; vpres corp affairs, Ameritech, 82-83; pres & chief exec officer, Ind Bell Tel Co Inc, 83-89; pres & chief exec officer, Ameritech Servs, 89-90. *Mem:* Medal of Merit, US Treas Dept, 84 & 85; Charles Whistler Award, 89; Benjamin Harrison Medallion Award, 90; Americanism Award, 91. *Mailing Add:* Indianapolis Power & Light One Monument Circle PO Box 1595 Indianapolis IN 46206-1595

HUMM, HAROLD JUDSON, MARINE BIOLOGY. *Current Pos:* prof, 67-82, dir, 67-73, EMER PROF, MARINE SCI INST, UNIV SFLA, 82- *Personal Data:* b Lorain, Ohio, Feb 26, 12; m 36; c 3. *Educ:* Univ Miami, BS, 34; Duke Univ, MS, 42, PhD(bot), 45. *Prof Exp:* Res investr, Marine Lab, Duke Univ, 42-45, from asst dir to dir, 45-49; dir oceanog inst, Fla State Univ, 49-54; assoc prof bot, Duke Univ, 54-65; prof biol, Queens Col, NC, 65-67. *Concurrent Pos:* Jacques Loeb assoc, Rockefeller Inst, 59-60; treas, Gulf Oceanog Develop Found, 68-; distinguished scholar, Marine Sci Inst, Univ SFla, 82- *Mem:* Int Phycol Soc; Phycol Soc Am. *Res:* Distribution, taxonomy and utilization of marine algae; marine bacteriology. *Mailing Add:* 13 E View Dr Brevard NC 28712

HUMMEL, DONALD GEORGE, ORGANIC CHEMISTRY. *Current Pos:* RETIRED. *Personal Data:* b St Louis, Mo, Oct 26, 25; m 50, Elizabeth Kalert; c 6. *Educ:* St Louis Univ, BS, 48; Boston Col, MS, 50; Kans State Univ, PhD, 58. *Prof Exp:* Asst, Boston Col, 48-50 & Kans State Univ, 50-51; res chemist, Olin Mathieson Chem Corp, 53-57; res chemist, Org Chem Dept, Jackson Lab, E I Du Pont de Nemours & Co Inc, 58-76, prod supvr, Chem, Dyes & Pigments Dept, 76-80, sr chemist, Chem & Pigments Dept, 80-85; pres, Donald G Hummel Inc, 85-95. *Concurrent Pos:* Consult, 85-95. *Mem:* Am Chem Soc; Sigma Xi. *Res:* Explosives; fluorocarbon compounds; fluorocarbon chemistry; gasoline additives; surfactants; ethylene oxide chemistry; environmental consulting. *Mailing Add:* 603 Amberly Rd Wilmington DE 19803

HUMMEL, F(LOYD) A(LLEN), CERAMIC CHEMISTRY. *Current Pos:* from asst prof to prof, 48-79, head dept, 63-67, EMER PROF CERAMICS, PA STATE UNIV, 79- *Personal Data:* b Chicago, Ill, Sept 28, 15; m 38; c 4. *Educ:* Univ Ill, BS, 37; Pa State Univ, MS, 48. *Honors & Awards:* Purdy Award, Am Ceramic Soc, 53, Meyer Award, 60, Bleininger Award, 83. *Prof Exp:* Res ceramist, Onondaga Pottery Co, Syracuse, NY, 37-41 & Corning Glass Works, Pa & NY, 41-44; res asst prof ceramics, Univ Ill, 44-45. *Concurrent Pos:* Consult, Lamp Bus Div, Gen Elec Co, 53-75; Universal Dental Co, Philadelphia, 57-72, Ferro Corp, 62-77. *Mem:* Am Chem Soc; fel Am Ceramic Soc; fel Mineral Soc Am; Mineral Soc Can; Brit Ceramic Soc; Sigma Xi. *Res:* Crystal chemistry; phase equilibria and its application to luminescence; mechanical and thermal properties of solids; inorganic pigments. *Mailing Add:* 819 Fairway Rd State College PA 16803-3413

HUMMEL, HANS ECKHARDT, CHEMICAL ECOLOGY, CHEMICAL COMMUNICATION. *Current Pos:* ASST PROF ENTOM & CHEM ECOL, DEPT ENTOM, UNIV ILL, URBANA, 74- *Personal Data:* b Heilbronn, Ger, Apr 30, 39; m 79. *Educ:* Univ Stuttgart, BS, 60; Univ Munich, MS, 64; Univ Marburg, PhD(insect biochem), 68. *Prof Exp:* Fel res & teaching asst physiol chem, Philipps Univ, Marburg, 64-70; res entomologist, Div Toxicol & Physiol, Univ Calif, Riverside, 70-73; res assoc ecol chem, Dept Chem, State Univ NY, Syracuse, 73-74. *Concurrent Pos:* Consult environ toxicol, 82- *Mem:* Entom Soc Am; Am Chem Soc; AAAS; Sigma Xi. *Res:* Chemical communication, inter and intraspecifically, among invertebrates, emphasis in insects, vertebrates, plants, by pheromones, allomones, kairomones, hormones; chemical ecology; bioassays; analytical techniques (chromatographic, spectrometric) for identifying submicrogram quantities of semiochemicals; environmental toxicology; integrated pest management. *Mailing Add:* J Leibig-Univ Phytopathologie Ludwigstr 21 35390 Giessen Germany

HUMMEL, JAMES ALEXANDER, COMPLEX VARIABLES, UNIVALENT FUNCTIONS. *Current Pos:* from asst prof to prof, 57-93, EMER PROF MATH, UNIV MD, COLLEGE PARK, 93- *Personal Data:* b Santa Monica, Calif, Dec 14, 27; m 50, Caroline Ludy; c Robert, John & Albert. *Educ:* Calif Inst Technol, BS, 49; Rice Univ, MA, 53, PhD(math), 55. *Prof Exp:* NSF fel, Stanford Univ, 55-57. *Mem:* AAAS; Am Math Soc; Math Asn Am; Sigma Xi. *Res:* Complex variables; univalent functions. *Mailing Add:* Dept Math Univ Md College Park MD 20742. *E-Mail:* jah@math.umd.edu

HUMMEL, JOHN PHILIP, NUCLEAR CHEMISTRY. *Current Pos:* RETIRED. *Personal Data:* b Blue Earth, Minn, July 29, 31; m 53; c 4. *Educ:* Univ Rochester, BS, 53; Univ Calif, PhD(chem), 56. *Prof Exp:* From instr to assoc prof, Univ Ill, Urbana, 56-67, prof chem & physics, 67-94, assoc head, Dept Chem, 71-94. *Mem:* Am Phys Soc. *Res:* Radiochemical studies of nuclear reactions induced by high energy x-rays; study of chemical effects on positron annihilation. *Mailing Add:* 1003 W William St Champaign IL 61821

HUMMEL, JOHN RICHARD, ATMOSPHERIC SCIENCE, ENVIRONMENTAL SCIENCE. *Current Pos:* prin investr, 88-91, DIR ENVIRON PHYSICS DIRECTORATE, SPARTA, INC, 91- *Personal Data:* b Kansas City, Mo, May 19, 51; m 81, Cynthia S Mark. *Educ:* Pa State Univ, BS, 73, MS, 75; Univ Mich, PhD(atmospheric sci), 78. *Prof Exp:* Res asst meteorol, Ionosphere Res Lab, Pa State Univ, 73-75; res scientist, Univ Mich, 75-78; res scientist atmospheric physics, Gen Motors Res Labs, 78-81, sr res scientist, 81-82; staff scientist, Opti Metrics, Inc, 82-85, sr scientist, 85-88. *Mem:* Am Geophys Union; Am Meteorol Soc; AAAS; Sigma Xi. *Res:* Climatology, radiative transfer, and environmental simulation. *Mailing Add:* 595 Great Elm Way Acton MA 01718. *E-Mail:* jhumel@aip.org

HUMMEL, JOHN WILLIAM, CONSERVATION TILLAGE SYSTEMS, SOIL PHYSICAL PROPERTIES SENSORS. *Current Pos:* AGR ENGR, AGR RES SERV, USDA, 76- *Personal Data:* b Grantsville, Md, Nov 1, 40; m 64, Judith C Minick; c John W Jr, Lisa M, Mark D & Lori R. *Educ:* Univ Md, BS, 64, MS, 66; Univ Ill, PhD, 70. *Prof Exp:* from asst prof to assoc prof agr eng, Univ Md, Col Park, 69-76. *Concurrent Pos:* Prof & agr engr, Univ Ill. *Mem:* Am Soc Agr Engrs; AAAS. *Res:* Sensors for measurement of soil physical properties; sensors and systems for site-specific crop management. *Mailing Add:* 376 Agr Engr Sci Bldg 1304 W Penn Ave Urbana IL 61801. *Fax:* 217-244-0323; *E-Mail:* jwh@sugar.age.uiuc.edu

HUMMEL, RICHARD LINE, CHEMICAL ENGINEERING, PHYSICAL CHEMISTRY. *Current Pos:* asst prof, 61-64, assoc prof, 64-76, PROF CHEM ENG, UNIV TORONTO, 76- *Personal Data:* b Dothan, Ala, Dec 27, 28; m 54; c 2. *Educ:* Purdue Univ, BS, 50; Iowa State Univ, PhD(phys chem), 62. *Prof Exp:* Engr in training, E I du Pont de Nemours & Co, 51-52, engr, 52-55; asst quantum mech, Inst Atomic Res, Ames, Iowa, 55-59; instr chem eng, Univ Mich, 59-60; res assoc quantum mech, Iowa State Univ, 60-61. *Mem:* Am Chem Soc; Am Inst Chem Engrs; Solar Energy Soc; Chem Inst Can. *Res:* Boiling catalysis to increase evaporation coefficients; mechanism of boiling; theoretical calculation of electronic spectra of catacondensed and pericondensed aromatic hydrocarbons. *Mailing Add:* Dept Chem Eng Univ Toronto Toronto ON M5V 1A4 Can

HUMMEL, ROBERT P, SURGERY. *Current Pos:* From instr to assoc prof, 59-77, PROF SURG, UNIV CINCINNATI, 77-, VCHMN DEPT, 84- *Personal Data:* b Bellevue, Ky, Sept 17, 28; m 54, Helen Beam; c 3. *Educ:* Xavier Univ, BS, 47; Univ Cincinnati, MD, 51. *Concurrent Pos:* Attend surgeon, C R Holmes Hosp, 60, Children's Hosp, 64, Univ Hosp, 65; chief staff, Univ Hosp, 92- *Mem:* Am Col Surgeons; Am Surg Asn; Alimentary Tract; Am Burn Asn. *Res:* Trauma; burns; surgical infections; breast disease. *Mailing Add:* 1073 Stratford Hill Dr Cincinnati OH 45230

HUMMEL, ROLF ERICH, ELECTRONIC MATERIALS. *Current Pos:* from asst prof to assoc prof, 64-74, PROF MAT SCI, UNIV FLA, 74- *Personal Data:* b Sindelfingen, Ger, July 21, 34; m 61; c 3. *Educ:* Univ Stuttgart, BS, 56, dipl physics, 60, Dr rer nat(physics, metall), 63. *Prof Exp:* Res assoc phys metall, Max Planck Inst Metals Res, 58-63. *Concurrent Pos:* Vis prof, Max Planck Inst Metals Res, Stuttgart, 71-72, Solar Energy Res Inst, 80, Solid Optics Lab, Paris, 81 & Univ Kyoto, Japan, 88 & Victoria Univ, Wellington, NZ, 95; vis scientist, Chinese Acad Sci, Bejing, 88. *Mem:* Am Inst Metall Eng; Am Phys Soc; Mat Res Soc. *Res:* Optical properties of metals and alloys; corrosion optics; electrotransport in thin films; electronic materials; ion implantation; thin film technology; differential reflection spectroscopy; porous silicon by spark-processing. *Mailing Add:* Dept Mat Sci & Eng Univ Fla Gainesville FL 32611. *Fax:* 352-392-6359; *E-Mail:* rhumm@mse.ufl.edu

HUMMEL, STEVEN G, CHLORIDE TRANSPORT GROWTH OF III-V COMPOUNDS, VAPOR LEVITATION EPITAXY. *Current Pos:* RES ASST, DEPT ELEC ENG, UNIV SOUTHERN CALIF, 87-; MEM TECH STAFF, HEWLETT-PACKARD, PALO ALTO, CALIF, 93- *Personal Data:* b Tarrytown, NY, Jan 23, 58. *Educ:* Rutgers Univ, BA, 80, MSEE, 86; Univ Southern Calif, PhD(elec eng), 93. *Prof Exp:* Sr staff technologist, AT&T Bell Labs, 80-83; mem tech staff, Bell Commun Res, 84-87. *Concurrent Pos:* Fel, Ctr Photonic Technol, 87-93; consult, Lam Res, Inc, 88-90. *Mem:* Inst Elec & Electronics Engrs; Am Phys Soc; Am Asn Crystal Growth. *Res:* Metal organic chemical vapor deposition of III-V compounds; optical and electrical characterization techniques; in-situ growth probes. *Mailing Add:* Hewlett-Packard 3500 Dear Creek Rd MS 26M-7 Palo Alto CA 94303. *Fax:* 650-857-2379; *E-Mail:* steve_hummel@hpl.hp.com

HUMMEL, THOMAS, OLFACTORY & PAIN RESEARCH. *Current Pos:* ASST PROF & ASSOC DIR, DEPT OTORHINOLARYNGOL, SMELL & TASTE CTR, UNIV PA, 96- *Personal Data:* m 84, Cornelia Stangl. *Educ:* Univ Erlangen, Ger, MD, 87, PhD(pharmacol), 94. *Honors & Awards:* Takasago Award, Europ Chemoreception Res Orgn, 96. *Mem:* Am Chemoreception Soc; Int Asn Study Pain; Am Soc Neurosci; Ger Soc Pharmacol & Toxicol; Ger Soc Physiol. *Res:* Electrophysiology and psychophysiology of the chemical senses; clinical applications. *Mailing Add:* Smell & Taste Ctr Univ Pa 3400 Spruce St Philadelphia PA 19104-7685. *Fax:* 215-349-5266; *E-Mail:* thummel@mail.med.upenn.edu

HUMMELER, KLAUS, PATHOLOGY, VIROLOGY. *Current Pos:* DIR, JOSEPH STOKES SR RES INST, 72- *Personal Data:* b Hamburg, Ger, Feb 23, 22; nat US; m 50; c 1. *Educ:* Univ Hamburg, MD, 48. *Prof Exp:* Instr pediat & pub health, 51-52, assoc pediat & virol, 52-55, from asst prof to assoc prof, 55-70, prof pediat, Univ Pa, 70-, chief div exp path, 66-; mem res staff, Children's Hosp, 50- *Concurrent Pos:* Prof, Wistar Inst, 81- *Mem:* Fel AAAS; Am Asn Immunologists; Royal Soc Med; Path Soc Gt Brit & Ireland; Am Asn Path. *Res:* Virus immunology; cell biology; electron microscopy. *Mailing Add:* Childrens Hosp Philadelphia 34th St & Civic Ctr Blvd Philadelphia PA 19104-4303. *Fax:* 215-590-3960

HUMMELS, DONALD RAY, ELECTRICAL ENGINEERING. *Current Pos:* asst prof, 70-75, assoc prof, 75-, PROF & HEAD ELEC ENG, KANS STATE UNIV. *Personal Data:* b Morris, Ill, June 30, 36; m 57; c 5. *Educ:* Ariz State Univ, BS, 67, MS, 68, PhD(eng), 69. *Prof Exp:* Sr engr, Motorola, Inc, 57-70. *Mem:* Inst Elec & Electronics Engrs. *Res:* Communication and information theory. *Mailing Add:* Dept Elec & Comput Eng Kans State Univ Manhattan KS 66506

HUMMER, DAVID GRAYBILL, THEORETICAL ASTROPHYSICS, LOW ENERGY ATOMIC PHYSICS. *Current Pos:* chmn, Inst, 73-74 & 77-78, FEL, JOINT INST LAB ASTROPHYS, UNIV COLO, BOULDER, 66- *Personal Data:* b Manheim, Pa, Nov 4, 34; m 61; c 1. *Educ:* Carnegie Inst Technol, BS, 57, MS, 59; Univ London, PhD(physics), 63. *Honors & Awards:* Von Humboldt Sr Scientist Award, 84. *Prof Exp:* Physicist, Gen Atomic Div, Gen Dynamics Corp, 57-59; vis fel, Joint Inst Lab Astrophys, Univ Colo, 63-64; lectr physics, Univ Col, Univ London, 64-66. *Concurrent Pos:* Mem, Interagency Coord Comt Astron, 75-77. *Mem:* Am Phys Soc; fel Royal Astron Soc; Int Astron Union; Am Astron Soc; Astron Soc of Pac. *Res:* Theory of spectral line shapes; radiative transfer; stellar atmospheres and accretion disks; experimental and theoretical atomic physics; numerical analysis; stellar opacities; equation of state. *Mailing Add:* 313 Alder Ln Boulder CO 80304

HUMMER, JAMES KNIGHT, ORGANIC CHEMISTRY. *Current Pos:* RETIRED. *Personal Data:* b Titusville, Pa, June 13, 26. *Educ:* Tufts Univ, BS, 46; Middlebury Col, MS, 50; Univ NC, PhD(chem), 56. *Prof Exp:* Instr chem, Col Wooster, 54-58; res fel, Univ Sydney, 58-59; mem steroid prog, Clark Univ, 59-60; asst prof chem, Bucknell Univ, 60-62; from assoc prof to prof chem, Lycoming Col, 62-68. *Concurrent Pos:* Teaching & res fel, Imp Col Sci & Technol, London, 70-71. *Mem:* Am Chem Soc; Royal Soc Chem. *Res:* Heterocyclics; steroids. *Mailing Add:* 2211 Fink Ave Williamsport PA 17701-1215

HUMMERS, WILLIAM STRONG, JR, INORGANIC CHEMISTRY. *Current Pos:* assoc prof, 58-65, PROF CHEM, THE CITADEL, 65- *Personal Data:* b Hackensack, NJ, Nov 1, 17; m 44; c 3. *Educ:* Washington & Lee Univ, BS, 41; Univ NC, PhD(chem), 51. *Prof Exp:* Chemist paint & pigments, Nat Lead Co, 46-48; asst, Univ NC, 48-51; fel, Mellon Inst, 51-54; chemist molybdenum compounds, Climax Molybdenum Co, 54-58. *Res:* Anhydrous metal halides; organometallic complexes; clay; clay complexes; molybdenum compounds; catalyst. *Mailing Add:* 159 Sea Marsh Dr Johns Island SC 29455-5505

HUMMERT, GEORGE THOMAS, PRODUCT DESIGN & DEVELOPMENT, PROJECT MANAGEMENT. *Current Pos:* DIR PROD ENG & RES, R E PHELM CO INC, 93- *Personal Data:* b Pittsburgh, Pa, Oct 23, 38; m 62; c 2. *Educ:* Carnegie-Mellon Univ, BSEE, 60, MSEE, 64, PhD(elec eng), 68. *Prof Exp:* Instrument engr, Hercules, Inc, 61-63, develop engr circuit design, 64-66; sr engr electrotechnol, Westinghouse Elec Corp, 68-80, mgr electromagnetics, Res & Develop Ctr, 80-89; dir electromagnetic applns, McNeal Schwendler Corp, 89-91. *Concurrent Pos:* Lectr electromagnetics, Univ Pittsburgh, 75-79. *Mem:* Inst Elec & Electronics Engrs; Soc Automotive Engrs. *Res:* Ignition systems for 2-stroke and 4-stroke engines for the lawn and garden industry. *Mailing Add:* 14 Inverness W Aiken SC 29803

HUMMON, WILLIAM DALE, POPULATION BIOLOGY, MEIOBENTHIC INVERTEBRATES. *Current Pos:* asst prof, 69-73, assoc prof, 73-79, PROF ZOOL, OHIO UNIV, 79- *Personal Data:* b Akron, Ohio, July 27, 32; m 58; c 2. *Educ:* Univ Mont, BA, 55, BS, 60, MS, 61; Univ Mass, PhD(zool), 69. *Prof Exp:* Res trainee zool, Systs Ecol Prog, Marine Biol Lab, Woods Hole, 67-69. *Concurrent Pos:* Instr, Olympic Col, 61-65; NATO fel marine lab, Dept Agr & Fisheries Scotland, Aberdeen, 74-75; Ohio Univ fac fel, 78-79. *Mem:* Am Soc Zool; Am Micros Soc; Soc Study Evolution; Ecol Soc Am; fel AAAS; Am Soc Limnol Oceanog. *Res:* Evolutionary and quantitative ecology of meiobeuthic communities, with emphasis on spatio-temporal zoogeography and systematics of gastrotricha; interactions between science and religion, with emphasis on evolution and the challenge of creationism. *Mailing Add:* Biol Sci Ohio Univ Athens OH 45701-2979

HUMPHERYS, ALLAN (STRATFORD), IRRIGATION, ON-FARM AUTOMATION OF IRRIGATION. *Current Pos:* RETIRED. *Personal Data:* b Idaho Falls, Idaho, Apr 4, 26; m 56; c 9. *Educ:* Utah State Univ, BS, 54, MS, 60. *Prof Exp:* Res asst canal & reservoir lining res, Agr Exp Sta, Utah State Univ, 54-58; agr engr irrig res, Agr Res Serv, USDA, 58-90. *Concurrent Pos:* Mem, Water Supply & Conveyance Comt, Am Soc Agr Engrs, 72-; chmn, Am Soc Civil Engrs, 84-87, mem, Comt Control Systs Water Pipelines, 75-87; mem, Int Comt Irrig & Drain Working Group, Mechanized Irrig, 77-, chmn, 79-; consult, On-Farm Auto Irrig, Argentina, 85. *Mem:* Am Soc Agr Engrs; Sigma Xi; Am Soc Civil Engrs; Int Comn Irrig & Drainage; Irrig Asn. *Res:* Control, conveyance and measurement of water; methods, hydraulic design and improvement of structures, facilities and systems for conveying, controlling and automatically applying irrigation water efficiently on farms. *Mailing Add:* 3771 N 3575 E Kimberly ID 83341

HUMPHREY, ALBERT S, PRODUCT & BUSINESS DEVELOPMENT, RE-ENGINEERING & PROJECT MANAGEMENT. *Current Pos:* CHMN, BUS PLANNING & DEVELOP INC, 70- *Personal Data:* b Kansas City, Mo, June 2, 26; m 82, Myriam de Baere; c Albert, Virginia, Jonathan, Heidi, Jonas, Roosje & Stephanie. *Educ:* Univ Ill, BS, 46; Mass Inst Technol, MS, 48; Harvard Bus Sch, MBA, 55. *Prof Exp:* Staff engr ECoast Tech Serv, Esso Stand Oil Co, 48-50; off chief chem officer, US Army Chem Corp, Chief Chem & Protective Group, 50-54; asst to pres, Penberthy Instrument Co, 54-55; chief prod planning, Boeing Airplane Co, 55-60; mgr, Value Anal Prog Small Aircraft Div, Gen Elec, 60-61; mgr res & develop planning, P R Mallory & Co, Inc, 61-64; mgr, Mgt Admin Improv Gen Dynamics, 64-65; sr consult & dir, Int Exec Seminar in Bus Planning, Stanford Res Inst, Calif, 65-70. *Concurrent Pos:* Consult var US & foreign bus; dir, Sanbros Ltd, Eng, Tower Lysprodukter a/s, Norway, Petras Petrochemische Anwendungssysteme GmbH, Ger, Visual Int Ltd, Eng, CHR Long Life Herbal Classics Inc, NJ; fac mem, Polytechnic Sch Bus & Mgt; vis prof, Newcastle upon Tyne; dir, Webb Corp Derby, East West Herbs Ltd, Kingham, Hidden Valley Ltd, Birmingham, UK, Bank Consultancy Group, Ltd, London, UK, Frigborg Instruments; secy, Randolph Mgmt Corp; consult, Off Advan Res & Technol, NASA, 65-70. *Mem:* Sci Res Soc Am; Sigma Xi; Am Inst Chem Engrs; Nat Bur Prof Mgt Consults; Brit Inst Dirs; British Inst Mkt. *Res:* Developed a method for inter-relating people in working parties which mimics the brain of the individual making it possible for a team of people from 2-21 to work together and think together at roughly the same speed as the individual working alone; application of the team work method to managing change in organizations and family units; creativity and product development programs; special project management system which eliminates organizational politics, stagnation and resistance to change. *Mailing Add:* Bus Planning & Develop Inc 1D Randolph Crescent Little Venice, Maida Vale London NW9 1DP England. *Fax:* 44-171-266-0039; *E-Mail:* humph@bpdev.demon.uk.co

HUMPHREY, ARTHUR E(ARL), BIOCHEMICAL ENGINEERING, BIOTECHNOLOGY. *Current Pos:* BIOTECHNOL CONSULT, 97- *Personal Data:* b Moscow, Idaho, Nov 9, 27; m 51, Shiela C Darwin; c Andrea L & Allyson D. *Educ:* Univ Idaho, BS, 48, MS, 50; Columbia Univ, PhD(chem eng), 53; Mass Inst Technol, MS, 60. *Hon Degrees:* DSc, Univ Idaho, 74; DEng, Lehigh Univ, 93. *Honors & Awards:* Donald L Katz Lectr Award, Univ Mich, 73; Food & Bioeng Award, Am Inst Chem Engrs, 75; Van Lanen Award, Am Chem Soc, 79, Marvin Johnson Award, 96; Founders Award, Am Inst Chem Engrs, 89, Van Antwerpen Award, 96; John Fritz Medal, Eng Founder Soc, 97. *Prof Exp:* Asst phys sci, Univ Idaho, 47-50 &

Columbia Univ, 50-52; from asst prof to prof chem eng, Univ Pa, 53-80, dean, Col Eng & Appl Sci, 72-80; provost & vpres, 80-86, prof chem eng, dir, Ctr Molecular Biosci & Biotechnol, Lehigh Univ, 80-92; dir, Biotechnol Inst, PA State Univ, 92-95, prof chem eng, 95-97. *Concurrent Pos:* Chem engr, Inst Coop Res, 54-58; NSF fel, Mass Inst Technol, 58-59; consult, Merck, Sharp & Dohme, Inc, 58-62; Sun Oil Co, 61-68; Merck Chem Co, 62-63; Int Minerals & Chem Co, 63-67, Fermentation Design, 66-, Squibb, 67- & Air Products, 71-86, & Hoffman LaRoche, 87-; Fulbright lectr, Tokyo, 63 & Univ NSW, 70; chmn atmospheric regeneration panel, Space Sci Bd, Nat Acad Sci, 66-68, mem food sci panel, Comn Undergrad Educ Biol Sci, 66; lectr, Tunghai Univ, 67; mem ad hoc working group on single cell protein, Protein Adv Group, Food & Agr Orgn, WHO, UNICEF, 69-; mem eng adv bd, NSF, 70-; mem, Franklin Inst; adj prof, Univ Pa, 80-84; dir & mem bd dirs, Carpenter Steel, Inc, 80-; T L Diamond prof biochem eng, Lehigh Univ, 86-92; vis prof biotechnol, Pa State Univ, 87. *Mem:* Nat Acad Eng; Am Soc Microbiologists; Am Chem Soc; Am Soc Eng Educ; fel Am Inst Chem Engrs (pres, 91-92); fel Am Inst Med & Biol Engrs; Int Asn Microbiol Soc; Sigma Xi; fel Soc Indust Microbiol; fel AAAS. *Res:* Enzyme engineering; air sterilization; media sterilization; kinetics of growth of cellular organisms; computerized fermenters; immobilized enzymes; recycle of wastes; author of numerous publications; granted 3 patents. *Mailing Add:* Pa State Univ 111 Fenske Labs University Park PA 16802-4400. *Fax:* 814-865-7846

HUMPHREY, BRIAN, CHEMISTRY, BIOCHEMISTRY. *Current Pos:* CHMN, DEPT CHEM & BIOCHEM, MONTCLAIR STATE COL, 85- *Personal Data:* b Dallas, Tex, Apr 13, 58. *Educ:* St Joseph Univ, BA, 80; Princeton Univ, PhD(chem), 84. *Mem:* Am Chem Soc; Electrochem Soc; Am Indust Soc. *Mailing Add:* 33 Washington Ave West Caldwell NJ 07006

HUMPHREY, CHARLES HARVE, ATMOSPHERIC PHYSICS. *Current Pos:* MEM STAFF, VISIDYNE INC, 76- *Personal Data:* b Brewer, Maine, Sept 5, 25; m 48, Phyllis; c Christine (Kabell) & Robert. *Educ:* Univ Calif, Los Angeles, AB, 47, MA, 49, PhD(physics), 56. *Prof Exp:* Asst physics, Univ Calif, Los Angeles, 51-53; res scientist, Missile & Space Div, Lockheed Aircraft Corp, 54-58 & Aeronutronic Div, Ford Motor Co, 58-62; staff scientist, Palo Alto Res Lab, Lockheed Missiles & Space Co, Calif, 62-71; scientist, Sci Applns, Inc, 71-74; mem staff, R&D Assocs, Santa Monica, Calif, 74-77. *Mem:* Am Phys Soc; Am Geophys Union. *Res:* Nuclear physics; reactor and plasma physics; atomic physics; weapons effects physics; atmospheric physics. *Mailing Add:* 219 Follen Rd Lexington MA 02173

HUMPHREY, DONALD GLEN, CYTOGENETICS. *Current Pos:* dean div natural sci & math, 70-74, mem fac biol, 74-84, EMER MEM FAC BIOL, EVERGREEN STATE COL, 84- *Personal Data:* b Ames, Iowa, Feb 28, 27; m 46, Eileen Wilson; c Ragan (Humphrey) & Holly (Snyder). *Educ:* Univ Iowa, BS, 49; Univ Wash, MS, 50; Ore State Univ, PhD(zool), 56. *Prof Exp:* From instr to asst prof biol, Ore Col Educ, 50-57; instr, Ore State Univ, 54-55, from asst prof to prof & chmn dept, 57-70, dir honors prog, 65-70, asst dean fac, 69-70. *Concurrent Pos:* Consult, Portland Curric Study, 58; dep dir, Am Quintana Roo Expeds, 65 & 66; panel mem & consult, Comn Undergrad Ed Biol Sci, NSF; NSF fac fel hist & philos sci, Harvard Univ, 67-68 & Sci & Pub Policy, Kennedy Sch Govt, Harvard Univ, 80-81. *Mem:* Fel AAAS; Sigma Xi. *Res:* Chromosomes of vertebrates, Amphibia, Reptilia and Aves; evolution of genetic systems; science and public policy; electron microscopy. *Mailing Add:* 3026 43rd Ct NW Olympia WA 98502

HUMPHREY, DONALD R, NEUROPHYSIOLOGY, NEUROANATOMY. *Current Pos:* asst prof to assoc prof, 71-80, PROF PHYSIOL, SCH MED, EMORY UNIV, 80-, DIR LAB NEUROPHYSIOL, 71- *Personal Data:* b Tahlequah, Okla, July 31, 35; m 61; c 2. *Educ:* San Jose State Univ, BA, 60; Univ Wash, PhD(physiol & biophys), 66. *Honors & Awards:* Hans Berger Res Award, Am EEG & Clin Neurophysiol Soc, 68. *Prof Exp:* USPHS staff assoc clin neurophysiol, Nat Inst Neurol Dis & Stroke, 66-68, staff neurophysiologist, Lab Neurol Control, 68-71. *Concurrent Pos:* Mem, NIH Study Sect, 77-81; consult, Nat Inst Neurol Commun Disorders & Stroke, NIH, 80- *Mem:* Am Physiol Soc; Soc Neurosci; Biomed Eng Soc; Am Asn Anatomy. *Res:* Cerebral cortical mechanisms in the control of movement and posture; neuromuscular control systems. *Mailing Add:* Dept Physiol Emory Univ Sch Med 1440 Clifton Rd NE Atlanta GA 30307-1053

HUMPHREY, EDWARD WILLIAM, surgery, physiology, for more information see previous edition

HUMPHREY, FLOYD BERNARD, MAGNETISM. *Current Pos:* RES PROF ELEC & COMPUTER & SYSTS ENG, BOSTON UNIV, 87- *Personal Data:* b Greeley, Colo, May 20, 25; m 55; c 4. *Educ:* Calif Inst Technol, BS, 50, PhD(chem), 56. *Prof Exp:* Mem tech staff, Bell Tel Labs, 55-60; res group supvr, Jet Propulsion Lab, Calif Inst Technol, 60-64, assoc prof elec eng, 64-71, prof elec eng & appl physics, 71-80; prof & head, dept elec eng, Carnegie-Mellon Univ, 80-87. *Mem:* Am Phys Soc; fel Inst Elec & Electronics Engrs; Am Vacuum Soc; Sigma Xi. *Res:* Magnetism and magnetic computer devices; thin films. *Mailing Add:* PO Box 722 Meredith NH 03253-0722

HUMPHREY, GEORGE LOUIS, physical chemistry; deceased, see previous edition for last biography

HUMPHREY, GORDON LAIRD, PHYSIOLOGY, PSYCHOLOGY. *Current Pos:* asst prof physiol, 71-76, ASST PROF PHYSIOL IN OTOLARYNGOL, UNIV ILL MED CTR, 74-; SR RES BIOLOGIST, RES RESOURCES CTR, BENJAMIN GOLDBERG RES CTR, 76- *Personal Data:* b Yuba City, Calif, Dec 2, 40; m 66; c 2. *Educ:* Willamette Univ, BA, 63; Univ Calif, Los Angeles, MA, 66, PhD(psychol), 68. *Prof Exp:* Actg asst prof psychol, Univ Calif, Los Angeles, 68; USPHS trainee, Brain Res Inst, 68-70, NIMH trainee, 70-71. *Mem:* AAAS; Soc Neurosci. *Res:* Neurophysiology of learning. *Mailing Add:* Res Resources Univ Ill 901 S Wolcott Chicago IL 60612

HUMPHREY, HAROLD EDWARD BURTON, JR, ENVIRONMENTAL HEALTH. *Current Pos:* ENVIRON EPIDEMIOLOGIST, MICH DEPT PUB HEALTH, 71- *Personal Data:* b Lansing, Mich, Aug 5, 40; m 63; c 2. *Educ:* Univ Mich, BS, 62, MS, 65; Mich State Univ, PhD(microbiol & pub health), 70. *Prof Exp:* Sci adv, Gov's Exec Off, State Mich, 69-70; asst prof environ sci, Mich State Univ, 70-71. *Concurrent Pos:* Dir, Kelmik Corp, 71-; US rep, Health Effects Comt, Int Joint Comn, 75-, Res Adv Bd, 79-; adj prof, Col Med, Mich State Univ, 80-; lectr, Sch Pub Health, Univ Mich, 81- *Mem:* Am Soc Microbiol; AAAS; Am Chem Soc; Sigma Xi. *Res:* Chemical contaminants in the environment, detection and evaluation of the effects of exposure on human health; chemical solid-liquid separation processes. *Mailing Add:* 815 Stuart Ave East Lansing MI 48823-3142

HUMPHREY, J RICHARD, PROCESS DEVELOPMENT FOR TITANIUM INVESTMENT CASTING, METAL-MATERIAL SCIENCE. *Current Pos:* TECH VPRES TITANIUM CASTINGS, SELMET INC, 83- *Personal Data:* b Clovis, NMex, Oct 21, 42; m 66; c 4. *Educ:* Univ Calif, Riverside, BA, 63. *Prof Exp:* Chemist anal chem, Atomics Int Div, Rockwell Int, 63-65; proj engr chem vapor deposition, San Fernando Labs, 65-67; solid state electrochemist, Mat & Device Develop, Gould Ionics, 67-69; tech dir titanium castings, Rem Metals Corp, 69-83. *Concurrent Pos:* Guest lectr, Linn-Benton Community Col, 70-71. *Mem:* Am Soc Metals; Metall Soc. *Res:* Electrochemical behavior of organo-titanium compounds, chemical vapor deposition process and solid state electrochemical devices; production of titanium castings, including thermoplastics, ceramics, melting processes, heat treatment and welding techniques; author of 14 technical papers; recipient of three patents. *Mailing Add:* 3836 Kalakala Circle S Salem OR 97306

HUMPHREY, JIMMY LUTHER, SEPARATION PROCESSES, DISTILLATION EXTRACTION. *Current Pos:* PRES, J L HUMPHREY & ASSOCS, 86- *Personal Data:* b Fulbright, Tex, Oct 24, 36; m 78; c 2. *Educ:* Univ Tex, Arlington, AS, 61; Tex A&M Univ, BS, 63; Univ Tex, Austin, PhD(chem eng), 67. *Prof Exp:* Res supvr, Eastman Kodak Co, 67-69, sr res engr, 69-72, environ coordr, 73-74, prod mgr, 75, energy mgr, 76-79; proj mgr, Argonne Nat Lab, 79-82; assoc head, Separations Res Prog, Univ Tex, Austin, 82-86. *Concurrent Pos:* Prin investr & sr lectr, Univ Tex, Austin, 82-86; prog adv bd, US Dept Energy, 83-; indust consult, Alcoa, Gas Res Inst, Combustion Eng, Proctor & Gamble & Gen Foods, 84-; proj rev panel, NSF, 84-; consult, plate distillation subcomt, Am Inst Chem Engrs, 84-86; adv bd, Pub Utility Comn Tex, 84-86. *Mem:* Fel Am Inst Chem Engrs; Am Chem Soc; NAm Membrane Soc; Am Filtration Soc; Am Soc Eng Educ; Int Aosorption Soc. *Res:* Specialize in performance and economics of leading-edge separation technologies; adsorption; membranes; hybrid processes. *Mailing Add:* 3605 Needles Dr Austin TX 78746

HUMPHREY, PATRICIA H, REPRODUCTIVE PHYSIOLOGY. *Current Pos:* RETIRED. *Personal Data:* b Elizabeth, NJ, Nov 9, 38; m 94; c 2. *Educ:* NMex State Univ, BS, 62; Purdue Univ, PhD(reprod physiol), 67. *Prof Exp:* From asst prof to assoc prof zool, Ohio Univ, 67-96. *Concurrent Pos:* Consult, Schering Corp, 67. *Mem:* Soc Study Reproduction. *Res:* Reproductive physiology in domestic pig, dairy cow and laboratory rat. *Mailing Add:* 3930 Marion Johnson Rd Albany OH 45710

HUMPHREY, PHILIP STRONG, ORNITHOLOGY. *Current Pos:* RETIRED. *Personal Data:* b Hibbing, Minn, Feb 26, 26; m 46; c 2. *Educ:* Amherst Col, BA, 49; Univ Mich, MS, 51, PhD(ornith), 55. *Prof Exp:* Res asst, Mus Zool, Univ Mich, 49-55, res assoc, 55-57; asst prof zool, Yale Univ, 57-62, asst cur ornith, Peabody Mus, 57-62; cur, Div Birds, US Nat Mus Natural Hist, Smithsonian Inst, 62-65, chmn, Dept Vert Zool, 65-67; chmn, Dept Zool, Univ Kans, 67-69, prof & dir, Mus Natural Hist, 67-95. *Concurrent Pos:* Curatorial assoc, Peabody Mus, Yale Univ, res fel, Saybrook Col; res assoc, Fla State Mus; Guggenheim mem fel; Rockefeller Found res award. *Mem:* Fel Am Ornith Union; fel AAAS; Soc Syst Zool. *Res:* Vertebrate ecology and epidemiology; tropical rain forest in Brazil; biological survey of the central Pacific; ecology and distribution of birds in Patagonia and Tierra del Fuego. *Mailing Add:* 1609 Hillcrest Rd Lawrence KS 66044

HUMPHREY, RAY EICKEN, ANALYTICAL CHEMISTRY. *Current Pos:* RETIRED. *Personal Data:* b La Harpe, Ill, Jan 27, 31; m 51; c 3. *Educ:* Carthage Col, BA, 52; Western Ill State Col, MS, 55; Univ Iowa, PhD(analytical chem), 58. *Prof Exp:* Analytical res chemist, Ethyl Corp Res Labs, Mich, 58-61; assoc prof, Sam Houston State Univ, 61-66, prof chem, 66-91. *Concurrent Pos:* Robert A Welch Found res grant, 63-71. *Mem:* Am Chem Soc. *Res:* Infrared spectra of charge-transfer complexes; determination of anions; ultraviolet study of the chemistry of mercury. *Mailing Add:* 137 Royal Oaks Rd Kerrville TX 78028

HUMPHREY, RONALD DEVERE, MICROBIAL PHYSIOLOGY. *Current Pos:* PROF BIOL, PRAIRIE VIEW A&M UNIV, 70- *Personal Data:* b Denver, Colo, Mar 31, 38; m 60; c 2. *Educ:* Colo State Univ, BS, 60, MS, 63; Univ Tex, Austin, PhD(microbiol), 70. *Honors & Awards:* Distiguished Serv Award, Tex Br, Am Soc Microbiol. *Concurrent Pos:* Fac res appointee, Argonne Nat Lab, Ill, 78 & Oak Ridge Nat Lab, 85. *Mem:* AAAS; Am Soc Microbiol; NY Acad Sci. *Res:* Microbial physiology; microbial genetics; microbial polysaccharide hydrolyzing enzymes; bacterial nitrogen fixation; bacteriophage enzymes. *Mailing Add:* Dept Biol Prairie View A&M Univ Prairie View TX 77446

HUMPHREY, RONALD MACK, MICROBIOLOGY. *Current Pos:* Res scientist bact, Univ, 54-58, res assoc radiobiol, Hosp, 58-63, assoc biologist, 63-69, PROF BIOPHYS, UNIV TEX M D ANDERSON HOSP & TUMOR INST, 69-, MEM GRAD FAC, BIOMED SCI, UNIV, 68-, ASHBELL SMITH CHAIR BIOPHYS, 80- *Personal Data:* b Abilene, Tex, Aug 13, 32; m 52; c 3. *Educ:* Hardin-Simmons Univ, BA, 53; Univ Tex, MA, 55, PhD(bact), 58. *Mem:* AAAS; Radiation Res Soc. *Res:* Radiobiology; radiation biophysics; mutagenesis and carcinogenesis. *Mailing Add:* Univ Tex MD Anderson Cancer Ctr Sci Park-Res Div PO Box 389 Smithville TX 78957

HUMPHREY, WATTS S, SYSTEM DESIGN, FINANCIAL MANAGEMENT. *Current Pos:* dir, Software Process Prog, 86-91, FEL SOFTWARE ENG INST, CARNEGIE-MELLON UNIV, 91- *Personal Data:* b Battlecreek, Mich, Jul 4, 27; m 54, Barbara Falou; c Katharine (Pickman), Lisa (Fish), Sarah (DeCamillo), Watts Jr, Peter, Erica (Jarrett) & Christopher. *Educ:* Univ Chicago, BS, 49, MBA, 51; Ill Inst Technol, MS, 50. *Honors & Awards:* Aerospace Software Eng Achievement Award, Am Inst Aeronaut & Astronaut, 93. *Prof Exp:* Elec engr, Fermi Inst, 49-51, Chicago Midway Labs, Univ Chicago, 51-53; mgr comput develop, Sylvania Elec Prods, 53-59; instr comput design, Northeastern Univ, 56-59; dir prog, IBM, 59-68, vpres, Systs Develop Div, 69, dir, Endicott Labs, 69-72, dir policy develop, 72-79, tech assessment, 79-82, prog qual, 82-86. *Concurrent Pos:* Chmn adv bd, Systs Res Inst, IBM, 73-82; reviewer, Inst Elec & Electronics Engrs Software & Comput, 84. *Mem:* Fel Inst Elec & Electronics Engrs; Asn Comput Mach. *Res:* Characterizing the software process, assessing the state of US software work, identifying key problems and issues, and initiating activities to address them, focus on process management, process definition; software engineering education. *Mailing Add:* Software Eng Inst Carnegie-Mellon Univ Pittsburgh PA 15213

HUMPHREYS, JACK BISHOP, TRAFFIC ENGINEERING, HIGHWAY SAFETY. *Current Pos:* from asst prof to prof, 66-92, EMER PROF CIVIL ENG, UNIV TENN, KNOXVILLE, 92- *Personal Data:* b Knoxville, Tenn, Dec 17, 33; m 84, Judy Millsaps; c Don & Wesley. *Educ:* Univ Tenn, BS, 55, MS, 62; Tex A&M Univ, PhD(civil eng), 67. *Honors & Awards:* Teetor Ed Award, 68. *Prof Exp:* Instr civil eng, Univ Tenn, 55-56 & 59-62; asst prof, Southwestern La Univ, 62-64. *Concurrent Pos:* Supporting mem, Hwy Res Bd, Nat Acad Sci-Nat Res Coun. *Mem:* Inst Transp Engrs; Am Soc Civil Engrs. *Res:* Highway safety as related to highway design, vehicle operation, driver competence and enforcement; temporary traffic control in construction and maintenance work zones; accident reconstruction. *Mailing Add:* 654 Watershaw Dr Friendsville TN 37737

HUMPHREYS, JAN GORDON, ENTOMOLOGY. *Current Pos:* Prof zool, 69-80, PROF ZOOL & BIOL, INDIANA UNIV, PA, 80- *Personal Data:* b Jackson, Ohio, Mar 24, 41; m 64; c 8. *Educ:* Ohio Univ, BS, 63, MS, 65; Va Polytech Inst, PhD(med entom), 69. *Concurrent Pos:* Mem bd dirs, Marine Sci Consort, 75-80. *Mem:* Sigma Xi; Soc Vector Ecologists. *Res:* Use of wildlife to monitor Lyme Disease; biology of squirrel fleas on the family Sciuridae; parasites of hyraxes in southern Africa. *Mailing Add:* Dept Biol WEY 325 Indiana Univ Pa Indiana PA 15705-0001

HUMPHREYS, KENNETH K, COST ENGINEERING, PROJECT ENGINEERING. *Current Pos:* RETIRED. *Personal Data:* b Pittsburgh, Pa, Jan 19, 38; m 61; c 4. *Educ:* Carnegie Inst Technol, Pittsburgh, Pa, BS, 55; WVa Univ, Morgantown, MSE, 68; Kennedy-Western Univ, Agoura Hills, Calif, PhD(eng mgt), 90. *Honors & Awards:* Award of Merit, Am Asn Cost Engrs Int, 93. *Prof Exp:* Res engr, Appl Res Lab, US Steel Corp, 59-65; from assoc dir to asst dir & cost engr, WVa State Bur Coal Res, 65-82; asst dean, prof & chmn mineral processing, Col Mineral & Energy Resources, WVa Univ, 70-81, adj prof, 81-93; eng consult, 93. *Concurrent Pos:* Consult, var indust firms & govt agencies, 65-81; dir, Am Asn Cost Engrs, 71, exec dir, 71-93. *Mem:* Fel Am Asn Cost Engrs; Int Cost Eng Coun (secy-treas, 76-); Mex Soc Cost & Econ Eng; fel Asn Cost Engrs UK; Nat Soc Prof Engrs; Coun Eng & Sci Soc Exec. *Res:* Cost and optimization engineering; coal utilization; coke production; fuel technology; ferrous metallurgy. *Mailing Add:* 23 Hidden Lake Dr Granite Falls NC 28630. *Fax:* 704-728-5287

HUMPHREYS, MABEL GWENETH, MATHEMATICS. *Current Pos:* from assoc prof to prof math & chmn dept, 50-73, Dana prof, 73-80, EMER DANA PROF MATH, RANDOLPH-MACON WOMAN'S COL, 80- *Personal Data:* b Vancouver, BC, Oct 22, 11; nat US. *Educ:* Univ BC, BA, 32; Smith Col, AM, 33; Univ Chicago, PhD(math), 35. *Prof Exp:* Instr math & physics, Mt St Scholastica Col, 35-36; from instr to asst prof math, Newcomb Col, Tulane Univ, 36-49. *Concurrent Pos:* Fac fel, Fund Adv Ed, 55-56; NSF fac fel, 62-63. *Mem:* Am Math Soc; Math Asn Am; Can Math Soc. *Res:* Linear algebra; theory of numbers. *Mailing Add:* 1824 Clayton Ave Lynchburg VA 24503

HUMPHREYS, ROBERT EDWARD, IMMUNOCHEMISTRY, BIOCHEMISTRY. *Current Pos:* asst prof, 75-78, assoc prof, 78-86, PROF PHARMACOL & MED, UNIV MASS MED SCH, 86- *Personal Data:* b New York, NY, Dec 24, 42; m 68, Barbara Kemp; c David J & Daniel M. *Educ:* Yale Col, BS, 64; Yale Grad Sch, PhD(biochem), 69; Yale Med Sch, MD, 70. *Prof Exp:* Intern, US Naval Hosp, Bethesda, 70-71; med officer, US Naval Med Res Inst, 71-73; res fel biochem, Harvard Univ, 73-75. *Concurrent Pos:* Anna Fuller Fund fel, 73-74; USPHS fel, 74-75; Am Cancer Soc, Mass Div, cancer res scholar, 76-79. *Mem:* Am Asn Immunologists. *Res:* Regulation antigen processing and presentation; protein folding; vaccine design. *Mailing Add:* Univ Mass Med Sch 55 Lake Ave Worcester MA 01605-0126. *Fax:* 508-856-5080; *E-Mail:* reh@umassmed.ummed.edu

HUMPHREYS, ROBERT WILLIAM RILEY, ADHESIVES CHEMISTRY, ORGANIC PHOTOCHEMISTRY. *Current Pos:* SR DIR CORP RES, NAT STARCH & CHEM CO, 93- *Personal Data:* b Ottawa, Ont, April 25, 51; m 80. *Educ:* Univ Western Ont, BSc, 74, PhD(chem), 78. *Prof Exp:* Fel chem, Univ Utah, 79-80; res chemist, Loctite Corp, 80-83; staff, Lever Res Inc, 83-93. *Mem:* Am Chem Soc. *Res:* Peroxide and hydroperoxide chemistry; autoxidation; organic and organometallic photochemistry; free radical chemistry including polymerization; chemistry of charge-transfer complexes; polymer modification. *Mailing Add:* Nat Starch & Chem Co 10 Finderne Ave Bridgewater NJ 08807

HUMPHREYS, ROBERTA MARIE, ASTRONOMY. *Current Pos:* from asst prof to assoc prof, 72-83, PROF ASTRON, UNIV MINN, 83- *Personal Data:* b Indianapolis, Ind, May 20, 44; m 76; c 1. *Educ:* Ind Univ, AB, 65; Univ Mich, MS, 67, PhD(astron), 69. *Honors & Awards:* George Taylor Award, 85; Humboldt Distinguished Sr Scientist Award, Fed Repub Ger. *Prof Exp:* Res assoc astron, Dyer Observ, Vanderbilt Univ, 69-70 & Steward Observ, Univ Ariz, 70-72. *Concurrent Pos:* Alfred P Sloan Found fel, 76-78; dir, Asn Univ Res Astron, 81-84; mem, NSF Astron Adv Comt, 81-84. *Mem:* Am Astron Soc; Int Astron Union; fel AAAS; Sigma Xi. *Res:* Galactic structure; stellar spectroscopy; infrared sources. *Mailing Add:* 594 Pond View Dr St Paul MN 55120

HUMPHREYS, SUSIE HUNT, CELL BIOLOGY, FOOD SCIENCE & TECHNOLOGY. *Current Pos:* SR RES SCIENTIST, KRAFT, INC, 83- *Personal Data:* b Jackson, Miss, June 15, 39; div; c 1. *Educ:* Univ Chicago, BS, 60, MS, 62; Harvard Univ, PhD(biol), 69. *Prof Exp:* Res biologist, Univ Calif, San Diego, 66-69; trainee, Salk Inst Biol Studies, 69-71; asst researcher biol, Pac Biomed Res Ctr, Univ Hawaii, 72-79; sr staff fel, NIH, 79-83. *Mem:* Am Soc Cell Biol; Inst Food Technologists; Electron Micros Soc Am. *Mailing Add:* HFF-156 CFSAN FDA 200 C St SW Washington DC 20204-0001. *Fax:* 202-260-0498

HUMPHREYS, THOMAS ELDER, PLANT BIOCHEMISTRY. *Current Pos:* RETIRED. *Personal Data:* b Lakewood, Ohio, Feb 10, 24; m 54. *Educ:* Ohio State Univ, BS, 49, MS, 50; Univ Pa, PhD(bot), 54. *Prof Exp:* Jr res biochemist, Univ Calif, 53-55; from asst biochemist to biochemist, Univ Fla, 55-92, prof bot, 68-80, prof, Dept Veg Crops, 80-92. *Mem:* Am Soc Plant Physiol; Sigma Xi. *Res:* Carbohydrate metabolism; sugar transport. *Mailing Add:* 4006 SW 21st St Gainesville FL 32608

HUMPHREYS, TOM DANIEL, ZOOLOGY, IMMUNOLOGY. *Current Pos:* exec dir, 86-88, CHMN, CELL, MOLECULAR & NEUROSCI GRAD PROG, CANCER RES CTR, 88-; PROF GENETICS & MOLECULAR BIOL, KEWALO MARINE LAB & CANCER RES CTR, UNIV HAWAII, 77- *Personal Data:* b Arlington, Tenn, June 22, 36; div; c 1. *Educ:* Univ Chicago, BS, 58, PhD(zool), 62. *Prof Exp:* NSF fel biol, Mass Inst Technol, 62-63; asst prof, 63-66; asst prof, Revelle Col, Univ Calif, San Diego, 66-71; assoc prof biochem, Kewalo Marine Lab Exp Biol, Pac Biomed Res Ctr, Univ Hawaii, 71-77. *Concurrent Pos:* Dir embryol, Marine Biol Lab, Woods Hole, Mass, 75-79; dir basic sci, Cancer Res Ctr, Hawaii, 86- *Mem:* Biophys Soc; Soc Develop Biol; Am Soc Cell Biol; Marine Biol Lab Corp. *Res:* Mechanisms of cell adhesion; invertebrate immune recognition. *Mailing Add:* Kewalo Marine Lab Univ Hawaii 41 Ahui St Honolulu HI 96813. *Fax:* 808-599-4817

HUMPHREYS, WALTER JAMES, biological structure; deceased, see previous edition for last biography

HUMPHRIES, ARTHUR LEE, JR, SURGERY. *Current Pos:* From instr to assoc prof, 60-70, PROF SURG, MED COL GA, 70- *Personal Data:* b Rock Hill, SC, 1928. *Educ:* The Citadel, BS, 48; Johns Hopkins Univ, MD, 52; Am Bd Surg, dipl, 62. *Concurrent Pos:* NIH res grant, 61- *Mem:* Transplantation Soc; Am Soc Artificial Internal Organs; Soc Univ Surg. *Res:* Transplantation; storage of dog kidney by hypothermic perfusion. *Mailing Add:* Med Col Ga Hosp 1120 15th St Augusta GA 30912

HUMPHRIES, ASA ALAN, JR, CELL BIOLOGY, ZOOLOGY. *Current Pos:* prof biol & vpres, 81-83, DEAN COL, TRANSYLVANIA UNIV, 81-, EXEC VPRES, 83- *Personal Data:* b Anniston, Ala, Sept 6, 24; m 49, 72; c 4. *Educ:* Emory Univ, AB, 48, MS, 49; Princeton Univ, AM, 52, PhD(biol), 53. *Prof Exp:* Asst biol, Emory Univ, 48-49, instr, 49-50; asst instr, Princeton Univ, 50-52; instr anat, Univ Va, 53-54; from asst prof to prof biol, Emory Univ, 54-81, chmn dept, 74-81. *Concurrent Pos:* NSF sr fel, Free Univ Brussels, 62-63; NATO sr sci fel, Lab Molecular Embryol, Naples, 71; Physiol Lab, Univ Cambridge, 78; scholar, Bellagio Study & Conf Ctr, Italy, 83. *Mem:* AAAS; Soc Develop Biol; Am Soc Cell Biol; Int Soc Develop Biol; Soc Study Fertility; Sigma Xi. *Res:* Embryology of amphibians; gametogenesis; control of cell division; heteroploidy; fertilization. *Mailing Add:* 2009 Des Cognet Lane Lexington KY 40502-3040

HUMPHRIES, ERVIN G(RIGG), AGRICULTURAL ENGINEERING. *Current Pos:* Res instr, 61-64, from asst prof to assoc prof, 64-73, PROF AGR ENG, NC STATE UNIV, 73- *Personal Data:* b Shelby, NC, Apr 26, 36; m 58; c 2. *Educ:* NC State Univ, BS, 58, MS, 60, PhD(agr eng), 64. *Concurrent Pos:* Indust consult food processing equip. *Mem:* Am Soc Agr Engrs; Sigma Xi. *Res:* Investigations of the interaction of biological and engineering systems as related to production, harvesting and storage of food and fiber; physical properties of biological materials pertinent to engineering design. *Mailing Add:* Dept Agr Eng Box 7625 NC State Univ Raleigh NC 27695-7625. *Fax:* 919-515-7760; *E-Mail:* humphries@eosncsu

HUMPHRIES, J O'NEAL, MEDICINE. *Current Pos:* PROF MED & CHMN, DEPT MED, SCH MED, UNIV SC, 79-, DEAN, SCH MED. *Personal Data:* b Columbia, SC, Oct 22, 31; m 54; c 3. *Educ:* Duke Univ, AB, 52; Johns Hopkins Univ, MD, 56. *Prof Exp:* Res fel cardiol, Sch Med, Johns Hopkins Univ, 56-57 & 61-62, St George's Hosp, Univ London, 60-61; from instr to assoc prof, Johns Hopkins Univ, 64-76, assoc prof, 76-78, prof med, 78-79. *Concurrent Pos:* Consult, Union Mem Hosp, 64-; consult, Vet Admin Hosp, 69-; chmn Subspecialty Bd in Cardiovascular Dis, 76-79. *Mem:* Am Fedn Clin Res; Asn Univ Cardiologists; fel Am Col Physicians; fel Am Col Cardiol; Am Clin & Climat Asn. *Mailing Add:* Sch Med Univ SC Columbia SC 29208

HUMPHRIES, JACK THOMAS, PHYSICS, NUCLEAR ENGINEERING. *Current Pos:* prof natural sci & technol & asst dean, 72-93, PROF NATURAL SCI, UNIV NFLA, 93- *Personal Data:* b Middlesboro, Ky, May 7, 29; m 51; c 2. *Educ:* Univ Ky, BS, 51; US Air Force Inst Technol, MS, 58; Univ Fla, PhD(nuclear eng), 66. *Prof Exp:* Physicist, Mat Lab, Wright Air Develop Ctr, Ohio, 51-53; proj officer reactor shield mat, Mat Lab, Wright Air Develop Ctr, USAF, 53-56, instr physics, USAF Acad, 58-59, asst prof, 59-63, tenure prof, 66-72, head dept, 70-71. *Concurrent Pos:* Honorarium lectr, Univ Colo, Colorado Springs, 66-68; vis scholar, Dakota State Col, 71; interim dean, Col Arts & Sci, 78-80. *Mem:* Sigma Xi; Am Asn Physics Teachers. *Res:* Control of nuclear rocket engines; applications of nuclear radiation; reactor shielding materials; computers in physics instruction; attitudes of students toward science; calculus-based physics curricula. *Mailing Add:* 4198 Paloma Point Ct Jacksonville FL 32217-4303

HUMPHRIES, JAMES EDWARD, JR, TEACHING ADMINISTRATION, TECHNOLOGY APPLICATIONS. *Current Pos:* assoc prof, 71-82, PROF & HEAD EARTH SCI, E TEX STATE UNIV, 82- *Personal Data:* b Shreveport, La, Aug 7, 40; m 63; c 1. *Educ:* Sam Houston State Univ, BS, 65, MEd, 66; Univ Okla, PhD(biogeog), 71. *Prof Exp:* Instr geog, Univ Okla, 70-71. *Mem:* Asn Am Geogr; Asn Arid Land Studies; Am Geog Soc. *Res:* Distribution and adaptation of Mesquite (Prosopis glandulosa) in humid environments; ethnobotany of native species in arid and semi-arid regions; appropriate technologies in developing nations. *Mailing Add:* Dept Earth Sci ETex State Univ ETex Sta Commerce TX 75428-9998

HUMPHRIES, LAURIE LEE, NUTRITION, MEDICINE. *Current Pos:* from asst prof to assoc prof, 81-91, PROF CHILD PSYCHIAT, COL MED, UNIV KY, 91- *Personal Data:* b Atlanta, Ga, Apr 26, 44; m 72; c 1. *Educ:* Emory Univ, BA, 66, MD, 73. *Prof Exp:* Resident adult psychiat, Emory Univ Sch Med, 73-75, fel child psychiat, 75-77, asst prof, 78-81. *Concurrent Pos:* Prin investr, zinc & eating dis, NIMH, 86-88, zinc deficiency in eating dis, McKnight Found, 86-90 & child & adolescent acad award, NIMH, 89- *Mem:* Am Acad Child & Adolescent Psychiat; Am Psychiat Asn; AMA; AAAS. *Res:* Study of nutritional factors, particulary zinc deficiency on anorexia nervosa and bulimia nervosa; medical complications of eating disorders. *Mailing Add:* Dept Psychiat Univ Ky Chambers Bldg Annex No 4 Lexington KY 40536-0226

HUMPHRIES, ROBERT GORDON, meteorology, for more information see previous edition

HUMPHRIES, STANLEY, JR, COMPUTER MODELING OF ELECTROMAGNETIC FIELDS & CHARGED PARTICLE DYNAMICS, DESIGN OF PULSED POWER SYSTEMS & PARTICLE ACCELERATORS. *Current Pos:* STAFF PHYSICIST, SANDIA NAT LABS, 77-; PROF ELEC ENG, UNIV NMEX, 81- *Personal Data:* b Paterson, NJ, Feb 25, 46; c Colin J & Courtney E. *Educ:* Mass Inst Technol, BS, 68; Univ Calif, MS, 70, PhD(nuclear eng), 71. *Prof Exp:* Staff physicist, Livermore Nat Lab, 71-72; researcher, Los Alamos Nat Lab, 72-73; asst prof, Cornell Univ, 73-77. *Concurrent Pos:* Consult, Naval Res Lab, 87-91, Los Alamos Nat Lab, 83-; pres, Acceleration Assocs, 88-; partner, Arc Eng, 91- *Mem:* Fel Am Phys Soc; fel Inst Elec & Electronics Engrs. *Res:* Have published 2 text books and over 120 papers in the fields of intense charged particle beams, accelerator applications, controlled fusion, pulsed power technology and ion sources. *Mailing Add:* 13407 Sunset Canyon NE Albuquerque NM 87111. *Fax:* 505-294-0222

HUMPHRIS, ROBERT R, electrical engineering, for more information see previous edition

HUNDAL, MAHENDRA S(INGH), MECHANICAL ENGINEERING. *Current Pos:* assoc prof, 67-77, PROF MECH ENG, UNIV VT, 77- *Personal Data:* b Syana, India, Nov 25 34; nat US; m 64; c 1. *Educ:* Osmania Univ, India, BE, 54; Univ Wis, MS, 62, PhD(mech eng), 64. *Honors & Awards:* R R Teetor Award, Soc Automotive Engrs, 67. *Prof Exp:* Design engr, Tata Iron & Steel Co, India, 55-60; asst prof eng, San Diego State Col, 64-67. *Concurrent Pos:* Fulbright award, 87. *Mem:* Am Soc Mech Engrs; Inst Noise Control Engrs; Sigma Xi. *Res:* Design methods; computer-aided design; modeling of dynamic systems; industrial noise control. *Mailing Add:* Dept Mech Eng Votey Bldg Univ Vt Burlington VT 05405

HUNDERT, IRWIN, PETROLEUM REFING, ENVIRONMENTAL TRAINING. *Current Pos:* VIS PROF CHEM ENG & ENVIRON SCI, NJ INST TECHNOL, 83- *Personal Data:* b New York, NY, Nov 9, 25; m 48; c 2. *Educ:* City Col New York, BChE, 45; NY Univ, MChE, 48. *Prof Exp:* Process & design engr, Heyden Chem Corp, 45-50; sr engr ref, supply & mkt, Chevron Corp, 50-83. *Concurrent Pos:* Consult, Chevron Corp, Amerada Hess Corp, Englehardt Corp & Intercontinental Hotel; prin investr, Alt Teaching Mat/Energy Balances; assoc, var precol progs. *Mem:* Sigma Xi; Am Inst Chem Engrs. *Res:* Energy production; hazardous waste; precollege activities. *Mailing Add:* 48 Dutch Rd East Brunswick NJ 08816

HUNDERT, MURRAY BERNARD, POLYMER CHEMISTRY, ORGANIC CHEMISTRY. *Current Pos:* RETIRED. *Personal Data:* b New York, NY, Sept 15, 19; m 48, Rose Kordish; c Eric & Steven. *Educ:* Brooklyn Col, BA, 40; NY Univ, MS, 43, PhD, 50. *Prof Exp:* Sr res chemist, US Indust Chems, Inc, 42-48; proj leader, Heyden-Newport Chem Corp, 48-50; tech dir, Crownoil Chem Co, Inc, 50-61 & Farnow, Inc, 61-62; from asst prof to prof chem, Fairleigh Dickinson Univ, 62-85, dep chmn, 63-65, chmn dept, 71-73 & 82-85. *Concurrent Pos:* Vis instr, NY Community Col, 57-62; consult; vis prof, Col Physicians & Surgeons, Columbia Univ, 81. *Mem:* AAAS; Am Chem Soc; Sigma Xi. *Res:* Polymer preparation and characterization; protective coatings, latexes, product development and synthetic organic chemistry. *Mailing Add:* 46 Wingate Dr Livingston NJ 07039-3518

HUNDHAUSEN, ARTHUR JAMES, THEORETICAL PHYSICS, ASTROPHYSICS. *Current Pos:* STAFF SCIENTIST, HIGH ALTITUDE OBSERV, 71- *Personal Data:* b Wausau, Wis, Aug 2, 36; m 68; c 2. *Educ:* Univ Wis, BS, 58, MS, 59, PhD(physics), 65. *Prof Exp:* Mem staff theoret div, Los Alamos Sci Lab, Univ Calif, 64-71. *Concurrent Pos:* Lectr, Univ Colo, 71- *Mem:* AAAS; Am Geophys Union; Am Astron Soc. *Res:* Observations and theoretical models of the interplanetary plasma and its interaction with the geomagnetic field; physical processes in tenuous plasmas. *Mailing Add:* 669 Linden Park Dr Boulder CO 80304

HUNDHAUSEN, JOAN ROHRER, MATHEMATICS. *Current Pos:* adj asst prof, 74-75, asst prof, 75-80, ASSOC PROF MATH, COLO SCH MINES, 80- *Personal Data:* b Pittsburgh, Pa; m 67; c 3. *Educ:* Duquesne Univ, BS, 58; Univ Wis, MS, 59; Carnegie-Mellon Univ, PhD(math), 67. *Prof Exp:* Instr math, Duquesne Univ, 59-61 & 62-63, asst prof, 64; staff mem, Los Alamos Sci Lab, Univ Calif, 67-71. *Concurrent Pos:* Adj prof, Univ NMex, 68-71; mem, Consortium Coun Undergrad Math & Its Appl, 80-83, Comt Placement Exams, Math Asn Am, 86-89, subcomt symbolic computation, Comt Undergrad Prog Math, 89-92, Comt Classroom Res Mat, 91-, Comt Minicourses, 92-; prin investr, Curric Develop Prog Calculus, NSF, 88-91; prog chmn, Math Div, Am Soc Eng Educ, 91-92, div chmn, 92-93. *Mem:* Am Math Soc; Sigma Xi; Asn Women Math; Math Asn Am; Am Soc Eng Educ. *Res:* Discrete function theory; differential equations; complex analysis; interface issues of mathematics and science/engineering; mathematics applied to physics/astrophysical phenomena. *Mailing Add:* 669 Linden Park Dr Boulder CO 80304

HUNDLEY, JOHN GOWER, CHEMICAL ENGINEERING. *Current Pos:* Engr res & develop, 53-57, asst proj engr, 57-59, proj engr, 59-61, proj engr res dept, Amoco Chem, 61-62, sr proj engr, 62-66, sr res engr, 66-67, group leader, 67-70, sect leader, Am Chem Corp, 70-85, RES ASSOC, AMOCO CHEM CO, STANDARD OIL CO, 85- *Personal Data:* b New Orleans, La, Feb 19, 29; m 58; c 2. *Educ:* Univ NDak, BS, 50; Univ Wis, MS, 51, PhD(chem eng), 53. *Mem:* Am Chem Soc. *Res:* Chemical process development; chemical plant design; process economics. *Mailing Add:* 4N159 Wild Rose Rd St Charles IL 60174

HUNDLEY, LOUIS REAMS, PHYSIOLOGY. *Current Pos:* RETIRED. *Personal Data:* b Greenwood, Va, May 22, 26; m 53, Katheryne Tindall; c Mary Louise. *Educ:* Va Mil Inst, BS, 50; Va Polytech Inst & State Univ, MS, 53, PhD(biol), 56. *Prof Exp:* Asst instr biol, Va Mil Inst, 50-51; wildlife biologist, Va Coop Wildlife Res Unit, 52-53; grad asst biol, Va Polytech Inst, 53-54 & Va Agr Exp Sta, 54-56; from asst prof to prof, Va Mil Inst, 56-90, actg head dept, 65-67. *Mem:* AAAS; Am Physiol Soc; Am Inst Biol Sci. *Res:* Fat-free body weight; gross body composition; nutrients in deer browse. *Mailing Add:* 4 Ringneck Rd Lexington VA 24450

HUNDLEY, RICHARD O'NEIL, THEORETICAL PHYSICS. *Current Pos:* prod mgr, 72-83, VPRES, R&D ASSOCS, 83- *Personal Data:* b Joliet, Ill, May 27, 35; m 57; c 3. *Educ:* Calif Inst Technol, BS, 57, MS, 59, PhD(physics), 63. *Prof Exp:* Consult, Rand Corp, 60-62, phys scientist, 62-72. *Concurrent Pos:* Mem, Army Sci Adv Panel, 72-78, Army Sci Bd, 78-80. *Mem:* AAAS; Am Phys Soc. *Res:* Quantum mechanics; quantum field theory; atomic and molecular physics; reentry physics; nuclear weapon effects; military systems research; laser physics; laser and satellite systems; electrooptic systems. *Mailing Add:* Rand Corp PO Box 2138 Santa Monica CA 90407

HUNEKE, HAROLD VERNON, MATHEMATICS. *Current Pos:* RETIRED. *Personal Data:* b Arnett, Okla, Aug 26, 17; m 48; c 2. *Educ:* Northwestern State Col, AB, 36; Univ Okla, MA, 41, PhD(math), 57. *Prof Exp:* Asst, Univ Okla, 39-42; head dept math, Northwestern State Col, Okla, 46-48; prof math, Univ Wichita, 51-60; assoc prof, Univ Okla, 60-67, prof math, 67-81. *Concurrent Pos:* Mem New Delhi staff, NSF, 69-71. *Mem:* Math Asn Am. *Res:* Changes in undergraduate and teacher education programs. *Mailing Add:* 517 S Flood Ave Norman OK 73069

HUNEKE, JOHN PHILIP, MATHEMATICS. *Current Pos:* from asst prof to assoc prof, 69-82, vchmn, 80-95, PROF MATH, OHIO STATE UNIV, 82-*Personal Data:* b Spokane, Wash, Apr 16, 42; m 65; c 4. *Educ:* Pomona Col, BA, 64; Wesleyan Univ, PhD(math), 67. *Prof Exp:* Dunham Jackson res instr math, Univ Minn, Minneapolis, 67-69, asst prof, 69-70. *Mem:* Am Math Soc; Math Asn Am. *Res:* Commuting functions; combinatorial topology; topological graph theory; topological dynamics. *Mailing Add:* 2086 Iuka Ave Columbus OH 43201

HUNEYCUTT, JAMES ERNEST, JR, WEAPON SYSTEM ANALYSIS. *Current Pos:* MATHEMATICIAN, APPL PHYSICS LAB, JOHNS HOPKINS UNIV, 82- *Personal Data:* b Gastonia, NC, Dec 14, 42; m 64. *Educ:* Univ NC, Chapel Hill, BS, 63, MA, 65, PhD(math), 68. *Prof Exp:* Asst prof math, NC State Univ, 68-73, assoc prof, 73-78; sr software engr, Hadron Inc, 78-82. *Mem:* Inst Elec & Electronics Engrs; Math Asn Am; Soc Indust Appl Math; Sigma Xi. *Res:* Linear error analysis; software development; vector measures and integration; probability; estimation; Kalman filtering. *Mailing Add:* Box 157 Bluemont VA 20135

HUNEYCUTT, MAEBURN BRUCE, mycology, for more information see previous edition

HUNG, GEORGE WEN-CHI, ANALYTICAL CHEMISTRY, PHYSICAL CHEMISTRY. *Current Pos:* ASSOC PROF CHEM DEPT, UNIV MONTEVALLO, AL, 84- *Personal Data:* b Penghu, Taiwan, Oct 14, 32; US citizen; m 63; c 2. *Educ:* Tamkang Col Arts & Sci, Taiwan, 62; Auburn Univ, PhD(anal chem), 70. *Prof Exp:* Asst instr chem, Tamkang Col Arts & Sci, 62-65; res assoc, Univ Tenn Med Units, 70-72; res fel & NIH trainee, St Jude Children's Res Hosp, Memphis, 72-73; res assoc toxicol & biomat, Ctr Health Sci, Univ Tenn, 73-76; res scientist & head chemist, 76-77, dir & res scientist, Woodson-Tenent Labs, Nat Health Labs, Inc, Memphis, 78-83. *Mem:* Am Chem Soc; Chem Soc Japan; AAAS; Am Soc Testing & Mat; fel Am Inst Chemists. *Res:* Trace and ultratrace analysis of inorganic and organic compounds in biological and environmental systems by atomic absorption spectrophotometry and gas-liquid and high performance liquid chromatography. *Mailing Add:* 2428 Mountain Run Birmingham AL 35244-3400

HUNG, JAMES CHEN, SYSTEMS & CONTROL ENGINEERING. *Current Pos:* VPRES, POLY-ANALYTICS INC, KNOXVILLE, TN, 81-; DISTINGUISHED SERV PROF, ELEC ENG DEPT, UNIV TENN, KNOXVILLE, 84- *Personal Data:* b Foochow, China, Feb 18, 29; nat US; m 58, Sufenne Hiuang; c John, Samuel & Stephen. *Educ:* Nat Taiwan Univ, BS, 53; NY Univ, MEE, 56, ScD(elec eng), 61. *Honors & Awards:* Anthony J Hornfeck Serv Award, Inst Elec & Electronics Engrs, 95. *Prof Exp:* Asst elec eng, NY Univ, 54-56, instr, 56-61, from asst prof to prof, 61-83. *Concurrent Pos:* Prin investr, NASA, 63-83, Army Res Off, US Army, 73-89; mem tech staff, IBM, Poughkeepsie, 67-68; eng consult, US Army Missile Command, 75-80; consult prof, Northwestern Polytech Univ, Xian, China, Chongging Univ & Southwest China Teachers Univ, 84-; assoc ed, Inst Elec & Electronics Engrs Trans Indust Electronics, 85-90, ed, 91-95, distinguished lectr, 94-, pres elect, 97; mem admin comt, Inst Elec & Electronics Engrs, 85-; consult investr, US Army, 89; hon prof, Nanjing Aeronaut Inst, 89- & Hunan Univ, 96- *Mem:* Fel Inst Elec & Electronics Engrs; Sigma Xi. *Res:* System analysis, development and design; control engineering; system instrumentation, measurement, testing and evaluation; digital information and data processing; navigation and guidance systems; robotics and automation; 180 publications. *Mailing Add:* Dept Elec & Comput Eng Univ Tenn Knoxville TN 37996-2100

HUNG, JAMES Y(UN-YANN), ENGINEERING MECHANICS, HEAT & MASS TRANSFER. *Current Pos:* PRES, HUNG INT ENTERPRISES INC, 91- *Personal Data:* b Tuinan, China, Oct 3, 35; m 62, Winifred H Wu; c Merit Y & Andy C. *Educ:* Cheng Kung Univ, Taiwan, BS, 58; Univ Mass, MS, 61; Univ Wis, PhD(eng mech), 68. *Prof Exp:* Assoc prof math & physics, Inst Paper Chem, 67-77; sr appln engr, Voith Inc, 78-83; sr res assoc, Tec Systs, 84-91. *Concurrent Pos:* Tech consult press & dryer fabrics, Appleton Mills & Lindsay Wire. *Mem:* Am Soc Mech Engrs; Am Soc Eng Educ; Tech Asn Pulp & Paper Indust. *Res:* Applied mechanics and mathematics; computer simulations; 25 years of research experience in paper, coating and ink drying. *Mailing Add:* 3511 N Bracken Dr Appleton WI 54911-8502. *Fax:* 920-734-5386

HUNG, KUEN-SHAN, ANATOMY, HISTOLOGY. *Current Pos:* from asst prof to assoc prof, 74-83, PROF ANAT, UNIV KANS MED CTR, 83- *Personal Data:* b Chia-Yi, Taiwan, Jan 13, 38; m 68; c 2. *Educ:* Nat Taiwan Univ, BS, 60; Univ Kans, PhD(anat), 69. *Prof Exp:* Teaching asst anat, Col Med, Nat Taiwan Univ, 61-64; teaching asst, Med Ctr, Univ Kans, 64-69; asst prof, Univ SDak, 69-71; asst prof path & anat, Univ Southern Calif, 71-74. *Concurrent Pos:* Gen res support grant, Univ SDak, 69-71; Am Lung Asn res grant, 74-76; NIH, 76-81; affil, Am Heart Asn, Kansas, 81-87, 90-91. *Mem:* Electron Micros Soc Am; Am Asn Anatomists; Am Soc Cell Biol. *Res:* Innervation of lungs; hypoxia induced pulmonary hypertension; pulmonary endocrine cells. *Mailing Add:* Dept Anat Univ Kans Med Ctrr 3901 Rainbow Blvd Kansas City KS 66160-7400

HUNG, PAUL LING-KONG, CATIONIC MONOMERS & POLYMERS FOR WATER TREATMENT, PRINTED CIRCUIT BOARD FABRICATION. *Current Pos:* MGR RES & DEVELOP, CPS CHEM INC, 91- *Personal Data:* b Hong Kong, Nov 5, 47; US citizen; m, Pao F Chen; c Harry D & Helen D. *Educ:* McGill Univ, BS, 70; Mass Inst Technol, MS, 73; Rutgers Univ, PhD(org chem), 81. *Prof Exp:* Mgr res & develop, M&T Chem, Elf Aquitaine Group, 82-90, Elf Atochem NA, 90-91. *Mem:* Am Chem Soc; Soc Plastics Engrs; Soc Advan Mat & Process Eng. *Res:* Syntheses and applications of materials, monomers and polymers for microelectronics, printed circuit board fabrication, radiation curing, water treatment, polyelectrolytes and adhesives; formulate coatings (high solids, water borne and hundred percent reactive); plastic applications by formulation of thermoplastic resins and additives for processing by injection molding, extrusion and calendering; electroplating chemicals and processes. *Mailing Add:* 130 Hill Hollow Rd Watchung NJ 07060. *Fax:* 908-755-5118

HUNG, PAUL P, VIROLOGY, MOLECULAR BIOLOGY. *Current Pos:* ASST VPRES, BIOTECHNOL & MICROBIOL DIV, WYETH-AYERST RES, 88- *Personal Data:* b Taipei, Formosa, Sept 30, 33; US citizen; m 56, Nancy K Clark; c Pauline, Eileen & Clark. *Educ:* Millikin Univ, BS, 56; Purdue Univ, MS, 58, PhD(biochem), 60. *Prof Exp:* Res asst biochem, Purdue Univ, 56-60; sr biochemist, Abbott Labs, 60-70, assoc res fel, 70-73, res fel, 73-79, head molecular virol & biol, 74-81; gen mgr, Genetics Div, Bethesda Res Labs, Inc, 81-82; dir, Microbiol Div, Wyeth Labs, 82-88. *Concurrent Pos:* Adj asst prof, Stritch Sch Med, Loyola Univ, Chicago, 68-72; vis res fel, Sch Med, Stanford Univ, 69-70; adj assoc prof, Stritch Sch Med, Loyola Univ, Chicago, 72-76; adj prof, Northwestern Univ Med Sch, Chicago, 76-; consult, UN Indust Develop Orgn, 82. *Mem:* Am Chem Soc; Am Soc Biol Chem; Am Asn Cancer Res; Am Soc Microbiol; AAAS; Am Inst Chem. *Res:* Nucleic acid; biosynthesis of antibiotics and carbohydrates; bacteriophages and oncogenic viruses; genetic engineering; vaccines; biopharmaceuticals. *Mailing Add:* Biotechnol & Microbiol Div Wyeth Ayerst Labs PO 8299 Philadelphia PA 19101-8299. *Fax:* 610-989-4588

HUNG, RU J, MICROGRAVITY FLUID MECHANICS, CRYOGENIC FLUID MANAGEMENT. *Current Pos:* PROF MECH ENG, UNIV ALA, HUNTSVILLE, 72- *Personal Data:* b Taiwan, China, June 17, 34; US citizen; m 66, Nancy Lin; c Elmer & Christine. *Educ:* Nat Taiwan Univ, BS, 57; Univ Osaka, MS, 66; Univ Mich, PhD(aerospace), 70. *Honors & Awards:* Nat Acad Sci Res Award; Res Award, Ministry Educ Japan; Res Award, Sigma Xi, Nat Aero Space Admin. *Prof Exp:* Nat Acad Sci res assoc, Ames Res Ctr, NASA, 71-72. *Concurrent Pos:* Prin investr, NASA, 72-, US Army Res Off, 76-78, 90-, Nat Acad Sci, 76-79 & NSF, 76- *Mem:* Assoc fel Am Inst Aeronaut & Astronaut; Am Geophys Union; Am Meteorol Soc; Nat Soc Prof Engrs; fel Royal Meteorol Soc. *Res:* Author or co-author of over 200 articles; space-based propulsion; cryogenic fluid management; fluid mechanics; heat transfer; computational fluid dynamics; propulsion; microgravity fluid mechanics; magneto hydrodynamics; plasma physics; numerical simulation of fog formation due to combustion related pollutants; satellite remote sensing; remote sensing of atmosphere; energy conversion. *Mailing Add:* Dept Mech Eng Univ Ala 4701 Univ NW Huntsville AL 35899. *Fax:* 205-895-6758; *E-Mail:* uahrjho1@asnuah.asn.net

HUNG, TONNEY H M, MECHANICAL ENGINEERING. *Current Pos:* team leader, Systs Analytical Directorate, US Army Weapons Command, 68-71, Syst Res Div, Res Develop & Eng Directorate, 71-75, prog dir, US Army Res Command, 75-77, chief aircraft armament team, 77-80, chief systs eng br, Fir Control & Small Caliber Weapons Systs Lab, Armament Res & Develop Command, 80-, SCI ADV, US ARMY JAPAN/XI CORPS. *Personal Data:* b Formosa, Nov 5, 32; m 65; c 1. *Educ:* Cheng Kung Univ, Taiwan, BS, 55; Kans State Univ, MS, 61, PhD(mech eng), 64. *Prof Exp:* Design & systs control engr, Taiwan Power Co, 56-59; asst fluid mech, Cheng Kung Univ, 59; res asst mech eng, Kans State Univ, 60-64; sr res engr, Appl Sci Dept, Deere & Co, 64-68. *Concurrent Pos:* Lectr, Univ Iowa, 68-69; mem Simulation Coun. *Mem:* Am Soc Mech Engrs; Sigma Xi. *Res:* Heat transfer systems dynamics control; ordnance systems science and design. *Mailing Add:* 7 Nuko Terr Randolph NJ 07869

HUNG, WILLIAM MO-WEI, POLYMER CHEMISTRY. *Current Pos:* STAFF RES SCIENTIST, CIBA VISION CORP, 87- *Personal Data:* b Chi-Kiang, China, Sept 17, 40; US citizen; m 68; c 2. *Educ:* Nat Chung-Hsing Univ, Taiwan, BS, 63; Univ Mass, Amherst, PhD(org chem), 70. *Prof Exp:* Res assoc, Ohio State Univ, 70-74; res chemist, Hilton-Davis Chem Co, 74-80, dir chem res, 80-84, sr res fel, 84-87. *Mem:* Am Chem Soc. *Res:* Organic synthesis, dye and intermediates; contact lens materials and selections. *Mailing Add:* c/o Tech Res Int 5000 McGinnis Ferry Rd Alpharetta GA 30201-3919

HUNG, YOU-TSAI JOSEPH, IRRIGATION ENGINEERING. *Current Pos:* from asst prof to assoc prof, 69-77, prof agr eng, 77-97, EMER PROF AGR ENG, CALIF STATE POLYTECH UNIV, ROMONA, 97- *Personal Data:* b Chunan, Taiwan, Aug 21, 32; m 61; c 3. *Educ:* Nat Taiwan Univ, BS, 56; Mich State Univ, MS, 64, PhD(agr eng), 69. *Prof Exp:* Hydraul engr, Taiwan Soil & Water Conserv Bur, 56-58; asst instr agr eng, Nat Taiwan Univ, 58-63, instr, 64-66; res asst, Mich State Univ, 66-68; civil engr, Mich Dept State Hwy, 68-69. *Concurrent Pos:* Consult, Agr Exp Sta, Hsinchu, Taiwan, 64-66, Irrig & Drainage Comt, Taiwan Sugar Coop, 65-66 & Litton Systs Inc, Calif, 71; mem, Renovated Water Use Study Comt, Calif State Polytech Col, 69-; consult, Ministry Educ, Repub China, 73. *Mem:* Am Soc Agr Eng; Am Soc Eng Educ; Hydraul Eng Soc China; Chinese Soc Agr Eng. *Res:* Soil-water-plant relationships; irrigation and drainage systems design; erosion controls. *Mailing Add:* Dept Agr Eng/Landscape & Irrigation Sci Calif State Polytech Univ 3801 W Temple Ave Pomona CA 91768-4056

HUNGATE, FRANK PORTER, RADIOBIOLOGY. *Current Pos:* RETIRED. *Personal Data:* b Cheney, Wash, June 6, 18; m 41; c 4. *Educ:* Univ Tex, AB, 40; Stanford Univ, PhD(biol), 46. *Honors & Awards:* IR 100 Award. *Prof Exp:* Instr zool, Univ Nev, 45; asst prof, Reed Col, 46-52; res scientist, Biol Sect, Gen Elec Co, 52-53, head plant nutrit & microbiol unit, 53-63; mgr radioecol oper, Hanford Labs, 63-65; mgr radioecol sect, Pac Northwest Lab, Battelle Mem Inst, 65-66, mgr plant physiol & agr sect, 66-68, staff scientist, Biol Dept, 68-82. *Concurrent Pos:* Instr, Univ Calif, Santa Barbara, 48; tech specialist, Int Atomic Energy Agency, Greece, 61-62; biol prog chmn, Joint Ctr, Grad Study, Wash, 67-73; affil assoc prof, Radiol Sci, Univ Wash, 75- *Mem:* AAAS; Genetics Soc Am; Radiation Res Soc; Soc Exp Biol & Med. *Res:* Radiation biology; genetics; transmutation effects; biochemical genetics in yeasts and molds; ion uptake and transport by plants; ecology; metabolism of actinides; genetic effects of microwaves; immunosuppression by blood irradiation; mutational effects from non-ionizing radiations; food irradiation. *Mailing Add:* 7763 Seward Park Ave S Seattle WA 98118

HUNGATE, ROBERT EDWARD, BIOLOGY. *Current Pos:* chmn dept, 56-62, prof bact, 56-73, EMER PROF BACT, UNIV CALIF, DAVIS, 73- *Personal Data:* b Cheney, Wash, Mar 2, 06; m 33; c 3. *Educ:* Stanford Univ, AB, 29, PhD(biol), 35. *Hon Degrees:* Dr, Univ Göttingen, 89. *Honors & Awards:* Fac Res Lectr, Univ Calif, Davis, 67. *Prof Exp:* Actg instr biol, Stanford Univ, 30-33, instr, 33-35; from instr to asst prof zool, Univ Tex, 35-43, assoc prof & res assoc, Biochem Inst, 43-45; from assoc prof to prof bact, State Col Wash, 45-56. *Concurrent Pos:* Guggenheim fel, 50; mem subcomt bloat, Nat Res Coun, 54; vis investr, EAfrica Vet Res Orgn, 57 & Univ Sheffield, 62-63; fac res lectr, Univ Calif, Davis, 67; Fulbright fel, NZ, 69. *Mem:* Am Soc Microbiol (pres, 71); Am Acad Microbiol. *Res:* Cohesion of water; carbohydrate and nitrogen nutrition of termites; biological decomposition of cellulose; nutrition of ruminant protozoa; biology and biochemistry of ruminant cellulose bacteria; growth of mammary cancers in eggs; rates of natural microbial processes; microbiology of acute indigestion and bloat in ruminants; microbiology of sludge; cultivation of strict anaerobes, synthesis in exergonic chemical reactions. *Mailing Add:* 801 Anderson Rd Davis CA 95616

HUNGER, HERBERT FERDINAND, ELECTROCHEMISTRY. *Current Pos:* RETIRED. *Personal Data:* b Vienna, Austria, Aug 25, 27; US citizen; m 55. *Educ:* Univ Vienna, PhD(chem), 55. *Honors & Awards:* Dept of Army Res & Develop Achievement Award, 62. *Prof Exp:* Res asst phys chem, Univ Vienna, 54-56; res chemist, US Army Electronics Res & Develop Command, Ft Monmouth, 56-86. *Concurrent Pos:* Mem, Fuel Cells Res & Develop Panel, President's Interdept Energy Study, 63. *Mem:* Nat Space Soc. *Res:* Fuel cells, hydrogen-oxygen, methanol, biochemical, ion-exchange membranes; direct production of electrical pulses from galvanic cells; mechanism of periodic electrode processes; solid electrolytes; ionic sensors; lithium nonaqueous electrolyte cells. *Mailing Add:* 18 Mark Dr Long Branch NJ 07740

HUNGER, ROBERT MARVIN, WHEAT PATHOLOGY & BREEDING FOR DISEASE RESISTANCE. *Current Pos:* asst prof, 82-87, ASSOC PROF PLANT PATH, OKLA STATE UNIV, 87- *Personal Data:* b Denver, Colo, Jan 14, 54; m 82; c 1. *Educ:* Colo State Univ, BS, 76, MS, 78; Ore State Univ, PhD(plant path), 82. *Mem:* Am Phytopath Soc; Sigma Xi. *Res:* Epidemiological aspects of several fungal and viral pathogens of wheat; development of wheat lines with resistance to diseases caused by these pathogens. *Mailing Add:* Dept Plant Path Okla State Univ Stillwater OK 74078-0001

HUNGERFORD, ED VERNON, III, NUCLEAR PARTICLE PHYSICS. *Current Pos:* assoc prof, 73-79, dept chmn, 80-88, PROF PHYSICS, UNIV HOUSTON, 79- *Personal Data:* b New Orleans, La, Feb 18, 39; m 64; c 2. *Educ:* Ga Inst Technol, PhD(physics), 67. *Prof Exp:* Physicist, Oak Ridge Nat Lab, 67-69; asst prof physics, Rice Univ, 70-73. *Concurrent Pos:* Prin investr, Dept Energy. *Mem:* Fel Am Phys Soc; AAAS. *Res:* Hyperon nuclear interactions; anti nucleon-nucleon interactions; electroweak interactions. *Mailing Add:* Dept Physics Univ Houston Houston TX 77004. *E-Mail:* hunger@uh.edu

HUNGERFORD, GERALD FRED, anatomy, for more information see previous edition

HUNGERFORD, HERBERT EUGENE, NUCLEAR ENGINEERING, RADIATION TRANSPORT & SHIELDING. *Current Pos:* from res asst to instr, 63-64, assoc prof, 64-68, prof, 68-82, EMER PROF NUCLEAR ENG, PURDUE UNIV, 83- *Personal Data:* b Hartford, Conn, Oct 3, 18; m 49. *Educ:* Trinity Col, Conn, BS, 41; Univ Ala, MS, 50; Purdue Univ, PhD(nuclear eng), 65. *Honors & Awards:* Presidential Citation for Significant Contrib to Advan Nuclear Sci & Technol, Am Nuclear Soc, 93. *Prof Exp:* Instr, Brent Sch, Philippine Islands, 41 & Choate Sch, 45-46; head, Dept Physics, Marion Mil Inst, 46-48; physicist & head group, Oak Ridge Nat Lab, 50-54, mem opers team aircraft reactor exp, 54-55; head, Shielding & Health Physics Sect, Atomic Power Develop Assocs, 55-62. *Concurrent Pos:* Consult var orgn. *Mem:* Am Nuclear Soc; Am Phys Soc; Health Physics Soc; Am Asn Physics Teachers; Am Soc Eng Educ. *Res:* Fast reactor shield design; new shield materials; radiation streaming; deep penetration of neutrons; stochastic neutron transport. *Mailing Add:* 2104 Fourth Ct SE Vero Beach FL 32962-7315

HUNGERFORD, KENNETH EUGENE, WILDLIFE ECOLOGY, MANAGEMENT. *Current Pos:* instr & dir, Naval Training Sch, 42-45, instr forestry & wildlife mgt, 46-47, from asst prof to prof wildlife mgt, 48-78, chmn acad, 78-81, EMER PROF WILDLIFE RESOURCES, UNIV IDAHO, 78- *Personal Data:* b Madison, Wis, May 5, 16; m 40, 74; c 3. *Educ:* Univ Idaho, BS, 38; Univ Conn, MS, 40; Univ Mich, PhD(wildlife mgt), 52. *Honors & Awards:* Arthur S Einarson Award, Wildlife Soc, 80. *Prof Exp:* Proj supvr, US Fish & Wildlife Serv, 40; biologist, State Fish & Game Dept, Idaho, 40-42. *Concurrent Pos:* Consult, NZ Forest & Range Exp Sta, 69 & Nat Taiwan Univ, Taipei, China, 74; mem, Idaho Water Resource Bd, 81- *Mem:* Wildlife Soc. *Res:* Ecological life history of the Idaho ruffed grouse; microenvironment, especially dew moisture; whitetailed deer in relation to habitat; environmental impact of animal populations on resource use; behavior of fossorial mammals. *Mailing Add:* 2005 Orchard Ave Moscow ID 83843

HUNGERFORD, THOMAS W, MATHEMATICS. *Current Pos:* chmn, 80-87, PROF, DEPT MATH, CLEVELAND STATE UNIV, 80- *Personal Data:* b Oak Park, Ill, Mar 21, 36; m 58, Mary A Ryan; c Anne E & Thomas J. *Educ:* Col Holy Cross, AB, 58; Univ Chicago, MS, 60, PhD(math), 63. *Prof Exp:* From instr to assoc prof math, Univ Wash, 63-80. *Mem:* Am Math Soc; Math Asn Am. *Res:* Algebra; mathematics education. *Mailing Add:* Dept Math Cleveland State Univ Cleveland OH 44115. *Fax:* 216-687-9366; *E-Mail:* hungerford@math.csuohio.edu

HUNKINS, KENNETH L, ARCTIC OCEAN, COASTAL & ESTUARINE STUDIES. *Current Pos:* Res asst, Lamont Geol Observ, Columbia Univ, 57-60, res scientist, 60-64, sr res scientist, 64-89, adj prof, 74-94, SPEC RES SCIENTIST, LAMONT-DOHERTY GEOL OBSERV, COLUMBIA UNIV, 89- *Personal Data:* b Lake Placid, NY, Mar 3, 28; m 85, Mei Be; c 2. *Educ:* Yale Univ, BS, 50; Stanford Univ, MS, 57, PhD, 60. *Concurrent Pos:* Chmn oceanog panel, Comt Polar Res, Nat Acad Sci-Nat Res Coun, 67-72; mem, Oceanog Adv Comt to US Navy, 71-77. *Mem:* Am Geophys Union; Sigma Xi; Am Meteorol Soc. *Res:* Physical oceanography and marine geophysics, with special interest in the Arctic Ocean. *Mailing Add:* Lamont-Doherty Earth Observ Palisades NY 10964. *E-Mail:* hunkins@ldeo.columbia.edu

HUNN, JOSEPH BRUCE, PHYSIOLOGY, FISHERIES. *Current Pos:* FISHERY BIOLOGIST, NAT FISH CONTAMINANT RES CTR, 87-; QUAL ASSURANCE OFFICER, COLUMBIA NAT FISH RES LAB, 91- *Personal Data:* b St Paul, Minn, Mar 12, 33; m 67, Susan Wazney; c Will & Suzy. *Educ:* St John's Univ, Minn, BA, 55; Mich State Univ, MS, 57, PhD(physiol), 63. *Prof Exp:* NIH res fel fish dis, Eastern Fish Dis Lab, WVa, 63-65; fishery biologist, Fish Control Lab, US Fish & Wildlife Serv, LaCrosse, Wis, 65-77; supvry fishery biologist, Hammond Bay Biol Sta, Millersburg, Mich, 77-80; fishery biologist, Columbia Nat Fish Res Lab, Columbia, Mo, 80-85, asst chief biologist, 85-87, spec invests, 87-90. *Concurrent Pos:* Adj prof, Sch Natural Resources, Univ Mo, Columbia, 90- *Mem:* AAAS; Am Fisheries Soc; Am Soc Zool. *Res:* Aquatic toxicology. *Mailing Add:* 2242 Bluff Blvd Columbia MO 65201. *Fax:* 573-876-1896

HUNNELL, JOHN WESLEY, FOOD TECHNOLOGY. *Current Pos:* mgr process & prod develop, 65-68, dir res & develop, 68-78, ASST VPRES, TECH SERVS, RIVIANA FOODS, INC, 78-, DIR RES, 80- *Personal Data:* b Chicago, Ill, July 23, 32; m 58; c 2. *Educ:* Univ Ill, BS, 53, MS, 54, PhD(food tech), 60. *Prof Exp:* Mgr com develop, Refrigerated Foods, Pillsbury Co, 60-62, sr scientist, 62-63; sr food technologist, Colgate-Palmolive Co, 63-65. *Mem:* Inst Food Technol; Am Asn Cereal Chemists; Am Oil Chemists Soc; Am Chem Soc; Sigma Xi. *Res:* Formulation, process and packaging development and commercialization of food products. *Mailing Add:* 411 Hunterwood Dr Houston TX 77024

HUNNICUTT, CHARLES A, AVIATION POLICY. *Current Pos:* ASST SECY TRANSP, AVIATION & INT AFFAIRS, DEPT TRANSP, 96- *Personal Data:* b LaGrange, Ga. *Educ:* Am Univ, BS, 72; Univ Ga, JD, 75, Vrije Univ Brussel, LLM, 76. *Prof Exp:* Staff, White House Presidential Personnel Off, 77; asst to dep asst secy commerce, 77-79; exec asst, Under Secy Commerce for Int Trade, 79-80; legal adv chairwoman, US Int Trade Comn, 80-87; partner, Robins, Kaplan, Miller & Ciresi, Washington, DC, 87-96. *Res:* Commercial aviation policy, including economic and regulatory issues. *Mailing Add:* US Dept Transp 400 Seventh St SW Rm 10232 Washington DC 20590. *Fax:* 202-493-2005

HUNNICUTT, RICHARD P(EARCE), METALLURGICAL ENGINEERING. *Current Pos:* vpres, 62-82, EXEC VPRES, ANAMET LABS, INC, 82- *Personal Data:* b Asheville, NC, June 15, 26; m 54, Susan Haight; c Barbara, Beverly, Geoffrey & Anne. *Educ:* Stanford Univ, BS, 51, MS, 52. *Prof Exp:* Res metallurgist, Res Labs, Gen Motors Corp, 52-55; head metall sect, Aerojet-Gen Corp, Div Gen Tire & Rubber Co, 55-57; head mat & processes, Eng Lab, Firestone Tire & Rubber Co, 57-58; supvr mat lab, Dalmo Victor Co, 57-62. *Mem:* Am Soc Metals; Am Welding Soc; Am Soc Testing & Mat; Am Inst Aeronaut & Astronaut; Nat Asn Corrosion Engrs. *Res:* Development of high strength-high temperature structural materials, especially rocket engine applications; friction; lubrication; wear; fracture studies and failure analysis of materials. *Mailing Add:* 2805 Benson Way Belmont CA 94002-2938. *Fax:* 510-887-8427

HUNNINGHAKE, GARY W, MEDICINE. *Current Pos:* assoc prof, 81-84, DIR PULMONARY DIS DIV, DEPT INTERNAL MED, UNIV IOWA COL MED & DEPT VET AFFAIRS CTR, IOWA CITY, 81-, PROF MED, 84-, DIR CRITICAL CARE PROG, 89- *Personal Data:* b Seneca, Kans, July 10, 46; m 68; c 3. *Educ:* St Benedicts Col, BS, 68; Kans Univ, MD, 72; Am Bd Internal Med, dipl pulmonary dis; Am Bd Allergy & Immunol, dipl. *Prof Exp:* Intern, Kans Univ Med Sch, 72-73, resident, Med Ctr, 73-74; clin assoc, Nat Inst Allergy & Infectious Dis, NIH, Bethesda, Md, 74-76, med officer, 76-77, sr investr, Pulmonary Br, Nat Heart, Lung & Blood Inst & consult, 77-81. *Concurrent Pos:* Mem, Clin Res Comt, Nat Inst Allergy & Infectious Dis, NIH, 74-77, chmn, 76-77; mem, Clin Res Ctr Comt, Univ Iowa, 81-83; mem prog comt, Allergy & Immunol Assembly, Am Thoracic Soc, 81-90; mem, Pulmonary Allergy Drugs Adv Comt, Food & Drug Admin, 84-86; assoc ed, Chest, 86-90, Am Rev Respiratory Dis, 89-; numerous grants, NIH & Dept Vet Affairs, 86-95. *Mem:* Am Fed Clin Res (pres, 86-87); Am Soc Microbiol; Am Asn Immunologists; Am Soc Clin Invest; Asn Am Physicians; Am Acad Allergy; Am Col Chest Physicians; Am Thoracic Soc (secy-treas, 91-92); Am Col Physicians; Soc Critical Care Med. *Res:* Lung immunology and host defenses, interstitial lung diseases, asthma, viral lung disease. *Mailing Add:* Dept Internal Med C33 GH Univ Iowa Col Med 200 Hawkins Dr Iowa City IA 52242-1081

HUNSAKER, DON, II, PSYCHOBIOLOGY, ECOLOGY. *Current Pos:* From asst prof to assoc prof, 64-67, PROF BIOL, SAN DIEGO STATE UNIV, 67- *Personal Data:* b Ft Worth, Tex, Apr 4, 30; c 4. *Educ:* Tex Tech Univ, BA, 52, MS, 57; Univ Tex, PhD, 60. *Concurrent Pos:* Vis prof biol, Colo State Univ, 65-70 & Univ Ariz, 70-73; coordr, US Peace Corps, Columbia Prog Ecol & Nat Parks, 70-72; pres, Environ Trust. *Mem:* Am Soc Ichthyol & Herpet; Herpetologists' League. *Res:* Behavior, speciation and vocalization of vertebrates; behavioral ecology of endangered species; fish and wildlife. *Mailing Add:* Dept Biol San Diego State Univ San Diego CA 92182-0002

HUNSICKER, HAROLD YUNDT, METALLURGY & PHYSICAL METALLURGICAL ENGINEERING, MATERIALS SCIENCE ENGINEERING. *Current Pos:* RETIRED. *Personal Data:* b Frankfort, Ind, Dec 22, 14; m 39; c 3. *Educ:* Purdue Univ, BSChE, 36; Case Inst Tech, MSMetE, 39. *Prof Exp:* Engr phys metall, Aluminum Res Labs, Alcoa, Cleveland, 36-48, asst div chief phys metall, 48-58, div chief, Alcoa Labs, New Kensington, 58-60, div mgr, Alcoa Labs, Alcoa Ctr, 60-77, consult, 77-80. *Concurrent Pos:* Consult, Pitman-Dunn Labs, Frankford Arsenal, 77-79. *Mem:* Fel Am Soc Metals; Am Inst Metall Engrs. *Res:* Developed aluminum alloys for automotive engine bearings, automotive, aerospace and architectural castings; advanced wrought products for automotive, aerospace, electrical and architectural industries; microstructural/property relationships for these aluminum products. *Mailing Add:* 508 Chester Dr New Kensington PA 15068-3304

HUNSINGER, BILL JO, ELECTRICAL ENGINEERING. *Current Pos:* ASSOC PROF ELEC ENG, UNIV ILL, 74- *Personal Data:* b Roanoke, Ill, Feb 23, 39; m 60; c 2. *Educ:* Univ Ill, BS, 61, PhD(elec eng), 70; Bradley Univ, MS, 66. *Prof Exp:* Res engr elec eng, Gen Elec Co, 61-67; res engr, Magnavox Co, 67-74. *Res:* Surface acoustic waves; ultrasonics; microwave devices; semiconductor devices; signal processing. *Mailing Add:* 1710 Hickery Dr Mahomet IL 61853

HUNSLEY, ROGER EUGENE, ANIMAL SCIENCE. *Current Pos:* EXEC SECY, AM SHORTHORN ASN, 83- *Personal Data:* b Pierre, SDak, Feb 21, 38; m 63; c 3. *Educ:* SDak State Univ, BS, 59; NDak State Univ, MS, 61; Iowa State Univ, PhD(animal nutrit), 67. *Prof Exp:* Field rep, Am Hereford Asn, 61-63; instr animal sci, Iowa State Univ, 64-67; from asst prof to assoc prof, Purdue Univ, 67-76, prof animal sci, 76-83. *Concurrent Pos:* Tech adv comt mem, NAm Limousin Found, 74-75. *Mem:* Am Soc Animal Sci; Int Livestock Coaches Asn. *Res:* Management practices; nutritional regimes and genetics in relationship to their effects on growth and body composition of red meat animals; evaluation of red meat animals and their products. *Mailing Add:* 9942 Harney Pkwy N Omaha NE 68114

HUNSPERGER, ROBERT G(EORGE), PHOTONIC DEVICES, MICROWAVE DEVICES. *Current Pos:* PROF ELEC ENG, UNIV DEL, 76- *Personal Data:* b Philadelphia, Pa, Mar 6, 40; m 58, Elizabeth J Thorpe; c Lisa M (Wilson). *Educ:* Drexel Univ, BSEE, 62; Princeton Univ, MSE, 63; Cornell Univ, PhD(appl physics), 67. *Prof Exp:* Mem staff res ctr, Burroughs Corp, 58-62; asst electronic circuits, Princeton Univ, 62-63; asst semiconductor lasers, Cornell Univ, 63-67; mem tech staff, Hughes Res Labs, 67-76. *Concurrent Pos:* Instr, Dept Eng-Phys Sci Exten, Univ Calif, Los Angeles, 68-76; consult, Hughes Aircraft Co, 78-87, Martin Marietta Corp, 81-83, Westinghouse Corp, 82-84, E I du Pont de Nemours & Co, Inc, 84-92, ISC Defense Systs, 85-87, Nat Inst Stand & Tech, 88-, Nat Technol Univ, 91- & Astro Power, Inc, 92- *Mem:* Fel Inst Elec & Electronics Engrs; AAAS; Int Platform Asn; Soc Photoinstrumentation Engrs; Optical Soc Am. *Res:* Electrical and optical properties of semiconductors and semiconductor devices, particularly photonic and microwave devices; integrated optics. *Mailing Add:* Dept Elec Eng Univ Del Newark DE 19716. *Fax:* 302-831-4316; *E-Mail:* hunsperg@udel.edu

HUNSTAD, NORMAN A(LLEN), MECHANICAL ENGINEERING. *Current Pos:* PRES, BEECHCREEK CORP, 87- *Personal Data:* b Pipestone, Minn, Aug 25, 24; m 50, Freda M Soukup; c Joseph, Mary & David. *Educ:* Univ Iowa, BS, 49. *Prof Exp:* Engr, Gen Motors Corp, 49-55, asst head, Fuels & Lubricants Dept, Res Lab, 55-87. *Mem:* Fel Soc Automotive Engrs; fel Soc Tribologists & Lubrication Engrs; fel Am Soc Testing & Mat; Sigma Xi. *Res:* Automotive lubricants. *Mailing Add:* BeechCreek Corp 6281 Little Creek Rd Rochester Hills MI 48306

HUNSTON, DONALD LEE, COMPOSITES, RHEOLOGY. *Current Pos:* SUPVRY PHYS SCIENTIST, NAT INST STAND & TECH, 80- *Personal Data:* b Springfield, Mo, July 27, 43. *Educ:* Kent State Univ, BS, 65, PhD(chem), 69. *Honors & Awards:* Am Inst Chem Award, 65; Gold Medal, Dept Com. *Prof Exp:* NIH fel, Northwestern Univ, 70-71; res chemist, Naval Res Lab, 71-80. *Mem:* Am Chem Soc; Soc Rheol; Am Inst Physics; Soc Advan Mat & Process Eng; Am Soc Composites; Adhesion Soc. *Res:* Relationship between molecular structure and the mechanical or chemical properties of macromolecules; fracture behavior of polymeric materials; molecular interactions of biological molecules; structure-property relations in polymer composites; fluid mechanics. *Mailing Add:* Polymer Div Nat Inst Stand & Tech Gaithersburg MD 20899. *E-Mail:* donald.hunston@nist.gov

HUNSUCKER, ROBERT DUDLEY, SPACE PHYSICS IONOSPHERE, RADIO PROPAGATION. *Current Pos:* from assoc prof to prof geophys, 71-87, EMER PROF GEOPHYS & SR CONSULT, GEOPHYS INST, UNIV ALASKA, 88-; SR PARTNER, RP CONSULTS, KLAMATH FALLS, OR, 95- *Personal Data:* b Portland, Ore, Mar 15, 30; m 56, 81, Phyllis M Hoover; c Edith, Jeanne & Cynthia. *Educ:* Ore State Univ, BS, 54, MS, 58; Univ Colo, PhD(elec eng), 69. *Honors & Awards:* Achievement Award, Region Six Pac Coast, Inst Elec & Electronics Engrs, 88. *Prof Exp:* Asst geophys, Univ Alaska, 58-59, from instr to asst prof, 60-64; physicist, Res Labs, Inst Telecommun Sci & Aeronomy, Environ Sci Serv Admin, Colo, 64-69, sr proj leader, 69-71. *Concurrent Pos:* Mem, US Comm G & H Int Union Radio Sci, 67- & working groups incoherent scatter, ionospheric sounders & propagation, 75-; prin investr, NSF grants, 71-88; vis sr scientist, AT&T Bell Labs, Murray Hill, NJ, 82-83; sr partner, PR Consults, Fairbanks, Alaska, 88-95; adj prof, Pa State Univ, 92-, Ore Inst Technol, 96-; ed-in-chief, Radio Sci. *Mem:* Fel Inst Elec & Electronics Engrs; fel AAAS; Am Geophys Union; Sigma Xi. *Res:* Physics and radio propagation investigations of the high and middle latitude ionosphere using incoherent scatter radar and other techniques; author and co-author of over 85 papers and 2 books. *Mailing Add:* R P Consults 7917 Gearhart St Klamath Falls OR 97601. *Fax:* 541-885-1666; *E-Mail:* hunsuckr@cdsnet.net, hunsuckr@oit.edu

HUNT, ANDREW DICKSON, PEDIATRICS. *Current Pos:* PROF PEDIAT, SCH MED, MERCER UNIV, 84-, ASSOC DEAN GLYNN-BRUNSWICK PROGS, 87- *Personal Data:* b Staten Island, NY, Oct 1, 15; m 40, Lotta H Mayberry; c George M, Elisabeth H, Judith P & Lotta R (Rosen). *Educ:* Haverford Col, BS, 37; Cornell Univ, MD, 41; Am Bd Pediat, dipl, 48. *Hon Degrees:* LHD, Northern Mich Univ, 78. *Prof Exp:* Intern, Hosp Univ Pa, 41-42, resident pediat, 42-43; asst instr, Sch Med, Univ Pa, 46-48, instr pediat, 48-50, assoc, 50-52, asst prof, 52; asst prof clin pediat, Col Med, NY Univ, 52-55, asst prof pediat, 55-59; assoc prof pediat, Sch Med & dir ambulatory serv, Med Ctr, Stanford Univ, 59-64; prof pediat & dean col human med, Mich State Univ, 64-77, actg dir health serv prog, 77-78, coordr med humanities prog, 78-84. *Concurrent Pos:* Chief resident, Children's Hosp, Philadelphia, 46-47, asst dir clins, 47-50, asst physician, 48-50, dir diag clin, 48-52; dir clins, 50-52, sr physician, 51-52; dir pediat serv, Hunterdon Med Ctr, Flemington, NJ, 52-59; asst vis physician, Bellevue Hosp, NY, 52-59; chmn adv coun, Comprehensive State Health Planning Comn, 68-; fel adolescent med, Sch Med, Stanford Univ, 81-82; fel, Ctr Advan Study Behav Sci, 87-88. *Mem:* AAAS; Soc Pediat Res; Am Pediat Soc; AMA; Am Acad Pediat. *Res:* Infectious disease; application of medical knowledge to society; medical education; adolescent medicine. *Mailing Add:* 201 Hermitage Way St Simons Island GA 31522-1717. *Fax:* 912-638-9626; *E-Mail:* hunt.a@gain.mercer.edu

HUNT, ANGUS LAMAR, physics; deceased, see previous edition for last biography

HUNT, ANN HAMPTON, STRUCTURE ELUCIDATION. *Current Pos:* sr phys chemist, 78-82, RES SCIENTIST, LILLY RES LABS, ELI LILLY & CO, 83- *Personal Data:* b Lexington, NC, Nov 4, 42. *Educ:* Univ NC, Greensboro, AB, 65; Duke Univ, PhD(phys chem), 70. *Prof Exp:* From instr to asst prof, Converse Col, 69-71; fel biochem, Univ Tex M D Anderson Hosp & Tumor Inst, 71-73; res fel biol chem, Harvard Med Sch, 75-78. *Concurrent Pos:* Proj dir, NSF res grant, 70-71; counr, Am Chem Soc, 85-; vis scientist, Scripps Res Inst, 92-93. *Mem:* AAAS; Am Chem Soc. *Res:* Nuclear magnetic resonance of natural products, including proteins. *Mailing Add:* Structural Chem Eli Lilly & Co 307 E McCarty St Indianapolis IN 46285

HUNT, ARLON JASON, LIGHT SCATTERING, SOLAR ENERGY CONVERSION. *Current Pos:* PHYSICIST, LAWRENCE BERKELEY LAB, 76- *Personal Data:* b Council Bluffs, Iowa, Oct 8, 39; m 71, Mary E Quinby; c 2. *Educ:* Univ Minn, BA, 63; Univ Ariz, MS, 71, PhD(physics), 74. *Honors & Awards:* Fulbright res scholar, Africa, 85. *Prof Exp:* Res assoc, Physics Dept, Univ Ariz, 68-74 & Optical Sci Ctr, 74-76. *Concurrent Pos:* Pres, Particle Technol Assoc, 79-; consult, 80-; prin, Thermalux LP, 89- *Mem:* Am Phys Soc; Am Optical Soc; Am Ceramic Soc; AAAS; Mat Res Soc. *Res:* Absorption and scattering of light by small particles; optical and physical properties of solids; solar energy conversion; instrumentation; microstructural materials-Aerogel. *Mailing Add:* 70-108 Lawrence Berkeley Lab Univ Calif Berkeley CA 94720. *E-Mail:* ajhunt@lbl.gov

HUNT, BOBBY RAY, ELECTRICAL ENGINEERING, COMPUTER SCIENCE. *Current Pos:* PROF ELEC ENG, UNIV ARIZ, 75-85, 89- *Personal Data:* b McAlester, Okla, Aug 24, 41; m 65; c 2. *Educ:* Wichita State Univ, BSc, 64; Okla State Univ, MSc, 65; Univ Ariz, PhD(systs eng), 67. *Prof Exp:* Staff mem systs res, Sandia Lab, NMex, 67-68; staff mem comput sci, Los Alamos Sci Lab, Univ Calif, 68-72; adj prof elec eng & comput sci, Univ NMex, 72-75; chief scientist, Defense Systs Group, Sci Appln Int Corp,

85-89. *Mem:* Fel Inst Elec & Electronics Engrs; fel Optical Soc Am. *Res:* Processing of images by digital computer; digital filtering; systems theory and applications in image processing. *Mailing Add:* Dept Elec & Comput Eng Univ Ariz Tucson AZ 85721

HUNT, C WARREN, APPLIED GEOLOGY. *Current Pos:* CONSULT GEOLOGIST, 48- *Personal Data:* b San Francisco, Calif, Dec 15, 24; Can citizen; m 50, Patricia McCallum; c Lucile G (Edwards), Malcolm I, Melinda & C W Schuyler. *Educ:* Calif Inst Technol, BS, 45. *Prof Exp:* Jr geologist, Stand Oil Co, Calif, 45; geologist, 46, Independent Explor Co, 47-48. *Mem:* Am Asn Petrol Geol; Can Inst Mining & Metall. *Res:* Oil, gas and mineral exploration; structural surface and subsurface geology; petroleum exploration; goldmine development; entrepreneur in development of oil, gas, coal and gold miner; author of 3 books. *Mailing Add:* 1119 Sydenham Rd SW Calgary AB T2T 0T5 Can. *Fax:* 403-244-2834; *E-Mail:* archeanc@freenet.catgory.ab.ca

HUNT, CARL E, PEDIATRICS. *Current Pos:* PROF & VCHMN DEPT PEDIAT, NORTHWESTERN UNIV MED SCH & HEAD DIV NEONATOLOGY, CHILDREN'S MEM HOSP, 75- *Educ:* Yale Univ, Dr, 65; Am Bd Pediat, cert pediat neonatology. *Res:* Respiratory control; Sudden Infant Death Syndrome. *Mailing Add:* Dept Pediat Med Col Ohio 3000 Arlington Ave PO Box 10008 Toledo OH 43699-0008. *Fax:* 419-381-3618

HUNT, CARLTON CUYLER, neurophysiology, for more information see previous edition

HUNT, CHARLES E, EXPERIMENTAL PATHOLOGY, NUTRITIONAL BIOCHEMISTRY. *Current Pos:* assoc dir comp med & path, 69-74, SR SCIENTIST, INST DENT RES, UNIV ALA, BIRMINGHAM, 69-, PROF COMP MED, 74-, PROF & DIR NUTRIT PATH, DEPT NUTRIT SCI, 78- *Personal Data:* b Riverside, Calif, Jan 10, 35; m 61; c 6. *Educ:* Wash State Univ, DVM, 59; Mass Inst Technol, PhD(nutrit, biochem), 67. *Prof Exp:* Intern, Rowley Mem Hosp, Springfield, 59-60; instr small animal med & surg, Auburn Univ, 60-62, Ala Heart Asn fel, 62-63; res assoc nutrit path, Mass Inst Technol, 63-66, asst prof, 66-68; assoc dir labs toxicol & path, Schick Pharmaceut, Inc, 68-69. *Mem:* Am Col Vet Path; Int Acad Path; Sigma Xi. *Res:* Pathology and biochemistry of copper; effects of fluoride, strontium, molybdenum, boron and lithium on tooth and bone in rats; adult onset obesity in mice; experimental atherosclerosis and diabetes. *Mailing Add:* Path-Toxicol Res Upjohn Co Bldg 300-1-132 Kalamazoo MI 49001-4940

HUNT, CHARLES EDMUND LAURENCE, PHYSICAL METALLURGY, MECHANICAL ENGINEERING. *Current Pos:* PVT CONSULT, 92- *Personal Data:* b Norwich, Eng, Aug 8, 35; Can citizen; m 58, Dorothy H Jamieson; c Murray Laurence, Graham Charles & Neil Edmund James. *Educ:* Univ BC, BASc, 57; Univ Waterloo, MASc, 67, PhD(mech eng), 70. *Prof Exp:* Jr res engr, Atomic Energy Can, Ltd, 57-59, opers engr, 59-65, develop engr, 65-67, res engr, 70-92. *Res:* Phase transformations in alloys, specifically directed towards zirconium base alloys; physical and mechanical properties of metal alloys and the effects of radiation on properties; effects of high temperature transients on nuclear fuel sheathing; release mechanisms of fission products from uranium dioxides particularly under abnormal conditions such as high temperature and oxidation by air or steam. *Mailing Add:* PO Box 958 Deep River ON K0J 1P0 Can

HUNT, CHARLES MAXWELL, environmental chemistry, fine particle measurement; deceased, see previous edition for last biography

HUNT, CURTISS DEAN, HUMAN BORON NUTRITION, HUMAN COPPER NUTRITION. *Current Pos:* RES BIOLOGIST, USDA AGR RES SERV GRAND FORKS HUMAN NUTRIT RES CTR, 87- *Personal Data:* b Scottsbluff, NB, Apr 28, 50; US citizen; m 86, Janet Ross; c Vanessa, Carilla, Renatta & Brian. *Educ:* Dakota Wesleyan Univ, BA, 72; Univ NDak, MS, 76, PhD(anat), 79. *Prof Exp:* Res assoc, Univ NDak, 79-81, vis asst prof anat, 81-82, res assoc, 82-85. *Concurrent Pos:* Adj asst prof, Univ NDak, 85- *Mem:* Am Inst Nutrit; Am Soc Bone & Mineral Res; Int Asn Bioinorg Scientists; Soc Exp Biol & Med; Tissue Cult Asn. *Res:* Determining boron essentiality, dietary requirement, utilization, interrelationships with other nutrients; physiological functions of elements found in trace amounts in foods. *Mailing Add:* USDA Univ Sta PO Box 9034 Grand Forks ND 58202-9034

HUNT, DAVID ALLEN, DESIGN & SYNTHESIS OF NOVEL INSECT CONTROL AGENTS, HETEROCYCLIC CHEMISTRY. *Current Pos:* sr res chemist, Chem Discovery, 89-91, GROUP LEADER, CHEM DISCOVERY, AGR RES DIV, AM CYANAMID CO, 91- *Personal Data:* b Huntington, WVa, Dec 4, 52; m 73, Susan L Sullivan; c Jessica R & Ashley L. *Educ:* Marshall Univ, BS, 73, MS, 75; Duke Univ, PhD(org chem), 79. *Prof Exp:* Sr chemist mass spectrometry, Union Carbide Corp, 79-80, sr chemist process develop, Agr Prod Div, 80-81; sr scientist org chem, Immunodiag Group, Becton Dickinson Res Ctr, 81-84; sr res chemist, Agr Res Div, PPG Industs, 84-88; tech mgr chem res & develop, Salsbury Labs, Solvay & Cie, 88-89. *Concurrent Pos:* Adj asst prof chem, Marshall Univ, 80-81; sci test question writer, Am Col Testing Prog, 89-90; adj prof chem, Col NJ, 97- *Mem:* Sigma Xi; Am Chem Soc; AAAS; NY Acad Sci; Int Soc Heterocyclic Chem. *Res:* Design and synthesis of novel heterocyclic systems which possess biological activity; development of novel synthetic methods; synthetic organometallic chemistry. *Mailing Add:* 9 Water Lily Way Newtown PA 18940. *Fax:* 609-275-3550; *E-Mail:* huntd@pt.cyanamid.com

HUNT, DAVID MICHAEL, NATURAL COMMUNITY CONSERVATION, OAK SYSTEMATICS & ECOLOGY. *Current Pos:* botanist-ecologist, 87, info mgr-steward 90-95, ASSOC ECOLOGIST, NATURE CONSERVANCY, 95- *Personal Data:* b Framingham, Mass, May 23, 59; m 89, Lori Durrance. *Educ:* Cornell Univ, BA, 81; Univ Ga, PhD(bot), 90. *Prof Exp:* Botanist-ecologist, Jason M Cortell & Assoc, 87-90. *Concurrent Pos:* Contract botanist, US Army 91-93, Mass Nat Heritage Prog, 93-94. *Res:* Preservation and classification of natural communities, systematics and ecology of Quercus series Laurifoliae, Nigrae and Marilandicae (red oaks), floristics of northeastern US, quantification of leaf shape, restoration ecology. *Mailing Add:* NY Natural Heritage Prog 700 Troy-Schectady Rd Latham NY 12110-2400. *Fax:* 518-783-3916

HUNT, DONALD F, ANALYTICAL BIOCHEMISTRY. *Current Pos:* from asst prof to assoc prof, 68-78, PROF CHEM, UNIV VA, 78-, UNIV PROF CHEM & PATH, 93- *Personal Data:* b Hyannis, Mass, Apr 25, 41; m 65, Linda Carson; c 2. *Educ:* Univ Mass, BS, 62, PhD(chem), 67. *Honors & Awards:* Charles H Stone Award, Am Chem Soc, 90, Chem Instrumentation Award, 97; Pehr Eaman Award, 92; Distinguished Contrib Award, Am Soc Mass Spectrometry, 94; Christian B Anfinsen Award, Protein Soc, 96. *Prof Exp:* NIH trainee chem, Mass Inst Technol, 67-68. *Mem:* Am Chem Soc; Protein Soc; Am Soc Mass Spectrometry. *Res:* Mass spectrometry; analytical biochemistry; development of new methods and instrumentation for the structural characterization of proteins, processed antigens, glycoproteins, oligosacharrides, and nucleic acids by mass spectrometry. *Mailing Add:* Dept Chem Univ Va Charlottesville VA 22901. *Fax:* 804-982-2781

HUNT, DONALD F(ULPER), ELECTRICAL ENGINEERING, COMPUTER ENGINEERING. *Current Pos:* assoc prof, 63-66, PROF ELEC ENG, POLYTECH INST, NEW YORK, 66- *Personal Data:* b Philadelphia, Pa, May 10, 25; m 61, Catherine Krumm; c Douglas. *Educ:* Univ Pa, BS, 48. *Prof Exp:* Instr elec eng, Univ Pa, 48-54. *Mem:* Inst Elec & Electronics Engrs. *Res:* Systems, computer applications. *Mailing Add:* Dept Chem Univ Va McCormick Rd Charlottesville VA 22901. *Fax:* 804-296-3159

HUNT, DONNELL RAY, AGRICULTURAL ENGINEERING, ENGINEERING EDUCATION. *Current Pos:* RETIRED. *Personal Data:* b Danville, Ind, Aug 11, 26; m 51, Dorothea May; c David & De Anne. *Educ:* Purdue Univ, BS, 51; Iowa State Univ, MS, 54, PhD(agr eng), 58. *Prof Exp:* From instr to assoc prof agr eng, Iowa State Univ, 51-60; from assoc prof to prof agr eng, Univ Ill, Urbana, 60-94, asst dean eng, 85-96. *Concurrent Pos:* Consult, FMC Corp, 62, Massey-Ferguson Ltd, 63 & US Steel Corp, 65-66 & var law firms & small mfrs; lectr, Univ Col, Dublin, 68-69. *Mem:* Am Soc Agr Engrs; Am Soc Eng Educ; Sigma Xi. *Res:* Optimization of farm field machine operations; mechanization of crop production; alternative tractor fuels; cooperative education. *Mailing Add:* 405 Ira Urbana IL 61802

HUNT, EARLE RAYMOND, PHYSICS. *Current Pos:* assoc prof, 67-75, PROF PHYSICS, OHIO UNIV, 75- *Personal Data:* b Petersburg, Va, Mar 7, 36; m 56; c 4. *Educ:* Rutgers Univ, BA, 58, PhD(physics), 62. *Prof Exp:* Res assoc physics, Duke Univ, 62-63, from instr to asst prof, 63-67. *Mem:* Am Phys Soc. *Res:* Solid state physics; chaos. *Mailing Add:* Dept Physics Ohio Univ Athens OH 45701

HUNT, EUGENE B, ELECTRICAL ENGINEERING. *Current Pos:* RETIRED. *Personal Data:* b Gary, SDak, Sept 21, 23. *Educ:* SDak State Univ, BS, 48; Kans State Univ, MS, 50; Purdue Univ, PhD, 55. *Prof Exp:* Instr elec eng, SDak State Univ, 48-49; asst prof, SDak Sch Mines & Technol, 50-53; res instr, Purdue Univ, 54-55; res specialist, Autonetics Div, NAm Aviation, Inc, 55-64; assoc prof elec eng, Calif State Col, Long Beach, 64-66; chmn dept, Calif State Col, Fullerton, 66-79, prof elec eng, Calif State Univ, 80-90. *Mem:* Am Soc Eng Educ; Inst Elec & Electronics Engrs. *Res:* Electronics; automatic control; networks; computers; communications. *Mailing Add:* Calif State Univ Fullerton CA 92634

HUNT, EVERETT CLAIR, MARINE ENGINEERING, SHIP DESIGN. *Current Pos:* CONSULT, 92- *Personal Data:* b Stamford, Conn, Dec 28, 28; m 52, Jay Kilby; c Gerilyn, Scott & Erik. *Educ:* US Merchant Marine Acad, BS, 51; Rennselaer Polytech Inst, MS, 58; Northeastern Univ, MS, 72; Eurotech Univ, DSc, 88. *Honors & Awards:* Bronze Medal, US Dept Transp, 83. *Prof Exp:* Eng officer, USN, 52-54; engr, Gen Elec Co, 54-65, proj mgr, 65-66, consult, 66-67, mgr eng, 67-69, mgr qual control, 69-75; dir, Sun Shipbldg Co, 75-79; prof eng, US Merchant Marine Acad, 79-84; prof eng & res dir, Webb Inst Naval Archit, 84-92. *Concurrent Pos:* Adj prof, Union Col, 70-75 & Widener Univ, 78-79; chmn, Inst Marine Engrs, 80-83. *Mem:* Inst Marine Engrs; Pan-Am Inst Naval Eng; Inst Indust Engrs. *Res:* Engineering marine power plants; ship propulsion systems; engineering economics; quality control; statistics. *Mailing Add:* PO Box 308 Warner NH 03278-0308. *E-Mail:* chunt@conknet.com

HUNT, FERN ENSMINGER, FOODS. *Current Pos:* RETIRED. *Personal Data:* b Mt Perry, Ohio, May 11, 26; m 53. *Educ:* Ohio State Univ, BS, 48, MS, 54, PhD(food, microbiol), 65. *Prof Exp:* Home economist, Ohio Edison Co, 48-52; asst food, Univ State Univ, 52-53, from instr to asst prof food & nutrit, Ohio Agr Res & Develop Ctr, 54-68, assoc prof food & equipment, 68-73, prof food & equipment, Ohio Agr Res & Develop Ctr, 73-80. *Mem:* AAAS; Am Soc Microbiol; Inst Food Technologists; Am Home Econ Asn; Sigma Xi. *Res:* Factors in cooking affecting organoleptic qualities of food; effect of freezing and thawing rates on microbial activity in frozen food; energy management in households. *Mailing Add:* 4692 Scenic Dr Columbus OH 43214-2519

HUNT, GARY W, x-ray crystallography, for more information see previous edition

HUNT, GEORGE LESTER, JR, ECOLOGY, MARINE ORNITHOLOGY. *Current Pos:* PROF BEHAV ECOL & MARINE ORNITH, SCH BIOL SCI, UNIV CALIF, IRVINE, 71- *Personal Data:* b Boston, Mass, Aug 10, 42; m 88. *Educ:* Harvard Univ, AB, 65, PhD(biol), 71. *Mem:* Fel AAAS; fel Am Ornith Union; Brit Ornith Union; Am Ecol Soc; Brit Ecol Soc; Am Soc Limnol Oceanog. *Res:* Ecology and reproductive biology of seabirds; coloniality and reproductive success; biological oceanography of seabirds; habitat selection; foraging behavior. *Mailing Add:* Dept Ecol & Evolutionary Biol Univ Calif Irvine CA 92697-2425. *Fax:* 714-824-2181; *E-Mail:* glhunt@uci.edu

HUNT, GRAHAM HUGH, ECONOMIC GEOLOGY. *Current Pos:* PROF GEOL & CHMN DEPT, UNIV LOUISVILLE, 74- *Personal Data:* b Melville, Sask, May 15, 30; m 56; c 3. *Educ:* Univ Man, BS, 53; Univ Alta, MS, 58, PhD(geol), 61. *Prof Exp:* Geologist, Hudson Bay Mining & Smelting Co, 51-56, Shell Oil Co, 57-58 & Mobil Oil Co, 61-64; prof geol, Brandon Col, 64-65, Odessa Col, 65-67 & Eastern Ky Univ, 67-74. *Concurrent Pos:* Consult geol map, Dept Mines, Can, 65-67. *Mem:* Nat Asn Geol Teachers. *Res:* Geologic research of Pre-Cambrian in western Canada; geology of Purcell rocks in British Columbia, Alberta and Montana; geology of Manitoba. *Mailing Add:* Dept Geol Univ Louisville 2301 S Third St Louisville KY 40292-0001

HUNT, GUY MARION, JR, NEUROANATOMY. *Current Pos:* from instr to asst prof, 45-46, assoc prof, 57-75, assoc prof neurol, 64-75, dir & electroencephlaographer, Neurodiag Lab, 64-81, chief, Neurol Sect, 73-81, PROF NEUROL & ANAT, MED CTR, LOMA LINDA UNIV, 75- *Personal Data:* b Battle Creek, Mich, Aug 26, 15; m 41; c 3. *Educ:* Col Med Evangelists, MD, 42, MS, 59; Emmanuel Missionary Col, BS, 46; Am Bd Psychiat & Neurol, dipl, 55. *Prof Exp:* Rotating intern, Los Angeles County Gen Hosp, 41-42. *Concurrent Pos:* Resident & fel, White Mem Hosp, 50-52, consult neurologist, 52-; active sr neurologist & attend neurologist, Loma Linda Univ Hosp. *Mem:* AMA; Am Acad Neurol; Sigma Xi. *Res:* Electron microscopy of the nervous system; anatomy, physiology and pathology of the choroid plexus; convulsive disorders; diseases of the basal ganglia. *Mailing Add:* Dept Neur Loma Linda Univ Loma Linda CA 92354

HUNT, HAROLD RUSSELL, JR, INORGANIC CHEMISTRY. *Current Pos:* RETIRED. *Personal Data:* b Evansville, Ind, Mar 22, 32; m 56; c 2. *Educ:* Harvard Univ, AB, 53; Univ Chicago, PhD(chem), 57. *Prof Exp:* From asst prof to assoc prof chem, Ga Inst Technol, 57-95. *Res:* Complex ions; mechanisms of reactions. *Mailing Add:* Sch Chem Ga Inst Technol Atlanta GA 30332

HUNT, HEMAN DOWD, PHOTOGRAPHIC CHEMISTRY. *Current Pos:* RETIRED. *Personal Data:* b Yakima, Wash, Feb 6, 19; m 41, Rhea E Harris; c Carol A, Donna R & Shirley D. *Educ:* Col Puget Sound, BS, 49; Univ Wash, Seattle, PhD(molecular biol), 52. *Prof Exp:* Sr chemist, Res Div, Photo-Prod Dept, E I du Pont de Nemours & Co, Inc, 52-65, res assoc, 65-82. *Mem:* Soc Photog Scientists & Engrs. *Res:* Vacuum ultraviolet spectroscopy of organic molecules; photographic optical sensitization mechanisms; new photosensitive systems; research and development of new photographic films. *Mailing Add:* 220 Shorewood Dr Webster NY 14580

HUNT, HURSHELL HARVEY, BIOMETRICS. *Current Pos:* ASSOC PROF BIOMET, DEPT BIOMET, MED UNIV SC, 74- *Personal Data:* b Wheeler, Tex, Apr 26, 30; m 59; c 4. *Educ:* Panhandle State Col, BS, 53; Okla State Univ, MS, 59, PhD(math & statist), 68. *Prof Exp:* Asst prof math, Okla Cent State Univ, 59-65; asst math & statist, Okla State Univ, 65-68; asst prof statist, Tex A&M Univ, 68-74. *Mem:* Sigma Xi; Biomet Soc; Am Statist Asn. *Mailing Add:* Med Univ SC 171 Ashley Ave Charleston SC 29425

HUNT, ISABELLE F, NUTRITION DURING PREGNANCY, DIET OSTEOPORSIS. *Current Pos:* PROF PUB HEALTH, UNIV CALIF, LOS ANGELES, 68- *Personal Data:* b Winnepeg, Man, 29. *Educ:* Univ Calif, Los Angeles, DPH, 68. *Mem:* Am Inst Nutrit; Am Pub Health Asn; Am Dietetic Asn; Sigma Xi. *Mailing Add:* Sch Pub Health Univ Calif Los Angeles CA 90024. *Fax:* 310-825-8440

HUNT, JAMES CALVIN, internal medicine, nephrology, for more information see previous edition

HUNT, JAMES HOWELL, EVOLUTIONARY ENTOMOLOGY. *Current Pos:* asst prof, 74-81, assoc prof, 81-94, PROF BIOL, UNIV MO, ST LOUIS, 94- *Personal Data:* b Memphis, Tenn, Oct 6, 44; div; c Noah, Tyler & Jesse. *Educ:* NC State Univ, BS, 66; La State Univ, MS, 69; Univ Calif, Berkeley, PhD(zool), 73. *Prof Exp:* Res assoc biol, Harvard Univ, 73-74. *Mem:* Entom Soc Am; Soc Study Evolution; Int Union Study Social Insects. *Res:* Laboratory and field studies on the evolution of sociality in hymenoptera, especially the role of trophic relationships among colony members, patterns of protein nutrition, demography, life history and caste determination. *Mailing Add:* Dept Biol Univ Mo St Louis MO 63121. *Fax:* 314-516-6233; *E-Mail:* jimhunt@umslvma.umsl.edu

HUNT, JAMES L, PHYSICS. *Current Pos:* assoc prof, 63-70, PROF PHYSICS, UNIV GUELPH, 70- *Personal Data:* b Guelph, Ont, Feb 23, 37; m 55; c 3. *Educ:* Queen's Univ, Ont, BA, 55; Univ Toronto, MA, 56, PhD(physics), 59. *Prof Exp:* Asst prof physics, Mem Univ, Nfld, 59-63. *Concurrent Pos:* Vis prof, Pa State Univ, 68-69. *Mem:* Can Asn Physicists; Am Asn Physics Teachers. *Res:* Molecular spectroscopy. *Mailing Add:* Dept Physics Univ Guelph Guelph ON N1G 2W1 Can

HUNT, JANET R, ZINC NUTRITION, IRON NUTRITION. *Current Pos:* chief dietitian, 78-87, RES SCIENTIST, HUMAN NUTRIT RES CTR, AGR RES SERV, USDA, 88- *Personal Data:* b Glendale, Ariz, Sept 23, 52; m 86, Curtiss; c Vanessa, Carilla, Renatta & Brian. *Educ:* Brigham Young Univ, BS, 73, MS, 75; Univ Minn, PhD(nutrit), 87. *Prof Exp:* Instr food & nutrit, Brigham Young Univ, 75-76; instr nutrit & dietetics, Univ Tex Health Sci Ctr, Dallas, 76-78. *Concurrent Pos:* Adj instr, Univ NDak, 82-91; chmn-elect, Coun Res, Am Dietetic Asn, 91-92, chmn, 92-93; chmn, Am Dietetic Asn & rep, Food & Nutrit Sci Alliance, 95-96. *Mem:* Am Dietetic Asn; Am Soc Nutrit Sci; Am Soc Clin Nutrit; Sigma Xi. *Res:* Zinc and iron bioavailability from diets; effects of dietary protein on mineral and bone metabolism; iron deficiency and behavior; radioisotope tracers to measure trace element absorption and retention. *Mailing Add:* Human Nutrit Res Ctr USDA-Agr Res Serv Grand Forks ND 58202. *Fax:* 701-795-8395

HUNT, JERRY DONALD, ORGANIC CHEMISTRY, INORGANIC CHEMISTRY. *Current Pos:* RES & DEVELOP ASSOC, GOODYEAR TIRE & RUBBER CO, 83- *Personal Data:* b Hastings, Nebr, Nov 11, 38; div; c Kristine & Wendy. *Educ:* Hastings Col, AB, 60; Iowa State Univ, MS, 63, PhD(org chem), 66. *Prof Exp:* Res scientist, Firestone Tire & Rubber Co, 65-68, group leader, 68-77, assoc scientist chem, 77-83. *Concurrent Pos:* Chmn, Akron Rubber Group, 92-93; alt area dir, Rubber Div, Am Chem Soc, 94- *Mem:* Am Chem Soc; Am Soc Testing & Mat. *Res:* Rubber chemistry; free radical chemistry; antioxidant and antiozonant chemistry. *Mailing Add:* 7355 Thatcher Ave NW North Canton OH 44720

HUNT, JOHN A, MOLECULAR GENETICS. *Current Pos:* assoc prof, 64-70, PROF GENETICS, UNIV HAWAII, 70- *Personal Data:* b Reading, Eng, June 22, 35; nat US; div; c Ian K & Tara M. *Educ:* Cambridge Univ, BA, 56, PhD(molecular biol), 60. *Prof Exp:* Fel biochem, Carlsberg Lab, Denmark, 59-60; mem sci staff, Nat Inst Med Res, Eng, 60-64. *Mem:* Genetics Soc Am; Soc Molecular Biol & Evolution. *Res:* Chemistry of genetic mutations affecting abnormal hemoglobins; biosynthesis of hemoglobin and transfer of genetic information in erythropoiesis; RNA synthesis; DNA sequence analysis in the evolution of Hawaiian Drosophila. *Mailing Add:* Dept Genetics Univ Hawaii 1960 E West Rd Honolulu HI 96822. *Fax:* 808-956-5506

HUNT, JOHN BAKER, INORGANIC CHEMISTRY. *Current Pos:* prog officer, Chem Dynamics, Div Chem, NSF, 83-84, prog dir, Chem Instrumentation, 84-87, prog dir, Inorg Chem, 87-90, dep div dir, 90-93, ACTG DIV DIR, DIV CHEM, NSF, 93- *Personal Data:* b Pine Bluff, Ark, Oct 20, 33; m 59, Patricia; c Joseph, Sharon & Timothy. *Educ:* Tulane Univ, BS, 55; Georgetown Univ, MS, 60; Univ Chicago, PhD(chem), 62. *Prof Exp:* Instr chem, US Naval Acad, 57-59; from asst prof to prof chem, Cath Univ Am, 62-85. *Mem:* Am Chem Soc; Am Soc Biochem & Molecular Biol. *Res:* Mechanisms of redox and substitution reactions of complex ions; bioinorganic chemistry. *Mailing Add:* Dept Chem Rm 1005 NSF Arlington VA 22230. *Fax:* 703-306-0545

HUNT, JOHN MEACHAM, PETROLEUM, GEOCHEMISTRY. *Current Pos:* chmn, dept chem, 64-74, sr res scientist, 74-84, EMER SCIENTIST, WOODS HOLE OCEANOG INST, 85- *Personal Data:* b Cleveland, Ohio, Dec 1, 18; m 47; c 2. *Educ:* Western Reserve Univ, AB, 41; Pa State Univ, MS, 43, PhD(org chem), 46. *Honors & Awards:* Treibs Medal, Geochem Soc, 82. *Prof Exp:* Asst petrol ref, Pa State Univ, 43-46, hon asst to Dean F C Whitmore, 46, instr chem, 46-47; sr res chemist, Carter Oil Co, 48-56, sect head, 56-63. *Concurrent Pos:* Lectr, Oil & Gas Consults Int, Tulsa, Okla, 83-96. *Mem:* Europ Asn Org Geochemists; Am Chem Soc; Am Asn Petrol Geol; fel Geochem Soc. *Res:* Application of geochemical techniques to oil and gas exploration; origin, migration and accumulation of petroleum; identification of petroleum source rocks and correlation of crude oils. *Mailing Add:* Dept Chem Woods Hole Oceanog Inst Woods Hole MA 02543

HUNT, JOHN PHILIP, PHYSICAL CHEMISTRY, INORGANIC CHEMISTRY. *Current Pos:* RETIRED. *Personal Data:* b Ann Arbor, Mich, Feb 2, 23; div; c Alan, Phyllis & Roberta. *Educ:* Univ Mich, BS, 44; Univ Chicago, PhD(chem), 50. *Prof Exp:* Mem staff, Clinton Labs, Oak Ridge, Tenn, 44-46; res assoc, Univ Chicago, 50-51; asst prof chem, Cornell Univ, 51-55; from assoc prof to prof, Wash State Univ, 55-90, emer prof chem, 90-97. *Mem:* Am Chem Soc; fel AAAS. *Res:* Inorganic reaction mechanisms. *Mailing Add:* N W 1325 Orion Dr Pullman WA 99163

HUNT, JOHN R, POULTRY NUTRITION. *Current Pos:* RETIRED. *Personal Data:* b Vancouver, BC, Apr 12, 28; m 53; c 3. *Educ:* Univ BC, BSA, 51; Wash State Univ, PhD(nutrit), 55. *Prof Exp:* Res asst nutrit, Wash State Univ, 51-55; res scientist, 56-74, head animal sci sect, Agassiz Res Sta, Can Dept Agr, 74-84, res scientist, 84- *Mem:* Poultry Sci Asn; Nutrit Soc Can; Can Soc Animal Sci. *Res:* Measurement of egg shell strength; effect of nutrition on the strength of the hen's egg shell; factors effecting the acid-base balance in the laying hen; effect of early nutrition on the performance of the broiler breeder; effect of pesticides on shell formation; mineral metabolism; feed restriction of layers; distribution of egg weight; rabbit nutrition; sudden death syndrome in broilers. *Mailing Add:* PO Box 138 Agassiz BC V0M 1A0 Can

HUNT, JOHN WILFRED, BIOPHYSICS, RADIATION CHEMISTRY. *Current Pos:* PHYSICIST, ONT CANC INST, 57-, from asst prof to assoc prof, 59-71, prof, 71-97, EMER PROF MED BIOPHYS, UNIV TORONTO, 97- *Personal Data:* b Regina, Sask, May 30, 30; div; c 5. *Educ:* Univ Sask, BSc, 52, MSc, 53; McGill Univ, PhD(physics), 56. *Honors & Awards:* Arturo Miolati Prize, 73. *Prof Exp:* Nat Cancer Inst Can fel, Univ London, 56-57.

Concurrent Pos: Gordon Richards Mem fel, 65-66, 82; mem, NAm Hyperthermia Group. *Mem:* Am Inst Ultrasound Med; Radiation Res Soc; NAm Hyperthermia Soc; Inst Elec & Electronics Engrs. *Res:* Initial processes of radiation chemistry studied by nanosecond and picosecond pulse radiolysis; reactions and yields of free radicals and ions in liquids, particularly for biologically important molecules; diagnostic ultrasound techniques, including basic studies in high-resolution scanning and development of transrectal and breast scanners, Doppler; development of ultrasound devices designed to generate heating patterns in the body; clinical studies of hyperthermia; simulation and measurement of heating in perfusing structure; analysis of heating using high intensity focused ultrasound beams. *Mailing Add:* Ont Cancer Inst Exp Therapeut & Dept Med Biophys Univ Toronto 500 Sherbourne St Toronto ON M4X 1K9 Can

HUNT, KATHARINE LOIS CLARKE, THEORY OF MOLECULAR INTERACTIONS & SPECTROSCOPY, NON-EQUILIBRIUM THERMODYNAMICS & NON-LINEAR KINETICS. *Current Pos:* from asst to prof chem, 79-92, UNIV DISTINGUISHED PROF, DEPT CHEM, MICH STATE UNIV, 79- *Personal Data:* b Akron, Ohio, June 15, 53; m 78, Paul M; c Laurel A. *Educ:* Mich State Univ, BS, 75; Cambridge Univ, Eng, PhD(chem), 78. *Prof Exp:* NSF fel, Dept Chem, Mass Inst Technol, 78-79. *Mem:* Am Chem Soc; Am Phys Soc; Sigma Xi. *Res:* Intermolecular forces, electric and magnetic susceptibilities, collision-induced spectroscopy, nonlinear optical processes, induction, dispersion and hyperpolarization effects. *Mailing Add:* Dept Chem Mich State Univ East Lansing MI 48824. *Fax:* 517-353-1793

HUNT, KENNETH WHITTEN, botany, conservation; deceased, see previous edition for last biography

HUNT, LAWRENCE BARRIE, ORNITHOLOGY, VERTEBRATE ECOLOGY. *Current Pos:* from assoc prof to prof zool, 67-89, EMER PROF, EASTERN ILL UNIV, 89- *Personal Data:* b Richmond, Ind, July 19, 32; m 55; c 2. *Educ:* Miami Univ, BA, 55; Univ Wis-Madison, MS, 60, PhD(zool, wildlife ecol), 68. *Prof Exp:* Instr zool & bot, Univ Wis-Kenosha, 62-67. *Mem:* Am Ornith Union; Wilson Ornith Soc; Asn Field Ornithologists. *Res:* Effects of pesticides on vertebrate populations and ecosystem accumulation; avian breeding behavior and habitat preference. *Mailing Add:* 51 Heather Dr Charleston IL 61920

HUNT, LEE MCCAA, OCEANOGRAPHY, GEOLOGY. *Current Pos:* tech asst, Mine Adv Comt, 60-62, exec secy, 62-74, exec secy, Army Countermine Adv Comt, 70-72 & Undersea Warfare Comt, 72-74, EXEC DIR, NAVAL STUDIES BD, NAT ACAD SCI, 74- *Personal Data:* b Clio, Ala, Aug 18, 26; m 51; c 2. *Educ:* Am Univ, BS, 56. *Prof Exp:* Pres & gen mgr, Southern Iron Corp, 56-58; res asst oceanog, Tex A&M Univ, 58-60. *Mem:* Marine Technol Soc. *Res:* Underwater acoustics, magnetics and explosive phenomena; naval weapons and weapons countermeasures design; oceanographic environmental studies. *Mailing Add:* 7715 Lookout Ct Alexandria VA 22306

HUNT, LEON GIBSON, mathematical statistics, operations research, for more information see previous edition

HUNT, LINDA MARGARET, DEVELOPMENTAL BIOLOGY. *Current Pos:* ASST PROF GEN BIOL, UNIV NOTRE DAME, 75- *Personal Data:* b Lexington, NC, Oct 25, 47. *Educ:* Univ NC, Greensboro, BA, 69, MA, 71; Univ Mich, MS, 73, PhD(zool), 75. *Concurrent Pos:* Coordr gen biol, Univ Notre Dame, 75- *Mem:* AAAS; Entom Soc Am; Sigma Xi; Am Soc Zoologists; Am Inst Biol Sci. *Res:* Developmental biology of hemiptera with emphasis upon both histological and endocrinological studies; developmental biology. *Mailing Add:* 148 Galvin Life Sci Bldg Notre Dame IN 46556

HUNT, LINDSAY MCLAURIN, JR, ORAL BIOLOGY. *Current Pos:* PROF RESTORATIVE DENT & DEAN, SCH DENT, VA COMMONWEALTH UNIV, 85- *Personal Data:* b Oklahoma City, Okla, Sept 19, 39; m 60; c 2. *Educ:* Okla Univ, BA, 61; Baylor Univ, DDS, 65, PhD(physiol), 71. *Prof Exp:* Dent intern, St Anthony Hosp, Oklahoma City, 67-68; asst prof dent res & coordr basic health sci dent, Sch Dent, Emory Univ, 71-73, from assoc prof to prof oral biol & chmn dept, 73-85. *Mem:* AAAS; Int Asn Dent Res; Am Asn Dent Schs; Am Dent Asn; fel Am Col Dent. *Res:* Calcium metabolism; pain. *Mailing Add:* Sch Dent Va Commonwealth Univ PO Box 980566 Richmond VA 23298

HUNT, LOIS TURPIN, CYTOLOGY, MICROBIOLOGY. *Current Pos:* jr res scientist, 66-68, SR RES SCIENTIST & PROTEIN DATA ED, ATLAS OF PROTEIN SEQUENCY & STRUCT STAFF, NAT BIOMED RES FOUND, 68- *Personal Data:* b Norfolk, Va, Jan 14, 33; div; c 1. *Educ:* Univ Kans, BA, 58; Univ Wash, MS, 61; Univ Md, College Park, PhD(cytol), 68. *Prof Exp:* Instr zool, Univ Md, College Park, 64-66. *Mem:* Soc Protozool; Coun Biol Educ; Soc Pharmacol & Environ Path; NY Acad Sci; Am Fisheries Soc; Sigma Xi. *Res:* Histopathology and protozoan parasites of freshwater fishes; biochemical evolution of organisms based on analyses of sequences of proteins; evolutionary relations of protein families. *Mailing Add:* 12317 Dalewood Dr Wheaton MD 20902-1121

HUNT, LOUIS ROBERTS, SYSTEMS & CONTROL, SIGNAL PROCESSING. *Current Pos:* PROF APPL MATH, UNIV TEX, DALLAS, 84-, PROF ELEC ENG, 88-, DIR, CTR FOR ENG MATH, 90- *Personal Data:* b Shreveport, La, Dec 5, 42; m 67; c 2. *Educ:* Baylor Univ, BS, 64; Rice Univ, PhD(math), 70. *Prof Exp:* From asst prof to prof math, Tex Tech Univ, 69-84. *Concurrent Pos:* Res engr, NASA Ames Res Ctr, 80-82. *Mem:* Am Math Soc; Soc Indust & Appl Math; Inst Elec & Electronics Engrs; Int Fedn Nonlinear Analysts. *Res:* Early work in several complex variables, in particular tangential Cauchy-Riemann equations; research in nonlinear systems and control involves controllability, observability and feedback linearization; interest in nonlinear sign processing. *Mailing Add:* Prog Math Sci EC 3-5 Univ Tex Richardson TX 75083-0688

HUNT, MAHLON SEYMOUR, GEODESY. *Current Pos:* RETIRED. *Personal Data:* b Cairo, Ill, Apr 1, 25; m 53; c 4. *Educ:* Wash Univ, AB, 49, MA, 52. *Prof Exp:* Cartogr, Aeronaut Chart & Info Ctr, Mo, 51-54, geodesist, 57-59; cartogr, US Naval Observ, Washington, DC, 54-57; geodesist, Air Force Cambridge Res Labs, Mass, 59-68, chief, Lunar Laser Observ, Ariz, 68-72, geodesist, Air Force Geophys Lab, Mass, 72-76. *Res:* Astronomy; geodetic instrumentation and techniques. *Mailing Add:* 1545 E Erie St Springfield MO 65804

HUNT, MICHAEL O'LEARY, FOREST PRODUCTS. *Current Pos:* asst prof, 60-69, assoc prof, 69-79, PROF WOOD SCI, PURDUE UNIV, WEST LAFAYETTE, 79-, DIR, WOOD RES LAB, 82- *Personal Data:* b Louisville, Ky, Dec 9, 35; c 3. *Educ:* Univ Ky, BS, 57; Duke Univ, MF, 58; NC State Univ, PhD(wood sci), 70. *Honors & Awards:* Gottschalk Mem Award, Forest Prod Soc, 84. *Prof Exp:* Prod engr, Wood Prod Div, Singer Co, 59-60. *Concurrent Pos:* Consult eng wood composites, 62. *Mem:* Soc Wood Sci & Technol; Forest Prod Soc; Am Soc Testing & Mat. *Res:* Use of wood and woodbase composite materials in structural systems; use, reuse and care of wood in historic preservation and restoration. *Mailing Add:* Dept Forestry Purdue Univ FPRD Bldg West Lafayette IN 47907-1200. *Fax:* 765-496-1344; *E-Mail:* mhunt@forest1.fnr.purdue.edu

HUNT, PAUL PAYSON, PHYSICAL CHEMISTRY. *Current Pos:* assoc prof, 65-68, PROF CHEM, FROSTBURG STATE COL, 68-, CHMN DEPT, 66- *Personal Data:* b Elkview, WVa, Dec 17, 30; m 55; c 3. *Educ:* Glenville State Col, BS & AB, 54; Univ Tenn, MS, 58, PhD(phys chem), 60. *Prof Exp:* Sr res chemist, Hercules Powder Co, Md, 59-65. *Mem:* Am Chem Soc; Sigma Xi. *Res:* Gas chromatography of hydrogen isotopes; high temperature kinetics of corrosive reactions; decomposition and stabilization studies of high-energy solid propellant ingredients. *Mailing Add:* 11707 Bedford Rd Cumberland MD 21502-9803

HUNT, RICHARD LEE, INORGANIC CHEMISTRY. *Current Pos:* PROF CHEM, MOREHEAD STATE UNIV, 91- *Personal Data:* b Lansing, Mich, Nov 1, 36; m 57; c 2. *Educ:* Antioch Col, BS, 59; Univ Chicago, PhD(chem), 63. *Prof Exp:* NSF fel, Imp Col, Univ London, 63-65; from asst prof to assoc prof chem, Calif State Univ, Long Beach, 65-80. *Mem:* Am Chem Soc; Royal Soc Chem. *Res:* Kinetics of oxidations; electron microscopy; structure determination of organometallic compounds; nuclear quadruple resonance. *Mailing Add:* UPO 979 Morehead State Univ Morehead KY 40351

HUNT, RICHARD STANLEY, FOREST PATHOLOGY. *Current Pos:* RES SCIENTIST FOREST PATH, CAN FORESTRY SERV, 73- *Personal Data:* b Victoria, BC, Apr 22, 44; m 68, S Carol Phillips; c Tony, Jeffrey & Meggan. *Educ:* Univ Victoria, BSc, 67; Univ Calif, Berkeley, PhD(plant path), 71. *Prof Exp:* Fel, Prairie Regional Lab, Nat Res Coun Can, 72-73. *Concurrent Pos:* Sr ed, Can J Plant Path. *Mem:* Am Phytopath Soc; Can Phytopath Soc. *Res:* White pine blister rust; disease control through silviculture; hazard rating; genetic selection and biotechnology; tomentosus root disease biology and control. *Mailing Add:* Pac Forest Ctr 506 W Burnside Victoria BC V8Z 1M5 Can. *Fax:* 250-363-0775

HUNT, ROBERT HARRY, PHYSICS. *Current Pos:* from asst prof to assoc prof, 64-77, assoc chmn dept, 75-78, prof, 77-95, EMER PROF PHYSICS, FLA STATE UNIV, 95- *Personal Data:* b Ann Arbor, Mich, June 13, 32. *Educ:* Univ Mich, BS, 54, MS, 55, PhD(molecular physics), 63. *Prof Exp:* Instr physics, Univ Mich, 63-64. *Mem:* Am Phys Soc. *Res:* High resolution infrared spectroscopy; molecular structure. *Mailing Add:* Dept Physics Fla State Univ Tallahassee FL 32306-3016

HUNT, ROBERT M, JR, VERTEBRATE PALEONTOLOGY. *Current Pos:* from asst prof to prof geol, 73-93, PROF MUS & GEOL, UNIV NEBR. *Personal Data:* b Cleveland, Ohio, July 18, 41; m 70; c 2. *Educ:* Col Wooster, BA, 63; Univ NMex, MS, 65; Columbia Univ, PhD(biol), 71. *Prof Exp:* Instr anat, Columbia Univ, 70-73. *Concurrent Pos:* Res assoc, Am Mus Natural Hist, NY, 73-93. *Mem:* Paleont Soc; Soc Vert Paleont; Soc Study Evolution. *Res:* Biostratigraphy of Miocene mammals of North America; functional anatomy of mammals; evolution and biogeography of carnivora. *Mailing Add:* Div Vert Paleont Univ Nebr Lincoln NE 68588-0549

HUNT, ROBERT NELSON, MUNICIPAL ENGINEERING, DINOSAUR PALEONTOLOGY. *Current Pos:* chmn, Dept Sci, 80-87, fac asn pres, 90-92, INSTR ENG, GRANDE PRAIRE REGIONAL COL, 74-, DINOSAUR PALEONT, 89- *Personal Data:* b Edmonton, Alta, Sept 9, 46; m 68, Patricia Bunting; c Scarlett & Nando. *Educ:* Univ Alta, BS, 68, PhD(physics), 74. *Prof Exp:* Instr eng & comput, Col Arts, Sci & Technol & Univ WI, Jamaica, 72-73 & Camrose Lutheran Col, 73-74. *Concurrent Pos:* Civil engr, Beairsto, Stewart & Weir Eng, Ltd, 79-85; consult, Microelectronics Ctr & lectr, Dept Elec Eng, Univ Man, 85, vis scientist, 85-86; Paleo trustee, Tyrell Mus Paleont, 91- *Mem:* Can Asn Physicists; AAAS. *Res:* Stable isotope studies; computer-aided control systems; computer-assisted design, manufacturing and engineering of printed circuit boards and very-large-scale integration gate arrays for custom design and semi-custom design; computer-aided design, manufacturing and engineering of chips and microelectronic devices. *Mailing Add:* 3500 Rock Creek Dr Raleigh NC 27609-7125. Fax: 403-539-2832

HUNT, ROBERT WELDON, MATHEMATICAL ANALYSIS, APPLIED MATHEMATICS. *Current Pos:* chmn dept, 87-90, PROF MATH, HUMBOLDT STATE UNIV, 77- *Personal Data:* b Portales, NMex, Nov 16, 35; m 55, 64, Bonnie J Dixon; c Robyn, Shawna, Robert, Tracy, Tanya, Talisha, Michael, Dylan, Ashley & Ciara. *Educ:* WTex State Univ, BS, 56; Univ Utah, MS, 58, PhD(math), 61. *Prof Exp:* Instr math, Univ Utah, 59-61; asst prof, Huntsville Br, Univ Ala, 61-62; assoc prof, Southern Ill Univ, 62-68 & Naval Postgrad Sch, 68-70; prof math & chmn dept, Calif State Col, Bakersfield, 70-77. *Concurrent Pos:* Consult, Marshall Space Flight Ctr, NASA, Ala, 62-67 & Douglas Aircraft Co, Calif, 64-65; vis prof, Calif State Univ, Los Angeles, 74-75 & Humboldt State Univ, 75-77. *Mem:* Am Math Soc; Math Asn Am; Sigma Xi. *Res:* Ordinary differential equations; oscillation properties and matrix forms; calculus of variations and its application to space and missile problems. *Mailing Add:* Humboldt State Univ Arcata CA 95521. *E-Mail:* rwh2@axe.humboldt.edu

HUNT, RONALD DUNCAN, COMPARATIVE PATHOLOGY, RESEARCH ADMINISTRATION. *Current Pos:* pathologist-in-chg, Animal Res Ctr, Harvard Med Sch, 63-72, chmn, Div Comp Path, New Eng Regional Primate Res Ctr, 65-76, assoc prof comp path & assoc dir, Animal Res Ctr, 72-77, dir Animal Res Ctr, 79-88, DIR, NEW ENG REGIONAL PRIMATE RES CTR, HARVARD MED SCH, 76-, PROF COMP PATH, 77- *Personal Data:* b Los Angeles, Calif, Oct 9, 35. *Educ:* Univ Calif, Davis, BS, 57, DVM, 59. *Honors & Awards:* Res Awards, Am Asn Lab Animal Sci, 67, 69 & 73; Charles River Prize, Am Vet Med Asn, 83. *Prof Exp:* Mem, US Army Vet Corps Inst Path, , 59-61, captain, 61-63. *Concurrent Pos:* Lectr, Mass Inst Technol, 64-81; affil pathologist, Angell Mem Animal Hosp, 66-75. *Mem:* Am Col Vet Path; Int Acad Path; Am Soc Exp Path; Am Vet Med Asn; NY Acad Sci. *Res:* Comparative pathology of human and animal diseases, especially of primates; herpesvirus diseases and metabolic bone diseases; author or co-author of over 150 publications. *Mailing Add:* New Eng Regional Primate Res Ctr Southborough MA 01772-1312. Fax: 508-460-0612

HUNT, ROY EDWARD, CHEMISTRY. *Current Pos:* RETIRED. *Personal Data:* b New York, NY, Sept 4, 18; m 47, Jeanette Riley; c William E, Deborah H, Donald R & David R. *Educ:* Brown Univ, ScB, 40; Univ Rochester, PhD(chem), 47. *Prof Exp:* Res assoc, George Washington Univ, 42-45; res assoc, Gen Elec Co, 47-48, asst mgr, Tech Personnel Div, 48-53, mgr tech recruiting sci doctorates, 53-54, supvr tech personnel, Knolls Atomic Power Lab, 54-60; assoc, Exec Personnel Dept, Booz Allen & Hamilton, 60-68, managing assoc, 68-80; vpres, Spencer Stuart & Assocs, 80-83. *Mem:* Am Chem Soc. *Res:* Vapor pressures of binary liquid mixtures; photochemical investigations of ketones; fluorescence of ketone vapors; ultraviolet filters; burning rates of double-base powder; flame-thrower ballistics. *Mailing Add:* HC-01 Box 58 Kattskill Bay NY 12844-9702

HUNT, STEVEN CHARLES, GENETIC-EPIDEMIOLOGY. *Current Pos:* Res instr, 80-82, from res asst prof to res assoc prof, 82-93, RES PROF MED, UNIV UTAH, 93- *Personal Data:* b Salt Lake City, Utah, 53; m 77; c 5. *Educ:* Univ Utah, BS, 76, PhD(med biophysics), 80. *Concurrent Pos:* Coun on Hypertension, Am Heart Asn. *Mem:* Am Soc Hypertension; Am Heart Asn. *Res:* Research on cause and prevention of early coronary disease and hypertension; separate genetic, common environment and sporadic causes; cellular ion transport and lipid abnormalities. *Mailing Add:* Res Park 410 Chipeta Way Rm 161 Salt Lake City UT 84108. Fax: 801-581-6862; *E-Mail:* steve@ucvg.med.utah.edu

HUNT, THOMAS KINTZING, ENERGY CONVERSION. *Current Pos:* CHMN & CHIEF SCIENTIST, ADVAN MODULAR POWER SYSTS INC, 91- *Personal Data:* b Boston, Mass, Oct 9, 37; m 64, Ann E Webster; c Jennifer A, David S, Diana K & Susan E. *Educ:* Pomona Col, BA, 59; Calif Inst Technol, MS, 61, PhD(physics), 64. *Prof Exp:* Res fel physics, Calif Inst Technol, 64; staff scientist, Sci Lab, Ford Motor Co, 64-88. *Concurrent Pos:* NSF fel, 59-61; res scientist & mgr, Environ Res Inst Mich, 89-96. *Mem:* Am Phys Soc; Am Asn Physics Teachers; AAAS; Sigma Xi. *Res:* Low temperature physics; superconductivity; energy conversion and storage. *Mailing Add:* 3420 Andover Rd Ann Arbor MI 48105

HUNT, THOMAS KNIGHT, SURGERY. *Current Pos:* asst prof, 65-69, PROF SURG, UNIV CALIF, SAN FRANCISCO, 69-, PROF AMBULATORY & COMMUNITY MED, 71- *Personal Data:* b Chicago, Ill, Aug 6, 30; c 3. *Educ:* Harvard Univ, BS, 52, MD, 56. *Honors & Awards:* Mallinckrodt Award, Harvard Univ, 53; James IV Traveller, Alpha Omega Alpha, 74. *Prof Exp:* Intern surg, Boston City Hosp, 56-57; resident, Univ Ore, Med Sch, 59-63, instr, 63-65. *Concurrent Pos:* Res fel hyperbaric oxygen unit, Dept Surg, Western Infirmary, Univ Glasgow, 64; dir, Gen Surg & dir, Surg Outpatient Dept, Univ Calif Hosp, 68- *Mem:* Am Asn Surg of Trauma (vpres); Am Surg Asn; Soc Univ Surgeons; Am Col Surgeons; Am Trauma Soc (pres, 80-82). *Res:* Wound healing; tissue gas determination; general and endocrine surgery. *Mailing Add:* Univ Calif Med Ctr 513 Parnassus Ave Rm 839 San Francisco CA 94143-0001

HUNT, V DANIEL, technology assessment, system concept development, for more information see previous edition

HUNT, WALTER ANDREW, ALCOHOLISM, DRUG ABUSE. *Current Pos:* CHIEF, NEUROSCI & BEHAV RES BR, NAT INST ALCOHOL ABUSE & ALCOHOLISM, 89- *Personal Data:* b Atlantic City, NJ, Mar 31, 45. *Educ:* Bethany Col, BS, 67; WVa Univ, MS, 69, PhD(pharmacol), 71. *Prof Exp:* Res scientist, Armed Forces Radiol Res Inst, 73-80, chief, Physiol-Psychol Div, 80-89. *Mem:* Res Soc Alcoholism; AAAS. *Res:* Neurochemistry. *Mailing Add:* Div Basic Res Willco Bldg Suite 402 6000 Executive Blvd Bethesda MD 20892-7003. Fax: 301-594-0673; *E-Mail:* whunt@willco.niaaa.nih.gov

HUNT, WILLIAM A(LFRED), HYDRAULIC ENGINEERING, FLUID MECHANICS. *Current Pos:* HKM CONSULT, 90- *Personal Data:* b Whitefish, Mont, Aug 8, 30; m 56; c 4. *Educ:* Mont State Univ, BS, 52; Univ Wis-Madison, MS, 53, PhD(hydraul eng), 60. *Honors & Awards:* Stephen D Bechtel Pipeline Engineering Award, Am Soc Civil Engrs, 78. *Prof Exp:* Res asst civil eng, Univ Wis-Madison, 52-53; instr, Mont State Univ, 55-58; res asst, Univ Wis-Madison, 58-60; from asst prof to assoc prof civil eng, Mont State Univ, 60-67, actg head, Dept Civil Eng & Eng Mech, 77-78, dir, Mont Water Resources Res Ctr, 78-82, prof civil eng, 67-90. *Concurrent Pos:* Eng consult, 60- *Mem:* Am Soc Civil Engrs; Am Water Works Asn. *Res:* Hydraulic transport of solids in pipelines; analysis and design of pipelines and distribution systems; hydraulic transients and control systems for water pipelines. *Mailing Add:* MSE HKM Consult Engr PO Box 1090 Bozeman MT 59771-1090

HUNT, WILLIAM B, JR, MEDICINE, IMMUNOLOGY. *Current Pos:* clin assoc prof, 78-90, CLIN PROF MED, EASTERN CAROLINA SCH MED, 90- *Personal Data:* b Lexington, NC, Sept 27, 27; m 50, Nancy Robinson; c 4. *Educ:* Wake Forest Col, BS, 48; Bowman Gray Sch Med, MD, 53; Am Bd Internal Med, dipl, 62, recert, 74; Am Bd Allergy, dipl, 66. *Prof Exp:* Instr med, NY Med Col, 59-60; res fel microbiol & immunol, Sch Med, Univ Va, 60-62, from instr to asst prof med, 65-67, assoc prof & asst dean, 67-75, dir, Respiratory Care Unit, 69-75; med dir cardiopulmonary serv, Craven Reg Med Ctr, 75-95. *Concurrent Pos:* Mem, T B Qual Assurance Comt, State NC; trustee, Nat Bd Respiratory Care. *Mem:* Fel Am Col Chest Physicians; fel Am Acad Allergy; Am Fedn Clin Res; fel Am Col Physicians; Am Thoracic Soc; Am Lung Asn. *Res:* Allergies; internal medicine; pulmonary disease. *Mailing Add:* PO Box 2157 New Bern NC 28560

HUNT, WILLIAM CECIL, ORGANIC CHEMISTRY. *Current Pos:* RETIRED. *Personal Data:* b Conemaugh, Pa, June 21, 23; m 48; c 4. *Educ:* Juniata Col, BS, 44; Univ Pa, MS, 49, PhD(org chem), 51. *Prof Exp:* Asst prof chem, Washington & Lee Univ, 50-51; fel protected metals, Mellon Inst, 51-53, sr fel, 53-57, admin fel, 57-59, head sci rels, 59-62; mgr lab facil, Celanese Corp Am, 62-64, mgr, Spec Projs Res Dept, 64-65; vpres & tech dir, Devoe & Raynolds Co, Inc, Ky, 65-66, vpres & tech dir, Celanese Coatings Co, 66-67, vpres technol & mfg, 67-68, vpres, Celanese Res Co, NJ, 68-71; vpres corp technol, Great Lakes Chem Corp, 71-80; pres, Syngene Corp, 81-87. *Mem:* Indust Res Inst; Am Chem Soc; Soc Plastics Eng. *Res:* Polyester resins. *Mailing Add:* 814 N Seven Lakes Apt 7 West End NC 27376

HUNT, WILLIAM DANIEL, ACOUSTIC CHARGE TRANSPORT DEVICES, SURFACE ACOUSTIC WAVE DEVICES. *Current Pos:* asst prof, 87-91, ASSOC PROF ELEC ENG, GA INST TECHNOL, 91- *Personal Data:* b Jackson, Miss, Dec 21, 54; m 91, Mary Hallisey; c Owen. *Educ:* Univ Ala, BS, 76; Mass Inst Technol, SM, 80; Univ Ill, Urbana-Champaign, PhD(elec eng), 87. *Prof Exp:* Engr, Govt Systs Div, Harris Corp, 76-78; staff engr, Bolt Beranek & Newman, Inc, 80-84. *Concurrent Pos:* Consult, Electronic Decisions Inc, 85-87 & United Technol Res Ctr, 88-90; NSF presidential young investr, 89; distinguished eng fel, Univ Ala, 94. *Mem:* Acoust Soc Am; Inst Elec & Electronics Engrs; Am Phys Soc; Am Soc Eng Educ; Sigma Xi. *Res:* New types of acoustic charge transport devices; new substrate materials for acoustic charge transport devices; surface acoustic wave propagation in AlGaAs heterostructures and in III-V compound semiconductors as they pertain to the performance of proposed acoustic charge transport devices; transducers for biomedical ultrasound tissue characterization. *Mailing Add:* Sch Elec Eng Ga Inst Technol Atlanta GA 30332-0250

HUNT, WILLIAM EDWARD, NEUROSURGERY. *Current Pos:* from instr to assoc prof, 52-64, PROF SURG & DIR, DIV NEUROL SURG, COL MED, OHIO STATE UNIV, 64- *Personal Data:* b Columbus, Ohio, Nov 26, 21; m 45; c 3. *Educ:* Ohio State Univ, BA, 43, MD, 45. *Prof Exp:* Resident gen surg, White Cross Hosp, Columbus, Ohio, 48-49; resident neurosurg, Barnes Hosp, St Louis, 49-50; fel, Washington Univ, 50-51; resident, Barnes Hosp, St Louis, 51-52. *Mem:* Cong Neurol Surg; Am Asn Neurol Surg; Am Col Surgeons; Neurosurg Soc Am; Soc Neurol Surg (secy); Sigma Xi. *Res:* Cerebral vascular disease and related fundamental problems; cerebral vascular physiology; sensory disorders and physiology; spinal cord injury. *Mailing Add:* 1000 Urlin Ave 2205 Columbus OH 43212-3341

HUNTE, BERYL ELEANOR, MATHEMATICS EDUCATION. *Current Pos:* asst prof & sr instr, Manhattan Community Col, City Univ NY, 64-66, assoc prof, 66-70, chmn, Dept Math, 66-67 & 70-73, prof math, 70-95, actg dean students, 85-86, actg dean acad affairs, 87, dean spec projs, Off Acad Affairs, 88-89, EMER PROF MATH, MANHATTAN COMMUNITY COL, CITY UNIV NY, 96- *Personal Data:* b New York, NY. *Educ:* Hunter Col, BA, 47; Columbia Univ, MA, 48; NY Univ, PhD, 65. *Prof Exp:* Instr math, Southern Univ, 48-51; teacher math, Bloomfield High Sch, 51-57 & Friends Sem, 57-62; asst prof math, Rockland Community Col, 62-63; instr math & supvr pract teachers, NY Univ, 64. *Concurrent Pos:* Deleg, Workshop Human Rels, PR Dept Educ, 65; speaker, Bur Math Educ, NY State Dept

Educ, 67; consult, William H Sadlier, Inc, 67-70; mem, Mid States Eval Team, 71-73 & 77; math consult Title I progs, NY State Educ Dept, 72; test supvr, Am Col Testing, 73 & 74; oral examr, Dept Civil Serv, State NY, 75; NSF rev panelist, 76; tech rev panelist, Div Equal Educ Opportunities, HEW, 77; fac fel, Off Acad Affairs, Cent Off, City Univ New York, 80-81; rev panelist, Dept Higher Educ, State NJ, 84, 85 & 87; assoc, Univ Seminar Higher Educ, Columbia Univ, 89-95; bd dirs, City Univ NY Acad Humanities & Sci, 91-, first vpres, 94-; bd dirs, UN Asn NY City, secy 80-86. *Mem:* NY Acad Sci; Am Math Soc. *Res:* Geometry; mathematics education; statistics and probability; educational opportunities; urban education. *Mailing Add:* 30 W 60th St New York NY 10023

HUNTEN, DONALD MOUNT, PLANETARY SCIENCES. *Current Pos:* prof, 77-88, REGENTS PROF PLANETARY SCI, LUNAR & PLANETARY LAB, UNIV ARIZ, 88- *Personal Data:* b Montreal, Que, Mar 1, 25; m 95, Isobel A Rubenstein; c Keith A & Mark R. *Educ:* Univ Western Ont, BSc, 46; McGill Univ, PhD(physics), 50. *Honors & Awards:* Pub Serv Medals, NASA, 77, 85 & 96; Space Sci Award, Am Inst Aeronaut & Astronaut, 80; Kuiper Prize Award, Am Astron Soc, 87. *Prof Exp:* Res assoc physics, Univ Sask, 50-52, from asst prof to assoc prof, 53-63; physicist, Kitt Peak Nat Observ, 63-77. *Concurrent Pos:* Ed, Can Asn Physicists, 61-63; prof physics, Univ Sask, 64-66; consult, NASA, 64-, vchmn, Sci Steering Groups, Pioneer-Venus Prog, 74-, mem, Space Sci Bd, 75-76 & 82-86, sci adv, Assoc Admin Space Sci. 76-77, mem, Adv Coun & Chmn, Space Sci Adv Comt, 78-; mem, Climatic Impact Comt, Nat Acad Sci, 72-75. *Mem:* Nat Acad Sci; Am Geophys Union; Am Astron Soc; Am Phys Soc. *Res:* Spectroscopy; earth's upper atmosphere and planetary atmospheres; photoelectric and spectroscopic instrumentation; planetary entry probes. *Mailing Add:* 3445 W Foxes Den Dr Tucson AZ 85745. *Fax:* 520-621-4933; *E-Mail:* dhunten@lpl.arizona.edu

HUNTER, ALAN GRAHAM, ANIMAL PHYSIOLOGY. *Current Pos:* from asst prof to assoc prof, 63-70, PROF REPROD & LACTATION, UNIV MINN, ST PAUL, 70- *Personal Data:* b Pawtucket, RI, Apr 1, 34; m 55; c 2. *Educ:* Univ RI, BS, 55, MS, 58; Mich State Univ, PhD(reprod physiol), 63. *Prof Exp:* Asst dairy sci, Univ RI, 55-58; res instr, Mich State Univ, 58-63. *Concurrent Pos:* Vis Prof, Cambridge Univ, 85. *Mem:* AAAS; Am Soc Animal Sci; Am Dairy Sci Asn; Brit Soc Study Fertil; Sigma Xi. *Res:* Protein constituents of semen and female reproductive cells and fluids and their physiological role in reproduction and lactation. *Mailing Add:* Dept Animal Sci Univ Minn 495 An Sc/VM St Paul MN 55108

HUNTER, ALICE S (BAKER), DIPTERA, DROSOPHILIDAE. *Current Pos:* assoc prof, 70-75, PROF BIOL SCI, UNIV OF PAC, 75- *Personal Data:* b New York, NY, Sept 11, 23; m 54; c Deborah & Linda C. *Educ:* Queen's Col, NY, BS, 44; Columbia Univ, MA, 46, PhD(zool), 52. *Prof Exp:* Instr biol, Johns Hopkins Univ, 48-50; res assoc chem & physiol, Fla State Univ, 50-53; chemist, Fla State Dept Agr, 53-54; res assoc physiol, Col Med, Univ Ill, 54-55; asst prof biol, Roosevelt Univ, 55-57; prof, Univ Andes, Colombia, 57-64; prof, Univ Centro-Occidental, Venezuela, 64-70. *Mem:* AAAS; Am Soc Zoologists; Entom Soc Am; Sigma Xi. *Res:* Taxonomy and ecology of Drosophila; soil arthropods-insects. *Mailing Add:* Dept Biol Sci Univ Pac Stockton CA 95211-0001

HUNTER, ARVEL HATCH, SOIL FERTILITY. *Current Pos:* vpres, 74-87, PRES, AGRO SERV INT INC, 87- *Personal Data:* b Rigby, Idaho, Dec 19, 21; m 46, Genavieve Webb; c 4. *Educ:* Brigham Young Univ, BS, 54; Ohio State Univ, MS, 55; NC State Univ, PhD(soil sci), 59. *Prof Exp:* Res instr soil chem, NC State Univ, 55-59, asst prof soil fertil, 59-60; asst prof soil fertil, Wash State Univ, 60-61; regional agronomist, Calif Chem Co, 61-64; regional dir, NC State Univ-AID Contract, 64-67, dir control lab, 67-74, AID vis assoc prof soil sci, NC State Univ, 69-74. *Concurrent Pos:* Owner, Custom Lab Equip Co, 69-90. *Mem:* Am Soc Agron; Soil Sci Soc Am. *Res:* Agronomy; analytical chemistry; soil fertility; soil analytical methods. *Mailing Add:* 840 Citrus Tree Dr Orange City FL 32763. *Fax:* 904-775-9890

HUNTER, BARRY B, MYCOLOGY, PLANT PATHOLOGY. *Current Pos:* PROF BIOL, CALIFORNIA STATE COL, PA, 68- *Personal Data:* b Turtle Creek, Pa, Apr 4, 39; m 63; c 3. *Educ:* California State Col, Pa, BS, 63, MEd, 69; Univ Minn, MS, 67; WVa Univ, PhD(plant path), 70. *Prof Exp:* Teacher high sch, 63-66. *Mem:* Am Phytopath Soc; Mycol Soc Am. *Res:* Soil microbial ecology of fungal pathogens as they relate to environmental, chemical and biological factors. *Mailing Add:* Biol Dept Calif Univ Pa Box 45 California PA 15419-1341

HUNTER, BYRON ALEXANDER, INDUSTRIAL ORGANIC CHEMISTRY, RUBBER CHEMISTRY. *Current Pos:* RES ASSOC, BRIGHAM YOUNG UNIV, 77- *Personal Data:* b Salt Lake City, Utah, Oct 15, 10; m 42, Margaret C Oleson; c Shirley A, James C, Robert B, Margaret E, Virginia J (Wendy), Sharman J, Heather E & Deborah L. *Educ:* Univ Utah, AB, 33, BA, 37, AM, 38, MS, 38; Ohio State Univ, PhD(org chem), 41, PhD(biochem), 42. *Honors & Awards:* Outstanding Achievement Award, Thermoplastics & Foams Div, Soc Plastics Engrs, 90; Thomas Midgley Award, Am Chem Soc, 90. *Prof Exp:* Asst chem, Iowa State Univ, 38-40; res chemist, Uniroyal Chem, Uniroyal Inc, 41-45, group leader org res, 45-48, sr res assoc, 58-75; prof chem, Univ Conn, Waterbury, 60-77. *Mem:* Am Chem Soc; Sigma Xi. *Res:* Agricultural chemicals; rubber accelerators and antioxidants; stabilization of synthetic rubber; blowing agents, rubber and plastics; organic hydrazine compounds; high molecular weight aliphatic compounds of nitrogen and sulfur; cement chemicals; soil chemicals; recipient of 67 US patents; cement water repellents; freeze-thaw breakup inhibitors. *Mailing Add:* 352 E 426 North St Alpine UT 84004-1424

HUNTER, CHRISTOPHER, APPLIED MATHEMATICS. *Current Pos:* dir appl math, 70-83, 89-95, prof, 70-91, MCKENZIE PROF MATH, FLA STATE UNIV, 91-, CHMN, 93- *Personal Data:* b Manchester, Eng, May 28, 34; m 61, Hilda M Salmon; c James, Alison, Rosemary & Andrew. *Educ:* Cambridge Univ, BA, 57, PhD(math), 60, ScD, 93. *Honors & Awards:* Bronwer Award, Div Dynamical Astron, Am Astron Soc, 94. *Prof Exp:* Res assoc math, Mass Inst Technol, 60-61, lectr, 61-62; res fel, Trinity Col, Cambridge Univ, 62-64; from asst prof to assoc prof, Mass Inst Technol, 64-70. *Concurrent Pos:* Consult, Avco, Tyco Labs; Joint Inst Lab Astrophys fel, Univ Colo, 76-77. *Mem:* Am Astron Soc; Soc Indust & Appl Math; Int Astron Union; Royal Astron Soc London. *Res:* Dynamics of stellar systems; applied analysis. *Mailing Add:* Dept Math Fla State Univ Tallahassee FL 32306-3027. *Fax:* 850-644-4053; *E-Mail:* hunter@math.fsu.edu

HUNTER, CYNTHIA L, CORAL REEF ECOLOGY. *Current Pos:* res asst, Dept Zool, 82-88, asst researcher, 89-92, RES ASSOC, DEPT BOT, HAWAII INST MARINE BIOL, UNIV HAWAII, 92- *Personal Data:* b Wichita Falls, Tex, Mar 28, 54; m 91. *Educ:* Calif State Univ, BS, 75; Univ SFla, MS, 80; Univ Hawaii, PhD(zool), 88. *Prof Exp:* Res assoc, Conserv Consults Inc, 76-78, Smithsonian Inst, 78-80; staff biologist, Mote Marine Lab, Fla, 80-82. *Concurrent Pos:* Lectr, Scientists in Sch, Hawaii Dept Educ, 87-88; researcher, Univ Guam, 88-89; consult, Oceans Alive Inc, 89- *Mem:* Soc Study Evolution; Sigma Xi; Western Soc Naturalists; Pac Sci Asn; Am Soc Zoologists. *Res:* Reproduction, genetics and ecology of corals; long term dynamics of coral reefs; biotoxicities for tropic pacific reef species. *Mailing Add:* Dept Bot Univ Hawaii 3190 Maile Way St John 101 Honolulu HI 96822. *E-Mail:* cindyh@uhunix.uhcc.hawaii.edu

HUNTER, DOUGLAS LYLE, STATISTICAL PHYSICS, CRITICAL PHENOMENA. *Current Pos:* from asst prof to assoc prof, 72-84, chmn dept, 74-78 & 81-90, PROF PHYSICS, ST FRANCIS XAVIER UNIV, 84-, CHMN DEPT, 96- *Personal Data:* b Belleville, Ont, Aug 29, 40; m 62, Paige Jeffrey; c Karen & Jennifer. *Educ:* Univ Alta, BSc, 62, MSc, 64; Univ London, PhD(theoret physics), 67. *Prof Exp:* Nat Res Coun Can fel & lectr physics, Univ Alta, 67-69; asst prof math, St Francis Xavier Univ, 69-70; assoc mathematician, Brookhaven Nat Lab, 70-72. *Concurrent Pos:* Vis assoc prof, Kings Col, Univ London, 78-79. *Mem:* Can Asn Physicists. *Res:* Statistical mechanical models of phase transitions; use of series expansions to deduce critical and correction-to-scaling behavior; series and computer simulation studies of magnetism, percolation, aggregation, polymers, self-avoiding walks, spin glasses. *Mailing Add:* Dept Physics St Francis Xavier Univ Antigonish NS B2G 2W5 Can. *Fax:* 902-867-2414; *E-Mail:* dhunter@stfx.ca

HUNTER, ERIC, MOLECULAR VIROLOGY, MOLECULAR GENETICS. *Current Pos:* from asst prof to assoc prof, 76-84, PROF MICROBIOL, UNIV ALA, BIRMINGHAM, 84-, ASSOC SCIENTIST, COMPREHENSIVE CANCER CTR, 76- *Personal Data:* b Guisborough, Eng, Aug 18, 48. *Educ:* Univ Birmingham, Eng, BSc, 69; Imp Cancer Res Fund & Brunel Univ, Eng, PhD(tumor immunol), 72. *Prof Exp:* Fel microbiol, Sch Med, Univ Southern Calif, 72-76. *Concurrent Pos:* fel cancer immunol, Cancer Res Inst, NY; Fel, Daymon Runyon Mem Fund Cancer Res; Nat Cancer Inst Res Career Develop Award, 80. *Mem:* Am Soc Microbiol; Am Soc Biol Chemists; AAAS; Am Soc Virol. *Res:* Organization and expression of retroviral genes, synthesis and processing of products of such genes, particularly glycoproteins, and assembly of these products into virus particles. *Mailing Add:* Dept Microbiol Univ Ala 845 19th St S BHS 256 Birmingham AL 35294-2170. *Fax:* 205-934-1640

HUNTER, FRANCIS EDMUND, JR, BIOCHEMISTRY, PHARMACOLOGY. *Current Pos:* asst pharmacol, 41-42, from instr to prof, 42-84, EMER PROF PHARMACOL, SCH MED, WASH UNIV, 84- *Personal Data:* b Alliance, Ohio, June 6, 16; m 40; c 2. *Educ:* Mt Union Col, BS, 38; Univ Rochester, PhD(biochem), 41. *Prof Exp:* Asst pharmacol & biochem, Univ Rochester, 38-41. *Mem:* Am Chem Soc; Am Soc Pharmacol & Exp Therapeut; Am Soc Biol Chem; Am Soc Cell Biol; Biophys Soc. *Res:* Phospholipids; sphingomyelin; barbiturates; oxidation of butyric and other fatty acids; oxidation of acetoacetic acid; tricarboxylic acid cycle; mechanisms of oxidative phosphorylation; mechanism of action of dinitrophenol; enzymatic activity and structural relationships in insolated mitochondria; glutathione-dependent enzymes. *Mailing Add:* 147 Timbercrest Rd Kirkwood MO 63122-7311

HUNTER, FRISSELL ROY, ZOOLOGY, COMPARATIVE PHYSIOLOGY. *Current Pos:* RETIRED. *Personal Data:* b Richmond, Va, Aug 28, 24; m 58, Ethel Harrison; c Venise & Ivan. *Educ:* Va Union Univ, BS, 47; Howard Univ, MS, 52; Univ Iowa, PhD(zool), 57. *Prof Exp:* Prof biol, Southern Univ, 57-63 & Fla Agr & Mech Univ, 63-64; prof biol & chmn div natural sci & math, Allen Univ, 64-65; prof biol, Fayetteville State Col, 65-69 & Atlanta Univ, 69-71; prof biol, Savannah State Col, 71-86 & 92-93, head, Dept Biol & Life Sci, 86-92. *Concurrent Pos:* Mem, Asn Southwestern Biologist, Ga Acad Sci. *Mem:* Am Soc Zool; Sigma Xi; Am Inst Biol Sci; AAAS; Sigma Xi. *Res:* Protozoan enzymology; drug effects on enzyme systems. *Mailing Add:* 10615 Gray Fox Way Savannah GA 31406-4415

HUNTER, GEOFFREY, QUANTUM CHEMISTRY. *Current Pos:* Nat Res Coun Can fel, 65-66, asst prof, 66-69, ASSOC PROF THEORET & PHYS CHEM, YORK UNIV, 69- *Personal Data:* b Manchester, Eng, Apr 23, 34; m 71. *Educ:* Royal Col Adv Technol, Eng, ARIC, 61; Univ Manchester, MSc, 62, PhD(theoret chem), 64. *Prof Exp:* Welch fel theoret chem, Rice Univ, 64-65. *Mem:* The Chem Soc; assoc Royal Inst Chem. *Res:* Chemical and relativistic quantum mechanics; theory of electromagnetic interactions; hardware systems. *Mailing Add:* Dept Chem York Univ Downsview ON M3J 1P3 Can. *Fax:* 416-736-5936; *E-Mail:* fs300022@sol.yorku.ca

HUNTER, GEORGE L K, organic chemistry, analytical chemistry, for more information see previous edition

HUNTER, GEORGE TRUMAN, PHYSICS. *Current Pos:* ADJ PROF PHYSICS, MIAMI UNIV, OXFORD, OHIO, 86- *Personal Data:* b Erie, Pa, May 10, 18; m 54, Mary Dodd; c Grace & Ross. *Educ:* Univ Tampa, BS, 39; Univ Fla, MS, 41; Univ Wis, PhD(physics), 49. *Hon Degrees:* DSc, Univ Tampa, 61. *Prof Exp:* Instr elec commun, Mass Inst Technol, 43-45; asst prof physics & electronics, US Naval Postgrad Sch, 45-49, assoc prof physics, 49-50; physicist, Int Bur Mach Corp, 50-53, asst to dir appl sci div, 53-55, ed consult, 56-57, consult exec develop, 57-59, proj coordr election processing activities, 59-61, mgr advan mgt control systs, 61, consult exec develop, 62, educ prog adminr, 62-68, consult, Univ Rels Dept, 68-71, prog adminr tech support, 71-72, sr educ indust mkt rep, Data Processing Div, 72-73, mgr APL, Syst Develop Div, 73-75; consult, 75-76. *Mem:* Am Phys Soc. *Res:* Education; executive development; applications of computing machinery. *Mailing Add:* 1203 Dana Dr Oxford OH 45056-2513

HUNTER, GORDON EUGENE, BOTANY. *Current Pos:* chmn dept, 67-74, PROF BIOL, TENN TECHNOL UNIV, 74- *Personal Data:* b Sharon, Pa, July 17, 30; m 55; c 3. *Educ:* Miss Col, BS, 56; Wash Univ, MA, 60, PhD(bot), 63. *Prof Exp:* Assoc prof biol, Murray State Col, 63-67. *Concurrent Pos:* NSF res partic col teachers, 64-66. *Mem:* Am Inst Biol Sci; Sigma Xi. *Res:* Morphology and taxonomy of Mexican and Central America Saurauia; taxonomy of the Dilleniaceae of Panama; chromosome numbers, biochemical systematics and trichome morphology of North American Vernonia; floristics and plant ecology of central Tennessee. *Mailing Add:* Rte 1 Box 592 Sparta TN 38583

HUNTER, HUGH WYLIE, PHYSICS. *Current Pos:* RETIRED. *Personal Data:* b Greeley, Colo, Apr 16, 11; m 37, Clare Dunn; c 2. *Educ:* Ind Univ, AB, 32, PhD(physics), 37. *Prof Exp:* Instr physics, Ind Univ, 37-38, res assoc, Univ Conn, 38-39, asst prof, 39-41; res assoc, Ind Univ, 41-42; asst prof, Univ Conn, 42-43; physicist, Div War Res, Univ Calif, 42-45, Manhattan Dist Proj, Calif Inst Technol, 45-46 & Naval Ord Test Sta, Pasadena, 46-47; asst prof physics, Univ Colo, 47-48; physicist, Tech Staff, US Naval Ord Test Sta, 48-51, assoc head res dept, 51-56, head propulsion dept, 56-59; sr scientist, Res Triangle Inst, NC, 59-65; head res dept, US Naval Weapons Ctr, 65-76. *Mem:* Assoc Am Phys Soc. *Res:* Spectroscopy; nuclear physics; underwater sound transmission; development of small mechanical devices; cyclotron construction and operation; solid propellants and propulsion. *Mailing Add:* 18192 Sencillo Dr Rancho Bernardo San Diego CA 92128

HUNTER, JAMES BRUCE, CHEMISTRY. *Current Pos:* RETIRED. *Personal Data:* b Kansas City, Mo, Dec 7, 15; m 43; c 3. *Educ:* Univ Ill, BS, 37; Univ Pa, PhD(chem eng), 42. *Prof Exp:* Res chemist, Atlantic Refining Co, 41-58, res suprv, 58-59; res chemist, J Bishop Co Platinum Works, Matthey Bishop Inc, 59-71, vpres res & develop, 71-78, vpres new technol develop, 78-80. *Mem:* Am Chem Soc. *Res:* Mass spectrometry; dewaxing; catalytic reactions; asphalt and light oil research; vaporization from aqueous solutions; evaluating failure of bituminous materials; isomerization; cracking catalysts; synthetic lubricants; hydrogen purification through palladium-silver membranes; platinum group chemicals, catalysts and devices. *Mailing Add:* 313 Echo Valley Lane Newtown Square PA 19073-2398

HUNTER, JAMES CHARLES, ELECTROCHEMISTRY, SOLID STATE CHEMISTRY. *Current Pos:* Electrochemist, 74-76, sr electrochemist, 76-79, staff electrochemist, 79-83, technol assoc, Battery Prod Div, Union Carbide Corp, 83-88, SR TECHNOL ASSOC, EVEREADY BATTERY CO, 88- *Personal Data:* b Salt Lake City, Utah, Nov 1, 46; m 73; c 3. *Educ:* Calif Inst Technol, BS, 68; Univ Calif, Santa Barbara, PhD(chem), 74. *Mem:* Electrochem Soc. *Res:* Electrode processes; structural chemistry and electrochemical activity of manganese dioxide; use of complex impedance techniques to study electrochemical processes. *Mailing Add:* 43869 Russia Rd Elyria OH 44035

HUNTER, JAMES EDWARD, PLANT PATHOLOGY, EPIDEMIOLOGY. *Current Pos:* assoc prof & head dept, 72-82, PROF PLANT PATH, NY STATE AGR EXP STA, CORNELL UNIV, 82-, DIR, 90- *Personal Data:* b Groveton, NH, Feb 2, 35; m 56; c 1. *Educ:* Univ NH, BA, 61, PhD(bot), 64. *Prof Exp:* Asst prof microbiol, Calif State Polytech Col, 64-65; assoc plant pathologist, Agr Exp Sta, Univ Hawaii, 65-72. *Mem:* Am Phytopath Soc; Am Inst Biol Sci; Am Soc Hort Sci. *Res:* Epidemiology of fungal and bacterial diseases of vegetables; control of plant diseases by chemicals and disease resistance. *Mailing Add:* 28 Denton Ave Geneva NY 14456

HUNTER, JAMES EDWARD, FOOD SCIENCE & TECHNOLOGY. *Current Pos:* CONSULT, 96- *Personal Data:* b Philadelphia, Pa, May 4, 45; m 68, Marilyn K Jones; c 2. *Educ:* Lehigh Univ, BS, 67; Univ Wis, MS, 69, PhD(biochem), 74. *Prof Exp:* Lab technician dermat, US Army, 69-71; nutritionist, Proctor & Gamble Co, 74-92, toxicologist, 92-95, regulatory affairs, 95-96. *Concurrent Pos:* Mem tech comt, Inst Shortening & Edible Oils, 81-93; mem, Am Heart Asn, Oral Health Comt, Int Life Sci Inst-Nutrit Found, 85-89; mem bd dirs, Greater Cincinnati Nutr Coun, 86-90; assoc ed, J Am Oil Chem Soc, 87-89; mem, Subcomt Fatty Acids & Health, Int Life Sci Inst, Nutrit Found, 89-92; mem, Human Nutrit Bd Sci Counselors, USDA, 90-92; mem bd dirs, Ohio Valley Sect, Am Oil Chem Soc, 90-93. *Mem:* Am Chem Soc; Sigma Xi; Am Soc Nutrit Sci; Am Oil Chemists; Int Life Sci Inst. *Res:* Availability of dietary trans fatty acids, omega-3 fatty acids from vegetable oils; iron availability in rats; effects of phytate; iron status and tissue ferritin levels; protein turnover; stability and induction of pyridoxal phosphate-dependent enzymes in vitamin B6 deficiency; effects of food processing conditions on nutritional quality; dietary fat and health; dietary trends. *Mailing Add:* 423 Flemidge Ct Cincinnati OH 45231-4015. *Fax:* 513-563-1810

HUNTER, JAMES H, AGRICULTURAL ENGINEERING. *Current Pos:* Asst agr eng, 55-57, asst prof, Exp Sta, 57-63, ASSOC PROF AGR ENG, UNIV MAINE, ORONO, 63- *Personal Data:* b Washburn, Maine, June 7, 31; m 55; c 4. *Educ:* Univ Maine, BSAE, 53, MSAE, 57; Univ Mass, Amherst, PhD(food & agr eng), 77. *Mem:* Am Soc Agr Engrs; Potato Asn Am. *Res:* Design, development and study of equipment; facilities and methods of handling potatoes. *Mailing Add:* PO Box 765 Presque Isle ME 04769

HUNTER, JAMES HARDIN, JR, ASTRONOMY, HYDRODYNAMICS. *Current Pos:* PROF ASTRON, UNIV FLA, 79- *Personal Data:* b Lafayette, Ind, Mar 24, 38; m 60, 80, Sandra Bragg; c James & Nathan. *Educ:* Kalamazoo Col, BA, 60; Univ Calif, Los Angeles, PhD(astron), 64. *Prof Exp:* Res staff astronr, Yale Univ, 64-65; asst prof astron, 65-70; from assoc prof to prof, Grad Sch, Univ SFla, 70-79. *Concurrent Pos:* Consult, Los Alamos Nat Lab, 84- *Mem:* Am Astron Soc; Int Astron Union. *Res:* Magnetohydrodynamics; star and galaxy formation; observational astronomy; galactic dynamics. *Mailing Add:* Dept Astron Univ Fla Gainesville FL 32611

HUNTER, JERRY DON, CELL BIOLOGY, CELL PHYSIOLOGY. *Current Pos:* asst prof zool, 66-70, ASSOC PROF BIOL SCI, UNIV TEX, EL PASO, 70- *Personal Data:* b Abilene, Tex, Oct 31, 35. *Educ:* Hardin-Simmons, BA, 58; Tex A&M Univ, MS, 60, PhD(zool), 66. *Prof Exp:* Res asst radioisotopes, Univ Tex M D Anderson Hosp & Tumor Inst, 58-59; instr biol, Howard Col, 60-62; asst prof, Muhlenberg Col, 65-66. *Mem:* Fel AAAS; Sigma Xi. *Res:* Effects of ionizing radiations on cells and tissues; applications of autoradiographic techniques in study of reproductive cell differentiation and effects of chemical inhibitors on cellular DNA synthesis. *Mailing Add:* Dept Biol Sci Univ Tex 500 W University Ave El Paso TX 79968-8900

HUNTER, JOHN EARL, BACTERIOLOGY. *Current Pos:* mem res staff, 59-65, SECT HEAD FOOD PROD DEVELOP, PROCTER & GAMBLE CO, 65- *Personal Data:* b Galesville, Wis, Dec 12, 29; m 52; c 3. *Educ:* Univ Wis, BS, 51, MS, 53, PhD(bact), 59. *Prof Exp:* Asst bact, Univ Wis, 51-53, 56-59. *Mem:* Am Soc Microbiol. *Res:* Microbial interactions; oral and food microbiology; food safety, science and technology. *Mailing Add:* 7615 View Place Dr Cincinnati OH 45224

HUNTER, JOHN ROE, MARINE BIOLOGY, ICHTHYOLOGY. *Current Pos:* Res fishery biologist, 62-88, div chief, Southwest Fisheries Ctr, 88-, CHIEF COASTAL FISHERIES, NAT MARINE FISHERIES SERV. *Personal Data:* b Los Angeles, Calif, Apr 11, 34; m 56; c 2. *Educ:* Univ Calif, Santa Barbara, BA, 56; Univ Wis, MS, 58, PhD(zool), 62. *Honors & Awards:* Gold Medal, US Dept Com, 80. *Concurrent Pos:* Adj prof, Scripps Inst Oceanog, Univ Calif, San Diego; scholar in residence, Bellagio Study & Conf Ctr, Rockefeller Found, Italy, 81; pres, Am Inst Fishery Res Biol, 87-88. *Mem:* Am Fishery Soc; Am Inst Fishery Res Biol. *Res:* Behavior and physiology of fishes in relation to the ecology and management of marine fish populations. *Mailing Add:* Southwest Sci Ctr Nat Marine Fisheries Serv PO Box 271 La Jolla CA 92038-0271

HUNTER, JOHN STUART, STATISTICS, ENGINEERING STATISTICS. *Current Pos:* prof, 68-84, EMER PROF STATIST & CIVIL ENG, PRINCETON UNIV, 85- *Personal Data:* b Holyoke, Mass, June 3, 23; m 52, Edna Martz; c Jean (Bartlett), William Mark & Anne (Robinson). *Educ:* NC State Col, BS, 47, MS, 49, PhD(exp statist), 54. *Honors & Awards:* Shewhart Medal, 70; Deming Medal, 86; S S Wilks Medal, 87. *Prof Exp:* Staff statistician, Am Cyanamid Co, NY, 54-57; res assoc statist, Tech Res Group, Princeton Univ, 57-59; mem staff, Army Math Res Ctr, Univ Wis, 59-61; assoc prof chem eng, Princeton Univ, 61-66; statistician in residence, Univ Wis, 66-67. *Concurrent Pos:* Founding ed, Technometrics, Am Statist Asn & Am Soc Qual Control, 59-64; mem staff, Nat Acad Sci, 75-76; mem, Comn Nat Statist, 77-81; chmn adv panel, Appl Math Ctr, Nat Bur Standards, 77-81; lectr, Nat Ctr Indust Sci & Technol, Dalian Inst Technol, People's Rep China, 81. *Mem:* AAAS; Royal Statist Soc; Am Inst Chem Engrs; Am Statist Asn (pres, 93); Inst Math Statist; Biomet Soc. *Res:* Experimental design in the engineering sciences, time series, production quality maintenance and improvement; development and application of multifactor experimental strategies for product design and manufacturing processes. *Mailing Add:* 503 Lake Dr Princeton NJ 08540

HUNTER, JOSEPH LAWRENCE, physics; deceased, see previous edition for last biography

HUNTER, JOSEPH VINCENT, ENVIRONMENTAL SCIENCES. *Current Pos:* instr, Rutgers Univ, 55-59, lectr, 59-62, from asst prof to prof, 62-78, dir, Grad Prog, 79-86, chmn, Dept Environ Sci, 82-93, distinguished prof, 83-93, EMER PROF ENVIRON SCI, RUTGERS UNIV, 93- *Personal Data:* b Brooklyn, NY, June 12, 25; m 57; c 5. *Educ:* St John's Univ, NY, BS, 47, MS, 49; Rutgers Univ, PhD(environ sci), 62. *Prof Exp:* Res chemist, Nopco Chem Co, NJ, 51-55. *Concurrent Pos:* Am Chem Soc lectr tour speaker, 70 & 71. *Mem:* Am Chem Soc; Water Pollution Control Fedn; Am Water Works Asn; Am Pub Health Asn; fel Am Inst Chem. *Res:* Stream oxygen dynamics; composition of waste waters and treatment plant effluents; source, distribution and fate of toxic and carcinogenic substances; industrial waste water treatment. *Mailing Add:* 13 Patton Dr East Brunswick NJ 08816

HUNTER, KATHERINE MORTON, MICROBIOLOGY, MEDICAL TECHNOLOGY. *Current Pos:* Asst microbiologist & teaching suprv, 67-71, educ coordr, 71-77, MICROBIOLOGIST, SCH MED TECHNOL, BAPTIST MED CTR, 71-, SPECIALIST MICROBIOLOGIST, 72-, PROG

DIR, 77- *Personal Data:* b Birmingham, Ala, Sept 16, 39; m 67; c 2. *Educ:* Ala Col, BS, 59; Emory Univ, MT, 60; Vanderbilt Univ, MA, 62, PhD(biol), 68. *Concurrent Pos:* Dipl, Am Bd Med Microbiol, 77-; clin asst prof path, Univ Ala Med/Dent Sch, Birmingham, 77- *Mem:* Am Soc Microbiol; Am Soc Clin Path; Am Pub Health Asn. *Res:* Microbial nutrition and antibiotics; clinical microbiology; microbiology of hospital environment. *Mailing Add:* Lab Baptist Med Ctr 800 Montclair Rd Birmingham AL 35213

HUNTER, KENNETH W, JR, IMMUNOLOGY, PARASITOLOGY. *Current Pos:* assoc vpres res, 89-95, PROF BIOL & MICROBIOL & DEAN GRAD SCH, UNIV NEV, RENO, 89-, VPRES RES, 95- *Personal Data:* b June 30, 50; m 70, Carol L; c Matthew & Michael. *Educ:* Ariz State Univ, BA, 72, MS, 73; Johns Hopkins Univ, ScD(immunol-parasitol), 77. *Prof Exp:* Res collab, Div Entom, Western Cotton Res Lab, Agr Res Serv, US Dept Agr, 73; John W Graham Fund Immunol Res grant, Johns Hopkins Univ, 75; vis res assoc, Malaria Res Proj, Agency Int Develop, Univ NMex, 76; fel, Infectious Dis Div, Uniformed Serv Univ Health Sci, F Edward Hebert Sch Med, 78-79, res asst prof, 79-82, assoc prof pediat & prev med/biometrics & dir pediat res, 82-86, adj assoc prof, 86-89. *Concurrent Pos:* Founder & exec vpres, Antech Consult, Inc, 82-89; chief scientist, Westinghouse Bio-Med Systs Co, 85-89; pres & chief exec officer, Biotronic Systs Corp, 86-89. *Mem:* AAAS; Am Asn Immunologists; Am Soc Trop Med & Hyg; Am Soc Clin Path; Asn Off Anal Chemists. *Res:* Gene regulation in leishmania; immunoregulatory functions in malaria; development of monoclonal antibodies for chemical haptens; somatic cell genetics-human hybridomas; biosensor and molecular electronics. *Mailing Add:* Univ Nev 239 Getchell Libr Reno NV 89557-0035. *Fax:* 702-784-6064; *E-Mail:* khunter@admin.scs.uhr.edu

HUNTER, LARRY RUSSEL, PRECISION MEASUREMENTS, FUNDAMENTAL SYMMETRIES. *Current Pos:* from asst prof to assoc prof, 83-91, PROF PHYSICS, AMHERST COL, 91- *Personal Data:* b Harvey, Ill, Apr 23, 53; m 82; c Virginia, Christopher & Elizabeth. *Educ:* Columbia Univ, BA, 74; Univ Calif, Berkeley, MA, 78, PhD(physics), 81. *Hon Degrees:* MA, Amherst Col. *Honors & Awards:* Res Award, Am Phys Soc, 90. *Prof Exp:* Asst, Hertz Lab Spectros, 81-82. *Concurrent Pos:* Sloan Found fel. *Mem:* Am Phys Soc. *Res:* Atomic physics and fundamental symmetries; parity violation; time reversal violation; local lorentz invarience. *Mailing Add:* Dept Physics Amherst Col Amherst MA 01002. *Fax:* 413-542-5821; *E-Mail:* lrhunter@amherst.edu

HUNTER, LAWRENCE WILBERT, MATERIALS SCIENCE ENGINEERING. *Current Pos:* PRIN STAFF CHEMIST, APPL PHYSICS LAB, JOHNS HOPKINS UNIV, 86- *Personal Data:* b London, Ont, July 15, 45; m 71; c 2. *Educ:* Carleton Univ, BSc, 67; Univ Wis-Madison, PhD(chem), 72. *Mem:* Sigma Xi; Am Ceramic Soc; Combustion Inst. *Res:* Theory of molecular collisions; kinetic theory of gases, polymer flammability and combustion; air-breathing propulsion; advanced structural materials. *Mailing Add:* Appl Physics Lab Johns Hopkins Univ Johns Hopkins Rd Laurel MD 20723-6099

HUNTER, LLOYD PHILIP, PHYSICS. *Current Pos:* prof, 63-81, EMER PROF ELEC ENG, UNIV ROCHESTER, 81- *Personal Data:* b Wooster, Ohio, Feb 11, 16; m 43; c 5. *Educ:* Wooster Col, BA, 39; Mass Inst Technol, BS, 39; Carnegie Inst Technol, MS, 40, DSc(physics), 42. *Prof Exp:* Asst physics, Carnegie Inst Technol, 39-40; res physicist, Westinghouse Elec Corp, 42-49, mgr solid state electronics, 49-51; sr physicist, Int Bus Mach Corp, 51-63, mgr res dept, 53-57, resident mgr, Poughkeepsie Res Lab, 58-60; dir component res & develop, IBM Corp, 61-62. *Concurrent Pos:* Res physicist, Radiation Lab, Univ Calif, 44-45 & Oak Ridge Nat Lab, 46-48; consult, Int Bus Mach Corp, 63- *Mem:* Fel Am Phys Soc; Fel Inst Elec & Electronics Engrs. *Res:* Development of magnetrons; photo and secondary electron emission; elasticity and physics of solids; development of calutron; physics of semiconductors and transistors; diagnostic ultrasound; contact electrification; nuclear fuel research. *Mailing Add:* 10 Schoolhouse Lane Rochester NY 14618

HUNTER, MALCOLM LLEWELLYN, JR, CONSERVATION BIOLOGY. *Current Pos:* LIBRA PROF CONSERV BIOL, UNIV MAINE, 78- *Personal Data:* b Dumariscotta, Maine, Sept 28, 52; m 89, Aram Calhoun. *Educ:* Univ Maine, BS, 74; Univ Oxford, PhD(zool), 78. *Concurrent Pos:* Mem, Species Survival Comn, World Conserv Union, 91-, Biodiversity Task Force-Pres Comm Environ Qual, 92-93; consult, World Wildlife Fund, Smithsonian Inst, USAID & US Forest Serv. *Mem:* Soc Conserv Biol; Wildlife Soc; Ecol Soc; Am Ornithologists' Union; Asn Study Animal Behav. *Res:* Integrating forest management and biodiversity and ecological integrity; design of ecological reserves. *Mailing Add:* Wildlife Dept Univ Maine Orono ME 04469-0001. *E-Mail:* mhunter@maine.edu

HUNTER, NORMAN ROBERT, CHEMISTRY CURRICULUM DEVELOPMENT. *Current Pos:* from asst prof to assoc prof, 74-87, PROF ORG SYNTHESIS, DEPT CHEM, UNIV MAN, 87-, ASSOC HEAD, 85- *Personal Data:* b Odessa, Ont, Nov 9, 41; m 64, Marie D Vansickle; c Andrew J & Jeffrey J. *Educ:* Carleton Univ, Ottawa, Ont, BSc, 65, MSc, 68; Univ NB, PhD(org chem), 70. *Prof Exp:* Fel, Dept Chem, Stanford Univ, 70-71 & Nat Res Coun Can, 71-72; sr med chemist, Merck-Frosst Labs, Montreal, Que, 72-74. *Mem:* Can Soc Chem; Int Union Pure & Appl Chem. *Res:* Development of synthetic methodology; selective oxidation processes; interconversion of fuels; oxidative processes in fatty acids; catalyst development; improvement of science teaching. *Mailing Add:* Dept Chem Univ Man Winnipeg MB R3T 2N2 Can. *Fax:* 204-275-0905

HUNTER, NORMAN W, CHEMICAL EDUCATION, HISTORY OF CHEMISTRY. *Current Pos:* from asst prof to assoc prof, 68-82, PROF CHEM, WESTERN KY UNIV, 82- *Personal Data:* b Toledo, Ohio, June 10, 31; m 53, Ronna L Smith; c Kevin, Becky S & Matthew. *Educ:* Univ Toledo, BSE, 53, MSEd, 61, EdD, 68. *Prof Exp:* Teacher, Mason Consol Schs, Erie, Mich, 53-56 & Washington Local Schs, Toledo, Ohio, 56-65. *Concurrent Pos:* Instr, Univ Toledo, 59-67. *Res:* History of science; computer-assisted instruction. *Mailing Add:* Dept Chem Western Ky Univ Bowling Green KY 42101

HUNTER, ORVILLE, JR, REFRACTORIES. *Current Pos:* VPRES RES, A P GREEN INDUST, INC, MEXICO, MO, 84- *Personal Data:* b Wellsville, Mo, Aug 20, 38; m 60; c 3. *Educ:* Univ Mo, Rolla, BS, 60; Alfred Univ, PhD(ceramics), 64. *Prof Exp:* Res assoc ceramics, Alfred Univ, 64; res asst, US Army Mat Res Agency, Watertown Arsenal, Mass, 64-66; from asst prof to prof ceramic eng, Iowa State Univ, 66-84. *Concurrent Pos:* Prof ceramic eng, Univ Mo, Rolla, 87. *Mem:* Am Ceramic Soc; Nat Inst Ceramic Engrs; Sigma Xi; Am Soc Testing & Mat. *Res:* High temperature mechanical and thermal properties; oxides; refractories. *Mailing Add:* 816 Bucks Run Columbia MO 65201

HUNTER, OSCAR BENWOOD, JR, medicine, for more information see previous edition

HUNTER, PRESTON EUGENE, ENTOMOLOGY, ACAROLOGY. *Current Pos:* RETIRED. *Personal Data:* b Tonganoxie, Kans, Nov 4, 27; m 51; c 2. *Educ:* Univ Kans, AB, 51, PhD(entom), 56. *Prof Exp:* Res fel entom, Univ Minn, 56-59; from asst prof to prof entom, Univ Ga, 59-89, head dept, 74-89. *Mem:* AAAS; Acarology Soc Am; Entom Soc Am; Sigma Xi. *Res:* Taxonomy and ecology. *Mailing Add:* 143 Beacham Dr Athens GA 30606

HUNTER, RALPH EUGENE, MARINE & COASTAL GEOLOGY. *Current Pos:* RETIRED. *Personal Data:* b Evansville, Ind, Jan 13, 35. *Educ:* Ind Univ, AB, 57; Johns Hopkins Univ, PhD(geol), 60. *Prof Exp:* Geologist, Bellaire Res Labs, Texaco, Inc, 60-63; asst geologist, Ill State Geol Surv, 64-67; geologist, US Geol Surv, 67-95. *Mem:* AAAS; Soc Econ Paleont & Mineral; Geol Soc Am; Int Asn Sedimentologists. *Res:* Sedimentology, especially sedimentary structures and petrography of sands and gravels of shallow marine, coastal and eolian origin. *Mailing Add:* Off Marine Geol 2441 Cowper St Palo Alto CA 94301

HUNTER, RICHARD EDMUND, PHYTOPATHOLOGY. *Current Pos:* RETIRED. *Personal Data:* b Jersey City, NJ, Jan 26, 23; m 46; c 3. *Educ:* Rutgers Univ, BS, 49; Okla State Univ, MS, 51, PhD, 68. *Prof Exp:* Asst plant pathologist, NMex State Univ, 51-55; agt, 58-65, res scientist, USDA, Stillwater, Okla, 65-72, Col Sta, Tex, 72-75, Byron, Ga, 75-79, location & res leader, W R Poage Pecan Field Sta, Brownwood, Tex, Agr Res Serv, 79-87. *Concurrent Pos:* From instr to assoc prof plant path, Okla State Univ, 58-72; regional ed, Pecan Quart, 77-79; mem Crop Adv Comt for Pecan & Hickory Germplasm, 84-87. *Res:* Etiology, epiphytology and control of pecan diseases; breeding disease resistance in pecans. *Mailing Add:* 3903 Glenwood Dr Brownwood TX 76801

HUNTER, ROBERT DOUGLAS, PHYSIOLOGICAL ECOLOGY. *Current Pos:* asst prof, 72-78, assoc prof, 79-92, PROF BIOL, OAKLAND UNIV, 93- *Personal Data:* b Lafayette, Ind, July 13, 44; m. *Educ:* Marietta Col, AB, 66; Syracuse Univ, PhD(biol), 72. *Prof Exp:* Res asst neurol, Cornell Med Ctr, Bellevue Hosp, New York, 66; res asst physiol ecol, Syracuse Univ & Marine Biol Lab, 68-72. *Concurrent Pos:* Hon res fel, Univ Glasgow, Scotland, 80; mem, Marine Biol Lab, Woods Hole; vis assoc prof biol, Simmons Col, 87-88. *Mem:* NAm Benthol Soc; Malacol Soc London; Am Malacol Union; Ecol Soc Am; Int Asn Great Lakes Res. *Res:* Lake acidification and molluscs; ecology of the zebra mussel, esp effects on unionids; effects of grazing by snails on attached microalgae. *Mailing Add:* Dept Biol Sci Oakland Univ Rochester MI 48309-4401. *Fax:* 248-370-4225; *E-Mail:* hunter@oakland.edu

HUNTER, ROBERT L, pathology, immunology, for more information see previous edition

HUNTER, ROBERT L, ANATOMY. *Current Pos:* RETIRED. *Personal Data:* b Delaware, Ohio, June 29, 21; m 44; c 4. *Educ:* Ohio Wesleyan Univ, BA, 43, MA, 49; Univ Mich, PhD(zool), 54. *Prof Exp:* Asst path, Sch Med, Washington Univ, 47-48; asst oncol, Sch Med, Univ Kans, 48-49; from instr to assoc prof anat, Med Sch, Univ Mich, 53-63; assoc prof, Sch Med, Stanford Univ, 63-66; chmn dept human anat, Sch Med, Univ Calif, Davis, 68-74, prof anat, 66- *Concurrent Pos:* Vis res prof, Univ Recife, 61; USPHS career develop award, 61-63; vis prof anat, Univ Helsinki, 71. *Mem:* AAAS; Histochem Soc (pres, 68-69); Am Asn Anatomists; Sigma Xi. *Res:* Histology; cytology; enzymology; histochemistry; starch-gel and acrylamide-gel electrophoresis. *Mailing Add:* Dept Human Anat Unif Calif 809 Plum Lane Davis CA 95616

HUNTER, ROBERT P, MATHEMATICS. *Current Pos:* assoc prof, 62-65, PROF MATH, PA STATE UNIV, 65- *Personal Data:* b Newark, NJ, Jan 30, 33; m 56; c 4. *Educ:* Univ Miami, BS, 54, MS, 56; La State Univ, PhD(math), 58. *Prof Exp:* Asst prof math, Univ Ga, 58-59 & 60-62; Sarah Moss Found fel, Oxford Univ, 59-60. *Concurrent Pos:* Vis prof, Univ London, 68-69. *Res:* Algebra; topology. *Mailing Add:* Dept Math Pa State Univ University Park PA 16802

HUNTER, ROY, JR, DEVELOPMENTAL BIOLOGY. *Current Pos:* DIR, FAC DEVELOP FELS PROG, MOREHOUSE SCH MED, 83- *Personal Data:* b Birmingham, Ala, Jan 7, 30; m 65; c 1. *Educ:* Morehouse Col, BS, 50; Univ Atlanta, MS, 53; Brown Univ, PhD(develop biol), 62. *Prof Exp:* Instr sci, Birmingham Baptist Col, 50-51; instr biol, Morgan State Col, 53-57; from asst prof to assoc prof, Morehouse Col, 61-64; assoc prof biol, Atlanta Univ, 64-68, prof, 64-70 & 73-81, chmn dept, 76-79. *Concurrent Pos:* Univ Ctr Corp res grant, Atlanta Univ, 64-65; prof & chmn biol dept, Morgan State Col, 70-73. *Mem:* Am Inst Biol Sci; Am Soc Zoologists; Nat Inst Sci; Sigma Xi; NY Acad Sci. *Res:* Notochordal cells of amphibian embryos and larvae, including their involvement in fibrillogenesis; environmental teratogenesis. *Mailing Add:* Morehouse Sch Med 720 Westview Dr SW Atlanta GA 30310

HUNTER, SAMUEL W, THORACIC SURGERY. *Current Pos:* RETIRED. *Personal Data:* b Ireland, Nov 13, 21; nat US; m 44; c 6. *Educ:* Cornell Univ, AB, 43; Univ Rochester, MD, 47; Univ Minn, MS, 56; Am Bd Surg, dipl, 55; Am Bd Thoracic Surg, dipl, 59. *Prof Exp:* From instr to asst prof, Univ Minn, St Paul, 55-77, clin assoc prof surg, Med Sch, 77- *Concurrent Pos:* Dir cardiac res lab, St Joseph's Hosp, 57-; mem comt hyperbaric oxygenation, Nat Acad Sci-Nat Res Coun. *Mem:* AAAS; fel Am Col Angiol; fel Am Col Surg; fel Am Col Chest Physicians. *Res:* Cardiac research, especially the atrioventricular block; use of the bipolar myocardial electrode; hyperbaric oxygenation; clinical application cardiac pacemakers; cardiac surgery of all phases, clinical and research. *Mailing Add:* 1175 Orchard Pl St Paul MS 55118-4119

HUNTER, STANLEY DEAN, ASTROPHYSICS. *Current Pos:* ASTROPHYSICIST GAMMA-RAY ASTROPHYS, NASA-GODDARD SPACE FLIGHT CTR, 85- *Personal Data:* b Phoenix, Ariz, Feb 4, 54; m 83; c 2. *Educ:* Univ Ariz BS(physics) & BS(math), 76; La State Univ, PhD(physics), 81. *Prof Exp:* Res assoc gamma-ray astrophys, Nat Res Coun, Goddard Space Flight Ctr, NASA, 81-83; res assoc x-ray astrophys, Inst Space & Astronaut Sci, Tokyo, 84. *Mem:* Am Phys Soc. *Res:* High energy (30 mega electron volts to 100 giga electron volts) gamma rays produced by astrophysical processes; probe of the matter distribution in the galaxy; generation by energetic point sources; design and construction of satellite and balloon experiments for imaging detection of gamma rays. *Mailing Add:* Goddard Space Flight Ctr NASA Code 662 Greenbelt MD 20771

HUNTER, SUSAN JULIA, OSTEOCLAST STRUCTURE FUNCTION, BONE PROTEOGLYCANS. *Current Pos:* AT DEPT MOLECULAR BIOL, PA STATE UNIV. *Educ:* Pa State Univ, PhD(physiol), 80. *Mailing Add:* Dept Zool Univ Maine 203 Murray Hall Orono ME 04469-0001. *Fax:* 207-581-2537

HUNTER, THOMAS HARRISON, INTERNAL MEDICINE. *Current Pos:* RETIRED. *Personal Data:* b Chicago, Ill, Oct 12, 13; m 43; c 5. *Educ:* Harvard Univ, AB, 35, MD, 40. *Prof Exp:* Asst physician med, Presby Hosp, 41-42; instr, Col Physicians & Surgeons, Columbia Univ, 42-47; from asst to assoc dean, Sch Med, Wash Univ, 47-53; dean, Sch Med, Univ Va, 53-65, chancellor med affairs, 65-70, prof med & sci, 70-81. *Concurrent Pos:* Mem, Comt Infectious Dis & Chemother, Nat Res Coun; mem, Nat Arthritis & Metab Dis Coun, NIH. *Mem:* Am Acad Arts & Sci; AAAS; Am Soc Clin Invest; Asn Am Med Cols (pres, 60). *Res:* Infectious diseases; antibiotics and bacterial endocarditis; human ecology. *Mailing Add:* PO Box 212 Keswick VA 22947-0212

HUNTER, TONY, MOLECULAR BIOLOGY, VIROLOGY. *Current Pos:* from asst prof to assoc prof, 75-82, PROF, SALK INST, SAN DIEGO, 82- *Personal Data:* b Ashford, Eng, Aug 23, 43; UK citizen; m 69, 92, Jennifer A Price; c Sean A Brocas. *Educ:* Cambridge Univ, Eng, BA, 65, MA, 66, PhD(biochem), 69. *Honors & Awards:* Cancer Res Award, Am Bus Found, 88; Katharine Berkan Judd Award, Mem Sloan Kettering, Cancer Ctr, 92; Hopkins Medal, Biochem Soc, 94; Gairdner Found Int Award, 94. *Prof Exp:* Res fel, Christ's Col, Cambridge, 68-71; res assoc, Salk Inst, San Diego, 71-73; res fel, Christ's Col, 73-75. *Concurrent Pos:* Adj assoc prof biol, Univ Calif, San Diego, 79-83, adj prof, 83-, Am Cancer Soc prof, 92- *Mem:* Fel Royal Soc London; fel Am Acad Arts & Scis; assoc mem Europ Molecular Biol Orgn. *Res:* Molecular mechanisms of malignant cellular transformation by viral and tumor oncogenes; properties of oncogenic proteins; mechanisms of growth control of mammalian cells; regulation of protein function by phosphorylation; cancer. *Mailing Add:* Salk Inst PO Box 85800 San Diego CA 92186-5800. *Fax:* 619-457-4765; *E-Mail:* hunter@salk.scz.sdsc.edu

HUNTER, W(ILLIAM) STUART, ORTHODONTICS, ANTHROPOLOGY. *Current Pos:* prof & chmn, Div Orthod, 68-92, EMER PROF, UNIV WESTERN ONT, 92- *Personal Data:* b Orillia, Ont, May 5, 27; m 96, June Farran; c Anne & Beth. *Educ:* Univ Toronto, DDS, 50; Univ Mich, MS, 55, PhD(anthrop, orthod), 59. *Prof Exp:* From asst prof to assoc prof dent, Univ Mich, Ann Arbor, 61-68. *Mem:* Am Asn Orthod. *Res:* Genetics; growth; twins; clefting lip/palate. *Mailing Add:* Fac Dent Univ Western Ont London ON N6A 5C1 Can

HUNTER, WILLIAM LESLIE, PLASTICS CHEMISTRY, SEMICONDUCTORS. *Current Pos:* RETIRED. *Personal Data:* b East Liverpool, Ohio, May 2, 28; m 51; c 3. *Educ:* Va Polytech Inst, BS, 50, MS, 57, PhD(phys chem), 60. *Prof Exp:* Res chemist, Basic Res Dept, Chemstrand Res Ctr, 59-62; asst prof phys & polymer chem, Va Polytech Inst, 62-68; mgr, Org Mat Sect, Mat Res Lab, Motorola Inc, 68-75, mem tech staff, Semiconductor Prod Sector, 75-89. *Mem:* Soc Plastics Eng; Am Chem Soc; Sigma Xi. *Res:* Plastic encapsulants for semiconductors. *Mailing Add:* 7714 E Davenport Dr Scottsdale AZ 85260

HUNTER, WILLIAM RAY, PHYSICAL OPTICS. *Current Pos:* PHYSICIST, SACHS-FREEMAN ASSOC INC, 82- *Personal Data:* b Ancon, CZ, Oct 22, 24. *Educ:* Univ Fla, BS, 48, MS, 49. *Honors & Awards:* Progress Medal, Photog Soc Am, 58. *Prof Exp:* Physicist, Col Geophys Inst, Alaska, 49-50 & US Naval Mine Countermeasures Sta, Panama City, Fla, 50-52; physicist, US Naval Res Lab, 52-80. *Concurrent Pos:* Assoc ed, J Optical Soc Am, 74-77. *Mem:* Fel Optical Soc Am; fel Am Phys Soc. *Res:* Optical properties in the vacuum ultraviolet; thin films; diffraction gratings photo emissive properties; vacuum ultraviolet detectors; particle radiation damage. *Mailing Add:* 6705 Caneel Ct Springfield VA 22152. *E-Mail:* 74443.1045@compuserve.com

HUNTER, WILLIAM SAM, PHYSIOLOGY, BODY TEMPERATURE REGULATION. *Current Pos:* ASSOC PROF DEPT PHYSIOL, SCH MED, SOUTHERN ILL UNIV, CARBONDALE, 75- *Personal Data:* b Amarillo, Tex, Sept 28, 40; m 72; c 2. *Educ:* Univ Okla, BS, 62, MS, 65; Mich State Univ, PhD(physiol), 71. *Prof Exp:* Res asst, Civil Aeromed Inst, 64-65; res engr physiol, NAm Rockwell Corp, 65-67; consult, Ford Motor Co Safety Div, 67-68; asst prof physiol, Sch Med, St Louis Univ, 71-75. *Mem:* AAAS; Am Physiol Soc; Soc Neurosci. *Res:* Thermoregulatory physiology; mechanisms of fever induction by blood borne pyrogens. *Mailing Add:* Dept Physiol Southern Ill Univ Med Sch Carbondale IL 62901-6512. *Fax:* 618-453-5861; *E-Mail:* hunter@qm.c___som.siu.edu

HUNTER, WILLIAM WINSLOW, JR, instrumentation, for more information see previous edition

HUNTER, WOOD E, organic chemistry, for more information see previous edition

HUNTING, ALFRED CURTIS, APPLIED PHYSICS. *Current Pos:* PRIN DEVELOP ENGR, HONEYWELL SEATTLE MARINE SYSTS CTR, 76- *Personal Data:* b Plainfield, NJ, Apr 30, 28; m 53; c 4. *Educ:* Swarthmore Col, BS, 49; Univ Mich, MS, 52, PhD(physics), 62. *Prof Exp:* Jr physicist, Brookhaven Nat Lab, 49-50; res asst, Eng Res Inst, Univ Mich, 50-54; res technologist, Field Res Lab, Mobil Oil Co, 54-57; sr res assoc, Res Inst, Univ Mich, 57-61; res specialist, Aerospace Div, Boeing Co, 61-69; sr engr, Equip Group, Tex Instruments Inc, 69-76. *Mem:* Am Phys Soc; Inst Elec & Electronics Engrs. *Res:* Modeling, analysis and simulation of engineering systems, including sonar systems and fiber-optic sensors; underwater acoustics; sonar signal processing. *Mailing Add:* 2357 Federal Ave E Seattle WA 98102

HUNTINGTON, CHARLES ELLSWORTH, ORNITHOLOGY. *Current Pos:* RETIRED. *Personal Data:* b Boston, Mass, Dec 8, 19; m 56, Louise Chapin Slater; c George S, William E, Katherine C & Sarah C. *Educ:* Yale Univ, BA, 42, PhD(zool), 52. *Prof Exp:* From instr to prof biol, Bowdoin Col, 53-86, dir sci sta, 53-89, chmn dept, 73-76. *Concurrent Pos:* NSF res grant, 58; Guggenheim mem fel, Oxford Univ, 63-64. *Mem:* AAAS; Asn Field Ornith (pres, 62-67); Am Ornith Union; Brit Ornith Union; Cooper Ornith Soc; Wilson Ornith Soc. *Res:* Population dynamics of sea birds, concentrating on long term study of Leach's Storm-Petrel. *Mailing Add:* RFD 2 Box 357 Harpswell ME 04079. *E-Mail:* chunting@polar.bowdoin.edu

HUNTINGTON, DAVID HANS, TECHNICAL COLLEGE ADMINISTRATION. *Current Pos:* RETIRED. *Personal Data:* b Westford, NY, Mar 19, 26; m 49; c 2. *Educ:* Cornell Univ, BS, 46, MS, 48, PhD, 53. *Prof Exp:* Teacher pub sch, NY, 48-51; asst agr eng, Cornell Univ, 51-53; from asst prof to assoc prof, Univ Maine, 53-61, asst to dean col agr, 57-61, from asst dean to assoc dean, 61-64; pres, State Univ NY Agr & Tech Col Alfred, 64-86. *Mailing Add:* 5470 Elm Valley Rd Alfred Station NY 14802

HUNTINGTON, HILLARD BELL, solid state physics; deceased, see previous edition for last biography

HUNTLEY, DAVID, HYDROGEOLOGY. *Current Pos:* PROF GEOL, SAN DIEGO STATE UNIV, 81- *Personal Data:* b San Mateo, Calif, Feb 28, 50; m 71. *Educ:* Univ Calif, Santa Barbara, BA, 72; Colo Sch Mines, PhD(geol eng), 76. *Prof Exp:* Res asst geol, Colo Sch Mines, 72-76; asst prof, Univ Conn, 76-78. *Mem:* Am Geophys Union; Nat Water Well Asn. *Res:* Geologic and geophysical techniques in ground water hydrology; numerical modeling of ground water flow; multiphase flow; hydrology of geothermal systems. *Mailing Add:* Dept Geol Sci 5300 Campanile Dr San Diego State Univ San Diego CA 92182-0002. *E-Mail:* dhuntley@geology.sdsu.edu

HUNTLEY, JIMMY CHARLES, FISH & WILDLIFE SCIENCE. *Current Pos:* FOREST BIOLOGIST, NAT FORESTS ALA, US FOREST SERV, 88- *Personal Data:* b Louisville, Miss, Nov 29, 46; m 68; c 2. *Educ:* Miss State Univ, BS, 69, MS, 77, PhD(biol sci), 80. *Prof Exp:* res wildlife biologist, Southern Forest Exp Sta, US Forest Serv, 78-86; wildlife biologist, Southern Region, Nat Forest Syst, 86-88. *Mem:* Wildlife Soc; Sigma Xi. *Res:* Effects of forestry management practices on wildlife habitat; wildlife habitat evaluation and classification; management of utility rights-of-way to reduce maintenance costs and improve wildlife habitat. *Mailing Add:* Nat Forest Syst 2946 Chestnut St Montgomery AL 36107

HUNTLEY, ROBERT ROSS, PREVENTIVE MEDICINE, FAMILY MEDICINE HEALTH ADMINISTRATION. *Current Pos:* prof & chmn dept, 70-89, EMER PROF COMMUNITY & FAMILY MED, SCH MED, GEORGETOWN UNIV, 89- *Personal Data:* b Wadesboro, NC, Sept 6, 26; m 76; c 5. *Educ:* Davidson Col, BS, 47; Bowman Gray Sch Med, MD, 51. *Prof Exp:* From intern to resident, Univ Hosp, Univ Mich, 51-53; pvt pract, 53-58; resident & fel med, NC Mem Hosp, Univ NC, 59-62; assoc dir prog develop, Nat Ctr Health Serv Res & Develop, 68-70. *Concurrent Pos:* Exec co-dir health adv comt, Appalachian Regional Comn, 65-66; from instr to assoc prof med & prev med, Sch Med, Univ NC, 59-70, asst prof health admin, Sch Pub Health, 67-70; Milbank fac fel, 64-70; mem health serv res study sect, NIH, 66-68; mem test comt prev med & pub health, Nat Bd Med Examr, 70-74; trustee, Am Bd Prev Med, 74-78; chmn health care technol study sect, Nat Ctr Health Serv Res, 78-82; adj prof, Health Admin, Univ NC, Chapel Hill, 89- *Mem:* Asn Teachers Prev Med (pres, 74-75); Am Fedn Clin Res; fel Am Pub Health Asn; Asn Dept Family Med; Am Geriatrics Soc; Soc Teachers Family Med. *Res:* Organization and delivery of health services, quality, distribution of resources; clinical epidemiology and studies useful for planning the rational allocation of health resources. *Mailing Add:* PO Box 190 Chapel Hill NC 27514-0190

HUNTOON, CAROLYN LEACH, PHYSIOLOGY. *Current Pos:* Head endocrinol lab, NASA Johnson Space Ctr, 68-74, head endocrine & biochem labs, 74-76, spec asst to dir, 76-77, chief, Space Metab & Biochem Br, 76-77, chief, Biomed Labs Br, 77-84, assoc dir, 84-87, dir, Space & Life Sci, 87-94, DIR, NASA JOHNSON SPACE CTR, 94- *Personal Data:* b Leesville, La, Aug 25, 40. *Educ:* Northwestern State Col, BS, 62; Baylor Univ, MS, 66, PhD, 68. *Hon Degrees:* Dr, Northwestern State Univ, 94. *Honors & Awards:* Arthur S Fleming Award; Career Achievement Award, Nat Civil Serv League; Paul Bert Award; Hubertus Strughold Award; Yuri Gagarin Medal, USSR Fedn Cosmonatuics, 87; Presidential Rank Meritorious Exec Award, 91; Outstanding Woman in Sci, Am Women in Sci; Lovelace Award, Am Astronaut Soc, 91, Space Flight Award, 94; Louis H Bauer Founders Award. *Mem:* Fel Aerospace Med Asn; Am Inst Aeronaut & Astronaut; Asn Bus & Prof Women; Am Physiol Soc; Endocrine Soc; Inst Acad Astronaut; fel Am Astronaut Soc. *Mailing Add:* NASA Johnson Space Ctr 2101 NASA Rd 1 Houston TX 77058-3607

HUNTOON, JACQUELINE E, FIELD GEOLOGY, NUMERICAL MODELLING GEOLOGIC PROCESSES. *Current Pos:* CONSULT, 88- *Personal Data:* b Encino, Calif, May 23, 59. *Educ:* Univ Calif, Santa Cruz, BS, 81; Univ Utah, Salt Lake City, MS, 85. *Prof Exp:* Geol field asst, US Geol Serv, Menlo Park, Calif, 82-; exploration geol, Shell Offshore Inc, New Orleans, 87; consult geologist, Penn State Univ, 87-88. *Mem:* Am Assoc Petrol Geologists; Geol Soc Am; Am Geophys Union; Soc Econ Paleontol & Mineral. *Res:* Evolution of sedimentary basin-current research focuses on the interaction of thermal mechanical tectonic processes with sedimentologic processes that are controlled by climate, topography, pre-existing lithology and paleogeography. *Mailing Add:* Dept Geol Eng Sci Mich Tech Univ 1400 Townsend Dr Houghton MI 49931

HUNTRESS, WESLEY THEODORE, JR, ASTROCHEMISTRY. *Current Pos:* dir, Solar Syst Explor Div, 90-93, ASSOC ADMIN, OFF SPACE SCI, NASA, 93- *Personal Data:* b Washington, DC, Apr 11, 42; m 73; c 1. *Educ:* Brown Univ, BS, 64; Stanford Univ, PhD(chem physics), 68. *Prof Exp:* Sr res scientist, Jet Propulsion Lab, Calif Inst Technol, 69-90. *Concurrent Pos:* Vis prof cosmochem, Dept Planetary Sci & Geophys, Calif Inst Technol, 89-90. *Mem:* AAAS; Am Chem Soc; Am Astron Soc; Am Phys Soc. *Res:* Ion cyclotron magnetic resonance; mass spectrometry; ion-molecule reactions in the gas phase; photo-ionization, photoexcitation and photodissociation phenomena in the gasphase; the production and reactions of molecular species in planetary atmospheres; comets and interstellar clouds. *Mailing Add:* 19828 Meredith Dr Rockville MD 20855

HUNTS, BARNEY DEAN, ELECTRONICS. *Current Pos:* RETIRED. *Personal Data:* b Rehoboth, NMex, July 23, 36; m 55; c 4. *Educ:* Univ Ariz, BSEE, 61; Univ Calif, Berkeley, MSEE, 62. *Prof Exp:* Electronic design engr, Gen Dynamics Corp, 62-66; dir microcircuits, Friden Res Lab, 66-69; mgr microelec res & develop, Singer Res Lab, Singer Co, 69-71, mgr microelec appl, Corp Res & Develop Lab, 71-74, dir, 74-77, sr dir advan technol, 77-; dir, Tech Develop, Allied Electronic Components, Morristown, NJ; pres, Circuit Technol Inc. *Mem:* Inst Elec & Electronics Engrs; Am Phys Soc; Indust Res Inst; AAAS. *Res:* Solid-state devices; electro-optics; microelectronics; system architecture; logic design; circuit design. *Mailing Add:* 145 Morris Ave Mountain Lakes NJ 07046

HUNTSBERGER, DAVID VERNON, STATISTICS. *Current Pos:* Instr, Iowa State Univ, 50-53, from asst prof to assoc prof, 53-62, prof, 62-80, EMER PROF STATIST, IOWA STATE UNIV, 80- *Personal Data:* b Harrisburg, Pa, July 22, 17; m 41; c 1. *Educ:* Bethany Col, WVa, BS, 47; WVa Univ, MS, 48; Iowa State Col, PhD(statist), 54. *Mem:* Fel Am Statist Asn; Int Math Statist; Int Asn Statist Phys Sci. *Res:* Preliminary tests of signficance; experimental design; engineering applications of statistics. *Mailing Add:* 1702 Maxwell Ames IA 50010

HUNTSBERGER, JAMES ROBERT, SURFACE CHEMISTRY, ADHESION. *Current Pos:* CONSULT, 82- *Personal Data:* b Harrisburg, Pa, Feb 4, 21; m 45, 85, Janet O'Connor; c Lynn, James R II, & Janet. *Educ:* Bethany Col, BS, 42; WVa Univ, PhD(chem), 49. *Prof Exp:* Res assoc, Fabrics & Finishes Dept, E I DuPont de Nemours & Co, Inc, 48-65, res fel, 65-74, res fel, Plastics Dept, 74-78, res fel reverse osmosis, 78-82. *Concurrent Pos:* Chmn, Gordon Res Conf Adhesion, 64; assoc ed, J Adhesion, 71-84. *Mem:* Am Chem Soc; Sigma Xi; Adhesion Soc (vpres, 80-81). *Res:* Organic finishes; adhesion; dispersion; mechanical properties of polymers and composites; reverse osmosis. *Mailing Add:* 501 Field Lane Owls Nest Wilmington DE 19807

HUNTSMAN, GENE RAYMOND, FISH BIOLOGY, POPULATION BIOLOGY. *Current Pos:* FISHERY BIOLOGIST, NAT MARINE FISHERIES SERV, US DEPT COM, 67- *Personal Data:* b East St Louis, Ill, Aug 12, 40; m 63, Susan A Deropp; c Glee E. *Educ:* Cornell Univ, BS, 62; Iowa State Univ, MS, 64, PhD(fishery biol), 66. *Prof Exp:* NIH fel, Univ Miami, 66-67. *Concurrent Pos:* From adj asst prof to adj assoc prof, NC State Univ, 70-83, adj prof, 84-; mem, NC Coastal Resources Comn, 74-83, NC Coastal Resources Adv Coun, 83-87; pres, Marine Fishery Sect, Am Fisheries Soc, 87-88. *Mem:* Am Fisheries Soc; Ecol Soc Am; Am Soc Limnol & Oceanog; Am Inst Fishery Res Biologists; Sigma Xi. *Res:* Population dynamics of coastal pelagic fishes; biology of deep water reef fishes; recreational fisheries. *Mailing Add:* 205 Blades Rd Havelock NC 28532. *Fax:* 919-728-8784

HUNTSMAN, LEE L, BIOMEDICAL ENGINEERING. *Current Pos:* from res asst prof to res assoc prof, Ctr Bioeng & Dept Mech Eng, 68-81, actg dir, 80, DIR, CTR BIOMED ENG, COL ENG & SCH MED, UNIV WASH, SEATTLE, 80-, PROF, 81- *Personal Data:* b Tacoma, Wash, June 11, 41. *Educ:* Stanford Univ, BS, 63; Univ Pa, PhD(biomed eng), 68. *Prof Exp:* NIH fel, Biomed Eng, Univ Pa, 63-68. *Concurrent Pos:* Mem bd dirs, Lawrence Med Systs, 80-85; Biomed Eng Soc, 84-87; Wash Res Found, 86-, Wash Exhib Sci & Technol, 87-; mem, Rocky Mountain Regional Heart Comt, Am Heart Asn, 81-85, Cardiovasc Study Sect, NIH, 83-85, Trinus adv bd, 87-; consult, Lawrence Med Systs, 80-89, CooperVision IOL, 83-85, Endosonics, 85-89, St Jude Med, 89-; grants, NIH prog proj, 89-94, W M Keck Found, 89-92 & Whitaker Found, 90-93. *Mem:* AAAS; Am Heart Asn; Biomed Eng Soc; Biophys Soc; Inst Elec & Electronics Engrs. *Res:* Bioengineering; heart; myocardial mechanics; ventricular performance; non-invasive measurements; ultrasound; doppler; technology transfer; numerous technical publications; granted 3 patents. *Mailing Add:* Ctr Bioeng Univ Wash Box 357962 Seattle WA 98195

HUNTSMAN, WILLIAM DUANE, ORGANIC CHEMISTRY. *Current Pos:* from asst prof to assoc prof, 51-61, chmn dept, 63-69, prof, 61-69, DISTINGUISHED PROF CHEM, OHIO UNIV, 69- *Personal Data:* b Dart, Ohio, Mar 1, 25; m 49; c 3. *Educ:* Ohio Univ, BS, 47; Northwestern Univ, PhD(chem), 50. *Prof Exp:* Res assoc chem, Northwestern Univ, 50-51. *Mem:* Am Chem Soc; The Chem Soc. *Res:* Thermal rearrangement reactions; catalytic hydrogenation; acid-catalyzed isomerization of hydrocarbons. *Mailing Add:* Dept Chem Clippinger Lab Ohio Univ Athens OH 45701

HUNTZICKER, JAMES JOHN, AIR POLLUTION, ATMOSPHERIC CHEMISTRY. *Current Pos:* from asst prof to assoc prof environ sci, 74-85, chmn, dept environ sci, 76-83, chmn, dept chem, biol & environ sci, 84-86, PROF ENVIRON SCI, ORE GRAD CTR, 85- *Personal Data:* b St Clair, Mich, Oct 23, 41; m 67; c 2. *Educ:* Univ Mich, BS, 63; Univ Calif, Berkeley, PhD(chem), 68. *Prof Exp:* Physicist, Lawrence Radiation Lab, Univ Calif, 68-69; guest prof physics, Free Univ Berlin, 69-70; actg asst prof, Indian Inst Technol, Kanpur, India, 71-72; res assoc environ health eng, Calif Inst Technol, 72-74, instr, 74. *Concurrent Pos:* Mem climatic impact assessment prog, Panel Aerosol Formation, Stratosphere Supersonic Transp Effluents, 73-75; consult, Environ Res & Technol Inc, 74-; exec vpres, Ore Grad Ctr, 86, pres, 87-, actg pres, 87-88. *Mem:* Am Chem Soc; Am Phys Soc. *Res:* Aerosol chemistry; air pollution chem. *Mailing Add:* 5170 NW Kaiser Rd Portland OR 97229

HUNZEKER, HUBERT LAVON, MATHEMATICS, COMPUTER PROGRAMMING APPLICATIONS. *Current Pos:* head dept, 68-71, prof, 68-84, EMER PROF MATH, MICH TECHNOL UNIV, 84- *Personal Data:* b Pawnee City, Nebr, Nov 12, 20; m 43; c 4. *Educ:* Nebr State Teachers Col, Peru, AB, 48; Iowa State Col, MS, 50; Univ Mich, PhD(math), 59. *Prof Exp:* Actg instr math, Ohio Univ, 50-52; asst, Willow Run Res Ctr, Univ Mich, 53; from instr to asst prof math, DePauw Univ, 53-57; asst, Univ Mich, 57-58; asst prof, Univ Nebr, 58-62; from assoc prof to prof, Univ Omaha, 62-68, chmn dept, 62-68. *Concurrent Pos:* Consult, Res Inst, Univ Mich, 58-59, CAAM consult, 84- *Mem:* Am Math Soc; Math Asn Am; Sigma Xi; Asn Comput Mach. *Res:* Trend analysis of time series. *Mailing Add:* 1489 County Trunk Hwy 6 La Crescent MN 55947-9755

HUNZICKER-DUNN, MARY, HORMONE ACTION, PROTEIN PHOSPHORATION. *Current Pos:* ASSOC PROF, DEPT MOLECULAR BIOL, NORTHWESTERN UNIV, 79- *Personal Data:* m. *Educ:* Univ Ill, PhD(physiol), 73. *Concurrent Pos:* Res career develop award, Biochem Endocrinol Study Sect, NIH; bd dirs, Soc Study Reprod, 87-90. *Mem:* Am Soc Biol Chemists; Endocrine Soc. *Res:* Camp regulation; protein phosphorylation; molecular mechanisms by which the gonadotropic hormones luteinizing hormone and follicle stimulating hormone regulate functions of ovarian follicles and corpora lutea; adenylyl cyclase enzyme and various protein kinases which mediate hormonal signals. *Mailing Add:* Molecular & Structural Biol Northwestern Univ Sch Med 303 E Chicago Ave Chicago IL 60611-3072. *Fax:* 312-503-0566

HUNZIKER, HEINRICH ERWIN, chemical physics, for more information see previous edition

HUNZIKER, RODNEY WILLIAM, ASTRONOMY. *Current Pos:* RETIRED. *Personal Data:* b Everett, Wash, May 9, 22; m 48; c Susan. *Educ:* Univ Wash, BS, 44; San Francisco State Col, MA, 50; Univ Calif, Berkeley, MA, 64; PhD, 77. *Prof Exp:* Prof phys sci, Calif State Univ, Chico, 55-88. *Concurrent Pos:* NSF sci fac fel astron, Univ Calif, Berkeley, 60-62. *Mem:* Astron Soc Pac. *Res:* Astronomical spectroscopy; abundances in high-velocity Type A stars; science education; concept formation in the physical sciences. *Mailing Add:* 3226 26th Ave W Seattle WA 98199

HUPE, DONALD JOHN, PARASITIC PROTOZOA, ENZYME INHIBITORS. *Current Pos:* dir, 90-91, SR DIR BIOCHEM, PARKE DAVIS PHARMACEUT, 91- *Personal Data:* b Newark, NJ, Nov 27, 44; m 69, Lynn Bitz; c Carol & Amedia. *Educ:* Rutgers Univ, BA, 68; Dartmouth Univ, PhD(chem), 72. *Prof Exp:* Teaching fel biochem, Brandeis Univ, 72-74; asst prof chem & biochem, Univ Mich, 74-80; res fel, Merck Inst Therapeut Res, 80-86, sr res fel biochem, 86-90. *Concurrent Pos:* Vis assoc prof, Rutgers Univ, 81-82; adj prof med chem, Univ Mich, 90- *Mem:* Am Soc Biol Chem; Am Chem Soc; NY Acad Sci. *Res:* Biochemistry and enzymology, particularly of parasitic protozoa; development of antiparasitic agents; study of mode of action of known antiparasitic agents; antimetastasis agents; nucleotide biosynthesis; antiviral agents. *Mailing Add:* Parke Davis/Warner Lambert 2800 Plymouth Rd Ann Arbor MI 48105-2495. *Fax:* 313-996-1355

HUPKA, ARTHUR LEE, PHARMACOLOGY. *Current Pos:* PROF & CHMN PHARMACOL, PONCE SCH MED, PR, 88- *Personal Data:* b South Bend, Ind, June 3, 40. *Educ:* Butler Univ, BA, 64, MS, 66; Univ Utah, PhD(pharmacol), 71. *Prof Exp:* Fel, Dept Biochem, Univ Utah, 71-73; asst prof pharmacol, Univ Nebr Med Ctr, Omaha, 73-78; from asst prof to assoc prof pharmacol, Sch Health Sci, Grand Valley State Cols, 81-88. *Mem:* Res Soc Alcoholism; NY Acad Sci. *Res:* Drug metabolism; alcoholism; pharmacokinetics. *Mailing Add:* W Va Sch Osteopath Med 400 N Lee St Lewisburg PR 24901

HUPP, EUGENE WESLEY, PHYSIOLOGY & ENVIRONMENTAL BIOLOGY. *Current Pos:* assoc prof, 65-69, PROF BIOL, TEX WOMAN'S UNIV, 69- *Personal Data:* b Knox Co, Nebr, Feb 23, 33; m 57, 88, Marion Barrett; c Stephen, Michael, Alice & Victoria. *Educ:* Univ Nebr, BS, 54, MS, 57; Mich State Univ, PhD, 59. *Prof Exp:* Asst & assoc scientist, Agr Res Lab, Atomic Energy Comn Proj, Tenn, 58-62; assoc prof, Biol Dept & Radiation Biol Lab, Tex A&M Univ, 62-65. *Mem:* Radiation Res Soc. *Res:* Effects of environmental agents on animals; reproductive physiology; laboratory animal management. *Mailing Add:* 2109 N Elm St Denton TX 76201

HUPPE, FRANCIS FROWIN, TECHNICAL MANAGEMENT, OPTICS. *Current Pos:* RETIRED. *Personal Data:* b Kansas City, Mo, Dec 11, 34; m 61, Dorothy Sweeney; c John, Susan & Michael. *Educ:* Rockhurst Col, BS, 56; Mass Inst Technol, MS, 59; Univ Wis, PhD(physics), 67. *Prof Exp:* Electronics engr, Bendix Aviation Corp, 59-60; instr math & physics, Rockhurst Col, 60-61; res physicist, E I Du Pont De Nemours & Co, 66-68, sr res physicist, 68, supvr, 68-69, res supvr, 69-71, div staff, 71-72, sr supvr, 72-74, mgr appl physics, 74-79, mgr instruments & control, 79-80, dir, Eng Physics Lab, 81-91. *Concurrent Pos:* Consult & freelance writer. *Mem:* Am Phys Soc; Sigma Xi. *Mailing Add:* 1401 Clive Circle Wilmington DE 19803. *Fax:* 302-764-0578; *E-Mail:* ffhuppe@strauss.udel.edu

HUPPERT, IRWIN NEIL, chemical engineering, for more information see previous edition

HUPPI, KONRAD E, CANCER RESEARCH. *Current Pos:* EXPERT, NAT CANCER INST, NIH, 84- *Personal Data:* b Abington, Pa, Nov 5, 55; US & Swiss citizen; 79, Joan Waldron; c Kristen, Katherine & John. *Educ:* Univ SFla, BA, 77; Univ Pa PhD(immunol), 84. *Prof Exp:* Asst trainer, Marineland, Inc, 76; res asst, Univ SFla, Col Med, 76-77, Basle Inst Immunol, 77-79, Inst Cancer Res, Fox Chase Cancer Ctr, 79-83. *Concurrent Pos:* Co-chmn, Chromasome 15, Int Mammalian Genome Soc, 89- *Mem:* Am Asn Immunol; Int Mammalian Genome Soc. *Res:* Characterization of genes involved in normal and neoplastic development of the immune system; rearrangement and organization of immunoglobulin genes; somatic mutation in oncogenes and tumor suppressor genes and the biological consequences of these alterations in hematological malignancies. *Mailing Add:* Nat Inst Cancer Lab Genetics Bldg 37 Rm 2B21 Bethesda MD 20892. *Fax:* 301-402-1031; *E-Mail:* huppi@helix.nih.gov

HUR, J JAMES, CHEMICAL & MATERIALS ENGINEERING. *Current Pos:* CONSULT, 84- *Personal Data:* b Greenville, Ohio, Aug 29, 20; m 44; c 4. *Educ:* Ohio State Univ, BChE, 42, MSc, 47. *Prof Exp:* Develop engr, Res & Develop Dept, Atlantic Richfield Co, 47-49; supv eng, 49-60, asst to vpres res, 60-65, planning dir, 65-69, mgr coordr & eval, 69-72, mgr prod supply, 72-73, mgr info systs & servs, 73-81, dir fed govt rels, 81-84. *Concurrent Pos:* Assoc prof, Drexel Univ eve sch, 57-68. *Mem:* Am Inst Chem Engrs; Int Asn Energy Econ. *Res:* Energy sources, corrosion; process design; information systems and research administration; environmental engineering. *Mailing Add:* 109 Harrells Ct Williamsburg VA 23185

HURA, GURDEEP SINGH, PETRI NET MODELING SYSTEMS, DISTRIBUTED COMPUTING & COMPUTER NETWORKS. *Current Pos:* MEM STAFF SCH APPL SCI, NANYANG TECHNOL UNIV, SINGAPORE. *Personal Data:* b Raipur, India, May 18, 50; m 76, Rajinder Kaur; c Devendra S & Mandeep S. *Educ:* Jalalpur Univ, India, BE, 72; Univ Roorkee, India, ME, 75, PhD(comput eng), 84. *Prof Exp:* Lectr electronics, Regional Eng Col, Kurukshetra, India, 74-83, asst prof, 83-84; fel comput sci, Concordia Univ, Montreal, 85; asst prof comput sci, Wright State Univ, Dayton, Ohio, 85-92. *Concurrent Pos:* Consult, BDM Inc, Dayton, Ohio, 88-90; chmn, Dayton Chap, Inst Elec & Electronics Engrs Comput Soc, 88-90, mem prog comt, Region 10 TENCON, 89-92 & Distrib Comput Syst, 90-92, chmn, overseas prog comt, Region 10 TENCON, 93; guest ed, spec issue Microelectronics & Reliability Int J, 91; reviewer/panelist, NSF, 91; region ed, Microelectronics & Reliability Int J; gen chmn, Elec Microelectronics Soc, Inst Elec & Electronics Engrs. *Mem:* Sr mem Inst Elec & Electronics Engrs; Asn Comput Mach. *Res:* Published over 80 scholarly research papers in various international journals and proceedings; presented invited papers in the areas of modeling, computer networks, distributed systems, graph theory, real time design and software systems. *Mailing Add:* Sch Appl Sci NTu Nanyang Ave Singapore 639798 Singapore. *Fax:* 65-791-9414; *E-Mail:* g.hura@ieee.org

HURAY, PAUL GORDON, COMPUTER SCIENCES, INORGANIC CHEMISTRY & MANUFACTURING EDUCATION. *Current Pos:* sr vpres res, 88-93, CAROLINA DISTINGUISHED PROF PHYSICS, UNIV SC, 93- *Personal Data:* b Knoxville, Tenn, Nov 3, 41; m 62, Susan Lyons; c William, Stephanie & Jennifer. *Educ:* Univ Tenn, BS, 64, PhD(physics), 68. *Honors & Awards:* IR 100, 82. *Prof Exp:* Physicist, Solid State Div, Oak Ridge Nat Lab, 64 & Univ NC, Chapel Hill, 68-69; from asst prof to prof physics, Univ Tenn, 69-81, assoc dean lib arts, 81-84, dir, 84-85, sr policy analyst, White House Off & Technol Policy, 85-87, dir, The Sci Alliance, 87. *Concurrent Pos:* Consult, Transuranium Res Lab, Chem Div, Oak Ridge Nat Lab, 70-85; chmn, Comput Res & Appln Comt, Fed Coord Coun Sci Eng & Technol, 86-89; mem, Acad Adv Bd, Indust Res Inst, 86-88; mem, White House Initiative Sci Adv Bd, Hist Black Cols & Univs, 85-88; consult, White House Sci Off, 87-; chmn, Acad Coal Intelligent Mfg Systs, 95-98. *Mem:* Am Phys Soc; AAAS; Sigma Xi. *Res:* Electronic and magnetic properties of transuranium elements; Mossbauer effect of iron, gold, uranium and neptunium isotopes; primary containment of transuranium elements for the purpose of nuclear waste disposal; high performance computing and communications. *Mailing Add:* Univ SC 300 S Main St Columbia SC 29208. *Fax:* 803-777-9557; *E-Mail:* huray@sc.edu

HURD, ALBERT EMERSON, MATHEMATICS. *Current Pos:* assoc prof, 71-82, PROF MATH, UNIV VICTORIA, BC, 82- *Personal Data:* b Montreal, Que. *Educ:* Univ Toronto, BASc, 53, MA, 57; Stanford Univ, PhD(math), 62. *Prof Exp:* CLE Moore instr math, Mass Inst Technol, 61-63; asst prof, Univ Calif, Los Angeles, 63-71. *Mem:* Can Math Soc. *Res:* Applications of nonstandard analysis to mathematical physics. *Mailing Add:* Dept Math Univ Victoria PO Box 3045 Victoria BC U8W 2V2 Can

HURD, COLIN MICHAEL, SOLID STATE PHYSICS, MATERIALS SCIENCE. *Current Pos:* RETIRED. *Personal Data:* b Hull, Eng, Mar 9, 37; Can citizen; m 60; c 3. *Educ:* Univ Hull, BSc, 58, PhD(physics), 61. *Prof Exp:* Fel chem, Inst Microstruct Sci, Nat Res Coun Can, 61-63, sr res officer chem, 63-81, prin res officer, 81-97. *Concurrent Pos:* Vis scientist physics, CRTBT, Grenoble, France, 68-69 & Fac Sci, Orsay, France, 77-78; vis prof physics, Univ Geneva, Switz, 74. *Res:* Numerical simulation of semiconductor devices. *Mailing Add:* Inst Microstruct Sci Nat Res Coun Can Ottawa ON K1A 0R9 Can. *Fax:* 613-957-8734; *E-Mail:* hurd@nrcphy1.phy.nrc.ca

HURD, CUTHBERT CORWIN, MATHEMATICS. *Current Pos:* CHMN, CUTHBERT CHURD ASSOCS, 74-; VIS SCHOLAR COMPUT SCI & RES PROF LITHOGRAPHY, 84-; CHMN SCI BD, CAMBRIDGE RES ASSOCS, 92- ; CHIEF SCIENTIST, NORTH POINT SOFTWEAR VENTURES, 93- *Personal Data:* b Estherville, Iowa, Apr 5, 11; m 41, Bettie J Mills; c Steven, Diana, Susan, Elizabeth & Victoria. *Educ:* Drake Univ, AB, 32; Iowa State Col, MS, 34; Univ Ill, PhD(math), 36. *Hon Degrees:* LLD, Drake Univ, 67. *Prof Exp:* From instr to asst prof math, Mich State Col, 36-42; dean, Allegheny Col, 45-47; tech res head, Union Carbide & Carbon Chem Corp, Oak Ridge, 47-49; dir appl sci dept, Int Bus Mach Corp, 49-53, dir appl sci div, 53-55, dir electronic data processing mach, 55-56, dir automation res, 56-60, dir indust process control systs, 60-61, spec asst vpres res, 61-62; chmn bd, Comput Usage Co, Inc, New York, NY & Palo Alto, Calif, 62-74; chmn, HCC, Inc, 74-90; chmn, Picodyne Corp, 78-86; chmn, Quintus Comput Systs, 84-89. *Concurrent Pos:* Past mem comput comt, Nat Res Coun; mem Textile Res Inst; Nat Res Coun del, Int Sci Radio Union; pres exec coun, Found Instrumentation, Educ & Res; mem develop bd, Mass Inst Technol; chmn comput sci adv comt, Stanford Univ; comput hist proj, Smithsonian Inst; adv comt, Ctr Comput Sci & Technol, Inst Appl Technol, Nat Bur Stand. *Mem:* Fel AAAS; Inst Mgt Sci (vpres, 53-54); Opers Res Soc Am; Psychomet Soc; Am Math Soc. *Res:* Asymptotic solutions to differential equations; probability distribution theory of functions of indirect measurements; numerical analysis as applied to high-speed computing machines; logical design of computing machines. *Mailing Add:* 332 Westridge Dr Portola Valley CA 94028

HURD, ERIC R, INTERNAL MEDICINE. *Current Pos:* CLIN PROF INTERNAL MED, SOUTHWESTERN MED SCH, UNIT TEX, DALLAS, 81-; ASSOC, BAYLOR ARTHRITIS CTR, BAYLOR UNIV MED CTR, 81- *Personal Data:* b Columbus, Kans, July 5, 36; m; c 3. *Educ:* Univ Tulsa, BS, 58; Univ Okla, MD, 62. *Prof Exp:* Intern, St John's Hosp, Tulsa, Okla, 62-63, resident internal med, 63-65; NIH fel, 65-67, from instr to prof, 67-81. *Concurrent Pos:* Sr attend physician, Parkland Mem Hosp, Dallas, 67-; mem, Am Rheumatism Asn Coop Clin Comt, 68-74; dir, Arthritis Clin, John Peter Smith Hosp, Ft Worth, 72-; consult rheumatology, Vet Admin Hosp, 72-, attend physician, 73-, chief rheumatology, 81-; mem, Med & Sci Comt, Arthritis Found, 82-, chmn, Prof Educ Comt, 88- *Res:* Rheumatoid arthritis; author of numerous publications. *Mailing Add:* Dept Int Med 712 N Washington No 200 Dallas TX 75246-5412. *Fax:* 214-826-0605

HURD, JAMES WILLIAM, PARTICLE ACCELERATORS, NUCLEAR DETECTORS. *Current Pos:* SR TECH STAFF MEM, TASC, 93- *Personal Data:* b Grand Rapids, Minn, Oct 13, 51; m 79, Linda S Townsend; c Ian & Alexander. *Educ:* Univ Ala, Huntsville, BS, 74; Rutgers Univ, MS, 77; Univ NMex, MBA, 87. *Prof Exp:* Teaching res asst, Dept Physics, Rutgers Univ, 74-77, accelerator engr, Nuclear Physics Lab, 77-79; sect leader, Los Alamos Nat Lab, 79-91; sect leader, Super Conducting Super Collider Lab, 91-93. *Mem:* Am Phys Soc; Inst Nuclear Mat Mgt. *Res:* Modeling and measurement of beam transports and accelerator systems; development of numerical and analytical models of transport elements; algorithms for accelerator operations; management of accelerator operations; management of physics research and development programs. *Mailing Add:* 654 Hummingbird Dr Indialantic FL 32903. *Fax:* 407-259-8605; *E-Mail:* jwhurd@aol.com

HURD, JEFFERY L, ELECTRON BEAM MICROANALYSIS, CRYSTAL GROWTH & CHARACTERIZATION. *Current Pos:* STAFF ENGR, IBM E FISHKILL, HOPEWELL JUNCTION, NY, 88- *Personal Data:* b Denver, Colo, July 31, 54. *Educ:* Colo Sch Mines, BS, 78; Univ Calif Berkeley, MS, 87. *Prof Exp:* Assoc scientist, Solar Energy Res Inst, 78-85; res asst, Lawrence Berkeley Lab, Calif, 85-88. *Concurrent Pos:* Teaching asst lab mat sci, Univ Calif, Berkeley, 86; Peer Rev Panel mem, Dept Energy Nat Photovoltaics Prog, 89-90. *Mem:* Electrochem Soc; Am Asn Crystal Growth; Mat Res Soc; Microbeam Anal Soc. *Res:* Silicon sheet crystal growth and characterization for photovoltaics; hydrothermal crystal growth of copper-indium-selenium; medium temperature CVD of BN films for semiconductor applications; characterization of gradient freeze galium-arsenide; microbeam analysis of ceramics and semiconductors; high temperature thermal properties; author of various publications. *Mailing Add:* IBM E Fishkill Z/40E 1580 Rte 52 Hopewell Junction NY 12533-6531

HURD, JON RICKEY, NUCLEAR STRUCTURE & SPECIAL NUCLEAR MATERIAL SAFEGUARDS. *Current Pos:* STAFF MEM, LOS ALAMOS NAT LAB, 84- *Personal Data:* b Columbus, Ohio, July 8, 45. *Educ:* Ohio State Univ, BSc, 68; Miami Univ Ohio, MSc, 73; Fla State Univ, PhD(nuclear physics), 79. *Prof Exp:* Fel low energy nuclear physics, Univ Pa, 79-81; fel nuclear physics, Univ Va, 81-84. *Mem:* Am Phys Soc; Am Asn Physics Teachers; Int Nuclear Mat Mgt. *Res:* Low energy nuclear resonance phenomena, intermediate energy nuclear physics and safeguards for special nuclear materials. *Mailing Add:* 2 Antigua Ct Santa Fe NM 87505

HURD, LAWRENCE EDWARD, ENTOMOLOGY. *Current Pos:* HEAD, DEPT BIOL, WASHINGTON & LEE UNIV, 93- *Personal Data:* b Syracuse, NY, Aug 13, 47; c 1. *Educ:* Hiram Col, BA, 69; Syracuse Univ, PhD(ecol), 72. *Prof Exp:* Fel, Cornell Univ, 72-73; from asst prof to prof ecol, Univ Del, 73-93. *Mem:* AAAS; Ecol Soc Am; fel Royal Entom Soc London; Entom Soc Am. *Res:* Ecosystem theory; regulation of community diversity; population regulation in predators. *Mailing Add:* Dept Biol Washington & Lee Univ Lexington VA 24450

HURD, MAGGIE PATRICIANNE, mycology, electron microscopy, for more information see previous edition

HURD, MARY KRUMBOLTZ, CIVIL ENGINEERING, CONCRETE CONSTRUCTION. *Current Pos:* ENG WRITER & CONSULT, 90-; PRES ENG PUBL, FARMINGTON, MICH. *Personal Data:* b Ralph W, Denise L & Holly L. *Educ:* Iowa State Univ, BS. *Honors & Awards:* Delmar L Bloem Distinguished Serv Award, Am Concrete Inst, 90, Arthur Y Moy Award, 94, Henry C Turner Medal, 95. *Prof Exp:* Assoc ed spec tech publs, Am Concrete Inst, 66-67, staff engr, 67-76, engr-writer & consult, 76-80; ed, Concrete Construct Mag, 81-83, eng ed, 83-90. *Mem:* Am Soc Civil Engrs; Precast/ Prestressed Concrete Inst; Soc Tech Commun; fel Am Concrete Inst. *Mailing Add:* 33742 Lyncroft Rd Farmington MI 48331-3647. *Fax:* 248-474-1369

HURD, PAUL DEHART, BIOLOGY, SCIENCE EDUCATION. *Current Pos:* prof, 51-71, EMER PROF SCI EDUC, STANFORD UNIV, 71- *Personal Data:* b Denver, Colo, Dec 25, 05; m 46; c 2. *Educ:* Univ Northern Colo, AB, 29, MA, 32; Stanford Univ, EdD(sci educ), 49. *Hon Degrees:* DSc, Drake Univ, 74, Ball State Univ, 79, Univ Northern Colo, 80. *Honors & Awards:* Apollo Award, NASA, 70. *Prof Exp:* Teacher pub sch, Colo, 29-39; chmn dept sci, Menlo Jr Col, Calif, 39-51. *Concurrent Pos:* Fac fel, Stanford Univ, Northeast Asia-US Forum Int Policy, 80- *Mem:* Nat Sci Teachers Asn; Nat Asn Biol Teachers; Nat Asn Res Sci Teaching; fel AAAS. *Res:* Biology curriculum; history of science teaching. *Mailing Add:* 549 Hilbar Lane Palo Alto CA 94303

HURD, PHILLIP WAYNE, ADHESIVES PRODUCT DEVELOPMENT, POLYMERIC PLASTICIZERS. *Current Pos:* SCIENTIST, GA PAC RES & DEVELOP, 96- *Personal Data:* b Norfolk, Va, Nov 13, 51; m 80; c 2. *Educ:* Baylor Univ, PhD(org chem), 85. *Prof Exp:* Res assoc, Tex A&M Univ, 84-85; sr res chemist, Dow Chem US Am, Freeport, Tex, 85-89; sr develop chemist, Chem Prod Div, Union Camp Corp, 89-96. *Mem:* Am Chem Soc. *Res:* New product development for rasin ester tackifiers used as hot melt and pressure sensitive adhesives. *Mailing Add:* 2605 Westchester Pkwy SE Conyers GA 30208-2480. *Fax:* 912-238-6726

HURD, RALPH EUGENE, NUCLEAR MAGNETIC RESONANCE. *Current Pos:* appl chemist, Nicolet Magnetics Corp, 80-83, MGR, RES & DEVELOP, GE NMR INST, 83- *Personal Data:* b Columbus, Ohio, May 19, 50; m 71; c 2. *Educ:* Calif State Col, San Bernadino, BA, 73; Univ Calif, Riverside, PhD(biochem), 78. *Prof Exp:* Res asst biochemist, Univ Calif, Riverside, 79-80. *Mem:* Am Chem Soc. *Res:* Application of nuclear magnetic resonance spectroscopy to biochemical problems, especially in the study of protein-nucleic acid interactions and structure. *Mailing Add:* GE Med Systs 47697 Westinghouse Dr Fremont CA 94539

HURD, RICHARD NELSON, REGULATORY AFFAIRS FOR NEW DRUG & BIOLOGIC PRODUCTS, MANAGEMENT OF CLINICAL RESEARCH. *Current Pos:* PRES, HURD & ASSOC. *Personal Data:* b Evanston, Ill, Feb 25, 26; m 50, Jocelyn Martin; c Melanie (Brown) & Suzanne (Benes). *Educ:* Univ Mich, BS, 46; Univ Minn, PhD(org chem), 56. *Prof Exp:* Group leader, Polyethylene Br, Res Div, Koppers Co, Inc, 56-57; res chemist, Org Res Dept, Mallinckrodt Chem Works, Inc, 57-64, group leader plastics additives res, Res Dept, Indust Chem Div, Mo, 64-66; group leader res dept, Com Solvents Corp, 66-69, sect leader, 69-71; mgr int sci affairs, G D Searle Int Co, 72-74, dir mfg & tech affairs, 74-77; vpres tech affairs, Elder Pharmaceut, 77-81; vpres res & develop, US Proprietary Drugs & Toiletries Div, Schering-Plough, Inc, 81-83; vpres sci affairs, Moleculon Inc, 83-88; vpres regulatory affairs, Pharmaco, 89; consult, Epoulon Inc, 88-89. *Mem:* Fel AAAS; Am Chem Soc; Sigma Xi; NY Acad Sci; Regulatory Affairs Prof Soc; Am Asn Pharm Scientists. *Res:* Macrolide and natural product syntheses; non-steroidal estrogens; thioamide syntheses and reactions; structures and properties of organic chelates and complexes; stabilization of polymeric systems; photo-chemotherapy; photobiology; investigative dermatology. *Mailing Add:* 2724 Crawford Ave Evanston IL 60201. *Fax:* 512-326-7725

HURD, ROBERT CHARLES, BACTERIOLOGY. *Current Pos:* RETIRED. *Personal Data:* b Mt Vernon, Wash, Mar 7, 22; m 50; c 4. *Educ:* Pac Univ, BS, 46; Wash State Univ, MS, 50, PhD(bact), 53. *Prof Exp:* Instr biol, Pac Univ, 46-48; res asst biol sci, State Col Wash, 48-53; instr microbiol, Gonzaga Univ, 53-57, head dept, 57-77, from asst prof to prof biol, 60-87. *Concurrent Pos:* Consult, bact. *Mem:* AAAS; Sigma Xi. *Res:* Pathogenic microbiology. *Mailing Add:* 3805 W Weile Ave Spokane WA 99208

HURD, SUZANNE SHELDON, BIOCHEMISTRY. *Current Pos:* scientist adminr, 69-81, DIR, DIV LUNG DIS, NAT HEART, LUNG & BLOOD INST, 77- *Personal Data:* b Elmira, NY, Dec 17, 39. *Educ:* Bates Col, BS, 61; Univ Wash, MS, 63, PhD(biochem), 67. *Prof Exp:* NIH fel biochem, Univ Calif, Berkeley, 67-69. *Mem:* Am Therapeut Soc. *Res:* Enzymology; muscle proteins; diseases of the heart and lung. *Mailing Add:* Nat Heart Lung and Blood In, Div Lung Diseases 2 Rock Ledge Ctr Rm 10122-6701 Rockledge Dr Bethesda MD 20892-7952

HURD, WALTER LEROY, JR, QUALITY ENGINEERING, QUALITY CONSULTING. *Current Pos:* PRIN, WL HURD ASSOC, 92- *Personal Data:* b 1919; m 41, Ann Cornell; c David, Caroline, Drew, Bruce & Kevin. *Educ:* Morningside Col, BA, 40; San Jose State Univ, MA, 78. *Honors & Awards:* EL Grant Award, 74, Am Soc Qual Control, EJ Lancaster Award, 84, Edwards Medal, 86. *Prof Exp:* Group oper officer, USAAF, 41-45; vpres-gen oper mgr, Philippine Airlines, 46-54; qual mgr, Nat Seal Div, Lockheed Corp, 55-58, reliability dept mgr & supvr, Missles Syst Div, 58-62, reliability div mgr, 63, reliability & qual eng div mgr, 63-65, reliability & qual mgr, Elec Div, 65-66, dir prod assurance, Space Syst Div, 66-78, corp dir, 78-86; chmn bd, Harrington Hurd & Rieker, 87-89; prin, Ernst & Young 89-91. *Mem:* Fel Am Soc Qual Control (pres, 77-78); Int Acad Qual; Asia Pac Orgn Qual (vpres, 85-); Nat Soc Prof Engrs; assoc fel Am Inst Aeronaut & Astronaut. *Res:* Delivered many papers nationally and internationally on aero and space quality and reliability, space industrialization and the use of near earth space resources. *Mailing Add:* 1012 Windmill Rd Dripping Springs TX 78620

HURDIS, EVERETT CUSHING, ORGANIC CHEMISTRY. *Current Pos:* asst prof, 62-69, ASSOC PROF CHEM, TEX WOMAN'S UNIV, 69- *Personal Data:* b Providence, RI, Feb 5, 18; m 46; c Helen, Cynthia, Holly & Sara. *Educ:* Brown Univ, ScB, 39; Princeton Univ, MA, 41, PhD(phys chem), 43. *Prof Exp:* Res chemist, US Rubber Co, NJ, 42-58; mgr styrene polymers group, Koppers Co, Pa, 58-62. *Concurrent Pos:* Lectr, Rutgers Univ, 48-49; instr, Fairleigh Dickinson Col, 50-52. *Mem:* Am Chem Soc; NY Acad Sci; fel Am Inst Chem. *Res:* Aromatic substitutions; redox indicators; polymer chemistry. *Mailing Add:* 621 E University Dr Denton TX 76201-2084

HURDLE, BURTON GARRISON, PHYSICS, ACOUSTICS. *Current Pos:* supvr res physicist & asst supt, 77-84, physicist & assoc supt, 84-89, SR SCIENTIST & CONSULT, ACOUST DIV, NAVAL RES LAB, WASHINGTON, DC, 89- *Personal Data:* b Roanoke, Va, Jan 2, 18; wid, Edith Hubbard; c Burton G Jr (deceased) & Allen H. *Educ:* Roanoke Col, BS, 41; Va Polytech Inst, MS, 43; Open Univ, UK, PhD, 88. *Honors & Awards:* Alan Berman Res Publ Award, 85. *Prof Exp:* Teaching asst, Math Dept, Va Polytech Inst & State Univ, 41-43; Res physicist, Sound Div, Naval Res Lab, Washington, DC, 43-47; res physicist, Eng Res Assoc, Arlington, Va, 47-49; res physicist, Sound Div, Naval Res Lab, Washington, DC, 49-56, supvr res physicist & head, Acoust Scattering Sect, Acoust Div, 56-70, supvr res physicist & head, Propagation Br, 70-76; vis scientist, Admiralty Res Lab, Teddington, Eng, UK, 76-77. *Mem:* Fel Acoust Soc Am; Sigma Xi. *Res:* Underwater acoustic propagation; scattering and noise; geophysics and physical oceanography of the ocean environment; author or co-author of over 25 publications. *Mailing Add:* 6222 Berkeley Rd Alexandria VA 22307. *Fax:* 202-404-7588; *E-Mail:* bhurdle@fenton.nrs.navy.mil

HURFORD, THOMAS ROWLAND, POLYMER CHEMISTRY, ANALYTICAL CHEMISTRY. *Current Pos:* Chemist, 67-69, tech rep polymer chem, 69-71, MKT REP PLASTICS, E I DU PONT DE NEMOURS & CO, INC, 72-, SALES & SALES MGT, 82- *Personal Data:* b Detroit, Mich, Nov 20, 41; m 64, Delores A Watts; c Matthew T & Mark T. *Educ:* Wayne State Univ, BS, 64, PhD(analytical chem), 67. *Mem:* Am Chem Soc. *Mailing Add:* 1001 Oriente Ave Greenville DE 19807-2260. *Fax:* 302-773-2500

HURKMAN, WILLIAM JAMES, MOLECULAR BIOLOGY, PLANT STRESS. *Current Pos:* res plant physiologist, 82-92, RES LEADER, CROP IMPROV & UTILIZATION RES UNIT, WESTERN REGIONAL RES CTR, 92- *Personal Data:* m 70, Marion F McGuckin; c Robert W. *Educ:* Univ Wis-Whitewater, BS, 70, Univ Wis-Milwaukee, MS, 74; Purdue Univ, PhD(plant physiol), 79. *Prof Exp:* Res assoc fel, Dept Bot & Plant Path, Univ Okla, 79-82. *Mem:* Am Soc Plant Physiologists. *Res:* Molecular biological techniques in conjunction with physiological and biochemical analyses; identify potential genetic mechanisms for tolerance to environmental stress to efficiently develop more tolerant crop plants. *Mailing Add:* 111 Appalachian Dr Martinez CA 94553

HURLBERT, BERNARD STUART, LABORATORY DESIGN. *Current Pos:* PRES, AQUA LIBRA ASSOCS, 88- *Personal Data:* b Yarmouth, NS, Oct 11, 30; m 52, 87, Glenna D Wolfe; c 3. *Educ:* Acadia Univ, BSc, 50 & 51; McGill Univ, MSc, 53; Univ NB, PhD(chem), 57. *Prof Exp:* Instr chem, Rochester Inst Technol, 57-59; res chemist, Wellcome Res Labs, 59-61, sr res chemist, 61-70, group leader, 70-80, sect head, 80-88. *Concurrent Pos:* Consult, 88- *Res:* Organic chemistry; nuclear magnetic resonance; laboratory design. *Mailing Add:* 6323 Mt Mitchell Rd Efland NC 27243

HURLBERT, ROBERT BOSTON, BIOCHEMISTRY. *Current Pos:* PROF BIOCHEM, UNIV TEX GRAD SCH BIOMED SCI, 67- *Personal Data:* b David City, Nebr, Aug 9, 26; m 55; c 4. *Educ:* Univ Nebr, BS, 47, MS, 49; Univ Wis, PhD(physiol chem), 52. *Prof Exp:* Am Cancer Soc fel, Kemiska Inst, Karolinska Inst, Sweden, 53-54; fel, Inst Cytophysiol, Copenhagen Univ, 54-55; instr biochem, McArdle Lab, Univ Wis, 55; from asst biochemist to assoc biochemist, 56-62, biochemist, Univ Tex M D Anderson Hosp & Tumor Inst Houston, 62-, prof biochem, 65- *Concurrent Pos:* From clin asst prof to clin assoc prof, Col Med, Baylor Univ, 56-67; assoc ed, Cancer Res, 68-80; mem adv comts, Am Cancer Soc, 66-71 & 79-82. *Mem:* Am Soc Biol Chemists; Am Asn Cancer Res; Am Soc Cell Biol. *Res:* Chemistry and metabolism of orotic acid; chromatography of ribonucleotides; biosynthesis of uridine nucleotides and cytidine nucleotides; synthesis of RNA and protein in isolated nuclei and nucleoli; chromatographic analysis of intra-cellular deoxynucleotides; mechanisms of action of antitumor drugs. *Mailing Add:* Univ Tex M D Anderson Cancer Ctr 8807 Manhatten St Houston TX 77096-2517

HURLBERT, STUART HARTLEY, LIMNOLOGY, BIOSTATISTICS. *Current Pos:* from asst prof to assoc prof, 70-78, PROF BIOL, SAN DIEGO STATE UNIV, 78- *Personal Data:* b Savannah, Ga, July 16, 39; m 65, Irene L Woo; c Allen H. *Educ:* Amherst Col, BA, 61; Cornell Univ, PhD(ecol), 68. *Honors & Awards:* G W Snedecor Award, Am Statist Asn, 84. *Prof Exp:* Instr zool, Cornell Univ, 66; res entomologist, 66-70, asst prof ecol & fel entom, Dept Entom, Univ Calif, Riverside, 70. *Concurrent Pos:* Vis prof, Univ Chile, 71-72. *Mem:* Fel AAAS; Ecol Soc Am; Am Soc Limnol & Oceanog; Am Soc Nature; Int Soc Theoret Appl Limnol; Int Soc Salt Lake Res. *Res:* Salamander migration; mathematical ecology; insecticides in aquatic ecosystems; predation and competition among freshwater zooplankters; limnology of the Central Andes; statistics; flamingo ecology; saline lakes; salton sea. *Mailing Add:* Dept Biol San Diego State Univ San Diego CA 92182-0057. *Fax:* 619-594-5676; *E-Mail:* shurlbert@sunstroke.sdsu.edu

HURLBURT, H(ARVEY) ZEH, CHEMICAL ENGINEERING. *Current Pos:* CONSULT, 85- *Personal Data:* b Kellogg, Idaho, Sept 2, 21; m 43, Lepick; c 8. *Educ:* Univ Tex, BA, 42, BS, 43, MS, 47; Mass Inst Technol, ScD(chem eng), 50. *Prof Exp:* Process engr, synthetic rubber div, US Rubber Co, 43-46; lab instr, Univ Tex, 46-47; asst, Mass Inst Technol, 47-49; dir res, Consol Chem Industs Div, 50-67, mgr, Peiser Labs, Stauffer Chem Co, 67-85. *Mem:* Am Chem Soc; Am Inst Chem Engrs; Sigma Xi. *Res:* Interphase resistance to mass transfer; inorganic chemical manufacture. *Mailing Add:* 7814 Santa Elena Houston TX 77061

HURLBURT, HARLEY ERNEST, NUMERICAL OCEAN MODELLING, OCEAN PREDICTION. *Current Pos:* OCEANOGR, NAVAL RES LAB, 77- *Personal Data:* b Bennington, Vt, Apr 12, 43. *Educ:* Union Col, Schenectady, BS, 65; Fla State Univ, MS, 71, PhD(meteorol), 74. *Honors & Awards:* Distinguished Scientist Medal, Int Liege Colloquium, 81; Kaminski Publ Award, Sigma Xi, 91. *Prof Exp:* Weather officer, USAF, 65-69; fel, Nat Ctr Atmospheric Res, 74-75; staff scientist, Jaycor, 75-77. *Concurrent Pos:* Prin investr, Off Naval Res, 75-77 & 84-; adj fac Marine Sci Univ Miss, Stennis Space Ctr 93-, meteorol Fla State Univ, Tallahassee, 95- *Mem:* Am Geophys Union; Am Meteorol Soc; The Oceanog Soc; Sigma Xi. *Res:* Developing the world's first 1/16th degree eddy-resolving global ocean prediction model for the US Navy; numerous articles in professional journals. *Mailing Add:* Naval Res Lab Code 7323 Stennis Space Center MS 39529-5004. *Fax:* 228-688-4759; *E-Mail:* hurlburt@nrlssc.navy.mil

HURLBUT, CORNELIUS SEARLE, JR, MINERALOGY, CRYSTALLOGRAPHY. *Current Pos:* Instr petrog, 31-33, from instr to prof mineral, 33-72, EMER PROF MINERAL, HARVARD UNIV, 72- *Personal Data:* b Springfield, Mass, June 30, 06; m 32, 56; c 3. *Educ:* Antioch Col, AB, 29; Harvard Univ, AM, 32, PhD(petrog), 33. *Honors & Awards:* Neil Miner Award, Nat Asn Geol Teachers, 66. *Concurrent Pos:* Guggenheim fel, 55; vis prof, Boston Col, 72-77. *Mem:* AAAS; fel Am Mineral Soc (secy, 44-59, pres, 63); Nat Asn Geol Teachers; Am Acad Arts & Sci; fel Geol Soc Am; Gemmological Asn Gt Brit. *Res:* Gemology. *Mailing Add:* Dept Earth & Planetary Sci Harvard Univ Cambridge MA 02138

HURLBUT, FRANKLIN CHARLES, PHYSICS. *Current Pos:* from lectr to assoc prof, 56-68, prof aeronaut sci, 56-91, EMER PROF AERONAUT SCI & MECH ENG, UNIV CALIF, BERKELEY, 91- *Personal Data:* b Los Angeles, Calif, July 20, 20; m 52, Marianne McKelvey; c Douglas & Catherine. *Educ:* Univ Calif, Los Angeles, AB, 41; Univ Calif, Berkeley, PhD(physics), 54. *Prof Exp:* Physicist, Appl Res Lab, Univ Calif, Berkeley, 42-44. *Concurrent Pos:* Consult, aerospace indust. *Mem:* Am Phys Soc; Am Inst Aeronaut & Astronaut. *Res:* Molecular and atomic interaction with solid surface; upper atmospheric aerodynamics. *Mailing Add:* 15 Tamalpais Rd Berkeley CA 94708

HURLEY, DAVID JOHN, DEVELOPMENTAL & NUTRITIONAL VETERINARY IMMUNOLOGY, MEMBRANE BIOPHYSICS OF PROTEIN-LIPID INTERACTION IN SIGNAL TRANSDUCTION. *Current Pos:* asst prof, 89-94, ASSOC PROF MICROBIOL, SDAK STATE UNIV, 94- *Personal Data:* St Paul, Minn, Mar 4, 53; m 77, Enid M Pohland; c Ian D, Katherine A & Christian A. *Educ:* Univ Wis-Milwaukee, BA, 77; Pa State Univ, PhD(microbiol- biophys), 88. *Honors & Awards:* Ernest L Buckley Award, SDak Govs Off, 93. *Prof Exp:* Clin cell biol assoc, Burn Reb Lab, St Marys Hosp, 76-81; res assoc vet sci, Pa State Univ, 86-89. *Concurrent Pos:* Immunol consult, Tri Biol Labs, State Col Pa, 84-88; dir cell anal lab, Ctr Cell Res, NASA Prog, Pa State Univ, 88-89; flow cytometry consult, Dept Molecular & Cell Biol, 88-89; dir, Anal Flourescent Ctr, SDak State Univ, 90-; flow cytometry consult, Dept Path, Sioux Valley Hosp, 91-93; vpres sci affairs, Sterling Technol, 92-; pres & chief exec officer, Rural Technologies Inc. *Mem:* Am Soc Microbiol; Am Asn Vet Immunol; Asn Med Lab Immunologists; Sigma Xi; Int Soc Anal Cytology. *Res:* Development and control of the immune response from the level of membrane interactions between leukocytes and invaders to the level of organismal pathogenesis. *Mailing Add:* Biol/Microbiol SDak State Univ Brookings SD 57007. *Fax:* 605-688-6003

HURLEY, FORREST REYBURN, INORGANIC CHEMISTRY. *Current Pos:* RETIRED. *Personal Data:* b Greene Co, Ohio, Jan 11, 21; m 42, Dorothy Hutchison; c Dennis, Pamela & Patrick. *Educ:* Ohio State Univ, BChE, 42, PhD(chem), 54. *Prof Exp:* Control chemist, Gen Chem Co, 42-44; res chemist, Monsanto Chem Co, 46-49; asst chem, Ohio State Univ, 50-51; res chemist, Battelle Mem Inst, 51 & Davison Chem Co, 54; res supvr, W R Grace & Co, 54-66; dir res, Cement Div, Martin Marietta Corp, 66-77; dir cement & concrete res, W R Grace & Co, 78-86. *Mem:* Fel AAAS; Am Chem Soc; Am Ceramic Soc. *Res:* Chemistry of nitrogen, phosphorus, lanthanides, magnesia and lime; catalysis; inorganic colloids; portland cement and concrete. *Mailing Add:* 1452 Rosemoor Rd Jamestown OH 43335-9553

HURLEY, FRANCIS JOSEPH, PARASITOLOGY. *Current Pos:* from asst prof to assoc prof, 60-71, PROF BIOL, STONEHILL COL, 71-, HEAD DEPT, 60- *Personal Data:* b Waltham, Mass, May 18, 27. *Educ:* Univ Notre Dame, AB, 49; Cath Univ Am, MS, 58, PhD(parasitol), 60. *Prof Exp:* Head dept sci high sch, NY, 54-56. *Mem:* Am Soc Parasitol. *Res:* Nematode parasites of vertebrates; parasitic immunology. *Mailing Add:* Stonehill Col 320 Washington St North Easton MA 02357-7800

HURLEY, FRANK LEO, BIOSTATISTICS. *Current Pos:* SR PARTNER, BIOMET RES INST, 73- *Personal Data:* b Lowell, Mass, Oct 25, 44; m 80. *Educ:* Georgetown Univ, BS, 66; Johns Hopkins Univ, PhD(biostatist), 70. *Prof Exp:* Lectr, Loyola Col, 67-70; asst prof biostatist, Sch Med, George Washington Univ, 70-73. *Concurrent Pos:* Asst prof biostatist, Sch Med, Georgetown Univ, 71- *Mem:* Am Statist Asn; NY Acad Sci; Biomet Soc; AAAS. *Res:* Applications of stochastic models; statistical methods. *Mailing Add:* 4515 Potomac Ave NW Washington DC 20007

HURLEY, HARRY JAMES, DERMATOLOGY. *Current Pos:* assoc prof, 62-68, PROF CLIN DERMAT, SCH MED, UNIV PA, 68- *Personal Data:* b Philadelphia, Pa, Oct 10, 26; m 50; c 5. *Educ:* St Joseph's Col, Pa, 43-45; Jefferson Med Col, MD, 49; Univ Pa, DSc(med), 58. *Honors & Awards:* Clark W Finnerud Award, Dermat Found, 91. *Prof Exp:* Instr dermat, Sch Med, Boston Univ, 54-55; instr, Sch Med, Univ Pa, 56-57, instr, Grad Sch Med, 56-58, assoc, 57-59; prof, Hahnemann Med Col, 59-62. *Concurrent Pos:* Consult, US Vet Admin, 59-; mem bd trustees, Dermat Found, 73-75, pres, 75-; mem, Am Bd Dermat, 74-84, exec dir, 93- *Mem:* Soc Invest Dermat; AMA; Am Col Physicians; Am Acad Dermat; Am Dermat Asn. *Res:* Physiology of the skin; sweat gland and vascular activity; experimental granulomagenesis. *Mailing Add:* 39 Copley Rd Upper Darby PA 19082

HURLEY, JAMES EDGAR, MICROBIOLOGY. *Current Pos:* assoc prof, 62-67, PROF BIOL, OKLA BAPTIST UNIV, 67-, CHMN DEPT, 68- *Personal Data:* b Morristown, Tenn, Sept 30, 29. *Educ:* Tusculum Col, BA, 50; Vanderbilt Univ, PhD(biol), 63. *Prof Exp:* Instr biol, Mid Tenn State Col, 53-54; instr microbiol, US Naval Med Sch, Bethesda, Md, 55-58; chief microbiologist, Washington Hosp Ctr, DC, 58-61. *Concurrent Pos:* Danforth assoc, 70-; vis prof, Univ Tex Cancer Ctr, Houston, 76. *Mem:* AAAS; Am Soc Microbiol; NY Acad Sci. *Res:* Physiology of algae in mass culture; taxonomy and physiology of the Bacteriodaceae; physiology of Euglena and Paramecium bursaria. *Mailing Add:* Dept Nat Sci Okla Baptist Univ 500 W University Shawnee OK 74801-2558

HURLEY, JAMES FREDERICK, LIE ALGEBRAS, ALGEBRAIC GROUPS. *Current Pos:* assoc prof, 71-82, PROF MATH, UNIV CONN, 82- *Personal Data:* b Kansas City, Mo, Apr 3, 41; m 66, Marie C Nespral; c Joseph J & Regina M. *Educ:* Ariz State Univ, BA, 61, MA, 63; Univ Calif, Los Angeles, PhD(lie algebras), 66. *Prof Exp:* Lectr math, Univ Calif, Riverside, 66-67, asst prof, 67-71. *Concurrent Pos:* Fulbright-Hays vis assoc prof, Ateneo de Manila Univ & De La Salle Univ, Philippines, 73; vis prof, NSF Scientists & Engrs Econ Develop Prog, Univ Philippines, Quezon City, 75-76; vis fel, Inst Advan Studies, Australian Nat Univ Res Sch Phys Sci, Canberra, 76 & Tsukuba Univ, Japan, 80; comt employ & educ policy, Am Math Soc, 85-89; vis fel, Max-Planck-Inst Math, 87; prin investr, Instr Lab Improv Grant, NSF, 88-90; grant, State Conn Elias House High Technol Prog, 89-91; acad specialist, US Info Agency, Philippine Sci Consortium, 89; data comt, Am Math Soc & Math Asn Am, 90-95; grant, NSF Curric Develop Math-Calculus, 91-93 & 92-97; teaching fel, Univ Conn, 95. *Mem:* Am Math Soc; Math Asn Am; Asn Advan Comput Educ; Sigma Xi. *Res:* Lie algebras; Chevalley algebras; Chevalley groups over rings; classical linear algebraic groups over rings; simple groups of Lie type; Kac-Moody Lie algebras. *Mailing Add:* Dept Math U-9 Univ Conn 196 Auditorium Rd Rm 111 Storrs CT 06269-3009. *E-Mail:* hurley@math.uconn.edu

HURLEY, JAMES R(OBERT), CHEMICAL ENGINEERING, ELECTRICAL ENGINEERING. *Current Pos:* RETIRED. *Personal Data:* b Milwaukee, Wis, May 9, 31; m 53; c 4. *Educ:* Univ Wis-Madison, BS, 53, MS, 61, PhD(chem eng), 63. *Prof Exp:* Res engr, Phillips Petrol Co, 53-57, develop engr, 57-58; eng analyst, Allis-Chalmers Mfg Co, 58-63, proj leader energy conversion, 63-64, group leader fuel cells, 64, sect mgr aerospace fuel cells, 64-67, dir mat res, 67; assoc prof mech eng, Marquette Univ, 69-74, lectr, 67-68; mgr, Advan Technol Power Systs Div, McGraw-Edison Co, 67-69, sr staff engr, 75-86. *Mem:* Inst Elec & Electronics Engrs. *Res:* Control theory; energy conversion; heat transfer. *Mailing Add:* McGraw-Edison Co 11131 Adams Rd Franksville WI 53126

HURLEY, JOHN STEVEN, MATERIALS CHARACTERIZATION, MICROSENSORS. *Current Pos:* ASSOC PROF ELEC ENG & SR RES SCIENTIST, CLARK ATLANTA UNIV, 94- *Personal Data:* b Orlando, Fla, Jan 10, 55. *Educ:* Fla State Univ, BS, 76, MS, 80; Howard Univ, PhD(elec eng), 91. *Prof Exp:* Assoc prof appl math, Hampton Univ, 90-92; assoc prof physics & mfg, Cent State Univ, 92; sr res scientist, Wright Patterson AFB, 92-94. *Concurrent Pos:* Res fel, Ohio Bd Regents, 93; dir, A-12 Beta Test Site, High Performance Comput & Embedded Appln Ctr, 96-; prin investr, NASA Jet Propulsion Lab, 97 & Dept Energy, 97. *Mem:* Sigma Xi; Inst Elec & Electronics Engrs; Am Phys Soc; Optical Soc Am. *Res:* Materials processing, assessment, characterization and design of microsensors. *Mailing Add:* PO Box 3290 Atlanta GA 30302-3290. *Fax:* 404-880-6923; *E-Mail:* jhurley@cau.edu

HURLEY, LAURENCE HAROLD, MICROBIAL BIOCHEMISTRY. *Current Pos:* GEORGE HITCHING CHMN, DRUG DESIGN, COL PHARM, UNIV TEX & ASST DIR, DRUG DYNAMICS INST, 81- *Personal Data:* b Birmingham, Eng, Jan 29, 44; US citizen; m 96, Terry Evers; c Bridget & Nicole. *Educ:* Bath Univ, BPharm, 67; Purdue Univ, PhD(med chem), 70. *Hon Degrees:* DSc, Bath Univ, 96. *Honors & Awards:* Volwiler Award, 89; Outstanding Investr Award, Nat Cancer Inst; Res Achievement Award, Am Pharm Asn; Med Chem Award, Am Chem Soc, 94. *Prof Exp:* Fel org chem, Univ BC, 70-71; asst prof med chem, Col Pharm, Univ Md, 71-73; from asst prof to prof, Col Pharm, Univ Ky, 73-81. *Concurrent Pos:* Chmn, NIH Bioorg & Nat Prod Study Sect; consult, Upjohn, Smith Kline, French Labs & Abbotts Labs. *Mem:* Am Chem Soc; Am Asn Cancer Res; Am Soc Pharmacog; Am Asn Col Pharm. *Res:* Mechanism of action of antitumor-antibiotics; drug-nucleic acid interactions; DNA damage and repair; molecular graphics and drug design. *Mailing Add:* Drug Dynamics Inst Col Pharm Univ Tex Austin TX 78712. *Fax:* 512-471-2746; *E-Mail:* clg_dna@mail.utexas.edu

HURLEY, MAUREEN, MICROBIOLOGY, CELL BIOLOGY. *Current Pos:* from asst prof to assoc prof, 66-70, PROF BIOL, XAVIER UNIV, LA, 71- *Personal Data:* b Boston, Mass. *Educ:* Emmanuel Col, Mass, BA, 43; Cath Univ Am, MS, 55, PhD(biol), 59. *Prof Exp:* Teacher prep sch, Xavier Univ, 50-54; teacher chem & biol, Blessed Sacrament Col, 58-66. *Concurrent Pos:* NSF fac fel, Med Sch, Johns Hopkins Univ, 69-70. *Res:* Medical microbiology; morphogenesis and differentiation in development. *Mailing Add:* Dept Biol Xavier Univ La 7325 Palmetto St New Orleans LA 70125-1056

HURLEY, NEAL LILBURN, GEOPHYSICS, GEOLOGY. *Current Pos:* RETIRED. *Personal Data:* b Long Beach, Calif, Aug 3, 28; m 64, Sandra Thurston; c Jill, Melissa & Kendra. *Educ:* Calif Inst Technol, BS, 49; Stanford Univ, MS, 51, PhD(geol, geophys), 53. *Prof Exp:* Geologist, US Geol Surv, 49; res geologist, Continental Oil Co, 51; geophysicist explor, Richfield Oil Corp, 56-67; chief geophysicist, Union Pac RR Co, 67-70; explor mgr, Champlin Petrol Co, 70-74, chief geologist, 74-79, mgr explor serv, 79-88. *Mem:* Soc Explor Geophys; Am Asn Petrol Geol. *Res:* Mechanics of earth deformation; groundwater motion; exploration seismology. *Mailing Add:* 535 Regentview Houston TX 77079-6908

HURLEY, PATRICK MASON, GEOCHRONOLOGY. *Current Pos:* from asst prof to assoc prof geol & geophys, Mass Inst Technol, 46-52, chmn fac, 58-60, prof, 53-81, EMER PROF GEOL & GEOPHYS, MASS INST TECHNOL, 81- *Personal Data:* b Hong Kong, China, Jan 12, 12; nat US; m 41, Margaret Macurda; c David, Peter & Pamela. *Educ:* Univ BC, BA & BASc, 34; Mass Inst Technol, PhD(econ geol), 40. *Honors & Awards:* Walter Bucher Medal, Am Geophys Union, 85. *Prof Exp:* Mining engr & geologist, Gold Mines, BC, 34-37; field asst, Geol Surv Can, 38; res assoc, Mass Inst Technol, 40-42, Nat Defense Res Comt, 42-45 & Univ Wis, 46. *Concurrent Pos:* Mem comts, Nat Res Coun. *Mem:* Fel Geol Soc Am; fel Am Geophys Union; Geochem Soc; Am Acad Arts & Sci; hon mem Geol Soc London. *Res:* Geological age measurement and application of nuclear physics to geology; radiogenic isotopes in research on the development of the earth's crust. *Mailing Add:* 260 Seaview Ct Apt 611 Marco Island FL 34145

HURLEY, ROBERT EDWARD, CHEMICAL ENGINEERING, CERAMICS. *Current Pos:* proj engr, Chem & Phys Lab, Radio Corp Am, NJ, 45-54, proj engr, Molded Prod Lab, 54-57, mgr ferrite eng, NJ, Ohio & Ind, 57-62, group leader, Ind, 62-68, MGR MAT ENG, CONSUMER ELECTRONICS DIV, RCA CORP, 68- *Personal Data:* b Cincinnati, Ohio, Oct 31, 11; m 41; c 4. *Educ:* Univ Cincinnati, BS, 35. *Prof Exp:* Analyst, Joseph E Seagram & Sons, Ind, 35-36, chief chemist, 40; chief chemist, Calvert Distilling Co, Md, 36-40; mem staff ord mil training, Training Div Ord, Aberdeen, Md & The Pentagon, 40-45. *Mem:* Am Chem Soc; Am Ceramic Soc; fel Am Ceramic Soc. *Res:* Water chemistry and industrial water treatment; paper technology and dynamic properties of paper; sintering of pure oxides; technology of ferrite manufacture. *Mailing Add:* 324 E 45th St Indianapolis IN 46205-1752

HURLEY, ROBERT JOSEPH, MARINE GEOLOGY, OCEANOGRAPHY. *Current Pos:* ENVIRON CONSULT, 76- *Personal Data:* b Boston, Mass, July 11, 29; m 52; c 2. *Educ:* Tufts Univ, BS, 51; Scripps Inst Oceanog, Univ Calif, San Diego, MS, 57, PhD(oceanog), 60. *Prof Exp:* Res geologist oceanog, Scripps Inst Oceanog, Univ Calif, San Diego, 54-59; res oceanogr, Bell Tel Labs, NJ, 60-61; from asst prof to assoc prof oceanog, Univ Miami, 61-67, prof, 67-72, assoc dean grad studies, 69-72; dir, Moss Landing Marine Labs, 72-76. *Concurrent Pos:* Dep dir off oceanol, Asst Secy Intergovt Comn Oceanog, UNESCO, Paris. *Mem:* Geol Soc Am; Am Geophys Union; Challenger Soc; Sigma Xi. *Res:* Morphology of the deep sea floor involving structure, geophysical investigations, sedimentary processes, ocean dynamics and the tectonic history of the ocean basins. *Mailing Add:* PO Box 305 Aptos CA 95001-0305

HURLEY, WALTER L, LACTATION BIOLOGY, REPRODUCTIVE BIOLOGY. *Current Pos:* asst prof, 82-88, assoc prof, 88-95, PROF, ANIMAL SCI LAB, UNIV ILL, 95- *Personal Data:* b Bethesda, Md, May 10, 50. *Educ:* Univ Md, BS, 72, MS, 75; Univ Ky, PhD(animal sci), 79. *Prof Exp:* Res assoc, Univ Wis, 80-82. *Mem:* Am Dairy Sci Asn; Am Soc Animal Sci; AAAS. *Res:* Study of mammary gland biology; function and control and the interactions between mammary function and neonate development. *Mailing Add:* Animal Sci Lab Univ Ill 1207 W Gregory Dr Urbana IL 61801

HURLEY, WILLIAM CHARLES, food science, biochemistry, for more information see previous edition

HURLEY, WILLIAM JORDAN, SYSTEMS MODELING & ANALYSIS, POLICY STUDIES. *Current Pos:* RES STAFF, INST DEFENSE ANALYSIS, 85- *Personal Data:* b Norwood, Mass, July 31, 43; m 70, Cleo Goers; c Elizabeth M, Michael F, David A & Brian J. *Educ:* Boston Col, BS, 65; Univ Rochester, PhD(physics), 71. *Prof Exp:* Res asst physics, Univ Rochester, 65-70; res assoc physics, Syracuse Univ, 70-72; res scientist, Ctr Particle Theory, Univ Tex, Austin, 72-75, res staff, Ctr Naval Analysis, 75-85. *Mem:* Am Phys Soc. *Res:* Studies, modeling and analysis in support of national security policy decisions. *Mailing Add:* 6332 Waterway Dr Falls Church VA 22044

HURLEY, WILLIAM JOSEPH, PHOTOGRAPHIC EMULSION TECHNOLOGY & PLASTIC FILMS, COATINGS & FINE PARTICLE TECHNOLOGY. *Current Pos:* Res chemist magnetic tape, E I du Pont de Nemours & Co, Inc, Wilmington, Del, 67-71, res chemist silver halide, Parlin, NJ, 71-73, res supvr silver halide chem, Parlin, NJ, 73-74 & Rochester, NY, 74-80, tech mgr magnetic mat, 83-86, venture mgr, 86-88, tech mgr, high performance films, Du Pont Electronics, Circleville, Ohio, 88-89, lab dir 89-93, mgr, corp tech staffing, 93-94, MGR, CORP NEW BUS DEVELOP, E I DU PONT DE NEMOURS & CO, INC, WILMINGTON, DEL, 94- *Personal Data:* b Philadelphia, Pa, July 26, 40; m 63, Rosemary A Gorman; c 4. *Educ:* Villanova Univ, BS, 62; Princeton Univ, PhD(chem), 67. *Prof Exp:* Develop mgr magnetic mat, PD Magnetics, BV, Neth, 81-83. *Mem:* Am Chem Soc. *Res:* Materials for magnetic recording media; silver halide emulsions for x-ray and graphic arts films; coating technology; interferometric and raman spectroscopy; polyester and polyimide films; laminates; fine particle technology; automotive finishes; research and technology management. *Mailing Add:* E I Du Pont De Nemours & Co Inc Exp Sta E326 Wilmington DE 19880. *Fax:* 302-695-7615

HURN, R(ICHARD) W(ILSON), MECHANICAL ENGINEERING. *Current Pos:* PRES, R-H TECH SERV, 79- *Personal Data:* b Henrietta, Tex, Jan 13, 19; m 45; c 2. *Educ:* Tex Tech Col, BS, 40; Univ Wis, MS, 47. *Honors & Awards:* Gold Medal, US Dept Interior, 67. *Prof Exp:* Petrol prod engr, Humble Oil Co, 40-48; supvr combustion res, Bartlesville Energy Res Ctr, 48-73, dir, Engine/Fuels Res, 73-79. *Concurrent Pos:* Ord Officer, destroyers,

USN, 42-46; consult alternative fuels, fuel behavior, engine fuel matching & engine fuel technol develop, fuel fires. *Mem:* Soc Automotive Engrs; Nat Soc Prof Engrs. *Res:* Combustion of hydrocarbon fuels; combustion reactions and engine emissions control; photochemical air pollution research; engine performance; engine/fuel interface; alternative fuels. *Mailing Add:* 800 SE Winding Way Bartlesville OK 74006

HURRELL, JOHN GORDON, BIOSENSOR CHEMISTRY & APPLICATION, NEW PRODUCT COMMERCIALIZATION. *Current Pos:* SR VPRES RES & DEVELOP OPERS, BOEHRINGER MANNHEIM CORP, 89- *Personal Data:* b Melbourne, Australia, Oct 13, 49; m 73, Ella; c 3. *Educ:* Univ Melbourne, BS, 71, PhD(immunochem & protein), 78. *Prof Exp:* Head immunochem res & develop, Commonwealth Serum Labs, Australia, 80-83; vpres res & develop, Allelix Inc, Toronto, 84-88; dir res & develop, Serono Diag, Woking, Eng, 88-89. *Concurrent Pos:* Tutor med biochem, Ormond Col, Univ Melbourne, 72-73. adj prof, Path Dept, 83-87; sr counr, Univ Col, Melbourne, 74-78; adj prof path & immunol dept, Monash Univ, 81-84; lectr grad biochem, Univ Melbourne, 82. *Mem:* Am Asn Immunologists; Am Diabetes Asn; Regulatory Affairs Profs Soc. *Res:* Transition of scientific discovery and technical innovation from the research laboratory to commercial products of medical value; electrochemical and optical biosensors; discoveries stemming from human gene research. *Mailing Add:* 9115 Hague Rd Indianapolis IN 46250-0457

HURRELL, JOHN PATRICK, SOLID STATE PHYSICS. *Current Pos:* mem tech staff, Aerospace Corp, 73-77, res scientist, 77-79, mgr, Device Physics Sect, 79-80, mgr galluim arsenide microelectronics, 80-84, mgr silicon microelectronics, 84-88, sr scientist, 88-91, PRIN SCIENTIST, ELECTRONICS TECHNOL CTR, AEROSPACE CORP, 91- *Personal Data:* b Sanderstead, Eng, Sept 17, 38; US citizen; m 63; c 3. *Educ:* Oxford Univ, BA, 60, MA, 64, DPhil(physics), 66. *Prof Exp:* Fel, Clarendon Lab, Oxford Univ, 64-66; mem tech staff, Bell Tel Labs, 66-68; asst prof, Univ Southern Calif, 68-73. *Mem:* Am Phys Soc; Inst Physics Eng; sr mem Inst Elec & Electronics Engrs. *Res:* Quantum electronics, atomic standards and magnetics; superconducting cryelectronics; silicon and gallium arsenide microelectronics. *Mailing Add:* PO Box 92957 Los Angeles CA 90009-2957

HURREN, WEILER R, PLASMA PHYSICS, SOLID STATE PHYSICS. *Current Pos:* PROF PHYSICS & HEAD DEPT, THE CITADEL, 80- *Personal Data:* b Salt Lake City, Utah, May 16, 35; m 60; c 5. *Educ:* Utah State Univ, BS, 59; Univ SC, MS, 62; Brigham Young Univ, PhD(physics), 68. *Prof Exp:* Asst prof physics, Western Ill Univ, 68-72, assoc prof & chmn dept, 72-77. *Mem:* Am Phys Soc; Sigma Xi. *Res:* Magnetic resonance. *Mailing Add:* 320 Molasses Lane Mt Pleasant SC 29464-2521

HURSH, JOHN W(OODWORTH), INERTIAL NAVIGATION, AUTOMATIC CONTROL & SATELLITE SYSTEMS. *Current Pos:* CONSULT, 85- *Personal Data:* b Duluth, Minn, Oct 8, 20; m 44; c 1. *Educ:* Harvard Univ, SB, 42, SM, 43, MES, 52. *Honors & Awards:* Gold Medal Award, NY Acad Sci, 67. *Prof Exp:* Res engr, USM Corp, 46-48, proj leader, 48-51; mem staff, Instrumentation Lab, Mass Inst Technol, 51-52, asst proj engr, 52-54, proj engr, 54-55, asst dir, 55-63, assoc dir, 63-73; div leader, Charles Stark Draper Lab, Inc, 75-85. *Res:* Inertial navigation systems; administration of scientific activities; instrumentation and satellite systems. *Mailing Add:* 35 Newbury Park Needham MA 02192

HURSH, ROBERT W(ILLIAM), MECHANICAL ENGINEERING. *Current Pos:* RETIRED. *Personal Data:* b Champaign, Ill, Mar 3, 16; m 47; c 2. *Educ:* Univ Ill, BS, 37; Ohio State Univ, MS, 39. *Prof Exp:* Asst, Univ Ill, 37-38; fel, Ohio State , 38-39; eng trainee, B F Goodrich Co, Ohio, 40, physicist, 40-43, tire construct engr, 43-46; develop engr, Owens-Ill Glass Co, NJ, 46-49, Lukens Steel Co, Pa, 49-54, Gen Elec Co, Ohio, 54-58 & NY, 58-60; dir res & develop, Hansen Mfg Co, 60-63; head mech div, Electromech Res Ctr, Repub Steel Corpr, 64-66; dir res & develop, Kinnear Corp, 67-70; indust hyg engr, Indust Comn Ohio, 70-77, mgr eng & indust hyg, 77-79, mgr tech res & eng, Div Safety & Hyg, 79-86. *Mem:* Am Soc Mech Engrs; Nat Soc Prof Engrs; Am Indust Hyg Asn. *Res:* Tires; process machinery; machinery products; electric insulation; fluid handling equipment; steel production and testing; industrial hygiene. *Mailing Add:* 983 Clubview Blvd S Columbus OH 43235

HURST, DAVID CHARLES, STATISTICS. *Current Pos:* assoc prof, 66-70, prof statist & chmn dept biostatist, Sch Med, 70-82, PROF STATIST, UNIV ALA, BIRMINGHAM, 70- *Personal Data:* b Bozeman, Mont, Aug 25, 28; m 54; c 2. *Educ:* Mont State Col, BS, 50; NC State Col, MS, 57, PhD, 62. *Prof Exp:* Asst statist, NC State Col, 53-57; assoc prof, Va Polytech Inst & State Univ, 66. *Mem:* Am Statist Asn; Inst Math Statist; Biomet Soc. *Res:* Statistical techniques; design of experiments; nonlinear estimation; biostatistics; research consulting; biomedical modeling. *Mailing Add:* Dept Biostatist & Biomath Univ Ala, Birmingham Univ Sta 1717 Seventh Ave S Birmingham AL 35294-0001

HURST, EDITH MARIE MACLENNAN, NEUROANATOMY. *Current Pos:* asst prof, Med Col Pa, 71-73, assoc prof, 73-76, PROF BIOL, EASTERN MICH UNIV, 76- *Personal Data:* b Detroit, Mich, Aug 1, 26; m 58; c 3. *Educ:* Wayne State Univ, BS, 48; Univ Mich, MA, 49, PhD(anat), 56. *Prof Exp:* Instr anat, Hahnemann Med Col, 56-60, asst prof, 66-71. *Mem:* Am Asn Anatomists. *Res:* Study of connections of cortical auditory areas by ablation experiments in monkeys; histological and chemical studies of rodent hypothalamus. *Mailing Add:* Dept Biol Eastern Mich Univ 316 Mark Jefferson Ypsilanti MI 48197-2211

HURST, ELAINE H, PHYCOLOGY, AQUATIC ECOLOGY. *Current Pos:* assoc prof, 66-69, PROF BIOL, NAZARETH COL, MICH, 69-, HEAD DEPT, 66- *Personal Data:* b St Joseph, Mich, Mar 4, 20; m 46; c 2. *Educ:* Western Mich Univ, BS, 43, MA, 55; Mich State Univ, PhD(mycol), 65. *Prof Exp:* Teacher, Milford Consol Schs, 43-44; teacher, Richland Rural Agr Sch, 44-46; instr biol, Western Mich Univ, 55-63, asst prof, 63-66. *Mem:* Am Micros Soc. *Res:* Growth of blue-green algae in culture and production of extra metabolites by these organisms; role of extra metabolites in ecology. *Mailing Add:* 3205 Hylle Ave Kalamazoo MI 49006

HURST, G SAMUEL, RADIATION PHYSICS, PHOTOPHYSICS. *Current Pos:* INDEPENDENT CONSULT, 88- *Personal Data:* b Pineville, Ky, Oct 13, 27; m 48; c 2. *Educ:* Berea Col, AB, 47; Univ Ky, MS, 48; Univ Tenn, PhD(physics), 59. *Hon Degrees:* Dr, Berea Col. *Honors & Awards:* IR-100 Touch Sensor & IR-100 One-Atom Detector Awards. *Prof Exp:* Sr physicist, Oak Ridge Nat Lab, Tenn, 48-66; prof physics, Univ Ky, 66-70; sr physicist, Oak Ridge Nat Lab, 70-85; prof, Univ Tenn, 85-88. *Concurrent Pos:* Vis res prof, Fla State Univ, 62-63; assoc prof, Univ Tenn, 63-; corp fel, Union Carbide & Martin Marietta Corps. *Mem:* Fel Am Phys Soc. *Res:* Laser and instrumentation applications; atomic and molecular physics; chemical kinetics-gas phase and photochemistry; atomic diffusion and mobility; one-atom detection; resonance ionization spectroscopy (RIS). *Mailing Add:* 2314 W Gallher Ferry Rd Knoxville TN 37932-2567

HURST, HARRELL EMERSON, MASS SPECTROMETRY, PHARMACOKINETICS. *Current Pos:* From instr to assoc prof, 78-91, PROF PHARMACOL & TOXICOL, SCH MED, UNIV LOUISVILLE, 91- *Personal Data:* b Somerset, Ky, Mar 4, 49; m 74, Carol Fathergill. *Educ:* Univ Ky, BS, 72, MS, 76, PhD(toxicol), 78. *Concurrent Pos:* Dir, Dept Pharmacol & Toxicol, Therapeut & Toxicol Lab, 82-; pres, Ohio Valley Regional Chap, Soc Toxicol, 86. *Mem:* Am Chem Soc; Am Soc Mass Spectrometry; Am Soc Pharmacol & Exp Therapeut; Soc Toxicol; Sigma Xi. *Res:* Analytical chemistry, pharmaco- and toxicokinetics, toxicological and pharmacological problems; techniques include gas chromatography-mass spectrometry, gas chromatography and high performance liquid chromatography for study of drug and chemical disposition in humans and animals. *Mailing Add:* Dept Pharmacol & Toxicol Univ Louisville 319 Abraham Flexner Way Louisville KY 40292-0457. *Fax:* 502-852-7868; *E-Mail:* hehurs01@ulkyvm.louisville.edu

HURST, HOMER T(HEODORE), AGRICULTURAL ENGINEERING. *Current Pos:* assoc prof, 55-60, PROF AGR ENG, VA POLYTECH INST & STATE UNIV, 60-, PROF ENVIRON & URBAN SYSTS, 77- *Personal Data:* b Lone Rock, Ark, Oct 25, 19; m 45; c 4. *Educ:* Ohio State Univ, BS, 50, MS, 51. *Prof Exp:* Instr agr eng, Ohio State Univ, 51-55. *Mem:* Am Soc Agr Engrs. *Res:* Accelerated structural research with full-scale buildings or large sections of homes and service structures. *Mailing Add:* 501 Milhurst St Blacksburg VA 24060

HURST, JAMES KENDALL, BIOCHEMISTRY. *Current Pos:* PROF CHEM, WASH STATE UNIV, 92- *Personal Data:* b Maquoketa, Iowa, Oct 17, 40; m 66; c 2. *Educ:* Cornell Col, BA, 62; Stanford Univ, PhD(phys chem), 66. *Prof Exp:* NIH career develop awards, Cornell Univ, 65-67 & 68-69; from asst prof to assoc prof, Ore Grad Ctr, 69-82, chmn dept, 78-82, prof chem, 78-92, vchair chem prog, 82-92. *Concurrent Pos:* Consult, McDonell-Douglas Res Labs, St Louis 78-79; vis prof, Inst de Phys Chem, Lausanne, Switz, 80 & 85. *Mem:* Am Chem Soc. *Res:* Oxidation-reduction reactions of coordination compounds and biological particles; leukocyte microbicidal mechanisms. *Mailing Add:* Dept Chem Fulmer Hall Wash State Univ Pullman WA 99164-4630

HURST, JEFFREY HENRY, CARDIOVASCULAR MEDICINE, NEUROPHARMACOLOGY. *Current Pos:* postdoctoral fel, 81-84, HEALTH SCIENTIST ADMINR, NAT HEART LUNG & BLOOD INST, NIH, 84- *Personal Data:* b July 24, 51. *Educ:* Dartmouth Col, AB, 73, PhD(pharmacol), 80. *Prof Exp:* Postdoctoral fel, Sch Med, Univ Md, 80-81. *Mem:* Am Soc Pharamacol & Exp Therapeut; Soc Neurosci; Int Brain Res Orgn. *Res:* Evaluation of fedderal grant application in atherosclerosis, vascular biology, blood disorders and transfusion medicine. *Mailing Add:* NHLBI 2 Rockledge Ctr Rm 7208 6701 Rockledge Dr Bethesda MD 20892-7924

HURST, JERRY G, PHYSIOLOGY. *Current Pos:* asst prof, 64-69, ASSOC PROF PHYSIOL, OKLA STATE UNIV, 69- *Personal Data:* b Belleview, Mo, Dec 8, 32; m 54; c 7. *Educ:* Hardin-Simmons Univ, BA, 54; Okla State Univ, MS, 63, PhD(physiol), 67. *Prof Exp:* Instr, Buckner Acad, Tex, 54-56; teacher, Pampa Sch Dist, 59-60. *Res:* Control of parathyroid hormone secretion rate; iodide metabolism in birds. *Mailing Add:* 1723 E Fourth Ave Stillwater OK 74074

HURST, JOSEPHINE M, HEMATOLOGY, ONCOLOGY. *Current Pos:* res assoc, 79-92, dept head res, 92-96, CONSULT, GOODWIN INST CANCER RES, FLA, 96- *Personal Data:* b Philadelphia, Pa, May 14, 38. *Educ:* Immaculata Col, Pa, AB, 60; St John's Univ, NY, MS, 62, PhD(hemat-physiol), 65. *Prof Exp:* Teaching asst hemat, St John's Univ, 60-62; res asst hemat, NY Univ, 62-63; instr biol, St Johns Univ, 63-65, asst prof hemat, Grad Sch, 66-71; res scientist hemat & oncol, NY Ocean Sci Lab, 71-72. *Concurrent Pos:* Res assoc hemat, Holt Radium Inst, Christie Hosp, UK, 65-66, Sch Med, Univ Bristol, UK, 66 & Med Dept, Brookhaven Nat Lab, 71-72; consult path & oncol, Cancer Lab, N Ridge Hosp, Fla, 82-83, actg head, 83-86; dir, SFla Biotherapeut Assocs, 87-88. *Mem:* Int Asn Breast

Cancer Res; Am Asn Cancer Res. *Res:* Control of differentiation proliferation of the hemopoietic stem cells; drug sensitivity of human tumor cells; development of metastatic human breast carcinoma model; controls of metastatic phenotype; hematopoietic changes associated with tumor growth and metastasis; growth controls of metastasis breast cancer. *Mailing Add:* Goodwin Inst Cancer Res Box 350443 Ft Lauderdale FL 33335. *E-Mail:* john@worldnet.att.net

HURST, PEGGY MORISON, INORGANIC CHEMISTRY. *Current Pos:* RETIRED. *Personal Data:* b Abington, Pa, May 15, 25. *Educ:* Wilson Col, AB, 46; Univ Wis, MA, 48, PhD(chem), 56. *Prof Exp:* From instr to prof chem, Bowling Green State Univ, 55-96. *Mem:* AAAS; Am Chem Soc; Sigma Xi. *Res:* Peroxy compounds of transition elements; history of science. *Mailing Add:* 134 Buttonwood Ave Bowling Green OH 43402-2810

HURST, REX LEROY, STATISTICS, COMPUTER SCIENCE. *Current Pos:* RETIRED. *Personal Data:* b Payson, Utah, Mar 10, 23; m 46; c 5. *Educ:* Utah State Univ, BS, 48, MS, 50; Cornell Univ, PhD, 52. *Prof Exp:* Asst prof appl statist, Utah State Univ, 52-55, assoc prof & head dept, 55-59, prof appl statist & comput sci & head dept, 60-; vis prof statist, Iowa State Univ, 59-60. *Mem:* Am Statist Asn; Biomet Soc. *Res:* Data analysis; experimental design; computer programming. *Mailing Add:* Dept Comput Sci Utah State Univ Logan UT 84322-4205

HURST, RICHARD WILLIAM, GEOLOGY, GEOCHEMISTRY. *Current Pos:* ASST PROF GEOL, CALIF STATE UNIV, LOS ANGELES, 77- *Personal Data:* b Rockville Centre, NY, Aug 2, 48. *Educ:* State Univ NY Stony Brook, BS, 70; Univ Calif, Los Angeles, PhD(geol), 75. *Prof Exp:* Res asst geochem, Earth Sci, State Univ NY Stony Brook, 69-70; res asst geol, Univ Calif, Los Angeles, 72-75; asst res geol, Univ Calif, Santa Barbara, 75-77. *Concurrent Pos:* Consult, Santa Monica Mountains Task Force, 74-; Penrose Grant, Geol Soc Am, 74; instr geol, Santa Barbara City Col, 75-78. *Mem:* Meteoritical Soc; Geol Soc Am; Geochem Soc; Am Geophys Union. *Res:* Geochronology of early archaean gneisses of Labrador; archaean crustal evolution; evolution of the Santa Monica mountains; environmental geology. *Mailing Add:* Dept Geol Calif State Univ 5151 St Univ Dr Los Angeles CA 90032-8000

HURST, ROBERT NELSON, ENVIRONMENTAL PHYSIOLOGY, SCIENCE EDUCATION. *Current Pos:* RETIRED. *Personal Data:* b Ogden, Utah, May 21, 30; m 49; c 3. *Educ:* Univ Utah, BS, 57; Harvard Univ, AMT, 58; Purdue Univ, MS, 64, PhD(physiol), 66. *Prof Exp:* Teacher, San Diego Unified Sch Dist, 58-63; from instr to asst prof biol, Purdue Univ, 63-67; assoc prof zool & educ, Univ Man, 67-69; asst prof, Purdue Univ, West Lafayette, 69-75, assoc prof biol, 75-93. *Concurrent Pos:* Area day consult, Biol Sci Curric Study, 65; vis scientist, Int Rice Res Inst, Los Banos, Philippines, 78-79. *Mem:* Am Inst Biol Sci; Nat Sci Teachers Asn; Int Audio-Tutorial Cong (pres, 72-73). *Res:* Seasonal behavior and bio-rhythmia of hybernating animals; simultaneous recording of physiological parameters; galvanic skin response; audio-tutorial instruction and learning theory. *Mailing Add:* 2844 Ashland St West Lafayette IN 47906

HURST, ROBERT PHILIP, ATOMIC PHYSICS, MOLECULAR PHYSICS. *Current Pos:* PROF PHYSICS, STATE UNIV NY, BUFFALO, 62- *Personal Data:* b Bozeman, Mont, May 30, 30; m 55, 93, Elaine C Schunk; c 4. *Educ:* Mont State Univ, BS, 52; Univ Tex, MA, 56, PhD(chem physics), 58. *Prof Exp:* Jr scientist, Gen Elec Co, 52-54; teaching asst, Univ Tex, Austin, 54-55, res asst, 55-58; fel, Univ Wis-Madison, 58-59; fel, Univ Ill, Urbana, 59-60; asst prof physics & chem, Univ Okla, 60-62. *Concurrent Pos:* Vis prof, Univ Sussex, Eng, 68-69 & Univ Tex, 76. *Mem:* Am Phys Soc; NY Acad Sci. *Res:* Irridiated uranium crystal structures; calculations in atomic and molecular quantum mechanics; computer profiles and momentum space; non-linear electric polarizabilities. *Mailing Add:* Dept Physics State Univ NY Buffalo Amherst NY 14260. *E-Mail:* phyhurst@acsu.buffalo.edu

HURST, ROBERT R(OWE), MEDICAL PHYSICS, RADIATION THERAPY PHYSICS. *Current Pos:* DIR MED PHYSICS, CLIN ENG & RADIOL, BOONE HOSP CTR, COLUMBIA, MO, 83- *Personal Data:* b Washington, Iowa, Sept 17, 37; c 3. *Educ:* Pa State Univ, BS, 60, MS, 62, PhD(nuclear physics), 64. *Prof Exp:* Asst, Pa State Univ, 60-64; from asst prof to assoc prof physics, Univ Mo-Columbia, 64-83. *Mem:* Am Phys Soc; Am Asn Physicists in Med; Am Asn Physics Teachers; Sigma Xi; Soc Magnetic Resonance in Med. *Res:* Magnetic resonance imaging. *Mailing Add:* Dept Med Physics Boone Hosp Ctr 1600 E Broadway Columbia MO 65201

HURST, VERNON JAMES, GEOLOGY, CRYSTALLOGRAPHY. *Current Pos:* prof geol & head dept, 61-66, chmn div phys sci, 66-69, RES PROF GEOL, UNIV GA, 69- *Personal Data:* b Glenmore, Ga, July 18, 23; m 50; c 2. *Educ:* Univ Ga, BS, 51; Emory Univ, MS, 52; Johns Hopkins Univ, PhD(geol), 54. *Prof Exp:* Geologist, Dept Mines, Mining & Geol, Ga State Geol Surv, 53-61. *Mem:* Fel Geol Soc Am; Geochem Soc; fel Mineral Soc Am; Soc Econ Geol; French Soc Mineral & Crystallog. *Res:* Crystal growth; saprolitization. *Mailing Add:* 1800 Ketterer St Waycross GA 31503

HURST, WILBUR SCOTT, PHYSICS. *Current Pos:* PHYSICIST, NAT BUR STANDARDS, 68- *Personal Data:* b Camden, NJ, May 20, 39; m 66; c 1. *Educ:* Albion Col, BA, 61; Univ Pa, MS, 63; Pa State Univ, PhD(physics), 68. *Mem:* Am Phys Soc. *Res:* Temperature metrology; stimulated raman spectroscopy. *Mailing Add:* Bldg 221 Rm B128 Nat Inst Standards & Technol Gaithersburg MD 20899

HURST, WILLIAM JEFFREY, ANALYTICAL CHEMISTRY. *Current Pos:* from assoc scientist to sr scientist, analytical group, Hershey Foods Corp, 76-81, group leader, 81-85, staff scientist, 86-93, SR STAFF SCIENTIST, HERSHEY FOODS CORP, 93- *Personal Data:* b West Palm Beach, Fla, Jan 12, 48; m 69, Deborah; c Heather & Jana. *Educ:* Ohio Univ, AB, 69; Youngstown State Univ, MS, 75; Columbia Pac Univ, PhD, 84. *Prof Exp:* Radiation safety officer, USAF, 69-72; instr environ sci, Muskingum Area Tech Col, Ohio, 72-73. *Concurrent Pos:* Instr, Chem Dept, Dickinson Col, 77-; chem res officer, Air Force Wright Aeronaut Lab, Air Force Mat Lab, Wright Patterson AFB, 81-; tech abstrutor, Preston Pub, 81-; adj asst prof chem, Lebanon Valley Col, 82-; instr, dept continuing educ, Hershey Med Ctr & clin comp med. *Mem:* Am Chem Soc; Inst Food Technologists; fel Am Inst Chemists; NY Acad Sci. *Res:* Analytical chemistry of compounds of nutritional or food safety emphasis and the use of high-performance liquid chromatography and its applicability to solve problems in that area; applications of laboratory autiomation. *Mailing Add:* Hershey Foods Corp 1025 Reese Ave Hershey PA 17033. *Fax:* 717-534-6132; *E-Mail:* wjh5200024@aol.com

HURT, ALFRED B(URMAN), JR, SYNTHETIC TEXTILE FIBERS ENGINEERING, CHEMICAL ENGINEERING. *Current Pos:* RETIRED. *Personal Data:* b NC, Sept 5, 20; m 49, Orla Abernathy; c Cheryl A (Radley). *Educ:* NC State Col, BChE, 47, MSEE, 50. *Prof Exp:* Instr elec eng, NC State Col, 48-49; sr tel engr, Rural Elec Authority, NC, 49-50; chemist, E I du Pont de Nemours & Co, 41-44, engr, 52-55, sr engr, 55-60, sr res engr, 60-66, eng assoc, 66-74, design supvr eng, 74-78, proj engr, 78-79. *Concurrent Pos:* Captain, comndg officer, USN Res Unit, 76-78. *Mem:* Inst Elec & Electronics Engrs. *Res:* Automatic impedance measurement; industrial instrumentation; synthetic textile process development and equipment design. *Mailing Add:* 173 South J E Gentry Rd Crumpler NC 28617

HURT, H DAVID, NUTRITION. *Current Pos:* DIR NUTRIT, QUAKER OATS CO, 80- *Personal Data:* b Del Norte, Colo, Jan 2, 41; m 62; c 2. *Educ:* Colo State Univ, BS, 64; Univ Conn, MS, 67; Cornell Univ, PhD(nutrit), 70. *Prof Exp:* Asst dir nutrit res, Nat Dairy Coun, 69-70, assoc dir, 70-72; head, Div Nutrit Sci, Campbell Soup Co, 72-78; assoc dir biochem & nutrit, Del Monte Corp, 78-80. *Mem:* Am Inst Nutrit; Inst Food Technol; Am Dietetic Asn. *Res:* Protein quality evaluation; bioavailability of nutrients in foods; nutrient retention of processed foods. *Mailing Add:* 14205 Burr Oak Rd Wamego KS 66547

HURT, JAMES EDWARD, physics, for more information see previous edition

HURT, JAMES JOSEPH, OPERATIONS RESEARCH, APPLIED MATHEMATICS. *Current Pos:* TECH FEL, STRUCT DYNAMICS RES CORP, 93- *Personal Data:* b Iowa City, Iowa, June 25, 39; m 61; c 3. *Educ:* Univ Iowa, BS, 61, MS, 63; Brown Univ, PhD(appl math), 67. *Prof Exp:* Asst prof math, Univ Iowa, 67-70; mathematician, Hq US Army Weapons Command & Rodman Labs, 72-76; sr staff mathematician, Deere & Co, 76-85; chief mathematician, Cognition, Inc, 85-89; sr partner, Hardy, Hurt & Coin, 89-93. *Mem:* Math Asn Am; Sigma Xi; Soc Indust & Appl Math; Asn Comput Mach; Am Math Soc. *Res:* Simulation of manufacturing process. *Mailing Add:* 2000 Eastman Dr Milford OH 45150

HURT, SUSAN SCHILT, ENVIROMENTAL TOXICOLOGY, ENVIROMENTAL SCIENCES. *Current Pos:* sr chemist agr res, 75-80, prod tech mgr, Govt Rel Agr Chem, 80-81, PROG MGR TOXICOLOGY, ROHM AND HAAS CO, 81-, PROG MGR ECOTOXICOL, 86- *Personal Data:* b Buffalo, NY, Aug 6, 47; c 3. *Educ:* Univ Mich, BSChem, 69; Univ Colo, PhD(org chem), 74; Am Bd Toxicol, dipl, 83. *Prof Exp:* Fel, Univ Colo, 74. *Mem:* Am Chem Soc; AAAS. *Res:* Design and synthesis of candidate herbicides; environmental/toxicological evaluation and risk assessment of pesticides and industrial chemicals, registration management. *Mailing Add:* 1528 Evans Rd Ambler PA 19002-1211

HURT, VERNER C, AGRICULTURAL ECONOMICS. *Current Pos:* asst prof & asst economist, Agr Econ Dept, Miss State Univ, 56-58, from assoc prof & economist to prof & economist, 60-71, asst dept head agr econ, 71-72, dept head, 72-87, DIR, AGR & FORESTRY EXP STA, MISS STATE UNIV, 87- *Personal Data:* b Yazoo City, Miss, Dec 19, 29; c 4. *Educ:* Miss State Univ, BS, 50, MS, 55; Okla State Univ, PhD, 61. *Prof Exp:* Auditor, Miss Dept Agr & Com, 55-56; res asst, Agr Econ Dept, Okla State Univ, 58-60. *Concurrent Pos:* Economist & statist consult, Fla Citrus Comn; statist & computer programmer & consult, Southern Interstate Nuclear Bd; chmn, Econ Adv Comt Dairymen Inc & Alternative Publ Comt, Am Agr Econ Asn, 76; econ consult, Econ Res Serv, USDA & Nat Fertilizer Develop Ctr, Tenn Valley Authority; adv economist, Nat Boiler Mkt Asn. *Mem:* Am Agr Econ Asn; Southern Agr Econ Asn (pres, 73-74). *Mailing Add:* 702 Cottonwood Dr Starkville MS 39759

HURT, WAVERLY GLENN, GYNECOLOGY & GYNECOLOGIC SURGERY, UROGYNECOLOGY. *Current Pos:* PROF OBSTET & GYNEC, MED COL VA, 69- *Personal Data:* b Richmond, Va, Sept 6, 38. *Educ:* Hampden-Sydney Col, BS, 60; Med Col Va, MD, 64. *Concurrent Pos:* Med dir, Ambulatory Surg Ctr, Med Col Va, 81- *Mem:* Fel Am Col Obstetricians & Gynecologists; Am Urol-Gynec Soc. *Res:* Urogynecology; gynecologic surgery; pelvic organ prolapse. *Mailing Add:* Dept Obstet & Gynec PO Box 980034 Med Col Va Richmond VA 23298-0034. *Fax:* 804-828-1792; *E-Mail:* wghurt@gems.vcu.edu

HURT, WILLIAM C, JR, MECHANICAL ENGINEERING. *Current Pos:* RETIRED. *Personal Data:* b Tuskegee, Ala, Dec 27, 07; m 36; c 3. *Educ:* Ala Polytech Inst, BS, 28, ME, 33. *Prof Exp:* Appln engr, Gen Elec Co, 31-36, mfg supt staff, 36-39, wage rate & planning, 39-40, design engr, Pittsfield Lab, 40-41, develop engr, 41-44 & 46-53, mgr & suprv adv process develop, 53-60, sr mech engr, mat eng div, 60-69, mat & tech lab, 69-70. *Concurrent Pos:* Eng Consult, Berkshire Community Col & Serv Corps Retired Execs. *Mem:* Am Soc Mech Engrs; Nat Soc Prof Engrs; Wire Asn Int. *Res:* Development of processes and material applications in area of electrical conductors; process developments; transformers and allied products. *Mailing Add:* 43 Arlington St Pittsfield MA 01201

HURTER, ARTHUR P, ENGINEERING ECONOMICS, LOGISTICS. *Current Pos:* Res assoc, Transp Ctr, Northwestern Univ, 62-65, assoc dir res, 65-69, from asst prof to assoc prof, 62-69, chmn dept, 70-90, PROF INDUST ENG & MGT SCI, NORTHWESTERN UNIV, 69-, PROF TRANSP, 90- *Personal Data:* b Chicago, Ill, Jan 29, 36; m 56, Florence E Kays; c Patricia L (Hoeksema) & Arthur E. *Educ:* Northwestern Univ, BS, MS & MA, 61, PhD(econ), 62. *Concurrent Pos:* Prof finance, Northwestern Univ, 65-; fac mem, Newspaper Mgt Ctr Univ, 90-; consult, Stand Oil Industs, Sears Roebuck & Ill Inst Natural Resources; chmn, Opers Res Soc Am; NSF res grants. *Mem:* Am Econ Asn; Inst Indust Engrs; Regional Sci Asn; Int Ref Orgn Forensic Med & Sci. *Res:* Author of over 60 books and papers on the integration of operations research and economics applied to facility location problems, plant and equipment investment and replacement, transportation, logistics, cost/benefit studies dealing with environment and energy, production/distribution problems-currently in newspaper industry. *Mailing Add:* 1505 W Norwood St Chicago IL 60660. *Fax:* 847-491-8005

HURTO, KIRK ALLEN, WEED SCIENCE, TURFGRASS MANAGEMENT. *Current Pos:* res scientist, Truegreen-Chemlawn, 81-85, sr res scientist & group mgr, 86-90, dir tech serv, 90-96, VPRES, TECH SERV, TRUGREEN-CHEMLAWN, 96- *Personal Data:* b Chicago, Ill, Nov 27, 51; m 75; c 2. *Educ:* Southern Ill Univ, BS, 74, MS, 75; Univ Ill, PhD(hort), 78. *Prof Exp:* Grad asst plant & soil, Southern Ill Univ, 74-75; grad asst turf, Univ Ill, Urbana, 75-78; asst prof plant & soil sci, Univ Mass, Amherst, 78-81. *Mem:* Am Soc Agron; Crop Sci Soc Am; Weed Sci Soc Am. *Res:* Turfgrass ecology and adaptation, weed competition and control, and herbicide activity in plants and soil environment. *Mailing Add:* Trugreen Chemlawn 135 Winter Rd Delaware OH 43015. *Fax:* 614-548-4860

HURTT, WOODLAND, PLANT PHYSIOLOGY. *Current Pos:* RETIRED. *Personal Data:* b Galena, Md, Feb 6, 32; m 59; c 2. *Educ:* Univ Md, BS, 55, MS, 57; Mich State Univ, PhD(crop sci), 62. *Prof Exp:* Fel biochem, Mich State Univ, 61-63; plant physiologist, Vegetation Control Div, USDA, Ft Detrick, 63-74, plant physiologist, Weed Physiol Lab, Sci & Educ Admin-Agr Res, 74-87; scientist, Dynamac, Int, 87-93. *Mem:* AAAS; Am Soc Plant Physiol; Weed Sci Soc Am; Sigma Xi; Plant Growth Regulator Soc Am. *Res:* Weed seed germination; promotion, inhibition, and physiology as affected by chemicals and environmental variables. *Mailing Add:* 11403 Eastwood Ct Hagerstown MD 27142-4019

HURTUBISE, ROBERT JOHN, ANALYTICAL CHEMISTRY. *Current Pos:* from asst prof to assoc prof, 74-83, PROF CHEM, UNIV WYO, 83-, HEAD DEPT, 93- *Personal Data:* b Chicago, Ill, June 7, 41; m 65, Paula Bockhage; c Tim, David & Suzanne. *Educ:* Xavier Univ, BS, 64, MS, 66; Ohio Univ, PhD(anal chem), 69. *Prof Exp:* Asst prof chem, Rockhurst Col, 69-71; suprv chem test, Pfizer Inc, 71-74. *Mem:* Am Chem Soc; Soc Appl Spectros; AAAS. *Res:* Luminescence analysis; chemical and physical separation methods; author of various publications. *Mailing Add:* Dept Chem Univ Wyo Box 3838 Univ Sta Laramie WY 82071-3838

HURVICH, LEO MAURICE, PSYCHOPHYSIOLOGY. *Current Pos:* prof, 62-79, EMER PROF PSYCHOL, INST NEUROL SCI, UNIV PA, 79- *Personal Data:* b Malden, Mass, Sept 11, 10; m 48, Dorothea Jameson. *Educ:* Harvard Col, BA, 32; Harvard Univ, MA, 34, PhD(psychol), 36. *Hon Degrees:* MA, Univ Pa, 72; DSc, State Univ NY, 89. *Honors & Awards:* Howard Crosby Warren Award, Soc Exp Psychologists, 71; Distinguished Sci Contrib Award, Am Psychol Asn, 72; Godlove Award, Int Soc Color Coun, 73; Edgar D Tillyer Award, Optical Soc Am, 82; Deane B Judd-Int Color Asn Award, 85; Hermann von Helmholtz Prize, Cognitive Neurosci Inst, 87. *Prof Exp:* Asst psychol, Harvard Univ, 36-37, instr, 37-40, res asst, Grad Sch Bus Admin, 40-47; res psychologist vision, Eastman-Kodak Co, 47-57; prof & chmn, Dept Psychol, Washington Square Col, NY Univ, 57-62. *Concurrent Pos:* Rep Am Psychol Asn, Optics Sect, Am Stand Asn, 53-54 & deleg, Inter Soc Color Coun, 55-79; Guggenheim fel, 64-65; chmn, Vision Tech Group, Optical Soc Am, 70-71; Troland Award Comt, Nat Acad Sci, 83-84; vis res prof, Columbia Univ, 71-72; vis prof psychol, Ctr Visual Sci, Univ Rochester, 74; mem vis comt, Psychol Dept, Mass Inst Technol, 77-83; assoc ed, J Optical Soc Am, 80-83; fel, Ctr Advan Studies Behav Sci, 81-82; MEC-NAS Comt Currency, 85-87; William James fel, Am Psychol Soc, 89; topical ed, Color Vision, Color Res & Appln, 91-92. *Mem:* Nat Acad Sci; Optical Soc Am; Soc Neurosci; Asn Res Vision & Ophthal; Soc Exp Psychologists; Am Acad Arts & Sci. *Res:* Sensory processes; psychophysics and psychophysiology of vision; color vision; neural coding. *Mailing Add:* 3815 Walnut St Philadelphia PA 19104-6196. *Fax:* 215-898-7301

HURVITZ, ARTHUR ISAAC, COMPARATIVE PATHOLOGY, IMMUNOPATHOLOGY. *Current Pos:* DIR RES & CHMN, DEPT PATH, ANIMAL MED CTR, NEW YORK, 71- *Personal Data:* b Newton, Mass, Nov 29, 39; m 61; c 2. *Educ:* Mich State Univ, BS, 62, DVM, 64; Univ Calif, Davis, PhD(comp path), 67; Am Col Vet Path, dipl. *Honors & Awards:* Small Animal Res Award, Ralston Purina. *Prof Exp:* Res assoc comp path, Rockefeller Univ, 67-69, asst prof, 69-71. *Concurrent Pos:* Adj asst prof immunol, Rockefeller Univ, 71-73; assoc scientist, Sloan-Kettering Inst Cancer Res, 71-73; adj asst prof, Col Physicians & Surgeons, Columbia Univ, 73-; consult, Off Dir, Bur Radiol Health, US Dept Health Educ & Welfare, 70-71. *Mem:* Am Vet Med Asn; Am Soc Exp Path; Int Acad Path; Am Col Vet Path. *Res:* Immunology; immunopathology; mechanisms of disease-correlating morphological with underlying molecular-biochemical alterations. *Mailing Add:* Animal Med Ctr 510 E 62nd St New York NY 10021-8383. *Fax:* 212-486-4226

HURWICZ, LEONID, ECONOMICS, STATISTICS. *Current Pos:* prof econ & math, 51-71, CURTIS L CARLSON PROF ECON & EMER REGENTS PROF, UNIV MINN, MINNEAPOLIS, 71- *Personal Data:* b Moscow, Russia, Aug 21, 17; nat US; m 44; c 4. *Educ:* Univ Warsaw, LLM, 38. *Honors & Awards:* Nat Medal Sci, 90. *Prof Exp:* Asst, Mass Inst Technol, 41; mem fac, Univ Chicago, 41-45; assoc prof econ & statist, Iowa State Col, 45-49; res prof econ & math statist, Univ Ill, 49-51. *Concurrent Pos:* Res assoc, Cowles Comn, 41-45, vis prof, 50; Guggenheim fel, 45; consult, Cowles Comn, 46-, Econ Comn for Europe, UN, 48, Rand Corp, 50-51 & US Bur Budget, 51-52; mem, Math Div, Nat Res Coun, 54-; fel, Ctr Advan Study Behav Sci, 55-56 & 58-59; vis prof, Stanford Univ, 58-59. *Mem:* Nat Acad Sci; Am Statist Asn; fel Economet Soc. *Res:* Economic organization in resource allocation; decision-making under uncertainty; dynamic models. *Mailing Add:* Dept Econs Univ Minn 271 19th Ave S Minneapolis MN 55455-0430

HURWITZ, ALEXANDER, COMPUTER SCIENCES. *Current Pos:* STAFF MEM COMPUT SCI, LOS ANGELES SCI CTR, IBM CORP, 65- *Personal Data:* b Syracuse, NY, Oct 16, 37; m 69; c 2. *Educ:* Univ Calif, Los Angeles, BA, 59, MA, 61, PhD(math), 65. *Mem:* Sigma Xi; Math Asn Am; Am Asn Artificial Intel; Asn Comput Mach. *Res:* Artificial intelligence; computer graphics. *Mailing Add:* 869 Santa Rita Ave Los Altos CA 94022

HURWITZ, CHARLES E(LLIOT), ELECTRICAL ENGINEERING, SOLID STATE PHYSICS. *Current Pos:* VPRES, LASERTRON, INC, 82- *Personal Data:* b Sioux City, Iowa, Nov 10, 37; m 59; c 3. *Educ:* Univ Mich, BSE, 59; Mass Inst Technol, SM, 60, PhD(elec eng), 63. *Prof Exp:* Staff mem, Lincoln Lab, Mass Inst Technol, 63-76, asst leader appl physics group, 76-78, assoc leader, 78-82. *Mem:* Am Phys Soc; Sigma Xi; Inst Elec & Electronics Engrs; sr mem Am Optical Soc. *Res:* Solid state devices; semiconductor lasers and detectors; guided-wave optics; electro-optical devices; fiber optics. *Mailing Add:* 42 Baskin Rd Lexington MA 02173-6929

HURWITZ, DAVID ALLAN, PHARMACOLOGY. *Current Pos:* CONSULT. *Personal Data:* b Lynn, Mass, Apr 17, 38; m 63; c 2. *Educ:* Mass Col Pharm, BS, 61, MS, 64, PhD(pharmacol), 69. *Prof Exp:* Pharmacologist, US Army Res Inst Environ Med, 65-70; from asst prof to assoc prof pharmacol, Univ NMex, 70-75; radiopharmacist, Pharmaco Nuclear, Inc, 75-80, pres, 80-81. *Mem:* AAAS; Sigma Xi. *Res:* Behavioral pharmacology; biochemical correlates of behavior, namely the relationships between animal behavior, brain biogenic amines, drugs, and environmental stresses, and the effects of one upon the others. *Mailing Add:* 652 Charles Pl Cleveland OH 44143

HURWITZ, JAN KROSST, ANALYTICAL CHEMISTRY. *Personal Data:* b Toronto, Ont, Apr 3, 24; m 48; c 2. *Educ:* Univ Toronto, BASc, 46, MA, 47, PhD(physics), 50. *Prof Exp:* Physicist & sr sci officer, Mines Br, Dept Mines & Tech Surv, Govt Can, 48-57; physicist & assoc res consult, Res Lab, US Steel Corp, 57-85. *Concurrent Pos:* Lectr, Univ Ottawa, 54-57 & Univ Pittsburgh, 63-70; consult & lectr, Pa State Univ, 87-88. *Mem:* Soc Appl Spectros (secy, 65-68, treas, 87-89); hon mem Spectros Soc Can (pres, 55-57); Iron & Steel Chemists Asn (secy-treas, 77, pres, 78 & 79); Am Soc Testing & Mat. *Res:* Emission spectroscopy; low pressure discharges; computer applications; development of certified chemical standard samples. *Mailing Add:* 109 Leslie Dr Monroeville PA 15146

HURWITZ, JERARD, MICROBIOLOGY. *Current Pos:* MEM STAFF & SLOAN KETTERING INST PROF, SLOAN KETTERING DIV, MED COL, CORNELL UNIV, 84- *Personal Data:* b New York, NY, Nov 20, 28; wid; c 4. *Educ:* Ind Univ, BA, 49; Western Res Univ, PhD(biochem), 53. *Honors & Awards:* Eli Lilly Award, 62; Brown-Hazen lectr, 72. *Prof Exp:* Res asst biochem, Western Res Univ, 49-50; Am Cancer Soc fel, Nat Med Res Coun, London, 53-54; NIH, 55-56; instr, Sch Med, Wash Univ, 56-58; asst prof, Sch Med, NY Univ, 58-60, assoc prof microbiol, 60-63; prof molecular biol, Albert Einstein Col Med, Bronx, NY, 63-65, prof & chmn, Dept Develop Biol & Cancer, 65-84. *Concurrent Pos:* Mem, Physiol Chem Study Sect, NIH, 64-68 & 81-84, Spec Viral Cancer Prog, 73-75; Charles Mickle fel award, Can, 67; Guggenheim fel award, Inst Pasteur, 68; mem study sect, Am Cancer Soc, 71-75; Fogarty scholar, 80; Louis & Bert Freeman Found prize res in biochem, NY Acad Sci, 82; Pfizer Sci award, 84-89; Guggenheim Mem Found fel, 86- *Mem:* Nat Acad Sci; Am Soc Biol Chemists; Am Acad Arts & Sci; fel NY Acad Sci. *Res:* Enzyme purification; synthesis of coenzymes; studies of electron transport, cytochromes and flavin enzymes; chemistry of hydroxy amino acids; nucleic acids; author or co-author of over 260 publications. *Mailing Add:* Mem Sloan Kettering Cancer Ctr 1275 York Ave PO Box 97 New York NY 10021. *Fax:* 212-717-3627; *E-Mail:* judshurwitz@ski.mskcc.org

HURWITZ, JULIA LEA, HIV VACCINE DEVELOPMENT, IMMUNOTHERAPY. *Current Pos:* asst mem, 88-93, ASSOC MEM, ST JUDE CHILDREN'S RES HOSP, 93- *Personal Data:* b Schenectady, NY, July 21, 54. *Educ:* Cornell Univ, BS, 76; Johns Hopkins Univ, PhD(immunol), 81. *Prof Exp:* Postdoctoral fel, Wistar Inst, 81-83, res assoc, 83-85; mem, Basel Inst Immunol, 85-88. *Concurrent Pos:* Prin investr, NIH, 84-85 & 92-; asst prof, Univ Tenn, 91-; asoc ed, J Immunol, 94-; adj prof, Univ Memphis, 96- *Mem:* Am Asn Immunologists. *Res:* Development of vaccines against HIV and against the human parainfluenza virus-type 1(h PIV-1); studying the effects of t-cell immunotherapy and antibody therapy on immunodeficient cancer and transplant patients. *Mailing Add:* St Judes Childrens Res Hosp 332 N Lauderdale Memphis TN 38101. *Fax:* 901-495-3107; *E-Mail:* julia.hurwitz@stjude.org

HURWITZ, LEON, AUTONOMIC PHARMACOLOGY. *Current Pos:* RETIRED. *Educ:* Univ Rochester, PhD(pharmacol), 53. *Prof Exp:* Prof pharmacol & chmn dept, Sch Med, Univ NMex, 72-87. *Res:* Physiology and pharmacology of smooth muscle; role of calcium in muscle contraction. *Mailing Add:* 8904 Harwood NE Albuquerque NM 87111

HURWITZ, MELVIN DAVID, ORGANIC CHEMISTRY. *Current Pos:* prof, 77-86, EMER PROF, CLOTHING & TEXTILES DEPT, UNIV NC, GREENSBORO, 86- *Personal Data:* b Medford, Mass, Dec 12, 17; m 43, Charlotte Krevitsky; c Judith, Michael & Sara. *Educ:* Harvard Univ, AB, 39; Univ Chicago, MS, 42; Cornell Univ, PhD(org chem), 48. *Honors & Awards:* Olney Medalist, Am Asn Textile Chemists, 86. *Prof Exp:* Res assoc, Billings Hosp, Chicago, 41-42; inspector powder & explosives, Elwood Ord Plant, 42; res assoc, Nat Defense Res Comt, 42-45; asst inorg chem, Cornell Univ, 45-47; res chemist, Rohm & Haas Co, 48-57, head textile prod develop lab, 57-61, head miscellaneous synthesis lab, 61-68, head textile chem lab, 68-73, mgr textile & leather chem res dept, 73-77. *Concurrent Pos:* Legal consult. *Mem:* Am Chem Soc; Sigma Xi; Am Asn Univ Prof; Am Asn Textile Chemists & Colorists; Fed Soc Coatings Technol. *Res:* Vitamin analyses; catalytic reductions; explosives; nitrogenous resins; organic fluorine chemistry; high polymers; organic coatings; textile chemicals; textile processing; leather chemicals; flammability; dyestuffs; protective clothing. *Mailing Add:* 5000 Robert Andrews Rd Greensboro NC 27406

HURWITZ, SOLOMON, MATHEMATICS. *Current Pos:* prof, 46-72, EMER PROF MATH, CITY COL NEW YORK, 72- *Personal Data:* b New York, NY, Apr 11, 07; m 37; c 2. *Educ:* City Col New York, BS, 27; Columbia Univ, MS, 29, PhD(math), 44. *Prof Exp:* Instr pub sch, NY, 27-42; instr math, Brooklyn Col, 42-46. *Concurrent Pos:* Instr div gen studies, Columbia Univ, 46-48; vis prof, Grad Summer Sch Teachers, Wesleyan Univ, 61-73. *Mem:* Am Math Soc; Math Asn Am. *Res:* A class of Dirichlet series; class of functions suggested by the zeta of Riemann. *Mailing Add:* 2806 Bedford Ave Brooklyn NY 11210-1238

HURYCH, ZDENEK, SOLID STATE PHYSICS, SURFACE PHYSICS. *Current Pos:* From asst prof to assoc prof, 68-77, PROF PHYSICS, NORTHERN ILL UNIV, 77- *Personal Data:* b Pelhrimov, Czech, July 19, 41; m 65; c 1. *Educ:* Charles Univ, Prague, MS, 63, PhD(physics), 67. *Mem:* Sigma Xi; Am Phys Soc. *Res:* Photoemission spectroscopy of solids and solid surfaces using synchrotron radiation; optical properties of solids; surface physics; vacuum ultraviolet radiation; electronic structure of solids; layered solids; semiconductors; thin films. *Mailing Add:* Dept Physics Northern Ill Univ DeKalb IL 60115

HUSA, DONALD L, SOLID STATE LOW TEMPERATURE, LIGHT WAVE SYSTEMS ENGINEERING. *Current Pos:* MEM TECH STAFF, AT&T BELL LABS, 81- *Personal Data:* b Hastings, Nebr, Sept 13, 40. *Educ:* Univ SC, BS, 62; Ohio State Univ, PhD(physics), 66. *Prof Exp:* Res assoc, Univ Pittsburgh, 67-70, res assoc, 70-79, res assoc prof, Stevens Inst Technol, 79-81. *Mem:* Am Phys Soc; Inst Elec & Electronics Engrs. *Res:* Engineering of lightwave systems. *Mailing Add:* 22 Tudor Dr Ocean Township NJ 07712

HUSA, WILLIAM JOHN, JR, ANALYTICAL CHEMISTRY. *Current Pos:* head phys sci div & chmn dept chem, 66-73, CHMN DIV NATURAL SCI & MATH & HEAD DEPT PHYS SCI, MID GA COL, 73- *Personal Data:* b Gainesville, Fla, Dec 16, 27. *Educ:* Univ Fla, BS, 48, MS, 51, PhD, 53. *Prof Exp:* Prof chem, Southwest Mo State Col, 53-66. *Res:* Spectrophotometry; chemical education. *Mailing Add:* PO Box 543 Cochran GA 31014-0543

HUSAIN, ANSAR, zoology, parasitology, for more information see previous edition

HUSAIN, KAZIM, NEUROTOXICOLOGY, ANTIOXIDANT SYSTEM. *Current Pos:* RES ASSOC, SCH MED, SOUTHERN ILL UNIV, 94- *Personal Data:* b Faizabad, India, June 10, 60; m 91, Sheeba Ahmad Zaida; c Sabiha & Samra. *Educ:* Lucknow Univ, BS, 79, MS, 81; Kanpur Univ, PhD(chem), 88. *Honors & Awards:* Jr Scientist Award, Asn Scientists Indian Origin Am, 97. *Prof Exp:* Jr fel, Indust Toxical Res Ctr, India, 82-85, sr fel, 85-87; scientist B, Defense Res & Develop, Esh, India, 87-92, scientist C, 92-94. *Concurrent Pos:* PhD examr biochem, Univ Bombay, 91-92; NIH postdoctoral fel, Sch Med, Southern Ill Univ, 94. *Mem:* Asn Physiologists & Pharmacologists India; Am Soc Toxicol. *Res:* Develop new antidotes for organophosphate toxicity; study delayed neurotoxicity of nere agents; find out biochemical markers for organophosphate-induced delayed neurotoxicity; mechanisms of nephro and ototoxicity and protection by chemoprotectants; antioxidant system; interaction of exercise and alcohol on antioxidant system of heart, brain, liver and testes. *Mailing Add:* Dept Pharmacol Sch Med Southern Ill Univ Springfield IL 62794-9230

HUSAIN, LIAQUAT, NUCLEAR CHEMISTRY. *Current Pos:* sr res scientist, 75-80, DIR LAB INORG & NUCLEAR CHEM, WADSWORTH CTR OF LABS & RES, NY STATE DEPT HEALTH, 80-; PROF, DEPT ENVIRON HEALTH & TOXICOL, STATE UNIV NY, ALBANY, 85- *Personal Data:* b Lucknow, India, July 12, 42; m 64; c 2. *Educ:* Univ Karachi, BS, 61, MS, 63; Univ Ark, PhD(nuclear chem), 68. *Prof Exp:* Asst lectr chem, Univ Karachi, 63-64; res assoc, Brookhaven Nat Lab, 68-70; lectr earth & space sci, State Univ NY Stony Brook, 70-75. *Concurrent Pos:* Adv, Pakistan Inst Nuclear Sci & Technol, 74-75 & 81 & Pakistan Upper Atmosphere Res Comn, 85 & 87. *Mem:* Am Chem Soc; AAAS; Am Geophys Union. *Res:* Atmospheric chemstry and physics; aerosol composition and transport; chemical reactions in clouds; acid rain; origin of tropospheric ozone; age determination of lunar rocks & meteorites; mechanisms of high-energy nuclear reactions; migration of radioactive isotopes from radioactive waste burial sites. *Mailing Add:* NY State Dept Health Wadsworth Ctr Albany NY 12201-0509

HUSAIN, SYED, PHARMACOLOGY, PHARMACY. *Current Pos:* asst prof, 76-81, ASSOC PROF PHARMACOL, MED SCH, UNIV NDAK, 81- *Personal Data:* b Hyderabad, India, Dec 9, 39; US citizen; m 68; c 3. *Educ:* Osmania Univ, BSc, 59; Univ Wis, BS, 65; Univ Mo, MS, 68, PhD(pharmacol), 71. *Prof Exp:* Res assoc pharmacol, Med Sch, Ind Univ, 71-74; biochem pharmacologist, SRI Int, 74-76. *Concurrent Pos:* Nat Inst Drug Abuse grant, 74-76 & 80-82; HEW grant, 74-76; Univ NDak Fac res grants, 76-77 & 78-79; NIH grant, 77-80. *Mem:* Int Soc Biochem Pharmacol; Sigma Xi; AAAS; Soc Exp Biol Med. *Res:* Disposition of anticoagulants and other drugs, their biliary and lymphatic excretion and metabolism; drug interactions with marijuana and cannabinoid effects on brain and testicular metabolism and function. *Mailing Add:* NIDA NIH 5600 Fishers La Rm 10-42 Univ NDak Sch Med Rockville MD 20857-0001

HUSAIN, SYED ALAMDAR, MATHEMATICS. *Current Pos:* assoc prof, 65-76, PROF MATH, UNIV WYO, 76- *Personal Data:* b Arrah, India, Feb 5, 31; nat US; m 63; c 5. *Educ:* Aligarh Muslim Univ, India, BA, 50; Univ Dacca, MA, 52; Univ Chicago, MS, 56; Purdue Univ, PhD(math), 59. *Prof Exp:* Lectr math, Brindaban Col, Bangladesh53-54 & Rajshahi Univ, Bangladesh, 54-55; instr, Purdue Univ, 56-59; asst prof, Seattle Univ, 59-60 & Univ Sask, 60-61; from asst prof to assoc prof, Univ Idaho, 61-64; vis prof, Aegean Univ, Turkey, 64-65. *Mem:* Am Math Soc. *Res:* Fourier analysis; divergent series and fixed point theorems. *Mailing Add:* 1233 Reynolds St Laramie WY 82070

HUSAIN, TAQDIR, PURE MATHEMATICS. *Current Pos:* RETIRED. *Personal Data:* b India, July 16, 29; m 59; c 3. *Educ:* Aligarh Muslim Univ, BA, 50, MA, 52; Syracuse Univ, PhD(math), 60. *Prof Exp:* Lectr math, Aligarh Muslim Univ, 52-53; res scholar, Tata Inst Fundamental Res, Bombay, India, 53-55; lectr, Forman Christian Col, Panjab, Pakistan, 55-57; asst, Syracuse Univ, 57-60, instr, 60-61; asst prof, Univ Ottawa, Can, 61-64; assoc prof math, McMaster Univ, 64-67, prof & chmn dept, 67-73 & 79-82. *Concurrent Pos:* Assoc ed, Can J Math, 79-86. *Mem:* Am Math Soc; Math Asn Am; Can Math Soc; NY Acad Sci. *Res:* Functional analysis; topological vector spaces; topological groups and spaces; Banach algebras, summability methods, real and complex analysis; author of six books. *Mailing Add:* 2018 Chevoit Ct Burlington ON L7P 1W8 Can

HUSAINI, SAEED A, food science, for more information see previous edition

HUSAR, RUDOLF BERTALAN, MECHANICAL ENGINEERING, AIR POLLUTION. *Current Pos:* assoc prof, 73-76, PROF MECH ENG, WASHINGTON UNIV, ST LOUIS, 73-, DIR CAPITA, 79- *Personal Data:* b Martonos, Yugoslavia, Oct, 29, 41; US citizen; m 67; c 2. *Educ:* Tech Univ, WBerlin, dipl eng, 66; Univ Minn, PhD(mech eng), 71. *Prof Exp:* Design technician, W Hofer, Heating, Ventilation Consult, 62-63; res asst, Tech Univ, WBerlin, 63-66; res asst, Univ Minn, 66-69, res assoc & fel, 69-71; res fel, Calif Inst Technol, 71-73. *Concurrent Pos:* Res fel, Univ Glasgow, Scotland, 65; vis prof, Meterol Inst, Univ Stockholm, 76; mem, Comt Sulfur Oxides, Nat Acad Sci, 78; Co-chmn, Interagency Comt Health & Environ Effects Advan Energy Technol, 78; mem, Coop Prog Develop & Appln Space Technol Air Pollution, Environ Protection Agency/NASA, 78; mem, Comn Atmospheric-Biosphere Interactions, Nat Acad Sci, 79-81. *Mem:* Am Meterol Asn; Air Pollution Control Asn; AAAS; Am Asn Aerosol Res; Ges Aerosolforschung. *Res:* Aerosol dynamics and plume studies of sulfur oxide kinetics; regional scale model of acid rain and optical effects; satellite imagery studies; historical trends of fuel use and concentrations for checks of the consistency in the systems's behaviour; visibility trends; environmental informatics. *Mailing Add:* 63 Ridgemoor Dr St Louis MO 63105

HUSBAND, ROBERT MURRAY, ORGANIC CHEMISTRY, CHEMICAL ENGINEERING. *Current Pos:* PRES, POLYPULP TECHNOL, 73- *Personal Data:* b Russell, Man, Oct 5, 19; m 50, Helen D Karantjieff; c Jon R & William D. *Educ:* Univ Sask, BA & BE, 44; McGill Univ, PhD(chem), 47. *Prof Exp:* Bristol Labs res fel streptomycin res inst, Ohio State Univ, 47-50; asst prof cellulose industs, Toronto, 50-52; res assoc wood chem, State Univ NY Col Forestry, Syracuse Univ, 52-55, assoc prof pulp & paper technol, 55-57; chief chem sect, Res Ctr, Consol Paper Corp, Ltd, 57-61; mgr cent res, Riegel Paper Corp, 61-69; dir res, R T Vanderbilt Co, Inc, 69-72. *Concurrent Pos:* Proj leader, Empire State Paper Res Assocs, 52-57; expert adv, Cent Am Inst Indust Invest & Technol, 72-73. *Mem:* Am Chem Soc; Tech Asn Pulp & Paper Indust; Can Pulp & Paper Asn; NY Acad Sci. *Res:* Chemistry of wood and its components, carbohydrates and phenols; wood pulping and pulp bleaching; oxidation of organic compounds; surface chemistry; paper structure and rheology; chemistry of paper-making. *Mailing Add:* 5285 Madison Ave Trumbull CT 06611. *Fax:* 203-261-4548

HUSBAND, ROBERT W, ENTOMOLOGY. *Current Pos:* assoc prof biol, Adrian Col, 64-73, chmn dept 71-80, chmn div sci, 73-75 & 88-90, PROF BIOL, ADRIAN COL, 73- *Personal Data:* b Hesperia, Mich, May 21, 31; m 55; c David O, Suzanne M & Linda C. *Educ:* Univ Mich, AB, 53; Western Mich Univ, MA, 60; Mich State Univ, PhD(zool), 66. *Prof Exp:* Instr radar intercept tech, USAF Intercept Sch, 55-58; teacher pub schs, Mich, 59-60; teaching asst zool, Mich State Univ, 60-64. *Concurrent Pos:* Mem, Cong Acarologists, 64-; res assoc entom, Univ Ga, 71-72; pres, Mich Ent Soc. *Mem:* Am Micros Soc (treas, 75-79); Entom Soc Am; Soc Syst Zool; Am Inst Biol Sci; Sigma Xi. *Res:* Mites associated with insects; bumblebees; taxonomy; ecology; zoogeography Acarina, Podapolipidae; author of more than 60 publications. *Mailing Add:* Dept Biol Adrian Col Adrian MI 49221

HUSBAND, THOMAS PAUL, WILDLIFE ECOLOGY. *Current Pos:* ASSOC PROF NATURAL RESOURCES SCI, UNIV RI, 77- *Personal Data:* b Flint, Mich, Jan 23, 50; m 70; c 4. *Educ:* Univ Mich, Flint, BA, 72; Mich State Univ, MS, 74, PhD(wildlife ecol), 77. *Concurrent Pos:* Res asst, NSF, 74-76. *Mem:* Wildlife Soc; Soc Am Foresters; Am Asn Univ Professors; Am Soc Mammalogists. *Res:* Population dynamics of wildlife; bioenergetics of mammals; primary and secondary productivity of terrestrial ecosystems; faunal inventory of Brazilian Atlantic forest; population ecology, genetics and behavior of mountain goats. *Mailing Add:* Dept Natural Resources Sci Univ RI Kingston RI 02881

HUSBY, FREDRIC MARTIN, ANIMAL NUTRITION, RUMINANT NUTRITION. *Current Pos:* ASST PROF ANIMAL SCI & NUTRIT, AGR EXP STA, UNIV ALASKA, 75- *Personal Data:* b Mt Vernon, Wash, Feb 16, 43; m 71; c 2. *Educ:* Wash State Univ, BS, 66, MS, 69, PhD(nutrit), 74. *Prof Exp:* Fel animal physiol & animal metab, Univ BC, 74-75. *Mem:* Am Soc Animal Sci; Am Soc Dairy Sci. *Res:* Evaluation of feedstuffs, Alaska grains and animal-fish byproducts for use by swine; management and production systems for swine, beef and sheep in a northern environment; forage utilization. *Mailing Add:* Dept Animal Sci Univ Alaska PO Box 757200 Fairbanks AK 99775-7200

HUSCII, LAWRENCE S, TOPOLOGY. *Current Pos:* assoc prof, 71-75, PROF MATH, UNIV TENN, KNOXVILLE, 75- *Personal Data:* b Hollis, NY, Feb 17, 42; m 68; c 2. *Educ:* St Francis Col, NY, BS, 63; Fla State Univ, MS, 64, PhD(math), 67. *Prof Exp:* Res asst math, Fla State Univ, 66-67; asst prof, Univ Ga, 67-69; from asst prof to assoc prof, Va Polytech Inst, 69-71. *Concurrent Pos:* Vis res scientist, Univ Zagreb, Yugoslavia, 76-77; Fulbright res scholar, 86; vis distinguished prof, Univ NC, Greensboro, 90-91. *Mem:* Am Math Soc. *Res:* Topology of manifolds; dynamics. *Mailing Add:* Dept Math Univ Tenn Knoxville TN 37996-0001

HUSCHILT, JOHN, THEORETICAL PHYSICS. *Current Pos:* RETIRED. *Personal Data:* b Kitchener, Ont, June 1, 31; m 55, Cornelia Ellen Kolb; c Mary Anne (Piaget), Ruth Marie (Rofulo), John Charles, Joseph Gabriel, Katherine Grace (Alari), Peter Nicholas, Paul Michael & Karen Margaret. *Educ:* Univ Toronto, BA, 52, MA, 53; Wayne State Univ, PhD(theoret physics), 63. *Prof Exp:* from asst prof to assoc prof physics, Univ Windsor, 53-94, actg chmn dept, 58-59. *Concurrent Pos:* Vis prof, Inst Theoret Physics, Univ Neurchatel, Switz, 70-71; Stuttgart, Ger, 79-80. *Mem:* Am Asn Physics Teachers; Am Phys Soc; Can Asn Physicists. *Res:* Attempting to clarify basic interactions of elementary particles and interactions with radiation by investigating these in a consistent, classical, fully relativistic framework analytically and by numerical calculations; applications of Clifford Algebras to theoretical physics. *Mailing Add:* Dept Physics Univ Windsor Windsor ON N9B 3P4 Can. *Fax:* 519-973-7075

HUSCHKE, RALPH ERNEST, METEOROLOGY. *Current Pos:* PRES, HUSCHKE ASSOCS, INC, 82- *Personal Data:* b Utica, NY, Nov 28, 29; m 48; c 2. *Educ:* Mass Inst Technol, BS, 46. *Prof Exp:* Prin asst, US Weather Bur, Conn, 48-51; field aide, Mass, 51-52; res staff mem meteorol, Div Indust Coop, Mass Inst Technol, 54-55; chief res prods br, Geophys Res Directorate, Air Force Cambridge Res Ctr, Mass, 56-59; eng specialist meteorol, Norair Div, Northrop Corp, Calif, 59-61; phys scientist, Rand Corp, 62-73, consult, 73-82. *Concurrent Pos:* Ed glossary meteorol, Am Meteorol Soc, Mass, 55-59; asst to dir ed film prog, 61-62; mem panel weather & climate modification, Nat Acad Sci, 65-66; assoc, Clin Consult Corp, 82- *Mem:* AAAS; Am Meteorol Soc; Am Geophys Union; Nat Coun Indust Meteorol. *Res:* Applied meteorological research and analysis; economic aspects of weather information; weather data processing; numerical simulation; military climatology; weather effects on systems and operations; forensic meteorology. *Mailing Add:* Six Admiralty Cross Coronado CA 92118

HUSEYIN, KONCAY, APPLIED MECHANICS, STABILITY THEORY. *Current Pos:* vis asst prof, Univ Waterloo, 69-71, res assoc prof solid mech, 71-72, assoc prof, systs design, 72-75, assoc chmn dept, 74-78, chmn systs design, 78-87, prof, 75-96, DISTINGUISHED EMER PROF SYSTS DESIGN, UNIV WATERLOO, 97- *Personal Data:* b Nicosia, Cyprus, Oct 7, 36; m 62, Tuncay; c Neyzar, Zuhal & Hulya. *Educ:* Istanbul Tech Univ, MSc, 60; Univ London, PhD(civil eng), 68, DSc(eng), 79. *Prof Exp:* Supvr civil eng, Tumpane Co, Inc, 61-64; asst prof, MidE Tech Univ, Ankara, 68-69. *Concurrent Pos:* NATO res fel, Alexander von Humboldt res fel & Nat Res Coun fel; vis prof, Inst Mech, Darmstadt Tech Univ, Ger, 78, 83 & 87-88; ed, Dynamics & Stability Systs; fel, CSME, 87. *Mem:* Am Acad Mech; Soc Natural Philos; Ger Asn Appl Math & Mech; Asn Mech Eng Can; fel Can Soc Mech Eng. *Res:* Elastic stability of conservative and non-conservative structural systems; general theory of stability of systems; bifurcation theory; nonlinear oscillations; catastrophe theory. *Mailing Add:* Dept Systs Design Univ Waterloo Waterloo ON N2L 3G1 Can. *Fax:* 519-578-2039

HUSHAK, LEROY J, AGRICULTURAL ECONOMICS. *Current Pos:* From asst prof to assoc prof, 68-78, PROF AGR ECON, OHIO STATE UNIV, 78- *Personal Data:* b Belle Plaine, Iowa, Sept 15, 39; m 80; c 1. *Educ:* Iowa State Univ, BS, 61; Univ Chicago, MA & PhD(econ), 68. *Concurrent Pos:* Vis scholar, US Dept Agr, 84-85. *Mem:* Am Agr Econ Asn; Am Econ Asn; Am Fisheries Soc; Asn Environ & Resource Economists. *Res:* Economics of agricultural trade, regional economics, fishery economics. *Mailing Add:* 238 Halligan Ave Worthington OH 43085

HUSIC, HAROLD DAVID, CARBON DIOXIDE AQUISITION & UTILIZATION BY PHOTOSYNTHETIC ORGANISMS. *Current Pos:* asst prof, 86-92, ASSOC PROF CHEM, LAFAYETTE COL, 92- *Personal Data:* b Lansdale, Pa, Nov 24, 55; m 84, Diane White; c Corey Christopher. *Educ:* Pa State Univ, BS, 77; Mich State Univ, PhD(biochem), 82. *Prof Exp:* Res assoc biochem, Mich State Univ, 82-86. *Mem:* Am Soc Biochem & Molecular Biol; Am Soc Plant Physiologists; Am Chem Soc. *Res:* Study of the enzyme carbonic anhydrase, especially as it applies to the acquisition of carbon dioxide by photosynthetic organisms. *Mailing Add:* Dept Chem Lafayette Col Easton PA 18042-1782. *Fax:* 610-250-9263; *E-Mail:* husicd@lafcol.lafayette.edu

HUSK, GEORGE RONALD, organometallic chemistry, polymer chemistry; deceased, see previous edition for last biography

HUSKEY, GLEN E, FOOD MICROBIOLOGY, BIOCHEMISTRY. *Personal Data:* b Hillsboro, Mo, Aug 9, 31; m 53; c 3. *Educ:* Univ Mo, BS, 56, MS, 57, PhD(food microbiol), 66. *Prof Exp:* Prod trainee plant opers, Fresh Milk & Ice Cream Div, Carnation Co, Tex, 57-58; plant mgr, Int Div, Foremost Dairies, Inc, Calif, 59-64; asst prof dairy technol & exten specialist, Ohio State Univ, 66-67; prin scientist, Pet Inc, 67-69, asst mgr corp qual assurance, 70-71, mgr, 71-74, vpres processing & mfg, Dairy Div, 74-82. *Mem:* Am Soc Qual Control; Am Dairy Sci Asn; Inst Food Technologists. *Res:* Implementation of a total quality control program for the food industry and/or total production management in the dairy industry. *Mailing Add:* 25521 Via Impreso Valencia CA 91355

HUSKEY, HARRY D(OUGLAS), COMPUTERS & MATHEMATICS, ELECTRICAL ENGINEERING. *Current Pos:* dir, Comput Ctr, Univ Calif, 68-77, prof, 68-85, chmn dept, 76-79, EMER PROF INFO SCI, UNIV CALIF, SANTA CRUZ, 85- *Personal Data:* b Whittier, NC, Jan 19, 16; m 39, 94, Nancy Grindstaff; c Carolyn Roxanne, Harry Jr & Linda. *Educ:* Univ Idaho, BS, 37; Ohio State Univ, MS, 40, PhD(math), 43. *Honors & Awards:* Pioneer Award, Inst Elec & Electronics Engrs Comput Soc, 82; Centennial Award, Inst Elec & Electronics Engrs, 84. *Prof Exp:* Asst math, Ohio Univ, 37-38; instr, Ohio State Univ, 41-43 & Univ Pa, 43-46; temp prin sci officer, Nat Phys Lab Eng, 47-48; temp prin officer, Nat Bur Stand, Washington, DC, 48-49, asst dir, Inst Numerical Anal, Univ Calif, 49-54; from assoc prof to prof math & elec eng, Univ Calif, Berkeley, 54-68, prof comput & info sci, 68-86. *Concurrent Pos:* Tech dir comput lab, Wayne Univ, 52-53; consult comput div, Bendix Corp, 54-63; Indian Inst Technol, India, 63-64 & 71; vis prof, Mass Inst Technol, 66; mem comput sci panel, NSF; Naval Res Adv Comt; consult comput for develop nations, UN; Von Humboldt award, 75; mem, NAS Comt to Adv Brazil on Comput Sci. *Mem:* Fel AAAS; fel Inst Elec & Electronics Engrs; fel Brit Comput Soc; Am Math Soc; fel Asn Comput Mach (vpres, 58-60, pres, 60-62). *Res:* Design and use of electronic digital computing machines and accessories; mathematical area of surfaces; solution of algebraic linear simultaneous equations. *Mailing Add:* 10 Devant Lane Bluffton SC 29910. *E-Mail:* hhuskey@hargray.com

HUSKEY, ROBERT JOHN, GENETICS. *Current Pos:* asst prof, 69-74, mem, Ctr Advan Studies, 69-71, ASSOC PROF BIOL, UNIV VA, 74-, ASSOC DEAN GRAD SCH ARTS & SCI, 83- *Personal Data:* b San Antonio, Tex, Dec 29, 38; m 60; c 2. *Educ:* Univ Okla, BS, 60, MS, 62; Calif Inst Technol, PhD(biol), 68. *Prof Exp:* Asst prof genetics, Syracuse Univ, 67-69. *Mem:* Genetics Soc Am; Soc Develop Biol; AAAS; Sigma Xi. *Res:* Development genetics of algae; physiology and genetic recombination in bacteriophage lambda. *Mailing Add:* Dept Biol Univ Va 229 Gilmer Hall Charlottesville VA 22903

HUSKINS, CHESTER WALKER, ORGANIC CHEMISTRY. *Current Pos:* RETIRED. *Personal Data:* b Lincoln Co, NC, Jan 2, 21; m 53; c 1. *Educ:* Davidson Col, BS, 48; Univ Fla, MS, 49. *Prof Exp:* Chemist, Fruit & Veg Lab, USDA, Fla, 49-52; chemist, Redstone Arsenal, US Army Missile Command, 52-59, chief org chem group, 59-62, explor res & develop, 62-70, prog mgr shoulder fired rocket propellant develop, Directorate Res, Develop & Eng Propellant Lab, 70-74, dir boron proj, Directorate Res, 74-80. *Concurrent Pos:* Tech projs officer, Weapons Data Exchange Agreements, Neth & Belg, 62-67; consult, 81- *Mem:* Am Chem Soc. *Res:* Solid rocket propellant development; propellant ingredient synthesis, characterization and evaluation; fluorine, polymer, ferrocene and carborane chemistry; synthesis of new boron compounds, development of pilot plant and manufacturing facilities for selected compounds. *Mailing Add:* 623 Owens Dr SE Huntsville AL 35801-1820

HUSNI, ELIAS A, cardiovascular surgery, for more information see previous edition

HUSON, FREDERICK RUSSELL, HIGH ENERGY PHYSICS. *Current Pos:* PHYSICIST, FERMI NAT ACCELERATOR LAB, 70- *Personal Data:* b Sheridan, Wyo, Nov 22, 36; m 55. *Educ:* San Diego State Col, BA, 59; Univ Calif, Berkeley, PhD(physics), 64. *Prof Exp:* Res assoc physics, Polytech Sch, Paris, 64-65; res assoc, Accelerator Lineaire Labs, Orsay, 65-66; scientist, Brookhaven Nat Lab, 66-70. *Mem:* Am Phys Soc; Sigma Xi; AAAS. *Res:* Experimental high energy particle physics. *Mailing Add:* PO Box 9674 The Woodlands TX 77387

HUSS, RONALD JOHN, MICROBIAL SCREENING & STRAIN IMPROVEMENT, FERMENTATION DEVELOPMENT. *Current Pos:* Group leader, 83-85, proj mgr, 86, DIR RES, BIO-TECH RESOURCES, INC, 86- *Personal Data:* b Ft Atkinson, Wis, Dec 3, 53; m 77. *Educ:* Univ Wis-Madison, BA, 75; Univ Ill, Champaign-Urbana, PhD(biochem), 85. *Concurrent Pos:* Lab mgr, Ladish Malting Co, 76-77. *Mem:* Am Chem Soc; Am Soc Plant Physiologists. *Res:* Microbial screening and strain improvement; fermentation development. *Mailing Add:* 1415 Michigan Ave Manitowoc WI 54220

HUSSA, ROBERT OSCAR, BIOCHEMISTRY. *Current Pos:* VPRES RES & DEVELOP, ADEZA BIO MED, SUNNYVALE, CALIF, 86- *Personal Data:* b La Crosse, Wis, Mar 15, 41; m 63; c 2. *Educ:* Univ Wis-Madison, BS, 64; Univ Hawaii, PhD(biochem), 68. *Prof Exp:* Res assoc pharmacol, Sch Med, Ind Univ, 68-69, instr, 69; instr, Med Col Wis, 69-72, asst prof, 72-77, assoc prof biochem & gynec & obstet, 78-84, prof, 84-86. *Concurrent Pos:* Am Cancer Soc grant, Sch Med, Ind Univ, 68-69 & Med Col Wis, 70-71; Human Life Found grants, Med Col Wis, 70-72, Nat Cancer Inst res grant, 74-76 & 77-78. *Mem:* Endocrine Soc; Am Soc Biol Chemists; Am Chem Soc; Tissue Cult Asn. *Res:* Synthesis of polypeptide, protein, glycoprotein, and steroid hormones; glycogen metabolism. *Mailing Add:* Adeza Bio Med 1240 Elko Dr Sunnyvale CA 94089. *Fax:* 408-745-0968

HUSSAIN, BADRUZZAMAN, MOTOR OPERATED VALVES, CONDITION MONITORING OF MACHINES. *Current Pos:* PROJ MGR ELECT, KCI ENG. *Personal Data:* m, Mahrukh Subhani; c Ayesha & Usama. *Educ:* Ned Univ Pakistan, BS, 83; Univ Ky, MS, 87; Ill Inst Technol, PhD(elec & comput), 91. *Mem:* Sr mem Inst Elec & Electronics Engrs. *Res:* Solving innovative problems of nuclear generating stations; motor operated valves; dynamic performance ac motors; distribution system network equipments. *Mailing Add:* 1401 Branding Lane No 255 Downers Grove IL 60515. *E-Mail:* kiran@xnet.com

HUSSAIN, FAZLE, FLUID MECHANICS, TURBULENCE. *Current Pos:* from asst prof to assoc prof, 71-73, distinguished univ prof, 85-89, PROF MECH ENG, UNIV HOUSTON, 76-, CULLEN DISTINGUISHED PROF, 89- *Personal Data:* b Dhaka, Bangladesh, Jan 20, 43; m 68, Rehana; c Shama. *Educ:* E Pakistan Univ Eng & Technol, BSc, 63; Stanford Univ, MS, 66, PhD(mech eng), 70. *Honors & Awards:* Tani Mem Lect, Asian Cong Fluid Mech, Singapore, 95. *Prof Exp:* Lectr, Dept Mech Eng, E Pakistan Univ Eng & Technol, 63-65; vis asst prof, Dept Mech, Johns Hopkins Univ, 69-71. *Concurrent Pos:* Consult var co & adv bds of tech comt; assoc ed, Turbulence in Liquids, Sci Press, 79- & Physics Fluids, Am Inst Physics, 80-84; Int Sci Comt, Asian Cong Fluid Mech, 79-; Freeman scholar, Am Soc Mech Engrs, 84, mem sci comt, Int Union Theoret & Appl Mech Symp, topological fluid mech, Cambridge Univ, 89; mem, Tech Comt Turb, Am Soc Chem Engrs, 87-91; assoc ed, J Fluids Eng, Am Soc Mech Engrs, 95-98; US Nat Comn Theoret & Appl Mech, 96-; Fl Oyn Comn, Am Inst Aeronaut & Astronaut, 97- *Mem:* Fel Am Soc Mech Engrs; fel Am Phys Soc; assoc fel Am Inst Aeronaut & Astronaut. *Res:* Turbulence, experimental, numerical, and analytical studies of turbulent shear flows, mixing layers, jets and wakes, and turbulence control; hydrodynamic stability; chaos; aerodynamics; aeroacoustics; biofluid mechanics; flow visulization; digital image processing; vortex dynamics; vortex chaos; separation phenomena. *Mailing Add:* Dept Mech Eng Univ Houston Houston TX 77204-4792. *Fax:* 713-743-4503; *E-Mail:* fhussain@uh.edu

HUSSAIN, MALEK GHOLOUM MALEK, ULTRAWIDEBAND RADAR & COMMUNICATION TECHNOLOGY, DIGITAL COMMUNICATIONS. *Current Pos:* DEAN, DIV PROF & TECHNOL PROGS, INTER-AM UNIV PR, 91- *Personal Data:* b Kuwait City, Kuwait, Oct 7, 53; m 84; c 2. *Educ:* Cath Univ Am, BEE, 77, MEE, 79, PhD(elec eng), 83. *Honors & Awards:* Sci Achievements Prize, Kuwait Found Advan Sci, 90. *Prof Exp:* From asst prof to assoc prof elec eng, Kuwait Univ, 83-90. *Concurrent Pos:* Consult, Signal Corps, Ministry Defense, Kuwait, 84-86, Gulf Coop Coun, Kuwait, 87-88; vis assoc prof, Univ Mich, Ann Arbor, 88-89. *Mem:* Sr mem Inst Elec & Electronics Engrs; Soc Kuwaiti Engrs. *Res:* Ultrawideband, impulse, radar and communication technology; antenna theory and design; signal propagation and scattering; signal processing; radar system design and simulation; adaptive array processing; neural networks and systolic array processing. *Mailing Add:* 1522 Cavalieri St Urb Belisa Rio Piedras PR 00927

HUSSAIN, MOAYYED A, FRACTURE MECHANICS, INTEGRAL EQUATIONS. *Current Pos:* MATHEMATICIAN, CORP RES & DEVELOP, GEN ELEC CO, 79- *Personal Data:* b Poona, India, Feb 25, 37; US citizen; m 66; c 2. *Educ:* Univ Poona, India, BE, 59; Renesselaer Polytech Inst, MS, 62, PhD(mech), 65. *Prof Exp:* Lectr mech, Col Eng, Univ Poona, India, 59-60; res asst aeronaut, Rensselaer Polytech Inst, 60-62; res engr appl math, US Army Watervliet Arsenal, 62-79. *Concurrent Pos:* Vis scientist, Math Res Ctr, Univ Wis-Madison, 66-67; adj assoc prof, Union Col, 72-74. *Mem:* Soc Indust Appl Math; Am Soc Mech Engrs; Am Comput Mach; Sigma Xi; Inst Elec & Electronics Engrs. *Res:* Mathematical physics; mechanics fracture; vibration; electromagnetic phenomenon; integral equations; dual series relations; finite element methods; finite difference methods; array synthesis. *Mailing Add:* Bldg K-1 Rm KWC434A Corp Res-Develop Gen Elec Co PO Box 8 Schenectady NY 12301. *Fax:* 518-387-5299

HUSSAIN, NIHAD A, FORCED & NATURAL CONVECTION, RADIATION. *Current Pos:* ASSOC DEAN, COL ENG, SAN DIEGO STATE UNIV, 81- *Personal Data:* b Basrah, Iraq, Jan 9, 41; m 64, Suzanne Quillen; c Juhaina, Samir & Shaun. *Educ:* Univ Baghdad, Iraq, BS, 62; Purdue Univ, MS, 65; Univ Notre Dame, PhD(mech eng), 69. *Prof Exp:* Grad asst heat transfer, Purdue Univ, 63-65; res assoc heat transfer, Univ Notre Dame, 65-69; from asst prof to prof heat transfer & fluid mech, San Diego State Univ, 69-81. *Concurrent Pos:* Design engr, Al Damalogy Consult Eng, Baghdad, Iraq, 62-63; res fel, NASA-Lewis Res Ctr, 73-75, USAF-Wright Patterson AFB, 75-76; consult, Geosci, Inc, Solana Beach, Calif, 72-73, Burroughs Corp, Rancho Bernardo, Calif, 75-76, Boekamp, Inc, San Diego, Calif, 80-84, Langley Corp, San Diego, Calif, 81-86, Calif Energy Comm, 89-; chmn, K-19 comt, Heat Transfer Div, Am Soc Mech Engrs, 87-90, rep, Nat Heat Transfer Conf Coord Comn, 90-93; rep, coun eng, Nat Mems Interest Comt, Am Soc Mech Engrs, 93- *Mem:* Sigma Xi; Am Soc Mech Eng; Am Soc Eng Educ. *Res:* Development of engineering correlations in the areas of combined free and forced convections in horizontal tubes; two phase buoyant plumes and in the areas of radiation in semi-transparent media. *Mailing Add:* 13026 Trigger St San Diego CA 92129. *Fax:* 619-594-6005

HUSSAIN, RIAZ, PHYSICS. *Current Pos:* from instr to assoc prof physics, 67-85, ASSOC PROF FINANCE, UNIV SCRANTON, 85- *Personal Data:* b Gujranwala, Pakistan, Jan 18, 37; US citizen; m 65, 78, Atiya Bokhari; c Paul A. *Educ:* Forman Christian Col, Lahore, Pakistan, BSc, 54; Univ Punjab, Lahore, Pakistan, MSc, 56; Johns Hopkins Univ, Md, PhD(physics), 73; Univ Scranton, MBA, 80; Lehigh Univ, Bethlehem, Pa, PhD(finance), 93. *Honors & Awards:* Fulbright fel, 60. *Prof Exp:* Lectr physics, Forman Christian Col, Lahore, Pakistan, 56-60. *Mem:* Am Asn Physics Teachers; Financial Analysts Fedn; Am Finance Asn. *Res:* Atomic spectroscopy; optical instrumentation; teaching of physics; portfolio theory; financial analysis. *Mailing Add:* 540 N Webster Ave Scranton PA 18510. *Fax:* 717-941-4342; *E-Mail:* hussain@uofs.edu

HUSSAIN, SYED TASEER, VERTEBRATE PALEONTOLOGY, FUNCTIONAL ANATOMY. *Current Pos:* from instr to assoc prof, 72-85, PROF ANAT, HOWARD UNIV, 85- *Personal Data:* b Lahore, Pakistan, Sept 18, 43; m 75. *Educ:* Panjab Univ, Lahore, BS, 63, BS hon, 64, MS, 65; Utrecht Univ, Holland, PhD(paleont), 69. *Prof Exp:* Fel vertebrate paleont, Am Mus Natural Hist, New York, 70-72; instr geol, NY Univ, 71-72. *Concurrent Pos:* Prin investr & proj dir, Cenozoic Mammals & Biostrat, Pakistan, 76-; res assoc, Smithsonian Inst, Washington, DC, 77-; guest scientist, Chinese Acad Sci, 82, US-India Exchange of Scientists Prog, 92; dir gen, Pakistan Mus Natural Hist, Pakistan Sci Found, 85-87. *Mem:* AAAS; Am Asn Anatomists; Soc Vert Paleont. *Res:* Mammalian evolution in Asia with particular interests in paleoecology, paleogeography, paleoclimates and climate changes and faunal migrations during the last sixty million years; science administration; educational administration; science education; climate change and human health. *Mailing Add:* Dept Anat Col Med Howard Univ Washington DC 20059

HUSSAINI, M YOUSUFF, COMPUTER APPLICATIONS. *Current Pos:* res scientist & sr staff scientist, 78-86, chief scientist, 86-92, DIR, INST COMPUT APPLNS SCI & ENG, 92- *Educ:* Univ Madras, BS & MS; Univ Calif, Berkeley, PhD(mech eng), 70. *Prof Exp:* From group chief to actg div head, Indian Space Res Orgn, 70-76; sr res fel, Nat Acad Sci-Nat Res Coun, 76-78. *Concurrent Pos:* Assoc ed, J Sci & Statist Comput, 88-91; ed-in-chief, Theoret & Comput Fluid Dynamics. *Mem:* Am Soc Mech Engrs; AAAS; Am Inst Aeronaut & Astronaut; Am Phys Soc; Soc Indust & Appl Math. *Res:* Author of numerous publications. *Mailing Add:* ICASE NASA Langley Res Ctr Mail Stop 132C Hampton VA 23665

HUSSAK, ROBERT EDWARD, POLYMER ENGINEERING, POLYMER CHEMISTRY. *Current Pos:* Mgr, Pigment Lab, STO Corp, 83-85, mgr plant qual assurance, 85-86, primary formulation chemist-Ger, 86-87, synthetic lab mgr, 87-90, CORP QUAL CONTROL/QUAL ASSURANCE GOVT REGULATIONS SAFETY MGR, STO CORP, 90- *Personal Data:* b Perth Amboy, NJ, Feb 15, 61. *Educ:* Bethany Col, BS, 83. *Res:* Waterspace coatings, paints, sealers and allied coating used primarily in the exterior insulation market and concrete/cement restoration market; environmental control-production related safety; toxicology. *Mailing Add:* 45 Quality Rd Rutland VT 05701

HUSSAMY, SAMIR, COLOR CHEMISTRY, DYES & PIGMENTS. *Current Pos:* PRES, INDUST CHEM, HILTON INDUSTS, EVINGTON, VA, 90- *Personal Data:* b Cairo, Egypt, Mar 18, 35; US citizen; m 60; c 1. *Educ:* Leeds Univ, dipl, 56, MS, 60; ETH Zurich, Switz, DSc(Tech), 68. *Prof Exp:* Asst mgr dyeing & finishing, Polytex Co, Egypt, 60-61; res chemist color chem, ETH Zurich, Switz, 62-67; res & develop chemist dye synthesis, Clayton Aniline Co, UK, 67-70; dir indust chem res, Klopman Div, Burlington Indusx, Inc, 70-87; sr scientist, Inst Textile Technol, Charlottesville, Va, 87-88; mgr & formulator indust org chems, Catawba-Charlab, Charlotte, NC, 88-90. *Concurrent Pos:* Consult, Indust Prod. *Mem:* Am Asn Textile Chemists & Colorists; Am Chem Soc; Swiss Asn Chemists & Colourists; Soc Dyers & Colourists. *Res:* Synthesis of dyes, pigments, polymers and textile auxiliaries; dispersion of dyes and pigments; preparation, dyeing, printing-discharge finishing of textile and industrial fabrics; chemical modification of polyester fibers; dyeing and printing of nomex; flame retardency of industrial and textile fabrics; liquid acid; basic and direct dyes; paper liquid dyes; granted 7 US patents. *Mailing Add:* 1008 White Pine Dr Lynchburg VA 24501. *Fax:* 804-239-5118

HUSSAR, DANIEL ALEXANDER, PHARMACY. *Current Pos:* From asst prof to prof, 66-75, dir dept, 71-75, dean fac, 75-84, REMINGTON PROF PHARM, PHILADELPHIA COL PHARM, 75- *Personal Data:* b Philadelphia, Pa, Feb 12, 41; m 67; c 3. *Educ:* Philadelphia Col Pharm & Sci, BS, 62, MS, 64, PhD(pharm), 67. *Mem:* Am Pharmaceut Asn; Am Col Pharm; Am Soc Hosp Pharmacists; Am Col Apothecaries; Drug Info Asn (treas, 72-74, pres, 77-78); Sigma Xi. *Res:* Aspects of antibiotic-metal ion interactions; protein-binding of drugs; drug interactions. *Mailing Add:* Philadelphia Col Pharm & Sci 600 S 43rd St Philadelphia PA 19104

HUSSELS MAUMENEE, IRENE E, OPHTHALMOLOGY, GENETICS. *Current Pos:* fel, Dept Med, Johns Hopkins Univ, 69-71, ophthal preceptorship, Wilmer Inst, Johns Hopkins Hosp, 69-71, from asst prof to assoc prof, 72-87, PROF OPHTHAL & PEDIAT, WILMER OPHTHAL INST, 87-, DIR, JOHNS HOPKINS HEREDITARY EYE DIS, 79- *Personal Data:* b Bad Pyrmont, Ger, Apr 30, 40. *Educ:* Univ Gottingen, MD, 64; Am Bd Ophthal, cert; Am Bd Med Genetics, cert. *Prof Exp:* Res asst, Univ Hawaii, 68; vis geneticist, Pop Genetics Lab, 68-69. *Concurrent Pos:* Consult, John F Kennedy Inst Visually & Ment Handicapped Children, 74-; dir, Low Vision Clin, Wilmer Inst, 77-88; vis prof, Fr Ophthal Soc, Paris & Fr Award Med, 88. *Mem:* AMA; Am Soc Human Genetics; Am Acad Ophthal; Asn Res Vision & Ophthal; Int Soc Genetic Eye Dis; Am Ophthal Soc; Pan Am Asn Ophthal. *Res:* Nosology and management in ophthalmic and general medical genetics; population genetics; computer application to genetic analysis; molecular genetics; over 200 publications on human genetics and eye diseases. *Mailing Add:* Johns Hopkins Hosp 600 N Wolfe St No 517 Baltimore MD 21205-2110

HUSSEY, ARTHUR M, II, GEOLOGY, MINERALOGY-PETROLOGY. *Current Pos:* from asst prof to assoc prof, 61-72, PROF GEOL, BOWDOIN COL, 72-, CHMN DEPT, 61- *Personal Data:* b Pittsburgh, Pa, Mar 9, 31; div; c 3. *Educ:* Pa State Univ, BS, 54; Univ Ill, PhD(geol), 61. *Prof Exp:* Vis asst prof geol, Purdue Univ, 60-61. *Concurrent Pos:* Mem, educ comt, Geol Soc Am, 90-, chmn, NE Sect. *Mem:* AAAS; Geol Soc Am; Geol Asn Can; Sigma Xi; Am Geophys Union. *Res:* Structural geology; igneous and metamorphic petrology, especially of the Northern New England Appalachians. *Mailing Add:* Dept Geol Bowdoin Col Brunswick ME 04011

HUSSEY, CHARLES LOGAN, ANALYTICAL CHEMISTRY, ELECTROCHEMISTRY. *Current Pos:* from asst prof to assoc prof, 78-87, PROF CHEM, UNIV MISS, 87- *Personal Data:* b San Diego, Calif, Dec 26, 47; m 71, Jolee Childs; c Charles T. *Educ:* Univ Miss, BS, 71, PhD(anal chem), 74. *Prof Exp:* Res chemist & lectr, F J Seiler Res Lab, Air Force Systs Command, USAF Acad, 74-78. *Mem:* Am Chem Soc; Electrochem Soc; Sigma Xi; Soc Electroanal Chem. *Res:* Molten salt electrochemistry; electrochemical studies of transition metal solutes in haloaluminate melts; electrodeposition; electroactive self-assembled monolayers; electrochemical nitration. *Mailing Add:* Dept Chem Univ Miss University MS 38677. *Fax:* 601-232-7300; *E-Mail:* chclh@chem1.olemiss.edu

HUSSEY, CLARA VERONICA, PATHOLOGY. *Current Pos:* RETIRED. *Personal Data:* b Milwaukee, Wis, Oct 24, 20. *Educ:* Mt Mary Col, BS, 47; Marquette Univ, MS, 50, MD, 61. *Honors & Awards:* Franklin V Taylor Award, Soc Eng Psychol. *Prof Exp:* Med technician, St Alban's Hosp, NY, 44-46; med technician, St Joseph's Hosp, Wis, 46-48; asst, Med Col Wis, 50-52, instr biochem, 52-64, from asst prof to prof path, 69-91; mem staff, Path Lab, Milwaukee Co Gen Hosp, 64-91. *Concurrent Pos:* Intern, Ind Univ, Med Ctr, 62; mem coun thrombosis, Am Heart Asn. *Mem:* Am Heart Asn; Int Soc Thrombosis & Haemostasis; Am Med Women's Asn. *Res:* Blood coagulation; study of hemorrhagic diseases regarding abnormalities and diagnostic tests. *Mailing Add:* 175 S Beaumont Ave Brookfield WI 53005

HUSSEY, EDWARD WALTER, ORGANIC CHEMISTRY, POLYMER CHEMISTRY. *Current Pos:* Chemist, E I du Pont de Nemours & Co, Inc, 65-76, sr res chem, 76-83, res assoc, 83-90, SR RES ASSOC, E I DU PONT DE NEMOURS & CO, 90- *Personal Data:* b Petaluma, Calif, Sept 3, 38; m 69, Anita Greenwald; c Laura, Claude, Christopher, Theresa & Stephen. *Educ:* Univ Nev, Reno, BS, 61, PhD(org chem), 65. *Mem:* Am Chem Soc. *Res:* Natural products; polymer science. *Mailing Add:* RR One Washington WV 26181

HUSSEY, KEITH MORGAN, GEOMORPHOLOGY. *Current Pos:* RETIRED. *Personal Data:* b Rock Island, Ill, Dec 2, 08; m 37; c 2. *Educ:* Augustana Col, AB, 36; La State Univ, MS, 39, PhD(geol), 40. *Prof Exp:* From instr to asst prof geol, Univ Houston, 40-46; assoc prof micropaleont, Univ Okla, 46-49; from assoc prof to prof geomorphol, Iowa State Univ, 49-79, head dept, 62-74. *Concurrent Pos:* Emer prof geomorphol, Iowa State Univ, 79- *Mem:* Fel Geol Soc Am; Am Asn Petrol Geol; Nat Asn Geol Teachers; fel Arctic Inst NAm; Am Geol Inst. *Res:* Photo interpretation; pediment development of Wyoming, Colorado and New Mexico piedmont areas; geomorphogeny of the Arctic Coatal Plain of Alaska; palynology of some Iowa coals. *Mailing Add:* 1910 Meadowlane Ave Ames IA 50010

HUSSEY, RICHARD SOMMERS, PLANT NEMATOLOGY. *Current Pos:* from asst prof to prof, 74-92, D W BROOKS DISTINGUISHED PROF NEMATOL, DEPT PLANT PATH, UNIV GA, 92- *Personal Data:* b Wheeling, WVa, Dec 18, 42; m 68; c 2. *Educ:* Miami Univ, AB, 65; Univ Md, MS, 68, PhD(plant path), 70. *Prof Exp:* Fel nematol, Dept Plant Path, NC State Univ, 70-73; chief nematologist, NC Dept Agr, 73-74. *Mem:* Fel Soc Nematologists; Sigma Xi; AAAS; fel Am Phytopath Soc; Coun Agr Sci & Technol. *Res:* Host-parasite relationships involving plant-parasitic nematodes; nematode management; plant resistance; nematode secretions; molecular basis of host-nematode interactions. *Mailing Add:* Dept Plant Path Univ Ga Athens GA 30602-7274

HUSSEY, ROBERT GREGORY, FLUID DYNAMICS. *Current Pos:* Asst physics, 57-62, from asst prof to assoc prof, 62-79, PROF PHYSICS, LA STATE UNIV, BATON ROUGE, 79-, ASSOC DEAN, COL BASIC SCI, 71- *Personal Data:* b Shreveport, La, May 15, 35; m 60; c 4. *Educ:* Univ Notre Dame, BS, 57; La State Univ, PhD(physics), 62. *Honors & Awards:* George B Pegram Award, Am Phys Soc, 82. *Mem:* Am Phys Soc; Am Asn Physics Teachers. *Res:* Flow of incompressible fluids; low Reynolds number flow. *Mailing Add:* Dept Physics & Astron La State Univ Baton Rouge LA 70803

HUSSIAN, RICHARD A, AGING, BEHAVIOR MODIFICATION. *Current Pos:* PSYCHOLOGIST & UNIT DIR, TERRELL STATE HOSP, 82- *Personal Data:* b Greensboro, NC, Aug 20, 52; m 79. *Educ:* Davidson Col, BA, 74; Univ NC-Greensboro, MA, 76, PhD(psychol), 78. *Prof Exp:* Psychologist, Evergreens, Inc, 78-80; psychologist, Guilford Co Ment Health, 80-82. *Concurrent Pos:* Ed, Int J Behav Geriat, 82-83; instr, Univ NC, Greensboro, 79-81, vis prof, 79-82; vis prof, Southwest Med Ctr, Dallas, Tex, 82- *Mem:* Am Psychol Asn; Asn Behav Analysis; Geront Soc Am. *Res:* Effects of environmental changes on the behavior of patients with progressive dementia. *Mailing Add:* 17601 Preston Rd Dallas TX 75252

HUSSON, SAMIR S, MANAGEMENT CONSULTING, SYSTEM & COMPONENT RELIABILITY. *Current Pos:* PRES & CONSULT, INT MGT SYST, 85- *Personal Data:* b Nazareth, Israel, June 5, 34; nat US citizen; m 57; c 1. *Educ:* Greenville Col, BS, 57; Mich State Univ, BSEE, 58, MS, 59. *Prof Exp:* Develop engr, IBM, 60-69, staff, Syst Res Inst, 69-72, sr engr design automation, 73-78, dir Tech Publ, 78-81, dir Quality Inst, 81-85. *Concurrent Pos:* Vis prof comput sci, Yale Univ, 72-73. *Mem:* Fel Inst Elec & Electronics Engrs; Comput Soc; Asn Comput Mach. *Res:* Micro programming system, concepts, organization and designs; microprogrammable systems architecture and implementation; numerous publications. *Mailing Add:* 9855 Bankside Dr Roswell GA 30076

HUSSONG, DONALD MACGREGOR, MARINE GEOPHYSICS. *Current Pos:* Res asst, Univ Hawaii, 66-68, jr geophysicist, 69-72, from asst geophysicist to assoc geophysicist, 72-82, GEOPHYSICIST & PROF, HAWAII INST GEOPHYS, 82-; UNIV HAWAII; SEAFLOOR SURV INT. *Personal Data:* b Paterson, NJ, Aug 31, 42; c 3. *Educ:* Princeton Univ, BSE, 64; Univ Hawaii, MS, 67, PhD(geol, geophys), 72. *Concurrent Pos:* Coordr, Nazca Plate Proj, Int Decade Ocean Explor, Univ Hawaii, 72-79; tech adv, UN comt Coord Joint Prospecting, 74-75; chmn & mem, Active Margins Panel, Int Prog Ocean Drilling, Joint Oceanog Insts Deep Earth Sampling, 77-80; comt chmn, Ocean Crystal Dynamics Planning Comt, 78-80; mem, Oceanog Proposal Rev Panel, NSF, 80-81 & planning comt, Ocean Drilling Prog, 85-; prin investr, Sea MARC II proj, 81- *Mem:* Am Geophys Union. *Res:* Marine geophysics related to the tectonic evolution of the oceanic crust using seismic refraction experiments with ocean bottom seismometers; submarine morphology and tectonics using side-scan sonar and swath bathymetry mapping. *Mailing Add:* 1929 Bonair Dr SW Seattle WA 98116

HUSSUNG, KARL FREDERICK, ORGANIC CHEMISTRY. *Current Pos:* From asst prof to assoc prof, 57-63, PROF CHEM, MURRAY STATE UNIV, 63- *Personal Data:* b Louisville, Ky, Feb 19, 31; m 53; c 4. *Educ:* Murray State Col, BS, 53; Univ Louisville, PhD(chem), 57. *Mem:* Sigma Xi; Am Chem Soc. *Res:* 2-pyrones, benzotriazoles and cancer chemotherapeutics. *Mailing Add:* 900 Meadow Lane Murray KY 42071-3311

HUST, JEROME GERHARDT, PHYSICS. *Current Pos:* Physicist thermodyn, 61-66, PHYSICIST SOLID STATE, NAT BUR STAND, 66- *Personal Data:* b Logan Co, NDak, May 21, 32; m 55; c 4. *Educ:* SDak Sch Mines & Technol, BS, 58, MS, 60. *Mem:* Am Soc Testing & Mat. *Res:* Thermophysical properties of solids; numerical data analysis; data evaluation and critical analysis; thermodynamic properties of fluids. *Mailing Add:* 222 Iroquois Dr Boulder CO 80303

HUSTED, JOHN EDWIN, GEOLOGY, NATURAL RESOURCES. *Current Pos:* res scientist, Eng Exp Sta, Ga Inst Technol, 58-63, head, Mineral Eng Group, 60-66, assoc prof geol, 63-67, res prof, 67-71, prof, 71-74, prof chem eng, 74-84, dir geol, 80-84, EMER PROF MINERAL ENG, SCH CHEM ENG, GA INST TECHNOL, 84-, EMER DIR, GA MINING & MINERAL RESOURCES INST, 84- *Personal Data:* b Lucasville, Ohio, Oct 12, 15; m 42, Kathryn Stewart; c Stewart W & Mary H (Ferraro). *Educ:* Hampden Sydney Col, BS, 39; Univ Va, MA, 42; Fla State Univ, PhD(geol), 70. *Prof Exp:* Sci teacher high sch, Va, 38-40; mem staff, US Geol Surv, 42, chemist, 42-44, geologist, 44-45; plant chemist, Consol Feldspar Corp, 45-46; instr geol & chem, Wash & Lee Univ, 46-48; jr geologist, Humble Oil & Ref Co, 48-49; assoc prof geol & head dept, Trinity Univ Tex, 49-51; res geologist, Va Iron Coal & Coke Co, 51-55; prin geologist, Battelle Mem Inst, 55-57; mem staff, Capital Univ, 58. *Concurrent Pos:* Consult, Va Iron Coal & Coke Co, 47-51, Slick-Morman Oil Co, 50-51, Transcontinental Oil Co, 52-55 & Battelle Mem Inst, 57-58; fel, NSF Sci Fac, 66-67; Civil Defense Exec Reserve, US Dept Interior, 69-90. *Mem:* Am Inst Mining, Metall & Petrol Eng; Geol Soc Am; Am Asn Petrol Geologists. *Res:* Mineral engineering; mineral and fuel resources; economic and structural geology; tectonophysics. *Mailing Add:* 2844 Woodthrush Dr Roanoke VA 24018-5043. *E-Mail:* rockman5@juno.com

HUSTED, RUSSELL FOREST, RENAL ION TRANSPORT. *Current Pos:* ASST RES SCIENTIST, DEPT MED, UNIV IOWA, 82- *Personal Data:* b Lafayette, Ind, Apr 4, 50; m 88, Ruth E Hurlburt; c Jacqueline & Randall. *Educ:* Colo State Univ, BS, 72; Univ Utah, PhD(pharmacol), 76. *Prof Exp:*

Fel, Dept Med, Univ Iowa, 76-79, asst res scientist, 79-81; asst prof, Dept Med, Univ Conn, 81-82. *Mem:* Sigma Xi; Soc Gen Physiol; Am Physiol Soc; Am Soc Nephrology; NY Acad Sci; AAAS. *Res:* Papillary collecting duct of the kidney exerts the final control of urine composition; transport of sodium, chloride, and acid by cultured cells isolated from rat collecting ducts is studied to determine the effects of steroids and the role of the kidney in the development of hypertension. *Mailing Add:* 317 Med Labs Iowa City IA 52242. Fax: 319-356-7893

HUSTON, ERNEST LEE, MATERIALS SCIENCE, METALLURGY. *Current Pos:* MGR ALLOY TECH, ENERGIZER POWER SYSTS, 92- *Personal Data:* b Uniontown, Pa, Mar 27, 40; m 76; c 2. *Educ:* Lafayette Col, BS, 62; Northwestern Univ, PhD(mat sci), 68. *Prof Exp:* Technician, Alcoa Res Labs, Aluminium Co Am, 60; res asst mat sci, Northwestern Univ, 63-68; res metallurgist, Paul D Merica Res Labs, Int Nickel Co, Inc, 68-72, energy systs sect mgr, Inco Res & Develop Ctr, 77-80; tech mgr, Ergenics Div, MPD Tech Corp, 80-84; pres, Ergenics Inc, 84-86, mgr spec projs, 86-92. *Concurrent Pos:* Consult, Tempel Steel Co Chicago, 67-68. *Mem:* AAAS; Am Soc Metals; Sigma Xi. *Res:* Phase equilibria; phase transformation; thermodynamics; magnetic alloys; magnetostriction; metal hydrides; photoelectrochemistry; getter alloys. *Mailing Add:* Energizer Power Systs Hwy 441 N Gainesville FL 32614

HUSTON, JEFFREY CHARLES, ENGINEERING MECHANICS, BIOMECHANICS. *Current Pos:* from asst prof to prof eng sci & mech, 76-90, PROF AEROSPACE ENG, ENG MECH & BIOMED ENG, IOWA STATE UNIV, 90- *Personal Data:* b Johnstown, Pa, Jan 30, 51; m 74, Patricia Lemmon; c Tiffany & Roger. *Educ:* Ill Inst Technol, BS, 72; WVa Univ, MS, 73, PhD(mech eng), 75. *Honors & Awards:* Teetor Award, Soc Automotive Engrs, 80; Michol Award, Am Soc Eng Educ, 84. *Prof Exp:* Mech engr res, Morgantown Energy Res Ctr, Energy Res Develop Admin, 75-76. *Concurrent Pos:* Lectr asst prof, WVa Univ, 75-76. *Mem:* Am Soc Mech Engrs; Am Soc Eng Educ; Soc Automotive Engrs; Sigma Xi; Nat Soc Prof Engrs; Biomed Eng Soc. *Res:* Biodynamics of human body motion; vehicles dynamics/recreational vehicles; multimedia engineering education. *Mailing Add:* 535 Valley West Ct West Des Moines IA 50265

HUSTON, JOHN LEWIS, PHYSICAL CHEMISTRY, INORGANIC CHEMISTRY. *Current Pos:* from asst prof to prof, 52-84, EMER PROF CHEM, LOYOLA UNIV CHICAGO, 84- *Personal Data:* b Lancaster, Ohio, Aug 19, 19; m 63, Mary Margaret Lally. *Educ:* Oberlin Col, AB, 42; Univ Calif, PhD(chem), 46. *Prof Exp:* From instr to asst prof, Ore State Col, 46-52. *Concurrent Pos:* Consult, Argonne Nat Lab, 65-89. *Mem:* Am Chem Soc; Sigma Xi. *Res:* Inorganic tracers; nonaqueous solvents; kinetics in solution; isotopic exchange reactions; xenon and synthetic inorganic chemistry; organic and inorganic fluorine chemistry. *Mailing Add:* 4401 Keeney Skokie IL 60076-3203

HUSTON, KEITH ARTHUR, RESEARCH ADMINISTRATION. *Current Pos:* EMER PROF, OHIO STATE UNIV, 89- *Personal Data:* b Cleveland, Ohio, Mar 18, 26; m 61. *Educ:* Univ Wis, BS, 49, MS, 50, PhD(dairy husb), 51. *Prof Exp:* Assoc prof exten dairy cattle breeding, Va Polytech, 51-54; assoc prof dairy cattle genetics, Kans State Univ, 54-63, prof dairy husb, 63-69, asst dir, Kans Agr Exp Sta, 69-71, prof & assoc dir, 71-75, adj prof vet path, 72; prof animal sci, Univ Minn, 75-79, dir, Agr Exp Sta, 75-79; dir-at-large, NCent Asn, State Agr Exp Sta, 79-89. *Concurrent Pos:* Adj prof dairy sci, Ohio State Univ, 79-89. *Mem:* AAAS; Am Soc Animal Sci; Am Dairy Sci Asn; Am Genetic Asn. *Res:* Dairy cattle breeding; pathological genetics. *Mailing Add:* 1689 Arthur Dr Wooster OH 44691-1537

HUSTON, MERVYN JAMES, PHARMACOLOGY. *Current Pos:* RETIRED. *Personal Data:* b Ashcroft, BC, Sept 4, 12; m 38; c 2. *Educ:* Univ Alta, BSc, 37, MSc, 40; Univ Wash, Seattle, PhD(pharmacol), 43. *Hon Degrees:* LLD, Dalhousie Univ, 82; DSc, Univ Alta, 88. *Honors & Awards:* Squibb Pan-Am Pharmaceut Award, 71; Stephen Leacock Award, 96. *Prof Exp:* From lectr to asst prof pharm, Sch Pharm, Univ Alta, 39-46, actg dir, 46-48, dir, 48-55, dean fac pharm, 55-78, emer prof, 78-91. *Concurrent Pos:* Chmn, Can Conf Pharmaceut Facs, 48-49; mem, Can Drug Adv Comt, 64-70; sci ed, Can J Pharmaceut Sci, 65-70, ed-in-chief, 70-78; mem coun, Int Pharmaceut Fedn, 67-70; pres, Can Found Advan Pharm, 69-70. *Mem:* Am Pharmaceut Asn; Can Pharmaceut Asn (pres, 68-69). *Res:* Effect of drugs on tissue respiration. *Mailing Add:* Fac Pharm Univ Alta Edmonton AB T6G 2N8 Can

HUSTON, NORMAN EARL, NUCLEAR PHYSICS, TECHNICAL MANAGEMENT. *Current Pos:* RETIRED. *Personal Data:* b Jefferson, Iowa, Jan 24, 19; m 43; c 3. *Educ:* Univ Calif, AB, 43; Univ Southern Calif, PhD(physics), 52. *Prof Exp:* Physicist, Radiation Lab, Univ Calif, 43-44; physicist, Atomics Int Div, NAm Aviation Corp, 47, res engr, 50-53, supt appl physics, 54-56, group leader instrumentation & control, 57-59, sr tech specialist, 60-61, chief tech oper, 61-62, dir radiation tech & instrumentation, 63-66; prof & dir Instrumentation Systs Ctr, Univ Wis-Madison, 66-84, emer prof nuclear eng & consult engr, 84. *Concurrent Pos:* Dir, Ocean Eng Labs, 67-70; mem comt, Interplay Eng in Biol & Med, Nat Acad Eng, 68-72; dir, Adv Ctr Med Technol & Systs, Univ Wis-Madison, 72-78; UN Expert on Mission Singapore Inst Stand & Indust Res, 72; mem fact finding team on instrumentation req on mission to Nat Res Ctr, Cairo, Egypt, NSF, 74 & workshop team on sci instrumentation & biomed eng on mission to Rome, Italy & Cairo, Egypt, NSF, 75, prof leader mgt systs labs instruments, Nat Res Ctr, Cairo, 76, consult, 75-76 & prof leader, Egypt Sci & Technol Proj, Nat Res Ctr, Agency Int Develop, Cairo, 77; mem adv team to Saudi Arabian Nat Ctr Sci & Tech, NSF, 81; consult, World Bank & Indonesian Ministry Educ & Cult, 83. *Mem:* Fel AAAS; Am Phys Soc; Am Nuclear Soc; fel Instrument Soc Am (secy, 78, pres, 79); fel Inst Measurement & Control. *Res:* Reactor physics; instrumentation and control; radiation effects; radiation instrumentation; gaseous discharges; technical marketing; biomedical engineering; research management. *Mailing Add:* 5025 Sheboygan Ave Madison WI 53705-2811

HUSTON, ROBERT JAMES, AERONAUTICAL ENGINEERING. *Current Pos:* RETIRED. *Personal Data:* b Riley Co, Kans, Apr 30, 31; m 52; c 1. *Educ:* Univ Kans, BS, 58, MS, 61; Stanford Univ, dipl sys, 72. *Honors & Awards:* NASA Except Serv Medal; Howard Hughes Award, Am Helicopter Soc. *Prof Exp:* Res engr helicopters verticle takeoff & landing, Flight Res Br, Langley Res Ctr, NASA, 58-70, asst br head helicopters, 70-72, proj mgr, Rotor Systs Res Aircraft Proj Off, 72-76, asst chief helicopters, Flight Res Br, 76-78, proj mgr risk anal, Graphite Fibers Risk Anal Prog, 78-80, mgr Rotorcraft Res & Technol, 80-85 & 86-88, actg asst dir aeronaut, NASA Hq, 85-86, spec asst to dir struct, 89-96. *Mem:* Am Helicopter Soc; Am Inst Aeronaut & Astronaut. *Res:* Flight dynamics of helicopter and vertical takeoff and landing aircraft. *Mailing Add:* Langley Res Ctr NASA Hampton VA 23665

HUSTON, RONALD L, DYNAMICS, BIOMECHANICS. *Current Pos:* From asst prof to prof, 62-70, head, Dept Eng Analysis, 69-75, DIR INST APPL INTERDISCIPLINARY RES, UNIV CINCINNATI, 71-, PROF MECH, 77- *Personal Data:* b Central City, Pa, Aug 5, 37; m 56, Barbara Howe; c Thomas R, Dryver R & Suzanne H (Phillips). *Educ:* Univ Pa, BS, 59, MS, 61, PhD(eng mech), 62. *Honors & Awards:* Teetor Award, Soc Automotive Engrs, 78. *Concurrent Pos:* Div dir, NSF, 78-79; actg sr vpres & provost, Univ Cincinnati, 82-83. *Mem:* Soc Automotive Engrs; Am Soc Mech Engrs; Am Soc Eng Educ; Am Inst Aeronaut & Astronaut; Am Soc Biomech. *Res:* Multibody mechanics; accident reconstruction; crash-victim simulation; applied mathematics; finite element theory; robotics; multibody dynamics; gearing and transmissions. *Mailing Add:* PO Box 210072 202G Old Ser Bldg Univ Cincinnati Cincinnati OH 45221-0072

HUSTRULID, WILLIAM A, rock mechanics, mineral engineering, for more information see previous edition

HUSZAR, GABOR, BIOCHEMISTRY, MALE INFERTILITY. *Current Pos:* asst prof, 75-80, ASSOC PROF OBSTET, GYNECOL & PEDIAT, MED SCH, 81-, DIR, UTERINE PHYSIOL UNIT, 79-, DIR, SPERM PHYSIOL, YALE UNIV, 83- *Personal Data:* b Budapest, Hungary; m 65; c 2. *Educ:* Med Univ Budapest, MD, 63. *Prof Exp:* Resident obstet & gynec, Univ Hosp, Med Univ Budapest, 63-66; res fel muscle biochem, Retina Found, Boston, Mass, 67-70, Boston Biomed Res Inst, 70-71 & biochem, Harvard Univ, 71-74. *Concurrent Pos:* Res fel neurol, Harvard Med Sch, 68-70; Mass Heart Asn res grant biochem, 70-71; Nat Inst Child Health & Human Develop spec fel, 71-74. *Mem:* AAAS; Am Chem Soc; Biophys Soc; Fedn Am Soc Biol Chemists; Soc Gynec Invest; Am Fertil Soc; Am Soc Androl. *Res:* Male fertility; myometrial contractility; biology and biochemistry of the uterine cervix; sperm fertility; human sperm physiology and biochemistry. *Mailing Add:* Sch Med Yale Univ 333 Cedar St New Haven CT 06510-3219

HUSZCZUK, ANDREW HUSZCZA, RESPIRATORY, METABOLIC & FITNESS EVALUATION EQUIPMENT CONTROL OF RESPIRATION IN VARYING METABOLIC STATES. *Current Pos:* DIR RES & DEVELOP, VACUMED, 93-; VOL RES PROF, CALIF STATE UNIV, LONG BEACH, 93- *Personal Data:* b Wilno, Poland, Oct 7, 39; m 88, Beata Brzezinska; c Paulina & Agata. *Educ:* Warsaw Polytech, MS, 64; Polish Acad Sci, PhD(physiol & neurophysiol), 72. *Prof Exp:* Sr res asst, Polish Acad Sci, 66-72, dir medipan sci instruments, 72-73, asst prof, 73-79; vis scientist, Univ Calif, Los Angeles, 79-82, res assoc, 82-88, assoc researcher, 88-93. *Mem:* Am Phys Soc; Am Heart Asn. *Res:* Physiology, role of muscular perfusion in stimulation of breathing during exercise and inhibition of breathing in sleep disorder (SIDS, sleep apnea); bioengineering, design of improved equipment for testing and evaluation of metabolism and fitness. *Mailing Add:* 940 E Third St No 13 Long Beach CA 90802. Fax: 805-654-8759; E-Mail: vacumed@compuserve.com

HUT, PIET, THEORETICAL ASTROPHYSICS, STELLAR DYNAMICS. *Current Pos:* mem, 81-84, PROF, INST ADVAN STUDY, PRINCETON, 85- *Personal Data:* b Sept 26, 52; Neth citizen. *Educ:* Univ Utrecht, Neth, BSc, 74, MSc, 77; Univ Amsterdam, PhD(astron), 81. *Prof Exp:* Res & teaching asst, Inst Theoret Physics, Univ Utrecht, Neth, 77-78 & Astron Inst, Univ Amsterdam, Neth, 78-81. *Concurrent Pos:* Sloan Found fel, 85; asst prof, dept astron, Univ Calif, Berkeley, 85; sr vis fel, Japanese Soc Prom Sci, 84S & 89. *Mem:* Int Astron Union; Am Astron Soc; Dutch Astron Union; Royal Astron Soc. *Res:* Theoretical astrophysics, especially stellar dynamics; impacts of comets and asteroids and their relation to mass extinctions; astrophysical computer science. *Mailing Add:* Inst Advan Study Princeton NJ 08540

HUTCHCROFT, ALAN CHARLES, ORGANIC CHEMISTRY. *Current Pos:* From asst prof to assoc prof, Rockford Col, 67-80, prof chem & chmn dept, 80-87, chair Div Sci, Math & Nursing, 87-96, GORDON H & VIOLET J BARTELS PROF, ROCKFORD COL, 84-,. *Personal Data:* b Greeley, Colo, Mar 17, 41; m 65, Elaine Goff; c Eric C & Sara E. *Educ:* Kalamazoo Col, BA, 63; Univ Mich, MS, 65, PhD(chem), 69. *Concurrent Pos:* Consult, Pierce Chem Co, 77- *Mem:* Sigma Xi; Am Chem Soc. *Res:* Ferrocene chemistry, including attempted synthesis and study of novel bridged ferrocene compounds. *Mailing Add:* Dept Chem Rockford Col Rockford IL 61108-2393. Fax: 815-226-4119; E-Mail: ahutchcroft@rockford.edu

HUTCHCROFT, CHARLES DENNETT, agronomy; deceased, see previous edition for last biography

HUTCHENS, JOHN OLIVER, toxicology; deceased, see previous edition for last biography

HUTCHENS, TYRA THORNTON, clinical pathology, nuclear medicine, for more information see previous edition

HUTCHEON, DUNCAN ELLIOT, SCIENCE EDUCATION. *Current Pos:* from asst prof to prof pharmacol & from instr to prof med, 59-91, EMER PROF PHARMACOL & MED, UNIV MED & DENT NJ, 91- *Personal Data:* b Kindersley, Sask, June 21, 22; nat US; wid; c R Gordon, Jean M (Daleo), Marcia L (Gale) & Megan M (Smith). *Educ:* Univ Toronto, MD, 45, BSc, 47; Oxford Univ, DPhil(pharmacol), 50; Am Bd Internal Med, dipl. *Honors & Awards:* Clin Investr Award, Am Col Clin Pharmacol. *Prof Exp:* Assoc prof pharmacol, Univ Sask, 50-53; sr pharmacologist, Pfizer Therapeut Inst, 53-56; resident med, Jersey City Med Ctr, 57-59; pres, Princeton Inst Environ Med, 80-88. *Concurrent Pos:* Ed, J Clin Pharmacol, 77-84, emer ed, 85-; ed, CINE Inc, 90- *Mem:* Ecol Soc Am; Soc Exp Biol & Med; fel Am Col Physicians; Am Soc Clin Pharmacol; Am Lung Asn. *Res:* Health effects and costs of atmospheric pollution. *Mailing Add:* MSB 1-657 Univ Med & Dent NJ Med Sch Newark NJ 07103. *Fax:* 973-982-4554

HUTCHERSON, JOSEPH WILLIAM, ATOMIC PHYSICS, APPLIED MATHEMATICS. *Current Pos:* RETIRED. *Personal Data:* b Scooba, Miss, Sept 12, 40; m 64; c 1. *Educ:* Univ Tenn, Chattanooga, BA, 62; Vanderbilt Univ, MS, 64, PhD(physics), 68. *Prof Exp:* Asst prof physics, Southern Missionary Col, 67-68 & Walla Walla Col, 68-69; asst prof math, Univ Tenn, Chattanooga, 69-75, assoc prof math, 75-90. *Mem:* Math Asn Am; Sigma Xi; Am Asn Univ Professors; Am Phys Soc. *Res:* Vacuum ultraviolet spectra of atoms and molecules. *Mailing Add:* 626 Greenslake Circle Rossville GA 30741

HUTCHERSON, R KENNETH, PLASMA PHYSICS. *Current Pos:* RES SCIENTIST, USN, 84- *Personal Data:* b Roanoke, Va, Apr 4, 61. *Educ:* Univ Va, BS, 83; Va Polytech Inst & State Univ, MS, 87. *Mem:* Am Phys Soc. *Mailing Add:* 2106 Broughton Dr Beverly MA 01915

HUTCHESON, DAVID PAUL, ANIMAL NUTRITION, BIOSTATISTICS. *Current Pos:* MEM STAFF, TEX AGR EXP STA, TEX A&M UNIV. *Personal Data:* b Ft Worth, Tex, Nov 5, 41; m 66; c 2. *Educ:* Tex A&M Univ, BS, 63; Univ Mo-Columbia, MS, 67, PhD(animal husb), 70. *Prof Exp:* Asst prof vet physiol & pharmacol, 70-73, assoc prof animal sci, Univ Mo-Columbia, 73-, biostatistician Sinclair Res Farm, 70- *Mem:* AAAS; Am Asn Animal Sci; Am Soc Vet Physiol & Pharmacol. *Res:* Design and theoretical models of protein and energy metabolism. *Mailing Add:* Animal-Agr Consult Inc PO Box 50367 Amarillo TX 79159

HUTCHESON, ELDRIDGE TILMON, III, BIOCHEMISTRY. *Current Pos:* LAB SUPVR, TEX STATE HEALTH DEPT, 94- *Personal Data:* b Atlanta, Tex, Dec 23, 42; m 66; c 1. *Educ:* Southwest Tex State Univ, BS, 66, MA, 68; Univ Tex, Austin, PhD(chem), 71; Am Bd Clin Chem, dipl, 77. *Prof Exp:* Clayton Found Biochem Inst fel, Univ Tex, Austin, 71; sr scientist & protein chemist, Flow Labs, Inc, 71-72; instr & NIH fel, Univ Tenn, Memphis, 72-73, asst prof biochem, Ctr Health Sci, 73-75; res chemist clin chem, Salem Vet Admin Med Ctr, 75-82; asst prof path, Sch Med, Univ Va, 77-82; consult, 82-93. *Concurrent Pos:* Res chemist connective tissue, Memphis Vet Admin Hosp, 73-75; dir, Biolabs Med Lab, Roanoke, 77-82. *Mem:* Am Asn Clin Chem; Am Chem Soc. *Res:* Protein structure and function; enzymology; collagen structure and function; clinical chemistry; nutrition. *Mailing Add:* 411 Storeywood Dr San Antonio TX 78213

HUTCHESON, HARVIE LEON, JR, PLANT ECOLOGY. *Current Pos:* From asst prof to assoc prof, 66-88, PROF BOT, SDAK STATE UNIV, 88- *Personal Data:* b Tipton, Okla, Oct 6, 37; m 60; c 2. *Educ:* Okla State Univ, BS, 60, MS, 63; Univ Okla, PhD(plant ecol), 65. *Concurrent Pos:* NSF res grant-in-aid, Biol Sta, Univ Okla, 66. *Mem:* Ecol Soc Am; Soc Range Mgt. *Res:* Grassland ecosystem analysis; vegetation in relation to geological materials. *Mailing Add:* Dept Biol SDak State Univ Box 2207b Brookings SD 57007-0001

HUTCHESON, KERMIT, BIOSTATISTICS. *Current Pos:* PROF STATIST, UNIV GA, 67- *Personal Data:* b Wrightsville, Ga, Dec 8, 29; m 50; c 3. *Educ:* Ga Southern Col, BS, 53; Univ Miami, MS, 57; Va Polytech Inst, PhD(statist), 70. *Prof Exp:* Instr math, Miami Univ, 59-61; asst prof, Radford Col, 62-67. *Mem:* Am Statist Asn; Sigma Xi. *Res:* Ecological diversity. *Mailing Add:* Dept Statist Univ Ga Athens GA 30602-4066

HUTCHESON, PAUL HENRY, APPLIED MATHEMATICS, COMPUTER SCIENCE. *Current Pos:* RETIRED. *Personal Data:* b Nashville, Tenn, Dec 7, 28; m 50; c 6. *Educ:* David Lipscomb Col, BA, 50; Peabody Col, MA, 51; Univ Fla, PhD(math chem), 60. *Prof Exp:* Instr math & chem, Fla Col, 51-54; asst prof math, Univ Tampa, 54-57; from asst prof to prof math, Mid Tenn State Univ, 60-95, dir, Comput Ctr, 63-78. *Concurrent Pos:* Asst prof, Space Inst, Univ Tenn, 64-68; consult, ARO, Inc, Arnold Air Force Sta, 58-70. *Mem:* Am Math Soc; Math Asn Am; Asn Comput Mach. *Res:* Linear elasticity; reflector design; remote sensing; landsat processing. *Mailing Add:* 921 DeJarnett Lane Murfreesboro TN 37130

HUTCHIN, RICHARD ARIEL, MATHEMATICAL PHYSICS. *Current Pos:* treas, 81-93, PRES, NOVON, INC, 93-; CONSULT, 80- *Personal Data:* b Lafayette, Ind, May 9, 46; div; c 3. *Educ:* Princeton Univ, AB, 67; Stanford Univ, MS, 68, PhD(physics), 70. *Honors & Awards:* Kusaka Physics Prize; Technol Achievement Award, Soc Photogram & Instrumentation Engrs. *Prof Exp:* Fel physics, State Univ NY, 70-72; staff scientist, Itek Corp 72-74, prin scientist, 75, sect mgr electrooptics, 75-76, dept mgr advan anal, 76-77, chief scientist, 77-79. *Mem:* Optical Soc Am; Sigma Xi; Soc Photogram & Instrumentation Engrs. *Res:* Compensated imaging through turbulence; electro-optical reconnaisance; space optics; optical computing; active optics; active mirrors; pattern recognition; high energy laser beam control; speckle interferometry; optical tracking and acquisition; unconventional imaging; laser defense systems. *Mailing Add:* 25436 Cumberland Lane Calabasas CA 91302. *Fax:* 818-880-5099; *E-Mail:* rahutchin@aol.com

HUTCHINGS, BRIAN LAMAR, MICROBIAL BIOCHEMISTRY. *Current Pos:* prof biol sci & chmn dept, Wright State Univ, 68-72, dean, Col Sci & Eng, 73-84, distinguished serv prof, 84-85, EMER PROF, WRIGHT STATE UNIV, 85- *Personal Data:* b South Jordan, Utah, June 11, 15; m 38; c Robert L, Barbara A, Stephen B & David C. *Educ:* Brigham Young Univ, BS, 38; Univ Wis, MS, 40, PhD(biochem), 42. *Prof Exp:* Asst, Univ Wis, 40-42; res chemist, Lederle Labs Div, Am Cyanamid Co, 42-49, head dept biochem, 49-52, asst dir chem & biol res, 52-56, dir biochem res, 56-65, sr res fel, 65-68. *Mem:* Fel AAAS; Am Chem Soc; Am Soc Biol Chemists; fel NY Acad Sci; Am Soc Microbiol; Soc Exp Biol & Med. *Res:* Chemistry of vitamins, anti-malarials and antibiotics; microbial transport; biochemistry of membranes. *Mailing Add:* 3228 S Espana Circle Aurora CO 80013-3729

HUTCHINGS, DONALD EDWARD, BEHAVIORAL TERATOLOGY. *Current Pos:* instr psychiat, 66-68, res assoc, 68-72, ASST PROF MED PSYCHOL, DEPT PSYCHIAT, COLUMBIA UNIV, 72-, ASST PROF MED PSYCHOL, DEPT PEDIAT, 75-; RES SCIENTIST, NY STATE PSYCHIAT INST, 74- *Personal Data:* b Chicago, Ill, Jan 9, 34; m 60; c 3. *Educ:* Lake Forest Col, BA, 59; Univ Chicago, MA, 63, PhD(psychol), 65. *Prof Exp:* From res scientist to sr res scientist, NY State Psychiat Inst, 63-74. *Concurrent Pos:* Adj asst prof, Dept Psychol, Columbia Univ, 66- & Barnard Col, 71- *Mem:* Am Psychol Asn; Teratol Soc; AAAS; Int Soc Develop Psychobiol; Sigma Xi. *Res:* Developmental behavior toxicology; effects of prenatal drug exposure on behavior of the offspring. *Mailing Add:* 722 W 168th St New York NY 10032

HUTCHINGS, JOHN BARRIE, ASTRONOMY. *Current Pos:* Fel astron, 67-69, RES SCIENTIST, NAT RES COUN CAN, 69- *Personal Data:* b Johannesburg, SAfrica, July 18, 41. *Educ:* Univ Witwatersrand, BSc, 62, BSc(Hons), 63, MSc, 64; Cambridge Univ, PhD(astron), 67. *Honors & Awards:* Beals Award, 82. *Mem:* Fel Royal Astron Soc; Am Astron Soc; Int Astron Union; Can Astron Soc; fel Royal Soc Can. *Res:* Optical and radio imaging and spectroscopy of quasi-stellar objects and active galaxies; optical and ultraviolet astronomy research into early type stars with particular interest in evolution, mass loss, rotation, masses and dimensions; x-ray sources and cataclysmic variables; space instrumentation including Hubble Space Telescope. *Mailing Add:* Dom Astrophys Observ 5071 W Saanich Rd Victoria BC V8X 4M6 Can. *E-Mail:* hutchings@dao.nrc.ca

HUTCHINGS, L(EROI) E(ARL), CHEMICAL ENGINEERING. *Current Pos:* RETIRED. *Personal Data:* b Northfield, Minn, Aug 3, 20; m 49; c 2. *Educ:* Univ Mich, BSE, 43, MS, 44; Northwestern Univ, PhD(chem eng), 48. *Prof Exp:* Process control engr, US Rubber Co, 43; res assoc, Univ Mich, 44-45; div dir process & prod res, Pure Oil Co, 48-61; assoc dir res, Great Lakes Res Corp, 61-65, mgr tech serv, Great Lakes Carbon Corp, 65-69; sr coordr eng res & develop, Universal Oil Prod Co, Des Plaines, 69-82. *Mem:* Am Chem Soc. *Res:* Petroleum coke; unit operations; hydrotreating. *Mailing Add:* 1002 W Gregory Mt Prospect IL 60056-2212

HUTCHINGS, WILLIAM FRANK, MECHANICAL ENGINEERING. *Current Pos:* proj engr, Genera Signal Corp, 70-71, mgr design eng, 71-76, mgr prod stand & develop, 76-82, dir res & prod develop, lightnin, 82-95, VPRES ENG, GENERA SIGNAL CORP, 95- *Personal Data:* b Rochester, NY, July 13, 38; m 64; c 3. *Educ:* Case Western Reserve Univ, BS, 60; Univ Rochester, MS, 69. *Prof Exp:* Design engr, Cornell Aeronaut Lab, 61-66; supv engr, Consol Vacuum Corp, 66-70. *Mem:* Am Soc Mech Engrs; Am Soc Metals. *Res:* Fluid dynamics of mixing along with the dynamics of mixing machinery; development of fluid mixers. *Mailing Add:* 19 Cannock Dr Fairport NY 14450

HUTCHINS, CLYDE, CHEMISTRY. *Current Pos:* TECHNOL SUPVR, E I DUPONT CO, 78- *Personal Data:* b Sprinfield, Vt, Feb 11, 51. *Educ:* Wesleyan Col, BA, 73; Cornell Univ, MA, 76, PhD(chem), 78. *Mem:* Am Chem Soc; Sigma Xi. *Res:* Chemistry. *Mailing Add:* E I Dupont Co Yerkes Plant PO Box 88 Buffalo NY 14207

HUTCHINS, GROVER MACGREGOR, ANATOMIC PATHOLOGY, AUTOPSY PATHOLOGY. *Current Pos:* from instr to assoc prof, 66-83, PROF PATH, JOHNS HOPKINS UNIV SCH MED, 83- *Personal Data:* b Baltimore, Md, Aug 17, 32; m 56, Loretta Bajkowska; c Diana, David & Sally. *Educ:* Johns Hopkins Univ, BA, 57, MD, 61; Am Bd Path, cert anat, 72 & pediat, 90. *Prof Exp:* Resident path, Johns Hopkins Hosp, 64-65; res fel, Scripps Clin & Res Found, 65-66. *Concurrent Pos:* Assoc dir autopsy path, 67-76, dir, 76- *Mem:* Col Am Pathologists; Am Heart Asn; Int Acad Pathologists; Soc Cardiovasc Path; Soc Pediat Path; Teratol Soc. *Res:* Studies in human cardiovascular, pulmonary and pediatric pathology. *Mailing Add:* Dept Path Johns Hopkins Hosp 600 N Wolfe St Baltimore MD 21287

HUTCHINS, GUDRUN A, TRANSMISSION ELECTROMICROSCOPY. *Current Pos:* CORP RES SCIENTIST, GEN ELEC, 90- *Personal Data:* b Berlin, Ger, July 20, 38. *Educ:* Brown Univ, BS, 59; Williams Col, MS, 62. *Prof Exp:* Res scientist, Sprague Elec Co, 60-90. *Mem:* Am Phys Soc; Micros Soc Am. *Mailing Add:* RD 1 Box 427 Pownal VT 05261

HUTCHINS, HASTINGS HAROLD, SR, pharmacy, for more information see previous edition

HUTCHINS, JOHN R(ICHARD), III, CERAMICS, PHYSICAL CHEMISTRY. *Current Pos:* CHMN, BD BAND TECH INC, 88- *Personal Data:* b Perth Amboy, NJ, May 6, 34; m 58; c 4. *Educ:* Rensselaer Polytech Inst, BS, 55. *Hon Degrees:* ScD, Mass Inst Technol, 59 & Rutgers Univ, 84. *Prof Exp:* Res asst ceramics, Mass Inst Technol, 55-58; res physicist, Knox Labs, Inc, NJ, 59-60; sr ceramist, Tech Staff Div, Corning Glass Works, NY, 60-61, res ceramist, 61-62, res assoc ceramics, 62-66, mgr mat res, 66-67, mgr surface chem res, Tech Staffs Div, 67-69, dir bio-org technol, 69-72, dir appl physics & biol, 72-73, vpres res & develop, 73-80, dir, 73-85, sr vpres, 80-85; exec vpres staffs, Siecor Corp, Hickory, NC, 85-88, exec vpres & dir technol & new bus develop, 88. *Concurrent Pos:* Dir, Cormedics Corp, NJ, Diag Res, Inc, NY, 71-72 & Genecor Inc, 82-85; mem, NY State Adv Coun on High Technol, 78-; mem, Nat Mat Adv Bd, 78-80; mem, Res & Develop Coun, Am Mgt Asn, Dir Indust Res & Technol Coun ITG, Electronic Indust Asn. *Mem:* AAAS; Am Chem Soc; Sigma Xi; fel Am Ceramic Soc; Brit Soc Glass Technol. *Res:* Gases in glass; ion selective electrodes; immobilized enzymes; chromatography; immunochemistry; optical waveguides; medical instrumentation; hypodermic syringe manufacture; solid state reactions; dissolution; glass ceramics, photosensitive glasses; refractories; specialty glasses and ceramics. *Mailing Add:* 1058 25th Ave Dr NW Hickory NC 28601

HUTCHINS, MARYGAIL KINZER, SURFACE CHEMISTRY, SPECTRAL ANALYSIS. *Current Pos:* ANALYTICAL CHEMIST, ICI ADVAN MAT, 86- *Personal Data:* b Los Angeles, Calif, Jan 17, 40; m 62; c R Owen & Richard J. *Educ:* Mt St Mary's Col, BA, 61; St Joseph's, MS, 77; Temple Univ, PhD(chem), 81. *Prof Exp:* Technician, Douglas Aircraft Co, 58-59; lit chemist, Richfield Res, Anaheim, 61-62; lit chemist, Thermophys Properties Res Ctr, 62-64; sci teacher, Cent Cath High Sch, Ind, 64-65; spectros technician, Purdue Univ, 65-66; nuclear magnetic resonance technician, Univ Notre Dame, 66-68; substitute teacher, Philadelphia Bd Educ, 68-69; instr, Dept Chem, Temple Univ, 69-71; technician, Drexel Univ, 71-72; lit chemist, Inst Sci Info, 72-73; teaching asst, St Joseph's Univ, 74-76; teaching asst & res asst, Temple Univ & Fels Res Found, 76-79, Pub Health Serv trainee & res assoc, 79-80, grad res assoc, 80-81; prod develop chemist, LNP Eng Plastics Corp, 81-86. *Mem:* Am Chem Soc; Sigma Xi; Fiber Soc; Soc Advan Mat & Process Eng; Soc Appl Spectros; NAm Thermal Analysis Soc. *Res:* Compositing of thermoplastics with fiber; nature of any coating required to better these composites; surface of and bulk polymer analyses. *Mailing Add:* 315 Anderson Rd King of Prussia PA 19406-1905. *Fax:* 610-363-4527

HUTCHINS, PHILLIP MICHAEL, PHYSIOLOGY, BIOMEDICAL ENGINEERING. *Current Pos:* from asst prof to assoc prof, 70-81, PROF PHYSIOL, BOWMAN GRAY SCH MED, 81-, DIR DEPT BIOMED ENG, 70- *Personal Data:* b Winston-Salem, NC, Aug 15, 42; m 64, Linda J Fulk; c 3. *Educ:* NC State Univ, BSEE, 64; Bowman Gray Sch Med, MS, 66, PhD(physiol), 69. *Prof Exp:* Assoc med, Harvard Med Sch, 69-70. *Concurrent Pos:* Res assoc, Peter Bent Brigham Hosp, 69-70; NASA & NC Heart Asn grants, 71-; Nat Heart & Lung Inst grant, 71- *Mem:* Am Heart Asn; Am Physiol Soc; Microcirc Soc; Biomed Eng Soc; Planetary Soc; Am Soc Gravitational & Space Biol. *Res:* Microcirculation and effects of oxygen; hypertension; hemorrhagic shock; pharmacology of the microcirculation; computers; medical instrumentation; gravitational (space) physiology; chronic cardiovascular monitoring; aging. *Mailing Add:* Physol & Pharmacol Bowman Gray Sch Med 300 S Hawthorne Rd Winston-Salem NC 27157. *Fax:* 910-716-7738

HUTCHINS, ROBERT OWEN, SR, ORGANIC CHEMISTRY. *Current Pos:* from asst prof to assoc prof, 68-79, PROF ORG CHEM, DREXEL UNIV, 79-, HEAD DEPT, 86- *Personal Data:* b Danville, Ill, Sept 25, 39; m 62, Mary G Kinzer; c Robert O Jr & Richard J. *Educ:* Univ Calif, Berkeley, BS, 61; Calif State Univ, Long Beach, MA, 62; Purdue Univ, PhD(chem), 67. *Honors & Awards:* Drexel Res Award, 82; Res Award, Am Chem Soc, Philadelphia Sect, 87. *Prof Exp:* NSF res fels, Univ Notre Dame, 66-68. *Mem:* AAAS; Am Chem Soc; Chem. *Res:* New synthetic techniques; conformational analysis and stereochemistry; asymmetric synthesis. *Mailing Add:* Dept Chem Drexel Univ Philadelphia PA 19104. *Fax:* 215-895-1265; *E-Mail:* hutchiro@ouvm.ocs.drexel.edu

HUTCHINS, SANDRA ELAINE, SPEECH & LANGUAGE PROCESSING, SIGNAL PROCESSING. *Current Pos:* PRES, NATURAL SPEECH TECHNOLOGIES, 84- *Personal Data:* b San Diego, Calif, Jan 22, 46. *Educ:* Univ Calif, San Diego, BA, 67, PhD(info & comput sci), 70. *Prof Exp:* Asst prof elec eng, Purdue Univ, 70-72; sr staff engr commun, TRW Defense & Space Systs, 72-77; eng mgr, Linkabit Corp, 77-79; dir speech processing, ITT Inc, 79-84. *Concurrent Pos:* NSF res grant, 71-72; instr, Loyola Marymount Univ, 73-74 & Univ Calif, Davis, Exten, 78- *Mem:* Inst Elec & Electronics Engrs; Asn Comput Mach. *Res:* Speech and language processing using computer software. *Mailing Add:* 12 Prospect Dr S Huntington Manor NY 11746. *Fax:* 516-549-7249; *E-Mail:* nst@li.net

HUTCHINS, WILLIAM R(EAGH), ELECTRONICS ENGINEERING, COMPUTER SYSTEMS. *Current Pos:* PRES & CONSULT, FUTURE CONCEPTS, 85- *Personal Data:* b New York, NY, Mar 23, 19; wid; c James A, Robert B & Janet G. *Educ:* Columbia Univ, BA, 39, BS, 40, MS(EE), 41. *Prof Exp:* Eng asst to Maj Edwin H Armstrong, Columbia Univ, 39-46; mgr & chief engr, E Anthony & Sons, Mass, 46-48; mgr, Adv Develop Dept, Missile Systs Div, Raytheon Co, 48-58; chief, ballistic missile defense br, ARPA, 58-59; sci liaison officer, Raytheon Co, 59-60; dir, eastern tech opers, Aerospace Corp, 61-65; vpres adv develop, Nat Co Inc, 65-66; systs consult, Sanders Assocs Inc, 66-69, mgr, S-3A, 69-71, mgr, Antisubmarine Warfare Systs, 71-72, tech dir, Systs Div, 72-73, mgr, Air Systs, 74-79, mgr, VHSIC, 79-81, mgr, Adv Electronic Warfare, 81-85. *Concurrent Pos:* Mem proj Lamplight, Off Naval Res, Exec Off Pres, 44-45; security resources panel, 47; consult, NY Eye & Ear Infirmary, 48-50; dir, mission area study on integrated air surveillance, USAF Systs Command, 74-75; bd chmn, Pub Info Network Inc, 90-96. *Mem:* Acoust Soc Am; assoc fel Am Inst Aeronaut & Astronaut; Inst Elec & Electronics Engrs. *Res:* Frequency modulation-continuous wave radar; acoustics, missile and defense systems; audio; audiometry; radio and microwaves. *Mailing Add:* Future Concepts Inc 5605 Brisbane Dr Chapel Hill NC 27514. *E-Mail:* hutch@rtpnet.org

HUTCHINSON, ALBERT L, ELECTRICAL ENGINEERING. *Current Pos:* sr tech assoc, 79-81, assoc mem tech staff, 81-82, MEM TECH STAFF, AT&T BELL LABS, 82- *Personal Data:* b Gention, Ga, June 16, 33; m 59, Sylvia M Tyson; c Sharmaine L, Wanda E & Albert L Jr. *Honors & Awards:* Newcomb Cleveland Prize, AAAS, 93; Electronics Lett Premium Award, Inst Elec & Electronics Engrs, 95. *Mem:* Inst Elec & Electronics Engrs; AAAS. *Res:* Contributed over 42 research papers and granted 5 patents. *Mailing Add:* AT&T Bell Labs 600 Mountain Ave New Providence NJ 07974-2008

HUTCHINSON, BENNETT BUCKLEY, FAR-INFRARED SPECTROSCOPY, SOLAR ENERGY. *Current Pos:* prof chem, 89-90, CHMN, NATURAL SCI DIV, PEPPERDINE UNIV, 90- *Personal Data:* b Honolulu, Hawaii, Aug 7, 42; m 70, Nancy Richardson; c Amy. *Educ:* Abilene Christian Col, BS, 63; Univ Tex, Austin, MA, 65; Ill Inst Technol, PhD(phys chem), 70. *Prof Exp:* Prof chem, Abilene Christian Univ, 70-89. *Concurrent Pos:* Vis prof chem, Univ Tex Austin, 79-80. *Mem:* Am Chem Soc; Am Asn Univ Professors; AAAS; Sigma Xi. *Res:* Preparation and far-infrared spectrum of transition metal coordination compounds often using stable metal isotopes to identify the metal-ligand stretching vibrations; use of concentrated solar energy to activate T1 O2 and decompose organic pesticides. *Mailing Add:* Natural Sci Div Pepperdine Univ Malibu CA 90263

HUTCHINSON, CHARLES E(DGAR), VERY LARGE SCALE INTEGRATION, COMPUTER AIDED DESIGN. *Current Pos:* dean, 84-94, PROF, THAYER SCH ENG, DARTMOUTH COL, 84- *Personal Data:* b Parkersburg, WVa, Dec 18, 35; m 60, Elva Butland; c Charles IV & John. *Educ:* Ill Inst Technol, BSEE, 57; Stanford Univ, MSEE, 61, PhD(elec eng), 63. *Prof Exp:* Res specialist, Autonetics Div, NAm Aviation, Inc, Calif, 63-65; prof elec eng, Univ Mass, Amherst, 65-84. *Concurrent Pos:* Lectr, Univ Calif, Los Angeles, 64-65. *Mem:* Inst Elec & Electronics Engrs; Am Soc Eng Educ. *Res:* Automatic control systems; stochastic processes; inertial navigation systems; computer processing; software quality; total quality management. *Mailing Add:* Thayer Sch Eng Dartmouth Col Hanover NH 03755. *Fax:* 603-646-2508; *E-Mail:* hutch@dartmouth.thayer.edu

HUTCHINSON, CHARLES F, REMOTE SENSING, GEOGRAPHIC INFORMATION SYSTEMS. *Current Pos:* asst prof geog, 81-89, chmn, Arid Lands Resource Sci Doctoral Prog, 83-93, DIR, ARIZ REMOTE SENSING CTR, ASSOC DIR, OFF ARID LANDS STUDIES UNIV ARIZ, 83-, ASSOC PROF ARID LANDS, 89-, CHMN, COMT REMOTE SENSING & SPATIAL ANALYSIS, 93-, PROF ARID LANDS STUDIES. *Personal Data:* b Riverside, Calif, Sept 22, 46; div; c Heather & Sydney. *Educ:* Univ Calif, Riverside, AB, 72, MA, 74, PhD(geog), 78. *Prof Exp:* Geog, Earth Resources Observ Syst, US Geol Surv, 76-78; tech staff, Jet Propulsion Lab, Calif Inst Technol, 78-80. *Concurrent Pos:* Gilbert F White fel, Resources Future, 88-89. *Mem:* Am Soc Photogram; Sigma Xi; Asn Am Geographers; AAAS. *Res:* Development and application of remote sensing and geographic information systems techniques; techniques for land resource inventory; famine early warning and vulnerable assessment. *Mailing Add:* 4101 E La Cadena St Tucson AZ 85718-6148. *Fax:* 520-621-3816; *E-Mail:* chutch@ccit.arizona.edu

HUTCHINSON, CHARLES S, JR, GEOLOGY. *Current Pos:* PUBL, GEOSCI PRESS, INC, 88- *Personal Data:* b Topeka, Kans, Oct 17, 30; m 56; c 2. *Educ:* Principia Col, BA, 52. *Prof Exp:* Ed-in-chief & corp secy, Burgess Pub Co, 55-65; ed-in-chief prof books, Reinhold Book Corp, 65-68 & Van Nostrand Reinhold Co, 68-70; pres & co-founder, Dowden, Hutchinson & Ross Inc, 70-83; publ geol, physics, math & statist, Van Nostrand Reinhold Co, 84-86. *Concurrent Pos:* Consult, Hutchinson Assoc, 87- *Mem:* Fel Geol Soc Am; Am Soc Petrol Geologists; Am Geophys Union; Soc Econ Paleontologists & Mineralogists. *Mailing Add:* 5520 N Camino Arenosa Tucson AZ 85718

HUTCHINSON, DONALD PATRICK, PLASMA & LASER PHYSICS. *Current Pos:* PHYSICIST, OAK RIDGE NAT LAB, 74- *Personal Data:* b Laurel, Miss, Jan 15, 47; m 67; c 2. *Educ:* Univ Miss, BS, 68; Mass Inst Technol, SM, 70, ScD(appl plasma physics), 74. *Mem:* Am Phys Soc; Am Optical Soc. *Res:* Development of CW and pulsed submillimeter lasers for use as plasma diagnostic tools. *Mailing Add:* 909 Woodsmoke Circle Knoxville TN 37922

HUTCHINSON, ERIC, COLLOID CHEMISTRY. *Current Pos:* RETIRED. *Personal Data:* b Morton, Eng, Dec 25, 20; nat US; m 42. *Educ:* Cambridge Univ, BA, 41, MA, 44, PhD(colloid chem), 45. *Prof Exp:* Lectr phys chem, Univ Sheffield, 45-46; Bristol Myers fel colloid chem, Stanford Univ, 46-48; asst prof phys chem, Fordham Univ, 48-49; from asst prof to assoc prof, Stanford Univ, 49-59, assoc exec head, Dept Chem, 58-62, prof, 59, acad secy, 74. *Concurrent Pos:* Fulbright lectr, Yokohama Nat Univ, 59-60; vis prof, Univ Sussex, 67. *Mem:* Am Chem Soc; Chem Soc. *Res:* Properties of interfacial monolayers; adsorption on surfaces; thermodynamics of colloidal electrolytes; microcalorimetry; science and public policy; studies of government support of scientific and technological research and development. *Mailing Add:* 138 Petercoutts Circle Stanford CA 94305-1684

HUTCHINSON, FRANKLIN, BIOPHYSICS, MOLECULAR BIOLOGY. *Current Pos:* instr radiol & physics, Yale Univ, 48-51, asst prof physics, 51-57, from assoc prof to prof biophys, 57-90, chmn dept, 60-63 & 67-69, chmn, Dept Molecular Biophys & Biochem, 73-76, EMER PROF BIOPHYS & BIOCHEM & SR RES SCIENTIST, YALE UNIV, 90- *Personal Data:* b Brooklyn, NY, Feb 29, 20; m 44, Edith Pringle; c Bruce, Franklin IV, Alexander & Candace. *Educ:* Mass Inst Technol, BS, 42; Yale Univ, PhD(physics), 48. *Prof Exp:* Staff mem, Radiation Lab, Mass Inst Technol, 42-45. *Concurrent Pos:* Guggenheim fel, King's Col, Univ London, 63-64. *Mem:* AAAS; Biophys Soc; Am Phys Soc; Radiation Res Soc. *Res:* Damage to DNA by physical and chemical agents; repair of DNA damage and the biological consequences of damage and of errors in repair; mutagenesis. *Mailing Add:* Dept Ther Radiol PO Box 208040 Yale Univ New Haven CT 06520-8040. *Fax:* 203-785-6309; *E-Mail:* hutchinsfa@maspo3.mas.yale.edu

HUTCHINSON, FREDERICK EDWARD, SOIL CHEMISTRY. *Current Pos:* RETIRED. *Personal Data:* b Atkinson, Maine, June 1, 30; m 52; c 2. *Educ:* Univ Maine, BS, 53, MS, 58; Pa State Univ, PhD, 67. *Prof Exp:* Instr soil chem, Univ Maine, 58, from asst prof to assoc prof soil fertil, 58-67, prof soil sci, 67-82, chmn, Dept Plant & Soil Sci, 71-72, dean, Col Life Sci & Agr, 72-75, vpres res & pub serv, 75-82; mem, Bd Int Food & Agr Develop, Dept State, Wash, DC, 82-85; dir, Ohio Agr Res & Develop Ctr, Ohio State Univ, Columbus, 85-86, vpres agr admin & dean, Col Agr, 86-89; sr vpres, Acad Affairs & Provost, Univ Maine, 89-92, pres, 92-97. *Mem:* Am Soc Agron; Soil Conserv Soc Am; Am Soc Hort Sci. *Res:* Nutrition of snap beans, sweet corn and peas; relationship of soil fertility to plant growth; lime requirement of specific soil types; chemical characteristics of selected soil types. *Mailing Add:* Off Pres Univ Maine 5703 Alumni Hall Orono ME 04469

HUTCHINSON, GEORGE ALLEN, ALGEBRA. *Current Pos:* RES MATHEMATICIAN, NIH, 67- *Personal Data:* b Brooklyn, NY, Apr 24, 36; m 69, Carol A Occhiogrosso; c Daniel, John & Andrew. *Educ:* Columbia Univ, BA, 58, MA, 60, PhD(math), 67. *Prof Exp:* Jr mathematician res & develop lab, US Army Signal Corps, NJ, 58; mem tech staff, IT&T Commun Systs, Inc, 62-64; asst prof math, Fairleigh Dickinson Univ, 64-65. *Mem:* Am Math Soc; Math Asn Am; Int Neural Network Soc. *Res:* Algebra, especially category theory, lattice theory and ring and modules; computer science; neural networks. *Mailing Add:* 1617 Rainbow Dr NIH Silver Spring MD 20905-4144. *Fax:* 301-402-1946; *E-Mail:* gah@helix.nih.gov

HUTCHINSON, GEORGE KEATING, COMPUTER SCIENCE, MANAGEMENT SCIENCES. *Current Pos:* CONSULT, HUTCHINSON ASSOCS, LTD. *Personal Data:* b Belfast, Maine, Nov 20, 32; m 58; c 5. *Educ:* Univ Maine, BS, 55; Carnegie Inst, MS, 56; Stanford Univ, PhD(mgt sci), 64. *Prof Exp:* Teaching asst mech drawing & anal geom, Carnegie Inst, 55-56; design engr, Lockheed Missiles & Space Co, 57-58, eng opers analyst, 58, from math analyst to sr math analyst, 58-62, proj leader & math engr, 62-66; asst prof indust eng & dir comput ctr, Tex Tech Univ, 66-68; assoc prof mgt info systs & dir comput ctr, 68-71, prof mgt info systs, Univ Wis, Milwaukee, 71-96. *Concurrent Pos:* Res asst, Western Data Processing Ctr, Stanford Univ, 59-60; consult var nat & int orgn, 68-; mem comt, Nat Acad Sci; US rep, Int Fedn Info Processing. *Mem:* AAAS; Asn Comput Mach; Oper Res Soc Am; Inst Elec & Electronics Engrs; Inst Mgt Sci. *Res:* Development and application of generalized simulation models to solve complex systems problems; management information systems; automation of manufacturing and production systems, CAM and CIM. *Mailing Add:* Hutchinson Assocs Ltd 3404 Colette Ct Mequon WI 53092

HUTCHINSON, GORDON LEE, BIOSPHERE-ATMOSPHERE EXCHANGE OF GASEOUS NITROGEN COMPOUNDS. *Current Pos:* SOIL SCIENTIST, AGR RES SERV, USDA, 65- *Personal Data:* b Yuma, Colo, Feb 6, 43; m 62, Ilene J Derry; c Stuart J, Angela D (Ewari) & Shane R. *Educ:* Colo State Univ, BS, 65, MS, 68; Univ Ill, PhD(soil sci), 73. *Honors & Awards:* Emil Truog Soil Sci Award, Soil Sci Soc Am, 74. *Mem:* Fel Am Soc Agron; fel Soil Sci Soc Am; Am Geophys Union; AAAS; Coun Agr Sci & Technol; Int Soc Soil Sci. *Res:* Biosphere-atmosphere exchange of ammonia and gaseous nitrogen oxides, its measurement and implications to agricultural productivity, biogeochemical nutrient cycles and contemporary environmental issues. *Mailing Add:* Agr Res Serv USDA PO Box E Ft Collins CO 80522. *Fax:* 970-490-8213; *E-Mail:* glhutch@lamar.colostate.edu

HUTCHINSON, HAROLD DAVID, ANIMAL NUTRITION. *Current Pos:* RETIRED. *Personal Data:* b Moneymore, Northern Ireland, Apr 15, 31; US citizen; m 57; c 2. *Educ:* Queen's Univ Belfast, BAgr, 53; Univ Ill, MS, 55, PhD(animal sci), 57. *Prof Exp:* Res asst animal sci, Univ Ill, 53-56, instr vet physiol, 56-57; swine nutritionist, Moorman Mfg Co, 57-64, head explor res, 64-67, head accessory prod develop & control coord, Res Dept, 67-71, dir res, 71-77, vpres & dir res, 77-92. *Mem:* AAAS; Am Soc Animal Sci. *Res:* Factors influencing amino acids requirements of swine; methods of controlling anemia in baby pigs; effects of feeding moldy grains to swine. *Mailing Add:* 2901 Curved Creek Rd Quincy IL 62301

HUTCHINSON, IAN HORNER, PLASMA PHYSICS. *Current Pos:* Res scientist, 76-79, at MASS INST TECHNOL, 79- *Personal Data:* b UK, June 7, 51. *Educ:* Cambridge Univ, BA, 72; Australia Nat Univ, PhD(plasma physics), 76. *Concurrent Pos:* Prof, Dept Nuclear Eng, Cambridge Col, 83- *Mem:* Am Phys Soc. *Mailing Add:* Mass Inst Technol NW17-186 Cambridge MA 02139

HUTCHINSON, JAMES HERBERT, JR, ORGANIC CHEMISTRY. *Current Pos:* PROF CHEM, MID TENN STATE UNIV, 69-, CHMN, DEPT CHEM, 92- *Personal Data:* b Jackson, Miss, Aug 7, 33; m 62, Betty R Scott; c James H III & Melinda. *Educ:* Univ Southern Miss, BS, 55; Univ Iowa, MS, 60; Auburn Univ, PhD(org chem), 68. *Prof Exp:* Res chemist, Ethyl Corp, La, 57-58; develop chemist, Geigy Chem Corp, Ala, 61-62; US Army Med Res & Develop Command, Dept Army grant, Ind Univ, Bloomington, 67-69. *Mem:* Am Chem Soc; Sigma Xi. *Res:* Heterocyclic chemistry; synthesis of physiologically active compounds. *Mailing Add:* Mid Tenn State Univ PO Box 196 Murfreesboro TN 37132. *Fax:* 615-898-5182; *E-Mail:* jhutchinson@a1.mtsu.edu

HUTCHINSON, JAMES R(ICHARD), ENGINEERING MECHANICS. *Current Pos:* from asst prof eng to prof civil eng, 64-93, EMER PROF CIVIL ENG, UNIV CALIF, DAVIS, 93- *Personal Data:* b San Francisco, Calif, June 1, 32; m 56, Patricia A Robinson; c Katherine L & William D. *Educ:* Stanford Univ, BS, 54, PhD(eng mech), 63; Univ Pittsburgh, MLitt, 58. *Prof Exp:* Engr, Atomic Power Div, Westinghouse Elec Corp, 54-58; res specialist, Lockheed Missiles & Space Co, 58-64. *Mem:* Am Soc Mech Engrs; Am Acad Mech; Sigma Xi. *Res:* Vibrations; structural dynamics; development of exact solutions for the vibration of solids such as cylinders, rectangular parallelepipeds, and hollow cylinders; comparison of these solutions with previous approximate beam plate and shell theories; research into the application of Boundary Element and Boundary Collocation Methods to vibration problems. *Mailing Add:* Dept Civil Eng Univ Calif Davis CA 95616

HUTCHINSON, JOAN PRINCE, MATHEMATICS, GRAPH THEORY. *Current Pos:* PROF MATH, MACALESTER COL, 90- *Personal Data:* b Philadelphia, Pa, Apr 19, 45; m 75, Stan Wagon. *Educ:* Smith Col, BA, 67; Univ Pa, MA, 71, PhD(math), 73. *Prof Exp:* John Wesley Young res instr math, Dartmouth Col, 73-75; asst prof, Tufts Univ, 75-76; prof math, Smith Col, 76-90. *Concurrent Pos:* NSF res grant, 77-79, 84-88; Benedict distinguished vis prof math, Carleton Col, 78-79; vis prof women, NSF, 89-90. *Mem:* Am Math Soc; Math Asn Am; Asn Women Math; Soc Indust & Appl Math. *Res:* Chromatic and topological graph theory; combinatorial analysis; graph algorithms; computer science theory. *Mailing Add:* Dept Math Macalester Col 1600 Grand Ave St Paul MN 55105-1899

HUTCHINSON, JOHN W(ENDLE), CIVIL ENGINEERING. *Current Pos:* RETIRED. *Personal Data:* b Williamstown, Ky, Dec 1, 27; m 50; c 7. *Educ:* Univ Ill, BS, 51, MS, 54, PhD(civil eng), 61. *Honors & Awards:* Teetor Award, Soc Automotive Engrs, 79. *Prof Exp:* Engr in training, Stephens-Adamson Co, Ill, 51; from instr to assoc prof civil eng, Univ Ill, 54-64; from assoc prof to prof, Univ Ky, 65-89. *Concurrent Pos:* Mem, Transp Res Bd, Nat Acad Sci-Nat Res Coun; sci adv, Int Ctr Transp Studies, Amalfi, Italy. *Mem:* Nat Acad Eng; Am Soc Civil Engrs; Int Ctr Transp Studies; Asn Asn Automotive Med; Inst Transp Engrs; Am Soc Eng Educ. *Res:* Highway materials, geometrics, safety and administration; traffic planning; accident reconstruction; vehicle dynamics. *Mailing Add:* 104 Tahoma Rd Lexington KY 40506

HUTCHINSON, JOHN WOODSIDE, APPLIED MECHANICS. *Current Pos:* Res fel, Harvard Univ, 63-64, asst prof struct mech, 64-68, assoc prof appl mech, 68-69, GORDON MCKAY PROF APPL MECH, HARVARD UNIV, CAMBRIDGE, MASS, 69- *Personal Data:* b Hartford, Conn, Apr 10, 39; m 64, Helle Vilsen; c Leif, David & Robert. *Educ:* Lehigh Univ, BS, 60; Harvard Univ, MS, 61, PhD (mech eng), 63. *Hon Degrees:* DSc, Royal Inst Technol, Stockholm, 85, Tech Univ Denmark, Copenhagen, 92. *Honors & Awards:* Irwin Medal, Am Soc Test Engrs, 82; Arpard L Nadai Award, Am Soc Mech Engrs, 91; Prager Medal, Soc Eng Sci, 91; Swedlow Award, Am Soc Test & Mat, 93. *Concurrent Pos:* Consult var industs; Guggenheim Found fel, 74; Defense Sci Res Coun, 80-; US Nat Comt, Theoret & Appl Mech, 81-89; exec comt, Appl Mech Div, Am Soc Mech Engrs, 90-95. *Mem:* Nat Acad Sci; Nat Acad Eng; fel Am Soc Mech Engrs; AAAS; Am Soc Test Engrs; Am Acad Arts & Sci. *Res:* Applied mechanics; solid mechanics and structures; plasticity, buckling and fracture; mechanics and micromechanics of engineered materials, including polycrystalline materials, composites, thin blind and multilayers; contributed articles to professional journals. *Mailing Add:* Gordon McKay Lab Pierce Hall No 315 Harvard Univ Cambridge MA 02138

HUTCHINSON, KENNETH A, ANALYTICAL CHEMISTRY, CHEMICAL ENGINEERING. *Current Pos:* RETIRED. *Personal Data:* b Dugger, Ind, Sept 8, 32. *Educ:* Wayne State Univ, BS, 55, MS, 56, PhD(anal chem), 60. *Prof Exp:* Instr anal chem, Wayne State Univ, 58-60; res chem engr, Detroit Edison Co, 60-69, engr, Water Systs Eng Div, 69-74, engr, Analytical Chem, 74-92. *Concurrent Pos:* Res compounder org chem, US Rubber Co, 59-60. *Mem:* Am Chem Soc; Air Pollution Control Asn; Sigma Xi; Am Soc Testing & Mat. *Res:* Gas chromatography; infrared spectrophotometry; gas analysis; rubber; paint; plastics; electrical insulation; research engineering of liquid alkali metals; asbestos analysis; scanning electron microscopy; x-ray diffraction spectrometry. *Mailing Add:* 2109 E Columbia Dansville MI 48819-9785

HUTCHINSON, PETER J, GROUND WATER CONTAMINATION & REMEDIATION, LAND FILL GEOLOGY. *Current Pos:* PRES & CHIEF EXEC OFFICER, HUTCHINSON GROUP LTD, 92-; ADJ PROF ENVIRON GEOL, UNIV PITTSBURGH, 92-, CHATHAM COL, 94- *Personal Data:* b New York, NY, Dec 11, 52; m 74, Cheryl Schosek; c Heather, Kelly & Jana. *Educ:* Syracuse Univ, BS, 74; Univ NMex, MS, 81; Univ Pittsburgh, PhD(environ geochem), 92. *Honors & Awards:* A I Levorsen Mem Award, Am Asn Petrol Geologists, 89. *Prof Exp:* Sr geologist, Exxon Co, 80-83; sr explor geologist, Primary Fuels Inc, 83-88; mgr geol hydrogeol, Chambers Develop Co, 88-92. *Concurrent Pos:* Vis prof geologist, Am Asn Petrol Geogogists, 93; vpres, Pittsburgh Geol Soc, 93-94. *Mem:* Am Asn Petrol Geologist; Am Inst Prof Geologists; Geol Soc Am; Nat Ground Water Asn; Soc Econ Paleontologists & Mineralogists; AAAS. *Res:* Modeling and predicting the impact of earthquakes effects on man; detection and remediation of groundwater contaminated and the impact these contaminants have upon the biosphere. *Mailing Add:* 5124 Scenic Dr Murrysville PA 15668. *Fax:* 412-733-7901

HUTCHINSON, RICHARD ALLEN, PHARMACY. *Current Pos:* assoc prof, 73-78, PROF & HEAD CLIN PHARM, UNIV ILL, 78- *Personal Data:* b Wayne, Mich, Jan 6, 42; m 67, Karen Sutton; c 3. *Educ:* Univ Mich, BS, 66, Pharm D, 67. *Prof Exp:* Resident clin pharm, Univ Mich, 68; instr clin pract, Wayne State Univ, 68-69; asst prof clin pharm, State Univ NY, Buffalo, 69-73. *Concurrent Pos:* Dir pharmaceut serv, Sinai Hosp, Detroit, Mich, 68-69; chief clin pract, E J Meyer, 69-70; chief clin pract, Buffalo Gen Hosp, 69-70, dir pharmaceut servs, 70-73. *Mem:* Am Soc Hosp Pharmacists; fel Am Col Clin Pharm; Am Asn Col Pharm. *Res:* Establishment and audit of minimum standards of clinical practice; justification of clinical pharmacy practice. *Mailing Add:* Dept Pharm Pract MC 886 Univ Ill Col Pharm Rm 164 833 S Wood St Chicago IL 60612. *Fax:* 312-996-0379; *E-Mail:* hutch@uic.edu

HUTCHINSON, RICHARD WILLIAM, GEOLOGY. *Current Pos:* Charles F Fogarty prof, 83-94, EMER CHARLES F FOGARTY PROF ECON GEOL, COLO SCH MINES, 94- *Personal Data:* b London, Ont, Nov 17, 28; m 51; c 4. *Educ:* Univ Western Ont, BSc, 50; Univ Wis, MS, 51, PhD(geol), 54. *Honors & Awards:* Barlow Gold Medal, Can Inst Mining & Metall, 72 & 79; Duncan Derry Gold Medal, Mineral Deposits Div Geol Assoc Can, 83; Silver Medal, Soc Econ Geol, 85; Jubilee Gold Medal, Geol Soc SAfrica, 88. *Prof Exp:* Geologist, Am Metal Climax, Inc, 54-64; from assoc prof to prof econ geol & mineral deposits, Univ Western Ont, 64-83. *Concurrent Pos:* Nat Res Coun Can res grant, 64-83; consult geologist, Callahan Mining Corp, NY, 64-70, Chevron Resources, 72-84, Utah Int, 84-; Geol Surv Can res grant, 65-69; NATO Res Coun res grant, 67-69, Nat Sci & Eng Res coun, Can Res grant, 64-83; coun, Geol Soc Am, 88-90. *Mem:* Soc Econ Geologists (pres, 83); Geol Soc Am; Can Inst Mining & Metall; Geol Asn Can; Soc Geol Appl; Prospectors & Developers Asn Can; Geol Soc SAfrica. *Res:* Descriptive geology on pegmatites and deposits of rare-element minerals in pegmatites; genesis and tectonic relationships of massive sulfide base metal ore deposits; origin of K-bearing marine evaporite deposits; metallogenic evolution of ore deposits; genesis of stratiform sulfide-rich tin lodes; geology and genesis of Precambrian gold deposits. *Mailing Add:* Dept Geol & Geol Eng Colo Sch Mines Golden CO 80401-1887. *E-Mail:* 105532.1563@compuserve.com

HUTCHINSON, ROBERT MASKIELL, GEOLOGY. *Current Pos:* from asst prof to assoc prof, 56-74, PROF GEOL, COLO SCH MINES, 74- *Personal Data:* b Trenton, NJ, Dec 24, 28; m 48; c 8. *Educ:* Princeton Univ, AB, 41; Univ Mich, AM, 48; Univ Tex, PhD(geol), 53. *Prof Exp:* Civil engr, Eng Dept, CEngr, US War Dept, Trinidad, BWI, 41-42; geologist, Strategic Minerals Div, US Geol Surv, 42-45, groundwater div, 45; instr geol, Univ Tex, 48-53; asst prof, Kans State Col, 53-56. *Concurrent Pos:* Geol Soc Am res grant, 52-55; NSF grant, 60-63. *Mem:* Geol Soc Am; Am Inst Prof Geologists; AAAS. *Res:* Igneous, metamorphic and structural petrology; economic geology, genesis and occurrence of metalliferous ore deposits associated with batholiths; time-space, time-span studies of Precambrian basement rocks of central Texas and Colorado Rocky Mountains; erosion rates in the Colorado Rocky Mountains during Precambrian time; economic geology of precious and base metal ore deposits; nuclear waste repository siting in Precambrian crystalline basement rocks; structural analysis of heavy oil reservoirs in overthrust belts. *Mailing Add:* Dept Geol Scis Colo Sch Mines Golden CO 80401

HUTCHINSON, THOMAS C, BIOLOGY, AGRICULTURE. *Current Pos:* PROF ENVIRON & RESOURCE STUDIES, TRENT UNIV, 91- *Personal Data:* b Sunderland, UK, Feb 18, 39; div; c Sally Louise. *Educ:* Victoria Univ Manchester, BSc, 60; Univ Sheffield, PhD(bot), 66. *Honors & Awards:* George Lawson Medal, Can Bot Asn, 83. *Prof Exp:* Sir James Knott fel, Univ Newcastle, 64-67; from asst prof to assoc prof bot, Univ Toronto, 67-71, assoc exec, Inst Environ Sci & Eng, 71-73, assoc dir, 73-76, prof bot, 74-91, chmn dept, 76-82, prof forestry, 78-91, grad coordr, 83-87. *Concurrent Pos:* Chmn, Can Water Pollution Res Coun, 74-75; consult, WHO, 74-; chmn heavy metal subcomt, Nat Res Coun, 77- & Nat Sci & Eng Coun, 81-82; dir, Rare Breeds Can, 92-; mem, Nat Sci & Eng Res Coun, Can, 93- *Mem:* Brit Ecol Soc; Ecol Soc Am; Can Bot Soc; Am Soc Agron; Arctic Inst NAm; fel Royal Soc Can. *Res:* Heavy metal toxicity; oil spill phytotoxicity; air pollution; acid rain phenomena; smelter metal studies on lead, arsenic, copper and nickel; tailings revegetation, metal tolerant grasses; algae; forest decline; climatic change on boreal forest. *Mailing Add:* Environ & Resource Studies Univ Trent Peterborough ON K9J 7B8 Can. *Fax:* 705-748-1636; *E-Mail:* thutchinson@trent.u.ca

HUTCHINSON, THOMAS EUGENE, HUMAN-MACHINE INTERFACE, ANALYSIS EYE CHARACTERISTICS BY COMPUTER OCULOMETER. *Current Pos:* assoc dean, 82-86, WILLIAM STANSFIELD CALCOTT, PROF, SCH ENG & APPL SCI, UNIV VA, 82- *Personal Data:* b York, SC, Aug 1, 36; m 59; Colleen Ray; c Rachel & Thomas E Jr. *Educ:* Clemson Univ, BS, 58, MS, 59; Univ Va, PhD(physics), 63. *Prof Exp:* Teaching asst, Univ Va, 60-61; res fel, AEC, 62; sr scientist, 3M Co, 63-66, res specialist, 66-67; assoc prof chem eng & mat sci, Univ Minn, 67-74, prof, 74-76; prof biomed & chem eng, Univ Wash, 76-82, assoc dean eng res, 82. *Concurrent Pos:* Consult for var orgns including 3M Co, RCA, North Star Res & Others, 67-73; chmn, Gordon Res Conf, 70; vis prof, Cavendish Lab, Cambridge, Eng, 71; sr res fel, Univ Glasgow, Scotland, 74-; chmn, Battelle Conf Microprobe Anal, 80; Thomas Jefferson vis scholar, Cambridge Univ, 92; fel, Downing Col, Cambridge Univ, 92. *Mem:* Electron Micros Soc Am; Am Vacuum Soc; sr mem Inst Elec & Electronics Engrs; sr mem Bioeng Soc; sr mem Biomat Soc; Am Asn Univ Prof. *Res:* Eye-computer interface systems which control computer function through eye position on the display; used to interface the handicapped to the outside world; determine eye function indicating intoxication, fatigue, etc; show psychological state in response to visual display images, sound and odor. *Mailing Add:* Univ Va Dept Syst Eng Sch Eng & Appl Sci Thornton Hall Charlottesville VA 22903. *Fax:* 804-982-2972; *E-Mail:* teh@virginia.edu

HUTCHINSON, WILLIAM BURKE, surgical cancer; deceased, see previous edition for last biography

HUTCHISON, CLYDE ALLEN, JR, PHYSICAL CHEMISTRY. *Current Pos:* asst, Metall Lab, Univ Chicago, 45-46, from asst prof to prof, 45-63, chmn dept, 59-62, Carl William Eisendrath prof, 63-69, Carl William Eisendrath distinguished serv prof, 69-83, EMER, CARL WILLIAM EISENDRATH DISTINGUISHED SERV PROF CHEM, ENRICO FERMI INST & DEPT CHEM, UNIV CHICAGO, 83- *Personal Data:* b Alliance, Ohio, May 5, 13; m 37, Sara J West; c Clyde A III, Sarah J (Dunn) & Robert W. *Educ:* Cedarville Col, AB, 33; Ohio State Univ, PhD(chem), 37. *Hon Degrees:* DSc, Cedarville Col, 53. *Honors & Awards:* Peter Debye Award, Am Chem Soc, 72. *Prof Exp:* Nat Res Coun fel, Dept Chem, Columbia Univ, 37-38, res assoc, Dept Chem, 38-39 & SAM Labs, 43-45; asst prof chem, Univ Buffalo, 39-45. *Concurrent Pos:* Res assoc, Manhattan Dist Proj, Dept Physics, Univ Va, 42-43; consult, Argonne Nat Lab, 46- & Los Alamos Sci Lab, 53-62; ed, J Chem Physics, 53-59; Guggenheim fel, Oxford Univ, 55-56 & 72-73; mem, Chem Panel, NSF, 60-63; mem vis comt, Brookhaven Nat Lab, 60-63 & Oak Ridge Nat Lab, 63-66; mem bd dirs, Ohio State Univ Res Found, 63-68; consult, Nat Bur Stand, 63-69; mem, Chem Eval Panel, USAF Off Sci Res, 66-70; mem vis comt, Argonne Nat Lab, 70- & Mass Inst Technol, 71-; Japan Soc Prom Sci vis prof, 75; mem, Eval Panel, Phys Chem Div, Nat Bur Stand, 77-80; Eastman prof, Univ Oxford, 81-82. *Mem:* Nat Acad Sci; Am Chem Soc; fel Am Acad Arts & Sci; Am Phys Soc. *Res:* Separation and tracer studies of isotopes; magnetic susceptibilities of heavy elements; electron paramagnetic resonance absorption; paramagnetism of triplet state organic molecules; organic crystals; application of electron magnetic resonance to protein structure determination. *Mailing Add:* 5550 South Shore Dr Univ Chicago 5735 Ellis Ave Chicago IL 60637. *Fax:* 773-702-0805

HUTCHISON, CLYDE ALLEN, III, MOLECULAR BIOLOGY, GENETICS. *Current Pos:* From asst prof to prof microbiol, 68-83, KENAN PROF MICROBIOL, SCH MED, UNIV NC, CHAPEL HILL, 83- *Personal Data:* b New York, NY, Nov 26, 38; div; c 3. *Educ:* Yale Univ, BS, 60; Calif Inst Technol, PhD(biophys), 69. *Honors & Awards:* NIH Merit Award, 87. *Concurrent Pos:* NIH grant, 69- & res career develop award, 73-78; vis scientist, Lab Molecular Biol, Med Res Coun, Cambridge, Eng, 75-76 & 87-88. *Res:* Mammalian genome organization; hemoglobin genes; long interspersed sequences (retroposons); directed mutagenesis using chemically synthesized DNA; DNA sequence analysis. *Mailing Add:* Dept Microbiol & Immunol Sch Med Univ NC Chapel Hill NC 27599. *Fax:* 919-962-8103; *E-Mail:* clude@mail.unc edu

HUTCHISON, DAVID ALLAN, FUEL & LUBRICANT CHEMISTRY. *Current Pos:* RES ADV, ETHYL CORP, 92- *Personal Data:* b Milwaukee, Wis, Oct 6, 47; m 74, Jean Kadish. *Educ:* Univ Wis-Milwaukee, BS, 69; Purdue Univ, PhD(org chem), 75. *Prof Exp:* Chemist res & develop, Explor Res-Lubrizol Corp, 75-79; sr chemist, Specialty Prod, Arco Petrol Prod Co, 79-81, mgr, Fuel Develop, 81-82, mgr engine oils res & develop, 82-85; sr res chemist, Amoco Petrol Additives Co, 85-92. *Concurrent Pos:* Consult lubrication & petrol additives, 97- *Mem:* Am Chem Soc; Am Soc Lubricant Eng; Soc Automotive Eng. *Res:* Fuel development; motor oils; industrial lubricants; lubricant additive development; railroad engine oil formulation. *Mailing Add:* 1622 Rocky Ford Rd Powhatan VA 23139

HUTCHISON, DAVID M, GEOLOGY. *Current Pos:* from asst prof to assoc prof, 67-78, PROF GEOL, HARTWICK COL, 78- *Personal Data:* b Chicago, Ill, Aug 3, 35; m 58; c 3. *Educ:* Beloit Col, BS, 57; Univ Mont, MS, 59; WVa Univ, PhD(geol), 68. *Prof Exp:* Asst geol, Mich State Univ, 59-62; instr, Flint Community Jr Col, 62-65; asst, WVa Univ, 65-66. *Mem:* Geol Soc Am. *Res:* Clay mineralogy; correlation of volcanic ash; provenance study of sand in sand dunes. *Mailing Add:* Dept Geol Hartwick Col Oneonta NY 13820

HUTCHISON, DORRIS JEANNETTE, MICROBIOLOGY. *Current Pos:* instr bact, Cornell Univ, New York, NY, 52-53, res assoc, 53-54, from asst prof to prof microbiol, 54-90, chmn biol unit, 68-74, assoc dir, 74-87, EMER PROF MICROBIOL, SLOAN-KETTERING DIV, GRAD SCH MED SCI, CORNELL UNIV, NEW YORK, NY, 90- *Personal Data:* b Carrsville, Ky,

Oct 31, 18. *Educ:* Western Ky State Col, BS, 40; Univ Ky, MS, 43; Rutgers Univ, PhD(microbiol), 49. *Prof Exp:* Res asst, Univ Ky, 40-42; instr biol, Russell Sage Col, 42-44; instr plant sci, Vassar Col, 44-46; res fel & asst, Rutgers Univ, 46-48; res assoc, 48-49; instr bot, Wellesly Col, 49-51; asst, Sloan-Kettering Inst Cancer Res, 51-56, assoc, 56-60, sect head drug resistance, 56-72, assoc mem, 60-69, actg chief, Div Exp Chemother, 65-66, chief, Div Drug Resistance, 67-72, co-head, Lab Exp Tumor Ther, 73-74, head, Lab Drug Resistance & Cyto-Regulation, 73-83, coordr field of educ, 75-81. *Concurrent Pos:* Fac fel, Vassar Col, 46; USPHS fel, 51-53; Philippe Found fel, 59; assoc dean, Grad Sch Med Sci, NY & asst dean, Grad Sch, Cornell Univ, Ithaca, 78-87; mem, Sloan-Kettering Inst Cancer Res, 69-90, Sloan-Kettering Cancer Ctr, NY, 84-90, emer mem, 90-; nat deleg dir, Am Cancer Soc, 86-90. *Mem:* AAAS; Am Soc Microbiol; Am Asn Cancer Res; fel Am Acad Microbiol; fel NY Acad Sci; Am Cancer Soc; Am Inst Nutrit; Genetics Soc Am; Soc Cryobiol. *Res:* Biochemistry; microbial antagonism; antibiotics, especially with tuberculosis; antimetabolites; mechanisms of resistance to antimetabolites in bacteria, mouse and human leukemia; enzymatic formation of citrovorum factor; pteridine metabolism. *Mailing Add:* Southgate Bronxville NY 10708

HUTCHISON, GEORGE B, EPIDEMIOLOGY. *Current Pos:* RETIRED. *Personal Data:* b Lexington, Ky, Oct 18, 22. *Educ:* Harvard Univ, AB, 43, MD, 51, MPH, 60. *Prof Exp:* Fel med, Lahey Clin, 52-55; asst med dir, Equitable Life Assurance Soc US, 55-56 & Health Ins Plan Gtr NY, 56-57; dir res, City Health Dept, NY, 57-59; from asst prof to assoc prof epidemiol, Sch Pub Health, Harvard Univ, 60-66; epidemiologist, Michael Reese Hosp, Chicago, 66-71; prof epidemiol, Sch Pub Health, Harvard Univ, 72-88. *Mem:* Fel Am Pub Health Asn; Am Statist Asn; World Med Asn; Asn Teachers Prev Med; NY Acad Med. *Res:* Epidemiologic study of effects of ionizing radiation and study of causes of cancer and other chronic diseases. *Mailing Add:* 115 St Francis Ct No 96 Louisville KY 40205

HUTCHISON, JAMES A, MYCOLOGY. *Current Pos:* from asst prof to assoc prof, 65-71, PROF BOT, DIV BIOL, ARK STATE UNIV, 71- *Personal Data:* b Salina, Kans, Jan 28, 30; m 53; c 2. *Educ:* Kans Wesleyan Univ, BA, 58; Univ Kans, MA, 60, PhD(bot), 63. *Prof Exp:* Asst prof biol, Southwest Col, Kans, 63-65. *Mem:* Mycol Soc Am; Med Mycol Soc Ams. *Res:* Zygomycetes, fungal agents causing disease in insects and/or fungi inhabiting the intestine of the ectotherms. *Mailing Add:* Ark State Univ PO Box 262 State University AR 72467-0262

HUTCHISON, JAMES E, CHEMISTRY. *Current Pos:* PROF, DEPT CHEM, UNIV ORE. *Concurrent Pos:* Chem grantee, Camille & Henry Dreyfus Found, 94. *Mailing Add:* Dept Chem Univ Ore Eugene OR 97403

HUTCHISON, JAMES ROBERT, PHYSICAL INORGANIC CHEMISTRY. *Current Pos:* from asst prof to prof, 73-90, CHMN DEPT, ALMA COL, 78-, TOWSLEY PROF CHEM, 90- *Personal Data:* b Smithville, Ohio, July 23, 40; m 63, Margaret Llewellyn; c Claire E, Robert L, David E & J Matthew. *Educ:* Wittenberg Univ, BS, 62; Princeton Univ, PhD(chem), 68. *Prof Exp:* From instr to asst prof chem, Swarthmore Col, 66-73. *Concurrent Pos:* Res assoc, Mass Inst Technol, 69-70; adj prof chem, Mich State Univ, 79-81; SERAPHIM fel, NSF-Proj SERAPHIM, Eastern Mich Univ, 86-87. *Mem:* Am Chem Soc; Sigma Xi. *Res:* Nuclear magnetic resonance of paramagnetic systems; kinetics and mechanisms of rearrangement reactions of metal complexes; nuclear magnetic resonance of metal nuclides; instructional uses of computers. *Mailing Add:* Dept Chem Alma Col 614 W Superior Alma MI 48801. *E-Mail:* hutchison@alma.edu

HUTCHISON, JEANNE S, MATHEMATICS. *Current Pos:* ASST PROF MATH, UNIV ALA, BIRMINGHAM, 70- *Personal Data:* b Newburgh, NY, Nov 13, 42; wid; c 1. *Educ:* Creighton Univ, BS, 64; Univ Calif, Los Angeles, MA, 67, PhD(math), 70. *Concurrent Pos:* Assoc dean nat sci & math, Univ Ala, Birmingham, 77-81. *Mem:* Am Math Soc; Math Asn Am. *Res:* Convexity. *Mailing Add:* 3612 Oakdale Rd Birmingham AL 35223

HUTCHISON, JOHN HOWARD, VERTEBRATE PALEONTOLOGY. *Current Pos:* Sr mus paleontologist, Univ Calif Mus Paleonnt, 66-84, asst res, 84-86, assoc res paleontologist, 86-93, adj prof, integrative biol, 90-93, EMER RES PALEONTOGIST, UNIV CALIF MUS PALEONT, 93- *Personal Data:* b Chicago, Ill, Dec 29, 39. *Educ:* Univ Fla, MS, 62; Univ Ore, MA, 64; Univ Calif, Berkeley, PhD(paleont), 76. *Mem:* Soc Vert Paleont; Am Soc Mammalogists; Soc Syst Zool; Am Soc Ichthyologists & Herpetologists; Soc Study Amphibians & Reptiles. *Res:* Systematics, morphology and ecology of recent and fossil moles, Talpidae, Mammalia; systematics, morphology and ecology of North American fossil turtles. *Mailing Add:* Mus Paleont Valley Life Sci Bldg Univ Calif Berkeley CA 94720

HUTCHISON, JOHN JOSEPH, ORGANIC CHEMISTRY, POLYMER CHEMISTRY. *Current Pos:* CHEMIST ENVIRON REGULATION, BASF AG, 70- *Personal Data:* b New York, NY, Nov 16, 39; m 64; c 2. *Educ:* Polytech Inst Brooklyn, BChE, 61, PhD(chem), 65. *Prof Exp:* Sr res scientist, Jet Propulsion Lab, NASA, 66-68; Humboldt Found res fel, Univ Heidelberg, 68-70. *Mem:* Am Chem Soc. *Res:* Organic chemistry of polymers, particularly polyurethanes. *Mailing Add:* Hans Willmannstra 8 67157 Wachenheim Germany

HUTCHISON, KENNETH JAMES, MEDICAL PHYSIOLOGY, NON-INVASIVE VASCULAR DIAGNOSIS. *Current Pos:* assoc prof, 69-76, PROF PHYSIOL, UNIV ALTA, 76-, SURG, 85-; SCI & RES ASSOC STAFF, UNIV ALTA HOSP, 84- *Personal Data:* b Portadown, Northern Ireland, June 23, 36; Can citizen; m 62; c 3. *Educ:* Queens Univ Belfast, MB, BCh & BAO, 61, MD, 66. *Prof Exp:* Tutor physiol, Queens Univ Belfast, 62-66, lectr, 66-69. *Concurrent Pos:* Med Res Coun Can fel, Univ Western Ont, 67-68; lectr, Northern Ireland Hosps Authority, 69; acting chmn physiol, Univ Alta, 77-78; vis scientist, Dept Surg, Univ Wash, 79-80. *Mem:* Brit Physiol Soc; Can Physiol Soc (treas, 85-88); fel Am Col Angiology. *Res:* Arterial hemodynamics; peripheral circulation; hemodynamics and atherosclerosis; non-invasive diagnosis of peripheral arterial disease; Doppler ultrasound spectral shape; B-mode measurement of arterial wall thickness. *Mailing Add:* Dept Physiol Univ Alta Edmonton AB T6G 2H7 Can

HUTCHISON, NANCY JEAN, GENETICS. *Current Pos:* Damon Runyon-Walter Winchell Cancer Fund fel, 82, NIH fel, 83-84, STAFF SCIENTIST, DEPT GENETICS, FRED HUTCHINSON CANCER RES CTR, 84- *Personal Data:* b Dallas, Tex, June 21, 50. *Educ:* Univ Tex, BA, 77; Univ Calif Irvine, PhD(develop & cell biol), 82. *Concurrent Pos:* Sci adv Fred Hutchinson Cancer Res Ctr Image Anal & chair Users Comt, 88-90; mem, Clin Sci Study Sect, Subcomt 1, NIH. *Mem:* Am Soc Cell Biol; Asn Women Sci; Am Soc Microbiol; AAAA. *Res:* Developmental and cell biology; genetics; numerous technical publications. *Mailing Add:* Dept Genetics AC136 Fred Hutchinson Cancer Res Ctr 1124 Columbia St Seattle WA 98104-2092

HUTCHISON, ROBERT B, ORGANIC CHEMISTRY. *Current Pos:* res mgr, Henkel Corp, Emery Group, 67-74, dir cent res, 74-78, dir corp res develop, 78-79, VPRES RES & DEVELOP, HENKEL CORP, EMERY GROUP, 79- *Personal Data:* b Freeport, Ill, June 14, 35; m 58; c 3. *Educ:* Kent State Univ, BS, 57; Univ Calif, Berkeley, PhD(org chem), 60. *Prof Exp:* Res chemist, Miami Valley Labs, Procter & Gamble Co, 60-63; asst prof chem, Bowling Green State Univ, 63-67. *Concurrent Pos:* USPHS grant, 65-69. *Mem:* Am Chem Soc; Soc Cosmetic Chem. *Res:* Structure studies of naturally occurring compounds; reaction study of compounds leading to electron deficient nitrogen species. *Mailing Add:* 10066 Whitebridge Ct Cincinnati OH 45242

HUTCHISON, THOMAS SHERRET, PHYSICS. *Current Pos:* RETIRED. *Personal Data:* b Scotland, Aug 12, 21; m 46; c 2. *Educ:* St Andrews Univ, BSc, 42, PhD(physics), 48. *Hon Degrees:* DSc, Queen's Univ, 85. *Honors & Awards:* Medal, Can Metal Physics Conf, 54. *Prof Exp:* Exp off, Admiralty Res Estab, 42-45; lectr, St Andrews Col, 48-49; sr sci off, Atomic Energy Res Estab, Eng, 49-50; assoc prof physics, Royal Mil Col Can, 50-54, head dept, 54-62, dean grad studies & res, 62-80, chmn, Div Sci, 72-80, prof physics, 54-86. *Mem:* Fel Brit Inst Physics; fel Am Phys Soc; fel Royal Soc Edinburgh. *Res:* X-ray diffraction; solid state physics. *Mailing Add:* Sibbit Rd RR 1 Kingston ON K7L 4V1 Can

HUTCHISON, VICTOR HOBBS, PHYSIOLOGICAL ECOLOGY, ZOOLOGY. *Current Pos:* prof zool & chmn dept, 70-81, GEORGE LYNN CROSS RES PROF, UNIV OKLA, 79- *Personal Data:* b Blakely, Ga, June 15, 31; m 52; c 4. *Educ:* NGa Col, BS, 52; Duke Univ, MA, 56, PhD(zool), 59. *Prof Exp:* Asst zool, Duke Univ, 54-57, instr, 58-59; from instr to assoc prof, Univ RI, 59-67, dir inst environ biol, 66-70. *Concurrent Pos:* Guggenheim fel, 65-66. *Mem:* Fel AAAS; Ecol Soc Am; Am Soc Ichthyologists & Herpetologists (pres, 88); Am Soc Zoologists; Am Physiol Soc; Soc Study Amphibians & Reptiles. *Res:* Physiological ecology; comparative physiology; metabolism and gas exchange in lower vertebrates; temperature relations; herpetology. *Mailing Add:* Dept Zool Univ Okla Norman OK 73019. *Fax:* 405-325-7560; *E-Mail:* vhutchison@ou.edu

HUTCHISON, WILLIAM FORREST, parasitology, preventive medicine, for more information see previous edition

HUTCHISON, WILLIAM MARWICK, ANALYTICAL CHEMISTRY. *Current Pos:* Chemist, Harshaw Chem Co, 40-46, analytical chemist, 50-63, mgr analytical serv, 63-67, sr analytical res assoc, Analytical Res Dept, 67-88, CONSULT, N & T HARSHAW, 88- *Personal Data:* b Cleveland, Ohio, Oct 18, 19; m 59; c 3. *Educ:* Ohio State Univ, BS, 50. *Mem:* Am Chem Soc. *Res:* Inorganic analytical chemistry. *Mailing Add:* 72 Kendal Dr Oberlin OH 44074

HUTH, EDWARD J, MEDICINE, SCIENTIFIC COMMUNICATION. *Current Pos:* from asst ed to ed, Annalg Internal Med, Am Col Physicians, 61-90, bk rev ed, 90-93, interim ed, 94-96, EMER ED, ANNALS INTERNAL MED, AM COL PHYSICIANS, 90- *Personal Data:* b Philadelphia, Pa, May 15, 23; m 57, Carol Monnik; c John E & James J. *Educ:* Wesleyan Univ, BA, 45; Univ Pa, MD, 47. *Honors & Awards:* Meritorious Award, Coun Biol Eds. *Prof Exp:* From intern to resident, Univ Pa Hosp, 47-51; asst instr pharmacol, Sch Med, 48-49; assoc med, 51-58, asst prof, 58-61. *Concurrent Pos:* From adj asst prof to adj assoc prof, Sch Med, Univ Pa, 65-74, adj prof med, 74- *Mem:* Europ Asn Sci Ed; master Am Col Physicians; World Asn Med Ed; Coun Biol Ed; fel Royal Col Physicians (Eng); hon mem Med Libr Asn. *Res:* Medical editing. *Mailing Add:* 1124 Morris Ave Bryn Mawr PA 19010-1712

HUTHNANCE, EDWARD DENNIS, JR, ALGEBRA, COMPUTER SCIENCE. *Current Pos:* AT MATH DEPT, MIDWESTERN STATE UNIV, WICHITA FALLS. *Personal Data:* b Macon, Ga, Aug 31, 42. *Educ:* Ga Inst Technol, BS, 64, MS, 66, PhD(math), 69. *Prof Exp:* Asst math, Ga Inst Technol, 64-66, instr, 68-69; asst prof, Newberry Col, 69-71, assoc prof, 71-, head dept, 69- *Mem:* Am Math Soc; Math Asn Am; Sigma Xi. *Res:* Modern, abstract algebra; generalizations of group theory; loop theory. *Mailing Add:* Dept Math Bloomsburg Univ Pa Bloomsburg PA 17815-1301

HUTJENS, MICHAEL FRANCIS, DAIRY SCIENCE, NUTRITION. *Current Pos:* PROF ANIMAL SCI & EXTEN DAIRY SPECIALIST, UNIV ILL, URBANA, 79- *Personal Data:* b Green Bay, Wis, Nov 21, 45; m 68, Carol; c Charles, Melissa, Matt, Michelle & Chris. *Educ:* Univ Wis-Madison, BS, 67, MS, 69, PhD(dairy sci, nutrit), 71. *Honors & Awards:* Midwest Young Exten Award, Am Asn Animal Sci, 84; DeLavel Exten Award, Am Dairy Sci Asn, 85, Appl Nutrit Award, 92. *Prof Exp:* From asst prof to prof animal sci, Univ Minn, 71-79. *Mem:* Am Dairy Sci Asn; Am Soc Animal Sci; Coun Agr Sci & Technol. *Res:* Dairy cattle nutrition, especially lipid and protein metabolism; mastitis detection with practical application. *Mailing Add:* 9 Hale Haven Ct Savoy IL 61874. *Fax:* 217-333-7088; *E-Mail:* hutjensm@idea.ag.uiuc.edu

HUTNER, SEYMOUR HERBERT, MICROBIOLOGY. *Current Pos:* Haskins adj prof biol, 70-78, EMER PROF IN RESIDENCE, PACE UNIV, 78-, EMER STAFF MEM, HASKINS LABS. *Personal Data:* b Brooklyn, NY, Oct 28, 11; m 37, Margarita S Santiago; c Reed A. *Educ:* City Col New York, BS, 32; Cornell Univ, PhD(microbiol), 37. *Hon Degrees:* DSc, St Francis Col, Brooklyn, NY, 86. *Prof Exp:* Res assoc physics, Mass Inst Technol, 35-36; technician, Labs & Res Div, State Health Dept, NY, 38-41; mem staff biochem & microbiol, 41-65, assoc res dir, Haskins Labs, 65-77. *Concurrent Pos:* Vis prof, Inst Microbiol, Univ Brazil, 63-; adj prof, Fordham Univ, 64-68; vis prof, Univ Brasilia, 70. *Mem:* Soc Protozool (pres, 61-62); Am Soc Microbiol; Am Chem Soc; Phycol Soc Am; corresp mem Brazilian Acad Sci; Biochem Soc. *Res:* Nutritional physiology of bacteria, algae, fungi and protozoa; chemotherapy of trypanosomatid diseases; biopterin metabolism; polyamine metabolism; cell-injury repair; cancer chemotherapy. *Mailing Add:* Haskins Labs Pace Univ One Place Plaza New York NY 10038-1502

HUTNIK, RUSSELL JAMES, FOREST ECOLOGY. *Current Pos:* from asst prof to prof, 57-86, EMER PROF FORESTRY, PA STATE UNIV, 86- *Personal Data:* b Register, Pa, Feb 9, 24; m 55; c 3. *Educ:* Pa State Univ, BS, 50; Yale Univ, MF, 52; Duke Univ, PhD(forestry), 64. *Prof Exp:* Res forester, Northeastern Forest Exp Sta, Pa, 50-57. *Concurrent Pos:* Consult elec utilities, USDA, 64- *Mem:* Soc Am Foresters; Ecol Soc Am; Am Inst Biol Sci; Sigma Xi; Am Soc Surface Mining & Reclamation. *Res:* Ecosystem dynamics; reclamation of disturbed land; impact of air pollution on forest ecosystems; vegetation management on right-of-way. *Mailing Add:* 1658 Princeton Dr State College PA 16803

HUTSON, JAMES CHELTON, REPRODUCTIVE IMMUNOLOGY, REPRODUCTIVE BIOLOGY. *Current Pos:* PROF, TEX TECH UNIV HEALTH SCI CTR, 76- *Personal Data:* b Leon, Iowa, May 14, 47; m 80; c 2. *Educ:* Peru State Col, BS, 69; Univ Nebr, MS, 74, PhD(anat), 76. *Mem:* Endocrine Soc; Am Asn Anatomists; Soc Study Reproduction Cell Biol. *Res:* How specific cell types of the immune system communicate with cells outside the immune system. *Mailing Add:* Dept Cell Biol & Biochem Tex Tech Univ Lubbock TX 79430. *Fax:* 806-743-2747; *E-Mail:* hejch@ttacs/.ttu.edu

HUTSON, RICHARD LEE, ELEMENTARY PARTICLE PHYSICS. *Current Pos:* Appointee, 67-69, MEM STAFF NUCLEAR PHYSICS, LOS ALAMOS SCI LAB, 69- *Personal Data:* b Pittsburg, Kans, Nov 25, 36; m 58; c 2. *Educ:* Univ Colo, BA, 60, PhD(nuclear physics), 67; Mass Inst Technol, SB, 63. *Mem:* Am Asn Physicists Med. *Res:* Study of medical applications of particle beams and accelerator technology. *Mailing Add:* 2497 36th St Los Alamos NM 87544

HUTSON, SUSAN MARY, STRUCTURE & FUNCTION OF AMINO ACID METABOLIZING ENZYMES, ENERGY METABOLISM. *Current Pos:* assoc prof biochem, 88-96, PROF BIOCHEM, BOWMAN GRAY SCH MED, WAKE FOREST UNIV, 96- *Personal Data:* b Boston, Mass, Aug 23, 48; m, Reidar Wallin; c 2. *Educ:* Vanderbilt Univ, BS, 70; Univ Wis-Madison, PhD(biochem), 76. *Prof Exp:* Amanvensis/stipendiat biochem, Univ Tromso, 80-82; asst prof physiol, Pa State Univ, Hershey, 83-87. *Concurrent Pos:* Adj prof, Dept Food, Nutrit & Food Serv Mgt, Univ NC, Greensboro, 96- *Mem:* Am Soc Biochem & Molecular Biol; Am Soc Nutrtit Sci; Int Soc Neurosci. *Res:* Key enzymes involved in the catabolism nutritionally essential amino acids, protein and energy metabolism. *Mailing Add:* Dept Biochem Wake Forest Univ Medical Center Blvd Winston-Salem NC 27157. *Fax:* 910-716-7671; *E-Mail:* shutson@bgsm.edu

HUTT, FREDERICK BRUCE, genetic resistance to disease in domestic animals; deceased, see previous edition for last biography

HUTT, MARTIN P, INTERNAL MEDICINE. *Current Pos:* from instr to asst prof, 57-80, PROF MED, SCH MED, UNIV COLO, DENVER, 80- *Personal Data:* b New York, NY, Sept 27, 26; m 49; c 4. *Educ:* NY Univ, MD, 49; Am Bd Internal Med, dipl, 58. *Prof Exp:* Instr med, Med Sch, Northwestern Univ, 55-57. *Concurrent Pos:* Consult, Vet Admin Hosp, Denver, 59- & Fitzsimmons Army Hosp, 65- *Mem:* Am Soc Nephrology. *Res:* Clinical nephrology. *Mailing Add:* 1395 S Jackson Denver CO 80210

HUTT, RANDY, MICROBIOLOGY, VIROLOGY & IMMUNOLOGY. *Current Pos:* MGR, IN VITRO TESTING & DEVELOP (QC), WYETH-LEDERLE VACCINES & PEDIAT, 95- *Personal Data:* b New York, NY, Dec 11, 47; div; c Jasmine & Gregory. *Educ:* State Univ NY, Buffalo, BA, 68; Univ Fla, MS, 72; Pa State Univ, PhD(microbiol), 77. *Prof Exp:* Lab technologist indust bacteriol, West Chem Co, 68-69; lab technologist clin bacteriol, Queen's Gen Hosp, 70; res scientist virol, Southwest Found Res & Educ, 77-79; mgr immunol & virol, Res & Develop Labs, Gibco Div, Dexter Corp, 79-80; mgr biol control, Schering Corp, 80-83, qual assurance coordr, interferon mfg proj team, 83-84, tech serv proj coordr, 84-85; dept head, tech support, Burroughs Wellcome Co, 86-88, dept head, compounding, filling & packaging, Sterile Prod Div, 88-95. *Mem:* Am Soc Microbiol; Parenteral Drug Asn; Mensa. *Res:* Basic virology research in vitro and in vivo; development of diagnostic tests; immunology; molecular virology; cell kinetics. *Mailing Add:* 21 Stockbridge Ave Suffern NY 10901. *E-Mail:* randyhutt@internetmail.pr.cyanamid.com

HUTTA, PAUL JOHN, CHEMICAL PHYSICS. *Current Pos:* RES SCIENTIST, BETZ LABS, 78- *Personal Data:* b Coaldale, Pa, Jan 20, 46; m 69; c 1. *Educ:* Pa State Univ, BS, 67; Lehigh Univ, MS, 69, PhD(physics), 74. *Prof Exp:* Lectr, 75-76, res assoc phys chem, Tex A&M Univ, 76-78. *Mem:* Am Phys Soc. *Res:* Study of transition metal complexes in aluminosiliates utilizing electron paramagnetic resonance, and infrared visible ultra violet spectroscopy with the intention of developing heterogeneous analogs to homogeneous analogs to catalysts. *Mailing Add:* 1224 Oakleaf Lane Warminster PA 18974

HUTTENLOCHER, DIETRICH F, ORGANIC CHEMISTRY, LUBRICATION ENGINEERING. *Current Pos:* chemist, 63-74, res assoc, 74-78, PROG MGR HERMETIC SYSTS, MAJOR APPLIANCE LABS, GEN ELEC CO, 78- *Personal Data:* b Oberlahnstein, Ger, June 27, 28; US citizen; m 61; c 2. *Educ:* Univ Buffalo, BA, 53; Univ Cincinnati, PhD(org chem), 58. *Prof Exp:* Teaching asst, Univ Cincinnati, 53-55; chemist, Texaco Res Labs, NY, 58-60 & SKF Industs, Pa, 60-63. *Mem:* Am Chem Soc; Am Soc Lubrication Eng; Am Soc Heat, Refrig & Air-Conditioning Eng. *Res:* Synthetic organic chemistry; lubricants and lubrication technology; chemistry of sealed refrigeration systems. *Mailing Add:* 32 Sterling Rd Louisville KY 40220

HUTTER, GEORGE FREDERICK, ORGANIC & POLYMER CHEMISTRY. *Current Pos:* RES CHEM, WESTVACO, 86- *Personal Data:* b Glen Ridge, NJ, Jan 7, 43. *Educ:* Rutgers Univ, BA, 71; Seton Hall Univ, MS, 74, PhD, 85. *Prof Exp:* Chemist, Inmont Corp/BASF, 71-78, sr chemist, 78-86. *Mem:* Assoc mem Sigma Xi; Am Chem Soc. *Res:* Synthesis of polymers and resins used as coatings and ink vehicles. *Mailing Add:* 968 Orange Grove Rd Charleston SC 29407

HUTTER, KOLUMBAN, MECHANICAL ENGINEERING. *Current Pos:* PROF, MECHANICS TECH INST, DARMSTADT, GER, 87- *Personal Data:* b St Gallen, Switz, Jan 22, 41; m 40, Anna B Faivre; c Bettina & Katja. *Educ:* Fed Inst Technol, Dipl Ing, 64; Cornell Univ, MS, 70, PhD, 73. *Honors & Awards:* Max-Planck-Forschungs Prize, 94; Alexander von Humboldt-Stiftung Award, 94. *Prof Exp:* Res scientist, Lab Hydraul Fed Inst Technol, 73-75, sr res scientist, 75-78, head phys limnol group, 78-83, dir res, 83-87. *Concurrent Pos:* Postdoctoral res fel, Johns Hopkins Univ, 74; vis prof, Tech Univ, Neth, 76 & 78, Univ Ariz, 79-80, 84-85, Univ Glasgow, 84; vis scientist, Univ EAnglia, Eng, 84, Fed Inst Technol, Zurich, 88-91; co-ed, J Glaciol, 84- *Mem:* Int Glaciol Soc; Int Soc Limnol; Soc Indust & Appl Math; Sigma Xi. *Mailing Add:* Bergstrasse 5 8044 Zurich 8044 Switzerland

HUTTER, ROBERT V P, PATHOLOGY, ONCOLOGY. *Current Pos:* dir, 70-73, CHMN, DEPT PATH, ST BARNABAS MED CTR, 73- *Personal Data:* b Yonkers, NY, May 25, 29; m 55; c 3. *Educ:* Syracuse Univ, BA, 50; State Univ NY, MD, 54. *Hon Degrees:* MA, Yale Univ, 69. *Prof Exp:* Intern, Yale Med Ctr, 54-55, resident, 55-56; resident path, Mem Ctr, NY, 56-58; asst attend pathologist, Mem Hosp, NY, 60-64, asst attend cytologist, 62-64, assoc attend pathologist, 65-68, attend pathologist, 67-68; chief path serv, Yale-New Haven Hosp, 68; prof path & dir anat path & cytopath, Sch Med, Yale Univ, 68-70; prof path & chmn dept, Col Med NJ, 70-73. *Concurrent Pos:* Asst vis pathologist, James Ewing Hosp, New York, 60-64, assoc vis pathologist, 65, attend pathologist, 67-68; consult, NY State Div Labs, 60, Mary Swift Tumor Clin & Registry, Butte, Mont, 64, West Haven Vet Admin Hosp, Conn, 67, St Peter's Gen Hosp, New Brunswick, NJ, 68, Lyndon B Johnson Trop Med Ctr, Am Samoa, Laurel Heights Hosp, Shelton, Conn, Windham Community Mem Hosp, Willimantic, 69 & Waterbury Hosp, 70; consult pathologist & cytopathologist, USPHS, NY, 61-68; prof clin oncol, Am Cancer Soc, 71-73. *Mem:* AAAS; AMA; Am Acad Forensic Sci; fel Col Am Path; Am Soc Cytol; hon fel Am Col Radiol; Am Cancer Soc (pres, 81-82); Soc Surg Oncol (pres, 86-87). *Mailing Add:* St Barnabas Med Ctr Old Short Hills Rd Livingston NJ 07039-5601

HUTTERER, FERENC, CLINICAL BIOCHEMISTRY, CLINICAL PATHOLOGY. *Current Pos:* PROF BIOCHEM & MOLECULAR PATH & CHMN DEPT, COL MED, NORTHEASTERN OHIO UNIV, 75- *Personal Data:* b Budapest, Hungary, Jan 27, 29; US citizen; m 53; c 1. *Educ:* Univ Szeged, MD, 53. *Prof Exp:* Prof clin chem, Mt Sinai Sch Med, 68-75. *Concurrent Pos:* Dir dept chem, Mt Sinai Hosp, 68-75. *Mem:* Fedn Am Soc Exp Biol; Asn Study Liver Dis; NY Acad Sci; AAAS. *Res:* Microsomal electron transfer system and its relation to human diseases, especially cholestasis and atherosclerosis; molecular pathology. *Mailing Add:* Northeastern Ohio Univ Col Med 4209 SR 44 PO Box 96 Rootstown OH 44272-0095. *Fax:* 330-325-2524

HUTT-FLETCHER, LINDSEY MARION, PATHOLOGY. *Current Pos:* from asst prof to assoc prof, 82-90, PROF DEPT COMP & EXP PATH, COL VET MED, DEPT IMMUNOL & MED MICROBIOL & DEPT PATH & LAB MED, COL MED, UNIV FLA, GAINESVILLE, 90- *Personal Data:* b Cardiff, South Wales, July 2, 47; nat US. *Educ:* Liverpool Univ, Eng, BSc, 68; Univ London, PhD(viral immunol), 73. *Prof Exp:* Res asst, Dept Virol, Lister Inst Prev Med, Univ London, Eng, 68-73; res assoc, Dept Bact & Immunol & Cancer Res Ctr, Univ NC, Chapel Hill, 76-77, res asst prof, 77-82. *Res:* Comparative and experimental pathology. *Mailing Add:* Univ Mo, Kansas City Sch Biol Sci 5100 Rockhill Rd Kansas City MO 64110-2499. *Fax:* 816-235-5158

HUTTLIN, GEORGE ANTHONY, PHOTOCONDUCTIVITY, PULSED-POWER. *Current Pos:* SUPVRY PHYSICIST, ARMY RES LAB, ADELPHI, MD, 92- *Personal Data:* b Abington, Pa, Mar 19, 47. *Educ:* La Salle Col, Philadelphia, BA, 69; Univ Notre Dame, MS, 72, PhD(nuclear physics), 75. *Prof Exp:* Physicist pulsed power, Dept Army, Harry Diamond Labs, 75-92. *Mem:* Am Phys Soc; Am Asn Physics Teachers; Inst Elec & Electronics Engrs; Percussive Arts Soc. *Res:* Numerical and analytical modeling; design and diagnostics of multi-terawatt, pulsed-power machines; nuclear structure studies through nuclear reactions induced by polarized deuteron beams; polarization of nuclear reaction; application of photoconductivity to the control of high-powered microwave and pulsed-power. *Mailing Add:* 10500 Truxton Rd Adelphi MD 20783

HUTTO, FRANCIS BAIRD, JR, FILTRATION & SEPARATION, CHEMICAL MICROSCOPY. *Current Pos:* PRES, TUTCO SCI CORP, 93- *Personal Data:* b Savannah, Ga, June 25, 26; m 52, Mary J Hall; c Frank, Madeline, Roger, Nancy, Ellen & Amy. *Educ:* Clemson Univ, BS, 48; Cornell Univ, MS, 50, PhD(chem), 52. *Prof Exp:* Sr res chemist, Res & Eng Ctr, Johns-Manville Corp, 52-61, from sect chief to sr sect chief, 61-69, res mgr, 69-72, sr res assoc, Res Ctr, Johns-Manville Prod Corp, 72-76; dir res & develop, Pabco Insulation Div, Fibreboard Corp, 76-92. *Mem:* Am Chem Soc; fel Am Inst Chem Engrs. *Res:* Calcium silicate chemistry as related to industrial insulation, fire proofing and fillers; filter aids and filtration; stress corrosion cracking testing. *Mailing Add:* 676 Peony Dr Grand Junction CO 81503

HUTTON, ELAINE MYRTLE, medical genetics, prenatal diagnosis, for more information see previous edition

HUTTON, HAROLD M, PHYSICAL CHEMISTRY, NUCLEAR MAGNETIC RESONANCE. *Current Pos:* assoc prof, 70-77, chmn dept, 83-93, PROF CHEM, UNIV WINNIPEG, 77- *Personal Data:* b Prince Albert, Sask, June 30, 37; m 63, Natalie A Yorkewich; c Julianne R (Klein) & Michelle A. *Educ:* Brandon Col, BSc, 58; Univ Man, MSc, 61, PhD(chem), 63. *Prof Exp:* Res assoc chem, Johns Hopkins Univ, 63-64; asst prof, Univ Man, 64-65; from asst prof to assoc prof, Brandon Univ, 65-70. *Concurrent Pos:* Adj prof, Univ Man, 74-78; vis scholar, Univ Ariz, 90-91. *Mem:* Fel Chem Inst Can; Soc Chem Indust; Int Union Pure & Appl Chem; Am Chem Soc. *Res:* Proton and carbon-13 magnetic resonance of organic and inorganic compounds for the determination of physical properties. *Mailing Add:* Dept Chem Univ Winnipeg Winnipeg MB R3B 2E9 Can. *Fax:* 204-775-2114; *E-Mail:* hutton@uwinnipeg.ca

HUTTON, JAMES ROBERT, MOLECULAR BIOLOGY. *Current Pos:* MGR, PURE CULT FERMENTATION FAC, UNIVERSAL BIOVENTURES; ASST PROF BIOL MARQUETTE UNIV, 75- *Personal Data:* b Lilbourn, Mo, Mar 22, 43; m 64; c 1. *Educ:* Univ Mo-St Louis, BS, 69; Univ Ill, MS, 71, PhD(biochem), 73. *Prof Exp:* Res fel biol, Harvard Med Sch, 73-75. *Concurrent Pos:* Am Cancer Soc fel, 73-75. *Mem:* Am Chem Soc; AAAS; Sigma Xi. *Res:* Organization and structure of DNA in chromosomes; molecular biology and control of gene expression; factors affecting polynucleotide-polynucleotide interactions. *Mailing Add:* 6143 N 60th St Milwaukee WI 53218-1606

HUTTON, JOHN JAMES, JR, EDUCATIONAL ADMINISTRATION. *Current Pos:* prof, Children's Hosp Med Ctr, 84-87, DEAN & PROF MED & PEDIAT, UNIV CINCINNATI, 87- *Personal Data:* b Ashland, Ky, July 24, 36; m 64; c 3. *Educ:* Harvard Univ, AB, 58, MD, 64. *Prof Exp:* Intern med, Mass Gen Hosp, 64-65; staff assoc biochem, Nat Heart Inst, 65-67; resident & instr med, Univ Ky, 67-68; sect chief mammalian genetics, Roche Inst Molecular Biol, 68-71; from assoc prof to prof med, Sch Med, Univ Ky, 71-80; prof med, Sch Med, Univ Tex, San Antonio, 81-84; chief Heniat, Vet Admin Hosp, San Antonio, 81-84. *Concurrent Pos:* Vis investr, Jackson Lab, 68-69; adj asst prof, Columbia Univ, 69-71; chief med serv, Vet Admin Hosp, Lexington, 74-80. *Mem:* AAAS; Am Soc Clin Invest; Am Soc Biol Chemists; Am Soc Hemat; Am Fedn Clin Res; Asn Am Physicians. *Res:* Mammalian molecular genetics. *Mailing Add:* Dean Col Med Univ Cincinnati Col Med PO Box 670555 Cincinnati OH 45267

HUTTON, KENNETH EARL, PHYSIOLOGY. *Current Pos:* from asst prof to assoc prof, 58-66, PROF BIOL, SAN JOSE STATE UNIV, 66- *Personal Data:* b Chicago, Ill, Apr 17, 28. *Educ:* Kalamazoo Col, AB, 51; Purdue Univ, MS, 52, PhD, 55. *Prof Exp:* Instr zool, Tulane Univ, 55-58. *Mem:* AAAS; Am Soc Zoologists; Sigma Xi. *Res:* Reptilian blood chemistry; blood and immunochemistry of fish. *Mailing Add:* Dept Biol Sci San Jose State Univ 1 Washington Sq San Jose CA 95192-0001

HUTTON, LUCREDA ANN, MATHEMATICS, MATHEMATICS EDUCATION. *Current Pos:* RETIRED. *Personal Data:* b Logansport, Ind, Jan 5, 26; c 2. *Educ:* Butler Univ, BA, 67; Purdue Univ, MS, 72; Ind Univ, Bloomington, EdD(math educ), 76. *Prof Exp:* From asst prof to assoc prof math, Ind Univ-Purdue Univ, Indianapolis, 76-95. *Concurrent Pos:* Dir res proj, Math Div, Indianapolis Pub Schs, 76-77, consult, 78-; math consult, Optical Apprenticeship Prog, Workmate, Inc, 77-78. *Mem:* Math Asn Am; Nat Coun Teachers Math; Am Math Asn Two Year Cols; Am Math Soc. *Res:* Effects of calculators and micro-computers in the teaching of mathematics; mathematics anxiety. *Mailing Add:* 10 N 400 W Lebanon IN 46052

HUTTON, THOMAS WATKINS, ORGANIC CHEMISTRY. *Current Pos:* CONSULT, 80- *Personal Data:* b Milwaukee, Wis, June 1, 27; m 54; c 3. *Educ:* Brown Univ, ScB, 50; Univ Wash, PhD, 54. *Prof Exp:* Asst, Univ Calif, 54-56; res scientist, Weyerhaeuser Co, 56-61; chemist, Rohm & Haas Co, Philadelphia, 61-80. *Mem:* Am Chem Soc. *Res:* Natural products; effect of ultraviolet light on organic compounds; photolysis of organic compounds; synthetic tanning agents; organic synthesis and coatings; adhesives; caulks. *Mailing Add:* 153 Woodview Dr Doylestown PA 18901-2923

HUTZ, REINHOLD JOSEF, REGULATION OF OVARIAN FUNCTION, ESTROGEN RECEPTOR REGULATION & TOXICOLOGY. *Current Pos:* asst prof, 86-92, ASSOC PROF, DEPT BIOL SCI, UNIV WIS, MILWAUKEE, 92-, GRAD PROG DIR, 93- *Personal Data:* b Salzburg, Austria, Mar 18, 56; m 83, Irene M O'Shaughnessy; c Erika, Michael & Peter. *Educ:* Loyola Univ, Chicago, BS, 78, MS, 80; Mich State Univ, PhD(physiol), 83. *Prof Exp:* Assoc, Wis Regional Primate Res Ctr, 83-86. *Concurrent Pos:* Affil scientist, Wis Regional Primate Res Ctr, 87-; consult ed, Am J Primatology, 89-; assoc adj prof obstet/gynec, Med Col Wis, 91-, assoc adj prof physiol, 96-; dep dir, NIEHS Biomed Sci Ctr, 97- *Mem:* AAAS; Am Physiol Soc; Am Soc Primatologists; Int Primatological Soc (treas, 92-96); Endocrine Soc; Soc Study Reproduction. *Res:* Regulation of ovarian function by steroids and growth factors; interaction between estrogen receptor and dioxins in reproduction. *Mailing Add:* 4830 N Bartlett Ave Whitefish Bay WI 53217. *Fax:* 414-229-3926

HUTZENLAUB, JOHN F, PHYSICS, MATHEMATICS. *Current Pos:* CONSULT ENGR, 80- *Personal Data:* b Derby, Conn, Oct 8, 18; wid; c 2. *Educ:* Rensselaer Polytech Inst, BS, 39; Mass Inst Technol, PhD(physics), 43. *Prof Exp:* Staff mem, Div Indust Coop, Mass Inst Technol, 42-44, proj engr, Instrumentation Lab, 44-50; tech dir exp eng, AC Spark Plug Div, Gen Motors Corp, 50-52; group leader res & develop, Lincoln Lab, Mass Inst Technol, 52-62, assoc div head eng, 62-63, div head eng, 63-80. *Res:* Experimental solid state physics; instrumentation; inertial navigation systems; automatic control systems; structural design. *Mailing Add:* 18230 NW Cornell Rd No F Beaverton OR 97006-7422

HUTZINGER, OTTO, ENVIRONMENTAL CHEMISTRY. *Current Pos:* CHMN ECOL CHEM & GEOCHEM DEPT, UNIV BAYREUTH, WGER; DIR, LAB ENVIRON & TOXICOL CHEM, UNIV AMSTERDAM, 74- *Personal Data:* b Vienna, Austria, Mar 14, 33; Can citizen; m 60; c 3. *Educ:* Fed Inst Chem, Vienna, Ing, 56; Univ Sask, MS, 63, PhD(org chem), 65. *Honors & Awards:* Sr Res Award, Alexander von Humboldt Found, Ger, 73; Frank R Blood Award, Soc Toxicol, 74. *Prof Exp:* Chemist, Ebewe Pharmaceuts, Austria, 53-58; res scientist, Synthesis of Drugs, Psychiat Res Unit, Univ Hosp, Univ Sask, 60-65; res biochemist metabolism, Univ Calif, Davis, 65-67; scientist, Indoles, Pesticides & Pollutants, Atlantic Regional Lab, Nat Res Coun Can, 67-74. *Concurrent Pos:* Lectr, Dalhousie Univ, 70-; dir, Lab Environ Chem, Univ Amsterdam, Holland, 74- *Mem:* Am Chem Soc; Chem Inst Can; Dutch Chem Soc; Soc Environ Toxicol & Chem; Sigma Xi. *Res:* Chemistry, metabolism and environmental breakdown of pesticides and pollutants; development of new analytical procedures. *Mailing Add:* Ecol Chem & Geochem Dept Univ Bayreuth Postfach 3008 95447 Bayreuth Germany

HUTZLER, JOHN R, ELECTRICAL INSULATION, DIELECTRICS & ACID RAIN. *Current Pos:* CHIEF OPER OFFICER & DIR, VA ACCELERATORS CORP. *Personal Data:* b New York, NY, Aug 8, 29; m 52; c 4. *Educ:* Fordham Univ, BS, 51; Rensselaer Polytech Inst, MS, 54. *Prof Exp:* Supvr chem, Gen Elec, 51-59; sr engr, Western Elec, 63-64; prod mgr, Union Carbide, 64-70; dir res & develop, Aerovox Inc, subsid RTE Corp, 71-90; pres, High Energy, Parkesburg, Pa. *Concurrent Pos:* Mem, Int Conf Large High Tension Elec Systs; technol consult. *Mem:* Inst Elec & Electronics Engrs; Illum Engrs Soc. *Res:* Lower cost, smaller size capacitors for electrical and electronic applications; high voltage capacitors; electronic scrubbing of flue gases to remove SO_2, NO_x, and small particals by 90-98% at low cost. *Mailing Add:* 80 Dutton Mill Rd Malvern PA 19355. *Fax:* 703-836-2878

HUTZLER, LEROY, III, CHEMICAL, SAFETY & ENVIRONMENTAL ENGINEERING. *Current Pos:* CONSULT, HUTZLER CONSULT SERV, 84- *Personal Data:* b Richmond, Va, Oct 18, 21; m 50, Helen Currier; c 4. *Educ:* Va Polytech Inst, BS, 42. *Prof Exp:* Chem engr, process develop & serv, Gen Elec Co, 42-47, chem engr & process supvr, 47-52, supvr, chem eng unit, 52-53, supvr, process eng lab, 53-61, supvr, adv mfg eng, 61-65, adv mfg engr mat & process, 65-68, mgr, process & equip develop, 68-72, environ engr, 72-83. *Mem:* Am Indust Hyg Asn; Am Acad Indust Hyg; Am Soc Safety Engrs. *Res:* Drying and vacuum treating processes for insulating materials; painting and metal finishing; wire manufacturing and insulating processes; plastics molding; industrial hygiene; environmental health. *Mailing Add:* 11 Biltmore Ave Providence RI 02908-3513

HUWE, DARRELL O, PARTICLE PHYSICS. *Current Pos:* asst prof, 66-70, ASSOC PROF PHYSICS, OHIO UNIV, 70- *Personal Data:* b Lemmon, SDak, Sept 22, 32; m 64; c 3. *Educ:* SDak Sch Mines & Technol, BS, 54; Univ Calif, Berkeley, PhD(physics), 64. *Prof Exp:* Res assoc physics, Univ Colo, 64-66. *Concurrent Pos:* Vis assoc prof, Am Univ Cairo, 75-77. *Mem:* Am Phys Soc; Sigma Xi. *Res:* Study of strong interactions among elementary particles using hydrogen bubble chamber. *Mailing Add:* 9 West Hills Dr Athens OH 45701-2255

HUXLEY, ANDREW (FIELDING), PHYSIOLOGY. *Current Pos:* Jodrell prof physiol, Univ Col, London, 60-69, Royal Soc res prof, 69-83, hon fel, 80, EMER PROF PHYSIOL, UNIV LONDON, 83- *Personal Data:* b London, Eng, Nov 22, 17; m 47, Jocelyn R; c Janet R, Stewart L, Camilla R, Eleanor (Brace), Henrietta C & Clare M (Peace). *Educ:* Cambridge Univ, Eng, BA, 38, MA, 41. *Hon Degrees:* Numerous from Europe & US univs. *Honors & Awards:* Nobel Prize, 63; Herter Lectr, Johns Hopkins Univ, 59; Jesup Lectr, Columbia Univ, 64; Forbes Lectr, 66; Croonian Lectr, Royal Soc, 67; Copley Medal, Royal Soc, 73; Hans Hecht Lectr, Chicago, 75; Sherrington Lectr, Liverpool Univ; Florey Lectr, 82; Decorated Order of Merit, 83; Blackett Mem Lectr, 84; Tarner Lectr, Trinity Col, Cambridge, 88; Maulana Abul Kalam Azad Mem Lectr, New Delhi, 91; C G Bernhard Lectr, Stockholm, 93; Grand Cordon of the Sacred Treas, 95. *Prof Exp:* Mem res staff, Anti-Aircraft Command, 40-42, admiralty, 42-45; fel, Trinity Col, Cambridge, 41-60, dir studies, 52-60, hon fel, 67-90, master, 84-90. *Concurrent Pos:* Demonstr, Cambridge Univ, 46-50, asst dir res, 51-59, reader biophys, 59-60; Fullerian prof, Roy Inst, London, 67-73; chmn, Med & Res Comt, Muscular Dystrophy Group, Gt Brit & N Ireland, 74-81, vpres, 81-; Centenary Coloquim lectr, Berlin Inst Physiol, 77; Cecil H & Ida Green vis prof, Univ BC, 80; hon fel, Imperial Col Sci & Tech, 80; trustee, Brit Mus Natural Hist, 81-90, sci mus, 84-88; 6th Ann Darwin lectr, 82; fel Queen Mary & Westfield Col, 87. *Mem:* Foreign assoc Nat Acad Sci; Royal Acad Eng; Indian Nat Sci Acad; Am Physiol Soc; Int Union Physiol Sci (pres, 86-93); Brit Biophys Soc; Royal Acad Med Belg; fel Royal Soc (pres, 80-85); Brit AAAS; Am Philos Soc. *Res:* Physiology of striated muscle; development of interference microscope and ultramicrotome. *Mailing Add:* Manor Field One Vicarage Dr Grantchester Cambridge CB3 9NG England

HUXLEY, HUGH E, MOLECULAR BIOLOGY, PHYSIOLOGY. *Current Pos:* PROF BIOL, BRANDEIS UNIV, 87- *Personal Data:* b 1924; m 66, Frances Maxon; c Olwen. *Educ:* Univ Cambridge, MA, 48, PhD(molecular biol), 52. *Hon Degrees:* DSc, Harvard Univ, 69, Univ Chicago, 74 & Univ Pa, 76, ScD, Leicester Univ, 89. *Honors & Awards:* Feldberg Prize, 63; Horwitz Prize, 71; Feltrinelli Prize, 74; Int Award, Gairdner Found, 75; Baly Medal, Royal Col Physicians, 75; Royal Medal, Royal Soc Eng, 77; E B Wilson Award, 83; Albert Einstein World Award of Sci, 87; Benjamin Franklin Medal, 90. *Prof Exp:* Sci staff, MRC Molecular Biol, Cambridge, UK, 54-87, dep dir, 77-87; dir, Rosenstiel Basic Med Sci Res Ctr, 88-94. *Concurrent Pos:* Extenal staff, Biophys Dept, Univ Col London, 56-62. *Mem:* Nat Acad Sci; Royal Soc London; Am Acad Arts & Sci. *Res:* Structural biology, especially mechanism of muscle contraction. *Mailing Add:* Brandeis Univ Rosenstiel Ctr 415 S St Waltham MA 02254. *Fax:* 781-736-2405; *E-Mail:* huxley@auriga.rose.brandeis.edu

HUXSOLL, DAVID LESLIE, VETERINARY MEDICINE. *Current Pos:* DEAN RES & ADVAN STUDIES, SCH VET MED, LA STATE UNIV, BATON ROUGE, 90- *Personal Data:* b Aurora, Ind, July 18, 36; m 59; c 2. *Educ:* Univ Ill, Urbana, BS, 59, DVM, 61; Univ Notre Dame, PhD(microbiol), 65. *Prof Exp:* Lab officer, Dept Vet Microbiol, Div Vet Med, Walter Reed Army Inst Res, 61-62, asst chief dept, 64-67, dep dir div, 66-67, chief, Dept Vet Med, Ninth Army Med Lab, Vietnam, 67-68, chief, Dept Vet Diag Serv, Div Vet Med, Vet Corps, Walter Reed Army Inst Res, 68-, dep dir, Div Vet Med, 72-; US Army Med Res Inst Infectious Dis. *Mem:* Am Vet Med Asn; Am Soc Microbiol; Wildlife Dis Asn; US Animal Health Asn. *Res:* Virus diseases of laboratory animals; infectious diseases of dogs; zoonotic diseases. *Mailing Add:* 5629 Riverbend Blvd Baton Rouge LA 70820

HUXTABLE, RYAN JAMES, PHARMACOLOGY. *Current Pos:* asst prof, 70-75, assoc prof, 75-79, PROF PHARMACOL, COL MED, UNIV ARIZ, 79- *Personal Data:* b Bristol, Eng, Sept 20, 43; US citizen; m 68. *Educ:* Bristol Univ, BSc, 64, PhD(chem), 68. *Prof Exp:* Tech officer chem, Mond Div, Imp Chem Indust, 67-68; res assoc chem, Univ Ill, 68-69; res assoc biochem, Duke Univ, 69-70. *Concurrent Pos:* Vis prof, Univ Montreal, 77, Univ Mex, 80 & Univ Florence, 81. *Mem:* Am Soc Pharmacol & Exp Therapeut; AAAS. *Res:* Pharmacology and biochemistry of taurine, with emphasis on involvement in epilepsy and cardiac dysfunctioning; cardiopulmonary toxicology of pyrrolizidine alkaloids. *Mailing Add:* Dept Pharmacol Univ Ariz Health Sci Ctr Tucson AZ 85724-0001

HUYER, ADRIANA (JANE), PHYSICAL OCEANOGRAPHY. *Current Pos:* res assoc phys oceanog, 75-79, from asst prof to assoc prof, 79-85, PROF OCEANOG, ORE STATE UNIV, 85- *Personal Data:* b Giessendam, Neth, May 19, 45; Can citizen; m 86, Robert L Smith. *Educ:* Univ Toronto, BSc, 67; Ore State Univ, MS, 71, PhD(oceanog), 74. *Prof Exp:* Sci officer phys oceanog, Marine Sci Directorate, Environ Can, 67-74, res scientist, 74-75. *Mem:* Am Geophys Union; AAAS; Am Meteorol Soc; Can Meteorol & Oceanog Soc. *Res:* Coastal upwelling; circulation over continental shelves, distributions of physical properties in the ocean. *Mailing Add:* Col Oceanog Ore State Univ Corvallis OR 97331-5503

HUYLEBROECK, MICHAEL R, DIABETIC FOOTCARE, WOUND CARE MANAGEMENT. *Current Pos:* CHIEF THERAPIST, INDIAN HOSP, USPHS, 81-, CHIEF CONSULT, 91-, CHIEF PROF OFFICER, 94- *Personal Data:* b Jersey City, NJ, Nov 30, 42. *Educ:* Ind Univ, BS, 66; Golden Gate Univ, MBA, 84. *Honors & Awards:* Commendation Medal Exemplary Serv, US Surgeon Generals Off, 89. *Prof Exp:* Staff therapist, Norfolk Va US Health Servs Hosp, 74-77; chief therapist, Philadelphia Outpatient Clin, 77-80; dep chief therapist, SF Pub Health Hosp, 80-81. *Mem:* Am Phys Ther Asn. *Mailing Add:* Indian Hosp USPHS White River AZ 85941. *Fax:* 520-338-1122; *E-Mail:* meh@wr.2phx@ihs

HUYSER, EARL STANLEY, ORGANIC CHEMISTRY. *Current Pos:* from asst prof to assoc prof, 59-66, PROF ORG CHEM, UNIV KANS, 66- *Personal Data:* b Holland, Mich, May 27, 29; m 52, Barbara Van Kolken; c Nancy, Thomas, David & Gretchen. *Educ:* Hope Col, AB, 51; Univ Chicago, PhD(org chem), 54. *Prof Exp:* Res fel, Univ Chicago, 54-55; res chemist, Dow Chem Co, 57-59. *Concurrent Pos:* Vis prof, State Univ Grottingen, 64-65; consult, Dow Chem Co & Dowell Schlumberger, Inc; vis scientist, Univ Wash, 81. *Mem:* Am Chem Soc. *Res:* Chemistry of free radical reactions; kinetic analysis of chain reactions; halogenation reactions; biochemical redox reactions; theoretical chemistry. *Mailing Add:* Dept Chem Univ Kans Lawrence KS 66044

HUZINAGA, SIGERU, THEORETICAL CHEMISTRY, PHYSICS. *Current Pos:* PROF CHEM, UNIV ALTA, 69- *Personal Data:* b Chanchun, Manchuria, May 23, 26; m 54; c 2. *Educ:* Kyushu Univ, BSc, 48; Kyoto Univ, DSc(physics), 59. *Prof Exp:* Assoc prof physics, Kyushu Univ, 58-65. *Mem:* Phys Soc Japan; Am Phys Soc. *Res:* Atomic and molecular structures. *Mailing Add:* Dept Chem Univ Alta Edmonton AB T6G 2J1 Can

HVATUM, HEIN, ELECTRONICS. *Current Pos:* res assoc, 58-60, asst dir, 65-72, SCIENTIST, NAT RADIO ASTRON OBSERV, 61-, ASSOC DIR, 72- *Personal Data:* b Tonsberg, Norway, Apr 17, 23; m 47; c 2. *Educ:* Chalmers Tech Univ, Sweden, MSc, 54, PhD, 58. *Prof Exp:* Asst electronics, res lab electronics, Chalmers Tech Univ, Sweden, 48-54, assoc prof, 54-58 & 60-61. *Mem:* Am Astron Soc; Inst Elec & Electronics Engrs. *Res:* Development and applications of electronics in radio astronomy. *Mailing Add:* 104 Lancaster Ct Charlottesville VA 22901

HWA, JESSE CHIA HSI, POLYMER CHEMISTRY. *Current Pos:* PRES, HWA INT, INC, 85- *Personal Data:* b Hankow, China, July 12, 24; nat US; m 49, Dolores Lowe; c Nancee, David & Nadine. *Educ:* St John's Univ China, BS & BS Hons, 45; Univ Ill, MS, 47, PhD(chem), 49. *Prof Exp:* Chemist, China Biol & Chem Co, 45-46; res chemist, Rohm & Haas Co, 49-55, group leader, 55-63; sr group leader, Stauffer Chem Co, 63-64, head org sect, 64-65, mgr polymer sect, 65-67, mgr polymer res dept, 67-71, mgr res planning, 71-77, dir develop, 77-82, corp proj dir, 82-84, tech dir electronic mat, 84-85. *Concurrent Pos:* Mem adv bd, Polymer Res Inst, Univ Conn, 71-82 & Mat Res Inst, Univ Mass, 81-83; mem comm macromolecular chem, Nat Res Coun, Nat Acad Sci, 72-77; tech comt Nat Asn Mfg, 75-78; mem bd dirs, Sci & Ed Soc, 82-; sr adv, Ministry Light Indust, China, 85- *Mem:* Am Chem Soc; Soc Plastics Eng; Chinese Am Chem Soc (pres, 81-85). *Res:* Industrial organic intermediates; surfactants; monomer and polymer synthesis; ion exchange resins; emulsion polymers; stereospecific polymers; polyvinyl chloride; surface chemistry; polymer physics; electronic materials; suspension and emulsion polymerization. *Mailing Add:* HWA Int Inc 54 Westhill Circle Stamford CT 06902. *E-Mail:* jchhwa@aol.com

HWA, RUDOLPH CHIA-CHAO, HIGH ENERGY PARTICLE AND NUCLEAR PHYSICS, COMPLEX SYSTEMS. *Current Pos:* dir, Inst Theoret Sci, 73-77 & 79-84, PROF PHYSICS, UNIV ORE, 74- *Personal Data:* b Shanghai, China, Nov 1, 31; nat US; m 62, 84; c 4. *Educ:* Univ Ill, BS, 52, MS, 53, PhD(elec eng), 57; Brown Univ, PhD(physics), 62. *Prof Exp:* Res asst prof, Univ Ill, 57-58; asst physics, Brown Univ, 58-62; res physicist, Lawrence Radiation Lab, Univ Calif, Berkeley, 62-64; mem, Inst Advan Study, 64-66; asst prof, Inst Theoret Physics, State Univ NY Stony Brook, 66-71; assoc prof physics & res assoc, Inst Theoret Sci, 71-74. *Concurrent Pos:* Ed, Int J Mod Physics & Mod Physics Lett, 85- *Mem:* Fel Am Phys Soc. *Res:* High energy physics; scattering and production processes; symmetries; structure of hadrons; quantum chromodynamics; quark-gluon plasma; heavy-ion collisions; chaos; phase transition. *Mailing Add:* Inst Theoret Sci Univ Ore Eugene OR 97403

HWANG, BRUCE YOU-HUEI, ORGANIC CHEMISTRY, MEDICINAL CHEMISTRY. *Current Pos:* CONSULT, CHEM & BIO PHARMACEUT, 94- *Personal Data:* b Taiwan, Jan 6, 36; US citizen; m 66; c 3. *Educ:* Nat Taiwan Univ, BS, 58; ETenn State Univ, MA, 61; Ohio State Univ, PhD, 65. *Prof Exp:* Sr med chemist, Smithkline Beecham Pharmaceutical, 65-69, assoc sr investr, 69-72, sr investr, 72-94. *Mem:* AAAS; Am Chem Soc; NY Acad Sci; fel Am Inst Chemists; Int Soc Study Xenobiotics. *Res:* Organic chemistry; drug metabolism; natural products; structure elucidation. *Mailing Add:* 1571 Horseshoe Trail Chester Springs PA 19425-1906. *Fax:* 610-827-1319; *E-Mail:* bhwang@concentric.net

HWANG, CHARLES C, FLUID MECHANICS, COMBUSTION. *Current Pos:* asst prof, 69-74, assoc prof, 74-93, PROF, DEPT MECH ENG, UNIV PITTSBURGH, 93- *Personal Data:* c 2. *Educ:* Nat Taiwan Univ, BS, 54; Kans State Univ, MS, 57; Harvard Univ, PhD(eng), 68. *Prof Exp:* Teaching asst, Nat Taiwan Univ, 54-55; res engr, Carrier Corp, 57-60; sr scientist, Avco Corp, 67-68; postdoctoral fel, Harvard Univ, 68-69. *Concurrent Pos:* Fac mem, Nat Inst Occup Safety & Health, 71- *Mem:* Am Soc Mech Engrs. *Res:* Modeling of energy systems, fluid-mechanics systems and combustion systems. *Mailing Add:* Dept Mech Eng Univ Pittsburgh Pittsburgh PA 15261

HWANG, CHERNG-JIA, SEMICONDUCTOR LASERS, FIBER OPTICS. *Current Pos:* PRES, OPTRONICS INT CORP, TAIWAN, 96- *Personal Data:* b Changhua, Taiwan, Oct 1, 37; US citizen; m 65, Elizabeth Y Shen; c Karen C & Dennis C. *Educ:* Nat Taiwan Univ, BS, 60; Univ Wash, MS, 64, PhD(elec eng), 66. *Prof Exp:* Mem tech staff, Bell Tel Labs, Murray Hill, 66-73; proj leader, Hewlett Packard Labs, Hewlett Packard Co, 73-77; pres & dir, Gen Optronics Corp, 77-88; vpres & dir, Laser Diode, Inc, Morgan Crucible Co, 88-90; chief exec officer, pres & dir, Appl Optronics Corp, 91-93; chief adv, Telecommun Labs, Ministry Transp & Communs, Taiwan, Repub China, 94-96. *Concurrent Pos:* Pres & dir, Photon Imaging Corp, 90-92. *Mem:* Am Phys Soc; Am Optical Soc; Soc Photo-Optical Instrumentation Engrs. *Res:* Application of super radiant diode array and fiber optic bundle in the development of high resolution printers; high power semiconductor laser fabrication and application; quantum well laser structure; strained-layer laser structure; application of high power lasers and fiber coupling technology in therapeutic and diagnostic medicine. *Mailing Add:* 170 Hill Hollow Rd Watchung NJ 07060

HWANG, CHING-LAI, MECHANICAL & INDUSTRIAL ENGINEERING. *Current Pos:* from asst prof to assoc prof, 64-73, PROF INDUST ENG, KANS STATE UNIV, 73- *Personal Data:* b Taiwan, Formosa, Jan 22, 29; m 54, Meilang Liu; c Grace, Frank & Jean. *Educ:* Taiwan Univ, BS, 52; Kans State Univ, MS, 60, PhD(mech eng), 62. *Prof Exp:* Instr, Ta-Tung Inst Technol, 54-58; asst prof eng & physics, Washburn Univ, Topeka, 62-65. *Concurrent Pos:* Guest prof, Tech Univ Denmark, 74-75. *Mem:* Am Soc Mech Engrs; sr mem Am Inst Indust Engrs; Japan Asn Automatic Control Engrs. *Res:* Decision theory; optimization techniques; operation research; published seven books and 125 journal articles. *Mailing Add:* Dept Indust Eng Kans State Univ Manhattan KS 66506

HWANG, FRANK K, statistics, discrete mathematics, for more information see previous edition

HWANG, HELEN H L, EXPERIMENTAL DESIGN, MARKET MEASUREMENTS & INFORMATION ANALYSIS. *Current Pos:* mem tech staff, 85-91, DISTINGUISHED MEM TECH STAFF, AT&T BELL LABS, 91- *Personal Data:* b Canton, China, Feb 3, 47; US citizen; m 71, Dah-Min; c Peter & Dick. *Educ:* Cheng Kung Univ, Taiwan, BS, 69; Kent State Univ, MS, 71; Univ Ill, PhD(statist), 82. *Prof Exp:* Lectr math, Nat Tsing Hua Univ, 73-78; asst prof statist, Northern Ill Univ, 82-84; mem tech staff, Bell Commun Res, 84-85. *Res:* Evaluate and characterize the performance of AT&T and other long distance carriers telephone networks, the work activities include designing of tests, sampling, analyzing data and modeling the results. *Mailing Add:* 11 Delwood Dr Holmdel NJ 07733

HWANG, HU HSIEN, ELECTRICAL ENGINEERING. *Current Pos:* PROF ELEC ENG, UNIV HAWAII, 66- *Personal Data:* b China, Dec 1, 23; US citizen; m 64, Elizabeth Woo. *Educ:* Chiao Tung Univ, BSc, 49; Lehigh Univ, MS, 57, PhD(elec eng), 59. *Prof Exp:* Instr elec eng, Lehigh Univ, 57-60; asst prof, Univ Windsor, 60-64; chmn, Dept Math, Chung Chi Col, Hong Kong, 61-62; assoc prof elec eng, Univ Windsor, 64-66. *Mem:* Inst Elec & Electronics Engrs. *Res:* Electromechanical energy conversion and systems analysis. *Mailing Add:* Dept Elec Eng Univ Hawaii 3540 Dole St Honolulu HI 96822. *Fax:* 808-956-3427

HWANG, HUEY-MIN, MICROBIAL DEGRADATION-BIOREMEDIATION, AQUATIC PHOTOCHEMISTRY. *Current Pos:* asst prof, 90-94, ASSOC PROF BIOL, JACKSON STATE UNIV, 94- *Personal Data:* b Taichung, Taiwan, Nov 18, 52; US citizen; m, Ching-Lee Liu; c Wayne W & Hank H. *Educ:* Nat Taiwan Normal Univ, BS, 75; Univ Ga, PhD(microbiol), 85. *Prof Exp:* Teacher biol, Yeong-Chuen Jr High Sch, Taipei, 78-79; grad teaching asst human anat, Univ Ga, 80, grad res asst microbiol ecol, 80-85, postdoctoral assoc, 86-89. *Concurrent Pos:* Res consult, Univ Ga, 87-89; vis scientist, Lawrence Berkeley Lab, 90-92, consult, Earth Sci Div, 93-; prin investr, Jackson State Univ, 90- *Mem:* Am Soc Microbiol; AAAS. *Res:* Bioremediation, aquatic photochemistry and environmental toxicology to investigate the fates and effect of contaminants and enrich the data base for restoring the quality of contaminated environments. *Mailing Add:* Biol Dept Jackson State Univ Jackson MS 39217. *Fax:* 601-968-2058

HWANG, JOHN DZEN, INFORMATION TECHNOLOGY, SYSTEMS ENGINEERING. *Current Pos:* GEN MGR, INFO TECHNOL AGENCY, CITY OF LOS ANGESLES, CALIF, 96- *Personal Data:* b Shanghai, China, Sept 8, 41; US citizen; m 67, Gloria Lum; c John, Andrew & Audrey. *Educ:* Univ Calif, Berkeley, BS, 64; Ore State Univ, MA, 66, PhD(math), 68; Harvard Bus Sch, PMD, 81. *Prof Exp:* Asst math, Ore State Univ, 65-68; opers researcher, Hq, US Army Materiel Command, 68-70, mathematician, Weapons Command, Ill, 70-71, res scientist, US Army Air Mobility Res & Develop Lab, Ames Res Ctr, Moffett Field, Calif, 71-75; prog mgr, Defense Commun Agency, Washington, DC, 75-82; dir telecom mgt, Fed Emergency Mgt Agency, Washington, DC, 82-87, dir systs eng, 87, 92, dir facil mgt, 92-93, assoc dir, 93-96. *Concurrent Pos:* Asst comput physics, Eng Exp Sta, Ore State Univ, 67-68; vis prof, US Army Logistics Mgt Ctr, Va, 69-70; mem, Army Math Steering Comt, 71-75; chmn, Comt Retail Comput Facil Issues, Army Mat Command Sci Comput Coun, 74-75 & Subcomt Opers Res, Army Math Steering Comt, 75; vchmn, Army Mat Command Sci & Eng Comput Coun, 75; consult to mgr, Nat Commun Syst, 78-82; adj prof, George Mason Univ, Va, 78-83; dir, Fed Emergency Mgt Agency, 81; fel, Harvard Univ, 81; adj prof, Am Univ, Washington, DC, 83-90; adj prof, Marymount Univ, Va, 91-92. *Mem:* Inst Elec & Electronics Engrs; NY Acad Sci; Opers Res Soc Am. *Res:* Information systems and telecommunications; defense material acquisition, particularly research and development management, decision risk analysis, military systems analysis; applied mathematics, particularly numerical algorithms for computational physics and mathematical systems theory; information technology for emergency management. *Mailing Add:* 2157 Moreno Dr Los Angeles CA 90039. *E-Mail:* jhwang@ita.ci.la.ca.us

HWANG, KAI, COMPUTER & ELECTRICAL ENGINEERING. *Current Pos:* PROF ELEC ENG & COMPUT SCI, UNIV SOUTHERN CALIF, 85- *Personal Data:* b Lan-Chou, China, Feb 28, 43; m 71; c 2. *Educ:* Nat Taiwan Univ, BS, 66; Univ Hawaii, MS, 69; Univ Calif, Berkeley, PhD(elec eng), 72. *Prof Exp:* From asst prof to assoc prof elec eng, Purdue Univ, 81-85. *Mem:* Inst Elec & Electronics Engrs; Asn Comput Mach. *Res:* Computer architecture; parallel processing arithmetic systems; advanced automation; information processing and computer applications. *Mailing Add:* Dept Elec Eng Univ Hong Kong Dokfulam Rd Hong Kong People's Republic of China

HWANG, LI-SAN, PHYSICAL OCEANOGRAPHY, ENGINEERING & RESEARCH MANAGEMENT. *Current Pos:* Mem tech staff, Nat Eng Sci Co Calif, 65-66, mem sr staff, 66-67, sr scientist, 67-71, assoc dir eng div, 71-72, dir eng div, 72-74, vpres eng div, 74-77, sr vpres eng div, 77-88, CHMN & PRES, TETRA-TECH, INC, 88- *Personal Data:* b Chikiang, China, Aug 12, 35; m 62; c 2. *Educ:* Nat Univ Taiwan, BS, 58; Mich State Univ, MS, 62; Calif Inst Technol, PhD(civil eng), 65. *Concurrent Pos:* Chmn & chief exec officer, Edward H Richardson Assocs, 81- *Mem:* Am Soc Civil Engrs; Am Geophys Union; Int Asn Hydraul Res; Am Nuclear Soc. *Res:* Harbor oscillation due to both periodic and dispersive waves; problem of water wave propagation in shallow water; problem of wave run-up; tsunami generation, propagation and coastal effects; container ships problems; scale model studies of harbor problems. *Mailing Add:* 1955 Kinclair Dr Pasadena CA 91107

HWANG, S STEVE, FLUID MECHANICS, HEAT TRANSFER & XEROGRAPHICS. *Current Pos:* Assoc scientist, Xerox, 67-70, scientist, 70-74, proj mgr & sr scientist, 74-84, SR MEM RES STAFF & PROJ MGR, WEBSTER RES CTR, XEROX, 84- *Personal Data:* b Taichung, Taiwan, Oct 28, 38; US citizen; m 72, Cecilia Chen; c Katherine, Jennifer & Victoria. *Educ:* Nat Taiwan Univ, BS, 62; Univ Rochester, MS, 65, PhD(mech & aerospace sci), 67. *Mem:* Am Soc Mech Eng; Sigma Xi; Soc Imaging Sci & Technol. *Res:* Novel color imaging systems including analysis, hardware development and integration; photoelectrophozesis; electronic printing; engineering research. *Mailing Add:* 11 Valley Green Circle Penfield NY 14526. *Fax:* 716-422-2126; *E-Mail:* steve_hwang@wb.xerox.com

HWANG, SAN-BAO, BIOCHEMISTRY, BIOPHYSICS. *Current Pos:* SR VPRES RES, ALTEON INC, 93- *Personal Data:* b Kaohsiung, Taiwan, Sept 8, 46; US citizen; m 70; c 2. *Educ:* Nat Taiwan Univ, BS, 69; Univ Calif, Berkeley, PhD(biophys), 76. *Prof Exp:* Fel physiol, Univ Calif, San Francisco, 76-78, res asst physiologist physiol, 78-79; sr res biophysicist, Merck Sharp & Dohme Res Lab, 79-83, res fel, 84-88, sr res fel, 88-91; dir, Cytomed Inc, 91-93. *Mem:* Biophys Soc; Am Soc Biochem & Molecular Biol; NY Acad Sci; AAAS. *Res:* Characterization of platelet-activating factor receptors; identification of receptor antagonists of platelet-activating factor; identification of various receptor subtypes and intracellular receptors of platelet-activating factor. *Mailing Add:* Alteon Inc 170 Williams Dr Ramsey NJ 07446. *Fax:* 201-934-8880

HWANG, SHY-SHUNG, FLUID MECHANICS, ENGINEERING SCIENCE. *Current Pos:* Assoc scientist, 67-70, scientist, 70-74, proj mgr & sr scientist, 74-84, PROJ MGR & SR MEM RES STAFF, XEROX CORP, 84- *Personal Data:* b Taichung, Taiwan, Oct 28, 38; m 72; c 3. *Educ:* Nat Taiwan Univ, BS, 62; Univ Rochester, MS, 66, PhD(fluid mech), 67. *Mem:* Am Soc Mech Engrs; Sigma Xi; Soc Photographic Scientists & Engrs. *Res:* Photoelectrophoresis; engineering research; electronic printing. *Mailing Add:* 11 Valley Green Circle Penfield NY 14526-1719

HWANG, SOON MUK, COMBUSTION CHEMISTRY, HIGH TEMPERATURE REACITON KINETICS. *Current Pos:* SR RES SCIENTIST, UNIV TOLEDO, 92- *Personal Data:* b Korea, Aug 15, 47; m 76, OK-Gyung Chai; c Yoon Jung & Yoon Jae. *Educ:* Sogang Univ, Korea, BS, 75; Univ Tex, Austin, PhD(phys chem), 88. *Prof Exp:* Sr researcher, Agency Defense Develop, 78-79; fel, Univ Tex, Austin, 88; vis res assoc, Max-Planck Inst, Fluid Dynamics, 89-90; res scientist, Case Western Res Univ, 90-91. *Mem:* Combustion Inst; Am Chem Soc. *Res:* Kinetic research for hydrogen and hydrocarbon pyrolysis oxidation and soot formation by using the laser absorption spectroscopy-shock tube technique; computer modeling for reaction systems to elucidate the information on combustion phenomena. *Mailing Add:* NASA Lewis Res Ctr MS 5-11 Cleveland OH 44135. *Fax:* 216-433-3000

HWANG, SUN-TAK, CHEMICAL ENGINEERING. *Current Pos:* prof & head, 82-93, PROF CHEM ENG, UNIV CINCINNATI, 82-, DIR, CTR EXCELLENCE MEMBRANE TECHNOL, 87- , PROF MAT ENG, UNIV IOWA, 73- *Personal Data:* b Taijon, Korea, June 24, 35; m 63; c 2. *Educ:* Seoul Nat Univ, BS, 58; Univ Iowa, MS, 62, PhD(chem eng), 65. *Prof Exp:* Instr fluid flow, Univ Iowa, 64-65, from asst prof to assoc prof, thermodyn transport processes, 66-73, prof mat eng, 73-82; res engr, Field Res Lab, Mobil Oil Corp, 65-66. *Mem:* Am Inst Chem Engrs; Am Chem Soc; NAm Membrane Soc. *Res:* Membrane separations. *Mailing Add:* Dept Chem Eng Univ Cincinnati Cincinnati OH 45221-0171

HWANG, WILLIAM GAONG, SATCOM SYSTEMS. *Current Pos:* asst vpres, 88-92, VPRES, SAIC, 93- *Personal Data:* b Shanghai, China, June 17, 49; US citizen; m 78; c 2. *Educ:* Calif Inst Technol, BS, 71; Cornell Univ MS, 74, PhD(appl math), 78. *Prof Exp:* Eng aide, Calif Dept Water Resources, 67, Calif Inst Technol, 68-69 & Sacramento Munic Utility Dist, 69-70; teaching asst eng, Cornell Univ, 71-76; mem staff, BDM Corp, 78-82; asst vpres, M/A-Com Linkabit, 82-88. *Mem:* Inst Elec & Electronics Engrs; Am Math Soc; Soc Indust & Appl Math; Armed Forces Commun & Electronics Asn. *Res:* Command, control, and communications systems analysis; satellite communications analyses; information systems and networking. *Mailing Add:* Sci Applns Int Corp T710 Goodridge Dr MS1-2-8 703 McLean VA 22102

HWANG, YU-TANG, POLYMERIZATION PROCESSES, POLYOLEFIN CATALYSIS. *Current Pos:* res assoc, 69-75, asst mgr, tech sect, 75-85, TECH PROJ MGR, QUANTUM CHEM, USI DIV, 85- *Personal Data:* b Tainan, Taiwan, May 20, 30; m 61; c 3. *Educ:* Univ Taiwan, BS, 54; Univ Mich, MS, 57, PhD(chem eng), 61. *Prof Exp:* Sr res engr, Pure Oil Co, Ill, 61-63, res scientist, 63-65; res assoc, Hawshaw Chem Co, 65-69. *Mem:* Am Chem Soc; Am Inst Chem Engrs; Sigma Xi. *Res:* Industrial catalysis; process research and development; polyethylene. *Mailing Add:* 1109 Mooreland Shorewood IL 60431-8613

HWU, MARK CHUNG-KONG, CHEMICAL ENGINEERING. *Current Pos:* RETIRED. *Personal Data:* b Canton, China, Nov 10, 26; m 60, Margaret A Po; c Katherine, Patrick, Susan & Peggy. *Educ:* Nat Taiwan Univ, BS, 51; Kans State Col, MS, 54; Univ Cincinnati, PhD(chem eng), 59. *Prof Exp:* Asst phys chem, Univ Cincinnati, 58-59, res assoc, 59-60, res assoc polymer characterization, 62; chief chem engr, Que Lithium Corp, Can, 60-61, tech adv, 61; asst prof chem eng, Univ NB, 61; chem engr, Chem Div, Union Carbide Corp, 62-67, proj scientist, 67-84, eng scientist, Chem Div & sr develop scientist, Polyolefins Div, 84-95. *Concurrent Pos:* Fel, Univ Cincinnati, 59-60; vis lectr, WVa Inst Technol, 64 & 66. *Res:* Polymerization of ethylene and associated fields; homopolymers and copolymers in high-pressure processes and low-pressure fluid bed processes; chemical engineering kinetics; high pressure and high temperature processing; process modelling, control and optimization; computer control of polyethylene processes. *Mailing Add:* 23 Camden Rd Belle Mead NJ 08502

HYATT, ABRAHAM, AEROSPACE ENGINEERING. *Current Pos:* CONSULT, PLANNING & MGT RES & DEVELOP PROGS IN AEROSPACE. *Personal Data:* b Ukraine, July 15, 10; US citizen; m 38; c 2. *Educ:* Ga Inst Technol, BS, 33. *Honors & Awards:* Distinguished Civilian Serv Award, USN. *Prof Exp:* Sr stress analyst, Glenn L Martin Co, 36-39; chief struct engr, McDonnell Aircraft Corp, 39-44; head airframe design res, Res Div, Bur Aeronaut, USN, 46-48, asst dir aeronaut systs, 48-54, dir, Res Div, 54-56, chief scientist, 56-58; asst dir propulsion systs, NASA, 58-60, dep dir launch vehicle systs, 60, dir prog planning, 60-63; consult space systs, Douglas Aircraft Corp & IBM Corp, 63-64; Hunsaker prof aeronaut & astronaut, Mass Inst Technol, 64-65; exec dir bus develop, N Am Rockwell Corp, 65-76. *Concurrent Pos:* USMC, 44-46; mem, Polaris sci adv bd, Navy Dept, 54-58; adv panel aeronaut, Dept Defense, 56-58; comt aircraft, missile & spacecraft aerodynamics, Nat Adv Comt Aeronaut, 56-58, spec comt space technol, 57-58; panel high altitude detection, President's Sci Adv Comt, 58; comt long range planning, Fed Coun Sci & Technol, 60 & USAF Sci Adv Bd, 60-63. *Mem:* AAAS; fel Am Inst Aeronaut & Astronaut; Am Nuclear Soc; Int Acad Astron. *Res:* Research and optimization of engineering systems principally involving aeronautical systems and manned space systems. *Mailing Add:* 18038 Blue Sail Dr Pacific Palisades CA 90272

HYATT, ASHER ANGEL, SCIENCE ADMINISTRATION, ORGANIC CHEMISTRY. *Current Pos:* exec secy, Med & Org Chem Fels Comt, 66-69, Med Chem Study Sect, 69-78, CHIEF, CHEM & RELATED SCI REV SECT, REFERRAL & REV BR, DIV RES GRANTS, NIH, 78- *Personal Data:* b London, Eng, July 31, 30; US citizen; m 57; c Anthony J & Victoria M. *Educ:* Univ London, BSc, 51, PhD(org chem), 54. *Prof Exp:* Demonstr, Queen Mary Col, Univ London, 52-54; res assoc, Mass Inst Technol, 54-55; res chemist, Brit Thomson-Houston, Eng, 55-56; dir, Nucleus Chem Labs, London, 56-57; res chemist, Ionics Inc, Mass, 57-58; sr org chemist, Monsanto Res Corp, 58-64; head org res, Collab Res Inc, 64-65, sr scientist, 65-66. *Mem:* AAAS; Am Chem Soc; Royal Inst Chem. *Res:* Research administration and management; peer review. *Mailing Add:* 5401 Westbard Ave Bethesda MD 20816

HYATT, DAVID ERNEST, INORGANIC CHEMISTRY, ORGANOMETALLIC CHEMISTRY. *Current Pos:* SR RES CHEMIST, ADA, 90- *Personal Data:* b Syracuse, NY, Nov 25, 42; m 65; c 2. *Educ:* Colgate Univ, AB, 64; Univ Ill, MS, 66, PhD(chem), 68. *Prof Exp:* Res chemist, Eastern Res Ctr, Stauffer Chem Co, 68-70; sr res chemist, Vulcan Mat Co, Colo, 70-72; sr proj engr & environ scientist, Colo Sch Mines Res Inst, 72-75, mgr, Analytical Serv Lab, 75-77; sr proj engr, Hazen Res, 77-81; res mgr, Chem & Metal Industs, 81-90. *Mem:* Am Chem Soc; Am Inst Mining & Metall Engrs; Am Soc Testing & Mat. *Res:* Boron hydride and carborane synthesis; homogeneous and heterogeneous catalysis systems; pollution abatement; minerals processing. *Mailing Add:* 1054 Cook St Denver CO 80206

HYATT, EDMOND PRESTON, CERAMIC ENGINEERING. *Current Pos:* RETIRED. *Personal Data:* b Joliet, Ill, Nov 15, 23; c 10. *Educ:* Univ Mo-Rolla, BS, 49, MS, 50; Univ Utah, PhD(ceramic eng), 56. *Prof Exp:* Instr, Brigham Young Univ, 50-54; co-founder, Electro-Ceramics Inc, 54, vpres opers, 57-63; ceramic eng consult, 70-90. *Mem:* Fel Am Ceramic Soc; Inst Ceramic Engrs; Int Soc Hybrid Microelectronics. *Mailing Add:* 21 E 400 S Orem UT 84058

HYATT, GEORGE, JR, dairy husbandry; deceased, see previous edition for last biography

HYATT, JOHN ANTHONY, SYNTHETIC ORGANIC CHEMISTRY. *Current Pos:* SR RES ASSOC, EASTMAN CHEM CO, EASTMAN KODAK CO, 75- *Personal Data:* b Harlan, Ky, Aug 21, 48; m 71, Julie Sarnoff; c Alice E. *Educ:* Wake Forest Univ, BS, 70; Ohio State Univ, PhD(chem), 73. *Prof Exp:* Res fel chem, Harvard Univ, 73-74. *Concurrent Pos:* Vis prof chem, ETenn State Univ, 82-83. *Mem:* Am Chem Soc; Sigma Xi; AAAS. *Res:* Synthetic chemistry of complex organic compounds; plant cell wall polysaccharide chemistry; synthetic photochemistry; cellulose chemistry; natural products chemistry. *Mailing Add:* 439 Forest Hills Dr Kingsport TN 37663-2200. *Fax:* 423-229-4558; *E-Mail:* usechnq3@ibmmail.com

HYATT, RAYMOND R, JR, multivariate statistics, computer graphics, for more information see previous edition

HYATT, ROBERT ELIOT, PHYSIOLOGY, INTERNAL MEDICINE. *Current Pos:* RETIRED. *Personal Data:* b Trenton, NJ, June 2, 25; m 52; c 2. *Educ:* Univ Rochester, AB, 47, MD, 50; Am Bd Internal Med, dipl. *Prof Exp:* Resident internal med, Sch Med, Wash Univ, 50-52, fel cardiol, 52-53; clin assoc, Nat Heart Inst, 53-55, investr respiratory physiol, 55-58; assoc chief med & dir cardiopulmonary lab, Beckley Mem Hosp, 58-62; consult & asst prof physiol, Mayo Clin, 62-67, assoc prof physiol, Mayo Grad Sch Med, Univ Minn, 67-71, assoc prof med, 71-73, prof med & physiol, 73-87. *Concurrent Pos:* Intern, Barnes Hosp, St Louis, 50-51, asst resident, 51-52. *Mem:* Am Physiol Soc; Am Thoracic Soc; Am Fedn Clin Res. *Res:* Physiology of ventilatory mechanics; lung growth and development. *Mailing Add:* 2978 Co Rd 120 NE Stewartville MN 55976

HYATT, ROBERT MONROE, SYSTEMS ENGINEERING. *Current Pos:* PRES & CHIEF EXEC OFFICER, INERTIAL MOTORS CORP, 94- *Personal Data:* b Orlando, Fla, July 14, 43; m 76; c 3. *Educ:* Univ Fla, BSEE, 65; Univ Dallas, MBA, 74. *Prof Exp:* Design eng electro-optics, Tex Instruments, 69-74; region mgr eng, Teccor, 74-75, Portescap, 75-77; gen mgr, Amco Enterprises, 77-78; vpres engr mkt, Transicoil Inc, 78-92; independent consult, 92-94. *Mem:* Inst Elec & Electronics Engrs; Am Helicopter Soc; Army Aviation Am; Soc Automotive Eng. *Res:* Electro magnetic device development; precision drive trains for position system. *Mailing Add:* 5702 Constitution Ct North Wales PA 19454

HYBL, ALBERT, BIOPHYSICS, CRYSTALLOGRAPHY. *Current Pos:* asst prof, 64-71, ASSOC PROF BIOPHYS, MED SCH, UNIV MD, BALTIMORE CITY, 71- *Personal Data:* b Iowa City, Iowa, Jan 8, 32; m 62; c 2. *Educ:* Coe Col, BA, 54; Calif Inst Technol, PhD(chem), 61. *Prof Exp:* Fel chem, Iowa State Univ, 61-64. *Mem:* AAAS; Am Crystallog Asn; Am Chem Soc; Biophys Soc; Sigma Xi. *Res:* Biological structures; molecular structure of organic compounds; structure of membranes and carbohydrates. *Mailing Add:* Dept Biophys Univ Md Med Sch Baltimore MD 21201

HYDE, BEAL BAKER, GENETICS, MOLECULAR BIOLOGY. *Current Pos:* chmn dept, 65-77, PROF BOT, UNIV VT, 65- *Personal Data:* b Dallas, Tex, June 26, 23; m 47; c 3. *Educ:* Harvard Univ, AB, 48, Am, 50, PhD(biol), 52. *Prof Exp:* Res assoc bot, Ind Univ, 51-54; assoc prof plant sci, Univ Okla, 54-61; NSF res fel, Calif Inst Technol, 61-64; vis assoc prof bot, Univ Tex, 64-65. *Concurrent Pos:* Mem staff, Inst Genetics, Copenhagen Univ, 71-72 & Plant Breeding Inst, Cambridge, Eng, 78-79. *Mem:* AAAS; Genetics Soc Am; Am Soc Cell Biologists; Sigma Xi. *Res:* Plant cytogenetics and cytochemistry; ultrastructure of nucleus. *Mailing Add:* Dept Bot Marsh Life Sci Bldg Univ Vt Burlington VT 05405-0068

HYDE, DALLAS MELVIN, ANATOMY, PULMONARY INFLAMMATION. *Current Pos:* from asst prof to assoc prof, 79-88, PROF & CHMN DEPT ANAT, PHYSIOL & CELL BIOL, SCH VET MED, UNIV CALIF, DAVIS, 88- *Personal Data:* b Mar 12, 45; m 77, Leigh West; c Mack & Roy. *Educ:* Univ Calif, Irvine, BA, 67, Whittier Col, MS, 72, Univ Calif, Davis, PhD(anat), 76. *Prof Exp:* Capt, USMC Res, 67-70; staff res assoc II, Sch Vet Med, Univ Calif, Davis, 72-74, Walter Foster Found fel, 74-76; asst prof, Dept Metab, Col Vet Med, Univ Fla, Gainesville, 76-79. *Concurrent Pos:* Mem, Grad Studies & Res Comt, Col Vet Med, Univ Fla, 76-78, Electron Micros Comt, 76-79, Student Advisement Comt, 76-79, Admis Comt, 77-79, Off Vet Med Educ Comt, 77-79; mem, Curric Comt, Grad Group Anat, Univ Calif, 80-81, mem, Health Sci Libr, Sch Vet Med, 80-81, chmn, Curric Comt, 81-83, grad adv, 83-85; Nat Res Serv Award sr fel, NIH, Nat Jewish Hosp, Denver, Colo, 85-86. *Mem:* Am Asn Anatomists; Am Asn Vet Anatomists; Am Asn Pathologists; Am Thoracic Soc; Micros Soc Am; Int Soc Stereology; Soc Quant Morphol. *Res:* Morphometric and morphologic evaluation of the mechanisms of pulmonary inflammation in response to inhale environmental pollutants and fibrogenic chemicals. *Mailing Add:* Dept Anat Physiol & Cell Biol Univ Calif Davis CA 95616-5224. *Fax:* 530-752-7690; *E-Mail:* dmhyde@ucdavis.edu

HYDE, DAVID RUSSELL, MOLECULAR GENETICS OF VISUAL TRANSDUCTION, MECHANISMS OF RETINAL DEGENERATION. *Current Pos:* asst prof, 88-95, ASSOC PROF, BIOL SCI, UNIV NOTRE DAME, 95- *Personal Data:* b Pittsburg, Pa, Sept 4, 58; m 81, Laura Schaefer; c Nathaniel, Brittany & Jordan. *Educ:* Mich State Univ, BS, 80; Pa State Univ, PhD(biochem & molecular biol), 85. *Prof Exp:* Vis instr genetics, Bucknell Univ, 83; res fel, neurogenetics, Div Biol, Calif Inst Technol, 85-88. *Mem:*

Genetics Soc Am; AAAS. *Res:* Molecular basis of visual transduction in Drosophila melanogaster using molecular biology, genetics, biochemical and electrophysiological approaches. *Mailing Add:* Dept Biol Sci Univ Notre Dame Notre Dame IN 46556. *E-Mail:* david.r.hyde.1@nd.edu

HYDE, EARL K, NUCLEAR CHEMISTRY, NUCLEAR PHYSICS. *Current Pos:* chemist, Nuclear Chem Div, Lawrence Berkeley Lab, Univ Calif, 49-72, dep head, 71-73, dep dir, 73-83, assoc dir-at-large, 84-86, SR STAFF SCIENTIST, LAWRENCE BERKELEY LAB, UNIV CALIF, 73-, EMER DEP DIR, 86- *Personal Data:* b Rossburn, Man, Aug 9, 20; US citizen; m 49; c 4. *Educ:* Univ Chicago, BS, 41, PhD(chem), 46. *Prof Exp:* Res assoc inorg war res proj, Univ Chicago, 42-44, jr chemist, Metall Lab, Manhattan Dist, 44-46; assoc chemist, Argonne Nat Lab, 46-49. *Mem:* Am Chem Soc; fel Am Phys Soc. *Res:* Chemistry of heavy elements; mechanisms of interaction of giga electron volt particles with complex nuclei studied by physical techniques; identification of new alpha emitting isotopes of short half life; radioactive isotopes produced by high energy spallation or fission reactions. *Mailing Add:* 852 Arlington Ave Berkeley CA 94707

HYDE, GEOFFREY, SATELLITE COMMUNICATIONS, RADIOPHYSICS. *Current Pos:* RETIRED. *Personal Data:* b Toronto, Ont, Apr 10, 30; US citizen; m 53; c 3. *Educ:* Univ Toronto, BSc, 54, MSc, 59; Univ Pa, PhD(elec eng), 67. *Prof Exp:* Engr power equip, Can Gen Elec Co, 53-55; engr antennas, Sinclair Radio Labs, Ltd, 55-57; engr antennas & radar, Avro Aircraft Ltd, 58-59; engr antennas & electromagnetic theory, Radio Corp Am, 59-65, engr radar systs, 67-68; sr staff scientist antennas & electromagnetic theory, Comsat Labs, 68-74, mgr propagation studies, 74-80, sr staff scientist & coordr, Corp Res Develop Prog, 80-84, asst to dir, 84-89; consult, 89-93. *Concurrent Pos:* Mem US Study Group 5, Int Radio Consult Comt, Int Telecommun Union, 74-, mem US deleg, Switz, 76, US deleg, France, 77 & subcomt chmn, US Study Group 5F, 78-; David Sarnoff fel, 65-67. *Mem:* Fel Inst Elec & Electronics Engrs; Int Scientists Radio Union; Am Inst Aeronaut & Astronaut. *Res:* Propagation of electromagnetic waves in non-ionized media; microwave antenna research and development; related areas of satellite communications systems and radio meteorology; related areas of electromagnetic theory; communications engineering and systems; radio engineering; radio physics. *Mailing Add:* 15116 Red Clover Dr Rockville MD 20853-1642

HYDE, JAMES STEWART, ELECTRON PARAMAGNETIC RESONANCE SPECTROSCOPY. *Current Pos:* PROF RADIOL & BIOPHYS, MED COL WIS, 75-, DIR NAT BIOMED ELECTRON SPIN RESONANCE CTR, 80- *Personal Data:* b Mitchell, SDak, May 20, 32; m 59; c 3. *Educ:* Mass Inst Technol, SB, 54, PhD(physics), 59. *Hon Degrees:* Dr, Jagiellonian Univ, Krakow, Poland, 89. *Prof Exp:* Asst, Lab Insulation Res, Mass Inst Tech, 55-59; res physicist, Varian Assocs, 59-64, mgr, Electron Paramagnetic Resonance Res, 64-75. *Concurrent Pos:* Adj prof biomed eng, Marquette Univ, 81- *Mem:* Fel Am Phys Soc; Biophys Soc; Soc Magnetic Resonance Med; Soc Magnetic Resonance Imaging; Radiol Soc NAm. *Res:* Electron paramagnetic resonance; electron nuclear double resonance; free radicals in liquids; spin-labels; spin resonance instrumentation; dynamics of macromolecular complexes; oxygen transport; physico-chemical properties of melanin; in-vivo magnetic resonance imaging and spectroscopy. *Mailing Add:* Biophys Res Inst Med Col Wis 8701 Watertown Plank Rd Milwaukee WI 53226-4801. *Fax:* 414-266-8515

HYDE, KENDELL HEMAN, MATHEMATICS. *Current Pos:* from asst prof to assoc prof, 69-78, PROF MATH, WEBER STATE COL, 78- *Personal Data:* b Afton, Wyo. *Educ:* Univ Wyo, BS, 59; Univ Utah, MS, 62, PhD(math), 69. *Prof Exp:* Asst prof math, Church Col Hawaii, 62-66. *Mem:* Math Asn Am; Asn Educ Data Systs. *Res:* Group theory. *Mailing Add:* 4840 S 1000 E Ogden UT 84403

HYDE, KENNETH E, INORGANIC CHEMISTRY. *Current Pos:* from asst prof to assoc prof, 68-78, PROF CHEM, STATE UNIV NY COL OSWEGO, 78- *Personal Data:* b Pittsburgh, Pa, July 26, 41; c 1. *Educ:* Carnegie-Mellon Univ, BS, 63; Univ Md, PhD(inorg chem), 69. *Prof Exp:* Instr chem, Univ Md, 67-68. *Concurrent Pos:* Grant-in-aids, State Univ NY Res Found, 69-71, 73-74, 77-78, Petrol Res Fund, 73-76 & Cottrell res grant, 76-78; vis assoc prof, State Univ NY Buffalo, 74-76; vis scientist, Inst Phys Chem, Univ Frankfurt, applications prog, Gen Elec Corp, Syracuse, 81-85; vis fac res partic, Oak Ridge Nat Lab, 90-91. *Mem:* Am Chem Soc; Sigma Xi. *Res:* Magnetic and thermal properties of inorganic complex compounds; kinetics and mechanisms of inorganic complexes in aqueous solutions; applications of computer systems to on-line data acquisition; connecting serial instruments to microcomputers. *Mailing Add:* 126 Sagamore Dr Liverpool NY 13090

HYDE, KENNETH MARTIN, BIOLOGY, WILDLIFE MANAGEMENT. *Current Pos:* DEPT CHEM, STATE UNIV NY, OSWEGO, 91- *Personal Data:* b Warren, Ohio, Aug 8, 43; m 63; c 3. *Educ:* Hiram Col, BA, 68; La State Univ, MS, 70, PhD(entom), 72. *Prof Exp:* Assoc prof, Pt Loma Nozarene Col, 73-80, chmn dept, 73-90, prof biol, 80-90. *Concurrent Pos:* Mem comt on pesticides, San Diego Qual Life Bd, 73-75 & Environ Health Sect, Comprehensive Health Planning Asn, Imperial, Riverside & San Diego Counties, 74. *Mem:* Sigma Xi. *Res:* Effects of chronic exposure of environmental contaminants on nervous systems of endemic mammals as monitored through the electroencephalogram. *Mailing Add:* Dept Chem State Univ NY Col Oswego Oswego NY 13126-3575

HYDE, RICHARD MOOREHEAD, MICROBIOLOGY, IMMUNOLOGY. *Current Pos:* from asst prof to prof, 65-90, DAVID ROSS BOYD PROF MICROBIOL, UNIV OKLA, 90-, VCHMN, 85- *Personal Data:* b Pierre, SDak, Feb 11, 33; m 53; c 3. *Educ:* Univ SDak, BA, 55, MA, 56; Univ Minn, PhD(immunol), 62. *Prof Exp:* Asst prof microbiol, San Francisco State Col, 60-62; from instr to asst prof, Univ Mo, 62-65. *Concurrent Pos:* Res assoc, Sch Dent, Univ of the Pac, 61-62; USPHS spec fel, Scripps Clin & Res Found, 68-69; spec fel, Univ Ill & Univ Dundee, 84. *Mem:* AAAS; Am Asn Immunologists; Am Soc Microbiol; Soc Exp Biol & Med; Reticuloendothelial Soc. *Res:* Innate immunity; medical education. *Mailing Add:* Dept Microbiol Univ Okla Health Sci Ctr PO Box 26901 Oklahoma City OK 73190. *Fax:* 405-271-3117

HYDE, RICHARD WITHERINGTON, RESPIRATORY PHYSIOLOGY. *Current Pos:* PROF MED & ENVIRON MED, UNIV ROCHESTER, 69- *Personal Data:* b Plainfield, NJ, Sept 6, 29; m 57, Susan Case; c 4. *Educ:* Yale Univ, BA, 53; Columbia Univ, MD, 57. *Prof Exp:* Intern & resident, Hosp Univ Pa, 57-60, asst prof, 65-69. *Concurrent Pos:* USPHS res fel physiol, Hosp Univ Pa, 60-64; estab investr, Am Heart Asn, 67-72. *Mem:* AAAS; Am Fedn Clin Res; Am Physiol Soc; Am Soc Clin Invest; Am Thoracic Soc; Am Heart Asn. *Res:* Respiratory gas exchange; aerosols; lung metabolism; pulmonary edema; lung nitric oxide production. *Mailing Add:* Pulmonary Unit Box 692 Univ Rochester Med Ctr Rochester NY 14642-8692

HYDE, WALTER LEWIS, PHYSICS, ACADEMIC ADMINISTRATION. *Current Pos:* RETIRED. *Personal Data:* b Minneapolis, Minn, May 30, 19; m 41, Elizabeth Sanford; c Lee, Lewis, Benjamin, Elizabeth & Rebecca. *Educ:* Harvard Univ, BS, 41, AM, 43, PhD(physics), 49. *Prof Exp:* Res physicist, Polaroid Corp, 43-46 & Baird Assoc, 48-50; sci liaison officer, Off Naval Res, London, 50-53; res physicist, Am Optical Co, 53-58, asst dir res, 58-60; dir develop, J W Fecker Div, 60-63; prof optics, Univ Rochester, 63-68; provost, NY Univ, Univ Heights Campus, 68-71, spec asst to pres, Univ, 71-72; exec dir, Conn Conf Independent Cols, 72-79 & Conn State Tech Cols, 79-84. *Concurrent Pos:* Mem, US Nat Comt, Int Comn Optics, 56-, vpres, 62-; dir, Inst Optics, 65-68. *Mem:* Optical Soc Am (pres, 70). *Res:* Optical instruments; polarized light; education policy. *Mailing Add:* 337 English Neighborhood Rd Woodstock CT 06281. *E-Mail:* lhyde@nec.com

HYDE, WILLIAM W, FORCE ENERGY ENGINEERING, RENEWABLE ENERGY ENGINEERING. *Current Pos:* ENG MGR, AUTOMOTIVE RES CORP, 79- *Personal Data:* b Twin Falls, Idaho, Jan 19, 46; m 63; c 2. *Educ:* Gen Motors Res Inst, BSME, 68; Univ Calif, BSEE, 71. *Prof Exp:* Eng mgr, Dept Defense, 71-75, NASA, 75-79. *Concurrent Pos:* Consult, Dept Defense, NASA, Gen Motors, Ford, Chrysler, DOW, Gen Dynamics, Gen Elec, Defense Advan Res Projs Agency, IBM & others, 79- *Mem:* Soc Automotive Engrs; Inst Elec & Electronics Engrs. *Res:* Advanced electrical power generator from natural forces and sources such as the electric field, magnetic field, gravitational field, solar, wind, nuclear; advanced research in automotive hydrogen propulsion systems using the above mentioned forces; issued 20 patents. *Mailing Add:* 1685 Whitney Idaho Falls ID 83402-1768

HYDER, DONALD N, RANGE SCIENCE. *Current Pos:* RANGE CONSULT, 78- *Personal Data:* b Crossville, Tenn, Apr 24, 21; m 48; c 3. *Educ:* Univ Idaho, BS, 47; Utah State Univ, MS, 49; Ore State Univ, PhD, 61. *Honors & Awards:* Outstanding Achievement Award, Soc Range Mgt, 73. *Prof Exp:* Asst range mgt, Utah State Univ, 47-48; range conservationist, Bur Land Mgt, US Dept Interior, Ore, 49-56; res agronomist, Sci & Educ Admin-Agr Res, USDA, 56-61, range scientist, 61-73, leader forage & range res, 73-76; retired, 76-78. *Mem:* Soc Range Mgt. *Res:* Range improvement; plant morphology; range management. *Mailing Add:* 1008 E Elizabeth Ft Collins CO 80524

HYDER, MONTE LEE, NUCLEAR CHEMISTRY, ANALYTICAL CHEMISTRY. *Current Pos:* SR ADV SCIENTIST, WESTINGHOUSE SAVANNAH RIVER CO, 89- *Personal Data:* b Maryville, Tenn, June 16, 36; m 64, Penelope Fletcher; c Robert, Edward & John. *Educ:* Rice Univ, BS, 58; Univ Calif, Berkeley, PhD(chem), 62. *Prof Exp:* Res chemist, Savannah River Lab, E I du Pont de Nemours & Co, Inc, 62-67, res supvr, 67-76, res mgr, 76-84, sr res assoc, 84-89. *Mem:* Am Chem Soc. *Res:* Radiation chemistry of aqueous solutions; nuclear fuel reprocessing; chemistry of uranium and transuranium elements; nuclear reactor safety. *Mailing Add:* 33 Longwood Dr Aiken SC 29803. *E-Mail:* mlhyder@srs.gov

HYDOCK, JOSEPH J, CHEMISTRY. *Current Pos:* SR CORROSION ENGR, FLUOR ENGRS, INC, 74- *Personal Data:* b Plains, Pa, Apr 13, 18; m 45; c 4. *Educ:* Univ Scranton, BS, 40; Univ Notre Dame, PhD(chem), 50. *Prof Exp:* Res assoc, Nat Defense Res Comt, 42-43; res chemist, Sinclair Res Labs, 49-54; sr res engr, Autonetics Div, NAm Aviation, Inc, 54-65; mem tech staff, Hughes Aircraft Co, Calif, 65-66 & Autonetics Div, NAm Rockwell Corp, 67-69; consult, Radkowski Assocs, 69-73; pres, QAS Corp, 73-74. *Concurrent Pos:* Consult design groups on corrosion. *Mem:* Am Chem Soc; Nat Asn Corrosion Engrs. *Res:* Lubrication; corrosion; radiation; materials; liquid metals; dielectric coolants. *Mailing Add:* 11832 Peacock Ct Garden Grove CA 92641-2590

HYERS, DONALD HOLMES, ANALYSIS, FUNCTIONAL EQUATIONS. *Current Pos:* RETIRED. *Personal Data:* b Los Angeles, Calif, Apr 1, 13; m 40, 87, Roberta Spicer; c Richard & Diane (Kert). *Educ:* Univ Calif, Los Angeles, AB, 33, MA, 34; Calif Inst Technol, PhD(math), 37. *Prof Exp:* Asst math, Calif Inst Technol, 36-37; fel mech eng, Nat Defense Res Comt, 42-44; instr, Univ Wis, 37-42; from assoc prof to prof math, Univ

Southern Calif, 44-78, head dept, 45-50, emer prof, 78. *Mem:* Am Math Soc; Soc Indust & Appl Math. *Res:* Functional analysis; nonlinear integral equations; applications to hydrodynamics; stability of functional equations. *Mailing Add:* 270 E 36th Ave Eugene OR 97405-4748

HYERS, THOMAS MORGAN, PULMONOLOGY, CRITICAL CARE MEDICINE. *Current Pos:* asst prof med & dir, Div Pulmonary, 82-85, PROF MED, ST LOUIS UNIV MED CTR, 85- *Personal Data:* b Jacksonville, Fla, June 16, 43; m 65, Elizabeth McLean; c Justin Barstow & Adam McLean. *Educ:* Duke Univ, MD, 68; Am Bd Internal Med, dipl, 74, cert pulmonary dis, 80, cert critical care med, 87. *Prof Exp:* Chief resident & instr med, Vet Admin Med Ctr, Univ Wash, Seattle, 74-75; fel pulmonary dis, Univ Colo, Denver, 75-76, res fel, Cardiovasc Pulmonary Res Lab, Health Sci Ctr, 76-77, asst prof med, 77-82. *Concurrent Pos:* Res assoc med, Vet Admin Med Ctr, St Louis, 79-82; dir, Nat Heart, Lung & Blood Inst, NIH grant, Scor Adult Respiratory Failure, 83-93; mem, Coun Thrombosis & Cardiopulmonary Dis, Am Heart Asn. *Mem:* Am Physiol Soc; Int Soc Thrombosis & Haemostasis; Am Fedn Clin Res; Am Heart Asn; Am Thoracic Soc; fel Am Col Physicians; fel Am Col Chest Physicians; AAAS; Asn Pulmonary & Critical Care Prog Divs (secy/treas, 90-95). *Res:* Pathogenesis of the adult respiratory distress syndrome; relationship of adult respiratory distress syndrome to multiple organ injury; interactions of protease inhibitors and various cytokines in modulating neutrophil activation; role of growth factors in the recovery of the acutely injured lung. *Mailing Add:* Div Pulmonary & Occup Med St Louis Univ Med Ctr PO Box 15250 St Louis MO 63110-0250. *Fax:* 314-577-8859; *E-Mail:* hyerstm@wpagate.slu.edu

HYLAND, JOHN R(OTH), GEOLOGICAL & CIVIL ENGINEERING. *Current Pos:* CONSULT, 80- *Personal Data:* b Cleveland, Ohio, Aug 25, 25; div; c 4. *Educ:* Colo Sch Mines, GeolE, 50. *Prof Exp:* Head eng geol sect, Ohio Dept Natural Resoucres, 51-54, asst chief shore erosion, 54-59, chief shore erosion & secy water ways comt, 59-61, asst chief Div Water, 61-63; consult, Found, G K Jewell Assocs, Ohio, 63-64; proj dir, Monongahela River Eng Proj, USPHS, Fed Water Pollution Control Admin, US Dept Interior, 64-68, staff engr spec control projs, 69, actg chief, Spec Control Prog Br, 69-71, chief indust wastes eval sect, Environ Protection Agency, 71-75; consult, 76-78; div engr, Ohio Div Reclamation, 78-80. *Mem:* Am Soc Civil Engrs; Water Pollution Control Fedn. *Res:* Wave energy and bottom deposits of Lake Erie; waterborne pollutants from mining and oil; automated monitoring for organic pollutants in water. *Mailing Add:* 1431 Oakmont Ave Erie PA 16505

HYLAND, KERWIN ELLSWORTH, JR, ENTOMOLOGY, PARASITOLOGY. *Current Pos:* from instr to assoc prof, 53-66, chmn dept, 65-68, PROF ZOOL, UNIV RI, 66- *Personal Data:* b York, Pa, Apr 7, 24; m 79, Irene Keymeulen; c John, Jeanne, Janet & Jeffrey. *Educ:* Pa State Univ, BS, 47; Tulane Univ, MS, 49; Duke Univ, PhD(zool), 53. *Prof Exp:* Asst zool, Duke Univ, 49-51; sci instr, Christchurch Sch, Va, 51-53. *Concurrent Pos:* Vis prof entom, Mich State Univ, 58-60; Fulbright res scholar, Prince Leopold Inst Trop Med, Belg, 60-61; vis prof, Univ Lovanium, Kinshasha, 64; USPHS spec res fel, Prince Leopold Inst Trop Med, Belg, 68-69, sr res prof, 69-; guest prof, Univ Instelling, Antwerp, Belg, 77 & 78. *Mem:* Am Soc Parasitol; Entom Soc Am; Wildlife Dis Asn; Acarological Soc Am; Soc Vector Ecologists; Am Soc Trop Med & Hyg; Int Soc Acarology. *Res:* Acarology; medical entomology; taxonomy; life histories and host-parasite relations of parasitic mites and ticks; epidemiology of Lyme disease and honeybee mites. *Mailing Add:* Dept Biol Sci Univ RI Kingston RI 02881-0816. *Fax:* 401-874-4256; *E-Mail:* ticklab@uriacc.uri.edu

HYLAND, SANDRA, INTEGRATED CIRCUIT PROCESSING, PHOTOVOLTAICS. *Current Pos:* SR STAFF OFFICER, NAT RES COUN, 94- *Personal Data:* b Minneapolis, Minn, Mar 23, 54. *Educ:* Rensselaer Polytechnic Inst, BS, 77; Rutgers Univ, MS, 79; Cornell Univ, PhD(mat sci), 91. *Prof Exp:* Res staff, Jet Propulsion Lab, 79-83; sr engr, IBM, 91-94. *Mem:* Soc Women Engrs; Mat Res Soc; Electrochem Soc. *Res:* Materials issues for US government; explosives detection; transportation security; semiconductor processing; structural materials. *Mailing Add:* 2101 Constitution Ave NW HA262 Washington DC 20418. *Fax:* 202-334-3718; *E-Mail:* shyland@nas.edu

HYLANDER, DAVID PETER, ORGANIC CHEMISTRY. *Current Pos:* RETIRED. *Personal Data:* b Chicago, Ill, Nov 2, 24; m 53; c 5. *Educ:* NCent Col Ill, BA, 49; Univ Ill, MS, 50. *Prof Exp:* From asst res chemist to assoc res chemist, Parke Davis & Co, 50-68, res chemist, 68-76; scientist, Warner-Lambert Co, 76-86. *Mem:* Am Chem Soc. *Res:* Synthetic organic, peptide and heterocyclic chemistry; bench scale to pilot plant development of synthe. *Mailing Add:* 219 Country Club Rd Holland MI 49423

HYLANDER, WILLIAM LEROY, PRIMATOLOGY, DENTAL RESEARCH. *Current Pos:* asst anat, 71-72, asst prof anat & anthrop, 72-74, ASSOC PROF ANAT & ANTHROP, DUKE UNIV, 74-; ASST PROF ORTHOD, UNIV NC, 75- *Personal Data:* b Chicago, Ill, Mar 5, 38; m 72. *Educ:* Univ Ill, BS, 61, DDS, 63; Univ Chicago, AM, 69, PhD(anthrop), 72. *Prof Exp:* Dent intern, Vet Admin Hosp, Ann Arbor, Mich, 63-64; pvt pract dent, Plymouth, 64-66. *Concurrent Pos:* Duke Univ Med Ctr res award, 75; NIH Res Career Develop Award, 76-81, NIH grant, 76-80; NSF grant, 76-79; assoc ed, J Phys Anthrop, 76-80. *Mem:* Int Asn Dent Res; Am Asn Phys Anthropologists; Am Soc Zoologists; Sigma Xi. *Res:* Analyzing the biomechanics of the primate craniofacial region utilizing histological, biometrical, radiographical, electromyographical and strain gage techniques. *Mailing Add:* Dept Biol Anthrop Anat Duke Univ PO Box 3170 Durham NC 27706-8001

HYLIN, JOHN WALTER, PLANT BIOCHEMISTRY, PESTICIDE SCIENCE. *Current Pos:* from asst prof to prof, 59-85, EMER PROF AGR BIOCHEM, UNIV HAWAII, 85- *Personal Data:* b Brooklyn, NY, Jan 28, 29; m 54, Valia Belkoff; c Edward C, Douglas E & Kenneth L. *Educ:* Marietta Col, AB, 50; Purdue Univ, MS, 53; Columbia Univ, PhD(bot), 57. *Prof Exp:* Asst, Delafield Hosp & Columbia Univ, 53-54; res assoc biochem, Univ Tenn, 57-58, instr, 58-59. *Concurrent Pos:* Ed-in-chief, Bull Environ Contamination & Toxicol, 65-75, assoc ed, 75-; Fulbright res fel, Denmark, 72-73; chmn dept, Univ Hawaii, 85-; IAEA expert, Korea, 87, Algeria, 90, Philippines, 93, Pakistan, 95, Ecuador, 95, Indonesia, 96. *Mem:* AAAS; Am Chem Soc; Sigma Xi; Am Inst Chem. *Res:* Pesticide metabolism; biosynthesis and metabolism of alkaloids and naturally occurring sulfur compounds; phytochemistry; dithiocarbamate fungicide behavior. *Mailing Add:* PO Box 6323 Incline Village NV 89450-6323

HYLTON, ALVIN ROY, ENVIRONMENTAL SCIENCES. *Current Pos:* TEACHER ENVIRON SCI, LAS VEGAS COMMUNITY COL, SOUTHERN NEV, UNIV NEV, LAS VEGAS, 88- *Personal Data:* b Los Angeles, Calif, Feb 19, 24. *Educ:* Iowa State Univ, BS, 50; Johns Hopkins Univ, ScD, 65; dipl, US Army Command & Gen Staff Col, 65. *Honors & Awards:* Enterprise Award, Midwest Res Inst Coun Prin Scientists, 74. *Prof Exp:* Res entomologist, US Army, Ft Detrick, Md, 62-64, asst dir biol res, 64-65, res & develop coordr, Army Res Off, 65-66, chem officer, First Infantry Div, Vietnam, 66-67, staff officer, Pentagon, Washington, DC, 68-69; sr biologist, Midwest Res Inst, 69-71, sr environ biologist, 71-72, head ecol assessments, 72-75, dir Denver opers, 75-76, dir prog develop, 77-84. *Concurrent Pos:* Rep for Chief, Res & Develop US Army to Armed Forces Pest Cent Bd, 65-66; chmn, Mid Continent Res & Develop Coun, 82-83; dir, Sales & Mgt Execs, 80-82. *Mem:* Entom Soc Am; Am Inst Biol Sci; Sigma Xi; Am Forestry Asn; Ecol Soc Am. *Res:* Insect pathology and physiology, particularly aging, fecundity and longevity in disease vectors; chemical and biological research and development programs; use and effects of herbicides; environmental studies and impact statements. *Mailing Add:* 501 Kennedy Dr Las Vegas NV 89110

HYMAN, ABRAHAM, ELECTRONICS, ELECTRICAL ENGINEERING. *Current Pos:* ENVIRON & SAFETY CONSULT, 95- *Personal Data:* b Brooklyn, NY, Mar 8, 24; m 55; c 3. *Educ:* Polytech Inst Brooklyn, BEE, 45; Newark Col Eng, MSEE, 54. *Prof Exp:* Develop engr, Int Tel & Tel Lab, 45-48, supvry elec engr, Fed Aviation Agency, 48-55; chief elec eng br, Med Equip Res & Develop Lab, 55-64, head electronics lab, USN Training Device Ctr, 64-66; tech adminstr electronics, US AEC, Brookhaven Nat Lab, 66-71; supvry indust hygienist, Occup Safety & Health Admin, US Dept Labor, 71-81, regional indust hygienist, 81-84; safety & health mgr, Unisys Corp, 84-95. *Concurrent Pos:* Consult, JFD Electronics Corp, 52-53, Sterling Electronic Corp, 53-55, Dakon Corp, 57-59, Int Electronics Corp, 59-60, Taffett Electronics Corp, 62-63 & Poison Control Ctr, Nassau County Med Ctr, NY; lectr, Dept Elec Sci, State Univ NY, Stony Brook, adj asst prof, dept allied health professions; adj prof, York Col, City Univ New York, 74-78 & Staten Island Col, City Univ New York, 83-; mem, bd dirs, Am Lung Asn; environ consult, Staten Island Col, City Univ. *Mem:* Inst Elec & Electronics Engrs; Sigma Xi; dipl Am Acad Environ Engrs. *Res:* Bio-medical engineering instrumentation, automation, transducers; radar, sonar and scoring trainers; signal analysis and synthesis; environmental and industrial hygiene; noise reduction; measurement of toxic substances; ventilation and engineering improvement; environmental and industrial hygiene; nine US patents. *Mailing Add:* 142 Claudy Lane New Hyde Park NY 11040

HYMAN, ARTHUR BERNARD, MEDICINE. *Current Pos:* RETIRED. *Personal Data:* b London, Eng, Aug 22, 05; US citizen; m 30; c 2. *Educ:* Univ London, MB, BS, 28; Am Bd Dermat, dipl, 45. *Prof Exp:* Prof clin dermat, Sch Med & in-charge teaching dermatopath, Postgrad Med Sch, NY Univ, 59-91. *Concurrent Pos:* Dermatopathologist, Beth Israel Hosp, 56-; chief serv skin & cancer unit & attend dermatologist, Univ Hosp, 58-; attend dermatologist, Vet Admin Hosp, 58- *Mem:* AMA; Am Acad Dermat. *Res:* Dermatology; dermatopathology. *Mailing Add:* 225 W 86th St New York NY 10024

HYMAN, BRADLEY CLARK, MOLECULAR EVOLUTION. *Current Pos:* ASST PROF BIOL, DEPT BIOL, UNIV CALIF, RIVERSIDE, 83- *Personal Data:* b San Diego, Calif, May 14, 52; m 75; c 2. *Educ:* Univ Calif, San Diego, BA, 74; Univ Calif, Los Angeles, PhD(biol), 80. *Prof Exp:* NIH fel, lab molecular biol, Univ Wis-Madison, 80-83. *Mem:* Am Soc Cell Biol. *Res:* Molecular genetics of yeast nuclear and mitochondrial DNA replication; mitochondrial genome diversity in non-free-living, pathogenic nematodes. *Mailing Add:* Univ Calif Dept Biol 900 University Ave Riverside CA 92521-0101

HYMAN, EDWARD SIDNEY, INTERNAL MEDICINE, PHYSIOLOGY. *Current Pos:* INDEPENDENT RESEARCHER, 90- *Personal Data:* b New Orleans, La, Jan 22, 25; m 56, Jean Simons; c Judith (Lidden), Sydney, Edward David & Anne. *Educ:* La State Univ, BS, 44; Johns Hopkins Univ, MD, 46. *Prof Exp:* Intern internal med, Barnes Hosp, Wash Univ, 46-47; fel med, Sch Med, Stanford Univ, 49-50, resident, Univ Hosps, 50-51; resident, Peter Bent Brigham Hosp, Harvard Univ, 51-53; clin instr, La State Univ, 53-55; investr, Touro Res Inst, 58-90. *Concurrent Pos:* Teaching fel, Harvard Med Sch, 52-53; dir artificial kidney, Charity Hosp, 53-55; NIH & Am Heart Asn res grants, 55-80. *Mem:* Am Physiol Soc; Biophys Soc; Am Soc Artificial Internal Organs; fel Am Col Physicians; Am Fedn Clin Res; AAAS; Am Soc Microbiol; Biomat Found. *Res:* Renal physiology; salt metabolism; physical chemistry of electrolytes; artificial kidney and heart; salt retaining hormone; delivery of medical care; bacteriuria; systemic coccal disease (a group of diseases with a common cause). *Mailing Add:* 3525 Pritania St Suite 220 New Orleans LA 70115

HYMAN, JAMES MACKLIN, NUMERICAL ANALYSIS, MATHEMATICAL PHYSICS. *Current Pos:* staff mem numerical analysis, 77-83, assoc chmn, Ctr Nonlinear Studies, 83-84, GROUP LEADER APPL MATH, LOS ALAMOS NAT LAB, 85- *Personal Data:* b Lakeland, Fla, Mar 20, 50; m 72; c 2. *Educ:* Tulane Univ, BS, 72; Courant Inst Math Sci, NY Univ, MS, 73, PhD(math), 76. *Prof Exp:* Res staff mem math, Courant Inst Math Sci, 76-77. *Mem:* Soc Indust & Appl Math. *Res:* Numerical methods and software for the approximate solution of partial differential equations. *Mailing Add:* Los Alamos Nat Lab MS 8284 Los Alamos NM 87545-0001

HYMAN, LLOYD GEORGE, EXPERIMENTAL HIGH ENERGY PHYSICS. *Current Pos:* from asst scientist to assoc scientist, 61-71, SR SCIENTIST, ARGONNE NAT LAB, 71- *Personal Data:* b New York, Mar 18, 28; m 58; c 4. *Educ:* Mass Inst Technol, BS, 53, PhD(physics), 59. *Prof Exp:* Res fel, Harvard Univ, 59-61. *Concurrent Pos:* Vis prof, Univ Tel-Aviv, Ramat-Aviv, Israel, 73-74. *Mem:* Fel Am Phys Soc; Fedn Am Sci. *Res:* High energy physics; neutrino interactions at high energies; Interactions in colliding beams; superconducting magnet design, construction, instrumentation and operation. *Mailing Add:* 303 N Ashland Ave LaGrange Park IL 60525

HYMAN, MELVIN, SPEECH PATHOLOGY, VOICE DISORDERS & HEARING AIDS. *Current Pos:* chmn, Dept Commun Dis, 52-81, prof speech, 52-85, EMER PROF PATH & AUDIOL, BOWLING GREEN STATE UNIV, 77-, CO-DIR, HYMAN SPEECH, LANG & HEARING CTR, 85- *Personal Data:* b US, June 20, 27; m 73, Joy A Kirk; c Ilana M. *Educ:* Brooklyn Col, BA, 49; Ohio State Univ, MA, 50, PhD(voice sci), 53. *Honors & Awards:* Pioneer Award, Am Speech-Lang-Hearing Asn, 92. *Concurrent Pos:* Consult, New Voice Club Northwest Ohio, 54-; mem, Diag Team, Toledo Cleft Palate Ctr, 55-; mem bd trustees, Am Cancer Soc, 61-; mem, Comt Stroke Rehab, Am Heart Asn, 62-; chmn bd trustees, Northwest Ohio Heart Asn, 77-; med staff, St Vincents & St Lukes Hosps. *Mem:* Fel Am Speech & Hearing Asn. *Res:* Voice problems, particularly those concerning contact ulcers, nodules, laryngectomy, cerebral palsy, cleft palate, aphasia, language retardation, stuttering and other areas of speech pathology and related psychology. *Mailing Add:* Hyman Speech Lang & Hearing Ctr 5950 Airport Hwy Suite 17 Toledo OH 43615. *Fax:* 419-865-7500

HYMAN, RICHARD W, BIOCHEMISTRY, MOLECULAR BIOLOGY. *Current Pos:* SCIENTIST, STANFORD DNA SEQUENCY CTR, 93- *Personal Data:* b San Francisco, Calif, Oct 22, 41. *Educ:* Univ Calif, Berkeley, BS, 62; Cornell Univ, MS, 64; Calif Inst Technol, PhD(chem), 70. *Prof Exp:* From asst prof to prof microbiol, PA State Univ Col Med, 73-88; res scientist, Syntax, 88-92. *Mem:* AAAS; Am Soc Biochem & Molecular Biol; Am Soc Microbiol. *Res:* Genomics; sequencing. *Mailing Add:* 1450 Oak Creek Dr Apt 307 Palo Alto CA 94304

HYMAN, SEYMOUR C, CHEMICAL ENGINEERING. *Current Pos:* RETIRED. *Personal Data:* b New York, NY, June 3, 19; m 45; c 2. *Educ:* City Col New York, BChE, 39; Va Polytech Inst, MS, 40; Columbia Univ, PhD(chem eng), 50. *Hon Degrees:* LLD, William Paterson Col, 85. *Prof Exp:* Chem engr, Ashland Oil Ref Co, 40-42 & US War Dept, NJ, 42- 47; from asst prof to prof & assoc dean sch technol, City Univ New York, 47-66, vchancellor campus planning & develop, 66-69, dep chancellor, 69-77, actg chancellor, 71; pres, William Paterson Col NJ, 77-85. *Mem:* Am Soc Mech Engrs; Am Inst Chem Engrs. *Res:* Heat transfer; fluid flow. *Mailing Add:* 6904 W Country Club Dr Sarasota FL 34243-3501

HYMAN, WILLIAM A, REHABILITATION. *Current Pos:* from asst prof to assoc prof, 72-83, head, Bioeng Prog, 79- 89, PROF BIOENG, TEX A&M UNIV, 83- *Educ:* Cooper Union, BS, 65; Columbia Univ, MS, 66, ScD, 70. *Prof Exp:* Res assoc, Mass Inst Technol, 69-72. *Concurrent Pos:* Adj prof, Baylor Col Med, 74-83; Consult, Optex Biomed, Houston, Tex Dept Ment Health & Ment Retardation, Tex Rehab Comn, Med Designs Inc, Azle, Med Training & Serv Int, Longmont, MedTek Develop Corp, Houston, Atlas Processing Co, Shreveport, United Airlines Serv Corp, Lakewood, US Army, US Gen Accounting Off, NSF & NIH; prin investr, NSF; mem, Comt Surg Implants & Med Devices, Am Soc Testing & Mat, Comt Sports Equip & Facil & Comt Forensic Sci. *Mem:* Am Soc Testing & Mat; Asn Advan Med Instrumentation; Biomed Eng Soc; Sigma Xi; Inst Elec & Electronics Engrs Eng Med & Biol Soc; Human Factors & Ergonomics Soc. *Res:* System safety in medical device design; rehabilitation engineering; clinical engineering; biomechanics. *Mailing Add:* Indust Eng Tex A&M Univ College Station TX 77843-0100

HYMANS, WILLIAM E, ORGANIC CHEMISTRY. *Current Pos:* Res chemist, Chem Res & Develop Ctr, FMC Corp, 67-78, regist specialist, 78-81, mgr tech serv, 81-85, prod mgr, 85-87, regist mgr, 87-90, DIR DEVELOP CHEM, FMC CORP, 90- *Personal Data:* b Detroit, Mich, Mar 30, 40; m 66; c 2. *Educ:* Cornell Univ, BA, 62; Ohio State Univ, PhD(org chem), 67. *Res:* Synthetic organic chemistry. *Mailing Add:* FMC Corp/Agr Chem Group Box 8 Princeton NJ 08543-0008

HYMER, WESLEY C, ENDOCRINOLOGY, CELL BIOLOGY. *Current Pos:* asst prof zool, 65-68, assoc prof biol, 68-73, PROF BIOCHEM & BIOPHYS, PA STATE UNIV, 73- *Personal Data:* b Ironwood, Mich, July 22, 35; m 61; c 4. *Educ:* Univ Wis, BA, 57, MS, 59, PhD(zool, biochem), 62. *Prof Exp:* Res fel, Lab Biochem, Nat Cancer Inst, 62-64, staff fel, 64-65. *Concurrent Pos:* NIH res career develop award, 69-74. *Res:* Hypothalamic regulation of the anterior pituitary; cytophysiology of separated adenohypophysial cells. *Mailing Add:* Ctr Cell Res Pa State Univ 207 S Frear Lab University Park PA 16802-0001. *Fax:* 814-865-2413

HYMES, DELL HATHAWAY, ANTHROPOLOGY, LIGUISTICS & NATIVE AMERICAN LANGUAGES. *Current Pos:* PROF ANTHROP & ENG, UNIV VA, 87-, COMMONWEALTH PROF ANTHROP & ENG, 90- *Personal Data:* b Portland, Ore, June 7, 27; m 54, Virginia M Dosch; c Robert P, Alison (Bowman), Kenneth D & Vicki (Unruh). *Educ:* Reed Col, BA, 50; Ind Univ, MA, 53, PhD, 55. *Prof Exp:* From instr to asst prof, Harvard Univ, 55-60; from assoc prof to prof, Univ Calif, Berkeley, 60-65; prof anthrop, Univ Pa, 65-72, prof folklore & ling, 72-88, prof sociol, 74-88, dean, Univ Grad Sch, 75-87, prof educ, 75-88. *Concurrent Pos:* Bd dirs, Soc Sci Res Coun, 65-67, 69-70 & 71-72; assoc ed, J Hist Behav Sci, 66-, Am J Sociol, 77-80 & J Pragmatics, 77-; Guggenheim fel, 69-70; Nat Endowment Humanities sr fel, 72-73. *Mem:* Fel Am Folklore Soc (pres, 73-74); AAAS; Am Anthrop Asn (pres, 83); Am Asn Appl Ling (pres, 86); Ling Soc Am (pres, 82); fel Am Acad Arts & Sci; fel Brit Acad. *Res:* Studies in Southwestern and Native American ethnolinguistics; language in culture and society; computers in anthropology; history of linguistics; foundations in socrolinguistics. *Mailing Add:* 205 Montvue Dr Charlottesville VA 22901-2022

HYMOWITZ, THEODORE, GENETICS, PLANT BREEDING. *Current Pos:* from asst prof to assoc prof, 67-76, PROF PLANT GENETICS, UNIV ILL, URBANA, 76- *Personal Data:* b New York, NY, Feb 16, 34; m; c 3. *Educ:* Cornell Univ, BS, 55; Univ Ariz, MS, 57; Okla State Univ, PhD(plant breeding, genetics), 63. *Honors & Awards:* Frank N Meyer Medal, 88; Funk Award, 90. *Prof Exp:* Fulbright scholar, Indian Agr Res Inst, New Delhi, 62-63; agronomist, IRI Res Inst, Campinas, Brazil, 64-66. *Concurrent Pos:* Partic, AID-Univ Ill coord soybean res prog, G B Pant Univ Agr & Technol, India, 67 & Nat Acad Sci-Romanian Acad Fac Exchange Prog, 69; Food & Agr Orgn consult soybean prod, Yugoslavia & Hungary, 73; consult biotechnol, Indonesia, 91. *Mem:* Fel AAAS; fel Am Soc Agron; Genetics Soc Am; Soc Econ Botanists; fel Crop Sci Soc Am; fel Linnean Soc London. *Res:* Plant introduction of chemurgic and forage crops; genetics and origin of Cyamopsis tetragonoloba; biosystematics and genetics of Glycine; origin of cultivated plants. *Mailing Add:* Dept Crop Sci Univ Ill 1102 S Goodwin Urbana IL 61801. *Fax:* 217-333-9817; *E-Mail:* soyui@ux1.cso.uiuc.edu

HYNDMAN, ARNOLD GENE, NEUROBIOLOGY. *Current Pos:* asst prof, 81-90, ASSOC PROF BIOL SCI, RUTGERS UNIV, 90- *Personal Data:* b Los Angeles, Calif, Oct 16, 52; c 4. *Educ:* Princeton Univ, AB, 74; Univ Calif, Los Angeles, PhD(biol), 78. *Prof Exp:* Teacher biol, Upward Bound Prog, Univ Calif, Los Angeles, 75-77, lectr, 78; fel, Ohio State Univ, 78-79; res fel, Univ Calif, San Diego, 79-81. *Concurrent Pos:* Dir minority adv prog teaching & res, Rutgers Univ, 83-90, assoc provost, 90- *Mem:* Soc Neurosci; Asn Res Vision & Ophthal; Sigma Xi. *Res:* Development of visual cells; intact retinal and purified monolayer cultures are used in the analysis of retinal cells; analysis includes the study of cellmorphology, survival, transmitter development and cellular metabolism. *Mailing Add:* Dept Biol Sci Rutgers Univ New Brunswick NJ 08903

HYNDMAN, DONALD WILLIAM, IGNEOUS PETROLOGY, GENERAL PETROLOGY. *Current Pos:* From asst prof to assoc prof, 64-72, chmn, 75-77, PROF GEOL, UNIV MONT, 72- *Personal Data:* b Vancouver, BC, Apr 15, 36; m 60, Shirley Boyes; c Karen & David. *Educ:* Univ BC, BASc, 59; Univ Calif, Berkeley, PhD(geol), 64. *Concurrent Pos:* Prin investr, NSF, 67-72, 78-80 & 83-86 & Nat Park Serv, 79-82; vis prof, Stanford, 77-78. *Mem:* Fel Geol Soc Am; fel Mineral Soc Am; Mineral Asn Can; fel Geol Asn Can; Sigma Xi; Am Geophys Union. *Res:* Igneous and metamorphic petrology; petrography; geochemistry; tectonics of Northern Rockies; granites of Idaho batholith; high-grade regional metamorphism and partial melting; alkaline igneous rocks; books on petrology and roadside geology. *Mailing Add:* Dept Geol Univ Mont Missoula MT 59812. *Fax:* 406-243-4028; *E-Mail:* dhyndman@selway.umt.edu

HYNDMAN, HARRY LESTER, ORGANIC & ANALYTICAL CHEMISTRY. *Current Pos:* RETIRED. *Personal Data:* b Springfield, Ill, Sept 23, 40; m 65, Kathleen R Skinner; c Debra, Thomas & Anna. *Educ:* Univ Ill, Urbana, BS, 62; Calif Inst Technol, PhD(chem), 68. *Prof Exp:* Sr res chemist, Monsanto Co, 68-75, res specialist, 75-77, sr res specialist, 77-81, res group leader, 81-82, sr res group leader, 83-93. *Concurrent Pos:* Secy, Regulatory Rev Comt, Soc Qual Assurance, 89-90, chmn, 90-92. *Res:* Agriculture chemical residue analysis; computer applications in chemistry; quality assurance. *Mailing Add:* 9310 Old Bonhomme Rd Olivette St Louis MO 63132

HYNDMAN, JOHN ROBERT, physical chemistry; deceased, see previous edition for last biography

HYNDMAN, ROY D, GEOPHYSICS, OCEANOGRAPHY. *Current Pos:* RES SCIENTIST, EARTH PHYSICS BR, DEPT ENERGY MINES RESOURCES, PAC GEOSCI CENTRE, 75- *Personal Data:* b Vancouver, BC, Feb 20, 40; m 69. *Educ:* Univ BC, BASc, 62, MASc, 64; Australian Nat Univ, PhD(geophys), 67. *Prof Exp:* Asst prof, 67-71; vis assoc prof, Univ BC, 71-72; assoc prof, Dalhousie Univ, 72-74; vis prof, Inst Phys Glove, Paris, 74-75. *Concurrent Pos:* Mem subcomts geomagnetism, seismol & physics of earth's interior, Nat Res Coun Can Assoc Comt & Int Heat Flow Comt; assoc ed, J Geophys Res & Marine Geophys Res; chmn, Joint Oceanogr Inst Deep Earth Sampling Downhole Measurement Panel. *Mem:* Can Geophys Union; Geol Asn Can; Am Geophys Union. *Res:* Continental and oceanic heat flow marine seismology; temperatures in the earth; magnetotellurics; general oceanic geophyiscal measurements; physical properties of rocks; marine geophysics. *Mailing Add:* Nat Res Can 9860 Saanich Rd Sidney BC V8L 4S2 Can. *Fax:* 250-356-6565

HYNE, JAMES BISSETT, CHEMISTRY. *Current Pos:* assoc prof, 60-63, first head chem, 63-66, dean, Fac Grad Studies, 66-89, PROF PHYS ORG CHEM, UNIV CALGARY, 65- *Personal Data:* b Dundee, Scotland, Nov 23, 29; m 58. *Educ:* St Andrews Col, BSc, 50, PhD(chem), 54. *Honors & Awards:* R S Jane Mem lectr, 77; Queen Elizabeth II Jubilee Medal, 77. *Prof Exp:* Fel chem kinetics, Nat Res Coun Can, 54-56; instr phys org chem, Yale Univ, 56-59; asst prof, Dartmouth Col, 59-60. *Concurrent Pos:* Res dir, Alta Sulphur Res, Ltd, 64-; consult, Oil, Gas & Sulphur, 78- *Mem:* Am Chem Soc; The Chem Soc; fel Chem Inst Can; Can Res Mgt Asn. *Res:* Fundamental and applied sulphur research; study of the chemical reaction of water with components of heavy oils during steam stimulated enhanced recovery. *Mailing Add:* Dept Chem Univ Calgary 2500 University Dr Calgary AB T2N 1N4 Can

HYNE, NORMAN JOHN, PETROLEUM GEOLOGY. *Current Pos:* From asst prof to assoc prof earth sci, 69-79, head dept, 72-79, PROF PETROL GEOL, UNIV TULSA, 79-; PRES, NJH ENERGY, 85- *Personal Data:* b Berwyn, Ill, Nov 17, 39; c 2. *Educ:* Pomona Col, BA, 61; Fla State Univ, MS, 65; Univ Southern Calif, PhD(marine geol), 69. *Mem:* Geol Soc Am; Soc Econ Paleontologists & Mineralogists; Am Asn Petrol Geol; Soc Petrol Engrs. *Res:* Sedimentation; petroleum geology. *Mailing Add:* 6338 E 98th St Tulsa OK 74137

HYNEK, ROBERT JAMES, ANALYTICAL CHEMISTRY. *Current Pos:* SUPVR PROCESS ENG, ENVIREX, INC, 82- *Personal Data:* b Phillips, Wis, Sept 7, 27; m 52; c 5. *Educ:* Carroll Col, Wis, BS, 51; Marquette Univ, MS, 59. *Prof Exp:* Chemist, Allis-Chalmers Mfg Co, Milwaukee, 51-52, group leader, sect leader & res chemist, Metals & Ultra High Purity Gases, 52-70; supvr pollution control lab, Autorol Corp, Milwaukee, 70-72, mgr pilot plant prog, 72-76, mgr process develop, 76-78, mgr process verification, 78-82. *Mem:* Am Chem Soc; Water Pollution Control Fedn. *Res:* Water and waste analysis; gas chromatography; elemental analysis. *Mailing Add:* W4946 Woodland Rd Bonduel WI 54107-8724

HYNES, HUGH BERNARD NOEL, FRESHWATER ECOLOGY. *Current Pos:* prof biol, 64-83, EMER PROF BIOL, UNIV WATERLOO, 83- *Personal Data:* b Devizes, Eng, Dec 20, 17; Can citizen; m 42, Mary Hinks; c Richard, Elisabeth (Grant), Andrew & Julian. *Educ:* Univ London, BSc & ARCS, 38, PhD(biol), 41, DSc, 58. *Hon Degrees:* DSc, Univ Waterloo, 87. *Honors & Awards:* Can Centennial Medal, 67; Hilary Jolly Award, Australian Limnol Soc, 84. *Prof Exp:* Field asst entom, Brit Ministry Agr, 41; entomologist locust control, Brit Colonial Agr Serv, Kenya, Ethiopia & Somalia, 42-46; lectr zool, Univ Liverpool, 47-58, sr lectr, 58-64; vis prof, Ind Univ, 62-63, Monash Univ, Australia, 71-72. *Concurrent Pos:* Sabbatical leave, Monash Univ, Australia, 71-72 & Univ Tasmania & Adelaide Univ, Australia, 78-79; vis prof, Addis Ababa Univ, Ethiopia, 73-74, Univ Louisville, 85. *Mem:* Royal Soc Can; Freshwater Biol Asn; Australian Limnol Soc; Int Soc Limnol; Can Soc Zool; NAm Benthol Soc. *Res:* Ecology of the desert locust and aquatic invertebrates, especially running water and pollution; Plecoptera; Amphipoda. *Mailing Add:* 127 Iroquois Pl Waterloo ON N2L 2S6 Can

HYNES, JOHN BARRY, ORGANIC CHEMISTRY. *Current Pos:* assoc prof, 68-72, prof pharmaceut chem, 72-80, PROF PHARMACEUT CHEM & ASSOC PROF BIOCHEM, COL PHARM, MED UNIV SC, 80- *Personal Data:* b Orange, NJ, Oct 24, 36; m 60; c 2. *Educ:* Colgate Univ, AB, 58; Duke Univ, PhD(chem), 61. *Prof Exp:* Res assoc chem, Duke Univ, 61-62; pres, Hynes Chem Res Corp, 62-68. *Mem:* Am Chem Soc; Am Soc Biol Chemists. *Res:* Synthesis of potential antagonists of folic acid metabolism; synthesis and evaluation of new potential chemotherapeutic agents, especially those targeted for the treatment of malaria, leprosy, fungal infections and cancer. *Mailing Add:* Dept Pharm Sci Med Univ SC Charleston SC 29425

HYNES, JOHN EDWARD, PHYSICS. *Current Pos:* CONSULT. *Personal Data:* b New Orleans, La, Sept 25, 40; m 67; c 2. *Educ:* La State Univ, BS, 62; Fla State Univ, MS, 66, PhD(solid state physics), 69. *Prof Exp:* Res assoc solid state physics, Fla State Univ, 68-69; sr physicist magnetic physics, Pitney Bowes, 69-77; vpres res & develop, EMI Data-Malco Plastics Inc, 77-87, vpres & gen mgr, Malco Security Magnetics, Owings Mill, 87- *Res:* Magnetic tape; magnetic materials; security systems encoding; code analysis; date entry devices. *Mailing Add:* 6417 Dear Park Rd Reisterstown MD 21136

HYNES, JOHN THOMAS, FOOD BIOCHEMISTRY. *Current Pos:* RETIRED. *Personal Data:* b Brooklyn, NY, Sept 6, 33; m 57; c 7. *Educ:* Manhattan Col, BS, 56. *Prof Exp:* Chemist, Kraft Inc, 56-59, res chemist, 59-68, sr chemist, 68-77, group leader, 77-85, sr res scientist, 81-84, sr group leader, 85-89, res prin, Res Ctr Kraft Gen Foods, 89-93. *Mem:* AAAS; Dairy Sci Asn; Inst Food Technol. *Res:* Chemistry of edible proteins; food enzyme control and utilization; effect of heat on protein denaturation; cheese research and development. *Mailing Add:* 840 Rolling Pass Glenview IL 60025

HYNES, MARTIN DENNIS, III, PHARMACOLOGY, PSYCHOPHARMACOLOGY. *Current Pos:* sr pharmacologist, Eli Lilly, 79-84, head cent nervous syst & endocrine res, 84-86, mgr pharmaceut proj, 86-87, dir clin res, Japan, KK, 87-90, dir qual assurance, 90-94, DIR PHARMACEUT PROJ MGMT, CENT NERVOUS SYSTS COMPOUNDS, LILLY RES LABS, 94- *Personal Data:* b Albany, NY, Dec 23, 49; m 82, Lynne W Miller; c 2. *Educ:* Providence Col, BA, 72; Univ RI, MS, 75, PhD(pharmacol), 78. *Prof Exp:* Asst pharmacol, Univ RI, 72-77; fel, Roche Inst Molecular Biol, 77-79. *Mem:* AAAS; Sigma Xi; Soc Neurosci; NY Acad Sci; Am Soc Pharmacol & Exp Therapeut. *Res:* Major interest in the area of the central nervous system; endocrine and clinical research. *Mailing Add:* Eli Lilly & Co Lilly Corp Ctr Indianapolis IN 46285. *Fax:* 317-276-5583

HYNES, RICHARD OLDING, CELL BIOLOGY, DEVELOPMENTAL BIOLOGY. *Current Pos:* from asst prof to assoc prof, Mass Inst Technol, 75-83, assoc head, 85-89, head, 89-91, PROF BIOL, MASS INST TECHNOL, 83-, INVESTR, HOWARD HUGHES MED INST, 88-, DIR, CTR CANCER RES, 91- *Personal Data:* b Nairobi, Kenya, Nov 29, 44; Brit & US citizen; m 66, Fleur Marshall; c Hugh & Colin. *Educ:* Univ Cambridge, BA, 66, MA, 70; Mass Inst Technol, PhD(biol), 71. *Honors & Awards:* Harvey lectr, 86. *Prof Exp:* Res fel, Imp Cancer Res Fund, London, 71-74. *Concurrent Pos:* Mem, Cell Biol Study Sect, NIH, 78-82; assoc ed, Cell, 78-, Develop Biol, 78-85, BBA Rev Cancer, 80-86, J Cell Biol, 84-85, Develop, 87-90 & Proc Roy Soc B, 90-93; hon res fel, Univ Col, London, 82-83; Guggenheim fel, 82-83; investr, Howard Hughes Med Inst, 87- *Mem:* Nat Acad Sci; Inst Med-Nat Acad Sci; Soc Develop Biol; fel Royal Soc; Am Asn Cancer Res; Int Soc Thrombosis & Haemostasis; fel AAAS; fel AAAS; Am Soc Cell Biol. *Res:* Molecular basis of cell adhesion and migration; structure-function relations of adhesion proteins. *Mailing Add:* Ctr Cancer Res Mass Inst Technol E17-227 Cambridge MA 02139

HYNES, THOMAS VINCENT, SOLID STATE PHYSICS, MATERIALS SCIENCE. *Current Pos:* Nat Acad Sci res fel, US Army, 73-74, staff physicist, Mat & Mech Res Ctr, 74-84, phys sci adminr, Mat Command, 85, chief, Ceramics Res Div, 85-90, dir, Technol Integration & Mgt Div, Mat Technol Lab, 86-90, mgr optical & electro optical mat, Mat Lab, 90-93, SR STAFF SPECIALIST, ELECTRO OPTICAL MAT, ARMY RES LAB, US ARMY, 93- *Personal Data:* b New Haven, Conn, Aug 11, 38; div; c Robert, Marya & Angeline. *Educ:* St Joseph's Col, BS, 59; St Louis Univ, PhD(physics), 68. *Prof Exp:* Physicist, E I du Pont de Nemours & Co, 60; physicist & Nat Acad Sci fel physics, US Army Mat & Mech Res Ctr, 68-70; Orgn Am States vis prof, Cath Univ Rio de Janeiro, 70-71, assoc prof, 71-73. *Concurrent Pos:* Lectr, Northeastern Univ, 90-93. *Mem:* Am Phys Soc; AAAS; Sigma Xi; Am Ceramics Soc; Mat Res Soc. *Res:* Electromagnetic properties of structural materials and structures; response of materials to ultra-short pulses of electromagnetic radiation; quantum mechanical properties of systems with nondiagonal density matrices; structure of glasses. *Mailing Add:* 39 Stanstead Pl Nashua NH 03063. *Fax:* 617-923-5113; *E-Mail:* thymes@msc.arl.army.mil

HYSELL, DAVID L, SPACE PLASMA PHYSICS. *Current Pos:* ASST PROF PHYSICS, CLEMSON UNIV, 94- *Educ:* Pa State Univ, BS, 87; Cornell Univ, PhD(elec eng), 92. *Prof Exp:* Postdoctoral, Cornell Univ, 92-94. *Res:* Theory and observation of plasma waves in the earths ionosphere with emphasis on radar remote sensing. *Mailing Add:* 205 Kinard Lab Clemson SC 29634

HYSLOP, NEWTON EVERETT, JR, INFECTIOUS DISEASES, CLINICAL IMMUNOLOGY. *Current Pos:* PROF MED & CHIEF, INFECTIOUS DIS SECT, TULANE UNIV MED CTR, 84- *Personal Data:* b Newton, Mass, Oct 14, 35; m 57; c 2. *Educ:* Harvard Col, AB, 57; Harvard Med Sch, MD, 61. *Prof Exp:* Intern & resident med, Mass Gen Hosp, 61-63; res assoc immunol, Lab Immunol, Nat Inst Allergy & Infectious Dis, NIH, 63-65; sr resident, Peter Bent Brigham Hosp, 65-66; clin & res fel infectious dis, Mass Gen Hosp, 66-68; vis scientist immunochem, Oxford Univ, UK, 68-69; instr, 69-71, asst prof med, Harvard Med Sch & Mass Gen Hosp, 71-85. *Concurrent Pos:* Investr, Howard Hughes Med Inst, 71-75; prin investr, Tulane-LSU AIDS Treatment Eval/Clin Trials Unit, 87- *Mem:* Am Asn Immunologists; fel Am Col Physicians; Am Soc Microbiol; fel Infectious Dis Soc Am. *Res:* Clinical aspects and chemotherapy of AIDS; immunochemistry and pathophysiology of hypersensitivity reactions to beta-lactam antibiotics (penicillins and cephalosporins) and other antimicrobials; factors regulating normal and abnormal chemotactic responses of human leukocytes. *Mailing Add:* Infectious Dis Sect Tulane Med Ctr 1430 Tulane Ave New Orleans LA 70112-9826

HYSLOP, PAUL A, BIOCHEMISTRY. *Current Pos:* SR PHARMACOLOGIST, LILLY RES LABS, ELI LILLY & CO, 88- *Personal Data:* b London, Eng, July 12, 52. *Educ:* Univ South Hampton, London, BMS, 76, PhD(physiol & biochem), 81. *Prof Exp:* Researcher, Scripps Clin & Res Found, La Jolla, Calif, 82-88. *Mem:* Am Soc Biochem & Molecular Biol. *Mailing Add:* 7556 Cherryhill Dr Indianapolis IN 46254

HYUN, KUN SUP, CHEMICAL ENGINEERING, POLYMER ENGINEERING. *Current Pos:* chem engr, Dow Chem Co, 66, res engr, 66-71, res specialist II, Styrene Molding Polymers Res & Develop, 71-76, res specialist II, 76-79, res assoc, 79-84, assoc scientist, saran & converted prod, 84-89, sr assoc scientist polymer processing technol, 89-93, res scientist thermoplastics processing & fab tech, 93-96, SR SCIENTIST, DOW PLASTICS, DOW CHEM CO, 97- *Personal Data:* b Seoul, Korea, Feb 25, 37; m 63, Sung Za Lee; c Eileen, Phillip & Paul. *Educ:* Seoul Nat Univ, BS, 59; Univ Mo, Columbia, MS, 62, PhD(chem eng), 66. *Prof Exp:* Res asst chem eng, Univ Mo, Columbia, 61-65. *Concurrent Pos:* Abstr, Chem Abstract Serv, 67-76. *Mem:* Am Inst Chem Engrs; Am Chem Soc; Sigma Xi; Soc Rheology; Soc Plastics Engrs; Korean Polymer Soc. *Res:* Polymer processing; melt rheology; characterization of polymers. *Mailing Add:* 613 Nakoma Dr Midland MI 48640. *Fax:* 517-636-0592; *E-Mail:* kshyun@dow.com

HYZER, WILLIAM GORDON, CLOSE-RANGE PHOTOGRAMMETRY, HUMAN VISIBILITY. *Current Pos:* CONSULT, 53- *Personal Data:* b Janesville, Wis, Mar 25, 25; m 49; c David, John & James. *Educ:* Univ Minn, BEE, 46; Univ Wis, BS, 48. *Honors & Awards:* DuPont Gold Medal, Soc Motion Picture & TV Engrs, 69; Coleman Award, Brit Inst Physics, 80; Hon Master Photog, Prof Photogr Am, 81; Payne Achievement Award, Am Acad Forensic Sci, 91. *Prof Exp:* Chief physicist, Parker Pen Co, 48-53. *Concurrent*

Pos: Contrib ed, Photomethods mag, 56-; lectr, Univ Wis, 60-; columnist, Res & Develop mag, 70-78 & Optical Eng J, 76-79; US nat deleg, Int Cong High Speed Photog & Photonics, 78-86; vis prof, Xian Inst Optics & Precision mech, People's Repub China, 79. *Mem:* Soc Motion Pictures & TV Engrs (vpres, 66-69); fel Soc Photo Optical Instrumentation Engrs; fel Am Acad Forensic Sci; Illum Eng Soc; Prof Photogr Am; NAm Photonics Asn (pres, 80-82). *Res:* Developed and publicized techniques of high speed photography and videography as they apply to scientific and industrial research; developed low-light-level visibility and photographic techniques for forensic applications. *Mailing Add:* 136 S Garfield Ave Janesville WI 53545

I

I, TING-PO, PHYSICAL CHEMISTRY, ANALYTICAL CHEMISTRY. *Current Pos:* sr res chemist, Pfizer Inc, 74-79, sr res investr, 79-83, prin res investr, 83-89, RES ADV, FERMENTATION PROCESS RES & DEVELOP, CTR RES, PFIZER INC, 89- *Personal Data:* b Yunnan, China, Feb 20, 41; m 69, Ai-Mei; c Shiao Lan & David I. *Educ:* Cheng-Kung Univ, Taiwan, BSc, 65; State Univ NY, Buffalo, PhD(phys chem), 72. *Honors & Awards:* Pfizer Res Achievement Award. *Prof Exp:* Res assoc phys org chem, Brandeis Univ, 72-74. *Mem:* Am Chem Soc; Am Inst Chemists; NY Acad Sci. *Res:* Aqueous and non-aqueous solution chemistry; purification and separation science, including solvent extraction, chromatography, crystal growth, membrane separation and supercritical fluid extraction; high performance liquid chromatography and thin layer chromatography; analytical process automation; bio-engineering produced compound recovery; continuous flow analysis; protein and peptide chemistry; biotechnology down stream processing; protein engineering; artificial intelligence; distrumental automation. *Mailing Add:* Pfizer Inc Eastern Pt Rd Bioprocess Res & Develop Bldg 118 Groton CT 06340. *Fax:* 860-441-3198; *E-Mail:* it@pfizer.com

IACHELLO, FRANCESCO, PHYSICS. *Current Pos:* PROF PHYSICS, YALE UNIV, 78-, J W GIBBS PROF J, 76-79 *Educ:* Torino Polytech, Italy, Dott Nucl eng, 64; Mass Inst Technol, PhD, 69; Univ Ferrara, Italy, PhD, 92; Chung Yuan Univ, China, PhD, 93; Univ Sevilla, Spain, PhD, 93. *Honors & Awards:* Akzo Prize, Dutch Acad Sci, 81; Wigner Medal, Group Theory & Fund Physics Founds, 90; Taormina Prize Arts & Sci, 91. *Prof Exp:* Fel, Niels, Bohr Inst, Copenhagen, Denmark, 65-71; assoc prof physics, Torino Polytech, Italy, 71-74; sr scientist, Kernfysisch Versneller Inst, Groningen, Neth, 74-76,; prof, Univ Groningen, Neth, 76-82. *Concurrent Pos:* Vis sr scientist, Argonne Nat Lab, 74 & 77; vis prof, Weizmann Inst Sci, 76 & 77, Univ Trento, Italy, 82 & 84. *Mem:* Fel Am Phys Soc; Europ Phys Soc; Ital Phys Soc; Dutch Phys Soc; AAAS. *Res:* Nuclear theory; physics. *Mailing Add:* Sloan Physics Lab Yale Univ PO Box 6666 New Haven CT 06511

IACOBUCCI, GUILLERMO ARTURO, BIO-ORGANIC CHEMISTRY. *Current Pos:* ADJ PROF CHEM, EMORY UNIV, 75- *Personal Data:* b Buenos Aires, Arg, May 11, 27; m 52; c 2. *Educ:* Univ Buenos Aires, MChS, 50, PhD(chem), 52. *Prof Exp:* Res chemist org chem, Res Labs, E R Squibb & Sons, Arg, 52-57; Guggenheim fel, Harvard Univ, 58-59; prof phytochem, Fac Pharm & Biochem, Univ Buenos Aires, 60-61; sr res chemist org chem, Squibb Inst Med Res, 62-67; sr res scientist, Fundamental Res Dept, Coca-Cola Co, 67-68 & Corp Res Dept, 68-70, head, Biochem Sect, 70-74, asst dir, Corp Res & Develop Dept, 74-87, mgr, Biochem & Basic Org Chem Group, 88-93. *Mem:* AAAS; Am Chem Soc; Am Soc Pharmacog; Sigma Xi; Int Union Pure & Appl Chem; Am Inst Chemists. *Res:* Chemistry of natural products. *Mailing Add:* 160 N Mill Rd NW Atlanta GA 30328-1837. *Fax:* 404-252-9481

IACOCCA, LEE A, SCIENCE ADMINISTRATION. *Current Pos:* RETIRED. *Personal Data:* b Allentown, Pa, Oct 15, 24; m 91, Darrien Earle; c Kathryn Lisa (Hentz) & Lia Antoinette (Nagy). *Educ:* Lehigh Univ, BS, 45; Princeton Univ, MSME, 46. *Hon Degrees:* Var from univs. *Prof Exp:* From mgt trainee to pres & chief oper officer, Ford Motor Co, 46-78; pres & chief operating officer, Chrysler Corp, 78-79, chmn bd dirs & chief exec officer, Chrysler Motors Corp, Chrysler Financial Corp & Chrysler Technol, 79-93, consult, Chrysler Corp, 93-94. *Concurrent Pos:* Chmn comt, Corp Support Joslin Diabetes Found; founder, Iacocca Inst Am Enterprise, Lehigh Univ; chmn, Iacocca Found; co-chmn, Gov Mich Comn Jobs & Econ Develop; emer chmn, Statue Liberty-Ellis Island Found; prin, Iacocca Partners, 94-; pres, Iacocca Assocs, Los Angeles. *Mem:* Nat Acad Eng; Soc Automotive Engrs. *Res:* Advancement of diabetes research; author of 2 publications. *Mailing Add:* 10880 Wilshire Blvd Suite 1400 Los Angeles CA 90020. *Fax:* 310-441-2651

IACONO, JAMES M, BIOCHEMISTRY, NUTRITION. *Current Pos:* chief, Lipid Nutrit Lab, Nutrit Inst, Beltsville Human Nutrit Inst, 70-75, dep asst, nat prog staff, 75-77, assoc adminr, Off Human Nutrit, 78-82, S&E, USDA, DIR WESTERN HUMAN NUTRIT RES CTR, AGR RES SERV, USDA, 82- *Personal Data:* b Chicago, Ill, Dec 11, 25; div; c Joseph, Lynn, Michael & Rosemary. *Educ:* Loyola Univ, Chicago, Ill, BS, 50; Univ Ill, Urbana, MS, 52, PhD(nutrit biochem), 54. *Prof Exp:* Res asst agr, Univ Ill, 50-53; asst chief, Physiol Div, US Army Med Nutrit Lab, Fitzsimmons Army Hosp, Denver, Colo, 54-57; from asst prof to assoc prof exp med & biol chem, Col Med, Univ Cincinnati, 58-70. *Concurrent Pos:* Vis prof, Inst Pharmacol, Med Sch, Univ Milan, Italy, 66-67; mem, Coun Arteriosclerosis & Coun Thrombosis, Am Heart Asn. *Mem:* AAAS; Am Chem Soc; Am Inst Nutrit; Am Soc Clin Nutrit; Am Oil Chemists Soc; fel Am Heart Asn; fel Am Inst Chemists. *Res:* Nutritional biochemistry; nutrient requirements; role of dietary fats in cardiovascular disease. *Mailing Add:* 480-1 Point Pacific Dr Daly City CA 94014. *Fax:* 650-756-5514

IADECOLA, COSTANTINO, NEUROSCIENCES. *Current Pos:* ASST PROF NEUROL, UNIV MINN, 90- *Personal Data:* b Aquino, Italy, Mar 15, 53; m 87; c 1. *Educ:* Univ Rome, MD & PhD(physiol), 77. *Honors & Awards:* McHenry Award, Hist Neurol, 90. *Prof Exp:* Instr physiol, Univ Rome, 78-79; instr neurol, Cornell Univ Med Col, 82-83, asst prof neurobiol, 84-86; neurol residency, 86-90. *Mem:* Am Physiol Soc; Neurosci Soc; Am Acad Neurol; Soc Cerebral Blood Flow. *Res:* Regulation of blood circulation to the brain with respect to intrinsic neural pathways and neuro transmitters, in health and in the disease state. *Mailing Add:* Dept Neurol Univ Minn Box 295 420 Delaware St SE Minneapolis MN 55455

IAFRATE, GERALD JOSEPH, PHYSICS OF NANOELECTRONICS, QUANTUM TRANSPORT. *Current Pos:* DIR, US ARMY RES OFF, 89- *Personal Data:* b Brooklyn, NY, Apr 8, 41; c 1. *Educ:* Long Island Univ, BS, 63; Fordham Univ, MS, 65; Polytech Inst Brooklyn, PhD(physics), 70. *Prof Exp:* Physicist, Inst Explor Res, 65-68; res phys scientist, Electronics Technol & Devices Lab, 68-85, prin scientist, 85-89. *Concurrent Pos:* Adj prof, Monmouth Col, 65-82, Ocean Co Col, 77-84, adj prof physics, Georgian Ct Col, 80-90; vis prof elec eng, NC State Univ, 86-, Physics Dept, Duke Univ, 90- *Mem:* fel Inst Elec & Electronics Engrs; fel Am Phys Soc; Am Asn Physics Teachers. *Res:* Physics of small dimensions; conceiving, planning and conducting avante-garde theoretical research in areas of ultra-small, ultra-fast device physics leading to the realization of ultra-high information processing systems for applications scenarios. *Mailing Add:* US Army Res Off PO Box 12211 Research Triangle Park NC 27709-2211. *Fax:* 919-549-4348

IAIZZO, PAUL ANTHONY, SKELETAL MUSCLE PATHOPHYSIOLOGY, THERMOREGULATION. *Current Pos:* sea grant trainee, Univ Minn, 79-81, res asst, 81-83, res assoc, 90-91, asst prof physiol, 92-96, ASST PROF ANESTHESIOL, UNIV MINN, 91-, ASSOC PROF ANESTHESIOL & PHYSIOL, 96- *Personal Data:* b Superior, Wis, Nov 26, 56; m 83, Margaret K (Hoyer); c Maria E, Jenna C & Hanna R. *Educ:* Univ Minn, BS, 78, MS, 80, PhD(physiol), 86. *Prof Exp:* NIH res fel, Mayo Clin, 86, asst prof anesthesiol, 88-90; Alexander von Humboldt fel, Tech Univ Munich, 87-88. *Concurrent Pos:* Dir res, Dept Anesthesiol, Univ Minn, 90-, dir malignant hyperthermia muscle biopsy ctr, 90-, assoc, Ctr Interfacial Eng, 92-; vis scientist, Mayo Clin, 90-92; consult, Augustine Med, Inc. 91-; guest prof, Univ Ulm, Ger, 93-; mem grad fac physiol, Univ Minn, 93-, grad fac bioeng, 93- & fac mem biomed interfacial eng, 94-; co-dir, Ctr Muscle & Muscle Dis, Univ Minn; adj fac, Master Physther Prog, Col St Catherine, Minn. *Mem:* Am Soc Anesthesiologist; Biophys Soc; Biomed Eng Soc. *Res:* Pathophysiology of human skeletal muscle; anesthetic effects on extrafusal and intrafusal skeletal muscle; role of elevated intracellular calcium on cell signalling, dystrophic processes and cell toxicity; physiology of thermoregulation; physiology of skin injury and subsequent wound healing. *Mailing Add:* Dept Anesthesiol PO Box 294 Univ Minn Minneapolis MN 55455. *Fax:* 612-626-2363; *E-Mail:* iaizz001@maroon.tc.umn.edu

IAMMARINO, RICHARD MICHAEL, PATHOLOGY. *Current Pos:* PROF PATH, WVA UNIV, 79- *Personal Data:* b Cleveland, Ohio, Aug 17, 26; m 52; c 4. *Educ:* John Carroll Univ, BS, 49; Loyola Univ Chicago, MD, 53. *Prof Exp:* Fel, Med Ctr, Univ Kans, 56-58; fel, Western Res Univ, 58-59; dir labs, St Alexis Hosp, Cleveland, Ohio, 59-63; assoc prof, Univ Pittsburgh, 63-79. *Concurrent Pos:* Sigma Xi fel, Univ Pittsburgh, 63-64. *Mem:* Am Asn Clin Chemists; Col Am Path; Acad Clin Lab Physicians & Scientists. *Res:* Clinical laboratory medicine, particularly plasma protein disorders, lipoproteins, acute phase protein reactants and alpha 1-antitrypsin; electrophoresis methodology. *Mailing Add:* WVa Univ Med Ctr PO Box 9122 Morgantown WV 26506-9122

IAMPIETRO, P(ATSY) F, PHYSIOLOGY. *Current Pos:* RETIRED. *Personal Data:* b Middleboro, Mass, Jan 5, 25; m 54; c 3. *Educ:* Univ Mass, BS, 49, MA, 51; Univ Rochester, PhD(physiol), 54. *Honors & Awards:* Hitchcock Award, Aerospace Med Asn, 74. *Prof Exp:* Chief environ physiol sect, Qm Res & Eng Ctr, 54-60; chief physiol lab, Civil Aeromed Inst, Fed Aviation Admin, 60-73; dir life sci, 73-82, dir, Air Force Off Sci Res, Far East, Tokyo, 83-85. *Concurrent Pos:* Adj prof zool & prof res physiol, Univ Okla, 62-73; consult, Nat Inst Environ Health Sci, 67-71; mem adv group aerospace res & develop, NATO, 75-82. *Mem:* Fel Aerospace Med Asn; Am Phys Soc; Sigma Xi; Am Polar Soc; Soc Exp Biol & Med. *Res:* Temperature regulation; acclimatization to heat and cold; tolerance to extreme environments; water and electrolytes; drugs. *Mailing Add:* 3803 Barrington Dr San Antonio TX 78217-4101

IANDOLO, JOHN JOSEPH, BACTERIAL PHYSIOLOGY, FOOD MICROBIOLOGY. *Current Pos:* Assoc prof biol, 67-80, prof path, 80-94, prof biol, 80-94, UNIV DISTINGUISHED PROF, DEPT PATH & MICROBIOL, KANS STATE UNIV, 94- *Personal Data:* b Chicago, Ill, Sept 26, 38; m 60; c 3. *Educ:* Loyola Univ Ill, BS, 61; Univ Ill, Urbana, MS, 63, PhD(microbiol), 65. *Honors & Awards:* Merit Award, NIH. *Concurrent Pos:* Mem consult bact & mycol study sect, NIH, 75-79; ed, Appl & Environ Microbiol. *Mem:* Am Soc Microbiol; Am Acad Microbiol. *Res:* Genetics and biosynthetic regulation of the staphylococcal enterotoxins. *Mailing Add:* Dept Path & Microbiol Kans State Univ Manhattan KS 66502. *E-Mail:* iandolo@vet.ksu.edu

IANNICELLI, JOSEPH, ORGANIC CHEMISTRY, MINERAL BENEFICIATION & SEPARATION. *Current Pos:* PRES & BD CHMN, AQUAFINE CORP, 71-; PRES & TECH DIR, AERO INSTANT SPRAY DRYING SERVS, 88-, VPRES & DIR, IMPEX CORP, 88- *Personal Data:* b New York, NY, Aug 5, 29; m 58, Betty Peterson; c Mark, Rex & Gina. *Educ:* Mass Inst Technol, SB, 51, PhD(org chem), 55. *Prof Exp:* Chemist,

Explosives Dept, E I du Pont de Nemours & Co, 51, res chemist, Dacros Res Lab, Textile Fibers Dept, 55-56, chemist, Tech Lab, Org Chem Dept, 56, Carothers Res Lab, 57-58, Pioneering Res Lab, Textile Fibers Dept, 58-60; res dir, J M Huber Corp, 60-68, asst tech dir, 68-69, tech dir, 69-71. *Concurrent Pos:* Co-investr, NSF Proj Magnetic Beneficiation, 74-; chief investr, Elec Power Res Inst, 80; consult, Consol, Goldfields Australia, Sydney, RioTinto, Madrid, Hoganes, Sweden. *Mem:* Am Inst Mining, Metall & Petrol Engr; fel Am Inst Chemists; Tech Asn Pulp & Paper Indust; Clay Minerals Soc; Am Chem Soc. *Res:* Synthetic penicillin analogs and intermediates; synthesis of fiber forming polymers; polyesters; irradiation chemistry; pyrolysis of organic compounds; mineral beneficiation; pigment modification; mining equipment; water purification systems; spray and flash dryers; high intensity magnetic separation of industrial minerals, metallic ores and coal; performed first mineral separation on high temperature superconducting magnet; granted more than 75 patents in the US and abroad. *Mailing Add:* 28 St Andrews Dr Jekyll Island GA 31527. *Fax:* 912-265-3000; *E-Mail:* aquafine@graphnet.net

IANUZZO, C DAVID, MUSCLE PHYSIOLOGY & BIOCHEMISTRY, EXERCISE PHYSIOLOGY. *Current Pos:* ADJ PROF, DEPT SURG, UNIV TORONTO, 87- *Personal Data:* Concord, NH, Oct 15, 38; c 4. *Educ:* Springfield Col, BS, 66; Wash State Univ, MS, 68, PhD(exercise physiol), 71. *Prof Exp:* Teaching asst, Wash State Univ, 66-67, res asst electron micros, 67-68, res asst exercise physiol, 68-71; asst prof biol & health sci, Boston Univ, 71-75; assoc prof, 75-80, prof biol & phys educ, York Univ, 81- *Concurrent Pos:* Res grants, Atkinson Charitable Found, 78-79, Health & Welfare, Can, 78-79 & 84-85, Nat Sci & Eng Res Coun, 78-85 & Ont & Can Heart Found, 84-85; consult, Civil Aviation Med, Health & Welfare, Can, 78-85; founder & pres, Bio-Clin Res Assays Ltd, 88- *Mem:* Can Soc Cell Biol; Am Physiol Soc; fel Am Col Sports Med; Sigma Xi. *Res:* Biochemical characteristics and adaptability of skeletal and cardiac muscle cells. *Mailing Add:* Deborah Res Inst Trenton & Pine Mill Rd Browns Mills NJ 08015-1799. *Fax:* 609-893-2441

IATROPOULOS, MICHAEL JOHN, COMPARATIVE & EXPERIMENTAL PATHOLOGY, TOXICOLOGY. *Current Pos:* HEAD REGULATORY PATH, AM HEALTH FOUND, 89-, PRES, LABPATH MGT, INC, 89. *Personal Data:* b Athens, Greece, Nov 8, 38; US citizen; m 66; c 2. *Educ:* Univ Tubingen, MD, 64, DrMed, 65. *Prof Exp:* Res assoc cytol, Brown Univ, 66-69, instr path, 69-71; resident path, Univ Mo, Columbia, 71-72; spec fel, Albany Med Col, 72-74, from asst prof to assoc prof toxicol, 74-78; head, Exp Path Dept, Med Res Div, Am Cyanamid Corp, 78-89. *Concurrent Pos:* Adj prof, NMex State Univ, 75-78 & Old Dominion Univ, Va, 81-; assoc ed, J Toxicol Path; prof path, NY Med Col, 91- *Mem:* Int Fedn Soc Toxicol Pathologists; Am Inst Biol Sci; Soc Toxicol Pathologists; Soc Toxicol; NY Acad Sci; Int Soc Xenobiotics; hon mem Japanese Soc Toxicol Path; fel Acad Toxicol Scis. *Res:* Tumor induction potential and safety evaluation of drugs, vaccines, medical devices, cosmetics, food additives, agricultural and chemical products; toxicology. *Mailing Add:* 6 Bruce Ct Suffern NY 10901. *Fax:* 914-357-6711

IATROU, KOSTAS, EUKARYOTIC GENE REGULATION, RNA METABOLISM. *Current Pos:* from asst prof to assoc prof, 81-90, PROF MOLECULAR BIOL, DEPT MED BIOCHEM, UNIV CALGARY, 91- *Personal Data:* b Athens, Greece, June 10, 46; m 68, Michelle; c John & Nikiforos. *Educ:* Univ Thessaloniki, Greece, BSc, 70; Univ Calgary, Alta, Can, PhD(med sci), 77. *Prof Exp:* Res fel molecular biol, Dept Cellular & Develop Biol, Harvard Univ, 77-80, res assoc, 80-81. *Concurrent Pos:* Med Res Coun Can Scholar, 81-85, scientist, 86-91; Alta Heritage Found Med Res Scholar, 81-91; chmn, Molecular Develop Biol Res Group, Fac Med, Univ Calgary, 89-91; mem bd dirs, Insect Biotech, Can, 90- *Mem:* Soc Develop Biol; Am Soc Cell Biol; Int Soc Develop Biologists; NY Acad Sci; Int Sericult Comn; Am Soc Virol. *Res:* Regulation of gene expression during insect oogenesis; evolution of eukaryotic multigene families; molecular biology of insect viruses. *Mailing Add:* Dept Med Biochem Fac Med Univ Calgary 3330 Hospital Dr NW Calgary AB T2N 4N1 Can. *Fax:* 403-270-0737; *E-Mail:* iatrou@acs.ucalgary.ca

IBANEZ, MANUEL LUIS, BIOCHEMISTRY, MICROBIOLOGY. *Current Pos:* PRES, TEX A&M UNIV, KINGSVILLE, 89- *Personal Data:* b Worcester, Mass, Sept 23, 35; m 70; c 4. *Educ:* Wilmington Col, BS, 57; Pa State Univ, MS, 59, PhD(microbiol), 61. *Prof Exp:* Asst prof biol, Bucknell Univ, 61-62; res fel biochem, Sch Med, Univ Calif, Los Angeles, 62; sr biochemist plant tech, Interam Inst Agr Sci, Orgn Am States, 62-65; assoc prof biol, Univ New Orleans, 65-77, chmn dept, 65-70, health sci coordr, 71-76, assoc dean grad sch, 78-82, assoc vchancellor acad affairs, 82-83, actg vchancellor acad affairs, 83-85, prof biol, 77-85, vchancellor Acad Affairs & Provost, 85-89. *Concurrent Pos:* NSF coop fel, 59-60. *Mem:* Am Soc Microbiol. *Res:* Bacterial photosynthesis; cacao seed physiology; phospholipids in chromatophore of Rhodospirillum rubrum. *Mailing Add:* Tex A&M Univ 700 University Blvd Kingsville TX 78363-8203

IBANEZ, MICHAEL LOUIS, pathology; deceased, see previous edition for last biography

IBELE, WARREN EDWARD, MECHANICAL ENGINEERING. *Current Pos:* Asst prof mech eng, Univ Minn, 53-56, assoc prof mech eng & thermodyn, 56-59, assoc dean, 67-75, dean, Grad Sch, 75-83, PROF MECH ENG, UNIV MINN, MINNEAPOLIS, 59- *Personal Data:* b New Orleans, La, Aug 17, 24; m 47. *Educ:* Tulane Univ, BS, 44; Univ Minn, MS, 47, PhD(mech eng), 53. *Concurrent Pos:* Field eng, Babcock & Wilcox Co, 47, Pratt & Whitney Aircraft Div, United Aircraft Corp, 57-58; eng educ & accreditation comt, Engrs Coun Prof Develop; chmn adv comt transit, Twin Cities Area Metrop Transit Comn. *Mem:* Fel Am Soc Mech Engrs; Am Soc Eng Educ; Sigma Xi. *Res:* Thermodynamics; power; fluid mechanics; heat transfer; transport properties. *Mailing Add:* Dept Mech Eng Rm 241 Univ Minn 111 Church St SE Minneapolis MN 55455

IBEN, ICKO, JR, ASTROPHYSICS, STELLAR EVOLUTION SINGLE & BINARY STARS. *Current Pos:* head dept astron, 72-84, prof, 72-89, DISTINGUISHED PROF ASTRON & PHYSICS, UNIV ILL, URBANA-CHAMPAIGN, 90- *Personal Data:* b Champaign, Ill, June 27, 31; m 56, Miriam G Fett; c Miriam C (Stark), Icko E, Benjamin C & Michael T. *Educ:* Harvard Univ, AB, 53; Univ Ill, MS, 54, PhD(physics), 58. *Honors & Awards:* George Darwin Lectr, Royal Astron Soc, 84; Henry Norris Russell lectr, Am Astron Soc, 89; Eddington Medal, Royal Astron Soc, 90. *Prof Exp:* Asst prof, Williams Col, 58-61; sr res fel, Calif Inst Technol, 61-64; from assoc prof to prof, Mass Inst Technol, 64-72. *Concurrent Pos:* Vis prof, Harvard Univ, 66, 68 & 70; vis fel joint inst lab astrophys, Univ Colo, Boulder, 71-72; Eberly Family Chair Astron & Physics, Pa State Univ, State Col, 89-90; vis prof physics & astron & mem, Inst Astron, Univ Hawaii, Manoa, 77; mem adv panel, Astron Sect of NSF, 72-74; univ scholar, Univ Ill, 85-88; vis comt, Nat Astron Optical Observ, 79-82; Telescope Allocation Comt, Cerro Tololo Inter Am Observ, 82-88; vis prof, Dept Earth Sci Astron, Col Arts & Sci, Univ Tokyo, 84; vis scientist, Astron Coun, USSR Acad Scis, 85; vis prof, Astron Dept, Univ Bologna, Italy, 86-, Inst Theoret Physics, Christian Albrechts Univ, Germany, 90, fac educ, Niigate Univ, Japan, 90; Guggenheim fel, 85-86, US & USSR exchange scholar, 85, sr vis fel Australian Nat Univ, 86, Univ Sussex, Eng ,86. *Mem:* Nat Acad Sci; Int Astron Union; Am Astron Soc; fel Japan Soc Prom Sci. *Res:* Stellar structure; evolution; pulsation; binary star evolution. *Mailing Add:* Dept Astron Univ Ill Urbana IL 61801

IBER, FRANK LYNN, MEDICINE. *Current Pos:* CHIEF, GASTROENTEROL DIV, HINES VET ADMIN HOSP, LOYOLA UNIV, 86- *Personal Data:* b Eaton, Ohio, Oct 28, 28; m 53; c 3. *Educ:* Miami Univ, BA & MA, 49; Johns Hopkins Univ, MD, 53. *Prof Exp:* Intern med, Johns Hopkins Hosp, 53-54, asst resident, 56-58, from instr to assoc prof, Johns Hopkins Univ, 58-68; prof, Tufts Univ, 68-73; prof med, Sch Med, Univ Md, Baltimore, 73- *Concurrent Pos:* Markle scholar; asst & USPHS fel, Postgrad Med Sch, Univ London, 58-59, resident, 59-60; consult, Liver Res Unit, Univ Calcutta; chief med, Lemuel Shattuck Hosp, 68-73; chief gastroenterol div, Baltimore Vet Admin Hosp & Univ Md Hosp, 73-85. *Mem:* Am Gastroenterol Soc; Am Asn Study Liver Dis; Am Physiol Soc; Am Soc Clin Nutrit. *Res:* Liver disease; protein disorders; biochemistry of human disease; alcoholism; human nutrition; aging nutrition. *Mailing Add:* 339 Selboure Riverside IL 60546

IBERALL, ARTHUR SAUL, PHYSICS OF COMPLEX SYSTEMS. *Current Pos:* PUBL, CRI-DE-COEUR PRESS, 91- *Personal Data:* b New York, NY, June 12, 18; m 40, Helene Rubenstein; c Eleanora (Robbins), Pamela (Rubin), Althea & Val (O'Conner). *Educ:* City Col New York, BS, 40. *Hon Degrees:* DSc, Ohio State Univ, 75. *Prof Exp:* Gen physicist instrumentation & measurement, Nat Bur Stand, 41-53; res dir instruments & aircraft accessories, Aro Equip Corp, 53-54; chief physicist res & develop, Rand Develop Corp, 54-64; pres, Gen Tech Serv, Inc, 64-81; vis scholar, Univ Calif, Los Angeles, 81-93; teaching grad course physics social systs, Univ Calif, Irvine, 93-94. *Concurrent Pos:* Consult, 53- *Mem:* Am Soc Mech Eng; NY Acad Sci; Am Phys Soc; Biomed Eng Soc; Sigma Xi. *Res:* Hydrodynamics; thermodynamics; molecular physics; biophysics; hydrology; control theory; instrumentation; physics of complex systems including behavior and social systems; physics of space; scientific systems analysis, physical, biological and social. *Mailing Add:* 5070 Avenida del Sol Laguna Hills CA 92653. *Fax:* 714-768-1963

IBERS, JAMES ARTHUR, INORGANIC CHEMISTRY, SOLID STATE CHEMISTRY. *Current Pos:* PROF CHEM, NORTHWESTERN UNIV, 65-, MORRISON PROF, 86- *Personal Data:* b Los Angeles, Calif, June 9, 30; m 51, Joyce A Henderson; c Jill T & Arthur A. *Educ:* Calif Inst Technol, BS, 51, PhD(chem), 54. *Honors & Awards:* Am Chem Soc Award in Inorg Chem, 78; Award Distinguished Serv Advan Inorg Chem, Am Chem Soc, 92, Linus Pauling Medal, 94. *Prof Exp:* NSF fel, Commonwealth Sci & Indust Res Orgn, Australia, 54-55; chemist, Shell Develop Co, 55-61 & Brookhaven Nat Lab, 61-64. *Mem:* Nat Acad Sci; Am Chem Soc; Am Acad Arts & Sci. *Res:* Coordination, solid state and bioinorganic chemistry; structural chemistry. *Mailing Add:* Dept Chem Northwestern Univ Evanston IL 60208-3113

IBRAHIM, A MAHAMMAD, materials engineering, polymers & composites, for more information see previous edition

IBRAHIM, ADLOY N, MICROBIOLOGY. *Current Pos:* from assoc prof to prof, 70-85, EMER PROF MICROBIOL, GA STATE UNIV, 85- *Personal Data:* b Egypt, Jan 4, 17; m 43; c 2. *Educ:* Cairo Univ, DVM, 39, dipl bact, 60; Univ Miami, MS, 64; Univ Pittsburgh, DSc(virol), 67. *Prof Exp:* Vet, 40-51; med rep, Parke, Davis & Co, Egypt, 51-61; teaching asst microbiol, Univ Miami, 61-64; fel virol, Grad Sch Pub Health, Univ Pittsburgh, 64-68; res virologist, Gulf South Res Inst, 68-70. *Mem:* Am Soc Microbiol; Am Soc Trop Med & Hyg; Tissue Cult Asn. *Res:* Degradation of hyaluronic acid by certain strains of Hemophilus influenzae; application of immunodiffusion methods to the antigenic analysis of dengue viruses; tumor immunology with emphasis on immunodiagnosis of human cancer. *Mailing Add:* 946 Bridgegate Dr NE Marietta GA 30068

IBRAHIM, BAKY BADIE, FLUID DYNAMICS, HEAT TRANSFER. *Current Pos:* sr engr, 76-86, FEL ENGR, WESTINGHOUSE ELEC CORP, 86- *Personal Data:* b Assiut, Egypt, Sept 18, 47; US citizen; m 78, Joanne Catanzarite; c Carolyn M & Lorene D. *Educ:* Assiut Univ, BS, 68; Kans State Univ, MS, 71 & PhD(mech eng), 75. *Honors & Awards:* George Westinghouse Signature Award. *Prof Exp:* Instr mech eng, Helwan Inst Technol, 68-69 & Kans State Univ, 71-75; asst prof, Bradley Univ, 75-76. *Mem:* Am Soc Mech Engrs. *Res:* Propose, design and conduct tests in the thermal and hydraulics area simulating different nuclear reactor components; fluid flow, fluid-solid interaction and fluid transients and instabilities; flow visualization. *Mailing Add:* 11496 Drop Rd North Huntingdon PA 15642. *Fax:* 412-476-6392; *E-Mail:* bakyi@aol.com

IBRAHIM, MEDHAT AHMED HELMY, POWER SYSTEMS, SYSTEMS ENGINEERING. *Current Pos:* prof elec eng, 80-91, PROF & CHMN, DEPT ELEC & COMPUT ENG, CALIF STATE UNIV, FRESNO, 91- *Personal Data:* b Alexandria, Egypt, Apr 25, 39; m 69. *Educ:* Cairo Univ, BSE, 61; Univ Mich, MSE, 65, MA, 68, PhD(elec eng), 69. *Prof Exp:* Instr elec eng, Cairo Univ, 61-63; asst res eng, Radiation Lab & asst lectr, Univ Mich, 65-69; lectr math, Eastern Mich Univ, 70; asst prof elec eng, Mich Technol Univ, 70-74; vis asst prof, Purdue Univ, 74-76; sr engr, Bechtel Power Corp, 76-80. *Concurrent Pos:* Vis scholar, Univ Mich, 78-79. *Mem:* Sr mem Inst Elec & Electronics Engrs; Am Soc Eng Educ; Sigma Xi. *Res:* Systems; control; computer applications. *Mailing Add:* Dept Elec & Comput Eng Calif State Univ Fresno CA 93612. *Fax:* 209-278-6297; *E-Mail:* medhati@csufresno.edu

IBRAHIM, MICHEL A, EPIDEMIOLOGY. *Current Pos:* assoc prof, 71-73, chmn, 75-82, PROF EPIDEMIOL, SCH PUB HEALTH, UNIV NC, CHAPEL HILL, 73-, DEAN, SCH PUB HEALTH, 82- *Personal Data:* b Egypt, Jan 28, 34; US citizen; m 62; c 4. *Educ:* Cairo Univ, MD, 57; Univ NC, MPH, 61, PhD(epidemiol), 64. *Prof Exp:* Hosp dir, Walaga Hosp, Egypt, 59-60; univ fel, Univ NC, 61-62, USPHS fel, 62-64; from asst to assoc prof med, State Univ NY Buffalo, 65-71. *Concurrent Pos:* Dep comnr health, Erie Co Dept Health, Buffalo, 68-71; chmn ed bd, Am J Pub Health, 74-; consult, Nat Inst Neurol & Commun Dis & Stroke, 77-; assoc ed, Am J Epidemiol. *Mem:* Fel Am Pub Health Asn; fel Am Heart Asn; Am Epidemiol Soc; fel Am Col Epidemiol. *Res:* Epidemiology of cardiovascular and cerebrovascular diseases; group psychotherapy and prognosis of coronary heart disease; community-based intervention studies for hypertension; health service planning and evaluation. *Mailing Add:* Pub Health Univ NC Chapel Hill NC 27599-8140

IBRAHIM, RAGAI KAMEL, plant biochemistry, plant tissue culture, for more information see previous edition

IBRAHIM, RAOUF A, NONLINEAR VIBRATING, RANDOM VIBRATION. *Current Pos:* PROF MECH ENG, WAYNE STATE UNIV, 87- *Personal Data:* b Meetghamr, Egypt, Feb 4, 40; US citizen; m 71, Sohari S Abd-El-Malik. *Educ:* Cairo Univ, Egypt, BS, 63, MS, 69; Edinburgh Univ, PhD(mech eng), 74. *Prof Exp:* Res engr, Egyptian Aerospace Org, 63-71; fel, Edinburgh Univ, 74-76; sr res engr, Sakr Factory Develop Indust, 76-79; sr engr, Shaker Res Corp, 79-81; from asst prof to prof mech eng, Tex Tech Univ, 80-87. *Concurrent Pos:* Fel, Brit Sci Res Coun, 74-76; adj asst prof, Cairo Univ, 76-78; mem tech comt vibration & sound, Am Soc Mech Engrs, 89-; invited lectr, Worchester Inst Technol, 87, Sandia Nat Labs, 88, Tex A&M Univ, 88, Mich State Univ, 88, Ga Inst Technol, 89, Univ Mich, 90, Southhampton Univ, 91, Univ Ill, 91 & 93, Off Naval Res; univ fac, Sandia Nat Lab, 87, US Tank Automotive Command, 89; prin investr, NSF, Battelle Mem Inst, Air Force Off Sci Res & Off Naval Res, 93- *Mem:* Am Soc Mech Engrs; assoc fel, Am Inst Aeronaut & Astronaut; Am Soc Eng Educ; Am Acad Mechanics. *Res:* Dynamic behavior of nonlinear systems under deterministic and random excitations analytically, numerically and experimentally, these include aeroelastic structures under supersonic speed, liquid-structure interaction and rotating machinery with friction; to explore complex cynamic characteristics that cannot be predicted by the linear theory of small oscillations; author of over 80 publications. *Mailing Add:* Dept Mech Eng Wayne State Univ 2100 W Eng Detroit MI 48202-3940. *Fax:* 313-577-8789; *E-Mail:* raouf_ibrihim@eng.wayne.edu

IBSEN, KENNETH HOWARD, BIOCHEMISTRY. *Current Pos:* asst prof, 63-71, ASSOC PROF BIOCHEM, SCH BIOL SCI & CALIF COL MED, UNIV CALIF, IRVINE, 71-, ASST DEAN, 88- *Personal Data:* b New York, NY, Feb 4, 31; m 58; c 2. *Educ:* Univ Calif, Los Angeles, BS, 54, PhD(physiol chem), 59. *Prof Exp:* Res biochemist, Sepulveda Vet Admin Hosp, Calif, 59-61; asst res physiol chemist, Univ Calif, Los Angeles, 61-64. *Mem:* AAAS; Am Soc Biol Chem; Am Chem Soc. *Res:* Regulation of energy metabolism; properties of regulatory enzymes. *Mailing Add:* Dept Biol Chem Univ Calif Col Med Irvine CA 92651

IBSER, HOMER WESLEY, PHYSICS. *Current Pos:* from asst prof to prof, 59-91, EMER PROF PHYSICS, CALIF STATE UNIV, SACRAMENTO, 91- *Personal Data:* b Ft Worth, Tex, Sept 17, 20; m 64, Tomiko Kaneko; c Hank & Maya. *Educ:* Nebr Wesleyan Univ, AB, 41; Univ Wis, MS, 48, PhD, 54. *Prof Exp:* Jr physicist, Manhattan Proj, 42-46; res assoc physics, Univ Wis, 54-55; asst prof, Northwestern State Col La, 55-58; assoc prof, Lincoln Univ Mo, 58-59. *Mem:* AAAS; Am Asn Physics Teachers. *Res:* Thermodynamics; nuclear physics; nuclear energy controversy. *Mailing Add:* Dept Physics Calif State Univ Sacramento CA 95819. *E-Mail:* hwi@saclink.csus.edu

ICE, GENE EMERY, X-RAY OPTICS, ANOMALOUS DIFFRACTION. *Current Pos:* from staff scientist to sr staff scientist, 79-94, STAFF SCIENTIST & GROUP LEADER, OAK RIDGE NAT LAB, 95- *Personal Data:* b Stillwater, Okla, Feb 14, 50; m, Rosalyn McKeown; c Gary S & Kelsey C. *Educ:* Harvey Mudd Col, BS, 72; Univ Ore, PhD(physics), 77. *Honors & Awards:* IR-100 Award, Indust Res & Develop Mag, 83; Outstanding Achievement Award, Metals & Ceramics, Dept Energy, 91. *Prof Exp:* Res assoc, Stanford Res Inst, 74, Univ Ore, 77-79. *Mem:* Am Phys Soc; Am Crystallog Soc; Mat Res Soc; Am Soc Metall Int; Micros Soc Am. *Res:* Develop and use advanced x-ray optics for the study of local structure in solid solution alloys and for the study of strain and microchemistry in materials. *Mailing Add:* 113 Hendrix Dr Oak Ridge TN 37830. *Fax:* 423-574-7659; *E-Mail:* gei@ornl.gov

ICE, RODNEY D, PHARMACY, NUCLEAR MEDICINE. *Current Pos:* PROF & MGR, OFF RADIATION SAFETY, GA INST TECHNOL, 85- *Personal Data:* b Ft Lewis, Wash, Apr 24, 37; m 58; c Randal D, Rex D & Ronald D. *Educ:* Univ Wash, BS, 59; Purdue Univ, MS, 65, PhD(bionucleonics), 67; Am Bd Health Physics, cert health physicist, 72. *Prof Exp:* Asst prof radiochem & radiation safety officer, Temple Univ, 67-69, assoc prof radiochem, 69-70; from assoc prof to prof pharm, Univ Mich, Ann Arbor, 70-76, dir radiopharmaceut serv, 70-75; prof pharm & dean, Univ Okla, Oklahoma City, 76-83; vpres, Eagle-Picher Industs, 85-92. *Concurrent Pos:* Consult, Philadelphia Tech Inst, 68-69, Philadelphia Pub Health Dept, 69-74 & Vet Admin Hosps, 72-74; chmn, Govt Adv Comt Ionizing Radiation, 73-74; US Pharmacopeia Comt of Rev, 81-90. *Mem:* AAAS; Am Pharmaceut Asn; Am Sci Affil; Health Physics Soc; Soc Nuclear Med. *Res:* Radiopharmaceutical development, dosimetry and design; boron neutron capture therapy; health physics. *Mailing Add:* 17516 Durbin Park Rd Edmond OK 73003. *Fax:* 404-853-9325

ICERMAN, LARRY, ADVANCED TECHNOLOGY & MANAGEMENT CONSULTING, PUBLIC POLICY. *Current Pos:* PRES, ICERMAN & ASSOCS, 89- *Personal Data:* b Muncie, Ind, Sept 22, 45. *Educ:* Mass Inst Technol, BS, 67; Univ Calif, San Diego, MS, 68, PhD(eng sci), 76; San Diego State Univ, MBA, 76. *Honors & Awards:* Spec Recognition Award for Energy Innovation, US Dept Energy, 85, Award for Energy Innovation, 86, 88. *Prof Exp:* Asst prof technol & human affairs, Washington Univ, 76-79, assoc prof, 79-80; dir, NMex State Univ Energy Inst, Las Cruces, 80-83; dir, NMex Res & Develop Inst, Santa Fe, 84-89. *Concurrent Pos:* Bd dirs, NMex Entrepreneurs Asn, 90-93, RhoMed Inc, 90-92, Trade, 90-, Permacharge Corp, 91-, Coronado Ventures Forum, 94- *Mem:* Am Inst Aeronaut & Astronaut; AAAS; Int Solar Energy Soc; Int Asn Hydrogen Energy; Am Chem Soc; Am Mgt Asn. *Res:* Technology, science, and policy; technology transfer and commercialization; defense conversion; renewable energy and energy conservation; energy analysis and economics. *Mailing Add:* 2999 Calle Cerrada Santa Fe NM 87505

ICHIDA, ALLAN A, MYCOLOGY, BACTERIOLOGY. *Current Pos:* from asst prof to assoc prof, 61-71, PROF BOT & BACT & CHMN DEPT, OHIO WESLEYAN UNIV, 71- *Personal Data:* b Seattle, Wash, Aug 26, 29; m 62; c 1. *Educ:* Ohio Wesleyan Univ, BA, 53; Univ Tenn, MS, 55; Univ Wis, PhD(bot), 60. *Prof Exp:* Res asst mycol, Univ Wis, 59-60, res assoc, 60-61. *Concurrent Pos:* Sci fac fel, NSF, 66-67; microbiologist, Agr Res Serv, USDA, 70-71. *Mem:* Am Soc Microbiol; Mycol Soc Am; Sigma Xi. *Res:* Ecology and taxonomy of aspergilli; ultrastructure of fungi. *Mailing Add:* 265 Cottswold Dr Delaware OH 43015

ICHIKAWA, SHUICHI, CHEMICAL & EXPERIMENTAL HYPERTENSION, CARDIOLOGY. *Current Pos:* PRES, CARDIOVASC HOSP CENT JAPAN, 89- *Personal Data:* b Tokyo, Japan, Aug 9, 43; m 72; c 4. *Educ:* Gunma Univ, MD, 69, PhD(hypertension), 78. *Prof Exp:* Fel hypertension, Univ Mo, 75-77; asst prof internal med, 2nd Dept Internal Med, Sch Med, Gunma Univ, 83-89. *Concurrent Pos:* Invited asst prof, 2nd Dept Internal Med, Sch Med, Gunma Univ, 89-, Col Med Care & Technol, 89- *Mem:* Am Physiol Soc; Soc Exp Biol & Med; Endocrine Soc. *Res:* Vascular reactivity and the involvement in the pathogenesis of hypertension; renin-angiotesin system. *Mailing Add:* Cardiovasc Hosp Cent Japan Hokkitsu-Mura Seta Gumma 377 Japan

ICHIKI, ALBERT TATSUO, IMMUNOLOGY. *Current Pos:* res assoc, 71-72, res asst prof immunol, 72-78, asst prof, 78-80, ASSOC PROF MED BIOL, DEPT MED BIOL, UNIV TENN MEM RES CTR, 80- *Personal Data:* b Lahaina, Hawaii, Sept 21, 36. *Educ:* Purdue Univ, BS, 58, MS, 61; Univ Calif, Los Angeles, PhD(microbiol), 69. *Prof Exp:* Grad res microbiol, Univ Calif, Los Angeles, 66-69; fel immunol, John Curtin Sch Med Res, Australia, 69-71. *Concurrent Pos:* NIH fel, USPHS, 69. *Mem:* Am Soc Hemat; AAAS; Am Asn Cancer Res; Sigma Xi; Int Soc Hematol. *Res:* Immunological evaluation of colorectal cancer and malignant melanoma patients; surface receptors on chronic myelogenous leukemia cells; isolation and characterization of colorectal tumor and malignant melanoma associated antigens. *Mailing Add:* Dept Med Biol Univ Tenn Med Ctr Knoxville TN 37920-1511

ICHINOSE, HERBERT, PATHOLOGY. *Current Pos:* MED DIR, DRAMATOPATH INC, 85- *Personal Data:* b Koloa, Hawaii, July 25, 31; m 55; c 4. *Educ:* Tulane Univ, BS, 53, MD, 57, dipl path, 62. *Honors & Awards:* Mellon Award, 64. *Prof Exp:* Rotating intern med path, Charity Hosp, New Orleans, 57-58; from instr to prof, Sch Med, Tulane Univ, 58-80, clin prof path, 80-85. *Concurrent Pos:* Nat Cancer Inst trainee, 58-62; jr attend pathologist, Charity Hosp, New Orleans, 58-63, vis pathologist, 63-69, sr vis pathologist, 69-; NIH grant, 62-63; Am Cancer Soc advan clin fel, 62-65. *Res:* Study of neoplasia; chemical carcinogenesis; dermatopathology. *Mailing Add:* 10555 Lake Forest Blvd Suite S-CDB New Orleans LA 70127-2708

ICHIYE, TAKASHI, physical oceanography; deceased, see previous edition for last biography

ICHNIOWSKI, CASIMIR THADDEUS, PHARMACOLOGY. *Current Pos:* RETIRED. *Personal Data:* b Baltimore, Md, Mar 4, 09; m 51; c 4. *Educ:* Univ Md, BS, 30, MS, 32, PhD(pharmacol), 36. *Prof Exp:* Asst pharmacol, Univ Md, 30-36; asst toxicologist, Chem Warfare Serv, Edgewood Arsenal, 36-38; pharmacologist, Warner Inst Therapeut Res, NY, 38-46 & Wyeth, Inc, Pa, 46-51; asst dean, Sch Pharm, Univ Md, Baltimore City, 68-74, Emerson prof pharmacol, 51-74. *Mem:* AAAS; Am Pharmaceut Asn. *Res:* Bioassays; stability of pharmaceuticals; absorption; drug combinations. *Mailing Add:* 625 Woodbine Ave Baltimore MD 21204

ICHNIOWSKI, THADDEUS CASIMIR, CHEMISTRY. *Current Pos:* From asst prof to prof, 61-96, coordr coop educ, Chem Dept, 80-92, EMER PROF CHEM, ILL STATE UNIV, 96- *Personal Data:* b Baltimore, Md, June 1, 33; m 59, Joan Pierce; c Mary E, Isabelle, Katherine & Rebecca. *Educ:* Wash Col, BS, 55; Purdue Univ, MS, 60, PhD(chem), 62. *Concurrent Pos:* Vis prof, Dow Chem Co, 80-81; dir, Univ Coop Prog, Ill State Univ, 87. *Mem:* Am Chem Soc. *Res:* Synthetic inorganic chemistry; inorganic polymers; cooperative education in chemistry; water soluble polymers. *Mailing Add:* 900 Randall Dr Normal IL 61761

ICKE, VINCENT, astrophysics, hydrodynamics, for more information see previous edition

ICKES, WILLIAM K, SPEECH PATHOLOGY, AUDIOLOGY. *Current Pos:* dir hearing & speech clin, 62-69, chmn dept speech & theatre arts, 69-76, PROF SPEECH PATH & AUDIOL, TEX TECH UNIV, 64- *Personal Data:* b Salt Lake City, Utah, Feb 4, 26; m 46; c 4. *Educ:* Univ Utah, BS, 48, MS, 49; Southern Ill Univ, PhD(audiol), 60. *Prof Exp:* Audiologist, Detroit Hearing Ctr, 50-52 & Mich Asn Better Hearing, 52-54; exec dir, Des Moines Hearing & Speech Ctr, 54-62. *Mem:* Fel Am Speech & Hearing Asn; Nat Rehab Asn. *Res:* Establishing psycho-physical thresholds, auditory; stuttering as a learned phenomenon; noise-induced hearing loss; industrial audiology. *Mailing Add:* 4306 57th St Lubbock TX 79413

IDDINGS, CARL KENNETH, THEORETICAL PHYSICS. *Current Pos:* assoc prof, 65-70, PROF PHYSICS, UNIV COLO, BOULDER, 70- *Personal Data:* b New York, NY, June 28, 33. *Educ:* Harvard Univ, AB, 55; Calif Inst Technol, PhD(physics), 60. *Prof Exp:* Res assoc theoret physics, Enrico Fermi Inst Nuclear Studies, Univ Chicago, 60-62; asst prof physics, Stanford Univ, 62-65. *Concurrent Pos:* Consult, Phys Res Lab, Space Tech Labs, 60. *Mem:* Am Phys Soc; Sigma Xi. *Res:* Elementary particle physics. *Mailing Add:* Campus Box 390 Boulder CO 80309-0390

IDDINGS, FRANK ALLEN, NUCLEAR SCIENCE, NONDESTRUCTIVE TESTING. *Current Pos:* CONSULT, 95- *Personal Data:* b Abilene, Kans, Jan 20, 33; m 54, Wanda Lee; c 4. *Educ:* Midwestern Univ, BS, 54; Univ Okla, MS, 56, PhD(anal chem), 59. *Honors & Awards:* Bausch-Lomb Sci Award, 51; Tutorial Award, Am Soc Nondestructive Testing, 85. *Prof Exp:* Instr chem, Univ Okla, 56-59; chemist, Esso Res Labs, La, 59-64; from asst prof to assoc prof, 64-75, prof nuclear sci, 75-85, asst dir, Nuclear Sci Ctr, La State Univ, Baton Rouge, 83-85; dir, Nondestructive Res & Testing Info Anal Ctr & Radiation Safety Off, Southwest Res Inst, San Antonio, 85-95. *Concurrent Pos:* Tech expert, Int Atomic Energy Agency, 71 & 83. *Mem:* Am Nuclear Soc; fel Am Soc Nondestructive Testing; Health Physics Soc; Sigma Xi. *Res:* Industrial radioisotope applications; liquid scintillation spectrometry; neutron activation analysis; nondestructive testing; neutron radiography; environmental monitoring. *Mailing Add:* 1635 Rob Roy Lane San Antonio TX 78251

IDE, CARL HEINZ, OPHTHALMOLOGY. *Current Pos:* From instr to assoc prof, 64-72, actg chief dept, 66-67, PROF OPHTHAL, SCH MED, UNIV MO, COLUMBIA, 72- *Personal Data:* b New York, NY, Nov 15, 28; m 62; c 2. *Educ:* NY Univ, BA, 52; Univ Hamburg, MD, 59. *Concurrent Pos:* Assoc ophthal, Mo Crippled Children's Serv, 65- *Mem:* AMA; Asn Res Vision & Ophthal; Am Col Surg; Ger Ophthal Soc. *Res:* Retinal surgery; clinical and experimental evaluation of grafts with preserved sclera; congenital abnormalities of the eye. *Mailing Add:* Univ Mo Inst Ophthal Columbia MO 65212

IDE, HIROYUKI, DRUG DEVELOPMENT IN JAPAN, RESEARCH & SCIENCE ADMINISTRATION. *Current Pos:* pres, Contract Labs, 85-95, FOUNDER & MEM BD, PANAPHARM LABS, 95- *Personal Data:* b Fukuoka, Japan, Mar 22, 33; m 56; c 2. *Educ:* Kyushu Univ, PhD(drug metab), 65. *Honors & Awards:* Prize Sci Technol, Japanese Govt, 77, 79 & 90. *Prof Exp:* Res fel oncol, Sch Med, Tufts Univ, 65-67, instr, 67-68; assoc prof hyg chem, Sch Pharmacol Sci, Fukuoka Univ, 68-71; dir drug develop, Hisamitsu Pharmaceut Co Ltd, 71-74, gen mgr, 74-80; pres, Contract Labs, Kyudo Co Ltd, 80-82. *Concurrent Pos:* Pres, Ide Off, 82- *Res:* Drug metabolism; pathology; toxicology. *Mailing Add:* Panapharm Lab Co Ltd Kurisaki-1285 UTO Kumamoto 80904 Japan

IDE, KAYO, APPLICATION OF DYNAMICAL SYSTEMS THEORY TO CLIMATE SYSTEMS, ESTIMATION THEORY & PREDICTION. *Current Pos:* Postdoctoral fel, 90-93, RES GEOPHYSICIST, UNIV CALIF, LOS ANGELES, 93- *Personal Data:* b Tokyo, Japan, Feb 10, 62. *Educ:* Nagoya Univ, Japan, BS, 84; Calif Inst Technol, MS, 85, PhD(aeronaut), 90. *Honors & Awards:* Amelia Earhart Award, Zonta Int, 84. *Mem:* Am Geophys Union; Am Meteorol Soc; Soc Indust & Appl Math. *Res:* Climate system and global change through observations, numerical models and analysis using dynamical systems theory as a main tool to identify fundamentals and reveal underlying processes. *Mailing Add:* Dept Atmospheric Sci Univ Calif Los Angeles CA 90095-1565. *Fax:* 310-206-5219; *E-Mail:* kayo@atmos.ucla.edu

IDE, ROGER HENRY, NUCLEAR CHEMISTRY, RESEARCH ADMINISTRATION. *Current Pos:* DEPT ENERGY TECH TEAM LEADER NUCLEAR TEST NEGOTIATIONS WITH USSR, 87- *Personal Data:* b Port Clinton, Ohio, July 8, 37. *Educ:* Wabash Col, BA, 59; Univ Calif, Los Angeles, PhD(nuclear chem), 64. *Prof Exp:* Chemist, Lawrence Livermore Lab, Univ Calif, 64-69, asst div leader, 69-72, test group dir, 72-76, asst assoc dir, 76-80, dep assoc dir, 80-87. *Res:* Interaction of artificial radionuclides with the environment; high energy fission yields. *Mailing Add:* 4627 Almond Circle Livermore CA 94550

IDELL-WENGER, JANE ARLENE, BIOCHEMISTRY, PHYSIOLOGY. *Current Pos:* ASST PROF PHYSIOL, COL MED, MILTON S HERSHEY MED CTR, PA STATE UNIV, 74-, ASST PROF MED, 81- *Personal Data:* b Halifax, Pa. *Educ:* Elizabethtown Col, BS, 65; Univ Minn, MS, 68, PhD(biochem), 70. *Prof Exp:* NIH fel pharmacol, Mayo Clin & Grad Sch Med, 70; USPHS fel, Univ Mich, 71, NIH fel biochem, 72-73. *Mem:* Am Physiol Soc; Biophys Soc; Asn Women in Sci; Int Asn Women Bioscientists; Am Heart Asn. *Res:* Myocardial and renal fatty acid metabolism in normal and ischemic conditions. *Mailing Add:* 111 Esheman Rd Lancaster PA 17601-5643

IDELSOHN, SERGIO RODOLFO, NUMERICAL METHODS. *Current Pos:* assoc prof, 75-80, PROF APPL MECH, UNIV ROSARIO, AGR, 80-; PROF COMP MECH, UNIV LITORAL, ARG, 89- *Personal Data:* b Parana, Arg, Nov 15, 47; m 71; c 3. *Educ:* Tech Sch, Parana, Arg, Dipl Tech, 65; Univ Rosario, Arg, Dipl Eng, 70; Univ Liege, Belg, PhD(comp mech), 74. *Prof Exp:* Sr scientist comp mech, Univ Liege, Belg, 71-74; dir res, Regional Res Ctr, Santa Fe, 85-87. *Concurrent Pos:* Prin res comp mech, Conicet, Arg, 81-; chmn, Comp Mech Lab, 81-; ed, Mecamica Computacional, 85; pres, Arg Asn Comp Mech, 85-; consult, several Arg Industs, 85-; vis prof, Inst Advan Study, Princeton, 87-88 & Univ Paris VI, France, 89-90. *Mem:* Int Asn Computational Mech; Am Soc Mech Eng. *Res:* Numerical methods in engineering; computational mechanics; fluid mechanics; aerodynamics; structural dynamics problems. *Mailing Add:* INTEC Guemes 3450 3000 Santa Fe Argentina

IDELSON, MARTIN, ORGANIC CHEMISTRY, PHOTOGRAPHIC CHEMISTRY. *Current Pos:* DEPT MGR, SHIPLEY CO, INC, 85- *Personal Data:* b Staten Island, NY, Aug 23, 28; m 57; c 2. *Educ:* Polytech Inst Brooklyn, BS, 52, PhD, 55. *Prof Exp:* With Children's Med Ctr, Boston, 54-57; scientist, Polaroid Corp, 57-65, sr scientist, 65-66, res group leader, 66-68, sr res group leader, 68-69, asst mgr, 69-70, res assoc, 70-75, res fel, Res Div, 75-85, dir dye chem, 80-85. *Concurrent Pos:* Instr, Northeastern Univ, 56-64. *Mem:* AAAS; Am Chem Soc; fel Soc Photog Scientists & Engrs. *Res:* Photographic chemistry; polymers; dyes. *Mailing Add:* 1603 Commonwealth Ave West Newton MA 02165-2800

IDEN, CHARLES R, BIOMEDICAL MASS SPECTROMETRY. *Current Pos:* instr, 77-80, asst prof, 80-92, RES ASSOC PHARMACOL, STATE UNIV NY, STONY BROOK, 74-, ASSOC PROF, 92- *Personal Data:* b NJ, 42. *Educ:* Lafayette Col, BA, 64; Johns Hopkins Univ, PhD(phys chem), 71. *Prof Exp:* Res fel, Johns Hopkins Univ, 71-72; res asst, Brookhaven Nat Lab, 72-74. *Concurrent Pos:* Consult, Brookhaven Nat Lab, 77-81 & County Suffolk, NY, 79-; vis scientist, Brookhaven Nat Lab, 82- *Mem:* Am Chem Soc; Am Soc Mass Spectrometry; AAAS. *Res:* Biomedical applications of mass spectrometry. *Mailing Add:* Grad Chem Bldg State Univ NY Stony Brook NY 11794-3400

IDIDUNNI, BOLA, HIGH TEMPERATURE OXIDATION & AQUEOUS CORROSION, ELECTRONIC PACKAGING. *Current Pos:* SCIENTIST & DEPT HEAD, SHELDAHL MICROPRODS, 84-; CONSULT, MAT CONSULT ASSOC, 86- *Personal Data:* b Lagos, Feb 23, 54; US citizen; c Sheeba, Quekan, Wura & Haile. *Educ:* Ohio State Univ, BS, 78, MS, 79, PhD(metall eng), 82. *Prof Exp:* Fel, Mining & Minerals Resources & Res Inst, 79-81; mat & metal eng, Systs Eng Assocs, 83-86. *Concurrent Pos:* Mem tech staff, AT&T Bell Labs, 86-94. *Mem:* Metall Soc; Electrochem Soc; Mat Res Soc; Am Soc Metals. *Res:* Thin films and stability of thin films in electronic applications, particularly as passive devices; fundamental oxidation and corrosion behavior of these films in processing environment characteristic of integrated circuit processing; packaging of electronic devices and effect of corrosion on such packages. *Mailing Add:* 1285 S Fordham St Longmont CO 80503. *Fax:* 303-651-2265; *E-Mail:* bola@sheldahl.com

IDLER, DAVID RICHARD, biochemistry; deceased, see previous edition for last biography

IDOL, JAMES DANIEL, JR, INDUSTRIAL CHEMISTRY, ORGANIC POLYMER CHEMISTRY. *Current Pos:* DIR & PROF II, CTR PACKAGING SCI & ENG, RUTGERS UNIV, 88-; FOUNDER & PRIN, JDI ASSOCS, 88- *Personal Data:* b Harrisonville, Mo, Aug 7, 28; m, Marilyn T Randall. *Educ:* William Jewell Col, AB, 49; Purdue Univ, MS, 52, PhD(chem), 55. *Hon Degrees:* DSc, Purdue Univ, 80. *Honors & Awards:* Modern Pioneer Award, Nat Asn Mfrs, 65; Chem Pioneer Award, Am Inst

Chemists, 68; Perkin Medal, Soc Chem Indust, 79; FG Ciapetti Award, Catalysis Soc NAm, 88. *Prof Exp:* Sr chemist, Standard Oil Co, Ohio, 55-56, proj leader, 56-59, res assoc, 59-62, res supvr, 62-65, res mgr, 65-77; vpres venture res & develop, Ashland Chem Co, 77-88; indust rel dir, Ohio State Univ, 88. *Concurrent Pos:* Lectr, var univs, 68-86; mem consult comt chem eng, Okla State Univ, 74-76, mem adv comt, Dept Chem, 78-88, Ohio State Univ, Purdue Univ & Tex A&M Univ, 79-81; mem & fel lectr, Am Inst Chemists, 80, mem bd dir, 81-83; chmn bd, Am Inst Chemists, 77-78; mem res & develop coun & packaging coun, Am Mgt Asn; mem Nat Res Coun Toxic Waste Handling & Energy Conserv. *Mem:* Nat Acad Eng; Am Chem Soc; Soc Plastic Engrs; fel Am Inst Chemists; Am Inst Chem Engrs; fel AAAS; Plastics Pioneers Asn; Int Union Pure & Appl Chem; Sigma Xi. *Res:* Vapor phase oxidation and catalysis; organic halogen compounds; monomer synthesis; organic process chemistry; separation processes; polymer synthesis and physical properties; plastics processing; barrier properties of polymeric materials. *Mailing Add:* Ctr Packaging Sci & Eng Rutgers Univ Piscataway NJ 08855

IDOURAINE, AHMED, NUTRITION, BIOCHEMISTRY. *Current Pos:* RES ASSOC, VERIGEN INC, 96- *Personal Data:* b Souk El Had, Algeria, Jan 22, 48; c Melissa Sarah. *Educ:* Nat Inst Agron, Algiers, BS, 77; Univ Ariz, Tucson, MS, 87, PhD(nutrit sci), 93. *Prof Exp:* Res team leader, Sonatrach, 77-83; postdoctoral, Harrington Arthritis Res Ctr, 94-96. *Concurrent Pos:* Adj fac, Gateway Community Col, Phoenix, 95. *Mem:* Inst Food Technologists; Am Asn Cereal Chemists; Sigma Xi; NY Acad Sci. *Res:* Protein chemistry, food composition and dietary fiber and other nutritional aspects of food; cartilage and chondrocytes and the way to halt tissue degeneration in osteoarthritic diseases. *Mailing Add:* Verigen 9535 E Double Rd Suite 300 Scottsdale AZ 85258. *Fax:* 602-314-5688; *E-Mail:* geneai@dancris.com

IDOUX, JOHN PAUL, ORGANIC CHEMISTRY. *Current Pos:* PROVOST & VPRES ACAD AFFAIRS, COASTAL CAROLINA UNIV, 94- *Personal Data:* b Houston, Tex, Feb 5, 41; m 66; c 4. *Educ:* Univ St Thomas, Tex, BA, 62; Tex A&M Univ, MS, 65, PhD(chem), 66. *Prof Exp:* Teaching & res assoc, Tex A&M Univ, 63-66; vis res assoc chem, Ohio State Univ, 66-67; asst prof, Northeast La State Col, 67-70; from asst prof to assoc prof, Univ Cent Fla, 70-77, asst dean, Col Natural Sci, 77-80, prof chem, 77-84, assoc dean, Col Arts & Sci, 80-84; dean, Col Arts & Sci & prof chem, Lamar Univ, 84-90, exec vpres, 90-94. *Mem:* AAAS; Am Chem Soc; Chem Soc; Sigma Xi. *Res:* Effect of structure on properties of organic compounds; model peptide bond chemistry; polymer supported catalyst systems; organofluoro chemistry; phase transfer catalysis. *Mailing Add:* Provost & Vpres Acad Affairs Coastal Carolina Univ PO Box 261954 Conway SC 29528-6054

IDRISS, IZZAT M, CIVIL ENGINEERING. *Current Pos:* dir, Ctr Geotech Modeling, 89-96, PROF CIVIL ENG, DEPT CIVIL ENG, UNIV CALIF, DAVIS, 89- *Educ:* Rensselaer Polytech Inst, BCE, 58; Calif Inst Technol, MS, 59; Univ Calif, Berkeley, PhD(civil eng), 66. *Honors & Awards:* Thomas A Middlebrooks Award, Am Soc Civil Engrs, 71, J James Croes Medal, 72, Walter L Huber Civil Res Prize, 75, Norman Medal, 77 & H Bolton Seed Mem Award & Lectr, 95. *Prof Exp:* Field engr, Moran, Proctor, Meuser & Rutledge, 58; from field engr to sr engr, Danes & Moore, 59-66 & 68-69; res engr, Dept Civil Eng, Univ Calif, Berkeley, 66-75; from proj engr to prin, vpres & dir, Woodward-Clyde Consults, Oakland & San Francisco, Calif, 69-82, managing prin, Orange Co, Los Angeles & Santa Barbara area offices & vpres, 82-87, sr consult prin & vpres, Oakland, Calif, 87-89. *Concurrent Pos:* Consult, several architect engrs & other firms, 66-69; lectr, Dept Civil Eng, Univ Calif, Berkeley, 66-75; consult prof, Dept Civil Eng, Stanford Univ, 78-82; adj prof, Dept Civil Eng, Univ Calif, Los Angeles, 84-86; mem, External Rev Panel, US Geol Surv, 90 & US Comt Large Dams, Comn Large Dams. *Mem:* Nat Acad Eng; Sigma Xi; Am Soc Civil Engrs; Earthquake Eng Res Inst; Seismol Soc Am. *Res:* Geotechnical earthquake engineering; soil mechanics and foundation engineering; earthfill and rockfill dam engineering; probabilistic applications to geotechnical problems; numerical modeling; author of various publications. *Mailing Add:* Dept Civil Eng Univ Calif Davis CA 95616. *Fax:* 530-758-1104; *E-Mail:* imidavis@aol.com

IDSO, SHERWOOD B, CLIMATOLOGY, REMOTE SENSING. *Current Pos:* RES PHYSICIST, AGR RES SERV, USDA, 67- *Personal Data:* b Thief River Falls, Minn, June 12, 42; m 63, Carolyn M Wakefield; c 7. *Educ:* Univ Minn, BPhysics, 64, MS, 66, PhD(soil sci), 67. *Honors & Awards:* Arthur S Flemming Award, 77. *Concurrent Pos:* Adj prof geog, Ariz State Univ, 80-, adj prof geol, 81- & adj prof bot & microbiol, 84- *Mem:* Am Meteorol Soc; Am Geophys Union; AAAS; Royal Meteorol Soc; Sigma Xi; Am Soc Agron. *Res:* Global climate, specializing in effects of carbon dioxide; remote sensing to detect plant water stress; schedule irrigations and predicting crop yields; serial fertilization effect of carbon dioxide on plants. *Mailing Add:* US Water Conserv Lab 4331 E Broadway Rd Phoenix AZ 85040

IDSON, BERNARD, CHEMISTRY. *Current Pos:* group leader res, 66-84, SR RES FEL, HOFFMANN-LA ROCHE, INC, 71- *Personal Data:* b Brooklyn, NY, Mar 23, 19; m 47; c Wendy & Todd. *Educ:* Brooklyn Col, BSc, 39; Polytech Inst Brooklyn, MSc, 43, PhD(chem), 52. *Prof Exp:* Res chemist, Reed & Carnrick, 39-44 & 46-50; res chemist & asst res dir, W Disinfecting Co, 51-52; res proj leader, Biocolloids Div, Gen Foods Corp, 52-56; res dir, Julius Schmid Inc, 56-60 & Dome Div, Miles Labs, 60-66. *Concurrent Pos:* Lectr, Polytech Inst Brooklyn, 52; vis prof, Columbia Col Pharmaceut Sci, 66-; sr res fel, Hottman La Roche, 66-84. *Mem:* Am Chem Soc; Am Inst Chem; Soc Investigative Dermat; Soc Cosmetic Chemists; Sigma Xi. *Res:* Heterocyclic chemistry; medicinal chemistry; organic, colloid and biological chemistry; natural polymers. *Mailing Add:* Dept Pharmaceut Rm 214 Univ Tex Sch Pharm Austin TX 78712-1070

IDZIAK, EDMUND STEFAN, FOOD MICROBIOLOGY. *Current Pos:* from asst prof to assoc prof, 65-78, dir, Sch Food Sci, 75-78, PROF MICROBIOL, MACDONALD CAMPUS, MCGILL UNIV, 78- *Personal Data:* b Montreal, Que, Sept 23, 35; m 63, Irene Idziak; c Stefan, Edmund, Margaretha & Christina. *Educ:* McGill Univ, BSc, 56, MSc, 57; Delft Univ Technol, DSc(microbiol), 62. *Prof Exp:* Bacteriologist, Food & Drug Directorate, Dept Nat Health & Welfare, 62-65. *Concurrent Pos:* Mem adv comt food safety assessment, Minister Nat Health & Welfare, 73-76; consult, Cent Health Lab, WHO, Cairo, Egypt, 81, Amalgamated Dairies Ltd, PEI Salmonella in Cheese Outbreak, 84, Minister, Nat Health & Welfare, Can, Eval Food Safety, Qual & Nutrit Prog, 85-86, Cent Health Lab, WHO, Mogadishu, Somalia, 87; mem, Food Safety Assessment Rev, Can, 85; food microbiol exchange expert, Nankai Univ, China, 85; food consult, Fermentation Indust. *Mem:* Inst Food Technologists; Am Soc Microbiol; Can Inst Food Technol; Can Soc Microbiol; Sigma Xi; Int Asn Milk, Food, Environ Sanitarians. *Res:* Interactions between spoilage and food poisoning microorganisms; microbiology of meat spoilage. *Mailing Add:* Dept Natural Resource Sci Microbiol McGill Univ 21111 Lakeshore Rd Ste Anne de Bellevue PQ H9X 3V9 Can. *Fax:* 514-398-7990; *E-Mail:* esi@nrs.mcgill.ca

IDZKOWSKY, HENRY JOSEPH, ENDOCRINOLOGY, EMBRYOLOGY. *Current Pos:* from asst prof to assoc prof, prof biol, 58-74, head dept, 68-74, EMER PROF BIOL, UNIV PITTSBURGH, JOHNSTOWN CAMPUS, 74- *Personal Data:* b Pittsburgh, Pa, Mar 19, 08; m 37; c 2. *Educ:* Univ Pittsburgh, BS, 32, MS, 33, PhD(biol), 36. *Prof Exp:* Teaching fel zool & Buhl Found fel, Univ Pittsburgh, 36-37; prof biol & head dept, St Francis Col, Pa, 37-45. *Mem:* Sigma Xi. *Res:* Biological effects of vitamin C; experimental embryology; host-donor relationships; endocrinology; gonad-adrenal relationships; larval transplants to adult Amphibia; ovarian implant; energy transfer relationships in freshwater ecosystems. *Mailing Add:* 1324 Christopher St Johnstown PA 15905-2149

IEYOUB, KALIL PHILLIP, ORGANIC CHEMISTRY. *Current Pos:* Lab instr, 59-62, from asst prof to assoc prof, 66-70, prof chem, 70-80, head dept, 80-87, dean, Col Sci, 87-88, VPRES ADMIN & STUDENT AFFAIRS, MCNEESE STATE UNIV, 88- *Personal Data:* b Lake Charles, La, Aug 21, 35; m 59; c 4. *Educ:* McNeese State Col, BS, 58; La State Univ, MS, 65, PhD(org chem), 67. *Concurrent Pos:* Consult. *Mem:* Am Chem Soc. *Res:* Chemistry of tertiary amides; study of the syntheses, reactions, and stereochemistry of these compounds; acid rain studies; geo-pressured, gas-thermal water studies; environmental studies. *Mailing Add:* PO Box 92455 MSU Lake Charles LA 70609

IEZZI, ROBERT ALDO, metal & organic coatings, packaging, for more information see previous edition

IFFLAND, DON CHARLES, ORGANIC CHEMISTRY. *Current Pos:* assoc prof, 56-59, chmn, Dept Chem, 68-78, PROF CHEM, WESTERN MICH UNIV, 59- *Personal Data:* b Blissfield, Mich, Nov 26, 21; m 44; c 2. *Educ:* Adrian Col, BS, 43; Purdue Univ, MS, 44, PhD(org chem), 47. *Hon Degrees:* DSc, Adrian Col, 73. *Prof Exp:* From asst prof to assoc prof chem, WVa Univ, 47-56; fel, Purdue Univ, 54-55. *Mem:* Am Chem Soc; Royal Soc Chem; Sigma Xi. *Res:* Aromatic and aliphatic amines; aliphatic nitro compounds; reaction of oximes and hydrazones; configuration of substituted diphenyls. *Mailing Add:* 3430 Northview Dr Kalamazoo MI 49004-3138

IFFT, EDWARD M, PHYSICS, ARMS CONTROL. *Current Pos:* DEP DIR, US ON-SITE INSPECTION AGENCY, 91- *Personal Data:* b Grove City, Pa, July 19, 37; m 67, Jeanne Felts; c John & Sharon. *Educ:* Antioch Col, BS, 60; Ohio State Univ, PhD(physics), 67. *Prof Exp:* Res assoc low temperature physics, Ohio State Univ, 65-67; phys sci officer, US Arms Control & Disarmament Agency, 67-73; dep dir, Off Arms Control & Disarmament, US State Dept, 73-78; chief, Int Prog Policy Office, US Nat Aeronaut & Space Admin, 78-81; dep state dept rep, US deleg Strategic Arms Reduction Talks, USSR, Geneva, 81-84; sr state dept rep, Nuclear & Space Talks, 85-91; sr state dept rep, Comprehensive Test Ban Treaty Negotiations, 94-96. *Concurrent Pos:* Mem US deleg, Strategic Arms Limitations Talks with Soviet Union, 69-78; exec secy, US-USSR agreement on space coop, 78-81. *Mem:* Am Phys Soc; Int Inst Strategic Studies. *Res:* Arms control; properties of liquid mixtures of helium-3 and helium-4 at low temperatures. *Mailing Add:* 6825 Wheatley Ct Falls Church VA 22042

IFJU, GEZA, FORESTRY. *Current Pos:* Asst prof, 64-71, PROF FORESTRY, VA POLYTECH INST & STATE UNIV, 71-, HEAD DEPT, 77- *Personal Data:* b Szeged, Hungary, Jan 26, 31; US citizen; m 60; c 7. *Educ:* Univ BC, BSF, 59, PhD(wood sci), 63; Yale Univ, MF, 60. *Hon Degrees:* Dr, Univ Forestry, Hungary, 90. *Honors & Awards:* Wood Award, 64; Marwardt Award, Forestry Prod Res Soc, 84. *Concurrent Pos:* Asst specialist & fel forest prod, Forest Prod Lab, Univ Calif, 63-64. *Mem:* Forest Prod Res Soc; Tech Asn Pulp & Paper Indust; Soc Wood Sci & Technol; Can Pulp & Paper Asn. *Res:* Wood science and technology; relationship between chemical constitution and strength behavior of wood; wood anatomy and physical properties of cell wall of woody plants. *Mailing Add:* 803 Broce Dr Blacksburg VA 24060

IGEL, HOWARD JOSEPH, PATHOLOGY, VIROLOGY. *Current Pos:* dir infectious dis & virol, 68-72, dir labs, 72-75, PROF & CHMN PATH & LAB MED, AKRON CHILDREN'S HOSP, 75- *Personal Data:* b Omaha, Nebr, May 10, 34; m 59; c 4. *Educ:* Creighton Univ, BS, 55, MD, 59. *Prof Exp:* Intern, St Joseph's Hosp, Omaha, Nebr, 59-60; resident path, Western Res Univ, 60-64; res pathologist-virologist, Nat Cancer Inst, 64-68. *Concurrent*

Pos: Nat Cancer Inst res fel, 61-64; assoc clin prof path, Case Western Res Univ; adj prof biol, Akron Univ & Kent State Univ; Nat Adv Panel, Food & Drug Admin, 82- *Mem:* AAAS; Am Asn Path; Am Soc Microbiol; Am Soc Clin Path. *Res:* Mouse leukemia and sarcoma viruses; virus-chemical cocarcinogenesis; in vitro systems of carcinogenesis; in vitro transformation of human cells; in vitro growth of human skin for grafting burn patients. *Mailing Add:* Dept Path Akron Childrens Hosp Med Ctr One Perkins Sq Akron OH 44308-1062

IGLAR, ALBERT FRANCIS, JR, ENVIRONMENTAL HEALTH, SANITARY ENGINEERING. *Current Pos:* from asst prof to assoc prof, 70-81, PROF ENVIRON HEALTH, ETENN STATE UNIV, 81- *Personal Data:* b New Kensington, Pa, July 17, 39; m 64, Loretta Streich; c 2. *Educ:* Carnegie-Mellon Univ, BS, 61; Univ Minn, Minneapolis, MPH, 66, PhD(environ health), 70. *Prof Exp:* Sanit engr I, Regional Off, Pa Dept Health, Meadville, 61-65, sanit engr II, Sewerage Sect, Cent Off, Harrisburg, 62-65; res fel environ health, Univ Minn, Minneapolis, 66-70. *Concurrent Pos:* Consult to numerous cos. *Mem:* Nat Environ Health Asn; Air Pollution Control Asn; Am Indust Hyg Asn. *Res:* Institutional solid waste management; treatment of coal gasification wastewater; land disposal of low level radiological waste; industrial hygiene; hazardous waste management. *Mailing Add:* Environ Health E Tenn State Univ PO Box 10001 Johnson City TN 37614-0002

IGLEHART, DONALD LEE, OPERATIONS RESEARCH, MATHEMATICAL STATISTICS. *Current Pos:* RETIRED. *Personal Data:* b Baltimore, Md, May 11, 33; m 61, Sheralee Hill; c Kent & Mark. *Educ:* Cornell Univ, BEngPhys, 56; Stanford Univ, MS, 59, PhD(math statist), 61. *Prof Exp:* Asst, Appl Physics Lab, Johns Hopkins Univ, 56-58; assoc prof, Cornell Univ, 61-67; prof opers res, Stanford Univ, 67-90, chmn, 85-90. *Concurrent Pos:* Nat Acad Sci-Nat Res Coun res fel, 61-62. *Mem:* Opers Res Soc Am; fel Inst Math Statist. *Res:* Mathematical theory of inventory; Markov processes; limit theorems in queueing theory; simulation methodology; weak convergence of probability measures. *Mailing Add:* 833 Tolman Dr Stanford CA 94305

IGLESIA, ENRIQUE, REACTION ENGINEERING, HETEROGENEOUS CATALYSIS. *Current Pos:* PROF CHEM ENG, UNIV CALIF, BERKELEY, 93- *Personal Data:* b Havana, Cuba, Aug 27, 54; US citizen; m 78; c 3. *Educ:* Princeton Univ, BSE, 77; Stanford Univ, MS, 79, PhD(chem eng), 82. *Prof Exp:* Prin investr catalysis res & develop, Corp Res Labs, Exxon Res & Eng, 81-93, sect head, 88-93. *Concurrent Pos:* Consult prof chem eng, Stanford Univ, 89-93. *Mem:* Am Chem Soc; Am Inst Chem Engrs; Mat Res Soc; NAm Catalysis Soc; Int Zeolite Asn. *Res:* Heterogeneous catalysis and its applications to petrochemical processing; mechanisms of surface reactions and engineering of catalytic materials and reactors. *Mailing Add:* Dept Chem Eng Univ Calif 103 Gilman Berkeley CA 94720. *Fax:* 510-642-4778; *E-Mail:* iglesia@ns144.cchem.berkeley.edu

IGLEWICZ, BORIS, STATISTICS. *Current Pos:* assoc prof, Temple Univ, 69-74, dir, PhD Prog, 70-76, chmn dept, 78-82, PROF STATIST, TEMPLE UNIV, 74-, DIR BIOSTATIST RES CTR, 93- *Personal Data:* b Omsk, Russia, Oct 11, 39; US citizen; m 73, Raja Brody; c David & Alana. *Educ:* Wayne State Univ, BS, 62, MA, 63; Va Polytech Inst, PhD(statist), 67. *Prof Exp:* Instr math, Mich Technol Univ, 63-64; asst prof statist, Case Western Res Univ, 67-69. *Concurrent Pos:* Fel Harvard Univ, 78, vis prof, 84-85. *Mem:* Inst Math Statist; Biomet Soc; fel Am Statist Asn; Int Statist Inst; sr mem Am Soc Qual Control; fel Royal Statist Soc. *Res:* Quality control; clinical trial models; survey sampling; robust methods; sequential analysis. *Mailing Add:* Dept Statist Speakman Hall Temple Univ Philadelphia PA 19122. *Fax:* 215-204-1501

IGLEWICZ, RAJA, ENVIRONMENTAL HEALTH & SCIENCES. *Current Pos:* sup & indust hygienist, 85-87, octg prog mgr, 89-90, RES SCIENTIST, NJ DEPT HEALTH, 87-88 & 91- *Personal Data:* b Nov 27, 45; US citizen; m 73, Boris; c David & Alana. *Educ:* Temple Univ, BS, 75, MS, 80. *Prof Exp:* Indust hygienist, NJ Dept Health, 80-84; consult, Gen Elec Co, 84-85. *Mem:* Am Indust Hyg Asn; Am Pub Health Asn. *Res:* Health hazards of elevated levels of carbon monoxide in ambulances and vehicles; AIDS issues in occupational settings, and the control of occupational health hazards in industrial settings; environmental and occupational health hazards from chromium contamination; occupational health hazards resulting from lead abatement in commercial and residential settings; evaluation of control technology used for lead abatement and paint removal. *Mailing Add:* 1912 Rolling Lane Cherry Hill NJ 08003

IGLEWSKI, BARBARA HOTHAM, MICROBIOLOGY. *Current Pos:* from instr to assoc prof, 68-79, PROF MICROBIOL, ORE HEALTH SCI UNIV, 79- *Personal Data:* b Freeport, Pa, Mar 23, 38; m 65; c 2. *Educ:* Allegheny Col, BS, 60; Pa State Univ, MS, 62, PhD(microbiol), 64. *Prof Exp:* Fel, Pa State Univ, 64-65, Univ Colo Med Ctr, 65-66 & Pub Health Res Inst, NY, 66-68. *Concurrent Pos:* Sr fel, Walter Reed Army Inst Res, 76-77; mem, Bacterial & Mycotic Dis Study Sect, NIH, 79-83, Res & Training Comt, Nat Cystic Fibrosis Found, 81-84 & Vaccine & Related Biol Prod Adv Comt, 81-82. *Mem:* Am Soc Microbiol. *Res:* Bacterial toxins and pathogenesis of gram negative bacteria, including Pseudomonas aeruginosa and Legionella pneumophila. *Mailing Add:* Dept Microbiol Univ Rochester Med Sch 601 Elmwood Ave Rochester NY 14642-0001

IGLEWSKI, WALLACE, VIROLOGY, MOLECULAR BIOLOGY. *Current Pos:* PROF, DEPT MICROBIOL-IMMUNOL, MED SCH, UNIV ROCHESTER 86- *Personal Data:* b Cleveland, Ohio, Aug 17, 38; m 65, Barbara Hotham; c Eric & William. *Educ:* Western Res Univ, BA, 61; Pa State Univ, MS, 63, PhD(microbiol), 65. *Prof Exp:* Fel virol, Med Sch, Univ Colo, 65-66; fel, Pub Health Res Inst City of New York, Inc, 66-68; from asst prof to prof microbiol, Med Sch, Univ Ore, 68-86. *Mem:* Am Soc Microbiol; Am Soc Virol. *Res:* Replication of RNA viruses, microbial toxins, somatic cell genetics, especially the translation and transcription of viral ribonucleic acid and the effects of virus multiplication on cellular metabolism; control of translation in eucaryotes; mechanism of intoxication of animal cells; ADP-Ribosylation in eucaryotic and procaryotic organisms. *Mailing Add:* Dept Microbiol & Immunol Univ Rochester Med Sch Rochester NY 14642. *Fax:* 716-473-9573

IGNARRO, LOUIS JOSEPH, PHARMACOLOGY, CELL BIOLOGY. *Current Pos:* PROF PHARMACOL, SCH MED, UNIV CALIF, 86-, ASST DEAN RES, 91- *Personal Data:* b Brooklyn, NY, May 31, 41; c 1. *Educ:* Columbia Univ, BS, 62; Univ Minn, PhD(pharmacol), 66. *Honors & Awards:* Res Award, Pharmaceut Mfrs Asn Found, 73; Res Award, Edward G Schlieder Found Educ, 73; Smith, Kline & French Award. *Prof Exp:* NIH fel, 66-68; res scientist pharmacol, Ciba-Geigy Corp, 68-72; asst prof to assoc prof, 72-78, prof pharmacol, Med Sch, Tulane Univ, 79-86. *Concurrent Pos:* Merck res grant, Tulane Univ, 73-74; Arthritis Found grant, 74-75; Nat Inst Arthritis, Metab & Digestive Dis grant, 74-77, 78-81 & 82-85; USPHS res career develop award, 75-80. *Mem:* Am Soc Pharmacol & Exp Therapeut; Soc Exp Biol & Med; Am Rheumatism Asn; Am Heart Asn; Am Soc Cell Biol; Sigma Xi; Am Soc Biochem & Molecular Biol; Am Physiol Soc. *Res:* Inflammation and arthritis; cyclic nucleotide research; bioregulation of human cell function; hormonal control mechanisms; free radicals and enzyme activation; nitric oxide metabolics; regulation of vascular and platelet function. *Mailing Add:* Dept Pharmacol Univ Calif Sch Med Los Angeles CA 90095-1735

IGNAT, DAVID WALTER, WAVES IN INHOMOGENEOUS PLASMA. *Current Pos:* ED NUCLEAR FUSION, INT ATOMIC ENERGY AGENCY, 96- *Personal Data:* b Painesville, Ohio, May 18, 41; m 68, Eleanor Peters; c Elizabeth (Bausch) & Emily. *Educ:* Carleton Col, BA, 63; Yale Univ, PhD(physics), 68. *Prof Exp:* Instr eng & appl sci, Yale Univ, 68-69; postdoctoral fel, Los Alamos Sci Lab, 69-71; res staff, Ctr Res Plasma Physics, Lausanne, Switz, 71-73; prog staff, US Dept Energy, Washington, DC, 73-77; sci staff, Plasma Physics Lab, Princeton Univ, 77-96. *Mem:* AAAS; Am Phys Soc. *Res:* Waves in inhomogeneous plasma; radio frequency heating and current drive in toroidal plasmas; dynamic modeling of tokamak plasmas; design study. *Mailing Add:* Int Atomic Energy Agency Box 100 Wagramerstrass 5 Vienna A-1400 Austria. *Fax:* 43-1-2060-29655; *E-Mail:* ignat@phoenix.princeton.edu

IGNATIEV, ALEX, SURFACE PHYSICS. *Current Pos:* from asst prof to assoc prof, 74-83, PROF PHYSICS & CHEM, UNIV HOUSTON, 83-, ASSOC DIR, MAGNETIC INFO RES LAB, 84- *Personal Data:* b Wehingen, Ger, Feb 14, 45; US citizen; m 67; c 2. *Educ:* Univ Wis, BS, 66; Cornell Univ, PhD(mat sci), 72. *Prof Exp:* Fel mat sci, State Univ NY, Stony Brook, 71-73. *Concurrent Pos:* Mem, Energy Lab, Univ Houston, 75-; lectr physics, Aarhus Univ, Denmark, 77-78; Fulbright sr scholar, 83; assoc dir, Space Vacuum Epitaxy Ctr, 86-88, dir, 88- *Mem:* Am Phys Soc; Am Vacuum Soc; Am Chem Soc; Int Solar Energy Soc. *Res:* Structure and properties of surfaces, including catalysis, two dimensional phase transitions, surface image, small particle structures, solar energy absorbing and reflecting coatings; epitaxial growth of thin film semiconductors by MBE/CBE, thin film high Tc superconductor materials. *Mailing Add:* Physics Dept Univ Houston Houston TX 77004

IGNIZIO, JAMES PAUL, operations research, for more information see previous edition

IGNOFFO, CARLO MICHAEL, ENTOMOLOGY, INVERTEBRATE PATHOLOGY. *Current Pos:* dir biol control, Insects Res Lab, Entom Res Div, 71-91, SUPVR INVERT PATH, AGR RES SERV, USDA, 91-; DIR BIOL CONTROL INSECTS RES LAB, ENTOM RES DIV, AGR RES SERV, USDA, 71- *Personal Data:* b Chicago Heights, Ill, Aug 24, 28; m 49, Florence F Mielcarek. *Educ:* Northern Ill Univ, BS, 50; Univ Minn, MS, 54, PhD(entom), 56. *Prof Exp:* Assoc prof entom, Iowa Wesleyan Col, 57-59; res entomologist, Agr Res Serv, USDA, 59-65; dir entom, Bioferm Div, Int Minerals Chem Corp, 65-67, dir entom, 67-71. *Concurrent Pos:* Mem, Int Comt Nomenclature Invert Viruses & Int; assoc ed, J Invertr Path Comt Standardization & Assay of Insect Pathogens. *Mem:* AAAS; Entom Soc Am; Soc Invert Path; Am Inst Biol Sci; Int Orgn Biol Control. *Res:* Insect pathogens and their effects on invertebrates and vertebrates; viruses, fungi and bacteria infecting insects; environ stability of entomas pathogens; sunlight-UV persistence; virulence of ferol and recombinant baculoviruses. *Mailing Add:* CIRL USDA ARS 1503 S Providence Rd Columbia MO 65203

IGO, GEORGE (JEROME), PHYSICS, NUCLEAR & PARTICLE PHYSICS. *Current Pos:* chmn dept, 77-80, PROF PHYSICS, UNIV CALIF, LOS ANGELES, 69- *Personal Data:* b Greeley, Colo, Sept 2, 25; m 53; c 1. *Educ:* Harvard Univ, AB, 49; Univ Calif, PhD(physics), 53. *Prof Exp:* Res assoc, Radiation Lab, Univ Calif, 52-53, Sloane Physics Lab, Yale Univ, 53-54; assoc physicist, Brookhaven Nat Lab, 54-56; assoc physics, Stanford Univ, 56-58; Fulbright fel, Univ Heidelberg, 58-59; staff scientist, Lawrence Radiation Lab, Univ Calif, 60-64; dir cyclotron inst, Tex A&M Univ, 64; mem vis staff, Los Alamos Sci Lab, 65-69. *Mem:* Am Phys Soc. *Res:* Nuclear physics; deep inelastic scattering; pp spin physics; relatuistic heavy ion physics. *Mailing Add:* Dept Physics 3174 Knudsen Hall Univ Calif Los Angeles CA 90024

IGUSA, JUN-ICHI, MATHEMATICS. *Current Pos:* from asst prof to assoc prof, 55-61, PROF MATH, JOHNS HOPKINS UNIV, 61- *Personal Data:* b Japan, Jan 30, 24; m 48; c 3. *Educ:* Tokyo Univ, BS, 45; Kyoto Univ, PhD, 53. *Prof Exp:* Asst math, Inst Statist Sci, 47-48; asst prof, Tokyo Univ Educ, 48-49 & Kyoto Univ, 49-53; res assoc, Harvard Univ, 53-55. *Concurrent Pos:* Mem, Inst Advan Study, Princeton, 59-60 & 70-71; guest, Inst Advan Study Sci, Paris, 64, Tata Inst, Bombay, 78; ed, Am J Math; vis prof, Harvard Univ, 81-82. *Mem:* Am Math Soc; Japan Math Soc. *Res:* Algebraic geometry connected with number theory. *Mailing Add:* 1409 Greencroft Lane Hunter Valley MD 21030

IH, CHARLES CHUNG-SEN, ELECTRO-OPTICAL DEVICES, ELECTRO-OPTICAL SYSTEMS. *Current Pos:* PROF ELECTRO-OPTIC DEVICES & SYST, DEPT ELEC ENG, UNIV DEL, 75- *Personal Data:* b Hankow, China, May 15, 33; US citizen; c 2. *Educ:* Nat Taiwan Univ, BSEE, 56; Lehigh Univ, MSEE, 59; Univ Pa, PhD(physics), 66. *Prof Exp:* Engr, Sperry Rand Univac, 59-63; mem tech staff, RCA Lab, 67-71; dir, Galor Lab, CBS Lab, 71-75. *Concurrent Pos:* Consult, Perkin Elmer Corp, 75, Naval Air Develop Ctr, Warminister, Pa, 80-81; IBM & Sperry Univac, 81; mem fac, IBM Res Ctr, Yorktown Heights, NY, 81. *Mem:* Optical Soc Am; Inst Elec & Electronics Engrs; Am Inst Physics; Soc Photo-Optical Instrumentation Engrs. *Res:* Holography applications related to color image preservation; holographic scanners and fiber optical communications. *Mailing Add:* Dept Elec Eng Univ Del Newark DE 19716-0001

IHA, FRANKLIN TAKASHI, MATHEMATICAL ANALYSIS. *Current Pos:* lectr, 74-79, INSTR, DIV MATH & NATURAL SCI, LEEWARD COMMUNITY COL, 79- *Personal Data:* b Honolulu, Hawaii, Dec 29, 37; m 71. *Educ:* Univ Hawaii, BA, 61, MA, 63; Univ Calif, Los Angeles, PhD(math), 69. *Prof Exp:* From instr to asst prof math, Univ Hawaii, 63-74. *Mem:* Am Math Soc; Math Asn Am. *Res:* Spectral theory of partial differential operators. *Mailing Add:* 1667 Lima St Honolulu HI 96819-2657

IHAS, GARY GENE, ULTRA-LOW TEMPERATURE PHYSICS. *Current Pos:* from assoc prof to assoc prof, 77-85, PROF PHYSICS, UNIV FLA, 85- *Personal Data:* b Hillsdale, Mich, Sept 5, 45; m 66; c 3. *Educ:* Calif Inst Technol, BA & BS, 67; Univ Mich, MA, 70, PhD(physics), 71. *Prof Exp:* Res physicist low temp, Kernforschungsanlage, Juelich, WGer, 71-73; vis asst prof physics, Ohio State Univ, 73-75, res assoc physics, 75-77. *Concurrent Pos:* Alfred P Sloan Found fel, 77-82. *Mem:* Am Phys Soc. *Res:* Surface effects in liquid helium; superfluid helium three; critical phenomena; impurities and excitations in liquid helium; nuclear demagnetization refrigeration. *Mailing Add:* Dept Physics Univ Fla Williamson Hall Gainesville FL 32611

IHDE, AARON JOHN, CHEMISTRY, HISTORY OF SCIENCE. *Current Pos:* from instr to prof, 42-80, chmn integrated lib studies, 63-70, EMER PROF CHEM, HIST SCI & INTEGRATED LIB STUDIES, UNIV WIS-MADISON, 80- *Personal Data:* b Neenah, Wis, Dec 31, 09; wid; c 2. *Educ:* Univ Wis, BS, 31, MS, 39, PhD(food chem), 41. *Honors & Awards:* Dexter Award, Am Chem Soc. *Prof Exp:* Res chemist, Blue Valley Creamery Co, Ill, 31-38; asst chem, Univ Wis, 39-41; instr, Butler Univ, 41-42. *Concurrent Pos:* Carnegie fel, Harvard Univ, 51-52; consult, Wis Food Stands Adv Comt, 55-67. *Mem:* AAAS; Am Chem Soc; Hist Sci Soc; Soc Hist Technol. *Res:* Metals, vitamins, and synthetic additives in foods; history of chemistry; biochemistry; social implications of science; science education. *Mailing Add:* Chem Bldg Univ Wis Madison WI 53706

IHDE, DANIEL CARLYLE, INTERNAL MEDICINE, MEDICAL ONCOLOGY. *Current Pos:* fel, Bethesda, Md, 73-75, sr investr, Vet Admin Med Oncol Br, Vet Admin Med Ctr, Washington, DC, 75-81, HEAD, CLIN INVEST MED ONCOL, NAT CANCER INST-NAVY MED ONCOL BR, NAVAL HOSP, BETHESDA, MD, 81- *Personal Data:* b Parsons, Kans, July 10, 43; m 68; c 2. *Educ:* Eastern NMex Univ, BS, 64; Stanford Univ, MD, 69. *Honors & Awards:* Commendation Medal, USPHS, 84. *Prof Exp:* Intern & resident internal med, NY Hosp, 69-71; resident & fel internal med & med oncol, Mem Hosp, NY, 71-73. *Concurrent Pos:* Prof med, Uniformed Serv Univ Health Sci, 85- *Mem:* Am Col Physicians; Am Soc Clin Oncol; Am Asn Cancer Res; Int Asn Study Lung Cancer. *Res:* Clinical investigations in cancer chemotherapy; staging and the natural history of human cancer; clinical-cell biologic correlation, particularly lung cancer mycosis fungoides and prostatic cancer. *Mailing Add:* 1686 Mason Knoll Ct St Louis MO 63131

IHLER, GARRET MARTIN, MOLECULAR BIOLOGY & HEMATOLOGY, MOLECULAR GENETICS INTRACELLULAR PATHOGENS. *Current Pos:* prof head dept, 76-95, PROF MED BIOCHEM, COL MED, TEX A&M UNIV, 76- *Personal Data:* b Milwaukee, Wis, Nov 4, 39; m 70; c 2. *Educ:* Calif Inst Technol, BS, 61; Harvard Univ, PhD(biochem), 67; Univ Pittsburgh, MD, 76. *Prof Exp:* NIH res fel biochem, Harvard Med Sch, 67-69; from asst prof to assoc prof biochem, Sch Med, Univ Pittsburgh, 71-76. *Mem:* Am Chem Soc; Am Soc Microbiol; Acad Clin Lab Physicians & Scientists; Am Soc Cell Biol; Am Soc Biol Chemists. *Res:* Enzyme therapy using red cells as carrier; Gaucher's disease; enzymology, especially RNA polymerase; macromolecules, especially DNA replication; protein synthesis; bacterial and phage genetics; genomic maps. *Mailing Add:* Dept Med Biochem & Genetics Tex A&M Univ Health Sci Ctr College Station TX 77843-1114. *Fax:* 409-847-9481

IHNAT, MILAN, ANALYTICAL CHEMISTRY. *Current Pos:* PAC SCIENTIST AGR FOOD RES CTR, 97- *Personal Data:* b Montreal, Que, Oct 1, 41; m 70; c 2. *Educ:* McGill Univ, BSc, 62, PhD(phys chem), 67. *Prof Exp:* Res assoc biophys chem, Columbia Univ, 66-69; res asst, McGill Univ, 69-71; res scientist anal chem, Chem & Biol Res Inst, Res Br Agr Can, 71-86, Land Resource Res Centre, 86-97. *Current Pos:* Asst prof, McGill Univ, 70-71. *Mem:* Am Chem Soc; Chem Inst Can; fel Asn Off Analytical Chemists; Spectros Soc Can. *Res:* Quantitative analytical methodology for the determination of macro and trace concentrations of metals and other inorganic constituents in biological materials; analytical atomic absorption, atomic emission and atomic mass spectroscopy; development of biological reference materials for chemical composition. *Mailing Add:* Pac Agr Food Res Ctr Agr Agr-Food Can Summerland BC V0H 1Z0 Can

IHNDRIS, RAYMOND WILL, ORGANIC CHEMISTRY. *Current Pos:* RETIRED. *Personal Data:* b Sterling, Ind, Apr 1, 20; m 42, Violet E Parrish; c Ray L & Robert B. *Educ:* Rollins Col, BSc, 55. *Prof Exp:* Chemist, Bur Entom & Plant Quarantine, USDA, 46-55, chemist, Pesticid Chem Res Br, Entom Res Div, 56-60; head, Sci Records Sect, Res Commun Br, Cancer Chemother Nat Serv Ctr, NIH, 60-67, sr info chemist, Toxicol Info Prog, Nat Libr Med, 67-76, info chem consult, 76-81. *Mem:* Am Chem Soc; Am Soc Info Sci. *Res:* Organic chemical abstracts system of nomenclature; synthetic organic insecticides and attractants; formulation of insecticides, repellants and attractants; information storage and retrieval of organic compounds by structural fragmentation. *Mailing Add:* 682 Granville Dr Winter Park FL 32789

IHRIG, JUDSON LA MOURE, PHYSICAL CHEMISTRY. *Current Pos:* from asst prof to assoc prof chem, Univ Hawaii, 52-72, dir, Lib Studies Prog, 73-79, chmn dept, 81-86, prof, 73-93, dir, Hon Prog, 87-95, EMER PROF CHEM, UNIV HAWAII, 93- *Personal Data:* b Santa Maria, Calif, Nov 5, 25; m 50, Gwendolyn A Montz; c Kristin & Neil M. *Educ:* Haverford Col, BS, 49; Princeton Univ, AM, 51, PhD(phys chem), 52. *Mem:* Am Chem Soc; Sigma Xi. *Res:* Transport properties of aqueous solutions; magnetochemistry; inhibition of chain reactions. *Mailing Add:* 386 Wailupe Circle Honolulu HI 96821

IHRKE, CHARLES ALBERT, GENETICS, PLANT BREEDING. *Current Pos:* asst prof genetics, Univ Wis, Green Bay, 69-75, assoc prof pop dynamics, 75-80, chmn dept, 84-88, ASSOC PROF HUMAN BIOL, UNIV WIS, GREEN BAY, 81-, CHMN DEPT, 94- *Personal Data:* b Oshkosh, Wis, June 9, 38; m 60, Carol Hinderman; c Craig & Christopher. *Educ:* Wis State Univ, BS, 60; Univ Nebr, Omaha, MS, 66; Ore State Univ, PhD(plant genetics), 69. *Prof Exp:* Instr biol, Onarga Mil Sch, 60-64. *Concurrent Pos:* Bd trustees, Bellin Col Nursing, 96- *Mem:* Am Soc Agron; Crop Sci Soc Am; Genetics Soc Am; Am Inst Biol Sci; Am Genetics Asn; Sigma Xi. *Res:* Investigations of environmental effects on genetic recombination; incidence of genetic disorders in some small United States populations. *Mailing Add:* 2201 Sunrise Ct Green Bay WI 54302. *Fax:* 920-465-2769; *E-Mail:* ihrkec@ kwgb.edu

IHRMAN, KRYN GEORGE, ORGANIC CHEMISTRY. *Current Pos:* RETIRED. *Personal Data:* b Kalamazoo, Mich, Nov 5, 30; m 64. *Educ:* Kalamazoo Col, BA, 52; Ohio State Univ, PhD(org chem), 57. *Prof Exp:* Res chemist, Ethyl Corp, 57-92. *Mem:* Am Chem Soc. *Res:* Organo-metallic synthesis involving transition elements; organic synthesis by organo-metallic catalysis; synthesis of polymer additives; synthesis of organic intermediates. *Mailing Add:* 60 Wakefield Dr Verona VA 24482

IHSSEN, PETER EDOWALD, GENETICS, FISH BIOLOGY. *Current Pos:* RES SCIENTIST FISHERIES GENETICS, FISHERIES BR, ONT MINISTRY NATURAL RESOURCES, 71- *Personal Data:* b Bremen, Ger, Jan 12, 39; m 64. *Educ:* Univ Man, BSc, 63; Univ Toronto, MSc, 66, PhD(zool), 71. *Mem:* Can Soc Zoologists; Genetics Soc Can; Am Fisheries Soc. *Res:* Application of quantitative and population genetics principles to fisheries problems; conservation of biodiversity of fishes; physiological and biochemical genetics of fish. *Mailing Add:* Ministry Natural Resources Box 5000 Maple ON L6A 1S9 Can

IJAMS, CHARLES CARROLL, CHEMICAL PHYSICS. *Current Pos:* RETIRED. *Personal Data:* b Jackson, Tenn, Dec 23, 13; m 47; c 1. *Educ:* Union Univ, Tenn, AB, 36; Vanderbilt Univ, MS, 37, PhD(phys chem), 41. *Prof Exp:* Asst chemist, Wolf Creek Ord Plant, Tenn, 41-42; chief chemist, Gulf Ord Plant, 42-43; asst prof chem, Union Univ, Tenn, 47-48; from assoc prof to prof physics & head dept, Memphis State Univ, 48-77. *Concurrent Pos:* Consult, USN Air Tech Training Command. *Mem:* Am Asn Physics Teachers. *Res:* Spreading of monomolecular films on water; solubility of gases in organic liquids; maintenance of sonar equipment. *Mailing Add:* 249 N Rose Rd Memphis TN 38117

IJAZ, LUBNA RAZIA, TECHNICAL MANAGEMENT, INDUSTRIAL PRODUCTION. *Current Pos:* CHMN, INT SOLAR & ELECTRONIC INDUST LTD, PAKISTAN, 83-, MANAGING DIR, 90- *Personal Data:* b Lahore, Pakistan, Mar 27, 40; US citizen; m 60; c Mansoor, Farouk, Atif, Mujeek & Neelaum. *Educ:* Peshawar Univ, BS, 57; Punjab Univ, MS, 60; Va Polytech Inst & State Univ, PhD(physics educ), 75. *Honors & Awards:* VERA Res Merit Award, 75, VERA Merit Award, 76; Nat Sci Teacher Award, AAAS & Sci Teachers Asn, 77; Int Women of Yr in Sci, 93; Albert Einstein Merit Award for Solar Tech Res, 95; Gold Medal of Hon for Solar Res Work, 95. *Prof Exp:* Asst prof physics, Va Polytech Inst & State Univ, Blacksburg, 75-79; pres, Solar Energy Educ & Res Corp, 80-83. *Concurrent Pos:* Vis solar scientist & lectr, Int Summer Col Physics & Contemp Needs, Nathiagali, 76 & 77; adj prof elec eng, Va Polytech Inst & State Univ, 79-83; prof physics, KFU, Saudi Arabia, 79-84. *Mem:* AAAS; Nat Sci Teachers Asn; Inst Elec & Electronics Engrs; Am Asn Physics Teachers. *Res:* Solar cell materials; thin film solar cells for photovoltaic energy conversion; developing solar photovoltaic module production facility and transfering electronic chip technology to Pakistan; US patent on solar cell. *Mailing Add:* 2236 Archer Rd Shawsville VA 24162. *Fax:* 540-382-5528

IKA, PRASAD VENKATA, PHYSICAL & MECHANICAL PROPERTIES, STRUCTURE-PROPERTY CORRELATIONS. *Current Pos:* NEW PROD DEVELOP MGR, RADIAC ABRASIVES, INC, 93- *Personal Data:* b Eluru, Andhra Pradesh, India, Apr 8, 58; m 87; c 2. *Educ:* Indian Inst Technol, Delhi, MS, 81; State Univ NY, MS, 83, PhD(polymer chem), 85. *Prof Exp:* Res engr indust res, Polymer Prod Develop, Norton Co, 85-88, sr res engr, 88-90, res supvr, Supv Polymer Res, 90-93. *Mem:* Am Chem Soc. *Res:* Product development research of polymer based abrasive products; structure-property correlationships of polymers in-general and thermosets-in-particular; polymer characterization tools to probe into polymer wear characteristics and degradation. *Mailing Add:* 1517 Westminster Dr No 103 Naperville IL 60563-9217

IKAWA, HIDEO, FLUID-AERODYNAMICS, ENDO-EXO ATMOSPHERIC FLIGHT MECHANICS. *Current Pos:* sr specialist, 87-95, PRIN ENGR, MIL AIRCRAFT SYSTS DIV, NORTHROP GRUMMAN CORP, 95- *Personal Data:* b Yanai-shi, Japan, May 8, 35; US citizen; m 58, Yoshiko Imai. *Educ:* Northrop Univ, BS, 62; Calif Inst Technol, MS, 64, PhD(aeronaut), 73. *Prof Exp:* Engr aerodyn, Gen Dynamics, Pomona, 62-63; engr S-II aerothermodyn, Space Div, Rockwell Int, 64-66, lead engr, 66-68, eng specialist aerothermodyn, Satellite Syst Div, 73-81, sr eng specialist flight mech, 81-85; sr res scientist, Aerojet Propulsion Inst, 86-87. *Concurrent Pos:* Invited vis prof, Inst Space & Aeronaut Sci, Univ Tokyo, 79-80. *Mem:* Am Inst Aeronaut & Astronaut. *Res:* Aerodynamic analysis, trajectory simulation and concept evaluation of endo-exoatmospheric flight vehicles such as aero assisted orbit transfer vehicle, maneuverable reentry research vehicle and transatmospheric vehicle. *Mailing Add:* 15722 Dawson Lane Huntington Beach CA 92647-2904. *Fax:* 562-942-6464

IKAWA, MIYOSHI, ALGAL & FUNGAL TOXINS, MARINE TOXINS. *Current Pos:* prof, 63-87, EMER PROF BIOCHEM & ADJ PROF ZOOL, UNIV NH, 87- *Personal Data:* b Venice, Calif, Feb 14, 19; m 50; c 2. *Educ:* Calif Inst Technol, BS, 41; Univ Wis, MS, 45, PhD(biochem), 48. *Prof Exp:* Res fel chem, Calif Inst Technol, 48-52; res scientist, Biochem Inst, Univ Tex, 52-56; from asst res biochemist to assoc res biochemist, Univ Calif, 56-63. *Mem:* Fel AAAS; Am Chem Soc; Int Soc Toxinol; Japan Asn Mycotoxicol. *Res:* Algal and fungal toxins; microbial. *Mailing Add:* 32 Mill Pond Rd 03824-2719 NH 03824

IKE, ALBERT FRANCIS, FOREST SOILS, ACADEMIC ADMINISTRATION. *Current Pos:* assoc prof outdoor recreation, 70-74, ASSOC DIR, UNIV GA INST COMMUNITY & AREA DEVELOP, 74- *Personal Data:* b East Orange, NJ, July 18, 32; m 56; c 2. *Educ:* Rutgers Univ, BS, 54; Cornell Univ, MS, 57; NC State Univ, PhD(soil sci), 69. *Prof Exp:* Soil Scientist soil surv, Monogahela Nat Forest, US Forest Serv, 59-60; res forester soils & tree nutrit, Southeastern Forest Exp Sta, US Forest Serv, Asheville, NC, 60-70. *Concurrent Pos:* Consult, Conserv Found, 73-74, US Army CEngr, 79, Nat Park Serv, 82. *Mem:* Soc Am Foresters; Sigma Xi. *Res:* Coastal Zone Management Planning, including carrying capacity estimates for Cumberland Island National Seashore; soil-site relations; soil variability; tree nutrition; land management planning and decision making; forest site evaluation; carrying capacity; natural resource policy analysis. *Mailing Add:* 302 Riverview Rd Athens GA 30606

IKEDA, GEORGE J, BIOCHEMISTRY. *Current Pos:* pharmacologist, Div Toxicol, Bur Foods, 75-84, SUPVRY PHARMACOLOGIST, DIV TOXICOL RES, CTR FOOD SAFETY & APPL NUTRIT, FOOD & DRUG ADMIN, 85- *Personal Data:* b Pahoa, Hawaii, Jan 9, 35; m 62, Paulina Basa. *Educ:* Univ Hawaii, BA, 57; Ore State Univ, MS, 60, PhD(biochem), 67. *Prof Exp:* Res asst phys & anal chem, Upjohn Co, 60-64; pharmacologist, Dept Drug Metab, Abbott Labs, 67-75. *Mem:* Am Chem Soc; Phytochem Soc NAm; AAAS; Sigma Xi; Soc Toxicol; Int Soc Study Xenobiotics. *Res:* Drug metabolism; intermediary metabolism; plant biochemistry; radiotracer methodology; pharmacokinetics. *Mailing Add:* Pharmacokinetics & Metab Br HFS-506 Food & Drug Admin 8501 Muirkirk Rd Laurel MD 20708

IKEDA, RICHARD MASAYOSHI, POLYMER SCIENCE. *Current Pos:* res chemist, E I du Pont de Nemours, & Co, Inc, 59-67, staff scientist, Film Dept, 67-73, res assoc, 73-76, res assoc, Cent Res & Develop Dept, 76-78, res supvr, 78-93, RES FEL, E I DU PONT DE NEMOURS & CO, INC, 93- *Personal Data:* b Long Beach, Calif, Feb 21, 34; m 55, Harriet Hitchner; c David M & Timothy P. *Educ:* Juniata Col, BS, 55; Univ Ill, PhD(phys chem), 58. *Prof Exp:* NSF fel, Harvard Univ, 58-59. *Mem:* Am Chem Soc; Am Phys Soc. *Res:* Chemical kinetics; polymer physics. *Mailing Add:* 39 Cedarwood Lane Chadds Ford PA 19317-9244. *Fax:* 302-695-8207; *E-Mail:* ikeda@esvax.dnet.dupont.com

IKEDA, ROBERT MITSURU, AGRICULTURAL CHEMISTRY. *Current Pos:* RETIRED. *Personal Data:* b Tracy, Calif, Feb 4, 25; m 51; c 3. *Educ:* Univ Calif, BS, 50, PhD(agr chem), 55. *Prof Exp:* Sr lab technician, Univ Calif, 50-55, jr res food technologist, 55-57; chemist, Fruit & Veg Chem Lab, USDA, 57-62; sr chemist, Philip Morris, Inc, 62-67, mgr, Anal Div, 67-69, mgr, Chem & Biol Div, 69-72, assoc prin scientist, 72-76, prin scientist, 76-88. *Mem:* Am Chem Soc; Inst Food Technol; Sigma Xi. *Res:* Isolation and identification of flavor constituents. *Mailing Add:* 1915 Southcliff Rd Richmond VA 23225

IKEDA, TATSUYA, MOLECULAR SPECTROSCOPY, TECHNOLOGY TRANSFER. *Current Pos:* PATENT ATTY, HOECHST-CELANESE CORP, 81- *Personal Data:* b Tokyo, Japan, Apr 1, 40; m 69, Hiroko; c Tatsuhiro, Eureka & Mika. *Educ:* Univ Tokyo, BE, 63; Univ Wis, Milwaukee, MS, 68; Mass Inst Technol, PhD(phys chem), 72. *Hon Degrees:* JD, Suffolk Univ, 81. *Prof Exp:* Mem staff petrol chem, Res & Develop Dept, Tonen Sekiyu Kagaku Co, 63-66; fel, Rice Univ, 72-74 & Univ Calif, Santa Barbara, 74-75; tech adv polymer chem, 74-81. *Concurrent Pos:* Gen counr, Burlex. *Mem:* Sigma Xi. *Res:* Microstructures of polymers; application of tunable dye laser and fixed-frequency laser to the study of electronic spectra of small molecules. *Mailing Add:* 6 Blackberry Lane Whitehouse Station NJ 08889-9692

IKEDA-SAITO, MASAO, STRUCTURE & FUNCTION OF METALLO PROTEINS. *Current Pos:* ASSOC PROF, DEPT PHYSIOL/BIOPHYS, CASE WESTERN RES UNIV, 89- *Educ:* Osaka Univ, PhD(biophys), 78. *Prof Exp:* Asst prof molecular spectros, Univ Pa, 81-89. *Mailing Add:* Dept Physiol/Biophys Rm E559 Case Western Res Univ 2109 Adelbert Rd Cleveland OH 44106-4970. *Fax:* 216-368-3952

IKEHARA, YUKIO, MOLECULAR CELL BIOLOGY. *Current Pos:* PROF BIOCHEM, SCH MED, FUKUOKA UNIV, 78-, DEAN, GRAD SCH MED, 91- *Personal Data:* b Kagoshima, Japan, Apr 11, 39; m 70, Miyuki Ishimatsu; c Kenichi, Makoto & Eri. *Educ:* Kyushu Univ, Japan, MD, 64, PhD(biochem), 69. *Prof Exp:* Fel biochem, Sch Med, Univ Ill, 69-71, Univ Wis, 71-72; assoc prof, Fukuoka Women's Univ, 72-73; assoc prof, Kyushu Univ Sch Pharm Sci, 73-78. *Concurrent Pos:* Vis prof, Sch Med, NY Univ, 80; mem, Japanese Soc Biochem & Japanese Soc Cellular Biol. *Mem:* Am Soc Cell Biol; AAAS. *Res:* Intracellular transport and modification of proteins; biogenesis and function of the Golgi complex; membrane anchoring of proteins; structure and function of ectoenzymes. *Mailing Add:* Dept Biochem Fukuoka Univ Sch Med 34 Nanakuma Jonan-ku Fukuoka 814-01 Japan. *Fax:* 81-92-864-3865

IKENBERRY, DENNIS L, PHYSICS. *Current Pos:* From asst prof to assoc prof, 65-77, PROF PHYSICS, CALIF STATE COL, SAN BERNARDINO, 77- *Personal Data:* b Glendale, Calif, Oct 14, 39; m 64. *Educ:* Occidental Col, BA, 61; Univ Calif, Riverside, PhD(physics), 65. *Concurrent Pos:* Res leave, Univ Utah, 69-71. *Mem:* Am Phys Soc. *Res:* Theoretical chemical physics; biophysics; air pollution and exercise. *Mailing Add:* Dept Comput Sci Calif State Univ San Bernardino CA 92407

IKENBERRY, GILFORD JOHN, JR, PLANT ANATOMY, PLANT DEVELOPMENT. *Current Pos:* assoc prof, 61-64, PROF BIOL, MCPHERSON COL, 64- *Personal Data:* b Fargo, NDak, Dec 26, 29; m 51; c 3. *Educ:* McPherson Col, BS, 52; Okla State Univ, MS, 56; Iowa State Univ, PhD(plant morphol), 59. *Prof Exp:* Asst prof, Mich State Univ, 59-61. *Concurrent Pos:* NSF sci fac fel biol, Yale Univ, 67-68. *Mem:* AAAS; Bot Soc Am; Am Soc Cell Biol; Am Inst Biol Sci; Sigma Xi. *Res:* Developmental anatomy of angiosperms; plant morphogenesis; somatic cell culture. *Mailing Add:* 1307 E Sharp St McPherson KS 67460-3736

IKENBERRY, LUTHER CURTIS, ANALYTICAL CHEMISTRY. *Current Pos:* RETIRED. *Personal Data:* b Franklin Co, Va, Jan 8, 17; m 43, Jeanette Fall; c Joyce, Beverly & Diana. *Educ:* Bridgewater Col, AB, 37; Va Polytech Inst & State Univ, MS, 40. *Honors & Awards:* Lundell-Bright Award, Am Soc Testing & Mat, 80, Merit Award, 82. *Prof Exp:* Analyst chem, Middletown Works, Armco Inc, 40-41, from chemist to sr chemist, Res Ctr, 41-68, supvr res chemist, 68-74, prin res chemist, 74-82. *Mem:* Am Chem Soc; Am Soc Testing & Mat. *Res:* Analytical methods using gas chromatography for trace impurities in the environment; laboratory automation of analytical chemical equipment; gas chromatography and mass spectrometry analysis of organic pollutants in air and water. *Mailing Add:* 314 N Marshall Rd Middletown OH 45042

IKENBERRY, RICHARD W, PLANT PATHOLOGY. *Current Pos:* from asst prof to assoc prof, 65-73, PROF BIOL, UNIV NEBR KEARNEY, 73- *Personal Data:* b Des Moines, Iowa, June 17, 37. *Educ:* Iowa State Univ, BS, 60, PhD(plant path), 64. *Prof Exp:* Instr bot & plant path, Iowa State Univ, 64-65. *Mailing Add:* 22 E 37th St Kearney NE 68847. *Fax:* 308-234-8157

IKENBERRY, ROY DEWAYNE, VERTEBRATE PHYSIOLOGY, HEMATOLOGY. *Current Pos:* DIR INSTITUTIONAL RES, MISS STATE UNIV, 92- *Personal Data:* b Raton, NMex, Apr 21, 40; m 60; c 2. *Educ:* Eastern NMex Univ, BS, 62; Tex Tech Univ, MS, 64; Univ Okla, PhD(zool), 69. *Prof Exp:* Instr biol, Eastern NMex Univ, 64-66; from asst prof to assoc prof biol, ETenn State Univ, 77-92. *Mem:* Sigma Xi. *Res:* Biosystematics of blood serum; reproductive studies of mammalian species; cardiovascular physiology of fishes and amphibians; mammalian pheromones. *Mailing Add:* Miss State Univ Starkville MS 39762-9990

IKEZI, HIROYUKI, HIGH POWER SOLITON GENERATION. *Current Pos:* SR TECH ADV APPL PHYSICS, GEN ATOMICS, 81- *Personal Data:* b Kochi, Japan, Apr 5, 37; US citizen; m 62; c 3. *Educ:* Univ Electrocommun, BS, 60; Tokyo Univ Educ, MS, 62; Nagoya Univ, PhD(physics), 68. *Honors & Awards:* Nishina Prize, Nishina Mem Found, Japan, 69. *Prof Exp:* Res assoc plasma physics, Inst Plasma Physics, Nagoya Univ, 62-68; asst prof physics, Univ Calif Los Angeles, 68-70; assoc prof plasma physics, Inst Plasma Physics, Nagoya Univ, 70-75; mem tech staff physics, Bell Lab, 75-81. *Concurrent Pos:* Consult, Gen Atomics, 69; vis scientist, Culham Lab, UK

Atomic Energy Authority, 71. *Mem:* Am Phys Soc. *Res:* Nonlinear plasma waves such as solitons, trapped particle effects and echoes; two dimensional electron system by using electrons on liquid helium; development of high-power microwave system employing soliton generation. *Mailing Add:* Gen Atomics PO Box 85608 San Diego CA 92186

IKONNÉ, JUSTUS UZOMA, biochemistry, for more information see previous edition

IKUMA, HIROSHI, PLANT PHYSIOLOGY. *Current Pos:* from asst prof to assoc prof bot, 65-75, chmn dept cellular & molecular biol, 76-78, PROF BIOL SCI, UNIV MICH, ANN ARBOR, 75- *Personal Data:* b Nishinomiya-Shi, Japan, Jan 23, 32; m 66; c 2. *Educ:* Kobe Univ, BSc, 56; Harvard Univ, AM, 58, PhD(biol), 62. *Prof Exp:* Res fel plant biochem, Johnson Res Found, Univ Pa, 62-65. *Mem:* Am Soc Plant Physiologists. *Res:* Respiratory properties of higher plant mitochondria; cellular regulation of plant growth and developmental processes; germination processes of onoclea fern spores. *Mailing Add:* Dept Biol 1121 Nat Sci Bldg Univ Mich Main Campus 830 N University Ave Ann Arbor MI 48109-1048

ILARDI, JOSEPH MICHAEL, PHYSICAL CHEMISTRY. *Current Pos:* Res chemist, Res Labs, 66-74, mgr phys chem sect, 74-78, MGR INORG PROCESS DEVELOP, FMC CORP, PRINCETON, 78- *Personal Data:* b New York, NY, Dec 11, 39; m 63; c 3. *Educ:* Fordham Univ, BS, 61, MS, 63, PhD(chem), 66. *Mem:* Am Chem Soc; Sigma Xi. *Res:* Nuclear and radiation chemistry of chelate compounds; high temperature studies of fluorapatite melt systems; crystallographic studies of system sodium carbonate, carbon dioxide, water. *Mailing Add:* 111 Skyline Dr Sparta NJ 07871-3436

ILDSTAD, SUZANNE T, IMMUNOLOGY, TRANSPLANTATION. *Current Pos:* PROF SURG, ALLEGHENY UNIV HEALTH SCI, 96-, DIR, INST CELLULAR THERAPEUT, 96- *Personal Data:* b Minneapolis, Minn, May 20, 52; m 71, David J Tollerud; c David J II & Suzanne K. *Educ:* Univ Minn, BS, 74; Mayo Med Sch, MD, 78; Am Bd Surg, dipl. *Prof Exp:* Resident gen surg, Mass Gen Hosp, Boston, 78-82 & 85-86; immunol fel, Transplant Biol Sect, Nat Cancer Inst, NIH, 82-85; clin fel pediat surg, Childrens Hosp Med Ctr, Cincinnati, 86-88; from asst prof to assoc prof, Dept Surg, Univ Pittsburgh, 88-94; prof & chief, Dept Surg, Childrens Hosp Med Ctr, 94; dir, Div Cell Therapeut, Univ Pittsburgh, 94-96. *Concurrent Pos:* Grantee, Univ Pittsburgh, 89-90 & 91-92, Am Cancer Soc, 90-91, NIH, 91-96 & 92-95, Univ Pittsburgh Med Ctr, 91-92, Juv Diabetes Found, 91-92, Nat Kidney Found, 91-92, Am Heart Asn, 92-95 & Am Diabetes Asn, 92-94; vis prof, Univ Minn, 91 & Childrens Mem Hosp, Univ Chicago, 92. *Mem:* Inst Med-Nat Acad Sci; fel Am Cancer Soc; AAAS; Am Acad Pediat; Am Asn Cancer Res; Am Asn Immunologists; Am Fedn Clin Res; Am Soc Clin Res; Am Soc Transplant Surgeons; Asn Acad Surgeons; Soc Clin Immunol; Surg Infection Soc. *Res:* Xenotransplantation; use of bone marrow to induce tolerance for solid organ transplants; targeted cellular therapies for opportunistic infections. *Mailing Add:* Allegheny Univ Health Sci Broad & Vine Sts MS 490 Philadelphia PA 19102

ILGEN, DANIEL RICHARD, PSYCHOLOGY. *Current Pos:* HANNAH PROF ORGN BEHAV, DEPT MGT & PSYCHOL, MICH STATE UNIV, EAST LANSING, 83- *Personal Data:* b Freeport, Ill, Mar 16, 43; m 65, Barbara Geiser; c Elizabeth A & Mark A. *Educ:* Iowa State Univ, BS, 65; Univ Ill, MA, 68, PhD(indust orgn psychol), 69. *Prof Exp:* Asst prof, Dept Psychol, Univ Ill, Urbana, 69-70; instr, Dutchess Co Community Col, Poughkeepsie, NY, 71-72; from asst prof to prof, Dept Psychol Sci, Purdue Univ, West Lafayette, Ind, 72-83. *Concurrent Pos:* Purdue Univ Found grant, 73-75, 76-77 & 81-82, US Army Res Inst grant, 74-82, Off Naval Res grant, 82-86 & 90-; vis assoc prof, Dept Mgt & Orgn, Univ Wash, Seattle, 78-79; Area head, Indust Orgn Psychol, 78-83. *Mem:* Soc Orgn Behav; Sigma Xi. *Res:* Organizational behavior and human performance; contributed chapters to books and articles to professional journals. *Mailing Add:* Dept Mgt & Psychol Univ Mich 135 Snyder East Lansing MI 48824-1020

ILIC, MARIJA, ELECTRICAL POWER SYSTEMS. *Current Pos:* SR RES SCIENTIST, MASS INST TECHNOL, 89- *Personal Data:* b Zajecar, Yugoslavia, Feb 11, 51; US citizen; m; c 2. *Educ:* Univ Belgrade, dipl elec eng, 74, MEE, 77; Washington Univ, St Louis, MSc, 79, DSc, 80. *Honors & Awards:* Presidential Young Investr Award, NSF, 84. *Prof Exp:* Asst prof elec eng, Drexel Univ, 81-82, Cornell Univ, 82-84; from asst prof to assoc prof elec eng, Univ Ill, Urbana, 86-89. *Concurrent Pos:* Vis assoc prof elec eng, Mass Inst Technol, 87-89. *Mem:* Inst Elec & Electronics Engrs. *Res:* Modeling and control design for interconnected electric power systems; impact of high technology on the operation of power systems and electromechanical and electronic devices; power electronics based motion control; economic incentives for efficient technologies. *Mailing Add:* Dept Elec Eng Mass Inst Technol 77 Massachusetts Ave Bldg 10-059 Cambridge MA 02139-4307

ILLANGASEKARE, TISSA H, GEOHYDROLOGY, NUMERICAL MODELING & COMPUTATIONAL METHODS. *Current Pos:* assoc prof, 86-90, PROF CIVIL ENG, UNIV COLO, BOULDER, 90- *Personal Data:* b Kandy, Sri Lanka, Feb 19, 49; US citizen; m 77, Paulis; c Samantha & Tushani. *Educ:* Univ Ceylon, Sri Lanka, BSc Hons, 71; Asian Inst Technol, MEng,74; Colo State Univ, Ft Collins, PhD(civil Eng), 78. *Prof Exp:* Instr civil eng, Univ Ceylon, 71-72; res assoc, Asian Inst Technol, 74; asst prof, Colo State Univ, 78-83 & La State Univ, 83-86. *Concurrent Pos:* Prin investr, NSF, Dept Energy, Environ Protection Agency, US Dept Interior & other orgn, 79-; mem, US Army Res Off; assoc ed, J Hydrol, 94- & J Contaminant Hydrol, 97- *Mem:* Am Geophys Union; Am Soc Civil Engrs; Nat Water Well Asn; Am Water Resources Asn; Am Inst Hydrol. *Res:* Transport and flow through porous media as applied to chemical and waste transport in ground water; global hydrology and greenhouse effect; flow in snow; dam stability; mathematical and numerical modeling of hydrolic systems. *Mailing Add:* 5222 Pinehurst Dr Boulder CO 80301-3791. *Fax:* 303-492-7317; *E-Mail:* illangas@gwater.colorado.edu

ILLIAN, CARL RICHARD, ANALYTICAL CHEMISTRY, PHARMACEUTICALS. *Current Pos:* VPRES TECH AFFAIRS, GENETIC INST, 89- *Personal Data:* b Trenton, NJ, Dec 31, 41; m 63; c 4. *Educ:* Rutgers Univ, BS, 63, MS, 67; Univ Kans, PhD(analytical pharm chem), 71. *Prof Exp:* Sr chemist, Ciba-Geigy Corp, 71-77; mem staff, Pharm Div, Pennwalt Corp, 77-88, dir qual control, Pharm Div, 80-88. *Mem:* AAAS. *Res:* Methods development for analysis of pharmaceuticals; high speed liquid chromatography; stability of pharmaceutical systems; quality control pharmaceutical systems. *Mailing Add:* 6 Meadowbrook Rd Derry NH 03038

ILLICK, J(OHN) ROWLAND, third world development, cartography & remote sensing; deceased, see previous edition for last biography

ILLINGER, JOYCE LEFEVER, polymer science, physical chemistry, for more information see previous edition

ILLINGER, KARL HEINZ, PHYSICAL CHEMISTRY. *Current Pos:* from instr to asst prof, 60-67, chmn dept, 82-86, ASSOC PROF CHEM, TUFTS UNIV, 67- *Personal Data:* b Nuernberg, Ger, May 4, 34. *Educ:* Univ Pa, AB, 56; Princeton Univ, MS, 58, PhD(phys chem), 60. *Prof Exp:* Res assoc chem, Princeton Univ, 59-60. *Mem:* Am Phys Soc; Am Chem Soc; NY Acad Sci. *Res:* Intermolecular forces and collisional perturbation of molecular spectra; experimental microwave and millimeter-wave spectroscopy; interaction between electromagnetic radiation and biological systems. *Mailing Add:* Chem Dept Tufts Univ Medford MA 02155-5555

ILLINGWORTH, GEORGE ERNEST, PHYSICAL ORGANIC CHEMISTRY, INDUSTRIAL CHEMISTRY. *Current Pos:* Res chemist, 62-74, mgr petrochem, 74-75, DIR BIOCHEM & CHEM RES, UNIVERSAL OIL PROD, INC, 75- *Personal Data:* b Somerville, Mass, Mar 11, 35; m 56; c 3. *Educ:* Loyola Univ, Los Angeles, BS, 56; Univ Calif, Los Angeles, PhD(org chem), 63. *Mem:* Am Chem Soc; Am Inst Chem; Sigma Xi. *Res:* Elucidation of mechanisms involved in free radical reactions; addition reactions; hydrocarbon oxidation processes; petrochemicals; surfactants; fragrance and specialty chemicals; rubber and petroleum additives, water treatment and purification systems; immobilized enzymes. *Mailing Add:* 807 W White Oak St Arlington Heights IL 60005-3027

ILLINGWORTH, KEITH, forest genetics, for more information see previous edition

ILLIS, ALEXANDER, CHEMICAL METALLURGY. *Current Pos:* RETIRED. *Personal Data:* b Hungary, Jan 16, 17; nat Can; m 44; c 1. *Educ:* St Francis Xavier Univ, BSc, 42. *Prof Exp:* Anal chemist, Int Nickel Co Can Ltd, 42-45, res chemist, 46-50, group leader, 50-64, sr res scientist, 64-66, tech asst to dir, 67-70, res mgr, 71-74, dir process technol, 74-82. *Mem:* Am Chem Soc; Chem Inst Can; Can Inst Mining & Metall; Am Inst Mining, Metall & Petrol Engr. *Res:* Extractive metallurgy of nickel, copper, cobalt and associated metals. *Mailing Add:* 3303 Don Mills Rd Apt 2802 Willowdale ON M2J 4T6 Can

ILLMAN, WILLIAM IRWIN, MYCOLOGY. *Current Pos:* RETIRED. *Personal Data:* b Chatham, Ont, Apr 10, 21; m 45; c 3. *Educ:* Univ Western Ont, BA, 43, MSc, 46, PhD, 61. *Prof Exp:* Jr res officer, Div Appl Biol, Can Nat Res Coun, 44-46 & 48-49; from lectr to adj prof bot, Carleton Univ, 49-92. *Mem:* Mycol Soc Am; Can Bot Asn. *Res:* Mold deterioration of material; mold fermentations; sexuality and nutrition of fungi in culture; wood pathology; taxonomy of wood inhabiting fungi; morphology of plants and the taxonomy of fungi and algae. *Mailing Add:* 2227 Reeves Crescent Ottawa ON K1H 7H3 Can

ILMET, IVOR, PHYSICAL CHEMISTRY, ANALYTICAL CHEMISTRY. *Current Pos:* assoc prof chem, State Univ NY Col Buffalo, 67-80. *Personal Data:* b Tartu, Estonia, Mar 29, 30; US citizen; m 56; c 2. *Educ:* NY Univ, AB, 56, PhD(phys chem), 61. *Prof Exp:* From instr to asst prof chem, Univ Conn, 61-67. *Mem:* AAAS; Am Chem Soc; Sigma Xi. *Res:* Structure and chemistry of organic charge-transfer complexes; solvent effects in spectrophotometry. *Mailing Add:* Chem Dept State Univ Col 1300 Elmwood Ave Buffalo NY 14222-1004

ILNICKI, RICHARD DEMETRY, WEED SCIENCE. *Current Pos:* RES PROF WEED SCI, RUTGERS UNIV, NEW BRUNSWICK, 58- *Personal Data:* b Proctor, Vt, Sept 1, 28; m 55, Helen Franek; c Deanna, Carolyn & Janet. *Educ:* Rutgers Univ, BS, 49, MS, 51; Ohio State Univ, PhD(agron, plant physiol), 55. *Prof Exp:* Asst farm crops, Rutgers Univ, 50-51; asst plant genetics, Conn Agr Exp Sta, 51; res asst agron, Ohio Agr Exp Sta, 51-55. *Concurrent Pos:* Vpres, Northeastern Weed Control Conf, 65-66, pres, 66. *Mem:* Am Soc Agron; Weed Sci Soc Am (secy, 73-74); Crops Sci Soc Am. *Res:* Weed control in agronomic and horticultural crops; life cycle studies of economically important weeds; uptake, translocation and degradation of herbicides in plants; use of adjuvants to increase herbicide efficiency; weed/crop competition. *Mailing Add:* 403 Georges Rd Dayton NJ 08810

ILOFF, PHILLIP MURRAY, JR, ORGANIC CHEMISTRY, INORGANIC CHEMISTRY. *Current Pos:* RETIRED. *Personal Data:* b State College, Pa, Jan 8, 21; m 54; c 2. *Educ:* Stanford Univ, BS, 48, PhD(org chem), 57. *Prof Exp:* Res chemist, Univ Calif, Berkeley, 52-56; res chemist, Callery Chem Co, Pa, 56-59; res chemist, Aerojet-Gen Corp Div, Gen Tire & Rubber Co, 59-62; asst prof chem, Whittier Col, 62-70; assoc prof chem, Piedmont Col, 70-74, prof chem & physics, 74-87, chmn, Div Nat Sci, 83-87. *Mem:* Am Chem Soc; Sigma Xi. *Res:* Terpenes; turpentines; organo-boron compounds; azo compounds; free radicals; boro-hydrides; synthesis of high energy fuels and propellants. *Mailing Add:* 991 S Todd St Jupiter FL 33458

ILTEN, DAVID FREDERICK, PHYSICAL CHEMISTRY. *Current Pos:* sr res assoc, 74-78, SYST ANALYST CONTROL DATA, UNIV REGENSBURG, 78- *Personal Data:* b Marshalltown, Iowa, July 24, 38; m 68; c Paul F, Stephan D & Eric T. *Educ:* Yale Univ, BA, 60; Univ Calif, Berkeley, PhD(chem), 64. *Prof Exp:* Alexander von Humboldt fel, Inst Phys Chem, Frankfurt, 64-66, Ger Res Asn res fel, 66-68; chemist, Fishkill Labs, IBM Corp, 68-72; res & teaching fel, Tech Univ Berlin, Ger, 72-74. *Mem:* NY Acad Sci; Am Chem Soc; Am Inst Chem Engrs; AAAS; Am Phys Soc; Sigma Xi; Am Stand Testing Mat. *Res:* Photochemistry of charge-transfer complexes; electron paramagnetic resonance; theoretical physical chemistry; biophysical chemistry; optimization of chemical production facilities; physical property data. *Mailing Add:* Dechema Eu Theordor-Heuss-Allee 25 60486 Frankfurt Germany. *Fax:* 49-69-622680

ILTIS, DONALD RICHARD, MATHEMATICS. *Current Pos:* from assoc prof to prof math, Willamette Univ, 72-81. *Personal Data:* b Leon, Iowa, Mar 28, 36; m 60; c 2. *Educ:* SDak Sch Mines & Tech, BS, 58; Stanford Univ, MS, 62; Univ Ore, PhD(math), 66. *Prof Exp:* Programmer, Gen Elec Co, 59-62; fel, Univ Toronto, 66-67; asst prof math, Univ NC, Chapel Hill, 67-72. *Mem:* Am Math Soc. *Res:* Abstract harmonic analysis; Banach algebras. *Mailing Add:* Williamette Univ Salem OR 97301-3922

ILTIS, HUGH HELLMUT, SYSTEMATIC BOTANY, BIOGEOGRAPHY. *Current Pos:* from asst prof to prof, 55-93, dir herbarium, 68-93, CUR HERBARIUM, UNIV WIS-MADISON, 55-, EMER PROF BOT & HERBARIUM DIR, 93- *Personal Data:* b Brno, Moravia, Czech, Apr 7, 25; nat US; div; c Frank S, Michael G, David H & John P. *Educ:* Univ Tenn, AB, 48; Washington Univ, St Louis, MA, 50, PhD(syst bot), 52. *Honors & Awards:* Presidential Citation, Mex, 88; Spec Conserv Award, Nat Wildlife Fed, 92; Pupa Medal, Univ Guadalajara, 94; Asa Gray Award, Am Soc Plant Taxon, 94; Spec Achievement Award, Soc Conserv Biol, 94; Spec Achievement Award, Bot Soc Am, 96. *Prof Exp:* From instr to asst prof, Univ Ark, 52-55. *Concurrent Pos:* Exped, Costa Rica, 49, 89, Mex, 60, 71-96, Peru, 62-63, Hawaii, 67, Equador, 77, USSR, 79, Venezuela, 91; res assoc, Mo Bot Garden, 91- & Bot Res Inst, Tex, 93- *Mem:* Fel AAAS; Am Inst Biol Sci; Am Soc Plant Taxon; Int Asn Plant Taxon; Bot Soc Am; Soc Study Species Biol; Bot Soc Mex; fel Linnaean Soc London; Ecol Soc Am; Soc Study Evolution; New Eng Bot Club. *Res:* Taxonomy and evolution of New World Capparidaceae; origins of agriculture and preservation of genetic diversity in cultivated plants, especially corn; human ecology, especially human needs and adaptations for natural environment, diversity and beauty; taxonomy and evolution of Zea mays and the teosintes; flora of Wisconsin; flora of Sierra de Manantlam, Jalisco, Mexico; preservation of biodiversity. *Mailing Add:* Dept Bot Univ Wis Birge Hall 430 Lincoln Dr Madison WI 53706

ILTIS, WILFRED GREGOR, BIOLOGY, MOSQUITOES. *Current Pos:* RETIRED. *Personal Data:* b Brno, Czech, Apr 20, 23; m 48. *Educ:* Univ Minn, BA, 57; Univ Calif, Davis, PhD(entomol), 66. *Prof Exp:* Assoc prof biol, San Jose State Univ, 68-89. *Concurrent Pos:* Fel, Sch Pub Health, Harvard Univ, 67-68. *Mem:* Ecol Soc Am; AAAS; Soc Vector Ecol; Am Mosquito Control Asn. *Res:* Biosystematics and physiological ecology of Culicidae, especialy the Culex pipiens complex; effect of social and political decisions on ecosystems and human survival. *Mailing Add:* 1043 Lick Ave San Jose CA 95110

IM, JANG HI, MATERIALS SCIENCE, FRACTURE MECHANICS. *Current Pos:* sr res engr polymer physics, Dow Chem Co, 76-79, proj leader, 79-83, res leader, microlayer coextrusion, 83-86, res assoc, polymer processing, 86-93, assoc scientist high performance fiber & composites, 94-96, ASSOC SCIENTIST, THIN FILM DIELECTRICS ELECTRONIC PACKAGING APPLNS, DOW CHEM CO, 97- *Personal Data:* b Seoul, Korea, June, 42; US citizen; m 73, Dong-Sook Kim; c Fred & Mike. *Educ:* Seoul Nat Univ, BS, 64; Mass Inst Technol, MSME, 71, ScD, 76. *Prof Exp:* Design engr machine design, Doerfer Eng & Design, 67-70. *Concurrent Pos:* Adj prof, Univ Ill, Chicago, 89- *Mem:* Sigma Xi; Korean Scientist & Engrs Asn Am; Am Phys Soc; Mat Res Soc; Soc Advan Mat & Process Eng; Am Soc Mech Engrs; Int Microelectronics & Packaging Soc. *Res:* Polymer structure to processing relationship; fracture mechanics of reinforced composite materials; microlayer coextrusion; liquid crystalline fibers and composites; polymer dielectric thin film applications to microelectronic devices. *Mailing Add:* New Businesses & Cent Res & Develop-Electronics 1712 Bldg Dow Chem Co Midland MI 48674

IM, UN KYUNG, CHEMICAL ENGINEERING. *Current Pos:* res engr, Amoco Chem Corp, 70-75, sr res engr, 75-78, res assoc, 78-81, sr proj mgr, 81-92, PLANT MGR, AMOCO CHEM CORP, WOOD RIVER, ILL, 92- *Personal Data:* b Seoul, Korea, June 27, 34; m 60; c 2. *Educ:* Univ Mo-Columbia, BS, 57; Univ Kans, MS, 59, PhD(chem eng), 70. *Prof Exp:* res engr, Butler Mfg Co, 57-58; process engr, Chungju Fertilizer Co, Korea, 59-60; chem engr, US Agency Int Develop, 60-67. *Mem:* Am Inst Chem Engrs; Am Chem Soc. *Res:* Thermodynamic properties of hydrocarbons, particularly phase behavior of multicomponent systems; transport properties of pure and mixed hydrocarbons; mathematical modeling of reaction systems; olefins technology. *Mailing Add:* 41 Country Club View Edwardsville IL 62025

IMAEDA, TAMOTSU, MYCOBACTERIOLOGY, LEPROLOGY. *Current Pos:* from asst prof to assoc prof, 70-75, PROF MICROBIOL, NJ MED SCH, UNIV MED & DENT NJ, 75- *Personal Data:* b Nogoya, Japan, Nov 9, 27; m 55; c 2. *Educ:* Third Nat Col, BS, 49; Kyoto Univ, MD, 53, PhD(cytol), 59. *Honors & Awards:* Sakurane Prize, Japanese Leprosy Asn, 63. *Prof Exp:* Res fel, leprosy res lab, Sch Med, Kyoto Univ, 53-54, asst dermat, Univ, 54-59; contract investr microbiol, Venezuelan Inst Sci Invest, 59-61, from assoc investr to investr, 61-70. *Mem:* Am Soc Microbiol; Int Leprosy Asn. *Res:* Genetic characteristics of mycobacteria. *Mailing Add:* 37 Manor Rd Livingston NJ 07039

IMBER, MURRAY, MECHANICAL ENGINEERING, HEAT CONDUCTION. *Current Pos:* PROF MECH ENG, POLYTECH INST NY, 58- *Personal Data:* b New York, NY; m 69, Elaine Burdett-Jenkins; c Sarah B. *Educ:* Univ Ill, BS, 51; Columbia Univ, MS, 53, DEngSc, 58. *Concurrent Pos:* Union Carbide fel. *Mem:* Fel Am Soc Mech Engrs; Am Soc Eng Educ; assoc fel Am Inst Aeronaut & Astronaut; Sigma Xi. *Res:* Non-linear heat transfer in solids; temperature measurements; determination of golf system and sports equipment characteristics; inverse problems. *Mailing Add:* Dept Mech Eng 333 Jay St Brooklyn NY 11201

IMBERSKI, RICHARD BERNARD, DEVELOPMENTAL GENETICS. *Current Pos:* asst prof, 67-73, ASSOC PROF ZOOL, UNIV MD, 73- *Personal Data:* b Amsterdam, NY, Nov 5, 35; m 67; c 2. *Educ:* Univ Rochester, BS, 59, PhD(biol), 66. *Prof Exp:* Teaching asst biol, Univ Rochester, 60-63, res trainee, 63-65; res assoc, Johns Hopkins Univ, 65-67. *Concurrent Pos:* NIH trainee, 65-67; sr fel sci, NATO, 70; vis investr, Univ Nijmegen, 70 & 73-74, Univ Leiden, 77. *Mem:* Genetics Soc Am; Soc Develop Biol; Int Soc Develop Biologists. *Res:* Developmental genetics; genetics of hormone production. *Mailing Add:* Dept Zool Univ Md College Park MD 20742

IMBODEN, JOHN BASKERVILLE, PSYCHIATRY. *Current Pos:* ASSOC PROF PSYCHIAT, JOHNS HOPKINS UNIV, 63-; PVT PRACT, 90- *Personal Data:* b Morrilton, Ark, Sept 17, 25; m, Anne; c John B Jr & Connie E. *Educ:* Univ Notre Dame, 44-46; Johns Hopkins Univ, MD, 50. *Prof Exp:* Psychiatrist in chief, Sinai Hosp Baltimore, 69-90. *Concurrent Pos:* Instr med, Johns Hopkins Univ, 58- *Mem:* AMA; Am Psychiat Asn; Am Psychoanal Asn. *Res:* Psychosomatic medicine; author of 30 papers in the field of psychomatic medicine, one book and several book chapters. *Mailing Add:* 600 Wyndhurst Ave Suite 225 Baltimore MD 21210-2414

IMBRIE, JOHN, INVERTEBRATE PALEONTOLOGY, PALEOCLIMATOLOGY. *Current Pos:* prof geol, 67-76, Henry L Doherty prof, 76-90, EMER HENRY L DOHERTY PROF OCEANOG, DEPT GEOL SCI, BROWN UNIV, 90- *Personal Data:* b Penn Yan, NY, July 4, 25; m 47; c 2. *Educ:* Princeton Univ, BA, 48; Yale Univ, MS, 49, PhD(geol), 51. *Hon Degrees:* DSc, Univ Edinburgh, Scotland, 89. *Honors & Awards:* MacArthur Prize fel, 81-85; William Smith lectr, Geol Soc, London, 84; Maurice Ewing Medal in Geophys, Am Geophys Union-USN, 86; Leopold von Buch Medal, Dutch Geol Asn, 90. *Prof Exp:* Asst prof geol, Univ Kans, 51-52; from asst prof to prof, Columbia Univ, 52-67, chmn dept, 66-67. *Concurrent Pos:* Vis res assoc, Lamont-Doherty Geol Observ, Columbia Univ, 71-; co-prin investr or prin investr, NSF, 71-; adj prof oceanog, Univ RI, 76-; MacArthur Prize fel, 81-85; mem, several permanent fed comts sci & sci policy & several ad hoc comts & panels. *Mem:* Nat Acad Sci; fel Geol Soc Am; Am Philos Soc; Am Acad Arts & Sci. *Res:* Paleoecology; biometrics; history of climate aimed at identifying the main mechanisms of climatic variability on time scales ranging from a month to 100,000 years. *Mailing Add:* Dept Geol Sci Brown Univ Providence RI 02912

IMBRIE, JOHN Z, MATHEMATICAL PHYSICS, FUNCTIONAL INTEGRALS. *Current Pos:* PROF MATH, UNIV VA, 91- *Personal Data:* b Englewood, NJ, May 16, 56; m 85, Marcia Moore; c John. *Educ:* Harvard Univ, AB, 78, AM, 79, PhD(physics), 80. *Prof Exp:* Jr fel, Harvard Soc Fel, Harvard Univ, 81-84, asst prof physics, 84-86, assoc prof physics & math, 86-91. *Concurrent Pos:* Vis mem, Courant Inst Math Sci, 86; res fel, Alfred P Sloan Found, 86-; Presidential Young Investr Award, 88- *Mem:* Am Phys Soc; Am Math Soc; Int Asn Math Physics. *Res:* Mathematical physics; phase transitions in quantum field theory and statistical mechanics; expansion methods and renormalization group methods; disordered systems. *Mailing Add:* Dept Math Univ Va Charlottesville VA 22903. *E-Mail:* ji2k@virginia.edu

IMBRUCE, RICHARD PETER, PULMONARY PHYSIOLOGY. *Current Pos:* DIR CLIN PHYSIOL, SECT CHEST DIS, NORWALK HOSP, 70-; ASSOC PROF RESPIRATORY THER, UNIV BRIDGEPORT, 78-; PRES, PNEUMEDICS CORP, 87- *Personal Data:* b New York, NY, Aug 27, 42; c 1. *Educ:* St Peter's Col, BS, 63; NY Univ, MS, 68, PhD(biol), 71. *Concurrent Pos:* Chmn subcomt on humidifiers & nebulizers, Am Nat Stand Inst. *Mem:* Am Asn Respiratory Ther; Am Thoracic Soc. *Res:* Computerized respiratory cardio-pulmonary monitoring; effect of pharmacological agents on airway dynamics. *Mailing Add:* Pneumedics Inc 25 Van Zant St Norwalk CT 06855

IMEL, ARTHUR MADISON, ORGANIC CHEMISTRY. *Current Pos:* RETIRED. *Personal Data:* b San Francisco, Calif, June 30, 32; m 57; c 2. *Educ:* Willamette Univ, BS, 54; Ore State Univ, MS, 58, PhD(org chem), 60. *Prof Exp:* Teaching fel chem, Ore State Univ, 54-59; sr res chem, Richmond Res Ctr, Stauffer Chem Co, 59-63; mgr res, Cent Processing Co, 63-64; prof, Northwest Nazarene Col, 64-68, head dept chem, 68-94. *Concurrent Pos:* Guest prof, Col Idaho, 74 & 81. *Mem:* Am Chem Soc. *Res:* Organic chemistry, especially structure and mechanism; photochemical reactions; structure biological activity relationships; organic phosphorus compounds. *Mailing Add:* Dept Chem Northwest Nazarene Col Nampa ID 83686-5897

IMHOF, WILLIAM LOWELL, SPACE PHYSICS, NUCLEAR PHYSICS. *Current Pos:* SR STAFF SCIENTIST PHYS RES, LOCKHEED MISSILES & SPACE CO, PALO ALTO, 56- *Personal Data:* b Oakland, Calif, Aug 17, 29; m 53. *Educ:* Univ Calif, Berkeley, BA, 51, MA, 53, PhD(nuclear physics), 56. *Prof Exp:* Res asst phys res, Radiation Lab, Univ Calif, Berkeley, 52-56. *Mem:* Sigma Xi. *Res:* Meson production by photons and protons; neutron and charged particle reactions; electrons and protons trapped in the earth's magnetic field. *Mailing Add:* 1130 Westfield Dr Menlo Park CA 94025

IMHOFF, DONALD WILBUR, ANALYTICAL CHEMISTRY, SPECTROSCOPY. *Current Pos:* RES ASSOC NUCLEAR MAGNETIC RESONANCE & INTERNAL REFLECTION SPECTROS, ETHYL CORP, 66- *Personal Data:* b West Salem, Ohio, Dec 8, 39; m; c 2. *Educ:* Manchester Col, BS, 61; Ohio State Univ, MS, 64, PhD(analytical chem), 66. *Mem:* Am Chem Soc. *Res:* Research and methods development utilizing nuclear magnetic resonance and internal reflection spectroscopies in support of the overall research and development programs. *Mailing Add:* 3048 Woodland Ridge Blvd Baton Rouge LA 70816

IMHOFF, EUGENE A, OPTICAL PROPERTIES. *Current Pos:* PROJ MGR, LYTEL INC, 85- *Personal Data:* b Chicago, Ill, Mar 16, 54. *Educ:* Miami Univ, BS, 76; Cornell Univ, MS, 79, PhD, 83. *Mem:* Am Phys Soc. *Res:* Optical Properties. *Mailing Add:* Lytel Inc PO Box 1300 Somerville NJ 08876

IMHOFF, JOHN LEONARD, INDUSTRIAL ENGINEERING. *Current Pos:* prof indust eng & head dept, 52-80, DIR, PRODUCTIVITY CTR, UNIV ARK, FAYETTEVILLE, 80- *Personal Data:* b Baltimore, Md, Feb 9, 23; m 48; c 3. *Educ:* Duke Univ, BS, 45; Univ Minn, MS, 47; Okla State Univ, PhD, 71. *Prof Exp:* Eng asst, Crosse & Blackwell Co, 40 & Am Rolling Mill Co, 41-43; asst prof indust eng, Univ Minn, 47-52. *Concurrent Pos:* Consult engr, 49- & US Army Ord Mgt Training Hq, Pentagon, 53; partic, AEC nuclear eng inst, Univ Calif, 58; adv nuclear eng inst, Argonne Nat Lab, 59; sci fel, Stanford Univ, 60-61; nat chmn, Nat Coun Indust Eng Dept Heads, 66-67; guid chmn for Ark, Engrs Coun Prof Develop, 71. *Mem:* AAAS; Am Soc Eng Educ; Am Soc Qual Control; Nat Soc Prof Engrs; fel Am Inst Indust Engrs; Sigma Xi. *Res:* Plant design; organization and controls; statistical analysis; operations research; data processing; engineering and nuclear materials; manufacturing processes. *Mailing Add:* 1619 Clark St Fayetteville AR 72701-3713

IMHOFF, MICHAEL ANDREW, ORGANIC CHEMISTRY. *Current Pos:* from asst prof to assoc prof, 70-79, PROF CHEM, AUSTIN COL, 79-, DEAN SCI, 93- *Personal Data:* b Los Angeles, Calif, Dec 4, 42; m 65, Janet R Broadhead; c Joshua & Elizabeth. *Educ:* Univ Calif, Riverside, BA, 64; Univ Colo, Boulder, PhD(chem), 69. *Prof Exp:* Res assoc & fel, NIH, 69-70. *Concurrent Pos:* Res grants, Robert A Welch Found, 72-81 & 86-88; vis prof, Ind Univ, 80; Rupert B Lowe chair chem, Austin Col, 94- *Mem:* Am Chem Soc; Sigma Xi. *Res:* Carbonium ion rearrangements, reactivities and stabilities; neighboring group participation in carbonium ion and free radical reactions; isotope effects. *Mailing Add:* Dept Chem Austin Col Sherman TX 75090-4440. *Fax:* 903-813-2420; *E-Mail:* mimhoff@austinc.edu

IMIG, CHARLES JOSEPH, PHYSIOLOGY. *Current Pos:* Asst, 46-51, instr, 51-52, res assoc, 52-54, asst prof, 54-58, ASSOC PROF PHYSIOL, UNIV IOWA, 58- *Personal Data:* b Waterloo, Iowa, Oct 14, 22; m 44; c 6. *Educ:* Coe Col, AB, 44; Univ Iowa, BS, 48, PhD(physiol), 51. *Honors & Awards:* Sci Exhibit Award, Am Cong Phys Med, 49 & 53. *Concurrent Pos:* Lederle med fac award, 55-57; Arthritis & Rheumatism Found fel, 52-55. *Mem:* Am Physiol Soc; Soc Exp Biol & Med. *Res:* Peripheral blood flow; microwaves; vascular muscle energetics. *Mailing Add:* Dept Physiol Univ Iowa Iowa City IA 52240

IMIG, THOMAS JACOB, NEUROBIOLOGY. *Current Pos:* PROF PHYSIOL, MED CTR, UNIV KANS, 85- *Personal Data:* b Omaha, Nebr, Jan 17, 45; m 84, Dianne Harrell; c 2. *Educ:* Pomona Col, BA, 67; Univ Calif, Irvine, PhD(biol), 72. *Mem:* Soc Neurosci; Asn Res Otolaryngol; Int Brain Res Orgn. *Res:* Mechanisms of directional hearing. *Mailing Add:* Dept Physiol Univ Kans Med Ctr Sch Med 39th & Rainbow Blvd Kansas City KS 66160

IMLAY, RICHARD LARRY, HIGH ENERGY PHYSICS. *Current Pos:* assoc prof, 79-83, PROF PHYSICS, LA STATE UNIV, BATON ROUGE, 83- *Personal Data:* b Lockport, NY, Sept 9, 40; m 78, Adena Bellegia; c Lauren E. *Educ:* Univ Md, BS, 62; Princeton Univ, PhD(physics), 67. *Prof Exp:* Instr physics & res assoc, Cornell Univ, 67-71; res assoc, Univ Wis-Madison, 71-75; asst prof physics, Rutgers Univ, 75-79. *Mem:* Am Phys Soc. *Res:* Colliding beams; weak decays; weak interactions. *Mailing Add:* Dept Physics & Astron La State Univ Baton Rouge LA 70803-4001

IMLE, ERNEST PAUL, PLANT PATHOLOGY. *Current Pos:* ASST DIR, INT PROGS DIV, AGR RES SERV, USDA, 71- *Personal Data:* b Marshall, Ill, Oct 15, 10; m 47; c 4. *Educ:* Purdue Univ, BSc, 33, MSc, 36; Cornell Univ, PhD(plant path), 42. *Prof Exp:* Asst bot, Purdue Univ, 34-36, asst botanist, 36-37; asst plant path, Cornell Univ, 37-41, instr, 42; assoc pathologist, Bur Plant Indust, Soils & Agr Eng, USDA, 42-44, pathologist, 45, sr pathologist, prin agriculturist & dir, Regional Rubber Exp Sta, Turrialba, Costa Rica, 45-54, botanist, Plant Introd Sect, 55-57; dir res, Am Cocoa Res Inst, 57-71. *Concurrent Pos:* Plant pathologist & res fel, Boyce Thompson Inst, 37-41; res adv, Ministry of Agr, San Salvador, 70-71. *Mem:* AAAS; Phytopath Soc; Mycol Soc; Soc Hort Sci; Soc Econ Bot. *Res:* Crop improvement and diseases of tropical crops; research and training needs in tropical agriculture; plant introduction; quarantine and germ plasm problems. *Mailing Add:* 10802 Bornedale Dr Adelphi MD 20783

IMMEDIATA, TONY MICHAEL, ORGANIC CHEMISTRY, POLYMER CHEMISTRY. *Current Pos:* RETIRED. *Personal Data:* b Riverside, NJ, June 1, 13; m 49; c 1. *Educ:* Philadelphia Col Pharm, BSc, 36; Univ Pa, MS, 37, PhD(chem), 40. *Prof Exp:* Res chemist, Sharp & Dohme Inc, 41-45; res chemist, Int Resistance Co, 45-49, develop chemist, 49-55, chief chem engr, 55-62, sr chem consult, 62-68; sr chem consult, TRW Inc, Philadelphia, 68-70, mgr org & inorg chem, 70-78. *Concurrent Pos:* Consult, 78- *Mem:* Am Chem Soc. *Res:* Development on materials, mainly polymers and plastics, for electronic components and hybrid circuits; organic research, synthesis of medicinals. *Mailing Add:* 401 Bellefonte Ave Wilmington DE 19809

IMMERGUT, EDMUND H(EINZ), SCIENCE PUBLISHING, POLYMER CHEMISTRY. *Current Pos:* ED DIR, HANSER PUBL, 80-, CONSULT ED, VCH PUBL, 80- *Personal Data:* b Vienna, Austria, Mar 23, 28; US citizen; m 55, Brita Hassel; c Ellen, Eva & Karin. *Educ:* Univ Calif, Berkeley, BS, 49; Polytech Inst Brooklyn, MS, 51, PhD(polymer chem), 54. *Prof Exp:* Res assoc cellulose chem, Inst Phys Chem, Sweden, 54-55; fel, Mass Inst Technol, 55-57; mgr explor res, Dunlop Res Ctr, Ont, Can, 57-59; ed chem, Intersci Publ Div, John Wiley & Sons, New York, NY, 59-65, head bk div, 65-69; vpres & ed-in-chief, Gordon & Breach Sci Publs Inc, 69-75; ed & dir prof educ book dept, Sci Am, 75-80. *Concurrent Pos:* Consult, Dunlop Res Ctr, Ont, Can, 59-79; adj prof, Polytech Inst Brooklyn, 62-74, fel; managing ed, Encycl Appl Physics, 87. *Mem:* AAAS; Am Chem Soc; Soc Plastics Engrs; Mat Res Soc; Am Phys Soc; fel NY Acad Sci. *Res:* Cellulose; fibers; elastomers; polymer chemistry. *Mailing Add:* 2 Sidney Pl Brooklyn NY 11201. *Fax:* 718-875-8613; *E-Mail:* cam2@aip.bitnet

IMMING, HARRY S(TANLEY), MECHANICAL ENGINEERING. *Current Pos:* RETIRED. *Personal Data:* b Newark, NJ, Jan 2, 18; m 49. *Educ:* Univ Mich, BS, 42; Stevens Inst Technol, MS, 58. *Prof Exp:* Aeronaut scientist, Nat Adv Comt Aeronaut, 42-48; assoc marine engr, US Naval Boiler & Turbine Lab, 48-50; asst proj engr, Curtiss-Wright Corp, 50-56; design engr, Walter Kidde & Co, 56-57; asst prof mech eng, Rutgers Univ, 57-60; equip design engr, Foster Wheeler Corp, 60-67; sr engr, C F Braun & Co, 67-70; sr engr, Ebasco Serv, Inc, Enserch Corp, 70-81. *Res:* Heat transfer and fluid dynamics; stress analysis as related to steam raising equipment for nuclear energy power plants. *Mailing Add:* 110 Midvale Terr Westfield NJ 07090

IMONDI, ANTHONY ROCCO, PHARMACOLOGY, TOXICOLOGY. *Current Pos:* mgr pharmacol, Adria Labs, 77-83, mgr strategic planning oncol, 83-84, dir res, 85-89, DIR PRECLIN DEVELOP, ADRIA LABS, 90- *Personal Data:* b Providence, RI, Aug 21, 40; m 63; c 4. *Educ:* Univ RI, BS, 62; Univ Maine, MS, 64, PhD(animal nutrit), 66. *Prof Exp:* Res assoc biochem, Med Col, Cornell Univ, 66-69; sr pharmacologist, Warren-Teed Pharmaceut, Rohm & Haas Co, 69-74, proj leader pre-clin res, 74-77. *Concurrent Pos:* USPHS res fel biochem, Walker Lab, Sloan-Kettering Inst Cancer Res, 67-69. *Mem:* AAAS; Am Soc Pharmacol & Exp Therapeut; Soc Exp Biol & Med. *Res:* Evaluation of preclinical pharmacology and toxicology for human drugs. *Mailing Add:* Pharmacia PO Box 16529 Columbus OH 43216-6529. *Fax:* 614-761-4518

IMORDE, HENRY K, EARTH SCIENCE. *Mem:* Selwyn G Blaylock Medal, Can Inst Mining & Metall, 91. *Mailing Add:* Xerox Tower Suite 1210 3400 de Maisonneuve Blvd W Montreal PQ H3Z 3B8 Can

IMPAGLIAZZO, JOHN, COMPUTER MODELING. *Current Pos:* ASSOC PROF COMPUT SCI, HOFSTRA UNIV, 85-, CHMN DEPT, 87- *Personal Data:* b Brooklyn, NY, July 25, 41. *Educ:* St John's Univ, BS, 64; State Univ NY, Stony Brook, MS, 66; Adelphi Univ, MS, 78, PhD(math), 83. *Concurrent Pos:* Mem, Two Yr Col Comput Curric Task Force, Asn Comput Mach, 86-, chair, 89-91; chair, Accreditation Comt Comput Sci, Asn Comput Mach, 91- *Mem:* Asn Comput Mach. *Mailing Add:* 2 Meadow Glen Rd Northport NY 11768-2710

IMPARATO, ANTHONY MICHAEL, SURGICAL RESEARCH, INTIMAL & NEOINTIMAL HYPEPLASIA. *Current Pos:* Instr anat, Col Med, NY Univ, 49-50, clin surg, 53-54 & surg, 54-56, from asst prof to assoc prof, 59-71, dir, Div Vascular Surg, 75-92, PROF SURG, POSTGRAD MED SCH, NY UNIV, 71- *Personal Data:* b New York, NY, July 29, 22; m 43, Agatha Petriccione; c Maria A (Phillips) & Karen E (Cotton). *Educ:* Columbia Univ, AB, 44; NY Univ, MD, 46; Am Bd Surg, dipl, 57 & 83. *Concurrent Pos:* From asst attend surgeon to assoc attend surgeon, NY Univ Hosp, 56-68, attend surgeon, 69-; from asst vis surgeon to assoc vis surgeon, 4th Surg Div, Bellevue Hosp, 56-68, vis surgeon, 69-; co-prin investr joint study Extracranial Arterial Occlusion, 62-72; consult, Paterson Gen Hosp, NJ, 59- & Norwalk Hosp, Conn, 76-; fel, Coun Cerebrovasc Dis, Am Heart Asn, 70;

consult surg, Manhattan Vet Admin Hosp, 72- & Lenox Hill Hosp. *Mem:* Int Cardiovasc Soc; Soc Clin Vascular Surg; fel Am Col Cardiol; fel Am Surg Asn; fel Am Col Surgeons; Soc Vascular Surg (pres, 84-85); Am Surg Asn; hon mem Australasian Col Surg; James IV Asn Surg (treas). *Res:* Gastric physiology, including autonomic innervation and intrinsic circulation; hemodynamic factors in atherosclerosis; toxicity of vascular contrast media; hemodynamic factors in atherosclerosis and postoperative intimal hyperplasia; evaluation of surgical procedures on cerebrovascular insufficiency states; data monitoring committee, North American symptomatic caroted endorterestomy trial and VA cooperative study 167, etiologic importance in development of stroke; evolution of caroted bifurcation atherosclerotic plague. *Mailing Add:* NY Univ Dept Surg 530 First Ave 6F New York NY 10016-6451. *Fax:* 212-263-7722

IMPERATO, PASCAL JAMES, INTERNAL MEDICINE, PREVENTIVE MEDICINE. *Current Pos:* DISTINGUISHED SERV PROF PREV MED & COMMUNITY HEALTH & CHMN DEPT, HEALTH SCI CTR, BROOKLYN, STATE UNIV NY, 78- *Personal Data:* b New York, NY, Jan 13, 37; m 77, Eleanor; c Alison, Gavin & Austin. *Educ:* St John's Univ, NY, BS, 58; State Univ NY Downstate Med Ctr, MD, 62; Tulane Univ, MPH & TM, 66. *Hon Degrees:* DSc, St John's Univ, 77 & Tulane Univ, 96. *Honors & Awards:* Meritorious Honor Award & Medal, US Agency Int Develop, 70, US Dept State, 71; Frank Babbot Award, Downstate Med Ctr, State Univ NY, 80; Spec Serv Award, Smallpox Eradication, USPHS, 87. *Prof Exp:* From intern to resident internal med, Long Island Col Hosp, New York, 62-65; Tulane Univ fel, Univ Valle, Colombia, 65; Glorney-Raisbeck fel, Tulane Univ, 65-66; med epidemiologist, Smallpox Eradication-Measles Control Prog, Ctr Dis Control, USPHS, Mali, 66-72; dir bur infectious dis control, New York City Dept Health, prin epidemiologist & dir immunization prog, 72-74, dir residency training prog pub health, 74-77, first dep health comnr, 74-77, comnr health, 77-78. *Concurrent Pos:* Trustee, Martin & Osa Johnson Safari Museum, 64-, Milton Helpern Libr Legal Med, 77-; consult, US Agency Int Develop, 74, Nat Res Coun, 85; lectr commun med, Mt Sinai Sch Med, 74-; asst attend physician, Dept Med, NY Hosp, 74-78; asst clin prof med, Med Col, Cornell Univ, 74-78, from asst clin prof to assoc clin prof pub health, 74-78, adj prof pub health, 78-; chmn, NY City Swine Influenza Immunization Task Force, 76-77, Bd Dirs NY City Health & Hosps Corp, 77-78, NY City Bd Health, 77-78, Exec Comt NY City Health Systs Agency & NY City Inter-Agency Health Coun, 77-78; mem bd dirs, Community Coun Greater New York, 77-78, Pub Health Res Inst, 77-78, Int Med Res Found, 78-79 & NY Heart Asn, 83-84; attend physician, Dept Med, State Univ Hosp, 78-, Kings Co Hosp, 78-; mem adv bd, Physicians Social Responsibility, 83-; dep ed, NY State J Med, 83-85, ed, 86-93; mem adv coun, NY Tech Col, 84-87; sr Fulbright Fel, Yemen Arab Repub, 85; ed, J Community Health, 85-; mem, NY State Bd Med, 85-95, vchmn, 91-93, chmn, 93-95; mem, Bd Zoning & Appeals, Plandome Heights, NY, 86-90, trustee, 90-92; chmn, Metrop NY City Area Syphilis Task Force, 90-91; mem, NY State Coun Grad Med Educ, 94. *Mem:* Am Soc Trop Med & Hyg; Am Col Physicians; Am Col Prev Med; African Studies Asn; Am Col Epidemiol. *Res:* International health, preventive medicine; health care administration, health risks; African history and traditional African medicine and african art; Acquired Immunodeficiency Syndrome; medical editing. *Mailing Add:* State Univ NY Health Sci Ctr 450 Clarkson Ave Box 43 Brooklyn NY 11203-2012. *Fax:* 718-270-2533; *E-Mail:* pascal_imperato@netmail.hscbklyn.edu

IMPERIAL, GEORGE ROMERO, NON-IMPACT ELECTRONIC PRINTING, PAPER TECHNOLOGY. *Current Pos:* MGR, ELECTRONIC COMMUN PAPERS & PRIN SCIENTIST, CORP RES CTR, INT PAPER CORP, 86- *Personal Data:* b Dumaguete City, Philippines, Apr 8, 29; m 56; c 3. *Educ:* Silliman Univ, Philippines, BSCh, 52; Pa State Univ, MS, 57, PhD(fuel sci), 62. *Prof Exp:* Chemist, Petrol Lab, Caltex, Inc, Manila, 53-55; res asst fuel sci, Pa State Univ, 57-61; mem tech staff, Appl Chem Group, Bell Tel Labs, Pa, 61-64; actg head, Dept Chem, Silliman Univ, Philippines, 64-65; res assoc fuel sci, Pa State Univ, 65-66; scientist & prog mgr, Res Ctr, Xerox Corp, 66-79; sr scientist, Tech Ctr, St Regis/Champion, 79-86. *Mem:* Am Chem Soc; Am Phys Soc; Soc Imaging Sci & Technol; Tech Asn Pulp & Paper Indust. *Res:* Surface and semiconductor chemistry; properties of carbons and graphites; protective coats; imaging processes; electrical and surface properties of polymers; polymer/elastomer properties and structure/adhesion; non-impact printing technologies; paper/media product develop for non-impact printing. *Mailing Add:* Timber Ridge 54 Redwood Dr Highland Mills NY 10930-9527

IMPINK, ALBERT J(OSEPH), JR, NUCLEAR ENGINEERING. *Current Pos:* from asst prof to assoc prof nuclear eng, 69-78, prof, 78-80, ADJ PROF NUCLEAR ENG, CARNEGIE-MELLON UNIV, 80- *Personal Data:* b Reading, Pa, Sept 4, 31; m 53; c 4. *Educ:* Villanova Univ, BME, 53; Mass Inst Technol, SM, 61, PhD(nuclear eng), 63. *Prof Exp:* Staff mem, Sandia Corp, 53-54; sr engr, Westinghouse Elec Co, 62-65, fel eng, 65-69. *Concurrent Pos:* Consult, Westinghouse Elec Corp, 69- *Mem:* Am Nuclear Soc; Sigma Xi. *Res:* Nuclear power reactors, reactor physics testing and operations; thermonuclear power reactors, feasibility and initial design. *Mailing Add:* 18 Bel Aire Rd Belmont PA 15626

IMSANDE, JOHN, GENETICS, PLANT PHYSIOLOGY. *Current Pos:* assoc prof genetics & biochem, 69-73, PROF GENETICS, IOWA STATE UNIV, 73- *Personal Data:* b Grass Range, Mont, June 14, 31; m 56; c 2. *Educ:* Univ Mont, BA, 53; Mont State Univ, MS, 56; Duke Univ, PhD(biochem), 60. *Prof Exp:* USPHS fel, Univ Calif, Berkeley, 60-61; lectr & vis fel, Princeton Univ, 61-62; from asst prof to assoc prof biol, Case Western Reserve Univ, 62-69. *Concurrent Pos:* Vis prof, Univ Queensland, Australia, 86-87. *Mem:* Am Soc Agron. *Res:* Genetics and biochemistry of dinitrogen fixation. *Mailing Add:* Dept Agron Iowa State Univ Ames IA 50011-2010

INADA, HITOSHI, ELECTRICAL ENGINEERING. *Current Pos:* MEM STAFF, LINCOLN LAB, MASS INST TECHNOL, 75- *Personal Data:* b Nara, Japan, Mar 10, 37; m 70, Misako Mochida; c Maki & Tetsu. *Educ:* Tokyo Elec Eng Col, BS, 60; Northwestern Univ, MS, 66, PhD(elec eng), 69. *Honors & Awards:* Award, Inst Elec & Electronics Engrs, 71. *Prof Exp:* Res engr, Toa Electronics Ltd, Tokyo, 60-64; res asst, Northwestern Univ, 64-69; asst prof elec eng, Univ Ill, Chicago, 69-75. *Concurrent Pos:* NSF res grant, Univ Ill, Chicago, 70-71; mem US Nat Comt, Int Union Radio Sci, Wash, 71. *Mem:* Inst Elec & Electronics Engrs; Inst Electronics & Commun Eng Japan; Optical Soc Am. *Res:* Electromagnetic wave scattering; radar systems; optical wave propagation through atmosphere; imaging technique. *Mailing Add:* Mass Inst Technol Lincoln Lab PO Box 73 Lexington MA 02173-0073. *Fax:* 781-981-0993

INAGAMI, TADASHI, BIOCHEMISTRY. *Current Pos:* from asst prof to assoc prof, 66-74, PROF BIOCHEM, SCH MED, VANDERBILT UNIV, 75- *Personal Data:* b Kobe, Japan, Feb 20, 31; m 61, Masako Araki; c Sanae & Mari. *Educ:* Kyoto Univ, BS, 53, MS, 60, DAgrSc, 63; Yale Univ, MS, 55, PhD(chem), 58. *Honors & Awards:* CIBA Award, Am Heart Asn, 85, Res Achievement Award, 95; SPA Award, Belg NSF, 86; Okamoto Int Award, 94; Bristol Myers Squibb Res Excellence Award, 95; Award Japan Acad, 96. *Prof Exp:* Res asst chem, Yale Univ, 57-59; instr, Hanazono Univ, Japan, 61-62; instr biochem, Sch Med, Nagoya City Univ, 62; res asst chem, Yale Univ, 62-63, res assoc molecular biophys, 63-66. *Mem:* Am Soc Biol Chem; Am Chem Soc; Am Heart Asn; Japanese Biochem Soc; Endocrine Soc; Am Soc Cell Biol; Neurosci Soc; Am Soc Hypertension; AAAS; Soc Exp Biol Med. *Res:* Biochemistry and hypertension; protein and peptide chemistry; cell biology. *Mailing Add:* Biochem Dept Sch F Med Sta 17 Vanderbilt Univ Nashville TN 37232. *Fax:* 615-322-3201

INAMINE, EDWARD S(EIYU), MICROBIOLOGY. *Current Pos:* RETIRED. *Personal Data:* b Honolulu, Hawaii, Nov 18, 26; m 52; c 4. *Educ:* Univ Hawaii, BA, 50; Wash State Univ, MS, 53, PhD(chem), 55. *Prof Exp:* Res assoc biochem, Col Med, Cornell Univ, 55-57; res chemist, Merck Sharp & Dohme Res Labs, NJ, 57-63, sr res chemist, 65-69, res fel, 69-73, sr res fel, 73-81, dir, 81-90; res biochemist, Western Regional Res Lab, Calif, 63-65. *Mem:* Am Chem Soc. *Res:* Natural products; microbial metabolism. *Mailing Add:* 376 Russel Ave Rahway NJ 07065

INANA, GEORGE, OPHTHALMOLOGY, HUMAN GENETICS. *Current Pos:* res assoc, Lab Molecular Genetics, Nat Inst Child Health & Human Develop, NIH, 80-82, Lab Molecular & Develop Biol, Nat Eye Inst, 82-83, Lab Ophthalmic Path, 83-85, chief, Sect Molecular Path, Lab Mech Ocular Dis, 85-89. *Personal Data:* b Tokyo, Japan, Sept 14, 47; US citizen. *Educ:* Johns Hopkins Univ, BA, 70; Univ Chicago, PhD(biochem), 77, MD, 78. *Prof Exp:* Intern, dept path, Stanford Univ Hosp, 78-79, resident, 79-80. *Mem:* AAAS; Asn Res Vision & Ophthal. *Res:* Molecular genetic investigations of human hereditary ocular diseases, including gyrate atrophy and retinoblastoma. *Mailing Add:* 6500 SW 133rd Dr Miami FL 33156

INCARDONA, ANTONINO L, VIROLOGY, NUCLEOPROTEIN STRUCTURE. *Current Pos:* assoc prof, 73-95, EMER ASSOC PROF MICRO & IMMUNOL, CTR HEALTH SCI, UNIV TENN, MEMPHIS, 96- *Personal Data:* b Johnstown, Pa, Mar 2, 36; m 60, Mary C Ludwig; c 4. *Educ:* Georgetown Univ, BS, 58; Univ Wis-Madison, MS, 60, PhD(biochem, phys chem), 62. *Prof Exp:* Mellon independent biophys fel, Mellon Inst, 62-65; asst prof chem, Fla State Univ, 65-73. *Concurrent Pos:* USPHS spec fel biol, Univ Calif, San Diego, 75-76. *Mem:* Am Soc Microbiol; Sigma Xi; Am Soc Biochem & Molecular Biol. *Res:* Characterization of protein-protein and protein-nucleic acid interactions and elucidating their role in the control of virus uncoating and assembly; theory of ultracentrifugation. *Mailing Add:* Dept Microbiol & Immunol Univ Tenn Memphis TN 38163

INCE, A NEJAT, COMMUNICATIONS SATELLITES & EARTH STATIONS, REMOTE SENSING. *Current Pos:* PROF, TECH UNIV ISTANBUL, 84-; PRES RES, MARMARA RES CTR, TURKISH SCI COUN, 90- *Personal Data:* b Bodrum, Turkey, Nov 16, 28; m 52; c 3. *Educ:* Birmingham Univ, UK, BSc, 52; Cambridge Univ, UK, PhD(electronics), 55. *Honors & Awards:* Int Commun Award, Inst Elec & Electronics Engrs, 79; Sci Award, Turkish Sci Coun, 82. *Prof Exp:* Div chief commun, Shape Tech Ctr, The Hague, Holland, 61-78; asst vpres advan develop, Western Union Tel Co, NJ, 78-79; dir res & develop, Pa Ctr Advan Studies, Cambridge, 79-81; prof telecoms, Istanbul Tech Univ, Turkey, 81-82; chief engr systs, Marconi Space & Defence Systs Ltd, UK, 82-83; secy gen res & develop, Turkish Sci Coun, 83-86; dept dir gen commun, Proj Off, PTT, Turkey, 87-90. *Concurrent Pos:* Mem, Avionics Panel, NATO Adv Group Aerospace Res & Develop, 68-, adv bd, Am Int Open Un, St Louis, Mo, 75-80, Europ Sci Found, 84-86 & NATO Sci Comt, Brussels, 85-87; adv, Europ Comn, Luxemberg, 79-81; bd mem, Aselsan Electronics Co, Ankara, 84-; pres space, Turkish Space Sci & Technol Comn, 90- *Mem:* Fel Inst Elec & Electronics Engrs; Int Acad Astronaut. *Res:* Satellite communications systems including propagation, modulation, multiple access, on-board processing, and system control; design and planning of automatically switched, stored-program controlled integrated services, digital networks; digital speech processing. *Mailing Add:* Burumcuk Sok 7/10 Cankaya Ankaara Turkey

INCE, SIMON, HYDRAULIC & WATER RESOURCES ENGINEERING, HYDROLOGY. *Current Pos:* PROF CIVIL ENG, HYDROL & WATER RESOURCES, UNIV ARIZ, 71- *Personal Data:* b Istanbul, Turkey, Nov 6, 21; Can citizen; m 61. *Educ:* Robert Col, Istanbul, BSc, 43; Univ Iowa, MS, 48, PhD(mech, hydraul), 53. *Prof Exp:* Instr math & civil eng, Robert Col, Istanbul, 43-46; asst to chief engr, Istanbul Off, Braithwaite & Co, 46-47; res asst hydraul, inst hydraul res, Univ Iowa, 48-50, res assoc mech & hydraul, 50-53; Nat Res Coun Can, 57-61, sr res officer, 61-63, head hydraul sect, 63-71. *Concurrent Pos:* Secy, assoc comt, waves & littoral drift, Nat Res Coun Can, 60-69; mem working group ice in navig waters, Can Comt Oceanog, 61-71; vis lectr, Univ Ariz, 63-64, vis prof, 65 & 66. *Mem:* AAAS; Am Water Resources Asn; Int Asn Hydraul Res; Am Soc Civil Engrs; Am Geophys Union; NY Acad Sci. *Res:* Hydrology and water resources development; coastal engineering; arid lands resources; history of science. *Mailing Add:* 2033 E Third St Tucson AZ 85719

INCE, WILLIAM J(OHN), ELECTRICAL ENGINEERING, SOLID STATE PHYSICS. *Current Pos:* asst group leader, Lab, Mass Inst Technol, 60-80, asst prof elec eng, Inst, 69-72, assoc group leader, 80-83, GROUP LEADER, LINCOLN LAB, MASS INST TECHNOL, 83- *Personal Data:* b London, Eng, Jan 19, 33; m 56, 87; c 4. *Educ:* Victoria Univ, Manchester, BSc, 55; Mass Inst Technol, SM, 65, PhD(elec eng), 69. *Prof Exp:* Engr, E M I Electronics Ltd, 55-59; sr engr, Raytheon Co, 59-60. *Mem:* Fel Brit Inst Physics; Inst Elec & Electronics Engrs. *Res:* Theoretical and experimental investigations of microwave circuits and components; microwave magnetics; interactions between electromagnetic energy and magnetic insulators; radar systems; communications systems. *Mailing Add:* Armour Dr Eastham MA 02642

INCH, WILLIAM RODGER, radiobiology; deceased, see previous edition for last biography

INCHIOSA, MARIO ANTHONY, JR, PHARMACOLOGY, TOXICOLOGY. *Current Pos:* assoc prof, 66-76, assoc dean acad affairs, 85-88, PROF PHARMACOL, NY MED COL, 76-, RES PROF ANESTHESIOL, 80-, DIR MD/PHD PROG, 81-, VCHMN PHARMACOL, 83- *Personal Data:* b Weehawken, NJ, Jan 9, 29; m 55, 77, Elisabeth H Stamm; c Maria, Mario & Andrew. *Educ:* Rutgers Univ, BS, 50, MS, 53; Univ Ill, PhD(physiol), 56. *Prof Exp:* Asst, Rutgers Univ, 51-53, Univ Ill, 53-56; resident res assoc pharmacol, Argonne Nat Lab, 56-58; sr res scientist physiol neuro-endocrine res unit, NY State Ment Hyg Dept, Willowbrook State Sch, 58-60; res assoc med, Harvard Med Sch, 60-66. *Concurrent Pos:* Assoc, Beth Israel Hosp, Boston, 60-66; prof pharmacol extraodinario, Univ Guadalajara, Autoomous, 84-85; vis prof pharmacol, Univ Lille, France, 86-88; consult, US Food & Drug Admin, 96-. *Mem:* Am Col Clin Pharmacol; Am Col Toxicol; Am Soc Pharmacol & Exp Therapeut; Int Soc Study Xenobiotics; Int Anesthesia Res Soc; Soc Cardiovasc Anesthesiol. *Res:* Biochemical and physiological importance of oxidation products of epinephrine in relation to involuntary muscle contraction; biochemistry of cardiac muscle proteins; doxorubicin cardiotoxicity. *Mailing Add:* Dept Pharmacol NY Med Col Valhalla NY 10595

INCROPERA, FRANK P, HEAT TRANSFER. *Current Pos:* from asst prof to assoc prof, 66-73, PROF MECH ENG, PURDUE UNIV, 73-, HEAD, SCH MECH ENG, 89- *Personal Data:* b Lawrence, Mass, May 12, 39; m 60, Andrea J Eastman; c Terri (Chapman), Donna (Dant) & Shaunna (Tefelski). *Educ:* Mass Inst Technol, SB, 61; Stanford Univ, MS, 62, PhD(mech eng), 66. *Honors & Awards:* Roe Award, Am Soc Eng Educ, 82, Westinghouse Award, 83; Alexander von Humboldt Stiftung, Fed Repub Ger, 87; Heat Transfer Mem Award, Am Soc Mech Eng, 88, Melville Medal, 88; Worcester Reed Warner Medal, 95. *Prof Exp:* Heat transfer specialist, Lockheed Missiles & Space Co, 62-64. *Concurrent Pos:* Prin investr heat transfer res grants, NSF & energy conversion grants, Dept Energy; consult, Alcoa, 3M & John Wiley & Sons. *Mem:* Nat Acad Eng; Am Soc Mech Engrs; Am Soc Eng Educ. *Res:* Heat transfer; electronic equipment cooling; manufacturing and material processing. *Mailing Add:* Sch Mech Eng Purdue Univ West Lafayette IN 47907

INCULET, ION I, ELECTRICAL ENGINEERING. *Current Pos:* dir environ eng, 66-68, PROF ELEC ENG, UNIV WESTERN ONT, 64-, DIR APPL ELECTROSTATICS RES CTR, 86- *Personal Data:* b Iasi, Romania, Feb 11, 21; m 51, Marion Elsie Smith; c Richard, Catherine & Diana. *Educ:* Bucharest Polytech, Romania, 44; Laval Univ, Que, M(eng sci), 62. *Hon Degrees:* DTechSc, Bucharest Univ, Romania, 93. *Honors & Awards:* Outstanding Achievement Award, Indust Appln Soc-Inst Elec & Electronics Engrs, 83; Centennial Medal, Inst Elec & Electronics Engrs, 84; Eng Medal, Nat Soc Prof Engrs, 84; T C Keefer Medal, Can Soc Civil Eng, 94. *Prof Exp:* Advan develop engr, Can GE, 48-56, mgr eng, 56-64. *Concurrent Pos:* Pres, Elstat Ltd, London, 72- *Mem:* Can Acad Eng; Inst Electrostatics Japan; Nat Soc Prof Engrs; fel Inst Elec & Electronics Engrs. *Res:* Published over 100 articles and granted numerous patents. *Mailing Add:* 81 Lloyd Manor Crescent London ON N6A 5B9 Can

INDECK, RONALD S, ELECTRICAL ENGINEERING, INFORMATION SCIENCE. *Current Pos:* from asst prof to assoc prof, 88-95, PROF ELEC ENG, WASHINGTON UNIV, 95- *Personal Data:* b Minneapolis, Minn, Dec 3, 58; m 80; c 3. *Educ:* Univ Minn, BS, 80, MS, 84, PhD(elec eng), 87. *Honors & Awards:* Presidential Young Investr Award, NSF & Int Exchange Award; Centennial Young Engr Key to the Future Award, Inst Elec & Electronics Engrs; Bausch & Lomb Hon Sci Award. *Prof Exp:* Res fel, Res Inst Elec Commun, Tohoku Univ, Japan, 87-88. *Concurrent Pos:* Mem, Local Prog Comt, Intermag Conf, Inst Elec & Electronics Engrs, 84-85, Secy, Magnetics Group, Twin Cities Sect, 86, vchmn, 87, chmn, Local Prog Comt, Intermag Conf, 88-92, vchmn, St Louis Combined Group, 89, session chmn, Intermag Conf, 90, chmn, St Louis Sect, Combined Chap, Inst Elec & Electronics Engrs, 90-, mem, Magnetics Soc Admin Comt, 91- *Mem:* Am Phys Soc; Inst Elec & Electronics Engrs. *Res:* Fundamental applied magnetic recording research; transducers and limitations of ultra-high density magnetic recording systems; author of 21 publications. *Mailing Add:* Dept Elec Eng Washington Univ St Louis MO 63130-4899. *Fax:* 314-935-7500; *E-Mail:* rsi@ee.wustl.edu

INDELICATO, JOSEPH MICHAEL, organic chemistry; deceased, see previous edition for last biography

INDERBITZEN, ANTON LOUIS, MARINE GEOLOGY, POLAR EARTH SCIENCE. *Current Pos:* dept asst dir res, 91-95, CHIEF, TECHNOL TRANSFER OFF, US GEOL SURV, 95- *Personal Data:* b Sacramento, Calif, Dec 9, 35; m 59, Patricia A Noland; c Daniel R, Heidi M, Rebecca S & Jennifer A. *Educ:* Stanford Univ, BS, 57; Univ Southern Calif, MA, 60; Stanford Univ, PhD(geol, geotechnol), 70. *Honors & Awards:* Antarctic Geog feature named in honor, Mt Inderbitzen, 94. *Prof Exp:* Eng geologist, Maurseth & Howe Found Engrs, 58-61; sr scientist oceanog, Lockheed Aircraft Corp, 61-72; dir marine opers, Univ Del, 72-77; sr staff scientist, MAR, Inc, 77-78; prog mgr appl geophys sci, NSF, 78-80, actg chief scientist, Ocean Drilling Progs, 80-81, prog dir, Sci Ocean Drilling, 81-83, assoc chief scientist, Polar Progs, 83-86, head, Antarctic staff, 86-91. *Concurrent Pos:* Instr, Loyola Univ, Calif, 59-60, San Diego City Col, 63-67 & Univ Calif, Los Angeles, 67-69 & 71; US-Japan Coop Prog in Natural Resources Marine Mining Panel, 82-90; USCG User Coun Working Group on Icebreaker Design, 84-86; US Deleg & NSF rep to the Antarctic Minerals Regime Negotiations, 87-91. *Mem:* Fel Geol Soc Am; Am Geophys Union. *Res:* Mass physical properties of marine sediments; sea floor stability; marine mining; instrumentation for sea floor exploration. *Mailing Add:* US Geol Surv 104 Nat Ctr Reston VA 22092. *Fax:* 703-648-5068; *E-Mail:* ainderbi@usgs.gov

INDICTOR, NORMAN, ORGANIC CHEMISTRY, POLYMER CHEMISTRY. *Current Pos:* from instr to assoc prof, 63-71, PROF CHEM, BROOKLYN COL, 72-, CHAIR, CHEM DEPT, 96- *Personal Data:* b Philadelphia, Pa, June 23, 32; m 59; c 1. *Educ:* Univ Pa, AB, 53; Columbia Univ, MA, 54, PhD(chem), 58. *Prof Exp:* Res chemist, Interchem Corp, NY, 58-59; res assoc chem, Princeton Univ, 59-61; res chemist, FMC Corp, NJ, 61-63. *Concurrent Pos:* Adj prof, Inst Fine Arts, NY Univ. *Mem:* Am Chem Soc. *Res:* Reaction mechanisms; technical aspects of the conservation of art objects. *Mailing Add:* Chem Dept Brooklyn Col City Univ New York Brooklyn NY 11210. *Fax:* 718-951-4607; *E-Mail:* norman@brooklyn.cuny.edu

INDUSI, JOSEPH PAUL, NUCLEAR SAFEGUARDS & ARMS CONTROL VERIFICATION. *Current Pos:* assoc chmn, Dept Advan Technol, 90-96, SCI STAFF, BROOKHAVEN NAT LAB, 73-, HEAD, SAFEGUARDS, SAFETY & NON-PROLIFERATION DIV, 86-, SR SCIENTIST, 96- *Personal Data:* b Ossining, NY, Apr 12, 42; m 78; c 1. *Educ:* Univ Bridgeport, BS, 65; State Univ NY, Stony Brook, MS, 69, PhD(appl math), 71. *Prof Exp:* Systs consult, Burndy Corp, 72-73. *Mem:* Inst Nuclear Mat Mgt; Health Physics Soc. *Res:* Development and application of mathematical models and optimization methods for analysis of nuclear material measurement, accountability systems, and physical protection systems; assessment methods of safeguard systems; development of arms control verification systems. *Mailing Add:* Dept Advan Technol Bldg 197-C Brookhaven Nat Lab Upton NY 11973. *Fax:* 516-344-7533; *E-Mail:* indusi@bnl.gov

INFANGER, ANN, MITOCHONDRIAL GENETICS. *Current Pos:* Instr, 56-59, assoc prof, 63-71, PROF BIOL, SETON HILL COL, 72- *Personal Data:* b Newark, NJ, Dec 20, 33. *Educ:* Seton Hill Col, BA, 55; Cornell Univ, PhD(genetics), 63. *Concurrent Pos:* Res grant, Gen Med Div, NIH, 63-69; dir, NSF grant coop prog col biol educ, 69-73. *Mem:* AAAS; Genetics Soc Am; Sigma Xi. *Res:* Cytoplasmic inheritance in Neurospora; mitochondrial genetics of Neurospora. *Mailing Add:* Dept Biol Seton Hill Col Greensburg PA 15601. *E-Mail:* infanger@setonhill.edu

INFANTE, ANTHONY A, BIOCHEMISTRY. *Current Pos:* asst prof, 67-72, assoc prof, 72-78, PROF BIOL, WESLEYAN UNIV, 78- *Personal Data:* b Philadelphia, Pa, June 29, 38; m 64; c 4. *Educ:* Temple Univ, BA, 59; Univ Pa, PhD(biochem), 63. *Prof Exp:* NIH res fel, 63-64; res assoc biochem, Inst Cancer Res, 64-67. *Concurrent Pos:* Am Cancer Soc fac res award, 75-80. *Mem:* Am Soc Biol Chemists; Soc Develop Biol. *Res:* Metabolism of ribonucleic acids and regulation of protein synthesis during embryonic development; DNA polymerases and regulation of DNA synthesis in eucaryotic cells; chemistry of muscle contraction; heat shock response in sea urchin embroys. *Mailing Add:* Dept Molecular Biol Wesleyan Univ Middletown CT 06459-0175. *Fax:* 860-685-2141

INFANTE, ETTORE F, APPLIED MATHEMATICS. *Current Pos:* prof math & dean, 84-91, SR VPRES ACAD AFFAIRS & PROVOST, INST TECHNOL, UNIV MINN, 91- *Personal Data:* b Modena, Italy, Aug 20, 38; m 84, Trudi C Miller; c Cecilia & Michael. *Educ:* Univ Tex, BA, 58, BS, 59, PhD, 62. *Prof Exp:* Asst prof mech eng, Univ Tex, Austin, 62-64; from asst prof to prof appl math, Brown Univ, 64-80. *Concurrent Pos:* Consult, Humble Oil & Refining Co, Tex, 64-65, NSF, 80-81; dir, Div Math & Comput Sci, NSF, 81-84. *Mem:* Soc Indust & Appl Math; Am Soc Mech Eng; Inst Elec & Electronics Eng; Am Math Soc; Sigma Xi. *Res:* Differential equations; stability theory; nonlinear control systems; elasticity and plasticity of porous media; vibrations; mathematical macroeconomics. *Mailing Add:* Acad Affairs 232 Morrill Univ Minn 100 Church Minneapolis MN 55455. *Fax:* 612-624-3814; *E-Mail:* infante@mailbox.mail.umn.edu

INFANTE, GABRIEL A, RADIATION CHEMISTRY, CANCER. *Current Pos:* asst prof, 74-76, assoc prof, 76-81, PROF CHEM, CATH UNIV PR, 81- *Personal Data:* b Habana, Cuba, Nov 3, 45; US citizen; m 69; c Gabriel Jr, Antonio & Francisco. *Educ:* Cath Univ PR, BS, 67; Univ PR, Mayaguez, MS,

69; Tex A&M Univ, PhD(chem), 73. *Prof Exp:* Instr chem, Cath Univ PR, 69-71; res fel, Tex A&M Univ, 71-73; fel, Carnegie-Mellon Univ, 73-74. *Concurrent Pos:* Dir biomed res prog, Cath Univ PR, 77-; mem, Adv Comt, Biomed Res Symp, 80, Radiation Study Sect, NIH, 80-84 & Liason Comt, Univ PR-NSF Resource Ctr Sci & Eng, 80- *Mem:* Am Chem Soc; Latin Am Chemists Fedn. *Res:* Radiosensitization characteristics of newly synthesized chemical compounds and the chemical basis of their actions; radiation chemical investigations and in vitro and in vivo tests of potential radio-chemotherapeutic agents. *Mailing Add:* Pontifical Catholic Univ PR 2250 Avenida Las Americas Ponce PR 00731. *Fax:* 787-840-4295

INFANTE, RONALD PETER, DIFFERENCE ALGEBRA. *Current Pos:* ASSOC PROF MATH, SETON HALL UNIV, 67- *Personal Data:* b Newark, NJ, Sept 10, 40; m 67; c 3. *Educ:* Rutgers Univ, AB, 61; Yale Univ, MA, 63, PhD(math), 73. *Prof Exp:* Instr, Newark Col Eng, 66-67. *Mem:* Am Math Soc; Math Asn Am. *Res:* Transcendental Galois theory of difference field extensions. *Mailing Add:* 1 Arnold Dr Randolph NJ 07869

INFELD, MARTIN HOWARD, PHARMACEUTICAL DOSAGE FORM DEVELOPMENT, NEW DRUG DELIVERY SYSTEMS. *Current Pos:* Sr chemist, Hoffmann-La Roche Inc, 69-74, sr scientist, 74-80, tech fel, 80-84, res investr, 84-87, res leader, 87-91, DIR, SOLID DOSAGE DEVELOP, HOFFMANN-LA ROCHE INC, 91- *Personal Data:* b New York, NY, Aug 3, 40; m 65; c 2. *Educ:* Columbia Univ, BS, 62; Univ Wis, MS, 67, PhD(pharm), 69. *Mem:* Am Asn Pharmaceut Scientists; Sigma Xi. *Res:* Development of new, stable and pharmaceutical dosage forms and development of new drug delivery systems. *Mailing Add:* 6 Tuers Pl Upper Montclair NJ 07043-2520

ING, HARRY, HEALTH PHYSICS, NUCLEAR PHYSICS. *Current Pos:* PRES, BUBBLE TECHNOL INDUST, 88- *Personal Data:* b China, July 5, 40; Can citizen; m 65; c 4. *Educ:* Univ Toronto, BASc, 65, MSc, 67, PhD(nuclear physics), 69. *Prof Exp:* res officer, Neutron Dosimetry, Atomic Energy Can Ltd, 69-88. *Concurrent Pos:* Vis scientist, Stanford Univ, 79-80; ed, J Health Physics, J Radiation Protection Dosimetry; adv mem, Nat Coun Radiation Protection & Measurements. *Mem:* Health Phys Soc; Can Asn Physicists. *Res:* Interaction of neutrons with nuclei; neutron spectra determination, experimentally and using Monte Carlo calculation; moderation of fission neutrons by ordinary materials; bubble damage polymer detector, space dosimetry. *Mailing Add:* Bubble Technol Indust Inc Hwy 17 Chalk River ON K0J 1J0 Can

ING, ROY T, PUBLIC HEALTH, EPIDEMIOLOGY. *Current Pos:* MED EPIDEMIOLOGIST, NAT CTR ENVIRON HEALTH, CTR DIS CONTROL, 79- *Educ:* Univ Calif, Los Angeles, BS, 69; Univ Calif, San Francisco, MD, 73; Johns Hopkins Univ, MPH, 75. *Mailing Add:* Ctr Dis Control 1600 Clifton Rd Atlanta GA 30333. *Fax:* 770-488-7310

ING, SAMUEL W(EI-HSING), JR, CHEMICAL ENGINEERING, PHYSICAL CHEMISTRY. *Current Pos:* RETIRED. *Personal Data:* b Shanghai, China, Sept 26, 32; US citizen; m 58; c 2. *Educ:* Mass Inst Technol, SB, 53, SM, 54, ScD(chem eng), 59. *Prof Exp:* Asst prof chem eng, Bucknell Univ, 58-59; sr engr, Raytheon Co, 59-60; physicist, Adv Semiconductor Lab, Gen Elec Co, 60-62, electronics lab, 62-64; sr scientist res labs, Xerox Corp, 64-71, prin scientist, 71-77, lab mgr, 77-93. *Mem:* Fel Am Inst Chem; Am Chem Soc; Soc Photog Scientists & Engrs; Sigma Xi. *Res:* Materials, chemistry and physics of semiconductors and devices; electrophotographic sciences. *Mailing Add:* 10 Chestnut Lane Bedford MA 01730

INGALLS, JAMES WARREN, JR, LIMNOLOGY & LAKE BASINS. *Current Pos:* instr microbiol, Long Island Univ, 51, from asst prof to prof, 52-82, chmn dept, 63-77, EMER PROF PHARMACOL, LONG ISLAND UNIV, 82- *Personal Data:* b Barre, Vt, July 31, 19; m 44; c 3. *Educ:* Univ Maine, BS, 42; NY Univ, MS, 49, PhD(parasitol), 53. *Prof Exp:* Asst zool, Univ Maine, 42; asst biol, NY Univ, 47-50. *Concurrent Pos:* Mem comm schistosomiasis, US Army, 45-46; vis asst prof, Einstein Col Med, 58-67; consult, Air Reduction Co, 66-71. *Mem:* AAAS; Sigma Xi; fel NY Acad Sci. *Res:* Practical political protection of lakes and lakeshore and forest residents. *Mailing Add:* PO Box 119 North Hudson NY 12855-0119

INGALLS, JESSE RAY, ANIMAL SCIENCE. *Current Pos:* From asst prof to assoc prof, 64-74, PROF ANIMAL SCI, UNIV MAN, 74- *Personal Data:* b Randolph, Vt, Apr 4, 36; m 63; c 3. *Educ:* Univ Vt, BS, 58, MS, 60; Mich State Univ, PhD(dairy nutrit), 65. *Mem:* Am Soc Animal Sci; Am Dairy Sci Asn; Can Soc Animal Prod; Am Forage & Grassland Coun. *Res:* Dairy nutrition; forage utilization; use of rape seed meal in dairy rations. *Mailing Add:* Dept Animal Sci Univ Man Winnipeg MB R3T 2N2 Can

INGALLS, PAUL D, NUCLEAR PHYSICS, UNDERWATER ACOUSTICS. *Current Pos:* PHYSICIST, APPL PHYSICS LAB, UNIV WASH, 78- *Personal Data:* b Hood River, Ore, May 18, 44. *Educ:* Univ Wash, BS, 66; Princeton Univ, PhD(nuclear physics), 71. *Prof Exp:* Res assoc, Univ Colo, 71-73; res fel, Calif Inst Technol, 73-76; vis asst prof physics, Univ Ore, 76-78. *Mem:* Am Phys Soc; Acoust Soc Am. *Mailing Add:* PO Box 2248 Kirkland WA 98083

INGALLS, ROBERT L, PHYSICS. *Current Pos:* from asst prof to assoc prof, 66-74, PROF PHYSICS, UNIV WASH, 74- *Personal Data:* b Spokane, Wash, June 15, 34; div; c Karen, Johanna (Bozich) & David. *Educ:* Univ Wash, BS, 56; Carnegie Inst Technol, MS, 60, PhD(physics), 62. *Prof Exp:* Instr physics, Carnegie Inst Technol, 61-63; res assoc, Univ Ill, 63-65, res asst prof, 65-66. *Concurrent Pos:* Vis scholar, State Univ Groningen, 72-73. *Mem:* Am Phys Soc; Fedn Am Sci; AAAS. *Res:* Synchrotron radiation; solid state physics; high pressure physics; Mossbauer effect. *Mailing Add:* Dept Physics Univ Wash PO Box 351560 Seattle WA 98195. *Fax:* 206-685-0635; *E-Mail:* sup@phys.washington.edu

INGALLS, WILLIAM LISLE, VETERINARY PATHOLOGY, VETERINARY MEDICINE. *Current Pos:* vpres, Columbus Serum Co, 52-74, secy, Col Vet Med, 77-78, assoc prof, 74-76, PROF VET PREV MED, COL VET MED, OHIO STATE UNIV, 76-, PROF VET COOP EXT, 76-, PROF ANIMAL SCI, 78- *Personal Data:* b Franklin Co, Ohio, Sept 28, 18; m 46; c 2. *Educ:* Ohio State Univ, DVM, 42, MS, 47. *Prof Exp:* Asst pathologist, State Lab, Ohio, 42-45; assoc animal pathologist, Exp Sta, Va Polytech Inst, 45-47; from instr to asst prof vet path, Ohio State Univ, 47-52. *Concurrent Pos:* Prof vet sci, Ohio Agr Res & Develop Ctr, Wooster, 76-, prof animal sci, 78-; health comnr, Pickaway Co, Circleville, Ohio, 88. *Mem:* Fel Vet Med Asn. *Res:* Bovine mastitis, bacteriology, pathology and trichomoniasis; protozoology; avian pathology; Newcastle disease; sulfaquinoxaline-swine-diseases. *Mailing Add:* 486 S Waggoner Rd Reynoldsburg OH 43068

INGALSBE, DAVID WEEDEN, food science, natural products chemistry; deceased, see previous edition for last biography

INGARD, KARL UNO, FLUID DYNAMICS. *Current Pos:* from asst prof to assoc prof, Mass Inst Technol, 52-66, prof physics, 66-91, prof aeronaut & astronaut, 71-91, EMER PROF PHYSICS & AERONAUT & ASTRONAUT, MASS INST TECHNOL, 91- *Personal Data:* b Gothenburg, Sweden, Feb 24, 21; nat US; m 48; c 4. *Educ:* Chalmers Univ Technol, Sweden, EE, 44, Techn lic, 48; Mass Inst Technol, PhD(physics), 50. *Hon Degrees:* Dr, Chalmers Inst Technol, Sweden, 79. *Honors & Awards:* Biennial Award, Acoust Soc Am, 54, Gold Medal, 97; Gustaf Dalen Medal, Sweden, 70; John Ericsson Medal, Am Soc Swed Engr, 72; Rayleigh Medal, Inst Acoust, UK, 81; Per Bruel Gold Medal, Am Soc Mech Engrs, 89. *Prof Exp:* Res engr, Nat Lab Defense, Stockholm, 45-46; dir, Acoust Lab, Chalmers Univ Technol, Sweden, 46-52. *Concurrent Pos:* Armstrong Cork fel, Mass Inst Technol, 50; Guggenheim fel, 59. *Mem:* Nat Acad Eng; fel Acoust Soc Am; fel Am Phys Soc; Inst Noise Control Eng; Sigma Xi. *Res:* Plasma physics; acoustics. *Mailing Add:* 22 Captains Way Gerrish Island Kittery Point ME 03905. *Fax:* 207-439-0578

INGBER, LESTER, STATISTICAL MECHANICS, GLOBAL ORGANIZATION. *Personal Data:* b Brooklyn, NY, Mar 26, 41; m 81, Louise. *Educ:* Calif Inst Technol, BS, 62; Univ Calif, San Diego, PhD(theoret nuclear physics), 66. *Prof Exp:* NSF postdoctoral fel, Univ Calif, Berkeley, 67-68, Univ Calif, Los Angeles, 68-69; asst prof physics, State Univ NY, Stony Brook, 69-70; asst res physicist, Univ Calif, San Diego, 70-72, dir, Learning to Learn, San Diego Exten, 72-73; pres, Phys Studies Inst, 70-78; prof physics, Naval Postgrad Sch, 86-89; prof math, George Washington Univ, 89-90. *Concurrent Pos:* Res asst, Niels Bohr Inst, 65; consult, Rand Corp, 65-66, Anser, 86-88; res assoc, Music Dept, Univ Calif, San Diego, 72-74, Physics Dept, 80-86; sr res assoc, Nat Res Coun, 85 & 89. *Mem:* Sigma Xi. *Res:* Statistical mechanics of neocortex (short term memory and electroencephalography), financial systems (interest-rate and trading models) and combat analyses (baselining simulations to exercise data); application of adaptive simulated annealing. *Mailing Add:* Lester Ingber Res 1020 S Wabash Ave Apt 5D Chicago IL 60605-2257. *E-Mail:* ingber@ingber.com

INGE, WALTER HERNDON, JR, ENVIRONMENTAL PHYSIOLOGY, MEDICAL WRITER. *Current Pos:* MED WRITER, 88- *Personal Data:* b Mobile, Ala, July 24, 33; wid; c Ruth G (Hardy) & Katherine L. *Educ:* Univ Ala, BS, 55; Univ Calif, Berkeley, MA, 65, PhD(physiol), 72. *Prof Exp:* Instr physiol, USAF Acad,Colo, 65-66; opers analyst, Weapons Effectiveness Test Div, Armament Test Ctr, Air Force, Eglin AFB, Fla, 70-71; proj officer biol & behav sci, Europ Off of Aerospace Res, London, 71-73, chief, Eng & Biotech Div, 73-75; res physiologist environ physiol, Aerospace Med Res Lab, Air Force, Ohio, 75-77; asst prof, Dept Health Sci, Sargent Col, Boston Univ, 77-83; prof, Emory Univ, 83-87; prof & chmn, Dept Physiol, St Ga Sch Med, 87-88. *Concurrent Pos:* US Rep, Working Party, Aerospace Physiol & Med & Working Party Effects Ionizing Radiations, Coun Europe, Strasbourg, France, 72-75; informal liaison, NASA Europ Space Res Orgn, 72-75; mem bd dirs, Nat Safety Training Found, Inc, 78-83; consult occup health & safety, Western Elec Co, 78-83. *Mem:* Am Med Writers Asn; Am Heart Asn; Am Mycol Asn. *Res:* Environmental physiology such as extremes of temperature, altitude, pressure, acceleration; occupational hazards and disabilities; exercise physiology; cardiopulmonary physiology. *Mailing Add:* 753-7 Houston Mill Rd NE Atlanta GA 30329. *Fax:* 404-325-0115; *E-Mail:* walteringe@worldnet.att.net

INGELS, FRANKLIN M(URANYI), ELECTRICAL ENGINEERING, MATHEMATICS. *Current Pos:* from instr to assoc prof, 64-76, PROF ELEC ENG, MISS STATE UNIV, 76- *Personal Data:* b New York, NY, Aug 7, 37; m 55; c 3. *Educ:* Univ Kans, BS, 60, MS, 62; Miss State Univ, PhD(elec eng), 67. *Prof Exp:* Engr, Oread Electronics Lab, Inc, 60-62; group engr, Dynatronics, Inc, 62-64. *Concurrent Pos:* Consult, Battelle Mem Inst, 77-78, 84-, FWG assoc, 89, SCI Systs, 80, 81, Gen Dynamics, 81; consult, Inst Defense Anal, 67, staff consult, Los Alamos Sci Lab, 67-; staff consult & sci adv, Mil Asst Command, Vietnam, 68; army consult, 85- *Mem:* Inst Elec & Electronics Engrs. *Res:* Communications and electronic systems; information theory and radar system analysis. *Mailing Add:* Dept Elec Eng Miss State Univ PO Box 2097 Mississippi State MS 39762

INGELS, NEIL BARTON, JR, BIOMEDICAL ENGINEERING, CARDIOVASCULAR PHYSIOLOGY. *Current Pos:* CONSULT ASST PROF MED, STANFORD UNIV MED CTR, CALIF, 79-, LECTR, DEPT ELEC ENG, 80- *Personal Data:* b Evanston, Ill, July 15, 37; m 59; c 2. *Educ:* Univ Ark, BSEE, 59; Santa Clara Univ, MSEE, 63; Stanford Univ, PhD(biomed eng), 66. *Prof Exp:* Systs designer guided missiles, Sperry Utah Eng Lab, 59-60; systs designer space satellites, Lockheed Missile & Space Co, 60-62; sr res assoc cardiovasc physiol, Palo Alto Med Res Found, 62-78. *Concurrent Pos:* Consult, Stanford Univ Sch Med, 74-, Alza Res, 78- *Mem:* Biomed Eng Soc; Am Heart Asn; Am Physiol Soc; AAAS. *Res:* Basic and clinical studies of heart function with special emphasis on cardiac muscle dynamics. *Mailing Add:* Bioeng/Physiol Dept Palo Alto Med Res Found 860 Bryant St Palo Alto CA 94301-2707. *Fax:* 650-324-2665

INGENITO, ALPHONSE J, PHARMACOLOGY. *Current Pos:* assoc prof 76-78, PROF PHARMACOL, E CAROLINA UNIV, 78- *Personal Data:* b Harrison, NJ, Oct 8, 32; m 62; c 4. *Educ:* St John's Univ, BS, 53; Rutgers Univ, MS, 60; NJ Med Col, PhD(pharmacol), 65. *Prof Exp:* From instr to assoc prof pharmacol, Albany Med Col, 65-76. *Mem:* AAAS; Am Soc Pharmacol & Exp Therapeut; Am Col Clin Pharmacol. *Res:* Actions of anti-hypertensive and other drugs on the central and reflex neural control of the cardiovascular system; role of endogenous opioid peptides in experimental hypertension. *Mailing Add:* Dept Pharmacol Sch Med ECarolina Univ Greenville NC 27834-2882. *Fax:* 919-816-3203

INGENITO, FRANK LEO, UNDERWATER ACOUSTICS. *Current Pos:* SACLANT UNDERSEA RES CTR, ITALY, 87- *Personal Data:* b Brooklyn, NY, Aug 15, 32; m 59. *Educ:* Univ Rochester, BS, 54; Brown Univ, PhD(physics), 67. *Prof Exp:* Physicist, Pratt & Whitney Div, United Aircraft Co, 59-61; res assoc physics, Mich State Univ, 66-68; res physicist, US Naval Res Lab, 68-87. *Mem:* Acoust Soc Am; Am Phys Soc. *Res:* Acoustic signal and ambient noise characteristics in shallow water. *Mailing Add:* 5031 Fulton St NW Washington DC 20016

INGERSOL, ROBERT HARDING, mammalogy, ecology; deceased, see previous edition for last biography

INGERSOLL, ANDREW PERRY, PLANETARY ATMOSPHERES. *Current Pos:* from asst prof to assoc prof, 66-76, PROF PLANETARY SCI, CALIF INST TECHNOL, 76- *Personal Data:* b Chicago, Ill, Jan 2, 40; m 61, Sarah Morin; c Jeremiah, Ruth (Wood), Marion, Minneola & George. *Educ:* Amherst Col, BA, 60; Harvard Univ, AM, 61, PhD(atmos physics), 65. *Honors & Awards:* Except Sci Achievement Award, NASA, 81. *Prof Exp:* Res fel atmosphere physics, Harvard Univ, 65-66. *Concurrent Pos:* mem, Summer Study Prog, Geophys Fluid Dynamics, Woods Hole Oceanog Inst, 65, 70-73, 76, 80, 92; chmn, Div Planetary Sci, Am Astron Soc, 89-90; mem, Spacecraft Exp Teams, Pioneer 10/11, Pioneer Venus, Nimbus 7, Voyager, Galileo, Mars Surveyor, Cassini. *Mem:* Am Astron Soc; fel Am Geophys Union; fel AAAS. *Res:* Dynamics of planetary atmospheres; solar system exploration by means of deep space probes; climates of earth and planets; geophysical fluid dynamics. *Mailing Add:* Div Geol & Planetary Sci Calif Inst Technol Pasadena CA 91125. *Fax:* 626-585-1917; *E-Mail:* api@gps.caltech.edu

INGERSOLL, EDWIN MARVIN, ZOOLOGY. *Current Pos:* RETIRED. *Personal Data:* b Minn, Dec 23, 19; m 48; c 4. *Educ:* Bemidji State Teachers Col, BS, 42; Univ Minn, MS, 49, PhD(zool), 54. *Prof Exp:* Assoc prof, Miami Univ, 51-70, asst chmn, Dept Zool & Physiol, 66-70, prof zool, 70-85, asst chmn dept zool, 75-85. *Mem:* Soc Parasitol. *Res:* Parasitology. *Mailing Add:* 502 Glenview Dr Oxford OH 45056

INGERSOLL, HENRY GILBERT, PHYSICAL CHEMISTRY. *Current Pos:* RETIRED. *Personal Data:* b Chestertown, Md, Sept 11, 15; m 43; c 5. *Educ:* Washington Col, Md, BS, 35; Univ Md, MS, 37; Mass Inst Technol, PhD(phys chem), 40. *Prof Exp:* Res chemist, E I du Pont de Nemours & Co, Inc, 40-51, sr res chemist, 51-74, res assoc, 74-79. *Mem:* Am Chem Soc. *Res:* Compressibility of hydrocarbons; physical structure of high polymers; mechanism of film and filament formation; heterogeneous catalysis. *Mailing Add:* 633 Horseshoe Hill Hockessin DE 19707-9570

INGERSOLL, RAYMOND VAIL, SEDIMENTARY GEOLOGY, TECTONICS. *Current Pos:* dept earth & space sci, 82-85, PROF GEOL, UNIV CALIF, 85- *Personal Data:* b New York, NY, June 17, 47; m 72, Mary M Amadeo; c Jennifer A (Ingersoll). *Educ:* Harvard Univ, AB, 69; Stanford Univ, MS, 74, PhD(geol), 76. *Honors & Awards:* A I Levorsen Award, Am Asn Petrol Geologists, 78. *Prof Exp:* Teacher phys sci, Putney Sch, Vt, 69-72; from asst prof to assoc prof geol, Univ NMex, 76-82. *Concurrent Pos:* Assoc ed, J Sedimentary Petrol, 84-88, Geol Soc Am Bulletin, 84-92. *Mem:* Fel Geol Soc Am; Int Asn Sedimentologists; Soc Sedimentary Geol; Sigma Xi; Am Geophys Union. *Res:* Sandstone petrology; turbidite sedimentation; basin analysis; plate tectonics. *Mailing Add:* Dept Earth Space Sci Univ Calif Los Angeles CA 90024. *Fax:* 310-825-2779

INGHAM, HERBERT SMITH, JR, SOLID STATE PHYSICS. *Current Pos:* RETIRED. *Personal Data:* b Los Angeles, Calif, Nov 15, 31; m 60; c 2. *Educ:* Rensselaer Polytech Inst, BS, 53; Carnegie Inst Technol, MS, 56, PhD(physics), 59; Hofstra Univ, JD, 82. *Prof Exp:* Engr, Photocircuits, Inc, 53; res asst, Carnegie Inst Technol, 53-58; assoc physicist, Res Ctr, Int Bus Mach Corp, 58-60; mgr res & develop, Metco Inc, 60-79, adminr patents & contracts, 79-83; sr patent atty, Perkin-Elmer, 83-96. *Mem:* Am Bar Asn. *Res:* Nuclear radiation effects in solids; ionic conductivity in crystals; vapor deposition, crystal growth; plasma and combustion flames, flame-spray materials and process; coating properties. *Mailing Add:* 1101 Prospect Ave Westbury NY 11590

INGHAM, KENNETH CULVER, PROTEIN SCIENCE. *Current Pos:* res scientist, 75-80, sr res scientist, Blood Res Lab, 80-85, HEAD, BIOCHEM DEPT, HOLLAND LAB, AM NAT RED CROSS, 85- *Personal Data:* b Ann Arbor, Mich, Feb 14, 42; m 63, Glenda Griswold; c 2. *Educ:* Eastern Mich Univ, BS, 64; Univ Colo, PhD(chem), 70. *Prof Exp:* Res assoc biophys, Mich State Univ, 70-72; staff fel, Nat Inst Arthritis, Metab & Digestive Dis, 72-75. *Concurrent Pos:* Res career develop award, NIH, 77-82. *Mem:* Biophys Soc; Am Phys Soc; Am Soc Biol Chemists; Protein Soc; Int Soc Biorecognition Technol. *Res:* Purification, structure and function of human plasma proteins; fluorescense probes of protein-protein interactions. *Mailing Add:* Biochem Dept Holland Lab Am Red Cross 15601 Crabs Branch Way Rockville MD 20855-2743

INGHAM, KENNETH R, PHYSICS, COMPUTER SCIENCE. *Current Pos:* CHMN BD & CHIEF EXEC OFFICER, ALLMEDIA SOLUTIONS, INC, 89- *Personal Data:* b Cambridge, Mass, Aug 26, 38; m 58; c 3. *Educ:* Boston Univ, BA, 60; Brandeis Univ, MA, 63, PhD(physics & astrophys), 67. *Prof Exp:* Staff engr, Res Lab Electronics, Mass Inst Technol, 63-67, res assoc, 67-71; res affil, 71-77; dir, Arts Bur, Protestant Guild for Blind, 71-73; founder & pres, ASI Teleprocessing, 69-78, chmn bd, 78-81; pres, founder, chief exec officer & treas, Jupiter Technol, Inc, 81-86, chmn bd & treas, 86-89; consult, Intel Corp, 89. *Concurrent Pos:* Sr consult, Mitre Corp, 67-69; consult, Comput Notation Braille Proj, Bur Educ Handicapped, Fla State Univ; consult, Mass Inst Technol, 72-73; consult, Inst Corp & Govt Strategy, 82-83; mem bd, Lexington Waldorf Sch; trustee, Carroll Ctr Blind, Stone Soup Arts Trust Inc, Christian Community, Inc; dir, Rudolf Steiner Libr Blind, Inc. *Mem:* Inst Elec & Electronics Engrs. *Res:* Speech analysis, generation, synthesis and recognition; computer use in artificial intelligent language translation especially punctiliographics such as Braille, word processing and text, data base formatting; packet switching network analysis; communications, telecommunication and data; Information Service Data Network standards; author of numerous professional and business publications. *Mailing Add:* 111 Gibbs St Newton Centre MA 02159-1927

INGHAM, MERTON CHARLES, PHYSICAL OCEANOGRAPHY, BIOLOGICAL OCEANOGRAPHY. *Current Pos:* RETIRED. *Personal Data:* b Stockton, Calif, Jan 9, 30; m 55; c 3. *Educ:* Ore State Univ, BS, 53, MS, 59, PhD(oceanog), 65. *Prof Exp:* Teacher jr high sch, Ore, 55-56 & sr high sch, 56-58 & 59-62; res oceanogr, Trop Atlantic Biol Lab, Bur Com Fisheries, 65-69; dir, Oceanog Unit, USCG, 69-72; chief, Atlantic Environ Group, Nat Marine Fisheries Serv, Nat Oceanic & Atmospheric Admin, 72-85, chief, Phys Oceanog Br, 85-92. *Res:* Fishery oceanography; descriptive physical oceanography. *Mailing Add:* 11 Hawthorne St South Dennis MA 02660

INGHAM, ROBERT KELLY, ORGANIC CHEMISTRY. *Current Pos:* from asst prof to assoc prof, 53-63, PROF CHEM, OHIO UNIV, 63- *Personal Data:* b Bristol, Va, Sept 26, 26; m 52. *Educ:* King Col, AB, 47; Iowa State Univ, PhD(chem), 52. *Prof Exp:* Res assoc chem, Iowa State Univ, 53. *Mem:* Am Chem Soc; Royal Soc Chem. *Res:* Chemistry of organophosphorus compounds; heterocyclic compounds; organometallic chemistry; biological action; chemical constitution. *Mailing Add:* 22 Northwood Dr Athens OH 45701-2978

INGHAM, STEVEN CHARLES, MICROBIOLOGY. *Current Pos:* ASST PROF, DEPT FOOD SCI, UNIV WIS-MADISON, 93- *Personal Data:* b Portland, Ore, Mar 6, 61; m 88, Barbara Halpin; c Owen J. *Educ:* Cornell Univ, BS, 83, MS, 85, PhD(food sci), 88. *Prof Exp:* Food technologist, US Army Natick Res & Develop Ctr, 85; asst prof, Dept Food Sci, La State Univ, 88-89; from asst prof to assoc prof, Dept Appl Microbiol & Food Sci, Univ Sask, 89-93. *Mem:* Inst Food Technologists; Int Asn Milk Food & Environ Sanitarians; Am Soc Microbiol. *Res:* Microbiological safety ramifications of modern food processing and packaging techniques; anaerobic microbiological techniques for evaluation of microbiological safety of foods. *Mailing Add:* Dept Food Sci Univ Wis 1605 Linden Dr Madison WI 53706. *Fax:* 608-262-6872

INGHRAM, MARK GORDON, PHYSICS. *Current Pos:* from instr to prof physics, Univ Chicago, 47-69, chmn dept, 59-70, assoc dean, Div Phys Sci, 64-71 & 81-85, Samuel K Allison Distinguished Serv Prof physics, 69-85, master & assoc dean col, 81-85, EMER PROF PHYSICS, UNIV CHICAGO, 85- *Personal Data:* b Livingston, Mont, Nov 13, 19; m 46, Evelyn Dyckman; c Cheryl A & Mark G III. *Educ:* Olivet Col, BA, 39; Univ Chicago, PhD(physics), 47. *Honors & Awards:* Smith Medal, Nat Acad Sci, 57. *Prof Exp:* Jr physicist, Univ Minn, 42; physicist, Manhattan Proj, Columbia Univ, 42-45; sr physicist, Argonne Nat Lab, 45-49. *Concurrent Pos:* Mem, Comt Sci & Pub Policy, Nat Acad Sci, 66-69. *Mem:* Nat Acad Sci; fel Am Phys Soc; Am Acad Art & Sci. *Res:* Nuclear physics, geophysics and chemical physics as studied using mass spectrometric techniques. *Mailing Add:* 3077 N Lakeshore Dr Holland MI 49424

INGLE, DONALD LEE, ANIMAL NUTRITION. *Current Pos:* sr res nutritionist, Am Cyanamid Co, 72-76, group leader nutrit & physiol, 76-81, mgr, Animal Indust Res, Agr Res Div, Nutrit & Physiol Res Dept, 81-82, mgr, Animal Indust Develop, 82-89, MGR INT REGULATORY AFFAIRS, ANIMAL INDUST DEVELOP, AM CYANAMID CO, 89- *Personal Data:* b Kendrick, Idaho, Sept 4, 36; m 66; c 3. *Educ:* Univ Idaho, BS, 58, MS, 68; Univ Ill, PhD(ruminant nutrit), 71. *Prof Exp:* Ext agr agent, Bonner Co, Idaho, 59-61; ext agr agent, Boundary County, Idaho, 61-65. *Concurrent Pos:* Res assoc, Dairy Sci Dept, Univ Ill, 71-72; co-adj fac human nutrit, Div Nursing, Trenton State Col, 73-78. *Mem:* Am Soc Animal Sci; Am Dairy Sci Asn; AAAS; Nutrit Today Soc; Am Inst Nutrit; Am Meat Sci Asn. *Res:* Improving growth and body composition of farm animals; mechanisms controlling fat deposition and lipid metabolism. *Mailing Add:* Int Animal Regulatory Affairs Am Cyanamid Co 3 Bridle Path Lawrenceville NJ 08540

INGLE, GEORGE WILLIAM, PHYSICAL CHEMISTRY, RESEARCH ADMINISTRATION. *Current Pos:* RETIRED. *Personal Data:* b Lynbrook, NY, May 11, 17; m 46, Jeannette Donaldson; c Grant M, William T, Susan M (Owen) & Jeanne F. *Educ:* Colgate Univ, AB, 38; Inst Paper Chem, MS, 40. *Prof Exp:* Control chemist, Plastic Div, Monsanto Co, 40-42, color physicist, 42-46, operating supt, Plant Labs, 46-49, group leader color res, 49-54, sect leader polystyrene process & prod develop, Res Dept, 54-60, asst dir res, 60-64, mgr res, Property & Stand Sect, 64-67, mgr res prod property develop, 67-68, dir tech liaison, 68-75; asst tech dir, Mfr Chemists Asn, 75-78; dir asn liaison nat & int, Chem Mfrs Asn, 78-85. *Concurrent Pos:* Chmn, Int Stand Orgn Tech Comt 61, 74-77. *Mem:* Am Soc Testing & Mat; Am Chem Soc. *Res:* Colorimetry; coloring of plastics; process and product development of polystyrene plastics; toxicity of plastics for food packaging; plastics waste management; industrial solid waste management; toxicity; toxic substances control legislation and regulation, United States and International. *Mailing Add:* 125 Mountain Rd Hampden MA 01036

INGLE, JAMES CHESNEY, JR, MICROPALEONTOLOGY, MARINE GEOLOGY. *Current Pos:* from asst prof to prof, 68-84, chmn dept, 82-86, W H PECK PROF EARTH SCI, STANFORD UNIV, 84- *Personal Data:* b Los Angeles, Calif, Nov 6, 35; m 58; c 1. *Educ:* Univ Southern Calif, BS, 59, MS, 62, PhD(geol), 66. *Honors & Awards:* Lewis G Weeks lectr, Univ Wis, 86; A I Levorsen Award, Am Asn Petrol Geol, 88. *Prof Exp:* Asst, Univ Southern Calif, 59-60; jr geologist, Shell Oil Co, 60; res assoc, Dept Geol & Allan Hancock Found, Univ Southern Calif, 61-67. *Concurrent Pos:* Res assoc, Los Angeles Co Mus, 63-; vis scholar, Inst Geol & Paleont, Tohoku Univ, Japan, 66-67; scientist, Leg 18, Deep-Sea Drilling Proj, 71, co-chief scientist, Leg 31, 73; geologist, US Geol Surv, 76-81; distinguished lectr, Am Asn Petrol Geologists, 86, Joint Oceanog Inst, 91; co-chief scientist, Leg 128, Ocean Drilling Prog, 89. *Mem:* AAAS; fel Geol Soc Am; Soc Econ Paleont & Mineral; Am Geophys Union. *Res:* Marine stratigraphy; biostratigraphy; marine geology; Cenozoic foraminiferal biostratigraphy and paleoceanography of the Pacific region; Cenozoic geology of the Pacific coast of North America. *Mailing Add:* Dept Geol & Environ Sci Sch Earth Sci Stanford Univ Mitchell B-70 Stanford CA 94305-2115. *Fax:* 650-725-0979; *E-Mail:* ingle@pangea.stanford.edu

INGLE, JAMES DAVIS, JR, CHEMICAL INSTRUMENTATION, TRACE ANALYSIS. *Current Pos:* PROF CHEM, ORE STATE UNIV, 71- *Personal Data:* b Chicago, Ill, Oct 9, 46; m 70; c 1. *Educ:* Univ Ill, Urbana-Champaign, BS, 68, Mich State Univ, PhD(anal chem), 71. *Mem:* Am Chem Soc; Soc Appl Spectros. *Res:* Instrumentation for the determination of trace amounts of inorganic and organic species with emphasis on environmental and clinical samples. *Mailing Add:* Dept Chem Ore State Univ 153 Gilbert Hall Corvallis OR 97331-4003

INGLE, JOHN IDE, DENTISTRY, ENDODONTICS. *Current Pos:* RETIRED. *Personal Data:* b Colville, Wash, Jan 19, 19; m 40, Joyce Ledgerwood; c Geoffrey, Schuyler & Leslie (Idemoxley). *Educ:* Northwestern Univ, DDS, 42; Univ Mich, Ann Arbor, MSD, 48; Am Bd Periodont, dipl, 51; Am Bd Endodont, dipl, 63. *Prof Exp:* Asst, Northwestern Univ, 42-43; from asst prof to prof periodont & endodont, Sch Dent, Univ Wash, 48-55, from actg exec officer to exec officer dept, 53-64; prof periodont & endodont & dean, Sch Dent, Univ Southern Calif, 64-72; sr prof assoc, Inst Med-Nat Acad Sci, 73-78; pres, Palm Springs Seminars, Inc, 78-89. *Concurrent Pos:* Mem dent educ rev comt, NIH, 70; mem adv comt dent health, Off Secy, HEW, 70-72; liaison comt dent educ & lic, Am Asn Dent Schs, 70-73; vis lectr, Univ Calif, Los Angeles, 80- & Loma Linda Univ, 81- *Mem:* Int Asn Dent Res; Am Asn Endodont; Am Dent Asn; Am Acad Periodont; fel Am Col Dent; fel Int Col Dent. *Res:* Periodontics; endodontics; author of one publication. *Mailing Add:* 18755 W Bernado Dr Suite 1231 San Diego CA 92127. *Fax:* 619-592-9646

INGLE, L MORRIS, PLANT PHYSIOLOGY, HORTICULTURE. *Current Pos:* from asst prof to assoc prof, 63-71, PROF HORT, WVA UNIV, 71- *Personal Data:* b Covina, Calif, July 28, 29; m 60; c 3. *Educ:* Univ Calif, Santa Barbara, AB, 51; Univ Calif, Davis, MA, 56; Purdue Univ, PhD(plant physiol), 60. *Prof Exp:* Asst plant physiologist, United Fruit Co, 59-62, assoc biochemist, 62-63. *Mem:* Am Soc Plant Physiol; Am Soc Hort; Sigma Xi. *Res:* Post-harvest physiology of fruits; plant growth regulators; carbohydrate and amino acid metabolism. *Mailing Add:* Plant Scis WVa Univ PO Box 6108 Morgantown WV 26506-0001

INGLEDEW, WILLIAM MICHAEL, BREWERY & GASOHOL MICROBIOLOGY, FERMENTATIONS. *Current Pos:* from asst prof to assoc prof agr microbiol, 70-79, assoc mem, Dept Microbiol, Sch Med, 78-92, PROF APPL MICROBIOL & FOOD SCI, UNIV SASK, 79- *Personal Data:* b Vancouver, BC, Mar 8, 42; m 66, Lynne; c Wade & Leanne. *Educ:* Univ BC, BSc, 65, PhD(microbiol), 69. *Prof Exp:* Nat Res Coun Can fel, Cellular Chem Dept, Coun Sci Res, Madrid, Spain, 69-70. *Concurrent Pos:* Nat Res Coun Can sr indust fel, Molson Res Lab, Montreal, 78-79; assoc, Exp Sta Viticult & Enology, Univ Calif, Davis, 83-84; ed-in-chief, Am Soc Brewing Chemists J, 88-92. *Mem:* Can Soc Microbiol; Am Soc Brewing Chemists; Master Brewers' Asn Am; Am Soc Microbiol; Soc Indust Microbiologists; Inst Brewing. *Res:* Brewing; production of alcohols from starch; heat resistance of microbes; utilization of spent industrial microbes; fuel alcohol; yeast nutrition; alcohol tolerance. *Mailing Add:* Dept Appl Microbiol & Food Sci Univ Sask 51 Campus Dr Saskatoon SK S7N 5A8 Can. *Fax:* 306-966-8898; *E-Mail:* ingledew@agric.usask.ca

INGLEHART, LORRETTA JEANETTE, PHYSICS. *Current Pos:* Assoc res scientist, 85-87, ASST PROF MAT SCI, JOHNS HOPKINS UNIV, BALTIMORE, 87- *Personal Data:* b Cleveland, Ohio, July 14, 47. *Educ:* Wayne State Univ, BS, 79, MS, 82, PhD, 84. *Concurrent Pos:* Prin investr, Bendix Corp, 79-81; vis prof, Physics Optic Lab, Sch Advan Physics & Chem, Paris, 84, 86 & 89; Fulbright scholar, France, 86; prof lectr physics, Am Univ Wash, 86-87; guest scientist, Nat Bur Stand, Gaithersburg, Md, 85- *Mem:* AAAS; Am Phys Soc; Optical Soc; Sigma Xi. *Res:* Physics. *Mailing Add:* 6105 Cheverly Circle Cheverly MD 20785

INGLES, CHARLES JAMES, BIOCHEMISTRY, MOLECULAR BIOLOGY. *Current Pos:* from asst prof to assoc prof biochem, 71-76, assoc prof med res, 76-81, PROF MED RES, UNIV TORONTO, 81- *Personal Data:* b Halifax, NS, Jan 31, 42; m 66; c 1. *Educ:* Univ Toronto, BSc, 64; Univ BC, PhD(biochem), 68. *Prof Exp:* Nat Res Coun Can fel biochem, Beatson Inst Cancer Res, Glasgow, 68-70; res biochemist, Univ Calif, San Francisco, 70-71. *Mem:* Can Biochem Soc. *Res:* Molecular biology of cellular differentiation; control of gene expression in eukaryotes. *Mailing Add:* Banting & Best Dept Med Res Univ Toronto 112 College St Toronto ON M5G 1L6 Can

INGLESSIS, CRITON GEORGE S, ORGANIC CHEMISTRY. *Current Pos:* PRES, FRINTON LABS, 60- *Personal Data:* b Piraeus, Greece, Apr 23, 30; US citizen; m 76; c 3. *Educ:* Colgate Univ, BA, 53; Clark Univ, PhD(chem), 58. *Prof Exp:* Res chemist, Vineland Chem Co, 59-60. *Mem:* AAAS; Am Chem Soc. *Res:* Synthetic organic chemistry; liquid crystals; herbicides. *Mailing Add:* 204 Winding Way Moorestown NJ 08057

INGLETT, GEORGE EVERETT, AGRICULTURAL CHEMISTRY, FOOD CHEMISTRY. *Current Pos:* sr food technologist, Inst Minerals & Chem Corp, 63-64, supvr natural prod chem, 64-65, mgr natural prod & food technol, 65-67; CHIEF CEREAL SCI & FOODS LAB, NORTHERN REGIONAL RES CTR, AGR RES SERV, USDA, 67- *Personal Data:* b Waltonville, Ill, Aug 3, 28; m 54, Marilyn J Fawley; c George D (deceased) & Carolyn J. *Educ:* Univ Ill, BS, 49; Univ Iowa, PhD(biochem), 52. *Honors & Awards:* Philadelphia Sect Award, Inst Food Tech, 81; Advan Appln Agr & Food Chem Award, Agr & Food Chem Div, Am Chem Soc, 83, Distinguished Serv Award, 85; R&D 100 Award, 93. *Prof Exp:* Asst biochemist, Univ Ill, 52-54; asst scientist cancer res, Nat Cancer Inst, 54-55; sr asst scientist air & water pollution control, Robert A Taft Sanit Eng Ctr, USPHS, 55-56; res chemist, Corn Prod Co, 56-60; sr res chemist, Griffith Labs, 60-63. *Concurrent Pos:* Adj prof food sci, Univ Ill, 77-; sr res scientist, supvr & mgr, Foods & Natural Prod Res, Int Minerals & Chem Corp, 63-67. *Mem:* Am Chem Soc; Inst Food Technologists; Am Asn Cereal Chem. *Res:* Inventor of OATRIM, a fat substitute contributing to the prevention of heart diseases and widely used in reduced-fat foods; innovations in corn sweeteners, intense sweeteners, corn milling and Z-TRIM, a food texturizer. *Mailing Add:* USDA Agr Res Serv Nat Ctr Agr Utilization Res Biopolymer Res Unit Peoria IL 61604. *Fax:* 309-681-6686; *E-Mail:* inglettge@ncauri.ncaur.gov

INGLIS, D R, nuclear physics; deceased, see previous edition for last biography

INGLIS, JACK MORTON, ECOLOGY. *Current Pos:* from instr to assoc prof, 58-76, PROF WILDLIFE & FISHERIES SCI, TEX A&M UNIV, 76- *Personal Data:* b Houston, Tex, Dec 31, 23; m 44; c 5. *Educ:* Tex A&M Univ, BS, 50, MS, 52, PhD(zool), 67. *Prof Exp:* Proj leader wildlife res, Tex Game & Fish Comn, 52-54; res biologist, Tex Agr Exp Sta, 54-58. *Concurrent Pos:* Scientist, Seregenti Res Inst, 71-72; ecol consult, Bechtel Power Corp, 73-78; vis prof, Univ Dar es Salaam, Tanzania, 79; consult wildlife, Tex Munic Power Agency, 81. *Mem:* Ecol Soc Am; Am Soc Mammal; Sigma Xi; Wildlife Soc; Animal Behav Soc. *Res:* Integration of wildlife management into ranching systems; habitat relationships and movements of white tailed deer; sociology of white-tailed deer; radioecology; wildlife conservation in developing countries. *Mailing Add:* 607 Old Jersey St College Station TX 77840

INGLIS, JAMES, SYSTEMS ENGINEERING, STATISTICS. *Current Pos:* mem tech staff, AT&T, 78-81, tech supvr, 81-87, dept head, 87-95, DIV MGR, AT&T, 95- *Personal Data:* b Cleveland, Ohio, June 19, 45; m 67, Carolyn Corcoran; c Jeffrey & Katherine. *Educ:* Amherst Col, BA, 67; Stanford Univ, MS, 68, PhD(statist), 73. *Prof Exp:* Mathematician, US Army Engr Div, Huntsville, 69-70; asst prof statist & biostatist, Univ Rochester, 72-78. *Mem:* Am Statist Asn; Comput Soc. *Res:* Data analysis; reliability; management. *Mailing Add:* AT&T 101 Crawfords Corner Rd Rm 2k-307 PO Box 3030 Holmdel NJ 07733-3030

INGOGLIA, NICHOLAS ANDREW, NEUROSCIENCE. *Current Pos:* PROF PHYSIOL & NEUROSCI, NJ MED SCH, 81- *Educ:* NY Univ, PhD(biol), 69. *Mailing Add:* Dept Physiol NJ Med Sch 185 S Orange Ave Newark NJ 07103-2757. *Fax:* 973-982-7950

INGOLD, DONALD ALFRED, ETHOLOGY, ORNITHOLOGY. *Current Pos:* ASSOC PROF BIOL, E TEX STATE UNIV, 69- *Personal Data:* b Columbus, Nebr, Dec 12, 34; m 58; c 4. *Educ:* Univ Nebr, Lincoln, BS, 58, MS, 61; Univ Wyo, PhD(zool), 69. *Prof Exp:* Asst prof biol, Sterling Col, 62-66. *Concurrent Pos:* Res fac grant, ETex State Univ, 71 & 75-78; consult, US Army corps Engr, 74-76. *Mem:* AAAS; Am Soc Mammal; Sigma Xi. *Res:* Avian ecology; ornithology; animal behavior. *Mailing Add:* 212 Brookhaven Terr Commerce TX 75428-2002

INGOLD, KEITH USHERWOOD, PHYSICAL ORGANIC CHEMISTRY. *Current Pos:* assoc dir, Div Chem, 77-90, RES OFFICER, NAT RES COUN, 55-, DIST SCIENTIST, STEACIE INST MOLECULAR SCI, 91- *Personal Data:* b Leeds, Eng, May 31, 29; Can citizen; m 56, Cairine Hodgkin; c Chris D, John H & Diana H. *Educ:* Univ London, BSc, 49; Oxford Univ, DPhil(phys chem), 51. *Hon Degrees:* DSc, Univ Guelph, Ont, 85, Univ St Andrews, Scotland, 89, Carleton Univ, Ont, 92; LLD, Mt Allison Univ, Sackville, NB, 87, McMaster Univ, Ont, 95, Dalhousie Univ, Halifax, NS, 96. *Honors & Awards:* Award Petrol Chem, Am Chem Soc, 68; Frank Burnett Dains Mem Lectr, Univ Kans, 69; Queen's Silver Jubilee Medal, 77; Award Kinetics & Mech, Am Chem Soc, 78, Pauling Medal, 88, Arthur C Cope Scholar Award, 92, James Flack Norris Award, 93; Medal, Chem Inst Can, 81, Syntex Award Phys Org Chem, 83; Centennial Medal, Royal Soc Can, 82; J A McRae Mem Lectr Chem, Queens Univ, 80; C I L Lectr, Acadia Univ, Wolfville, Nova Scotia, Can, 87; Imp Oil Lectr, Univ Western Ont, 87; Douglas Hill Mem Lectr, Univ Hong Kong, Japan, 88; Rayson Huang Lectr, Univ Hong Kong, Japan, 88; Alfred Bader Award in Org Chem, Can Soc Chem, 89; Sir Christopher Ingold Lectr Award, Royal Soc Chem, UK, 91; Alfred Bader Award in Org Chem, Can Soc Chem, 89. *Prof Exp:* Fel chem, Nat Res Coun, 51-53; Defense Res Bd fel, Univ Br Columbia, BC, 53-55. *Concurrent Pos:* Vis scientist, Chevron Res Corp, Calif, 66, Exxon Res & Develop Co, NJ, 72, Univ Adelaide, Australia, Univ Sci & Med Grenole & Univ Bordeaux, France, Leiden Univ, Holland, 93; vis prof, Univ Col, Univ London, 69 & 72, Univ Western Ont, 75, Univ Bologna, 75, Univ St Andrews, 77 & Univ Frieberg, Essen, Dusseldorf, 89 & 90; vis lectr, Japan Soc Prom Sci, 82; adj prof, Dept Chem, Brunel Univ, UK, 83-94, Dept Chem & Biochem, Univ Guelph, Ont, Can, 85-87; vis fel, Australian Nat Univ, Canberra, 87; mem, Frontiers Free Radicals & Radical Traps, Tex A&M Univ, 89; Van Arkel vis prof, Leiden Univ, Holland, 92; adj res prof, Carleton Univ, Ottawa, 91-; lectr, NSF, Repub China, 92 & Chem, Univ Western Ont, 93. *Mem:* Am Chem Soc; fel Chem Inst Can; Royal Soc Chem; fel Royal Soc Can; fel Royal Soc London; Can Soc Chem (vpres, 85-87, pres, 87-88). *Res:* Kinetics and mechanisms of free radical reactions in solution and in biological systems. *Mailing Add:* 72 Ryeburn Dr Gloucester ON K1V 1H5 Can

INGRAHAM, JOHN CHARLES, PLASMA PHYSICS. *Current Pos:* MEM STAFF, LOS ALAMOS SCI LAB, 70- *Personal Data:* b Seattle, Wash, Nov 15, 36. *Educ:* Mass Inst Technol, SB, 58, PhD(physics), 63. *Prof Exp:* From instr to asst prof physics, Mass Inst Technol, 63-68; sci specialist, Edgerton, Germeshausen & Grier, Inc, 68-70. *Mem:* Am Phys Soc; Sigma Xi. *Res:* Plasma physics; microwave techniques; atomic and molecular physics. *Mailing Add:* 304 Venado Los Alamos NM 87544

INGRAHAM, JOHN LYMAN, MICROBIOLOGY. *Current Pos:* asst prof enol, 58-62, from assoc prof to prof, 62-89, EMER PROF BACT, UNIV CALIF, DAVIS, 89- *Personal Data:* b Berkeley, Calif, Sept 22, 24; m 50; c 2. *Educ:* Univ Calif, BS, 47, PhD(microbiol), 51. *Prof Exp:* Res scientist microbiol, Stine Lab, E I du Pont de Nemours & Co, 51-56; chemist, Western Regional Lab, USDA, 56-58. *Concurrent Pos:* Guggenheim fel, 65-66. *Mem:* AAAS; Am Soc Microbiol (pres, 92-93); Sigma Xi. *Res:* Microbial physiology and genetics. *Mailing Add:* 7535 Cheryl Lane Fair Oaks CA 95628

INGRAHAM, JOSEPH STERLING, IMMUNOLOGY. *Current Pos:* from asst prof to assoc prof, Ind Univ, 54-69, prof microbiol, 69-87, prof immunol, 80-87, EMER PROF, IND UNIV, INDIANAPOLIS, 87- *Personal Data:* b Grand Rapids, Minn, Nov 13, 20; m 89, Ruth A Cornish; c Loring J, Mary E, Lisa (Krieg) & Christy (Krieg). *Educ:* Univ Minn, BA, 43; Univ Chicago, SM, 47, PhD(biochem), 50. *Prof Exp:* Res chemist, Armour & Co, 43-46; instr biochem, Univ Chicago, 50-54. *Concurrent Pos:* Vis asst prof microbiol, Sch Med, Univ Colo, 61; vis scientist, Pasteur Inst, Paris, 62 & 77. *Mem:* Am Chem Soc; Am Soc Microbiol; Am Asn Immunol; Soc Exp Biol & Med; AAAS; French Soc Immunol. *Res:* Fate of radioactive labeled antigens in vivo; formation of antibody homologous to simple hapten groups; antibody formation by individual cells; allotypy of antibodies; antigen-antibody reactions. *Mailing Add:* Dept Microbiol/Immunol Ind Univ 635 Barnhill Dr Indianapolis IN 46223

INGRAHAM, LLOYD LEWIS, PHYSICAL CHEMISTRY, ORGANIC CHEMISTRY. *Current Pos:* asst prof enzyme chem, 58-59, assoc prof biophys, 59-65, PROF BIOPHYS, UNIV CALIF, DAVIS, 65- *Personal Data:* b Berkeley, Calif, Jan 24, 20; m 47; c 2. *Educ:* Univ Calif, BS, 42; Univ Calif, Los Angeles, PhD(chem), 49. *Prof Exp:* Chemist, Assoc Oil Co, 42-44; chemist, Western Regional Res Lab, USDA, 49-58. *Concurrent Pos:* Guggenheim fel, Harvard Univ, 55-56; NSF sr fel, Copenhagen Univ, 64-65. *Mem:* Sigma Xi. *Res:* Biochemical kinetics and mechanisms. *Mailing Add:* PO Box 202 Woodland CA 95695-0202

INGRAHAM, RICHARD LEE, THEORETICAL PHYSICS. *Current Pos:* RES PROF PHYSICS, NMEX STATE UNIV, 60- *Personal Data:* b Des Moines, Iowa, Aug 29, 23; m 51, 55; c 2. *Educ:* Harvard Univ, BS, 47, MA, 50, PhD(physics), 52. *Prof Exp:* Asst, Inst Advan Study, 52-54; instr math, Univ Conn, 54-55; asst prof physics, Johns Hopkins Univ 55-56; res assoc, Univ Md, 56-57; assoc prof, NMex State Univ, 57-59; assoc prof, Tech Inst Aeronaut, Brazil, 59-60; dept biol, San Jose State Univ. *Concurrent Pos:* Sheldon prize traveling fel from Harvard Col, 48-49; Fulbright fel, Paris, 50-51; consult, US Naval Res Lab, 56-57. *Mem:* Sigma Xi. *Res:* Quantum field theory; group theory and elementary particles; conformal relativity. *Mailing Add:* Dept Physics Dept 3-D NMex State Univ PO Box 3001 Las Cruces NM 88003

INGRAHAM, THOMAS ROBERT, PHYSICAL CHEMISTRY, AIR POLLUTION. *Current Pos:* RETIRED. *Personal Data:* b Sydney, NS, Dec 7, 20; m 49. *Educ:* Dalhousie Univ, BSc, 43, MSc, 45; McGill Univ, PhD(chem), 47. *Prof Exp:* Prof chem, Loyola Col, Concordia Univ, 47-51; res scientist metall, Mines Br, Mines & Tech Surv, 53-54; head res, Mines Br, Energy, Mines & Resources, 54-72; dir technol, Environ Protection, 72-78; dir progs, Natural Sci & Eng Res Coun, 78-84. *Concurrent Pos:* Fel, Univ Toronto, 51-53. *Mem:* Fel Chem Inst Can; fel Metall Soc-Am Inst Mining, Metall & Petrol Engrs; Air Pollution Control Asn; NAm Thermal Anal Soc (pres, 72). *Res:* Metallurgical thermodynamics; heterogeneous chemical kinetics; air pollution control technology. *Mailing Add:* 7 Opeongo Rd Ottawa ON K1S 4K9 Can

INGRAM, ALVIN JOHN, ORTHOPEDIC SURGERY. *Current Pos:* assoc prof, 60-71, prof orthop surg & chmn dept, 71-78, EMER PROF & CHMN, COL MED, UNIV TENN, 78- *Personal Data:* b Jackson, Tenn, Mar 31, 14; m 43; c 3. *Educ:* Univ Tenn, BS & MD, 39, MS, 47. *Prof Exp:* Intern, Univ Mich Hosp, Ann Arbor, 39-40, asst resident surg, 40-41; fel orthop surg, Campbell Clin, Memphis, 41-42 & 46-47, mem staff, 47-67, dep chief of staff, 67-69; consult, Orthop Surg, Richards Med Co, 84-90. *Concurrent Pos:* Med dir, Crippled Children's Hosp, 48-61, chief of staff, 61-71; med dir, Les Passes Cerebral Palsy Treatment Ctr, 53-56; mem staff, Baptist Mem Hosp, exec comt med staff, 69-70, chmn orthop dept, 70-72, pres med staff, 73; chief of staff, Campbell Clin, 70-77, emer chief, 77-; mem Am Bd Orthop Surg, pres, 76-78; emer staff mem, St Joseph Hosp, LeBonheur Children's Hosp & Methodist Hosp. *Mem:* Inst Med-Nat Acad Sci; Am Acad Orthop Surgeons; Am Orthop Asn (pres, 73); Int Soc Orthop & Traumatology; Am Acad Cerebral Palsy (pres, 58); Am Bd Orthop Surg (pres, 75 & 76). *Mailing Add:* 190 Belle Mead Lane Memphis TN 38117

INGRAM, ALVIN RICHARD, ORGANIC POLYMER CHEMISTRY. *Current Pos:* RETIRED. *Personal Data:* b Enfield, NH, May 16, 18; m 42, Virginia E Long; c Carl & Richard. *Educ:* Univ NH, BS, 40; Northeastern Univ, MS, 42; Univ Pittsburgh, PhD(org chem), 55. *Honors & Awards:* Outstanding Tech Achievement Award, Atlantic Richfield Corp, 82. *Prof Exp:* Chemist, Gen Chem Defense Corp, WVa, 42-43; fel, Mellon Inst, 43-44; res proj leader, Johnson & Johnson, NJ, 44-48; fel, Mellon Inst, 48-53; chemist, tech coordr & group leader, Koppers Co, Inc, 53-58, mgr, Expandable Polymers Res Group, Koppers Co & Sinclair-Koppers Co, 58-73; mgr, Dylite Polymer Res Group, Arco Polymers Co & Arco Chem Co, 74-84. *Concurrent Pos:* Res consult, Arco Chem Co, 84-90. *Mem:* Am Chem Soc; Soc Plastics Indust. *Res:* Synthesis and application of thermoplastic and thermoset polymers; polystyrene bead foams; amino acids; plaster of paris; orthopedic bandages; organic reactions; granted 43 patents. *Mailing Add:* 1106 Cardinal Dr West Chester PA 19382-7804

INGRAM, DAVID CHRISTOPHER, ION IMPLANTATION, ION BEAM EQUIPMENT. *Current Pos:* ASSOC PROF PHYSICS, OHIO UNIV, 89- *Personal Data:* b Nottingham, Eng, Sept 9, 53; m 79; c 4. *Educ:* Salford Univ, BS, 75, MS, 76, PhD(elec eng), 80. *Prof Exp:* Res fel, Atomic Energy Res Estab Harwell, 79-82; sr scientist, Universal Energy Syst, 82-87; chief scientist, Whickam Ion Beams Systs Ltd, 87-89, gen mgr, 89. *Concurrent Pos:* Vis res fel, Univ Durham, 87-90; consult, 89- *Mem:* Mat Res Soc; Am Soc Metals; Am Phys Soc; Am Vacuum Soc; Inst Physics; Bohmische Phys Soc. *Res:* Application of ion beams to materials for modification and analysis; deposition of diamond-like carbon and diamond coatings. *Mailing Add:* Dept Physics & Astron Ohio Univ Athens OH 45701

INGRAM, FORREST DUANE, NUCLEAR & BIOPHYSICS, ASTRONOMY. *Current Pos:* PROF PHYSICS, ROCK VALLEY COL, 85- *Personal Data:* b Lafayette Co, Wis, Jan 17, 38; m 65; c 3. *Educ:* Wis State Col, Platteville, BS, 59; Univ Iowa, MS, 61, PhD(physics), 68. *Prof Exp:* From instr to asst prof physics, Wis State Univ, Platteville, 62-65; instr physiol & biophys, Univ Iowa, 68-75, res scientist, Cardiovasc Ctr, 75-80; asst prof pediat, Baylor Col Med, 80-85. *Concurrent Pos:* Lectr-consult, Oak Ridge Inst Nuclear Studies, 66-69; vis asst prof internal med, Univ Tex Health Sci Ctr Dallas, 75-; vis scientist, Univ Nijmegeu, Neth, 79; res opportunity award, NSF, 93 & 94. *Mem:* fel Royal Micros Soc; Am Phys Soc. *Res:* Electron microprobe studies of the distributions of soluble ions in soft biological tissue; studies of the final state Coulomb interactions resulting from three body breakup reactions involving charged reaction products. *Mailing Add:* Rock Valley Col Div Phys Sci 3301 N Mulford Rockford IL 61114-5699. Fax: 815-654-4438; E-Mail: faps3di@rvcux1.rvc.cc.il.us

INGRAM, GERALD E(UGENE), CIVIL ENGINEERING. *Current Pos:* RETIRED. *Personal Data:* b Phoenix, Ariz, Mar 8, 28; m 54; c 3. *Educ:* Univ Ariz, BSCE, 49; Purdue Univ, MSCE, 57, PhD(civil eng), 61. *Prof Exp:* Asst county engr, Pinal County Hwy Dept, Ariz, 49-50, county engr, 52-55; instr civil eng, Purdue Univ, 55-60; assoc prof & chmn dept, Univ Denver, 60-63; mgr advan res & develop, Arinc Res Corp, 63-64; mem prof staff systs anal, ctr advan studies, Tempo-Gen Elec Co, 64-71; mgr reliability progs, Adcon Corp, 71-74; sr engr reliability eng, Advan Reactor Systs Dept, Gen Elec Co, 75-85. *Concurrent Pos:* Instr, Engrs Sch, Ft Belvoir, Va, 50-52; consult, Hq USAF Opers Anal Off, 61-65; consult engr, 74-75 & 85- *Mem:* Am Soc Civil

Engrs; Nat Soc Prof Engrs; Am Astron Soc; Am Concrete Inst; Soc Exp Stress Anal. *Res:* Probabilistic approaches to analysis and design of structural and other type systems; basic technology associated with systems effectiveness analysis with emphasis on reliability; efficient techniques for safety reliability and risk analysis of nuclear power plant systems. *Mailing Add:* 13575 Howen Dr Saratoga CA 95070

INGRAM, GLENN R, COMPUTER SCIENCE. *Current Pos:* ASSOC DIR COMPUT, CENT AM MISSION, NAT BUR STAND, 78- *Personal Data:* b Terry, Mont, Apr 25, 28; m 81; c 2. *Educ:* Mont State Col, BS, 52, MS, 54; Wash State Univ, PhD(math), 62. *Prof Exp:* From instr to assoc prof math, Mont State Col, 52-65, dir comput ctr, 62-65; engr, Mont Hwy Dept, 54-55; asst comput analyst, Wash State Univ, 57-62; assoc prog dir comput sci, NSF, Washington, DC, 65-66, prog dir comput facs, 66-69, actg head off comput activ, 69-70; assoc prof comput sci & dir comput ctr, Wash State Univ, 70-73; chief tech appl div, Nat Inst Educ, 73-75; chief comput serv & technol, Energy Res & Develop Admin, 75-78. *Concurrent Pos:* Consult, NSF; mem steering comt, Comput in Undergrad Curricula. *Mem:* Asn Comput Mach; Soc Indust & Appl Math; Inst Elec & Electronics Engrs. *Res:* Applied mathematics; numerical analysis. *Mailing Add:* 18417 Kingshill Rd Germantown MD 20874

INGRAM, JOHN (WILLIAM), JR, taxonomic botany, for more information see previous edition

INGRAM, JOHN MICHAEL, MATHEMATICS. *Current Pos:* PROF, DEPT MATH, CALIF STATE UNIV, SACRAMENTO, 82- *Personal Data:* b Sylacauga, Ala, Nov 6, 52. *Educ:* Univ Fla, BS, 75, MS, 77; N Tex State Univ, PhD(math), 81. *Mem:* Am Math Soc. *Res:* Mathematics. *Mailing Add:* 3027 Hobart Ct Sacramento CA 95864-5632

INGRAM, JORDAN MILES, biochemistry; deceased, see previous edition for last biography

INGRAM, LONNIE O'NEAL, MICROBIAL PHYSIOLOGY, INDUSTRIAL MICROBIOLOGY. *Current Pos:* from asst prof to assoc prof, 72-81, PROF MICROBIOL, UNIV FLA, 82- *Personal Data:* b Greenwood, SC, Dec 30, 47; m 68, Vickie Webb; c Erin, Thomas & Kenneth. *Educ:* Univ SC, BS, 69; Univ Tex, Austin, PhD(bot), 71. *Honors & Awards:* Distinguished Serv Award, USDA. *Prof Exp:* Fel microbiol physiol, Oak Ridge Nat Lab, Biol Div, 71-72. *Mem:* Soc Indust Microbiol; Am Soc Microbiol; Sigma Xi. *Res:* Relationship of lipids in the cell membrane to cellular functions; the effects of alcohols and other lipophilic agents on membranes; role of membranes in alcohol tolerance; production of alcohol by zymomonas and yeasts; regulations of glycolysis; molecular biology of alcohol production; glycolytic enzymes. *Mailing Add:* Dept Microbiol Univ Fla 3052 McCarty Hall PO Box 110700 Bldg 981 Gainesville FL 32611. *Fax:* 352-486-4953

INGRAM, MARYLOU, MEDICAL RESEARCH. *Current Pos:* DIR, INST CELL ANALYSIS & PROF MED & BIOMED ENG, UNIV MIAMI SCH MED, 77- *Personal Data:* b Ashtabula, Ohio, June 14, 20; div. *Educ:* Western Reserve Univ, BA, 42, MS, 43; Univ Rochester, MD, 47. *Prof Exp:* Asst biol, Western Reserve Univ, 42-43; from instr to asst prof radiation biol, Sch Med & Dent, Univ Rochester, 46-55, assoc prof radiation biol & biophys, 59-71; med scientist & res assoc bio-med eng, Jet Propulsion Lab, Calif Inst Technol, 71-75; staff med scientist, Health Div, Los Alamos Sci Lab, Univ Calif, 75-77. *Concurrent Pos:* From asst to sect head, Atomic Energy Proj, Univ Rochester, 46-71, proj physician, 47-65, instr med, Sch Med & Dent, 53-61, sr instr, 61-71; consult, Nat Cancer Inst, 57-60 & Armed Forces Radiobiol Res Inst, 64-; NIH resident res collabr, Jet Propulsion Lab, Calif Inst Technol, 71-72, John A Hartford Found grant, 72-75; res collabr, Brookhaven Nat Lab, 70-74; clin prof path, Sch Med, Univ Southern Calif, 71-75; mem, Nat Coun Radiation Protection & Measurements, 73-79 & Environ Radiation Mgt & Control Adv Comt, 79- *Mem:* Soc Exp Biol & Med; Radiation Res Soc; Am Inst Biol Sci; Anal Cytol Soc; Am Soc Hemat; Sigma Xi. *Res:* Analytical cytology; mammalian and human hematology; biological effects of radiation clinical medicine. *Mailing Add:* 371 Patrician Way Pasadena CA 91105-1027

INGRAM, PETER, BIOPHYSICS. *Current Pos:* SR PHYSICIST, DREYFUS LAB, RES TRIANGLE INST, 63- *Personal Data:* b London, Eng, Nov 14, 38; US citizen; m 59; c 3. *Educ:* Univ Southampton, BSc, 59, PhD(physics), 63. *Honors & Awards:* Cecil Hall Award, Ecectron Micros Soc Am, 89. *Concurrent Pos:* Adj asst prof path, Duke Univ, 81- *Mem:* Electron Micros Soc Am; Microbeam Analysis Soc. *Res:* Analytical electron microscopy; morphology of natural and synthetic polymers, ultrastructure of biological tissue; scanning and transmission electron microscopy and x-ray analysis, especially of submicron cellular inclusions, intracellular elemental distributions and quantitative analytical and imaging techniques. *Mailing Add:* PO Box 12194 Research Triangle Park NC 27709

INGRAM, RICHARD GRANT, PHYSICAL OCEANOGRAPHY. *Current Pos:* From asst prof to assoc prof phys oceanog, Inst Oceanog, 72-87, chmn Ctr, 79-84, PROF METEOROL, MCGILL UNIV, 87- *Personal Data:* b Warrington, Eng, Feb 15, 45; Can citizen; m 70. *Educ:* McGill Univ, BSc, 65, MSc, 67; Mass Inst Technol, PhD(oceanog), 71. *Concurrent Pos:* Exec coun, Inter-Univ Res Group Oceanog, Que, 71- *Mem:* Am Geophys Union; Am Meteorol Soc; Can Meteorol Oceanog Soc. *Res:* Estuarine dynamics; coastal oceanography; mixing and entrainment processes in under-ice plumes and coastal waters. *Mailing Add:* Dept Meteorol McGill Univ 805 Sherbrooke St W Montreal PQ H3A 2K6 Can

INGRAM, ROLAND HARRISON, INTERNAL MEDICINE, PULMONARY DISEASES. *Current Pos:* PROF MED, EMORY-CRAWFORD LONG HOSP, 92- *Personal Data:* b Birmingham, Ala, Mar 10, 35; m 61; c 1. *Educ:* Univ Ala, BS, 57; Yale Univ, MD, 60. *Hon Degrees:* AM, Harvard Univ, 80. *Prof Exp:* Dir, Respiratory Div, Sch Med, Emory Univ, 67-73; dir, Respiratory Div, Med Pulmonary Dis, Brigham & Women's Hosp, 73-92. *Concurrent Pos:* Parker B Francis prof med, Harvard Med Sch, 79-92; dir, Respiratory Div, Beth Israel Hosp, 80-85. *Mem:* Asn Am Physicians; Am Soc Clin Invest; Am Physiol Soc; Am Thoracic Soc (pres, 82-83). *Res:* Respiratory and cardiopulmonary physiology; pulmonary & critical care medicine problems. *Mailing Add:* Dept Med Emory Crawford Long Hosp 550 Peachtree St NE Suite 6183 Atlanta GA 30365

INGRAM, ROY LEE, GEOLOGY. *Current Pos:* From asst prof to assoc prof, Univ NC, Chapel Hill, 47-57, chmn dept, 57-64 & 74-79, prof, 57-91, EMER PROF GEOL, UNIV NC, CHAPEL HILL, 91- *Personal Data:* b Mamers, NC, Mar 12, 21; m 44, Jacqueline Sparks; c Keith S & Karen A. *Educ:* Univ NC, BS, 41; Univ Okla, MS, 43; Univ Wis, PhD(geol), 48. *Mem:* Geol Soc Am; Soc Econ Paleont & Mineral; Am Asn Petrol Geol; Int Peat Cong. *Res:* Sedimentation of ancient and modern sediments; marine geology; clay mineralogy; peat resources. *Mailing Add:* 601 Oteys Rd Chapel Hill NC 27514. *E-Mail:* rlingram@email.unc.edu

INGRAM, SAMMY WALKER, JR, ORGANIC CHEMISTRY. *Current Pos:* RETIRED. *Personal Data:* b Easonville, Ala, Nov 17, 33; m 60; c 2. *Educ:* Jacksonville State Col, BS, 55; Univ Tex, PhD(org chem, math), 59. *Prof Exp:* Asst prof chem, Jacksonville State Col, 59-62, assoc prof sci & head, Dept Chem, 62-64; asst prof chem, Univ Ala, 64-65; prof, Troy State Univ, 65; Dept Chem, Livingston Univ. *Mem:* Am Chem Soc. *Res:* Isomerization of the 2-bromo-2-butenes; isomerization of haloalkenes by means of transition element complex ions; adamantine and its compounds; natural products. *Mailing Add:* 126 Woodland Circle Troy AL 36081

INGRAM, VERNON MARTIN, BIOCHEMISTRY. *Current Pos:* assoc vis prof, 58-59, assoc prof, 59-61, PROF BIOCHEM, MASS INST TECHNOL, 61- *Personal Data:* b Breslau, Ger, May 19, 24; m 50; c 2. *Educ:* Univ London, BSc, 43 & 45, PhD, 49, DSc, 61. *Honors & Awards:* William Allen Award, Am Soc Human Genetics, 67. *Prof Exp:* Asst lectr chem, Birkbeck Col, Univ London, 47-50; fel, Rockefeller Inst, 50-51; Coxe fel, Yale Univ, 51-52; mem sci staff, Med Res Coun, Cavendish Lab, Cambridge Univ, 52-58. *Concurrent Pos:* Lectr, Col Physicians & Surgeons, Columbia Univ, 61-73. *Mem:* Am Acad Arts & Sci; Am Chem Soc; Brit Biochem Soc; The Chem Soc; fel Royal Soc. *Res:* Human and animal hemoglobins, their chemistry and the control of their biosynthesis; development of erythropoiesis in embryos; DNA methylation; biochemical mechanisms in Alzheimers disease; molecular basis of mental retardation in Downs syndrome. *Mailing Add:* Dept Biol Rm 56-601 Mass Inst Technol 77 Massachusetts Ave Cambridge MA 02139-4307

INGRAM, WILLIAM THOMAS, CONTINUUM THEORY OF TOPOLOGY. *Current Pos:* PROF MATH & CHMN MATH & STATIST, UNIV MO, ROLLA, 89- *Personal Data:* b McKenzie, Tenn, Nov 26, 37; m 58, Barbara Gordon; c William, Kathie & Mark. *Educ:* Bethel Col, Tenn, BA, 59; La State Univ, MS, 61; Auburn Univ, PhD(math), 64. *Prof Exp:* Instr math, Auburn Univ, 61-63; from instr to prof math, Univ Houston, 64-89. *Mem:* Am Math Soc; Math Asn Am. *Res:* Point set topology, particularly problems concerned with tree-like continua. *Mailing Add:* Dept Math & Statist Univ Mo Rolla MO 65409-0020. *E-Mail:* ingram@umr.edu

INGRATTA, FRANK JERRY, COMMERCIAL MUSHROOM PRODUCTION. *Current Pos:* Exten horticulturist, Ont Ministry Agr & Food, 72-75, res scientist, 75-83, chief res scientist, Hort Res Inst Ont, 83-90, ASST DEP MINISTER, HERICULTURAL DIV, MINISTRY AGR, FOOD & RURAL AFFAIRS, 94- *Personal Data:* b Chatham, Ont, Can, Aug 30, 49. *Educ:* Univ Guelph, BSc, 71, MSc, 74; Univ Toronto, PhD(fungal physiol), 84. *Mem:* Can Soc Hort Sci; Am Soc Hort Sci; Int Soc Hort Sci; Agr Inst Can; Can Mushroom Growers Asn. *Res:* Commercial production technologies for Agaricus bisporus mushrooms and greenhouse vegetable crop production; crop management; energy conservation. *Mailing Add:* 69 Monticello Crescent Guelph ON N1G 4P4 Can

INGRUBER, OTTO VINCENT, chemistry, electrochemistry; deceased, see previous edition for last biography

INGUVA, RAMARAO, CONDENSED MATTER PHYSICS, STATISTICAL MECHANICS. *Current Pos:* from asst prof to assoc prof, 78-92, PROF PHYSICS, UNIV WYO, 92-; NAT RES COUN ASSOC, MICOM REDSTONE ARSENAL, 87- *Personal Data:* b Chinamuttevi, India, Dec 6, 41; m 64; c 1. *Educ:* Osmania Univ, India, BSc, 60, MSc, 62; Univ Colo, PhD(physics), 69. *Prof Exp:* Res assoc theoret physics, Stanford Univ, 69-70; fel, Tata Inst Fundamental Res, Bombay, India, 70-78. *Concurrent Pos:* Consult, McAdams, Roux & O'Connor & Co, Denver, 81; vis scientist, Explor Res Div, Conoco Inc, 85-86. *Mem:* Sigma Xi; NY Acad Sci; Am Phys Soc. *Res:* Ground state properties of quantum fluids; dielectric properties of heterogeneous layered media such as oil shales; microwave heating of oil shales; critical phenomena; information theory and statistical mechanics; nonlinear optics. *Mailing Add:* Dept Physics Univ Wyo PO Box 3905 Laramie WY 82071

INGWALL, JOANNE S, BIOENERGETICS. *Current Pos:* ASSOC PROF PHYSIOL & BIOPHYS, DEPT MED, HARVARD MED SCH & DIR, NMR LAB/BIOCHEMIST, BRIGHAM & WOMEN'S HOSP, 84- *Personal Data:* b Syracuse, NY, Oct 23, 41; m 63. *Educ:* Le Moyne Col, NY, BS, 63; Cornell Univ, PhD(biophys chem), 68. *Honors & Awards:* Louis N Katz Basic Sci Res Award, Am Heart Asn, 72. *Prof Exp:* Nat Heart & Lung Inst trainee, Cardiovasc Res Inst, Univ Calif, San Francisco, 68-69 & 71; fel, Stanford Res Inst, 69-71; clin asst prof physiol, Sch Dent, Univ Pac, 72-73; asst res biochemist cardiol, Univ Calif, San Diego, 73-74, asst prof in residence med cardiol, 74-76; asst prof physiol, Dept Med, Harvard Med Sch & mem assoc staff, Peter Bent Brigham Hosp, 77-83. *Concurrent Pos:* Muscular Dystrophy Asn Am fel, Sch Dent, Univ Pac, 72-73. *Mem:* Biophys Soc; Am Heart Asn; Fedn Am Socs Exp Biol; Am Soc Cell Biol; Soc Magnetic Res Med. *Res:* Muscle biochemistry, especially regulation of cardiac energy metabolism. *Mailing Add:* Brigham & Women's Hosp NMR Lab Rm 209 221 Longwood Ave Boston MA 02115-5817. *Fax:* 617-732-6900

INGWALSON, RAYMOND WESLEY, INDUSTRIAL ORGANIC CHEMISTRY. *Current Pos:* OWNER, PRO CHEM CO, 74-, CONSULT, 77- *Personal Data:* b Rockford, Ill, Mar 13, 12; m 39; c 1. *Educ:* Carthage Col, BA, 35; Univ Fla, MS, 48, PhD(chem), 52. *Prof Exp:* Inspector, Vol Ord Works, 42-43; chemist, Chem Div, W F & Johns Barnes Co, 43-46; res chemist, Tenn Prod & Chem Corp, 52-63; res supvr, Velsicol Chem Corp, 63-74. *Concurrent Pos:* Consult, Velsicol Chem Corp, 75-; vis assoc prof, Fla Technol Univ, 75-76, adj assoc prof, 76-77. *Mem:* Am Chem Soc. *Res:* Photochlorination and oxidation of hydrocarbons; synthesis of biological chemicals and organic intermediates; specialty chemicals-processes: plasticiers, synthetic lubricants, ultraviolet absorbers, esterification, oxidation, chlorination. *Mailing Add:* 686 Barrington Circle Winter Springs FL 32708

INHABER, HERBERT, RISK ANALYSIS, ENVIRONMENTAL QUALITY INDICES. *Current Pos:* PRIN SCIENTIST, WESTINGHOUSE SAVANNAH RIVER CO, AIKEN, SC, 91- *Personal Data:* b Montreal, Que, Can, Jan 25, 41; m 96, Donna Ponce. *Educ:* McGill Univ, BSc, 62; Univ Ill, MS, 64; Univ Okla, PhD(physics & math), 71. *Prof Exp:* Assoc physicist, US Steel Corp, 64-65; sci adv sci policy, Sci Coun Can, 71-72; policy analyst, Can Dept Environ, 72-77; sci adv, Atomic Energy Control Bd, Can, 77-80; sr staff mem, Oak Ridge Nat Lab, 80-84; pres, Risk Concepts Inc, 84-87; pres & chief scientist, Light Fantastic Inc, 86-88; exec scientist, Nus Corp, Gaithersburg, Md, 87-88; exec scientist, Ecol & Environ Corp, Lancaster, NY, 88-91. *Concurrent Pos:* Sessional lectr physics, Carleton Univ, 74-80; vis lectr hist sci, Yale Univ, 75-76; columnist, Oak Ridger, 81-; mem, Comt Technol Safety, Scientists & Engrs for Secure Energy, 83-; consult, Technol Energy Corp, 84 & Tenn Valley Authority & Martin Marietta Energy Systs, 85; bd dirs, Am Nuclear Soc. *Mem:* AAAS; Air Pollution Control Asn; Health Physics Soc; fel Am Nuclear Soc; Soc Risk Anal; Am Soc Testing & Mat. *Res:* Risk analysis of energy systems; measurement and analysis of environmental quality; probabilistic risk analysis in nuclear energy and other fields; determining the bottom line or lines of technological effects on human and environmental well-being. *Mailing Add:* 26 Timberidge Dr North Augusta SC 29841

INHORN, STANLEY L, PATHOLOGY. *Current Pos:* Intern med, Univ Wis, 53-54, resident path, 56-60, from instr to assoc prof, 59-69, asst dir Wis State Lab Hyg, 60-66, dir, 66-79, chmn dept, 78-81, PROF PREV MED & PATH, UNIV WIS-MADISON, 69-, MED DIR, WIS STATE LAB HYG, 79- *Personal Data:* b Philadelphia, Pa, Aug 1, 28; m 54, Shirley Sherburne; c Lowell F, Marcia C & Roger C. *Educ:* Western Reserve Univ, BS, 49; Columbia Univ, MD, 53. *Honors & Awards:* Papanicolaou Award, 81. *Concurrent Pos:* Consult, Vet Admin Hosp, 62-; NIH res grant, 63-66; Children's Bur res grant cytogenetics, 66-81. *Mem:* Am Asn Path; Am Soc Clin Path; Am Soc Cytol; Am Soc Human Genetics; fel Am Pub Health Asn. *Res:* Cancer cytology; clinical laboratory improvement programs. *Mailing Add:* Dept Path State Lab Hyg Univ Wis Sch Clin Ctr 465 Henry Mall Madison WI 53706-1578. *Fax:* 608-262-3257

INIGO, RAFAEL MADRIGAL, NEURAL NETWORKS. *Current Pos:* assoc prof, 79-86, PROF ELEC ENG, UNIV VA, 86- *Personal Data:* b Madrid, Spain, June 18, 32; m 61, Eliana Soto; c Paulina & Alvaro. *Educ:* Valparaiso Tech Univ, Chile, Ing Elec, 57; Univ Va, MS, 65, DSc, 66. *Honors & Awards:* Halliburton Educ Found Award, 78. *Prof Exp:* From asst prof to prof elec eng, Valparaiso Tech Univ, 61-68; from assoc prof to prof elec eng, Va Mil Inst, 68-78. *Concurrent Pos:* Invited prof, Univ Navarra, Spain, 74-75; vis prof, Univ Va, 78-79; Helen Wessel fel. *Mem:* Inst Elec & Electronics Engrs; Sigma Xi. *Res:* Application of machine vision and neural networks to control, guidance and robotics. *Mailing Add:* Dept Elec Eng Univ Va Thornton Hall Charlottesville VA 22901. *Fax:* 804-924-8818; *E-Mail:* rmi@virginia.edu

INKLEY, SCOTT RUSSELL, INTERNAL MEDICINE. *Current Pos:* RETIRED. *Personal Data:* b Cleveland, Ohio, Mar 8, 21; m 43, Josephine Newcomer; c 4. *Educ:* Western Reserve Univ, MD, 45. *Prof Exp:* Instr med, Sch Med, Univ Hosps, Case Western Res Univ, 51-54, sr instr, 54-55, asst prof, 55-66, assoc clin prof, Sch Med & physician, Univ Hosps, 66-71, assoc prof, 71-75, prof med, Sch Med & Physician, chief staff, 78-82, pres & chief exec officer, Univ Hosps, Cleveland, 82-86. *Concurrent Pos:* Physician in chg outpatient dept, Case Western Reserve Univ, 62-; dir pulmonary function lab & dir dept inhalation ther, Univ Hosps Cleveland, 65-77, chief staff, 78-82. pres & chief exec officer, 82-86. *Mem:* Fel Am Col Physicians; fel Am Col Chest Physicians; Cent Soc Clin Invest; Am Fedn Clin Res; Am Thoracic Soc; Sigma Xi. *Res:* Cardio-pulmonary disease. *Mailing Add:* County Line Rd Chagrin Falls OH 44022

INMAN, CHARLES GORDON, ORGANIC & INORGANIC PIGMENT CHEMISTRY. *Current Pos:* RES MGR, PIGMENTS DEPT, CIBA-GEIGY CORP, 79- *Personal Data:* b New York, NY, Apr 12, 29; m 54; c 3. *Educ:* Rensselaer Polytech Inst, BS, 51; Mass Inst Technol, MS, 53. *Prof Exp:* Res chemist, Durez Plastics, Inc, 53-54 & Hooker Chem Corp, 56-57; chemist imp dept, Hercules, Inc, 57-65, res supvr coatings & specialty prod dept, 65-73, asst supt res & develop, Coatings & Specialty Prod Dept, 73-79. *Mem:* Am Chem Soc. *Res:* Azo and chelate pigments. *Mailing Add:* RR 1 Box 1372 Ft Edward NY 12828-9733

INMAN, DANIEL JOHN, MECHANICAL ENGINEERING, VIBRATION ANALYSIS DESIGN. *Current Pos:* SAMUEL HERRICK PROF ENG & SCI MECH, VA TECH INST, 92- *Personal Data:* b Shawano, Wis, May 10, 47; m 82, Catherine Little; c Jennifer W, Angela W & Daniel J. *Educ:* Grand Valley State Univ, BS, 70; Mich State Univ, MA, 75, PhD, 80. *Prof Exp:* Instr physics, Grand Rapids Educ Park, Mich, 70-76; res asst, Mich State Univ, East Lansing, 76-79 & 79-80, instr, 78-79; tech staff, Bell Labs, Whippany, NJ, 78; prof, State Univ NY, 80-92. *Concurrent Pos:* Dir, Mech Systs Lab, Buffalo, 84; presidential young investr, NSF, 84-89; consult, Kistler Instrument Corp, Amherst, NY, 85; adj prof, Brown Univ, Providence, 86; chair, Mech & Aeronaut Dept, State Univ NY, 89-92; distinguished lectr, Am Soc Mech Engrs, 95-97. *Mem:* Fel Am Soc Mech Engrs; assoc fel Am Inst Aeronaut & Astronaut; Inst Elec & Electronics Engrs; Am Acad Mech Soc; Soc Exp Mech; Soc Eng Sci. *Res:* Vibration and acoustics; smart material systems and structures; experimental vibration analysis; actuator development for vibration suppression; damping. *Mailing Add:* Dept Eng Sci & Mech Va Tech Inst Blacksburg VA 24061-0219. *Fax:* 540-231-4574; *E-Mail:* dinman@vt.edu

INMAN, DOUGLAS LAMAR, COASTAL OCEANOGRAPHY, GEOTECHNICAL SCIENCE. *Current Pos:* asst, Univ Calif, 47-48, assoc marine geologist, 58-53, asst prof marine geol, 53-57, assoc prof, 57-65, prof oceanog, 65-80, founding dir, Ctr Coastal Studies, Scripps Inst Oceanog, 80-87, PROF OCEANOG, UNIV CALIF, SAN DIEGO, 87- *Personal Data:* b Guam, Marianas Islands, July 7, 20; US citizen; m 46, 80, Patricia M Masters; c John, Scott & Bryce. *Educ:* San Diego State Col, BA, 42; Univ Calif, MS, 48, PhD(oceanog), 53. *Honors & Awards:* Int Coastal Eng Award, Am Soc Civil Engrs, 88; Ocean Sci Educ Award, Off Naval Res, 89. *Prof Exp:* Asst phys geol, San Diego State Col, 40-42, instr, 64. *Concurrent Pos:* Guggenheim fel, 61; consult coastal oceanog, expert witness & arbitrator. *Mem:* Fel Geol Soc Am; Am Asn Petrol Geologists; Am Geophys Union; AAAS. *Res:* Coastal oceanography; nearshore sediment transport; waves; effect of waves on beaches; beach and nearshore processes. *Mailing Add:* Scripps Inst Oceanog Univ Calif San Diego La Jolla CA 92093. *Fax:* 619-534-0300; *E-Mail:* dinman@ucsd.edu

INMAN, FRED WINSTON, NUCLEAR PHYSICS. *Current Pos:* chmn dept, 67-75, PROF PHYSICS, MANKATO STATE UNIV, 67- *Personal Data:* b Mountain Home, Ark, Mar 30, 31; m 55; c 2. *Educ:* Univ Calif, AB, 53, MA, 55, PhD(physics), 57. *Prof Exp:* Prof physics & chmn dept, Howard Payne Col, 57-63, chmn div sci & math, 63-64; assoc prof physics, Univ Pac, 64-67. *Mailing Add:* 12 Valley View Pl Mankato MN 56001

INMAN, JOHN KEITH, PROTEIN CHEMISTRY, BIOCONJUGATE CHEMISTRY. *Current Pos:* RES BIOCHEMIST, LAB IMMUNOL, NAT INST ALLERGY & INFECTIOUS DIS, 65- *Personal Data:* b St Louis, Mo, May 21, 28; m 54, Jeanne Jaques; c Nancy I (Villadsen), Louise I (Capon) & Keith E. *Educ:* Calif Inst Technol, BS, 50; Harvard Univ, PhD(biochem), 56. *Honors & Awards:* Director's Award, NIH, 78. *Prof Exp:* Res biochemist labs, Mich Dept Health, 56-60, dir, Div Biochem, Ortho Pharmaceut Corp, Div Johnson & Johnson, 60-63; NIH spec fel, Sch Med, Johns Hopkins Univ, 63-65. *Concurrent Pos:* Biotechnol consult. *Mem:* AAAS; Fedn Am Socs Exp Biol; Am Asn Immunol; Am Chem Soc. *Res:* Synthesis of immunomodulators; antibody specificity; immunochemistry; synthesis and design of bioconjugate macromolecules as biological response modifiers for potential therapeutic use in treatment of infectious diseases, allergy, cancer and autoimmune disorders; design of bioconjugating reagents and strategies. *Mailing Add:* Lab Immunol Rm 11N311 Bldg 10 Nat Inst Allergy Infectious Dis Bethesda MD 20892. *Fax:* 301-496-0222; *E-Mail:* jinman@nih.gov

INMAN, ROBERT DAVIES, RHEUMATOLOGY & IMMUNOLOGY. *Current Pos:* assoc prof, 83-89, PROF MED & IMMUNOL, UNIV TORONTO, 89- *Personal Data:* b Toronto, Can, Mar 6, 49; m 71, Straughn Eastman; c Susan, David & Kathryn. *Educ:* Yale Univ, BA, 71; McMaster Univ, MD, 74. *Prof Exp:* Asst prof, Cornell Univ, 79-83. *Concurrent Pos:* Fel, Cornell Univ, 77-79. *Mem:* NY Acad Sci; Am Asn Immunol; Am Col Rheumatology. *Res:* Infection, autoimmunity and immunogenetics; interaction of infection and immunogenetics in arthritis and autoimmunity. *Mailing Add:* Dept Med Rheumat Dis Unit Toronto Western Hosp 399 Bathurst St Toronto ON M5T 2S8 Can

INMAN, ROSS, DNA REPLICATION, ELECTRON MICROSCOPY. *Current Pos:* assoc prof biophys, 67-69, PROF BIOPHYS & BIOCHEM, UNIV WIS-MADISON, 70- *Personal Data:* b Adelaide, Australia, Nov 4, 31; m 57; c 3. *Educ:* Univ Adelaide, BSc, 56, Hons, 57, PhD(molecular biol), 60. *Prof Exp:* Fel molecular biol, Med Sch, Stanford Univ, 60-64; res fel, Univ Adelaide, 64-67. *Concurrent Pos:* NIH grant, 67-; Am Cancer Soc grant, 70-; consult, Australian Govt, 82- *Res:* Structure and function of nucleic acids. *Mailing Add:* Biophys Lab Univ Wis Madison WI 53706

INNANEN, KIMMO A, ASTROPHYSICS. *Current Pos:* from asst prof to assoc prof physics, York Univ, 66-73, actg chmn dept, 84-85, dean pure & appl sci, 86-94, PROF PHYSICS, YORK UNIV, 73- *Personal Data:* b Kirkland Lake, Ont, Mar 12, 37; m 64, Sandra; c Sally, Kristopher & Andrew. *Educ:* Univ Toronto, BASc, 59, PhD(astron), 64; Univ Waterloo, MSc, 60. *Hon Degrees:* PhD, Univ Turku, Finland, 95. *Prof Exp:* Lectr astron, Western Ont Univ, 63-64, asst prof, 64-66. *Concurrent Pos:* Chmn bd, Inst Space & Terrestrial Sci, Innovation York, 87-88. *Mem:* Am Astron Soc; Royal Astron Soc Can; Can Astron Soc. *Res:* Galactic structure; stellar and planetary dynamics. *Mailing Add:* Dept Physics & Astron York Univ North York ON M3J 1R1 Can

INNERARITY, TOM L, LIPOPROTEIN METABOLISM. *Current Pos:* SR SCIENTIST BIOCHEM, GLADSTONE FOUND LAB CARDIOVASC DIS, UNIV CALIF, SAN FRANCISCO, 79- *Personal Data:* b Durant, Okla, Oct 29, 43. *Educ:* Univ Okla, PhD(biochem), 70. *Mailing Add:* Gladstone Inst PO Box 419100 San Francisco CA 94141-9100. *Fax:* 415-285-5632

INNERS, JON DAVID, GEOLOGY. *Current Pos:* geologist, 73-79, ASSOC STATE GEOLOGIST, BUR TOPOG & GEOL SURV, PA DEPT CONSERV & NATURAL RESOURCES, HARRISBURG, 89- *Personal Data:* b York, Pa, July 1, 42; m 68, Martha Hudson; c Rebecca, Brant & Margaret. *Educ:* Susquehanna Univ, AB, 64; Univ Mass, Amherst, PhD(geol), 75. *Prof Exp:* Soils engr, Pa Dept Transp, Dist 6-0, St Davids, Pa, 69-70 & 72-73; geologist soil conserv, USDA, Amherst, 71-72. *Mem:* Soc Indust Archeol. *Res:* Areal geology of the central Appalachians; geotechnical evaluation of bedrock and surficial mapping units; economic geology of anthracite. *Mailing Add:* Bur Topog & Geol Surv Pa Dept Conserv & Natural Resources PO Box 8453 Harrisburg PA 17105. *E-Mail:* inners.jon@a1.denr.state.us

INNES, DAVID LYN, PHYSIOLOGY, GASTROENTEROLOGY. *Current Pos:* dir res, Mercer Univ, 80-82, dir, Off Protection Res Risks & asst provost, Med Affairs, 85-93, PROF PHYSIOL, SCH MED, MERCER UNIV, 80-, ASST VPRES HEALTH & BIOSAFETY, 93- *Personal Data:* b Cleveland, Ohio, Dec 19, 41; m 64, Janet L Koons; c 2. *Educ:* Ohio Wesleyan Univ, BA, 64; Univ Cincinnati, MS, 66; Ohio State Univ, PhD(physiol), 69. *Prof Exp:* Instr physiol, Ohio State Univ, 69-70; from asst prof to assoc prof physiol, Temple Univ, 70-80. *Concurrent Pos:* Adj prof, Univ Col, Mercer Univ. *Mem:* AAAS; Am Soc Zool; Sigma Xi; Am Physiol Soc; Am Gastroenterol Asn; Am Asn Lab Animal Sci. *Res:* Gastrointestinal and neural endocrinology; nuclei within the brain controlling gastrointestinal and/or metabolic-endocrine functions of the body and their mechanisms of action; mechanisms of gastric stress ulceration. *Mailing Add:* Sch Med Mercer Univ 1550 College St Macon GA 31207-0001. *Fax:* 912-752-2547

INNES, IAN ROME, PHARMACOLOGY. *Current Pos:* RETIRED. *Personal Data:* b Portgordon, Scotland, July 14, 16; m 40, 82; c 3. *Educ:* Aberdeen Univ, MB, ChB, 37, MD, 55. *Prof Exp:* Lectr physiol, Aberdeen Univ, 48-58; from asst prof to assoc prof pharmacol, Univ Man, 58-64, head dept pharmacol & therapeut, 67-82, prof, Fac Med, 64-87. *Concurrent Pos:* Res assoc, Harvard Med Sch, 57; Can Heart Found res fel, 60; chmn, Man Drug Stand & Therapeut Comt, 72-88. *Mem:* Am Soc Pharmacol & Exp Therapeut; Pharmacol Soc Can; Brit Pharmacol Soc; Brit Physiol Soc. *Res:* Cardiovascular and autonomic physiology and pharmacology; therapy of cardiomyopathy and myocardial infarction. *Mailing Add:* 704 Oak St Winnipeg MB R3M 3R7 Can

INNES, JOHN EDWIN, INDUSTRIAL ORGANIC CHEMISTRY. *Current Pos:* CYTEC IND 93- *Personal Data:* b Philadelphia, Pa, Apr 3, 38; m 60; c 2. *Educ:* Ursinus Col, BS, 60; Univ Del, PhD(org chem), 64; Ohio Univ, MBA, 85. *Prof Exp:* Chemist, Am Cyanamid Co, 64-72, group leader org chem, 72-76, prod supt, 76-77, tech dir, Marietta Plant, 77-88, plant mgr, 88-92. *Mem:* Am Chem Soc; Sigma Xi. *Mailing Add:* 3525 Popla Neck Rd Pittsville MD 21850

INNES, KENNETH KEITH, CHEMICAL PHYSICS, MOLECULAR PHYSICS. *Current Pos:* prof chem, 69-79, actg vpres, Acad Affairs, 74-75, DISTINGUISHED PROF, STATE UNIV NY BINGHAMTON, 79- *Personal Data:* b Fayette, Mo, June 6, 28; m 52; c 2. *Educ:* Cent Col, Mo, AB, 47; Brown Univ, MS, 49; Univ Wash, Seattle, PhD(phys chem), 51. *Prof Exp:* Nat Res Coun Can fel, 51-53; asst prof chem, Univ Okla, 53-55; assoc prof, Vanderbilt Univ, 55-62, prof, 62-69. *Concurrent Pos:* Guggenheim fel, 61-62; mem adv panel chem, NSF, 65-69, sr fel, 67-68; mem petrol res fund adv bd, Am Chem Soc, 73-75; vis prof, Univ Toronto, 75-76. *Mem:* Am Chem Soc; fel Am Phys Soc. *Res:* Molecular spectroscopy and structure. *Mailing Add:* 304 Robin Lane Vestal NY 13850

INNES, WALTER RUNDLE, PARTICLE PHYSICS. *Current Pos:* MEM STAFF, STANFORD LINEAR ACCELERATOR CTR, 79- *Personal Data:* b Stamford, Conn, Dec 29, 45; m 66; c 2. *Educ:* Calif Inst Technol, BS, 67; Univ Calif, San Diego, MS, 69, PhD(physics), 74. *Prof Exp:* Res assoc particle physics, Fermi Nat Accelerator Lab, 74-78. *Mem:* Am Phys Soc. *Res:* Hyperon beta decay; dihadron, dilepton, and upsilon production; electron positron colliding beam physics; search for fractional charge states; studies of Z bosons; CP violation in B meson decay. *Mailing Add:* MS 61 Stanford Linear Accelerator Ctr PO Box 4349 Stanford CA 94305

INNES, WILLIAM BEVERIDGE, CATALYSIS, OXIDES OF NITROGEN. *Current Pos:* PRES, PURAD INC, 64- *Personal Data:* b Cambria, Calif, Mar 8, 13; m 38, Dorothy Rundle; c 4. *Educ:* Univ Calif, BS, 37; Univ Iowa, MS, 39, PhD(phys chem), 41. *Prof Exp:* Asst, Univ Iowa, 39-41; res chemist, Champion Paper & Fibre Co, Ohio, 41-43 & Am Cyanamid Co, 43-44; res scientist, SAM Labs, Columbia, 44-45; sr chemist, Am Cyanamid Co, 45-55, group leader, 55-58, res assoc, 58-64. *Mem:* Air Pollution Control Asn; Am Chem Soc. *Res:* Surface phenomena; adsorption and pore structure; catalysis, vehicle exhaust treatment; thermocatalytic detectors, instrumentation; oxides of nitrogen, photochemical smog; stratospheric ozone depletion; economics of air pollution regulations. *Mailing Add:* Purad Inc 724 Kilbourne Dr Upland CA 91784. *E-Mail:* 74020.2171@compuserve.com, noxnox@aol.com

INNIS, GEORGE SETH, MATHEMATICS, SYSTEMS ANALYSIS. *Current Pos:* CONSULT, 90-; MGR DEVELOP, IQ CORP, 91- *Personal Data:* b Victoria, Tex, Jan 7, 37; m 58; c 2. *Educ:* Univ Tex, BA, 58, MA, 61, PhD(math), 62. *Prof Exp:* Res asst physics & math, Defense Res Lab, Univ Tex, 57-58, res scientist, 58-60 & 62, asst univ, 58-59, spec instr, 60-62; Nat Acad Sci-Nat Res Coun fel, Harvard Univ, 62-63; asst prof math, Rice Univ, 63-64; asst prof math, Univ Tex, 64-67, res scientist physics & math, Defense Res Lab, 64-67; staff mem, Los Alamos Sci Lab, 67-68; assoc prof math & dir comput serv, Tex Tech Univ, 68-71; assoc prof math & dir systs anal, Nat Resource Ecol Lab, Colo State Univ, 71-73; assoc prof, Utah State Univ, 73-76, prof fisheries & wildlife & adj prof math, 76-86, dept head, 80-86. *Concurrent Pos:* Res mathematician, Tracor Corp, 60-61; consult, Antioch Col, 70-72, NSF, Washington, 70- & W F Sigler & Assocs, Logan, Utah, 74- *Mem:* AAAS; Wildlife Soc; Sigma Xi; Ecol Soc Am; Soc Comput Simulation. *Res:* Complex variables; signal processing; acoustics; applications of quantitative techniques to ecological problems including the development of simulation languages and mathematical theories addressed to specific needs. *Mailing Add:* Develop IQ Software Corp 400 N Loop 1604W San Antonio TX 78232

INNISS, DARYL, REACTION MECHANISM, SURFACE ANALYSIS. *Current Pos:* MEM TECH STAFF, AT&T BELL LABS, 88- *Personal Data:* b St Thomas, VI, June 15, 61; US citizen; m 83; c 2. *Educ:* Princeton Univ, AB, 83; Univ Calif, Los Angeles, PhD(chem), 88. *Mem:* Am Ceramic Soc; Nat Orgn Prof Advan Black Chemists & Chem Engrs. *Res:* Chemical reaction theory is applied to the fracture of silica fibers; the contribution of the chemical environment to the failure mechanism is explored. *Mailing Add:* Lucent Tech Bell Labs Rm 1A-122 600 Mountain Ave Murray Hill NJ 07974

INNISS, WILLIAM EDGAR, MICROBIOLOGY. *Current Pos:* from asst prof to assoc prof, 63-80, PROF BIOL, UNIV WATERLOO, 80-, ASSOC DEPT CHMN, 89- *Personal Data:* b Toronto, Ont, Feb 25, 36; m 58, Sheila Stewart; c Catherine & Michael. *Educ:* Univ Toronto, BSA, 58, MSA, 59; Mich State Univ, PhD(microbiol), 61. *Prof Exp:* Microbiologist, Biochem Res Lab, Dow Chem Co, Mich, 61-63. *Concurrent Pos:* Vis prof, Univ Calif, Davis, 73. *Mem:* Am Soc Microbiol; Can Soc Microbiol. *Res:* Microbial physiology; environmental and physiological activities of psychrotrophic and psychrophilic microorganisms; microbial activity in cold environments; effect of toxicants on microorganisms; macromolecular synthesis and metabolism. *Mailing Add:* Dept Biol Univ Waterloo Waterloo ON N2L 3G1 Can. *Fax:* 519-746-0614; *E-Mail:* weinniss@sciborg.uwaterloo

INOKUTI, MITIO, RADIATION PHYSICS. *Current Pos:* resident res assoc, Agronne Nat Lab, 63-65, physicist, 65-73, sr physicist, environ res div, 73-95, GUEST SCIENTIST, PHYSICS DIV, AGRONNE NAT LAB, 95- *Personal Data:* b Tokyo, Japan, July 6, 33; m 60, Makiko Omori; c Mika I (Cusick). *Educ:* Univ Tokyo, BS, 56, MS, 58, PhD(appl physics), 62. *Prof Exp:* Instr math physics, Univ Tokyo, 60-62; res assoc, Dept Chem & Mat Res Ctr, Northwestern Univ, 62-63. *Concurrent Pos:* Vis fel, Joint Inst Lab Astrophys, Univ Colo, 69-70; mem comt average energy required produce & ion pair, Int Comn Radiation Units & Measurements, 73-79, vchmn comt stopping power, 76-; mem gen comt, Int Conf Physics Electronics & Atomic Collisions, 73-77, adj officer exec comt, 77-79; assoc ed, Radiation Res, 76-79; vis prof, Inst Space & Aeronaut Sci, Univ Tokyo, Japan, 78-79, Odense Univ, Denmark, Tokyo Inst Technol, Japan, 89, GSF Res Ctr, Neuherber, Ger, 96 & Nara Women's Univ, 96; counr, Radiation Res Soc, 78-81; corresp, Comments Atomic & Molecular Physics, 82-; mem, Int Comn Radiation Units & Measurements, 85- *Mem:* Fel Am Phys Soc; Radiation Res Soc; fel Brit Inst Physics; Phys Soc Japan; Int Radiation Physics Soc; Sigma Xi. *Res:* Theoretical problems concerning action of ionizing radiations on molecular substances, especially primary elementary processes. *Mailing Add:* Argonne Nat Lab 9700 S Cass Ave Argonne IL 60439. *Fax:* 630-252-3903; *E-Mail:* inokuti@anl.gov

INOMATA, AKIRA, THEORETICAL PHYSICS. *Current Pos:* from asst prof to assoc prof, 67-84, PROF PHYSICS, STATE UNIV NY ALBANY, 84- *Personal Data:* b Tochigi, Japan, May 13, 31; m 58; c 2. *Educ:* Kyushu Univ, BS, 56, MS, 58; Rensselaer Polytech Inst, PhD(physics), 64. *Prof Exp:* Res physicist, Benet Res Labs, 64-67. *Concurrent Pos:* Vis lectr, State Univ NY, 66-67; adj assoc prof, Rensselaer Polytech Inst, 78; vis prof, Univ Munich, 81. *Mem:* Am Phys Soc; Phys Soc Japan. *Res:* Neutrinos in general relativity; geometric models for hadrons; de Sittar and conformal symmetries; gauge theory; path integrals; strong-gravity; monopoles. *Mailing Add:* Dept Physics State Univ NY 1400 Washington Ave Albany NY 12222

INOSE, HIROSHI, DIGITAL COMMUNICATIONS SYSTEMS, ROAD TRAFFIC CONTROL SYSTEMS. *Current Pos:* DIR GEN, NAT CTR SCI INFO SYSTS, 87- *Personal Data:* b Tokyo, Japan, Jan 5, 27; m 60, Mariko Tsuchiya. *Educ:* Univ Tokyo, BEng, 48, PhD(elec eng), 55. *Honors & Awards:* Int Commun Award in Hon of Hernand & Susthenes Behn, Inst Elec & Electronics Engrs, 82, Alexander Graham Bell Medal, 94; Person of Cult Merit, Japanese Govt, 85, Order of Cult, 91. *Prof Exp:* Engr, Toshiba Corp, 54-55; assoc, Univ Pa, 56-58; from assoc prof to prof elec eng, Univ Tokyo, 56-86, dir, Comput Ctr, 77-81, dean eng, 86-87. *Concurrent Pos:* Consult, Bell Tel Labs, 57; vis prof, Univ Mich, 69, Rheinische-Westfalische Tech Sch, 74; vpres int affairs, Inst Elec & Electronics Engrs Commun Soc, 80-81; Sherman Fairchild distinguished scholar, Calif Inst Technol, 82; chmn, Comt Sci & Technol Policy, Orgn Econ Coop & Develop, 83-87, Comt Info Comput & Commun Policy, 87-90; chmn, Indust Technol Coun, 90-; mem, Radio Wave Regulatory Coun, 90-, Nat Sci Coun, 92- *Mem:* Foreign assoc Nat Acad Sci; foreign assoc Nat Acad Eng; foreign mem Royal Acad Eng UK; foreign mem Royal Swed Acad Eng Sci; fel Inst Elec & Electronics Engrs; foreign mem Am Philos Soc. *Res:* Digital communications and time slot interchange for digital telephone switching, a key technology for integrated service digital networks; road traffic control. *Mailing Add:* 39-9 Jingumae 5-chome Shibuya-Ku Tokyo 150 Japan. *Fax:* 81-3-3942-0285

INOUE, MICHAEL SHIGERU, INDUSTRIAL ENGINEERING. *Current Pos:* asst to the pres, Kyocera Northwest, Inc, 82-83, mgr consumer prod, 83-84, mgr corp planning & admin, 84, vpres admin & secy, 84-87, VPRES TECHNOL & PLANNING, KYOCERA INT, INC, 87- *Personal Data:* b Tokyo, Japan, June 27, 36; m 65, Mary L Shuhart; c Stephen, Rosanne, Marcus, Joanne & Suzanne. *Educ:* Univ Dayton, BS, 59; Ore State Univ, MS, 64, PhD(indust eng), 67. *Prof Exp:* Res engr, appl res lab, Black & Decker Mfg Co, 61-62, sr res engr, 62-64; teaching asst physics, indust eng & elec eng, 64-65, from instr to prof indust eng, Ore State Univ, 64-82; pres, Productive Resources, Inc, 77-82. *Concurrent Pos:* Prin investr res proj, Nat Marine Fisheries Serv, 68-70, Educ Coord Coun, 70-71 & Sea-Grant Activities, 71-75; consult, minicomput mgt syst, 73-82, microprocessor-based syst design, 79, educ consult, qual circle implementation, 80-, Forest Prod Exportation, 81-; vis prof, Kyoto Univ, Japan, 74, Monterrey Inst Technol, Mexico, 76, Latvia Grad Inst, USSR, 79, Costa Rica Inst Technol, 82; invited speaker, Ore Productivity Conf, 85. *Mem:* Inst Indust Engrs; Sigma Xi; Am Ceramic Soc; World Decision Inst. *Res:* Systems analysis; systems design and systems science; computer sciences; operations research; management science; data processing; computer simulation languages and models; organizational productivity and technology; sea-food harvesting and processing techniques; corporate planning and decision processes. *Mailing Add:* 5154 Via Playa Los Santos San Diego CA 92124-1555

INOUE, SHINYA, CELL BIOLOGY, MICROSCOPY. *Current Pos:* sr scientist, 80-86, DISTINGUISHED SCIENTIST, MARINE BIOL LAB, WOODS HOLE, 86-, INSTR, 87- *Personal Data:* b London, Eng, Jan 5, 21; US citizen; m 52, Sylvia McCandless; c 5. *Educ:* Tokyo Imp Univ, Rigakushi, 44; Princeton Univ, MA, 50, PhD(biol), 51. *Hon Degrees:* MA, Dartmouth Col, 62. *Honors & Awards:* Brown-Hazen Award for Outstanding Contrib to Basic Life Sci, 88; E B Wilson Award, Am Soc Cell Biol, 92; Distinguished Scientist Award, Micros Soc Am, 95. *Prof Exp:* Instr micros & submicros anat, Dept Anat, Sch Med, Univ Wash, Seattle, 51-53; asst prof biol, Tokyo Metrop Univ, 53-54; from res assoc to assoc prof, Dept Biol, Univ Rochester, 54-59; prof cytol & chmn dept, Dartmouth Med Sch, 59-66, John Laporte Given prof, 65-66; prof biol & dir, Prog Biophys Cytol, Univ Pa, 66-82, grad group chmn, 77-79. *Concurrent Pos:* Consult, Am Optical Co, 54-60, Hamamatsu Photonics Kabushki Kaisha, 88-, Nikon Corp, Tokyo, 94-; scholar in cancer res, Am Cancer Soc, 55-58; chmn, Dept Anat, Dartmouth Med Sch, 59-63; instr, Woods Hole Marine Biol Labs, 62-65, mem bd trustees, 73-79 & 81-84; corp mem, Marine Biol Lab, 62-, trustee, 70-77, 81-85, 92-; John Simon Guggenheim fel, 71-72; adj prof, Univ Pa, 82-89; pres, Universal Imaging Corp, 84-87, bd mem, 87- *Mem:* Nat Acad Sci; Soc Gen Physiologists (pres, 69-70); fel Am Acad Arts & Sci; Am Soc Cell Biol; Biophys Soc; hon fel Royal Micros Soc; fel AAAS; Micros Soc Am; Sigma Xi; Optical Soc Am. *Res:* Mechanisms of mitosis, cell division and their contols; molecular and structural organization of cytoplasm and nucleoplasm in living cells; development of new biophysical approaches and instruments for fine structure analysis directly in living cells; physical optics; video microscopy. *Mailing Add:* Marine Biol Lab Woods Hole MA 02543

INOUYE, DAVID WILLIAM, ECOLOGY. *Current Pos:* asst prof, 76-81, ASSOC PROF ZOOL, UNIV MD, 81- *Personal Data:* b Philadelphia, Pa, Jan 7, 50; m 69, Bonnie A Gregory; c Brian & Kevin. *Educ:* Swarthmore Col, BA, 71; Univ NC, Chapel Hill, PhD(zool), 76. *Concurrent Pos:* NATO fel ecol, Bot Inst, Univ Wien, 77-78; mem bd trustees, Rocky Mt Biol Lab, 78-95; dir, Univ Colo Mountain Res Sta, 88-90. *Mem:* AAAS; Soc Study Evolution; Animal Behav Soc; Sigma Xi; Ecol Soc Am; Bot Soc Am. *Res:* Plant-animal interactions; pollination ecology; plant-ant mutualisms; plant population biology. *Mailing Add:* Dept Zool Univ Md College Park MD 20742. *Fax:* 301-314-9358; *E-Mail:* di5@umail.umd.edu

INOUYE, MASAYORI, MEMBRANE BIOCHEMISTRY. *Current Pos:* PROF BIOCHEM & CHMN DEPT, UNIV MED & DENT NJ, 87- *Educ:* Osaka Univ, Japan, PhD(biochem), 63. *Prof Exp:* Prof biochem & chmn dept, State Univ NY, Stony Brook, 81-87. *Res:* Regulation of gene expression. *Mailing Add:* Dept Biochem Univ Med & Dent NJ Robert Wood Johnson Med Sch 675 Hoes La Piscataway NJ 08854-5635. *Fax:* 732-235-4783

INSALATA, NINO F, MICROBIOLOGY, BACTERIOLOGY. *Current Pos:* assoc bacteriologist, Gen Foods Res Ctr, 53-60, sr microbiologist, 60-67, sect head, Post Div, 67-73, lab mgr, 71-73, res assoc, Res Ctr, 73-75, AREA MGR MICROBIOL, CENT RES, GEN FOODS CORP, 75- *Personal Data:* b Brooklyn, NY, Aug 6, 26; m 49; c 1. *Educ:* St John's Univ, BSc, 48, MSc, 50. *Honors & Awards:* Res Achievement Award, Gen Foods Res Comt, 73. *Prof Exp:* Chem bacteriologist, Nat Distillers Prod Corp, 49-53. *Concurrent Pos:* Mem subcomt sampling & methodology, USPHS, 64-75; assoc referee standardization microbiol test methods, Asn Off Anal Chemists, 64-75; prin investr, USPHS Contract, 66-67; US Food & Drug Admin res contract, 69-71; mem comn, Microbiol of Foods, Nat Acad Sci, Nat Res Coun; assoc referee, Am Asn Cereal Chemists & Am Off Anal Chemists; mem, Food Hyg Comn, Codex Alimentarius; mem subcomt microbiol standards for foods, Am Pub Health Asn; mem USDA salmonella comn, Am Asn Vet Lab Diagnosticians; consult, US Food & Drug Admin, USDA, Communicable Dis Ctr, USPHS, Am Pub Health Asn, Nat Fisheries Inst, Nat Food Protection Comt & pharmaceut & cosmetics industs; mem, Nat Referral Ctr, Libr Cong; co-chmn, Interagency Comn Compendium Microbiological Methods for Foods, Am Pub Health Asn, 71-75; mem subcomt, Microbiol Food Protection, Am Pub Health Asn, 74-75; tech advr, US Food & Drug Admin, Int Standards Orgn, Berlin, 80 & Paris, 81. *Mem:* Am Soc Microbiol; Soc Indust Microbiol; NY Acad Sci; Inst Food Technol; Int Asn Milk, Food & Environ Sanitarians. *Res:* Development of rapid microbiological test methods; incidence and survival studies with C1 Botulinum; methodology of recovery of Salmonellae, Staphylococci, Streptococci and fecal enterocci and development of fluorescent-antibody methods; environmental health aspects of industrial bioengineering and good manufacturing practices. *Mailing Add:* 4 Sleator Dr Ossining NY 10562

INSCOE, MAY NILSON, INSECT PHEROMONES. *Current Pos:* RETIRED. *Personal Data:* b Geneva, Ill, May 16, 25; m 54, Joseph K; c 4. *Educ:* Wheaton Col, Ill, BS; Northwestern Univ, MS, 48, PhD(org chem), 51. *Prof Exp:* Teacher chem & physics, Tarsus Koleji, Turkey, 49-50; instr phys chem, Wellesley Col, 51-52; asst prof chem, Am Col Girls, Turkey, 52-54; chemist, Nat Bur Stand, Washington, DC, 54-66 & Beltsville Agr Res Ctr, Agr Res Serv, USDA, 66-95. *Mem:* Am Chem Soc; Entom Soc Am. *Mailing Add:* 10007 Thornwood Rd Kensington MD 20895-4228

INSEL, ARNOLD J, ANALYSIS & FUNCTIONAL ANALYSIS, OTHER MATHEMATICS. *Current Pos:* From asst prof to assoc prof, 69-87, PROF MATH, ILL STATE UNIV, 87- *Personal Data:* b Danbury, Conn, Jan 30, 40; m 69, Barbara Blais; c Thomas & Sara. *Educ:* Univ Fla, BA, 60, MA, 62; Univ Calif, Berkeley, PhD(math), 69. *Mem:* Am Math Soc; Math Asn Am. *Res:* Harmonic analysis; topological groups; linear algebra. *Mailing Add:* Dept Math Ill State Univ Normal IL 61790-4520. *Fax:* 309-438-5866; *E-Mail:* insel@math.ilstu.edu

INSEL, PAUL ANTHONY, RECEPTOR BIOLOGY & PHARMACOLOGY. *Current Pos:* from asst prof to assoc prof med, 78-87, PROF PHARMACOL & MED, UNIV CALIF, SAN DIEGO, 87- *Personal Data:* b New York, NY, Nov 22, 45; m 77; c 2. *Educ:* Univ Mich, MD, 68. *Prof Exp:* Intern, Harvard Unit, Boston City Hosp, 68-70; clin assoc med officer, Nat Inst Child Health & Human Develop Geront Res Ctr, NIH, 70-74; res fel, Cardiovasc Res Inst, Univ Calif, San Francisco, 74-77, asst prof med, 77-78. *Concurrent Pos:* Asst med, Johns Hopkins Univ, 71-74; assoc, Cardiovasc Res Inst, Univ Calif, San Francisco, 77-78; estab investr, Am Heart Asn, 77-82; master res, Inserm, France, 81, 86; mem US-France coop cancer res, NIH, 81; mem, Pharmacol Study Sect, NIH, 82-86. *Mem:* Am Soc Clin Invest; Am Soc Biol Chemists; Am Soc Pharmacol & Exp Therapeut; Am Soc Cell Biol; Endocrine Soc; Coun High Blood Pressure Res. *Res:* Mechanisms of action of adrenergic receptors and regulation of those receptors by target cells; cardiovascular disorders. *Mailing Add:* Dept Pharmacol & Med 0636 Univ Calif San Diego La Jolla CA 92093

INSELBERG, ALFRED, applied math, multi-dimensional multivariate visualization, for more information see previous edition

INSELBERG, EDGAR, DEVELOPMENT PHOTOSYNTHESIS. *Current Pos:* ASSOC PROF BIOL, WESTERN MICH UNIV, 66- *Personal Data:* b Athens, Greece, June 15, 30; nat US; m 56, Rachel Marzan; c 1. *Educ:* Cornell Univ, BS, 53; Univ Ill, MS, 54, PhD, 56. *Prof Exp:* Res asst, Univ Ill, 53-56; dir res, Na-Churs Plant Food Co, Ohio, 56-61; res assoc photosynthesis, Univ Pittsburgh, 61-63, fel, Space Prog, 63-65; res scientist, Volcani Inst, Israel, 65-66. *Concurrent Pos:* Consult, 61- *Mem:* Am Soc Agron; Am Soc Plant Physiol; Am Soc Photobiol. *Res:* Earshot development in corn; methodology and statistics of radioassay; photosynthesis: flash spectroscopy of algae; flash spectroscopy of algae. *Mailing Add:* Dept Biol Sci Western Mich Univ Kalamazoo MI 49008-5050. *E-Mail:* ed.inselberg@wmich.edu

INSKEEP, EMMETT KEITH, REPRODUCTIVE PHYSIOLOGY, ENDOCRINOLOGY. *Current Pos:* From asst prof to assoc prof, 64-73, PROF ANIMAL PHYSIOL, WVA UNIV, 73- *Personal Data:* b Petersburg, WVa, Jan 11, 38; m 60, Ansusan Presby; c Todd K & Thomas C. *Educ:* WVa Univ, BS, 59; Univ Wis, MS, 60, PhD(endocrinol), 64. *Honors & Awards:* Nat Asn Animal Breeders Res Award, 81; Am Soc Animal Sci Physiol & Endocrinol Award, 87. *Concurrent Pos:* Sect ed, Am Soc Animal Sci J, 72-74. *Mem:* Am Soc Animal Sci; Endocrine Soc; Soc Study Reproduction (pres, 92-93); Brit Soc Study Fertil. *Res:* Control of ovulation in mammals; prostaglandins in uterine and ovarian tissues in relation to luteal function and life span; follicular maturation and ovulation in ruminants. *Mailing Add:* Div Animal & Vet Sci WVa Univ Morgantown WV 26506-6108. *Fax:* 304-293-2232; *E-Mail:* einskeep@wvu.edu

INSKEEP, GEORGE ESLER, CHEMISTRY. *Current Pos:* RETIRED. *Personal Data:* b Wilmington, Del, Dec 25, 18; m 55, Kathryn Hadley. *Educ:* Pa State Col, BS, 40; Univ Ill, MS, 41, PhD(org chem), 43. *Prof Exp:* Asst chem, Univ Ill, 41-43, spec asst, US Off Rubber Res contract, 43-45; res chemist, Firestone Plastics Co, 45-50 & E I du Pont de Nemours & Co, 50-61; res chemist, Philip Morris, Inc, 61-66, asst patent off, 66-84. *Mem:* Am Chem Soc; Sci Res Soc Am. *Res:* High polymer chemistry; plastics characterization; smoke chemistry. *Mailing Add:* Rte 1 Box 2460 Kilmarnock VA 22482

INSKEEP, RICHARD GUY, PHYSICAL CHEMISTRY. *Current Pos:* assoc prof, Univ Hawaii, 61-65, chmn dept, 62-71, prof, 65-85, EMER PROF CHEM, UNIV HAWAII, 85- *Personal Data:* b East Liberty, Ohio, Mar 11, 23; m 51. *Educ:* Miami Univ, Ohio, AB, 44; Univ Ill, MS, 47, PhD(phys chem), 49. *Prof Exp:* Res engr, Dept Fuels, Battelle Mem Inst, 45-46; asst phys chem, Univ Ill, 46-48; fel chem, Univ Minn, 49-51; instr, Brown Univ, 51-53; from asst prof to assoc prof, Univ Vt, 53-61. *Concurrent Pos:* NSF sci fac fel, Tech Univ Denmark, 58-59; vis prof, Univ BC, 74-75; vis scholar, Stanford Univ, 82-83. *Mem:* Am Chem Soc. *Res:* Molecular spectroscopy; complex ions; resonance Raman spectroscopy. *Mailing Add:* 2545 The Mall Univ Hawaii Honolulu HI 96822-1888

INSKIP, ERVIN BASIL, PROCESS CHEMISTRY, ANALYTICAL CHEMISTRY. *Current Pos:* Chemist analytical chem, Mallinckrodt Inc, 63-65, sr chemist, 65-70, supvr tantalum process technol, 70-74, group leader, res & develop process chem, 74-77, MGR RES & DEVELOP, PROD DEVELOP, MALLINCKRODT INC, 77- *Personal Data:* b Nebo, Ill, Oct 27, 41; m 65; c 2. *Educ:* Southern Ill Univ, BS, 63. *Mem:* Chem Soc. *Res:* Analytical chemistry in chemical process control; niobium and tantalum benefication, iodine chemistry, iodine in disinfection of water; derivatives of p-aminophenol-manufacturing methods and applications; monomer stabilization. *Mailing Add:* 213 W Second St Trenton IL 62293

INSKIP, HAROLD KIRKWOOD, ORGANIC CHEMISTRY. *Current Pos:* from res chemist to res supvr, 52-61, staff scientist, 61-66, RES ASSOC, ELECTROCHEM DEPT, E I DU PONT DE NEMOURS & CO, 66- *Personal Data:* b Buffalo, NY, Nov 7, 22; m 49; c 3. *Educ:* Yale Univ, BS, 44, MS, 48, PhD(org chem), 52. *Prof Exp:* Asst & instr org chem, Univ Ill, 50-52. *Mem:* Am Chem Soc. *Res:* Vinyl polymerization. *Mailing Add:* 38 Bridle Brook Lane Newark DE 19711-2061

INSLEY, ROBERT H(ITESHEW), CERAMICS. *Current Pos:* RETIRED. *Personal Data:* b Washington, DC, June 20, 23; m 47, Betty Hughes; c 3. *Educ:* Hamilton Col, BA, 49; Pa State Col, MS, 52. *Honors & Awards:* Ross Coffin Purdy Award, Am Ceramic Soc, 66; Award of Merit, Am Soc Testing & Mat, 83. *Prof Exp:* Asst mineral, Pa State Col, 49-52; petrographer, Ceramic Div, Champion Spark Plug Co, 52-58, sr res engr, 58-68, mgr ceramic res, 68-73, asst dir res & eng, 73-75, dir res & develop 75-87. *Mem:* Fel Am Ceramic Soc; Am Soc Mineralogists; Sigma Xi; fel Am Ceramic Soc; fel Am Soc Testing & Mat. *Res:* Petrography of ceramic raw materials and finished products; high temperature investigations of oxides; semiconductors; glass to metal seals. *Mailing Add:* 4 Robbers Row Hilton Head Island SC 29928. *E-Mail:* insleybob@aol.com

INTAGLIETTA, MARCOS, BIOENGINEERING. *Current Pos:* from asst prof to assoc prof bioeng, 66-76, PROF BIOENG, UNIV CALIF, SAN DIEGO, 76- *Personal Data:* b Buenos Aires, Arg, Aug 10, 35. *Educ:* Univ Calif, Berkeley, BS, 57; Calif Inst Technol, MS, 58, PhD(appl mech), 63. *Prof Exp:* Estab investr, Los Angeles County Heart Asn, Calif Inst Technol, 64-66. *Concurrent Pos:* Dir, Int Inst Microcirculation; Hoffman La-Roche Int fel. *Mem:* Microcirculatory Soc (pres, 85-86); Am Physiol Soc; Soc Biorheology. *Res:* Transport phenomena; instrumentation at the microscopic level; microcirculatory physiology. *Mailing Add:* AMES Bioeng Dept Univ Calif San Diego 9500 Gilman Dr La Jolla CA 92093

INTEMANN, GERALD WILLIAM, PARTICLE PHYSICS. *Current Pos:* head dept, 80-90, PROF PHYSICS, UNIV NORTHERN IOWA, 80-, DEAN, COL NATURAL SCI, 90- *Personal Data:* b North Bergen, NJ, Jan 12, 43; c 3. *Educ:* Stevens Inst Technol, BS, 64, MS, 66, PhD(particle physics), 68. *Prof Exp:* Asst prof physics, State Univ NY, Binghamton, 68-72; from asst prof to assoc prof physics, Seton Hall Univ, 72-80. *Concurrent Pos:* Vis physicist, Argonne Nat Lab, 83. *Mem:* Am Phys Soc; Am Asn Physics Teachers; Sigma Xi; AAAS. *Res:* Theoretical investigation of multi-quark states; phenomenological studies of strong and electromagnetic decays of hadrons which are bound states of heavy quarks. *Mailing Add:* Dept Physics Univ Northern Iowa Cedar Falls IA 50614. *Fax:* 319-273-2993; *E-Mail:* intemann@uni.edu

INTEMANN, ROBERT LOUIS, THEORETICAL PHYSICS. *Current Pos:* From asst prof to assoc prof physics, Temple Univ, 64-84, asst dean, Col Lib Arts, 71-81, chmn dept, 85-90, PROF PHYSICS, TEMPLE UNIV, 84- *Personal Data:* b North Bergen, NJ, Feb 23, 38; m 64, Peter; c 1. *Educ:* Stevens Inst Technol, BE, 59, MS, 61, PhD(physics), 64. *Mem:* AAAS; Am Phys Soc; Am Asn Physics Teachers; Sigma Xi. *Res:* Theoretical atomic physics; inner shell processes in atoms; atomic collisions; radiation theory. *Mailing Add:* Dept Physics Temple Univ Philadelphia PA 19122

INTERRANTE, LEONARD V, INORGANIC CHEMISTRY, MATERIALS CHEMISTRY. *Current Pos:* at DEPT CHEM, RENSSELAER POLYTECH INST, 85- *Personal Data:* b Brooklyn, NY, Apr 6, 39; m 59; c 2. *Educ:* Univ Calif, Riverside, AB, 60; Univ Ill, PhD(inorg chem), 64. *Prof Exp:* NSF fel, Univ Col, Univ London, 63-64; asst prof inorg chem, Univ Calif, Berkeley, 64-68; inorg chemist, Corp Res & Develop, Gen Elec Co, 68-85. *Concurrent Pos:* Consult, indust, Heineman-Butterworths Publ Co; ed, Am Chem Soc, Chem of Mat. *Mem:* Am Chem Soc; Royal Soc Chem; fel AAAS; Am Ceramic Soc; Mat Res Soc. *Res:* Synthesis and solid state properties of coordination compounds; synthesis, electrical and magnetic properties of donor-acceptor complexes; organometallic chem vapor deposition; development of organometallic precursors to ceramic materials. *Mailing Add:* Chem Dept Rensselaer Polytech Inst Troy NY 12181

INTRES, RICHARD, MOLECULAR BIOLOGY, MOLECULAR DIAGNOSTICS. *Current Pos:* HEAD MOLECULAR BIOL, DEPT PATH, BERKSHIRE MED CTR, PITTSFIELD, 91- *Educ:* Windham Col, BA, 78; Wesleyan Univ, PhD, 86. *Honors & Awards:* Nat Res Serv Award, 90-91. *Prof Exp:* Asst staff scientist, May & Baker Ltd, Dagenham, Essex, Eng, 78-79; res scientist, Norwich-Eaton Pharmaceut, Inc, 79-81; Peterson fel biochem, Wesleyan Univ, 83, res asst, 83-86; res assoc, Dept Biochem & Biophys, Howard Hughes Med Inst, Univ Calif, San Francisco, 86-87; asst scientist res & develop, Bionique Lab, Inc, Saranac Lake, NY, 87-89; res scientist, W Alton Jones Cell Sci Ctr, Lake Placid, NY, 89-91. *Concurrent Pos:* Asst prof, Dept Molecular Genetics & Microbiol, Med Ctr, Univ Mass, Worcester. *Mem:* Am Soc Cell Biol; Asn Res Vision & Ophthal; Am Asn Clin Chem; Asn Molecular Path. *Res:* Tissue culture; cell culture; cell separation; electron microscopy; immunofluorescence; DNA amplification technology; molecular pathology. *Mailing Add:* Berkshire Med Ctr Dept Path 725 North St Pittsfield MA 01201. *Fax:* 413-447-2097

INTRILIGATOR, DEVRIE SHAPIRO, SPACE PHYSICS. *Current Pos:* SR RES PHYSICIST, CARMEL RES CTR, 79-, DIR, SPACE PLASMA LAB, 80- *Personal Data:* b New York, NY; m 63, Michael; c Kenneth, James, William & Robert. *Educ:* Mass Inst Technol, SB, 62, SM, 64; Univ Calif, Los Angeles, PhD(planetary & space physics), 67. *Prof Exp:* Res asst cosmic ray group, Physics Dept, Mass Inst Technol, 60; consult physicist, Inst Physics, Univ Milan, 61; physicist, Cosmic Ray Br, Air Force Cambridge Res Labs, 62-63; asst res geophysicist, Inst Geophys & Planetary Physics, Univ Calif, Los Angeles, 67; Nat Acad Sci-Nat Res Coun resident res assoc, Space Sci Div, Ames Res Ctr, NASA, 67-69; res fel physics, Calif Inst Technol, 69-72, asst prof, 72- 80, mem, Space Sci Ctr, 78-83; mem staff, Stauffer Hall Sci, Univ Southern Calif, 74-77, asst prof physics, 77-79. *Concurrent Pos:* Vis assoc physics, Calif Inst Technol, 72-73; consult, NASA, Nat Oceanic & Atmospheric Admin & Jet Propulsion Lab, 83-86; chmn, Comn Solar Terrestrial Res, Nat Res Coun, Nat Acad Sci, 83-86; mem, Geophys Res Bd, Geophysics Study Comn, NSF Div Atmospheric Sci, 83-86; US Nat Repr, Sci Comn Solar-Terrestrial Physics, 83-86. *Mem:* Am Geophys Union; Am Phys Soc; AAAS. *Res:* High energy nuclear physics; plasma physics; astrophysics; participant pioneers 10/11 missions to outer planets; Pioneer Venus Orbiter; Pioneers 6, 7, 8 and 9 heliocentric missions; many articles in professional journals. *Mailing Add:* Carmel Res Ctr PO Box 1732 Santa Monica CA 90406. *Fax:* 310-453-2983

INTURRISI, CHARLES E, PHARMACOLOGY. *Current Pos:* from asst prof to assoc prof, 69-78, PROF PHARMACOL, MED COL, CORNELL UNIV, 78- *Personal Data:* b Waterbury, Conn, Apr 15, 41; m 66; c 1. *Educ:* Univ Conn, BS, 62; Tulane Univ, MS, 65, PhD(pharmacol), 67. *Honors & Awards:* Litchfield lectr, Oxford Univ, 82. *Prof Exp:* Res assoc chem pharmacol, Nat Heart Inst, 67-69. *Mem:* AAAS; NY Acad Sci; Am Soc Pharmacol & Exp Therapeut. *Res:* Biochemical pharmacology; relationship of disposition of narcotics and antagonists to pharmacologic effects and development of tolerance. *Mailing Add:* Dept Pharmacol Cornell Univ Med Col 1300 York Ave New York NY 10021-4896

INUI, THOMAS S, MEDICINE. *Current Pos:* PROF & CHMN, AMBULATORY CARE & PREV DEPT, HARVARD UNIV, 92- *Personal Data:* b Baltimore, Md, July 10, 43; m 96, Nancy Stowe; c Tazo Stowe. *Educ:* Haverford Col, BA, 65; Johns Hopkins Univ, MD, 69, ScM, 73; Am Bd Internal Med, dipl, 72. *Honors & Awards:* mem, Inst Med Nat Acad Sci, 90. *Prof Exp:* Intern, Johns Hopkins Hosp, 69-70, asst resident med, 70-71, sr asst resident, 71-72, chief resident, 73-74, instr, Dept Med Care Orgn, Sch Hyg & Pub Health, Johns Hopkins Univ, 73-76; chief med, USPHS Indian Hosp, Albuquerque, NMex, 74-76, physician-in-chief, 74-76; asst prof, Univ Wash, 76-80, from assoc prof to prof med & health serv, 80-92, head, Div Gen Internal Med, 86-92. *Concurrent Pos:* Carnegie-Commonwealth Clin scholar, Johns Hopkins Univ, 71-73; instr, Dept Med, Sch Med, 73-74; dir, Robert Wood Johnson Clin Scholars Prog, Univ Wash, 77-; chief, Med Comprehensive Care Unit, Seattle Vet Admin Med Ctr, 76-86, dir, Health Serv Res & Develop Ctr, 76-82, co-dir, Health Serv Res Training Prog, 79-86; assoc mem, Hastings Ctr, 81-; nat coun mem, Soc Gen Internal Med, 83-86; chief, Gen Internal Med Sect, Harborview Med Ctr, Seattle, 86-; mem, Med Res Serv Coop Studies Eval Comt, Vet Admin, 88-91; assoc ed, J Gen Internal Med; correspondent, Comt Human Rights, Nat Acad Sci. *Mem:* Inst Med-Nat Acad Sci; Am Pub Health Asn; Soc Gen Internal Med (pres-elect, 86-89); Am Fedn Med Res; fel Am Col Physicians. *Res:* Author or co-author of over 160 publications. *Mailing Add:* Harvard Univ 126 Brookline St 2nd Flr Boston MA 02215. *E-Mail:* tinui@warren.med.harvard.edu

IOACHIM, HARRY L, PATHOLOGY, ONCOLOGY. *Current Pos:* from asst prof to assoc prof, 62-72, CLIN PROF PATH, COL PHYSICIANS & SURGEONS, COLUMBIA UNIV, 72-; PROF PATH, MED COL, CORNELL UNIV, 90- *Personal Data:* b Bucharest, Rumania, Oct 22, 24; US citizen; m 54; c 2. *Educ:* Cultura-Lyceum, Bucharest, Rumania, BS, 44; Fac Med, Univ Bucharest, MD, 51. *Prof Exp:* Chief pathologist, First Surg Clin, Fac Med, Univ Bucharest, 54-61, asst prof path, Dept Path, 56-61; chief res cancer, Inst Cancer, Paris, France, 61-62. *Concurrent Pos:* Health res career award, City New York Health Res Coun, 66; attend-on-staff path, Lenox Hill Hosp, 68-; grant cancer res, Nat Cancer Inst, 67, 70, & 73-, & Am Cancer Soc, 82-; ed, Pathobiol Ann, Raven Press, 70-80; dir dept path, Med Col, Cornell Univ, 82- *Mem:* Int Acad Path; NY Acad Sci; Am Asn Cancer Res; Am Asn Immunol; Harvey Soc. *Res:* Cancer immunology, lung cancer, ovarian cancer; cancer pathology; etiology and mechanisms of leukemia; author 3 books on pathology and AIDS. *Mailing Add:* Dept Path Lenox Hill Hosp 100 E 77th St New York NY 10021-1882

IODICE, ARTHUR ALFONSO, BIOCHEMISTRY. *Current Pos:* RES SCIENTIST, MASONIC MED RES LAB, 75- *Personal Data:* b Rome, NY, Nov 7, 28. *Educ:* Columbia Col, AB, 50; State Univ NY Upstate Med Ctr, PhD(biochem), 58. *Prof Exp:* Jane Coffin Childs Mem Fund fel biochem, Univ Calif, Berkeley, 58-60, res assoc, 60-62; res assoc, Biochem Div, Inst Muscle Dis, 62-65, asst mem, 65-69, assoc mem, 69-74. *Mem:* AAAS; NY Acad Sci; Am Heart Asn. *Res:* Roles of the lysosomal and neutral proteases in protein turnover and in muscular dystrophy; intracellular uptake of quinidine and other antiarrhythmic agents by cardiac tissues; isolation and characterization of myocytes. *Mailing Add:* Masonic Med Res Lab Utica NY 13501-1787. *Fax:* 315-735-5648

IONA, MARIO, COSMIC RAY PHYSICS, PHYSICS WRITING. *Current Pos:* from asst prof to prof physics, Univ Denver, 46-85, coordr, Inter-Univ High Altitude Labs, 48-62, coordr, High Altitude Lab, 62-82, EMER PROF PHYSICS, UNIV DENVER, 85- *Personal Data:* b Berlin, Ger, June 17, 17; nat US; m 49, Nancy Mossman; c Steven & Ann. *Educ:* Univ Vienna, PhD(physics), 39. *Honors & Awards:* Distinguished Serv Citation, Am Asn Physics Teachers, 71; Robert A Milliken Lectr Award, Am Asn Physics Teachers, 86. *Prof Exp:* Int Student Serv fel, Univ Uppsala, 39-41; from res asst physics to instr, Univ Chicago, 41-46. *Concurrent Pos:* Consult, Denver Res Inst 55-77; asst coord, NSF Summer Inst High Sch Teachers, 58, coord phys, In-serv Inst High Sch Teachers, 58-59; consult, Denver Pub Schs, 62-65, 76- & summer inst col teachers, Univ Saugar, India, 66; vis prof, Univ Northern Colo, 70; consult, Jefferson Co Pub Schs, 73 & Adams Co Sch Dist R12, 85; consult, J Sci & Children, Nat Sci Teachers Asn, 75-, J Sci Scope, 82- & J Sci Teacher, 85-95 & J Physics Teacher, Am Asn Physics Teachers, 63-65 & 70- *Mem:* Fel AAAS; Am Phys Soc; Am Asn Physics Teachers; Nat Sci Teachers Asn. *Res:* Nuclear physics; cosmic rays; electronics; science education. *Mailing Add:* Dept Physics Univ Denver Denver CO 80208-2238. *Fax:* 303-871-4405; *E-Mail:* miona@du.edu

IONESCU, DAN, COMPUTERS, ELECTRICAL ENGINEERING. *Current Pos:* ASST PROF COMPUT CONTROL, UNIV OTTAWA, 85- *Personal Data:* b Oravita, Romania, July 23, 43; Can citizen; m 69; c 2. *Educ:* Polytech Inst Bucharest, Dipl Eng, 66, DrSci, 82; Univ Timisoara, Dipl Math, 82. *Mem:* Sr mem Inst Elec & Electronics Engrs; Soc Indust & Appl Math; Am Math Soc; NY Acad Sci. *Res:* Multivariable control; robust control; artificial intelligence in control; expert systems for process control; learning in control. *Mailing Add:* Dept Elec Eng 770 King Edward Ottawa ON K1N 6N5 Can

IONESCU, LAVINEL G, PHYSICAL CHEMISTRY, BIOCHEMISTRY. *Current Pos:* PROF PHYS CHEM, FED UNIV SANTA CATARINA, BRAZIL, 78- *Personal Data:* b Varset, Yugoslavia, May 19, 43; US citizen. *Educ:* Univ NMex, BS, 64, MS, 66; NMex State Univ, PhD(chem), 70. *Prof Exp:* NSF fel, NMex State Univ, 71; asst prof, NMex Highlands Univ, 72-75; asst prof chem, Univ Detroit, 75-78. *Concurrent Pos:* USPHS fel, Univ Calif, Santa Barbara, 71-72. *Mem:* AAAS; Sigma Xi; Am Chem Soc. *Res:* Thermodynamics; kinetics; application of physical chemical principles in the elucidation of basic biologic processes; noble gases, micelles, membranes, respiratory pigments, clathrates and radioactive exchange. *Mailing Add:* Rua Venancio Aires 139 Viamao Taruma Brazil

IONESCU TULCEA, CASSIUS, PROBABILITY STATISTICS, MATHEMATICAL ANALYSIS. *Current Pos:* PROF MATH, NORTHWESTERN UNIV, 66- *Personal Data:* b Bucarest, Roumania, Oct 14, 23; US citizen. *Educ:* Univ Bucarest, MS, 46; Yale Univ, PhD(math), 59. *Honors & Awards:* Prize, Roumanian Acad Sci, 57. *Prof Exp:* Instr math, Univ Bucarest, 46-51, from asst prof to assoc prof, 52-57; res assoc, Yale Univ, 57-59, vis lectr, 59-61; assoc prof, Univ Pa, 61-64; prof, Univ Ill, Urbana, 64-66. *Res:* Research monographs on probability and statistics, lifting theory and Hilbert Spaces; set theory and topology; game theory; mathematical economics; mathematics of gambling. *Mailing Add:* Dept Math Northwestern Univ Evanston IL 60208

IORILLO, ANTHONY J, AVIATION ENGINEERING. *Current Pos:* RETIRED. *Personal Data:* b Southington, Conn, Feb 12, 38; m; c 4. *Educ:* Calif Inst Technol, ME, 59, MS, 60. *Honors & Awards:* Lawrence A Hyland Patent Award, 70; Spacecraft Design Award, Am Inst Aeronaut & Astronaut, 71. *Prof Exp:* Chmn bd, Am Mobil Satellite Corp, 96. *Concurrent Pos:* Fulbright scholar, Politecnico, Turin, Italy, 61; mem, Air Force Sci Adv Bd & Defense Commun Agency Sci Adv Group. *Mem:* Nat Acad Eng. *Mailing Add:* Am Mobil Satellite Corp 551 Paseo Miramar Pacific Palisades CA 90272

IORNS, TERRY VERN, ANALYTICAL CHEMISTRY. *Current Pos:* res chemist, 77-87, VPRES, PROD PLANNING, AXION SYSTS INC, 87- *Personal Data:* b Kenosha, Wis, Apr 15, 44. *Educ:* Northwestern Univ, BA, 66; Univ Wis, PhD(chem), 70. *Prof Exp:* Fel chem, Univ Calif, Los Angeles, 70-71; instr chem, Syracuse Univ, 71-72; supvr chem methods, Phillips Petrol Co, 72-77. *Mem:* Am Chem Soc; Sigma Xi. *Res:* Automation of chemical methods of analysis including wet chemical and combustion methods; application of computers to chemical analysis. *Mailing Add:* 6334-46 E Viewmont Mesa AZ 85215

IOVINO, ANTHONY JOSEPH, PHYSIOLOGY. *Current Pos:* PROF BIOL, LONG ISLAND UNIV, 56-, DIR DIV SCI, 77- *Personal Data:* b Brooklyn, NY, Apr 25, 25; m 49; c 1. *Educ:* St John's Univ, NY, BS, 46, MS, 52; NY Univ, PhD(biol), 59. *Prof Exp:* Instr biol, St John's Univ, NY, 49-56. *Mem:* AAAS; NY Acad Sci; Sigma Xi. *Res:* Endocrinology. *Mailing Add:* 170 Powerhouse Rd Roslyn Heights NY 11577

IP, CLEMENT CHEUNG-YUNG, BIOCHEMISTRY. *Current Pos:* CANCER RES SCIENTIST, BREAST CANCER, ROSWELL PARK MEM INST, 75- *Personal Data:* b Hong Kong, Aug 21, 47; m 72. *Educ:* McGill Univ, BSc, 69; Univ Wis-Madison, PhD(biochem), 73. *Prof Exp:* Res assoc endocrinol, State Univ NY Upstate Med Ctr, 73-75. *Mem:* Am Asn Cancer Res. *Res:* Nutritional modification of mammary carcinogenesis. *Mailing Add:* Dept Oncol Roswell Park Cancer Inst 666 Elm St Buffalo NY 14263-0001

IP, MARGOT MORRIS, ENDOCRINOLOGY, CANCER RESEARCH. *Current Pos:* CANCER RES SCIENTIST, ROSWELL PARK CANCER INST, 75- *Personal Data:* b Toronto, Ont, Mar 10, 43; m 72, Clement. *Educ:* Univ Toronto, BA, 65; Harvard Sch Pub Health, MS, 67; Univ Wis-Madison, PhD(biochem), 72. *Prof Exp:* Fel nutrit biochem, Univ Wis-Madison, 72-73; res assoc endocrinol, Upstate Med Ctr, Syracuse, 73-75. *Mem:* Am Asn Cancer Res; Am Inst Nutrit; AAAS; Endocrine Soc. *Res:* Endocrinology of neoplastic tissues; breast cancer. *Mailing Add:* Dept Exp Therapeut Roswell Park Cancer Inst Buffalo NY 14263-0001. *Fax:* 716-845-5865

IP, STEPHEN H, BIOPHYSICS. *Current Pos:* PRES & CHIEF OPER OFFICER, CYTOMED INC, FRAMINGHAM, MASS, 89- *Personal Data:* b China, Feb 9, 49. *Educ:* Bridgewater Col, BA, 70; Univ Va, PhD(biochem & biophys), 76. *Prof Exp:* NIH fel hemat & oncol, Med Sch Univ Pa, assoc scientist, 76-79; group leader cancer biol, Ortho Diag Systs, Inc, Cambridge, Mass, Johnson & Johnson subsid, mgr technol develop, 79-84; dir res, T Cell Sci, Inc, vpres & corp officer technol develop, 84-89. *Concurrent Pos:* Adj vis assoc prof path, Med Sch, Columbia Univ, 82-84. *Mem:* Am Asn Immunologists; Am Asn Exp Hemat; Am Chem Soc; Am Asn Clin Chemists. *Res:* Bone marrow transplantation; blood transfusion and immuno-hematology; author of numerous scientific articles. *Mailing Add:* CytoMed 11 Singing Hills Sudbury MA 01776-1051

IP, WALLACE, CYTOSKELETON STRUCTURE & FUNCTION, ELECTRON MICROSCOPY. *Current Pos:* ASSOC PROF ANAT & CELL BIOL, SCH MED, UNIV CINCINNATI, 85- *Personal Data:* b Hong Kong, Dec 29, 48; US citizen; m; c 1. *Educ:* Ill Inst Technol, PhD(cell biol), 77. *Concurrent Pos:* Estab investr, Am Heart Asn. *Mem:* Am Soc Cell Biol. *Res:* Structure and assembly of intermediate filaments. *Mailing Add:* Dept Anat & Cell Biol Col Med Univ Cincinnati 231 Bethesda Ave ML521 PO Box 670521 Cincinnati OH 45267-0521. *Fax:* 513-558-4454

IPPEN, ERICH PETER, QUANTUM ELECTRONICS. *Current Pos:* prof, Dept Elec Eng & Comput Sci, 80-87, ELIHU THOMSON PROF ELEC ENG, MASS INST TECHNOL, 87-, PROF PHYSICS, 96- *Personal Data:* b Fountain Hill, Pa, Mar 29, 40; m 66, Dorothea Swansen; c Erich & Jason. *Educ:* Mass Inst Technol, SB, 62; Univ Calif, Berkeley, MS, 65, PhD(elec eng), 68. *Honors & Awards:* R W Wood Prize, Optical Soc Am, 81; Edward Longstreth Medal, Franklin Inst, 82; Morris Leeds Awards, Inst Elec & Electronics Engrs, 83; R V Pole Lectr, Optical Soc Am, 88; Walter Schottky lectr, RWTH Aachen, Ger, 89; Harold E Edgerton Award, Int Soc Optical Eng, 89. *Prof Exp:* Mem tech staff, Bell Labs, Holmdel, NJ, 68-80. *Concurrent Pos:* Vis prof, Dept Elec Eng & Comput Sci, Mass Inst Technol, 78; NSF spec rev panels, 80, 85 & 87; mem adv comt, Lasers & Electro Optics Soc, Inst Elec & Electronics Engrs, 82-85, chmn, Fel Eval Comt, 85-86; mem prog comt, Conf Picosecond Electronics & Opto-electronics, Optical Soc Am, 85 & 87; Humboldt award, 86; mem, Air Force Studies Bd, Nat Acad Sci, 86-92, Comt Optical Data Collection, 87, chmn, Sect Eng, 90-93 & Class Appl Sci & Eng, 93-96; mem, Lincoln Lab Adv Bd, Mass Inst Technol, 90-; bd, Optical Soc Am, 96- *Mem:* Nat Acad Sci; Nat Acad Eng; fel Am Acad Arts & Sci; fel Inst Elec & Electronics Engrs; fel Optical Soc Am; Arthur L Shawlow Prize, Am Phys Soc, 97. *Res:* Development of sub-picosecond and femtosecond optical techniques; application to studies of ultrafast processes in materials; extension of picosecond techniques to semiconductor optical electronics and signal processing in optical waveguides; author of over 200 publications. *Mailing Add:* Dept Elec Eng Bldg 36 Rm 319 Mass Inst Technol 77 Massachusetts Ave Cambridge MA 02139

IPPEN-IHLER, KARIN ANN, bacterial genetics; deceased, see previous edition for last biography

IPSER, JAMES REID, THEORETICAL ASTROPHYSICS. *Current Pos:* AT PHYSICS DEPT, UNIV FLA. *Personal Data:* b New Orleans, La, July 13, 42; m 65; c 2. *Educ:* Loyola Univ, La, BS, 64; Calif Inst Technol, MS, 67, PhD(physics), 69. *Prof Exp:* Fel physics, Calif Inst Technol, 69-70; actg asst prof astron, Univ Wash, 70-71. *Mem:* Am Astron Soc; Am Phys Soc; Int Astron Union. *Res:* Theoretical astrophysics and applications of general relativity to astrophysical problems. *Mailing Add:* Dept Physics Univ Fla Williamson Hall Gainesville FL 32611

IQBAL, ZAFAR, NEUROCHEMISTRY, NEUROSCIENCES. *Current Pos:* asst prof neurol & neurosci, 82-85, assoc prof neurol, 89-95, ADJ PROF NEUROL & NEUROSCI, MED SCH, NORTHWESTERN UNIV, 95- *Personal Data:* b Lucknow, India, July 12, 46; US citizen. *Educ:* Univ

Lucknow, BS, 61, MS, 63; All-India Inst Med Sci, PhD(biochem), 72. *Prof Exp:* Jr res fel biochem, Coun Sci & Indust Res, India, 63-66; res scholar, Directorate-Gen Health Serv, India, 66-67; res fel, Coun Sci & Indust Res, 67-68; asst res officer, Indian Coun Med Res, 68-71; res assoc & investr physiol, Sch Med, Ind Univ, Indianapolis, 72-77, asst prof med biophys, 77-79, asst prof biochem, 79-82; assoc prof pharmacol, Chicago Med Sch, 85-88. *Concurrent Pos:* FIDIA Res Found Award, 87; UN Develop Prog award, 87 & 93; vis prof, Dept Biochem, Postgrad Inst Med Res & Educ, India, 87; mem, Inst Neurosci, Northwestern Univ, Ctr Develop Biol & Amyolateral Sclerosis Res Ctr, 89-; advan study award, NATO, 90; health sci specialist, Vet Admin Cent Off Med Res Serv, Washington, 95- *Mem:* Int Brain Res Orgn; Int Soc Neurochem; Soc Neurosci; Am Soc Neurochem; Biophys Soc; Am Physiol Soc; Soc Exp Biol & Med; Sigma Xi; NY Acad Sci; Asn Scientists Indian Origin Am; AAAS. *Res:* Chemical exploration of developing nervous system; characterization of enzymes, proteins and polypeptides associated with the axoplasmic transport system; calmodulin associated neurobiological processes; role of polyamines in neuronal signal transduction; molecular biology of neuromuscular disorders; contributor or editor of several books. *Mailing Add:* Northwestern Univ Sch Med PO Box 11538 Chicago IL 60611-0538. *Fax:* 202-275-6649

IRANI, KEKI B, ELECTRONICS. *Current Pos:* assoc res engr, Inst Sci & Technol, 61-62, from asst prof to assoc prof elec eng, 62-67, PROF ELEC ENG, UNIV MICH, ANN ARBOR, 67- *Personal Data:* b India. *Educ:* Univ Bombay, BE, 47; Univ Mich, MSE, 49, PhD, 53. *Prof Exp:* Res & develop engr, Philips Telecommun Industs, Neth, 50-56; from asst prof to assoc prof elec eng, Univ Kans, 56-60. *Mem:* Sr mem Inst Elec & Electronics Engrs; Sigma Xi. *Res:* Computers; large-scale systems. *Mailing Add:* 2785 Parkridge Dr Ann Arbor MI 48103-1732

IRANI, N F, PHYSICAL CHEMISTRY. *Current Pos:* SR RES CHEMIST, RES LABS, EASTMAN KODAK CO, 68- *Personal Data:* b Haifa, Israel, July 20, 34; m 60; c 2. *Educ:* Am Univ Beirut, BS, 55, MS, 60; Univ NC, Chapel Hill, PhD(phys chem), 66. *Prof Exp:* Chmn, Sci Sect, Nat Col Chouifat, Lebanon, 55-60; instr chem, Am Univ Beirut, 60-61; sr res chemist, Westvaco Corp, SC, 66-68. *Mem:* Am Chem Soc. *Res:* Adsorption of dispersants on colloidal particles; solid liquid interface; characterization of polymers involved in adsorption on a colloidal substrate. *Mailing Add:* 10 Enfield Dr Pittsford NY 14534

IRANI, RIYAD RAY, PHYSICAL CHEMISTRY. *Current Pos:* chief exec officer, Occidental Petrol Corp, 83-91, chmn, 83-94, chief operating officer, Occidental Petrol Corp, 84-91, pres, 84-94, CHMN & CHIEF EXEC OFFICER, OCCIDENTAL PETROL CORP, 91-; CHMN, CAN OCCIDENTAL PETROL CORP, 87- *Personal Data:* b Beirut, Lebanon, Jan 15, 35; nat US; m 56; c 3. *Educ:* Am Univ Beirut, BS, 53; Univ Southern Calif, PhD(phys chem), 57. *Prof Exp:* Res chemist, Monsanto Chem Co, 57-60, group leader, 60-63, sr res group leader, Monsanto Co Mo, 63-67; assoc dir, T R Evans Res Ctr, Diamond Shamrock Corp, 67-69, dir res, 69-73; vpres res & develop, Olin Corp, 73-74, sr vpres, 74-76, pres & chief operating officer, 78-80, exec vpres, Chem Group, 77-83. *Mem:* Am Chem Soc; Sigma Xi. *Res:* Ionic solutions; theory of liquids; physical properties of powders; complex ion formation; thermodynamics; phosphorous compounds chemistry. *Mailing Add:* Occidental Petrol Corp 10889 Wilshire Blvd Los Angeles CA 90024

IRAUSQUIN, HILTJE, BIOCHEMISTRY, NUTRITION. *Current Pos:* sr staff fel, 78-81, rev toxicologist, 81-85, GROUP LEADER, FOOD & DRUG ADMIN, 85- *Personal Data:* b Neth, Jan 14, 37; US citizen; div; c 2. *Educ:* Univ Amsterdam, BS, 58, MS, 64, PhD(biochem), 69. *Prof Exp:* Surv dir nutrit, Cent Health Lab, Curacao, Neth Antilles, 64-67; res asst, Royal Trop Inst, Amsterdam, 69; res assoc cell biol, Children's Hosp Nat Med Ctr, Washington, DC, 69-72; biomed indexer, Nat Libr Med, Bethesda, Md, 75-77; res assoc, Univ Md, 77-78. *Mem:* AAAS; NY Acad Sci; Soc Toxicol; Sigma Xi; Am Chem Soc. *Res:* Metabolism of artificial sweeteners and their interactions with glucose homeostasis; regulatory mechanism of enzyme activity; safety of food additives; database management and priority ranking; toxicology; food safety. *Mailing Add:* Div Toxicol HFF 156 US Food & Drug Admin 200 C St SW HFS-227 Washington DC 20204

IRBY, BOBBY NEWELL, SCIENCE EDUCATION. *Current Pos:* RETIRED. *Personal Data:* b Meridian, Miss, Mar 17, 32; m 53; c 1. *Educ:* Univ Wash, Seattle, BA, 57; Univ Miss, MS, 62, DEd, 67. *Prof Exp:* Teacher pvt sch, Miss, 57-58; head, Dept Sci, Pub Sch, 59-64; instr chem, Northeast La State Col, 64-65; from asst prof to prof sci educ, Univ S Miss, 67-92, head dept, 69-92. *Concurrent Pos:* Prin investr, Miss-Ala sea grant, Marine Educ Curric Proj, 79, 80 & 81; dir, Dept Educ Inserv Marine Educ Proj, Miss, 81. *Mem:* AAAS; Am Chem Soc; Nat Sci Teachers Asn; fel Am Inst Chem. *Res:* Vapor pressures of the methylacetylenes; effect of ion hydrate size and shape on the surface interaction between metal ions and highly porous materials; science curriculum development and teacher education. *Mailing Add:* 231 Highpoint Diamond Head MS 39525

IRBY, WILLIAM ROBERT, MEDICINE. *Current Pos:* assoc med, 56-58, from asst prof to prof, 58-92, EMER PROF MED, MED COL VA, VA COMMONWEALTH UNIV, 92- *Personal Data:* b Blackstone, Va, May 31, 23; m 50, Catherine Connaughton; c Catherine B (Wellford), Bonnie L (Williams) & William Robert Jr. *Educ:* Hampden-Sydney Col, AB, 43; Med Col Va, MD, 48. *Prof Exp:* Trainee arthritis, Nat Inst Arthritis & Metab Dis, 53-54. *Concurrent Pos:* Arthritis med consult, USPHS, 64-72; arthritis prog consult, Arthritis Found, 66-72, chmn educ comt, 67-72; dir, Arthritis Clin, Med Col Va. *Mem:* AMA; master, Am Col Rheumatology; Nat Soc Clin Rheumatol; fel Am Col Physicians. *Res:* Bone and joint changes observed in patients undergoing renal transplantation and hemodialysis. *Mailing Add:* Box 980647 Richmond VA 23298. *Fax:* 804-828-4670

IRELAND, CAROL BEARD, PHYSICAL CHEMISTRY. *Current Pos:* Res chemist, Exp Sta, 75-90, SUPVR TECHNOL SERV, E I DU PONT DE NEMOURS & CO, INC, 90- *Personal Data:* b Southington, Conn, July 6, 48; m 73. *Educ:* Earlham Col, AB, 70; Univ Ill, Urbana-Champaign, PhD(chem), 74. *Mem:* Am Chem Soc; Sigma Xi. *Res:* Use of physical chemical techniques to characterize and improve elastomeric materials; gas chromatography and gas chromatography/mass spectrometry methods development. *Mailing Add:* Dupont Exp Sta PO Box 80-268 Wilmington DE 19880-0268

IRELAND, GORDON ALEXANDER, CLINICAL PHARMACY. *Current Pos:* CLIN PHARMACIST, BALTIMORE VET ADMIN MED CTR, 76- *Personal Data:* b Belfast, Northern Ireland, Feb 13, 44; US citizen. *Educ:* Univ Md, BS, 73; Univ Minn, PharmD, 76. *Prof Exp:* Asst pharm, Univ Md, 73-74, asst prof clin pharm, Sch pharm, 76- *Concurrent Pos:* Consult, Shangri-La Nursing Home, 78-; pharmacist consult, McGilvray's Pharm, 78-80. *Mem:* Am Pharmaceut Asn; Am Asn Cols Pharm; Am Soc Hosp Pharmacists. *Res:* Pharmacokinetics of medications especially in the patient with liver disease. *Mailing Add:* 35 Chestnut Hill Lane St Louis MO 63119

IRELAND, HERBERT O(RIN), CIVIL & GEOTECHNICAL ENGINEERING. *Current Pos:* From asst to prof civil eng, 46-79, EMER PROF CIVIL ENG, UNIV ILL, 79- *Personal Data:* b Buckley, Ill, June 12, 19; m 41, Mary L Austin; c Orin L, Marin F & Jeanne L. *Educ:* Univ Ill, BS, 41, MS, 47, PhD(civil eng), 55. *Honors & Awards:* Fourth Across Can Lectr, Nat Res Coun Can, 67. *Concurrent Pos:* Consult, geotech probs; mem, US Nat Coun Soil Mech & Found Eng. *Mem:* Fel Am Soc Civil Engrs; fel Geol Soc Am; Am Rwy Eng Asn; Sigma Xi. *Res:* Soils and foundations; foundation and retaining wall behavior. *Mailing Add:* RR 1 Box 185C Gilman IL 60938

IRELAND, JAMES, REPRODUCTIVE BIOLOGY, ENDOCRINOLOGY. *Current Pos:* PROF ANIMAL SCI & PHYSIOL, MICH STATE UNIV, 77- *Personal Data:* b Clarksville, Tenn, June 30, 47; m 67; c 2. *Educ:* Austin Peay State Univ, BS, 69; Univ Tenn, PhD(animal sci), 75. *Honors & Awards:* Young Investr Award, Soc Study Reproduction, 77. *Concurrent Pos:* NIH & Ford Found fel, 76-77 & Univ Mich fel, 77; prin investr, Nat Inst Child Health & Human Develop, 79-91; NSF & USDA grants, 79-91; invited lectr, twenty univs incl Univ Wis, WVa Univ, Yale Univ, Dublin, Nebr Univ & Ohio State Univ, 85; NIH sr fel, Yale Sch Med, 87; dir, Ctr Animal Prod & Toxicol, 90-91. *Mem:* Soc Study Reproduction; Endocrine Soc. *Res:* Hormonal regulation of ovarian follicular development; published over 100 scientific articles. *Mailing Add:* Dept Animal Sci Mich State Univ East Lansing MI 48824

IRELAND, ROBERT ELLSWORTH, ORGANIC CHEMISTRY. *Current Pos:* PROF ORG CHEM, CALIF INST TECHNOL, 65-, PROF & CHMN CHEM DEPT, 87- *Personal Data:* b Cincinnati, Ohio, Apr 12, 29; div; c 2. *Educ:* Univ Wis, PhD(org chem), 54. *Prof Exp:* NSF fel & res chemist, Univ Calif, Los Angeles, 54-56; instr chem, Univ Mich, 56-59, from asst prof to assoc prof, 59-65. *Concurrent Pos:* Consult, Merrell Nat Labs, 72-; mem adv ed bd, J Am Chem Soc, 72- & Org Synthesis, 75- *Mem:* Am Chem Soc; The Chem Soc; Swiss Chem Soc. *Res:* Synthetic organic chemistry relative to natural products. *Mailing Add:* 1255 N Gulfstream Ave No 1001 Sarasota FL 34236-8905

IRENE, EUGENE ARTHUR, MATERIALS SCIENCE. *Current Pos:* DEPT CHEM, UNIV NC, 82- *Personal Data:* b Brooklyn, NY, Oct 22, 41; m 64, MaryAnn Felice; c Michael & Christina. *Educ:* Manhattan Col, BS, 63; Rensselaer Polytech Inst, PhD(solid state chem), 72. *Honors & Awards:* Callinan Award, Electrochem Soc, 88. *Prof Exp:* Proj scientist, Rocket Propulsion Lab, USAF, 63-66, instr electronics, Electronics Training Ctr, 66-68; commun officer, Defense Commun Agency, Dept of Defense, 68-69; res staff mem solid state chem, T J Watson Res Ctr, IBM Corp, 72-82. *Mem:* Mat Res Soc; Electrochem Soc; Am Vacuum Soc. *Res:* Thin films, particularly dielectrics for field effect transistor applications, including preparation, mechanical properties, optical properties, electrical properties, electron microscopy and ellipsometry for structure of thin films and oxidation kinetics. *Mailing Add:* Dept Chem CB3290 Univ NC Chapel Hill NC 27599-3290. *Fax:* 919-962-2388; *E-Mail:* gene_irene@unc.edu

IRETON-JONES, CAROL S, MARKETING NUTRITION SERVICES, MANAGEMENT OF MAJOR CORPORATE INITIATIVES. *Current Pos:* clin nutrit network mgr, 91-95, PRIN & OWNER, PREFERRED NUTRIT THERAPISTS, 95-; DIR NUTRIT PROG MGT, CORAM HEALTHCARE, 97- *Personal Data:* b Ft Worth, Tex, Sept 5, 56; m 86, James D; c Lauren K & Kristen L. *Educ:* Tex Tech Univ, BS, 78; Tex Woman's Univ, MS, 82, PhD(nutrit), 88. *Honors & Awards:* Outstanding Serv Award, Am Diabetic Asn, 93; Recognized Young Dietitian of the Year, Am Dietetian Asn, 94. *Prof Exp:* Res dietitian, SW Med Ctr, Univ Tex, 82-91. *Concurrent Pos:* Nutrit consult, Good Nutrit for Good Living, 82-; lectr, Tex Woman's Univ, 89-, Sch Allied Health, SW Med Ctr, Univ Tex, 91-; chairperson, Dietitians Nutrit Support, 97- *Mem:* Am Dietetic Asn; Am Soc Clin Nutrit. *Res:* Discovery of energy requirements of hospitalized patients through development of Ireton-Jones energy equations; investigation of energy requirements of individuals in many situations. *Mailing Add:* 2329 Highland Heights Lane Carrollton TX 75007. *E-Mail:* dreijrd@ibm.net

IREY, NELSON SUMNER, PATHOLOGY. *Current Pos:* pathologist, Registry Tissue Reactions to Drugs, 65-78, CHMN, DEPT ENVIRON & DRUG-INDUCED PATH, ARMED FORCES INST PATH, 78- *Personal Data:* b Lewisburgh, Pa, July 18, 11; m 40; c 5. *Educ:* Univ Pittsburgh, BS, 35, MD, 38. *Prof Exp:* Chief, Dept Path, 97th Gen Hosp, Frankfurt, WGer,

50-54, Letterman Gen Hosp, 54-60 & Walter Reed Gen Hosp, 61-65. *Concurrent Pos:* Clin prof path, Sch Med, George Washington Univ, 67-; prof lectr, Dept Forensic Sci, Grad Sch Arts & Sci, George Washington Univ, 75-76. *Mem:* Fel Am Soc Clin Pathologists; fel Am Col Physicians; fel Col Am Pathologists; Soc Pharmacol & Environ Pathologists (pres, 74-75); Int Acad Pathologists. *Res:* Adverse reactions to drugs. *Mailing Add:* Armed Forces Inst Path Washington DC 20306

IREY, RICHARD KENNETH, MECHANICAL ENGINEERING. *Current Pos:* from asst prof to assoc prof, 64-69, PROF MECH ENG, UNIV FLA, 69- *Personal Data:* b Hackensack, NJ, Dec 11, 36; c 3. *Educ:* Rose Polytech Inst, BSME, 58; Purdue Univ, MSME, 62, PhD(mech eng), 64. *Prof Exp:* Test & res engr, E I du Pont de Nemours & Co, Inc, 58-60. *Mem:* Am Soc Mech Engrs. *Res:* Cryogenic heat transfer; thermophysical properties; statistical thermodynamics; radiation heat transfer. *Mailing Add:* 10030 NW 44th Terr Apt 108 Miami FL 33178

IRFAN, MUHAMMAD, RADIATION PHYSICS, MEDICAL PHYSICS. *Current Pos:* from asst prof to assoc prof, 64-81, PROF PHYSICS, MEM UNIV NFLD, 81- *Personal Data:* b Meerut, India, Jan 7, 33; Can citizen; m 68; c 2. *Educ:* Univ Punjab, Pakistan, BSc, 52; Univ Dacca, MSc, 54; Glasgow Univ, PhD(physics), 62. *Prof Exp:* Demonstr physics, Univ Karachi, 55-57, lectr, 58; attache res, Univ Montreal, 62-64. *Concurrent Pos:* Nat Res Coun Can fel, 62-63, radiation control officer & chmn radiation control comt, Mem Univ, Nfld, 69-74, 75-78; consult, UN Develop Prog, Pakistan, 81. *Mem:* Am Phys Soc; Int Radiation Physics Soc; Can Asn Physicists; Can Radiation Protection Asn. *Res:* Nuclear reactions, especially those induced by fast neutrons; scintillation counters for gamma rays; measurements of radioactivity in water samples, in air, and like problems; neutron activation analysis; beta dosimetry (medical physics). *Mailing Add:* 15 Paddy Dobbin Dr St John's NF A1A 4V3 Can

IRGENS, ROAR L, MICROBIOLOGY. *Current Pos:* RETIRED. *Personal Data:* b Trondheim, Norway, Oct 15, 30; US citizen; m 58, Barbara Ann Southwell; c Heidi & Leif. *Educ:* Univ Ill, BS, 57, PhD(microbiol), 63. *Honors & Awards:* Antarctica Serv Medal, NSF, Dept Navy, 87; Antarctic Marine Bacterium named in honor if, Polarobacter Irgensii, 96. *Prof Exp:* Res asst waste treatment, Univ Ill, 63-65; chemist, Minn State Dept Health, 65-66; from asst prof to assoc prof res teaching, Southwest Mo State Univ, 66-77, prof biol, 77-91. *Concurrent Pos:* Sabbatical leave, Gottingen, Ger, 72-73. *Mem:* Am Soc Microbiol. *Res:* Microbiology of waste treatment; antarctic marine bacteria. *Mailing Add:* 437 Klickitat Dr La Conner WA 98257

IRGOLIC, KURT JOHANN, RESEARCH ADMINISTRATION, SYNTHETIC FUELS. *Current Pos:* Fel chem, Tex A&M Univ, 64-66, from asst prof to assoc prof, 66-77, assoc dir energy, Ctr Energy & Mineral Resources, 75-86, PROF INORG CHEM, TEX A&M UNIV, 77- *Personal Data:* b Hartberg, Austria, Sept 28, 38; m 64; c 1. *Educ:* Univ Graz, PhD(inorg anal chem), 64. *Concurrent Pos:* Prog coordr res, Off Univ Res, Tex A&M Univ, 73-75. *Mem:* Am Chem Soc. *Res:* Synthetic chemistry of organic compounds of arsenic, selenium and tellurium; metal ion extraction with organic arsenic compounds; isolation and characterization of arsenic and releniune compounds from biological systems; mass spectrometry of organometallic compounds; element specific detectors for high pressure liquid chromatography; inductively coupled argon plasma emission spectrometry; trace element and trace element compound determinations in environmental materials. *Mailing Add:* Inst Analytical Chem Universitsplatz Karl Franzens Univ Graz A 8010 Graz Austria

IRGON, JOSEPH, ENERGETICS, CATALYSIS. *Current Pos:* prin scientist radiant energy sci, 73-80, PRIN SCIENTIST & CONSULT ENERGETICS, J IRGON & ASSOCS, 80- *Personal Data:* b Polonnoe, Russia, Dec 30, 19; US citizen; m 48; c 3. *Educ:* Northeastern Univ, BS, 43; Mass Inst Technol, PhD(phys chem), 48. *Prof Exp:* Res assoc chem eng, Chem Warfare Serv Develop Lab, Mass Inst Technol, 43-45; proj leader phys chem, Cent Labs, Gen Foods Corp, 48-52; dept head space sci, Reaction Motors, 52-56; vpres res & develop space & ocean sci, Fulton-Irgon Corp, 56-62; pres ocean sci & technol, Proteus, Inc, 62-69; vpres res & develop ocean sci, Ocean Recovery Systs, 69-73. *Concurrent Pos:* Coffin fel, Mass Inst Technol, 46-48; consult energy, Stauffer Chem Corp, 56-59, Allied Chem Corp, 58-59, McGraw Edison Co, 63-65, Union Carbide Corp, 63-66; USN, 64-66 & Pakistan Govt, 75-77; consult dir res, Energy Technol Inc, 79-83. *Mem:* Am Chem Soc; Am Soc Mech Engrs. *Res:* Development and/or extension of basic principles large-scale collection and conversion of radiant energy; integrated waste-to-energy systems; computer assisted catalysis of oxidation/reduction processes; human chemical warfare test participation and current long term evaluation of effects. *Mailing Add:* 144 Emmans Rd Flanders NJ 07836-9042

IRIBARNE, JULIO VICTOR, PHYSICAL CHEMISTRY. *Current Pos:* RETIRED. *Personal Data:* b Buenos Aires, Arg, Nov 11, 16; m 57; c 1. *Educ:* Univ Buenos Aires, DChem, 42. *Prof Exp:* Mem staff phys & inorg chem, Univ Buenos Aires, 45-53; indust consult & chemist, 53-55; assoc prof phys chem, Univ Buenos Aires, 56-57, head inst atmospheric physics, 57-66, prof meteorol, 58-66; from assoc prof to emer prof physics, Univ Toronto, 66-84. *Concurrent Pos:* Fel, Inst Phys Res Rio de Janeiro, Brazil, 53- & Imp Col, London, 65-66. *Mem:* AAAS; Am Meteorol Soc; Can Meteorol Soc; Can Asn Physicists; Am Geophys Union. *Res:* Cloud physics; atmospheric electricity; aerosol physics; atmospheric chemistry. *Mailing Add:* 29 Banstock Dr Willowdale ON M2K 2H5 Can

IRICK, GETHER, JR, PHOTOCHEMISTRY, CATALYSIS. *Current Pos:* From chemist to sr res chemist, Tenn Eastman Co, 60-70, res assoc, 70-78, sr res assoc, 78-90, RES FEL, TENN EASTMAN CO, 90- *Personal Data:* b Stone, Ky, Jan 29, 36; m 80, Sarah Wilson; c Timothy A, Steven R, Sarah E, Lucinda J & Jerry A. *Educ:* Eastern Ky State Col, BS, 57; Univ Louisville, PhD(org chem), 60. *Mem:* AAAS; Am Chem Soc; Sigma Xi; Am Asn Textile Chem & Colorists. *Res:* Synthesis and photochemistry of dyes and stabilizers for synthetic polymers; oxidation hydrogenation carbonylation catalysis. *Mailing Add:* 113 S Patrick Dr Gray TN 37615-2217

IRICK, PAUL EUGENE, APPLIED STATISTICS, INFORMATION SCIENCE. *Current Pos:* RETIRED. *Personal Data:* b Greenville, Ohio, Nov 4, 18; m 58; c 5. *Educ:* Purdue Univ, BS, 40, MS, 45, PhD(statist), 50. *Prof Exp:* Assoc prof statist, Purdue Univ, 54-56; res statistician hwy engr, Nat Res Coun, 56-57, asst dir spec projs hwy res, Transp Res Bd, 68-82. *Concurrent Pos:* Vpres, Engr Index, Inc, 70-74, pres, 74-76. *Mem:* Am Statist Asn. *Res:* Scientific and technical information systems. *Mailing Add:* 484 Windmill Point Rd Hampton VA 23664

IRIE, REIKO FURUSE, ONCOLOGY, CANCER. *Current Pos:* res oncol cancer immunol, 71-77, from asst prof to assoc prof, 77-84, PROF SURG, SCH MED, UNIV CALIF, LOS ANGELES, 84- *Personal Data:* b Japan, Sept 11, 40; m 68; c 1. *Educ:* Nat Ochanomizu Univ, Japan, BS, 63; Nat Niigata Univ, Japan, MD, 72. *Prof Exp:* Researcher immunol, Virol Div, Nat Cancer Inst, Japan, 66-71. *Mem:* Am Asn Cancer Res. *Res:* Immunobiology of cancer; immunotherapy and immunodiagnosis of human cancer. *Mailing Add:* John Wayne Cancer Inst 2200 Santa Monica Blvd Santa Monica CA 90404

IRISH, DONALD EDWARD, PHYSICAL CHEMISTRY, VIBRATIONAL SPECTROSCOPY. *Current Pos:* from lectr to assoc prof, Univ Waterloo, 57-71, prof chem, Univ Waterloo, 71-96, chmn dept, 77-83, exec dir, Fac Sci Found, 85-90, EMER PROF CHEM, UNIV WATERLOO, 96- *Personal Data:* b Uxbridge, Ont, June 14, 32; m 56, Shirley (Chandler); c 4. *Educ:* Univ Western Ont, BSc, 55; McMaster Univ, MSc, 56; Univ Chicago, PhD(chem), 62. *Honors & Awards:* Union Carbide Award for Chem Educ, Chem Inst Can, 90. *Prof Exp:* Teacher tech sch, Ont, 56-57. *Concurrent Pos:* Vis fac, Bell Tel Labs, Inc, 63; guest mem staff, Sch Chem, Univ Newcastle, 70-71; exchange scientist, Nat Res Coun Can-Nat Sci Res Ctr, France, 76; vis prof, Univ Karlsruhe, WGer, 83, Dept Sci & Indust Res, Lower Hutt, NZ, 85, Univ Queensland, Australia, 85 & Univ Geneva, Switz, 92. *Mem:* Chem Inst Can; Royal Soc Chem; Electrochem Soc; Spectros Soc Can. *Res:* Raman and infrared spectroscopy; constitution and processes in electrolyte solutions; high temperature aqueous chemistry; Raman spectroscopy at electrode surfaces. *Mailing Add:* Dept Chem Univ Waterloo Waterloo ON N2L 3G1 Can. *Fax:* 519-746-0435; *E-Mail:* dirish@sciborg.uwaterloo.ca

IRISH, JAMES DAVID, PHYSICAL OCEANOGRAPHY, OCEAN ENGINEERING. *Current Pos:* RES SPECIALIST, WOODS HOLE OCEANOG INST, 91- *Personal Data:* b Bay City, Mich, Dec 7, 43; m 65, Peggy Ann Thompson. *Educ:* Antioch Col, BS, 67; Univ Calif, San Diego, MS, 69, PhD(oceanog), 71. *Prof Exp:* Res asst tides, Scripps Inst Oceanog, Univ Calif, San Diego, 67-71, assoc marine instrumentation, 71-72; res asst prof internal waves, Dept Oceanog, Univ Wash, 72-79, oceanographer, Appl Physics Lab, 74-79; res scientist, Univ NH, 79-83, res assoc prof, Dept Earth Sci, 83-91, Dept Ocean Eng, 85-91. *Mem:* Marine Technol Soc; Am Geophys Union; Oceanog Soc. *Res:* Tides, tidal dissipation and internal tides; internal wave behavior and the effect on acoustic propagation, wind driven shelf circulation; marine instrumentation and satellite data telemetry; sediment transport, bottom boundary layer dynamics. *Mailing Add:* MS No 17 Woods Hole Oceanog Inst Woods Hole MA 02543. *E-Mail:* jirish@whoi.edu

IRISH, JAMES MCCREDIE, III, RENAL PHYSIOLOGY. *Current Pos:* ASST PROF PHYSIOL, MED CTR, WVA UNIV, 78- *Personal Data:* b Portland, Maine, Sept 30, 43. *Educ:* State Univ NY, New Paltz, BS, 70; Univ Ariz, PhD(physiol), 75. *Concurrent Pos:* Nat Kidney Found renal fel, Med Ctr, Univ Kans, 75-76 & USPHS renal fel, 76-78. *Mem:* Am Physiol Soc; Am Soc Nephrol. *Res:* Organic anion and cation transport mechanisms in the kidney. *Mailing Add:* Riverside Med Bldg 375 E Park Ave No 3C Durango CO 81301-5042

IRITANI, W M, HORTICULTURE, PLANT PHYSIOLOGY. *Current Pos:* RETIRED. *Personal Data:* b Denver, Colo, Apr 29, 23; m 54; c 3. *Educ:* Univ Minn, BS, 51; Univ Idaho, MS, 53; Univ Ill, PhD(hort), 58. *Prof Exp:* Assoc hort, Univ Idaho, 58-68; prof & horticulturist, Wash State Univ, 68-89. *Concurrent Pos:* Fulbright grant to Japan; sabbatical, Neth 81, Scotland, 87. *Mem:* Am Soc Hort Sci; Potato Asn Am (pres, 84-85); Europ Potato Asn; Asian Potato Asn. *Res:* Physiology and post-harvest problems of potatoes. *Mailing Add:* 506 N 66th Seattle WA 98103

IRMITER, THEODORE FERER, food chemistry; deceased, see previous edition for last biography

IRONS, EDGAR T(OWAR), COMPUTER SCIENCE. *Current Pos:* CHIEF SCIENTIST, FRANKLIN ELECTRONIC PUBL, MT HOLLY, NJ, 92- *Personal Data:* b Detroit, Mich, Oct 11, 36. *Educ:* Princeton Univ, BSE, 58; Calif Inst Technol, MS, 59. *Prof Exp:* Mem tech staff comput res, Inst Defense Anal, 61-69; from assoc prof to prof comput sci, Yale Univ, 69-80, dir res, Interactive Syst Corp, 80-84; pres, Slater Tower Ltd, 84-92. *Concurrent Pos:* Vis lectr, Princeton Univ, 65-66. *Mem:* Asn Comput Mach. *Res:* Communication between man and digital computers; computer languages; compilers; operating systems. *Mailing Add:* Franklin Electronic Publ One Franklin Plaza Burlington NJ 08016-4907

IRONS, GORDON ALEXANDER, MATERIALS SCIENCE ENGINEERING. *Current Pos:* from asst prof to assoc prof, 80-89, chair, 91-94, PROF MAT SCI & ENG, MCMASTER UNIV, 89-, NAT SCI & ENG RES COUN PROF, 96- *Personal Data:* b Toronto, Ont, Aug 12, 50; m 90, Diane Crouchman; c Derek, Matthew & David. *Educ:* Univ Toronto, BASc, 73; McGill Univ, MSc, 75, PhD(metall eng), 78. *Honors & Awards:* Henry Marion Howe Medal, Am Soc Metals, 82; John Chipman Award, Iron & Steel Soc, Am Inst Mining Metall & Petrol Engrs, 83. *Prof Exp:* Res metallurgist, Noranda Technol Ctr, Noranda Minerals Inc, 78-79. *Mem:* Iron & Steel Soc; Metall Soc Can Inst Mining & Metall; Minerals Metals & Mat Soc; Am Soc Metals. *Res:* Transport phenomena and modeling of metallurgical and materials processing, including gas and solids injection processes, steelmaking, refining, smelting-reduction, and submerged arc smelting. *Mailing Add:* Dept Mat Sci & Eng McMaster Univ Hamilton ON L8S 4L7 Can. *Fax:* 905-526-8404; *E-Mail:* ironsga@mcmaster.ca

IRONS, MARGARET JEAN, cell biology, retina, for more information see previous edition

IRONS, RICHARD DAVIS, TOXICOLOGY, CELL BIOLOGY. *Current Pos:* PATHOLOGIST IMMUNOPATH, CHEM INDUST INST TOXICOL, 76- *Personal Data:* b Oakland, Calif, Sept 30, 47; m 79; c 3. *Educ:* Univ Pac, BA, 68; Univ Calif, MT, 70; Univ Rochester, PhD(toxicol), 75; Am Bd Toxicol, cert, 80. *Prof Exp:* Fel path, Strong Mem Hosp, Rochester, NY, 74-76. *Concurrent Pos:* Adj prof, Duke Univ Sch Med; mem, Ad Hoc Study Sect Immunol & Toxicol, NIH, 79, 81-82, permanent mem toxicol, 83-87, chmn, Toxicol Study Sect, 86-87, mem, EPA Health Effects Rev Panel, 87- *Mem:* AAAS; Am Asn Pathologists; Fedn Am Socs Exp Biol; Soc Toxicol; Reticuloendothelial Soc. *Res:* Myelotoxicity and immunopathology; molecular aspects of the effects of chemical agents on the cytoskeleton; regulation of cell growth and differentiation; leukemogenesis. *Mailing Add:* Dept Molec Toxicol Environ Health Sci Univ Colo Health Sci Ctr C-235 4200 E Ninth Ave Denver CO 80262-0001

IRR, JOSEPH DAVID, GENETICS. *Current Pos:* res genetic toxicologist, Haskell Lab, 81-84, sr res geneticist & cent res & develop biotechnol, 84-86, RES ASSOC, MED PROD DEPT, DUPONT MERCK PHARMACEUT, 77-; PRO LIFE & HEALTH SCI, UNIV DEL, 81- *Personal Data:* b Pittsburgh, Pa, Sept 19, 34. *Educ:* Univ Pittsburgh, BS, 62; Univ Calif, Santa Barbara, PhD(microbial genetics), 67. *Prof Exp:* NIH fel, Univ Wash, 67-69; from asst prof to assoc prof biol, Marquette Univ, 69-75; NSF fel, 70-74, Peter M Stanka Found fel, 71-74, March of Dimes fel, 74-75, NIH fel, 75-77. *Concurrent Pos:* Res fel, Harvard Med Sch-Mass Gen Hosp, 74-77; vis prof, Univ Hamburg, WGer, 76; vis scientist, Mass Inst Technol, 77; adj assoc prof genetics, Univ Del, 78-81. *Mem:* Genetics Soc Am; Am Soc Microbiol; Environmental Mutagen Soc; Genetic Toxicol Asn. *Res:* Genetic control mechanisms; gene expression in human cells, cellular therapy. *Mailing Add:* 386 Briar Lane Newark DE 19711

IRSA, ADOLPH PETER, MASS SPECTROMETRY, PHYSICAL CHEMISTRY. *Current Pos:* RETIRED. *Personal Data:* b New York, NY, Dec 9, 22; m 53; c 1. *Educ:* City Col New York, BS, 47; Adelphi Col, MS, 55. *Prof Exp:* Chemist mass spectrometry, Hydrocarbon Res Inc, 47-49, Brookhaven Nat Lab, 49-87. *Mem:* Am Chem Soc; Am Soc Mass Spectrometry. *Res:* Isotope effects; biomedical mass spectrometry; ion molecule reactions; analytical mass spectrometry. *Mailing Add:* 79 Morton Blvd Plainview NY 11803-5627. *E-Mail:* erehwon@worldnet.att.net

IRVIN, HOWARD BROWNLEE, CHEMICAL ENGINEERING, ECONOMICS. *Current Pos:* RETIRED. *Personal Data:* b Pittsburgh, Pa, Oct 21, 19; m 48; c 1. *Educ:* Pa State Col, BS, 42, MS, 46; Purdue Univ, PhD(chem eng), 49. *Prof Exp:* Res asst fluids, Pa State Col, 42-46; engr, Phillips Petrol Co, 48-66, sect mgr process design, 66-72, sr design engr, 72-86. *Mem:* Am Inst Chem Engrs; Am Chem Soc. *Res:* Process design and evaluation of plants for manufacture of polymers, petrochemicals and fertilizers. *Mailing Add:* 1927 Polaris Dr Bartlesville OK 74006-6113

IRVIN, HOWARD H, POLYMER CHEMISTRY. *Current Pos:* PRES, HOWARD H IRVIN & ASSOCS, 82- *Personal Data:* b Munich, Ger, Nov 19, 18; nat US; m 43; c 2. *Educ:* Rose Polytech Inst, BS, 43. *Hon Degrees:* DEng, Rose Hubean Inst, 87. *Prof Exp:* Metal inspector, Inland Steel Co, Ind, 43; asst to dir res, Marbon Chem Div, Borg-Warner Chem, 59-65, exec vpres, 65-69, pres, Marbon Int, 69-74, vpres eastern hemisphere, 74-79, vpres external technol, 80-81. *Mem:* Am Chem Soc; Am Soc Testing & Mat; Soc Plastics Indust; Tech Asn Pulp & Paper Indust. *Res:* Development of synthetic rubbers and special resins used in rubber compounding; electrical insulation materials; adhesives; adhesive for elastomers; special resins; administration; plastics and paint resins. *Mailing Add:* 175 N Harbor Dr Apt 3203 Chicago IL 60601-7344

IRVIN, JAMES DUARD, BIOCHEMISTRY. *Current Pos:* from asst prof to assoc prof, 73-83, PROF CHEM, SOUTHWEST TEX STATE UNIV, 83- *Personal Data:* b Grand Island, Nebr, Sept 24, 42; m 63; c Miriam & David. *Educ:* Gonzaga Univ, Wash, BS, 65; Mont State Univ, PhD(chem), 70. *Prof Exp:* Res assoc biochem, Univ Tex, Austin, 70-73. *Concurrent Pos:* Grants, Res Corp, 74-75, Robert A Welch Found, 74-84 & Pub Health Serv, 78-81, 86-88. *Mem:* Am Chem Soc; Am Soc Biochem & Molecular Biol. *Res:* Eukaryotic protein synthesis; antiviral and toxic proteins; ribosomes inactivating proteins. *Mailing Add:* Dept Chem Southwest Tex State Univ San Marcos TX 78666. *Fax:* 512-245-2374

IRVINE, CYNTHIA EMBERSON, STELLAR SPECTROSCOPY, PRE-COLLEGE SCIENCE ENRICHMENT. *Current Pos:* pres, 82-86, dir educ, 85-86, RES SCIENTIST, MONTEREY INST RES ASTRON, 72-; PROJ LEADER, GEMINI COMPUT, 87- *Personal Data:* b Washington, DC, Aug 14, 48; m 71, Nelson; c 2. *Educ:* Rice Univ, BA, 70; Case Western Reserve Univ, PhD(astron), 75. *Prof Exp:* Res assoc, US Naval Postgrad Sch, 75-81. *Concurrent Pos:* Consult, 84-85; instr, Monterey Peninsula Col, 85-86; consult & thesis adv, US Naval Postgrad Sch, 85-86. *Mem:* Am Astron Soc; Optical Soc Am; Inst Elec & Electronics Engrs. *Res:* Design and implementation of trusted computer system; design of applications to run on trusted systems; operating systems; software engineering. *Mailing Add:* Naval Post Grad Sch Code CSIC Monterey 1107 Sawmill Gulch Rd Pebble Beach CA 93943

IRVINE, DONALD GRANT, GEOGRAPHIC & GEOCHEMICAL TOXICOLOGY, ALTERNATIVE & COMPUTERIZED BIOASSAYS DEVELOPMENT. *Current Pos:* RETIRED. *Personal Data:* b Victoria, BC, Oct 28, 30; m 54, Isabelle F Davis; c Ian D, Rosalee A & Kenneth D. *Educ:* Univ BC, BA, 52, MA, 54; Univ Sask, PhD(biol psychiat), 81. *Prof Exp:* Res asst zool, Univ BC, 53-54; res asst physiol, Dept Physiol, Univ Sask, 54-58; res scientist, Psychiat Res Div, Sask Health, 58-83; res scientist, Toxicol Res Ctr, Univ Sask, 83-90, sr res scientist, 90- *Concurrent Pos:* Prin investr, var projs, Nat Health, Can, 67-71, Med Res Coun Can, 70-73, Schizophrenia Biol Res Found, 71 & Wildlife Toxicol Fund, 86-90; res assoc psychiat, Univ Sask, 69-72; adj prof toxicol, Fac Grad Studies & Res, Univ Sask, 85-, actg dir, Toxicol Res Ctr, 88-89. *Mem:* Soc Toxicol Can; Can Biochem Soc; Can Soc Clin Chemists; Soc Environ Toxicol & Chem; Am Soc Testing & Mat; World Asn Theoret Chemists. *Res:* Geographic, geochemical and hydrogeochemical factors in toxicoses and related diseases of man, animals and plants; use of minature organisms, computers and automation in developing alternative bioassays and bioindicators for toxicity. *Mailing Add:* 51 Campus Dr Saskatoon SK S7N 5A8 Can. *Fax:* 306-931-1664

IRVINE, DONALD MCLEAN, DAIRY SCIENCE. *Current Pos:* CONSULT, BIO-QUEST. *Personal Data:* b Toronto, Ont, Mar 22, 20; m 58; c 4. *Educ:* Ont Agr Col, BSA, 42; Univ Wis, MSc, 50, PhD(dairy sci), 56. *Honors & Awards:* Pfizer Award, Am Dairy Sci Asn. *Prof Exp:* Lectr dairy eng, Ont Agr Col, Univ Guelph, 46-47, head dept, 55-66, prof dairy sci, 55-85; instr, Univ Wis, 48-55. *Concurrent Pos:* Consult. *Mem:* Am Dairy Sci Asn; Int Food Technol; Nat Dairy Coun; Can Inst Food Technol. *Res:* Cheese mechanization; cheese food products; cheese varieties; enzymes. *Mailing Add:* 107 College Ave W Guelph ON N1G 1S3 Can

IRVINE, GEORGE NORMAN, PHYSICAL BIOCHEMISTRY. *Current Pos:* CONSULT, 79- *Personal Data:* b Calgary, Alta, Apr 6, 22; m 45, Joyce Johnstone; c Duncan & Donald. *Educ:* Univ Man, BSc, 43; McGill Univ, PhD(chem), 49. *Honors & Awards:* William F Geddes Mem Award, Am Asn Cereal Chemists, 78; Neumann Medal, Arbeitsgemeinschaft Getreideforsch, Ger, 78. *Prof Exp:* Res chemist, Can Grain Comn, 45-63, dir, Grain Res Lab, 63-78. *Concurrent Pos:* Adj prof, Univ Man. *Mem:* Am Asn Cereal Chemists; fel Chem Inst Can. *Res:* Chemical kinetics; enzymes; wheat pigments; quality factors in durum and bread wheat; milling and baking technology; flour quality. *Mailing Add:* 994 Cottontree Close Victoria BC V8X 4E9 Can

IRVINE, JAMES BOSWORTH, PHYSICAL CHEMISTRY, MINERALOGY. *Current Pos:* PRES, ROCKREATION, INC, 82- *Personal Data:* b Lexington, Ky, Apr 15, 14; m 37, Martha Campbell; c 2. *Educ:* Univ Ky, BS, 37. *Prof Exp:* Anal chemist, Naval Stores, Hercules Powder Co, 37-38; anal & develop chemist, Textile Auxiliaries, O F Zurn Co, 38-41; textile chemist, Collins & Aikman Corp, 41-45; chemist textile auxiliaries, Quaker Chem Prods Corp, 45-47, group leader, Customer Serv & Textile Auxiliaries, 47-52, dir, New Prod Develop, 52-58, Textile Process Develop, 58-60 & Tech Sales Develop, 60-64, process engr, Quaker Chem Corp, 64-82. *Mem:* Am Chem Soc; Am Asn Textile Chem & Colorists; Friends Mineral. *Res:* Textile auxiliaries and processes; physical sciences. *Mailing Add:* 3508 Starmount Dr Greensboro NC 27403

IRVINE, JAMES ESTILL, PLANT PHYSIOLOGY. *Current Pos:* at RES EXTEN CTR, TEX A&M AGR CTR. *Personal Data:* b Charlottesville, Va, Feb 2, 28; m 51; c 3. *Educ:* Univ Miami, Fla, BS, 51, MS, 52; Univ Va, PhD(biol), 57. *Prof Exp:* Asst prof biol, Bridgewater Col, 53-54; instr, Univ Va, 55-56; plant physiologist & dir, US Sugarcane Lav, Sci & Educ Admin-Agr Res, USDA, 57- *Mem:* Am Soc Plant Physiol; Am Soc Agron; Asn Trop Biol; Int Soc Sugarcane Technol. *Res:* Photosynthetic efficiency; leaf physiology; cold tolerance; pre- and post-harvest changes in sugarcane quality; tropical agriculture. *Mailing Add:* Tex A&M Agr Res Exten Ctr 2415 E Hwy 83 Weslaco TX 78596

IRVINE, MERLE M, PHYSICS. *Current Pos:* RETIRED. *Personal Data:* b San Francisco, Calif, Jan 5, 24; m 45; c 4. *Educ:* Mont State Univ, BS, 50; Lehigh Univ, MS, 52, PhD(physics), 55. *Prof Exp:* Instr physics, Lehigh Univ, 52-55; mem tech staff, Bell Labs, 55-61, supvr, 61-63, dept head, 63-71, dir, 71-84. *Mem:* Am Asn Physics Teachers; Asn Comput Mach; Am Phys Soc; Inst Elec & Electronics Engrs. *Res:* Cathode sputtering in glow discharges; digital computers; electromagnetic theory; plasma physics; data management systems. *Mailing Add:* 511 S Willson Ave Bozeman MT 59715

IRVINE, STUART JAMES CURZON, CRYSTAL GROWTH, INFRARED DETECTORS. *Current Pos:* PROF MAT CHEM, NORTH EAST WALES INST, 93- *Personal Data:* b Broadstairs, Kent, UK, May 14, 53; m 74, Caroline Stagy; c Tim, Alex & Michael. *Educ:* Loughborough Univ Technol,

UK, BSc, 74; Univ Birmingham, UK, PhD(metall & mat sci), 78. *Prof Exp:* Res fel, Dept Phys, Univ Birmingham, UK, 77-78; higher sci officer, Royal Signals & Radar Estab, Ministry Defence, UK, 78-80, sr sci officer, 80-84, prin sci officer, 84-90; asst mgr, Array Prod Res, Sci Ctr, Rockwell Int, 90-93. *Concurrent Pos:* Tutor physics, Open Univ, 79-82; guest ed, J Crystal Growth, 81-85; UK rep, Int Adv Comt for Eurocryst. *Mem:* Am Asn Crystal Growth; Mat Res Soc; fel Inst Phys; Brit Asn Crystal Growth. *Res:* Growth of narrow and wide band gap II-VI semiconductors using metal organic vapor phase epitaxy; ultra violet and laser stimulation of epitatial growth processes; optical in site monitoring. *Mailing Add:* North East Wales Inst Plas Coch Mold Rd Wrexham Clwyd LL11 2AW Wales. Fax: 44-1978-293212; E-Mail: irvines@newi.ac.uk

IRVINE, T NEIL, GEOLOGY. *Current Pos:* PETROLOGIST, GEOPHYS LAB, WASHINGTON, DC, 72- *Personal Data:* b Manitoba, Can, Jan 5, 33; m 62; c 1. *Educ:* Univ Man, BSc, 53, MSc, 56; Calif Inst Technol, PhD(geol), 59. *Prof Exp:* Asst prof geol, McMaster Univ, 59-62; petrologist, Geol Surv Can, 62-72. *Mem:* Geol Soc Am; Am Geophys Union. *Res:* Petrology and geochemistry of ultramafic rocks. *Mailing Add:* 3225 Coquelin Terr Chevy Chase MD 20815

IRVINE, THOMAS FRANCIS, HEAT TRANSFER, FLUID MECHANICS. *Current Pos:* dean, 61-72, PROF MECH ENG, STATE UNIV NY STONY BROOK, 72- *Personal Data:* b Northmont, NJ, June 25, 22; m 66; c 2. *Educ:* Pa State Univ, BS, 46; Univ Minn, MS, 51, PhD(mech eng), 56. *Prof Exp:* From instr to assoc prof mech eng, Univ Minn, 50-59; prof, NC State Univ, 59-61. *Concurrent Pos:* Ed transl jours: Heat Transfer-Soviet Res, 69-, Heat Transfer-Japanese Res, 72- & Previews Heat & Mass Transfer, 74-; co-ed, Advances in Heat Transfer, 60; vis prof, Tech Univ Munich, 68, Univ Florence, 85; vis scientist, Boris Kidric' Inst, Belgrade, 72. *Mem:* Fel Am Soc Mech Engrs; fel AAAS; fel Int Ctr Heat & Mass Transfer. *Mailing Add:* 161 Mills Pond Rd St James NY 11780

IRVINE, WILLIAM MICHAEL, PLANETARY SCIENCE, RADIO ASTRONOMY. *Current Pos:* assoc prof astron & physics, 66-69, head astron prog & chmn, Five Col Astron Dept, Univ Mass, Amherst, Hampshire, Smith & Mt Holyoke Cols, 66-76; PROF PHYSICS & ASTRON, UNIV MASS, AMHERST, 69- *Personal Data:* b Los Angeles, Calif, Aug 31, 36; m; c 4. *Educ:* Pomona Col, BA, 57; Harvard Univ, MA, 58, PhD(physics), 61. *Prof Exp:* Physicist, Smithsonian Astrophys Observ & res fel & lectr, Harvard Col Observ, 62-66. *Concurrent Pos:* NATO fel astron, 61-62; mem bd trustees, NE Radio Observ Corp, 67-79, vchmn, 68-73; sr fel, Int Res & Exchanges Bd, Sweden, 73-74; chmn, Div Planetary Sci, Am Astron Soc, 73-74; assoc ed, Icarus, 76-; vis prof, Kanazawa Inst Technol, Japan, 77; vis prof & chmn sci comn, Onsala Space Observ, Chalmers Univ Technol, Sweden, 79-81; vis prof, Japanese Nat Astron Observ, 90. *Mem:* Am Phys Soc; Am Astron Soc; Am Geophys Union; Int Astron Union; Int Sci Radio Union; Int Soc Study Origin Life. *Res:* Light scattering and radiative transfer in planetary atmospheres and surfaces; spectral line radio astronomy. *Mailing Add:* Dept Physics & Astron Univ Mass Amherst MA 01003

IRVING, CHARLES CLAYTON, BIOCHEMISTRY. *Current Pos:* RETIRED. *Personal Data:* b Memphis, Tenn, Oct 12, 32; m 54; c 5. *Educ:* Memphis State Univ, BS, 53; Univ Tenn, MS, 55, PhD(chem), 57. *Prof Exp:* Asst chem, Univ Tenn, 56-57; res fel physiol chem, Univ Minn, 57-59; from asst prof to prof biochem, Med Units, Univ Tenn, Memphis, 60-93, prof uriol, 76-93. *Concurrent Pos:* Res biochemist, Vet Admin Hosp, 60-93. *Mem:* AAAS; Am Chem Soc; Am Soc Biol Chem; Am Asn Cancer Res. *Res:* Chemical carcinogenesis; drug metabolism. *Mailing Add:* 701 Ridge Rd Heber Springs AR 72543

IRVING, EDWARD, PALEOMAGNETISM. *Current Pos:* res scientist, 81-92, EMER SCIENTIST, PAC GEOSCI CTR, 92- *Personal Data:* b Colne, Eng, May 27, 27; m 57, Sheila A Irwin; c Kathryn, Susan, Martin & George. *Educ:* Cambridge Univ, BA, 50, MA, 53, ScD, 65. *Hon Degrees:* DSc, Carleton Univ, 79, Mem Univ Nfld, 86. *Honors & Awards:* Gondwanaland Medal, Mining, Geol & Metallog Inst India, 65; Logan Medal, Geol Asn Can, 75; Walter Bucher Medal, Am Geophys Union, 79; Wilson Medal, Can Geophys Union, 84; Alfred Wegener Medal, Europ Union Geosci, 95. *Prof Exp:* From res fel to sr fel geophys, Australian Nat Univ, 54-64; sr sci officer geomagnetism, Dominion Observ, 64-66; prof geophys, Univ Leeds, 66-67; res scientist geomagnetism, Earth Physics Br, Dept Energy Mines & Resources, Can, 67-81. *Concurrent Pos:* Adj prof, Carleton Univ, Ottawa, 75-77 & Univ Victoria, 85-96. *Mem:* Fel Royal Astron Soc; fel Am Geophys Union; fel Royal Soc Can; fel Geol Asn Can. *Res:* Paleomagnetism and its application to geological and geophysical problems. *Mailing Add:* Pac Geosci Ctr 9860 W Saanich Rd PO Box 6000 Sidney BC V8L 4B2 Can

IRVING, ELIZABETH L, OPTOMETRY. *Current Pos:* POSTDOCTORAL FEL, EYE RES INST CAN, UNIV TORONTO, 95- *Personal Data:* b Can, May 6, 60. *Educ:* Univ Waterloo, Dr, 83, MS, 89, PhD(vision sci), 94. *Honors & Awards:* Alice Wilson Award, Royal Soc Can, 94. *Prof Exp:* Pvt pract, Humbolt, Sask, 83-84; res asst, Sch Optom, Univ Waterloo, 85-86, lab demonstr, 87-93, optom clin supvr, 85-95. *Concurrent Pos:* Postdoctoral fel, Med Res Coun Can, 94-96. *Mem:* Asn Res Vision & Ophthal. *Res:* Research in adaptations of eye and visual system to environmental influences; monocular adaptations in binocular vision; adaptations in refractive development. *Mailing Add:* Eye Res Inst Can Toronto Hosp 399 Bathurst St Toronto ON M5T 2S8 Can

IRVING, FRANK DUNHAM, FORESTRY. *Current Pos:* from instr to assoc prof, 55-66, PROF FORESTRY, UNIV MINN, ST PAUL, 66- *Personal Data:* b Plainfield, NJ, July 30, 23; m 48; c 3. *Educ:* Rutgers Univ, BS, 48; Univ Minn, BS, 49, MF, 50, PhD(forestry), 60. *Prof Exp:* Dist game mgr, Wis Conserv Dept, 50-55. *Mem:* Soc Am Foresters; Wildlife Soc; Sigma Xi. *Res:* Southeastern Minnesota hardwood management; patterns of administrative organization in forestry and wildlife management; techniques of prescribed burning. *Mailing Add:* 1745 Tatum St St Paul MN 55113

IRVING, GEORGE WASHINGTON, JR, BIOCHEMICAL PHARMACOLOGY. *Current Pos:* RETIRED. *Personal Data:* b Caribou, Maine, Nov 20, 10; m 38, Frances Connell; c George W III & Mary C (Fitzpatrick). *Educ:* George Washington Univ, BS, 33, MS, 35, PhD(biochem), 39. *Honors & Awards:* Honor Award, Am Inst Chem, 69; Honor Award, Am Leather Chem Asn, 69. *Prof Exp:* Lab asst, Nat Bur Stand, 27-28; lab asst, Bur Chem, USDA, 28-35, jr chemist, Bur Entom & Plant Quarantine, 35; res fel biochem, George Washington Univ Med Sch, 36-38 & Cornell Univ Med Col, 38-39; asst chem, Rockefeller Inst, 39-42; biochemist southern regional res lab, Bur Agr & Indust Chem, USDA, La, 42-43, sr biochemist, 43-44, sr biochemist, Agr Res Ctr, Md, 44-46, prin chemist & head div biol active compounds, 46-47, asst chief, agr & indust chem, Washington, DC, 47-53, chief biol sci br, Mkt Res Div, Agr Mkt Serv, 53-54, dep adminstr, Agr Res Serv, 54-64, from assoc adminstr to adminstr, 64-71; consult, 71-72; res assoc, Fedn Am Soc Exp Biol, Bethesda, Md, 72-77; consult, 78-93; sr res, 78-88, exec vpres agr res, Inst Bethesda, Md, 82-84; exec vpres, Inter-Life Scis Int, 86-89; dir, Friends Agr Res, Beltsville, 85- *Concurrent Pos:* Lectr, USDA Grad Sch, 46-52 & med sch, George Washington Univ, 47-54; trustee, The Nutrit Found, 56; mem, Expert Comt Food Additives, Joint Food & Agr Orgn, WHO, UN, Geneva, Switz, 76-77; chmn bd, The Nutrit Found, 83-84; Assoc ed, Hexagon, 84. *Mem:* AAAS (vpres, 62); Am Chem Soc; Am Soc Biochem & Molecular Biol; Inst Food Technol; Sigma Xi; Am Inst Chemists. *Res:* Biochemistry of pituitary hormones; plant and animal proteolytic enzymes; chemistry of plant proteins; chemistry of antibiotics and plant growth regulators; toxicological evaluation of food additives. *Mailing Add:* 9707 Old Georgetown Rd No 2316 Bethesda MD 20814-1727

IRVING, JAMES P, CHEMICAL ENGINEERING. *Current Pos:* RETIRED. *Personal Data:* b New York, NY, Apr 28, 36; m 63; c 3. *Educ:* Univ Notre Dame, BS, 57; Univ Northwestern, MS, 59; Yale Univ, DEng, 66. *Prof Exp:* Res engr, Jet Propulsion Lab, Calif Inst Technol, 59-61; res engr, Chevron Res Co, 65-68, sr res engr, Chevron Oil Field Res Co, 68-71, sr eng assoc, 71-72, prod eng, 72-73; mgr systs & eng serv, Stand Oil Co, Calif, 73-75, mgr oil recovery, 75-78, mgr planning, Mgt Planning & Develop Staff, 78-80, mgr reservoir eng, 80-81, Western Region coordr prod, Chevron USA, 81-83, vpres prod res, Chevron Oil & Fuel, Lahbra Co, pres, 83-85, gen mgr prod, Southern Region, Chevron USA, 87-92; gen mgr, Human Resources Overseas, 92-95. *Mem:* Am Inst Chem Engrs. *Res:* Assisted recovery techniques. *Mailing Add:* 6001 Bollinger Canyon Rd PO Box 5046 San Ramon CA 94583

IRVING, PATRICIA MARIE, PHYSIOLOGICAL ECOLOGY. *Current Pos:* VPRES ENVIRON SYSTS & TECHNOL, BATTELLE MEM INST, 92- *Personal Data:* b Kenosha, Wis, May 28, 50. *Educ:* Dominican Col, BS, 72; Univ Wis-Milwaukee, MS, 75, PhD(bot), 79. *Honors & Awards:* Wolf Vishniac Mem Excellence Award, 85. *Prof Exp:* Res assoc, Argonne Nat Lab, 74-79, asst ecologist, 79-86, ecologist, 86-88, assoc, White House Coun Environ Qual, 88-90, dir, Nat Acid Precipitation Assessment Prog, 91-92. *Concurrent Pos:* Instr, Milwaukee Area Tech Col, 76; ecologist, M H Gabriel & Assocs, 78-79; adj prof, Northern Ill Univ, 81-83; US rep UN-ECE Conv Transboundry Air Pollution Task Force Terrestrial Effects, 87-; US rep Int Meeting Acid Rain Coord, 89- *Mem:* Ecol Soc Am; Fedn Am Scientists; AAAS. *Res:* Causes, effects and control strategy options for pollution; effects of environmental stress on ecosystems; environmental economics. *Mailing Add:* Battelle Pac NW Labs Univ Progs PO Box 999 K6-98 Richland WA 99352

IRWIN, ARTHUR S(AMUEL), engineering mechanics; deceased, see previous edition for last biography

IRWIN, CHARLES EDWIN, JR, PEDIATRICS, ADOLESCENT MEDICINE. *Current Pos:* Clin scholar, Robert Wood Found, 74-77, DIR ADOLESCENT MED & PROF PEDIAT & VICE CHMN, DEPT PEDIAT, SCH MED, UNIV CALIF, SAN FRANCISCO, 77- *Personal Data:* b Medford, Mass, Dec 15, 45; m 79, Nancie N Kester; c Seth Kester. *Educ:* Hobart Col, BS, 67; Dartmouth Med Sch, BMS, 69; Univ Calif, San Francisco, MD, 71. *Honors & Awards:* Res award, Soc Adolescent Med, 83; Nat Youth Law Ctr Award, 88. *Concurrent Pos:* Dir, Interdisciplinary Adolescent Health Training Prog, Health & Human Serv training grant, 77-, Nat Adolescent Health Info Ctr, 93-, Policy & Info Ctr Mid Childhood & Adolescence; int hon lectureship, Swedish Soc Med, 96. *Mem:* Soc Adolescent Med; Ambulatory Pediat Asn; Am Acad Pediat; Am Pub Health Asn; Am Venereal Dis Asn; Soc Pediat Res; Soc Res Child Develop; Am Pediat Soc. *Res:* Health behaviors of adolescents; compliance and self care in adolescents; adolescent reproductive health problems; risk-taking behaviors in adolescence; evaluation of preventive health services in adolescent in managed care settings. *Mailing Add:* Dept Pediat Univ Calif San Francisco CA 94143. Fax: 415-476-6106; E-Mail: cirwin@itsa.ucsf.edu

IRWIN, DAVID, ONCOLOGY, HEALTH SCIENCES ADMINISTRATION. *Current Pos:* spec expert genetics, Nat Inst Gen Med Sci, NIH, 83-84, exec secy molecular biol, Div Res Grants, 84-85, health sci admin grant rev, 85-89, CHIEF, NAT CANCER INST, 89- *Personal Data:* b Leeds, Eng, Oct 17, 45; US citizen; m 69, Pauline G Yeoman; c Melissa & James. *Educ:* Univ Leeds, BSc, 69, PhD, 74. *Prof Exp:* Postdoctorate fel surg, Harvard Med Sch, 73-75, instr, 75-79; asst biochemist, Mass Gen Hosp, 75-79; sr res scientist, George Washington Univ Med Ctr, 79-83. *Concurrent Pos:* Lectr biol, Boston Univ, 73-75; vis prof, Univ Mass, Boston, 77-79, St George's Med Sch, Grenada, 81-83; vis asst prof, Northern Va Community Co, 84-85; freelance ed, Cambridge Sci Abstr, 85-87. *Mem:* Am Asn Cancer Res; Biochem Soc; Am Soc Cell Biol; AAAS. *Res:* Molecular biology and regulation of cellular growth in normal and neoplastic tissues. *Mailing Add:* Res Pro Sect Grants Revi Br 6130 Executive Blvd Bethesda MD 20892-0001

IRWIN, DAVID MICHAEL, MOLECULAR EVOLUTION, GENE EXPRESSION. *Current Pos:* ASST PROF CLIN BIOCHEM, UNIV TORONTO, 91- *Personal Data:* b Dingwall, Scotland, Dec 15, 60; Can citizen; m 93, Min Wang. *Educ:* Univ Guelph, BSc(Hon), 82, Univ BC, PhD(genetics), 86. *Prof Exp:* Fel, Univ Calif, Berkeley, 87-91. *Mem:* AAAS; Int Soc Molecular Evolution; Molecular Biol & Evolution Soc. *Res:* Origin of new genes; evolution of ruminant stomach lysozyme genes and the origin of glucagon-like peptides. *Mailing Add:* Univ Toronto 100 College St Toronto ON M5G 1L5 Can. *Fax:* 416-978-4108; *E-Mail:* irwin@medac3.med.utoronto.ca

IRWIN, GEORGE RANKIN, PHYSICS, MECHANICAL ENGINEERING. *Current Pos:* RETIRED. *Personal Data:* b El Paso, Tex, Feb 26, 07; m 33; c 4. *Educ:* Knox Col, AB, 30; Univ Ill, MS, 33, PhD, 37. *Hon Degrees:* DEng, Lehigh Univ, 77. *Honors & Awards:* Timoshenko Medal, Am Soc Mech Engrs; Gold Medal, Am Soc Mech. *Prof Exp:* Physicist, US Naval Res Lab, 37-67; prof mech, Lehigh Univ, 67-72; prof mech eng, Univ Md, Col Park, 72-94. *Concurrent Pos:* Vis prof, Univ Ill, 61 & 62. *Mem:* Nat Acad Eng; Am Soc Mech; Am Soc Mech Engrs; hon mem Am Soc Testing & Mat; Soc Exp Mech. *Res:* Fracture mechanics. *Mailing Add:* 7306 Edmonson Rd College Park MD 20740

IRWIN, GLENN WARD, JR, endocrinology, internal medicine, for more information see previous edition

IRWIN, HOWARD SAMUEL, SYSTEMATIC BOTANY, PLANT ECOLOGY. *Current Pos:* CONSULT, 91- *Personal Data:* b Louisville, Ky, Mar 28, 28; m 79, Anne I Lieb; c Elizabeth & Dorothy. *Educ:* Univ Puget Sound, BA, 50, BEd, 52; Univ Tex, PhD(trop bot), 60. *Hon Degrees:* DSc, Fordham Univ, 77. *Honors & Awards:* Willdenon Medal, Berlin Bot Garden, 79; Prof Hort Award, Am Hort Soc, 91. *Prof Exp:* Fulbright English & biol, Queen's Col, Georgetown, Guyana, 52-56; res assoc trop bot, NY Bot Garden, 60-63, assoc cur, 63-66, cur & herbarium adminr, 66-68, head cur, 68-71, exec dir inst mgt, 71-72, exec vpres, 72-73, pres, 73-78; vchancellor, Long Island Univ, 79-83; dir, Clark Bot Garden, Albertson, NY, 83-91. *Concurrent Pos:* Adj prof bot, City Univ New York, 71-78; NSF grantee, 64-78; prof, Columbia Univ, 68-78. *Mem:* Fel NY Acad Sci; Sigma Xi; Asn Trop Biol (secy-treas, 63-64); Am Soc Plant Taxonomists (pres, 71-72); Asn Systs Collections (pres, 73-75). *Res:* Systematics of neotropical Cassia, Mimosa; flora of planalto do Brasil. *Mailing Add:* PO Box 846 Truro MA 02666. *Fax:* 508-349-3656

IRWIN, JOHN (HENRY) BARROWS, astronomy, for more information see previous edition

IRWIN, JOHN CHARLES, PHYSICS, RAMAN SCATTERING. *Current Pos:* From asst prof to assoc prof, 65-78, chmn, 80-88, PROF PHYSICS, SIMON FRASER UNIV, 78- *Personal Data:* b Rossburn, Man, June 3, 35; m 86, Sandra Stover; c 4. *Educ:* Univ BC, BASc, 58, PhD(physics), 65. *Concurrent Pos:* Nat Res Coun Can grant, 65-; mem bd mgt, BC Res Coun, 74-77. *Mem:* Can Asn Physicists; Am Phys Soc; Mat Res Soc. *Res:* Roman scattering studies of solids: dielectrics, semiconductors, metals and superconductors. *Mailing Add:* Dept Physics Simon Fraser Univ Burnaby BC V5A 1S6 Can. *Fax:* 604-291-3592; *E-Mail:* irwin@sfu.ca

IRWIN, JOHN DAVID, NOISE & VIBRATION CONTROL. *Current Pos:* prof, 69-93, EARLE C WILLIAMS EMINENT SCHOLAR & PROF ELEC ENG, AUBURN UNIV, 93- DEPT HEAD, 69- *Personal Data:* b Minneapolis, Minn, Aug 9, 39; m; c 3. *Educ:* Auburn Univ, BS, 61; Univ Tenn, MS, 62, PhD(elec eng), 67. *Honors & Awards:* Centennial Medal, Inst Elec & Electronics Engrs, 84. *Prof Exp:* Supvr & mem tech staff, Bell Tel Labs, 67-69. *Mem:* Fel Inst Elec & Electronics Engrs; Indust Electronics Soc (pres 80-81); Educ Soc (pres, 89-90); Am Soc Eng Educ. *Res:* Author or co-author of books on industrial noise, computer logic and engineering circuits. *Mailing Add:* Dept Elec Eng Auburn Univ Auburn AL 36849-5201

IRWIN, JOHN MCCORMICK, MATHEMATICS. *Current Pos:* PROF MATH, WAYNE STATE UNIV, 65- *Personal Data:* b Peking, China, Nov 11, 29; US citizen; m 56; c 4. *Educ:* Purdue Univ, BS, 53; Univ Kans, MA, 56, PhD(math), 60. *Prof Exp:* From asst prof to assoc prof math, NMex State Univ, 60-65. *Concurrent Pos:* Co-recipient, NSF res grant, 61-64. *Mem:* Am Math Soc; Math Asn Am. *Res:* Algebra, specifically infinite Abelian groups and differential equations; applied math. *Mailing Add:* 748 Moorland Grosse Pointwoods Grosse Point MI 48236-1129

IRWIN, LAFAYETTE K(EY), mechanical metrology, applied mechanics; deceased, see previous edition for last biography

IRWIN, LOUIS NEAL, NEUROBIOLOGY, NEUROCHEMISTRY. *Current Pos:* PROF & CHMN BIOL SCI, UNIV TEX, EL PASO, 91- *Personal Data:* b Big Spring, Tex, Jan 8, 43; m 67, Carol Crumrine; c Sean, Anthony & Brian. *Educ:* Tex Tech Univ, BA, 65; Univ Kans, PhD(biochem, physiol), 69. *Prof Exp:* NIH trainee, Parsons State Hosp, Kans, 69-70; asst prof biol, Col Pharmaceut Sci, Columbia Univ, 70-73; asst prof physiol, Sch Med, Wayne State Univ, 73-76; assoc biochemist, E K Shriver Ctr, 76-79; prof biol, Simmons Col, 80-91. *Concurrent Pos:* Staff scientist, Neurosci Res Prog, Mass Inst Technol, 77-78. *Mem:* AAAS; Soc Neurosci; Am Soc Neurochem; Sigma Xi; Int Soc Neurochem; Soc Integrative & Comp Biol. *Res:* Molecular neurobiology; biochemical correlates of brain organization and function; developmental neurochemistry. *Mailing Add:* Biol Sci Univ Tex El Paso TX 79968. *Fax:* 915-747-5808; *E-Mail:* lirwin@utep.edu

IRWIN, LYNNE HOWARD, HIGHWAY ENGINEERING, PAVEMENT DESIGN & EVALUATIONS. *Current Pos:* ASSOC PROF ENG, CORNELL UNIV, 73- *Personal Data:* b Los Angeles, Calif, May 4, 44; m 65; c 3. *Educ:* Univ Calif, BS, 65, MS, 66; Tex A&M Univ, PhD(civil eng), 73. *Prof Exp:* Asst prof eng, Calif State Univ, 66-69; res assoc, Tex A&M Univ, 69-72. *Concurrent Pos:* NSF fel, 69-71; hwy engr, US Forest Serv, 79-80; res engr, Cold Regions Res & Eng Lab, US Army Corps Engrs, 80. *Mem:* Asn Soc Civil Engrs; Asn Asphalt Pavement Technologists; Am Rd & Transp Builders Asn. *Res:* Structural evaluation of pavements using nondestructive deflection testing; recycling of pavements, surfaces and bases, using chemical stabilization; development of computer programs for calculation of moduli of elasticity of pavement layers. *Mailing Add:* Dept Agr Eng 104 Riley-Robb Hall Cornell Univ Ithaca NY 14853-0001

IRWIN, MARY JANE, APPLICATION SPECIFIC PROCESSOR DESIGN, ELECTRONIC CAD TOOLS. *Current Pos:* From asst prof to assoc prof, 77-89, PROF COMPUT SCI & ENG, PA STATE UNIV, 89- *Personal Data:* b Cairo, Ill, July 14, 49; m 66, Vernon; c John. *Educ:* Memphis State Univ, BS, 71; Univ Ill, MS, 75, PhD(comput sci), 77. *Concurrent Pos:* Prin investr, NSF, 89-94; distinguished lectr, Inst Elec & Electronics Engrs Comput Soc, 90-92, publ bd, 92-93, bd gov, 93-; Cent Res Agency Bd Dirs, Comput Res Asn, 91-94; ed, Inst Elec & Electronics Engrs Comput, 91- *Mem:* Am Comp Mach; Spec Interest Group Archit Comput Syst (secy-treas, 85-91); Spec Interest Group Design Automation; Inst Elec & Electronics Engrs Comput Soc. *Res:* Computer architecture design and the development of electronic CAD tools to support the design process; published technical papers on a wide range of topics; digital signal processing architecture; electronic CAD tools for module generation and logic synthesis; high speed arithmetic; massively parellel processor design. *Mailing Add:* Pa State Univ University Park University Park PA 16802

IRWIN, MICHAEL EDWARD, ENTOMOLOGY, SYSTEMATICS. *Current Pos:* from asst prof to assoc prof, 74-89, dir, Ctr Econ Entom, 90-93, PROF ENTOM & PLANT PATH, UNIV ILL & ILL NAT HIST SURV, 84- *Personal Data:* b Los Angeles, Calif, Aug 10, 40; m 71. *Educ:* Univ Calif, Davis, BS, 63; Univ Calif, Riverside, PhD(entom), 71. *Prof Exp:* Res entomologist surv entom, Univ Calif-Univ Chile, 66-67; asst spec entom, Univ Calif, Riverside, 70-71; sr prof officer entom, Nat Mus, Pietermaritzburg, SAfrica, 71-74. *Concurrent Pos:* Mem, Int Soybean Prog; Travel Award, Entom Soc Am, 80; prog mgr, Plant/Pests Interactions, USDA Nat Res Initiative Competitive Grants, 90; dir, Ctr Econ Entom, Ill Nat Hist Surv, 90- *Mem:* Entom Soc Am (secy, 78); Can Entom Soc; Am Inst Biol Sci; AAAS; Int Asn Ecol; Sigma Xi. *Res:* Epidemiology of plant viruses by insect vectors; long distance movement of insects; biosystematics of Therevidae (Insecta Diptera). *Mailing Add:* 1107 S Busey Ave Urbana IL 61801-4831

IRWIN, PETER ANTHONY, WIND ENGINEERING, FLUID MECHANICS. *Current Pos:* PRIN, ROWAN WILLIAMS DAVIES & IRWIN, INC, 86- *Personal Data:* b Thetford, Eng, Aug 10, 45; Can citizen; m 70; c 2. *Educ:* Southampton Univ, UK, BSc, 67, MSc, 69; McGill Univ, PhD(fluid mech), 74. *Honors & Awards:* Two Merit Awards, Asn Consult Engrs Can; Gzowski Medal Award, 95. *Prof Exp:* Sci officer aerodyn, Royal Aircraft Estab, Farnborough, UK, 68-71; res officer wind eng, Nat Res Coun Can, 74-80; dir tech serv, Morrison Hershfield Ltd, 80-86. *Concurrent Pos:* Mem, Standing Comt Struct Design, Can Nat Bldg Code. *Mem:* Can Soc Civil Engrs; Eng Inst Can; Am Soc Civil Engrs. *Res:* Response of buildings, bridges and structures to wind; aerodynamics; fluid mechanics; turbulence; aeroelasticity; airborne pollution studies; snow loading and drifting. *Mailing Add:* Rowan Williams Davies & Irwin Inc 650 Woodlawn Rd W Guelph ON N1K 1B8 Can

IRWIN, PHILIP GEORGE, PHYSICAL ORGANIC CHEMISTRY. *Current Pos:* PRES, PRESTIGE CHEM INC, 83- *Personal Data:* b Duquesne, Pa, Nov 20, 34; m 61; c 6. *Educ:* Duquesne Univ, BS, 56; Purdue Univ, MS, 58; Pa State Univ, PhD(org chem), 62. *Prof Exp:* Res chemist, Gulf Res & Develop Co, 62-65; appl res, US Steel Corp, 65-69; group leader synthetic resin res, Picco Resins, Hercules Inc, 69-80; tech dir, Ameron Ind Coatings, 80; tech mgr, Ga-Pac Corp, 82-83. *Concurrent Pos:* Consult. *Mem:* Am Chem Soc. *Res:* Resin and chemical synthesis; chemical modification of polymers; new product and process research; polymer and chemical research in adhesives, printing inks, toners, paper size, film, coatings. *Mailing Add:* RR1 PO Box 1034 Box 1034 Ruffs Dale PA 15679

IRWIN, RICHARD STEPHEN, COUGH, ASTHMA. *Current Pos:* assoc prof med, 79-82, PROF MED, UNIV MASS MED SCH, 82- *Personal Data:* b New London, Conn, Nov 15, 42; m 69, Diane Northrop; c Rachel, Sara, Catherine & Rebecca. *Educ:* Tufts Univ, BS, 64; Tufts Sch Med, MD, 68; dipl, Nat Bd Med Examiners, 69, Am Bd Internal Med, 72, Am Bd Pulmonary

Med, 74, Am Bd Critical Care Med, 87. *Prof Exp:* Internship med, Tufts New England Med Ctr, 68-69; residency, 69-70; fel cardioresponse physiol, Columbia Presby Hosp, 70-72; asst prof med, Brown Univ, 74-79. *Concurrent Pos:* Dir, Div Pulmonary & Critical Care Med, 79- *Mem:* Fel Am Col Chest Physicians; Am Thoracic Soc; Am Col Chest Physicians; Am Col Physicians; Nat Asn Med Dirs Respiratory Care; Soc Crit Care Med; fel Am Col Physicians. *Res:* The pathophysiology, pathogenesis, diagnosis and treatment of cough and the diagnosis and treatment of asthma; interactions of the gastrointestinal and respiratory systems. *Mailing Add:* Univ Mass Med Ctr 55 Lake Ave N Worcester MA 01655. Fax: 508-856-3999

IRWIN, ROBERT COOK, MATHEMATICS, COMPUTER SCIENCES. *Current Pos:* MEM TECH STAFF, MITRE CORP, 71- *Personal Data:* b Hastings, Nebr, Oct 25, 29; m 60; c 1. *Educ:* Univ Nebr, BS, 51; Univ Calif, MA, 58; Univ Ariz, PhD(math), 63. *Prof Exp:* Engr, Int Bus Mach Corp, 54-56; mem staff, Lincoln Lab, Mass Inst Technol, 58-59; mem tech staff, Mitre Corp, Mass, 59-67; sr res mathematician, Dikewood Corp, NMex, 67-71. *Concurrent Pos:* Lectr, Univ Colo, 64-67. *Mem:* Math Asn Am; Am Math Soc. *Res:* Systems science; numerical analysis; computer science. *Mailing Add:* PO Box 183 Monument CO 80132-0183

IRWIN, WILLIAM EDWARD, PLASTICS CHEMISTRY. *Current Pos:* RETIRED. *Personal Data:* b Reading, Pa, Sept 26, 26; m 50; c 3. *Educ:* Kutztown State Col, BS, 48; Columbia Univ, MA, 54; Pa State Univ, PhD(org chem), 62. *Prof Exp:* Chemist prod develop, Armstrong World Industs, Inc, 62-64, res supvr, 64-69, sr res scientist, 69-73, unit mgr, 73-82, res assoc, 82-89. *Mem:* Am Chem Soc; fel Am Soc Testing & Mat. *Res:* Chemical and physical property studies of plastic materials. *Mailing Add:* 3139 Parker Dr Lancaster PA 17601-1640

IRWIN, WILLIAM ELLIOT, BIOCHEMISTRY, FOOD TECHNOLOGY. *Current Pos:* USA REP, PALATNIT GMBH, 89- *Personal Data:* b Ferndale, Mich, Nov 1, 28; m 48; c 2. *Educ:* Western Mich Univ, BS, 50; Univ Notre Dame, MS, 65, PhD(biochem), 70. *Prof Exp:* Chem buyer, R P Scherer Corp, 50-55; tech serv mgr, Miles Labs, Inc, 55-65, dir prod develop, 55-89. *Concurrent Pos:* Dir, Food Protein Coun, 71-73. *Mem:* AAAS; Am Chem Soc; Am Asn Cereal Chemists; Inst Food Technologists. *Res:* Development of economical, biologically efficient, protein foods; protein, carbohydrate enzyme mechanisms. *Mailing Add:* 1501 Dogwood Dr Elkhart IN 46514

ISA, ABDALLAH MOHAMMAD, MICROBIOLOGY, IMMUNOLOGY. *Current Pos:* asst prof, 69-73, ASSOC PROF IMMUNOL, MEHARRY MED COL, 73- *Personal Data:* b Bassa, Palestine, June 15, 38; m 62; c 3. *Educ:* Am Univ Beirut, BS, 60; Univ Calif, Berkeley, MA, 66; Univ Calif, San Francisco, PhD(microbiol), 68. *Prof Exp:* Asst, Univ Calif, Berkeley, 63-65; asst, Univ Calif, San Francisco, 66-68, Fight for Sight, Inc fel, Med Ctr, 68-69. *Concurrent Pos:* Fight for Sight, Inc grant, Meharry Med Col, 69-72; Res Corp grant, 70-73; spec asst, Off Exec Vpres Near Eastern Affairs, Meharry Med Col. *Mem:* AAAS; Europ Dialysis & Transplant Soc; Transplantation Soc; Am Asn Immunologists. *Res:* Immunology of trachoma and other Chalamydia agents; transplantation immunology, especially the rejection reaction and the role of the thymocyte and bone marrow-derived cells in rejection; cellular immunology; role of the suppressor cell in tumor immunity. *Mailing Add:* Dept Biol Sci Tenn State Univ 3500 J A Merritt Blvd Nashville TN 37209-1561

ISAAC, PETER ASHLEY HAMMOND, PULP & PAPER TECHNOLOGY. *Current Pos:* group leader, Am Cyanamid Co, 76-79, planning mgr, 79-81, sales mgr, 81-82, opers mgr, 82-83, bus develop mgr, 83-84, mkt mgr elastomer, 84-86, mkt mgr, Urethane Chem, 86-87, MGR BUS DEVELOP, AM CYANAMID CO, 87- *Personal Data:* b Grimsby, Lincolnshire, Eng, Jan 25, 45; m 72; c 2. *Educ:* Cambridge Univ, BA, 67, MA, 71; Carnegie-Mellon Univ, PhD(org chem), 72; Rutgers Univ, MBA, 76. *Prof Exp:* Res chemist, 72-74, group leader paper prod res, Minerals & Chem Div, Engelhard Minerals & Chem Corp, 74-76. *Concurrent Pos:* Chmn, Mkt Comt, Polyurethane Mfrs Asn. *Mem:* Am Chem Soc. *Res:* Application of inorganic materials in paper coating and filling; mineralogy, synthetic inorganic chemistry, colloid and surface chemistry; polymers and plastics. *Mailing Add:* 2218 Cortelyou Rd Charlotte NC 28211-3838

ISAAC, RICHARD EUGENE, MATHEMATICS. *Current Pos:* PROF MATH, LEHMAN COL, 69- *Personal Data:* b New York, NY, Jan 2, 34; m 63; c 1. *Educ:* Cornell Univ, BA, 55; Univ Calif, Berkeley, PhD(math), 59. *Prof Exp:* Fulbright fel math, Poincare Inst, Paris, 59-60; instr, Fordham Univ, 61; res assoc, Yeshiva Univ, 61-62; asst prof, Hunter Col, 62-69. *Concurrent Pos:* Vis asst prof, Cornell Univ, 64-65. *Mem:* Am Math Soc. *Res:* Probability theory and related fields; analysis. *Mailing Add:* Dept Math Lehman Col City Univ New York Bronx NY 10468-1589

ISAAC, ROBERT A, ANALYTICAL CHEMISTRY. *Current Pos:* dir, Soil & Plant Anal Lab, Coop Exten Serv, 80-87, DIR AGR SERV LABS, UNIV GA, 87- *Personal Data:* b Georgetown, SC, Feb 19, 36; m 66; c 3. *Educ:* Col Charleston, BS, 58; Clemson Univ, MS, 62, PhD(anal chem), 66. *Prof Exp:* Teacher high sch, SC, 58-60; chemist, Savannah River Lab, E I Du Pont de Nemours & Co, Inc, 62-63; head anal chem dept, Tenn Corp, 66-68. *Concurrent Pos:* Assoc referee, Asn Off Anal Chemists, 66-; analytical chemist, Univ Ga, 68- *Mem:* Am Soc Agron; Am Chem Soc; fel Am Inst Chem; Sigma Xi; Soc Appl Spectros. *Res:* Analytical methodology for the analysis of major and micronutrients in soils and plant tissue; use of atomic absorption and plasma emission spectroscopy along with automated analytical techniques. *Mailing Add:* Soil & Plant Analysis Lab 2400 College Station Rd Athens GA 30605-3636

ISAAC, WALTER, psychophysiology; deceased, see previous edition for last biography

ISAACKS, RUSSELL ERNEST, BIOCHEMISTRY, NUTRITION. *Current Pos:* from asst prof to res assoc prof biochem, 65-83, RES PROF, MED SCH, UNIV MIAMI, 83-; RES CHEM RES SERV, VET ADMIN HOSP, MIAMI, 65- *Personal Data:* b Humble, Tex, July 25, 35; m 54; c 2. *Educ:* McNeese State Col, BS, 57; Tex A&M Univ, MS, 59; PhD(biochem), 61. *Prof Exp:* Res asst nutrit, Tex A&M Univ, 56-61; scientist, USPHS, HEW, Md, 61-64; res chem, res serv, Vet Admin Hosp, Dallas, 64-65. *Mem:* AAAS; Sigma Xi; Poultry Sci Asn; Am Chem Soc; Am Physiol Soc; Am Zool. *Res:* Metabolism and function of organic phosphates in oxygen transport of red blood cells of birds, reptiles, amphibians, and fishes; membrane transport. *Mailing Add:* 8965 SW 115th Terr Miami FL 33156

ISAACS, CHARLES EDWARD, IMMUNOLOGY OF HUMAN MILK, ANTIVIRAL COMPOUNDS IN BLOOD. *Current Pos:* RES SCIENTIST, NY STATE INST BASIC RES, 78- *Personal Data:* b Brooklyn, NY, Oct 26, 49; m 77; c 2. *Educ:* State Univ NY, Stony Brook, BS, 70; Rutgers Univ, PhD(microbiol), 77. *Prof Exp:* Postdoctoral fel, Roche Inst Molecular Biol, 77-78. *Concurrent Pos:* Adj asst prof, Dept Pediat, Mt Sinai Sch Med, 78-; prin investr, Nat Inst Heart, Lung & Blood, 88- *Mem:* Am Inst Nutrit; AAAS; NY Acad Sci; Int Soc Res Human Lactation. *Res:* Antiviral and antibacterial in humans. *Mailing Add:* Protein Chem Lab Inst Basic Res 1050 Forest Hill Rd Staten Island NY 10314-6330

ISAACS, GERALD W, AGRICULTURAL ENGINEERING. *Current Pos:* prof & chmn, 81-91, EMER PROF, AGR ENG DEPT, UNIV FLA, 91- *Personal Data:* b Crawfordsville, Ind, Sept 3, 27; m 48, Phyllis Seaton; c David, Donald, Susan & Linda. *Educ:* Purdue Univ, BSEE, 47, MSEE, 49; Mich State Univ, PhD(agr eng), 54. *Honors & Awards:* Silver Medal, Max Eyth Gesellschaft, 66; Massey Ferguson Gold Medal, Am Soc Agr Engrs. *Prof Exp:* Asst, Purdue Univ, 47, instr, 48-52; asst, Mich State Univ, 52-54; from asst prof to prof agr eng, Purdue Univ, 54-81, head dept, 64-81. *Concurrent Pos:* Consult, var farm equip mfrs, 58-; guest prof, Hohenheim Agr Univ, 63 & 74, Friederich Wilhelms Univ, Bonn, 92. *Mem:* Fel Am Soc Agr Engrs (pres, 82-83); Am Soc Eng Educ. *Res:* Grain storage; grain drying; solar energy utilization. *Mailing Add:* Dept Agr Eng Univ Fla Gainesville FL 32611

ISAACS, GODFREY LEONARD, MATHEMATICAL ANALYSIS. *Current Pos:* from assoc prof to prof, 68-86, EMER PROF MATH, LEHMAN COL, CITY UNIV NEW YORK, 86- *Personal Data:* b Cape Town, SAfrica, Feb 9, 24. *Educ:* Univ Cape Town, BSc, 44, MSc, 45; London Univ, PhD(math), 50. *Prof Exp:* Lectr math, Univ Natal, 46-47 & Birkbeck Col, London, 48-49; lectr, Univ Witwatersrand, 52-55, sr lectr, 55-59, prof, 60-67; vis prof, State Univ NY Stony Brook, 67-68. *Concurrent Pos:* Nuffield fel res assoc, Univ Col, London, 59-60; Carnegie Corp Traveling grant, 66; fac res fel, City Univ New York, 70. *Mem:* SAfrican Math Asn; Am Math Soc; Math Asn Am; NY Acad Sci. *Res:* Summability; integration; Fourier series; set theory. *Mailing Add:* 3111 N Ocean Dr Apt 1206 Hollywood FL 33019

ISAACS, HUGH SOLOMON, MATERIAL SCIENCE, ELECTROCHEMISTRY. *Current Pos:* METALLURGIST, BROOKHAVEN NAT LAB, 74- *Personal Data:* b Johannesburg, SAfrica, Aug 13, 36; US citizen; m 59; c 2. *Educ:* Univ Witwatersrand, BSc, 58; Imp Col Sci Technol, DIC, 61; Univ London, PhD(metal corrosion), 64. *Honors & Awards:* H E Armstrong Medal & Prize, Imp Col Sci & Technol, 64; Sam Tour Award, Am Soc Testing & Mat, 83; Uhlig Award, Electrochem Soc Inc, 93. *Prof Exp:* Vis sci oxidation metals, UK Atomic Energy Authority, Harwell, 63-64; res scientist metall, Atomic Energy Bd, SAfrica, 64-67; asst metallurgist, Brookhaven Nat Lab, 67-72; assoc metallurgist, Oak Ridge Nat Lab, 72-74. *Concurrent Pos:* Adj prof, Univ NY, 77-80 & 90. *Mem:* Electrochem Soc; Nat Asn Corrosion Engrs. *Res:* Corrosion and electrochemical kinetics at solid and liquid electrolyte interfaces. *Mailing Add:* Brookhaven Nat Lab Upton NY 11973

ISAACS, I MARTIN, FINITE GROUPS, GROUP REPRESENTATIONS. *Current Pos:* assoc prof, 69-71, PROF MATH, UNIV WIS-MADISON, 71- *Personal Data:* b New York, NY, Apr 14, 40. *Educ:* Polytech Inst Brooklyn, BS, 60; Harvard Univ, AM, 61, PhD(math), 64. *Prof Exp:* Instr math, Univ Chicago, 66-68, vis asst prof, 68-69. *Concurrent Pos:* Sloan res fel, 71-73; vis prof, Univ Calif, Berkeley, 73-74 & 89; hon fel, Oxford Univ, Eng, 84. *Mem:* Am Math Soc; Math Asn Am. *Res:* Theory of finite groups and their characters. *Mailing Add:* Dept Math Univ Wis Madison WI 53706

ISAACS, LESLIE LASZLO, EXPERIMENTAL SOLID STATE PHYSICS, THERMODYNAMIC PROPERTIES. *Current Pos:* ASSOC PROF CHEM ENG, CITY COL NEW YORK, 74-, ASSOC DEAN SCH ENG, 88- *Personal Data:* b Berehovo, Czech, Aug 5, 33; US citizen; m 62; c 2. *Educ:* Columbia Univ, BSc, 55; Mass Inst Technol, PhD(phys chem), 60. *Prof Exp:* Fel metal physics, Mellon Inst, 60-65; mem metall div, Argonne Nat Lab, 65-71; vis fac chem, Univ Wash, Seattle, 72-74. *Mem:* Am Phys Soc; Am Inst Chem Eng; Am Chem Soc; Mat Res Soc. *Res:* Properties of materials; low temperature physics; thermodynamics of coal chars; catalysis; thermodynamics, materials science. *Mailing Add:* Dept Chem Eng City Col New York NY 10031-9198

ISAACS, PHILIP KLEIN, POLYMER CHEMISTRY. *Current Pos:* RETIRED. *Personal Data:* b 1927; m 53; c 3. *Educ:* Bard Col, BA, 48; Columbia Univ, MA, 50; Univ Cincinnati, PhD, 51. *Prof Exp:* Res chemist, Dewey & Almy Div, W R Grace & Co, 51-58, group leader, 58-62, res assoc, Res Div, 63-66; res assoc, Machteshim Chem Co, Israel, 66-68; head, Textile Finishing Dept, Israel Fibers Inst, 68-74; vis scientist, Weizmann Inst Sci,

74-75; chief technologist, Off Chief Scientist, Ministry Com & Indust, Israel, 75-86; res chemist, Israel Fiber Inst, 87-92. *Concurrent Pos:* Sr lectr, Sch Appl Sci, Hebrew Univ, 69-75; UN fel, 71; vis scientist, Casali Inst, Hebrew Univ, 81-86. *Mem:* Am Chem Soc. *Res:* Polymer modification; latex applications; flame retardancy of textiles; surface chemistry; crosslinking of polymers; plastic coatings for foods; halogenated polymers; adhesives. *Mailing Add:* 2 Dov Kimchi St Jerusalem 92549 Israel

ISAACS, TAMI YVETTE, PHOTOCHEMISTRY, PHYSICAL ORGANIC CHEMISTRY. *Current Pos:* ASST PROF CHEM, COL NOTRE DAME, MD, 80- *Personal Data:* b Elizabeth, NJ, Feb 17, 52; m; c 3. *Educ:* Rensselaer Polytech Inst, BS, 74; Johns Hopkins Univ, MA, 76, PhD(org chem), 80. *Prof Exp:* Lectr chem, Essex Community Col, Baltimore County, 76-79; asst prof, Rider Col, Lawrenceville, NJ, 80. *Concurrent Pos:* Adj prof, Towson State Univ, Md, 81-82; researcher, Johns Hopkins Univ, 81-83. *Mem:* Am Chem Soc; Sigma Xi. *Res:* Organic photochemical reactions, including mechanisms and using various methods to increase control of the products formed. *Mailing Add:* 6006 Berkeley Ave Baltimore MD 21209-4014

ISAACSON, ALLEN, PHYSIOLOGY, BIOPHYSICS. *Current Pos:* ASSOC PROF BIOL, WILLIAM PATERSON COL, NJ, 69- *Personal Data:* b Brooklyn, NY, Jan 15, 32; m 59; c 2. *Educ:* City Col New York, BS, 53; Harvard Univ, AM, 54; NY Univ, PhD(biol), 62. *Prof Exp:* Jr engr, Amperex Electronics Corp, 55-56; proj engr, Kollsman Instrument Corp, 56-58; res asst biophys, Sloan-Kettering Inst Cancer Res, 58-60; res assoc physiol, Inst Muscle Dis, 60-62, asst mem, 62-69. *Concurrent Pos:* Instr biol sci, Fairleigh-Dickenson Univ, 67-71; NSF res partic, biochem & biophys, Ore State Univ, 70, 71 & 75, Neurol Dept, Columbia Univ, 82; post-doctoral res, Inst Muscle Dis, Muscular Dystrophy Asn, 72 & 73 & Physiol Dept, Downstate Med Ctr, State Univ NY, 74. *Mem:* Fel AAAS; Am Physiol Soc; Soc Gen Physiol; Biophys Soc; Nat Asn Biol Teachers; Health Physics Soc. *Res:* Excitation-contraction coupling of muscle; kinetics of calcium and zinc movements in skeletal muscle; radiation safety; radioisotope applications; caffeine and related drug effects on the integrity of membranes of muscle. *Mailing Add:* Dept Biol William Paterson Col 300 Pompton Rd Wayne NJ 07470. *Fax:* 973-595-3414

ISAACSON, DAVID, NUMERICAL METHODS, SCIENTIFIC COMPUTING. *Current Pos:* ASSOC PROF MATH, RENSSELAER POLYTECH INST, 80- *Personal Data:* b New York, NY, Oct 22, 48; m 71; c 2. *Educ:* NY Univ, BA, 70, MS, 72, PhD(math), 76. *Prof Exp:* Lectr math, NY Univ, 74-75; lectr, Rutgers Univ, 75-76, asst prof, 76-80. *Mem:* Am Math Soc; Math Asn Am; Soc Indust & Appl Math; Sigma Xi; Inst Elec & Electronics Engrs. *Res:* Numerical and analytical methods for approximating the spectral properties of Schrodinger; energy; operators; mathematical problems in cardiology. *Mailing Add:* Dept Math & Comput Sci Rensselaer Polytech Inst Troy NY 12180

ISAACSON, DENNIS LEE, ENTOMOLOGY, REMOTE SENSING. *Current Pos:* PROG MGR, NOXIOUS WEED CONTROL, ORE DEPT AGR, 90- *Personal Data:* b Los Angeles, Calif, May 5, 42; m 66; c 2. *Educ:* Portland State Univ, BS, 69; Ore State Univ, MS, 72, MAg, 75. *Prof Exp:* Entomologist biol control weeds, Ore Dept Agr, 74-78; sr analyst, Environ Remote Sensing Applns Lab, Ore State Univ, 78-90. *Concurrent Pos:* Proj leader, Pac NW Regional Comn, 74-75 & 75-76; contract adminr, Bur Land Mgt, US Dept Interior, 75-76; World Bank consult, Gadhah Mada Univ, Indonesia, 87. *Mem:* Am Soc Photogram & Remote Sensing. *Res:* Vegetation inventories by application of remote sensing techniques; distribution and abundance of plant species; insect-plant interactions with special interest in biological weed control. *Mailing Add:* 9000 Helmick Rd Monmouth OR 97361

ISAACSON, EUGENE, APPLIED MATHEMATICS, NUMERICAL METHODS. *Current Pos:* asst, NY Univ, 44, from asst prof to prof, 49-89, actg chief, AEC Comput & Appl Math Ctr, 52-53, assoc dir, 58-65, chmn, Comput Ctr, 63-73, EMER PROF MATH, NY UNIV, 89- *Personal Data:* b Brooklyn, NY, June 14, 19; m 47, Muriel Lewenstein; c David & Eli L. *Educ:* City Col New York, BS, 39; NY Univ, MS, 41, PhD(math), 49. *Prof Exp:* Comput operator, US Bur Stand, 43. *Concurrent Pos:* Chmn ed comt, J Math of Computation, 66-74, mem bd assoc ed, 75-; vis prof & actg chmn dept comput sci, City Col New York, 70-71; consult, US Army CEngrs; managing ed, Soc Indust Appl Math J Numerical Anal, 80-86; prin investr, NASA grant, 83-89; trustee, Univ Space Res Asn, 84-90. *Mem:* Am Math Soc; Math Asn Am; Soc Indust & Appl Math. *Res:* Applied mathematics; waterwaves; numerical analysis; climatology; meteorology. *Mailing Add:* Courant Inst Math Sci New York Univ 251 Mercer St New York NY 10012

ISAACSON, EUGENE I, PHARMACEUTICAL CHEMISTRY, ORGANIC CHEMISTRY. *Current Pos:* assoc prof, 69-74, PROF PHARMACEUT CHEM, COL PHARM, IDAHO STATE UNIV, 74- *Personal Data:* b Wilson, Wis, June 30, 33; m 53; c 3. *Educ:* Univ Minn, BS, 56, PhD(pharmaceut chem), 63. *Prof Exp:* Asst prof pharmaceut chem, Col Pharm, Univ Tex, Austin, 63-69. *Mem:* Am Pharmaceut Asn; Acad Pharmaceut Sci; Am Asn Cols Pharm; NY Acad Sci; fel Am Inst Chemists. *Res:* Synthesis and structure-activity-relationships among cholinergic and anti-cholinergic agents; psychopharmacologic agents; anticonvulsants. *Mailing Add:* Col Pharm Idaho State Univ Pocatello ID 83209

ISAACSON, HENRY VERSCHAY, ORGANIC POLYMER CHEMISTRY. *Current Pos:* sr res chemist, 69-76, RES ASSOC, RES LABS, EASTMAN KODAK CO, 77- *Personal Data:* b Chicago, Ill, Nov 11, 39; m 66; c 2. *Educ:* Univ Ill, Urbana, BS, 61; Univ Minn, Minneapolis, PhD(org chem), 69. *Prof Exp:* Chemist, Sinclair Res Labs, 61-65. *Mem:* Am Chem Soc. *Res:* Synthesis of polymers; emulsion polymerization; electrophotographic toners; modification of polymers. *Mailing Add:* 1260 Holley Rd Webster NY 14580

ISAACSON, LAVAR KING, MECHANICAL ENGINEERING, THERMODYNAMICS. *Current Pos:* instr mech eng, 57-58, from asst prof to assoc prof, 61-70, PROF MECH ENG, UNIV UTAH, 70- *Personal Data:* b Provo, Utah, July 15, 34; m 61; c 3. *Educ:* Univ Utah, BS, 56, PhD(mech eng), 62. *Prof Exp:* Engr, Sperry Utah Co, 57. *Concurrent Pos:* Res specialist, Space & Info Systs Div, NAm Aviation, Inc, 63-64; proj mgr, Elec Power Res Inst, 74-75, prog mgr, 75-76. *Mem:* Inst Aeronaut & Astronaut; Am Soc Eng Educ; Sigma Xi. *Res:* Reactive boundary layers; combustion gas dynamics; nonequilibrium thermodynamics; turbulent flow. *Mailing Add:* Dept Mech Eng Univ Utah 3210 Merrill Eng Salt Lake City UT 84124-1107

ISAACSON, MICHAEL, CIVIL ENGINEERING. *Current Pos:* MEM STAFF, DEPT CIVIL ENG, UNIV BC, VANCOUVER, 76-, PROF & HEAD DEPT. *Educ:* Univ Cambridge, BA, 71, MA, 75, PhD, 75. *Honors & Awards:* R A McLachlan Award, Asn Prof Engrs & Geoscientists, BC, 92; Camille A Dagenais Award, Can Soc Civil Engrs, 92. *Prof Exp:* Mem code design offshore prod struct tech comt, Can Stand Asn, comt environ forces int, Ship & Offshore Struct Cong. *Concurrent Pos:* Consult in field; assoc ed, Can J Civil Eng, Int J Offshore & Polar Eng. *Mem:* Am Soc Civil Engrs; Can Soc Civil Engrs; Eng Inst Can; Int Asn Hydraul Res; Int Soc Offshore & Polar Engrs. *Res:* Research in coastal and ocean engineering. *Mailing Add:* Dept Civil Eng Univ BC Vancouver BC V6T 1Z4 Can

ISAACSON, MICHAEL SAUL, ELECTRON PHYSICS, ELECTRON MICROSCOPY. *Current Pos:* at DEPT PHYSICS, CORNELL UNIV. *Personal Data:* b Chicago, Ill, July 4, 42; m 65; c 2. *Educ:* Univ Ill, BS, 65; Univ Chicago, SM, 66, PhD(physics), 71. *Honors & Awards:* Burton Award, Electron Micros Soc Am, 76. *Prof Exp:* Staff scientist, Brookhaven Nat Lab, 70-73; asst prof physics, Univ Chicago & Enrico Fermi Inst, 73- *Concurrent Pos:* Consult, Coates & Welter Instrument Corp, 71-73 & Siemens A G, 76; adv, Annual Scanning Microscope Symp, Ill Inst Technol Res Inst, 74-77; ed adv, J Ultramicros, 75- & Electron Micros Soc Am Bull, 77-; Alfred P Sloan res fel, 75-; mem organizing comt, 9th Int Cong Electron Micros, Toronto, 1978, 75-; adv, SEM, Inc, 78- *Mem:* Radiation Res Soc; Electron Micros Soc Am; Am Asn Physics Teachers; Biophys Soc. *Res:* Development of new advanced electron optical systems and techniques, and the illucidation of new principles for use in increasing the limits of ultrastructure research by means of electrons. *Mailing Add:* Sch Appl Physics 210 Clark Hall Cornell Univ Ithaca NY 14853-0001

ISAACSON, PETER EDWIN, BIOSTRATIGRAPHY, PALEOECOLOGY. *Current Pos:* asst prof, 78-83, PROF GEOL, COL MINES, UNIV IDAHO, 83- *Personal Data:* b Seattle, Wash, Mar 29, 46; m 79; c 2. *Educ:* Univ Colo, BA, 68; Ore State Univ, PhD(geol), 74. *Honors & Awards:* Fulbright Res Fel, Czech, 87. *Prof Exp:* Adj asst prof geol, Univ Mass, Amherst, 74-78; res assoc, Amherst Col, 74-78. *Concurrent Pos:* Vis asst prof, Franklin & Marshall Col, 75; exchange scientist, Eastern Europe Prog, Nat Acad Sci, 82, 90. *Mem:* Asn Paleontol Agr; Geol Soc Am; Soc Econ Paleontologists & Mineralogists; Int Paleontol Union. *Res:* Biostratigraphic and paleo-depositional modelling of Paleozoic-age rock sequences. *Mailing Add:* Dept Geol Univ Idaho 375 S Line St Moscow ID 83843-4140

ISAACSON, RICHARD ALLEN, GRAVITATION, COMPUTATIONAL PHYSICS. *Current Pos:* PROG DIR, GRAVITATIONAL PHYSICS, 73- *Personal Data:* b New York, NY, Oct 6, 41. *Educ:* Columbia Col, AB, 62; Stanford Univ, MS, 65; Univ Md, PhD(physics), 67. *Prof Exp:* Asst prof physics, Ill Inst Technol, 68-73; mgr, Sci Prog, Nat Ctr Supercomput Applns, Univ Ill, Champaign-Urbana, 86-87. *Concurrent Pos:* Mgr, Sci Prog, Nat Ctr Supercomput Applns, Univ Ill, Champaign Urbana, 86-87. *Res:* Cosmology; relativistic astrophysics; general relativity; gravitational radiation. *Mailing Add:* Physics Div Rm 1015-33 NSF 4201 Wilson Blvd Arlington VA 22230. *Fax:* 703-306-0566; *E-Mail:* isaacson@nsf.gov

ISAACSON, RICHARD EVAN, MICROBIOLOGY. *Current Pos:* ASSOC PROF, UNIV ILL, URBANA, 89- *Personal Data:* b Chicago, Oct 25, 47; m 70, Barbara L Southon; c William J, Amanda J & Daniel E. *Educ:* Univ Ill, BS, 69, PhD, 74. *Prof Exp:* Microbiologist, Nat Animal Dis Ctr, Ames, Iowa, 74-78; asst prof, Univ Mich, Ann Arbor, 78-83; mgr, Pfizer Inc, Groton, Conn, 83-89. *Concurrent Pos:* NIH grant, 79, USDA grant, 82, 90 & 93; ed, Recombinant DNA Vaccines, Rationale & Strategies, 92. *Mem:* AAAS; Am Soc Microbiol; Am Acad Microbiol; Sigma Xi. *Res:* Discovery and development of first federally licensed recombinant DNA vaccine. *Mailing Add:* Vet Pathobiol Univ Ill 2001 S Lincoln Ave Urbana IL 61801-6199

ISAACSON, ROBERT B, polymer chemistry, organic chemistry, for more information see previous edition

ISAACSON, ROBERT JOHN, ORTHODONTICS, ANATOMY. *Current Pos:* PROF & CHMN DEPT ORTHOD, VA COMMONWEALTH UNIV, 87- *Personal Data:* b Flushing, NY, July 12, 32. *Educ:* Univ Minn, Minneapolis, BS, 54, DDS, 56, MSD, 61, PhD(anat), 62. *Prof Exp:* From asst prof to prof dent, Sch Dent, Univ Minn, Minneapolis, 62-77, chmn, Orthod

Div, 65-77; prof & chmn, Dept Growth & Develop, Sch Dent, Univ Calif, San Francisco, 77-87. *Concurrent Pos:* Mem grad fac, assoc mem dent & anat & dir res training prog, Univ Minn-Minneapolis, 63-77, lectr, Sch Dent, 64-77. *Mem:* Int Asn Dent Res. *Res:* Quantitation of loads in relation to skeletal changes in orthodontics, teratogenesis and cleft lip and palate; facial skeletal growth and dental occlusion. *Mailing Add:* Dept Orthod Med Col Va Va Commonwealth Univ PO Box 980566 Richmond VA 23298-0566

ISAACSON, ROBERT LEE, BEHAVIORAL NEUROSCIENCE. *Current Pos:* DISTINGUISHED PROF PSYCHOL, STATE UNIV NY, BINGHAMTON, 78- *Personal Data:* b Detroit, Mich, Sept 26, 28; m 75, Ann Watson; c Gunnar, Lars, Mary Ingrid & Mary Christina. *Educ:* Univ Mich, BA, 50, MA, 54, PhD(psychol), 58. *Prof Exp:* Instr psychol, Univ Mich, Ann Arbor, 58-60, from asst prof to prof, 60-68; prof psychol & neurosci, Univ Fla, 68-77, grad res prof, 77-78. *Concurrent Pos:* Dir, NSF Res Participation Prog for Col Teachers Psychol, 61-64; dir, Ctr Neurobiol Sci, 70-78; mem biol sci training review comt, NIMH, 70-74; mem Neurol A Study Sect, NIH, 76-80; dir, Ctr Neurobehav Sci, 78-84; co-dir, Ctr Develop Psychobiol, 93- *Mem:* Am Physiol Soc; Soc Neurosci; Int Soc Behav Neurosci. *Res:* Effects of brain lesions and hormones on behavior; limbic system, drug actions and behavior; neurotoxicology, effects of toxins or hypoxia on brain structure due to alteration in microvasulature. *Mailing Add:* Dept Psychol State Univ NY Binghamton NY 13902-6000. *E-Mail:* isaacson@binghamton.edu

ISAACSON, STANLEY LEONARD, MATHEMATICAL STATISTICS. *Current Pos:* sales mgr, Gendler Stone Prod Co, 56-64, vpres, 64-80, pres, 80-86, GEN MGR, GENDLER AGGREGATES CO, 86- *Personal Data:* b Baltimore, Md, Jan 31, 27; m 52, Annette Gendler; c Rita, Irving & Marcia. *Educ:* Johns Hopkins Univ, BA, 45, MA, 47; Columbia Univ, PhD(math statist), 50. *Prof Exp:* Jr instr math, Johns Hopkins Univ, 45-47; asst, Off Naval Res Contract, Columbia Univ, 49-50; asst prof statist, Iowa State Col, 50-55; sr statistician, Westinghouse Elec Corp, Pa, 55-56. *Concurrent Pos:* Vis prof, Stanford Univ, 53-54; lectr, Drake Univ, 56-59; corp secy, 87-90, dir, CIM Tech, Inc, 87- *Mem:* Am Statist Asn; Inst Math Statist. *Res:* Statistical decision theory; industrial application of statistics. *Mailing Add:* 4706 Lakeview Dr Des Moines IA 50311

ISAAK, DALE DARWIN, CELLULAR IMMUNOLOGY, VIRAL ONCOLOGY. *Current Pos:* ASSOC & PROF, MOLECULAR BIOL, UNIV WYO, 85-97. *Personal Data:* b Bismarck, NDak, July 2, 48; m 70; c 2. *Educ:* Eastern Mont Col, BS, 70; Mont State Univ, MS, 73, PhD(microbiol), 76. *Prof Exp:* Cancer res scientist I viral oncol, Roswell Park Mem Inst, 76; res assoc cellular immunol, Harvard Sch Public Health, 76-79; asst & assoc prof Med Microbiol & Immunol, Kirksville Col Osteop Med, 79-85. *Concurrent Pos:* Adj asst prof, Northeast Mo State Univ; prin investr res grant, NIH, 79-82, Am Osteop Asn, 79-83 & NSF, 80-83, 85-89, Am Cancer Soc, 93-96. *Mem:* Am Soc Microbiol; Reticuloendothelial Soc; Sigma Xi; Am Asn Immunol. *Res:* Elucidation of processes involved in lymphocyte differentiation into subpopulation; the role of major histocompatibility complex-coded proteins in lymphocyte interactions; epigenetic factors involved in malignant transformation of lymphocytes by leukemia viruses, retro virus induced apoptosis. *Mailing Add:* Dept Molecular Biol Univ Wyo PO Box 3944 Laramie WY 82071-3944. *E-Mail:* isaak@plains.uwyo.edu

ISAAK, ROBERT D(EETS), ELECTRICAL ENGINEERING, UNDERWATER ACOUSTICS. *Current Pos:* RETIRED. *Personal Data:* b Spokane, Wash, Jan 1, 21; m 44, Margie Allen; c Robert A, Marilynn (Ludwig) & James D. *Educ:* Univ Colo, BS, 43, MS, 49. *Prof Exp:* Test engr, Gen Elec Co, 43-44; infrared radar, USN Aircorp, 44-47; instr elec eng, Univ Colo, 47-52; sect head underwater acoust, US Naval Electronics Lab, 52-64, div head, Sonic Sonar & Countermeasures, 64-68; dir eng, Honeywell Marine Systs Ctr, 68-79, advan prog mgr, 81-85, chief sci consult, 85-86, sci tech adv, Honeywell-Elac, Kiel, WGer, 79-81. *Mem:* Inst Elec & Electronics Engrs. *Res:* Acoustic communication between submarines; active and passive means of detecting submarines; digital computers and digital signal processing techniques as applied to sonar devices; acoustic warfare techniques; numerous patents in areas of signal processing, communications and ocean engineering. *Mailing Add:* 7111 35th Ave NW Seattle WA 98117

ISACHSEN, YNGVAR WILLIAM, GEOLOGY. *Current Pos:* assoc geologist, 58-74, PRIN GEOLOGIST, NY STATE GEOL SURV, 74- *Personal Data:* b Oslo, Norway, Mar 16, 20; nat US; m 44; c Eric John & Clark Edward. *Educ:* Syracuse Univ, BA, 42; Washington Univ, St Louis, MA, 49; Cornell Univ, PhD(geol), 53. *Honors & Awards:* Photog Interpretation Award, Am Soc Photogram, 74. *Prof Exp:* Instr geol, Lafayette Col, 49-51; dist geologist Colo plateau, AEC, 53-57; radioactive minerals expert, UN Tech Asst Mission, Turkey, 57; prof geol, State Univ NY Col Plattsburgh, 57-58. *Mem:* Fel AAAS; fel Geol Soc Am; Soc Econ Geol; Am Geophys Union; Int Basement Tectonics Asn. *Res:* Metamorphic, igneous, structural, economic geology and neotectonics of New York including remote sensing of natural resources; geology of impact craters; geology of uranium in Colorado Plateau, Colombia and Turkey. *Mailing Add:* New York Geol Surv State Educ Dept Albany NY 12230. *Fax:* 518-486-3696; *E-Mail:* yisachse@museum.nysed.gov

ISACKS, BRYAN L, SEISMOLOGY. *Current Pos:* ASSOC PROF GEOL SCI, CORNELL UNIV, 71- *Personal Data:* b New Orleans, La, July 25, 36; m 58; c 3. *Educ:* Columbia Univ, AB, 58, PhD(seismol), 65. *Prof Exp:* Res asst seismol, Lamont Geol Observ, Columbia Univ, 62-65, res assoc, 65-68; res geophysicist, Earth Sci Labs, Environ Sci Serv Admin Res Labs, US Dept Com, 68-71. *Mem:* Am Geophys Union; Soc Explor Geophys; Seismol Soc Am. *Res:* Analysis of seismicity; seismicity of island arc regions; deep-focus earthquakes. *Mailing Add:* Dept Geol Cornell Univ 2122 Snee Hall Ithaca NY 14853-1504

ISADA, NELSON M, ENGINEERING, STRUCTURAL DYNAMICS. *Current Pos:* RETIRED. *Personal Data:* b Dao, Philippines, July 29, 23; m 52; c 3. *Educ:* Univ Mich, BS, 50, MS, 52, PhD(eng), 56. *Prof Exp:* Engr, Smith, Hinchman & Grylls Inc, Mich, 55-56, Giffels & Vallet Inc, 56-57 & Harley-Ellington-Day Inc, 57; asst prof graphics & mech, Syracuse Univ, 57-59; from assoc prof to prof shock & vibration, State Univ NY, Buffalo, 59-93. *Concurrent Pos:* Consult, Konski Engrs, 57-59, Nat Gypsum Res Lab, 60-61, Bell Aerosysts Co, 63-64, Electronic Assocs Inc, 65-66 & lawyers in Niagara Frontier, 66-; res assoc, Cornell Aeronaut Lab, 63- *Mem:* Am Soc Civil Engrs. *Res:* Vehicle ride; crash mechanics; shock; vibration; structural dynamics; ultrasonics; earthquake engineering. *Mailing Add:* Dept Mech Eng State Univ NY Jarvis Hall Buffalo NY 14260-0001

ISAKOFF, SHELDON ERWIN, MATERIALS SCIENCE ENGINEERING. *Current Pos:* RETIRED. *Personal Data:* b Brooklyn, NY, May 25, 25; m 46, Anita Ginsburg; c Peter D. *Educ:* Columbia Univ, BS, 45, MS, 47, PhD(chem eng), 52. *Honors & Awards:* Inst Lectr Award, Am Inst Chem Engrs, 84; Reilly Lectr, Notre Dame Univ, 89. *Prof Exp:* Res engr, Eng Res Lab, E I du Pont de Nemours & Co, Inc, 51-54, res supvr, 55-58, res mgr appl physics, 58-60, asst dir, Mech Res Lab, 61-62, dir, Eng Mat Lab, 63-69, dir, Eng Physics Lab, 70-73, asst dir eng res & develop, 74, dir, 75-90. *Concurrent Pos:* Dir, Am Inst Chem Eng, 77-79; adv, NSF, Univ Pa, Columbia Univ. *Mem:* Nat Acad Eng; fel Am Inst Chem Engrs (vpres, 89, pres); Am Chem Soc; fel AAAS. *Res:* Heat transfer; fluid mechanics; process dynamics and process control; polymer processing; engineering materials. *Mailing Add:* RD 1 102 Center Mill Rd Chadds Ford PA 19317

ISAKS, MARTIN, PHYSICAL ORGANIC CHEMISTRY. *Current Pos:* asst prof, 65-71, ASSOC PROF ORG CHEM, UNIV MASS LOWELL, 71- *Personal Data:* b Riga, Latvia, Sept 24, 35. *Educ:* Purdue Univ, BS, 57; Iowa State Univ, MS, 60; Univ Cincinnati, PhD(chem), 63. *Prof Exp:* Res fel org chem, Ga Inst Technol, 63-64; res assoc, Brown Univ, 64-65. *Concurrent Pos:* Vis prof, Univ Toronto, 82-84. *Mem:* AAAS; Am Chem Soc; Chem Soc; Sigma Xi; Am Asn Univ Profs. *Res:* Carbenes; oxidation mechanisms; acidity functions; Hammett equation; cyclopentadienones; reaction mechanisms; photochemistry. *Mailing Add:* Dept Chem Univ Mass-Lowell Lowell MA 01854

ISAMAN, FRANCIS, PHYSICS. *Current Pos:* PRES, CELTIC INDUSTS, INC, VAN NUYS, 65- *Personal Data:* b Lewiston, Idaho, Jan 18, 30; m 56, Virginia A; c Scott A. *Educ:* Univ Utah, BA, 51; San Fernando Valley State Col, MS, 68. *Prof Exp:* Res engr, Hughes Aircraft Co, 54-57; asst to mgr, Electronics Div, Statham Instruments Inc, 57-60; pres, Pac Telemetry Systs, Inc, 60-62; mgr, Instrument Div, Scionics Corp, 62-64; res engr, Rocketdyne Div, NAm Aviation, Inc, 64-65. *Res:* Electronics and materials science. *Mailing Add:* Celtic Industs Inc 551 Fifth St No D-1 San Fernando CA 91340-2247

ISARD, HAROLD JOSEPH, medicine, radiology; deceased, see previous edition for last biography

ISAYEV, AVRAAM ISAYEVICH, INJECTION MOLDING, POLYMER & COMPOSITE PROCESSING. *Current Pos:* assoc prof, 83-87, PROF, DEPT POLYMER ENG, UNIV AKRON, 87-; DIR, MOLDING TECHNOL CTR, INST POLYMER ENG, 90- *Personal Data:* b Privolnoe, Azerbaijan, USSR, Oct 17, 42; US citizen; m 69, Lubov Dadasheva; c Daniela. *Educ:* Azerbaijan Inst Oil Chem, Baku, MS, 64, Inst Electronic Mach Bldg, Moscow, MS, 75; Inst Petrochem Synthesis, USSR Acad Sci, PhD(polymer eng), 70. *Honors & Awards:* Silver Medal, Inst Mat, London, 97. *Prof Exp:* Res assoc, State Res Inst Nitrogen Indust, 65-66; res assoc, Inst Petrochem Synthesis, Acad Sci Moscow, 70-76; sr res fel, Israel Inst Technol, 77-78; sr res assoc, Cornell Univ, 79-83. *Concurrent Pos:* Vis prof, Univ Aachen, Ger, 86, Univ Linz, Austria, 93 & IPF, Dresden, Ger, 97; prog chmn, Polymer Processing Soc, Soc Plastics Engrs, 87 & 94; expert witness, US House Reps, 88. *Mem:* Soc Plastics Engrs; Polymer Processing Soc (treas, 89-91); Soc Rheology; Am Chem Soc; NY Acad Sci; Am Ceramic Soc. *Res:* Polymer and composite processing; rheo-optics and rheology of polymers and oil products; constitutive equations and process modeling; self-reinforced composites based on liquid crystalline polymers; processing and decrosslinking of polymers with aid of high power ultrasound and recycling; editor of 3 books, published over 150 articles and issued 20 patents. *Mailing Add:* Inst Polymer Eng Univ Akron Akron OH 44325-0301. *Fax:* 330-258-2339; *E-Mail:* aisayev@uakron.edu

ISBELL, ARTHUR FURMAN, ORGANIC CHEMISTRY. *Current Pos:* RETIRED. *Personal Data:* b Lubbock, Tex, Feb 12, 17; m 42; c 3. *Educ:* Baylor Univ, BA, 37; Univ Tex, MA, 41, PhD(chem), 43. *Prof Exp:* Lab asst chem, Baylor Univ, 36-37; analytical chemist, First Tex Chem Mfg Co, 37-39; instr chem & quiz-master, Univ Tex, 39-42; res chemist, Gen Mills, Inc, Minn, 43-50; chief chemist, Buckman Labs, Inc, Tenn, 50-51; sr res chemist, Monsanto Chem Co, Ala, 51-53; from asst prof to assoc prof chem, Tex A&M Univ, 53-61, prof, 61-77. *Mem:* Am Chem Soc; Am Inst Chemists; Am Asn Univ Profs; Sigma Xi. *Res:* Synthesis of anticonvulsants; amino acids; quinoline derivatives; surface active agents; organo-phosphorus compounds; indexing of scientific information. *Mailing Add:* 800 Delma Circle Bryan TX 77802

ISBELL, JOHN ROLFE, MATHEMATICS. *Current Pos:* PROF MATH, STATE UNIV NY BUFFALO, 69- *Personal Data:* b Portland, Ore, Oct 27, 30; m 60; c 3. *Educ:* Univ Chicago, BS, 51; Princeton Univ, PhD(math), 54. *Prof Exp:* Fel, NSF Inst Adv Study, 56-57; asst prof math, Univ Wash, Seattle, 57-59, from assoc prof to prof, 59-65; prof, Case Western Res Univ, 65-69. *Mem:* Am Math Soc. *Res:* Categories; topology; theory of games. *Mailing Add:* Dept Math Diefendorf Hall State Univ NY Buffalo NY 14214-3093

ISBELL, RAYMOND EUGENE, ORGANIC CHEMISTRY. *Current Pos:* assoc prof, Florence State Univ, 65-68, prof, 68-74, coord chem dept, 71, PROF CHEM, UNIV N ALA, 74-, HEAD DEPT, 73- *Personal Data:* b Colbert Co, Ala, Jan 13, 32; m 53; c 2. *Educ:* Florence State Col, BS, 53; Univ Ala, MS, 57, PhD(phys chem), 59. *Prof Exp:* Lab instr, Univ Ala, 56-57; chemist, Interior Ballistics Res, Rohm & Haas Co, 58-60 & Chem Process Res, 60; res chemist, Fundamental Res Br, Tenn Valley Authority, 60-65, proj leader, 65. *Mem:* Am Chem Soc. *Res:* Mechanism of organic reactions. *Mailing Add:* 101 Hiram St Sheffield AL 35660-1739

ISBERG, CLIFFORD A, ELECTRICAL ENGINEERING, COMPUTER SCIENCE. *Current Pos:* PROD PLANNER COMPUT, MEMOREX CORP, SANTA CLARA, 71- *Personal Data:* b Tomahawk, Wis, May 25, 35; m 57; c 5. *Educ:* Univ Alaska, BS, 57; Stanford Univ, MS, 58, PhD(elec eng), 65. *Prof Exp:* Adv engr, IBM Corp, 59-70; sr res engr, Comput Synectics, 70; consult, Comput Performance, 70-71. *Concurrent Pos:* Sr res engr, SRI Int, 70- *Mem:* AAAS; Asn Comput Mach; Inst Elec & Electronics Engrs; Sigma Xi. *Res:* Computer systems performance; automata theory; metamathematics; formal linguistics; simulation. *Mailing Add:* SRIIAH 333 Barnswood Ave BS 266 Menlo Park CA 94025

ISBERG, RALPH, MOLECULAR BIOLOGY, MICROBIOLOGY. *Current Pos:* PROF, MOLECULAR BIOL DEPT, TUFTS UNIV. *Honors & Awards:* Eli Lilly & Co Res in Microbiol Immunol Award, Am Soc Microbiol, 93. *Mailing Add:* Dept Molecular Biol Tufts Univ 136 Harrison Ave Boston MA 02111-1800

ISBIN, HERBERT S(TANFORD), CHEMICAL ENGINEERING. *Current Pos:* prof, 50-83, EMER PROF CHEM ENG, UNIV MINN, MINNEAPOLIS, 83- *Personal Data:* b Seattle, Wash, Dec 8, 19; m 48, Katherine Brudnoy; c Ira M, Sharon G, Neil W & Rena. *Educ:* Univ Wash, BS, 40, MS, 41; Mass Inst Technol, ScD, 47. *Honors & Awards:* Tech Achievement Award, Thermal Hydrual Div, Am Nuclear Soc. *Prof Exp:* Chem engr, Md Res Labs, 43-45; res assoc chem eng, Mass Inst Technol, 45-47; chem engr, Hanford Works, Gen Elec Co, 47-50. *Concurrent Pos:* Mem, Nuclear Safety Res Rev Comt, Nuclear Regulatory Comn. *Mem:* AAAS; Am Inst Chem Engrs; Am Soc Eng Educ; Am Chem Soc. *Res:* Two-phase flow; nuclear safety; radiation chemistry. *Mailing Add:* 2815 Monterey Pkwy Minneapolis MN 55416-3959. *E-Mail:* isbin001@maroon.tc.umn.edu

ISBISTER, ROGER JOHN, POLYMER CHEMISTRY. *Current Pos:* Res chemist, 68-74, GROUP LEADER PACKAGING POLYMERS, MORTON-NORWICH PROD, INC, 74- *Personal Data:* b Waterville, Maine, May 18, 42; m 64; c 2. *Educ:* Colby Col, BA, 64; Univ Colo, Boulder, PhD(org chem), 68. *Mem:* Am Chem Soc. *Res:* Small ring organic nitrogen compounds; polymer latices; barrier films and foils; gel permeation chromatography. *Mailing Add:* 14817 Dogwood Lane Woodstock IL 60098-9756

ISBRANDT, LESTER REINHARDT, PHYSICAL CHEMISTRY, NUCLEAR MAGNETIC RESONANCE. *Current Pos:* staff chemist, 73-77, ANALYTICAL SECT HEAD, PROCTER & GAMBLE CO, 77- *Personal Data:* b Chicago, Ill, Jan 29, 46; m 67; c 1. *Educ:* Northern Ill Univ, BS, 67; Mich State Univ, PhD(phys chem), 72. *Prof Exp:* Staff chemist, Gulf Res & Develop Co, 72-73. *Concurrent Pos:* Lectr, Xavier Univ, 75. *Mem:* Am Chem Soc. *Res:* Application of nuclear magnetic resonance spectroscopy to organic and inorganic chemical systems for molecular structure identification and characterization. *Mailing Add:* 9 Edgewood Dr Summit NJ 07901

ISEBRANDS, JUDSON G, WOOD SCIENCE & TECHNOLOGY, PHYSIOLOGY OF PLANTS & TREES. *Current Pos:* TREE PHYSIOLOGIST, FORESTRY SCI LAB, N CENT FOREST EXP STA, US FOREST SERV, 69- *Personal Data:* b Los Angeles, Calif, Oct 20, 43; m 65; c 2. *Educ:* Iowa State Univ, BS, 65, PhD(wood sci & technol), 69. *Mem:* Soc Am Foresters; Tech Asn Pulp & Paper Indust; Int Asn Wood Anat; Soc Wood Sci & Technol; Bot Soc Am. *Res:* Physiology of forest trees; application of statistics to forestry research. *Mailing Add:* 5985 County Rte K Rhinelander WI 54501

ISELER, GERALD WILLIAM, MATERIALS SCIENCE. *Current Pos:* MEM RES STAFF MAT SCI, MASS INST TECHNOL LINCOLN LAB, 66- *Personal Data:* b Port Hope, Mich, May 23, 38; m 60; c 3. *Educ:* Northwestern Univ, BS, 61, PhD(sci eng), 66. *Mem:* Am Phys Soc. *Res:* Luminescence due to isoelectronic centers in II-VI compounds; donor levels in compound semiconductors; crystal growth of nonlinear optical materials and indium phosphide and their optical and electrical properties. *Mailing Add:* 26 State St Chelmsford MA 01824

ISELIN, DONALD G, CIVIL ENGINEERING. *Current Pos:* CONSULT, 85- *Personal Data:* b Racine, Wis, Sept 5, 22. *Educ:* US Naval Acad, BS, 45; Rensselaer Polytech Inst, MSc, 48. *Prof Exp:* Vpres, Raymond Kaiser Engrs, 81-84, sr vpres, 85. *Mem:* Nat Acad Eng; fel Am Soc Mil Engrs (pres, 78-79); hon mem Am Inst Architects; Am Soc Civil Engrs. *Mailing Add:* 2695 Sycamore Canyon Rd Santa Barbara CA 93108. *Fax:* 805-969-5165

ISELY, DUANE, PLANT TAXONOMY, ECONOMIC BOTANY. *Current Pos:* sr seed analyst, Ala Dept Agr, 43-44, exten assoc, 44-46, from asst prof to prof, 46-81, DISTINGUISHED PROF, IOWA STATE UNIV, 81- *Personal Data:* b Bentonville, Ark, Oct 24, 18; m 40, Mary Faden; c Karl & Deanna S. *Educ:* Univ Ark, BA, 38, MS, 39; Cornell Univ, PhD(econ & taxon bot), 42. *Honors & Awards:* Award, Asn Off Seed Anal, 65. *Prof Exp:* Asst, Univ Ark, 38-39; asst bot, Cornell Univ, 40-42, instr, 42-43. *Concurrent Pos:* Ed, Iowa State J Res, 78-87. *Mem:* Soc Econ Bot; Asn Off Seed Anal (pres, 53); Int Asn Plant Taxonomists; Am Soc Plant Taxon. *Res:* Leguminosae of the United States, a taxonomic summary; plant taxon; economic utilization of legumes; history of botany; history of biology. *Mailing Add:* Dept Bot Iowa State Univ Ames IA 50011

ISENBERG, ALLEN (CHARLES), PHARMACEUTICAL CHEMISTRY, INFORMATION SCIENCE. *Current Pos:* assoc ed, 70-73, info scientist, 73-78, sr assoc ed, 78-87, SR ED, CHEM ABSTR SERV, 87- *Personal Data:* b Philadelphia, Pa, Aug 18, 38; m 67. *Educ:* Temple Univ, BSc, 60; Univ Wis, MSc, 62, PhD(pharmaceut chem), 65. *Prof Exp:* Res asst pharmaceut chem, Univ Wis, 60-65; res assoc med chem, Univ Calif, 65-66; vis asst lectr pharmaceut chem, Univ Strathclyde, 66-67; asst prof pharmacog & pharmaceut chem, Temple Univ, 67-70. *Mem:* Am Chem Soc. *Res:* Chemical information science; chemical nomenclature. *Mailing Add:* Chem Abstr Serv Columbus OH 43210

ISENBERG, HENRY DAVID, MEDICAL MICROBIOLOGY. *Current Pos:* microbiologist, 54-69, attend microbiologist, 69-77, PROF LAB MED, ALBERT EINSTEIN COL MED, 87-, CHIEF MICROBIOL, LONG ISLAND JEWISH MED CTR, 77- *Personal Data:* b Giessen, Ger, Mar 9, 22; nat US; m 48, Lila Groseman; c Ina P & Gerald A. *Educ:* City Col New York, BS, 47; Brooklyn Col, MA, 51; St John's Univ, NY, PhD, 59; Am Bd Med Microbiol, dipl, 68. *Honors & Awards:* Becton-Dickinson Award, Am Soc Microbiol, 79, Alexander Sunnenwirth Mem Lectr, 89; Kimble Award, 80; Distinguished Achievements Clin Microbiol Award, NY City Br, Am Soc Microbiol, 91; Prof Recognition Award, Am Bd Med Microbiol, 94. *Prof Exp:* Asst dir labs, Labs of Dr A Angrist, 47-54; asst prof orthop surg, State Univ NY Downstate Med Ctr, 62-65, clin assoc prof, 65-71; prof clin path, Sch Basic Sci, State Univ NY Stony Brook, 71-89; clin prof microbiol & immunol, Sch Med, Univ SFla, 82-87. *Concurrent Pos:* Res assoc, Sloan-Kettering Inst Cancer Res, 59-63; consult, Health Care Facil Serv, Health Servs & Ment Health Admin, 68-73; prof lectr orthop surg, State Univ NY Downstate Med Ctr, 71-; ed, J Clin Microbiol, Am Soc Microbiol, 75-79, Critical Reviews Microbiol, 78-82 & ed-in-chief, J Clin Microbiol, 79-89; chair, Am Bd Med Microbiol, 76-79; ed chief, Clin Microbiol Procedures Handbook, Am Soc Microbiol, 89-; consult, Biomed Opers & Res Br, NASA, 90- *Mem:* Fel NY Acad Sci; fel Am Inst Chem; fel Asn Clin Sci; Am Bd Med Microbiol; fel Am Acad Microbiol; assoc fel NY Acad Med; fel Infectious Dis Soc. *Res:* Microbial metabolism; host-parasite relationships; mineral deposition; antibiotics; automation; nosocomial disease. *Mailing Add:* Div Microbiol Long Island Jewish Med Ctr 270-05 76th Ave New Hyde Park NY 11042-1433. *Fax:* 718-962-6410

ISENBERG, IRVING HARRY, WOOD ANATOMY. *Current Pos:* tech assoc, Inst Paper Chem, 37-38, res asst wood technol, 38-41, instr wood technol, 38-55, res assoc, 41-55, group leader wood technol, 41-46, group leader wood technol & fiber micros, 46-53, instr fiber micros, 46-55, assoc prof wood technol & fiber micros, 55-73, res assoc wood technol & fiber micros, 55-73, EMER ASSOC PROF WOOD TECHNOL & FIBER MICROS, INST PAPER CHEM, 73- *Personal Data:* b Buffalo, NY, Sept 11, 09; m 41, Doris Koehnke; c William, Ilene & John. *Educ:* State Univ NY, Syracuse, BS, 31, MS, 32; Univ Calif, Berkeley, PhD(plant biochem), 36. *Hon Degrees:* MS, Lawrence Univ, 73. *Prof Exp:* Asst, State Univ NY Col Environ Sci & Forestry, Syracuse, 31-32; Pac SW Forest & Range Exp Sta, US Forest Serv, Univ Calif, 32-34, tech asst forestry, 35-37. *Concurrent Pos:* Consult, 73-83; instr, Fox Valley Tech Inst, 75-76; vis prof, Inst Paper Chem, 79. *Mem:* Soc Am Foresters; Tech Asn Pulp & Paper Indust; Int Asn Wood Anat. *Res:* Pulp and paper microscopy; wood structure and fiber identification; wood chemistry; wastewater treatment. *Mailing Add:* 115 E Winnebago St Apt 212 Appleton WI 54911

ISENBERG, JAMES ALLEN, LONG-TIME BEHAVIOR OF SOLUTIONS OF EINSTEINS EQUATIONS, NONLINEAR PARTIAL DIFFERENTIAL EQUATION STUDIES OF PROBLEMS IN DIFFERENTIAL GEOMETRY. *Current Pos:* from asst prof to assoc prof, 82-93, PROF MATH & PHYSICS, UNIV ORE, 93- *Personal Data:* b Boston, Mass, Mar 14, 51; m 89, Jillian Bowling. *Educ:* Princeton Univ, AB, 73; Univ Md, PhD(physics), 79. *Prof Exp:* Fel, Dept Appl Math, Univ Waterloo, 79-80, Dept Math, Univ Calif, Berkeley, 80-82. *Concurrent Pos:* Vis asst prof math, Rice Univ, 83-84, Univ Minn, 85; Nat Ctr Sci Res fel, Univ Paris, 86; vis assoc prof math, Univ Calif, San Diego, 88; fel, Ctr Math Anal, Canberra, 88-89, Inst Theoret Physics, Santa Barbara, 93 & Erwin Schrodinger Inst, Vienna, 94; Max Planck Inst Gravitational Physics, 96. *Mem:* Am Phys Soc; Am Math Soc; Soc Gen Relativity & Gravitation. *Res:* Behavior, in time, of solutions of Einstein's equations; use of heat-like partial differential equations to study the relationship between topology and geometry. *Mailing Add:* 717 Amelia Brownsville OR 97327. *E-Mail:* jim@newton.uoregon.edu

ISENBERG, LIONEL, ENERGY SYSTEMS ENGINEERING, LIQUID SYNTHETIC FUELS. *Current Pos:* RETIRED. *Personal Data:* b Detroit, Mich, Feb 26, 25; m 49; c 3. *Educ:* Univ Calif, Los Angeles, BS(chem) & BS(elec eng), 50; Alexander Hamilton Inst, MBA, 70. *Honors & Awards:* Presidential Award for Innovation, 71 & 72. *Prof Exp:* Plant mgr chem, Prudential Chem Co, 50-55; asst div mgr struct mat, Aerojet-Gen Corp, 55-63; mgr tech transfer, Rockwell Int, 63-71; mgr energy prog, Fairchild

Industs, 76-80; tech mgr syst eng, Jet Propulsion Lab, Calif Inst Technol, 80-90. *Concurrent Pos:* Consult, Proj Gold Eagle, USAF, 65; pres, IR Assocs, 70-90. *Mem:* Assoc fel Am Inst Aeronaut & Astronaut; Am Inst Chem Engrs; Am Chem Soc; fel Am Inst Chemists; AAAS; Sigma Xi. *Res:* Heat transfer and insulation systems, especially nuclear cryogenic and ultra high temperatures; synthetic fuels, liquid natural gas transport and storage; ablative systems; acoustic control; chemical process; netted computer systems; space nuclear power; author of two books, over 180 publications and over 50 patents. *Mailing Add:* 1205 Sunbird Ave La Habra CA 90631

ISENBERG, NORBERT, ORGANIC CHEMISTRY. *Current Pos:* from asst prof to assoc prof, Univ Wis-Parkside, 64-69, actg chmn div sci, 68-69, chmn, 69-71, 73-76, prof chem, 69-90, EMER PROF CHEM, UNIV WIS-PARKSIDE, 90- *Personal Data:* b Saarbruecken, Ger, June 17, 23; nat US; m 50, Edith Sternheim; c Ralph, Mark, Jon & Lori. *Educ:* Columbia Univ, BA, 48, MA, 50; Rensselaer Polytech Inst, PhD(org chem), 63. *Prof Exp:* Asst chem, Columbia Univ, 49-50; from instr to assoc prof, Skidmore Col, 50-64, dir NSF undergrad res prog, 60-63. *Concurrent Pos:* Fel oncol, Univ Wis, 63-64; vis prof, Univ Wis-Madison, 71-72. *Mem:* Fel AAAS; Am Chem Soc; Sigma Xi; NY Acad Sci. *Res:* Organic sulfur compounds; heterocyclic compounds; synthetic organic chemistry; precipitation with thioacetamide; undergraduate research projects. *Mailing Add:* 4118 Pennington Lane Racine WI 53403

ISENECKER, LAWRENCE ELMER, MATHEMATICS. *Current Pos:* RETIRED. *Personal Data:* b Cleveland, Ohio, Feb 8, 24. *Educ:* Xavier Univ, Ohio, LittB, 46; West Baden Col, PhL, 50, STL, 58; Cath Univ Am, MS, 54, PhD(math), 62. *Prof Exp:* Teacher math, Loyola Acad, Ill, 50-52; from asst prof to assoc prof, Xavier Univ, Ohio, 63-96. *Mem:* Am Math Soc; Math Asn Am. *Res:* Mathematical analysis; foundations of mathematics. *Mailing Add:* PO Box 139 Clarkston MI 48347

ISENHOUR, THOMAS LEE, ANALYTICAL CHEMISTRY. *Current Pos:* DEAN, KANS STATE UNIV, 87- *Personal Data:* b Statesville, NC, Jan 29, 39; m 60; c 2. *Educ:* Univ NC, BS, 61; Cornell Univ, PhD(anal chem), 65. *Honors & Awards:* Am Award Anal Chem, 83. *Prof Exp:* Asst prof chem, Univ Wash, 65-69; assoc prof, Univ NC, Chapel Hill, 69-74, chmn dept, 75, prof chem, 74-; dean, Chem Dept, Utah State Univ, 84-87. *Concurrent Pos:* Sloan res fel, 71; I M Kolthoff vis prof, Hebrew Univ, 81. *Mem:* Am Chem Soc; Pattern Recognition Soc. *Res:* Computerized chemical information processing, search and retrieval system, molecular structure encoding; computerized learning machines: application to pattern recognition and interpretation in mass, infrared, and gamma-ray spectra; metal chelate mass spectrometry. *Mailing Add:* Duquesne Univ Dept Chem Mellon Hall Pittsburgh PA 15283

ISENOR, NEIL R, PHYSICS. *Current Pos:* RETIRED. *Personal Data:* b Dutch Settlement, NS, Jan 6, 32; c 3. *Educ:* Acadia Univ, BSc, 54; McMaster Univ, MSc, 55, PhD(physics), 59. *Prof Exp:* Lectr physics, Univ NB, 55-56; asst prof, Bishop's Univ, Can, 59-61; from asst prof to prof physics, Univ Waterloo, 61-92, assoc dean, 76-77, chmn dept, 77-82. *Concurrent Pos:* Nat Res Coun Can res grant, 62-; vis res assoc, Univ Rochester, 65; vis res fel, Univ NSW, 82-83 & Macquarie Univ, 88-89. *Mem:* Am Phys Soc; Can Asn Physicists; Optical Soc Am. *Res:* Laser interactions with matter; quantum optics. *Mailing Add:* 564 Woolwick St Waterloo ON N2J 4G8 Can

ISENSEE, ALLAN ROBERT, SOIL SCIENCE, PLANT PHYSIOLOGY. *Current Pos:* PLANT PHYSIOLOGIST, BELTSVILLE AGR RES SERV, USDA, 67- *Personal Data:* b Sparta, Wis, Dec 25, 39; m 64; c 2. *Educ:* Wis State Univ, Stevens Point, BS, 62; Univ Wis-Madison, MS, 65, PhD(soils), 68. *Mem:* Am Soc Agron; Weed Sci Soc Am; Am Chem Soc; Sigma Xi. *Res:* Persistence and absorption of pesticides in soil; influence of soil and pesticide properties on plant uptake of pesticides; development and use of model ecosystems to determine the fate and behavior of pesticides in the aquatic environment. *Mailing Add:* US Dept Agr Bldg 050 BARC-West Beltsville MD 20705

ISENSEE, ROBERT WILLIAM, ORGANIC CHEMISTRY. *Current Pos:* RETIRED. *Personal Data:* b Portland, Ore, Nov 2, 19; m 43, Beth Cingcade; c Nancy (Paff) & Elaine (Baker). *Educ:* Reed Col, BA, 41; Ore State Col, MA, 43, PhD(org chem), 48. *Prof Exp:* Res chemist, Hercules Powder Co, Del, 43-44, indust chemist, Va, 44-45; instr chem, Ore State Univ, 47-48; from asst prof to prof, San Diego State Univ, 48-82, chmn dept, 58-61. *Mem:* Am Chem Soc. *Res:* Synthesis of organic heterocycles; catalytic hydrocarbon oxidation; fine chemicals; explosives; synthesis of a new amino alcohol derived from quinazoline; acid-base equilibria studies. *Mailing Add:* 5036 Art San Diego CA 92115

ISERI, OSCAR AKIO, PATHOLOGY. *Current Pos:* PROF PATH, SCH MED, UNIV MD, BALTIMORE, 74-; STAFF PATHOLOGIST, VET ADMIN HOSP, 74- *Personal Data:* b Thomas, Wash, Aug 23, 27; m 61, Anna M; c 3. *Educ:* Antioch Col, BS, 52; Harvard Univ, MD, 56; Am Bd Path, dipl, 64. *Prof Exp:* Intern internal med, King County Hosp, Seattle, Wash, 56-57; asst resident, Univ Wash, 57-58, trainee exp path, 58-61, res instr path, 61-62; USPHS res fel, Mallory Inst Path, Boston City Hosp, 62-64, asst pathologist, Inst, 64-69; from asst prof to assoc prof path, Tufts Univ, 64-74. *Concurrent Pos:* Lectr, Harvard Med Sch, 65-74; asst physician path, Boston City Hosp, 65-69, assoc vis physician, 69-74; assoc pathologist, Mallory Inst Path, 69-74. *Mem:* AAAS; Am Asn Pathologists; Int Soc Stereology; Electron Micros Soc Am; Am Asn Study Liver Dis; Int Acad Path. *Res:* Ultrastructural and chemical pathology; liver and gastro-intestinal pathology. *Mailing Add:* DVA Med Ctr Univ Maryland Sch Med Ctr Baltimore MD 21201-1524. *Fax:* 410-605-7911

ISERSON, KENNETH VICTOR, EMERGENCY MEDICINE, BIOETHICS. *Current Pos:* assoc prof, 81-91, DIR, ARIZ BIOETHICS PROG, UNIV ARIZ COL MED, 90-, PROF SURG MED, 91- *Personal Data:* b Washington, DC, Apr 8, 49; m 73, Mary Lou Sherk. *Educ:* Univ Md Col Park, BS, 71; Univ Md, Baltimore, MD, 75; Univ Phoenix, Tucson, MBA, 87. *Prof Exp:* Clin assoc prof emergency med, Scott & White Clin, Tex A&M Col Med, 80-81. *Concurrent Pos:* Chair, Univ Med Ctr Bioethics Comt, Univ Ariz Col Med, 86-; chmn pract mgt comt, Am Col Emergency Physicians, 87-89; mem, Coun Med Soc, Am Med Asn, 88-; bioethics fel, Univ Chicago, 90-91. *Mem:* Am Col Emergency Physicians; AMA; Soc Acad Emergency Med; Wilderness Med Soc; Soc Health & Human Values; Soc Bioethics Consult; Nat Asn Advs Health Professions. *Res:* Health policy and bioethics; rapid blood warming. *Mailing Add:* Dept Surg Emergency Med Sect PO Box 245707 1501 N Campbell Ave Tucson AZ 85724. *Fax:* 520-626-2480

ISGUR, BENJAMIN, soil conservation; deceased, see previous edition for last biography

ISGUR, NATHAN, THEORETICAL SUBATOMIC PHYSICS. *Current Pos:* Fel physics, 74-76, from asst prof to assoc prof, 76-82, PROF PHYSICS, UNIV TORONTO, 82; THEORY GROUP LEADER, CONTINUOUS ELECTRON BEAM ACCELERATOR FACIL, 90- *Personal Data:* b Houston, Tex, May 25, 47; m 84, Karin Bergsagel. *Educ:* Calif Inst Technol, BS, 68; Univ Toronto, PhD(physics), 74. *Honors & Awards:* E W R Steacie Prize, Natural Sci Eng Res Coun, Can,; Rutherford Medal, Royal Soc Can, 89. *Mem:* Can Asn Physicists; Am Inst Physics; Can Inst Particle Physics; fel Royal Soc Can; fel Am Phys Soc. *Res:* Quantum chromodynamics; weak interactions; theories of elementary interactions. *Mailing Add:* Continuous Electron Beam Accelerator Facility 12000 Jefferson Ave Newport News VA 23606. *Fax:* 757-249-7002; *E-Mail:* isgur@cebaf.gov

ISH, CARL JACKSON, chemistry; deceased, see previous edition for last biography

ISHAM, ELMER REX, PLASMA PHYSICS, SOLID STATE PHYSICS. *Current Pos:* from asst prof to assoc prof, 65-75, asst pres, 77-79, PROF PHYSICS, SAM HOUSTON STATE UNIV, 75-, DIR RES, 67-, ASST TO PRES, 79- *Personal Data:* b Bovina, Tex, July 26, 35; m 56; c 2. *Educ:* Tex A&M Univ, BS, 58, MS, 61, PhD(physics), 65. *Prof Exp:* Instr physics, Tex A&M Univ, 61-64, instr math, 64-65. *Mem:* Am Phys Soc. *Res:* Theoretical plasma physics; luminescence of solids. *Mailing Add:* 2736 Lake Shore Dr Waco TX 76708

ISHAQ, KHALID SULAIMAN, ORGANIC CHEMISTRY. *Current Pos:* Fel lipids res, Univ NC, Chapel Hill, 68-70, instr, 70-73, asst prof, 73-80, ASSOC PROF MED CHEM, UNIV NC, CHAPEL HILL, 80- *Personal Data:* b Basra, Iraq, Jan 16, 33; US citizen; m 68. *Educ:* Am Univ Beirut, BS, 56; Univ Minn, Minneapolis, PhD(med chem), 69. *Mem:* Am Chem Soc; Am Asn Pharmaceut Scientists. *Res:* Lipid chemistry; anti-tumor agents; antiviral agents. *Mailing Add:* Sch Pharm Univ NC Chapel Hill NC 27514

ISHERWOOD, DANA JOAN, GEOCHEMISTRY. *Current Pos:* Geochemist, 77-86, sr analyst, 86-94, DIR CONG AFFAIRS, LAWRENCE LIVERMORE LAB, 94- *Personal Data:* b Lewiston, NY; m 70, William. *Educ:* San Francisco State Univ, BS, 64; Univ Colo, PhD(geol), 75. *Concurrent Pos:* Sci cong fel, Am Geophys Soc, 85-86. *Mem:* AAAS; Am Geophys Soc; Soc Women Geographers; Grad Women Sci. *Res:* Geochemistry of radionuclides in natural systems; soil geochemistry; rock weathering processes; groundwater pollution. *Mailing Add:* 370 La Encinal Orinda CA 94563. *Fax:* 510-422-4116; *E-Mail:* isherwood1@llnl.gov

ISHERWOOD, WILLIAM FRANK, GEOTHERMAL RESOURCES, CONTAMINANT HYDROGEOLOGY. *Current Pos:* proj leader, 87-91, DIV LEADER, LAWRENCE LIVERMORE NAT LAB, 91- *Personal Data:* b Stoneham, Mass, Apr, 30, 41; m 70, Dana J Isherwood. *Educ:* Princeton Univ, AB, 63; Univ Utah, MS, 67; Univ Colo PhD(geol sci), 75; Golden Gate Univ, MBA, 82. *Prof Exp:* Geophysicist, Geophys Polar Res Ctr, Univ Wis, 65-67, Stanford Res Inst, 67-70, Nat Oceanic & Atmospheric Admin, 71-73 & US Geol Surv, 73-77; chief geothermal eval, US Geol Surv, 77-79, dep conserv mgr, geothermal conserv div, 79-83; sr geophysicist, Geothermex Inc, 83-87. *Concurrent Pos:* Bd dirs, Geothermal Resources Coun, 83-91; chair, res comt, Am Alpine Club. *Mem:* Am Geophys Union; Nat Water Well Asn. *Res:* Using geophysical methods for evaluation and understanding of geothermal systems; industrial ecology applied to energy systems; developing and applying advanced technologies to environmental cleanup and monitoring. *Mailing Add:* 37 La Encinal Orinda CA 94563. *Fax:* 510-422-3000; *E-Mail:* isherwood2@llnl.gov

ISHIDA, HATSUO, SURFACE SPECTROSCOPY, COMPOSITE INTERFACE. *Current Pos:* Postdoctoral res assoc, Case Western Res Univ, 77-78, sr res assoc, 79, asst prof phys chem, 79-83, assoc prof, 84-87, PROF MACROMOLECULAR SCI, CASE WESTERN RES UNIV, 88- *Personal Data:* b Kosai, Japan, Dec 16, 48; m 75; c 2. *Educ:* Doshisha Univ, Japan, BS, 71, MS, 73; Case Western Res Univ, PhD(macromolecular sci), 76. *Concurrent Pos:* Dir, CR Newphor Polymer Composite Processing, Case Western Res Univ, 80-; gen chmn, Int Conf Composite Interfaces, 83- *Mem:* Am Chem Soc; Soc Appl Spectros; Japan Soc Polymer Sci; Processing Soc; Am Composite Soc; Soc Advan Mat & Process Eng. *Res:* Molecular characterization techniques to investigate structure of composite interfaces, coatings on metals, and structural changes during processing of composites; synthesize and characterize organic ferro-magnetic polymers. *Mailing Add:* Dept Macromolecular Sci Case Western Res Univ 10900 Euclid Cleveland OH 44106

ISHIDA, TAKANOBU, ISOTOPE EFFECTS, STABLE ISOTOPE SEPARATION. *Current Pos:* FAC MEM, CHEM DEPT, STATE UNIV NY, STONY BROOK, 79- *Personal Data:* b Kyoto, Japan, Mar 22, 31; m 64, Michiko Horiguchi; c Nobuyuki & Emi. *Educ:* Kyoto Univ, BS, 53, MS, 55; NY Univ, MS, 58; Mass Inst Technol, PhD(nuclear eng), 64. *Prof Exp:* Res assoc chem, Brookhaven Nat Lab, 64-66, Belfer Grad Sch Sci, Yeshiva Univ, 66-68; from asst prof to assoc prof chem, Brooklyn Col, 68-74, prof chem, 74-79. *Concurrent Pos:* Res collabr, Brookhaven Nat Lab, 66-; res grant, AEC, Energy Res & Develop Admin & Dept of Energy, 71-; vis assoc prof, Univ Rochester, 73-74, vis prof, 74-79; vis scholar, Max Planck Inst Chem, Mainz, 86. *Mem:* Am Chem Soc; Am Phys Soc. *Res:* Separation of stable isotopes; statistical mechanics of isotope effects and condensed phase. *Mailing Add:* Chem Dept State Univ NY Stony Brook NY 11794-3400. *Fax:* 516-632-7960; *E-Mail:* tishida@sbccmail.bitnet; tishida@ccmail.sunysb.edu

ISHIDA, YUKISATO, BIOCHEMISTRY, NEUROSCIENCES. *Current Pos:* researcher pharmacol, 77-85, SR RESEARCHER PHYSIOL, MITSUBISHI KASEI INST LIFE SCI, 85- *Personal Data:* b Tokyo, Japan, July 7, 48; m 74, Shizuko Ishimoto; c Yukiaki & Satoshi. *Educ:* Toyama Univ, BS, 71; Univ Tokyo, MS, 74, PhD(pharmacol), 83. *Prof Exp:* Asst prof vet pharmacol, Fac Agr, Univ Tokyo, 75-77. *Concurrent Pos:* Vis asst prof, Dept Physiol Biophys, Col Med, Univ Cincinnati, 84-86; vis scientist, Inst Cell Biol, Swiss Fedn Inst Technol, ETH, Honggerberg, 89. *Mem:* Corresp mem Am Physiol Soc; fel Japan Pharmacol Soc; fel Japan Physiol Soc; fel Japan Soc Smooth Muscle Res; Japan Soc Vet Med. *Res:* Energy metabolism of smooth muscle; phosphagen content and tension of muscle; identification of mitochrondrial creatine kinase in smooth muscle; cardiovascular physiology and pharmacology. *Mailing Add:* Mitsubishi Kasei Inst Life Sci Machida Tokyo 194 Japan. *Fax:* 81-427-24-6314; *E-Mail:* yishida@libra.ls.m-kagaku.co.jp

ISHIHARA, KOHEI, HEAT TRANSFER. *Current Pos:* ENG CONSULT, SR ENG CO, 93- *Personal Data:* b Kyoto, Japan, Apr 9, 41; m 65, Atsuko Hori; c Mariko, Hiroki, Emi & Yumi. *Educ:* Kyoto Univ, BS, 65; Okla State Univ, MS, 67, PhD(chem eng), 71. *Prof Exp:* Res engr polymer extrusion, Toyobo Co, 71-72; res engr heat transfer, Chicago Bridge & Iron Co, 72-75 & Heat Transfer Res, Inc, 75-91; sr staff engr, R M Parsons Co, 91-93. *Mem:* Am Inst Chem Engrs; Japan Heat Transfer Soc. *Res:* Condensation and convection heat transfer; single and two-phase flow; numerical analysis of fluid flow. *Mailing Add:* 1835 Vistillas Rd Altadena CA 91001. *Fax:* 626-794-7273

ISHIHARA, TERUO (TERRY), MECHANICAL & AEROSPACE ENGINEERING. *Current Pos:* RETIRED. *Personal Data:* b Ogden, Utah, Apr 9, 27; m 52; c 5. *Educ:* Wash State Univ, BS, 49; Univ Calif, Berkeley, teaching cert, 51; San Jose State Col, MS, 58; Univ Ariz, MS, 66, PhD(mech eng), 69. *Prof Exp:* Jr mech engr, US Naval Air Missile Test Ctr, Calif, 51-53; res analyst, Northrop Aircraft Corp, 53-54; teacher math, jr high sch, Calif, 54-55; mech engr, Lawrence Radiation Lab, 55-59; instr eng, San Jose City Col, 59-61; instr math, Monterey Peninsula Col, 61-63; asst prof mech eng, Univ Mo, Columbia, 66-70; assoc prof mech eng, Rose-Hulman Inst Technol, 70-80; prof mech eng & technol, Saginaw Valley State Col, 80- *Mem:* AAAS; Am Soc Eng Educ; Am Soc Mech Engrs; Am Asn Univ Professors. *Res:* Applied mathematics; applications of optimization theory; educational methods in the teaching of engineering; numerical analysis; digital computer applications; engineering mechanics; thermodynamics; heat transfer. *Mailing Add:* 20 W Tonto Dr Sedona AZ 86351

ISHII, DOUGLAS NOBUO, MOLECULAR BASIS OF NERVE DEVELOPMENT & REGENERATION, PATHOGENESIS OF DIABETIC NEUROPATHY. *Current Pos:* assoc prof, 86-89, PROF PHYSIOL & PROF BIOCHEM & MOLECULAR BIOL, COLO STATE UNIV, FT COLLINS, 89- *Personal Data:* b Santa Anita, Calif, July 30, 42; m 82, Wendy A Nute; c Jordon, Gregory & Aaron. *Educ:* Univ Calif, Berkeley, BA, 67; Stanford Univ PhD(pharmacol), 74. *Prof Exp:* Instr pharmacol, Univ Pac, San Francisco, 68-70; fel neurobiol, 74-76; from asst prof to assoc prof pharmacol, Columbia Univ, New York City, 76-85. *Concurrent Pos:* Res career develop award, NIH, 78; prin investr grants, Nat Inst Neurol & Communicative Dis & Stroke, NIH, 78-, ad hoc mem, Neurol B Study Sect, 81, site rev team, Cancer Therapeut Prog Rev Comt, Nat Cancer Inst, 83 & 86, spec reviewer, Neurol C Study Sect, 87, mem, Special Prog Proj Rev Comt, Nat Inst Child Health & Human Develop, 87, spec reviewer, Exp Cardiovasc Sci Study Sect, 89; ad hoc consult, Develop Neurosci Panel, NSF, 85, 88 & 89. *Mem:* Soc Neurosci; Am Soc Pharmacol & Exp Therapeut; AAAS; Am Diabetes Asn; Tissue Cult Asn. *Res:* Neurobiology of insulin and insulin-like growth factors; peripheral nerve development and regeneration; new theory for pathogenesis of diabetic neuropathy has been developed and is under test. *Mailing Add:* Physiol Dept Colo State Univ Ft Collins CO 80523-0001. *Fax:* 970-491-7569

ISHII, T(HOMAS) KORYU, ELECTRICAL ENGINEERING, MICROWAVES. *Current Pos:* from asst prof to assoc prof, 59-64, PROF ELEC ENG, MARQUETTE UNIV, 64- *Personal Data:* b Japan, Mar 18, 27; m 58, Eiko B Ishida; c Mutsumi M, Naomi B, Megumi M & Mayumi M. *Educ:* Nihon Univ, Tokyo, BS, 50, DEng, 61; Univ Wis, MS, 57, PhD(elec eng), 59. *Honors & Awards:* Inst Elec & Electronics Engrs TC Burnam Awards, 69, Centennial Awards, 84. *Prof Exp:* Elec engr, Japan Naval Res Lab, 45 & Japan Broadcasting Corp, 49; instr elec eng, Nihon Univ, Tokyo, 50-56. *Mem:* Inst Elec & Electronics Engrs. *Res:* Microwave applications and electronics; millimeter circuit; millimeter wave amplification, detection and generation; masers and lasers; industrial sensors. *Mailing Add:* Dept Elec Eng Marquette Univ Milwaukee WI 53233

ISHIKAWA, HIROSHI, DIFFERENTIATION. *Current Pos:* PROF ANAT, DEPT ANAT, SCH MED, JIKEI UNIV, 80- *Personal Data:* b Tokyo, Japan, Nov 11, 41; m 68, Yoshiko; c Mayumi & Takaki. *Educ:* Jikei Univ, BMed, 68, DMed, 72. *Honors & Awards:* Prize of Japan Endocrine Soc, Japan Endocrine Soc, 74. *Prof Exp:* Asst anat, Dept Anat, Sch Med, Showa Univ, 72-73, lectr, 73-74; asst prof, Dept Anat, Sch Med, Tohoku Univ, 74-80. *Concurrent Pos:* Med examr, Tokyo Med Examiner's Off, 72-76 & 80-; researcher, Found Advan Int Sci. *Res:* Functional and morphological studies on the differentiation of anterior pituitary cells in vivo and in vitro. *Mailing Add:* Dept Anat Sch Med Jikei Univ 3-25-8 Nishishinbashi Minato-ku Tokyo 105 Japan. *Fax:* 81-3-3261-9484

ISHIKAWA, SADAMU, MEDICINE, PHYSIOLOGY. *Current Pos:* ASSOC PROF MED, SCH MED, TUFTS UNIV, 71-; DIR, PULMONARY LAB, ST ELIZABETH MED CTR, 81- *Personal Data:* b Osaka, Japan, July 6, 32; m 61; c 1. *Educ:* Kyoto Med Col, MD, 57. *Prof Exp:* From asst prof to assoc prof path, Univ Man, 67-71; physician in charge pulmonary function, Cent Blood Gas & Lung Physiol Labs, Boston City Hosp, 71-73. *Concurrent Pos:* Dir, Pulmonary Function Lab, Lemuel Shattuck Hosp, 73-80. *Mem:* Am Thoracic Soc; fel Am Col Chest Physicians. *Res:* Ecology of man, adaptation of lung and heart to abnormal environment; air pollution and emphysema; structure-function of aging lung. *Mailing Add:* 736 Cambridge St Boston MA 02135

ISHIMARU, AKIRA, ELECTRICAL ENGINEERING. *Current Pos:* From asst prof to assoc prof, 58-65, PROF ELEC ENG, UNIV WASH, 65- *Personal Data:* b Fukuoka, Japan, Mar 16, 28; US citizen; m 56, Yuko; c John, Jane, James & Joyce. *Educ:* Univ Tokyo, BS, 51; Univ Wash, PhD(elec eng), 58. *Honors & Awards:* Achievement Award, Inst Elec & Electronics Engrs, 68, Centennial Medal, 84, Distinguished Achievement Award, 95. *Concurrent Pos:* Vis assoc prof, Univ Calif, Berkeley, 63-64; consult, Boeing Co, Wash, 59- & Jet Propulsion Lab, 64-; ed, Radio Sci, Am Geophys Union, 79-82; mem comn, Int Sci Radio Union; Inst Elec & Electronics Engrs; ed, Waves In Random Media, Inst Physics, UK. *Mem:* Nat Acad Eng; Inst Elec & Electronics Engrs; Int Union Radio Sci. *Res:* Antenna pattern synthesis; propagation and antennas; plasmas; waves in random and turbulent media; bioengineering applications; remote sensing; space communications; ultrasound imaging. *Mailing Add:* Dept Elec Eng Univ Wash Box 352500 Seattle WA 98195-0001. *Fax:* 206-543-3842

ISHIMARU, HAJIME, PHYSICS. *Current Pos:* res assoc, 72-75, assoc prof, 75-84, PROF, NAT LAB HIGH ENERGY PHYSICS, JAPAN, 84-; PROF, GRAD UNIV, 88- *Personal Data:* b Sapporo, Japan, Feb 21, 40; m 69, Masako Kodera; c Dan & Goh. *Educ:* Hokkaido Univ, BS, 63; Tohoku Univ, MS, 65, DE, 80; Nagoya Univ, DS(physics), 68, DSc, 70. *Honors & Awards:* Vacuum Tech Award, Vacuum Soc Japan, 79-82; Remarkable Patent Award, Ministry Sci & Tech, Tokyo, 83 & 85; Albert Nerken Award, 94. *Prof Exp:* Res assoc, Tokyo Univ, 69-72. *Concurrent Pos:* Consult, Synchrotron Radiation Res Ctr, Hsinchu, Taiwan, 86- & Superconductive Super Collider Lab, Dallas, 91- *Mem:* Am Vacuum Soc; Japan Vacuum Soc; Japan Light Metal Soc; Japan Appl Physics Soc. *Res:* Particle accelerator; vacuum science and technology; space vacuum technology. *Mailing Add:* High Energy Accelerator Res Org 1-1 Oho Tsukuba Ibaraki 305 Japan. *Fax:* 81-298-64-3182; *E-Mail:* ishimaru@kekux1.kek.jp

ISHIZAKA, KIMISHIGE, IMMUNOLOGY, IMMUNOCHEMISTRY. *Current Pos:* CONSULT PHARMACEUT DIV KIRIN BREWERY, JAPAN, 96- *Personal Data:* b Tokyo, Japan, Dec 3, 25; m 49; c 1. *Educ:* Univ Tokyo, MD, 48, DrMedSci(immunol), 54. *Honors & Awards:* Passano Found Award; Paul Ehrlich & Ludwig-Darmstaedter Prize, WGer; Int Award, Gairdner Found, Can; Emperor's Award, Japan; Borden Award, Asn Am Med Cols; Achievement Examr, Am Col Physicians. *Prof Exp:* Res mem, NIH, Tokyo, 50-53, chief, Div Immunoserol, 53-62; from asst prof to assoc prof microbiol, Univ Colo, Denver, 62-70, chief, Div Serol, Children's Asthma Res Inst & Hosp, 62-63, dir, Dept Basic Sci, 63-70; prof med & microbiol, Sch Med, Johns Hopkins Univ, 70-81, dir, Sub-dept Immunol & prof immunol & med, 81-89; pres & sci dir, La Jolla Inst Allergy & Immunol, Calif, 89-96. *Concurrent Pos:* Res fel chem, Calif Inst Technol, 57-59; res fel microbiol, Johns Hopkins Univ, 59; mem, Adv Comt Immunol, WHO. *Mem:* Foreign assoc Nat Acad Sci; Am Asn Immunol; hon fel Am Acad Allergy; Soc Exp Biol & Med; fel AAAS. *Res:* Molecular bases of hypersensitivity reactions; immunochemical and physicochemical properties of human antibodies, especially reaginic antibodies; regulation of the immunoglobulin-E response. *Mailing Add:* 1659-15 Zao Hango Yomagata 990-23 Japan

ISHIZAKA, TERUKO, IMMEDIATE HYPERSENSITIVITY, ALLERGIES. *Current Pos:* From assoc prof to prof microbiol, 70-81, from assoc prof to prof med, 72-81, PROF IMMUNOL & MED, JOHNS HOPKINS UNIV, 79- *Personal Data:* b Sept 28, 26; c 1. *Educ:* Tokyo Women's Med Sch, MD, 49; Univ Tokyo, PhD, 55. *Honors & Awards:* Passano Found Award, USA, 72; Gairdner Found Int Award, Can, 73; First Sci Achievement Award, Inst Asn Allergology, 73; Borden Award, Asn Am Med Cols, 79. *Concurrent Pos:* Res mem, Dept Serol, NIH, Tokyo, 51-57, Dept Immunoserol, 59-62; res fel, div chem & chem eng, Calif Inst Technol, 57-59 & dept microbiol, Sch Hyg & Pub Health, Johns Hopkins Univ, 59; res immunologist, Children's Asthma Res Inst & Hosp, Denver, 62-70. *Mem:* Japanese Soc Bacteriol; Japanese Soc Allergy; Am Asn Immunologists; hon mem Am Acad Allergy; AAAS; Am Soc Exp Path; Int Col Allergol; hon mem Span Soc Allergy & Clin Immunol; hon mem Venezuelan Soc Allergy & Immunol. *Res:* Immediate hypersensitivity, allergies. *Mailing Add:* Kirin Brewery Co 26-1 Jingumae 6-Chome Shibuya Tokyo Japan 150-11

ISIED, STEPHAN SALEH, INORGANIC CHEMISTRY. *Current Pos:* from asst prof to assoc prof, 75-83, PROF INORG CHEM, RUTGERS UNIV, 83- *Personal Data:* b Jerusalem, Jordan, Aug 4, 46. *Educ:* Am Univ Beirut, BS, 67, MS, 69; Stanford Univ, PhD(inorg chem), 74. *Honors & Awards:* Camille & Henry Dreyfus Award; Rutgers Excellence in Res Award. *Prof Exp:* Teaching asst inorg & phys chem, Am Univ Beirut, 68-69; teaching & res asst inorg & anal chem, Stanford Univ, 70-73; postdoctoral bioinorg chem, Univ Calif, Berkeley, 74-75. *Mem:* Am Chem Soc. *Res:* Intramolecular electron transfer in electron transfer proteins; the role of amino acids and peptides in electron mediation; reactivity of coordinated small molecules. *Mailing Add:* Dept Chem Rutgers Univ New Brunswick NJ 08903

ISIHARA, AKIRA, CONDENSED MATTER PHYSICS. *Current Pos:* VCHMN & PRES, JIDELO, BARDSTOWN, INC, 91- *Personal Data:* b Kofu, Japan; US citizen; m 53, Ikuko; c 4. *Educ:* Univ Tokyo, DSC, 52. *Prof Exp:* Res assoc statist physics, Univ Tokyo, 52-55; res assoc statist physics, Univ Md, 55-58; from assoc prof to prof statist physics, Polytech Inst NY, 58-64; prof, State Univ NY, Buffalo, 64-90, chmn, Dept Phys, 77-87. *Concurrent Pos:* Consult, Oak Ridge Nat Lab, 62-69, NAm Rockwell, 60-65 & Boeing Sci Lab, 60-63; vis prof, Vander Waals Lab, Univ Amsterdam, 77, Free Univ Brussels, 71 & Univ Rochester, 70-71; vis scholar, Harvard Univ, 87; adj prof physics, Univ Louisville, 92- *Mem:* Fel Am Phys Soc. *Res:* Transport and many body phenomena in 2D electron systems; polymer physics; condensed matter physics; many body theory. *Mailing Add:* Jideco of Bardstown Inc 901 Withrow Ct Bardstown KY 40004

ISKANDER, FELIB YOUSSEF, TRACE ELEMENT MEASUREMENT, RADIOCHEMISTRY. *Current Pos:* Radio chemist, 83-85, res assoc, 85-90, MGR, NUCLEAR ANALYTICAL SERV, UNIV TEX, 90- *Personal Data:* b Assiout, Egypt, Sept 19, 49; m 72, Soheir A Maximoss; c Maryana & Vivian. *Educ:* Cairo Univ, Egypt, BS, 71, MS, 73; Wash State Univ, MS, 82, PhD(chem), 83. *Concurrent Pos:* Fac mem, Dept Chem, Austin Community Col, 89- *Mem:* Am Chem Soc; Am Nuclear Soc; Egyptian Pharmaceut Soc; Asn Off Anal Chemists Int. *Res:* Innovative approaches to solve problems associated with trace element measurement in food, geological deposites and environment samples using radioanalytical method of analysis. *Mailing Add:* Univ Tex PRC-NETL-No 159 Austin TX 78712. *Fax:* 512-471-4589; *E-Mail:* f.iskander@mail.utexas.edu

ISKANDER, SHAFIK KAMEL, FRACTURE MECHANICS, FINITE ELEMENTS. *Current Pos:* engr, Oak Ridge Nat Lab, 72-77, head solid mech sect, Comput Sci Div, 77-82, resident engr Ger, US Nuclear Regulatory Comn, 82-86, SR DEVELOP STAFF MEM, METALS & CERAMIC DIV, OAK RIDGE NAT LAB, 86- *Personal Data:* b Cairo, Egypt, Dec 15, 34; US citizen; m 62, Horia F Soliman; c Marianne & Yousef. *Educ:* Cairo Univ, Egypt, BMechEng, 56, MSc, 67; Univ Tenn, PhD(eng mech), 72. *Prof Exp:* Head tech off eng, Gen Indust Co, Gimoc, Egypt, 58-62; head mat testing unit eng, Nat Inst Stand, 62-68; instr eng sci & mech, Col Eng, Univ Tenn, 69-72. *Concurrent Pos:* Consult, govt & pvt industs, 58-68; instr, Mech Eng Dept, Cairo Univ, 58-68; researcher, Bundesanstalt fur Mat Res, WBerlin, Ger, 62-64; assoc prof, Eng Sci & Mech Dept, Univ Tenn, 72-82. *Mem:* Am Soc Mech Engrs; Soc Exp Stress Anal; Sigma Xi; Am Metals Soc Int; Am Soc Testing & Mat. *Res:* Effects of neutron irradiation on fracture and mechanical properties of nuclear pressure vessel steels, including their crack arrest behavior; computation mechanics including finite elements. *Mailing Add:* 103 Berwick Dr Oak Ridge TN 37830-7834. *Fax:* 423-574-5118; *E-Mail:* ski@stc10.ctd.ornl.gov

ISKAROUS, MOENES ZAHER, ASIC DESIGN, ROBOTICS. *Current Pos:* STAFF DESIGN ENGR, INTEL CORP, 97- *Personal Data:* b Cairo, Egypt, Nov 5, 64; m 91, Nevine R Elmasry; c Mark M & Mina M. *Educ:* Ain Shams Univ, Cairo, Egypt, BSc, 87; Vanderbilt Univ MSc, 92, PhD(elec eng), 95. *Prof Exp:* Control systs engr, Team Int, Egypt, 88-89; design engr, Reem Res & Electronic Mfg, Egypt, 89-90; staff design engr, C-Cube Microsysts, 95-97. *Concurrent Pos:* Expert witness, Riddell Williams Bullitt & Walkinshaw Law Off, 91; adj prof elec eng, Tenn State Univ, 95. *Mem:* Inst Elec & Electronics Engrs; Robotics & Automation Soc. *Res:* Very large scale integration architecture design including modeling, performance analysts and validation; robotics including controller design; intelligent control algorithms with neural networks and neuro fuzzy networks with applications in human service; patentee in field. *Mailing Add:* 1072 Reed Ave No 57 Sunnyvale CA 94086. *E-Mail:* moenes@hotmail.com

ISLAM, M SAFIQUL, WATER-SOLUBLE POLYMERS, WATER TREATMENT CHEMICALS. *Current Pos:* chemist, Mayo Chem Co, 91-96, SR CHEMIST, CALLAWAY CHEM CO (MAYO DIV), 96- *Personal Data:* b India, Jan 14, 54: US Citizen; m 89, Fahamida Arzoo; c Fahad & Nadia. *Educ:* Rajshahi Univ, BS, 76, MS, 78; Auburn Univ, PhD(chem), 86. *Prof Exp:* Assoc, Southern Methodist Univ, 86-90; res assoc, Coatings Res Inst, 90-91. *Mem:* Am Chem Soc. *Res:* Research and development on different water-soluble polymers, chelating agents, scale and corrosion inhibitors, cleaning compounds and proprietory formulations for water treatment. *Mailing Add:* 3629 Naturewalk Trail Marietta GA 30060

ISLAM, MIR NAZRUL, FOOD SCIENCE, NUTRITION. *Current Pos:* from asst prof to assoc prof, 74-88, PROF FOOD SCI & NUTRIT, UNIV DEL, 88- *Personal Data:* b Barisal, Bangladesh, Jan 1, 47; m 70, Sara Asvat; c Najmul & Mansoor. *Educ:* Dacca Univ, BSc, 66, MSc, 67; La State Univ, PhD(food sci), 72. *Prof Exp:* Lectr biochem & nutrit, Dacca Univ, Bangladesh, 67-69; asst prof food & nutrit, Southern Univ, La, 72-74. *Concurrent Pos:* Consult, Int Paper Co, Tuxedo, NY, 76-77, Shoregood Corp, Federalsburg, Md, 78- & Container Corp Am, Oaks, Pa, 81-, Int Am Develop Bank, 90-91; distinguished vis prof, Univ Panama, 80-81; Fulbright prof, Univ Sao Paulo, Brazil, 89. *Mem:* Inst Food Technologists; Am Asn Cereal Chemists; Nutrit Today Soc; Am Dietetic Asn. *Res:* Post-harvest preservation; product development and utilization of halophyte crops; tropical fruits; awarded US patents. *Mailing Add:* Dept Animal & Food Sci Univ Del Newark DE 19717. *Fax:* 302-831-2822; *E-Mail:* islam@udel.edu

ISLAM, MOHAMMED N, OPTICS. *Current Pos:* ASSOC PROF ELEC ENG & COMPUT SCI, UNIV MICH, ANN ARBOR, 92- *Personal Data:* b Newark, NJ, Feb 8, 60. *Educ:* Mass Inst Technol, BSEE, 80, MSEE, 82, ScD, 85. *Honors & Awards:* Adolph Lomb Medal, Optical Soc Am, 92. *Prof Exp:* Tech mem, Systs Eng & Antenna Design Groups, IBM, 78-79; staff mem, Femtosecond Laser Lab, AT&T Bell Labs, 83, consult, 83-85; res scientist, Photonics Switching Res Dept, 85-92. *Concurrent Pos:* Mem, Spec Studies Physics Group, Lawrence Livermore Nat Lab, 82-83, consult, 85-; mem, Prog Comt Integrated Photonics Res, Int Soc Optical Eng, 91-93, chair, 94. *Mem:* Int Soc Optical Eng. *Res:* Ultrafast fiber switching devices and systems; granted 7 US patents. *Mailing Add:* Dept Elec Eng & Comput Sci Univ Mich 1301 Beal Ave Ann Arbor MI 48109

ISLAM, MUHAMMAD MUNIRUL, THEORETICAL HIGH ENERGY PHYSICS. *Current Pos:* from asst prof to assoc prof, 67-75, PROF PHYSICS, UNIV CONN, 75-; FAC MEM, PHYS DEPT, STATE UNIV NY, POTSDAM. *Personal Data:* b Chittagong, Bangladesh, May 18, 36; m 62; c 1. *Educ:* Univ Dacca, BSc, 56, MSc, 57; Univ London, PhD(theoret physics), 61. *Prof Exp:* Res asst theoret physics, Imp Col, Univ London, 61-62; res assoc high energy physics, Brown Univ, 62-65, asst prof res, 65-67. *Concurrent Pos:* Vis scientist, Saclay Nuclear Res Ctr, France, 74-75. *Mem:* Am Phys Soc. *Res:* Scattering of elementary particles, their interactions and structure. *Mailing Add:* Dept Phys Univ Conn 2152 Hillside Rd Storrs CT 06268

ISLAM, NURUL, PLANT PHYSIOLOGY, AGRONOMY. *Current Pos:* ENVIRON SCIENTIST, ELEC STAFF DIV, USDA RURAL ELECTRIFICATION ADMIN, 81- *Personal Data:* b Bogra, Bangladesh, Dec 13, 39; m 71, Haq; c Samrina, Shakil & Sharmina. *Educ:* Univ Dacca, BAgr, 60, MAgr, 61; Tuskegee Inst, MAgr, 65; WVa Univ, PhD(plant physiol), 69. *Prof Exp:* Res asst bot, EPakistan Agr Res Inst, Dacca, 61-62; instr agr, Pakistan-Japan Training Inst, 63; annotator, WVa Univ, 68-69, planner, Div Water Resources, WVa Dept Natural Resources, 69-75, chief planning, 75-81. *Mem:* Am Soc Agron. *Res:* Environmental physiology of crops with respect to day length, temperature, and plant growth substances. *Mailing Add:* 357 Copperfield Lane Herndon VA 20170. *Fax:* 202-720-7491

ISLEIB, DONALD RICHARD, PLANT PHYSIOLOGY. *Current Pos:* exec secy, Mich Toxic Substance Control Comn, 80, DIR, BEAN/COWPEA COLLABORATIVE RES SUPPORT PROG, MICH STATE UNIV, 81- *Personal Data:* b Paterson, NJ, June 2, 27; m 51; c 3. *Educ:* Rutgers Univ, BS, 51, MS, 52; Iowa State Univ, PhD, 54. *Prof Exp:* Asst chem weed control & plant physiol, Rutgers Univ, 51-52 & Iowa State Univ, 52-54; assoc prof farm crops, Mich State Univ, 54-61; agr res mgr, Frito-Lay, Inc, 61-65 & Int Minerals & Chem Corp, 65-71; from sci adv to dir, Mich Dept Agr, 71-74, chief dep dir, 74-79. *Mem:* Potato Asn Am (pres, 66); Am Soc Agr; Crop Sci Soc. *Res:* Special emphasis on crop plants and chemicals used in crop production. *Mailing Add:* 5400 Park Lake Rd East Lansing MI 48823

ISLER, GENE A, ANIMAL SCIENCE. *Current Pos:* CONSULT, KALMBACH FEEDS, 91- *Personal Data:* b Marion, Ohio, Apr 13, 40; m 68; c 2. *Educ:* Ohio State Univ, BS, 62, MS, 66, PhD(animal sci), 69. *Prof Exp:* Exten specialist animal sci, Ohio State Univ, 69-91. *Mem:* Am Soc Animal Sci. *Res:* Swine genetics; swine performance testing; adjustment factors for growth; swine ultrasonics. *Mailing Add:* 3555 Chapman Rd Delaware OH 43015

ISLER, RALPH CHARLES, ATOMIC SPECTROSCOPY, PLASMA PHYSICS. *Current Pos:* RES STAFF MEM, OAK RIDGE NAT LAB, 76- *Personal Data:* b Pittsburgh, Pa, Apr 23, 33; m 58; c 3. *Educ:* Univ Pittsburgh, BS, 55; Johns Hopkins Univ, PhD(physics), 64. *Prof Exp:* Instr physics, Johns Hopkins Univ, 62-64; res assoc, Columbia Univ, 64-66; from asst prof to prof, Univ Fla, 66-78. *Mem:* Fel Am Phys Soc. *Res:* Spectroscopic research as applied to plasmas; rocket studies of planetary atmospheres and low energy ion-atom and ion-molecule collisions; level-crossing spectroscopy. *Mailing Add:* Fusion Energy Div Oak Ridge Nat Lab PO Box 2009 Oak Ridge TN 37831-8072. *Fax:* 423-576-7926; *E-Mail:* smtp%isler@fedc04.fed.ornl.gov

ISLES, DAVID FREDERICK, MATHEMATICS. *Current Pos:* Asst prof, 63-69, ASSOC PROF MATH, TUFTS UNIV, 69- *Personal Data:* b Rahway, NJ, Sept 23, 35; m 64. *Educ:* Princeton Univ, AB, 57; Mass Inst Technol, PhD(math logic), 64. *Mem:* Am Math Soc. *Res:* Mathematical logic. *Mailing Add:* Dept Math Tufts Univ Medford MA 02155-5555

ISLEY, JAMES DON, RESEARCH ADMINISTRATION. *Current Pos:* jr engr, Tenn Eastman Co, Eastman Kodak, 51, engr archit, 53-58, mech engr, 53-60, sr indust engr, 60-65, sr group engr, 66-68, sr supv engr, mat handling engr, eng div, 69-83, MGR ENG SERV, EASTMAN CHEM DIV, TENN EASTMAN CO, EASTMAN KODAK, 83- *Personal Data:* b Kingsport, Tenn, May 7, 28; m 54; c 2. *Educ:* Va Polytech Inst, BS, 51. *Prof Exp:* First lieutenant artillery, US Army, 51-53. *Concurrent Pos:* Chmn task group, Chemists Mfg Asn, 69-72; chmn, Am Soc Mech Engrs, MH14 Comt, 82-85. *Mem:* Am Inst Indust Engrs. *Res:* Design of pilot plants; expansion and development of research facilities. *Mailing Add:* 1713 Longview St Kingsport TN 37660

ISMAIL, AMIN RASHID, PERSONAL COMPUTERS - HARDWARE & SOFTWARE, MICROPROCESSOR CONTROLLERS. *Current Pos:* From instr to asst prof, 78-90, ASSOC PROF ELECTRONICS, UNIV DAYTON, 90- *Personal Data:* b Bombay, India, Mar 18, 58; m 90. *Educ:* Univ Dayton, BS, 78, MS, 81. *Concurrent Pos:* Consult, Sch Eng, Univ Dayton, 77-85, instr, Spec Progs, 77-89; dir, Microcon Int, 81-87; instr, Kettering Col Med Arts, 81, Air Force Inst Technol, 82; consult, Milmar Century Corp, 90- *Mem:* Am Soc Eng Educ; Inst Elec & Electronics Engrs; Asn Comput Mach. *Res:* Conducted research and development of an aircraft relay life-test system for the United States Air Force; co-author of three books on microprocessors and digital electronics. *Mailing Add:* Dept Electronic Eng Univ Dayton 300 College Park K1-341 Dayton OH 45469

ISMAIL, MOURAD E H, ORTHOGONAL POLYNOMIALS & SPECIAL FUNCTIONS. *Current Pos:* PROF MATH, UNIV SFLA, 87- *Personal Data:* b Cairo, Egypt, Apr 27, 44; Can & Egyptian citizen; m 69, Thanaa M Rashed. *Educ:* Cairo Univ, BSc, 64, Univ Alta, MSc, 69, PhD(math), 74. *Prof Exp:* Demonstr math, Dept Math, Fac Sci, Cairo Univ, 64-68; asst scientist, Math Dept & Res Ctr, Univ Wis-Madison, 74-75; fel & vis lectr, Univ Toronto, 75-76; asst prof appl math, McMaster Univ, 76-78; from asst prof to prof math, Ariz State Univ, 78-88. *Concurrent Pos:* Univ SFla distinguished scholar, 92-93. *Mem:* Am Math Soc; Soc Indust & Appl Math; Math Asn Am. *Res:* Orthogonal polynomials and their applications to spectra of Jacobi matrices; birth and death processes and queueing theory; special functions and infinite divisibility problems. *Mailing Add:* Dept Math Univ SFla Tampa FL 33620. *Fax:* 813-974-2700

ISMAN, MURRAY, ENTOMOLOGY. *Current Pos:* PROF, UNIV BC. *Honors & Awards:* Gordon Hewitt Award, Entom Soc Can, 91. *Mailing Add:* Univ BC Vancouver BC V6T 1Z2 Can

ISOM, BILLY GENE, malacology, aquatic toxicology, for more information see previous edition

ISOM, GARY E, PHARMACOLOGY, NEUROTOXICOLOGY. *Current Pos:* assoc prof, Purdue Univ, 80-83, dir, Div Sponsored Progs, 88-95, assoc head, Dept Pharmacol, 92-96, PROF TOXICOL, SCH PHARM & PHARMACEUT SCI, PURDUE UNIV, 83-, ASSOC VPRES RES, 95- *Personal Data:* b Twin Falls, Idaho, June 21, 46; m 67, Sharon J; c Randy E, Jeffrey A & Christina M. *Educ:* Idaho State Univ, BS, 69; Wash State Univ, PhD(pharmacol), 73. *Prof Exp:* Res asst pharmacol, Wash State Univ, 69-70; fel pharmacol, Am Found Pharmaceut Educ, 70-71; partic molecular pharmacol, NIH & Am Soc Pharmacol & Exp Therapeut, 71; fel pharmacol, Burroughs-Welcome Co, 71-73; clin clerkship, Wash State Univ, 73; from asst prof to assoc prof pharmacol, Idaho State Univ, 73-80. *Concurrent Pos:* Pharmaceut Mfgrs Asn res grant, 73-75; mem, US Pharmacopeia Conv, 75-80; regist pharmacist, Idaho; prin investr, NIH grants, 78- *Mem:* Am Soc Pharmacol & Exp Therapeut; Sigma Xi; Soc Toxicol; Am Asn Col Pharm; Soc Neurosci; Soc Res Adminr. *Res:* Selective vulnerability of the nervous system to neurotoxicants; neurotoxicology of cyanide. *Mailing Add:* Dept Med Chem & Molecular Pharmacol Sch Pharm Purdue Univ West LaFayette IN 47907-1968. *E-Mail:* geisom@sps.purdue.edu

ISOM, HARRIET C, DIFFERENTIATION, VIRUS TRANSFORMATION. *Current Pos:* from asst prof to assoc prof, 76-87, PROF MICROBIOL, PA STATE UNIV COL MED, 87- *Personal Data:* b 1947; m 70; c 1. *Educ:* Bryn Mawr Col, AB, 69; Univ Ill, MS, 71, PhD, 73. *Prof Exp:* NIH fel microbiol, Univ Pa Sch Med, 73-74, Pa plan scholar, 74-76, assoc, 76. *Concurrent Pos:* Assoc mem grad fac, Pa State Univ Col Med, 76-82, mem grad fac, 82- *Mem:* Am Soc Microbiol; AAAS; Sigma Xi; NY Acad Sci; Am Asn Cancer Res; Am Soc Virol; Tissue Cult Asn; Am Soc Cell Biol; Am Soc Biol Chemists. *Res:* Viral transformation of differentiated cells to determine the virus genes involved in converting, in particular normal adult mondividing liver cells to replicating tumorogenic cells; effects of virus infection and transformation on expression of liver proteins. *Mailing Add:* Dept Mircobiol & Immunol Pa State Univ Hershey Med Ctr PO Box 850 Hershey PA 17033-0850. *Fax:* 717-531-4133

ISOM, JOHN B, pediatrics, neurology, for more information see previous edition

ISOM, MORRIS P, AERONAUTICAL ENGINEERING, APPLIED MATHEMATICS. *Current Pos:* ASSOC PROF AEROSPACE ENG, POLYTECH INST NEW YORK. *Personal Data:* b Miami, Fla, Mar 12, 28; m 56; c 3. *Educ:* Harvard Col, BA, 52; Mass Inst Technol, MS, 56; Princeton Univ, PhD(aerospace & mech sci), 64. *Prof Exp:* Res engr, Mass Inst Technol, 53-55; asst proj eng fluid mech, Wright Aeronaut Div, Curtis-Wright Corp, 57-58; res assoc, Princeton Univ, 58; res analyst strategic & defense systs, Hudson Inst, 62-64; assoc prof aeronaut & astronaut, NY Univ, 64-, asst chmn dept, 67- *Concurrent Pos:* Consult, Hudson Inst, 64-66, Sikorsky Aircraft, 67-69 & US Army, 70- *Res:* Aerodynamics. *Mailing Add:* Dept Aerospace Studies 6 Metro Tech Ctr Polytech Inst New York 333 Jay St Brooklyn NY 11201-2990

ISOM, WILLIAM HOWARD, AGRONOMY, FIELD CROPS. *Current Pos:* RETIRED. *Personal Data:* b Hurricane, Utah, Oct 30, 17; m 48, Helen J Onyett; c Peggy J (Teague), Claudia L (Laureski) & William T. *Educ:* Utah State Univ, BS, 40, MS, 51; Cornell Univ, PhD(plant breeding, genetics), 55. *Prof Exp:* Res agronomist, Agr Res Serv, USDA, 55-60; farm adv, Coop Exten, Univ Calif, Riverside, 60-62, exten agronomist, 62-73, agriculturist, 73-88, lectr plant sci, 74-88. *Mem:* Am Soc Agron; Sigma Xi; AAAS. *Res:* Flax breeding and improvement; field crops; dry edible legumes; agricultural extension; developed new varieties of chickpea. *Mailing Add:* 5313 Falkirk Ave Riverside CA 92506

ISON-FRANKLIN, ELEANOR LUTIA, PHYSIOLOGY, ENDOCRINOLOGY. *Current Pos:* from asst prof to assoc prof physiol, 63-71, assoc dean gen admin, 70-72, assoc dean acad affairs, 72-80, PROF PHYSIOL, COL MED, HOWARD UNIV, 71-, DIR CARDIOVASC RES LAB, 80- *Personal Data:* b Dublin, Ga, Dec 24, 29; m 65; c 1. *Educ:* Spelman Col, Atlanta, AB, 48; Univ Wis-Madison, MS, 51, PhD(zool), 57. *Prof Exp:* Instr biol, Spelman Col, 48-49 & 51-53; asst zool, Univ Wis, 50-51, res asst zool, 55-57; instr biol, Spelman Col, 51-53; asst prof physiol, Sch Vet Med, Tuskegee Inst, 57-60, assoc prof physiol, Carver Found, 60-63. *Concurrent Pos:* Porter physiol lectr, Am Physiol Soc, 67-74; vis prof Harvard Med Sch, 77-78; co-prin investr, NASA grant NAG 2-250, 83-86. *Mem:* Am Physiol Soc; Am Heart Asn; Am Soc Hypertension; Sigma Xi; Fedn Am Socs Exp Biol. *Res:* Cardiovascular physiology; cardiac dynamics and hypertension. *Mailing Add:* Dept Physiol & Biophys Howard Univ Col Med 520 W St NW Washington DC 20059

ISPHORDING, WAYNE CARTER, GEOCHEMISTRY, MINERALOGY. *Current Pos:* Assoc prof, 66-78, PROF CRYSTALLOG & MINERAL, UNIV S ALA, 78- *Personal Data:* b Willow Grove, Pa, Sept 26, 37; m 59; c 3. *Educ:* Univ Fla, BS, 62, MS, 63; Rutgers Univ, PhD(geol), 66. *Concurrent Pos:* Grants, Army Res Off, NSF, Nat Oceanic Atmospheric Admin. *Mem:* Geol Soc Am; Am Asn Petrol Geol; Soc Econ Paleont & Mineral; Am Inst Prof Geologists. *Res:* Application of computer techniques to sediment analysis; engineering properties of tropical soils; paleogeographic studies of the upper Tertiary of eastern United States; geochemistry of Laterites in Yucatan; genesis and petrology of palygorskite-sepiolite clays; heavy metal chemistry of estuarine sediments. *Mailing Add:* Dept Geog & Geol Univ SAla 307 University Dr Mobile AL 36688-0001

ISQUITH, IRWIN R, PROTOZOOLOGY, ECOLOGY. *Current Pos:* from asst prof to assoc prof, Fairleigh Dickinson Univ, 68-76, chmn, Dept Biol Sci, 82-93, assoc dean, 93-96, PROF BIOL, FAIRLEIGH DICKINSON UNIV, 76- *Personal Data:* b Brooklyn, NY, Jan 23, 42; m 64; c 2. *Educ:* Brooklyn Col, BS, 62; NY Univ, MS, 64, PhD(biol), 66. *Prof Exp:* Asst cur, Acad Nat Sci, Philadelphia, 66-68. *Mem:* AAAS; Am Soc Protozool; NY Acad Sci; Sigma Xi. *Res:* Taxonomy, genetics and evolution of protozoa, especially the ciliate, Blepharisma; ecology; biomagnetics. *Mailing Add:* Sch Natural Sci Fairleigh Dickinson Univ 1000 River Rd Teaneck NJ 07666

ISRAEL, HAROLD L, pulmonary diseases; deceased, see previous edition for last biography

ISRAEL, HARRY, III, DENTISTRY, PERIODONTICS. *Current Pos:* DIR DENT RES, CHILDREN'S MED CTR, DAYTON, 76- *Personal Data:* b Dayton, Ohio, Sept 30, 34; m 60; c 2. *Educ:* Univ Mich, Ann Arbor, BA, 56; Western Reserve Univ, DDS, 60; Univ Pa, MSc, 69; Univ Ala, Birmingham, PhD(anat), 71. *Prof Exp:* NIH fels, Boston Univ Hosps, 61-62, Philadelphia Gen Hosp-Univ Pa, 62-63 & Univ Ala, 69-70; res assoc growth & genetics, Fels Res Inst, 65-68, sr investr, 68-71, chief dent res sect, 71-76. *Concurrent Pos:* Assoc clin prof, Wright State Univ, Sch Med, 76- *Mem:* Am Dent Asn; Am Acad Periodont; AAAS; Am Inst Nutrit; Int Asn Dent Res; Am Soc Clin Nutrit; Int Col Dentists. *Res:* Growth and aging in the human cranio-facial skeleton; nutriton and oral-facial development; cranio-facial congenital malformation; periodontal disease. *Mailing Add:* 111 W First St Suite 917 Dayton OH 45402

ISRAEL, HERBERT WILLIAM, PLANT CYTOLOGY, PLANT PATHOLOGY. *Current Pos:* NIH post doctoral fel, Dept Bot, Cornell Univ, 63-64, res assoc lab cell physiol, growth & develop, 64-69, sr res assoc, 69-72, sr res assoc, Dept Plant Path, 72-93, VIS SCIENTIST, CORNELL UNIV, 93- *Personal Data:* b Chicago, Ill, July 17, 31; m 53, Ruth M Goetz; c Lynn M (Walter), Carla A (Niesen) & William J. *Educ:* Concordia Teachers Col, Ill, BS, 53; Univ Wis, MS, 60; Univ Fla, PhD(bot, zool), 62. *Prof Exp:* Chmn, Dept Sci, Luther High Sch, Ill, 53-60; NSF fel, Univ Wis-Madison, 59-60; Nat Defense Educ Act fel, Turtox Scholar, Univ Fla, 60-62, res assoc, 63; vpres & treas, H&I Agritch, Inc, 92-96. *Concurrent Pos:* Partic, Academic Year Inst, NSF, 59; Hatch New York res grants, Coop State Res Serv, USDA, 74, 77, 79 & 83, spec prog grant, 73; cong sci fel & space fel, Am Phys Soc, 93-94; NSF res grant, 76, 79 & 81; res grant, Comp Res Grant Off, Sci Educ Admin, USDA, 79, 81 & 89; assoc ed, Phytopath, 80-83; bd regents, Concordia Univ, 86-95, vchmn, 92, chmn, 93-95; regent mem, Concordia Univ Syst, 92-95, bd regents, Concordia Col, 95- *Mem:* AAAS; Am Inst Biol Sci; Sigma Xi; Am Phytopath Soc; Bot Soc Am; Nat Asn Biol Teachers. *Res:* Cellular ultrastructure; virology; pathogen-host, primary interactions; developmental morphology; plant embryology and morphogenesis; plant and animal physiology; plant genetics; plant pathology. *Mailing Add:* Room 314 Plant Sci Bldg Rm 314 Cornell Univ Ithaca NY 14853

ISRAEL, MARTIN HENRY, COSMIC-RAY ASTROPHYSICS. *Current Pos:* From asst prof to assoc prof, Washington Univ, 68-75, dean fac arts & sci, 88-94, vchancellor, 94-95, PROF PHYSICS, WASHINGTON UNIV, ST LOUIS, 75-, VCHANCELLOR ACAD PLANNING, 95- *Personal Data:* b Chicago, Ill, Jan 12, 41; m 65, Margaret Mitouer; c Elisa J & Samuel L. *Educ:* Univ Chicago, SB, 62; Calif Inst Technol, PhD(physics), 69. *Honors & Awards:* Except Sci Achievement Award, NASA, 80. *Concurrent Pos:* Alfred P Sloan Found fel, 70-72; prin investr, Heavy Nuclei Exp on High Energy

Astron Observ-3, 71-89; mem, exec comt, Div Cosmic Phys, Am Phys Soc, 75-77 & 79-82, balloon study comt, Nat Acad Sci, 75, space astron and astrophys comt, 76-79, mgt opers group high energy astrophys div, Am Astron Soc, 82-84, sub-panel for cosmic rays, space & astrophys plasmas & physics surv comt, Nat Acad Sci, 83-85 & space & earth sci adv comt, NASA, 85-88; chmn, exec comt, Bevalac Users Group, 75, chmn, Div Dosmic Physics, Am Physics Soc, 80-81, chmn, nat org comt, 19th Int Cosmic Ray Conf, 82-85, particle astrophys superconducting magnet definition team, NASA, 85-88; assoc dir, McDonnell Ctr Space Sci, Washington Univ, St Louis, 82-87, actg dean fac arts & sci, 87-88; mem, Struct & Eval Universe Subcomt, NASA, 96- Mem: Fel Am Phys Soc; Am Astron Soc; Am Asn Univ Professors; AAAS. Res: Cosmic ray physics; very heavy nuclei; electrons; observations using electronic detectors on satellites and high-altitude balloons. Mailing Add: Campus Box 1080 Washington Univ St Louis MO 63130-4899. Fax: 314-935-5188; E-Mail: mhisrael@hilltop.wustl.edu

ISRAEL, STANLEY C, PYROLYSIS MASS SPECTROMETRY, REACTION MECHANISMS. Current Pos: From instr to assoc prof, 68-80, PROF CHEM, UNIV LOWELL, 80-, DEPT HEAD, 92- Personal Data: b Brooklyn, NY, Dec 30, 42; m 66; c 1. Educ: Parsons Col, BS, 65; Lowell Technol Inst, PhD(chem), 70. Honors & Awards: A L Lipschitz Award, 87; Phoenix Award, Am Chem Soc, 89, Polymer Distinguished Serv Award, 93. Concurrent Pos: Assoc ed, Fire Res; consult, Optimers Co & Polymer Technol Corp; vis prof, Univ Utah, 75-77, dir chem res, Flammability Res Ctr, Univ Utah, 76-77; prin investr numerous grants & contracts; mem, Div Polymer Chem, Am Chem Soc, treas, 79-84, chmn, 89, Div Org Chem, Div Chem Educ; consult, chem indust & legal profession. Mem: AAAS; Am Chem Soc; NY Acad Sci; Am Asn Univ Profs; Am Soc Mass Spectrometry; Sigma Xi. Res: Pioneering the techniques of direct-pyrolysis-chemical ionization mass spectrometry for the study of the reactions and mechanisms of thermal decomposition of polymeric materials; identification and characterization of materials by high temperature pyrolysis; surface characterization of fine fibers and lens like curved surfaces by laser contact angle gonionmetry; author of over 70 papers and patents. Mailing Add: Dept Chem Univ Mass 1 University Ave Lowell MA 01854. Fax: 978-934-8003; E-Mail: israels@woods.uml.edu

ISRAEL, WERNER, THEORETICAL PHYSICS. Current Pos: FEL, CAN INST ADVAN RES, 86-; ADJ PROF, UNIV VICTORIA, 97- Personal Data: b Berlin, Ger, Oct 4, 31; m 58, Inge Lee; c Pia L & Mark A. Educ: Univ Cape Town, BSc, 51, MSc, 54; Trinity Col, Dublin, PhD(math), 60. Hon Degrees: DSc, Queens Univ, Kingston, Ont, 87, Dr, Univ Tours, France, 94. Honors & Awards: Medal Achievement Physics, Can Asn Physicists, 81; Killam Mem Prize, Can Coun, 84; Dr Tomalla Prize, Tomalla Found Gravitational Res, 96; Officer Order Can, 94. Prof Exp: Lectr math, Univ Cape Town, 55-56; res scholar theoret physics, Dublin Inst Advan Studies, 56-58; from asst prof to prof math, Univ Alta, Edmonton, 58-72, prof physics & univ prof, 72-96. Concurrent Pos: Vis prof, Dublin Inst Advan Studies, 66-68; mem, Int Comt Gen Relativity & Gravitation, 71-80; Sherman Fairchild distinguished scholar, Calif Inst Technol, 74-75; sr visitor, Dept Appl Math & Theoret Physics, Univ Cambridge, 75-76; maitre de recherche assoc, Inst Henri Poincare, Paris, 76-77; vis prof, Univ Berne, 80, Univ Kyoto, 86; mem, Comn Math Physics, Int Union Pure & Appl Physics, 84-88; vis fel, Gonville & Caius Col, Cambridge, 85. Mem: Int Astron Union; fel Royal Soc Can; Can Asn Physicists; Can Astron Soc. Res: General relativity; cosmology; statistical mechanics; black hole physics. Mailing Add: Dept Physics of Astron Univ Victoria Victoria BC V8W 3P6 Can

ISRAEL, YEDY, PHARMACOLOGY. Current Pos: PROF PHARMACOL, SCH MED, UNIV TORONTO, 70- Personal Data: b Temuco, Chile, Sept 19, 39; m 62; c 2. Educ: Univ Chile, biochemist, 62; Univ Toronto, PhD(biochem, pharmacol), 65. Honors & Awards: Award, Med Soc Chile, 70; Jellinek Award, 80. Prof Exp: NIH int fel biochem, Nat Heart Inst, 65-66; from asst prof to prof, Univ Chile, 66-69. Concurrent Pos: Head, Dept Biochem, Addiction Res Found, Ont, 81- Mem: Am Soc Pharmacol; Soc Neurosci; Pharmacol Soc Can. Res: Mechanisms of psychotropic drug action; alcoholic liver disease; alcoholism. Mailing Add: 1020 Locust St Rm 275 Philadelphia PA 19107

ISRAELACHVILI, JACOB NISSIM, CHEMICAL & NUCLEAR ENGINEERING. Current Pos: PROF, DEPT CHEM & NUCLEAR ENG & MAT, UNIV CALIF, SANTA BARBARA, 86-, ASSOC DIR, MAT RES LAB, 93- Educ: Univ Cambridge & Christ's Col, BA, 68, PhD, 71. Honors & Awards: Pawsey Medal, Australian Acad Sci, 77, Matthew Flinders Lectr Medallist, 86; David Syme Prize, 84; Goodyear Lectr, Case Western Res Univ, 86, Langmuir Lectr, 93; Debye Lectr, Cornell Univ, Am Chem Soc, 87; AT&T Fel Lectr, Duke Univ, 89; Kurt Wohl Lectr, Univ Del, 90; John Manson/Frederick Fowkes Mem Lectr, Lehigh Univ, 91; A E Alexander Lectr, Royal Australian Chem Inst, 92; Arne Brandstorm Lectr, Chalmers Univ, Sweden, 95. Prof Exp: Postdoctoral res, Dept Surface Physics, Univ Cambridge, 71-72; res fel, Europ Molecular Biol Orgn, Biophysics Inst, Univ Stockholm & Karolinska Inst, 72-74; from res fel to prof fel, Inst Advan Studies, Australian Nat Univ, 74-86, head, Dept Appl Math, 84-85. Concurrent Pos: Fel, Australian Acad Sci, 82; mem coun, Int Asn Colloid & Interface Scientists, 83; fel, Royal Soc London, 88; vchmn, Gordon Res Conf Org Thin Films, 88; lectr surface sci, Univ Fla, 94. Mem: Foreign assoc Nat Acad Eng; fel Australian Acad Sci. Res: Intermolecular and intersurface forces in complex fluid systems; use of Surface Forces Apparatus for directly measuring forces between surfaces in liquids and vapours; interfacial phenomena. Mailing Add: Dept Chem & Nuclear Eng & Mat Dept Univ Calif Santa Barbara CA 93106

ISRAELS, LYONEL GARRY, HEMATOLOGY, ONCOLOGY. Current Pos: From lectr to asst prof biochem, Univ Man, 54-59, from asst prof med to prof 59-88, actg chmn internal med, 78-79, DISTINGUISHED PROF INTERNAL MED, UNIV MAN, 88-; SR SCIENTIST, MAN CANCER TREATMENT & RES FOUND, 92- Personal Data: b Regina, Sask, July 31, 26; m 50; c Sara & Jared. Educ: Univ Sask, BA, 46; Univ Man, MD, 49, MSc, 50; FRCPC, 54. Concurrent Pos: Mem bd, Nat Cancer Inst Can, 67-78, mem, Adv Res Comt, 83-87; dir, Man Inst Cell Biol, 69-73; mem, Med Res Coun Can, 73-75; exec dir, Man Cancer Treatment & Res Found, 73-92. Mem: Nat Cancer Inst Can (pres, 76-78); Can Soc Hemat (pres, 74); Can Soc Clin Invest (pres, 68); Am Soc Clin Invest. Res: Chemotherapy of malignant tumors; biological effects of alkylating agents, bilirubin synthesis and heme metabolism; studies on vitamin K. Mailing Add: 100 Olivia St Winnipeg MB R3E 0V9 Can

ISRAELSEN, C EARL, HYDROLOGY, EROSION CONTROL. Current Pos: Asst res engr, Eng Exp Sta, Utah State Univ, 60-63, res engr, Utah Water Res Lab, 66-68, assoc prof civil & environ eng, 68-78, dir interam ctr integral develop land & water resources, Utah State Univ-Orgn Am States, Venezuela, 70-72, PROF CIVIL & ENVIRON ENG, UTAH WATER RES LAB, UTAH STATE UNIV, 78- Personal Data: b Hyrum, Utah, Apr 21, 28; m 53, Marilyn Hilton; c Ronald, Brent, Margie, Brian, Linda, Cheri, Juli & Kyle. Educ: Utah State Univ, BS, 59; Univ Ariz, PhD(hydrol & water res), 68. Concurrent Pos: Assoc dir, Int Off Water Educ, 83-92, dir, training adv irrig syst mgt proj, Pakistan, 86-88; training adv, Main Syst Mgt Proj, Egypt, 89-91. Res: Physical hydraulic modelling; evaporation reduction by use of monolayers; measurement of streamflow by capacitance methods; weather modification in mountainous areas using silver iodide; saline water studies; erosion control during construction; development of water education materials for public schools; development of state water atlas; performance evaluation of erosion control products and practices; water-science education. Mailing Add: Utah Water Res Lab Utah State Univ Logan UT 84322-8200. Fax: 435-750-3663

ISRAELSTAM, GERALD FRANK, PLANT PHYSIOLOGY. Current Pos: RETIRED. Personal Data: b Johannesburg, SAfrica, Jan 19, 29; Can citizen; m 53; c 1. Educ: Univ Witwatersrand, BSc, 51, BSc, 53; Univ London, Eng, PhD(bot), 63. Prof Exp: Lectr bot, Univ Col, Ft Hare, SAfrica, 57-60; lectr biol, Medway Col Technol, Eng, 60-61; lectr plant physiol, Birmingham Univ, Eng, 63-64; assoc prof plant physiol, Scarborough Col, Univ Toronto, 64-94. Mem: Can Soc Plant Physiol; Soc Exp Bot. Res: Mechanism of action of plant growth substances. Mailing Add: 53 Sanddrift Sq Scarborough ON M1E 4N5 Can

ISRAILI, ZAFAR HASAN, HYPERTENSION, MEDICINAL CHEMISTRY. Current Pos: asst prof med & chem, 70-75, assoc prof chem, 74-78, ASSOC PROF MED, EMORY UNIV, ATLANTA, 75-, PROF CHEM, 78- Personal Data: b Sambhal, India, July 2, 34; US citizen; m 70; c 3. Educ: Aligarh M Univ, India, BSc, 51, MSc, 53; Univ Kans, PhD(med chem), 68. Prof Exp: Lectr chem, Aligarh M Univ, 53-54, sr res scholar chem, 54-57; res asst & sci officer radiation chem, Atomic Energy Comn, India, 57-61; sr res chemist, Inst Pharmaceut Chem, Alza Corp, Kans, 69-70; res pharmacologist, Vet Admin Med Ctr, 79-87. Concurrent Pos: Fel, Dept Med Chem, Univ Kans, 68-69; mem sci staff, Grady Hosp, Atlanta, 74-; assoc ed, Drug Metab Rev, 74-; res grant, Merck, Sharpe, & Dohme, 77-; mem res serv, Vet Admin Hosp, 78-87; res grants, Nat Cancer Inst, 78-81 & Nat Inst Aging, 80-82, Vet Admin, 79-87. Mem: Am Asn Cancer Res; Am Soc Clin Pharmacol & Therapeut; Am Soc Pharmacol & Exp Therapeut; Soc Exp Biol & Med; Am Chem Soc; Interam Soc Clin Pharmacol Therapeut; Am Aging Soc; Am Heart Asn; Int Soc Study Xenobiotics; Int Soc Hypertension Blacks. Res: Drug metabolism; clinical pharmacology and toxicology; hypertension; medicinal chemistry; analytical biochemical methods; aging; cancer chemotherapy. Mailing Add: 3567 Cloudland Dr Stone Mountain GA 30083

ISSAQ, HALEEM JERIES, ANALYTICAL CHEMISTRY. Current Pos: SCIENTIST ANALYTICAL CHEM, FREDERICK CANCER RES & DEVELOP CTR, 72- Personal Data: b Haifa, Palestine, Feb 19, 36; US citizen; m 75, Alberta Salim; c Sameer. Educ: Robert Col, BS, 65; Technion-Israel Inst Technol, MS, 68; Georgetown Univ, PhD(anal chem), 72. Concurrent Pos: Assoc ed, J Liquid Chromatography. Mem: Am Chem Soc; Soc Appl Spectros; Sigma Xi; Electrophoresis Soc. Res: Role of trace metals in cancer; detection of differences of trace metals between cancerous and non-cancerous serum and tissue; detection and identification of trace chemicals by thin layer and liquid chromatography; solvent effects and selectivity optimization in liquid chromatography; methods development; capillary zone electrophoresis application in the biomedical field. Mailing Add: NCI Frederick Cancer Res Fac PO Box B Bldg 469 Frederick MD 21702-1201. Fax: 301-846-1438

ISSEKUTZ, BELA, JR, PHYSIOLOGY. Current Pos: prof, 67-83, EMER PROF PHYSIOL, DALHOUSIE UNIV, 83- Personal Data: b Kolozsvar, Hungary, Dec 24, 12; nat Can; m 41, Anne-Marie Knuman; c Andrew & Thomas. Educ: Univ Szeged, MD, 36. Hon Degrees: Dr habil, Univ Budapest, 42; DSc. Prof Exp: Instr pharmacol, Univ Szeged, 36-38; from asst prof to assoc prof pharmacol, Univ Budapest, 38-45; prof physiol & head dept, Univ Szeged, 45-56; vis scientist physiol, Max Planck Inst, Heidelberg, WGer, 56-57; vis scientist & res grant, Smith Kline & French Lab, Pa, 57-58; head dept biochem, Res Div, Lankenau Hous, Philadelphia, 59-61; head dept physiol, 61-67. Concurrent Pos: Hoffman-LaRoche fel physiol, Univ Basel, 37; Hungarian State fel pharmacol, Univ Berlin, 38-39 & Univ Gottingen, 43; vis prof physiol & head dept, Univ Greifswald, 55-56. Mem: Am Physiol Soc; Can Physiol Soc. Res: Endocrine and nervous regulation of metabolism; mode of action of thyroxine and insulin; exercise metabolism; obesity. Mailing Add: 4 Warwick Lane Halifax NS B3M 4J3 Can

ISSEL, CHARLES JOHN, VETERINARY VIROLOGY, EPIDEMIOLOGY. *Current Pos:* WRIGHT-MARKEY PROF EQUINE INFECTIOUS DIS, UNIV KY, 90- *Personal Data:* b San Francisco, Calif, Mar 25, 43; m 64, Patricia Sowerwine; c Mark & Laurie (Tarver). *Educ:* Univ Calif, Berkeley, AB, 65; Univ Calif, Davis, DVM, 69; Univ Wis-Madison, MS, 71, PhD(vet sci), 73. *Prof Exp:* Vet med officer, USDA, Plum Island, 73-74; from asst prof to prof vet virol, La State Univ, 74-90. *Mem:* AAAS; Am Vet Med Asn; Am Soc Microbiol; Am Asn Equine Practitioners; Am Soc Virol. *Res:* Epidemiology diagnosis and control of viral diseases of horses and wildlife. *Mailing Add:* Dept Vet Sci Univ Ky Gluck Equine Res Ctr Lexington KY 40546-0099. *Fax:* 606-257-8542; *E-Mail:* cissel@pop.uky.edu

ISSELBACHER, KURT JULIUS, MEDICINE, BIOCHEMISTRY. *Current Pos:* instr, Harvard Med Sch, 56-58, assoc, 58-60, from asst prof to prof, 60-72, CHMN EXEC COMT, DEPTS MED, HARVARD MED SCH, 68-, MALLINCKRODT PROF MED, 72- *Personal Data:* b Wirges, Ger, Sept 12, 25; nat US; m 55, Rhoda Solin; c 4. *Educ:* Harvard Univ, AB, 46, MD, 50. *Honors & Awards:* Distinguished Achievement Award, Am Gastroenterol Asn, 85, Friedenwald Medal, 85; Merit Award, Nat Inst Diabetes, Digestive & Kidney Dis, NIH, 88; John Phillips Mem Award, Am Col Physicians, 89. *Prof Exp:* Intern med, Mass Gen Hosp, 50-51, from asst resident to resident, 51-53; clin instr, Sch Med, Johns Hopkins Univ, 53-54 & Sch Med, George Washington Univ, 54-56. *Concurrent Pos:* Fel, Harvard Med Sch, 51-53; clin investr, Nat Inst Arthritis & Metab Dis, 53-56; asst, Mass Gen Hosp, 56-58, chief, Gastroenterol Unit & Res Lab, 57-88, from asst physician to assoc physician, 58-66, physician, 66-, chmn, Comt Res, 67-70, dir, Cancer Ctr, 87-; chmn, Cancer Comt, Harvard Univ, 72-87; ed-in-chief, Harrison's Prin Internal Med, 90- *Mem:* Nat Acad Sci; Inst Med-Nat Acad Sci; Am Gastroenterol Asn (vpres, 72-73, pres-elect, 73-74, pres, 74-75); Soc Exp Biol & Med; Am Soc Biol Chemists; fel Am Acad Arts & Sci; Am Soc Clin Invest (vpres, 71); Asn Am Physicians (vpres & pres-elect, 76-77, pres, 77); fel NY Acad Sci; Am Asn Cancer Res; hon mem Harvey Soc; Am Col Physicians; Am Fedn Clin Res. *Res:* Biochemical basis for normal and disturbed function of the intestinal tract and liver; cellular changes in malignancy. *Mailing Add:* 20 Nobscot Rd Newton Centre MA 02159

ISSEROFF, HADAR, IMMUNOLOGY, ZOOLOGY. *Current Pos:* from asst prof to assoc prof, 68-78, PROF BIOL, STATE UNIV NY COL BUFFALO, 78- *Personal Data:* b Newark, NJ, Dec 24, 38; m 60, Eileen C Reifler; c Raanan & Chari (Biton). *Educ:* Brooklyn Col, BS, 60; Purdue Univ, MS, 63, PhD(microbiol), 66. *Prof Exp:* Teaching assoc biol, Purdue Univ, 61-63; NIH fel physiol of parasites, Rice Univ, 66-68. *Concurrent Pos:* Fel & grant, State Univ NY Res Found, State Univ NY Col Buffalo, 69 & 70; res grants, United Health Found Western NY, 70-72, NIH, 71-74, 76-83 & Edna McConnell Clark Found, 79-81; vis prof, Med, Sch, Univ Tel Aviv, 75; vis scientist & prof, Roswell Park Mem Inst, 83, 87-88 & 90- *Mem:* Fel AAAS; Am Physiol Soc; Am Soc Parasitol; Am Soc Zool; Sigma Xi. *Res:* Symbiology; proline in fascioliasis and schistosommiasis; proline as a regulator of bile duct morphogenesis; electron microscopy of larval trematodes; pheromones regulating population growth in molluscs; molecular basis of immuo-endocrine interactions in schistosomiasis; suppression of the immune response by schistosomiasis at the genomic level. *Mailing Add:* 58 Redwood Terr Williamsville NY 14221-2412. *Fax:* 716-878-4009; *E-Mail:* isseroffh@snybufvacs.snybuf.edu

ISSEROW, SAUL, materials science, materials engineering, for more information see previous edition

ISSITT, PETER DAVID, IMMUNOHEMATOLOGY, TRANSFUSION MEDICINE. *Current Pos:* ASSOC PROF PATH, DUKE UNIV MED CTR, 89-, DIR, MHS PROG, TRANSFUSION MED, 92- *Personal Data:* b London, Eng, Jan 29, 33; m 85, Linda Israel; c John & Patrick. *Educ:* Inst Med Lab Sci, AIMLS, 55, FIMLS, 57; Inst Biol, LIBiol, 68, MIBiol, 78, MRCPath, 77, FIBiol, 85, CB, 85, FRC Path, 89; Columbia Pac Univ, PhD, 87. *Honors & Awards:* Ivor Dunsford Mem Award, Am Asn Blood Banks, 74, Emily Cooley Award, 86, Grove-Rasmusson Award, 91; Zoutendyk Medal, SAfrican Inst Med Res, 87; Outstanding Res Award, Am Soc Clin Path, 95. *Prof Exp:* Supvr immunohemat, St Mary's Hosp, London, Eng, 58-62; supvr hemat & immunohemat, Peace Mem Hosp, Watford, Eng, 62-64; res fel immunohemat, New York Blood Ctr, 64-68; gen mgr, Spectra Biol Div, Becton-Dickinson Co, 68-71; asst prof res surg immunohemat, Paul I Hoxworth Blood Ctr, Univ Cincinnati, 71-77, dir labs, 71-81, assoc prof, 77-81; sci dir, SFla Blood Serv, Miami, 81-89; assoc prof med, Univ Miami, 81-89. *Concurrent Pos:* Examnr, New York Bd Health-Immunohemat, 65-68; sr sci consult, Spectra Biol Div, B-D Diag, 75-80; assoc ed, J Transfusion, Am Asn Blood Banks, 76-81 & 84-94; assoc prof med lab sci, Fla Int Univ, 81-89; chmn grants rev comt, Nat Blood Found, 89-92; sci prog comt, Am Asn Blood Banks, 91-94. *Mem:* Am Asn Blood Banks; Inst Med Lab Sci; Brit Inst Biol; Int Soc Blood Transfusion; Royal Col Pathologists; Brit Blood Transfusion Soc. *Res:* Investigation of human blood group systems as they pertain to genetics, immunology and biochemistry; investigation of hemolytic disorders caused by blood group autoantibodies; quantitation of human blood group antigens; investigation of polymorphisms of human blood groups. *Mailing Add:* Transfusion Serv Duke Univ Med Ctr PO Box 2928 Durham NC 27710. *Fax:* 919-681-8969

ISTOCK, CONRAD ALAN, ANIMAL ECOLOGY, POPULATION GENETICS. *Current Pos:* PROF & HEAD DEPT ECOL & EVOLUTIONARY BIOL, UNIV ARIZ, 84- *Personal Data:* b Aug 31, 36; m 61; c 2. *Educ:* Wayne State Univ, AB, 59; Univ Mich, MA, 61, PhD(zool), 64. *Prof Exp:* Asst prof zool, Univ Ill, 64-65; from asst prof to prof biol, Univ Rochester, 65-84. *Concurrent Pos:* Vis prof, Biol Sta, Univ Mich, 74, 75, 78 & 80. *Mem:* AAAS; Ecol Soc Am; Am Soc Naturalists (secy 83-86); Gen Soc Am; Soc Study Evolution. *Res:* Population ecology; intraspecific and interspecific competition in animal populations; insect and microbiol population genetics; evolutionary theory. *Mailing Add:* Dept Ecol Univ Ariz 1600 E University Blvd Tucson AZ 85721-0001

ISTRE, CLIFTON O, JR, AUDIOLOGY. *Current Pos:* PVT PRACT, 71- *Personal Data:* b Jennings, La, Sept 17, 32; m 56; c 3. *Educ:* Univ Ala, MA, 56; Ind Univ, PhD(hearing), 65. *Prof Exp:* From asst prof to assoc prof otolaryngol, Med Sch, Tulane Univ, 71-82. *Concurrent Pos:* Consult, USPHS & USAF. *Mem:* Acoust Soc Am; Am Speech & Hearing Asn; assoc fel Am Acad Ophthal & Otolaryngol. *Res:* Noise and human hearing; electronystagmorphy and hearing. *Mailing Add:* 1472 S College Rd Lafayette LA 70503

ITABASHI, HIDEO HENRY, NEUROPATHOLOGY, FORENSIC NEUROPATHOLOGY. *Current Pos:* from assoc prof to prof, 71-93, EMER PROF PATH & NEUROL, SCH MED, UNIV CALIF, LOS ANGELES, 93- *Personal Data:* b Los Angeles, Calif, July 7, 26; m 52, Yoko Osawa; c Mark & Helen. *Educ:* Boston Univ, AB, 49, MD, 54; Am Bd Path, dipl & cert neuropath, 66. *Prof Exp:* Intern, Univ Mich Hosp, 54-55, resident neurol, 55-58; assoc res neurologist, Univ Calif, San Francisco, 58-60, clin instr psychiat & neurol, Med Ctr, 60-64, asst clin prof, 64-65; asst prof neurol, Med Sch, Univ Mich, Ann Arbor, 65-68, asst prof path, 66-68, assoc prof neurol & path, 68-71. *Concurrent Pos:* Nat Inst Neurol Dis & Blindness spec fel neuropath, 58-60; electroencephalographer, State Dept Ment Hyg, Sonoma State Hosp, Calif, 59-60; asst neuropathologist, Langley Porter Neuropsychiat Inst, Calif, 60-65; consult neuropath, San Francisco Gen Hosp, 64-65, Dept Chief Med Examr-Coroner, Los Angeles Co, 77-; consult neurol, Ypsilanti State Hosp, Mich, 66-71; consult, Vet Admin Hosp, Ann Arbor, 69-71; attend, Wadsworth Gen Hosp Vet Admin, Los Angeles; consult path, Sepulveda Vet Admin Hosp, 77- *Mem:* Am Asn Neuropath; Am Acad Neurol; Am Acad Forensic Sci; Nat Asn Med Examrs. *Res:* Electron microscopy of human muscle and degenerative, viral disorders of the central nervous system; neuropathology of dementias and amnestic disorders and head and neck trauma. *Mailing Add:* 1000 W Carson St Torrance CA 90502-2004

ITAKURA, KEIICHI, MOLECULAR BIOLOGY. *Current Pos:* assoc res scientist, 76-78, SR RES SCIENTIST BIOL, CITY OF HOPE NAT MED CTR, 78- *Personal Data:* b Tokyo, Japan, Feb 18, 42; m 70; c 2. *Educ:* Tokyo Col Pharm, BS, 65, PhD(pharm sci), 70. *Prof Exp:* Fel chem, Nat Res Coun Can, 71-74; sr scientist, Calif Inst Technol, 74-76. *Concurrent Pos:* Vis scientist, Nat Res Coun Can, 74-75; co-prin investr, Genentech, Inc, 76-; prin investr, Calif Inst Technol, 77-, vis assoc, 78-; prin investr, NIH, 78-81. *Res:* Chemical synthesis of nucleic acids for the study of molecular biology. *Mailing Add:* Dept Molecular Biol City Hope Nat Med Ctr 1500 E Duarte Rd Duarte CA 91010

ITANO, HARVEY AKIO, BIOCHEMISTRY. *Current Pos:* prof dept path, 70-88, EMER PROF DEPT PATH, SCH MED, UNIV CALIF, SAN DIEGO, 88- *Personal Data:* b Sacramento, Calif, Nov 3, 20; m 49, Rose N Sakemi; c Wayne, Glenn & David. *Educ:* Univ Calif, BS, 42; St Louis Univ, MD, 45; Calif Inst Technol, PhD(chem), 50. *Hon Degrees:* DSc, St Louis Univ, 87. *Honors & Awards:* Lilly Award Biol Chem, Am Chem Soc, 54; Minot lectr, AMA, 55; Harrington lectr, Univ Buffalo, 63. *Prof Exp:* Intern, City of Detroit Receiving Hosp, 45-46; Am Chem Soc fel, Calif Inst Technol, 46-48, NIH fel, 48-50; sr asst surgeon, Nat Cancer Inst, 50-54, surgeon, 54-56, sr surgeon, Nat Inst Arthritis & Metab Dis, 56-58, med dir, 58-70, chief sect chem genetics, Lab Molecular Biol, 62-70. *Concurrent Pos:* Res fel chem, Calif Inst Technol, 50-52, sr res fel, 52-54; vis prof, Osaka Univ, 61-62, Univ Chicago, 65, Univ Calif, San Francisco, 67; fel, Japan Soc Prom Sci, Okayama Univ, 83-84. *Mem:* Nat Acad Sci; Am Soc Biochem & Molecular Biol; Am Soc Hemat; AAAS; Int Soc Hemat; Am Chem Soc. *Res:* Abnormal hemoglobins; chemical modification of amino acids and proteins; heme degradation; oxidative degradation of hemoglobin; chemically induced hemolytic anemia; heme ligands; sickle-cell anemia. *Mailing Add:* Dept Path Sch Med Univ Calif San Diego La Jolla CA 92093-0506. *E-Mail:* hitano@ucsd.edu

ITANO, WAYNE MASAO, ATOMIC & MOLECULAR PHYSICS, ATOMIC FREQUENCY STANDARDS. *Current Pos:* PHYSICIST, TIME & FREQUENCY DIV, NAT INST STAND & TECHNOL, 79- *Personal Data:* b Pasadena, Calif, June 1, 51; m 83, Christine Yoshinaga; c Nicole & Michelle. *Educ:* Yale Univ, BS, 73; Harvard Univ, MA, 75, PhD(physics), 79. *Honors & Awards:* Gold Medal, Dept Com, 85; Stratton Award, Nat Inst Standards & Technol, 89. *Concurrent Pos:* Secy-treas, Laser Sci Topical Group, Am Phys Soc, 90-93; sci & technol agency fel, Commun Res Lab, Tokyo, 90. *Mem:* Fel Am Phys Soc; Optical Soc Am. *Res:* Atomic and molecular hyperfine structure and g-factors, radio frequency and optical spectroscopy of stored ions; radiation-pressure cooling of atoms and ions, atomic frequency standards; strongly coupled non-neural plasmas. *Mailing Add:* Nat Inst Stand & Technol 325 Broadway St Boulder CO 80303-3328. *Fax:* 303-497-7375; *E-Mail:* witano@nist.gov

ITAYA, STEPHEN K, VISUAL SYSTEM DEVELOPMENT, NEUROANATOMY. *Current Pos:* ASSOC PROF & CHAIR, UNIV S ALA, 87- *Personal Data:* b Cleveland, Ohio, Jan 11, 47; m 73, Patricia Williams; c 2. *Educ:* Washington Univ, St Louis, BA, 68; Univ Tenn, PhD(anat), 74. *Prof Exp:* From postdoctoral to asst prof, Univ Iowa, 74-84; asst prof, Univ Ill, Chicago, 84-87. *Mem:* Soc Neurosci. *Res:* Structural and functional development of the mammalian visual system. *Mailing Add:* Dept Biomed Sci Univ SAla UCOM 6000 Mobile AL 36688. *Fax:* 334-380-2711; *E-Mail:* sitaya@usamail.usouthal.edu

ITEN, LAURIE ELAINE, DEVELOPMENTAL BIOLOGY. *Current Pos:* ASST PROF BIOL, PURDUE UNIV, WEST LAFAYETTE, 77- *Personal Data:* b Los Angeles, Calif, Jan 5, 47; m 77. *Educ:* Univ Calif, Irvine, BSc, 71, PhD(biol), 75. *Prof Exp:* Fel develop biol, Ctr Pathobiol, Univ Calif, Irvine, 75-76 & Dept Avian Sci, Univ Calif, Davis, 76-77. *Concurrent Pos:* Nat Inst Child Health & Human Develop fel, 75-76; Am Cancer Soc fel, 76-77; prin investr, NSF res grant, 77-83. *Mem:* Int Soc Develop Biologists; Soc Develop Biol; Am Soc Zoologists; AAAS. *Res:* Pattern formation during animal development. *Mailing Add:* Dept Biol Sci Purdue Univ West Lafayette IN 47907-1968

ITIABA, KIBE, biochemistry, physiology, for more information see previous edition

ITIL, TURAN M, PSYCHIATRY, NEUROLOGY. *Current Pos:* CLIN PROF, NY UNIV, MED CTR, 93- *Personal Data:* b Bursa, Turkey, Aug 12, 24; m 55, Ellen; c Kurt Z & Yasmin (Le Bars). *Educ:* Istanbul Univ, MS, 43, MD, 48; Univ Erlangen, Venia Legendi, 63; Ger Bd Psychiat & Neurol, dipl, 60. *Prof Exp:* Intern med, Istanbul Univ Hosps, 47-48; intern, Seferihisar Mil Hosp & Workers Hosp, Istanbul, 49; resident surg & internal med, Neuropsychiat Clin, Univ Tubingen, 49-50, resident neurol, 50-51, resident psychiat, 51-52, asst neurol, Col Med & resident child psychiat, 52-53; resident neuropath, Neuropsychiat Clin, Univ Erlangen, 53, instr psychiat, Col Med & res assoc neurol & psychiat, 53-55, instr psychiat & EEG, neuropsychiatrist, dir out-patient dept & chief EEG dept, 55-62; assoc prof psychiat & neurol, Sch Med, Univ Mo, Columbia, 62-64, from assoc prof to prof psychiat, 64-73, from asst chmn to assoc chmn dept, 68-73; res prof, NY Med Col, 74-92. *Concurrent Pos:* Assoc chmn, Mo Inst Psychiat, 62-63, sr psychiatrist & prin res scientist, 63-65, chief sect EEG & clin neurophysiol, 65-73, chief sect psychopharmacol, 67-73; co-investr, USPHS Res Grants, 63-66 & 70-75, proj dir, 63-68 & 66-68, prin investr, 71-75; pvt docent, Univ Erlangen, 63-; consult, Clin EEG Lab, St Louis State Hosp, 64-65 & 69; docent, Istanbul Univ, 67-; mem, Am Schizophrenia Found; prin scientist, Int Asn Psychiat Res, 73-; res psychiatrist, Vet Admin Hosp, Montrose, NY, 74-83; chmn, HZI Res Ctr, Inc, 74-, NY Inst Med Res, 84- *Mem:* Am Col Neuropsychopharmacol; Am Soc Med Psychiat; Acad Psychosom Med; Am Psychiat Asn; Am Psychopath Asn; Am Psychiat Electrophysiol Asn (pres, 92-). *Res:* Electroencephalography; psychopharmacology; neurology; drugs for psychiatric patients using computer-analyzed model; electrophysiological markers to predict the outcome of psychiatric patients during drug treatment; biological diagnosis of psychiatric syndromes, treatment of therapy resistant depression and schizophrenia. *Mailing Add:* 150 White Plains Rd Tarrytown NY 10591. *Fax:* 914-631-3514

ITKIN, IRVING HERBERT, ALLERGY. *Current Pos:* RETIRED. *Personal Data:* b New York, NY, Aug 1, 17; m 42; c 3. *Educ:* Ind Univ, Bloomington, AB, 35, MD, 39. *Prof Exp:* Intern, Kings Co Hosp, Brooklyn, 39-41; resident, Mt Sinai Hosp, NY, 41-42; attend & chief allergy clin, Worcester Mem Hosp, 47-59; chief dept asthma-allergy, Nat Jewish Hosp Denver, 59-69; dir, Div Clin Immunol, Hahnemann Univ, 69-82, prof med, 69-90. *Concurrent Pos:* Asst, Mass Gen Hosp, 49-59; asst clin prof, Univ Colo, 61-66, asst prof, 66-69; vpres, Sect Allergy, AMA, 64-65. *Mem:* AMA; fel Am Col Physicians; fel Am Acad Allergy & Immunol. *Res:* Inhalation challenge in asthma; Candida Albicans as an allergen; chemical mediators of hypersensitivity; exercise in asthma; role of infection and antibiotics in asthma. *Mailing Add:* 11 Lechwick Rd Palm Beach Gardens FL 33418

ITO, HIROSHI, CHEMISTRY. *Current Pos:* RES SCIENTIST, ALMADEN RES CTR, IBM, SAN JOSE, CALIF. *Honors & Awards:* Soc Polymer Sci Award, Japan, 90; Coop Res Polymer Sci & Eng Award, Am Chem Soc, 92. *Mailing Add:* IBM Almaden Res Ctr 650 Harry Rd San Jose CA 95120-6001

ITO, JUNETSU, MICROBIOL GENETICS, BIOTECHNOLOGY. *Current Pos:* PROF MED MICROBIOL, COL MED, UNIV ARIZ, 83- *Personal Data:* b Oct 25, 35; m 66, Eiko Tatsumi; c Hiroko I & Marie I. *Educ:* Kyoto Univ, Japan, PhD(biochem), 67. *Concurrent Pos:* Assoc, Scripps Clin & Res Found, La Jolla, Calif. *Mem:* Am Soc Biochem & Molecular Biol; Protein Soc. *Res:* DNA polymerase superfamily to apply for molecular phylogeny of living organisms, evolutionary studies of DNA polymerases; US patentee. *Mailing Add:* Dept Microbiol & Immunol Col Med Univ Ariz Tucson AZ 85724-0001. *E-Mail:* ito@aruba.ceit.arizona.edu

ITO, KEITH A, BACTERIOLOGY, FOOD SCIENCE. *Current Pos:* DIR MICROBIOL & PROCESSING, NFPA, 75-, ASST MGR, WESTERN RES LAB, 79-, VPRES, 81- *Personal Data:* b Sebastopol, Calif, Mar 21, 39. *Educ:* Univ Calif, Berkeley, BA, 61. *Mem:* Am Soc Microbiol; Soc Appl Bacteriol; Inst Food Technologists. *Res:* Growth and resistance of clostridium botulinum, food spoilage; thermal processing of foods. *Mailing Add:* Western Res Lab 6363 Clark Ave Dublin CA 94568-3097

ITO, PHILIP J, HORTICULTURE & PLANT BREEDING, TROPICAL FRUITS & NUTS. *Current Pos:* Assoc horticulturist, 64-80, PROF & HORTICULTURIST, UNIV HAWAII, HILO, 80- *Personal Data:* b Kapaa, Kauai, Hawaii, Mar 11, 32; m 60, Carole K Nakaguma; c Ann, Bryan & Caryn. *Educ:* Univ Hawaii, BS, 58; Univ Minn, PhD(veg breeding), 64. *Concurrent Pos:* Consult trop fruits & nuts; Fulbright grant. *Mem:* Am Soc Hort Sci. *Res:* Tropical and subtropical fruit and nut breeding and culture. *Mailing Add:* 127 Anela St Hilo HI 96720. *Fax:* 808-969-7923

ITO, SUSUMU, ELECTRON MICROSCOPY, CYTOLOGY. *Current Pos:* assoc, 60-64, from asst prof to assoc prof, 64-69, PROF ANAT, HARVARD MED SCH, 69- *Personal Data:* b Stockton, Calif, July 27, 19; m 48; c 4. *Educ:* Fenn Col, BS, 50; Western Reserve Univ, MS, 51, PhD, 54. *Hon Degrees:* MS, Harvard Univ, 66. *Prof Exp:* Asst zool, Western Reserve Univ, 52-54; USPHS fels, 54-58; instr anat, Med Col, Cornell Univ, 58-60. *Mem:* Am Soc Cell Biol; Electron Micros Soc; Tissue Cult Asn; Am Gastroenterol Asn; Am Asn Anatomists. *Res:* Electron microscopy of biological material; cell biology; correlation of fine structure with function; gastrointestinal tract; gastric mucosal repair; carbonic anhydrase localization. *Mailing Add:* Dept Neurobiol Harvard Med Sch 220 Longwood Ave Boston MA 02115-6092

ITO, TAKERU, BIOCHEMISTRY. *Current Pos:* RETIRED. *Personal Data:* b Tokyo, Japan, May 10, 28; US citizen; m 59, Lois C Johnson; c Miki A (Derrico), Elizabeth L & Bronwyn A N. *Educ:* Trinity Univ, Tex, BS, 54; Okla State Univ, MS, 56; Univ Calif, Berkeley, PhD(biochem), 58. *Prof Exp:* Asst prof physiol chem & res assoc nutrit, Ohio State Univ, 62-67; prof biol, E Carolina Univ, 67-93. *Concurrent Pos:* Univ fel, Univ Pa, 58-60; USPHS fel, Osaka Univ, 61-62. *Mem:* Sigma Xi. *Res:* Microbial iron metabolism; essential fatty acids; oxidative phosphorylation in animal and plant mitochondria and in microorganisms. *Mailing Add:* 4511 Pinckney Pl Raleigh NC 27604

ITO, Y(ASUO) MARVIN, ENGINEERING MECHANICS. *Current Pos:* Res asst engr, Univ Calif, Los Angeles, 63-65, res engr, 65-68, asst prof eng, 68-75, ADJ PROF ENG, UNIV CALIF, LOS ANGELES, 75- *Personal Data:* b Los Angeles, Calif, July 4, 40; m 65; c 2. *Educ:* Univ Calif, Los Angeles, BS, 63, MS, 65, PhD(eng), 68. *Concurrent Pos:* NSF grants, 69-72; res fel, Harvard, 71-72. *Mem:* Am Acad Mech; Am Soc Mech Engrs. *Res:* Solid mechanics, especially physical theories of inelastic solids and composites and computational approaches. *Mailing Add:* 11260 Overland Ave Unit 15A Culver City CA 90230

ITOGA, STEPHEN YUKIO, COMPUTER SCIENCE. *Current Pos:* ASST PROF COMPUT SCI, UNIV HAWAII, 75- *Personal Data:* b Honolulu, Hawaii. *Educ:* Cornell Univ, BS, 65, ME, 66; Univ Calif, Los Angeles, PhD(syst sci), 73. *Prof Exp:* Mem tech staff, TRW Systs, TRW Inc, 66-75. *Concurrent Pos:* Mem staff, Fairchild Test Systs, 81-82. *Mem:* Asn Comput Mach; Soc Indust & Appl Math; Inst Elec & Electronics Engrs. *Res:* Programming methodology; software systems. *Mailing Add:* 3015 Kahalda Dr Honolulu HI 96822

ITOH, TATSUO, MICROWAVES, MILLIMETER WAVES. *Current Pos:* PROF ELEC ENG, UNIV CALIF, LOS ANGELES, 91- *Personal Data:* b Tokyo, Japan, May 5, 40; m 69, Seiko Fukumori; c Akihiro & Eiko. *Educ:* Yokohama Nat Univ, BS, 64, MS, 66; Univ Ill, PhD(elec eng), 69. *Prof Exp:* Res assoc fel elec eng, Univ Ill, 69-71, res asst prof, 71-76; sr res engr, Stanford Res Inst, 76-77; assoc prof elec eng, Univ Ky, 77-78; from assoc prof to prof elec eng, Univ Tex, Austin, 78-90. *Concurrent Pos:* Consult, Hughes Aircraft Co, 79-94; vis prof, Nat Defense Acad, Japan, 91; distinguished lectr, Inst Elec & Electronics Engrs, Australia; chmn, Comn D, Int Sci Radio Union, 93-96 & Long Range Planning Comt; vis prof, Univ Leeds, UK. *Mem:* Int Sci Radio Union; fel Inst Elec & Electronics Engrs; Inst Electronics; Info & Commun Engrs, Japan. *Res:* Millimeter wave circuit; field theory. *Mailing Add:* Dept Elec Eng Univ Calif Los Angeles CA 90024-1594

ITON, LENNOX ELROY, PHYSICAL CHEMISTRY, SURFACE SCIENCE. *Current Pos:* Fel solid state sci, 75-77, ASST CHEMIST SOLID STATE SCI, ARGONNE NAT LAB, US DEPT ENERGY, UNIV CHICAGO, 78- *Personal Data:* b St Vincent, WI, Jan 3, 49; UK citizen; m 80. *Educ:* McGill Univ, BSc, 70; Princeton Univ, PhD(chem), 76. *Mem:* Am Chem Soc; AAAS; Sigma Xi; Am Phys Soc. *Res:* Electron paramagnetic resonance; nuclear magnetic resonance; x-ray spectroscopic absorption techniques for electronic, dynamic, structural and chemical characterizations of surfaces; adsorbates and heterogeneous catalysts. *Mailing Add:* Mat Sci Div Argonne Nat Lab 9700 S Cass Argonne IL 60439-4803

ITTEL, STEVEN DALE, INORGANIC CHEMISTRY. *Current Pos:* chemist, 74-79, RES SUPVR, E I DU PONT DE NEMOURS & CO, INC, 79- *Personal Data:* b Hamilton, Ohio, Nov 8, 46; m 68; c 2. *Educ:* Miami Univ, Ohio, BS, 68; Northwestern Univ, Evanston, PhD(inorg chem), 74. *Prof Exp:* Chemist, Dept Health & Human Serv, USPHS, 68-70. *Mem:* Am Chem Soc; Catalysis Soc. *Res:* Homogeneous catalysis; olefin polymerization; activation of carbon; metal vapor synthesis; use of phosphorus ligands to control organometallic reactions through steric and electronic effects. *Mailing Add:* Chalfonte 2802 Landon Dr Wilmington DE 19810-2213

ITURRIAN, WILLIAM BEN, NEUROPHARMACOLOGY. *Current Pos:* asst prof, 67-71, ASSOC PROF PHARMACOL, UNIV GA, 71- *Personal Data:* b Hudson, Wyo, May 17, 39; m 65; c 4. *Educ:* Univ Wyo, BS, 62; Ore State Univ, PhD(pharmacol), 68. *Prof Exp:* Asst pharmacol, Wash State Univ, 62-63; asst, Ore State Univ, 64-66, res assoc, 66-67. *Mem:* Soc Neurosci; Int Soc Develop Psychobiol; Am Soc Pharmacol & Exp Therapeut. *Res:* Behavioral pharmacology; response of the immature nervous system to drugs or noise. *Mailing Add:* Dept Pharmacol Univ Ga Col Pharm Athens GA 30602-2356

ITZKAN, IRVING, MEDICAL APPLICATIONS OF LASERS. *Current Pos:* SR SCIENTIST, LASER BIOMED RES CTR, MASS INST TECHNOL, 85- *Personal Data:* b Brooklyn, NY, Dec 4, 29; m 57, Annette Brodsky; c Harry & Seth. *Educ:* Cornell Univ, BEngPhys, 52; Columbia Univ, MSEE,

61; NY Univ, PhD(physics), 69. *Prof Exp:* Engr, Sperry Rand Corp, 57-69; optics comt chmn, Avco Everett Res Lab, 69-85. *Mem:* Am Soc Laser Med & Surg; Optical Soc Am. *Res:* Use of lasers in medicine for diagnosis and treatment of disease. *Mailing Add:* Mass Inst Technol 6-014 Spectro Lab 77 Massachusetts Ave Cambridge MA 02139. *Fax:* 617-253-4513

ITZKOWITZ, GERALD LEE, MATHEMATICS. *Current Pos:* from asst prof to assoc prof, 71-93, PROF MATH, QUEENS COL, NY, 94- *Personal Data:* b Brooklyn, NY, June 2, 38; m 67, Adele Karp; c Zev & Ari. *Educ:* Mass Inst Technol, BS, 60; Univ Rochester, MA, 63, PhD(math), 65. *Prof Exp:* Asst math, Univ Rochester, 60-64; lectr, State Univ NY, Buffalo, 64-65, asst prof, 65-71. *Concurrent Pos:* Assoc investr, NSF grant, 66-67; instr, NSF, Inst High Sch Teachers, 86-87. *Mem:* Math Asn Am; Am Math Soc. *Res:* Harmonic analysis and extensions of Haar measure and other invariant integrals on groups; embedding theorems for topological groups, density character; functional equations; integration theory; uniform spaces and uniformities on topological groups. *Mailing Add:* Dept Math Queens Col City Univ New York Flushing NY 11367

IULIUCCI, JOHN DOMENIC, TOXICOLOGY, DRUG DEVELOPMENT. *Current Pos:* vpres preclin develop, 90-95, VPRES, DRUG DEVELOPMENT, ARIAD PHARMACEUT, 95- *Personal Data:* b Camden, NJ. *Educ:* Temple Univ, BS, 67, MS, 70, PhD(pharmacol), 73; Am Bd Toxicol, dipl. *Prof Exp:* Scientist toxicol, Warner-Lambert Co, 72-75; supvr, Adria Labs Inc, 75-77, mgr toxicol, 77-84; dir preclin, Clin & Regulatory Affairs, Centocor, Inc, 84-86, dir toxicol & pharmacol, 86-90. *Mem:* Environ Mutagen Soc; Soc Toxicol; Am Col Toxicol; Teratology Soc. *Res:* Safety evaluation of new investigational drugs intended for human use; preclinical acute, subacute and chronic toxicity; carcinogenic potential; teratology; reproduction toxicology; mutagenicity; pharmaceutical formulation development; worldwide regulatory affairs; clinical trials. *Mailing Add:* Ariad Pharmaceut 26 Landsdowne St Cambridge MA 02139

IUVONE, PAUL MICHAEL, NEUROCHEMISTRY, NEUROPHARMACOLOGY. *Current Pos:* from asst prof to assoc prof pharmacol, Emory Univ, 78-90, asst prof ophthal, 80-86, dir, Pharmacol Grad Prog, 85-88, ASSOC PROF OPHTHAL, SCH MED, EMORY UNIV, 86-, PROF PHARMACOL, 90- *Personal Data:* b New York, NY, Sept 4, 51; m 79; c 3. *Educ:* Univ Fla, BS, 72, PhD(neurosci), 76. *Honors & Awards:* Nat Res Serv Award, NIMH, 76. *Prof Exp:* Fel pharmacol, NIMH, 76-78. *Mem:* Am Soc Neurochem; Int Soc Neurochem; Am Soc Pharmacol & Exp Therapeut; Asn Res Vision & Ophthal; AAAS; Soc Neurosci. *Res:* Cellular and systems approaches to neurotransmitter function; retinal cell biology and neurotransmitters; neurotransmitter receptors and second messengers; dopamine in brain function and dysfunction. *Mailing Add:* Dept Pharmacol Emory Univ Sch Med Atlanta GA 30322-3090

IVAN, MICHAEL, animal nutrition, animal physiology, for more information see previous edition

IVANETICH, RICHARD JOHN, OPERATIONS RESEARCH, INFORMATION SYSTEMS. *Current Pos:* res staff mem, 75-84, asst dir, Syst Eval Div, 84-90, DIR, COMPUT & SOFTWARE ENG DIV, INST DEFENSE ANALYSIS, 90- *Personal Data:* b San Francisco, Calif, Feb 12, 41; m 66; c 2. *Educ:* Univ Calif, Berkeley, BS, 63; Harvard Univ, PhD(physics), 69. *Prof Exp:* Asst prof physics, Harvard Univ, 69-74. *Mem:* Asn Comput Mach; Inst Elec & Electronics Engrs Comput Soc. *Res:* Defense systems, operations, and policy analysis; primarily concerned with computer and information systems; command, control and communication systems and procedures, modeling and simulation; crisis management; strategic and theater nuclear systems. *Mailing Add:* 1801 N Beauregard St Alexandria VA 22311. *Fax:* 703-845-6848; *E-Mail:* rivan@ida.org

IVANKOVICH, ANTHONY D, ANESTHESIOLOGY. *Current Pos:* PROF & CHMN ANESTHIOL, RUSH MED COL, RUSH-PRESBY ST LUKE'S MED CTR, 80- *Personal Data:* b Delrljaca, Yugoslavia, Mar 25, 39. *Educ:* Univ Zagreb Med Sch, Yugoslavia, MD, 63; Am Bd Anesthesiol, dipl, 71. *Prof Exp:* Instr anesthesiol, Univ Chicago, Pritzker Sch Med, 69; asst prof, Loyola Univ, Stritch Sch Med, 70-71; prof, Univ Ill, Lincoln Sch Med, 75-80. *Concurrent Pos:* Attend anesthesiologist, Loyola Univ Hosp, 70-71; consult, Suburban Tuberc Sanitorium, Hinsdale, Ill, 70-71; attend & dir anesthesia res, Michael Reese Med Ctr, 71-74; chief, Operating Rm Serv, 801st Gen Hosp, US Army Res, 71-73, chief surg, 73-74 & assoc chief, 74-76; lectr anesthesiol, Loyola Univ, Stritch Sch Med, 71-81; chmn, Ill Masonic Med Ctr, 74-80; consult, Shriner's Hosp Crippled Children, 77-82. *Mem:* AMA; Am Soc Anesthesiologists; Int Anesthesia Res Soc; Am Heart Asn; Sigma Xi; Am Col Chest Physicians; Am Pain Soc. *Res:* Neurosurgical and cardiovascular clinical anesthesia, pain treatment, cerebral blood flow, pharmacology of digitalis and anti-hypertensive drugs, patient monitoring and safety in the operating room. *Mailing Add:* Rush-Presby St Luke's Med Ctr 1653 W Congress Pkwy Off 741 Jelke Chicago IL 60612

IVANOV, IGOR C, ION ASSISTED SYNTHESIS OF MATERIALS, ARTIFICIAL INTELLIGENCE IN DATA INTERPRETATION. *Current Pos:* staff analyst, 88-91, assoc mgr Auger electron spectros & Fourier transform infrared spectros, 91-93, ASSOC MGR ELECTRON BEAM SERVS, CHARLES EVANS & ASSOCS, 93- *Personal Data:* b Seymchan, Russia, Feb 22, 59; US citizen; m, Helen Volk; c 2. *Educ:* St Petersburg State Univ, BS, 74, MS, 75, MS, 80, PhD(mat sci), 82. *Prof Exp:* Sr scientist, Cent Physics Res Inst, 84-88. *Res:* Novel deposition processes involved use of low-energy metal plasma; artificial intelligence applications for automatic emission spectroscopy, Fourier transform infrared spectroscopy and mass spectroscopy spectra data reduction. *Mailing Add:* 3932 Churchill Dr Pleasanton CA 94588. *Fax:* 510-426-5534; *E-Mail:* igori@aol.com

IVANOV, VADIM O, LIGAND-RECEPTOR INTERACTION, REGULATION OF CELL GROWTH. *Current Pos:* RES ASSOC, ORE STATE UNIV, 96- *Personal Data:* b Chelyabinsk, Russia, June 22, 58; m 80, Svetlana Schigreva; c Anton & Andrei. *Educ:* Tomsk Med Inst, BS, 81, MD, 81; USSR Cardiol Ctr, PhD(biochem), 85. *Prof Exp:* Scientist, USSR Cardiol Ctr, 84-89, head res group, 89-91; proj mgr, Americard, joint venture, 91-93; res assoc, Linus Pauling Inst, 93-94, head res group, 94-96. *Res:* Cellular mechanisms of atherosclerosis; involvement of receptor-mediated metabolism of plasma lipoproteins; biology of smooth muscle and micronutrients. *Mailing Add:* 960 NW Tenth Corvallis OR 97330. *Fax:* 541-737-5077; *E-Mail:* vadim.ivanov@orst.edu

IVANOV, VLADIMIR N, T CELL DEVELOPMENT, REGULATION OF APOPTOSIS. *Current Pos:* RES SCIENTIST, MEM SLOAN-KETTERING CANCER CTR, 95- *Personal Data:* b Baku, Russia, Nov 17, 46; m 74, Xenia B; c Tatyana & Darya. *Educ:* Russ Acad Sci, PhD(biochem), 77. *Hon Degrees:* DSc, Russ Acad Sci, 91. *Prof Exp:* Scientist & sr staff scientist, Inst Gen Genetics, Moscow, 81-90; sr staff scientist, Inst Gene Biol, Moscow, 90-91; vis scientist, Univ Strasbourg, France, 91-93; res scientist, Univ Miami, 93-95. *Mem:* Am Asn Immunologists; Fedn Am Socs Exp Biol. *Res:* Gene regulation during t-cell development, activation and programmed death. *Mailing Add:* Mem Sloan-Kettering Cancer Ctr 1275 York Ave New York NY 10021. *Fax:* 212-794-4019; *E-Mail:* v-ivahou@ski.mskcc.org

IVANSO, EUGENE V, PHYSICAL METALLURGY. *Current Pos:* RETIRED. *Personal Data:* b Braddock, Pa, Dec 8, 08; m 38, 52; c 1. *Educ:* Case Inst Technol, BS, 31, MS, 32. *Prof Exp:* Instr math, Case Inst Technol, 31-32; field engr & mgr elec sound equip, Cleveland Sound Equip Co, 32-34; res metallurgist alloy develop, Brush Beryllium Co, 34-36; phys metallurgist, Bundy Tubing Co, 36-40; chief metallurgist, corrosion & foundry, Wyandotte Chem Corp, 40-44; mgr alloy sales & field eng nickel alloys, Steel Sales Corp, 44-52; vpres & dir, Commercial Lab, Detroit Testing Lab, Inc, 52-55, dir & consult, 55-65; assoc dir, Appl Mgt & Tech Ctr, Wayne State Univ, 65-74. *Concurrent Pos:* Vpres, March Corp, 55-65. *Res:* Constitution of beryllium-copper alloys; internal stresses in aluminum alloys; desulfurization of cast iron; investigations in mechanism of galvanic corrosion; surface tension of molten metals; diffusion of metals; high temperature and room temperature corrosion of all types alloys and effects of properties; educational up-dating of industrial and professional personnel in science, technology and management; administration. *Mailing Add:* 911 Lakepointe Ave Grosse Pointe MI 48230

IVASH, EUGENE V, THEORETICAL PHYSICS. *Current Pos:* from asst prof to assoc prof, 52-66, PROF PHYSICS, UNIV TEX, AUSTIN, 66-, RES SCIENTIST, CTR NUCLEAR STUDIES, 67- *Personal Data:* b Windsor, Ont, July 24, 25; nat US; m 53; c 3. *Educ:* Univ Mich, BS, 45, MS, 47, PhD(physics), 52. *Prof Exp:* Asst physics, Univ Mich, 47-52. *Concurrent Pos:* Res scientist, Nuclear Physics Lab, 52-67; res partic, Oak Ridge Nat Lab, 55-57, consult, 57-58; tech adv, Chulalongkorn Univ, Bankok, 58-59; lectr, Cambridge Univ, 59; vis scientist, Lawrence Radiation Lab, Univ Calif, 61; consult, Gen Atomic Div, Gen Dynamics, 63. *Mem:* Am Phys Soc; Am Asn Physics Teachers. *Res:* Nuclear physics; quantum mechanics; microwave spectroscopy; plasma physics. *Mailing Add:* Dept Physics Univ Tex Austin TX 78712

IVASHKIV, EUGENE, PHARMACEUTICS, CHEMISTRY. *Current Pos:* RETIRED. *Personal Data:* b Ukraine, Mar 21, 23; US citizen; m 53; c 2. *Educ:* Ukrainian Polytech Inst, Ger, BSForestry, 50; Columbia Univ, BSChem, 57; Polytech Inst Brooklyn, BSChemEng, 59; Newark Col Eng, MSChemEng, 63. *Honors & Awards:* Quality/Productivity Innovation Award, Squibb, 87. *Prof Exp:* Sr res scientist, Squibb Inst Med Res, 57-92, res fel, 63-92, sr res leader, 89-92. *Mem:* Am Inst Chem Engrs; NY Acad Sci; Ukrainian Engrs Soc Am (pres, 72-74); Shevchenko Sci Soc. *Res:* Development of new methods for following the biosynthesis of antibiotics, microbial and enzymatic conversion of steroids, for drugs in dosage forms, residual methods, bioavailibility of drugs, metabolites; extraction, separation and purification, kinetic studies and characterization of new products; modern instrumentation, automation. *Mailing Add:* 239 E Fifth St New York NY 10003

IVATURI, RAO VENKATA KRISHNA, NUTRITION EDUCATION, INTERNATIONAL NUTRITION. *Current Pos:* ASST PROF NUTRIT, IND STATE UNIV, 86- *Personal Data:* b Madras, India, Jan 20, 60; m 88. *Educ:* Andhra Pradesh Agr Univ, BS, 81; Kans State Univ, MS, 83; Univ Nebr, PhD(nutrit), 86. *Prof Exp:* Coordr nutrit, Univ Nebr, Lincoln, 85-86. *Concurrent Pos:* Nutrit consult, WCent Ind Econ Develop Dist Inc, 86-; sem leader, Weight Mgt Clin, Oper Weight Loss, Adult Fitness Prog, Ind State Univ, 86-, coordr-World Food Day, World Food Day Teleconf, 86 & 88 & prin investr res projs, 86-; Fullbright-Hays partic, Fullbright-Hays: Group to Brazil, 91. *Mem:* Am Inst Nutrit; Fedn Am Socs Exp Biol; Sigma Xi; Soc Nutrit Educ. *Res:* Dietary sugars and their interactions with minerals in humans; nutrition education research with senior citizens; investigating factors that affect food consumption in young adults; nutrition education research in the developing countries. *Mailing Add:* Dept Home Econ Ind State Univ Terre Haute IN 47809-0001

IVENS, MARY SUE, MEDICAL MYCOLOGY, INFECTIOUS DISEASES. *Current Pos:* CLIN PROF MED, LA STATE UNIV MED CTR, 72-; ASSOC PROF NATURAL SCI, DILLARD UNIV, 72- *Personal Data:* b Maryville, Tenn, Aug 23, 29. *Educ:* Tenn State Univ, BS, 49; Tulane Univ Sch Med, MS, 63; La State Univ Med Ctr, PhD(microbiol & mycol), 66. *Prof Exp:*

Res asst nuclear med, Oak Ridge Nat Lab, 49-51; dir, Microbiol Lab, Lewis-Gale Hosp, Roanoke, Va, 53-57; res mycologist, Ctr Dis Control, Atlanta, Ga, 57-60; res assoc med, Med Ctr, La State Univ, 66-72, instr microbiol, 68-72. *Concurrent Pos:* Res asst, Baroness Erlanger Hosp, Chatanooga, Tenn, 52-53; dir, Mycol Lab, Med Ctr, La State Univ, 63-72, lectr, Sch Dent, 68-70; consult, Conf Ctr Mycotic Sera, WHO, 69, Med Mycol, Charity Hosp, New Orleans, 66-; prin investr NSF grants, Med Ctr, La State Univ, 68-72, clin prof med, 72-; prin investr NIH grants, Dillard Univ, 76-; Macy fel, Marine Biol Lab, Woods Hole, Mass, 78. *Mem:* Int Soc Human & Animal Mycol; Med Mycol Soc Am; Am Soc Microbiol; AAAS; Sigma Xi; Infectious Dis Soc Am. *Res:* Immunology of the systemic mycoses; biochemical characterization of fungal skin testing antigens; mechanisms of infectious diseases. *Mailing Add:* 408 Berclair Ave New Orleans LA 70123

IVERS, DREW RUSSELL, RESEARCH ADMINISTRATION. *Current Pos:* DIR PLANT RES, LAND O'LAKES, INC, 88- *Personal Data:* b Vincennes, Ind, Aug 12, 46; m 68; c 3. *Educ:* Purdue Univ, BS, 68; Iowa State Univ, PhD, 74. *Prof Exp:* Res assoc, Iowa State Univ, Ames, 72-74; res mgr, Cargill, Inc, 74-76. *Concurrent Pos:* Mem bd, Nat Soybean Variety Rev, 77-86 & Nat Plant Genetic Resources Bd, Washington, DC, 82-88; chmn, Basic Soy Res Comt, Am Seed Trade Asn, 87-89. *Mem:* Crop Sci Soc Am; Am Seed Trade Asn; Nat Coun Com Plant Breeders. *Res:* Soybean breeding methods; awarded 12 patents. *Mailing Add:* 110 Bicentennial Ct Webster City IA 50595

IVERSEN, EDWIN SEVERIN, FISH BIOLOGY. *Current Pos:* assoc prof fisheries biol, 56-74, PROF BIOL & LIVING RESOURCES, ROSENSTIEL SCH MARINE & ATMOSPHERIC SCI, UNIV MIAMI, 74- *Personal Data:* b Ferndale, Mich, Dec 4, 22; m 58; c 2. *Educ:* Univ Wash, BS, 49, MS, 53; Tex A&M Univ, PhD(biol oceanog), 61. *Prof Exp:* Fishery res biologist, Fishery Res Inst, Univ Wash, 48-52 & US Fish & Wildlife Serv, Hawaii, 53-56. *Mem:* Am Fisheries Soc; Am Inst Fishery Res Biol; World Maricult Soc. *Res:* General marine fishery biology; population dynamics; marine parasites; mariculture. *Mailing Add:* 427 Majorca Ave Miami FL 33134

IVERSEN, GUDMUND R, APPLIED STATISTICS. *Current Pos:* fac assoc, Inst Social Res & asst prof sociol, Univ Mich, 69-72, assoc prof, 72-77, PROF STATIST & CONSULT STATISTICIAN, CTR SOCIAL & POLICY STUDIES, SWARTHMORE COL, 72- *Personal Data:* b Norway, Sept 14, 34; US citizen; m 62, 74, Roberta Rehner; c 4. *Educ:* Univ Mich, AM, 60 & 61; Harvard Univ, PhD(statist), 69. *Prof Exp:* Instr math, Eastern Mich Univ, 61-62; res assoc sociol, Univ Oslo, 62-64. *Mem:* Am Statist Asn; Am Sociol Asn. *Res:* Sociological methodology; application of statistics to the social sciences. *Mailing Add:* Dept Math & Statist Swarthmore Col Swarthmore PA 19081. *E-Mail:* iversen@cs.swarthmore.edu

IVERSEN, JAMES D(ELANO), AEROSPACE ENGINEERING. *Current Pos:* From instr to assoc prof, 56-70, PROF AEROSPACE ENG, IOWA STATE UNIV, 70- *Personal Data:* b Omaha, Nebr, Apr 1, 33; m 60; c David & Philip. *Educ:* Iowa State Univ, BS, 56, MS, 58, PhD, 64. *Concurrent Pos:* Opers analyst, USAF, NASA; chmn, Dept Aerospace Eng, Iowa State Univ, 87-90; vis prof, Univ Aarhus, Denmark, 91-93. *Mem:* Fel Am Inst Aeronaut & Astronaut; Am Soc Eng Educ; Am Geophys Union; Am Soc Civil Engrs. *Res:* Aerodynamics; micrometeorology; aeolian geology. *Mailing Add:* 4523 Westbend Dr Ames IA 50014

IVERSON, A EVAN, COMPUTER VISION, IMAGE EXPLOITATION. *Current Pos:* SR SCIENTIST, SCI APPLICATIONS INT CORP, 90- *Personal Data:* b Stanley, NDak. *Educ:* Univ NMex, BS; Univ Ariz, MS, PhD(appl math). *Prof Exp:* Scientist, Los Alamos Nat Lab, 77-90. *Mem:* Soc Indust & Appl Math; Appl Computational Electromagnetics Soc. *Res:* Mathematical modeling of physical systems, numerical analysis, signal and image processing and computer vision; over 20 publications in these areas. *Mailing Add:* SAIC 101 N Wilmont Suite 400 Tucson AZ 85711

IVERSON, F KENNETH, STEEL PRODUCTION. *Current Pos:* Vpres & gen mgr, Vulcraft Div, Nucor Corp, 62-63, group vpres, 63-65, pres, 65-84, chmn & chief exec officer, 84-96, CHMN, NUCOR CORP, 96- *Personal Data:* b Downers Grove, Ill, Sept 18, 25. *Educ:* Cornell Univ, BS; Purdue Univ, MS. *Hon Degrees:* Dr, Univ Nebr & Purdue Univ. *Honors & Awards:* Nat Medal Technol, 91. *Concurrent Pos:* Dir, Wachovia Corp, Wal-Mart Stores & Wikoff Color Corp. *Mem:* Nat Acad Eng. *Res:* Low-cost steel production; author of numerous technical and business articles. *Mailing Add:* Nucor Corp 2100 Rexford Rd Charlotte NC 28211. *Fax:* 704-362-4208

IVERSON, JOHN BURTON, VERTEBRATE BIOLOGY, HERPETOLOGY. *Current Pos:* From asst prof to assoc prof, 78-88, PROF BIOL, EARLHAM COL, 89-; ADJ CUR HERPET, FLA STATE MUS, UNIV FLA, 77- *Personal Data:* b Omaha, Nebr, Oct 4, 49; m 71, Sheila Jelinek; c 2. *Educ:* Hastings Col, BA, 71; Univ Fla, MS, 74, PhD(zool), 77. *Concurrent Pos:* Prin investr, Sigma Xi grant, 77-78, Theodore Roosevelt Mem Fund, 77-78 & Am Philos Soc, 78, NSF, 80-82, 84, 91-93 & 93-94, US Fish & Wildlife Serv Grant, 81-83 & 85; asst investr, BLM grant, 77-78. *Mem:* Am Soc Ichthyologists & Herpetologists; Herpetologists League; AAAS; Ecol Soc Am; Soc Studies Amphibians & Reptiles. *Res:* Herpetology, specifically systematics and ecology of freshwater turtles; ecology and behavior of large herbivorous Iguanine lizards in the American tropics; reproductive strategies of turtles. *Mailing Add:* Dept Biol Earlham Col Richmond IN 47374. *Fax:* 765-983-1497; *E-Mail:* johni@earlham.edu

IVERSON, KENNETH EUGENE, APPLIED MATHEMATICS. *Current Pos:* RETIRED. *Personal Data:* b Camrose, Alta, Dec 17, 20; m 46; c 4. *Educ:* Queen's Univ, Can, BA, 50; Harvard Univ, AM, 51, PhD(appl math), 54. *Hon Degrees:* Hon degree, York Univ, Toronto, 97. *Honors & Awards:* Harry Goode Award, Am Fedn Info Processing Soc, 75; Tueing Award, Asn Comput Mach, 79. *Prof Exp:* Instr appl math, Harvard Univ, 54-55, asst prof, 55-60; res staff mem, Sci Ctr, IBM Corp, 60-71, IBM fel, 71-80; I P Sharp assoc, Toronto, Can, 80-87. *Mem:* Nat Acad Eng. *Res:* Automatic computers and programming. *Mailing Add:* 70 Erskine Ave Toronto ON M4P 1Y2 Can. *Fax:* 416-488-7559; *E-Mail:* kei@interlog.com

IVERSON, LAURA HIMES, HEALTH POLICY ANALYSIS. *Current Pos:* Res assoc, 85-87, SR RES ASSOC HEALTH CARE, INTERSTUDY CTR AGING & LONG TERM CARE, 87- *Personal Data:* b Michigan City, Ind, Apr 25, 60; m 82; c 1. *Educ:* Carleton Col, BA, 82; Univ Southern Calif, MSG & MPA, 85. *Mem:* Sigma Xi; Geront Soc Am; Am Pub Health Asn; Am Pub Aging. *Res:* Improved financial planning and long term health care services to the elderly; author of numerous publication and articles related to long term care financing, medicare HMOs and case management. *Mailing Add:* 2464 Elm Dr White Bear Lake MN 55110

IVERSON, RAY MADS, BIOLOGY. *Current Pos:* PROF BIOL SCI, FLA ATLANTIC UNIV, 72- *Personal Data:* b Tremonton, Utah, Nov 3, 27; m 53; c 3. *Educ:* Reed Col, BA, 51; Stanford Univ, PhD, 57. *Prof Exp:* Asst prof zool, Univ Miami, 58-64, assoc prof, 64-66, prof, 66-72. *Mem:* AAAS; Sigma Xi. *Res:* Cellular physiology. *Mailing Add:* 8818 SE Sharon St Hobe Sound FL 33455

IVERSON, SCOTT, STRATEGIC PLANNING, HEALTH SYSTEMS ENGINEERING. *Current Pos:* ASSOC PROF INDUST ENG & CO-DIR PEMM, UNIV WASH, 83- *Personal Data:* b San Leandro, Calif, Oct 4, 48; m 72, Kathryn McLeod; c Kristen. *Educ:* Univ Calif, Davis, BS, 70; San Jose State Univ, MS, 72; Univ Colo, Boulder, PhD(aerospace eng), 74; Dublin Univ, Ireland, MSc, 77. *Prof Exp:* Systs engr, Pratt & Whitney Aircraft, Hartford, Conn, 72; asst prof civil eng, Calif Polytech State Univ, 74-75, indust eng, Bogazic Univ, Istanbul, Turkey, 75-77 & systs develop, Trinity Col, Dublin Univ, Ireland, 77-78; assoc prof civil eng, Univ NC, Charlotte, 78-83. *Concurrent Pos:* Vis prof, Nat Univ Singapore, 81-82. *Mem:* Nat Coun Systs Eng; Inst Indust Eng; Am Soc Eng Educr; Opers Res Soc Am. *Res:* Optimal allocation of scarce resources amongst competing needs in health care, manufacturing and environmental organization. *Mailing Add:* Dept Indust Eng Box 352650 Univ Wash Seattle WA 98195

IVERSON, STUART LEROY, MAMMALIAN ECOLOGY, RADIATION ECOLOGY. *Current Pos:* SR ASSOC, IVERSON & ASSOCS, 96- *Personal Data:* b Albert Lea, Minn, Oct 12, 39; m 62, Alice Berhow; c Scott & Christopher. *Educ:* St Olaf Col, BA, 61; Univ NDak, MA, 63; Univ BC, PhD(zool), 67. *Prof Exp:* Group leader ecol, Environ Res Br, Whiteshell Labs, Atomic Energy Can Ltd, 67-77, head, Ecol Res Sect, 77-81, Environ Res Br, 81-83, sr adv exec vpres, Head Off, Res Co, 83-84, head radiation, Appl Res Br, 85-93, dir, Whiteshell Initiative, 93-96. *Mem:* Ecol Soc Am; Am Soc Mammal. *Res:* Use of radiation for food preservation, crosslinking and other industrial processes; mammalian population ecology and physiological ecology; long term environmental implications of methods of radioactive waste management; technology commercialization; international technology transfer. *Mailing Add:* 122 Burrows Rd Pinawa MB R0E 1L0 Can. *Fax:* 204-753-2610; *E-Mail:* iversons@granite.mb.ca

IVES, DAVID HOMER, ENZYMOLOGY, BIOCHEMISTRY. *Current Pos:* From asst prof to assoc prof, 62-69, PROF BIOCHEM, OHIO STATE UNIV, 69- *Personal Data:* b Rockford, Ill, Apr 6, 33; m 56, Jean E Seldon; c Laura J (Lino) & Eric G. *Educ:* Cornell Col, AB, 55; Univ Minn, PhD(physiol chem), 60. *Concurrent Pos:* Nat Cancer Inst fel, Univ Wis, 60-62; NIH & NSF res grants. *Mem:* Am Soc Biochem & Molecular Biol; fel Am Sci Affil; Am Chem Soc; Protein Soc. *Res:* Enzyme regulation and mechanism; structure/function relationships. *Mailing Add:* Dept Biochem Col Biol Sci Ohio State Univ 484 W 12th Ave Columbus OH 43210. *Fax:* 614-292-6773; *E-Mail:* ives.1@osu.edu

IVES, JEFFREY LEE, ORGANIC CHEMISTRY, MEDICINAL CHEMISTRY. *Current Pos:* MED CHEMIST, PFIZER, INC, 78- *Personal Data:* b Torrington, Conn, Feb 6, 51; m 74; c 1. *Educ:* Colgate Univ, BA, 73; Yale Univ, MS, MPhil & PhD, 78. *Mem:* Am Chem Soc. *Res:* Synthesis of pharmacologically active agents involving the design and discovery of new organic reactions and transformations. *Mailing Add:* 80 Goose Hill Dr Chester CT 06412-1229

IVES, JOHN (JACK) DAVID, MOUNTAIN GEOECOLOGY. *Current Pos:* prof geog & chairperson, 89-93, prof mountain geoecol, 94-97, EMER PROF MOUNTAIN GEOECOL, UNIV CALIF, DAVIS, 97-; RES PROF, CARLETON UNIV, 97- *Personal Data:* b Grimsby, Eng, Oct 15, 31; Can citizen; m 54, Pauline A Cordingley; c Nadine E (Thurston), Anthony R, Colin H & Peter R. *Educ:* Univ Nottingham, BA, 53; McGill Univ, PhD(geog), 56. *Prof Exp:* Asst cur geog, Sub-Arctic Res Lab, McGill Univ, 55, dir geog, Res Lab & asst prof, Univ, 57-60; asst to dir & chief, Div Phys Geog, Geog Br, Can Dept Mines & Tech Surv, 60-63, dir, 64-67; dir, Inst Arctic & Alpine Res, Univ Colo, Boulder, 67-79, prof geog, 67-89. *Concurrent Pos:* Mem subcomt glaciers, Nat Res Coun, 60-67; mem, Can Comt, Int Geog Union, 61-63, secy-treas 64-67; chmn, Nat Adv Comt Geog Res, 65-67; alpine site coordr, Tundra Biome, Int Biol Prog, 69-73; founder & ed, J Arctic & Alpine Res, 69-81 & J Mountain Res & Develop, 81-; chmn, US Directorate

Proj, Human Impacts Mountain Ecosyts, 74-, Int Geog Union Comn, Mountain Geoecol, UN Univ Proj, Highland-Lowland Interactive Syst, 74-90, UN Univ Mountain Ecol & Sustainable Develop, 90-; John Simon Guggenheim mem fel, 76-77; vis prof, Bern Univ, Switz, 76-77; chmn, Int Geog Union Comm Mountain Geoecol, 88-; hon mem, Yunnan Acad Soc Sci, China, 94- *Mem:* Glaciol Soc; Asn Am Geographers; Int Mountain Soc (pres, 80-); Arctic Inst NAm; Cent Himolayan Environ Asn. *Res:* Geomorphology with emphasis on processes of deglaciation and effects of erosion by glacier melt-water; investigation of history of recession of the last major ice sheets; glaciology; coordination of interdisciplinary studies on mountain geoecology; permafrost studies in alpine areas; natural hazards in mountain regions; renewable natural resources in mountain regions, Nepal, China, Thailand, South America and USSR. *Mailing Add:* 412 Thessaly Circle Ottawa ON K1H 5W5 Can. *Fax:* 530-752-9592

IVES, MICHAEL BRIAN, CORROSION, SURFACE TREATMENT. *Current Pos:* from asst prof to assoc prof, 61-72, assoc dean eng, 79-88, PROF MAT SCI & ENG, MCMASTER UNIV, 72- *Personal Data:* b Bournemouth, Eng, Sept 30, 34; m 61, Daina Skrapa. *Educ:* Bristol Univ, BSc, 57, PhD(physics), 59. *Prof Exp:* Res metall engr, Carnegie Inst Technol, 58-61. *Concurrent Pos:* Sabbatical leave, Univ Milan, 67-68; Alexander Von Humboldt Found teaching fel, vis prof, Max Planck Inst Iron Res, Dusseldorf, 75, Japan Soc Prom Sci, 79, Univ Erlangen, Nurnberg, 83 & EPFL, Switz, 89-90. *Mem:* Fel Am Soc Metals Int; Nat Asn Corrosion Engrs Int. *Res:* Localized corrosion of metals and alloys, dissolution of crystals; alloy development; materials for sulfuric acid induction. *Mailing Add:* Dept Mat Sci & Eng McMaster Univ 1280 Main St W Hamilton ON L8S 4L7 Can. *E-Mail:* ives@mcmaster.ca

IVES, NORTON C(ONRAD), AGRICULTURAL ENGINEERING. *Current Pos:* CONSULT AGR ENGR, 61- *Personal Data:* b Rolfe, Iowa, Mar 6, 17; m 42; c 7. *Educ:* Iowa State Univ, BS, 38, MS, 39, PhD, 59. *Prof Exp:* Exten agr engr, Univ Minn, 39-44 & Iowa State Univ, 44-45; chief dept agr eng, Inter-Am Inst Agr Sci, Costa Rica, 45-53; agr engr, USDA, Iowa State Univ, 53-61. *Mem:* AAAS; Am Soc Agr Engrs; Soil Conserv Soc Am; Sigma Xi. *Res:* Farm structures; grain drying and storage investigations; crop processing; farmstead engineering. *Mailing Add:* RR 1 Rolfe IA 50581

IVES, ROBERT SOUTHWICK, CHEMISTRY. *Current Pos:* TREAS, CONTOUR CHEM CO, 60- *Personal Data:* b Salem, Mass, July 7, 13; m 40; c 7. *Educ:* Univ Maine, BS, 33. *Prof Exp:* Chemist, Lever Bros Co, 37-41 & F C Huyck & Sons Co, 41-43; res chemist, Sylvania Elec Corp, 43-47; lab dir, Esselen Res Corp, 47-52; pres, Ives Lab, 52-58; dir res, Ludlow Papers, Inc, 58-60. *Mem:* Am Chem Soc; Tech Asn Pulp & Paper Indust; Am Asn Textile Chemists & Colorists. *Res:* Research and development of plastics; adhesives; functional paper coatings and textiles. *Mailing Add:* 127 Eastern Ave PO Box 8008 Gloucester MA 01931-8008

IVESON, HERBERT TODD, CHEMISTRY. *Current Pos:* RETIRED. *Personal Data:* b Mirror, Alta, Sept 28, 15; m 42; c 3. *Educ:* Univ Ill, BS, 37, MS, 40. *Prof Exp:* From res chemist to sr chemist, Glidden Co, 40-51, indust consult, 51-58; mgr lecithin prod, Cent Soya Co, Inc, 58-62, div prod mgr, 62-64, div prod adminr, 64-65, mgr indust applns, 65-70; qual assurance mgr, Glidden-Durkee Div, SCM Corp, Joliet, 70-81. *Mem:* Am Chem Soc; Am Oil Chemists Soc; Sigma Xi. *Res:* Design of radio frequency induction heating units; ionization from hot filaments; development of products from fats, oils and lipids; lecithin product showing increased efficiency in chocolate viscosity reduction; method of producing a non-break bleached oil; edible emulsifiers. *Mailing Add:* 219 Clinton St Elmhurst IL 60126-2908

IVETT, REGINALD WILLIAM, INDUSTRIAL CHEMISTRY. *Current Pos:* RETIRED. *Personal Data:* b Stockton, NY, Oct 27, 15; m 43. *Educ:* Allegheny Col, AB, 36; Purdue Univ, MS, 39, PhD(phys chem), 41. *Prof Exp:* Res chemist, Hercules Powder Co, 41-43, res supvr, 43-49, res mgr, 49-63, dir develop, Fibers Dept, 63-68; patent coordr, Hercules, Inc, 68-83. *Mem:* Am Chem Soc. *Res:* Fiber science; polymer applications; research administration; rosin and terpene chemicals. *Mailing Add:* 536 Kerfoot Farm Rd Woodbrook Wilmington DE 19803-2444

IVEY, DON LOUIS, CIVIL ENGINEERING. *Current Pos:* asst, 60-63, PROF CIVIL ENG, TEX A&M UNIV, 71-, ASST DIR, TEX TRANSP INST, 76-; PRES, SCI INQUIRY INC, 76- *Personal Data:* b Ft Worth, Tex, Nov 17, 35. *Educ:* Lamar State Col, BS, 60; Tex A&M Univ, MS, 62, PhD(struct eng), 64. *Honors & Awards:* Kummer lectr, Am Soc Testing & Mat, 79. *Prof Exp:* Asst res eng, Tex Transport Inst & resident engr, Struct Res Lab, 63-69. *Concurrent Pos:* Res engr & head, Hwy Safety Res Ctr & Safety Div, Tex Transp Inst, 71-76. *Mem:* Am Concrete Inst; Am Soc Testing & Mat. *Res:* Highway safety engineering; concrete technology; reinforced lightweight structural concrete design practices; vehicle handling and stability; collision dynamics; tire pavement friction; highway geometrics; highway safety structures. *Mailing Add:* CE/TTI Bldg Safety Dir Tex A&M Univ College Station TX 77843

IVEY, DONALD GLENN, PHYSICS, POLYMER PHYSICS. *Current Pos:* from asst prof to assoc prof, Univ Toronto, 49-63, prin, New Col, 63-74, vpres, Instnl Rels, 80-84, prof, 63-87, EMER PROF PHYSICS, UNIV TORONTO, 87- *Personal Data:* b Clanwilliam, Man, Feb 6, 22; m 44; c 3. *Educ:* Univ BC, BA, 44, MA, 46; Univ Notre Dame, PhD(physics), 49. *Prof Exp:* Demonstr math & physics, Univ BC, 43-46; res assoc physics, Univ Notre Dame, 46-49. *Concurrent Pos:* Secy & treas, Can High Polymer Forum, 53-55, chmn, 58. *Mem:* Am Phys Soc; Am Asn Physics Teachers; Can Asn Physicists. *Res:* Physical properties of solid polymers. *Mailing Add:* 34 Yewfield Cres Don Mills ON M3B 2Y6 Can

IVEY, E(DWIN) H(ARRY), JR, PETROCHEMICALS MANUFACTURE, PROJECT MANAGEMENT. *Current Pos:* gen mgr, 70-72, CONSULT & PRES, E H IVEY & CO, INC, 72- *Personal Data:* b Galveston, Tex, Apr 19, 21; m 84; c 6. *Educ:* Agr & Mech Col, Tex, BSChE, 41, MSChE, 47. *Prof Exp:* Instr chem, Agr & Mech Col, Tex, 42-43, instr chem eng, 46-47; res & develop engr, Houdry Process Corp, 47-50; res & develop engr, Dow Chem Co, 50-52, asst supt, Light Hydrocarbons Dept, 53-55, supt, 55-66, proj mgr, Dow Chem Nederland, 66-67, hydrocarbons tech mgr, Dow Chem Europe, Switz, 67-68; consult & proj mgr, P R Olefins Co, 68-70. *Mem:* Am Chem Soc; Am Inst Chem Engrs. *Res:* Project management; petrochemical manufacture in Europe and North America. *Mailing Add:* 8415 Laurelhurst San Antonio TX 78209-2015

IVEY, ELIZABETH SPENCER, ACOUSTICS. *Current Pos:* PROVOST, MACALESTER COL, 90- *Personal Data:* b Schenectady, NY, Apr 21, 35; m 57, 82; c 5. *Educ:* Simmons Col, BS, 57; Harvard Univ, MAT, 59; Univ Mass, PhD(mech eng acoust), 76. *Prof Exp:* Prof physics, Simmons Col, 58-59, Bucknell Univ, 60-63 & Colo State Univ, 64-68; assoc dean fac, Smith Col, 82-85, Louise Wolff Kahn Chair, 85, prof physics, 69-83, chair dept, 83-90. *Concurrent Pos:* Vis prof, Yale Univ, 82. *Mem:* Acoust Soc Am; AAAS; Am Asn Physics Teachers. *Res:* Study of noise propagation in urban and suburban situations; sound attenuation by building-size barriers; diffraction, absorption and scattering processes; ground vibrations due to urban rail transportation systems; attenuation of loud sounds by helmets. *Mailing Add:* Provost Off Univ Hartford 200 Bloomfield Ave West Hartford CT 06117

IVEY, HENRY FRANKLIN, LUMINESCENCE. *Current Pos:* RETIRED. *Personal Data:* b Augusta, Ga, June 16, 21; m 48, Sylvia Berg; c Stephen D & Lisa A (Lobel). *Educ:* Univ Ga, AB, 40, MS, 41; Mass Inst Technol, PhD(physics), 44. *Prof Exp:* Asst physics, Univ Ga, 40-41; mem staff, Radiation Lab, Mass Inst Technol, 42-45; sr engr, Nat Union Radio Corp, NJ, 45-46; res engr, Lamp Div, Westinghouse Elec Corp, 46-52, adv engr, 53-56, res sect mgr, 56-61, res eng consult, 61-63, adv scientist, Res Labs, 63-69, mgr optical physics, 69-74, adv scientist technol assessment, Res Labs, 74-86. *Mem:* Am Phys Soc; hon mem Electrochem Soc; Optical Soc Am; fel Inst Elec & Electronics Engrs. *Res:* Color centers in alkali halides; cathode ray tube screens; thermionic electron emission; phosphors; space charge; electroluminescence; laser materials; lamps. *Mailing Add:* 9259-B Jamison Ave Philadelphia PA 19115

IVEY, MARVIN L(EE), PHYSICAL GEOLOGY, HYDROGEOLOGY. *Current Pos:* RETIRED. *Personal Data:* b Orlando, Fla, Jan 17, 32; m 53, Bette R Perry; c Marvin L Jr & Susan R (Restani). *Educ:* Univ Fla, BSE, 53, MEd, 57, EdD(educ & geol), 61; Stetson Univ, JD, 78. *Prof Exp:* High sch teacher, Fla, 53-54; asst geol, Univ Fla, 56-59; instr geol, St Petersburg Jr Col, 59-64, chmn dept natural sci, 64-75 & 77-84, asst div dir sci, 75-77, prof geol, 84-91. *Concurrent Pos:* Dir officer instr, Tampa USAR Sch, 75-77; atty, 87-94. *Mem:* Fel AAAS; Geol Soc Am; Nat Asn Geol Teachers; Nat Asn Res Sci Teaching; Nat Sci Teachers Asn; Am Inst Prof Geologists. *Res:* Local investigations into ground water conditions and associated problems of erosion, sink-holes and caverns. *Mailing Add:* 14452 Hillview Dr Largo FL 33774. *E-Mail:* i0653@aol.com

IVEY, MICHAEL HAMILTON, MEDICAL PARASITOLOGY. *Current Pos:* assoc prof prev med & pub health, Sch Med, from assoc prof to prof lab practice & chmn dept parasitol & lab practice, Sch Health, 67-72, PROF MICROBIOL & IMMUNOL, HEALTH SCI CTR, UNIV OKLA, 73- *Personal Data:* b Auburn, Ala, Jan 24, 30; m 52; c 2. *Educ:* Ala Polytech Inst, BS, 51; Univ NC, MSPH, 53, PhD, 56. *Prof Exp:* Asst prof microbiol, Univ Mo, 56-62; fel, Tulane Univ, 62-63. *Concurrent Pos:* Fel, China Med Bd, 57; consult to Saigon Med Sch, AMA Proj, 68-75. *Mem:* AAAS; Am Soc Microbiol; Am Soc Parasitol; Am Soc Trop Med & Hyg. *Res:* Host-parasite relationships; immunology; pneumocystis. *Mailing Add:* Dept Microbiol & Immunol Univ Okla Col Med PO Box 26901 Oklahoma City OK 73126-0901

IVEY, ROBERT CHARLES, CHEMICAL PHYSICS, PETROLEUM ENGINEERING. *Current Pos:* VPRES & GEOPHYSICIST, LAJET GEOPHYS, INC, 81-; PRES, SOFT SEARCH, 86- *Personal Data:* b Portland, Ore, Aug 3, 43; m 67; c 2. *Educ:* Abilene Christian Univ, BS, 65; Univ Tex, Austin, PhD(phys chem), 69. *Prof Exp:* Lectr chem & comput sci, Univ Tex, El Paso, 68-69; asst prof, Abilene Christian Univ, 69-77, chmn, Dept Physics & dir observ, 71-81, prof physics, 77-86. *Concurrent Pos:* Welch Found grant electron diffraction res, 72-81; co-owner, CSA Software Co; consult & vpres res & develop, GeoNuclear Consults, Inc; consult independent oil & gas explor. *Mem:* Am Asn Physics Teachers; Am Inst Mech Engrs. *Res:* Electromagnetic geophysics, nuclear well logging, petroleum formation evaluation research; electron diffraction of gases; applications of group theory in quantum mechanics; scattering theory; determination of the structures of gas phase radicals. *Mailing Add:* 1202 Estates Dr Apt A Abilene TX 79602

IVINS, BRUCE EDWARDS, VACCINE RESEARCH & DEVELOPMENT, HOST-PARASITE RELATIONSHIPS. *Current Pos:* RES MICROBIOLOGIST, BACT DIV, US ARMY MED RES INST INFECTIOUS DIS, FT DETRICK, 80- *Personal Data:* b Apr 22, 46; m, Mary D Betsch; c Andrew & Amanda. *Educ:* Univ Cincinnati, BS, 68, MS, 72, PHD(microbiol), 76. *Prof Exp:* Lab asst clin microbiol, Cincinnati Gen Hosp, 75; fel, Dept Bact & Immunol, Univ NC, Chapel Hill, 76-78; teaching & res assoc, Dept Microbiol, Uniformed Servs Univ Health Scis, 78-80. *Concurrent Pos:* Instr microbiol, Dept Bact & Immunol, Univ NC, 77, lab inst med microbiol, 78; lab instr med microbiol, Dept Microbiol, Uniformed Servs Univ

Health Scis, 78-79, instr pathogenic microbiol, 79. *Mem:* Am Soc Microbiol; Sigma Xi; Int Soc Vaccines. *Res:* Development and testing of prototype vaccines for various bacterial diseases of humans; investigation of live recombinant vaccines and chemical vaccines employing new adjuvants for safety and efficacy. *Mailing Add:* 622 Military Rd Frederick MD 21702-8243. *Fax:* 301-619-2152; *E-Mail:* bruce_ivins@detrick.army.mil

IVINS, MARSHA S, SPACE TRAVEL, AEROSPACE ENGINEERING. *Current Pos:* Engr, Crew Sta Design Br, NASA-Lyndon B Johnson Space Ctr, 74-80, mission specialist shuttle flight STS-32, 90, shuttle Atlantis flight, 92, ENGR FLIGHT SIMULATION, NASA-LYNDON B JOHNSON SPACE CTR, 80-, ASTRONAUT, 85- *Personal Data:* b Baltimore, Md, Apr 15, 51. *Educ:* Univ Colo, BS, 73. *Mem:* Exp Aircraft Asn. *Mailing Add:* CB Astronaut Off Johnson Space Ctr NASA Houston TX 77058

IVINS, RICHARD O(RVILLE), chemical engineering, for more information see previous edition

IVORY, JOHN EDWARD, PHYSICS. *Current Pos:* RETIRED. *Personal Data:* b Buffalo, NY, May 8, 29; m 57, Gertrude Costello; c 3. *Educ:* Canisius Col, BS, 50; Univ Notre Dame, MS, 52, PhD(physics), 54. *Prof Exp:* Physicist aerodyn, Bell Aircraft Corp, 54-55; asst prof physics, Col St Thomas, 55-56, chmn dept, 56-60; res physicist thermoelec, US Naval Res Lab, 60-68; physist, Off Naval Res, Chicago Br, 68-81; consult, Naval Res Lab, 87-94. *Concurrent Pos:* Lectr, Univ Md, 61-68; adj prof, Harper & Triton Col, 81-84; adj prof, Col DuPage, 84-85; assoc prof, Ind Univ, 86-87; vis assoc prof, Ind Univ, 88 & 89. *Mailing Add:* 302 S Dwyer Arlington Heights IL 60005-1642. *E-Mail:* johnei@aol.com

IVORY, THOMAS MARTIN, III, BIOLOGY, MICROBIOLOGY. *Current Pos:* proj mgr ecol, 73-81, MGR WESTERN REGION, ESE, NUS CORP, 81- *Personal Data:* b Corpus Christi, Tex, Aug 24, 43; m 72; c 1. *Educ:* Univ Utah, BA, 65, MS, 67, PhD(biol), 73. *Prof Exp:* Res asst limnol, Univ Utah, 65-67; environ health officer, USN Med Serv Corp, 67-70; res asst limnol, Univ Utah, 70-73. *Mem:* Am Soc Limnol & Oceanog. *Res:* Limnology; primary productivity of fresh water lakes; phyxology; environmental microbiology; in stream flow requirements of aquatic organisms; environmental permit studies for mining projects. *Mailing Add:* 3072 S Grape Way Denver CO 80222

IVY, JOHN L, EXERCISE PHYSIOLOGY. *Current Pos:* from asst prof to assoc prof, 82-89, PROF KINESIOLOGY & PHARMACOL, UNIV TEX, 89-, DIR, EXERCISE SCI LABS, 89- *Personal Data:* b Portsmouth, Va, Dec 26, 45. *Educ:* Old Dominion Univ, BS, 70; Univ Md, MS, 73, PhD(phys educ), 76. *Prof Exp:* Res assoc, Human Performance Lab, Ball State Univ, 76-78; asst prof phys educ & pharmacol, Univ SC, 80-82. *Concurrent Pos:* Nat Res Serv Award, NIH, 78-80; Judy Spence Frank fel, Univ Tex, 87-91. *Mem:* Fel Am Col Sports Med; Am Physiol Soc; Sigma Xi; Am Diabetes Asn. *Mailing Add:* Exer Physiol Lab Univ Tex Belmont 222 Austin TX 78712

IWAMOTO, HARRIET S, FETAL PHYSIOLOGY, GENE THERAPY. *Current Pos:* ASSOC PROF PEDIAT, PHYSIOL & BIOPHYS, UNIV CINCINNATI, 90- *Personal Data:* b Buffalo, NY, Sept 8, 53; m 83; c 1. *Educ:* Univ Ill, BS, 75; Univ Calif, San Francisco, PhD(physiol), 80. *Prof Exp:* Vis asst prof pediat, Brown Univ, 83-84; asst prof physiol, Univ Calif, San Francisco, 84-89. *Mem:* Am Physiol Soc; Soc Pediat Res. *Mailing Add:* Div Neonatology Childrens Hosp Med Ctr 3333 Burnet Ave Cincinnati OH 45229-3039. *Fax:* 513-636-7868; *E-Mail:* harriet.iwamoto@chmcc.org

IWAMOTO, REYNOLD TOSHIAKI, ANALYTICAL CHEMISTRY. *Current Pos:* from asst prof to assoc prof, 56-65, PROF CHEM, UNIV KANS, 65- *Personal Data:* b Honolulu, Hawaii, Nov 20, 28; m 51; c 3. *Educ:* Univ Hawaii, BS, 50, MS, 52; Harvard Univ, PhD(chem), 56. *Prof Exp:* Instr chem, Princeton Univ, 55-56. *Mem:* Am Chem Soc. *Res:* Electrochemical, spectral and magnetic resonance studies of the nature and behavior of inorganic species in nonaqueous media; porphyrin redox chemistry. *Mailing Add:* 818 W 22nd St Lawrence KS 66046

IWAMOTO, TOMIO, ICHTHYOLOGY, SYSTEMATICS. *Current Pos:* CUR ICHTHYOL, CALIF ACAD SCI, 72- *Personal Data:* b Los Angeles, Calif, July 16, 39; m 71; c 3. *Educ:* Univ Calif, Los Angeles, AB, 61; Univ Miami, MS, 68, PhD(marine sci), 72. *Prof Exp:* Biologist, Pascagoula Fishery Sta, US Bur Comm Fisheries, 62-65; instr fisheries, Ore State Univ, 71-72. *Concurrent Pos:* Prin investr, NSF grant, 75-90; consult, Environ Mgt & Res, 78- *Mem:* Am Soc Ichthyologists & Herpetologists; Ichthyol Soc Japan; Indian Soc Ichthyol; Systematic Zool; Sigma Xi. *Res:* Biology of deep-sea fishes, particularly grenadier family Macrouridae. *Mailing Add:* Ichthyol Calif Acad Sci San Francisco CA 94118

IWANIEC, TADEUSZ, QUASICONFORMAL MAPPINGS, PARTIAL DIFFERENTIAL EQUATIONS. *Current Pos:* PROF MATH, SYRACUSE UNIV, 86- *Personal Data:* b Elblag, Poland, Oct 9, 47; m 71; c 1. *Educ:* Univ Warsaw, Habilitation, 79, PhD(math), 75. *Prof Exp:* From asst to assoc prof, Univ Warsaw, 71-81; assoc prof math, Polish Acad Sci, 81-83. *Concurrent Pos:* Vis prof math, Univ Lomonoff, Moscow, 78-79, Univ Bonn, 79, Univ Piza, 81, Univ Helsinki, 82, Univ Mich, Ann Arbor, 83-84, Univ Tex, Austin, 84-85 & Courant Inst, 85-86. *Mem:* Am Math Soc. *Res:* Quasiconformal analysis and related problems in non-linear elliptic equations, complex functions and differential geometry; complex functions and differential geometry; harmonic analysis. *Mailing Add:* 100 Acorn Path Syracuse NY 13210

IWASA, KUNI H, BIOPHYSICS. *Current Pos:* BIOPHYSICIST, NAT INST DEAF & COMM DIS, NIH, 91-, ACTG SECT CHIEF, 96- *Personal Data:* b Tokushima, Japan, Nov 26, 44; US citizen; m 73; c 3. *Educ:* Osaka City Univ, BSc, 67; Nagoya Univ, MSc, 69, PhD(physics), 74. *Prof Exp:* Killam fel chem, Dalhousie Univ, 75-76; res assoc chem, Ind Univ, 76-77; vis fel, Univ Ljubljana, 77-78; res assoc chem eng, Rice Univ, 78-79; chemist biophys, NIMH, 79-83; biophysicist, Nat Inst Neurol Dis & Stroke, NIH, 83-85 & 86-91; physicist, Ctr Drugs & Biol, Fed Drug Admin, 85-86. *Mem:* Am Chem Soc; Biophys Soc; Am Phys Soc. *Res:* Excitable membrane; thermodynamical study of polyelectrolytes. *Mailing Add:* NIH Bldg 9 Rm 1E120 Bethesda MD 20892-0922. *E-Mail:* kiwasa@helix.nih.gov

IWASA, YUKIKAZU, ELECTRICAL ENGINEERING. *Current Pos:* SR SCIENTIST SUPERCONDUCTIVITY, FRANCIS BITTER NAT MAGNET LAB, MASS INST TECHNOL, 64- *Personal Data:* b Kyoto, Japan, Feb 15, 38; m 69; c 2. *Educ:* Mass Inst Technol, SB, SM(mech eng) & SM(elec eng), 62, EE, 64, PhD(elec eng), 67. *Honors & Awards:* Oyama Mem Award, 84; M Hetényi Award, 87; Cryog & Brit Cryog Coun Prize, 90. *Mem:* AAAS. *Res:* Applied superconductivity; materials, magnets and devices. *Mailing Add:* Francis Bitter Nat Magnet Lab Rm NW14-3101 Mass Inst Technol 77 Massachusettes Ave Cambridge MA 02139

IWASAKI, IWAO, METALLURGY, CHEMISTRY. *Current Pos:* TECH COUNR, MITSUBISHI MAT CORP, JAPAN, 91- *Personal Data:* b Tokyo, Japan, Feb 6, 29; m 72, Junko Ikegami; c Eiji, Yoko & Miwa. *Educ:* Univ Minn, BS, 51, MS, 53; Mass Inst Technol, ScD(metall), 57. *Hon Degrees:* Dr Eng, Tohoku Univ, Japan, 61. *Honors & Awards:* A M Gaudin Award & A F Taggart Award, Soc Mining Engrs of Am Inst Mining, Metall & Petrol Engrs, 81; R H Richard Award, Am Inst Mining, Metall & Petrol Engrs, 86. *Prof Exp:* Asst prof metall, Univ Minn, 57-59; group leader, Nippon Steel Corp, Japan, 59-63; assoc prof, Univ Minn, Minneapolis, 63-66, prof metall, 66-91. *Mem:* Nat Acad Eng; Mining Inst Japan; Resources Processing Soc Japan; Am Inst Mining, Metall & Petrol Engrs. *Res:* Mineral processing, ore flotation, flocculation, hydrometallurgy, iron ore agglomeration and reduction; solid waste treatment; grinding media wear; chlorination and segregation roasting; water treatment methods. *Mailing Add:* Mitsubishi Materials Corp Central Research Inst 1-297 Kitabukuro-cho Omiya 330 Japan. *Fax:* 81-48-644-8608; *E-Mail:* iwasaki@omiya.mmc.co.jp

IWASAWA, KENKICHI, mathematics, for more information see previous edition

IWATSUKI, SHUNZABURO, ORGAN TRANSPLANTATION, LIVER & BILIARY DUCT SURGERY. *Current Pos:* PROF SURG, UNIV PITTSBURGH, 87- *Personal Data:* b Nagoya, Japan, May 24, 40; m 72, Jeanette. *Educ:* Nagoya Univ, MD, 65, PhD(med sci), 72. *Concurrent Pos:* Staff mem, Presby Univ Hosp, 81, Children's Hosp Pittsburgh, 81. *Mem:* Am Surg Asn; Transplantation Soc; Am Soc Transplantation. *Res:* Liver transplantation; hepatic cancer. *Mailing Add:* Univ Pittsburgh Med Ctr 3601 Fifth Ave Pittsburgh PA 15213. *Fax:* 412-648-3184

IWIG, MARK MICHAEL, WHEAT & CORN BREEDING. *Current Pos:* Res sta mgr, 77-86, dir, Dept Cereal Seed Res, 86-89, DIR, DEPT NAM CORN BREEDING, PIONEER HI-BRED INT, 89- *Personal Data:* b Topeka, Kans, Feb 6, 51; m 73; c 3. *Educ:* Baker Univ, BS, 73; Purdue Univ, MS, 75, PhD(plant breeding & genetics), 77. *Mem:* Agron Soc Am; Crop Sci Soc Am. *Res:* Development of new improved cultivars of soft red winter wheat, hard red winter wheat, hard res spring wheat and new improved corn hybrids of North America. *Mailing Add:* 5950 S Winwood Dr Johnston IA 50131. *Fax:* 515-253-2125

IYENGAR, DORESWAMY RAGHAVACHAR, PHYSICAL CHEMISTRY, SURFACE CHEMISTRY. *Current Pos:* RETIRED. *Personal Data:* b Nanjangud, India, July 3, 30; m 66, Kowsalya Garudachar; c 2. *Educ:* Univ Mysore, BSc, 51; Univ Madras, MSc, 54; Univ Miami, PhD(chem), 63. *Prof Exp:* Lectr chem, Univ Mysore, 51-56; Du Pont fel, Lehigh Univ, 62-64, US Army Signal Corps fel, 64-65; phys scientist, Frankford Arsenal, Pa, 65-66 & Army Mat Res Agency, Mass 66-67; res assoc prof chem, Lehigh Univ, 67-70; sr res chemist, Cent Inorg Res Lab, Sherwin-Williams Co, 70-71; staff scientist & leader, Pigments Lab, 71-75; prof consult, 75; res assoc, Dispersions Pigments Div, Basf Wyandotte Corp, 75-80, sr res assoc & head, Dispersions Characterization, 81-86; tech mgr, Flint Ink Corp, 86-90, consult. *Concurrent Pos:* Prof chem, Roosevelt Univ, 72-75. *Mem:* Am Chem Soc; fel Royal Soc Chem; fel Am Inst Chem; fel Tech Surface Coatings. *Res:* Heterogeneous catalysis; surface chemistry of metals; oxides; semiconductors and pigments; adsorption and chemisorption; neutron inelastic scattering from surfaces; adsorbed species by electron spin resonance; corrosion and stress corrision; studies on pigments and coatings; dispersions and emulsions; printing inks and lithography. *Mailing Add:* 1474 Hidden Creek S Saline MI 48176

IYENGAR, RAVI SRINIVAS V, PHARMACOLOGY, MOLECULAR BIOLOGY. *Current Pos:* assoc prof, 86-90, PROF, DEPT PHARMACOL, MT SINAI SCH MED, 90- *Personal Data:* b Bombay, India, June 16, 51; US citizen; m 77, Rama Narayanan; c Radha & Rupa. *Educ:* Bombay Univ, BSc, 71, MSc, 73; Univ Houston, MS, 75, PhD(biophys sci), 77. *Prof Exp:* Fel, Baylor Col Med, 77-80, from asst prof to assoc prof, 80-86. *Concurrent Pos:* Prin investr, NIH, 80-; ed, J Biol Chem, 91- *Mem:* Am Soc Biochem & Molecular Biol; Endocrine Soc; AAAS. *Res:* Molecular mechanisms of hormone and neurotransmitter signaling through G protein dependent cell surface signaling systems; gene isolation; biochemical and physiological characterization of components of signaling systems; modified genes of signaling systems as therapeutic agents; signal transduction. *Mailing Add:* Dept Pharmacol Mt Sinai Sch Med PO Box 1215 New York NY 10029. *Fax:* 212-831-0114; *E-Mail:* liyengar@msvax.mssm.edu

IYER, HARIHARAIYER MAHADEVA, GEOPHYSICS, SEISMOLOGY. *Current Pos:* geophysicist, 67-80, SUPVRY GEOPHYSICIST, US GEOL SURV, 80- *Personal Data:* b Kerala, India, June 21, 31; US citizen; m 72; c 2. *Educ:* Univ Kerala, BSc, 51, MSc, 53; Univ London, PhD(oceanog), 59. *Honors & Awards:* Krishnan Mem Gold Medal, Indian Geophys Union, 66. *Prof Exp:* Sci officer oceanog, Indian Naval Phys Lab, Cochin, 53-60; Sverdrup Mem fel inst geophys & planetary physics, Univ Calif, San Diego, 60-61; Gassiot fel seismol, Brit Meteorol Off, Bracknell, 61-63; sci officer seismol, Bhabha Atomic Res Ctr, Bombay, 63-67. *Concurrent Pos:* Consult inst geophys & planetary physics, Univ Calif, San Diego, 62 & 64; mem, Dept Energy Consortium Active & Passive Seismic Methods for Geothermal Explor, 77; USA-India exchange scientist, 78; UN expert, seismology, 81; consult, Regional Govt Azores, 83; fel, Indo-US Subcomt Educ & Cult, Nat Geophys Inst, Hyderabad, India, 85-86; adv, Wadan Inst, Himalayan Geol, India, 90; mem, Working Group Microseisms, Int Asn Seismol & Physics Earths. *Mem:* Fel Asn Explor Geophysicists India; Int Asn Seismol & Physics Earths Interior; Seismol Soc Am; Am Geophys Union. *Res:* Structure and evolution of the earth's crust and mantle; mapping the heterogeneous structure of the earth's crust and upper mantle using seismic tomography; imaging magma chambers using seismic tomography; physics and evolution of volcanic and geothermal systems; geothermal exploration using seismic techniques; microseismic, seismic and earthquake prediction; induced seismicity associated with dams and reservoirs; author of 70 publications including six in books. *Mailing Add:* 697 Gilbert Ave Menlo Park CA 94025

IYER, RAJUL V, microbiology, for more information see previous edition

IYER, RAM R, PIPE STRESS ANALYSIS, FINITE ELEMENT ANALYSIS. *Current Pos:* sr staff engr, Sun Co, 83-87, sr proj engr, 87-89, mgr contracts, 89-91, MGR EQUIP ENG, SUN CO, 91- *Personal Data:* b Pallavaram, India, Apr 17, 53; m 82, Rupa Iyer; c Amrit & Tara. *Educ:* Bangalore Univ, India, BE, 74; Indian Inst Sci, ME, 76; Brooklyn Polytech, DE, 78; Drexel Univ, MBA, 86. *Prof Exp:* Res assoc, Ctr Regional Technol, 77-78; design engr, SunTech, Inc, 78-83. *Concurrent Pos:* Chmn subcomt mats piping & pressure vessels, Am Soc Mech Engrs, Del Valley Chap, 85-90. *Mem:* Am Soc Civil Engrs; Am Soc Mech Engrs. *Res:* Pipe stress analysis; pipe support design; earthquake resistant design of concrete structures; design of petroleum and petrochemical plants; vibration and fatigue evaluation of rotating equipment and finite element analysis of mechanical and structural components. *Mailing Add:* 7 Bon Air Dr Marlton NJ 08053. *Fax:* 215-497-6295; *E-Mail:* rriyer@aol.com

IYER, RAMAKRISHNAN S, ENVIRONMENTAL & REGULATORY COMPLIANCE. *Current Pos:* ENVIRON SPECIALIST, DYNMCDERMOTT PETROL OPERS, INC, 92- *Personal Data:* b Shivaganga, India, Feb 26, 47; US citizen; m 78, Maria; c Evelina & Melissa. *Educ:* Univ Bombay, India, BS, 67, MSc, 69; ETex State Univ, MS, 75. *Prof Exp:* Process qual engr, Teccor Electronics, Inc, 79-81; hybrid process engr, Motorola, Inc, 81-82; failure analysis engr, NCR Corp, 83-85; sr prod engr, Unisys, Inc, 85-87; sr reliability engr, Medtronic, Inc, 87-88; sr reliability engr, 88-90, sr mfg engr, Compaq Comput Corp, 90-91. *Concurrent Pos:* Mem, Int Soc Hybrid Microelectronics, 81-87. *Mem:* Am Chem Soc; Am Soc Qual Control. *Res:* Investigate new chemical solvents or methods to replace freon as a cleaning solvent since freon is an ozone depletor; freon solvent replacement in organic extration methods during analytical testing for environmental compliance to Environmental Protection Agency and state regulatory requirements. *Mailing Add:* Manage Cell Syst Northern Telecom Inc 2221 Lakeside Blvd Richardson TX 75082

IYER, RAVI, PASSIVATION & INSULATOR RESEARCH ON III-V SEMICONDUCTORS, OPTICAL CHARACTERIZATION & KINETIC STUDIES. *Current Pos:* MEM STAFF, MICRON, 92- *Personal Data:* b Kumbakonam, India, July 13, 58; m 85; c 1. *Educ:* Regional Eng Col, BTech, 79; Colo State Univ, MS, 84, PhD(elec eng), 91. *Prof Exp:* Res asst solar energy, Colo State Univ, 81-84, res asst semiconductors, 85-87, res assoc, 87-89, postdoctoral semiconductors, 89-92. *Res:* Development of a suitable insulator on InP for MIS technology; kinetics of SiO_2 deposition from silane and plasma O_2; passivation of III-V semiconductors and characterization using photoluminescence and raman spectroscopy. *Mailing Add:* Micron 8000 S Federal Way MS 306 Boise ID 83707-0006

IYER, SAVITRI VENKATESWARAN, GENERAL RELATIVITY. *Current Pos:* Vis asst prof, Dept Physics, 93-96, ASST PROF, DEPT PHYSICS, STATE UNIV NY, GENESEO, 96- *Personal Data:* b Madras, India, July 24, 63; m 91, Madan V Shastri; c Gaurav V. *Educ:* Univ Madras, India, BSc, 84; Indian Inst Technol, India, MSc, 86; Iowa State Univ, MS, 89; Univ Pittsburgh, PhD(physics), 93. *Mem:* Am Phys Soc. *Mailing Add:* 464 Countess Dr West Henrietta NY 14586. *E-Mail:* iyer@uno.cc.geneseo.edu

IYPE, PULLOLICKAL THOMAS, CELL BIOLOGY, CANCER. *Current Pos:* PRES & OWNER, BIOL RES FAC & FACIL, 85- *Personal Data:* b Kottayam, India. *Educ:* Univ Madras, BSc, 55; Univ Baroda, India, MSc, 58, PhD(zool), 61. *Prof Exp:* Demonstr zool, Univ Baroda, 58-61; sci officer biochem, Regional Res Lab, India, 61-65; Damon Runyon fel carcinogenesis, McArdle Lab, Madison, Wis, 65-68; sci officer, Regional Res Lab, India, 68-69; scientist, Paterson Lab, Christie Hosp, Eng, 69-77; sect head carcinogenesis, Frederick Res Ctr, Nat Cancer Inst, 77-85. *Concurrent Pos:* Lectr, Univ Manchester, 72-77. *Mem:* Am Asn Cancer Res; Brit Asn Cancer Res; Brit Soc Cell Biol; AAAS. *Res:* Cellular aspects of chemical carcinogenesis using model systems to analyze the early events, especially the control of cell proliferation, during malignant transformation of epithelial cells. *Mailing Add:* Biol Res Facil Inc 10075-20 Tyler Pl Ijamsville MD 21754-8753. *Fax:* 301-831-8842

IZANT, ROBERT JAMES, JR, PEDIATRIC SURGERY. *Current Pos:* from asst prof to assoc prof, PROF PEDIAT SURG, CASE WESTERN RES UNIV, 72- *Personal Data:* b Cleveland, Ohio, Feb 4, 21; m 47; c 3. *Educ:* Amherst Col, BA, 43; Western Reserve Univ, MD, 46. *Honors & Awards:* Belle Sherwin Award. *Prof Exp:* From intern to resident gen surg, Univ Hosps, Cleveland, 46-52; resident pediat surg, Boston Childrens Hosp, 52-55; asst prof, Ohio State Univ, 55-58. *Mem:* Am Col Surg; Am Pediat Surg Asn (pres, 87-88); Am Asn Surg Trauma; Am Burn Asn; Am Acad Pediat; Sigma Xi. *Res:* Congenital malformations, malignancies and trauma in infants and children. *Mailing Add:* 2275 Harcourt Dr Cleveland OH 44106

IZATT, JERALD RAY, LASERS, SPECTROSCOPY. *Current Pos:* prof, 81-96, EMER PROF PHYSICS & FOUND COALITION PROF, UNIV ALA, TUSCALOOSA, 96- *Personal Data:* b Preston, Idaho, Sept 22, 28; m 51, Mary A Fassler; c Richard A, James A, Peggy J, Nancy L & Joseph A. *Educ:* Univ Utah, BS, 52; Johns Hopkins Univ, PhD(physics), 60. *Prof Exp:* Analyst, digital comput prog, Douglas Aircraft Co, Inc, 52-53; engr weapon syst anal, Westinghouse Elec Corp, 54-55; res scientist, Electro-Optical Systs Anal, Northrop Space Labs, 60-61; from asst prof to prof physics, NMex State Univ, 61-70; vis prof physics, Laval Univ, 70-71, prof, 71-81. *Concurrent Pos:* Consult, 61-; vis scientist, Cambridge Res Labs, USAF, 67-68, Max Planck Inst Solid State Physics, 79-80, Univ Regensburg, 92; adj prof, NMex State Univ, 70-75; vis scholar, Univ Utah, 89-90; adj prof mat sci, Univ Ala, Birmingham & Huntsville, 88-96. *Mem:* Optical Soc Am; Sigma Xi. *Res:* Infrared and submillimeter lasers; molecular spectroscopy; optical techniques for industrial inspection; non-linear effects in optically pumped gases. *Mailing Add:* Dept Physics Univ Ala Tuscaloosa AL 35487-0324. *E-Mail:* jizatt@ua1vm.ua.edu

IZATT, REED MCNEIL, INORGANIC CHEMISTRY, METAL SEPARATIONS. *Current Pos:* from asst prof to assoc prof, 56-64, PROF CHEM, BRIGHAM YOUNG UNIV, 64- *Personal Data:* b Logan, Utah, Oct 10, 26; m 49; c 6. *Educ:* Utah State Univ, BS, 51; Pa State Univ, PhD, 54. *Honors & Awards:* Separation Sci & Technol Award, Am Chem Soc, 96. *Prof Exp:* Fel chem, Mellon Inst, 54-56. *Mem:* AAAS; Am Chem Soc; Sigma Xi. *Res:* Thermodynamics of coordination compounds in aqueous solutions; selective transport of cations across liquid membranes using macrocycles; heats of mixing at elevated temperatures and pressures. *Mailing Add:* Dept Chem Brigham Young Univ Provo UT 84602-1022

IZEN, JOSEPH M, EXPERIMENTAL ELEMENTARY PARTICLE PHYSICS. *Current Pos:* asst prof, 91-94, ASSOC PROF, UNIV TEX, DALLAS, 94- *Personal Data:* b Brooklyn NY, Nov 14, 56. *Educ:* Cooper Union, BS, 77; Harvard Univ, AM, 78, PhD(physics), 82. *Prof Exp:* Res assoc, Univ Wis, 82-85; asst prof, Univ Ill, 86-91. *Concurrent Pos:* Eli Lilly teaching fel, 87-88; US spokesperson, Beijing Spectrometer Collab, 91-; vis assoc prof physics, Colo State Univ, 94-96. *Mem:* Am Phys Soc. *Res:* Experiments observing the high energy annihilation of electrons and positrons; physics of charm and bottom quarks and the tau lepton. *Mailing Add:* Dept Particle Physics Univ Tex Dallas PO Box 830688 Richardson TX 75083. *Fax:* 972-883-2848; *E-Mail:* joe@utdallas.edu

IZENOUR, GEORGE C(HARLES), ELECTRICAL ENGINEERING. *Current Pos:* dir, Electomech Lab, Drama Sch, 46-77, from assoc prof to prof theatre eng, 50-77, EMER PROF THEATRE ENG, YALE UNIV, 77- *Personal Data:* b New Brighton, Pa, July 24, 12; m 37; c 1. *Educ:* Wittenberg Univ, AB, 34, MA, 36. *Hon Degrees:* DFA, Wittenberg Univ, 60. *Prof Exp:* Lighting dir, Fed Theatre, 37-39; Rockefeller Found res fel & founder, Electromech Lab, Drama Sch, Yale Univ, 39-43; res engr, Airborne Instruments Lab, Off Sci Res & Develop, Columbia Univ, 43-46. *Concurrent Pos:* Consult, US State Dept, Brazil, 57; grantee award, Ford Found, 60, grant, 67. *Mem:* AAAS. *Res:* Electromechanical-electronic aspects of control systems as they affect the theatre and television. *Mailing Add:* Box 2903 Westville Sta New Haven CT 06515

IZMAILOV, ALEXANDRE, LASER PHYSICS. *Current Pos:* SR SCIENTIST, VISIBLE GENETICS INC, 95- *Personal Data:* b Uralsk, Russia, Jan 22, 57; Can citizen; m 80, Svetlana Alimova; c 2. *Educ:* St Petersburg Univ, Russia, MSc, 79, PhD(optics, lasers), 83. *Prof Exp:* Sr sci researcher, St Petersburg Univ, 90-95. *Concurrent Pos:* Consult, Advan Sci Consult, De La Rosa & De La Rosa, 96-97 & Univ Toronto, 97. *Mem:* Optical Soc Am; Soc Photo-Instrumentation Engrs. *Res:* Development and investigation of new dye and solid state lasers; multicolor lasers with several independently tunable emission lines; application of lasers in spectroscopy, biophysics and opthalmology; investigation of liquid crystals. *Mailing Add:* 114 Longboat Ave Toronto ON M5A 4G3 Can. *Fax:* 905-542-8673; *E-Mail:* izmailov@visgen.com

IZOD, THOMAS PAUL JOHN, FIBER FINISHING, FLUORO-CHEMICAL RESEARCH. *Current Pos:* MGR EXPLOR RES, RES & DEVELOP, ALLIED CORP, 85- *Personal Data:* b London, UK, Apr 12, 45; US citizen; m 69; c 3. *Educ:* London Univ, UK, BSc, 66; Oxford Univ, DPhil(phys chem), 69. *Prof Exp:* Teaching fel, res, Harvard Univ, Cambridge,

Mass, 69-71; res assoc phys chem, St Andrews Univ, Scotland, 71-74; group leader res, Union Carbide Corp, Tarrytown, NJ, 74-78; technol mgr, res & develop, Waters Assoc, Millipore Corp, 78-82; sr res group leader, res & develop, Polaroid Corp, 82-85. *Mem:* Am Chem Soc; Royal Chem Soc. *Res:* Chemical surface modification of polymers and inorganic surfaces; characterization of these surfaces such as adsorption catalysis; techniques for making small (colloidal) particles and mechanisms for stabilizing particles in aqueous and non-aqueous media. *Mailing Add:* Allied Signal Corp PO Box 31 Petersburg VA 23804

IZQUIERDO, RICARDO, laser processing, for more information see previous edition

IZUI, SHOZO, AUTOIMMUNOLOGY, IMMUNOPATHOLOGY. *Current Pos:* res fel immunol, WHO/IRIC, 73-74, asst immunol, Div Hemat, 74-77, chg res immunol, Div Hemat, 81-84, Dept Path, 84-87, PROF ADJ IMMUNOL, DEPT PATH, FAC MED, UNIV GENEVA, 87- *Personal Data:* b Kanazawa, Japan, Jan 22, 46; m 77; c 2. *Educ:* Univ Tokyo, MD, 70. *Hon Degrees:* Dr, Univ Geneva, 83. *Prof Exp:* Res assoc immunopath, Scripps Clin & Res Found, USA, 77-78, asst Mb I immunopath, 78-79, Mb II immunopath, 79-81. *Mem:* Am Asn Immunologists. *Res:* Genetic, cellular and molecular investigation on immunopathogenesis of spontaneous murine model of autoimmune diseases, especially systemic lupus erythematosus. *Mailing Add:* Dept Path CMU One rue Michel Servet 1211 Geneva 4 Switzerland 1211

IZYDORE, ROBERT ANDREW, ORGANIC & PHARMACEUTICAL CHEMISTRY. *Current Pos:* assoc prof, 71-80, PROF CHEM, NC CENT UNIV, 80- *Personal Data:* b McKeesport, Pa, July 13, 43; div; c Robert R & Kenneth M. *Educ:* Pa State Univ, BS, 65; Duquesne Univ, PhD(org chem), 69. *Prof Exp:* US Army Res Off-Durham Res Assoc, Duke Univ, 69-71. *Concurrent Pos:* Instr, Pa State Univ, McKeesport, 68-69. *Mem:* Am Chem Soc; Sigma Xi. *Res:* Synthesis and chemistry of azo compounds and their cyclo-addition products; synthesis of pharmacologically active compounds; synthesis of novel organic heterocyclic compunds. *Mailing Add:* 311 Hubbard Chem Bldg NC Cent Univ Durham NC 27707. *Fax:* 919-560-5135; *E-Mail:* rizydore@wpu.nccu.edu

IZZO, JOSEPH ANTHONY, JR, mathematics; deceased, see previous edition for last biography

IZZO, PATRICK THOMAS, CHEMISTRY, PHARMACEUTICAL CHEMISTRY. *Current Pos:* RETIRED. *Personal Data:* b Beverly, Mass, May 10, 18; m 53; c 2. *Educ:* Fordham Univ, BS, 42, MS, 44; Columbia Univ, PhD(chem), 47. *Prof Exp:* Fel, Mass Inst Technol, 47-48; res chemist, Lederle Labs, Am Cyanamid Co, 48-91. *Concurrent Pos:* Instr, Rockland Community Col, Suffern, NY, 72- *Mem:* Am Chem Soc. *Res:* Organic chemistry; anti-infective agents; central nervous system agents. *Mailing Add:* 5 Rollins Ave Pearl River NY 10965-1812